ALL MUSIC GUIDE

The best CDs, albums & tapes

The experts' guide to the best releases from thousands of artists in all types of music

EDITOR: MICHAEL ERLEWINE

ASSOCIATE EDITOR: SCOTT BULTMAN

ASSISTANT EDITOR: STEPHEN THOMAS ERLEWINE

MILLER FREEMAN INC.

San Francisco

ACKNOWLEDGEMENTS

This book would not have been possible without the guidance of Andrew Gun McIver and Ven. Khenpo Karthar Rinpoche.

Special thanks to Rick Clark and Ron Wynn. Thanks to Paul Attinello, Harry Bernstein, Tom Dorsaneo, Terry Hounsome, Neal Umphred, Kit Kieffer, Opal Louis Nations, Jack Levin, Peter Lee (editor of *Living Blues* magazine), Bob Koester (of Delmark Records), John DeBlaiso, Paul Hartman, Marjorie Ellen Ruhlmann, Thomas C. Terry (TCT), and Jeff Tamarkin.

To our production staff ...

Special thanks to Vladimir Bogdanov, Malinda McCain, and Forest Ray. Thanks to Tavia Hobart, Iotis Erlewine, Annie Erlewine, Phillip Erlewine, Tom Bridges, David McCarthy, Kristina Shapar, Cathy Howe, Linda Kent, Andrew Larrick, Alison Oldfield, Sara Sytsma, John Wichman, and Morgen Erlewine.

And to all the Matrix staff ...

Margaret Erlewine, Stephen Erlewine, Douglas Dixon, Ludmila Lobenko, Franz Sturm, Walter Crockett, Kevin Fowler, Pat Dorset, Susan Munn, Mary King, Brian Guthrie, and Viniita Hutchinson.

From Scott Bultman ...

I would especially like to thank my parents — William and Kathryn Bultman — for their love and support and for teaching me that I could do whatever I set my mind to. Also a big thanks to Jackie for encouraging me to chase my dreams.

Published by Miller Freeman Inc., Book Division, 600 Harrison Street, San Francisco, CA 94107

Portions of Jas Obrecht's sidebars are exclusive, copyrighted excerpts from his book-in-progress, *Early Blues: The Music Before Robert Johnson;* used by permission.
Billboard Chart ratings used with the permission of Records Research, Inc.
DOWN BEAT star-rating system used with permission of DOWN BEAT magazine.
Cover Design: Tom Erlewine

Library of Congress Catalog Card Number 92-60948
ISBN 0-87930-264-X
Printed in the United States of America
First printing October 1992

92 93 94 95   6 5 4 3 2 1

DEDICATION & FOREWORD

I'd like to dedicate this book to...

...the spirit of the 60s and the music scene in Ann Arbor, Michigan, at that time.

...my wife Margaret — I was lucky enough to find her back there and then.

... our four children — Iotis, Anne, May, and Michael Andrew.

Music, whatever else it may or may not be, is a great healing force. It is the best medicine for the soul that I have ever found, and it comes in all flavors. In my case, the more upset I am by life, the more music I listen to. And it takes some special music to cure those stubborn heartaches, which is how the *All-Music Guide* came into being.

A simple examination of my checkbook dates makes it clear that I buy more music when my life is in turmoil than otherwise. During the period when my aging parents died, I bought and listened to a whole lot of music. If it's true that music is the best medicine for an aching heart, what I most needed at that time was some *very* good music.

But a lot had changed since the 60s, when I was a full-time musician. For one thing, almost 20 years had passed and the recordings I knew just were not around anymore. What I needed was to hear the music I most remembered and maybe try some new stuff too. I set out to find it.

By trial and error I did find some. But I made a lot of mistakes along the way, wasting my time and hard-earned money on worthless recordings, re-record-ings, bad sound—you name it. I needed guidance and searched, with some success, through the many books and magazines available on music for more information. In a last-ditch effort to track down the best recordings for different artists, I called the experts themselves—music writers. This worked. They do know their stuff. I started finding some of the music that I craved.

Sharing this information with those around me, it soon became clear that I am not alone. Many people want to know where the good music is or how to venture into new music categories without fear of wasting both time and money guessing at music. This book is intended as an offering to music listeners everywhere. The driving force behind compiling the *All-Music Guide* has always been my own need for the book, and I intend to be a major user.

–Michael Erlewine

CONTENTS

CONTENTS

ALL-MUSIC GUIDE DATABASE

The *All-Music Guide* is more than this book. It is an ongoing database project, the largest collection of substantive album reviews ever assembled. In fact, the 23,000 albums listed in this book represent a rather small subset (albeit the most important one) of a much larger collection of over 100,000 albums and reviews. The entire *All-Music Guide* database will be made available in 1993 as a consumer CD-ROM for computer users, and as an on-line service in record stores across the country.

We welcome your feedback. Perhaps we have left out some of your favorite albums, and/or included ones that you don't consider essential. Let us know about it. We welcome criticism, suggestions, additions, and/or deletions. The *All-Music Guide* is a continuing project. Perhaps you are expert on the complete output of a particular artist or group and would like to participate in future editions of this book and/or our larger computer database. We would be glad to hear from you. Call or write

All-Music Guide
315 Marion Avenue
Big Rapids, MI 49307
616/796-3437
FAX 616/796-3060
A division of Matrix Software

INTRODUCTION

The *All-Music Guide* represents the combined effort of over eighty experienced music writers to point out the most important artists and their best music. Most are well-known reviewers. Aside from producing scores of liner notes, they also write for magazines like *Rolling Stone, Goldmine, Detail, Pulse, Request, Billboard, Music Express, Mix, Agent/Manager, Spin, Musician, CD-Review, Rock & Roll Disc,* and many others.

Starting with extensive lists of musicians in their area of expertise, each writer picked the artists they felt should be in the book. These lists were then combined to create a master list for each genre of the most frequently selected artists. Master lists were then submitted to genre editors, further refined and commented upon, and then given to at least one other editor for still more criticism, additions, and suggestions. The final result is in your hands, the 23,000+ top albums selected from a database of over 100,000 albums.

HOW TO USE THIS BOOK

This book is organized by sections and, within each section, by artist. The general index at the back of the book allows you to locate any particular artist. The following information is provided for each artist.

ARTIST NAME

QUICK MUSIC TYPE To make it easy to see at at glance what types of music an artist plays, we have included these short phrases at the beginning of each bio. A description of these music types is at the beginning of the particular section (except Classical).

BIOGRAPHY A quick view of the artist's biographical details and, for major artists, something about their place in music is included.

MAJOR ALBUMS These are the 23,000+ albums selected by a group of experts from a group of over 100,000. An album listed here (even one without a bullet or comment) is considered an important recording by one or more of our experts. It's worth a listen. Undistinguished albums are not included here.

KEY TO SYMBOLS ○ ● ☆ ★

○ LANDMARK RECORDINGS Albums marked with an open circle are singled out as landmark or career turning points for the particular artist. These are classic albums—prime stuff. A landmark recording is either a pivotal recording that marked a change in their career or a high point in their recording output.

☆ ESSENTIAL COLLECTIONS Albums marked with a star should be part of any beginning collection of the genre. Often, these are also a good first purchase (filled Star). By hearing these albums, you can get a good overview of the entire genre. These are must-hear and must-have recordings. You can't go wrong with them.

● ★ FIRST PURCHASE Albums marked with either a filled star or a filled circle should be your first purchase. This is where to begin to find out if you like this particular artist. These albums are representative of the best this artist has to offer. If you don't like these picks, chances are this artist is not for you. In the case where an artist (like Miles Davis) has a number of distinct periods, you will find an essential pick marked for each period. It might be best to start with an earlier album (the albums are listed chronologically when possible) and work up to the later ones.

CLASSICAL RECORDINGS The classical section uses a separate rating system, which is explained on the facing page.

MISSISSIPPI JOHN HURT   1893-1966

Acoustic country blues. An exquisite country blues singer and guitarist with a subtle voice and refined finger-picking guitar style, Hurt recorded in the 20s and again in the 60s. Both periods are well worth hearing: acoustic country blues with real technical clarity that is also comforting and easy to listen to. He never made a recording not worth hearing. With a gospel flavor in his blues, Mississippi John Hurt projects a sense of dignity and kindliness through all of his recordings. If you have trouble with the frequent heaviness of many blues players, you may find Hurt refreshing. He is one of a kind, and a kind one at that. –JME

Today / VANGUARD   1966
A fine 60s album. –JME

○ **Immortal Mississippi John Hurt / VANGUARD**   1967
The best of Hurt's 60s "rediscovery-era" recordings. –MH

The Best of Mississippi John Hurt / VANGUARD   1971
A great double-album collection of 60s Hurt. –JME

★ **1928 Sessions / YAZOO / DB 5**   1988
Justifiably legendary, with gentle grace and power on these understated masterpieces of finger-picked guitar and vocals. This is the one to get. These are the early (1928) recordings, which are very fine. –JME & MH

RATINGS In addition, many albums will have additional rating information that may prove of value to readers. Ratings in the charts (top 100 albums) are listed when available. This lets you know that the album was a hit, climbing the *Billboard* charts to the position indicated. A #1 hit is as good as it gets. For jazz fans, we have included albums that have attained five stars on the now-famous DOWN BEAT rating system. Here are some of the main sources of those:

DOWN BEAT awards a rating of one to five stars, with five stars being the best. These ratings appear along with the initials "DB" following the label name.

BILLBOARD CHARTS An indication of how high on the *Billboard* music charts the album rose. Look for the initials "BB" followed by the number the recording reached on the *Billboard* charts.

GOLD/PLATINUM RECORDS Gold or platinum recordings are mentioned in the editors' comments when applicable.

HOW TO USE THIS BOOK

ALBUM TITLE The name of the album as it appears on the original when possible. Very long titles have been abbreviated, or repeated in full as part of the comment, where needed.

RECORD LABEL Record labels have always been useful in locating albums. However, in today's ever-changing music scene, many albums tend to appear on more than one label. As for label numbers, forget it. They change so fast that we have not included them here. If you are searching for a title, it is best to look up albums by artist name and album title.

COMMENTS Album comments are brief, due to space limitations. We hope they can provide details of value in album selection.

COMMENT AUTHORS The initials of each comment's author are given at the end of the comment. A list of these authors can be found in the table of contents and inside the front cover.

CLASSICAL RATING SYSTEM

The classical section uses a different star-rating system than elsewhere in the book, since here we have individual compositions that are performed by many different groups rather than unique albums.

○ An open circle marks the beginning of an individual composition, and additional performances of that piece are listed underneath, but are unmarked. It is important to note that multiple performances of a classical piece are listed *in order of preference* by the reviewers. In other words, the first performance listed is the pick, the second is the next best, and so on.

☆ Stars here indicate the most popular compositions for the composer, and should be part of any comprehensive collection of classical music.

Major/Minor—Listings in major keys are indicated with a capital letter (A, B, C, etc.) and minor pieces in lower case (a, b, c). Thus Mozart's "Great" mass in C minor would be listed as "Mass in c," and so on.

MISSISSIPPI JOHN HURT   1893-1966

Acoustic country blues. An exquisite country blues singer and guitarist with a subtle voice and refined finger-picking guitar style, Hurt recorded in the 20s and again in the 60s. Both periods are well worth hearing: acoustic country blues with real technical clarity that is also comforting and easy to listen to. He never made a recording not worth hearing. With a gospel flavor in his blues, Mississippi John Hurt projects a sense of dignity and kindliness through all of his recordings. If you have trouble with the frequent heaviness of many blues players, you may find Hurt refreshing. He is one of a kind, and a kind one at that. –JME

Today / VANGUARD   1966
A fine 60s album. –JME

○ **Immortal Mississippi John Hurt** / VANGUARD   1967
The best of Hurt's 60s "rediscovery-era" recordings. –MH

The Best of Mississippi John Hurt / VANGUARD   1971
A great double-album collection of 60s Hurt. –JME

★ **1928 Sessions** / YAZOO / DB 5   1988
Justifiably legendary, with gentle grace and power on these understated masterpieces of finger-picked guitar and vocals. This is the one to get. These are the early (1928) recordings, which are very fine. –JME & MH

YEAR OF RELEASE The year of an album's first release (and/or recording) is included where available in all cases except jazz. Jazz dates refer to the recording date, unless marked with an "i" (date of issue/release), or an "r" (date when reviewed in DOWN BEAT or *Cadence* magazines). We have made every attempt to verify album dates. However, we apologize in advance for any inadvertent mistakes. If you have more accurate information, please write us.

3

ABOUT THE EDITORS

Here are the people whose combined talents in music make this book possible. Included with the biographies are "desert island" lists — the artists, groups, and recordings the editors would take with them to a deserted island. Note that the editors' initials, appearing after their names, show up throughout the book with the recordings on which they have commented.

MICHAEL ERLEWINE   JME

Michael Erlewine is the editor of the *All-Music Guide*. In 1965 he helped form the Prime Movers Blues Band in Michigan, the first such band, and a pace-setter; he was the lead singer and played amplified harmonica. The original band included a number of now well-known musicians, including Iggy Pop (drums), "Blue" Gene Tyranny (piano; now a well-known avant-garde classical composer), Jack Dawson (bass; became bass player for Siegal-Schwall Blues Band), and Michael's brother Daniel Erlewine (lead guitar; now monthly columnist for *Guitar Player* magazine). Michael has extensively interviewed blues performers, both in video and audio, and, along with his band, helped shape the first few Ann Arbor Blues Festivals.

Today, Michael is a computer programmer and the director of Matrix Software. The *All-Music Guide*, aside from this book, is being prepared as a CD-ROM for home computers and as an on-line service in record stores across the country. In addition to its music operations, Matrix Software is the largest center for astrological programming and research in the Western hemisphere. Michael has been a practicing astrologer for almost 30 years and has an international reputation in that field.

Michael Erlewine is active in Tibetan Buddhism and serves as the director of Heart Center Karma Thegsum Chöling, a main center in North America for the translation, transcription, and publication of texts and teachings of the Karma Kagyu Lineage of Tibetan Buddhism.

J. S. Bach _____ (Keyboard works and cantatas)
       The Art of Fugue (Die Kunst der Fuge) (Archive)
Big Walter Horton _____ *Chicago: The Blues Today –*
       Vol. 3 (Vanguard)
Grant Green _____ *The Complete Blue Note Recordings*
       of Grant Green, with Sonny Clark (Mosaic)
Wolfgang Amadeus Mozart _____ (Anything in E flat)
       Divertimento in E Flat, K. 563 (CALIG)
Erik Satie _____ *Mass for the Poor*
       (And almost all the piano music)
Aaron Neville _____ (The early Minit and Parlo recordings)
       Tell It like It Is ... Great Golden Classics (Collectables)
William Clarke _____ *Blowin' like Hell & Serious*
       Intentions (Alligator)
John Coltrane _____ (Early and mid-period)
       Blue Train (Blue Note); *My Favorite Things* (Atlantic)
Miles Davis _____ (Early and mid-period)
       Kind of Blue (Columbia); the Prestige recordings
       (*Walkin', Bag's Groove, Cookin', Relaxin', Steamin'*)

Aside from the individual artists and composers listed above, I also depend on certain genres of music for my musical diet. Here are several of them:

Funk or Soul Jazz of all kinds _____
       Jimmy Smith, Stanley Turrentine, Shirley Scott, Richard "Groove" Holmes, Jimmy McGriff, Jack McDuff
Country and Folk _____
       Artists such as Kitty Wells, Jimmie Rodgers, early Hank Lochlan, Joan Baez, Gordon Lightfoot, Doc Watson, and Hank Williams.
Classic Rock _____
       Last, but not least, how could I live without the singles from artists and groups such as Jerry Butler, the Shirelles, Brenton Wood, Barbara Lewis, Shep and the Limelites, the Heartbeats, the Five Satins, the Skyliners, the Penguins, the Fleetwoods, the Platters, the Flamingos, the Drifters, and Santo and Johnny.

SCOTT BULTMAN   SWB

Scott Bultman is the associate editor of the *All-Music Guide*. He began his musical career in high school, playing guitar in a band with classmates, at the birth of MTV and the music-video generation. He attended the University of Michigan, taking art, music, and film classes. He took an extended leave in New Zealand and Australia, seeking the roots of the great Aussie rock sound of bands such as Midnight Oil, Australian Crawl, Split Enz, and others. Back at the University of Michigan, he pursued both a film/video degree and a music degree specializing in electronic music composition. Scott played in the University's Javanese gamelan ensemble for two years and gained music industry experience working in a record store and for a local concert promoter. After graduation, Scott built a MIDI-based electronic music studio and wrote and distributed MIDI software for Atari computers. He pursues an interest in MIDI recording and software and publishes the *Electronic Alliance* newsletter to support local electronic musicians.

Beatles _____ *Rubber Soul*
James Brown _____ *30 Greatest Hits 1954-1978*
Crowded House _____ *Wood Face*
Jimmy Cliff _____ *Reggae Greats*
Prefab Sprout _____ *Jordan: The Comeback*
Midnight Oil _____ *10-9-8-7-6-5-4-3-2-1*
Various Artists _____ *16 Gospel Greats*
Billie Holiday _____ *The Billie Holiday Story - Vols. 1-3*
David Sylvian _____ *Secrets of the Beehive*
Pennies from Heaven _____ *Soundtrack*

4

Ambrosia...(Self-titled)
Squeeze...*Argy Bargy*

STEPHEN ALDRICH   SA

Stephen Aldrich has spent a decade at WLAV-FM radio in Grand Rapids, MI, hosting everything from oldies shows to the long-running alternative new-music show "Clambake." He is also a musician who works with a wide variety of groups, including pioneering Michigan punk rockers such as the Infections and Profile recording artists such as Euro-K. Aldrich has written and photographed for a number of publications. He is a contributor to *Music Review*, a Michigan entertainment monthly.

Scott Walker...*Scott 1-4*
John Coltrane...*Any Impulses*
Frank Sinatra...*Ring-A-Ding-Ding*
Duke Ellington.....................*The Blanton-Webster Band*
Beach Boys...*Pet Sounds*
Bill Evans.............*Trio albums with LaFaro and Motian*
The Byrds..............................*Younger than Yesterday*
Jefferson Airplane............................*Surrealistic Pillow*
Only Ones..(Self-titled)
Tim Buckley..*Starsailor*
Moby Grape...*1st*
Miles Davis

GEORGE BEDARD   GB

George Bedard is not only a great rock guitarist; he is sensitive to the history of the music and addresses the challenge of taking the music to a higher level. Bedard excels at the music of the Beatles and the Byrds and such blues legends as B. B. King, T-Bone Walker, and Otis Rush. Bedard's interest embraces the golden era of country & western as well as jazz. He and his group the Bonnevilles have received awards. Bedard's current group, a trio known as the Kingpins, has been called "the best rockabilly pickers on the planet."

MYLES BOISEN   MB

Myles Boisen graduated from Western Washington University in 1979 with a self-designed major in 20th-century media and contemporary art. He is active in the San Francisco area and has several recordings of jazz and improvised music. He is record review editor of *Roots & Rhythm*, has contributed to *Down-Home Guide to the Blues* and the *San Francisco Weekly* magazine, and is editor for and contributor to the newsletter of the *Improvised Music Association*.

Fred Frith..*Gravity*
Captain Beefheart & the Magic Band....*Trout Mask Replica*
Orvette Coleman..........................*Dancing in Your Head*
Burundi...(Traditional music)
Link Wray..........................(Any, the earlier the better)
Nina Rota..............................(Any Fellini soundtrack)
MX-80 Sound...*Hard Attack*
Barry Altschul.............*You Can't Name Your Own Tune*
Charles Mingus..........*The Complete Candid Recordings*
Rakotozafy................*Famous valiha-madagasikara IV*
Mahmoud Ahmed.................................*Ere Mela Mela*
Atlantic........*A Rhythm & Blues Saxophone Anthology*

JOHN BOOK   JB

John Book was a DJ and station manager for his high school radio station while writing record reviews for the "The B-Side

Report." In 1989 he began writing for *Hot Stops* magazine and *Psychedelic Hemisphere* and has had reviews and a feature article published in *Goldmine*. His work has appeared in *Fringe* (Japan), *Metal Assault* (Canada), and *Rock around the World*. He contributes to *Curious Goods, DiscRespect, Lintfit*, and *Maximum Rock 'n' Roll* and publishes his own magazine, *Intensity*.

The Beatles..*Abbey Road*
Pink Floyd.............................*The Dark Side of the Moon*
Funkadelic........................*One Nation under a Groove*
Sunday Manoa...3
Rolling Stones................................*Exile on Main Street*
Public Enemy............*It Takes a Nation of Millions ...*
Melvins Gluey.......................................*Porch Treatments*
James Brown...*Star Time*
Mr. Bungle..*Mr. Bungle*
K. D. Lang...*Ingenue*
Richard Pryor.............................*Bicentennial Nigger*
Various Artists...*Woodstock*

ROB BOWMAN   RB

Rob Bowman is a journalist and musicologist living in Toronto. He was the first person to teach courses on rock and R & B at a Canadian university. He has written about music extensively since 1971 and has twice been nominated for Grammy Awards, once for coproducing *The Otis Redding Story* and again for his liner notes accompanying *The Complete Stax/Volt Singles 1959-1968*. He hosts a weekly radio show, teaches in the music department at York University, sits on Grammy and Juno committees, continues to write freelance, and plugs away at a book on Stax Records.

James Brown...*Star Time*
Otis Redding...............................*The Otis Redding Story*
Al Green.....................................*Greatest Hits 1 & 2*
Aretha Franklin...................(Rhino-Atlantic boxed set)
Bob Dylan...*Biograph*
Van Morrison............................*St. Dominic's Preview*
Velvet Underground........*Velvet Underground and Nico*
The Band...*To Kingdom Come*
Parliament........*Funkadelic Mothership Connection*
The Meters-Neville Brothers..........................*Yellow Moon*
Miles Davis...*Kind of Blue*
Muddy Waters................................(Chess boxed set)

RICK BUECHE   RAB

Rick Bueche is a music expert and researcher at Motown Records. He has collected Motown recordings since the 60s, interviewed numerous Motown artists, and writes freelance for several Louisiana publications.

Diana Ross and the Supremes..........(Motown anthology)
The Four Tops....................................(Motown anthology)
The Temptations................................(Motown anthology)
Martha Reeves and the Vandellas........(Motown anthology)
Smokey Robinson and the Miracles......(Motown anthology)
Marvin Gaye.....................................(Motown anthology)
Marvin Gaye...*What's Goin' On*
Pointer Sisters...*Break Out*
Supremes...*Right On*
The Four Tops...*Reach Out*
Stevie Wonder.......................................*Love Songs*
Mary Wells........*Compact Command Performances*

BIL CARPENTER   BC

Bil Carpenter is a music researcher and expert on gospel music. He has worked for the Smithsonian Institute, edited the *Journal of Gospel Music*, and written freelance for *Goldmine*, the *Journal of Gospel Music*, *Living Blues*, the *Washington New Observer*, *Rejoice*,and *American Gospel*.

Laura Lee	*Love More than Pride*
Fleetwood Mac	*Rumours*
Dionne Warwick	*Make Way for Dionne*
Bruce Springsteen	*Born in the USA*
Tom Petty	*Damn the Torpedos*
Natalie Cole	*Natalie*
Aretha Franklin	*Sparkle*
Various Artists	*Stax Singles 1959-1968*
Captain and Tennille	*Song of Joy*
Rufus Featuring Chaka Khan	(Self-titled)
Bob Dylan	*Slow Train Coming*
Willie Nelson	*Always on My Mind*

KENNETH M. CASSIDY   KMC

Ken Cassidy is a freelance video producer, music consultant, critic, and researcher for ASCAP. He has written record and theater reviews for *Good Times*, published an article in *Goldmine*, done video reviews for *North Shore Today*, and has extensive experience in recorded music.

Beatles	*Meet the Beatles*
Bob Dylan	*Blood on the Tracks*
Frank Sinatra	*Songs for Swinging Lovers*
Fred Astaire	*Starring Fred Astaire*
The Byrds	*Younger than Yesterday*
Rolling Stones	*Between the Buttons*
The Kinks	*Something Else by the Kinks*
The Band	(Self-titled)
Phil Ochs	*Chords of Fame*
John Lennon	*Plastic Ono Band*
Ella Fitzgerald	*The Songbooks*
Motown	*The Motown Story: The First Decade*

RICK CLARK   RC

Rick Clark has appeared in *Billboard*, *Music Express*, *Request*, *Mix*, *Agent/Manager*, *Rock & Roll Disc*, *Digital Audio*, *Goldmine*, and *Rolling Stone*, among others. He is a songwriter with chart success, a musician (bass, keys, vocals), producer, and, since 1969, has worked in many styles, with many artists, touring and handling session work.

Marvin Gaye	*What's Goin' On*
Stax	(Boxed set)
Alantic R & B	(Boxed set)
Bruce Cockburn	
The Byrds	
Big Star	
Van Morrison	
The Kinks	
Badfinger	
Bob Dylan	
Neil Young	
The Beatles	
Creedence Clearwater Revival	

BILL DAHL   BD

Bill Dahl is a freelance music journalist for the Chicago Tribune, *Living Blues*, *Goldmine*, and many others. He is a contributor to the *Blackwell Guide to Soul Recordings*, *T•I•N•A* (a biography of Tina Turner), and *Rock 'n' Roll Trivia*, as well as an author of numerous album and CD liner notes and a former blues and oldies radio DJ.

Jerry Lee Lewis	*Greatest Hits*
Fats Domino	*They Call Me the Fat Man*
Ricky Nelson	*Legendary Masters – Vols. 1 & 2*
Chuck Berry	(Chess boxed set)
Elvis Presley	*Sun Sessions*
Freddy King	*Just Pickin'*
Wilson Pickett	*Greatest Hits*
Otis Redding	*Otis Redding Story*
Junior Walker	*Shotgun/Roadrunner*
Muddy Waters	(Chess boxed set)
Carl Perkins	*Best of Carl Perkins*
Little Richard	*Specialty Sessions*

HANK DAVIS   HD

Hank Davis is a musician and a freelance writer for *Goldmine*, *Living Blues*, *Country Sounds*, and *Discoveries*. He has written liner notes for Capitol, Sun, Bear Family, Charly, EMI, Polygram, Krazy Kat, Edsel, and Mercury.

The Band	*The Band*
The Beatles	*Magical Mystery Tour*
Bobby Blue Bland	*Here's the Man*
Fats Domino	*They Call Me the Fat Man*
Hank Davis	*Crazy Living*
Percy Mayfield	*Poet of the Blues*
Thelonious Monk	*Tokyo Concerts*
Hank Wiliams	(Original singles collection)
Jerry Lee Lewis	*Classic* (complete Sun recordings)
Charlie Rich	*Original Hits & Midnight Demos*
Various Artists: Sun Records	*The Country Years*
Les Paul	*Legend & Legacy*

MICHAEL P. DAWSON   MPD

Michael P. Dawson is a freelance writer for *Goldmine*, *Musician*, and *Option*. His many feature articles in *Goldmine* cover Gentle Giant, Cuneiform, Procol Harum, Marillion, Keith Emerson, Can, Firesign Theatre, and Yes.

Frank Zappa	*Uncle Meat*
Jethro Tull	*A Passion Play*
King Crimson	*Lizard*
Emerson, Lake & Palmer	*Brain Salad Surgery*
Yes	*Tales from Topographic Oceans*
Gentle Giant	*Octopus*
Stravinsky	*The Rite of Spring*
Varese	*Amériques*
Eric Dolphy	*Out to Lunch*
John Coltrane	*The Major Works of John Coltrane*
Fripp and Edno	*No Pussyfooting*
The Lemon Pipers	*Green Tambourine*

ROBERT DEFREITAS   RDF

Robert DeFreitas is an avid Kiss collector and a lover of rock music.

DONNA DICHARIO   DDC

From 1989 to 1991, Donna DiChario was rock critic and weekly columnist for the Rochester, NY, Democrat and Chronicle. She has written for *Rock & Roll Disc* since 1989.

Bob Dylan	*Blood on the Tracks*
Pink Floyd	*Dark Side of the Moon*
Guns 'n' Roses	*Appetite for Destruction*
Fleetwood Mac	*Rumours*
Jimi Hendrix	*Are You Experienced?*
Jeff Beck	
Ray Charles	
Miles Davis	
The Beatles	
Led Zeppelin	
Sinead O'Connor	
Stevie Ray Vaughan	

JOHN DOUGAN   JD

John Dougan has been writing about music since Quicksilver Messenger Service released *Happy Trails*. He has been pop critic for the Springfield, MA, Daily News and an editor for the *Boston Edge*. His work has appeared in numerous magazines and journals, including *Spin*, *In These Times*, *Option*, *Asymptote*, City Pages, and the *Utne Reader*. He is now a contributor to *Rock & Roll Disc*, where he co-authors the monthly column "Sounding Off." Originally from the eastern US, he now lives in Minneapolis, where he remains a fan of the Ramones and the Boston Celtics.

Al Green	*Call Me*
Ramones	*Rocket to Russia*
Sun Ra	*Anything*
Lee Perry	*Build the Ark and Open the Gate*
Muddy Waters	(Chess boxed set)
Miles Davis	*Aghanda*
George Jones	*Best of 1955-1967*
Sex Pistols	*Never Mind the Bollocks*
Aretha Franklin	*Spirit in the Dark*
Van Morrison	*It's Too Late to Stop Now!*
Clash	*London Calling*
Rolling Stones	*Exile on Main Street*

BRUCE EDER   BE

Bruce Eder is a reviewer, feature writer, and researcher for *Goldmine*, *Video Magazine*, and *Current Biography*. He has contributed to *Village Voice*, *Newsday*, *V Magazine*, *Aquarian Weekly*, *New York Arts Weekly*, *Our Town*, *Interview Magazine*, and *Video Review*. He has worked on a variety of film, laser-disc, and music productions, including the reissues of a great many CDs (soundtracks in particular); has contributed to the *Rolling Stones Singles Collection* and the *Bo Diddley London Sessions*; and is vice president of the Society for British Music, a soundtrack expert, and producer for Sony Special Products.

Elvis Presley	*The Sun Sessions*
Buddy Holly	(Self-titled)
Sparkletones	*Collection*
Beatles	*Please Please Me*
Rolling Stones	*Got Live If You Want It*
Bo Diddley	*Bo Diddley's Beach Party*
Ralph Vaughan Williams	*Symphony no. 2*
	(Sir John Barbirolli and the Halle Orchestra)

Genesis	*Selling England by the Pound*
Yardbirds	*Having a Rave-Up*
Chris Squire	*Fish out of Water*
Bernard Herrmann	*Obsession* (soundtrack)
Yes	*Close to the Edge*

THE ERLEWINE FAMILY

Music is very much a part of the extended Erlewine family, many of whom contributed to make this book possible. In addition to Michael (editor of the *All-Music Guide*) and all those listed in the acknowledgements who helped produce the book, the following Erlewines were editors.

DAN ERLEWINE   RDE

Dan Erlewine is a veteran guitar repairer who has worked for such players as Mike Bloomfield, Ted Nugent, Jerry Garcia, and Albert King (whose guitar "Lucy" he built in 1972). After producing the "Dan Erlewine Guitar Hospital" series of videotapes on guitar repair in 1984, he began writing a monthly repair column for *Guitar Player* magazine in 1985. Based on the success of his these columns, in 1990 he produced an internationally successful book, *Guitar Player Repair Guide*, for *Guitar Player*'s parent company, Miller Freeman Publications. Dan is now the resident repair research expert for Stewart-MacDonald's Guitar Shop Supply in Athens, OH, a leading company in the guitar field.

John Hiatt	*Slow Turning*
B. B. King	*Live at the Regal*
Billie Holiday	*The Quintessential Billie Holiday*
Nat King Cole Trio	*Trio Days* (Capitol Jazz Classics – Vol. 8)
Bud Powell	*Amazing Bud Powell* (Blue Note – Vols. 1 & 2)
James Booker	*New Orleans Piano Wizard: Live!*
Elmore James	*I Need You*
Delbert McClinton	*Live from Austin*
T-Bone Walker	*Dirty Mistreater*
Magic Sam	*West Side Soul*
Albert King	*The Big Blues*
Robert Johnson	*King of the Delta Blues*

MEREDITH ERLEWINE   ME

Meredith Erlewine is the daughter of Guitar Player columnist Daniel Erlewine. She is a junior at Ohio University, a bicyclist, and a lover of live music.

The Beatles
David Bowie
The Rolling Stones
Phish
Bob Dylan
Neil Young
Mudhoney
Public Enemy
The Grateful Dead
Donald Fagen
The Red Hot Chili Peppers
Jimi Hendrix

IOTIS ERLEWINE   IME

Iotis Erlewine is a sophomore at the University of Michigan, a bass player, and, like all the Erlewine family members, an avid music buff.

Paul Simon	*Graceland*
Bob Dylan	*Desire/Blood on the Tracks*

Sting...................................*Dream of the Blue Turtles*
J. S. Bach
Bob Marley
John Coltrane
R. E. M.
The Beatles
The Chieftains
Ella Jenkins
John Denver (early)
Hoi Polloi

MICHAEL ANNE ERLEWINE   MAE

Anne Erlewine is a high school senior in Big Rapids, MI, a pianist, and the 1991 Michigan state cross-country running champion.

Grateful Dead..........*Skeletons from the Closet* (The best of)
Simon and Garfunkel.........................*Collected Works*
10,000 Maniacs......................................*In My Tribe*
Beatles...*White Album*
U2..*Joshua Tree*
George Winston......................................*December*
Jimmy Smith.......................*Back in the Chicken Shack*
Rolling Stones...*Hot Rocks*
R. E. M..*Lifes Rich Pageant*
Tracy Chapman................................*Tracy Chapman*
The Police............................*Every Breath You Take*
Ella Jenkins..............................(Any children's albums)
The Singles

STEPHEN THOMAS ERLEWINE   STE

Tommy Erlewine is the assistant editor of the *All-Music Guide*, a freelance music writer, and a DJ at WCMU in Ann Arbor. He is a sophomore at the University of Michigan.

The Beatles
Bob Dylan
The Rolling Stones
Howlin' Wolf
Chuck Berry
Prince
Miles Davis
Public Enemy
Led Zeppelin
The Velvet Underground
The Replacements
Bob Wills and His Texas Playboys

COLIN ESCOTT   CE

Colin Escott is a Toronto-based music journalist whose book, *Good Rockin' Tonight: The Sun Records Story*, is published by St. Martin's Press. He has written many liner notes for Polygram, Rhino, MCA, CBS, Bear Family, RCA, Atlantic, Rounder, and Time-Life.

The Blue Sky Boys....................*The Blue Sky Boys*
Jimmy Giuffre Three.................*Train and the River*
Howlin' Wolf............................*The Howlin' Wolf Box*
Django Reinhardt.............................*QHCF Souvenirs*
Hank Williams...........*The Original Singles Collection*
The Stanley Brothers................................*1949-1952*
Fairground Attraction...........*First of a Million Kisses*
Lester Young..............................(Time-Life boxed set)

Jimmy Reed.................................*I'm Jimmy Reed*
Merle Travis...................*The Merle Travis Guitar*
Los Lobos...................*La Pistola y el Corazon*
Jerry Lee Lewis...................*Live at the Star Club*

PHIL FINK   PF

Phil Fink has been the host of "Shalom America" since 1966, providing the Cleveland, OH, area with Jewish music, news, and information. Proficient in Hebrew and Yiddish, he is able to add a word or two about the meaning of the music he plays. Phil is also a Jewish humorist, telling stories about Jewish people throughout the US and Canada.

JOHN FLOYD   JF

John Floyd has written reviews, essays, and articles in *Musician, Rock and Roll Confidential, The Journal of Country Music, MD, Rock & Roll Disc, Goldmine*, The Minneapolis City Pages, Spectrum Weekly, *Buzz, It's Hip*, and *Memphis Magazine*. He is associate editor for The Memphis Flyer, an alternative-news weekly.

The Band....................................*The Band*
Sly and the Family Stone.........*There's a Riot Goin' On*
Bob Dylan.............................*Blonde on Blonde*
Marvin Gaye...........................*What's Goin' On*
James Brown.....................*Live at the Apollo '62*
Elvis Costello............................*This Year's Model*
Rolling Stones.......................*Beggar's Banquet*
The Clash..............................*London Calling*
The Who......................................*Who's Next*
Stevie Wonder............................*Talking Book*
Bruce Springsteen..........................*The River*
Derek and the Dominoes.......*Layla/Assorted Love Songs*

NILES J. FRANTZ   NJF

Niles Frantz is the host of "Comin' Home," a program of blues and related music on Jazz 90, the Temple Public Radio Network — circulation 230,000 in the Pennsylvania, New Jersey, and Delaware areas. He has written for *Living Blues; Blues & Rhythm: The Gospel Truth; Juke Blues; Philadelphia People*; and *Tempo*, the Jazz 90 listener guide.

Muddy Waters...........................(Chess boxed set)
Albert Collins.............*The Complete Imperial Recordings*
T-Bone Walker..*The Complete T-Bone Walker 1940-1954*
Bessie Smith.............*The Complete Recordings – Vol. 1*
Blind Willie McTell..............*The Early Years, 1927-1933*
Jimmy Yancey..................*Chicago Piano – Vol. 1*
Joe Louis Walker....................................*The Gift*
Jimi Hendrix...*Stages*
Prince.................................*Sign o' the Times*
Stevie Ray Vaughan..................................*In Step*
Brian Eno......................*Another Green World*
Fela Kuti......................................*Upside Down*

ROBERT GORDON   RG

Robert Gordon writes for most major music publications, is publisher and editor of *Asymptote* literary magazine, and received the 1991 Handy Award, "Keeping the Blues Alive in Journalism." He directed and edited the blues documentary video *All Day and All Night* and has made music videos for Mojo Nixon, Tav Falco's Unapproachable Panther Burns, and the Flat Duo Jets, among others. He is writing a documentary on the continuing impact of music in Memphis.

Jerry Jeff Walker	*Ridin' High*
Big Star	*3rd*
Rufus Thomas	*Walkin' the Dog*
K. C. and the Sunshine Band	*That's the Way I Like It*
Freedy Johnston	*Can You Fly*
Bob Dylan	*New Morning*
The Replacements	*Let It Be*
Cuban Classics 2	*Dancing with the Enemy*
Furry Lewis	*Live at the Gaslight*
Dan Penn	*Skin*
Louvin Brothers	*Live at Red River Ranch*
King Curtis	

TOM GRAVES   TG

Tom Graves is the editor of *Rock & Roll Disc* and has been published in *Musician* and *Rolling Stone*.

DAN HEILMAN   DH

Dan Heilman has writen about music professionally since 1982. He has edited several music magazines and is a former music editor for the Minneapolis City Pages. His work has appeared in *Billboard, The Village Voice, Rock & Roll Confidential*, Minneapolis Star Tribune, *Rock & Roll Disc, BuZZ, Artpaper*, and *Cake*.

Elvis Presley	*Elvis Is Back!*
Bruce Springsteen	*Live 1975-1985*
The Beatles	*With the Beatles*
Bob Dylan	*Highway 61 Revisited*
Johnny Cash	*The Sun Years*
Elvis Costello	*This Year's Model*
Public Enemy	*It Takes a Nation of Millions …*
Louis Prima	*The Wildest!*
Frank Sinatra	*September of My Years*
The Who	*Quadrophenia*
Rolling Stones	*Exile on Main Street*
The Kinks	*The Kink Kronicles*

JEFF HANNUSCH   JH

A native of Canada now living in New Orleans, Jeff Hannusch has written liner notes for over 100 albums, including *They Call Me the Fat Man, Antoine "Fats" Domino*, and *The Legendary Imperial Recordings*. Hannusch won the 1986 American Book Award for *I Hear You Knockin': The Sound of New Orleans*. He has been published in *Billboard, Rolling Stone*, USA Today, and *Goldmine*, among others.

BOB HINKLE   BH

Bob Hinkle is president of Zoom Express, a media and marketing company for children's and family products (partnered with BMG Kidz). He was the president of Bob Hinkle Management and of The Children's Group, which managed and/or released Tom Chapin, Red Grammer, and Classical Kids. He has written, performed, and produced music, promoted concerts, and managed the J. Geils Band, Harry Chapin, Manfred Mann, Naked Eyes, and others.

Red Grammer	*Teaching Peace*
Uncle Fred Miller	*Let Your Inside Out*
Lois LaFond	*One World*
Miles Davis	*Sketches of Spain*
Classical Kids	*Beethoven Lives Upstairs*
Peter Combe	*Chopsticks*
Glenn Bennett	*I Like My Music with a Beat*

Handel	Messiah (London SO & Chorus)
The J. Geils Band	*Freeze Frame*
Ray Charles	*Genius + Soul = Jazz*
Flatt and Scruggs	*Live at Carnegie Hall*
Stan Freeberg	*Stan Freeberg Presents the United States of America*

TERRI HINTE   TH

Terri Hinte is a 19-year music business veteran who has been Director of Press & Public Information for Berkeley's Fantasy Records since 1979. Her longtime love for Brazilian music led to extensive travel throughout Brazil. In the mid 80s, she managed several North American tours for Azymuth, Fantasy's Rio-based jazz fusion trio.

MARK A. HUMPHREY   MH

Mark Humphrey has been a freelance journalist since 1979. Until 1984, he was a frequent contributor to *Frets*, an acoustic stringed instrument magazine. His reviews and profiles have appeared in *The Los Angeles Reader, Old Timey Music*, Los Angeles Daily News, *Guitar Player, Esquire, Journal of Country Music, Playboy*, and others. Since 1983, he has been a regular contributor to *Record Roundup*; has written liner notes for Robert Wilkins' *Memphis Gospel Singer, Blue Flame: A Sun Blues Collection* and for the forthcoming reissue of Muddy Waters' '70s CBS recordings. He is writing a booklet for a Lightnin' Hopkins and Otis Spann Mosaic reissue; has written "Prodigal Sons: Son House and Robert Wilkins," for the International Conference on African-American Music and Literature, on religion versus secularity in African-American music. He is a singer, songwriter, and guitarist.

Howlin' Wolf	*Change My Way*
Bob Wills and the Texas Playboys	*Bob Wills Anthology*
Joseph Spence	*Good Morning, Mr. Walker*
Bill Monroe	*Country Music Hall of Fame* (series)
Jimmie Rodgers	*America's Blue Yodeler, 1930-1931*
Doc Watson	(Self-titled – first Vanguard album)
Hank Williams	*Rare Demos: First to Last*
The Falcons	*I Found a Love*
Roy Harris	*Symphony no. 3*
The Ventures	*Batman Theme*
Roscoe Holcomb	*The High Lonesome Sound*

JULIAN KATZ   JK

Julian Katz (son of Michael Katz, below) attends the Rhode Island School of Design, majoring in illustration.

The Minutemen	*Double Nickels on the Dime*
No Means No	*Wrong*
The Beastie Boys	*Paul's Boutique*
Bad Brains	*Rock for Light*
The Red Hot Chili Peppers	*Uplift Mofo Party Plan*
Funkadelic	*Maggot Brain*
fIREHOSE	*Ragin', Full On*
Nick Cave and the Bad Seeds	*Your Funeral, My Trial*
Fishbone	*Fishbone*
Tom Waits	*Frank's Wild Years*
James Brown	*In the Jungle Groove*
Dead Kennedys	*Give Me Convenience or Give Me Death*

MICHAEL KATZ   MK

Michael Katz, father of Julian Katz, is an emergency room physician in the San Francisco Bay area. He has no formal training or particular talent in music, but was not prevented from forming a psychedelic rock & roll band in 1966, the San Francisco-based Anonymous Artists of America.

Charles Mingus	*Jazz at Antibes* (Atlantic)
Buddy Holly	*From the Original Master Tapes* (MCA)
Gerry Mulligan and Chet Baker	*Pacific Jazz Recordings*
Mozart	Don Giovanni (Giulini/EMI)
The Beatles	*Beatles for Sale*
Elvis Costello	*My Aim Is True*
The Rolling Stones	*Between the Buttons*
Elvis Presley	*Sun Sessions*
Ike and Tina Turner	*Best Of*
Giuseppe Verdi	*La Traviata* (Callas)
(Soundtrack)	*The Big Easy*
(Soundtrack)	*Repo Man*

KIT KIEFER   KK

Kit Kiefer is formerly the managing editor of *Goldmine*. He wrote *They Called It Rock: The Goldmine Oral History of Rock 'n' Roll* and has written *Goldmine* articles on many rock & roll groups.

Benny Goodman Sextet	*Slipped Disc*
Paul Kelly and the Messengers	*Under the Sun*
Warren Zevon	*Warren Zevon*
The Blasters	*The Blasters*
Ry Cooder	*Paradise and Lunch*
Phil Cunningham	*Airs and Graces*
Dave Edmunds	*DE7*
Richard/Linda Thompson	*I Want to See the Bright Lights*
Nick Lowe	*Pure Pop for Now People*
Graham Parker	*Squeezing Out Sparks*
Tommy Keene	*Places That Are Gone*
dBs	*Sound of Music*

CUB KODA   CK

Cub Koda is a founding member of the Brownsville Station hard-rock group. He is a freelance writer for *Goldmine*, a contributor to *Rock 'n' Roll Disc*, and a compiler and annotator for Rhino Records.

Merle Travis	*The Merle Travis Guitar*
Jimmy Reed and Eddie Taylor	*Ride 'em on Down*
Carl Perkins	*Original Sun Greatest Hits*
Chuck Berry	*Is on Top*
Bo Diddley	*Bo Diddley's Beach Party*
Jerry Lee Lewis	*Live at the Star Club*
Howlin' Wolf	*Moanin' in the Moonlight*
Chet Atkins	*Finger-Style Guitar*
Travis Wammack	*That Scratchy Guitar from Memphis*
Nolan Strong and the Diablos	*Fortune of Hits – Vol. 1*
Spike Jones	*Thank You, Music Lovers!*
Hound Dog Taylor and the Houserockers	

LINDA KOHANOV   LK

With interests ranging from worldbeat to jazz, rock, and the classical avant-garde, Linda Kohanov is a versatile critic and contributor for a number of national magazines. In addition to writing reviews and artist profiles for *Jazz Times*, *New Age Journal*, and *Free Spirit*, she serves as the contemporary instrumental columnist for *Pulse*, the "Contempo" column (popular jazz) for *Jazziz*, and the "Worldbeat" column for *CD- Review*. (Some of her material in this book was derived

from articles and reviews previously published in *Pulse* and *CD-Review*). Kohanov has a degree in music from Miami University and has played the viola with regional orchestras and chamber music groups in Ohio and Florida. She worked as a program director, producer, and announcer at several radio stations, including seven years at the Florida fine arts station WUWF-FM in Pensacola and, currently, on-air host at classical station KUAT-FM and jazz station KUAZ-FM in Tuscon. Her interest in Middle Eastern percussion techniques has led to live and recorded performances on frame drum and other percussion instruments, including collaborations with her husband, composer/synthesist Steve Roach.

Arvo Pärt	*Tabula Rasa*
Suso Saiz	*Simbolos*
Steve Roach	*Dreamtime Return*
John Coltrane	*A Love Supreme*
Djivan Gasparyan	*I Will Not Be Sad in This World*
Hamza El Din	*Eclipse*
Alan Hovhaness	*Shalimar*
K.D. Lang	*Ingenue*
Terry Riley	*Salome Dances for Peace*
Bartok	*Concerto for Orchestra*
Miles Davis	*Kind of Blue*
Ali Akbar Khan	*Signature Series – Vol. 1*

PAUL KOHLER   PK

Paul Kohler, an expert on jazz and rock fusion, has studied guitar and music theory since 1980.

Allan Holdsworth	(All albums)
Eric Johnson	*Tones*
Frank Gambale	*Live!*
Steve Morse	*High Tension Wires*
Michael Brecker	(All albums)
Chick Corea	*Three Quartets*
Claus Ogerman	*Cityscape* (Featuring Michael Brecker)
Bill Connors	*Step It!*
Al DiMeola	(All albums)
Bob Berg	*Short Stories*
Bill Bruford	*One of a Kind*
Tony Williams	*Believe It!*

LAWRENCE LAPKA   LL

Larry Lapka is a record collector, music critic, and publisher of the award-winning music fanzine *Hear Again*.

The Monkees	*Headquarters*
The Beatles	*Magical Mystery Tour*
Paul Revere and the Raiders	*Spirit of '67*
The Dave Clark Five	*Glad All Over Again* (compilation)
Herman's Hermits	*Herman's Hermits XX* (compilation)
Cheap Trick	*Live at Budokan*
Elvis Costello	*This Year's Model*
Grassroots	*Let's Live for Today*
The Supremes	*Where Did Our Love Go?*
R. E. M.	*Out of Time*
Sly and the Family Stone	*There's a Riot Going On*
Simon and Garfunkel	*Bookends*

ROBERT LEAVER   RVR

Robert Leaver is the director of Round World Music, a record store specializing in contemporary and traditional African, Arabic, Asian, Latin, and Caribbean music. Round World

Music works with EJs and does mail order.

Bob Dylan	*Blonde on Blonde*
Franco et le TPOK Jazz	*20th Anniversary (1976)*
Marvin Gaye	*What's Goin' On?*
Beethoven	*Piano Sonata, op. 3*
Marcus Garvey	*Garvey's Ghost*
Monguito Presents Laba Sosseh	*Salsa Africana*
Sweet Talks	*Hollywood Highlife Party*
John Coltrane	*Afro-Blue*
Yousson N' Dour	*Immigrées*
Zalko Langa Langa	*Papa Omar*
Coulde Cloule	*The Preacher*
Salif Keita	*Soro*
Burning Spear	

RICHARD LIEBERSON   RL

Richard Lieberson is a working guitarist with recordings on Flying Fish. He is now part of Vince Giordano's Nighthawks (a big band specializing in 20s/30s arrangements) and has a broad background in country, country blues, vintage-through-60s jazz, and many R&B styles and artists. He is the author of *Old-Time Fiddle Tunes for Guitar* and his work has appeared in *Jazz Guitars*, *Guitar Player*, and *Country Musicians*. He has written various liner notes.

Sam Cooke	*Night Beat*
The Davis Sisters (Skeeter and Betty Jack)	(RCA 45s)
Coleman Hawkins	*Hollywood Stampede*
Goldie Hill	(Decca 45s)
Sheila Jordan	*Duets with various bassists*
Percy Mayfield	*Best of Percy Mayfield*
Lefty Frizzel	
The Nat King Cole Trio	
Le Mystère des Voix Bulgares	
Paul Desmond quartets with Jim Hall	
Charles Brown with Johnny Moore's Three Blazers	
The Bill Evans Trio with Scott LaFaro and Paul Motian	

KIP LORNELL   KL

Kip Lornell, who works on music projects for the Smithsonian Institute, has a doctorate in ethnomusicology, a master's in folklore, and a bachelor's degree in cultural studies. He is the author of *Introducing American Folk Music*; *Leadbelly: King of the Twelve String Guitar*; *Virginia's Blues; Country and Gospel Records: 1902-1943*; and *Happy in the Service of the Lord: Afro-American Gospel Quartets in Memphis*. He has received many grants, nominations, and awards, has been a consultant and contributor for many publications, and has written reviews, media productions, and liner notes.

John Coltrane	*A Love Supreme*
Sonny Boy Williamson	(Chess boxed set)
Charlie Patton	*Founder of the Delta Blues*
McCoy Tyner	*Sama Luchea*
Kid Creole	(First album)
Robert Johnson	(Columbia boxed set)
Uncle Dave Macon	(County album)
Rolling Stones	*Her Majesty's Satanic Request*
Incredible String Band	*The Big Huge*
Talking Heads	*Remain in Light*
Pearls before Swine	*These Things Too*
Julie Wilson	*Kurt Weil Songbook*

DAVID NELSON MCCARTHY   DNM

From an early age, David McCarthy sang in a church choir and played guitar. He received a bachelor's degree in music from the University of Michigan; studied jazz and improvisational music; taught guitar; and, in 1980, attended the Naropa Institute in Boulder, CO, studying with core faculty Bill Douglas and Jerry Granelli and taking seminars with Charlie Haden, John Abercrombie, and Oregon (including classical guitar with Ralph Towner). In 1981, he served as teaching assistant to the head of the Naropa Music Department and played professionally from 1983 to 1989. He studied mainstream jazz in New York City with Renard Hoover and Jack Wilkins and is cofounder of the avant-garde band Mosaic Art Ensemble (1983) and chamber jazz ensemble Soundworks (1987).

J. S. Bach	*Well-Tempered Clavier (Book II)* (Leonhardt)
Mozart	Late Symphonies (39, 40, 41)
Christopher Parkening	*Parkening Plays Bach*
John Williams	*First Meditations*
Monk/Coltrane	*Monk/Trane*
Parker	*Complete Savoy Recordings*
Abercrombie/Towner	*Sargasso Sea*
John Coltrane	*Love Supreme*
John Coltrane	*Ballads*
Jim Hall/Bill Evans	*Intermodulation*
Paul Desmond/Jim Hall	*Complete Quartet Recordings* (Mosaic Set)

DENNIS MACDONALD   DMAC

Dennis MacDonald was a DJ and music director for WMHS-AM and, from 1974 to 1978, for WMHB FM. His nickname, "Decibel Dennis," was given to him by a listener based on music he aired. Following six years as manager and buyer for four record stores in Boston, he became the director of operations and buyer for Roundup Records. He writes reviews for *Record Roundup*.

James Brown	*Star Time*
Creedence Clearwater Revival	*Willie and the Poorboys*
Everly Brothers	*Cadence Classics: Their 20 Greatest Hits*
Buddy Holly	*From the Original Master Tapes*
Howlin' Wolf	(Chess boxed set)
Los Lobos	*How Will the Wolf Survive*
Roxy Music	*Stranded*
Doug Sahm	*Sir Douglas Quintet*
Richard and Linda Thompson	*Shoot Out the Lights*
Hank Williams	*40 Greatest Hits*
Lucinda Williams	(Self-titled)

BRIAN MANSFIELD   BM

Brian Mansfield writes on Country music for *Music Row* and on Christian music for *Inside Music*. His work has appeared in *Spin*, *Country America*, *Request*, and *CD-Review*.

The Beatles	*Meet the Beatles*
Elvis Presley	*The Sun Sessions*
Bruce Springsteen	*Born to Run*
Van Morrison	*Astral Weeks*
The Swan Silvertones	*Love Lifted Me*
George Jones	*Anniversary: Ten Years of Hits*
The Neville Brothers	*Neville-ization*
The Ramones	*Rocket to Russia*
Marvin Gaye	*Let's Get It On*

Russ Taff	(Self-titled)
The Flamingos	(Anything)
King Curtis	*Live at the Fillmore West*

PETER MEYER   PM

Peter Meyer is the classical import buyer for Schoolkids Records in Ann Arbor, MI, and an avid classical music collector. He worked as a jazz drummer during the 60s.

Sibelius	*Symphony no. 2* (Pierre Monteux)
Elgar	*Enigma Variations*
Mendelssohn	*Midsummer Night's Dream* (Maag)
J. S. Bach	*Cantata no. 106* (Leonhardt)
Mozart	*Mass in c* (Celibidache)
Schubert	*Wanderer Fantasy* (Richter)
Robert Schumann	*Fantasia in C, op. 17*
J. S. Bach	*Chaconne* (Michelangeli)
Mahler	*Symphony no. 3* (Horenstein)
Mahler	*Symphony no. 9* (French NO)
Beethoven	*Symphony no. 3* (Hunt CD 363)
	Symphony no. 9 (Hunt CD 357) (Furtwängler)

RICHARD MEYER   RM

Richard Meyer's second album, *The Good Life!*, was just released nationally. As an active performer on the Greenwich Village scene, he has promoted many musicians and booked the SpeakEasy Musicians' Co-op, including a series of live radio broadcasts. As editor of *The Fast Folk Musical Magazine* (1986-1992), he has produced nearly 40 live and studio albums. He is a lighting/scenery designer for theater with 85 productions to his credit.

Ella Fitzgerald	*The 50s Songbook Series*
Hirth Martinez	*Big Bright Street*
Orleans	(Self-titled)
Elvis Presley	*The 50s Masters*
Elvis Is Back	*Chrysalis/Definition*
Manitas De Plata	*Juerga*
Bob Dylan	*Blonde on Blonde/Basement Tapes/ Bootleg Series*
The Beatles	

DAVID A. MILBERG   DAM

David Milberg was a DJ and radio/TV station executive, now an attorney and vice president of a national consulting/ management company. He produced his own nationally syndicated oldies show on 130 stations in the 1980s, "Rare and Scratchy Rock & Roll," and owns more than 60,000 records, including the largest Christmas collection this side of the North Pole. His work has appeared in *Goldmine*, *Broadcasting*, and *Illinois Entertainer*.

John Stewart	*California Bloodlines*
Earl Bostic	*Greatest Hits*
Jimmy Buffett	*A1A*
Herb Alpert and the Tijuana Brass	*SRO*
The Everly Brothers	*Greatest Hits*
Bruce Springsteen	*Welcome to Asbury Park*
Eagles	*Desperado*
Jim Croce	*I Have a Name*
Beach Boys	*Surf's Up*
The Lettermen	*Greatest Hits*
Duane Eddy	*Greatest Hits*
Sheb Wooley/Ben Colder	*Greatest Hits*

DAN MORGENSTERN   DM

Dan Morgenstern is a renowned jazz expert. From 1958 to 1961, he was the New York correspondent for *Jazz Journal*; from 1962 to 1963, the editor of *Metronome*; from 1964 to 1973, the editor of *DOWN BEAT*. He also produced jazz concerts for TV and has lectured at Brooklyn College and the Peabody institute. In 1976, he was appointed director of the Rutgers University Institute of Jazz Studies. Since then he has been editor for the *Journal of Jazz Studies* and the *Annual Review of Jazz Studies*. He has won four Grammy Awards for liner notes, has written the book *Jazz People* (ASCAP-Deems Taylor Award in 1977), has published many articles, and translated Joachim Berendt's *Das neue Jazzbuch*.

MICHAEL G. NASTOS   MGN

Michael G. Nastos writes syndicated previews, reviews, and opinion columns on jazz, blues, and other music. He was named one of the top five midwest critics by readers of *Arts Midwest* newsletter in 1988 and #1 Jazz Critic in the SEMJA Music Poll in 1990. He writes for *DOWN BEAT*, *Cadence*, *Coda*, *Jazz Forum*, *Swing Journal*, *Arts Midwest*, and *Jazz News International*, and is a freelance writer of artists' biographies, interviews, jazz festival and concert programs, and liner notes. He is an instructor and guest lecturer at the University of Michigan and Washtenaw Community College.

John Coltrane	*Africa Brass I/II*
Roseanna Vitro	*A Quiet Place*
Muddy Waters	(Chess boxed set)
Jack Kerouac	*Collection*
Santana	*Lotus*
Linton Kwesi Johnson	*In Dub*
Steve Reich	*Music for 18 Musicians*
Captain Beefheart	*Bat Chain Puller*
Ramsaan Roland Kirk	*Complete*
Larry Young	*Complete Blue Note*
Arthur Blythe	*Lenox Avenue Breakdown*
Eddie Palmieri and Cal Tjader	*El Sonido Nuevo*

JAS OBRECHT   JO

Jas Obrecht is associate editor of *Guitar Player* and author of *Blues Guitar: The Men Who Made the Music*.

Jimi Hendrix Experience	*Electric Ladyland*
Robert Johnson	*The Complete Recordings*
Bob Marley	*Legend*
Miles Davis	*Chronicle*
	(The Complete Prestige Recordings, 1951-1956)
Muddy Waters	(Chess boxed set)
Patti Smith Group	*Wave*
Hank Williams	*The Original Singles Collection*
Blind Willie Johnson	*Praise God I'm Satisfied*
Son House	*Son House and the Great Delta Blues Singers, 1928-1929*
Bob Dylan	*Bringing It All Back Home*
Billie Holiday	*The Quintessential Billie Holiday*
U2	*War*

CHRISTINE OHLMAN   CO

Christine Ohlman is a singer, songwriter, guitarist, record collector, and music historian with a particular interest in southern ("deep") soul music. She recently became a contributing reviewer for *The Record Round-Up*. Performing remains her first love; she fronts her own trio,

Rebel Montez. As vocalist with G. E. Smith and the Saturday Night Live Band, during the 1991-1992 season she could be seen singing her heart out beside bandleader Smith.

Bobby "Blue" Band
James Carr
Dinah Washington
Sam Cooke
Aretha Franklin
Al Green
Etta James
Billie Holliday
Wilson Pickett
Otis Redding
Irma Thomas
James Brown

JIM O'NEAL   JON

Jim O'Neal is the founder of *Living Blues: A Journal of the African-American Blues Tradition*.

BUZ OVERBECK   BO

Born of show-business parents (a bandsinger/radio personality and a vaudeville entertainer), Buz Overbeck started playing professionally at age 15. He studied at the Cincinnati College/Conservatory of Music and became the show drummer at Cincinatti's Gaiety Theater, the last of the authentic vaudeville/burlesque houses. He worked with Pete Fountain in New Orleans in the early 60s, then as a freelance studio, recording, and show drummer in Hollywood. He also led his own bands and was in great demand due to his ability to play all types of music, including big band, jazz, country & western, polka, continental, and shows. He toured with the Freddy Martin orchestra in the 70s, then formed his own jazz/rock-fusion band and later was featured with various show bands. He is well-informed on the playing and career of Buddy Rich.

Duke Ellington	*Ellington Uptown*
Judy Garland	*Judy at Carnegie Hall – Vols. 1 & 2*
Miles Davis	*(Any Gil Evans collaboration)*
Gershwin	*Porgy and Bess*
Gary Burton	*Artist's Choice*
Barbra Streisand	*Yentl*
Giacomo Puccini	*La Bohème*
Frank Sinatra	*It Might As Well Be Swing*
Elton John	*Live in Australia*
Billie Holiday	*Lady in Satin*
J. S. Bach	*St. Matthew's Passion*
Wynton Marsalis	*Live at Blues Alley*

RICHARD PACK   RP

Richard Pack is a freelance writer for publications in the UK, US, and Canada, including *Blackbeat* and *It Will Stand*. He is writer and editor for *Soul Survivor*, has written liner notes for Big Bear and Kent, and is writing a book, *Detroit Soul: The Golden Years 1963-1969*.

Doris Duke	*I'm a Loser*
Tim Buckley	*Blue Afternoon*
Swamp Dogg	*Total Destruction to Your Mind*
Laura Lee	*That's How It Is*
Darrell Banks	*Darrell Banks Is Here!*
Temptations	*Wish It Would Rain*
Millie Jackson	*Still Caught Up*

Sam Dees	*The Show Must Go On*
Hesitations	*Soul Superman*
Fairport Convention	*What We Did on Our Holidays*
Soul Children	*Friction*
J. J. Barnes and Steve Manch	*Rare Stamps*

BARRY LEE PEARSON   BLP

Dr. Barry Pearson has written two books and over 40 other publications on traditional and popular African-American music — the bulk of his work deriving from well over 100 taped interviews with blues performers. He has written the books *Sounds Good to Me: The Bluesman's Story*, *Virginia Piedmont Blues: The Lives and Art of Two Virgina Blues Men* (covering the relationship between life-story and repertoire), and (forthcoming) *Blues and African-American Community Life* (covering the relationship between blues artists and other African-American institutions and community events). He is an English professor at the University of Maryland, works with the Smithsonian Folklife Festival and the Library of Congress Folklife Center, is president of the National Council for the Traditional Arts, and as a musician has toured for the Arts America Program in Africa and South and Central America.

Elmore James	*The Sky Is Crying*
Sleepy John Estes	*Sleepy John Estes, 1929-1940*
The Soul Stirrers	*The Original Soul Stirrers, Featuring Sam Cooke*
Joe Tex	*The Best of Joe Tex*
Bo Diddley	*Go Bo Diddley*
John Lee Hooker	*Alone*
Waylon Jennings	*Just to Satisfy You*
Magic Sam	*West Side Soul*
Junior Wells	*Hoodoo Man Blues*
Assorted Gospel	*Ain't That Good News*
Jimmy Jarlton and Tom Darby	*Darby and Tarlton*
Henry Thomas	*Texas Worried Blues: A Complete Recorded Works, 1927-1929*

J. POET   JP

J. Poet is a San Francisco-based world music expert. He has written for *Pulse, Music Independent, Rock 'n' Roll Disc, Culture Concrete, It's Hip*, and is a regular contributor to the *Daily Californian, BAM*, Bay Guardian, *The City*, East Bay Guardian, *Goldmine*, SF Weekly, *Rock 'n' Roll Confidential, In These Times*, and Ward Report's *Music Monthly*.

BOB PORTER   BP

Bob Porter is a legendary jazz and R & B producer for Atlantic Records — an acknowledged master, with some of the most important albums in the history of these genres to his credit.

Joe Turner	*Boss of the Blues*
Jazz at the Philharmonic	*Blues from Chicago*
Gene Ammons	*Boss Tenor*
Dexter Gordon	*Our Man in Paris*
Count Basie	*Breakfast Dance & Barbecue*
Albert King	*I'll Play the Blues for You*
Jimmy Smith	*Midnight Special*
Illinois Jacquet	*Jacquet's Got It*
Lester Young	*Keynote Masters*
Ben Webster	*King of the Tenors*
Duke Ellington	*Piano in the Background*
Charlie Parker	*Master Takes*

BRUCE BOYD RAEBURN   BR

Bruce Boyd Raeburn is the curator of the Hogan Jazz Archive
at Tulane University and is working on a study of early
American jazz historians. He is a professional drummer with
various rock, R&B, and jazz groups and serves on the
National Park Service Jazz Advisory Commission, which
studies ways to commemorate the early development of jazz
in New Orleans. Dr. Raeburn's upbringing (son of a
bandleader and a jazz vocalist) and musical experience have
given him extremely eclectic tastes. He advocates the
broadest possible appreciation of American vernacular music
as essential to understanding any particular aspect of it.

Jelly Roll Morton and His Red Hot Peppers	*The King of New Orleans Jazz*
Brian Jones	*... Presents the Pipes of Pan in Joujouka*
The Chieftains	*Bonaparte's Retreat*
Giants of Jazz	*Louis Armstrong*
The Byrds	*Sweetheart of the Rodeo*
Mahalia Jackson	*The Great Mahalia Jackson*
Charlie Parker	*The Complete Savoy Studio Sessions*
Boyd Raeburn and His Orchestra	*Jewells*
My Bloody Valentine	*Loveless*
John Coltrane	*A Love Supreme*
Captain Beefheart	*Trout Mask Replica*

CHIP RENNER   CR

Chip Renner is an avid collector of folk, country, Irish,
acoustic, bluegrass, and blues, and alternative music. He is
music reviewer for the *Inde Nightowl* (a publication covering
folk, country, Irish, and bluegrass music) and is working on a
radio show that will provide in-depth reviews of albums and
independent artists.

New Grass Review	*Barren County*
Tony Rice	*Cold on the Shoulder*
Nanci Griffith	*The Last of the True Believers*
Dick Gaughan	*Handful of Earth*
Luca Bloom	*Riverside*
Guy Clark	*Old Friends*
Robert Earl Keen	*West Textures*
David Mallett	*For a Lifetime*
Tom Russell Band	*Poor Man's Dream*
Peter Case	*The Man with the Blue Postmodern*
Tommy Sands	*Singing of the Times Gene*
Parsons	*Kindling*

JOHN STORM ROBERTS   JSR

John Storm Roberts is the founder and president of Original
Music, for ten years a world music mail-order source and
record label. He is the author of *Black Music of Two Worlds*
and *The Latin Tinge* and has recorded and/or compiled two
dozen African, Caribbean, and other recordings. As a writer,
he has appeared regularly in the US and overseas as a
contributor to *The Village Voice* and *High Fidelity*.

TOM ROLAND   TR

Tom Roland is a Nashville-based writer and producer for the
Unistar Radio Network Solid Gold Country national radio
show and the author of the *Billboard Book of Number One
Country Hits*. He has been published in *Country Song
Roundup* and *Country Rhythms*.

WILLIAM RUHLMANN   WR

Bill Ruhlmann has been the associate editor of *Relix*
magazine and a regular contributor to *Goldmine*. He is the
author of *The History of the Grateful Dead, The Doors*,
and a recently published book on Led Zeppelin. He has
written liner notes for Relix, Columbia, Epic, and Bear Family.

The Beatles	*Sgt. Pepper's Lonely Hearts Club Band*
Bob Dylan	*Blonde on Blonde*
Jackson Browne	*Late for the Sky*
Hank Williams	*24 Greatest Hits*
Leonard Cohen	*Songs of Leonard Cohen*
Bruce Springsteen	*The Wild, the Innocent, and the E Street Shuffle*
Elvis Costello	*This Year's Model*
David Massengill	*The Great American Bootleg Tape*
Maggie and Terre Roche	*Seductive Reasoning*
Elvis Presley	*The Sun Sessions*
Van Morrison	*Astral Weeks*
Woody Guthrie	*Dust Bowl Ballads*

MAX SALAZAR   MS

Max Salazar wrote on Afro-Cuban music history for *Latin
New York* magazine from 1973 to 1976. He has written
biographies, concert reviews, and record reviews for *The
Village Voice, Melody Maker, Clave, Mira, Latin Times*,
and *Musician Magazine*. He hosted "The Latin Musician"
radio show from 1974 to 1989 and is senior writer and
musicologist for *Latin Beat* magazine.

MARY SCANLAN   MKS

Mary Scanlan has a doctorate in piano pedagogy from the
University of Illinois and master's and bachelor's degrees in
piano performance from the Universities of Iowa and
Wisconsin, respectively. She has studied piano with many
greats, including Paul Badurka-Skoda, and harpsichord with
Robert Conant. She has given many workshops and lectures
and served as staff pianst for the Chicago Civic Symphony;
pianist for the Lieder and Chamber Music program (Yale
Summer Festival); recital accompanist for the National
Association of Teachers of Singing and National Federation of
Music Clubs; lieder accompanist in Rome, Munich, Paris,
Dusseldorf, Nürnberg, and Wiesbaden; and lecture-recitalist
at the National Festival of Music by Women Composers. A
1989 grant to research women composers resulted in recitals
devoted to music by women and an article on Catherine
Comet for *Music Editor's Journal*. She was awarded a 1992
NEH grant to study American music in Boston.

Johannes Brahms	*Piano Concerto no. 1 in d* (Arrau)
Johannes Brahms	*Piano Concerto no. 2 in B flat* (Richter)
Don Shirley	(Any recordings)
Benjamin Britten	*Serenade* (Peter Pears/Dennis Brain)
Antonin Dvořák	*Piano Trios* (Ax/Kim/Yo Yo Ma)
Charles Martin Loeffler	*La Mort de Tintagiles*
Claude Debussy	*Piano Preludes* (Gieseking)
Béla Bartók	*Sonata for Two Pianos and Percussion*
Franz Liszt	*Années de Pèlerinage* (Berman)
Richard Strauss	*Four Last Songs* (Schwarzkopf/Norman)
J. S. Bach	*Mass in b* (Netherlands Chamber Choir)
Maurice Ravel	*Piano Concerto in G* (Michelangeli)

GENE SCARAMUZZO   GS

Gene Scaramuzzo is based in New Orleans, LA. Since 1980, he has been deeply involved in the Caribbean and African music scenes, interviewing and researching. He has a special interest in the music of Trinidad, Tobago, and the French Antilles islands of Guadeloupe and Martinique, and is the only English-language writer providing in-depth coverage of the French Antilles music scene. Since 1980, Gene has hosted a bi-weekly radio program, "The Caribbean Show," on New Orleans radio station WWCZ. From 1980 to 1991, he was associate editor and columnist on Caribbean and Rhythmatic music for *Wavelength*, a New Orleans music magazine. Since 1985, he has written a column for *The Beat* called "The Other Caribbean" and has written freelance articles on Caribbean and African music for many publications, including the New Orleans daily newspaper. He is Caribbean music advisor for the New Orleans Jazz and Heritage Festival and Festival International de Louisiana and the editor and annotator for Rounder compilations on zouk and soca.

Louis Armstrong	*Louis Armstrong and Earl Hines*
Duke Ellington	*The Blanton-Webster Band*
Count Basie	*The Complete Decca Recordings*
Benny Goodman	(Self-titled)
Lester Young	*Giants of the Tenor Sax*
Coleman Hawkins	*Body and Soul*
Charlie Parker	*Master Takes*
Dizzy Gillespie	*Dizziest*
Bud Powell	*Jazz Giant*
Miles Davis	*Dig*
Billie Holiday	*The Legacy (1933-1958)*
Sarah Vaughan	*The Early Years*

"BLUE" GENE TYRANNY   BGT

Robert Sheff, aka "Blue" Gene Tyranny, has composed and performed avant-garde music for 30 years, writing over 60 works for various ensembles of electronic and acoustic instruments and voices. He has produced and recorded many albums of music by other composers, published articles on contemporary music, and composed over 30 soundtracks for film and video productions. He writes for *Music with Roots in the Ether* and *Music beyond the Boundaries* and his compositions have been reviewed in *Sonic Transports*, *Soundpieces 2: Interviews with American Composers*, and *Talking Music: Conversations with Five Generations of American Experimental Composers*. He has received a New York Foundation for the Arts Fellowship in Composition.

RICHARD SKELLY   RS

Richard Skelly is popular music reporter and reviewer for the Central New Jersey Home News in New Brunswick, NJ, and a contributor to *Goldmine, Sing Out!, Music Retailing, Independent Music Producers Society Journal, National Academy of Songwriters' Songtalk, Relix,* and *Living Blues*. He is host of "The Low Budget Blues Program" on WRSU-FM, the radio station of Rutgers University.

ROGER STEFFENS   RMS

Roger Steffens is founding editor of *The Beat*. He has been co-host of "Reggae Beat" (1979-1987) and "Reggae Beat International" (1983-1987), heard on 130 radio stations worldwide. He lectures widely on the life of Bob Marley.

DAVID SZATMARY   DS

David Szatmary recently completed a major revision of his book, *Rockin N Time* (a social history of rock & roll) and is at work on a similar history of jazz. He has managed a chain of record stores and has written for numerous publications.

Sex Pistols	*Never Mind the Bollocks*
Jimi Hendrix	*Hendrix Concerts*
Thelonious Monk	*Modern Jazz Giants*
AC/DC	*Highway to Hell*
Elvis Presley	(Self-titled; first)
Sonny Rollins	*Worktime*
Lou Reed	*New York*
Wildman Fischer	*An Evening with Wildman Fisher*
Roy Buchanan	*Live Stock*
Little Richard	*Little Richard's Greatest*
Charlie Parker	*Dial Material*
Bob Dylan	*Freewheelin'*

JEFF TAMARKIN   JT

Jeff Tamarkin has been an editor and writer for *Goldmine* since 1981. He is formerly the editor of CMJ's *College Media Journal, Relix, Modern Recording & Music,* and *Grateful Dead Comix*. He is a columnist for *Tower Pulse!* magazine, a contributor to *Music Alive*; has contributed to *Billboard, Circus, Hit Parader,* and many other publications; has written the books *Billy Joel: From Hicksville to Hitsville* and *Bruce Springsteen: Born in the USA;* has contributed to the *Guinness Companion to Popular Music* and is a consultant for many other books. His liner notes include *Way Back* (Jive Five); *Sons of Mercury* (Quicksilver Messenger Service); *The Best of Jesse Colin Young; Sandie Shaw: The Collection; Jefferson Airplane Loves You;* and *The Best of CMJ*. He is on the Rock & Roll Hall of Fame Nominating Committee and a compiler of the album *Garage Sale!*

The Beatles	(All)
Elvis Presley	*Top 10 Hits*
Grateful Dead	*Live/Dead*
The Beach Boys	*Pet Sounds*
Rolling Stones	(Up to 1972)
Elvis Costello	*Best of Elvis Costello*
Frank Sinatra	*The Capitol Years*
Marvin Gaye	*Anthology*
Jefferson Airplane	*Jefferson Airplane Loves You*
Stan Getz	*Best of the Verve Years*
NRBQ	*Peek-a-Boo (Best of)*
Buck Owens	(Rhino boxed set)

BOB TARTE   BT

Bob Tarte writes regular columns on world music for *The Beat* and *Yellow Silk* (a journal of the erotic arts) and has written for *Electronic Musician, The Whole Earth Review,* and the Boston Globe. His book of short fiction, *Duplicity,* in collaboration with photographer Steven R. Milanowski, is published by GRAM/University of Washington Press.

Nick Drake	*Five Leaves Left*
3 Mustaphas 3	*Soup of the Century*
Captain Beefheart and His Magic Band	*Lick My Decals Off, Baby*
Edgar Bergen	*Teaches You Ventriloquism*
Van Morrison	*Astral Weeks*

Ikhwani Safaa Musical Club	*Taarab 2: The Music of Zanzibar*
King Sunny Ade	*Aura*
Neil Young	*Everybody Knows This Is Nowhere*
Can	*Ege Bamyasi*
Sona Diabate	*Girls of Guinea*
Eek-A-Mouse	*U-Neek*

DAVID VINOPAL   DV

David Vinopal says, "For 40 of my 48 years I have loved country music; that means I wasted the first eight." He is author of *The Country Music Funbook*, a trip through country music history in a question/answer format. His article "Same Train, Different Time," about country music stars and fans, was published in *Shaping the Shorter Essay*. He has played with a number of country bands, including the Country Cousins, Rainbow Rhythm Boys, Sleepy Hollow Express, Rural Rhythm Boys, Vin & Earl, and the Mellow Ds. He teaches technical writing at Paul Smith's College and is co-authoring a book about vintage Gibson acoustic guitars.

Merle Haggard	*Same Train, a Different Time*
Roy Acuff	"Great Speckled Bird"
Delmore Brothers	*In Memory – Vol. 1*
Bill Boyd	*Bill Boyd's Cowboy Ramblers*
Hank Snow	*Travelin' Blues*
Louvin Brothers	*The Louvin Brothers*
Stanley Brothers	*Folk Song Festival*
E. C. and Orna Ball	*E. C. Ball*
Jethro Burns/Tiny Moore	*Back to Back*
George Jones and Tammy Wynette	*The King and Queen of Country*
Doc Watson	*The Doc Watson Family*
Ricky Skaggs	*Waiting for the Sun to Shine*

TOM WILSON WEINBERG   TW

Under the name Tom Wilson, Tom Wilson Weinberg has released two albums, *Gay Name Game* and *All-American Boy*. He travels and performs widely and now focuses on musical theater. His show *Get Used to It* played off-Broadway in 1992. He is at work on a musical.

STEPHEN WINICK   SW

Stephen Winick is a regular contributor to *Dirty Linen* and *Sing Out!* magazines and has made many radio appearances presenting Celtic folk music. He has a master's degree in folklore and folklife from the University of Pennsylvania, where he lectures on the folklore of Britain and Ireland.

BILL WIRTHS   BW

Formerly a special education teacher and pro-wrestling manager, comedian ("Rev. Billy C. Wirtz") and gospel specialist Bill Wirths was born in Aiken, SC. He records for Hightone Records and has listened to and loved gospel music all his life.

Patsy Cline	*Greatest Hits*
Elvis Presley	*Golden Records – Vol. 1*
Dixie Hummingbirds	*Best of the Dixie Hummingbirds*
Swan Silvertones	*Best of the Swan Silvertones*
Sensational Nightingales	*Best of the Sensational Nightingales*
Five Blind Boys of Mississippi	*Best of the Five Blind Boys of Mississippi*

Brother Dave Gardner	*Kick Thy Own Self*
Hank Williams	(Boxed set)
Otis Spann	*Otis Spann Is the Blues*
Various	*Doo Wop Delights*
Moon Mulligan	*Seven Nights to Rock*

CHARLES S. WOLFE   CW

Charles S. Wolfe is an expert on folk and country music. He has produced and annotated over 50 albums and has been nominated for Grammy Awards three times. He is the author of *Grand Old Opry: The Early Years*; *Tennessee Strings*; *The Illustrated History of Country Music*; *Kentucky Country: Folk and Country Music of Kentucky*; *Everybody's Grandpa*; and a contributor to the *Grove Dictionary of American Music*; *Encyclopedia of Southern Music*; and *Country: The Music and the Musicians*. He is a freelance writer for *American Music, The Journal of Country Music, Pop Music Yearbook, Country Music Magazine, Bluegrass Unlimited*, and is associated with the Tennessee Folklore Society.

CARLO T. WOLFF   CTW

Carlo T. Wolff is a rock critic from Cleveland.

Thelonious Monk	*Brilliant Corners*
Duke Ellington	*The Blanton-Webster Band*
Minutemen	*Double Nickels on the Dime*
Nick Drake	*Five Leaves Left*
David Forman	*Arista*
Bob Dylan	*Highway 61 Revisited*
Otis Redding	*The Immortal Otis Redding*
AC/DC	*Back in Black*
Thin White Rope	*Exploring the Axis*
Nine Inch Nails	*Pretty Hate Machine*
Bonnie Raitt	*Nick of Time*
Elvis Presley	*The Sun Sessions*

RON WYNN   RW

Ron Wynn is the editor of the *New Memphis Star*, a bi-weekly music magazine, and the former chief critic for *The Memphis Commercial Appeal* and the Bridgeport Post. He has contributed to *Rock & Roll Confidential, The Boston Phoenix, Living Blues, Rejoice* and is the author of *The Tina Turner Story*.

Duke Ellington
John Coltrane
Miles Davis
Aretha Franklin
Marvin Gaye
James Brown
Dinah Washington
B. B. King
Ray Charles
The Swan Silvertones
Charlie Pride
Carlos Santana

ROCK, POP & SOUL

Ask 20 people for a definition of rock & roll and you'll get 20 different answers, for everyone has their own idea of what the music is and what it should do. And that's good, because if rock & roll could be defined with a simple, concise description, it would've died sometime in the mid 60s. Rock & roll defies categorization: you can't trace its origins back to one particular source, you can't define its content with words like "rebellion" or "sexuality," and you can't pinpoint its sensibility with one clever catch phrase.

More than any other genre of 20th century music, rock & roll has stood the test of time on the strength of its diversity — the diversity of the countless producers, engineers, songwriters, vocalists, and musicians who create the stuff. The hierarchy in anyone's personal history of rock & roll is predestined to include dozens of eclectic names and song titles. And the things people think rock & roll should do vary as wildly as the artistic approaches of the Beatles and the Rolling Stones. Some think it should be full of rebellion, anger, and venom, and they point to the early work of the Who, the Rolling Stones, or the Sex Pistols or to the rantings of some contemporary agit-popster. Others may see it as a vehicle for romantic expoundings, positing their arguments with an armful of doo-wop singles and the complete works of Phil Spector. Still others may argue that the music is simply a White bastardization of Black blues and R&B; these people can point to just about any post-50s group and make a convincing argument.

But rock's origins aren't so easily defined. Many critics and historians credit Jackie Brenston's "Rocket 88," recorded in 1951 at Sam Phillips's Sun Studio in Memphis, TN, as the first "rock & roll" record. Its driving beat, over-amped guitar riffs, blaring horns, and automobile-as-sexual-metaphor theme lend weight to this theory. But what about the blues-laced prewar country work of Jimmie Rodgers or the vivid imagery and pathos in the oeuvre of Hank Williams? What about the prewar and postwar gospel that provided much of the foundation for not only rock & roll but for blues, R&B, and soul? What about the swaggering jump-blues that proliferated in the Midwest and on the West Coast during the 40s and early 50s? What about the Delmore Brothers' choogling, revved-up acoustic country? What about the high, mournful wail of Bill Monroe and the Stanley Brothers? What about the raucous assault of blues pioneers such as Howlin' Wolf, Muddy Waters, Little Walter Jacobs, and Sonny Boy Williamson?

The diversity of rock's origins may explain why the Rock, Pop, & Soul chapter of the *All-Music Guide* is the most variegated section of the book. With over 20 critics applying their opinions and critical idiosyncrasies to the canon of 20th century popular music, the variety of music highlighted is certain to be eclectic, to say the least. Whatever your personal definition of rock & roll may be, that eclecticism is necessary, if only to give an accurate overview of what's out there. It also means, however, that not every starred or bulleted album is going to fill everyone's needs. Someone may think Michael Bolton is a pockmark on the face of contemporary pop; someone else may think he's inherited the White-soulman traditions of Van Morrison or the Rascals. Whatever your opinion, in the pages of this section there's a bulleted album recorded by Bolton. We realize no one is going to agree with every critical assessment found in this chapter, and no one should; if they do, they probably aren't asserting their own personality quite as strongly as they should. And some may squabble that we've included contemporary and vintage soul, doo-wop, and jump-blues within the rock and pop section. But without the artists who've worked and continue to work in those genres, the rock & roll section of any book (or record store) would be considerably smaller — and far less interesting.

What this chapter should do, however, is act as a guidepost for the curious, a map to guide readers through areas of music they may not find on their own. You may already know about a lot of the music discussed here, but maybe you'll find a record that somehow slipped through the cracks of popularity. Or maybe you're interested in tracking down the finest album by an obscure New York noise band or an overlooked doo-wop quintet. Odds are, you'll find them both somewhere within these pages. Keep in mind, though, that regardless of how painstakingly the *All-Music* editors have worked at making this a definitive portrait of what's good in rock, pop, and soul, it is not definitive — there's no way any one book ever could attain that goal. But if it makes one person purchase an album by an artist they've never heard of, if it makes somebody decide once and for all to dig into the roots of American music to find out where the Rolling Stones got all those cool old songs, the *All-Music Guide* has accomplished its task. You, the reader, will be the final judge of its success.

— John Floyd

ABBA

Pop, Dance-pop. During the 70s, ABBA's slick light Euro-pop made them one of the world's most successful acts, particularly outside of America. Each of the members had already enjoyed some professional success, previous to the band's formation. The spirited debut single, "Waterloo," won ABBA much recognition when they won the 1974 Eurovision Song Contest. From there, ABBA scored a seemingly endless string of predominately bouncy pop hits, featuring well-crafted catchy melodies (some quite good) and the band's distinctive (but occasionally shrill) multilayered vocals, which highlighted female singers Agnetha Ulvaeu and Anni-Frid Lyngstad-Fredriksson.

Of the 14 American Top 40 pop hits, "Dancing Queen" was ABBA's biggest, hitting #1 in 1976. –RC

○ **Singles: The First Ten Years / POLYGRAM**   1982
ABBA scored a string of hit singles from the early 70s to the early 80s, (far more outside the US than within) because of their talent for constructing bouncy, catchy, well-produced tunes with light romantic lyrics. This 23-track collection contains all their best work. –WR

GREGORY ABBOTT

Urban R&B. Abbott's silken croon has roots in the romantic splendor of Marvin Gaye (with whom he understudied), and his 1986 debut comes off like a would-be successor to Gaye's *Let's Get it On.* –JF

○ **Shake You Down / CBS**   1986
Great soul can come from the most unlikely of places. Abbott was a Wall Street researcher with the same silky croon as Marvin Gaye. He and some friends set up a home studio and produced the huge 1986 hit, "Shake You Down," the best thing from his debut. –JF

ABC

Dance-pop. ABC was formed in 1980, when singer Martin Fry teamed up with Stephen Singleton and Mark White, who were members of the group Vice Versa. Their stylish debut, featuring Fry's cartoonishly overwrought delivery backed up by a dramatically lush dance/synth-pop sound, scored well with high-profile singles like "The Look of Love (Part One)" (#18), and "Poison Arrow" (#25). Except for a quick sidestep into a harder rocking middle-period Roxy Music-influenced effort with *Beauty Stab,* ABC has increasingly streamlined their sophisticated dance/pop. Their biggest hits have been "Be Near Me" (#9), "(How to Be A) Millionaire" (#20), and "When Smokey Sings" (#5), a tribute to Smokey Robinson. –RC

How to Be a Zillionaire / MERCURY   1985
Darkly humorous dance grooves incorporate some hip-hop. The album contains the hit "Be Near Me." –RC

Alphabet City / MERCURY   1987
Possibly ABC's best album effort — soulful, sleek, modern dance music. –RC

○ **Absolutely ABC - Best Of / POLYGRAM**   1990
Singer/songwriter Martin Fry's Bowie/Roxy vocal affectations and sweeping productions (aided by Mark White) are showcased to great effect on this fine anthology that contains all of this act's essential dance-pop hits. –RC

Abracadabra / MCA   1991
Production and dance grooves are more atmospheric, while borrowing from the mid-70s Philly soul arrangements. –RC

PAULA ABDUL   *b* 1962

Dance-pop. Abdul studied sportscasting at Cal State Northridge and became a Los Angeles Lakers cheerleader while still in her teens. She was spotted by the Jacksons, who hired her as their choreographer. She choreographed videos for ZZ Top, the Pointer Sisters, Duran Duran, and Janet Jackson before launching a pop singing career in 1987. –BC

○ **Forever Your Girl / VIRGIN**   1989
Choreographer-turned-diva Abdul debuts with this upbeat collection of dance-pop that yielded a string of Top 40 hits, including four #1 smashes — "Straight Up," "Cold Hearted," "Opposites Attract," and "Forever Your Girl." –DDC

Spellbound / VIRGIN   1991
This sophomore set produced another string of hits, with the danceable "The Promise of a New Day" and "Rush Rush," both reaching #1. –RC

THE A-BONES

Rock & roll. Hailing from Brooklyn, NY, the A-Bones play sloppy and greasy rock with a maniacal intensity. Named after a song by the Trashmen and fronted by vocalist Billy Miller and drummer Miriam Linna, the A-Bones started life as an offshoot to their earlier, rockabilly-tinged combo, the Zantees. Their love for the awesomely arcane is reflected in the choice of material they cover ("Go, Go, Go for Louie's Place") and the original songs they've added to the underbelly of rock's history. They were most recently seen rocking their brains out in the science fiction cult movie, *I Was a Teenage Mummy.* No two ways about it, the A-Bones are definitely a noise combo to be reckoned with. –CK

○ **The Life of Riley / NORTON**   1991
An album chock-full of stupid, greasy, stompin', wack-oid rock & roll by America's premier grease-pit combo. Atonal highlights include "El Kabong," "Go Go Go for Louie's Place," and drummer Miriam Linna's lyrical scream-fest, "Go Betty Go." –CK

I Was a Teenage Mummy / NORTON   1992
Music from the original motion picture soundtrack of this black & white sci-fi cult-classic for the 90s. Titles include "Mark of the Squealer," "Little Egypt," "The Fez Man Walks," and "Mum's the Word." –CK

AC/DC

Hard rock. When Australia's AC/DC blasted onto the music scene during the mid 70s, they were loud, crude, salacious (did I mention LOUD?), and audiences all over the world ate up their scorch-the-earth policy toward rock & roll. The bazooka roar of the Young brothers' twin guitars and Bon Scott's snarling vocals (they were labeled "crotchgrind" by Chuck Eddy) made them one of the most popular hard-rock bands in the world (with the platinum albums to prove it). Even on a bad night they were very nearly the equals of the Stones or the Who on their best.

The band nearly fell apart when singer Bon Scott died in 1980, but they rallied around his successor Brian Johnson, who managed to sound like Scott with an even greater vocal boom. In the 90s they show no inclination toward lowering the decibels. –TG

High Voltage / ATLANTIC   1976
AC/DC kicked things off properly by blowing away the girders with their concussion bomb skronk. Raw, raunchy, and fun-o-plenty, with songs like "The Jack" guaranteed to offend every woman in listening radius. –TG

Let There Be Rock / ATLANTIC   1977
A great followup that proved these Aussies would be a nasty itch for a long time. Great meltdown boogie on songs like "Let There Be Rock," "Problem Child," and "Whole Lotta Rosie." –TG

If You Want Blood You've Got It / ATLANTIC   1978
Although the sound engineering lacks, rock & roll still ain't much more in your face than this. Fans had known what a great live band AC/DC was, and this was the album that proved it to everyone else. Collects the best tracks from the early years and spits them back louder than bejeezus. –TG

○ **Highway to Hell / ATLANTIC**   1979
A classic of hard-rock/heavy metal noise-grunge-skronk-pillage-and-burn. Earlier AC/DC albums had great riffs and killer chords, but *Highway to Hell* proved the boys could write too. Not a clinker on this thudfest, and songs like "Highway to Hell" and "Girls Got Rhythm" have appropriately become rock staples. –TG

★ **Back in Black / ATLANTIC**   1980
Following Bon Scott's death, AC/DC came back with reinforcements and released another truly great hard-rock album. Brian Johnson ups the ante with his own tough-as-tacks vocals. Robert "Mutt" Lange's production on *Back in Black* remains one of the most powerful in all of hard rock. All in all, this is great diamond-hard, full-throttle rock & roll. –TG

Dirty Deeds Done Dirt Cheap / ATLANTIC   1981
An odds-'n'-sods collection of earlier Bon Scott-era tracks, worth it alone for the unforgettable title track. –TG

ROCK, POP & SOUL GENRES AND SUBGENRES

These genre/subgenre descriptions are intended to give the reader a feel for the school of music an artist may have worked within. Since many artists have crossed the line from one style to another over the course of their careers, when artists are mentioned within genres, it is merely intended to illuminate an aspect of the artist's sound.

R&B (RHYTHM AND BLUES) — A term that originated during the 40s, was initially a Black pop synthesis of big-band jump-blues, Tin Pan Alley, swing, and early rock & roll. R&B submerged into soul as that genre gained prominence during the 60s. Examples: Johnny Ace, La Vern Baker, Ray Charles, and Fats Domino.

ROCKABILLY — The mating of hillbilly country and Delta blues, Rockabilly, found its first expression at Sun Studios in Memphis, TN, during the mid 50s. The genre was usually built around small ensembles (string bass; lean, economical, rhythm-heavy electric guitar; minimal drum work; acoustic guitar; supporting an addled singing style (sometimes with hiccupping, stuttering vocals) set in a highly reverberant audio mix. Examples: Elvis Presley, Carl Perkins, Jerry Lee Lewis, Gene Vincent, Wanda Jackson, Eddie Cochran.

ROCK & ROLL (ROCK'N'ROLL) — Like the word "jazz," "rock & roll" was basically a euphemism for sexual intercourse. Rock's emphasis on rhythm, gritty (occasionally abrasive) instrumental sounds, and often salacious lyrical themes underscored the genre's roots in sexuality and things impulsive and earthy. Since the beginning, rock's visceral energy has provided an expression for the young at heart, the rebellious, or anyone looking for some kind of release. Musically, rock & roll drew liberally from Black blues and R&B and from White pop, folk, and country. Like R&B, rock & roll's grooves made for great dance-party music. Examples: Chuck Berry, Bob Seger, and Bruce Springsteen.

In the mid 60s, a less dance-oriented, more concert-oriented style of rock & roll emerged, which was usually given the title "rock." Rock music that had specialized leanings was usually indicated by hyphenated subgenre titles such as country-rock, folk-rock, blues-rock, and so forth.

ROOTS-ROCK — The term is usually applied to an acoustic/electric style of rock that draws more obviously from various American music traditions like country, blues, R&B, and folk. Examples: Dave Edmunds, John Hiatt, Stray Cats, Spanic Boys, and the Blasters.

POP — Pop (an abbreviation of the word "popular") music exists for mass-market appeal. Ideally, the intention of pop music is to achieve instant memorability. Most pop music is developed from a well-structured combination of repetitive melody and lyrical lines (referred to as "hooks") that convey messages of varying importance. Pop is even more chameleon-like than rock in the way it can exist in a seemingly endless array of styles while maintaining its essential structural qualities. Generally pop's spiritual home is Top 40 and middle-of-the-road adult radio formats.

Although pop is rarely more than a fairly pleasant diversion, at its best it can possess powerful sentiment and melodic invention that transcend mere craftsmanship; consider, for example, a deceptively simple song like the Beatles'

"Yesterday." Examples: Bread, the Carpenters, Culture Club, Neil Diamond, Michael Bolton, Art Garfunkel, Lionel Richie, Sade, Simply Red, Dionne Warwick, and Swing Out Sister.

Rock/pop — Basically, this description is applied to a commercially accessible blend of pop-song craftsmanship and production values, which still incorporates elements of rock's immediacy. Artists who have delved into this approach include Bon Jovi, Peter Frampton, Fleetwood Mac, Billy Joel, the Guess Who, Extreme, and World Party.

DOO-WOP — During the 50s doo-wop evolved from various Black R&B vocal groups; later, it crossed over to White acts as well, particularly in Northeastern cities. The name doo-wop referred to the application of nonsensical words sung in harmony, usually behind a lead vocal line. Many of the best artists from this genre created absolutely poetic moments with their arranged phonetics. Examples: The Moonglows, the Ravens, Dion & the Belmonts, and the Crests.

MOTOWN — The Detroit record label Motown rose to prominence in the 60s, with a clean, stylized Black pop sound that young White America bought by the truckloads. It was perfect radio music that utilized elements of gospel and sophisticated pop-song craftsmanship, delivered with snappy arrangements that lacked some of the rougher musical aspects of Southern soul music. Examples: The Temptations, the Four Tops, Smokey Robinson & the Miracles, the Supremes, and Martha & the Vandellas.

SOUL — In the American South (particularly in Memphis, TN, and Muscle Shoals, AL), the urgency found in Black gospel and rock helped transform R&B into a grittier, more immediate style known as soul. As the name implies, soul comes straight from the heart and articulates secular concerns and desires with gospel intensity, no matter whether in Sam & Dave's joyous statement of purpose, "Soul Man," Otis Redding's reflective "(Sittin' On) The Dock of the Bay," Wilson Pickett's sexy boast, "I'm a Midnight Mover," or Aretha Franklin's feminist anthems "Respect" or "Think."

British Invasion — While America was embracing light teen-idol pop during the early 60s, British youth were undergoing a pop and rock revolution, inspired by stateside sounds like blues, country, American pop, and garage-rock. Among the scores of emerging bands, the Beatles and the Rolling Stones best exemplified the diversity of these absorbed influences and created a totally fresh, vibrant sound that reawakened pop and rock from their dormancy. The collective effect was empowering to a generation of post-WWII adolescents, who were beginning to question the expectations of their elders in a Cold War climate.

Both the Beatles and the Rolling Stones initially recorded material that reflected their American influences, but eventually they became formidable sources of original work.

Examples — Peter & Gordon, Gerry & the Pacemakers, Herman's Hermits, and Billy J. Kramer & the Dakotas to rougher rock-oriented acts like the Yardbirds, Them, the Kinks, the Animals, and the Who.

FOLK/ROCK — When Bob Dylan infused his provocative imagistic folk music with a rough and tumble blues-influenced rock & roll sound, he laid the groundwork for taking rock beyond mere boy/girl issues into weightier thematic possibilities.

It was the Byrds, however, who defined what is commonly known as the folk-rock sound. Their distinctive, chiming folk-influenced rhythm-guitar sound (dominated by Rickenbacker 12-string electric guitars) and clean vocal harmony work (coupled with their soaring arrangements of songs by Dylan and Pete Seeger, as well as traditional folk copyrights and originals) have influenced generations of artists. During the mid 60s, many artists (particularly on the West Coast) followed the Byrds's lead, especially the Turtles, the Beau Brummels, and singer/songwriter P. F. Sloan. The Plimsouls and Tom Petty & the Heartbreakers are more recent examples of folk-rock-influenced artists.

BLUES/ROCK — Blues-rock generally stays true to the initial song forms and themes of blues, set in a rock band context. Usually the no-nonsense groove-oriented arrangements feature improvisary work by a lead instrument, developing ideas from blues scales and tonalities. Examples: Stevie Ray Vaughan, Rory Gallagher, Roy Buchanan, Canned Heat, and early ZZ Top.

R&B/ROCK — This rock subgenre displays more of the swing groove sensibilities of R&B. Horns are also not an uncommon element of the sound. Examples: Delbert McClinton, the J. Geils Band, Van Morrison, and Southside Johnny.

TEX-MEX — Also known as Tejano music, this genre originated in Texas. Tex-Mex, which began in the 1700s, draws from Spanish and Mexican folk music traditions. Over the last 30 years, Tex-Mex has brought in elements of country, rock and R&B. Examples: Joe King Carrasco, Ry Cooder, David Lindley, Doug Sahm, and the Texas Tornadoes.

PSYCHEDELIC — During the 60s, various rock artists sought to broaden the parameters of musical expression through mind-expanding drugs. Psychedelic rock attempted to convey the spirit of these altered states. Examples: Pink Floyd, Jimi Hendrix, Blue Cheer, Jefferson Airplane, Quicksilver Messenger Service, and later-period Beatles.

COUNTRY-ROCK — Country informed rock music from its inception, but it wasn't until the late 60s that rock artists aggressively sought to put their sound back into country. Gram Parsons was a primary facilitator in the creation of what was to be known as country-rock. His presence in the Byrds helped generate the first important album of this subgenre, *Sweetheart of the Rodeo*. Examples: Flying Burrito Brothers, Poco, Pure Prairie League, Linda Ronstadt, and the Eagles.

ART-ROCK/CLASSICAL-ROCK/PROG-ROCK — During the late 60s, many artists were inspired by the Beatles' renaissance approach to making rock a more serious art form. Art-rock, or classical-rock, was the result of realizing those intentions. Groups like the Moody Blues, Procol Harum, Genesis, Gryphon, and Emerson, Lake & Palmer incorporated extended classically structured compositions or grand orchestrally influenced arrangements with rock instrumentation. Thematically, many of these groups reached for lofty sentiment as well. Progressive rock came on the heels of art-rock with a more aggressive, occasionally dissonant style that borrowed from the spirit of hard rock. Examples: King Crimson, Yes, and later Rush.

SINGER/SONGWRITER — The singer/songwriter school fused elements of folk music with pop-song-craftsmanship. Artists like Carole King, James Taylor, Cat Stevens, and Joni Mitchell reached millions of listeners with their soft acoustic-based soft-pop introspections during the early 70s.

POWER-POP/ANGLO-POP — As rock attempted to get heavier and more serious toward the top of the 70s, various artists continued to mine the super-melodic pop/rock sensibilities of the British Invasion. Power-pop and Anglo-pop are basically interchangeable terms used to describe this approach. Generally the sound features fine harmonies and a full mid-period Beatles or Byrds-influenced guitar sound. Unlike most rock & roll or R&B, much of the groove takes a back seat to the melodies. Examples: Badfinger, Big Star, Shoes, the Raspberries, Michael Penn, the dB's, Bill Lloyd, and the Posies.

FUNK — Funk took the gritty appeal of soul and stripped it down to its most basic visceral rhythmic form. James Brown was the master of distilling his sound into bare-bones one-chord grooves that were stretched out over simple riffs. Sly & the Family Stone explored funk's earthiness as well. During the 70s the Ohio Players, Parliament/Funkadelic, the Brothers Johnson, and Bootsy Collins were some of funk's more prominent players.

SOUTHERN ROCK — This regional form emerged in the early 70s with such artists as the Allman Brothers, Lynyrd Skynyrd, Charlie Daniels Band, Wet Willie, Marshall Tucker Band, and Atlanta Rhythm Section. Thematically, Southern rock addresses the feelings and concerns of those in the American South. Musically, Southern rock draws from the music indigenous to that part of the country, such as gospel, soul, R&B, folk, and some jazz. This music was very much geared toward a high level of improvisation, which managed to maintain a strong sense of groove. Twin lead guitar lineups (with slide guitar) were not uncommon.

GARAGE-ROCK — Rock & roll didn't start out as some highbrow musical conceit, and garage-rock's determined anti-virtuosity underscored that its music was something practically anyone could generate. After all, many of rock & roll's greatest songs featured almost idiot-proof riffs and chord changes, no matter whether it was the Kingsmen's "Louie Louie," the Kinks' "You Really Got Me," Them's "Gloria," or the Ramones' "I Wanna Be Sedated." Garage-rock's amateurism and reckless energy helped pave the way for other genres like punk and alternative rock.

HARD ROCK/HEAVY METAL — The introduction of guitar distortion during the mid 60s created a common ground for blues-influenced rock and psychedelia. The result was an aggressive riff-oriented rock sound. The wider tonalities offered by distortion and fuzz tone, coupled with the larger, more aggressive role of drums and bass, helped bring about hard rock. The Yardbirds set the stage perfectly for the development of this sound, with their experimental sounds and increasingly unconventional arrangements. The Who also laid the groundwork with their anarchic approach to rhythm and their thick choral guitar voicings. Led Zeppelin, Cream, Jimi Hendrix, Steppenwolf, and Deep Purple expanded on the form. Over the years, artists like Van Halen, Blue Oyster Cult, Aerosmith, Bad Company, Scorpions, AC/DC, Tesla, and Guns N' Roses have carried on the spirit of hard rock/heavy metal.

As hard rock became denser and more aggressive-sounding, fans began groping for a way to describe the new attitudes. The designation heavy metal emerged, originating from William Burrough's *Naked Lunch* and later used in Steppenwolf's biker anthem "Born to be Wild." Black Sabbath, with their stripped-down half-speed themes of gloom and doom, laid the groundwork for metal as a stage for the exploration of themes concerning evil.

Thrash incorporated the raw energy of punk and the themes and thick tonalities of heavy metal into a high-speed style. Motörhead was one of the standard bearers for thrash. Over the course of the 80s and 90s, the music evolved further into speed-metal and death-metal, essentially upping the ante in the departments of speed, unintelligibility, and dark subject matter.

HARDCORE — This subgenre mixed elements of punk and thrash into an even more aggressive sound. Examples: Hüsker Dü, Suicidal Tendencies, the Misfits, Bad Brains, Dead Kennedys, and Meat Puppets.

FUSION — During the mid 70s, fusion captured the imagination of certain jazz and prog-rock artists who desired a musical platform to showcase their compositional and musical technique. With few exceptions, fusion lacked any vocal augmentation. In many ways, it was a close cousin to prog-rock; the only real difference came with the jazz chops that certain musicians brought to the genre. Examples: Return to Forever, the Mahavishnu Orchestra, Al Dimeola, and the Dixie Dregs.

PUNK — As rock became more diffuse in the 70s, it also lost much of its primal potency. Punk's willfully confrontational amateurism spat in the face of the pretense that rock had begun to embrace. The movement found much of its roots in the raw aggression of 60s and early 70s groups like MC5, New York Dolls, the Stooges, Velvet Underground, and early Who. Gone were the lengthy lead-instrumental breaks, and in their place was a jack-hammer-beat minimalism that made its point and got out of the way. The Ramones, Richard Hell & the Voidoids, the Sex Pistols, the Buzzcocks, and Clash represented the peak of this spirit.

NEW-WAVE — New-wave emerged in the late 70s with its art-pop-meets-fashionably-punk-ish style. Some vital bands emerged from this scene, such as the Cars, Pere Ubu, Split Enz, and Devo. Many of the artists possessed a sound that had affected vocals; clipped, clean arrangements; and rhythm parts. By the beginning of the 80s, the term new-wave had become such a catch-all for anything that looked left of mainstream rock/pop that it lost resonance as a meaningful designation. Even the Knack and Tom Petty & the Heartbreakers were marketed as such at one point.

ALTERNATIVE ROCK/POP — As new-wave mutated into meaninglessness, the designation alternative rock or pop came to represent music that was more attuned to the college radio market than to Top 40 or mainstream FM rock. Examples: R.E.M., Echo & the Bunnymen, Sonic Youth, and Mojo Nixon, the La's, Julian Cope, XTC, Psychedelic Furs, and the Cocteau Twins.

SKA-REVIVAL — Ska originated in Jamaica during the 60s. The Skatalites and Toots & the Maytals were the most successful exponents of that sound. Around 1980 there was a resurgence of artists in Britain who embraced ska's energetic nervous grooves. The Two-Tone record label was the heartbeat of that sound, with groups like English Beat, Specials, Madness, and Selector.

DISCO — While undanceable hard rock and introspective singer/songwriters seemed to reign during the first half of the 70s, the predominately gay Manhattan discotheque (French for "record library") scene increasingly gained prominence as the purveyors of the type of music eventually called disco, which set out to celebrate one thing: dancing. One of disco's signature qualities was its steady kick-drum-heavy beat. By the late 70s, the genre had become essentially a producer's medium, where the singer's personality was secondary to the groove. Gamble & Huff's glossy production style helped score a considerable number of hits for artist like the O'Jays, Harold Melvin & the Blue Notes, the Intruders, and the Three Degrees. Giorgio Moroder's clinical synth-heavy approach launched Donna Summer's career. (Summer eventually went beyond disco into major pop success.) In 1977 disco reached its commercial zenith with the 24-million-selling soundtrack to the movie *Saturday Night Fever*, which featured the Bee Gees, Tramps, Tavares, KC & the Sunshine Band, Kool & the Gang, MFSB, and others. Other significant disco artists included Shalamar, George McCrae, Chic, Village People, Sister Sledge, Sylvester, and Barry White. Disco's dominance of the late-70s popular-music landscape was so pervasive that even the sound of such artists as Herbie Hancock and the Rolling Stones incorporated its thumping grooves.

DANCE/DANCE-POP — At the top of the 80s, disco had more than worn out its welcome with many people, so disco's rigid 4/4 groove was replaced by more elastic rhythms and varied synth and other instrumental arrangements. Like disco, much dance-pop is a producer's medium. In a sense, disco never died; it just changed clothes. Over the course of the 80s and 90s, this form of music has remained extremely popular. Examples: Michael Jackson, Janet Jackson, Prince, Madonna, Paula Abdul, and Whitney Houston.

URBAN R&B — Urban R&B blended jumpy grooves like hip-hop and new-jack-swing into classic R&B song structures. Many of these artists are quite adept at covering smooth dance-oriented music as well as romantic ballads. Examples: Luther Vandross, Gregory Abbott, Johnny Gill, and Vanessa Williams.

TECHNO-POP/DANCE — Techno's roots can be traced to the 70s synthesizer experiments of Tangerine Dream, Kraftwerk, and Brian Eno. David Bowie and Roxy Music aided in the cool, arty pop sensibilities that have informed this subgenre. Examples: Ultravox, Depeche Mode, Blue Nile, Human League, Yello, New Order, and Marc Almond.

Radio format terms.

AOR — The emergence of progressive free-form FM rock radio in the renaissance period of the late 60s provided an outlet for many developing artists like Cream, the Doors, Jefferson Airplane, the Who, Janis Joplin, Jimi Hendrix, Crosby, Stills & Nash, and many more. These artists didn't cater to the standard 3-minute hit-single song format but opted instead for extended improvisations and unconventional song structures and arrangements. It was these characteristics of the artists that were played on FM rock stations that helped coin the AOR, or album-oriented rock.

MOR — MOR stands for middle-of-the-road. Most MOR stations feature a style of music that is usually heavy on ballads and light upbeat pop.

CHR — CHR (contemporary hits radio) came into prominence in the early 80s. Essentially a very tightly formatted equivalent to AM's Top 40s sound, CHR came at a time when MTV was beginning to affect the musical tastes of the youth market. Consequently, CHR helped the careers of artists like Thomas Dolby, Simple Minds, and Naked Eyes, while featuring a considerable amount of dance-pop.

For Those About to Rock / ATLANTIC   1981
For Those About to Rock We Salute You is another masterwork from the Brian Johnson period. The title song has become the group's signature track and is featured in AC/DC concerts with pyrotechnics galore. A must for those who don't mind staring into the face of deafness. –TG

74 Jailbreak / ATLANTIC   1984
Actually an EP of Bon Scott-period material but nonetheless some of AC/DC's best and most blistering blues. In particular the title song and an incendiary "Baby, Please Don't Go" are worth the admission. –TG

The Razor's Edge / ATLANTIC   1991
The band unarguably slipped a few notches in the late 80s, but *The Razor's Edge* brought them back into the 90s with a vengeance. Great hooks, great sound, and a great single, "Money Talks." Whoever said they sold out? –TG

ACCEPT

Heavy metal. Impressive and aggressive heavy metal from Germany that has continued to stay strong, even with the departure of an essential vocalist. Once considered an underground group, they may have been one of the first bands to introduce speed-metal to Americans. –JB

Restless and Wild / CBS   1983
Accept created what would eventually become speed-metal with "Fast As a Shark." Very influential. –JB

Restless and Wild / Balls to the Wall / CBS   1986
A packaging of their two best albums, but omitting a couple of key songs. –JB

ACCUSED

Thrash. Accused is a band from Seattle that combines punk and hardcore with slight metal influences. Their first EP was independently released in 1984; in 1987 Combat Records signed them. –JB

More Fun Than ... / RELATIVITY   1987
More Fun Than an Open Casket Funeral is the best album the band has ever done, and the best of punk and metal combined. An essential album for those getting into the Seattle music scene for the first time. –JB

JOHNNY ACE   1929-1954

R&B. One of the more tragic 50s R&B heroes. Ace (John Alexander) was a fixture on the Memphis Beale Street blues scene, playing with Bobby Bland and Roscoe Gordon in the fabled Beale Streeters. He struck out solo in the early 50s, recording the gorgeous, stark ballad "Pledging My Love" in 1954, and died playing Russian roulette on Christmas Eve 1954. –JF

Memorial Album / MCA   1974
The greatest hits from this ill-fated Memphis blues pianist. Includes the posthumous smash "Pledging My Love." –BD

BARBARA ACKLIN   b1944

R&B, Southern rock. Acklin began singing background vocals at Chess in the mid 60s. Signing with Chicago's Brunswick label (where she was a receptionist), Acklin debuted on the R&B charts in 1968 as Gene Chandler's duet partner before stepping out on her own later that year with the brassy "Love Makes a Woman," her biggest R&B and pop hit. Acklin was also a prolific composer at Brunswick, writing or cowriting hits for Jackie Wilson and the Chi-Lites. –BD

Love Makes a Woman / BRUNSWICK   1968
Unrepresented on CD as yet. This is 60s Chicago soul songstress Acklin's debut album, with her irresistible title-track smash. –BD

Seven Days of Night / BRUNSWICK   1969
More excellent late-60s soul from Brunswick's top female artist — includes "Just Ain't No Love" and "Am I the Same Girl," both R&B hits. –BD

BRYAN ADAMS   b1959

Rock/pop. Canadian artist Bryan Adams is one of mainstream rock's biggest hitmakers with his style of Heartland rock — a rhythm-guitar-heavy sound that implies roots in the Byrds and the Stones. With his raspy lower tenor, he has a classic rock & roll voice. His grasp of creating memorable melodic and simple lyrical hooks has earned him an enormous string of hits including "Cuts Like a Knife" (#15), "Run to You" (#6), "Summer of 69" (#5), "Heat of the Night" (#6), "Heaven" (#1), and "(Everything I Do) I Do it for You," the #1 hit from the movie *Robin Hood.* –RC

Cuts Like A Knife / A&M   1983
A Top Ten breakthrough album in America for this Canadian rocker, carried by the strength of "Straight from the Heart" (his first US single) and the title track. –DDC

Reckless / A&M   1985
Radio-friendly pop-rock driven by Adams's trademark gravelly vocals that spawned three Top Ten hits, including "Heaven," "Run to You," and a duet with Tina Turner on "It's Only Love." –DDC

Waking Up the Neighbours / A&M   1991
Features the mega hit "(Everything I Do) I Do It for You" from the movie *Robin Hood - Prince of Thieves.* –DDC

FAYE ADAMS

R&B. The heavily gospel-influenced chanteuse scored three chart-topping R&B hits in 1953-1954. From Newark, NJ, Adams joined Joe Morris's band in 1952 as featured singer. A year later, she was a star, thanks to her moving ballad "Shake a Hand" on Al Silver's New York-based Herald label. The song has proven an R&B standard, covered by the likes of Little Richard and Ruth Brown. Two more #1 R&B hits followed in rapid succession: "I'll Be True" (covered by Bill Haley and the Comets) and "Hurts Me to My Heart." She later moved to Imperial, and stirred up some action with "Keeper of My Heart" in 1957, before returning to the church. –BD

Golden Classics / COLLECTABLES   1990
This gospel-influenced vocalist's 50s hits, most notably the powerful "Shake a Hand." –BD

OLETA ADAMS

Urban R&B. The youngest daughter of a minister, Oleta's first musical experience was in the choir of her father's church. Discovered by Tears for Fears while performing solo in a Hyatt Regency lounge in Kansas City, MO, she was featured prominently on their *Seeds of Love* album. Tears for Fears member Roland Orzabal went on to produce her 1990 debut album, *Circle of One*, featuring the hit "Get Here." She was a 1991 Grammy nominee. –SWB

Circle of One / POLYGRAM   1990
The former backing vocalist for Tears for Fears performs very well on her debut album, establishing her as a singer to watch. Soothing and deep vocals with a heavy gospel influence, featuring the hits "Get Here" and the relaxing "Rhythm of Life." –JB

HASIL ADKINS   b1936

Rockabilly. A crazed rockabilly one-man band, Adkins has been recording in a tarpaper shack in the hills of West Virginia since the mid 50s. The absolutely crudest and wildest of all rock & rollers, Hasil's lyrics stray as far from the standard 50s clichés as you can get. Songs about eating peanut butter on the moon, chopping girls' heads off and mounting them on his wall, and doing something called the "hunch" are typical lyrical fare for Adkins. Combining a three-octave voice that can go from sub-glottal Elvis moans to blood-curdling screams that can freeze the blood with an over-amplified guitar that sounds like a gigantic rubber band, there is nothing in pop music that sounds anything like Hasil Adkins, a true rock & roll primitive. –CK

○ **Out to Hunch / NORTON**   1986
All the lunatic classics: "She Said," "Chicken Walk," "No More
Hot Dogs," "The Hunch," "We Got a Date" and the mind-
boggling arrangements of "Memphis" and "High School
Confidential." Not for the faint of heart. −CK

The Wild Man / NORTON   1987
His 80s recordings, just as crazy. −CK

Chicken Walk / DEE-JAY JAMBOREE   1988
More crazed 50s-early 60s sides. (Import) −CK

ADOLESCENTS

Hardcore. Wild Los Angeles hardcore band fronted by guitarist
Rikk Agnew. The band released its first album in 1981,
disbanded and re-formed in 1986 with Agnew, singer Tony
Montana, and bassist Steve Soto. The group again disbanded
in 1989. −DS

○ **Adolescents / FRONTIER**   1981
Seminal 80s West Coast punk outfit led by guitarist Rikk
Agnew. −DS

Live 1981 and 1986 / TRIPLE X   1989
Excellent live record that samples both periods of the
California mosh masters. −DS

AEROSMITH

Hard rock. Boston's Aerosmith is a riff-heavy American
synthesis of Led Zepplin, the Yardbirds, and the Rolling
Stones. During their rise to prominence as album rock kings
in the mid 70s, Aerosmith managed to produce an impressive
collection of hard-rock classics like "Dream On," "Walk This
Way," "Back in the Saddle," and "Sweet Emotion."
By the end of the 70s, FM album-rock had become a cynical
stale format, and arena rock groups like Aerosmith became
the subject of derision among arbiters of the ascending punk
and new-wave movements. By then, ensuing personal
conflicts and drug problems had weakened Aerosmith's
creative power, anyway.
Nevertheless, Aerosmith had the good fortune to make the
most of a second chance at success. This was fueled by two
very different sources. Rap artists Run-D.M.C. scored a huge
hit version of Aerosmith's "Walk This Way" in 1986, and the
rise of FM classic-rock radio fed a market nostalgic for
something more edgy and organic than synth-pop acts like
Tears for Fears, Wham!, and Duran Duran.
The newly sober Aerosmith seized the moment and produced
two highly successful albums with *Permanent Vacation* and
Pump, which ranks with *Rocks* as their best work. −RC

Aerosmith / CBS   1973
The debut from this Boston band shows a sensitive side with
their best-known ballad, "Dream On." But the focus remains
on it's raw, aggressive garage-rock style amply displayed on
"Mama Kin," "One Way Street," and "Make It." −DDC

Get Your Wings / CBS   1974
Aerosmith took the Yardbird's classic "Train Kept a Rollin'"
and made it their own with Steven Tyler's blistering vocals
and Joe Perry's ace guitar work. −DDC

○ **Toys in the Attic / CBS**   1975
A solid slice of classic 70s raunch and roll. Aerosmith defined
grunge-rock with their best and now-classic "Sweet Emotion"
and "Walk This Way." −DDC

○ **Rocks / CBS**   1976
After defining their style on *Toys in the Attic*, they perfected it
here. −DDC

★ **Greatest Hits / CBS**   1980
A solid collection of hits, including their stellar Beatles
remake "Come Together." All hits, no misses. −DDC

Permanent Vacation / GEFFEN   1987
On their first major success after choosing the clean and sober
route and switching to Geffen Records, Aerosmith begins to
regain its rock edge with "Dude (Looks Like a Lady)" and
"Rag Doll." −DDC

Music Map

50s R&B THROUGH SOUL AND FUNK TO 90s DANCE POP

| **50s R&B** |
| James Brown — Ray Charles |
| Sam Cook — Charles Brown |

| **60s Soul** |
| James Brown — Otis Redding |
| Sam & Dave — Wilson Pickett |
| Aretha Franklin |

| **Late 60s Funk** |
| James Brown — Sly & The Family Stone |

| **Funk 70's** |
| Funkadelic — Parliament |
| George Clinton — Bootsy Collins |

| **70s Soul** |
| Curtis Mayfield — Issac Hayes |
| The Chi-Lites — The Stylistics |
| Harold Melvin & the Blue Notes — The O' Jays |
| The Spinners — Rufus |

| **Disco (mid to late 70s)** |
| Chic — Donna Summer |
| Bee Gees — Sisters Sledge |

| **80s Dance** |
| Michael Jackson — Madonna — The Gap Band |
| Cameo — Prince — The Time |

| **90s Dance** |
| Michael Jackson — Madonna — Janet Jackson — Keith Sweat |
| Guy — Bell Biv Devoe — Bobby Brown — Another Bad Creation |
| Boyz II Men — Paula Abdul |

○ **Pump / GEFFEN**   1989
Loaded with great tunes, from the risqué "Love in an
Elevator" to the controversial "Janie's Got a Gun" to the
melodic "What It Takes." Their best later-period work. −DDC

AFGHAN WHIGS

Punk, alternative rock. Although initially they sounded a lot
like the Replacements, Cincinnati's Afghan Whigs decided to
crank up the amps and let the riffing do the talking. −JD

○ **Up in It / SUB POP**   1990
More pop than you'd expect from a Sub Pop release, this is still
loud & hard riff-raunch with a thick, unyielding sound. −JD

AGENT ORANGE

Hardcore. A trio from Fullerton, CA, which specialized in the
unlikely combination of punk and surf music. Cemented by
vocalist/guitarist Mike Palm, Agent Orange released its first
album in 1981 amid the California hardcore craze. −DS

Living in Darkness / POSHBOY   1981
Hard-driving debut of this echoey 80s hardcore band. −DS

○ **This is the Voice / RES**   1986
The best example of this twangy version of California punk,
showcasing the guitar and vocals of Mike Palm. −DS

AGITPOP

Alternative rock. From upstate New York, this trio sounds a lot like the Minutemen but they eschew politics for the more traditional rock fare of good times — not necessarily a bad thing, even in the 90s. –BE

○ **Open Seasons / TWINTONE**   1988
Spirit over sonic perfection. A spare trio making great adventurous rock. –RG

Stick It / TWINTONE   1989
Forays into roots rock, Agitpop style. –RG

AGNOSTIC FRONT

Hardcore. One of the most influential hardcore bands from New York, they formed in the early 80s and gained a massive following within the hardcore and metal crowds. –JB

○ **Cause for Alarm / RELATIVITY**   1986
An album that presented hardcore to many metal listeners for the first time. Politically aware and frighteningly true, they're not a metal band but they demonstrated the kinds of things metal lacked back then. –JB

Victim in Pain / RELATIVITY   1986
Continues to be an influence for many hardcore and punk bands. –JB

Liberty & Justice for All / RELATIVITY   1987
The album contained a slight influence from metal, and thus sold quite well within the metal community. –JB

Live at CBGB / RELATIVITY   1989
Agnostic Front the way they should be enjoyed, in concert, with full support from the crowd. The band's last album before their temporary hiatus. –JB

AIR SUPPLY

Pop. Russell Hitchcock and Graham Russell make up this Australian pop duo who had many hits with their soft ballads. The Top Ten hits "Lost in Love," and "Even the Nights Are Better" were radio staples of the 80s. Although Hitchcock and Russell disbanded in 1988, they reunited in 1991. –IME

○ **Greatest Hits / ARISTA / BB 7**   1983
This self-explanatory collection includes "Lost in Love" (#3), "The One That You Love" (#1), "Every Woman in the World" (#5), "All out of Love" (#2), "Sweet Dreams" (#5), "Making Love out of Nothing at All" (#2), "Even the Nights Are Better" (#5), and many more soft-pop hits. –RC

THE ALARM

Alternative rock. An English foursome, the Alarm (inspired by U2's lofty dispatches) initially generated a rock-heavy acoustic guitar-based rock, loaded with anthemic melodies and issue-oriented lyrics. Later the band switched to electric guitars and developed a more mainstream/alternative sound that earned them an audience among the MTV set. Even though the Alarm has been quite popular in England, they've only had one pop chart hit stateside with the #77 "Presence of Love." –RC

○ **Standards / CAPITOL**   1990
Solid anthology covers everything from early aggressive topical folk/rock anthems ("Matching On," "The Stand") to more mainstream rock hits like "Strength" and "Sold Me Down the River." –RC

ARTHUR ALEXANDER   *b 1942*

R&B, soul. Alexander was one of the first true singing songwriting stars of "country-soul," a genre that wed Southern Black R&B singers to songs written in a country format and played basically by White musicians. Alexander's "You Better Move On" (#2-1962), was the first hit to come out of Rick Hall's fledgling Muscle Shoals studio. Alexander's work was immediately appreciated by his peers in the business; those who have covered his tunes (self-penned or otherwise)

read like a Who's Who from both sides of the Atlantic — "Anna" (Beatles); "Soldiers of Love" (Beatles and Marshall Crenshaw); "Burning Love" (Elvis Presley); "Set Me Free" (Joe Tex, Esther Phillips, Percy Sledge). The Rolling Stones' cover of "You Better Move On" led to valuable contacts for Rick Hall, and the resulting business enabled him to build the new FAME studio. It was the start of the whole Muscle Shoals sound, and Alexander's career was one of its cornerstones. He went on, after a brief retirement, to record for both Warner Brothers and Buddah.

"Anna (Go to Him)," one of Alexander's best-known tunes, epitomizes the anguished, haunting tone of his music. From the onset, the heavily echoed piano and tortured vocal set a mood that is soulful, mysterious, a little spooky, and totally mesmerizing. His work is essential to any country-soul collection. –CO

Arthur Alexander / WARNER   1972
Vintage country-soul, produced by Tommy Cogbill. Includes semi-autobiographical "Rainbow Road" plus the original version of Elvis Presley's "Burning Love." (Out of print) –CO

☆ **Greatest Hits / ACE**   1991
Reissue of the great Dot recordings plus his rare early Judd sides. Includes "Anna (Go to Him)," "Soldiers of Love," "Go Home Girl," and "You Better Move On." Haunting, soulful, essential. –CO

ALICE IN CHAINS

Heavy metal. From being a total glam band to becoming one of the hottest bands out of the Seattle scene, Alice in Chains created good-time heavy metal by using what was good from the past and moving forward to make their own sound. –JB

○ **Facelift / CBS**   1990
Members of this band used to be in glam bands, but now they offer the crunch of heavy metal with the class of Seattle "grunge." The new wave of heavy metal in the 90s. –JB

LEE ALLEN   *b 1926*

R&B. The blasting tenor saxophone of Lee Allen was every bit as integral a factor in the sizzling sound of the 50s New Orleans R&B as were the well-documented contributions of Fats Domino, Lloyd Price, and Little Richard. As a key member of the studio band at Cosimo's, Allen played his searing solos that sparked hundreds of Crescent City classics. Allen's wallpaper-peeling sax solos are instantly identifiable — check out Richard's "Slippin' and Slidin'" and "Tutti Frutti" for irrefutably exciting evidence.

But despite his sax mastery, Allen failed to sustain a brief solo career. Signing with Al Silver's New York-based Ember label, he managed one decent-sized hit in 1958, the rocking instrumental "Walkin' with Mr. Lee," while the second-line scorcher "Boppin' at the Hop" inexplicably never received any national airplay.

When the New Orleans sound shifted to a funkier beat, Allen's muscular sound fell out of favor on the local recording scene. But he hasn't been idle — Allen has toured extensively with Domino over the years, as well as working with a variety of young rockers (including the Blasters) who revere his blistering sound. –BD

○ **Walkin' with Mr. Lee / CBS**   1958
New Orleans's leading tenor sax man during the 50s, with his only solo album. Hot rockin' instrumentals. –BD

GREGG ALLMAN BAND   *b 1947*

Southern rock. Gregg Allman is the lead vocalist and keyboardist of the Allman Brothers Band. Fans of the Allman Brothers should find this solo work generally satisfying. –RC

○ **Laid Back / POLYGRAM**   1973
Debut solo album showcases Allman's soulful, earthy keyboard work and leathery drawl to good effect. "These Days" and the reworked Allman Brothers Band standard, "Midnight Rider" are exceptional. –RC

Playin' Up a Storm / POLYGRAM   1977
Weaker material, but the playing and singing more than compensate. –RC

I'm No Angel / CBS   1987
Title track was a comeback hit. Allman's voice is distanced in the mix by a little too much reverb. The band tracks are particularly hot. –RC

Just Before the Bullets Fly / EPIC   1988
Another solid journeyman outing. As on *I'm No Angel*, this release suffers from overly wet mixes. "Demons" is a highlight. –RC

THE ALLMAN BROTHERS BAND

Southern rock. The Allman Brothers Band was the major instigator of the Southern-rock genre of the 70s and one of the major rock acts of the first half of that decade; it continues to be popular today. In its original configuration, the group consisted of Duane Allman (b Nov 20, 1946-d Oct 29, 1971) on guitar; Gregg Allman (b Dec 08, 1947) on organ and vocals; Dickey Betts (b Dec 12, 1943) on guitar and vocals; Berry Oakley (b Apr 04, 1948-d Nov 11, 1971) on bass; and Butch Trucks and Jaimo (b John Lee Johnson, Jul 08, 1944) on drums. This sextet was a showcase for the twin-guitar work of Duane Allman and Dickey Betts and for the bluesy singing of Gregg Allman. It cut three albums between 1969 and 1971. *Live at the Fillmore East*, the Allmans' breakthrough third album, went gold four days before bandleader Duane Allman was killed in a motorcycle accident. The group continued as a quintet, finishing its fourth album, *Eat a Peach* (1972), which was a major success. After bassist Oakley was also killed in a motorcycle accident, the group was augmented with bassist Lamar Williams (b 1947-d Jan 1983) and pianist Chuck Leavell to complete its fifth album, *Brothers and Sisters*, which topped the charts and spawned the #2 single "Ramblin' Man." But the group split up in acrimony after the release of *Win, Lose or Draw* in 1975.

The Allmans re-formed in 1978, this time returning to the sextet format, with Allman, Betts, Trucks, and Jaimo being joined by guitarist Dan Toler and bassist David Goldflies for the gold-selling *Enlightened Rogues* (1979). Two more albums, *Reach for the Sky* and *Brothers of the Road* (for which David Toler replaced Jaimo and Mike Lawler was added on piano), were released before the band split again.

Following the release of a boxed-set retrospective, *Dreams*, in 1989, the Allmans again re-formed, and to date they have released two more albums and toured extensively. –WR

○ **The Allman Brothers Band / POLYGRAM**   1969
The Allmans' aggressive synthesis of blues, rock, jazz, and gospel made an impressive entrance on this 1969 debut, with soon-to-be-standards like "Whipping Post" and the dynamic moody "Dreams." Highlights like "Don't Want You No More," "It's Not My Cross to Bear," "Black Hearted Woman," and "Trouble No More" are further reasons why this was one of the greatest bands to ever emerge from the American South. –RC

○ **Idlewild South / POLYGRAM / BB 38**   1970
The Allmans' second effort may not have been quite as strong as their powerful debut, but *Idlewild South* had more than a handful of gems with songs like the celebratory "Revival," the earthy "Midnight Rider," and the instrumental "In Memory of Elizabeth Reed," with its soaring twin-guitar counterpuntal melodies. –RC

☆ **At Fillmore East / POLYGRAM / BB 13**   1971
The double-disc *Allman Brothers Band at Fillmore East* is one of rock's greatest live albums, featuring amazing interplay within highly dynamic arrangements. Most of the tracks exceed ten minutes, yet the Allmans never stumble. "Hot 'Lanta," "In Memory of Elizabeth Reed," and "Statesboro Blues" are highlights. Contrary to claims that these are untouched performances, *Fillmore East* actually was a skillfully edited document (courtesy of producer Tom Dowd) taken from a run of shows at Bill Graham's Fillmore. (Mobile Fidelity offers an audiophile version in a mock-road-

case style package, complete with photos and notes from Tom Dowd.) –RC

● **Eat a Peach / POLYGRAM / BB 4**   1972
Half of *Eat a Peach* consists of more fiery improvisations from the *Live at the Fillmore* dates, in the form of the "Mountain Jam." Even though this was released after Duane Allman's fatal motorcycle accident, the studio sides include some tracks showcasing his soaring lead work. Creatively, the band was in peak form with great tracks like "Ain't Wastin' Time No More" (#77), "Melissa" (#86), "One Way Out" (#86), "Stand Back," "Blue Sky," and the delicate acoustic guitar instrumental "Little Martha." (Also available on Mobile Fidelity) –RC

Beginnings / POLYGRAM / BB 25   1973
Beginnings is nothing more than the first two albums on a single disc. Since its release, Polygram has done a markedly improved remastering job, releasing each album separately. –RC

Enlightened Rogues / POLYGRAM / BB 9   1979
After six years of spotty albums, the Allmans made a strong comeback with this Tom Dowd-produced effort. Gregg Allman is in fine voice, and the band kicks up some sparks throughout. Some of the material is a little weak, but "Crazy Love," a duet by Bonnie Bramlett and Dickie Betts, is a highlight. –RC

○ **Dreams / POLYGRAM**   1989
This is a thoughtfully compiled boxed set, containing highlights throughout the Allman Brothers' entire career, as well as solo projects and early pre-Allman recordings. A booklet, with generous annotation and photos, is provided. The remastering is a noticeable improvement over initial CD releases of the Allman catalog. If you've got the bucks for a boxed set, this is a worthwhile acquisition for completists and those looking for a comprehensive introduction. –RC

○ **Seven Turns / CBS / BB 53**   1989
After a nine-year absence, the Allmans return with a vengeance on *Seven Turns*, with tracks like the hard-swinging opener, "Good Clean Fun" and the powerful blues-rock work-out "Gambler's Roll." The Dickey Betts-penned title track, a mystical take on life, is the album's spiritual highlight, while "True Gravity" is the musical peak, ranking with "In Memory of Elizabeth Reed" as one of the band's best instrumentals. Overall, *Seven Turns* is their strongest album since 1972's *Eat a Peach*. –RC

Shades of Two Worlds / CBS   1991
Weaker than *Seven Turns*, *Shades of Two Worlds* still has its moments, particularly the extended rave-up "Kind of Bird." "Bad Rain" and "Nobody Knows" are two other highlights. –RC

DUANE ALLMAN   1946-1971

Southern rock. During his brief career, the late Duane Allman managed to become one of rock's greatest guitarists, with his liquid, yet visceral electric lead and slide guitar playing. Allman's consistently high caliber of recorded work as a session sideman (particularly at Rick Hall's Fame Studio in Muscle Shoals) for artists like Wilson Pickett, King Curtis, and Clarence Carter, and in his role in the groundbreaking Allman Brothers Band and Derek & the Dominos, has understandably inspired thousands of guitarists.

Allman's star was still rising when his life was tragically cut short by a motorcycle accident in October of 1971. He was just 24 years old. –RC

○ **Anthology / POLYGRAM**   1972
A superb collection of Duane's work with the Allmans, as well as many great session gigs. –DH

Anthology - Vol.2 / POLYGRAM   1973
More great guitar work in tandem with Aretha Franklin, Wilson Pickett, and others. –DH

MARC ALMOND   b1959

Techno-pop. Marc Almond, the rather unsteady-sounding lead singer of the early-80s techno-cabaret/pop unit Soft Cell, generated a rather popular solo career in England with his fairly bleak, decadent Euro-pop. –RC

Singles 1984 - 87 / SOME BIZZARE   1987
A compilation of Almond's solo work. –SA

○ **Stars We Are / PARLOPHONE**   1988
Accessible "big-pop"; a fine introduction to Almond. –SA

Jacques / SOME BIZZARE   1989
Almond sings Jacques Brel. –SA

Memorabilia / MERCURY   1991
A compilation of solo material and Soft Cell sides. –SA

HERB ALPERT   b 1935

Pop. Trumpeter Herb Alpert started in rock & roll, working with Jan & Dean and others. He took a $200 demo of the instrumental *Twinkle Star*, overdubbed bullfight crowd noises, retitled it *The Lonely Bull*. It became his first gold record. Shortly thereafter Alpert formed A&M Records with Jerry Moss as well as a studio group named the Tijuana Brass. The TJB scored consistently on both the single and album charts over the next ten years, with five albums going to #1. Alpert's laidback vocal style later found mega-success with the smash "This Guy's in Love with You," trading original Latin-flavored style for straight MOR. –CK

The Lonely Bull / A&M   1962
The early breakthrough sound of the TJB featuring the title track and the cream of Los Angeles session players. –CK

○ **Classics - Vol. 1 / A&M**   1987
All the high points from the ten-year dominance of Alpert and the Tijuana Brass; includes "A Taste of Honey," "Spanish Flea," and others. –CK

Classics - Vol. 20 / A&M   1987
This set features Alpert's solo hits from "This Guy's in Love with You" to "Rise." –CK

ALTERED IMAGES

Alternative pop. Altered Images was a British power-pop group formed in 1979 and led by film actress Claire Grogan. The group lasted until 1984, their biggest success coming with the UK Top Three hit "Happy Birthday" in 1981. –WR

○ **Happy Birthday / CBS**   1981
Their debut album contains their first UK hit, the title track, produced by Martin Rushent of Joy Division fame. –WR

DAVE ALVIN

Roots-rock. Most neo-rockabilly artists merely mimic the music without expanding its vocabulary or its creative horizons. Dave Alvin is the exception that proves the rule. From his teeth-cutting days with the now-defunct Blasters (which featured Dave's brother Phil on vocals) up to his current solo career, Alvin has used rockabilly and country as a springboard (as opposed to sole inspiration) for his sympathetic and precise songwriting, which tackles some of the same issues as John Mellencamp's. He's also one hell of an axe slinger. –JF

○ **Romeo's Escape / EPIC**   1987
After leaving the roots-rock Blasters, Dave Alvin, the group's primary songwriter and guitarist, decided to give country a go. His hoarse shout of a voice made him a tough sell, and the songs on *Romeo's Escape*, his sole Nashville album, have yet to be plundered and they should be. Dwight Yoakam lifted his arrangement of "Long White Cadillac," a Blasters song, in 1989, and Joe Ely covered "Every Night About This Time" in 1992. (George Jones should.) Alvin's a natural storyteller, with a strong perspective on history that makes him perfect for country — even if country's not perfect for him. –BM

★ **Blue Blvd / HIGHTONE**   1991
The former guitarist/songwriter of the Blasters has his solo debut, singing his own songs. As with the Blasters, it's the songs that impress most, notably here "Fourth of July" and "Border Radio." –WR

PHIL ALVIN

Rock/pop. Phil Alvin was the lead singer of the Blasters in the early 80s. He released an eclectic solo album, *Un "Sung" Stories*, in 1986, with backing from the Dirty Dozen Brass Band and Sun Ra and the Arketra. –WR

○ **Un "Sung" Stories / WARNER**   1986
Leaving the Blasters, lead singer Phil Alvin moved back in time from that band's rockabilly approach to jazz and jump-blues styles, employing the Dirty Dozen Brass Band and Sun Ra & His Arkestra on songs by Cab Calloway and others. –WR

AMAZING BLONDEL

Prog-rock. A progressive-rock trio who came at the music in a decidedly retrograde manner, playing originals based on pre-19th-century musical forms (madrigals, chamber music, etc.) on authentic instruments and reproductions. The results were eloquent, stunning in their textures and timbre, but decidedly unrocklike even by the standards of the time. John David Gladwin was the trio's musical mainspring, and when he left in 1972, the duo that remained carried on with one good album before losing direction and inspiration. The group moved through a succession of labels from Bell to Island — where they did their best work — over to DJM. –BE

○ **England 72 / ISLAND**   1972
A staggeringly beautiful collection of love songs and odes to nature, all with distinctly pre-20th-century (indeed, pre-19th-century) feel. Exquisitely sung and played. (Out of print) –BE

Blondel / ISLAND   1973
A less wide-ranging followup, as a duo rather than a trio. Decidedly more limited musically but still possessing some hauntingly beautiful moments. (Out of print) –BE

THE AMAZING RHYTHM ACES

R&B rock, country rock. One of the first and best Southern country-rock bands, the Aces were formed out of Jesse Winchester's backup band in 1974 and produced six albums bristling with rock, bluegrass, hardcore honky-tonk country, Western swing, and R&B. They scored their biggest hit with "Third Rate Romance"; supplied country singer Mel McDaniel with his hits "Big Old Brew" and "Anger and Tears"; and had minor hits with "The End Is Not in Sight (The Cowboy Song)" and "Burning the Ballroom Down." After three albums, they disbanded in 1981. Lead singer and songwriter Russell Smith pursued a solo career. –KK

○ **Stacked Deck / ABC**   1975
The Aces' first and still their best, *Stacked Deck* produced "Third Rate Romance," the country chart hit "Amazing Grace (Used to Be Her Favorite Song)," and sparkling covers of "Life's Railway to Heaven" and Charlie Rich's "Who Will the Next Fool Be." –KK

Too Stuffed to Jump / ABC   1976
The followup to *Stacked Deck* is worth having solely for "The End Is Not in Sight" and is solid throughout even with the atrocious cover art. –KK

How the Hell Do You Spell Rhythum? / WARNER   1980
The band goes out in tighter-than-tight style, covering "Futher on Down the Road," Delbert McClinton's "Object of My Affection," and Van Morrison's "Wild Night" and introducing the original version of "Big Ole Brew." –KK

AMBITIOUS LOVERS

Alternative rock. A surprisingly accessible rock group led by "no wave" guitarist Arto Lindsay (b May 28, 1953) and Peter Scherer that still manages to express Lindsay's odd combination of Brazilian, pop, and avant-garde styles. –WR

○ **Greed / ATLANTIC**   1988
The wonder was that certified noisemaker Arto Lindsay, in cahoots with Peter Scherer, could make an album this accessible. Which is to say, for an avant-garde/artsy outfit like this one, there sure are a lot of melodies and love lyrics. But

there's still enough noise (courtesy of sidemen like John Zorn and Living Colour's Vernon Reid) to keep things strange. –WR

AMBROSIA

Art-rock, rock/pop. Ambrosia, a 70s Los Angeles group, synthesized art-rock with a relatively slick West Coast pop sound, especially toward the end of their career. They produced a few multi-format hits with "Biggest Part of Me" (#3), "How Much I Feel" (#3), "Holding on to Yesterday" (#17), and "You're the Only Woman" (#13). –RC

○ **Ambrosia / 20TH CENTURY**   1975
A wonderful debut album, produced by Alan Parsons. Top-notch mid-70s art rock, with great musicianship. Features "Holdin' on to Yesterdays" and "Nice, Nice, Very Nice." –SWB

Somewhere I've Never Travelled / 20TH CENTURY 1976
Their second album is more in the symphonic realm but just as good as their debut. –SWB

One Eighty / WARNER   1980
Contains their biggest pop hits, "Biggest Part of Me" and "You're the Only Woman." –SWB

AMERICA

Rock/pop. This light singer/songwriter pop trio scored big with their Neil Young-like #1 hit "Horse with No Name." America generated several more harmony-laden acoustic hits before enlisting Beatles producer George Martin, who gave the band a fuller sound, while maintaining their soft pop approach. –RC

○ **History - Greatest Hits / WARNER**   1975
A nice roundup of their peak years (1971-1975), including tracks like "A Horse with No Name" (#1), "I Need You" (#9), "Ventura Highway" (#8), "Tin Man" (#4), "Lonely People" (#5), "Sister Golden Hair" (#1), and more. –DH

Encore: More Greatest Hits / RHINO   1991
This followup to their *Greatest Hits* contains "The Border" (#33), "Right Before Your Eyes" (#45), "Today's the Day" (#23), and "You Can Do Magic" (#8). The rest of the tracks are album sides or previously unreleased material. –ED

AMERICAN MUSIC CLUB

Alternative rock. A traditional-sounding rock band in these postmodern times? Well, American Music Club, led by Mark Eitzel, may be an anomaly, but its a pretty engaging proposition on record. Eitzel's songwriting is very straightforward: good people living through hard times, and he's very much the agreeable populist. His bandmates add to this mix by playing no-nonsense bare bones rock & roll that, if slightly derivative of blues/rock structures, is also loaded with enough panache. Smart and direct, a fine American band. –JD

California / FRONTIER   1988
Stark-sounding, highly personal songs that cemented the reputation of band leader Mark Eitzel. –SA

United Kingdom / DEMON FIEND   1990
Studio and live tracks; this import CD also includes the entire *California* album. –SA

○ **Everclear / ALIAS**   1991
More expansive production, arrangements without watering down the quality of Eitzel's material; brilliant album. –SA

ANACRUSIS

Thrash. Anacrusis was formed in the late 80s in their home of St. Louis and is one of the more diverse metal bands of the 90s, employing more sophisticated harmonies and melodies while retaining their aggressive edge. –JB

○ **Manic Impressions / WARNER**   1991
St. Louis hits the metal map with this album. Alternative and progressive, *Manic Impressions* is everything metal should be. Not thrash- or speed-metal but could appeal to both punk and alternative music listeners. –JB

AL ANDERSON   *b* 1947

Rock & roll. Anderson started with a local Connecticut band, the Wildweeds, in the late 60s, scoring with the hit, "No Good to Cry." He joined NRBQ in 1971. In addition to work with the band, he has released the odd solo album over the years, most strongly connected to his love and mastery of country music. –CK

○ **Party Favors / TWINTONE**   1962
NRBQ's brilliant guitarist and vocalist steps out on his solo debut, a lively, if somewhat disappointing effort from one of rock's undiscovered greats. –JT

IAN ANDERSON   *b* 1947

Art-rock. Ian Anderson, the lead singer/songwriter of the 70s English art-rock ensemble Jethro Tull, was also featured on the flute in the band's highly arranged settings. His hollow tone and use of echo delays are quite distinctive. –RC

○ **Walk Into Light / CAPITOL**   1983
Anderson's mix of folk and rock works best in Jethro Tull's group setting, although one is hard-put to distinguish this album from parts of Tull's two-decade output. –BE

JON ANDERSON   *b* 1944

Art-rock. Jon Anderson's cherubic tenor voice is one of English art-rock band Yes's most distinctive elements. As a lyricist, Anderson has generally been mystically obscure, at times sounding as though he was more fascinated with the sound of the words than with their actual thematic coherence. Nevertheless, he was one of art-rock's most aggressive conceptualizers. Aside from Yes, Anderson has engaged in numerous side projects, including several successful outings with synth-whiz Vangelis. –RC

○ **Olias of Sunhillow / ATLANTIC**   1976
This Yes vocalist's debut solo album is his most pleasing. A near-impressionist piece of music, with elements of mysticism and science fiction interwoven like a lost "tale from Topographic Oceans." (Import) –BE

LAURIE ANDERSON   *b* 1950

Avant-garde. A member of the NYC "loft artists" scene in the early 70s, Anderson first started as a sculptor, enhancing her performance-art exhibits by writing and performing music to go along with it. Quirky and unconventional, Anderson has remained a cult figure with strong ties to pop music's alternative scene. –CK

○ **Big Science / WARNER**   1982
Anderson employs a variety of musical and sound effects (including voice alteration) on this condensation of her mammoth performance-art piece *United States I-IV*, but it is her stories and unusual observations (many of them seriocomic) that really catch the ear. When the album appeared, nothing like it had ever been heard before, and little has been since. –WR

Mister Heartbreak / WARNER   1984
Anderson becomes more musically involved, using a broad range of backup musicians who include Adrian Belew, Nile Rodgers, and Peter Gabriel. But it's still her spoken observations that carry the record. –WR

United States Live / WARNER   1984
The complete performance piece that first gained Anderson attention is a grab bag but its still full of funny and fascinating individual moments, spread across five records. –WR

Strange Angels / WARNER   1989
On her first new studio album in five years, Anderson ups the musical ante by actually singing on many tracks. It has the effect of reducing her impact, though this remains an unusually inventive and interesting record. –WR

LEE ANDREWS & THE HEARTS

R&B. Specializing in smooth ballads, this Philadelphia R&B

vocal quintet notched three hits in 1957-1958. Andrews formed the Hearts in 1953, and they debuted the next year on the Rainbow label. Chess picked up their first big seller, "Long Lonely Nights," from the tiny Mainline label in 1957. Mainline also originally issued their biggest hit for Chess, "Teardrops." Moving to United Artists, the group charted for the last time in 1958 with the typically polished "Try the Impossible." Andrews and a shifting lineup of Hearts continued to record through the 60s. –BD

Gotham Recording Sessions / COLLECTABLES
More attractive 50s doo-wop harmonies. –BD

○ **Biggest Hits / COLLECTABLES**   1981
Classy 50s doo-wop, heavy on dreamy ballads. –BD

RUBY ANDREWS   b 1947

Soul. Ruby Andrews's tuneful late 60s sides established her as a seductive Windy City soul singer. Andrews debuted on the Zodiac label in 1967 and scored her biggest seller, *Casanova (Your Playing Days are Over)* the same year. Successful followups on Zodiac included *You Made a Believer (Out of Me)* in 1969 and *Everybody Saw You* the next year. Andrews recently cut some bluesy material for Ichiban, with the outrageous Swamp Dogg producing. –BD

○ **Casanova / COLLECTABLES**
Includes the Zodiac Records hits. 60s recordings. –RP

Kiss This / ICHIBAN   1991
Produced by Swamp Dogg. Different from the *Casanova* album, but just as good. –RP

ANGEL CITY

Hard rock. The roaring Australian combo enjoyed hit status during the late 70s in their homeland but have never broken in the States. It's hard to see why: their jagged hard rock is remarkably similar to fellow Aussies AC/DC, who share the same love of clever melodies and concise (read: short) musical statements. –JF

Face to Face / CBS   1980
This roaring Australian combo displays their AC/DC-cum-punk hearts on a powerful US debut. –JF

○ **Beyond Salvation / CHRYSALIS**   1990
After a lengthy absence, Angel City returns with a new moniker (The Angels from Angel City) and a decent album made great by the horny "Dogs Are Talking." –JF

THE ANGELS

Pop. One of the leading girl-groups of the early 60s, thanks to the #1 hit "My Boyfriend's Back." With Linda Jansen as lead and sisters Jiggs and Barbara Allbut providing harmony, the Orange, NJ, trio signed with Caprice Records in 1961 and hit with "'Til." Jansen was replaced by Peggy Santiglia (b May 4, 1944) and the trio signed with Mercury's Smash subsidiary in 1963, cutting the bouncy "My Boyfriend's Back" at the height of the girl-group craze. "I Adore Him" proved mildly successful later that year. –BD

And the Angels Sing / CAPRICE   1962
Nice compilation of their earlier, pre-hit material. –CK

○ **My Boyfriend's Back / COLLECTABLES**   1963
Their major hit and 11 other solid girl-group performances, including the quirky "Love Me Now." In and out of print. –CK

ANGRY SAMOANS

Punk. Dorky, high-speed, shock-punk group who later turned more psychedelic. Band included critic Gregg Turner. –JD

Inside My Brain / TRIPLE X   1980
A great punk-era artifact with no redeeming social value! –JD

○ **Gimme Samoa: 31 Garbage-Pit Hits / PVC**   1987
Great overview; includes live and unreleased tracks. –JD

Yesterday Started Tomorrow / TRIPLE X   1987
Less thrashy. Good psychedelic neo-visionism. –JD

ANIMAL LOGIC

Rock/pop. This trio is composed of ex-Police percussionist Stewart Copeland (b July 16, 1952), ex-Return to Forever bassist Stanley Clarke, and singer/songwriter Deborah Holland. Copeland's innovative licks are everywhere, giving Animal Logic a fusion/pop sound with Police grooves. –RC

○ **Animal Logic / CAPITOL**   1989
The innovative Copeland and virtuoso Clarke team up with the frustratingly average Holland for this debut. Nevertheless, there are some fine moments (melodically and performancewise) in "There's a Spy (In the House of Love)," "Someday We'll Understand," "Elijah," "Winds of Santa Ana," and "I Still Feel for You." The followup effort *Animal Logic II* highlights the band's worst elements. –RC

THE ANIMALS

British Invasion, psychedelic. One of the bands originating from England's active R&B scene during the first half of the 60s, the gritty sound and appearance of the Animals was a definite contrast to much of the British Invasion's well-scrubbed pop. Like the Rolling Stones, the Animals drew much of their early material from the catalogs of American Black R&B and blues artists.

Under the guidance of producer Mickie Most, whose credits also included Jeff Beck, Herman's Hermits, and Donovan, the Animals scored well with a number of great songs, including "We Gotta Get out of This Place" (#13 pop), "Don't Let Me Be Misunderstood" (#15 pop), and the #1 "House of the Rising Sun."

Ego problems (particularly between lead singer Eric Burdon and keyboardist Alan Price) and drug abuse resulted in a number of personnel changes, ultimately making the band essentially the backup for Burdon's increasingly psychedelic vision. At one point, then-future Police guitarist Andy Summers was in the lineup.

The group became Eric Burdon and the Animals in 1966 and produced several wonderfully trippy hits with "Sky Pilot" (#14 pop), "Monterey" (#25 pop), and "San Franciscan Nights" (#9 pop).

In 1969 Burdon closed shop and hooked up with harmonica player Lee Oskar and Los Angeles nightclub band Night Shift, retitling the band War. During his brief time with them, Burdon hit big with the #3 "Spill the Wine." Since then, the Animals have knocked off a couple of fairly respectable reunions. –RC

Best of the Animals / ABKCO
A curiously flat-sounding collection of major songs, easily available but supplanted by the preferred British import *The Complete Animals.* –BE

○ **Animalization / POLYGRAM**   1966
A dazzling collection of the group's more ambitious album tracks, mostly sophisticated blues-based rock. –BE

☆ **The Complete Animals / EMI**   1990
A brilliant-sounding 2-fer of outtakes and extended versions of some songs, plus all the hits. (Import) –BE

● **Best of - Vol. 2 / POLYGRAM**   1991
The Best of Eric Burdon & the Animals - Vol. 2 is a surprisingly hard-rocking collection from this group's psychedelic period. Excellent songs. –BE

PAUL ANKA   b 1941

Pop, singer/songwriter. Hugely successful vocalist from 1957 into the 80s, as well as writer of several venerable pop music standards. The young native of Ottawa, Canada, took the US by storm in 1957 with his rock-slanted ballad "Diana," a #1 smash on ABC-Paramount Records. Dramatic renditions of "You Are My Destiny," "Lonely Boy," "Put Your Head on My Shoulder," and "Puppy Love" elevated the youth to teen-idol status over the next three years. Moving to RCA in 1962, the maturing Anka continued to chart regularly, although some of his most notable 60s copyrights were bequeathed to others

— he wrote "My Way" for Frank Sinatra as well as the theme for TV's "Tonight Show." Anka returned to the top pop slot in 1974 with the controversial million-seller "(You're) Having My Baby," cut in Muscle Shoals and issued on United Artists, and he enjoyed several followup smashes, many featuring vocalist Odia Coates. –BD

○ **30th Anniversary Collection / RHINO**　　　　　1989
The best package of Anka's early teen-idol hits, featuring "Diana," "Puppy Love," "Put Your Head on My Shoulder," and "You Are My Destiny." –CK

ADAM ANT　　　　　　　　　　　　　　　　♭1954

New-wave. Adam & the Ants debuted with the *Dirk Wears White Socks* album in 1979; in early 1980 two original members split to eventually form Bow Wow Wow while leader Adam Ant (born Stuart Goddard) created a new lineup. In 1982 Adam Ant went solo, earning his biggest sales. Ant's popularity dipped steadily throughout the rest of the decade, rebounding slightly in spring 1990 with a #17 hit, "Room at the Top." –BC & STE

○ **Kings of the Wild Frontier / EPIC**　　　　　　1980
Combining pounding tom-toms (from two drummers and drum kits) and a guitar style adapted from Ennio Morricone movie soundtracks with a visual motif borrowed from pirates and Native Americans, Adam & the Ants had a brief run as Britain's top band in the wake of the punk/power-pop days of the late 70s. This second album, was their apex, featuring the signature tune "Antmusic." –WR

Friend or Foe / CBS　　　　　　　　　　　1982
As a solo artist Adam Ant struck gold in the US with this album, which adopts the same musical style as that of the Ants and features the hit "Goody Two Shoes" and a version of the Doors' "Hello, I Love You." –WR

ANTHRAX

Heavy metal. New York's Anthrax has become one of the most innovative bands in speed-metal. Their debut album was released in 1983 with Scott Ian and Dan Spitz on guitar, Neil Turbin on vocals, Charlie Benante on drums, and Danny Lilker on bass. Turbin and Lilker soon left, replaced by Frank Bello (bass) and Joey Belladonna (vocals). Their next album captured the moment of the uprising of thrash- and speed-metal, still with a heavy punk influence.

With the release of *Among the Living*, 1987 became *the* year for the band —the album appealed to its buyers and became their first gold album. They have toured Europe, Japan, and as part of the MTV Headbanger's Ball Tour and the first Clash of the Titans tour package.

Many bands have tried to capture the essence and intensity of Anthrax, but none of them had the lasting power. They continue to be an influence for many heavy metal bands and will be for years to come. –JB

Spreading the Disease / POLYGRAM　　　　　1985
Spreading the Disease demonstrates that a speed-metal band can still have a knack to create a song accessible for pop audiences. An essential Anthrax album. –JB

☆ **Among the Living / POLYGRAM**　　　　　　1987
"The" Anthrax album to have, a high point in speed-metal history. Harsh, powerful, and strong; flawless from beginning to end. –JB

I'm the Man / POLYGRAM　　　　　　　　1987
An EP consisting of a few non-album tracks and some live material. The title track pokes fun at rap, the Beastie Boys, Metallica, the Mentors, and themselves. Anthrax was the first heavy metal band to experiment with rap. –JB

Persistence of Time / POLYGRAM　　　　　1990
Second best to *Among the Living*, the band makes strong political statements without sounding preachy. –JB

Attack of the Killer B's / POLYGRAM　　　　1991
The band gets loose on this one. A compilation of B-sides, covers, and rejects. Shows a lighter side of Anthrax. –JB

APACHE DANCERS

Alternative rock. This male/female duo (Tom Durbin and Bernadette Colomine) dishes out an oddball synthesis of rockabilly-influenced roots rock, country, and early Velvet Underground. This stuff would be good soundtrack music for a Russ Meyers flick. –RC

○ **War Stories / CAPITOL**　　　　　　　　　1990
A bizarre husband/wife team (she sings in French while he sounds like a thoroughly addled Merle Haggard wannabe). They do an appealingly bad voodoo gumbo of swampy rockabilly (i.e., Cramps, Panther Burns), Nico-era Velvet Underground, and devolved Creedence licks. Uneven but fun for fans of fringe trash-rock. Highlights include: "You're the Reason," "Merle's Cravate," "Last Night I Was a Bad Person's Plaything," and "I Dreamed of Hank Williams." –RC

ARANBEE POP SYMPHONY ORCHESTRA

Alternative pop. A large studio group assembled by original Rolling Stones manager Andrew "Loog" Oldham, doing overblown arrangements of material held in the Stones' publishing catalog. –CK

○ **Today's Pop Symphony / CBS**　　　　　　　1991
A silly, fatuous but entertaining attempt to blow 60s pop-rock up to "classical" size with, among other things, Wagner colliding with Otis Redding. Keith Richards signed his name as producer, but Stones manager Andrew "Loog" Oldham probably had more to do with it. –BE

ARGENT

Rock/pop, art-rock. Ex-Zombies keyboardist Rod Argent (b June 14, 1945) formed Argent in 1969. Like the Zombies, Argent was capable of some excellent melodies even when indulging in more extended art-rock forays. Rod Argent had as many chops as Keith Emerson, able to pull out all the stops when needed, but he seemed to have a greater understanding of the value of economy in note selection. Guitarist Russ Ballard (b Oct 31, 1947) was equally tasty, and Argent's rhythm section, bassist Jim Rodford (b July 7, 1945) and drummer Rob Henrit (b May 2, 1945), delivered all the right fire and dynamics. Their self-titled debut and sophomore effort *Ring of Hands* are standouts.

Argent's one huge hit, "Hold Your Head Up," went to #1. After Argent's demise, Ballard went on to a moderately successful solo career. Both Ballard and Argent became successful producers. Henrit and Rodford went on to join the Kinks. –RC

○ **Anthology - Greatest Hits / CBS**　　　　　1974
"Hold Your Head Up" and other well-crafted rockers. –DH

JOAN ARMATRADING　　　　　　　　　　♭1950

Singer/songwriter. Reared in England, Armatrading taught herself to play piano and guitar. She appeared in the 1970 production of *Hair* and later formed a folk duo with Pam Nestor. As a singer/songwriter, Armatrading's very personal style has earned her a cult following. –BC

○ **Joan Armatrading / A&M**　　　　　　　　1976
Her third album was the one most people fell in love with, attracted by her Caribbean-flavored singing of articulate romantic lyrics and Glyn Johns's tasteful folk/rock production, especially on "Love and Affection." –WR

Show Some Emotion / A&M　　　　　　　1977
A companion piece to *Joan Armatrading*, this lovely album contains the title track, "Warm Love," and "Willow." –WR

To the Limit / A&M　　　　　　　　　　1978
She began to up the musical ante with a more rock-oriented approach, and her songs also took a more argumentative tone, especially in the critical "Barefoot and Pregnant." –WR

● **Track Record / A&M**　　　　　　　　　1983
A reasonable best-of that samples Armatrading's first decade of recording. –WR

○ **The Key / A&M**　　　　　　　　　　　1983

The best of Armatrading's later albums, which took on a much harder rock edge. Steve Lillywhite produced, and Armatrading provided some good uptempo material, including "Drop the Pilot" and "(I Love It When You) Call Me Names." –WR

The Shouting Stage / A&M   1988
Astoundingly well-done light rock and pop. "Stronger Love" and "Devil I Know" are the best cuts. –BC

ARMORED SAINT

Heavy metal. Possibly one of the most underrated heavy metal bands today, Armored Saint began playing in the garages of Los Angeles in 1982. Their first record label pretty much ignored them, despite incredible success on stage in the US and Europe. The death of guitarist Dave Prichard in 1990 almost closed the book on the Armored Saint story, but the band rebounded into an upsurge of sales after re-signing to Metal Blade Records. –JB

Delirious Nomad / CAPITOL   1985
A powerful set of songs, *Delirious Nomad* was able to get a few underground hits on the radio. –JB

○ **Symbol of Salvation / WARNER**   1991
Their latest album following the death of guitarist David Prichard. Awesome American heavy metal, tighter than before and already considered to be the band's best. –JB

P. P. ARNOLD   b 1946

R&B. P. P. Arnold moved to England from America in 1965 as a member of the Ikettes, backing Ike and Tina Turner. She stayed on and made a name for herself as a soul singer on Andrew Oldham's Immediate Records label. –BE

○ **P. P. Arnold Collection / SONY SP**   1991
Transplanted American R&B singer hits it big with achingly soulful ballads. A 60s curio and more, especially "The First Cut Is the Deepest." –BE

ART OF NOISE

Techno-pop. Anne Dudley, Gary Lanagan, and J. J. Jeczalik were members of producer Trevor Horn's in-house studio band in the early 80s before they formed Art of Noise, a techno-pop group whose music was an amalgam of studio gimmickry, tape splicing, and synthesized beats. After earning a cult following in the latter half of the 80s (as well as scoring two Top 40 hits) the Art of Noise broke up in 1990. –STE

○ **The Best of the Art of Noise / POLYGRAM**   1988
All of the Art of Noise's best tracks are here, including "Close (To the Edit)," "Legacy," and a cover of Prince's "Kiss" with Tom Jones on lead vocals. –STE

ARTFUL DODGER

Power-pop. An above-average 70s guitar-driven power-pop quintet. –RC

○ **Honor Among Thieves / CBS**   1976
Raspberries-style exuberant 60s-influenced guitar pop-rock with a little early Aerosmith tossed in for roughness. This is the best release available, but their out-of-print self-titled debut is worth seeking out too. –RC

ASHFORD & SIMPSON

R&B, soul. Nikolas Ashford and Valerie Simpson have two careers, as songwriters and as performers, with the former seemingly more important than the latter until the mid 80s. The two met in 1964 and scored their first songwriting hit in 1966 with Ray Charles's recording of their "Let's Go Get Stoned." After a period at Scepter Records, they moved to Motown, where they wrote hits for the duo of Marvin Gaye and Tammi Terrell ("Ain't Nothing Like the Real Thing," "You're All I Need to Get By"). When Diana Ross left the Supremes for a solo career, Ashford and Simpson wrote "Reach out and Touch Somebody's Hand" for her. Their own performing career was launched in 1973 with *Keep*

It Comin' on Motown and *Gimme Something Real* on Warner Bros. Their first success came in 1977 with the gold-selling *Send It,* which contained the Top Ten R&B hit "Don't Cost You Nothing." *Is it Still Good to Ya,* a second gold album, contained the #2 R&B hit "It Seems to Hang On" in 1978. *Stay Free,* their third straight gold album, contained "Found a Cure," another R&B smash that also made the Top 40 on the pop chart. *A Musical Affair,* 1980, featured the hit "Love Don't Make It Right," but was not as successful as previous efforts. Meanwhile, A&S continued to work with other artists, scoring successes with Ross, Chaka Khan ("I'm Every Woman"), and Gladys Knight. Their own career saw a resurgence in 1984 with *Solid,* which went gold and produced the R&B #1 "Solid" (#12 on the pop charts), "Outta the World," and "Babies." –WR

Is it Still Good to Ya / WARNER   1978
The disco arrangements are a little dated, but this is still Ashford & Simpson's best 70s album, as their two similar voices intertwine on a collection of songs about devoted love, among them the title track and "It Seems to Hang On." –WR

○ **Solid / CAPITOL**   1984
Ashford & Simpson have always been the prime representatives in R&B of the joys of wedded bliss, and this extended valentine is their most consistent set as well as their biggest hit ever. –WR

ASIA

Rock/pop, prog-rock. Veterans from King Crimson (John Wetton, b July 12, 1949), Yes (Steve Howe, b Apr 8, 1947; Geoff Downes), and Emerson, Lake & Palmer (Carl Palmer, b Mar 20, 1947) shoot for a synthesis of art-rock and mainstream rock and generally end up with a lot less. Their self-titled debut effort, however, became a #1 success in 1982. Their followup album, *Alpha,* reached #6. After a few more albums, the group called it quits in 1985. –RC

○ **Then & Now / GEFFEN / BB 114**   1990
This compilation includes all of their Top 40 hits — "Heat of the Moment" (#4), "Only Time Will Tell" (#17), "Don't Cry" (#10), and the #34 "The Smile Has Left Your Eyes" — as well as some unreleased tracks. –ED

THE ASSOCIATION

Rock/pop. Between 1966 and 1969, the Association was one of the most successful practitioners of romantic light pop. The band's smooth Lettermen-like harmonies helped make songs like "Cherish" (#1 pop), "Never My Love" (#2 pop), and "Everything That Touches You" (#10 pop) staples of adult easy-listening formats and elevators throughout the planet. Before the Association, founding member Terry Kirkman had actually performed coffeehouses with Frank Zappa for several years.

Their first hit, the upbeat "Along Comes Mary" (#7 pop), met with resistance from radio programmers, afraid that the song was about marijuana. The exuberant "Windy," on the other hand, easily sailed all the way to #1, becoming the band's biggest seller. Interestingly, "Windy" (which knocked Aretha Franklin's "Respect" out of the top slot) was originally written as a waltz. Attempts to infuse a more progressive "rock" sound with "Six Man Band" (#47 pop) were met with indifference from the public. That was to be their last hit.

The Association ground on until 1972, when the death of bassist Brian Cole, plus the poor commercial response to their Columbia Records debut, *Waterbeds in Trinidad,* provided impetus for the band's dissolution. The band has managed a few reunions, most notably the 1980 HBO reunion special, and a moderate hit "Dreamer" (#66) on Elektra. –RC

○ **Songs That Made Them Famous / PAIR**
Beyond the hits, all of which are included here ("Windy," "Cherish," "Along Comes Mary"), the Association made stunning orchestral folk/pop that still makes the listener feel good. –JT

Greatest Hits / WARNER   1969
At only 13 songs, this is concise but not definitive. –JT

ATHEIST

Heavy metal. Atheist is mid-80s progressive death-metal with an edge. Intelligent? Brutal? It's all of that and then some, as well as highly original. —JB

Piece of Time / CAROLINE 1990
Changes the thought of what death-metal can be. Roger Patterson was considered one of the top bass players and one of the top musicians in the genre, but unfortunately he died before the recording of their second album. —JB

○ **Unquestionable Presence / WARNER** 1991
Twisted and in-depth lyrics, music that travels into the worlds of death-metal, progressive metal, and jazz. Wonderful bass work from new bassist Tony Choy. Atheist's best so far, this will be hard to top. —JB

ATLANTA RHYTHM SECTION

Rock/pop, southern rock. Atlanta Rhythm Section formed out of remnants of Roy Orbison's Candymen backup group and the smooth rockers the Classics IV around 1970. Manager/producer Buddy Buie (who had also handled Classics IV) gave the group a glossy production sheen, while nonstop touring helped to build their following. Slicker and more melodic than most Southern rock bands of the genre, they scored consistently on both the album and singles charts during their decade together. —CK

○ **Best of / POLYGRAM** 1982
This well-compiled anthology not only covers ARS's biggest radio hits, but it does a good job of highlighting key album tracks that showcase their sophisticated style of Southern rock. Included are "Spooky" (#17), "Imaginary Lover" (#7), "So into You" (#7), "Georgia Rhythm" (#68), "Jukin'" (#82), "Do It Or Die" (#19), "Angel (What in the World's Come over Us)" (#79), "Doraville" (#35), and more. —RC

ATLANTIC STARR

Disco, urban R&B. Eight men and one woman make up the band that was formed by the Lewis brothers (Wayne, Johnathan, and David) in 1976. Their early music was upbeat and disco-oriented, but after signing with A&M and gaining the Commodores' producer James Carmichael, they became known for their string-laden pop-soul ballads. —BC

○ **Classics - Vol. 10 / A&M** 1987
Excellent soft soul and mid-tempo R&B cuts from the 70s and early 80s, including "When Love Calls." —BC

All in the Name of Love / WARNER 1987
A judicious combo of modern R&B and pop, including their hit "Always." —BC

Love Crazy / WARNER 1992
Lush ballads, especially "Masterpiece." —BC

AUDIENCE

Rock/pop, art-rock. Audience's unusual blend of Keith Gimmel's sax work and Howard Werth's woody lead vocals gave the band's arty pop a distinctive sound. Internal friction caused the group to break up after their second album, but during their brief existence this English group, enjoyed two minor hits with "Indian Summer" off of the 1971 debut *House on the Hill*, and "Stand by the Door" from their second album, *Lunch*. —RC

○ **House on the Hill / CAROLINE** 1971
For their debut, producer Gus Dudgeon imbues Audience with a thick art-pop sound recalling Roxy Music, Jethro Tull, and his work with early Elton John. It contains the moderate hit "Indian Summer." "You're Not Smiling," "Jackdaw," a version of Screamin' Jay Hawkins's "I Put a Spell on You" and the title cut are the highlights. Their followup album, *Lunch* is generally a waste except for the single "Stand by the Door." —RC

PATTI AUSTIN   b 1948

Urban R&B. Patti Austin can sing anything, which may explain why she was a child star, then a successful studio singer, before becoming a pop/R&B success in 1983 with her #1 duet with James Ingram, "Baby, Come to Me." But since then she has moved toward jazz singing, and she has the voice to triumph there too. —WR

Every Home Should Have One / WARNER 1981
Quincy Jones-produced pop album featuring "Baby, Come to Me," which became a belated hit when it was featured on "General Hospital," two years after the album came out. —WR

○ **The Real Me / WARNER** 1988
And how! Austin tackles standards such as "Smoke Gets in Your Eyes" and "They Can't Take That Away from Me," and succeeds brilliantly. Her version of Comden, Green, and Bernstein's "I Can Cook, Too" is enough by itself to make this a pick. —WR

AVERAGE WHITE BAND

Soul, funk. This Glasgow, Scotland, sextet achieved much success during the 70s with their blue-eyed soulful funk. Bonnie Bramlett (of Delaney & Bonnie) jokingly bestowed the band with their name. During their prime, AWB's solid grooves and overall chemistry were anything but average. Their biggest hits came in 1975 with "Cut the Cake" (#10), "School Boy Crush" (#33), "If I Ever Lose This Heaven" (#39) and "Pick up the Pieces," which hit #1 pop at the top of the year. The band members have worked as session sidemen for artists ranging from Chaka Khan to Paul McCartney and Badfinger. —RC

○ **Average White Band / ATLANTIC** 1974
Average White Band's self-titled third album was also their best. It contained their biggest and best hit, "Pick up the Pieces," as well as "Keepin' It to Myself." —DH

AZTEC CAMERA

Alternative pop. More a creative outlet for Glasgowian Roddy Frame than a proper group, Aztec Camera has specialized in lush, acoustic-based cerebral pop, reaching their apex on *High Land, Hard Rain*, their 1983 debut. —JF

○ **High Land, Hard Rain / WARNER** 1983
Intelligent and detailed, if somewhat overambitious, debut showcasing vocalist/songwriter Roddy Frame's catchy and wordy acoustic-based pop songs. Imagine a folky version of Elvis Costello, with better guitar chops, and you've got the picture here. None of the Camera's other albums have come close to matching this release. —JF

B. T. EXPRESS

Funk, disco. Formed in Brooklyn, NY, around 1972, as the Brooklyn Transit Express, they had a big-band hard-disco sound with various funk elements and proved to have more creativity than most disco groups. Consequently, as disco faded, so did they. —BC

○ **Golden Classics / CBS**
Contains "Do It (Till You're Satisfied)," and a few other dance hits. —DH

THE B-52'S

Alternative pop, dance-pop. Athens, GA, has been a hotbed of alternative talent for quite a while, but the town's rise to cutting-edge musical prominence was aided in no small part by the 1976 formation of the B-52's, a wildly unorthodox party band that featured a guitarist with a five-string Mosrite electric and two mini-skirted, go-go-booted female singers (Kate Pierson and Cindy Wilson) who sported extremely bouffant hairdos.

The recklessly exuberant self-titled Warner debut was a left-field success, selling tons of copies with little radio support. The followup, *Wild Planet*, picks up where *The B-52's* left off, with mixed results; nevertheless, it enjoys even greater success.

A dance-mix EP and two subsequent albums (*Mesopotamia*

and *Whammy!*) provide further variations on the band's sound, but the "fun" sounds increasingly forced.
Guitarist Ricky Wilson passed away in 1985 from AIDS, before the release of the uneven *Bouncing off the Satellites*. With drummer Keith Strickland taking over Wilson's guitar duties, the B-52's returned from an extended break and put out the hugely successful *Cosmic Thing*. Produced by Don Was and Nile Rodgers, *Cosmic Thing* successfully sythesized the band's wacky energy with just the right amount of streamlining. –RC
○ **The B-52's / WARNER**   1979
It's all here on the debut album: the "Secret Agent Man" drum/guitar tracks that compel the feet to dance, topped by shrill female vocals and the brash speak-singing of Fred Schneider giving forth with some of the strangest non sequiturs as though he were an overexcited carnival barker. Includes "Planet Claire" and the hit "Rock Lobster." –WR
Wild Planet / WARNER   1980
Wild Planet is more of the same, as the B-52's celebrate the joys of living in your own "Private Idaho" and the wonders of quiche lorraine. –WR
Cosmic Thing / WARNER   1989
Belatedly, and despite the death of their musical leader Ricky Wilson, the B-52's found enormous commercial success with this album, which effectively recapitulates their zany virtues, especially on the two Top Three hits "Love Shack" and "Roam." –WR

BABE RUTH

Art-rock. This hard-hitting art-rock group from the early 70s enjoyed a moderate cult following. Babe Ruth featured powerful lead singer Jenny Hann, whose style was similar to that of Julie Driscoll. –RC
○ **First Base / ONE WAY**   1973
A fine hard-rock outing with progressive tinges and the gutsy vocals of Jenny Haan. Includes a version of Zappa's "King Kong." –MPD

BABES IN TOYLAND

Hardcore. The screeching, often atonal sound of this all-female Minneapolis trio prompted critics to tag their sound "foxcore." Considered authentic cathartic crunch by many, and aimless noise by others, Babes in Toyland are developing a very strong following in Europe. –DH
○ **Spanking Machine / TWINTONE**   1990
A scabrous, brutal debut that sent shock waves through the underground scene. Kat Bjelland's guitar is a rampaging string machine, while her vocals pin you to the wall. Not for the weak or fainthearted. –DH & JD
To Mother / TWINTONE
An EP followup that's strong but not life-changing. –JD

BABY ANIMALS

Rock/pop. Australian hard pop-rock quartet Baby Animals is fronted by Suze DeMarchi, who at times can deliver her lines with the intensity of Chrissie Hynde or Concrete Blonde's Johnette Napolitano. –RC
○ **Baby Animals / RCA**   1991
Solid mainstream rock with an edge (Concrete Blonde and Pretenders, diluted with Pat Benatar). Two standout tracks in "Painless" and "One Word." Produced by Mike Chapman (Blondie, the Sweet, Pat Benatar). –RC

BABYFACE

Urban R&B. With his friend Antonio Reid, Babyface formed a Cincinnati-based band, the Deele, in the early 80s. They were introduced by members of Midnight Star to Solar Records executive Dick Griffey, who put them to work producing music for Carrie Lucas, the Whispers, and Dynasty. Since then, they've produced hits for Sheena Easton, Pebbles, Paula Abdul, and others. –BC

○ **Tender Lover / CBS**   1990
Youthfully ecstatic balladry. –BC

THE BABYS

Rock/pop. The Babys (formed 1976) were a moderately successful mainstream pop-rock outfit from England. Their debut failed to live up to advance hype concerning their visual appeal and Raspberries-meets-Free concept.
Their hits included "If You've Got the Time" (#88), "Isn't It Time" (#13), "Every Time I Think of You" (#13), "Back on My Feet Again" (#33), and "Turn and Walk Away" (#51).
The Babys disbanded in 1981. Lead singer John Waite (b Jul 4, 1954) went on to enjoy one of the biggest hits of 1984 with the #1 "Missing You." Lead guitarist Wally Stocker (b Mar 17, 1954) joined Air Supply's road band, and keyboardist Jonathon Cain went to work with Journey. –RC
○ **Anthology / CAPITOL**   1981
A good collection of the group's efficient mainstream pop-rock. –DH

BACHMAN-TURNER OVERDRIVE

Rock/pop. Bachman-Turner Overdrive, formed by two expatriates of Canada's the Guess Who, Randy Bachman and C. F. Turner, specialized in no-nonsense blue collar rock & roll. In fact, part of the band's name came from the trucking industry magazine *Overdrive.* This isn't to say that BTO was without musical sophistication, certainly evidenced in the jazzy "Lookin' Out for No. 1." The band's initial demos were rejected by over two dozen record labels before Mercury picked them up.
Several of the band's radio tracks became substantial hits, particularly "Takin' Care of Business" (#12 pop) and the #1 hit "You Ain't Seen Nothing Yet," which had a stuttering vocal hook inspired by the speech impediment of the band's first manager, Gary Bachman. –RC
Not Fragile / POLYGRAM   1974
Featuring the #1 "You Ain't Seen Nothing Yet." The band's best noncompilation album. –DDC
○ **Best of B.T.O. (So Far) / POLYGRAM**   1976
Everything you need to hear, at the height of their popularity. No-frills hard-driving 70s rock. –DDC

BAD BRAINS

Hardcore. Certainly the most interesting group spawned during the early-80s hardcore era. This DC-based group, led by vocalist H. R. and guitarist Dr. Know, specialized in blazing, yet conventionally structured punk and Rastafarian reggae. An influential outfit. –JF
○ **I Against I / SST**   1986
Slick production helped the Brains make the most satisfying metal/reggae record of their career. Dr. Know's guitar is pushed way up front in the mix, and the funkier back beat (replacing the hardcore speed blur) kicks every track (especially "Return to Heaven") into high gear. –JD

BAD COMPANY

Rock & roll. Supergroups usually don't enjoy lengthy fruitful careers, but Bad Company was a highly successful exception, producing a string of hit records from 1974 to 1982. Paul Rodgers and Simon Kirke of Free, Boz Burrell from King Crimson, and Mott the Hoople's Mick Ralphs delivered Bad Company's sparse, crunchy hard-rock.
Their self-titled debut, recorded in ten days, exuded an appealing unpolished sound at a time when a lot of rock seemed to be trading its visceral essence for arty pretention. After their second album (*Straight Shooter*), Bad Company began to lose some of its freshness, opting for a more processed sound.
Bad Company broke up in 1983, but by the late 80s, a new lineup with Kirke and Ralphs emerged. Brian Howe filled Rodgers's slot. Even though this lineup produced some

substantial rock hits, the band's sound is disappointingly interchangeable with a load of other professional radio rock acts. –RC

Bad Company / ATLANTIC 1974
A powerhouse debut, including "Can't Get Enough," "Ready for Love," and the title track. –DH

Straight Shooter / ATLANTIC 1975
Their hot streak continues with "Feel Like Makin' Love." A fine followup. –DH

○ **10 from 6 / ATLANTIC** 1985
A concise, if overly brief collection of hits. –DH

BAD EXAMPLES

Rock & roll. Currently one of the Windy City's hottest attractions, boasting the prolific songwriting skills of lead singer Ralph Covert and incendiary lead guitar from John Duich. Formed in 1987, the band issued a cassette, *Meat: the Bad Examples*, the next year. Covert's "Not Dead Yet," one of the group's most popular numbers, was covered by Styx on their *Edge of the Century* album. The Bad Examples' debut CD on the Water Dog label, *Bad is Beautiful*, was released in 1991, and a live set is due shortly. Bassist Tom "Pickles" Piekarski formerly played with John Prine. –BD

○ **Bad is Beautiful / WATER DOG**
With leader Ralph Covert writing a virtual raft of standout songs and John Duich adding blistering guitar, this Chicago quartet is ready to tackle the national rock market. –BD

BAD MANNERS

Ska-revival. The English group Bad Manners, formed in 1980 and featuring lead singer Buster Bloodvessel, arrived as part of the early 80s ska revival, with groups like the English Beat, Madness, and the Specials. –RC

○ **Bad Manners / MCA** 1981
The American debut of these silly ska revivalists, who burst upon the scene with more serious-minded groups such as the Specials and the Selecter. –DS

BAD RELIGION

Punk. Southern California high-speed punkers, turned scouts-down hard-rock punkers. –JD

How Can Hell Be Any Worse / EPITAPH 1982
Durable standard Southern California hardcore post punk with brains. –JD

○ **Into the Future / EPITAPH** 1983
Slightly spacey but more direct and hard-hitting. –JD

No Conviction / EPITAPH 1989
Smarter and more involving but doesn't kick as hard as *Into the Future*. –JD

BADFINGER

Anglo-pop. Paul McCartney discovered Badfinger's demo and signed them to the Beatles' Apple label. Originally known as the Iveys, Badfinger got their name from Apple exec Neil Aspinall. Paul McCartney had lobbied for Home, and Lennon wanted them to be called Prix.
McCartney penned their first hit, "Come and Get It" (#7), which was featured (along with a couple of their other songs) in the movie *The Magic Christian*, as well as on their debut, *Magic Christian Music*.
It was with Badfinger's next two albums, *No Dice* and *Straight Up*, that the image of the band as a poor man's Beatles (using McCartney songs) began to evaporate, as they forged a unique sound that generated a series of classic hits. –RC

Magic Christian Music / APPLE 1970
Magic Christian Music is Badfinger's uneven debut. The band hadn't found their *sound* yet. Nevertheless, tracks like "Come and Get It" and "Maybe Tomorrow" gave power-pop fans a good taste of this band's potential. –RC

○ **No Dice / APPLE** 1970

Badfinger's distinctive melodic abilities, great vocals, and solid ensemble work on *No Dice*, was a strong case that this quartet could stand on it own, apart from Apple's shadow. "I Can't Take It," "Midnight Caller," the beautifully romantic "We're for the Dark," and "No Matter What," (one of the greatest pop singles ever), are among *No Dice*'s many highlights. –RC

● **Straight Up / APPLE** 1971
George Harrison and Todd Rundgren took turns producing Badfinger's third album, *Straight Up*, which produced two international hits with the gorgeous "Day After Day" and the wall-of-sound pop/rock masterpiece "Baby Blue." Badfinger forges a unique sound with their sweeping, strained high harmonies, thick, edgy rhythm guitar parts, and a drumming style that featured an exaggerated hi-hat attack on the backbeat. Check out "Take It All," "Sometimes," and the powerful "It's Over" for examples. –RC

Ass / APPLE / BB 122 1973
A step down from Badfinger's two previous classics. *Ass* was the final kiss-off on the Beatles' rapidly deteriorating Apple Record label. In spite of some fairly inconsequential tracks, "Apple of My Eye" (the single), "Icicles," "I Can Love You," and the first half of the "I Want You/She's So Heavy" rip, "Timeless," more than redeem this release. –RC

Badfinger / WARNER / BB 161 1974
Tentatively titled *For Love or Money*, this was an unfortunate rush job that, in spite of it all, generated a handful of fine songs. Produced by Chris Thomas (Beatles, Roxy Music, Pink Floyd), Joey Molland's darkly meditative "Give it Up," "Andy Norris," and "Island" are fine contributions. "Lonely You," "Shine On," and "Song for a Lost Friend" showcase Pete Ham's emotive lower tenor and his considerable melodic skills. On the down side, "Matted Spam" is a horrible attempt at marrying soul with their sound, and "I Miss You" has enough sugar in it to put Paul McCartney into a coma. Regardless of that, fans of the band will be glad to know that an import CD can be obtained. –RC

○ **Wish You Were Here / WARNER / BB 148** 1974
After many professional and personal distractions, Badfinger refocused their creative energies and, with producer Chris Thomas, created one of their finest albums. The urgent fanfare of the opening track, "Just a Chance," sets the make-it-or-break-it undercurrent here. This features two impressive medleys, "In the Meantime/Some Other Time" and "Meanwhile Back at the Ranch/Should I Smoke," which features stately horn backing by the Average White Band. (Import) –RC

● **Best of Badfinger - Vol. 2 / RHINO** 1989
A decent attempt at chronicling the last half of their career, which included one of the great lost pop-rock albums of the 70s, *Wish You Were Here*. With the exception of important tracks like Joey Molland's "Love Time" and Pete Ham's "Dennis," *Wish* ... is well represented. Key tracks from the self-titled Warner debut are included, as well as several sides from the never-released *Head First*. Also included are the only two tracks worth having from their 1979 album *Airwaves*. Until the Warner albums get released on CD stateside (which is doubtful), this is the only place you can get these fine tracks. –RC

PHILIP BAILEY   ♭1951

Soul. The falsetto-singing co-lead vocalist in Earth, Wind & Fire, Philip Bailey launched a solo career during the band's hiatus, resulting in his hit duet with Phil Collins, "Easy Lover," in 1985. He also makes gospel records. –WR

○ **Chinese Wall / CBS** 1984
Phil Collins produced this rock/soul workout, with the sweet-voiced Bailey equally at home on lush ballads and uptempo dance floor numbers. Features the Collins-Bailey duet "Easy Lover," which was a #2 hit. –WR

ANITA BAKER   b 1957

Urban R&B. A smoky-voiced soul singer from Detroit who was a member of Chapter 8, then launched an extremely successful solo career in the mid 80s. −WR

The Songstress / ELEKTRA   1983

Not too many people heard it at the time of its release, but this album contains Baker's characteristically tasteful arrangements and remarkably evocative singing. Reissued by Elektra. −WR

○ **Rapture / ELEKTRA**   1986

Baker invented a new musical genre, "quiet storm," with this gorgeous album of love ballads sung in her compelling voice. Contains "Caught up in the Rapture" and the Top Ten hit "Sweet Love." −WR

Giving You the Best That I Got / ELEKTRA   1988

Baker topped the charts with this worthy followup to *Rapture*, which contains the hit title song and "Just Because." −WR

GINGER BAKER   b 1940

Prog-rock. Ginger Baker was the fiery drummer for the late-60s power trio Cream. As a young drummer, Baker embraced jazz and R&B, playing with some of England's finest traditional big bands. While Baker was fully capable of laying down a straight groove, the most distinctive element of his style was in his melodic arrangement-oriented phrasing. After Cream disbanded, Baker formed Ginger Baker's Air Force, which contained three drummers, and also worked in the ill-fated Blind Faith.
Baker moved to Lagos, Nigeria, and built the country's first 16-track studio. Paul McCartney's *Band on the Run* was recorded there. Even though Baker has had a low profile since the late 70s, his recent solo works, which predominately explore African rhythms, are among his best recorded performances. −RC

○ **Middle Passage / POLYGRAM**   1990

With producer Bill Laswell, mixing African drummers (Ayib Dieng, Mou Gueye, Magette Fall) with fusioneers (Bernie Worrell, Jonas Helborg, Nicky Skopelitis) and bassists (Jah Wohble and Laswell) to land in a "middle passage" of worldbeat. Not bad at all. −MGN

LAVERN BAKER   b 1929

R&B. Baker was one of R&B's finest singers, scoring twenty pop hits between 1955 and 1966, including duets with Jackie Wilson and Jimmy Ricks. Baker's career momentum was constantly hurt by White artists covering versions of her songs and having bigger hits. In spite of that, she managed to score some sizable hits with a series of noveltyish records containing titles like "Tweedle Dee," "Voodoo Voodoo," "Jim Dandy," and "Jim Dandy Got Married." "I Cried a Tear" was her sole Top Ten record. −RC

Lavern Baker / ATLANTIC   1955

Includes her hits "Tweedlee Dee" and "Jim Dandy." Some formulaic material (like "Tra-La-La," an obvious attempt at recapturing "Tweedly Dee"), but some good stuff too. −GB

○ **Sings Bessie Smith / ATLANTIC**   1959

From the sassy punch of "Gimmie a Pigfoot," the album's opener, to "Preaching the Blues" at the end, the performances on this CD swing with a vibrant confidence. All in all, this is a great disc for those looking for an intoxicating blend of R&B and jazz. −RC

● **Soul on Fire - Best of LaVern Baker / ATLANTIC**   1991

This well-annotated collection rounds up every important hit Baker had with Atlantic, and a few choice rarities as well. −JF

Live In Hollywood / RHINO   1992

Recent recordings show Baker can still belt out a song. She's returned to the jazz and jazzy blues sound of her youth. −RW

MARTY BALIN   b 1942

Rock/pop. Lead singer and cofounder of Jefferson Airplane,

Marty Balin's aching tenor was the centerpiece of some of their most reflective recordings as well as a few hits, including his self-penned "Miracles," which went #3 for Jefferson Starship. In 1978, Balin left for a solo career that leaned more toward MOR pop than rock. His singles include "Hearts" (#8), "Atlanta Lady (Something About You Love)" (#28), and "What Love Is" (#63). −RC

Better Generation / GWE

His smooth-as-silk voice as inviting as ever, Balin showcases new material and remakes a couple of Airplane favorites on this 1991 recording. −JT

○ **Balince - A Collection / RHINO**   1991

Drawing from his days as a lead vocalist for both Jefferson Airplane and Starship and from his solo recordings, this best-of also includes five unreleased tracks. −JT

HANK BALLARD & THE MIDNIGHTERS   b 1936

R&B. Though born in Alabama, Ballard moved to Detroit at an early age, forming a doo-wop group called the Royals by age 16. He signed to King label in early 1953. Mid-size chart hits followed, and the group's name was changed to the Midnighters to avoid confusion with labelmates the Five Royales when "Work with Me Annie" became a national hit. Banned because of "explicit" lyrics, the song spawned a flurry of answer records (some by Ballard himself), most of them hitting the R&B charts as well. The hits kept coming throughout the early 60s, but the flipside of one of them became a national hit when Chubby Checker rerecorded "The Twist," spawning a national craze. Ballard's best records are informed by Gospel-style harmonies and gritty guitar work, usually played by Alonzo Tucker. −CK

Twistin' Fools / KING   1962

All the Hank Ballard twist songs — compare with Chubby Checker and draw your own conclusions. −GB

★ **20 Hits / KING**   1977

Part of a great reissue series from several years back, this has all their R&B and Hot 100 hits including "Work with Me Annie," "The Twist," and those from the early 50s when they were still known as the Royals. −GB

○ **What You Get ... / CHARLY**   1985

What You Get When The Getting Gets Good is a best-of collection featuring "Finger Poppin' Time," "Work with Me Annie," "Let's Go, Let's Go, Let's Go," "The Twist," and "Annie Had a Baby." It's Detroit R&B at its best. −CK

BANANARAMA

Dance-pop. This female dance-pop trio came on the scene just as MTV was becoming an influential force in the early 80s. Bananarama's first recordings were with English artists Fun Boy Three. Their slight airy vocal sound and strong grooves have earned them a number of hits, including "Shy Boy" (#83), "Robert De Niro's Waiting" (#95), "Cruel Summer" (#9), "The Wild Life" (#70), "Love in the First Degree" (#48), "I Heard a Rumour" (#4), and "I Can't Help It" (#47). −RC

Deep Sea Skiving / POLYGRAM   1983

Though this was not their American breakthrough, it was their biggest UK success, hitting the Top Ten and featuring the hits "Really Saying Something," "Shy Boy," and "Na Na Hey Hey Kiss Him Goodbye." It establishes the formula for the group's success, with its untrained unison trio singing and pop exuberance. The amateurishness of the singers was what made them so appealing. −WR

Bananarama / POLYGRAM   1984

The group adopted a more glamorous fashion style for this album, which finally brought them US success with the Top Ten "Cruel Summer." Also included "Robert De Niro's Waiting." −WR

True Confessions / POLYGRAM   1986

Bananarama scored its biggest US hit with this third album, earning gold sales with the #1 single "Venus." −WR

○ **Greatest Hits Collection / LONDON**   1988
Contains "I Heard a Rumour" and other similar smashes. –DH

BAND OF SUSANS

Alternative rock. An often-changing lineup does not interfere with this New York City band's love of guitars. Often loud and brash, their triple-guitar attack has a solid rock & roll base, nowhere near as pretentious as Glenn Branca nor as discordant as Sonic Youth. –BE

○ **Love Agenda / ENIGMA-RESTLESS**   1989
Their cover of the Rolling Stones' "Child of the Moon" is a must-hear. –RG

The World & the Flesh / RESTLESS   1991
Triple-guitar attack — a sea of six-strings. –RG

THE BAND

Rock & roll, folk/rock. Composed of four Canadians and one American, the Band first came together in Toronto in the early 60s as Ronnie Hawkins's backup group. Hawkins recorded nine 45s for Roulette between 1959 and 1963. Drummer Levon Helm plays on all nine, guitarist Robbie Robertson and bass player Rick Danko can be heard on the last three, pianist Richard Manuel on the last two, and organist Garth Hudson plays on the final outing only. Leaving Hawkins collectively in early 1964, they called themselves the Levon Helm Sextet, Levon and the Hawks, and (for a brief spell) the Canadian Squires, releasing two singles before becoming Bob Dylan's backup ensemble for his crazed electric tour of North America, Australia, and Europe in the fall of 1965 through the spring of 1966. (After a couple of gigs, Levon headed back to Arkansas.)

Playing with Dylan had a profound influence on the Band. Woodshedding for two years in Woodstock, NY, they released their debut album, *Music from Big Pink*, in late summer 1968. Over the succeeding eight years, the Band stood completely apart from everything else happening in rock & roll. There was no precedent for what they did and there have been no antecedents. Ironically, given that they were four-fifths Canadian, their music embodied an essence of Americana that no one else in rock & roll has approached. Chief writer, Torontonian Robbie Robertson, wrote about the South, the land, rural America, tradition, and the value and richness of heritage and blood ties. The settings for his songs took place in cornfields, during the Civil War, and at carnivals at the edge of town. He was most concerned with displaced people and the passing of a way of life. Sonically, the Band was equally unique. Hudson played accordion, sax, and organ; drummer Levon Helm doubled on mandolin and guitar; pianist Manuel drummed whenever Helm was out front; bassist Rick Danko played fiddle when they needed a rural or "old-timey" feel; guitarist Robbie Robertson had a pinched, economical style that kept one teetering on the edge with tension. As a unit, they quite consciously avoided any of the current trends. They didn't want their voices to blend, because that is what everyone else was doing; they wanted their piano to sound like a funky old upright, not like a brand spanking new Yamaha Grand; and so on. In the process they created some of the most ethereal and evocative music imaginable. –RB

☆ **Music from Big Pink / CAPITOL / BB 30**   1968
Everything about the Band's debut album, *Music from Big Pink*, flew in the face of the current ethos of rock & roll in 1968. For example, the disc opens in an unusual fashion, with a ballad, the Richard Manuel/Bob Dylan composition "Tears of Rage." There is not a guitar solo on the album, and this was a time when Jeff Beck, Eric Clapton, and Jimi Hendrix ruled the world. There was a lot of harmony singing that was deliberately ragged: together but not together — community, where the people that made up the community could be individuals. And then there were the songs, enigmatic tales such as "The Weight," "Chest Fever," and the first released version of Bob Dylan's "I Shall Be Released." An

unbelievably strong debut. (Also available as a Mobile Fidelity Ultradisc) –RB

☆ **The Band / CAPITOL / BB 9**   1969
Big Pink had been a fine, even superior debut; *The Band* was their masterpiece. Robbie Robertson's songwriting had grown by leaps and bounds. As players, all five musicians had reached a completely new level of ensemble cohesion. The sum was very much greater than the parts, and the parts were as good as any that existed. The album's single, "Up on Cripple Creek," became the Band's first and only Top 30 release. It was one of several songs on the album that had an "old-timey" feel. Other highlights on this masterpiece include "Rag Mama Rag," "The Night They Drove Old Dixie Down," and "King Harvest." –RB

Stage Fright / CAPITOL / BB 5   1970
Stage Fright was a reaction to a level of adulation that the Band members were unprepared for. It was conceived as a lighter, less serious, more rock & roll type of album. The final product ended up somewhat darker, as the Band themselves were going through a number of changes. "The Shape I'm In" and "Stage Fright" tell the story well. Some of the original feeling manifests itself in romps such as "Strawberry Wine" and "W. S. Walcott Medicine Show." –RB

Cahoots / CAPITOL / BB 21   1971
Cahoots was the first album recorded at Albert Grossman's Bearsville Studios in Woodstock. The sessions were difficult, as the studio was still having the bugs worked out and the Band was experiencing internal problems. Robertson's songs had become much more difficult; the structures, chord changes, and arrangements were increasingly complex. Despite these factors, the album has a number of gems, including "Life Is a Carnival" with its great Allen Toussaint horn arrangement, Dylan's "When I Paint My Masterpiece," a duet between Richard Manuel and Van Morrison entitled "4% Pantomime," "The River Hymn," and "Where Do We Go from Here." –RB

☆ **Rock of Ages / CAPITOL / BB 6**   1972
Recorded on New Year's Eve 1971/72, this was the Band's last gig for a year and a half. Allen Toussaint was brought in again to write horn arrangements for many of the Band's classics. The results were inspired. Highlights are many, but of particular note are a cover of the Four Tops's "Baby Don't Do It" and a live recording of a track that had earlier been relegated to B-side status only, "Get up Jake." –RB

○ **Northern Lights - Southern Cross / CAPITOL / BB 26**
1975
The first studio album of Band originals in four years, in many respects *Northern Lights - Southern Cross* was viewed as a comeback. It also can be seen as a swan song. The album was the Band's finest since their self-titled sophomore effort. Totaling eight songs in all, on this album the Band explores new timbres, utilizing for the first time 24 tracks and what was (then) new synthesizer technology. "Acadian Driftwood" stands out as one of Robertson's finest compositions, the equal to anything else the Band ever recorded. –RB

☆ **The Last Waltz / WARNER / BB 16**   1978
The Band's farewell gig was held at Winterland in San Francisco on Thanksgiving 1976. Guests from all periods of their career were invited to participate. The luminaries included Bob Dylan, Van Morrison, Neil Young, Joni Mitchell, Muddy Waters, Eric Clapton, and Paul Butterfield. The four-hour concert was one of the most spectacular in rock history. Two hours of it were released on this 3-LP (now 2-CD) set. Utilizing horns one more time, this was the gig of the Band's life and one of the greatest in rock history. We are privileged that it exists in a form where we can hear it as often as we want. –RB

● **To Kingdom Come / CAPITOL**   1991
If (and only if) you have it in your budget for just *one* Band set, *To Kingdom Come (The Definitive Collection)* provides a good collection of their best songs, presented in remastered

form. Even though the sequencing is chronological, experiencing these songs out of the context of their original albums may be disconcerting for some. In other words, the best way to *hear* this great group is to start with their first two albums, then move on to *Rock of Ages*, and so on. Nevertheless, this is an exceptionally solid overview. –RC

BANGLES

Rock/pop. This all-female Los Angeles quartet has produced some exhilarating music, utilizing impressive four-part vocal work on their generally buoyant power-pop arrangements. At their harmonic best, the Bangles projected the exuberance of the Mamas & Papas, approaching the rich density of the Byrds.

Their first major label effort, *All over the Place*, is an absolute gem. Even though the Bangles achieved much greater success, with subsequent efforts, the band's charm became increasingly sanded out.

After the group disbanded in late 1989, primary lead singer Susanna Hoffs pursued a rather uninspiring solo career. –RC

○ **All Over the Place / CBS**   1984
Featuring the Bangles's rich harmonies and slightly ragged folk/pop-rock ensemble work, *All Over the Place* is an absolute gem. Highlights like "Hero Takes a Fall," "Dover Beach," "James," "Tell Me," "Live," and "Going Down to Liverpool" easily make this their best album. –RC

Different Light / CBS   1986
The Bangles' most successful album, *Different Light* presented the band with a more polished sheen, depended on a lot more outside material from professional songsmiths. Prince penned the slight (but tuneful) "Manic Monday," which became their first big hit. That was followed by the novelty-ish "Walk Like an Egyptian," their first #1 hit. The highlights, however, went to an inspired reading of Jules Shears's "If She Knew What She Wants" (a #29 hit) and a bouncy version of Big Star's "September Gurls." –RC

● **Greatest Hits / CBS**   1990
Greatest Hits is just that, including a great version of Simon & Garfunkel's "Hazy Shade of Winter," a hit from the *Less Than Zero* soundtrack that's not found on their other albums. Another previously unreleased track is a workmanlike reading of the Grassroots chestnut "Where Were You When I Needed You." The highlights off of their weakest album, *Everything*, are provided, rendering that album inconsequential. It would've been nice if Sony had utilized the space available on CD to include more essential album tracks from their first two albums, like "September Gurls," "Live," and "James." As collections go, this is a logical place to start, but *All Over the Place* is their most appealing album. –RC

THE BAR-KAYS

Soul, funk. Even though four group founders were killed in a 1967 plane crash along with Otis Redding, the Bar-Kays came back to reign as one of the top R&B outfits of the 70s. The original Bar-Kays were a Memphis instrumental combo that scored an R&B hit in 1967 on Volt with the rousing "Soul Finger." Guitarist Jimmy King, organist Ronnie Caldwell, drummer Carl Cunningham, and saxist Phalon Jones perished with Redding, leaving trumpeter Ben Cauley and bassist James Alexander to re-form the group. After honing their chops with session work at Stax, the new Bar-Kays kicked off a long string of R&B smashes in 1976 with "Shake Your Rump to the Funk" on Mercury. –BD

Animal / POLYGRAM
One of their top-selling releases. –RW

○ **Soul Finger / VOLT**   1967
The Bar-Kays were being trained as a second generation Booker T and the MG's, largely by MG drummer Al Jackson. *Soul Finger* was their first album coming off the success of the their debut single, the group-written title cut. The album is in the classic Memphis soul instrumental vein; sparse arrangements, accentuated low-end, walloping snare drum, and slightly delayed backbeat with horns taking the place of vocals. *Soul Finger* was the only album made by this particular version of the group. –RB

Gotta Groove / VOLT   1969
After the plane crash in December 1967, trumpeter Ben Cauley and bass player James Alexander regrouped, forming a second edition of the Bar-Kays. *Gotta Groove* was the new group's first release. Modelled on earlier Bar-Kays work, the album is totally instrumental, including covers of the Mar-Keys's "Grab This Thing" and the Beatles's "Yesterday" and "Hey Jude." No standout cuts but plenty of fine, hard-driving slices of Memphis instrumental soul. –RB

Money Talks / STAX   1978
Prototype southern funk and hot R&B licks. –RW

Best of the Bar-Kays / STAX   1988
A nice overview of this major Stax band in their second incarnation. –RW

RICHARD BARONE

Rock/pop. In the early 80s, Richard Barone was the lead singer/songwriter and guitarist of the Bongos, a New Jersey-based pop-rock band that garnered critical acclaim but ran into record company problems. He launched a solo career in 1987 with the release of *Cool Blue Halo*. –WR

○ **Cool Blue Halo / PST-LINE**   1987
Former Bongos leader Richard Barone writes and sings wonderful pop songs in a mid-60s, Beatlesque manner. On this live album, he assembled an unusual backup band (featuring cellist Jane Scarpantoni) to play some new songs, Bongos favorites, and logical covers like "Cry Baby Cry." –WR

Primal Dream / MCA   1990
Barone's first full-fledged studio solo album is long on stirring and beautifully arranged rockers, with some striking guitar work. The touchstone is still *Beatles '65*, but Barone updates it, and his tunes are irresistible. –WR

SYD BARRETT   b 1946

Psychedelic. Roger "Syd" Barrett founded and was the lead singer, main songwriter, and lead guitarist for Pink Floyd. He left the band in 1968 and released two solo albums in 1970 (a third from outtakes was subsequently released), but he's been inactive in music ever since. –WR

○ **The Madcap Laughs / CAPITOL**   1970
While this collection bears similarities to the songs found on *The Piper at the Gates of Dawn*, the only Pink Floyd album Barrett contributed to significantly, it nevertheless comes across more as a session of run-throughs and demos than as a finished record. Its very roughness is its charm, undercutting the whimsy of the songs with Barrett's ultimate strangeness. –WR

BARRY & THE REMAINS

Rock/pop. The Remains, fronted by Barry Tashian, were a blistering, shake 'em down rock & roll teen combo, probably the finest Boston had to offer in the mid 60s; they seemed poised for national stardom after signing to Epic for their debut album. Success eluded them, however, and they fell victim to the label's massive "Bosstown sound" promo campaign, which backfired for all groups signed to Epic at that time. The Remains became cult favorites with 60s collectors, with varied compilations appearing on foreign labels over the years. –CK

○ **The Remains / CBS**   1967
A topflight garage band in this classic collection, painstakingly remastered. –BE

LOU ANN BARTON

Blues/rock. Barton is arguably the queen of the Austin, TX, roadhouse R&B/blues scene. Her recordings on Antone are well worth seeking out. –RC

○ **Read My Lips / ANTONE**   1989
Barton's lascivious delivery of roadhouse R&B chestnuts by Hank Ballard, Slim Harpo, and others is hotter than four-alarm chili on a Texas summer night. Members from the Fabulous Thunderbirds, Stevie Ray Vaughan's band, and other Austin heavy-hitters ensure that songs like "Sexy Ways," "Shake Your Hips," "You Can Have My Husband," "Sugar Coated Love," and "Rocket in My Pocket" have the right amount of grease. Absolutely great stuff! –RC

BASIA

Rock/pop. Born and raised in Poland, Basia (born Basia Trzetrzelewska) sang in the group Matt Bianco before she launched a light-jazz/pop solo career in the late 80s. –ED

Time and Tide / EPIC   1987
Good mix of pop-soul, with Brazilian overtones on "Astrud," a tribute to Astrud Gilberto. –KMC & BC

○ **London Warsaw New York / CBS**   1989
Melodic pop-jazz. Includes "Cruising for Bruising" and "Baby You're Mine." –KMC

MARTHA BASS & FONTELLA

R&B. They are progressive gospel singers, although Fontella is better known for her R&B hit "Rescue Me." –MGN

○ **From the Root to the Source / SOUL NOTE**   1980
Traditional and gospel music updated. Quintessential music, with Amina Myers on piano. –MGN

BATHORY

Heavy metal. During the 80s Bathory was one of the best groups in the black-metal genre, full of devilish stories that push the limits of good taste. –JB

○ **Under the Sign ... / NEW RENAISSANCE**   1987
When it comes to the dark and evil side of the world, Bathory was one of the best bands to do it in both words and gloomy music, and *Under the Sign of the Black Mark* is one of the few black-metal albums that'll still leave chills. –JB

BAUHAUS

Alternative rock. One of the originators of gloom-and-doom electronic rock, the British group included Peter Murphy on vocals, Daniel Ash on guitar, and the Haskins brothers, David Jay and Kevin, for the rhythm section. The band formed in 1978 and gained notoriety the next year with the single, "Bela Lugosi's Dead." After achieving chart success and adopting a brighter sound, the group disbanded in July 1983, as Ash and Kevin Haskins re-formed into Tones on Tail and later, with David Jay Haskins, into Love and Rockets. –DS

In the Flat Field / NESAK   1981
Captures the brooding bleakness of early Bauhaus. –DS

Mask / BEG   1981
In this followup to *In the Flat Field*, Bauhaus matures by creating an album that stands on its own rather than a collection of scattered hits strung together with not-so-strong fillers. Feedback-driven looped guitars, fuzz bass, and Peter Murphy's ever-haunting, commanding vocals help to create their best album. More raw than their later material yet nicely refined, next to their first. Includes "The Passion of Lovers" and "Kick in the Eye." –JK

The Sky's Gone Out / A&M   1982
An upbeat, commercially successful Bauhaus LP (#4 in the UK) that includes a remake of Bowie's "Ziggy Stardust" and a three-part mini-opera, "The Three Shadows." –DS

○ **Swing the Heartache: The BBC Sessions / RCA**   1989
A posthumous collection of five sessions on English BBC, some from John Peel's famous show, on which Bauhaus abandoned hits such as "Bela Lugosi" and "Dark Entries" to experiment with different songs and revamp certain

prereleased material. The loose, live-recorded format suits this group, whose creative and skilled musicianship is highlighted on this recording. "God in an Alcove" and "Swing the Heartache" are rendered much better here. A better greatest-hits album than the double set *1979-1983.* –JK

BE BOP DELUXE

Art-rock. This English quartet (formed in 1972) blended art-rock with early techno-rock. Lead singer/guitarist Bill Nelson's detached singing and the band's metallic productions gave them a cold sound, that seemed to suit their futuristic fantasy themes. Nelson's elegant lead-playing rivaled Pink Floyd's David Gilmour for sheer power, even though his tone lacked Gilmour's warmth. Since Be Bop's demise in 1979, Nelson has enjoyed a moderately successful career in England as a solo artist and producer. –RC

○ **Raiding the Divine Archive ... / CAPITOL**   1991
Raiding the Divine Archive - Best of Be Bop Deluxe is a smartly assembled overview of arty-sci-fi-rock outfit (heavier on the rock), led by Bill Nelson, one of the most powerfully elegant lead guitarists of the 70s. The band was an early experimenter of techno-rock. Dense clinical production (sometimes recalling mid-period Roxy Music), further underscored by Nelson's cold detached vocals, occasionally does a poor job of drawing the listener into appreciating the band's real musical strengths. –RC

THE BEACH BOYS

Rock/pop. The Beach Boys are the most successful and important American band of the rock music era. They were formed in 1961 in Hawthorne, CA, around the three Wilson brothers: Brian (b Jun 20, 1942), Dennis (b Dec 4, 1944 - d Dec 28, 1983), and Carl (b Dec 21, 1946). Additional members were Mike Love, the Wilsons's cousin (b Mar 15, 1941), and Al Jardine (b Sep 3, 1942). From the start, the focus of the group's music was Brian, who combined a fascination with vocal harmony in the Four Freshmen mold with a love of Chuck Berry derived rock & roll. Added to that was the subject matter of middle-class teenage life in southern California — surfing, cars, and girls.

The result was massive popular success for the group, starting with their first chart entry, "Surfin'," in 1962. "Surfin' Safari" was their first Top 20 hit the same year, and "Surfin' USA" reached #3 in 1963, while the album of the same name went to #2 and became the first of eight straight gold albums for the Beach Boys over the next two years.

Most of the music was written and produced by Brian, who retired from touring in 1964 to concentrate on this aspect of the band's career. After several replacements, the group settled on Bruce Johnston (b Jun 24, 1944) This led to a dichotomy between Brian and the rest of the Beach Boys that continues to this day. Brian's music became progressively more sophisticated and less like the teen anthems of the first hits as the 60s wore on, until, with the 1966 recordings *Pet Sounds* and the #1 single "Good Vibrations," they had become elaborate studio creations taking months to perfect.

Brian was unable to finish *Smile*, the followup to *Pet Sounds*, and the other members of the band came to assert more say in the recorded music from 1967 on, as their commercial fortunes declined. In 1974 they enjoyed a resurgence in popularity, topping the charts with *Endless Summer*, a compilation of their 60s hits, and in 1976 they scored with a new album, *15 Big Ones*, again produced by Brian. Subsequent recordings have been uneven, though the Beach Boys scored a #1 hit with "Kokomo" in 1988, the same year Brian Wilson launched a solo career. –WR

Best of the Beach Boys - Vol. 1 / CAPITOL   1966
Satisfactory but unexceptional collection of early hits, mastered with substandard sound. –BE

☆ **Pet Sounds / CAPITOL**   1966
The group's most well realized, ambitious, and well-produced album, a wistful, bittersweet, achingly beautiful foray into post-teenage angst ("God Only Knows," "Wouldn't It Be Nice,"

"That's Not Me") and uncertainty ("Don't Talk"), augmented with one hit rock single ("Sloop John B."). –BE

Sunflower / CBS   1970
The group's first 70s album, and a highpoint for all concerned, from the transcendental doo-wop music of "This Whole World" to the simple pleasantries of "Add Some Music." –BE

○ **Surf's Up / CBS**   1971
Its title notwithstanding, this album has less to do with surfing than with the band coming to terms with aging and with changing audiences — environmentalism shares space alongside the title track, a poignant, serious masterpiece of modern pop music. –BE

Holland / CBS-CARIBOU   1972
A failed effort to renew the group's sound with a change of venue (to Holland) that is salvaged largely by the presence of one great rock number ("Sail on Sailor") and a conceptual piece ("California Saga") that has a phenomenal middle section. –BE

Beach Boys In Concert / CBS-CARIBOU   1973
With virtually no audience presence on this early-70s live album, it's a good deal less exciting than either of their Capitol live recordings. But some of the concert renditions ("Don't Worry Baby") are superior to the studio originals, and the record as a whole is consistently rewarding. –BE

Endless Summer / CAPITOL   1974
A notable collection, as the record that sparked the commercial revival of the band's fortunes during the 70s, although all of the material on it has been remastered in superior form on other Capitol CDs. –BE

Spirit of America / CAPITOL   1975
A followup to *Endless Summer*, much weaker in content, but its near-repeat success helped put the group back in the spotlight. –BE

15 Big Ones / CBS-CARIBOU   1976
A return to simplicity and the group's roots, complete with a hit Chuck Berry cover ("Rock and Roll Music") and a lot of songs about beaches, babes, and amusement parks. It was a hit too. –BE

M.I.U. Album / CBS   1978
The group's last halfway-good album, sparked by pleasant singing, some unexpected rock cover versions, and funny wordplay by Brian Wilson. –BE

Ten Years of Harmony 1970-1980 / CBS   1981
An adequate collection of their best 1970-1980 period music, but missing some tracks. –BE

○ **Surfin' USA / Surfer Girl / MOBILE FID.**
State-of-the-art audiophile CD of the group's first two albums, brilliant sounding and unbelievably vivid in its textures. Possibly the ultimate surf-music experience on CD. –BE

Surfin' Safari/Surfin' USA / CAPITOL   1990
Mindless fun in the sun. A first flash of pop genius. –BE

○ **Little Deuce Coupe/All Summer Long / CAPITOL**   1990
Both of these albums are highlighted by exquisitely soaring harmonies over a solid rock beat — their title tracks represent the high point of the group's work with car songs and seasonal anthems, respectively. As a 2-fer CD, it's indispensible. –BE

Surfer Girl/Shut Down - Vol. 2 / CAPITOL   1990
The group's surf sound added a good deal of romanticism and sentimentality with *Surfer Girl*, along with more elegant harmonies. *Shut Down - Vol. 2*, by contrast, was probably the most accomplished and successful collection of car songs ever recorded. It's almost all macho swagger, which is set to an infectious beat. –BE

Beach Boys Concert/Live in London / CAPITOL   1990
Two shows from five years apart which feature the group at their most exciting. The *Live in London* material is more ambitious, drawing principally on their post-1965 repertory, but the group is remarkably consistent in its sense of fun in

both shows. *Concert* may be a little too lightweight by modern standards, but it is also an amazingly coherent and accomplished document, capturing "Fun, Fun, Fun," "Little Deuce Coupe," and other early hits in performance for posterity, much as *Live in London* preserves "Barbara Ann," "Good Vibrations," "Darlin'," and more. –BE

☆ **Today!/Summer Days / CAPITOL**   1990
The Beach Boys began growing up on these two albums — *The Beach Boys Today!* and *Summer Days (& Summer Nights!!)*, which feature more mature sentiments ("She Knows Me Too Well") and more confident expressions ("California Girls") in complex vocal and instrumental arrangements that anticipate the beauty of *Pet Sounds*. –BE

Beach Boys' Party!/Stack-O-Tracks / CAPITOL   1990
Party was a fake "live" album, put together as a stop-gap release while the group worked on more complicated material. It yielded one monster hit ("Barbara Ann") amid its informal kidding of the Beatles, Dylan, and the Beach Boys themselves. *Stack-O-Tracks* was a bizarre but welcome effort by Capitol to milk the group's catalog, a music-minus-one-style release featuring nothing but the backing tracks to the group's more well known songs — and it worked, not only as good listening on its own terms but also for what it revealed about the complexity of the band's singing. These two records are best for hardcore fans but can be enjoyed by anybody. –BE

Smiley Smile/Wild Honey / CAPITOL   1990
Smiley Smile was considered something of a bummer when it appeared in late 1967, but its languid, moody, spaced-out psychedelia has aged extremely well, and today it has lots more fans. *Wild Honey* was a successful attempt at White soul; while it will never rival Hall & Oates or the Righteous Brothers for romanticism, it is an effective digression for the Beach Boys, yielding one major hit in "Darlin'." –BE

Friends/20/20 / CAPITOL   1990
Friends is a very mildly druggy, lighthearted foray into the meaning of life ca. 1968, with a glow of California serenity suffusing nearly every good-natured note. *20/20* is an odd collection of hits ("Do It Again"), leftovers from the psychedelic masterpiece *Smile* ("Cabinessence"), at least one track coauthored by Charles Manson ("Never Learn Not To Love"), and other flotsam and jetsam from the tail-end of the group's stay at Capitol — and it *all* works as rock and psychedelia. –BE

Lost and Found 1961-62 / DCC   1991
An odd collection of very early pre-Capitol session tapes, featuring the sounds of the group at work, experiments that anticipate their minimalist psychedelia of 1967, and the best-sounding version of their debut single "Surfin'" that anyone ever heard. –BE

★ **Absolute Best - Vol. 1 / CAPITOL**   1991
The early hits and their best-known songs ("Surfin' USA," "Fun, Fun, Fun," etc.), and a good anthology from that standpoint — but none of all the really interesting stuff from the albums and B-sides. It's also a little too predictable, making it okay for the unadventurous. –BE

☆ **Absolute Best - Vol. 2 / CAPITOL**   1991
The second half of this collection is much more interesting than the first, containing as it does some of their most offbeat celebrated tracks. –BE

THE BEARS

Alternative pop. In 1987, guitarist Adrian Belew (whose previous credits included Frank Zappa, Talking Heads, and King Crimson) formed the Bears with a few friends he'd known before he became a hot hired gun for alternative music stars. The Bears's quirky Anglo-pop/rock (similar to XTC's unorthodox song constructions and changes) fused seamlessly with Belew's bizarre tonal washes and occasionally dissonant leads.

After the second album, *Rise and Shine*, Belew returned to his own solo work, which has since reflected the tunefulness of the Bears as opposed to his more jarring earlier work; the remaining Bears continue as a trio called the Psychodots. –RC

○ **The Bears / PRIMITIVE MAN**   1987
Fans of XTC/Squeeze-style oddball pop-rock will love this debut. The band's punchy arrangements and vocals and Belew's peculiar guitar gymnastics shine on super-melodic tracks like "Figure It Out," "None of the Above," and "Honey Bee." –RC

Rise & Shine / PRIMITIVE MAN   1988
The songs aren't as strong as those on their debut, but *Rise & Shine* is still a good showcase for fans of Belew's playing. –RC

THE BEATLES

British Invasion, rock & roll, psychedelic. The most successful and significant rock group in history, the Beatles were formed in Liverpool, England, in the late 50s by John Lennon (b Oct 9, 1948 - d Dec 8, 1980), Paul McCartney (b June 18, 1942), and George Harrison (b Feb 25, 1943). Ringo Starr (b July 7, 1940) joined the group in 1962 in time for their first formal recordings.

The Beatles ingested every popular music style of their day — the raucous rock & roll of Jerry Lee Lewis and Little Richard, the more sophisticated rock/pop of Buddy Holly, the soul of Motown and the Phil Spector-produced girl groups, the pop/R&B of the Isley Brothers and Larry Williams, the country-rock style of Carl Perkins, the pop-schmaltz of Broadway show tunes — and synthesized them into a style of their own, most importantly, a style expressed in the original songwriting of Lennon and McCartney. And that was only the beginning. By a year or so into their recording career, the Beatles had begun to throw off their influences and forge new directions in popular music.

They were also, at the outset, the teenage heartthrobs of their day. "Beatlemania" struck Great Britain in 1963 and the rest of the world in 1964 and, in a sense, never let up throughout the rest of the 60s. Though the teen-phenomenon aspect of their career became less intense in 1966 (by which time, inevitably, new teen dreams had cropped up), the Beatles made a successful transition to an older audience without sacrificing longtime fans. In part this was because they were so successful that they redefined the terms of success in the music business, and in part it was because they managed to be on top of, if not ahead of, popular trends.

Unlike even the most successful musical artists, who tend to achieve a number of hits in a given style and then base their reputations and their careers on that, the Beatles changed rapidly and went from success to success. Their early records were short, bouncy tunes of love, filled with harmony and exuberance. But by late 1964, melancholy and doubt had begun to surface, along with an increased musical sophistication and the use of different instrumentation. By 1965 their style had expanded to include the timeless ballad "Yesterday," performed with a string quartet, and the band that released the single "Penny Lane"/"Strawberry Fields Forever" in 1967 was almost unidentifiable in appearance as well as music, as the lovable moptops of 1964. The only thing the two had in common was that the music was still amazingly good.

Though the Beatles defined yet another genre of music — "art-rock" — with their work of 1967, they returned to a simpler style in their final years of existence, albeit one that gave greater space to the individual talents of the band members. The formula sound of the Beatles was long gone by 1968, replaced by four different, imaginative musicians still moving in new directions. Unfortunately, the evident musical differences were mirrored in personal and business differences, and the Beatles broke up in 1970.

The music, however, remains, and just as the Beatles absorbed the styles they heard while growing up, so a generation of musicians has grown up absorbing the Beatles,

and their influence is palpable in virtually every rock record made since. –WR

☆ **Please Please Me / EMI**   1963
Nearly 30 years after its release, the Beatles' first album still stands not only as a blueprint for what the group itself would accomplish in the next three years, but for what a large part of popular music would sound like from then on. Listening now, one revels anew at the songwriting of John Lennon and Paul McCartney (songs include "I Saw Her Standing There"), their remarkable harmonies and solo singing, and the encyclopedia of pop and rock they offer from other sources — especially light pop and hard R&B (like the show-stopping closer, Lennon's take on the Isley Brother's "Twist and Shout"). The CD reissue is in the original mono, but Mobile Fidelity has issued the album in stereo. –WR

☆ **With the Beatles / CAPITOL**   1963
In only a few months, and despite a torrid schedule, the Beatles demonstrated enormous growth on their second album (growth and change would be constants throughout their remarkable career). From the forceful "It Won't Be Long" to the bouncy "All My Loving," their original songs have made a leap, especially in ensemble playing, and the covers again offer a broad range, from Broadway show music ("Till There Was You" from *The Music Man*) to two great Motown songs ("You Really Got a Hold on Me" and "Money"). The CD reissue is in mono, while Mobile Fidelity has issued it in stereo. –WR

Meet the Beatles / CAPITOL   1964
When the US subsidiary of their UK label, Capitol Records, finally decided to issue a Beatles album, they took both sides of the group's current single "I Want to Hold Your Hand," pulled "I Saw Her Standing There" from *Please Please Me*, and culled nine of the 14 tracks from *With the Beatles* for this release. They also performed some studio gimmickry, supposedly to make the music sound more pleasing to American ears. The album is great anyway. –WR

Beatles' Second Album / CAPITOL   1964
The other five tracks from *With the Beatles*, the B-sides of three singles, "She Loves You," and two newly recorded songs (one a raucous version of Little Richard's "Long Tall Sally") make up the cobbled-together contents of Capitol's second US Beatles album. The shuffling doesn't matter a bit, since the overall quality of the Beatles output is so high. –WR

☆ **A Hard Day's Night (UK) / EMI**   1964
Maybe it was all the success of the previous year, but on their third (UK) album, the Beatles sound positively triumphant, roaring through exciting songs like the title tune, "Can't Buy Me Love," and "Any Time at All." On their first album to be entirely self-written, it's the material (produced under incredible pressure) that continues to impress. "I Should Have Known Better," "If I Fell," "And I Love Her" — these are songs a generation can sing word-for-word decades later. At the same time, one can hear around the edges the beginnings of Lennon's darker side and individual voice, as more than once he refers to something he can't stand. "I'll Cry Instead" is almost bitter. *A Hard Day's Night's* freshness has not dated an hour. –WR

Something New / CAPITOL   1964
Capitol Records initially did not have the rights to *A Hard Day's Night*, issued in the US as a soundtrack by United Artists, the company that released the film. Instead, Capitol cobbled together a competing record containing eight of the 14 songs from the UK version, two songs from a UK EP, and a German language version of "I Want to Hold Your Hand." –WR

☆ **Beatles for Sale / CAPITOL**   1964
In a sense, this fourth UK album is a step back for the Beatles as they return to the eight-originals-with-six-covers formula of their first two albums. Fatigue is clearly setting in. But some of the originals are gems, especially Lennon's "No Reply" and "I'm a Loser," songs confirming his sense of anguish. The covers of Chuck Berry, Carl Perkins, and Little

Richard are, once again, inspired recastings of formative material for the group. −WR

Beatles '65 / CAPITOL 1964
Dave Dexter Jr (a name which will live in infamy) "assisted" the Beatles by pulling eight tracks from *Beatles for Sale*, one from *A Hard Day's Night*, and both sides of the latest Beatles single ("I Feel Fine"/"She's a Woman") for the creation of this album. −WR

Early Beatles / CAPITOL 1965
Capitol acquired the rights to the Beatles material on which it had passed in 1963, and so issued this album, which consists of 11 of the 14 tracks from *Please Please Me*. −WR

Beatles VI / CAPITOL 1965
Capitol strikes again, using the remaining six tracks from *Beatles for Sale*, four newly recorded songs (two of them covers of Larry Williams hits), and the B-side of a single, to create another "new" Beatles album. −WR

☆ **Help! (UK) / EMI** 1965
Their fifth UK album contained seven songs used in a film plus seven other songs and marked a move to a softer, more reflective style. The lyrics are more prominent and thoughtful, and the sound more often features slow tempos, acoustic guitars, and other instruments. Here Lennon continued to cry for "Help!" and bitterly declared "You've Got to Hide Your Love Away" over a strummed acoustic. Here McCartney took a bluegrass/country turn in "I've Just Seen a Face" and achieved his biggest ballad with "Yesterday" (singing before a string quartet). Once again, the Beatles had exhibited remarkable growth and pointed the way for all of pop music to follow. −WR

Help! - Original Soundtrack (US) / CAPITOL 1965
Things got even more confusing (if possible) on the American release front when Capitol began to adopt similar titles for its albums while still monkeying with the contents. Capitol's *Help!* is a true soundtrack, as it includes only the seven Beatles tracks actually heard in the film, and the album is filled out with music from the film score by Ken Thorne. −WR

☆ **Rubber Soul (UK) / CAPITOL** 1965
Although the Beatles' sixth (UK) album is less consistent than some of their other releases, it has its share of memorable songs, among them Lennon's "Norwegian Wood," "Nowhere Man," and "In My Life" and McCartney's "Michelle." Again, the sound is softer and more sophisticated than any of the group's 1964 material. −WR

Rubber Soul (US) / CAPITOL 1965
In its by-now-familiar style, Capitol Records took the UK *Rubber Soul*, cut four songs, added two culled from Side 2 of the UK *Help!*, and emerged with a 12-track US version. −WR

Yesterday ... and Today / CAPITOL 1966
Those of you keeping score will note that some tracks are still unaccounted for, and here they are on a "new" Capitol album, its 11 tracks containing those four lost *Rubber Soul* tracks, two more from the second side of *Help!*, both sides of the 1965 single "We Can Work It Out"/"Day Tripper," and three new songs taken from the next UK Beatles album, then being recorded. −WR

☆ **Revolver (UK) / CAPITOL** 1966
Those three songs swiped for *Yesterday ... and Today* were the least of another astonishing leap in songwriting and production that introduced "Eleanor Rigby," "Yellow Submarine," "She Said, She Said," "Good Day Sunshine," "For No One," "Got to Get You into My Life," and "Tomorrow Never Knows." If McCartney was becoming a consummate pop craftsman with a command of horns and strings, Lennon was delving into a drugged psyche while experimenting with tape loops and strange sounds. And George Harrison, whose unprecedented three songs were led by "Taxman," was finally flowering into a first-rate songwriter. −WR

Revolver (US) / CAPITOL 1966
In preparing *Revolver* for US release, Bill Miller simply cut the

three songs already used on *Yesterday ... and Today*, resulting in an 11-song version. −WR

Collection of Beatles' Oldies / PARLOPHONE (UK) 1966
In the UK, where singles frequently did not appear on albums, this album culled 16 popular Beatles tunes from 1963 to 1966. The Beatles' first greatest-hits album. −WR

☆ **Sgt. Pepper's Lonely Hearts Club Band / CAPITOL** 1967
The Beatles' finest album is a song cycle full of childlike whimsy and irresistibly catchy songs. Its playfulness belies an amazingly fluid arrangement of melodies, lyrics, and sounds that flow together into a whole, creating its own magical world. An open-ended embrace of light pop, hard-rock, Indian music, swing, classical music, and blues, the album makes the case for musical unity-in-diversity, seemingly gathering all that came before it into surprising yet perfect combinations. The Beatles only occasionally approached this achievement in isolated moments afterwards, and nobody else even came close, then or since. −WR

☆ **Magical Mystery Tour / CAPITOL** 1967
Six songs from the group's TV film *Magical Mystery Tour*, plus their three 1967 singles. Especially notable among them is "Penny Lane"/"Strawberry Fields Forever," perhaps the most impressive two-sided hit ever recorded. And with songs like "All You Need Is Love," "Hello Goodbye," "The Fool on the Hill," and the title track, the rest of the album isn't too shabby, either. −WR

☆ **The Beatles / CAPITOL** 1968
In their later recordings, the Beatles largely eschewed the elaborate arrangements and instrumentation of 1967 in favor of returning to the simpler sound of the four-piece band. They did not, however, return to the ensemble style of 1964, rather serving as backup to one of four leaders, depending on who wrote the song. On this sprawling double album, already apparent individual styles gain ascendency; likewise, musical styles are not so much combined as separated out in pastiche form — the Beach Boys pop of "Back in the USSR," the blues of "Yer Blues," the folk of "Rocky Raccoon," the hard rock of "Birthday," the schmaltzy pop of "Good Night." The musical facility is amazing but also seems near-parodic. −WR

Yellow Submarine / CAPITOL 1969
There are really only four new songs here, and even they predate the material on *The Beatles*, but this is a pleasant enough soundtrack album, dominated by the musical score written by Beatles producer George Martin. −WR

☆ **Abbey Road / CAPITOL** 1969
The Beatles' last unified statement finds them going out at a peak of musical achievement, from Lennon's "Come Together" to Harrison's "Something," with McCartney dominating the Side 2 medley that finds the group rocking out in fine style. *Abbey Road* is the best-selling Beatles album ever. −WR

Hey Jude (or The Beatles Again) / CAPITOL 1970
The first US Beatles compilation album, this gathers singles and stray tracks dating back to 1964 and features the first LP (and live stereo) releases of such songs as "Paperback Writer," "Lady Madonna," and "Hey Jude." −WR

○ **Let It Be / CAPITOL** 1970
Flawed, botched, and overproduced by Phil Spector, the final new Beatles album to be released (most of it was recorded prior to *Abbey Road*) nevertheless included the title song, "The Long and Winding Road," an abbreviated version of "Get Back," and such lovely tunes as "Two of Us," which, for one last time, presented Paul McCartney and John Lennon and their acoustic guitars, harmonizing together. −WR

★ **1962-1966 / CAPITOL** 1973
A 26-track double-album of the Beatles' greatest hits up through 1966. Though it is primarily devoted to singles, the collection also includes a few key album tracks. −WR

★ **1967-1970 / CAPITOL** 1973
Twenty-eight songs from the second half of the Beatles' career, focusing on the hits but also including key album tracks. −WR

Rock & Roll Music / CAPITOL 1976

Music Map
Rock-British Invasion To America & Back-'64 to '67

Roots-American Blues
Robert Johnson — Sonny Boy Williamson
Jimmy Reed — Elmore James
Muddy Waters — Howlin' Wolf
B. B. King — Willie Dixon

Roots–50s Rock/R&B
Elvis Presley — Little Richard — Jerry Lee Lewis
Buddy Holly — Everly Brothers — Gene Vincent

Roots-Music Hall Shuffle
Vera Lunn
Lonnie Donegan

British Invasion Rock '64-'69
The Rolling Stones
The Who — The Kinks — John Mayall — Fleetwood Mac
The Animals — The Yardbirds

American Garage Bands
Post-Beatles era: 1964-1969
The Shadows of Knight
The Leaves
The Seeds
The 13th Floor Elevators
The Chocolate Watch Band
The Barbarians
The Sonics
The Outsiders
Count Five
Blues Magoos
? & the Mysterians
The MC5
Iggy & the Stooges
The Sir Douglas Quintet

British Invasion Rock/Pop '64-'67
The Beatles
The Hollies — Dave Clark 5 — Gerry & the Pacemakers — Herman's Hermits
The Searchers — Freddie & the Dreamers — Billy J. Kramer & the Dakotas
The Zombies — Manfred Mann — The Troggs — The Spencer Davis Group

American Pop Bands
Post-Beatles era: 1964-1967
Gary Lewis & the Playboys — The Grass Roots
The Five Americans — The Beau Brummels
The Monkees — The Box Tops

Folk Rock
Bob Dylan — The Byrds
Mouse & the Traps — The Lovin' Spoonful
Mamas & the Papas — Simon & Garfunkel
Donovan — Sonny & Cher

A double-pocket compilation emphasizing the Beatles' more uptempo material (and hence, their earlier work). All tracks are previously released, though "I'm Down" makes its first appearance on LP. (Later released as two single albums.) —WR

○ **Live at the Hollywood Bowl / CAPITOL**   1977
Previously unreleased live performances culled from shows at the Hollywood Bowl in 1964 and 1965. The screaming never stops, but the group's musical talent and personal charm shine through. —WR

Love Songs / CAPITOL   1977
Two albums of Beatles ballads, starting with "Yesterday," and including some of the best romantic music of the 60s. All tracks previously released. —WR

Rarities / CAPITOL   1980
Songs never released on album, or in stereo, or in alternate versions, make up this collector's album of oddities. (Not to be confused with Parlophone's album of the same name [PCM 1001, UK], an entirely different album, which contains only tracks not previously released in England on LP.) —WR

Reel Music / CAPITOL   1982
A 14-track selection of previously released songs used in various Beatles movies. —WR

20 Greatest Hits / CAPITOL   1982
The Beatles reached the #1 position on the *Billboard* magazine singles chart 20 times. Here are those songs. —WR

☆ **Past Masters - Vol. 1 / CAPITOL**   1988
When EMI and Capitol released the Beatles' recordings on

compact disc, it was decided to issue the albums in their original British formats in both the UK and the US. The British albums frequently did not contain singles released by the Beatles at the same time, and there were other odd tracks not included on albums. Thus two discs were necessary to gather the stray material (some of which included their biggest hits). This first volume, for example, running from 1962 to 1965, contains "She Loves You," "I Want to Hold Your Hand," and "I Feel Fine." —WR

☆ **Past Masters - Vol. 2 / CAPITOL**   1988
Completing the CD release of the Beatles' complete EMI/Capitol catalog, this disc contains "We Can Work It Out," "Paperback Writer," "Lady Madonna," "Hey Jude," "Get Back," "Let It Be," and other later Beatles songs. —WR

THE BEAU BRUMMELS

Rock/pop, folk/rock. The Beau Brummels, from San Francisco, enjoyed a brief run on the Top 40 pop charts in 1965 with a bracing blend of Brit Invasion pop and West Coast folk/rock. Sylvester Stone (later of Sly & the Family Stone) produced the band's first two albums, as well as their biggest hits, "Laugh Laugh" (#15) and "Just a Little" (#9). The fatalistic "You Tell Me Why," the band's last Top 40 hit, and the aggressive Byrds-like rocker "Don't Talk to Strangers" (#52) revealed the Beau Brummels to be a group possessing much depth. Unfortunately, the band's label (Autumn) folded at the end of 1965.

Two subsequent albums on Warner, *Triangle* and *Bradley's*

Barn, are out of print but are worth seeking out. In 1973, Leo Kottke recorded a fine version of "You Tell Me Why" (minus the bridge) for his album *Ice Water*. In 1975 the Beau Brummels re-formed for an impressive reunion on Warner, then called it quits. —RC

Triangle / WARNER   1967
A beautiful venture by the surviving trio into a more authentic form of folk and country-rock, with a repertoire that recalls the more famous Everly Brothers classic, *Roots*. —BE

○ **Best of the Beau Brummels / RHINO**   1987
Probably the best (and best-sounding) anthology covering their golden years, although it lacks their brilliant, later country-based work at its best. —BE

THE BEAUTIFUL SOUTH

Alternative pop. A British quintet formed by Paul Heaton (b May 9, 1962) after the demise of the Housemartins in 1988, characterized by sweet, jazz-pop arrangements that belie their witty, caustic lyrics. They had three albums on Elektra as of 1992. —WR

○ **Welcome to the Beautiful South / ELEKTRA**   1990
The difference between the catchy light pop that constitutes the Beautiful South's music and the bitter, pessimistic lyrics innocently sung by Paul Heaton is so great it constitutes a kind of malevolent seduction. But that's the point. —WR

BECK, BOGERT & APPICE

Hard rock. This early-70s hard rock trio comprised ex-Yardbird lead-guitarist Jeff Beck and two former Vanilla Fudge members in drummer Carmine Appice and bassist Tim Bogert.
Beck, Bogert & Appice pushed Cream's concept of free-for-all interplay into new realms of lumbering excessiveness. They only had one album Stateside, but there was a much-sought-after live-in-Japan effort, which has finally been included (in part) on Beck's *Beckology* boxed set. —RC

○ **Beck Bogert & Appice / CBS**   1973
Guitar virtuoso Beck toys with hard rock, supported by bassist Tim Bogert and drummer Carmine Appice. Includes a cover of Stevie Wonder's "Superstition." —DDC

JEFF BECK   b 1944

Hard rock, fusion. Utterly distinctive and certainly one of the most important electric lead guitarists in rock history, Jeff Beck was the wildcard element that gave the post-Clapton Yardbirds work its futuristic quality. His pioneering experiments with feedback and various effects, particularly on the classic "Shapes of Things," influenced thousands of musicians.
After leaving the Yardbirds, Beck went on to a highly successful solo career that produced an excellent debut (*Truth*), featuring Rod Stewart on vocals, Ron Wood (bass), Nicky Hopkins (keys), and Mickey Waller (drums). The next few albums contained fine moments with Stewart and replacement vocalist Bobby Tench, but during the mid 70s Beck switched gears and released the instrumental jazz/rock fusion *Blow by Blow*, generating his greatest commercial success. Further efforts to delve into that style were less notable, but even when the material wasn't up to par, Beck's liquid, yet impulsive style has been generally amazing. —RC

● **Truth / EPIC**   1968
Along with Led Zeppelin's self-titled first album, Jeff Beck's *Truth* is considered the primo primer for what came to be known as heavy metal. Fusing the thunderous rhythm section of Ron Wood on bass and Mickey Waller on drums with his paint-blistering lead guitar and Rod Stewart's gravel-and-whiskey vocals, Beck's visionary approach to blues and rock & roll influenced practically every rock band that followed on both sides of the Atlantic. Although Beck could be unpredictable and eclectic (witness his straightforward, acoustic reading of "Greensleeves"), *Truth* features the

smoking "Beck's Bolero," "Rock My Plimsoul," and the wah-wah pièce de résistance, "I Ain't Superstitious." —TG

Beck-Ola / EPIC   1969
A year after Jeff Beck recorded *Truth*, he came back with the even heavier *Beck-Ola*. Although the songwriting seems diluted, and the addition of Nicky Hopkins on piano added spice in all the wrong places, *Beck-Ola* is still a gut-slamming good time. Notable tracks include "Spanish Boots" and "Plynth (Water Down the Drain)." —TG

Rough and Ready / CBS   1971
After Jeff Beck nearly died in a car crash, he came back in 1971 with a new group and a new sound, reflecting his more introspective state of mind. Although the firepower and guitar blasts are still there, he burns cooler. With the help of the jazzy Max Middleton on piano, Beck created one of rock's most haunting set pieces, "Raynes Park Blues." Other highlights include the dynamic ballad "Jody" and the hard grinding rock groove of "I've Been Used." —TG & RC

Jeff Beck Group / CBS   1972
Continuing with the same group lineup as on *Rough and Ready*, *Jeff Beck Group* was slagged off by critics for Steve Cropper's admittedly lazy production. However, several of the songs hold up masterfully, including the skronky "Ice Cream Cakes," the superlative redo of Don Nix's "Going Down," and the beautifully sad and wistful instrumental, "Definitely Maybe." Beware of early, poor-sounding versions. —TG

★ **Blow by Blow / CBS**   1975
When Jeff Beck announced that he was working on an all-instrumental album, few but his legion of guitar fans could have predicted the far-reaching impact of this pivotal rock/jazz fusion album. Teamed with the Beatles' ex-producer, George Martin, Beck singlehandedly created a new subtext for rock & roll. With his virtuosity and taste at an all-time peak, Beck let loose with unforgettable tracks such as the Roy Buchanan-inspired "Cause We've Ended As Lovers" and the percolating "Freeway Jam." One of rock's great instrumental works. —TG

Wired / CBS   1976
Nearly *Blow by Blow*'s equal. Although Beck doesn't venture any further musically, Charles Mingus's "Goodbye Pork Pie Hat" is worth the price alone. (Available on Mobile Fidelity's Ultradisc) —TG

Jeff Beck's Guitar Shop / CBS   1989
A guitar hero in his prime, full of fury and finesse, with topnotch support from Terry Bozzio and Tony Hymas. —JO

○ **Beckology / CBS**   1991
Covering everything from his earliest (and terrific) tracks with the Tridents through his spot-on interpretation of Santo & Johnny's "Sleep Walk," *Beckology* features great remastering, smart packaging (resembling a vintage Fender tweed guitar case), and the essential Yardbirds and solo years material. The set (55 tracks in all) also collects the best material from weaker albums such as *Flash* and *There and Back*. A definitive overview of Beck's career would have included his work as a sideman with artists like Stevie Wonder, Rod Stewart, and Donovan; nevertheless, *Beckology* is as comprehensive a collection as one will find on this innovative guitarist. —TG & RC

GEORGE BEDARD   b 1952

Rockabilly, blues/rock. While other youngsters in the 60s were listening to British Invasion bands and wishing they were on the Ed Sullivan show, a young George Bedard was in his basement teaching himself guitar, playing along with records by blues legends Howlin' Wolf, B. B. King, and Muddy Waters. By the early 70s Bedard was teaming up with blues harpist/guitarist Steve Nardella to form the Silvertones, one of the finest Ann Arbor, MI, blues/rockabilly bands of the 70s. Combining genres is a path Bedard has pursued relentlessly, working in groups both as soloist and sideman, covering a wide range of styles from country to jazz to rockabilly and back to his first love, the blues. There's not much Bedard can't play extremely well in any of these idioms, his style always informed by taste and economy. Though his solo recordings have been few, George Bedard remains a guitar hero's guitar hero. —CK

○ **Upside! / SCHOOLKIDS** 1992
Bedard's debut album features great originals and a rollicking textbook approach to everything from rockabilly to T-Bone Walker-style blues. Worth it just for the explosive solo on "What a Shame." —CK

THE BEE GEES

Pop, disco. The Bee Gees' lengthy career has been one of the most successful in all of popular music. Their history could be broken down into two periods, pre- and postdisco. From 1967 to 1972, the Bee Gees (built around brothers Barry, Maurice, and Robin Gibb) produced 13 Top 40 pop hits, which were ornate, lush, and somewhat sentimental. More than most self-contained writing teams, the Bee Gees were adept at creating memorable melodies.

As if the first phase wasn't more success than most artists could hope to attain, the Bee Gees pulled out of a three-year dormancy, courtesy of the rising disco movement, and cashed in big with the Arif Mardin-produced *Main Course*, which contained the hits "Jive Talking" (#1) and "Nights on Broadway" (#7).

The Bee Gees were then asked to supply material for Robert Stigwood's film *Saturday Night Fever*. Their dominance on the soundtrack, coupled with the film's phenomenal success (over 30 million units sold), made the band quite wealthy. The followup album, the disco-heavy *Spirits Having Flown*, contained three #1 hits with "Love You Inside Out," "Tragedy," and "Too Much Heaven." With the death of disco, the group's fortune has subsided, although they have scored a few solid chart successes. —RC

○ **Bee Gees Gold - Vol. 1 / RSO** 1976
Some great post-Beatles pop from the Bee Gees' first fertile era. —DH

Bee Gees Greatest / POLYGRAM 1979
The cream of their stunning string of late-70s hits. —DH

Tales from the Brothers Gibb / POLYGRAM 1990
An exhaustive 4-disc boxed set that contains too much for anyone but hardcore fans. —DH

BEL CANTO

Alternative pop. This chamber-rock trio from Norway offers an authentic medieval sound based almost exclusively on the modern techniques of synthesis, with original music that expresses a stream of loss and sorrow from the past. Almost all their songs are built on a specific type of energy: female power, or the power of the earth, sometimes both destructive and hysterical. Bel Canto has an elaborate orchestration, utilizing a wide range of instruments. —VB

White-Out Conditions / NETTWERK 1988
Bel Canto's first album is refreshing and intriguing. Although it's uneven, it is definitely more than just a search for a new style. —VB

○ **Birds of Passage / CAPITOL** 1990
Completely professional material, well composed and performed. —VB

ADRIAN BELEW

Alternative pop. This avant-garde guitar slinger cut his teeth with Frank Zappa and became a critical darling during his stint in the 80s with Talking Heads and the re-formed King Crimson. He has released albums both as a solo artist and with the late-80s band, the Bears. —JF

Mr. Music Head / ATLANTIC 1989
Former King Crimson member Belew shines on his own, with aggressive guitar work framing a set of thoughtful alternative rockers. —DDC

○ **Inner Revolution / ATLANTIC** 1992
Belew uses his well-developed one-man-band and state-of-the-studio abilities to produce a Beatle pastiche record that ranks with the best of such Fab Four idolaters as Todd Rundgren, the Raspberries, and ELO, and that's no mean feat. He can sing (almost) like John Lennon and play guitar like George Harrison. His sturdy songwriting makes this much more than just a successful genre exercise. —WR

BELL BIV DEVOE

Urban R&B. Former members of New Edition struck pay dirt with their 1990 debut, which crossed over into the White pop charts in addition to dominating the R&B world. Their outside production efforts have resulted in hit debuts by the R&B groups Another Bad Creation and Boyz II Men. —JF

○ **Poison / MCA** 1990
BBD describe their style as "R&B on the smooth tip with a hip-hop feel," and that's just what you'll find on this hugely successful debut. Equally adept at sumptuous ballads and big-beat dance thumpers, BBD have taken Teddy Riley's new-jack innovations to both a wider audience and a new creative plateau. —JF

CHRIS BELL

Anglo-pop. Memphis singer/songwriter Chris Bell cofounded the influential power-pop quartet Big Star in 1971, with Alex Chilton. Bell left the group before the release of their second album, *Radio City*, to pursue a solo career. He died in an automobile accident on Dec 27, 1978. It wasn't until 1992 that Bell's work was released in an album form. —RC

○ **I Am the Cosmos / RYKODISC** 1992
A collection of the late Chris Bell's solo work, mostly demos. The title track is a brilliant downer (Big Star and Badfinger at half-speed) that opens the album. "You and Your Sister" is a gorgeous heartbreaker, rendered with delicate acoustic guitars and Mellotron and guest vocalist Alex Chilton. Not everything Bell undertakes is so fragile. "I Don't Know" (and its later, inferior incarnation "Get Away"), "Make A Scene," and "Fight at the Table" are relentless rockers. Bell's voice may be an acquired taste for some, as it occasionally gets a little whiney. When it does connect with the music, the results can be quite affecting, particularly on "You and Your Sister," "Speed of Sound," and the title track. Ryko has done a great job remastering these tapes, and the packaging is a first-rate labor of love. —RC

WILLIAM BELL   b 1937

R&B, soul. William Bell was one of the first artists signed to the Stax label during its fledgling years in Memphis, and he greatly influenced the "Stax sound" as both performer and writer. His self-penned "You Don't Miss Your Water" (1961) almost defined the genre known as country-soul, with the unmistakable gospel feel of Bell's elegant, lilting vocal over a country-church piano figure. It was this perfect marriage of styles that became Bell's trademark at Stax and opened the door for others — most notably Otis Redding (who initially mined the same country-soul vein) — to follow. With the ascent of Redding, Bell's star began to fade somewhat. He continued to record (the beautiful, string-laden "I Forgot to Be Your Lover" in 1968) and, most importantly, to write — (his own "Tribute to a King," written after Redding's death, and Albert King's "Born under a Bad Sign," both cowritten with Booker T. Jones). After Stax's collapse in 1975, Bell moved to Mercury, where he scored his first-ever million-seller with "Trying to Love Two." Bell continues to live and work in Memphis. —CO

○ **Soul of a Bell / ATLANTIC** 1967
The 1967 debut album of Stax's resident balladeer, loaded with Memphis soul ballads and an occasional raver. —BD

Best of William Bell / STAX 1988

Post-Atlantic work from the late 60s and early 70s. Includes Bell's playful duets with Judy Clay. —BD

THE BELMONTS

Doo-wop. Bronx-based vocal group that enjoyed a string of national hits from 1958 to 1960, with Dion DiMucci as lead singer. After Dion went solo, the Belmonts carried on as a trio and managed several more chart entries in the early 60s. Carlo Mastrangelo (b Oct 5, 1938) sang lead on the group's first and biggest post-Dion hit in 1961 on the Sabrina label, "Tell Me Why." The group also included Angelo D'Aleo and Freddie Milano. —BD

○ **Cigars Acappella Candy / ELEKTRA**   1972
New York City street-corner doo-wop. New recordings. —HD

JESSE BELVIN   1933-1960

R&B. An influential, silky-voiced R&B crooner and songwriter from the 50s, best known for his 1956 hit "Goodnight My Love" and for writing the Penguins' hit "Earth Angel." —JF

... But Not Forgotten / UNITED
Terrible sound quality, but this old LP features the balladeer's best-known mid-50s work for Modern Records. —BD

○ **Blues Balladeer / SPECIALTY**   1990
Loaded with previously unissued gems. Belvin's introspective, subdued vocals are delightful. —BD

PAT BENATAR   b 1953

Rock/pop. Originally trained as an opera singer, Pat Benatar decided to apply her considerable lung power to rock. Beginning with her first recording in 1979, Benatar adopted the persona of a tough, no-nonsense woman, which helped make her one of the most popular female performers of the 80s. Much of the material was written by Benatar and/or her guitarist husband Neil Giraldo. *True Love* (1991) was a departure for Benatar. It is a collection of blues tunes, with backing provided by Roomful of Blues. Time will tell whether this is a permanent change in direction. —KMC

In the Heat of the Night / CHRYSALIS   1979
This debut album features her trademark power-pop song "Heartbreaker." —DDC

Crimes of Passion / CAPITOL   1980
She won the Best Rock Vocal Performance - Female for her revival of the Young Rascals 1966 hit "You Better Run." —DDC

○ **Best Shots / CAPITOL**   1989
Multi-Grammy winner Benatar has vocal range to spare on this hits collection, including her rockers "Heartbreaker," "Fire and Ice," and "Hell Is for Children." —DDC

True Love / CAPITOL   1991
Benatar's stab at the blues, mixing traditional standards with three new songs, none suited to her power-pop style. Still, this gives diehard fans a chance to hear Benatar's vocals in a different context. —DDC

BROOK BENTON   1931-1988

R&B. Silky smooth: that was Brook Benton's byword from his first record to his very last, as the singer parlayed his rich baritone pipes into seven #1 R&B hits and eight Top Ten items.

Stints on the gospel circuit preceded Benton's first secular session for Okeh in 1953, but his career didn't begin to take off until he teamed with writer/producer Clyde Otis. Benton cowrote and sang hundreds of demos for other artists before frequent collaborator Otis signed his friend to Mercury; together they pioneered a lush, violin-studded variation on the standard R&B sound, which beautifully showcased Benton's intimate vocals.

Benton crashed the top spot on the R&B charts in early 1959 with his moving "It's Just a Matter of Time," then rapidly encored with three more R&B chart-toppers — "Thank You Pretty Baby," "So Many Ways," and "Kiddio." Pairing with

Mercury labelmate Dinah Washington, their delightful repartee on "Baby (You've Got What It Takes)" and "A Rockin' Good Way" paced the R&B lists in 1960.

The early 60s were a prolific period for Benton, but he left Mercury a few years later and bounced between labels before reemerging with the atmospheric Tony Joe White ballad "Rainy Night in Georgia" on Cotillion in 1970. Benton later made a halfhearted attempt to cash in on the disco craze, but his hitmaking reign was at an end long before his death in 1988. —BD

Anthology / RHINO
A slightly more modest version than the *40 Greatest*. —HD

○ **40 Greatest Hits / POLYGRAM**   1989
Everything you need to know about Benton. Bluesy, sexy pop music. Includes the duets with Dinah Washington. —HD

BERLIN

Rock/pop. This Los Angeles-based synth-pop group made up of Terri Nunn, John Crawford, and Rob Brill topped the charts in 1986 with "Take My Breath Away." Nunn left for a solo career in 1987. —WR

○ **Pleasure Victim / GEFFEN**   1982
Berlin pulled three dance-pop hits from this album, which successfully combined synth-beats with the sexy vocals of Terri Nunn, especially on the uninhibited "Sex (I'm A ...)." —WR

Count Three and Pray / GEFFEN   1986
Berlin's third album, their last before the departure of Terri Nunn for a solo career, contains their #1 hit, the ballad "Take My Breath Away," which was featured in the film *Top Gun.* —WR

CHUCK BERRY   b 1926

Rock & roll. It's impossible to give the reader a suitable description of Chuck Berry's rock & roll, and you really don't need one: the innovations he brought to the music, his dazzling, lucid lyrics, a guitar lick that everyone who's ever picked up a guitar has attempted to duplicate, vocals that place you dead-center into his detailed vignettes, can be heard everywhere. They are ingrained in rock's collective conscience, from the 60s shimmy of the Beatles up to the latest heavy metal raving.

The St. Louis-born Berry brought his unique stylings to pianist Johnnie Johnson's jump-blues boogie trio in 1953; he quickly became the band's leader and began filtering Johnson's tinkly, omnipresent piano runs into his guitar style. In 1955 Muddy Waters suggested that Berry pass a demo tape to Chess-label head Leonard Chess. Chess jumped on a Berry original called "Ida May" (based on an age-old country tune), changed the name to "Maybellene" and gave Berry his first hit in 1955. The song's choogling guitar sound, flowing lyrics, and tight, driving rhythm laid the groundwork for an amazing string of hits that have inspired generations. "Johnny B. Goode," "Too Much Monkey Business," "Little Queenie," "Carol," "Sweet Little Sixteen," "Back in the USA," "Roll over Beethoven," and dozens more just like them dealt with everything from tragicomic social drama and teen love and heartbreak to urban protest, all the while giving rock & roll a good deal of its language and most of its style.

A list of rock & rollers who've used Berry's hits for their own jump pads reads like a Who's Who: the Rolling Stones, the Beatles, the Beach Boys, the Yardbirds, Bob Dylan, Bruce Springsteen; the list is endless. Chuck Berry hasn't made a worthwhile record in decades and slops through concerts with only a paycheck on his mind. But if it weren't for Berry's legacy, books like the one you're reading would be considerably smaller. —JF

○ **Berry Is on Top / CHESS**   1959
Berry's best 50s Chess album (his third) features many of his biggest hits, plus atmospheric instrumentals like "Blues for Hawaiians." —CK

☆ **St. Louis to Liverpool / CHESS**   1964
This album, recorded and issued after Berry's 1964 prison

release, is one of the decade's finest albums, a concise shot of brilliance that includes such career-defining statements as "You Never Can Tell," "No Particular Place to Go," and "Nadine." –JF

★ **Great Twenty-Eight / CHESS**   1982
A single-disc compilation of Berry's original Chess greats, every one a gem: "Maybellene," "Johnny B. Goode," "Roll over Beethoven," "Sweet Little Sixteen," and "Little Queenie" are the music the Beatles and others cut their teeth on. Beyond essential. –CK

☆ **Chess Box / CHESS**   1988
A 3-CD box of Berry's career at Chess, from 50s classics to mid-70s chart entries, and all the high spots in between. –CK

DICKEY BETTS   ♭1943

Southern rock. Best known as the guitarist for the Allman Brothers Band, Dickey Betts has made recordings as a solo artist and bandleader during his tenure with the Allmans and during that band's hiatuses, notably leading Great Southern in the 70s and the Dickey Betts Band in the 80s. –WR

○ **Highway Call / POLYGRAM**   1974
Betts has made occasional solo albums, starting with this one, which picks up from the country-rock style of his Allmans hit "Ramblin' Man." There's a lot of tasty guitar set in ensemble arrangements also featuring steel guitar and the prominent fiddle of Vassar Clements. –WR

Pattern Disruptive / CBS   1988
After a long layoff, Betts cut this blistering guitar rock album in a style strongly reminiscent of the Allman Brothers Band. In fact, his band contains pianist Johnny Neel and second guitarist Warren Haynes, both of whom would join the next edition of the Allmans when they re-formed; Allmans drummer Butch Trucks guests. –WR

BIG AUDIO DYNAMITE

Alternative rock. Organized by Mick Jones (b Jun 26, 1955) after he left the Clash, this band prominently featured video artist Don Letts. It was reorganized with Letts in 1991 as Big Audio Dynamite II. –WR

○ **This is Big Audio Dynamite / CBS**   1985
Since Mick Jones was the more melodic, pop force in the Clash, it was some surprise that the band he formed after that group's demise was such an unusual mix of synthesized drumming and spoken-word tape inserts, although beneath all the gimmicky sounds (or perhaps accentuated by them) were Jones's often winning songs. –WR

THE BIG BOPPER   1930-1959

Rock & roll. Legendary as one of the three rock greats to die in the tragic 1959 Clear Lake, IA, plane crash that also claimed the lives of Buddy Holly and Ritchie Valens, the Big Bopper (born Jiles Perry Richardson) had just established himself as a rock hitmaker with the rollicking "Chantilly Lace." Born in the heart of Texas, Richardson grew up in Beaumont and changed his first name to Jape. He broke into show biz as a DJ over KTRM radio, where he coined the nickname "The Big Bopper." He began recording for Mercury in 1957, his animated baritone scaling pop playlists the next year with "Chantilly Lace" — easily his top seller — and the equally raucous novelty "Big Bopper's Wedding." Richardson wrote "White Lightning," a huge country hit for George Jones, and Johnny Preston's #1 one smash "Running Bear." –BD

○ **Hellooo Baby! The Best of ... / RHINO**
Hellooo Baby! The Best of the Big Bopper, 1954-1959 is a single-CD compilation of the Bopper's finest, including "Chantilly Lace," "Little Red Riding Hood," and "The Big Bopper's Wedding." It's wild and fun. –CK

BIG BROTHER & THE HOLDING COMPANY

Psychedelic. Fronted by one of rock's most charismatic female singers, Janis Joplin, Big Brother & the Holding Company

(formed 1965 with Joplin joining in 1966) was one of the premier groups of the late-60s San Francisco rock scene. Joplin's fiery performances and the band's inspired blues-rock intensity are best captured on *Cheap Thrills*. –RC

☆ **Cheap Thrills / CBS / BB 1**   1968
Cheap Thrills is a masterpiece of utterly raw psychedelic blues-based rock from the peak of the 60s San Francisco rock scene. Joplin works up a fever unlike anything she ever did on subsequent albums. Her delivery of "Ball and Chain" is a must-hear. Anyone who thinks Guns n' Roses mastered hard electric blues-grunge hasn't heard Big Brother's James Gurley and Sam Houston Andrews duke it out on tracks like "Ball and Chain," "Summertime," and "Combination of the Two." *Cheap Thrills* also features the hit "Piece of My Heart." –RC

BIG COUNTRY

Alternative rock. Scottish group Big Country burst onto the 1982 rock scene with a uniquely expansive twin-guitar sound (of ex-Skids Stuart Adamson and Bruce Watson) that at times recalled bagpipes. Bassist Tony Butler (whose credits included the Pretenders and Pete Townshend) and drummer Mark Brzezicji (also Townshend) provided an aggressively supple rhythmic foundation.
The Chris Thomas-produced debut effort "Harvest Home" didn't chart, but *The Crossing*, cinematically produced by the innovative Steve Lillywhite, captured the band's sonic vision perfectly. It contains the band's first (and only significant stateside) hit "In a Big Country" (#17 pop).
Big Country followed *The Crossing* with an EP containing the fine "Wonderland" (#86 pop), which basically echoed the spirit of "In a Big Country." In England, meanwhile, Big Country scored a brief string of hits, gaining enough popularity to sell out two nights at London's Wembley Stadium in December of 1984. This was further aided by the release of the album *Steeltown*, which entered British charts as #1. After an 18-month layoff, Big Country released *The Seer*. "Look Away" was a 1986 British hit, but only received moderate attention on US rock radio. The rather generic *Peace in Our Time*, released in 1988 on a new label (Reprise), was a misguided redirection of their sound, ditching most of the qualities that made the band so appealing. –RC

○ **The Crossing / MERCURY**   1983
One of the most unique and exciting debut rock releases of the early 80s. Producer Steve Lillywhite (U2, Simple Minds) aided in the band's larger-than-life sound and grand themes. The album contains expansive hits, including "In a Big Country" and "Fields of Fire." Other highlights are "Chance" and "Harvest Home." –RC

The Seer / MERCURY   1986
Continues their trademark sound to a fine effect. Contains the hit "Look Away." –RC

BIG DIPPER

Alternative rock. This Boston quartet featured ex-members of Dumptruck, the Embarrassment, and the Volcano Suns. Their strong sense of humor combined well with their slightly skewed rock licks, making them an accessible post-punk band. Their major label debut fell flat, and the band just fell out. –BE

○ **Heavens / HOMESTEAD**   1987
Perhaps the quintessential quirky power-pop, this album has a harder edge. Big Dipper inspires laughter and air guitar playing. –RG

○ **Craps / HOMESTEAD**   1988
Quirkier than *Heavens* but less powerful. In spite of being more melodic than *Heavens*, it's more abstruse, yet it's worthy of the repeated listenings it requires. –RG

BIG SHOULDERS

Blues/rock. Utilizing an unusually vast array of influences, Big Shoulders has cut a pair of albums for Rounder that are difficult to categorize, encompassing rock, blues, jazz, and ethnic origins. Vocalist/keyboardist Ken Saydak and harpist Ron Sorin are veterans of the Chicago blues circuit. –BD

○ **Big Shoulders / ROUNDER**   1989
The eclectic, blues-influenced Chicago quintet's impressive debut, featuring keyboardist Ken Saydak's gravelly vocals. –BD

Nickel History / ROUNDER   1991
More ambitious genre-mixing — everything from polkas to Percy Mayfield. –BD

BIG STAR

Anglo-pop. Like many American cities, during the 60s and early 70s, Memphis, TN, developed a coterie of young musicians who cut their teeth on the sounds of the British Invasion. Nevertheless, the sounds many of these players developed went far beyond replicating their influences. As with practically everything that has ever been created through the cultural filters in the mid-South, this music generally possessed a distinctive edge and a knack for getting to the soul of the subject matter, in spite of the apparent absence of any indigenous sounds.
Big Star was the premier band from this collection of local pop Anglophiles. From 1971 to 1975, Big Star released three brilliant albums that synthesized the influences of groups like the Beatles, the Kinks, and the Byrds with their own style of upside-down harmonies and angular ensemble work.
It is fair to say that, in spite of almost nonexistent commercial success, Big Star has been an important influence on many of the post-punk/power-pop bands since the late 70s. Among those bands who owe a debt to Big Star are R.E.M., the Replacements, the Posies, Game Theory, the Bangles, Teenage Fanclub, and Primal Scream.
With the demise of Big Star, lead singer Alex Chilton (also once the frontman for the Box Tops), went on to pursue a renegade solo career that has taken him full circle from untamed reckless garage rock to his earthy mid-Southern musical R&B roots.
Chris Bell, who shared vocal and writing credits on the first album, died (1978) before he was able to release his solo work. Bell's sound was equally idiosyncratic, remaining distinctly flavored with the British sound. Most of his work has since been released on a Rykodisc collection called *I Am the Cosmos.* –RC

☆ **Third/Sister Lovers / RYKODISC**   1978
Basically an Alex Chilton solo project, aided by remaining bandmate Jody Stephens (drums) and a slew of Memphis players. Chilton, frustrated at the music biz and career let-downs, enlisted Jim Dickinson (renegade producer genius) to aid in this creative tightrope walk without a net. The result is a listening experience that's as uncompromisingly harrowing as Neil Young's *Tonight's the Night.* Not for the casual listener, but essential in any serious rock listener's collection. –RC

★ **#1 Record/Radio City / FANTASY**   1992
Their first two albums (1972, 1973), loaded with amazing songs and performances. Mid-period Beatles, Kinks, and Byrds turned inside out and regurgitated into an utterly unique sound. A must-own for any lover of Anglo-pop/rock. –RC

BIG WHEEL

Heavy metal, alternative rock. These Kentucky rockers stay within the confines of alternative metal, creating songs with some depth and lots of crunch. Lead singer Peter Searcy abandons the teen angst of his former outfit Squirrel Bait for more studied expression. –BE

East End / GIANT   1989
Metalish rock with an alternative bent. –RG

BIRTHDAY PARTY

Heavy metal, alternative rock. The gnarled, noisy, metallic, bluesoid garage-rock of Birthday Party makes them one of

Australia's finest bands. Features Nick Cave. Formerly called Boys Next Door. –JD

○ **Prayers on Fire / NESAK**   1981
Howling, hellacious mangled art-noise. Sure-fire. –JD

Junkyard / NESAK   1982
Slightly less confrontational but no less disturbing. –JD

Drunk on the Pope's Blood / IMP   1982
An extremely harrowing live EP, with Lydia Lunch. –JD

ELVIN BISHOP   *b* 1942

Blues/rock, southern rock. This blues guitarist, a member of the Paul Butterfield Blues Band from 1965 to 1968, made a series of Southern-rock albums for Capricorn in the 70s. He now cuts blues records for Alligator. –WR

○ **Let It Flow / CAPRICORN**   1974
The best of Bishop's Southern-rock records, featuring the seven-minute "Travelin' Shoes" and guests Dickey Betts, Toy Caldwell, Sly Stone, and more. –WR

Struttin' My Stuff / CAPRICORN   1975
Features the hit single "Fooled Around and Fell in Love," sung by Mickey Thomas. –WR

Best of Elvin Bishop/Crabshaw Rising / EPIC   1975
Though the title must by now be considered suspicious, this is a good compilation of Bishop's first solo material from the early 70s. –WR

Don't Let the Bossman ... / ALLIGATOR   1991
On *Don't Let the Bossman Get You Down,* Bishop projects a good-natured, humorous persona in the extended spoken-word sections of his songs, but still finds time to play a lot of tasty blues guitar. –WR

STEPHEN BISHOP   *b* 1951

Pop, singer/songwriter. Bishop has made a career out of light MOR pop songs that range from romantic to humorously quirky. A number of his songs have ended up on movie soundtracks like *Animal House, Summer Lovers, Unfaithfully Yours,* and *Tootsie.* His biggest pop hits include "Save It for a Rainy Day" (#22), "On and On" (#11), and "Everybody Needs Love" (#32). –RC

○ **Best of Bish / RHINO**
Contains "On and On," "Save It for a Rainy Day," and other lesser hits. –DH

BLACK

Alternative rock. Black is singer Colin Vearncomb from Liverpool, who gained notice on the independent-label scene in England in the mid 80s with the singles "Wonderful Life" and "Everything's Coming up Roses," songs that matched uplifting, melodic music to dark lyrics. –WR

○ **Wonderful Life / A&M**   1987
This smoky-voiced singer/songwriter, whose sophisticated jazz-pop songs and dramatic vocal delivery place him somewhere between Bryan Ferry and Morrissey, hits his peak with the driving "Everything's Coming up Roses" (not the Jule Styne song). –WR

THE BLACK CROWES

Rock & roll. This Atlanta quintet brought the barroom grunge of the Faces, Rolling Stones, and Humble Pie to the charts with their wildly successful 1989 debut. –JF

○ **Shake Your Money Maker / DEF AMERICAN**   1990
The best ideas on the Crowes's debut are all about 20 years old, but when those ideas are replicas of vintage Stones and Faces, timelessness is not an issue. The mix of throttling rockers and acoustic ballads doesn't flow with the grace of *Beggar's Banquet,* but the best songs here — "Twice As Hard," "She Talks to Angels," "Could I've Been So Blind" — act as anchors for a strikingly confident debut. –JF

Southern Harmony ... / DEF AMERICAN   1992

On *The Southern Harmony & Musical Companion* the Crowes avoid the sophomore slump by taking the best elements of their debut and fleshing them out (and giving the rhythm section and keyboards more room to breathe). The Stones/Faces/Humble Pie comparisons are still relevant, but the band's own identity flourishes on such songs as "Remedy," "Black Moon Creeping," and "Sting Me." –JF

BLACK FLAG

Punk. Following the footsteps of California punks like the Germs and the Avengers, Greg Ginn and Black Flag took a look around their sun-drenched hometown and got pissed — pissed about the suntans, pissed about suburban decadence, pissed for the sake of being pissed. They released a few decent singles and an EP on Ginn's SST label and, in 1981, released an album (*Damaged*) that channeled their aggression and hostility through a molten mix of cranky guitars and Henry Rollins's manic vocals. On "Rise Above" and "Six Pack," Rollins expressed the nihilism, cynicism, and outrage of Cali youths better than any of his hardcore peers (and with more humor, as well). The group made the fatal mistake of sticking around too long, though, and after influencing hundreds of similarly disillusioned minds — and forging a career that evolved into self-parody — the group called it quits in 1987. –JF

○ **Damaged / SST**   1981
A devastating barrage of piss and noise that is a benchmark of West Coast punk. (CD includes their EP *Jealous Again*.) –JF

The First Four Years / SST   1984
Rounds up all their early singles, EPs, and compilation cuts. "Nervous Breakdown" and a rewrite of "Louie Louie" are included. –JF

Wasted ... Again / SST   1987
A solid collection of some of their greatest hits, including the best cuts from their lame later albums. –JF

BLACK FLAMES

Urban R&B. This late-80s vocal quartet took a then-novel approach, combining hip-hop fashion with a sweet sound that took its cues from such 70s groups as the Stylistics and the Chi-Lites; they even had a hit with a cover of the Chi-Lites' "Are You My Woman?" This approach was slicked up and turned to gold by such 1991 phenomenons as Boyz II Men and Another Bad Creation. –DH

○ **Black Flames / CBS**   1988
Contains a good remake of "Are You My Woman" by the Chi-Lites. –DH

BLACK OAK ARKANSAS

Southern rock. 70s Southern perennials from (where else) Black Oak, AR. Best-known for wildman vocalist Jim Dandy Mangrum, who predated the posturing of David Lee Roth. –JF

○ **The Best of Black Oak Arkansas / ATLANTIC**   1977
Good collection. Includes a live version (from 1973's *Raunch N' Roll*) of LaVern Baker's 1957 hit "Jim Dandy" and the best tracks from the group's debut album. –RC

BLACK SABBATH

Heavy metal. Originally formed as Earth in 1968 in Birmingham, England, with John "Ozzy" Osbourne (vocals), Tony Iommi (guitar), Terry "Geezer" Butler (bass), and Bill Ward (drums). They changed their name to Black Sabbath and were signed to Warner Brothers, who released their self-titled debut in the summer of 1970. Over the next five years they became one of the top hard-rock bands around, but by 1975 the band started having problems, mainly with Osbourne, who wanted to change the band's sound. Their later albums with Osbourne didn't sell well (partly due to the current love for disco and the rising of punk rock), and like any band who had been around for over five years, they were called dinosaurs.

Osbourne left in 1979. His replacement was Ronnie James Dio, an American vocalist who had done some work with Rainbow and Elf. Dio's brief but impressive stint with the band brought out two successful studio albums and a live album. By 1983 Dio left, replaced by former Deep Purple vocalist Ian Gillan. One album later, Bill Ward was replaced by ELO drummer Bev Bevans. It was also around this time that fans were getting weary of everchanging vocalists, and Sabbath's popularity was never again like it was in the early 70s. After 17 years Warner dropped them from the roster, but they have since been signed to I.R.S. and have released two albums so far. Dio has recently joined Sabbath again after his band called it a day. –JB

○ **Black Sabbath / WARNER**   1968
Their debut album set the tone with the title cut, "The Wizard," "Wasp," and "Warning." –CK

○ **Paranoid / WARNER**   1971
Their second and perhaps best album, featuring the title track, "Iron Man," "War Pigs," and "Fairies Wear Boots." –CK

Masters of Reality / WARNER   1971
Sabbath's third album, no less potent than the first two. It includes "Into the Void," "Children of the Grave," and "Lord of This World." –CK

Black Sabbath - Vol. 4 / WARNER   1972
A surprisingly song-oriented set of cynical boogie. –JF

★ **We Sold Our Souls for Rock 'n' Roll / WARNER**   1976
A solid 16-track sampler (over 70 minutes) from the band's first six albums. The perfect place to start. –JF & CK

BLACKFOOT

Southern rock. A Southern rock band consisting of Charlie Hargrett, Jackson Spires, Greg Walker, and Ricky Medlocke. Three of the members had Indian bloodlines, hence the group's name. With a sound that owed a large stylistic debt to the more musical Lynyrd Skynyrd, Blackfoot cashed in on the last gasp of Southern rock's brief flourishing. After numerous personnel changes, Medlocke still tours and records with a version of the band. –CK

○ **Strikes / ATLANTIC**   1978
This features Blackfoot's best-known songs, "Train, Train" and "Highway Song." The last gasp of Southern-rock. –CK

THE BLASTERS

Roots-rock. Among the rock bands that emerged from the Los Angeles scene in the early 80s, the Blasters were the most roots-conscious, producing a sound akin to 50s rockabilly and other 20-year-old musical styles. The group was led by the Alvin brothers (Phil, who sang and played rhythm guitar, and Dave, who played lead guitar and wrote songs) and included John Bazz (bass), Bill Bateman (drums), and Gene Taylor (piano).

The group issued the album *American Music* on the local Rolling Rock label, then switched to Slash for *The Blasters*, which was included in a distribution deal with Warner Brothers. They drew national attention in 1982, when the album reached the Top 40. The Blasters released a live EP of rock & roll covers later that year, then returned in 1983 with *Non Fiction*, which was dominated by Dave Alvin's songs. Those songs, steeped in rock, country, and blues traditions, also commented trenchantly on the current state of the American dream in much the same way Bruce Springsteen was doing at the time. They earned the Blasters greater critical respect, though sales did not expand. When *Hard Line* (1985) was also a sales disappointment, Dave Alvin decamped to join X. Phil Alvin kept the band going by hiring another guitarist, Hollywood Fats (Michael Mann), who died a few months later. Dave Alvin returned for a few gigs, then former X guitarist Billy Zoom took his place, but the Blasters had ceased to become a full-time entity. Phil Alvin released a solo album in 1986, then went back to school. Dave Alvin has so far released two solo albums. –WR

○ **The Blasters Collection / SLASH**   1991

One of the leading American "roots" bands of the 80s, this group's anthemic no-frills rock music sounds purer and more real than ever in the post-Milli Vanilli age. −JT

BLIND FAITH

Rock & roll. The calculated grafting of ex-Cream members Eric Clapton (guitar, vocal) and Ginger Baker (percussion) to ex-Traffic Steve Winwood (keys, guitar, vocal), and bassist/violinist Rick Grech of the popular Brit group Family brought the term "supergroup" to new levels of hype. No doubt, the talent involved in this amalgamation was quite impressive, but the cynical marketing minds behind this appropriately named fabrication failed to consider natural group chemistry. The volatile personalities in the lineup helped ensure that Blind Faith would more than likely be nothing more than an interesting one-off.
In spite of unrealistic pressure to live up to fan expectations, Blind Faith delivered an album that at times almost made good on its perceived potential. It still holds up today as a listening experience, thanks to Clapton's inspiring "Presence of the Lord," Winwood's reading of Buddy Holly's "Well All Right," and his own plaintive "Can't Find My Way Home."
The band's auspicious live US debut, selling out Madison Square Garden, soured within a matter of weeks, and Blind Faith became yet another historical footnote in the ongoing marriage of commerce and artistic expression. −RC
○ **Blind Faith / RSO-POLYGRAM**   1969
The only album released by this supergroup. The formula pays off with the haunting "Can't Find My Way Home" and the art-rock of "Sea of Joy." (Also available on Mobile Fidelity) −DDC

BLONDIE

New-wave, dance-pop. Blondie started out in the mid-70s punk/new-wave scene in New York City, along with bands such as the Ramones and Talking Heads. They would eventually be the most commercially successful new-wave band. Their breakthrough came with their third album, the Mike Chapman-produced *Parallel Lines.* It contained the rock-disco smash "Heart of Glass." This, along with Debbie Harry's movie-star good looks, propelled the band to stardom. They would continue to ride high on the charts for the next few years with an eclectic mix of hits, including the reggae-flavored "The Tide is High" and the rap "Rapture." The group disbanded in 1983 with various members pursuing solo careers. −KMC
○ **Blondie / CHRYSALIS**   1975
The great 60s girl groups go surfin' in peroxide and run into a bunch of punks with brains. Rock & roll hadn't been this much fun in years. −JT
Plastic Letters / CHRYSALIS   1977
Not as startlingly original as the debut, but the followup was proof that Blondie was no one-album wonder. −JT
○ **Parallel Lines / CHRYSALIS**   1978
Blondie goes image busting and proves it knows how to create mini-pop masterpieces. Debbie Harry's finest performance on record. −JT
● **Best of Blondie / CHRYSALIS**   1981
All of the hits, and that's the best way to hear this creative singles band. −JT

BLOOD, SWEAT & TEARS

Pop, fusion. One of the first rock bands to integrate jazz-influenced horns into their sound, Blood, Sweat & Tears burst onto the pop playlists with three million-sellers in 1969. Keyboardist Al Kooper, once a member of the Royal Teens ("Short Shorts"), formed the group in 1968, but soulfully raspy vocalist David Clayton-Thomas was up front when they scored their first smash for Columbia in 1969, a revival of Brenda Holloway's "You've Made Me So Very Happy." "Spinning Wheel" and Laura Nyro's "And When I Die" made it

three giants in a row for the band. Clayton-Thomas went solo in 1972 but returned two years later. −BD
○ **Child Is Father to the Man / CBS**   1968
Brilliant debut effort, seamlessly conceptualized and directed by Al Kooper. Wonderfully arty dynamic production and performances dignify a great batch of songs written by Kooper, Randy Newman, Harry Nilsson, Tim Buckley, Gerry Goffin, and Carole King. −RC
Blood, Sweat & Tears / CBS   1969
The followup to *Child Is Father to the Man* is the band's most successful release. Kooper is gone, replaced by the histrionic David Clayton-Thomas. Big-band arrangements with some rock pretentions dominate here. Contains the hits "And When I Die," "God Bless the Child," "You've Made Me So Very Happy," and "Spinning Wheel." Of the post-Kooper albums, this is the best. (Also available on Mobile Fidelity) −RC
Greatest Hits / CBS   1972
Self-explanatory collection. −RC

LUKA BLOOM

Singer/songwriter. Born Barry Moore in Ireland, Bloom produced several albums before carpal tunnel syndrome stopped his finger-picking guitar style. He came to the New Jersey/New York area, changed his name, and developed an open-tuning guitar style. His brother is the legendary Christy Moore. −CR
○ **Riverside / WARNER**   1990
This great songwriter and guitarist has enough help on this album to make it sound good, without taking anything away from his music. A must-have. −CR

BLOOMFIELD-KOOPER-STILLS

Blues/rock, psychedelic. Mike Bloomfield, Al Kooper, and Stephen Stills −ED
○ **Super Session / CBS**   1968
Al Kooper was the mastermind behind this appropriately named album, one side of which features his "spontaneous" studio collaboration with Mike Bloomfield and the other a session with Stephen Stills. The recordings have an off-the-cuff energy that displays the inventiveness of the two guitarists to best advantage. The best-selling recording of Bloomfield's career, it inspired the followup *The Live Adventures of Mike Bloomfield and Al Kooper.* (Also available on Mobile Fidelity). See also the Blues section. −JT

BLUE AEROPLANES

Alternative rock. A sometimes expanded Bristol quintet fueled by the poetic lyrics of Gerard Langley. Releasing its first album in 1984, the band specialized in intelligent lyrics recited over a sound that ranged from pop to danceable funk. −DS
○ **Swagger / CAPITOL**   1990
An excellent example of the clear-headed pop produced by the group. Guest artists include Michael Stipe of R.E.M. −DS

BLUE CHEER

Psychedelic. The late 60s was a big time for hard-rock trios, but one of the first, and certainly the most extreme, was Blue Cheer, a San Francisco band whose moniker was also the name of a desirable type of LSD.
Their brain-numbing version of Eddie Cochran's "Summertime Blues" is a hallmark of heavy metal excess. The band's first two crash-and-burn albums (*Vincebus Eruptum* and *Outsideinside*), amateurishly produced by the group's manager, ex-Hell's Angel Abe "Vovo" Kesh, gave a new meaning to the word *loud.* Their subsequent efforts increasingly degenerated into fairly undistinguished hippie rock wanderings. −RC
○ **Louder Than God - Best of Blue Cheer / RHINO**   1988
The fact that this collection is only available on vinyl may be a drawback for some folks, but (on one level) Blue Cheer, in all

its grungy glory, makes even more sense on 8-track than on CD, so what's the complaint? After all, this one has "Just a Little Bit," and the Polygram disc doesn't. If you can find their first two albums, *Vincebus Eruptum* and *Outsideinside* (only on out-of-print vinyl), then you will have all the Blue Cheer you'll ever need. —RC

Good Times Are So Hard To Find / POLYGRAM 1990
Good Times Are So Hard To Find (The History of Blue Cheer) is an overview spanning Blue Cheer's entire catalog. If only their first two albums of over-the-top psychedelic distorto-blare had been represented a little more. —RC

BLUE MAGIC

Soul. Utilizing slick, dreamy vocal harmonies, the Philadelphia group Blue Magic proved to be a popular R&B attraction during the early and mid 70s. With Theodore Mills handling lead vocals, Blue Magic scored a pair of giant hits for Atco in 1974 — the ethereal "Sideshow," which topped the R&B charts, and "Three Ring Circus." The group remained on soul playlists into the 80s. —BD

○ **Magic of the Blue - Greatest Hits / OMNI** 1974
Classy, clear Norman Harris arrangements from this Philadelphia vocal group of the 70s. Bobby Eli produced this warm love music, done at Sigma sound and featuring "Sideshow." —BC

BLUE NILE

Techno-pop. Unlike most acts during the 80s, who depended on synthesizers and drum machines for their sound, Blue Nile managed to create a sound that was haunting, steely cool, romantic, and melancholy. Sonically, their albums are the stuff audiophiles love. —RC

○ **A Walk across the Rooftops / A&M** 1984
This Scottish trio's 1984 debut, originally on Linn Records, is a beautifully atmospheric collection of synth-heavy songscapes. The dichotomy between the cool synthesized musical washes (with periodic percolating drum machine parts) and the yearning, passionate (yet strangely disconnected) vocals is engaging. This album could have been the soundtrack to Jonathon Pryce's lonely quenchless dreams in the Terry Gilliams movie *Brazil*. The Linn version sounds superior to the A&M release. —RC

Hats / A&M 1989
The followup to *Walk* ... was five years in the making. The songs aren't as memorable, but the results are still coolly haunting. "The Downtown Lights" and "Headlights on Parade" are among the standout tracks. —RC

BLUE ÖYSTER CULT

Rock & roll. Seminal hard-rockers epitomized the good and the bad of the 70s heavy metal. Their best work is ambitious, intelligent, and rocking, in a strangely sensual kind of way. —JF

Blue Öyster Cult / CBS 1972
Their debut bogs down under some stupid lyrics, but mostly this is a complex and powerful set. —JF

Tyranny & Mutation / CBS 1973
Blue Öyster Cult's second album sports better lyrics and sharper hooks, culminating in the thunderous "I'm on the Lamb But I Ain't No Sheep." —JF

○ **Agents of Fortune / CBS** 1976
This bid for mainstream success trades the murky appeal of their early stuff for more coherent themes, crisper production, and ringing guitars. "True Confessions" and "Don't Fear the Reaper" may be their best moments. —JF

Spectres / CBS 1977
The followup to *Agents of Fortune* doesn't break any new ground lyrically or musically, but it's a solid, workmanlike effort. Includes the AOR staple "Godzilla." —JF

BLUE RODEO

Rock & roll, folk/rock. Canadian artists Blue Rodeo incorporate elements of the Band, mid-period Beatles, Buffalo Springfield, and Bob Dylan to a fine effect. Worth seeking out for those who share those influences. —RC

Outskirts / ATLANTIC 1987
A strong debut. —RC

○ **Casino / ATLANTIC** 1991
Their best album yet, produced by Pete Anderson (Dwight Yoakam, Michelle Shocked). —RC

THE BLUES BROTHERS

Pop, soul. During the late 70s, "Saturday Night Live" twosome Dan Aykroyd and the late John Belushi, as Elwood and Jake Blues, employed the services of Stax rhythm-section players Steve Cropped and Duck Dunn, as well as Letterman band leader Paul Shaffer, for a run-through on some soul classics. As a "Saturday Night Live" skit, this was fun. Musically, the best thing that can be said about the Blues Brothers is that they inspired a new audience to look for the real thing. —RC

Briefcase Full of Blues / ATLANTIC 1978
Not for blues purists. Just a fun collection, including the rave-up "Hey Bartender." —DDC

○ **Best of the Blues Brothers / ATLANTIC** 1982
A solid collection, this includes hits "Rubber Biscuit" (#37), "Soul Man" (#14), and "Gimme Some Lovin'" (#18), plus music from the *Blues Brothers* soundtrack. —ED

THE BLUES PROJECT

Blues/rock, folk/rock. The Blues Project was New York's first "underground" group. In 1965 guitarist Danny Kalb, who was well established as a player on various Elektra Records folk and early folk-rock and blues albums, played on an Elektra Records sampler called *The Blues Project.* Soon after, he hooked up with Steve Katz (a guitarist with Elektra's Even Dozen Jug Band), Andy Kulberg (a flutist and bassist), Tommy Flanders (singer and harmonica player), Al Kooper came in on keyboards, guitar, and vocals, with Andy Kulberg on drums and Roy Blumenfeld on bass. This septet quickly built up a reputation for its mix of rock, jazz, classical, and electric blues on numbers such as "Night Time Is the Right Time," "Flute Thing" (which became popular on progressive FM radio stations), and "Catch the Wind." Kooper exited the band after the third album and went on to join the more jazz-oriented Blood, Sweat & Tears, into which Katz quickly followed. The Blues Project also lost Kalb (to ill health) and continued in name only for another album and another year or two. A late-70s Central Park reunion album recorded by the original sextet attracted a lot of attention but generated little musical excitement. The three original Verve albums and Rhino's best-of are the records that count. —BE

Live at Cafe Au GoGo / POLYGRAM 1966
Arguably the first artistically successful live rock album of the mid 60s. A fine showcase for the band's many talents. —BE

○ **Projections / VERVE** 1966
A groundbreaking record, that mixed blues and light jazz with an electric-rock sensibility as solid as in any band at that time. —BE

● **No Time Like the Right Time / RHINO** 1969
No Time Like the Right Time - The Best of the Blues Project is the best anthology of the band ever likely to be done. It encompasses their wealth of high points in better sound than ever. —BE

BLUES TRAVELER

Blues/rock. This NY-based rock quartet is led by harmonica player and vocalist John Popper. Known for extended jamming, they were signed by A&M, which issued their debut album in 1990. —WR

○ **Blues Traveler / A&M** 1990
Blues Traveler's loose jam structures on basic blues riffs mark

them as a band in the tradition of such predecessors as the Grateful Dead. Unlike that communal effort, however, this group has a distinct focal point in virtuoso harmonica player and vocalist John Popper, who keeps things from meandering too much. –WR

EDDIE BO   b 1930

R&B. A New Orleans journeyman pianist remembered for his 1961 hit "Check Mr. Popeye" on the Ric label. –JF

○ **Check Mr. Popeye / ROUNDER**   1979
Engaging early-60s New Orleans R&B from a prolific pianist, with a classic title track that spawned a local "Popeye" dance craze. –BD

BODEANS

Roots-rock. The BoDeans are led by Sammy Llana and Kurt Neumann, guitarists, singers, and songwriters from Wakesha, WI, who play tight, well-arranged guitar rock on their several albums for Slash/Warner Brothers. –WR

○ **Love & Hope & Sex & Dreams / SLASH**   1986
On this debut album, Llanas and Neumann are at their best on songs like "Fadeaway," where their sweet-and-sour harmonizing rules over a bouncing rock arrangement full of twangy guitars. There is just enough fidelity to basic rock & roll, and the right number of individual twists to mark the group's considerable promise. –WR

ANGELA BOFILL   b 1954

Urban R&B. This Bronx native sang with Ricardo Morero & the Group and the Dance Theater of Harlem chorus before her 1978 debut. With her strong, distinctive alto, she has carved a niche as an outstanding interpreter of soul ballads. –BC

○ **Best of Angela Bofill / ARISTA**   1986
Lazy, jazz-styled soft soul from the 70s and 80s. –BC

TOMMY BOLIN   1951-1976

Hard rock. Tommy Bolin achieved his greatest notoriety in Deep Purple, filling the position of founding member lead-guitarist Ritchie Blackmore, who had left the band to form Rainbow. Previously Bolin had worked with Zephyr, Billy Cobham, and James Gang. After Deep Purple folded in 1976, Bolin went solo, releasing two albums. Of particular note was Bolin's slide work. He passed away in Miami in 1976. –RC

Teaser / CBS   1975
A scattershot collection, but Bolin's forceful slide work on "The Grind" is worth the hunt. --RC

○ **Private Eyes / CBS**   1976
A solid showcase for Bolin's no-nonsense lead work in a focused package. –RC

Ultimate - The Best of Tommy Bolin / GEFFEN   1989
An overkill boxed set memorializing this late guitarist. Completists will be disappointed that some of Bolin's *Teaser* best moments are not included. –RC

MICHAEL BOLTON   b 1954

Pop. Gravelly-voiced singer/songwriter who writes adult-contemporary/pop songs and sings covers of R&B standards. Bolton fronted the mainstream rock band Blackjack in the late 70s and early 80s. –BC

○ **The Hunger / CBS**   1987
His best set. R&B covers and grooving pop, including the hits "That's What Love Is All About" and "(Sittin' On) The Dock of the Bay." –BC

Time, Love & Tenderness / CBS   1991
Light rock-styled Top 40, with some R&B. Includes the title track and "Love Is a Wonderful Thing." –BC

BON JOVI

Rock/pop. One of the most successful teen-geared groups of the last decade. The Jersey-bred group honed their skills as an opening act on the arena circuit until the mid 80s, when the band added some pop to their lite-metal riffs, and frontman Jon Bon Jovi (born Jon Bongiovi) took advantage of the possibilities of MTV and became the sex symbol for prepubescent girls across the globe. –JF

○ **Slippery When Wet / MERCURY**   1986
Bon Jovi delivers a hook-laden rock album with several of their biggest hits, including "Livin' on a Prayer" and the rocker-as-cowboy opus "Wanted Dead or Alive." –DDC

New Jersey / MERCURY   1988
While less instantly catchy than *Slippery When Wet*, this offers many of Bon Jovi's trademark radio-friendly melodies and lyrics that appeal to their faithful following. –DDC

JON BON JOVI

Rock/pop. The lead singer of Bon Jovi. –ED

Blaze of Glory / MERCURY   1990
Music inspired by the film *Young Guns II.* Jon Bon Jovi goes solo here with these cowboy/Wild West rockers and ballads, with substantial guest support from guitarist Jeff Beck. –DDC

GARY US BONDS   b 1939

R&B, rock/pop. After moving to the Norfolk, VA, area as a child, young Gary Anderson began plying his vocal wares, first in church, later with a local group called the Turks. When he was not yet 21, he was approached by local record producer Frank Guida to join his tiny Legrand label. Guida changed Anderson's name to US Bonds, hoping the first release would get extra airplay by disc jockeys mistaking it for a public service announcement. The result was the classic "New Orleans," combining rock-combo raunch with impassioned, scorched soul-singing that set the stage for all that would follow. Guida double- and triple-tracked Bonds's voice, and the resulting murky production gave all the hits (including "Quarter to Three," "Not Me," "School is Out," and "Dear Lady Twist") a party-in-outer-space quality all their own. Though he's kept recording, making a couple of excellent solo albums over the last decade, Bonds is best seen today dotting the landscape of oldies-shows the world over, singing the songs that made him famous. –CK

Dedication / RAZOR EDGE-EMI   1981
Bruce Springsteen, a long-time fan, helped revitalize Bonds's career in the 80s by working with him on two albums. This, the first, is the better one, including Springsteen's songwriting and vocals on "This Little Girl." –WR

○ **School of Rock 'n' Roll / RHINO**   1990
Gary US Bonds was one of the few people trying to make honest rock & roll in the early 60s, and *School of Rock 'n' Roll: The Best of Gary US Bonds* captures his successes, among them his signature song, "Quarter to Three." –WR

KARLA BONOFF   b 1952

Singer/songwriter. By the time Karla Bonoff had released her self-titled debut album, she had already developed quite a reputation as an introspective songwriter, landing several cuts on albums by Linda Ronstadt, Bonnie Raitt, and Nicolette Larson. On her solo work, Bonoff trod the same general late-70s Southern California turf as Ronstadt, with less authority. Her biggest hit was the #19 "Personally," off of her third album, *Wild Heart of the Young.* –RC

○ **Karla Bonoff / CBS**   1977
Contains a couple of songs that Linda Ronstadt recorded. A pleasant but not a very strong or distinctive singer, Bonoff surrounded herself with the cream of the mid-70s California rock/pop players for this solid debut effort. Ronstadt/Eagles fans will no doubt like this one. –RC

Restless Nights / CBS   1979
Wild Heart of the Young / CBS   1982
Restless Nights and *Wild Heart of the Young* continue in the

same general vein of the debut, but fail to add any new developments. –RC

THE BONZO DOG BAND

Rock/pop, psychedelic. The Bonzo Dog Band (formed in 1965 as the Bonzo Dog Doo-Dah Band) specialized in a peculiarly British absurdist humor and satire that drew from an odd blend of 20s cabaret music, 50s rock & roll, and 60s psychedelia. –RC

Best of the Bonzo Dog Band / RHINO 1974
A well-chosen overview of the playful late-60s British absurdists' work. The precursor to Monty Python. Fans of Python should check this out. –RC

BOOK OF LOVE

Techno-pop. Synth-dance music quartet from New York featuring the breathy vocals of Susan Ottaviano. They got their start with the club hit "Boy" in 1985 and have since recorded three albums for Sire/Warner Bros. –WR

○ **Book of Love / SIRE** 1986
Book of Love plays synthesizer-based dance-pop with an edge. The music is sweeter and lighter than much of this genre, and vocalist Susan Ottaviano has a matter-of-fact phrasing style that keeps it all from getting too sweet. –WR

BOOKER T. & THE MG'S

R&B, soul. The percolating bass of Duck Dunn, the razor-sharp leads and ringing chords of Steve Cropper, the thick, oozing organ runs of Booker T. Jones, and the deadlocked drum thwap of Al Jackson — known collectively as Booker T. and the MG's — epitomized the sound of Memphis soul. As the house band for the legendary Stax studio, the MG's played on nearly every song released on the label and influencing both other Memphis musicians (such as Willie Mitchell's Hi musicians) and New Orleans luminaries like the Meters. Cropper's choked guitar style had an impact on everyone from Pete Townshend and Eric Clapton to Robert Cray. There's a sameness in the work of the MG's that makes some of their albums blur together, but you will find no better soundtrack for house parties, romancing, or tooling down the interstate. –JF

Doin' Our Thing / RHINO-ATLANTIC
Rhino once again put together a classy reissue from the vaults of Atlantic Records. Highlights from this solid album include the title track, "Let's Go Get Stoned," and "You Keep Me Hanging On." –STE

Hip Hug-Her / RHINO-ATLANTIC 1967
Great album cover and songs — "Groovin'," "Soul Sanction," "Double or Nothing," and the classic title track are just the beginning of the wealth of terrific Memphis soul available on this album. –STE

○ **McLemore Avenue / STAX** 1970
An instrumental reconstruction of *Abbey Road*. The title is derived from the street where Stax was located, and the cover art is a better Beatles parody than anything on *The Rutles*. –JF

★ **Best of Booker T. & the MG's / ATLANTIC** 1989
The title says it all. Includes "Green Onions," "Hip Hug-Her," "Groovin'," and "Jellybread." The only one it's missing is "Time Is Tight," which is on Stax's *Best of Booker T. & the MG's*. –JF

THE BOOMTOWN RATS

New-wave, rock/pop. An Irish punk quintet (1975-1986) led by singer/songwriter Bob Geldof (b Oct 5, 1954). Their early work had the energy and attitude of punk, but on later records (including several UK hits), an increased musical sophistication put them closer to the pop-rock mainstream. Geldof left for a solo career in 1986, ending the band. –WR

The Boomtown Rats / MERCURY 1977
The Rats posed as a punk group on their debut, but they were always a little too tight to make the tag stick. Still, "Looking Out for No. 1" and "Mary of the 4th Form," both of which made the UK charts, had the right energy and the right attitude. –WR

○ **The Fine Art of Surfacing / CBS** 1979
Lead singer Bob Geldof hit his peak as a Ray Davies-influenced writer of story-songs on this album, which retained the group's early force while displaying an increased sophistication, especially on the signature song "I Don't Like Mondays." –WR

PAT BOONE   b 1934

Pop. He was clean-cut, polite to his elders, and glorified the nutritional value of milk. To folks who hated everything the new music stood for, Pat Boone was the perfect 50s rock & roller. But no matter how music historians judge the career of Pat Boone, nobody can dispute his enormous sales figures. The well-scrubbed crooner in the white buckskin shoes sold many millions of copies of his sanitized R&B covers during the 50s, helping to facilitate acceptance of rock & roll in the pop marketplace.

Boone's family ties are impressive — he's related to frontier legend Daniel Boone through bloodlines and to country great Red Foley through marriage to his daughter. After debuting on the small Republic imprint in 1954, Boone signed with Dot and took the pop world by storm over the next couple of years with covers of R&B items by Fats Domino, Little Richard, the El Dorados, the Flamingos, Ivory Joe Hunter, and too many others to list here.

With his college-boy good looks and an affinity for smooth ballads, Boone crossed over into TV and films, scoring #1 hits in 1957 with "Love Letters in the Sand," from the movie *Bernardine*, and the theme from the movie *April Love*, both of which he starred in.

"Moody River" marked Boone's last chart-topper in 1961, although he gamely tackled everything from novelty rockers ("Speedy Gonzales") to surf songs ("Beach Girl") to sustain his success. These days, you're most likely to encounter Boone and his family (which includes Debby Boone of "You Light Up My Life" fame) on the contemporary Christian circuit or doing work for charitable organizations, the white bucks and crewcut long since retired. –BD

★ **Best of Pat Boone / MCA** 1957
Most of Boone's chaste items are represented here. Lots of memories. –HD

○ **Jivin' Pat / BEAR FAMILY** 1986
All of Boone's rockers — cover versions of Fats Domino, Little Richard, et al. Includes a revealing set of liner notes. You won't find these elsewhere unless you have an enormous singles collection. –HD

Greatest Hits / CURB 1990
Nothing fancy. A minimal collection of Pat's 50s hits. –HD

EARL BOSTIC   1913-1965

R&B. Bostic began as a jazz player in the big-band jazz era of the 20s and 30s. In the early 40s he worked with Cab Calloway, Lionel Hampton, and others. He pioneered the hard-driving R&B sax sound of the early 40s. Bostic's band was a training ground for many great artists, including John Coltrane, Stanley Turrentine, Bill Doggett, Mickey Baker, and others. Jazz great Art Blakey says, "Nobody knew more about the saxophone than Bostic, I mean technically, and that includes Bird." Bostic had a #1 R&B hit with "Flamingo." This is hard-rockin', raunchy R&B saxophone at its best. –JME

○ **The Best of Earl Bostic / KING** 1957
A nice cross-section of this fiery alto saxist's 50s output, including his hits "Sleep" and "Flamingo." –BD

Alto Magic in Hi-Fi / KING 1958
More swinging standards. –BD

Let's Dance with Earl Bostic / KING 1958
Take this alto-sax legend up on the invitation! –BD

Dance Music from the Bostic Workshop / KING 1988

Includes an astonishing display of sax technique over a torrid R&B beat on the breathtaking "Up There in Orbit." –BD

Bostic for You / KING   1988
Bostic's blistering renditions of old dance numbers transcend R&B and jazz barriers. –BD

BOSTON

Rock/pop. During the late 70s, Boston dominated AOR (album-oriented rock) FM with their dense multilayered guitars and vocals. The self-titled debut effort, which was basically constructed from band leader Tom Scholz's basement demos, eventually sold over 6 1/2 million copies. "More Than a Feeling," their first single, is a perfect encapsulation of Boston's sound. After a two-year wait, Boston's followup, *Don't Look Back*, basically replicated the debut's formula. By then, Scholz was gaining a reputation as an obsessive perfectionist, further underscored by the seven-year wait for the group's third album, *Third Stage*.
During this time, Scholz applied his previous background as a senior product designer for Polaroid and started Scholz Research & Development, which marketed popular professional-musician outboard gear, like the Rockman. –RC

○ **Boston / CBS**   1976
The album that virtually defined 70s FM rock, selling over six million copies. Featuring the smash hits "More Than a Feeling," "Peace of Mind," and "Let Me Take You Home Tonight." –DDC

Don't Look Back / EPIC   1978
Continued success with their rock formula, highlighted by the hit title track. –DDC

Third Stage / MCA   1986
A chart-topping comeback after a seven-year hiatus and a lineup reshuffling that left only singer Brad Delp and guitarist/producer Tom Scholz from the original band. Hits include "Amanda" and "We're Ready." –DDC

BOURGEOIS TAGG

Alternative pop. Brent Bourgeois and Larry Tagg specialized in smart, Beatlesque pop in the style of their apparent mentor, Todd Rundgren. Their biggest hit, 1987's "I Don't Mind at All," was produced by Rundgren. –DH

○ **Yoyo / POLYGRAM**   1987
Produced by Todd Rundgren, this contains the hit single "I Don't Mind at All." –DH

BOW WOW WOW

Alternative pop. Bow Wow Wow was a quartet organized by UK manager Malcolm McLaren (best known as the mastermind behind the Sex Pistols) at the start of the 80s. McLaren matched the trio of musicians who had constituted Adam Ant's Ants (Matthew Ashman, b 1962, guitar; Leigh Gorman, b 1961, bass; and David Barbarossa, b 1961, drums) with teenage singer Annabella Lwin (b Oct 31, 1965), retaining the earlier group's African-derived drum sound. In 1983 Lwin quit the group for a solo career, and the remaining three changed their name to the Chiefs of Relief. Both Lwin and the Chiefs issued their own albums. –WR

○ **I Want Candy / RCA**   1982
This album largely recompiles Bow Wow Wow's first album, plus its *Last of the Mohicans* EP. As such, it includes the hits "Go Wild in the Country," "I Want Candy," and "Louis Quatorze" and presents the band's urgent, rhythmic sound at its most consistent. –WR

DAVID BOWIE   b 1947

Alternative rock. Although he succeeded as a singer, musician, songwriter, and film and stage actor, David Bowie's chief artistic accomplishment may have been his astute manipulation of his own image as a star. When he achieved international fame in the early 70s, Bowie brought a new, highly conscious approach to stardom that involved the

frequent creation of new personae. No wonder that when he made his film acting debut in 1976, he seemed so good at it: acting was what a large part of his career was about. Born in Brixton, South London, as David Jones, the singer was already playing in bands by his late teens. He changed his name to avoid confusion with Davy Jones of the Monkees. His early-60s work was rock and blues oriented, then he turned to an Anthony Newley-style expressive show-music approach. But his breakthrough British hit "Space Oddity" (1969) was a folkie ballad about an astronaut who doesn't come home. By the time of *Hunky Dory* (1971), Bowie had turned again more toward rock, using the first of many strong collaborators, guitarist Mick Ronson.
It was Bowie's concept album *The Rise and Fall of Ziggy Stardust and the Spiders from Mars* (1972) that made him a giant star in England, where he adopted the image of his fantasy rocker, with bright red hair and futuristic stage suits. In America, "Space Oddity" became a belated hit in 1973, the year Bowie "retired" from stage work only to return in 1974 with an even more elaborate stage show. More an established star than a real record-seller in the US, Bowie finally hit #1 with "Fame" (cowritten by John Lennon and Luther Vandross) in 1975. The late 70s found him collaborating with electronics whiz Brian Eno. He made a major commercial comeback in 1983 with *Let's Dance*, produced by ex-Chic coleader Nile Rodgers. Bowie's work in the 80s was inconsistent, but as late as 1990 he was still able to tour the US, playing football stadiums. This was supposedly his farewell tour (again) before he turned full attention to a group project, Tin Machine. But by 1992 it seemed likely he would return to solo work. –WR

Space Oddity / RYKODISC / BB 16   1969
Originally titled *Man of Words Man of Music*, this release was a transitional effort from Bowie's earlier Anthony Newley affectations on Decca. Tracks range from the Bob Dylan-influenced future-shock epic "Cygnet Committee" to lightweight rockers like "Janine." This includes "Space Oddity," Bowie's first major single and the highlight of this album. –RC

○ **The Man Who Sold the World / RYKODISC**   1970
After the theatrical acoustic leanings of *Space Oddity*, Bowie undertook a dark foray into British hard rock that at times attempted Cream-style free-for-alls, particularly "She Shook Me Cold." The strangely dense, bass-heavy production (courtesy of Tony Visconti), coupled with Bowie's disturbing imagery, provided some powerful moments. Musically, Tin Machine's discordant roots can be found here. One of Bowie's better efforts. –RC

☆ **Hunky Dory / RYKODISC**   1972
This followup to *The Man Who Sold the World* found Bowie lightening his sound considerably. Some of his most memorable songs are found on this classic: the catchy pop classic "Changes" (a theme song of sorts), the beautifully expansive "Life on Mars," the moody dynamics of "Quicksand," "The Bewlay Brothers," and "Oh, You Pretty Things." –RC

☆ **Ziggy Stardust ... / RYKODISC**   1972
Regarded by many to be Bowie's best album, Bowie took the melodicism developed on *Hunky Dory* and beefed it up with a punchy, rigid, freeze-dried "rock" setting. It's a perfect setting for Bowie's concept of a plastic rock star, Ziggy Stardust. *The Rise and Fall of Ziggy Stardust and the Spiders from Mars*, without a doubt, was an important defining effort for the glam-rock movement. –RC

Aladdin Sane / RYKODISC   1973
Rocks harder than *Ziggy Stardust ...* but flirts pretty closely at times with cabaret death (courtesy of pianist Mike Garson). "Watch That Man" is a fine rocker that manages to draw inspiration from the Stones' *Exile on Main Street*, while not totally abandoning the tight-assed rhythmic stiffness inherent in the glam sound. Other highlights: "Jean Genie," "Cracked Actor," and "Panic in Detroit." –RC

Pin Ups / RYKODISC   1973

Bowie covers a selection of personal favorite songs from the 60s by the Yardbirds, the Kinks, the Who, Pink Floyd, and more. It's an affectionate tribute that makes more of a case for Bowie's excellent taste than for his ability to transcend the original versions. Contains the hit "Sorrow." –RC

Diamond Dogs / RYKODISC   1974
Ambitious smudge of an album. Nevertheless contains some standouts in the lean, riff-heavy hit "Rebel Rebel," the fatalistic futurism of "1984" (an early discoish harbinger of his Thin White Duke era), and the title track. –RC

Young Americans / RYKODISC   1975
Bowie affects Philly Soul and a hodgepodge of other things. Ace sidemen can't save this spotty album, but the title track and "Fame" (cowritten by John Lennon) became worldwide hits. –RC

Station to Station / RYKODISC   1976
A transitional effort that bridges Bowie's clinical pop/disco persona to the icy psychosis and dissonance of this next phase, working with Brian Eno. Almost as ill formed as *Diamond Dogs* (particularly the title track), but the Top Ten hit "Golden Years" and "TVC15" are highlights. –RC

Low / RYKODISC   1977
The first of several efforts with ex-Roxy Music sound painter Brian Eno, *Low* is a willful departure from Bowie's pop persona. Short songs make their point and get out of the way on the first half, followed by four dense synth-instrumental soundscapes. –RC

○ **Heroes / RYKODISC**   1977
Echos *Low*'s half-sung/half-instrumental approach, this time with longer songs (given a maniacal musical accompaniment by King Crimson's Robert Fripp) and chillingly desolate soundscapes. The brilliant title track features one of Bowie's most passionate performances. Those who like discordant rock should be in heaven with "Beauty and the Beast," "Joe the Lion," and "Blackout." –RC

Stage / RYKODISC   1978
A great double-disc live document of Bowie's *Heroes* tour, with Disc 1 focussing on *Ziggy Stardust* and *Station to Station* material and Disc 2 featuring *Low* and *Heroes*. –RC

○ **Lodger / RYKODISC**   1979
The third installment with Eno returns Bowie to a more conventional (but not necessarily more commercial) song structure. Production isn't so sharp sounding as *Heroes*, but it has many engaging moments, particularly the hopeful "Fantastic Voyage" and the goofy "D.J.," plus "Boys Keep Swinging," and the hyperdrive of "Look Back in Anger." –RC

○ **Scary Monsters / RYKODISC / BB 12**   1980
One of the better post-*Low* efforts. Contains the hits "Fashion" and "Ashes to Ashes," and the dissonant rocker "It's No Game (Part 1)." Robert Fripp provides a wonderfully jarring racket on "It's No Game (Part 1)," the Tom Verlaine-penned "Kingdom Come," and several others. Pete Townshend guests on "Because You're Young." CD includes four bonus tracks, a nice version of Kurt Weill and Bert Brecht's "Alabama Song," an instrumental that could've come off of *Low*, and 1979 re-recordings of "Space Oddity" and "Panic in Detroit" of interest only to hardcore fans. –RC

Let's Dance / CAPITOL   1983
Bowie guns for big pop success and gets it on this outing, somehow deftly sidestepping appearances of being a sell-out. The title track, "China Girl," and "Modern Love" achieve international chart success. This album also includes a nice reworking of Metro's "Criminal World." –RC

○ **Sound & Vision / RYKODISC**   1989
An extravagantly produced 3-CD-plus CDV (video mini-disc) boxed set that digs deeper than *Changesbowie*. This features much previously unavailable stuff but comes up short on certain primary radio tracks. Good complement to *Changesbowie*, in spite of a little track duplication. –RC

★ **Changesbowie / RYKODISC**   1990

Except for the substitution of a "Fame '90" remix over the original #1 hit, this is a great sampling of big cuts from all of Bowie's many phases, from "Space Oddity" to "Ashes to Ashes." While Bowie has had some classic albums, the uninitiated should start here. –RC

THE BOX TOPS

Rock/pop, soul. If you forget about the Rascals and the Righteous Brothers, the Memphis-based Box Tops are the finest blue-eyed soul group. Lead singer (and former Big Star honcho) Alex Chilton had a tough, swaggering voice that belied his teenage years, sounding at times as if he were in a cutting match with the young Steve Winwood. Producers Chips Moman and Dan Penn surrounded Chilton with a crack American studio band, giving the music more muscle and deep funk than you'll ever find in "Mary Mary." Instead of knocking off pimply, lightweight teen-fodder, the Box Tops managed to add another link in the Memphis soul chain, mixing blues, Beatlesque pop, and the sound of Stax, Hi, and Goldwax. And unlike the Monkees, the Box Tops benefited from top-notch material: Dan Penn and Spooner Oldham's "Cry Like a Baby" and " I Met Her in Church"; Wayne Thompson's "The Letter" and "Soul Deep"; and the occasional Chilton-penned nugget, such as "I Must Be the Devil." The group's heyday was brief — two years, tops — but their music remains a staple on oldies stations and has retained its vitality for over two decades. –JF

○ **The Ultimate Box Tops / WARNER**   1987
Everything you need by this blue-eyed soul combo. Includes "The Letter," "Cry Like a Baby," and "Soul Deep." –JF

BILLY BRAGG   *b* 1957

Singer/songwriter. At home with both socialist-geared political dogma and heartbroken love songs, Bragg has blended the one-man and-a-guitar attack of early Dylan with the passion and big-rock attitude of the Clash and the Jam. His thick British accent may be the reason his clever Costello-esque work hasn't made it big in the States. –JF

☆ **Talking with the Taxman / ELEKTRA**   1986
Bragg's one-man approach is fleshed out on *Talking with the Taxman About Poetry*, his second longplayer. "Levi Stubb's Tears" and "The Marriage" include subtle percussion and horn flourishes; "Greetings to the New Brunette" is cushioned in layers of overdubbed acoustic guitars. That makes it Bragg's most satisfying album musically, but the witty, plaintive songs listed above — in addition to "Ideology" and "The Warmest Room" — make it a stirring and evocative lyrical statement as well. –JF

★ **Back to Basics / ELEKTRA**   1987
This disc brings together Bragg's first three releases (*Life's A Riot with Spy vs. Spy*, *Brewing Up with Billy Bragg*, and the *Between the Wars* EP) and offers the best introduction to his confessional songwriting and uncompromising politics. Highlights include "A New England," "The Busy Girl Buys Beauty," and "A Lover Sings." –JF

Workers Playtime / ELEKTRA   1988
Bragg's first attempt at working with a full band could be better — most of the songs are mopey and depressing, and some of his socialist manifestos are tiresome and dogmatic. Still, cuts like "She's Got a New Spell," "Must I Paint You A Picture," and "Little Time Bomb" are excellent, and "Waiting for the Great Leap Forward" is a humble and humorous explanation of Bragg's motives and intentions, both political and emotional. –JF

○ **Don't Try This at Home / ELEKTRA**   1991
With full-blown production by the likes of Johnny Marr, and with musical assistance from R.E.M., this would seem like a blatant stab at the postmodern marketplace. Maybe so, but the thrust of his band turns "Accident Waiting to Happen" and "North Sea Bubble" into throttling rockers and makes "Sexuality" his best single. There are also several gorgeous

ballads, "Tank Park Salute" and "Wish You Were Here" among them. –JF

The Peel Sessions Album / STRANGE FRUIT   1992
Because Bragg started his career as a solo act, these live-in-the-studio radio transcriptions don't offer anything you can't find on *Back to Basics*. But fanatics will enjoy the occasional lyric deviations, and "A13 Trunk Road to the Sea" (a rewrite of "Route 66" with British directions) is a keeper. –JF

BRAND X

Prog-rock, fusion. A British jazz fusion band that existed between 1976 and 1982. Former members include John Goodsall, Percy Jones, and Genesis drummer Phil Collins. –PK

Livestock / CAROLINE   1977
A live album with nice compositions, featuring Phil Collins and John Goodsall. –PK

Masques / CAROLINE   1978
Jazz/rock-infused with John Goodsall's guitar. An interesting blend of sounds, with Percy Jones on bass. –PK

○ **Product / CAROLINE**   1979
An excellent fusion album of mostly instrumentals, with a few vocals by Phil Collins. –PK

Is There Anything About / PASSPORT   1982
The last release from this legendary jazz/rock band. –PK

● **X-Trax / PASSPORT**   1987
An excellent 13-track compilation CD with tracks from all their albums. A great selection of material. –PK

LAURA BRANIGAN   ♭1957

Pop, dance-pop. Laura Branigan is a singer and, increasingly, an actress from Brewster, NY, who first gained notice when she became a backup singer for Leonard Cohen in 1977. Branigan achieved considerable popular success in the early 80s by applying her big, powerful voice to translated versions of Eurodisco hits. She was less successful with subsequent recordings in the second half of the 80s, though by then she had begun to appear on television and in films. –WR

○ **Laura Branigan / ATLANTIC**   1982
Branigan's big, expressive voice is the draw here, placed in dramatic musical settings that show it off to best advantage, especially on "Gloria," her breakthrough hit and stirring pop performance. –WR

Branigan 2 / ATLANTIC   1983
"Solitaire" is the inevitable "Gloria" followup, but the album also shows unusual range, including a version of the Who's "Squeeze Box" and the dramatic ballad "How Am I Supposed to Live without You," which was a minor hit for Branigan and a much bigger hit a few years later for Michael Bolton. –WR

BRAVE COMBO

Alternative rock. A fun band from Texas that helped fuel the accordion renaissance with offbeat polkas, Tex-Mex, world music, and pop amalgams. –MB

○ **Musical Varieties / ROUNDER**   1987
An expanded CD program of their formative recordings from the early years on the Four Dots label. World music romps, with lots of accordion and well-intended humor. –MB

Polkatharsis / ROUNDER   1987
Their first Rounder album has better sound, but a shakeup in personnel altered the focus a bit. Still lots of jovial world-fusion here. –MB

Humansville / ROUNDER   1988
More slick and less memorable as a result — but not without moments of greatness and humorous covers. –MB

A Night on Earth / ROUNDER   1990
This one focuses more on Latin pastiches, their specialty. –MB

BREAD

Pop. Bread produced an impressive string of ultra-light pop

hits from 1970 to 1976, ten of which were Top 20 pop. In spite of their rather syrupy constitution, Bread had a knack for highly crafted melodies that possessed memorable hooks. "It Don't Matter to Me," with its multiple key and time-signature changes, is a tour de force in that genre. David Gates, the writer for all their hits, delivered the goods vocally with a silky tenor that had heart. –RC

○ **Anthology / ELEKTRA**   1985
"Make It with You," "If," "Baby I'm-a Want You," and many other fine-tuned pop gems. –DH

BREEDERS

Alternative pop. This female trio is a side project for members of Pixies, Throwing Muses, and Perfect Disaster. –IME

○ **Pod / NESAK**   1990
A fine collective effort from women normally reduced to supporting roles in their respective regular groups. –SA

EDIE BRICKELL & NEW BOHEMIANS

Rock/pop. Edie Brickell was born around 1966 in the Oak Cliff section of Dallas. She attended Southern Methodist University for a year and a half before drinking up enough courage in a bar one night in 1985 to get up onstage with a local band, the New Bohemians. She joined the band and wrote songs over the next year as the band changed and evolved. They finally settled on the personnel of Brad Houser (bass), Kenny Withrow (guitar), and Matt Chamberlain (drums), before taking off for Rockfield Studios in Wales to record their debut album.

That album, *Shooting Rubberbands at the Stars*, revealed Brickell to be a songwriter with a unique perspective and a singer with an intimate, conversational style. The album was hailed by critics and became a massive hit, selling over a million copies and producing the Top Ten hit "What I Am." –WR

○ **Shooting Rubberbands at the Stars / GEFFEN**   1988
Lead singer Brickell is charmingly unique on this album of light pop with thoughtful lyrics. Featuring the hit "What I Am." –DDC

Ghost of a Dog / GEFFEN   1990
An overlooked followup that found Brickell expanding on her offbeat vocals. –DDC

THE BROTHERS JOHNSON

Rock/pop, soul. George and Louis Johnson were backup guitarists for Bobby Womack, David Ruffin, and the Supremes. They were session men on some of Billy Preston's early-70s albums, and after they worked on a Quincy Jones set, he began producing them. Their masterful, hard, funky guitar playing set the tone for a lot of late-70s soul on cuts like "I'll Be Good to You" and "Stomp." –BC

○ **Classics - Vol. 11 / A&M**   1987
All of their big funk hits and jazz-tinged soul ballads, like "Strawberry Letter 23" and "I'll Be Good to You." –BC

BOBBY BROWN   ♭1969

Urban R&B. The foremost purveyor of New Jack Swing and a former member of New Edition, Brown had major late-80s/early-90s hits with "Every Little Step" and "Don't Be Cruel." –DH

☆ **Don't Be Cruel / MCA**   1988
Ex-New Edition vocalist Brown released a dud debut in 1985, but his followup *Don't Be Cruel*, produced by new jack kingpin Teddy Riley, was a monster hit and a brilliant statement of Brown's creative purpose. The title cut brought a level of sensitivity into new jack, and "My Prerogative" is one of the greatest dance-groove anthems produced in the late 80s. And the man can smoke on the ballads. –JF

JAMES BROWN   ♭1928

R&B, soul, funk. When the smoke clears, James Brown will be seen as probably the most influential African-American singer of recent times. Certainly, he is preeminent in terms of chart placings, and his influence on today's Black music is beyond question — it's literally in the grooves, thanks to the magic of sampling.

Brown's career stretches across forty years — thirty-five or more as a recording artist — so it makes no sense to talk about his style, because it inevitably evolved. He knew something different from the beginning, though ("Please, Please, Please" was not an ordinary record ca. 1956). The difference was urgency; he went back beyond the gospel progressions of Ray Charles to primordial rhythms and wordless vocals. It was African-American music in the purest sense.

By the mid 60s, with hits like "Papa's Got a Brand New Bag" and "I Got You," Brown had ceased fooling with conventional R&B and had ceased trying to cross over into the pop market (as he had with "Prisoner of Love," etc.) He found his groove and he turned it loose. The creative juices began to get a little watered down as the disco era dawned, but, between the mid 60s and the mid 70s, James Brown was a force unto himself. Musically and politically, he was the dominant Black musician of the day, an importance that subsequent developments have only served to heighten. –CE

★ **Live at the Apollo / POLYGRAM / BB 2**   1963
An astonishing record of James and the Flames tearing the roof off the sucker at the mecca of R&B theatres, New York's Apollo. When King Records owner Syd Nathan refused to fund the recording, thinking it commercial folly, Brown singlemindedly proceeded anyway, paying for it out of his own pocket. He had been out on the road night after night for a while, and he knew that the alchemy magic that was part and parcel of a James Brown show was something no record had ever caught. Hit follows hit without a pause — "I'll Go Crazy," "Try Me," "Think," "Please Please Please," "I Don't Mind," "Night Train," and more. The affirmative screams and cries of the audience are something you've never experienced unless you've seen the Brown Revue in a Black theatre. If you have I need not say more; if you haven't, suffice it to say that this should be one of the very first records you ever own. –RB

☆ **James Brown's Funky People - Part 1 / POLYGRAM** 1988
James Brown the entrepreneur, writing and producing superlative slices of funk for various members of his Revue. These two volumes (see below) include hits and great misses by Lyn Collins, Vicki Anderson, Marva Whitney, Maceo & the Macks, Bobby Byrd, Fred Wesley & the JB's, and so on. Part 1 highlights include Collins's powerhouse Top Ten hit "Think (About It)" and the JB's first two hits, "Gimme Some More" and "Pass the Peas." –RB

☆ **James Brown's Funky People - Part 2 / POLYGRAM** 1988
More of the above, including Bobby Byrd's 1971 hits "I Know You Got Soul" and "Hot Pants - I'm Coming, Coming, I'm Coming." Delves into some more obscure tracks, such as Hank Ballard's "From the Love Side." –RB

★ **Star Time / POLYGRAM**   1991
One of the great boxed sets of all time; over four CDs, Brown's recorded legacy is traced from "Please Please Please" in 1956 through his 1984 duet with Afrika Bambaataa, "Unity Pt. 1." With 71 tracks in all, the set places the #1 R&B artist ever in his proper perspective as the prime progenitor of funk, one of the architects of soul, and the Godfather of Rap. To have done any one of these things would have been a bid for immortality, having done all three makes him a god. Four CDs at once is virtually too rich for one sitting. The well-written liner notes provide three different perspectives on Brown's career. A cornerstone of any great collection. –RB

☆ **Love Power Peace / POLYGRAM**   1992
James Brown with the then newly formed JB's — the maestro's second great band including Bootsy Collins, Phelps Collins, Jabo Starks, Bobby Byrd, and Fred Wesley. *Live at the Apollo* had caught James Brown, the 50s gospel/rhythm and blues singer; *Love Power Peace - Live at the Olympia, Paris*

1971 captures James the funkster. In the early 70s Brown turned up the funk, recording such litanies for Black America as "Ain't It Funky Now," "Sex Machine," "Give It Up or Turn It Loose," "Super Bad," "Get Up, Get into It, Get Involved," and "Soul Power." They are all here, along with revved white-hot versions of the early- and middle-period classics. The ferocity of this band is nearly too much for the heart. Brown had planned to release this as a triple album in 1971. When several band members left shortly after it was recorded, Brown switched from King to Polydor Records, leading him to scrap the record at the time and record a new studio album instead. Thank God for the CD revolution, as in 1992 Polygram decided to make the recording available for the first time. Ain't it funky now indeed. –RB

JOE BROWN   ♭1941

Rock/pop. Cockney Joe Brown was one of England's top guitar talents of the early 60s. He made his name playing lead on records like Billy Fury's *The Sound of Fury* before striking out on his own with his band, the Bruvvers. Joe Brown and the Bruvvers were a loud, dexterous topflight band whose main problem was repertoire — when they weren't doing great songs like "Picture of You" (a fave of the young Paul McCartney), they wasted their time on silly novelty tunes. Brown recorded well into the 70s but has been most successful as a stage actor. –BE

○ **Hits 'N' Pieces / PRT**   1988
A somewhat regrettable collection, with "Picture of You" and three or four other worthwhile tracks surrounded by tuneless Cockney novelty dross. Still, it is the only collection of Brown's work, but more of his live recordings would've been better. See also the collection, *Roots of British Rock*. (Import) –BE

MAXINE BROWN

R&B, soul. An underrated 60s R&B chanteuse from New York responsible for the original "Oh No Not My Baby." With an early gospel background, Brown waxed her first secular hit, "All in My Mind," for the tiny Nomar label in 1960, and quickly encored with "Funny." Switching to Wand Records, Brown recorded some fine uptown-style R&B, including the charming and often-covered "Oh No Not My Baby" in 1964. Teamed with labelmate Chuck Jackson, Brown scored another hit the following year with a duet revival of Chris Kenner's "Something You Got." Brown later recorded for a variety of firms into the early 70s. –BD

○ **Golden Classics / COLLECTABLES**
One of the underrated soul queens of the 60s. Smoldering vocals and uptown production. –BD

SHIRLEY BROWN   ♭1947

R&B, soul. Shirley Brown was one of the first singers to make use of the soulful "love rapping" popular among Black singers in the early 70s. –BC

○ **Woman to Woman / STAX**   1974
In the gritty, loudmouth style of rapping dialog songs popular at the time, her songs either spoke directly to a "no-good man" or to the "bitch" who was trying to take him away from her. The term "rapping" shouldn't be confused with modern hip-hop. This was more a talk-rap style of soul singing. –BC

Timeless / MALACO   1990
Less inspiring than her early material but still of the same style. What makes the music worthwhile is Brown's shrill, husky vocals and sense of drama, making even the lamest dialog sound interesting. –BC

DUNCAN BROWNE

Prog-rock. British singer and guitarist who emerged from Andrew Oldham's Immediate label in the late 60s, with a sound that embraced the most lyrical elements of Paul McCartney, Donovan, and the Moody Blues. Later a member of the power-pop band Metro on Sire Records, and most recently a composer of film music. –BE

○ **Give Me Take You / CBS**   1968
A lush, introspective work that is lacking in excitement but exquisitely produced and arranged. Chock-full of haunting, McCartneyesque melodies. –BE

JACKSON BROWNE   b 1948

Singer/songwriter. As one of the guiding lights from the sensitive 70s singer/songwriter school of pop, Jackson Browne (along with Joni Mitchell) gave the word "introspection" new meaning with his earnest musical epistles from the inside. Like Mitchell and James Taylor (somewhat), Browne provided a weighty soundtrack for scores of apprehensive 60s kids who were trying to come to grips with growing up and finding their place in the world.

Without a doubt, his first four albums are loaded with gems, even if his melodies tend to have a sameness. Browne has always attracted stellar sidemen for his records, many of whom can also be found on records by Linda Ronstadt and James Taylor.

During his career, Browne has proven himself to be a very capable producer for Warren Zevon and Greg Copeland.

Hardcore Browne fanatics will claim their hero ceased to perform to their expectations after his million-selling 1977 opus *The Pretender;* but, his greatest commercial success took place from that album on. Granted, his highest charting single, the lightweight #4 hit, "Somebody's Baby," was quite a departure from his previous work, but maybe Browne needed a breather.

In 1982 Browne's California rock/pop phase ended and he returned with the more topical *Lawyers in Love,* which produced a hit with the title track. Subsequent albums have increasingly addressed global issues over the self-absorbed ruminations of his earlier work. –RC

☆ **Jackson Browne / ELEKTRA**   1972
Jackson Browne's debut album was the accomplished work of a veteran singer/songwriter who'd been kicking around the music business for years. Its songcraft is extremely well developed, and Browne comes off as the kind of wordsmith who never has to strain for a rhyme or limit his imagination to his verbal facility. "Doctor My Eyes," the album's hit, is full of wordplay from the title on, and it's typical. Browne sings in a warm, conversational voice, and his music suggests rock without really working up a sweat. –WR

For Everyman / ELEKTRA   1973
This is a less consistent collection than the debut. Some of its songs are old examples of promising juvenilia ("These Days"), originally written for others ("Take It Easy"), or somewhat coy ("Ready or Not"). Nevertheless, there is the stunning title track, and Browne's overall songwriting ability remains impressive. –WR

☆ **Late for the Sky / ELEKTRA**   1974
This album is both a reconfirmation of Browne's ability to make words do whatever he wants and something of a musical dead end — people who think all of Browne's songs sound alike are thinking of this record. People who think of him as a profound pessimist are too, what with another death song, "Fountain of Sorrow," and another apocalypse song, "Before the Deluge," to add to the Browne collection. But "The Late Show" is his best-realized love song yet, and even if he is a doom-monger, he's so good at it! –WR

☆ **The Pretender / ELEKTRA**   1976
Browne turns to Bruce Springsteen's producer, Jon Landau, and is rewarded with his best-recorded album, one on which he seeks a way out of the gloom in such songs as "The Fuse," though there may be no more cynical view of middle-class suburban life than the album's title track. –WR

★ **Running on Empty / ELEKTRA**   1978
On the surface, this is the album for anyone who ever had the urge to say, "Hey, Jackson, lighten up!" It's a live album of previously unrecorded songs, several of them covers or co-compositions, its overriding theme "life on the road." But as the title track suggests, even that life is no more than a temporary escape, and the equally famous medley "The Load-Out/Stay" tells us that the singer wants to stay onstage rather than face life off of it. –WR

Lawyers in Love / ELEKTRA   1983
After managing to sound romantically mawkish on 1980's *Hold Out,* Browne returned with this album. It showed he has a weird sense of humor when he puts his mind to it. –WR

World in Motion / ELEKTRA   1989
On *World in Motion,* Browne continued fleshing out his idealogical discourse on the sins of America committed during the Reagan era. This time out, his bold human-rights brush strokes more often than not seemed truly committed to reaching people, as opposed to browbeating them. Highlights include "Anything Can Happen," "Enough of the Night," Little Steven's "I Am A Patriot," and an amazing statement of forgiveness in the face of injustice called "My Personal Revenge." –RC

BROWNSVILLE STATION

Rock & roll. A Detroit-area rock & roll band formed in 1969 by guitarist Cub Koda. Original members also included Mike Lutz (guitar), T. J. Cronley (drums), and Tony Driggins (bass). Initially influenced by Chuck Berry, Bo Diddley, Jerry Lee Lewis, and other 50s rockers, their early albums included inspired covers and genre-faithful originals. The group hit pay dirt in late 1973 with their #3 hit, the Koda-penned "Smokin' in the Boy's Room." After disbanding the group in 1979, Koda went on to a career as a solo recording artist (see separate entry) –STE

○ **No B. S. / WARNER**   1970
Their debut album, featuring pedal-to-the-metal renditions of "Road Runner," "Rumble," and "Be Bop Confidential." –STE

Brownsville Station / PRIVATE STOCK   1977
Their next-to-last album, featuring the cult favorite "The Martian Boogie." –STE

BOB BROZMAN

Blues/rock. Brozman came to prominence in the ranks of underground comics artist Robert Crumb's Cheap Suit Serenaders, a cheerfully reactionary band that reveled in the musical hokum of the 78-RPM era. Bob's talents on Hawaiian slide guitar, blues guitar, ukelele, and other delightful anachronisms gave authenticity to Cheap Suit's sound. His later solo projects are fun, technically astounding updates of Delta blues, early jazz, and vintage Hawaiian music, often aided by the rarely heard stride piano stylings of George Winston. –MB

Hello Central - Give Me Dr. Jazz / ROUNDER   1985
Bob enlists George Winston and others to faithfully re-create the 78-RPM era, focusing on early-jazz standards, hokum and blues. –MB

○ **Devil's Slide / ROUNDER**   1988
Blues, Hawaiian, calypso, hot jazz — slide wizard Bob can do it all with startling authenticity and humor. This CD compilation has five cuts from his *Hello Central* album to boot. –MB

JACK BRUCE   b 1943

Prog-rock. In the pantheon of great rock bassists, Jack Bruce certainly stands tall. His forceful yet elastic technique and his trademark wide tonality and phrasing are utterly unique. As a rock bassist, Bruce incorporated a jazz sensibility by giving the instrument freedom to voice itself beyond merely holding down the pulse with the drummer.

Along with Eric Clapton (guitar, vocals) and Ginger Baker (percussion), Bruce pioneered the hard-rock trio concept, complete with extended free-for-all jams. Bruce has also done exemplary work with the Tony Williams Lifetime, Alexis

Korner, the Graham Bond Organization, John Mayall's Bluesbreakers, Carla Bley, Robin Trower, Frank Zappa, West, Bruce & Laing, and the Golden Palominos.

Bruce (with cowriter Pete Brown) penned most of Cream's biggest numbers. As a solo singer/songwriter, Bruce integrated an eclectic sampling of music, ranging from folk to classical overtones to jazz/rock fusion, all focused through a rather impenetrable arty filter. –RC

○ **Songs for a Tailor / POLYGRAM / BB 55**   1969
There's not a weak song on this first and most accessible solo album. "Theme for an Imaginary Western" (also made popular by Mountain) is one of the finest songs Bruce has ever recorded. Musically, this is more subdued and keyboard-oriented than Bruce's work with Cream. –RC

Harmony Row / ATCO   1971
Bruce's third effort is a much more challenging listen, possessing more complicated arrangements and impenetrable lyrics than *Songs for a Tailor*. Among the album's many highlights is the aggressive multi-time-signature rock of "You Burned the Tables on Me" and the haunting "Victoria Sage." –RC

● **Willpower / POLYGRAM**   1989
Willpower is a well-compiled overview of Bruce's entire solo output, with choice unreleased tracks. This is the place to start if you are budgeting one disc of his music for your collection. Otherwise, get *Songs for a Tailor*. –RC

BILL BRUFORD   b 1948

Art-rock. Bruford was one of art-rock's most influential drummers, due to his distinctively tight snare-drum sound and detailed percussion work in the group Yes. In August 1972 Bruford left Yes for King Crimson, where he increasingly became fascinated with the application of Simmons electronic drums. –RC

○ **One of a Kind / CAROLINE**   1979
This British drummer's best Jazz/rock fusion done with spirit and originality. –MGN

Master Strokes 1978-85 / CAROLINE   1986
A very well put-together compilation. –MGN

All Heaven Broke Loose / CAROLINE   1991
A very good effort with his *Earthworks* group. –MGN

PEABO BRYSON   b 1951

Soul, urban R&B. This smooth-voiced soul ballad singer is known both for his solo successes and for duets with Natalie Cole, Roberta Flack, and Regina Belle. –WR

○ **The Peabo Bryson Collection / CAPITOL**   1984
A best-of covering Bryson's Capitol years, 1978-1983, much of it given over to his collaboration with Roberta Flack, including the hits "Tonight, I Celebrate My Love" and "You're Lookin' Like Love to Me." –WR

Straight from the Heart / ELEKTRA   1984
Good mix of slow and uptempo tunes, including the definitive Bryson ballad, "If Ever You're in My Arms Again." –WR

ROY BUCHANAN   1939-1988

Blues/rock. Buchanan's reputation as a hot-shot guitarist extends back to the beginnings of rock & roll itself. On the road and recording with Dale Hawkins by his teens, Buchanan became the law of the land around the Washington, DC, area by the mid to late 60s. His use of the Fender Telecaster, using high harmonic squeals in place of feedback and distortion, was part and parcel of rock guitar's vocabulary by the early 70s. A reluctant superstar, Buchanan's later work became more unfocused as his career waned, but his unique stylings remain etched into his best records. –CK

○ **Roy Buchanan / POLYGRAM**   1972
His debut album, with a skunk-hot stage band. Buchanan's guitar sizzles on tracks like "Haunted House," "Sweet Dreams," and "The Messiah Will Come Again." –CK

Second Album / POLYGRAM   1973
More blues-based than his debut, with great stretched-out jams showcasing some of his best playing. –CK

That's What I Am Here For / POLYGRAM   1973
Excellent blues-rock guitar, including the riveting Hendrix tribute "Hey Joe." –DS

● **Livestock / POLYGRAM**   1975
Brilliant live blues-rock guitar by the legend who turned down the Rolling Stones. A must for guitar-hero fans. –DS

When a Guitar Plays the Blues / ALLIGATOR   1985
An excellent example of this blues-rock guitar virtuoso's recent work. –DS

LINDSEY BUCKINGHAM   b 1948

Rock/pop. A singer/songwriter, guitarist, arranger, and producer who achieved prominence as the guiding force in Fleetwood Mac, 1975-1987. He has recorded three solo albums. –WR

○ **Law and Order / WARNER**   1981
Buckingham's studio mastery is placed in the service of a collection of carefully arranged pop confections not unlike the work he was doing with Fleetwood Mac at the time. A good example is the haunting "Trouble," a Top Ten hit. –WR

THE BUCKINGHAMS

Rock/pop. If everyone on the northwest side of Chicago who claims to have hung out with the Buckinghams during their heyday had faithfully bought all their releases, the rock group might have sold more records than the Beatles.

Popular attractions while still in high school, the quintet changed its name from the Pulsations to the Buckinghams to reflect the British Invasion craze and signed with Chicago's USA Records in 1966. Backing Dennis Tufano's buoyant lead vocals with prominent harmonies and punchy soul-styled brass, the group came across the wistful "Kind of a Drag," and in short order, the Buckinghams had a million-selling pop chart-topper on their hands. They quickly graduated to recording for Columbia.

As long as songwriter Jim Holvay supplied more material of the same high quality as "Kind of a Drag," the Buckinghams were sitting pretty. Holvay cowrote "Don't You Care," "Hey Baby (They're Playing Our Song)," and the pseudo-psychedelic "Susan," and they all proved to be major hits for the band. The group's R&B roots surfaced on a vocal adaptation of Cannonball Adderley's jazz standard "Mercy, Mercy, Mercy," their second-biggest hit.

But the Buckinghams' fortunes soon changed drastically — one of the top-selling rock groups of 1967, they managed only one hit after early 1968, and by 1970 the group was kaput. Two original members, guitarist Carl Giammarese and bassist Nick Fortuna, have since revived the Buckinghams for oldies tours. –BD

○ **Mercy Mercy Mercy (A Collection) / CBS**   1991
These mid-60s hitmakers from Chicago hold up well with their neat blend of pop and soul. All of their hits and more can be found on this 18-song anthology. –JT

TIM BUCKLEY   1947-1975

Singer/songwriter. Tim Buckley's mournful wail, his synthesis of folk and jazz, and his haunting melodies seemed decidedly out of step with much of the music that was popular at the end of the 60s. Discovered by Frank Zappa manager Herb Cohen, Buckley was signed to Elektra, where he cut several albums. Two of his best from that period, *Goodbye and Hello* and *Happy Sad*, were produced by ex-Lovin' Spoonful Jerry Yester. In 1970 Buckley moved to Cohen's Straight Records and released *Blue Afternoon*, an album that lived up to its title.

Buckley dropped out after 1971's *Starsailor* and became a taxi driver and chauffeur for a while. He returned with a new direction on *Greetings from L. A.*, which featured a down-and-dirty collection of funk rock. In 1975 Buckley died of an accidental drug overdose, mistaking a mix of heroin and morphine for cocaine. –RC

Goodbye ... and Hello / ELEKTRA 1967
Promising debut, produced by Jerry Yester of the Lovin' Spoonful. Contains the much-covered track "Morning Glory." A favorite of Buckley fans. –RC

○ **Blue Afternoon / RHINO** 1969
Buckley's atmospheric melancholy folk/jazz shines on the first four tracks, "Happy Time," "Chase the Blues Away," "I Must Have Been Blind," and "The River." Those tracks alone make this worth having. –RC

Greetings from L.A. / RHINO 1972
A grittier rock approach supports Buckley's plunge into eroticism. Buckley's uncaged wailing, plus his lyrical urgency, conveys a great deal of sexual tension and an absence of inner peace. Intense stuff — considered by many to be his best. –RC

● **Dream Letter - Live in London / ENIGMA** 1990
A live double-disc set capturing Buckley's jazzy folk and passionate mega-octave vocal in fine form. Lee Underwood (guitar), David Friedman (vibes), and Danny Thompson (bass) provide empathetic support. –RC

BUFFALO SPRINGFIELD

Folk/rock, country rock, rock & roll. Few American groups have produced a wealth of talent like that of Buffalo Springfield. Over a 19-month period, during 1967 and 1968, Buffalo Springfield released three impressive albums; the second one, *Again*, is their masterpiece. In that brief time, they produced a handful of classics, among them "For What It's Worth" (#7 pop) and "Bluebird" (#58 pop). Buffalo Springfield possessed three strong songwriters (with distinctly different yet complementary styles) in Richie Furay, Stephen Stills, and Neil Young.

Even more than the Byrds, Buffalo Springfield's sound was undeniably American, drawing from rock, folk, and country. The intense clash of creative energies, however, finally caused the demise of the band in May of 1968. Stephen Stills went on to Crosby, Stills & Nash. Neil Young joined them briefly for *Déjà Vu*, then went on to pursue an erratic solo career with periods of great success and brilliant music. After Springfield, Jim Messina and Richie Furay founded the country-rock group Poco. After Poco, Messina recorded a string of hits during the 70s with Kenny Loggins, as Loggins & Messina. During the late 80s, Messina and Furay reunited for a one-off Poco album. –RC

Buffalo Springfield / ATLANTIC 1966
Their strong debut contains the Stephen Stills classic "For What It's Worth" and Neil Young's "Nowadays Clancy Can't Even Sing." "Sit Down I Think I Love You" and "Go and Say Goodbye" are also highlights. –RC

☆ **Buffalo Springfield Again / ATLANTIC** 1967
By far their best effort. Stills, Furay, and Young each contribute some great songs: the hits "Bluebird," "Mr. Soul," and "Rock & Roll Woman," plus standouts like "A Child's Claim to Fame," "Hung Upside Down," "Broken Arrow," "Everydays," and "Expecting to Fly." Essential stuff for any good rock & roll collection. –RC

Last Time Around / ATCO 1968
Their last album showcases a couple of gems in Furay's "Kind Woman" and Young's "On the Way Home." –RC

○ **Best of ... Retrospective / ATLANTIC** 1969
Best of Buffalo Springfield ... Retrospective is a decent sampler for the uninitiated. Contains all their hits and some key album tracks but it isn't comprehensive enough to be essential. –RC

BUFFALO TOM

Alternative rock. These alternative rockers with a guitar-heavy sound have endured a lot of comparisons with Dinosaur Jr. *Birdbrain*, their second album, established Buffalo Tom's own style more firmly. –DH

○ **Birdbrain / RCA** 1990
A well-produced eccentric batch of underground rock, featuring "Sunflower Suit." –DH

JIMMY BUFFETT   b 1946

Singer/songwriter, country rock. Buffett is a country/folk/pop singer/songwriter whose songs strongly reflect his Gulf Coast origins: beach bums, booze, sailing, hedonism, and sly humor. He has built up an enormous regional following of fans, who call themselves "Parrotheads." –WR

A-1-A / MCA 1974
A little hardworking for a beachcomber, Buffett released a second album in 1974. It was his most perfect evocation of noncareerist hedonism yet, even if its most telling song, "A Pirate Looks at Forty," was unusually thoughtful for a party animal. –WR

Living and Dying in 3/4 Time / DUNHILL 1974
Jimmy Buffett was already on the second edition of his Coral Reefer Band by the time his third album rolled around. He had also firmly established his Gulf Coast beach-bum/poet persona, but he hadn't written a classic song until "Come Monday," which put him, and the album, on the map. –WR

Havana Daydreamin' / MCA 1976
Buffett's best overall collection of songs yet bears the influence of Steve Goodman, who wrote "This Hotel Room" and cowrote "Woman Goin' Crazy on Caroline Street." But a personal favorite is Buffett's own "My Head Hurts, My Feet Stink, and I Don't Love Jesus." –WR

○ **Changes in Latitudes, Changes in Attitudes / MCA** 1977
Buffett's biggest all-time seller contains his biggest hit single, "Margaritaville." It's also a peak in terms of songwriting, both for the artist himself and in his covers of the work of Steve Goodman and Jesse Winchester, among others. Funny, wistful, and celebratory, the album is the definitive statement of Buffett's world view. –WR

Son of a Son of a Sailor / MCA 1978
If this album was a slight step down from its predecessor, it was almost equally successful commercially, and it contained its share of terrific material, notably the uptempo hit "Cheeseburger in Paradise" and one of Buffett's older songs, "Livingston Saturday Night." –WR

Last Mango in Paris / MCA 1985
Buffett's rapid recording schedule tended to outrun his muse in the late 70s and early 80s, resulting in some uneven albums with occasional good songs. This time he came up with a far more consistent collection, including three entries on the country charts: "Gypsies in the Palace," "If the Phone Doesn't Ring, It's Me," and "Please Bypass This Heart." –WR

● **Boats, Beaches, Bars & Ballads / MCA** 1992
This 4-CD, 72-track anthology is essential for "Parrotheads" (Buffett fans) who don't miss his concerts but aren't so hardcore that they have to own every single thing Buffett ever released. Each disc revolves around a theme (Boats, Beaches, Bars, Ballads). All of his hits and popular album tracks are here, as well as some previously unreleased material. The box includes the Parrothead Handbook, a 64-page booklet that provides a well-assembled collection of photos, reflections from Buffett, and explanations of his songs. The sound on this set is first-rate. –RC

THE BUGGLES

Alternative pop. The short-lived synth-pop duo Buggles (formed 1979) earned the distinction of having the first video ever played on MTV, with the international hit "Video Killed the Radio Star" (#40). Made up of Geoff Downes and Trevor Horn (b July 15, 1949), Buggles joined up with Yes in 1980 and released *Drama*. Horn went on to become a very successful techno-pop producer (*Frankie Goes to Hollywood*), while Downes joined the art-pop supergroup Asia. –RC

○ **The Age of Plastic / ISLAND** 1980

A debut techno-pop effort for *Drama*-era Yes members Trevor Horn and Geoff Downes. Includes "Video Killed the Radio Star," which MTV appropriately used to christen its channel. –RC

CINDY BULLENS   ♭1953

Rock/pop. A rock singer/songwriter who appeared in *Grease* and sang backup with Elton John before cutting three albums of her own. –WR

○ **Desire Wire / UNITED ARTISTS**   1978
One of the great lost rock albums of the 70s, Cindy's debut release is full of tough, passionate, incredibly catchy rock & roll played to the hilt and sung with fire. Bullens followed it up with *Steal the Night* in 1979. Ten years later, she made *Cindy Bullens*, and they're almost as good, though no one noticed. So life is unfair. Search those used-record stores for any of them. –WR

SONNY BURGESS   ♭1931

Rockabilly. Sonny Burgess is one of the wildest rockers to record for the legendary Sun label in Memphis. He and his band the Pacers came out of Newport, AR, with a hard-rocking style that, unlike that of most rockabillies, owed little to nothing in the way of a stylistic debt to country music. With his red-dyed hair, matching stage suit and guitar, and wild stage performances, Burgess and the Pacers made mincemeat of the competition on many of the early-50s rock & roll package tours. Though his Sun releases never brought him much in the way of commercial success, Sonny's recordings nonetheless remain landmarks of the early rockabilly style. Currently touring and recording with other Memphis alumni in the Sun Rhythm Section, the rockin' flame that is Sonny Burgess refuses to be snuffed out. –CK

○ **We Wanna Boogie / ROUNDER**   1990
Savage rockabilly from one of the wildest artists in the 50s Sun Records stable. Slashing guitar and chaotic vocals. –BD

● **The Classic Recordings 1956 1959 / BEAR FAMILY**   1991
Sonny's complete output for Sun spread over two CDs. Wild and crazed, featuring Burgess's spitfire guitar and booming vocals, and the relentless drive of the Pacers in support. –CK

SOLOMON BURKE   ♭1936

R&B, soul. Musically and corporeally imposing, Burke was almost as important as he says he was. His account of how he invented soul music is entertaining if fanciful, but even when SB's BS count is lowered, there is no doubt he was present at the creation of 60s soul music — and at least partially responsible for it.
Starting as "Solomon the Boy Wonder Preacher" in Philadelphia, he had been recording for six years when he finally broke through with "Just out of Reach" in 1961. Burke's best recordings probably date from the early 60s, when he was working with producer Bert Berns. Songs like "Cry to Me," "I'm Hanging up My Heart for You," "Goodbye Baby," and "The Price" collectively formed the keynote address for soul music. Some of the arrangements sound unnecessarily ornamented today, but the passion Burke brought to those recordings was that of the Boy Wonder Preacher. Live, he's still impressive, as recent recordings attest. –CE

Soul Alive / ROUNDER   1985
Captures masterfully the intensity of Burke's sweaty and raucous stage show. –JF

A Change is Gonna Come / ROUNDER   1986
This, Solomon Burke's best latter-day recording, spotlights his gospel training. –JF

○ **The Bishop Rides South / CHARLY**   1988
When Burke left Atlantic, he signed with New York City's Bell Records. Bell wisely sent Solomon down to Muscle Shoals. Two 1969 hits, covers of "Uptight Good Woman" and "Proud

Mary," resulted, along with a slew of classic Southern soul covers. –RB

● **Home in Your Heart / RHINO-ATLANTIC**   1992
Home in Your Heart - The Best of Solomon Burke is a 41-track two-disc set that covers Burke's Atlantic recordings from 1961 to 1968. Seventeen of those tracks charted. All are superior examples of country-soul and gospel-soul. –RB

T-BONE BURNETTE   ♭1945

Singer/songwriter, folk/rock, country rock, roots-rock. T-Bone Burnette may not be a household word, but he has managed to attain a kind of creative freedom that many more successful artists never see. A virtual Renaissance man, Burnette has produced some great albums for Bruce Cockburn, Los Lobos, Elvis Costello, and Marshall Crenshaw. As a singer/songwriter, he has released a number of albums that have made him somewhat of a critic's darling.
Burnette first gained notoriety with the Alpha Band (after a stint in Bob Dylan's Rolling Thunder Revue) during the middle and late 70s. Among their three albums, *Spark in the Dark* most successfully sidestepped the band's tendency for heavy-handed Christian moralizing. That preachy quality has surfaced periodically in Burnette's solo work; nevertheless, it is Burnette's intelligent spiritual grounding that has also informed his artistry's many strengths.
Stylistically, Burnette has primarily drawn from folk, country, and roots rock, but he has infused other elements, creating some provocative combinations of music. –RC

○ **Truth Decay / TAKOMA**   1980
The first album after his stint with the Alpha Band. A great mix of Texas roadhouse R&B/blues-based rock, with hard-folk acoustic instrumental augmentation. Thematically, *Truth Decay* was a refreshing departure from some of the Alpha Band's relentless moralizing. Burnette still took some heavy-handed shots on songs like "Madison Ave" and "House of Mirrors," but the presence of tracks like the gritty rocker "Boomerang," "Talk Talk Talk Talk Talk," and "Love at First Sight" makes this a must-own for lovers of Dylanish rock. –RC

Trap Door (EP) / WARNER   1982
From his clever reading of the Marilyn Monroe standard "Diamonds Are a Girl's Best Friend," to stunning folk/rock originals like "Hold On Tight" and "I Wish You Could Have Seen Her Dance," to the thoughtful closer "Trap Door," this EP is Burnette's most consistently satisfying release. Too bad it wasn't a full-length album. Too bad it's not out on CD yet. –RC

Proof through the Night / WARNER   1983
Truth Decay and *Trap Door* had earned Burnette loads of critical praise, but this followup featured strong performances (by an all-star lineup) and impressive production, although tracks like "Hefner and Disney" and "The Sixties" were smug, overreaching concept pieces (recalling the Alpha Band's later work) that undermined the overall strength of this release. –RC

T-Bone Burnette / DOT   1986
Recorded digitally, straight to 2-track, Burnette's self-titled Dot Records release is a heartfelt, low-key affair, featuring flawless country-folk musicianship and a strong collection of originals and covers. Among the highlights are "River of Love," "Shake Yourself Loose," and a version of Tom Waits's "Time." –RC

● **The Criminal under My Own Hat / CBS**   1992
On his first album in four years, Burnette adopts a spare instrumentation dominated by Marc Ribot's angular guitar work to complement a set of close-to-the-bone lyrics that strip love of sentimentality, castigate politicians and evangelists, and, as the album title (echoed in the song "Criminals") attests, do not spare the songwriter himself. The result is a gripping record in the best tradition of Burnette's mentor, Bob Dylan. –WR

KATE BUSH   ♭1958

Prog-rock, alternative pop. A preeminent singer/songwriter with a unique sound and style since her emergence with

"Wuthering Heights" in 1978. Bush's high keening voice has mellowed into a beautifully lyrical instrument, while her music and lyrics define the meaning of sensuousness in subject and feeling, especially in the late 80s. Her music is tasteful, intelligent, and stimulating beyond the libido. Her major inspiration was the Beatles, and her mentor, Pink Floyd's David Gilmour. It shows in the exquisite lyricism and timbral qualities of her work. −BE

The Kick Inside / CAPITOL   1978
An amazing debut album. Strident and surprisingly mature for a twenty-year-old. Includes "Wuthering Heights." −BE

Lionheart / CAPITOL   1978
Diffuse as compared with her debut, this second album, *Lionheart* suffers from unfocused artistic sensibilities and production and overall weak lyrics, despite some pleasant melodies. "Oh England My Lionheart" is the strongest track, followed by "Wow." −BE

Never for Ever / EMI-USA   1980
Something of a comeback, *Never for Ever* recast Bush in a fiercer musical persona, exploring facets of the dark side of human nature ("The Wedding List") and of tragic melodrama ("Babooshka"). −BE

The Dreaming / CAPITOL   1982
Bush's fourth album is a personal exploration of mysticism and magic and their effect on the mind of the beholder. It's difficult to absorb and, lacking the poetic qualities of her previous work, it's for serious fans only. −BE

☆ **Hounds of Love / CAPITOL**   1985
A sexy, sensual masterpiece, embracing love, sex, guilt, and the quest for psychic wholeness within a framework of rich melodies, stunning timbres, and a perfectly developed sense of the dramatic. An outstanding album of the entire decade. −BE

● **The Whole Story / EMI-USA**   1986
A well-thought-out cross-section of the representative tracks from her first five albums, remixed and remastered in some cases. A great way to start on her music. −BE

○ **The Sensual World / CBS**   1989
The world of sexuality and guilt and the divisions between the sexes — Bush's followup to *Hounds of Love* lacks the concise structure of the earlier record, but the individual songs stand out, especially the sensual title track. −BE

○ **This Woman's Work (1978-1990) / EMI**   1990
The complete Kate Bush collection as of 1990, assembling all six full-length albums plus two CDs' worth of rare B-sides and limited-release singles that are often as finely produced as her albums. The only problem is the hefty price tag and the inclusion of a booklet that has photos but virtually no information on any of the songs. (Import) −BE

THE BUSH TETRAS

Punk. Early-80s NY-based, post punk rock group led by singer Cynthia Sley and guitarist Pat Place. −WR

○ **Better Late Than Never, 1980-1983 / ROIR**   1989
The Bush Tetras made a few independent label EPs in New York in the early 80s and then disappeared forever. The music was simple and relentless, as were the chanted messages of songs such as the seminal "Too Many Creeps." This was punk minimalism down to the point of amateurishness but no less compelling because of it. This belated compilation contains more than everything they put out — there are unissued demos never heard before. −WR

JERRY BUTLER   b 1939

R&B, soul. It would be safer to talk about Jerry Butler's careers than about his career. Up from Mississippi, he joined Curtis Mayfield in the Impressions around 1957. They began recording the following year and broke through with *For Your Precious Love,* touted by some as the first soul record. Inevitably, he went solo and fell — or was pushed — into the pop mainstream. Reunited with Mayfield (the latter as a

writer), Butler announced his return with *He Will Break Your Heart* in 1960. His subsequent recordings for Vee-Jay trod the turf where pop and R&B meet and are variable; the best are excellent.

After Vee Jay went broke in 1966, Butler signed with Mercury and was soon placed with the team of Gamble and Huff, who produced him in Philadelphia. Jerry Butler's mellow baritone and the sweet Philly sound were a winning combination, as attested by pop and R&B hits like "Only the Strong Survive" and "Hey, Western Union Man." After the Gamble and Huff deal dissolved in 1970, Butler's career went slowly downhill. Deals with Motown and even Gamble and Huff's Philadelphia International label couldn't deliver the goods. There's something for everyone in Butler's prolificacy, but unfortunately little of it is available to sample. −CE

Ice on Ice / MERCURY
The Ice Man Cometh / MERCURY   1969
Ice on Ice and *The Ice Man Cometh* are two of his best late-60s albums, produced by the Gamble/Huff team. They've been out of print for years, but snap them up if you can find them. −JF

● **Best of Jerry Butler / RHINO**   1977
An excellent 18-song overview of his solo hits and his first recordings with the Impressions. It could use a few more of his later hits. −JF

☆ **Iceman: The Mercury Years / POLYGRAM**   1992
A glorious 44-song double-disc set collecting Butler's best Mercury sides, with several previously unreleased songs and alternate mixes. Crummy liner notes, though. −JF

THE BUTTHOLE SURFERS

Punk. The art-rock punk band from hell. Funny, abrasive, and only occasionally tuneful. Always surprising. −JD

○ **Butthole Surfers / ALTERNATE TENTACLES**   1983
Their best album, randy and wild. Smart, stupid, and outrageous all at the same time. It may be out of print. −JD

Psychic ... Powerless ... / TOUCH & GO   1985
New-age drug music on *Psychic ... Powerless ... Another Man's Sac.* −JD

Rembrandt Pussyhorse / TOUCH & GO   1986
Chunky, cranky, out-of-control pop. −JD

Hurdy Gurdy Man / ROUGH TRADE   1990
Their college-radio hit. −JD

THE BUZZCOCKS

Punk. First-wave punks from Manchester, England, led by songwriter Pete Shelley, who combined his penchant for desolate love songs with the three-minute roar of the Sex Pistols. −JF

Singles Going Steady / I.R.S.   1979
A magnificent collection of their first eight British singles, both A- and B-sides. Infectious melodies and buzzsaw guitars carry Shelley's finest set of brokenhearted rockers. −JF

○ **Operator's Manual: The Buzzcocks Best / I.R.S.**   1991
A 25-song set that duplicates 11 songs from the *Singles* album. It also contains the best of their three albums, only one of which was released in the US, and showcases a different side of the band. −JF

THE BYRDS

Folk/rock, psychedelic, country rock. Outside of the Beatles and the Rolling Stones, there hasn't been a group from the 60s whose sound has been so widely influential. Their trademark bell-like jangle of 12-string electric guitar and rich harmonies has been internalized by artists like Tom Petty, R.E.M., Big Star, Fairport Convention, the Church, the Bangles, and the Eagles, as well by as much of today's country music.

Before the advent of the British Invasion, Jim (later Roger) McGuinn, Chris Hillman, David Crosby, and Gene Clark were active in the Los Angeles folk scene. By fusing the energy of the Beatles and the weightier lyrical concepts developed by Bob Dylan, the Byrds were conceived, and folk/rock was born. Over the course of their existence, the Byrds pioneered many musical frontiers, breaking ground in futuristic space-rock and country-rock.

Through all their endeavors, the only constant in their many lineup changes was Roger McGuinn. After the band's demise in 1973, McGuinn released a series of solo efforts.

Like Buffalo Springfield, many of the Byrds members went on to even-greater success. David Crosby helped form Crosby, Stills & Nash. Chris Hillman, along with Gram Parsons, formed the Flying Burrito Brothers. Hillman also has continued to have much success in the country field with the Desert Rose Band. Parsons managed two fine albums on Warner before dying in 1973 of a drug overdose. Gene Clark, one of the band's finest songwriters, had a sporadic solo career; *Echoes* is a dignified compilation of his highlights. Clark died in 1991. –RC

☆ **Mr. Tambourine Man / CBS**   1965
An incredibly focused debut, featuring a smart blend of well-chosen song covers and originals, plus the band's trademark 12-string electric sound and transcendent harmonies. The title track and Gene Clark's "I'll Feel a Whole Lot Better," as well as "All I Really Want to Do," are hits. Two highlights, "I Knew I'd Want You" and "Here without You," reveal Clark as the most mature songwriter in the band at this point. –RC

○ **Turn! Turn! Turn! / CBS**   1966
Continuing in the vein of their debut, this has lots of electrified folk-song covers (Dylan, Seeger, traditional) and Gene Clark shines on "Set You Free This Time" (curiously omitted from the box), "If You're Gone," and the expansive "The World Turns All Around Her." –RC

○ **Fifth Dimension / CBS**   1966
Clark left during the recording of this, but David Crosby and Jim McGuinn more than fill the void. The 12-string sound is much more experimental, with McGuinn and Crosby drawing inspiration from jazz and Indian music. Though this album isn't so strong as *Turn! Turn! Turn!* and *Mr. Tambourine Man*, some of their greatest moments are found here in the powerful, hymnlike "5 D," the breathtakingly beautiful psychedelia of "Eight Miles High," or the playful hit "Mr. Spaceman." Other tracks of note are the psychedelic "I See You" (later cut by Yes on their debut), "What's Happening?!?!," and the orchestrated folky "Wild Mountain Thyme." –RC

☆ **Younger Than Yesterday / CBS**   1967
Overall a stronger album than *Fifth Dimension*, even though some of the psychedelia lacks much sustaining impact ("C.T.A.-102," "Mind Gardens"). Chris Hillman makes strong contributions, writing or cowriting five of the 11 tracks. Among them are the tongue-in-cheek hit "So You Want to Be a Rock'N'Roll Star" and the spirited "Have You Seen Her Face." Also includes the hit version of Dylan's "My Back Pages." –RC

★ **The Byrds' Greatest Hits / CBS**   1967
Even though this collection only covers the first half of their career, it contains more primo stuff than *20 Essential Tracks* (see below). The mastering here isn't quite as good as that on the boxed set. –RC

○ **The Notorious Byrd Brothers / CBS**   1968
A classic psychedelic opus, drawing from the space-rock of *Younger ...* and *Fifth ...* while hinting at the country-rock to come with cuts like "Change Is Now" and "Old John Robertson." The 12-string electrics are downplayed. Production techniques like phasing, vari-speed vocals, sound effects, and baroque string and horn arrangements play a bigger role, while the melodies and vocal execution is much spacier. Highlights include Carole King's yearning "Goin' Back," "Draft Morning," "Dolphins Smile," and "Wasn't Born to Follow" (featured in the movie *Easy Rider*). –RC

☆ **Sweetheart of the Rodeo / CBS**   1968
The Byrds made this groundbreaking country-rock classic with the songwriting aid of new member Gram Parsons. "One

Hundred Years from Now" features some incredibly fine guitar and pedal steel work from Clarence White and Lloyd Green, respectively. Versions of Dylan's "Nothing Was Delivered" and "You Ain't Going Nowhere" are pure magic, and renditions of the Louvin Brothers' "The Christian Life" and William Bell's "You Don't Miss Your Water" are standouts too. –RC

Dr. Byrds & Mr. Hyde / CBS   1969
Not one of their best but this contains two notable tracks in "This Wheel's on Fire" and "King Apathy III." There is a continued country influence but rock still predominates. –RC

○ **Ballad of Easy Rider / CBS**   1969
Another beautiful gem with hardly a weak cut. "Gunga Din," with its delicate arpeggios, is one of the finest moments by a later incarnation of the Byrds. By this time, their characteristic 12-string sound was all but gone. –RC

Untitled / CBS   1970
Originally a double-record set (one live LP/one studio) and now on single CD, this contains their last hit of any substance, "Chestnut Mare." The studio tracks are uneven, but tracks like the reflective "Just a Season," "Truck Stop Girl," stop "All the Things" and much of the live stuff make this set worth having, if only for Clarence White's remarkable guitar playing. –RC

In the Beginning / RHINO   1978
A collection of pre-*Tambourine Man* Byrds. Fans might find interest in early versions of "Mr. Tambourine Man," "I Knew I'd Want You," "You Showed Me" (a Byrds original the Turtles scored with), and Gene Clark's "For Me Again." –RC

Never Before / MURRAY HILL   1987
A compilation of previously unreleased sides and alternative versions. The stereo remix of "Mr. Tambourine Man" contains too much spread on the soundstage. The alternative take of "Eight Miles High" and an extended version of "Psychodrama City" will appeal to hardcore fans. The boxed set, however, has since included most of these tracks. Good liner notes and a great picture in the booklet. –RC

○ **The Byrds / CBS**   1990
A thoughtfully compiled 4-CD boxed set that features great sound from remastered and remixed tracks. The remixes generally manage to maintain the essential integrity of the original tracks, but there are some that entirely miss the spirit, like "Just a Season" and a toothless "Why" (which, by the way, is *not* the sought-after version found on the B-side of "Eight Miles High.") Regardless, a must-own for anyone interested in finding out about one of America's greatest groups. –RC

○ **Twenty Essential Tracks from the Box Set / CBS**   1991
That may have been the case for the first sixteen cuts, but why include the four 1990 reunion tracks, when there's much better material left on the box? An okay choice for the budget-minded; that's about it. –RC

DAVID BYRNE   b 1952

Alternative rock, prog-rock. The former lead singer/songwriter and guitarist of Talking Heads, David Byrne has written theatre and film scores (Academy Award winner for *The Last Emperor*), acted and directed (*True Stories*), compiled a series of samplers of South American music, and launched a solo career with Rei Momo in 1989. –WR

The Catherine Wheel / WARNER   1981
This is Byrne's score for a Broadway dance production choreographed and directed by Twyla Tharp. Its sound — with herky-jerky rhythms and unusual noises, along with Byrne's own vocals and odd lyrics on many songs — will be familiar to Talking Heads fans. As originally released, only the cassette version contained the full 73-minute score, though an abridged songs-from LP was also issued. –WR

Music for the Knee Plays / ECM-SIRE/WARNER   1985
This music was composed for use in segments of Robert Wilson's opera *The Civil Wars.* Byrne uses a variety of stately horn charts and recites impressionistic lyrics between and

over them. The album concludes with the hilariously absurd "In the Future." –WR

Sounds from True Stories / SIRE 1986
Stylistically all over the map, this set of songs for Byrne's film (not to be confused with the Talking Heads album *True Stories*) ranges from the cowboy hoedown of "Cocktail Desperado" to a short piece for reeds written by Meredith Monk. Members of the Heads turn up, as does the Kronos Quartet. –WR

○ **Rei Momo / LUAKA BOP-SIRE** 1989
On his first full-fledged solo album, Byrne indulges his fascination with Latin and South American musical styles, employing a variety of native musicians but mixing up the sounds to suit his own distinctly non-purist vision and singing over the tracks the same kind of witty, oddball lyrics found on Talking Heads albums. (When released, the cassette version contained three more tracks than the LP.) –WR

C & C MUSIC FACTORY / CLIVILLES & COLE

Dance-pop. Techno-rap hip-hop dance conglomeration. –JF

○ **Gonna Make You Sweat / CBS** 1990
Their hit pop-hip-hop singles are all here — "Gonna Make You Sweat (Everybody Dance Now)," "Here We Go," and "Things That Make You Go Hmmm ...." –BC

Clivilles & Cole's Greatest Remixes - Vol. 1 / CBS 1991
New remixes of "Things That Make You Go Hmmm ..." and other hits, three new songs, and a cover of U2's "Pride (In the Name of Love)." Also some material by the Cover Girls and Seduction. –BC

THE CADILLACS

R&B, doo-wop. Equally adept at polished ballads or torrid rockers, the Cadillacs were one of New York's top doo-wop groups. The Harlem quintet signed with Josie in 1954 and debuted with the beautiful "Gloria," but with Earl Carroll's (b Nov 2, 1937) prominent energetic lead vocals, the Cadillacs became known for humorous jump material and hot choreography after "Speedoo" hit big for them in 1956. Tapping into the novelty R&B market pioneered by the Coasters, the Cadillacs cut a load of great rockers during the late 50s, such as "Peek-A-Boo" and "Please, Mr. Johnson," and performed in the quickie flick *Go, Johnny, Go!* in 1959. Carroll left to join the Coasters in 1958 but the group persevered, eventually signing with Mercury. Carroll has re-formed the Cadillacs in recent years. –BD

☆ **The Best of the Cadillacs / RHINO** 1990
One of the top novelty R&B groups of the mid 50s. Sizzling rockers and a handful of doo-wop ballads. –BD

J. J. CALE   b 1938

Singer/songwriter, blues/rock. Oklahoma-born songwriter and guitarist known for his laidback style. He wrote several songs — "After Midnight," "Cocaine" — recorded by Eric Clapton. –WR

○ **Special Edition / POLYGRAM** 1984
Sinuous rhythms, conversational singing, and, most of all, intricate, bluesy guitar playing characterize Cade's performances of his own songs. This compilation, covering 11 years of recording, includes the songs Eric Clapton, who borrowed heavily from Cale's style in his 1970s solo work, made famous: "After Midnight" and "Cocaine." –WR

JOHN CALE   b 1940

Alternative rock, art-rock. A former member of the Velvet Underground (for whom he played viola), Cale has moved between the worlds of rock and avant-garde classical music since launching a solo career in 1969. He also worked as producer for a variety of punk and new-wave artists. –WR

○ **Paris, 1919 / REPRISE** 1973
John Cale's third solo album possessed a rare beauty,

demonstrating that the classically trained avant-garde rock & roll viola player could, when he wished, make melodic pop music with a lush elegance. –WR

Slow Dazzle / ISLAND 1975
On the second installment of a trilogy made for Island in the mid 70s, Cale played (as one song title had it) "Dirtyass Rock & Roll," anticipating the coming punk movement. *Slow Dazzle* includes Cale's drastic reconstruction of "Heartbreak Hotel." –WR

Honi Soit ... / A&M 1981
Cale's first studio album in six years was an excellent pop-rock collection paced by its leadoff track, "Dead or Alive." –WR

Music for a New Society / PASSPORT 1982
Cale's calmest collection of music since *Paris, 1919* contains an excellent version of "Close Watch," as well as the haunting "Chinese Envoy." –WR

THE CALL

Rock & roll. The Call, a California-based quartet featuring the passionate singing and writing of Michael Been, incorporated the fire of the Clash and the organic earthy soul of the Band to deliver their spiritually rooted, socially aware themes. –RC

Reconciled / ELEKTRA 1986
Features the hit "Everywhere I Go" — Christian mysticism with a nervy edge. One of their best efforts. –RC

Let the Day Begin / MCA 1989
The title cut was a major rock hit in spite of poor retail distribution. Other highlights include the rude rough-and-tumble rock of "Same Ol' Story." –RC

○ **Red Moon / MCA** 1990
Pressured for new product, Been rose to the occasion, creating some of his most affectingly passionate music, particularly in the stirring title cut, as well as "What's Happened to You" (reminiscent of the Band), "Like You've Never Been Loved," "This Is Your Life," and "Floating Back." The organic style of production works beautifully with the music. –RC

● **Walls Came Down ... / POLYGRAM** 1991
Walls Came Down - Best of the Mercury Years is a great collection of the band's early career. Contains the fiery debut "The Walls Came Down." Compiled by Been. –RC

CAMEL

Art-rock. The British art-rock band Camel features reflective melodies within the context of extended instrumental workouts. Guitarist Andrew Latimer has been Camel's creative mainstay throughout their many incarnations, which have included keyboardists Pete Bardens and Kit Watkins. –ED

Rain Dances / DERAM 1977
Rain Dances, Camel's fifth release, offers the most consistent and representative package in their saga. This is the band at its best. The addition of Caravan cofounder Richard Sinclair proves profitable, as do a few colorist touches by Brian Eno on "Elke." Mel Collins's woodwinds are among the highlights, especially on *Tell Me* and the title track. From beginning to end, this project flows gracefully. –ED

○ **I Can See Your House from Here / DERAM** 1979
Although not an honest representation of the band's character, this is undoubtedly their most popular work. The one-time addition of American Kit Watkins produces some fine keyboard lead work. Rupert Hines's resourceful production and appearances by Phil Collins and Mel Collins round out this strong import release. "Survival" and "Who We Are" feature some fine orchestrations, and guitarist Latimer delivers some exceptional lead work on the album's closer, "Ice." –ED

Dust and Dreams / CAMEL PRODUCTIONS 1991
As with *Nude* and *The Snow Goose*, Camel continues refining their concept album approach, here based on Steinbeck's *The Grapes of Wrath*. Latimer maintains a symphonylike coherence throughout, with subtle character-based themes.

Guest vocalist Mae McKenna has a hand in "Rose of Sharon," a gem of lyrical and musical depth. This recent album was produced and packaged by Latimer himself and may be harder to find than their others. (Available from Camel Productions, PO Box 4876, Mt. View, CA 94040.)—ED

CAMEO

Funk. This funk group from Los Angeles was originally formed as the New York City Players in 1974. Members included Wayne Cooper, Tomi Jenkins (vocals), Larry Blackmon (drums), and Gregory Johnson (keyboards), but by 1985 Johnson and Cooper had left the group, and Nathan Lefenant was added. Hits include "Candy" and "Word Up." —IME

Cameosis / POLYGRAM 1980
Searing rhythms and horn charts. —RW

○ **She's Strange / POLYGRAM** 1984
An edgy, humorous funk vehicle. —RW

★ **Word Up / POLYGRAM** 1986
The definitive 80s R&B/funk album. —RW

G. C. CAMERON

Soul, Motown. G. C. Cameron was one of the most underrated of the Motown artists. He came to fame as lead singer for the Spinners in the late 60s. It's Cameron's voice on the group's only big Motown hit, "It's a Shame," in 1970. When the group defected to Atlantic Records in 1972, Cameron remained with Motown, where he launched an unsuccessful solo career. Today he records in England. —RAB

○ **You're What's Missing in My Life / MOTOWN**
Produced by Brian Holland, this was Cameron's best work. Lush orchestration. (Out of print) —RAB

CAMPER VAN BEETHOVEN

Alternative rock. During the mid to late 80s, Camper Van Beethoven (from California) plundered everything from country, Indian music, jangly alternative guitar rock, psychedelia, folk, and progressive rock with considerable ease. All of this was irreverently tossed together with refreshing humor. Thematically, these left-field pop iconoclasts were just as eclectic, with oddball originals like "Take the Skinheads Bowling" (a college-radio hit) and song covers by artists as diverse as Sonic Youth, Ringo Starr, Pink Floyd, and the Status Quo. —RC

○ **Telephone Free ... / ROUGH TRADE** 1985
Telephone Free Landslide Victory. "Quirky," "eccentric," "eclectic" — all those words were used often to describe this marvelous debut by Camper Van Beethoven. The Middle East meets C&W, and skinheads go bowling. A howl. —JT

● **Camper Van Beethoven / PITCH-A-TENT** 1986
Their third album is the apex of their creativity — stunning musicianship, witty lyrics, and a musical melting pot. Alternative rock at its most alternative. (The CD includes their 1987 EP *Vampire Can Mating Oven*). —JT

II & III / PITCH-A-TENT 1986
Similar to the debut — well played but not so humorous or sharp. —JT

RAY CAMPI

Rockabilly. Campi recorded a handful of classic sides in Texas during the late 50s and later staged a comeback via Ronny Weiser's Rollin' Rock revivalist label. Born in New York, Campi relocated to Austin and cut his debut single for TNT in 1956, "Caterpillar"/"Play It Cool." He cut "Ballad of Donna & Peggy Sue" for Dot before moving to Los Angeles in 1959 and signing with Colpix. After a long layoff when he became a junior high school teacher in Los Angeles, Campi's 1980 return to vinyl on Rollin' Rock, "Rockin' at the Ritz," kicked off a series of releases that celebrate the timeless charm of savage rockabilly rhythms. —BD

○ **Gone Gone Gone! / ROUNDER** 1986
Latter-day, retro-rockabilly from a performer active at the genre's beginnings. —BD

CAN

Avant-garde. Experimental avant-garde combo from Germany. Through their numerous albums released from 1968 to the late 70s, Can paved the way for scores of postpunk groups, including Public Image Ltd. and Joy Division. —JF

Monster Movie / ENIGMA-RESTLESS 1969
Beat-heavy and guitar-driven drones dominate Can's second album. A taste of the tranced eclecticism to come. —MB

Tago Mago / ENIGMA-RESTLESS 1971
All of their seemingly disparate influences are balanced and blended here, with the addition of vocalist Damo Suzuki. —MB

Ege Bamyasi / ENIGMA-RESTLESS 1972
Funky, urgent, and experimental at their 1972 peak, this documents a band that is still ahead of our time. —MB

Future Days / ENIGMA-RESTLESS 1973
Long, jazzy excursions with few vocal moments. Uncharacteristic but engaging. —MB

Soon over Babaluma / ENIGMA-RESTLESS 1974
The band at its most stripped-down potency. But without Damo, they have a new sound. —MB

Unlimited Edition / ELEKTRA 1976
Studio outtakes from Can's history up to 1975. Fascinating electronic and ethnic musical excursions. —MB

Saw Delight / ELEKTRA 1977
This effort is a nice mix of trance/groove instrumentals, ethnic sampling, and silly vocals in English. —MB

○ **Cannibalism 1 / ENIGMA-RESTLESS** 1978
A sampler of early tracks up to 1974. Many of their most focused grooves and stylistic extremes are here. —MB

CANNED HEAT

Blues/rock. A hard-luck blues band of the 60s, founded by Al Wilson and Bob Hite. They seemed to be on the right track and played all the right festivals (including Monterey and Woodstock, making it very prominently into the documentaries about both) but somehow never found a lasting audience. Wilson died under mysterious (probably drug-related causes) circumstances in 1970, and Hite carried on with various reconstituted versions of the band until his death in 1981, from a heart seizure just before a show. —BE

○ **Best of Canned Heat / CAPITOL** 1972
An okay collection that is really all anyone but the most serious fan needs to have. The EMI British import version has superior sound quality and content. —BE

CANNIBAL CORPSE

Heavy metal. New York's Cannibal Corpse is one of the most extreme examples of death-metal. Song titles like "Butchered at Birth" and "A Skull Full of Maggots" pretty much tell the story. —JB

○ **Butchered at Birth / CAROLINE** 1991
Death-metal and grindcore taken to the extreme; the album has been banned in parts of Europe and the US. —JB

THE CAPITOLS

Soul. The energetic Detroit-based Capitols capitalized on mid-60s R&B dance fever with one of the most memorable entries of the genre, "Cool Jerk." Successful local producer Ollie McLaughlin signed the trio — lead singer Sam George, Donald Norman (who wrote most of the group's material under his real surname of Storball), and Richard Mitchell — to his Karen logo, and the irresistible "Cool Jerk" made them an overnight sensation. After a couple more chart entries later that year, the trio faded quickly. George was murdered on March 17, 1982. —BD

○ **Golden Classics / COLLECTABLES**
Dance-oriented mid-60s Detroit soul, with the notable classic "Cool Jerk." –BD

THE CAPRIS

Doo-wop. The only major Capris hit, the romantic "There's a Moon Out Tonight," is a New York street-corner harmony classic. Doo-wop was back in fashion by 1961, and it was no longer limited to R&B aggregations. Led by Nick Santo (born Nick Santamaria in 1941), the Capris named themselves after the Isle of Capri in Italy. The Queens, NY, natives originally cut "There's a Moon Out Tonight" for the obscure Planet imprint in 1958, but when the song was reissued on Lost Nite (and eventually on Old Town) it became a national smash its second time around in early 1961. After many moons out of the spotlight, the Capris came back triumphantly in 1981 with an album on Ambient Sound and an appearance on the PBS-TV series "Soundstage." –BD

○ **There's a Moon out Again! / AMBIENT SOUND**   1982
Recorded in 1982, live to two-track, here's a perfect example of what a great modern-day doo-wop album should be. –CK

CAPTAIN BEEFHEART   *b* 1964

Alternative, psychedelic. Drawing from gut-bucket Delta blues, free jazz, bare-boned rock, and the dissonance of 20th-century avant-garde chamber music, Captain Beefheart (born Don Van Vliet) and the Magic Band never sold many records, but they influenced many alternative artists, including Devo, XTC, Pere Ubu, and Sonic Youth.
Beefheart, an accomplished multi-instrumentalist, exhibited a vocal range that (some claim) spanned seven-and-a-half octaves, at times sounding like an utterly crazed incarnation of Howlin' Wolf. The first lineup of the Magic Band included Ry Cooder, and some of their first recordings on A&M were actually produced by future Bread founder David Gates.
Longtime friend and occasional musical cohort Frank Zappa signed Beefheart to his Straight label, allowing them complete artistic freedom. The result was the groundbreaking *Trout Mask Replica*.
Since then, Beefheart has put out a dozen albums, either with the Magic Band, with Zappa, or solo. Among those highlights are *Clear Spot, Bat Chain Puller, Doc at the Radar Station*, and *Ice Cream for Crow*. –RC

★ **Trout Mask Replica / REPRISE**   1969
Originally released and produced by Frank Zappa as a double album on his Bizarre/Straight label, *Trout Mask Replica* is the definitive Captain Beefheart album. To some, it is just plain weird, perhaps even anti-music. To others, it is blues with a warp or rock & roll at the absolute cutting edge. Deeply rooted in blues and jazz, the Captain taught each member of the Magic Band their extremely complex individual parts over the course of a year. Playful and challenging at the same time, rhythmically kinetic, poetically beautiful, it is an absolute masterpiece. –RB

Lick My Decals Off Baby / ENIGMA   1970
The bookend release to *Trout Mask Replica*, this time produced by the Captain himself. Sample title "The Smithsonian Institute Blues (The Big Dig)" should give you a sense that this is not an ordinary rock & roll record. Just a shade less essential than *Trout Mask Replica*. –RB

○ **Mirror Man / ONE WAY**   1971
An early version of the Captain's Magic Band, recorded live in Los Angeles probably in 1968 (the cover says 1965, but that is undoubted erroneous). Stunning extended versions of four Beefheart originals, including his Robert Johnson-inspired "Tarotplane." –RB

Spotlight Kid/Clear Spot / WARNER   1972
The Spotlight Kid (1972) and *Clear Spot* (1973) have been released on one CD. The Captain became slightly more accessible on these two early-70s releases, accenting the rock & roll ingredients. Slide guitar abounds on some of the most asymmetrical riffs imaginable throughout *The Spotlight Kid*. The lyrics are just as playful. *Clear Spot* is the Captain at his most balanced — accessible without deserting the avant-garde. "Big-Eyed Beans from Venus" became one of his all-time classics. –RB

Shiny Beast (Bat Chain Puller) / ENIGMA   1978
The Captain's comeback album, with the second edition of the Magic Band. As good as *Clear Spot* or *The Spotlight Kid*, with a slightly different temperament and a touch of synthesizer. –RB

☆ **Doc at the Radar Station / VIRGIN**   1980
The masterpiece of the Captain's late-70s/early-80s resurrection. This time, the new Magic Band had coalesced into an ensemble of frightening power. Cross-rhythms abut each other in some of the most hyperkinetic settings imaginable. There's not a weak song or performance to be found. Buy this. –RB

CAPTAIN & TENNILLE

Pop. Vibrant, relentlessly upbeat harmonies made Captain (born Daryl Dragon, Aug 27, 1942) & Tennille (born Toni Tennille, May 8, 1943) stars during the latter half of the 70s. Dragon, dubbed the "Captain" because of his distinctive headgear, had played keyboards with the Beach Boys prior to teaming with his wife. Their first hit on A&M, the buoyant "Love Will Keep Us Together," was a million-selling chart-topper in 1975, and a reissue of their 1974 single "The Way I Want to Touch You" also went gold. The couple hung three more gold records in their den in 1976 — "Lonely Night (Angel Face)," "Shop Around," and Willis Alan Ramsey's "Muskrat Love" — and that was enough for ABC-TV to install them as hosts of their own variety program. "Do That to Me One More Time" was the last #1 item for the pair in 1979. –BD

○ **Captain & Tennille's Greatest Hits / A&M**   1977
A solid collection of all of their mid-70s hits. –STE

CARCASS

Grindcore. England's Carcass assisted in a revival of the death-metal genre while introducing the new grindcore style. –JB

○ **Symphonies of Sickness / RELATIVITY**   1989
Hi-tech grindcore. Very fast and very wicked; not for the squeamish. An introduction to grindcore. –JB

MARIAH CAREY   *b* 1970

Pop, dance-pop. In 1990 mainstream, soulful pop-diva Mariah Carey came onto the scene with quite a splash, due to her stratospheric mega-octave vocal range — à la Minnie Ripperton. With the aid of considerable promotional muscle from her label (Sony), Carey has become one of the most successful female singers of the 90s. –RC

○ **Mariah Carey / CBS**   1990
Carey sold over five million copies of her debut, which featured ballads and R&B hits like the Grammy-winning "Vision of Love." –DDC

Emotions / CBS   1991
Carey continues to crank out the hits with her blend of dance, pop, and R&B. The album includes the smash hits "Emotions" and "Make It Happen." –DDC

BELINDA CARLISLE   *b* 1958

Pop. Former lead singer of the early-80s all-female group, the Go-Go's, Belinda Carlise has taken her fresh-faced vibrato-laden sound from her bouncy girl-group pop into a more mainstream direction. She has continued to do well on the singles charts with "Mad about You" (#3), "I Get Weak" (#2), and the #1 "Heaven Is a Place on Earth." –RC

○ **Heaven on Earth / MCA**   1987
Her commercial peak, containing "I Get Weak," "Circle in the Sand," and the title track. –DH

ERIC CARMEN   *b* 1949

Rock/pop. Eric Carmen was the lead vocalist and songwriter of the Raspberries, an early-70s band heavily influenced by mid-60s pop, especially the Beatles. For his 1975 self-titled debut album, Carmen looked even farther into the past, to the early 20th century. His two hit singles, the heavily produced ballads "All by Myself" and "Never Gonna Fall in Love Again," were based on pieces by Russian classical composer Serge Rachmaninoff. The rest of the album and Carmen's subsequent, less commercially successful albums were a pastiche of classic pop styles. Carmen didn't enjoy a big commercial success again until 1987's "Hungry Eyes," from the "Dirty Dancing" concert tour. –KMC

Eric Carmen / ARISTA   1975
Carmen achieved far greater success with his debut solo album than he ever had with his old group, the Raspberries. In part this was because, freed from the restrictions of leading a rock band, he could indulge his taste in big, lush ballads. That's what he did here, especially on the album's three Top 40 hits, one of which, "All by Myself," was a gold-selling #2 hit. –WR

○ **The Best of Eric Carmen / ARISTA**   1988
This album lacks Carmen's 1988 hit "Make Me Lose Control," but it does sample six of the eight singles-chart entries he enjoyed from 1975 to 1980, plus interesting album cuts such as "Hey Deanie," the Shaun Cassidy hit written by Carmen, and, of course, his comeback hit, "Hungry Eyes," from the *Dirty Dancing* soundtrack. –WR

KIM CARNES   ♭1945

Pop, singer/songwriter. The raspy-voiced singer's atmospheric #1 smash, "Bette Davis Eyes," was cowritten by Jackie DeShannon. Carnes was once a member of the New Christy Minstrels with Kenny Rogers, who gave her welcome exposure in 1980 with their duet "Don't Fall in Love with a Dreamer." Later that year, a Carnes cover of the Miracles' "More Love" was a smash. She scored numerous pop hits throughout the decade and experimented with country in 1988. –BD

○ **Mistaken Identity / CAPITOL**   1981
A successful pop-rock album, featuring the smash "Bette Davis Eyes," which held the top position on the pop charts for nine weeks. –BC

THE CARPENTERS

Pop. Between 1969 and 1981, the brother-and-sister duo, comprising Richard (b Oct 15, 1946) and Karen Carpenter (b Mar 2, 1950 - d Feb 4, 1983), made twenty sweet trips to the Top 40 singles charts with their ultra-sweet light pop featuring Karen's wholesome, even-tempered alto voice. During the first half of the 70s, the Carpenters were one of pop's most successful acts with twelve Top Ten hits, including "Top of the World" (#1), "(They Long to Be) Close to You" (#1), "We've Only Just Begun" (#2), "Rainy Days and Mondays" (#2), "Superstar" (#2), "Hurting Each Other" (#2), "Yesterday Once More" (#2), "For All We Know" (#3), and "Sing" (#3). –RC

○ **Yesterday Once More / A&M**   1985
A 2-CD set with 27 songs. Includes mostly their big hits, like "We've Only Just Begun" and "Mr. Postman," but there are a few sleeper cuts too. –BC

JAMES CARR   ♭1942

R&B, soul. Considered to be among the very greatest of "deep" Southern male soul singers, James Carr's succession of R&B hits on the Memphis Goldwax label were all gems of "country" soul, that wonderful 60s marriage of Southern Black R&B vocalists with songs written in a country format and played mostly by White musicians. Carr's dark, gospel-inflected style, marked by a subtle, rich voice that is almost frightening in its intensity and range, has been compared to that of Otis Redding and Percy Sledge; many reviewers would class him above even these formidable peers. "At the Dark End of the Street," the first songwriting collaboration between Dan Penn and Chips Moman, is Carr's undisputed masterpiece. Also

recorded by Aretha Franklin, Clarence Carter, Linda Ronstadt, and Ry Cooder, it is the quintessential country-soul take on adulterous love.
Carr's career initially was short; Goldwax ceased operation in 1969, and Carr cut only one other single for Atlantic in 1971; however, he has recently emerged from retirement with a new album on Goldwax. His work stands at the apex of 60s soul — with Aretha, Otis, Percy, and Wilson — essential stuff! –CO

☆ **You Got My Mind Messed Up / VIVID SOUND**
A somewhat pricey Japanese import, with its companion *A Man Needs a Woman*, of all the great Goldwax gems. Includes the classic "At the Dark End of the Street," the achingly beautiful "These Ain't Raindrops," plus 19 more. Until a cheaper reissue comes along, this is absolutely essential. –CO

A Man Needs a Woman / VIVID SOUND
Companion Japanese import to *You Got My Mind Messed Up*, this completes the Goldwax sides. Two selections from Carr's first album, plus nine more — includes the great "Pouring Water on a Drowning Man." No duplication of titles with *You Got My Mind Messed Up*. Again, pricey but essential. –CO

Take Me to the Limit / GOLDWAX   1991
Carr's comeback, on a resurrected Goldwax label. Doesn't quite live up to his 60s stuff — maybe nothing could — but it is good contemporary Southern soul in the classic vein, and it's great to have him back! –CO

WYNONA CARR   ♭1924

R&B. One of the top gospel artists on the Specialty label during the early 50s, Carr later made some fine R&B. Born in Cleveland, Carr moved to Detroit and joined Rev. C. L. Franklin's New Bethel Baptist Church Choir. She began cutting gospel as Sister Wynona Carr for Los Angeles-based Specialty in 1949, enjoying success with "The Ball Game." Carr went secular in 1955, rocking out on "Boppity Bop (Boogity Bop)" and "Nursery Rhyme Rock." Her lone R&B chart item in 1957, the bluesy "Should I Ever Leave Again," was covered by rockabilly great Gene Vincent. –BD

○ **Jump Jack Jump! / SPECIALTY**   1985
The ex-gospel singer's secular rockers from the mid 50s. –BD

PAUL CARRACK   ♭1951

Rock/pop. Despite a distinctive, soulful singing style, British keyboardist Paul Carrack's most popular work has not been done under his own name. He is the voice on Ace's "How Long," Squeeze's "Tempted," and Mike & the Mechanics' "The Living Years." Carrack finally began to score his own hits in the late 80s. –WR

○ **One Good Reason / CAPITOL**   1987
The third of Carrack's four solo albums of the 80s is the best-realized showcase for his soulful vocals. It produced four singles-chart entries, the most successful of which was the Top Ten hit "Don't Shed a Tear," Carrack's first big hit under his own name. –WR

JIM CARROLL   ♭1950

Alternative rock, singer/songwriter. New York poet and rock & roll frontman Carroll published *The Basketball Diaries*, an influential book of poetry, and recorded during the early 80s, bringing his cryptic, junkie-framed lyrics to jagged, Big Apple punk. "People Who Died" was his only hit. –JF

○ **Catholic Boy / ATLANTIC**   1980
Inspired by beat poets, basketball, and the New York street hustle, Carroll took his tales from the printed pages to the punk-rock stage. –JT

THE CARS

New-wave, rock/pop. The Cars were one of the most popular rock bands in America between 1978 and 1985. Formed in Boston in 1976, the quintet was Rick Ocasek (guitar and vocals), Ben Orr (bass and vocals), Greg Hawkes (keyboards),

Elliot Easton (guitar), and David Robinson (drums). Their 1978 debut album *The Cars*, which typified their sleek sound — new-wave energy matched to tight rhythms, disembodied vocals by Ocasek and Orr, and an affection for the sound of 60s bubblegum music, was an immediate success, spawning the singles "Just What I Needed" and "My Best Friend's Girl." After turning out million-selling albums in 1979 (*Candy-O*), 1980 (*Panorama*), and 1981 (*Shake It Up*), the group members took a breather for solo albums before returning for their biggest album yet, *Heartbreak City* (featuring the hits "You Might Think," "Magic," and "Drive") in 1984. *Door to Door* (1987) marked a falloff in the band's popularity, and they split soon after, with Ocasek so far the most prominent solo star. –WR

☆ **The Cars / ELEKTRA**   1978
On the heels of new-wave, this debut album for the Cars was a mechanized rock delight, its music spare and precise yet undeniably catchy, with sly references to the Beatles and Tommy James & the Shondells. Ocasek's and Orr's vocals sounded oddly dispassionate, as if they were being sung in a foreign language. –WR

★ **Greatest Hits / ELEKTRA**   1985
Ultimately, the Cars were a singles band. Here are those singles, including the biggest ones, "Drive," "Shake It Up," "You Might Think," and "Tonight She Comes." –WR

CARLENE CARTER

Rock & roll, country rock. Carlene Carter, daughter of June Carter, continued the musical tradition of the Carter Family while expanding beyond the realms of traditional country into rock and pop. Her best solo efforts have reflected the charm of the band Rockpile (thanks in no small part to ex-husband Nick Lowe's input as producer) and rockabilly. –RC

○ **Musical Shapes / WARNER**   1980
This is Carter's masterpiece to date. Great songs and production that could easily fit into today's climate of country radio. –CK

CLARENCE CARTER   b 1936

R&B, soul. A blind soul singer whose numerous hits of the late 60s and early 70s epitomized the Muscle Shoals rhythm & blues sound, Carter hit the big time with his Atlantic single "Patches" (1970) and won a lasting place in the annals of Southern soul with others like "Slip Away" and "Too Weak to Fight." In 1981 Carter broke out of a dry spell with the Venture album *Let's Burn,* featuring a track called "Workin' (On a Love Building)" which set the theme for much of what was to follow: robust, lascivious lovemaking boasts. More recent tracks such as his salacious reworking of Tampa Red's "Love Me with a Feeling" and the jukebox favorite "Strokin'" (too risqué for some radio stations) further solidified the carnal Carter image. Still primarily a soul/R&B singer, Carter has incorporated more hard blues elements in his music recently than in the Muscle Shoals days, despite his new and unblues-minded penchant for playing and programming all the instruments on his albums. –JON

The Best of Clarence Carter / ICHIBAN / BB 13   1972
A selection of Carter's lascivious recent output on Ichiban Records. –BD

○ **Snatchin' It Back / RHINO-ATLANTIC**   1992
Snatchin' It Back - The Best of Clarence Carter is a great compilation, spotlighting Carter's stellar guitar work and trademark vocals on classics like "Slip Away," "Too Weak to Fight," and "Lookin' for a Fox." His great "Tell Daddy" (covered by Etta James as "Tell Mama") is included. Dave Marsh contributes the liner notes. Soul music at its funky best, and *the* compilation to own if you're a Carter fan. –CO

PETER CASE

Singer/songwriter, folk/rock, country rock, roots-rock. A Los Angeles journeyman rocked with the early-80s LA band the

Plimsouls before taking off on a pseudo-folkie singer/songwriter solo career. –JF

Peter Case / GEFFEN   1986
Case's debut suffers from diverse stylistic jumps, but its best songs (seven, by my count) are compassionate, intelligent, and intriguing. –JF

○ **The Man with the Blue ... / GEFFEN**   1989
On *The Man with the Blue Postmodern Fragmented Neo-traditionalist Guitar*, Case sticks to one style, a Mellencampish rocker oozing with compassion. This beats the debut through the range of Case's lyrical concerns and his intense vocals. –JF

THE CASTELLES

R&B, doo-wop. Sporting the high tenor lead of George Grant, the Philadelphia-based Castelles cut a series of beautiful doo-wop items during the mid 50s. The group was formed in 1949 and signed with Grand Records in 1953, debuting with "My Girl Awaits Me." Specializing in ballads such as "This Silver Ring" (written by 60s soul producer Jerry Ragovoy) and "Heavenly Father," the Castelles briefly moved to Atco in 1956 before calling it quits. –BD

○ **Sweet Sounds of the Castelles / COLLECTABLES**   1987
Dreamy mid-50s Philly doo-wop. –BD

NICK CAVE

Alternative rock. New-wave vocal interpreter Nick Cave assembled the Bad Seeds after his previous band, the Birthday Party, fell apart. Literate, bluesy, and arty, this is post punk with ambitions. –JD

The First Born Is Dead / HOMESTEAD   1986
Recorded with the Bad Seeds, this album contains angst directly influenced by early American folk-blues. –JD

○ **From Her to Eternity / ENIGMA-RESTLESS**   1988
Desperate and ominous, this is a chilling love letter. –JD

Kicking Against the Pricks / HOMESTEAD   1988
All covers, all unique, all recorded with the Bad Seeds. More rock of your worst nightmare. –JD

THE CAVEDOGS

Power-pop. This Boston trio incorporates early Who, Badfinger, Beatles, and Big Star into an updated, hard-hitting, Anglo-power-pop sound. –RC

○ **Joyrides for Shut-Ins / CAPITOL**   1988
Exuberant early-Who-style melodic bash-ola rock. Good songs and loads of attitude make this a fine choice for lovers of guitar-heavy Anglo-pop-rock. –RC

THE CELLOS

Doo-wop. A five-man group formed in 1955 in Manhattan, influenced by local high school stars (the Kodoks, the Crests, the Schoolboys, and the Keynotes). After-school harmonizing led to the Cellos making a $4 demo, which in true Hollywood movie tradition got them a recording contract! Though their moment in the spotlight was relatively brief, hitting the charts with their first single — "Rang Tang Ding Dong (I Am the Japanese Sandman)" — their street-corner sound nonetheless exemplifies New York doo-wop in its earliest stages. –CK

○ **Rang Tang Ding Dong / RELIC**   1992
An excellent CD compilation of all their best Apollo sides, including unreleased material. Contains the title cut, plus "Juicy Crocodile," "The Be Bop Mouse," and "You Took My Love." –CK

CELTIC FROST

Heavy metal. The eccentric heavy metal band Celtic Frost was influential until they adopted normal metal clothed in a glam image. Their early albums feature their best work. –JB

To Mega Therion / NOISE   1986
Avant-garde heavy metal, with ventures into thrash- and

death-metal. Arguably their best album, along with *Morbid Tales*. —JB

○ **Morbid Tales/Emperor's Return / NOISE** 1988
These two records, considered two of the best of the 80s, made a big impact on thrash- and death-metal. Essential. —JB

EXENE CERVENKA

Folk/rock, roots-rock. Exene (Christine) Cervenka was the co-lead singer and songwriter of the Los Angeles punk group X for most of the 80s. When the band took a hiatus in 1987, Cervenka turned to a solo career. She has thus far released two albums in more of a folk-rock style on Rhino. —WR

○ **Old Wives' Tales / RHINO** 1988
Exene Cervenka's first solo album after the breakup of X is closer in spirit to the folkie-country album she and some friends made as the Knitters than to the punk-rock throttle of her former band. Acoustic guitars and calm singing of highly poetic lyrics are the order of the day, and Cervenka makes a smooth transition to singer/songwriter. (The followup, 1990's *Running Sacred*, is more of the same and also recommended.) —WR

PETER CETERA b 1944

Pop. Cetera was a vocalist, bassist, and songwriter with Chicago from 1967 to 1985, singing lead on many of the group's major ballad hits. He then launched a solo career that has resulted in more hits in the same style. —WR

○ **One More Story / WARNER** 1988
Cetera launched his solo career playing music very close to the soaring ballads of his days with Chicago. He switched gears on this album, working with Madonna producer Patrick Leonard on a more uptempo approach that lost none of his usual melodic feel for its dance rhythms. —WR

CHAD & JEREMY

Pop, British Invasion. This soft-pop duo from England arrived during the first wave of the British Invasion in 1964. Their image and sound echoed (but was softer than) Peter & Gordon, who already had a couple of big hits under their belts when Chad & Jeremy scored with their debut "Yesterday's Gone" (#21). "A Summer Song," their second single, broke the US Top Ten at #7. Several other hits followed, and Chad & Jeremy became fixtures on TV shows like "Hullabaloo." In keeping with the times, they released one of the first "concept" albums, *Of Cabbages and Kings*, in 1967. They broke up shortly thereafter, with Jeremy pursuing an acting career and Chad continuing in music. —RC

○ **Best of Chad & Jeremy / KTEL** 1985
A poor-sounding rip-off budget CD. Wait for the Capitol and Columbia best-of's coming in 1992. —JT

EUGENE CHADBOURNE

Avant-garde. Eugene Chadbourne is perhaps the most unusual guitarist playing today, fusing elements of country, folk, blues, rock, and free jazz into a challenging, impressive, and downright *weird* postmodern amalgam. —ED

Country Protest / FUNDAMENTAL-SAVE 1985
The warped guitarist/vocalist/deconstructionist puts original political tunes and covers of several 60s staples through his horror-show wringer. Experimental to the max. —JT

Corpses of Foreign War / FUNDAMENTAL-SAVE 1986
Radical protest tunes radically rendered, with members of the Violent Femmes helping out. —JT

Vermin of the Blues / FUNDAMENTAL-SAVE 1987
With backing from frantic Austin rockers Evan Johns & the H-Bombs, and originals like "Fried Chicken for Richard Speck" meeting covers of Count Basie and the Count 5, this is Eugene at his most perverse. —JT

○ **LSD C&W / FUNDAMENTAL-SAVE** 1987
The ultimate Chadbourne, featuring medleys of the Beatles,

Roger Miller, and Burl Ives, plus much more insanity filtered through post-avant-garde brilliance. —JT

Dear Eugene / PLACEBO 1987
Dear Eugene, What You Did Was Not Very Nice, So I Am Going to Kill... is live, solo, extremely cool. Who else would construct a Bacharach/Manson tune? —JT

There'll Be No Tears Tonight / FUNDAMENTAL 1987
Country fans expecting straight, faithful versions of these covers of Roger Miller, Hank Williams, and Merle Haggard will be in shock. Imagine honky-tonk as free jazz, and that's what you'll get. —JT

CHAGALL GUEVARA

Rock & roll. Formed by a trio of iconoclasts from the contemporary Christian music biz, Chagall Guevara is an idiosyncratic blend of very sophisticated songwriting (in its lyrics and arrangements) delivered with an exhilarating punkish aggressiveness.
Lead vocalist Steve Taylor spews out the kind of well-aimed venom that made early Graham Parker so fine. All this is backed up by a thickly orchestrated wall of guitars and a bash-ola rhythm section. —RC

○ **Chagall Guevara / MCA** 1991
This audacious self-titled debut is fiercely passionate, intelligent, and darkly humorous. Matt Wallace (The Replacements, Faith No More) produced this album without the use of any digital reverbs or samples, just miking natural room sounds. Performancewise, Chagall's guitar-heavy delivery is predisposed toward dissonance, falling somewhere in the cracks between progressive AOR and conservative college/alternative rock. —RC

CHAIRMEN OF THE BOARD

R&B, soul. One of the most dynamic acts to emerge on Holland/Dozier/Holland's Invictus label after the legendary songwriters exited Motown. Lead Norman "General" Johnson had previously fronted the Showmen, who hit in 1961 with "It Will Stand," cut in New Orleans. Johnson's pinched, intense vocal delivery powered the pleading "Give Me Just a Little More Time," the first smash for the Chairmen in late 1969, although Danny Woods handled lead duty on the group's biggest R&B seller, "Pay to the Piper." Johnson, who wrote "Patches" for the group's first album only to see Clarence Carter score the hit, departed in 1974 to start a solo career. —BD

○ **Greatest Hits / HDH** 1973
Driving Detroit soul of the late 60s/early 70s. General Johnson's pungent lead vocals give this quartet a unique sound. Their notable hit was 1970's "Give Me Just a Little More Time." —BD

THE CHALLENGERS

Rock/pop, rock & roll. This West Coast instrumental group, firmly rooted in the surf style of Dick Dale and the Ventures, cashed in on the surf and hot-rod music craze of the early 60s. Their albums became staples of the 99-cent bargain bins for years afterward but are now highly sought-after collector's items. —CK

○ **Surfbeat / VAULT** 1963
Their debut album is a good representation of the band. Out of print and highly collectible in its original colored-vinyl format. —CK

Surfing / VAULT 1963
Their second album: gas & go instrumentals reverbed to the max. Companion piece to the above. —CK

THE CHAMBERS BROTHERS

R&B, psychedelic, soul. Originally a Black gospel group from Mississippi, the Chamber Brothers packed up and moved to California and became active in the developing folk and blues movements. Their biggest claim to fame was the 11-minute psychedelic epic "Time Has Come Today," which was a #4 pop hit in 1967. In spite of their gospel roots and their tendency to cover soulful standards like "I Can't Turn You Loose" (#37) and "People Get Ready," the Chamber Brothers' sound gravitated more toward a spirited raw rock approach than toward R&B. –RC

○ **Greatest Hits / CBS** 1971
Contains only two hits, the endless 1968 psychedelic garage-grunge hit "Time Has Come Today" plus "I Can't Turn You Loose," which doesn't touch Otis Redding's fiery version. Most of this doesn't hold up too well, but it is the best sampler available. –RC

CHAMELEONS

Alternative pop. A Manchester, UK, intellectual pop outfit that was slightly ahead of its time. Writing stylish, moody guitar-swirled pop, the Chameleons set the stage for numerous UK bands to come, never really reaping the benefits of their (often much better) music. –JD

○ **Script of the Bridge / STATIK** 1983
With dark, dense but heavily melodic songs equaling the strength of Echo & the Bunnymen and Joy Division, this is a largely undiscovered 80s classic. –SA

What Does Anything Mean? Basically? / STATIK 1985
Their second studio album solidly sustains the *Script* formula. –SA

CHAMPAIGN

Urban R&B, soul. Champaign took its name from its home city of Champaign, IL. The group was an interracial septet comprising singers Pauli Carman and Rena Jones, guitarist Howard Reeder, keyboardists Michael Day and Dana Walden, bassist Michael Reed, and percussionist Rocky Maffitt. The group hit a commercial peak with its 1981 debut album, *How 'Bout Us*, whose title track was a hit single (Top Five in the UK and on the US R&B chart). Followups included *Modern Heart* (1983) (which includes the #2 R&B hit "Try Again") and *Woman in Flames* (1984), featuring the R&B Top Ten hit "Off and On Love." –WR

○ **How 'Bout Us / CBS** 1981
Smooth, well-crafted pop-R&B topped by the creamy vocals of Pauli Carman and Rena Jones. This debut is a pop hybrid that sounds very promising, though the group never followed through adequately. –WR

JAMES CHANCE & THE CONTORTIONS

New-wave. An acerbic player influenced by Ornette Coleman, rock saxophonist Chance was the darling of NYC's late-70s new-wave scene. –DMAC

○ **Buy the Contortions / ZE** 1979
A wacky fusion of off-kilter rock and the Ornette Coleman-influenced saxophonist Chance. Lots of fun, but it's for special tastes. Includes "Contort Yourself" and "I Don't Want to Be Happy." –MGN

Live in New York / ROIR 1981
Top-notch rock from the new-wave period. –MGN

GENE CHANDLER b 1937

Soul. A Chicago soul journeyman who worked under the tutelage of Curtis Mayfield during the mid 60s. Chandler's understated, balladesque style is best heard on his 1962 Vee Jay hit, "Duke of Earl." –JF

● **Duke of Earl / BLACK TULIP** 1962
The sound quality isn't top-notch, but this budget-priced CD contains the Chicagoan's classic early-60s work for Vee Jay and Constellation Records. –BD

The Gene Chandler Situation / MER 1970
Slick Chicago soul from 1970. Includes the smash "Groovy Situation." –BD

CHANGE

Urban R&B, soul. An Italian and American group formed by producer Jacques Fred Petrus; Luther Vandross was featured on their early albums. –ED

○ **The Glow of Love / WARNER** 1980
Elegant dance-music arrangements with feathery leads from Luther Vandross. Includes Change's only Top 40 hit, "A Lover's Holiday." –RW

CHANNELS

Doo-wop. The obscure New York doo-wop quintet hit it sorta big in 1956 with "The Closer You Are," recorded for the Beltone label. –JF

○ **Greatest Hits / RELIC** 1990
Velvety 50s New York doo-wop, led by the distinctive falsetto of Earl Lewis. –BD

THE CHANTELS

R&B, doo-wop. An early female R&B quartet led by powerhouse vocalist Arlene Smith, whose vocals on their 1957 hit "Maybe" remain some of the most moving ever recorded. –JF

○ **Best of the Chantels / RHINO** 1990
One of the leading girl groups of the late 50s, distinguished by Arlene Smith's impassioned leads. –BD

HARRY CHAPIN 1942-1981

Singer/songwriter. Singer/songwriter Harry Chapin made a solid career out of essentially setting short stories to music. His most popular tracks were "Taxi" (#24), "W.O.L.D." (#34), "Cat's in the Cradle" (#1), and "Sequel" (#23), which was a followup to the story in "Taxi."
Chapin's music possessed a folksy intimacy, further enhanced by the stirring chamber-style string work. His voice, while limited, conveyed the sincerity of his feelings, in spite of his heavy-handed tendency to proselytize. Chapin did put his money where his mouth was, devoting much of his time and income to aid the hungry and socially disenfranchised. During his career, he raised over five million dollars for various causes. Chapin died in an auto accident on July 16, 1981, while on his way to do a benefit. –RC

Heads & Tales / ELEKTRA 1972
Chapin's breakthrough album, with "Taxi." –DH

○ **Anthology of Harry Chapin / ELEKTRA** 1985
A fine summing-up, featuring "Cat's in the Cradle," "Taxi," and others. –DH

TRACY CHAPMAN b 1964

Singer/songwriter. Tracy Chapman was the most successful folk-based performer to emerge in the 80s. Born in Cleveland, she won a scholarship to the Wooster School in Connecticut, then attended Tufts University. She began singing on street corners and in coffeehouses in the Boston area, then she signed with Elektra Records after graduating from college.
Chapman cut her debut album, prominently featuring her throaty alto and acoustic guitar, with minimal added instrumentation. Her songs were closely observed tales of lower-class life (the hit "Fast Car") and political rhetoric ("Talkin' 'Bout a Revolution"), sung compellingly. Released on April 1, 1988, *Tracy Chapman* became a #1 international hit, selling three million copies in the US and a reported 6 1/2 million more overseas. Chapman toured extensively behind it, including a series of Amnesty International benefits around the world. She won three 1988 Grammy Awards, including Best New Artist. *Crossroads*, her second album, was released in 1989 and was also a million-seller. Her third album, *Matters of the Heart*, was released in 1992. –WR

○ **Tracy Chapman / ELEKTRA** 1988
With her choked voice and acoustic guitar, Tracy Chapman reawakened social awareness and demonstrated the power of

folk music on her debut album, singing of homelessness and desperation and "Talkin' 'Bout a Revolution." Contains the Top Ten hit "Fast Car." –WR

CHARLATANS UK

Alternative pop. This English quintet emerged from the Manchester club scene in the late 80s/early 90s with organ-laced, 60s-style psychedelic pop music. –DDC

○ **Some Friendly / BEGGARS BANQUET**   1990
This British band combines 60s psychedelia with a 90s mentality, creating a strong retro-groove. –DDC

RAY CHARLES   ♭1930

R&B, soul. The seminal 50s Atlantic recordings of Ray Charles virtually defined the very essence of soul, and his radical early 60s R&B/country synthesis helped immeasurably to bridge the gap between the two idioms. If he isn't a certifiable genius, as is often claimed, Ray Charles is certainly one of the most influential musical figures of the 20th century.
Completely blind by age seven, Charles mastered the piano in his teens and, by 1948, was already recording in a Nat Cole/Charles Brown-derived style. But Charles hit upon a daring concept of combining joyous gospel rhythms with secular lyrics just about the time he signed with Atlantic, turning the musical world on its collective ear in the process. With his jazzy combo in place, Brother Ray sat down at the 88s and began racking up the hits during the mid 50s — "I've Got a Woman," "Hallelujah, I Love Her So," and, in 1959, the wondrous "What'd I Say," combining the call-and-response structure of the church with the sexually charged message of the blues. The number one R&B seller also showcased Charles's pioneering use of the electric piano.
When Charles signed with ABC-Paramount in 1960, he shifted gears entirely, delving deep into pop and country in his own inimitable style. Ray Charles epitomizes the soul idiom with his gospel-soaked vocals and keyboards, even though his recent recording activities have generally been confined to the country field (with the exception of those ubiquitous Diet Pepsi TV ads). –BD

Soul Brothers / ATLANTIC   1959
An early glimpse of the jazz side of Charles, with vibist Milt Jackson. –HD

Genius + Soul = Jazz / DCC   1961
A reissue of a memorable early-60s big-band session that produced the instrumental hit "One Mint Julep." –HD

○ **Modern Sounds ... / RHINO**   1962
Modern Sounds in Country & Western Music is historically important, and considered by most critics to be a classic, but I've always had mixed feelings about it. Charles's interpretations of songs previously recorded by Hank Williams, Eddy Arnold, Floyd Tillman, and Don Gibson are superb, but so often the arrangements by Marty Paich, Gerald Wilson, and Gil Fuller threaten to drown him in a sea of lachrymose bric-a-brac. "I Can't Stop Loving You" and "You Don't Know Me" were Top Ten pop and R&B. –RB

Live / ATLANTIC   1973
The intensity of the original hits, enhanced even further by the energy of a very responsive audience. –HD

☆ **His Greatest Hits - Vols. 1 & 2 / DUNHILL**   1987
These discs contain 40 tracks from Charles's ABC-Paramount tenure, covering the years 1960 through 1972. While under contract with ABC, Charles placed 51 singles on the *Billboard* charts. Most of the important ones are included here, alongside a few judiciously chosen album cuts. Styles range from country-soul to jazz to stone R&B. Digitally remixed and remastered by Charles and Steve Hoffman, the sound is a joy. Absolutely recommended. –RB

★ **The Birth of Soul / ATLANTIC**   1991
On three CDs, *The Birth of Soul* contains every R&B recording Ray Charles waxed while at Atlantic between 1952 and 1959. The early recordings are in the Charles Brown/Nat King Cole

"Sepia Sinatra" vein. The later recordings go a long way toward defining the birth of soul. Robert Palmer has contributed a superb set of liner notes, contextualizing both Charles and the recordings. The sound is state of the art. This is essential seminal American music. –RB

CHARTS

R&B, doo-wop. Despite never cracking *Billboard*'s R&B charts, "Deserie" by the Charts endures as a doo-wop classic. Formed in 1956, the group's manager, musician Les Cooper, got the Harlem quintet a contract with Danny Robinson's Everlast imprint. Fronted by Joseph Grier, the Charts released the mellow "Deserie" in 1957, backed with the rocking "Zoop." After a few more 45s for Everlast, the Charts disbanded in 1958. –BD

○ **Greatest Hits / COLLECTABLES**   1981
Late-50s harmonies from this talented Harlem doo-wop group. –BD

CHEAP TRICK

Rock & roll, power-pop. This Rockford, IL, quartet arrived at a time (the mid-70s) when FM rock was skidding toward its nadir and punk was emerging. With their audacious debut, Cheap Trick seemed like the panacea for those who loved melodic Anglo-rock and the crash-and-burn of *Live at Leeds*-period Who. Imagewise, Cheap Trick seemed to have their cake and eat it too, with their loony dicotomy of pretty boys and geeks. Rick Nielson's amphetamine nerd personna, with his formidable chops as a lead guitarist and songwriter, flew in the face of popular poseur guitar heros. For their second album, *In Color*, Cheap Trick did an about-face and delivered a collection of concise power-pop songs. Ever since, they've vacillated between mainstream hard rock and power ballads, with mixed results. –RC

☆ **Cheap Trick / CBS**   1977
A raucous debut loaded with brain-crunching rude noises and attitude, plundering all the right stuff (Beatles, Who, the Move). All this supports some primo rockers like "Hot Love," "He's a Whore," "Taxman, Mr. Thief," and "Oh Candy," which ranks as one of the great lost rock singles of the 70s. Subsequent albums sound tame next to this one. Without a doubt one of their best. –RC

In Color / CBS   1977
Their second album ditches boistcrous performances in favor of super-tight pop-rock, with hooks galore. All the same influences are there; it's just more mannered. The lightweight "I Want You to Want Me" became their first hit. Also check out "Big Eyes," "Clock Strikes Ten," and "You're All Talk." – RC

Heaven Tonight / CBS   1978
Since Cheap Trick had dispensed with the straight medicine after an excellent debut, this third album recalibrates the band's pop smarts with an impressive handful of tunes. "Surrender," in particular, is a classic. The band wears its good taste well, with a fine cover of the Move's "California Man." –RC

● **Live at Budokan / CBS**   1979
This concert album broke them into mass success, featuring improved performances of "I Want You to Want Me" and a thunderous reading of Fats Domino's "Ain't That a Shame." Any fan of this band should own this one. –RC

Dream Police / CBS   1979
With the big time upon them, Cheap Trick went for bigger-production sounds. Fortunately, it worked most of the time. The paranoid title cut is an effective, highly orchestrated rocker. Other notable tracks are the appealingly melodic (albeit wimpy) "Voices" and the no-frills rock of "I Know What I Want," complete with a great chorus you can shout to. In spite of its strengths, *Dream Police* marks the beginning of the band's creative decline. –RC

Next Position Please / CBS   1983
This release, produced by Todd Rundgren, is Trick's last

decent album, opening with a great Robin Zander original "I Can't Take It." "Borderline," "Next Position Please," and "Younger Girls" are all strong, but the Rundgren-penned "Heaven's Falling" is magnificent. –RC

Greatest Hits / CBS   1991
Hardly a passable collection, certainly not definitive by any standard. Nevertheless, it'll be good for those who prefer the band's more recent cookie-cutter hits, like "The Flame" and "Can't Stop Falling in Love." –RC

CHUBBY CHECKER   b 1941

R&B, rock/pop. He taught America how to twist. Not just the kids, who always learned the latest steps, but everyone — from society matrons and jetsetters to the proverbial man in the street.

Rock & roll was becoming complacent when Chubby Checker came along in 1960 with his note-for-note remake of Hank Ballard and the Midnighters' "The Twist" and got it moving again. The husky Philadelphia lad, known as Ernest Evans until Dick Clark's wife decided he resembled Fats Domino, had already waxed a few 45s for the local Parkway label, including a novelty called "The Class" that found him imitating Fats, Elvis, and even the Chipmunks. But it was "The Twist," a #1 hit not once but twice (in 1960 and 1961), that made him an international celebrity.

Checker quickly became the nation's leading dance specialist, introducing "The Hucklebuck," "The Fly," "Pony Time," and "Limbo Rock" to the gyrating masses and successfully recycling his initial routine into "Let's Twist Again" and "Slow Twistin'." While racking up monster sales figures for Parkway, Checker starred in a couple of quickie exploitation films, *Twist around the Clock* and *Don't Knock the Twist*, later trying his hand at folk songs when the twist fad finally began to fade. The British Invasion led to some lean years for Checker although he got a little revenge by charting with a cover of the Beatles tune "Back in the U.S.S.R." in 1969. But he continued to put on a high-energy show that inevitably led to that classic million-seller — and Chubby Checker proved every time out that he was still the king of the Twist. –BD

Chubby's Dance Party / KTEL-QWIL
The only CD by the Twist King currently in print. Probably not the original Cameo-Parkway versions. –BD

○ **Greatest Hits / EVEREST RECORD GROUP**   1972
The long out-of-print two-LP set contains all of the early-60s twist and related dance workouts that made this Philadelphian a star. –BD

CHER   b 1946

Rock/pop. After untying the knot with Sonny Bono in 1974, Cher developed into a pop icon of a magnitude many times brighter than during her 60s duet days with her husband. Even while married to Sonny, Cher was hitting the charts as a solo act with "Bang Bang (My Baby Shot Me Down)" in 1966 and "You Better Sit Down Kids" in 1967, both on Imperial, and her output on Kapp included the 1971 #1 hit "Gypsys, Tramps & Thieves." The gold records continued with "Half-Breed" in 1973 and "Dark Lady" in 1974, both chart-toppers on MCA. 1979's "Take Me Home" was Cher's last smash for eight years, but she wasn't idle, starring in the acclaimed motion pictures *Silkwood* and *The Witches of Eastwick* and winning the 1987 Best Actress Oscar for her role in *Moonstruck*. Cher roared back in 1989 with "After All," a duet with Peter Cetera, and the anthemic solo outing "If I Could Turn Back Time," both on Geffen. Whether she's hawking memberships for a health-club chain or tearing up a concert stage, Cher endures as one of the nation's premier celebrities. –BD

Heart of Stone / GEFFEN   1989
One of the most mature albums of Cher's career, focusing on relationships from a 40 year-old's perspective rather than a teenager's. Cuts include "If I Could Turn Back Time," "Just Like Jesse James," and a duet with Peter Cetera, "After All." –BC

○ **Bang Bang - My Baby Shot Me Down ... / EMI**   1991
Bang Bang - My Baby Shot Me Down - The Best of Cher collects more than twenty of Cher's 60s solo cuts on the Imperial label. There is the Motown-styled "Dream Baby," but it's mostly folk-pop including little-known gems like the pensive "She's Not Better Than Me." –BC

THE CHI-LITES

Soul. Ultra-smooth ballads were the specialty of the Chi-Lites, and they were one of the Windy City's hottest soul exports throughout most of the 70s. Changing their name from the Hi-Lites, the quartet reformed for a number of local firms before hitting in 1969 on Brunswick with "Give It Away." Lead Eugene Record's (b Dec 23, 1940) floating tenor caressed the R&B chart-toppers "Have You Seen Her" in 1971 and "Oh Girl" the next year, and the group scaled the soul playlists regularly through 1976, when Record went solo. Founding member Marshall Thompson keeps the group active today. –BD

○ **Greatest Hits / RHINO**   1992
Outstanding collection containing everything you need, including the hits "Oh Girl" and "Have You Seen Her." –JF

CHIC

Disco, funk. Chic was the best and most influential disco band of the latter half of the 70s, earning hits with both their own records and the outside productions of coleaders Nile Rodgers and Bernard Edwards. Beginning their career as the Big Apple Band, the group changed their name to Chic in 1977 after Walter Murphy & the Big Apple Band had a #1 hit with "A Fifth of Beethoven." Along with the change in name came a change in music, from fusion to disco. Edwards (bass), Rodgers (guitar), and Tony Thompson (drums) hired Norma Jean Wright and Alfa Anderson to sing, and they recorded a demo of "Dance Dance Dance." Atlantic picked it up in late 1977 after a series of rejections from other record labels; the single sold a million copies in one month, catapulting Chic into the forefront of the disco scene. After Wright left for a solo career, Luci Martin joined the band. Chic's biggest hits — "Le Freak" (#1), "I Want Your Love" (#7), and the "Good Times" (#1) — came in 1978-1979, and as disco started to fade, so did the group's popularity. Still, Chic's influence was apparent throughout the 80s; "Good Times" alone spawned Queen's hit "Another One Bites the Dust" (a complete rip-off), and Sugarhill Gang used the record as the foundation for "Rapper's Delight," arguably the first rap single. Nile Rodgers was one of the most successful producers of the early 80s, scoring hits with David Bowie's *Let's Dance*, Madonna's *Like A Virgin*, and Mick Jagger's solo debut, *She's the Boss*. Edwards's solo productions weren't as consistent as Rodgers's, but the Power Station's album (which featured Tony Thompson on drums) was a hit. Chic re-formed in 1992, but failed to recapture the fire of its glory days. –STE

☆ **Dance Dance Dance - Best of Chic / ATLANTIC**   1991
You think disco was nothing more than assembly-line funk and freeze-dried beats? Then you need to step into the crisp grooves and walloping boogie found on this stunning collection of Chic's 70s recordings. Such hits as "Good Times," "Dance Dance Dance," and "Le Freak" used the stylistic innovations of James Brown and Sly Stone as a blueprint for a new era of funk. Bernard Edwards's basslines are so provocative they seem to talk, while Nile Rodgers's skeletal guitar runs hark back to Steve Cropper's slashing style. Sure, the songs don't say much. Sure, the dance mixes collected here ramble on after about six minutes. But once you step into these grooves — grooves that influenced an entire generation of artists from David Byrne to Prince — you will realize that these were indeed good times. –JF

CHICAGO

Rock/pop. A rock band with a prominent horn section, Chicago was one of the most popular American groups of the 70s. By the second half of the decade, they were best known for ballads like "If You Leave Me Now." Their success continued with such material through the late 80s. –WR

Chicago Transit Authority / CBS 1969
The first rock & roll band to successfully integrate a horn section into its sound, Chicago (fresh from years on the Midwest bar circuit) demonstrated a wide versatility on its debut. The band seemed capable of playing everything from lounge music to hard rock, and here it mixed ballad material with gritty funk and psychedelic guitar, often on the same song. This time capsule of late-60s popular music features the hits "Does Anybody Really Know What Time It Is?," "Beginnings," and "Questions 67 And 68." –WR

Chicago II / CBS 1970
With its second double album (now on one CD), Chicago became even more ambitious and even more successful, mounting the extended "Suite for a Girl in Buchannon," from which were excerpted the hit singles "Make Me Smile" and "Colour My World." "25 or 6 to 4" is also featured on this album. –WR

Chicago V / CBS 1972
The group's avant-garde roots are explored on the set-opening "A Hit by Varèse," while the album also includes the autobiographical "Alma Mater" and the hits "Saturday in the Park" and "Dialogue." –WR

● **Chicago IX - Chicago's Greatest Hits / CBS** 1975
The biggest hits of Chicago's first five years of recording, including "Just You 'N' Me," "Feelin' Stronger Every Day," "Wishing You Were Here," "Call on Me," and "(I've Been) Searchin' So Long." –WR

Chicago - Greatest Hits-Vol. 2 / CBS 1981
This album chronicles Chicago's gradual transformation in the second half of the 70s into a group that produced big ballads, usually sung by Peter Cetera. And here they are, starting with "If You Leave Me Now" and continuing with "Baby, What a Big Surprise" and the nostalgic "Old Days." –WR

Greatest Hits - 1982-1989 / WARNER 1989
Chicago returned from a career dip in 1982 with "Hard to Say I'm Sorry" and continued to hit with power ballads, among them "Hard Habit to Break" and "You're the Inspiration," all sung by Peter Cetera. But the streak continued after Cetera departed in 1985, as Jason Scheff stepped in and Chicago went on to score hits like "Will You Still Love Me?," "I Don't Wanna Live without Your Love," and "Look Away," which are all heard here. –WR

○ **Group Portrait / CBS** 1991
If the two *Greatest Hits* collections don't look like adequate places to go, yet you want to have some Chicago in your collection, then *Group Portrait* is an extremely comprehensive boxed set that chronicles all the hits and important album tracks. You'll probably never find a more complete history on the band than that provided in the set's booklet. –RC

CHICKASAW MUDD PUPPIES

Alternative rock. Imagine a rickety-front-porch-style White blues duo filtered through Captain Beefheart and Michael Stipe (of R.E.M.), and you'd have Chickasaw Mud Puppies (Brant Slay, vocals, harmonica, stomp board, washboard, cowbell; Ben Reynolds, vocals, guitar, bass). So far, Stipe has assisted in production, teaming up with blues legend Willie Dixon for the fine *8-Track Stomp*. –RC

○ **8-Track Stomp / POLYGRAM** 1991
An improvement over their oddly engaging EP *White Dirt*, *8-Track Stomp* (produced by Willie Dixon and Michael Stipe) marries their "stomp music" to some better songs like "Superior," "Cold Blue," and "Moving So Fast." –RC

THE CHIFFONS

Pop. One of the few girl-groups not produced by Phil Spector, maybe because they didn't need him. These NYC gals talked tough and to the point about the intricacies of the heart, the ones filled with love and the ones sliced in half. Their best 60s hits are high points of the genre. –JF

○ **Best of the Chiffons / LAURIE**
Everything you need by this delicious ensemble, including some undeservedly obscure gems. –JF

TONI CHILDS

Singer/songwriter. Born in Orange, CA, Toni Childs grew up in a variety of locations around the US and lived in London for four years, where she had a song-publishing deal with Island Music. She then moved to Los Angeles, where she became involved with David Ricketts (of David + David) and collaborated on the soundtrack for the film *Echo Park* (1986). Her debut album, *Union*, was recorded in London, Paris, Los Angeles, and Africa, and reflected an interest in the music of Zimbabwe as well as more conventional singer/songwriter styles. It earned her an opening spot on a Bob Dylan tour and a Grammy nomination for Best Female Rock Vocal, as well as reaching #67 in the charts. Childs's followup, *House of Hope*, was released in 1991. –WR

○ **Union / A&M** 1988
Making her presence felt in the new wave of female singer/songwriters, Childs contrasts her vulnerable, dreamlike lyrics with a powerhouse booming alto voice. Includes the single "Don't Walk Away." –DDC

ALEX CHILTON

Alternative rock, rock & roll. Over the course of the last 25 years, Alex Chilton's artistic career has run the gamut from singing on classic Top Ten records with the Memphis, TN, group the Box Tops ("The Letter," #1; "Cry Like a Baby," #2) to creating willfully chaotic solo outings with very limited commercial appeal. During the early 70s, Chilton helped form Big Star (with singer/songwriter Chris Bell). In spite of nonexistent sales, Big Star received much critical acclaim, influencing a generation of the post punk/power-pop movement. Chilton's later solo efforts ranged from ramshackle garage rock to tight Memphis-style R&B. –RC

○ **19 Years - A Collection / RHINO** 1988
Except for the 1969 track "Free Again," this anthology focuses on Chilton's post-*Radio City* Big Star work. It contains five tracks from the disconcerting classic Big Star *Third/Sister Lovers* album. *19 Years* is no doubt an acquired taste, but in the world of safe-rock radio, Chilton's willful artistry contains the raw essence of the true renegade spirit of rock & roll, regardless of how he hits or misses. Check out "Rock Hard," "My Rival," "No Sex," "Bangkok," and "You Can't Have Me," which contains the telling lyric "You can't have me. Not for free!" Also includes sendups of the Seeds' garage-rock standard "Can't Seem to Make You Mine" and the Troggs hit "With a Girl Like You." –RC

CHINA CRISIS

Rock/pop, prog-rock. A melodic, ethereal rock quartet founded in 1979 by British musicians Gary Daly and Eddie Lundon, sometimes including ex-Steely Dan member Walter Becker as a player and producer. –WR

○ **Flaunt the Imperfection / WARNER** 1985
Despite the title, China Crisis achieved a cool perfection with this synthesized pop confection, an album of gorgeously arranged midtempo tunes that were calmly reminiscent of later Roxy Music. Some of that sophistication was doubtless due to producer Walter Becker. –WR

THE CHOCOLATE WATCH BAND

Rock & roll, psychedelic. A legendary ensemble of the 60s, the Chocolate Watch Band's psychedelic punk/garage sound evoked the Rolling Stones at their bluesiest and mixed it up with sitars, bells, flutes, and an enviable array of hooks. –BE

○ **Best of the Chocolate Watch Band / RHINO** 1983
A classic, too-little-known collection built on hooks by Brian

Jones and Dave Davies, with punk enthusiasm and dope's most beguiling side effects. —BE

LOU CHRISTIE   b 1943

Rock/pop. Lou Christie's shrieking, falsetto-soaked vocals led to prolonged pop stardom through the 60s. Born Lugee Sacco, Christie began recording in 1960 in Pittsburgh. "The Gypsy Cried," cut in 1962, was released on the local C&C logo and leased to Roulette, where it proved to be Christie's first sizable hit. After encoring for Roulette the next year with "Two Faces Have I," Christie moved to MGM and scored a million-seller in 1966 with the ambitious chart-topper "Lightnin' Strikes." The daring "Rhapsody in the Rain" was another major hit the same year. Christie returned to the Top Ten for the last time in 1969, with "I'm Gonna Make You Mine," on the bubblegum-oriented Buddah label. He remains a dynamic attraction on the oldies circuit. —BD

○ **Enlightnin'ment: The Best of... / RHINO**   1991
A solid collection that contains "Lightnin' Strikes," "Two Faces Have I," and others. —DH

THE CHURCH

Alternative rock. The Church, from Australia, combines a moddish Bowie-ish delivery with Byrds and midperiod Beatles arrangements that dip into psychedelia. "Under the Milky Way" has been their biggest hit so far. —RC

○ **Starfish / ARISTA**   1988
Engaging alternative rock, appealing to a wider range of listeners than their previous output. This album crystallizes the intensely atmospheric layers of bassist Steve Kilbey's lead vocals with swirling guitar work from Peter Koppes and Marty Wilson-Piper, yielding a Top 40 US hit with "Under the Milky Way." —DDC

Gold Afternoon Fix / ARISTA   1990
The dreamlike essence prevails again as a hypnotic backdrop for the band's cryptic lyrics. —DDC

Priest = Aura / ARISTA   1992
The Australian quartet returns to their earlier sound with less structured alternative-rock tracks. —DDC

CINDERELLA

Rock & roll. Philadelphia's Cinderella is definitely a blues-based metal band, one that actually listened to Willie Dixon, Howlin' Wolf, Muddy Waters, and Sonny Boy Williamson instead of stealing all their licks from Zeppelin and Stones records. They received a major-label deal with the help of their close friend, Jon Bongiovi. Cinderella instantly became a success through their great songs and addictive music videos, and they continue to be a force in metal. —JB

○ **Long Cold Winter / POLYGRAM**   1988
A commercial breakthrough for Cinderella, producing three Top 40 singles "Don't Know What You Got (Till It's Gone)," "The Last Mile," and "Coming Home." Cinderella's sound has grown bluesier, more like Led Zeppelin than Bon Jovi, and the songs are better. —STE

CIRCLE JERKS

Hardcore, punk. The Circle Jerks were one of the first West Coast hardcore bands. Smartass ex-Black Flag vocalist Keith Morris was one of the genre's funnier mouthpieces, when his homophobia didn't get in the way. —JF

○ **Group Sex / FRONTIER**   1980
Fast and loud debut by this early California thrash combo, offering the best intro to their pungent social commentary and bad jokes. —JF

ERIC CLAPTON   b 1945

Rock & roll, blues/rock. Upon the release of his first solo album in 1970, Eric Clapton had already invented the role of guitar hero. Starting out in England's Yardbirds, Clapton played pure blues. When the group recorded the pop song "For Your Love"

and moved to the blues-purist territory of John Mayall's Bluesbreakers. Clapton left Mayall to form the supergroup Cream with Jack Bruce and Ginger Baker, where they combined blues structures with overpowering volume and long improvised solos. After two one-shot supergroups, Blind Faith and Derek & the Dominos, Clapton retreated from six-string heroics for his solo records of the 70s. His new records were heavily inspired by the Band and J. J. Cale, featuring laidback rock with hints of blues, country, and reggae; songs became more important than the solos. The albums Clapton has made since 1974 are almost interchangeable stylistically, though the quality varies greatly. In the 80s, Clapton's studio sound became slicker in the hands of Phil Collins, without producing many chart smashes. At the end of the decade Clapton began playing more guitar, playing better than he has since the days of Derek & the Dominos. —STE

○ **Eric Clapton / RSO**   1973
The band of Delaney & Bonnie backed Clapton on his first solo outing. Naturally, the results are much closer to Delaney and Bonnie than to Cream. Though Clapton sings about "Blues Power," the heart of this album is in rock & roll. —STE

● **461 Ocean Boulevard / RSO**   1974
Clapton returned from a break in recording to do the best solo album he ever made. *461 Ocean Boulevard* is laidback yet never boring, because Clapton sings and solos equally well. Clapton kept trying to remake this album, but he never recaptured its charming ambience. —STE

○ **Slowhand / POLYGRAM**   1977
After a spell of tepid albums, Clapton made a comeback with a recording that strongly recalls *461 Ocean Boulevard.* Certain influences became more pronounced (a country feel on "Lay Down Sally" and the cover of J. J. Cale's "Cocaine"), the blues sound heartfelt, and the guitar sounds as if it had taken a shot of adrenaline. One of his best efforts. (Also available on Mobile Fidelity.) —STE

Just One Night / POLYGRAM   1980
For once, Clapton's backing band (including guitarist Albert Lee) pushes him into recording an interesting, listenable live album. Worth the extra expense of a double set. —STE

☆ **Crossroads / POLYGRAM**   1988
A 4-CD boxed set that follows Clapton from his Yardbird days to peddling Michelob on slick TV commercials. Following every different musical path Clapton traveled in his career, the box is a musical autobiography, detailing both his strengths and weaknesses and revealing many insights. Plenty of unreleased songs are on *Crossroads*, including tracks from an aborted second Derek & the Dominos album. A truly remarkable set. —STE

Journeyman / WARNER   1989
While the songs are not always first-rate, Clapton is playing better than he has since the early 70s. Clapton's best album of the 80s. —STE

Unplugged / WARNER   1992
This acoustic live performance on MTV's *Unplugged* program allowed Clapton to stretch out from the normal rock style. Includes a wonderful skiffle/swing time. —ED

THE DAVE CLARK FIVE

British Invasion. For a very brief time in 1964 it seemed that the biggest challenger to the Beatles phenomenon was the Dave Clark Five. Between 1964 and 1967, the Dave Clark Five made the Top 40 seventeen times, with memorable hits like "Glad All Over" (#6), "Bits and Pieces" (#4), "Because" (#3), and a remake of Bobby Day's "Over and Over" (#1). They made more appearances on "The Ed Sullivan Show" than any other English act.
One of the elements that set the band apart from their British contemporaries was their larger-than-life production and their loud stomping drum sound.
Unlike many artists of the time, bandleader Dave Clark managed and produced the band, negotiating a much higher royalty rate than artists of that period usually received.

The Dave Clark Five eventually fell out of step with changing times and called it quits in 1970. –RC

○ **Glad All Over Again / EPIC**   1975
Their best hits package. –LL

GENE CLARK   1941-1991

Folk/rock, country rock. As a founding member of the Byrds, Clark was inducted into the Rock & Roll Hall of Fame in 1991, a few months before his death. Born in Tipton, MO, in a musical family, Clark was surrounded by bluegrass and country but joined the clean-cut folk boomers, the New Christy Minstrels at, 18. After hearing the Beatles, Clark quit the Minstrels and went to Los Angeles, where a fortuitous meeting with Roger McGuinn led to the forming of the Byrds. Clark wrote some of the best early Byrds songs, one of which, "Feel a Whole Lot Better," Tom Petty recorded in 1990. Clark was the first Byrd to fly in 1966, and his subsequent solo career flickered with moments of brilliance — he was one of the seminal figures of folk-rock and country-rock. –MH

● **Echoes / CBS**
Contains six songs with the Byrds, the entire Gosdin Brothers album, and two unreleased tracks. This is a nice companion piece to the Byrds box. –KMC

Gene Clark with the Gosdin Brothers / SONY SP   1967
Clark's solo debut, recorded with the Gosdin Brothers. –KMC

White Light / A&M   1971
Good Dylanesque songs. Nice subtle production by Jesse Ed Davis, low-key and lyrical. (Import) –KMC

No Other / LINE   1974
A slightly overproduced but interesting album. (Import) –KMC

So Rebellious a Lover / RHINO   1987
Clark's last album, recorded with Carla Olson of the Textones. A good mix of folk and country. –KMC

○ **Roadmaster / EDSEL**   1988
Includes two songs from the early-70s original Byrds that are much better than anything on the ill-fated Byrds reunion album of 1973. A must for fans of Clark-era Byrds. (Import) –KMC

Silhouetted in Light / LINE   1992
A very good 15-track live CD featuring Gene Clark and Carla Olson at their best. The sound is good and the song selection impressive. Pick up this import — highly recommended. –CR

GENE CLARK & CARLA OLSON

Folk/rock. Gene Clark was a member of the Byrds in the 60s and then went on to projects with the Dillards, the Gosdin Brothers, and several solo albums. Carla Olson is a guitarist and pianist from Los Angeles. –CR

So Rebellious a Lover / RAZOR & TIE
This reissue features three extra cuts, but that's not what is best about it. The combination of Carla Olson and Clark's voices is great. They come together on "The Drifter," "Deportee," and "Don't It Make You Want to Go Home." The CD has a real country/folk sound. Let's hope for more gems from the archives. –CR

PETULA CLARK   ♭1932

Pop. By the time Petula Clark made her debut on American pop charts in 1964, she had already developed quite a career as an actress and singer throughout Europe, appearing in over 20 films and selling several million records.
"Downtown" is the song that broke her Stateside and placed her firmly in the #1 spot, displacing the Beatles's "I Feel Fine." Not only was she the first female artist from England to land that chart position, but her second record, "I Know a Place," went to #3. Only Cyndi Lauper has equaled that impressive an entry on her first two singles. Despite the competition, "Downtown" won the Grammy for Best Rock & Roll Recording in 1965. Over the next three years, Clark scored fifteen Top 40 pop hits.

Music Map

Early Rock Through Punk To Hardcore

50s American Rock n' Roll
Chuck Berry — Little Richard — Link Wray

60s British Rock
The Beatles — The Rolling Stones
The Kinks — The Who

60s American Garage Rock
The Kingmen — The Standells — Count Five
? and the Mysterians — Chocolate Watch Band

Art Garage (late 60s)
Velvet Underground

Late 60s American Garage Punk
The Stooges — MC5

Folk Garage
Neil Young

Early 70s American Proto-Punk
New York Dolls

Mid-70s American Punk
The Ramones — Richard Hell
Patti Smith — Television

Mid 70s British Punk
The Sex Pistols — The Damned
The Buzzcocks — The Clash

Metal/Thrash
Motorhead

80s AMERICAN HARDCORE
Black Flag — Dead Kennedys
Bad Brains — Circle Jerks
Misfits — Husker Du

Grindcore
Carcass — Napalm Death

Thrashcore
Helmet — Prong

Even though Clark's English origins helped her ride in on the first wave of the British Invasion, her music was definitely geared more towards the adult market. –RC

○ **Greatest Hits / GNP CRESCENDO**   1986
This import collection is much crisper and more vibrant-sounding than the domestic releases. All the major US hits are here, plus some British and European chart successes never heard in the US. –BE

THE CLASH

Punk, alternative rock. The Clash, 1976-1986, was the most accomplished band to come out of the British punk rock scene of the 70s. The group was formed by guitarist and singer Joe Strummer (b Jan 21, 1955), guitarist and singer Mick Jones (b Jun 26, 1955), bassist Paul Simonon (b Dec 15, 1955), and drummer Terry Chimes — replaced in 1977 by Topper Headon (b May 30, 1955). They first gained national recognition opening for the Sex Pistols, the other major punk band. But unlike the Pistols, the Clash had a straightforward earnestness to go with their punk anger. Their music was similarly simple, loud, and abrasive.

In December 1979, the Clash released *London Calling*, a critically acclaimed double album that found them expanding their musical style from punk to a more eclectic approach. The album spawned a single in the title song, which became their biggest UK single during their existence, getting to #11, while the album hit #9 in the UK and was their first real US success at #27. "Train in Vain (Stand by Me)" from the album was the Clash's first US chart single, reaching #23.

Sandinista!, a triple-LP set released in December 1980 took their eclecticism to new lengths. The album got to a disappointing #19 in the UK but was a surprisingly strong #24 in the US. The Clash again grazed the Top 40 in the UK with the album's "The Magnificent Seven" in May 1981.

Their next, *Combat Rock* (1982), was a straightforward rock collection that was their last album with the original personnel and their most popular. It hit #2 in the UK and #7 in the US (where it sold a million copies), and its singles "Should I Stay or Should I Go?" and "Rock the Casbah" were hits on both sides of the Atlantic. Meanwhile, Headon left the band in July 1982, and Jones was fired by Strummer and Simonon in September 1983. He formed Big Audio Dynamite. Strummer and Simonon reorganized and added new members, releasing *Cut the Crap* in the fall of 1985, but by the start of 1986, the Clash was no more. –WR

Give 'Em Enough Rope / EPIC   1978
In retrospect, Sandy Pearlman's production brings a welcome coherence to the Clash's sound, though they sound as aggressive as ever on such songs as "Safe European Home," "English Civil War," and "Tommy Gun." The most moving song is Mick Jones's "Stay Free," however, which may say more about the punk aesthetic than about any of Joe Strummer's angry rants. –WR

☆ **The Clash / EPIC**   1979
The revised US version of the Clash's first album, containing most of the vital punk anthems of that record, plus such later tunes as "White Man in Hammersmith Palais" and "I Fought the Law." This and the sole Sex Pistols album, *Never Mind the Bollocks, Here's the Sex Pistols*, tell the story of English 70s punk rock. –WR

★ **London Calling / EPIC**   1980
"What are we gonna do now?" asks Joe Strummer at the start of "Clampdown," one of this album's songs. But by the time you get to that track, it's already clear that the Clash have solved that problem by taking a giant step toward making craftsmanlike rock without sacrificing the urgency that made them punk leaders. From the title track through the reggae, rock, and pop tracks that follow, this is one of the premier albums of its time. –WR

Combat Rock / EPIC   1982
The Clash are still a little too individual to be as straight ahead a rock group as much of this album implies they are, but you can't fault a collection that contains the rock energy of "Should I Stay or Should I Go?" and the absurdist danceability of "Rock the Casbah." –WR

Story of the Clash - Vol. 1 / EPIC   1988
A 2-disc, 28-track compilation that ranges over the Clash catalog somewhat haphazardly; maybe hits like "Rock the Casbah" were being saved for a *Volume 2* that never came. Still, this is some of their essential music. –WR

○ **Clash on Broadway / CBS**   1991
A 3-disc, 63-track compilation that treats the catalog coherently and chronologically, with all the major songs included. It's a pricey boxed set, but if you want one album that covers the Clash's career, this is it. –WR

THE CLASSICS IV

Rock/pop. This Atlanta-based group had a brief (but

impressive) run on the *Billboard* charts during the late 60s with their easygoing soft-pop style. Million-sellers like "Spooky" (#3), "Traces" (#2), and "Stormy" (#5), along with "Everyday with You Girl" (#19), have continued to rotate endlessly on adult- and contemporary-radio formats and oldies stations. Guitarist J. R. Cobb and producer Bobby Buie cowrote most of the band's material. They later went on to form the Atlanta Rhythm Section, who also landed a hit with a redone version of "Spooky" (#17) in 1979. –RC

○ **The Very Best of the Classics IV / EMI** 1988
Everything you need to know about these MOR performers, who wrote the book on the mellower side of rock before adult-contemporary became a true category. The various members either played with Roy Orbison or went on to form the Atlanta Rhythm Section. –LL

OTIS CLAY   ♭1942

Soul. Otis Clay made most of his best-known records in Memphis during the early 70s, but he's still universally hailed as Chicago's deep-soul king. In a city filled to overflowing with legendary blues artists, Clay has become the proud standard-bearer for Chicago's enduring soul tradition.

Like so many of his contemporaries, Clay's intense vocal style reflects a gospel background. He made the secular jump in 1965, signing with Chicago's One-derful Records and issuing a series of gospel-tinged soul records that were a lot grittier than the customary Windy City soul sound. Clay inaugurated Atlantic's Cotillion subsidiary in 1968 with a supercharged cover of the Sir Douglas Quintet's "She's About a Mover," produced by Rick Hall in Muscle Shoals shortly before the singer joined forces with Hi Records boss Willie Mitchell. With the relentlessly driving Hi Rhythm Section in tow, Clay waxed his biggest seller in 1972, "Trying to Live My Life without You," later covered very successfully by Bob Seger.

Although Clay's tenure on Hi may have been his most commercially potent, he's steadily recorded and gigged ever since. He is a genuine hero in Japan, where he's recorded two sizzling live albums filled with the churning grooves, punchy horns, and searing vocals that inevitably characterize the best deep soul — no matter where it's recorded. –BD

○ **Soul Man - Live in Japan / BULLSEYE BLUES** 1985
The greatest live soul performer, backed by the Hi rhythm section. –RP

Trying to Live My Life without You / HI UK 1987
UK import. Hi tracks. The title song is the original version of the Bob Seger hit. –RP

Got to Find a Way / P-VINE   1990
A Japanese import featuring nineteen early Chicago tracks from 1965-1967. –RP

THE CLEFTONES

Doo-wop. This Harlem-based quartet led by Herb Cox made a splash in 1961 with the "Heart and Soul." –JF

○ **Best of the Cleftones / RHINO**   1990
The careening "Heart and Soul" was their only hit (1961), but doo-wop nuts will love this entire set. –JF

GEORGE CLINTON   ♭1940

Soul, funk. George Clinton scored a few solo hits on Capitol in the early 80s, but as the president of Parliament, P. Funk, Funkadelic, Bootsy's Rubber Band, and other outfits, Clinton set a new agenda for Black music during the 70s. He combined theater, sci-fi, and funk glossolalia into something that was uniquely his own. On record he loses some of his impact, but it's still the ultimate boom-box music. That Motown passed on him says much for the stripe of Clinton's music. –CE

○ **Computer Games / CAPITOL**   1982
Former Parliament and Funkadelic leader George Clinton made a major comeback under his own name with this album, whose irresistible grooves, vocal choruses, and absurd

humor were essentially identical to the music of Funkadelic's salad days. Were you wondering where that "woof-woof" cheer heard on Arsenio Hall and at Black concerts came from? Check out "Atomic Dog." —WR

R&B Skeletons in the Closet / CAPITOL   1986
Clinton's second and third solo albums had their moments, but he didn't reach the peak of danceable madness of which he is truly capable again until this record, which contains the strange but wonderful "Do Fries Go with That Shake?" Despite its title, it's not a collection of oldies. —WR

CLOSE LOBSTERS

New-wave. A Scottish quartet who released their first album in 1987. Delivering snappy-sounding New Wave, the band features singer Andrew Burnett, guitarists Graeme Wilmington and Tom Donnelly, and the rhythm section of Bob Burnett and Stewart McFayden. —DS

○ **Headache Rhetoric / CAPITOL**   1989
The best effort of the underrated guitar-driven popsters. —DS

THE CLOVERS

Doo-wop. One of the earliest doo-wop vocal groups, formed in the late 40s in Washington, DC. Original members were Buddy Bailey, Matthew McQuater, Hal Lucas Jr, and Harold Winley. Bobby Mitchell replaced Bailey by the time the group was signed to the fledgling Atlantic label in 1950. The Clovers racked up 13 Top Ten R&B hits between 1951 to 1954, all showcasing their solid harmonies and unerring rhythmic verve. After a few years between hits, they scored again in 1959 with their biggest, "Love Potion No. 9." The Clovers went their separate ways by 1961, but they will always be revered by hardcore doo-wop fans the world over. —CK

○ **Love Potion No. 9 / CAPITOL**   1991
The Best of the Clovers - Love Potion No. 9 features their later sides for United Artists including the classic title track. —CK

★ **Down in the Alley / ATLANTIC**   1991
Down in the Alley - Best of the Clovers is an excellent compilation of their best and earliest sides, including "Nip Sip," "Don't You Know I Love You," and "One Mint Julep." —CK

THE COASTERS

Doo-wop. Possibly the most popular doo-wop group of the 50s, the Coasters started on the West Coast as the Robins, scoring hits under the writing-and-production helm of Jerry Lieber and Mike Stoller. When Atlantic signed Lieber and Stoller as a production team, the group split into two factions; the core of the group became the Coasters and moved to New York to record, while the Robins continued on the West Coast to diminishing acclaim. The Coasters' hits, some of the most finely crafted, well-written, and hilarious in the genre, continued throughout the rest of the decade. Carl Gardner's sly leads and Bobby Nunn's bass singing defined their sound through numerous personnel changes. When their time on the charts came to an end a number of "Coasters" groups suddenly proliferated (much like the Drifters), many of them still dotting the landscape of a million oldies shows and still singing those classic songs. —CK

★ **Greatest Hits / ATLANTIC**   1988
Though several Coasters compilations exist on the market, this features all their hits ("Searchin'," "Yakety Yak," "Along Came Jones," etc.) while showcasing the best of their more obscure sides like "The Shadow Knows." —CK

○ **Anthology / RHINO-ATLANTIC**   1992
Anthology is an excellent collection for those looking for more than the basic greatest hits package. Typical of Rhino packages, this set is thoughfully assembled and well-sequenced. —ED

EDDIE COCHRAN   1938-1960

Rock & roll, rockabilly. As with his friend and contemporary Buddy Holly, Cochran's star has continued to shine ever more

brightly since his untimely death. Partially this is because of his "image" — the brash, flamboyantly dressed, hot-guitar-picking, teenage smart-aleck rebel — but the substance is there too. A fine guitarist (I cite the guitar breaks on "Twenty Flight Rock" and "Jeannie Jeannie Jeannie," just to name a couple) and fine songwriter (especially in collaboration with his friend and producer Jerry Capehart), Cochran's best work captured the spirit of its time (the late 50s) so perfectly it can never seem dated: Cars, girls, teenage rebellion, and angst distilled into 2 1/2 minute gems of ringing guitars, throbbing bass (his were among the first rock & roll records to exploit the electric bass's distinctive character), and growling, drawling vocals. Especially influential in Britain (where he was on tour when he was killed), echoes of Cochran's work (and sometimes his songs) have surfaced in the records of the Who, Rod Stewart, the Clash, Neil Diamond, the Stray Cats, and many, many others. —GB

☆ **Legendary Masters Series / CAPITOL**   1990
The definitive single-disc collection of Cochran's best: "Summertime Blues," "Cut Across Shorty," "Something Else," "Come On Everybody," and "Twenty Flight Rock." All the hits; all the feeling. —CK

BRUCE COCKBURN   b 1945

Singer/songwriter. Over the course of his lengthy career, Bruce Cockburn has gone from plaintive singer/songwriter folk to aggressive world beat, rock, and even some jazz. Thematically, Cockburn has gone from deeply introspective musings to human rights activism, all filtered through a distinctly mystical Christian point of view. Cockburn's poetic lyrics are consistently many cuts above those of most artists who choose to tackle this kind of weighty subject matter.
In his native Canada, Cockburn has won many Juno Awards (the equivalent to the Grammys). Overseas, he has quite a following, but stateside Cockburn has only managed two significant forays onto the radio playlists, 1980's "Wondering Where the Lions Are" (#21) and "If I Had a Rocket Launcher," his 1984 response to injustices he witnessed while in Central America.
Most recently, Cockburn has signed with Sony, releasing the fine T-Bone Burnette-produced "Nothing but a Burning Light," which recalls his earlier folkie style. —RC

Further Adventures of Bruce Cockburn / ESD   1976
More electric guitar and diverse instrumental backup. Some of the material tends to drag, but "Prenons La Mer" and "Can I Go with You" sparkle with Cockburn's stunning guitar interplay and strong melodies. "Laughter" and "Rainfall" are standouts too. —RC

○ **In the Falling Dark / CBS**   1976
The followup to *Joy Will Find a Way* possesses some Cockburn standards in "Festival of Friends," the propulsive folk-jazz of "Silver Wheels," the meditative "Lord of the Starfields," and the title cut. The lyrics involve increasingly complex mystical Christian metaphors. Cockburn's exceptional guitar technique is showcased on the instrumental "Water into Wine." —RC

○ **Dancing in the Dragon's Jaws / CBS**   1980
Cockburn's first Stateside success produced a #21 pop hit with "Wondering Where the Lions Are," but there is much better material to be found here on one of his best albums. The lyrics tend to be spacier, and, musically, Cockburn begins to aggressively synthesize Third World rhythms with his singer/songwriter-style folk. —RC

● **Humans / CBS**   1980
This followup to isn't as accessible as *Dancing in the Dragon's Jaws,* but it's possibly Cockburn's most brilliant artistic statement, where the struggles of the general human condition and (more personally) a divorce cause this Christian mystic to dig deep and grapple with more down-to-earth issues. With some of his most powerfully poetic lyrics he maintains a fine balance between lofty intentions and grave disillusions. Musically, it is a heady dose of worldbeat folk. —RC

Inner City Front / CBS   1981
Transitional self-produced effort featuring more musical diversity, from the techno-dirge of "The Strong One" to the reggaelike "Justice." "Loner" provides a dramatic highlight. Cockburn's human rights concerns and his left-of-center politics dominate over more mystical fascinations for the first time. –RC

Stealing Fire / CBS   1984
Features a more streamlined, sophisticated rock sound. "If I Had a Rocket Launcher" became a powerful left-field AOR hit in 1984. "Lovers in a Dangerous Time" and "Nicaragua" are highlights. "Maybe the Poet," is a low point, being the highbrow artistic equivalent to Barry Mann's hideous, self-congratulatory ode to the value of pop-song craftsmen, "Who Put the Bomp (In the Bomp, Bomp, Bomp)." But it's a fine album overall. –RC

○ **Trouble with Normal / CBS**   1985
Another consistently strong effort. Cockburn's brainy lyrics occasionally border on the didactic, but the imagery is usually brilliant. "Waiting for the Moon" is one of his most beautiful songs. The title cut is released in two totally different versions; the True North rendition is preferable. –RC

○ **Waiting for a Miracle / TRUE NORTH**   1987
This double-CD best-of collection is geared around Cockburn's Canadian singles — an odd approach, considering that much of his strongest material never enjoyed radio airplay. Because of that, *Waiting for a Miracle (Singles 1970-1987)* isn't definitive, but it is a very good collection. This is mainly because Cockburn is practically incapable of writing a bad song. Nevertheless, Cockburn has yet to receive the kind of treatment he deserves for a collection. *Waiting for a Miracle* is the best overview of Cockburn's music, by default. (Import) –RC

Big Circumstance / CBS   1989
Cockburn tries to balance the edge-rock approach of recent work with more reflective earlier sounds. He's the most successful at illuminating big issues when he's focusing on his personal backyard (on "Understanding Nothing," "Don't Feel Your Touch") rather than the "Tibetan Side of Town." Surprise element: Cockburn displays rare flashes of humor. –RC

Nothing but a Burning Light / CBS   1991
This T-Bone Burnett produced effort finds Cockburn returning to the more introspective quiet spirit of his earlier work, including his most open Christian expressions in years, particularly "Cry of a Tiny Babe," a Cockburn-style Christmas story, and "Somebody Touched Me." "One of the Best Ones" is classic reflective Cockburn. Although not one of his best albums, it's a nice breather from the relentless heaviness of his last few efforts. –RC

JOE COCKER   b 1944

Rock/pop. After starting out in the late 50s as an unsuccessful British pop singer (working under the name Vance Arnold), English soul/rock singer Cocker found his niche in the pubs of England with his superb backing group, the Grease Band. Worldwide success soon followed with a brace of fine recordings based around Cocker's fine interpretive skills. Cocker's first peak of success came when Leon Russell organized the Mad Dogs & Englishmen tour, featuring Cocker and over 40 others. Problems with alcohol (both on stage and off) reduced Cocker's once-powerful voice to a croaking rasp, but he has survived, still scoring hits into the early 80s. It's unlikely we've heard the last of him, since the man still seems capable of making any song his own. –CK

○ **With a Little Help from My Friends / A&M** 1969
The album that foisted Joe Cocker on an unsuspecting public is full of tasteful, raucous covers, Cocker's trademark hysterical vocals, and outstanding studio backing by pros like Jimmy Page and Steve Winwood. –TG

☆ **Joe Cocker! / A&M**   1969
The rare sophomore effort that was an improvement over the first, with great tracks (and vocals) like "Delta Lady" and "She Came In through the Bathroom Window." Arguably Cocker's most soulful album. –TG

○ **Mad Dogs & Englishmen / A&M**   1970
Superb document of Cocker's high-energy 1970 tour that included about a zillion musicians and hangers-on. All the goods are here, and many consider this Cocker's last great moment. Check out Mobile Fidelity's audiophile version. –TG

● **Classics - Vol. 4 / A&M**   1987
A solid collection from his 1967-1976 peak. Includes "Feeling Alright," "You Are So Beautiful," and "With a Little Help from My Friends." –DH

COCTEAU TWINS

Alternative pop. This Scottish group features Harold Budd, Elizabeth Fraser, Robin Gutherie, and Simon Raymonde. –BC

○ **Blue Bell Knoll / CAPITOL**   1988
This, the first Cocteau Twins regular studio album to be released in the US, is typical of their earlier UK output: keyboards and guitars swirl together into sonic landscapes, over which (or rather, buried within which) Elizabeth Fraser sings in a high, ethereal voice reminiscent of Kate Bush and Jane Siberry, the difference being that the lyrics are utterly unintelligible. The result is classy mood music that might appeal to the new crop of Enya fans. –WR

Heaven or Las Vegas / CAPITOL   1990
The song structures are more discernible, as are the lyrics, which perhaps makes this a little less mysterious than most Cocteau Twins albums, and a little more accessible, if also less characteristic. –WR

MARC COHN

Singer/songwriter. This husky-voiced singer/songwriter and pianist from Cleveland released his self-titled debut album in 1991, including the Top 20 hit "Walking in Memphis." and won the 1991 Grammy for Best New Artist. –WR

○ **Marc Cohn / ATLANTIC**   1991
The singer/songwriter album of 1991, and an auspicious debut for a writer of soulful, keenly observed lyrics, who sings them passionately. –WR

LLOYD COLE & THE COMMOTIONS   b 1956

Alternative rock. Scottish singer/songwriter Lloyd Cole formed the Commotions, who served as his backup band, in Glasgow in 1983. The group featured guitarist Nick Clark, bassist Lawrence Donegan, keyboard player Blair Cowan, and drummer Steven Irvine. Heavily influenced by Bob Dylan and the Band, Cole and the Commotions developed a familiar-sounding but distinctive folk/rock sound, highlighted by Cole's literate lyrics. The group signed to Polydor in 1984, and scored a series of UK hits, including "Perfect Skin." In 1989, he split the band and moved to New York, where he recorded *Lloyd Cole*, his debut solo album, with New York Session players such as Voidoid and Lou Reed guitarist Robert Quine (releasing it in 1990). Cole has garnered considerable critical acclaim, but so far has failed to make a commercial impact in the US. –WR

○ **Rattlesnakes / CAPITOL**   1984
Cole's debut album reflects his Glasgow surroundings in its observations but also incorporates a Dylanish attitude toward them, while the Commotions prove to be a cohesive backup unit. –WR

NATALIE COLE   b 1950

Urban R&B, dance-pop. Natalie Cole is an eclectic soul singer, pianist, and songwriter, and the daughter of Nat King Cole. –BC

Inseparable / CAPITOL   1975
A fine sample of Chicago-style keyboard soul. –BC

Thankful (Original Master Recording) / CAPITOL 1977
Her finest hour, encompassing jazz and soul. –BC

Natalie Live! / CAPITOL 1978
Raucous, lowdown, gospel-style shouting. –BC

Everlasting / ELEKTRA 1987
Fine 80s Top 40 and light-jazz music. –BC

○ **Collection / CAPITOL** 1988
Her 70s belting hits. –BC

● **Unforgettable with Love / ELEKTRA** 1991
Her urbane interpretations of her father's classics. Impressive personnel and subdued jazz vocalizing. –BC

BOOTSY COLLINS   b 1951

Funk. William "Bootsy" Collins is one of funk's most influential bassists. He cut his teeth in James Brown's band in the late 60s, then jumped on George Clinton's P-Funk mothership. Along the way he's made a number of weird and wiggy albums, both on his own and with his Rubber Band, which at times take the funk patterns of Brown and Clinton into new territory. –JF

○ **Ahh ... The Name Is Bootsy, Baby! / WARNER** 1977
His second album is a fine introduction into Bootsy's bizarre and throbbing funky fairy-tale world. –JF

Bootsy? Player of the Year / WARNER 1978
Funny jokes, tight ballads, and loads of elastic funk make this album necessary for enthusiasts. (Out of print) –JF

● **What's Bootsy Doin'? / CBS** 1988
This pounding set is Collins's best work, with plenty of grooves for the brain and the booty. –JF

THE COLLINS KIDS

Rockabilly. By the time Lawrence (b 1944) and Lawrencine (b 1942) Collins were eleven and thirteen, respectively, they were already tearing it up on country package shows, recording for Columbia Records, and performing on national TV almost weekly. Older sister Lorrie held up the cowgirl fringe-rustling-against-nylons teenage-sensuality department; kid brother Larry was a bundle of hyperkinetic energy, bopping all over the place while laying down exciting, twangy guitar breaks learned firsthand from the "King of Doublenecked Mosrite," Joe Maphis. The Collins's recordings as time went on veered from mawkish brother/sister country-style duets to white-hot rockabilly, and they were just reaching their peak when Lorrie eloped, effectively breaking up the act. Revered by rockabilly collectors the world over, their filmed television appearances and recordings arc testimony to the fact that the Collins Kids weren't just "good for their age," they were just plain good, period. –CK

○ **Hop Skip & Jump / BEAR FAMILY** 1991
A 2-CD boxed set covering the Kids' entire career. –CK

PHIL COLLINS   b 1951

Rock/pop. Phil Collins's ascent to the status of one of the most successful pop and adult-contemporary singers of the 80s and beyond was probably as much of a surprise to him as it was to many others. Balding and dimimutive, Collins was almost 30 years old when his first solo single, "In the Air Tonight," became a #2 hit in his native UK (the song was a Top 20 hit in the US). Between 1984 and 1990, Collins had a string of 13 straight US Top Ten hits.

Long before any of that happened, however, Collins was a child actor/singer who appeared as the Artful Dodger in the London production of *Oliver!* in 1964. (He also has a cameo in *A Hard Day's Night,* among other films.) He got his first break in music at the end of his teens, when he was chosen to be a replacement drummer in the British art-rock band Genesis in 1970. (Collins maintained a separate jazz career with the band Brand X, as well.) Genesis was fronted by singer Peter Gabriel. They had achieved a moderate level of success in the UK and the US, with elaborate concept albums, before Gabriel abruptly left in 1974. Genesis auditioned 400 singers without success, then decided to let Collins have a go.

The result was a gradual simplifying of Genesis's sound and an increasing focus on Collins's expressive, throaty voice. *And Then There Were Three ...* went gold in 1978, and *Duke* was even more successful. Collins made his debut solo album *Face Value* in 1981, which turned out to be a bigger hit than any Genesis album. It concentrated on Collins's voice, often in stark, haunting contexts such as the piano-and-drum dirge "In the Air Tonight," which sounded like something from John Lennon's debut solo album, *John Lennon/Plastic Ono Band.* Collins's continuing solo work has not meant the end of Genesis. In fact, he balances group and solo careers with enormous success. In 1992 Genesis released *We Can't Dance* and an began an extensive tour, and it seems likely that Collins's double success will continue. –WR

○ **Face Value / ATLANTIC** 1981
Collins proves himself a passionate singer (and distinctive drummer) with a gift for both deeply felt ballads and snarling rockers. His debut album transformed him from the frontman of Genesis to a solo star who happened to be in Genesis too. Contains "In the Air Tonight" and "I Missed Again." –WR

No Jacket Required / ATLANTIC 1985
From ballads like the #1 "One More Night" to uptempo funk like the #1 "Sussudio," another tour de force in what was by now one of the most identifiable styles in pop music. The 1985 Grammy winner for Album of the Year. –WR

But Seriously / ATLANTIC 1989
This chart-topping fourth album contains "Another Day in Paradise," "I Wish It Would Rain Down," "Do You Remember?," and "Something Happened on the Way to Heaven," all Top Five hits. –WR

COLOR ME BADD

Urban R&B. An early-90s vocal quartet specializing in sensual urban R&B, yet able to sing all varietys of soul well. –BC

○ **C.M.B. / WARNER** 1991
Their debut album includes the hit "I Wanna Sex You Up," which is innovative from an instrumental perspective. –BC

SHAWN COLVIN   b 1958

Singer/songwriter. A NY-based singer/songwriter who first gained notice singing backup to Suzanne Vega, then signed with Columbia Records. Colvin's debut album, *Steady On,* won the 1990 Grammy Award for Best Folk Album. –WR

○ **Steady On / CBS** 1989
Sharp production, surprising arrangements, and Shawn Colvin's alternately breathy and ringing vocals give the best possible forum to her astute reflections on life and love. The album's roots go into rock and country as well as folk. –WR

COMMANDER CODY

Country rock. This Texas ensemble (formed in Ann Arbor, MI)was a good-time blend of roadhouse country swing, rockabilly, and anything else conducive to guzzling mass quantities of Lone Star beer. You could say they were the perfect band for pot-smoking truckers. They scored one big hit with "Hot Rod Lincoln" (#9) in 1972. –RC

Lost in the Ozone / MCA 1971
Their remarkable debut album went from gospel to the Andrews Sisters to Eddie Cochran, and was a hoot from top to bottom. –JT

Hot Licks, Cold Steel & Trucker's Favorites / MCA 1972
Their second studio album features a collection of odes to truckers and 50s rock & roll that found Cody and the boys getting in gear. –JT

Very Best of (... plus) / SEE FOR MILES 1986
More tracks than their US best-of and costlier, but this collection provides a grand overview of one of the saving graces of 70s rock. (Import) –JT

Deep in the Heart of Texas / MCA 1991
The Airmen were at their best onstage, and this 1973 set caught them at the peak of their game. –JT

○ **Best of Commander Cody - Too Much Fun / MCA**
Not only could they play the hell out of their instruments, but
C. C. and his Lost Planet Airmen were a virtual melting pot of
American music — country, R&B, rockabilly, western swing.
And always too much fun. —JT

THE COMMODORES

Soul, funk, pop. The Commodores got their start by being the
opening act for the Jackson 5. Largely through the prolific
lyrics of Lionel Richie, the band broke out nationally in the
mid 70s. Their initial success was mainly with dance tunes,
but in the late 70s Richie began turning out love ballads such
as "Easy," "Still," and "Three Times a Lady." His departure for
solo stardom crippled the band, but not before they had one
more huge success with "Nightshift" in 1985. Today the group
plays state fairs and oldies venues. Members included Lionel
Richie (replaced in 1984 by J. D. Nicholas), Thomas McClary
(who left in 1984), Ronald LaPread, William King, Walter
Orange, and Milan Williams. —RAB

The Commodores / MOTOWN   1977
A strong set of Lionel Richie songs. Their best album, with
"Easy" and "Brick House." —RAB

○ **Greatest Hits / MOTOWN**   1978
A representative collection released at the group's peak, it
features "Easy," "Three Times a Lady," "Brick House," and
"Just to Be Close to You." —RAB

Nightshift / MOTOWN   1985
Strong production by Dennis Lambert. The band's only hit
after Lionel Richie left the group, with the Marvin Gaye tribute
title track. —RAB

CONCRETE BLONDE

Alternative rock. Built around the throaty lead vocals and spare
pulsing bass work of Johnette Napolitano and the crunchy
guitar execution of former Sparks member Jim Mankey,
Concrete Blonde occasionally displays some of the raw fire of
the early Pretenders. Their more recent efforts have enjoyed
some significant alternative-radio exposure. —RC

Free / CAPITOL   1989
This sophomore effort is an improvement over their slapdash-
sounding debut, with punchier arrangements supporting
Johnette Napolitano's throaty dramatics. Highlights include
the forceful "God Is a Bullet" and the poppish "Happy
Birthday." —RC

Bloodletting / CAPITOL   1990
Moodier than *Free.* "Joey" is the band's first hit. —RC

○ **Walking in London / I.R.S.**   1992
Continues in a vien similar to that on *Bloodletting.* Contains
"Ghost of a Texas Ladies Man." —RC

ARTHUR CONLEY   *b* 1946

Soul. A protegé of Otis Redding and, like Redding, a musical
disciple of Sam Cooke. Conley cowrote (with Redding) and
sang "Sweet Soul Music," one of the true anthems of the 60s.
Based on Cooke's "Yeah, Man," the record was sweet and hot at
the same time, witha readily identifiable horn intro and lyrics
that immortalized the soul stars of the day. Conley, although
signed to Atco, toured overseas with the Stax/Volt Revue and
later joined the Soul Clan with Atlantic label-mates Wilson
Pickett, Solomon Burke, Don Covay, Ben E. King, and Joe Tex.
He has lived in France for a number of years. —CO

The Soul Clan / ATLANTIC
Conley with Covay, Burke, King, and Tex. Includes "Soul
Meeting" with Bobby Womack on guitar. Out of print. —CO

○ **Sweet Soul Music / ATLANTIC**   1967
The title track is a real killer! Conley sounds young but
assured, and the Otis Redding production is solid throughout.
Includes "Let Nothing Separate Us" and "I Can't Stop." —CO

THE CONNELLS

Alternative rock. This North Carolinian rock quartet, led by

brothers Mike and David Connell has a jangly guitar sound.
Their debut album, *Darker Days,* was released on Black Park
in 1986. —WR

○ **One Simple Word / TEEVEE TOONS**   1990
In the course of four albums, the Connells have evolved their
own style within the jangling guitar-rock sound so prevalent
in alternative bands of the 80s. Mainly it's been a matter of
writing more distinctive songs and having them sung by
guitarist George Huntley so they sink in. This is their first
album to cross over from the category of "promising" to the
beginnings of a fulfillment of that promise. —WR

THE CONTOURS

R&B, Motown. One of Berry Gordy's earliest discoveries at
Motown, the hard-rocking Contours cultivated a new
generation of fans when their "Do You Love Me" was featured
in the 1987 hit movie *Dirty Dancing.* Led by gravelly-voiced
Billy Gordon, the quintet scored an R&B chart-topper in 1962
with the rollicking "Do You Love Me" on Gordy's label, then
smoothed out their sound just a bit for the mid-60s soul
classics "First I Look at the Purse" and "Just a Little
Misunderstanding." Dennis Edwards, who joined the group
well after "Do You Love Me," was recruited to replace David
Ruffin as lead of the Temptations in 1968. —BD

○ **Do You Love Me / MOTOWN**   1962
A rough-edged, early-60s Motown group that deserves more
than its enduring one-hit status for "Do You Love Me." —BD

TOMMY CONWELL & THE YOUNG RUMBLERS

Rock & roll. These mainstream heartland rockers hail
from Philadelphia. —RC

○ **Guitar Trouble / CBS**   1990
Conwell creates straightahead and blues-influenced garage-
rock, with Bruce Hornsby adding piano and organ on "I'm
Seventeen." —DDC

RY COODER   *b* 1947

Blues/rock, roots-rock. Since his self-titled 1970 debut, Ry
Cooder has drawn deeply from rich North American
colloquial music and prerock genres like Tex-Mex, Hawaiian,
gospel, vaudeville, country, ragtime, Caribbean, and blues.
His passion for dignifying these sounds, plus his earthy
emotive guitar technique and choice of stellar sidemen
(particularly drummer Jim Keltner), have made for some
great albums, especially 1974's *Paradise and Lunch.* Cooder
has a knack for inventive song selections, juxtaposing old
material with new in a fashion that sometimes illuminates
both. It is his understanding of these earlier musical genres
that informs Cooder's rock sensibilities with a unique sound,
particularly on slide guitar.
Besides his solo efforts, Cooder has worked with the Rolling
Stones, Taj Mahal, Gordon Lightfoot, Captain Beefheart, John
Hiatt, Randy Newman, and Little Feat, and produced the solid
R&B Rounder debut of his backup singers Bobby King and
Terry Evans. Cooder has also done extensive soundtrack work
(some with Jim Dickinson) for movies, some of which are *The
Long Riders, Goin' South, Southern Comfort, Crossroads,* and
Paris, Texas. More recently, Cooder is working with John Hiatt,
Jim Keltner, and Nick Lowe under the moniker of Little
Village. —RC

Ry Cooder / REPRISE   1971
His debut serves as a neat prototype, with its Sleepy John
Estes and Woody Guthrie covers. It also introduces a most
talented musician in its leader. But it's still a prototype; the
best was yet to come. —JT

Into the Purple Valley / REPRISE   1972
Cooder perfects his snaky slide guitar technique and
introduces exotic ethnic elements on his second album. An
American traditional music celebration. —JT

Boomer's Story / WARNER   1972
Largely laidback and bluesy, this album features a number of
paeans to an America long lost. —JT

☆ **Paradise and Lunch / REPRISE**   1974
Working with an intriguing collection of veteran musicians, the master musician and archivist turns in a stunning set of timeless remakes and new compositions. –JT

Chicken Skin Music / WARNER   1976
Hawaiian traditional music meets Leadbelly and Ben E. King on Cooder's gospelization of rock & soul. –JT

Show Time / WARNER   1977
Recorded live in 1976, Cooder cooks and struts his stuff on this grand tour of his abilities. The great Flaco Jimenez is on accordion. –JT

Jazz / WARNER   1984
A tribute to Dixieland, with a stopover at the blues hotel. Joseph Byrd's arrangements on tunes by Bix Beiderbecke, Joseph Byrd's, Joseph Spence, et al., are inspired. –JT

○ **Get Rhythm / WARNER**   1987
Self-producing this time, Cooder gets the old rock & roll right. Johnny Cash and Chuck Berry are pretty darn funky. Cooder can still play slide guitar like no one else. –JT

SAM COOKE   1935-1964

R&B, soul. Possessing arguably the most glorious voice in Black music, Cooke was never entirely sure what to do with it. Purists prefer his work with the Soul Stirrers (1950-1956) where the gospel edges were untrammeled by any concession to the pop market. When he began recording pop and R&B for Keen and, subsequently RCA, the results varied widely among supper club music, teen ballads, early-60s pop, and proto-soul. That's why the *Live at the Harlem Square* set is important; it captures the way Cooke performed for a Black audience and shows why virtually every soul singer from the 60s and beyond cited him as a primary influence.

For the majority of his years in secular music, Cooke burdened himself with producers for whom the R&B market was at best a secondary consideration. Even the dippiest material is redeemed to an extent by his voice and phrasing, but his unqualified successes are fewer than we might have hoped for. Cooke's death in 1964 meant that he never lived to see his own prophecy, "A Change Is Gonna Come," become truer than he would ever have believed. –CE

★ **The Man and His Music / RCA**   1986
The ultimate Sam Cooke collection, and really the only one worth owning, covering his post-1957 career from his pop music breakthrough ("You Send Me") to his final impassioned soul statement, "A Change Is Gonna Come" (which is included in its seldom-heard uncut version). Few stones are left unturned, the sound is clean and sharp, and the tragedy of Cooke's early death is recalled with each play of this collection. –BE

☆ **Live at the Harlem Square Club / RCA**   1989
Long believed lost, this live album — rejected for release in 1963 by Cooke's managers, who wanted to broaden his appeal to White listeners — captures Cooke playing to a largely Black crowd, and it couldn't be more different from his *At the Copa* live album. A hot, sweaty performance, with Cooke and a proper band luxuriating in his most soulful material in its most wrenching and impassioned form. –BE

RITA COOLIDGE   b 1944

Pop. Coolidge sang in her father's church and backed up Delaney & Bonnie and Joe Cocker before launching a solo career in 1969. Her adult-contemporary, laidback style touches on blues, gospel, pop, and R&B elements. –BC

○ **Classics - Vol. 5 / A&M**   1987
Fine cuts from every style Coolidge has recorded, including the hits "(Your Love Has Lifted Me) Higher and Higher," "We're All Alone," and "You." –BC

ALICE COOPER   b 1948

Hard rock, rock/pop. During the first half of the 70s, Alice

Cooper (born Vincent Furnier, son of a preacher), made a name for himself as the king of gross-out, horror hard-rock, touring with guillotines, boa constrictors, and mutilated baby dolls, among other shock props. Fortunately, Cooper's theatrical hard-rock anthems generally weren't upstaged by his performance antics, thanks to smart choices of song covers and crafty plunderings of showtune melodies. Songs like "I'm Eighteen" (#21) and "School's Out" (#7) are among some of rock's finest expressions of teen discontent. Cooper fired his original classic lineup in 1974 to pursue a solo career that, while giving him his biggest chart hits, reduced him to an odd middle-of-the-road balladeer. He returned to his old schtick with blood and guts in the late 80s, enjoying something of a comeback. –RC

Love It to Death / WARNER   1971
Features the classic "Eighteen." Other standouts: "Caught in a Dream," "Long Way to Go," and "Black Juju." The best studio album by Cooper. –RC

Killer / WARNER   1971
Contains the hits "Under My Wheels" and "Be My Lover." Some of the more theatrical pieces undermine the album's strengths. –RC

School's Out / WARNER   1972
The title cut is a Top Ten hit. One of Cooper's best albums. –RC

○ **Alice Cooper's Greatest Hits / WARNER**   1974
A good collection of hit singles and key album tracks but not definitive. –RC

Welcome to My Nightmare / ATLANTIC   1975
Cooper's solo artist debut contains "Only Women Bleed." It's the best of his solo efforts. –RC

LES COOPER   b 1931

R&B, rock & roll. A longtime denizen of New York's doo-wop scene, Cooper's only major hit was the 1962 instrumental "Wiggle Wobble." The Norfolk, VA, native was a member of the Empires and the Whirlers, and managed the Charts, before signing with Danny Robinson's Everlast imprint and cutting a vocal called "Dig Yourself" with his band, the Soul Rockers. Ironically, it was the flip side (a pounding instrumental called "Wiggle Wobble," featuring prominent King Curtis-styled tenor sax by ex-Charts lead singer Joe Grier) that gave Cooper his only chart ride. Followup efforts included the similar "Let's Do the Boston Monkey" for Enjoy. –BD

○ **Wiggle Wobble / COLLECTABLES**   1963
Cooper's soulful vocals and Joe Grier's yakety-sax combine for some scorching early 60s R&B. –BD

JULIAN COPE

Alternative pop. By the time Julian Cope called it quits with the Teardrop Explodes in 1982, he had already acquired something of a legendary status in English alternative pop, as a wildly creative oddball who fell somewhere between Syd Barrett and Jim Morrison. His solo albums blended 60s psychedelia, synth-pop, and garage rock into a wonderfully twisted stew, with his dry vocal delivery way up in the mix. Subject matter ranges from acid-tinged ruminations to unique manifestos on the state of the planet.

Each of his efforts is worth seeking out, but *Peggy Suicide* is an ambitious project that consolidates Cope's many strengths to great effect. –RC

○ **Saint Julian / ISLAND**   1987
Former Teardrop Explodes leader Julian Cope adopted a harder, more direct rock style for his solo work, making it more accessible and bringing out the qualities of his commanding baritone. –WR

● **Peggy Suicide / POLYGRAM**   1991
Peggy Suicide is Cope's idiosyncratic and complexly layered treatise on the state of the earth. Initially inspired by a vision that involved his own self-created mythological characters

(Peggy Suicide as Mother Earth, Pollutio as destructive siren), Cope expands his cosmic tragedy beyond the larger political, social, and ecological issues with a healthy dose of mesmerizing psychedelic state-of-the-mind profiles. The unpolished production quality gives *Peggy Suicide* a more immediately believable delivery. Cope juxtaposes pure garage-rock next to marimbas, loopy keyboard sounds, and loose-limbed percussion into a spellbinding tapestry. Among the many highlights are the ominous AIDS/death epic "Safesurfer" and "Drive, She Said," which is a trashy synthesis of Bowie's Velvet Underground sendups. –RC

CORROSION OF CONFORMITY

Punk. This North Carolina band was one of the first to address political issues. They began in the early 80s with lots of support within the punk community for their hardcore sound. By the end of the decade they adopted thrash-metal. –JB

○ **Animosity / CAROLINE**   1985
Their most popular work to date, with a lot of punk and hardcore overtones. Like Agnostic Front, they introduced a lot of metal listeners to punk and hardcore, and this was the album that did it. –JB

Blind / RELATIVITY   1991
One of the best bands in hardcore turns around and moves into the thrash world with excellent results. Heavy like Metallica yet still capturing that punk edge. –JB

ELVIS COSTELLO   b 1955

Singer/songwriter, alternative rock. The most evocative, innovative, and wildly gifted songwriter since Bob Dylan, Elvis Costello is a remarkably brilliant and complex personality. From the angry young mannerisms of his initial work through the sophistication of his later stuff, Costello has confounded and intrigued audiences with songs that offer highly personal takes on love and politics, often (as on *Armed Forces*) blurring the divisions between those elements. The stylistic diversity of his oeuvre reflects his refusal to limit himself within the structures of pop music. And while our determination has rendered some of his more recent work insufferably erratic and stuffy, his fascinatingly deft lyricisms remain some of the most individualistic and significant of the rock era. Although there are two best-ofs in his catalog, his strengths are most apparent on the original long-players.

☆ **My Aim Is True / CBS / BB 32**   1977
Elvis Costello's debut album is a pop landmark that indicates the future that may exist for the spirit of punk in the wider genre of rock music. Backed by the American group Clover (featuring then-future Doobie Brother John McFee but not harmonica player Huey Lewis), Costello displays all the characteristics that would serve him throughout his career: a caustic wit he uses to savage himself and others, a broad imagination — "(The Angels Wanna Wear My) Red Shoes" is one of the best pieces of rock whimsy ever written, an unsentimental but compelling sense of romance ("Alison"), and an astonishing verbal facility, all enmeshed with a pop encyclopedist's musical knowledge. One of the greatest first albums in pop history. –WR

☆ **This Year's Model / CBS / BB 30**   1978
Backed by his road band, the Attractions, his music becomes harder on the edges, suiting perfectly the bitterness of Costello's best song-for-song set. –JF

★ **Armed Forces / CBS / BB 10**   1979
Lavishly produced by Nick Lowe, and masterfully programmed, this is Costello's most political album and his most melodic. His bitterness is somewhat subdued, but his passion informs every song. –JF

Get Happy! / CBS / BB 11   1980
This brisk 20-song set is Costello's take on soul music. Many of the songs are remarkable but just as many fall flat. –JF

Taking Liberties / CBS / BB 28   1980
An interesting jumble of British B-sides and previously

unreleased material. Stylistically diverse, and occasionally sublime. –JF

Almost Blue / CBS / BB 50   1981
Costello's country record, produced by veteran Nashville producer Billy Sherrill. Not one of Costello's best, but it shows an interesting side of his musical sensibilities, even as it makes his shortcomings as a singer more obvious. –SWB

Trust / CBS / BB 28   1981
Some of the songs are too obtuse to really stick, but the Attractions turn the best of them into edgy and brittle mini-masterpieces. –JF

☆ **Imperial Bedroom / CBS / BB 30**   1982
This ornately orchestrated and lush set is Costello's version of *Blood on the Tracks*. It's a musically sophisticated and emotionally devastating tour through the crumbling heart of an incurable romantic. –JF

Punch the Clock / CBS / BB 24   1983
An upbeat set of fairly clear and concise pop songs, supplemented by some punchy horn charts. –JF

○ **King of America / CBS / BB 39**   1986
Although this is linked thematically to *Imperial Bedroom*, Costello's newfound clarity and the mostly acoustic accompaniment distinguish it from anything in his canon. Remarkable. –JF

Blood & Chocolate / CBS   1986
A hard-rocking but inconsistent set made worthwhile by "I Want You," "I Hope You're Happy Now," and "Next Time Round," all emotional stunners. –JF

Girls Girls Girls / CBS   1989
Elvis Costello assembled this compilation himself. It is highly idiosyncratic, not the least of its peculiarities being that the CD and cassette versions differ considerably. Costello describes a vague concept in his notes, but the collection of songs (47 on the CDs, 51 on the cassettes) seems a jumble. At least he demonstrates that songs from different periods work well together. A large part of Costello's oeuvre, including some of his best work, is represented. –WR

○ **Spike / WARNER / BB 32**   1989
Throughout his career Elvis Costello has always been prolific; thus it was surprising, even given the change in record labels for the US, when he took a whole 20 months between *Blood & Chocolate* and this followup. But the musical growth he exhibits makes the wait worthwhile. The musical settings range from the stark folk of "Tramp the Dirt Down" to the pop sprightliness of "Veronica" (a collaboration with Paul McCartney that became Costello's first American Top 20 hit) and the New Orleans jazz sound of "Deep Dark Truthful Mirror," featuring the Dirty Dozen Brass Band. The lyrics are among his best. –WR

Mighty Like a Rose / WARNER   1991
The lyrical concerns here are cumbersome and pretentious, and the music is ponderous and indulgent. But a few decent songs — especially "The Other Side of Summer" — make this 1991 set worthwhile. –JF

PAUL COTTON   b 1943

Country rock. This rock guitarist cofounded Illinois Speed Press (two albums on Epic), then joined Poco in 1971, replacing Jim Messina. He left that group in the mid 80s and issued the solo debut *Changing Horses* in 1989. –WR

○ **Changing Horses / CAPITOL**   1990
On this solo outing, Cotton abandons the country leanings of his former band for a more straightforward rock approach that benefits from his tasty guitar playing and grainy voice. (Includes a remake of his Poco hit "Heart of the Night.") –WR

COUNTRY JOE & THE FISH

Folk/rock, psychedelic, country rock. Led by Country Joe McDonald (b Jan 1, 1942) and Barry Melton (b 1947) this psychedelic country/folk/rock group (based in Berkeley, CA)

formed in the mid 60s. Their anthem was the anti-war satire "I-Feel-Like-I'm-Fixin'-to-die Rag." –WR

○ **Collected Country Joe & the Fish / VANGUARD**   1987
CJ & the F are well represented on *Collected Country Joe & the Fish (1965-1970)*, a 19-track compilation that traces their development from a politically oriented folk-jugband ensemble to a politically oriented rock and soul band. Most of the material comes from 1967, the band's high-water mark, and the centerpiece is the still cutting "I-Feel-Like-I'm-Fixin'-to-Die Rag." –WR

DAVE COUSINS

Folk/rock, prog-rock. Leader/founder of the Strawbs, Dave Cousins may be the most talented Dylan-influenced songwriter to come out of England. His work fairly resounds of both rebellion and antiquity, as though he were writing protest songs of the 18th or 19th centuries. Haunting melodies abound, carried by his raspy and sincere voice. It's beautiful sound is marred only by the same problem that plagued the Strawbs — his difficulty in finding proper musical backup and settings. –BE

○ **Two Weeks Last Summer / A&M**   1972
Almost a lost Strawbs album, with moments of stately, haunting beauty and a wonderful title tune but harsh and unmelodic a little too often. (Out of print import) –BE

Old School Songs / PVC   1980
A mixed bag of songs that lacks the excitement of Cousins's electric recordings but is more pleasing with repeated listenings. (Out of print) –BE

COWBOY JUNKIES

Alternative rock. Low-key quartet from Toronto comes off like a country group with a lava-lamp rhythm section, but occasionally the songwriting of Michael Timmins and the eerie vocals of his sister Margo produce strangely fascinating moments. –JF

○ **The Trinity Session / RCA**   1988
Recorded with one microphone in an abandoned church, their second album achieves a haunting ambience. –JF

Black Eyed Man / RCA   1992
The Cowboy Junkies stick with their style of low-key songs steeped in country blues. Songwriter and guitarist Michael Timmins writes story-songs full of rain and street life and regret, and they are movingly sung by Margo Timmins. Two Townes Van Zandt songs, including his classic "To Live is to Fly," fit right in. –WR

THE CRAMPS

Alternative rock. They made their arrival during the first wave of punk-rock, but this New York (via Cleveland, OH) quartet (two guitars, drums, vocals, no bass) found their inspiration in the bizarre sounds of rockabilly and surf guitar and the seedy side of American junk-culture. At their best, the Cramps managed to pay homage to their musical heroes without aping them. –JF

○ **Songs the Lord Taught Us / I.R.S.**   1980
Their first album is a brillant tribute to their inspirers. It's well-chosen covers mingle with ferocious originals. –JF

○ **Psychedelic Jungle / A&M**   1981
Contains the second album (not as wild as the first but still a ton of fun) and their debut EP material, featuring the epochal "Human Fly" and a pulverizing cover of Roy Orbison's "Domino." –JF

Smell of Female / CAPITOL   1983
A live EP of new material that is a tad lackluster. "Call of the Wighat" conjures the fire of the old days, and "I Ain't Nothin' but a Gorehound" is a career-defining anthem. –JF

● **Bad Music for Bad People / A&M**   1984
A solid collection of singles, B-sides, and album cuts. A decent introduction made great by "Drug Train" and "New Kind of Kick." –JF

CRAZY BACKWARDS ALPHABET

Prog-rock. A Henry Kaiser one-off, with drummers John French and Michael Maksymenko and bassist Andy West (Dixie Dregs). –MB

Crazy Backwards Alphabet / SST   1987
Heavy chops and creativity from this expansive supergroup, with Henry Kaiser. Some hilarious cover versions. –MB

CRAZY HORSE

Rock & roll. A hard-rock trio consisting of bassist Billy Talbot, drummer Ralph Molina, and guitarist Danny Whitten. They are known best as the on-again, off-again backup band for Neil Young, though they have recorded occasional albums themselves. Frank Sampedro replaced Whitten after his death in 1973. The current band is Talbot, Molina, singer Sonny Mone, and guitarist Matt Piucci. –WR

○ **Crazy Moon / RCA**   1978
The trio of Molina, Talbot, and Sampedro is frequently joined by compatriot Neil Young on an album of hard rock with a sound not unlike that produced by them on Young's records. –WR

THE CRAZY WORLD OF ARTHUR BROWN

Rock/pop, psychedelic. Arthur Brown (b Jun 24, 1944) formed the Crazy World of Arthur Brown with Vincent Crane (organ) and Drachen Teaker (drums) in his native England in the mid 60s. They were a one-hit wonder with "Fire," though Brown has continued to record since and appeared in the film *Tommy*. –WR

○ **The Crazy World of Arthur Brown / POLYGRAM**   1985
Brown came on like a British verison of Screamin' Jay Hawkins in 1968, when he launched his first and only hit by intoning "I am the god of hellfire." That song, "Fire," is on the album, and it's reason enough to recommend it. –WR

CREAM

Prog-rock, psychedelic. Eric Clapton (guitar), Jack Bruce (bass) and Ginger Baker (drums) were all veterans of the British blues scene by the time they formed Cream in late 1966, but their brand of highly amplified, free-form playing took the music to new directions that a band like the Yardbirds could only dream of. They were one of the first bands to legitimatize jamming on stage, with each member a solid soloist in his own right; Baker's solo on "Toad" being a constant highlight of their live show. Their original material (much of it written by Bruce) strayed far from their blues roots, in a more pop direction, expanding their audience in the bargain. When they called it quits in 1969, rock critics mourned their demise, but their two principal contributions (being rock's first "supergroup" and helping to lay the foundation for heavy metal) live on. –CK

Fresh Cream / RSO / BB 39   1966
Cream's debut album was largely rooted in the blues, and included here highly-charged versions of such standards as Willie Dixon's "Spoonful," Muddy Waters's "Rollin' and Tumblin'," and bassist Jack Bruce's "N.S.U." — took on a whole new life on stage. On this record they sound somewhat flat and uninspired. (Fans of the band will want to obtain the gold disc from DCC Compact Classics, as it offers amazing detailing of the instrumentation set in a deep soundstage.) –RB

○ **Disraeli Gears / RSO / BB 4**   1967
Cream's sophomore effort was a substantial step forward. Interestingly, part of the reason seems to be that they stopped covering American blues musicians and started writing their own psychedelic blues-based hybrids. "Sunshine of Your Love" was the big AM radio hit and "Tales of Brave Ulysses," "Strange Brew," and "Swlabr" received substantial FM play. –RB

○ **Wheels of Fire / POLYGRAM**   1968
Wheels of Fire was a two-album set, one disc recorded in the studio, the second disc recorded on stage in San Francisco. Side 3 contains the definitive live version of what became

Clapton's signature piece, Robert Johnson's "Crossroads," plus a version of "Spoonful" that clocks in just short of seventeen minutes. On such pieces, Cream approached blues-based rock with a jazz aesthetic, using the song as a framework to begin and end a performance. The strength of the performance is in the improvisation. When it worked, as it does on "Spoonful," they were brilliant. When it didn't, as on side 4's "Traintime" and "Toad," the band became excess incarnate. The studio disc contained their second Top Ten single, Jack Bruce's "White Room," as well as a stunning cover of Albert King's "Born under a Bad Sign." Other tracks, particularly those written by Ginger Baker, do not hold up. (DCC's gold-plated CD sounds marvelous, using, for the first time ever, the original master tape. The original foil and day-glo artwork was restored, as was a previously unreleased version of "Passing the Time.") –RB

Goodbye / RSO 1969
As the title implies, this is Cream's farewell. By the time it was issued, the band had broken up. Three studio recordings that were left were coupled with extended live versions of "I'm So Glad," "Politician," and "I'm Sitting on Top of the World." The live tracks burn. Clapton, Bruce, and Baker each take credit for one of the studio tracks. Clapton's cut, "Badge," was cowritten by George Harrison and remains what was surely the prettiest melody to ever grace a Cream recording. –RB

○ **Live Cream - Vol. 2 / RSO** 1969
More live Cream concentrating on material from their *Disraeli Gears* and *Wheels of Fire* albums plus an extended workout on Freddie King's "Hideaway." –RB

★ **Strange Brew - The Very Best of Cream / RSO** 1971
What the title implies, all the finest tracks from the band's four studio albums. The best was brilliant. –RB

☆ **Live Cream - Vol. 1 / RSO** 1981
Cream was a band born to the stage. I think this is their most consistently brilliant album. Four of the five cuts appeared on *Fresh Cream*. The fifth, "Lawdy Mama," is a traditional blues piece that makes its first appearance here. All but "Lawdy Mama" are given extended jazz-based treatment. The dialog among the three musicians as the jams develop is fascinating. Foreground and background seem to dissolve as all three musicians take charge, using the full range of their instruments. Performances like this single-handedly raised the stakes of musicianship in rock. –RB

THE CREATURES

Alternative pop. The Creatures are a subset of Siouxsie and the Banshees consisting of singer Siouxsie Sioux (born Susan Dallion, May 27, 1957) and drummer Budgie (born Peter Clarke, Aug 21, 1957). –WR

○ **Boomerang / GEFFEN** 1989
If you like Siouxsie and the Banshees, you'll like this spin-off, which features Siouxsie singing over elaborate percussion tracks. –WR

CREEDENCE CLEARWATER REVIVAL

Rock & roll. Even though Creedence Clearwater Revival hailed from the San Francisco area, the band's soul, which was steeped in R&B, rockabilly, blues, and stripped-down rock & roll, made it hard to believe they came from anywhere but the Mississippi Delta. At that time, Bay Area rock was dominated by bands like the Grateful Dead, Quicksilver Messenger Service, and Jefferson Airplane, whose idea of economical arrangements and a tight rhythmic pocket hardly existed.
John Fogerty, the band's lead vocalist/lead guitarist, brought a kind of passion to rock & roll that few recorded artists have ever delivered. Not only that, but his songwriting contributions to rock have unquestionably placed him in the ranks of American music legends like Chuck Berry, Willie Dixon, and Carl Perkins. Creedence's rhythm section, with Stu Cook (bass), Doug Clifford (drums), and Tom Fogerty (rhythm guitar), made every note count, doing for rock what Booker T. and the MG's did for Memphis soul.

Any lover of real, earthy rock should own most of Creedence's catalog, since this is the meat-and-potatoes of any decent rock collection. Then again, it is unimaginable that any lover of rock & roll could be unaware of this band. –RC

Creedence Clearwater Revival / FANTASY 1968
The band's unique swampy crunch was already well developed on this fine debut. It opens with a riveting version of Screamin' Jay Hawkins's hit "I Put a Spell on You." A gritty psychedelic version of Dale Hawkin's creation "Suzy Q" was Creedence's first hit. –RC

Bayou Country / FANTASY 1969
John Fogerty's songwriting voice gains new focus, particularly in "Proud Mary," the band's most popular song, and "Penthouse Pauper." "Bootleg" features a powerfully spare groove, and "Born on the Bayou," with its rock-solid pulse and economical lead guitar work, is one of the band's better attempts at stretching out. Nevertheless, the long jams found here cause the album to lose some steam. –RC

○ **Willy & the Poor Boys / FANTASY** 1969
Not a weak cut here, just more hits like "Down on the Corner" and the relentless wrong-side-of-the-tracks railing of "Fortunate Son." By the time of *Willy*, this California band had captured the spirit of the South more believably than most bands from that region. Versions of "The Midnight Special," "Cotton Fields," and instrumentals like the down-home "Poorboy Shuffle" and "Side O' the Road," with its Booker T. groove, helped underscore that perception. –RC

○ **Green River / FANTASY** 1969
Fogerty tightens things up with this great collection of songs. Contains the truly great hits "Green River," "Lodi," and "Bad Moon Rising." "Wrote a Song for Everyone," "Cross-tie Walker," and "Tombstone Shadow" are classic Fogerty. There's a super version of "The Night Time is the Right Time." –RC

○ **Cosmo's Factory / FANTASY** 1970
"Ramble Tamble" and a masterful version of "I Heard It through the Grapevine" may run a little too long, but the remainder of the album is letter-perfect. Pointing out highlights here is useless. Most of these tracks were hits as well. –RC

Pendulum / FANTASY 1970
Creedence loses some steam here by wasting too much time on lengthy groove numbers like "Pagen Baby," "Born to Move," and "Rude Awakening #2," a horrible attempt at creating something serious-sounding, and an irritating waste of time. In spite of these miscalculations, most bands could only hope for as many good songs like "Have You Ever Seen the Rain?," "Hey Tonight," "It's Just a Thought," "Molina," and "(Wish I Could) Hideaway." –RC

Mardi Gras / FANTASY 1972
Maybe Fogerty was running out of steam, but in the name of democratization, each of the other band members got to toss in their creative licks on this album. After so many great albums, this one sounds half-hearted. Only "Sweet Hitch-Hiker," "Someday Never Comes," and a cover of the Ricky Nelson tune "Hello Mary Lou" recall the band's earlier magic. –RC

★ **Chronicle - Vol. 1 / FANTASY** 1976
Essential disc for any serious lover of rock & roll. Contains almost all of the Creedence hits, plus a generous helping of key album tracks. –RC

The Royal Albert Hall Concert / FANTASY 1980
This solid no-frills live document covers many of the band's hits, plus time for some meat-and-potatoes groove-jammin' with ten minutes of "Keep on Chooglin'." It beats the dismal *Live in Europe* by a long shot. –RC

☆ **Chronicle - Vol. 2 / FANTASY** 1986
A well-compiled set that fills in most of the gaps left by Vol. 1. Sin of omission: Where's "Bootleg" ?! –RC

Creedence Clearwater Revival / TIME-LIFE
A very good made-for-TV anthology. Good liner notes. The

mastering lacks some of the definition and presence found on the Fantasy discs. –RC

MARSHALL CRENSHAW   b1954

Singer/songwriter, rock/pop, rock & roll. When Marshall Crenshaw's debut burst onto the 1982 music scene, his tight well-crafted songs (part Buddy Holly/part Beatles) and exuberant performances were a fresh breeze at a time when robotic pop by Human League and Tony Basil, as well as soulnumbing ballads like Lionel Richie's "Truly," reigned on the airwaves. He even managed a Top 40 hit with the timeless-sounding "Someday, Someway."

Crenshaw's albums have been mostly enjoyable. Only on 1989's *Good Evening* does Crenshaw seem creatively adrift. –RC

○ **Marshall Crenshaw / WARNER / BB 50**   1982
His incredible debut revealed Crenshaw to be a fully formed songwriter in the Beatles and Buddy Holly super-melodic pop tradition. Like the work of those influences, the best material here seems timeless. "Someday, Someway" (#36) was a moderate hit, even though it (and others like "Cynical Girl," "Girls," "The Usual Thing," and "Mary Anne") seemed written in stone. Crenshaw does include one fine cover of "Soldier of Love," recorded originally by Arthur Alexander and later by the Beatles. Criticism: Why has Warner chosen not to include Crenshaw's fine B-sides as bonus tracks from this period on this or his other CDs? –RC

● **Field Day / WARNER / BB 52**   1983
For those expecting a repeat of his fine debut effort, Crenshaw made an unexpected left turn and sought out in-demand producer Steve Lillywhite, whose credits (Psychedelic Furs, XTC, U2, Ultravox) read like an alternative-rock Who's Who. The heavily treated drum sounds and walls of guitar may have initially put off some fans, but *Field Day* demonstrated that Crenshaw was making impressive strides as a songwriter and musician. "Whenever You're on My Mind" (a great single that should've been a hit), "Our Town," "All I Know Right Now," and "Monday Morning Rock" are highlights. –RC

○ **Downtown / WARNER**   1985
With the help of producer T-Bone Burnette and a handful of session sidemen, Crenshaw delivered a strong collection of originals and covers. Highlights include a version of Ben Vaughn's "I'm Sorry (But So Is Brenda Lee)" and Crenshaw's own "The Distance Between." This is one of Crenshaw's best efforts. –RC

Mary Jean & 9 Others / WARNER   1987
Not quite as strong as his first three full-length albums, *Mary Jean* does possess some standout tracks in "Calling Out for Love (At Crying Time)," a version of Peter Case's "Steel Strings," and the title cut. Produced by Don Dixon, whose credits include the Smithereens. –RC

Life's Too Short / MCA   1991
Crenshaw changes labels and brings on producer Ed Stasium (Cavedogs, Living Colour, Smithereens). The result is a more vibrant, harder-rocking sound. Highlights include "Better Back Off," "Don't Disappear Now," "Face of Fashion," and "Fantastic Planet of Love." This is his strongest release since *Downtown*. –RC

THE CRESTS

Doo-wop. One of the most successful integrated doo-wop groups, the Crests waxed the classic ballad "16 Candles" in 1959. Formed in 1956, they began recording the next year for Joyce, where they inched onto the pop lists with "Sweetest One." Moving to the brand-new Coed logo, Johnny Maestro's (b May 7, 1930) warm tenor made "16 Candles" a national smash, and pop/R&B hybrids like "The Angels Listened In" and "Step by Step" also did well. Maestro went solo in 1960, scoring the next year with "Model Girl" on Coed, while the Crests attempted to survive on their own. Maestro eventually reclaimed stardom as leader of Brooklyn Bridge, an 11-piece aggregation that hit with "Worst That Could Happen" in 1968. –BD

○ **The Best of the Crests / COED**
All the hits, including the classic "16 Candles." Out of print and highly collectible. –CK

CRICKETS

Rock & roll. After the tragic death of Buddy Holly, his band, the Crickets, regrouped and continue to record and tour to this day. Drummer Jerry Allison and bassist Joe B. Mauldin had split from Holly shortly before his death, and with ex-Holly guitarist Sonny Curtis and vocalist Earl Sinks, they continued to record for Brunswick and Coral, notably the original versons of "I Fought the Law" and "More Than I Can Say." Moving to Liberty in 1961 with Jerry Naylor as their new singer, the Crickets recorded for Liberty into 1965 without having a hit of their own. Allison and Curtis were prolific session musicians, backing Bobby Vee, Eddie Cochran, Johnny Burnette, and the Everly Brothers in addition to Holly. With a lineup of Allison, Mauldin, and Gordon Payne, the Crickets garnered airplay in 1988 with "T-Shirt," a bouncy number produced by lifelong Holly fan Paul McCartney. –BD

○ **Liberty Years / CAPITOL**   1991
Thirty-one cuts of post-Buddy Holly material from his band the Crickets, who endured into 1965 on Liberty Records. Their energetic pop-rock sound often mirrored whatever trends were happening at the time. –BD

CRIME & THE CITY SOLUTION

Alternative rock. Believers in and purveyors of the myths of the gothic American South, CCS is a spin-off of Nick Cave's Birthday Party. Mostly Aussies living in Britain, they developed from a sparse, bluesy group into a somewhat arch, unfeeling rock thing. –BE

○ **Just South of Heaven / RESTLESS**   1985
Aussies with a gothic vision of the American South. –RG

Paradise Discotheque / ELEKTRA   1990
Disjointed elements of folky dance music, gothic rock, and the blues. A different but listenable stew. –RG

JIM CROCE   1943-1973

Singer/songwriter. A singer/songwriter whose enormous pop success of the early 70s was cut short by his death in a plane crash. A Philadelphia native who had worked the coffeehouse circuit for almost ten years when he was signed to ABC Records in 1971, Croce had a warm singing voice that served him well on his comic uptempo hits ("You Don't Mess Around with Jim," "Bad, Bad Leroy Brown") as well as his sincere ballads ("Operator"). The latter became predominant after his death, with "I Got a Name," "Time in a Bottle," and "I'll Have to Say I Love You in a Song," all of which were posthumous Top Ten hits. –WR

You Don't Mess Around with Jim / COMMAND   1972
Debut of love songs and gimmicky story tunes. –BC

○ **Photographs & Memories ... / ATLANTIC**   1974
Photographs & Memories - His Greatest Hits is a compilation containing Croce's best songs and biggest hits, including the #1 hits "Bad, Bad Leroy Brown" and "Time in a Bottle." –WR

STEVE CROPPER   b1941

Soul. Probably the best-known soul guitarist in the world, Cropper came to prominence in the early 60s, first with the Mar-Keys ("Last Night"), then as a founding member of Booker T. & the MG's. A major figure in the Southern soul movement of the 60s, Cropper made his mark not only as a player and arranger (most notably on classic sides by Otis Redding, Sam & Dave, and Wilson Pickett) but as a songwriter as well, cowriting the classic "In the Midnight Hour." After the breakup of the MG's, Cropper spent most of the 70s producing Jeff Beck and Mitch Ryder, among others. In the 80s he rode the classic Stax sound (which he helped shape) back to popularity with a new audience when actors John Belushi and Dan Aykroyd tapped him for service in the Blues Brothers, a

"Saturday Night Live" skit that stretched into several albums and a movie. –CK

○ **With a Little Help from My Friends / STAX** 1971
Like Booker T. & the MG's, with a focus on guitar instead of organ. Hard-driving; great horns. A great dose of Memphis soul. –RG

DAVID CROSBY ♭1941

Singer/songwriter, rock/pop. Crosby was an original member of the groundbreaking 60s Los Angeles band, the Byrds. During his time with them, Crosby's smooth harmonic capabilities and airy lead-vocal style provided a major ingredient in their distinctive sound. He also wrote or cowrote some wonderfully trippy songs during his stint with them, including "Lady Friend" (#82), "Everybody's Been Burned," "Draft Morning," "Dolphins Smile," "Why," "Eight Miles High" (#14), "What Happening?!?!," and "I See You," a song Yes recorded on their debut album.

Crosby left the Byrds and helped found the richly harmonic, mellow acoustic-rock trio Crosby, Stills & Nash in 1968. They enjoyed enormous success in their first few years, but solo projects and Crosby's notorious drug problems (and subsequent late-80s celebrity cleanup) resulted in the band's sporadic output. In 1989 Crosby released *Oh Yes I Can*, along with a best-seller autobiography. –RC

○ **If I Could Only Remember My Name / ATLANTIC** 1971
On his first solo album, the velvet-voiced hippie crooner invited half of Northern California to join him. It's vintage Crosby, ranking with the best of CSNY group efforts. –JT

Oh Yes I Can / A&M 1989
His post-rehab reintroduction to the world of creativity finds a reflective Crosby still in fine voice and trying a few new things with his music. –JT

CROSBY & NASH

Rock/pop, folk/rock, singer/songwriter. This subset of Crosby, Stills, Nash & Young featured David Crosby (b Aug 14, 1941) and Graham Nash (b Feb 2, 1942) relying on their sweet harmonies and strong songwriting. The duo lasted from 1972 to the more-or-less permanent re-forming of Crosby, Stills & Nash in 1977. –WR

Crosby and Nash / ATLANTIC 1972
Nash and Crosby's first duo album after the demise of Crosby, Stills, Nash & Young produced a Top 40 hit, "Immigration Man." It also featured the excellent "Southbound Train," demonstrating the viability of C&N as a separate harmonic unit. –WR

○ **Wind on Water / MCA** 1975
Among the finest of the splinter albums to come out of the CSNY camp, this album was paced by Crosby's leadoff track, the moving "Carry Me," and by its closer, the vocal showcase "To the Last Whale." –WR

CROSBY STILLS & NASH (AND YOUNG)

Rock/pop, folk/rock, singer/songwriter. Crosby, Stills & Nash, expatriates of the Byrds, Buffalo Springfield, and the Hollies, respectively, became musical ambassadors of the Woodstock Generation, selling millions of albums along the way.

Their distinctive, tight, airy harmonies and soft acoustic-rock sound seemed effortless, in spite of the incredibly volatile nature of the band's personalities. Neil Young, formerly of Buffalo Springfield, came on board for their second album, *Déjà Vu*. His presence gave the band more edge and some of the album's highlights. Young's response to the 1970 National Guard killings of four Kent State students inspired "Ohio" (#14 pop), one of the group's best songs.

Nash compiled tapes of the band's live output and released the double-record set *Four Way Street*, which became a #1 album. When Young left, Crosby Stills & Nash got back together, their sound intact, and released *CS&N*, which produced the #7 hit "Just a Song Before I Go." It was another five-year wait before

they got around to doing a followup, *Daylight Again*. *Allies*, featuring live material, came out in 1983.

By this time, Crosby's long-running drug addiction was causing major problems within the group. In August of 1983, he was found guilty of cocaine possession and illegally carrying a gun and sentenced by a Texas judge.

Since then Crosby has cleaned up, written a best-seller about life as a star wrestling with his demons, and released his best solo album, *Oh Yes I Can*. Crosby, Stills, Nash & Young reunited, for the first time in fifteen years to record *American Dream*. –RC

☆ **Crosby, Stills & Nash / ATLANTIC** 1969
The group's debut album is a scintillating blend of personal poetry, topical politics, and splendid, spare production. "Suite: Judy Blue Eyes" caught everybody's ear, but every track here is worthwhile, and the success of the album can be measured by the fact that every song here could have been a single or a B-side. "Marrakesh Express," "Pre-Road Downs," and "Lady of the Island" stand out. –BE

★ **Déjà Vu / ATLANTIC** 1970
This was the group's triumph, displaying a broader musical scope than that found on the CSN debut record. Each of the four members contributed high-quality material, with Stills turning in the leadoff track, "Carry On," Nash contributing such standards as "Teach Your Children" and "Our House," Crosby presenting the title track, and Young adding the characteristic "Helpless." There was also the hit version of Joni Mitchell's "Woodstock." Flawless harmonies, thoughtful lyrics, accomplished playing: this is state-of-the-art 70s rock music and continues to be the best explanation of CSN&Y's enormous stature and enduring legacy. –WR

Four Way Street / ATLANTIC 1972
This expanded version of the original double live album by CSN&Y is now an indispensible part of any collection, with additional Neil Young and Graham Nash material (and even a version of "King Midas in Reverse," the old Hollies tune) that any serious listener will want. Some of the extended guitar jams between Stills and Young ("Southern Man") go on longer than strict musical sense would dictate, but it seemed right at the time, and they capture a form that was far more abused in other hands after this group broke up. –BE

CSN / ATLANTIC 1977
A fair and somewhat slick reprise, highlighted by "Dark Star." A valiant attempt to re-create the good spirits of the first album amid the malaise of the 70s. –BE

Replay / ATLANTIC 1980
Although this is a decent anthology of their hits and most well-known album tracks, with a few remixes, it's no substitute for the first album. –BE

○ **CSN (Boxed Set) / ATLANTIC** 1991
Seventy-seven tracks make up this four-CD boxed-set retrospective of the various permutations of Crosby, Stills & Nash (and Young) from 1968 to 1990. The set is dotted with fine unreleased tracks from abortive album sessions plus good choices of both solo work and well-known material. For a neophyte, it may be on the long side, but seasoned fans can welcome this lavish tribute. The sound quality alone justifies its purchase. –WR & BE

CHRISTOPHER CROSS ♭1951

Pop. Cross (born Christopher Geppert) came out of the blue in 1980 with his self-titled debut of slight soft-pop. He managed to clean up at the following year's Grammys, beating out previous record-holder Frank Sinatra with a total of five awards. That album generated several substantial hits with "Ride Like the Wind" (#2), "Never Be the Same" (#15), "Say You'll Be Mine" (#20), and the transcendent "Sailing," which went #1 and won Song of the Year. Cross briefly continued his success with several more hits like "Think of Laura" (#9), "All Right" (#12), and the #1 "Arthur's Theme (The Best That You Can Do)," from the movie *Arthur*, before sinking from sight.

Cross's last album, the 1988 release *Back of My Mind*, failed to chart, indicating that what fan base he had enjoyed no longer existed. –RC

○ **Christopher Cross / WARNER / BB 6**   1980
This Michael Omartian-produced collection of light-pop, which featured the atmospheric "Sailing," cleaned up at the 1980 Grammy presentations. Cross's rather thin tenor is given ample support from Michael McDonald, Don Henley, guitarist Eric Johnson, and other Los Angeles "A"-list session pros. –RC

CROWDED HOUSE

Rock/pop. In 1985, New Zealand-born Neil Finn was left with the task of continuing with Split Enz after the departure of his brother (and founding member) Tim Finn. He opted instead to dissolve the Enz. Taking drummer Paul Hester with him, he formed a stripped-down trio with bassist Nick Seymour. After years of writing Split Enz's synth-pop hits like "I Got You" and "One Step Ahead," Neil concentrated on well-crafted, melodic songs and transparent production. This new Australian band was dubbed Crowded House for the state of congestion in the Los Angeles bungalow the band shared while recording with producer/keyboardist Mitchell Froom. Their self-titled 1986 debut album was a sleeper hit that waited until the third single, "Don't Dream It's Over," before jumping into the Top Ten. An excellent live act, Crowded House made quite a splash that year. Although their next two albums didn't match the chart success of the first, the consistently high level of quality has earned them many fans and critic's darling status. Tim Finn joined the band briefly for the *Woodface* album and tour. –SWB

● **Crowded House / CAPITOL**   1986
Their Top 40 debut is loaded with highly melodic, anglo-pop gems. Strong, upbeat songwriting and vocal harmonies from this talented trio, featuring the hits "Don't Dream It's Over" and "Something So Strong." –SWB

Temple of Low Men / CAPITOL   1988
Darker and more introspective, this still has fine songwriting and performances, including a guest appearance from Richard Thompson. Highlights include "Into Temptation," "Better Be Home Soon," and "When You Come." –SWB

○ **Woodface / CAPITOL**   1991
Reaching a new level of craft, this album has the great melodies of their first, the soul-searching depth of the second, and the great vocal harmonies of the reunited Finn brothers. A close contender for their most essential album. –SWB

THE CULT

Hard rock. Singer Ian Astbury formed the Southern Death Cult in England in 1982 as a doom-rock band. Reorganized in 1983 with guitarist Billy Duffy as Death Cult, by 1984 the rock quartet, quickly moving toward heavy metal, had become simply the Cult. Their hard-rock set *Electric* (1987) was a commercial breakthrough. –WR

○ **Electric / SIRE**   1987
After four years of evolving from a goth-rock band with two longer names (Southern Death Cult, Death Cult), the Cult emerged on this Rick Rubin production as a full-fledged heavy metal band. Billy Duffy pulls out monstrous guitar riffs and lead singer Ian Astbury declaims like a latter-day Jim Morrison. Contains "Love Removal Machine." –WR

CULTURE CLUB

Pop. Culture Club was a successful pop-rock group of the early 80s, led by singer Boy George O'Dowd (b Jun 14, 1961). It was as well known for O'Dowd's flamboyant fashion sense as it was for its music, but when it was hot, it was hot: Culture Club racked up six straight Top Ten hits in 1983-1984.
The group was formed in London in 1981. In addition to O'Dowd, it consisted of bassist Mikey Craig (b Feb 15, 1960), guitarist Roy Hay (b Aug 12, 1961), and drummer Jon Moss (b Sep 11, 1957). They topped the charts with their debut single,

"Do You Really Want to Hurt Me." The band's visual flair helped them in the US, where music video had recently become an important promotional tool, and the single hit #2 Stateside by early 1983.
Culture Club's music was light, bouncy pop, topped by O'Dowd's appealing tenor. It was anything but outrageous, although O'Dowd's elaborate costumes made the group seem more daring than it was. *Kissing to be Clever*, their debut album, was a million-seller and included "I'll Tumble 4 Ya," another Top Ten hit. The fall of 1983 brought a second album, *Colour by Numbers*, and more hits: "Church of the Poison Mind," "Karma Chameleon" (a #1), and "Miss Me Blind."
Unfortunately, the group's very novelty was its undoing. The third album, *Waking Up with the House on Fire* (1984) went platinum by momentum but its singles were not big hits, and the fourth album, *From Luxury to Heartache*, was a relative flop in 1986, the same year O'Dowd's heroin addiction became a matter of public knowledge. In 1987 O'Dowd cleaned up, split up Culture Club, and embarked on a solo career. –WR

○ **Kissing to Be Clever / ATLANTIC**   1982
Appealing lightly synthesized 80s pop music, featuring the infectious ballad hit "Do You Really Want to Hurt Me." –WR

Colour By Numbers / ATLANTIC   1983
More melodic bouncy pop led by Boy George's engaging singing on "Karma Chameleon" and other songs. –WR

THE CURE

Alternative rock. The Cure has become one of the most popular groups to emerge from Great Britain's post-punk gloom-rock trend of the late 70s, though it took a relatively long time to achieve its present prominence. Amid a variety of personnel changes, the constant in the group has been singer, songwriter, and guitarist Robert Smith (b Apr 4, 1957), whose teased hair and black eyeliner dominate the group's look. He formed the Cure as a trio in 1976 with Laurence Tolhurst (drums) and Michael Dempsey (bass). After some work for an independent label (including the single "Killing an Arab," based on Albert Camus's novel *The Stranger*), they released their first album, *Three Imaginary Boys*, in 1979.
In January 1980, Dempsey left and was replaced by Simon Gallup. More albums followed at yearly intervals, with the fourth, *Pornography*, finally breaking the UK Top Ten. The fifth album, *The Top*, became another UK Top Ten in 1984, a year that also produced the album *Concert - The Cure Live*. In 1985, *The Head on the Door* became the band's biggest UK hit yet, reaching # 7; it also broke the US Top 100 list.
By 1986 the Cure had expanded to a quintet. In addition to Smith, Tolhurst (now on keyboards), and Gallup, the group had Port Thompson on guitar and Boris Williams on drums. That year a compilation album, *Standing on a Beach - The Singles*, hit # 4 in the UK; in America it went gold in early 1987, finally establishing the Cure in the US.
In 1987 they released the double album *Kiss Me, Kiss Me, Kiss Me*, another success, and added Roger O'Donnell on keyboards. (Tolhurst subsequently departed.) In 1989 *Disintegration* produced the Cure's first big US single, "Love Song" (#2). The album itself hit #12 and went platinum. *Wish*, released in the spring of 1992, entered the US charts at #2. –WR

○ **Standing on a Beach - The Singles / ELEKTRA**   1986
The Cure's gloom-and-doom (but danceable) greatest hits, 1979-1985. Though not hits in the US, these helped set the stage for the group's later Stateside success. –WR

Kiss Me, Kiss Me, Kiss Me / ELEKTRA   1987
The Cure's breakthrough US success, a double album containing "Why Can't I Be You?," "Just Like Heaven," and "Hot Hot Hot!!!" –WR

Disintegration / ELEKTRA   1989
The Cure became a top-selling group in the US with this album, which sold a million copies and contains their #2 hit, "Love Song." –WR

Wish / ELEKTRA   1992
Early notices for this album suggested that Robert Smith and company were getting more optimistic. To be sure, "Doing the Unstuck" contains the lyric "Kick out the gloom," but the chorus to that song is more ambiguous: "It's a perfect day to throw back your head and kiss it all goodbye." In fact, much of this album, from its dirge-like tempos to Smith's just-off-key vocals, bespeaks the depressed state typical of the Cure. There are oddly bouncy pop songs here and there too ("Friday I'm in Love") but the Cure remains the band its fans love to mope to. –WR

CYRKLE

Rock/pop. Cyrkle's biggest hit in 1966, "Red Rubber Ball," was cowritten by Bruce Woodley, a member of the Seekers, and Paul Simon. With Tom Dawes and Don Dannemann as lead vocalists, the folk-tinged group managed by Beatles manager Brian Epstein came together at a Pennsylvania college and signed with Columbia. After "Red Rubber Ball" bounced up the charts, the group encored with another major seller, "Turn-Down Day." They made their last pop-chart appearance in late 1967. –BD

○ **Red Rubber Ball (A Collection) / CBS**   1966
Basically a two-hit wonder of the mid 60s ("Red Rubber Ball," "Turn-Down Day"), the Cyrkle had Beatles and Paul Simon connections and were themselves fine examples of lightweight folkie pop. Everything of note they ever did is on this album. –JT

D.O.A.

Punk. A seminal Vancouver-based hardcore combo who shared common ground with the early Clash in both their lyrical commitment and their cogent musical structure. –JF

○ **Bloodied but Unbowed / CD PRESENTS**   1984
A compilation (1978-1983) capturing the wild, uninhibited exuberance of these Vancouver punksters. –DS

DICK DALE & DEL-TONES

Rock & roll. Through his staccato guitar attack and his revolutionary use of reverb, Dick Dale invented the surf-guitar genre in the early 60s. Although his singles never broke outside of California, "Miserlou," "Surf Beat," and "Let's Go Trippin'" remain some of the most influential instrumentals in rock history. –JF

○ **King of Surf Guitar - Best of Dick Dale / RHINO**   1989
From "Miserlou" on down, the best Dale document. –DH

ROGER DALTREY   b 1945

Rock/pop. Lead singer of the British rock group the Who, 1962-1982 (plus a reunion tour in 1989). He launched a parallel solo career in 1973 with the album *Daltrey* and has also worked as a film and television actor. –WR

Daltrey / TRACK (MCA)   1973
For his first solo album, Daltrey turned to Dave Courtney, who wrote the lyrics to all the songs and coproduced with Adam Faith, who wrote some of the music. The album turned out to be something of a showcase and springboard for the main composer, Leo Sayer; nevertheless, it demonstrates Daltrey's versatility as a singer outside a strictly hard-rock context. –WR

○ **Best Bits / MCA**   1982
A best-of from Daltrey's 1973-1980 work on MCA, including "Avenging Annie" and "Say It Ain't So Joe." –WR

Under a Raging Moon / ATLANTIC   1985
Starting with Pete Townshend's "After the Fire," Daltrey moved to more of a hard-rock sound. When his solo career no longer needed to stand in contrast to his work with the Who. As that song indicates, he isn't afraid to invoke the old group's spirit. –WR

THE DAMNED   b 1976

Punk. This English punk-rock band formed in 1976, consisting of Dave Vanian on vocals, Brian James on guitar, Captain Sensible (Ray Burns) on bass, and Rat Scabies (Chris Millar) on drums. The first UK punk band to release an album, for a brief moment they seemed poised to steal the thunder away from their rival Sex Pistols. The Damned continued into the 80s with only Vanian and Scabies left from the original lineup. –CK

○ **The Light at the End of the Tunnel / MCA**   1987
This 27-track double album traces the history of this seminal British punk band from 1977 to 1986, following its development from energetic thrashers to more mainstream rock musicians. –WR

Final Damnation / ENIGMA-RESTLESS   1989
Chronicles the Damned's reunion concert, June 13, 1988, for a final run-through of the best material. –WR

DANNY WILSON   b 1987

Alternative pop. This Scottish trio, made up of brothers Gary and Kit Clark and Ged Grimes, took its name from the Frank Sinatra film *Meet Danny Wilson.* They released two albums on Virgin before breaking up in 1990. –WR

○ **Meet Danny Wilson / ATLANTIC**   1987
Wistful and sensitive, with jazzy, melodic music, this Scottish trio group's sometimes sounds like Ray Davies of the Kinks fronting Steely Dan. In other words, they're really great, especially on the single "Mary's Prayer." –WR

DANZIG

Heavy metal. Fronted by Glenn Danzig, former vocalist for the Misfits and Samhain, this late-80s/early-90s band delivers a bluesy, 70s-style death-metal. –JB

○ **Danzig / DEF AMERICAN**   1988
Glenn Danzig's debut album with his new band. Some incredibly dark and morbid lyrics, including such songs as "Twist of Cain" and "Mother." –JB

Danzig II - Lucifuge / WARNER   1990
Possibly Glenn Danzig's most interesting work to date, with incredible drumming from Chuck Biscuits. Features "Blood & Tears," "Devil's Plaything," "Long Way Back from Hell," and "Snakes of Christ." –JB

Danzig III - How the Gods Kill / DEF AMERICAN   1992
Danzig's most accessible album to date, with songs that could even cross over into mainstream audiences. Glenn Danzig's vocals aren't as raw as they used to be; they're rather more defined and toned down like a real heavy metal vocalist. John Christ's guitar playing is great throughout, and it shows his progression from the band's debut. Cover artwork is by H. R. Giger. –JB

TERENCE TRENT D'ARBY   b 1962

Urban R&B, rock/pop. Expatriate American D'Arby was one of the most distinctive newcomers of the late 80s, blending the swagger and attitude of Sly Stone and Prince with a penchant for Rolling Stones crunch and Sam Cooke soul. His pretensions are sometimes hard to bear, but he's helped expand the boundaries of both rock and R&B. –JF

○ **Introducing the Hardline ... / CBS**   1987
Introducing the Hardline According to Terence Trent D'Arby is a strong debut by this young, cocky Black British singer, who wrote virtually every note on this pop album, played a multitude of instruments, and claimed that it was the most important one since the Beatles' *Sgt. Pepper.* Hits included "If You Let Me Stay," "Dance Little Sister," "Sign Your Name," and the #1 "Wishing Well." His first album is a curious mixture of old and new styles. Although the production is quite modern, D'Arby shows his roots in the work of older artists, borrowing a page or two from Michael Jackson and Stevie Wonder, while James Brown appears to have had the strongest influence on D'Arby's stage presence. –RB

BOBBY DARIN   1936-1973

Rock/pop, singer/songwriter. He established himself with early rock hits such as "Dream Lover" and "Splish Splash," but Bobby Darin wanted to be the next Sinatra. He never made it that far, but his canon contains a few gems that should appeal to followers of early rock & roll and bel-canto big-band belting. –JF

☆ **Ultimate Bobby Darin / WARNER**   1988
Offers a thorough look at Darin's rock and pop hits, including "Mack the Knife," "Dream Lover," "Splish Splash," and the breathtaking "Beyond the Sea." –JF

Capitol Collectors Series / CAPITOL   1989
A compilation of Darin's mid-60s singles, songs that showcase Darin's diversity even if the majority of the set leans heavily on his pop material. Comprehensive liner notes, intelligent track selection, and great fidelity make this worth picking up. –STE

DARK ANGEL

Thrash. One of the original Bay Area thrash/speed-metal bands from the early 80s . –JB

○ **Darkness Descends / RELATIVITY**   1986
One of the top thrash/speed-metal albums of all time. It's dark, evil, and gloomy, from the band that inspired a generation of copycats. Features original vocalist Don Doty. –JB

Time Does Not Heal / RELATIVITY   1991
On one of the best thrash albums of 1991, the band deals with personal topics to create a psychologically disturbing album. –JB

DASH RIP ROCK

Roots-rock. Taking their name from a character on the television show "The Beverly Hillbillies," this Louisiana trio released its first record in 1986. Hailing from Baton Rouge, the group features vocalist and guitarist Bill Davis backed by bassist Ned Hickel and drummer Fred LeBlanc. –DS

○ **Not of This World / MAMMOTH**   1990
A showcase for the propulsive rockabilly/R&B menu served by the Louisiana rockers. –DS

VANESSA DAVIS BAND

Blues/rock. High-energy vocalist Vanessa Davis has been a Chicago favorite since 1978, which is when the aspiring singer joined forces with a group formerly known as the Blues Twisters. After establishing themselves on the local circuit, they formed their own Spectra label in 1981 to release a sultry version of Johnny "Guitar" Watson's "One Kiss." By the time they cut *Fast Forward*, their 1984 debut album, the band was moving away from swinging jump-blues to concentrate on originals. Their 1990 release, *One Heart*, is even more of a departure, Davis singing movingly of her own life, with rock-oriented support from her veteran band (including Dick Vonachen on guitar and saxophonist Doug Cannon). –BD

Fast Forward / SPECTRA   1984
R&B/blues-oriented debut album. Includes the band's rendition of Johnny "Guitar" Watson's "One Kiss" and plenty of intense rockers. –BD

○ **One Heart / SPECTRA**   1990
Driving blues-influenced rock from one of Chicago's top club acts; a concept album, with Davis singing about her own youth. –BD

SPENCER DAVIS GROUP

British Invasion. His ferocious soul-drenched vocals belying his tender teenage years, Stevie Winwood powered the Spencer Davis Group's three biggest US hits during their brief life span as one of the British Invasion's most convincing R&B-based combos.
Guitarist Davis formed the band with Winwood on organ, his brother Muff Winwood on bass, and drummer Peter York. Signing on with producer Chris Blackwell, the quartet got their first hit (the blistering "Keep On Running") from

another of Blackwell's acts, West Indian performer Jackie Edwards. After topping the British charts in 1965, the song struggled on the lower reaches of the US Hot 100.
The group's two hottest sellers were self-penned projects. "Gimme Some Lovin'" and "I'm a Man" were searing showcases for the adolescent Winwood's gritty vocals and blazing keyboards and the band's pounding rhythms. Although they burned up the charts even on this side of the ocean in 1967, the quartet never capitalized on their fame with an American tour. At the height of their power, Winwood left to form Traffic, leaving Davis without his dynamic front man. The bandleader focused on producing other acts, including a Canadian ensemble called the Downchild Blues Band during the early 80s. –BD

○ **Best of the Spencer Davis Group / EMI**   1985
Contains "Gimme Some Lovin'" and many good lesser-known songs. –DH

HANK DAVIS

Roots-rock. Writer Hank Davis has had a string of rockabilly, rock & roll, and country-influenced records. –ED

○ **Crazy Living / RELAXED RABBIT**
Early-80s bluesy rockabilly and country. An underproduced Sun-style sound. (Import) –ED

Songs of Animals and Imagination / FOLKWAYS
Simple folk songs and countryish children's music. –ED

Stompin' at the Dead Moose / DUCKTAIL
A 17-track 70s anthology of rockabilly, hillbilly, and primitive rock & roll. Bizarre but humorous packaging. (Import) –ED

New York Country Rock / REDITA   1988
A set of 24 tracks of obscure 45s, demos, and 50s and 60s tracks with sparse, guitar-based sounds. (Import) –ED

TYRONE DAVIS   b 1938

Soul. Perennially a ladies' choice, Tyrone Davis just seems to naturally appeal to women. That's not to say that gents haven't bought his churning Chicago soul records too — his impressive hit-making career harks back to 1968, and there's no end in sight.
His mentor, noted singer Harold Burrage, coached his charge well, and Davis debuted on wax in 1965 as "Tyrone the Wonder Boy" on the local Four Brothers logo. Far more wondrous were Davis's classy efforts for Chicago's Dakar label, commencing with the remorseful R&B chart-topper "Can I Change My Mind" in 1968, continuing with "Is It Something You've Got" in 1969, and the million-selling classic "Turn Back the Hands of Time" in 1970. With Willie Henderson producing, the cats at Dakar were forging a fresh, vital new Chicago soul sound, and Tyrone Davis was right there at its forefront.
Davis remained with Dakar into 1976, his warm, assured vocals powering the likes of "I Had It All The Time" and "Turning Point," before moving over to Columbia without missing a beat. These days, Tyrone hops from one label to the next, seemingly with each new release — but he's still no stranger to the urban contemporary charts, and the women still love him. What more could he possibly ask for? –BD

○ **Greatest Hits / CBS**   1972
A little short on running time, this is, nevertheless, the best CD representation for now, showcasing the Chicago soulman's 1968-1975 Dakar output. –BD

BOBBY DAY   1932-1990

Doo-wop. An important cog in Los Angeles's doo-wop community during the 50s, Day wrote three often-covered early rock classics in 1957-1958. Day was part of the Hollywood Flames, one of the area's top R&B vocal groups, and briefly part of Bob and Earl, later to hit without Day on "Harlem Shuffle." Day formed his own group, the Satellites, in 1957, cutting the original "Little Bitty Pretty One" for Class Records. A nearly identical cover by Thurston Harris beat the original out, so Day countered with the driving "Rockin' Robin" in 1958, an R&B chart-topper. Its flip, "Over and Over," was a hit in its own right, although the Dave Clark Five's 1965 revival is better remembered today. Day waxed a few more hits for Class in 1959, including "That's All I Want" and a derivative "The Bluebird, the Buzzard & the Oriole," flitting from label to label during the 60s. –BD

Best of Bobby Day / RHINO
This 14-song vinyl release included out-of-print "Rockin' Robin" as well as Day's other major recordings. –JT

○ **The Original Rockin' Robin / ACE**   1991
Bobby Day's "Rockin' Robin" remains a classic. That and 25 other original recordings show up on this solid British import. –JT

MORRIS DAY

Dance-pop, funk. Lead singer of the R&B group the Time (1981-1984), Day launched a solo career in 1985, following his success in the Prince film *Purple Rain.* Day has since taken on other acting assignments and participated in a Time reunion in 1990. –WR

○ **The Color of Success / WARNER**   1985
Dance grooves augmented by Day's elastic tenor and his comic gigolo persona in the Time mold. Features the hit "The Oak Tree." –WR

Daydreaming / WARNER   1987
Day hooks up with old Time mates Jimmy Jam and Terry Lewis (now producers) for the #1 R&B hit "Fishnet" and other danceable songs. –WR

THE DB'S

Anglo-pop. Among the alternative bands who emerged during the 80s, the dB's clever songs, quirky vocals, and unique arrangements and production made them arguably the best practitioners of the smart power-pop movement that drew much inspiration from Big Star, the Move, the Byrds, and the Beatles, for example.
Regardless, principle singer/songwriters Chris Stamey (formerly of the North Carolina band Sneakers, and Alex Chilton sideman) and Peter Holsapple forged a sound together on their two Scott Litt-produced albums (*Stands for Decibels, Repercussion*) that was truly distinctive. Stamey left to pursue a solo career, releasing several EPs and a couple of albums, of which *Fireworks* (released in 1991) is arguably his best.
After Stamey's departure, Holsapple forged ahead with the dB's, releasing *Like This* and *The Sound of Music,* two solid albums that delved deeper into a more Americanized roots/pop sound.
In early 1991, Holsapple and Stamey got together and released *Mavericks,* a charming collaboration that featured a cover of Gene Clark's "Here without You," as well as some great originals like "Angels," "The Child in You," and "Geometry." –RC

● **Stands for Decibels / I.R.S.**   1981
Influences like the Beatles, Big Star, and the Move are detectable, but the dB's creatively synthesized those sounds into something unique and personal, with wonderfully twisted melodies, inside-out harmonies, herky-jerky grooves, and quirky arrangements. Every track is noteworthy. –RC

Like This / RHINO   1984
With Stamey gone, the trio (fronted by Peter Holsapple) dropped some of the band's previous eccentricities and got down to a more rootsy rock & roll approach, even touching on a little country. The melodies are still as catchy as ever. –RC

○ **Repercussion / CAPITOL**   1987
Their second effort is more polished, but none of their distinctive charm is missing. Consistently fine material from top to bottom. –RC

The Sound of Music / MCA   1987
Sound of Music continues the rootsy pop direction pursued on *Like This.* Even though it is a little weaker than its predecessor,

there are some fine standout tracks like "I Lie," "Working for Somebody Else," and the folk-like Holsapple-Syd Straw duet, "Never Before and Never Again." –RC

DEAD CAN DANCE

Alternative pop. Originally from Australia, this group has a purely European sound (Gregorian chants, Celtic, neo-gothic). Their songs are of lost beauty, regret, and sorrow, inspiration and nobility, and of the everlasting human goal of attaining a meaningful existence. –VB

Spleen and Ideal / PHANTOM   1985
Well balanced in terms of both mood and style, this album brings you the whole new world of hopeless hope and aimless urge and search. –VB

Within the Realm of a Dying Sun / NESAK   1987
Probably their most subtle and intelligent album. Touches the deepest levels of our identity. –VB

Serpent's Egg / NESAK   1988
An interesting combination of Slavonic and European medieval music. –VB

○ **Aion / PHANTOM**   1990
True medieval sound combined with all the variety of modern studio techniques. Not an imitation at all; just enriched with an old musical tradition. –VB

● **A Passage in Time / RYKODISC**   1991
This anthology offers a sampling of their best work. –VB

DEAD KENNEDYS

Hardcore, punk. Next to Black Flag and X, Jello Biafra's Dead Kennedys were the longest lasting of West Coast hardcore groups. Their music challenged everything and offended everybody, and Biafra's self-righteous morality made him a post-punk role model for thousands of pissed-off kids. In the late 80s, Biafra became a spokesperson for the indecency of music censorship. When the group disbanded in 1987, Biafra continued with the band Lard. –JF

☆ **Fresh Fruit for Rotting Vegetables / ALT. TEN.**   1981
The DK's 1980 debut was as important to the West Coast hardcore scene as the Sex Pistols's *Bollocks* was to disenfranchised British punks. Despite a few clunkers, *Fresh Fruit* is an explosive and scalding blast of political and social fury, underpinned by Jello Biafra's wise-ass vocals and Klaus Flouride's pseudo-surf guitar wailing. Most of the band's best songs are here. –JF

In God We Trust, Inc. / ALTERNATE TENTACLES   1981
DK's anti-religion 7-song EP varies from all other material in thrashy-metallic nature. Each song is a speedy, essentially unintelligible gem of punk lore with super dominating guitars and heavier drums. Includes "Religious Vomit" and "Dog Bite" and culminates in a cover of the classic "California Uber Alles" entitled "We've Got a Bigger Problem Now," dealing with Ronald Reagan instead of Jerry Brown. –JK

Plastic Surgery Disasters / ALT. TEN.   1982
Their second effort, capturing their frenetic live set full of mayhem and confusion but with an underlying feeling of greatness. Nonconformist, anti-establishment sentiment eloquently made sensible by talented frontman Jello Biafra. Punk at its best, musically and lyrically, with "Terminal Preppie," "Government Flu," and "Winnebago Warrior." –JK

○ **Give Me Convenience or Give Me Death / ALT. TEN.**   1987
A useful compilation in that it not only collects many essential nonalbum cuts but rounds up the best material from the otherwise desultory followups to *Fresh Fruit.* –JF

DEAD MILKMEN

Alternative rock, punk. Funny guys from Philadelphia whose satire and good-natured humor too often gets the better of them. Playing a melodic strain of radio-friendly pop, the Milkmen seem more outrageous than they really are. In fact, they come off like an occasionally funny party guest who keeps cracking jokes, hoping you'll laugh at one of them. –JD

○ **Big Lizard in My Backyard / ENIGMA-RESTLESS**   1985
You can hardly refer to any Dead Milkmen album as a classic, but *Big Lizard* comes close. Stupid, sophomoric, and quite tuneful, this is when the jokes were still funny or, at the very least, still worth listening to. Features "Bitchin' Camaro" and the tastelessly funny "Takin' Retards to the Zoo." –JD

BILL DEAL & THE RHONDELS

R&B, rock & roll. Combining soul-inflected vocals with brassy, uptempo R&B-inspired grooves, Bill Deal & the Rhondels remain favorites on the Carolina "beach music" circuit to this day. The group was part of the Norfolk, VA, scene during the early 60s, and Deal played organ on Jimmy Soul's 1963 smash "If You Wanna Be Happy" on Legrand Records. The Rhondels apparently preferred reviving R&B obscurities to writing their own material, and it paid off — in 1969 their supercharged remake of the Maurice Williams hit "May I" gave the group their first hit, and they followed it up with a pair of blasting Tams covers, "I've Been Hurt" and "What Kind of Fool Do You Think I Am," all on the Heritage logo. The Rhondels charted for the final time in early 1970 with "Nothing Succeeds like Success." –BD
○ **Best of Bill Deal & the Rhondels / RHINO**   1986
Contains their biggest and best hit, a cover of "May I," first released by the Zodiacs. –DH

DEATH

Heavy metal. Formed in 1983, Florida's Death (formerly called Mantas) may possibly be the most influential band in the death-metal and grindcore genres. –JB
○ **Scream Bloody Gore / RELATIVITY**   1987
Probably the first band to influence what is now known as "grindcore." Death-metal taken to the next level. A classic. –JB

DEATH ANGEL

Heavy metal. Technical speed-metal from San Francisco with a decent hard-rock influence. The band started in the early 80s when drummer Andy Galeon was only nine years old, and split up in 1991. –JB
○ **Ultra-Violence / ENIGMA**   1987
San Francisco thrash. None of the band members were yet eighteen years old at the time of release (drummer Andy Galeon was only 14!). Deep lyrics, fantastic musicianship — one of the best thrash/speed-metal albums of the 80s. –JB
Act III / GEFFEN   1990
This album shows a band that has matured, even including acoustic guitars in their sound. The band had great potential and possibilities at the time of its release, but they split up due to personal and musical differences. –JB

DEBARGE

Dance-pop. Motown hoped this family act would turn into another Jackson 5. Specializing in soft-pop tunes such as "All This Love" and "Time Will Reveal," family members include Eldra, Mark, Randy, Bunny, and Bobby. After hitting big with Richard Perry's "Rhythm of the Night," El began receiving accolades for his fine tenor vocals and was singled out for a solo career in 1986. He went on to further success while the remainder of the family floundered at other record companies. –RAB
Rhythm of the Night / MCA-MOTOWN   1985
Their best Motown album, with the #1 title track. –RAB
○ **Greatest Hits / MOTOWN**   1986
All of their Motown work. Most were Top 40 hits. –RAB

CHICO DEBARGE

Dance-pop. Brother to the singing DeBarge family, Chico launched a promising solo career on Motown in the late 80s. Despite a hit single and a hit debut album, his career was sidelined by imprisonment on a drug charge. –RAB
○ **Chico Debarge / MOTOWN**   1986

His best album for Motown. A fine start, but his brushes with the law and eventual imprisonment stifled his success. Includes the funky hit "Talk to Me." –RAB

EL DEBARGE   ♭1964

Dance-pop. Emerged from his family act in 1986 with a hit solo album and several single releases. Like that of his troublesome sibling, his career was sidetracked by brushes with the law. He now records for Warner Brothers. –RAB
○ **El Debarge / MOTOWN**   1986
His first and, to date, his best solo album. Includes "Who's Johnny" from the "Short Circuit" soundtrack. –RAB

JOEY DEE & STARLITERS   ♭1940

R&B, rock & roll, pop. Joey Dee led the house band at New York's Peppermint Lounge, immortalizing the joint in his 1961 chart-topper "Peppermint Twist." Born Joseph DiNicola in Passaic, NJ, Dee teamed with veteran producer Henry Glover to cut "Peppermint Twist" for Roulette, and the huge hit led to a starring role in the film *Hey, Let's Twist.* Most of Dee's hits, including a supercharged revival of the Isley Brothers hit "Shout" in 1962, were firmly in the Twist mode, although he took a successful stab at a softer sound that year with a Johnny Nash tune, "What Kind of Love Is This." Dee gave several future stars early breaks with the Starliters, notably the Ronettes, three-quarters of the Young Rascals, and Jimi Hendrix. Dee is still active on the oldies circuit. –BD
○ **Best of Joey Dee & Starliters ... / RHINO**   1990
Best of Joey Dee & Starliters - Hey Let's Twist is a representative early-60s compilation by the man who made the "Peppermint Twist" a national craze. –BD

DEEP PURPLE

Hard rock, heavy metal. Formed in 1968, Deep Purple's initial success was on Bill Cosby's Tetragrammaton label with remakes of Joe South's "Hush" (#4) and Neil Diamond's "Kentucky Woman" (#38). When Tetragrammaton went under shortly afterward, Deep Purple switched to Warner, with a change in lineup, including the addition of dramatic lead singer Ian Gillan.
Their first effort on Warner, John Lord's *Concerto for Group and Orchestra*, was a ponderously overblown affair that died a quick death in the marketplace. From there on out, the band pursued a hard-rock direction, generating their greatest successes in *Machine Head*, *Burn*, and the live double record set *Made in Japan*. In 1975 Deep Purple earned the dubious distinction of being named the "world's loudest band" in the *Guinness Book of World Records.*
Much of Deep Purple's appeal during their heyday (from 1970's *In Rock* to 1972's *Made in Japan*) came from the lightning-fast duels between keyboardist Jon Lord and lead guitarist Ritchie Blackmore.
Deep Purple successfully carried on after Blackmore, Gillan, and bassist Roger Glover departed (at different times), with a lineup featuring ex-Trapeze member Glen Hughes (bass, vocals), Tommy Bolin (lead guitar, vocals), and David Coverdale (lead vocals). Coverdale would later front the popular MTV/AOR band Whitesnake. –RC
○ **Deep Purple / TETRAGRAMMATON**   1969
Worthwhile mainly for their psychezilla cover of Joe South's "Hush," which pits Ritchie Blackmore's flame-throwing guitar bursts against Jon Lord's chugging organ. –TG
○ **Deep Purple in Rock / WARNER**   1970
The album on which Deep Purple decided they were rockers after all and turned up the amps to prove it. Ian Gillan on vocals (added at this time) became the archetype for heavy metal screamers thereafter. Check out "Speed King," "Bloodsucker," and "Flight of the Rat" for your daily dose of high voltage. –TG
○ **Fireball / WARNER**   1971
Fireball solidified the band's reputation as purveyors of maximum-dosage heavy metal. Ritchie Blackmore steals the

show with a wall of grinding chords and greased-lightning lead flourishes. At this juncture the band began to challenge Led Zeppelin's position as hard rock's most successful act. –TG

★ **Machine Head / WARNER**   1972
The definitive 70s heavy metal album, with each locomotive song ("Highway Star," "Space Truckin'") blasting off like World War III. The highlight is the AOR staple "Smoke on the Water," which has a mandatory riff for anyone owning a guitar. It still fries ears twenty years after the fact. –TG

○ **Made in Japan / WARNER**   1973
Not only could they kick buns in the studio but they could stir up a hornet's nest on stage too. This double album (one CD) set recorded in Japan includes most of their best material ("Highway Star," "Smoke on the Water") and pushes the metal envelope even further. Ritchie Blackmore is in peak form throughout. –TG

○ **When We Rock ... / WARNER**   1975
When We Rock, We Rock & When We Roll, We Roll is a solid, if incomplete collection from their 1968-1974 peak years. –DH

DEF LEPPARD

Hard rock, rock/pop. Def Leppard's catchy, guitar-driven, power-pop/rock was one of the most imitated styles of the 80s. Leppard's hit albums are polished syntheses of heavy, hummable guitar riffs, memorable pop melodies, and simple teen-oriented lyrics. Originally the band (Joe Elliot, vocals; Pete Willis, guitar; Steve Clark, guitar; Rick Savage, drums; Rick Allen, drums) was associated with the new wave of British heavy metal bands, releasing two albums (*On through the Night* and *High 'N' Dry*) that made a small impact on the US. Robert "Mutt" Lange produced *High 'N' Dry*, which contained the seeds of the signature Leppard sound. Before the recording of their next album, Pete Willis left and was replaced by Phil Collen, who used to play in the glam-rock band Girl. *Pyromania*, released in 1983, was a monster success selling over 6.5 million copies in the US and featuring three Top 40 hits ("Photograph," "Rock of Ages," and "Foolin'"). The album showcased the refinement of Def Leppard's twin-guitar attack, where both parts worked together to create a huge sound instead of merely repeating the riff. In 1984 the group made two attempts to record a followup, one with the exhausted Lange and another with Jim Steinman, both ending with the dismissal of the producer. On New Year's Eve, Allen lost his left arm in an auto accident. Despite this, the band wanted Allen in the group; he was equipped with a customized electronic drum kit to ease his playing. In 1987 the long-awaited *Hysteria* (also produced by Lange) was released. Although *Hysteria* was a bigger success than *Pyromania*, it took a considerable amount of time for it to gain its sales — after 49 weeks, the album reached #1. Recording for the followup to *Hysteria* was under way when Clark was found dead in his apartment after a drinking binge in January 1991. Def Leppard continued the album, with Collen playing all the guitars. *Adrenalize* shot to the top of the charts upon its release in April 1992. Vivian Campbell, former guitarist for Whitesnake, was announced as Clark's replacement in spring of 1992. –STE

○ **Pyromania / MERCURY**   1983
Although Def Leppard's first two workmanlike metal albums, *On Through the Night* and *High 'n' Dry*, had already established the band in both England and the US, it was *Pyromania* that broke the sound (and sales) barrier for them. *Pyromania*'s acute emphasis on pop sensibilities in songs like "Photograph" and "Rock Rock ('Til You Drop)" over numbing thonk made the album a huge crossover success with the more conservative AOR market. MTV video saturation with key *Pyromania* songs didn't hurt either. (Also available as a Mobile Fidelity Ultradisc) –TG

☆ **Hysteria / POLYGRAM**   1987
If *Pyromania* was great pop-metal, *Hysteria* upped the ante a few more notches. With dense, elaborate instrumental layering and meticulous engineering, the album became

known almost as much for its production values as for its terrific music. Drummer Rick Allen, who lost an arm in an automobile accident, adds an even harder core of bottom end with his specially rigged drum kit. As hardhitting as it is slicksounding, *Hysteria* became the standard-bearer for pop metal with anthemic tracks like "Rocket" and "Pour Some Sugar on Me." One of the masterpieces of the 80s that renewed the faith, for many, in sensible hard rock. –TG

Adrenalize / MERCURY   1992
The jury may still be out on *Adrenalize*, but with the band's misfortunes (guitarist Steve Clark died of a drug overdose), they can be forgiven for slipping a bit after the mega-success of *Hysteria*. That's not to dismiss *Adrenalize*, however, which still has a heaping helping of Leppard's patented Brit-pop crash-and-burn fusion. –TG

DEL FUEGOS

Roots-rock. Originally including Dan and Warren Zanes (who have the vocalist and guitarist duties, respectively), bassist Tom Lloyd, and drummer B. Woody Giessmann, this Boston-based band pounds out Rolling Stones-style rock. After critics panned the 1987 album *Stand Up*, Giessmann left the group. The band added horns for a more Stax-oriented sound on *Smoking in the Fields*. Guest appearances on their albums include James Burton and Tom Petty (*Stand Up*) and Rick Danko (*Smoking*). –DS

○ **The Longest Day / WARNER**   1984
An explosive garage-meets-roots-rock debut from the Boston rockers. –DS

Stand Up / WARNER   1987
A tone-downed, more bluesy effort. Includes guests James Burton and Tom Petty. –DS

DEL LORDS

Roots-rock. No-nonsense New Yorkers who deliver their rock & roll with no frills or fancy stuff. Ex-Dictator Scott Kempner writes plainspoken, socially conscious songs, and the crunching riffs make the best of them ring like minor classics. –JF

Frontier Days / EMI   1984
Their debut sports a low-budget sound but manages to capture their frenzied enthusiasm. Some of their best work. –JF

○ **Based on a True Story / ENIGMA**   1988
Kempner expands his songwriter range, but it's the celebratory party-man anthems like "The Cool and the Crazy" that make this the group's best work. –JF

Lovers Who Wander / ENIGMA   1990
The band's most ambitious work, with complex songs and a sound that expands on their previous attack. –JF

DELANEY & BONNIE

Rock/pop, blues/rock. Delaney Bramlett (b Jul 1, 1939) and his wife Bonnie (b Nov 8, 1944) recorded a series of blues and country influenced albums in the late 60s and early 70s. A variety of musicians played in Delaney and Bonnie's band, including Eric Clapton, Dave Mason, Duane Allman, Leon Russell, Rita Coolidge, Jim Gordon, Bobby Whitlock, and Carl Radle; Clapton, Gordon, Whitlock, and Radle formed Derek & the Dominoes after performing together on Delaney & Bonnie's 1969-70 tour. Delaney and Bonnie's records were a strong influence on Eric Clapton's style in the 70s. The group broke up after the Bramlett's marriage collapsed in 1972. –KMC

○ **On Tour / ATLANTIC**   1970
Recorded with Eric Clapton, *On Tour* features Delaney & Bonnie's blend of country, rock, blues, and gospel. Includes "I'm Coming Home." –KMC

The Best of Delaney & Bonnie / RHINO   1972
A good overview of their brief career. –KMC

THE DELFONICS

Soul. A sweet ballad-oriented Philadelphia vocal trio, who proved highly popular in the late 60s and early 70s. Lead singer William Hart's high-pitched tenor effortlessly sailed into falsetto range on their first hit in 1968, "La-La-Means I Love You," a typically smooth ballad filled with swirling strings. Hart and co-producer Thom Bell wrote most of the group's early smashes, including the majestic "Didn't I (Blow Your Mind This Time)" in 1970. The group's hitmaking reign ended in 1974. –BD

○ **The Best of the Delfonics / ARISTA**   1990
Slick late-60s Philly soul with lush production and polished harmonies. –BD

DELL-VIKINGS

R&B, doo-wop. One of the first integrated acts during rock & roll's infancy, the Dell-Vikings recorded a beloved classic in 1956, "Come Go with Me." The quintet was formed at Pittsburgh's Air Force Serviceman's Club in 1955 while the members were stationed there. They recorded their immortal "Come Go with Me," written by bass singer Clarence Quick, in the basement of a local deejay and sold the master to tiny FeeBee Records. When given national distribution on Dot, the upbeat tune proved a monster hit. Upon their discharge, four members split to form a new "Del Vikings" on Mercury, hitting in 1957 with "Cool Shake." Kripp Johnson, meanwhile, stayed with Dot, assembling a new lineup of "Dell-Vikings" that included a young Chuck Jackson. and hitting at precisely the same time with "Whispering Bells." All the confusion about the two groups may have ultimately sunk both, since those were the last hits for either lineup. –BD

○ **Dell-Vikings / COLLECTABLES**   1988
Solid hits by one of doo-wop's first integrated groups. –BD

THE DELLS

Soul, doo-wop. After nearly four decades of recording an incredible legacy of hits, the Dells have made only one personnel change in their entire professional career. Perhaps that's why the venerable R&B vocal group can boast such a remarkably consistent track record.
The quintet from Chicago's south suburbs has weathered stylistic shifts from doo-wop and soul to disco and urban contemporary, and every permutation in between. Their harmony remains as striking as ever, with Marvin Junior's earthshaking lead enduring as the group's focal point.
Signing with Vee Jay in 1955, their creamy vocal blend on "Oh, What a Night" gave the Dells their first major R&B hit the next year, but it would be nearly a decade before they returned to the winner's circle with another dreamy classic, "Stay in My Corner." By then Chicago's R&B sound had changed drastically — doo-wop was dead and soul was king — but the Dells adapted effortlessly, regularly scaling the charts for the Chess subsidiary Cadet with "There Is," "Always Together," "Give Your Baby a Standing Ovation," and a marathon remake of "Stay in My Corner" that afforded Junior's booming baritone room to roam.
Seemingly an indestructible force (turning up on the R&B charts as recently as 1984), the succinct harmonies of the Dells span entire generations of R&B history. –BD

Dells vs. the Dramatics / MCA
A vocal delight. Two great late-60s/early-70s soul groups, including two tracks featuring both groups together. –RP

Oh, What a Night / VEE JAY   1959
Earlier doo-wop classics by the venerable Windy City R&B vocal group. This showcases their impeccable harmony on the gorgeous title track and similar fare. –BD

○ **There Is / MCA**   1968
Rich 1966-1968 Chicago soul with little of the overproduction that marred the powerful R&B quintets of the later Chess output. –BD

JOHN DENVER   ♭1943

Singer/songwriter, pop, folk/rock. A fan of folk music by the Chad Mitchell Trio, Joan Baez, and others in the 60s, Denver sang their songs in coffeehouses. He later joined the Mitchell Trio before going solo in 1969. From 1974-1975 Denver scored four #1 hits, including "Thank God I'm a Country Boy," "Sunshine on My Shoulders," and "Annie's Song." His commercial fortunes declined in the early 80s. –BC

○ **John Denver's Greatest Hits - Vol. 1 / RCA**   1974
A good collection of his early (and best) era, 1969-1973. –DH

An Evening with John Denver / RCA   1975
His homey appeal at its most effective, in concert. –DH

John Denver's Greatest Hits - Vol. 2 / RCA   1977
More pop, less folk, and more hits. –DH

John Denver's Greatest Hits - Vol. 3 / RCA   1984
Not many hits, but notable 80s tracks. –DH

DEPECHE MODE

Techno-pop. In 1980 Depeche Mode (the name means "fast fashion") was formed in Basildon, Essex, England, by Andy Fletcher (b Jul 8, 1961), Martin Gore (b Jul 23, 1961), Vince Clarke, and Dave Gahan. All four played synthesizers, and Gahan sang. They were signed to tiny Mute Records in England in 1982 (distributed by Sire/Warner Bros. in the US) and scored two Top 20 hits, "New Life" and "Just Can't Get Enough," and a Top Ten album, *Speak and Spell*, by the end of the year. At that point, Clarke quit and was replaced by Alan Wilder. The band's style — pop songs with ominous lyrics sung in Gahan's distinct baritone and backed by intricate synthesized dance music — did not change, and its commercial success continued as well.
The group only gradually built a following in the US, finally breaking the Hot 100 with "People Are People," which reached #13 in 1985. The first album to reach the American Top 100 albums was *Black Celebration* in 1986; then *Music for the Masses* went gold in 1987. By 1989 Depeche Mode was big enough in the US to play a concert at the Rose Bowl in California, and that show was recorded for the live album *101*. But it wasn't until the 1990 album *Violator* and the single "Enjoy the Silence" that Depeche Mode made the Top Ten in the US. By then, they'd also conquered the rest of the world and become one of the most popular "modern" or "alternative" rock groups of the 80s and early 90s. –WR

Speak & Spell / WARNER   1981
Vince Clarke's only album with Depeche Mode is dominated by him (he wrote nine of 11 tracks), and the band was never this imaginative or infectious again. Especially notable is the UK Top Ten hit, "Just Can't Get Enough," which remains the best single track they ever recorded. –WR

Some Great Reward / SIRE   1984
Depeche Mode's most consistent post-Clarke album contains some of its most provocative material, notably "Blasphemous Rumours" and "Master and Servant," which concern, respectively, religion and sexual domination. –WR

○ **Catching Up with Depeche Mode / SIRE**   1985
A US-only compilation that's a well-put-together best-of, from the band's early singles to its current state. If you want to know what Depeche Mode is about, this is the record that will tell you. –WR

DEREK & THE DOMINOS

Rock & roll, blues/rock. Eric Clapton and members of Delaney & Bonnie formed this group for one album and tour, producing one of the greatest albums in rock & roll history. The Dominoes played R&B, rock & roll, and blues that didn't sound like White boys pretending they were Black — it sounded real. Duane Allman sat in on the *Layla* sessions, contributing some beautiful playing. A second album was attempted but never finished; the remains of these sessions can be found on Clapton's *Crossroads*. –STE

☆ **Layla (& Other Assorted Love Songs) / RSO**   1970
Quite simply, this is Eric Clapton's finest moment and a real blues album. All of the songs are tortured love songs, tough and sensitive. Clapton and Allman play brilliantly, the best they ever have. −STE

RICK DERRINGER   b 1947

Rock/pop, rock & roll. As a lead guitarist, Rick Derringer (born Rick Zehringer) was the frontman for the McCoys, a group of mid-60s pop-rockers who recorded the #1 million-seller "Hang On Sloopy." The McCoys linked up with Texas guitarist Johnny Winter, and Derringer began producing and backing up Winter and his brother Edgar.
Derringer's solo debut, *All American Boy*, generated his only hit with the 1974 #23 "Rock and Roll Hootchie Koo." In 1976 he formed Derringer, a hard-rock quartet that enjoyed moderate success. More recently, Derringer has produced Weird Al Yankovic's pop parodies. −RC
○ **All American Boy / COLUMBIA**   1973
Derringer's first solo album, featuring great songwriting and performing, with his own version of his classic "Rock & Roll Hootchie Koo." −CK

SUGAR PIE DESANTO   b 1935

R&B, soul. DeSanto's earthy approach was suited equally to R&B and blues, and she cut both for Chess during the 60s. Discovered by bandleader Johnny Otis, who was responsible for her debut sides on Federal, DeSanto scored her biggest R&B seller, "I Want to Know," for producer Bob Geddins of Veltone in 1960. After she signed with Checker, her 1964 "Slip-In Mules (No High Heel Sneakers)" — the answer to Tommy Tucker's "High Heel Sneakers" — sold well, and a 1966 duet with Etta James, "In the Basement," also garnered spins. DeSanto wrote material for many of her labelmates before returning to the San Francisco Bay area in the 70s. −BD
○ **Down in the Basement / MCA**   1989
Saucy, bluesy, mid-60s R&B with a soulful edge. She had a Top Ten hit in 1960 with "I Want to Know." −BD

DESCENDENTS

Punk. One of Southern California's finest hardcore-era bands, the Descendents liberally sprinkled pop on their typically mega-volume ceaseless-rush-of-guitar sound. Also, they featured a terrific lead singer in Milo Aukerman. Essential listening for fans of the late-70s/early-80s post-punk mosh scene. −JD
Somery / SST
A solid career overview. −JD
○ **Milo Goes to College / NEW ALLIANCE**   1982
Indisputably their best. Fast, furious, and funny, the Descendents never sounded this unabashedly joyous again. Essentially a farewell record (lead singer Milo was actually going to college), its songs are great slice-of-life tales of bored middleclass life in the perpetually sunny environs of LA. −JD
Bonus Fat / NEW ALLIANCE   1985
A compilation of their first (and superb) EP plus assorted tracks. You'll never find a better culinary tune than "I Like Food." −JD
Liveage / SST   1987
Great gig live in Minneapolis. −JD

JACKIE DESHANNON   b 1944

Singer/songwriter, rock/pop. Primarily known for writing songs recorded by the Byrds, Bruce Springsteen, the Searchers, Brenda Lee, and Marianne Faithful, plus the Grammy-winning Kim Carnes hit "Betty Davis Eyes," DeShannon also enjoyed a sporadic solo artist career. She generated two Top Ten hits with her own "Put a Little Love in Your Heart" (#4) and a cover of Burt Bacharach and Hal David's "What the World Needs Now" (#7). She was one of the few artists who had the privilege of being a warmup act on the first Beatles US

tour. She has worked with Jimmy Page, Van Morrison, Ry Cooder, and an early incarnation of the Crusaders. Over the course of her artistic career, DeShannon's music has ranged from early folk/ rock to gospelish pop. −RC
Jackie DeShannon / SUNSET   1965
This album features DeShannon's hit version of Hal David and Burt Bacharach's "What the World Needs Now Is Love," but also included is DeShannon's rendition of her own standard, "When You Walk in the Room," and a co-composition with Randy Newman, "She Don't Understand Himlike I Do." −WR
Put a Little Love in Your Heart / IMPERIAL   1969
DeShannon cowrote her second Top Ten hit, the title track, with Jimmy Holiday and Randy Myers, and this album contains more of the fruit of their collaboration, including the followup, a Top 40 hit called "Love Will Find a Way." −WR
New Arrangement / CBS   1975
Excellent updating of DeShannon's sound. Includes her co-composition "Bette Davis Eyes," which Kim Carnes took to the top of the charts six years later. −WR
○ **Best of Jackie DeShannon / RHINO**   1991
This album is a fine roundup of her best moments as a singer and a writer. −DH

MINK DEVILLE   b 1950

Rock/pop, blues/rock. From 1977 to 1985, NYC singer and guitar slinger Willy DeVille recorded six albums with his band, Mink DeVille. Willy wrote street-tough songs but was a romantic at heart, showing his inspiration to be closer to Ben E. King and the Drifters than to Lou Reed. Mink DeVille got lumped in with other bands in the burgeoning NYC punk underground, which perhaps helped the band get gigs but also made them misunderstood. 1987 saw Willy recording under his name on his third major label but all seven of these releases (along with a Capitol compilation, *Savoir Faire*) remain out of print. The self-titled debut (*Mink DeVille*) and *Savoir Faire* were briefly available on CD but these also remain out of print. Both are worth seeking out in used-record stores. −DMAC
○ **Mink DeVille / CAPITOL**   1977
Energetic, no-holds-barred, smoking rock with R&B roots. Excellent. (Out of print) −DS
Return to Magenta / CAPITOL   1978
Followup to DeVille's self-titled debut. (Out of print) −DS

DEVO

Alternative pop. Made up of two sets of brothers, Mark and Bob Motherbaugh and Jerry and Bob Casale. One of the first new-wave groups to get mass-market attention, this Akron, OH, band had its own philosophy, "de-evolution" — a sci-fi/satirical view of postmodern cultural values, complete with strange costumes and behavior. Their sound was appropriately nervous and jerky, with a heavy emphasis on synthesizers. Their debut album, *Q: Are We Not Men? A: We Are Devo!*, was produced by Brian Eno and featured a great cover of the Rolling Stones' "Satisfaction." After a less interesting second album, they rebounded with the self-produced album *Freedom of Choice*, containing the hit "Whip It." As one of new-wave's most cartoonish and successful bands, they helped define the genre with a minimalistic synth sound and a nihilistic attitude. Although each successive album provided a new look and theme, their sound became more glossy and less challenging, heading toward straight synth/dance-pop grooves. While both sets of brothers remain musically active on soundtrack work like "Pee Wee's Playhouse" and the theme for "Davis Rules," most Devo discs of late have been repackaged/remix efforts, live recordings, or instrumental works. −SWB
○ **Q: Are We Not Men? A: We Are Devo! / WARNER**   1978
All the mechanized, herky-jerky rhythms, and quirky lyrics that first gained attention for Devo are here, among them "Jocko Homo," "Mongoloid," and their drastic recasting of "(I Can't Get No) Satisfaction." −WR

Freedom of Choice / WARNER   1980
Devo's dance-floor triumph, "Whip It," plus more electro-pop delights. −WR

DHARMA BUMS

Alternative rock. Maturing from a solid but ordinary rock band, this Portland quartet plays with feeling and intensity that is exciting, even if they break no new ground. −BE

○ **Bliss / FRONTIER**   1990
Dark but accessible alternative-rock. −RG

NEIL DIAMOND   *b* 1941

Pop. Neil Diamond may never grace the pages of most music publications, and he's never been a presence on television, but it's obvious by the staggering number of Top 40 hits he's amassed (over 35) that there's an audience out there that doesn't need to be hyped, eager to sell out his shows and buy his music.
A veteran of the Brill Building school of songcrafting (he wrote the Monkees hits "I'm a Believer" and "A Little Bit Me, a Little Bit You"), Diamond's early (and most of his best) hits were cut on the Bang label. At the time, Diamond borrowed from gospel and folk, which he delivered with simple but distinctive acoustic guitar chord patterns as musical hooks. The hits kept coming when Diamond switched over to the Uni label, but this was a transitional period, blending the early upbeat Bang song sensibilities with weightier dramatic material, such as the "African Trilogy" suite and "I Am I Said." Upon signing a $5,000,000 deal with Columbia in 1973, Diamond plunged headfirst into a series of overwrought MOR records (most notably the insubstantial soundtrack for the movie *Jonathon Livingston Seagull*), which sold by the truckloads. His 1978 duet with Barbra Streisand on "You Don't Send Me Flowers" (#1) was a million-seller.
In 1979 Diamond starred in *The Jazz Singer* (a remake of an old Al Jolson flick) and provided the songs for the soundtrack. "America," a song from that soundtrack, became Diamond's most requested song Stateside. His last big hit was "Heartlight" (#4), which charted in 1982. It was inspired by the movie *E.T.*
Diamond is still a successful concert draw, even though his recorded output has slowed down considerably. −RC

Hot August Night / MCA   1972
This double-record set is the album that established Diamond's reputation as a live performer. Containing passionately performed versions of his biggest hits up to this time, it sold the best of any album he'd had so far, going gold the month of its release. −WR

His 12 Greatest Hits / MCA   1974
Actually, this is 12 songs that were hits for Diamond on Uni between 1969 and 1972. "Cracklin' Rosie" is here, along with Diamond's other chart-topper of the period, "Song Sung Blue." Note, however, that "Sweet Caroline" and "Holly Holy" are presented in live versions, not the original studio tracks. To hear the former, you'll have to buy *Sweet Caroline, Others* (MCA 94037), while for the latter, it's *Touching You, Touching Me* (MCA 93071). −WR

Beautiful Noise / CBS   1976
A beautifully recorded concept album about Diamond's own emergence from the Brooklyn streets and from the Brill Building's Tin Pan Alley. Produced by Robbie Robertson. −WR

○ **The Greatest Hits 1966-1992 / COLUMBIA**   1992
Columbia has been Diamond's label since 1973, and it acquired the rights to his Bang material of 1966-1968. But MCA still controls the recordings from 1968-1973. That's why (although you won't find out by reading the album cover) this two-disc, 37-track retrospective consists of the original versions of such hits as "Cherry, Cherry" (1966) and "You Don't Bring Me Flowers" (1978) but covers the middle period with re-recordings and live renditions of 13 of Diamond's

biggest hits. As such, this collection gets only a qualified recommendation. −WR

DIAMONDS

Rock/pop, R&B, doo-wop. One of the leading cover groups of the mid 50s, the Diamonds adapted current R&B hits into pop gold of their own. Hailing from Toronto, the Canadian quartet signed with Mercury in 1955 and immediately zoomed up pop playlists with covers of the Teenagers' "Why Do Fools Fall in Love," the Willows' "Church Bells May Ring," and their biggest hit of all, a sanitized version of the Gladiolas hit "Little Darlin'." Fronted by David Somerville, the quartet hit with an original, the smooth dance outing "The Stroll." After weathering major personnel changes, the Diamonds notched their last hit in 1961. Somerville remains active as a solo, while various aggregations billed as the Diamonds populate the oldies scene. −BD

○ **Best of the Diamonds / RHINO**
"Little Darlin'," "The Stroll," and some of their lesser hits are all here. −DH

THE DICKIES

Alternative rock. The Dickies started as a rock fusion band known as "Jerry's Kids" in the mid 70s and gained popularity for their speeded-up metal/bubblegum/punk, especially in England where they toured with the Jam and the Stranglers. They have covered songs made popular by Paul Simon, Barry McGuire, and the Monkees. They're more a comedy band than a rock band per se, because of their treatment of material. −LL

○ **We Aren't the World! / RELATIVITY**   1986
An excellent cassette-only collection of their tunes. −LL

THE DICTATORS

Rock & roll. A punk-rock group that predated punk by a few years and was something of a comedy group as well, the Dictators were formed in the Bronx in 1974 by Handsome Dick Manitoba (born Richard Blum Jan 29, 1954), Ross the Boss (b Jan 3, 1954), Scott Kempner (b Feb 6, 1954), Andy Shernoff (b Apr 19, 1952), Mark Mendoza, and Ritchie Teeter (b Mar 16, 1951). They recorded three albums before breaking up in 1978. −WR

○ **Go Girl Crazy / CBS**   1975
These punk progenitors and rock & roll comedians made only one great album, but it continues to stand up as both a celebration of the joys of three-chord rock and a sendup of the same. −WR

BO DIDDLEY   *b* 1928

Rock & roll, R&B. Bo Diddley (born Ellas Otha Bates McDaniels) is one of the most influential R&B artists of all time. His music resists classification to this day. Though some critics dismiss him as a one-riff artist, nothing could be farther from the truth. His trademark rhythm (based on equal parts "hambone" beat and sanctified church shout) has many variations, textures, and subtleties, which reveal themselves to the listener with concentrated listening. Though his chart hits were few, the scope and breadth of his influence, both here and abroad, are wide indeed. A major innovator in guitar sounds and designs and a galvanizing live performer with a powerful singing voice and personality to match, his induction to the Rock & Roll Hall of Fame was no less than his due. The only musician in history to have a specific beat named after him, Bo Diddley stands as a true American music original. −CK

Bo Diddley/Go Bo Diddley / CHESS
Diddleys first and second albums on one CD. −CK

Bo Diddley's Beach Party / CHECKER   1963
A blistering live album. Currently out of print but well worth any search. −CK

☆ **The Chess Box / CHESS**   1990
A two-CD boxed-set overview of Diddley's music. The perfect place to start. −CK

Rare & Well Done / CHESS — 1992
Contains unissued and rare sides. The perfect companion piece to *The Chess Box*. –CK

DIED PRETTY

Alternative pop. A moody Australian group who use the sound of the Byrds, Tom Petty, and R.E.M. as a base for their own swirling, atmospheric rock. Vocalist Ronald Peno at times is a dead ringer for Joy Division's Ian Curtis. –JF

○ **Free Dirt / WHAT GOES ON** — 1986
Easily their best. Not a bad track. –JD

DINOSAUR JR

Alternative rock. This acclaimed underground band from Amherst, MA, is really a vehicle for vocalist and guitarist J. Mascis, whose songwriting shows the influence of everyone from Neil Young and the Meat Puppets to the Velvet Underground and Sonic Youth. The band's minimalist attack also incorporates elements of heavy metal and surf guitar. –JF

○ **Dinosaur / HOMESTEAD** — 1985
Great angst-ridden songs. Tense, with a Neil Young flavor. –RG

Green Mind / WARNER — 1991
Some good stuff. Less tense; more flippant. –RG

DION — ♭1939

Doo-wop, rock & roll. Doo-wop was just as seductive a musical force in the Bronx as it was in Harlem, and young Dion DiMucci fell under its spell as a lad. With his pompadoured good looks and clear, powerful pipes, he was a natural for rock & roll stardom.

Dion and his vocal group, the Belmonts, joined the fledgling Laurie label in 1958 and immediately hit with the upbeat "I Wonder Why." After scoring two major pop smashes with "A Teenager in Love" and the pop standard "Where or When," Dion and the Belmonts went their separate ways.

Vocal group harmonies remained integral to Dion's sound even after going solo, from his initial 1960 hit, "Lonely Teenager," through his swaggering macho classics "Runaround Sue" and "The Wanderer" (still two of the most requested items on any oldies playlist). Moving to Columbia in 1963, Dion's output took on a distinctly bluesier tone with remakes of the Drifters' "Ruby Baby" and "Drip Drop" before a recurring problem with heroin forced him to take an extended hiatus from show biz.

America was rocked to its foundations by a series of tragic political assassinations in 1968, and Dick Holler's moving tribute "Abraham, Martin and John" inspired Dion to mount a comeback with the folk-style song. Since then, he's made several more acclaimed returns to action as a rocker between stints as a contemporary Christian performer, and now fittingly enjoys the status of a revered rock legend. –BD

☆ **Greatest Hits / CBS** — 1982
A solid compilation of Dion's solo sides, including "Donna the Prima Donna," "Ruby Baby," and others. –CK

★ **24 Golden Greats / ARISTA** — 1983
A sampling of every phase of Dion's career, from the late 50s to the early 70s. –DH

Yo Frankie / ARISTA — 1989
A solid streetwise effort. –DH

○ **Bronx Blues: The Columbia Recordings / CBS** — 1991
In the mid-60s, Dion turned away from teen-idol doo-wop material and cut several sides in a solid R&B/blues/folk vein. The best of those sides are collected here. –CK

DION & THE BELMONTS — ♭1939

Doo-wop, rock & roll. Like many teenagers from the 50s, Dion DiMucci (b Jul 18, 1939) developed his singing style from singing on street corners with neighborhood friends. Dion possessed a believable soulfulness in his delivery that enabled him to transcend the scads of doo-wop groups of the late 50s

and early 60s. In 1957 Dion & the Timberlanes released their first single, "The Chosen Few" (Mohawk Records, then Jubilee Records). The band changed its name to Dion & the Belmonts (named after a Bronx avenue), signed to Laurie Records, and released their first big hit, the #22 "I Wonder Why." 1959 and 1960 were golden years for Dion & the Belmonts, with the million-selling hits "A Teenager in Love" (#5) and "Where or When" (#3).

In September 1960 Dion & the Belmonts parted ways. The Belmonts scored two more Top 40 hits with "Tell Me Why" (#18) and "Come On Little Angel" (#28). Meanwhile, Dion went solo and enjoyed a substantial string of thirteen Top 40 hits between 1960 and 1963. "Runaround Sue," "The Wanderer," and "Ruby Baby" were among the eight that went Top Ten. –RC

☆ **Everything You Always Wanted To Hear / LAURIE**
The best overall collection of their classic sides. Includes "Teenager in Love," "Where or When," and "I Wonder Why." White New York doo-wop at its best. –CK

DIRE STRAITS

Rock & roll. In 1977 disco reigned and the new-wave/punk movements were heralding the death of tired FM rock. It was then that Dire Straits came along with a unique blend of atmospheric blues-flavored rock and literate Dylanesque story-type lyrics. Singer/songwriter and lead guitarist Mark Knopfler's dry, low-key vocal delivery and economical, clean guitar playing immediately hit a nerve with the public, and the group's self-titled debut effort went #2, aided by the driving #4 hit "Sultans of Swing."

Aside from *Communique*, the band's sophomore effort, Dire Straits increasingly developed a cinematic approach to songwriting and production. *Love over Gold* is a particular highlight. It was only a natural sidestep for Knopfler to score the highly acclaimed soundtracks for *Local Hero* (1983) and *The Princess Bride* (1987). *Alchemy*, a double-record live set was released in 1984.

In 1985 *Brothers in Arms* was released, becoming one of the biggest internationally selling albums of the 80s. The song "Money for Nothing" became free advertising for MTV, with the hook "I want my MTV."

Knopfler undertook various side projects, including the Notting Hillbillies and a fine duet album with Chet Atkins (*Neck and Neck*). Six years after the release of *Brothers in Arms*, *On Every Street* was released. –RC

★ **Dire Straits / WARNER** — 1978
Even after all the success, the debut is the best example of the intricate style of Dire Straits, dominated by the electric finger-picking of guitarist Mark Knopfler, his smoky voice and poetic lyrics. Features their first hit, "Sultans of Swing." –WR

○ **Making Movies / WARNER** — 1980
The third album displays Knopfler's expanding ambitions as a songwriter with, as the title suggests, a cinematic sweep on such songs as "Tunnel of Love" and "Romeo and Juliet." –WR

○ **Love over Gold / WARNER** — 1982
The fourth Dire Straits album is their most atmospheric effort, featuring the spacious title track as well as the epic "Telegraph Road," with an extended guitar workout at its conclusion. –RC

Brothers in Arms / WARNER — 1985
Their biggest-selling album, containing the mega-hit "Money for Nothing" as well as "Walk of Life" and "So Far Away." –WR

○ **Money for Nothing / WARNER** — 1988
This best-of collection contains Dire Straits' biggest hits as well as some key album tracks. "Sultans of Swing," "Walk of Life," "Money for Nothing," plus a live version of "Telegraph Road" from *Love over Gold* are among the highlights. Even though this may be a fairly representative sampler, listening to their better albums in their entirety is the best way to hear this band. –RC

DIVINYLS

Hard rock, rock/pop. This Australian band, built around Christina Amphlett's hiccuping vocals and Mark McEntee's rude grunge-guitar work, made an impressive debut with *Desperate*, a record that blends the thick chorusy guitar sound of the Pretenders with a punkish hard-rock recklessness.
On their first album for Virgin Records, *Divinyls* (1991), Amphlett's naughty-girl/sexual-fetish persona is brought to the fore with the Top Ten ode to auto-eroticism, "I Touch Myself." –RC

Desperate / CAPITOL   1983
Raw, ugly noises abound on this, their best studio album. Good songs too! Highlights include "Take a Chance," "Only Lonely," and "Boys in Town." –RC

○ **Essential / CAPITOL**   1987
Good compilation. Contains key radio tracks, but some great album sides are omitted. Still, a good place to start. –RC

Divinyls / ATLANTIC   1991
Only a couple of tracks of note: the highly song-crafted ode to auto-eroticism, "I Touch Myself" (their biggest hit), and "Make Out Alright." –RC

THE DIXIE DREGS

Fusion. This Georgia-based instrumental fusion band developed quite a following during the late 70s with their musical chops, band chemistry, and complicated (but solidly melodic) compositions, primarily written by guitarist Steve Morse. –RC

Best of the Dixie Dregs / GRAND SLAM
A decent selection of their best work while signed to Capricorn. Includes "Cruise Control," a live version of "Refried Funky Chicken," and a healthy sampling off of *What If.* –RC

Free Fall / POLYGRAM   1977
A potent debut that presents the Dregs's melodic instrumental fusion to fine effect. –JO

○ **What If / POLYGRAM**   1978
Of all the albums by the Dregs, this is the one to get. Steve Morse's melodies have an otherwordly elegance on songs like "Night Meets Light." The band plays with just the right amount of restraint. Ken Scott's production is, at turns, atmospheric and immediate. "Take It off the Top" is a fine rocker. –RC

Night of the Living Dregs / POLYGRAM   1979
A good half-live, half-studio set. –JO

DON DIXON

Roots-rock, anglo-pop. Don Dixon led the North Carolina rock group Arrogance for 14 years, then became a producer for a variety of 80s alternative bands, notably R.E.M. and the Smithereens, before launching a solo career as a singer/songwriter. He also works extensively with his wife Marti Jones. –WR

○ **Most of the Girls Like to Dance ... / ENIGMA**   1985
Dixon put together *Most of the Girls Like to Dance but Only Some of the Boys Like To* out of demos cut from 1981-1984. It's a kind of best-of from a man with a pure pop sensibility and a wicked sense of humor when it comes to matters romantic. (The 1986 CD version adds two songs to make a total of 16.) –WR

Romeo at Juilliard / ENIGMA   1987
Dixon's domestic debut featured more of his skewed songs, and here he was aided and abetted by such compatriots as Mitch Easter and Marti Jones (who is his wife). –WR

Chi Town Budget / ENIGMA   1988
An intimate live album featuring many of the best songs from the two previous albums. –WR

DR. BUZZARD'S ORIGINAL SAVANNAH BAND

Pop, disco. Dr. Buzzard's Original Savannah Band was one of the most original musical ensembles of the disco era. They were formed in the Bronx in 1974 by Stony Browder Jr (b 1949), his brother August Darnell (Thomas Browder, b 1951), singer Cory Daye (b 1952), Andy Hernandez (b 1950), and Mickey Sevilla (b 1953). The concept of the group was the re-creation of a 30s dance band à la Cab Calloway, with witty lyrics and a disco beat. –WR

○ **Dr. Buzzard's Original Savannah Band / RCA**   1976
Dr. Buzzard introduced a big-band sheen to 70s dance music with the hit "Cherchez la Femme" and the rest of this charmingly neo-retro album. –WR

DR. FEELGOOD

Blues/rock, punk. This UK pub-rock band, formed in 1971, benefited from the mid-70s punk movement. It featured guitarist Wilko Johnson and vocalist Lee Brilleaux (b 1948). Johnson left the band in 1977. –WR

Down by the Jetty / UNITED ARTISTS   1975
Dr. Feelgood's debut album is on a par with the early Rolling Stones albums as a demonstration of R&B fervor. Every track burns. (Import) –WR

○ **Malpractice / CBS**   1975
Guitarist Wilko Johnson's songs shine against such inspired covers as "Riot in Cell Block #9." And his Stonesy playing takes no prisoners. –WR

Sneakin' Suspicion / CBS   1977
Wilko Johnson's last album with Dr. Feelgood continues to be dominated by his tough guitar playing, though fewer of his songs are heard. –WR

DR. HOOK

Country rock, pop. This American country-rock band was originally named Dr. Hook and the Medicine Show. Formed in New Jersey in 1968, the original members included Ray Sawyer (b 1937), Dennis Locorriere (b 1948), Bill Francis, John David, and George Cummings. First coming to prominence with material written by Shel Silverstein, the looniness of their stage show transferred to records well, reaching its peak with the mega-hit "The Cover of the *Rolling Stone*" in 1972. They mellowed their style on record, hitting the charts with ballads as the decade wore on, but they were still crazy in live performances. Sawyer continues to front versions of the band to this day on various oldies package shows. –CK

Sloppy Seconds / CBS   1972
At their raunchy, early best, featuring "The Cover of the Rolling Stone." –DH

○ **Greatest Hits / CAPITOL**   1987
Includes "Sexy Eyes," "Sylvia's Mother," "Only Sixteen," "When You're in Love with a Beautiful Woman," and "Cover of the *Rolling Stone*." –ED

DR. JOHN   b 1940

R&B, rock & roll. Dr. John (born Mac Rebennack) honed his skills playing 50s sessions during the heyday of New Orleans R&B. His solo work has alternately paid homage to his inspirations and incorporated those influences into his own distinct rhythmic roux. –JF

Gumbo / ATLANTIC   1972

● **Ultimate Dr. John / WARNER**   1987
An adequate overview of the Doctor's Atlantic recordings, including the 1973 hit "Right Place Wrong Time." –JF

○ **Gris Gris / ALLIGATOR**   1987
A haunting and creepy set infused with voodoo imagery from the bayous and acid-tinged variations on New Orleans R&B structures. –JF

JOHN DOE   b 1954

Roots-rock, punk. Bassist and co-lead singer of the Los Angeles punk-rock group X during the 80s, John Doe launched a solo career when the group took a hiatus in 1987. He has also scored as an actor in such films as *Great Balls of Fire*. –WR

○ **Meet John Doe / GEFFEN** 1990
From the rock-out sound, slashing guitars, and near-howl of the unison singing, not to mention the temper of the lyrics, the leadoff track, "Let's Be Mad," could be by X, Doe's former band. Elsewhere on his debut solo album he takes a less punky approach, but this is still a charged, rocking record. –WR

BILL DOGGETT b 1916

R&B, rock & roll. Organist Bill Doggett cut one of the biggest-selling instrumentals of all time in 1956 with the two-part "Honky Tonk." He formed his first band in 1938 and sold the entire outfit to Lucky Milinder for a soda two years later. Doggett worked extensively with Millinder and Louis Jordan and recorded with Ella Fitzgerald before striking out on his own. He signed with King in Cincinnati around 1953, churning out a slew of sizzling instrumentals with Clifford Scott on tenor sax, Billy Butler on guitar, and Doggett on organ, notably "Ram-Bunk-Shush" in 1957 and, in 1958, "Leaps and Bounds" and the often-covered "Hold It." Doggett continues to tour and record — he was recently featured on a disc by the King All-Stars, a distinguished group of alumni from the famous label. –BD

Dance a While / KING 1958
Sizzling R&B-based instrumentals. –BD

○ **Everybody Dance to the Honky Tonk / KING** 1958
The hugely influential jazz-laced R&B quartet plays their classic two-part instrumental and several more groovers, with guitarist Billy Butler and saxist Clifford Scott incendiary throughout the album. –BD

Hold It / KING 1959
The title instrumental is a classic. –BD

The Doggett Beat for Happy Feet / KING 1988
Doggett's fatback organ cooks in tandem with Butler's licks and Scott's sax. –BD

DOKKEN

Heavy metal. Formed in Sacramento, CA, in the late 70s, Dokken's claim to fame was the harmonious vocals of Don Dokken and the engaging guitar work of George Lynch. Although their strength was heavy metal, they weren't afraid to record ballads, which brought them attention across the world. They soon toured around the world and became an important American metal band in the 80s, gathering a few hits along the way before splitting up in 1989 due to "personal indifferences." Don Dokken went solo and Lynch formed the Lynch Mob. –JB

○ **Under Lock & Key / ELEKTRA** 1985
Melodic heavy metal played by a band that spawned a lot of copycats, both in sound and image. The album features strong vocals from Don Dokken and not-too-flashy guitar playing from George Lynch. –JB

Beast from the East / ELEKTRA 1988
The band's only live album, recorded in Japan. They do their best material. Unfortunately, it was their last as a band. –JB

THOMAS DOLBY b 1958

Alternative pop, dance-pop. Dolby's upbeat dance-pop made him a synthesizer pioneer in the early 80s. He had several hits with "She Blinded Me with Science" and "Hyperactive." –IME

● **The Golden Age of Wireless / CAPITOL** 1983
This contains Dolby's biggest hit, the humorously quirky "She Blinded Me with Science." Highlights include "Radio Silence," "Europa and the Pirate Twins," "Windpower," "One of Our Submarines," and "Airwaves" — a track that should've been a single. All in all, this is a very solid collection of early-80s synth-pop. –RC

○ **The Flat Earth / CAPITOL** 1984
A departure from the style of his debut, this moody and atmospheric album adds jazz and Joni Mitchellesque elements to warm his synth textures. Only one cut, the single "Hyperactive," features the hard dance beats of his early hits. –SWB

FATS DOMINO b 1929

R&B, rock & roll. New Orleans has produced many musical legends over the years but none have created a sound that was more recognizable, more influential, or more profitable than Fats Domino. Beginning with "The Fat Man" in 1949, Domino had an enviable run of chart success, selling more than 65 million records and chalking up 23 gold records. Although he's become a rock & roll deity — he was one of the first Rock & Roll Hall of Fame inductees — Domino made his name playing the same New Orleans R&B he'd always played. His best recordings were made for the Imperial label between 1949 and 1963. Of his scores of hits, "Ain't That a Shame," "Blueberry Hill," "I'm Walking," "Whole Lot of Lovin'," and "I'm Ready" were among the biggest. EMI's *They Call Me the Fat Man*, a 100-track boxed set, concisely chronicles Domino's sound and story. –JH

Fats Is Back / REPRISE 1968
Producer Richard Perry's successful update of Domino's sound, complete with two most effective Beatles covers. (Out of print) –BE

● **My Blue Heaven - Best of Fats Domino / CAPITOL** 1990
A crisp, well-thought-out collection that says it all. –BE

☆ **They Call Me the Fat Man / CAPITOL** 1991
Hardcore lovers of Fats Domino's rolling boogie-style piano playing and easy Cajun-inflected tenor voice (if they're ready to chunk down the change for a boxed set) should find this 4-CD, 100-song compilation (which includes all of his Imperial hits) a thorough baptism. Sonically, this set is very impressive. Many times when old tracks are cleaned up during remastering, the life gets processed out, but that's not evident here. The 84-page booklet is a fan's delight, with first-rate annotation and plenty of photos. –RC

THE DOMINOES

R&B, doo-wop. Though they were often billed on records as Billy Ward & the Dominoes, Ward was, in fact, not their lead singer. But as group leader and musical director, he sure knew how to pick them, as evidenced by the back-to-back tenures of frontmen Clyde McPhatter and Jackie Wilson. Originally formed in 1950, the Dominoes were one of the first groups to infuse their music with a strong gospel flavor, changing the sound of R&B vocal-group stylings forever and influencing everyone from Nolan Strong to Smokey Robinson in the process. –CK

☆ **The Dominoes Featuring Clyde McPhatter / KING** 1958
The first album for King collects a dozen of their best sides, including "The Bells" and "Have Mercy Baby" –CK

DON & DEWEY

R&B, doo-wop. Wailing in tandem like twin Little Richards, Don & Dewey cut numerous blistering rockers for Specialty from 1957 to 1959 without registering a single hit, only to see other acts revive their songs to much greater acclaim. Don Harris (b 1938) and Dewey Terry (b 1938) were born and raised in Pasadena, CA, joining a group called the Squires and recording for Vita before branching off on their own. Their Specialty output included the savage rockers "Jungle Hop," "Koko Joe" (written by Sonny Bono), and "Justine," the latter pair later covered by the Righteous Brothers. Don & Dewey's Specialty discography also includes the original "I'm Leavin' It Up to You," a hit for Dale & Grace; "Big Boy Pete," ditto for the Olympics; and "Farmer John," the Premiers' only smash. Don laid down his guitar for a violin during the 60s and, billed as "Sugarcane" Harris, sawed his rocked-out fiddle beside John Mayall and Frank Zappa. –BD

☆ **Don & Dewey / SPECIALTY** 1974
A solid best-of collection featuring the original versions of "Farmer John," "Koko Joe," and "Justine." –CK

DON & JUAN

Doo-wop. New York doo-woppers Roland Trone and Claude Johnson crafted one astonishing single ("What's Your Name") in 1962, then drifted into obscurity. –JF

○ **What's Your Name - Golden Classics / COLLECTABLES**
The title cut, a hit during the early 60s doo-wop revival, is the one to keep, but there's enough here to keep doo-woppers happy. –JF

DONOVAN
♭1946

British Invasion, folk/rock, singer/songwriter. Donovan (born Donovan Leitch), initially touted as the "British Invasion's Bob Dylan," recorded such topical tracks as "The Universal Soldier" and "Catch the Wind" in 1965. However, a new manager, Allen Klein (later to work with the Rolling Stones and the Beatles), and a new producer, Mickie Most (who also cut hits for the Animals, Herman's Hermits, and Jeff Beck), revealed that Donovan was much better suited to synthesizing folk with mystical hippie-pop. Between 1965 and 1969, Donovan scored a series of memorable hits, including "Sunshine Superman" (#1), "Mellow Yellow" (#2, containing a Paul McCartney cameo), "Hurdy Gurdy Man" (#5, with Jeff Beck), and "Atlantis" (#7) –RC

Sunshine Superman / CBS 1966
Probably the singer/songwriter's best album, embracing folk, blues, and a druggy psychedelia, and driven by crisp rhythm guitars (especially on the title track). It starts to sound the same after a bit, but at its release, even this was a point of recommendation — it set a hazy, drugged-out mood. The use of the mono master helps, because it's punchier. –BE

A Gift from a Flower to a Garden / EPIC 1968
A blast from hippie past — a flower-decorated double album made up of precious trippy music spiced with a haunting melody or two ("Wear Your Love like Heaven"). –BE

Hurdy Gurdy Man / CBS 1968
For this performer, this is a hard-rocking album, driven by some loud electric guitar subbing for sitar, which dresses up the plainer folk melodies and turns the title tune into a near-classic. –BE

○ **Greatest Hits / EPIC** 1969
Entertaining but flawed collection of Donovan's psychedelic-era hits, fleshed out with too-languid rerecordings of his pre-CBS folk successes, including "Colours." It's unfortunate that the producers used the stereo versions, which don't sound nearly as good as the mono. –BE

Classics Live / GREAT NORTHERN
Fresh stage recordings of Donovan's 60s hits, well produced and arranged, and laced with a certain amount of humor from the passage of time and the druggy sensibilities behind them. "Sunshine Superman" is an intrinsically good song, although the infectious beat of the original Mickie Most production is missed in spite of the good playing. –BE

THE DOOBIE BROTHERS

Rock/pop. The Doobie Brothers ("doobie" being slang for a marijuana joint) straddled FM rock and Top 40 pop better than most bands of the 70s, with their good-time grooves and melodies and solid musicianship. During the first part of their career (1970 to 1975), the Doobie Brothers scored with a batch of radio classics in "Listen to the Music" (#11), "Long Train Running" (#8), "China Grove" (#15), and the #1 hit "Black Water." With the arrival of soulful Steely Dan singer and keyboardist Michael McDonald, the Doobie Brothers took on a

mellower, more sophisticated musical direction, giving passing nods to jazz and light funk along the way. "Takin' It to the Streets" (#13) showcased McDonald's contribution to fine effect. The 1977 album *Living on the Fault Line* is an artistic pinnacle of the band's new direction, but the #1 followup, *Minute by Minute*, was a much bigger success, containing hits "What a Fool Believes" and the title cut.
By the time *One Step Closer* was released in 1980, the Doobies' brand of slick California pop reached the saturation point in fern bars across the land. The fact that Michael McDonald's aching vocals seemed to appear on every record from the West Coast ensured overkill. The band called it quits in 1981. The pre-McDonald lineup re-formed in 1987 and enjoyed a successful comeback. –RC

Captain & Me / WARNER 1973
Their best early album, featuring "China Grove." –DH

○ **Best of the Doobies / WARNER** 1976
A formidable bunch of hard-rock hits from 1972-1976. –DH

Best of the Doobies - Vol. 2 / WARNER 1981
The best of the Michael McDonald era. –DH

THE DOORS

Rock & roll. An American rock band consisting of Jim Morrison (vocals), Robbie Krieger (guitar), John Densmore (drums), and Ray Manzarek (organ and keyboard bass). Starting as a frat/R&B band on campus at UCLA, they evolved into something resembling performance art under the sway of poet and vocalist Morrison. His lyrics, free-form associations, and demonic stage energy were startling to pop audiences of the time, earning the band much chart success and a devoted following. When Morrison died in 1971, the band became a legendary icon of its time, one that has continued unabated thanks to their frequent rotation on classic-rock-format radio and to Oliver Stone's film based on their career. –CK

☆ **The Doors / ELEKTRA** 1967
One of the most remarkable debut albums in rock history introduced the powerful singing of Jim Morrison, his provocative lyrics, and the group's spare, direct guitar/organ sound. "Light My Fire" became an instant standard but the album also contained such Doors classics as "Break On Through (To the Other Side)," "Twentieth Century Fox," and, of course, that Oedipal odyssey "The End." (DCC Compact Classics has a gold disc that offers superior fidelity.) –WR

Waiting for the Sun / ELEKTRA 1968
Singles like "Hello, I Love You" and "The Unknown Soldier" are on *The Best of the Doors* (see below), but many of the standouts on this album are gentle songs like "Summer's Almost Gone," "Yes, the River Knows," and "Wintertime Love," which demonstrate that Morrison & Co. can be lyrical without losing their power. –WR

The Soft Parade / ELEKTRA 1969
Probably the most underrated Doors collection because its addition of horns and strings ("Wishful Sinful") turns it into a more exploratory album than their more basic music usually attempted. But "Tell All the People" is the group at its most revolutionary, and the long title track is among its most ambitious. This included the hit "Touch Me" as well as "Wild Child," one of their best rockers. –WR

Morrison Hotel/Hard Rock Cafe / ELEKTRA 1970
A bluesy, hard-rock album that nevertheless contains some of Morrison's most visionary poetry. –WR

L.A. Woman / ELEKTRA 1972
Morrison's final testament shows him at the height of his ability to bring striking images to the lyrics of rock music, and the group produces some of its most trancelike music. –WR

★ **The Best of the Doors / ELEKTRA** 1985
A well-chosen, 19-track compilation balancing the radio hits with the longer, more complex song poems. It's a good sampler (and contains enough of the good tracks from

Strange Days that we didn't bother to list that album separately), but this is one group for whose the whole story. you need to hear—WR

In Concert / ELEKTRA   1991

The Doors could be erratic live, as this double CD shows. Still, it's a fair example of their in-concert charms. —JT

LEE DORSEY   1924-1986

R&B, soul. The effervescent approach of Lee Dorsey perfectly summarizes the infectious charm of early-60s New Orleans R&B. Dorsey specialized in good-humored music with a touch of second-line funk thrown in to make it all the more irresistible.

Although he had already waxed a couple of singles, Dorsey caught the country by total surprise in 1961 with his deceptively simply nursery-rhyme-style "Ya Ya" on Bobby Robinson's Fury label. Arranged by prolific New Orleans pianist Allen Toussaint, the track proved an R&B chart-topper and a major pop hit to boot.

Dorsey's laconic vocal charms served him well on "Ya Ya" and the Earl King-penned followup "Do Re Mi," and the mid 60s found him working with Toussaint on the funky smashes "Ride Your Pony" and "Working in the Coal Mine," this time for Amy Records. It's little remembered that Dorsey was responsible for the original 1970 version of Toussaint's "Yes We Can," revived to much greater acclaim by the Pointer Sisters (who tacked on an extra "Can").

From all accounts, Dorsey remained an exceedingly humble R&B star who preferred tinkering with cars to extensively touring the country. He died of emphysema in 1986. —BD

Golden Classics / COLLECTABLES

Covers Dorsey's Allen Toussaint-produced mid-60s soul hits as well as some earlier material on the Relic set. —BD

○ **Ya Ya / RELIC**   1962

Terrific overview of the good-humored New Orleans singer's early-60s classics for Bobby Robinson's Fury label. Direct-from-masters sound quality. —BD

LAMONT DOZIER   b 1941

Soul, Motown. A prolific Detroit R&B composer who doubled as a soul singer in the early 70s. As one third of the fabulously successful writing and production team of Holland-Dozier-Holland, Lamont Dozier was directly responsible for numerous hits by the Supremes, the Miracles, Marvin Gaye, Junior Walker, and many other Motown acts. After the trio exited Motown in 1968 and formed their own Invictus and Hot Wax labels, Dozier revived his long-dormant singing career by notching an R&B hit in 1972 with "Why Can't We Be Lovers." Moving to ABC, Dozier enjoyed three more major soul smashes in 1973 and 1974, including "Trying to Hold On to My Woman" and "Fish Ain't Bitin'." —BD

○ **Inside Seduction / ATLANTIC**

New recordings from an outstanding R&B/soul composer-and-performer. —RW

THE DRAMATICS

Soul. Popular Detroit R&B vocal aggregation that scored numerous hits for Volt and maintained their momentum through the disco era. The early Dramatics lived up to their billing with the emphatic vocals of Ron Banks (b May 10, 1951) powering the funky "Whatcha See Is Whatcha Get," their first big-seller in 1971, and the R&B chart-topping ballad "In the Rain" the next year. The quintet was just as successful later in the decade, signing with ABC in 1975 and scoring repeatedly throughout disco-fever days. —BD

○ **The Best of the Dramatics / STAX**   1974

A solid compilation that includes the hits "Whatcha See Is Whatcha Get" (#9), "In the Rain" (#5), "Fell for You" (#45), and other equally good but lesser-known tracks. —ED

THE DREAM ACADEMY

Alternative pop. A lush pop trio from Great Britain, featuring

Nick Laird-Clowes, Gilbert Gabriel, and Kate St. John, that scored a #7 single in 1986 with "Life in a Northern Town." —WR

○ **The Dream Academy / WARNER**   1985

Classical influences (and not a little of *Sgt. Pepper*-era Beatles) can be heard on this lovely pop album, much of it co-produced by Pink Floyd's David Gilmour. Contains the hits "Life in a Northern Town" and "Love Parade." —WR

THE DREAM SYNDICATE

Psychedelic. A Los Angeles-based "paisley underground" psychedelic-rock band of the 80s, led by Steve Wynn. —WR

○ **Tell Me When It's Over: The Best of ... / RHINO**   1992

These 15 tracks contain the cream of the crop of this Los Angeles band's independent- and major-label work. Among the highlights are "When You Smile," "Tell Me When It's Over," and "Halloween" off of their 1982 Ruby/Slash EP *Days of Wine and Roses*. The fine remastering captures their dense Velvet Underground-style rock in all its trashy glory. The booklet is loaded with a detailed history, many photos, lyrics, and track and personnel listings. —RC

THE DRIFTERS

R&B, doo-wop. The Drifters were the longest-lasting of the 50s doo-wop groups simply because they were the best. What other vocal group from those days produced such 20th-century marvels as Clyde McPhatter and Ben E. King? What other group survived numerous personnel changes and changes in audience tastes, keeping their name in the charts for 12 straight years? Doo-wop is certainly full of mythological groups, celebrated as much for their obscurity as their musi;, the Drifters are the group that turned the myth into fact.

Clyde McPhatter was already an R&B star when Atlantic's Ahmet Ertegun signed him in 1953, thanks to his work with Billy Ward's Dominoes. After leaving them, McPhatter assembled a group to support his glorious, soaring vocals, and in 1953 the Drifters landed their first hit with Jesse Stone's "Money Honey." A slew of meticulously recorded classics followed; "Let the Boogie Woogie Roll," "Such a Night," "Honey Love," and "White Christmas" are among the best. McPhatter took off for a solo career in 1954 but was amply replaced by Johnny Moore, who was on hand when the group recorded three of their finest songs: "Ruby Baby," "Your Promise to Be Mine," and "Adorable."

Drifters manager George Threadwell disbanded the group in 1958 and found an ensemble called the Crowns, who had a lead singer named Ben E. King; a new Drifters was born. Under the wings of Jerry Leiber and Mike Stoller, this new outfit established their own identity in 1959 with the Latin-tinged "There Goes My Baby," a tour de force for King and the first R&B song to include strings, which ushered in a new era of Black music, known as soul. King departed in 1960, but thanks to a string of songs written by the likes of Doc Pomus and Mort Shuman, the Drifters, with Rudy Lewis and Johnny Moore taking leads, became a veritable hit factory. "Save the Last Dance for Me," "On Broadway," "Up on the Roof," and "This Magic Moment" all helped define the sound of soul music and define an era, with their tugging romanticism, dancing strings, and musical innovation and sophistication. —JF

The Drifters' Golden Hits / ATLANTIC   1968

A basic collection of later hits. —ED

○ **Let the Boogie Woogie Roll ... / ATLANTIC**   1988

Let the Boogie Woogie Roll - Greatest Hits is the definitive account of the early group (1953-1958) and Clyde McPhatter's greatest sides. —BE

★ **All-Time Greatest Hits & More ... / ATLANTIC**   1988

All the Greatest Hits & More - 1959-1965 is a towering and magnificent collection of some of the best popular R&B ever done this side of Sam Cooke. —BE

DRIVIN' N CRYIN'

Rock & roll. This Georgia quartet boldly mixes country and bluegrass tunes alongside pedal-to-the-metal hard rock and, more often than not, manages to pull it off. It's an over-amped 90s version of the Buffalo Springfield style of earthy rock eclecticism. –RC

Scarred but Smarter / POLYGRAM 1986
Their debut boldly mixes everything from countryish sendups to death-rock. It almost works. Certainly it's an engaging listen. Highlights: "Stand Up and Fight for It," "Another Scarlet Butterfly," and "Saddle on the Side of the Road." –RC

Whisper Tames the Lion / POLYGRAM 1987
The juxtaposing of diverse genres continues, with greater success. Produced by Anton Fier (Grapes of Wrath, Joe Henry). –RC

Mystery Road / ISLAND 1989
New guitarist Buren Fowler adds more punch to the band's sound. Kevn Kinney's mature songwriting grasp of various genres is shown to great effect, from reckless rockers like "Toy Never Played With" to more laidback tracks like "Peacemaker." –RC

○ **Fly Me Courageous / POLYGRAM** 1991
This Atlanta quartet's most fully realized synthesis of aggressive hard rock, country-rock, and folk/rock. Visceral production by Geoff Workman. Standout tracks include the hyperdrive of "Rush Hour" and "Lost in the Shuffle," as well as "Around the Block Again," "Chain Reaction," "Build a Fire," and the title cut. –RC

THE DUKES OF STRATOSPHEAR

Psychedelic. The Dukes of Stratosphea, (conceived in 1987) are the psychedelic alter-personalities of the English alternative pop-rock band XTC. –RC

○ **Chips from the Chocolate Fireball / GEFFEN** 1987
Fans of late-60s psychedelia will love this affectionate Rutlesesque collaboration between XTC (posing as the Dukes) and producer John Leckie (Posies, Let's Active, House of Freaks). *Chips from the Chocolate Fireball* is loaded with playful tips of the hat to artists like the Move, the Electric Prunes, early Pink Floyd, the Yardbirds, Spirit, the Zombies, the Beach Boys, and (of course) the Beatles. By the way, this is a compilation of the Dukes's *25-O-Clock* EP and the full-length album *Psonic Psunspot*. –RC

THE DUPREES

Doo-wop. Specializing in updated renditions of 40s and 50s pop fare, the Duprees had a classy sound that harked back to an earlier era. Formed as the Parisians in Jersey City, they were discovered by George Paxton, who ran Coed Records in New York. Paxton convinced the quartet to change their name, and they hit big their first time out in 1962 with a polished revival of Jo Stafford's "You Belong to Me." Most sides cut for Coed were in the same big-band mold, including "My Own True Love" and "Have You Heard." Lead singer Joe Canzano (b Apr 3, 1943) left the group in 1964, and the Duprees moved to Columbia the next year with minimal success. –BD

○ **You Belong to Me / COED** 1962
Debut album, featuring the title track hit and 11 other doo-wop classics done in typical early-60s NYC production style. –CK

Have You Heard / COED 1963
Second album, companion piece to *You Belong to Me.* –CK

DURAN DURAN

Alternative pop, dance-pop. The major teen-pop band of the 80s (Nick Rhodes, keyboards; John Taylor, bass; Andy Taylor, guitar; Roger Taylor, drums) formed in 1978 in Birmingham, England, although the final lineup was not set until the addition of Simon Le Bon (vocals) in 1980. Taking their name from a character in the Jane Fonda film *Barbarella*, their style of dance music was quickly drawn into the new romantic movement of the British punk/new-wave scene. These so-called haircut bands were inspired to their fashion-centered

look and hip-synthesizer, neo-disco style by bands like Roxy Music. Duran Duran's lush arrangements and distinct vocal sound, combined with an aggressive new-wave, funk-rhythm section caught the attention of the mass market. But it was their visual appeal and exotic/erotic videos for "Girls on Film," "Hungry like the Wolf," and "Rio" on the newborn MTV that catapulted them into concert arenas and multi-platinum stardom. Although unabashed teen idols, the members tried to gain more critical respect with sideline efforts like Power Station (for John and Andy Taylor) and Arcadia (for LeBon, Roger Taylor, and Rhodes). After these experiments, the band went through a series of lineup changes and artistic wanderings as their teenage fans began to outgrow them. But none of their later works were as successful as *Rio* or *Seven and the Ragged Tiger*. With the end virtually in sight, the band released the hits/retrospective package *Decade* and one final studio album before they finally dissolved. –SWB

○ **Decade - Greatest Hits / CAPITOL** 1989
All their hits "Hungry like the Wolf" (#3), "Rio" (#14), "Is There Something I Should Know" (#4), "Union of the Snake" (#3), "The Wild Boys" (#2), "Notorious" (#2), "I Don't Want Your Love" (#4), and the #1s "The Reflex" and "A View to a Kill" in a well-selected package. –DH

BOB DYLAN   b1941

Singer/songwriter, folk/rock, rock & roll, country rock. The greatest songwriter of his generation and a figure of incalculable influence on popular music from the 60s on, Bob Dylan is also (with the possible exception of Elvis Presley) the most important individual ever in rock music.

Dylan came from Minnesota to New York City in 1961, at the age of 19, as an acolyte of folksinger Woody Guthrie, although he had played rock music in the late 50s. He met Guthrie (who was slowly dying in a hospital) and was quickly taken up by the New York folk community. He signed to Columbia Records and, in March 1962, released his first album, *Bob Dylan*, consisting largely of folk-blues covers. By this time, however, he had begun to write original songs, many in the philosophical/political style of his Greenwich Village compatriots (though far superior in quality), the best early example being "Blowin' in the Wind." Many of these songs were on Dylan's second album, *The Freewheelin' Bob Dylan*, released in May 1963. That summer, the popular folk group Peter, Paul & Mary took "Blowin' in the Wind" to #2 in the national charts. Thereafter, Bob Dylan songs became favorites among many pop and folk performers. As the result of such exposure, *Freewheelin'* became a chart hit in September 1963. Dylan followed with two albums in 1964, the heavily protest-oriented *The Times They Are A-Changin'* and the more introspective *Another Side of Bob Dylan*. In 1965, he began recording and playing concerts with rock musicians, which vastly increased his following but also led to controversy within the folk community. His singles "Like a Rolling Stone" and "Positively 4th Street" were Top Ten hits, as were the albums *Bringing It All Back Home* and *Highway 61 Revisited*, and the "folk/rock" sound of his music could be heard on any number of other artists' records, many of them written by Dylan himself. Dylan undertook a world tour in 1966 to promote the double album *Blonde on Blonde*, which featured the #2 single "Rainy Day Women #12 & 35." That summer he was in a motorcycle accident and he withdrew from public view for a year and a half, meanwhile recording the informal material later released as *The Basement Tapes*.

When Dylan returned to action in early 1968, it was with the quieter *John Wesley Harding* album, followed in 1969 by the country-flavored *Nashville Skyline* and its Top Ten single "Lay Lady Lay." Critics expecting Dylan's more complex work were disappointed and they savaged his two-disc *Self-Portrait* in 1970, though most saw *New Morning*, released only a few months later, as a return to form.

Dylan was not much heard from in the early 70s (he played at

George Harrison's Bangladesh benefit concert in 1971, and in 1973 he appeared in the film *Pat Garrett and Billy the Kid* and wrote its score), but he returned in 1974 with a national concert tour and the #1 album *Planet Waves*. This was followed in 1975 by *Blood on the Tracks*, regarded by many as his best collection of the decade. The same year, Dylan organized a roving band of musicians as the Rolling Thunder Revue and toured the Northeast, later appearing in other parts of the country in 1976.

A film crew was part of the entourage, and Dylan put together a sprawling film, *Renaldo & Clara*, released in 1978. With that done, he went on an international tour and released a new album, *Street-Legal*. In 1979, Dylan converted to Christianity and released the first of three overtly religious albums, *Slow Train Coming*.

The religious fervor became less apparent by the time of *Infidels* in 1983, and Dylan has released several excellent albums since, while touring more or less continually. The 80s and early 90s have also seen the welcome legitimate release of much previously unissued vintage Dylan material (some of it widely available on bootlegs). –WR

Bob Dylan / CBS   1962
For the most part, Bob Dylan's debut album positions him as an interpretive singer of rural folk songs, and already influential at that. The Animals found "House of the Rising Sun" on this album, while Led Zeppelin borrowed "In My Time of Dyin'." But the most striking track is the Dylan original "Song to Woody," his tribute to Woody Guthrie, which leaves no doubt he intends to carry on in his mentor's footsteps. –WR

☆ **The Freewheelin' Bob Dylan / CBS**   1963
The most important collection of original songs issued in the 60s. "Don't Think Twice, It's All Right," "Girl from the North Country," "A Hard Rain's A-Gonna Fall," "Masters of War," and, especially, "Blowin' in the Wind" have long since become standards, and their sheer range, from bitter protest to wry romantic regret, is astonishing, not to mention the absurd apocalyptic humor of some of the album's other tracks. The songs were so strong that they put across Dylan's limited, rough vocal style at a time when such a voice normally would have seemed completely unacceptable in a professional singer. *The Freewheelin' Bob Dylan* transformed the notion of what "good" singing was. –WR

☆ **Another Side of Bob Dylan / CBS**   1964
The first of two transitional albums in which Dylan moved beyond protest, and then beyond folk music. Here, in songs like "Chimes of Freedom" and "My Back Pages," he suggested that social issues were much more complicated than the increasingly polarized times made them seem. His lyrics, meanwhile, also became more complicated and poetic. Other singers would mine this album for hits with "All I Really Want to Do" and "It Ain't Me, Babe." –WR

☆ **The Times They Are A-Changin' / CBS**   1964
Dylan devoted most of his third album to hard, uncompromising topical or "protest" songs, starting with the anthemic title track and continuing through "The Lonesome Death of Hattie Carroll," "Ballad of Hollis Brown," "Only a Pawn in Their Game," and "With God on Our Side." –WR

☆ **Bringing It All Back Home / CBS**   1965
Dylan added a bluesy rock-band backing for the first half of this album, and the lyrics of the new songs are compendiums of allusions and witticisms — "Subterranean Homesick Blues," "Maggie's Farm," "Mr. Tambourine Man," "It's All Right, Ma (I'm Only Bleeding)." Even the love songs achieve a new poetic height — "She Belongs to Me," "Love Minus Zero/No Limit," "It's All Over Now, Baby Blue." –WR

☆ **Highway 61 Revisited / CBS**   1965
Dylan only upped the ante, making more extensive use of a crack backup band including Al Kooper and Michael Bloomfield to play his signature song, "Like a Rolling Stone," and other articulate, poetic, and incredibly bitter songs,

notably "Ballad of a Thin Man" and "Desolation Row." The gold-disc version possesses a fuller bottom end, and you can hear instruments in the mix with greater detail than ever before, particularly all of Harvey Brooks's bass parts (including his mistakes) and kick drum. (The gold disc available from DCC Compact Classics offers improved fidelity and the complete original artwork.) –WR

☆ **Blonde on Blonde / CBS**   1966
The bitterness was transmuted into humor and absurdity on this remarkable album, on which Dylan's gush of wordplay seems endlessly inventive, his wit razor sharp, and his world-weariness overwhelming. The music, meanwhile, has coalesced into a rock backing that continues to influence every musician who hears it. –WR

★ **Greatest Hits / CBS**   1967
A 10-song retrospective of the work of the most impressive — and most protean — singer/songwriter of the period 1963 to 1966. Please note that, while this album is listed as the "pick" of this period of Dylan's career due to its general accessibility, a full understanding of the popular music of the 60s is impossible unless the listener is familiar with its three predecessors. *Greatest Hits* combines folk-protest standards like "Blowin' in the Wind" and "The Times They Are A-Changin'" with his folk/rock hits "Like a Rolling Stone" and "Rainy Day Women #12 & 35." –WR

☆ **John Wesley Harding / CBS**   1968
A quieter, simpler album than those Dylan had made in the mid 60s, this "comeback" record nevertheless contained open-ended, parable-like songs, the most memorable of which has turned out to be "All Along the Watchtower." –WR

Nashville Skyline / CBS   1969
Dylan reached a sales peak with this album of simple, country-inflected songs (including "Lay Lady Lay"). –WR

○ **New Morning / CBS**   1970
While retaining some of the bucolic, sunny outlook of his recent work, Dylan partially turned back to a grittier rock sound (Al Kooper again in the mix) and to the more ironic, poetic lyrics of his mid-60s songs. –WR

☆ **Bob Dylan's Greatest Hits - Vol. 2 / CBS**   1971
A grab-bag of material dating back to 1963, this sprawling two-disc set is notable for its rarities, especially the 1971 single "Watching the River Flow" and the 1963 live performance of "Tomorrow Is a Long Time." –WR

Planet Waves / CBS   1974
A companion work to its predecessor, *New Morning*, this first album to be recorded with Dylan's backup group, the Band, mixes pronouncements of marital and familial contentment with severe criticisms of the singer himself and others. Contains "Forever Young." –WR

★ **Blood on the Tracks / CBS**   1975
A stunning, mature statement, in which the songwriter faced the conflicting elements of his life, the uncertainties of life in general, and the virtues of kindness and generosity. Incidentally, he also invented new songwriting structures and composed some of the most appealing music of his career. Still perhaps Dylan's most listenable and compelling album, this best represents his post-60s work. –WR

☆ **Basement Tapes / CBS**   1975
A two-disc set of ad hoc performances from 1967, albeit refurbished slightly for this release, *The Basement Tapes* provides the missing link between Dylan's long, poetic songs of the mid 60s and the shorter, more direct songs of the late 60s. Some of the songs had already become well known: "Too Much of Nothing," "Tears of Rage," "This Wheel's on Fire," and "You Ain't Goin' Nowhere." –WR

☆ **Desire / CBS**   1976
A rough-and-tumble collection cut with a band Dylan was assembling for the Rolling Thunder tour. "Hurricane" recounts the tale of an unjustly imprisoned boxer, "Romance in Durango" and "Black Diamond Bay" are short stories in

song, and "Sara" is a last plaintive plea from the singer to his wife. –WR

Street Legal / CBS   1978

Using a big band assembled for a world tour, Dylan presents a group of songs, some of which are as imagistic — and as bitter — as his mid-60s material. Particularly notable are the tone poem "Changing of the Guards" and the desperate but moving "Senior." –WR

☆ **Masterpieces / CBS (JAPAN)**   1978

The best-organized Dylan retrospective ever done up to this time, *Masterpieces* spends three LPs (now two CDs) thoroughly presenting Dylan's best work from 1962 to 1976, including several rare singles never before released on an album. (Import) –WR

Slow Train Coming / CBS   1979

Among Dylan's best-played (members of Dire Straits participate) and best-produced recordings, this album reflects Dylan's religious conversion. At its best, on "Gotta Serve Somebody" and "When You Gonna Wake Up," the album presents cautionary messages similar to those Dylan had served up throughout his career. –WR

Infidels / CBS   1983

Dylan emerged from his overt references to Christianity with his sense of moral outrage reawakened. He expressed it in songs defending Israel and unions on this impassioned collection, which also includes "Jokerman," as impressive a piece of socially conscious poetry as he'd ever produced, and the love songs "Sweetheart Like You" and "Don't Fall Apart on Me Tonight." –WR

○ **Biograph / CBS**   1985

A five-LP, three-CD retrospective of Dylan's first 20 years of recording, with an emphasis on presenting some of the mountain of unreleased songs that began leaking out unofficially in the late 60s. The only reason this massive, brilliantly executed album is not listed as an essential pick is its expense — in fact, it's not a bad place to start in trying to appreciate the whole of Dylan's achievement. –WR

Empire Burlesque / CBS   1985

Dylan's strongest song collection since *Blood on the Tracks*, this album also benefits from excellent backup work by members of Tom Petty's Heartbreakers, among others, and a remix by dance expert Arthur Baker. Dylan himself sounds unusually engaged as well, especially on such songs as "Emotionally Yours" (later an R&B hit for the O'Jays) and the moving autobiographical folk ballad "Dark Eyes." –WR

☆ **Oh Mercy / CBS**   1989

This stunning album demonstrated that, after more than 25 years, Dylan was perfectly capable of writing songs of topical concern, high poetry, and unflinching self-examination to match any of his best work of the 60s and 70s. –WR

☆ **Bootleg Series - Vols. 1-3 / CBS**   1991

The floodgates opened with the release of this 58-song collection of outtakes and unreleased songs from throughout Dylan's career, an outpouring that demonstrated what all the bootleggers and their customers had known all along: that Dylan's throwaways were better than everyone else's keepers. It's amazing to think that, while turning out some of the most impressive albums of his time, Dylan was holding back material often equally good. –WR

(E)

Singer/songwriter, pop. Virginia singer/songwriter and multi-instrumentalist, (E) projects a humorously idiosyncratic loser (Woody Allen-meets-Brian Wilson in the sandbox) mentality. In fact, (E)'s wistful melancholy and tainted hopefulness, as well as his delicately quirky melodicism and dense production smarts, recall the reclusive Beach Boy's better moments. –RC

○ **A Man Called (E) / POLYGRAM**   1992

A Man Called (E) is a wonderful collection of pop gems, tapped from the soul of Beach Boys' *Pet Sounds*, *Tumbleweed*

Connection-era Elton John, *White Album* Beatles, and early Todd Rundgren. (E) performed practically every instrument in this keyboard-rich production. Highlights from this impressive debut are "Hello Cruel World," "Fitting in with the Misfits," and "Are You and Me Gonna Happen." –RC

THE EAGLES

Rock/pop, country rock. The Eagles were among the most successful rock groups of the 70s, and their blend of country, folk, and rock continues to sell well in catalog. The group's four original members were Los Angeles session and group veterans assembled by producer John Boylan in 1970 as backup musicians for Linda Ronstadt on her *Silk Purse* album. They then served as her backup band for two years. The four were Glenn Frey (b Nov 6, 1948), guitarist; Bernie Leadon (b Jul 19, 1947), who played banjo and mandolin; Randy Meisner (b Mar 8, 1948) on bass; and Don Henley (b Jul 22, 1947) on drums. All four sang, though Henley and Frey took most leads. Signed to Ronstadt's label, Asylum, they issued their first album, *Eagles*, in June 1972. It was a moderate hit (going gold a year and a half later) and produced the Top 40 hits "Take It Easy" (written by Frey and Jackson Browne), "Witchy Woman" (#9), and "Peaceful Easy Feeling."

The second Eagles album, a semi-concept album called *Desperado* (1973) that emphasized an "outlaw" image, was somewhat less successful. For their third album, *On the Border* (1974), the group added guitarist Don Felder. This was a breakthrough record, going gold in three months and producing the #1 hit "Best of My Love," which didn't top the charts until almost a year after the album's release, just in time to set up their fourth album. *One of These Nights* (1975), the first of four straight albums to top the charts, featured the title track, "Lyin' Eyes" and "Take It to the Limit," all Top Ten hits.

The Eagles released a greatest-hits album in 1976 (it now stands at 12 million sales, the best-selling hits record of all time) and suffered the loss of Leadon, who was replaced by former James Gang leader Joe Walsh (b Nov 20, 1947). At the end of the year, they released *Hotel California*, which has now sold nine million copies. Its hits included the ominous title track, "New Kid in Town," and "Life in the Fast Lane."

In 1977 Meisner left the band and was replaced by former Poco member Timothy B. Schmit (b Oct 30, 1947). It took the Eagles until the fall of 1979 to complete *The Long Run*, another million-seller, featuring the chart-topper "Heartache Tonight" and Top Ten successes in the title track and "I Can't Tell You Why." The next year saw the release of a live album, but by 1981 the Eagles had split up. All five members have since released solo albums, the most successful of which have been by Henley and Frey. –WR

On the Border / ELEKTRA   1974

A transitional Eagles album (and their commercial breakthrough), this contained songs like "Already Gone" and "James Dean" (cowritten by Jackson Browne) that hark back to their earlier uptempo rock style, but also "Best of My Love" and Tom Waits's "Ol' 55," ballads that showed off their harmonies and won them a whole new audience. –WR

★ **Their Greatest Hits 1971 - 1975 / ELEKTRA**   1976

The reason this is such a great greatest-hits album is that it includes almost all the best tracks from the Eagles' first four albums, eight Top 40 hits including the #1s "Best of My Love" and "One of These Nights," plus the favorites "Tequila Sunrise" and "Desperado." Only *On the Border* is such a strong album that it needs a separate listing; otherwise, this is the essential Eagles for the period. –WR

☆ **Hotel California / ELEKTRA**   1977

A concept album about the dissipated life of Southern California rock stars, from being the "New Kid in Town" to living "Life in the Fast Lane" to holing up in the "Hotel California" and fearing it's all been "Wasted Time" and turning to "The Last Resort." This album and Pink Floyd's *The*

Wall are aural versions of *A Star is Born* for the rock generation. –WR

Eagles Greatest Hits - Vol. 2 / ASYLUM   1982
This will save you from having to buy *The Long Run*, an inconsistent album best remembered for its hit songs, all of which are here, along with the ones from *Hotel California*. –WR

STEVE EARLE

Country rock, singer/songwriter. When Steve Earle released his 1986 debut *Guitar Town*, he had already developed quite a reputation as an exceptional singer/songwriter in the Nashville music community. Nevertheless, that album's tough-as-nails lyrical and musical delivery immediately made Earle an outsider for the generally polite country radio format. With each subsequent album, Earle has integrated a harder rock sound, helping him gain entrance on FM rock playlists. –RC

○ **Guitar Town / MCA**   1986
Steve Earle rode a suspiciously rocking band into Nashville and up to the top of the country charts with this album, after which it was decided he was just a little too extreme for the country market, which means this record is "on the edge" in more ways than one. –WR

Copperhead Road / UNI   1988
Earle finally got around to rerecording his early classic "The Devil's Right Hand" on an album that is a potent combination of hillbilly attitude and rude rock & roll. Irish punk-folksters the Pogues pitch in on some of the proceedings. The title track became Earle's first FM rock hit. –WR & RC

The Hard Way / MCA   1991
Some of Earle's best songwriting is on this album. The anthemic "The Other Kind" is a classic. On "Country Girl," Earle and his band (The Dukes) do their best NRBQ grooves. "Billy Austin" is a compassionate character sketch of a Native American on death row. Former Lone Justice lead singer Maria McKee offers vocal support on this album. On the down side, the subtleties of these songs are occasionally buried under a sea of cinematic production. Earle sometimes sounds too tired to emote anything, and the heavily compressed mix doesn't help matters. Regardless, fans of rock that contains well-written lyrics might enjoy this. –RC

JACK EARLS

Rockabilly. One of the more obscure names in the annals of Sun Records, Jack Earl's lone original single, "Slow Down" (covered by rock group the Paladins), is one of the shining crude examples of rockabilly. Never comfortable as a full-time musician, Earls moved from Memphis to Detroit to work full-time at the Chrysler plant, a job he maintains to this day. Occasionally playing and recording for small collector-oriented labels, Earls has a cracked mountain tenor that is still intact and capable of scraping the paint off walls any time he feels like it. –CK

○ **Let's Bop / BEAR FAMILY**   1990
Complete collection of Earl's Sun recordings, raw rockabilly at its finest. –CK

EARTH, WIND & FIRE

Funk, urban R&B, dance-pop. Earth, Wind & Fire was the most successful R&B group of the 70s. EW&F was founded by Maurice White (b Dec 19, 1942) and his brother Verdine (b Jul 25, 1951) in Chicago in 1969, and they released their self-titled debut album on Warner Brothers in 1970. After the 1972 release of the second album, *The Need of Love*, White reorganized the group, bringing in Philip Bailey (b May 8, 1951) as co-lead singer for the recording of the third album, *Last Days and Time* on Columbia. EW&F encapsulated many strains of Black pop from before their time. Their high-pitched harmony vocals called to mind groups such as the Temptations, while their funkiness was reminiscent of Sly and the Family Stone, and their horn section sometimes evoked the work of James Brown and others. Over this, Maurice White laid his own brand of African-inspired kalimba music for a thorough synthesis that nonetheless bore a particular musical stamp unique to Earth, Wind & Fire.

The band began to break through with its fourth album, *Head to the Sky*, in 1973. This album contained EW&F's first R&B Top Ten hit, "Mighty Mighty," and became their first gold album. It was followed by *Open Our Eyes*, which went to #15 in the pop charts and contained the R&B hit "Kalimba Story." EW&F's breakthrough to a mass audience, however, came in 1975 with the release of *That's the Way of the World*, the soundtrack to a film in which the group appeared. Led by its gold-selling #1 single, "Shining Star," the album topped the pop charts.

Equally successful were the partially live *Gratitude* (1975), *Spirit* (1976), *All 'n All* (1977), *The Best of Earth, Wind & Fire - Vol. 1* (1978), and *I Am* (1979). Several albums in the early 80s did almost as well, but after the relative failure of *Electric Universe* in 1983, EW&F disbanded. It re-formed for the 1987 release *Touch the World*. –WR

○ **That's the Way of the World / CBS**   1975
Sleekly produced 70s pop/R&B, highlighted by the stirring "Shining Star" and the atmospheric title track. –WR

★ **Best of Earth, Wind & Fire - Vol. 1 / CBS**   1978
Hits compilation covering 1973-1978. –WR

I Am / CBS   1979
The gorgeous ballad "After the Love Has Gone" and the bouncy "Boogie Wonderland" (featuring the Emotions) lead this consistent collection. –WR

SHEENA EASTON   b 1959

Pop, dance-pop. Easton came onto the pop scene in 1980 as an overnight sensation from England, due to her #8 UK hit "Modern Girl" (it later reached #18 stateside). Her first American hit, "Morning Train (Nine to Five)," went to #1 for two weeks. During the early 80s, Easton released a series of light dance-pop hits, but in 1984 she began to pursue hit material with more erotic implications, as in "Strut" (#7) and the Prince-penned "Sugar Walls" (#9). She dueted with Prince on "U Got the Look" (#2), off of his *Sign o' the Times* album in 1987. Easton has released several more singles and, in 1991, pursued an acting stint on Broadway with *Les Miserables*. –RC

○ **Greatest Hits / CAPITOL**   1989
Easton's biggest and best tracks, including "Morning Train (Nine to Five)," "For Your Eyes Only," "Telefone (Long Distance Love Affair)," "Strut," and "Sugar Walls." –STE

EASYBEATS

Anglo-pop, British Invasion. Although thought of as Australia's answer to the Beatles, this mid-60s band also owed a little bit to the Kinks — and their sound anticipated the Pretenders. A tight guitar-driven brand of R&B based rock was their forte, and few groups anywhere played or wrote it ("Friday on My Mind") better. –BE

○ **Absolute Anthology / EMI**
A 2-CD package from Australia, with ear-stunning sound and two hours of golden classics. The collection of choice. –BE

Best of the Easybeats / RHINO   1985
A well-devised collection that pales in sound and content next to its Australian competitor. –BE

ECHO & THE BUNNYMEN

Alternative rock, techno-pop. Formed in 1978, Echo & the Bunnymen integrated the drama of the Doors and some psychedelia with the syntho-pop feel favored in the early 80s. Lead singer Ian McCulloch's (b May 5, 1959) self-absorbed agitation and the band's forceful delivery earned them a substantial devoted alternative-music following in the UK and Stateside. –RC

○ **Crocodiles / WARNER**   1980
Arguments rage about these guys, but I prefer this — their

debut — when their pop was spacier, moodier, and less coherent; in other words, before they started reading their press clippings. —JD

DUANE EDDY   b 1938

Rock & roll. One of the 50s most influential guitarists, and one of the more distinct: unlike other guitarslingers of the era, Eddy forged a sound based on minimalism (and lots of twangy reverb). His best hits ("Rebel Rouser," "Movin' and Groovin'," "Peter Gunn") feature simple reverb-drenched guitar riffs that usually provide a backdrop for a wailing sax. Eddy's chart run was brief (from 1958 to 1960), but his style is embedded in rock's fiber and continues to shape many young players. —JF

○ **Have Twangy Guitar, Will Travel / MOTOWN**   1959
Debut album, featuring "Rebel Rouser," "Ramrod," "Detour," "Three Thirty Blues," and "The Stalker." The album that inspired thousands of guitarists worldwide. —CK

☆ **$1,000,000 Worth of Twang / MOTOWN**   1960
Solid best-of collection of Duane's earliest hits, including "Rebel Rouser," "Movin' & Groovin'," "Ramrod," and "Forty Miles of Bad Road." —CK

Compact Command Performances / MOTOWN   1988
Respectable overview of Eddy's output. —ED

DAVE EDMUNDS   b 1944

Roots-rock. This Welsh roots-rocker has maintained an infatuation with 50s rock for nearly thirty years, from his 60s days with Love Sculpture up to his 70s-80s work with Nick Lowe and Rockpile. He's never cared much about innovation or creativity, but his best albums stand heads above your garden-variety roots-rehashes. —JF

Tracks on Wax 4 / ATLANTIC   1978
A piledriving set of new written-to-orders and covers, powered by Edmunds's dexterous vocals and the bar-band boogie of Rockpile. —JF

○ **Repeat When Necessary / ATLANTIC**   1979
His creative breakthrough mines the usual retro-terrain, only the nuevo-oldies are the best he's ever had. Both Edmunds's and Rockpile's finest moment. —JF

THE EDSELS

Doo-wop. A brief encounter with fame came for the Edsels (from the tiny mill town of Campbell, OH) when they did the doo-wop masterpiece "Rama Lama Ding Dong," its success coming only after diligent record collectors made the record a hit some three years after its release. —CK

○ **Rama Lama Ding Dong / RELIC**   1992
A complete 16-track collection of the group's best sides, including the title track, one of the great nonsense doo-wop sides of all time. —CK

DENNIS EDWARDS   b 1943

Motown, soul. A former member of the Temptations, Edwards broke from the group for a mildly successful solo career in 1983. —RAB

○ **Don't Look Any Further / MOTOWN**   1985
Excellent production by Dennis Lambert. Edwards has never sounded better, with the Top 20 "Aphrodisiac" and the smash title track. —RAB

JONATHAN EDWARDS   b 1946

Singer/songwriter. This Minnesota singer/songwriter's claim to fame was the lightly upbeat ditty "Sunshine" (#4). Even though he was unable to match the success of that song, Edwards released a string of albums to a small but devoted following. His more recent efforts reflected a return to his bluegrass roots. —RC

○ **Jonathan Edwards / ATLANTIC**   1971
His light acoustic folk-pop debut includes the hits "Sunshine" and "Everybody Knows Her." —RC

EINSTÜRZENDE NEUBAUTEN

Alternative rock. The German-based industrial group (their name means "collapsing new buildings") brought new meaning to the genre by creating a roaring wall of noise, using many "found" instruments. Their music hinges on the drama wrenched from banging sheets of metal and oil drums, among other junkyard elements, with hammers, wrenches, and other tools. Guitars squeal in white-noise abandon, and their vocals sometimes conjure your worst nightmares. —JF

○ **Strategies Against Architecture / HOMESTEAD**   1974
Radical noisy primitivism. Occasionally stunning. —JD

2 X 4 / ROIR   1984
Live noise with power tools. Fun! —JD

Vol. 2 - Strategies Against Arch / ELEKTRA   1984
Radical, noisy primitivism, part two. —JD

ELECTRIC FLAG

Blues/rock. A horn-dominated rock band led by guitarist Michael Bloomfield (b 1944 - d 1981) and featuring drummer and vocalist Buddy Miles, bassist Harvey Brooks (born Goldstein), and vocalist Nick Gravenites. Whereas later, more successful horn-based groups like Chicago and Blood, Sweat & Tears worked from jazz and pop influences, the Electric Flag used the Stax/Volt sound, James Brown, and B. B. King's large groups as role models. Bloomfield left after their first album, with Miles taking over the leadership role for the second album. They re-formed with Bloomfield in 1974 for one quick album released to scant acclaim, but its influence as a trendsetter far exceeds its record sales. —CK

○ **A Long Time Comin' / CBS**   1968
Ex-Butterfield Band guitarist/drummer Miles and others put this soul-rock band together in 1967. This debut is a testament to their ability to catch fire and keep on burnin'. —JT

ELECTRIC LIGHT ORCHESTRA

Rock/pop. Formed in 1971 from the ashes of one of Britain's greatest eccentric rock bands, the Move, the Electric Light Orchestra drew heavily from the ornately lumbering "I Am the Walrus"-period Beatles. This is shown to extreme effect on their oddly engaging debut, *No Answer*. Of particular note is the track "10538 Overture." Move expatriates Roy Wood, Jeff Lynne, and Bev Bevan formed the initial nucleus of ELO, but multi-instrumentalist Wood split after *No Answer* to form the bizarrely 50s-influenced Wizzard. Their sophomore release, *ELO II*, retained some of the off-key crunch of the debut, but it is clearly a transition to what became a very slick, highly orchestrated pop-hit factory. Between 1975 and 1981, ELO managed 17 Top 40 hits, among which were "Evil Woman" (#10), "Telephone Line" (#7), "Don't Bring Me Down" (#4), "Hold on Tight" (#10), "Shine a Little Love" (#8) and the wonderful "Can't Get It Out of My Head" (#9). ELO also scored a #24 hit with "Do Ya," which was the Move's only Stateside chart hit. ELO increasingly became a side project to leader Jeff Lynne's successful outside artist productions, which included Brian Wilson, Dave Edmunds, Tom Petty, the Traveling Wilburys, Randy Newman, and George Harrison. —RC

○ **No Answer / EPIC**   1972
Their most lively album, this debut is driven by Roy Wood's manic musical sensibilities. An energetic offshoot of the Move's final album. —BE

○ **On the Third Day / EPIC**   1973
ELO's sound came togther here, hooked around rocked-up classics and Jeff Lynne's guitar. —BE

Face the Music / EPIC   1975
Superb production and a good song lineup featuring "Evil Woman" and "Strange Magic." —BE

A New World Record / EPIC   1976
A superbly crafted and dark-hued body of songs, all melodic and delectable. —BE

○ **Olé ELO / EPIC** 1978
The early hits, marred only by the unnecessary cutting of "Roll Over Beethoven." –BE

● **Afterglow / EPIC** 1990
For sound and content, the best collection ever likely to be done. –BE

ELEVENTH DREAM DAY

Alternative pop. A stunning guitar band that grafts relationship angst onto a swirling intoxicating cushion of electric string damage. Easily one of the (if not *the*) most underrated bands currently in the alternative/independent-label scene. With the strength and sass derived from the formidable pair of Rick Rizzo and Janet Beveridge Bean, who make this country-flavored punk amalgam work hard. –JD

○ **Lived to Tell / ATLANTIC** 1991
The overlooked album of 1991, *Lived to Tell* exhibits all of Eleventh Dream Day's strengths without ever sounding forced or generic. Sad, combative, and rageful, this is a triumphant spiritual record that reveals more on repeated plays. –JD

LORRAINE ELLISON

Soul. A Philadelphia-born gospel singer (with the Ellison Sisters) turned soul diva, Ellison is best known for the poignant, apocalyptical "Stay with Me" (1966), a virtuoso display of vocal pyrotechnics written and produced by Jerry Ragovoy, which instantly garnered Ellison a cult following among her peers in the business.
Ellison's stunning soprano, her phrasing by turns ethereal and triumphant, soars above Ragovoy's equally intense arrangements. Her technical perfection in the higher registers infuses each syllable with a purity that has rarely been equaled in the genre. –CO

Lorraine Ellison / WARNER 1974
Gospel-tinged effort includes a fine cover of Jimmy Cliff's "Many Rivers to Cross." Out of print. –CO

○ **Stay with Me / LINE** 1985
Produced by Jerry Ragovoy. Includes title track, covered by Terry Reid; "Try (Just a Little Bit Harder)," covered by Janis Joplin; "You Don't Know Nothing About Love," covered by Irma Thomas. Few soul albums have ever matched the intensity of this! –CO

JOE ELY   b 1947

Country rock. In the 70s, C&W was full of artists referred to as "outlaws," mavericks who bucked the stodgy Nashville music establishment by writing their own songs, recording with their road bands, and producing their own records. The genre produced a slew of acts, but it was Lubbock, TX, native Joe Ely who best epitomized the form. And unlike most of that era's big names, Ely remains a viable artist.
He got his start back in the early 70s, working with Butch Hancock and Jimmie Dale Gilmore in a group called the Flatlanders. Their only album didn't go far, and the group broke up. (The album was reissued in 1990 on Rounder.) Around the mid 70s, Ely formed an eclectic group that was able to swing from Cajun and western to honky-tonk stomps and rockabilly; they were signed to MCA in 1977. Ely released an eponymous debut that year, using songs written by ex-Flatlanders Butch Hancock and Jimmie Dale Gilmore and throwing in some of his own road-worn, oddly poetic originals. The next year brought *Honky Tonk Masquerade*, the cornerstone of Ely's legacy and one of modern country's most ambitious albums. Further albums (especially *Live Shots*, recorded during his European tour with the Clash) brought Ely to the attention of rock fans and netted ecstatic reviews in country and pop magazines (but, mysteriously, no hits were produced).
Ely was dropped by MCA in 1983 and woodshedded until 1987, when the independent Hightone label signed him and released *Lord of the Highway*. Another Hightone album followed, before Ely (whose influence was being felt in the new

breed of country neo-traditionalists) re-signed with MCA and released another live set. He's yet to top his late-70s achievements, but Ely remains an energetic and passionate live performer and an occasionally inspired songwriter. Writing him off could be perilous. –JF

○ **Live Shots / SOUTH COAST / BB 159** 1980
Ely partakes of the musical diversity of his hometown, Lubbock, TX, freely mixing country, rock, Tex-Mex, and hard honky-tonk music in excellent songs he writes himself or borrows from his friend Butch Hancock. This is a live best-of covering his first three albums, recorded on tour in England. –WR

Lord of the Highway / HIGHTONE 1987
After a long recording layoff, Ely picked up where he'd left off in 1984 with this typical collection, whose best songs — "Me and Billy the Kid" and "Are You Listenin' Lucky?" — were Ely originals. –WR

THE EMBARRASSMENT

Alternative rock. The Embarrassment grasped the sharp, witty possibilities of post-punk and had the ability to play with force. Many New York bands in the early 80s wished they were this Wichita group. –BE

○ **God Help Us / RES** 1990
Solid alternative rock. Cult status. –RG

EMERSON, LAKE & PALMER

Art-rock. By the end of the 60s, many artists became swept up in the wake of the Beatles and their aggressive exploration of the possibilities of pop and rock. In the minds of many young, schooled musicians who found release in rock's energy, expanding the form by incorporating motifs and highly arranged extended compositions seemed an appealing notion. The results of this concept became known as art-rock. Depending on your point of view, Emerson, Lake & Palmer was guilty of encouraging solo indulgence, or they delivered some of the genre's better moments. Pianist Keith Emerson had already met much success in Britain with his theatrical pyrotechnics in the Nice. Greg Lake was the vocalist/bassist for the explosively dark King Crimson, and percussionist Carl Palmer backed up the heavy blues-based Atomic Rooster, a band that also contained eventual Fleetwood Mac member Christine McVie.
Months before the arrival of Emerson, Lake & Palmer's self-titled debut, expectations began running high about what the band would contribute to the expansion of rock. The debut was impressive, ranging from delicate acoustic piano and guitar interplay to explosive free-for-alls, but with the second album (*Tarkus*) it became obvious that the band often placed an enormous amount of finesse on playing to the back of the bleachers, rather than focusing that energy into a consistently satisfying musicality.
Nevertheless, Emerson, Lake & Palmer became a staple of FM rock radio during the 70s, even scoring a couple of hits with "Lucky Man" (#48) and "In the Beginning" (#39). –RC

○ **Emerson Lake & Palmer / ATLANTIC** 1970
Lively, ambitious, largely successful debut album, made up of daring instrumentals ("Three Fates" and "The Barbarian") and romantic ballads ("Lucky Man"), showcasing three very daunting talents. "Take a Pebble" is rewarding and pretentious enough to have been a Moody Blues track, except that the Moodies could never solo like Keith Emerson. The trio would never be as concise or precise in their work again. –BE

Trilogy / ATLANTIC 1972
A major improvement over their second album (the convoluted concept effort *Tarkus*) and the group's first success with adapting the music of Aaron Copland ("Hoedown"), which became something of a signature of theirs. The title track is a romantic, almost torch-song number, while "The Endless Enigma" is a curious mixture of pomp and mysticism. –BE

○ **Brain Salad Surgery / ATLANTIC**   1973
Science-fiction rock, virtually a soundtrack to a non existent film. Well produced and overpowering, but fully rewarding only on the tracks that fall outside the concept. –BE

● **The Atlantic Years / ATLANTIC**   1992
This double-disc set is a solid two-and-a-half hours' overview of ELP's career highlights, including "The Endless Enigma (Parts 1 & 2)," "Fugue," "Knife-Edge," "Take a Pebble," "Lucky Man," "From the Beginning," "Fanfare for the Common Man," "Still ... You Turn Me On," Greg Lake's "Father Christmas," and excerpts from *Pictures at an Exhibition*. –ED

EMF

Techno-pop. A British quintet that combines funky dance rhythms with a guitar sound, releasing its first album in 1991. The band includes guitarist/songwriter Ian Dench, singer James Atkin, drummer Mark Decloedt, Zac Foley, and sampler Derry Brownson. The group attributes its sound to such influences as the Smiths, the Cure, and Echo & the Bunneymen. –DS

○ **Schubert Dip / CAPITOL**   1991
Their debut album fuses dance music and rock. Includes the hit "Unbelievable." –DS

THE EMOTIONS

Soul, dance-pop. A trio of sisters with a strong gospel base, the Emotions (based in Chicago) were one of the leading female R&B acts of the 70s. Lead singer Sheila Hutchinson and her sisters Wanda and Jeanette were only teenagers when they crashed the soul charts in 1969 with the engaging "So I Can Love You," but they sang gospel as children and enjoyed secular fame locally before signing with Memphis-based Volt and working with producers Isaac Hayes and David Porter. When Stax folded in 1975, the group hooked up with Maurice White of Earth, Wind & Fire, an association that led to the #1 pop/R&B hit "Best of My Love" in 1977. –BD

Flowers / CBS   1976
Earth, Wind & Fire's Maurice White produced the excellent choral effect of this group. –RAB

○ **Rejoice / CBS**   1977
The finest late-70s soul collection available. –RAB

EN VOGUE

Urban R&B. This California female quartet became an unexpected crossover smash when their *Born to Sing* debut produced four 1991 #1 singles. The 1992 followup, *Funky Divas*, expanded their audience and led some critics to call the dance-floor divas the "new Supremes." –JF

○ **Born to Sing / ATLANTIC**   1990
A youthful unit with classic girl-group chops. –RW

ENCHANTMENT

Soul. This Detroit group, formed in 1966, only hit it big in 1977 with the glorious ballad, "Gloria." –BC

○ **Golden Classics / COLLECTABLES**
A good collection of soul hits. –RW

ENGLAND DAN & JOHN FORD COLEY

Pop. Successful mid- to late-70s soft-pop duo. England Dan is Dan Seals, brother of Seals & Croft's Jim Seals. –RC

○ **Best of / ATLANTIC**   1979
Contains "I'd Really Like to See You Tonight" (#2), "Nights Are Forever without You" (#10), "We'll Never Have to Say Goodbye Again" (#9), and "Love Is the Answer" (#10). –DH

THE ENGLISH BEAT

Ska-revival. Next to the Specials, the racially mixed English Beat were the best of the "2-Tone" ska-revival bands that flourished in late-70s England, mixing bluebeat shimmy with punk sensibilities. –JF

☆ **I Just Can't Stop It / I.R.S.**   1980
A diverse, energetic, and incessantly danceable debut, marked by percolating rhythms and an admirable loathing of England's right-wing government. –JF

Wha'ppen? / A&M   1981
The rhythms, although less vigorous, incorporate other aspects of Third-World boogie and tackle more global social concerns. –JF

Special Beat Service / A&M   1982
More jangly pop here, epitomized by the stunning "Save It for Later" and the slinky "I Confess." –JF

What Is Beat? / A&M   1983
This compilation entices the owners of the albums with some previously unreleased live tracks and a couple of great remixes, but it's not definitive. –JF

BRIAN ENO   *b*1948

Art-rock. See the Contemporary Instrumental section for Brian Eno's biography. –ED

Here Come the Warm Jets / EDITIONS EG   1973
Eno's solo debut features complex but tight pop songs with bizarre and often hilarious lyrics, which puncture the treated guitar and keyboard textures. –JF

Taking Tiger Mountain (By Strategy) / CAROLINE   1974
They lack the vibrant and energetic rock-laced enthusiasm of *Here Come the Warm Jets*, but these experimentations within the pop format give art-rock a good name. –JF

★ **Another Green World / EDITIONS EG**   1975
Eno's masterpiece. Containing a sumptuous aural mélange of dense ambient instrumental snippets and rich, often beautiful pop melodies, this is one of those albums that should be enjoyed in one concentrated sitting. –JF

Before and After Science / EDITIONS EG / BB 171   1977
A thrashing partial return to more basic song structures, punctuated by the exhilarating "King's Lead Hat." –JF

○ **Desert Island Selection / EDITIONS EG**   1989
A CD-only survey of Eno's first four albums, with songs hand-picked and annotations written by Eno himself. –JF

Wrong Way Up / WARNER   1990
After nearly floating away on an ambient sea, Eno returned with this mildly engaging set of relatively conventional pop songs, which was written and performed in collaboration with John Cale. –JF

ENYA

Alternative pop. Enya (Eithne Ni Bhraonain) is from Gweedore, County Donegal, Ireland, which she left in 1980 to join the Irish band Clannad, the group that already featured her older brothers and sisters. She stayed with Clannad for two years, then left, hooking up with producer Nicky Ryan and lyricist Roma Ryan, with whom she recorded film and television scores. The result was a successful album of TV music for the BBC. Enya then recorded *Watermark* (1988), which featured her distinctive, flowing music and multi-overdubbed trancelike singing; the album sold four million copies worldwide. It was followed by *Shepherd Moons* (1991), which confirmed Enya's status as a new-age superstar. –WR

○ **Watermark / GEFFEN**   1988
The US was a little slower than the rest of the world to admire Enya's blend of ethereal multi-tracked vocals and subtly flowing music than the rest of the world, but this album's single, "Orinoco Flow (Sail Away)," which topped the charts elsewhere, was a Top 25 hit, and the album went gold. –WR

Shepherd Moons / REPRISE   1991
More of Enya's textured music, and with this album, the US succumbed. As of this writing (July 1992), *Shepherd Moons* had been at #1 on *Billboard* magazine's New-Age Albums chart for 21 weeks and had sold over a million copies. –WR

ERASURE

Techno-dance. A British pop duo formed in 1985 by ex-Depeche Mode and Yaz synthesizer player/songwriter Vince Clarke and singer Andy Bell. –WR

○ **Wonderland / SIRE** 1986
No matter who the singer is, Vince Clarke's inventive synthesizer music is immediately identifiable. Here the former Depeche Mode/Yaz leader does his electronic wonders behind emotive singer Andy Bell (who bears a certain vocal resemblance to Yaz's Alison Moyet). Clarke's irresistible music is the best argument there is for synthesizers, and Bell is an appealing front man. –WR

The Innocents / WARNER 1988
Erasure emerged from the dance clubs with this gold-selling US breakthrough album, which contains the Top 15 hits "A Little Respect" and "Chains of Love." –WR

ROKY ERICKSON

Rock & roll. Aside from Syd Barrett, the Austin, TX, native Erickson is rock's most notorious looney-toon. After forming the 13th Floor Elevators, the quintessential acid-rattled 60s punk band, Erickson embarked on a solo career that has explored his emotional crumbling (due mostly to his nasty penchant for LSD). He's spent several years in institutions, and his voluminous and scattered solo catalog reflects the peculiarities of his vision. At its best, Erickson's music is truly scarifying. –JF

○ **You're Gonna Miss Me / RESTLESS**
Erickson's peculiar rock vision has been too schizophrenic to produce one essential album. *You're Gonna Miss Me - The Best of Roky Erickson* rounds up the finest cuts from Erickson's solo career, from a remake of "Bermuda" up to the slashing "Don't Slander Me" and "Don't Shake Me Lucifer." An alternately rocking and frightening compilation, with fine liner notes by John Morthland. –JF

THE ESCORTS

Soul. Many live albums have been recorded behind prison walls, but few by actual inmates. Discovered by producer George Kerr, the Escorts were incarcerated at Rahway State Prison in New Jersey when they began recording for the Alithia imprint. The seven-member group scored four R&B hits during 1973 and 1974. Lead singer Reginald Hayes later recorded as a solo artist. –BD

○ **All We Need Is Another ... / COLLECTABLES**
All We Need is Another - Golden Classics features fine uptempo soul tunes and good ballads. This is a collection of soul hits by an underrated local unit. –RW

ESQUERITA   d1986

Rock & roll. With a six-inch pompadour, brocaded shirts, rhinestone shades, and a rhythmic, belligerent style of piano playing, Esquerita was the original Little Richard, years before Mr. Penniman tutti-frutti'd his way to stardom. Working around the Dallas-New Orleans circuit in the early 50s, Esquerita's shot at the big time came when Capitol Records decided they needed their own version of Little Richard, after signing their answer to Elvis, Gene Vincent. The resulting recordings, though smartly produced, stand as some of the most untamed and unabashed sides ever issued by a major label. Long revered by rock & roll fans the world over, they make Little Richard's Specialty sides look highly disciplined by comparison. Though Esquerita continued to record in a tamer style through the 60s, his Capitol sides stand as a monument to the potential of rock & roll's lunatic power and the off-kilter genius of Esquerita. –CK

I Never Danced Nowhere! / CHARLY
These 17 tracks were cut in New Orleans in 1962. Not as essential as the Capitol material, but fun. (Import) –JT

Esquerita / CAPITOL 1984

Exact reproduction of the rare 1959 debut album — once a valued collector's item and still a gas. (Import) –JT

○ **Capitol Collectors Series / CAPITOL** 1990
One of the great lost rock & roll wildmen, Esquerita was as crazed as Little Richard (to whom he was an inspiration musically and visually). All of his key Capitol tracks can be found on this 28-song CD. –JT

GLORIA ESTEFAN/MIAMI SOUND MACHINE   b1957

Pop, dance-pop. More than any other pop group, Miami Sound Machine and lead singer Gloria Estefan (b Jan 9, 1957) have brought Latin American (particularly Cuban) music into the mainstream. They originated out of the Miami Cuban community, and many of their early recordings were sung in Spanish. Their hits have included "Conga" (#10), "Bad Boy" (#8), "Words Get in the Way" (#5), "Anything for You" (#1), "1-2-3" (#9) and "Rhythm Is Gonna Get You" (#5). –RC

○ **Let It Loose / CBS** 1987
The group was still billed as "Gloria Estefan & Miami Sound Machine" on this album, which showed the singer and her bandleader husband, Emilio, retaining the jazzy, Latino flavor of their earlier music while moving determinedly into the pop mainstream and incidentally positioning Gloria as a superstar. Such goals were reached by a record that sold two million copies, went Top Ten, and produced the hits "Rhythm Is Gonna Get You," "Betcha Say That," "Can't Stay Away from You," "Anything for You," and "1-2-3." –WR

Cuts Both Ways / EPIC 1989
Dispensing with the "Miami Sound Machine" name, Estefan continued to successfully to mix Latin-tinged dance numbers with strong ballads on this million-selling Top Ten solo album, which included "Don't Wanna Lose You," "Get On Your Feet," and "Here We Are." –WR

Into the Light / CBS 1991
With this successful album, Estefan demonstrated that she had recovered from her serious accident of 1990. The album contains the telling hit "Coming Out of the Dark" but showed her moving even farther toward the middle of the road and sacrificing her younger fans in the process — most of the singles from this album performed better on the Adult Contemporary charts than on the Hot 100. –WR

MELISSA ETHERIDGE

Singer/songwriter, roots-rock. Etheridge is a forceful singer/songwriter who has done well on rock and alternative formats (as well as with certain markets of the female community), with her blend of acoustic and electric roots folk/rock. Among her more notable cuts are "Similar Features," "Bring Me Some Water," "Brave and Crazy," "2001," and "Ain't It Crazy." –RC

○ **Melissa Etheridge / ISLAND** 1988
A powerful debut with occasionally strident performances. Includes "Bring Me Some Water," a fine acoustic rocker. "Similar Features," a scathing indictment of a former lover, is a standout. –RC

Brave & Crazy / ISLAND 1989
A little more laidback offering than her self-titled debut, including reflective numbers like "Testify" and "You Used to Love to Dance." There are a few acoustic rockers like "My Back Door," "Skin Deep," and "Let Me Go." –RC

Never Enough / ISLAND 1992
Nothing here matches the raw power of "Bring Me Some Water," but this outing blends the thoughtful virtues of *Brave & Crazy* with the more rocking elements of her debut. Etheridge also synthesizes urban-dub rhythms and rap on tracks like "2001" (a single) and "Must Be Crazy for Me." Also includes the single "Ain't It Heavy." –RC

EURYTHMICS

Rock/pop, dance-pop. Formed in December 1980 out of the ashes of the British band the Tourists, Eurythmics (comprising Dave Stewart and Annie Lennox) initially embraced the cool, clinical, synth-heavy sound of German ensembles like Kraftwerk or Can.

The musical element that immediately set Eurythmics apart from other techno artists was Lennox's powerful yet subtle voice, which could be extremely icy or soulful, depending on the requirements of the material. Stewart's production skills and multiinstrumental strengths usually provided all the right support.

Visually, Lennox toyed with androgyny as aggressively as David Bowie. As the 80s wore on, Eurythmics progressively infused soul and garage-rock into their sound, producing an impressive string of hits. "Sweet Dreams (Are Made of This)" (#1), "Here Comes the Rain Again" (#7), "Would I Lie to You?" (#5), and a duet with Aretha Franklin, "Sisters Are Doing It for Themselves" (#18), are among their hits. –RC

Sweet Dreams (Are Made of This) / RCA   1983
Their breakthrough second album. Much commotion was caused by the MTV video clip for the hit title track, which played up vocalist Annie Lennox's androgynous image. –DDC

Touch / RCA   1983
The followup to the success of *Sweet Dreams* showed a more confident Lennox and Stewart, ready to expand their stylistic range. Contains the Top 40 hits "Here Comes the Rain Again," "Who's That Girl," and "Right by Your Side." –SWB

○ **Greatest Hits / ARISTA**   1991
Whether cool and sophisticated or impassioned and soulful, this duo of singer Annie Lennox and guitarist Dave Stewart creates stylish and compelling rock. –DDC

THE EVERLY BROTHERS

Rock/pop, rock & roll. Don (b 1937) and Phil (b 1939) were sons of guitarist Ike Everly, said to be a teacher of finger-picking legend Merle Travis. As children, the brothers starred on an early radio program with their parents, going solo when their folks retired in the 50s. After recording in a country-duo style for Columbia with scant results, they switched to rock & roll on the Cadence label and had an immediate smash with "Bye Bye Love," going on to score over 25 Top 40 pop hits between 1957 and 1964. Their unerring harmonies melded well with crisp arrangements featuring top Nashville session players (among them Chet Atkins) and a bountiful supply of top-notch material, most of it coming from the prolific pens of Felice and Boudleaux Bryant. By the late 60s, the strain of touring, lack of record sales, and drug problems were all leading to their eventual and much-publicized split in 1973. Both recorded solo albums without success and reunited in 1983 to much critical acclaim, recording new material and touring with superb backup from a band led by guitarist Albert Lee. A major influence on any White rock & roll group singing two-part harmon, from the Beatles on down, they continue to impress and delight fans the world over. –CK

Songs Our Daddy Taught Us / RHINO   1958
Retro music 50s style but surprisingly hip. –BE

○ **The Everly Brothers / RHINO**   1958
The definitive album, with exquisite harmonies, a great beat, and teen-angst sentiment galore. –BE

○ **Fabulous Style of the Everly Brothers / RHINO**   1960
Their best album. One of the most listenable rock records of the 50s. –BE

The Very Best of the Everly Brothers / WARNER   1965
An odd but satisfying collection of their Warner-era hits grouped with new recordings of their Cadence hits. A fun way to spend 31 minutes. –BE

○ **Roots / WARNER**   1968
The best album of their Warner Bros. period, and the most well crafted of the numerous breakthrough country-rock albums of the late 60s. (Out of print) –BE

★ **Cadence Classics - Their 20 Greatest Hits / RHINO**   1986
Some of the best rock & roll ever recorded. Tough, melodic, innocent, and inventive. A road map for the Beatles' sound. –BE

EVERYTHING BUT THE GIRL

Pop. A British pop duo with light jazz overtones, formed by Tracey Thorn (b Sep 26, 1962) and Ben Watt (b Dec 6, 1962) in 1983. –WR

○ **Idlewild / SIRE**   1988
Thorn and Watt made a couple of albums with a cocktail-jazz backup and one with strings before trying a small unit for the intimate songs of their most accessible recording. The setting is perfect for such moving compositions as "Love Is Here Where I Live" and "Apron Strings." Start here, then go on to the rest of this remarkable group's catalog. –WR

EX

Punk. Ugly, abrasive, radical-activist punk primitives from Holland. –JD

○ **Pokkeherrie / ROCKABILLY**   1985
Primal leftist politics meet primal mega-loud guitar. Stunning. –JD

EXCITERS

R&B, doo-wop. Despite the presence of lone male Herb Rooney, the Exciters made some of the best girl-group records of the early 60s. Led by vibrant-voiced Brenda Reid, the originally all-female quartet came from Jamaica, NY, as the Masterettes. After signing on with saxist Al Sears as their manager, they switched their name to The Exciters and cut "Tell Him" in 1962 for United Artists. Produced by Jerry Leiber and Mike Stoller, the brilliant uptown soul effort proved a major smash. Reid's roaring pipes were expertly spotlighted on the followups "He's Got the Power," "Get Him," and their original reading of "Do-Wah-Diddy," immortalized later that year by Manfred Mann. The group later appeared on Roulette, Band, Shout, and RCA. Reid and Rooney were married for a time, and Reid now performs with her children backing her. –BD

○ **Tell Him / CAPITOL**   1991
Girl-group R&B with full-fledged, violin-laden productions backing Brenda Reid's soul-drenched lead vocals. –BD

EXPOSÉ

Dance-pop. This trio of female singers includes Ann Curless, Jeanette Jurado, and Gioia Bruno. It is primarily a vessel for the production skills and musical material of Miami-based produce, Lewis A. Martinee, who runs the Pantera Group there. –BC

○ **Exposure / ARISTA**   1986
Exposure (recorded at Criteria Studios) featured the #1 soft-pop hit "Seasons Change," which brought out the tender elements of their style. Also several dance cuts: "Come Go with Me" and "Point of No Return." –BC

EXTREME

Rock/pop, hard rock. This Boston band (originating in the late 80s) possesses an eclectic range of musical influences spanning from sensitive acoustic ballads to lounge jazz to mainstream rock. Nuno Bettencourt became one of the new guitar heroes of the early 90s. –JB

○ **Extreme II: Pornograffitti / A&M**   1991
MTV-ready mainstream pretty-boy hard rockers or sensitive acoustic balladeers, singing lounge-lizard schmaltz — candy mint or breath mint? Exceptional lead-guitar chops by Nuno Bettencourt, who also carries fine vocal work with lead singer Gary Cherone. Contains the hits the left-field acoustic "More Than Words," and "Hole Hearted." "Song for Love" should have been an AOR hit. –RC

THE FABULOUS THUNDERBIRDS

Blues/rock. The Fabulous Thunderbirds are one of the finest examples of Texas roadhouse R&B/electric blues. The original lineup featured the taut lead guitar work of Jimmie Vaughan

(Stevie Ray's brother). Kim Wilson, the band's frontman, is a master of rude harmonica playing. After years of fine album releases and endless gigging, this journeyman Austin band hit it big in 1986 with the #10 title cut off of the Dave Edmunds-produced *Tuff Enuff*. Since then they've continued to enjoy a string of hits, including a remake of Sam & Dave's "Wrap It Up" (#50), "Stand Back" (#76), and "Powerful Stuff" (#65), featured in the Tom Cruise film *Cocktail*. In 1990 Vaughan left the group and was replaced by Kid Bangham and Duke Robillard. −RC

○ **The Fabulous Thunderbirds / CAPITOL**   1979
Their debut album, with the original lineup of Wilson, Vaughn, Buck, and Ferguson stompin' through a roadhouse set of covers and genre-worthy originals. One of the few White blues albums that work. −CK

What's the Word / CAPITOL   1980
Second album, equally powerful. Some of their best, including the off-kilter "Los Fabulous Thunderbirds" and "Running Shoes." −CK

Tuff Enuff / CBS   1986
Their breakthrough success. The title track and soul covers pointthe band in a new, more mainstream direction. −CK

● **Essential / CAPITOL**
Nice compilation of the early Chrysalis albums on one CD. −CK

FACES

Rock & roll. After lead singer/guitarist Steve Marriott left Small Faces for Humble Pie in 1969, the remaining members shortened their name and enlisted Jeff Beck Group lead singer Rod Stewart. They disbanded in 1975. −RC

○ **A Nod Is As Good As a Wink / PIONEER**   1971
The Faces' third release with Rod Stewart became their most successful outing, thanks to the ragged-but-right raveup "Stay with Me," a #17 hit. Other highlights include a ramshackle version of "Memphis" and "Too Bad," one of this band's best rockers. (Import) −RC

Snakes & Ladders (Best of) / PIONEER   1976
The best available overview of the Faces. Includes "Pool Hall Richard," "Cindy Incidentally," and "Stay with Me." (Import) −RC

DONALD FAGEN   b 1948

Rock/pop. One of the founding members of Steely Dan, keyboardist Fagen pursued a solo career after the group disbanded. Since the 1982 release of *The Nightfly*, which scored a #26 hit with "I.G.Y. (What a Beautiful World)," Fagen has been fairly inactive, contributing music to an occasional film and writing a column for *Premiere* magazine in the mid 80s. In the early 90s Fagen toured with the New York Rock & Soul Revue and was preparing his second solo album. −STE & IME

○ **The Nightfly / WARNER**   1982
For his debut solo album after leaving Steely Dan, Fagen turned in a typically sophisticated jazz-pop collection tied to a lyrical theme concerning the late 50s and early 60s. One song takes the Kennedy administration's slogan, "The New Frontier," as a title, while another, "The Goodbye Look," is set in Cuba around the time of Castro's takeover. Steely Dan lovers will feel right at home. −WR

FAIRPORT CONVENTION   b 1966

Folk/rock. Founded in 1967, Fairport Convention was the first British ensemble to successfully meld authentic folk stylings with competent (and even virtuoso) rock playing, and their early albums with guitarist Richard Thompson and singer Sandy Denny are indispensable parts of any serious mainline rock collection. Their work since *Full House*, featuring a floating membership, is more uneven, and later records such as *Gladys' Leap* are less interesting, despite Ric Sanders's ornate electric fiddle playing. −BE

○ **Fairport Convention / COTILLION**   1968
A bracing and riveting debut that embraces folk/rock, with Richard Thompson and Ian Matthews on board. −BE & WR

What We Did on Our Holidays / CARTHAGE   1969
Their second album introduces Sandy Denny, singing "I'll Keep It with Me." Dazzling traditional folk, highlighted by "She Moved through the Fair." −WR & BE

☆ **Unhalfbricking / CARTHAGE**   1969
Richard Thompson and Sandy Denny at their Fairport peak; three Dylan tunes, including the hit "Si Tu Dois Partir," and Denny's "Who Knows Where the Time Goes." This is worth owning just for the apocalyptic "A Sailor's Life." −WR & BE

Leige and Lief / A&M   1970
This was Sandy Denny's exit album, highlighted by the scintillating "Tam Lin" and "Matty Groves." Voted the Best Folk Album of All Time by the readers of Britain's *Folk Roots* magazine. Features Thompson and Denny along with fiddler Dave Swarbick. −SW & BE & WR

Full House / CARTHAGE   1970
Richard Thompson's swan song with the band. By and large, worthwhile for fans of his guitar playing. −BE

● **Fairport Chronicles / POLYGRAM**   1976
A well-chosen early best-of collection. −WR

Tippler's Tales / BEAT GOES ON   1978
Some of their finest traditional song performances are here, from yet another lineup. Singer/guitarist Simon Nicol, the only original Fairporter left, begins to take a more active role. −SW

Heyday / CARTHAGE   1987
Songs rescued from radio broadcasts. All gems, and full of surprises. −BE

FAITH NO MORE

Alternative rock, heavy metal. Faith No More began in the early 80s in San Francisco under the name Faith No Man, which featured vocalist Courtney Love. With the rest of the band not pleased with her style, she was let go, and Chuck Mosely became the new vocalist. After the name change to Faith No More, the band was approached by Ruth Schwartz to do an album for her brand-new label, Mordam. With word of mouth, the album sold quite a few copies. Slash Records now expressed interest and signed them up.
In 1988 vocalist Mosely was causing friction within the rest of the band and was quietly let go. The hunt for a new singer was on, and they found him in Michael Patton, from another Bay Area band, Mr. Bungle. −JB

○ **The Real Thing / WARNER**   1989
An unusual combination of heavy metal, rap, and hard rock, appealing to head-bangers and popsters alike. −DDC

Angel Dust / SLASH   1992
Quite diverse and eclectic, with its range of styles going from lounge jazz to power-pop and all-out industrial grindcore. The songwriting shows a lot of talent, especially from Mike Patton, whose vocal range is used to its full potential on this album, the band's fourth. −JB

MARIANNE FAITHFULL   b 1947

Rock/pop. Faithfull gravitated into the London pop scene with model looks and a sweet singing voice. She was discovered by Rolling Stones manager Andrew "Loog" Oldham and was romantically involved for a period with Mick Jagger. Her early work was influenced by the Stones, while her later work, affected by years of pain and substance abuse, was the rock equivalent of Edith Piaf's music, sort of pop-cabaret singing with a throaty delivery. −LL

Marianne Faithfull's Greatest Hits / ABKCO   1969
Her early-60s hits. −BC

○ **Broken English / POLYGRAM**   1979
After a lengthy absence, Faithfull resurfaced on this 1979 album, which took the edgy and brittle sound of punk-rock and gave it a shot of studio-smooth dance rock. Faithful's

whiskey-worn vocals perfectly match the bitter and biting "Why'd Ya Do It" and revitalize John Lennon's "Working Class Hero." –JF

○ **Strange Weather / POLYGRAM**   1987
Faithfull's 1987 release recast her as a nicotine-stained chanteuse, approaching such standards as "Boulevard of Broken Dreams" and "Penthouse Serenade" with a ravaged, world-weary demeanor that recalls the latter-day recordings of Billie Holiday. She also tackles some blues and jazz material and turns "As Tears Go By" into the gut-wrenching torch ballad neither the Stones nor Faithfull could ever have done in the 60s. A dark, challenging masterpiece. –JF

Blazing Away / POLYGRAM   1990
Live disc recorded at the Brooklyn St. Anne's Cathedral. With a song list that stretches back to her 60s singles, this is something of a career overview. But the wisdom and maturity she applies to the material — both old and new — make this a document that attests to Faithfull's continued vitality and brave artistic commitment. –JF

TAV FALCO & PANTHER BURNS

Rockabilly, roots-rock, alternative rock. The Memphis-based Panther Burns are a vehicle for Falco's plundering of rock and blues history, offering twisted takes on obscure rockabilly and blues songs and suggesting what the Cramps would sound like if they were from the South. –JF

Sugar Ditch Revisited / NEW ROSE   1985
Controlled neo-rockabilly and neo-soul. Included is a great version of Mack Rice's "Money Talks." –RG

○ **Life Sentence / TRIPLE X**   1991
Tav's best in years. Rockabilly meets tango (and does not make chaos). –RG

THE FALCONS

R&B, soul. Often credited as having cut the first true soul record in 1959 with "You're So Fine," a host of 60s soul stars called themselves Falcons at one time or another, including founder Eddie Floyd, Wilson Pickett, Sir Mack Rice, and 100 Proof Aged in Soul's Joe Stubbs. Originally an integrated R&B group headed by Floyd, the Falcons debuted on Mercury in 1955. Under the production aegis of Robert West, the Falcons' sound became more gospel-based as time passed, and with Stubbs as lead, the seminal "You're So Fine" was a major hit in 1959. Pickett screamed the gospel-fired ballad "I Found a Love" to national prominence on West's LuPine label in 1962, backed by guitarist Robert Ward's Ohio Untouchables. When Pickett went solo shortly thereafter, the members went their separate ways. West recruited another group, the Fabulous Playboys, who took over the Falcons name, but with little success. –BD

○ **I Found a Love / RELIC**
A more incendiary collection, thanks to the addition of Wilson Pickett as the Falcons' front man. –BD

You're So Fine / RELIC
Prototypical early Detroit soul from this rough-edged vocal group that featured Eddie Floyd and Joe Stubbs. –BD

GEORGIE FAME

British Invasion, rock/pop. Remember his hit "Yeh Yeh"? Fame, the ex-leader of Blue Flames, sings hip blues/jazz/rock/pop. Still sounds fresh; not affected by pop trends. Neat guy. –MGN

○ **Cool Cat Blues / RHINO**   1991
Better known for rock/pop, Fame makes a decent, sometimes worthy jazz statement. –RW

CHRIS FARLOWE   b 1940

British Invasion. British R&B singer of the mid 60s discovered and heavily boosted by Mick Jagger, who produced Farlowe's best and most successful sides. Alas, he lacked the commercial look needed for success. –BE

○ **Soulful Chris Farlowe ... / CBS**   1991
Soulful Chris Farlow - The Immediate Collection is Farlowe's strongest work, featuring soulful and very powerful renditions of Mick Jagger/Keith Richards songs, spiced with other covers. –BD

FATES WARNING

Heavy metal. Fates Warning (from Connecticut) specializes in a style of mainstream power-metal with progressive, melodic grooves. –JB

○ **No Exit / CAPITOL**   1988
Progressive metal with a lot of power and harmony. Their hardest album. –JB

Parallels / WARNER   1991
Fans of Queensrÿche's *Empire* album will enjoy this melodic album, the band's most accessible work to date. Engineered with the "Q-Sound" process. –JB

FEAR

Punk. A Los Angeles-based punk-rock quartet of the early 80s led by Lee Ving, who also gained success as an actor. –WR

○ **The Record / SLASH**   1982
Fierce punk-rock, Los Angeles 80s variety, distinguished by the raw vocals of lead singer Lee Ving. –WR

CHARLIE FEATHERS   b 1932

Rockabilly. Charlie Feathers was one of the first country artists to record for Sam Phillips at the legendary Sun studios. He was there at the birth of rock & roll. Marketed during his tenure at the label strictly as a country artist, Feathers went on to record a superb collection of singles for labels like Meteor, King, Kay, and Philwood, all in a highly charged rockabilly vein. Championed by the European rockabilly collector community in the early 70s, he has continued recording for a variety of labels — not varying, only improving, his original 50s style. Charlie Feathers is a superb stylist. His voice is a consummate instrument, full of nuances uniquely his own, whether he's rocking up a storm or singing the most mournful of country ballads. Though never commercially successful, Charlie Feathers nonetheless remains a shining example of raw American music at its finest. –CK

Charlie Feathers / ELEKTRA   1977
Recent recordings with Sun alumni. –CK

Live in Memphis / BARRELHOUSE   1979
Loose early-70s recordings. Great, but unfortunately out of print. –CK

○ **Rock-A-Billy / ZUZAZZ**   1991
Superb collection of rare and unissued sides, 1954-1973, showcasing Feathers's mastery of rockabilly and country material. (Import) –CK

THE FEELIES

Alternative pop. A New Jersey band fueled by the twin guitars of Glenn Mercer and Bill Million. Since their debut in 1980, the group has produced a sound that combines elements of the Byrds and Velvet Underground under several names besides the Feelies, including the Trypes and Yung Wu. –DS

○ **Crazy Rhythms / A&M**   1980
The debut of the New Jerseyites fluctuates between folk/rock and Velvet Underground fuzz. –DS

The Good Earth / TWINTONE   1986
A folkish entry with an occasional stinging guitar by the band that re-formed as the Feelies with this album. Coproduced by Peter Buck. –DS

BRYAN FERRY   b 1945

Alternative rock. Bryan Ferry has been recording solo albums since Roxy Music's early- to mid-70s heyday, in a bizarre and confounding hodgepodge of styles. His first few solos incorporated mostly eclectic covers that wander everywhere from early rock and soul hits up to Dylan and Beatles tunes; musically, they share a lot of common ground with his full-time group. −JF

Another Time, Another Place / WARNER   1974
Same concept, different songs, as the suave Ferry recasts "Smoke Gets in Your Eyes," Sam Cooke, and several country standards. −WR

○ **These Foolish Things / WARNER**   1974
As a side project during his Roxy Music tenure, Ferry recorded this album of drastic rearrangements of a variety of standards, most of them from the 60s. The Beatles, the Rolling Stones, and especially Bob Dylan never sounded like this before. −WR

Boys and Girls / WARNER   1985
With the second (and presumably final) disbanding of Roxy Music, Ferry turned full time to his solo career, so this album is more of a followup to 1982's *Avalon*, the last Roxy album, than to 1978's *The Bride Stripped Bare*, the previous Ferry solo release. It brilliantly continues the ethereal dance-floor charm of *Avalon*. −WR

Bête Noire / WARNER   1987
Enlisting Madonna producer Patrick Leonard to assist, Ferry matches his studiedly languorous vocals to densely percussive dance tracks. −WR

5TH DIMENSION

Pop. They didn't sound anything like an R&B group, and their soaring, lighter-than-air harmonic blend frequently proved more palatable to pop audiences than to Black record buyers. But do not suggest, even for a second, that the 5th Dimension was in any way lacking in soul.
Formed as the Versatiles in 1965, the slick quintet changed its name at the request of Johnny Rivers, who had just signed them to his brand new label, Soul City. Up-and-coming songwriter Jimmy Webb supplied the group with their first pop smash "Up, Up and Away," in 1967, and the group's monumental rise mirrored the song's high-flying imagery. Another prolific composer, Laura-Nyro, handed the 5th Dimension several megahits, notably "Stoned Soul Picnic" and "Wedding Bell Blues," but their biggest seller hailed from the groundbreaking musical *Hair*. The Grammy-winning "Aquarius/Let the Sunshine In" held down the #1 slot on the pop lists for six weeks in 1969.
After several more hits, Marilyn McCoo and Billy Davis Jr, who had married while part of the group, successfully branched off as a duo, while Lamonte McLemore, Ron Townson, and Florence LaRue kept the 5th Dimension on the soul charts, losing a head-to-head battle with Diana Ross for hit status on "Love Hangover" in 1976. −BD

○ **Anthology 1967-1973 / RHINO**
Complete compilation representing the best of this California soul quintet. −RAB

FINE YOUNG CANNIBALS

Alternative pop, dance-pop. British pop-rock trio formed in the mid 80s by guitarist Andy Cox (b Jan 25, 1956) and bassist David Steele (b Sep 8, 1960), both former members of the English Beat, along with singer Roland Gift. −WR

Fine Young Cannibals / I.R.S.   1985
Roland Gift's vocals are the find here, backed by the R&B/pop music provided by Ex-Beat members Andy Cox and David Steele. −WR

○ **The Raw and the Cooked / I.R.S.**   1989
FYC rode to massive success on the tender-and-terrified singing of Roland Gift and the neo-Motown sheen of the #1 hits "She Drives Me Crazy" and "Good Thing." −WR

TIM FINN   b 1952

Alternative pop. This singer/songwriter and keyboardist was

born in Te Awamutu, New Zealand. Influenced by his Catholic upbringing and the joyous communal singalongs of the native Maori people, Finn founded the 70s art-rock band Split Enz. Leaving in 1983 for a solo career, he joined his brother Neil's band, Crowded House, for their *Woodface* album and tour. His light melodic songs and soaring vocals, while influenced by classic British pop, reflect his unique homeland at the bottom of the world. −SWB

Escapade / A&M   1983
His solo debut. Finn broke from Split Enz to exorcise these charming, light, melodic pop songs that didn't quite fit the band's style. Sweet and sappy, his soaring vocal style and introspective lyrics make this worthwhile. −SWB

Big Canoe / ATLANTIC   1988
Much production glitz here from producer Nick Launay, competing for attention with Finn's voice and songs. A very melodic and musical second solo effort; the highlights include "Don't Bury My Heart" and "Hyacinth." −SWB

○ **Tim Finn / CAPITOL**   1989
His most recent is his most sparsely produced effort. Supported by Los Angeles session musicians and producer Mitchell Froom (Crowded House), Finn is as accessible here as he's ever been. Great melodies, well-turned phrases, and seamless backing vocals from brother Neil Finn of Crowded House, make this one his best. −SWB

FIRE MERCHANTS

Fusion. Rock band formed by ex-Brand X guitarist John Goodsall and Genesis drummer Chester Thompson. −PK

○ **Fire Merchants / ENIGMA**   1989
Uptempo rock fusion. It is a well-executed album. −PK

FIREFALL

Rock/pop, country rock. When Firefall was formed in 1974, their pedigree included the Flying Burrito Brothers, the Byrds, and Spirit. Their first album (arguably their best) was a very commercial blend of tight harmonies and acoustic/electric, country-flavored pop/rock. Subsequent albums mined that approach, producing hits like "You Are the Woman" (#9), "Just Remember I Love You" (#11), and "Strange Way" (#11). −RC

Firefall / RHINO-ATLANTIC   1976
Includes hits "You Are the Woman" and "Cinderella." This debut effort was their best album. −RC

○ **Best of Firefall / ATLANTIC**   1981
A greatest-hits collection that includes almost all the essential tracks. −RC

WILD MAN FISCHER   b 1945

Alternative. A mentally disturbed street singer discovered by Frank Zappa. He recorded a double album for Zappa's Bizarre label, some of it with Zappa and the Mothers of Invention, the rest of it solo, giving full vent to nonmetrical original material. He recorded again for the Rhino label in 1977. An acquired taste to be sure, Fischer may surface again. −CK

○ **An Evening with Wild Man Fischer / BIZARRE**   1969
Fischer (aka Larry) proves to be the epitome of the bizarre. Includes the classics "Merry-Go-Round" and "The Taster." For those who lust for the unique. −DS

Nothing Scary / RHINO   1984
Fischer's most recent effort shows he hasn't changed. −DS

FISHBONE

Funk, ska-revival, hardcore, punk. Fishbone is the late-80s amphetamine equivalent to Sly & the Family Stone (with a healthy dose of eccentric Frank Zappa-style humor) and early Bus Boys. Originating in Los Angeles, Fishbone tosses ska, hard funk, and hardcore rock into a socially aware stew that, like Sly Stone, blends equal parts of optimism and despair into their intelligently streetwise delivery.

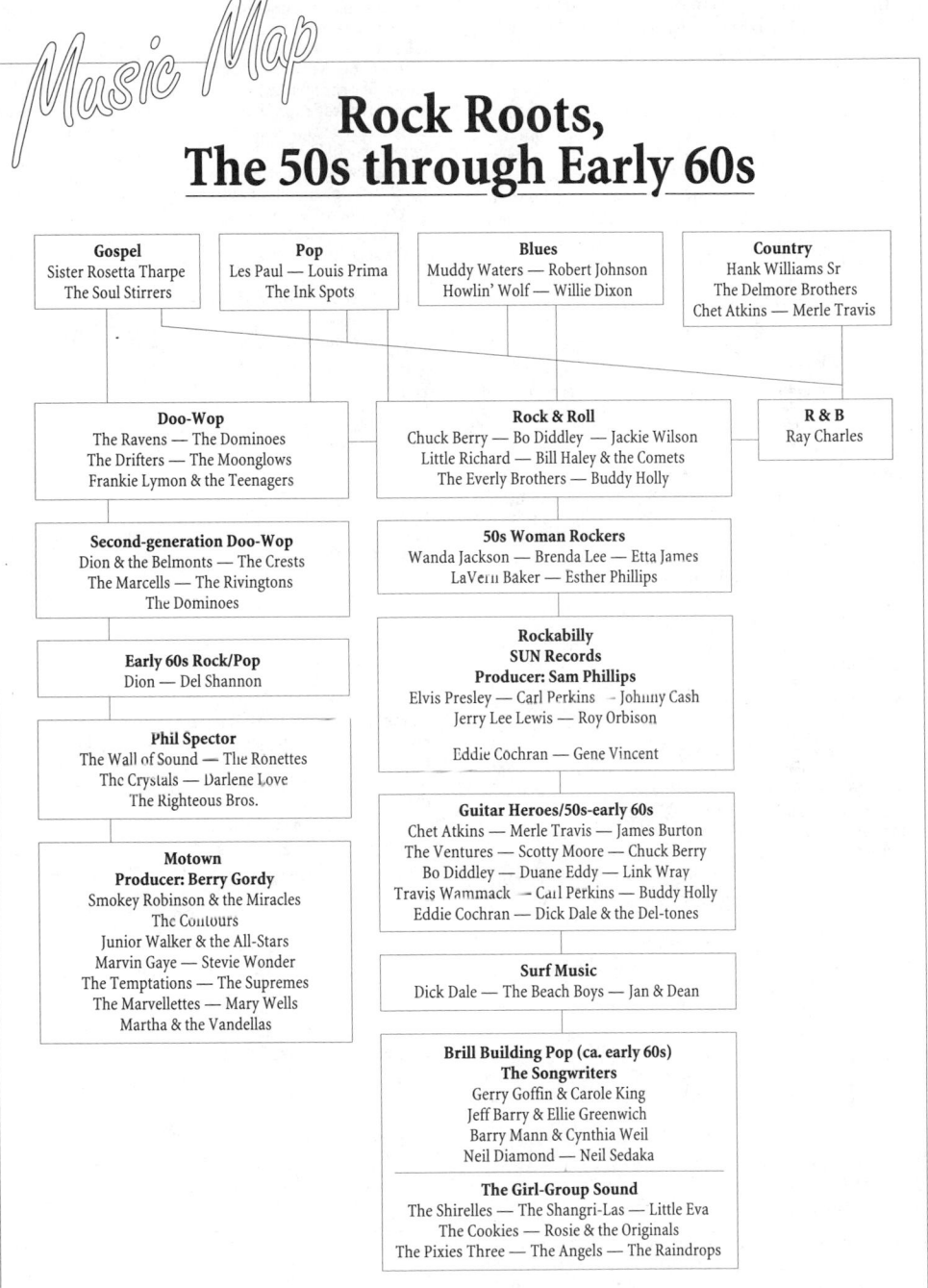

Rock Roots, The 50s through Early 60s

Gospel	Pop	Blues	Country
Sister Rosetta Tharpe The Soul Stirrers	Les Paul — Louis Prima The Ink Spots	Muddy Waters — Robert Johnson Howlin' Wolf — Willie Dixon	Hank Williams Sr The Delmore Brothers Chet Atkins — Merle Travis

Doo-Wop
The Ravens — The Dominoes
The Drifters — The Moonglows
Frankie Lymon & the Teenagers

Rock & Roll
Chuck Berry — Bo Diddley — Jackie Wilson
Little Richard — Bill Haley & the Comets
The Everly Brothers — Buddy Holly

R & B
Ray Charles

Second-generation Doo-Wop
Dion & the Belmonts — The Crests
The Marcells — The Rivingtons
The Dominoes

50s Woman Rockers
Wanda Jackson — Brenda Lee — Etta James
LaVern Baker — Esther Phillips

Early 60s Rock/Pop
Dion — Del Shannon

**Rockabilly
SUN Records
Producer: Sam Phillips**
Elvis Presley — Carl Perkins — Johnny Cash
Jerry Lee Lewis — Roy Orbison

Eddie Cochran — Gene Vincent

Phil Spector
The Wall of Sound — The Ronettes
The Crystals — Darlene Love
The Righteous Bros.

Guitar Heroes/50s-early 60s
Chet Atkins — Merle Travis — James Burton
The Ventures — Scotty Moore — Chuck Berry
Bo Diddley — Duane Eddy — Link Wray
Travis Wammack — Carl Perkins — Buddy Holly
Eddie Cochran — Dick Dale & the Del-tones

**Motown
Producer: Berry Gordy**
Smokey Robinson & the Miracles
The Contours
Junior Walker & the All-Stars
Marvin Gaye — Stevie Wonder
The Temptations — The Supremes
The Marvellettes — Mary Wells
Martha & the Vandellas

Surf Music
Dick Dale — The Beach Boys — Jan & Dean

**Brill Building Pop (ca. early 60s)
The Songwriters**
Gerry Goffin & Carole King
Jeff Barry & Ellie Greenwich
Barry Mann & Cynthia Weil
Neil Diamond — Neil Sedaka

The Girl-Group Sound
The Shirelles — The Shangri-Las — Little Eva
The Cookies — Rosie & the Originals
The Pixies Three — The Angels — The Raindrops

The band's hyperkinetic arrangements are well married to their music. All in all, Fishbone is great for those who like their music to be funky and provocative at the same time. —RC

Fishbone / CBS 1985
What a debut! Fierce, funny, and ferocious. —JD

○ **Truth and Soul / CBS** 1988
A blend of Sly Stone's *Stand* and *There's a Riot Goin' On*, equal parts optimism and despair, *Truth and Soul* is Fishbone's strongest release to date. Their hyperenergetic rhythms and arrangements might take a few listens before sinking in, but it soon becomes apparent that the message and the music are well married. Rarely does the busy instrumentation get in the way of the vocals. The intelligently streetwise lyrics possess a sense of outrage rooted in a spirituality that doesn't come off

as self-righteous. A great album for those who want their music to be funky and provocative at the same time. –RC

The Reality of My Surroundings / CBS   1991
Needs editing but contains some inspiring moments. –JD

FIVE AMERICANS

Rock/pop. With Michael Rabon as lead singer, the Dallas-based group scaled the charts in 1967 with "Western Union," a catchy rocker produced by Dale Hawkins of "Suzy-Q" fame. The Five Americans had enjoyed pop success the year before with "I See the Light," and after the success of "Western Union" on Abnak Records, they encored with "Sound of Love" and "Zip Code." –BD

○ **Western Union / SUNDAZED**   1968
A one-hit wonder (with "Western Union," 1967), the Five Americans nonetheless recorded several other lost pop gems. A full 20 of them are compiled here. –JT

THE FIVE KEYS

Doo-wop. A seminal pre-rock vocal group best remembered for the 1951 hit "The Glory of Love." Not quite as rollicking as most doo-woppers, the Keys were steeped more in the traditions of the Ink Spots. –JF

Capitol Collectors Series / CAPITOL   1989
Worthwhile companion volume to *The Aladdin Years*, containing all of their Top 100 singles — "Ling Ting Tong," "Wisdom of a Fool," "Let There Be You," and "Out of Sight, Out of Mind" — as well as lesser-known tracks like "I Wish I'd Never Learned to Read" and "My Pigeon's Gone." –STE

○ **The Aladdin Years / CAPITOL**   1991
Early 50s doo-wop with a highly polished, easy-on-the-ears sheen from the *Legends of Rock & Roll Series*. Heavy on the ballads, with a few uptempo items. –BD

THE FIVE ROYALES

Doo-wop. The North Carolina-based Five Royales practically defined Black vocal group singing in the 50s, with their early sides cut for Apollo as well as their latter-day hits on King. Johnny Tanner's vocals anticipated the sound of Southern soul singing, and Lowman Pauling's stinging guitar licks influenced everyone from Steve Cropper to Eric Clapton. –JF

The Real Thing / CHARLY
A stellar collection of the band's King recordings, including the stomping "The Slummer the Slum" and the original versions of "Think" and "Dedicated to the One I Love." –JF

The Five Royales Sing for You / KING   1959
An exact reproduction of their best original album. Not many hits, but the obscurities will keep you interested. –JF

★ **Sing "Baby Don't Do It" / RELIC**   1987
Definitive overviews of the band's early days at Apollo, slamming their gospel-trained ensemble singing into suggestive gutbucket lyrics by Lowman Pauling. Both this album and *Sing "Laundromat Blues"* contain informative liner notes. –JF

☆ **Sing "Laundromat Blues" / RELIC**   1987
With the companion album, *Sing "Baby Don't Do It,"* this is the essential collection of their work. –JF

THE FIVE SATINS

Doo-wop. Fred Haven and the Five Satins were New Haven, Connecticut's favorite doo-wop sons. Their 1956 hit "In the Still of the Night" gave rock & roll one of its first cuddle anthems and set the tone for several tasty followups. –JF

○ **In the Still of the Night / RELIC**
Everything you need from this sumptuous and smoochy late-night doo-wop quintet. The title cut is a work of art worth listening to over and over. –JF

THE FIVE STAIRSTEPS

Soul, pop. The Five Stairsteps were a Windy City family affair

initially consisting of four brothers and a sister; later on, five-year-old Cubie Burke toddled aboard, and even mom and pop got into the act. Curtis Mayfield discovered the group at a talent contest, and they debuted in 1966 on his Windy C logo with the tender "You Waited Too Long," their first hit. Lead singer Clarence Burke Jr was only 15 years old in 1966, yet his attractive leads on "World of Fantasy" and "Come Back" displayed a wealth of emotion. The group enjoyed its biggest pop hit in 1970 with the classic "O-o-h Child" for Buddah. After a few years apart, the group re-formed and notched a final hit, "From Us to You," on George Harrison's Dark Horse label in 1976. Four of the Burkes recorded as the Invisible Man's Band, scoring a sizable seller in 1980 with "All Night Thing," and bassist Keni Burke has recorded as a solo artist. –BD

○ **Greatest Hits / COLLECTABLES**
This hits package examines the pubescent Chicago soul group from their mid-60s beginning through their 1970 bubblegum soul hit "O-o-h Child." –BD

THE FIXX

Alternative pop, prog-rock. Originally formed in 1980 as the Portraits, the Fixx was one of many early-80s techno-pop groups that rode the wave of video exposure on the new MTV channel. –RC

○ **One Thing Leads to Another - Greatest Hits / MCA**   1989
All their hits, including "One Thing Leads to Another" (#4), "Are We Ourselves" (#15), "The Sign of Fire" (#32), "Secret Separation" (#19), "Stand or Fall" (#76), and "Saved by Zero" (#20). –LL

ROBERTA FLACK   b 1939

Urban R&B, soul. Flack has made a career out of giving composed readings of ultra-smooth ballads. The urbane restraint of her music has attracted plenty of light commercial jazz and romantic urban R&B. Flack's biggest include "The First Time Ever I Saw Your Face" (#1), "Killing Me Softly with His Song" (#1), "Feel like Making Love" (#1), and "Making Love" (#13), as well as duets with Donny Hathaway "Where Is the Love" (#5) and "The Closer I Get to You" (#2). –RC

○ **The Best of Roberta Flack / ATLANTIC**   1981
Showcases her biggest ballads, like "First Time Ever I Saw Your Face" (#1), "Feel Like Making Love" (#1), "Killing Me Softly with His Song" (#1), as well as her duets with Donny Hathaway including "Where Is the Love" (#5) and "The Closer I Get to You" (#2). –BC

Born to Love / CAPITOL   1983
A duet set with Peabo Bryson on which they sing mood songs like "Tonight, I Celebrate My Love" and "You're Lookin' like Love to Me." –BC

THE FLAMIN' GROOVIES

Rock & roll. The second-largest surviving original San Francisco band doesn't sound like the Dead or the Airplane. The Groovies, under original lead singer Roy Loney or lead guitarist Cyril Jordan, are a hard-rocking outfit into Little Richard, Chuck Berry, the Beatles, the Byrds and — amazingly — the Lovin' Spoonful. They've been at it 25 years and are still plugging away, and most of the music is priceless. –BE

Supersnazz / EPIC BN-26487   1969
Flawed, but a good debut album. Roots-rock played with a vengeance. –BE

Shake Some Action / SIRE   1976
This and *The Flamin' Groovies Now!* are the greatest "British Invasion" albums ever, done a decade late by a California band. Go figure. (Out of print) –BE

The Flamin' Groovies Now! / SIRE   1978
See the review of *Shake Some Action.* (Out of print) –BE

○ **Greatest Grooves / WARNER**   1989

Stylistically, a staggering assembly of covers and retro-originals. Loud and beautiful. –BE

THE FLAMINGOS

Doo-wop. One of the few doo-wop groups who made it to the 60s, this Chicago group could swing from the slow-dance groove of "I Only Have Eyes" to house-party rockers like "Jump Children." –JF

○ **Best of the Flamingos / RHINO**
A splendid collection of smooth doo-wop. Includes "I Only Have Eyes for You" and the gorgeous "The Vow." Beautiful stuff. –JF

BELA FLECK & THE FLECKTONES

Fusion. A highly original banjo stylist, Fleck has played traditional bluegrass, newgrass (with the New Grass Revival), and his own innovative material. He has been in high demand as a session player. –DV

○ **Bela Fleck & the Flecktones / WARNER**   1990
After disbanding New Grass Revival, Bela Fleck began re-creating the role of the banjo in the same way Charlie Parker redefined the role of the saxophone. But Fleck may be the least innovative member of this quartet: Howard Levy gets chromatics from his blues harp, Victor Wooten picks banjo rolls on his bass, and Roy "Future Man" Wooten plays a Frankenstein-monster drum-machine/guitar synthesizer. For all the flash, there's little pretense; the group's astonishing musicianship keeps an "aw-shucks" accessibility that lets everybody follow the melody while they marvel. –BM

Flight of the Cosmic Hippo / WARNER   1991
The Flecktones owe more to bop than to bluegrass, and here the group finally names its style "blu-bop." Which is why *Cosmic Hippo* topped the jazz, not the country, chart. The Flecktones continue to make it look easy, adding banjo power chords to "Turtle Rock" and reworking Lennon-McCartney's "Michelle." –BM

FLEETWOOD MAC

Blues/rock, rock/pop. Fleetwood Mac, formed in 1967, initially began as one of Britain's great blues-influenced rock ensembles. Over the course of many lineup changes and a relocation to Los Angeles in 1974, "Big Mac" evolved into one of the most successful pop/rock units in commercial music history.

During the early years, Fleetwood Mac endured a succession of unstable (but brilliant) lead-guitarist/singer/songwriters in Peter Green, Danny Kirwan, and Jeremy Spencer. Green and Spencer eventually jumped ship for cultish religious pursuits, and Kirwan (who ended up in a psychiatric hospital) was fired in 1972 for refusing to go on stage at a Munich gig. Green, in particular, wrote some classics in "Oh Well" (#55), "Black Magic Woman" (later a #4 hit for Santana), and "The Green Manalishi (With the Two-Pronged Crown)." Danny Kirwan contributed many of the standout tracks on albums like *Bare Trees,* including the haunting "Dust," the ethereal "Sunny Side of Heaven," and the propulsive title track.

Bob Welch, a Los Angeles resident, was brought on board in 1971. During his time with Fleetwood Mac, Welch penned some standouts as well, like "Hypnotized" and "Sentimental Lady." During all these changes, drummer Mick Fleetwood, bassist John McVie, and vocalist and keyboardist Christine McVie (also a fine songwriter) provided the glue for the proceedings.

In January of 1975 Welch left, and engineer and producer Keith Olsen turned the band on to a tape of Lindsey Buckingham and Stevie Nicks (who had previously released a much-sought-after debut on Polydor called *Buckingham Nicks*). They were hired onto Fleetwood Mac, and the rest is history.

Fleetwood Mac, the first album featuring the new lineup, became a goldmine, eventually hitting #1 in November 1976, fifteen months after its release. After much inner turmoil,

Fleetwood Mac put out *Rumours,* which topped charts around the world and became one of the biggest albums in history. Mac never duplicated the impact of *Rumours,* but subsequent albums (*Tusk, Fleetwood Mac Live, Mirage, Tango in the Night*) have been substantial successes.

Buckingham (who left in 1987) and Nicks have enjoyed solid solo careers, and Christine McVie had a #10 hit in 1984 with "Got a Hold on Me" from her self-titled solo album. "Dreams" (#1), "Don't Stop" (#3), "Sara" (#7), "You Make Loving Fun" (#9), "Hold Me" (#4), "Tusk" (#8), and "Go Your Own Way" (#10) are some of the band's many hits. –RC

○ **English Rose / EPIC**   1969
Under the direction of Peter Green, Fleetwood Mac is heard as a British blues group, though its most notable performances are on Green's original tunes "Black Magic Woman" and "Albatross," both British hits. –WR

Then Play On / WARNER   1969
More heavy blues-rock, featuring the Green hit "Oh Well." –WR

○ **Bare Trees / WARNER / BB 70**   1972
On *Bare Trees,* Fleetwood Mac married the gritty electric blues-rock of their earlier incarnations to the classic pop sensibilities that would later become fully realized in 1975's *Fleetwood Mac.* Bob Welch's "Sentimental Lady" and Christine McVie's soulful "Spare Me a Little of Your Love" are highlights. Danny Kirwin revealed an ability to compose highly melodic material that didn't constrain the band's legendary musical chemistry. –RC

Mystery to Me / WARNER   1973
At this point, Fleetwood Mac is a mainstream rock band whose songs alternate between guitarist/singer Robert Welch and keyboard player/singer Christine McVie. –WR

○ **Heroes Are Hard to Find / WARNER**   1974
Welch's peak as a songwriter (with new highs by Christine McVie) is also his swan song with the group. - WR

☆ **Fleetwood Mac / WARNER**   1975
The addition of Lindsey Buckingham and Stevie Nicks, plus the increasing quality of Christine McVie's songs, results in massive success. This #1 album, one of the finest collections of pop-rock in the decade, contains the hits "Rhiannon," "Over My Head," and "Say You Love Me." –WR

☆ **Rumours / WARNER**   1977
Among the best-selling albums of all time, this brilliant song cycle about the travails of love features "Dreams," "Don't Stop," "Go Your Own Way," and "You Make Loving Fun." –WR

○ **Tusk / WARNER**   1979
In some ways even more impressive than *Rumours,* this two-record set (fit on one CD by editing the hit "Sara,") is full of unusual arrangements and striking instrumental passages, plus a wealth of topflight songwriting. –WR

Mirage / WARNER   1982
A tuneful, tastefully produced album that makes up in songcraft ("Hold Me," "Gypsy") what it lacks in the anguished passion that was once Fleetwood Mac's stock in trade. –WR

Tango in the Night / WARNER   1987
Buckingham's final effort with the group strongly features his dramatic production techniques and striking guitar playing on his own "Big Love" and Christine McVie's terrific "Little Lies," among other tracks. –WR

● **Greatest Hits / WARNER**   1988
A well-chosen best-of. The cassette version has three more tracks than the LP. –WR

THE FLEETWOODS

Pop, doo-wop. An ultra-smooth White pop vocal trio that, in the late 50s, recorded some of the most delicate hits of the rock era. –JF

○ **Best of the Fleetwoods / RHINO**   1990
Contains "Come Softly to Me," "Mr. Blue," and other creepily pristine sides. –DH

FLESH EATERS

Alternative rock. A West Coast post-punk outfit led by pseudo-beat artist Chris D(esjardins), which included at various times many Los Angeles cult figures. At their best, they walked the line separating the Cramps and the Gun Club. –JF

○ **Greatest Hits - Destroyed by Fire / SST**   1987
Great career overview. Relentless and exciting. –JD
Prehistoric Fits - Vol. 2 / SST   1990
More greats. Tough to say no to. –JD

THE FLESHTONES

Alternative rock. Peter Zaremba'a post-punk 60s-rock revival band from Los Angeles on I.R.S. Records. –ED

○ **Living Legends Series / I.R.S.**   1989
A great overview of their I.R.S. work, including choice cuts from their second album, powerful singles, and some unreleased goodies. –JF

FLIPPER

Alternative rock. These San Francisco-based grunge boys were hardcore's most deliberately slovenly group, making feedback-drenched music that droned at a dreary pace. Their early singles ("Love Canal," "Ha Ha Ha," "Getaway") are essential West Coast punk nuggets. –JF

○ **Generic Album / SUBTERRANEAN**   1982
Slower-than-death riffing, screamed vocals, and the great "Sex Bomb." What a delight! –JD
Blowin' Chunks / ROIR   1990
A good live album. –JD

FLO & EDDIE

Rock/pop. The duo of former Turtles and Mothers of Invention lead singers and radio personalities Mark Volman (b Apr 19, 1947) and Howard Kaylan (b Jun 22, 1947). The name is an abridged version of their original monicker, "the Phlorescent Leech & Eddie," used during their Mothers days. –WR

○ **Illegal, Immoral and Fattening / CBS**   1975
Flo & Eddie are both impressive singers and very funny comedians, and both aspects of their talent are on display here, from the pop sheen of "Rebecca" to the sidesplitting return of the Sanzini Brothers. –WR
The History of Flo & Eddie & the Turtles / RHINO   1983
A three-record boxed set that traces the history of the duo back to Westchester High School through their hits with the Turtles to their present comic-musical adventures. –WR

A FLOCK OF SEAGULLS

New-wave. A Liverpool new-wave group with a name derived from the novel *Jonathan Livingston Seagull*, featuring lead singer/keyboard player Mike Score (b Nov 5, 1957), his brother Ali (drums), Paul Reynolds (guitar), and Frank Maudsley (drums). They formed in 1979, hit with "I Ran (So Far Away)" in 1982, split up in 1986, and have since re-formed. –WR

○ **A Flock of Seagulls / JIVE**   1982
A Flock of Seagulls scored one big hit, "I Ran," in the driving, quick-tempo dance style that characterized most of their work. It's here, along with several similar tracks. –WR

FLOTSAM & JETSAM

Heavy metal. Great speed-metal from Arizona, with a heavy rhythm section; still an underground favorite. Original bassist Jason Newsted is now a member of Metallica. –JB

Doomsday for the Deceiver / METAL BLADE   1987
The classic debut album from this Arizona quintet. Great songwriting and bass playing from Jason Newsted, who eventually left and joined Metallica. –JB

○ **No Place for Disgrace / ELEKTRA**   1988
A different taste of American thrash. Their major-label debut didn't hold back from anything: strong vocals, magnificent

guitars, and excellent songs. Includes a cover of Elton John's "Saturday Night's Alright (For Fighting)." –JB

EDDIE FLOYD   b 1935

Soul. Equally valuable to the Stax empire as a songwriter and a vocalist, Eddie Floyd cut an acknowledged Memphis soul treasure in 1966 with his #1 R&B smash "Knock on Wood" — and quite a few others around the same time that were just as incendiary. He was also a founding member of the Falcons, a Detroit-based vocal group that also spawned Wilson Pickett. –BD

○ **Knock on Wood / ATLANTIC**   1967
Essential 1966 collection from one of the hottest singers and writers at Stax. "Knock on Wood" is a Memphis soul classic, and Floyd's covers often outshine the originals. –BD
Soul Street / STAX   1974
A worthwhile set. Funk's Memphis soul. –BD
Chronicle - Greatest Hits / STAX   1978
A disc spanning Floyd's early output and his softer post-1968 work for Stax. Pumping Memphis grooves back Floyd's energetic vocals. –BD

THE FLYING BURRITO BROTHERS

Country rock. The Flying Burrito Brothers was formed in October of 1968 from Byrd expatriates Chris Hillman, Sneaky Pete Kleinow, Gram Parsons, and (later) Michael Clarke, all fresh from recording what was arguably the most important seminal country-rock album — the Byrds's *Sweetheart of the Rodeo*. The Burritos took that concept and focused it into a brilliantly soulful country-rock sound.
Primary lead singer/songwriter Gram Parsons was capable of displaying heartbreaking vulnerability, as evidenced in tracks like "Hot Burrito #1." Parson's influence and the band's overall concept literally laid the groundwork for many artists like the Eagles, Emmylou Harris, and much of today's cutting-edge country music. Parsons died of heart failure following a drug overdose in 1973, at the Joshua Tree Inn in Joshua Tree, CA. His solo followup, *Grievous Angel*, was posthumously released in January 1974. Burrito Brothers cofounder Chris Hillman later formed the Desert Rose Band, which has scored numerous country hits. –RC

★ **The Gilded Palace of Sin / A&M**   1969
The birth of country-rock. Gram Parsons and Chris Hillman, aided by Sneaky Pete Kleinow and Chris Ethridge, create a hybrid by combining rock attitude with country sentiments and change the course of popular music. Really. –WR
The Flying Burrito Brothers / A&M   1971
On their first post-Parsons album, the Burritos (now led by Hillman and Rick Roberts, and with future Eagle Bernie Leadon replacing Ethridge) make an honest step forward in country-rock. Includes the Roberts song "Colorado." –WR
☆ **Farther Along / A&M**   1988
Farther Along: The Best of the Flying Burrito Brothers is an excellent 21-track, 65-minute compilation of the Burritos. –WR

DAN FOGELBERG   b 1951

Singer/songwriter. When singer/songwriter and multi-instrumentalist Dan Fogelberg arrived in 1973 with his debut *Home Free*, reflective soft-folk/pop was making big inroads into a baby-boomer mass market that was coming of age.
Fogelberg had the good fortune to be previously acquainted (from his University of Illinois days in 1971) with ascending artist manager and industry power-broker Irving Azoff, who was managing R.E.O. Speedwagon at the time. Azoff took on Fogelberg and brought in Joe Walsh (another artist client of Azoff's) to produce the sophomore effort *Souvenirs*. It became Fogelberg's first chart success, generating a #31 hit with "Part of the Plan."
During the 70s and early 80s, Fogelberg became a mainstay on FM rock stations and soft adult-contemporary formats, easily managing to share air space with artists like the Eagles,

Linda Ronstadt, Jimmy Buffett, and Jackson Browne. "Longer" (#2), "Same Old Lang Syne" (#9), and "Leader of the Band" (#9) were big hits indicative of Fogelberg's thoughtful mellow sound. His attempts at rock have generally failed to score as successfully, particularly the 1988 release *Exiles*. –RC

○ **Home Free / COLUMBIA**   1973
This debut, recorded in Nashville and produced by Norbert Putnam, is a nice blend of haunting acoustic-guitar-based numbers ("Stars," "Be on Your Way"), some supported by tasteful string-section work ("To the Morning," "Wysteria," "Hickory Grove"). There are also a few country/light-rock items in "Anyway I Love You," "Long Way Home (Live in the Country)," and "More Than Ever." –RC

Souvenirs / COLUMBIA   1975
This Joe Walsh-produced effort includes Fogelberg's first hit "Part of the Plan." Overall, this isn't as strong as the debut. –RC

○ **Netherlands / COLUMBIA**   1977
Fogelberg returns to Norbert Putnam for this effort, which ranges from the heavily orchestrated, highly dramatic title cut to light CSN-style folk/rock like "Once Upon a Time." One of Fogelberg's better albums, in spite of his tendency for grandiose statement. –RC

Twin Sons of Different Mothers / COLUMBIA   1978
This album contains duets with flutist Tim Weisberg. It's a nice diversion, featuring a good remake of the Hollies hit "Tell Me to My Face." There are some pleasant instrumental numbers here. Fogelberg scored a hit with "The Power of Gold" (#24). –RC

○ **Phoenix / COLUMBIA**   1979
Fogelberg's highest-charting album (#3) features his widest stylistic stretches, between the ultra-sentimental acoustic hit "Longer," to extended rockish numbers like "Face the Fire," "Wishing on the Moon," and the title cut. –RC

○ **The Innocent Age / COLUMBIA**   1981
An ambitious song cycle, detailing the experience of coming of age. Several of Fogelberg's biggest hits ("Leader of the Band," "Same Old Lang Syne," "Hard to Say," and "Run for the Roses") are on this set. –RC

● **Greatest Hits / COLUMBIA**   1982
Even though this collection fails to address much of his best non-single material, most of his obvious hits are here (heavy on the sentimental), making this a fairly safe starting place for someone wanting to get into Fogelberg. –RC

○ **High Country Snows / COLUMBIA**   1985
A well-recorded foray into more traditional acoustic country music. –RC

JOHN FOGERTY   b1945

Rock & roll. John Cameron Fogerty achieved fame as the lead singer/songwriter and guitarist in Creedence Clearwater Revival and has since gone on to a chart-topping solo career. Born in Berkeley, CA, Fogerty and his brother Tom organized the group that would become Creedence as the Golliwogs in the late 50s. As Creedence, they released nine Top Ten singles, all written by Fogerty, between 1969 and 1971, starting with the standard "Proud Mary." They also scored eight gold albums between 1968 and 1972, all fueled by Fogerty's simple, driving rock songs and his burly baritone, intoning deceptively poetic ("Bad Moon Rising") and even political ("Fortunate Son") lyrics.
Creedence split up in 1972. Fogerty at first confused his considerable following by releasing an album of covers, on which he played all the instruments, under the name the Blue Ridge Rangers in 1973. This was followed by a formal solo album, *John Fogerty*, in 1975, and then silence for more than nine years while the artist worked out business problems with Creedence's old label. But Fogerty returned at the end of 1984 with a Top Ten single, "The Old Man down the Road," and a #1 album, *Centerfield*. *Eye of the Zombie* was a less successful followup in 1986. –WR

Blue Ridge Rangers / FANTASY   1973
Fogerty as a one-man country band paying tribute to his honky-tonk roots. –JT

○ **Centerfield / WARNER**   1985
The comeback album that proved the ex-Creedence firebrand still knew how to rock and make it count. Includes "The Old Man down the Road" (#10), "Rock and Roll Girls" (#20), and "Centerfield" (#44). –JT

FOGHAT

Rock & roll. Formed in 1971, Foghat enjoyed a string of successful albums with their brand of hard blues-based boogie rock. Biggest hits included "Slow Ride" (#20), "Third Time Lucky (First Time I Was a Fool)" (#23), "I Just Want to Make Love to You" (#33), "Driving Wheel" (#34), and "Stone Blue" (#36). –RC

○ **Best of Foghat / RHINO**   1990
Excellent blue-collar rock featuring "Slow Ride" and "Fool for the City." –DH

FOLLOW FOR NOW

Rock & roll, funk. Five Black men from Atlanta who, on their 1991 debut, suggested that Living Colour wasn't the only Black group determined to expand rock's vocabulary. –JF

○ **Follow for Now / CAPITOL**
Rock conventions in a hip-hop context, giving both a kick in the head. Highly recommended. –RG

STEVE FORBERT   b1955

Singer/songwriter. Mississippi-born Forbert was one of the better received folk-based singer/songwriters of the late 70s. In recent years, he has written hits for country artists as well as continuing to record albums himself. –WR

○ **Alive on Arrival / CBS**   1978
Forbert takes the folk/rock singer/songwriter format, already 13 years old at this point, and gives it a fresh, exuberant, almost punkish appeal. –WR

Jackrabbit Slim / NEMPEROR   1979
Forbert's more elaborately produced second album continues the songwriting quality of his first and includes his #11 hit single "Romeo's Tune." –WR

Streets of This Town / GEFFEN   1988
Coming back after a six-year layoff, Forbert displays a previously unheard edge of bitterness that only deepens his thoughtful lyrics. And he rocks harder than ever. –WR

FORCED ENTRY

Thrash. The small community of Mountlake Terrace, WA, is what the three-piece Forced Entry calls home. During their inception in the mid 80s, there was no active thrash-metal scene in the Seattle area. The band decided to change that situation with their musically diverse songs and intelligent lyrics. They are currently considered a major factor in the Seattle metal community. –JB

○ **Uncertain Future / RELATIVITY**   1989
They changed the world of thrash with their debut album in 1989. Eerie power chords, awesome vocals, a tremendous bass guitar sound — for an album recorded on a low budget, the sound is impressive. An album that has yet to be appreciated by the masses. –JB

As Above So Below / RELATIVITY   1991
More complex than *Uncertain Future* but just as good. The guitar playing of Brad Hull needs to be heard. –JB

FOREIGNER

Hard rock, rock/pop. Foreigner was formed in 1976 by Mick Jones (ex-Spooky Tooth) and Ian McDonald (ex-King Crimson). The band was an instant success with the release of their debut album in 1977, which showcased the talents of guitarist Jones and lead singer Lou Gramm. Jones and Gramm also wrote most of the band's material. The songs, mainly hard rock, boasted strong melodies and memorable guitar riffs. The band never strayed far from this formula but, to keep things fresh, added some interesting touches. For example, Junior Walker's sax on "Urgent" and the gospel vocals of Jennifer Holliday and the New Jersey Mass Choir on "I Want to Know What Love Is" helped elevate these songs above the ordinary. Gramm left the band in the late 80s for a solo career. Foreigner recruited a new lead singer but Gramm's writing and distinctive vocals are sorely missed. –KMC

Foreigner / ATLANTIC   1977
No-nonsense rock & roll catapulted the band's debut all the way to the top of the charts with the hits "Cold As Ice" and "Feels like the First Time." –DDC

Double Vision / ATLANTIC   1978
Building on the success of the first album, this followup yielded the Top 20 hits "Hot Blooded," "Double Vision," and "Blue Morning, Blue Day." –DDC

○ **4 / ATLANTIC**   1981
A #1 album on the strength of Lou Gramm's powerhouse vocals and the band's synth-pop texturing. This album produced several major hits, including "Urgent," which featured a sax solo by Junior Walker, and "Waiting for a Girl like You." –DDC

● **Records / ATLANTIC**   1982
All the band's early (including those from 4) radio-friendly hits are here in this collection of straightahead rock & rollers. Includes "Waiting for a Girl like You," "Hot Blooded," and more. –DDC

FOUR TOPS

Motown. After passing through five record labels in almost a decade, the Four Tops finally broke big-time on Motown in 1965 with "I Can't Help Myself." Like many Motown acts, they provided the soundtrack for an era — they were in that heavy rotation on the radio. Immaculately rehearsed, choreographed, and outfitted, they epitomized Motown's value system. With a lead vocal from Levi Stubbs, a Motown backing track, and a Holland-Dozier-Holland song, you had an almost guaranteed hit. Even after H-D-H quit, the hits kept coming; even after the Tops quit Motown, the hits still kept coming, but there is no doubt about where the classic recordings reside. At their best, they were about as soulful as Motown got. More surprisingly, the original group is still together. Reach out — they're still there. –CE

○ **Four Tops / MOTOWN**   1964
An excellent debut album. –RAB

○ **Four Tops Second Album / MOTOWN**   1965
Twelve masterpieces from Motown songwriters Holland-Dozier-Holland. –RAB

○ **Reach Out / MOTOWN**   1967
Pure Motown magic here, with "Reach Out, I'll Be There," "Bernadette," and "Walk Away Renee." –RAB

★ **Anthology / MOTOWN**   1974
This 1973 album is representative of their Motown work. –RAB

Best of the Four Tops (1972-1976) / MCA
This has all their Dunhill hits, like "One Chain Don't Make No Prison." –RAB

PETER FRAMPTON   ♭1950

Rock/pop. After years of toiling away as an exceptional journeyman guitarist and singer during the late 60s and early 70s, Peter Frampton struck mega-platinum with a double live album entitled *Frampton Comes Alive.* The huge success of that album, coupled with Frampton's pretty-boy looks, almost overshadowed his elegantly melodic musicianship.
The Herd was Frampton's first successful group, but he gained much visibility with the heavy English boogie band Humble Pie. Frampton left just when Humble Pie was becoming a major concert draw, and he released a great 1972 debut solo

effort titled *Wind of Change,* following with the strong *Frampton's Camel, Somethin's Happening,* and *Frampton.*
Frampton Comes Alive was a neat summation of Frampton's first four solo albums; it also became the biggest-selling live rock album in history. Frampton's next studio album, *I'm in You,* was a hit, but a series of poor career moves (such as appearing in the ill-conceived movie *Sgt. Pepper's Lonely Hearts Club Band*) and a tragic auto accident undermined his momentum. Frampton continues to release periodic albums and tours regularly. –RC

● **Frampton Comes Alive / A&M**   1976
Fueled by Frampton's voice-box guitar technique and accessible radio-friendly pop-rock songs like "Show Me the Way" and "Baby I Love Your Way," the double album *Frampton Comes Alive* became the biggest-selling live album in rock history, topping the ten million mark. It's a sensible place to start, since Frampton seems to be in his element here, and the song selection includes the cream of his first four albums. –DDC

○ **Classics - Vol. 12 / A&M**   1989
This overview of Frampton's work may not be definitive but it is a nice sampler that includes all of his hits, plus some favorite album tracks. –RC

CONNIE FRANCIS   ♭1938

Pop. Considered the leading pop female singer of her era, Connie Francis usually sang of her latest broken heart with a teardrop in her voice. The Newark, NJ, native started performing as a child, signing with MGM Records in 1955, but she suffered two years of bombs before the torch ballad "Who's Sorry Now" shot up the charts in 1958. Although she specialized in sobbing tales of woe, Francis proved she could rock with Neil Sedaka's "Stupid Cupid" in 1958 and "Lipstick on Your Collar" the next year. Francis scored two #1 hits in 1960 — the twangy "Everybody's Somebody's Fool" and "My Heart Has a Mind of Its Own," and she branched into acting with a starring role in *Where the Boys Are,* the archetypal spring-break movie. "Don't Break the Heart That Loves You" was Francis's last pop chart-topper in 1962, but she continued to rank high in the pop pantheon throughout the decade, with forays into ethnic and country idioms. –BD

Italian Favorites / MGM
The best of Connie's early "international theme" albums. –CK

Live at the Sahara in Las Vegas / MGM
Lat- 60s live album, with Francis in peak form. –CK

○ **Very Best of Connie Francis / MGM**   1986
Though many best-of's exist on the market, this one leans more heavily toward her earlier rock & roll hits. –CK

FRANKIE GOES TO HOLLYWOOD

Dance-pop. Under the production hand of Trevor Horn, this Liverpool group took the "hi-NRG" dance sound into British and American charts in 1984 with the homoerotic "Relax" and the politically trenchant "Two Tribes." The group, however, was a victim of overhype, and by the time their debut album was released, Frankie's fad had worn thin. –JF

○ **Welcome to the Pleasuredome / ISLAND**   1984
Upbeat British dance music with melodramatic vocals and lyrics that are sexually and politically provocative. The sound of Frankie Goes to Hollywood swept Britain in the years 1983-1985. Here is the wide-screen debut double album, containing the hits "Relax," "Two Tribes," "The Power of Love," and the title track. –WR

ARETHA FRANKLIN   ♭1942

Soul. Appositely dubbed "Lady Soul," Aretha Franklin made several false starts before finding consistent artistic direction. It was only when she began integrating her gospel phrasing and passion (heard in its embryonic form on the Chess album) into secular material that she, like Ray Charles before her, elevated herself from the ranks of the also-rans. There were hints of what was to come in her Columbia recordings, but the flowering of Aretha Franklin coincided with her arrival at Atlantic.

From the moment "I Never Loved a Man" broke through in early 1967, Aretha rarely put a foot wrong for five or six glorious years. When she went wrong, it was usually because of her poor choice of other people's songs to record, but even then, Aretha could sometimes turn dross into gold. By the late 70s, though, the partnership with Atlantic had become stale, and it took a deal with Arista to recharge her chart career. She still has the vocal chops, but many consider that market considerations alone will ensure she will never surpass the artistic high-water mark of her early Atlantic recordings. –CE

Aretha Arrives / ATLANTIC 1967
Her second Atlantic album features hip "Aretha-fied" covers from Sinatra's "That's Life" to Question Mark & the Mysterians' "96 Tears." A great record utilizing King Curtis and the Muscle Shoals musicians heard on most of Aretha's classic Atlantic work. Includes "Baby I Love You." –GB

I Never Loved a Man ... / ATLANTIC 1967
I Never Loved a Man (The Way I Love You) is Franklin's first Atlantic album — an electrifying breakthrough in her somewhat stymied (Columbia) career. The Muscle Shoals sound featured here became legendary. –GB

Lady Soul / ATLANTIC 1968
Great personnel again — King Curtis, Bobby Womack, Frank Wess, and others, including a guest spot by Eric Clapton. Several classic songs, including the lesser-known "Ain't No Way" by Carolyn Franklin and the hits "Chain of Fools" and "Natural Woman." –GB

Aretha Now / ATLANTIC 1968
1968 release with more good covers and the hit "Think." –GB

Aretha's Greatest Hits / ATLANTIC 1971
Includes her most important Atlantic hits plus lesser pop covers ("Let It Be," "Call Me") in about 50/50 proportion. –GB

Hey Now Hey ... / ATLANTIC 1973
Hey Now Hey (The Other Side of the Sky) was just about Franklin's last gasp before succumbing to disco. This odd album, with its cheesy junkie artwork contains some gems — notable are a poignant cover of Bernstein's "Somewhere," a sparkling "Moody's Mood," and the beautiful Carolyn Franklin composition "Angel." –GB

☆ **30 Greatest Hits / ATLANTIC** 1986
Contains all of her essential Atlantic hits; a matchless catalog of soul vocalizing that will never be topped. –GB

☆ **The Queen of Soul / RHINO** 1992
This 4-CD, 86-track collection is a comprehensive look at Franklin's soul genius. All of her great Atlantic hits are here, as well as many key performances. –ED

FREDDIE & THE DREAMERS

British Invasion. Freddie & the Dreamers were the clowns of the British Invasion, playing their pop music for laughs while the other groups of the time were dead serious. Lead singer Freddie Garrity (b Nov 14, 1940) began playing in skiffle groups in the late 50s, switching to rock & roll in the early 60s. After the Beatles broke the American market wide open, Freddie & the Dreamers followed in the flood of acts that tried to duplicate the overwhelming success of the Beatles. The group's hits were more numerous in the UK than in America, where they had only one Top Ten hit, the #1 "I'm Telling You Now." As 1965 turned into 1966, the group stopped charting in the US and the hits began to dwindle in the UK; by 1968 the original group disbanded. Garrity continues to tour with a new version of the Dreamers. –STE

○ **Best of Freddie & the Dreamers / EMI** 1992
Yes, "I'm Telling You Now" is here, and so is "Do the Freddie," an absurd attempt at fashioning a dance craze, but so are "How about Trying Your Luck with Me," "When I'm Home

with You," and "Brown and Porters (Meat Exporters) Lorry." In other words, it's more than a definitive collection, with 25 tracks (many previously unreleased in the US) and a comprehensive discography. –STE

FREE

Hard rock. Free, an English quartet formed in 1968 with Paul Rodgers, Andy Fraser, Paul Kossoff, and Simon Kirke, took the then-popular heavy British blues-rock sound and stripped it down to a hard yet open minimalistic sound.

Rodgers quickly earned a reputation as one of the greatest singers of the genre, able to deliver lyrics with gritty dark sensuality as well as playful toss-offs. Drummer Simon Kirke was the hard-rock equivalent to soul music's Al Jackson, speaking volumes with a no-nonsense groove. Paul Kossoff's wide sustain leads and rhythm work filled in the band's sounds, allowing Andy Fraser great freedom to pursue his inventive style of very spare, open but melodic bass playing.

The band's sound coalesced into some great moments, particularly the #4 hit "All Right Now," "Fire and Water," and "The Stealer." After some lineup changes and an uneven final album (*Heartbreaker*) in 1973, Free disbanded. Rodgers and Kirke went on to form Bad Company. Fraser and Kossoff released spotty solo efforts, and Kossoff died of heart failure on March 19, 1976. –RC

○ **Best of Free / A&M** 1973
A solid compilation showcasing "All Right Now" and other semi-hits. –DH

FRENCH-FRITH-KAISER-THOMPSON

Avant-garde. Frank French, Fred Frith, Henry Kaiser, and Richard Thompson. –ED

○ **Live Love Larf & Loaf / RHINO** 1987
Master guitarists meet master bassist and master the art of making eclectic, intriguing, otherworldly rock, and more. –JT

Invisible Means / WINDHAM HILL 1990
Less stunning than their first album, but you can't go wrong if daring, innovative guitar playing intrigues you. –JT

GLENN FREY b 1948

Rock/pop. Frey, previously a singer/songwriter and guitarist in the Eagles, launched a solo career upon the band's demise, starting in 1982. He also worked as a TV actor on "Miami Vice," "Wiseguy." –WR

○ **The Allnighter / MCA** 1984
Frey breaks with the old Eagles sound on his second solo album, much of which has a bluesy, rocking feel. Includes the hits "Smuggler's Blues" and "Sexy Girl." –WR

ROBERT FRIPP b 1946

Prog-rock. Once a member of the British band King Crimson, this avant-garde guitar virtuoso began recording solo albums during the latter part of King Crimson's seven-year hiatus. Fripp, in addition to his solo efforts, founded a guitar school in the mid 80s, and in 1991 he released an album with his new rock band Sunday All Over the World. –ED

○ **No Pussyfooting / CAROLINE** 1973
His collaboration with Brian Eno. A musical landscape made up of sedate guitar feedback echoed, repeated, and otherwise treated by tape recorder. Today this would be classified under "new-age." The followup, *Evening Star*, is similar. –WR

● **Exposure / CAROLINE** 1979
Though Fripp uses words like "commercial" and "MOR" to describe this music, and though parts of it contain more-or-less conventional pop-rock music, Fripp introduces a variety of tape loops and edits, vocal fragments and sound experiments, resulting in a unique musical sound collage. Guest artists include Phil Collins, Brian Eno, Daryl Hall, and Peter Gabriel. –WR

Let the Power Fall ... / CAROLINE   1981
Let the Power Fall (An Album of Frippertronics).
"Frippertronics" is the name Robert Fripp gives to his
instrumental pieces constructed with an electric guitar and a
tape recorder. It is characterized by long-lined instrumental
passages with sustained notes that reverberate in interesting
repetitions and variations. –WR

THE FUGS

Alternative rock. A New York City rock/comedy group formed
in the mid 60s by beatnik poets Ed Sanders and Tuli
Kupferberg. They got their act together while running a way-
off-Broadway rock theater presentation *NYC* for over 900
performances, filled with scatological satire and crudely
performed music. Barely able to sing or play their
instruments, the Fugs nonetheless scored big with college
audiences when their first album was reissued by the tiny ESP
label in 1966. Successful throughout the end of decade
(eventually signed to Frank Sinatra's Reprise label!), the Fugs's
brand of humor and music exerted an influence on bands as
diverse as the Velvet Underground and Frank Zappa's Mothers
of Invention. –CK

○ **The Fugs / ESP**   1965
Their debut effort, which combines leftist politics, William
Blake, and beatnik sensibilities. Necessary if you want to
understand the hippies and acid rock. –DS

The Fugs / ESP - DIS   1966
More politically minded insanity. –DS

It Crawled into My Hand, Honest / REPRISE   1968
Features the classic "Wide, Wide River." –DS

Tenderness Junction / REPRISE   1968
Listen especially to the live "Exorcising Evil Spirits from the
Pentagon." –DS

BOBBY FULLER FOUR   d1966

Rock & roll. Fuller was Buddy Holly's greatest disciple: both
were Texans who loved the sound of ringing Stratocasters;
they both knew good hooks when they heard them; and both
died at the apex of their careers. Fuller is best remembered for
the charging 1965 hit "I Fought the Law" and the followup
"Let Her Dance." An undeservedly overlooked mid-60s
highlight. –JF

○ **Best of Bobby Fuller Four / RHINO**   1986
He fought something and it won, but while he was around
there were few bands that could churn out rock & roll this raw
and determined. –JT

I Fought the Law / KRLA King of the Wheels / ACE 1990
The first two albums by the legendary 60s rockers, with bonus
tracks. For collectors only. (Import) –JT

Live at PJ's Plus! / ACE   1991
Killer live show plus assorted rarities, by the ultimate 60s
garage band. (Import) –JT

FUN BOY THREE

Alternative pop. UK trio of Terry Hall, Neville Staples, and
Lynval Golding, a subset of the Specials, formed when that
group split in 1981. Fun Boy Three had six UK Top 20 singles
before they split in 1983. –WR

○ **The Fun Boy Three / CHRYSALIS**   1982
Hall sings lead and Staples and Golding chant behind him on
the group's beat-heavy ballads on such hits as "It Ain't What
You Do ...," on which they are joined by Bananarama. –WR

Waiting / CHRYSALIS   1983
David Byrne-produced second album contains the Boys' own
version of their song "Our Lips Are Sealed," a hit for the Go-
Go's. –WR

FUNKADELIC

Funk, psychedelic, soul. Funkadelic was the more politicized of
George Clinton's psycho-funk spinoffs. Where Parliament
offered the butt-tugging ecstasy of "Tear the Roof off the
Sucker" and "Flashlight," Funkadelic tackled racial conflict
("You and Your Folks, Me and My Folks"), government
corruption (*America Eats Its Young*), and the power of the
boogie (*One Nation under a Groove*). They were never the
singles act Parliament turned out to be, but Funkadelic
tackled tougher issues and made them wiggle and wobble as
surely as anything that ever bore Clinton's stamp. –JF

○ **Funkadelic / WESTBOUND**   1971
The music is serious but George Clinton is as tongue-in-cheek
as ever. The album opens up with his voice, proposing "If you
will suck my soul, I will lick your funky emotions," and
proceeds in and out of that vein for forty minutes. This album
is raw and pure funk, with often twangy guitars and deep, low
yet prominent bass lines. It takes the quirky, basic groove of
the Meters and renders it heavy, grungy, while maintaining
the straightfaced humor that Clinton has made famous. –JK

☆ **Maggot Brain / WESTBOUND**   1971
The best early Funkadelic record. There's some indulgent stuff
here that may conjure some art-rock nightmares, but at its
best — "You and Your Folks, Me and My Folks" — this is a
brave and pioneering recording. –JF

Free Your Mind ... / WESTBOUND   1972
Not quite as promising as its title and classic cover would
indicate, *Free Your Mind and Your Ass Will Follow* is full of
faux religious rambling and spacey studio overdubs and
effects, yet still manages to pull it off in the endearing Clinton
style of blending soul, heavy metal, gospel, and bad sci-fi
movies, coming up with gems such as "Friday Night, August
the Fourteenth," and "Funky Dollar Bill." –JK

Funkadelic's Greatest Hits / WESTBOUND   1975
Excellent collection of the early years. "You and You're Folks"
isn't here, but it does rescue the best cuts from their spotty
early records. Out of print; not on CD. –JF

Hardcore Jollies / WARNER   1976
Major-label debut lacks the manic drive of the early stuff, but
tightens the grooves and adds some sharp melodies. –JF

★ **One Nation under a Groove / WARNER**   1978
Clinton's supreme goodfoot manifesto, and for the first time
in his career he pulls off a start-to-finish masterstroke. –JF

○ **Uncle Jam Wants You / WARNER**   1979
Doesn't keep moving like its immediate predecessor, but this
is where you'll find "Not Just Knee Deep," a wonderful piece of
erotic esoterica. –JF

BILLY FURY   b1941

Rock/pop, British Invasion. England's best rock singer of the
pre-Beatles era. Born in Liverpool, Fury was the most talented
of England's Elvis clones and near-clones of the very early 60s,
and also wrote some of his own songs. A strong singer with a
very suggestive stage presence, Fury also had the benefit of a
fine backing band, including rockabilly guitarist Joe Brown.
His recordings from 1963 onward, backed by the Tornadoes
(of "Telstar" fame) lack this power, but Fury still made the
charts through the mid 60s, and, prior to his death in the mid
80s, retained the respect and admiration of the British rock
establishment he helped to form. –BE

○ **The Sound of Fury / POLYGRAM**   1988
The best rock album recorded in England before the rise of
the Beatles (Andy White, the guest drummer on "Love Me
Do," plays the skins on this too). A hard-rocking gem, driven
by Fury's powerful voice and Joe Brown's superb guitar. This
reissue has ten bonus tracks. –BE

PETER GABRIEL   *b* 1950

Prog-rock. Peter Gabriel was one of the founding members of Genesis when it was formed in 1965. Gabriel left Genesis in 1975 to pursue an idiosyncratic but highly successful solo career. He initially drew from the art-rock sounds of his time with Genesis but increasingly infused worldbeat and extremely dissonant rock, and eventually some R&B, into his sound.

Gabriel has always surrounded himself with first-class producers (Bob Ezrin, Robert Fripp, Daniel Lanois, Steve Lillywhite), who could sonically push the envelope into new frontiers. Thematically Gabriel's lyrics progressively abandoned the journey through the dark side of the psyche in favor of reaching out with awareness-elevating sentiment. That transition helped expand Gabriel's audience significantly in 1986 with the multi-platinum hit album *So*, which peaked at #2.

Gabriel's hits include "Solsbury Hill" (#68) (#84 live version), "Games without Frontiers" (#48), "Shock the Monkey" (#29), "Sledgehammer" (#1), "In Your Eyes" (#26), and "Big Time" (#8). –RC

○ **Peter Gabriel / ATCO**   1977

His strong debut, produced by Bob Ezrin (Pink Floyd, Alice Cooper), features the hit "Solsbury Hill," which addressed Gabriel's breakup with Genesis. The sound reflects some of Genesis's art-rock sensibilities ("Moribund the Burgermeister"), while charting some more accessible styles (in Gabriel's eccentric fashion) like the fairly straightahead rock of "Modern Love." Other highlights include the portentous "Here Comes the Flood" and "Humdrum." –RC

Peter Gabriel / ATLANTIC   1978

King Crimson's Robert Fripp produced this followup. Overall, this effort is more uneven, but there are some real highlights in the form of "D.I.Y." and the aggressively dissonant rocker "On the Air." –RC

★ **Peter Gabriel / GEFFEN**   1980

On this, the third of three self-titled efforts, Gabriel teams up with producer Steve Lillywhite (XTC, Psychedelic Furs, U2) and produces a masterpiece. From the chilling opener, "Intruder," to "Biko," an impassioned tribute to murdered South African poet and activist Steven Biko, Lillywhite's experimental (and very left-of-center) approach to sound is a perfect match for Gabriel's convoluted tales from the dark side of human nature. Arguably Gabriel's best work thus far. –RC

○ **Security / GEFFEN**   1982

Produced by David Lord and Gabriel, this is really a transitional album, borrowing from the heavily treated approach to sound found on the Lillywhite work while embracing more worldbeat rhythms. The music is less dissonant. Thematically, Gabriel picks up the human rights thread he started with "Biko" on "Wallflower." "Kiss of Life" suggests a hopefulness emerging in his work. Includes the hit "Shock the Monkey." –RC

Plays Live / GEFFEN   1983

Gabriel has always been an excellent performer. This live set is excellent proof, in spite of some slight post-gig doctoring. Nevertheless, most of these songs work best in the arid confines of the studio atmosphere. –RC

Birdy - Music from the film / GEFFEN   1985

This instrumental work was Gabriel's first major soundtrack undertaking. Fans of Gabriel's texturous arrangements and melodies (some here are drawn from earlier material) should check out this fine work. (Import) –RC

☆ **So / GEFFEN**   1986

After a four-year layoff from his last studio album (*Security*), Gabriel returns with his most upbeat record, infusing funk, world beat, and gospel. The more accessible production, by Daniel Lanois (U2) and Gabriel, helps make this album a worldwide commercial success. Includes the hits "In Your Eyes," "Sledgehammer," "Big Time." –RC

○ **Passion / GEFFEN**   1989

For the soundtrack for Martin Scorsese's film *The Last Temptation of Christ,* Gabriel drew inspiration from field recordings of musicians in the Middle East, fusing those recordings with his own atmospheric sound tapestries for a powerful collection of music. –RC

Shaking the Tree / GEFFEN   1990

This is an odd best-of collection. True, it includes his hits, but Gabriel isn't merely a singles artist. As a result, there are many important album tracks that would be glaring omissions in a well-rounded picture of Gabriel's artistry. The title, no doubt, is an indicator of the tossed-off nature of this set. –RC

GALACTIC COWBOYS

Prog-rock. Houston's Galactic Cowboys blend strong Beatlesque four-part harmonies with extended grunge-meets-art-rock song constructions. The band, along with producer Sam Taylor, imbues the sound and arrangements with a fine blend of playful humor and serious sentiment. –RC

Galactic Cowboys / GEFFEN   1991

This strong debut manages to incorporate four-part *Abbey Road*-style Beatles harmonies with extended multisectional Metallica-like heavy-metal ensemble work. There are many standout tracks on this collection, including "I'm Not Amused," "My School," "Why Can't You Believe in Me," "Sea of Tranquillity," and the affecting crunch-rock ballad of "Someone for Everyone." –RC

DIAMANDA GALAS

Punk. Harsh, assaultive art-punk with quasi-operatic delivery. Not for the fainthearted. –JD

○ **Divine Punishment / ENIGMA-RESTLESS**   1988

Compelling but brutal. An ugly, brooding masterpiece. –JD

Divine Punishment/Saint of the Pit / RES   1988

A worthwhile compilation, but a tad over-long. –JD

Plague Mass ... / ELEKTRA   1991

Plague Mass (1984 - End of the Epidemic). A howling metaphor for the AIDS era. –JD

GALAXIE 500

Alternative pop. While many bands picked up on the Velvet Underground's more rocking traits, this Boston-based trio reveled in their slower doings. Sparse and not upbeat, they are not dour either. –BE

○ **Today / ROUGH TRADE**   1988

Working the slow side of the Velvet Underground. Melodic and intense. –RG

THE ERIC GALES BAND

Blues/rock, psychedelic. When guitarslinger Eric Gales arrived on the scene in 1991 with his self-titled debut album, he was only 16, the product of a family of professional musicians. It's older brother (and bassist) Eugene Gales who provided much of the history and musical discipline behind Eric's Hendrix-influenced excursions. –RC

○ **The Eric Gales Band / ELEKTRA**   1991

Heavy Hendrix-influenced mainstream AOR debut. In spite of some weak material, there are a few highlights with "Resurrection," the hit "Sign of the Storm," and the instrumental "High Anxiety." –RC

RORY GALLAGHER   *b* 1949

Blues/rock. Irish blues-rock guitarist and singer Rory Gallagher is surely one of the most exciting of the British blues acts to be seen live, and his recorded output over the years guarantees him a prominent place among the British blues stars. –RS

Live in Europe / POLYDOR   1972

Live recordings of many of his best tunes. –MGN

Rory Gallagher/Live! / POLYDOR   1972
Tattoo / POLYDOR   1973
Studio recording done with a quartet. Every cut is solid. –MGN
● **Irish Tour '74 / CIR**   1974
Double-album set recorded live at various venues in Ireland. Loaded with Gallagher's best material. A great album. –MGN
○ **Calling Card / CAPITOL**   1976
His best studio album. The Irish blues-rock guitarist plays like there's no tomorrow, even on mid-tempo tracks. He's an unsung hero on the guitar. –MGN

GAME THEORY

Alternative pop. Led by Scott Miller, an Alex Chilton-influenced singer/songwriter, Game Theory produces smart alternative Anglo power-pop, full of engaging quirky melodies and fairly obscure lyrics.
On the down side, Miller's voice can get a little whiney, and his earnest approximations to pitch (reminiscent of the Scruff's Steve Burns) may be an acquired taste for some. However, their Mitch Easter-produced albums, *Big Shot Chronicles*, *Real Nighttime*, and *Lolita Nation* are worth seeking out.
Big Star or dB's fans should love this band. Then again, they probably know about Game Theory already. –RC
Real Nighttime / RESTLESS   1985
The band's first effort with Mitch Easter (R.E.M., Let's Active) producing. Miller's Alex Chilton fixation comes to the fore here, and it generally works nicely. "24" was a breezy alternative college hit. Other highlights include "Curse of the Frontierland," with its Big Star-influenced guitar figure and the delicately reflective "If and When It All Falls Apart." –RC
Big Shot Chronicles / RESTLESS   1986
The band's sound and Miller's songwriting are more aggressive here, delivering an appealingly punchy power-pop sound. A fine album with many tracks to recommend. "I've Tried Subtlety" is a strong, over-amped T-Rex rocker, while "Like a Girl Jesus" shines with Easter's wholly psychedelic production touches. "Erica's World" is a wonderfully quirky rocker, and "Regenisraen" showcases the band's harmonic capabilities. –RC
○ **Tinker to Evers to Chance / RESTLESS**   1990
For the uninitiated, this collection of highlights from 1982 to 1989 is the best place to start, containing a healthy selection from their later Mitch Easter-produced albums. –RC
Lolita Nation / RESTLESS   1991
Many fans of the band claim that this is a creative peak for Game Theory. *Lolita Nation* is loaded with odd juxtapositions of experimental sounds and spoken passages. The material, while dazzling in places, is rather inconsistent. "The Real Sheila" and "We Love You, Carol and Alison" are highlights, and both of them are found on *Tinker*.... –RC

GANG OF FOUR

Punk. Militant UK punk group featuring Jon King, Hugo Burnham, Andy Gill, and Dave Allen, formed in Leeds in 1977. They made several critically successful albums before splitting in 1984. They were re-formed by King and Gill in 1991. –WR
★ **Entertainment! / WARNER**   1979
With their machine-shop rhythms, harsh guitar attacks, and chanted, unmelodic lyrics, GoF is anything but easy listening. But in songs such as "Damaged Goods" and "At Home He's a Tourist," their caustic messages perfectly match the musical lockstep, and both become nearly irresistible — in other words, pop music. –WR
Songs of the Free / WARNER   1982
Gang of Four fill out their sound with background vocals and rhythmic variety; most of all, the anguished singing begins to border on the passionate. –WR
○ **Brief History of the Twentieth Century / WARNER**   1990
A well-chosen 20-song compilation taken from the band's four studio albums and miscellaneous singles, ca. 1979-1983. –WR

THE GAP BAND

Funk. This Southern combo bopped around throughout the 70s, offering a rather pedestrian variety of boogie funk. After scaling down and retooling their sound, the Gap Band netted numerous hits with a big mod-funk sound that recalled everyone from Sly Stone to George Clinton and Rick James. –JF
○ **Strike a Groove / PST**
A remixed collection from 1983 that contains the best of the Gap band's late-70s recordings. Tepid at times, but cuts like "Knucklehead Funkin'" are definitely in the groove. (Out of print) –JF
● **Gap Gold (Best of the Gap Band) / POLYGRAM**   1987
This brief but thorough best-of contains every major hit netted by the revamped, latter-day Gap Band, including such dance crushers as "You Dropped a Bomb on Me" and "Early in the Morning." –JF

JERRY GARCIA   b 1942

Rock & roll. A singer/songwriter and guitarist in the Grateful Dead, Garcia has also worked extensively as a solo and in other configurations, starting in 1972. –WR
● **Garcia / GRATEFUL DEAD**   1972
In essence, this is a Grateful Dead record, featuring, as it does, the band's leader/singer/guitarist, its drummer, and its lyricist. Except for the few instrumental/experimental cuts, the material has been incorporated into the Dead's concert repertoire. In fact, this is a perfect followup to the folk/rock song albums the Dead produced in 1970, *Workingman's Dead* and *American Beauty*, albums the band itself has never really followed up. –WR
Reflections / GRATEFUL DEAD   1976
Again, a Dead album in everything but name, with several tracks featuring the entire band, perhaps most memorably on "It Must Have Been the Roses." –WR
Cats under the Stars / ARISTA   1978
The first real "Garcia Band" album is paced by songs that would not sound out of place at a Dead concert. As a matter of fact, the album has garnered increased interest in the 90s as the Dead added the leadoff track "Rubin and Cherise" to its repertoire. –WR
Almost Acoustic / GRATEFUL DEAD   1988
Garcia got his start in bluegrass, and here he assembles the Jerry Garcia Acoustic Band (some of whom he started playing with) to handle a live set full of Jimmie Rodgers, Mississippi John Hurt, and traditional mountain music. –WR
○ **Jerry Garcia & David Grisman / ACOUSTIC DISC**   1991
A guitar-and-mandolin duet album, exquisitely produced, with this pair trying a variety of styles from Garcia's "Friend of the Devil" to the ambitious instrumental "Arabia." –WR

ART GARFUNKEL   b 1941

Pop. As the airy choirboy half of Simon & Garfunkel, Art Garfunkel reached his greatest solo success between 1973 and 1978 with lushly produced soft-pop hits like "All I Know" (#9), "I Shall Sing" (#38), "Second Avenue" (#34), "I Only Have Eyes for You" (#18), "Breakaway" (#39), and " (What A) Wonderful World" (#17), recorded with James Taylor and Paul Simon. Garfunkel also reunited with Simon in 1975 for the #9 hit "My Little Town." –RC
○ **Garfunkel (Best Of) / COLUMBIA**   1990
This is a good overview of Garfunkel's solo work. Most of his airplay tracks are included here. –RC

THE GARRETT-SAHM-TAYLOR BAND

Blues/rock, R&B/rock. Not surprisingly, this group is also called "the Formerly Brothers," since all three members are alumni of other noted organizations (Paul Butterfield's Better Days, the Sir Douglas Quintet, Canned Heat, etc.). It was formed on an ad hoc basis after a chance gig at the Edmonton Folk Festival in 1986. –WR

○ **Return of the Formerly Brothers / RYKODISC**   1991
Blues and Cajun music are the touchstones on this loose set of
standards played with a bar-band enthusiasm. Queen Ida
guests on two cuts. –WR

DANNY GATTON

Rockabilly. In the early 50s, Gatton was a teen guitar prodigy,
with a style that incorporated the flashy calisthenics of Jimmy
Bryant, Joe Maphis, and Cliff Gallup (equal parts rockabilly
fire and honky-tonk dazzle). –JF

○ **Unfinished Business / NRG**   1987
Perhaps the most underrated guitarist there is. Gatton does it
all, and dazzles at every turn. –JT

88 Elmira St. / ELEKTRA   1991
His first major-label recording after decades of flooring
unsuspecting audiences. Gatton's guitar work is simply
astounding. –JT

Redneck Jazz / NRG   1991
Just like the title says. The music on this album is required
listening for those who think they've heard it all. –JT

MARVIN GAYE   1939-1984

Motown. He wanted to do it all, from standards to lubricous
make-out music — and by his track record he came close.
The most troubled of Tamla-Motown's talented stable, Gaye
came to the label from the usual background of gospel groups
and R&B quartets. He broke through in 1962 with dance-floor
specials, but his gentle tenor voice was better suited
elsewhere. His music slowly evolved, although the Motown
quality controllers ensured that its commerciality rarely
slipped.
Gaye's gloriously paranoid interpretation of "I Heard It
through the Grapevine" gave him the clout he needed to
reshape his career. He worked up some concept albums (most
notable, *What's Going On* and *Let's Get It On*), which swiftly ran
the gamut from ecological concerns to soft-core porn) and
then watched his career fall apart. Divorces, financial woes,
and record-label troubles conspired to send Gaye, never an
emotionally strong or stable man anyway, into a tailspin that
ended tragically when he was shot by his father in 1984. –CE

Moods of Marvin Gaye / MOTOWN   1966
One of his better 60s albums. –RAB

★ **What's Going On / MOTOWN / BB 6**   1971
Shortly after Marvin Gaye turned 30, he became the first
Motown artist with a measure of creative control. *What's
Going On* was the result, surely Marvin's finest moment and,
along with a number of *great* Stevie Wonder's early-70s releases,
one of a handful of *great* Motown albums. A concept album,
What's Going On chronicled a multitude of societal ills.
Ironically, Motown owner Berry Gordy did not want to release
it. He was convinced it held no commercial potential. Gordy
couldn't have been more wrong: *What's Going On* catapulted
Marvin Gaye into superstardom. Three #1 singles were pulled
from the album: the title song, "Mercy Mercy Me (The
Ecology)," and "Inner City Blues (Make Me Wanna Holler)."
This was the first album where Marvin overdubbed his voice
multiple times, creating a one-man vocal group. The result
was a level of timbral integration in the harmonies that
became a Gaye trademark. –RB

☆ **Let's Get It On / MOTOWN / BB 2**   1973
Let's Get It On is one of the most erotic recordings known to
mankind. Inspired by Gaye's obsession with a teenage girl,
Janis Hunter, who would later become his second wife, Side 1
is a self-contained suite. Side 2, including "You Sure Love to
Ball," is nearly pornographic. Over time, five songs would
chart from the album, including one of his concert standards,
"Distant Lover." –RB

★ **Anthology / MOTOWN**   1974
With *Anthology* you can get an overview of Gaye's Motown
work without having to plunk the money down for *The*

Marvin Gaye Collection boxed set. The 2-CD set contains most
of his major hits (although not his #1 hit, "Let's Get It On"),
including "Inner City Blues (Make Me Wanna Holler)," "Mercy
Mercy Me (The Ecology)," "I Heard It through the Grapevine,"
"Trouble Man," "I'll Be Doggone," "What's Going On," "Hitch
Hike," "Can I Get a Witness," and "Pride and Joy," as well as his
numerous duets with Kim Weston and Tammi Terrell, like
"Ain't No Mountain High Enough," "Ain't Nothing like the Real
Thing," "It Takes Two," and "Your Precious Love." –ED

Here, My Dear / MOTOWN / BB 26   1979
On one of the stranger releases in popular music, *Here, My
Dear*, Gaye stands emotionally naked. Over the course of this
two-album set, Marvin chronicles the dissolution of his
marriage (to company president Berry Gordy's sister Anna).
The level of detail is nearly painful as Marvin accuses Anna of
keeping him from seeing his son, having a restraining order
issued against him, and holding their separation up for
ransom. Marvin also tells us of his cocaine habit and his
obsession with prostitutes. In a trace of irony not lost on the
singer, Anna received all royalties from the album as per their
divorce agreement. Upon hearing it, she reportedly
contemplated suing for invasion of privacy. –RB

○ **Midnight Love / COLUMBIA / BB 7**   1982
Gaye's comeback album contains its share of fluff but "Sexual
Healing" is one of the greatest R&B singles of all time. Black
radio felt that way as well; the song stayed #1 for ten weeks,
remaining on the charts for a total of 27 weeks. –RB

Marvin Gaye & His Women / MOTOWN   1988
All the great duets with Mary Wells, Tammie Terrell, Kim
Weston, and Diana Ross. –RAB

○ **The Marvin Gaye Collection / MOTOWN**   1990
According to the Joel Whitburn chart books, Marvin Gaye is
the seventh most successful R&B artist ever. This is the
definitive Marvin Gaye anthology. The four CDs are arranged
thematically. The first disc contains 20 Top 20 chart hits, from
1962's "Stubborn Kind of Fellow" to 1982's "Sexual Healing."
The second CD is made up of 25 duets, many of them hit
singles sung by Gaye in tandem with Mary Wells, Kim Weston,
Tammi Terrell, and Diana Ross. The third, entitled *Rare, Live
and Unreleased*, is a little less consistent, although Gaye's
version of the "Star Spangled Banner" from the 1983 NBA All-
Star Game is a wonder to behold. The fourth disc showcases
Marvin the "balladeer." It is the weakest of the four, in my
estimation. The sound on the collection is quite good, and the
booklet, although a little brief and breezy, is adequate. –RB

GLORIA GAYNOR   b 1949

Disco. Gaynor sang with the Soul Satisfiers band before being
discovered at the Wagon Wheel in New York in the early 70s.
Probably the first "disco queen," Gaynor helped popularize,
through her music, the "segue" or "extended mix" that came
to represent disco music. Her 1979 cut, "I Will Survive,"
became a woman's anthem in the vein of Helen Reddy's "I Am
Woman." She continues to thrive as a major star in Europe,
although not here. –BC

Greatest Hits / POLYGRAM   1982
Her disco hits, from "Never Can Say Goodbye" to "I Will
Survive." –DH

PAUL GAYTEN   b 1920

R&B. An overlooked but important 50s R&B pianist from New
Orleans. His recordings for Specialty and Chess (many of
which feature the vocals of Anne Gayten) bridge the gap
between Midwestern jump-blues and the sounds of Bourbon
Street. In the 60s he was a talent scout for Chess. –JF

○ **Chess King of New Orleans/The Chess Years / MCA**   1989
Sizzling mid-50s New Orleans R&B from this veteran. –BD

GEAR DADDIES

Country rock, rock & roll. Minneapolis country-rock poppers
highlighted by the uncompromising songwriting of Martin
Zellar. –JF

○ **Billy's Live Bait / POLYGRAM**   1990
A gloomy but far more expansive followup, supported by top-notch angst-peddlers like "Time Heals" and "Sonic Boom." –JF

Let's Go Scare Al / POLYGRAM   1990
A compassionate and rocking debut that evokes the small-town blues of this Austin and Minneapolis quartet. –JF

J. GEILS BAND

Rock & roll, R&B/rock, rock/pop. The J. Geils Band from Boston (formed 1967) embraced the idioms of doo-wop, blues, and R&B at a time when many of their peers were diving headfirst into psychedelia. While everyone else grew their hair out, many of the Geils Band slicked their hair back into greasers. Jerome Geils was the band's lead guitarist, but it was Peter Wolf (Blankfield), a former WBCN-FM Boston DJ, who was the group's captivating frontman.

During the 70s, the J. Geils Band toured incessantly and enjoyed the occasional near-hit album or single, but the band struck multi-platinum with *Freeze Frame* (#1) in 1982, one of the biggest albums of that year. Excellent video exposure on the fledgling MTV helped considerably. With success came numerous problems, including substance abuse. A live album, *Showtime* (#23), followed before Wolf jumped ship for a spotty solo career. The group's first post-Wolf studio effort (*You're Getting Even While I'm Getting Odd*) was a major stumble chartwise (#80), and the group disbanded shortly afterwards. "Freeze Frame" (#4), "Centerfold" (#1), "Love Stinks" (#38), "Looking for a Love" (#33), "Give It to Me" (#30), and "Must Of Got Lost" (#12) are some of the band's hits. –RC

○ **J. Geils Band / ATLANTIC**   1970
Their debut paid homage to the likes of Otis Rush, John Lee Hooker, and Motown through blistering covers, but originals such as "Wait" and "What's Your Hurry" more than hold their own. Magic Dick steals the show on this one. –JF

☆ **Monkey Island / ATLANTIC**   1977
One of the great lost albums, *Monkey Island* is where the Geils Band make the blues their own. It's an elaborately produced, adventurous set that analyzes their commerical failure and looks for answers to hard-to-ask questions. Unlike their 1972 live album *Full House*, *Monkey Island* refuses to pander to blues conservatists or boogie-rock hammerheads; the album is steeped in the kind of pathos and bitterness that infuse the Stones' *Sticky Fingers*. The album flopped, but it remains the group's most personal statement. –JF

Sanctuary / EMI   1978
The Geils sound is retooled into a streamlined shuffle that owes much to production and songwriting floriation of keyboardist Seth Justman. Their soul and blues chops are still apparent, but they've worked them into a sound that manages to elaborate on the experiments of *Monkey Island* while still paying homage to their early days. –JF

Love Stinks / CAPITOL   1980
The title cut brought the band an across-the-board hit, and the near new-wave production touches don't get in the way of the crack rhythm section or Geils's tasty leads. A new sound for a new decade. –JF

○ **Best of the J. Geils Band / ATLANTIC**   1980
Pulling the decent material from this otherwise unspectacular mid-70s albums makes this an adequate sample of the band's achievements. It's the best place to sample such minor hits as "Must Of Got Lost" and "Give It to Me." –JF

○ **Freeze Frame / CAPITOL**   1981
A stylistic retread that nonetheless cemented the band's newfound popularity, thanks to the naggingly catchy "Centerfold" and the nuevo-funky "Flamethrower." "Piss on the Wall" and "Rage in the Cage" are blistering rockers. –JF

● **Packed Fair and Square / RHINO**   1992
Packed Fair and Square covers the J. Geils Band's entire career on Atlantic and EMI, from their earlier rough and tumble R&B influenced sound, to mainstream rock/poppers. This double-disc set includes 41 tracks. –ED

BOB GELDOF   *b* 1954

Rock/pop. Though Dublin-born Geldof has scored successes in music both with his group the Boomtown Rats and as a solo artist, Bob Geldof remains best known for his charitable activities, especially his organizing of Live Aid in 1985. –WR

○ **Deep in the Heart of Nowhere / ATLANTIC**   1986
On his first solo album, Geldof sheds the new-wave sound of the Boomtown Rats for a more straightforward classic Brit-rock approach, notably on the leadoff single, "This Is the World Calling" and on the "Waterloo Sunset" sequel, "Love like a Rocket," which features Eric Clapton. –WR

Vegetarians of Love / ATLANTIC   1990
Geldof investigates his Irish folk roots, reveals himself to be a Dylan acolyte, and sends up his "Saint Bob" image on this varied and ambitious second album. –WR

GENERAL PUBLIC

Rock/pop, ska-revival. This UK duo of vocalist Dave Wakeling (b Feb 19, 1956) and "toaster" Ranking Roger (b Feb 21, 1961) was formed from the split of the English Beat in 1983. General Public released two albums before they split. –WR

○ **All the Rage / I.R.S.**   1984
The vocal duo from the English Beat turn in an album of passionate pop-rock, little of which bears the ska style of the parent group. Most effective are the uptempo, Motown-style songs, especially the Top 30 hit "Tenderness." –WR

GENERATION X   1978-1981

Punk. An early London punk band (1978-1981) featuring Billy Idol and Tony James (later to form Sigue Sigue Sputnik). Often criticized as being too commercially minded, Gen X was definitely the smoothest and most pop-oriented of their rebellious crowd. Their first album is considered the best, with the US version offering a slightly improved song set. Their third and last, *Kiss Me Deadly*, was more an Idol/James project than a band effort and was produced by Keith Forsey, who shaped Idol's solo sound. This album contained an early version of "Dancing with Myself," which was eventually Idol's first big solo pop success. As to whether they were a band of crass opportunists or true champions of the punk spirit, Billy Idol's career and Sigue Sigue Sputnik's dubious distinction of having the first advertisement on a pop record speak volumes. –SWB

○ **Generation X / CAPITOL**   1978
Generation X had punk attitude and subject matter on their debut album, which includes their answer song to the Who, "Your Generation," and the generic "One Hundred Punks." But the group's music already had more of a melodic mainstream rock sound than punk's raw assault, and frontman Billy Idol's snarl was straight out of Elvis Presley. –WR

Kiss Me Deadly / CAPITOL   1981
Idol and bassist Brian James rehearse for their post-Gen X careers, respectively as a solo artist and as the leader of Sigue Sigue Sputnik. This album contains the dance hit "Dancing with Myself." –WR

GENESIS

Art-rock, rock/pop. In the band's original incarnation, the heart and soul of Genesis was singer Peter Gabriel. Gabriel's unique stage presence, involving costumes and bizarre pantomime antics, illustrated the surrealistic story lines of the band's eerie epics. Spooky support for these remarkable performances came from Tony Kaye's churning organ and Mellotron and Steve Hackett's unusual synthesizerlike guitar textures. Gabriel's decision to leave Genesis came when the band was at its artistic peak, following 1974's *The Lamb Lies Down on Broadway*. Surprisingly, the remaining quartet found a world-class singer within its own ranks: drummer Phil Collins. With Collins at the helm, Genesis made two solid studio albums before Steve Hackett also quit. Reduced to a trio, the band turned to a mixture of empty pomp and trivial pop, but an example of the latter ("Follow You Follow Me") gave Genesis their first American hit single. The group's success was consolidated as Collins began to guide their music in a funkier and more commercial direction. By the mid 80s, Genesis (which by now bore little resemblance to the art-rock ensemble of bygone days) was regularly scoring smash hit after smash hit, with Collins enjoying a similarly successful solo career on the side. –MPD

Foxtrot / ATLANTIC 1972
On its fourth album, Genesis's ambitious music finally starts to show individual identity and accomplishment, mixing elaborate arrangements with stirring rhythms and highly poetic lyrics. Contains "Watcher of the Skies" and the 22-minute "Supper's Ready." –WR

○ **Selling England by the Pound / ATLANTIC** 1973
One of the best examples of 70s British art-rock, this album incorporates a variety of styles, showcasing the musical dexterity of the players as well as the lyrics to story-songs like "I Know What I Like (In Your Wardrobe)," the first Genesis British hit. –WR

● **The Lamb Lies Down on Broadway / ATLANTIC** 1974
This, the last Genesis album with Peter Gabriel, is a sprawling two-disc thematic album concerning a character named Rael. Keeping with that theme, it includes pastiches of Broadway show music, plus the group's typical mixture of folk, rock, and classical influences. If this is not the first Gabriel Genesis album to buy, it ultimately may prove the most satisfying. –WR

And Then There Were Three / ATLANTIC 1978
The birth of the modern Genesis, a pop-rock trio led by singer/drummer Phil Collins, playing tightly constructed, short, catchy songs. The best of the bunch here is "Follow You, Follow Me," a hit on both sides of the Atlantic. (The first Genesis gold album in the US.) –WR

○ **Abacab / ATLANTIC** 1981
Genesis had perfected its rhythmic, densely chorded, passionate trio music with this, their first US million-seller and Top Ten hit, which includes the Top 40 singles "Abacab," "No Reply at All," and "Man on the Corner." –WR

Invisible Touch / ATLANTIC 1986
The biggest Genesis hit to date, this multi-million-selling release features five Top Five hits, including the #1 title track, "Throwing It All Away," "Land of Confusion," "Tonight, Tonight, Tonight," and "In Too Deep." –WR

GENTLE GIANT

Art-rock. Gentle Giant (formed 1970) brought art-rock to new levels of mathematical complexity. Their pseudo-medieval arrangements and dissonant instrumental voicings dominated most of their albums, but later efforts found the band simplifying their sound into something less daunting. Radio consultant Lee Abrams worked with the group's last album, *Civilian*, which failed commercially while alienating their cult following with its more mainstream sound. Lead singer Derek Shulman has since gone on to a successful career as a major-record-label executive. –RC

Octopus / COLUMBIA 1973
The dull, small-sounding production of this album tends to mask the power of some of the material. However, mathematically inclined art-rockers may find pleasure in tracks like "The Advent of Panurge," "Raconteur Troubadour," and "Knots," with its complicated vocal-round interplay. –RC

○ **Free Hand / CAPITOL-ONE WAY** 1975
In spite of the band's continuing fascination with rhythmic complication, *Free Hand* contains a more rockish feel. "On Reflection" and "His Last Voyage" are nice showcases for the band's vocal arrangements and considerable dynamic performance skills. –RC

BARBARA GEORGE   b 1942

R&B, soul. George's "I Know (You Don't Love Me No More)"

topped the R&B charts in 1961 and has proven a popular cover item ever since. The New Orleans native had never been in the studio before she brought her extremely catchy melody to Harold Battiste's fledgling A.F.O. label. Benefiting from her pleasing, unpolished vocal and a melodic cornet solo by Melvin Lastie, the tune caught fire, vaulting high on pop playlists. Amazingly, nothing else George did ever dented the charts, although she waxed some listenable followups for A.F.O. and Sue. –BD

○ **I Know / COLLECTABLES** 1962
Catchy New Orleans R&B from the early 60s with coy and charming vocals by George. –BD

GEORGIA SATELLITES

Rock & roll. An Atlanta-based rock quartet featuring guitarists Dan Baird and Rick Richards, bassist Rich Price, and drummer Mauro Magellan. Formed in 1980, they scored a surprise hit with "Keep Your Hands to Yourself" in 1987. They split up after the relative failure of their next two albums. –WR

○ **Georgia Satellites / ELEKTRA** 1986
Dirty Rolling Stones-like guitar grunge played by Rick Richards and topped by the adenoidal singing of Dan Baird. Especially enjoyable on the hits "Keep Your Hands to Yourself" and "Battleship Chains." –WR

GERRY & THE PACEMAKERS

British Invasion. The second group out of the Liverpool starting gate in the early 60s, Gerry and the Pacemakers shared manager Brian Epstein and producer George Martin with the Beatles and even got their hand-me-down material — their first (UK) hit was "How Do You Do It," a song the Fab Four had declined to release. It was a #1 for Gerry.

The group was formed in 1959 by singer and guitarist Gerry Marsden (b Sep 24, 1942), with his brother Freddie (b Oct 23, 1940) on drums and Les Chadwick (b May 11, 1943) on bass. Pianist Les Maguire (b Dec 27, 1941) completed the lineup in 1961. They followed the same path to success as the Beatles, including making trips to Hamburg and hooking up with Epstein and Martin. And shortly after the Beatles topped the charts with "Please Please Me," Gerry and the Pacemakers did so with "How Do You Do It."

Like the Beatles, the group went over to America in 1964 and debuted on the "Ed Sullivan Show," resulting in a hit with their ballad "Don't Let the Sun Catch You Crying." Like the Beatles, they then made a movie (theirs was called *Ferry Cross the Mersey*). But unlike the Beatles, Gerry and the Pacemakers faltered commercially after 1964 and failed to develop musically the way their Liverpool neighbors did. As a result, they split up in 1966, with Gerry going solo. By 1975, he had put together a new Pacemakers group and toured on the oldies circuit, his voice still appealing and the Mersey Beat still bouncing. –WR

○ **The EP Collection / SEE FOR MILES** 1987
A truly definitive collection, with all the hits and the most interesting non-hits. Includes the ultra-rare live *Gerry in California* concert recording from 1966. (Import) –BE

Best of ... - The Definitive Collection / CAPITOL 1991
The title promises more than it really delivers in content, if not sound. It'll do for the casual listener. –BE

GIBSON BROTHERS

Rockabilly. Rockabilly and blues from the same bottle that killed Robert Johnson. A group of Ohio-based adopted Memphians, whose revolving lineup frequently includes ex-members of Pussy Galore. –BE

Big Pine Boogie / HOMESTEAD 1988
If rotgut whiskey were music ... –RG

○ **Dedicated Fool / HOMESTEAD-GIANT/POSITIVE** 1989
Grunge-a-billy to the hilt. –RG

GILES-GILES-FRIPP

Prog-rock. Trio formed late in 1967 by future King Crimson alumni Robert Fripp, Michael Giles, and Peter Giles. Their sound was a mix of elegant psychedelia and light jazz, rather akin to the Moody Blues. With the addition of Ian McDonald, Greg Lake, and Peter Sinsfield, the trio evolved into King Crimson. –BE

Cheerful Insanity / DECCA 1982
The Cheerful Insanity of Giles, Giles, and Fripp is trippy light psychedelia, highlighted by Fripp's spacy, searing "Erudite Eyes" and the light pop "Little Children." –BE

JOHNNY GILL   b 1967

Urban R&B. Born in Washington, DC, Johnny Gill was discovered by singer Stacy Lattisaw after singing in his family's group Wings of Faith from age five. His solo career began in 1983 with the Top 30 R&B single "Super Love." In duo with Lattisaw, he scored an R&B Top Ten hit in 1984 with "Perfect Combination." In 1988 Gill joined New Edition, replacing Bobby Brown. In 1989 he sang on two R&B hits: "Where Do We Go from Here," a #1 by Stacy Lattisaw, and "One Love," by George Howard. Gill finally scored as a solo singer in 1990 with the release of his album *Johnny Gill*, which sold a million copies, topped the R&B chart, and made the Top Ten in the pop chart. –WR

Chemistry / ATLANTIC 1985
It's worth having merely for the awesome pop ballad "Half Crazy." –BC

○ **Johnny Gill / MOTOWN** 1990
Gill's long-in-coming solo breakthrough, featuring the hits "Rub You the Right Way," "My, My, My," and "Fairweather Friend." –WR

DAVID GILMOUR   b 1944

Prog-rock. David Gilmour, lead guitarist of Pink Floyd, is one of rock's most distinctive players with his use of echoes, delays, and distorted sustain. His solo efforts have done well, with his self-titled debut reaching #29 and followup *About Face* hitting #32 on the charts. –RC

David Gilmour / CBS 1978
Heavily atmospheric guitar rock in the tradition of his Pink Floyd work. –DDC

○ **About Face / CBS** 1984
More accessible than its predecessor, *About Face* is less about mood and more about well-crafted rock. Many highlights grace this underappreciated effort, including "Blue Light," "Love on the Air," and "All Lovers Are Deranged," which was cowritten with Pete Townshend. –DDC

GLASS EYE

Alternative rock. One of the most creative bands in alternative rock, Glass Eye both defines and defys the genre. With coleaders who have radically different sensibilities, this Austin band is sometimes very edgy, sometimes quite melodic, and usually sounds like no one else. –BE

○ **Beat by Nature / RES** 1988
Very edgy, angular pop. Deconstructed? Visionary! –RG

Christine / RES 1988
This EP features a version of Simon & Garfunkel's "Cecilia" and other tracks from the *Beat by Nature* sessions. –RG

THE GO-BETWEENS

Alternative rock. This Australian quintet was founded as a duo in 1977 by Robert Forster and Grant McLellan. The first of their six albums was released in 1982. When they broke up in 1990, Forster went solo and McLellan joined Steve Kilby in Jack Frost. –WR

○ **Tallulah / BIGTIME** 1987
The addition of violinist and oboist Amanda Brown makes a crucial difference in the Go-Betweens sound on this fifth album, giving it the elegance and pop sheen to back Forster and McLellan's intelligent, acerbic lyrics with the irony they deserve. –WR

16 Lovers Lane / CAPITOL 1988
A more acoustic but still lush collection of adult love songs from the Go-Betweens. –WR

THE GO-GO'S

Rock/pop. Formed in the late 70s, the Go-Go's were the first successful all-female band of the 80s. Their 1981 debut, *Beauty and the Beat*, was a collection of infectious pop songs written and played by the group. It yielded two hit singles, the classic "Our Lips Are Sealed" and "We Got the Beat." They recorded two more albums before splitting up in 1985 to pursue solo careers. –KMC

○ **Greatest / A&M** 1990
An adequate collection of hits, including "Our Lips Are Sealed" (#20), "We Got the Beat" (#2), "Vacation" (#8), and "Head over Heels" (#11). –DH

GODLEY & CREME

Rock/pop, art-rock. Kevin Godley and Lol Creme, two former members of 10CC, have found a niche with very ambitious and artsy pop albums, often conceived as self-contained narratives. The closest they've come to mass popularity was on 1985's *The History Mix*, which scrambled a number of 10CC hits and contained the soaring single "Cry." –DH

○ **The History Mix - Vol. 1 / POLYDOR** 1985
The duo's most accessible collection (available only on import), containing the hit "Cry." –DH

THE GOLDEN PALOMINOS

Alternative rock. This progressive project band from New York, led by drummer Anton Fier, features an ever-changing lineup of current alternative players. At various times, the Golden Palominos have included Michael Stipe of R.E.M., John Lydon, Richard Thompson, Chris Stamey, Jack Bruce, Arto Lindsay, Carla Bley, Bob Mould, Syd Straw, and others. –IME

○ **Visions of Excess / CELULLIOD** 1985
A great eclectic mix of alternative rock songcraft and great musicianship from Jack Bruce, Richard Thompson, and others. Syd Straw shines on "(Kind of) True" and so does Michael Stipe on "Omaha." –SWB

Blast of Silence / CELULLIOD 1986
Anton Fier, Syd Straw, T-Bone Burnette serve up a fine selection of tracks with a country-rock slant, including a Lowell George cover and Peter Holsapple's "Diamonds." –SWB

Drunk with Passion / ATLANTIC 1991
Fier and Bill Laswell are joined by Stipe, Thompson, Carla Bley, and former Hüsker Dü singer/songwriter and guitarist Bob Mould on this album. –WR

BOBBY GOLDSBORO   b 1941

Vocal, pop. Singer/songwriter Bobby Goldsboro began his career in the early 60s as a guitarist in Roy Orbison's band. After departing for a solo career, Goldsboro's success has been marked by a long string of sentimental ballads, the most famous being "Honey," which held the #1 spot for five weeks. Other hits included "See the Funny Little Clown" (#9), "Little Things" (#13), "Autumn of My Life" (#19), "Watching Scotty Grow" (#11), and "The Straight Life" (#36). –RC

○ **Best of Bobby Goldsboro - Honey / CAPITOL** 1991
A definitive 23-track collection of all the Bobby Goldsboro you'll ever need. –STE

GONG

Prog-rock. Avant-garde jazz-rock group originally fronted by Daevid Allen, former member of Soft Machine. The original lineup released a trilogy of trippy, whimsical albums in the late 60s-early 70s, centered around mythological tales on the planet Gong. Several personnel changes saw a shift in the band's direction, most notable when guitarist Allan Holdsworth joined their ranks. Gong released quirky, highly stylized concept albums into the early 80s. –CK

Camembert Electrique / CAROLINE 1971
An early Gong phase with Daevid Allen. A bit wacky, but a lot wonderful. –MGN

○ **Expresso / COL-VIRGIN** 1976
A studio album of excellent instrumental jazz/rock from percussionist Pierre Moerlen's band, featuring guitarist Allan Holdsworth's fluid guitar. –MGN

Gong Est Morte, Vive Gong / TAPIOCA 1977
Recorded live at the Hippodrome in Paris. Wildly eclectic, with Daevid Allen. –MGN

● **Live Etc / CAROLINE** 1977
A live 2-fer of wild acid-tinged music from 1973-1975 concerts, with Daevid Allen, Steve Hillage, and Tom Blake. An essential album. –MGN

Expresso II / CAROLINE 1978
French/German instrumentalists. Includes guitarist Allan Holdsworth and percussionist Pierre Moerlen. Very attractive music. –MGN

ROSCOE GORDON   b1934

R&B. Memphis pianist Gordon recorded prolifically in the 50s for Sun, Duke, Chess, and RPM. He is best remembered for his role in the Beale Streeters, who also included Bobby Bland and Johnny Ace. –JF

Best of Roscoe Gordon - Vol. 1 / ACE 1980
Primitive early-50s Memphis-recorded tracks. Originally issued on the RPM label. (Import) –HD

Keep On Doggin' / MR.R&B 1981
A scholarly compilation of Roscoe's singles from his early-50s R&B to mid-60s soul. (Import) –HD

No More Doggin' / CHARLY 1983
Roscoe's early-60s sides for the Vee Jay label. (Import) –HD

○ **Let's Get High / CHARLY** 1990
Sensational Memphis R&B by this Sun alumnus. 50s recordings of this rhythmic piano-led combo. (Import) –HD

LESLEY GORE   b1946

Rock/pop. Her strident teenage-slanted tunes made Lesley Gore one of the biggest pop stars of the mid 60s. Born in New York City and raised in New Jersey, Gore was discovered by jazz-great Quincy Jones, then a producer at Mercury Records. Her tear-stained "It's My Party" and revengeful "Judy's Turn to Cry" charged along over buoyant beats and proved giant hits in 1963. The change-of-pace ballad "You Don't Own Me" was another smash the same year, but Gore's forte was relentlessly upbeat material such as the impossibly giddy "Sunshine, Lollipops and Rainbows" in 1965. –BD

○ **Anthology / RHINO**
Superlative compilation of Leslie's best sides, including "It's My Party," "Judy's Turn to Cry," and "You Don't Own Me." –CK

GRACE POOL

Alternative pop, folk/rock. A New York-based melodic folk-rock quintet founded in 1983 by singer Elly Brown (b ca. 1960) and guitarist Bob Riley (b ca. 1955). –WR

○ **Grace Pool / REPRISE** 1988
Synthesizers and guitars are mixed to provide a catchy musical bed for the ethereal singing of Elly Brown on a series of well-constructed pop songs. –WR

LOU GRAMM   b1950

Rock/pop. Lou Gramm was the powerful lead singer for the mainstream hard-rock group Foreigner. During his solo career, Gramm has found continuing success with conservative power ballads like "Midnight Blue" (#10). –RC

○ **Ready or Not / ATLANTIC** 1987
Top-notch vocals propel these Foreigner-reminiscent rockers, including the hits "Midnight Blue" and "Ready or Not." –DDC

GRAND FUNK RAILROAD

Hard rock, rock/pop. In spite of the fact that Grand Funk Railroad was almost universally reviled by the critical community, FM rock radio and millions of hard-rock fans couldn't get enough. Conceived as a trio in 1968, Grand Funk got signed by Capitol after the label caught them live at the 1969 Atlanta Pop Festival. Unlike Cream or the Jimi Hendrix Experience, Grand Funk dispensed with wild interplay and focused on good-time boogie grooves and no-nonsense workmanlike arrangements. Their first album, *On Time* (#27), featuring Mark Farner's earnestly untrained tenor and buzz-saw guitar, Mel Schacher's buffalo-fart bass, and Don Brewer's bashola drumming, was an immediate hit.
The self-titled followup (#11) stripped down the band's sound to utter basics, but the third effort, *Closer to Home* (#6), showed the band utilizing strings and sound effects to widen their sound. By 1970 the band had sold more albums than any other American band. They broke the Beatles' record at Shea Stadium in 1971.
The band became a four-piece in 1973, and Todd Rundgren produced the hit albums *We're an American Band* (#2) and *Shinin' On* (#5). The Jimmy Ienner-produced *All the Girls in the World Beware!!!* (#10) continued their winning streak. Subsequent releases did progressively worse, and the band formally disbanded in 1983. –RC

More of the Best / RHINO 1991
This set does a decent job of picking key tracks not found on the *Capitol Collectors Series.* Included is the fuzz bass heavy "Paranoid" and boogie numbers like "Are You Ready" and "Got This Thing on the Move." Fans may wish for a more incisive selection from their first three albums. –RC

○ **Capitol Collectors Series / CAPITOL** 1991
Of the albums available on CD, this is the place to start. All of Grand Funk's hits are here: the classic "We're an American Band," Todd Rundgren's perverse production of "Loco-Motion," their thudding remake of the Animals's "Inside Looking Out," the epic "Closer to Home/I'm Your Captain," "Heartbreaker," and other big favorites. –RC

EDDY GRANT   b1948

Rock/pop. Grant was a member of the London group the Equals during the 60s; after they broke up, he established Coach House Studios in London in 1973 and founded the Ice Records label in 1974. He made records throughout the late 70s, gaining a following in the UK. In 1982 he hit big with "Electric Avenue" in the US. While Grant has not been able to repeat the success of "Electric Avenue" in the US, he remains a large figure in other countries. –STE

Walking on Sunshine / EPIC 1979
The title cut was a monster hit, while "Living on the Frontline" and "The Frontline Symphony" were also gems. –RW

○ **Killer on the Rampage / CBS / BB 10** 1983
In his Barbados recording studio, Eddy Grant doesn't play reggae music so much as dance-oriented music with thoughtful lyrics. His big US hit, "Electric Avenue," had a new-wave beat and a message about poverty. The rest of his album is also toe-tapping and timely. –WR

Barefoot Soldier / CAPITOL 1990
The popular term by the 90s is "world music," which is as good as any for Grant's bouyant sound, matched to the tough anti-apartheid message of the album's hit "Gimme Hope Jo'anna." –WR

GRASS ROOTS

Roots-rock, Rock/pop. A Top 40 band with folk/rock and light soul influences, looked down on as a largely faceless studio-spawned ensemble created by the songwriting/production team of Steve Barri and P. F. Sloane. But their sound was powerful as well as marketable, and their best song, "Let's Live for Today," contains the roots of Bruce Springsteen's sound and image. –BE

○ **Anthology - 1965-1975 / RHINO** 1991
A 2-CD set that contains "Midnight Confessions," "Let's Live for Today," and more. Extraordinary sound and brilliantly annotated. –BE

THE GRATEFUL DEAD

Psychedelic, country rock. The Grateful Dead are the longest-lived of the San Francisco "acid rock" groups of the 60s. In the 90s, after more than 25 years in action, the Dead were still playing to enough satisfied customers on the road (most of them "Dead heads") to make them one of the top-grossing concert acts in the music business.
The group was formed in 1965 by bluegrass enthusiast Jerry Garcia (b Aug 12, 1942) on guitar and vocals, Ron "Pigpen" McKernan (b Sep 8, 1945 - d Mar 8, 1973) on vocals and organ, Bob Weir (b Oct 16, 1947) on guitar and vocals, classical music student Phil Lesh (b Mar, 15, 1945) on bass and vocals, and Bill Kreutzmann (b Apr 7, 1946) on drums. From the beginning, they brought together a variety of influences, from Garcia's country background to Pigpen's feeling for blues (his father was an R&B radio DJ) and Lesh's education in contemporary "serious" music. Add to that the experimentation encouraged at some of the group's first performances at novelist Ken Kesey's "acid test" parties — multimedia events intended to replicate (or accompany) the experience of taking the then-legal drug LSD — and you had a musical mixture of styles often played with extended improvisational sections that could go off in nearly any direction.
They signed with Warner Brothers in 1967, experiencing some difficulties early on with the restrictions of standard recording practices and the company's interest in producing a conventionally commercial product. As a result, the group's first few albums were somewhat tentative but showed promise for the future, especially with the key additions of Mickey Hart as a second drummer in 1967 and Garcia's old friend Robert Hunter as the band's lyricist.
The Dead finally hit their stride with the release of *Live/Dead*, a double album, in 1969. (They were always more comfortable on stage than in the studio.) Two studio albums in 1970, *Workingman's Dead* and *American Beauty*, found them exploring folk/rock and more tightly constructed song forms and, along with extensive touring, won them a much larger audience.
The second half of the 70s found the Dead recording a series of commercially oriented albums for Arista, then concentrating on road work for the better part of the 80s. *In the Dark*, released in 1987, was their first studio album in seven years. It sold a million copies and produced the band's first Top Ten hit in "Touch of Grey." The Dead continued to tour, notably doing shows with Bob Dylan, and at the start of the 90s, they began to release vintage material on their own Grateful Dead Merchandising label. –WR

☆ **Live/Dead / WARNER** 1969
Long, trancelike songs with allusive lyrics (such as the classic "Dark Star") and R&B workouts featuring Pigpen's bluesy voice characterize this album, which is the basic document in the early Dead catalog — it's what most fans would like them to sound like every night. –WR

☆ **Workingman's Dead / WARNER** 1970
A folk/rock, tightly arranged Dead, singing (in harmony!) some of their best songs from "Uncle John's Band" to "Casey Jones." –WR

★ **American Beauty / WARNER** 1970
Workingman's Dead, part 2 - more of the songs that have served as the band's basic repertoire ever since these albums were released. Includes "Box of Rain," "Friend of the Devil," "Sugar Magnolia," "Ripple," and, of course, "Truckin'." –WR

Terrapin Station / ARISTA 1977
The best of the early Arista albums, containing the extended "Terrapin Station" suite. –WR

In the Dark / ARISTA 1987
The comeback, with "Touch of Grey," "West L.A. Fadeaway," and "Black Muddy River." For anyone who wondered how these old hippies could have such a following 20 years after the hippies disappeared, here's the answer. –WR

DOBIE GRAY b 1943

R&B, rock/pop. Journeyman soul singer, composer, and actor Gray has had a checkered career, scoring hit records in two different decades, acting on Broadway, and appearing in the Los Angeles production of *Hair*. –CK

○ **In Crowders / COLLECTABLES** 1965
Uptown soul from the mid 60s. Gray's commanding baritone delivery is well showcased. –BD

AL GREEN b 1946

R&B, soul. Born in 1946 in Forest City, AR, and growing up in Grand Rapids, MI, Al Green became the premier soul singer in the 70s, in the process being the last great purveyor of a music whose time had come and gone. When he was thirteen, Green started singing with a family gospel group, the Greene Brothers. By 1967 he was singing secular and solo, scoring a #5 R&B/#41 pop hit with "Back Up Train" on the Hot Line Music Journal label. Touring the chitlin circuit on the strength of the record, Green found himself playing the same bill in Midland, TX, as Memphis trumpeter and producer Willie Mitchell. Mitchell signed Green to Memphis's Hi Records, and, as they say, the rest is history.
Between 1970 and 1977, Green placed 23 records on the R&B charts and 18 on the pop charts, including seven Top Tens. The Green/Mitchell/Hi rhythm-section sound was incredibly consistent, making most of the albums listed below somewhat interchangeable. The records are ultra cool; there is little overt sweat. Green's phrases are disjointed, generally behind the beat, always surprising. At regular intervals he dips into his unreal falsetto. Soft girl backup singing is employed, as is a string orchestra. Drummers Al Jackson and Howard Grimes eschew the cymbals, replacing them with a ride pattern on the tom-toms. All of this is executed in the context of compositions by Mitchell, Green, Jackson, and guitarist Teenie Hodges such as "Love and Happiness," "Take Me to the River," "Let's Stay Together," and "Tired of Being Alone." Green became "born again" in 1976, splitting from Mitchell a year later and electing to record gospel music only for most of the next decade and a half. In 1985 he reunited with Mitchell for the album *He Is the Light*. –RB

○ **I'm Still in Love with You / MOTOWN / BB 4** 1972
Album #3 sees Green exploring country soul with an achingly beautiful take on Kris Kristofferson's "For the Good Times." The hits were the title song and "Look What You Done for Me." –RB

○ **Let's Stay Together / MOTOWN** 1972
Green's second album for Hi and the first of a string of brilliant releases. The title song was the big hit but an extended version of the Bee Gees's "How Can You Mend a Broken Heart" remained a staple for years. –RB

○ **Call Me / MOTOWN / BB 10** 1973
Three R&B Top Ten hits; the title song, "Here I Am (Come and Take Me)," and "You Ought to Be with Me" dominate what is probably his finest album. Once again he tackles some country-soul, turning in moving versions of Hank Williams's "I'm So Lonesome I Could Cry" and Willie Nelson's "Funny How Time Slips Away." Green also returns to the gospel vein on "Jesus Is Waiting." –RB

Livin' for You / MOTOWN / BB 24 1973
A cut below the albums listed above, *Livin' for You* is still mighty fine. The title cut and "Let's Get Married" were both Top Ten R&B hits. –RB

Al Green Explores Your Mind / MOTOWN / BB 15 1974
Only one hit single this time out with "Sha-La-La (Make Me

Happy)." *Explores Your Mind* also contains what may have become Green's best-known song, "Take Me to the River." –RB

★ **Greatest Hits - Vol. 1 / MOTOWN / BB 17**   1974
The title says it all, ten songs that define Southern soul in the mid 70s. –RB

○ **Love Ritual / MCA**   1974
Don't let the title lead you into thinking that these are second-rate leftovers, because this album *Love Ritual: Rare & Previously Unreleased 1968-1976* (originally compiled for the British Demon label) is loaded with gems. Highlights are hard to pin down, but one surprise is a spirited version of the Beatles's "I Want to Hold Your Hand;" it should've been a single. Every track except "Ride Sally Ride" has been digitally remixed from the original multi-tracks. The sound is great, being faithful to the spirit of Willie Mitchell's production and mixing style, and the disc includes detailed liner notes. All in all, Green fans should pick up on this. –RC

Is Love / MOTOWN / BB 28   1975
Two more Top Ten hits with "L-O-V-E (Love)" and "Oh Me, Oh My (Dream's in My Arms)." –RB

☆ **Greatest Hits - Vol. 2 / MOTOWN / BB 134**   1977
As good as *Volume 1*, augmented by non-chart items that might have been hits anyway, like "Love and Happiness," "Take Me to the River," and "For the Good Times." –RB

○ **The Lord Will Make a Way / HI**   1980
One of my favorite gospel albums by Rev. Green. The R&B and pop hits were stopped coming but the sacred peaks were the equal of any of his secular material. In 1992 Green was still performing the title song and "In the Holy Name of Jesus." –RB

○ **Higher Plane / HI**   1981
Another superior sacred recording, most notable for a stellar version of the Impressions' "People Get Ready." –RB

○ **He Is the Light / A&M**   1985
At the time of writing, this was Green's last truly great recording. Back with Willie Mitchell, the Hi rhythm section, and the Memphis Horns, Green has great material and delivers the goods. –RB

One in a Million / CBS   1990
Some of his best gospel moments. –BC

GREEN ON RED

Alternative rock. A California band with a shifting lineup anchored by singer/songwriter and guitarist Dan Stuart, Green on Red evolved from the neo-psychedelic "paisley underground" band of the early 80s to a country-rock duo by the decade's end. –WR

○ **This Time Around / POLYGRAM**   1989
The tight production of Glyn Johns keeps things from getting too sloppy in these barroom ballads and raveups that mix country, folk, and rock, all keyed to Dan Stuart's appealing voice and desperate lyrics. –WR

VERNON GREEN & THE MEDALLIONS

R&B, doo-wop. The Medallions, a Los Angeles doo-wop quartet with a predilection toward songs about speedy cars, formed in 1953. Their first single, "The Letter"/"Buick '59," on the Dootsie Williams Dootone label, was a regional hit, coupling a dreamy ballad with a joyriding rocker complete with automotive sound effects by the group. (Encores in the same vein included "Speedin'," "Pushbutton Automobile," and "Coupe DeVille Baby;" there was even a "'59 Volvo"!). –BD

○ **Golden Classics / COLLECTABLES**
This Los Angeles doo-wop aggregation specialized in "rocking car songs" during the mid 50s. –BD

CLIVE GREGSON & CHRISTINE COLLISTER

Singer/songwriter, folk/rock. Clive Gregson and Christine Collister were the most moving UK folk/rock duo to emerge since Richard and Linda Thompson. Gregson (b Jan 4, 1955) was the founder of Any Trouble, a rock quartet, in Manchester

in 1975. The band's sound, and Gregson's songwriting and singing, reminded some of Elvis Costello, and Any Trouble was signed by Stiff, Costello's label. The band made several well-remembered but poor-selling albums, then split up. Gregson made a solo album, *Strange Persuasions*, in 1985, then hooked up with Collister. Gregson first introduced Collister into Richard Thompson's band (Gregson was backup guitarist at the time), then they began performing as a duo. Their songs, all written by Gregson, are wry tales of the ins and outs of love, sung in Collister's heartbreaking voice. –WR

○ **Mischief / RHINO**   1988
Clive Gregson's songs treat romance with ironic charm: "We're Not Over Yet" is a compendium of reasons why they ought to be over, and "Everybody Cheats on You" is about more than just romantic infidelity. Christine Collister gives the songs a depth that often keeps them from being a bit too glib and clever, as do the folk-pop arrangements. –WR

A Change in the Weather / RHINO   1990
The self-insight continues in Gregson's lyrics, but the concerns are expanded. Collister does a fine job covering "Tryin' to Get to You." –WR

JOE GRUSHECKY & HOUSEROCKERS

Rock & roll. When Pittsburgh-based Joe Grushecky's band the Iron City Houserockers turned up on MCA Records in 1979, their driving bar-band rock & roll and working-class lyrics earned them critical kudos but also made them Johnny-come-latelies in a crowded field headed by Bruce Springsteen and including Bob Seger, John Cafferty, and John Mellencamp. Nevertheless, they managed to release four albums through 1983. –WR

○ **Rock & Real / ROUNDER**   1989
Grushecky's songs of tough urban life are made all the more compelling by his rough voice and the aggressive playing of his band, though he can also turn tender on such songs as "Daddy's Little Angel." –WR

GRYPHON

Art-rock. An English all-instrumental electric folk band, originally similar to Pentangle in their electricism (and, not coincidentally, signed to the same label, Transatlantic). They subsequently developed a more intense playing style and went electric, eventually hooking up with Yes for one US tour. Wind player Richard Harvey, who was classically trained and had a parallel career in movie music, was one of the more notable members, while Ernest Hart's rippling keyboards and guitarist Graeme Taylor's classically wrought elegance were key elements of the band's sound. –BE

○ **Red Queen to Gryphon Three / ARISTA**   1974
Apocalyptic electric folk/rock, utilizing traditional melodies pumped up and with heavily amplified organ and synthesizer and highly animated recorder and flute. The effect is rather Yes-like, sans vocals. This album achieves a *Close to the Edge*-style finale with the track "Checkmate." –BE

THE GTO'S

Rock/pop. The GTO's were a "groupie group" made up of young women familiar to musicians in the Los Angeles area. Most prominent among them was Miss Pamela who, as Pamela Des Barres, wrote the kiss-and-tell memoir *I'm with the Band*. –WR

○ **Permanent Damage / ERATO**   1969
Frank Zappa produced this combination of light pop songs and involved discussions of the ups and downs of groupie life. It's a sort of musical comedy documentary on record and, without doubt, unique. –WR

THE GUESS WHO

Rock/pop. A Winnipeg, Canada, band called Chad Allen & the Reflections (formed 1962) enjoyed some success with a couple of regional 1963 hits ("Tribute to Buddy Holly," "Shy Guy") but quickly shifted over to the new British Merseybeat style and recorded a version of Johnny Kidd & the Pirates's "Shakin' All Over." The song became a #1 Canadian hit. As a publicity stunt, the record label (Quality) listed the artist as "Guess Who?," implying that it might be some big English act ghosting on the side. The ploy worked, and the American label Scepter picked them up, taking the record to #22. At the label's request, the Reflections changed their name to the Guess Who.

The band couldn't generate a followup hit, and it wasn't until 1968, when they met producer Jack Richardson, that things began looking up. Richardson mortgaged his house to help them record what became the album *Wheatfield Soul*. One of the tracks, "These Eyes," went to #6 Stateside, beginning a long string of excellent pop/rock hits.

1970 and 1971 were banner years for the Guess Who, with a pair of hit albums, *American Woman* (#9) and *Share the Land* (#14). During this time, they displayed a highly developed level of melodic skills. Burton Cummings had developed a compelling vocal style, and new lead guitarists Kurt Winter and Greg Leskiw forged out a distinctive sound. The band scored a few more hits before breaking up in 1975. Cummings went on to experience an uneven solo career after landing a million-selling #10 hit with his debut single, "Stand Tall." –RC

Canned Wheat / RCA   1975
The group's second album, and probably their best long-player, with a couple of hits surrounded by some lyrical, well-crafted album tracks. –BE

○ **Track Record / RCA**   1988
A perfect collection, covering the band's whole history on two CDs. Includes the hits "These Eyes" (#6), "Laughing" (#10), "Undun" (#22), "No Time" (#5), "American Woman/No Sugar Tonight" (#1), "Share the Land" (#10), and the noveltyish "Clap for the Wolfman" (#6). –BE

GUN CLUB

Rock & roll. Los Angeles group led by Jeffrey Lee Pierce picked up on the Cramps's rockabilly fetish, added some blues and John Fogarty stylings, and crafted a blistering 1981 debut ("Fire of Love"). –JF

○ **Fire of Love / WARNER**   1981
Jeffrey Lee Pierce's fusion of punk energy and blues-based themes is linked to (but also derivative of) the Cramps's punk/rockabilly springboard. Pierce's group never matched that band's manic intensity but *Fire of Love* is worthwhile listening for those interested in how the influence of John Fogerty filtered into punk. And with "Sex Beat" and "Jack on Fire," Pierce came up with two minor classics of early-80s West Coast rock. –JF

GUNBUNNIES

Anglo-pop. The Arkansas band Gunbunnies produce a literate, earthy blend of Anglo-pop and rock from the American South (as opposed to Southern rock). –RC

○ **Paw Paw Patch / VIRGIN**   1990
There are so many wonderful, smart Southern pop/rock songs on *Paw Paw Patch* that it's a shame this effort got lost in the cracks. Lead singer Chris Maxwell writes like Elvis Costello soaked with a healthy dose of indigenously flavored pragmatism. Jim Dickinson's (Big Star, the Replacements) subtle minimalist production is wonderfully musical and egoless, stepping out of the way for the band to breathe, yet adding little touches here and there that speak volumes. –RC

GUNS N' ROSES

Hard rock. Guns N' Roses emerged from the swamp of the hard-rock and heavy metal bands inhabiting LA during the mid 80s to become the most successful and influential hard-rock band of the 80s and early 90s. G N' R's rock & roll is hard Stones/Aerosmith guitar boogie played with honesty and a vicious punk spirit, and it often displays a surprising musical diversity. Axl Rose's vocals are unmistakable, varying from a

soft murmur to a harsh, grating roar; Slash and Izzy Stradlin's guitars complemented each other better than any guitar team since Keith Richards and Mick Taylor; the rhythm section of Duff "Rose" McKagan on bass and Steven Adler on drums provided the band with a loose swing. Formed from the splinters of various LA bands in 1985, G N' R played numerous gigs before releasing any recordings. Their hard work eventually led to the independent release of the *Live ?!&@ Like a Suicide* EP in 1986. Geffen signed the band after a bidding war between major labels.

The Guns N' Roses debut album, *Appetite for Destruction*, was released in August of 1987 to little notice. Supported with a solid year of touring (including opening for Aerosmith, where G N' R frequently blew their heroes off the stage), the album began to climb the charts in 1988, hitting #1 over a year after its release. (*Appetite* would eventually sell over five million copies.) In December of 1988 *G N' R Lies*, a combination of the earlier *Live* EP and four new recordings, was released. The four new songs, featuring country and blues musical themes centered around an acoustic guitar, were a departure from the brutal, fast rock of *Appetite*.

Sessions for the sequel to *Appetite* began in 1989 but were aborted, starting in earnest the next year. Adler was fired from the band in October of 1990 because of his sub-par performance on the new material and was replaced by Matt Sorum from the Cult. Keyboardist Dizzy Reed was added to the band during recording. In no time, the new album became *two* new albums, *Use Your Illusion I* and *II*, scheduled for release in spring of 1991. Recording for the *Illusions* dragged on throughout the year, pushing the release all the way back to September. The *Illusions*, essentially two halves of a double album (four albums' worth of material), debuted at #1 and #2, (*II* and *I*, respectively) and showed that the band had continued to grow musically. As Guns N' Roses prepared for a tour to support the albums, founding member Stradlin left the band in early 1992 amidst deep personal conflict. He was replaced by Gilby Clarke. –STE

☆ **Appetite for Destruction / GEFFEN**   1987
Aggressive, brash, and well-executed hard rockers and ballads that never stray from their chosen target. This major-label debut is one of the finest examples of late-80s hard rock. "Welcome to the Jungle," "Sweet Child O' Mine," and "Paradise City" were key tracks from this classic. –DDC & RC

★ **Use Your Illusion I / GEFFEN**   1991
Use Your Illusion I and *II* is full of the goods that made Classic Rock, namely classic, forceful band chemistry and an uncompromising spirit that approach staples like the Stones' *Exile on Main Street*, Led Zeppelin's *IV*, or Aerosmith's *Rocks*. These two separately (but simultaneously) released volumes were a neat sidestep from the indulgent double-album concept. Musically, the band has never sounded better or rawer. Lyrically, W. Axl Rose still spews out enough venom to offend half the planet, but you'd have to listen hard to catch it through the band-heavy sound mix. Nevertheless, Rose has seasoned his railings with some insights that the world around him isn't hopeless. In spite of his sloppy target shooting, his raw sentiments and delivery are bracing compared to the bulk of rock bands pounding the circuits. Highlights on volume 1 are "Right Next Door to Hell," "November Rain," "Perfect Crime," "You Ain't the First," and "Don't Cry." Volume 2's standout tracks are "Civil War," "You Could Be Mine," "Locomotive," "Breakdown," and "Pretty Tied Up." Of the two albums, the first one is the better choice, but fans of hard rock should get both. –RC

Use Your Illusion II / GEFFEN   1991
(See entry above.) –DDC

GUY

Urban R&B. By bringing the minimalist swagger of hip-hop into the arena of 80s-style funk and soul, Guy (led by *wünderkind* Teddy Riley) forged a new R&B sound that continues to dominate the genre. Riley has been one of the most respected and sought-after hitmakers of the last decade, producing records for everyone from Heavy D. to Michael Jackson. —JF

☆ **Guy / MCA** 1988
Their debut was a monster hit, yielding such hits as "Groove Me" and "Spend the Night." Essential for those wondering why contemporary R&B sounds like it does. —JF

STEVE HACKETT

Prog-rock. The former guitarist for Genesis has recorded many albums since 1975; he left the group in 1977. —ED

○ **Voyage of the Acolyte / CAROLINE** 1976
A stunning solo debut recorded while Hackett was still a member of Genesis. Features Phil Collins and Mike Rutherford. —MPD

Please Don't Touch! / CAROLINE 1978
Hackett's first post-Genesis album, featuring Richie Havens and Chester Thompson. —MPD

Spectral Mornings / CAROLINE 1979
A fine effort, featuring "Ballad of the Decomposing Man" and the title track. —MPD

Defector / CAROLINE 1980
A good followup to *Spectral Mornings*, including "Two Vamps as Guests" and "Hammer in the Sand." —MPD

BILL HALEY 1925-1981

Rock & roll. The Bill Haley and the Comets recording of "Rock around the Clock," which topped the charts for eight weeks in 1955, is remembered as the beginning of the rock era. Though it also represented Haley's peak as a performer, his career had begun some time before and would continue for a long time after.
Born in Michigan, Haley began leading Western-swing bands under various names in the late 40s, slowly starting to incorporate elements of R&B. Soon after he began recording for Essex in the early 50s, his backup band was called the Comets. He hit #15 in the charts in 1953 with "Crazy Man Crazy," a rock & roll song he'd written. Haley signed to Decca in 1954 and went to #12 with "Shake, Rattle and Roll." In 1955 Haley hit with "Dim, Dim the Lights," "Mambo Rock," and "Birth of the Boogie," but it was "Rock around the Clock," previously recorded and released as a B-side in 1954 and reissued as the theme song for the movie *Blackboard Jungle*, that became his biggest hit. At that time the band consisted of Haley on guitar and vocals, Danny Cedrone on lead guitar, Joey D'Ambrose on sax, Billy Williamson on steel guitar, Johnny Grande on piano, Marshall Lytle on bass, and Dick Richards on drums.
Following the success of "Rock around the Clock," Haley and the Comets placed nine more records in the Top 40 over the next three years, among them the Top Tens "Burn That Candle" and "See You Later, Alligator." Haley was largely eclipsed as the king of rock & roll by Elvis Presley and other flamboyant performers who followed him from 1956 on; nevertheless, he continued to perform overseas and in oldies shows in the US, and "Rock around the Clock" even got back into the Top 40 in 1974. —WR

○ **From the Original Master Tapes / MCA** 1985
The best-sounding Haley collection, but its 20 songs are probably ten more than anyone but the most hardcore fan needs. —BE

HALL & OATES

Rock/pop. Daryl Hall first recorded as a member of Kenny Gamble and the Romeos and later became a session man at Sigma studios in Philly. He also recorded one album with the rock group Gulliver. John Oates played with Gulliver too, and when it disbanded in 1972, Hall and Oates signed with Atlantic as a duo. Their biggest hits have (for the most part) been a blend of blue-eyed soul and dance-pop. They enjoyed their greatest success during the first half of the 80s. —RC

Voices / RCA 1980
This is the album that took Hall and Oates from being a successful 70s pop duo to being one of the four biggest singles acts of the 80s (the others: Michael Jackson, Prince, and Madonna). The sound is a wonderful pop pastiche, from the Beatlesque "How Does it Feel to Be Back" to the neo-Philadelphia soul of the hits "Kiss on My List" and "You Make My Dreams." (Also available on Mobile Fidelity.) —WR

Private Eyes / RCA 1981
More bouncy, soulful rock & roll, led by the #1 hits "Private Eyes" and "I Can't Go for That (No Can Do)." —WR

H2O / RCA 1982
From the Motown beat of "Maneater" to the lush ballad "One on One," Hall & Oates continue to make the top pop of the early 80s. Also contains "Family Man." —WR

○ **Rock 'n' Soul Part 1 - Greatest Hits / RCA** 1983
The best of Hall and Oates, 1974 to 1983, including their biggest 70s hits, "She's Gone," "Sara Smile," and "Rich Girl," plus the 80s chart-toppers and two new hits: "Say It Isn't So" and "Adult Education." —WR

Big Bam Boom / RCA 1984
This ast of the major Hall & Oates albums of the 80s features more of their patented soul-rock sound on the hits "Out of Touch" and "Method of Modern Love." —WR

HALO OF FLIES

Alternative rock. Destructo, psycho-grunge from Minneapolis with big fuzzed-up guitars. —JD

○ **Amphetamine Reptile / AMPHETAMINE REPTILE**
The ultimate CD anthology. A veritable grunge-rock orgy! —JD

STUART HAMM

Fusion. Bassist Hamm has performed with Steve Vai and Joe Satriani. He currently leads his own band performing rock-fusion material. —PK

○ **Radio Free Albemuth / RELATIVITY** 1988
A great mix of musical styles on this debut. Bass players, check this one out! —PK

Kings of Sleep / RELATIVITY 1989
Album of great instrumental rock material with bass guitar in the spotlight. —PK

Urge / RELATIVITY 1991
This release of intrumental and vocal tracks features a mixture of rock, funk, and rap. With guest guitarist Eric Johnson. —PK

PETER HAMMILL

Prog-rock. Hammill's work as the leader of English prog-rockers Van Der Graaf Generator was always notable for its heavy moods and raw emotion. His solo work is even more intense, whether he's delivering a lump-in-the-throat ballad, railing with fury and scorn, or indulging his habit of using the studio as a combination confessional and psychiatric couch. Hammill's lyrics are always incomparably literate, passionate, and thought-provoking; his music is equally so. —MPD

○ **The Future Now / CAROLINE** 1978
Premier rock with ethnic rhythms. Frustration turns into high art. The title cut, "Energy Vampires," and "Mediaeval" are particularly earthshaking. All originals. —MGN

Vision / IMPORT 1978
Compilation of recordings from 1971-1975. Includes the campy "Imperial Zeppelin" and "Nadir's Big Chance," top early-period Hammill. —MGN

PH 7 / CAROLINE 1979
Excellent followup. "Handicap and Equality" and "Factory X" easily rank with his best. Hamill is unique. —MGN

COL. BRUCE HAMPTON

Alternative rock, southern rock. Equal parts psychedelicized

Allman Brothers and boogiefied Grateful Dead (with a dash of Commander Cody thrown in), Col. Bruce Hampton and the Aquarium Rescue Unit have capitalized on the nuevo-hippie movement that's been sweeping the country. The Atlanta-born Hampton has been kicking around the Southern music circuit since the early 60s; as the Hampton Grease Band, he released *Music to Eat* in 1969. After 70s-era stints in the New Ice Age and the Late Bronze Age, Hampton formed the AQR, an eclectic congregation that's adept at everything from country-swing jazz to meltdown Southern boogie and over-amped gospel bluegrass. −JF

○ **Arkansas / LANDSLIDE**   1984
This "Southern Captain Beefheart" misses, but this Colonel (Ret.) is original. −RG

THE HAPPY MONDAYS

Alternative pop. The Happy Mondays, formed in 1981, stand at the vanguard of the late-80s/early-90s Manchester scene, which featured British psychedelicized dance music. Driven by the lyrics of vocalist Shaun Ryder, the band successfully combines funk, psychedelic sounds, and 70s Labelle-like soul. −DS

○ **Bummed / ELEKTRA**   1988
The second album by the band, *Bummed*, established the group as premier dance rockers and helped publicize the Manchester scene internationally. −DS

HAPPY THE MAN

Art-rock. Happy the Man, originating from the Washington, DC/Maryland region, created an art-rock style during the late 70s and early 80s that featured the atmospheric synthesizer work of Kit Watkins. They were primarily an instrumental band. Their first two albums were produced by Ken Scott, whose credits included David Bowie and Dixie Dregs. −RC

○ **Retrospective / EAST SIDE DIGIT**
A collection of spirited progressive rock by America's answer to Gentle Giant. −MPD

JOHN WESLEY HARDING

Alternative rock. This modern-day folk-rocker with a sense of humor has his roots in the music of Bob Dylan, Phil Ochs, and others. −BC

○ **It Happened One Night / RHINO**   1988
Harding's debut, recorded live. Album includes "Headful of Something" and "The Night He Took Her to the Fairground." −BC

Here Comes the Groom / WARNER   1989
Harding's second album presents him at his cantankerous best. −DH

ROY HARPER   ♭1941

Folk/rock, blues/rock. Harper came out of the UK in the mid-60s folk boom in the wake of Bob Dylan's success with songs filled with poetic insight and anger. Guest appearances on his albums over the years by the cream of British Rock (including Jimmy Page, Ian Anderson, Bill Bruford, and Paul McCartney) should have given Harper a larger following, but he has never translated the admiration of his contemporaries into anything beyond cult status. Led Zeppelin's "Hats Off to Harper" was dedicated to Roy. −CK

Come Out Fighting Ghengis Smith / CBS   1967
From Harper's early period. Conservative compared to his later work, but no less vital. −MGN

Lifemask / EMI-HARVEST   1973
Album with Jimmy Page. Side 1 has five tracks; side 2 includes "The Lord's Prayer" suite. −MGN

○ **Flashes from ... / EMI-HARVEST**   1974
Flashes from the Archives of Oblivion. 14 tracks recorded at various concerts in England. Some of his most influential work. An obscene cover photo. −MGN

Valentine / EMI-HARVEST   1974
Includes "Male Chauvinist Pig Blues" and "Magic Woman (Liberation Reshuffle)," which is dedicated to Harper's mates in Led Zeppelin. −MGN

When an Old Cricketer Leaves ... / CHRYSALIS   1975
When an Old Cricketer Leaves the Crease is a premiere American release. Seven cuts written by Harper. Band mates include Bill Bruford and Chris Spedding. This is arresting folk/rock. −MGN

WEE WILLIE HARRIS

Rock & roll. In the first wave of rock & roll, England could only offer pale Elvis imitations or ancient pop singers masquerading as such. One exception to the rule was Wee Willie Harris. Dying his hair all manner of colors and wearing larger-than-life stage jackets that looked like the coat hanger was still inside, tight drainpipe trousers, and a huge polka-dot bow tie, Harris understandably stood out from the rest of the pack. Coming from the Three I's coffeehouse circuit in Soho, Harris had a love for hard American rock & roll and an ability to perform it with unrelenting energy that kept him actively performing and recording from the mid 50s onward, working everything from nostalgia packages to cruise ships across the Atlantic — anyplace where his humorous and dynamic stage show could have a forum. −CK

○ **Wee Willie Harris / SEE-FOR-MILES**
The best account of this singularly British phenomenon. (Import) −BE

GEORGE HARRISON   ♭1943

Rock/pop. As lead guitarist for the Beatles, George Harrison provided the band with a lyrical style of playing in which every note really mattered. Unlike Clapton, or many of his other English guitar peers, Harrison's style that wasn't steeped in American blues but often delivered a very real soulfulness. Harrison also developed a uniquely silky slide guitar sound during his last Beatles days.

Harrison has always been a rather weak singer, but as a songwriter he wrote some classics, both as a Beatle and as a solo artist. His greatest moment of artistic triumph was the triple album *All Things Must Pass* (#1), which Harrison coproduced with the legendary Phil Spector. Both that album and the single "My Sweet Lord" gave Harrison the distinction of being the first Beatle to top the charts after their breakup. In 1971 Bright Songs, publisher of the Chiffons hit "He's So Fine," sued Harrison for plagiarism and won. More hits followed, but Harrison's albums increasingly sounded like afterthoughts. The 1979 album *George Harrison* (#14) and 1987's comeback *Cloud Nine* (#10) were worthwhile exceptions.

In 1988 Harrison, Bob Dylan, Tom Petty, Jeff Lynne, and Roy Orbison formed the Traveling Wilburys, who have since released two very successful albums. −RC

○ **All Things Must Pass / CAPITOL**   1970
An exquisitely produced album, encompassing rock, mysticism, blues, and folk music under one cover. Every note is memorable. −BE

Concert for Bangladesh / CAPITOL   1972
A unique live document showcasing Harrison near his best, with ex-Beatle Ringo Starr, Eric Clapton, and many other superstars. It has less-than-perfect sound but overall fine re-creations of his best work, with work by Bob Dylan as an added bonus. −BE

The Best of George Harrison / CAPITOL   1976
The Harrison material is matched with some Beatles numbers in a good but routine collection. −BE

Cloud Nine / WARNER   1987
A great collection of bright, hard-rocking numbers, even embracing gospel. −BE

Best of Dark Horse 1976-1989 / WARNER   1989
The best of a less-than-satisfying era. The only way to take it in. −BE

WILBERT HARRISON   ♭1929

R&B, rock & roll. Harrison cut the classic version of "Kansas City" in 1959. The Charlotte, NC, native's laconic vocal style first turned up on Henry Stone's Rockin' label in 1952, and he progressed to Deluxe, Chart, and Savoy before landing on Bobby Robinson's Fury imprint in 1959. With Jimmy Spruill wildly wringing out slashing bent notes on his guitar, Harrison's rocking revival of the Jerry Leiber/Mike Stoller classic "Kansas City" (first cut by Little Willie Littlefield in 1952) topped both the pop and R&B charts. Subsequent Fury 45s (including the sequel "Goodbye Kansas City") undeservedly bombed, and Harrison plied his trade for a time as a one-man band. But he wasn't through — "Let's Work Together," a slight rewrite of his Fury-era "Let's Stick Together," vaulted up the charts in 1970 after being recut for Sue. Like his other best-seller, "Let's Work Together" was prime cover material — for the likes of Canned Heat and Bob Dylan. And once again, he was unable to follow it up with anything of equal potency. –BD

Kansas City / RELIC   1965
Harrison's toughest late-50s/early-60s output for Fury Records, many in stereo for the first time. –BD

○ **Greatest Classic R&B Hits / RCA-GRUDGE**   1989
The only available CD for Harrison's late-60s material, long after his 1959 classic "Kansas City." –BD

DEBBIE HARRY   ♭1945

Pop, dance-pop. Singer/actress who was the lead vocalist in the new-wave group Blondie, 1974-1982. Harry launched a solo singing career in 1981, as well as acting on stage and film, but she retired in 1983 to nurse seriously ill companion (and Blondie guitarist) Chris Stein. Stein recovered, and Harry returned to action in 1985. –WR

Kookoo / CHRYSALIS   1981
Harry teams up with Chic for bass-heavy dance rock, notably on the hit "Backfired." –WR

Rockbird / GEFFEN   1986
A return to the trashy, bubblegum-rock style of early Blondie, featuring the hit "French Kissin'." –WR

○ **Once More into the Bleach / CHRYSALIS**   1988
A compilation disc containing Blondie and Debbie Harry solo hits in remixed, extended dance versions. –WR

GRANT HART

Alternative rock. Grant Hart was co-lead singer, songwriter, and drummer for the critically lauded punk-rock group Hüsker Dü from 1981 to 1987. He launched a solo career in 1988 and, in 1989, formed the group Nova Mob. –WR

○ **Intolerance / SST**   1989
A one-man-band album of driving (but not punk) rock, much of it sounding Dylanesque. Many of its lyrics seem to refer to the acrimonious breakup of Hart's old group. –WR

ANNIE HASLAM

Art-rock. Former lead singer of Renaissance, with a three-octave vocal range and a penchant for art-rock. –ED

○ **Annie Haslam / CBS**
A hauntingly beautiful and personal collection that borders on art song rather than art-rock. Gorgeous musical texture and dazzling performances from this singer. –BE

DONNY HATHAWAY   1945-1979

Soul, R&B. Smooth, velvety-voiced crooner Hathaway played with the Ric Powell Jazz Trio and did session work with Stax and others before joining Atlantic as a solo artist in 1970. –BC

○ **Best of Donny Hathaway / ATCO**   1984
A hits compilation including "The Ghetto" and "Givin' Up Your Love Is Like (Givin' Up the World)," as well as the hit duets with Roberta Flack "Where Is the Love" and "You've Got a Friend." –BC

RONNIE HAWKINS & HAWKS   ♭1935

Rockabilly, rock & roll. A rockabilly singer who formed the original backing band, the Hawks, while attending the University of Arkansas. After auditioning unsuccessfully for Sun in 1957, he started working regularly in Canada the following year, eventually taking up permanent residence there. After one release on the Canadian Quality label, he signed with Roulette in New York in 1959, having hits with "Forty Days" and "Mary Lou." The live fervor of Hawkins (known as "Mr. Dynamo") & the Hawks's show continued in Canada after all the original members except Levon Helm headed back to the US. Hawkins quickly hired Canadian players Robbie Robertson, Garth Hudson, Rick Danko, and Richard Manuel as the new Hawks. They stayed with him until 1963, but later became Bob Dylan's backing group and went on to a career of their own as the Band. Hawkins has remained a legend in Canada, recording unrepentant rockabilly sides and gigging constantly. He's still the original Mr. Dynamo, capable of shaking the walls down any old time he feels like it. –CK

○ **The Best of Ronnie Hawkins & His Band / RHINO**
A good overview of the Hawks's best sides. –CK

SCREAMIN' JAY HAWKINS   ♭1929

R&B. Though capable of more conventional blues, sentimental ballads, and R&B, Screamin' Jay Hawkins will be forever remembered for the wild songs and onstage theatrics of his self-created brand of voodoo jive. His act has often featured him emerging from a casket to sing his best-known hit, "I Put a Spell on You." Other novelties, ranging from "Feast of the Mau Mau" to "Constipation Blues," may have stereotyped his talent, but on the other hand, his idiosyncracies have brought him TV and movie appearances that would have eluded him had he played his music straight. Regardless of style, Hawkins's recordings still display a remarkable voice, which would have been used for opera had Screamin' Jay had his way. –JON

Cow Fingers & Mosquito Pie / CBS
Surreal R&B (including "I Put a Spell on You") from the 50s, delivered with Robesonian pipes. –MH

○ **Voodoo Jive: Best Of / RHINO**
50s and 60s sides, including labels other than Okeh. –MH

HAWKWIND

Art-rock. British acid-rockers who have as much responsibility as Pink Floyd for having created the genre. –DMAC

○ **In Search of Space / ONE WAY**   1971
Psychedelic rangers from England go one up on Pink Floyd and Tangerine Dream, and maybe Sun Ra too. Their best studio date. –MGN

Hawkwind / UNITED ARTISTS   1975
Includes their best-known hit, "Silver Machine." –MGN

ISAAC HAYES   ♭1942

Soul, R&B, funk. From the tough urgency of the Stax studio (for whom he was a prolific writer and arranger), Isaac Hayes went on to develop an overwrought style that utilized the potential of the album. To that point, most R&B and soul albums had been a mixture of two-and-a-half minute singles and filler. Hayes concocted mini-symphonies of extraordinary length, which, allied with his visual presence (shaved head, designer African clothes, shades, and bizarre jewelry), made him more than a musician: he became an instantly recognizable cultural icon in early-70s Black music. One album title, *Black Moses*, was probably Hayes's own succinct self-appraisal. Some might argue that his legacy is better represented by his workaday compositions and his arrangements, which include Sam & Dave's immortal "Soul Man" and "Hold On, I'm Coming." –CE

Best of Isaac Hayes / ENTERPRISE   1975
A deep voice and an impeccable sense of the groove add up to some of the best R&B music of the early 70s. −WR

○ **Best of Vol. 1 / STAX**   1986
Best of Vol. 2 / STAX   1986
These two compilations dutifully boil down Isaac Hayes's sometimes long-winded albums to their essential parts — in other words, they're both singles collections, highlighted by 70s landmarks such as "Theme from *Shaft*" and "By the Time I Get to Phoenix." Fanatics may want to investigate *Hot Buttered Soul* and *Black Moses*. −JF

JUSTIN HAYWARD   b 1946

Rock/pop. Justin Hayward's rich emotive baritone and elegantly tasteful lead-guitar work were among Moody Blues's greatest appeals. Hayward's solo projects have not approached the level of success he's had with the Moodies; however, *Blue Jays*, a 1975 duo effort with Moody Blues bassist John Lodge, became a worldwide million-seller. −RC

○ **Songwriter / POLYGRAM**   1977
A lyric and occasionally mystical work, with a sense of wonder abounding. Beautifully produced. −BE

JEFF HEALEY BAND

Blues/rock. This Canadian blues-rock trio features Jeff Healey, a blind electric lead guitarist. −RC

○ **See the Light / ARISTA**   1989
An assured first effort that contains the hits "Angel Eyes" and "Confidence Man." −DH

HEART

Rock/pop. This Seattle band, led by sisters Ann and Nancy Wilson, has been a staple on FM rock-radio ever since their first hit in 1976, "Crazy on You," which went to #35. It was lead singer Ann Wilson's powerful voice that gave the band an immediate appeal. Heart synthesized Led Zeppelin-style riff-heavy rock and shades of folk. Over the years, the band has continued to churn out hit after hit. In spite of a recent resurgence in the band's popularity, their hits are sounding increasingly formulaic.
"Magic Man" (#9), "Barracuda" (#11), "Straight On" (#15), "What about Love" (#10), "Never" (#4), "These Dreams (#1), "Alone" (#1), "There's the Girl" (#12), and a remake of Aaron Neville's "Tell It like It Is" (#8) are a few of their hits. −RC

Dreamboat Annie / CAPITOL   1976
Their striking first album was one of the top-selling debuts ever. −DH

○ **Greatest Hits/Live / CBS**   1980
The live tracks are unnecessary but the hits are top-notch. −DH

THE HEARTBEATS

R&B, doo-wop. Lead singer James "Shep" Sheppard cowrote a series of velvety doo-wop ballads for the Heartbeats during the mid 50s; one entry, "A Thousand Miles Away," was a huge R&B seller in 1956. The Queens, NY, quintet began their string of street-corner classics with "Crazy for You" and "Darling How Long," culminating with "A Thousand Miles Away." The Heartbeats recorded for Hull, Rama, Roulette, Gee, and Guyden before packing it in. In 1961, the lead singer formed a new trio, Shep & the Limelites, and scored on the charts with a heartwarming sequel to his first hit, "Daddy's Home," for Hull. "Our Anniversary" also sold well for the trio the next year, but they broke up soon thereafter. Sheppard was found dead in his auto on the Long Island Expressway in 1970. −BD

○ **Best of the Heartbeats / RHINO**   1990
A silky smooth New York quintet from the mid 50s. This album includes five tracks by lead James Sheppard's early-60s vocal trio, Shep & the Limelites. −BD

RICHARD HELL & THE VOIDOIDS

Punk. Some people will tell you Richard Hell was the main catalyst behind the birth of New York punk and its sensibilities. That's hardly true, but he's been around forever and did influence a number of budding punks (the Sex Pistols among them). In 1971, Hell and former high school buddy Tom Verlaine formed a group called the Neon Boys, who later became Television; he also cofounded the Heartbreakers with ex-New York Doll Johnny Thunders. In 1976 Hell formed the Voidoids, a caustic congregation that included guitarists Ivan Julian and Robert Quine and soon-to-be Ramones drummer Marc Bell. Hell's apocalyptic lyrics were steeped in alienated poetry, and his anguished howl of a voice set the pattern for scores of Bowery rockers. −JF

○ **Blank Generation / WARNER**   1977
Hell's debut isn't a masterpiece but it manages to re-create the intensity and exhilaration of the burgeoning days of American punk. "Love Comes in Spurts" defines Hell's romantic outlook, and the title cut is a classic piece of angst rock. −JF

Destiny Street / RELATIVITY   1982
It took five years for Hell to follow his debut, but *Destiny Street* is a moderately successful extension of *Blank Generation*. Some of the energy from the old days had disappeared, but Hell compensates with some fine ballads and another screwball classic, "The Kid with the Replaceable Head." −JF

R.I.P. / ROIR   1984
Since Hell didn't record all that much, this cassette collection of live tracks and studio outtakes is an illuminating collection of antiques and curios. −JD

HELLOWEEN

Heavy metal. This German-bred band began in the early 80s with heavy Judas Priest and Scorpions influences, but by the mid 80s they became an influence for bands who wanted a powerful form of heavy metal without playing too fast or being too rough-edged. −JB

○ **Keeper of the Seven Keys, Part 1 / RCA**   1987
Power metal from Germany with a lot of technical aspects, the 13-minute track "Helloween" still remains as interesting as it was when it first came out. Later efforts aren't as satisfying, but anything released before this album is recommended as well. −JB

HELMET

Alternative rock. Featuring ex-Band of Susans Page Hamilton, Helmet has a take on what is traditionally called heavy metal that is extreme, grinding, and relentless, sometimes more than one can reasonably handle at one sitting. But the churning wad of guitars, slower-than-muck backbeat, and harsh shouted vocals make for a pretty intimidating display of contemporary power-rock, even if it is a pose. −JD

○ **Meantime / INTERSCOPE**   1992
Crude, loud, simplistic thrash and bash that sounds like Black Flag and Black Sabbath. In fact, "Give It" could be the best Sab song they never recorded. With its intensity and directness, this is the best Helmet available, and doubtlessly all you'll need. −JD

JIMI HENDRIX   1942-1970

Hard rock, psychedelic, blues/rock. Jimi Hendrix was one of rock's greatest pioneers on the electric guitar. Hendrix fused funky R&B with hard rock, developing and mastering fresh approaches to using feedback, distortion, and various sound effects. As a result of his early immersion in Muddy Waters, Elmore James, B. B. King, and Chuck Berry, as well as his work with the Isley Brothers and King Curtis, Hendrix's rhythm guitar style utilized soul and blues licks and chord inversions as a starting place for many of his songs.
Much has been said about Hendrix's guitar playing, but he was also a formidable songwriter, using sensually trippy lyrics that sometimes drew inspiration from Dylan. "Purple Haze," "Fire," "Little Wing," "The Wind Cries Mary," and "Angel" are a few of Hendrix's classic titles.

Along with Cream, Hendrix's group the Jimi Hendrix Experience (with Mitch Mitchell on drums and Noel Redding on bass) is the most important trio to ever come out of the rock era. After the demise of the Experience in July of 1969, Hendrix pursued a hard, funkier (slightly less imaginative) sound with Band of Gypsys, featuring Buddy Miles and Billy Cox. They released one self-titled live album in May of 1970. On September 18, 1970, Hendrix passed away due to complications brought on from a drug overdose.

In spite of Hendrix's important place in the history of rock, and his great album sales, pop radio was resistant to much of his sound. Pop radio only had one Top 40 hit, a fiery version of Dylan's "All along the Watchtower," which peaked at #20. Other hits were "Crosstown Traffic" (#52), "Purple Haze" (#65), "Foxy Lady" (#67), "Up from the Skies" (#82), "Freedom" (#59), and "Dolly Dagger" (#74). –RC

☆ **Are You Experienced? / REPRISE / BB 5**   1967
From the dissonant fanfare of "Purple Haze" to the hypnotic closing cadence of the title track, the Jimi Hendrix Experience's audacious debut built upon the experimental hard-rock groundwork of groups like the Yardbirds, focusing it through a ferociously interactive trio format. Hendrix fused spacey Dylan-influenced imagery with R&B-derived song structures and chordal voicings to create an unique style. Tracks like "Fire," "Foxy Lady," "Manic Depression," the haunting "The Wind Cries Mary," and "May This Be Love" make this disc essential for any rock collection. –RC

☆ **Axis: Bold As Love / WARNER / BB 3**   1967
Continuing Hendrix's groundbreaking streak, this time matching his guitar pyrotechnics with a more refined collection of originals. The album features gorgeously unconventional ballads like "Little Wing," "Castles Made of Sand," "One Rainy Wish," and "Bold As Love," which shone alongside hyperspace rockers like "You Got Me Floatin'," "Up from the Skies," and the psychedelic hard jazz-rock free-for-all of "If 6 Was 9." –RC

Smash Hits / WARNER / BB 6   1968
Smash Hits is a solid collection of his most popular radio tracks, as well as featuring the bluesy "Red House" and "Stone Free," which were not found on previous albums. –RC

★ **Electric Ladyland / WARNER / BB 1**   1968
Hendrix's funky psychedelia reached a zenith on *Electric Ladyland*, one of the greatest albums of the rock era. His aggressively otherworldly production did as much for advancing the possibilities of recorded music as Phil Spector's "Wall of Sound" did in the early 60s. Hendrix's imaginatively fiery guitar work (and the Experience's brilliant interplay) here became the textbook source of inspiration for generations of musicians. Among *Electric Ladyland*'s many highlights are "Voodoo Child (Slight Return)," with its kamikaze lead guitar work, the transcendentally dense "Burning of the Midnight Lamp," the searing remake of Dylan's "All along the Watchtower," and the beautifully spacey "1983 ... (A Merman I Should Turn to Be)." –RC

○ **Band of Gypsies / CAPITOL / BB 5**   1970
Hendrix, sans the Experience, hooked up with bassist Billy Cox and drummer Buddy Miles to record this hard electric funk outing live at the Fillmore East in New York on Dec 31, 1969. While the rhythm section may have lacked the chops for wild free-form excursions, they provided Hendrix with a no-nonsense groove for his funkier R&B experiments. "Machine Gun," the album's highlight, features some of Hendrix's greatest playing. His dramatically violent soundscapes convey the horror of the war experience, with brilliantly controlled use of feedback and rapid-fire bursts of notes. –RC

The Cry of Love / REPRISE / BB 3   1971
The posthumously released *The Cry of Love* revealed Hendrix turning toward a more subdued, less psychedelic style, with songs like "Night Bird Flying" and "Angel." Hendrix does deliver a few strong rockers with "Freedom," "Ezy Ryder," and "Astro Man." –RC

○ **Jimi Hendrix in the West / REPRISE / BB 12**   1972
The live set features great versions of "Little Wing" and "Red House," but the highlight of the album goes to a ferocious version of "Johnny B. Goode" that borders on definitive. –RC

The Essential Jimi Hendrix / WARNER / BB 114   1978
This double-disc set covers Hendrix's work with the Experience, as well as some posthumous tracks. The selection seems pretty obvious, but if you are considering dropping the money on this, you ought to simply get his first three albums and listen to these songs the way they were intended to be heard. –RC

The Essential Jimi Hendrix - Vol. 2 / WARNER   1979
A fairly interesting compilation that includes such items as Band of Gipsys' "Machine Gun" and a live version of Hendrix roaring through "Gloria," as well as the famous Woodstock performance of "Star Spangled Banner" and the Monterey Pop Festival rave-up of "Wild Thing." –RC

Live at Winterland / RYKODISC   1987
Live at Winterland is one of the best representations of Hendrix's live prowess. The great playing is further enhanced by a top-notch mastering job. –RC

○ **Radio One / RYKODISC**   1989
Just when it seemed that the only way to hear more unreleased Hendrix was to put up with doctored Alan Douglas releases, Ryko pulled this live 1967 BBC gem out of the hat. Includes versions of "Day Tripper," "Killing Floor," "Love or Confusion," "Purple Haze," and "Fire," among other tracks. Definitely worth getting, but only after you have purchased all of the other Hendrix albums recommended in this section. –RC

Stages / WARNER   1991
Four-CD boxed set of concerts: Stockholm 1967, Paris 1968, San Diego 1969, and Atlanta 1970. –JO

DON HENLEY   b 1947

Singer/songwriter, rock/pop. His work with the Eagles was grounded in misogyny, contempt, and narcissism, but Don Henley's solo work is uniformly brilliant. His first three discs are loaded with searing, politically charged rockers and ballads of enormous depth and compassion. Who would've believed it? –JF

I Can't Stand Still / ELEKTRA   1982
A crisply produced and well-conceived debut, highlighted by "The Unclouded Day," "Johnny Can't Read," and "Dirty Laundry." –JF

○ **Building the Perfect Beast / GEFFEN**   1984
His commercial breakthrough, defining his solo formula with songs like "The Boys of Summer" and "All She Wants to Do Is Dance," which respond to political and romantic breakdowns. –JF

● **End of the Innocence / GEFFEN**   1989
A conceptual elaboration on his *Beast* album, this frames some wonderfully sarcastic rockers around "The Heart of the Matter," one of the finest ballads of the 80s. –JF

HENRY COW

Prog-rock. Henry Cow was one of the best-known and most widely traveled English bands of the prog-rock era (though only a cult favorite in the US). Their music has aged amazingly well over the last 20 years due to diverse influences (Oliver Messiaen, Kurt Weill, Frank Zappa, and Soft Machine were a few), uncompromising creativity, and a blend of spontaneity, intricate structures, philosophy, and humor. The group's identity changed from album to album as members came and went. This turnover was one factor in the consistent vitality of Henry Cow; another was the dedicated core of the band — the serious, politicized trio of Tim Hodgkinson, (keyboards, vocals, and reeds), Chris Cutler (drums and vocals), and Fred Frith (guitar, vocals, and various other instruments) who appear on the albums recorded from 1973-1978. Other longtime members included multireedist Lindsay

Cooper, bassist John Greaves, and German singer Dagmar Krause. Together, their sound was so mercurial and daring that the band had few imitators.

Since the demise of Henry Cow in the late 70s, its members have mostly worked in Europe with rock-based or improvising ensembles. Over the years they have reunited in various units. −MB

○ **Legend / EAST SIDE DIGITAL**   1973
The first of their Virgin trilogy. A bold statement of humor and complexity, with a nod to Frank Zappa. −MB

Unrest / EAST SIDE DIGITAL   1974
Cow furthers their commitment to improvisation and sonic experimentation. −MB

In Praise of Learning / EAST SIDE DIGITAL   1975
A collaboration with Slapp Happy, this progressive and political operetta ended the group's influential Virgin period, pointing the way to future projects. −MB

Concerts / COMPENDIUM   1976
A 2-fer of various compositions and improvisations that document the group's busy life on the road in 1974-1975. With Robert Wyatt guesting on one side. −MB

Western Culture / INTERZONE   1979
One side each by members Tim Hodgkinson and Lindsay Cooper. Not a truly collective effort but a good reunion in the Cow tradition. −MB

HERMAN'S HERMITS

British Invasion. Herman's Hermits was one of the most successful bands from the mid-60s British Invasion, a product of producer Mickie Most's hit factory. During their four-year run on the charts (1964-1968), they scored 18 Top 40 hits. Nine of their eleven Top Ten hits were consecutive. A couple of their biggest hits, "Mrs. Brown You've Got a Lovely Daughter" (#1) and "I'm Henry the VIII, I Am" (#1), were rearranged versions of old English pub-songs. Most also maximized the band's older-audience appeal by having them do versions of Sam Cooke's "Wonderful World" (#4) and Frankie Ford's "Sea Cruise." Herman (born Peter Noone, Nov 5, 1947), the band's cute frontman, delivered the material with a light, likable quality. The Hermits' highly melodic, bouncy sound in many ways embodied the pop side of the British Invasion, as they were practically incapable of delivering rock with any believable conviction. −RC

The EP Collection / SEE FOR MILES   1990
This 22-track CD also features most of the major 'erman 'its, with a handful of obscurities thrown in. (Import) −JT

○ **The Collection / CASTLE COMMUNICATIONS**   1990
All of the hits by Peter Noone and company, with room to spare for some nice surprises. (Import) −JT

THE HESITATIONS

R&B, soul. Cleveland vocal group the Hesitations specialized in soulful treatments of blatantly pop melodies, epitomized by their biggest R&B smash, a stirring 1968 rendering of the theme from the movie *Born Free.* Although their initial bow on the R&B charts in 1967 was titled "Soul Superman," the Hesitations were best known for items like "The Impossible Dream" and "Who Will Answer," hardly typical soul fare. Lead singer George "King" Scott died from a gunshot wound in February of 1968. −BD

○ **Solid Gold / KAPP**   1968
The pop-oriented R&B group sports soaring harmonies on this vinyl release. −BD

RICHARD X. HEYMAN

Anglo-pop. Richard Heyman is a virtual one-man mid-60s-style band. Fans of mid-period Beatles, Byrds, and Kinks should seek out Heyman's releases. −RC

○ **Hey Man! / WARNER**   1991
Heyman delivers a fine collection of largely self-performed tunes. His drumming is particularly fine, especially on

"Sidetracked." "Falling Away" is a great power-pop song in the classic mid-60s Anglo tradition. Other standouts include the Byrds/Petty-ish "In the Scheme of Things," the upbeat rocker "Private Army," the Beatley "Loud," and "Bad Business in Town." −RC

JOHN HIATT   *b* 1952

Singer/songwriter, roots-rock, country rock. One of the longest-gestating singer/songwriters of the last quarter-century, and one of the best, John Hiatt left his native Indianapolis in 1970 (after high school) to go to Nashville and write songs. He signed up with Epic Records and made two albums, *Hangin' Around the Observatory* (1974) and *Overcoats* (1975), which demonstrated his powerful songwriting ability but didn't draw customers. He signed to MCA in Los Angeles in the late 70s and released *Slug Line* (1979) and *Two Bit Monsters* (1980), still without gaining a commercial following. Then came a stint on Geffen that produced *All of a Sudden* (1982), *Riding with the King* (1984), and *Warming Up to the Ice Age* (1985). All increased his visibility without really breaking through.

But in 1987, Hiatt went into the studio with old friends Ry Cooder and Nick Lowe, plus drummer Jim Keltner, and came out with his first chart album, *Bring the Family.* That album's two followups, *Slow Turning* (1988) and *Stolen Moments* (1990), have demonstrated Hiatt's maturity as a writer and his flowering as a performer, resulting in some of the best singer/songwriter rock of the era. In 1992, Hiatt again teamed with Cooder, Lowe, and Keltner, this time in a group called Little Village that released a well-received debut album.

John Hiatt's songs have been covered by Rick Nelson, Dave Edmunds, the Searchers, Three Dog Night, Conway Twitty, Maria Muldaur, Rodney Crowell, Bob Dylan, the Neville Brothers, and many others. −WR

Riding with the King / GEFFEN   1984
One half of Hiatt's best Geffen album is played by him and Scott Matthews, while the other half features a band including Paul Carrack and Nick Lowe. But what matters is the songs: Hiatt's trenchant observations on life and love, especially the perceptive and painfully funny "She Loves the Jerk." −WR

★ **Bring the Family / A&M**   1987
Not only is the small-band playing impeccable, but this is Hiatt's best collection of songs, which is saying a lot for so talented a writer. "Memphis in the Meantime" is a knowledgeable look at the fame game, "Your Dad Did" perfectly skewers domestic life, and "Have a Little Faith in Me" is a touching evocation of persistent love. And that's just three of them. −WR

○ **Slow Turning / A&M**   1988
Only a notch below *Bring the Family,* with such strong songs as "Drive South" and the wild criminals-on-the-loose song "Tennessee Plates." −WR

DAN HICKS & HIS HOT LICKS

Rock/pop. Formed in 1968, this San Francisco group was an anomaly in the burgeoning acid-rock scene, with their campy folky style of Western swing, jazz, ragtime, cabaret, and Andrews Sisters-style vocals, courtesy of Sherry Snow and Tina Natural. They disbanded in 1974. −RC

○ **Where's the Money / MCA**   1971
Strong live outing. Showcases Hicks's dry tongue-in-cheek delivery and his band's chemistry to good effect. −RC

Striking It Rich / MCA   1972
Hicks' most solid studio outing. −RC

Last Train to Hicksville / MCA   1973
Almost as good as *Striking It Rich.* Some exceptional playing, but the songs aren't quite up to snuff. −RC

WILLIE HIGHTOWER

R&B, soul. Teaming with veteran producer Bobby Robinson, Hightower cut some fine soul during the 60s. The Gadsden,

AL, native traveled the gospel circuit before going secular, waxing his first singles for Robinson's Enjoy logo. Hightower's soulful version of the folk standard "If I Had a Hammer" turned some heads, but he didn't scale the R&B charts until 1969 when "It's a Miracle" proved a decent seller on Capitol. –BD

○ **Golden Classics / COLLECTABLES**
Gospel-drenched, emotionally charged 60s soul. –BD

JESSIE HILL   b 1932

R&B. Loose and wild, Jessie Hill cut a New Orleans party classic with his crazed "Ooh Poo Pah Doo." The two-sided single, a 1960 Allen Toussaint production on Minit, has Hill shouting the nearly unintelligible lyrics over a strong Crescent City groove, while the flip is an instrumental featuring saxist David Lastie. Hill cut several more boisterous outings with Toussaint at the helm before heading to the West Coast, where he made a disappointing album for Blue Thumb in 1970. –BD

○ **Golden Classics / COLLECTABLES**
Good-time New Orleans R&B from the early 60s, produced by prolific pianist Allen Toussaint. –BD

STEVE HILLAGE

Prog-rock. A guitarist with the bands Gong and Egg as well as other similar 70s prog-rock bands. –ED

○ **L / CAROLINE**   1976
Heavy glissando guitar jazz-rock with Don Cherry. Essential statement. –MGN

Green / CAROLINE   1978
An album from this guitarist in his prime, with compositions by Miquette Giraudy. –MGN

Rainbow Dome Music / BLUE PLATE   1979
An album of two extended pieces. Absolute music in a new-age mode. A must-buy. –MGN

PETER HIMMELMAN

Singer/songwriter, rock/pop. Minnesota native Peter Himmelman was the leader of a rock/pop quintet called Sussman Lawrence that made two independent albums in the early 80s and earned him comparisons to such new-wave singer/songwriters as Elvis Costello and Joe Jackson. The group became Himmelman's backup band for the release of his debut album, *This Father's Day* (1986), which earned him a contract with Island Records. He followed with *Gematria* (1987), *Synesthesia* (1989), and *Strength to Strength* (1991). By the last release, he had moved to Epic Records. –WR

Synesthesia / POLYGRAM   1989
Inventive drum tracks highlight Himmelman's spare arrangements of songs that express a personal, poetic world view full of struggle and vulnerability. –WR

○ **From Strength to Strength / EPIC**   1991
"Woman with the Strength of 10,000 Men" is Himmelman's song of romantic devotion, but it's only one of the driven performances on an album whose song titles — "Crushed," "Midnight Walk in the Ruins" — express its sense of anguish and desperation. –WR

HINDU LOVE GODS

Rock & roll. Warren Zevon and a Michael Stipe-less R.E.M. engage in playful electric blues-rock romps, plus some left-field song covers. Spirited playing and singing throughout make this effort fresher than many rock releases. –RC

Hindu Love Gods / WARNER   1990
Includes a great version of Prince's "Raspberry Beret." The production is immediate-sounding, generating the feel of a band knocking around in a rehearsal hall. There are plenty of charged versions of blues standards by Robert Johnson, Willie Dixon, and Muddy Waters, and the Love Gods also charge through a fun rendition of Terry Anderson's "Battleship Chains." –RC

EDDIE HINTON

Soul/R&B. Muscle Shoals musician turned singer/songwriter, with an Otis Redding-influenced vocal style. –RP

○ **Very, Extremely Dangerous / CAPRICORN**   1978
A Muscle Shoals recording of searching, Southern soul. –RP

Letters from Mississippi / ZANE   1987
Continues where the *Dangerous* album left off. Great stuff. –RP

Cry & Moan / BUL   1991
Raw 90s blue-eyed soul. –RP

ROBYN HITCHCOCK   b 1952

Alternative pop. British avant-garde singer/songwriter Robyn Hitchcock built up a large cult following and critical acclaim for his highly poetic, if somewhat obscure, songs, especially after his work began to be more generally available in the US after 1985. Born in London, Hitchcock formed the Soft Boys with Andy Metcalfe and Morris Windsor in 1976; the band continued until 1981, when Hitchcock released his first solo album, *Black Snake Diamond Role.* This was followed by *Groovy Decay* (1982) and *I Often Dream of Trains* (1984). In 1984 Hitchcock formed a backing band called the Egyptians, consisting of Metcalfe, Windsor, Otis Horns Fletcher, and Roger Jackson, and began playing concerts for the first time in two and a half years. The first recorded output of this band, and the first US Hitchcock album, was *Fegmania!* (1985). It was followed by the live album *Gotta Let This Hen Out!* (1985), *Element of Light* (1986), and a compilation called *Invisible Hitchcock* (1986), all of which built up Hitchcock's following to the point that he was signed to A&M Records, resulting in his major-label debut *Globe of Frogs* (1988), which reached #111. *Queen Elvis*, Hitchcock's second A&M album, reached #139 in 1989. He then made *Eye* (1990), an acoustic solo album released on Twin/Tone Records. –WR

● **Fegmania! / WARNER**   1985
Hitchcock's first record with the Egyptians (reconstituted Soft Boys). *Fegmania* is a strong pop record that plays down his derivative Syd Barrettisms. Snappy, tuneful, and to the point, it's Hitchcock pursuing his muse succinctly, and succeeding. –JD

Gotta Let This Hen Out / RELATIVITY   1985
A fine live album that serves as a career overview. Because the band rocks more than usual, even the grim and pretentious numbers sound less irritating. A great sampling from an inconsistent performer. (Import) –JD

○ **Globe of Frogs / A&M**   1988
As indicated above, Hitchcock has a considerable catalog, but neophytes might wish to begin with this relatively recent collection, which finds him playing in a folk/rock style while singing highly imagistic lyrics, the tone of which can be suggested by noting some of the titles: "Tropical Fish Mandala," "Sleeping with Your Devil Mask," and "The Shapes between Us Turn into Animals." Hitchcock is an original lyricist, well worth hearing, if not an acquired taste. –WR

Queen Elvis / A&M   1989
Hitchcock earned some radio play for this album's lead-off track, "Madonna of the Wasps," which, like several tracks here, features the distinctive guitar of R.E.M.'s Peter Buck. –WR

ALLAN HOLDSWORTH   b 1948

Prog-rock. A British electric guitar fusion virtuoso who began playing with progressive rock bands Gong and Soft Machine in the 70s. A sideman with the Tony Williams Lifetime, Bill Bruford, and Chuck Mangione. Melodically, Holdsworth's precise style draws much inspiration from jazz horn phrasing. His most recent albums feature the Synth-axe, a guitarlike synthesizer controller. –SWB

Velvet Darkness / CBS   1976
Holdsworth's first solo album includes several exceptional acoustic guitar pieces. –PK

○ **Metal Fatigue / ENIGMA** 1985
A terrific album by a most innovative guitarist and composer. First-class. –PK

● **Atavachron / ENIGMA** 1986
Atavachron was a landmark album in the history of modern rock guitar instrumentals, because it marked the first time Holdsworth used a Synth-axe guitar/synthesizer. Incredible sounds and textures. –PK

Secrets / ENIGMA 1989
A masterpiece from start to finish. Nice chord changes and wonderful solos. The album includes a mix of guitar and Synth-axe. –PK

THE HOLLIES

Rock/pop, British Invasion. The Hollies's string of hits through much of the 60s is one of the most impressive of that decade. Like countless other British beat groups, they were drawn at the outset to American R&B, but their trademark vocal style from the Clarke, Hicks, and Nash front line, coupled with a unique and distinctive rhythm section, caused the Hollies to pull away from the pack quickly. Drawing on the songs of Graham Gouldman and ultimately their own, the group would reach its creative peak prior to losing the services of Graham Nash. The Nash-less Hollies continued through the 70s, charting huge international hits, and creating worthy albums. Still, the Hollies of the mid 60s contributed some of the most vital pop music of the era. –SA

○ **All-Time Greatest Hits / CURB** 1990
A 12-rack all-singles compilation that includes the Hollies's biggest US hits on both Liberty ("Bus Stop," "Stop, Stop, Stop") and Epic Records from 1964 to 1975. –WR

Epic Anthology / CBS 1990
Epic Anthology: From the Original Master Tapes!. A 20-track compilation that picks up when the Hollies signed with Epic in 1967 and presents their biggest hits plus select album tracks and rarities through 1975. Includes "Carrie-Anne," "He Ain't Heavy, He's My Brother," "Long Cool Woman (In a Black Dress)," and "The Air That I Breathe." –WR

● **Treasured Hits & Hidden Treasures / EMI** 1992
The Hollies - Treasured Hits & Hidden Treasures is a 3-CD, 54-track anthology that gathers all of the group's EMI hits ("Bus Stop," "Stop Stop Stop," etc.), plus some previously unreleased tracks. Most tracks have been remixed from the original master tapes. Fortunately, the original spirit has been maintained. A very thoughtfully compiled set, which gives the listener a real sense of this group's many virtues. –RC

BRENDA HOLLOWAY   b 1946

Motown. This sultry 60s addition to the Motown roster waxed several memorable ballads for the firm. One of Motown's first Los Angeles signings, Holloway's Tamla debut, "Every Little Bit Hurts," was a soaring ballad that sailed up the pop charts in 1964, while Smokey Robinson wrote and produced Holloway's 1965 smash "When I'm Gone." The voluptuous vocalist opened several concerts for the Beatles on their 1965 US tour, including their Shea Stadium show. In 1967 Holloway cowrote and recorded the original version of "You've Made Me So Very Happy," later a gigantic hit for Blood, Sweat & Tears. –BD

○ **Greatest Hits & Rare Classics / MOTOWN** 1991
A wonderful compilation of her best Motown releases, plus some unreleased material. –RP

BUDDY HOLLY   1936-1959

Rock & roll. An enormously important and influential performer, Holly started in his native Texas doing country music with boyhood friend Bob Montgomery, eventually adding R&B numbers to the set list after meeting Elvis Presley. He recorded early rockabilly sides in Nashville, but success didn't come until he formed the Crickets and recorded in Norman Petty's studios, producing the #1 hit "That'll Be the Day" in 1957. Holly and Petty, continued to experiment in the studio, utilizing different forms of echo ("Peggy Sue"), double-tracking ("Words of Love"), and close-miking techniques, now commonplace in the industry. After his death, much of Holly's earlier pre-Crickets music was overdubbed by Petty, using the Fireballs to keep up with the fan demand for more product. Though his moment in the spotlight lasted barely eighteen months, and the movie version of his life story only got it about half right, Buddy Holly's music still sounds fresh and continues to influence to this day. –CK

☆ **Complete / MCA** 1979
Contains every note Buddy Holly every recorded. This six-LP box is essential for hardcore fans. –JF

For the First Time Anywhere / MCA 1983
Powerful undubbed rockabilly sides. –CK

★ **From the Original Master Tapes / MCA** 1985
A 20-track best-of with superlative sound. –CK

Something Special ... / ROLLER COASTER 1986
Something Special from Buddy Holly is an import of more undubbed material from 1956. –CK

HOLLYWOOD FLAMES

R&B, doo-wop. Long-lasting Los Angeles doo-wop aggregation with a very fluid personnel roster. Bobby Day was one of the group's founders in 1950, and they recorded prolifically for Hollywood, Specialty, Lucky, Swingtime, Money, and other firms before cutting their one major hit, the rocking "Buzz Buzz Buzz," in 1957 for Ebb Records. Earl Nelson, who was later half of Bob and Earl, sang lead on the tune, and some of their subsequent Ebb 45s were rocking novelties. Day went on to solo success with "Rockin' Robin," and the group managed one more chart item, "Gee," for Chess in 1961 with Donald Height as lead. –BD

○ **Buzz Buzz Buzz / SPECIALTY**
Rockers and doo-wop from this respected West Coast 50s R&B vocal group, including the Top Ten "Buzz Buzz Buzz." –BD

HOLSAPPLE-STAMEY

Power-pop, singer/songwriter. Peter Holsapple and Chris Stamey were two of the principal singer/songwriters from the alternative power-pop band, the dB's. Much of the music from this collaboration is thoughtfully upbeat, guitar-driven folk-pop, with a few stylistic tips of the hat to the Byrds, Big Star, and mid-period Beatles. –RC

○ **Mavericks / RHINO** 1991
A charming low-key power-pop effort, "Geometry" is a perfect Gary Lewis & the Playboys-style sendup. "Angels" is pure power-pop magic. The softer acoustic numbers, "Close Your Eyes" and "Anymore," recall the duo's work on Repercussions. –RC

HONEY CONE

Soul. Signing to Holland-Dozier-Holland's Hot Wax label, Honey Cone came together in Los Angeles in 1969 and immediately rolled out one hit after another in a slickly produced, lighthearted soul style. All three members were veterans of the West Coast studio scene, and their experience paid off when "Want Ads" and "Stick-Up" proved back-to-back R&B chart-toppers in 1970, with "Want Ads" also pacing the pop lists. Both hits, along with the Latin-tinged "One Monkey Don't Stop No Show," were cowritten by coproducer General Johnson, who was taking a breather from his frontman role with Chairmen of the Board. –BD

○ **Greatest Hits / HDH [FANTASY]** 1990
All their hits. –RP

HONEYCOMBS

British Invasion. A quintet whose principal claim to fame rests with the 1964 transatlantic hit single "Have I the Right," and the fact that their drummer was a woman, one Ann "Honey" Lantree. Their sound was a mix of folk and pop, marred by a somewhat soft approach to playing that was occasionally compensated by a memorable hook. –BE

○ **Honeycombs / PRT**
An enjoyable collection, including their two major hits, "Have I the Right?" and "I Can't Stop." It suffers only from a certain sameness and a thinness to the sound. (Import) –BE

All Systems Go / PRT   1965
A followup record that will probably disappoint all but their diehard fans. If you own the first, you'll want this one. (Import) –BE

THE HONEYDRIPPERS

Rock/pop. The Honeydrippers were an ad hoc group put together by ex-Led Zeppelin lead singer Robert Plant and Atlantic Records executive Ahmet Ertegun to record a mini-album of 50s and 60s oldies in 1984. –WR

○ **Honeydrippers - Vol. 1 / ES PARANZA**   1984
Five-song EP features Robert Plant singing such oldies as the hit remake of "Sea of Love," with a backup that includes Nile Rodgers, Jeff Beck, and Jimmy Page. –WR

THE HOODOO GURUS

Alternative rock, anglo-pop. Australian kings of garage Anglo-pop/rock, the Hoodoo Gurus have provided the 80s alternative music scene with a handful of fine trashy, tuneful classics in "Bittersweet," "Poison Pen," "Like Wow - Wipeout," "What's My Scene," "Come Anytime," and "Where Nowhere Is," among others. They incorporated the grunge of the Cramps with the 60s melodic pop-smarts of groups like the Kinks and the Turtles. –RC

○ **Stoneage Romeos / A&M**   1984
Their debut effort is 60s garage-punk heaven. Highlights include the rave-ups "Let's All Turn On" and "Tojo"; "Dig It Up," a Cramps-style rocker; "My Girl," a slice of 60s girl/boy guitar-pop; and the grunge-ola "I Was a Kamikaze Pilot." Highly recommended. –RC

● **Mars Needs Guitars / ELEKTRA**   1985
This is the album that gave this Aussie band their break on the American college music market, thanks to some classic tracks, "Bittersweet," "Poison Pen," "Death Defying," and "Like Wow-Wipeout." The production is a little unfocused, lacking some of the punch the material demands and the trashy sparks of *Stoneage Romeos.* Nevertheless, the songs reflect considerable growth in the band's vision. –RC

○ **Blow Your Cool! / ELEKTRA**   1987
The Gurus alternate between appealing tuneful updates of Turtles-style guitar-pop ("Good Times," "What's My Scene") and wild workouts like "Where Nowhere Is" and "Hell for Leather." The anthemic "I Was the One" is a standout. The Bangles assist on backup harmonies on this effort. All in all, a solid effort. –RC

Magnum Cum Louder / RCA   1989
The Gurus continue their once-every-two-year release schedule with this consistent effort that showcases vocalist Dave Faulkner's solid songwriting. "Come Anytime" is primo Gurus and the moody "Shadow Me" is also a highlight. Even though *Magnum Cum Louder* doesn't shine as brightly as previous efforts, it's still a stronger album than many efforts by groups mining this genre. –RC

Kinky / RCA   1991
One of the band's very best releases. *Kinky* portrays a band straddling their playful 60s garage rock aesthetic with issues of adulthood, all the while playing as fiercely as ever. –RC

THE HOOTERS

Rock/pop. This regionally popular Philadelphia band, formed in 1978, incorporated folk, ska, reggae, and Heartland rock into a rather mainstream sound. During the mid 80s, the Hooters enjoyed a streak of hits and MTV exposure with "All You Zombies" (#58), "And We Danced" (#21), "Day by Day"

(#18), "Where Do the Children Go" (#38), "Johnny B" (#64), and "Satellite" (#61). –RC

○ **Nervous Night / COLUMBIA / BB 12**   1985
Fairly mainstream pop-rock debut, which produced their four biggest hit singles. –RC

BRUCE HORNSBY & THE RANGE   b 1954

Rock/pop. Virginia-born pianist Bruce Hornsby distinguished himself in the late 80s and early 90s as a thoughtful songwriter, an excellent performer, and a ubiquitous sideman for numerous fellow performers — he even joined the Grateful Dead on a part-time basis after the death of their keyboard player Brent Mydland in 1990.
His debut album with the Range, *The Way It Is* (1986), produced three Top 20 hits, reached #3, and landed the group the Grammy for Best New Artist that year. –WR

○ **The Way It Is / RCA**   1986
One of the best collections of new songs released in the 1980s, performed to perfection by a versatile band led by a seasoned (if new to the listener) artist. The songs provide an American panorama, in terms both of landscape and social mores. This is smart, compassionate music for thinking adults ... and you can dance to it too. Includes "The Way It Is" and "Mandolin Rain." –WR

Scenes from the Southside / RCA   1988
The Way It Is, part two, featuring some wonderful story songs, not only on the hits "Jacob's Ladder" and "The Valley Road" but also "Defenders of the Flag" and "The Road Not Taken." Hornsby continues to mine a rich American vein on this album. –WR

A Night on the Town / RCA   1990
Hornsby's third album found him trying to break out of his signature sound into other areas. It was less successful than its predecessors but, along with the pianist's extensive session work, it signaled his determination to tackle new musical challenges. –WR

HOT TUNA

Blues/rock, rock & roll, folk/rock. Hot Tuna (formed in October 1970) was an offshoot group led by Jefferson Airplane guitarist Jorma Kaukonen and bassist Jack Casady. The group's self-titled debut was a live recording that covered versions of old blues songs by Rev. Gary Davis and Jelly Roll Morton, as well as some originals that became required listening for those inclined toward the Airplane or Grateful Dead's more laidback material.
By the third album, *Burgers*, Hot Tuna increasingly drew upon their rock background, performing extended jams built around Casady's wide, lumbering bass sound and Kaukonen's tastefully texturous lead work. Even though the band seemed perpetually stuck in medium tempo, they were quite capable of generating sparks, which made them a popular concert draw for a number of years. –RC

○ **Hot Tuna / RCA / BB 30**   1970
This live set includes some solid originals, in particular the instrumental "Mann's Fate" and versions of tunes by Mississippi John Hurt and Rev. Gary Davis. Exceptionally tasteful acoustic guitar work by Jorma Kaukonen. Highlights are "Hesitation Blues" and "Death Don't Have No Mercy." –RC

● **Burgers / RCA / BB 68**   1972
On this third effort, Hot Tuna electrified its initial acoustic country-blues direction and turned in some blistering jams with "Sea Child" and "Sunny Day Strut." "Water Song" is a gorgeous instrumental, featuring some wonderful acoustic guitar and electric bass interplay. David Crosby guests on background vocals. "Keep On Truckin'" was a moderate underground FM hit. –RC

HOTHOUSE FLOWERS

Alternative rock. At the end of the 80s, Ireland's Hothouse Flowers was one of the most popular groups on the British

Isles, with their larger-than-life blend of U2 and Van Morrison. Liam O'Maonlai fronts the band with a commanding passionate vocal presence, but sometimes their overwrought mega-production sound tends to reduce them to a variation of Commitments-style soul. Their first album, *People*, contains some fine moments with "Don't Go," "Forgiven," "Yes I Was," and the single "I'm Sorry." –RC

○ **People / POLYGRAM**   1988
Irish sensation shoots for the big mystical picture, not unlike U2. Musically owes more to Van Morrison and various R&B rock influences. This debut is fairly solid from start to finish. Highlights are the prayerful "Forgiven," the affirmative "Yes I Was," and the exuberant hit single "I'm Sorry." –RC

HOUSE OF FREAKS

Alternative rock. House of Freaks, a guitar/drum duo originally from Virginia, creates an intelligent, urgent style of alternative rock/pop, drawing on all sorts of Americana subject matter and images. Musically, the duo created a tension with this basic lineup that drew the listener into the material; however, they have certain songs that begged for a real band treatment. In 1990, House of Freaks left Rhino Records for major-label waters (Giant Records) and released the fine *Cakewalk*, featuring an expanded lineup. –RC

Monkey on a Chain Gang / RHINO   1988
This Virginia duo delivers a fine debut with literate alternative-rock songs. The sparce production works to great effect. Good alternative choice to *Tantilla*. –RC

All My Friends / RHINO   1989
An EP loaded with more good songs and performances. The jazzy "You Can't Change the World Anymore" is an effective stylistic departure. –RC

○ **Tantilla / RHINO**   1989
John Leckie's production tries to make the most of this guitar/drum duo's sound, but he can't hide its limitations. Nevertheless, *Tantilla* contains a load of smartly twisted songs with good melodies. Lead singer Bryan Harvey delivers each song with just the right passion. –RC

HOUSEMARTINS

Alternative pop. The Housemartins were formed in Hull, England, in 1984 (they made much of their origins) and included singer/guitarist Paul Heaton (b May 9, 1962), bassist Stan Cullimore (b Apr 6, 1962), drummer Hugh Whitaker (the only one, it was revealed later, actually from Hull), and Ted Key. The Housemartins hit in the UK, while suffering adverse press and personnel conflicts that eventually convinced them to split in 1988. Heaton went on to form the Beautiful South. –RC

○ **London 0 Hull 4 / ELEKTRA**   1986
The Housemartins had a bouncy pop-rock sound that was reminiscent of the British beat groups of the mid 60s. This album is full of catchy tunes, though the lyrics are sometimes more serious than the music might suggest. –WR

THELMA HOUSTON

Motown, soul, disco. Houston was a protégé of composer Jimmy Webb in the late 60s. In spite of a fairly constant recording output, Houston's distinctively vigorous pipes have rarely appealed to the masses. Her biggest hit was the gold disco single "Don't Leave Me This Way" from her 1977 *Any Way You Want It* album on the Gordy label. –BC

○ **Best of Thelma Houston / MOTOWN**   1991
Encompasses her Motown career. –RAB

WHITNEY HOUSTON   b 1963

Pop, dance-pop. Coming from a solid musical background, this daughter of soul singer Cissy Houston and cousin of Dionne Warwick debuted in 1985. Her first album, *Whitney Houston*, was the first in *Billboard* chart history by a woman to enter at #1; it went on to sell 14 million copies. She scored heavily on

MTV with classy videos, helping to break the "color barrier" originally knocked down by Michael Jackson. Her second album, *Whitney*, was just as popular, scoring seven consecutive #1s in the US, shattering the previous record held by the Beatles. With pure pop music melded to stunning beauty, Houston's star shines bright whether she is singing ballads, uptempo dance material, the national anthem, or cola commercials. –CK

○ **Whitney Houston / ARISTA**   1985
Her debut contained the #1 hits "Saving All My Love for You," "How Will I Know," and "Greatest Love of All." It's her most consistent effort. –DH

STEVE HOWE

Prog-rock. Guitarist Steve Howe is mostly known for his work with the band Yes. Howe also was a member of Asia and GTR and has appeared on many albums as a sideman. Howe's playing embraces jazz, rock, folk, country, classical, and world music. –PK

Beginnings / ATLANTIC   1975
This excellent 1975 solo album from this ex-Yes guitarist contains vocal and instrumental material, with Howe playing everything but the kitchen sink. –PK

The Steve Howe Album / ATLANTIC   1979
Instrumental and vocal material with excellent acoustic guitar pieces. –BC

○ **Turbulence / RELATIVITY**   1991
An all-instrumental album featuring Howe on multiple guitars. A masterpiece! –PK

JIMMY HUGHES

R&B, soul. Jimmy Hughes established producer Rick Hall's fledgling Fame studio as an R&B mecca with his 1964 blues ballad "Steal Away." The ex-gospel singer hooked up with Hall in 1962 but it wasn't until the explosive "Steal Away" was issued on the Fame label that his career took off. With an intense, crying vocal style that was perfect for deep soul ballads, Hughes scored with the pleading "Why Not Tonight" in 1967, although the untypically uptempo "Neighbor, Neighbor" proved another giant hit. Hughes broke away from Hall and recorded an album for Volt before retiring from performing in the mid 70s. –BD

Steal Away / VEE JAY   1965
A classic pleading Rick Hall-produced ballad leads off this impressive debut album by the Alabama singer. Available only on vinyl. –BD

○ **Why Not Tonight / ATCO**   1967
It's criminal that this Muscle Shoals soul classic isn't on CD — aching, atmospheric lovelorn ballads and the ominous pounding hit, "Neighbor, Neighbor." –BD

Something Special / VOLT   1968
Hughes in Memphis — fine, underrated Southern soul. –BD

HUMAN LEAGUE

Dance-pop, techno-pop. The Human League scored a number of hits in the 80s that crossed the line between post-new-wave rock and dance-pop, though that was a very different style from the music the group played at first. The Human League was formed in Sheffield, England, in 1977 by synthesizer players Martin Ware (b May 19, 1956) and Ian Marsh (b Nov 11, 1956), along with Addy Newton and singer Philip Oakey (b Oct 2, 1955). Newton was soon replaced by Adrian Wright and the lineup held for the first two Human League albums, *Reproduction* (1979) and *Travelogue* (1980).

Ware and Marsh left the Human League in October 1980 (they subsequently formed Heaven 17). Oakey and Wright recruited bassist Ian Burden (b Dec 24, 1957) and backup singers Joanne Catherall (b Sep 18, 1962) and Susanne Sulley (b Mar 22, 1963), resulting in a much more pop-sounding version of the band. Synth player Jo Callis (b May 2, 1955) was added to the group.

The Human League's third album, *Dare*, was its commercial and international breakthrough. Released in October 1981 in the UK and in February 1982 in the US, it went to #1 in England and #3 in the US, largely on the strength of the single "Don't You Want Me," which topped the charts in both countries. Subsequent hits in 1982 and 1983 included "(Keep Feeling) Fascination" and "Mirror Man."
Hysteria (1984), was far less successful, and the group agonized over a followup. *Crash* appeared in 1986, produced by Jimmy Jam and Terry Lewis (responsible for Janet Jackson's *Control*, among other hits). Largely a studio creation, it was nevertheless successful, producing the #1 hit "Human." The Human League's sixth album, *Romantic?*, was released in 1990. –WR

Dare / A&M 1981
Martin Rushent's fresh, clean production keeps the synthesized music from being too cluttered, while Philip Oakey's voice is used for its self-consciously melodramatic effect and contrasted with the untrained singing of Joanne Catherall and Susanne Sulley. The hits are "Don't You Want Me" and (in England) "The Sound of the Crowd," "Love Action (I Believe in Love)," and "Open Your Heart," but the album also works as a consistent piece. –WR

○ **Greatest Hits / A&M** 1988
This well-chosen best-of contains the Human League's UK and US hits from 1978 ("Being Boiled") to 1986, including the chart-toppers "Don't You Want Me" and "Human" and such non-album singles as "(Keep Feeling) Fascination" and "Mirror Man." It's a study in 80s dance-pop. –WR

HUMAN RADIO

Rock/pop. This eclectic, arty rock/pop band from Memphis synthesizes everything from Beatles, Sly Stone, Frank Zappa, Steely Dan, and Todd Rundgren into a rhythmically aggressive, ultra-melodic sound.
"Me and Elvis," the first single off of their self-titled debut, is a wonderfully jaundiced Memphian's-eye story about the town's relentless icon. Unfortunately, that first impression made this journeyman band look more like a novelty act. –RC

○ **Human Radio / COLUMBIA** 1990
This debut, produced by David Kahne (Bangles, Fishbone) and David Leonard (The Rave-Ups), skillfully blended quirky power-pop ("Hole in My Head") with aggressive art-rock, ("N.Y.C.") and trashy funk ("My First Million"). All this sounds like the work of one band, and a good one at that. –RC

HUMAN SWITCHBOARD

Alternative rock. Keyboard-driven angst-pop from a great post-punk band. –JD

○ **Who's Landing in My Hangar? / I.R.S.** 1981
A gripping album full of hurt and neurosis and great, great songs. Their only studio album. –JD

HUMBLE PIE

Rock & roll, hard rock. When Humble Pie was formed in 1969, there was much excitement about the possibilities. After all, its founding members came from very popular English bands. Humble Pie comprised vocalist and guitarist Steve Marriott, previously with the Small Faces; Greg Ridley, former bassist for Spooky Tooth; Peter Frampton, the Herd's frontman and guitarist; and drummer Jerry Shirley of Little Women.
The band's initial albums (on Andrew Oldham's Immediate Records) were surprisingly laidback and melodic. 1971 turned out to be the band's breakthrough to major success, due to a hard and loud double live album, *Performance - Live at the Fillmore*, which went to #21. Frampton left shortly thereafter to pursue a successful solo career, and Humble Pie progressively turned toward an over-amped boogie style of rock. During the next two years, Humble Pie made three more forays onto the album charts with *Smoking* (#6), *Eat It* (#13), and *Lost and Found* (#37), an anthology of their earlier Immediate label work.

In spite of substantial album popularity, Humble Pie never had a major single, with their only chart titles being "I Don't Need No Doctor" (#73) and "Hot 'N' Nasty" (#52). The group disbanded in 1981, and Steve Marriott later passed away. –RC

○ **Safe As Yesterday Is / COLUMBIA** 1969
Even though many think of Humble Pie as a boogie-rock band, their first two efforts, originally released on Immediate Records, possessed a healthy dose of tasty acoustical instrumentation. Steve Marriott and Peter Frampton applied themselves, through months of rehearsals, and came up with a solid collection of songs. Even though *Safe As Yesterday Is* is a little stronger than the pastoral *Town and Country*, both albums are worth seeking out. In 1972, they were sold as a double-record set titled *Lost and Found*, which is now out of print. –RC

Rock On / A&M / BB 118 1971
By 1971 Humble Pie had taken on a much harder electric direction. Of their post-Immediate studio albums, this is probably their best. (Also available on Mobile Fidelity.) –RC

○ **Performance: Rockin' at the Fillmore / A&M /** 1971
This live, extended-play effort, recorded at the Fillmore, showcased the band in its element, with Steve Marriott's stratospheric wail and Peter Frampton's lyrical lead work in fine form. Frampton split to pursue a successful solo career after this album. –RC

● **Classics, Vol. 14 — Humble Pie / A&M** 1987
If you are looking for the one place to go for Humble Pie, this best-of collection covers the essentials, such as "I Don't Need No Doctor," "Stone Cold Fever," "30 Days in the Hole," "Hot 'N' Nasty," "C'mon Everybody," and "Take Me Back." –RC

IAN HUNTER   b 1946

Rock & roll. Hunter's post-Mott the Hoople work (most of it done in collaboration with guitarist Mick Ronson) has remained true to the boogie roots of his old group, while expanding his beautifully expressed romantic concerns. –JF

Ian Hunter / CBS 1975
A spotty debut, but "Once Bitten Twice Shy," "Who Do You Love," and "I Get So Excited" rank with the best Mott the Hoople material. –JF

You're Never Alone ... / CHRYSALIS 1979
Hunter's post-punk return on *You're Never Alone with a Schizophrenic* salutes the genre he helped spawn and brings that old Mott crunch to a fine set of energetic, if somewhat dated rock & roll. –JF

○ **YUI Orta / MERCURY** 1989
Overlooked upon its release, this is Hunter's most lyrically ambitious and mature disc, with tight rockers and melancholy ballads working gloriously off one another. –JF

HUNTERS & COLLECTORS

Alternative rock. This Australian collective has taken its penchant for American R&B and blended it with the righteousness of Midnight Oil. –BE

○ **Human Frailty/Living Daylight / I.R.S.** 1986
Touching the "new sensitivity" before its time, laying it over rhythmic soul. –RG

HÜSKER DÜ

Hardcore, alternative rock. From their faster-than-thou hardcore beginnings to their mature but intense major-label output, this Minneapolis trio epitomized the independent-rock ethic of the 80s. They made drastic improvements with each release, and their best albums juggle the screaming self-examinations of Bob Mould with the biting pop-romanticisms of Grant Hart. The mix won over some mainstream rockers along with independent-rock hipsters. –JF

Metal Circus / SST 1983
This five-songer, which followed a furiously paced debut, hinted that the confines of hardcore punk couldn't contain the group's collective vision. –JF

☆ **Zen Arcade / SST**   1984

Its four sides are linked by a muddled travelog concept, but this is a remarkable synthesis of hardcore sensibilities and rock & roll themes. "Turn on the News" may be their finest moment. –JF

★ **New Day Rising / SST**   1985

From its thin and distorted production to the rich, tugging melodies, this one-ups *Zen Arcade* through its front-to-back consistency. –JF

☆ **Flip Your Wig / SST**   1985

They finally got the professional production they've always deserved. While it's not the frontal assault of *New Day Rising*, the songs continue to get better, both lyrically and melodically. –JF

Candy Apple Grey / WARNER   1986

The band's major-label debut coincidentally happens to be their most lyrically optimistic. Musically, it reiterates *Flip Your Wig*. –JF

Warehouse: Songs & Stories / WARNER   1987

Their last album was another double set. There are some fine songs here but too many of them are buried amid the fluff. Necessary for fans, though. –JF

BRIAN HYLAND   b 1943

Pop. Initially aiming his output at teens, Brian Hyland grew up fast and cut a serious cover of "Gypsy Woman," a hit by the Impressions that went gold in 1970. The Queens, NY, native enjoyed his biggest hit at the tender age of 16 — the tongue-twisting "Itsy Bitsy Teenie Weenie Yellow Polkadot Bikini," a cute ditty snapped up by Kapp Records after it was issued on the little Leader logo. Hyland moved to ABC-Paramount and already sounded more adult by the time "Sealed with a Kiss" hit in 1962. A string of solid sellers, including "The Joker Went Wild" in 1966, preceded his remake of "Gypsy Woman," produced by Del Shannon and released on Uni. –BD

○ **Greatest Hits / RHINO**

Everything from "Itsy Bitsy Teenie Weenie Yellow Polka Dot Bikini" to "Gypsy Woman." –LL

JANIS IAN   b 1951

Singer/songwriter, folk/rock. A folk/pop singer/songwriter who gained fame at 16 for her socially conscious ballad "Society's Child" and scored all over again at 24 with "At Seventeen." Lately she is living and writing songs in Nashville. –WR

○ **Janis Ian / FORECAST**   1967

An amazingly precocious set of songs, including the civil rights anthem "Society's Child" and songs touching on religion, prostitution, politics, and other urban concerns, all from the viewpoint of an intelligent teenager. –WR

Stars / ONE WAY   1974

From precocity to an accelerated maturity, Ian ruefully comments on the fame business in the title track, then turns deeply romantic on "Jesse," a hit for Roberta Flack. –WR

Between the Lines / CBS   1975

"At Seventeen" is only one of a group of beautifully written, tastefully performed, and very moving songs. –WR

ICEHOUSE

Alternative pop. Though it has had varying personnel, Icehouse is essentially a vehicle for the work of Australian Iva Davies (May 22, 1955). Davies formed the first version of the band under the name Flowers in 1980 and began scoring hits in Australia with the group's first single, "Can't Help Myself." *Icehouse* was the name of the Flowers's first album, but the group changed its name as it went international, to avoid conflicts with another band. They first reached the US charts in 1981 with "We Can Get Together" but did not score a substantial hit until 1988, when "Crazy" went to #14. This was followed by the Top Ten hit "Electric Blue," which was written by John Oates. –WR

○ **Man of Colours / CAPITOL**   1987

The US debut finds Davies, whose baritone suggests both David Bowie and Bryan Ferry, fronting a cohesive, synthesized pop sound on the hits "Crazy" and "Electric Blue." –WR

Great Southern Land / CHRYSALIS   1989

This ten-track compilation album of Icehouse's greatest hits of the 80s reveals the band's chameleonlike pop talent. British art-rock is the touchstone, though the group can also rock out. –WR

BILLY IDOL   b 1955

New-wave, hard rock, rock/pop. Billy Idol represents the bridge between punk-rock and hard-rock/metal, a logical enough connection that somehow seemed unlikely until he made the transition. Idol left Sussex University in 1976 to join the punk movement, specifically the group of rabid Sex Pistols fans called the Bromley Contingent. Many of the members formed their own bands, and Idol began Generation X with Tony James. Generation X became a moderate success during the punk heyday of the late 70s, especially in England, with Idol on snarling lead vocals.

When the band split in 1981, Idol went to New York and hooked up with manager Bill Aucoin (who had handled Kiss, among others). This resulted in Idol's grooming as more of a mainstream rock figure. His debut album, *Billy Idol*, came out in 1982 and spent two years on the charts as the result of such video hits as "White Wedding" and "Hot in the City." But it was Idol's second album, *Rebel Yell*, that was his big breakthrough, selling two million copies and spawning hits in the raucous title track and the ballad "Eyes without a Face." Idol followed it up with *Whiplash Smile* in 1986 and *Charmed Life* in 1990. –WR

○ **Rebel Yell / CAPITOL**   1983

Tight rock arrangements featuring Steve Stevens's slashing guitar playing and Idol's vocal sneer. The dance-rock of "Rebel Yell" is alternated with power-ballads like "Eyes without a Face" for a well-rounded pop package. –WR

Vital Idol / CAPITOL   1987

Dance remixes of Idol's hits, plus a live cover of "Mony Mony" that topped the charts. –WR

THE IMPRESSIONS

R&B, soul. The first Impressions hit, "For Your Precious Love," was an anachronism when released in 1958. Jerry Butler's robust, yearning vocal was a throwback to deep-South gospel, and Curtis Mayfield's arrangement was decidedly barebones. But this song also precipitated the changes coming in R&B; you can hear the groundwork for soul music being laid, from the melisma of Butler's phrasing to Mayfield's skeletal guitar. The song literally flew in the face of then-popular doo-wop formulas.

Butler left the group in 1960, but the pared-down trio, led by Mayfield, cut a path that altered the R&B map. Mayfield's high falsetto and the trade-off vocals of Fred Cash and Sam Gooden framed a new kind of R&B: smooth and graceful, at times lilting, soaked in the history of gospel, and, thanks to Mayfield's lyrical examinations of racism and urban decay, the catalyst for the wave of socially aware Black hits recorded in the 70s.

The group's hits varied from supple statements of affirmation ("It's All Right," "People Get Ready") and romantic declarations ("Talking about My Baby," "I'm So Proud") to songs that were sociopolitical ("Choice of Colors," "This Is My Country") or mystical ("Gypsy Woman"). Mayfield's outside production work yielded similar-sounding hits for the likes of Major Lance, Walter Jackson, and Billy Butler (and sound of the Impressions was imitated by the likes of the Viscounts and the Knight Brothers). Their chart run ended by the late 60s, as did Mayfield's Midas touch; after recording the brilliant *Superfly* in 1972, his talents ran dry. Nonetheless, Mayfield's reputation as one of soul's supreme innovators cannot be exaggerated. –JF

○ **Greatest Hits / MCA**   1965
A skimpy but solid collection of Curtis Mayfield's early-60s soul landmarks. Includes "It's All Right" and "Gypsy Woman," defining the formula of early-60s soul. –JF

INDIGO GIRLS

Singer/songwriter, folk/rock. The Indigo Girls (Amy Ray and Emily Saliers) have earned a devoted following with their thoughtful, introspective lyrics (rich in religious metaphor), sensitive folky delivery, and earthy harmonies. The dichotomy between Ray's edgier, rock-influenced delivery and Saliers's soft, reflective style creates enough tension to keep their concept interesting. –RC

○ **Indigo Girls / EPIC**   1989
This major-label debut is a strong showcase for this duo's harmonic skills and songwriting virtues. "Closer to Fine" (#52) was a moderate hit. Emily Saliers's "History of Us" is particularly affecting. Other highlights include "Secure Yourself," "Tried to Be True," and "Kid Fears," which featured R.E.M. vocalist Michael Stipe on backups. Hothouse Flowers also provide support. –RC

INFECTIOUS GROOVES

Heavy metal, funk. This underground supergroup (featuring Mike Muir of Suidical Tendencies and ex-Jane's Addiction drummer Stephen Perkins) is a provocative synthesis of funk and metal. –JB

○ **The Plague That Makes Your Booty Move / CBS**   1991
This supergroup combines funk, metal, and a little bit of everything else, including an appearance by Ozzy Osbourne. A party record for the 90s. –JB

JAMES INGRAM   *b* 1956

Urban R&B, pop. Ingram began performing with the band Revelation Funk in the early 70s, moving from Akron, OH, to Los Angeles in 1973. During the 70s, Ingram supported Ray Charles on the road with backup vocals and piano, played keyboards behind the Coasters on Dick Clark's oldies revues, and was Leon Haywood's musical director. After hearing a demo of him singing "Just Once," Quincy Jones asked Ingram to perform on his new album. Released in 1980 on *The Dude*, the #17 "Just Once" was Ingram's first success, resulting in three Grammy nominations — Best New Artist, Best Pop Male Vocal, and Best R&B Vocal — winning in the two latter catagories. Throughout the 80s, Ingram had steady popular success singing duets, but all of his solo albums failed to make a dent in the charts; in 1990 he scored his first solo hit, "I Don't Have the Heart." –STE

○ **Power of Great Music - Best of / WARNER**   1991
Includes his Top 40 duets — "Yah Mo B There" (#19, recorded with Michael McDonald), "Somewhere Out There" (#2, recorded with Linda Ronstadt), "Baby, Come to Me" (#1, recorded with Patti Austin), and his first solo hit, "I Don't Have the Heart" (#1) — as well as songs that have scored the urban charts. –RW

THE INTRIGUES

Soul. A slick trio that served up funky Philly soul during the early 70s. Their biggest hit in 1969 on the Yew label, "In a Moment," was slickly arranged and produced by Bobby Martin and Thom Bell, although its flip, "Scotchman Rock," was a rocking throwback to simpler times. The Intrigues's lush 1971 hit on Yew, "The Language of Love," was coproduced by Van McCoy. After an extended absence from the R&B charts, the trio reemerged from the shadows in 1985 with "Fly Girl." –BD

○ **Golden Classics / COLLECTABLES**
Slickly produced Philly R&B from the late 60s and early 70s with smooth harmonies and crisp arrangements. –BD

THE INTRUDERS

Soul. One of the earliest hitmaking vehicles for producers Kenny Gamble and Leon Huff, the Intruders were a leading R&B act from the mid 60s to the mid 70s. Fronted by Samuel "Little Sonny" Brown, the Intruders hit in 1966 with "(We'll Be) United" and the next year with "Together" on Gamble Records. Their breezy "Cowboys to Girls" and "Love Is like a Baseball Game" garnered plenty of pop crossover action in 1968, and their slick cover of the Dreamlovers hit "When We Get Married" scored in 1970. The quartet enjoyed their last two important R&B hits in 1973 — "I'll Always Love My Mama (Part 1)" and "I Wanna Know Your Name" — before switching to Gamble and Huff's TSOP logo. –BD

○ **Super Hits / CBS**   1973
A fine collection of hits by the 70s Gamble/Huff-produced soul team who brought you "Cowboys to Girls" and "Love Is like a Baseball Game." –JF

INXS

Rock/pop. During the 80s this Australian sextet transformed from a danceable new-wave band to a strong rock & roll singles band. Even at the beginning of their career they were too tough for new-wave — they had to compete with the legacy of AC/DC and the likes of Midnight Oil in the Australian pubs. Consequently INXS has always been more of a rock & roll band than a pop band. –STE

Shabooh Shoobah / ATLANTIC   1982
The best of INXS's early work. Slowly the post-punk synthesizers were being replaced with groove, as "The One Thing" proves. "Don't Change" still smacks of the early 80s, but in a positive way: the synthesizer eerily repeats itself over Michael Hutchence's cold vocals. –STE

Listen like Thieves / ATLANTIC   1985
INXS completes its transition into an excellent rock & roll singles band with this album. Unfortunately the new configuration works only for three songs: "What You Need," "Listen like Thieves," and "Kiss the Dirt (Falling Down the Mountain)." Yet these three songs are so strong (especially "What You Need") that the album cannot be dismissed completely. The album is worth its price just for "What You Need," a strong Stonesy groove with Michael Hutchence singing warmer than he ever has. –STE

○ **Kick / ATLANTIC**   1987
INXS's finest work, this is a strong album full of hit singles. "Need You Tonight" and "Devil Inside" were chart and dance smashes, along with several other tracks. INXS is a bit like the Rolling Stones in that they produce rock & roll music with a strong beat and catchy melodies, not to mention the overall sexuality of the music. –STE

X / ATLANTIC   1990
The followup to the smash *Kick* isn't quite as successful as its predecessor yet it packs quite a punch. Although "Suicide Blonde," "The Stairs," "Bitter Tears," and "Disappear," are as good as anything on *Kick*, the album suffers from songs that sound too similar. –STE

IRON BUTTERFLY

Psychedelic, heavy metal. Formed in 1966, Iron Butterfly performed a heavy, minor-key style of psychedelic rock/pop. Their debut album *Heavy* was a promising start but the followup effort, *In a Gadda Da Vida* (#4) became the biggest-selling album in Atlantic Records history until the advent of Led Zeppelin. This was primarily due to the 17:05-minute title track, which became a staple on the emerging progressive-FM-rock format. An edited version became a #30 hit. The followup album, *Ball*, did one better at #3.
Besides "In-a-Gadda-Da-Vida," Iron Butterfly charted with "Soul Experience" (#75), "In the Time of Our Lives" (#96), and "Easy Rider (Let the Wind Pay the Way)" (#66), from the movie *Easy Rider*. The band attempted a reunion in 1975 with

two albums, the #138 *Scorching Beauty* and *Sun and Steel*, before breaking up again. –RC

○ **In A Gadda Da Vida / ATLANTIC**   1968
The title song, in all its glory, is all you need. –DH

IRON CITY HOUSEROCKERS

Rock & roll. After years of toiling in the Pittsburgh bar scene, Iron City Houserockers, fronted by Joe Grushecky, made a brief splash in the early 80s with their Springsteenish blue-collar Heartland rock. –RC

○ **Love's So Tough / MCA**   1979
Tough, R&B-based rock from the heartland. –DS

Have a Good Time (But Get Out Alive) / MCA   1980
More driving blues/rock fused with Springsteen-type plitics from the Iron City Houserockers. –DS

IRON MAIDEN

Heavy metal. From their origins as a bar band in the mid 70s to the present, England's Iron Maiden has become one of the most imitated bands in heavy metal. The man who has held the group together through the rough times is bassist Steve Harris. Some of their theatrics were somewhat tacky in the early days, but by the late 70s they were already gaining a respectable following. EMI released their self-titled debut album in 1980, featuring Paul Di'Anno on vocals and Dave Smith on guitar. In the US, the album was released on Harvest.
The band's second album helped them gain a huge following all over Europe and America, but within the band there were problems. Out went Di'Anno and in came Bruce Dickenson, former vocalist for the band Samson. Another change was the addition of guitarist Adrian Smith (replacing Dennis Stratton), and it was this lineup (along with drummer Clive Burr) that took them over the top. The band's impact has been immense, selling millions, and their sound has easily distinguished them from other bands. –JB

○ **Iron Maiden / CAPITOL**   1980
The debut album that started it all for this band. Many of the songs remain all-time metal classics, including "Sanctuary" and "Running Free." –JB

○ **The Number of the Beast / CAPITOL**   1982
The first Maiden album to feature ex-Samson vocalist Bruce Dickenson. This is one powerful album with some great guitar work from Dave Murray and Adrian Smith and fantastic bass playing from Steve Harris. This is the album that brought the band success in the US, and it features the classics "Run to the Hills" and the title track. –JB

● **Piece of Mind / CAPITOL**   1983
The first Maiden album to feature drummer Nicko McBrain. *Peace of Mind* is easily one of their best efforts. Lead guitarists Adrian Smith and Dave Murray play their most creative work here, and the whole band is in top form. –JB

Powerslave / CAPITOL   1984
Iron Maiden gets more into lyrical themes this time around, featuring the 13-minute classic "Rime of the Ancient Mariner." –JB

CHRIS ISAAK   b 1956

Rock/pop, singer/songwriter. Unlike most modern singers whose work recalls vintage rock & roll, Chris Isaak manages to capture the subtle energy and tension of that music without parodying its mannerisms or excesses. "Wicked Game" — and indeed the entire *Heart Shaped World* album from which it was drawn — is among the better rock & roll recordings of the past decade.
There is an undeniable similarity between Isaak's vocals and the work of Roy Orbison, but it goes far beyond range or timbre. Although Orbison is remembered largely for his operatic ballads, his music was grounded in the blues and country mix that was prevalent at Sun records, where he began. Similarly, Isaak brings a biting intensity and dramatic

tension to his vocals. And despite its modernity, Isaak's instrumental backup is surprisingly restrained and minimalist. –HD

○ **Heart Shaped World / REPRISE**   1989
The album that really broke Isaak through to a mainstream audience, this features the title cut, "I'm Not Waiting," "Wrong to Love You," a driving rendition of "Diddley Daddy," and the surprise #6 hit "Wicked Game." Brooding and intense. –CK

ISLEY BROTHERS

R&B, soul, funk. They're still at it: recording artists since 1957, and hitmakers for almost as long. Inevitably, their music has changed, but this group's chief claim to fame remains their secularization of gospel call-and-response. They found that particular groove on "Shout" (cut for RCA in 1959), later followed by "Twist and Shout" on Wand in 1962 — definitely one of the ballsier twist records. Four years in the commercial wilderness followed before they signed with Tamla and came up with "This Old Heart of Mine."
They didn't work long on the Motown assembly line, though, and in 1969 revived their own T-Neck Records. Twenty years later they were still grinding out hits on the label, although their first T-Neck smash, "It's Your Thing," remains their biggest. Brothers have come and gone, as have sidemen — including Jimi Hendrix at one point. Still, the family that plays together stays together, although the group trading as the Isley Brothers today includes elements of Isley-Jasper-Isley (two younger brothers and a cousin), who had a hit with "Caravan of Love" in 1985. –CE

The Complete UA Sessions / EMI-USA   1991
After the Isleys left Scepter, they recorded for United Artists for a year, a period that produced no hits but a wealth of muscular R&B. Although there's some overlap with the first volume of Rhino's anthology, this one's essential for fans of the Isleys. –STE

○ **Isley Brothers Story - Vol. 1 / RHINO**   1991
Rhino's two Isley Brothers compilations provide the definitive portrait of the group. *Vol. 1: Rockin' Soul (1959-1968)* focuses on the Isleys's R&B beginnings, including both parts of "Shout," "This Old Heart of Mine (Is Weak for You)," and "Twist and Shout." –STE

● **Isley Brothers Story - Vol. 2 / RHINO**   1991
Isley Brothers Story - Vol. 2: The T-Neck Years (1969-1985). The Isley Brothers founded their own record label, T-Neck, in 1969, and along with the new label came a new direction and sound for the group. Funkier and harder, the Isleys charted more frequently than ever before in their career, including "That Lady" (#6), "Fight the Power" (#4), and the #2 "It's Your Thing." This completes the picture that *Vol. 1* began and is essential for any collection of early-70s soul. –STE

ERNIE ISLEY

Funk, hard rock, soul. Isley's Hendrixesque guitar style added hard-rock grit to 70s Isley Brothers hits such as "Who's That Lady" and "Fight the Power." –JF

○ **High Wire / ELEKTRA**   1990
An astonishingly diverse solo debut by the Isley's axeman, full of screaming guitars, tight riffs, ear-tugging melodies, and evocative vocals. –JF

IT BITES

Rock/pop, alternative rock. This British band combines the art-rock flair of 70s bands like Genesis and 10CC with a pop-metal guitar bite. Melodic, quirky, well-crafted rock. –SWB

○ **Eat Me in St. Louis / GEFFEN**   1989
Basically a greatest-hits collection, this album takes two from *The Big Lad in the Windmill* and some the import *Once around the World.* –SWB

IT'S A BEAUTIFUL DAY

Psychedelic. It's a Beautiful Day (formed 1967) featured the custom-made five-string violin work of former Utah Symphony member David LaFlamme, who also sang and wrote much of the material with his wife Linda. —RC

○ **It's a Beautiful Day / SAN FRANCISCO SOUND /**   1969

Even though *It's a Beautiful Day*'s lyrical content was basically hippie fluff, this debut was a production tour de force that sonically captured many of the distinctive elements of the San Francisco sound. The leadoff track, "White Bird" (#118), became an FM rock-radio classic. Other highlights included "Hot Summer Day," "Girl with No Eyes," "Wasted Union Blues," and "Bulgaria." This domestic CD, which is hard to find, is sold at the top end of the import price scale, which might have been acceptable if the complete cover art (inside and out) and informative liner notes had been included. In spite of those drawbacks, the remastering is exceptional. —RC

JACKIE & THE STARLITES

Doo-wop. Diminutive Jackie Rue's histrionic lead tenor distinguished the brief recording career of Jackie and the Starlites. They debuted in 1960 with their best-known ballad "Valerie" on Bobby Robinson's Fury label. After a few followups for Robinson, which included the solid-selling "I Found Out Too Late," the group recorded for another New York outfit, Hull/Mascot, before disbanding. Rue died of a drug overdose in the late 60s or early 70s. —BD

○ **Valerie / RELIC**

Greasy Harlem doo-wop in all its late-50s glory from this unjustly obscure aggregation. —BD

JACKSON 5

Motown. The Jackson 5 was Motown's last great pop group and among the most successful singles acts of the 70s. The group consisted of five brothers — Jackie (b May 4, 1951), Tito (b Oct 15, 1953), Jermaine (b Dec 11, 1954), Marlon (b Mar 12, 1957), and Michael Jackson (b Aug 29, 1958). They grew up in Gary, IN, and were first organized as a group by their father, Joe Jackson, in 1966. In essence, the group was a vocal ensemble centered on Michael, who, though the youngest, was clearly the most talented. The group came to the attention of Motown and was signed in 1969. Their first four singles, "I Want You Back," "ABC," "The Love You Save," and "I'll Be There," all hit #1 in 1970; "Mama's Pearl" and "Never Can Say Goodbye" each got to #2 in 1971. In 1972 Motown launched both Michael Jackson and Jermaine Jackson as solo acts, and the group's efforts were gradually less successful in the following years, though "Dance Machine" was a #2 hit in 1974. In 1975 Jackie, Tito, Marlon, and Michael signed to Epic Records, adding brother Randy (b Oct 29, 1961) and became the Jacksons (the name the Jackson 5 was owned by Motown). (Although Jermaine stayed at Motown, he would rejoin the group in 1984.) —WR

☆ **Anthology / MOTOWN**   1976

This three-LP set contains all 18 of the Jackson 5's pop-chart hits, plus solo hits by Jermaine and Michael, among its 33 cuts. It's the definitive collection and a good sampler of the sound of pop/R&B, ca. 1969-1975. —WR

CHUCK JACKSON   b 1937

Soul, R&B. Chuck Jackson first hit as a member of the Dell-Vikings (1957-1959) before striking out on his own with a string of soulful pop classics ("I Don't Want to Cry," "Any Day Now") on Wand, a subsidiary of Scepter, during the early 60s. With a delivery by turns sophisticated and hoarsely sexy, he was part of a group of singers, Ben E. King among them, whose gospel-tinged style predated and influenced the singing of 60s soul men like Wilson Pickett. Jackson continues to be very active; in 1992 he received the prestigious Pioneer Award from the Rhythm and Blues Foundation. His work is well documented on Capricorn's boxed set, *The Scepter Records Story.* —CO

○ **Golden Classics / COLLECTABLES**

All the Wand Records hits, including "Any Day Now" and "I Don't Want to Cry." —RP

Good Things / KENT   1991

Twenty-four tracks, hits and unreleased material, from Wand Records. (Import) —RP

DEON JACKSON   b 1946

Soul. Still in his teens when he began recording, Deon Jackson's 1966 smash "Love Makes the World Go Round" was an engaging piece of soft Detroit soul. The Ann Arbor, MI, product caught the ear of Detroit producer Ollie McLaughlin, who began recording him for his Carla label in 1962. Jackson's first couple of singles ended up on Atlantic with little commercial feedback, but when he cut "Love Makes the World Go Round" for Carla in 1965, he was an overnight sensation. Nothing else Jackson did equaled its success, although "Love Takes a Long Time Growing" and "Ooh Baby" were solid-selling encores. Jackson's lilting vocal style has served him well over the last 15 years as a lounge entertainer in suburban Chicago. —RP

○ **Golden Classics / COLLECTABLES**

All the Carla hits. 60s recordings. —RP

FREDDIE JACKSON   b 1956

Urban R&B, soul. A former member of Mystic Merlin and backup singer for Melba Moore and Evelyn King, among others. Jackson had solo hits in the mid 80s. —ED

○ **Rock Me Tonight / CAPITOL**   1985

An album that in the 80s launched this singer who rivaled to Luther Vandross for male R&B supremacy. Includes the hits "You Are My Lady" (#12), "He'll Never Love You (Like I Do)" (#25), and the #18 title track. —RW

Just like the First Time / CAPITOL   1986

An excellent followup, featuring "Jam Tonight" (#32). —RW

Don't Let Love Slip Away / CAPITOL   1988

Slick and smooth, but he retains a soul/gospel flavor. —RW

JANET JACKSON   b 1966

Dance-pop, rock/pop. Janet Jackson is the ninth and last child in the musically talented Jackson family that includes the Jackson 5, Michael Jackson, and Jermaine Jackson. Janet Jackson performed on stage with her brothers at the age of seven. At ten, she acted in the TV series "Good Times" and was later seen in "Diff'rent Strokes" and "Fame." She released her first album, *Janet Jackson,* in 1982 and her second, *Dream Street,* in 1984, but neither of these records was notably successful. Then, in 1985, Jackson turned to the production team of Jimmy Jam and Terry Lewis (formerly of the Time) for the album *Control,* which, ironically, emphasized the artist's new maturity and independence, even though most of the songs were co-compositions of the three. *Control* was a massive hit: it topped the charts, selling more than four million copies, and spawned five Top Ten hits, including the #1 "When I Think of You." The followup, *Rhythm Nation 1814,* did even better, spawning seven Top Ten hits, among them the #1s "Miss You Much," "Escapade," and "Black Cat." In 1991 Jackson signed a new recording contract with Virgin Records for a reported $32 million. —WR

○ **Control / A&M**   1986

Jam and Lewis tailor their contemporary dance-pop to the emerging personality of Jackson, who is attempting to take "Control" of her life on this record. In the course of that attempt, she comes across as an aggressive, independent woman, notably on "What Have You Done for Me Lately." But the album is primarily a production showcase; it may be tailored to Jackson's persona, but the real artists are Jam and Lewis. —WR

Rhythm Nation 1814 / A&M   1989

Jam and Lewis have more beats up their sleeves, and the

singer's own personality is even more submerged than it was on *Control*, but this is the height of 80s dance-pop. —WR

JERMAINE JACKSON
b 1954

Motown, soul. When his brothers left Motown in 1975, Jermaine remained on the label for a shot at solo success. His career has been spotty, with his best work being the 1980 *Let's Get Serious* collaboration with Stevie Wonder. —RAB

Let's Get Serious / MOTOWN   1979
This is his finest solo Motown album; produced by Stevie Wonder. —RAB

○ **Greatest Hits & Rare Classics / MOTOWN**   1991
Encompassing his Motown career, some cuts are quality, some mundane. —RAB

JOE JACKSON
b 1955

New-wave, rock/pop. Although Joe Jackson initially appeared to fit in neatly with such new-wave singer/songwriters as Elvis Costello and Graham Parker when he appeared in the late 70s, he has displayed a much broader range on his numerous record releases since. Born in Burton-on-Trent, England, Jackson studied music as a youth and earned a piano scholarship to the Royal College of Music, which he attended from 1971 to 1974.
Look Sharp!, his debut album released in March 1979, featured a fast-paced, guitar-driven rock style, with Jackson spitting out sometimes bitter, sometimes vulnerable lyrics, notably on the single "Is She Really Going Out with Him?," which hit #21 in the US. The album got to #20 and went gold. *I'm the Man*, an album in the same style released in October, got to #22.
Jackson then began the first of his many changes of style. *Beat Crazy*, released in the fall of 1980, marked a sharp turn toward reggae and a drop in Jackson's commercial fortunes. *Joe Jackson's Jumpin' Jive* (1981) contained big-band and jump-blues standards from the 40s. In 1982 Jackson moved to New York City, adopting some of the sophisticated style of Cole Porter and some of the small-band jazz music found in the city's clubs for *Night and Day*, released in June. The album was Jackson's biggest hit, going to #4 and producing the hit singles "Steppin' Out" and "Breaking Us in Two."
Jackson composed a film soundtrack, *Mike's Murder*, in 1983, then made *Body and Soul* in a style similar to *Night and Day*. It hit #20 and included the Top 15 hit "You Can't Get What You Want (Till You Know What You Want)." In 1985 Jackson composed music for the Japanese film *House of the Poet*. Some of the music was later released on his album *Will Power*. Jackson's 1986 album was the three-sided *Big World*, which reached #34. *Will Power*, issued in 1987, was an instrumental album combining classical and jazz styles. It was followed in 1988 by the double *Live 1980/1986* and the soundtrack to the film *Tucker*. After his next pop album, *Blaze of Glory* (1989), did not succeed commercially, Jackson jumped to Virgin Records, which issued *Laughter and Lust* (1991). —WR

Look Sharp! / A&M   1979
Hyperactive new-wave rock overlaid with the intelligent, caustic world view of a man as angry as any punk, but far more perceptive. Includes the hit "Is She Really Going Out with Him?" —WR

● **Night and Day / A&M**   1982
Since Jackson has already demonstrated his broad musical tastes by turning from rock to "jumpin' jive" on his last album, that he was able to incorporate Latin, dance, and sophisticated ballad styles into his music wasn't so surprising. But that he could do it all so well was delightful. Includes "Steppin' Out" and "Breaking Us in Two." (Also available on Mobile Fidelity.) —WR

○ **Big World / A&M**   1986
A brilliant collection of songs, running over an hour, finds Jackson as biting as ever as he surveys the world, but also tenderly reflective on "Home Town." —WR

○ **Laughter & Lust / VIRGIN**   1991
Jackson's work has sometimes been too didactic for its own

good, but on *Laughter & Lust* he managed to balance the agenda with a nice blend of humor and heart. His perpetual disdain for the pop music industry found full flower in "Hit Single," in which Jackson finds himself in "pure pop heaven," where angels only want to hear the hits, but not "the whole damn album." Other highlights are the classic acidic Jackson-style rocker "Obvious Song," the hyperkinetic "Jamie G," a faithful remake of Fleetwood Mac's "Oh Well," and Jackson's ode to the dynamics of love in "Stranger Than Fiction." —RC

MICHAEL JACKSON
b 1958

Motown, dance-pop. As part of the Jackson 5, a group made up of his brothers, Michael Jackson was among the most popular singing stars of the 70s. On his own, he was the biggest pop star of the 80s. Jackson was always the visual and vocal focus of the Jackson 5, who broke through to national success on the Motown label in 1970, when he was 11, with the first of four straight #1 hits, "I Want You Back." Jackson was also promoted as a solo artist, and he scored his first hit, the #4 "Got to Be There," in 1971. Subsequent hits included his remake of "Rockin' Robin" and "Ben" in 1972.
Jackson's and the Jackson 5's fortunes declined somewhat after the early 70s, and the group moved to Epic at mid-decade, with Michael temporarily abandoning his solo career and subsuming his group leadership to other members of what was now called the Jacksons. The group gradually built back its popularity by writing its own material. Jackson returned to solo work in 1979 with *Off the Wall*, a mature combination of driving dance songs ("Don't Stop 'Til You Get Enough") and feelingly sung ballads ("She's Out of My Life") that outsold any previous group or solo effort, and spawned four Top Ten hits.
Jackson again recorded and toured with the Jacksons, but his next album, *Thriller* (1982), became a musical phenomenon. It was the biggest-selling album of all time, moving 20 million copies in the US alone and including seven Top Ten hits. Clearly Jackson had grown beyond his brothers, but he stayed with them for one more album and tour in 1984.
His followup album, *Bad* (1987), accompanied by a solo world tour, sold six million copies domestically. Only six of its seven singles hit the Top Ten (one stopped at #11), but five in a row hit #1.
In late 1991 Jackson returned with *Dangerous*, which, by mid-1992, had sold four million copies and spawned the hits "Black and White," "Remember the Time," "In the Closet," and "Jam," no doubt with more to come. Jackson's second world tour, launched in Europe in June 1992, was expected to continue into 1993. —WR

○ **Off the Wall / EPIC**   1979
If you were listening to the Jacksons's *Destiny* from the previous year, maybe you were less surprised than many that Michael Jackson was capable of making an album this accomplished and assured. From the first moments, he seems bursting with the wide range of music included, from the first side's clutch of irresistible dance tracks ("Don't Stop 'Til You Get Enough," "Rock with You," "Working Day and Night") to the light pop and ballads ("She's out of My Life," "Off the Wall") of Side 2. Throughout, Jackson's flexible tenor coos and growls by turns, always goosing the songs along. Deservedly a massive hit, this is less dated today than much of the dance music of that era. —WR

★ **Thriller / EPIC**   1982
What impresses after a decade is Jackson's range of musical expression, one that touches the schmaltzy pop of Paul McCartney (his duet partner on "The Girl Is Mine") on one side and the hard rock of Van Halen (whose lead guitarist, Eddie Van Halen, is heard on "Beat It") on the other, with plenty of mainstream rock/pop and dance music in between. It's no accident that the record found a home in so many record collections — there's good music here for everyone. And of course, by summing up the state of pop music, Jackson also redefined it — this was a high-water mark for pop music never equaled since, even in his subsequent music. —WR

○ **Anthology / MOTOWN**   1986
Michael Jackson's greatest hits (1971-1975) emphasize his waif-like charm and youth (he was 13 when the first of these songs appeared) in ballads such as "Got to Be There," "Ben" (even if it is a love song to a rat), and "I Wanna Be Where You Are." The upbeat cover of "Rockin' Robin" is equally appealing. –WR

○ **Bad / EPIC**   1987
A partially successful attempt to remake *Thriller*. Interestingly, Jackson did not turn to a softer, more broadly commercial approach but instead upped the dance-rock ante. Songs such as "Dirty Diana" and "Smooth Criminal" found him striding forward in terms of rhythm and beat. And with seven hit singles out of ten tracks (five at #1), this, like *Thriller*, is in effect a Michael Jackson greatest-hits record, covering 1987-1989. –WR

Dangerous / EPIC   1991
Wisely, Jackson altered his creative process here, jettisoning producer Quincy Jones in favor of Teddy Riley and bringing in several songwriting collaborators. The result is an updated dance-floor success (the drums are way up in the mix), though the songwriting sometimes seem schematic. When Jackson is left more or less to himself, he is less R&B-oriented, notably on the pop ballad "Heal the World" (not yet a major hit at this writing, but soon to be) and the guitar-driven rock/pop song "Black or White" (a Stones riff, though taken at a tempo the Stones never attempted). Rather than resting on his laurels, Jackson continues to work hard to maintain and further the quality of his work. –WR

MILLIE JACKSON   *b* 1944

R&B, soul. Millie Jackson's salaciously uncensored raps have earned her a reputation as an X-rated soul artist who isn't afraid to tell it like it is. The Georgia native moved to New Jersey as a teenager, where she began singing. Debuting on wax in 1970 for MGM, Jackson moved to Spring Records the next year and embarked on a long string of soul hits, including "Ask Me What You Want" and "My Man, a Sweet Man" in 1972 and "Hurts So Good" the following year. Very few of Jackson's R&B chart items crossed over to pop playlists, but her ribald commentaries remain a staple of urban contemporary fare. –BD

Caught Up / SPRING   1974
A concept album based on a love triangle. Outrageous raps between tracks. –RP

○ **Still Caught Up / SOUTHBOUND**   1990
Even better than *Caught Up*! A stronger story line and dynamite production on this reissue of a 1975 recording. –RP

PYTHON LEE JACKSON

Rock & roll. This is actually vocalist Rod Stewart recording with an Australian instrumental group under a pseudonym before he achieved major stardom. They scored one hit, "In a Broken Dream," which was reissued in 1972 to cash in on Stewart's solo success. –CK

○ **In a Broken Dream / GNP**
Featuring Rod Stewart's vocals on three tracks, including the title track. –LL

WALTER JACKSON   1939-1983

R&B, soul. Soul crooner who made his first recordings in the mid 60s for the Okeh label. Such hits as "Welcome Home" and "My Ship Is Coming In" represent the cream of his career. –JF

○ **Walter Jackson's Greatest Hits / CBS**   1987
All the Okeh hits — stunning vocals from this greatly underrated soul balladeer. –RP

WANDA JACKSON   *b* 1937

Rockabilly. Fact: Wanda Jackson was the greatest female rockabilly singer of the late 50s/early 60s. Starting out as a

Decca country singer in 1954, Oklahoma-born Wanda began her rock & roll career with Capitol in 1956 at age 18. Her trademark growl on the raveup "Fujiyama Mama" sounds like she gargled with nitroglycerine: explosive stuff. The Rhino compilation is evenly divided into Wanda's rocking sides, nine tracks cut between 1956-1960, with the remaining nine songs representing some of her best country output of 1958-1970. (For more of Wanda's rockabilly sides, seek out either the French Capitol *Only Rock & Roll* double-album set or the British Charly double album, *Let's Have a Party*.) –DMAC

Early Wanda Jackson / BEAR FAMILY   1983
This vinyl import reaches back before Jackson's rockabilly and presents her earliest sides, from 1954-1957. –JT

○ **Best of Wanda Jackson / RHINO**   1987
Perhaps the greatest of the rockabilly women, Wanda Jackson later turned to pure country. Rhino's *Best of Wanda Jackson - Rockin' in the Country* presents the best of both eras here on this 18-track collection. –JT

THE JACKSONS

Dance-pop. The Jacksons was the new name adopted by the Jackson 5 in 1975 when they signed to Epic Records, both because Motown Records owned the name Jackson 5 and because the group personnel changed, with Jermaine Jackson leaving and being replaced by Randy Jackson. This version of the group continued until 1983, when Jermaine rejoined his brothers for a tour and an album, *Victory*. By 1989 Michael and Marlon had departed, leaving the Jacksons a quartet consisting of Jermaine, Jackie, Tito, and Randy. –WR

The Jacksons / CBS   1976
Epic turned the Jacksons over to Philly soul producers Kenny Gamble and Leon Huff for this smooth, danceable label debut featuring the discofied hit "Enjoy Yourself." –WR

○ **Destiny / CBS**   1978
The Jacksons are finally turned loose to write and produce themselves, and the result is their best (non-hits collection) ever. The dance tracks still sound fresh ("Blame It on the Boogie," "Shake Your Body (Down to the Ground)"), and the ballads are heartfelt and smooth. This album is a dry run for Michael Jackson's adult solo career. –WR

Triumph / CBS   1980
An excellent followup, featuring the hits "Can You Feel It" and "Heartbreak Hotel." –WR

MICK JAGGER   *b* 1943

Rock/pop. Lead singer/songwriter for the Rolling Stones. After occasional forays away from the group, especially into acting, Jagger finally launched a full-fledged solo career in 1985. –WR

○ **She's the Boss / CBS**   1985
Jagger employs a Who's Who including Herbie Hancock, Pete Townshend, and Jeff Beck for an album that replaces the familiar sound of the Stones with a more sophisticated but no less hard-rock sound. And the voice *is* familiar. Features the hit "Just Another Night." –WR

THE JAM

Punk, rock & roll. First-wave mod punks, led by Paul Weller, began as energetic Who clones but quickly became one of England's most distinct and proudly British combos. Weller's songwriting — alternately political and romantic — invited comparisons with Pete Townshend and Ray Davies, but the band's unflagging energy (and the deadlocked rhythm section of bassist Bruce Foxton and skin-basher Rick Buckler) made them a hit on the then-burgeoning punk scene. Although they never scored a hit in America, by 1980 the group had become British superstars, topping that country's charts with nearly every single. In the mid 80s, just as the group was branching out into soulful new territory, Paul Weller called a halt to the group and quickly formed the Style Council. Foxton and Buckler also struck out on the solo path, but with tepid results. –JF

In the City / POLYDOR 1977
A spunky and abrasive debut that mixes a mod's penchant for soul grooves with some fine piss-and-vinegar originals. –JF

Gift / POLYDOR 1982
A blatant stab at expanding their soul roots. Pretty spotty, really, but "Town Called Malice," "Ghosts," and "Just Who Is the 5 O'Clock Hero?" are among the band's best work. –JF

Dig the New Breed / POLYDOR 1982
A live hodgepodge culled from material from 1977-1982. A rocking affair that's not bad, as far as live albums go. –JF

○ **All Mod Cons / POLYDOR** 1978
This, their third album, expands their sound and includes some of Weller's most ambitious songs, like "To Be Someone," "The Place I Love," and "Down in the Tube Station at Midnight." –JF

○ **Setting Sons / POLYDOR** 1979
A rough-edged concept album about lost friendships, set to the war-torn angst of "Private Hell," "Burning Sky," and "The Eton Rifles." –JF

○ **Sound Affects / POLYDOR** 1980
A return to the expansive sound and love-and-politics of *All Mod Cons*, highlighted by the snarling "Pretty Green," "Set the House Ablaze," and "Start!," a fiery rewrite of the Beatles hit "Taxman." –JF

★ **Snap! / POLYDOR** 1983
A generous overview of the band's best, including many British-only singles that are musts for fans. Start with this one. –JF

COLIN JAMES

Blues/rock. A Canadian blues-rock guitarist whose sound places him somewhere between ZZ Top's slickness and Stevie Ray Vaughan's grit. –RC

○ **Colin James / ATLANTIC** 1988
Impressive debut by the blues-drenched guitarist. Includes the wrenching gem, "Voodoo Thing." –DS

Sudden Stop / ATLANTIC 1990
A solid, stylistically varied followup by this Canadian guitarist. –DS

JAMES GANG

Hard rock, rock & roll. At the top of the 70s, Joe Walsh (James Gang lead guitarist and singer) blasted onto the music scene as the new kid on the block to watch. Walsh's distinctive staggered lead guitar phrasing, bare-boned boogie riff-work, and tonal integrity immediately earned him high marks, and stories of Walsh upstaging Jimi Hendrix during their warmup slots with the Experience spread like wildfire.
Walsh backed up the buzz with the James Gang's second album, *Rides Again*, which was a tour de force of dynamic, hard trio rock. What James Gang drummer Jim Fox and bassist Dale Peters lacked in inventive fire (à la Cream or Jimi Hendrix Experience), they made up for in providing a rock-solid foundation for Walsh's soaring guitar flights and wide chordal sound washes.
After one more studio effort, *Third*, and a live album, Walsh split and went solo, leaving the James Gang to flounder around and produce a couple of minor FM rock hits before falling apart. –RC

○ **The Best of the James Gang / MCA** 1973
A good collection of their innovative hard rock, featuring "Walk Away" and "Funk 49." –DH

RICK JAMES   *b* 1952

Funk. Considered somewhat of a renegade, Rick James burst on the scene in the late 70s with a blend of rock and soul music he called "punk funk." His lyrics usually encouraged drug use and illicit sex. –RAB

Come Get It! / MOTOWN 1978
An excellent debut set. Very risqué for its time, with "Mary Jane." –RAB

○ **Street Songs / MOTOWN** 1981
His best work to date, with "Super Freak" and "Give It to Me Baby." –RAB

● **Greatest Hits / MOTOWN** 1986
The best of his "punk funk." Includes "Super Freak," "Give It to Me Baby," and "You & I." –RAB

TOMMY JAMES & THE SHONDELLS   *b* 1947

Rock/pop. During the last half of the 60s, Tommy James & the Shondells were one of America's most successful pop acts, generating 14 Top 40 hits between 1966 and 1969. James formed the original Shondells at the age of twelve, in 1960. In 1963, they recorded a Jeff Barry-Ellie Greenwich song called "Hanky Panky" for the Snap label. Two years later, a Pittsburgh DJ picked up on the song and made it into a regional hit. James and the original Shondells parted ways because the band members didn't want to relocate from Indiana, and James formed a new Shondells by taking on a group called the Raconteurs. In 1966 they signed to Morris Levy's Roulette, which reissued "Hanky Panky" (it became a #1 million-seller).
For the next two years, they embodied lightweight chewy pop with hits like "I Think We're Alone Now" (#4) and "Mirage" (#10). The group developed a heavier sound with the percussive 1968 hit "Mony Mony" (#3). In keeping with the times, they became more psychedelic, best captured in their #1 "Crimson and Clover." The Shondells continued to chart until James left for a moderately successful solo career in 1970. James's biggest hit was the #4 "Draggin' the Line." The Shondells changed their name to Hog Heaven to no appreciable success. During the 80s, the Shondells's material enjoyed a resurgence of popularity among various pop and rock artists. Joan Jett scored with "Crimson and Clover," while Billy Idol's version of "Mony Mony" and Tiffany's "I Think We're Alone Now" took turns at the #1 position in November of 1987. –RC

○ **Anthology / RHINO** 1989
James and his band had a remarkable string of hits from the mid 60s to the early 70s, largely because of an uncanny ability to keep current with fast-changing pop trends, from their first garage-band hit, "Hanky Panky," to their psychedelicized songs like "Crimson and Clover." Even more remarkable, the music holds up entertainingly today, and this well-annotated, 27-track compilation contains all the hits and more. –WR

VINNIE JAMES

Singer/songwriter, folk/rock. This folk/rock guitarist was influenced by the music of Bob Dylan and Jackson Browne. He moved to Southern California in 1986 and formed a band, Rumbletown. His music fits along with that of the Cowboy Junkies and Michael Penn. –BC

○ **All American Boy / RCA** 1991
T-Bone Burnette supervised preproduction on this great debut. Al Kooper played keyboards and Aronoff supplied drums. Standout cuts: "Black Money," "Hey Geronimo," and "Walking on Stone." –CR

JAN & DEAN

Rock/pop. A surf-music duo dating from the late 50s, when they were a harmony duo. Wilder and less inhibited than the Beach Boys, Jan Berry and Dean Torrence were also less talented, but their music holds up equally to that of the Beach Boys from the same era, mostly by virtue of its manic kinetic energy. –BE

○ **Surf City - The Best of Jan & Dean / CAPITOL** 1990
The definitive collection of all their hits — their most resilient material. Surf music ethos, from the silly to the sublime. –BE

JANE'S ADDICTION

Alternative rock. Jane's Addiction were one of the most hotly pursued rock bands when they gained notice in Los Angeles in the mid 80s, with record companies at their feet. Flamboyant frontman Perry Farrell, formerly of the band Psi Com, has an undeniable charisma and an interest in provocative art (he designed the band's album covers) and Jane's Addiction plays a hybrid of rock music — metal with strains of punk, folk, jazz, or you-name-it.

The quartet comprising Farrell, bassist Eric Avery, drummer Stephen Perkins, and guitarist Dave Navarro) had already released their debut album as well, in the form of a live recording from the Roxy in Hollywood. Finally, Warner Brothers won the bidding war and released *Nothing Shocking* in 1988. The band's abrasive sound and aggressive atttitude (typified by the nude sculpture on the cover) led to some resistance, but Jane's Addiction began to break through to an audience: the album spent 35 weeks in the charts.

Ritual de lo Habitual followed in 1990 and was the band's commercial breakthrough, reaching the Top 20 and going gold. Jane's Addiction headlined the 1991 Lollapalooza Tour, one of the few successful summer road shows that year, but at the end of it, the group split. −WR

Nothing's Shocking / WARNER   1988
The cover (a sculpture of two naked females joined at the hips with their hair ablaze) screams that this is an artsy album, and it is. Jane's Addiction, thanks to frontman Perry Farrell, brings *art* to hard rock. Instead of provoking, the ambitions mostly irritate. Farrell's voice wears thin after a few songs, and it's not helped much by the post-Zeppelin stumble of the band — Navarro is no Jimmy Page. When the music is acceptable, the lyrics are annoyingly self-conscious, making the whole thing implode. Still, if *Nothing's Shocking* is absorbed in concentrated spurts instead of an hour-long session, there are some high points to be found, particularly "Summertime Rolls" and the Lou Reed rip, "Jane Says." −STE

○ **Ritual de lo Habitual / WARNER**   1990
Throughout the first half of *Ritual*, Jane's Addiction manages to groove, creating the best rock & roll of their short career. In particular the two Bo Diddley knock-offs ("Stop!" and the single "Been Caught Stealing") sound tight, but on the second half the indulgent ten-minute songs are hauled out, beginning with the insufferable *menage à trois* magnum opus "Three Days." Still, the band manages to salvage the album with "Classic Girl," one of their best songs. −STE

JAPAN

Alternative pop. Japan was part of the short-lived "new romantic" movement in British pop. Members of Japan included brothers David Sylvian and Steve Jansen (original family name "Batt, b 1958 and 1959, respectively), Mick Karn (b 1958), Richard Barbieri (b 1957), and Rob Dean (b 1959). Precursors to new-age music, Japan combined Eastern influences with synth-pop overlay, giving them a staunch UK following that has never translated into US chart success. −CK

○ **Gentlemen Take Polaroids / CAROLINE**   1980
First fully realized album in the group's latter-day phase. −SA

○ **Tin Drum / CAROLINE**   1981
A highly atmospheric effort strongly influenced by folk music of their namesake country; an early-80s classic. −SA

Oil on Canvas / VIRGIN   1983
An outstanding live album focusing on *Tin Drum* and *Polaroids*-era material. −SA

Exorcising Ghosts / VIRGIN   1984
A compilation of Virgin-era material. −SA

JAY & THE AMERICANS

Rock/pop, doo-wop. Jay and the Americans were a vocal group from Brooklyn formed by New York University students John ("Jay") Traynor, Kenny Vance (b Dec 9, 1943), Sandy Deane (b Jan 31, 1940), and Howie Kane (b Jun 6, 1942). Marty Sanders (b Feb 28, 1941) joined in 1961, the year before they scored their first hit, "She Cried." Traynor left the group after the hit and was replaced by David Blatt (b Nov 2, 1938), who took the

name "Jay Black." The group scored six more Top 40 hits through the end of 1965, all based around Black's dramatic (and near-operatic) tenor, among them the Top Fives "Come a Little Bit Closer" and "Cara Mia." They slowed down a little after that but came back in 1969 with a gold-selling version of "This Magic Moment" (the old Drifters hit). In total, they placed 18 records in the Hot 100.

The group personnel altered in the late 60s and early 70s. Then-future Steely Dan members Donald Fagen and Walter Becker played in the backup group for a time. Vance recorded solo and eventually found success as a musical director of movies. Black kept the band going on the oldies circuit. When last heard at a benefit concert in New Jersey at the start of the 90s, he could still hit those high notes in "Cara Mia." −WR

All Time Greatest Hits / RHINO   1986
Concise 1986 vinyl collection of key hits. −JT

○ **Come a Little Bit Closer / CAPITOL**   1990
Jay Black possesses one of the most remarkable voices in rock & roll. On *Come a Little Bit Closer - The Best of Jay & the Americans*, an exhaustive 28-song collection, you get all of the hits in superb fidelity, and plenty of bonuses. −JT

THE JB'S

R&B, soul, funk. Maceo Parker joined James Brown's fabled band in 1964, Alfred "Pee Wee" Ellis joined the fold two years later, and Fred Wesley came on board in 1968. Ellis cowrote such classics as "Cold Sweat" and "Say It Loud - I'm Black and I'm Proud," and both he and Wesley at various points were musical director of the JB's. Parker was immortalized in Brown's famous incantation "Maceo, come blow your horn." Ellis also served as musical director for Van Morrison, while Wesley and Parker were part of the Parliament/Funkadelic gang at their peak in the mid and late 70s. The three of them have recorded in various permutations as Maceo and All the King's Men, Maceo and the Macks, the JB's, Fred Wesley and the New JB's, Fred Wesley and the Horny Horns, the JB Horns and simply under any one of their individual names. In the 80s and early 90s, with the resurgence of interest in James Brown and Parliament/Funkadelic, the three horn men have been involved in a plethora of recordings. (Note: All of the albums made by Parker, Ellis, and Wesley in their various permutations have been included here; the artist credited with the album appears at the end of the review.) −RB

Doing Their Own Thing / HOUSE OF THE FOX   1970
Recorded and released after a mutiny by most of James Brown's late-60s band, *Doing Their Own Thing* contains 12 slabs of superb early-70s style funk. Mostly instrumental, radio play for the album and subsequent singles appears to have been blocked by Brown himself. (Credited to Maceo Parker.) −RB

○ **Doing It to Death / PEOPLE / BB 77**   1973
Extended live "funkafizing" including a ten-minute version of the #1 R&B hit "Doing It to Death." Written, produced, and arranged by James Brown. −RB

Damn Right I Am Somebody / PEOPLE / BB 197   1974
More of the same sparse, cutting-edge funk, including a Top 40 R&B hit in the title cut. (Credited to Fred Wesley & the JB's.) −RB

○ **Breakin' Bread / PEOPLE**   1974
The last of the Fred Wesley and the JB's albums. "Breakin' Bread" and "Makin' Love" charted R&B. The funk is still much in evidence, although some new twists and turns manifest themselves on the "rapped" title cut. (Credited to Fred Wesley & the New JB's.) −RB

○ **A Blow for Me, A Toot for You / ATLANTIC / BB 181** 1977
Produced by George Clinton and Bootsy Collins and recorded with the company of much of the P-Funk Mob, *A Blow for Me, A Toot for You* showcases a new, slinkier, more produced and less hard-edged edition of the J. B. Horns. The lead cut, a remake of Parliament's "Up for the Down Stroke," received a little R&B airplay. (Credited to Fred Wesley and the Horny Horns.) −RB

New Friends / ANTILLES   1990

Wesley and Parker in the company of jazz musicians Gerri Allen, Anthony Cox, and Robin Eubanks. This is by far the jazziest of Fred, Maceo, and Pee Wee's recordings, covering the likes of Thelonious Monk, Duke Ellington, and Dizzy Gillespie. Wesley also proves himself to be a fine jazz writer, "For the Elders" being particularly notable. (Credited to Fred Wesley.) –RB

The JB Horns / GRAMAVISION   1990

On an album made up of eleven originals, the three horn men turn in a fine, if undistinguished mix of jazz and funk. Worth hearing just for Fred's rapping, the gently swinging "Mother's Kitchen," and the sly "Everywhere Is Out of Town." (Credited to Fred Wesley w/ Pee Wee and Maceo.) –RB

● **For All the King's Men / 4TH & BROADWAY**   1990

Produced by Bill Laswell and Bootsy Collins, this five-cut CD EP includes Wesley, Parker, Bobby Byrd, Bootsy Collins, and Sly Stone on one cut. "Let 'Em Out" is a paean to free James Brown. That and "Sax Machine" appear in two different versions. Hilarious and serious-as-a-heart-attack funk all at once. (Credited to Maceo Parker.) –RB

Roots Revisited / VERVE   1990

Ellis, Wesley, and Parker in the company of jazz keyboardist Don Pullen and Bootsy Collins. The first of a string of new recordings, *Roots Revisited* is half jazz, half soul, with a little funk thrown in for good measure. It's the first time these three have played jazz on record. The album includes wonderfully invigorating versions of Charles Mingus's "Better Get It in Yo' Soul" and the Impressions's "People Get Ready." (Credited to Maceo Parker.) –RB

Mo' Roots / VERVE   1991

The second *Roots* installment, *Mo' Roots* was cut minus Pullen and Collins, leaning a little more toward the instrumental soul side. Three fine originals in conjunction with covers of Ray Charles, Marvin Gaye, Otis Redding, Horace Silver, and Lionel Hampton. (Credited to Maceo Parker.) –RB

JEFFERSON AIRPLANE / STARSHIP

Folk/rock, psychedelic, hard rock. Jefferson Airplane (formed July 1965), along with the Grateful Dead, Quicksilver Messenger Service, and Big Brother & the Holding Company, spearheaded the San Francisco rock sound of the 60s and the idealistic hippie message of free drugs and free sex. Compared to many of the Bay Area statements of flower power and peace, Jefferson Airplane always possessed a darker, more revolutionary image. Frontperson Grace Slick (b Oct 30, 1939) was a more-than-willing outspoken mouthpiece.

Musically, the band ranged from reflective acoustic gems (revealing their folk origins) to explosive excursions into psychedelia. Their performance of "Volunteers" at the legendary Woodstock festival was a highlight.

At the top of the 70s, Jefferson Airplane formed the RCA-distributed Grunt Records, on which they released their subsequent albums as well as albums by Papa John Creach and Hot Tuna. During this time, their counterculture tirades began to sound as tiring as the nagging, parental "Establishment."

In 1974 they become the Jefferson Starship. Their 1975 album *Red Octopus* became their biggest-selling album to date, generating lead singer Marty Balin's #3 hit "Miracles." Shortly thereafter, Grace Slick took a leave absence until 1981. Singer Mickey Thomas (formerly with Elvin Bishop) joined in 1979 and helped usher the band into further mainstream rock-radio success.

After long-time band leader Paul Kantner left Jefferson Starship in 1984, the band dropped the first word in its name. At that point it consisted of Mickey Thomas, Grace Slick, guitarist Craig Chaquico (b 1955), bassist Pete Sears, and drummer Donny Baldwin. This unit immediately scored with the #1 hits "We Built This City" and "Sara" and the million-selling album *Knee Deep in the Hoopla*. Sears had left by the

time of the 1987 followup, *No Protection*, which featured the #1 "Nothing's Gonna Stop Us Now" and the Top Ten "It's Not Over ('Til It's Over)." Slick then departed, and the remaining trio recruited keyboard player Mark Moragan and bassist Brett Bloomfield for the 1989 album *Love among the Cannibals*, which featured the Top 20 hit "It's Not Enough." In 1991, when RCA released a Starship greatest-hits album, the one new track on the album had been recorded by Thomas and studio musicians, leading to doubt that Starship remained a functioning band. –WR

Takes Off / RCA   1966

The original group's pre-Grace Slick debut album, really closer in spirit to the Mamas & Papas in some respects, as a kind of folk-pop album. Signe Anderson and Marty Balin handle most of the vocals, and the instrumental textures are largely acoustic (Jorma Kaukonen contributes some excellent playing, however) and the political sensibilities are almost nonexistent. –BE

After Bathing at Baxter's / RCA   1967

The group's attempt to re-create the psychedelic drug experience as pure music fails in part — the material is too disjointed and the stretch for the listener (except in certain states of mind) is too great for the record to be enjoyable. But as an experiment, *Baxter's* is dazzling in its intensity and the playing is superb. –BE

☆ **Surrealistic Pillow / RCA**   1967

Their groundbreaking folk-based psychedelic album hit like a shot heard round the world. From "White Rabbit" and "Somebody to Love" to the sublime "3/5 of a Mile in 10 Seconds," the sensibilities are fierce, the material is melodic, and the performances, sparked by new member Grace Slick on most of the lead vocals, are magnificent and inspired. –BE

Crown of Creation / RCA   1968

An impressive but meandering journey through the drugged-out sensibilities of 1967. The science-fiction content gives it some cohesiveness, but not enough. (Also on Mobile Fidelity) –BE

Bless Its Pointed Little Head / RCA   1969

A rough but very representative live album that succeeds where the *Baxter's* album failed in capturing the mood of psychedelic music in performance. The music is intense and driving, and the only unfortunate element of the album is that it dates from a period after Marty Balin's songs had largely been dropped from their set. –BE

Volunteers / RCA   1969

The band's most political album is a somewhat dated statement but also a very joyous and rewarding one. "We Can Be Together" is still a compelling anthem. (Also available as a Mobile Fidelity Ultradisc) –BE

Thirty Seconds over Winterland / RCA   1973

Well-produced document of the final days of the Airplane before it evolved into the Jefferson Starship. The singing and playing are all inspired, and the repertory is surprisingly melodic, considering the direction in which the group had been going. The highlight is a live version of the science-fiction anthem "Have You Seen the Saucers." –BE

Early Flight / RCA   1974

A beguiling collection of bluesy, druggy, and idealistic leftovers from the group's recorded output, partly supplanted by *2400 Fulton Street*, and sure to be further devalued by the upcoming boxed set, but still a handy little disc to have around. –BE

Slick & Kantner / Jefferson Starship / RCA   1974

From precocity to an accelerated maturity, Ian ruefully comments on the fame business in the title track, then turns deeply romantic on "Jesse," a hit for Roberta Flack. –WR

☆ **Red Octopus / RCA**   1975

The masterpiece, and a massive seller, too. Grace Slick sings expressively, especially on "Fast Buck Freddie" and "Play on Love," but the real story is the integration of Marty Balin fully

148

into the band, and again he brings a timeless ballad along in the hit "Miracles." −WR

Freedom at Point Zero / RCA   1979
Amazingly enough, the band survives the departure of Grace Slick and Marty Balin, adding Mickey Thomas on vocals and scoring hits with "Jane" and Kantner's "Girl with the Hungry Eyes." −WR

Gold / RCA   1979
Well-chosen best-of covering the years 1974-1979, after which the band personnel changed significantly. −WR

Modern Times / RCA   1981
Slick comes back for one song, and "Find Your Way Back" becomes a hit. Also included is "Stairway to Cleveland," as gutsy a statement of purpose as any in rock. −WR

Knee Deep in the Hoopla / RCA   1985
Keyboard arrangements dominate here, along with Thomas's soaring vocals, with Grace Slick along mostly for counterpoint (though her showcase is the stirring "Rock Myself to Sleep") on the hits "We Built This City" and "Sara." −WR

● **2400 Fulton Street - An Anthology / RCA**   1987
A more-than-adequate retrospective on the group (at least until the boxed set anticipated for late 1992 arrives), with every major song and a lot of oddball favorites as well, all remastered from sources far superior to those used on the original albums. Some of it will be redundant (virtually the whole *Surrealistic Pillow* album is here) but the quality and the order of the programming is rewarding. −BE

○ **Greatest Hits (10 Years & Change 1979-1991) / RCA**   1991
The Mickey Thomas era, half of it is also the Paul Kantner era, the choices reflecting taste ("Stranger" and "Layin' It on the Line" are included) rather than strict chart rankings (hits like "Be My Lady" and "Tomorrow Doesn't Matter Tonight" are missing). −WR

GARLAND JEFFREYS   b 1944

Singer/songwriter, rock & roll. Multi-ethnic singer/songwriter who also performs in a variety of styles, especially rock and reggae, and has gained considerable critical acclaim during a career dating back to the 60s. −WR

○ **Ghost Writer / A&M**   1977
Rock, reggae, and jazz mix on this album of striking urban songs that are both confessional and confrontational. Includes "Wild in the Streets." −WR

Escape Artist / EPIC   1981
Members of the Rumour and the E Street Band, among other top session people, give Jeffreys a sharp 80s rock sound on his typically well-written songs. Includes a cover of "96 Tears" that became a moderate hit. −WR

JELLYFISH

Power-pop. In 1990 Jellyfish became a buzz band in certain circles of the music industry for their power-pop direction, which was essentially a lukewarm Squeeze/Beatles/Beach Boys synthesis marketed with silly Alice in Wonderland-style psychedelic outfits. −RC

○ **Bellybutton / ATLANTIC**   1990
The beginning of the 90s brought a resurgence in Anglo-pop bands, and Jellyfish's debut, *Bellybutton*, was one of the best releases of that style. Highlights on this fine album are the Squeeze-influenced "Baby's Comin' Back," the hit single, "The King Is Half-Undressed," and "I Wanna Stay Home," a beautiful pop ballad that draws its melodic and arrangement smarts from McCartney and Burt Bacharach. −ED

JESTERS

Doo-wop. The archetypal New York street-corner group, with soaring falsetto and stirring harmonies. With Adam Jackson and Lenny McKay sharing lead duties, the Jesters recorded several classics of the doo-wop genre for Winley in 1957 and 1958, including "So Strange" and "The Plea." Jackson recast

the group in 1960 for their last Winley releases, including an accurate remake of the Diablos tune "The Wind." −BD

○ **Best of the Jesters / COLLECTABLES**
Falsetto-drenched late-50s NYC street-corner doo-wop. −BD

JESUS JONES

Alternative pop. Composer, producer, guitarist, and vocalist Mike Edwards leads this British alternative pop/rock/funk quintet. −BC

Liquidizer / CAPITOL   1989
Sampling, synths, and political lyrics all find a home in this electrifying techno-pop debut album. Many of the cuts are from original demos. Includes "Info Freako" and "Broken Bones." −DDC & BC

○ **Doubt / CAPITOL**   1991
A step forward from their debut, with swirling Beatlesque melodies surrounding clever, often political lyrics as on their hit "Right Here, Right Now." −DDC

JESUS & MARY CHAIN

Alternative rock. This Scottish combo burst out of East Kilbraid in 1984 with a style that piled thick gobs of squalling guitars over tugging Beach Boy harmonies and the lyrical cynicism of Velvets-era Lou Reed. Brothers Jim and William Reid eventually toned down the feedback just a tad — replacing their rhythm section with a drum machine — and have managed to keep their sound fresh, primarily through clever melodies and the occasional inspired lyric hook. −JF

○ **Psychocandy / WARNER**   1985
The fuzzy, super-loud release that introduced JMC to American audiences. −JF

● **Automatic / WARNER**   1989
The drum-machine beats are too stiff, but this set contains their best songs, including the sorta-hit "Head On." −JF

Darklands / WARNER   1989
The subdued, depressing followup to "Psychocandy." −JF

Barbed Wire Kisses / WARNER   1991
A singles and rarities collection that fills in some gaps of this productive band's catalog. −JF

JETHRO TULL

Hard rock, prog-rock. Centered around wildman flutist, singer, songwriter Ian Anderson, Jethro Tull has been churning out an oddball synthesis of British Isles folk and progressive hard rock since the late 60s. During their heyday (the 70s), Tull became one of the biggest concert draws, due to Anderson and the band's clownish stage antics and their amazingly complex interplay.
Their earlier albums, *This Was* (#62), *Stand Up* (#20), and *Benefit* (#11), laid the groundwork for Tull's success, but it was 1971's *Aqualung* (#7) that put them over the top.
Not unlike many bands attempting to take rock to new levels through extended pieces, Tull released two back-to-back albums (*Thick As a Brick, Passion Play*) containing one musical piece on each. Unlike many of those bands, both of these albums went to #1.
Jethro Tull also managed a couple of hits with "Living in the Past" (#11) and "Bungle in the Jungle" (#12). The band continues to release albums and tour. −RC

This Was / CHRYSALIS / BB 62   1969
Tull incorporated jazz, folk, and blues-based rock into this impressive debut, which included "Dharma for One," "My Sunday Feeling," and "Song for Jeffrey." −RC

Stand Up / CAPITOL / BB 20   1969
Tull's second album was as impressive as *This Was*. Anderson's flute dominates this outing. The instrumental "Bouree" became a signature song for the band's early sound. Other highlights included "A New Day Yesterday," "Fat Man," and "Nothing Is Easy." (Also available as a Mobile Fidelity Ultradisc) −RC

Benefit / CHRYSALIS / BB 11   1970

Benefit was almost as strong as *Stand Up*. Anderson had yet to take the group into the realm of extended pieces. "Teacher," "Nothing to Say," and "A Time for Everything" are particularly nice. –RC

○ **Aqualung / CAPITOL / BB 7**   1971

It was with *Aqualung* that Tull became a staple on FM rock radio, thanks to dynamic riff-heavy tracks like "My God," "Hymn 43," "Locomotive Breath," "Cross-eyed Mary," "Wind-Up," and the title track. Thematically, many of these songs were vehicles for Anderson's railings about how organized religion had restricted man's relationship with God. –RC

Thick As a Brick / CAPITOL / BB 1   1972

Only during the early 70s would a rock album containing a single extended piece of music ever go to #1 on the pop charts. *Thick As a Brick* accomplished that feat, in part due to featuring some of Tull's most memorable melodies and arrangements. The anticipation created from the success of *Aqualung* also helped matters. Much of the initial part of this piece still holds up, but the last half loses focus. (Also available as a Mobile Fidelity gold disc) –RC

● **Living in the Past / CHRYSALIS / BB 3**   1972

Living in the Past was essentially an anthology of key tracks from Tull's first five albums. Included are extended live tracks as well as popular numbers like "Christmas Song," "Song for Jeffery," "Hymn 43," and their biggest hit, "Living in the Past" (#11). The CD version has curiously omitted two of Tull's better early tracks — "Teacher" and "Bouree." Besides "Hymn 43," *Living in the Past* doesn't include any key tracks from *Aqualung.* –RC

Minstrel in the Gallery / CAPITOL / BB 7   1975

Minstrel in the Gallery was Tull's most successful exercise in synthesizing Elizabethan folk with prog-rock. –RC

M.U. - The Best of Jethro Tull / CHRYSALIS   1976

M.U. is a decent sampling of hits and album picks, but not definitive. –RC

Songs from the Wood / CHRYSALIS / BB 8   1977

On *Songs from the Wood*, Tull's aggressive rock interplay and Ian Anderson's fascination with early folk melodies from the British Isles produced a particularly appealing collection of songs. "Cup of Wonder," and The Whistler" are particularly successful. –RC

○ **A / CHRYSALIS / BB 30**   1980

With the addition of ex-Roxy Music violinist and keyboardist Eddie Jobson and ex-Fairport Convention bassist Dave Pegg, Tull produced their most overt (and fully realized) folk/rock album. "Batteries Not Included," "Black Sunday," and "Crossfire" are highlights. –RC

20 Yrs - Highlights / CHRYSALIS   1988

This is a distilled version of tracks taken from Tull's boxed set. Broken down into four parts, it includes a smattering of hits, live tracks, and some key album sides. It might not be definitive, but it does give the listener a good idea of the band's musical range. –RC

JOAN JETT   ♭1960

Rock & roll. She once led the Runaways, but Jett's solo career has been as distinguished and rewarding as Chrissie Hynde's (and less pretentious as well). She never goes beyond basic two-guitar, three-chord rock & roll, but her sometimes masterful songwriting and unbridled enthusiasm are essential to all but the most pointy-headed intellectuals. Her best work has been out of print since the mid 80s. –JF

Bad Reputation / BOARDWALK   1981

Her debut suffers from a lack of one coherent sound, but it's an impassioned homage to her glitter-and-punk roots. –JF

I Love Rock & Roll / BOARDWALK   1981

The title track was an inescapable hit in 1981, and Jett's new band, the Blackhearts, gave her a big crunching hard-rock sound. Could've used some better songs though. –JF

○ **Album / MCA**   1983

With her best set of songs and big-time production, this is an astonishing statement of purpose, full of gritty Rolling Stones-like boogie and a cover of Sly Stone's "Everyday People" that works better than you'd think. But it's all spectacular. –JF

★ **The Glorious Results of a Misspent Youth / MCA**   1984

Another masterful blast of fury and celebration, which shifts from a blazing cover of the Runaway's "Cherry Bomb" to her best song, "I Got No Answers." Besides the Pretenders's early work, *Glorious Results* ... ranks with the best rock of the 80s, focused through a female point of view. –JF

Up Your Alley / CBS   1988

"I Hate Myself for Loving You" is a strikingly complex take on relationships and was a hit, but aside from a whopping cover of Chuck Berry's "Tulane," this album is pretty thin. –JF

Good Music / CBS   1989

The production's a bit heavy but Jett's formula is still a winner. "Black Leather" and the title cut are fine rock anthems. –JF

Hit List / CBS

This one sidesteps the issue of poor songwriting by offering a full set of covers ranging from Roy Orbison to the Sex Pistols. It's all powerful, but it's also a step backward. –JF

Notorious / CBS

Jett finally conceives an album where the ballads work as well as the barnburners. Includes a collaboration with Paul Westerberg of the Replacements. –JF

JIVE FIVE

R&B, soul, doo-wop. One of the groups that was a major instigator in the move from 50s R&B to 60s soul, the Jive Five produced several outstanding hits for the New York Belton label during the early 60s. –JF

○ **My True Story / RELIC**

These hard-hitting doo-woppers testify on the title cut, "What Time Is It," and on "Hully Gully Callin' Time." Eugene Pitts is one of the era's most evocative singers. –JF

BILLY JOEL   ♭1949

Rock/pop, singer/songwriter. When pianist, singer, and songwriter Billy Joel came along in 1973 with his major-label debut *Piano Man* (#27), he was perceived as an American alternative to *Tumbleweed Connection*-period Elton John. Both of them tended toward ornate and grand-sounding melodies and progressions, but Joel's musical attack was more assertive, and lyrically, he was a straight-shooter with somewhat of a chip on his shoulder. Joel's music embraces classic Brill Building and Broadway schools of song structure while drawing from the Paul McCartney side of the Beatles and genres like street-corner doo-wop and early 60s pop.

Joel's first hit, "Piano Man" (#25), portrayed him as a guy who endured the lounge-lizard circuit as an observer passing through. On his followup hit, "The Entertainer" (#34), the punkish pragmatism of his personality is further defined. It is an attitude, along with his decidedly non-rock melodies, that doesn't sit well with critics, but Joel's dynamic shows and his finely tuned compositional skills attracted a hardcore fan base.

Joel's initial success began to diminish until he hooked up with producer Phil Ramone (Paul Simon, Julian Lennon) and recorded the mega-platinum *The Stranger*. That album began a string of huge hit singles and albums that remains unabated.

"Just the Way You Are" (#3), "My Life" (#3), "You May Be Right" (#7), "It's Still Rock and Roll to Me" (#1), "Tell Her about It" (#1), "Uptown Girl" (#3), and "You're Only Human (Second Wind)" (#9) are among Joel's numerous chart successes. –RC

○ **Piano Man / CBS**   1973

Joel presents a personal perspective of middle-class teen life in the suburbs ("Captain Jack," "The Ballad of Billy the Kid")

followed by life in a cocktail lounge ("Piano Man"), and concludes, "Worse comes to worst, I'll get along." But his already apparent sense of melody and supple singing voice indicate much more promise than that. —WR

Streetlife Serenade / CBS 1974
Extending a mean streak he'd already revealed more than once, Joel looks upon the starmaking machinery that broke him the year before and scorns it. But he has such a gift for the putdown, notably in "Los Angelenos" and "The Entertainer," and the melodies are so good that you can't help singing along and agreeing with him. If you didn't already, that is. —WR

○ **Turnstiles / CBS** 1976
Billy Joel's best, most consistent, most accessible record, even if not his best seller. From "Say Goodbye to Hollywood," which signals his return to the Big Apple with a drumbeat borrowed from the Ronettes, through the Sinatra ballad "New York State of Mind," the reflective "Summer, Highland Falls," and the hilarious "Miami 2017," Joel has never been more imaginative or more tuneful. Of course, "Angry Young Man" shows him to be as mean-spirited as ever, but the music carries even that one home. This record was the prototype to a virtual hit assembly line. —WR

○ **The Stranger / CBS** 1977
The breakthrough to superstardom. Actually, all the hits are included in *Greatest Hits - Vols. I & II*, so the only reason this record is even listed is because of the album track "Scenes from an Italian Restaurant," which remains one of Joel's most compelling story-songs. —WR

Glass Houses / CBS 1980
Billy Joel's response to punk, which, being a snotty kid himself, he felt a certain affinity with, and which allowed his usual belligerence unusually free rein (an aspect of his work that can be tolerated only because it is unflinchingly honest and as often directed at himself as at others). Again, most of the best songs are on the greatest hits but this is the only place you can get "Sometimes a Fantasy." —WR

An Innocent Man / CBS 1983
A brilliant evocation of popular styles of the early 60s, from doo-wop to R&B, that is much more than a period exercise because it obviously is so deeply felt and because it is so well executed. And no one has sounded quite so guilty as the singer of the title track, whether he realized it or not. —WR

★ **Greatest Hits - Vols. 1 & 2 (1973-1985) / CBS** 1985
Long overdue, and exactly what it says it is. —WR

DAVID JOHANSEN   b 1950

Rock & roll. The former lead singer with the New York Dolls, David Johansen went on to a solo career but failed to rise above cult status despite some fine albums. His live 1982 release, *Live It Up*, contains a great Animals medley that almost broke him into a wider market, but a persona change under the moniker "Buster Poindexter" put Johansen over the top, with a big dance hit, "Hot Hot Hot." Subsequent efforts as Poindexter have lacked the freshness of the original concept, which drew from Caribbean dance grooves and 30s and 40s swing and cabaret styles. —RC

○ **David Johansen / BLUE SKY** 1978
True, the best songs here ("Frenchette," "Funky but Chic," "Girls") are the ones Johansen brought with him from the Dolls. What's intriguing about his solo debut, though, is how well he pulls off ballads like "Donna" and "Pain in My Heart." And Johnny Rao's guitar work *almost* compensates for the absence of Johnny Thunders, the Dolls' guitarist. —JF

● **Live It Up / BLUE SKY** 1982
A scorching live set from 1982 that also works as a career-defining best-of. Johansen drives his roadhouse band through a few old Dolls hits, the best cuts from his solo albums, and a medley of Animals hits that damn near outstrips the originals. And don't miss the two Motown covers. —JF

ELTON JOHN   b 1947

Rock/pop. Elton John was the single most successful pop artist of the 70s, and he continued to score hits for decades after his initial reign of popularity. Born Reginald Dwight in Pinner, England, he showed an early aptitude for the piano and received classical training, winning a scholarship to the Royal Academy of Music at the age of 11. But after six years he turned to pop music, and struggled as a songwriter, sideman, and member of unsuccessful groups for the rest of the 60s.

During this period, he hooked up with lyricist Bernie Taupin through a newspaper advertisement, and the two were signed as songwriters to publisher Dick James, who was to have a tremendous impact on John's early career.

A debut album sponsored by James, *Empty Sky*, flopped in 1969, but in 1970, with the album *Elton John* and the single "Your Song," Elton John took off, scoring especially well in America. For the next five years, his output — and the sales that material racked up — was enormous. John always had an ability to hit with ballads like the wistful "Daniel," then turn around and rock as hard as the Rolling Stones on a song like "Saturday Night's Alright for Fighting." There hardly seemed a day from 1972, when "Rocket Man" began a streak of 16 straight Top 20 hits (15 of which went Top Ten), to 1976, when John took a breather, that his songs were not dominating the airwaves and the record charts.

The late 70s seem to have been a period of recovery and indecision for the singer, but by 1980 he had settled into making one well-crafted album a year, and many of them tossed off hits, if not with such consistency as before. "Little Jeannie" (1980), "I Guess That's Why They Call It the Blues" and "Sad Songs (Say So Much)" (both 1984), and "Nikita" (1986) all showed John could still hit the upper reaches of the charts, especially with his trademark ballads. The late 80s again saw a slowing in John's record success, but by the start of the 90s he had gone public about drug and alcohol problems he said were behind him, and he looked poised for a new start. —WR

Elton John / MCA 1970
Ironically, Elton John's breakthrough album (and US debut) is uncharacteristic of his other work, heavily featuring Paul Buckmaster's dramatic string arrangements. John is never overwhelmed by strings or choirs and turns in some powerful performances. Contains "Your Song." —WR

Madman across the Water / MCA 1971
One of John's best-ever collections of songs, containing "Levon," "Tiny Dancer," and the title track, all of which survive in the memory better than they did in the charts. (Also available as a Mobile Fidelity gold disc) —WR

☆ **Tumbleweed Connection / MCA** 1971
Elton John's followup was a thematic album about the American Old West (a Taupin fascination) that allowed John to rock out on several numbers. There are no hits here (!) but the album stands up well two decades later on. (Also available on Mobile Fidelity) —WR

Honky Chateau / MCA 1972
Notable not only for the hits "Honky Cat" and "Rocket Man" but also for "I Think I'm Gonna Kill Myself" and "Mona Lisas and Mad Hatters." The first of John's seven US #1 albums. (Also available on Mobile Fidelity) —WR

☆ **Goodbye Yellow Brick Road / MCA** 1973
Almost certainly Elton John's biggest seller, save his first greatest hits collection. The hits on this sprawling double-disc set include "Saturday Night's Alright for Fighting," the title track, and "Bennie and the Jets," and the album tracks include "Love Lies Bleeding" and "Candle in the Wind" (which became a hit 15 years later in a live version). (Mobile Fidelity's reissue has superior sound and is on one disc; MCA's version two discs.) —WR

★ **Greatest Hits / MCA** 1974
A virtual time capsule of the pop music of the first half of the 70s. —RW

ELTON JOHN

Captain Fantastic ... / MCA   1975
Bernie Taupin's most ambitious lyrical effort, *Captain Fantastic & the Brown Dirt Cowboy* is an autobiographical song cycle that also drew an unusually strong musical effort from John, resulting in perhaps his strongest overall record since *Tumbleweed Connection*. –WR

☆ **Greatest Hits - Vol. 2 / MCA**   1977
More of the hottest hit streaks of the decade, including such otherwise non-album singles as "Lucy in the Sky with Diamonds" and "Philadelphia Freedom." –WR

A Single Man / MCA   1978
An unusually well-crafted album, and the beginning of John's comeback. "Part-Time Love" was the hit, but "Madness" and the instrumental "Song for Guy" were musical highlights. –WR

21 At 33 / MCA   1980
An ambitious songwriting effort featuring Tom Robinson's collaboration on "Sartorial Eloquence" and Gary Osborne's on "Little Jeannie," though the best songs are by the returning Bernie Taupin: "Chasing the Crown" and "Two Rooms at the End of the World." –WR

Too Low for Zero / GEFFEN   1983
With Taupin (and his old band) on board full time, John turned out one of his best 80s albums — one full of remorse ("Cold As Christmas") and fierce reaffirmation ("I'm Still Standing"), not to mention such irresistible tunes as "Kiss the Bride" and "I Guess That's Why They Call It the Blues." –WR

Greatest Hits - Vol. 3 (1979-1987) / GEFFEN   1987
The best of the Geffen years is very good indeed. –WR

EVAN JOHNS & HIS H-BOMBS   b 1955

Rock & roll, rockabilly. Johns (b 1955) had fronted several bands in the Virginia/DC locale, coming to the attention of guitarist Danny Gatton and eventually doing vocals and writing the title track to Gatton's *Redneck Jazz* album. He formed the H-Bombs late 70s, recording an eponymous four-song EP on the tiny Deco label, one of the last 10-inch records issued in America. After moving to Austin, TX, Johns joined the LeRoi Brothers in the early 80s. Johns was nominated for a Grammy for guesting on the *Big Guitars from Texas* album, a compilation of Austin's best. He re-formed the H-Bombs, carnival barker voice and crazed guitar chops intact, and has continued into the 90s with a spate of frenzied, off-kilter albums ever since. –CK

○ **Evan Johns & the H-Bombs / JUNGLE**   1986
Recorded between 1983 & 1985 and including Springsteen mates Garry Tallent and Danny Federici, this is the Texan band at its most brutal. –JT

Rollin' through the Night / ALT. TEN.   1986
Bar-band bliss, originally recorded in 1982. –JT

Bombs Away! / RYKODISC   1989
Still toasty, these Texan madmen drop the big one on this massive roots-rock riot. –JT

Rockit Fuel Only / RYKODISC   1991
Few bands these days are as unpretentious and downright dangerous as Johns & friends. Not a cut here that doesn't cook. –JT

ERIC JOHNSON

Fusion, rock & roll. Very few post-Hendrix guitarists can match Eric Johnson's six-string magic. There's no hint of anger, angst, or sloppiness in any of his playing; instead, each note, each phrase, demonstrates his obsession with tone. Joyous celebrations, his solos seem to grow more magnificent with each listening.
For years esteemed players proclaimed Eric Johnson one of rock's most imaginative and tasteful guitarists. Despite the praise, Johnson labored in relative obscurity in Austin, TX, until the 1986 release of *Tones*. His goal was to produce music that entertains and heals, and his playing married deep emotion to mind-boggling finesse. The album's collage of

guitar tones ran from purest-of-pure Strat to Hendrix-approved psychedelia and majestic, violinlike textures. Johnson spent nearly two years producing his 1990 followup, *Ah Via Musicom*. Full of fire, light, and swirling thunder, it's an artistic triumph, as powerful a statement for Eric Johnson as *Electric Ladyland* was for Jimi Hendrix. –JO

○ **Tones / WARNER**   1986
A landmark guitar recording. –JO

Ah Via Musicom / CAPITOL   1990
Strong songs and exquisite tones. –JO

JESSE JOHNSON

Funk, hard rock. This former guitarist with the Time broke from the old to perfect his own variety of hard-rocking funk. –JF

Jesse Johnson's Revue / A&M   1985
Modeled on Prince & the Revolution's *Purple Rain.* –BC

○ **Shockadelica / A&M**   1986
Ten-piece band. A duet with Sly Stone on "Crazay." This is mostly light funk and dance music that ends with bare acoustic guitar on "Black in America." –BC

Every Shade of Love / A&M   1988
Contains eight tracks, all harder edged, akin to latter-day Jimi Hendrix. –BC

MARV JOHNSON   b 1938

R&B, Motown. Johnson played an important role in the founding of the Motown empire, with his "Come to Me" the first release on Berry Gordy's Tamla label in 1959. The tuneful high-pitched tenor's impressive effort was snapped up by United Artists, who promptly issued his two biggest Gordy-produced hits, "You Got What It Takes" (first waxed by Bobby Parker on Vee Jay) and "I Love the Way You Love." Johnson stayed with UA into the early 60s before returning home to Gordy in 1965 and staying to 1968. –BD

○ **Marvelous Marv Johnson / COLLECTABLES**   ·
Pre-Motown tracks, many written and produced by Berry Gordy. –RP

JON & VANGELIS

Prog-rock. Yes singer Jon Anderson and Greek synth composer Vangelis teamed up in the 80s for a pop-music experiment –ED

○ **Short Stories / POLYGRAM**   1980
Their first collaboration. Ethereal and melodic. –MPD

Friends of Mr. Cairo / POLYGRAM   1981
A surprisingly funky second effort from this duo. Includes "State of Independence," later a Donna Summer hit. –MPD

Best of Jon & Vangelis / POLYGRAM   1984
A sampling of their work, including "Friend of Mr. Cairo" and "State of Independence." –MPD

GRACE JONES   b 1952

Dance-pop. Entertainer and model Grace Jones has a European flair but a hard, stilted singing style. Jones is on the cutting edge of reggae-style dance music, although commercial success evades her. –BC

○ **Nightclubbing / POLYGRAM**   1981
A funk album that merges reggae roots and R&B styles. –BC

Slave to the Rhythm / POLYGRAM   1985
An audio biography of Grace Jones, produced by Trevor Horn, is a sonic treat along the lines of Yes's *90125* or Frankie Goes to Hollywood's first album (both produced by Horn). The music ranges from slick R&B runaway grooves to striking audio montages, interrupted occasionally by conversation about Jones's life. Serious ear candy! –SWB

HOWARD JONES   b 1955

Rock/pop. Adept at overdubbing himself into a one-man band through his use of synthesizers and drum machines, Jones scored consistently on the charts in the early 80s with an inoffensive pop style on tunes like "New Song" (#27), "No One Is to Blame" (#5), and "Things Can Only Get Better" (#4). –CK

Human's Lib / ELEKTRA 1984
Howard Jones's debut album is almost entirely performed on synthesizers. The material on *Human's Lib,* like all of the following albums, is very inconsistent; Jones either writes hits or flops, with very little in between. Containing two of Jones's best songs, "New Song" and "What is Love?" –IME

○ **Dream into Action / ELEKTRA** 1985
This album shows the synthesizer pop idol at the height of his creativity — *Dream into Action* is definitely the most interesting of Jones's albums. It contains some of his best songs — "Things Can Only Get Better," "Life in One Day," and "No One Is to Blame." The CD includes two bonus tracks, "Bounce Right Back" and "Like to Get to Know You Well," both of which are worthwhile additions. –IME

LINDA JONES   1944-1972
Soul. A word in support of an artist who will probably be passed over by 999 listeners out of a thousand. Her biggest hit, the tastefully restrained "Hypnotized," came on the Loma subsidiary of Warner Brothers in 1967, but her later recordings for Turbo were probably the most gloriously histrionic soul records of all time. She started at a climax and worked up from there, transforming a ballad like "Let It Be Me" with her towering fury. It was pure gospel — and then some. Jones was already ill with diabetes when she cut those records, and she died in 1972 after collapsing backstage at the Apollo. –CE

○ **Hypnotized / CBS** 1989
Twenty tracks, all the hits plus early singles. –RP

Your Precious Love / SEQUEL 1991
Best of the Turbo label tracks. Superior sound quality. (Import) –RP

MARTI JONES
Singer/songwriter. This Ohio-based singer and former member of Color Me Gone went solo under the tutelage of producer Don Dixon (now her husband). With Dixon she made four albums (1984-1990) interpreting the best of current songwriters. –WR

○ **Unsophisticated Time / A&M** 1984
Jones applies her smoky alto to a group of ironic love songs, the best of them written by producer Don Dixon. –WR

Any Kind of Lie / RCA 1990
After proving herself an ideal interpreter for the more literate songwriters of the day (Elvis Costello, Peter Holsapple, etc.), Jones writes most of her own material here (with Don Dixon). And it's just as good as, if not better than the covers. –WR

RICKIE LEE JONES   b 1954
Singer/songwriter. A singer/songwriter who emerged in 1979 with a million-selling album and the Top Ten hit "Chuck E's in Love." Born in Chicago, Jones grew up in Arizona and Washington state and was taught music by her father. Moving to Los Angeles in 1973, she started as a performer by doing rhythmic "beat" monologs. She began to gain notice after hooking up with singer/songwriter Tom Waits in 1977, and in 1979 Little Feat leader Lowell George recorded her "Easy Money" on his debut solo album. Signed to Warner Brothers, Jones recorded her own debut, *Rickie Lee Jones* (a combination of folk, jazz, and rock styles), its lyrical songs populated by bohemian characters and sung in Jones's slightly slurred voice. It hit #3, and Jones won the Best New Artist Grammy for 1979.
She returned in 1981 with the even more ambitious *Pirates,* which hit #5 and went gold. *Girl at Her Volcano* was a 1983 EP made up mostly of cover songs. Jones's next full-length album was *The Magazine,* which hit the Top 50 in 1984. In the second half of the 80s, Jones married and gave birth to a daughter.

She returned to recording with the Top 40 *Flying Cowboys* in 1989, and in 1991 she released another record of covers, *Pop Pop.* –WR

☆ **Rickie Lee Jones / WARNER** 1979
One of the most impressive debuts for a singer/songwriter ever, this infectious mixture of styles not only features a strong collection of original songs (the hits are "Chuck E's in Love" and "Young Blood," but "Danny's All-Star Joint" and "Coolsville" are just as good) but also a singer with a savvy, distinctive voice that can be streetwise, childlike, and sophisticated, sometimes all in the same song. –WR

Pirates / WARNER 1981
If the songs are less immediately accessible than on Jones's first album, repeated listenings are likely to lead to even greater rewards. Open-ended song structures allow Jones to explore more fully her closely observed portraits of lowlife characters, and her singing remains entrancing. –WR

JANIS JOPLIN   1943-1970
Blues/rock, R&B/rock, hard rock. Janis Joplin was one of the greatest White female singers to take on the blues. Hailing from Texas, Joplin journeyed to San Francisco in 1963 to sing, playing infrequent gigs with Jorma Kaukonen or Roger Perkins. She returned to Austin in 1966 to sort out her life, briefly giving up singing and making plans for marriage. Nevertheless, word that the Bay Area band Big Brother & the Holding Company was looking for a singer lured Joplin back. With Big Brother, Joplin wowed audiences with her intensity and aching vulnerability.
Cheap Thrills, a doctored-up live collection, topped a million sales. It contained incredible performances by Joplin and the band, particularly "Ball and Chain," "Summertime," "Combination of the Two," and the #12 hit "Piece of My Heart." On *Cheap Thrills,* the guitar interplay of Sam Andrew and James Gurley are among the finest examples of the psychedelic Bay Area style ever committed to disc. Joplin left for a solo career and released 1969's *I Got Dem Ol' Kozmic Blues Again Mama!* (#5), which featured the track "Try (Just a Little Harder)." Joplin assembled the Full-Tilt Boogie Band and began recording the followup album. Unfortunately, Joplin's crippling drug and alcohol addiction got to her, and she was found dead Oct 4, 1970, at the Landmark Hotel in Hollywood, of an accidental heroin overdose.
Pearl, which was Joplin's nickname, was assembled out of the sessions that had been recorded, and it went to #1 for nine weeks. The album produced a #1 hit, as well, with a version of Kris Kristofferson's "Me and Bobby McGee." (See also Big Brother & the Holding Company.) –RC

I Got Dem Ol' Kozmic Blues Again Mama / CBS 1969
Joplin's only solo album to be released during her lifetime heavily employs horns and an R&B band feel, but the dominant sound remains Joplin's impassioned singing on such songs as "Try." –WR

○ **Pearl / CBS** 1971
Backed by a tight rock band, Full Tilt Boogie, Joplin puts her mark on everything from the bluesy "Cry Baby" to her hit version of Kris Kristofferson's "Me & Bobby McGee." –WR

● **Greatest Hits / CBS** 1973
Well-chosen best-of gathers together tracks from Big Brother and the Holding Company and solo material. –WR

THE JORDANAIRES
Pop. A trio best known for backing Elvis Presley on his RCA recordings, the Jordanaires also had a furtive recording career of their own, with some beautifully subtle and expressive work when they weren't making ill-advised covers. –BE

Big Country Hits / CBS
Not what one would necessarily look for from this group, but with some worthwhile moments for those who appreciate their sound. –BE

Monster Makers / STOP
The grotesque cover, intended as a joke, hides some superb music making. The hauntingly beautiful rendition of the country-gospel number "Skip-A-Rope" is possibly their best record ever. (Out of print) –BE

○ **Tribute to Elvis' Favorite Spirituals / STEP ONE**
They sang on his originals; now they sing without him. –HD

MARGIE JOSEPH   b 1950

R&B, soul. Classy, Southern soul singer who recorded for Okeh, Stax, Atlantic, and Cotillion during the 60s and 70s. The Mississippi product debuted on Okeh in 1967 with some brassy R&B before moving to Volt at the turn of the decade. Joseph specialized for a time in lushly orchestrated revivals of R&B classics, including the Supremes hit "Stop! In the Name of Love" and Al Green's "Let's Stay Together." Notching her biggest hit on Atlantic in 1974 with "My Love," she collaborated the next year with the Philly vocal group Blue Magic on "What's Come over Me." –BC & BD

○ **Margie Joseph Makes a New Impression / VOLT-STAX**
Superb Southern soul lamentations from the late 60s. –BC

JOURNEY

Rock/pop. During its 14-year existence (1973-1987), Journey altered its musical approach and its personnel extensively while becoming a top touring and recording band. The only constant factor was guitarist Neal Schon (b Feb 27, 1954), a music prodigy who had been a member of Santana in 1971-1972. The original unit, which was named in a contest on KSAN-FM in San Francisco, featured Schon, bassist Ross Valory, drummer Praire Prince (replaced by Aynsley Dunbar), and guitarist George Tickner (who left after the first album). Another former Santana member, keyboard player and singer Gregg Rolie, joined shortly afterwards. This lineup recorded *Journey* (1974), the first of three moderate-selling jazz-rock albums given over largely to instrumentals.
By 1977, however, the group decided it needed a strong vocalist/frontman and hired Steve Perry (b Jan 22, 1953). The results were immediately felt on the fourth album, *Infinity* (1978), which reached #21 in the charts and had sold a million copies by the end of the year. (By this time, Dunbar had been replaced by Steve Smith.) *Evolution* (1979) was similarly successful, as was *Departure* (after which Rolie was replaced by Jonathan Cain). After a live album, *Captured* (1981), Journey released *Escape*, which broke them through to the top ranks of pop groups by scoring three Top Ten hit singles, all ballads featuring Perry's smooth tenor: "Who's Crying Now," "Don't Stop Believin'," and "Open Arms." The album topped the charts and had sold seven million copies by 1989.
Frontiers (1983), featuring the hit "Separate Ways," was another big success, after which Perry released a successful solo album, *Street Talk* (1984). When the group got back together to make a new album, Valory and Smith were no longer in the lineup, and *Raised on Radio* (1986) was made by Schon, Perry, and Cain, who added other musicians for a tour. This, however, was the end of Journey, as Perry and Cain went off to form Bad English. –WR

Infinity / CBS   1978
The first album with vocalist Steve Perry. "Wheel in the Sky" was the band's first US charting single, followed by "Anytime" and "Lights." It was the beginning of their climb up the charts with the trademark tenor of Steve Perry. –DDC

Evolution / CBS   1979
Journey got major US radio airplay with "Just the Same Way," "Lovin', Touchin', Squeezin'," and "City of Angels." –DDC

Escape / CBS   1981
Jonathan Cain (ex-Babys keyboardist) replaced Gregg Rolie on the band's most popular album to date. On the strength of the hits "Who's Crying Now" and "Don't Stop Believin'," this album spent more than a year in the Top 20. –DDC

○ **Journey's Greatest Hits / CBS**   1988
A collection of Journey's 70s and 80s radio staples. The band's best-known rockers and ballads, including "Open Arms," "Who's Crying Now," "Any Way You Want It," and "Separate Ways (Worlds Apart)," are here. –DDC

JOY DIVISION

Alternative rock. This four-piece outfit from Manchester is arguably the most important of all post-punk groups. Lead vocalist Ian Curtis sang of despair and self-loathing (and world-loathing) in a dramatic and uncompromising croon that sometimes evoked the torment of vintage Sinatra. The music was similarly determined. Underpinned by throbbing, minimalist bass, thrashing drums, and skeletal, metallic guitar, Joy Division pushed the envelope of punk rock's creative barriers and set the pattern for most of the gloom-and-doom British rock of the 80s. Curtis hung himself in 1980, which underscored his desolate lyricism. The remaining members went on to form New Order. Everything Joy Division recorded should be heard. –JF

☆ **Unknown Pleasures / WARNER**   1979
Their debut is a stark, almost Gothic, masterpiece of emotional destruction and inner pain, expressed both lyrically and musically. –JF

○ **Closer / WARNER**   1980
An even gloomier set on their second album, released just after Curtis's death. Guitars take a back seat to swirling layers of synthesizer, while Curtis's lyrics expand to examine the decay of not only the heart but society. –JF

Still / WARNER   1981
A double album that contains nine worthwhile studio outtakes, a live version of the Velvet Underground's "Sister Ray," and ten cuts from a 1980 gig. Of interest only to hardcore fans. –JF

● **Substance / WARNER**   1988
Collecting some riveting and rare material previously available only on singles and compilations, this offers a more diverse portrait of the band and works as both an introduction and a supplement to the original release. –JF

JUDAS PRIEST

Heavy metal. Judas Priest (the name is derived from Bob Dylan's "The Ballad of Frankie Lee and Judas Priest") is no doubt one of the most influential heavy metal bands to find its origins in the early 70s in England. The group consisted of vocalist Rob Halford, guitarists K. K. Downing and Glenn Tipton, bassist Ian Hill, and drummer Alan Moore, and they released their debut album in 1974. It only did well in their native country, but when they released the followup in 1976, some US radio stations gave it airplay. They soon signed with CBS, and it was there they gained worldwide appeal.
Unleashed in the East, recorded live in Japan in 1978, became one of the group's best-selling albums in the US, but 1981's *Point of Entry* put them over the top. Even if they had never recorded an album again, Judas Priest's sound (from the vocals of Halford to the double attack of Tipton and Downing) influenced a generation of new bands who can proudly claim the Priest as their primary influence. –JB

Sad Wings of Destiny / RCA   1976
Vintage Judas Priest from the mid 70s, an excellent example of British heavy metal coming into its own and of a band beginning to gain acceptance on both sides of the Atlantic. Includes "The Ripper" and "Victim of Changes," the latter of which demonstrates the full vocal range of Rob Halford. –JB

Unleashed in the East (Live In Japan) / CBS   1979
Recorded live in Japan, this was the album that helped Judas Priest finally break through in America with support from critics and radio airplay. The album is an exceptional live performance. The songs chosen are a good example of their material from the 70s. –JB

○ **Point of Entry / CBS** 1981
Point of Entry finally made Judas Priest a major-league success. With well-written songs, solid musicianship from the entire band and powerful vocals from Rob Halford, Judas Priest helped define heavy metal in the 80s. Includes "Heading out to the Highway," "Hot Rockin'," and "Don't Go." –JB

JULES & THE POLAR BEARS

Rock/pop. This late-70s quartet became a critics' favorite on the strength of Jules Shear's songwriting, which combined Beatles hooks with 70s sophistication. Their 1978 debut, *Got No Breeding*, was their finest number; from there one is best off with Shear's solo work. –DH

○ **Got No Breeding / CBS** 1978
A cult favorite, reissued on CD. –DH

DON JULIAN & THE MEADOWLARKS

R&B, doo-wop. An integrated group, formed at Los Angeles's Fremont High School, that cut some fine doo-wop during the mid 50s. With Julian's pleasingly cool lead vocals featured, the Meadowlarks recorded for RPM and Dootone, scoring a regional seller for the latter in 1955 with the smooth ballad "Heaven and Paradise." The Meadowlarks could rock too — "I Got Tore Up," also on Dootone, is a driving jump with rolling piano behind the quartet. As lead singer of the Larks, Julian hit the charts with "The Jerk" a decade later. –BD

○ **Golden Classics / COLLECTABLES**
Mid-50s Los Angeles doo-wop, with Julian supplying the floating leads. –BD

ROB JUNGKLAS

Singer/songwriter, rock & roll. A singer/songwriter from Memphis, Rob Jungklas imbues the well-worn topics of love and dynamics between the genders with a richly metaphorical style of lyricism. Musically, Jungklas ranges from reflective acoustic numbers to edgy melodic rock. –RC

○ **Work Songs for a New Moon / RCA** 1988
On *Work Songs for a New Moon*, Jungklas abandoned the edgey big-rock production found on his debut (*Closer to the Flame*), in favor of a mellower acoustic/electric style of music. Jungklas still sounds like an obsessive romantic, but there are a number of times when the album's mystical quasi-Christian imagery exuded a rich depth that approach Bruce Cockburn's most spiritually illuminating moments. –RC

JUNIE

Funk. Junie Morrison was a keyboardist and vocalist with the Ohio Players and Parliament/Funkadelic during the 70s. His solo efforts showcased his earthy, funky style. –ED

○ **Bread Alone / COL. SPEC. PROD** 1980
Lovers of earthy funk should check out this appealingly homemade effort in which Junie Morrison plays all the instruments. Morrison's singing is particularly affecting here. –RC

HENRY KAISER

Avant-garde. Guitarist Henry Kaiser is a prolific member of the San Francisco Bay Area music scene, as well as being a globally recognized leader of the "second generation" free improvisers who came of age in the 70s. His earliest musical inspiration came from the spiky sounds of English improvising guitarist Derek Bailey and the many guitarists in Captain Beefheart's Magic Band; later on Kaiser absorbed the subtle string textures of the American blues stylists and traditional music of Asia, particularly India, Korea, and Vietnam. His initial recordings documented solo projects and spontaneous groupings with other energetic improvisers like Fred Frith, the ROVA Saxophone Quartet, pianist Greg Goodman, and vocalist Diamanda Galas. Kaiser's restless creativity unearthed many new and unconventional electric guitar techniques during these years, and he combined these innovations with a strong sense of logic and concise development, often aided by sophisticated sound-processing devices. Recently Kaiser's projects have tended toward the rock sound of the 60s and 70s, with a special fascination for the music of the Grateful Dead. But he has simultaneously explored American folk along with the folk music of Vietnam and Madagascar. –MB

Lemonfish Tweezer / CUNEIFORM
A retrospective of Henry's boundary-smashing solo projects from the mid 70s on. –MB

Tomorrow Knows Where You Live / VICTO
Improvised guitar duos with O'Rourke and solos of orchestral richness. –MB

Aloha: Studio Solo / METALANQUAQE 1981
His first major statement of purpose as a multi-faceted soloist, leader, and producer. A 2-fer. –MB

Devil in the Drain / SST 1987
His most fully realized instrumental solo work. Fantastic structures from various creative directions on guitar and synclavier. –MB

● **With Enemies ... / SST** 1987
A CD compilation of Henry Kaiser and Fred Frith's guitar duo records. *With Enemies like These, Who Needs Friends?* is a masterpiece of studio improvisation and innovative guitar techniques. –MB

Re-Marrying for Money / SST 1988
Improvised rock with San Francisco's Stench Brothers on bass and drums. An encyclopedia of twisted guitar playing. –MB

Those Who Know History Are Doomed / SST 1988
Eclecticism reigns supreme here, on his first full exploration of pop music covers and Grateful Dead-style jamming. –MB

Heart's Desire / RECKLESS 1990
A live tribute to the psychedelic era, with the versatile Henry Kaiser Band rocking nonstop. –MB

○ **Hope You Like Our New Direction / RECKLESS** 1991
From Buddy Holly to Beefheart, Virginia to Viet Nam, this musical tour takes you to every corner of Kaiser's wonderful world. Lots of surprises. –MB

KANSAS

Prog-rock, rock/pop. This progressive rock group from Topeka featured Steve Walsh on keyboards, Phil Ehart on percussion, Rich Williams on guitar, Robby Steinhardt on violins, Dave Hope on bass, and Kerry Livgren on piano. They opened on the last Doors tour and were signed by Don Kirshner in 1974. Their music tended to be influenced by British groups such as Moody Blues and Yes. –BC

Kansas / CBS 1975
An encouraging debut reflecting an infatuation with English art-rock. –RC

Leftoverture / CBS 1976
The rock hit "Carry on Wayward Son" catapulted Kansas (and this album) into the big arena rock circuit. –RC

Song for America / CBS 1976
The title cut comprises some beautiful passages. While they never really attained the intensity of art-rock bands like Yes, this album is possibly Kansas's most fully realized artistic effort at testing the possibilities of the genre. –RC

○ **Best of Kansas / CBS** 1984
Contains the essential rock radio hits "Dust in the Wind," "Carry On Wayward Son," and "Point of Know Return," as well as improved remastering from the original tapes. –RC

In the Spirit of Things / MCA 1988
Pink Floyd producer Bob Ezrin gives Kansas a sonically impressive sound. Fans of orchestral mainstream rock will like this, particularly "One Man, One Heart," "One Big Sky," "House on Fire," and "The Preacher." Ex-Dixie Dregs guitarist Steve Morse and vocalist Steve Walsh shine. –RC

JORMA KAUKONEN   b 1940

Rock/pop, folk/rock. Guitarist, singer, and songwriter Jorma Kaukonen was born and grew up in Washington, DC, where he first turned to the guitar. He lived in the San Francisco Bay Area in the early 60s, playing backup to singer Janis Joplin in local clubs. In 1965 Kaukonen became a founding member of Jefferson Airplane, which soared to fame in 1967. Though Kaukonen's songs and vocals were not prominently featured in the band, his distinctive guitar-playing was crucial to its sound.

With bassist Jack Casady, Kaukonen formed a spinoff duo from the group in 1970 called Hot Tuna, and this became his primary musical vehicle after Jefferson Airplane split in 1973. Hot Tuna recorded a series of albums on which Kaukonen sang and played guitar through 1978. After that, Kaukonen worked as a soloist and with such groups as Vital Parts (1980), and he recorded occasional albums. Kaukonen reunited with Casady in Hot Tuna during the 80s, and both participated in the 1989 reunion of Jefferson Airplane. A Hot Tuna reunion album appeared the following year. –WR

○ **Quah / RELIX**   1974
Brilliant acoustic album, with Tom Hobson, of Kaukonen originals and folk blues standards, the highlights being the beautiful "Genesis" and the Rev. Gary Davis's "I'll Be All Right" and "I Am the Light of This World." –WR

Magic / RELIX   1985
Acoustic live album including such folk/blues favorites as "Walkin' Blues" and Kaukonen's Jefferson Airplane tunes "Embryonic Journey" and "Good Shepherd." –WR

KC & THE SUNSHINE BAND

Disco, pop. In the early 70s, two White men, Harry "KC" Casey (b Jan 31, 1951) and Richard Finch (b Jan 25, 1954), created a racially integrated disco band that based its music on various soul styles. They became one of the most commercially successful groups of the early disco era. –BC

○ **Best of KC & the Sunshine Band / RHINO**   1990
A percussive mix of steel drums, whistle flutes, and funky group harmonies on this most soulful disco. Includes all of their hits — "Get Down Tonight," "Please Don't Go," "That's the Way (I Like It)," "I'm Your Boogie Man," "(Shake, Shake, Shake) Shake Your Booty," and KC's solo hit, "Give It Up." –BC

PAUL KELLY & THE MESSENGERS   b 1940

Folk/rock. A muscular Australian folk-rock combo led by Kelly, a songwriter whose eye for detail and ability to transfer the listener into his world rivals Graham Parker's and (sometimes) Elvis Costello's. Kelly's best songs contain the episodic character of Bob Dylan's but with the rocking thwack of John Mellencamp and the occasional flash of the writer Raymond Carver. (Kelly's *So Much Water, So Close to Home* album takes its title and the inspiration for its title track from a Carver short story.) –JF & KK

● **Gossip / A&M**   1987
Their US debut offers 17 sublime examples of Kelly's compassionate and witty songwriting as well as the group's flexibility and charm. Highlights include "White Train," the gentle "Renwick Bells," "Darling It Hurts," and "Don't Ever Harm the Messenger." –JF & KK

○ **Under the Sun / A&M**   1988
This covers a lot of stylistic ground, including rockabilly, country, and punk throwbacks. A beautifully arranged set that runs the gamut from Hoodoo Gurus-style raveups ("Dumb Things") to country-rock shuffles ("To Her Door") and pointed social criticism ("Bicentennial"), not to mention the golden title track. –JF & KK

So Much Water, So Close to Home / A&M   1989
A somewhat light release, but Kelly's writing continues to dazzle with a song written from the perspective of an abused wife and a touching interpretation of a Raymond Carver story. –JF

Comedy / DOCTOR DREAM   1992
A diverse, startling record full of everything from folky social protest ("From Little Things Big Things Grow") to gorgeous pop ("Brighter"), with a dazzling out-of-left-field homage to Jimmie Dale Gilmore's "Dallas from a DC-9" ("Sydney from a 727"). –KK

EDDIE KENDRICKS   1940-1991

Motown, urban R&B. The silky tenor of the Temptations emerged as a solo artist in 1971. Under the production of Frank Wilson, he released several pop hits — including "Boogie Down" (#2), and the #1 "Keep On Truckin' (Part 1)" — predominantly dance hits. –RAB

People Hold On / MOTOWN   1972
A good Frank Wilson production. –RAB

Eddie Kendricks / MOTOWN   1973
His most successful Motown album. –RAB

○ **At His Best / MOTOWN**   1977
Not all of his best, but most of it. –RAB

CHRIS KENNER   1929-1976

R&B. Kenner wrote a number of enduring New Orleans R&B classics, although subsequent cover versions eclipsed all but "I Like It Like That," his Grammy-nominated greatest hit in 1961. Kenner cowrote "Sick and Tired" with Fats Domino and charted with it in 1957 on Imperial, but Domino's version blew it out of the water. Signing with Joe Babashak's Instant label, Kenner's "I Like It like That," "Land of 1000 Dances," and "Something You Got" sported Allen Toussaint's rolling piano behind Kenner's raw vocals.

"Land of 1000 Dances" was Kenner's last hit in 1963, although Wilson Pickett would soon immortalize it anew. –BD

● **I Like It like That - Golden Classics / COLLECTABLES**
Vocalist Kenner's early 60s sides for Instant, with Allen Toussaint laying down rolling piano behind him, represent New Orleans R&B at its most infectious. –BD

○ **Land of 1000 Dances / ATLANTIC**   1965
Slashing soul by the writer of the title cut. One of the great forgotten albums. –DS

NIK KERSHAW   b 1958

Rock/pop. This British singer/guitarist had a hit with "Wouldn't It Be Good." Clever synth-filled pop songs. –ED

○ **Human Racing / MCA / BB 70**   1984
His debut, although rough around the edges, showed talent and promise; includes "Wouldn't It Be Good." –SWB

The Riddle / MCA   1984
Kershaw's second album, containing a remixed "Wouldn't It Be Good," finally garnered some deserved attention. The rest is his unique style of well-crafted synth-pop. –SWB

CHAKA KHAN   b 1953

Funk, urban R&B, soul. The lead singer of the R&B band Rufus from 1972 to 1978. Since 1978 she has released several solo albums. The Grammy-winning Khan has also done vocal work for Prince, Steve Winwood, David Bowie, and Quincy Jones. –WR

○ **I Feel for You / WARNER**   1984
Smoothly produced funk outing features the Prince-composed title track, an R&B #1, and two more R&B Top 20 hits, "This Is My Night" and "Through the Fire." –WR

Life Is a Dance (The Remix Project) / WARNER   1989
In lieu of a desperately needed greatest hits-album, we'll have to settle for this reconfiguration of such Khan hits as "I'm Every Woman" and "Clouds." –WR

KID CREOLE & THE COCONUTS

Disco, pop. Born in Haiti as Darnell Browder in 1951, Creole and his brother Stoney formed Dr. Buzzard's Original Savannah Band in the 70s. Later, they created Coconuts with the help of Andy Hernandez. Much of their music is a campy blend of disco and Latin American influences. –BC

○ **Off the Coast of Me / ANTILLES**   1980
Mixing disco, Caribbean music, and strains of big-band jazz, Kid Creole engages in a self-deprecating dialog with his backup singers, the Coconuts, who dismiss him as "Mister Softee" and plead, "Can you get me into Studio 54?" on this hilarious debut album. –WR

Fresh Fruit in Foreign Places / ZE   1981
Musical gumbo of esoteric lilting, jazzy laidback disco, an acquired taste. –BC

Wise Guy / SIRE   1982
The ongoing adventures of Kid Creole continue on this bouncy collection that produced three British Top Ten hits, including "Annie, I'm Not Your Daddy" and "I'm a Wonderful Thing, Baby." –WR

JOHNNY KIDD & THE PIRATES

Rock & roll, British invasion. Pioneering British hard-rock act in the pre-Beatles era, Kidd (real name Fred Heath) and his backing trio the Pirates had a lean, loud, muscular approach to R&B that strongly influenced the Who and the Small Faces, among other bands. When they weren't recording dross like "The Birds and the Bees" at EMI's behest, they were making history with original numbers like "Shakin' All Over" (Heath wrote it) and a brilliant set of (mostly unreleased at the time) R&B covers. Pirates guitarist Mick Green later became well known in his own right. Kidd was in the process of reviving the group in the mid 60s when his life was ended in a car crash. –BE

○ **Hits & Rarities / SEE FOR MILES**   1983
This collection is the best of three now available. It contains the strongest of Kidd's singles plus superb vault finds. Considered too rough for release in the 60s, they hold up splendidly. (Import) –DE

GREG KIHN

Rock/pop. A record store clerk made good, San Franciscan Greg Kihn plays 60s-soaked pop with a smirk, loading up his tunes with so many British Invasion quotes you'll become dizzy keeping up. Although his hit-making days have passed, the earnest and likable Kihn still doggedly plays his squeaky-clean pop-rock with panache. –ED

○ **Kihnsolidation (The Best of Greg Kihn) / RHINO**
All his best are here. The CD version features 5 bonus tracks. –ED

JOHN KILZER

Singer/songwriter, rock & roll, R&B/rock. Memphian John Kilzer blends Heartland rock, R&B, and folk into a highly literate style. –RC

○ **Memory in the Making / GEFFEN**   1988
This strong debut presents Kilzer as a literate mainstream rocker. The single "Red Blue Jeans," "Green, Yellow & Red" (which Rosanne Cash cut on her *King's Record Shop*), and the title track are standouts. –RC

Busman's Holiday / GEFFEN   1991
On this sophomore effort, Kilzer invests himself in a moody blend of Memphis/New Orleans R&B and folk/rock filtered through a reverberant gauzy Dire Straits-like production by Patrick Moran. It's unfortunate that this sonic approach undermines the album's numerous virtues by burying Kilzer's distinctively ragged voice and his provocative lyrical imagery. –RC

BEN E. KING   b 1938

R&B. Swirling strings, subtly shaded orchestrations, and Ben E. King's assured baritone were a blueprint for uptown soul success during the early 60s.
King and his vocal group, the Five Crowns, were in the right

place at the right time when, in 1959, the manager of the Drifters decided to sack his entire group and solicit replacements. As new lead singer for the Drifters, King crooned the soulful smashes "There Goes My Baby," "Save the Last Dance for Me," and "I Count the Tears" before heading out on his own in 1960.
The vocalist's own Atco singles mirrored the sumptuous production of his Drifter sides, and "Spanish Harlem," "Don't Play That Song (You Lied)," and the R&B chart-topping "Stand by Me" were all huge successes. King remained with Atco through 1969, then triumphantly returned to Atlantic in 1975 with another #1 soul hit, "Supernatural Thing (Part 1)."
With the re-release of "Stand by Me" as the theme to the 1986 film of the same name, King was in demand all over again, the stirring song improbably scaling the charts for a second time, despite being a quarter-century old. –BD

○ **Ultimate Collection / ATLANTIC**
The rich baritone of this ex-Drifter lead is matched by the majestic, violin-drenched, uptown soul arrangements on these early 60s classics. –BD

BOBBY KING & TERRY EVANS

R&B, soul. Bobby King and Terry Evans have been Ry Cooder's backup singers since the late 70s. As frontmen, they deliver passionate soul performances, at times recalling Sam & Dave. –RC

○ **Live & Let Live / ROUNDER**   1988
Anyone predisposed to raw R&B should love *Live & Let Live*, which is produced by Ry Cooder. Their earthy delivery is shown to fine effect on tracks like the Sam & Dave-style rave-up "Just A Little Bit," the haunting "Let Love Begin," and a slow-burn remake of Dan Penn and Chip Moman's "Dark End of the Street." Cooder plays some remarkable guitar throughout this album. –RC

CAROLE KING   b 1942

Singer/songwriter. During the early 70s, the singer/songwriter movement emerged as a reflective, folky alternative to rock and pop. Among the genre's more notable avatars were James Taylor, Joni Mitchell, Cat Stevens, and Carole King.
Unlike many of the other artists, King was well grounded in the pop songcrafting tradition, primarily from her tenure as a writer during the glory days at the Brill Building in New York. It was while she was at the Brill Building, beginning in 1958, that King met Neil Diamond and Paul Simon and began a very successful string of collaborations with Gerry Goffin, whom she would later marry. To list all of those hits would fill a page, but classics like "Up on the Roof," "(You Make Me Feel Like) A Natural Woman," "Will You Still Love Me Tomorrow," "The Locomotion," "Don't Bring Me Down," "Hey Girl," "One Fine Day," "Pleasant Valley Sunday," "Some Kind-A-Wonderful," and "You've Got a Friend" are just a few.
In 1962 King scored a #22 hit as a solo artist with "It Might As Well Rain until September." With guitarist Danny Kortchmar and her second husband, bassist Charles Larkey, King formed the City, releasing an album titled *Now That Everything's Been Said* on Lou Adler's Ode label. The project fell apart and King focused on her solo career in 1970 with *Writer: Carole King.* That album went nowhere, but its followup, *Tapestry,* became one of the biggest-selling albums of the 70s, holding the #1 position for fifteen weeks and remaining on the charts for 302 consecutive weeks. *Tapestry,* which featured a blend of old King standards and new compositions, fused the introspection of the singer/songwriter genre with a warm, homey soulfulness and believable passionate delivery.
Since then, King's intimate delivery and quality work have given her a long, rewarding career. In 1987, King was inducted into the Songwriters Hall of Fame.
"It's Too Late"/"I Feel the Earth Move" (#1), "So Far Away" (#14), "Sweet Seasons" (#9), "Jazzman" (#2), and "Nightingale" (#9) are a few of her many hits. –RC

☆ **Tapestry / CBS / BB 1**   1971
In the world of popular music, the word "classic" gets bandied
about like the word "improved" on ad campaigns, ceasing to
mean anything after a while. *Tapestry*, however, is a *classic*, no
two ways about it. King (already a very successful songwriter)
assembled a collection of her best-known songs, plus some
new ones, and gave them intimate heartfelt readings. King's
voice had a warm earthy quality, with just the right amount of
urgency. Listing highlights is fairly pointless, as the whole
album is stunning. –RC

○ **Music / ODE / BB 1**   1971
Without the reserve of self-penned standards to draw upon,
Music lacked the powerful resonance of its predecessor,
Tapestry. Nevertheless, songs like "Sweet Seasons," "Brother
Brother," "Some Kind of Wonderful," and "Song of Long Ago"
make this one of her better efforts. –RC

Fantasy / CBS / BB 6   1973
By this time, King's work was recalling the detached
craftmanship of her days as a professional tunesmith. As a
result, many of her post-*Tapestry* efforts lacked a certain sense
of emotional investment in their performances. Regardless,
Fantasy (an improvement over the previously released
Rhymes and Reasons) produced three hits with "Believe in
Humanity" (#28), "Corazon" (#37), and "You Light Up My
Life" (#67). Other highlights included "A Quiet Place to Live"
and "Directions." –RC

○ **Really Rosie / CBS / BB 20**   1975
This winning soundtrack collaboration for a children's TV
special (with children's author Maurice Sendak) was a return
to form for King. *Really Rosie* contains some of King's best
solo material. This is an enjoyable listening experience for
children and adults alike. –RC

Thoroughbred / CBS / BB 3   1976
After a series of solid but unexceptional albums, King re-
collaborated with her first husband Gerry Goffin and
produced her best album since *Tapestry*. Like *Tapestry*, much
of *Thoroughbred* reflected a rich soulfulness. The only thing
lacking was *Tapestry*'s amazing collection of standards. The
emotive "Only Love Is Real" became a substantial hit. –RC

● **Her Greatest Hits / CBS / BB 47**   1978
All of King's major hits are here, plus a few key album tracks.
It's a decent starting place for the uninitiated, but *Tapestry* is a
richer listening experience. –RC

Pearls - Songs of Goffin and King / CAPITOL   1980
King reprises the early-60s pop gems she wrote with Gerry
Goffin, with fine results. –DH

KING CRIMSON

Art-rock. If the Moody Blues provided a heavenly Mellotron-
soaked soundtrack for millions of late-60s cosmic rockers,
King Crimson (formed in 1969) balanced the scales with
disturbingly dense and explosive sonic trips into the dark
side. Even when the band was playing something relatively
peaceful, there was a sense that something wasn't
quite settled. Founded by guitarist Robert Fripp and
saxophonist Ian McDonald, the group burst forth with an
ornate, majestic, savage sound and an approach that owed a
great deal to modern jazz. McDonald left after the first tour,
followed by the rest of the band, except for Fripp, who re-
formed the band in ever-changing configurations up through
1974, when the final breakup came. The latter-day King
Crimson (with Adrian Belew on guitar with Fripp) is the most
daring version but has virtually no connection with the
original except its name. –BE & RC

★ **In the Court of the Crimson King / CAROLINE**   1969
Definitive debut album, which was almost too good (it took
years for them to come up with a record as concise and
distinctive), an orchestrated vision of apocalyptic doom
dominated by Ian McDonald's Mellotron, Greg Lake's dignified
voice, and the ferocious guitar playing of Robert Fripp. The
latter would be the only survivor onto subsequent albums. –BE

○ **In the Wake of Poseidon / CAROLINE**   1970
A more carefully produced and better crafted but more diffuse
second album Fripp took over the keyboard as well as all the
compositional chores, with help from Gustav Holst (*The
Planets*). –BE

○ **Larks' Tongues in Aspic / CAROLINE**   1973
The new King Crimson debuts, with a violin (courtesy of
David Cross) now sharing center stage with Fripp's guitar, and
the Mellotron pushed somewhat into the background. The
material itself is the most experimental that Fripp had come
up with up to that time, and John Wetton's vocals were the
strongest since the departure of Greg Lake in 1970. –BE

Red / CAROLINE   1974
Some final thoughts before Fripp pulled the plug on Crimson
— the material is longer, the playing more ferocious, and the
whole album seems rushed toward the breaking point of
dissolution for the band. The culmination of five years of
doom-rock. –BE

Starless and Bible Black / CAROLINE   1974
An intriguing followup, stretching out the instrumental forms
somewhat and experimenting with all manner of subject
matter from experimental live tracks to songs built around
paintings ("The Night Watch"). –BE

Discipline / CAROLINE   1981
The new King Crimson, harder and heavier. –BE

○ **Beat / WARNER**   1982
A superior mid-80s followup with better material. –BE

Three of a Perfect Pair / CAROLINE   1984
The final chapter? Don't bet on it, but this would be a good
way to end, if so. –BE

○ **Frame by Frame / CAROLINE**   1991
Frame by Frame is a four CD box set, compiled by band leader
Robert Fripp, that does a good job providing primo samples
of each of Crimson's musical periods. Sonically, the excellent
remastering makes this the best this band has ever sounded
on disc. Three of the discs cover their studio work, while the
fourth is a collection of live work, spanning the band's entire
career. Enclosed is a richly detailed diary (written by Fripp)
of Crimson's entire history, plus interviews with band
members, and glowing and hateful reviews from critics.
Typical of Crimson, precious little of the music on this set
would qualify for casual listening. However, those whose taste
run towards the dark side of prog-rock will find this set
rewarding. –RC

KING DIAMOND

Heavy metal. King Diamond, former vocalist for the influential
black-metal band Mercyful Fate, continues to conceptualize
upon themes of evil in a theatrical manner, both in the studio
and on stage. –JB

○ **Abigail / ROADRACER**   1987
Any King Diamond is good, but this is a top-notch
performance. Excellent playing, powerful vocal effects, and a
believable (and eerie) story line. Comparable to his days with
Mercyful Fate. –JB

KING'S X

Hard rock. Known as the Edge since 1981, this Houston, TX,
trio became King's X in 1986. Featuring Ty Tabor's lyrical
guitar work, Jerry Gaskill's forceful drumming, and Doug
Pinnick's emotive lead singing and distinctive bass work
(sometimes on 12-string bass), King's X is a dense
instrumental fusion between hard rock and prog-rock.
Vocally, King's X exhibits a knack for rich three-part
harmonies that, at times, recall *Abbey Road*-period Beatles.
Thematically, they range from *Wizard of Oz*-style fantasy
imagery to more complex spiritual (particularly Christian)
metaphors. –RC

Out of the Silent Planet / MEGAFORCE   1988
Out of the Silent Planet (named after the first book of Christian

writer C. S. Lewis's space fantasy trilogy) was a brilliant debut for King's X, featuring memorable melodies and sweeping harmonies. This debut's over-the-top performances and well-defined arrangements earned this band a substantial following from both metal and prog-rock audiences early on. –RC

○ **Faith Hope Love by King's X / MEGAFORCE**   1990
Faith Hope Love was King's X's commercial breakthrough effort, containing the hit "It's Love." –RC

KINGFISH

Rock/pop. Kingfish is a San Francisco-influenced band featuring Bob Weir (at times), Dave Torbert, Matthew Kelly, Robby Hoddinott, and Chris Herolo. –CR

○ **Kingfish / GRATEFUL DEAD**   1976
A side project of Grateful Dead guitarist Bob Weir, Kingfish was a hot little bar band that stayed close to rock's roots. Very strong song selection featuring "Jump for Joy," "Lazy Lightning," "Wild Northland," "Big Iron," "Goodby Yer Honor," "Asia Minor," and more. Besides Weir, players on this release include Dave Torbert, Matthew Kelly, Robby Hoddinott, and Chris Herold. This album featured jams to challenge the Dead's but also knew when to come back to earth. –JT & CR

Alive in Eighty Five / RELIX   1989
Good songs — good crowd. –CR

Live 'n' Kickin' / JET   1989
Good sound on ten well-performed songs. –CR

KINGSMEN

Rock & roll. The rock & roll band from Portland, OR, whose one big hit "Louie, Louis" defined the garage-band style and became one of the all-time classics. The original lineup included Jack Ely (lead singer and guitar), Lynn Easton (drums), Mike Mitchell (lead guitar), Bob Nordby (bass), and Don Galucci (piano). –CK

○ **Best of Kingsmen / RHINO**   1989
All the hits; great sound. –CK

THE KINKS

British Invasion, Rock/pop. Formed in 1963, the Kinks were one of the most influential groups to emerge from the first wave of the British Invasion.
The band's rather sloppy, but energetic ensemble work, coupled with singer/songwriter Ray Davies's (b Jun 21, 1944) distinctly British point of view and excellent song sense, plus American producer Shel Talmy, generated a substantial body of classic albums. They were a thoroughly British garage-rock bridge (practically devoid of the overt American blues fascination practiced by the Animals or Rolling Stones) for those who desired an alternative to the bright clean tunefulness of the Beatles.
The Kinks's first Stateside hit, "You Really Got Me" (#7), was built around what must be one of rock's most memorable (and influential) guitar riffs. Davies quickly followed suit with the similar (and equally fine) "All Day and All of the Night" (#7). Davies's intelligently barbed take on the British class system increasingly dominated their themes. Eventually, the Kinks gravitated toward conceptual albums. *Arthur, Or the Decline and Fall of the British Empire* (released 1969, #105) was one of the first rock operas. *Lola versus Powerman and the Money-go-round* (1970, #35) would produce their last hit for many years, with "Lola" (#9), a song about a transvestite. A label change to RCA found the band increasingly doing conceptual albums, with fairly spotty results and diminishing sales. Regardless of some good material, the band sounded stale on record compared to their earlier work.
In 1977 the Kinks signed with Arista and gradually enjoyed some substantial hits, including the 1983 hit "Come Dancing" (#6), which tied the highest charting record of their career, 1965's "Tired of Waiting for You." –CK

You Really Got Me / RHINO / BB 29   1964

The highlight of this rather spotty debut (consisting of a sampling of originals and covers Kinks churned out at gigs) was, without a doubt, the title track, which single-handedly pioneered riff-oriented hard rock. "Stop Your Sobbing," a song later recorded by Pretenders, was also a standout track, but producer Shel Talmy's "Bald Headed Woman" was an absolute low point. –RC

Kinda Kinks / RHINO / BB 60   1965
Album #2 featured a rewrite of "You Really Got Me," with the equally fine "All Day and All of the Night" (#7). Ray Davies, however, delivered a strong set of tunes that went beyond riff-rockers with the exuberant "Come On Now," and "You Shouldn't Be Sad." His penchant for memorable melodies emerged with tracks like "Something Better Beginning" and "Tired of Waiting for You." –RC

☆ **Kink-Size/Kinkdom / RHINO**   1965
This Rhino reissue contains Kinks's third and fourth albums, *Kink-Size* (#13) and *Kinkdom* (#47), respectively, plus some non-album sides from the same period. *Kink-Size* featured the hit "Set Me Free" (#23), another Kinks classic, as well as "Everybody's Gonna Be Happy." By the release of *Kinkdom*, the Kinks had developed an instantly identifiable sound, built around Davies's wavering lower tenor and the group's airy falsetto background vocals and ragged garage-rock-like ensemble work. "Dedicated Follower of Fashion" (#36), a noisy dance-hall rocker, was a wonderful poke at a Carnaby Street fop in his "frilly nylon panties." Other hits included "Who'll Be the Next in Line" (#34) and "A Well Respected Man" (#13). This disc also includes the assertive "I'm Not Like Everybody Else," (originally written as a pitch for the Animals, and the B-side to "Sunny Afternoon"). –RC

○ **The Kink Kontroversy / PRT / BB 47**   1966
This great album is still only available as a British import. The Kinks sludge out some fine trashy rockers with "Where Have All the Good Times Gone" (later re recorded by Van Halen) and "Till the End of the Day" (#50), a moderate hit. Other highlights included "It's Too Late," "You Can't Win," and "I'm on an Island." –RC

Live Kinks / WARNER / BB 162   1967
Outside of the Rolling Stones' *Got Live If You Want It* and the Beatles' *Live at the Hollywood Bowl*, this is the only readily available concert document of a British Invasion-era band, complete with all of the screaming fans. The Kinks slog through a version of "The Batman Theme," "I'm on an Island," "Milk Cow Blues," and a smattering of hits. –RC

○ **Face to Face / REPRISE / BB 135**   1967
Face to Face was another extraordinary Kinks album, this time featuring the hit "Sunny Afternoon" (#14) and other gems like "Holiday in Waikiki," "Fancy," "Too Much on My Mind," and "Rainy Day in June." –RC

○ **Village Green Preservation Society / WARNER**   1968
On *The Kinks Are the Village Green Preservation Society*, Ray Davies's eye for the little lyrical details that speak volumes about everyday people hit a zenith. Initially inspired by Dylan Thomas's portrayal of an indolent Welsh village (*Under the Milkweed*), this was Kinks's finest conceptual album. Their first album produced without Shel Talmy, it projected an unassuming, low-key quality. It is amazing that this album failed to dent the charts. Fortunately, Warner has released it on CD. Highlights include "Picture Book," "Animal Farm," "Big Sky," "Johnny Thunder," "Wicked Annabella," and the title track. –RC

○ **Something Else by the Kinks / WARNER / BB 153**   1968
The followup to *Face To Face* was equally impressive, featuring the wistful "Waterloo Sunset," one of Davies's finest compositions. Other highlights included "Situation Vacant," "David Watts," "Love Me Till the Sun Shines," and Dave Davies's "Death of a Clown." Highly recommended! –RC

Arthur / WARNER / BB 15   1969
After the commercial disaster of *Village Green Preservation Society*, Ray Davies turned his attentions to collaborating on a

TV musical titled *Arthur (Or the Decline and Fall of the British Empire)* with writer Julian Mitchell. Even though the show got canned, the album received much acclaim, placing the Kinks back on the charts. "Victoria" (#62) became a moderate hit. Other highlights included "Brainwashed," "Australia," "Shangri-la," and the title cut. –RC

☆ **Lola ... / WARNER / BB 35**   1970
Thanks to the #9 hit single "Lola" (about an encounter with a transvestite), *Lola vs. the Powerman & the Money-go-round, Part One* became a comeback of sorts for the Kinks. Overall, this album is a Davies-eye view of life as an artist coping with the road ("This Time Tomorrow") and the music industry, which includes blackly humorous portrayals of the musician's union ("Get Back in Line"), music publishers ("Denmark Street"), making it big ("Top of the Pops"), and greed ("Money-go-round"). This might be a whinefest from a successful pop artist, but his observations aren't that far off base. Musically, The Kinks still had their ragged delivery, but they increasingly employed more acoustic instrumentation, giving the arrangements a slightly folky quality at times. –RC

Muswell Hillbillies / RHINO / BB 10   1971
For their first outing on the RCA label, the Kinks adopted a more laidback rootsy sound that even sported traces of country ("Holloway Jail") and dancehall/cabaret theater styles ("Skin and Bones," "Holiday," "Alcohol"). "Twentieth Century Man" is a nice medium-tempo rocker but lacking the reckless fire of their earlier efforts. –RC

Everybody's in Show-Biz / RHINO / BB 70   1972
One half of this release is a document of the Kinks' spirited live slopfest, including versions of "Top of the Pops," "Holiday," and the "Banana Boat Song." The other half contains a couple of gems like "Celluloid Heroes," "Sitting in My Hotel," as well as "Motorway," and "Maximum Consumption." –RC

☆ **The Kink Kronikles / WARNER / BB 94**   1972
Anyone wanting a well-chosen sampler of the best Kinks work, from half of their stay at Reprise, should start here. Many of the essential tracks are here. –RC

○ **Kinks' Greatest - Celluloid Heroes / RCA / BB 144**   1976
This is a good collection comprising the cream of the Kinks' RCA years. It includes "Sitting in My Hotel," Twentieth Century Man," "Alcohol," and "Everybody's a Star." –RC

○ **Come Dancing with the Kinks / ARISTA / BB 159**   1986
A sampling of the their Arista years (1977-1986). Most of the essential tracks are here, including all of their hits from that period. "Come Dancing," "A Rock 'n' Roll Fantasy," "Juke Box Music," "Destroyer," and "(Wish I Could Fly Like) Superman" are among the titles found here. –RC

★ **Greatest Hits - Vol. 1 / RHINO**   1989
If you are going to budget only for one Kinks disc, this is the one to get. It features all of their biggest 60s chart hits, plus some key B-Sides. Nevertheless, their albums from this period feature many fine album cuts worth having, so consider this an excellent primer but not a definitive package. –RC

KEVN KINNEY

Singer/songwriter. Kinney is a member of Drivin' N Cryin'. He released a solo project of acoustic folk music. –CR

○ **MacDougal Blues / ISLAND**   1990
One of the finest albums released in 1990. Kinney's songwriting talent lies in telling stories that pull the listener into his songs (as quirky as they sometimes are). His voice is by no means smooth, yet it has an engrossing quality. The music will amaze you. His backing band includes Peter Buck of R.E.M. (dulcimer, mandolin, guitar), Buren Fowler (guitar, pedal steel, banjo), Tim Nielsen (bass, mandolin), John Keane (guitar, electric slide guitar, bass, banjo), and others; they do a fantastic job. Very, very highly recommended. –CR

KISS

Hard rock, heavy metal. Paul Stanley (born Stanley Harvey Eisen), Ace Frehley (born Paul Frehley), Gene Simmons (born

Chiam Whitz), and Peter Criss (born Peter Crisscuola) formed Kiss in New York City, mid 1973. Taking their cue from Alice Cooper and the New York Dolls, the boys applied kabuki makeup and wreaked havoc with their shared passion for good loud hard rock. Signed to the newly formed Casablanca in 1974, they released their debut album and two others within a year.
With three albums under their belt, they gained a foothold on the arena rock circuit, dazzling audiences with a stage show built as much around smoke bombs, floating drum risers, flashpots, and outrageousness as around the music itself. At the height of their popularity in 1978, the members of the band released simultaneous solo albums with similar covers showing that member's face. All were good, but Frehley's outsold the others.
In the 80s, with lower-quality albums, a possible breakup was rumored. Criss was replaced by Eric Carr; Frehley left one album later, replaced by Vinnie Vincent. Kiss also ditched the makeup in a marketing about-face. Vincent left shortly thereafter, replaced briefly by Mark St. John and later by Bruce Kulick. This lineup brought Kiss to a new generation of fans, but at the peak of this new popularity, Carr died of brain cancer in 1991. Not to give up, Kiss recorded *Revenge*, some citing it as their best work in 15 years. Kiss's major influence in heavy metal is obvious in many of today's young bands. –JB

Kiss / POLYGRAM   1974
Their debut album, featuring future stage staples "Deuce," "Strutter," and "Firehouse." –JB

○ **Alive! / POLYGRAM**   1975
The definitive document of the band's power as a live act. Includes "Rock & Roll All Night," "Hotter Than Hell," and "Let Me Go, Rock & Roll." –JB

Destroyer / POLYGRAM   1976
Produced by Bob Ezrin and featuring the classic, "Detroit Rock City," as well as "Beth," "Do You Love Me?," and "Shout It Out Loud." –JB & RDF

● **Double Platinum (Greatest Hits) / POLYGRAM**   1978
The best of the band's early years, including "Beth," "Cold Gin," and "She." –DH

○ **Smashes, Thrashes & Hits / POLYGRAM**   1989
Companion volume to the above from their later makeup-less period. Includes "Lick It Up," "Let's Put the X in Sex," and "Love Gun." –DH

Revenge / POLYGRAM   1992
Their heaviest album since *Creatures*, containing "Heart of Chrome" and "God Gave Rock & Rock to You II." –RDF

THE KLF

Techno-pop. This English dance-pop troupe initially gained much notoriety for their liberal use of sampled performances in their recorded work. –JB

○ **White Room / ARISTA**   1991
Formerly known as Justified Ancients of Mu Mu, aka The Jams and the Timelords, the Kopyright Liberation Front (KLF) created dance music with as many samples as possible without getting busted. *White Room* is their major KLF debut and contains "Justified and Ancient," a surprise hit with Tammy Wynette on vocals. –JB

THE KNACK

Power-pop, new-wave. This Los Angeles band (formed 1978) made a nod to the 60s power-pop sound, pushing the image of themselves as the American Beatles on their debut album cover. All experienced musicians, they didn't try to hide their attempt to market their way to the top. Cleverly crafted pop songs like their smash hit "My Sharona," which sold over five million copies, were aimed straight at the teen-pop market. "Good Girls Don't," another song from the same album, was another strong hit. Their subsequent albums tried to repeat this initial success, even using blatant carbon copies of previous songs, but failed as the Beatles comparisons began to fade. After the third album, the Knack folded: with some members staying together as the Game, while vocalist Doug Fieger started the band Taking Chances. In the 90s, the band has re-formed with a new drummer, Billy Ward, but has so far not made much of a splash. −SWB

○ **Get the Knack / CAPITOL**   1979
New-wavish pop with the hit "My Sharona." With "Good Girls Don't" and "Maybe Tonight," one gets the feeling that they may have had the talent to do more than just update early Fab Four and 60s bubblegum rock. −SWB

GLADYS KNIGHT & THE PIPS   b 1944

R&B, Motown, soul, pop. Gladys Knight's career began when she won first prize at Ted Mack's Original Amateur Hour as a child. At the age of seventeen she had her first hit record, along with her brother and two cousins, who were known as the Pips. Their career really took off when they signed with Motown in 1966. Moving over to Buddah Records in 1973, they scored another string of hits. Gladys Knight now performs as a soloist and records for MCA. The Pips are retired; members include: Merald Knight, Edward Patten, and William Guest. −RAB

If I Were Your Woman / MOTOWN   1971
Gladys at her soulful best. −RAB

○ **Anthology / MOTOWN**   1986
Atlanta family group Gladys Knight and the Pips had been performing together for fourteen years before signing with Motown in 1966. This compilation more than adequately covers this period of the Pips's career. Working primarily with producer Norman Whitfield from 1967 to 1969, the group created such Motor City classics as "Everybody Needs Love," "I Heard It through the Grapevine," "The End of Our Road," and "Friendship Train." From 1970 through 1973 the Pips worked with a variety of Motown producers concentrating on ballads. Although perhaps a little less consistent, there was no shortage of hits, the most notable being 1970's "If I Were Your Woman" and 1973's "Neither One of Us (Wants to Be the First to Say Goodbye)." The downside of this compilation is that both the liner notes and the mastering for CD are substandard. −RB

● **Soul Survivors ... / RHINO**   1990
Soul Survivors - The Best of Gladys Knight & the Pips picks up where the Motown anthology left off, containing the most important singles that Gladys Knight and the Pips recorded for Buddah, Columbia, and MCA from the early 70s into the late 80s. The Buddah tracks, highlighted by the Jim Weatherly-written "Midnight Train in Georgia" and "Best Thing That Ever Happened to Me," contain some of Gladys's most impassioned vocal performances. −RB

JEAN KNIGHT   b 1943

Soul, R&B. Knight filed her claim to fame in 1971 with her sassy #1 R&B hit, "Mr. Big Stuff." Knight had previously recorded for Houston producer Huey Meaux, but it was her 1970 sojourn to Malaco Studios in Jackson, MS, that would make her a star. There she cut the teasing "Mr. Big Stuff," a #2 pop smash on Stax. Immediate followups included the similarly funky "You Think You're Hot Stuff." Knight returned to prominence in 1985 with her cover of Rockin' Sidney's wildly popular zydeco novelty "My Toot Toot." −BD

○ **Mr. Big Stuff / STAX**   1971
Funky and hard-hitting, recorded at Malaco Studios. −RP

BUDDY KNOX   b 1933

Rockabilly. The brand of Texas rockabilly that Buddy Knox cooked up around 1957 wasn't quite as raw as that of his Memphis cohorts at Sun, but it was just as commercially potent. Knox sported a light, almost gentle vocal style, and his band, the Rhythm Orchids, obliged with upbeat backing that suited him well. Formed at West Texas State University, the Rhythm Orchids also included Jimmy Bowen on upright bass, and it was Bowen's equally lighthearted vocal on "I'm Stickin' with You" that originally graced the flip side of Knox's first smash, "Party Doll." Roulette Records astutely picked up the master from the tiny Triple-D logo, separated the sides, and the fledgling firm enjoyed two giant hits for the price of one. "Party Doll" soared to the very top of the pops, and Knox encored with the equally tuneful "Rock Your Little Baby to Sleep" and "Hula Love," which he performed in the 1957 rock flick *Jamboree*. Knox waxed the fine rockabilly-based "Swingin' Daddy," "Devil Woman," and a cover of Ruth Brown's "Somebody Touched Me" for Roulette before moving to Liberty and hitting with a pop-flavored rendition of the Clovers's song "Lovey Dovey" in 1960. Over three decades later, the Texas rocker remains a popular act on the oldies front. −BD

○ **Best of Buddy Knox / RHINO**   1990
Gentle, catchy Texas rockabilly with a pop slant. −BD

CUB KODA   b 1948

Rock & roll, blues/rock, rockabilly. Founder and leader of the rowdy 70s rock group Brownsville Station ("Smokin' in the Boy's Room," "The Martian Boogie"), Koda has gone on to a solo career as a high-spirited archivist of obscure rock, blues, country, and R&B songs and artists. As a producer, Koda unearthed the "world's worst bar band," King Uszniewicz & the Uszniewicztones (see separate entry); as the frontman for Hound Dog Taylor's resurrected Houserockers, he recorded two raucous albums that are encyclopedic in their array of blues songs and styles. But perhaps Koda's most lasting contribution to music is as a writer of liner notes and the long-running "Vinyl Junkie" column for the record-collecting magazine *Goldmine*. −KK

○ **Cub Koda & the Points / FAN CLUB**   1980
Koda's first solo album after Brownsville Station. Highlights include "Jail Bait" and "Welcome to My Job." −STE

It's the Blues / FAN CLUB   1982
An intense, eclectic, wonderfully played set with the Houserockers. Lots of fun and 100% true to its title. −KK

Cub Digs Chuck / GARAGELAND   1989
Koda's tribute album to Chuck Berry, featuring blistering versions of "Johnny B. Goode," "Maybellene," and others. −STE

● **Live at B.L.U.E.S. 1982 / WOLF**   1991
Powerful blues with the Houserockers, raw and loud, with Koda shining on slide. Special appearance by Chicago legend Eddie Clearwater. −KK

Cub Digs Bo / GARAGELAND   1992
Koda's tribute album to Bo Diddley, including powerhouse renditions of "Mumblin' Guitar," "Roadrunner," and "Background to a Music." −STE

KOOL & THE GANG

Funk. One of the leading funk outfits of the 70s and 80s, with gold and platinum platters galore. Formed by bassist Robert "Kool" Bell (b 1950) as the Jazziacs in Jersey City, the Gang also featured his brothers Robert and Ronald Bell. The crew signed with De-Lite Records in 1969 and began churning out massively funky grooves, hitting full stride in 1973-1974 with "Jungle Boogie," "Hollywood Swinging," and "Higher Plane." The Gang topped the soul charts in 1979 with the high-stepping disco favorite "Ladies Night," — the same year they hired J. T. Taylor as their new lead singer. "Celebrate!" a staple of every respectable wedding reception of the last dozen years, went platinum for the group in 1980, and their non-stop string of incendiary successes stretched into the mid 80s with "Fresh" and "Cherish." Taylor went solo in 1988. −BD

○ **Spin Their Top Hits / POLYGRAM**   1978
The best of Kool & the Gang's early hits, including the jangly funk classic "Jungle Boogie." −CK

Greatest Hits & More / POYDOR   1988
The best of their later-era hits, featuring "Cherish" and the anthemic "Celebrate!" –CK

AL KOOPER   b 1944

Rock & roll, blues/rock, rock/pop. Over the last thirty years, Al Kooper has managed to involve himself in many creative aspects of popular music. As a songwriter, Kooper cowrote the #1 hit for Gary Lewis & the Playboys, "This Diamond Ring." Bob Dylan's "Like a Rolling Stone" and album *Highway 61 Revisited* benefited from Kooper's rolling Hammond B3 organ work. Kooper also played French horn and keys on the Rolling Stones' "You Can't Always Get What You Want." Kooper founded Blood, Sweat & Tears, producing and performing on their classic debut *The Child Is Father to the Man* (#47). He also did side projects with Stephen Stills and Michael Bloomfield, most notably *Super Session* (#12). As a producer, Kooper discovered Lynyrd Skynyrd, and produced their first three albums. Kooper's solo output has always been sporadic, due to the many other projects on his plate. More recently, Kooper has relocated to Nashville, where he produces and can be seen playing with the blues-rock band the Blue Bloods. –RC

○ **Super Session / CBS**   1969
A glorified jam session utilizing the talents of Michael Bloomfield and Stephen Stills. The album that started the trend. –CK

Live Adventures of Kooper & Bloomfield / CBS   1969
More jamming, this time at the Fillmore, with guest appearances by Elvin Bishop and Carlos Santana. –CK

KRAFTWERK

Techno-pop. The forebears of synthesizer rock, this German quartet brought their cold electronic music to the American charts with the 1975 hit "Autobahn." They're acknowledged today as one of the progenitors of 90s electro-dance-pop. –JF

○ **Autobahn / ELEKTRA**   1974
A cold, hypnotic album, the title song of which was an unlikely hit. –DH

BILLY J. KRAMER & THE DAKOTAS   b 1943

British Invasion. At the outset of the British Invasion in 1964, Billy J. Kramer with the Dakotas was one of the hottest bands of the movement's initial wave. Beatles manager Brian Epstein paired young Liverpool vocalist Kramer with the Dakotas and gave them a surefire hit — the Lennon/McCartney composition "Do You Want to Know a Secret?," which established the group in England. The group broke in America with the two-sided smash "Little Children"/"Bad to Me" in 1964 on Imperial, the latter another Lennon/McCartney effort. Their next two smashes, "I'll Keep You Satisfied" and "From a Window," were also penned by the prolific duo, although Kramer's last US hit, "Trains and Boats and Planes," was written by Burt Bacharach and Hal David. The group appeared in the popular 1964 movie *The T.A.M.I. Show*, but by 1967 the musicians and Kramer had gone their separate ways, the vocalist recording as a solo in Britain. –BD

○ **Best of Billy J. Kramer / CAPITOL**   1991
A strong collection that presents all of his best — including a number of songs written by John and Paul Beatle — are here in excellent sound. –BE & JT

LENNY KRAVITZ

Rock/pop, psychedelic. Stealing from a list of influences too long to mention (Lennon, Bowie, Velvet Underground, and Prince, for starters), multi-instrumentalist and songwriter Lenny Kravitz produces pleasant, catchy pop soaked in late-60s/early-70s rock & soul. On his 1989 self-produced debut, *Let Love Rule*, Kravitz played the majority of the instruments, a gutsy move that gained him considerable notice in the press along with modest sales. Kravitz skirted the sophomore slump with 1991's *Mama Said*, which gave him a wider audience and a #2 hit, "It Ain't Over 'Til It's Over." –STE

Let Love Rule / VIRGIN   1989
Kravitz played the majority of the instruments on this self-produced debut of catchy retro-pop. Kravitz's talent unfortunately does not extend past music, and the album features some embarassingly sophomoric lyrics (the least of which are from his ex-wife Lisa Bonet) that wreck some of his better songs. –STE

○ **Mama Said / VIRGIN**   1991
Intended to be a harrowing song cycle about the disintegration of Kravitz's marriage to actress Lisa Bonet, Kravitz doesn't understand there is quite a difference between saying he's in pain and illustrating he's in pain. Yet, the album *sounds* good, as Kravitz steals from nearly every major pop artist and style since 1966, making for some enjoyable ear candy (including the #2 hit single "It Ain't Over 'Til It's Over") yet nothing challenging or haunting. Kravitz again plays the majority of the instruments, with Slash (Guns N' Roses) contributing some fine guitar to "Always on the Run" and "Fields of Joy." –STE

KREATOR

Thrash. Kreator began in the early 80s in their native Germany, and as thrash- and speed-metal picked up momentum so did the following for Kreator. Their music remains a heavy influence for many metal bands, both for new acts and Kreator's contemporaries. –JB

○ **Pleasure to Kill / NOISE**   1986
Dark speed-metal with a passion for death. Influential. –JB

● **Terrible Certainty / NOISE**   1987
Angry speed-metal from Germany, with their tightest and harshest album to date. One of the best from the 80s. –JB

Endless Pain / NOISE   1989
Essential speed-metal album from the mid 80s when they were still a trio. –JB

L.T.D.

R&B, funk. Horn-based R&B/funk band originating in North Carolina, formed in 1968. Jeffrey Osborne was the lead vocalist until his departure in 1980; he was replaced by Andre Ray and Leslie Wilson in 1980. L.T.D. is an acronym for Love, Togetherness, and Devotion. –BC

○ **Classics - Vol. 27 / A&M**   1987
70s hard-funk and orchestrated ballads like "Love Ballad" (#20) and "(Every Time I Turn Around) I'm in Love Again" (#4). –BC

SLEEPY LA BEEF   b 1935

Rockabilly. This Rockabilly journeyman has a bodacious baritone voice and a slashing and primitive guitar style, but he's never broken out of his status as a cult performer. –JF

○ **Nothin' but the Truth / ROUNDER**   1987
The only CD currently available of this gentle rockabilly giant is a typically rocking affair. –BD

THE LA'S

Alternative pop. This unique alternative pop-rock band from Liverpool draws heavily from the folky acoustic/electric side of mid-60s Brit pop — à la Hollies and Searchers. –RC

○ **The LA's / POLYGRAM**   1991
One of the strongest debuts on the 1991 alternative music scene. "There She Goes" was a hit single with its appealing mid-60s-influenced Brit Invasion sound and interweaving hooks. Most of the album should be a joy to hear for fans of alternative Anglo-pop. Highlights include "Son of a Gun," "Way Out," "Freedom Song," and "I.O.U." –RC

LABELLE

R&B, soul, funk. A girl-group from Philadelphia, formed in

1962. Initially known as the Bluebelles, and then Patti LaBelle and the Bluebelles, the group's personnel consisted of Patti LaBelle, Cindy Birdsong, Sarah Dash, and Nona Hendryx. The quartet scored six R&B hits from 1962 through 1967 before Birdsong departed to join Diana Ross and the Supremes. Continuing as a trio, for the next seven years the group languished in obscurity. British manager Vicki Wickham remade their image in the early 70s and shortened the name to LaBelle. Decked out in ersatz futuristic garb, the threesome appeared as whirling dervishes delivering an explosive gospel/funk hybrid. Between late 1974 and late 1976, LaBelle enjoyed five R&B hits, the first, "Lady Marmalade," reaching the #1 spot on the R&B and pop charts. LaBelle split up in early 1977. –RB

○ **Nightbirds / EPIC / BB 7**   1974
The finest of the three LaBelle albums, *Nightbirds* was recorded in New Orleans with funk meister Allen Toussaint handling the production chores and, one assumes, members of the Meters taking care of the session work. Worth the price of admission for the Bob Crewe-written "Lady Marmalade" alone, the album veers between the strutting New Orleans, horn-laden singles and more mainstream pop material. –RB

PATTI LABELLE   b 1944

Soul, R&B, pop. Born Patricia Holt in Philadelphia, Patti LaBelle has enjoyed a 30-year-plus career, having sung early 60s girl-group material, soul, funk, and 80s ballad and dance music. From 1962-1976 she was a founding member of both Patti LaBelle & the Blue Belles and LaBelle. She began her solo career in 1977. Over the ensuing six years, she scored a number of lower-rung R&B hits with Epic, coming into her own on Gamble and Huff's Philadelphia International label in 1984 with the #1 R&B hit, "If Only You Knew." She has been a consistent chartmaker ever since, renowned for a gospel-trained voice with stunning power and range, capable of exhilarating aural gymnastics. One of the most gifted, idiosyncratic voices in R&B. –RB

Patti LaBelle / CBS   1977
A funky solo debut with incendiary readings of "You Are My Friend" and "Since I Don't Have You." –BC

○ **Best of Patti LaBelle / CBS**   1982
Emotive songs, like "Lady Marmalade," "You Are My Friend," and "Joy to Have Your Love." –BC

Winner in You / MCA   1986
Her first MCA album. Pop crossover, with her Michael McDonald duet "On My Own." –BC

Be Yourself / MCA   1989
Urban R&B, with some cuts produced by Prince. –BC

Burnin' / MCA   1991
Warm ballads, with guests Gladys Knight and David Peaston, and a Labelle reunion. –BC

ART LABOE

Rock/pop. A California disc jockey who popularized the "oldies but goodies" format in radio. Though compilation albums of older material are now commonplace, Laboe was among the first (if not *the* first) to license material from several labels for the first successful "oldies" albums to hit the market. –CK

Oldies but Goodies - Vol. 1 & 2 / ORIGINAL SOUND
The first two albums in this multi-volume series lean heavily toward both doo-wop and R&B classics and obscurities. Out of print but worth the search, as they are both excellent compilations. –CK

MAJOR LANCE   b 1941

R&B, soul. Few vocalists better epitomize the breezy danceability of 60s Chicago soul than whippet-thin Major Lance. Local deejay Jim Lounsbury discovered the loose-limbed singer and arranged his first contract with Mercury in 1959, but Lance needed expert guidance — and he received plenty from innovative producer Carl Davis after joining the

Okeh label in 1962. Armed with exceptional dance material by Curtis Mayfield and the brass-heavy, often Latin-tinged charts of Jonny Pate, Lance blasted off with "The Monkey Time" and "Hey Little Girl" in 1963 and followed with the mysterious "Um Um Um Um Um Um" and "The Matador" the next year. When the influence of Mayfield and Davis dimmed, the hits became lesser in magnitude, and Lance left OKeh in 1968, bouncing from Dakar to Curtom to Volt with moderate success. Lance did a three-year prison stretch from 1978 to 1981 for drug dealing, but has been sighted on stage recently. –BD

○ **Major Lance's Greatest Hits / OKEH**   1978
This Chicago-based soul crooner was Curtis Mayfield's finest discovery, cutting many Impressions-like hits that captured that group's effervescent spirit and a good deal of its groove appeal. All of Lance's major hits — "Monkey Time," "Um, Um, Um, Um, Um, Um," and "Gotta Getaway" — are included here. –JF

DANIEL LANOIS

Alternative pop. Canadian Daniel Lanois has made a name for himself as a producer of very ambient albums. He has worked on successful projects with U2, Bob Dylan, the Neville Brothers, and Chris Whitley. Since his relocation to New Orleans, his thoughtful solo work reflects his fascination with the French Cajun rhythms. –RC

○ **Acadie / WARNER**   1989
Producer Lanois imbues this solo debut with his trademark otherworldly ambience on classics like "Still Water" and "Amazing Grace." Originals like the mystical "The Maker" and the soft French folk melodicism of "O Marie" are other highlights. –RC

LARKS

Soul, R&B, doo-wop. After the demise of his previous doo-wop aggregation, the Meadowlarks, Don Julian assembled a new trio, called them the Larks, and cashed in on the Money label in 1965 with a floating soul dance number, "The Jerk." It was a huge R&B and pop hit, but numerous spinoffs, including "Soul Jerk," "Jerk Once More," and "Keep Jerkin'," went nowhere. –BD

○ **The Jerk / COLLECTABLES**
Floating, three-piece, Impressions-style harmonies on a dance-heavy program. –BD

DENISE LASALLE   b 1939

R&B, soul. Lasalle started her career as a short-story writer but later wrote songs. Her husband Bill Jones took her to Willie Mitchell's Hi studios in Memphis, where she recorded excellent Southern soul with bluesy overtones. –BC

○ **On the Loose / WESTBOUND**   1973
A prime example of her Memphis work, with Bowlegs Miller arrangements. Featuring "Man Sized Job" and "Breaking Up Somebody's Home." –BC

Still Trapped / MALACO   1990
Still talkin' trash and backin' it up in a blues setting. –BC

LATIMORE   b 1939

Soul, R&B, funk, disco. Deep-voiced Latimore's sultry mid-70s output for Miami's Glades label was a steamy marriage of soul and blues. Initially billed as Benny Latimore, the Tennessean began recording for Miami mogul Henry Stone in 1965, and his late-60s Dade singles are solid deep-soul. Dropping his first name on Glades, Latimore finally found stardom in 1973 with a jazzy reading of T-Bone Walker's "Stormy Monday." He topped the soul lists in 1974 with the anguished "Let's Straighten It Out," a simmering soul/blues hybrid, and encored with the incendiary "Keep the Home Fires Burnin'" the next year. Most of Latimore's Glades sides were produced in Miami by Steve "Everyday I Have to Cry" Alaimo, and when he wasn't cutting his own hits, Latimore acted as a house pianist for parent TK Records. Latimore moved to Malaco during the 80s, his appeal undiminished. –BD

More, More, More / GLADES   1974
Includes his biggest hit, "Let's Straighten It Out." –RP

○ **Good Time Man / MALACO**   1985
Their essential album. Perfection! –RP

The Only Way Is Up / MALACO-MUSCLE SHOALS   1991
Southern soul, 90s-style. –RP

STACY LATTISAW   b1966

Soul, urban R&B. Teenage soul singer Lattisaw had three Top 40 hits ("Let Me Be Your Angel," "Love on a Two Way Street," "Miracles") from 1980 to 1983. –STE

○ **Let Me Be Your Angel / ATLANTIC**   1981
Sweet, G-rated soul, her best teen release. –BC & RW

Perfect Combination / ATLANTIC   1984
With Johnny Gill, a good match of current R&B stars when they were teens. –RW

CYNDI LAUPER   b1950

Rock/pop. As a guitarist, Lauper gigged with several bands in the 70s before cofounding Blue Angel in 1977, which released a highly acclaimed rock & roll album on Polydor three years later. She went solo in 1983 and became a musical and MTV sensation with her her pop-feminist song "Girls Just Want to Have Fun" and her tender ballad "Time after Time." She won the 1984 Grammy for Best New Artist. –BC & DDC

○ **She's So Unusual / CBS**   1984
Her best effort with the excellent ballad "Time after Time" and the nutty dance cut "Girls Just Want to Have Fun." Cool remakes of "Money Changes Everything" and Prince's "When You Were Mine." –BC

True Colors / CBS   1986
Includes the Top Five title track ballad and her Top 20 faithfully remade cover of Marvin Gaye's "What's Going On." Also includes the harder-edged "Change of Heart." –DDC

LEAVING TRAINS

Alternative rock. . Self-styled politically incorrect hicks from California, the Trains's slophouse blues-inflected punkoid noise raunch can be alternately liberating and sophomoric. Led by "Falling" James Moreland, these guys are the quintessential mixed bag, but (at least early on) made some righteous, funny, self-depreciating rock. –JD

○ **Kill Tunes / SST**   1986
A sizzling little platter that focuses on country/folk leanings with a fiery edge. Not quite uncontrolled. It's still as close to an undeniable record as they've ever made. –JD

F**k / SST   1987
Their last really consistent record. Doomed to commercial failure, the title was much loved by anti-corporate rock snobs. It's still countrified, just sloppier, and is hampered by an 11-minute freakout "What the President Meant to Say." –JD

LED ZEPPELIN

Blues/rock, hard rock. In 1968 the Yardbirds's commercial glory days were well behind them. The groundbreaking band had been the nurturing ground for some of the greatest guitarists of the rock era: Eric Clapton, Jeff Beck, and Jimmy Page. It was Page (the last of the three to come on board) who, along with manager Peter Grant, sensed a change in the times and sought to create a heavier, more aggressive sound for the developing album-oriented market.

Initially called the New Yardbirds, Led Zeppelin got its name from a Keith Moon (the Who's drummer) catchphrase ("going down like a lead zeppelin") concerning encountering bad gigs. From the outset, Led Zeppelin (Jimmy Page, guitar; Robert Plant, vocal; John Paul Jones, bass and keys; John Bonham, drums) caused a stir with their incredibly heavy yet dynamic sound, their questionable plundering of old blues standards,

and Plant's agitated banshee wail of a voice. Their audacious self-titled debut, which went #10, displayed one of the greatest rock production jobs of all time, with its fine balance of room ambience and powerful immediacy. Throughout much of the 70s, Led Zeppelin reigned as the world's most successful rock band, breaking concert records and releasing ten Top Ten albums, eight of which went #1 or #2. In spite of their huge success, Led Zeppelin only had one Top Ten single, with the #4 "Whole Lotta Love." "Stairway to Heaven," the most requested song ever on rock radio, was never officially released as a single. Over the years, many bands have tried (and failed) to capture the raw power and sonic qualities of Led Zeppelin, but it was the band's shared vision that achieved their sound. They understood that enough to call it quits when Bonham died on Sept 25, 1980. –RC

☆ **Led Zeppelin / ATLANTIC**   1969
Led Zeppelin's debut album provided a blueprint for its overall approach — hard rock with ornate guitar textures and powerful riffs, topped by singer Robert Plant's high-pitched singing on roaring rockers like "Good Times Bad Times" and "Communication Breakdown," plus drawn-out blues performances like "Dazed and Confused." –WR

☆ **Led Zeppelin II / ATLANTIC**   1969
Perhaps the definitive heavy metal album, featuring "Whole Lotta Love." –WR

○ **Led Zeppelin III / ATLANTIC**   1970
After the bone-crunching hard rock of *Led Zeppelin II*, Page, Plant, Bonham, and Jones tracked a collection of more acoustic-flavored numbers. Songs like "Gallows Pole" and "Bron-Y-Aur Stomp" were essentially their trademark rockers played on folk instruments, but the reflective "That's the Way" and "Tangerine" indicated a new maturity. A handful of heavy riff-rockers like "Immigrant Song," "Out on the Tiles," "Celebration Day," and the hard blues raveup "Since I've Been Loving You" more than rounded out this solid (but transitional) effort. –RC

★ **Led Zeppelin 4 / ATLANTIC**   1971
The perfect mixture of Zeppelin's trademark heavy rock, plus some old-time rock & roll and the band's folkie influences, all of which culminated in its greatest song, "Stairway to Heaven." –WR

Physical Graffiti / ATLANTIC   1975
A lengthy two-disc set whose bluesy workouts (plus such new explorations as the Middle Eastern "Kashmir") mark it as the most "Zeppelinish" of Led Zeppelin albums. –WR

○ **Led Zeppelin Boxed Set / ATLANTIC**   1990
This 4-CD, 54-track collection, compiled by Robert Plant, Jimmy Page, and John Paul Jones, contains material from all nine of Led Zeppelin's studio albums as well as some previously unreleased cuts, all sequenced in a loosely chronological order. Most of the essential tracks are here, but the main reason to get this set (if you are a fan of this band) is the stunning remastering job. Zeppelin's CD reissues had drawn quite a bit of fire for their terrible sound (particularly *Houses of the Holy*). Many, in fact, had been made off of substandard safety tapes. (Only their self-titled debut escaped such sonic mutilation on a CD reissue.) This is a pricey set but worth the money since it's the only way to hear their essential tracks, the way they were intended to be heard. –RC

ALBERT LEE   b1943

Country rock, rockabilly. Lee is an English guitarist, highly proficient in a multitude of styles but primarily gifted in country and rockabilly picking. The ultimate sideman on countless sessions over the last two decades, his Telecaster twangings have graced the recordings of Eric Clapton, Jerry Lee Lewis, and Emmylou Harris, to name just a few. Also notable as the music director when the Everly Brothers reunited a few years back, Lee has released a few solo albums of his own in the last few years, all of them informed by his clean, articulate picking. –CK

Hiding / A&M   1979
Standard country-rock album. (Out of print) –JT

Country Guitar Man / MAGNUM   1986
This collection of Lee's early-70s work with Head, Hands, & Feet is fairly remarkable, particularly Lee's guitar work. (Import) –JT

Speechless / MCA   1987
One of the guitar world's best-kept secrets, the former Everly Brothers and Emmylou Harris sideman explores his roots in this instrumental jewel. Albert Lee coproduced this album. Very clean sound, very good cover of "Arkansas Traveler" featuring Lee on guitar, mandolin and piano; Jim Cox, Greg Humphrey, Sterling Biff Ball, and Chad Wackerman. –JT & CR

○ **Gagged but Not Bound / MCA**   1988
The master musician plays unworldly guitar on this acoustic/electric country-rock and traditional-oriented masterpiece. Exquisitely recorded. –JT

Black Claw & Country Fever / LINE   1991
This collection of late-60s material is raw yet engaging; the musicianship is stunning. (Import) –JT

BRENDA LEE   b 1944

Rock/pop. One of the most popular female vocalists of her time, with 50 Hot 100 entries between 1957 and 1973. The classic little girl with the big voice, Lee started as a child prodigy on the radio in her native Georgia at the age of five. She started recording and appearing on television by 1955. The most versatile of crossover performers, few can jump from rockabilly to country to novelty rockers to world-weary ballads as well as she. She went back to recording country by the early 70s, with consistent hits in that marketplace ever since. Still performing and recording, the voice and style of Brenda Lee continues to be an American music treasure. –CK

☆ **Anthology 1956-1980 / MCA**   1991
A 40-song, two-CD collection that proves Lee was the best White female rock singer of the pre-Beatles 60s. By the time she turned 18, Lee had hit the pop Top Ten 11 times. All of those cuts are here, from the innocently salacious "Sweet Nothin's" to the string-laden "I'm Sorry" and her remake of Earl "Fatha" Hines's "You Can Depend on Me." Her best country singles "Johnny One Time" and "Big Four Poster Bed" are also included. The compilers wisely passed over some minor hits in favor of obscure sides like the odd rockabilly "Let's Jump the Broomstick," a cover of Edith Piaf's "If You Love Me (Really Love Me)," and "Is It True?" a middling hit from 1964, which features guitarist Jimmy Page (who is 11 months older than Lee). *Anthology* thoroughly traces Lee's development as a vocalist, from early-childish exuberance to mature, graceful phrasing. –BM

LAURA LEE   b 1945

Soul. Laura Lee sang with the Meditations Singers gospel group in the 50s, but she's primarily known as a tough 60s soul singer whose salty sense of humor is aimed mostly at the men in her life. Her music laid the groundwork for artists like Millie Jackson and Denise LaSalle to expand this proud, sexy, brash-talking corner of "women's" soul music. Lee had a country/soul romantic side as well, as shown on her splendid version of the Penn-Oldham classic "Uptight Good Man." One of the most gifted and overlooked soul singers of the 60s and 70s. –CO & BC

Greatest Hits / HDH[FANTASY]   1990
An originator. Raps and bedroom politics on these 70s recordings. –RP

○ **That's How It Is - Chess Years / MCA**   1990
Her 60s Chess recordings. Bone-chilling vocals. –RP

● **Greatest Hits / HDH-FANTASY**   1991
Hot Wax artist Laura Lee took the spirit of the feminist movement and gave it a hard-hitting R&B setting. Assertive

titles like "Wedlock Is a Padlock," and "Rip Off" won her more acceptance on R&B stations. "Women's Love Rights," included here, dented the Top 40 charts at #36. –RC

THE LEFT BANKE

Rock/pop. Formed in 1966, the Left Banke's ornate pop/rock manifested two major hits with the #5 "Walk Away Renee" and the #15 "Pretty Ballerina." The band's songwriter and keyboardist Michael Brown left the Left Banke shortly thereafter, forming Stories with vocalist Ian Lloyd. –RC

○ **There's Gonna Be a Storm: 1966-1969 / MERCURY**   1992
This intelligently compiled 26 track collection includes the classic baroque-pop hits "Walk Away Renee," "Pretty Ballerina," and "Desiree." –ED

JOHN LENNON   1940-1980

Singer/songwriter, rock & roll, rock/pop. John Lennon was a singer, songwriter, guitarist, record producer, author, actor, filmmaker, artist, and political spokesman, and one of the greatest figures in postwar popular music. Lennon was born in Liverpool, England, and became involved in music in the 50s. The group he founded as the Quarrymen eventually evolved into the Beatles, and from 1963 to 1970 they were the most successful rock group in history. Lennon, the group's leader, played an important part in that success, writing and singing many of its biggest hits and best songs.

Lennon began to record and perform outside the group in 1969, usually in the company of his wife, avant-garde artist Yoko Ono. The early Lennon-Ono records (and films and performance events) were experimental in nature, but as Lennon turned to recording as a solo performer, his work was more accessible to pop audiences, though his lyrical concerns were frequently political or scathingly personal. His first formal solo album was *John Lennon/Plastic Ono Band* in 1970, and he followed this with *Imagine* (1971), *Sometime in New York City* (1972), *Mind Games* (1973), *Walls & Bridges* (1974), and *Rock & Roll* (1974). Most of his recordings sold well, with *Walls & Bridges* topping the charts along with its single, "Whatever Gets You through the Night."

Lennon, who had separated from Ono in 1973, was reconciled with her in 1975 and thereafter retired from music to raise their son Sean. He and Ono reemerged with the album *Double Fantasy* in 1980, and had plans for further recordings and performances at the time he was assassinated. –WR

Live Peace in Toronto 1969 / APPLE   1969
Impromptu concert appearance, with Lennon singing a few rock & roll oldies plus his then-new single, "Cold Turkey," backed by guitarist Eric Clapton. Also 17+ minutes of Yoko Ono screaming and singing over guitar feedback. –WR

☆ **John Lennon/Plastic Ono Band / CAPITOL**   1970
A stark, harrowing set of songs in which Lennon recounts the horrors of his childhood ("Mother," "Working Class Hero"), the disillusionment of his adulthood ("I Found Out"), and his loss of faith in all idols ("God") including "Beatles." This album is one of rock's most personal — and most ambitious — statements. –WR

☆ **Imagine / CAPITOL**   1971
In addition to the justly revered title track (a #3 hit), this eclectic pop album also contains "Jealous Guy" (later a hit for Roxy Music) and "Gimme Some Truth" (later adopted by such punk rockers as Generation X). –WR

Walls and Bridges / CAPITOL   1974
Craftsmanlike pop-rock featuring the uptempo #1 hit "Whatever Gets You through the Night," its Top Ten followup, "#9 Dream," and some lovely album tracks. –WR

○ **Shaved Fish / CAPITOL**   1975
Though superseded by *The John Lennon Collection* (see below), this greatest-hits album is the only place to find such singles as "Cold Turkey" and "Happy Xmas (War Is Over)." –WR

Double Fantasy / CAPITOL 1980
On an album made shortly before his death, Lennon explores his retirement, his artistic rebirth, and his relationship with his family on such songs as "(Just Like) Starting Over," "Woman," and "Watching the Wheels," all of which were Top Ten hits. Lennon's songs are interspersed with surprisingly accessible contributions from Ono. –WR

Milk & Honey / POLYGRAM 1984
Posthumous followup to *Double Fantasy*, featuring sometimes rough takes of perhaps unfinished songs that nevertheless sparkle with Lennon's wit and exuberance, among them the Top Five hit "Nobody Told Me." (Again, Ono's songs are interspersed with Lennon's contributions.) –WR

Live in New York City / CAPITOL 1986
A rare concert performance from 1972, containing live versions of "Instant Karma," "Come Together," "Imagine," and other favorites. –WR

Imagine: John Lennon / CAPITOL 1988
A two-disc set containing a selection of Lennon's work with the Beatles and as a solo artist. This is the original soundtrack album. –WR

● **The John Lennon Collection / CAPITOL** 1990
Six of the seven Lennon tracks from *Double Fantasy*, plus nine of his best songs from 1969 to 1974, among them the singles "Give Peace a Chance," in its only LP appearance, and "Instant Karma!" –WR

☆ **Lennon / CAPITOL** 1990
Lennon is given a solid boxed-set treatment with this four-CD, 73-track collection. The set is so complete that there is essentially no need to go out and obtain any of his albums on disc. *Lennon* runs chronologically, from the Plastic Ono Band's "Give Peace a Chance," to "Grow Old with Me" from 1984's *Milk and Honey*. All the best stuff from *Live Peace in Toronto 1969* is here, as well as his live (with Elton John) versions of "I Saw Her Standing There" and "Lucy in the Sky with Diamonds." The book contains a generous collection of photos and lyrics to all of the songs. The A-to-Z color-coded index is overkill in lieu of any track information detailing where and when the songs were cut and who played on them. –RC

JULIAN LENNON *b* 1963

Rock/pop. Julian Lennon (son of Beatle John Lennon and Cynthia Twist) has had the mixed blessing of choosing a vocation that placed him firmly in his father's shadow. Lennon's similar vocal and melodic style on his successful #17 debut *Valotte* (in 1984) heightened the comparisons. Since then Lennon's albums haven't sold as well, but his releases have revealed increasing artistic growth. –RC

○ **Valotte / ATLANTIC** 1984
A strong debut showcasing Julian's remarkable vocal resemblance to his dad. –DH

LEVEL 42

Rock/pop, funk. This Manchester pop-funk band has been led by bassist Mark King since 1972. The lineup also features Phil and Boon Gould, and Mike Lindup. Their first singles were on the Elite label and their biggest hit was "Something about You" in 1986. In 1987 the Goulds left the band, to be replaced by Alan Murphy and Gary Husband. –BC

○ **Level Best / POLYGRAM** 1989
This hits CD draws heavily from *Running in the Family* (1987) and *World Machine* (1985) but offers a good introduction to this band. –SWB

LEVERT

Soul. As the offical offspring of the O'Jays, LeVert is a trio from Philadelphia who combine the sweet harmonies that their fathers provided with the "rope-a-dope" style that will keep them in the spotlight in the 90s. Great music all around, and

powerful vocals from Gerald LeVert, who also has his own solo album. –JB

○ **Big Throwdown / ATLANTIC** 1987
A great vocal group that brings back the style of the groups from the late 60s and early 70s. Lots of smooth vocals from Gerald LeVert, including the irresistible "Casanova." –JB

Just Coolin' / ATLANTIC 1988
More good dance tunes and powerful ballads. Rapper Heavy D is featured on the title track. –JB

GERALD LEVERT

Soul. Lead singer from the group LeVert. –ED

○ **Private Line / ATLANTIC** 1991
LeVert's first solo effort seems more relaxed and smoother than his past work. Great material and lots of ballads, including one with his father Eddie LeVert (of the O'Jays). –JB

BARBARA LEWIS *b* 1943

R&B, soul. From a Detroit-area musical family (both parents had bands in the 30s and 40s), Barbara Lewis was writing songs at the age of nine. And she could sing! She wrote all the songs on her first album *Hello Stranger* and had a major hit in 1963. Other classic Lewis hits include "Baby, I'm Yours" and "Make Me Your Baby." Even with only a few big hits, Lewis has achieved almost a cult status among her admirers. There is something unique about her songs and singing — an enchantment — that goes right to the heart. –JME

○ **Golden Classics / COLLECTABLES**
Smooth, snappy soul. 60s recordings. –RP

GARY LEWIS & THE PLAYBOYS *b* 1946

Rock/pop. An American rock group formed in 1964 by the son of comedian Jerry Lewis. After landing a gig at Disneyland, they were immediately signed to Liberty Records and handed over to pop production genius Snuff Garrett. Utilizing the best songwriters and studio players available, Garrett fashioned five Top Five hits in a matter of 18 months (15 in the Hot 100 by 1969) around Lewis's meager abilities, sometimes augmenting his voice in the studio with backup singers doubling his part. Lewis pretty well held his own against the British Invasion, but the combination his draft call in late 1966 and the rising tide of psychedelia put his days on the charts to an end. Still active on the oldies circuit, he fronts various backup bands under the name the Playboys. –CK

○ **Legendary Masters Series / CAPITOL** 1990
One of the most engaging pop acts of the mid 60s, the Playboys benefited from strong songwriting (Al Kooper cowrote "This Diamond Ring") and studio personnel (courtesy of Leon Russell). It's still light, catchy pop with the enjoyable, unaffected vocals of Gary Lewis on top, and still fun. –WR

HUEY LEWIS & THE NEWS *b* 1950

Rock/pop. Before the formation of the News, Huey Lewis (born Hugh Cregg) had been part of the San Francisco band Clover from 1976 to 1980. During that time Clover (sans Lewis) backed up Elvis Costello on his debut *My Aim Is True*. Lewis also did session sideman work on Nick Lowe's *Labour of Lust* and Dave Edmunds's *Repeat When Necessary*. Clover broke up in 1979 after bandleader John McFee split to join the Doobie Brothers.
Lewis returned to a day gig and started jamming at a local Marin County bar called Uncle Charlie's. It was there that the nucleus of the News was formed out of visiting musicians, many of whom had previously backed up Van Morrison.
The News's self-titled debut failed to sell, but "Do You Believe in Love" went to #7. Their second album, *Picture This*, rose to #13 and produced a couple of moderate hits with "Hope You Love Me Like You Say You Do" (#36) and "Workin' for a Livin'"

(#41). The next album, *Sports*, went multi-platinum and generated a number of hits.

Between albums the News scored a # 1 hit, "The Power of Love," from the movie *Back to the Future*. Their followup album, *Fore* (#1), included five Top Ten hits: "Stuck with You" (#1), "Jacob's Ladder" (#1), "Hip to Be Square" (#3), and "Doing It All (For My Baby)" (#6). In 1988 the News released *Small World*. –RC

Picture This / CAPITOL   1982
Their second album broke through with the hits "Workin' for a Livin'" and "Do You Believe in Love." –DDC

○ **Sports / CAPITOL**   1983
Their brand of spirited, no-frills rock & roll, featuring the hits "I Want a New Drug," "The Heart of Rock & Roll," and "Walkin' on a Thin Line," helped sell more than seven million copies of this album. –DDC

Fore! / CAPITOL   1986
More pop-rock featuring the hits "Stuck with You," "Jacob's Ladder," and "Hip to be Square." –DDC

JERRY LEE LEWIS   b 1935

Rock & roll. Jerry Lee Lewis, the self-proclaimed "Killer," is a man of prodigous appetites and talent. Egocentric and self-absorbed, Jerry Lee is the last of the original 50s wildmen. A child prodigy who quickly mastered his instrument, Lewis claims to have no influences, but his stylistic quirks point to boogie-woogie master Cecil Gant and country-piano man Moon Mullican. After being run out of Nashville (where he was told he could be signed if he strummed a guitar instead), he came to Memphis, where his audition tape got him hooked up to Sam Phillips's Sun label. In the space of four singles released in a year's time, the Killer was suddenly running neck and neck with Elvis for King of Rock & Roll honors.

When Lewis married his 13-year-old cousin in 1958, his career promptly ground to a halt, leaving him to ckc out a bleak existence in the honky-tonks of America. It took 12 years of his life to fight his way back, but Lewis is nothing less than American music's consummate survivor, and his reemergence (via the country charts, with a string of smashes) was no less than his due.

There are few originals in 50s rock & roll, most taking their cue from Elvis or Little Richard, but Lewis is one of the major stylists in the history of American popular music — period. His distinctive piano style is tightly woven into the fabric of that instrument, while his vocal style is easily recognizable as well, whether tackling a mournful country weeper or storming through his prodigious catalog of rock & roll/R&B favorites, putting his individual stamp on each and every one. As he'll be the first to tell you, there is simply no one quite like the Killer. We shall not see the likes of him again in our lifetime. –CK

★ **18 Original Sun Greatest Hits / RHINO**   1984
Solid single-disc collection of the records that got Lewis into the Rock & Roll Hall of Fame on the first ballot; "Whole Lotta Shakin' Goin' On," "Great Balls of Fire," "High School Confidential," and "Breathless" being merely the tip of the iceberg. –CK

☆ **Classic / BEAR FAMILY**   1990
Eight-disc boxed set of Lewis's complete output for Sun Records. Along with Muddy Waters's Chess recordings, Louis Armstrong's *Hot Fives & Sevens*, and Hank Williams's undubbed MGM sides, this box comprises one of the finest bodies of American music ever recorded. –CK

☆ **Live at the Star Club / RHINO**   1992
The Killer at his storming best, dragging his backup group, the Nashville Teens, by the scruff of the neck through a blazing set that earmarks this recording as one of the finest live albums ever made. –CK

The Greatest Live Shows on Earth / BEAR FAMILY   1992
Combining two live albums originally issued in the 60s, Lewis proves that the onslaught of the British Invasion hadn't

lowered his rocking quotient one single bit. Blazing performances. –CK

JIMMY LIGGINS

R&B. Important West Coast jump-blues guitarist and vocalist (and younger brother of Joe Liggins) who became one of Specialty's first success stories in the late 40s and early 50s, thanks to such hits as "Cadillac Boogie," "Teardrop Blues," and "I Can't Stop It." His 1953 recording of "Drunk" is one of the greatest drinking songs you'll ever hear. –JF

○ **His Drops of Joy / SPEED**
Swinging West Coast jump-blues of the late 40s, with a slightly harder edge than his older brother Joe's sound. –BD

JOE LIGGINS

R&B. Jimmy Liggin's older brother was also a Specialty hitmaker, but his first hits (including "The Honeydripper") came on Exclusive during the mid 40s. The pianist signed with Specialty in 1950 and placed several songs in *Billboard*'s Black charts. "Pink Champagne," "Frankie Lee," and "Little Joe's Boogie" were his biggest hits with the label. –JF

○ **Joe Liggins & the Honeydrippers / SPEED**
Bouncy, danceable early-50s jump-blues by this pianist's brassy combo. CD version has nine bonus cuts. –BD

DAVID LINDLEY   b 1944

Tex-Mex, rock & roll, blues/rock. You may remember listening to these great Jackson Browne albums from the 70s and thinking, "This guy not only writes and sings great songs, but he's an incredible guitar player and does great arrangements." Well, he did write and sing great songs, but the guitar playing and arrangements are by David Lindley, Los Angeles studio musician extraordinaire. Starting in 1981, Lindley has put out several albums under his own name with his always-changing band, El Rayo-X. He has wide-ranging musical influences: Tex-Mex, zydeco, reggae, blues, and rock & roll. His specialty seems to be taking a song and playing it in the style of a completely different genre of music, for example, a maniacal surf-music version of "Do Ya' Wanna Dance?" or a version of "I Fought the Law" with musicians from Madagascar. His own compositions are sometimes quite wonderful and always at least peculiar and droll. When he plays guitar (and often instruments of his own design), it's as good as it gets. If you grew up on 50s, 60s, and 70s rock & roll, this guy is the best thing going. –MK

El Rayo-X / ELEKTRA   1981
His debut album. Highly recommended! –MK

○ **Very Greasy / ELEKTRA**   1988
His best. Unconditionally recommended. –MK

A World out of Time / SHANACHIE   1992
Lindley and Henry Kaiser travel to Madagascar, where they record and play with some of that country's best musicians. Great world music. –MK

LISA LISA & CULT JAM

Dance-pop. Sweet-tempered pop-funk from the Latin trio of Lisa Valez, Mike Hughes, and Alex Moseley. –BC & DH

Lisa Lisa & Cult Jam w/ Full Force / CBS   1985
Here's their debut, recorded with Full Force. –BC

○ **Spanish Fly / CBS**   1987
A Full Force production featuring the #1s "Head to Toe" and "Lost in Emotion." –BC

Straight to the Sky / CBS   1989
This includes the Top 40 hit "Little Jackie Wants to Be a Star." –BC

LITTLE ANTHONY & THE IMPERIALS

R&B, doo-wop. Formed in 1957, Little Anthony & the Imperials specialized in dramatic pop ballads. Fronted by tenor Anthony Gourdine (b Jan 8, 1941), the Imperials charted with "Going Out of My Head" (#6), "Hurt So Bad" (#9), "Take Me Back" (#16), "Tears on My Pillow" (#4), and "I'm on the Outside Looking In" (#15). –RC

○ **Best of ... / SPECIAL MUSIC**   1989
A generous helping of hits from "Tears on My Pillow" to "Goin' Out of My Head." –DH

LITTLE FEAT

Blues/rock, rock & roll, country rock. Little Feat was formed in 1970 when Frank Zappa encouraged his guitarist Lowell George to start his own band, after hearing George's original "Willin'." With Zappa bass player Roy Estrada in tow, George enlisted drummer Richie Hayward (formerly of Fraternity of Man) and keyboardist Billy Payne. The band's name came from Jimmy Carl Black's (of the Mothers of Invention) kidding about George's shoe size. Their first albums blended blues, country, and rock with gritty finesse. *Sailin' Shoes* (their second album) is loaded with fine songs and the rudest rock they ever commited to tape.

With *Dixie Chicken* (considered by many to be Little Feat's best album), they added Kenny Gradney on bass and Sam Clayton on congas. The result was a New Orleans style of rhythmic gumbo and George's incredible slide guitar work. The title cut sums up many of the band's virtues, possessing a rubbery groove, off-kilter instrumental parts, and a classic, dryly humorous Lowell George tale. Subsequent albums increasingly sanded off the rough edges in favor of an eccentric fusionlike equivalent to the late-70s Doobie Brothers.

Little Feat disbanded in April 1979 and Lowell George set out for a solo career, releasing the album *Thanks, I'll Eat It Here* (#71). On June 29, 1979, George was found dead of a heart attack brought on from drug abuse.

In 1988 Little Feat reunited with former Pure Prairie League singer and guitarist Craig Fuller filling George's slot. Since then, the band has regained its status as a solid concert draw and has released several albums. –RC

Little Feat / WARNER   1971
Debut album finds Lowell George's songwriting, singing, and playing style in place on his signature song, "Willin'," as well as "Truck Stop Girl" and "Crazy Captain Gunboat Willie." –WR

★ **Sailin' Shoes / WARNER**   1972
A near-peak of songwriting ("Easy to Slip," "Cold, Cold, Cold," "Sailin' Shoes") distinguishes this second album, on which the band finds a perfect second-line groove and Lowell George sings and plays with blues authority. –WR

☆ **Dixie Chicken / WARNER**   1973
A reconfigured group adds greater depth to the percussion, along with a rhythm guitarist who frees Lowell George to slide his way to heaven, and the songs — especially the title track, "Two Trains," and "Fat Man in the Bathtub" — are among George's best. –WR

Feats Don't Fail Me Now / WARNER   1974
Whereas earlier albums were carried by Lowell George, this one finds the band as a whole at a writing and performing peak, with Bill Payne and Paul Berrere especially standing out on such songs as "Rock and Roll Doctor," "Oh Atlanta," and "Skin It Back." –WR

Waiting For Columbus / WARNER   1978
Excellent double-disc live album. –WR

Hoy-Hoy / WARNER   1981
Compilation of best songs and odds and ends makes a good wrap-up to the Lowell George years. –WR

LITTLE RICHARD   b 1935

Rock & roll. With a six-inch-high pompadour topping a face dripping with eyeliner and pancake makeup, Little Richard (born Richard Wayne Penniman, 1935) came out of his native Macon, GA, to become one of the first Black artists not only to cross over to the national White pop charts, but to do it with an uncompromising set of recordings that virtually defined the inherent danger and wildness of rock & roll. Few records explode off a turntable the way the likes of "Tutti Frutti," "Long Tall Sally," "Rip It Up," "Lucille," or "Good Golly Miss Molly" do and Richard's banshee shrieks and propulsive beat (usually provided by crack New Orleans session players) were catnip to a young White audience who had never heard before a Black gospel singer sing with the brakes off. The hits kept coming, but by the late 50s Richard had quit show business to become a minister. The lure of success (his and the then-emerging Beatles) brought him back, recording dreadful remakes of his earlier hits for one label after another into the 70s and becoming a staple of the talk show circuit with his flamboyant costumes and chatter. The 90s now find him revitalized, making movie appearances and television commercials and recording new material. Though his claim to be "the architect of rock & roll" may be disputed by some, any list of pioneering rock & rollers that doesn't include Little Richard near the top has just become too damn sophisticated for its own good. –CK

★ **18 Greatest Hits / RHINO**   1985
The one definitive package to own. –CK

The Formative Years 1951-53 / BEAR FAMILY   1989
Early Richard, pre-"Tutti Frutti." –CK

○ **Specialty Box Set / SPECIALTY**   1991
Check out this beautiful three-CD boxed set of all the important Specialty sides. –CK

LITTLE RIVER BAND

Rock/pop. Little River Band (formed 1975) enjoyed an impressive string of hits during the late 70s and early 80s with their rather mellow harmony-laden MOR pop. The original lineup included lead singer Glenn Shurrock; guitarists Rick Furmoru, Beeb Birtles, and Graham Goble; Rugo McLachlan on bass; and Derek Pellicci on drums. Later members included David Briggs (guitar), George McArdle (bass), and lead singer John Faraham. –RC & LL

○ **Greatest Hits / CAPITOL**   1983
All of their best — "Reminiscing" (#3), "Lady" (#10), "Lonesome Loser" (#6), "Cool Change" (#10), "The Night Owls" (#6), and "Take It Easy on Me" (#10). –LL

LITTLE STEVEN & THE DISCIPLES OF SOUL

Rock & roll. Steven Van Zandt (b ca. 1951) grew up in the same south New Jersey shore scene as Bruce Springsteen and Southside Johnny Lyon and was closely associated with them. He was a member of Springsteen's band Steel Mill in 1969-1970 and the Bruce Springsteen band in 1971. He then worked with Southside Johnny, but rejoined Springsteen in the E Street Band in early 1975. This group went on to massive success, and Van Zandt worked closely with Springsteen, coproducing *The River* and *Born in the U.S.A.* while also producing and writing material for Southside Johnny and Gary US Bonds. In 1982, Van Zandt organized Little Steven and the Disciples of Soul, which released *Men without Women.* He left the E Street Band under amicable circumstances in April 1984. In 1985 he organized the Top 40 hit single "Sun City," featuring a multitude of pop stars protesting apartheid in South Africa. –WR & JF

○ **Men without Women / EMI**   1982
Little Steven's first album is a White-soul triumph, full of well-formed ballads, tough Stones-ish rockers, and the swagger and attitude of vintage Southside Johnny (for whom Van Zandt has produced and written). In effect, this is Van Zandt leading the E Street Band — Max Weinberg (d), Garry Tallent (b), Danny Federici (organ) — plus such other Northeast cronies as pianist Kevin Kavanaugh of the Asbury Jukes, ex-Rascals Felix Cavaliere and Dino Danelli, ex-Plasmatic Jean Beauvoir, and the La Bamba horn section. The result is a big sound that plays searing music. "Forever" was the album's closest thing to a hit, but its power and emotion still sound fresh a full decade after its release. –JF & WR

Voice of America / EMI   1984

The band has been pared down slightly, but the sound is just as big. This time Van Zandt has big issues on his mind, too, from the "disappeared" of South America to "Solidarity"; the best track is the plaintive anthem "I Am a Patriot." –WR

LITTLE VILLAGE

Rock & roll. An early-90s "supergroup" composed of string wizard Ry Cooder, tunesmith John Hiatt, English bassist Nick Lowe, and session drummer extraordinaire Jim Keltner. All four musicians originally played as a unit in 1987 on Hiatt's breakthrough album *Bring the Family*. In that context, all but Hiatt were sidemen. Four years later they collectively wrote and recorded their self-titled debut CD. Although the record was a bit of a disappointment, the live shows were superb. –RB

○ **Little Village / REPRISE**   1992

Given the personnel in the band, Little Village's first album was a somewhat uneven disappointment. That said, Ry Cooder has yet to make a truly poor recording and there is much here of merit. Particularly great is "Big Love" and the loose-limbed "The Action." –RB

LITTLE WILLIE JOHN   b 1937

R&B. He's never received the accolades given to the likes of Sam Cooke, Clyde McPhatter, and James Brown, but Little Willie John ranks as one of R&B's most influential performers. His muscular high timbre and enormous technical and emotional range belied his early age (his first hit came when he was 18), but his mid-50s work for Syd Nathan's King label would play a great part in the way soul music would sound. Everyone from Cooke, McPhatter, and Brown to Jackie Wilson, B. B. King, and Al Green has acknowledged his debt to this most overlooked of rock and soul pioneers.

His debut recording, a smoking version of Titus Turner's "All around the World" from 1955, set the pattern for a remarkable string of hits: "Need Your Love So Bad," "Suffering with the Blues," "Fever," "Let Them Talk," and his last, "Sleep," from 1961. His version of "Fever" was copied note for note by Peggy Lee and Elvis Presley, both of whom had bigger hits with it; John's version, however, remains definitive. His second hit, "Need Your Love So Bad," contains one of the most intimate, tear-jerking vocals ever caught on tape.

John had a volatile temper, fueled by a taste for liquor and an insecurity regarding his slight height (5 ft 4 in). He was known to pack a gun and knife; in 1966, he stabbed a man and was sent to the Washington State penitentiary, where he died of pneumonia in 1968. James Brown recorded a tribute album to John that year, and his material has been recorded by scores of artists from the Beatles to Fleetwood Mac to the Blasters. Nevertheless, Little Willie John remains a stranger to most listeners and has never received the respect his talent deserves. –JF

● **Grits and Soul / CHARLY**   1985

Since there isn't a definitive Willie John collection available anywhere, this 16-song sampler will have to do. Includes all the major hits but overlooks many hidden nuggets. –JF

○ **Mister Little Willie John / KING**   1987

His third King long-player is one of the 50s finest albums. "You're a Sweetheart" is an R&B landmark. –JF

Talk to Me / SING   1988

Reissue of John's second King album includes the title hit, "Person to Person," and the exquisite "There Is Someone in This World for Me." –JF

Sure Things / KING   1990

Another vintage reissue. It features his gorgeous reading of Billy Eckstine's "A Cottage for Sale" and the original version of "I'm Shakin'," which the Blasters covered on their debut. –JF

LIVING COLOUR

Hard rock, fusion, funk. A New York-based hard-rock group formed by guitarist Vernon Reid as part of the fusion-oriented Black Rock Coalition artists group and supported early on by

Mick Jagger. Their in-your-face approach, combining Hendrixian guitar with punk-rock fervor, has earned them across-the-board hits and a broad-based audience. –CK

○ **Vivid / EPIC**   1988

Living Colour broke through on this debut album with their mixture of heavy metal, guitar heroics (courtesy of Vernon Reid), and thoughtful, sometimes scathing lyrics, suggesting a new direction for hard rock. This Top Ten million-selling album included the songs "Cult of Personality," "Open Letter (To a Landlord)," and the Top Forty hit "Glamour Boys." –WR

Time's Up / CBS   1990

A powerful, uncompromising sophomore effort, featuring the radio hits "Type" and "Pride" as well as the provocative "Elvis Is Dead" and "Love Rears Its Ugly Head." –WR

BILL LLOYD   b 1955

Power-pop. As a solo artist, Bill Lloyd (half of country duo Foster & Lloyd) displays his real passion: finely crafted Anglo-power-pop/rock — à la Byrds, Big Star, Badfinger — a must for any lover of this kind of music. –RC

○ **Feeling the Elephant / DB**   1986

Originally released in 1986 on the Throbbing Lobster label, *Feeling the Elephant* was to be the debut for Lloyd's solo career until he got sidetracked with the successful country duo Foster & Lloyd. Lloyd might do country justice, but on *Feeling the Elephant*, his Anglo-pop/rock roots are everywhere to be found. From the urgent drive of "This Very Second," the album's opener, to the spacey melancholy of "Everything's Closing Down," the album exuberantly draws from the best elements of the Byrds, Big Star, Badfinger, mid-period Beatles, and early Who. Highlights include "It'll Never Get Better Than This" and "Lisa-Anne." –RC

NILS LOFGREN   b 1951

Rock & roll, rock/pop. Nils Lofgren formed Grin in 1969, a group with much promise and little financial success. During the 70s and early 80s, Lofgren pursued a spotty solo career while contributing some fine work with Neil Young. Lofgren joined up with Bruce Springsteen's band in 1986. A new deal with Minnesota label Rykodisc produced the moderate-hit album *Silver Lining* in 1991. –RC

○ **Nils Lofgren / RYKODISC / BB 141**   1975

After dismantling Grin in 1974, Lofgren signed a solo deal with A&M, releasing a self-titled debut that neatly showcased his strengths as a singer/songwriter and multi-instrumentalist. His reading of Carole King's wistful chestnut "Goin' Back" is a highlight, as are fiery originals like "Keith Don't Go" (a tribute to the Stones' Keith Richards) and "Rock & Roll Crook," with its wonderfully convoluted twin-guitar interplay. "Back It Up" is another gem. –RC

Cry Tough / A&M   1976

Lofgren's only other worthwhile record. A little forced on the songwriting side but delivered with enough panache to make it work. –JD

Nils / A&M / BB 54   1979

Lofgren rebounded, after several spotty albums, with this effort, which featured some of the strongest writing in his career, particularly "Shine Silently," "A Fool like You," "Steal Away," and the powerful ballad "No Mercy." –RC

Wonderland / MCA   1983

Unfortunately, this one got totally buried. "Across the Tracks," the single, should have been given the push it deserved. A remake of Bobby Womack's "It's All Over Now" is another highlight. –RC

KENNY LOGGINS   b 1948

Rock/pop. Singer, songwriter, and guitarist Kenny Loggins was born in Everett, WA, and moved to Los Angeles in his teens. He got a job as a staff writer and wrote four songs used on a Nitty Gritty Dirt Band album in 1970, among them the hit "House at Pooh Corner." This brought him to the attention of former Poco member Jim Messina, now a staff producer at CBS, who intended to produce Loggins's debut album. The two ended up in a duo, however, and Loggins & Messina made a series of successful albums during the 70s.

Loggins & Messina broke up in 1976, and Loggins went on to solo stardom with such million-selling albums as *Celebrate Me Home*, *Nightwatch* (which included the hit "Whenever I Call You Friend"), and *Keep the Fire*, all in the cheerful, sensitive style he had displayed in Loggins & Messina. Loggins also became known as the king of the movie soundtrack song, scoring Top Ten hits with "I'm Alright" (from *Caddyshack*), "Footloose" (from *Footloose*), "Danger Zone" (from *Top Gun*), and "Nobody's Fool" (from *Caddyshack II*). His own albums sold less well (and came less frequently) through the 80s. —WR

Celebrate Me Home / COLUMBIA / BB 27   1977
Features hit single "I Believe in Love" (#66). "Lady Luck," "Why Do People Lie," and the title cut are highlights on this relatively light MOR debut. —RC

Nightwatch / COLUMBIA / BB 7   1978
This super-slick sophomore effort was Loggins's biggest chart success, aided in no small part by the singles "Whenever I Call You Friend" (#5), which featured a duet with Stevie Nicks, and "Easy Driver" (#60). "Wait a Little While," and remakes of the Doobies hit "What a Fool Believes" and Billy Joe Royal's "Down in the Boondocks" were further highlights. —RC

Keep the Fire / COLUMBIA / BB 16   1980
Produced by Tom Dowd (Rod Stewart, Aretha Franklin, Allman Brothers), Loggins beefs up his sound a little with "Love Has Come of Age." He also enjoys more hits with "This Is It" (#11) and the title cut (#36). —RC

○ **Kenny Loggins Alive / COLUMBIA / BB 11**   1980
This extended live effort arrived on the wings of Loggins's #7 hit "I'm Alright," off the movie soundtrack of *Caddyshack*. The concert version included here is much better, stripped of some of the cute studio tricks found on the single. Most of the material comes from previously released studio tracks, which are given faithful (but livelier) readings. —RC

High Adventure / COLUMBIA / BB 13   1982
Loggins continued his successful string of hit albums with this release. A light mainstream rock duet with Journey lead singer Steve Perry titled "Don't Fight It," reached #17, while Loggins turned in a couple of MOR hits with "Heart to Heart" (#15) and "Welcome to Heartlight" (#24). As with all of his albums to this point, his sound is pleasant and well crafted. Loggins later enjoyed success with songs featured on soundtracks to the films *Caddyshack II*, *Top Gun*, and *Footloose*. —RC

LOGGINS & MESSINA

Rock/pop. Kenny Loggins and Jim Messina were the most successful pop-rock duo of the first half of the 70s. Loggins was a staff songwriter who had recently enjoyed success with a group of songs recorded by the Nitty Gritty Dirt Band when he came to the attention of Messina, a record producer and former member of Buffalo Springfield and Poco. Messina agreed to produce Loggins's first album, but somewhere along the way it became a duo effort that was released in 1972 under the title *Kenny Loggins with Jim Messina Sittin' In*. The album was a gold-seller that stayed in the charts more than two years.

In the next four years, Loggins & Messina released a series of gold or platinum albums, most of which hit the Top Ten. They were all played in a buoyant country-rock style with an accomplished band. *Loggins and Messina* (1972) featured the retro-rock hit "Your Mama Don't Dance." *Full Sail* (1973), *On Stage* (a double live album, 1974), and *Mother Lode* (1974) all hit the Top Ten. *So Fine* was an album of 50s cover songs. The pair's last new studio album, *Native Sons*, came out at the start of 1976.

Loggins and Messina split for two solo careers by the end of that year, their catalog completed by a greatest-hits album, *Best of Friends*, and a live record, *Finale*. —WR

○ **Best of Friends / CBS**   1976
Collects their biggest hits from "Your Mama Don't Dance" onward. —DH

LONE JUSTICE

Roots-rock, folk/rock. Lone Justice in its original form, ca. 1983, was a quartet based in Los Angeles and featuring singer Maria McKee (b 1964), guitarist Ryan Hedgecock (b ca. 1960), bassist Marvin Etzioni, and drummer Don Heffington. The group played in a country-rock style on its debut album, *Lone Justice* (1985). By the time of the second album, *Shelter* (1986), it had turned more toward mainstream rock and become a sextet, with only McKee and Hedgecock remaining from the original unit. Then Lone Justice broke up, and McKee went on to a solo career. —WR

○ **Lone Justice / GEFFEN**   1985
Maria McKee has one of those aching, little-girl voices (not unlike Stevie Nicks's), and it's heard to great effect on these country-rock tunes, especially Tom Petty and Mike Campbell's "Ways to Be Wicked." —WR

LONG RYDERS

Roots-rock, country rock. A 60s revisionist band from the early 80s. The West Coast-based Long Ryders, led by vocalist Sid Griffin, blended Gram Parsons country and Bob Dylan rock & roll with their own everyman anthems. They netted a minor hit in 1984 with "Looking for Lewis and Clark" and broke up in 1988. —JF

Native Sons / RCA-FRONTIER   1984
Updating the Byrds and Gram Parsons. —RG

○ **State of Our Union / ISLAND**   1985
American country-tinged rock & roll. —RG

LONGHOUSE

Singer/songwriter, pop. A New York-based pop-rock group led by Lisa Herman, whose sound is characterized by extensive vocal harmonies provided by as many as six backup singers. Formed in 1985, they released their debut album in 1988. —WR

○ **Longhouse / WARNER**   1988
Lisa Herman represents the logical evolution of the doo-wop street-corner harmony style into an intricate vocal chorus, with her own alto up front, echoing the emotive style of Laura Nyro. And all in the service of a strong collection of catchy pop-rock songs with deeply emotional lyrics. One of the most auspicious debuts of the 80s. —WR

LOOP

Alternative pop, psychedelic. Late-80s British band with moody/ambient guitar meditations. —ED

○ **Fade Out / ROUGH TRADE**   1984
Masters of one-chord throb-rock. Borrows heavily from the Spacemen 3 formula, still most excellent. —SA

Eternal / CHAPTER 22   1989
Collected singles sides, CD bonus tracks, and more. —SA

A Gilded Eternity / RCA   1990
Runner-up to *Fade Out* in a similar formula. —SA

LOS LOBOS

Rock & roll, Tex-Mex. Members: David Hidalgo on guitar, Conrad Lozano on bass, Cesar Rosas on guitar, Louie Perez on drums, and Steve Berlin on sax. High school buddies who grew up in a Chicano barrio, they formed the band in 1973, emphasizing Mexican folk songs and acoustic playing. Now they've merged their traditional Mexican stylings with electric guitars and both country and blues elements. —BC

○ **... And a Time to Dance / WARNER**   1983
Only seven songs but a perfect summation of what the band does and why it's important. A perfectly seamless fusion of Tex-Mex, R&B, and rock & roll, with powerhouse covers of the Ritchie Valens hit "Come On, Let's Go" and the norteño classic "A Te Dejo en San Antonio" thrown in for good measure. —KK

● **How Will the Wolf Survive? / SLASH** 1984
A broader spectrum of music without a measure of the all-out joy of ... *And a Time to Dance*, *How Will the Wolf Survive?* features at least two raveup rockers ("Don't Worry Baby" and "I Got Loaded"), an irresistible shuffle ("Evangeline"), two traditional Mexican numbers ("Seranata Norteña" and "Corrida #1") and a stirring title tune. Well rounded and fully realized. –KK

By the Light of the Moon / WARNER 1987
A very gentle, very Catholic album summed up by the trilogy of sad songs ("River of Fools," "The Mess We're In," "Tears of God") that closes out the album. –KK

LOVE

Psychedelic, rock/pop. Love was one of the most interesting bands to emerge from the mid-60s Los Angeles rock scene, with their trippy blend of folk/rock, psychedelia, hard rock, and bluesy R&B. "My Little Red Book," a Bert Bacharach and Hal David song, was Love's first hit, peaking at #52. That was followed by their only Top 40 hit, "7 and 7 Is" (#33), which was off of their second album, *Da Capo*. Their third album, *Forever Changes*, was a light psychedelic masterpiece, featuring band leader Arthur Lee's playful imagery and entrancingly convoluted melodies. However, their remaining efforts weren't as fully realized, with Love undergoing a number of stylistic and personnel changes. –RC

Love / ELEKTRA 1966
A grand debut and a prime piece of 60s "folk/rock." Love didn't peak for another couple of years but this proves they were one of Los Angeles's hottest bands in the mid 60s. –JT

Da Capo / ELEKTRA 1967
A beautiful but at times pretentious record (due to the 19-minute closing song.) Love's second album includes a few choice tracks. –JT

☆ **Forever Changes / ELEKTRA** 1967
Nothing less than a work of genius, Love's third album still shows up on many all-time-best lists. Arthur Lee's most inspired creation, it's everything that progressive, psychedelic folk/rock could have been. –JT

Best Of - Golden Archive Series / RHINO 1980
Well-chosen collection of Love's most celebrated tracks makes a case for Arthur Lee and company as one of the most creative, intense West Coast 60s rock bands. –JT

LOVE & ROCKETS

Alternative rock. Formed from the ashes of the English art-punk posers, Bauhaus, Love & Rockets (named after the comic book) became huge by playing a kind of folky postmodern rock, rife with inscrutably pretentious lyrics. Perfect fodder for the dress-in-black college crowd, who read a lot of French Symbolist poetry. –JD

○ **Seventh Dream of Teenage Heaven / RCA** 1986
An album filled with the dark, acoustic-driven work hinted at in their previous group, Bauhaus. –SA

Love & Rockets! / BEGGARS BANQUET 1990
Features their only US hit, "So Alive." –SA

LOVERBOY

Hard rock, rock/pop. This Canadian commercial hard-rock quintet was a mainstay on FM rock stations during the early 80s. –RC

○ **Big Ones / CBS** 1988
Loverboy's biggest and best hits, including "Turn Me Loose" (#35), "Lovin' Every Minute of It" (#9), "This Could Be the Night" (#10), "Hot Girls in Love," "Heaven in Your Eyes," and "Working for the Weekend" (#29). –ED

LYLE LOVETT ♭1957

Singer/songwriter. Lyle Lovett represents the increasing diversity of country music as it recovers from a commercial slump in the 80s. Highly literate (he has degrees in journalism and German from Texas A&M), the Houston-born singer comes from the eclectic tradition of Western swing, as filtered through the work of such wry 70s songwriters as Guy Clark and Townes Van Zandt. Lovett has a dry but absurdly hilarious sense of humor, as expressed on his first recorded song, "If I Had a Boat." ("And if I had a pony, I'd ride him on my boat.") But he also writes bitingly of love relations, as in "God Will," in which the singer tells his lover that God will forgive her, but he won't, "and that's the difference between God and me."
Despite some success in the country market and a Grammy award in the country category, it has been questionable since at least Lovett's second album, *Pontiac*, that his music could be categorized as country. But it's so multi-generic, with elements of folk, jazz, blues, and, lately, gospel, that it's hard to say exactly where it fits. At bottom, he's a singer/songwriter — and an amazingly imaginative one at that. –WR

Lyle Lovett / MCA 1986
Lyle Lovett has an ironic overview of the world, expressed in songs he sings with the dead seriousness of the true comic. But he also has a finely defined sense of romantic troubles that sometimes isn't funny at all. Songs like "God Will" and "If I Were the Man You Wanted" mark him as one of the best new writers of the decade. –WR

● **Pontiac / MCA** 1987
Lovett's best overall collection of songs includes the gently absurd "If I Had a Boat," the subtly murderous "L.A. County," and the Henny Youngman-style "She's No Lady," among other gems. –WR

○ **Lyle Lovett & His Large Band / MCA** 1989
On his third album, Lovett continues to explore a synthesis of country and big band. Includes his version of Tammy Wynette's country classic on "Stand By Your Man" and the bittersweet "I Married Her Just Because She Looks Like You." –RC

Joshua Judges Ruth / MCA 1992
Lovett's fascination with gospel emerges on his latest. –ED

THE LOVIN' SPOONFUL

Folk/rock, rock/pop. The Lovin' Spoonful, a major 60s folk-influenced quartet led by John Sebastian and Zal Yanovsky, made a fair bid to become New York's answer to the Byrds but never overcame their Top 40 radio image and several internal problems. Their catalog had been badly abused until 1990 (lost tapes, etc.), but the best-of collection and the early albums reveal flashes of sophistication, humor, and style of near-Beatlesque proportions. –BE

○ **Anthology / RHINO**
The only good-sounding and well-structured collection currently available. This contains all the essentials. –BE

Daydream / ONE WAY 1966
Blues, hard rock, and folk-pop, topped off by the achingly gorgeous "You Didn't Have to Be So Nice." –BE

NICK LOWE ♭1949

Alternative pop, power-pop, rock & roll. From his groundbreaking early 70s work with Brinsley Schwartz to his brilliant outside production gigs or his role in Rockpile, Nick Lowe has remained a singular figure in British rock. He fosters a true love for pop conventions, but his sardonic wit always guarantees that even the most conventional-sounding ditties bulge with his off-kilter perspectives. –JF

● **Pure Pop for Now People / CBS** 1978
A masterpiece from a year that was full of them. This offers the best glimpse into his sometimes demented and ear-catching world. –JF

Labour of Lust / CBS 1979
The grooves are tighter here than before, mixing the roots-rock sensibilities of Rockpile with his love of a good pop hook. Contains several minor hits, including "Cruel to Be Kind." –JF

○ **Basher: The Best of Nick Lowe / CBS**　　　1989

A superb collection spanning Lowe's solo career, with a smattering of Rockpile's sides tossed in. A fine introduction, but start with *Pure Pop for Now People*. —JF

Party of One / WARNER　　　1990

After years of dull and sometimes insipid albums, Lowe bounced back with this tight and funny offering. —JF

LUDICHRIST

Thrash. Considered to be an avant-garde crossover metal band, Ludichrist was one of the best-selling bands on Combat Records before it broke up. Three of its members eventually formed Scatterbrain, who are now signed to Elektra. —JB

○ **Immaculate Deception / RELATIVITY**　　　1986

Demented speed-metal and hardcore — strong, twisted, and sometimes funny. —JB

LYDIA LUNCH　　　♭1959

Alternative rock. A punk poet/actor who records sexually charged confrontational music loaded with clashing guitars. —JD

○ **Queen of Siam / TRIPLE X**　　　1980

Her laconic slur of a voice has never sounded sexier and her off-key rendition of "Spooky" is so lazily erotic it nearly sucks the life out of you. A putrid classic of style and substance. —JD

LUSH

Alternative rock. Few bands live up to their names; Lush, however, does so in spades. Paced by Miki Berenyi's paper-thin voice (so thin you'll think she's on a respirator), Lush literally builds it's music on a mountain of strummed guitars that approximates a rush of lava. Strong songwriting removes any tedium. —JD

○ **Gala / WARNER**　　　1990

A little of it goes a long way, but this is where Lush shines. By this time, their pop craft was developed enough to warrant repeated listenings. Fans of folkie-style guitar, albeit with a touch more volume, will love this. —JD

FRANKIE LYMON & THE TEENAGERS　　1942-1968

Doo-wop. Frankie Lymon (b 1942 - d 1968) & the Teenagers were a New York doo-wop group consisting of Joe Negroni, Herman Santiago, Jimmy Merchant, and Sherman Garnes but centered around the extraordinary talents of their lead singer, thirteen-year-old Frankie Lymon. Lymon wrote their first big hit, "Why Do Fools Fall in Love." His wise-beyond-his-years vocal and performing abilities not only made the Teenagers a group several notches above the competition but made Lymon the first Black teenage pop star. Though only together for a brief 18-month period, Lymon & the Teenagers exerted an enormous influence, spawning several "kid" vocal groups and providing initial inspiration to Berry Gordy to model his entire Motown production approach around Lymon's original vocal style. Inexplicably, the group split into two factions at the height of their success, and neither had a hit again. Lymon died from a drug overdose at age 26. Diana Ross, Smokey Robinson, Len Barry, and his principal protégé, Michael Jackson (whose early recordings with the Jackson 5 are virtual re-creations of the early Lymon sound, merely updated) all show the influence of Frankie Lymon & the Teenagers's groundbreaking work. —CK

Live, Rare & Unreleased / LIVE GOLD

A collection of 17 rare tracks. This isn't for everyone but will thrill the Lymon aficionado. —JT

Frankie Lymon & Teenagers / MURRAY HILL　　　1987

This out-of-print five-record boxed set was obviously aimed at the hardcore fan and collector, and should be sought by those with more than a passing interest. —JT

○ **Best of Frankie Lymon & the Teenagers / RHINO**　　1990

Frankie Lymon wrote "Why Do Fools Fall in Love" at 13 and led his group, the Teenagers, to a brief stardom. They remain one of the finest examples of New York vocal group singing, and all of the essentials are on this album. —JT

LOUIE LYMON & THE TEENCHORDS

R&B, doo-wop. Led by Lewis Lymon, the little brother of the far more successful Frankie Lymon, the Teenagers-soundalike, Teenchords, cut some solid singles beginning with 1956's "I'm So Happy" for the Fury logo. They also appeared in the 1957 movie *Jamboree*. —BD

○ **I'm So Happy / RELIC**　　　1992

Right off master tapes, this CD collects their complete output for Bobby Robinson's Fury label, 1956-1958. It features the title track, "Honey Honey," "Lydia," "I'm Not Too Young to Fall in Love," and "Your Last Chance." Classic examples of the early-50s "kiddie group" sound. —CK

BARBARA LYNN　　　♭1942

R&B, soul. A bluesy southpaw guitarist from Beaumont, TX, Barbara Lynn Ozen wrote her own ticket to hitdom with the 1962 smash "You'll Lose a Good Thing," an R&B chart-topper. Texas producer Huey Meaux brought Lynn to Cosimo's studio in New Orleans to cut the atmospheric downbeat tune, her debut single on the Jamie label. Followups included the bouncy "Oh! Baby (We Got a Good Thing Goin')" — better remembered through the Rolling Stones' faithful cover — and her minor 1966 hit on the often-covered "You Left the Water Running." Lynn remains active, currently recording for Antone's. —BD

You'll Lose a Good Thing / JAMIE　　　1962

Twelve tracks (ten composed by Barbara Lynn). Produced by Huey Meaux. —RP

Here Is Barbara Lynn / OVAL　　　1976

Reissues of 1968 Atlantic recordings produced by Huey Meaux and influenced by Motown. (Import) —RP

○ **Barbara Lynn / GOODTHING**　　　1989

Seventeen comprehensive tracks that cover all the labels and all the hits. (Import) —RP

LYNYRD SKYNYRD

Southern rock. From the time of their initial 1970 Sheffield, AL, demos to their tragic plane crash on Oct 20, 1977, the Jacksonville, FL, band Lynyrd Skynyrd fused the spirit of rock & roll with the truth and lyrical directness of great country music.

Lynyrd Skynyrd possessed a highly arranged approach to organizing their material. They also featured a powerful lead guitar triumvirate in Allen Collins, Gary Rossington, and Ed King (later replaced by Steve Gaines), which augmented lead singer/songwriter Ronnie Van Zant's no-nonsense tales of the common man's exploits.

Skynyrd was discovered playing in an Atlanta club by Blood, Sweat & Tears founder Al Kooper in 1972. Kooper signed them to his new Sounds of the South record label and released *Pronounced Leh-Nerd Skin-Nerd* (#27), which included the classic "Freebird" (#19-1975/#38-1977), one of the most requested songs in rock history.

The band, which drew heavily from the hard English blues-rock sound (Free, Cream, Stones), had the good fortune to have a fan in the Who's Pete Townshend, who requested that Skynyrd open for the 1973 *Quadrophenia* tour. As a result, the band developed a strong fan base early in their career.

"Sweet Home Alabama" (#8) from *Second Helping* (#12) was the band's biggest single. Other singles included "Saturday Night Special" (#27), "What's Your Name" (#13), "Double Trouble" (#80), and "You Got That Right" (#69).

Survivors of the 1977 plane crash played in various amalgamations (Rossington-Collins Band, Allen Collins Band, etc.). Lynyrd Skynyrd re-formed for a Tribute tour in 1987. Since then, they have released two albums for Atlantic. —RC

☆ **Pronounced Leh'Nerd Skin-Nerd / MCA / BB 27**   1973

With the release of this debut album, Skynyrd was immediately recognized as one of the South's premier bands. The album's highlight is "Freebird," a song that over time has become one of the most requested rock songs in the history of radio. "Simple Man," "Gimmie Three Steps," and "Tuesday's Gone" are several other standards from this classic album. Producer Al Kooper has remastered the CDs of this album, *Second Helping*, and *Nuthin' Fancy* to his specifications. All of these are budget priced, making this an exceptional deal. –RC

☆ **Second Helping / MCA / BB 12**   1974

Their appropriately titled followup to their debut was equally impressive, containing their highest-charting hit, "Sweet Home Alabama" (#8). Unlike many albums, where the hit is the highlight, *Second Helping* is chock full of great tunes like "Working for MCA," "Call Me the Breeze," "Don't Ask Me No Questions," and "Ballad of Curtis Loew." (Also available as a Mobile Fidelity Ultradisc) –RC

Nuthin' Fancy / MCA / BB 9   1975

Frazzled by too much endless roadwork and too little songwriting preparation, *Nuthin' Fancy* is a step down from its impressive predecessor, *Second Helping*. Nevertheless, "Saturday Night Special," the album's opener, is a classic rocker. Other standouts include the Free-style "On the Hunt," "Whiskey Rock-A-Roller," and "Am I Losin'." –RC

Gimme Back My Bullets / MCA / BB 20   1976

On their first production with the legendary Tom Dowd (Rod Stewart, Eric Clapton, Allman Brothers), Skynyrd sounds relatively uninspired, even as they indignantly call for a return to platinum status with the Free-influenced title cut. Nevertheless, Van Zant's gift for plain-speaking lyrics and the band's undeniable chemistry help this record hold up better than many late-70s AOR rock acts. –RC

One More from the Road / MCA / BB 9   1976

Recorded at Atlanta's Fox Theater and produced by Tom Dowd, Skynyrd returned to their original three-guitar lineup concept with the addition of Steve Gaines. Some might complain that *One More* failed to capture the energy of the band's shows, but overall it ranks as one of rock's finest live releases. Unfortunately, MCA abridged the CD, cutting out some key tracks and dialog. –RC

☆ **Street Survivors / MCA / BB 5**   1977

The addition of lead guitarist and singer Steve Gaines goaded Ronnie Van Zant and the band into a dramatic rebirth. *Street Survivors* featured tighter songs, strong melodies, and an exciting element of vocal interplay between Van Zant and Gaines ("You Got That Right"). The contrast between Gaines's clean lead style, Collins's flash, and Rossington's thick-toned lyrical phrasing is something to behold. Without a doubt, Skynyrd's most cohesive body of work since *Second Helping*. –RC

First ... & Last / MCA / BB 15   1978

Pre-Al Kooper Skynyrd, recorded in Muscle Shoals, may not be their best work, but it shows without a doubt that this Jacksonville band was already heads and shoulders above many major-label bands, even before they were signed. –RC

Gold & Platinum / MCA / BB 12   1979

Compiled by Gary Rossington and Allen Collins after their tragic 1977 plane crash, *Gold & Platinum* contains most of the band's essential tracks. It would've been nice if annotations had been included, but this is a good primer. –RC

★ **Lynyrd Skynyrd (Boxed Set) / MCA**   1991

This attractively packaged and well-chosen collection of the band's most popular tracks also includes early demos and other unreleased tracks. –RC

LYRES

Alternative rock. Led by garage-rock king Jeff "Monoman" Connolly, the Lyres are the Savoy Brown of the punk era, simply because of the band's ever-changing lineup (something like 30-40 members). Playing classic Farfisa-driven junk-riffing with manic glee, the Lyres are one of Boston's enduring rock legacies, and rightly so. –JD

○ **On Fyre / ACE OF HEARTS**   1984

Simply, their best. For fans of that trebly 60s shit-rock sound and Stooges-style destructo lurch, this is what it sounds like all revved up and ready to go. –JD

Lyres Lyres / ACE OF HEARTS   1986

Not as immediately engaging as *On Fyre* but this could well be the world's first *mature* garage-rock record. A bit slowed down and more emotionally complex, it's a departure in a genre known primarily for speed and sweat. –JD

MAD LADS

Doo-wop, soul. Vocal group who recorded for Stax in the late 60s, achieving little chart success, but establishing a cult following among Southern soul-fetishists. Their first (and best) hit for Stax was 1968's "Whatever Hurts You." –JF

○ **Greatest Hits / COLLECTABLES**

The best from 1965 to 1968, from this connoisseur's vocal group, including five hits. –RP

Best of the Mad Lads / STAX   1984

Two late hits, with no track duplication with their *Greatest Hits*. –RP

MADNESS

Ska-revival. Madness was a British septet formed in 1976. They gained fame in the late-70s ska-revival along with such bands as the Specials and the Beat. Unlike those contemporaries, however, the group had a comic, pop edge that turned it into a well-loved popular singles group. Members were Graham "Suggs" McPherson, vocals; Chas Smash, backup vocals; Chris Foreman, guitar; Mike Barson, keyboards; Lee Thompson, saxophone; Mark Bedord, bass; and Dan Woodgate, drums. The first of their 13 UK Top Ten hits was "One Step Beyond" in 1979.

Though the group's British subject matter and approach tended to preclude American success, Madness did manage one US Top Ten hit, "Our House," in 1983. The group disbanded in 1986. –WR

Absolutely / SIRE   1980

Their early, ska-influenced material, featuring such UK hits as "Baggy Trousers," "Embarrassment," and "Return of the Las Palmas 7." –WR

○ **Madness / GEFFEN**   1983

A US compilation album released to coincide with the success of "Our House." It includes that hit, its followup, "It Must Be Love," and such UK successes as "Tomorrow's Just Another Day," "Shut Up," "House of Fun," and "Grey Day." –WR

MADONNA   b 1958

Pop, dance-pop. The most controversial female artist of the last thirty years has never received her critical due in spite of massive worldwide success. Her unabashed sexual confidence, her canny marketing sense, her support of gay causes, her interracial relationships, and her consistent exposing of the hypocrisy of our male-dominated society have made her the scorn of critics and social commentators; she's been lambasted everywhere, from *Rolling Stone* to "Entertainment Tonight." But Madonna's music deserves to be heard on its own terms. She's been a trailblazing and innovative force in dance-pop. The formula she set with her first album has been mimicked by some of the hottest acts of 80s and 90s, including Janet Jackson and Paula Abdul. Her celebrity and notoriety, however, would be as vacuous as Cher's if her music weren't so good — if it didn't ring in the ears and stick in the brain like all classic pop should. –JF

Madonna / SIRE   1983

This debut took a while to catch the world's attention with hits like "Lucky Star," "Burning Up," and "Holiday," but there was something unique about this pop singer's style. –SWB

Like a Virgin / SIRE   1984

With monster hits like "Material Girl," "Dress You Up," and the title track, this album exploits the traits that defined her then-budding persona. –JF

True Blue / SIRE 1986

A staggering album from an artist known for hot singles. The hits include "Papa Don't Preach," "Open Your Heart," and "True Blue." "Live to Tell," her best, is also to be found here. –JF

Like a Prayer / SIRE 1989

Not as consistent as her *True Blue* album but a diverse and ambitious set, including "Keep It Together," a wonderful single. –JF

☆ **Immaculate Collection / SIRE** 1990

A 70-minute singles package that establishes once and for all Madonna's absolute mastery of the pop single. –JF

MAGAZINE

Punk. An arty angst-rock combo formed in 1978 by former Buzzcocks vocalist Howard Devoto. Before breaking up in 1981, the group recorded one devastating single, 1978's "Shot by Both Sides." –JF

○ **Real Life / CAROLINE** 1978

A vital album which fired the first shot in defining the UK post-punk scene. A period classic. –SA

The Correct Use of Soap / CAROLINE 1980

Only a shade less brilliant than their debut. Outstanding work from guitarist John McCeoch. –SA

After the Fall / I.R.S. 1982

A US compilation that includes non-LP single sides. –SA

THE MAIN INGREDIENT

R&B, soul. Originally formed in 1964 as the Poets, this New York soul group (Donald McPherson, Luther Simmons Jr, and Tony Sylvester) recorded for Red Bird before changing their name in 1966. After McPherson's death in 1971, Cuba Gooding became the lead singer, and the band scored three Top 40 hits, including "Everybody Plays the Fool," which went to #3. –BC & STE

○ **All-Time Greatest Hits / RCA**

Lushly orchestrated, smooth Philly-soul hits like "Everybody Plays the Fool." –BC

YNGWIE MALMSTEEN

Hard rock, heavy metal. By age twenty-one Yngwie Malmsteen had become one of the most admired guitarists on the planet. Raised in Sweden, the 19-year-old moved to California in 1983 and within two years had debuted on vinyl with Steeler, cut two albums with Alcatrazz, and self-produced a pair of much-lauded solo releases. Onstage, he was energy incarnate, tossing his Strat high in the air and catching it one-handed, playing with his teeth, and offering his instrument in symbolic sacrifice to the gods of feedback. The young Swede's technique was brilliant, with sheer speed and picking control surpassed by few others. Solos were the heart of his art: roaring masterpieces, they cast high-drama melodies more closely related to Bach and Paganini than to any rock forebears. An injured picking hand has slowed his career in recent years. –JO

○ **Rising Force / POLYGRAM** 1984

Sheer speed, dazzling execution. Result — the birth of the guitar hero. –JO

MAMA CASS 1941-1974

Rock/pop. After the Mamas & the Papas split up, Cass Elliot found success on her own with several sizable sellers. Her first solo smash in 1968, "Dream a Little Dream of Me," still featured the group's support, but her 1969 hit on Dunhill, "Make Your Own Kind of Music," proved Cass could do it on her own. Insisting on dropping her "Mama" nickname, Elliot

developed into a popular TV personality and nightclub act before succumbing to a heart attack in 1974. –BD

○ **Mama's Big Ones - Best of Mama Cass / MCA** 1971

A good compilation of Cass Elliot's hits, including "It's Getting Better" (#30), "Make Your Own Kind of Music" (#36), and "Dream a Little Dream of Me" (#12). –STE

THE MAMAS & THE PAPAS

Rock/pop. The leading California-based vocal group of the 60s, the Mamas & the Papas epitomized the ethos of mid to late 60s pop culture: live free, play free, and love free. Their music, built around radiant harmonies and a solid electric-folk foundation, was gorgeous on its own terms, but a major part of its appeal lay in the easygoing Southern California lifestyle it endorsed.

Founder and leader John Phillips came out of early rock roots and a partly successful folk career, as did Cass Elliott and Denny Doherty, while Phillips's wife Michelle was an ex-model who also sang. They got together out of several failed folk groups just as the music was going electric, pulled up stakes in New York and headed west, where they signed with Lou Adler and wowed the world with a song called "California Dreamin'."

Phillips was a pop poet with a commercial edge, and a good arranger. The group had enviable chart success, lived well, and indulged themselves lavishly yet retained credibility with the counterculture. But it all came apart in a couple of years, as the quartet's intertwining romantic entanglements, coupled with their chemical excesses (detailed in separate books by John and Michelle Phillips), strangled their ability to work. By 1971 they were a fond memory, although a reconstituted version of the quartet has done well on the oldies circuit in the late 80s and early 90s. –BE

If You Can Believe Your Eyes and Ears / MCA 1966

Radiant, full-length album. Superb songs. –BE

Deliver / MCA 1967

That they do, with some brilliant covers. –BE

16 Greatest Hits / MCA 1970

A great overview of the music from this group, one of the founders of the California sound in the late 60s. This is a good collection of their unforgettable electric folk/pop songs, including "Monday, Monday" and "California Dreaming." –ED

Monterey International Pop Festival / MCA 1971

A live concert curio, with uneven performances and recording quality, but it is unique. –BE

○ **Creeque Alley / MCA** 1991

Creeque Alley - History of the Mamas & the Papas is the ultimate, unbeatable anthology. –BE

MELISSA MANCHESTER b 1951

Pop. Melissa Manchester sang commercial jingles at 15 and later became a member of Bette Midler's Harlettes. With partners Peter Allen and Carole Bayer Sager, she wrote several modern-day adult standards. Manchester specialized in MOR hits, especially power ballads, thanks to her night-club background and her affiliation with Barry Manilow and Bette Midler. From 1975 to 1982, Manchester charted with "Midnight Blue" (#6), "Don't Cry out Loud" (#10), "Just You and I" (#27), "Just Too Many People" (#30), and the upbeat "You Should Hear How She Talks about You" (#5). –BC & RC

○ **Greatest Hits / ARISTA** 1983

Her own classic cuts like "Come In from the Rain" and "Fire in the Morning." –BC

MANFRED MANN

British Invasion, prog-rock. A British rock quintet led by keyboard player Manfred Mann (born Michael Lubowitz, Oct 21, 1940). They scored 13 British and two American Top Ten hits between 1963 and 1969. The biggest was the #1 "Do Wah

Diddy Diddy," before Mann disbanded and reemerged in the 70s with Manfred Mann's Earth Band. –WR

Roaring Silence / WARNER   1976
A later edition of Mann's band, which had a 70s hit with Bruce Springsteen's "Blinded by the Light" (on this album). –WR

○ **Best of Manfred Mann / CAPITOL**   1992
For a guy who claimed to be a jazz buff and to despise pop, Manfred Mann (the keyboard player) sure knew a pop hit when he heard one. And here they are, including "Do Wah Diddy Diddy" and "Pretty Flamingo." –WR

MANHATTANS

Doo-wop, R&B, soul. A venerable soul quintet from New Jersey, whose career has spanned the dawn of soul and the death of disco, although they have steadfastly preferred ballads over the years. Led initially by George Smith, who died in 1970, the Manhattans first charted in 1965 with "I Wanna Be (Your Everything)." After a string of solid R&B sellers on Carnival and DeLuxe, Gerald Alston replaced the late Smith and the group moved to Columbia. In 1976 they struck pay dirt with the elegant platinum-selling ballad "Kiss and Say Goodbye," which topped both the pop and soul lists. Several more huge R&B hits preceded their uplifting 1980 gold record "Shining Star," and still more followed. –BD

The Manhattans Doing Their Thing / UPFRONT
Worth a search for this mid-60s harmonic R&B. –BC

Manhattans / CBS   1976
Smooth and mellow mid-70s soul, such as "Kiss and Say Goodbye." –BC

○ **Greatest Hits / CBS**   1980
Other soul ballads from the mid 70s. –BC

BARRY MANILOW   *b* 1946

Pop, singer/songwriter. Barry Manilow just can't get any respect. He's been at the butt end of a million remarks regarding what's wrong with radio. Only recently has another act taken that honor away from him, in the form of fellow Arista labelmates Milli Vanilli. At least Manilow could play and sing. It's Manilow's sugary romantic MOR ballads, fortified with throw-in-the-kitchen-sink productions, that have always rankled detractors. Nevertheless, that never kept him from selling over fifty million records worldwide. The biggest successes, among his many hits, include "Mandy" (#1), "Could It Be Magic" (#6), "I Write the Songs" (#1), "Looks Like We Made It" (#1), "Can't Smile without You" (#3), "Weekend in New England" (#10), "Copacabana (At the Copa)" (#8), "Ships" (#9), "Somewhere in the Night" (#9), and "I Made It through the Rain" (#10). –RC

Live / ARISTA / BB 1   1977
Live was Manilow's only #1 album. The performances are so seamless that it's practically a faithfully performed greatest-hits album. It includes the hit "Daybreak." –RC

● **Greatest Hits - Vol. 1 / ARISTA / BB 7**   1978
Manilow had a slew of albums but essentially he is a singles artist. This first *Greatest Hits* collection is the place to start, for those desiring an introduction to one of the most successful MOR singers of all time. Among the songs included in this collection are "Mandy," "Looks Like We Made It," "Can't Smile without You," "Tryin' to Get the Feeling Again," and "Daybreak." –RC

○ **Greatest Hits - Vol. 2 / ARISTA / BB 30**   1983
Includes "Could It Be Magic," "This One's for You," "Weekend in New England," "Copacabana (At the Copa)," and "I Write the Songs." –RC

Greatest Hits - Vol. 3 / ARISTA
Vol. 3 isn't as consistently strong as the first two, since it consists mainly of his less successful tracks. This set contains "The Old Songs," "Memory," "Let's Hang On," "Somewhere Down the Road," "I Made It through the Rain," and his Top Ten version of Ian Hunter's "Ships." –RC

PHIL MANZANERA   *b* 1951

Prog-rock. Guitarist Phil Manzanera (born Jan 31, 1951) provided Roxy Music with a wide range of sounds from tonally dissonant chordal washes to elegantly understated melody lines. In many ways, Manzanera approached the guitar texturally, not unlike King Crimson's Robert Fripp. Apart from Roxy Music, Manzanera has involved himself in a number of solo and collaborative projects. –RC

Listen/Now / POLYDOR   1975
Studio album. Same feel but not as urgent as the *801 Live* album. Guests include Mel Collins (sax), Eddie Jobson (violin), Lol Creme and Kevin Godley (from 10CC), and Dave Mattacles. Rock music that stands the test of time. –MGN

○ **801 Live / CAROLINE**   1976
Instrumentals and somber vocalizing with a band whose virtuosity is unmatched. 801 consisted of Brian Eno, Phil Manzanera, and keyboardist Francis Moukman, powered by the fabulous drummer Simon Philips in his early period. Reprises of the Kinks "You Really Got Me," "Miss Shapiro," and Eno's "Baby's on Fire." Explosive music. –MGN

● **Diamond Head / CAROLINE**   1990
With the help of fellow Roxy Music bandmates and Quiet Sun, Manzanera produced his most diverse solo effort. Much of this release is instrumental, but Brian Eno and Robert Wyatt (formally of Soft Machine) pitch in on the bulk of the vocals. Musically, *Diamond Head* falls between Brian Eno's early synthetic-rock efforts and Roxy Music's mid-70s dissonant forays. Highlights include "Frontera," (sung in Spanish by Wyatt), "Big Day," and "Miss Shapiro." –RC

THE MAR-KEYS

Soul. Before Booker T. & the MG's, there were the Mar-Keys, who literally laid the groundwork for the Memphis Sound with their powerfully economic early R&B instrumental sound. They enjoyed only one real hit with the #3 "Last Night," which was released in 1961 on Satellite Records, the predecessor to Stax.
Besides including Steve Cropper and "Duck" Dunn in the lineup, the Mar-Keys also had Wayne Jackson, who later formed the Memphis Horns, and Don Nix, who had a fairly successful career as a solo artist and producer. –RC

○ **Back to Back / ATLANTIC**   1967
A smoldering live set featuring the Mar-Keys (aka the Memphis Horns), recorded in Europe during the 1967 Stax/Volt Revue. (Credited to the Mar-Keys and the MG's.) –JF

THE MARCELS

Doo-wop. This Pittsburgh quintet waxed "Blue Moon," a doo-wop masterpiece, in 1961. –JF

● **Best of the Marcels / RHINO**   1990
An outstanding vocal ensemble that is exceptional on nonsense/novelty tunes like "Blue Moon." –RW

○ **Summertime / RELIC**   1992
One of the finest and purest doo-wop albums available, this features 24 a cappella performances and served as the legendary audition tape that got the group signed to their first recording contract. Great singing, arrangements, and performances. –CK

BOBBY MARCHAN   *b* 1930

R&B, doo-wop. An energetic New Orleans vocalist who was the lead singer with Huey "Piano" Smith's Clowns and one of R&B's most outlandish transvestites, who had the ability to sing authentically as either a male or a female. He was also a member of the early R&B group the Tick Tocks. He went solo in 1960. –JF & BC

○ **Golden Classics / COLLECTABLES**
A collection of falsetto doo-wop and Southern soul balladry from the 60s. –BC

TEENA MARIE   b 1957

Motown, funk, dance-pop. This protègè of Rick James was one of Motown's most successful White artists. Her sound was so soulful that the company concealed her identity for her first album. She went on to become an accomplished writer and producer as well, and has always been a big album-seller. Today she records for Epic. –RAB

○ **Teena Marie's Greatest Hits / MOTOWN**   1985
The highlights of her career, including "I Need Your Lovin'" (#37) and "Square Biz" (#50). –RAB

Greatest Hits / EPIC   1991
More recent material, featuring "Lovergirl" (#4), "Jammin'" (#81), and "Ooo La La La" (#85). –RAB

MARILLION

Art-rock. British art-rock revivalists similar to Genesis. They formed in 1983 and lead singer split from the band in 1990 for a solo career. –ED

○ **Misplaced Childhood / CAPITOL**   1988
A masterpiece of articulate and emotional lyrics with exciting and colorful musical settings. The songs form a continuous album-length suite. –MPD

Thieving Magpie (la Gazza Ladra) / CAPITOL   1988
A fine double-CD live set from their 1984 and 1987 tours. Fish's last recording with Marillion. Named for the Rossini piece they open their shows with. –MPD

Fugazi / CAPITOL   1989
Gut-wrenchingly powerful lyrics and dynamic prog-rock performance. A classic! –MPD

MARK-ALMOND

Rock/pop. This mellow folk/jazz ensemble, formed in 1970 by singer and guitarist Jon Mark and multi-instrumentalist Johnny Almond, basically had two notable FM tracks from their six-album career, which were the 11-minute "The City" and "One Way Sunday." –RC

○ **Best of Mark-Almond / RHINO**   1980
Smartly compiled sampler of this English group's blend of light jazz, folk, and a hint of rock. Contains most of their first two albums. Highlights include "The City" and "One Way Sunday." –RC

CHRIS MARS

Alternative rock. Surprise! Ex-Replacements drummer and all-around quiet guy becomes pop-rock auteur. Mars's skills are hardly anything to marvel at, but his ability to do so many things well is. This is energetic pop with a dry cutting wit and Mars proves there is life after being kicked out of a great band. –JD

○ **Horseshoes and Hand Grenades / SMASH**   1992
Sure, it could use a little editing, but this is a strong debut album. With songs like "Popular Creeps" and "Reverse Status," Mars has created a gem of a pop record. What's amazing is that no one thought he would do it. –JD

THE MARSHALL TUCKER BAND

Southern rock. One of the major Southern-rock bands of the 70s, the Marshall Tucker Band was formed in Spartanburg, SC, in 1971 by singer Doug Gray; guitarist Toy Caldwell (b 1948); his brother, bassist Tommy Caldwell (b 1950 - d Apr 4, 1980); guitarist George McCorkle; drummer Paul Riddle; and reed player Jerry Eubanks. The group's style combined rock, country, and jazz, and featured extended instrumental passages on which lead guitarist Toy Caldwell shone. The band was signed to Capricorn Records and released its debut album, *The Marshall Tucker Band*, in March 1973. They gained recognition through a tour with the Allman Brothers Band and found significant success during the course of the 70s, with most of their albums going gold. Their peak came

with the million-selling album *Carolina Dreams* and its Top 15 single "Heard It in a Love Song" in 1977. The band was slowed down by the death of Tommy Caldwell in a car accident in 1980, and it faded from the album charts after 1982. Toy Caldwell left for a solo career, and by the early 90s, Marshall Tucker consisted of Doug Gray, Jerry Eubanks, guitarist Rusty Milner, bassist Tim Lawter, drummer Ace Allen, and pianist Don Cameron. –WR

○ **The Marshall Tucker Band / AJK**   1973
The Marshall Tucker Band was never better than on its debut, mixing country picking with R&B rhythms and writing topflight songs like "Take the Highway" and "Can't You See." –WR

○ **Searchin' for a Rainbow / AJK**   1975
For their fourth album, Marshall Tucker's synthesis of country and Southern rock found its most fully realized expression, particularly on tracks like "Fire on the Mountain" and the title track. Along with their debut, this is Marshall Tucker's best studio effort. –RC

● **Greatest Hits / AJK / BB 67**   1977
If you are looking for a place to start with this band, *Greatest Hits* covers all the main bases. Included are "Can't You See" (#75), "Heard It in a Love Song" (#14), "Fire on the Mountain" (#38), and "This Ol' Cowboy" (#78). –RC

MARVELETTES

Motown. This quintet came to Motown in 1961 after placing as finalists in their Inkster, MI, school talent contest. They were 16 years old when their first record, "Please Mr. Postman," zoomed to the #1 spot. Their finest work came in the mid 60s under the production of Smokey Robinson. Although they were overshadowed by the Supremes, their vocal styling was representative of the classic girl-group phenomenon of the 60s. By 1967 they were reduced to a trio, finally disbanding in 1970. Members included Gladys Harton (who left in 1967, and was replaced by Ann Bogan), Wanda Young, Juanita Cowart (left in 1962), Georgeanne Gordon (left in 1963), and Katherine Anderson. –RAB

○ **Anthology / MOTOWN**   1975
This traces the group's Motown history, including the hits "Beechwood 4-5789," "Don't Mess with Bill," "The Hunter Gets Captured by the Game," "Please Mr. Postman," "That's How Heartaches Are Made," "Too Many Fish in the Sea," and many others. –RAB

MARVIN & JOHNNY

R&B, doo-wop. Marvin Phillips was a constant presence in this swinging pair, but the role of his duet partner, Johnny, was variously held down by Emory Perry (who also handled the sax solos on many of their records), Carl Green, and even Marvin himself via overdubs. Phillips had recorded as a solo before teaming with Jesse Belvin in 1953 and hitting the R&B charts with "Dream Girl" for Specialty Records. Marvin recruited Perry for a series of rocking duets for Specialty, RPM, Aladdin, and other West Coast concerns. They cut the classic ballad "Cherry Pie" and its rocking hit flip, "Tick Tock," for RPM in 1954. –BD

○ **Cherry Pie / KENT**
A solid R&B duo, good on remakes, ballads, uptempo music, or novelty numbers. Forgettable sound quality. –RW

MARY JANE GIRLS

Rock/pop. Members Joanne McDuffie, Candice Ghant, Kim Wuletick, and Yvette Marine were originally the backup singers for Rick James's concerts and records. He produced admirable dance hits for them in the 80s, but as his fortunes declined, so did theirs, and they disbanded. –BC

○ **Only Four You / MOTOWN**   1985
Outstanding club music produced by Rick James, with the Top Ten hits "In My House" and "Wild & Crazy Love." –RAB

MARY'S DANISH

Alternative rock. A Los Angeles sextet that sounds like X and features vocalists Julie Ritter and Gretchen Seager and ex-Three O'Clock guitarist Louis Gutierrez. –DS

○ **There Goes the Wondertruck ... / ELEKTRA**   1989
A propulsive debut, which showcases tension-filled harmonies and churning punk with a country tinge. –DS

Circa / MORGAN CREEK   1991
Not so consistent or well produced as their debut, *Circa* is not a good introduction to Mary's Danish, but those who know (and therefore love) their first album and live shows, with their energetic country-seasoned funk & roll (Sly Stone-meets-Lyle Lovett-meets-ZZ Top-with-female singers), will appreciate it. –JK

DAVE MASON   *b* 1946

Rock/pop. Mason was a founding member of the influential late-60s group Traffic. He provided some of that group's best material on their first three albums, particularly "You Can All Join In" and "Feelin' Alright," a song that has been covered by numerous artists, including Joe Cocker and Three Dog Night. Mason left Traffic in 1970 and went solo, enjoying sporadic success during the 70s with his style of light melodic rock/pop. –RC

○ **Alone Together / MCA / BB 22**   1970
Mason's debut solo album remains his best effort, due to well-crafted tracks like the hit "Only You Know & I Know" (#42) and an appealing easygoing rock sound that presents a nice blend of acoustic and electric instrumentation. –RC

Let It Flow / CBS / BB 37   1977
On *Let It Flow* Mason delivered a super-slick bid for radio-friendly pop. He succeeded with three hits, "So High (Rock Me Baby and Roll Me Away)" (#89), "Let It Go, Let It Flow" (#45), and the richly harmonic "We Just Disagree" (#12). –RC

MATERIAL

Funk, avant-garde. Material began in the creative ferment of the late 70s, grafting many progressive trends onto a foundation of soulful dance beats. Bassist Bill Laswell has kept the concept and the funky bottom end going since then, producing diversely accessible and experimental studio projects with stellar lineups of jazz, soul, rock, avant-garde, and world-music figures. –MB

● **Memory Serves / CELLULOID**   1981
A peak statement from their expansionist phase, which combines a hard-funk foundation with wild New York improvisation and jazz writing. –MB

One Down / ELEKTRA   1982
A more commercialized attempt along the lines of *Memory Serves.* –MB

○ **Seven Souls / ATLANTIC**   1989
This collaboration with William S. Burroughs and many international names works like a charm. It contains lots of strong underground grooves with Burroughs's unmistakable prose. –MB

Third Power / POLYGRAM   1991
An awesome grouping of jazz, ethnic, soul, and new music stars that take their Material identity to the extremes. –MB

MATERIAL ISSUE

Rock. A hard power-pop trio from Illinois, who draw much musical inspiration from early Who. Lyrically, they stay focused on adolescent love songs. –RC

○ **International Pop Overthrow / POLYGRAM**   1991
Produced by Jeff Murphy of Shoes, this major label debut contained some power-pop gems like "Renee Remains the Same," "Dianne," "Valerie Loves Me," and the title cut. Fans of Cheap Trick and early Who should love much of this. Also check out their self-titled EP, which preceded this album. –RC

JOHN MAYALL   *b* 1933

Blues/rock. John Mayall is a major British blues bandleader who sings and plays harmonica, guitar, and keyboards. His bands, starting in London in 1963, have featured some of the most successful rock musicians of the 60s and 70s. Approaching the age of 60, Mayall continues to play and record frequently. –WR

☆ **Bluesbreakers with Eric Clapton / POLYGRAM**   1966
One of the seminal blues albums of the 60s with the Bluesbreakers, capturing Clapton on a series of blues standards, after the pop leanings of the Yardbirds and before the heavy indulgence of Cream. –WR

Turning Point / POLYGRAM   1969
Mayall at a live peak with a band featuring Jon Mark and John Almond. –WR

CURTIS MAYFIELD   *b* 1942

R&B, soul. Few have had as much influence on Black music, in as many fields of endeavor, as Curtis Mayfield, starting from his early days with the Impressions back in 1958. His sinewy guitar work has become so woven into the basic fabric of R&B guitar that more people know the style than know the man who invented it. He was the first to exhibit racial pride, singing about it on hit singles with the Impressions in the early 60s through 70s. He scored big with the soundtrack to the blaxploitation film *Superfly* in 1972; by this time he had already been running his own record company for four years. Mayfield wrote hits for everyone from Major Lance to Jerry Butler. He continues to persevere today despite the tragic accident that almost took his life in 1990. Curtis Mayfield's stardom is assured by his massive talent. –CK & CE

○ **Superfly / BUDDAH**   1973
Music from the film. Contains some of Mayfield's best, most incisive work. –CK

Of All Time - Classic Collection / CURTOM   1974
A good wrapup of his solo career hits, focused rightly on Mayfield's astoundingly high, reedy voice and massive songwriting chops. –CK

There's No Place like America / CURTOM   1989
Soul music with a message. This is one of Mayfield's most anthemic works to date. –CK

MAZE w/FRANKIE BEVERLY

Soul. Bandleader Frankie Beverly formed the group in 1971 as Raw Soul. After a move to California, they combined their native Philly sound with laidback California-rock arrangements, creating their own distinctive hybrid. –BC

○ **Lifelines - Vol. 1 / CAPITOL**
Includes "Joy and Pain," among other early hits from the 70s. –BC

Silky Soul / WARNER   1990
A comeback album of smooth soul. –BC

MAZZY STAR

Alternative pop, psychedelic. David Roback, veteran of the California paisley-underground group Rain Parade, and singer Hope Sandoval, from Going Home, undertake a cold, reverberant alternative-folk sound, with occasional forays into electric psychedelia –RC

○ **She Hangs Brightly / CAPITOL**   1990
Roback and Sandoval slog through a collection of Velvet Underground-style psychedelia and comatose folk. Sandoval's pleasantly detached vocal delivery complements the cold, highly reverberant production. Good for encouraging numb disconnection from the planet. –RC

MC5

Rock & roll. Detroit rock & roll band whose musical and political stance helped sow the seeds of the British punk movement of the late 70s. Original members included Wayne Kramer (guitar), Rob Tyner (vocals), Bob Gaspar (drums), Pat Burrows (bass), and Fred "Sonic" Smith (guitar). They played around their native Detroit ca. 1966 as the Motor City Five. Both Gaspar and Burrows, who had shaped much of the band's early rhythmic drive, left before the band ever recorded and were replaced by Dennis Thompson (drums) and Michael Davis (bass). After two local singles went nowhere, manager John Sinclair (of the revolutionary White Panther Party) got them signed to Elektra, who recorded them live at Detroit's Grande Ballroom, where they enjoyed a fanatical local following. Troubles with the album's lyrical content (based in large part around the band's sex, drugs, and rock & roll revolutionary rhetoric) and Sinclair's conviction on drug charges saw the band toning down its image for their second album, released on Atlantic. By the time their third album was released in 1971, the band was plagued by drugs and personal problems, and they broke up shortly thereafter. Though never commercially successful, the MC5 personified the Detroit high-energy sound and approach to rock & roll, and their style lives on in the work of punk and alternative bands around the world. –CK

★ **Kick Out the Jams / ELEKTRA** 1969
The band in full cry at the Grande Ballroom, 1968; one of the most exciting live albums ever recorded. Highlights include the title track (uncensored on CD), "Ramblin' Rose," and "Borderline." –CK

○ **Back in the U.S.A. / RHINO-ATLANTIC** 1970
Their second album. Not so wild but still exciting. Great original material, like "Shakin' Street" (featuring vocal by Fred "Sonic" Smith), "The American Ruse," "The Human Being Lawnmower," and "Looking at You," which featured some fiery lead guitar work by Wayne Kramer. –RC

High Time / RHINO-ATLANTIC 1971
Their last studio album, with "Sister Anne" and "Baby, Won't Ya" as principal highlights. –CK

Babes in Arms / ROIR 1983
Rare and unreleased sides. This includes their first singles, unavailable on album. –CK

PAUL MCCARTNEY   b 1942

Rock/pop. In the decade and a half after the demise of the Beatles in 1970, Paul McCartney has become one of the most successful figures in popular music. Though he had more trouble scoring hits after the mid 80s, McCartney embarked on a triumphant world tour in 1989 and premiered his first classical work, *Paul McCartney's Liverpool Oratorio*, in 1991.
Born in Liverpool, McCartney teamed with John Lennon and George Harrison in the 50s to form the nucleus of the Beatles, who scored unprecedented worldwide success in the 60s, much of it fueled by McCartney's melodic songs. The bass player and singer was a musical chameleon, equally capable of performing the most tender love song, the most schmaltzy show tune, or the most raucous rocker, on command.
McCartney scored a film (*The Family Way*) in 1966 but otherwise restricted his musical activities to the group until the end of the 60s, when he launched his solo career with *McCartney*. In the early 70s, he formed a new group, Wings, and toured while recording frequently. Every new album hit the Top Ten, as did nearly every single, such that McCartney and Wings ranked tenth among the Top 20 album artists of the decade and second among the Top 20 singles artists, according to *Billboard* statistics. McCartney finally began to cool off in sales terms after the #1 album *Tug of War* in 1982, but artistically he continued to challenge himself, writing his own motion picture, *Give My Regards to Broad Street* (1984), and entering into a writing collaboration with Elvis Costello that resulted in hits for both of them. –WR

McCartney / CAPITOL 1970
McCartney's handmade solo debut has a rough-hewn, off-hand quality that invites the listener into his highly melodic,

sometimes whimsical musical imagination. The best songs include "That Would Be Something" (lately revived by the Grateful Dead!), "Teddy Boy" (a Beatles outtake), and "Maybe I'm Amazed" (later a hit in a live 1977 version). –WR

Ram / CAPITOL 1971
While lacking the polish of his later efforts, McCartney's second post-Beatles effort is brimming with melodies and intriguing ideas. Ultimately, it seems unfinished, but along the way one is treated to the delights of "Uncle Albert/Admiral Halsey" (a #1 hit), "Heart of the Country," and "Back Seat of My Car." –WR

☆ **Band on the Run / CAPITOL** 1973
On his best post-Beatles album, McCartney uses his mastery of studio technique and gift for musical juxtaposition — from symphonic touches to hard rock to melodic acoustic music — in a wonderful collection of well-constructed songs, including the Top Ten hits "Helen Wheels," "Band on the Run," and "Jet." –WR

Venus & Mars / CAPITOL 1974
A highly polished band album featuring the #1 hit "Listen to What the Man Said," as well as "Letting Go" and "Venus and Mars/Rock Show," which served to introduce the McCartney & Wings world tour of 1975-1976. –WR

★ **Wings Greatest / CAPITOL** 1978
Most of McCartney & Wings's biggest hits, 1971-1978, among them the singles "Another Day," "Live and Let Die," "Junior's Farm," "Hi, Hi, Hi," and "Mull of Kintyre," which had not previously appeared on an album. –WR

Back to the Egg / CAPITOL 1979
A smart, hard-rocking set that never got the credit due it. –DH

McCartney II / CAPITOL 1980
Returning to an all-solo format, McCartney comes up with his best new studio album since *Band on the Run*, though ironically the album's hit is a live band version of "Coming Up," tossed in as a bonus. –WR

○ **Tug of War / CAPITOL** 1982
McCartney turns to Beatles producer George Martin for a carefully constructed blockbuster album that features the #1 duet with Stevie Wonder, "Ebony and Ivory," and the Top Ten hit "Take It Away," plus McCartney's tribute to John Lennon, "Here Today." –WR

All the Best / CAPITOL 1987
Unfortunately, this second greatest-hits collection repeats many of the tracks from the first. But it does add the singles "C Moon" and "Goodnight Tonight" (previously unavailable on an album) and some of the bigger 80s hits, such as "Say Say Say" and "No More Lonely Nights." –WR

Flowers in Dirt / CAPITOL 1989
A well-constructed comeback album on which McCartney collaborates with Elvis Costello for the Top 30 hit "My Brave Face," recalls his father on "Put It There," rocks out on "Figure of Eight," and turns in one of those lovely McCartney ballads on "This One." –WR

○ **Unplugged (The Official Bootleg) / CAPITOL** 1991
A delightful acoustic performance in which McCartney resurrects some Beatles classics, some oldies, and some of his less well known solo songs in a live setting. –WR

COUNTRY JOE MCDONALD   b 1942

Singer/songwriter, folk/rock. This politically oriented folk-rock singer/songwriter from Berkeley, CA, led the band Country Joe and the Fish and has since worked as a solo. –WR

Thinking of Woody Guthrie / VANGUARD 1969
McDonald proves to be an adept Guthrie interpreter on his debut solo album, recorded with the cream of Nashville session men. –WR

The First Three EPs / DECAL 1987
The first recordings by Country Joe and the Fish (1965-1966) and his early solo material (1971). Includes "I-Feel-Like-I'm-Fixin'-to-Die Rag," "Superbird," and "Tricky Dicky." –WR

Classics / FANTASY 1989
A compilation of McDonald's generally less political work of the second half of the 70s. –WR

○ **The Vanguard Years (1969-1975) / VANGUARD** 1990
McDonald worked with Vanguard on this 18-track solo career overview, which effectively demonstrates the range of his singing and writing talent. –WR

Superstitious Blues / RYKODISC 1991
This excellent comeback album finds McDonald in acoustic mode, accompanied by Jerry Garcia for some strong picking on a thoughtful collection of songs. –WR

MCDONALD & GILES

Art-rock. After Ian McDonald and Michael Giles dropped out of King Crimson at the end of the band's first US tour in 1969, they formed a short-lived duo that featured eccentric, oddly relaxed art-rock with a lot of heart. If ever this genre was capable of producing charming music, this is it. McDonald subsequently went on to Foreigner, whence he made his fortune. –BE & RC

○ **McDonald & Giles / ATLANTIC** 1971
This self-titled one-off (a Japanese import) by three expatriates of King Crimson is one of the great lost albums for fans of the art-rock genre. The whimsical themes and wonderfully creative musical interplay between the Giles brothers (Mike and Peter) and Ian McDonald keep this album from being bogged down in some of the ponderous elements of that style. Steve Winwood also guests on organ. "Suite in C," with its playful cut-and-paste motifs, and the extended concept piece "Birdman" are standouts. –RC

MICHAEL MCDONALD b 1952

Rock/pop. There was a time during the early 80s when Michael McDonald's earnest soulful upper baritone seemed to appear on half the hits coming out of the West Coast, including ones by Christopher Cross, Nicolette Larson, Kenny Loggins, Toto, Donna Summer, Steely Dan, and hit duets with James Ingram and Patti LaBelle. McDonald's vocal presence was most felt as lead singer for the Doobie Brothers between 1975 and 1982 on hits like "What a Fool Believes" (#1) and "Taking It to the Streets" (#8). –RC

○ **If That's What It Takes / WARNER** 1982
Sweet, romantic blue-eyed soul, containing "I Gotta Try" (#44) and "I Keep Forgettin' (Every Time You're Near)" (#4). –BC

ROGER MCGUINN b 1942

Folk/rock, rock & roll. Before he helped found the influential mid-60s group the Byrds, McGuinn (born Jim McGuinn) had been active as a sideman for Bobby Darin and folk artists like the Limeliters, the Chad Mitchell Trio, and Judy Collins.
With the Byrds, McGuinn forged the distinctively bright 12-string Rickenbacker electric sound, which has inspired groups too numerous to name.
His solo work hasn't risen to the level of his best work with the Byrds, but highlights include his self-titled debut, *Cardiff Rose,* and his 1991 comeback effort, *Back from Rio.* –RC

Back from Rio / ARISTA 1991
This comeback effort put McGuinn together with Tom Petty & the Heartbreakers, former Byrds Chris Hillman and David Crosby, and other guest artists eager to pay tribute, like Michael Penn and Timothy B. Schmit. "King of the Hill" was a substantial FM rock hit. Other highlights include Elvis Costello's "You Bowed Down" and a fine version of Jules Shear's "If We Never Meet Again." The mainstream AOR production values make McGuinn sound like he's guesting on a Tom Petty record — which is not a bad thing, just an observation. –RC

○ **Born to Rock & Roll / COLUMBIA** 1992
A well-chosen overview of McGuinn's post-Byrds solo work,
including "American Girl," "I'm So Restless," "Lover of the Bayou," "My New Woman," and "Peace on You." –RC

MALCOLM MCLAREN b 1946

Dance, alternative pop. He's been an artist, a clothing designer, a boutique owner, a personal manager (the New York Dolls, the Sex Pistols), a producer (Adam and the Ants, Bow Wow Wow), a songwriter, and finally a recording artist himself. –WR

Duck Rock / ISLAND 1983
An amazingly eclectic collection of world music mixed with urban hip-hop, featuring the dance hit "Buffalo Gals." –WR

○ **Fans / POLYGRAM** 1984
Selections from *Madame Butterfly* and *Carmen* recast as dance music — a wildly imaginative musical mixture, sometimes hauntingly beautiful. –WR

Waltz Darling / CBS 1989
More stunning musical juxtapositions — *The Blue Danube* with bass playing by Bootsy Collins and a guitar solo by Jeff Beck, and more. –WR

DON MCLEAN b 1945

Singer/songwriter. A singer/songwriter of a fiercely independent character, McLean dominated radio and record sales for weeks in 1971-1972 with his epic-length Buddy Hollyesque hit "American Pie." –BE

○ **American Pie / CAPITOL** 1971
The album that made McLean famous. The title track is the only real rocker, but the rest is intelligently produced and at times quite haunting, if a little angst ridden. –BE

Greatest Hits Then & Now / CAPITOL 1987
An acceptable collection, with few surprises. –BE

● **The Very Best of Don McLean ... / EMI** 1992
The Very Best of Don McLean, Favorites & Rarities. Fans of Don McLean should be thrilled with this comprehensive digitally remastered 42-track, double-disc set covering his hits, like "American Pie," "Castles in the Air," "Vincent," and "Everyday." There are also 18 previously unreleased tracks. Also included is an excellent set of liner notes, track annotations, and numerous photos from McLean's collection. –RC

JAMES MCMURTRY

Singer/songwriter. With a voice as dry as a summer in his native Texas, singer/songwriter James McMurtry (son of famous author Larry McMurtry) is a first-rate storyteller, drawing from classic folk traditions and left-of-center poetic metaphors that rarely sound overreaching. –RC

○ **Too Long in the Wasteland / COLUMBIA** 1989
On this impressive debut, McMurtry delivers a finely rendered series of musical snapshots that, at times, does for the drifters, dreamers, and losers of small-town America what Lou Reed did for the Big Apple — the Heartland as a wasteland. The characters that populate "Angeline" and "Terry" are portrayed with dignity, in a way that makes the listener care about what is being said. McMurtry's offhand vocal delivery is as dry as a Texas drought. This is one of the finest major-label singer/songwriter releases in years. –RC

CLYDE MCPHATTER 1932-1972

R&B. Along with Ray Charles and Sam Cooke, Clyde McPhatter was one of the most influential and important vocalists to emerge in the 50s. His unusually high, muscular vocals brought gospel fervor and sexual passion to the early-50s hits of Billy Ward's Dominoes, with whom McPhatter cut the showstopping "Have Mercy Baby" and "The Bells." Ahmet Ertegun signed him to Atlantic in 1953, after McPhatter and Ward parted company, and assembled the Drifters around his gorgeous soprano. His solo career began in 1955, while he was serving in the Army; "Treasure of Love," "Without Love," and "A Lover's Question" were his best solo hits. He had some minor success with Mercury in the 60s but died in obscurity in 1972. —JF

☆ **Deep Sea Ball ... / ATLANTIC**   1991
Deep Sea Ball - Best of Clyde McPhatter. This 19-track compilation contains all of the top hits that McPhatter scored between 1956 and 1959. He also charted singles on MGM and Mercury, but the bulk of his best-remembered work is here, including "A Lover's Question" and "Treasure of Love." —WR

MEAT LOAF   b 1946

Rock/pop. A rock singer (real name: Marvin Lee Aday) with a full, dramatic voice; also an actor who shot to fame with the multi-platinum album *Bat Out of Hell* in 1977. —WR

○ **Bat Out of Hell / CBS**   1977
Meat Loaf's powerful, passionate voice serves as the messenger for Jim Steinman's over-the-top rock songs, which treat teenage angst in practically Wagnerian terms, while Todd Rundgren provides a clean, well-articulated Wall of Sound production in this kitsch masterpiece, which includes "Two Out of Three Ain't Bad" and "Paradise by the Dashboard Light." —WR

MEAT PUPPETS

Hardcore. One of the weirdest groups from the 80s, and one of the more challenging, this Tempe, AZ, trio has confounded audiences and alternative standard-bearers by honing a singular style based on a genre (hardcore) that thrives on conformity. Their 1981 debut single was standard loud/fast punk, but by their second album the Pups became confident enough to flaunt their influences and their ambitions; traces of Captain Beefheart, Neil Young, ZZ Top, and Blue Öyster Cult seeped through the din of Curt Kirkwood's whining vocals and inventive guitar figures. Their sound has since become more streamlined, but they remain a unique and often-brilliant group, one of the best the 80s produced. —JF

Meat Puppets 2 / SST   1983
Sounds like country, reads like post-punk. —RG

○ **Up on the Sun / SST**   1985
Mellow. If they'd stayed in the heat any longer they'd have melted. —RG

● **Huevos / SST**   1987
Punk ZZ Top wannabees. —RG

Mirage / SST   1987
A bit forced but generally a mellow aura with driving rhythms. —RG

Forbidden Places / LONDON   1991
Less contemplative lyrically. A tighter fusion of their disparate musical sides. —RG

MEGADETH

Thrash. Megadeth formed in 1983 after Dave Mustaine left Metallica and moved to Los Angeles, where he met bassist Dave Ellefson. With guitarist Chris Poland and Gar Samuelson, they landed a contract with Combat Records, releasing their debut album in 1985. They became the first thrash band signed to Capitol Records. The next two albums on that label did extremely well, putting them among the top thrash bands with Metallica, Slayer, and Anthrax. Their music was very tight and the lyrics showed depth and intelligence. As far as Megadeth's impact on the world of heavy metal, they've lasted through many personnel changes and substance-abuse problems, while many other metal bands have since come and gone. —JB

○ **Killing Is My Business ... / RELATIVITY**   1985
Killing Is My Business ... And Business Is Good! is the album that started it all for ex-Metallica guitarist Dave Mustaine and his new band. This is a lot rawer than *Peace Sells ... But Who's Buying?*. —JB

★ **Peace Sells ... But Who's Buying? / CAPITOL**   1986
From the politics of war to the politics of the environment,

Megadeth covered them all on an album that brought them from cult status to the eyes and ears of the mainstream. *Peace Sells ... But Who's Buying?* is considered to be one of the best thrash albums of the 80s. —JB

Countdown to Extinction / CAPITOL   1992
Countdown to Extinction is proof that good ol' thrash can still survive in the 90s. Strongly written songs, wonderfully executed playing from the entire band, and believable lyrics ranging from suicide ("Skin O' My Teeth") to the destruction of civilization as we know it ("Ashes in Your Mouth"). Arguably the band's best since their *Peace Sells... But Who's Buying?*. —JB

THE MEKONS

Punk, alternative rock. This critically acclaimed band, led by Jon Langford and Tom Greenhaigh, was founded in Leeds as a punk outfit in 1977 and later metamorphosed into a countryish unit by the mid 80s. Now they're more mainstream, but still highly eclectic. —WR

○ **Fear & Whiskey / SIN**   1985
Country and folk played in an irreverent rock style like that later adopted by the Pogues, but even looser. (Import) —WR

New York / RELATIVITY   1987
An unusually tight version of the band (courtesy of drummer Steven Goulding, formerly of the Rumour) in live performances recorded in 1986 and 1987. Low fidelity, high energy. —WR

Mekons Rock 'n' Roll / A&M-TWINTONE   1989
The Mekons make like an alternative rock band. They're not, but they do make a lot of noise and have a lot of fun on this typically shambling impersonation. —WR

MELANIE

Folk/rock, singer/songwriter. Melanie is a folksinger who hit the charts after going electric with some sophisticated pop, rock, and gospel sounds. A product of the Woodstock-era counterculture, she was little more than a flower child with a raspy voice and uninteresting acoustic guitar sound, but she did some interesting covers of the Rolling Stones and Phil Ochs, as well as some intelligent originals. In 1972 her album *Gather Me* gave her a major hit with the suggestive "Brand New Key," and a good followup with the inspirational "Ring the Living Bell." Her later material matured rapidly into sophisticated and stylized pop music. —BE

○ **Best of Melanie / RHINO**   1990
A trip back to hippiedom at its most sincere and precious. It includes the #1 hit, "Brand New Key." —BE

JOHN COUGAR MELLENCAMP   b 1951

Rock & roll. Indiana native John Mellencamp is the American small-town boy who made good, selling millions of records while wresting artistic control from the record label and, all along, never disowning his Heartland roots. Unlike Springsteen, who has been lionized as a practically flawless all-American rocker for most of his career, Mellencamp seems utterly human, bullheaded, idealistic and preachy, indulgent, and very capable of sticking his foot in his mouth.
In 1971 Mellencamp formed a glam-rock band called Trash. It basically went nowhere but his admiration for David Bowie's music led him to the artist's manager, Tony DeFries of MainMan Mgmt. DeFries landed Mellencamp a deal at MCA. When the album *Chestnut Street Incident* was released, Mellencamp discovered his last name had been changed to Cougar, courtesy of DeFries. That event is the beginning of a series of humiliating record-biz miscalculations that (not unlike Tom Petty) caused Mellencamp to cut an image as a regular guy out to beat the system.
In 1982 Mellencamp (as John Cougar) scored the rock equivalent of winning a state lottery by selling five million copies of *American Fool* (#1), which produced two huge hits, "Jack and Diane" (#4) and "Hurts So Good" (#1).

Like anyone from the underbelly of the American middle class who wins big, Mellencamp underwent a running battle, trying to figure out how to stay sane while hanging onto the jackpot and trying to figure out why the gnawing vacuum deep inside him wouldn't go away.
Ever since then, Mellencamp's albums have been public airings of the American Dream come true, undergoing an initiation through the Book of Lamentations. (In 1983 he added Mellencamp back to his name. In 1991 Mellencamp dispensed with the Cougar moniker all together.)
Mellencamp's sound, while firmly rooted in rock, became increasingly earthy and acoustic until 1991's *Whenever We Wanted*, which was musically a return to a harder-edged sound. –RC

American Fool / RIVA / BB 1   1982
One of the biggest albums in 1982, *American Fool* established Mellencamp (then known as John Cougar) as a major star. His fatalistic ode, "Jack and Diane," and the radio rock sleezfest "Hurts So Good" were major hits. Even though Mellencamp was occasionally a clumsy lyricist, his small-town punk image, believable intentions, and rhythm guitar-heavy rock were embraced by millions throughout the American Heartland. –RC

Uh-Huh / RIVA / BB 9   1983
After the mega-platinum *American Fool*, Mellencamp roughened up his sound and began adopting a more topical stance with hits like "The Authority Song," "Pink Houses," and the Stones-ish-sounding "Crumblin' Down." –RC

○ **Scarecrow / RIVA / BB 2**   1985
Recorded at his home studio in Indiana, *Scarecrow* reflected Mellencamp's concern over the plight of the American farmer. The title track is one of the most fully realized statements of purpose in his artistic career. However, there are times when Mellencamp bludgeons the listener with heavy-handed polemics that lack focus. On the plus side, *Scarecrow* was loaded with great rock-radio singles like "Lonely Ol' Night," "R.O.C.K. in the U.S.A.," "Rumbleseat," and "Small Town." The raw noisy production did a good job of enhancing the sparks in Mellencamp's excellent band. –RC

★ **Lonesome Jubilee / MERCURY / BB 6**   1987
Here Mellencamp infused his Heartland rock with a strong dose of acoustic and country instrumentation in the form of fiddle, accordian, hammer dulcimer, dobro, banjo, and pedal steel. Thematically, he attempted to flesh out the big statements that predominated his previous album *Scarecrow*. In spite of the fact that Mellencamp's admonitions (with almost Biblical undertones) are delivered with the proselytizing earnestness of the recently converted, *Jubilee*'s spirited performances and memorable melodies make this one of his best efforts. Highlights include "Check It Out," "Paper in Fire," "Rooty Toot Toot," and "Cherry Bomb." –RC

Big Daddy / POLYGRAM / BB 7   1989
Mellencamp went deeper into acoustic-dominated rock with *Big Daddy*, an album where his focus was fine-tuned through smaller, personalized settings and stories. As a result, *Big Daddy* contained some of Mellencamp's best material, with tracks like "Jackie Brown," "Mansions in Heaven," "Void in My Heart," and "Sometimes a Great Notion." *Big Daddy* is his most subdued album (except for such tracks as his remake of the Hombres's "Let It Out (Let It All Hang Out)," "Martha Say," and his #15 hit whinefest "Pop Singer"). This was Mellencamp's first self-produced effort. The sounds are great but sometimes his vocals are buried way too deeply into the mix ("Mansions in Heaven") to be clearly intelligible. –RC

○ **Whenever We Wanted / POLYGRAM**   1991
Two years after Mellencamp released *Big Daddy*, he returned (sans the name Cougar) with electric guitars blaring away on material that represented the thematic extremes of his career. On "Get a Leg Up," (obviously concocted for radio airplay), Mellencamp resorted to his snotty *American Fool* personna, while on tracks like "Now More Than Ever," "Love and Happiness," and the title track he mined the concerns of his

more recent work. "I Ain't Ever Satisfied" (not the Steve Earle song) pretty much summed up Mellencamp's mortality-aware desire to have it every way. All in all, this is a very strong album, and a must for fans of Mellencamp's brand of forthright Heartland rock. –RC

MELLO-KINGS

Doo-wop. Although White, the Mello-Kings from New York had no trouble sounding like an R&B group on their only national hit for Herald Records in 1957, "Tonite, Tonite." Bob Scholl took lead honors on the ballad, written by Billy Myles. Although they recorded for Herald into 1961, the Mello-Kings never repeated their initial success. –BD

○ **Tonite Tonite / RELIC**
Some Mello memories. –MH

HAROLD MELVIN & THE BLUE NOTES

R&B, soul, doo-wop. Starting out in 1954 in Philadelphia as a doo-wop group with Harold Melvin as lead singer, the Blue Notes first recorded for the New York-based Josie label two years later. They debuted on the R&B charts in 1960 on the Val-ue label with "My Hero." A 1965 release, "Get Out," with a lead vocal by John Atkins, also charted R&B Top 40 on Landa. But it was not until 1972, when drummer Teddy Pendergrass took over lead vocal chores and the group came under the wing of Kenny Gamble and Leon Huff and their Philadelphia International label, that Harold Melvin and the Blue Notes became consistent chart-makers.
Pendergrass's vocals smoldered with sensuality. Combined with the smooth group harmonies that had always been a Blue Note trademark, Gamble and Huff's superior writing, and lush productions, the superb TSOP house band records, such as "I Miss You," "If You Don't Know Me by Now," and "The Love I Lost" were staples on both Black and White radio from 1972 to 1975. Pendergrass went solo in 1975 and the Blue Notes' glory days came to an end. Recording subsequently for a number of labels (including ABC, Source, MCA, and Philly World), Harold Melvin and the Blue Notes hit the R&B charts another ten times, often with lead vocals by Sharon Paige. Three of those 45s permeated the Top 20, one of which (1977's "Reaching for the World") reached as high as #6. The latter was the only one of the Blue Notes' post-Pendergrass recordings to break the Pop Hot 100. –RB

○ **To Be True / PHILADELPHIA INT.**   1975
The best of their original albums, containing many hits and no filler. Out of print; not on CD. –JF

★ **Collector's Item / CBS**   1976
Rounds up such hits as "Wake Up Everybody," "Bad Luck," "If You Don't Know Me by Now," and "The Love I Lost," all benchmarks of an era. –JF

MEMBERS

Punk, ska-revival. Rock & roll is loaded with one-shot bands that supernova, and the Members are such an entity. Punks with a fondness for speedy pop and reggae-style backbeats, they released only one fine record and a bunch of mediocre ones. –JD

○ **At the 1980 Chelsea Night Club / BLUE PLATE**   1991
The only Members album worth owning, *Chelsea Nightclub* plays into the band's strengths and is loaded with their strongest songwriting (e.g., "Stand Up and Spit," "Off-Shore Banking Business"). –JD

MEN AT WORK

Rock/pop. The Australian band Men at Work might still be a sensation relegated to the down under if it weren't for MTV's constant airing of their humorously oddball videos in America's heartland and FM radio's awareness that it was in dire need of some fresh faces. Men at Work's bar-band, Police-like pop-rock did have its share of hooks, particularly the sax line on their #1 international debut hit "Who Can It Be Now?"

Their next single, "Down Under," went #1 as well. Both of those tracks came off of *Business as Usual*, which held the #1 spot for 15 weeks in 1982.
Their followup, *Cargo*, peaked at #3 and produced two more big hits with "Overkill" (#3) and the topical "It's a Mistake" (#6). A two-year layoff effectively killed the band's momentum, and their third album, *Two Hearts*, only reached #50. —RC

○ **Business As Usual / CBS** 1982
Their smash debut contains "Who Can It Be Now" and "Down Under." —DH

MERCYFUL FATE

Heavy metal. During the early 80s, Mercyful Fate was one of the first to seriously touch upon themes of evil. —JB

○ **Melissa / CAROLINE** 1983
A heavy Black Sabbath influence lingers on this album, some of the music even sounding like early Dokken. The vocal range King Diamond has (and the way he uses it) is still astonishing and has yet to be matched. —JB

● **Don't Break the Oath / RDR** 1984
The feeling of being doomed still lingers with every listen of this very influential black-metal band from Denmark. This is vocalist King Diamond's tour de force. —JB

The Beginning / RDR 1987
A compilation of the band's earlier material not found on their two albums. —JB

METALLICA

Heavy metal. Out of a love of British heavy metal and hard rock from the early 70s, guitarist James Hetfield and drummer Lars Ulrich formed Metallica in late 1981 with guitarist Lloyd Grant. For a long time there was no bass player, but when Grant left and was replaced by guitarist David Mustaine, bassist Ron McGovney also joined the group. In 1982, Mustaine, Hetfield, and Ulrich moved to San Francisco to work with bassist Cliff Burton. Sometimes playing his bass like a guitar, Burton's style was unique.
As time went on, they replaced Mustaine with Kirk Hammet (of Exodus), and went to New York to record their debut album in late 1983. Successful tours across the US helped Metallica get their name and music to the masses, and in 1984 they recorded a second album. Just as that album was selling well, Metallica signed with Elektra, and the album was re-pressed on that label. Music magazines started calling this band someone to look out for.
In early 1986, Metallica released *Master of Puppets*, their best album to date. Soon they were the next big thing and having the time of their lives. Unfortunately, on a tour in Sweden, their tour bus slid off the road and bassist Cliff Burton was killed. Metallica found bassist Jason Newsted, who left his band in Arizona to join them. This lineup has held to this day, and they have become one of the biggest bands in heavy metal — period. Their influence on thrash-metal bands around the world is too huge to ignore. —JB

○ **Kill 'Em All / ELEKTRA** 1983
The origins of modern thrash-metal are here. One can hear traces of Judas Priest, the Scorpions, and Motörhead on some of the songs. The Elektra reissue also features two non-LP tracks from a European 12-inch single not found on the original album. —JB

Ride the Lightning / ELEKTRA 1984
Concise, direct, and to the point. Originally released by the independent Megaforce label, this led to their being signed by Elektra. —JB

☆ **Master of the Puppets / ELEKTRA** 1986
The album that put thrash-metal into the spotlight and into the mainstream. Flawless. This is one of the best albums of the 80s — period. Also the last album to feature bassist Cliff Burton. —JB

And Justice for All / ELEKTRA 1988
The most sophisticated album in their career. This is also the first full-length release to feature ex-Flotsam & Jetsam bassist Jason Newsted. The thin sound quality stops this from being a masterpiece. —JB

★ **Metallica / ELEKTRA** 1991
Longtime fans may call this one a sellout but that's hardly the case. Instead, the group has increased the bottom end of their sound and keeps the riff-per-song limit down to about two. This may keep *Metallica* from alienating staunch metal-haters, but it's the quality of the songs — hits such as "Enter Sandman" and the ballad "Nothing Else Matters," but also "Holier Than Thou" — that has made this their most successful (and best) album to date. —JF

THE METERS

R&B, funk. The top instrumental band in New Orleans during the late 60s and much of the 70s, both on their own and as a session crew (formed in 1966). Keyboardist Art Neville, guitarist Leo Nocentelli, bassist George Porter Jr, and drummer Zigaboo Modeliste played on numerous sessions for producer Allen Toussaint before they climbed the R&B charts themselves in 1969 with "Sophisticated Cissy" and "Cissy Strut" on the Josie label. They remained with Josie into the early 70s, issuing more funky hit instrumentals such as "Look-Ka Py Py" and "Chicken Strut" before spending the mid 70s with the major labels Reprise and Warner. The quartet went their separate ways in 1977 but sometimes re-form for the New Orleans Jazz & Heritage Festival. —BD

○ **Look-Ka Py Py / ROUNDER** 1969
Brilliant small-combo R&B with a great mix of New Orleans second-line beat, funk, and R&B inflections. —RW

Good Old Funky Music / ROUNDER 1979
Unissued material from the Meters's Josie heyday in the late 60s and early 70s. Some good moments but there's too much filler. —BD

GEORGE MICHAEL   b 1963

Pop, dance-pop. Yorgos Kyriatou Panayioutou (George Michael) achieved fame in the duo Wham! in his native UK in 1982. Through 1986, he and his partner, Andrew Ridgeley, scored hit after hit in a variety of styles from rap to uptempo pop to slow ballads. As songwriter and lead singer, Michael gradually overshadowed the group, and by the time they split, he was ready for a massively successful solo career. This began with the 1987 album *Faith*, which featured a series of chart-topping hit singles and sold more than seven million copies. That Michael had not achieved a similar critical success was evident from the title of his followup album, *Listen without Prejudice - Vol. 1*, which, though it sold a million copies, included two Top Ten hits, and hit #2, must be considered a major commercial disappointment. With *Vol. 2* apparently shelved, Michael contributed several songs to the charity album *Red Hot + Dance* in 1992, and one of them, "Too Funky," was streaking up the charts as we went to press. —WR

○ **Faith / CBS** 1987
George Michael certainly looked like the biggest pop star to emerge in the second half of the 80s when he released this debut album after his years in Wham! It wasn't just that the record topped the charts for 12 weeks and sold seven million copies and that six of its nine tracks were Top Ten hits (four #1s, a #2, and a #5); it was that Michael, who wrote, arranged, and produced, seemed to have a broad understanding of all aspects of pop, from the rockabilly of the title track and the heartfelt ballad "Father Figure" to the R&B dance grooves of "I Want Your Sex" (indeed, the album also got to #2 on the Black charts.) —WR

Listen without Prejudice - Vol. 1 / CBS 1990
Michael's followup to the massive success of *Faith* found him turning inward, trying to gain critical acclaim as well as sales.

Listen without Prejudice is not an entirely successful effort; Michael has cut back on the effortless hooks and melodies that crammed not only *Faith* but also his singles with Wham!, and his socially concious lyrics tend to be heavy-handed. Yet the highlights — the light, Beatlesque harmonies of "Heal the Pain," the plodding #1 "Praying for Time," "Waiting for That Day," and the Top Ten "Freedom 90" — make a case for his talents as a pop craftsman. –STE

MIDNIGHT OIL

Alternative rock. An Australian quintet formed in 1978 and led by singer Peter Garrett. Other members: Peter Gifford, bass (replaced by Bones Hillman in 1987); Martin Rotsey, guitar; James Moginie, guitar and keyboards; and Rob Hirst, drums. The group came up playing for the surf crowd in Sydney bars but always had a serious, political side. Its first three albums, *Midnight Oil* (1978), *Head Injuries* (1979), and *Place without a Postcard* (1981), were released only in Australia. (They appeared in the US in 1990.) Midnight Oil's first two US releases, *10,9,8,7,6,5,4,3,2,1* (1983) and *Red Sails in the Sunset* (1985) had only modest sales, but *Diesel and Dust* (1988) was a major hit, selling a million copies and featuring the Top 20 hit "Beds Are Burning." *Blue Sky Mining* went gold in 1990, and Midnight Oil released an album of concert recordings dating from 1982 to 1990, *Scream in Blue Live*, in 1992. –WR

○ **10,9,8,7,6,5,4,3,2,1 / CBS** 1983
Midnight Oil's first album to have full-scale production, this album effectively brings out the band's driving rock sound, Peter Garrett's impassioned vocals, and the band's forthright political standpoint. They've recorded better-*sounding* records but have never sounded better. –WR & JD

● **Diesel & Dust / CBS** 1988
On a thematic album about the plight of Aborigines in Australia, this is Midnight Oil's most focused and compelling music. Its single most impressive song, "The Dead Heart," works powerfully, both as agit-pop and as moving rock music. Also included is the anthemic hit single "Beds Are Burning." –WR

Blue Sky Mining / CBS 1990
Very close to *Diesel & Dust* — only with less aggression. It's still a solid record. –JD

STEVE MILLER

Rock/pop, psychedelic, blues/rock. For my money, the best of the hippie-era San Francisco bands. Maybe that's because the Steve Miller Band actually hailed from Texas, and Miller and early blues vocalist Boz Scaggs were blues fanatics who dabbled in psychedelic song structures and not vice versa. In the 70s Miller turned his tight blues machine into one of the decade's greatest and most consistent hit machines. His recent stuff, however, has been sloppy and desultory, save one fine return to the blues. –JF

○ **Children of the Future / CAPITOL / BB 134** 1968
Recorded in England with producer Glyn Johns (the Who, the Faces), this debut effort presented Miller as someone who was not only immersed in the blues but also fascinated with sound effects and sequencing, not unlike the Moody Blues or Pink Floyd. As a whole, this album flows nicely. Among the album's many highlights are "Baby's Callin' Me Home" (written by Boz Scaggs), "Stepping Stone," "Roll with It," "Junior Saw It Happen," and the spacey Mellotron-heavy ballad "In My First Mind." –RC

○ **Sailor / CAPITOL / BB 24** 1968
Less than six months after *Children of the Future*, Miller's solid followup proved that he wasn't a flash in the pan. Like its predecessor, *Sailor* dabbled in neat segues and effects, but to a lesser degree. Miller shines on the gently acoustic "Quicksilver Girl" and haunting "Dear Mary." *Sailor* has a couple of great rockers with "Living in the U.S.A." (Miller's first hit at #94) and "Dime a Dance Romance," penned by soon-to-be-departing member Boz Scaggs. –RC

○ **Brave New World / CAPITOL / BB 22** 1969
From the anthemic opening title cut, accelerating through to the crash-and-burn closer, "My Dark Hour" (a #126 hit featuring Paul McCartney ghosting on drums, bass, and vocals under the pseudonym of Paul Ramon), *Brave New World* is a tour de force. Other standout tracks include Miller's atmospheric "Seasons," "Kow Kow," and "Space Cowboy," an FM rock classic. –RC

○ **Your Saving Grace / CAPITOL / BB 38** 1969
This effort is a little more subdued than *Brave New World*, with cuts like "Baby's House" and "Feel So Glad." However, Miller does lay down an authoritative groove on "Don't Let Nobody Turn You Around," while "Little Girl" features some excellent, tasty lead guitar work. Miller also included a spacey reworking of "Motherless Children." Lonnie Turner's daft "Last Wombat in Mecca" is the album's only low point. Considering this was the fourth album Miller released in two years, the weakness is hardly worth mentioning. –RC

○ **Number Five / CAPITOL / BB 23** 1970
For this effort Miller went to Nashville, among other places, and recorded a wide range of material that covered everything from waxing poetic about eating hot chili to railing at the industrial military complex. In spite of this album's uneven material, it possesses many strong tunes, including "Going to Mexico," "Good Morning," and "Going to the Country" (a #69 hit). It also includes "Steve Miller's Midnight Tango," which charted at #117. –RC

Recall the Beginning ... / CAPITOL / BB 19 1972
After the miserable album *Rock Love*, Miller rebounded somewhat with *Recall the Beginning - A Journey from Eden*. One side is largely throwaway stuff, but the other half features a string of dreamy compositions that culminates with the haunting "Journey from Eden." "Love's Riddle," another track from that grouping, is also fine. –RC

★ **Anthology / CAPITOL / BB 56** 1972
This is a smartly assembled best-of collection that provides a good introduction to Miller's work up to this point. Those interested in digging deeper than this should check out *Brave New World*, *Sailor*, *Children of the Future*, and *Your Saving Grace*, in that order. –RC

The Joker / CAPITOL / BB 2 1973
While not so strong as some of his earlier work, *The Joker's* title cut (built off of a simple guitar riff) was Miller's first hit #1 single. "Sugar Babe" and "Something to Believe In" were also highlights. Nevertheless, Miller's focus on basic catchy material laid the groundwork for his incredibly successful late-70s albums. –RC

○ **Fly like an Eagle / CAPITOL / BB 3** 1976
In his effort to create the ultimate playable album, Miller reincorporated his interest in spacey sound effects and neat segues and synthesized them with a batch of tightly crafted light pop/rock tunes. The result generated a load of seamless hits like "Take the Money and Run," "Rock & Me," and the title track. –RC

○ **Book of Dreams / CAPITOL / BB 2** 1977
Recorded at the same time as *Fly like an Eagle*, this album repeated the same formula, with the same big results. Hits included "Jet Airliner" (a slight reworking of an old R&B tune by Paul Pena), "Jungle Love," and "Swingtown." –RC

★ **Greatest Hits 1974-1978 / CAPITOL / BB 18** 1978
This collection remains, to this day, Miller's most consistent-selling catalog item. It includes all of the hit singles and important album tracks from his biggest albums. –RC

Living in the 20th Century / CAPITOL / BB 66 1986
Miller does a half-assed return to his blues roots with this outing, which was dedicated to Jimmy Reed. Among the more promising numbers was "Nobody But You Baby," but heavily processed rhythm tracks marred what might have been a strong album. –RC

Born 2B Blue / CAPITOL / BB 18 1988
After a string of incredibly spotty albums, Miller quits noodling around with synthesizers and gimmicky effects and knuckles down with a smooth collection of jazz standards. Utilizing the formidable talents of vibe player Milt Jackson, Phil Woods (alto sax), and Ben Sidran (keys and coproduction), Miller creates an album that is playful and sophisticated. While his guitar playing is downplayed, Miller shines on "Just a Little Bit," "God Bless the Child," and the swinging "Red Top." –RC

MINISTRY

Hardcore, alternative rock. From their early days as one of the innovators of industrial music to becoming a major force in alternative music, Ministry continues to cross metal, synthesizers, and heavy dance rhythms to create a music that can only be compared to an air battle gone bad, all held together by Al Jourgensen. –JB

Everyday Is Halloween / WAX TRAX
More technical music and industrial metal from Ministry, when they were still considered a bit "danceable." The album has influenced many industrial bands of today. –JB

Twelve Inch Singles (1981-1984) / WAX TRAX 1987
All of their best-known songs from their independent-label days. Early techno-industrial music from the early 80s. –JB

● **The Land of Rape and Honey / WARNER** 1988
Considered to be one of Ministry's best albums, this is the one that crossed them over from the industrial/alternative scene and into the heavy metal crowds. Very heavy and enjoyable from start to finish. –JB

○ **In Case You Didn't Feel... / WARNER** 1990
A live album recorded during their most recent tour, *In Case You Didn't Feel Like Showing Up (Live)* demonstrates that a band that used a lot of technological wizardry in the studio is fully capable of playing its music on stage. Also available as a home video on Warner/Reprise. –JB

MINUTEMEN

Punk, alternative rock. At their best, the Minutemen made eclecticism seem as effortless as breathing: in songs that seldom lasted more than a minute (hence their name), this San Pedro, CA, trio touched on everything from jazz and funk to anarchist punk, bohemian beat poetry, and 70s dinosaur rock. Their songs (mostly written by either vocalist and guitarist D. Boon or bassist and vocalist Mike Watt) seethed with political outrage; their wry sense of humor (often pointed at themselves) separated them from the dead-serious punk brats on the West Coast, as did the diversity of their music. Their career was cut short in 1985 when Boon died in a car crash. Watt and MM drummer George Hurley formed fIREHOSE in 1986. –JF

● **Double Nickels on the Dime / SST** 1984
A double-disc set that remains their finest moment. It was here that the music, activism, and band chemistry coalesced in a forceful document of rage during the Reagan era. Boon's guitar sputters, clanks, and cajoles, while Watt and Hurley explode in rhythmic splendor. –JD

○ **3-Way Tie (For Last) / SST** 1985
Their last album shows maturing political involvement and a refinement of musical skills, melding their punk roots with folk's expressionism. –RG

Project: Mersh / SST 1985
The title stands for "commercial," meaning cool horns and some Mike Watt vocals. –RG

THE MISFITS

Hardcore. This influential early hardcore group took the Damned's infatuation with horrific themes and became one of the genre's legendary groups. Frontman Glenn Danzig

formed Samhain (and later, the group Danzig) following the 1983 breakup of the Misfits. –JF

Evilive / PLAN 9 1984
Live gore with laughs. –JD

○ **Walk among Us / WARNER** 1988
Steeped in sophomoric gore, with relentless guitars and Danzig's growl. –JD

● **The Misfits / PLAN 9** 1988
A great compilation, which is lean and mean and thankfully tosses out a lot of Glenn Danzig's goofball schlock-violence drooling. As a band, the Misfits simply rampage through these 20 tracks, outtakes, and assorted stuff. The most Misfits for the dollar. –JD

MISSING PERSONS

Rock/pop. Los Angeles-based quintet, 1980-1986, featuring former members of Frank Zappa's band, including drummer Terry Bozzio, Warren Cuccurillo, Patrick O'Hearn, Chuck Wild, and lead singer Dale Bozzio. –WR

○ **Best of Missing Persons / CAPITOL** 1987
The two main qualities of this band, heard on this compilation taken from their three albums and one EP, are the untutored singing of Dale Bozzio and the technical facility of the musicians, expressed in the inventive guitar and keyboard arrangements. High-quality 80s rock. –WR

MISSION OF BURMA

Punk. This Boston group pioneered the indie-rock ethic in the early 80s, during their brief stint with the Ace of Hearts label. Their music combined avant-garde experimentation with post-punk dynamics, creating a roaring din of wailing guitars and tribal percussion. A major influence on many mid-80s bands, including R.E.M. –JF

Signals, Calls, and Marches / ACE OF HEARTS 1981
"That's When I Reach for My Revolver" is a must-hear punk anthem. –RG

Vs. / ACE OF HEARTS 1982
Assaulting and musically sound. A great American punk album. –RG

○ **Mission of Burma / RYKODISC** 1987
The essential collection of Burma's artful punk rock on one disc. Revised for greater clarity, this thing burns from start to finish, with Roger Miller wielding his guitar like a lethal weapon. –JD

MR. BUNGLE

Alternative rock. A side project for Faith No More's lead singer Mike Patton, with his previous group. –RC

○ **Mr. Bungle / WARNER** 1991
Mike Patton, incognito as Vlad Drac, dishing out a relentlessly disturbing sonic collage that reeks of decay of all sorts. Ideal for those who like their music complicated-sounding but find Frank Zappa too upbeat. –RC

MR. FIDDLER

Funk. A funk combo formed in 1990 by former P-Funkers Joseph and Thomas Fiddler. –JF

○ **With Respect / ELEKTRA** 1990
Awesome debut by brothers Joseph and Thomas Fiddler, one-time members of Funkadelic, who outstrip Father George with a bodacious collection of witty, shoulder-rolling funk. –JF

MR. MISTER

Rock/pop. This Los Angeles-based pop/rock quartet came out of nowhere in 1985 with a #1 sophomore release, *Welcome to the Real World*, which produced three huge hits in "Broken Wings" (#1), the anthemic "Kyrie" (#1), and "Is It Love" (#8). –RC

○ **Welcome to the Real World / RCA** 1985
Here are the major pop hits "Broken Wings," "Kyrie," and

"Is It Love" from this band of session musicians and songwriters. –KMC

JONI MITCHELL   b 1943

Singer/songwriter. One of the most important artists to emerge from the singer/songwriter era of the early 70s. Mitchell first gained notice as a songwriter when her "Both Sides Now" was recorded in a hit version by Judy Collins in 1968. That same year, Mitchell released her debut album, *Joni Mitchell.* It was followed by *Clouds* in 1969 and *Ladies of the Canyon* in 1970, the latter containing the much-covered songs "Big Yellow Taxi" and "Woodstock." *Blue,* her 1971 album, was her first to hit the Top 20 and has now sold over a million copies. *For the Roses* in 1972 was Mitchell's first gold album and included her first Top 40 hit, "You Turn Me On, I'm a Radio."

Mitchell's 1974 album, *Court and Spark,* was a commercial breakthrough, hitting #2, producing two hit singles, selling a million copies, and being nominated for several Grammys. She followed it with a live album, *Miles of Aisles,* that duplicated its success. From the mid 70s on, Mitchell's work became more complicated and less folk/pop-oriented. *Hejira,* for example, paired her acoustic guitar with the bass improvisations of Jaco Pastorious, and *Don Juan's Reckless Daughter* contained impressionistic sidelong songs. Her most experimental album was *Mingus* (1979), which found her setting lyrics to the last tunes written by jazz composer Charles Mingus, at his request. The live *Shadows and Light* (1980), recorded with jazz guitarist Pat Metheny, also leaned in this direction.

Since 1982, Mitchell has adopted a slightly more accessible approach in a series of albums that take into consideration contemporary pop sounds. They have gained critical respect and sold moderately well. –WR

Joni Mitchell / WARNER   1968
David Crosby produced this debut album, on which Mitchell sings in a formal, restrained style and writes in a wordy, poetic style, which is nevertheless touching on such songs as "I Had a King" and "Michael from Mountains." –WR

Clouds / WARNER   1969
Contains Mitchell's version of "Both Sides Now," as well as the exuberant "Chelsea Morning" and such vulnerable love songs as "I Don't Know Where I Stand." Grammy Award-winner for best folk performance. –WR

Ladies of the Canyon / REPRISE   1970
Contains several Mitchell standards, including "For Free," "Big Yellow Taxi," "Woodstock," and "The Circle Game." –WR

★ **Blue / REPRISE**   1971
An extraordinarily revealing study in romance and dependency that begins with the girlish infatuation of "All I Want" and ends with the downcast but determined "The Last Time I Saw Richard." The spare music is dominated by Mitchell's newly expressive singing and her guitar and dulcimer work. –WR

For the Roses / ASYLUM   1972
Mitchell rails against the music industry and defends the position of the artist in isolation, at the same time moving toward more of a pop sound, notably on the Top 25 hit "You Turn Me On, I'm a Radio." –WR

☆ **Court and Spark / ASYLUM**   1974
Mitchell's commercial peak came with this polished collection, which features the backup of a clutch of jazz-oriented session aces. "Help Me" was a Top Ten hit, and "Free Man in Paris" reached #22. –WR

Hejira / ASYLUM   1976
Spare recordings prominently featuring the bass of Jaco Pastorius. Mitchell sings of life on the road, literally and figuratively. –WR

Mingus / ASYLUM   1979
Mitchell sets lyrics to Charles Mingus's last melodies in collaboration with the composer and a Who's Who of prominent jazz musicians. –WR

MOBY GRAPE

Folk/rock, psychedelic, country rock. There was no shortage of rock & roll in San Francisco in the late 60s. The Grateful Dead, the Jefferson Airplane, Big Brother and the Holding Company — the names go on and on. Moby Grape was, for a short while, one of the great ones. With a triple-guitar attack, the Grape presented taut, deftly arranged rock tunes, eschewing the jam-all-night approach of their contemporaries. They handled a ballad as well as a blistering rocker, and they weren't afraid to throw a country lick or a sweet harmony into the mix.

A combination of overhype and internal disarray killed the Grape after several years, and they never recaptured the brilliance of that debut. But 25 years later most of the original members were still working together, their brief discography regarded highly by a battery of loyal fans. –JT

○ **Moby Grape / SAN FRANCISCO SOUND**   1967
Some consider this 1967 debut to be the most impressive of the San Francisco rock revolution. Not a wasted moment, and the Grape do jam. –JT

Moby Grape '83 / SAN FRANCISCO SOUND   1985
The Grape go country-rock and pull it off. –JT

MODERN ENGLISH

Alternative pop. British punk quintet from Colchester formed in 1979 and featuring singer and guitarist Robbie Grey, guitarist Gary McDowell, bassist Mick Conroy, keyboard player Stephen Walker, and drummer Richard Brown. By 1990 personnel changes had left the group a trio of Grey and Conroy, with keyboardist, guitarist, and singer Aaron Davidson. –WR

○ **After the Snow / SIRE**   1983
Modern English had evolved into a synthesizer-driven power-pop band by the release of this second album, which features their signature hit, "I Melt with You." Ignore the 1990 remake on Tee Vee Toons. –WR

MOLLY HATCHET

Southern rock. These Jacksonville, FL, Southern boogie boys had the good fortune to emerge at the time of Lynyrd Skynyrd's untimely demise. The group lacked a songwriter as complex and intelligent as Ronnie Van Zandt, but songs like "Flirtin' with Disaster" made them AOR favorites during the late 70s/early 80s. –JF

○ **Greatest Hits / EPIC**   1985
Nice collection of their best-known tunes. Some of Southern rock's finest moments. –CK

MOMENTS

R&B, soul. 70s soul vocal group. One of the most consistent R&B aggregations of the 70s, the Moments enjoyed a string of major hits throughout the decade. The Hackensack, NJ, trio introduced themselves and the Stang label with "Not on the Outside" in 1968, and topped the R&B charts in 1970 with the gold-plated "Love on a Two-Way Street," produced by Sylvia Robinson (one half of Mickey and Sylvia). Other major soul smashes by the Moments included "If I Didn't Care" and "All I Have" in 1970, "Sexy Mama" in 1973, and another #1 R&B item, "Look at Me (I'm in Love)," in 1975. Members Harry Ray, Al Goodman, and William Brown changed their billing to Ray, Goodman & Brown in 1978 and topped the soul lists the next year with the slickly harmonized "Special Lady" on Polydor. The renamed trio remained potent soul hitmakers through the 80s. –BD

○ **Greatest Hits / CHESS**   1977
Collects "Love on a Two-Way Street," "Sexy Mama," and other worthy tracks. –DH

EDDIE MONEY   b 1949

Rock/pop. Since his 1977 self-titled debut, Eddie Money (born

Edward Mahoney) has enjoyed a long career as a purveyor of mainstream guitar-heavy pop/rock. His hits include "Baby, Hold On" (#11), "Two Tickets to Paradise" (#22), "Shakin'" (#63), "Take Me Home Tonight" (#4), "I Wanna Go Back" (#14), "Think I'm in Love" (#16), and "Walk on Water." –RC

○ **Greatest Hits - Sound of Money / CBS**   1989
Money's albums are often uneven combinations of solid tracks and filler. This collection has all the hits with none of the misses, including "Baby Hold On," "Two Tickets to Paradise," and "No Control." –DDC

THE MONKEES

Rock/pop. To nonmusical TV executives, aware that the pop market was exploding in 1965, the idea of auditioning cute actors to star in a show featuring a fabricated group called the Monkees (Davy Jones, Michael Nesmith, Peter Tork, and Mickey Dolenz) seemed like marketing genius. The public agreed, and the show was a huge success for several years. The Monkees could sing, and Mike Nesmith actually was a singer/songwriter, and guitarist. They also had access to the best material the professional songwriting world had to offer, covering songs by Neil Diamond, Goffin & King, Harry Nilsson, David Gates, Boyce & Hart, Mann & Weil, Leiber & Stoller, Paul Williams, and many more. As a result, the Monkees were a veritable pop-hit machine, charting with "Last Train to Clarksville" (#1), "I'm a Believer" (#1), "A Little Bit Me, a Little Bit You" (#2), "Daydream Believer" (#1), "Valerie" (#3), "Pleasant Valley Sunday" (#3), "I'm Not Your Stepping Stone" (#20), and many others. After the initial success, the Monkees lobbied for more artistic control and got it. The result, *Headquarters*, was #1 on the charts and the album went gold. Nevertheless, the high quality of material soon diminished and, with the demise of the show, the Monkees called it quits in 1971.
Michael Nesmith went solo and recorded some fine country-rock albums, scoring a hit with "Joanne" (#21). He also became very involved in video production, forming the Pacific Arts Corporation in 1977.
A well-orchestrated Monkees campaign returned the band and their show to new popularity in 1986, thanks in part to much MTV coverage. In August 1986, seven of their albums returned on the charts. Rhino Records released an extensive four-CD boxed set in 1991. –RC

The Monkees / ARISTA   1967
Their debut album, and every bit a winner. Prefab or not, there's some classic pop-rock here. –JT

More of the Monkees / ARISTA   1967
Album #2 contains some killer garage-rock among the fluffy novelties. Not the American Beatles, but a Top 40 gem anyway. –JT

Headquarters / ARISTA   1967
Their third album and the first to feature the band as a band playing their own instruments. Not so striking as the first two but a good Monkees album. –JT

Pisces, Aquarius ... / COLGEMS COM-104   1967
Much of the charm has worn off by the fourth album, *Pisces, Aquarius, Capricorn & Jones, Ltd.*, but in its place is some real experimentation. –JT

★ **Then & Now ... The Best of the Monkees / ARISTA**
The best of the single-CD collections, with 25 tracks, most of them true Monkees classics. –JT

○ **Listen to the Band / RHINO**   1991
A four-CD boxed set that includes every Monkees track a fan could want, and probably much more. Excessive, but a collector's dream. –JT

Live 1967 / RHINO
Still believe the Monkees didn't play their own music? This concert recording proves otherwise, and you know what? They played well! –JT

Missing Links / RHINO
A fine selection of rarities and oddities that every Monkee maniac with more than a passing interest should own. –JT

Missing Links 2 / RHINO
More outtakes and obscurities. Although it's not so interesting as the first volume, true fans shouldn't hesitate to pick it up. –JT

MICHAEL MONROE

Hard rock. As the vocalist for glam-revisionists Hanoi Rocks, Michael Monroe was a unique frontman: Instead of modeling himself after Robert Plant (as most hard-rock shouters do), he came off like a West Coast version of Johnny Thunders with the lung power of David Johansen. Their sleaze-and-decadence stance predated the attitude of Guns N' Roses by several years. –JF

○ **Not Fakin' It / MERCURY**   1989
An energetic hard-rock collaboration between Steve Van Zandt and this ex-Hanoi Rocks vocalist. Full of three-chord rebel rockers and a sharp grasp of leftist politics. –JF

CHRIS MONTEZ   b 1943

Rock/pop, rock & roll. One of the leading rockers in the Los Angeles Hispanic community after the tragic death of Ritchie Valens, Chris Montez later mellowed out under the tutelage of Herb Alpert and tallied several MOR-style hits. His first smash was on Monogram in 1962, "Let's Dance." It was a grinding rocker with roller-rink organ. Montez changed his attitude after signing with A&M. With Alpert producing, Montez adopted an easygoing approach on "Call Me," "The More I See You," and "Time after Time," all solid sellers in 1966. The formula quickly faded, however, and his final chart entry came the following year with "Because of You." –BD

○ **All-Time Greatest Hits / DCC**
Montez began as a Ritchie Valens-style rocker and reemerged as a crooner of pop ballads in the mid 60s. He excelled at both styles, each of which is amply documented here. –JT

MONTROSE

Heavy metal. After leaving the Edgar Winter Group in 1972, guitarist Ronnie Montrose decided to form his own band, so he called a young singer by the name of Sammy Hagar to join his new project. Hagar left in 1975 to do his own solo project, but the band continued with other singers and various lineups before splitting up in the early 80s. Ronnie Montrose now performs as a solo artist and does session work from time to time. –JB

○ **Montrose / WARNER**   1973
The first album that still rocks as hard as it did way back in 1973, featuring the vocals of Sammy Hagar. –JB

Paper Money / WARNER   1974
The second album from Montrose with Hagar as vocalist, just as good as their self-titled debut. Great collection of songs. –JB

Warner Brothers Presents ... Montrose / WARNER   1975
Some of the best guitar work Ronnie Montrose has ever done, with Bob James on vocals. Contains such songs as "Matriarch," "Black Train," "All I Need," and "Twenty Flight Rock." –JB

RONNIE MONTROSE

Heavy metal. Guitarist and vocalist who first backed Van Morrison and gained acclaim as a guitarist with Edgar Winter. Formed a self-named band in 1973 that included Sammy Hagar. –DS

Jump on It / WARNER   1976
Hard-rockin' album produced by Edgar Winter, which includes vocalist Bob James. –DS

○ **Speed of Sound / CAPITOL**   1988
Perfect showcase for guitar whiz Montrose, who wails against

an unlikely backdrop of ex-Mitch Ryder drummer Johnny Bee Badanjek and the sound of synthesizers. −DS

Mutatis Mutandis / CAPITOL   1991
Out of his many solo albums, *Mutatis Mutandis* remains one of his best efforts. −JB

MOODY BLUES

British Invasion, art-rock. Formed in Birmingham, England, as an R&B quintet in 1963, the Moody Blues originally consisted of Denny Laine (guitar), Mike Pinder (piano), Ray Thomas (harmonica), Graeme Edge (drums), and Clint Warwick (bass). The band emerged in 1965 with a soulful cover of an American R&B number called "Go Now," which topped the charts in both England and America. They toured with the Beatles and seemed poised for stardom, but none of their subsequent records made any impact. The quintet soon returned to playing the ballroom circuit, discovering at the same time that their management had filched much of their prior earnings. Amid these crises, Laine — who, after a furtive solo career and a tour with Ginger Baker, became Paul McCartney's lead guitarist in Wings — and Warwick were voted out of the group. In their places came Justin Hayward (guitar) and John Lodge (bass).
The Moody Blues 1966 records were heavily influenced by the Beatles, very upbeat, and unsuccessful. But in 1967 they were asked to record a stereo demonstration record with a major production budget, and came up with *Days of Future Passed*. Built around the concept of a day represented by rock songs, which were bridged by sweeping orchestral passages, this record yielded two major hits, "Tuesday Afternoon" and "Nights in White Satin," of which the latter became their signature tune. The Moodies established themselves as the pop mystics of the Summer of Love, their music blossoming on a series of impeccably produced albums in pseudo-classical glory, driven by Pinder's lush Mellotron orchestrations, Haywards and Lodge's multilayered guitars, Thomas's flute, and a great beat from Graeme Edge, when he wasn't reciting overblown poetry. Although many critics looked down on them, the band was very popular with college-age listeners and broadened the spectrum of rock sounds, thus paving the way for such art-rock outfits as King Crimson, Yes, and Emerson, Lake & Palmer.
In 1973, after seven albums, the Moodies decided to take a five-year hiatus devoted to solo projects. Pinder exited permanently following the 1978 comeback album, *Octave*, and was replaced by ex-Yes keyboard player Patrick Moraz. At this point, they became less interesting — Hayward could be relied on for passionate love songs, Lodge for driving but predictable rockers, and Thomas for his mysticism, which sounded woefully out of place in the 80s, but except for an occasional hit like 1986's nostagia-laden "In Your Wildest Dreams" (itself a look back at their own history), little of the new material stood out. The Moodies were reduced to the status of an arena oldies act. −BE

Magnificent Moodies / POLYGRAM   1966
The R&B version of the band. A little somber at times but with some major triumphs, including "Go Now" and the Barry-Greenwich number "I've Got a Dream," which is a pretty fair Four Tops imitation. −BE

○ **Days of Future Passed / POLYGRAM**   1968
An alternately overblown and superbly crafted piece of psychedelic mood music which established this band's new sound. (Also available as a Mobile Fidelity Ultradisc) −BE

○ **In Search of the Lost Chord / DERAM**   1968
An overtly mystical work, facing the mysterious East and laden with sound effects that seem sillier today than they did 25 years ago. But beneath those excesses are a handful of memorable tunes ("Ride My See Saw," "Legend of a Mind") and gorgeous arrangements ("Visions of Paradise"), which make this one of the most successful records ever issued by the band. −BE

○ **On the Threshold of a Dream / DERAM**   1969
Science-fiction elements dominate the theme of this concept album, all about intellect vs. emotion. The material lacks the simple melodic beauty of *Lost Chord*, but makes up for it somewhat with a production tour de force called "The Dream" and the surrounding "Have You Heard." −BE

○ **A Question of Balance / POLYGRAM**   1970
A return to form, and to mysticism, as the group plunges into a Lewis Carroll-like array of symbolic rock songs, all seemingly in search for some mystical meaning in life. All of it is a little pretentious but enjoyable, and "Tortoise and the Hare" became one of their best rock numbers on stage, while "Question" became something of an FM hit. −BE

○ **To Our Children's Children / THRESHOLD**   1970
A beautifully produced, somewhat languid theme album built around mystical concepts of time and the perception of its passage, *To Our Children's Children's Children* features the song "Gypsy," which became one of the group's most requested concert numbers (interestingly, it is said to have been inspired by the TV character Dr. Who), and the haunting and mysterious "Watching and Waiting." −BE

○ **Every Good Boy Deserves Favour / POLYGRAM**   1971
Probably the strongest single album of the group's history, with the Mellotron sound developed to its richest and most distinct, and guitarist Justin Hayward contributing one classic number ("The Story in Your Eye"). The overall attempt at profound statement here is balanced by a beautifully dense production and some very majestic tunes ("My Song," "Emily's Song," etc.). −BE

● **Seventh Sojourn / POLYGRAM**   1972
The group's hardest-rocking album of their post-R&B period, constructed around Graeme Edge and John Lodge's driving beat and generally a much leaner sound from Mike Pinder's Mellotron. At the time it was hailed as a breakthrough for the band, although it proved to be their last album for six years, and ultimately the most enduring material proved to be Lodge's "I'm Just a Singer in a Rock 'n' Roll Band" and Hayward's "New Horizons," two numbers completely opposite in terms of orientation, one a driving rock number and the other a romantic ballad. −BE

This Is the Moody Blues / POLYGRAM   1974
A double CD containing what purports to be the best of the group's material from 1967 through 1972 but really more a compendium of tracks that were popular on the radio. There are enough holes to make it worth overlooking for the serious listener. −BE

Caught Live + 5 / POLYGRAM   1977
An interesting if not completely successful live recording from a 1970 Royal Albert Hall concert, which leaves something to be desired sonically, and padded out with leftover songs from their unfinished 1970 album. Originally released to reintroduce the group after their five-year layoff, ahead of the release of the *Octave* album. (Out of print) −BE

Octave / POLYGRAM   1978
The band's comeback album, well written and well produced, with a strong selection of material and a leaner, more muscular sound than their earlier albums. This was their last completely effective record and marked Mike Pinder's exit from the band as well as the point where Hayward and Lodge pretty much took over the songwriting chores. −BE

VAN MORRISON   b 1945

R&B/rock, singer/songwriter. For years, the works of Leadbelly, Robert Johnson, Hank Williams, Howlin' Wolf, Jimmie Rodgers, and other legends of American folk-music forms have inspired subsequent generations of artists to capture the blues within themselves. Many artists may have the style or inflections down textbook perfect, but with an end result as insubstantial and hollow as the false-fronted buildings of a Hollywood movie set; no matter how much the outside had been dirtied up, investigation usually reveals that the place had truly never been lived in. Irishman Van Morrison is one of those truly gifted artists who goes way beyond the props. There seems to be an almost mystical connection between the soul of the blues and his voice and vision. As a result, Morrison's blues aren't limited to any one form of music; he takes in all that moves him.

While fronting the group Them in the mid 60s, Morrison's intense passion set him apart from the generally poppy British Invasion sound, with songs like "Mystic Eyes" (#33), "Here Comes the Night" (#24), and the classic "Gloria" (#93-1965/#71-1966).

Morrison went solo in 1967 and scored a #10 hit with "Brown Eyed Girl." In 1968 he signed with Warner Brothers and released the brilliant debut *Astral Weeks*, a synthesis of jazz and folk. Cut in 48 hours, it defied pop-radio airplay with its lengthy open-ended compositions. Morrison followed with a series of R&B-influenced albums, many of which are some of the greatest albums ever released in the rock era.

Much of Morrison's music has aged very gracefully, largely due to his commitment to artistic vision rather than fads or trends. Over the years, his work has mellowed with dignity, getting deeper into Christian mystical spirituality. –RC

☆ **Astral Weeks / WARNER**   1968
Recorded in a concentrated burst over a couple of days, *Astral Weeks* is one of the most uncompromising albums ever recorded by a major artist. Containing eight cuts that were more like impressionistic sound renderings than conventional melodic song structures, *Astral Weeks* treated the social outsiders that populated its grooves (the transvestite in "Madame George" or the dealer in "Slim Slow Rider") with dignity and compassion. Morrison's free-associative wail, over a sympathetic rhythm section that predominately drew from folk and jazz, made *Astral Weeks* an album that defied passive listening. His intonation might vary too much for some ears, but if you really *listen*, his soulful vocal flights will (as Dylan said concerning the function of art) practically stop time. Bassist Richard Davis's lyrical counterpoint and Modern Jazz Quartet drummer Connie Kay's sensitive rhythmic shadings are among this album's most stunning musical elements. Listing highlights is practically pointless, as *Astral Weeks* should be taken as a whole. –RC

☆ **Moondance / WARNER / BB 29**   1970
After *Astral Weeks*, Morrison switched gears for *Moondance*, a flawless collection of more accessible R&B-rooted material, which drew from easygoing swing ("These Dreams"), upbeat shuffles ("Come Running"), and gospel-influenced song structures like "Crazy Love," and "Caravan," the latter a celebration of radio that didn't pander to that medium's more self-congratulatory nature. The jazzy title cut is a classic, as is "Into the Mystic," a song that essentially encapsulated Morrison's artistic bent. *Moondance*'s tasteful production imbued the music with a timeless quality. –RC

His Band and the Street Choir / WARNER / BB 32   1970
A noticeable step down from the amazing *Moondance*, primarily in the sense that some of the material and performances lack Morrison's characteristic edge. Nevertheless, Morrison's immersion into R&B helped produce his highest-charting track, "Domino" (#9), as well as two lesser hits, "Blue Money" (#23) and "Call Me Up in Dreamland" (#95). –RC

Tupelo Honey / WARNER / BB 27   1971
The pastoral *Tupelo Honey* was another fine Morrison album, which ranged from the R&B rock of "Wild Night" (#28) to the folky gospel of the title cut, a heavenly love letter. –RC

☆ **Saint Dominic's Preview / WARNER / BB 15**   1972
Rarely has there ever been so joyous a rocker as "Jackie Wilson Said (I'm in Heaven When You Smile)" (#61), with its brilliantly arranged cascading horn lines. That's just one of many delights found here. From the inspirational title cut's tale of resolve to the primally prayerful "Listen to the Lion," *Saint Dominic's Preview* stands as one of Morrison's finest

albums. This is one of the few Warner reissues that actually was given a fine remastering for CD. –RC

☆ **It's Too Late to Stop Now / WARNER / BB 53**   1974
This dynamic double-disc set finds Morrison covering everything from his early work with Them, through *Astral Weeks*, to his early-70s Warner hits and album tracks. Morrison is in great vocal form, and the band, the Caledonia Soul Orchestra, is exceptionally hot. Any fan of Morrison's should own this one. –RC

Veedon Fleece / WARNER / BB 53   1974
His most willfully introspective album since *Astral Weeks*, *Veedon Fleece* (written in Ireland) is almost a classic, full of delicately rendered reflections and more open-ended vocal excursions. Morrison runs out of steam slightly during the second half of the proceedings, but not enough to keep this from being a pretty magical album. Highlights are "You Don't Pull No Punches but You Don't Push the River," "Fair Play," "Linden Arden Stole the Highlights," "Streets of Arklow," and "Comfort You." –RC

A Period of Transition / WARNER / BB 43   1977
On paper, the collaboration of Morrison with Dr. John looked awfully good. While *A Period of Transition* failed to live up to the potential, it did have some wonderful songs, like "Heavy Connection" and "It Fills You Up" (a particular favorite). The flat-sounding mixes tend to rob the sparks out of the music, making some of this album's more expressive moments sound forced. –RC

Wavelength / WARNER / BB 28   1978
The self-produced *Wavelength* marked an improvement over *A Period of Transition*, producing a near-hit (#42) with the title cut. Other highlights included "Santa Fe," cowritten with Jackie DeShannon. –RC

Into the Music / WARNER / BB 43   1979
Five years after Van's last great album (*Veedon Fleece*), he returned with one of his finest albums, *Into the Music*, which fused the earthly with the spiritual. Highlights included "Bright Side of the Road," "Full Force Gale," "Angelou," and a version of "It's All in the Game." Not the first place to go to discover Morrison, but a masterful album, nonetheless. –RC

Beautiful Vision / WARNER / BB 44   1982
Beautiful Vision improved upon its meandering predecessor, *Common One*, first by having some stronger melodies, and second by having a song as mystically upbeat as "Cleaning Windows." –RC

Poetic Champions Compose / POLYGRAM / BB 90   1987
The hypnotic string arpeggios and rolling rhythms of "The Mystery," the gentle exhortation of "Did Ye Get Healed," and even reverberant cocktail-jazz instrumentals like "Spanish Steps" help make the meditative *Poetic Champions Compose* one of Morrison's better albums during the late 80s. –RC

Live at Grand Opera House Belfast / POLYGRAM   1988
Not so fiery as *It's Too Late to Stop Now*, but an enjoyable set, featuring "It's All in the Game," "Cleaning Windows," and other tracks from this period. –RC

☆ **Avalon Sunset / POLYGRAM / BB 91**   1989
Avalon Sunset's evocative melodies and almost prayful sentiments make this one of Morrison's finest albums during the 80s. Some might find this album's rich orchestration a little too close to easy listening, but repeated listenings reveal it adds a quiet dignified elegance and atmospheric unity to the proceedings not unlike the strings on Marvin Gaye's trancendent *What's Going On*. "I'm Tired Joey Boy," "Orangefield," "Have I Told You Lately," "I'd Love to Write Another Love Song," and the supplicatory "When Will I Learn to Live in God" are among the many highlights. *Avalon Sunset* is the mature, timeless work of an artist beyond fashion. –RC

● **The Best of Van Morrison / POLYGRAM**   1990
This is a strong collection of many of Van Morrison's best songs. Of particular note is the inclusion of "Wonderful Remark," previously only available on *The King of Comedy* soundtrack. That alone makes this worth having. Many

of the key Them tracks are here ("Gloria," "Here Comes the Night"), as is Morrison's classic "Brown Eyed Girl." Even though it's a strong sampler, it fails to draw a complete-enough picture of the depth of his work. Sonically, this CD is quite impressive. –RC

Enlightenment / POLYGRAM / BB 62   1990
Morrison dispensed with the super-reflective spirit that dominated many of his albums from the 80s and returned to a more relaxed, almost playful effort with *Enlightenment*. "In the Days before Rock 'n' Roll" is a particular highlight. Not one of his best albums, but a nice change of pace. –RC

☆ **Bang Masters / CBS**   1991
Excellent sound and packaging of Morrison's work at Bert Bern's Bang label. The tracks range from the morose "T. B. Sheets," to his pop standard "Brown Eyed Girl." This is a must for fans who want to go deeper than just obtaining his obviously classic albums. –RC

MORRISSEY   ♭1959

Alternative pop. Steven Morrissey was the lead singer in the successful British post-punk band, the Smiths, from their formation in 1982 until they disbanded in 1987. He has since pursued an almost equally successful solo career. –WR

○ **Viva Hate / WARNER**   1988
Morrissey pairs with Stephen Street for an album very much in the mold of his Smiths work, i.e., melodic rock dominated by jangly guitar serving as a musical bed for the singer's idiosyncratic lyrical interests and unconcerned delivery on such songs as "Everyday Is like Sunday" and "Hairdresser on Fire." –WR

Kill Uncle / WARNER   1991
Clive Langer and Alan Winstanley provide a pop production dominated by keyboards for this typically catchy collection, with typically off-kilter songs like "(I'm) The End of the Family Line." –WR

STEVE MORSE BAND

Fusion. Guitarist and composer Steve Morse was the leader and main composer for his band the Dregs during the late 70s and early 80s. He went on to join the band Kansas for two albums in addition to leading his own group, the Steve Morse Band. –PK

○ **The Introduction / ELEKTRA**   1984
Solo debut album of instrumental fusion rock from the former guitarist with the Dregs/Dixie Dregs. *Introduction* features an excellent mix of styles and top-notch playing. Guitarist Albert Lee guests on this effort. Highlights include the hyperdrive "Cruise Missile," "General Lee," and the anthemic title track. –PK

Stand Up / ELEKTRA   1985
A rock/jazz/country blend and an excellent mix of instrumental and vocal material, with a cameo by guitarist Eric Johnson and guest vocalists. –PK

Southern Steel / MCA   1991
Uptempo, hard-hitting, instrumental rock virtuosity. Morse always delivers. –PK

THE MOTELS

New-wave, rock/pop. By the time the Motels scored with their 1982 hit album *All Four One* (#16), they had spent ten years in Los Angeles's alternative scene, going through enough lineup changes (particularly drummers) to make Spinal Tap proud. Fronted by the dramatic Martha Davis (b Jan 15, 1951), the Motels eventually succumbed to a West Coast mainstream rock sound, courtesy of producer Val Garay and a handful of session pros. The formula worked commercially, landing hits with "Only the Lonely" (#9), "Suddenly Last Summer" (#9), "Take the L (Out of Lover)" (#52), "Remember the Nights" (#36), and "Shame" (#21), before they ground to a halt in the mid 80s. –RC

○ **Best of the Motels - No Vacancy / CAPITOL**   1990

Features all of their mid-80s hits, like "Only the Lonely" and "Suddenly Last Summer." –LL

MOTHER LOVE BONE

Hard rock, heavy metal. This Seattle quintet formed after two celebrated groups (Green River and Malfunkshun) split up in early 1988. Their sound, consisting of hard rock, punk, and a slight sense of psychedelia, impressed many, and eventually Polygram signed them, a deal rumored to be the highest given for any Seattle band.
Mother Love Bone spent the latter half of 1989 recording their debut album, with plans for a wide tour, until lead singer Andrew Wood's drug use led to his early death at age twenty-four.
Mother Love Bone without Wood was unimaginable since he was the driving force behind it, so it was announced that the band would not continue. The album was released in late 1990 and sold well in spite of the fact there was no band to back it up. Eventually Gossard and Ament did a tribute album to Wood with Soundgarden vocalist Chris Cornell. –JB

Shine / POLYGRAM   1989
An EP that contributed to the buzz about the Seattle music scene. –JB

○ **Apple / POLYGRAM**   1990
The first and last album by a band that almost made it. Comparisons to Led Zeppelin, Deep Purple, and Marc Bolan can be made from the abundance of strong material and great vocals from Andrew Wood. This group could've reached the level that Nirvana gained in 1991. –JB

MÖTLEY CRÜE

Hard rock. Formed in Los Angeles in 1981, Mötley Crüe members Frank Ferrano (aka Nikki Sixx), Vincent Neil Wharton (Vince Neil), Thomas Lee Bass (Tommy Lee), and Robert A. Deal (Mick Mars) found each other through ads they ran in local music papers. The Crüe's image — lots of leather and makeup to give the music impact — was already set in this early stage. In 1982 the band signed with Elektra, and toured extensively throughout 1984. Musically they continued to get better and a year later they scored a nationwide hit with a remake of Brownsville Station's teen anthem "Smokin' in the Boys' Room." In 1991, after their eight years of hard work had payed off, they put together *Decade of Decadence*, a celebration of their first ten years. Mötley Crüe helped pave the way for many bands in the 80s, and the state of heavy metal would have been weaker without them. In 1992 Vince Neil was fired and the band vowed to continue without him. –JB

Too Fast for Love / ELEKTRA   1981
Sleazy heavy metal before all the hype took over their home of Los Angeles. Their debut album, remixed from the original on their own Leathur label. –JB

○ **Shout at the Devil / ELEKTRA**   1983
Possibly the best mainstream heavy metal band of the 80s, with their best album to date. –JB

● **Decade of Decadence / ELEKTRA**   1991
A collection of some of their hits and the best of their album material. –JB

MOTÖRHEAD

Punk, thrash, hard rock. English metal band formed in 1975. Led by bassist Ian "Lemmy" Kilminster, the band was originally named Bastard but soon changed to Motörhead (American slang for speed freak), a name that suited their style of playing very well. Along with guitarist Larry Wallis and drummer Lucas Fox, Lemmy and the boys brought the concept of the power trio to new heights, using the bass almost as a lead instrument behind a wall of noise emanating from the other two instruments. They attracted a huge following in England during the late-70s punk-rock era with their combination of breakneck speed and deafening volume.

Though Lemmy remains as the only original member (having revamped the lineup several times over), and their style hasn't progressed much in almost 20 years, their hardcore fans wouldn't have it any other way. –CK

○ **Ace of Spades / PROFILE**   1980
The forefathers of thrash, with one of their better-known albums. *Ace of Spades* features guitarist "Fast" Eddie Clark, who later left and formed Fastway. Highlights include "(We Are) The Road Crew" and the title track. –JB

○ **Orgasmatron / SINCLAIR**   1986
For *Orgasmatron*, Motörhead enlisted producer Bill Laswell, who assisted the band in achieving a dense wall of sound, which was a little too compressed sounding. Highlights on *Orgasmatron* are "Built for Speed," "Deaf Forever," and the title track, an incredible aural sludgefest that borders on psychedelic. –RC

● **No Remorse / ROADRACER**   1990
No Remorse is a solid collection (in spite of the omission of the band's Chiswick recordings), consisting of key album, EP, and single tracks. Included are Motörhead standards like "Killed By Death" and "Please Don't Touch." Unfortunately, this Roadracer reissue of the 1984 release omits "Leaving Here," and "Louie Louie." Overall, *No Remorse* is a great intro to the band's earlier thrash sound. –RC

○ **1916 / CBS**   1991
Produced by Pete Solley and Ed Stasium, *1916* is Motörhead's most diversified effort, including humorous sendups like "Ramones" (a tribute to the New York speed punkers) and "Angel City" (a love letter to Los Angeles), as well as grim topics, like the dying World War I soldier's perspective in the title track. Motörhead manages to cover all this territory without ever losing their basic sonic integrity. All in all, *1916* is arguably this band's finest release thus far. –RC

MOTT THE HOOPLE

Rock/pop, rock & roll. Originally a Herefordshire, England, band named Silence, Mott the Hoople was signed to Island in 1969 by A&R man Guy Stevens, who suggested that they change their name (inspired by a Willard Manus novel) and dump their lead singer, Stan Tippens, in their search for a stronger identity. Tippens was made road manager (he later worked for the Pretenders), and Ian Hunter (an engineering apprentice) was brought in to sing and play piano. Stevens, in turn, became the band's manager and producer. Between 1969 and 1972, Mott cut four albums, two of which contained some great rock & roll. Nevertheless, the band's future looked bleak, due to diminishing sales with each release. A happenstance pairing with ascending glam-rock star David Bowie caused a fortuitous turn of events, which culminated in a new record deal (Columbia) and sound. The result of their collaboration was the Bowie-produced *All The Young Dudes*, a blatant glam sendup. The title cut became Mott's first hit, and in the time one could say the words "image makeover," Mott was camping it up, teetering around the stage in makeup and cartoonish platform shoes. Their followup effort, *Mott*, was the band's finest artistic statement, loosely addressing the travails of rock "stardom." After that, Mott began to lose its focus, and the departure of lead singer/songwriter Ian Hunter hastened the band's demise. They eventually broke up in 1976. Hunter went on to enjoy a moderately successful cult following with his solo career. As a songwriter, he scored some substantial hits with artists like Great White ("Once Bitten Twice Shy") and Barry Manilow ("Ships"). –RC

● **Mott the Hoople / ATLANTIC / BB 185**   1969
Mott the Hoople, with its hard-rock variation of Dylan's *Blonde on Blonde* sound, stands as one of the band's better efforts. This debut sported some fine originals, particularly "Backsliding Fearlessly" and "Rock and Roll Queen," as well as some unusual (but hip) song covers, like Sonny Bono's "Laugh at Me" and Doug Sahm's "At the Crossroads." The Kinks's garage-riff standard "You Really Got Me" got a high-

octane instrumental treatment. Only on the middle section of the lengthy "Half Moon Bay," does *Mott the Hoople* lose momentum. The fidelity on this disc (and *Brain Capers*) rivals the sound of a good vinyl import version. –RC

● **Brain Capers / ATLANTIC**   1971
After a couple of fairly dismal efforts, Mott rebounded with one of the great lost hard-rock albums of the 70s. Released with practically no fanfare whatsoever, *Brain Capers* sank without a trace. Certainly, in the decade that produced Styx and Journey, *Brain Capers* (from the audaciously titled "Death May Be Your Santa Claus," to the closing "The Wheel of the Quivering Meat Conception") convincingly drew a line in the sand, revealing most everything called "rock" to be a fraud. Some of this was due, in part, to the return of Guy Stevens at the production helm. Among the album's highlights are versions of Dion's "Your Own Backyard," the Youngblood's "Darkness Darkness," and Ian Hunter's powerful "The Journey," "Sweet Angeline," and the previously mentioned "Death ...." –RC

All the Young Dudes / COLUMBIA / BB 89   1972
Just as Mott was about to pack it in due to their amazing lack of public acceptance, David Bowie entered the picture, and with the recording of a few cannily conceived songs, containing strong gay allusions (Bowie's "All the Young Dudes" and Mott's "Sucker" and "One of the Boys"), Mott went from potential has-beens to avatars of the glam-rock movement. The Bowie-produced album contained a version of Lou Reed's "Sweet Jane" and Mick Ralph's "Ready for Love," one of his finest bits of writing to date. As on many albums of that genre, the production sounds tight-assed, stiff, and dry. Nevertheless, Mott makes the proceedings rock fairly convincingly. –RC

○ **Mott / COLUMBIA / BB 35**   1973
Regarded by many to be their finest album, this self-produced effort was a loosely conceived concept album about the ups and downs of rock & roll success. *Mott* contained two UK hits with "All the Way from Memphis" and "Honaloochie Boogie." Other highlights were "The Ballad of Mott the Hoople," "Whizz Kid," "Violence," and "Drivin' Sister." The sound of this reissue is a little on the muddy side. Nevertheless, of their Columbia-period albums, this is the one to get. –RC

BOB MOULD   b c. 1

Alternative rock, hardcore. Guitarist, singer, songwriter, and former coleader of the acclaimed Minnesota punk-rock group Hüsker Dü, Mould released two solo albums (1989, 1990) and has now formed a new group, Sugar. –WR

○ **Workbook / ATLANTIC**   1989
Mould takes a less raucous, more coherent approach than on his Hüsker Dü work for this solo debut, which combines somewhat pessimistic lyrics with majestic guitar parts matched to a prominent cello. –WR

MOUNTAIN

Hard rock. Founded in 1969 by Cream producer, bassist, and vocalist Felix Pappalardi and 250-pound vocalist and lead guitarist Leslie West (from the Long Island group the Vagrants), Mountain specialized in bottom-heavy mid-tempo hard rock. The band was rounded out by organist Steve Knight and drummer Corky Laing's George-of-the-jungle-style pounding. West's distinctive sustain-drenched lead sound and economical phrasing made him one of the most emulated guitarists at the turn of the 70s.

During their brief existence, Mountain hit the charts with *Mountain Climbing* (#17) (which included the #21 hit "Mississippi Queen"), *Nantucket Sleighride* (#16), and *Flowers of Evil* (#35). –RC

Mountain Climbing / LEGACY / BB 17   1970
This includes the hit "Mississippi Queen." All in all, this is Mountain's strongest studio effort. –RC

○ **The Best of Mountain / COLUMBIA / BB 72**   1973

This collection contains most of the band's recorded highlights, except for the curious omissions of "Dreams of Milk and Honey" (off of the debut *Leslie West - Mountain*) and "Silver Paper" (off of *Mountain Climbing*). Included are "Mississippi Queen" (#21), "The Animal Trainer and the Toad" (#76), "For Yasgur's Farm" (#107), and their version of Jack Bruce's "Theme for an Imaginary Western." –RC

THE MOVE

Power-pop. A quintet of mod-poseurs from Birmingham, the Move wasted a lot of their time working on image and squandered some great music. Whether playing merry psychedelic odes ("Flowers in the Rain") or pumping their guitar amperage and attack to planet-cracking levels, they always had something worthwhile to say and play before they evolved into the Electric Light Orchestra. –BE

★ **Shazam / A&M** 1970
The single most accomplished album ever to be recorded by any of the 60s Birmingham rock bands, a mixture of expansive progressive rock worthy of the Beatles and high-energy music honed and developed by years of jamming on stage, not quite like any other sound of the era. "The Last Thing on My Mind," "Cherry Blossom Clinic Revisited," and the rest of the record all manages to sound like Byrds performances pumped up with about 1000 amps of electricity and laced with Beatlelike vocals. (Import) –BE

○ **Message from the Country / ONE WAY** 1971
A weak collection of original material, not very well recorded originally, which is highlighted by an even more strident imitation-Beatles approach. –BE

○ **Best of the Move / A&M** 1974
Not quite what it says it is (not enough from *Shazam* is included) but this anthology does include the weird ("Night of Fear") and trippy ("Flowers in the Rain") singles and odd album sides that helped establish the Move's reputation for eccentricity. –BE

ALISON MOYET b 1961

Alternative pop, dance-pop. A bluesy-voiced British singer who gained recognition in the synth-pop duo Yaz in the early 80s. She's had three solo albums since, all of which were big UK hits. –WR

○ **Alf / CBS** 1984
Moyet's debut attempted a gradual transition from the electronic-pop backgrounds of her Yaz work. She succeeded to the tune of three UK hits — "Love Resurrection," "All Cried Out," and "Invisible." –WR

MUDHONEY

Alternative rock. Noisemakers from Seattle with a penchant for 70s hard rock and post-punk thrash. Mark Arm's searing vocals provide the fuel for this guitar-driven rock. –JF&ME

Superfuzz Bigmuff (& Early Singles) / SUB POP 1988
A treasure chest of early singles. The Honeys at their most furious and fine. This EP keeps the overextended riffing and hyper-vocalizing down to a minimum, focusing on maximum-torque metallic garage raunch. A release that provides as much bite as bark. –JD&ME

○ **Mudhoney / SUB POP** 1989
This is a collection of catchy tunes sure to make your mother cringe. –ME

SHIRLEY MURDOCK

Soul. Roger Troutman (aka Roger) had Toledo gospel singer Murdock join his group, Zapp, after hearing her sing. In the late 80s, she struck out on her own and had a hit with "As We Lay." –ED

Let There Be Love! / ELEKTRA
She only needs promotion to be a superstar. –RW

○ **Shirley Murdock / ELEKTRA** 1986
A shocker in its time. Marvelous vocals. –RW

Woman's Point of View / ELEKTRA 1988
As good a soul shouter and confessional singer as anyone active today. –RW

ELLIOTT MURPHY b 1949

Folk/rock, alternative rock, singer/songwriter. A New York-based folk-rock singer/songwriter who emerged with the acclaimed *Aquashow* in 1973 and has since built a cult following in the US and Europe. –WR

○ **Aquashow / POLYGRAM** 1973
Highly literate songs played with an instrumentation (rock band, harmonica, piano, and organ) and in a manner strongly reminiscent of mid-60s Bob Dylan. The lyrics provide a telling portrait of suburban life. –WR

Just a Story from America / COLUMBIA 1977
Murphy travels to England for a streamlined rock sound featuring session aces such as guitarist Mick Taylor and drummer Phil Collins. But it's the songs, such as "Drive All Night," "Rock Ballad," and the title tune, that make the album a standout. –WR

Party Girls/Broken Poets / COURTISANE 1984
Backed by a seasoned three-piece band, Murphy again turns in a high-quality rocking collection, spearheaded by "Three Complete American Novels" and "Blues Responsibility." (Import) –WR

Milwaukee / EMIS 1986
Murphy adopts a more contemporary rock sound (with production on two tracks by Talking Head Jerry Harrison) for songs often touching on hard and desperate themes. –WR

PETER MURPHY

Alternative rock. Former Bauhaus singer carries on with Gothic synth-rock on solo albums. –ED

○ **Deep / RCA** 1990
Contains Murphy's dramatic alternative rock hit "Cuts You Up." Forceful grooves and thick (somewhat dissonant) arrangements and production propel material reminiscent of David Bowie's work with Brian Eno. –RC

MY BLOODY VALENTINE

Alternative rock. An Irish band that specializes in ultra-loud, grindingly simple pop, which sounds almost completely indebted to Sonic Youth and their ilk. After a protracted life as a critically acclaimed (and slightly overrated) independent-label mainstay, My Bloody Valentine broke out with their strongest release (oddly enough, their first on a major label), which played into their strengths as hyper-amped tunesmiths with a touch of the poet — that is, when you could understand the lyrics. –JD

○ **Loveless / WARNER** 1991
Forget the early stuff when their style was still metamorphosing — this is the big payoff. Grindingly assaultive, the big guitars of this monstrous, larger-than-life hunk of lush pop sink into you from Track 1. –JD

THE MYSTICS

Doo-wop. Doc Pomus and Mort Shuman wrote "Hushabye," this Brooklyn quintet's only big hit, for the Laurie label in 1959. With Phil Cracolici as lead, "Don't Take the Stars" barely charted later that year. The Mystics made an impressive comeback in 1981 with an album on Ambient Sound and a starring role in a doo-wop-drenched episode of PBS-TV's award-winning musical program "Soundstage." –BD

○ **16 Golden Classics / COLLECTABLES**
Late-50s/early-60s Italian-American doo-wop from the street corners of Brooklyn, NY. –BD

NAKED EYES

Dance-pop. This quintessential early-80s MTV synth-pop duo, made up of Pete Byrne (vocals) and Rob Fisher (keyboards), hit it big with "Promises, Promises" and a remake of Dionne Warwick's "Always Something There to Remind Me" (#8). −RC

○ **Best of Naked Eyes / CAPITOL**   1991
Everything you need by this duo, including the hits "Promises, Promises" and "Always Something There to Remind Me," as well as the key album tracks. The CD includes three bonus songs −LL

NAPALM DEATH

Hardcore. One of the most influential grindcore bands from England. −JB

○ **Harmony Corruption / RELATIVITY**   1990
The kings of grindcore. Disturbing lyrics and fast-paced music with no remorse. Essential. −JB

Death by Manipulation / RELATIVITY   1991
A compilation of three EPs from their home of England. −JB

GRAHAM NASH   b 1942

Singer/songwriter, country rock. One third of Crosby, Stills & Nash and cofounder of the Hollies, the Manchester-born Nash has long been famed for his high harmony singing and quirky songwriting. −BE

○ **Songs for Beginners / ATLANTIC**   1971
A moving, personal work, filled with lovely nuances and ideas and even lovelier melodies. −BE

JOHNNY NASH   b 1940

Rock/pop, reggae. Native-Texan Johnny Nash experienced his first chart success in 1958 with the #23 hit "A Very Special Love." By the end of the 60s, Nash had begun recording in Jamaica and formed his own record labels, Joda and Jad. He became one of the first artists to bring reggae into the pop mainstream, with the 1968 #5 hit "Hold Me Tight," 1972's #1 "I Can See Clearly Now," and a 1973 #12 version of Bob Marley's "Stir It Up." −RC

○ **I Can See Clearly Now / CBS**   1972
West Indian music for a pop audience, rhythmic and melodic. Nash helped open the mass-market doors to reggae. The title song and "Stir It Up" are winners. −HD

NATIONAL HEALTH

Prog-rock. National Health is one of those rare English progressive bands whose classic mid-70s output still sounds fresh today. Their sound prospered on imaginative linear musicality, often in a jazzy format that emphasized extended instrumental solos. In keeping with the collaborative spirit of the times, National Health had an ever-changing lineup, sharing members with other influential groups like Hatfield and the North, Henry Cow, Matching Mole, and others. −MB

○ **Complete / EAST SIDE DIGIT**   1990
A compilation of progressive rock efforts from this classic UK group. Their jazz sensibilities have kept their music fresh for 20 years. −MB

THE NAZZ

Power-pop, psychedelic. The Nazz (named after a Yardbirds song, "The Nazz Are Blue") was a Philadelphia-based quartet formed in 1967 by guitarist and songwriter Todd Rundgren, bassist Carson Van Osten, drummer Thom Mooney, and vocalist and keyboard player Robert "Stewkey" Antoni. Rejecting the free-form psychedelic rock and hippie fashions of the day, the group harked back a couple of years to the British Invasion, performing short, catchy pop songs, mostly written by Rundgren (sometimes with a hard-rock edge), and sporting suits and Beatle haircuts. They released their debut album, *Nazz*, in 1968 and scored a minor hit single with Rundgren's plaintive ballad "Hello, It's Me" in 1969 (it recharted in 1970, and Rundgren had a Top Five hit with a new version in 1973). Critics and a growing audience were charmed but the Nazz fell apart in 1969, largely because of

Rundgren's ascendancy. Predictably, he went on to the greatest success after the split. −WR

○ **Best of Nazz / RHINO**   1984
Contains good examples of the band's powerful uptempo material ("Open My Eyes"), the kind of Rundgren ballad material that defined the group to its pop audience ("Hello, It's Me"), and some interesting covers ("Kicks," a previously unreleased "Train Kept A-Rollin'"). −WR

NEGATIVLAND

Alternative rock. San Francisco Bay Area smart-guys who spend off-hours from their respectable 9-5 jobs creating sound sculptures and collages that include everything from sampled beats to TV news loops. Creative, difficult, and definitely not for those who think music should be solely about music. −JD

Escape from Noise / SST   1987
With superstar backup (including avant-gardist Fred Frith), Negativland completely destroys traditional pop by reinventing the form via spliced-together "found" sounds and in-studio hijinks. −JD

○ **Helter Stupid / SST**   1989
A galvanizing record that takes the piss out of media hysteria and the way assumptions are turned into "fact." As much a thesis on contemporary culture as anything else. −JD

BILL NELSON

Prog-rock. As the guiding light of Bebop Deluxe, the Yorkshire-born Nelson was a guitar hero who combined the passionate excess of Jimi Hendrix with a cold, calculated intellectualism. As a solo artist, he often forsakes the guitar entirely in favor of keyboards and splicing tape, crafting a body of work that ranges from thumping funk (of a cerebral sort) to synth-pop and ambient murmurs. −MPD

Das Kabinet/La Belle et Bete / CAPITOL   1981
Two excellent soundtrack projects on one CD. −MPD

○ **Love That Whirls ... / COCTEAU**   1981
Love That Whirls (Diary of a Thinking Heart) is infectious synthesizer-driven pop. −MPD

Quit Dreaming & Get On the Beam / CAPITOL   1981
One of Nelson's rockier efforts, similar to his work with Red Noise. −MPD

Summer of God's Piano / CAPITOL   1984
The first volume of *Trial by Intimacy*, a four-disc collection of short instrumental pieces. −MPD

Vistamix / CBS   1984
A ten-song compilation. −MPD

RICKY NELSON   1940-1985

Rock & roll. Ricky Nelson made it a little safer for "respectable" American teenagers to rock. When 16-year-old Ricky cut his debut single in 1957 — a timid cover of Fats Domino's "I'm Walkin'," allegedly on a dare from his girlfriend — the sneering image of Elvis Presley was still taboo in many households. Nelson, the nonthreatening, cleancut youth, commanded the perfect vehicle for spreading his rocking message — his family's beloved TV sitcom, "The Adventures of Ozzie and Harriet."

With a genuine passion for Sun-style rockabilly and the searing lead-guitar work of Joe Maphis initially and later the brilliantly inventive James Burton (from "Believe What You Say" on), Ricky signed with Imperial later that in 1957. He waxed one incendiary rocker after another, including "Stood Up," "Waitin' in School," and "It's Late." He introduced them via those TV airwaves, thus ensuring gold record status well into the 60s.

As the demand for unrelenting rock & roll slowly faded, Ricky's sound softened as well, with smoother material such as "Never Be Anyone Else But You" in 1959 and his 1961 chart-topper "Travelin' Man." A much-publicized name switch to Rick on his twenty-first birthday reflected that maturity.

But Nelson never forgot his roots, not even during the lean mid 60s on Decca, when he ran dry of fresh material and revived too many old Tin Pan Alley standards that should have stayed buried. Returning triumphantly to the top in 1972 with the introspective *Garden Party*, Rick Nelson proved emphatically that he was more than just another teen-idol hunk, right up to his fatal plane crash on New Year's Eve of 1985. Like his idols at Sun, this kid was born to rock — and showed America that it was no sin. –BD

Garden Party / MCA 1972
This comeback introduced Nelson to a new generation. –BD

★ **Legendary Masters Series / CAPITOL** 1990
Nelson at his early (1957-1960) best. His youthful vocals are backed by fiery rockabilly pioneers Joe Maphis and James Burton. –BD

☆ **Best of Rick Nelson - Vol. 2 / CAPITOL** 1991
This continues the showcase of Nelson's triumphant reign on Imperial through 1962. A fascinating smattering of unissued alternate takes is included amidst all the hits. –BD

MICHAEL NESMITH   b 1943

Country rock. You'll get very little argument that Michael Nesmith's songs are the highlights of the Monkees's catalog. If given a chance on his own, Nesmith might have beat Gram Parsons in a race to invent country-rock. When he ceased to be "Monkee Mike," Nesmith created rootsy country music, unaffected by the often cynical approach of numerous contemporaries.

Nesmith's stature as an outside producer grew, and he eventually shed much of the country influence of his writing before ultimately shelving his musical career entirely. What remains is a sizable body of solo work that too few have investigated. Now that it is readily available again, it would be well worth the effort to check out. –SA

Newer Stuff / RHINO 1989
This compilation of later solo material is often glossy and overreaching but still quite impressive. –JT

○ **The Older Stuff / RHINO** 1991
Post-Monkees country-oriented material is proof that at least one member of the "pre-fab four" possessed genuine musical talent. –JT

AARON NEVILLE

R&B, soul. Although Neville is often compared to singer Sam Cooke in terms of sheer vocal refinement, he has a voice and style uniquely his own. Today he is well known as part of the New Orleans sound of the Neville Brothers. Yet, aside from the 1967 #1 R&B hit "Tell It Like It Is," few have heard his incredible early solo recordings. Many of the first recordings of Aaron Neville, in the early and mid 60s, were arranged, produced, and often written by the brilliant Allen Toussaint — another talent only now being really appreciated. Most of these sides were cut for the Minit (and later) Parlo labels. Songs like "She Took You for a Ride" and "You Think You're So Smart" on Parlo are masterpieces. While his more recent work, including that with Linda Ronstadt, makes for pleasant listening, it lacks the sheer persuasion of his early songs. Aaron has re-recorded his early work often, and it is important to hear the originals. The early sides of Aaron Neville are just waiting to be heard. –JME

Like It 'Tis / MINIT
Excellent vinyl compilation of Neville's early-60s Allen Toussaint-produced Minit singles, including the amusingly macabre 1960 rocker "Over You." –BD

Show Me the Way / CHARLY 1989
Here are 22 of his early Minit recordings, many of them incredible. –JME

My Greatest Gift / ROUNDER 1990

Arranged and coproduced by Allen Toussaint. A funky mixed bag (dating from the late 60s to the mid 70s), which has some nice moments. –BD

○ **Tell It Like It Is / COLLECTABLES** 1991
Eleven of Neville's best Parlo cuts, including those mentioned above, on one CD. His biggest solo smash from 1966, plus more songs in the same style. Sublime stuff. –BD

Warm Your Heart / A&M 1991
This new set finds Neville's wavering vocals as elegant as ever on a ballad-oriented program. –BD

ART NEVILLE   b 1937

R&B, soul. New Orleans vocalist and keyboardist. As a founding member of the Meters and Neville Brothers, Neville helped immeasurably to shape the contemporary New Orleans funk sound. Neville's first band, the Hawketts, tasted local success in 1954 with the carnival perennial "Mardi Gras Mambo" on Chess. He cut some nice solo singles for Specialty during the late 50s, notably "Cha Dooky-Doo," as well as contributing two choruses of storming piano to Jerry Byrne's 1958 classic "Lights Out." "All These Things," a gentle ballad, also did well locally in 1962 on the Instant logo. He assembled the Meters in the mid 60s and the instrumental quartet proved the Crescent City's answer to the MG's until their 1977 breakup. That's when Art and his siblings formed the Neville Brothers, and today they reign as the leading musical export from New Orleans. –BD

○ **That Old Time Rock 'n' Roll / SPECIALTY**
Young Art in his late-50s New Orleans piano-rocking stage — terrific! –BD

THE NEVILLE BROTHERS

R&B, soul, funk. After more than two decades of performing together and alone, the Nevilles returned to their home turf, New Orleans, in 1977. The music they began making was grounded in that city's rhythms and folklore. Individually, the first Neville to get on record was Art, who joined the Hawketts and scored with "Mardi Gras Mambo" (1955) and on his own with "Cha Dooky-Doo" (1958). Then Aaron made his mark with "Over You" (1960) and the anthemic "Tell It Like It Is" (1966). The details of how Art, Aaron, Charles, and Cyril passed through the Meters, the Wild Tchoupitoulas, and other outfits to form their family band would defy a genealogist, and their less-than-successful debut on Capitol suggested that it was hardly worth the trouble. But then came *Fiyo on the Bayou* on A&M in 1981. Since then, the brother have gone from strength to strength, plundering their New Orleans heritage and combining it with an eclectic mix of material to produce music that is virtually without category. Exposure in the band has finally enabled Aaron Neville to gain recognition as one of the truly great, eccentric voices in Black music. *Rolling Stone* and then Linda Ronstadt offered their seals of approval, with the result that the brothers are now both funky and chic. –CE

○ **Fiyo on the Bayou / A&M** 1981
A brilliant updating of New Orleans R&B sound to include strains of Cajun, rock, and reggae on standards ranging from "Hey Pocky Way" to "The Ten Commandments of Love" and "Sitting in Limbo." –WR

★ **Treacherous ... / RHINO** 1986
Treacherous - A History of the Neville Brothers (1955-1985) traces the recorded careers of the four brothers' solo efforts, plus the Wild Tchoupitoulas and their more recent group work. Essential to a complete understanding of the Nevilles and New Orleans music in general. –WR

NEW EDITION

Urban R&B, dance-pop. This soul quintet, based on the Jackson 5 concept, featured Mike Bivins, Bobby Brown, Ralph Tresvant, Ronald Davoe, Johnny Gill, and Ricky Bell. They started out under the guidance of the starmaker Maurice Starr as a youthful group with high-pitched sugar ballads and innocent funk. They quickly emerged as a mature soul group and have done many solo projects. The group is currently on hiatus. –BC

Under the Blue Moon / MCA   1986
New Edition's terrific harmonies on a doo-wop album of 50s love ballads. –BC

Heart Break / MCA   1989
Jimmy Jam and Terry Lewis production that completed the group's transistion from boys to men. Johnny Gill replaced Brown at this time. Includes the hits "If It Isn't Love" and "Can You Stand the Rain." –BC

○ **Greatest Hits - Vol. 1 / MCA**   1991
A good collection of radio-ready hits, including their biggest single, "Cool It Now." –DH

NEW KIDS ON THE BLOCK

Dance-pop. Members Donnie Wahlberg, Danny Wood, Jon Knight, Jordan Knight, and Joe McIntyre were born between 1969 and 1973 in Boston. They were discovered by Maurice Starr in 1985 while performing as Orgi Nynik. They signed to Columbia in 1986, and became a sensation among the pre-teen crowd during the late 80s with their style of light blue-eyed soul/pop and dance-pop. –BC

○ **Hangin' Tough / CBS**   1989
Good songs collected by New Kids mastermind Maurice Starr highlight this smash, including "I'll Be Loving You (Forever)," "You Got It (The Right Stuff)," "Please Don't Go Girl," and the title track. Tight, warm, even soulful harmony on the ballads. –DH & BC

Step by Step / CBS   1990
In an attempt for some respect, the group wrote some cuts on *Step by Step*, a more serious, harder-sounding album. Although the title track was #1 for three weeks and the followup, "Tonight," went Top Ten, they couldn't replicate the success of *Hangin' Tough*. –BC

NEW ORDER

Techno-pop. A Manchester-based British rock band made up of Bernard Sumner (b Jan 4, 1956), guitar; Peter Hook (b Feb 13, 1956), bass; Stephen Morris (b Nov 28, 1957), drums; and Gillian Gilbert (b Jan 27, 1961), keyboards. The first three were members of Joy Division until the suicide of leader Ian Curtis. The group is currently on hiatus, with Sumner in the band Electronic, and Hook in Revenge. –WR

Power Corruption and Lies / WARNER   1983
Synthesized dance music at moderate tempos, plus calmly sung, distanced lyrics, makes for an entrancing effect. –WR

Low Life / WARNER   1985
New Order's messages are no less dire here, but the tempos are faster, the singing more engaged, and the melodies more distinct. In fact, "Love Vigilantes" is positively catchy. –WR

○ **Substance / WARNER**   1987
A collection of New Order singles — some of their best work — little of which had previously turned up on albums or in the US. –WR

THE NEW RIDERS OF THE PURPLE SAGE

Country rock. A country-rock group that spun off from the Grateful Dead in 1969, originally featuring John Dawson (b 1945), David Nelson, and Dead members Jerry Garcia (b Aug 1, 1942), Mickey Hart (b Sep 11, 1943), and Phil Lesh (b Mar 3, 1940). The band continues today, with Dawson the only original member left. –WR

New Riders of the Purple Sage / CBS   1971
An album for anyone who liked the sagebrush country-rock of the Grateful Dead's *Workingman's Dead* and *American Beauty* albums, dominated by John Dawson's songs and Jerry Garcia-like voice. –WR

○ **Best of the New Riders of the Purple Sage / CBS**   1976

A good selection from the group's Columbia catalog, featuring "Glendale Train," "Panama Red," and other favorites. –WR

THE NEW YORK DOLLS

Punk, rock & roll, hard rock. The New York Dolls were the bridge between the Rolling Stones, the MC5, and the Sex Pistols and the punk-rock movement of the late 70s. Their highly charged, reckless, guitar-heavy sound and lead singer David Johansen's fey stage antics, coupled with the group's inclination toward androgyny, made for a nice diversion in 1973, when their self-titled Todd Rundgren-produced debut came out. Unfortunately, the Dolls were too raw for most of the public, including those who claimed to love rock & roll. As a result, the band became more of a media event and critics' darlings.

The Shadow Morton-produced followup, *Too Much Too Soon*, proved that the Dolls were more than a one-shot wonder. It included a wonderful version of Archie Bell & the Drells's "There's Gonna Be a Showdown." The Dolls lost their deal with Mercury Records and were briefly managed by the outrageous Malcolm McLaren (who later handled the Sex Pistols). They eventually broke up in 1977. Of the five, Johansen has enjoyed the most success as a solo artist, later under the pseudonym Buster Poindexter. –RC

★ **The New York Dolls / POLYGRAM**   1973
Their debut suffers from Todd Rungren's murky production, but "Personality Crisis," "Pills," and "Frankenstein" manage to break through the clutter. –JF

☆ **Too Much Too Soon / MERCURY**   1974
Their second (and last) album mixes well-chosen soul/R&B covers with a slew of striking Johnny Thunders-David Johansen originals. Good enough to make their early demise even more regrettable. –JF

RANDY NEWMAN   b 1943

Singer/songwriter. Randy Newman, nephew of Lionel and Alfred Newman (Hollywood arrangers and heads of 20th Century Fox Pictures), was already steeped in a rich creative environment when he chose to pursue music as a career. Newman's first attempt as a solo artist was the 1961 Dot single "Golden Gridiron Boy," which was produced by Pat Boone. Even though the record went nowhere, Newman embarked on a successful songwriting career, with songs cut by the Fleetwoods, Jerry Butler, Cilla Black, Judy Collins, Manfred Mann, Nilsson, and Three Dog Night, among others.

Since 1968, when he released his self-titled Warner Bros. debut, Newman has employed a seductive blend of ragtime, rolling Fats Domino-style rock & roll, blues, and classic Hollywood cinema-style melodies (with a touch of Stephen Foster), which has been effective in luring the listener into the twisted mindsets of the characters that populate many of his songs. Since Newman often sang from the protagonist's point of view, he rarely wasted time moralizing his position. In 1978, Newman's tongue-in-cheek acerbity produced a hit with "Short People" (#2), off of *Little Criminals* (#9), but it also rankled many, who thought the single was mean-spirited. Even Newman's fans began to wonder about the literalness of his sentiment with the 1979 album *Born Again* (#41), which mercilessly skewered each of the protagonists represented. In 1982 Newman did the soundtrack for the movie *Ragtime*, beginning a successful career in film scoring. Newman has continued to sporadically release solo albums that are many cuts above the average release. –RC

☆ **12 Songs / WARNER**   1970
Randy Newman's droll humor and ability to render ludicrous settings (through the eyes of protagonists who were obviously not playing with full decks) made *12 Songs* an instant classic to the handful of people lucky enough to hear it. The bare-bones production, along with assistance from guitarist Ry Cooder, gave the record a homey immediacy. Highlights are hard to single out but "Mama Told Me Not to Come" (later a

hit for Three Dog Night), "Yellow Man," "Lucinda," and "Uncle Bob's Midnight Blues" are great. −RC

Randy Newman Live / REPRISE / BB 191 1971
This live set basically reprises much of his first two albums, without adding much to their interpretation. There are a few new tunes, the only standout being a song that Frank Sinatra passed on, called "Lonely at the Top." −RC

.☆**Sail Away / WARNER / BB 163** 1972
Sail Away was Newman's first synthesis of his satirical writing and his impressive orchestral arrangement skills. The result was one of his very best albums. The title cut was a brilliantly twisted take on slaves coming on a ship from Africa, set to a score that owed much to Stephen Foster. "Burn On," Newman's sentimental-sounding ode to the polluted Cuyahoga River (in Cleveland, OH), and his perverse "You Can Leave Your Hat On" (later popularized by Joe Cocker in the movie *9 1/2 Weeks*) are among the many great songs to be found on *Sail Away*. −RC

★ **Good Old Boys / WARNER / BB 36** 1974
On *Good Old Boys*, Newman increasingly focused his obsessions on the South, but his slant seemed to be rooted more in Steppin' Fetchit and Shirley Temple *Little Rebel* Hollywood films than in reality. As distorted as viewing things through that particular lens may be, the South in *Good Old Boys* is undeniably poignant. "Louisiana 1927" is an affecting account of a spring flood, while "Marie" (a love song from a drunk) is one of the most touching songs written in popular music. The grand, sweeping melodies and arrangements are quite simply beautiful. Newman's sloppy, soulful mumble and understated piano keep this effort from tumbling into drippy sentimentality. A great record. −RC

Little Criminals / WARNER / BB 9 1977
On *Little Criminals*, Newman's penchant for satirically illuminating the quirks in human nature earned him a million-selling #2 hit with "Short People," a song that dealt with the issue of bigotry. It also earned him the loathing of thousands of short people who failed to get the message. Aside from that controversy, *Little Criminals* was relatively tame by Newman standards. "Baltimore," "Sigmund Freud's Impersonation of Albert Einstein in America," and "Rider in the Rain" were among the standout tracks. −RC

Trouble in Paradise / WARNER / BB 64 1983
After the mean-spirited 1979 release *Born Again*, Newman regrouped and came out with *Trouble in Paradise*, an album that employed more lyrical subtlety and was more successful at skewering its terminally character-disordered targets ("Christmas in Capetown," "Song for the Dead," "My Life Is Good"). "The Blues," a dryly humorous duet with Paul Simon, was a moderate hit at #51. "I Love L.A." failed to chart, in spite of extensive exposure. Musically, Newman downplayed the timeless feel of his best work in favor of a trendier, clean West Coast-pop sound. As a result, this effort doesn't age so well. *Trouble in Paradise* may not be Newman's best work, but fans will enjoy it. −RC

Land of Dreams / WARNER / BB 80 1988
After a five-year layoff, Newman returned with the solid *Land of Dreams*, an album that was by turns gentle and reflective ("Something Special," "Falling in Love") or subtly scathing. Among the topics explored in *Land of Dreams* are Newman's childhood memories in New Orleans ("Dixie Flyer," "New Orleans Wins the War"), a beautifully twisted ode to patriotism ("Follow the Flag"), and an explanation from a father to his son ("I Want You to Hurt Like I Do"), concerning the passing down of abusive ways. The cynical "It's Money That Matters" barely dented the charts at #80. Interestingly, Jeff Lynne helped produce this album; only two albums earlier, Newman was skewering Lynne's band ELO for representing some of the worst elements of the music biz. −RC

THUNDERCLAP NEWMAN

Rock/pop. UK pop trio, 1969-1970, organized by Who guitarist Pete Townshend and featuring keyboard player Andy Newman (b ca. 1943), singer/drummer John "Speedy" Keen, and guitarist Jimmy McCulloch (b 1953 - d Sep 27, 1979). One-hit wonders with Keen's UK #1 "Something in the Air." −WR

Hollywood Dream / POLYGRAM 1969
Thunderclap Newman seized the sound of an era with their 1973 hit, "Something in the Air," as beautiful a call for pacifism as you'll ever hear. That song is included on this expanded version of their Pete Townshend-produced debut, which features a strange but enticing mix of off-kilter originals and clever covers (such as the Dylan nugget "Open the Door Homer"). −JF

OLIVIA NEWTON-JOHN   b 1947

Pop, dance-pop. Olivia Newton-John ranks at #12 in chart researcher Joel Whitburn's ranking of the most successful singles artists of the 70s. The biggest of her 15 Top Ten hits, "Physical," came in the 80s, when it spent ten weeks at #1. Born in Cambridge, England, but raised in Australia, she returned to her native country after winning a talent contest at 16 and spent several years struggling before she scored a Top Ten UK hit in 1971 with a cover of Bob Dylan's "If Not for You." But it was not until 1973 that Newton-John made her real American breakthrough with the first of five straight gold-selling Top Ten hits, "Let Me Be There." She scored two #1 albums in 1974 and 1975 with *If You Love Me, Let Me Know* and *Have You Never Been Mellow*. (Newton-John's simultaneous success on the country charts and her winning of Grammy and Country Music Association awards in country categories were controversial in Nashville.)
Newton-John's career cooled in 1976 and 1977, but in 1978 she appeared in the film version of the retro-50s musical *Grease*, which not only added to her hit total but also moved her image from sweetness and innocence to a more aggressive posture. She capitalized on the change and on the disco wave for songs like the sexually provocative "Physical," and enjoyed a new vogue as a dance-pop singer in the early 80s. Her last Top Ten hit, "Twist of Fate" was in 1984, also the year Newton-John married actor Matt Lattanzi. She has since released the gold-selling *Soul Kiss* in 1985, *The Rumour* in 1988, and released *Warm and Tender* (1989), an album of children's lullabies. −WR

○ **Back to Basics ... / GEFFEN** 1992
An artist well-defined by her hit singles, Olivia Newton-John has had a stylistically varied career, as is illustrated on *Back to Basics: The Essential Collection 1971-1992*, a set that ranges from her teary ballad "I Honestly Love You" to that bouncy paean to getting horizontal, "Physical." Fans may quibble that such hits as "Let Me Be There" and "Make a Move on Me" are not included, but Newton-John's two greatest-hits albums are out of print, and this is the only collection to combine both her good-girl and bad-girl personae. −WR

NICE

Art-rock. Formed in 1967, Nice was keyboardist Keith Emerson's theatrical testing ground before he formed Emerson, Lake & Palmer in 1970. The group never really sold Stateside, but their audacious stage antics and extended trashings of classical pieces made them popular in Europe. −RC

Ars Longa Vita Brevis / CBS
Leonard Bernstein, Bach, and Sibelius interpreted through a musical lens forged by Brubeck, Monk, and a mad keyboard player named Keith Emerson. −BE

○ **Nice / CBS** 1969
Their final statement, with rippling organ passages and a great lineup of songs, plus 20 minutes of a legendary Fillmore live gig. −BE

STEVIE NICKS   b 1948

Rock/pop. A singer/songwriter who gained fame as a member of Fleetwood Mac starting in 1975 and launched a concurrent solo career in 1981, resulting in five gold or platinum albums through 1991. −WR

Bella Donna / ATLANTIC 1981

Nicks's major attributes — her passionately ragged voice and emotionally vulnerable songwriting — are much in evidence on her debut solo album, given a clean rock production by Jimmy Iovine. Includes "Stop Draggin' My Heart Around" (with Tom Petty & the Heartbreakers), "Edge of Seventeen," and "Leather and Lace" (a duet with Don Henley). –WR

○ **Timespace: Best of Stevie Nicks / ATLANTIC** 1991

All the hits, some well-selected album tracks, and two new ones on a generous best-of. –WR

NICO d 1988

Avant-garde. German-born Christa Paffgen was a model and actress who turned to singing and joined the rock group the Velvet Underground, appearing on their first album, before turning to a solo career in 1968. –WR

○ **Chelsea Girl / POLYGRAM** 1968

Nico's distanced, German-accented voice is presented over austere strings and, in one case, electric guitar on a series of songs reminiscent of her work with the Velvet Underground and written by Velvets John Cale and Lou Reed. Other songs (some unrecorded elsewhere) were written by a young Jackson Browne. –WR

Desert Shore / REPRISE 1970

John Cale produces, arranges, and plays almost all the instruments on this atmospheric collection of songs well suited to Nico's droning delivery. –WR

Live Heroes / PERFORMANCE 1986

A six-track mini-album, four songs recorded live, including David Bowie's title track, which is perfectly suited to the Nico treatment. –WR

THE NIGHTHAWKS

Blues/rock. A hard-driving DC-based bar band with strong Chicago blues roots. Formed in 1972 by harpist and vocalist Mark Wenner and guitarist Jimmy Thackery, the band earned a reputation as a solid outfit through more than a decade of touring and recording projects with John Hammond and former members of Muddy Waters's band. Thackery left in 1986, but Wenner regrouped around longtime members Jan Zukowski on bass and Pete Ragusa on drums. *Trouble,* their recent release on Powerhouse, is a blend of blues, R&B, and rock influences, with a typically energetic sound born in thousands of one-night stands across the country. –BD

○ **Jacks & Kings / ADELPHI** 1977

Classic material and stirring playing. A must-find. –MGN

Side Pocket Shot / ADELPHI 1977

A studio album with the Rhythm King's Horns. Another solid album. –MGN

10 Years Live / VARRICK 1982

A highly recommended 2-fer that celebrates their decade together. –MGN

WILLIE NILE b 1949

Rock & roll. A New York-based singer/songwriter whose 1980 debut album sparked much critical attention and the usual Bob Dylan comparisons, but which really anticipated the jangly guitar-rock revival later led by such acts as R.E.M. Willie Nile reemerged in 1991 with *Places I Have Never Been* on Columbia. –WR

○ **Willie Nile / ARISTA** 1980

Strong songs full of urban observations, sung with urgency in Nile's high, thin voice and backed by guitar-driven music and the propulsive drumming of ex-Patti Smith group member Jay Dee Dougherty. It all adds up to one of the best debut albums of the early 80s. –WR

HARRY NILSSON b 1941

Rock/pop, singer/songwriter. Though he is best known as a singer, Harry Nilsson first gained recognition as a songwriter

in the mid 60s, when his songs were recorded by the Ronettes, the Modern Folk Quartet, and the Monkees. By the time Three Dog Night took his "One" into the Top Five, Nilsson had released two albums of his own on RCA. Neither of them was a hit, but Nilsson did score with his cover of Fred Neil's "Everybody's Talkin'" when it was used as the theme song of the film *Midnight Cowboy.* Nilsson wrote his own film and television scores and in 1970 made an album of songs written by Randy Newman. His career was not helped by his disinclination to undertake live appearances.

Nevertheless, Nilsson broke commercially with his late-1971 album, *Nilsson Schmilsson,* which contained his version of Badfinger's "Without You," a #1 hit, and his own novelty number, "Coconut," which also hit the Top Ten. *Son of Schmilsson,* another appealing collection, was successful the following year. Nilsson's next album was a collection of standards sung against an orchestra conducted by noted 50s arranger Gordon Jenkins, *A Little Touch of Schmilsson in the Night.*

Nilsson had always been a favorite of the Beatles (he was sometimes rumored to be joining the group), and he engaged in projects with Ringo Starr (a film called *Son of Dracula*) and John Lennon (who produced Nilsson's *Pussy Cats*) in the mid 70s. After Lennon's murder, Nilsson became an outspoken advocate of gun control and devoted much of his time to the cause. In the early 90s, he was holding showings of his art in galleries and starting a comeback in music. –WR

Pandemonium Shadow Show / RCA 1967

It's no wonder that Nilsson was taken up by members of the Beatles after they heard this album, which demonstrated that the singer understood better than most the eclectic whimsy that had given birth to *Sgt. Pepper's Lonely Hearts Club Band* better than most. Contains the bittersweet "1941" and "Cuddly Toy," which was covered by the Monkees. –WR

Sings Newman / RCA 1970

Nilsson turns out to be a wonderful interpreter of the work of Randy Newman, his light voice making Newman's satiric humor even drier than when the composer himself sang the songs. –WR

Nilsson Schmilsson / RCA 1971

Nilsson's most successful album was a bouncy Richard Perry production, whose catchy songs were deepened by the singer's puckish humor. Contains the hits "Without You," "Jump into the Fire," and "Coconut." –WR

Son of Schmilsson / RCA 1972

The humor is starting to take over on this followup but the songs are still entertaining, and the session players, including "George Harrysong" and "Richie Snare," make for a great backup band. Contains the hits "Spaceman" and "Remember (Christmas)," as well as the ultimate putdown song, "You're Breaking My Heart." –WR

A Little Touch of Schmilsson in the Night / RCA 1973

Nilsson was nearly a decade ahead of Linda Ronstadt and other nouveau crooners in hiring a conductor/arranger of the pre-rock era (in this case Gordon Jenkins) and recording an album of standards before a full orchestra. And he did it better than most, proving to be a marvelous interpreter of songs like "What'll I Do?" and "Makin' Whoopee!" His version of "As Time Goes By" became a minor hit. –WR

○ **All-Time Greatest Hits / RCA** 1978

Nilsson's albums tended to hang together well, but that didn't keep him from throwing off singles, at least in the late 60s and early 70s. This collection contains all ten of his chart singles (including "Everybody's Talkin'"), plus his version of his song "One," which was a hit for Three Dog Night. –WR

NINE INCH NAILS

Alternative rock. Led by psuedo-artist and industrial-dance honcho Trent Reznor, nine inch nails became the Nirvana of the industrial-dance scene by grafting sampled sounds onto jackboot rhythms crammed to the max with ugly, scratchy guitar and hoarsely shouted vocals. Music to dance to when the big one drops. –JD

○ **Pretty Hate Machine / TEEVEE TOONS** 1989
So far the only nine inch nails release, but with its stunning reconstruction of Queen's "Get Down, Make Love" (done as a kind of S&M drone/shout), this is the apotheosis of their terror dance music. –JD

NIRVANA

Alternative rock. The surprise success of 1991. This Seattle-based trio released an album in 1988 on SubPop and gained some underground notoriety. But their DGC major-label debut, *Nevermind*, anchored by the pulverizing single "Smells like Teen Spirit," broke the platinum barrier and made the band big-time stars. Vocalist and guitarist Kurt Cobain has emerged as a postmodern anti-hero. –JF

○ **Nevermind / GEFFEN** 1991
Loud, wild, tuneful, and essential rock, despite its unexpectedly mega-popular stars. –JD

MOJO NIXON

Alternative rock, rock & roll. Mojo Nixon parlayed an irrepressible personality, a wicked sense of humor, and a taste for high-energy rockabilly into success on a series of novelty albums, and even a place as an MTV VJ. The latter was surprising, since Nixon had first gained notice for a song on his and Skid Roper's second album, *Frenzy* (1986), called "Stuffin' Martha's Muffin," an ode to the joys of intimate contact with MTV VJ Martha Quinn.
The song was typical of Nixon's lyrical approach, which he followed with relentless mirth through the course of four albums on which Roper (a mostly silent partner) contributed incidental instrumental backup. *Bo-Day-Shus!!!* (1987), for example, contained "Elvis Is Everywhere," one of the more outrageous tributes to the King. Debunking famous names came more naturally to Nixon, however, and *Root Hog or Die* was introduced by the *National Enquirer*-headline leadoff song "Debbie Gibson Is Pregnant with My Two Headed Love Child." Gibson didn't comment, but when Nixon (now separated from Roper) issued his first solo album, *Otis*, containing the song "Don Henley Must Die," the ex-Eagle was heard to say that the singer needed a laxative. –WR

Frenzy / IRS 1986
Arguably the duo's best album, highlights include "I'm Living with the Three-Foot Anti-Christ," "The Amazing Bigfoot Diet," and two songs any working musician should understand, "Where the Hell's My Money" and "I Hate Banks." By the way, the *Get Out of My Way* mini-LP, which included some of Mojo's Christmas tunes, is also part of the *Frenzy* CD. –RC

Bo-Day-Shus!!! / IRS 1987
On *Bo-Day-Shus!!!*, Nixon and Roper want you to know that "Elvis Is Everywhere" (but you knew that anyway — right??). They explore the junk-food underbelly of American culture with thoughtful odes like "B.B.Q.U.S.A.," "I'm Gonna Dig Up Howlin' Wolf," and "We Gotta Have More Soul." Declarative odes like "I Ain't Gonna Piss in No Jar" and "Don't Want No Foo-Foo Haircut on My Head" are indications of Mojo and Skid's sensitivity to politically correct issues. –RC

Root Hog or Die / IRS 1989
With the help of producer Jim Dickinson and a few sidemen, Skid Roper and Mojo Nixon plow through thoughtful numbers like "Debbie Gibson Is Pregnant with My Two-Headed Love Child," "She's Vibrator Dependent," and "Louisiana Liplock." Nixon indulges his Elvis fixation with "(619) 239-KING," and a version of "This Land Is Your Land" mutates into a pitch for Mojo World. –RC

○ **Unlimited Everything / ENIGMA** 1990
This fairly complete overview of Nixon and Roper's most popular work is a good place to start for the uninitiated. –RC

Otis / IRS 1991
After *Root Hog or Die*, Mojo went solo and enlisted a primo

group of rude rock sidemen from the Del-Lords, X, Beat Farmers, and Dash Rip Rock. Nixon did a good job making the transition from the bare-bones duo approach to a full band. His putdown of "serious" pop rockers like Don Henley ("Don Henley Must Die") gained quite a bit of publicity. –RC

NOTTING HILLBILLIES

Country rock. Formed by Dire Straits guitarist Mark Knopfler (b 1949), this acoustic group showcased the fingerpicking skills of several friends in a primarily country-rock format, with the influence of Knopfler's idol Chet Atkins looming large. –CK

○ **Missing ... / WARNER** 1990
Missing ... Presumed Having a Good Time is a superb collection with strong country leanings. Melodic and memorable. –HD

NRBQ

Rock & roll, roots-rock. Formed in 1967 in Florida as New Rhythm & Blues Quintet, the original lineup included pianist Terry Adams, guitarist Steve Ferguson, bassist Joey Stampinato, vocalist Frank Gadler, and drummer Tom Staley. After recording two albums for Columbia (including one with Carl Perkins), which went nowhere, guitarist Al Anderson joined in 1971. Ferguson and Gadler were replaced by drummer Tom Ardolino and the Whole Wheat Horns. This versatile and witty quartet is at home with everything from atonal jazz to rockabilly to country swing to pop jangle to roadhouse R&B. But they don't always give eclecticism a good name; although there's something worth hearing on each of their albums, the Q's humor is often corny, and their penchant for indulging their every artistic whim means that even their best albums are padded with silly hokum. They've been doing the same stuff for nearly 30 years and have amassed a fanatical cult following. And at times, NRBQ can sound like the greatest rock band in the world. –CK & JF

Scraps / ROUNDER 1972
A spotty album that contains a few necessary gems, like "Magnet" and "It's Not So Hard." –JF

All Hopped Up / ROUNDER 1977
A fairly consistent and ballsy offering, containing early classics such as "Ridin' in My Car" and "That's Alright." –JF

○ **NRBQ at Yankee Stadium / POLYGRAM** 1978
Another winner, sporting three snazzy covers and nine of their best originals. –JF

Kick Me Hard / ROUNDER 1979
A decent mix of tough rockers and cheesy pop. –JF

○ **Tiddlywinks / ROUNDER** 1980
Stunning. Minimizes the foolishness and ups the ante with at least seven swinging and clever hard-pop nuggets. –JF

Grooves in Orbit / RHINO 1983
The same old thing, really, but "When Things Was Cheap" is their only political moment and "Rain at the Drive-In" is charming in a naive sort of way. –JF

Tap Dancin' Bats / ROUNDER 1983
Their most successful slice of goofball novelty numbers. –JF

RC Cola & a Moon Pie / ROUNDER 1986
An abridged version of *Workshop*, one of their finest early albums. Includes some previously unreleased and rare material. –JF

Lou and the Q / ROUNDER 1986
Silliness abounds on this wacky meeting of the "Q" with pro-wrestling manager Lou Albano. –JT

God Bless Us All / ROUNDER 1987
A live album that offers an energetic glimpse at what the "Q" can do on stage. –JF

★ **Peek-A-Boo - Best of NRBQ (1969-1989) / RHINO** 1990
A masterfully executed compilation of nearly every worthwhile song they've done. Could be the only "Q" you'll need. –JF

NUCLEAR ASSAULT

Heavy metal. This New York quartet specializes in over-the-edge speed metal. –JB

○ **Game Over / RELATIVITY**   1986
Their debut, a classic speed-metal album of the 80s. Dark, realistic, and also funny. Raw, with a punk mentality. –JB

TED NUGENT   ♭1948

Hard rock. Nugent started in a local Detroit teen band, the Lourds, and formed the Amboy Dukes in late 1965 or early 1966. He scored his first hit with "Journey to the Center of Your Mind" in 1968. Several albums using the Amboy Dukes tag followed, with the personnel changing with almost every album. Nugent went solo in 1975, marking his greatest success to date with one album after another in the charts, then put his solo career on hold to become a member of the group Damn Yankees in 1990. A powerful, high-decibel guitarist, Nugent's energy more than makes up for whatever subtleties he lacks. –CK

○ **Double Live Gonzo / CBS**   1978
This is the ultimate document of Nugent's mountain-man persona. –DH

THE NUTMEGS

R&B, doo-wop. The floating lead tenor of Leroy Griffin distinguished the Nutmegs's 1955 R&B smash "Story Untold," an East Coast doo-wop classic. Hailing from New Haven, CT, the quintet signed with Herald Records and debuted with "Story Untold." Another smooth ballad issued later that year, "Ship of Love," also scaled the R&B charts. The Nutmegs made several more solid singles for Herald but without recapturing their initial success. –BD

○ **Greatest Hits / RELIC**
Fine East Coast doo-wop, including the classic "Story Untold" and "The Ship of Love," only available on vinyl for now. –BD

LAURA NYRO   ♭1947

Singer/songwriter. While Laura Nyro remains best known for providing hit material for a number of late-60s acts, it's a mystery why she never had a smash of her own. Essential college-dorm-room listening for the era, and often bagged as a sort of East Coast answer to Joni Mitchell, in reality Nyro was in a class by herself.
Nyro's songs were steeped in classic R&B and framed in stark settings, her vocal gymnastics often accompanied only by her own piano work. Any doubts as to where her music came from were erased by the album *Gonna Take a Miracle*, a brilliant collection of soul covers recorded with the resurrected LaBelle, it was also one of the first albums of all-outside material by a major rock-era songwriter. In the 70s Nyro became more reclusive, releasing only the occasional album letting us in on a bit of her home life. Even now, the promise of new Laura Nyro material is still cause for much hope. –SA

The First Songs / CBS   1967
A collection given over to the more conventional, if high-quality early Nyro songs that later became hits (and standards) in the hands of other performers. The album includes "Wedding Bell Blues," "Stoney End," and "And When I Die." –WR

★ **Eli and the Thirteenth Confession / CBS**   1968
The hits (for others) keep coming — "Sweet Blindness," "Eli's Comin'," and "Stoned Soul Picnic" are all here, sung by their author — but Nyro not only proves herself a powerful singer in her own right, comfortable in styles from jazz to gospel/R&B to stark balladry, she also begins to turn to a more introspective, personal writing and singing which no one will be able to replicate. –WR

☆ **New York Tendaberry / CBS**   1969
A stunning musical journey through love, loss, religion, and

eroticism, by turns passionate, inspired, and suicidal, this is Nyro's most accomplished, most idiosyncratic record, and one of the greatest singer/songwriter works ever made. Using a wide vocal range and her often delicate piano work with deftly added instrumental touches, Nyro creates an aural landscape that spans the extremes of human emotion. It's not listed as her "pick" album only because it's not the place to start; rather, it's the logical conclusion of her musical development. –WR

Gonna Take a Miracle / CBS   1971
A joyous change of pace, this album presents inspired readings of pop/R&B hits of the 60s, songs like "Jimmy Mack" and "Nowhere to Run," produced by creamy-smooth soul producers Gamble & Huff and sung rapturously by Nyro, with gorgeous backing by Patti Labelle, Sarah Dash, and Nona Hendryx. –WR

Smile / CBS   1976
This warm comeback album is Laura Nyro's *Double Fantasy*, a return to action by a mature artist, who retains her emotional power but has worked through her problems and beaten back her demons to emerge as a "Sexy Mama." –WR

BILLY OCEAN   ♭1950

Soul/R&B. Born in Trinidad, Billy Ocean emigrated to the UK as a child. He worked as a tailor while pursuing music on the side in the 60s, then broke through with the Motown-flavored "Love Really Hurts without You," which hit #3 in the UK in 1976. Ocean continued to have UK hits through the end of the 70s but didn't achieve mass success in the US until 1984, when "Caribbean Queen (No More Love on the Run)" became a #1 hit, the first of seven Top Ten hits over the next four years. –WR

○ **Greatest Hits / JIVE**   1989
Contains his cool 80s disco hits "Caribbean Queen" and "Get outta My Dreams, Get into My Car" and piano-based ballads like "There'll Be Sad Songs to Make You Cry." –BC

SINÉAD O'CONNOR   ♭1967

Alternative rock. From Dublin, Ireland, Sinéad O'Connor came onto the music scene in 1987 with a powerful image of a woman who could express great sensitivity while not losing any qualities of inner strength. In public, O'Connor's seemingly audacious pronouncements about the state of the world around her may have put off those unaccustomed to a woman so forthright with her feelings; nevertheless, it's that courageousness that has endeared her to millions of fans. O'Connor's second album, *I Do Not Want What I Haven't Got*, was a worldwide hit. Musically, O'Connor draws from hard synth-rock, Celtic folk, and funk. Her dramatic alto explores sound in much the same way Peter Gabriel applies varied tonal dynamics. –RC

○ **The Lion & the Cobra / CHRYSALIS**   1987
The Lion and the Cobra was an impressive showcase for this Dubliner's vocal and writing skills. On this self-produced effort, O'Connor incorporates bits of hard rock, folk, synth-pop, and light funk onto standout tracks like "I Want You (Hands on Me)," "Jerusalem," and "Mandinka," a wonderful synth-rocker. –RC

● **I Do Not Want What I Haven't Got / ENSIGN**   1990
O'Connor's debut might have been a strong showing, but her followup, *I Do Not Want What I Haven't Got*, was a stunner. Her songwriting skills were much more incisive and, vocally, O'Connor exhibited a greater range of interpretive skills. Highlights include "The Emperor's New Clothes," "I Am Stretched on Your Grave," "Jump in the River," "Black Boys on Mopeds," and the international hit "Nothing Compares 2 U," which was penned by Prince. –RC

THE OHIO PLAYERS

R&B, funk. Originally formed in 1959 as an instrumental R&B group, the Ohio Untouchables (as they were then known) provided backup on the Falcons's records. After the

Untouchables broke up, two of the members (Clarence "Satch" Satchell and Marshall "Rock" Jones) formed a new outfit called the Ohio Players and began working as the house band at Compass Records. In the early 70s, the Ohio Players had a steady stream of funky, sexual hit singles, including the #1s "Fire" and "Love Rollercoaster." As the decade progressed, their sound gradually transformed into a throbbing disco pulse and their sales slowly tapered off. –STE

○ **Ohio Players Gold / POLYGRAM** 1976
A strong overview of their biggest hits and best moments, including "Fire" (#1), "Fopp" (#30), "Skin Tight" (#13), and the shattering "Love Rollercoaster" (#1). –STE

OINGO BOINGO

Alternative rock. Led the the wide-ranging musical talent of Danny Elfman (who would go on to score film and TV projects ranging from *Batman* to "The Simpsons"), Los Angeles's Oingo Boingo carved out a respectable reputation among the new-wave set with a quirky pop style that owed a heavy debt to bands like XTC. –DH

○ **Best O' Boingo / MCA**
Captures their peculiar-yet-catchy style well. –DH

THE O'JAYS

Soul, R&B, doo-wop. Kenny Gamble and Leon Huff's most consistent and durable hitmaking soul group played an essential role in the early years of disco. Gospel-trained vocalist Eddie Levert remains a critically neglected master of pumping, sweat-soaked soul testifying. –JF

★ **Greatest Hits /**
Doesn't have as many songs as *Collector's Item*, but everything here is a winner. –JF

○ **Back Stabbers / PHILADELPHIA I** 1972
Their first and greatest album strikes a balance between searing social drama ("992 Arguments" and the title cut) and sumptuous slow-dance ballads. (Out of print) –JF

Ship Ahoy / CBS 1974
This hit-packed set from 1973 contains the colossal hit "For the Love of Money" and other essentials. –JF

Collectors Item / CBS 1977
A generous but poorly programmed hits package. –JF

MIKE OLDFIELD ♭1953

Prog-rock, art-rock. Multi-instrumentalist Mike Oldfield's musical roots were in English folk, but his claim to fame primarily rests on his 1974 instrumental opus "Tubular Bells" (#7). The newly formed Virgin Records allowed Oldfield a year to complete his concept, which required him to record 80 tracks of himself playing 28 instruments, and ended up running 49 minutes. The track became the theme for the movie *The Exorcist*, and the album *Tubular Bells* rose to #3. Even though Oldfield hasn't charted stateside since, he's enjoyed a moderately successful career in England. –RC

○ **Tubular Bells / ATLANTIC** 1973
The original new-age instrumental, originally mistaken for progressive rock — its melodic invention remains beguiling, long after the druggy haze of the 60s/70s ambience of its origins has faded. –BE

Hergest Ridge / ATLANTIC 1974
A well-made followup, with a strange, otherworldly quality in evidence. –BE

OLYMPICS

R&B, doo-wop. A sub-Coasters R&B group scored in 1958 with the great novelty hit "Western Movies." In 1965 they recorded the original version of "Good Lovin'," later covered by the Rascals. Despite the rumors, they were not the same group as the Marathons ("Peanut Butter"). –JF

○ **All-Time Greatest Hits! / DCC** 1991
Somewhat more comprehensive than their Rhino package,

this 26-track gem is the definitive homage to this good-time R&B crew. –JT

OMAR & THE HOWLERS

Blues/rock. A hard electric blues/rock band out of Austin, TX, stirring up Howlin' Wolf with Creedence. –RC

○ **I Told You So / AUS** 1984
The rawest disc from this R&B-based band. –DS

100 PROOF (AGED IN SOUL)

Soul, funk. As part of legendary songwriting trio Holland-Dozier-Holland's early-70s Hot Wax/Invictus Records artist roster, 100 Proof's gritty soul reflected more of a Stax sensibility than a Motown one. "Somebody's Been Sleeping in My Bed" was their biggest hit, going #8 pop. –RC

○ **Greatest Hits / HDH-FANTASY** 1990
Great tracks and great sound quality. An Eddie Holland production. –RP

ALEXANDER O'NEAL ♭1953

R&B, soul, dance-pop. This Minneapolis soul man cut his teeth in the Time but was bounced (for looking "too Black") before they signed with Warner Brothers. His tough, ballsy voice has the same grain and range as Otis Redding's. Like that master, O'Neal is comfortable with pumping dance-floor burners and slinky couch-cuddlers. He's certainly the best singer Jimmy Jam and Terry Lewis have ever produced, and the strength of his material and his robust voice make him a candidate for Greatest Soul Singer of the last ten years. –JF

☆ **Hearsay / CBS** 1987
After a tentative debut, O'Neal rebounded with a masterly set, linked by the background chatter of a party but pushed to the limits of brilliance by Jam and Lewis's best production and O'Neal's versatility and power. –JF

All Mixed Up / CBS
Lengthy and intelligently programmed set of remixed hits, culled most from *Hearsay*. –JF

★ **All True Man / CBS** 1990
Rounds out O'Neal's personality — and surpasses *Hearsay* — with better songs and sharper production. –JF

THE ONLY ONES

Punk. One of the punk era's most underrated bands. Led by scuzzy romantic Peter Perrett, the Only Ones played not-so-fast guitar rock lifted from numerous listenings to the New York Dolls. Although traditional (actually downright conservative) in their approach to rock craft, their skill with a pop song was then matched only by the Undertones. –JD

○ **Peel Sessions / DUTCH EAST WAX** 1978
The essential compilation. Includes the classic "Another Girl, Another Planet," as well as about a dozen more of Perrett's gloomy, sardonic takes on romantic life. Pop so wry it'll make you giddy. –JD

Live in London / SKYCLAD 1990
Essentially a greatest-hits live package, this contains much of the aforementioned tracks but adds bits and some hots-on guitar spuzz. –JD

ORB

Alternative rock, art-rock. The brainchild of guitarist and vocalist Jimmy Cauty and Alex Patterson. The duo delivers challenging psychedelic electronics. –DS

○ **Huge Ever Growing ... / WAU! MR MODO** 1989
Pink Floyd-like space music with a variety of water noises. *A Huge Ever Growing Pulsating Brain That Rules from the Centre of the Ultraworld* is suited to those interested in psychedelia and the bizarre. –DS

ROY ORBISON 1936-1989

Rock & roll, pop, rockabilly. Roy Orbison was the most unlikely of early rock & rollers, the physical and charismatic antithesis of Elvis Presley, Jerry Lee Lewis, and Little Richard. But he forged a style that was as singular as any in rock, assuming the role of pop's master paranoic. He cut some rockabilly for Sun in the late 50s, but it's his string of brilliant 60s hits, produced with Frank Foster for Monument, that established Orbison's formula. His best singles delve into the darkest areas of a soul torn by romantic confusion and terror; "Only the Lonely" and "Running Scared" epitomize Orbison's near-operatic ballad formula. Although he also recorded some convincing and tough rock ("Oh, Pretty Woman," "Candy Man"), his reputation rests on his bleak, uncompromising broken-heart laments, which have influenced rockers from Del Shannon to Bruce Springsteen and Elvis Costello. After spending most of the 70s and 80s on the oldies circuit, Orbison revived his career through an association with a group called the Traveling Wilburys. He died in 1989, just weeks after releasing *Mystery Girl*, the album that put him back on the charts. –JF

☆ **All-Time Greatest Hits / MONUMENT**　　　　1976
The All-Time Greatest Hits of Roy Orbison is an essential collection. It rounds up 20 of the Big O's best 60s recordings, with some fine album tracks thrown in. –JF

★ **For the Lonely ... / RHINO**　　　　　　　　1988
For the Lonely: Roy Orbison Anthology (1956-1965) offers the usual Monument hits along with a few Sun tunes — 18 in all. Buyers beware: The vinyl version contains more cuts than the CD. –JF

○ **Mystery Girl / ATLANTIC**　　　　　　　　　1989
Roy's comeback is remarkable in that every song, from "You Got It" and "She's a Mystery to Me" to "The Only One," proves that the formula of his 60s stuff is still vital 30 years later. An album that really deserved a followup. –JF

☆ **The Sun Years 1956-58 / BEAR FAMILY**　　　1989
Contains Orbison's complete Sun output, featuring many undubbed recordings and the pile-driving "Domino." –JF

The Legendary Roy Orbison / CBS　　　　　　1991
While the Rhino set, *For the Lonely: Roy Orbison Anthology (1956-1965)*, is the most essential single-disc release of Orbison's work, *The Legendary Roy Orbison* tries to flesh out the picture considerably with a 4-CD, 75-track boxed set. It may be overkill for some, and certain tracks feel like pointless inclusions, but fans who want more than just a hits collection should like this set. The enclosed booklet contains a wealth of photos and the annotation is passionate and informative. –RC

JEFFREY OSBORNE

Urban R&B, soul. Until 1980, Osborne was the lead vocalist of L.T.D. Throughout the 80s, he had a string of Top 40 hits: "Don't You Get So Mad" (#25), "Stay with Me Tonight" (#30), "You Should Be Mine (The Woo Woo Song)" (#13), and "Love Power" (#12), a duet with Dionne Warwick. –STE

○ **Jeffrey Osborne / A&M**　　　　　　　　　1982
A pivotal, career-establishing R&B statement from this love stylist. –RW

Stay with Me Tonight / A&M　　　　　　　　1983
A fine title cut and a good overall session. –RW

Only Human / ARISTA　　　　　　　　　　　1990
This is the comeback, which returned Osbourne to the R&B forefront. –RW

OZZY OSBOURNE　　　　　　　　　　　　♭1948

Heavy metal. The former lead singer of Black Sabbath has carved out a thriving solo career in spite of — or maybe because of — a knack for creating controversy with his lyrics and his behavior. Osbourne's sound is basic and to the point, crafted almost strictly for teenage headbangers, who remain his most loyal followers. While his lyrics rarely hold any relevance for anyone over 17, he is to be admired for his skills as a bandleader who is able regularly to mine talent on the order of his brilliant one-time guitarist, the late Randy Rhoads. –DH

○ **Diary of a Madman / CBS / BB 16**　　　　　1981
This sophomore effort from the former Black Sabbath vocalist was his finest solo release to date. Osbourne's singing on the album stands up throughout, and guitarist Randy Rhoads (a primary songwriter on this album) became one of the first guitar heroes of heavy metal in the 80s with his fiery playing. (Rhoads died five months after the release of this album in a bizarre airplane accident.)–JB

Speak of the Devil / CBS / BB 14　　　　　　1982
A live album recorded from Osbourne's 1982 tour, featuring powerful new versions of Black Sabbath classics. It caused a minor controversy, since his Sabbath (with Ronnie James Dio as vocalist) released their first live album (*Live Evil*) at the same time, also with early Black Sabbath material. Ozzy's band at the time featured drummer Tommy Aldridge (now with House of Lords), Night Ranger guitarist Brad Gillis, and bassist Rudy Sarzo, later a member of Whitesnake. (Sarzo was also a founding member of Quiet Riot, an early incarnation of which featured a young guitarist named Randy Rhoads.) –JB

THE OUTLAWS

Southern rock. This Tampa, FL, quintet, formed in 1974, mixed Eagles-style harmonies and country-rock with a Southern rock twin-lead-guitar attack. They scored two minor hits with 1975's "There Goes Another Love Song" (#34) and the 1980 remake of "(Ghost) Riders in the Sky" (#31). –RC

Lady in Waiting / ARISTA　　　　　　　　　1976
Their best studio album, in which Hughie Thomasson leads the band through a flurry of Southern-style raveups. (Out of print) –DDC

○ **Bring It Back Alive / ARISTA**　　　　　　　1978
This fiery Southern rock guitar army led by Hughie Thomasson excels live — especially here, on an extended version of the band's trademark song, "Green Grass and High Tides." –DDC

THE OUTSIDERS

Rock/pop. The Outsiders started in Cleveland, OH, as a garden-variety bar band led by guitarist and songwriter Tom King. The addition of vocalist Sonny Geraci infused the band with new life. Signed to Capitol Records in 1967, the group scored big with the single "Time Won't Let Me," their finest moment.

Personnel changes and management conflicts stalled the band's career but not before they had racked up several hits. –CK

○ **Capitol Collectors Series / CAPITOL**　　　　1991
All their best in one neat little package. Includes "Time Won't Let Me," "Respectable," and "Girl in Love." –CK

THE OYSTER BAND

Folk/rock. A British folk-rock band of the late 80s and early 90s, specializing in contemporary dance rhythms (played by a rock rhythm section) yet retaining a traditional English folk flavor. Members are John Jones (melodeon, accordion), Ian Telfer (fiddle, viola, concertina), Alan Prosser (guitar, mandolin), Chopper (bass), and Russell Lax (drums). –WR

Wide Blue Yonder / POLYDOR　　　　　　　1987
The Oysters turn in some highly political material here, leading off with "The Generals Are Born Again" and covering Billy Bragg's "Between the Wars," but the love songs are just as fervent, notably "The Oxford Girl." It all barrels along at quick tempos, with much intricate playing and full-voiced singing; this is stirring stuff. –WR

○ **Ride / POLYGRAM**　　　　　　　　　　　　1989
"New York Girls" is a rollicking square-dance workout about prostitutes, which asks the musical question, "Can you dance the polka?" On the same album, the Oysters cover New Order's electro-rock "Love Vigilantes." And, somehow, it all sounds like English folk music. –WR

From Little Rock to Leipzig / RYKODISC   1991
With their infectious music and dance beats, it stands to reason the Oyster Band would be terrific live. They are and it shows here, on a collection of their best originals plus such wide-ranging covers as Phil Ochs's "Gonna Do What I Have to Do" and the old Bobby Fuller hit "I Fought the Law." –WR

OZARK MOUNTAIN DAREDEVILS

Rock/pop, country rock, Southern rock. This Missouri sextet (formed in 1973) employed an eclectic blend of influences ranging from bluegrass, country-rock, and Southern boogie to pop. –RC

○ **Best of Ozark Mountain Daredevils / A&M**
A solid selection of their best, featuring "If You Want to Get to Heaven" and "Jackie Blue." –DH

P-FUNK ALL STARS

Funk. This 1982-1983 conglomeration is another offshoot from George Clinton's Parliament/Funkadelic empire. –ED

○ **Urban Dancefloor Guerillas / CBS**   1983
A no-nonsense, butt-thumping George Clinton spinoff. Not many standouts, but "Copy Cat" is a great reply to "Atomic Dog." –JF

PABLO CRUISE

Rock. During the last half of the 70s, Pablo Cruise (formed in 1973 with members from It's a Beautiful Day, Stoneground, and Santana) landed a string of hits. Their sound contained polite amounts of rock and light West Coast pop/funk. Their hits include "Whatcha Gonna Do?" (#6), "Love Will Find a Way" (#6), "Don't Want to Live without It" (#21)" –RC

○ **Classics - 26 / A&M**
Their greatest hits, including "Whatcha Gonna Do" and "Love Will Find a Way." –KMC

JIMMY PAGE   b 1944

Hard rock, rock/pop. James Patrick Page is one of the most successful rock guitarists to come out of England in the 60s. Born in Heston, Page was playing recording sessions in London studios while still in his teens, and his guitar can be heard on many of the records made there in the mid 60s. Page turned down an initial offer to join the Yardbirds, then changed his mind and worked with the group until its demise in 1968. He then formed Led Zeppelin, which was the predominant hard-rock/heavy-metal band in popular music until 1980. After the group split, Page was less active, though he formed another hard-rock quartet, the Firm, in the mid 80s. He released his own solo album in 1988. In the 90s, while deflecting Zeppelin reunion rumors, he was working on an album with Whitesnake singer David Coverdale. –WR

○ **Outrider / GEFFEN**   1988
Page's debut solo album is a heavy guitar treat employing a varying cast of sidemen, including drummer Jason Bonham and Page's old Led Zeppelin partner Robert Plant, who co-writes and sings one song. –WR

Session Man - Vol. 1 / A.I.P.-BOMP   1989
Prior to his tenure in the Yardbirds and Led Zeppelin, Jimmy Page played numerous recording sessions in England. This is a compilation of his work from 1963 to 1968, including a solo single, some previously unreleased Yardbirds material, and various obscure British artists. –WR

Session Man - Vol. 2 / A.I.P.-BOMP   1991
With more obscure acts than the previous volume, it also includes such name artists as Brenda Lee and Billy Fury, plus a live Yardbirds cut. –WR

THE PALADINS

Rock & roll. Bluesy rockers with a touch of punk, led by guitarist Dave Gonzalez. –DH & CK

Years Since Yesterday / ALLIGATOR   1988
Their debut album for the label, chock-full of great material, honed by years on the club circuit. –CK

○ **Let's Buzz / ALLIGATOR**   1990
A good, raucous introduction to their sound. Features material ranging from rockabilly to blues to Tex-Mex influences and a great version of Juke Logan's title song. –CK

ROBERT PALMER   b 1949

Rock/pop. British singer (and occasional songwriter), with a strong taste for R&B, Caribbean, New Orleans, and other rhythmic styles. He made a series of well-received albums in the 70s but finally broke through commercially in the 80s, singing in the Duran Duran project band Power Station and later on his own with his *Addicted to Love* in 1986. –WR

Sneakin' Sally through the Alley / POLYGRAM   1973
On his debut solo album, Palmer employs members of the Meters and Little Feat for a musical gumbo enriched by his husky, percussive voice. –WR

Pressure Drop / POLYGRAM   1975
Palmer's own songs (especially the silky "Give Me an Inch" and "Work to Make It Work") and the backing of Little Feat help make this a worthy followup to *Sally*. –WR

Some People / POLYGRAM   1976
Palmer's "Keep in Touch," "Man Smart, Woman Smarter," and "Spanish Moon" (the latter by Little Feat's Lowell George) pace *Some People Can Do What They Like*, another terrific collection. –WR

Double Fun / POLYGRAM   1978
Palmer produces and writes more songs than usual, resulting in the hit "Every Kinda People" and a somewhat lighter, more pop approach. –WR

Secrets / POLYGRAM   1979
Palmer scores his biggest hit single of the 70s with the uptempo rocker "Bad Case of Loving You (Doctor, Doctor)" on an album that also includes a wonderful version of Todd Rundgren's ballad "Can We Still Be Friends." –WR

Clues / POLYGRAM   1980
A move toward fast-paced electronic dance-rock. It's successful about half the time, especially on Palmer's UK hits "Looking for Clues" and "Johnny and Mary." (Rod Stewart Xeroxed "Johnny and Mary" for his hit "Young Turks" the following year.) –WR

Maybe It's Live / ISLAND   1982
Five oldies recorded in concert and five new songs, among them Palmer's first big UK hit, "Some Guys Have All the Luck." (Rod Stewart had a US hit version two years later.) –WR

Riptide / POLYGRAM   1985
Palmer's commercial breakthrough, much of it in the hard-rock style of his one-shot band Power Station, and featuring the hits "Discipline of Love," "Addicted to Love" (a #1 hit), "Hyperactive," and "I Didn't Mean to Turn You On." –WR

○ **Addictions - Vol. 1 / POLYGRAM**   1989
Thirteen-track compilation containing Palmer's biggest hits, not only the ones on Island but also the Power Station singles and "Simply Irresistible," from Palmer's first EMI album. –WR

PARAGONS

Doo-wop. A New York quintet with Julius McMichael's distinctive high tenor up front, the Paragons were in the forefront of New York street-corner harmony in 1957. Their Winley label debut "Florence"/"Hey Little School Girl" paired a tender ballad with a torrid jump, and several Winley followups also racked up solid regional sales. –BD

○ **Meet the Jesters / RELIC**
Outstanding 50s doo-wop. –MH

MICA PARIS

Dance-pop, soul. A big-voiced British soul chanteuse. –JF

So Good / POLYGRAM   1989
Her American debut with "My One Temptation" and "Nothing Hits Your Heart Like Soul Music." On the latter, she sounds amazingly like Natalie Cole on her early Capitol records. –BC

○ **Contribution / POLYGRAM**   1990
British soul diva's second album is a tour de force highlighted by the sumptuous single "South of the River." –JF

GRAHAM PARKER   b 1950

Singer/songwriter, rock & roll. A British singer/songwriter who emerged from the pub-rock/punk scene of the mid 70s to garner critical acclaim for his strong songwriting, playing much of it backed by his band, the Rumour. –WR

○ **Howlin' Wind / POLYGRAM**   1976
Parker comes across as both tough-minded and optimistic (maybe the word is "determined") on his debut album, on which he sings with conviction against the cohesive backing of the Rumour. –WR

○ **Heat Treatment / POLYGRAM**   1976
Essentially *Howlin' Wind - Vol. 2*, as Parker and the Rumour demonstrate that their initial burst of high-quality songs can extend to a second album, in the same year as their debut. –WR

★ **Squeezing Out Sparks / ARISTA**   1979
Older and more bitter, Parker delves deeper into his demons, and the Rumour just plays harder. Parker's best album, and one of the best albums of the decade. –WR

The Up Escalator / ARISTA   1980
On his last album with the Rumour, Parker goes for mainstream rock success, employing the widescreen production style of Jimmy Iovine and such guests as Bruce Springsteen. It didn't sell, but it was a great try. –WR

Another Grey Area / ARISTA   1982
Parker begins to make his peace with human imperfection (though he can still be sharp-tongued) and starts to look for love ("It's All Worth Nothing Alone"), backed by a smooth session band and a clean Jack Douglas production, which cool his usual fire without putting it out. –WR

The Real Macaw / ARISTA   1983
Parker finds love, and manages to write about it without losing his usual wit ("Last Couple on the Dance Floor"). He also re-employs Rumour guitarist Brinsley Schwartz and goes back to the uptempo pub rock of his 70s albums. –WR

RAY PARKER JR   b 1954

Urban R&B, dance-pop, soul. Highly successful R&B vocalist through the 80s. His career peaked in 1984 with his monstrously popular movie theme "Ghostbusters." Born in Detroit, Parker built an enviable reputation as an ace Los Angeles session guitarist. He formed Raydio in 1977 and immediately hit with "Jack and Jill" on Artista, and his assured mid-tempo approach resulted in heavy pop airplay on "You Can't Change That" in 1979 and the 1981 R&B chart-topping "A Woman Needs Love (Just Like You Do)." Going solo the next year, Parker continued to rack up the sales for Arista, culminating with a gold record for "Ghostbusters," a #1 pop and R&B item. Parker continues to record in an urban contemporary vein. –BD

○ **Greatest Hits / ARISTA**   1982
Contains "The Other Woman," among his other hits. –DH

ROBERT PARKER   b 1930

R&B, soul. Parker's dance raver "Barefootin'" was one of the biggest hits to come out of New Orleans during the mid 60s. Parker played sessions as a saxophonist back in 1949 with the legendary pianist Professor Longhair, and his 1959 solo debut for Ron, "All Night Long," was a scorching two-part instrumental. But Parker's under-utilized vocal talents suddenly emerged in 1966, when his highly infectious "Barefootin'" became a giant hit on tiny Nola. Only one other

Parker single, "Tip Toe," charted the next year, but Parker remains a popular attraction in his hometown. –BD

○ **Barefootin' / COLLECTABLES**
Originally issued in 1987 on vinyl by England's Charly, this collection includes Parker's main claim to fame, the 1967 R&B and pop dance smash "Barefootin'"; its flip side, "Let's Go Baby (Where the Action Is)"; both sides of a 1969 single Parker cut for Silver Fox; and a number of 70s recordings the erstwhile sax player waxed for Sansu Enterprises. Much of the CD, including the title cut, is infectious New Orleans R&B of a high caliber, but other tracks find Parker attempting to cut mainstream funk and disco, usually with less-than-inspiring results. If possible, find the Charly release, because Collectables, in their typically shoddy manner, do not bother to provide songwriting credits, let alone track credits or liner notes. My policy is buy Collectables only if there is no other anthology of the same material issued anywhere else in the world, no matter what the price difference. –RB

VAN DYKE PARKS   b 1941

Singer/songwriter. Composer, arranger, producer, and musician Van Dyke Parks has had a varied career in popular music without ever getting near the popular mainstream. Parks worked as a songwriter in the early 60s and became a producer, handling such mid-60s acts as Harpers Bizarre. He was enlisted by Beach Boy Brian Wilson to write lyrics for what turned out to be an abortive album project called *Smile* (now one of the legendary lost albums of the 60s), resulting in such songs as the hit "Heroes and Villains." Parks released his own album, the eclectic *Song Cycle*, to critical acclaim and minimal sales in 1968. He then did session work with a variety of artists, not releasing his second album, *Discover America*, which revealed his immersion in Trinidadian music, until 1972. *Clang of the Yankee Reaper*, another eclectic collection, followed in 1975. But Parks maintained his "day job" — film work on scores by Ry Cooder and others, writing and arranging for Shelley Duvall's children's TV series, and other pursuits. Finally, in 1984, came the brilliant *Jump!*, a concept album based on the Uncle Remus tales of Joel Chandler Harris. It was followed in 1989 by *Tokyo Rose*, which concerned the state of American-Japanese relations. –WR

★ **Song Cycle / WARNER**   1968
Parks demonstrated an audacious musical imagination on this debut album, which effectively deployed a full orchestra, along with electric instruments, balalaikas, accordions, and an "authentic folk choir," plus nature sounds and God knows what else to produce a unique soundscape. A unique piece of music and a stunning accomplishment. –WR

Discover America / WARNER   1972
Parks turns to the music of Trinidad here, especially as it was heard in the 40s, which means tributes to "Bing Crosby" and "The Four Mills Bros.," not to mention "G-Man Hoover" and "FDR in Trinidad," played on steel drums and other indigenous instruments. A charming, idiosyncratic genre exercise. –WR

○ **Jump! / WARNER**   1984
An exhilarating song cycle based on the Uncle Remus tales. It incorporates the styles of Stephen Foster, ragtime, 30s movie-soundtrack music, you name it, all in the service of playful, touching lyrics that correspond to the source material, without actually aping it. A delight from start to finish. –WR

Tokyo Rose / WARNER   1989
One can hear "America" as played on a Japanese koto on this history of relations between East and West, which covers everything from the "Trade War" to baseball with Parks's typically eclectic and broad musical imagination. A charming album. –WR

PARLIAMENT

R&B, doo-wop, soul, funk. Parliament started as a doo-wop group centered around a barber shop owned and operated by

George Clinton in New Jersey in the late 50s. One 45 was released on the APT label before Clinton and company headed off to Detroit. Updating their sound to reflect the innovations of Motown, Parliament had a (#3 R&B/#20 pop) hit with "(I Wanna) Testify" for Revilot in 1967. Leaving Revilot before the group's contract had legally expired, Clinton lost the right to the name for a few years.

Putting his backup band up front, Clinton signed with Detroit's Westbound label and called the group Funkadelic. By 1971 Clinton regained title to the original name and shortened it to Parliament, while still recording as Funkadelic as well. Parliament's records tended to be more R&B dance-oriented, while Funkadelic leaned toward the psychedelic side of rock & roll.

Parliament was signed first to Invictus and then to Casablanca. In the mid and late 70s, they were at the forefront of funk music, playing crazed shows that included spaceships landing on stage and articulated Clinton's acid-tinged funk cosmology, where the pro-funk and anti-funk forces battled it out. Characters such as Sir Nose D'Void of Funk were routinely forced to give up the funk and dance at the end of Parliament's concerts. Hits included "Up for the Down Stroke," "Chocolate City," "Tear the Roof Off the Sucker (Give Up the Funk)," and "Flash Light." Group members included Fuzzy Haskins, Bernie Worrell, Bootsy Collins, Fred Wesley, Maceo Parker, Eddie Hazel, Gary Shider, and Michael Hampton. Offshoots included the P-Funk All-Stars, Bootsy's Rubber Band, the Brides of Funkenstein, Fred Wesley & the Horny Horns, and Parlet. –RB

☆ **Up for the Down Stroke / CASABLANCA**   1974
The first album by Clinton's revamped Parliament remains a perfect introduction, although its best songs are on their *Greatest Hits*. –JF

Clones of Dr. Funkenstein / CASABLANCA   1976
The band's most funkadelic-like concept album is worthwhile mostly for the great "Sexy Body" and "Dr. Funkenstein." –JF

☆ **Mothership Connection / POLYGRAM**   1976
Another brilliant album. Takes James Brown and Sly Stone into an entirely different, but definitely related galaxy. –JF

☆ **Funkentelechy ... / POLYGRAM**   1977
Funkentelechy vs. the Placebo Syndrome offers an even better introduction to the group than the singles collection, by presenting the most intelligible and rhythmically unstoppable glimpse into Clinton's P-Funk world. –JF

Motor Booty Affair / CASABLANCA   1978
Another concept album, only this time the concept is about water and not being able to swim and not wanting to swim. This album is worth hearing, in spite of its occasional Frank Zappa-isms. –JF

● **Greatest Hits (The Bomb) / POLYGRAM**   1984
A solid if scanty assortment of their best singles. –JF

GRAM PARSONS   1946-1973

Country rock. Parsons is considered the founder of country-rock. Like Hank Williams, Parsons lived hard and died young, but not before leaving behind a fine recorded legacy. This included stints with the International Submarine Band, the Byrds, the Flying Burrito Brothers, and finally as a solo artist. Parsons strove to break down the barriers between country and rock. He stripped country music down to its basics, while making its concerns more contemporary. For his two solo albums on Reprise, he is backed up by, among others, Elvis Presley's band and Emmylou Harris. The duets with Harris are superb. Harris has since gone on to re-record most of Parsons's material on her solo albums. His influence has also been acknowledged by the Rolling Stones, Elvis Costello, Dwight Yoakam, and Rodney Crowell. In his field, Parsons is the artist all others must be measured against. His music fits comfortably into any rock or country fan's collection. –KMC

Gram Parsons / SHILOH   1968
His first recordings, with the International Submarine Band. Considered by many to be the first country-rock album. Originally titled "Safe at Home." (Out of print) –KMC

☆ **GP/Grievous Angel / WARNER**   1973
1973 & 1974. His two classic solo albums on one CD. Country-rock at its best, featuring Emmylou Harris. –KMC

Gram Parsons & the Fallen Angels / SIERRA   1973
A good live document of Parsons's last tour. Recorded at radio station WLIR in New York. –KMC

ALAN PARSONS PROJECT

Prog-rock. Engineer/producer (Beatles, Ambrosia) Alan Parsons and his colleague, songwriter and lyricist Eric Woolfson, formed this band in 1975. Throughout their career, they have recorded concept albums (including adaptations of Poe and Asimov books), with a revolving cast of session musicians. 1982's *Eye in the Sky* was their greatest success; the title track charted at #3 on the pop charts and the album went platinum. –ED

○ **Tales of Mystery & Imagination / POLYGRAM**   1976
The Alan Parsons Project's first and best album (if not its most popular one) interprets the ominous poems and stories of Edgar Allan Poe. Heavy on synthesized keyboards and dramatic choral parts, it's rock soundtrack music minus the film. The group went on to make a series of similar followups, notably including *I Robot* and *Eye in the Sky*, but this is the place to start. –WR

Best of Alan Parson Project - Vols. 1 & 2 / ARISTA   1988
These two volumes collect the high points of their later albums, including tracks from *I Robot, Turn of a Friendly Card*, and *Eye in the Sky*. –SWB

LES PAUL   B 1915

Pop. The history of recorded music would have been different, much different, if it were not for the pioneering efforts of guitarist and inventor Les Paul. He started as a country musician, working radio spots in the early 30s as Rhubarb Red. Bitten by the jazz bug early on, he formed the Les Paul Trio in 1936, working for bandleader Fred Waring through the end of the decade. By the 40s, his experimenting with guitars and recording gear. He was among the first to build a solid-body electric and certainly the first to popularize the idea; his Gibson Les Paul models of the 50s now all highly sought-after collector's items. He was the first to pioneer multi-track recording and overdubbing, the use of tape echo, phase shifting, etc., changed the sound of popular music forever, most notably on the recordings made in the early 50s with his wife, vocalist Mary Ford. Paul is a consummate player, arranger, engineer, and entertainer, his inventions are only part of what makes him one of the giants of American music. –CK

★ **Early Les Paul / CAPITOL**
Strictly guitar wizardry here. The best of his 40s and 50s Capitol sides. Stunning. –HD

The Les Paul Trio / LASERLIGHT
A radio performance ca. 1947. –HD

☆ **The Legend and the Legacy / CAPITOL**   1991
Beautiful 4-CD boxed set of all of Les and Mary's best Capitol recordings, with the bonus of numerous unissued songs and a track-by-track commentary by Les in the accompanying booklet. A must have. –CK

FREDA PAYNE   b 1945

Soul, pop. A Detroit soul/jazz/pop vocalist. Multitalented and beautiful, Payne crashed the soul and pop playlists in 1970 with a series of powerful sides for Holland-Dozier-Holland's Invictus imprint. Payne's early musical experience was quite varied, and she debuted on the jazz-oriented Impulse! label in 1965. Her 1970 blockbuster, "Band of Gold," made Payne a pop star with its strident message and insistent bassline, and she encored with "Deeper & Deeper." The controversial antiwar anthem "Bring the Boys Home" proved her biggest R&B seller the next year. Payne hosted a TV gabfest during the 80s. –BD

○ **Greatest Hits / HDH-FANTASY**   1991
Includes the classic "Band of Gold" and other post-modern Holland-Dozier greats. –RAB

PEACHES & HERB

R&B, soul, pop. R&B duet from Washington, DC. The sweet harmonies of two different women billed as Peaches allowed Herb Fame to bridge the 60s soul era and 70s disco days resulting in major hits for Peaches & Herb in both decades. The original pairing — Fame and Francine Barker — burst onto the soul scene in 1966 with the charming "Let's Fall in Love" on Columbia's Date subsidiary. Covers of the Five Keys's "Close Your Eyes" and Ed Townsend's "For Your Love" gave the duo two sizable R&B sellers the next year. By the turn of the decade, the original Peaches & Herb were hit-making history, but after an extended hiatus, Fame considered Linda Green to be ripe for the picking as his new Peaches, and they actually bettered the earlier incarnation in sales. "Shake Your Groove Thing" went gold on Polydor in 1978, and the cooing, slow-dance classic "Reunited" went platinum the following year, topping both the R&B and pop lists. –BD

○ **Peaches & Herbs' Greatest Hits / EPIC**
A vinyl collection of the lovey-dovey DC duo's late-60s finest — includes "Reunited" and "Let's Fall in Love." –BD

PEARL JAM

Alternative rock, heavy metal. Pearl Jam was formed in 1990, originally as Mookie Blaylock. Members Jeff Ament and Stone Gossard were once part of the Seattle punk/grunge band known as Green River. With their separation, Ament and Gossard formed Mother Love Bone with friend Andrew Wood, whose own band Malfunkshun had split up as well. Mother Love Bone released a well-received EP and was ready to release their debut album when Wood died in a coma caused by an overdose. Ament and Gossard chose not to continue Mother Love Bone any further, but as a tribute, they formed a one-time side project (with Soundgarden vocalist Chris Cornell and drummer Matt Cameron) called Temple of the Dog, a band that featured a vocalist from San Diego named Eddie Vedder. With the project complete, Ament, Gossard, and Vedder decided to join forces and become a new band, who were immediately signed by a major label without any underground/college support. –JB

○ **Ten / CBS**   1991
Includes "Jeremy." –ED

ANN PEEBLES   b1947

Soul. Ann Peebles was the queen of Willie Mitchell's Memphis-based Hi Records roster during the 70s, when Al Green was its undisputed king. Sung in a voice as bittersweet as it is riveting, her always-dramatic recordings include one undisputed masterpiece, "I Can't Stand the Rain," cited as a favorite by John Lennon and most recently covered by Tina Turner. Other covers abound — Robert Palmer took "I'm Gonna Tear Your Playhouse Down," and Bette Midler claimed "Breakin' Up Somebody's Home." Backed by the brilliant Hi rhythm section and flawlessly produced by Mitchell, Peebles sang and wrote (often in partnership with husband Don Bryant) of the feminine perspective on the darker side of love — sometimes untrusting love, but love, for better or worse. Her work represents, with elegance and grit, some of the best of Memphis soul. –CO

○ **Greatest Hits / MCA**
Backed by the vaunted Hi rhythm section and produced by Willie Mitchell. Includes her original "Come to Mama" and "I Can't Stand the Rain." These are classics of the 70s Memphis soul idiom. –BD

TEDDY PENDERGRASS   b1950

R&B, soul, pop. In 1970 Pendergrass joined Harold Melvin and the Blue Notes as their drummer and lead vocalist; he sang on all of the group's Top 40 hits. Pendergrass left the group in 1976 and scored eight Hot 100 hits before he suffered an auto accident that left him partially paralyzed. He made a comeback two years later with *Heaven Only Knows*, which did not fare all that well commercially despite "Hold Me," a Top 50 duet with a young Whitney Houston. Subsequent albums also did not sell particularly well. –STE

○ **Greatest Hits / PHILADELPHIA INTNL**   1984
His best husky-voiced erotic soul ballads. –BC

Truly Blessed / ELEKTRA   1990
An inspirational album of R&B anthems and love songs for the 90s. –BC

PENGUINS

Doo-wop. West Coast doo-woppers, led by vocalists Curtis Williams and Cleve Duncan. "Earth Angel," from 1954, was their biggest hit. –JF

Earth Angel / ACE
A 21-track anthology from the Du Tone label. A deeper look at the group's 50s sides and style, built around the title track that sold five million copies worldwide. (Import) –HD

○ **Golden Classics / COLLECTABLES**
Unadorned West Coast doo-wop from the originators of "Earth Angel." Back-seat music. –HD

MICHAEL PENN

Anglo-pop. Penn draws heavily from late-period Beatles, Byrds, Badfinger, Dylan, and early Todd Rundgren for his ultra-melodic power-pop sound. In 1989 Penn (older brother of actor Sean) scored with the hits "No Myth" and "This and That." –RC

○ **March / RCA**   1989
A solid debut album, with the hit "No Myth." –KMC

PENTAGONS

Doo-wop. The Pentagons hit the pop charts twice in 1961 before fading into obscurity. The San Bernadino, CA, quintet's best seller, "To Be Loved (Forever)," was issued on Donna Records, while "I Wonder (If Your Love Will Ever Belong to Me)" came out a few months later on Jamie. –BD

○ **Golden Classics / COLLECTABLES**
Attractive R&B vocal group harmonies. –BD

PERE UBU

Avant-garde. Named for the French absurdist play by Alfred Jarry, Pere Ubu was one of the most important and long-lived bands of the punk/new-wave era (formed in September 1975 in Cleveland). The current edition of the band features original members David Thomas (vocals) and Scott Krauss (drums). Another current member, Tony Maimone (bass), joined the group in 1976. Pere Ubu was organized by Thomas and fellow rock journalist Peter Laughner (guitar, bass) for the purpose of recording the apocalyptic single "30 Seconds over Tokyo." By spring of 1976, Pere Ubu had recorded a second single, "Final Solution," and traveled to New York, where they gained exposure. The band was then reorganized, minus Laughner, who died the following year. Mercury Records signed Pere Ubu and issued their debut album, *The Modern Dance*, in February 1978. Its combination of uncompromising rock, featuring odd noises and Thomas's high-pitched singing, earned the group critical hosannas and commercial indifference beyond a loyal cult, a situation that would continue for most of their existence. That existence was fitful. Pere Ubu was dropped by Mercury and signed to Chrysalis, which released *Dub Housing* and *New Picnic Time* (both 1979), after which the group split again. But they were back to release *The Art of Walking* in 1980 (on Rough Trade). *360 Degrees of Simulated Stereo* (1981) was an archival live album, and *Song of the Bailing Man* (1981) was the last album before another split. 1985 saw the release of a compilation, *Terminal Tower*, and in 1987, Pere Ubu was reorganized, releasing the slighly more commercially accessible albums *The Tenement Year* (1987), *Cloudland* (1989), and *Worlds in Collision* (1991). –WR

The Modern Dance / BLANK   1978
Aggressive punk rock, punctuated by found sounds and noises and topped by Thomas's remarkably affecting near-falsetto shriek. It's not easy listening, but it's powerful and daring, and has lost none of its impact since release. –WR

● **Terminal Tower / TWINTONE**   1985
The songs on *Terminal Tower - An Archival Collection*, many of them taken from Pere Ubu's first singles, demonstrate what helped make them one of the most original and challenging bands of the American New Wave of the 70s. Be warned that songs like "30 Seconds over Tokyo" and "Final Solution" will have a polarizing effect on the listener: either this on-the-edge rock is just what you've been looking for, or it isn't. –WR

○ **Tenement Year / CAPITOL**   1987
Since the re-formed version of Pere Ubu reins in (slightly) the group's more extreme tendencies, this album, which nevertheless presents David Thomas's unique vision and the band's somewhat off-kilter approach to rock more or less intact, may be the place for neophytes to get their feet wet with a highly unusual group. This one should give you the idea — then you're on your own. –WR

CARL PERKINS   ♭1932

Rockabilly, rock & roll. The history of rock & roll guitar would have a gigantic gaping hole without the pioneering efforts of Carl Perkins. He taught Eric Clapton and George Harrison how to play, years before he met either one, and the early Beatles albums were peppered with their versions of Perkins rockabilly classics. Born dirt-poor and ambitious, Perkins started playing the honky-tonks in his native Tennessee with his brothers, fusing elements of hillbilly music with Black blues. He started recording for the Sun label a few months after Elvis, but he was cast as a straight country singer, albeit a fine one, in the Hank Williams mold. Every great singer needs a great lead guitarist, and Carl found one in himself, his combination of fingerpicking chording and rapid spitfire licks becoming instantly recognizable. Turned loose to rock out at his third session, Perkins did just that, producing the ultimate rockabilly anthem, "Blue Suede Shoes." Hitting the #1 slot on the pop, R&B, and country charts, Carl's future seemed assured when he almost perished in a car accident, just as Elvis became a worldwide phenomenon. Minor hits followed (now all acknowledged as classics of the genre), but Carl's star was on the wane. After becoming a member of the Johnny Cash TV show in the 60s (writing hits for Cash and others in the country field), he experienced a comeback when England went rockabilly crazy in the early 70s. Elected to the Rock & Roll Hall of Fame on the second ballot, Carl Perkins keeps on pickin', the ultimate rockabilly survivor. –CK

Blue Suede Shoes & Other Great / RHINO
Selected early work. Very intense and driving music. –HD

★ **Original Sun Greatest Hits / RHINO**   1986
Essential, primal rockabilly. Includes "Everybody's Trying to Be My Baby," "Matchbox," "Honey Don't," "Boppin' the Blues," "Glad All Over," and the original "Blue Suede Shoes." –HD

Dixie Fried / CHARLY   1986
24 original Sun tracks. –HD

Honky Tonk Gal / ROUNDER   1989
Quirky, obscure, and offbeat. A much deeper look into Perkins's Sun period, with emphasis on hillbilly roots. –HD

Jive after Five - Best of Carl Perkins / RHINO   1990
His later CBS work, much of it excellent. –HD

☆ **The Classic / BEAR FAMILY**   1990
Simply the most comprehensive collection imaginable. Five CDs, including all of his essential Sun tracks and alternate takes. All the 1958-1962 CBS sides, plus his 1963-1964 Decca sessions. Indispensable for the serious fan and completist. –HD

JOE PERRY PROJECT

Hard rock. After leaving Aerosmith in 1979, lead guitarist Joe Perry released a couple of moderately successful exercises in Stones/Yardbirds-influenced hard rock. –RC

○ **Let the Music Do the Talking / CBS**   1980
Guitar-driven rock recorded during his temporary alienation from Aerosmith. Heavy metal guitar riffs supported by a stellar rhythm section. –DDC

PERSUADERS

Soul. This 70s soul group is best remembered for their 1971 hit "Thin Line between Love and Hate," which the Pretenders revived in 1984. –JF

○ **Thin Line between Love & Hate / COLLECTABLES**   1974
A gritty soul unit, adept at tragic encounter tunes. The title song is a soul anthem. –RW

THE PERSUASIONS

R&B, soul. A cappella singing has been part of the African-American musical tradition since the days of slavery. Despite the recent success of the hi-tech a cappella group Take 6, the tradition has suffered a steady decline to the point where it is rare even in gospel circles. The Persuasions, though, are resolutely a cappella. Their chart successes have been minimal (two fleeting R&B entries in 1974-1975), but they carry forward the tradition without appearing ossified. Airplay will probably always elude them — and with it the really big breakthrough — but their music has been a consistently enjoyable sidebar, and never one that has simply reeked of revivalism. –CE

Acapella / STRAIGHT-REPRISE   1969
The first Persuasions release, recorded live in Los Angeles. The sound is a little two-dimensional, but to my way of thinking, this recording captures the spirit of joy in live harmonizing, which is the very essence of the Persuasions. Includes great takes on the Temptations's "Don't Look Back" and the Drifters's "Up on the Roof," making manifest the intrinsic connection between 50s doo-wop and 60s group singing. –RB

○ **We Came to Play / CAPITOL / BB 189**   1971
Better produced than their debut, *We Came to Play* continues what became a formula for the Persuasions — covering 50s and 60s classics (the latter most usually taken from the Motown and Curtis Mayfield portfolios), the occasional Tin Pan Alley standard, and judiciously chosen rock/pop covers. In the 70s, a cappella singing was a lost art that the Persuasions were determined to keep alive. –RB

Street Corner Symphony / CAPITOL / BB 88   1972
On this, their highest-charting recording, the Persuasions give more of the same, including gorgeous reworkings of Bob Dylan's "The Man in Me" and the Impressions's "People Get Ready." –RB

We Still Ain't Got No Band / MCA / BB 178   1973
Maintaining their high level of consistency, the Persuasions shy away from Motown here and delve into the blues, tackling Jimmy Hughes's "Steal Away" and a medley of Jimmy Reed's "Baby What You Want Me to Do" and "Bright Lights, Big City." Superb. –RB

● **Chirpin' / ELEKTRA**   1977
After two ill-advised albums for A&M with instruments, the Persuasions returned to their a cappella roots. No longer popular enough to chart, the music was in no way diminished. Highlights include a swinging version of the gospel standard "It's Gonna Rain" and a dramatic reading of Tony Joe White's "Willie and Laura Mae Jones." –RB

PET SHOP BOYS

Dance-pop. This British duo of Neil Tennant and Chris Lane has had an unerring flair for lush, dance-oriented pop. Since the early 80s, they have done well with their droll synth-heavy dance pop. Their biggest hits have been "West End Girls," "What Have I Done to Deserve This?," "Opportunities," and their playful medley of U2's "Where the Streets Have No Name" and "Can't Take My Eyes Off of You." –BC

○ **Discography ... / CAPITOL**   1991
Discography - The Complete Singles Collection is an overview of their chart-toppers in the 1985-1990 period, including a collaboration with Dusty Springfield. –BC

PETER & GORDON

British Invasion. As part of the first wave of the British Invasion, Peter Asher (b Jun 22, 1944) and Gordon Waller (b Jun 4, 1945), as Peter & Gordon, recorded a number of highly successful, lushly orchestrated pop singles that blended Phil Spectorish production sensibilities with Everly Brothers-style harmonies. Their hits included "I Go to Pieces" (#9), "World without Love" (#1), "Lady Godiva" (#6), "Woman" (#14), "To Know You Is to Love You" (#24), and a version of Buddy Holly's "True Love Ways" (#14). –RC

The Best of Peter & Gordon / RHINO   1991
A duo who synthesized Beatles and Everly Brothers harmonies into a wonderfully seamless string of mid-60s British Invasion lite-pop hits. They are all contained here, with great sound and well-rendered liner notes. –RC

TOM PETTY & THE HEARTBREAKERS   ♭1953

Rock & roll. A rock group formed in Los Angeles ca. 1975 by Florida-bred Petty. He has melded a Byrds-influenced guitar style with a Springsteenian sense of epic rock drama to make himself one of the top American rockers. The Heartbreakers, featuring Mike Campbell on guitar, Benmont Tench on keyboards, and Stan Lynch on drums, are simply one of America's finest rock & roll bands. –DH

Tom Petty & the Heartbreakers / MCA   1977
Originally released on Denny Cordell's Shelter label, the 1976 self-titled debut was a real sleeper until the single "Breakdown" (#40) became Petty's first hit almost a year and a half later. This album's release coincided with the advent of the punk and new-wave movements. The lean, edgy production and arrangements only enhanced that perception, in spite of the fact the the songs clearly drew inspiration from the Byrds and 60s Anglo-rock. Among the highlights are the gritty riff-rocker "Strangered in the Night" (which guests Dwight Twilley), "American Girl" (a song so shamelessly influenced by the Byrds that even Roger McGuinn covered it), "Hometown Blues" (later covered by Rosanne Cash), and "The Wild One, Forever." –RC

You're Gonna Get It! / GONE GATOR / BB 23   1978
Not quite so strong as the debut, *You're Gonna Get It* exhibited a denser, Rickenbacker-heavy guitar sound. Petty's voice was practically buried in the mix, particularly on the rockers. Nevertheless, this album does have some great songs, particularly "I Need to Know" (#41), and "Listen to Her Heart" (#59). Each of the first two CDs clocks in at around thirty minutes' playing time. It would've been nice if Petty were true enough to his well-advertised principles (concerning giving consumers value for their money) to fit these two albums on one disc when he re-released them on his own Gone Gator label. –RC

★ **Damn the Torpedoes / MCA / BB 2**   1980
Petty switched producers to Jimmy Iovine, and together they created the masterful *Damn the Torpedoes*. For once, Petty's voice was up front in the mix, giving him much more character. The band never sounded so full or punchy before this. *Torpedoes* opens with a seamless string of great rockers, "Refugee" (#15), "Here Comes My Girl" (#59), and "Even the Losers." Other highlights include "Century City" and "Don't Do Me Like That" (#10). (Also available as a Mobile Fidelity Ultradisc version) –RC

○ **Hard Promises / MCA / BB 5**   1981
Pre-album publicity made much of the fact that Petty was

taking issue with his big bad record label (MCA) over gouging his fans with a list-price increase on this album. Petty won, reinforcing the notion that he was a principled people's artist. The aptly titled *Hard Promises* became another platinum hit. Even though *Hard Promises* is a slight step down from its predecessor, there is plenty of strong material. "The Waiting," one of Petty's finest songs, is the stylistic epitome of his Byrds fixation. Other standouts include the rockers "Kings Road," "A Thing about You," and the darkly humorous "Something Big." –RC

Long after Dark / MCA / BB 9   1982
The highlights of this album, "Straight into Darkness," "Change of Heart" (#21), "Deliver Me," and "You Got Lucky" (#20), may be some of Petty's best, but much of *Long After Dark* suffers from weak melodies and flat-sounding production. –RC

Pack Up the Plantation - Live! / MCA   1985
A solid-as-a-brick live set, featuring incredible symbiotic playing from all the Heartbreakers. –CK

Let Me Up (I've Had Enough) / MCA / BB 20   1987
After the failed *Southern Accents*, Petty and company return to a fairly straightahead collection of rock & roll. Except for a handful of strong tunes like the free-associative rocker (cowritten with Dylan) "Jammin' Me," "Runaway Trains," and "My Life/Your World," much of this album feels like the product of an uninspired band. –RC

○ **Full Moon Fever / MCA**   1989
Recorded as a casual side project, Petty's first solo album possessed more flashes of brilliance than most of his albums put together. It also produced four hits, with "Free Fallin'" (#7), "A Face in the Crowd" (#46), "Runnin' Down a Dream" (#23), and "I Won't Back Down" (#12). Another highlight was a great remake of the Byrds's "I'll Feel a Whole Lot Better." Petty ought to moonlight more often. –RC

Into the Great Wide Open / MCA   1991
This is Petty's first Heartbreakers album after his multi-platinum solo effort, *Full Moon Fever*. The band sounds a little more lively than on the previous two efforts, and the material is generally better than much of their previous two studio albums. However, *Full Moon Fever* is a stronger album, overall. –RC

PFM

Prog-rock. Italy's leading progressive-rock outfit of the early 70s, who would've remained a purely Italian phenomenon had it not been for their being signed by Emerson, Lake & Palmer to the latter's Manticore label. Their sound was more distinctly rooted in the pre-classical era than that of their Germanic counterparts. In addition to electric keyboards (synthesizers, etc.), they also relied on violin and flute (recorder, actually) as major components of their music. Their name, by the way, was short for Premiata Forneria Marconi, the name of the bakery that originally sponsored them. –BE

○ **Photos of Ghosts / MANTICORE**   1987
Their phantasmagorical debut English-language album (sung phonetically, natch), filled with beautifully melodic, classically based songs; strong inclinations toward psychedelia; and a refreshingly open and airy sound, distinct from the thick Germanic textures of competing classical rock bands. (Out of print) –BE

SAM PHILLIPS   ♭1923

Singer/songwriter, rock/pop. Sam Phillips the singer, not the former head of Sun Records, is a California-based singer/songwriter, whose 1987 debut album, *The Turning* (released under her given name of Leslie Phillips) was a contemporary Christian recording issued by Myrrh and produced by fellow Christian and then-future husband T-Bone Burnette. He also handled the boards for Phillips's two secular albums, which have garnered considerable critical praise. –WR

○ **The Indescribable Wow / ATLANTIC**   1988
T-Bone Burnette surrounds Phillips's voice, which has both a little-girl bounce and a teenage ache in it, with neo-60s pop arrangements on songs whose lyrics are often more serious than the inevitably cute-sounding production. But that only means that, once the music has seduced you, the words surprise you. –WR

Cruel Inventions / ATLANTIC   1991
A somewhat less accessible but nevertheless impressive followup. –WR

WILSON PICKETT   b1941

Soul. The Wicked Pickett, as he dubbed himself, first achieved a measure of success as the apoplectic lead tenor on the Falcons's "I Found a Love" in 1962. Fleeting success followed (his original of "If You Need Me" was scooped up by Solomon Burke), before he signed with Atlantic Records in 1964. After a couple of false starts, he was shipped down to Memphis and came back with "In the Midnight Hour." It was followed by similarly compelling entries such as "Don't Fight It," "634-5789," "Mustang Sally," and a hysterical revival of Chris Kenner's mid-tempo shuffle, "Land of 1000 Dances." Scouring old albums, one will also notice that Pickett never lost his feel for a slow ballad, despite his reputation as the prince of the dance floor.
Some have charged that Pickett went on to reduce spontaneous emotion to a cliché, and most of his later records certainly reinforce that notion, but at his considerable best, Pickett was an immensely compelling performer at any tempo. The hit movie *The Commitments* hinted broadly at the esteem in which vintage Pickett is held. Sampled at his best, he was a titan. –CE

☆ **A Man and a Half ... / RHINO-ATLANTIC**   1992
A Man and a Half - The Best of Wilson Pickett is a double-disc set that collects the absolute cream of Pickett's early sides with the Falcons and all the highlights of his successful alliance with the Atlantic label. With "Mustang Sally," "In the Midnight Hour," "Ninety Nine & a Half," "Hey Jude," "Land of a 1000 Dances," "You're So Fine," and "634-5789" all included, this excellent compilation should be one of the cornerstones of anybody's soul collection. –CK

PINK FLOYD

Prog-rock, psychedelic. Practically from its inception in 1965, Pink Floyd was on the cutting edge of psychedelic rock experimentalism, utilizing feedback, sound effects, light shows, unorthodox lyrical themes, and spacey productions. It was band member Syd Barrett (b Jan 6, 1946) who gave the band its moniker, inspired by Georgia bluesmen Pink Anderson and Floyd Council. Barrett's trippy songwriting on their debut album, *The Piper at the Gates of Dawn* (UK #6) (which included the #5 English hit "See Emily Play"), set the band even further apart from most bands of the time. Barrett, however, left the band due to psychological deterioration encouraged by drug abuse, leaving bassist Roger Waters (b Sep 9, 1944) to take over the primary songwriting duties. The band's sonic explorations achieved focus with 1973's seamless *The Dark Side of the Moon* (#1), an album that firmly placed them in the big time. Followup albums *Wish You Were Here* (#1), *Animals* (#3), *The Wall* (#1), and *The Final Cut* (#6) enjoyed phenomenal success.
Waters reveals an increasingly vitriolic spirit in his conceptual themes as he addressed the breakdown of individual dignity in the face of a perceived Orwellian post-WWII social order. It should be said that guitarist Dave Gilmour's (b Mar 6, 1946) soaring guitar work and songwriting contributions on *The Wall's* "Comfortably Numb" gave him a high profile in the band. After *The Final Cut*, Waters and the band acrimoniously split up in 1983, leaving them to pursue various solo efforts, with moderate success.
Gilmour re-formed Pink Floyd in 1987 with drummer Nick

Mason (b Jan 27, 1945) and keyboardist Rick Wright (b Jul 28, 1945), releasing *A Momentary Lapse of Reason* (#3), which sparked a flurry of lawsuits between Waters and the band over the ownership of the name. While the album lacks the thematic bite of Waters's input, the band's sound is intact, helping the album become a worldwide hit. –RC

The Piper at the Gates of Dawn / CAPITOL   1967
The debut album combines long, group-written, largely instrumental compositions with shorter, whimsical, eclectic pop songs written by lead singer and guitarist Syd Barrett (his only full-length album appearance with the group). A wonderful evocation of the distinctly British take on 60s psychedelic music. (Note: Avoid the out-of-print LP version *Pink Floyd*, Tower 5093, which abridges the original UK album.) –WR

○ **Ummagumma / CAPITOL**   1969
A two-disc set, the first disc containing a definitive live set, the second experimental contributions from each of the band members. –WR

Meddle / CAPITOL / BB 70   1971
With *Meddle*, Pink Floyd instrumentally arrived at an airy ensemble sound, which would eventually find full flower on their 1973 classic *The Dark Side of the Moon*. This approach is particularly evident on "Echoes," a periodically languorous jam that takes up one half of the album. Nevertheless, there are enough sonic concepts and pleasant melodies at work on this album to make it worthwhile to the Floyd fan looking to dig deeper than *The Dark Side of the Moon* or *The Wall*. (Also available as a Mobile Fidelity Ultradisc) –RC

Relics / CAPITOL   1971
A singles collection from the Syd Barrett era, containing the British hits "Arnold Layne" and "See Emily Play," among other psychedelic nuggets. –WR

★ **The Dark Side of the Moon / CAPITOL**   1973
Pink Floyd's instrumental prowess and mastery of sound effects, married for the first time to bassist Roger Waters's lyrics about madness, "Time," "Money," and other concerns make for the most impressive mood music of the decade (and sales of 25 million copies so far). (Also available as a Mobile Fidelity gold disc) –WR

Wish You Were Here / CBS   1975
A concept album paying tribute to Syd Barrett ("Shine on You Crazy Diamond") and lambasting the music industry ("Have a Cigar"). –WR

☆ **The Wall / CBS**   1979
This is Roger Waters's two-disc meditation on the travails of a rock star, whose unhappy life causes him to build a psychological barrier between himself and the rest of the world. Contains the #1 hit "Another Brick in the Wall (Part 2)" and the concert favorite "Comfortably Numb" (cowritten by David Gilmour). (Also available as a Mobile Fidelity gold-disc) –WR

The Final Cut / CBS   1983
A Roger Waters solo album in all but name, containing the composer's response to Britain's Falklands War in the form of a massive condemnation of war and government. –WR

A Momentary Lapse of Reason / CBS   1987
A David Gilmour solo album in all but name, heavily featuring the kind of atmospheric instrumental music and Gilmour guitar sound typical of the Floyd before the now-departed Roger Waters took over but lacking Waters's unifying vision and lyrical ability. –WR

PINK SLIP DADDY

Alternative rock, rockabilly, punk. They have an appreciation for the finer things in 60s rock — like colored vinyl, records that play from the inside out, and the roots of punk. Ben Vaughn plays in and produces this band. –BE

○ **Antidisestablishmentarianism / SKYCLAD**
Rockabilly roots with punk (Cramps) energy and a humorous undertone throughout. –RG

THE PIRATES

Rock & roll. Originally organized as the trio backing Johnny Kidd, this band continued working long after the latter's death in a mid-60s automobile accident. Behind lead guitarist Mick Green, who has played with just about everybody over the years (most recently on Paul McCartney's Russian album, *Choba B CCCP*), they embraced their punk roots in the late 70s and early 80s and still do a great show, even without a "real" lead singer. –BE

○ **Out of Their Skulls / WARNER**   1977
Well representative of the latter-day group. Includes both live and studio material, with a savage "Shakin' All Over" as the highlight, and some loud and wonderfully grungy rockabilly. (Out of print) –BE

GENE PITNEY   *b* 1941

Rock/pop. Between 1961 and 1968, Gene Pitney's seamless pop sound scored sixteen Top 40 hits, with songs like "Town without Pity" (#13), "Only Love Can Break a Heart" (#2), "(The Man Who Shot) Liberty Valance" (#4), "It Hurts to Be in Love" (#7), and "I'm Gonna Be Strong" (#9).
Pitney, with his expressive tenor voice, was one of the few artists who successfully bridged the gap from early-60s light-pop to the British Invasion sound. Much of this came from his extensive music-industry background as a producer, engineer, and songwriter, penning hits for Ricky Nelson, the Crystals, Roy Orbison, and others. He also worked with producer Phil Spector and had a knack for identifying upcomers like Al Kooper and Randy Newman.
Pitney's shrewd business sense, coupled with the compliance of manager/publisher Aaron Schroeder, positioned him to record with much more favorable artistic control and greater participation in publishing and royalties. –RC

○ **Anthology 1961-1968 / RHINO**   1986
The voice still sounds surreal, like no one else in pop music, and this collection of hits exudes class. Emotional, pained, stunning. Pitney is a master — rock's Caruso. –JT

THE PIXIES

Alternative rock. This aggressive Boston quartet led by caterwauling vocalist Blackie Francis is one of the finest groups produced during the postmodern era of American rock. That they're also one of the more pretentious and precious can sometimes be overlooked — or, at least, ignored — amid the slashing mix of Francis's banshee-shriek vocals and Joey Santiago's chainsaw guitar. Since their 1987 debut, the Pixies have become college-radio icons. –JF

Come On Pilgrim / ELEKTRA   1987
The band's debut EP is an erratic and tentative first stab but "Bone Machine" is a keeper, and bassist Kim Deal offers a unique and refreshing love song in "Gigantic." –JF

○ **Surfer Rosa / ELEKTRA**   1988
Steve Albini's production on *Pilgrim*'s long-player followup adds more muscle to the Pixies's scratchy sound; Blackie Francis responds with a melodic but thrashing set of anguished howls, arty rave-ups, and some of Deal's best vocals. –JF

● **Doolittle / ELEKTRA**   1989
Their first release on Elektra cohesively blends cacophony with moments of shimmering melodic splendor — witness "Wave of Mutilation." This is also where you'll find the Pixies's finest stab at blatant guitar pop, "Here Comes Your Man." Gil Norton's production lacks Albini's gritty edge but places more emphasis on the deadlocked rhythm section. –JF

Bossanova / ELEKTRA   1990
For longtime fans, this was a disappointing followup to *Doolittle*; the guitar abrasion is reduced to a mere roar, and many of Francis's songs go nowhere. Nevertheless, "Blown Away," "Velouria," and "All over the World" work as second-string cuts, and "Havalina" is the band at their most quiet and lovely. –JF

○ **Trompe le Monde / ELEKTRA**   1991
A return to the rave-up squall of *Surfer Rosa* and the concise, dry-witted songwriting of *Doolittle*. From the opening blasts of the title cut and "Planet of Sound," up through tough vamps like "Subbacultcha" and "Head On" (a Jesus and Mary Chain cover), *Trompe* suggests the Pixies have found a way to elaborate on their sound and approach without sacrificing its bite or its relevance. –JF

PLANET PATROL

Urban R&B, funk, dance-pop. This Arthur Baker-produced group kicked in the era of minimalist electronic hip-hop, using the raw soul vocals of Herb Jackson as an anchor. –JF

☆ **Planet Patrol / TOMMY BOY**   1983
Early-80s collection of Arthur Baker and Afrika Bambaataa's groundbreaking hip-hop creations, with some Todd Rundgren and Gary Glitter covers thrown in for spice. Electro-funk at its best. –JF

ROBERT PLANT   *b* 1948

Hard rock, rock/pop. British hard-rock/heavy-metal singer Robert Plant had released a couple of singles and worked with a number of bands before he hooked up with Jimmy Page's New Yardbirds, subsequently renamed Led Zeppelin, around the time of his 20th birthday in 1968. For the next 12 years, Plant was one of the biggest rock stars on the planet. He gradually developed as a singer, branching out into other styles within Zeppelin's hard-rock framework, and he blossomed as a songwriter as well.
Plant launched a solo career in 1982 with the album *Pictures at Eleven*, a gold-selling hit. He did even better the following year with *The Principle of Moments*. It sold a million copies, included the Top 20 hit "Big Log," and led to his first post-Zeppelin concert tour. Surprisingly, Plant then organized a one-off mini-album, *The Honeydrippers - Vol. One*, recording some rock oldies with a superstar pickup band. He faced greater consumer resistance with his third solo album, *Shaken 'n' Stirred*, perhaps because joint appearances with Page led an audience to desire for a Zeppelin reunion. To an extent, Plant fed that desire with *Now and Zen*, which sampled Zeppelin tracks and featured Page. It was another million-seller. Plant's 1990 followup, *Manic Nirvana*, went gold. –WR

Pictures at Eleven / ATLANTIC   1982
The directions in which Plant seemed to be heading in the later Zeppelin records — toward lighter, more melodic music, tempered with sometimes odd rhythms — are continued on his first solo album, which finds him singing more and screaming less. It wasn't Led Zeppelin, but then, that was the whole point. –WR

○ **Principle of Moments / ATLANTIC**   1983
Plant reinvents rock and pop oldies in much the way Led Zeppelin recast old blues songs. "Other Arms" recasts "Lay Down Your Arms," as Plant declares, "I'm not a prisoner of the big parade," while "In the Mood" retools an old pop theme. The playing is propulsive (thanks to guest drummer Phil Collins) and Plant's singing unusually supple. –WR

Now and Zen / ATLANTIC   1988
Robert Plant hires a new band, prominently featuring keyboardist Phil Johnstone, and also adds a backup singer for a fuller sound. At the same time, the appearance of Jimmy Page on "Tall Cool One," a Top 25 hit, casts a glance back at Plant's Led Zeppelin days. –WR

THE PLATTERS

R&B, doo-wop. During the 50s and early 60s, this Los Angeles vocal quartet, featuring the soaring tenor of lead singer Tony Williams (b Apr 15, 1928), successfully straddled the line between teen and adult audiences with their romantically charged material. The Platters charted 35 Top 100 hits while on Mercury Records. Their hits, many of which were penned by manager Buck Ram, included "Only You (And You Alone)"

(#5), "The Great Pretender" (#1), "My Prayer" (#1), "Twilight Time" (#1), "Smoke Gets in Your Eyes" (#1), "Harbor Lights" (#8), "(You've Got) The Magic Touch" (#4), and "Enchanted" (#12). −RC

☆ **Magic Touch - An Anthology / MERCURY** 1991
Double-disc set of all their best sides, including "The Great Pretender," "Smoke Gets in Your Eyes," "Only You," "Harbor Lights," and the title track. Great annotation and impeccable sound. All compilations should be done this well. −CK

POCO

Country rock, rock/pop. Founded by Jim Messina and Richie Furay during the dying days of Buffalo Springfield, with Randy Meisner (who dropped out shortly before the recording of their first album), Rusty Young, and George Grantham, the band built a solid reputation in Los Angeles as an innovative country-rock ensemble. Their first album, *Pickin' Up the Pieces*, was one of the strongest debut records of its era, a blend of country and western influences, Beatlesque harmonies, and mainstream rock, all within one cover. They began developing a major national reputation with the release of their second album, *Poco*, at the same time that the group's membership entered what proved to be a virtually constant state of flux. By the mid 70s, the band had become an established fixture in the middle reaches of the national charts but Messina and Furay were long gone. The band continued recording well into the late 70s on MCA after leaving Epic, and their following was strong enough to justify a posthumous live album from Epic at the same time. The original quintet, which never did get to record, finally went into the studio under the auspices of RCA in the late 80s. −BE

Pickin' Up the Pieces / EPIC 1969
Their debut album, which is as accomplished as anything by Buffalo Springfield, also recalls the Beatles and the Byrds in its musical orientation. (Out of print) −BE

Poco / EPIC 1970
The second Epic album has a slightly harder sound than the debut. It reflects the results of an additional eight months of work, plus a fresh membership change. −BE

Deliverin' / CBS 1971
The first of two live albums, and consisting of entirely new material — a major country-rock success, capturing not only the lyricism and upbeat approach of the band, but also the infectiously positive attitude of its fans. −BE

From the Inside / CBS 1971
A most unusual record, produced by Memphis guitarist Steve Cropper. Much harder-edged than the rest of the group's output, this album is much more a solid rock album and relies less on the harmony sound than their other records. −BE

Good Feelin' to Know / CBS 1972
The title track is a failed attempt at a hit single, but the record as a whole is a much more pure rock album than they were known for. −BE

○ **Forgotten Trail (1969 - 1974) / EPIC** 1986
This definitive 2-CD collection is full of wonderful moments and great songs, so it is the obvious starting point. −BE

Crazy Loving - Best of Poco 1975-1982 / MCA 1989
An anthology of the group's second era, distilling the strongest tracks from those seven years. −BE

Legacy / RCA 1989
A reunion of the original quintet for a warmly nostalgic, crisply played collection. −BE

THE POGUES

Alternative rock. The Pogues combined traditional folk of all stripes (with an emphasis on Irish folk) with rock muscle, producing some of the most original and remarkable music of the 80s. Originally known as Pogue Mahone (Gaelic for "kiss my ass"), the group (Shane MacGowan, vocalist and songwriter; Philip Chevron, guitar; Spider Stacy, tin whistle;

Andrew Ranken, drums; James Fearnley, accordion; Darryl Hunt, bass; Jem Finer, banjo; Terry Woods, mandolin) formed in 1982. The Elvis Costello-produced *Rum Sodomy & the Lash* proved MacGowan was a gifted songwriter and earned the band several UK hits. Original bassist Caitlin O'Riordan left the band in 1985 and married Costello; O'Riordan was replaced by Hunt. The Pogues signed to Island, releasing *If I Should Fall from Grace with God*, arguably their best album, in 1988. MacGowan's health began to deteriorate due to drug use, culminating in a breakdown in the fall of 1990. Since then, Joe Strummer has toured with the band; the future of MacGowan in the Pogues is uncertain. −STE

Red Roses for Me / ENIGMA 1984
A very raw but enjoyable debut. −SW

○ **Rum Sodomy and the Lash / STIFF** 1985
A triumph, produced by Elvis Costello. Shane MacGowan has never sounded so intense nor has the band played with such authority. A classic melding of punk-era-defined sensibilities and the magic of Celtic traditionalism. Features a stirring version of Eric Bogle's classic "And the Band Played Waltzing Matilda." (Import) −JD

○ **If I Should Fall from Grace ... / POLYGRAM** 1987
If I Should Fall from Grace with God, The Pogues's third album, is another fiery, eclectic meld of traditional Celtic music and rock played with punk venom. The band can barely keep up with the breakneck pace of songs like "Bottle of Smoke," which is what makes the album so appealing. Overall, this album has more of a rock spirit than *Rum Sodomy and the Lash*, and MacGowan's songs show significant strides in quality. −STE

● **Essential Pogues / ISLAND** 1991
Essential Pogues doesn't cover *Red Roses for Me* or *Rum Sodomy and the Lash*, so it isn't the definitive collection. However, it does capture the majority of the highlights from their Island albums and functions as a good introduction to the band. One complaint: the tedious extended remix of "Yeah, Yeah, Yeah, Yeah, Yeah" was included instead of the punchy, energetic original single. −STE

POI DOG PONDERING

Alternative rock. A strange mélange of folk, Third World, Celtic, Hawaiian, and punk, which made some ripples on the 1989 self-titled debut of this Austin, TX, octet. When people talk about the splintering of the mainstream in popular music, this is what they mean. −DH

○ **Poi Dog Pondering / CBS** 1987
Not so precious as some of their other work. This album, their major-label debut, is certainly whimsical, but it contains enough assertiveness to make their folk-rock worldbeat engaging. −JD

BUSTER POINDEXTER b 1950

Pop, R&B/rock. "Buster Poindexter" is the pseudonym rock singer David Johansen adopted in the mid 80s for a semi-comic nightclub-singer act he began to perform. Eschewing his hard-rock solo career (which followed a stint as lead singer of the New York Dolls), Johansen turned up at the New York club Tramps in a tuxedo, with a band he dubbed the Banshees of Blue, and sang pop standards, jump blues, and various novelty material. Eventually, the act won him a record contract, resulting in a few albums on RCA, but it was basically a live attraction. Since then, Johansen has pursued an acting career, though he maintains the Buster persona, appearing, for example, in the Catskills in the summer of 1992. −WR

○ **Buster Poindexter / RCA** 1987
You can't experience Buster Poindexter's campy nightclub act on a studio recording, but you can get a sense of the material by listening to the Caribbean dance strains of "Hot Hot Hot" and the Wynonie Harris hit "Good Morning Judge." There are also a couple of good songs by one David Johansen. −WR

THE POINTER SISTERS

Soul, urban R&B, pop. Versatile Ruth, Anita, June, and Bonnie Pointer regularly scored pop and soul hits throughout the 70s and 80s in a chameleonic variety of styles. Formed in Oakland, with their first successes for Blue Thumb Records blending funky rhythms with a novel nostalgic attitude (beginning with their 1973 revival of Allen Toussaint's "Yes We Can Can"), leading up to their first #1 R&B item in 1975, "How Long (Betcha' Got a Chick on the Side)."

Bonnie signed with Motown in 1978 and kicked off her own string of R&B hits with "Free Me from My Freedom/Tie Me to a Tree (Handcuff Me)." (June and Anita also tried the solo route during the 80s, without leaving the fold.)

By 1979, when the remaining trio covered Bruce Springsteen's "Fire," the Pointers were headed in a more contemporary direction on the Planet label, and "He's So Shy" (1980), "Slow Hand" (1981), "Automatic," and the anthemic "Jump (For My Love)" (the last two both 1984) were savvy ditties that blazed trails across the R&B and pop charts. −BD

○ **Break Out / RCA**   1983
This hit package, produced by Richard Perry, includes "I'm So Excited," "Jump," and "Neutron Dance." −RAB

POISON

Rock/pop, heavy metal. A hard-rock quartet consisting of singer Bret Michaels, guitarist C. C. Deville, bassist Bobby Dall, and drummer Rikki Rockett, Poison was formed in Harrisburg, PA, in 1983, though the band members relocated to Los Angeles early on, where their highly visual approach (drummer Rockett was also a hairdresser who advised them on clothes, hair, and makeup) made them favorites in the city's glam-rock underground. C. C. Deville left the band in early 1992. −WR

Look What the Cat Dragged In / CAPITOL   1986
Glam-metal gets revived with the Los Angeles group, Poison, who turned many heads with their hook-filled songs as well as their looks. Although subsequent albums were more diverse, this one was loose and fun without a care for safety. Includes their first hit, "Talk Dirty to Me." −JB

○ **Open Up & Say ... Ahh! / CAPITOL**   1988
This, the group's most popular album, presents its taste for straightforward hard rock ("Nothin' but a Good Time"), for acoustic ballads ("Every Rose Has Its Thorn"), and for its roots in simple pop-rock ("Your Mama Don't Dance"). −WR

Flesh & Blood / CAPITOL   1990
On their third album, vocalist Bret Michaels puts in his best performance. "Unskinny Bop" and the anthemic "Something to Believe In" were both Top Ten hits. −JB

Swallow This Live / CAPITOL   1991
A two-disc concert release that captures Poison in all its excess (six-and-a-half-minute drum solo, nine-and-a-half-minute guitar solo) and hard-rock glory, with live versions of the hits that are better produced and more impassioned than the original studio cuts. −WR

THE POLICE

Rock/pop. In 1977, Sting (a British ex-schoolteacher born Gordon Sumner) and Stewart Copeland (a young drummer from the US) met up with guitarist Andy Summers (of Soft Machine), and the three formed the final lineup of the Police — the rock group that would later take the early 80s by storm. The band's debut album, *Outlandos d'Amor*, which sported jazz and reggae rhythms in a rock/pop format, was released in 1978. The album, with such classic songs as "Roxanne," was popular with college radio, marking the beginning of the band's ascent to fame. The followup, *Regatta de Blanc*, was released the next year; with its bouncy, lively songs, it hit #1 in the UK for four weeks. *Zenyatta Mondatta*, released in 1980, achieved the same success on the UK charts and became the band's first album to place into the US Top Ten. *Ghost in the Machine* was a success as well, and in 1983 *Synchronicity* was

released and went multi-platinum. It hit #1 on the US charts for 12 weeks and won three Grammy Awards, including Song of the Year for the single "Every Breath You Take." In 1985 the three band members split to pursue solo careers, reuniting in 1986 to release *Every Breath You Take - The Singles*, which featured a remake of "Don't Stand So Close to Me." −IME

Outlandos d'Amour / A&M   1978
The Police's first album, although fairly rough, is still an impressive first effort. Although "Can't Stand Losing You" was their first hit (it made the Top 50), the best-known track on this album is definitely "Roxanne," still a favorite among college-radio stations. The influence of the punk era on this album is evident, as is bass player Sting's jazz background. A great deal of fun. −IME

Regatta de Blanc / A&M   1978
The very title, *Regatta de Blanc* (rough French for "White reggae"), describes the style of the Police's second album. This speedy mix of reggae and mainstream rock spawned two #1 UK hits with "Message in a Bottle" and "Walking on the Moon." The reggae influence is most noticeable in the rhythms, especially on the tracks "Bring On the Night," "Walking on the Moon," and "The Bed's Too Big without You." −IME

○ **Zenyatta Mondatta / A&M**   1980
This album, although a bit rough around the edges, marks a transitional point in the band's career. "Don't Stand So Close to Me" became a #1 hit on the UK charts, and the band edged further into the mainstream. The sound became more pop oriented on this album, with songs like "De Do Do Do, De Da Da Da" and "Canary in a Coalmine," although they retained their unique sense of rhythm. For a good introduction to early Police, this album is a wise choice. −IME

Ghost in the Machine / A&M   1981
One of the Police's best songs, "Every Little Thing She Does Is Magic" (#3), is featured on this album, but as a whole, *Ghost in the Machine* is bland. Besides being poorly mixed (the music overpowers the vocals), the songs lack the musical simplicity and direction that is so appealing in the earlier albums. −IME

★ **Synchronicity / A&M**   1983
A departure from early Police, this album completed the band's transition into mainstream pop while, at the same time, becoming more musically refined. *Synchronicity* had the complexity of *Ghost in the Machine* without the boredom. The Police get louder and angrier, making this a stronger, more driving album. *Synchronicity* contains some of the band's most well-known work: "Every Breath You Take," which went #1 on both the US and the UK charts; "Wrapped around Your Finger"; and "King of Pain." The pinnacle of the band's career, it went multi-platinum and secured the Police's claim to the title of "Rock-gods" in the early 80s. With the exception of Andy Summers's "Mother," there is not a bad song on the album. The CD contains the bonus track "Murder by Numbers." (Also available as a Mobile Fidelity UltraDisc) −IME

○ **Every Breath You Take - The Singles / A&M**   1986
A collection of singles from the five Police albums, this provides a consistent sampling of some of the Police's best work, from "Roxanne" to "Every Breath You Take." It's a good overview of the band's work and an excellent place to get an introduction to their music. This also includes a 1986 remake of "Don't Stand So Close to Me," featuring all three members of the band. −IME

PONTIAC BROTHERS

Rock & roll, rock/pop. When they finally broke free from their Rolling Stones obsession, the Pontiac Brothers proved to be a guitar-loving, humorous, slightly twisted roots-rock band, with more rock than roots. Features Ward Dotson, formerly of the Gun Club. −BE

○ **Johnson / RCA**   1988
This great rock album defines the band's own sound: part Rolling Stones, part Replacements. −RG

THE POSIES

Power-pop. This Seattle-based power-pop quartet is influenced by the Move, Big Star, Badfinger, and the Beatles. The songwriting and harmonic skills of Jonathon Auer and Kenneth Stringfellow are particularly striking, at times sounding like Graham Nash-period Hollies. –RC

Failure / POPLLAMA   1988
Failure is worth looking up, not so much because it represents a mature work but because it's a nice diamond-in-the-rough portrait of a band with a deep creative resource and a strong sense of pop history. –RC

○ **Dear 23 / GEFFEN**   1990
From the Move-influenced "My Big Mouth" to the delicate, wistful "Everyone Moves Away," through tracks that would do Badfinger or Big Star proud, like "Apology," "Golden Blunders," and "Suddenly Mary," *Dear 23* is Anglo-rock/pop heaven. John Leckie's larger-than-life production might be a little overwhelming at times, but overall it highlights this band's gorgeous harmonies and arrangements to great effect. –RC

Suddenly Mary / GEFFEN   1991
Besides containing one of *Dear 23*'s finer songs, *Suddenly Mary* boasts two bonus tracks, the off-center pop of "Spite & Malice" and (the big surprise) a faithful remake of Big Star's "Feel." It's a damn good version too. Big Star fans will relish this remake. –RC

POSSESSED

Heavy metal. Possessed was one of the best death-metal bands from the Bay Area but came to an end when the ideas went no further. Personal conflict and differences with guitarist Larry Lalonde broke up the band to the dismay of fans and critics. Lalonde eventually played with the short-lived Blind Illusion and now finds a home in the funk/punk/metal band Primus. –JB

○ **Seven Churches / RELATIVITY**   1985
Ugly death/black-metal from San Francisco. Very dark, very evil; the next best thing to the end of the world. –JB

PREFAB SPROUT

Alternative pop. Prefab Sprout, featuring singer/songwriter Paddy McAloon, are an adult-alternative/smart-pop quartet from England, who integrate their music with a Steely Dan-like sophistication in an airy bed of texturous synth-work and acoustic instrumentation. –RC

● **Two Wheels Good / CBS**   1985
A strong album debut of atmospheric, breathy, and clever pop music, with Thomas Dolby's tight production. Earthy and ethereal at the same time. Released overseas as *Steve McQueen*, but with a different name for the US version due to protests from the actor's estate. –SWB

From Langley Park to Memphis / CBS   1988
A good but inconsistent record, with shining tracks like "The Golden Calf," "Cars and Girls," and "I Remember That." Paddy McAloon begins to explore his fixation with pop icons like Elvis and Springsteen. A must for fans. –SWB

○ **Jordan: The Comeback / EPIC**   1990
A stunning masterwork with 19 tracks (over 70 minutes) tied together by recurrent themes of God and Elvis. This one is stylistically all over the map — gospel, soul, rock, and pop. Pop songwriting with acknowledged influences from Jimmy Webb and Paul McCartney. –SWB

ELVIS PRESLEY   1935-1977

Rock & roll, rock/pop. Elvis Presley astonished the White culture of the American 50s with his overt sexuality and synthesis of hopped-up hillbilly music spot welded to the Blackest of blues sources. Preachers railed against it, parents hated it, teenage boys emulated it, and girls went hog-wild in ecstasy over it. It took the world by storm, and while his visual and musical styles had their cultural antecedents in Hollywood and the Mississippi Delta, no one had ever seen anything like him before.

At some point in 1953, the 19-year-old Presley entered Sam Phillips's Sun studios and cut a vanity disc under the auspices of its being a gift for his mother. Truth be known, Elvis (too proud to risk rejection at a formal audition) developed the ploy in hopes of being discovered. By July of 1954, Presley was in the studio again, laying down a series of recordings that transformed Western culture, achieving effortlessly what others would spend their careers pursuing in vain.

In 1955, after no commercial success of major consequence, virtually every label of standing was bidding for his services, including Atlantic, who (with a predominantly Black roster) were prepared to hock their entire assets to sign the unproven singer. His contract was eventually sold to RCA Victor under the guidance of Colonel Tom Parker, a former carnival hustler who aided in Presley's meteoric rise to the top and just as easily assured his slide into mediocrity.

In 1957, at the height of his success, he was drafted into the army, only to return two years later into a world of grade-Z movies and equally abominable soundtrack albums that exhibited only periodic flashes of his original brilliance.

In December of 1968, on his first-ever television special, Elvis (recently married and a father extolling family virtues) took the NBC stage sweating, greasy, and passionate, growling his way nervously through his past, rediscovering his roots, and reinventing his persona as the King of Rock & Roll.

To cap this achievement, he returned to Memphis and recorded there for the first time since 1955. The resulting recordings were the most mature and passionate of his career. This was followed by a much-ballyhooed conquest of Las Vegas, the town that chased him out in 1956. By the end of 1970, after a two-year run of hits and another wall full of gold records, Elvis Presley was the single most successful entertainer in the world. But with worldwide success came the personal problems that would eventually overwhelm him. During the last few years of his life, Presley stumbled onto stages around the country to croon his former glories, an unreliable entertainer, bloated beyond belief, a parody of his former self.

On June 26, 1977, Elvis was presented with a plaque commemorating his two-billionth record pressed by RCA. Less than two months later, on August 16, he died at Graceland, the victim of the progressively toxic effects of the veritable cornucopia of prescription drugs he had been taking for a decade or more. Whether his death was accidental, planned, or staged has been tabloid-magazine fodder ever since. What *is* certain is that, within days of his death, every record and tape on the planet earth with his name on it had been purchased by someone, somewhere. The real merchandising of Elvis Presley had begun in earnest ... –NU & RC & CK & STE

☆ **Elvis Presley / RCA / BB 1**   1956
While RCA had the material, they opted to play it safe and combine five Sun outtakes with seven new recordings and release the Hillbilly Cat's first album. This is a great way to begin a career! The best material here is on a par with the Sun singles. While "Blue Suede Shoes" is a cultural cornerstone of sorts, hearing Elvis's version of Clyde McPhatter's "Money Honey" is still, after four decades, revelatory. –NU

☆ **Elvis / RCA / BB 1**   1956
A solid rock & roll album that almost any rocker of the 50s could claim as their best album. While there are some excellent rhythm numbers ("Rip It Up," "Paralyzed," and too-country "When My Blue Moon Turns to Gold Again"), the album's standout is the panting "Love Me." –NU

☆ **Elvis' Christmas Album / RCA / BB 1**   1957
This combines the four tracks from the *Peace in the Valley* EP with recordings of seasonal standards and popular Christmas classics (Elvis does outstanding versions of "Blue Christmas" and covers the Drifters's arrangement of "White Christmas"). But the album comes together with the lascivious "Santa

Claus Is Back in Town," penned by Leiber and Stoller *at the sessions* so Elvis could have something original on the album. The definitive rock & roll Christmas album of the period, it stands with *A Christmas Gift to You from Phil Spector* as the very best of its genre. –NU

☆ **His Hand in Mine / RCA / BB 13** 1961
An amazing gospel record, in no small part because the gospel music sounds like rock & roll (which is not meant as a slight toward gospel music). You do not need to believe to be moved! The album is as much a showcase for the Jordanaires as it is for Elvis, who takes obvious delight in the ensemble vocals. –NU

How Great Thou Art / RCA / BB 18 1966
Between 1966 and 1968, Elvis recorded just enough studio material to fill one complete secular album and *How Great Thou Art*, a far more polite (and slightly surreal) reading of traditional religious material than the previous outing, a half-dozen years earlier. The performances throughout are superb, the sound impeccable; this actually beat *Sgt. Pepper* as the Best Engineered Album of 1967 in the Grammys! This album is also much closer to mainstream gospel and may not be so immediately accessible to the unconverted; don't let that steer you away from an otherwise great record. –NU

☆ **NBC TV Special / RCA** 1969
After years of making abysmal movies, Presley appeared before a live audience, scared to death. That he more than rose to the challenge is evidenced here, a masterly performance highlighted by the jam-session segment with DJ Fontana and Scotty Moore, where Presley plays electric guitar and knocks out drop-dead versions of "Baby, What You Want Me to Do" and "Tiger Man." –CK

☆ **In Person ... / RCA** 1970
When Elvis and the Colonel decided it was time to start appearing live again, they assembled a crackerjack band (featuring guitarist James Burton) and took on Vegas full bore. Easily the King's best live album, the highlights on *In Person (At the International Hotel, Las Vegas, NV)* include "Johnny B. Goode," the "My Babe/Mystery Train/Tiger Man" medley, and "Suspicious Minds." –CK

Elvis Country / RCA / BB 12 1971
Elvis Country was the second album from the June 1970 sessions. It is Elvis's best single album from the 70s and one of his very best ever. Every performance has something to offer; one can argue about the outstanding selection, although I tend away from the pleading of "I Really Don't Want to Know" to the raving "(I Washed My Hands In) Muddy Water." Even "Snowbird" is sung with passion! –NU

☆ **A Golden Celebration / RCA / BB 80** 1984
This box is what the first one should have been, with six albums of unreleased material: Sun outtakes, Elvis's complete television appearances from 1956, more exhilarating stuff from the "68 NBC Special." The packaging is a great leap forward, the sound impeccable, the selections of value both aesthetically and historically. Recommended to everyone; desperately needed on CD. –NU

☆ **Reconsider Baby / RCA** 1985
Since Elvis's death in 1977, the market has been inundated with an array of repackages, most of them artless, pointless and, a fan might wish, profitless. Part of the 50th Anniversary celebration, *Reconsider Baby* offered little that was new, but the concept — Elvis as an R&B singer — was overdue. The selection is impossible to argue with, the programming perfect, and the album makes its argument aptly. –NU

☆ **Number One Hits / RCA** 1987
Number One Hits contains 18 #1 records from the charts of *Billboard*, who somehow didn't rank "Crying in the Chapel," "In the Ghetto," "Burning Love," and "Way Down" as chart-toppers, although other national surveys did. In fact, according to RCA, every copy of "Way Down" was sold out within days after Presley's death, not just here but all over the planet, and somehow, amazingly, it didn't even make the magazine's Top Ten! –NU

☆ **The Complete Sun Sessions / RCA** 1987
The place where rock & roll begins. "That's All Right," "Baby, Let's Play House," "Mystery Train," "Milkcow Blues Boogie," and "Good Rockin' Tonight," plus fascinating outtakes like "When It Rains, It Really Pours." The cornerstone of any rock & roll collection, and great notes by Peter Guralnick too. –CK

★ **The Top Ten Hits / RCA** 1987
Each of Elvis's 37 Top Ten hits (again according to *Billboard*) on two CDs. I suppose if you want the *big* hits, this is the one to have. I'd like to see a companion volume of all the hits that made #11 to #40; that would be interesting ... –NU

☆ **The Memphis Record / RCA** 1987
Coming hot off the heels of his breakthrough NBC special in 1968, Presley returned to Memphis to record for the first time in 12 years and laid down 20 tracks in the space of four days. He was hot, he was inspired, and it's all here. –CK

○ **Essential Elvis: The First Movies / RCA** 1988
A great collection of movie-soundtrack alternates, including great, eye-opening versions of "Jailhouse Rock" and "Got a Lot of Livin' to Do." –HD & CK

Stereo '57 (Essential Elvis - Vol. 2) / RCA 1988
The second volume of *Essential Elvis* offers Elvis in binaural stereo from the January 1957 sessions that produced several hits. (RCA Victor generously filled the disc out with mono masters of the remaining songs to give the consumer a complete version of the sessions.) This is a lot of fun; the gaffes are numerous, obvious, and hilarious, and for ears raised on multi-track recording, it must be amazing to hear an entire record recorded live in the studio! –NU

☆ **Million Dollar Quartet / RCA** 1990
For years available only as a poor-fidelity bootleg, this is Elvis jamming in the Sun studios with Carl Perkins, Jerry Lee Lewis, and others on a set of primarily gospel and hillbilly material. Loose as a goose, with a true jam-session spirit to it, it offers a fascinating glimpse of one of the few times Presley let his true musical soul come up for air with somebody (Sam Phillips) there to record it. –CK

☆ **King of Rock 'n' Roll - Complete 50s' Masters / RCA** 1992
A casual Elvis fan wanting to assemble a decent overview of the King's 50s sides could probably sweat it down to the *Sun Sessions* CD and Volume 1 of the *Top Ten Hits* compilation. But for those of you who take your 50s Presley seriously, *The King of Rock 'n' Roll - The Complete 50s' Masters* is absolutely essential. For the hardcore Elvis fan, the booklet and CD graphics for this five-disc set provide incentive enough to justify its purchase. The liner notes by Presley expert Peter Guralnick are passionate, contagious in their enthusiasm, and filled with a real sense of history, time, and place. The treasure-trove of unpublished photos, session information and Elvis memorabilia accompanying the booklet text is no less inspiring. But it's the music (140 tracks in all) that's the real meat and potatoes of this set. Every studio track cut during the 50s — the seminal Sun sides, the early RCA hits, movie soundtracks, alternates, live performances, rarities (including both sides of the long-lost acetate he cut for his mother back in 1953) — it's all here in one gorgeous package. Soundwise, this box makes any of the previous issues of this material pale by comparison, the proper (non-reverbed) inclusion of the Sun masters being a particular treat. This is no mere rehash of what's been around a dozen times before — there's a lot of thought and care behind this package, and no serious fan of American rock & roll should consider a collection complete without it. –CK

BILLY PRESTON *b* 1946

R&B, soul. It's advantageous to get an early start on your chosen career, but Billy Preston took the concept to extremes. By age ten, he was playing keyboards with gospel diva Mahalia Jackson, and two years later, in 1958, he was featured in Hollywood's film bio of W. C. Handy, *St. Louis Blues*, as young Handy himself.

Preston was a prodigy on organ and piano, recording during the early 60s for Vee-Jay and touring with Little Richard. He was a loose-limbed regular on the mid-60s ABC-TV "Shindig" series, proving his talent as both vocalist and pianist, and he built an enviable reputation as a session musician, even backing the Beatles on their *Get Back* and *Let It Be* albums.

That impressive Beatles connection led to Preston's big break as a solo artist with his own Apple album, but it was his early-70s soul smashes "Outa-Space" and the high-flying vocal "Will It Go Round in Circles" for A&M that put Preston on the permanent musical map. Sporting a humongous Afro and an omnipresent gap-toothed grin, Preston showed that his enduring gospel roots were never far removed from his joyous approach, less so now than ever. –BD

○ **Best of Billy Preston / A&M**
Contains several fun pop hits, including "Will It Go Round in Circles" and "Outa-Space." –DH

THE PRETENDERS

Rock/pop. The Pretenders, fronted by singer/songwriter Chrissie Hynde, released their 1980 self-titled debut at the height of the punk/new-wave movement. Hynde's bracing, tough-as-nails female take on rock & roll and permutations of love, coupled with the band's inspired musical aggression, stood out in a market flooded with alienated, torn-shirt posturing. Sonically, the Pretenders were a tuneful fusion of mid-60s Anglo rock and late-70s punk energy.

After their sophomore effort, *Pretenders II*, the band's distinctive guitarist, James Honeyman Scott, died as a result of drug addiction, as did bassist Pete Farndon, who had been previously fired for incompatibility. Reeling from the losses, the Pretenders released the fine *Learning to Crawl*, which possessed a less aggressive, more melodic sound.

Over the course of their career, the Pretenders have softened their sound, but Hynde's honest (occasionally awkward and outspoken) search for personal growth has provided many provocative songs. –RC

○ **Pretenders / SIRE**   1980
Chrissie Hynde's tough-girl persona, allied with the aggressive onslaught of Pete Farndon, James Honeyman Scott, and Martin Chambers, makes this the top debut album of its year and prime evidence of the enlivening influence punk had on mainstream rock. –WR

Pretenders II / SIRE   1981
A well-named followup, since this album successfully repeats the formula of the debut, from its punky leadoff track, "The Adultress," to its catchy pop-rock single, "Talk of the Town," and even to its Kinks cover, "I Go to Sleep." But if you liked the first one ... –WR

Learning to Crawl / SIRE   1983
Half the band is dead, Chrissie Hynde has taken time off to have a baby, and the world has changed. The Pretenders are now a front for Hynde, solo artist, an adult rock singer/songwriter and, on such songs as "Middle of the Road," "Back on the Chain Gang," and "My City Was Mine," a damn good one too. –WR

Get Close / SIRE   1986
By now, Hynde is writing songs to her child and taking on social issues. But the chiming guitars are gorgeous, and Hynde's caught-in-the-throat voice has never been more expressive. –WR

★ **Singles / SIRE**   1987
Though the singles-only format makes the Pretenders sound more pop-oriented than they were, especially in the beginning, this album essentially addresses the legacy of punk in the 10 years after its peak, tracing a heritage back to mid-60s Merseybeat and forward to a more rock-based pop music. It also makes the case for Chrissie Hynde as a major artist. –WR

LLOYD PRICE   ♭1933

R&B. Having taken New Orleans by storm in 1952 with his

often-covered #1 R&B hit "Lawdy Miss Clawdy" and a raft of sizzling encores, Lloyd Price yearned for new horizons in 1958, when he signed with ABC-Paramount Records. Price wanted to be a pop star, and it didn't take him long to achieve his goal.

Price's pleading style worked brilliantly on his initial New Orleans sides for Specialty Records, resulting in a string of 1952-1953 R&B hits, but his later ABC output left the second-line rhythms behind in favor of prominent female choruses and giant supper-club-style horn sections. His socko reading of the old Crescent City chant "Stagger Lee" deservedly topped the R&B and pop lists in 1958, and he followed it with the utterly pop-styled "Personality" and "I'm Gonna Get Married," another pair of R&B #1s that sported no hint of Price's New Orleans roots.

As the 60s dawned, Price insisted on interpreting a variety of Tin Pan Alley standards on his albums, although "Come into My Heart" and "Lady Luck," both hits, swung with a brassy, R&B-based drive. Price formed his own Double-L logo in 1963, issuing hits by Wilson Pickett and one for himself — a Vegas-oriented treatment of "Misty." Price seemed to prefer the business end of show biz after that, rather than focusing on his singing career. –BD

Lawdy! / SPECIALTY
Only five years earlier than the pop hits, but what a difference! Wonderful New Orleans R&B, including the memorable "Lawdy Miss Clawdy." –HD

○ **Greatest Hits / CAPITOL**   1990
Price's biggest hits, vintage 1957-1959, like "Personality" and "Stagger Lee." Catchy, brassy, and over-arranged. –HD

PRIMUS

Alternative rock. San Francisco's Primus began in the mid 80s as a straightforward rock band, but as time went on, its members incorporated their own influences, including punk rock, thrash, speed-metal, and funk. The music has a party atmosphere to it, with its lyrics being humorous as well as fun. They are considered to be more of an alternative band, but they've been able to cross over to the metal field with their unique form of music. –JB

○ **Suck on This / CAROLINE**   1990
Originally released on their own Prawn Song label (a parody of Led Zeppelin's Swan Song Records), this is their debut, recorded live in a small club and featuring all of the greatness this trio has. Hard, thrashy funk and punk with a sense of humor. The reissue on Caroline sounds a little muddy. Find the original vinyl pressing on Prawn, which sounds more like a CD than the CD. –JB

Frizzle Fry / CAROLINE   1990
Their first studio album, although some of the songs seem rushed. –JB

● **Sailing the Seas of Cheese / ATLANTIC**   1991
The band's major-label debut, featuring an appearance by Tom Waits on "Tommy the Cat" (originally found on *Suck on This*). Guitarist Larry Lalonde, formerly with Possessed and Blind Illusion, shows his death-metal roots on some of the songs on this album. –JB

PRINCE   ♭1958

Rock/pop, funk, R&B, psychedelic. Minneapolis mega-star, producer, and hit songwriter Prince became one of the most important and successful pop figures of the 80s, due to his immense talent at synthesizing an eclectic spread of musical genres into a singularly identifiable sound of his own. Prince drew from artists as diverse as Little Richard, James Brown, Joni Mitchell, Jimi Hendrix, Sly Stone, and the Beatles, from the goofy, hard funk of George Clinton and Bootsy Collins, and from genres like 60s psychedelic Anglo-pop and 70s urban-soul and jazz.

Thematically, Prince audaciously smeared sexual symbols with the same finesse with which he blended musical styles, with results that ranged from provocative to playful. Early efforts, like *Dirty Mind* (#45) and the aptly titled *Controversy* (#21), did well, in spite of outraging certain quarters of the public with his aggressive androgyny and explicit imagery. Prince's first major breakthrough came in 1982 with the album *1999* (#9), which contained the hit title track and "Little Red Corvette" (#6). His 1984 followup, *Purple Rain*, stayed at #1 for 24 weeks, in part from extensive MTV exposure and the movie of the same name. A semi-autobiographical take on Prince's life (starring Prince), the film broke him into superstardom.

Besides a high-profile artistic career, Prince has penned hits for artists like the Bangles and Sheena Easton, and he's done three movies, *Under the Cherry Moon*, *Sign o' the Times*, and *Graffiti Bridge*, as well as music for *Batman*.

Since then, Prince has continued restlessly to meld various sounds into a funky stew. In spite of occasionally spotty results, Prince has blessed the mainstream Top 40 with some great cutting-edge pop. Among Prince's many hits are "When Doves Cry" (#1), "Let's Go Crazy" (#1), "Purple Rain" (#2), "Kiss" (#1), "Raspberry Beret" (#2), "U Got the Look" (#2), "Alphabet St." (#8), and "I Could Never Take the Place of Your Man" (#10). –RC

For You / WARNER   1978
Prince's debut is a fairly conventional blend of erotic funk, highlighted by the horny "Soft and Wet" and subverted by too much mediocre material. –JF

Prince / WARNER   1979
The followup makes his rock leanings more apparent, culminating in the Hendrix guitar-driven single "I Wanna Be Your Lover." –JF

☆ **Dirty Mind / WARNER**   1980
A delirious, hard-on masterpiece, dedicated to the joy of sex. The guitars are revved up a few notches, the funk has more muscle, and the songs make explicit just how unique (and sometimes twisted) Prince's vision can be. –JF

Controversy / WARNER   1981
Synthesizers move to the forefront and, though the sound is riveting, and while "Do Me, Baby" and the title cut are among his best, this is a tad short on decent songs. –JF

☆ **1999 / WARNER**   1982
Double-album mingling of politics and sex features Prince's sturdiest dance grooves and his first crossover hits ("Little Red Corvette," "Delirious," and the title track). This album is a near-masterpiece. –JF

☆ **Purple Rain / WARNER**   1984
Upon its release, the soundtrack from Prince's big-screen debut sounded as if his artistry had blossomed fully. Today it remains essential for the singles, like "When Doves Cry" and "Let's Go Crazy." Elsewhere, it retreads familiar ground. –JF

Parade / WARNER   1986
Another soundtrack (from Prince's second film, *Under the Cherry Moon*) that boasts some strong singles ("Kiss," "Mountains," and "Anotherloverholenyohead") and some dreary, neo-psychedelic filler. –JF

★ **Sign o' the Times / PAISLEY PARK**   1987
A two-disc, one-man-band romp through everything he does best, from galvanizing grooves (one of which was recorded with the Revolution) to some slinky smoochers, which show for the first time sympathy and genuine affection for his romantic objects. This is Prince's greatest album. –JF

The Black Album / BOOTLEG   1988
Recorded in 1987 but shelved in favor of *Lovesexy*, *The Black Album* is a sinister funk-fest, long on the boogie but short on anything really remarkable. –JF

Lovesexy / PAISLEY PARK   1988
Lovesexy was a better album, anyway. It's not perfect, but it does find Prince attempting to make clear his philosophy, which likens sex to godliness and vice versa. It doesn't fully convince, but "Anna Stasia" and "I Wish U Heaven" should keep you interested. –JF

☆ **Diamonds and Pearls / PAISLEY PARK**   1991
Out of nowhere, Prince suddenly regathers his strengths, assembles the New Power Generation, the best band of his career, and shimmies and strolls through his best album since *Times*. An eclectic yet seamless attestation of Prince's vitality in the 90s. –JF

JOHN PRINE   b 1946

Singer/songwriter. He's from the Bob Dylan school of talented folkies who love to play with words. But unlike most Dylanites, Prine also evokes the sly, dry humor of Woody Guthrie, and his brokenhearted laments are never chauvinistic and only seldom wallow in self-pity. If he's never made one album as great as prime Dylan, that's because he isn't Dylan; he makes great albums that flaunt his own personality, not the personality of his inspirations. –JF

☆ **John Prine / ATLANTIC / BB 154**   1971
A revelation upon its release, this album is now a collection of standards: "Illegal Smile," "Hello in There," "Sam Stone," "Donald and Lydia," and, of course, "Angel from Montgomery." Prine's music, a mixture of folk, rock, and country, is deceptively simple, like his pointed lyrics, and his easy vocal style adds a humorous edge that makes otherwise funny jokes downright hilarious. –WR

Sweet Revenge / ATLANTIC   1973
A bold and brilliant stab at (almost) straight country that tempers Prine's cynical streak with the tone of a jaded humorist and social commentator. –JF

Common Sense / ATLANTIC   1975
A brash album, full of aggressive rock rhythms and morose tunes. Even the Chuck Berry cover, "You Never Can Tell," is shot full of melancholy. –JF

☆ **Bruised Orange / ASYLUM-OH BOY / BB 116**   1978
Despite some brilliant songs, Prine's followup albums to his stunning debut were uneven until this, his fifth, produced by his friend Steve Goodman. Here, Prine's always fine-tuned sense of absurdity once again collides with his ability to depict pain sympathetically for a whole album, typified by "That's the Way That the World Goes 'Round," a neat statement of his philosophy, and "Sabu Visits the Twin Cities Alone," perhaps the best depiction ever written of life on the road in the entertainment business. –WR

Storm Windows / OH BOY   1980
A relaxed effort, defined by straightforward love songs and subdued vocals. Modest but quite nice. –JF

German Afternoons / OH BOY   1986
Another straight country set, but unlike *Sweet Revenge*, this is a sleepy-town stroll, highlighted by some beautiful ballads and snappy accompaniment by the New Grass Revival. –JF

★ **The Missing Years / OH BOY**   1991
Prine took five years between his ninth studio album and this, his tenth — enough time to gather his strongest body of material in more than a decade. From the caustic "All the Best" to the cliché compilation "It's a Big Old Goofy World," Prine's gifts for emotional revelation and off-the-wall humor are on display in abundance, and he's aided by excellent production (courtesy of Heartbreaker Howie Epstein) and strong backup musicians. *The Missing Years* won the 1991 Grammy Award for Best Contemporary Folk Album. –WR

PROCOL HARUM

Art-rock, rock & roll. Formed in 1967, Procol Harum incorporated a weighty classicism into their sound, with occasional traces of R&B and rock & roll. This British group was originally formed around the core of lyricist Keith Reid and singer/songwriter Gary Brooker, who hailed from the R&B club band the Paramounts. Their first collaboration, the stately "A Whiter Shade of Pale," was loosely built off of Bach's "Air on a G String." A band was formed (named after Reid's cat), and in short order, Procol Harum had a record deal and an international hit on their hands. Part of the success of the band's sound was due to Matthew Fisher's stately organ work and Robin Trower's lyrical blues-based lead-guitar playing, which appeared on Procol's second and third albums — *Shine on Brightly* and *A Salty Dog*.

In spite of further lineup changes (eventually incorporating most of the Paramounts), Procol Harum went on to enjoy even greater chart success during the early 70s, particularly *Live in Concert with the Edmonton Symphony Orchestra* (#5). By this time, the band seemed to be trading on its past glories, with flashes of their earlier brilliance briefly resurfacing on their 1974 release *Exotic Birds and Fruit* (#86). Procol Harum eventually broke up in 1977, after the spotty *Something Magic*. –RC

○ **Procul Harum / DERAM / BB 47**   1967
Their spectacular debut showed remarkable songwriting and became a late-60s classic, due to the immense popularity of "A Whiter Shade of Pale," which made their reputation. –CK

○ **Shine on Brightly / A&M / BB 24**   1968
Procol's ambitious sophomore effort expanded upon their symphonic-style rock, particularly the 18-plus-minute conceptual opus "In Held 'Twas In I." The title track was another highlight. –RC

○ **A Salty Dog / A&M / BB 32**   1969
Procol's synthesis of blues and grand classically inspired melodies reached an apex on their third album. The tasteful production featured sweeping orchestrations, subtle sound effects, and dynamic arrangements. *A Salty Dog* became one of Procol's signature numbers. (Also available on Mobile Fidelity) –RC

Home / A&M / BB 34   1970
With Matthew Fisher gone, Procol embraced a harder, more rock-oriented approach best displayed on the herky-jerky riff-rocker "Whiskey Train," a Robin Trower showcase. (Also available on Mobile Fidelity) –RC

Live in Concert / A&M / BB 5   1972
With the help of the Edmonton Symphony Orchestra (Canada), Procol Harum does an impressive job re-creating their more stately numbers, complete with sound effects and a full choir. "Conquistador" became a #16 hit. (Also available as a Mobile Fidelity gold disc) –RC

● **Classics - Vol. 17 / A&M**   1987
This best-of collection covers the hits, plus a decent collection of album tracks. –RC

PRONG

Heavy metal. Could be the perfectly named heavy metal band. From the ashes of New York speed-thrash, Prong plays slower, stripped-down metal without the egregious marketing flourishes (i.e., sexism, satanism). Perhaps a tad derivative, Prong makes up for its lapse in stylistic originality with speed and power. –JD

○ **Force Fed / RELATIVITY**   1988
Brutal and bloody, Prong achieves maximum riff thrust here as Tommy Victor's guitar penetrates the wall-of-steel sonic boom. A dense and forceful album, which is worth many headbangs. –JD

THE PSYCHEDELIC FURS

Alternative rock. The Psychedelic Furs, whose name belies their punk-influenced music, were formed in England in 1977 by brothers Richard Butler (vocals) and Tim Butler (bass), along with saxophone player Duncan Kilburn and guitarist Roger Morris. By the time they released their self-titled debut album in 1980, the group had become a sextet, adding guitarist John Ashton and drummer Vince Ely. That album, featuring Butler's hoarse voice (the tone of which suggested John Lydon without the sneer) was a bigger hit in England, where it reached the Top 20, than in the US.

Talk Talk Talk (1981) did better, reaching the US Top 100 and producing two British singles-chart entries, one of which was "Pretty in Pink," later also a hit in the US when a new version

was used as the title song of a film. *Forever Now* (1982) saw the band reduced to a quartet with the departure of Kilburn and Morris. The rest moved to the US, turned to producer Todd Rundgren, and scored a US Top 50 hit with "Love My Way." Ely then left, and the remaining trio of the two Butlers and Ashton made *Mirror Moves* (1984), the biggest Psychedlic Furs hit yet.

The film *Pretty in Pink* helped spread their name further before the release of their next album, *Midnight to Midnight* (1986), which consequently got to #12 in the UK and the Top 30 in the US and included the Top 30 US hit "Heartbreak Beat." *Book of Days* (1989) marked the return of Vince Ely but was a considerable commercial disappointment. *World Outside* (1991) also failed to find an audience. –WR

The Psychedelic Furs / CBS   1980
This auspicious debut finds the sextet turning out thick, noisy rock (especially in the saxophone-guitar combination) through which Richard Butler's voice cuts like a buzzsaw. Best track: "Imitation of Christ." –WR

○ **Talk Talk Talk / CBS**   1981
An even better followup makes explicit the Furs's connection to the Velvet Underground (their name comes from the Velvets' song "Venus in Furs"). Their strongest overall collection, this includes the original (superior) version of "Pretty in Pink," "Dumb Waiters," and the definitive Psychedelic Furs song, "Into You like a Train." –WR

Forever Now / CBS   1982
Actually, Todd Rundgren's much-vaunted clean, sharp production style has very little effect on the Furs's sound, which is still pretty noisy and still dominated by Butler's hoarse, slightly scornful voice on such songs as "Love My Way," "President Gas," and the title track. –WR

● **All of This and Nothing / CBS**   1988
Not a perfect Furs compilation, but this 12-track look back does contain the notable tracks from the albums *Mirror Moves* and *Midnight to Midnight*, plus some of the necessary ones from the albums listed above and a good new song, "All That Money Wants." –WR

PSYCHIC TV

Alternative rock. They're one of the weirdest products of post-punk music. The former shaman of the group Throbbing Gristle, Genesis P-Orridge conceived this group in 1982 as a youth cult which would espouse the theories of "The Temple ov Psychick Youth." Ex-Gristler Peter Christopherson and Alex Fergusson helped flesh out this skewed industrial vision, which eventually mutated in the late 80s into British acid-house dance drone. –JF

○ **Towards Thee Infinite Beat / WAX TRAX!**   1975
Although it's unvarying, this is a good place to start. –JD

PUBLIC IMAGE LTD.

Alternative rock. Public Image Ltd. (PiL) originally was a quartet led by singer John Lydon (formerly Johnny Rotten b Jan 31, 1956) and guitarist Keith Levene, who had been a member of the Clash in one of its early lineups. The band was filled out by bassist Jah Wobble (John Wordle) and drummer Jim Walker. It was formed in the wake of the 1978 breakup of Lydon's former group, the Sex Pistols. For the most part, it devoted itself to droning, slow-tempo, bass-heavy noise rock, overlaid by Lydon's distinctive, vituperative rant.

The group's debut single, "Public Image," was more of an uptempo pop-rock song, however, and it hit the UK Top Ten upon its release in October 1978. The group itself debuted on Christmas Day, shortly after the release of its first album, *Public Image*. Neither the single nor the album was released in the US.

Metal Box, the band's second UK album, came in the form of three 12-inch, 45 RPM discs in a film cannister. It was released in the US in 1980 as the double album *Second Edition*. (By this time, PiL was a trio consisting of Lydon,

Levene, and Wobble.) The third album, not released in the US, was the live *Paris in the Spring* (1980). Lydon and Levene, plus hired musicians, made up the group by the time of *The Flowers of Romance* (1981), the much-acclaimed fourth album, which reached #11 in the UK.

In 1983, PiL scored its biggest UK hit, when "This Is Not a Love Song" reached #5. By this time, however, Levene had left, and the name from here on would simply be a vehicle for John Lydon. A second live album, *Live in Tokyo*, appeared in England in 1983.

1984 saw the release of *This Is What You Want ... This Is What You Get*, only PiL's third album to be released in the US, though it now had six albums out. It marked the start of Lydon's move toward a more accessible dance-rock style, a direction that would be pursued further in *Album* (1986) (also called *Cassette* or *Compact Disc*, depending on the format), notably on the hit "Rise," as well as on *Happy?* (1987) and *9* (1989). In 1990, PiL released the compilation album *The Greatest Hits, So Far*, and in 1991 came the new album, *That What Is Not*. –WR

Second Edition / WARNER   1980
A two-disc deconstruction of traditional rock music, its tempos steady but slow, its bass track mixed high as in a reggae dub album, and Lydon's droning voice, with its scornful lyrics, wafting in the back. It is what PiL called it at the time, "anti-rock & roll," and it's fascinating. –WR

The Flowers of Romance / WARNER   1981
The drums are loud and sharp, and Lydon wails like some sort of Middle Eastern street singer on this forbidding but rewarding album. –WR

This Is What You Want ... / ELEKTRA   1984
Lydon adds keyboards, horns, and even a violin, double-tracks his vocals, and writes shorter songs with faster tempos. *This Is What You Want ... This Is What You Get* doesn't quite add up to a pop album but you can dance to it. Contains the UK hit "This Is Not a Love Song." –WR

Album/Compact Disc/Cassette / ELEKTRA   1985
Hot guitars and 4/4 time signatures make this sound more like a hard-rock album than anything Lydon's done since the Sex Pistols. And the hit single "Rise" is actually a catchy number, believe it or not. –WR

○ **Greatest Hits So Far / VIRGIN**   1990
Fourteen tracks, recorded between 1978 and 1990, that trace PiL from the punk energy of the first single, "Public Image" (not previously released in the US), through the anti-rock of "Death Disco" and "Flowers of Romance" to the almost-pop of "This Is Not a Love Song" and "Rise" and the best of the late-80s material. –WR

PULNOC

Alternative rock. This Czechoslovakian ensemble, a descendant of the outlawed underground group Plastic People of the Universe, is a synthesis between early-70s art-rock and early Velvet Underground. –RC

○ **City of Hysteria / ARISTA**
Pulnoc comprises ex-members of the important underground Communist-era Czechoslovakian band, the Plastic People of the Universe. This impressive debut, mostly sung in their native tongue, skillfully synthesizes Velvet Underground garage/art-rock with late-60s European progressive music. The lyrics are printed in English. –RC

PURE PRAIRIE LEAGUE

Country rock. Pure Prairie League fused singer/songwriter pop with mellow country-rock. They scored several hits from the mid 70s to early 80s, with "Let Me Love You Tonight" (#12), "I'm Almost Ready" (#34), "Still Right Here in My Heart" (#28), and their most popular track, "Amie" (#27). –RC

Bustin' Out / RCA / BB 34   1972
Bustin' Out was this band's most distinctive album, featuring very bright, thin-sounding acoustic guitars and dramatic

string arrangements, courtesy of David Bowie's lead player Mick Ronson. "Amie" became a standard of sorts for the college coffeehouse crowd. Other highlights include "Jazzman," "Early Morning Riser," "Boulder Skies," "Call Me Tell Me," and "Angel," a song originally recorded on J. D. Blackfoot's *The Ultimate Prophecy*. –RC

○ **Amie & Other Hits / RCA**   1981
This best-of collection contains all the hits and most of the essential album cuts, including a healthy sampling from *Bustin' Out*. –RC

JAMES AND BOBBY PURIFY

R&B, soul. James (b May 12, 1944) and Bobby (b Sep 2, 1939) of this Southern soul duo were not actually brothers but cousins. James Purify and Robert Lee Dickey joined forces for some classic Southern soul duets during the mid 60s. Producer Papa Don Schroeder brought the soulful Floridians to Muscle Shoals in 1966 to record at Rick Hall's Fame studios, and the result was the gorgeous mid-tempo "I'm Your Puppet." The Dan Penn/Spooner Oldham ballad proved their biggest hit for the Bell label, although "Let Love Come between Us" and their revival of the Five Dutones's "Shake a Tail Feather" also made some major noise in 1967. When Bobby mutinied, James went it alone for a while before recruiting a new Bobby (Ben Moore), and they picked up right where the old duo left off. –BD

○ **100% Purified Soul / CHARLY**   1988
A fine album collection (not issued on CD at the time of writing), containing the Purifys's chart hits for Bell. Light and understated, with less fire and brimstone when compared with Sam & Dave, but worthy nonetheless. –RB

PURSUIT OF HAPPINESS

Alternative rock. Canadian hard-pop rockers led by lovesick singer/songwriter Moe Berg, who has written some of the most ravaged (yet hilarious) love songs in recent memory. –JF

Love Junk / CAPITOL   1988
Produced by Todd Rundgren, their debut is cynical but catchy. Contains "I'm an Adult Now." –DH

○ **One Sided Story / CAPITOL**   1990
For their second album, Pursuit of Happiness continued to mine Berg's nakedly hung-up vision of the battle of the sexes. When Berg's obviously male protagonists aren't waxing loopy idealisms, they are engaging in darkly humorous exasperations over feminine nature. "Two Girls in One," "All I Want," "Shave Your Legs," and "Little Platoons" are highlights. Todd Rundgren was brought on board again to produce. Fans of Rundgren's style of power-pop should love this return. –RC

PYLON

Alternative rock. The group that put Athens, GA, on the musical map in the early 80s, thanks to their arty, angular dance-rock. Vanessa Briscoe's clipped melodies figured into the early sound of the B-52's, and her chopped lyrics and the band's minimalist punch influenced R.E.M. (who later covered Pylon's "Crazy"). The group broke up in 1983, but re-formed in 1989 for an album and a tour. –JF

○ **Hits / DB**   1977
Since they had no hits, the title is more than a little ironic, but this collection is the best of Pylon's a quirky college-educated dance-pop. With a blistering rhythm section and quirky singer in Vanessa Briscoe, this gets better with age. –JD

Chain / SKY   1991
This picks up where they left off in the mid 80s. –RG

QUEEN

Hard rock, rock/pop. Queen was a quartet that combined elements of hard rock, heavy metal, and art-rock, adding other styles along the way for an often-majestic sound that also contained a distinct element of campy humor. The group was formed in England in 1971 by singer Freddie Mercury (born as Frederick Bulsara, Sep 5, 1946 - d Nov 24, 1991), guitarist Brian May (b Jul 19, 1947), bassist John Deacon (b Aug 19, 1951), and drummer Roger Taylor (b Jul 26, 1949). They released their first album, *Queen*, in 1973, and it first reached the charts in the US (going gold in 1977). It wasn't until the following year that Queen broke through in its native country, getting a Top Ten hit with "The Seven Seas of Rhye" and reaching the album chart with *Queen II*. *Sheer Heart Attack*, later the same year, was a substantial hit on both sides of the Atlantic (a #2 UK hit with "Killer Queen," #12 in the US).

The biggest of Queen's early albums, however, was *A Night at the Opera* (1975), which topped the UK chart, made the Top Five in the US, and included the gold-selling single "Bohemian Rhapsody," the longest-running UK #1 in 18 years and voted the best song of all time in radio polls (in 1992, bolstered by an appearance in the film *Wayne's World*, it would be a hit all over again in the US). *A Day at the Races* (1976) was also a substantial hit, though it couldn't match its predecessor.

Queen turned to a harder rock approach for 1977's *News of the World*, which included the Top Five hit "We Are the Champions," still a sporting-event favorite. *Jazz* (1978) and *Live Killers* (1979) were successful, if less substantial albums, but Queen took a sharp stylistic turn for *The Game* in 1980 and was rewarded with two uncharacteristic #1 hits, the rockabilly-tinged "Crazy Little Thing Called Love" and the disco-rock "Another One Bites the Dust."

Though Queen scored gold in the US with the subsequent releases *Hot Space* (1982) and *The Works* (1984), the group was in a gradual commercial decline throughout the 80s. It returned to gold-selling status with *Innuendo* in 1991, but singer Freddie Mercury died of AIDS in November of that year. That set off a sales bonanza in Europe and, belatedly, in the US, with a giant benefit concert held in Mercury's honor at Wembley Stadium in England in April 1992. Posthumous releases began to appear, with a boxed set promised. −WR

Sheer Heart Attack / ELEKTRA 1974
An effective demonstration of the range of Queen's musical tastes, from the guitar pyrotechnics of "Brighton Rock" to the vocal histrionics of "Killer Queen" and the on-the-road diary "Now I'm Here." −WR

A Night at the Opera / ELEKTRA 1975
In case there was any doubt that Queen was devoted to over-the-top effects, this massively overdubbed combination of hard rock and opera, paced by May's monster guitar riffs and Mercury's million-voiced choir and emotive solo singing, should have erased it. Contains "Death on Two Legs," "You're My Best Friend," and, of course, "Bohemian Rhapsody." −WR

News of the World / ELEKTRA 1977
In the balance between Queen's operatic tendencies and its desire to rock out, the rock side once again gained an upper hand on this release. Not that the bombast lessened, but songs like "We Will Rock You" were actually dry runs for the stripped-down approach of *The Game* and even "We Are the Champions" was a ballad. Well, almost. −WR

The Game / ELEKTRA 1980
The basic elements of Queen's approach, from May's heavy guitar to Mercury's vocal army, were in attendance here, but the album owes its success to its novelties, especially "Another One Bites the Dust" and "Crazy Little Thing Called Love." −WR

○ **Greatest Hits / ELEKTRA** 1981
They may not have started out that way, but by 1981 Queen definitely was perceived as a singles act. This record gathers their biggest US/UK hits, 1973-1981, including the collaboration with David Bowie, "Under Pressure." −WR

QUEENSRŸCHE

Prog-rock, heavy metal. Formed in early 1981, two years later they released a self-titled four-song EP with decent results from the durability of Geoff Tate's voice (easily comparable to Don Dokken or Iron Maiden's Bruce Dickenson), and the great sound of Michael Wilton (guitar), Chris DeGarmo (guitar),

Eddie Jackson (bass), and Scott Rockenfeld (drums). It sold well, and in 1984 they recorded their first full-length album. They experimented with keyboards and synthesizers, but their use of these instruments was unlike the methods used by other heavy metal and hard-rock bands. In 1988, *Operation: Mindcrime* (a concept album) was released and suddenly Queensrÿche had arrived. −JB

○ **Operation Mindcrime / CAPITOL** 1988
Seattle's best kept secret is let out of the box with a concept album that brought comparisons of Pink Floyd and the Who. Fantastic lyrics with a great story line and powerful playing by the band, and powerful vocals by Geoff Tate, finally noticed by fans a year after its release. −JB

Empire / CAPITOL 1991
An album by a band who know what they want and how to get it. Masterfully produced (recorded digitally), this is the one that made the band international superstars. −JB

QUESTION MARK & THE MYSTERIANS

Rock & roll. Originally formed in Flint, MI, in 1962, this group took its name from the obscure science-fiction movie, "The Mysterians." They recorded the anthemic "96 Tears" for the local Spanish music label Pa-Go-Go in 1966. It was immediately picked up for national consumption by Cameo-Parkway, going on to be one of the most covered garage band classics of the 60s. Lead singer Question Mark (real name listed as both Rudy Martinez and Reeto Rodriguez) continues to front a version of the band on oldies package shows across the US. −CK

○ **96 Tears / CAMEO-PARKWAY** 1967
A true garage-band classic, featuring the title track and 11 others straight from the band's set list. (Out of print.) −CK

QUICKSILVER MESSENGER SERVICE

Psychedelic. The band that became Quicksilver Messenger Service originally was conceived as a rock vehicle for folk singer/songwriter Dino Valenti (b Nov 7, 1943), author of "Get Together." Living in San Francisco, Valenti had found guitarist John Cipollina (b Aug 24, 1943 - d May 29, 1989) and singer Jim Murray. Valenti's friend David Freiberg (b Aug 24, 1938) joined on bass, and the group was completed by the addition of drummer Greg Elmore (b Sep 4 1946) and guitarist Gary Duncan (b Sep 4, 1946).

They debuted at the end of 1965 and played around the Bay Area and then the West Coast for the next two years, building up a large following but resisting offers to record that had been taken up by such San Francisco acid-rock colleagues as Jefferson Airplane and the Grateful Dead. Quicksilver finally signed to Capitol toward the end of 1967 and recorded their self-titled debut album, which appeared in 1968 (by this time, Murray had left). *Happy Trails*, its 1969 followup, was recorded live. After its release, Duncan left the band and was replaced for *Shady Grove* (1970) by British session pianist Nicky Hopkins. By the time of its release, however, Duncan had returned, along with Valenti, making the group a sextet. This version of Quicksilver, prominently featuring Valenti's songs and lead vocals, lasted only a year, during which two albums, *Just for Love* and *What about Me*, were recorded. Cipollina, Freiberg, and Hopkins then left, and the remaining trio of Valenti, Duncan, and Elmore hired replacements and cut another couple of albums before disbanding. There was a reunion in 1975, resulting in a new album and a tour, and in 1986, Duncan revived the Quicksilver name for an album that also featured Freiberg on background vocals. −WR

Happy Trails / CAPITOL 1969
Quicksilver was heard at its best on this partially live album, which contained a 25-minute version of Bo Diddley's "Who Do You Love." −WR

○ **Sons of Mercury (1968-75) / RHINO** 1991
The thorough two-disc best-of contains Quicksilver's most familiar material from its various lineups, plus some rarities.

The only thing keeping this from being essential is the exclusion of the complete live version of "Who Do You Love," over a single edited version. –WR

THE RADIATORS

Rock & roll. A New Orleans-based sextet formed in 1978 and consisting of Ed Volker (keyboards, vocals), Dave Malone (guitar, vocals), Camile Baudoin (guitar, vocals), Reggie Scanlan (bass), Frank Bua (drums), and Glenn Sears (percussion). The group combines a blues-based style of jam-rock derived from the Grateful Dead with indigenous New Orleans rhythms such as second-line parade cadence. After building up a large regional following and releasing two independent albums, the group was signed to Epic Records in 1987. –WR

○ **Law of the Fish / CBS**   1987
The cohesive band feel of the Radiators is emphasized on this well-produced major-label debut. The groups that influenced them (especially Little Feat and the Allman Brothers Band) are obvious — but how many bands are good enough to suggest such comparisons? –WR

Zig-Zaggin' through Ghostland / CBS   1989
There's a slightly more aggressive approach here, but, in essence, the Radiators's albums are all of a piece, probably because the group had been together so long when they got signed. Some of the material here dates back to 1979, but it sounds fresh as well as seasoned. –WR

GERRY RAFFERTY   b 1947

Pop. Scottish artist Gerry Rafferty founded the band Humblebums in 1968 and later on became the coleader of Stealers Wheel, who produced the hits "Stuck in the Middle with You," and "Star." As a solo artist, Rafferty experienced international success with the sax-driven "Baker Street" in 1978. Rafferty enjoyed a string of pleasant light pop hits through the early 80s. –BC & LL

○ **City to City / CAPITOL**   1978
Includes "Baker Street" and "Right Down the Line." With sax by Raphael Ravenscroft. –LL

Best of Gerry Rafferty ... / CAPITOL   1989
Best of Gerry Raggerty - Right Down the Line is an okay but incomplete greatest-hits package. Missing several of his best tunes. –LL

RAIN PARADE

Psychedelic. Early-80s West Coast psychedelic revival band — part of the Paisley Underground movement. Much of the material was mildly trippy and hypnotic. –RC

Emergency 3rd Rail Power Trip / RES   1983
Popular band among the West Coast Paisley Underground movement during the early 80s. They drew inspiration from 60s California 12-string pop, as well as from the Velvet Underground. Pleasantly trippy, in a sleepwalking kind of way. Highlights: "1 Hr 1/2 Ago," "What She's Done to Your Mind," and "This Can't be Today." –RC

RAINCOATS

Alternative rock. Folk-punk, feminist in orientation, from the first wave of post-punk. Essential music from the late 70s and early 80s, too often ignored. –JD

○ **The Raincoats / ROUGH TRADE**   1979
Their ebullient debut is vibrant and enthralling. It is truly wonderful. (Out of print) –JD

Kitchen Tapes / ROI   1980
Live tracks; thoroughly entertaining. –JD

BONNIE RAITT   b 1949

Blues/rock, rock/pop, singer/songwriter. In 1989, Bonny Raitt, singer/songwriter and guitarist, finally hit major success, after almost twenty years of performing, with the aptly titled

Nick of Time (#1). The album came at a time when the market was ready for something earthy, and fortunately Capitol Records, who had just signed Raitt, had the foresight to encourage her love of sexy folk-blues, R&B, and intelligently thoughtful sentiment. Raitt, who has always championed quality songwriters like John Prine, John Hiatt, Terry Adams, Jackson Browne, and Jerry Williams, is quite an accomplished songwriter herself, penning songs for *Nick of Time* that equal anything she has covered.

Before Raitt's late-80s success, she had enjoyed a few moderate successes and a respectable cult following. By 1986, with the release of *Nine Lives*, Raitt's career seemed to be stagnating, and Warner Bros. (her label of fifteen years) cut her loose.

Raitt's soulful guitar playing, particularly slide, has sadly been overlooked. Lesser male guitar players have graced the covers of major music magazines. Hopefully, her time of recognition in that area will arrive as well. –RC

Bonnie Raitt / WARNER   1971
By the time Raitt had recorded this impressive self-titled debut, she had developed quite a set of blues chops playing with artists like Mississippi Fred McDowell, Howlin' Wolf, and other blues greats. In fact, she enlisted Chicago bluesmen Junior Wells and A. C. Reed to aid in the proceedings, which are relaxed and earthy. A fine record. –RC

★ **Give It Up / WARNER / BB 138**   1972
Raitt's sophomore release is a classic. Of all the albums from her days with Warner, this is the one that put together her folky singer/songwriter sensitivities with her love for country-blues. *Give It Up*, which took thirteen years to go gold, showcased an intelligent song selection, with tracks by Jackson Browne ("Under the Falling Sky"), Eric Kaz ("Love Has No Pride"), and Joel Zoss (Been Too Long at the Fair"). Her self-penned "Love Me like a Man" highlighted her impressive guitar technique. –RC

Takin' My Time / WARNER / BB 87   1973
Raitt continued her streak of quality albums with *Takin' My Time*. Like her previous efforts, Raitt drew from the cream of the songwriting crop. Randy Newman's "Guilty" and Jackson Browne's "I Thought I Was a Child" are highlights. –RC

Streetlights / WARNER / BB 80   1974
This album was undermined by slick production and unnecessary orchestration. At the time, Raitt seemed to be fighting the production by Jerry Ragovoy. Versions of Joni Mitchell's "That Song about the Midway" and Allen Toussaint's "What Is Success" are the main highlights of the album. –RC

Homeplate / WARNER / BB 43   1975
A return to form. Raitt shines with some great songs, particularly "Good Enough," "Your Sweet and Shiny Eyes," and "Run Like a Thief." –RC

Sweet Forgiveness / WARNER / BB 25   1977
One of Raitt's lesser efforts. Her version of Del Shannon's "Runaway" (#57) was a moderate hit, in spite of the fact that it's pretty lifeless-sounding. Even though the production isn't quite as slick as *Streetlights*, the relatively weak selection of material is this album's failing. –RC

The Glow / WARNER / BB 30   1979
With the success of "Runaway," Warner felt it was time to take Raitt all the way by pairing her up with hit producer Peter Ascher (Linda Ronstadt, James Taylor). Gone is the natural earthiness Riatt possessed on her first albums. In its place was an airbrushed slickness — from the cover photo all the way down to the grooves. A rendition of Isaac Hayes and David Porter's "Your Good Thing" and an original, "Standing by the Same Old Love" are among *The Glow*'s few highlights. The single off this album was a Robert Palmer song, "You're Gonna Get What's Coming" (#73). –RC

○ **Green Light / WARNER / BB 38**   1982
Raitt dumps the slick stuff and goes for the grit with this energetic set, featuring her band, which included keyboardist

Ian MacLagan, whose credits included the Stones and Faces. Raitt's sensitive electric slide-guitar work was finally up front in the mix. It's one of her very best albums. Raitt does spirited versions of NRBQ's "Green Light" and "Me and the Boys." Other standouts include the wreckless rockers "Willya Wontcha" and "I Can't Help Myself." "River of Tears" is a powerful track that Raitt has dedicated to the memory of Little Feat's Lowell George in shows over the years. –RC

★ **Nick of Time / CAPITOL** 1989
Few comebacks have been as celebrated as Raitt's multi-platinum hit *Nick of Time*, an album that included some of her strongest performances as a musician and singer. The determined "I Will Not Be Denied" seemed to say it all. Her poignant self-penned title cut revealed Raitt as a mature songwriter, on the level of the best writers whose work she had covered. She dug deep with some solid roadhouse R&B in "Love Letter," "Road's My Middle Name," and "Real Man." Her playful version of John Hiatt's "Thing Called Love" was another highlight. All in all, this is a very seamless album. Highly recommended. –RC

○ **The Bonnie Raitt Collection / WARNER** 1991
A good (not great) sampler of Raitt's years at Warner, and a good starting place. –RC

○ **Luck of the Draw / CAPITOL** 1991
Raitt followed *Nick of Time* with *Luck of the Draw*, another great album. Among the album's many highlights are "I Can't Make You Love Me" and a duet with Delbert McClinton on "Good Man, Good Woman." –RC

THE RAMONES

Punk. With a crisp, militaristic shout of "1-2-3-4" introducing a sonic barrage the likes of which had never been heard, the Ramones declared that rock & roll had become fatuous and ostentatious, embarrassingly prissy, and way too serious. They cranked up the volume, took out the stuffing, and let it be known that henceforth endless solos, pseudo-poetry, and concept albums were being relegated to the dustbin, to be mocked and scorned as digressions.

Perhaps all this quartet from Queens, NY, was really doing was reminding those who had strayed that simple is often best, that the first rockers had the right idea (just get a guitar and make some noise with it), that one should not have to study in a conservatory to play rock. The Ramones stripped it back to the basics, a few chords and some d-u-m-b words, and before they knew it they'd been congratulated — and blamed — for inventing something called punk-rock.

Nearly two decades later they were still at it, the Kings of Doofus, true to their original vision. Maybe they weren't able to rid the world of the scholarly approach to rock after all, but they sure "shook it up good." –JT

End of the Century / SIRE 1980
The Ramones as produced by Phil Spector. Not a disaster but not all it should've been. –JT

Animal Boy / SIRE 1986
The Ramones get d-u-m-b again and score with a back-to-basics roaring set. –JT

● **Ramones Mania / SIRE** 1988
The best of the Ramones, or, how to pack 30 songs onto one CD — not all of their "hits" but a crash course in stripped-down genius. –JT

☆ **All the Stuff & More - Vol. 1 / SIRE** 1990
The first two albums, *Ramones* and *Leave Home*, condensed onto one CD, plus bonus tracks. Punk-rock begins here. The cartoon kings of Queens at their most primitive and threatening. Rock's mainstream didn't know what hit it. –JT

☆ **All the Stuff & More - Vol. 2 / SIRE** 1991
The third and fourth albums, *Rocket to Russia* and *Road to Ruin*, combined the present Ramones at their peak on one CD plus bonus tracks. Includes "Rockaway Beach," "Teenage Lobotomy," "I Wanna Be Sedated," power ballads, even a

(gasp!) "country" tune, and other fine examples of Ramonedom. –JT

WILLIS ALAN RAMSEY

Singer/songwriter. Few artists have sustained a devout cult following off of only one album as Willis Alan Ramsey has. In a way, it's understandable. Ramsey's 1972 self-titled debut, on Denny Cordell's Shelter label, contained some real gems: "Satin Sheets," "Ballad of Spider John," "Painted Lady," and "Muskrat Love," a song that became a huge hit for Captain & Tennille. –RC

☆ **Willis Alan Ramsey / DCC** 1972
One of the great (and sadly overlooked) albums of the 70s, Willis Alan Ramsey's self-titled debut had great impact among Austin's progressive country-folk songwriters. Although best known as the writer of "Muskrat Love," which Captain & Tennille took to the Top Ten, Ramsey's muse was rooted much deeper in American lore and folk music. Influences from Robert Johnson to Jimmie Rodgers to Woody Guthrie can be felt if not actually heard on these eleven highly original tracks. Unfortunately, Ramsey, a unique talent with a clear and idiosyncratic artistic vision, hasn't been heard from since. –TG

RARE EARTH

Motown, rock/pop. Rare Earth started life as the Sunliners, a premier bar band of the Detroit circuit. Rumored to know over 5000 songs, their penchant for jamming "psychedelic" versions of Motown tunes caught the ear of session-man Dennis Coffey, who got them signed to the label's Rare Earth subsidiary in 1969. The group's name changed at the same time. Their formula worked like a charm throughout the 70s, with their best sides produced by Motown staffer Norman Whitfield. Massive personnel changes led to an eventual breakup. Drummer and lead vocalist Pete Rivera is still active on oldies shows, while an ersatz version of the group with two original members mines a similar circuit. –CK

2 Classic Albums: Get Ready/Ecology / MOTOWN 1988
Though no definitive greatest hits package currently exists, this CD repackage of their first two albums contains a number of them, such as "Get Ready" and "(I Know) I'm Losing You," and serves their memory well. –CK

○ **Greatest Hits & Rare Classics / MOTOWN** 1991
Motown's premier rock group. This CD includes all singles releases. –RAB

THE RASCALS

R&B, rock/pop. The Young Rascals from New York (formed 1965) successfully integrated soul and rock into a sound that earned the band considerable success on pop and R&B radio formats with songs like "Good Lovin'" (#1 — a remake of the Olympics 1965 R&B hit), "Groovin'" (#1), "People Got to Be Free" (#1), "A Beautiful Morning" (#3), and "How Can I Be Sure" (#4), as well as other hits, many of which were penned by keyboardist Felix Cavaliere (b Nov 29, 1944) and vocalist and percussionist Eddie Brigati. The Young Rascals possessed an explosive rhythm section with jazz drummer Dino Danelli (b Jul 23, 1945) and guitarist Gene Cornish (b May 14, 1945). "Young" was dropped from the band name, as they wanted to portray a more serious image. As the Rascals progressively immersed themselves in indulgent album projects like *Freedom Suite* (#17), their audience shrank. The band called it quits in 1972, after dismal success with their last three albums, *Search and Nearness* (#198), *Peaceful World* (#120), and *The Island of Real* (#180), which were actually pretty good, but their audience had left them. –RC

Time Peace - Greatest Hits / ATLANTIC 1968
Arguably the greatest greatest-hits album of the 60s. A White-soul classic. –BE

Ultimate Rascals / WARNER 1986
A somewhat impressive collection marred only by substandard sound. –BE

☆ **Anthology (1965-1972) / RHINO**   1992
Anthology is the most comprehensive overview of one of the greatest bands of the 60s. All 18 of their hits as well as important album cuts (including tracks from their Columbia releases) are here on this two-CD, 44-track set. –RC

THE RASPBERRIES

Power-pop. Led by Eric Carmen (b Aug 11, 1949), the Raspberries (from Cleveland, OH) brought out their exuberant Beatles-style Anglo-pop and matching outfits at a time in the early 70s when art-rock, concept albums, and serious "statements" were being heralded. It was a time when pop for pop's sake was decidedly uncool. Capitol Records accentuated the band's teenybopper appeal by marketing their self-titled debut with a raspberry-scented scratch-and-sniff sticker on the cover. The band's dynamic first single, "Go All the Way" (#5), was a huge hit. –RC

○ **Capitol Collectors Series / CAPITOL**   1991
Delightful and exciting old-style Top 40 rock, played like it mattered (which it did). Weighty enough to stand the test of time. –BE

RATT

Heavy metal. Los Angeles quintet Ratt gained a lot of acceptance in the early to mid 80s with the MTV-friendly style of their glam-influenced mainstream hard rock. –JB

Out of the Cellar / ATLANTIC   1984
The first album by Los Angeles's Ratt, it brought them instant success and a number of memorable hits. The cover featured actress Tawny Kitaen. –JB

○ **Invasion of Your Privacy / ATLANTIC**   1985
They may have been influenced by Aerosmith but at this stage Ratt were recording songs that were powerful as well as masterful hits. This album also showed they were a lot more than a hit-making machine. –JB

● **Ratt & Roll 8191 / ATLANTIC**   1991
A greatest-hits package with the best of Ratt's impressive ten-year (and still counting) career. –JB

THE RAVE-UPS

Psychedelic, folk/rock, country rock. Ever since the mid 80s, the Rave-Ups (based in Los Angeles) have delivered a smart blend of folk/country-rock with occasional touches of psychedelia. Jim Podrasky, the band's lead-singer/guitarist, pairs hooky, memorable melodies with intelligently abstruse lyrical images. –RC

○ **Chance / EPIC**   1990
This is currently the only album available by this fine band, who deliver a revved-up blend of Buffalo Springfieldish folk/rock, with slight country influences and a touch of psychedelia. David Leonard's (John Mellencamp, Prince) immediate-sounding production gives a nice urgency to the band's performances. "She Says (Come Around)" was a great single, which didn't get exposure. Other highlights include "For the Loser (Hallelujah)," "Hamlet Meets John Doe," and "The Best I Can't." Their 1988 Epic release, *The Book of Your Regrets*, or their releases on the Fun Stuff label — *Town + Country* and the *Class Tramp* EP — are well worth getting, if you can find them. –RC

LOU RAWLS   b 1935

Soul, pop. When Chicago-born Lou Rawls croons a soulful love song, his deep-hued pipes rumble with simmering passion. Rawls did the usual gospel apprenticeship before breaking out on a landmark jazz album with pianist Les McCann's trio for Capitol that launched his secular career. But it took Rawls a while to establish himself as a soul artist — perhaps he was perceived as a little too sophisticated and jazzy (although his uncredited responses on Sam Cooke's "Bring It on Home to Me" certainly proved he could wail). "Love Is a Hurtin' Thing" instantly changed that notion when it topped the R&B charts

in 1966, and the unyielding "Dead End Street" and "Your Good Thing (Is About to End)" perpetuated his success. After memorably delivering Bobby Hebb's powerful "A Natural Man" in 1971, Rawls joined forces with Philadelphia producers Kenny Gamble and Leon Huff in 1976, emerging with the silky "You'll Never Find Another Love like Mine," another gigantic R&B and pop smash tailor-made for nattily sweeping across the classiest disco dance floors. The disco era's long gone now, but Rawls maintains elegantly. He's still as cool as cool can be. –BD

● **Stormy Monday / CAPITOL**   1962
His best early album, with the Les McCann Jazz Trio. –BC

Live! / CAPITOL   1965
A jazz combo setting with blues standards. –BC

○ **All Things in Time / PHILADELPHIA INTNL**   1976
Fine Philly-sound disco and warm romantic ballads. –BC

At Last / CAPITOL   1989
A return to jazz roots and standard songs. –BC

Greatest Hits / CAPITOL   1990
Jazzy 60s hits. –BC

It's Supposed to Be Fun / CAPITOL   1990
Bluesy jazz material. –BC

JAMES RAY   b 1941

Soul. 1960s R&B vocalist. The Washington, DC, native's 1962 hit, "If You Gotta Make a Fool of Somebody," inspired a raft of covers, while one of his lesser-known efforts, "I've Got My Mind Set on You," provided George Harrison with a recent big-seller. Ray's pop-slanted R&B output for Caprice Records, including his less successful followup "Itty Bitty Pieces," was arranged by pianist Hutch Davie. All three of the songs cited above were written by prolific New York tunesmith Rudy Clark. –BD

○ **Golden Classics / COLLECTABLES**
An overlooked R&B stylist whose best songs were triumphs of form over thin lyrics. –RW

CHRIS REA   b 1951

Singer/songwriter, rock & roll. After a string of dull albums in the 70s, Rea released a pair of late-80s/90s albums that were astonishing in many ways, revealing the passion of the best kind of singer/songwriter and a rocker's heart that conjures images of everyone from Springsteen to Mark Knopfler. And he's one hell of an evocative vocalist. –JF

New Light through Old Windows / ATLANTIC   1988
A decent assortment of cuts from his early albums. –JF

○ **Road to Hell / ATLANTIC**   1989
The title only hints at the horror that lurks in this album's message. "Texas," "Looking for a Rainbow," and "You Must Be Evil" pick apart the atrocities of our society, while "Let's Dance" offers some much-needed tension release. A modern masterpiece. –JF

Auberge / ATLANTIC   1991
This one can't help but stand in the shadow of *Road to Hell*; it lacks that set's thematic cohesion. But it's still a hefty testament to the singularity of Rea's world vision. –JF

THE RECORDS

Rock/pop. A UK quartet, active from 1979 to 1982, employing a jangly-guitar, 60s-pop approach. The band was led by songwriter and guitarist Will Birch and also featured John Wicks, Phil Brown, and guitarist Huw Gower. Their first album, *Shades in Bed*, was released in the US as *The Records* and featured the minor hit single "Starry Eyes." Gower left, replaced by American Jude Cole for *Crashes* (1980). Their last album, *Music on Both Sides* (1982), featured a quintet of Birch, Wicks, Brown, Dave Whelan, and Chris Gent. –WR

○ **The Records / VIRGIN**   1979
Virtually every song here is a catchy guitar-driven pop song with sweet harmonies, from the single "Starry Eyes" through

"Teenarama" and "Another Star." The album includes a bonus record containing the Records's versions of such oldies as the Kinks's "See My Friends" and Spirit's "1984." −WR

RED HOT CHILI PEPPERS

Alternative rock. A quartet with varying personnel, anchored by lead singer Anthony Kiedis and bassist Flea (born Michael Balzary), the Red Hot Chili Peppers play a hybrid rock incorporating punk, funk, rap, and metal. Though the mixture was ahead of its time when the group was first organized in the early 80s in Los Angeles, the music industry has since caught up to it, which earns the group the right to call itself the forerunner of an approach now adopted by such acts as Living Colour and Faith No More, and also means the Peppers themselves have finally hit the big time. In 1988 guitarist Hillel Slovak died of an overdose and the band reorganized, with John Frusciante on guitar and Chad Smith on drums. This lineup scored a commercial breakthrough with *Mother's Milk*, which went gold after its release in 1989. They ascended to real star status with the release of *Blood Sugar Sex Magik*, which sold two million copies and included the Top Ten hit "Under the Bridge." In mid 1992, Frusciante left the group and was replaced by Arik Marshall. −WR

Freaky Styley / CAPITOL   1985
Funk-rock explosion on this George Clinton production. Standouts include "Blackeyed Blonde," the Dr. Seuss satire "Yertle the Turtle," and a cover of Sly Stone's "If You Want Me to Stay." −BC

Uplift Mofo Party Plan / CAPITOL   1987
The Peppers's best album before they crossed over into the mainstream and their last album with the original band members. Includes "No Chump Love Sucker" and "Fight like a Brave." −ME & BC

Mother's Milk / CAPITOL   1989
While *Mother's Milk* is not their most adventurous or best release, it's a good album, which expanded the Red Hot's cult. Mainstream listeners were attracted to the band in large part because of their cover of Stevie Wonder's "Higher Ground," the best song on *Mother's Milk*. Other highlights include "Knock Me Down," "Taste the Pain," "Nobody Weird like Me," and "Sexy Mexican Maid." −ME & STE

○ **Blood Sugar Sex Magik / WARNER**   1991
It isn't just that the world has finally come around to the Peppers's funk-rock mixture, it's that, with the help of producer Rick Rubin, they've found a focus and that, as musicians, they've reached a sufficient level of competence to execute their ideas. The result is their best album, containing the hit "Under the Bridge." −WR

LEON REDBONE

Folk-pop. Leon Redbone's renderings of ragtime, blues, and early folk chestnuts have earned him a solid cult following ever since the early 70s. However, his noveltyish appearance and deadpan delivery (however memorable) sometimes undercut the depth of the traditions he explores. −RC

On the Track / WARNER   1976
Debut album contains a typical collection of campy oldies ("Ain't Misbehavin'," "Lulu's Back in Town"), accompanied by a varied cast including folkie Don McLean and jazz stars Milt Hinton and Ralph McDonald. −WR

Leon Redbone Live / GREENE-STONE   1985
A live setting is just about ideal for a performer like Redbone, and he does not disappoint on this two-record set, which features "Diddy Wah Diddy," "Champagne Charlie," and other favorites. −WR

○ **Red to Blue / AUGUST**   1985
Redbone's best overall album veers from country to jazz to folk to blues. Backup includes members of Vince Giordano's old-time jazz band, Dr. John, David Bromberg, and the Roches on songs ranging from "Lovesick Blues" to Bob Dylan's "Living the Blues," and with two Redbone originals, as well. −WR

OTIS REDDING   d1967

Soul. We are left to guess the direction Otis Redding's music would have taken had he lived. His last hit, the gently affecting "Dock of the Bay," pointed away from the impassioned soul ballads with which he'd made his name and strayed further yet from the Little Richard imitations with which he'd begun his career.

Like many others during the mid 60s, Redding discovered what was special about his music in Memphis. He had been recording sporadically and unsuccessfully for three or four years when he arrived at Stax and cut "These Arms of Mine." It gave us everything we could expect from him for the next few years: the almost exaggeratedly impassioned vocals couched in the sparse elegance of the Stax/Volt rhythm and horn sections. Wrenching ballads such as "I've Been Loving You" and "That's How Strong My Love Is" were judiciously mixed with uptempo stomps like "Mr. Pitiful" and "Respect." The individual albums inevitably contain some duds, but Otis rarely fired blanks on his singles.

Redding's appearance at the Monterey Pop Festival and on the West Coast club circuit was beginning to spread word of his music beyond the traditional confines of the R&B market when he was tragically killed in a plane crash in December 1967. −CE

Dock of the Bay / ATLANTIC   1962
Includes the posthumously released classic title track plus the great "Ole Man Trouble." −CO

Pain in My Heart / ATLANTIC   1964
Redding's first release. Includes the title track, a deep-soul gem, plus "These Arms of Mine" and "Security." −CO

The Great Otis Redding Sings Soul Ballads / ATCO 1965
Redding's second album includes "Mr. Pitiful," "That's How Strong My Love Is," "Chained and Bound." He moves out of the country-soul genre into his own stompin' thing. −CO

In Person at the Whiskey a Go Go / ATCO   1965
Redding captured live in 1966, at the peak of his form! (Out of print.) −CO

☆ **Otis Blue - Otis Redding Sings Soul / ATCO**   1965
Pretty essential if you can only afford individual albums. Three Sam Cooke covers, including "Shake" and "A Change Is Gonna Come" are included, as well as "I've Been Loving You Too Long," "Satisfaction," and the original version of "Respect." −CO

☆ **Dictionary of Soul / ATLANTIC**   1966
If you can only afford one Redding album, start here. Includes "Try a Little Tenderness," "My Lover's Prayer," "Fa-Fa-Fa-Fa (Sad Song)." One of the best album covers ever! −CO

The Soul Album / ATLANTIC   1966
Includes "Chain Gang," "Good to Me," and "Cigarettes and Coffee." −CO

Live in Europe / ATLANTIC   1967
Ten of Redding's biggest hits, live before an ecstatic audience. Includes "Respect," "I Can't Turn You Loose," "Try a Little Tenderness," etc. Soul rave-up! −CO

King & Queen / ATLANTIC   1967
Eleven duets by the undisputed ruler and his consort Carla Thomas. Includes "Tramp" and "Lovey Dovey." Sweet and soulful! −CO

The Immortal Otis Redding / ATLANTIC   1968
His later sides, including the wonderful "I've Got Dreams to Remember" and the super-funky "Hard to Handle." Produced by Steve Cropper. Redding on the border of a new soul frontier as a writer and performer, before his untimely death. −CO

Love Man / ATLANTIC   1969
Includes the heart-fixin' title track, plus "Free Me," "Look at That Girl," "Direct Me." −CO

Tell the Truth / ATLANTIC 1970
Another posthumously released collection, including "The Match Game" and "Tell the Truth." –co

★ **The Otis Redding Story / ATLANTIC** 1987
A few previously unissued tracks, plus *all* the hits, from "These Arms of Mine" (1962) through "Dock of the Bay" (1967). A magnificent tribute to a magnificent career. It's a little expensive but it'll completely rock your soul! –co

Remember Me / STAX 1992
Twenty-two previously unreleased tracks, finished and unfinished, from the Stax vaults. Includes outtakes, remakes, cover tunes, and some very tasty never-before-heard originals. A historically important release covering all of Otis's remaining studio material. –co

LOU REED　　　　　　　　　　　　　　　　♭ 1942

Alternative rock, rock & roll. Lou Reed would be important even if his career had ended with the passing of the Velvet Underground. It didn't though, and Reed has forged a rich and varied solo career spanning some twenty albums. Not everything he has released has been great but the best is formidable, and most is worth investigating. Equally interested in poetry and guitar/bass/drums rock & roll, Reed has always felt that rock & roll can be made interesting and valid for those over 40. Just as authors and film directors are supposed to get better at their craft as they get older, why not rock & roll musicians? Similarly, books and films routinely deal with subject matter other than the "I love you, you love me" school, so why not rock & roll? Reed's solo career is proof that such goals are attainable.

Born in Brooklyn, Reed guided the Velvet Underground from 1965 to 1970. His first, eponymously titled solo album came out in 1972. From his second album, *Transformer*, came his only chart hit in "Walk on the Wild Side." Peaking in popularity in the mid 70s with the *Rock 'n' Roll Animal* and *Sally Can't Dance* albums, Reed became increasingly hostile, frustrated, and erratic. Cleaning himself up in the 80s, from 1982's *The Blue Mask* through 1992's *Magic and Loss*, he has made some of the finest, most engaging non-formulaic rock music ever conceived. –RB

Lou Reed / RCA 1972
Reed's first solo album, with "Walk It & Talk It," "Wild Child," and "Lisa Says" being particular standouts. –CK

○ **Transformer / RCA / BB 29** 1972
Produced by David Bowie and Mick Ronson, *Transformer* has a lushness and beauty to its production and arrangements that Reed's material had never before received. The hit single "Walk on the Wild Side" was a fluke brought about by the actions of one fill-in disc jockey at the BBC. The song chronicles several personages from Andy Warhol's Factory retinue, including speed-freaks and transvestites giving head; it is boggling to this day that it got by AM radio programmers. Other Reed classics such as "Vicious" and "Satellite of Love" get similar treatment. –RB

☆ **Berlin / RCA / BB 98** 1973
Relations between Bowie and Reed had been strained during the recording of *Transformer*, so for his third solo album Reed hired Canadian studio whiz Bob Ezrin. Ezrin and Reed concocted a brilliant album-length concept loosely constructed around the song "Berlin" from Reed's first solo album. Reed, of course, wrote the basic songs (several stemming back to demos recorded but not released by the Velvet Underground), and Ezrin and Allan MacMillan wrote orchestral arrangements for each track. Recording in London, Ezrin assembled a dream band including Jack Bruce, Steve Winwood, Aynsley Dunbar, and, from Detroit, two relatively unknown guitar heroes, Steve Hunter and Steve Wagner. Reed's writing and singing has never been better. He acts his way through the personas of Jim, Caroline, and the narrator. At the time of release, reviews were generally less than kind. A number of reactionary writers thought that

orchestration automatically meant somehow compromising one's authenticity. Others found the level of depression and vitriol in the story more than they wanted to bear. Over time most would concede this is one of the great albums of 70s rock & roll. –RB

Rock 'n' Roll Animal / RCA / BB 45 1974
Retaining guitarists Hunter and Wagner from the *Berlin* sessions, Reed hired a rhythm section consisting of Prakash John on bass, Pentti Glan on drums, and Ray Colcord on keyboards. Two shows were recorded at New York's Academy of Music in 1973. Behind Reed the band produced fierce near-heavy-metal twin-guitar apotheosis for ninety minutes. Just under half of the concert made it onto this album. An FM radio staple at the time, *Rock 'n' Roll Animal* includes searing versions of the Velvet Underground classics "Sweet Jane," "Heroin," "White Light/White Heat," and "Rock 'n' Roll," plus "Lady Day" from *Berlin*. –RB

○ **Lou Reed Live / RCA / BB 62** 1975
Most of the rest of the above-mentioned concert. Three songs from *Transformer*, two songs from *Berlin*, and the Velvet's "I'm Waiting for the Man." Just a shade less visceral than *Rock 'n' Roll Animal*. –RB

○ **Coney Island Baby / RCA / BB 41** 1976
Coney Island Baby was an album of renewal for Reed. The year 1974 had witnessed one of his worst albums ever in *Sally Can't Dance*, and, early in 1975, in reaction to a career spinning out of control, he had released the lyric-less sonic feedback assault of *Metal Machine Music*. *Coney Island Baby* was a return to peak songwriting form. The title track reflected Reed's early love of doo-wop. It is probably the grandest love song of his career. "Kicks" is a rather frightening internal study of a diseased mind that eventually turns to murder. As with most of Reed's writing in the 60s and 70s, he draws no conclusion; he simply paints a picture. –RB

Street Hassle / ARISTA / BB 89 1978
Reed's second album for Arista has a few weak spots but most of it, including the 11-minute title song, is unmitigated brilliance. The sound is rather odd as Reed began experimenting with Manfred Schunke's binaural recording process. Some tracks on the album are part live and part studio while others are near totally live or totally studio. *Street Hassle* includes Reed's tongue-in-cheek take on racial stereotypes, "I Wanna Be Black," and a quite strange reinterpretation of the Velvet Underground's "Real Good Time Together." –RB

☆ **The Blue Mask / RCA / BB 169** 1982
Reed took nearly two years off at the end of the 70s to dry out and clean up. When he did return to recording it was with a vengeance. In an odd quirk of fate Reed had re-signed with RCA and he had also gone back to a lineup of two guitars, a bass, and drums. *The Blue Mask* sounds immaculate. The guts of Reed's sound are still present in no uncertain terms but there is also a richness to the finished mix that is striking. The bass player, Fernando Saunders, became Reed's right-hand man for the next several years, and guitarist Robert Quine was Reed's ideal foil for this and the subsequent *Legendary Hearts*. The result was Reed's best album since *Berlin*. His songwriting had taken a quantum leap since cleaning up. The maturity was inspiring, as was the breadth of the material. (Import) –RB

○ **Legendary Hearts / RCA / BB 159** 1983
Continuing with Quine and Saunders, coupled with a different drummer in Fred Maher, Reed delivered his second superb album in a row. This was a more subdued affair than *The Blue Mask* but the writing was no less impressive. –RB

New Sensations / RCA 1984
After a few challenging (and critically acclaimed) albums, Reed dispensed with densely literate (and dissonant) excursions into the dark side of the human psyche and delivered a solid upbeat (and at times humorous) collection of accessible rock & roll. Reed celebrated love ("I Love You

Suzanne"), poked fun at power-plays between the genders ("My Red Joystick"), and, as the title track suggested, generally looked forward with optimism. Reed's dirty-electric rhythm, Fernando Saunders's elastic bass work and Fred Maher's forceful drumming provide a solid bed of ragged but tight ensemble work behind Reed's dry narratives. –RC

★ **New York / SIRE**   1989
Reed's first album in three years hailed another peak in his recording career. In the past he had always painted pictures of any given social situation. Positive or negative, he had never stated a point of view. On *New York* he rails. Sporting a new band, including bass virtuoso Rob Wasserman and Reed's brother-in-law guitarist Mike Rathke, Reed indicts everyone from slum lords to polluters. *New York* contains, perhaps, his finest writing. –RB

☆ **Songs for Drella / SIRE**   1990
Reed and former Velvet Underground partner John Cale reunite to create a song cycle based around the life of Velvet's mentor Andy Warhol. Recorded with just the two of them, the range of sound and mood is masterful. Reed's ballads give way to angst-ridden feedback-charged guitar freakouts. This is an astonishingly moving album. –RB

Magic and Loss / SIRE   1992
The third installment in what feels loosely like a trilogy. This time out Reed tackles death itself as his theme, having recently experienced the loss of two friends. A number of reviewers and fans have attacked the recording, claiming it is too depressing. Reed's irrefutable response is that if books and films are able to deal with death, why not popular songs and rock & roll. I'm on Reed's side. As an addendum, the man deserves brownie points for giving Little Jimmy Scott a cameo vocal on "Power and Glory." –RB

Between Thought and Expression / RCA   1992
For those whose pocketbook can handle a boxed set as an introduction to an artist's work, this 3-CD, 45-track set, compiled by Reed himself, is intelligently conceived and executed, spanning his 17-album career with the Arista and RCA labels. *Between Thought and Expression - The Lou Reed Anthology* is a generous selection of outtakes and other previously unreleased material. The box contains extensive liner notes, providing many fine quotes from Reed, who clarifies numerous factual "corrections" made by others concerning his mythology. Sonically, *Between Thought and Expression* is a great improvement over previous reissues of Reed's solo material from this period. –RC

MARTHA REEVES & THE VANDELLAS   b 1941

Motown. Perhaps the perfect product of the Motown machine, Martha Reeves was working as a secretary at the label, occasionally doubling as a demo singer, when she was called upon to do some background vocals for Marvin Gaye. That chance was parlayed into a recording deal for Motown's Gordy subsidiary, and her breakthrough came with her second record, "Come and Get These Memories." There were the inevitable comparisons with the Supremes, but Martha was an incomparably earthier singer than the slinky Ms. Ross, as witnessed by her storming leads on "Heatwave" and, especially, "Dancing in the Street." It was, as the Motown brass well knew, perfect party music, and it was a vein they mined successfully for several more years. The Vandellas came and went, and chart success grew increasingly elusive as the 60s closed, with the result that Martha left the label in 1972 to sign with MCA. Despite the fact that her Martha Reeves set was the most expensive album released to that point (1974), it failed to recharge her career, which has been largely confined to reprising her old hits — where the magic transcends mere nostalgia. –CE

○ **Anthology / MOTOWN**   1974
Motown's epic girl-group has material equal to, or better than anything done by the Supremes. –RAB

★ **Martha & the Vandellas Greatest Hits / MOTOWN** 1987

The one definitive package to own, with all their biggest and best, including "Come and Get These Memories," "Heat Wave," and "Dancing in the Streets." –CK

R.E.M.

Alternative rock, rock/pop. Contrary to *Rolling Stone's* belief, R.E.M. is not currently America's greatest rock & roll band; it is America's greatest pop band. Their sensibilities stem from the chiming guitar of Velvet Underground and the Byrds, not Chuck Berry and the Rolling Stones. With the *Chronic Town* EP and *Murmur,* R.E.M. ushered in the era of alternative college rock. R.E.M.'s quiet, chiming guitars, mumbled vocals, and a hushed rhythm section replaced roaring punk rock. Legions of imitators followed in R.E.M.'s footsteps but, by that point, R.E.M. had moved forward. Around the 1987 album, *Document,* vocalist Michael Stipe started singing clearly. Pete Buck's guitar became more muscular and bassist Mike Mills and drummer Bill Berry gained new strength. The change in sound brought mass success, earning them a Top Ten single, "The One I Love." *Green* continued their mass-market acceptance, but the album that really broke them through was 1991's *Out of Time,* an album that garnered more Grammy nominations in 1992 than anyone else's. –STE

☆ **Murmur / I.R.S.**   1983
All of R.E.M.'s imitators base their homages on this strange, eerie album. Out of all of R.E.M.'s albums, none have the mood this one has — it is the aural equivalent of the creeping kudzu on the cover. The music belongs to no time — the guitars and rhythms may have their roots in 60s pop and folk but the vocals couldn't have been produced before 1977 and punk-rock. –STE

○ **Reckoning / I.R.S.**   1984
The guitar still rings and chimes, the vocals still mumble, but the rhythm section is brought toward the front of the mix — the sound is brighter. While the mood has changed (it isn't out of time like *Murmur*), the songs are better — nothing on *Murmur* had the power of "(Don't Go Back To) Rockville" and "So. Central Rain." –STE

○ **Lifes Rich Pageant / I.R.S.**   1986
This is not R.E.M.'s most successful album but it captures the band at an important crossroads. The ringing guitars of *Murmur* and *Reckoning* remain ("Fall on Me," "Flowers of Guatemala," "What If We Give It Away?") but the bombastic directness of their next two albums, *Document* and *Green,* is anticipated with tracks like "Just a Touch," "Begin the Begin," and their cover of "Superman." An important transitional album. –STE

Dead Letter Office / I.R.S.   1987
For the fans: a collection of B-sides and outtakes, including a drunken cover of Roger Miller's "King of the Road" and three Lou Reed songs. An entertaining album that will leave the unconverted scratching their heads and the fans delighted. The CD version includes their fine 1982 debut EP *Chronic Town.* –STE

○ **Document / I.R.S.**   1987
The breakthrough. R.E.M.'s first Top Ten (hell, their first Top 40) single, "The One I Love," is included, as is the anthem "It's the End of the World As We Know It (And I Feel Fine)." Those two songs illustrate the difference in the band — loud guitars, driving rhythms, and clear (well, at least clearer) vocals. "It's the End of the World ..." may be unintelligible but Stipe's vocals are audible throughout the album, even though the lyrics are murky. –STE

● **Eponymous / I.R.S.**   1988
Basically a singles collection from R.E.M.'s first five albums, *Eponymous* gives the listener a sense of R.E.M.'s change from a folk-rock band to a rock band. The songs are intelligently selected, distilling most of the best moments from three successful albums and the minor disaster of their third album, *Fables of the Reconstruction.* Included is the original single of "Radio Free Europe," different mixes of "Gardening

at Night" (where it is actually possible to hear the vocal) and "Finest Worksong," and the previously unreleased (and unspectacular) "Romance." (Note: An import collection, *The Best of R.E.M.*, doesn't have the rarities but has 16 songs, including the remainder of *Eponymous* plus many other important songs from their I.R.S. years. Worth the couple of extra dollars for the beginner.) –STE

○ **Green / WARNER** 1988
Fables of the Reconstruction may be R.E.M.'s worst album, but *Green* is their most disjointed and strange recording. Alternating between eerie acoustic numbers and all-out guitar rave-ups, there is no cohesion here. Nevertheless, there is some good material: the goofy "Stand," the veiled confessions of "Hairshirt" and "World Leader Pretend," the guitar workout of "Turn You Inside Out," the mocking "Pop Song 89," and the charming untitled eleventh track. –STE

○ **Out of Time / WARNER** 1991
In contrast to the directness of *Green* and *Document*, this may seem like a return to the abstractness of the early years, yet this is not the case. *Out of Time* is among R.E.M.'s best work — a mature, balanced, graceful collection of pop songs quite different from *Murmur* and *Reckoning*. Buck, Berry, and Mills switch instruments frequently, keeping the music fresh and exciting. –STE

RENAISSANCE

Art-rock. Classical-rock ensemble, driven by Annie Haslam's three-octave voice and John Tout's piano. They always lacked excitement and presence but made up for it with their melodies. When those went, so did they. –BE

○ **Tales of 1001 Nights - Vol. 1 / WARNER** 1979
An intelligently programmed collection of highlights from their Sire years. –BE

REO SPEEDWAGON

Rock/pop. Midwestern rock band, including vocalist Kevin Cronin, guitarist Gary Richrath, and drummer Alan Gratzer, who determinedly stuck to the concert circuit until they were finally rewarded with a string of early-80s hits. –DH

Hi-Infidelity / CBS 1982
The band's breakthrough album with the masses. Heavy on the syrupy ballad formula that brought them success. –CK

○ **The Hits / CBS** 1988
This collects their chart hits and some old favorites. –DH

Decade of Rock & Roll '70-80 / CBS 1988
A well-chosen recap of REO's dues-paying years. –DH

THE REPLACEMENTS

Rock & roll. Minneapolis band the Replacements blasted onto the scene with a perfectly inspired blend of irreverence, sloppiness, and heart, the stuff from which great rock & roll is created.
Paul Westerberg, the band's primary singer/songwriter, has produced an impressive body of work that ranges from moronically inspired rock to reflective numbers possessing heartbreaking vulnerability. No others from the post-punk age have worn such an interesting and complex heart on their torn-up sleeve or used an imperfect voice to such great advantage. On their initial releases (*Sorry Ma, Forgot to Take Out the Trash*, *Stink*, and *Hootenanny*), the band puked out frantic song-bites (many less than two minutes long) with clown punk titles like "I Hate Music," "Shiftless When Idle," "White and Lazy," "F*** School," and "God Damn Job."
Let It Be, their fourth release, reflected a new maturity while not sacrificing their spirit of reckless fun. The next two efforts, *Tim* and *Pleased to Meet Me* (produced by Jim Dickinson), maintained the magic.
Since then, the Replacements have had some lineup changes and softened their ragged-but-right sound with *Don't Tell a Soul* (which produced a #1 rock hit in "I'll Be You") and the more acoustic-oriented followup *All Shook Down.*

They were called "the last great band of the 80s" by *Musician*. You'd better believe it. –RC & JF

Sorry Ma ... / TWINTONE 1981
Sorry Ma, Forgot to Take Out the Trash is a thrashy, Ramones-like debut. "Johnny's Gonna Die," "I'm in Trouble," and "Takin' a Ride" hint at things to come. –JF

Hootenanny / TWINTONE 1983
A hodgepodge of hard rock, country, punk — everything. It's patchy, but "Color Me Impressed," "Willpower," and "Within Your Reach" are among their best. –JF

☆ **Let It Be / TWINTONE** 1984
This is where they realized their potential and consolidated their diversity into a masterpiece that screams, cries, comforts, and antagonizes. Highlights include "Unsatisfied," one of Westerberg's finest songs and vocal performances, as well as the reckless swinging "I Will Dare," and the playful "Androgynous." –JF

○ **Tim / SIRE** 1985
Their major-label debut isn't a great leap forward but their raggedness is retained, and Westerberg contributes anthems of rebellion and insecurity, like "Bastards of Young" and "Hold My Life." Also included is a hard-rockin' nod to alternative radio (with Alex Chilton), "Left of the Dial." –JF

★ **Pleased to Meet Me / SIRE** 1987
Pared down to a trio, the band offers a complex set of ballads and guitar blazers and continues its examination of the effects of rock stardom. Producer Jim Dickinson (Ry Cooder, Big Star) gives the group a piledriver sound, like a boombox with the loudness up to ten. "Alex Chilton," a hard-rocking ode to Big Star's founder; "Can't Hardly Wait," with its great Memphis groove and Box Tops-style horn and string parts; and the haunting "Skyway" are among this album's highlights. –JF

○ **Don't Tell a Soul / SIRE** 1989
The full-blown production made some cry sell out, but *Don't Tell a Soul* contained a heightened level of melodicism that produced some wonderful moments, particularly the expansive "Darlin' One," "Talent Show," "Achin' To Be," and their first #1 AOR hit, "I'll Be You." With that song, Westerberg practically achieved the magic he so much admired on Big Star's records. If *Don't Tell a Soul* hadn't been a Replacements album, its appealingly sloppy melodic power-pop would have, more than likely, earned rave reviews. This contains their most desolate work, highlighted by "I'll Be You" (their first #1 AOR hit), "Talent Show," the expansive psychedelia of "Darlin' One," and the creepy "Rock & Roll Ghost." –JF

All Shook Down / SIRE 1990
More a Westerberg solo album than a band effort, this is a delicate, acoustic-based set, which finds him finally facing the perils of adulthood. But don't worry, he hasn't become a Jackson Browne-ian simp. –JF

PAUL REVERE & THE RAIDERS

Rock/pop. In 1959, two natives of Caldwell, ID, met and decided to form a band. Paul Revere (b Jan 7, 1942) and Mark Lindsey (b Mar 9, 1942) called their group the Downbeats, after the jazz magazine. At first the group was largely instrumental, featuring Revere's pounding roadhouse piano (in the style of Jerry Lee Lewis) and Lindsey's sax playing. The band was renamed Paul Revere & the Raiders in 1960, after a pressing plant owner suggested Revere ought to capitalize on his memorable name.
Their first single was an instrumental called "Beatnick Sticks," a takeoff on "Chopsticks." Their third single, an instrumental called "Like Long Hair" (#38) was their first national hit, getting them played on Dick Clark's "American Bandstand." Eventually Clark became one of the most important people in furthering the band's career.
Columbia signed the band, and Terry Melcher was given the job of producing them and toughening up their sound. Beginning with "Steppin' Out" (#46), the band had a long

stretch of substantial hits, aided by their residency on Dick Clark's "Where the Action Is" TV show.

Melcher managed to get songwriters Barry Mann and Cynthia Weil to give the Raiders an antidrug song, "Kicks" (#4) (originally written for the Animals) and it became one of their biggest hits. Mann and Weil supplied the #6 followup, "Hungry."

Other hits included "Good Thing" (#4), "Him or Me — What's It Gonna Be?" (#5), "Indian Reservation" (#1), "Just like Me" (#11), and "The Great Airplane Strike" (#20). Mark Lindsey concurrently pursued a solo career, scoring a #9 hit with "Arizona" during the latter part of the Raiders's existence. Paul Revere continued to perform with a modified lineup of Paul Revere & the Raiders. –RC

○ **Legend of Paul Revere / COLUMBIA**   1990

This two-CD anthology, with 55 songs, may be a lot more Raiders than the average fan would want. But go for it and be amazed at how consistently strong this rocking band from the Great Northwest was. Includes all the hits. –JT

REZILLOS

Punk, fusion. One of Scotland's great punk bands, the Rezillos came on like gangbusters with a hip attitude, a revved-up band (featuring soon-to-be Human Leaguer Jo Callis) and the remarkable pipes of Ms. Fay Fife. With a flair for garish 60s pop-art artifacts (something I'm positive influenced the B-52s), the Rezillos were decidedly less serious than their punk contemporaries, but their debut album *Can't Stand the Rezillos* is a cheesy classic. –JD

○ **Can't Stand the Rezillos / SIRE**   1978

Wild, untempered, popish punk. One of the best outcomes of the new-wave era. –DS

CLIFF RICHARD & THE SHADOWS   *b* 1940

Rock/pop. Britain's first great rock success, Cliff Richard (real name Harry Webb) rose to fame in 1958 with a hot-rocking single called "Move It," backed by a quartet called the Shadows (originally the Drifters), led by guitarists Hank Marvin and Bruce Welch. At its best, their sound (although a little too sterile in the studio) had a dynamism lacking in virtually all of the competition on that side of the pond, and although they later softened that sound, for a while, at least, the Sceptered Isle had a topflight rock act. Richard has continued recording into the 90s and even scored a hit in America in the 70s with "Devil Woman." A born-again Christian for 30 years, he has also recorded religious songs on the Light label. –BE

○ **Cliff Richard & the Shadows / EMI**

Cliff Richard & the Shadows rock out like nobody's business on this classic live album (arguably rock's first authorized and professionally recorded concert album). Recorded in February 1959 at EMI in front of 500 screaming fans, the sound is raw and raunchy by British standards of the time. (Import) –BE

KEITH RICHARDS   *b* 1943

Rock & roll. One of the few White guitarists with strong blues roots who has been able to take the form to new places, Richards's contribution to the vocabulary of rock guitar cannot be overestimated. His heavy reliance on Delta blues open tunings (mostly played on guitars with only five strings) has provided licks that are part and parcel for any player who wants to get the joint rocking and the dance floor packed. Though much has been made of his lifestyle, and time has reduced his voice to a sore-throated husk, it is as a guitarist and songwriter that Richards will ultimately establish his reputation. –CK

○ **Talk Is Cheap / ATLANTIC**   1988

Richard's lone solo album includes "Take It So Hard," "Struggle," "I Could Have Stood You Up," and "Make No Mistake," with a classic Hi Rhythm Section groove and featuring great guest vocals by Sarah Dash. (Also available as a Mobile Fidelity gold-disc) –CK

LIONEL RICHIE   *b* 1949

Pop. Emerging from his college band the Commodores in 1981, Lionel Richie has become the most successful love-song writer of the current pop generation. Between 1978 and 1985 he wrote and produced seven #1 hits for himself, the Commodores, Kenny Rogers, and Diana Ross. His classics include "Endless Love," "Lady," "Hello," and "Three Times a Lady." –RAB

Lionel Richie / MOTOWN   1982

A dynamic solo debut album, featuring "Truly," "You Are," and "My Love." –RAB

○ **Can't Slow Down / MOTOWN**   1983

His finest to date. Includes "Hello," "Running with the Night," "Stuck on You," and "Penny Lover" — all Top Ten hits. –RAB

Dancing on the Ceiling / MOTOWN   1987

Although not as solid as his first two albums, this does have several hits, including the title track, "Ballerina Girl," and "Love Will Conquer All." –RAB

JONATHAN RICHMAN/THE MODERN LOVERS   *b* 1951

Alternative pop. Jonathan Richman (b 1951) is a certifiable rock weirdo. In 1971 he and the Modern Lovers cut some demos for Warner Bros. (produced by John Cale) that funneled the influence of the Velvet Underground into the twisted vision of a high-school geek. Those demos were finally released in 1976, but everything he's done since then has pushed the parameters of cuteness into theme albums (*Jonathan Goes Country*, etc.), amplifying Richman's lighthearted approach. –JF & CK

★ **The Modern Lovers / RHINO**   1976

This is a reissue of the 1971 John Cale-produced demos that unknowingly precipitated what would eventually become punk-rock. As he states on "Roadrunner," he's in love with the modern world but also with girls. His odes to a lack of love make for a cogent debut. –JF

○ **Jonathan Richman & the Modern Lovers / RHINO**   1977

Richman's second collection of Modern Lovers, over which he was billed (eventually, the group name would be dropped) had a lighter rock & roll sound than the first. In fact, as often as not, Richman played acoustic guitar. And his lyrical concerns had similarly lightened up, to the point of childlike whimsy on such songs as "Hey There Little Insect" and "Here Come the Martian Martians." But the focus was still Richman's unabashed vocalizing (the word "sings" is put in quotes on the back cover), giving the whole album an amateurish charm. –WR

Rock 'N' Roll ... / BERSERKLEY   1977

Rock 'N' Roll with the Modern Lovers. Richman branches out to Japanese music, a "South American Folk Song," and even "Egyptian Reggae" (the last earning him a UK Top 5 hit), but the real highlight on *Rock 'N' Roll with the Modern Lovers* is that ode to a totaled car, "Dodge Veg-O-Matic." –WR

RIDE

Alternative rock. Trancelike vocals and dance grooves, coupled with walls of ambient distorto-guitar, are this Manchester, England, quartet's stock in trade. In the style of Echo & the Bunnymen, psychedelic dance-pop filtered through early Pink Floyd psycho-drone. –RC

Smile / WARNER   1980

The first two EPs from Britain's Creation label on one American collection. Sonically muddier than *Nowhere* (if that can be possible), but the tuneful crash-and-burn of "Like a Daydream" is one of their best. –RC

○ **Nowhere / WARNER**   1990

Rackety, reverberant, psychedelic drone-rock from Manchester, England. Fans of hypnotic detached singing against numbing waves of dissonance should find this somewhat interesting, particularly the throbbing "Polar Bear," the lumbering yet airy "Vapour Trail," the fairly accessible

"Taste," and the reckless "Here and Now." The title cut is an effective fusing of early Pink Floyd sonic freakout and industrial noise sludge. –RC

STAN RIDGWAY

Alternative rock. Ridgway is the former lead singer of eclectic post-punk Los Angeles group Wall of Voodoo (1977-1983). He scored a minor hit with "Mexican Radio" and released three solo albums between 1986 and 1991. –WR

○ **Mosquitos / GEFFEN** 1989
Ridgway is as much a storyteller as a songwriter, and the stories are wildly imaginative on this album. The sometimes exotic musical settings effectively evoke the literary landscapes Ridgway's near-spoken vocals describe. –WR

ZOOGZ RIFT

Alternative rock. Zoogz Rift is a Zappaesque cult icon from California. Portrait of the fringe artist as misanthrope. Airy but tuneful. –JD

○ **Looser Than Clams / SST** 1986
Their greatest-hits album is lean and mean and a great place to start. –JD

Idiots on the Miniature Golf Course / SST 1987
A good title and smartass rock to match it. –JD

THE RIGHTEOUS BROTHERS

R&B, rock/pop. The Righteous Brothers vocal duo consists of Bill Medley and Bobby Hatfield (both b 1941). Generally regarded as the popular originators of "blue-eyed soul," they originally formed as the Paramours in a stronger doo-wop style, eventually tackling harder R&B material in a more gospel-oriented fashion, prompting the name change. Early recordings featured the hit "Little Latin Lupe Lu," written by Medley. It quickly became a garage-band staple of the 60s, successfully covered by both the Kingsmen and Mitch Ryder. With producer Phil Spector, they went on to score Top Ten hits consistently with classic ballad material like "You've Lost That Lovin' Feelin'" and "Unchained Melody," the latter featured prominently in the movie *Ghost*. Even with label and production changes, the hits kept coming through the end of the 60s, when they went their separate ways. They reunited in 1974-1975, had another Top Ten smash with "Rock and Roll Heaven," and are still performing today to appreciative audiences. Their 21 entries on the *Billboard* Hot 100 chart and contribution to the music making their eventual induction into the Rock & Roll Hall of Fame a given. –CK

Live 1967 / LIVE GOLD
Great live performance from Anaheim Stadium, running the gamut from familiar hits to doo-wop and gospel favorites. With dynamic singing and energetic backing, this one catches them pretty much at the top of their form. –CK

○ **Anthology 1962-74 / RHINO** 1989
Excellent two-CD retrospective covering the hits from the early Moonglow R&B sides up to "Rock and Roll Heaven." The definitive overview. –CK

BILLY LEE RILEY   *b* 1933

Rockabilly. Rockabilly singer and multi-instrumentalist. An alumni of Sun Records, Riley was one of the most crazed, unabashed rockers that label had to offer — and in the company of Jerry Lee Lewis, Carl Perkins, and Sonny Burgess, that's saying a lot. Proficient at harmonica, guitar, bass, and drums, Riley contributed as a sideman to many a classic Sun session, and his combo the Little Green Men (most notably guitarist Roland Janes and drummer J.M. Van Eaton) in time became the Sun house band. Riley went on to record for a number of labels in a variety of styles, especially effective with blues. Though never commercially successful, Riley's Sun recordings of "Flying Saucer Rock 'n' Roll" and "Red Hot" (both covered in wooden renditions by Robert Gordon) remain landmarks of the genre. –CK

○ **Classic Recordings / BEAR FAMILY** 1990
All the classic Sun sides, plus later Memphis recordings in a brilliant 2-CD set. Raw rockin' at its finest. –CK

JOHNNY RIVERS   *b* 1942

Rock/pop. Johnny Rivers, intent on getting a break in the music business, left his Baton Rouge home for New York and Nashville. It is DJ Alan Freed who suggested the name change to Rivers, since he originated from the Delta South.
After a series of moves and song cuts and a stint with Louie Prima, Rivers gained attention on the Los Angeles club scene, particularly the Whiskey a Go-Go, where he recorded his #12 debut, *Johnny Rivers at the Whiskey a Go-Go*, for Imperial Records. Versions of Chuck Berry's "Memphis" and "Maybellene" hit #2 and #12, respectively, launching a series of live hit singles that reflect his tendency to draw from the blues and old rock & roll.
Rivers scored with the #3 "Secret Agent Man," capitalizing on the then-current fascination with foreign espionage. After that he increasingly turned his attentions to a lusher MOR formula with #1 "Poor Side of Town," "Baby I Need Your Lovin'" (#3), "The Tracks of My Tears" (#10), and the haunting "Summer Rain" (#14). During the 70s, Rivers had a comeback with several remakes of old rock hits, as well as a #10 hit with the romantic "Swayin' to the Music (Slow Dancin')."
Besides his artistry, Rivers displayed good commercial instincts by discovering and signing the 5th Dimension and assisting the career of writer Jimmy Webb.
Rivers continues to perform, sounding like he hasn't aged a day since his biggest hits. –RC

○ **Anthology / RHINO**
One of the great interpretive singers in rock & roll. Rivers made every song his own, and this 2-CD package is proof that he rarely faltered. –JT

THE RIVIERAS

Rock & roll. A South Bend, IN, rock & roll band whose one big hit was one of the last great gasps of pure American rock & roll before the British Invasion took over the charts. Original members Otto Nuss (organ), Doug Gean (bass), Marty "Bo" Fortson (vocals and guitar), Joe Pennell (guitar), and Paul Dennert (drums) were local teen ballroom heroes. They recorded a supercharged version of the Joe Jones R&B semi-hit "California Sun" featuring a powerful drum intro and the now-famous signature guitar and organ riff. The song became a hit in the midst of the first flush of Beatlemania, only nudged out of the #1 spot on the national charts by "I Want to Hold Your Hand." Although several equally fine 45s and two albums followed, the band's relatively young ages, coupled with numerous personnel changes caused by the draft and the changing musical climate, caused the band to break up by 1966. Nuss, Gean, and Fortson reunited the Rivieras in the mid 80s, recording and doing local shows, sounding as great as ever. Though their time in the spotlight was brief, their one big hit continues to define for future generations everything that's pulsatingly great about American teen-band rock & roll. –CK

○ **California Sun / SONET**
Import reissue of their first album. –CK

Campus Party / RIVIERA 1984
Second album; classic frat-band sound. Out of print and impossibly rare but worth the search at any cost. –CK

THE RIVINGTONS

Doo-wop. The Rivingtons were a West Coast vocal group featuring Al Frazier, Carl White, John "Sonny" Harris, and Turner "Rocky" Wilson Jr. Though they are best known for their string of early 60s novelties, the Rivingtons in reality had a rich tradition of doo-wop in their background, going back to their original recordings for Federal as the Lamplighters in 1953. They did extensive backup group work throughout the

50s between their own stray releases under a number of different names; the Sharps (singing on the original "Little Bitty Pretty One" and "Over and Over" by Thurston Harris), the Tenderfoots, the Rebels (they do all the backups on the Duane Eddy hits), the Four after Fives, the Crenshaws. They even sang backup on Paul Anka's first record, credited as the Jacks! In 1962 they became the Rivingtons and hit pay dirt with their first record, the self-penned "Pa Pa Ooh Mow Mow," one of the truly great rock & roll songs to make a virtue of sheer gibberish. They hit the charts again a year later with "The Bird's the Word," capitalizing on a current West Coast dance fad that teenagers were doing to "Pa Pa Ooh Mow Mow." A landlocked surf-teen combo from Minnesota called the Trashmen combined the two songs, revved up the beat to warp factor nine, and scored a massive hit with "Surfin' Bird." Despite no further chart success, their place in rock & roll history (both for the classic performances they recorded and for being the inspiration behind one of the great noise-rock anthems of all time) is assured. –CK

○ **Liberty Years / CAPITOL**   1991
An excellent 23-track CD with detailed notes and great sound, featuring both sides of all their original-issue 45s (including the insane followup "Mama Ooh Mow Mow") plus all the tracks from their lone Liberty album, *Doin' the Bird*. –CK

ROBBIE ROBERTSON   b 1943

Singer/songwriter. Chief songwriter and lead guitarist of the Band. After dissolving the Band in late 1976, Robertson acted in and produced *Carny*, wrote and/or chose the music for the soundtracks of Martin Scorsese's *Raging Bull*, *King of Comedy*, and *The Color of Money*, and in 1987 released his first solo album. Relatively inactive in the late 80s, Robertson's second solo album, *Storyville*, was not released until 1991. –RB

○ **Robbie Robertson / GEFFEN**   1987
Robbie Robertson's first solo album, released eleven years after the Band called it quits at *The Last Waltz*, found the singer-guitarist mining radically new territory. Hiring Daniel Lanois as coproducer, Robertson crafted an album that owed very little to the Band's roots-Americana sound. Instead Robertson opted for a quirky, enigmatic modern approach, using drum programs, the stick, and guest musicians such as U2, Peter Gabriel, and Bill Dillon. If the album had a weakness, it was in the vocal department. Robertson had only sung lead on a couple of songs with the Band. His reedy ghost of a voice can be quite effective but wears a bit thin over the course of a whole album. Ultimately that is a minor complaint, as the songwriting, arrangements, playing, and sound-painting are superb. Highlights: "Broken Arrow" and "Somewhere Down the Crazy River." –RB

Storyville / GEFFEN   1991
Robertson's second album was four years in the making. Once again he set out to explore an approach and sound markedly different from any of his previous work. The album is conceptual, roughing out a story over ten songs set in New Orleans' legendary turn-of-the-century Storyville red-light district. Coproduced by Robertson, Stephen Hague, and Gary Gersh, the record was recorded in New Orleans with members of the Neville Brothers, Mardi Gras Indians, the Meters, and the Zion Harmonizers. Legendary New Orleans arranger Wardell Quezergue crafted stunning horn charts. More aggressive than Robertson's first solo release, *Storyville* is perhaps a little less mysterious and enigmatic. –RB

DUKE ROBILLARD

Blues/rock. A founding member of the nine-piece Roomful of Blues, Robillard left to pursue a solo career in the early 80s, eventually replacing Jimmie Vaughan in the Fabulous Thunderbirds a decade later. Totally fluent in blues, rockabilly, early rock & roll, and blues-based jazz, Robillard is one of the idiom's finer guitarists. –CK

Swing / ROUNDER   1988
Superior small-group swing, featuring saxophonist Scott

Hamilton and his group. This is a bit out of the ordinary for this performer, but it's well titled and well executed. –BP

○ **Duke Robillard & the Pleasure Kings / ROUNDER**   1989
Trio recordings featuring fine T-Bone Walker-influenced guitar and vocals from the leader, mostly containing original compositions. This is good for what it is, but it seems to lack the punch that larger instrumentation might provide. –BP

SMOKEY ROBINSON & THE MIRACLES   b 1940

Motown. Bob Dylan called him "America's greatest living poet." Certainly, he was — and is — one of America's greatest living voices; he has brought his thrilling high tenor to a wide variety of material, most of it marked by his innate good taste. Smokey Robinson's association with Motown founder Berry Gordy goes back to the late 50s, when Gordy produced and cowrote the singles that the Miracles recorded for Chess and Roulette. Subsequently, the Miracles were one of the first acts to record for Tamla — and one of the first to break; "Shop Around" was a hit in 1960 and was followed by 38 more before Robinson quit the group in 1972. He also wrote for other acts (including "The Way You Do the Things You Do" and "My Girl" for the Temptations and "My Guy" and "Two Lovers" for Mary Wells).
Perhaps Robinson's masterpiece was "Tracks of My Tears," which he recorded with the Miracles. Its success was all the more surprising because the group had largely confined themselves to dance-oriented novelties before then. Robinson's contributions to Motown as an artist, writer, and producer were rewarded with a vice presidency, although the group's momentum was sagging. Their career was temporarily bolstered in 1970 when "Tears of a Clown" (cut three years earlier) became their first #1 pop hit. Robinson went solo two years later, and his solo albums trace the journey of a man who peaked early in life but has never lost the creative spark. –CF

Going to a Go-Go / MOTOWN   1965
Their best 60s album by far. –RAB

☆ **Anthology / MOTOWN**   1973
Detroit vocal group the Miracles were a fixture at Motown from day one. Driven by Robinson's superior writing and smooth, silky falsetto, the Miracles placed a stunning 48 singles on the *Billboard* charts, 39 of those with Smokey in tow. All but six are included on this collection. Songs such as "Ooh Baby Baby," "The Tracks of My Tears," and "The Tears of a Clown" define much that was good about the 60s. As usual with Motown's reissues, the sound is substandard and there is no decent set of liner notes. But this is the only way you can hear this essential material. –RB

TOM ROBINSON

Punk, alternative rock. Robinson emerged amid the British punk explosion with overtly political lyrics and a punkish pop sound. A former London folkster, he released his most successful album *Power in the Darkness* in 1978, which included the minor hit "2-4-6-8 Motorway." After a tamer followup inappropriately produced by Todd Rundgren, Robinson formed the short-lived, more electronic sounding Sector 27 in 1980. The singer subsequently abandoned his political messages for more commercial rock in a series of albums during the 80s. –DS

○ **Power in the Darkness / HARVEST**   1978
Angry British political punk at its best. –DS

TRB Two / HARVEST   1979
A good followup to a brilliant debut. –DS

MAGGIE AND TERRE ROCHE

Singer/songwriter. A duet from deepest New Jersey, a pair of folkies who debuted with one well-produced record but didn't hit their stride until they found a freer sound and a third sister, forming the Roches. –BE

○ **Seductive Reasoning / SONY SP**   1975
A very well produced folk-rock album that is unexceptional

but clearly sung and harmonized, very pleasant in its modest way. –BE

THE ROCHES

Singer/songwriter. Maggie, Terre, and Suzy Roche harmonize magnificently and share a quirky sense of humor that informs their songs. Most of the time it works, and their music is always interesting to listen to. –BE

○ **Roches / WARNER** 1979
An extraordinary debut record with ringing, soaring harmonies rubbing up against a beautiful and spare instrumental sound. A powerful piece of work. –BE

Keep On Doing / WARNER 1982
This is a comeback after the bizarre misstep of their second album. –BE

Another World / WARNER 1985
Their most unabashedly lyrical album. A bracing work that, alas, isn't as daring as their debut. –BE

A Dove / MCA 1992
An update from the singing sisters finds them living in the urban jungle and overcoming romantic expectations in favor of self-reliance, though not without regret and not, thank God, without moments of humor and absurdity. For the most part, the trio's folkie past has given way to a rock-pop approach on this album. –WR

ROCKPILE

Roots-rock. A quartet formed by Dave Edmunds and Nick Lowe in the mid 70s and famed for their live shows displaying an inspired command of basic rock & roll and distinctive originals. –BE

○ **Seconds of Pleasure / CBS** 1980
An oddly disappointing album considering the talent involved. This record seemed like a breath of fresh air in 1980 with its basic redefinition of rock & roll. The Everly Brothers covers now hold up best. –BE

TOMMY ROE b 1942

Rock/pop. Widely perceived as one of the archetypal bubblegum artists of the late 60s, Tommy Roe cut some pretty decent rockers along the way, especially early in his career — many displaying some pretty prominent Buddy Holly roots.
In fact, Roe's initial pop smash, 1962's chart-topping "Sheila," was quite reminiscent of Holly's "Peggy Sue," utilizing a very similar throbbing drum beat and Roe's hiccuping vocal. The singer had previously cut the song for the smaller Judd label before remaking it in superior form for ABC-Paramount. The infectious "Everybody" — another hot item the next year — was waxed in Muscle Shoals at Rick Hall's Fame studios, normally an R&B-oriented facility (it's not widely known that Roe wrote songs for the Tams, a raw-edged soul group from his Atlanta hometown).
Once Roe veered off on his squeaky-clean bubblegum tangent, he stuck with it for the rest of the decade. His lighthearted "Sweet Pea" and "Hooray for Hazel" burned up the charts in 1966, and he was still at it three years later when he waxed his biggest hit, "Dizzy," and "Jam Up Jelly Tight." –BD

○ **Greatest Hits / MCA**
With "Sheila," "Dizzy," and the rest, this is the place to start and finish. –DH

THE ROLLING STONES

Rock & roll. The Rolling Stones are the definitive rock & roll band and, by now, the longest-lived rock & roll band to remain consistently popular throughout their (30-year) career. The group came together in London, where singer Mick Jagger (b Jul 26, 1943) and guitarist Keith Richards (b Dec 18, 1943), who had been grade school classmates, joined with guitarist Brian Jones (b Feb 28, 1942 - d Jul 3, 1969) and a rhythm section then consisting of pianist Ian Stewart, bassist

Dick Taylor, and drummer Mick Avory (later of the Kinks) at a debut show at the Marquee on July 12, 1962. Taylor was replaced soon after by Bill Wyman (b Oct 24, 1936), and Avory eventually by jazz drummer Charlie Watts (b Jun 2, 1941).
The Rolling Stones played an eight-month residency at the Crawdaddy Club in 1963, during which they signed a management contract with Andrew "Loog" Oldham (who demoted Ian Steward to road manager) and a recording contract with Decca. The group was devoted to playing Chicago blues and its offshoots, notably the rock & roll of Chuck Berry, and its early records were either covers of such music or extremely derivative originals. The Stones' first single, for example, was a cover of Berry's "Come On." It was followed by "I Wanna Be Your Man," a song written for the Stones by John Lennon and Paul McCartney.
The Stones' first really successful single, however, was a version of Buddy Holly's "Not Fade Away," which reached #3 in England and became their first American chart entry. Their next five UK singles all hit #1, and by 1965 they had established themselves as second only to the Beatles as the most popular British rock group, a position they held until the Beatles broke up.
The important factor setting the Stones apart from their lesser competition was that they successfully moved from being a blues-rock cover band to being a band that performed primarily original pop-rock material with a blues base. Jagger and Richards turned into a songwriting team as early as 1964, and by 1965 such Stones hits as "The Last Time" and "(I Can't Get No) Satisfaction" were scoring on both sides of the Atlantic.
The Stones toured extensively in the mid 60s, with their success partially attributable to frontman Mick Jagger, who became the most prominent lead singer in rock. They followed many of the trends of the 60s as the decade wore on, and their involvement with drugs curtailed their ability to play in the US after 1966. By that time, like the Beatles and others, their musical horizons had expanded to include a variety of eclectic styles. Unlike the Beatles, however, the Stones were never really comfortable with psychedelia, and after their 1967 *Sgt. Pepper* knock-off, *Their Satanic Majesties Request*, they returned to a more basic hard-rock style on the single "Jumpin' Jack Flash" and the album *Beggars Banquet*.
In 1969 the Stones reemerged as a concert attraction after firing Brian Jones (who died shortly after) and hiring guitarist Mick Taylor (b Jan 17, 1948), who in turn was replaced by Ron Wood (b Jun 1, 1947) in 1976. They released the single "Honky Tonk Women" and the album *Let it Bleed* and embarked on an American concert tour that culminated in the disastrous Altamont Festival. Despite that debacle, after the Beatles' split the following year, the Stones were undisputed in their claim to being "the greatest rock & roll band in the world."
In the 70s, the Stones toured every three years and released a series of million-selling, chart-topping albums, despite guitarist Keith Richards's descent into heroin addiction. The drug problem came to a head when Richards was arrested in Toronto in 1977. He subsequently cleaned up, however, and took a more active role in the Stones' creative efforts, resulting in improved albums in the late 70s and early 80s.
The Stones played a world tour from 1981-1982 and continued actively into the mid 80s, but when Jagger made a solo album in 1985 and then refused to tour behind the Stones' 1986 *Dirty Work* album, their long career together seemed to be over. Richards reluctantly began work on a solo album and publicly voiced his anger. Jagger released a second solo album in 1987 and toured Japan as a solo in 1988, but by the time of the release of Richards's solo album, *Talk Is Cheap*, the Stones were in discussions about a reunion. A new album, *Steel Wheels*, was recorded and released in 1989, accompanied by another world tour lasting into 1990. As of mid 1992, the Stones had signed a new deal with Virgin Records (apparently without Bill Wyman), but Jagger was working on another solo album. –WR

Rolling Stones (British import) / LON   1964
The imported edition of the group's first album is superior in sound to the American version, with some curious differences in the songs as well ("Tell Me" runs longer). –BE

The Rolling Stones / ABKCO   1964
The group's debut album, a bit bluesier and more acoustically textured than the sound they later became famous for, with the influence of Slim Harpo and Muddy Waters getting equal time with Chuck Berry and Bo Diddley. "Carol," "King Bee," and "Route 66" are just a few of the indispensable highlights. –BE

☆ **12 X 5 / ABKCO**   1965
A much more rock-oriented album than their debut, *12 X 5* is the album that solidified the group's Chuck Berry and Bo Diddley-based sound, and on which guitarists Keith Richards and Brian Jones first flexed their muscles. –BE

December's Children / ABKCO   1965
A much more artful release, compiled from various singles and album sessions. The blues material is subservient to rock numbers like "Get Off of My Cloud" and elegant R&B such as "You Better Move On." –BE

Out of Our Heads / ABKCO   1965
The first of the American patchwork albums, assembled from sessions on two continents and some London concerts, and it all works — "Satisfaction" was the hit, but "I'm Alright" was a concert favorite for years. –BE

☆ **Rolling Stones Now! / ABKCO**   1965
The group's second album is a louder blues record, moving toward rock, with Mick Jagger beginning to stretch out as a vocalist and the band hardening its sound. "Everybody Needs Somebody to Love" and "Mona" are among the best parts of a near-perfect record. –BE

☆ **Aftermath / ABKCO**   1966
The group's most accomplished studio record of the 60s, and the first to feature all Jagger-Richards originals. The sound also expands here to embrace the mild psychedelic/Eastern sound of "Paint It Black," and the barrier bursting 10-minute-plus "Goin' Home," highlighted by Brian's workout on blues harp. –BE

Aftermath (British) / LONDON   1966
The British import of this album is superior to the American, with a different stereo sound mix and a longer version of "Out of Time" than have ever been heard officially in the US. –BE

Big Hits - Vol. 1 / ABKCO   1966
Big Hits - Vol. 1 (High Tide & Green Grass) is a concise collection of the group's early hits, without any surprises. –BE

☆ **Between the Buttons / ABKCO**   1967
A spaced-out, trippy mix of psychedelia, vaudeville, and Dylan homages that has worn well despite the inclusion of two hits ("Let's Spend the Night Together" and "Ruby Tuesday") that had nothing to do with the rest of it. A self-conscious album, and very theatrical. –BE

Their Satanic Majesties Request / ABKCO   1967
Underrated psychedelic venture by the Stones, who seem to lack confidence in their abilities and material (and lacked a producer at the time as well). The dross is balanced out by a couple of minor hits ("2000 Light Years from Home," "She's a Rainbow") and a couple of brilliant album tracks ("2000 Man" and "Citadel"). –BE

☆ **Beggar's Banquet / ABKCO**   1968
The group's newly matured sound came together on this album, a mixture of blues and politics that proved almost too controversial to release at the time. "Salt of the Earth," "Parachute Woman," "Street Fighting Man," and "Jigsaw Puzzle" make it worthwhile. –BE

☆ **Let It Bleed / ABKCO**   1969
A coda to the Brian Jones era, and the start of the Mick Taylor era, with a dazzling collection of numbers ("Gimme Shelter," "Midnight Rambler," "Love in Vain," "You Can't Always Get

What You Want," "Let It Bleed," etc.), most of which figured prominently in the group's subsequent tour. –BE

☆ **Get Yer Ya-Ya's Out / ABKCO**   1970
This live album, released largely to counteract the effect of the bootleg *Liver Than You'll Ever Be*, captured the new-era Stones in their top form, doing all of the key material from their preceding pair of albums. –BE

☆ **Sticky Fingers / CBS**   1971
A ballsy, bluesy masterpiece made up of leftovers and works in progress from the preceding two years, including "Wild Horses," "Brown Sugar," and "Sister Morphine." –BE

☆ **Exile on Main Street / CBS**   1972
Originally rock's most musically successful double album, this epic collection has aged magnificently. Includes the hit "Tumbling Dice," as well as "Rocks Off," "Happy," "Rip This Joint," and "Sweet Virginia." –BE

○ **Hot Rocks / LONDON**   1972
This import double-disc anthology contains their biggest hits on London, as well as many of their most popular album tracks. A stereo version of "Satisfaction" is the highlight, and worth the price, even though the US mono version is also pretty cool. –BE

● **Hot Rocks 1964-1971 / ABKCO**   1972
A straightforward hits package (1964-1971), and a radio programmer's dream. Includes "Satisfaction," "Gimme Shelter," "Brown Sugar," and many more of their greatest hits and album tracks. –BE

● **More Hot Rocks / ABKCO**   1972
Highlighted by a unique stereo edition of "It's All Over Now." Often thought of as secondary, this anthology is really a lot more interesting than *Hot Rocks*. –BE

○ **Some Girls / CBS**   1978
This album was received at the time as the toughest piece of music the Stones had cut since the early 70s. Today it sounds a bit thin; "When the Whip Comes Down" and "Respectable" do rock out but without the authority or energy you should expect from these guys. Nonetheless, it's an interesting piece of work, from the minimalist disco of "Miss You" up to the pulsating pseudo new-wave of "Shattered." And "Before They Make Me Run" is Keith Richards's most endearing vocal since "Happy." –JF

○ **Tattoo You / CBS**   1981
They've reclaimed some of the energy lacking on *Some Girls*, but this is still a slight album; it rocks just hard enough to keep the faithful within the fold but lacks the energy of the old days. "Start Me Up" is an infectious single, and "Black Limousine" is a return to twelve-bar blues, but it's the ballads ("Waiting on a Friend," "Worried about You") that keep this one afloat. –JF

☆ **Singles Collection: The London Years / ABKCO**   1989
The best individual collection of their classic hits ever assembled, for sound and content. –BE

Steel Wheels / CBS   1989
The band's best album of the 80s, embracing blues, classic rock, and even psychedelia ("Continental Drift"). –BE

HENRY ROLLINS

Punk, alternative rock. Ex-Black Flag shouter Henry Rollins now fronts a hard-rock/trash band that doesn't deviate from the formula that was successful for his previous band: loud, simple blues-rock with touches of funk, which provides a foundation for Rollins's lyrical vituperation. Loud, hard, and direct, this is the new face of hard rock: more aggressive and explosively cathartic. –JD

Big Ugly Mouth / TEXAS HOTEL   1965
A spoken-word record. –JD

○ **Hot Animal Machine / TEXAS HOTEL**   1966
A good solo effort, raw and powerful. This CD includes the EP *Drive By Shootings*. –JD

☆ **Turned On / QUARTER STICK**   1990
A perfect example of the Rollins Band at work, recorded live in Vienna, Austria, in 1989 with some of his best songs from that era. Recorded digitally, but the CD treats the entire recording as one track. –JB

ROMANTICS

Rock/pop. These power-poppers from the Motor City netted such 80s hits as "What I Like about You" and "Talking in Your Sleep." –JF

○ **What I Like about You ... / CBS**   1991
What I Like about You (& Other Romantic Hits). The title track was their finest hour but there are a couple of other hits here too. –DH

ROMEO VOID

Alternative rock. A post-punk quintet formed in San Francisco in 1979, consisting of singer Debora Iyall (b 1956), bassist Frank Zincavage, guitarist Peter Woods, drummer Jay Derrah (replaced by John Stench and then Larry Carter), and saxophone player Ben Bossi. They released several albums on 415 Records (distributed by CBS) 1981-1984. Iyall then left for a solo career. –WR

It's a Condition / 415   1981
Iyall's distanced vocal style, plus the group's steady beat, make sentiments such as "Love Is an Illness" believable. Iyall is the Mae West of punk rock: When she says, "Talk dirty to me," it doesn't sound as though she cares whether you do or not. –WR

○ **Benefactor / CBS**   1982
"I might like you better if we slept together," Iyall sings in "Never Say Never," and so coins her ultimate putdown line, which is, typically, in the form of a come-on. –WR

LINDA RONSTADT   b 1946

Country rock, pop. Coming out of the Los Angeles folk music coffeehouse circuit in the mid 60s with her original group, the Stone Poneys, Ronstadt was an early proponent of the country-rock movement spearheaded by groups like Poco and the Eagles, who were originally her backup band. With wide-ranging tastes and spot-on intonation, the sweet-voiced Ronstadt has dealt with many different styles in the intervening years with great popular success. –DH

☆ **Heart like a Wheel / CAPITOL**   1974
Ronstadt's breakthrough album, and her most perfectly realized. Solid from top to bottom, featuring the title track, "When Will I Be Loved?," "Desperado," and "You're No Good." Essential. –CK

● **Greatest Hits - Vol. 1 / ELEKTRA**   1976
A concise collection of her chart successes. –DH

Greatest Hits - Vol. 2 / ELEKTRA   1980
Her next dozen hits, more formulaic in content, but bigger on the charts. –CK

What's New / ASYLUM   1983
Some of Ronstadt's best work to date — her first collaboration with bandleader Nelson Riddle (40s and 50s standards). –CK

○ **A Retrospective / CAPITOL**   1989
A nice compilation of primarily country-influenced, pre-hit material. –CK

DIANA ROSS   b 1944

Motown, disco, pop. Diana Ross, protégé of Motown president Berry Gordy, stepped out of the Supremes in 1970 for a solo career that has included successes on record, stage, and film. As lead singer of the Supremes and as a soloist, she has had more #1 records than any other female artist in history. She left Motown for RCA in 1981, a move that diminished her record-selling power. Today she is back at Motown searching for a new musical identity. Her voice is one of the most recognizable in history. –RAB

Ain't No Mountain High Enough / MOTOWN   1970
An excellent Ashford & Simpson collection. –RAB

Boss / MOTOWN   1979
Great dance material again by Ashford & Simpson. –RAB

Diana / MOTOWN   1980
A funky Chic production. –RAB

Swept Away / RCA   1985
Her best post-Motown album. –RAB

○ **Anthology / MOTOWN**   1986
All of her solo material. The best album available on Diana Ross. –RAB

DAVID LEE ROTH   b 1955

Hard rock. David Lee Roth was the original vocalist for Van Halen. Known as "Diamond Dave" due to his sometimes overdone attitude on stage and off. He left Van Halen for a solo career, meeting with immediate success in 1985 with his cover of the Beach Boys hit "California Girls." Throughout the years his solo band has featured a great set of musicians, including one-time Frank Zappa and Alcatrazz guitarist Steve Vai and former Talas bassist Billy Sheehan, who now is comfortable in his own band Mr. Big. Roth's popularity has somewhat dwindled in recent years, but his work with Van Halen will always remain a heavy influence for metal bands around the world. –JB

○ **Eat 'Em & Smile / WARNER**   1986
This flamboyant frontman is flanked by bassist Billy Sheehan and guitar-shredder Steve Vai, blazing the solo trail with these big and bawdy rockers, like "Goin' Crazy!" –DDC

ROULETTES

British Invasion. An underrated British band, featuring future Argent alumnus Russ Ballard on lead guitar. They were originally formed as a backing group for vocalist Adam Faith, whose records, although few in number, were of a very high caliber and had some of the musical virtues evident in the better-known work of the Beatles and the Searchers: soaring harmonies behind strong lead vocals, crisp guitar playing, and a knack for memorable hooks. –BE

○ **Best of the Roulettes /**
A superb collection of singles, B-Sides, and album tracks. All are enjoyable and memorable, especially the track "I'll Remember Tonight." (Import) –BE

Stakes & Chips / EMI
An unusual album, marred only by some ill-chosen cover versions. (Import) –BE

ROXETTE

Rock/pop. Swedish singing duo with a decidedly pop singles edge (late 80s & 90s). Features guitarist and songwriter Per Gessle and vocalist Marie Fredriksson. They worked as solo performers (Gessle doing guitar-driven pop, Fredriksson as a jazz-oriented chanteuse) before teaming up. They have scored on American charts with several smart, upbeat guitar-driven hits. –DH

Look Sharp / CAPITOL   1989
A fun, dynamic debut, featuring the hit singles "The Look" (#1), "Dressed for Success" (#14), "Listen to Your Heart" (#1), and "Dangerous" (#2). –DH

○ **Joyride / CAPITOL**   1991
Their second album, featuring infectious, solid song construction from Gessle and dynamite singing from Fredriksson. "Knock on Every Door," "Watercolours in the Rain," and the title track are among the highlights. –CK

ROXY MUSIC

Alternative rock. Roxy Music scored enormous success in its native England in the 70s, first as a leader of the glam-rock movement and later for its sophisticated sound. The group was formed in London in 1971 around lead singer Bryan Ferry (b Sep 26, 1945). Personnel came and went until the group solidified by the time of its 1972 debut album with a lineup of Ferry, reed player Andy Mackay (b Jul 23, 1946), guitarist Phil Manzanera (b Jan 31, 1951), keyboardist Brian Eno (b May 15, 1948), and drummer Paul Thompson (b May 13, 1951). The band's original bassist, Graham Simpson, left during the album sessions and was replaced initially by Rik Kenton, though the group employed a series of bassists throughout its career.

Roxy Music was a Top Ten UK hit in the summer of 1972, spinning off the Top Ten single, "Virginia Plain." *For Your Pleasure* (1973) did even better, getting to #4. Eno had left the band by the time it made its third album, *Stranded* (going on to an extensive career as a solo artist and record producer), and was replaced by Eddie Jobson (b Apr 28, 1955), who played violin and keyboards. *Stranded* was another UK hit, going to #1, and it was followed by *Country Life*, Roxy Music's first album to sell in even modest numbers in the US. *Siren* (1975) contained the American Top 30 hit "Love Is the Drug" (#2 in the UK).

At the point of American commercial breakthrough, however, Roxy Music disbanded, with Ferry, Mackay, Manzanera, and Jobson going off to solo careers. The group re-formed in 1978, minus Jobson, and recorded *Manifesto* (1979), after which Thompson left. The remaining trio released *Flesh and Blood* and *Avalon* (the latter was Roxy's only US gold album), albums made in a smooth, melodic art-rock style before the group folded again in 1983. –WR

For Your Pleasure / WARNER / BB 193   1973
For Your Pleasure, Roxy's schizophrenic second album, vacillates between campy rockers like "Do the Strand" and "Editions of You" (both UK hits) and creepy mood pieces like "In Every Dream Home a Heartache" (an ode to an inflatable sex doll) and the title cut, which showcases lead singer Bryan Ferry's goulish croon over an instrumental track that would work well on "Twin Peaks." –RC

○ **Stranded / WARNER / BB 186**   1973
On *Stranded*, their first album without sound-manipulator Brian Eno, Roxy affected a more sophisticated, self-absorbed stance with elegant numbers like "A Song for Europe" and "Psalm." Roxy's penchant for fine oddball pop-rockers continued with "Street Life" (a #9 UK hit), "Amazona," and the soaring "Serenade." –RC

☆ **Country Life / WARNER / BB 37**   1974
Arguably their best album, *Country Life*'s everything-and-the-kitchen-sink art-rock production and steely dissonance reached a pinnacle with tracks like the "The Thrill of It All," "All I Want Is You," and "Casanova." "Out of the Blue," one of their finest songs, showcased Eddie Jobson on a powerfully phase-shifted violin solo. The beautifully unsettling "Bitter-Sweet" reflected Bryan Ferry's flirtation with Germanic melodicism and fascist imagery. –RC

○ **Siren / WARNER / BB 50**   1975
Siren provided Roxy Music with their first international hit, the coolly funky "Love Is the Drug" (#30). Except for "Sentimental Fool," "Both Ends Burning," and "Whirlwind," most of this album fails to deliver the power or memorable melodies of either *Country Life* or *Stranded*. –RC

Viva! / WARNER / BB 81   1976
While their studio work is the place to start with this group, this is a good live set. –RC

Flesh + Blood / WARNER / BB 35   1977
Flesh + Blood finds Roxy making a further transition away from dissonant arrangements. The sleepwalking delivery of "In the Midnight Hour" is oddly fascinating, as is the discoish streamlining of the Byrds's classic "Eight Miles High." Nevertheless, many of the originals lack any memorable qualities. –RC

● **Greatest Hits / ATCO**   1977
For anyone looking for an intro to Roxy's important earlier sides, this 1977 best-of collection is an essential primer. –RC

○ **Manifesto / WARNER / BB 23**   1979
After a four-year layoff, Roxy shed their aggressively dense rock sound and returned with a more streamlined (but still weird) danceable pop. Detractors claimed that the band had lost their edge, but *Manifesto* introduced Roxy Musi to a new audience looking for a sophisticated alternative to generic late-70s disco. Highlights include "Angel Eyes," "Dance Away," and the title cut. –RC

☆ **Avalon / WARNER / BB 53**   1982
From the beautifully longing romanticism of Bryan Ferry's melodies to the dreamy soundscapes rendered by Rhett Davies, Roxy Music, and Bob Clearmountain, *Avalon* is fashion-plate cool, yet somehow exudes a weird, intoxicating kind of detached soulfulness that makes this one of the most elegant-sounding releases ever committed to disc. –RC

○ **Atlantic Years 1973-1980 / ATCO**   1983
Atlantic Years 1973-1980 provides the cream of *Flesh + Blood* and *Manifesto* (as well as a couple of key tracks from Roxy's earlier work on Reprise). Overall it lacks the substance of the original 1977 Atco *Greatest Hits* package, which was an essential showcase for their earlier work. –RC

○ **Street Life/Hits / WARNER**   1986
This compilation is a more general (not entirely satisfactory) overview of Roxy tracks and Bryan Ferry's urbane dance-pop hits. –RC

ROYAL CRESCENT MOB

Alternative rock. A fun, high-spirited, funky rock & roll band from Columbus, OH. –ME

○ **Omerta / MOVING TARGET**   1987
Awesome! As close as you'll come to one of their energetic live shows. The Mob at their best! –ME

Spin the World / WARNER   1989
The better of the Mob's two big-label albums. –ME

ROYAL TEENS

Rock & roll. The Royal Teens hit pop pay dirt in 1958 with a catchy novelty rocker called "Short Shorts" on the ABC-Paramount label. Future Four Seasons mainstay Bob Gaudio was the group's pianist, while ex-Three Friends front man Joe Villa joined as vocalist in late 1958 and Al Kooper briefly passed through the ranks in 1959. Despite a brief appearance in the 1958 film "Let's Rock," ABC followups like "Harvey's Got a Girl Friend" and "Big Name Button" failed to match the excitement of "Short Shorts." The group notched their last pop hit in 1959 with "Believe Me," after moving to Capitol. –BD

○ **Short Shorts: Golden Classics / COLLECTABLES**
Good-humored late-50s rock & roll with a solid beat. –BD

DAVID RUFFIN   1941-1991

Motown. After an unsuccessful solo career in the early 60s, David Ruffin joined the Temptations in 1964. It was his gruff vocals and soaring falsetto that made classic hits for the group such as "My Girl," "I Wish It Would Rain" and "Ain't Too Proud to Beg." He was fired from the group in 1968 and launched a mildly successful solo career in 1969. His drug problems were his biggest hindrance, an addiction that finally claimed this gifted singer's life in 1991. –RAB

My Whole World Ended / MOTOWN   1969
Solid debut. Some great moments. –RP

Who I Am / MOTOWN   1975
Songs and production by Van McCoy, and includes "Walk Away from Love." –RP

Everything's Coming Up Love / MOTOWN   1976
The second Van McCoy album, even better than first one he produced for Ruffin. –RP

○ **At His Best / MOTOWN**   1978
Ten tracks of his biggest soul hits. –RP

JIMMY RUFFIN   b 1939

Motown.. The older brother of the Temptations' lead singer David Ruffin, Jimmy enjoyed several huge hits himself in the mid 60s for Berry Gordy's Soul label. Ruffin first signed with another Motown subsidiary, the short-lived Miracle, in 1961, but it was his convincing vocal on "What Becomes of the Brokenhearted" that made him a star in 1966. He encored with "I've Passed This Way Before" and "Gonna Give Her All the Love I've Got," In 1970 he briefly teamed with David (by then a solo) as the Ruffin Brothers and cut a duet remake of Ben E. King's "Stand by Me." He staged an impressive comeback in 1980 on RSO Records with a major pop hit, "Hold On to My Love," that was produced by Robin Gibb of the Bee Gees. –BD

○ **Sings Top Ten / MOTOWN**   1966
His classic ballads, including "What Becomes of the Brokenhearted" are here. –RP

Ruff 'n Ready / MOTOWN   1969
More of the same as *Sings Top Ten*, without the big hits. –RP

MASON RUFFNER

Blues/rock. Guitarist and singer. Working out of New Orleans for the past few years, Ruffner's style owes much to blues but has a slashing rock-tinged bent all his own. –CK

○ **Gypsy Blood / CBS**   1969
Ruffner showcased in a variety of styles, with "I Don't Care No More" being a particular standout. –CK

RUFUS & CHAKA KHAN

Funk, urban R&B, dance-pop. Personnel included Chaka Khan on lead vocals, Bobby Watson, Kevin Murphy, Andre Fischer, and David "Hawk" Wolinsky. One of the groundbreaking funk bands of the 70s, Rufus was formed in 1970 by Murphy. Khan replaced the original female lead, Paulette McWilliams, in 1972. Over the next decade, Khan's strident vocals and unique vocal arrangements (accompanying herself on playbacks) and the band's earthy style defined the group on cuts like "Tell Me Something Good," "Once You Get Started," and "At Midnight (My Love Will Lift You Up)." Khan left in 1984 for a full-time solo career she had started part-time in 1980. The band did mostly instrumentals before disintegrating without a potent lead singer like Khan. –BC

Rags to Rufus / MCA / BB 4   1974
From the hard-funk opener of "You Got the Love" (#11) to the Stevie Wonder-penned "Tell Me Something Good" (#3), *Rags to Rufus* is a fine showcase for Chaka Khan's amazing vocals. Even though it's not one of their best albums, fans will definitely enjoy this effort. –RC

○ **Rufusized / MCA / BB 7**   1975
With the addition of guitarist/songwriter Tony Maiden, Rufus delivers one of their best albums. It features the hits "Once You Get Started" (#10) and "Please Pardon Me (You Remind Me of a Friend)" (#48). –RC

Rufus Featuring Chaka Khan / MCA   1975
Rufus continued their string of successful albums with this 1975 release, featuring the mellow soul of "Sweet Thing," a #5 million-seller, as well as jolting funk tunes like "Dance Wit Me." –BC

Ask Rufus / ABC / BB 12   1977
This solid album includes "Hollywood" (#32) and "At Midnight (My Love Will Lift You Up)" (#30). –RC

Stompin' at the Savoy (live) / WARNER   1982
Double record — three sides of live hits and one side of new studio cuts, including "Ain't Nobody." –BC

THE RUNAWAYS

Rock & roll. Rock & roll band featuring vocalist Cherie Currie

and guitarists Joan Jett and Lita Ford. Organized by producer Kim Fowley in 1976, their raw, punkish style became a cult item in Japan and Europe, but unfortunately never connected with any kind of mainstream success stateside until Jett and Ford each went solo. –CK

The Runaways / MERCURY   1976
Their debut album, produced by mentor Kim Fowley, loaded with excitement and featuring the classic "Cherry Bomb." (Japanese import) –CK

○ **Queens of Noise / MERCURY**   1977
Their definitive statement, with Joan Jett taking over lead-singing chores on six of the ten tracks. The title cut says it all. (Japanese import) –CK

TODD RUNDGREN   b 1948

Rock/pop. Over the course of his lengthy career, Todd Rundgren (b Jun 22, 1948) has created some of popular music's finer moments, as well as some of its most frustrating. He has proven to be a master of great pop melodies (with influences from Beatles to Philly Soul) and heartfelt lyrical sentiment, while also releasing albums of tedious prog-rock that only a diehard fan could care about. At times Rundgren's productions seemed to have existed independently of the music, rather than enhancing it; nevertheless, Rundgren is an influential Renaissance man in the history of rock.

Rundgren's first taste of success came with the psychedelic pop-rock group Nazz, in 1967. "Hello, It's Me" (#71/#66) charted twice, while the heavily phased riff-rocker "Open My Eyes" became a signature tune of sorts.

Rundgren left Nazz (future Cheap Trick guitarist Rick Nielson was his replacement) and pursued a solo career with the 1971 debut *Runt.Something/Anything*, Rundgren's third album, was his finest showcase as a songwriter.

It was during this time that Rundgren began making a name for himself as an innovative producer. Over the years he has worked on projects for Badfinger, New York Dolls, Foghat, Patti Smith, Cheap Trick, XTC, Meat Loaf, and others. In 1974 Rundgren formed Utopia, a quartet that helped fulfill his prog-rock tendencies. By the late 70s, Rundgren was actively exploring the medium of rock video, opening his own computer video studio in Woodstock, NY. He continues to produce various artists and to release solo albums that enjoy a solid cult success. –RC

Runt / RHINO / BB 185   1970
Runt, Todd Rundgren's debut, might have been a little uneven, but its homemade production, spirited arrangements, and great tunes like "We Gotta Get You a Woman," and "I'm in the Clique," made this one of the most appealing albums of his career. –RC

Runt: Ballad of Todd Rundgren / RHINO   1971
Rundgren's sophomore release didn't contain the flashes of brilliance found on *Runt*, but "Be Nice to Me," "Parole," and "Remember Me" are standouts on this relatively low-key effort. –RC

☆ **Something/Anything? / RHINO / BB 29**   1972
From beginning to end, *Something/Anything?* is Rundgren's best album, featuring the hit singles "I Saw the Light," and "Hello, It's Me." There are also a load of gems like "It Wouldn't Have Made Any Difference," "Wolfman Jack," and "Couldn't I Just Tell You," one of the finest power-pop tracks ever cut. Rundgren plays every instrument and sings all the parts on three-fourths of this self-produced release. Even though Rundgren had flashes of brilliance after *Something/Anything?*, he never came up with an album with performances and material as consistently satisfying. –RC

A Wizard a True Star / RHINO / BB 86   1973
Rundgren's keen sense for writing tight pop songs is almost nowhere to be found on this over-the-top production job. That's not to say that *A Wizard a True Star* doesn't have its virtues. Rundgren's take on *Peter Pan*'s "Never Never Land" is otherworldly, and his Philly-soul medley is quite fine.

"International Feel" and "Just One Victory" are other standout tracks. –RC

Faithful / RHINO   1976
One half of this outing features Rundgren delivering almost letter-perfect versions of 60s classics like "Good Vibrations" and "Rain," which are impressive in their attention to detail but sound strangely lifeless. On the other half of the album, he delivers some of his best work since *Something/Anything?*, particularly on "Black & White" and "When I Pray." –RC

Hermit of Mink Hollow / RHINO / BB 36   1978
By the release of this album, Rundgren had ditched the homemade charm of *Something/Anything?* for a warbly hard-rock/pop sound. Tracks like "Determination," "Out of Control," "You Cried Wolf," and "Fade Away" best exemplify that approach. "Can We Still Be Friends" became a #29 hit. –RC

Ever Popular Tortured Artist Effect / RHINO   1983
This album, one of Rundgren's best do-it-yourself efforts of the 80s, contains his #63 hit "Bang the Drum All Day" and a swell remake of Small Faces's "Tin Soldier." –RC

● **Anthology (1968-1985) / RHINO**   1986
Anthology is a fairly comprehensive overview of Rundgren's entire career, starting with "Open My Eyes," by Nazz, and including "Something to Fall Back On," from Rundgren's 1985 solo album *A Cappella*. All of his radio hits are included, as well as many important album tracks. Nevertheless, there are several key tracks missing, like "Wolfman Jack," "International Feel / Never Never Land," and Nazz's "Forget All about It" and "Hang On Paul." Like all of Rundgren's reissues on Rhino, *Anthology* has been given a first-class remastering job. –RC

An Elpee's Worth of Productions / RHINO   1992
Essentially a scrapbook of Rundgren's productions with artists like Patti Smith, Meatloaf, New York Dolls, Grand Funk Railroad, Pursuit of Happiness, XTC, and more. The diversity of artists makes a nice case for Rundgren's wide range of taste, but many of the selections seem odd choices, considering that better material existed on those albums. –RC

RUSH

Prog-rock. Inspired by Cream, Led Zeppelin, and Jimi Hendrix, the Toronto, Canada, power trio Rush formed in 1969, comprising guitarist Alex Lifeson (b Aug 27, 1953), bassist Geddy Lee (b Jul 29, 1953), and original drummer John Rutsey — later replaced by Neil Peart (b Sep 12, 1952). Their first few albums were rather pedestrian hard rock, but the addition of Peart in 1974 prodded the group into a more complicated, heavy art-rock mode: King Crimson and Yes meet Led Zeppelin.

"The Trees," metaphorically addressing the Québec secessionist movement (off of 1978's #47 *Hemispheres*) became a controversial rock-radio hit. The 1980 album *Permanent Waves* (#4), containing two substantial AOR hits with "Freewill" and "Spirit of the Radio" (#51), marked the beginning of a golden period for the band, which peaked with the #3 followup *Moving Pictures*.

Rush briefly flirted with a more synthesized sound, sublimating the band's natural interplay. Fortunately, recent albums indicate Rush is back in top form with *Presto* and *Roll the Bones*. –RC

2112 / MERCURY / BB 61   1976
Rush's first successful stab at a concept album. Like many of Rush's albums during the 70s, this one deals with a futuristic scenario where an individual triumphs over an impersonalized high-tech society. –RC

A Farewell to Kings / MERCURY / BB 33   1977
Rush continues to explore their sci-fi fantasy themes and lofty concepts with this effort, which featured "Closer to the Heart," a substantial FM rock hit that also went #76 pop. –RC

○ **Archives / MERCURY / BB 121**   1978
This is a good compilation of Rush's first three albums,

including their first hits "Working Man," "Fly by Night," and "In the Mood." –RC

Permanent Waves / MERCURY / BB 4   1980
The cumulative effect of endless tours and obvious growth with each studio effort, Rush hit it big with this effort, delivering with their best material to date. "Spirit of the Radio" (#51), "Freewill," and "Entre Nous" (#110) were big FM rock hits. "Jacob's Ladder" was another highlight. –RC

☆ **Moving Pictures / MERCURY / BB 3**   1981
On *Moving Pictures*, Rush's aggressive prog-rock hit a zenith, with challenging playing that never became formless or devoid of good melodic integrity. The trio's active ensemble work reached new levels of interplay. "Tom Sawyer," "Limelight," "Red Barchetta," and the instrumental "YYZ" are standouts. –RC

Exit Stage Left / MERCURY / BB 10   1981
A good live collection, possibly the best of their three such releases. –RC

Signals / MERCURY / BB 10   1982
The third in a trio of great albums. "Digital Man" and "Analog Kid" are powerful riff-rockers. "New World Man" was a #21 hit, and "Subdivisions" was an FM rock favorite. The soundstage lacks some of the ambience found on *Moving Pictures*, but the performances still pack quite a punch. –RC

Power Windows / MERCURY   1985
An improvement over the sterile techno-crap of the 1984 release *Grace under Pressure*. "Big Money" recalls the highlights of *Moving Pictures*, while "Manhattan Project" and "Territories" also shine. –RC

Presto / ATLANTIC   1990
Presto, Rush's 13th album of new studio material, and their first for Atlantic, showed this Canadian trio coming out from under a succession of bloodless-sounding techno-excursions (*Grace under Pressure, Hold Your Fire*) and going for a much more open, accessible sound. From beginning to end, the arrangements reflect more straightahead rock playing than on any of their other albums. *Presto* contains some of Neil Peart's best lyrics, and along with *Moving Pictures*, smartly presents many of Rush's virtues in their best light. –RC

★ **Chronicles / MERCURY**   1991
Anyone wanting an essential overview of this Canadian band's prog-rock work should start here. All of their FM rock hits and most of the important album tracks are here. –RC

Roll the Bones / ATLANTIC   1991
Roll the Bones continues with the organic-sounding hard prog-rock spirit of *Presto*, and it's equally fine. After many years of albums and touring, it's obvious that Rush has maintained its edge as a musical unit. The playing and material are primo throughout. Highlights include "Neurotica," "Big Wheel," "Ghost of a Chance," and the title cut. –RC

LEON RUSSELL   b 1941

Singer/songwriter, rock/pop. Leon Russell has had a widely varied career as an artist, a songwriter, a record label owner, a producer, and an in-demand session sideman. As part of Phil Spector's "Wall of Sound" wrecking crew, Russell played on hits by the Crystals. He also played on Herb Alpert's *Taste of Honey* and the Byrds's *Mr. Tambourine Man* and played and arranged tracks for Gary Lewis & the Playboys. Russell also toured with Delaney & Bonnie and briefly with Paul Revere & the Raiders when Revere was drafted. Russell organized Joe Cocker's Mad Dogs & Englishmen tour, which led him to tours with Bob Dylan, Eric Clapton, and the Rolling Stones, and a performance at George Harrison's Concert for Bangladesh.

In 1970 Russell formed Shelter Records with English producer Denny Cordell. The label eventually released albums by Willis Alan Ramsey, Dwight Twilley, and Phoebe Snow, among others. In October 1971, the Carpenters had a huge hit with Russell's "Superstar." (Years later, another composition, "This Masquerade," became a career-making hit for George Benson.)

All of this visibility set the stage for Russell's lucrative solo career, which fused gospel, blues, country, rock, and light jazz behind his quirky warble of a voice. Russell had seven Top 40 albums, with 1972's *Carney* peaking at #2 for four weeks. "Tightrope" (#11), "Lady Blue" (#14), and a double-sided single remake of Hank Williams's "Roll in My Sweet Baby's Arms"/"I'm So Lonesome I Could Cry" (#78) are a few of Russell's hits. In 1992, he released a comeback effort, *Anything Can Happen.* –RC

○ **Leon Russell / DCC / BB 60**   1970
Russell's self-titled debut features his strongest set of songs and performances, with tracks like "A Song for You," "Dixie Lullaby," "Shoot Out at the Plantation," and "Delta Lady," which became one of Joe Cocker's early signature songs. The CD includes a brief version of Dylan's "Masters of War." As with all of Russell's DCC-label CD releases, the mastering is excellent. –RC

○ **And the Shelter People / DCC / BB 17**   1971
Released hot on the heels of his Mad Dogs & Englishmen tour with Joe Cocker, Russell released this spirited outing, which included covers of tunes by George Harrison ("Beware of Darkness") and Dylan ("It's a Hard Rain Gonna Fall," "It Takes a Lot to Laugh, It Takes a Train to Cry") and some fine originals: "Alcatraz," "Home Sweet Oklahoma," "Stranger in a Strange Land" (an FM hit), and the title cut. The CD includes three bonus versions of Dylan tunes. –RC

Carney / DCC / BB 2   1972
Carney became Russell's highest charting album with the aid of the oddball #11 hit "Tightrope." Also included is "This Masquerade," a song that later became an international hit for George Benson. "If the Shoe Fits" is a great putdown of pop-star sycophants. Other highlights include "Manhattan Island Serenade" and "Cajun Love Song." –RC

Hank Wilson's Back / THRIVAL   1975
A skewed but interesting Hank Williams tribute album, with capable country backing. –CK

Leon Live / THRIVAL   1975
A solid concert offering which showcases Russell's strengths (and weaknesses) as a live performer, with A-1 support throughout. –CK

● **Best of Leon Russell / THRIVAL / BB 40**   1976
This is a straightforward hits and key-album-tracks collection, including "Lady Blue," "Tightrope," "A Song for You," "This Masquerade," and "Stranger in a Strange Land," among others. –RC

RUTS

Punk, ska-revival. One of the most unjustly ignored English bands of the late 70s. High-velocity punk tempered with reggae. –JD

○ **Crack / CAROLINE**   1979
Find it and buy it. This is an overlooked gem of speedy guitars and reggae skank! –JD

MITCH RYDER & THE DETROIT WHEELS   b 1945

Rock & roll. Mitch Ryder & the Detroit Wheels blended the Motown soul sound with over-revved Midwestern rock & roll. Mitch Ryder's (born William Levise) gutsy soul shouting and superhuman screams were some of the most electrifying sounds to charge AM radio in the mid 60s, landing somewhere between the Rascals' Felix Cavaliere and Wilson Pickett. The Wheels sported two strong lead guitarists in Joe Cubert and Jim McCarty (later in Cactus and Detroit), and they were pushed along by one of the great unsung rock drummers of all time, John ("Johnny Bee") Badanjek.
It was producer Bob Crewe who signed the band to his New Voice label, releasing a string of high-octane raveups in "Jenny Take a Ride" (#10), "Little Latin Lupe Lu" (#17), "Devil with a Blue Dress On/ Good Golly Miss Molly" (#4), "Sock It to Me-Baby!" (#6), and "Too Many Fish in the Sea" (#24). In spite of all the hits and visibility, Mitch Ryder & the Detroit Wheels

were victims of the era, making loads of money for Crewe and New Voice, but ending up broke. –RC

☆ **Rev-Up ... / RHINO**   1989
Rev-Up: Best of Mitch Ryder & the Detroit Wheels. Perhaps the most raucous White soul band of the 60s, Ryder and the Detroit Wheels scored a series of hits, 1966-1968, by souping up rock and R&B ravers to fever pitch. This is hard party music. –WR

SADE   b 1959

Pop. Born Helen Folsade Adu, she grew up on Nina Simone and Billie Holiday records. She attended St. Martin's College in London and worked as a model before fronting a jazz band named the Pride. The other members are cofounder Stuart Matthewman on sax and guitar, Andrew Hale on keyboards, and Paul Denmon on bass guitar. Adu holds the distinctive throaty, smoldering voice of a chanteuse. –BC

○ **Diamond Life / CBS**   1984
Her debut included "Smooth Operator," "Your Love Is King," "Hang On to Your Love," and "When Am I Gonna Make a Living." –BC

Stronger Than Pride / CBS   1988
Still moody but more funky than past material. –BC

DOUG SAHM   b 1942

Tex-Mex. Since his days with the Sir Douglas Quintet in the 60s, Doug Sahm has been preaching the gospel of Texas music traditions. He's mastered everything from barrio Latin rock to Western swing to shuffle blues to doo-wop to Cajun, yet his work always bears his distinctive stamp. He's recorded a ton of albums with a wide array of sidemen and, regardless of style, his laconic, reefer-headed vision comes through. Everything he's recorded is worth hearing but most of it has been out of print for decades. But the stuff that's in print offers an adequate estimation of the beautiful music he's made for the last 30 or so years. –JF

● **Juke Box Music / ANTONES**   1988
Sahm shimmies and strolls through this set of doo-wop and R&B covers. A gorgeous slow-dancing gem. –JF

○ **Best of Doug Sahm: Atlantic Sessions / RHINO**   1992
In 1972 Atlantic bought out Sahm's contract with Mercury, giving him the freedom to create an all-star ensemble of musicians. Throughout the year Sahm recorded with the likes of Bob Dylan, Dr. John, and David Bromberg, producing a typically rich body of work that was released on two albums in late 1973. Rhino has collected various cuts from the albums, adding five previously unreleased tracks (on CD only), giving an excellent portrait of Sahm's music. –STE

SAM & DAVE

Soul. Stax duo Sam & Dave recorded some of the finest examples of the Memphis sound, with their gutsy call-and-response delivery. Samuel Moore (b Oct 12, 1935), son of a church deacon, and Dave Prater (b May 9, 1937) grew up singing gospel. By the time they met in December of 1961 at a Miami club, both of them had spent time in various gospel groups and were getting into secular music.
Miami music-biz entrepreneur Henry Stone began recording the duo for his local Alston and Marlin labels, eventually getting a deal on Morris Levy's Roulette. When their contract at Roulette expired, Stone turned to Atlantic impresario Jerry Wexler, who signed Sam & Dave immediately. Wexler took them to Jim Stewart (co-owner of Stax) and offered Sam & Dave to be released on the label, with the understanding that Atlantic owned the masters. With the help of Stax songwriter team David Porter and Isaac Hayes, Sam & Dave cut a string of truly classic tracks with "Soul Man" (#2), "I Thank You" (#9), "Hold On, I'm Comin'" (#21), "When Something Is Wrong with My Baby" (#42), "You Don't Know Like I Know" (#90), "You Got Me Hummin'" (#77), and others.
By the early 70s, Sam & Dave were sick of each other. Sam went solo as Sam Moore, and Dave enlisted Sam Daniels to

continue the duo, which led to an acrimonious legal situation. On April 9, 1988, Dave Prater tragically died in an automobile accident. –RC

I Thank You / RHINO-ATLANTIC   1968
Straight reissue of an original Atlantic album, one of Sam & Dave's better efforts. Highlights include "Wrap It Up," "These Arms of Mine," "Don't Turn Your Heater On," "If I Didn't Have A Girl like You," and the #9 title track. –STE

Can't Stand Up for Falling Down / EDSEL   1984
A 16-track import consisting of mainly Atlantic recordings, 1968-1971, with only two duplicates with the Atlantic anthology. –RP

☆ **An Anthology of Sam & Dave ... / ATLANTIC**   1990
An Anthology of Sam & Dave: The Stax/Volt Years, a double-disc set, is the best Sam & Dave have sounded on disc. Very little tape hiss is evident, while the top end is not sacrificed; the bass sounds full and warm. All the essential tracks (like "Soul Man," "Hold On, I'm Comin'," "When Something Is Wrong with My Baby," and "I Thank You,") are here, as well as rarities. Great liner notes too. –RC

SAM THE SHAM & THE PHARAOHS

Rock & roll. This mid-60s Dallas party band blended Tex-Mex and Memphis-rooted rock & roll for hits like "Wooly Bully" (#2), "Li'l Red Riding Hood" (#2), "Ju Ju Hand" (#26), "Ring Dang Doo" (#33), and "The Hair on My Chinny Chin Chin" (#22). –RC

○ **Best of Pharaohization / RHINO**
This one gets the nod for a great selection of songs. –DH

CARLOS SANTANA   ♭1947

Rock/pop, fusion. Santana is the name of a band that has successfully married elements of blues, rock, and Latin music and enjoyed international acclaim for more than two decades. It is also the name of the guitarist, Carlos Santana, who has led that band and made other recordings over the same period of time.
In its original manifestation, the Santana Blues Band was a group of equals, with Carlos named as leader only because of a musicians union requirement that such a designation be made. The group was formed in San Francisco in the mid 60s and first gained recognition in the same dance halls that hosted the psychedelic rock groups of the era, although, with its Latin and African roots, Santana never quite fit in with the psychedelic sound. The group came under the direction of promoter Bill Graham and had already scored a contract with Columbia when it appeared at the Woodstock Festival in August 1969. Personnel at that time, in addition to Carlos, included Gregg Rolie (vocals and keyboards), Dave Brown (bass), Mike Shrieve (drums), Armando Peraza (percussion and vocals), and Mike Carabello and Jose Areas (percussion). *Santana,* the debut album, was a massive success, including the #4 hit "Evil Ways." *Abraxas* (1970) did even better, topping the charts for six weeks and featuring the hits "Black Magic Woman" and "Oye Como Va." For *Santana III* (1971), the group expanded to a septet with the addition of guitarist Neal Schon, though an additional six sidemen were listed in the album credits. This album was #1 for five weeks.
Guitarist Santana released a live duet album with drummer and vocalist Buddy Miles (later a member of Santana) in 1972; then came the fourth Santana Band album, *Caravanserai,* on which different musician credits were listed for each track, none of them including bassist Dave Brown or percussionist Mike Carabello. The album was a Top Ten hit. Carlos released another duet album in 1973 with guitarist John McLaughlin (the two shared a guru), followed by *Welcome,* credited to "The New Santana Band," its only remaining original members being Santana, Mike Shrieve, Armando Peraza, and Jose Areas (Rolie and Schon had decamped to found Journey). In subsequent years, "Santana" for the most part referred to Carlos and a band of hired musicians playing in the established Santana style, while the leader also made

occasional solo albums that varied the style somewhat. In 1992, Santana ended his long association with Columbia and signed to Polydor, which set up a custom label for him, calling for him to sign his own new acts. –WR

○ **Santana / CBS**   1969
A brilliant combination of rock with Latin and African influences, prominently featuring the organ playing and husky vocals of Gregg Rolie; the energetic, precise drumming of Mike Shrieve; and, especially, the soaring, immediately identifiable guitar sound of Carlos Santana. Justifiably a massive hit and the prototype for an assembly line of similar records. Contains "Evil Ways" and "Soul Sacrifice." –WR

★ **Abraxas / CBS**   1970
Excellent continuation of the first album, with songwriting credits to four of the six band members, plus a terrific version of Tito Puentes's "Oye Como Va." The hit was a cover of the Fleetwood Mac song "Black Magic Woman." (Also available as a Mobile Fidelity gold disc version) –WR

Santana III / CBS   1971
Completes a trilogy of tightly constructed, exciting band albums filled with percolating, multirhythmic percussion and fiery guitar work. The last album that is the work of the Woodstock-era Santana band. –WR

Love Devotion Surrender / CBS   1973
A fiercer confrontation than the title would suggest, this jazz fusion album (recorded with Mahavishnu and John McLaughlin) contains excellent versions of John Coltrane's "A Love Supreme" and "Naima," plus a couple of McLaughlin originals. It's really more McLaughlin's show, but the contrast in guitar styles is fascinating. –WR

○ **Viva Santana! / CBS**   1988
A lovingly assembled three-disc retrospective set that collects the best of the Santana band, along with many interesting rarities. –WR

SAPPHIRES

R&B, doo-wop. A Philadelphia-based trio with two chart items. With Carol Jackson as lead and George Gainer and Joe Livingston supplying harmony, the Sapphires signed with Swan and hit with "Who Do You Love" in 1964. A year later, they returned to the charts with "Gotta Have Your Love" on ABC-Paramount. –BD

○ **Who Do You Love / COLLECTABLES**   1983
Mid-60s Philly-group R&B. The album includes the hit title track from 1964. –BD

JOE SATRIANI   ♭1956

Hard rock, fusion. Originally a drummer, Satriani switched to the guitar at the age of 14 when Jimi Hendrix died. Thinking he could make a living by teaching the guitar, he took music theory classes in high school and learned there was more to playing music than making sounds. Satriani's friend Steve Vai decided to take lessons and eventually went on to play with Frank Zappa, Alcatrazz, David Lee Roth, and Whitesnake. Guitarists around the US started hearing about this great musician from California, and in the early 80s Satriani had Kirk Hammett and Larry LaLonde as students.
Satriani was soon noticed by the heavy metal audience, partly because of the fame of guitarists he taught. Satriani has a style all his own, and he is regarded as one of the best guitarists working today. –JB

Joe Satriani / RUBINA
Ultra-rare (fewer than 500 copies were pressed) five-song EP produced by Satriani. All of the sounds were created with a guitar. A cult classic. –PK

Not of This Earth / RELATIVITY   1987
Major debut from this San Francisco guitarist. An eclectic mixture of sounds and styles. –PK

Dreaming #11 / RELATIVITY   1988
Live mini-CD featuring 20 minutes of fiery guitar playing. Intense! –PK

○ **Surfing with the Alien / RELATIVITY**   1988
Hard-hitting, intense, and foot-to-the-floor guitar playing. All instrumental. –PK

Flying in a Blue Dream / RELATIVITY   1989
His first album to feature Satriani's vocals, with a total playing time of over 66 minutes. –PK

BOZ SCAGGS   ♭1944

Rock/pop. Boz Scaggs got his start in 1959, playing with Steve Miller in the Dallas, TX, band, the Marksmen. It was Miller who taught Scaggs guitar. Scaggs and Miller eventually formed the Steve Miller Band, with Scaggs leaving after their classic second album, *Sailor. Rolling Stone* editor Jann Wenner helped Scaggs secure a solo artist deal with Atlantic. Scaggs' self-titled debut (produced by Wenner) failed to sell in spite of critical praise and the presence of sidemen like Duane Allman on the album. A deal with Columbia in 1970 was more fruitful, with each of Scaggs' album's selling in increasing numbers. In 1976 Scaggs achieved major stardom, thanks to the elegant urban pop of *Silk Degrees.* Over the next five years, he released a string of sophisticated R&B-influenced pop hits. In recent years, Scaggs' output has been very sporadic, as he became a restaurant owner in San Francisco. –RC

○ **Boz Scaggs / ATLANTIC**   1969
Produced by Jann Wenner, and featuring crack accompaniment by the Muscle Shoals house band, Scaggs' solo debut is a near-masterwork, mingling the pathos and heartbreak of vintage honky-tonk with the celebration and release of Southern soul. The highlights of the album also flaunt its diversity: "Loan Me a Dime," an extended blues dirge, which features some of Duane Allman's finest work, and "Waiting on a Train," Scaggs' marvelous revamping of Jimmie Rodgers's classic hobo song. –JF

Moments / CBS   1971
Scaggs' first album for Columbia is so low-key you barely notice the magic conjured on this set of introspective ballads. That is, until you really *listen.* –JF

○ **My Time / CBS**   1972
Scaggs's last rock & roll gasp. The ballads that would become his trademark are already surfacing, but you need this one for "Full-Lock Power Slide" and "Dinah Flo," two scorching rockers that give this album the muscle it needs. –JF

○ **Silk Degrees / CBS / BB 2**   1976
Scaggs reached his commercial peak with this elegant collection of soulful urban pop, thanks to hits like the ultra-smooth disco of "Lowdown" (#3), the revved-up "Lido Shuffle" (#11), and "We're All Alone," Scaggs' finest ballad. (Also available as a Mobile Fidelity Ultradisc) –RC

● **Hits / CBS**   1990
In spite of the inclusion of "Dinah Flo," *Hits!* primarily focuses on Scaggss 80s pop hits like "Lowdown," "Jojo," "Break Down Dead Ahead" and "Look What You've Done to Me." –BC

SCARLETS

Doo-wop. A 50s R&B vocal group. Before vocalist Fred Parris formed his Five Satins, he was lead singer of the Scarlets, a New Haven, CT, group that cut four highly prized singles for Bobby Robinson's Red Robin label from 1954 to 1955, notably "Dear One." –BD

○ **Golden Classics / COLLECTABLES**
Dreamy 50s East Cost doo-wop by the group who developed into the Five Satins. –BD

SCATTERBRAIN

Thrash. Scatterbrain, formed out of the ashes of Ludichrist, specializes in an intelligent and oddly humorous brand of speed-metal. –JB

○ **Here Comes Trouble / RELATIVITY**   1990
Former Ludichrist members go extra bonkers with this brouhaha of speed-metal, thrash, and total lunacy, even a

slight classical influence. Contains a cover of Cheech & Chong's "Earache My Eye." Illustration on the cover done by artist Robert Williams. –JB

SCHOOL OF FISH

Alternative rock. This Boston-based college-aged quintet outclassed their postmodern contemporaries with a striking, hook-laden 1991 debut. –JF

○ **School of Fish / CAPITOL**
A remarkably confident debut by four Bostonian collegiates who've concocted a sound that bites like the Replacements, casts hooks like vintage Cheap Trick, and beats the hell out of any other postmodern buzz band of the last three years. –JF

SCORPIONS

Heavy metal. A German metal band formed in 1970 by Rudolf and Michael Schenker; also included vocalist Klaus Meine, bassist Lothar Heimberg, and drummer Wolfgang Dziony. The original lineup stayed intact for three years, until Michael quit in 1973 to join UFO. The band broke up briefly and was re-formed at the end of the same year by Rudy Schenker with Meine; guitarist Uli Roth, bassist Francis Buchholz, and drummer Jorgen Rosenthal (replaced in 1975 by Rudy Lenners). Lenners was replaced in 1977 by Herman Rarebell. Roth left to form Electric Sun in 1978, replaced by Matthias Jabs, the two of them in and out of band during the 80s. Undoubtedly the biggest group to come out of Germany, the Scorpions have survived in a genre not noted for longevity, cutting several classic sides along the way. –CK

Tokyo Tapes / RCA   1978
Tokyo Tapes pulled this German band out of obscurity and into the spotlight. A quality sampling of their early material and a performance that is considered one of the band's best. Includes "All Night Long," "Back Stage Queen," and "Flight to the Rainbow." –JB

○ **Lovedrive / POLYGRAM**   1979
Well-written songs and powerful singing from Klaus Meine are some of the reasons given for calling *Lovedrive* one of the best Scorpions ever. Rudolf Schenker and Matthais Jabs provide many of this album's highlights, with lots of great guitar. –JB

Blackout / POLYGRAM   1982
The band experiments with pop smarts in a few of the songs, while retaining the solid hard-rock sound they have molded over the years. *Blackout* provided this German band with their first major hit, "No One like You" (#65). –JB

JACK SCOTT   ♭1936

Rockabilly. Jack Scott sounded tough, like someone you wouldn't want to meet in a dark alley unless he had a guitar in his hands. When he growled "The Way I Walk," wise men (and women) stepped aside.

Despite his snarling rockabilly attitude, Scott hailed from Ontario, Canada, and grew up near Detroit, developing a love for hillbilly music along the way. His first sides for ABC-Paramount in 1957 exhibited a profound country-rock synthesis, and after moving to the Carlton label, Scott hit the charts the next year with the tremulous ballad "My True Love," backed by his vocal group, the Chantones. Flip it over, however, and you have the hauling rocker "Leroy," all about some wacked-out tough guy who's content to remain behind the bars of his local jail.

Scott's pronounced emphasis on acoustic guitar distinguishes atmospheric rockers like "Goodbye Baby," "Go Wild Little Sadie," "Midgie," and "Geraldine." But his principal pop success came with tears-in-your-beer country-based ballads — "What in the World's Come Over You" and "Burning Bridges" were massive smashes on Top Rank in 1960, and he recorded an entire album's worth of Hank Williams covers for the firm the same year.

Scott continued to vacillate between cowboy crooner and

rough-edged rocker throughout the 60s, recording for Capitol and Groove. He still occasionally turns up on the oldies circuit, and he still looks and sounds like a man you seriously don't want to mess with. −BD

○ **Greatest Hits / CAPITOL**
This collects the cream of Scott's late 50s hits. −DH

GIL SCOTT-HERON   b 1949

Fusion. Gil Scott-Heron has had a prime influence on contemporary African-American popular music. He attended Lincoln and Johns Hopkins University, and wrote two novels, highly popular among Black college students, *The Vulture* and *The Nigger Factory.* He began working with musician Brian Jackson on putting music to his oral narratives and monologs. His 1972 release *Small Talk at 125th and Lenox* attracted underground attention, while the followup *Pieces of a Man* was a major hit. Throughout the 70s and early 80s, Heron's commentaries on racism, injustice, and inequality, with side trips on jazz, romance, and family life, were very popular among jazz fans with left-wing views as well as rock, R&B, and pop audiences. Although disputes with Arista over artistic direction and production control have resulted in very few Scott-Heron recordings in recent years, he continues to tour and give interviews. −RW

Winter in America / STRAFIA EAST   1973
A poignant album that has stood the test of time. "The Bottle," "H2O-Gate Blues," and the title track are among the poet/activist's greatest works. Brian Jackson plays sympathetic electric and acoustic piano. −MGN

○ **The Revolution Will Not Be Televised / RCA**   1975
Heavy-handed right-on statements that still have impact over 20 years later. Slightly to overtly funky music for the most perfect tribute to "Lady Day" and John Coltrane. The righteously angry "Whitey on the Moon" is included. −MGN

From South Africa to South Carolina / ARISTA 1975
Includes "Johannesburg" and "Summer of 1942." Pretty solid and pretty funky. −MGN

● **Best of Gil Scott-Heron / ARISTA**   1984
An exemplary firebrand poet whose raps and lyrics influenced the entire hip-hop generation, yet who has said his own influence was jazz. −RW

SCRATCH ACID

Hardcore. Psycho hardcore screaming from Texas. −JD

○ **Berserker / TOUCH & GO**   1987
Loud, crazed, and fast. Cool and corrosive! −JD

SCRAWL

Alternative rock. A trio who relied on a scratchy Wire-like sound on its first album, *"He's Drunk."* By intelligently delineating the woman's role in alternative rock culture, Scrawl has won many hearts. −DH

○ **He's Drunk / ROUGH TRADE**   1989
A good debut, which is angry without being strident. −DH

SCREAMING TREES

Alternative rock. From Washington state, this band rocks their psychedelia hard. Instead of being revivalists, they make the genre contemporary. The many spin offs of this band indicate the creativity — and tension — within it. −BE

Invisible Lantern / SST   1988
Solid neo-psychedelic pop. −RG

○ **Uncle Anesthesia / CBS**   1991
Major-label bucks don't detract from their punch. −RG

SEA LEVEL

Fusion, Southern rock. Three members of this 70s seven-piece ensemble hailed from the Allman Brothers Band, including Chuck Leavell (C. Leavell, get it?), current keyboardist for the Rolling Stones). They created an appealing fusion of jazz,

blues, and rock. Even though Sea Level never achieved great success, they managed a #50 hit with the 1978 single "That's Your Secret." −RC

Sea Level / CAPRICORN   1977
The debut album contains most of their best material, bright guitar, and keyboard-based instrumentals. Chuck Leavell shines on five of his tunes. Jimmy Nalls plays sweet guitar. Their first and best album. Some vocals, nicely crafted on "Nothing Matters but the Fever." −MGN

○ **Best of Sea Level / POLYGRAM**   1977
An excellent compilation for this short-lived spinoff form the Allman Brothers band. With Chuck Leavell and guitarist Jimmy Nalls. −MGN

SEAL

Dance-pop. This singer from England (born in Nigeria) has a soulful, funky pop style that could easily be compared to Lenny Kravitz , with less of Kravitz's psychedelia. Seal's self-titled debut album featured the Top 20 hit "Crazy." −ED

○ **Seal / WARNER**   1991
This debut album features great dance music, some acoustic tunes, and moody ballads, all with the irresistible "Zang Tumb Tumb" mystique, courtesy of producer Trevor Horn. −JB

SEALS & CROFTS

Singer/songwriter, pop. The 70s were big years for this soft acoustic-pop duo, who had previously enjoyed success with the late-50s/early-60s group, the Champs (remember "Tequila"?). From 1971 to 1978, Jim Seals (b Oct 17, 1941) and Dash Crofts (b Aug 14, 1940) charted 14 times with hits like "Summer Breeze" (#6), "Diamond Girl" (#6), "Hummingbird" (#20), "We May Never Pass This Way Again" (#21), "I'll Play for You" (#18), "You're the Love" (#18), and "Get Closer" (#6). Besides their pleasant tenor harmonies, both of them were multi-instrumentalists, showcasing instruments like mandolin and fiddle on some of their material. −RC

○ **Greatest Hits / WARNER**   1975
This album has all their hits, including "Summer Breeze," "Hummingbird," "We May Never Pass This Way (Again)," and "Diamond Girl," and "When I Meet Them." −DH

THE SEARCHERS

British Invasion. The Searchers (formed in 1961) came on the first wave of the British Invasion in 1964, with a million-selling hit, "Needles and Pins" (#13), written by Jack Nitzsche and Sonny Bono (of Sonny & Cher). The "Needles and Pins" jangling guitar arrangement was a Merseybeat forerunner to the 12-string Rickenbacker sound of the Byrds. Subsequent hits capitalized on that sound, as well as on the band's slightly husky vocals. Other hits included a #3 remake of the Clovers's "Love Potion #9" (another million-seller), a version of Jackie DeShannon's "When You Walk in the Room" (#35), "Don't Throw Your Love Away" (#16), "Some Day We're Gonna Love Again" (#34), "Bumble Bee" (#21), and "What Have They Done to the Rain" (#29). They enjoyed a brief comeback in 1980 with the self-titled Sire debut, which included a bouncy version of Big Star's "September Gurls." To this day, the Searchers continue as an active touring unit. −RC

○ **It's the Searchers / EAST WEST**
Their best and most representative album. Major hits surrounded by their unique renditions of folk and rock standards, including some surprising Phil Spector covers. A seminal British invasion album. (Import) −BE

● **Greatest Hits / RHINO**   1985
An okay way to whet the appetite, but not the definitive collection. −BE

SEATRAIN

Rock/pop. This late-60s/early-70s California-based fusion ensemble, formed by former Blues Project members Andy

Kulberg (bass/flute) and Roy Blumenfeld (drums), is probably best known for their 1971 hit "13 Questions" (#49). Their first albums spotlighted violinist Richard Greene, whose credits included bluegrass legend Bill Monroe and the Jim Kweskin Jug Band. The title cut from *Marblehead Messenger*, produced by George Martin (Beatles, America), charted at #108. –RC

○ **Seatrain / ONE WAY**   1970
This country-rock gem features the remarkable vocals of Peter Rowan, genre-stretching psychedelic guitar from Richard Greene, and the thoughtful songwriting of Andy Kulberg, ex-Blues Project. The album holds up well. –JT

JOHN SEBASTIAN   b 1944

Singer/songwriter, folk/rock, pop. Born in New York City, the son of a classical harmonica player, John Sebastian grew up in the Greenwich Village coffeehouses and was a popular sideman to various folk artists prior to forming the folk-rock band, the Lovin' Spoonful, for which he served as lead singer and songwriter in the mid 60s. When the Spoonful broke up, Sebastian went solo, appearing at the Woodstock Festival in 1969 and releasing the Top 20 *John B. Sebastian* album in 1970. Subsequent efforts were less successful, but in 1976 Sebastian scored a #1 hit with "Welcome Back," the theme song from the TV series "Welcome Back, Kotter." Sebastian has continued to tour and play on occasional sessions, though he has not released a new album since the 70s. –WR

John B. Sebastian / REPRISE   1970
A strong debut solo album spotlighting Sebastian's warm voice and optimistic, melodic folk-pop songwriting. –WR

Cheapo-Cheapo Productions ... / REPRISE   1971
Cheapo-Cheapo Productions Presents Real Live is an exuberant solo appearance at which Sebastian's humor and wit are at their apex. A wide variety of songs, from old folk-blues standards to Spoonful favorites. Makes you wish you'd been there. –WR

○ **Best of John Sebastian / RHINO**   1989
A 16-track selection from Sebastian's solo albums 1970-1976, including the hit "Welcome Back." –WR

NEIL SEDAKA   b 1939

Pop. An excellent songwriter, Sedaka came from a doo-wop background (working with an early version of the Tokens). He sharpened his skills with Juilliard training, and enjoyed much success with a number of pre-Beatles-era hits. Though the British Invasion stopped the flow of hits, he reentered the charts in the mid 70s with a string of chart-toppers that extended into the following decade. A major influence on Elton John, Sedaka continues performing today. –CK

○ **All-Time Greatest Hits / RCA**
Includes "Calendar Girl," "Happy Birthday, Sweet Sixteen," "Breaking Up Is Hard to Do," and other sprightly pop numbers. –DH

All-Time Greatest Hits - Vol. 2 / RCA
Companion volume to the above, equally fine. –DH

THE SEEDS

Psychedelic, rock & roll. The Seeds (formed in 1965 in Southern California) produced five albums of magically limited garage-psychedelia extolling the virtues of sex and drugs and drugs and sex. Sky Saxon, the band's self-absorbed singer and songwriter, evidently understood arrested development quite well, making the Seeds records a pretty enjoyable 60s punk sleazefest.
The urgent trashola snarl (and corny "Rawhide"-style backup vocals) of "Pushin' Too Hard" (#36) probably their best song, was later affectionately covered by Alex Chilton as the B-side of his "Bangkok" single. Both of those songs can be found on their self-titled debut. Even though subsequent albums recycled the basic formula of the Seeds, their second album, *A Web of Sound*, is worth checking out. –RC

○ **Seeds / GNP-CRESCENDO**   1966
Punk sneers, cheesy organ, and an attitude. A garage-band classic. –BE

A Web of Sound / GNP-CRESCENDO   1966
A more ambitious, but less successful venture into teenage rages and lusts. –BE

THE SEEKERS

Folk/rock, pop. During the 60s, this quartet from Australia deftly bridged folk vocal-ensemble work with shades of British Invasion pop. Their stirring harmonies and memorable melodies earned them a series of big hits, as first the Seekers (on Capitol) and, with a totally different lineup, as the New Seekers on Elektra. Their biggest hits were "Georgy Girl" (#2), "I'll Never Find Another You" (#4), and the #7 "I'd Like to Teach the World to Sing (In Perfect Harmony)," a song that also became a theme song for a Coca-Cola ad campaign. Their work on Capitol is their best. –RC

Come the Day / COLUMBIA   1971
Their best album, with their biggest hit and the Simon-Woodley songs. Also includes a killer rendition of Tom Paxton's "The Last Thing on My Mind." US title is *Georgy Girl*. (Out of print) –BE

○ **The Seekers / EMI**   1990
A compilation featuring over one hour of hits and key album tracks on this British import. Completely comprehensive, with the best sound ever. –BE

● **Capitol Collectors Series / CAPITOL**   1992
The Seekers' rich folky harmonies, fronted by the clear alto of Judith Durham, are given an excellent presentation on this 23-song anthology. All of their Capitol hits are here, including "Georgy Girl," "A World of Our Own," "Come the Day," and "I'll Never Find Another You." Typical of *Capitol Collectors Series* reissues, this set contains ample annotation, track info, and photos. –RC

BOB SEGER   b 1945

Rock/pop. At his best, Detroit rocker Bob Seger has produced some incredibly clearheaded music speaking to and about the working class's fleeting joys, shortchanged dreams, and grinding existence. Many of the people who populate Seger's material possess some kind of resolve and dignity. Seger grew up as one of these people, and he's never really forgotten it. Musically, Seger's influences range from Chuck Berry to the Creedence Clearwater Revival, the Rolling Stones, and Bob Dylan to Bruce Springsteen and the Eagles, all merged together in a Heartland rock stew.
Seger's first hit was the 1969 heavy soulful stomper "Ramblin' Gamblin' Man" (#17). For years after that, he consistently landed regional Top Ten hits that never saw the light of day anywhere else in the country. That was until the release of 1976's *Live Bullet*, a great concert album that encapsulated Seger's career to that point with an impassioned delivery. It became his first million-seller, charting at #34. His next two studio efforts, *Night Moves* (#8) and *Stranger in Town* (#4), were artistic highlights. By this time, Seger had become a major arena attraction. He stumbled on the mediocre *Against the Wind*, reducing once-effective sentiment to hack wordplay, but he regained his focus on *The Distance*. His latest effort, *The Fire Inside*, is solid but fails to mine any new territory. Blessed with a voice that could sing the phone book and sound great, Seger has even scored hits with his most pedestrian work. Nevertheless, he has created a body of work that, at its best, celebrates the spirit of rock in the face of mortality with a hard-won wisdom. –RC

☆ **Ramblin' Gamblin' Man / CAPITOL / BB 62**   1969
The title track on Seger's Capitol debut is one of the all-time great rock & roll stompers with its bone-crunching 2- and 4-drum groove and gospel-choir backup. Other highlights include the incredibly hard-rocking antiwar track "2 + 2 = ?," and "Down Home," a rude harmonica-driven rocker that

sports an absolutely addled rhythm section. In spite of some cornball psychedelic-period mixes, *Ramblin' Gamblin' Man*, with its reckless over-the-top delivery, is Seger's hardest-rocking album. Throughout many of these tracks, Seger wails like a banshee. Seger's later rock hits sound absolutely tame next to this stuff. –RC

Smokin' O.P.'s / CAPITOL / BB 180   1972
Smokin' O.P.'s was a fine showcase for Seger's workmanlike rock & roll approach. "Heavy Music," an original, became a huge Detroit hit. Other highlights included Seger's versions of such standards as "Bo Diddley," "Let It Rock," and "Turn on Your Lovelight." –RC

Beautiful Loser / CAPITOL / BB 131   1975
After several years of relative obscurity, Seger emerged with this rather reflective effort. The hard-rocking "Katmandu," however, was a substantial hit in the Midwest. –RC

Live Bullet / CAPITOL   1976
A blistering live show from Cobo Hall, containing raucous versions of early material like "Nutbush City Limits" and "Get Out of Denver" as highlights. –CK

★ **Night Moves / CAPITOL / BB 8**   1976
Seger's breakthrough album, a classic of blue-collar rock, featuring such standouts as the wistful "Mainstreet" (#24), the no-frills rock of "Rock and Roll Never Forgets" (#41), and the title track (a #4 hit), a reflective coming-of-age masterpiece. Throughout, Seger believably details the characters in his songs with compassion. –RC

☆ **Stranger in Town / CAPITOL / BB 4**   1978
It's not quite as strong as *Night Moves*, but *Stranger in Town* continues Seger's streak of great songwriting and performance. Highlights include the relentless rockers "Hollywood Nights" (#12) and "Feel like a Number." Seger's facility with the ballads "Still the Same" (#4) and "We've Got Tonight" (#13) produced substantial hits. –RC

Against the Wind / CAPITOL / BB 1   1980
Against the Wind became Seger's first #1 album, producing the hits and key album-rock-radio tracks, "Fire Lake" (#6), "You'll Accomp'ny Me" (#14), "The Horizontal Bop" (#42) and the #5 title cut. However, after two fine albums, Seger's lyrical abilities and melodic skills began to reveal a cookie-cutter sameness. His singing still had plenty of passion. –RC

Nine Tonight / CAPITOL   1981
Features the title-track contribution to the *Urban Cowboy* movie soundtrack and an affective cover of "Trying to Live My Life without You." –CK

The Distance / CAPITOL / BB 5   1983
The Distance was a strong rebound after the spotty *Against The Wind*, featuring his rocking Chuck Berry-like auto worker's tribute, "Makin' Thunderbirds," the resolute rock anthem "Even Now" (#12), and a fine version of Rodney Crowell's "Shame on the Moon"(#2). –RC

SELECTER

Ska-revival. An interracial ska group which emerged during the late-70s two-tone era, spearheaded by the Specials. –JF

○ **Too Much Pressure / CHRYSALIS**   1980
Extremely danceable propulsive fusion of 70s British punk and Jamaican ska music. –DS

Selected Selecter Selections / CHRYSALIS   1989
Greatest hits from their two studio albums. –DS

SEPULTURA

Heavy metal. An excellent speed-metal band from Brazil. –JB

Morbid Visions / ROADRACER   1985
America's first listen to what Brazil had to offer in the world of thrash. Before this, most bands were only known through trading tapes or demos in the underground. Sound quality isn't too good, though. –JB

○ **Beneath the Remains / ROADRACER**   1989
Excellent thrash that immediately goes into the conciousness

Power Pop

The Sixties
British Influences The Beatles — The Kinks — The Move
American Influences The Byrds — Nazz
The Seventies Badfinger — Big Star The Raspberries — Stories Dwight Twilley — Cheap Trick Shoes
The Eighties The dB's — R.E.M. Let's Active — Smithereens Hoodoo Gurus — The Bangles Crowded House
The Nineties The Posies — Material Issue — Matthew Sweet Cavedogs — Jellyfish — Teenage Fanclub

of the listener. The first metal band from Brazil to gain international acclaim. –JB

THE SEX PISTOLS

Punk. Geez, what's left to say? Let it suffice that vocalist Johnny Rotten and the Sex Pistols shook the dust off the fat and complacent late-70s rock scene, using their buzzsaw minimalism to deflate the pomposity that had engulfed rock's then-reigning champions. Their political nihilism and fuck-you attitudes (derived mostly from the Stooges, the MC5, and the New York Dolls) set England — and later America — on fire, demonstrating that anyone could play in a rock band, even if you couldn't dazzle like Clapton or jet-set like the Stones. They burned out faster than the Dolls, but the best music from the Sex Pistols is as caustic and vibrant today as it was back in the days when Yes and Jethro Tull were all the rage. –JF

☆ **Never Mind the Bollocks / WARNER**   1977
Never Mind the Bollocks (Here's the Sex Pistols) is a delightfully vulgar and viscerally pulverizing debut. Everything you need is here, including "God Save the Queen," "Pretty Vacant," "Holidays in the Sun," and "Anarchy in the U.K." –JF

The Great Rock & Roll Swindle / VIRGIN   1979
The soundtrack to a muddled film from 1979. Loaded with rubbish, but there are some live and studio cuts that should be heard. (Import) –JF

Flogging a Dead Horse / VIRGIN   1980
This collects the band's seven British singles. Some duplicates with *Never Mind the Bullocks*, but the B-sides can't be found elsewhere. (Import) –JF

CHARLIE SEXTON   ♭1969

Rock/pop. Sexton was a Texas-boy guitar wizard, playing behind Joe Ely by age 13 and going on to work with Bob Dylan, Keith Richards, Ron Wood, and former Eagle Don Henley. Sexton's good looks and technical wizardry had him pegged to be the next big thing coming out of Texas behind Stevie Ray Vaughan and the Fabulous Thunderbirds, but he was done in by overproduced albums and scathing reviews from the rock critics. He recently formed the band Archangel with members of Stevie Ray's Double Trouble. –CK

○ **Pictures for Pleasure / MCA**   1980
His debut album, with solid songs and playing. –CK

Charlie Sexton / MCA
An about-face, with more emphasis on Sexton's guitar playing and Texas roots. –CK

THE SHADOWS

British Invasion. Originally Cliff Richard's backing band, this British quartet began recording on their own in 1960 and had a major hit with the instrumental "Apache." They were built around guitarists Hark Marvin and Bruce Welch, with an ever-changing rhythm section (Jet Harris and Tony Meehan, the original bassist and drummer, were the most famous, and went on to success on their own in the early 60s). Often erroneously thought of as England's answer to the Ventures, the Shadows's sound was polished, crisp, clean, and metallic, making up for its inherent sterility and lack of soul with a knack for drawing out melodies in their most haunting form. They continue to record in the 90s. –BE

○ **20 Golden Greats / EMI**   1977
As fine a cross-section of their best work that has been (or ever will be) assembled. Highlighted by "Apache," but with lots of other fun. (Import) –BE

THE SHAGGS

Alternative. In 1969 the Shaggs, comprising three sisters Dorothy, Betty, and Helen Wiggin, entered a Revere, MA, recording studio under the encouragement and financial support of their father Austin Wiggin. The recording engineer, upon hearing the band, tactfully suggested that they weren't ready to be a recording unit, but their father insisted on catching the band on tape "while they were hot." The result of this session, their first album, was called *Philosophy of the World.* Their followup effort, the appropriately titled *Shaggs' Own Thing,* actually reflects some growth in the area of technical facility.
Depending on your point of view, this is the most hilarious-sounding mish-mash of ineptitude ever committed to CD, or it's an unconscious musical realization of everything great naive American art desires to be, believably innocent. Either way, you'll either love them or hate them. –RC

○ **Philosophy of the World / ROUNDER**   1969
This release compiles the Wiggins sisters' (otherwise known as the Shaggs) two releases *Philosophy of the World* and *Shaggs' Own Thing.* Anyone with unconventional tastes interested in taking a harrowing trip into the twilight zone of naive Americana pop should check this out. –RC

SHAKIN' PYRAMIDS

Rockabilly. This British rockabilly trio from the early 80s bashed madly at acoustic guitars and wrote some pretty decent originals. They released their only album in America. –JF

○ **Skin 'Em Up / VIRUS**   1981
Explosive bopping and mostly acoustic set from this Glasgow trio, which helped define the short-lived rockabilly revival of the early 80s. –DS

SHAM 69

Punk. 1977 agit-punks led by loudmouth frontman Jimmy Pursey. They outlived many of their contemporaries. –JF

Tell Us the Truth / SIRE   1978
Rough raw explosions from one of the most popular British punk bands. One side is live. –DS

That's Life / POLYDOR   1978
A good followup to their debut *Tell Us the Truth,* this one includes "Hurry Up Harry." –DS

The Game / POLYDOR   1980
A more experimental effort by these punkers. –DS

○ **Live and Love / LINK**   1987
A blazing 1979 live set, capturing these Hersham punks at their best. Includes many of their hit UK singles. –DS

THE SHANGRI-LAS

Rock & roll. Street-tough and smart, the Shangri-Las were like nothing that had come before in the history of rock & roll female groups. Hailing from Queens, NY, the group comprised two sets of sisters (one set identical twins, at that). They cranked out 11 hits in the space of two years, all of them enduring classics of the girl-group genre. Masterminded by oddball writer and producer George "Shadow" Morton, these narratives have a disturbing edge — tales of girls who run away from home, doomed girls who go all the way with bad boys; the spectre of death hangs over most of their songs. Eerie and creative production makes fatalistic melodramas such as "I Can Never Go Home Anymore" (1965) truly haunting — and the girls' voices, ranging from New York-snotty to wistful and breathy, are ideally utilized.
The epitome of "biker girls in heat," their live presentation devastated audiences on package shows, while their offstage antics left a string of trashed hotel rooms, tour buses, and male groupies in their wake. The formula of teen-biker melodramas with a tough-as-nails image worked like a charm until they were eclipsed by the progressive rock movement of the late 60s. –CK & GB

☆ **Golden Hits / POLYGRAM**   1987
Includes all the eerie three-minute melodramas from one of the all-time great girl groups. "Leader of the Pack," "Remember," "I Can Never Go Home Anymore," and "Past, Present, and Future." –GB

DEL SHANNON   1934-1990

Rock & roll. Del Shannon (born Charles Westover) came out of Grand Rapids, MI, in 1961 with a sound that no one had ever heard before. A rocker by inclination in a time when rock was supposedly dead, his first single, "Runaway," became a monster hit and a half with its catchy guitar hooks, great beat, and Shannon's strong yet vulnerable vocal (which leaped to falsetto range without compromising his manliness).
Shannon had several followup hits, none quite as memorable or driving, and in 1963 also became the first American artist to cover a Beatles song ("From Me to You"). By 1964, however, he began concentrating equally on songwriting and production, and wrote "I Go to Pieces," a romantic rocker that became a hit for Peter and Gordon. He made numerous attempts at finding a new and successful sound, signing with Liberty, which was able to sell his records in England and other parts of Europe but not Stateside. An attempt at updating his sound, first with Andrew "Loog" Oldham, and later with Dave Edmunds and Tom Petty as producers, met with very limited success. In the mid 80s, however, Shannon seemed poised for a comeback when "Runaway" emerged as a hit in an updated version by Todd Rundgren from the TV show "Crime Story." Unfortunately, just as he was completing a comeback album on MCA, Shannon took his own life. –BE

○ **I Go to Pieces / EDSEL**   1986
A British import and an indispensable complement to the Rhino hits package. Sixteen important tracks, capturing Shannon's sound at its most achingly beautiful. –BE

★ **Greatest Hits / RHINO**   1990
An almost-perfect collection of his best tracks from the US catalog. The gaps can (and should) be filled by his album *I Go to Pieces.* –BE

The Liberty Years / CAPITOL   1991
While not the place to start, this is a good collection of Del Shannon's late-60s recordings. Only one of these songs hit the charts ("The Big Hurt" reached #94) but they are worth hearing. –STE

ELLIOTT SHARP

Avant-garde. Sharp is a reigning member of the electric guitar avant-garde, an unrestrained improviser, and a theory-minded composer who bases much of his work on mathematical models. He is a frequent contributor to the New York new music scene and has toured with the Knitting Factory crew. He performs solo and leads his own bands. –MB

○ **In the Land of Yahoos / SST**   1987
Elliott's "pop" album, made as sort of a joke, features lots of sampled vocals on top of dance-club beats. It's certainly his most accessible: his other recordings have more of his trademark guitar turbulence and mathematically oriented compositional style. –MB

JULES SHEAR

Singer/songwriter, rock/pop. Singer/songwriter Shear (born in Pittsburgh) is best known for hits he's written for others, notably "All through the Night" for Cyndi Lauper and "If She Knew What She Wants" for the Bangles. He has been a member of the groups the Funky Kings, Jules and the Polar Bears, and the Restless Sleepers in addition to making solo albums. He was also an early host of the successful MTV series "Unplugged." –WR

The Third Party / CAPITOL   1989
Shear sings his songs with no more accompaniment than the acoustic guitar of Marty Willson-Piper of the Church. The results are stark but impressive. –WR

○ **The Great Puzzle / POLYGRAM**   1991
Full-band production gives a pop sheen to Shear's excellent songs, notably the ballad "We Were Only Making Love." –WR

THE SHELLS

Doo-wop. Recording for the tiny Johnson label, the Shells cut some fine doo-wop during the late 50s. With Nate Bouknight as lead singer, the Shells debuted with "Baby Oh Baby" in 1957 and continued to wax impressive 45s without much commercial interest. Three years later, record collectors Donn Fileti and Wayne Stierle promoted the track anew, and it actually hit the pop charts on its second time around. By 1962, when the quintet cut "Happy Holiday," Ray Jones had taken over as lead. –BD

○ **Golden Classics / COLLECTABLES**
Tasty late-50s R&B group harmonies. –BD

THE SHEPPARDS

Doo-wop. This seminal six-piece outfit from Chicago, centered around the twin lead vocals of Millard Edwards and Murrie Eskridge, had few hits, but their Apex and Constellation recordings from the late 50s/early 60s are pre-soul gems. –JF

☆ **Golden Classics / COLLECTABLES**
Obscure but absolutely brilliant 60s vintage recordings that walk the line between R&B and soul. Contains some of the most gorgeous ballads ever sung. –JF

THE SHIRELLES

Rock & roll. The premier female vocal group of the late 50s/early 60s, the Shirelles was one of the very few groups who wrote their own material. Led by Shirley Alston, the girls started singing as the Poquellos in high school at parties, etc. A friend hooked them up with her mother, who had music business connections. The result was their first record and first hit, "I Met Him on a Sunday." The hits flowed steadily from then on, all becoming enduring classics and staples of oldies station formats to this day. The Shirelles are still active on the revival circuit. –CK

☆ **Anthology, 1959-1967 / RHINO**   1988
One of the most consistently creative and diverse of the 60s girl-groups, the Shirelles were a hit-making machine. "Soldier Boy," "Dedicated to the One I Love," "Will You Still Love Me Tomorrow," and 13 others can be found here. –JT

SHIRLEY & LEE

R&B. Shirley Goodman's (b Jun 19, 1936) screechy vocals and Leonard Lee's (b Jun 29, 1936 - d Oct 23, 1976) bluesy retorts added up to R&B gold during the 50s for the young Crescent City duo. The teenagers' debut on Aladdin, the Dave Bartholomew-produced "I'm Gone," was a major R&B hit in 1952. Shirley and Lee caught fire in 1955-1956 with three rocking smashes: "Feel So Good," the R&B chart-topping "Let the Good Times Roll," and "I Feel Good," all written by Lee. The pair stayed on Aladdin into 1959 before moving to Warwick and re-doing "Let the Good Times Roll." The "Sweethearts of the Blues" broke up after a few 1962-1963 singles for Imperial. In 1974 Goodman returned under the sobriquet of Shirley and Company with a #1 R&B smash, the disco-fied "Shame, Shame, Shame," for producer Sylvia Robinson on the Vibration logo. –BD

☆ **Legendary Masters / CAPITOL**   1990
The "Sweethearts of the Blues" in all their glory, with "Let the Good Times Roll" and more. –DH

EVERETT SHOCK

Alternative rock. Vocalist and lyricist Everett Shock has worked in relative isolation since his formative years as part of the San Francisco Bay Area scene that spawned NAME and his partners Henry Kaiser, Erling Wold, and Bob Adams. Shock's deadpan delivery can be compared with that of David Byrne or Rich Stim (of MX-80). This is in contrast to his subtle lyrical humor and genre-busting musical settings. –MB

○ **Ghost Boys / SST**   1988
A slice of wonderful weirdness evolved from the San Francisco-based band NAME. Some of the most poetic lyrics ever written can be heard here. –MB

MICHELLE SHOCKED   *b* 1962

Singer/songwriter. A postmodern feminist folkie whose career has incorporated blitzspeed-punk and 40s swing, Michelle Shocked's eclectic folk is in the grand neo-tradition of acoustic performers in the post-post-punk era. –JD

Texas Campfire Tapes / POLYGRAM   1986
Recorded live around a campfire on a Walkman, her debut is a wildly overrated but interesting introduction to her talents. –JD

○ **Short Sharp Shocked / POLYGRAM**   1988
With the great miss-you song "Anchorage," this is Shocked's strongest record from start to finish. Rich and evocative, there's hardly a clinker in the bunch. Special credit to Pete Anderson for a sympathetic production job. –JD

Captain Swing / POLYGRAM   1988
Whoa, stop right there. Read the title. This is swing music like your parents listened to. That's right, Goodman, Herman, the lot. Includes "On the Greener Side." –JD

SHOES

Power-pop. If there was a band that typified all that was good about that post-punk permutation known as power-pop, it was the Shoes. This Zion, IL, quartet burst from their studio home with a string of terrific records that took Beatles-inspired pop and sprinkled it liberally with their own airy melodies and steady, sturdy playing. –JD

Black Vinyl Shoes / PVC   1978
A homemade demo that became their first national release, this is a dazzling collection of pop songs driven by thick sheets of guitar and warm, emotive singing. –JD

Present Tense / ELEKTRA   1979
Their major-label debut suffers from a bit of overwhelming postproduction, but there's not enough interference to ruin this great collection of tunes. –JD

○ **Shoes Best / BLACK VINYL**   1987
A 22-song compilation, this is a wonderfully comprehensive

overview of this wonderful band. Good liner notes by former *Trouser Press* head honcho Ira Robbins. —JD

SHONEN KNIFE

Alternative rock. Japan's greatest rock band. The members are three women, enamored of punk, jangly guitars, and 60s kitsch. Essential! —JD

○ **Pretty Little Baka Guy / Live In / ROCKVILLE**   1986
Their best combines great songs and a great attitude. Life-sustaining. —JD

Shonen Knife / GIANT   1990
Early sides, sung mostly in Japanese. Super! —JD

712 / ROCKVILLE   1991
A little sleeker but still terrific. —JD

SHOWMEN

Doo-wop, soul. Norman "General" Johnson's first group was based in New Orleans, but their best hit — "It Will Stand," from 1961 — became a rock & roll anthem with global appeal. In the 70s, Johnson led the Chairmen of the Board ("Give Me Just a Little More Time"). —JF

○ **It Will Stand / COLLECTABLES**   1988
The hottest sides by this New Orleans outfit led by General Johnson (later with the Chairmen of the Board). The title cut is rock's greatest anthem of affirmation and neccessity. —JF

SHRIEKBACK

Alternative rock. A UK dance-rock band, 1982-1989, with varying personnel. The only constant member was keyboard player Barry Andrews, a former member of XTC. The original lineup was a trio also featuring former Gang of Four bassist Dave Allen and guitarist and vocalist Carl Marsh. They reached the US charts with their first album, *Care*, in 1983, and the UK charts with their second, *Jam Science*, in 1984. *Oil & Gold* (1985), *Big Night Music* (1987) and *Go Bang!* (1988) also made the lower reaches of the US charts, but the group's real home was in discos devoted to the kind of electronic, industrial-noise dance music of such peers as Ministry. Hits include "Nemesis" and "My Spine (Is the Bassline)." —WR

○ **The Dancing Years / POLYGRAM**   1990
An idiosyncratic compilation devoted to remixes and extended dance versions and lacking some of the group's best-known songs, though it *is* very danceable and gives a good sense of what Shriekback sounded like. If possible, find the UK import *The Infinite*, a good best-of, covering the early years. —WR

JANE SIBERRY

Singer/songwriter. This Canadian singer/songwriter has been compared to both Joni Mitchell and Laurie Anderson, perhaps because she mixes traditional folk styles with various electronic effects and because of quirky lyrics that border on humor. —WR

Jane Siberry / EAST SIDE DIGITAL   1980
Siberry's first (low-budget) recording is her most conventional and folk-oriented, but already she is warning us that "Writers Are a Funny Breed" and is showing the offbeat perspective that will charm listeners later on. —WR

○ **No Borders Here / WINDHAM HILL-OPEN AIR**   1984
The sound has a new-wave rock energy. The songs poke fun at "Extra Executives" as well as the artist, who muses that she'd probably be famous by now if she weren't such a good waitress. —WR

Bound by the Beauty / REPRISE   1989
Siberry has by now mastered an ability to make her unorthodox song forms (changing time signatures, surprising alterations of melody) work for her, and she's struck a balance between revealing too much and too little in her lyrics, so that such songs as "The Life Is the Red Wagon" really do reveal all the levels she's given it. And "Everything Reminds Me of My Dog" is one of the funniest and best songs of the year. —WR

SILOS

Folk/rock. This critically acclaimed New York outfit, led by ex-Vulgar Boatman Walter Salas-Humara and former Bob member Bob Rupe, produces Bohemian folk-rock jangle. —JF

○ **Cuba / RECORD COLLECT**   1987
One of the great independent-label rock albums of the late 80s. Decidedly American, anthemic, personal car music. —RG

Silos / RCA   1990
Well-crafted and smooth, but lacks the punch of *Cuba*. —RG

CARLY SIMON   ♭1945

Singer/songwriter, pop. Simon, who possesses an airy, somewhat unsteady alto, was one of the more popular female artists of the 70s, presenting a blend of singer/songwriter introspection and slick pop-smarts.

After working with her sisters in a music group (The Simon Sisters) and experiencing a false solo-artist start in 1966, Simon's career took a turn for the better with her self-titled debut. It produced a #10 hit in "That's the Way I've Always Heard It Should Be," "Anticipation" (#13). The followup, *Hotcakes*, was practically a duet album with then-husband James Taylor (they split in 1982). With her third effort, *No Secrets*, Simon linked up with producer Richard Perry, resulting in a #1 album that included her politely snotty putdown hit, "You're So Vain."

Simon has continued to enjoy periodic chart success in recent years. Her hits include "Nobody Does It Better" (#2), "The Right Thing to Do" (#17), "Haven't Got Time for the Pain" (#14), "You Belong to Me" (#6), "Jesse" (#11), and "Coming Around Again" (#18). —RC

○ **The Best of Carly Simon / ELEKTRA**   1975
Good collection from Simon's most popular period, including "Anticipation," "That's the Way I've Always Heard It Should Be," and "You're So Vain." —CK

SIMON & GARFUNKEL

Singer/songwriter, folk/rock. Between Paul Simon's (b Oct 13, 1941) warm lower tenor and Art Garfunkel's (b Nov 5, 1941) sweet, airy choirboy upper tenor, Simon and Garfunkel's delicate harmonic interplay (coupled with Simon's brilliant songcraftsmanship) earned them the distinction of being the most successful folk/pop duo of the 60s and early 70s. As early as 1955, the twosome were seriously working on music together and registering their originals at the Library of Congress. Under the moniker Tom & Jerry, they landed a deal (while in high school) on the Big label in 1957. Their first single, "Hey Schoolgirl" reached #49 nationally, landing them a spot on "American Bandstand."

They went to separate colleges in 1959 but continued to release singles as solo artists under various pseudonyms. In 1964 Simon traveled to England and became active in the folk scene. While there, he met up with the vacationing Garfunkel, and they became Simon & Garfunkel. Shortly thereafter, Tom Wilson brought them to Columbia.

Their first album, *Wednesday Morning, 3 AM*, was a pretty straightforward folk effort, blending originals with song covers. It failed to make an impression on the marketplace. Without informing the duo, Wilson took a track called "Sounds of Silence" off the album, added electric guitars, drums, and bass, and remixed it as a single. It soared to the #1 position for two weeks and boosted their debut up to #30. The album *Sounds of Silence*, featuring the electrified title track, hit #21. It included three other hit singles, "I Am a Rock" (#3), "Homeward Bound" (#9), and "The Dangling Conversation" (#25). By this time, Paul Simon's writing was being mentioned in the same breath as Dylan and Lennon/McCartney, but much of his best writing was yet to come.

Their next three albums, *Parsley, Sage, Rosemary and Thyme* (#4), *Bookends* (#1 for seven weeks), *Bridge over Troubled Water* (#1 for ten weeks), and the soundtrack album from the movie *The Graduate* (#1 for nine weeks) were huge artistic and commercial successes. The duo broke up during the recording of *Bridge over Troubled Water*. Simon had become increasingly frustrated with Garfunkel's absence while Art pursued a career in movie-acting.

Bridge over Troubled Water, its #1 hit title track, and Simon and Garfunkel cleaned up at the 1971 Grammy Awards. Other hits include "Mrs. Robinson" (#1 for three weeks), "The Boxer" (#7), "Cecilia" (#4), "Fakin' It" (#23), "Scarborough Fair/Canticle" (#11), "At the Zoo" (#16), "A Hazy Shade of Winter" (#13 — later a hit for the Bangles), "El Condor Pasa" (#18), and the #9 "My Little Town," recorded as a reunion single in 1975 and released on Simon's solo *Still Crazy after All These Years*. –RC

● **Greatest Hits / CBS** 1972
Nothing much more than what it says, although the live tracks are interesting. –BE

☆ **Collected Works / CBS** 1981
This 3-CD set is the only way to get the original albums with the best sound that's ever likely to turn up. –BE

JOE SIMON   *b* 1943

Soul. His plaintive baritone equally conversant with R&B and country phrasing, Joe Simon married the two genres with startling success during the late 60s, adapting Nashville material to the soul sound and repeatedly coming up a winner. Simon began recording in the Bay Area, but a switch in recording sites (first to Muscle Shoals for Vee Jay and then to Nashville, upon signing with deejay John Richbourg's Sound Stage 7 label in 1966) heightened his national appeal. With easy access to prime country-oriented material, Simon soon found his true calling, scoring major hits with "Nine Pound Steel," "(You Keep Me) Hangin' On," and the #1 R&B smash "The Chokin' Kind," penned by Music Row tunesmith Harlan Howard.

Still dabbling in country covers after switching to the Spring imprint in 1970, Simon was even more successful when assigned to Philadelphia wizards Kenny Gamble and Leon Huff, who produced the moody "Drowning in the Sea of Love" the next year. Simon tried his hand at disco in 1975 with the sizzling "Get Down, Get Down (Get on the Floor)" and "Music in My Bones," two of the most palatable artifacts of the era. Simon eventually retired from active performing to devote his life to the church. –BD

○ **Golden Classics / COLLECTABLES**
Simon had good minor hits, most of which are here. –DH

PAUL SIMON   *b* 1942

Singer/songwriter. Paul Simon's career has been distinguished by a constant search for new musical styles — a constant musical exploration. Because of this, all of Simon's albums sound different; there is no representative album. Toward the end of Simon and Garfunkel's career, Simon began experimenting with different forms of music from around the world, a trend that blossomed when Simon went solo. From reggae and R&B to South African and Brazilian music, Simon has gone all over the map musically. Although he began his career by emulating Bob Dylan lyrically, by the time Simon started recording solo, he had developed his own distinct style. Simon's early-70s albums are classic singer/songwriter albums, with more musical variety than the genre usually exhibits. He then drifted into a severe dry spell, producing a few good songs between 1976 and 1985. With the release of *Graceland* in 1986, Simon's writer's block was eliminated with the help of some new musical influences. –STE

☆ **Paul Simon / WARNER** 1972
Backing away from the heavy production of the last Simon & Garfunkel album, Paul Simon's first solo outing is a quiet affair based around acoustic guitar. "Mother and Child Reunion," a successful experiment with reggae, is included as is "Me and Julio Down by the Schoolyard"; the great Stephane Grappelli guests on "Hobo's Blues." Many of Simon's finest songs are found here. –STE

☆ **There Goes Rhymin' Simon / WARNER** 1974
Simon listened to R&B when he was growing up, and on *Rhymin' Simon* he returns to those roots. At times the results are some true R&B, and even gospel ("Loves Me like a Rock" recorded with the Dixie Hummingbirds), but mainly there is a lot of beautiful, sophisticated pop, shaded with blues ("St. Judy's Comet" and "Something So Right.") Not as fully realized as *Paul Simon*, but there is much rewarding listening to be found. –STE

☆ **Still Crazy after All These Years / WARNER** 1975
Replacing the guitar with the piano as the primary instrument, Simon produced a quiet, introspective Grammy-winning album centering around love lost. Simon reunites with Garfunkel on "My Little Town," a track that sounds nothing like old S&G songs. *Still Crazy* doesn't much resemble Simon's two previous albums; it is a serious, somber album with none of the light touches present on *Paul Simon* and *Rhymin' Simon*. –STE

☆ **Graceland / WARNER** 1986
Graceland is immediately accessible because the music is exotic yet familiar. As Simon says in the liner notes, he was drawn to South African music because it sounded "like 50s rock & roll of the Atlantic Records school of simple three-chord pop." Simon put his own melodies and lyrics to South African rhythms and chords, producing a remarkable hybrid. Simon's songs are some of his best, recovering from a ten-year dry spell. Los Lobos guests on "All Around the World." *Graceland* is not only Simon's best album but one of the classic rock & roll albums. –STE

● **Negotiations & Love Songs 1971-1986 / WARNER** 1988
A good sampler of Paul Simon's personal favorites and hits. Many of his frequent changes in style are captured here, as are the highlights of the *One Trick Pony* and *Hearts and Bones* albums. –STE

Rhythm of the Saints / WARNER 1990
Simon moved from Africa to Brazil and produced an album that resembles *Graceland*, yet is harder to grasp. The songs are more oblique than *Graceland*'s and the music is harder to absorb in one listen. After a couple of repeat listenings, the album begins to take shape, and melodies emerge under the heavy percussion. It's necessary to put some time into this album, but the results are well worth it. –STE

In Central Park / WARNER 1991
Simon plays all the favorites from his African and Brazilian albums and recasts some old favorites in these settings. Sometimes the results are thought-provoking (Bridge over Troubled Water" and "Sound of Silence") other times severely faulted ("Kodachrome" and "Cecilia"), yet the album is immensely entertaining and listenable. –STE

SIMPLE MINDS

Alternative rock. Simple Minds was conceived in 1977 out of the remains of the Glasgow, Scotland, band Johnny & the Self-Abusers. Their initial albums were rather dissonant, moody, synth-heavy dance-music excursions that enjoyed increasing popularity in the British Isles, due to the band's incessant touring. The 1982 album *New Gold Dream (81, 82, 83, 84)* (UK #3) spent a year on the British charts and produced three hit singles; the followup, *Sparkle in the Rain*, was a #1 hit in England. In 1984, lead singer Jim Kerr's marriage to Chrissie Hynde of the Pretenders became a pop-media event. Nevertheless, it wasn't until the band recorded a nonoriginal track, "Don't You Forget about Me" (#1), for the 1985 brat-pack film *The Breakfast Club* that the group began making a big impression Stateside. During that time, Simple Minds played at the historic Live Aid benefit in Philadelphia. Their next album, *Once Upon a Time* (#10), featured a clean, radio-friendly production by Bob Clearmountain and Jimmy Iovine and generated a few Top 40 hits.

Subsequent efforts have included a fine live album and a couple of dramatically produced studio releases that continue the band's hopeful humanitarian themes. –RC

New Gold Dream (81-82-83-84) / A&M / BB 69   1982
New Gold Dream (81-82-83-84) was the first effort (after many spotty earlier releases) to exhibit a focused collection of strong songs. The material, overall, is a coolly elegant style of synth-rich dance-pop. Among the album's highlights are "Promised You a Miracle," "Glittering Prize," and the title song. –RC

☆ **Sparkle in the Rain / A&M / BB 64**   1984
On *Sparkle in the Rain*, Simple Minds assembled the best songs of their career and brought in producer Steve Lillywhite (XTC, Psychedelic Furs, U2) to help articulate their vision. The result was the best album of their career, thus far. Lillywhite's sweeping cinematic soundscapes perfectly suited grand songs like "WaterFront," "Book of Brilliant Things," "Up on the Catwalk," "East of Easter," and a version of Lou Reed's "Street Hassle." "Kick Inside of Me" rocks harder than anything the band has ever done. Highly recommended! –RC

Once Upon a Time / A&M / BB 10   1985
On the wings of the popular 1985 *Breakfast Club* soundtrack hit, Simple Minds enlisted in-demand producers Jimmy Iovine and Bob Clearmountain and released the ready-made-for-American-FM-radio *Once Upon a Time*. In spite of the fact that this album generated three hits with "Alive & Kicking" (#3), "Sanctify Yourself" (#14), and "All the Things She Said" (#28), Simple Minds had lost the inspirational edge they had attained on *Sparkle in the Rain*. –RC

Live in the City of Light / A&M / BB 96   1987
Simple Minds has a reputation as an excellent live unit, and this well-recorded 1986 set done in Paris is a testament to that fact. With the help of extra sidemen (background vocalists, computer programmer, and violinist) Simple Minds runs through a wide sampling of their best material. –RC

Street Fighting Years / A&M   1989
This album has its moments, but singer/songwriter Jim Kerr's heavy-handed moralizing and the bloated Cecil B. deMille-style production job practically sank this album. There are a few decent tunes here, however, with "Belfast Child," and "This Land Is Your Land," Lou Reed guesting. –RC

SIMPLY RED

Pop. This R&B sextet based in Manchester, England, is led by red-headed singer Mick Hucknall (b Jun 8, 1960). –WR

○ **Picture Book / ELEKTRA**   1985
The band finds a steady R&B groove reminiscent of 60s Stax house band the MG's, and, as with the MG's, it's all in the service of a big-voiced soul singer, in this case a British redhead. Features the US #1 "Holding Back the Years" and the UK Top 20 "Money's Too Tight (To Mention)." –WR

A New Flame / ELEKTRA   1989
Although Hucknall tries to resurrect soul in his own original songs, he's most successful at evoking the past, notably on Simply Red's second #1, a remake of Harold Melvin and the Blue Notes' "If You Don't Know Me by Now." –WR

SIOUXSIE & THE BANSHEES

Alternative rock. This British punk-rock band is led by singer Siouxsie Sioux (b Susan Dallion, May 27, 1957) and bassist Steve Severin (guitarist and drummer have varied over the years). They started in London in 1976, releasing their first album, *The Scream*, in 1978. Gradually they became established through frequent albums and tours, as their sound became more accessible. By 1992, Sioux was singing on the soundtrack of *Batman Returns*. –WR

○ **The Scream / GEFFEN**   1978
By waiting until punk essentially had blown over to sign a contract, the Banshees had a clear field for their harsh rock attack, and plenty of time to prepare it. The result is this fierce debut, which fulfills the promise of punk and suggests (unlike most of its progenitors) that it has a future. –WR

Juju / GEFFEN   1981
They're shifting gradually toward a more straightforward rock sound, but the Banshees also add Middle Eastern touches here. Contains the British hits "Spellbound" and "Arabian Knights." –WR

Once Upon a Time/The Singles / GEFFEN   1981
This compilation of UK singles (some appearing on LP for the first time) emphasizes the more pop sound of Siouxsie and the Banshees. Still not easy listening, though. –WR

Hyaena / GEFFEN   1984
Siouxsie and the Banshees's first album to benefit from a major-label push in the US (and make the charts) finds them taking a more melodic, expressive approach and even covering the Beatles' "Dear Prudence." Old fans howled, but there was a lot of new fans. –WR

Through the Looking Glass / GEFFEN   1987
Well-selected album of rock and pop cover songs, including everything from Sparks's "This Town Ain't Big Enough for Both of Us" to "Strange Fruit." –WR

THE SIR DOUGLAS QUINTET

Tex-Mex. Texas had always had its own brand of rock & roll — a little bit o' country, a little bit o' blues, with a heapin' helpin' o' hot sauce poured over the top. Doug Sahm was no stranger to the studio when he formed the Sir Douglas Quintet in 1964; he'd been at it since the age of six and already possessed an encyclopedic knowledge and innate understanding of those local flavors when the band cut its first big hit, "She's About a Mover."

The ingredient that set the Quintet apart was Tex-Mex, that curious, joyous, irresistible, danceable, festive feast that married the jumpy Mexican *conjunto* to good ol' rock & roll. With Augie Meyers on the organ and a rhythm section that couldn't stop cookin', Sir Doug Sahm let it be known that good-time music was alive and kickin' in San Antone.

After the Quintet itself dissolved, Sahm went on to cut numerous solo albums and collaborations, spreading the Tex-Mex influence. In the late 80s he and Meyers teamed up with two of their mentors, Freddy Fender and Flaco Jimenez, to form the Texas Tornados, keeping that high and happy sound alive. –JT

○ **Sir Doug's Recording Trip / EDSEL**
An incredible 30-song sampling of his Quintet and solo years, featuring most of the hits, some rare delicacies, and an educational set of notes by Ed Ward. (Import) –JF

Best of Doug Sahm & Sir Douglas ... / POLYGRAM   1990
Best of Doug Sahm & Sir Douglas Quintet. This is not as thorough as *Sir Doug's Recording Trip*, but it's easier to find and gives you 22 essential tracks in sterling digital fidelity. –JF

SISTER SLEDGE

R&B, disco. Four Philadelphia sisters who began singing professionally in 1974; contemporary pop and dance music performers. Though lead singer Kathie has a husky voice, theirs is a smooth sound true to their hometown. –BC

○ **The Sister Sledge Collection / ATLANTIC**   1992
From all of their great early Atco sides, on up to their early-80s work. Liner notes and photos. –BC

SISTERS OF MERCY

Alternative rock. A Leeds outfit, headed by lyricist Andrew Eldritch, that started with pounding heavy metal in its 1982 debut EP and since then has moved steadily toward danceable pop-funk. –DS

○ **Vision Thing / ELEKTRA**   1990
Guitar-based pop fueled by the bright-sounding sensibilities of ex-Generation X axeman Tony James. –DS

SKID ROW

Heavy metal. This New Jersey quintet Skid Row has become one of the premier players in the mainstream heavy-metal genre during the 90s. –JB

Skid Row / ATLANTIC 1989
With enough exposure, Skid Row became impossible to ignore. The beginning of a good band. —JB

○ **Slave to the Grind / ATLANTIC** 1991
Skid Row's impressive second album, with some great rockers, a nice ballad or two, and even a heavy venture into thrash. One of the best metal albums of 1991. —JB

SKIDS

Punk, alternative rock. A Scottish quartet which emerged with a raw-edged sound in 1978. Cemented by singer and writer Richard Jobson and featuring the guitar of Stuart Adamson, the band recorded two albums of propulsive rock before changing to a more art-rock sound. The Skids disbanded in 1981, guitarist Adamson forming Big Country. —DS

○ **Scared to Dance / CAROLINE** 1979
Jagged, hook-laden punk from Scotland, including the anthemic title song. —DS

SLADE

Hard rock. England's greatest working-class hard-rock band. Although they succumbed to the mid-70s glitter fad and failed to live up to US/UK mega-hype, Slade kicked out plenty of ferocious jams structured around a simple yet sound principle: minimal chord progressions played at maximum volume. With vocalist Noddy Holder's larynx-shredding howl and their purposely misspelled song titles ("Cum on Feel the Noize"), Slade loudly and proudly flew in the face of fashion and good taste. True proto-punk/metal pioneers. —JD

Sladest / POLYGRAM 1973
All the British hits that bombed in America. —LL

○ **Keep Your Hands Off My Power Supply / CBS** 1984
Heavy-metal grunge-rock at its best. —LL

SLAYER

Heavy metal. Slayer, a quartet with a passion for death-metal and Alice Cooper-like makeup, formed in Los Angeles in 1981. By concentrating on songwriting and musicianship, they molded a unique style of aggressive speed-metal, using lyrical themes ranging through nuclear weapons, death, and the overall dismal feeling of everyday life. Slayer remain one of the most influential thrash/speed-metal bands from the first wave of the early 80s. —JB

○ **Hell Awaits / ENIGMA** 1985
The fear of being in hell is explored on this classic album, right up there with *Reign in Blood.* —JB

★ **Reign in Blood / WARNER** 1986
One of the best albums in thrash/speed-metal, if not the best. Proof that playing fast doesn't result in monotonous boredom. Slayer's major-label debut. —JB

Seasons in the Abyss / WARNER 1990
Their best since *Reign in Blood.* —JB

Decade of Aggression - Live / DEF AMERICAN 1991
A double-length set with all of Slayer's great songs done in the only way the band should be experienced: in concert. The best-sounding live speed-metal album so far. —JB

PERCY SLEDGE   ♭1941

Soul. "When a Man Loves a Woman" existed long before Michael Bolton ever came on the scene — it's hard to believe that anyone could be unaware of Percy Sledge's original version of the song. As the first Southern soul recording to top both the R&B and pop charts in 1966, the emotionally supercharged ballad was a groundbreaker, and Sledge's remarkably anguished performance ranks as an unrivaled masterpiece of the soul genre.
Sledge often seems to teeter on the verge of tears on his best Atlantic label releases of the late 60s. A product of the musically fertile area around Muscle Shoals, AL, Sledge recorded "When a Man Loves a Woman" and the equally

moving followups "It Tears Me Up," "Out of Left Field," and "Take Time to Know Her" with the same session aces that played on most Muscle Shoals classics of the period.
By the turn of the decade, Sledge's well had run dry, although he's recorded off and on ever since. —BD

☆ **It Tears Me Up - The Best of Percy Sledge / RHINO** 1992
This stunning compilation from the vaults of Atlantic Records spotlights the voice that gave us the original version of "When a Man Loves a Woman." Lesser-known hits like "It Tears Me Up," "Take Time to Know Her," and "Warm and Tender Love" are equally wonderful, and all are included in this must-have package. Great liner notes by Dave Marsh. Soul music just doesn't get any more heart-wrenching than this. Absolutely essential! —CO

SLEEP

Heavy metal. Sleep formed in the late 80s in Southern California with a craving to combine punk with the slower grooves of hard rock. The end result is a nerve-racking recipe of heavy music that doesn't fit any one musical genre. —JB

○ **Volume One / VERY SMALL**
Taking their cue from bands like Fu Manchu, Melvins, and, most notably, Black Sabbath, California's Sleep performs sludgy rock with a slight metal edge that never goes over the speed limit. —JB

P. F. SLOAN

Singer/songwriter, folk/rock. During the mid 60s, P. F. Sloan was a popular songwriter whose memorable lyrical and melodic hooks landed him many cuts. Some of his compositions were anthemic folk-rockers that addressed certain socially relevant topics. Among his more popular songs are "Eve of Destruction" (recorded by Barry McGuire), "Let Me Be" (Turtles), "Must to Avoid" (Herman's Hermits), "Secret Agent Man" (Johnny Rivers), "Where Were You When I Needed You," and "Things I Should Of Said" (both recorded by the Grass Roots). As a solo artist, Sloan recorded some fine folk-rock tracks. —RC

○ **Precious Times - Best of P. F. Sloan / RHINO**
Best known as a songwriter, especially for "Eve of Destruction," "You Baby," and "Let Me Be," Sloan also recorded some excellent folk-rock of his own. His Dunhill sides from 1965-1966 are featured on this collection. —JT

The Grass Roots / BIG BEAT 1988
This import takes the best of Sloan's own recordings and combines them with his compositions as recorded by the Grass Roots. —JT

SLY & THE FAMILY STONE   ♭1944

Soul, funk. Sylvester Stewart came charging out of the psychedelic environs of San Francisco in 1967 with a band — and a sound — that made good on the communal spirit most acid-scorched bands only talked about. The Family Stone was rock's first fully integrated group: men and women, Black and White, they refused to play the music-business game of racial and sexual segregation, mixing rock and R&B until, as critic Dave Marsh pointed out, "you couldn't find where one began and the other left off."
Songs such as "Everyday People" explained Stone's desire to mix everything up, while "I Want to Take You Higher" and "Dance to the Music" made explicit the community of the Family Stone. But Stone's optimism began to sour in the wake of Dr. Martin Luther King's assassination and the return of segregation, and his music took on a chilling tone. The dizzy glee of "Hot Fun in the Summertime" gave way to the scathing "Thank You (Falettinme Be Mice Elf Agin)" and *There's a Riot Goin' On.* Eventually, his career bogged down under a shroud of drug problems. But Sly Stone's stamp is as indelibly placed on pop music as James Brown's, and his influence can be heard and felt in the work of Kool and the Gang, Prince, George Clinton, and dozens of others. —JF

Dance to the Music / EPIC / BB 142   1968
Sly's second album reached the lower echelons of *Billboard's* album charts due to the quintessential psychedelic soul single, "Dance to the Music." The rest of the album is uneven, early, and tentative, with the full funk being a little further around the bend. −RB

Life / EPIC / BB 195   1968
The Family Stone's third album was a step forward with a harder drum sound, sharper horn lines, and more focused writing. Despite these developments, *Life* failed to yield a hit single ("Plastic Jim," "Life," and "M'Lady" were all fine candidates). −RB

☆ **Stand! / EPIC / BB 13**   1969
The album on which Sly's integrationalist vision paid big dividends. Four of the record's seven songs, including "I Want to Take You Higher" and "Everyday People," charted as singles. The group contained Blacks and Whites, men and women; voices and instruments careened off one another in one apocalyptic vision of community. At the time, such an album seemed to be the clarion call of a new day. Brilliant. −RB

○ **Greatest Hits / EPIC / BB 2**   1970
This greatest-hits package was released as a stopgap while Sly was taking two years to record *There's a Riot Goin' On*. It's what you would expect from a greatest-hits package, with the addition of two newly recorded monster-hit singles, "Hot Fun in the Summertime" and "Thank You (Falettinme Be Mice Elf Agin)." −RB

☆ **There's a Riot Goin' On / EPIC / BB 1**   1971
Sly gets darker and funkier. By *Riot*, Sly was a bona fide superstar. His personal behavior became more erratic, and his songwriting became more eclectic and adventurous. There is no precedent for such a record; songs were conceived from the rhythm up, and often left in sparse, naked, seemingly semi-finished form. Sly's earlier hit, "Thank You (Falettinme Be Mice Elf Agin)" is slowed down, turned inside out, and retitled "Thank You for Talkin' to Me Africa." The result is an extremely personal stab at exorcism that takes the listener through the new reality of Black and White America in the early 70s. Mesmerizing. The album's most accessible songs, "Family Affair" and "Runnin' Away," were R&B and pop hit singles, the former reaching the #1 spot on both charts. −RB

○ **Fresh / EPIC / BB 7**   1973
Stripped down and funky, minus thumb-popping bass whiz Larry Graham (who had left to found Graham Central Station), Sly turned in a fine album. One Top Ten R&B hit resulted with "If You Want Me to Stay," while two other songs, "Frisky" and "If It Were Left Up to Me," also received substantial airplay on Black radio. In the wake of Sly's politics on *Riot* and his increasingly erratic personal and concert behavior, most pop-radio programmers seemed to grow leery of the Family Stone. The first single, "If You Want Me to Stay," reached #12 pop, but it was to be the last Sly Stone record to receive any significant pop success. −RB

Small Talk / EPIC / BB 15   1974
A new bass player and drummer signaled a toned-down Family Stone sound. Partially in keeping with changes in much of popular music in the early 70s, and maybe the result of marriage and a child, Sly became more introspective, quieter, calmer, even employing a string section on various cuts. Less exhilarating album than earlier efforts, there is still much of merit here, including the Top Ten R&B hit "Time for Livin'." −RB

● **Anthology / CBS**   1981
Repeats some cuts from *Greatest Hits* but also includes highlights from *Riot* and *Fresh*. But you should hear those albums in their entirety. −JF

THE SMALL FACES

British Invasion. America remembers them only for their hit "Itchycoo Park," but the Small Faces were one of England's most wonderful bands of the mid 60s, and their music remains some of the most valuable of the era. The diminutive mods came out roaring in 1965, basing their sounds around American R&B, but unlike countless of their contemporaries, the Small Faces were not about to merely mimic American soul sounds. The group was a powerhouse instrumental unit capped off by the incredible vocals of Steve Marriott. They stayed largely within the R&B-based formula through their stay at Decca. As thrilling as these sides often were, recording time was often rushed between live dates, and, as a result, the band never really had a chance to discover its studio potential during its stay at that label.

That situation changed when the Small Faces hooked up with Andrew "Loog" Oldham's Immediate in 1967. From the outset, the band created some of the most brilliant pop records of the day, far outdistancing their early work. They worked with expanded instrumentation, both live and in the studio, and also began to feature the voice of bassist Ronnie Lane, whose flat, cockney delivery was used brilliantly to contrast with Marriott's. The album *Ogden's Nut Gone Flake* was the pinnacle of their work; unfortunately, it was also their last album. A brief reunion, sans Lane, in the mid 70s added nothing to the band's legacy, but the Small Faces' work of the previous decade would have been hard to equal. With the group's often-confusing discography now sorted out on recent CD issues, it's time to rediscover a terrific band. −SA

★ **Ogden's Nut Gone Flake / CBS**   1968
A concept album with soul. A lot of great songs, and an off-center Cockney personality. A classic. −BE

○ **There Are but Four Small Faces / CBS**   1968
The Steve Marriott-Ronnie Lane songwriting team spreads its wings, and the band grinds and crunches its way through a collection of excellent (but not outstanding) songs, including the psychedelic anthem "Itchycoo Park." −BE

Small Faces / POLYGRAM   1988
A testament to greatness. The declaration of true Cockney rebel Steve Marriott singing out against the world. −BE

From the Beginning / POLYGRAM   1989
The early history of the band, at this time a quartet of earnest White soul shouters. −BE

SMASHING PUMPKINS

Alternative rock. From Chicago, the next big "indie-rock thang." The Pumpkins actually play pretty effective loud pop with a tinge of sub-pop-grunge. The only problem is that they show a bit too much artifice in their rock for my taste. Provided their pretentiousness doesn't get the better of them, this could be one snappy little combo. −JD

○ **Gish / CAROLINE**   1991
A fine, fine debut album that follows a simple structural philosophy: fast songs good, slow songs not-so-good. Snazzy sound courtesy of hip independent producer Butch Vig. −JD

PATTI SMITH   b 1946

Alternative rock. Patti Smith is a poet and rock singer who first gained notice when reading her poetry at gatherings in New York City in the early 70s. By 1974 Smith had edged toward music by reading with the backup of electric guitarist and rock critic Lenny Kaye, notably on her independent-label single, "Piss Factory." By 1975 Smith had organized a band that was playing in such clubs as the punk birthplace in New York, CBGB's, and she earned a contract with Arista Records. This resulted in the release of *Horses*, a critically acclaimed album that featured her songs, sometimes melded to dramatic readings, and such rock oldies as "Land of 1,000 Dances." *Radio Ethiopia* was both mainstream-rock-oriented and more experimental, depending on which track you played. With 1978's *Easter*, Smith was definitely moving in a more commercial direction, especially by pairing with Bruce Springsteen for the hit single "Because the Night." That marked the high point of Smith's rock career. *Wave* (1979) found her waving goodbye; she married ex-MC5 guitarist Fred "Sonic" Smith and retired from the music business. Her return came with the promising 1988 album *Dream of Life*, but she was not back to full-time duty. –WR

☆ **Horses / ARISTA** 1975

One of the more successful matings of poetry and rock, this landmark changed the role of women in rock and paved the way for rock without excess. –JT

Radio Ethiopia / ARISTA 1976

Her disjointed second album takes the focus off of Smith's words and shifts it to her excellent band. Intelligent rock & roll, minus a bit of the edge. –JT

Easter / ARISTA 1978

Although it contained the hit cover of Springsteen's "Because the Night," Smith's writing was weaker on this third album. The group burns though. –JT

WARREN SMITH 1933-1980

Rockabilly. For sheer, heartfelt vocalizing abilities, of all the folks who stood in front of the microphone at Sun studio, Warren Smith may have been the most talented. Equally adept at storming rockabilly and the most gut-wrenching of country ballads, Smith always sang it from the heart, without giving in to phony rasping or histrionics. Though typecast as strictly a rocker, Smith left Sun and achieved minor success in the 60s as a country singer, his first love. –CK

☆ **The Classic Recordings 1956-59 / BEAR FAMILY** 1992

Smith's entire output (31 tracks in all) for Sun Records. Includes the rockabilly classics "Rock & Roll Ruby," "Ubangi Stomp," and "Miss Froggie," as well as heartfelt country performances on "The Darkest Cloud," "I'd Rather Be Safe than Sorry," and "Goodbye Mr. Love." No Sun collection can really be considered complete without adding this one to the list. –CK

SMITHEREENS

Power-pop. Pat DiNizio (vocals, guitar), Jim Babjak (guitar), Mike Mesaros (bass), and Dennis Diken (drums) make up the Smithereens, formed in New Jersey in 1980 when DiNizio answered an ad placed by the three others. The band plays in a 60s British Invasion rock & roll style, DiNizio's songs overtly evoking that era. The Smithereens gigged around the New York area and recorded a couple of EPs on small labels in the early 80s, then scored a record contract with the independent Enigma, which issued *Especially for You* in 1986. It stayed on the charts nearly a year. Its followup, *Green Thoughts* (1988), also showed staying power in the charts, producing the AOR radio hit "Only a Memory." The Smithereens reached the pop Top 40 with "A Girl like You" from their third album *11* in 1989. A fourth album, *Blow Up*, stirred college and AOR radio interest for the track "Top of the Pops" in 1991, but it was less of a sales success. –WR

Beauty & Sadness / ENIGMA 1983

The Smithereens' second EP is an impressive collection of melodic guitar-driven power-pop, particularly the title cut. Fans of the band should seek this out, but the uninitiated will get a better picture of the band with *Especially for You* and *Green Thoughts*. –RC

● **Especially for You / ENIGMA** 1987

On *Especially for You*, Smithereens achieved a near-perfect blend of exuberant rockers and moody excursions. Don Dixon's production captured the band's exciting chemistry, while keeping lead singer Pat DiNizio up front in the mix, on this, their best album. "Behind the Wall of Sleep" and "Blood and Roses" were big college-music favorites, helping pave the way for greater success. Other highlights included "Strangers When We Meet," "Time and Time Again," "Groovy Tuesday," and "Alone at Midnight." –RC

○ **The Smithereens Live / RESTLESS** 1987

This CD is a great document of Smithereens's live power. Everyone plays impeccably, and the song selection is mint, with a version of "Beauty & Sadness" that surpasses the original and a knocked-out rendition of the Who chestnut "The Seeker." To enhance the authenticity of the gig experience, the mix is loaded with the kind of fatiguingly brittle midrange that only a veteran live engineer could achieve. –RC

○ **Green Thoughts / CAPITOL** 1988

The followup to *Especially for You* was another impressive batch of power-pop rockers. "Only a Memory" and "House We Used to Live In" were FM rock hits. Again, Dixon's production demonstrated his empathy for the band's sound. Other highlights included "Something New," "Drown in My Own Tears," and the title track. –RC

11 / CAPITOL 1989

On *11*, Smithereens employed alternative hard-rock producer Ed Stasium (Cavedogs, Living Colour) to beef up their sound. The result was a thick guitar-riff-heavy sound. The approach helped "A Girl like You" become a big rock and MTV hit but, taken as a whole, *11* lacked the dynamics and natural soundstage that made their earlier work so fresh-sounding. "Yesterday Girl," "Baby Be Good," and "A Girl like You" are highlights, though. –RC

Blow Up / CAPITOL 1991

An improvement over *11*, *Blow Up* displays Stasium's state-of-the-art power-rock production and a greater range of material. The soulful "Too Much Passion" was a hit, as was "Top of the Pops." –RC

THE SMITHS

Alternative rock. The Manchester-based rock quartet was formed in 1982, featuring (Steven) Morrissey, vocals (b May 22, 1959); Johnny Marr, guitar (b Oct 31, 1963); Andy Rourke, bass; and Mike Joyce, drums (b Jun 1, 1963). The center of the group's appeal was Morrissey's sometimes absurd, sometimes oddly touching lyrics, which he sang calmly, as though they contained ordinary pop sentiments. Marr led the band's musical attack, which leaned heavily on conventional guitar-based pop-rock with a 60s bent, emphasizing all the more the singer's unusual lyrics. The group disbanded in August of 1987. –WR

The Smiths / WARNER 1984

The Smiths make ear-pleasing, catchy pop-rock, and it seduces the listener into paying attention to Morrissey's dead-pan lyrics, which are deliberately self-pitying, sometimes caustic, and usually funny. "Reel around the Fountain" is a classic, and the album also contains the UK singles "Hand in Glove" and "What Difference Does it Make?" –WR

The Queen Is Dead / WARNER 1986

A harder-rock approach, with Morrissey putting more passion into his delivery on a collection of typically provocative songs, including "Bigmouth Strikes Again," "The Boy with the Thorn in His Side," "Vicar in a Tutu," and "Some Girls Are Bigger Than Others." –WR

○ **Louder Than Bombs / WARNER** 1987

Nearest thing to a Smiths greatest-hits album, this two-disc album contains 24 tracks, recorded between 1983 and 1987, including such favorites as "William, It Was Really Nothing" and "Please Please Please Let Me Get What I Want." –WR

PHOEBE SNOW b 1952

Singer/songwriter, pop. This pop-jazz singer/songwriter with a broad, melismatic contralto voice broke through in 1975 with her debut album on Shelter, then made several albums for Columbia and Atlantic despite legal and personal difficulties that distracted her from her career. She returned to recording on Elektra in 1989 after an eight-year layoff and was also part of Donald Fagen's New York Rock and Soul Revue. –WR

○ **Phoebe Snow / DCC** 1974

A wondrous folk, pop, and jazz album of Snow's original songs and some well-chosen covers, all showcasing her one-of-a-kind voice. Includes the Top Five hit "Poetry Man." –WR

It Looks like Snow / CBS 1976

The cover songs start to overwhelm the originals, but when Snow is able to bring such powerful interpretations to "Don't Let Me Down," "Shakey Ground," and "Teach Me Tonight," who could complain? –WR

SOCIAL DISTORTION

Punk, rock & roll. An early high mark in California punk. Actually, with their 1977-era power chords and an artistic scope that was comfortable enough to include Johnny Cash covers, this Fullerton, CA, band came on like a throwback to British punk groups like Stiff Little Fingers and the Vibrators. They were also able to move their chunky punk rock into the mainstream without cutting back on the energy, the power chords, or the nihilism. And that's something few West Coast hardcore bands can claim. –JF

○ **Mommy's Little Monster / TRIPLE X**   1983
Their debut is full of wailing guitars, sharp lyrics, tugging melodies, and snarling vocals. –JF

Prison Bound / ENIGMA-RESTLESS   1988
The release of lthis album brought acoustic guitars, ballads, and a cautious step toward the rock mainstream that makes their music of use for more than just hardcore nihilists. –JF

○ **Social Distortion / CBS**   1990
Their major-label debut repeated the winning formula of *Prison Bound* — Ramones meet the Blasters meet Johnny Thunders — but with better production. –JF

● **Somewhere between Heaven and Hell / CBS**   1991
Social Distortion wallows in rock & roll rebellion and fatalism. The combination of urgent lyrics and unbeatable riffs make this their best album. –JF

THE SOFT BOYS

Alternative rock. A punk outfit formed around Robyn Hitchcock and Kimberly Rew. Their hard sound was balanced by Hitchcock's dark, nasty sense of humor, reminiscent of both Syd Barrett and the filmmaking Hitchcock. (Alfred) –BE

○ **Underwater Moonlight / RYKODISC**   1980
Wry, savage humor permeates this near-virtuoso album. Extraordinarily well played, especially the guitars. –BE

SOFT MACHINE

Prog-rock. Named after a William Borroughs novel, Soft Machine (formed 1966) was one of the most exciting prog-rock bands to emerge from England during the late 60s. Their first two albums were brilliantly whimsical fusions of jazz and hard psychedelia. Robert Wyatt's inventive drumming and appealingly unstable tenor rasp of a voice enhanced the band's oddball musical attack, as did Michael Ratledge's off-center keyboard parts, Hugh Hopper's distorto-splat bass work and Kevin Ayers's manic lead guitar work. After their second album, the Soft Machine adopted a more pronounced instrumental space-jazz approach. After their appropriately titled *Third*, the group's lineup began to change dramatically. Subsequent albums became less interesting. –RC

Third / CBS   1970
This album marks the beginning of their penchant for long, jazz-influenced pieces, and the end of the youthful, madcap era. –MB

Live at the Proms 1970 / RECKLESS   1988
A masterful exposition of their more serious jazz side. –MB

☆ **Volumes 1 & 2 / BIG BEAT**   1989
Their influential early recordings, combining Bonzo Dog Band's zaniness with a strong progressive vision in concise song structures. (Import) –MB

SONIC YOUTH

Alternative rock. When Sonic Youth began as a downtown New York band in the early 80s, they rejected most traditional rock & roll formalities such as Western tuning and song structure. With screwdrivers randomly stuck into their guitar necks, the quartet created discordant, droning, mantralike songs, which were quietly forceful. As they matured, their material became more accessible and the songs more conventional, even as they retained their discordance. By the early 90s, Sonic Youth was approaching mainstream acceptance.

The band (Kim Gordon, bass and vocal; Thurston Moore, guitar and vocal; Lee Ranaldo, guitar; Steve Shelley, drums) had several releases before their sound crystallized. *Sonic Youth*, *Confusion Is Sex*, *Kill Yr Idols*, and *Sonic Death* document a band learning to express their complex ideas. These releases are often coarse and brash, sometimes unlistenable, and frequently startling in their power.

The band's cult following continued to grow throughout the late 80s, culminating in a major-label contract with Geffen Records. The corporate machine helped them develop a still-larger following. After their Geffen debut, 1990's *Goo*, Sonic Youth rested for two years. Their past indicates that a pause to regroup is usually followed by a burst of new creativity. –RG

Bad Moon Rising / HOMESTEAD   1985
On *Bad Moon Rising*, the songs gained a focus so that moods and styles which formerly had spread scross several releases could be accomplished in one album. –RG

○ **EVOL / SST**   1986
EVOL ("love" spelled backwards) is composed of catchy rhythms and melodies, even some hooks; however, a menacing darkness remained, even dominated. Vocals were split pretty evenly between Gordon and Moore. *EVOL* remains a high point for the band, with provocative songs that force us, even after punk, to question what was commonplace in pop. Features "Green Light" and "Expressway to Yr Skull." –RG

Sister / SST   1987
Sister found them largely embracing the rock aesthetic, though with little sacrifice to their own code. The album retains its menace and punkish attitude while totally rocking out. It's sort of the other side of the *EVOL* coin. They achieve a similar end, but instead of using spacious and brooding songs, they play hard, succinct, and tight. The CD features the bonus track "Master Dik." –RG

● **Daydream Nation / ENIGMA**   1988
Daydream Nation is a double album that warrants its indulgences; if the songs run long, they're worth it. When "Total Trash" devolves into a furious jam, its cacophony is beautiful, surpassed only by the surprise return to structure. The appeal of the "Teenage Riot" single brought the band a greater audience, and, if it seems to compromise their stance, in the context of the album it makes perfect sense. –RG

Goo / GEFFEN   1990
Though *Goo* is not a sellout, it didn't advance the band in the leaps their previous few albums had. Mostly it sounds like *Daydream Nation* rehashed. Includes "Tunic," "Dirty Boots," and "Kool Thing." –RG

THE SONICS

Rock & roll. A rock & roll band from Tacoma, WA, whose original members were Gerry Roslie (lead singer and piano/organ), Andy Parypa (guitar), Larry Parypa (bass), Bob Bennett (drums), and Rob Lind (saxophone). Forming in the wake of the early-60s success of local favorites the Kingsmen and the Wailers (whose Etiquette label they recorded for), the Sonics combined the classic Northwest-area teen-band raunch with early English band grit (particularly influenced by the Kinks), relentless rhythmic drive, and unabashed 50s-style blues-shouting for a combination that still makes their brand of rock & roll perhaps the raunchiest ever captured on wax. Lead singer Gerry Roslie was no less than a White Little Richard, whose harrowing soul-screams were startling even to the Northwest teen audience, who liked their music powerful and driving with little regard to commercial subtleties. With hit after hit on the local charts (and influencing every local band that ever took the stage), the band inexplicably was never able to break out nationally, leaving their sound largely undiluted for mass consumption.

Breaking up in the late 60s (after one ill-fated album attempt to water down their style for national attention), the Sonics continue today to be revered by 60s collectors the world over for their unique brand of rock & roll raunch. –CK

○ **Here Are the Ultimate Sonics / ETIQUETTE**
Combining all the tracks from their first two Etiquette albums, three tracks from the label's Christmas album, live tracks, and an alternate take of "The Witch," this compilation more than lives up to its title. The definitive overview. –CK

SONNY & CHER

Pop. Sonny & Cher proved one of the magical musical combinations of the 60s, with their wisecracking repartee providing counterpoint to a series of adoring hit duets. Sonny Bono (b Feb 16, 1935) started out at Los Angeles-based Specialty Records as a songwriter in the late 50s. While working sessions with legendary producer Phil Spector, Bono met and married background singer Cher (born Cherilyn Lapierre, May 20, 1946) and formed a duet with his new wife. Neither was blessed with an outstanding vocal range, but no matter — they went gold in 1965 with the pop chart-topper "I Got You Babe" on Atco and did well with "Baby Don't Go" on Reprise. At the same time, both enjoyed success separately — Sonny with "Laugh at Me" for Atco, Cher with "All I Really Want to Do" and "Bang Bang (My Baby Shot Me Down)" on Imperial. "The Beat Goes On" in 1967 and "All I Ever Need Is You" four years later presaged the pair's anointment as popular TV variety-hour hosts from 1971 to 1974 (the year they were divorced). Since then, Cher has gone on to mega-stardom on record and on the silver screen. Sonny, meanwhile, was elected mayor of Palm Springs, CA. –BD

○ **The Beat Goes On / ATCO**   1975
They were the ultimate "hip luv" couple of the 60s and their many hits are still fun to listen to. "I Got You Babe," "Laugh at Me," and the title track are three of the 21 original recordings included on this definitive collection. –JT

SOUL ASYLUM

Alternative rock, rock & roll. Loud, proud, and ready to kick out numerous jams, Soul Asylum didn't get the press of their Minneapolis contemporaries (i.e., Hüsker Dü and the Replacements) but they are worthy to stand in that company. Screamingly good pop, smart songwriting, and an unself-conscious attitude that's easy to love. –JD

Made to Be Broken / TWINTONE   1986
Early Soul Asylum blitzkreig-raunch at its best. Sure, it sounds a little like Hüsker Dü. But only a little. –JD

Clam Dip and Other Delights / TWINTONE   1989
A great EP with a very funny cover. Loud, fun, and funky. –JD

○ **Hang Time / A&M**   1989
More of a riff record than usual, this is the strongest collection of Dave Pirner songs in one place. Lenny Kaye's production does a good job of translating the roar of Pirner and lead guitarist Dan Murphy to tape. A great place to start. –JD

● **And the Horse They Rode On / POLYGRAM-A&M**   1990
Thanks to Steve Jordan's live production approach and some great material, *And the Horse They Rode On* is this Minneapolis quartet's best effort. Among this album's many highlights are "Veil of Tears" (a nice Stones riff), the spastic hyper-drive of "Spinnin'," the ugly funk of "Something Out of Nothing," and the dynamic rocker "Nice Guys (Don't Get Paid)." –RC

SOUL CHILDREN

R&B, soul. This mixed vocal group was formed by Isaac Hayes and David Porter (songwriters and producers) in Memphis in 1968. –RP

Friction / STAX   1974
Seven cheating songs with long raps and adult lyrics. –RP

○ **Chronicle / STAX**   1979

A best-of collection from 1968 to 1978. Every track is an R&B hit. –RP

Soul Children/Genesis / STAX   1990
Great value on this import reissue of two original albums. –RP

SOUL II SOUL

Urban R&B. The best of the current pack of British retro-soul groups, Soul II Soul (led by DJ, producer, and vocalist Jazzie B) blends elements of 70s Motown and Philly soul with the easy-groove approach favored by Loose Ends and the incessant thump of Chicago house music. –JF

Keep On Movin' / VIRGIN   1988
The group's debut (originally titled *Club Classics Vol. One* in Europe) contains their finest single, "Keep On Movin'," and "Back to Life" but is padded by stilted raps and plodding beat fodder. –JF

○ **Vol. II: 1990 - A New Decade / VIRGIN**   1990
A better album but a deceptive one: even the best songs here don't intoxicate as thoroughly as "Keep On Movin'," but within the context of the album itself, each plays a vital part. In other words, this is a genuine *album*, and not a pastiche of singles. –JF

SOUNDGARDEN

Heavy metal. One of the strange things about the Seattle sound is none of the bands are actually very similar in style. Soundgarden, Pearl Jam/Mother Love Bone, Mudhoney, and Nirvana all sound grungy and have recorded on the Sub Pop label, but they play quite differently. What distinguishes Soundgarden is their tempo — a slow, churning, hypnotic grind. Chris Cornell shrieks above the heavy 70s-style metal guitar played by Kim Thayil over the methodical groove of Hiro Yamamoto's bass and Matt Cameron's drumming — as if Robert Plant fronted a Black Sabbath with a more rhythmic kick. On the strength of the cult following they had gained from a series of independent releases, Soundgarden signed with A&M, releasing the moderately successful *Louder than Love* in 1989. 1991 brought the release of *Badmotorfinger*, an excellent album, which sold respectably yet had its thunder stolen by the astonishing success of Nirvana's *Nevermind*. –STE

Ultramega OK / SST   1988
A noticeable improvement from their EPs, Soundgarden's first full-length release is an impressive mixture of slow Zeppelin/Sabbath-style riffs updated for a new generation with even more murkiness. Cornell's vocals can be irritatingly overblown and the band can be unfocused (hear their cover of Howlin' Wolf's "Smokestack Lightning"), but the whole thing sounds fresh. –STE

Louder Than Love / A&M   1989
The first major-label release from Soundgarden is a step down from the independent *Ultramega OK*, as Thayil's guitar drowns in the murkiness of the production that Cornell tries to bellow through. It's uneven, but there are some staple Soundgarden songs that are among their best, including "Full on Kevin's Mom," "Hands All Over," "Ugly Truth," and the extraordinarily stupid "Big Dumb Sex." –STE

Screaming Life / Fopp / SUB POP   1990
A reissue of two early (1987 and 1988) EPs, which capture the band in its formative stages. Worth any true fan's time. –STE

○ **Badmotorfinger / A&M**   1991
Soundgarden's most accessible and accomplished album captures the band stretching out and successfully experimenting. Unlike those on the previous *Louder Than Love*, the songs have varied tempos and textures, along with memorable riffs. With Cornell singing better than he ever has on a Soundgarden album, the band has delivered a set of songs that now stands as their signature statement. –STE

THE SOUP DRAGONS

Alternative rock. This Scottish quartet released its debut album in 1986. Initially heavily influenced by the Buzzcocks, by 1990 the band moved toward the dance-club sound. –DS

○ **Hang-Ten! / WARNER**   1986
Raw, fast, punkish pop that is propelled by the twin guitars of Jim McCulloch and Sean Dickson, who also doubled as vocalist. –DS

Lovegod / POLYGRAM   1990
Psychedelicized dance music, which includes the hit remake of the Rolling Stones' "I'm Free." –DS

JOE SOUTH   ♭ 1940

Singer/songwriter, pop. By the time Joe South hit as a solo artist, he had become a veritable jack-of-all trades, being a country DJ and an in-demand session guitar player, providing electric guitar for Simon & Garfunkel's hit "Sounds of Silence." As a producer, he produced Billy Joe Royal, who scored with two South compositions, "Down in the Boondocks" (#9) and "I Knew You When" (#14). South also penned "Hush," a #52 hit for Royal and a #4 hit for the British band Deep Purple.
South signed to Capitol Records in 1968 and released his debut, *Introspect* (#117), with the single "Birds of a Feather." It didn't chart but earned a #23 hit for the Raiders. The second single off of that album, "Games People Play" (#12), was his first big solo hit, and it established South as a rather preachy straight-talking Southern artist. His followup singles were "Walk a Mile in My Shoes" (#12), "Don't It Make You Want to Go Home" (#41), and "Fool Me" (#78).
In 1971 South had his greatest songwriting success when country singer Lynn Anderson landed a worldwide million-selling hit with "Rose Garden" (#3), which Elvis Presley and many other artists recorded as well. Except for a few relatively obscure mid-70s solo albums, South dropped out and hasn't been heard from since. –RC

Best Of Joe South / RHINO   1990
Contains all his late-60s pop gems, including "Games People Play" and "Walk a Mile in My Shoes." –DH

JOHN DAVID SOUTHER   ♭ 1946

Singer/songwriter. This Detroit-born songwriter, singer, and guitarist is best known for the cover versions of his songs found on Linda Ronstadt albums and his hit co-compositions with members of the Eagles ("Best of My Love," "New Kid in Town," "Heartache Tonight"). Also a member of the Souther, Hillman, Furay Band in the mid 70s. –WR

John David Souther / ELEKTRA   1972
It may be that the only thing that kept Souther from becoming a major star in the 70s was that his friends the Eagles beat him to the country-rock style demonstrated on this album, which features "The Fast One" and "Run like a Thief," both recorded by Linda Ronstadt. –WR

○ **Black Rose / ELEKTRA**   1976
Excellent album steeped in the Southern California country-rock sound of the 70s, with all the usual suspects (Danny Kortchmar, Waddy Wachtel, Kenny Edwards, and Russ Kunkel, and producer Peter Asher — all Ronstadt veterans — plus Glenn Frey and Don Henley from the Eagles) in place on such songs as "Faithless Love," "Simple Man, Simple Dream," and "Silver Blue." –WR

You're Only Lonely / CBS   1979
Souther finally scored a hit single with the 50s-ish title track, and the album also includes such lovely ballads as "White Rhythm and Blues," as well as the solo version of the Souther, Hillman, Furay song "Trouble in Paradise." –WR

SOUTHSIDE JOHNNY & THE ASBURY JUKES

Rock & roll. A ragtag collection of Jersey-shore bar-band vets led by harmonica-playing, late night-voiced "Southside" Johnny Lyon. The Jukes coalesced under the direction, production, and songwriting assistance of Miami Steve Van Zandt and Bruce Springsteen and churned out a string of superb albums that merged horn-driven R&B raveups with

strong original material. Some seldom-heard Springsteen-written chestnuts show up on the Jukes's albums, including "The Fever," "Love on the Wrong Side of Town," "When You Dance," and the ravishing "Hearts of Stone." The group fell apart when guitarist Billy Rush left, but then re-formed for a stunning comeback album, *Better Days.* –KK

I Don't Want to Go Home / CBS   1976
The Jukes's debut and an R&B revivalist's delight, capped by splendid duets with Lee Dorsey ("How Come You Treat Me So Bad?") and Ronnie Spector ("You Mean So Much to Me"). –KK

This Time It's for Real / CBS / BB 85   1977
Southside Johnny's sophomore release was another strong collection of early-60s R&B- and doo-wop-influenced rock/pop. To underscore those elements, *This Time It's for Real* features guest appearances by the Drifters, the Coasters, and the Five Satins. Highlights include "Without Love," "Love on the Wrong Side of Town," and the title track. –RC

Hearts of Stone / CBS   1978
The most successful merger of old R&B with modern songwriting and sensibilities in the Jukes's catalog. "Hearts of Stone" features more great Van Zandt originals ("Got to Be a Better Way Home," "This Time Baby's Gone for Good") and Springsteen's knockout title tune. –KK

● **Having a Party / EPIC**
The highlights of this New Jersey band's first few albums, plus a fine remake of Sam Cooke's "Having a Party." It's a great starting place for the uninitiated. –RC

○ **Better Days / MCA**   1991
A comeback album that by all rights shouldn't be this good, "Better Days" reunites Southside Johnny with his old cohorts Springsteen and Van Zandt and some special guests (Jon Bon Jovi, Flo and Eddie) for 11 bittersweet originals capped by the gorgeous soul ballad "It's Been a Long Time." –KK

SPANDAU BALLET

Dance-pop. This British dance-pop group was part of the "new romantic" wave of the early 80s, scoring several hits with uptempo, synth-drenched balldas. –ED

○ **Singles Collection / CHRYSALIS**   1985
Traces the group's development from the melodramatic, "new-romantic" dance-pop style of "To Cut a Long Story Short" to the lush ballad "True." Spandau Ballet always went in for big effects, but they became more subtle as they went along. –WR

SPANIC BOYS

Roots-rock. Spanic Boys are a father/son duo from Milwaukee who specialize in driving roots-rock, with an alien Everly Brothers-influenced vocal harmony sound. –RC

○ **Spanic Boys / ROUNDER**   1990
Good collection of rockabilly-based, 50s-style rock. –DS

Strange World / ROUNDER   1991
More rockin' rawness from Milwaukee's finest. –DS

SPANKY & OUR GANG

Pop. Sort of a poor man's Mamas & Papas, Elaine "Spanky" McFarlane and her bandmates hit the heights of the charts in the late 60s with pop/folk/rock radio-ready tunes like "Sunday Will Never Be the Same," "Like to Get to Know You," and "Lazy Day." Being true folkies at heart, the group had a major protest song, "Give a Damn," that was banned on many radio stations. After breaking up in the early 70s (and briefly reuniting in 1975), McFarlane became a in-demand backup singer, working with many stars, including Roger McGuinn. Now, she is a member of the touring-only Mamas & Papas, where she fills the musical void left by Mama Cass Elliott. –JJ

○ **Best of Spanky & Our Gang / RHINO**
A good collection of their pop hits, including "Sunday Will Never Be the Same," "Lazy Day," and "Like to Get to Know You." –ED

SPARKLETONES

Rockabilly. Five 16-year olds from Spartanburg, SC, the Sparkletones were one of the finest rockabilly acts ever to record. Mostly their style was fast and spirited, with a frenetic energy that made most of the competition (even Elvis) seem geriatric by comparison. Singer and guitarist Joe Bennett's "Black Slacks" remains their defining song, but everything they did was worthwhile. –BE

○ **Black Slacks / MCA**
This topflight collection does not contain everything, but the ten best songs this rockabilly quintet left behind are here. As fine as any Elvis collection of 1956. (Out of print) –BE

SPARKS

Rock/pop. An American pop-rock group led by two brothers Ron (keyboards) and Russell Mael (vocals), with varying backup. They were especially popular in the mid 70s in England, where the singles "This Town Ain't Big Enough for Both of Us," "Amateur Hour," and "Beat the Clock," and the albums *Kimono My House* and *Propaganda* all hit the Top Ten. –WR

○ **Kimono My House / ISLAND** 1974
Sparks specializes in keyboard-based pop songs with clever, ironic lyrics (by Ron Mael), sung in a near-falsetto by Russell Mael. Examples include "Here in Heaven" (in which a disappointed, dead Romeo sings to a still-living Juliet who "broke our little pact"), "Thank God It's Not Christmas," and the UK hits "This Town Ain't Big Enough for Both of Us" and "Amateur Hour." –WR

Propaganda / ISLAND 1974
More of Ron's wit ("Don't Leave Me Alone with Her," "Who Don't Like Kids") and Russell's operatic singing with catchy rock backings, though it's hard to get the jokes without the lyric sheet. –WR

Number One In Heaven / ELEKTRA 1979
After flirting with hard rock, Sparks turned to disco producer Giorgio Moroder and scored three UK hits, "Tryouts for the Human Race," "Beat the Clock," and "The No. 1 Song in Heaven," all in an aggressive electro-dance rock style. –WR

Angst in My Pants / ATLANTIC 1982
Sparks turns to power-pop and scores their first US singles chart entry with the hilarious "I Predict" on an album that also includes such novelties as "Eaten by the Monster of Love." –WR

Sparks in Outer Space / ATLANTIC 1983
"Cool Places," an uptempo duet with ex-Go-Go Jane Wiedlin (and #49 hit) paces this collection, perhaps Sparks's biggest US seller. –WR

THE SPECIALS

Ska-revival. Jerry Dammers and the Specials kicked off the 2-Tone fad in late-70s England, where the hyperactive bounce of bluebeat met the energy and concise punch of punk. Their influence was widespread and culturally significant, in that most of the bands on Dammer's 2-Tone label (including the Specials) were racially mixed. –JF

The Specials / CHRYSALIS 1979
Mixing stinging political fury with rambunctious dance rhythms, their debut is a delight for activists and dance fiends. –JF

○ **Singles Collection / CAPITOL** 1991
This rounds up some choice material from the otherwise patchy followups. "Ghost Town" is their best song and "Free Nelson Mandela" comes close. –JF

BENNY SPELLMAN ♭1938

R&B, soul. New Orleans R&B vocalist. His deep bass voice booms through loud and clear on many early-60s Allen Toussaint productions, but Benny Spellman enjoyed a major hit of his own in 1962, "Lipstick Traces (On a Cigarette)."

Spellman spent some time with Huey "Piano" Smith and the Clowns before signing with Minit, where Toussaint utilized his deep pipes to full advantage as a backing vocalist behind Ernie K-Doe on "Mother-in-Law" and countless others. The Rolling Stones covered "Fortune Teller," the flip-side of this hit. Spellman recorded through much of the 60s, his "Word Game" turning up on Atlantic in 1965, before he took a day gig as a beer salesman. –BD

○ **Fortune Teller / COLLECTABLES**
Infectious and influential early-60s New Orleans R&B. Spellman's low-pitched vocals, perfectly produced by pianist Allen Toussaint. –BD

ALEXANDER SPENCE ♭1946

Singer/songwriter, psychedelic. The former drummer of the Jefferson Airplane and ex-guitarist from Moby Grape (and key songwriter for both) recorded his one-and-only solo album after a near-breakdown in 1969. –BE

○ **Oar / CBS** 1969
An odd but compelling mixture of blues, folk, and psychedelic influences, rather like a cross between the Band and Syd Barrett. –BE

THE SPINNERS

Doo-wop, soul, disco. There were plenty of Philly-soul groups that were as good as the Spinners, but none of them were better. They never cut anything as searing as the O'Jays's "For the Love of Money"; Teddy Pendergrass brought more eroticism to the hits of the Blue Notes; and they never matched the breathy, helium croon of the Stylistics's Russell Tompkins. What the Spinners and producer Thom Bell did was consolidate the best elements of Philly-soul into a hit-making machine that could be as topical ("Ghetto Child"), romantic ("Could It Be I'm Falling in Love"), and blistering ("I'm Coming Home") as anything Gamble and Huff ever whipped up for Eddie LeVert and Teddy Pendergrass. And Spinners lead vocalist Philippe Wynne had a voice that damn near outflanked anyone for versatility and sheer gospel slow-burn; think of him as soul's answer to Claude Jeter, with the mental imbalance of James Carr.

The group didn't last as long as their slick-soul contemporaries: Wynne left the fold in 1977 and they never found a suitable replacement. (Wynne died of a heart attack in 1984 while performing in San Francisco.) Most of their work is still in print, and urban stations regularly program the hits from the Spinners's glory years. If you think pure soul singing died in the 60s (and some people do), a session with the Spinners should change your mind. –JF

☆ **A One of a Kind Love Affair ... / ATLANTIC** 1991
Spanning from their first single, "That's What Girls Are Made For" in 1961, to their last charting single more than twenty years later, *One of a Kind Love Affair - The Anthology* is the definitive collection of the Spinners. The bulk of the 2-CD compilation is the Spinners's work with Thom Bell during the mid 70s, easily the best work they ever recorded and arguably the finest Philly-soul singles. All of the Spinners's major hits are here, as are excellent, informative liner notes (including complete personnel, discography). –STE

SPIRIT

Rock/pop, psychedelic. Of all the unusual musical groups that graced the West Coast in the late 60s, Spirit (formed in 1967) was certainly one of the most peculiar, both visually and musically. At a time when psychedelic music was in its most dissonant and disorganized state, the band performed elegantly quirky music with a kind of disciplined restraint. Except for the band's biggest hit, "I Got a Line on You" (#25), from *The Family That Plays Together* (#22), Spirit never really was a rock band in the usual sense; rather they were an ensemble of musical iconoclasts who sometimes embraced rock's abandon. The unique sustain-drenched lead-work of Randy California (b Randy Wolfe, Feb 20, 1951) and the forcefully melodic percussion playing of his stepfather Ed Cassidy (b May 4, 1931) were readily identifiable signatures for Spirit's ambient fusion of jazz, rock, and folk. –RC

Spirit / EDSEL / BB 31   1968
This is a strong debut by this quartet, featuring "Fresh Garbage," "Elijah," "Mechanical World," and "Uncle Jack." (Import). –RC

○ **Family That Plays Together / EDSEL / BB 22**   1969
Lou Adler's unusual production, coupled with Marty Paich's ethereal orchestrations, on songs like "Aren't You Glad," "It Shall Be," "Poor Richard," and "Silky Sam" gave Spirit's music a quality of icy distance. The only other band that comes to mind who employed such otherworldly arrangements was Love, with their masterful *Forever Changes*. This is a wonderful album worth getting. (Import) –RC

Clear Spirit / EDSEL / BB 55   1969
Previous to the recording of this album, Spirit had been working on music for a soundtrack for the movie *The Model Shop. Clear* reflected that effort with an odd blend of off-the-wall (occasionally goofy-sounding) rock-influenced songs and strangely sparse instrumentals (with titles like "Ice" and "Clear"). Highlights include "Dark Eyed Woman" (#118), "Policeman's Ball," "Give a Life, Take a Life" and "New Dope in Town." (Import). –RC

○ **12 Dreams of Dr Sardonicus / EPIC / BB 63**   1971
One of Spirit's most successful albums, containing "Nature's Way" (#111), "Mr. Skin" (#92), "Animal Zoo" (#97), and "Nothin' to Hide." (Also available as a Mobile Fidelity Ultradisc) –RC

★ **Time Circle (1968-1972) / COLUMBIA**   1991
A generous helping of practically everything Spirit accomplished in their years on Lou Adler's Ode Records and Epic Records. The collection is sonically satisfactory (although the Mobile Fidelity version of *Dr. Sardonicus* sound stronger), and there are generous, informative liner notes. –RC

SPLIT ENZ

New-wave, alternative pop. This New Zealand art-rock (and later synth-pop) band was formed in 1972 by art student and guitarist Phil Judd and singer/keyboardist Tim Finn. Their stylistic influences seem to include Roxy Music, Genesis, and the post-*Sgt. Pepper* Beatles. They were known for their wild costumes and haircuts as much as for their eccentric blend of British dancehall and rock music. After Phil Judd left the band in 1977, he was replaced by Tim's younger brother Neil, and the Finn brothers took the band in a more commercial direction. Pleasing melodic pop with some still-lingering offbeat impulses made their middle-period albums enjoyable. Neil's budding songwriting talent garnered attention with the pop hit "I Got You" from the 1979 *True Colours* album (also the world's first laser-etched album, whose surface is covered with prismatic designs). He went on to write several of the band's better-known hits like "One Step Ahead" and "History Never Repeats," but the band never received much chart success. Tim left for a solo career in 1983, and Neil carried on for one more album before disbanding the Enz and forming the trio Crowded House. –SWB

True Colours / A&M   1980
This New Zealand band's most cohesive pop statement, and their most successful American release. Clever pop songs with synthesizer textures. Neil Finn comes into his own as a writer in his brother's band. –SWB

○ **History Never Repeats (Best Of Split Enz) / A&M** 1987
All the best songs from their American albums are here, although many other great songs can be found on their import CDs. A good place to get acquainted with the band; the fans already have the albums. –SWB

SPOOKY TOOTH

Blues/rock, hard rock. Few bands in the late 60s rivaled England's Spooky Tooth for delivering bone-breaking heavy-

metal blues. Fronted by two fine blues-influenced lead singers, Gary Wright and Mike Harrison, and sparked by the lyrical crunch of lead guitarist Luther Grosvenor, Spooky Tooth produced a couple of great albums in *Spooky Two* (#44) and *The Last Puff* (#84). Wright split in 1970 after the horrible experimental-music effort *Ceremony* and went on to a briefly successful solo career with *Dream Weaver*. –RC

○ **Spooky Two / A&M**   1969
Their best album, includes the definitive "Evil Woman." With organist Gary Wright. –MGN

DUSTY SPRINGFIELD   b 1939

Soul, pop. The greatest female soul singer to come out of England's beat boom, Dusty Springfield (born Mary O'Brien) started with the folk trio, the Springfields, before going solo. With a big, powerful voice and a passionate full-bodied delivery, she was an overwhelming musical presence during the mid 60s and even held her own on stage with the best of Motown's acts. Her later material veered toward pop, but in 1970 she cut the classic White soul album *Dusty in Memphis*. –BE

Golden Hits / POLYGRAM   1966
A fair representation of her mid-60s hits, with major gaps. The imported CDs are preferable. –BE

☆ **Dusty in Memphis / RHINO-ATLANTIC**   1969
A sultry, subtle, soulful classic, key in any collection. –BE

● **The Silver Collection / PHILIPS**   1988
Twenty-four songs, encompassing her British and American chart history for the 60s. Superb sound. –BE

BRUCE SPRINGSTEEN   b 1949

Rock & roll, singer/songwriter. It could be argued that Bruce Springsteen has never made a wrong artistic move. His spirit is embedded in rock traditions that are as varied as singles on a jukebox: Woody Guthrie, Chuck Berry, Elvis, Buddy Holly, Phil Spector, Bob Dylan, the Rolling Stones — the bedrock of rock history. From his first album in 1973 up to 1987's *Tunnel of Love*, Springsteen has continually improved, tightening his strengths, growing with his vision, and proudly proclaiming a sense of purpose that's nearly unrivaled in rock.
He established a set of characters on his first two albums who grappled with the pain of adolescence, the reluctance to embrace adulthood, and the conflicting emotions of heartache and romance. But instead of succumbing to eternal adolescence, he let those characters grow and become adults who faced the grime and ecstasy of their lives in admirably uncompromising terms, all of which are realistic and fascinating, all of them outgrowths of the complexities of his own personality, and all of them unique in the pantheon of rock drama.
He treats his women with compassion and charity; his men try to maintain honor in a society bereft of that concept; and the settings in which they are placed reflect Springsteen's awareness of and contempt for an America that chews up and spits out its working class without care or concern. That he's managed to do this consistently without any lapse in quality or sureness of vision is remarkable. That he's done it without becoming a chest-thumping agit-pop irritant, but rather a performer whose concerts and albums are cathartic celebrations of ecstasy and release, is reason enough to call him the greatest American rocker of the last two decades. –JF

Greetings from Asbury Park NJ / CBS   1973
The songs, laced with Dylanistic wordplay, are gorgeous street vignettes fused with romance, idealism, and a true sense of wonder. –JF

The Wild, the Innocent ... / CBS   1973
The Wild, the Innocent & the E Street Shuffle is a subtle masterpiece. The grooves are tougher, revealing the R&B heart that *Greeting from Asbury Park* stifled, and the songs are long enough to let him develop his characters and their situations. –JF

☆ **Born to Run / CBS** 1975
A bombastic masterpiece. His breakthrough is a testament not only to the sound of Phil Spector's 60s hits, but to the romanticism, the longing, and the determination of those hits. The title cut and "Thunder Road" are anthems that deserve that status. –JF

☆ **Darkness on the Edge of Town / CBS** 1978
The flip side of *Born to Run*. The idealism of those characters turns into stark terror once they hit adulthood. This is where Springsteen's reputation as a working-class mouthpiece is based, but there's much more here than that. –JF

★ **The River / CBS** 1980
In many ways his best album, balancing the dashed dreams of *Darkness on the Edge of Town* with the hope of *Born to Run*, but it trades the Spectorian wallop for a taut, frat-rock sound that is alternately wiry, delicate, and full-blown. –JF

☆ **Nebraska / CBS** 1982
A set of acoustic demos offering ravaged tales of despair, defeat, and defiance. –JF

☆ **Born in the U.S.A. / CBS** 1984
The album that pushed him into superstar status ironically examines the dirty underbelly of America in both political and domestic terms. The big, catchy, hard-slamming rock & roll that carries the lyrics only adds to the irony. –JF

○ **Live 1975-1985 / CBS** 1986
A career-defining three-disc live collection. Among the three or four greatest boxed sets ever issued. –JF

☆ **Tunnel of Love / CBS** 1987
A moody and dark inquiry, which asks why people fall in love, why they get married, why they lose faith in the people closest to them, and why they even bother. Required listening for anyone contemplating the altar. –JF

Chimes of Freedom / CBS 1988
A four-song live EP from his 1988 tour, which includes a riveting version of Dylan's "Chimes of Freedom" and an acoustic rendering of "Born to Run." –JF

☆ **Human Touch / CBS** 1992
☆ **Lucky Town / CBS** 1992
Because they failed to repeat the massive success of *Born in the USA*, and because they eschewed the working-class posturing of his most famous work, many critics claimed *Human Touch* and *Lucky Town* offered proof that Springsteen had lost his creative foothold. Nothing could be further from the truth. Rather than letting a cast of desolate losers and struggling optimists do his talking, Springsteen forced *himself* to do it. They're both strikingly personal and confessional albums that analyze the difficulties of making commitments, the necessity of making those commitments. *Human Touch*, his first proper recording without the E Street Band, continues the conversation started on *Tunnel of Love* through the pleading urgency of "Soul Driver" and the forthright admissions on "Real World." Musically, the set balances E Street retreads ("Roll of the Dice," "All or Nothin' at All") with taut soul grooves and slashing hard rock, emphasizing Springsteen's astonishing guitar playing. *Lucky Town*, recorded chiefly by Springsteen, with occasional assistance from E Street keyboardist Roy Bittan, is the thematic antithesis of Dylan's *Blood on the Tracks*, an album devoted to the requisiteness of love and romance and how empty lives are without that love and romance. *Lucky Town* offers living proof that Bruce Springsteen's grappling with domestic bliss and superstardom is just as enlightening as his struggle to attain them. –JF

SQUEEZE

Rock/pop. Squeeze is a British pop-rock quintet that serves as a forum for the songs of its lead singer Glenn Tilbrook (b Aug 31, 1957) and his partner, guitarist Chris Difford. The duo formed Squeeze in 1974 with keyboardist Jools Holland (b Jan 24, 1958) whose bubbly personality made him a natural

frontman, bassist Harry Kakouli (replaced by John Bentley after the first album), and drummer Gilson Lavis (b Jun 27, 1951). They reached the UK Top 20 in 1978 with the single "Take Me I'm Yours," but really broke through the following year, when their second album, *Cool for Cats*, produced two UK Top Ten hits in the title track and the Difford-sung "Up the Junction." *Argybargy*, their third album, was a moderate success in 1980 (and their first US chart entry), but their next milestone came in 1981 with *East Side Story*, an album for which Holland was replaced by former Ace lead singer Paul Carrack (b Apr 22, 1951), who sang lead on "Tempted," Squeeze's first US chart single. The album, which hit the UK Top 20, also featured a #4 British hit, "Labelled with Love." As it turned out, Carrack left after the one album, replaced by Don Snow (b Jan 13, 1957) for *Sweets for a Stranger*, after which Squeeze disbanded. They re-formed in 1985 with Tilbrook, Difford, Holland, and Lavis, plus Keith Wilkinson on bass, to release *Cosi Fan Tutti Frutti* and then, in 1987, *Babylon and On*, which featured "Hourglass," a Top 20 hit on both sides of the Atlantic. *Frank* came out in 1989, followed in 1990 with the live album *A Round and a Bout*, which finished Squeeze's contract with A&M. They then signed to Warner Bros. and released *Play* in 1991. –WR

Argybargy / A&M 1980
Upbeat, cleverly crafted pop-rock with decidely British themes. Tilbrook's guitar work and Jools Holland's keyboards shine as Squeeze moves from being pub-rockers to critics' darlings. –SWB

○ **East Side Story / A&M** 1981
Their US breakthrough album featured the hit "Tempted," sung and written by Paul Carrack (of the 70s band Ace), who was Squeeze's keyboardist for this one album. This is the album that sparked the comparisons of Difford/Tilbrook to Lennon/McCartney. A broader pop style with classical overtones and a country influence courtesy of producers Elvis Costello and Dave Edmunds. Great songs. –SWB

○ **Singles 45 & Under / A&M** 1982
Twelve early Squeeze singles and one non-album track ("Annie Get Your Gun"). This is classic Squeeze, the songs that made them. Includes "Tempted," "Black Coffee in Bed," and "Another Nail for My Heart." –SWB

Sweets from a Stranger / A&M 1982
Still riding high on the success of *East Side Story*, Squeeze continues to write perky, upbeat tunes, but with the blue-eyed soul influence of the quickly departed Paul Carrack, they begin their move away from their classic sound. The hit "Black Coffee in Bed" sounds amazingly like a Paul Carrack song, perhaps an attempt to duplicate the success of Carrack's "Tempted." –SWB

○ **Cosi Fan Tutti Frutti / A&M** 1985
After *Sweets from a Stranger* and the Difford/Tilbrook solo effort, this re-formed Squeeze (with Jools Holland returning on keyboards) makes a move in another direction, with a less overt soul influence. High pop-craft and experimentation. Laurie Latham's technicolor/cinerama production makes this their most glossy album. Keith Wilkinson takes over on bass. –SWB

● **Classics - Vol. 25 / A&M** 1987
A 19-cut sampler of their 1978-1987 work, and the 25th CD in A&M's 25th anniversary reissue of the best material on the label. Six cuts overlap with the *Singles 45 & Under* package, but the other 13 tracks make this a worthwhile companion for those not up to buying the original albums. At 72+ minutes, this is a bargain. –SWB

Babylon and On / A&M 1987
Yet another step back to their classic sound, this time rewarded with minor chart success. Squeeze regains their drive and perkiness, firing on all cylinders. –SWB

BILLY SQUIER b 1950

Hard rock, rock/pop. This hard-rock guitarist played with Jimi

Hendrix and Johnny Winter early in his career. Billy Squier joined the Sidewinders in 1973 and later started Piper; he went solo in 1979 and scored his biggest hit, "Rock Me Tonight" in 1984. –BC

○ **Don't Say No / CAPITOL**   1981
Far and away the most consistent and solid work from this hard-rock singer/songwriter and guitarist. This studio-polished debut plays like a greatest-hits album. Includes "In the Dark," "The Stroke," and "Lonely Is the Night." –DDC

CHRIS SQUIRE   ♭1948

Prog-rock. Bassist and a cofounder of Yes, with an original and very distinctive style on his instrument, Squire may have the greatest critical respect of any of his fellow Yes men. He hasn't pursued his solo career as aggressively as Steve Howe or Jon Anderson, but he does have a single album of his own to his credit. –BE

○ **Fish Out of Water / ATLANTIC**   1975
Almost a lost Yes album, with more expressive lyrics than the band is known for. Tasteful orchestrations and guitar/bass playing by Squire which is superb much of the time, with (surprise!) an underproduced feel. (Import) –BE

SQUIRREL BAIT

Thrash. Sadly defunct thrash-pop band from Louisville, KY, Squirrel Bait (especially lead singer Peter Searcy) sounded a bit like the Replacements only with the throttle *always* to the floor. As they got older they tempered their assault (sigh, don't we all), but they continued to make good records. –JD

○ **Squirrel Bait/Skag Heaven / HOMESTEAD**
All of their work on compact disc. Hüsker Dü/Replacements-inspired, you bet. But this is still great, if overlooked and too-soon forgotten indie-pop. –JD

THE SQUIRRELS

Power-pop. Focused around Rob Morgan of the Seattle group Young Fresh Fellows, their inspired ransackings of oddball pop songs and goofy originals are a great antidote for those who think pop & roll is overdue for a healthy dose of irreverence. Jonathon Auer of the Posies provides production and engineering support. –RC

○ **What Gives? / PLANET**   1987
Seattle trash-pop renegades plunder everything from the gospel standard "We Are One in the Spirit" and the Buoys's horrendous ode to cannibalism ("Timothy"), to Gilbert O'Sullivan's fluffy "Get Down" and the Mindbenders's "Game of Love." Bill Withers's "Lean on Me" is given an inspired death-rock plundering. Jon Auer aids in the inspired goofiness. *Mad Magazine* rock. –RC

THE STANDELLS

Rock & roll. A 60s Los Angeles-based rock group. The Standells had the greasy garage-band sound down to perfection, and their pounding ode to Boston's "Dirty Water" was a huge hit in 1966. Prior to hitting national playlists, the band had recorded for MGM and Liberty and appeared in the 1964 movie *Get Yourself a College Girl.* Signed to Capitol's Tower subsidiary, drummer Dick Dodd's snarling vocal and pounding backbeat made "Dirty Water" (produced by Ed Cobb of the Four Preps, who were about as far opposed to the Standells' approach as could possibly be), their top-seller. Three subsequent 1966-1967 Standells singles also charted, but the quartet fell apart before the end of the decade. –BD

○ **Best of the Standells / RHINO**
Most 60s punk bands could barely fill an album side with decent material. This 18-song compilation is a tribute to the vitality of the Standells's raunch-and-roll attack, including not only their one hit ("Dirty Water") but salacious essentials ranging from the swaggering "Sometimes Good Guys Don't Wear White" to the horny wail of "Barracuda." –JF

LISA STANSFIELD   ♭1965

Dance-pop. A retro-disco British diva who brought sweet 70s soul back to American charts with her huge first hit, "All Around the World," from 1990. –JF

○ **Affection / ARISTA**   1989
Stansfield's voice serves this retro-disco material extremely well, best exemplified by the hits "All around the World" and "You Can't Deny It." An impressive debut. –STE

Real Love / ARISTA   1991
Another strong effort from Stansfield. –STE

THE STAPLE SINGERS

Soul. The Staple's story goes all the way back to Winona, MS, in 1915. It was then and there that patriarch Roebuck Staples entered the world. A contemporary and familiar of Charley Patton, Roebuck quickly became adept as a solo blues guitarist, entertaining at local dances and picnics. Gradually drawn to the church, by 1937 he was singing and playing guitar with a spiritual group based out of Drew, MS, the Golden Trumpets. Moving to Chicago four years later, he continued playing gospel music with the Windy City's Trumpet Jubilees. A decade later Pops Staples (as he had become known) presented two of his daughters, Cleotha and Mavis, and his one son, Pervis, in front of a church audience, and the Staple Singers were born.

The Staples recorded in an older, slightly archaic, deeply Southern spiritual style first for United and then for Vee Jay. Pops and Mavis Staples shared lead vocal chores, with most records underpinned by Pops's heavily reverbed Mississippi cottonpatch guitar. In 1960 the Staples signed with Riverside, a label that specialized in jazz and folk. With Riverside and later Epic, the Staples attempted to move into the then-burgeoning White folk boom. Two Epic releases, "Why (Am I Treated So Bad)" and a cover of Stephen Stills's "For What It's Worth," briefly graced the pop charts in 1967.

In 1968 the Staples signed with Memphis-based Stax. The first two albums, *Soul Folk in Action* and *We'll Get Over*, were produced by Steve Cropper and backed by Booker T and the MG's. The Staples were now singing entirely contemporary "message" songs such as "Long Walk to D.C." and "When Will We Be Paid." In 1970 Pervis Staples left, and was replaced by sister Yvonne Staples. Even more significantly, Al Bell took over production chores. Bell took them down the road to Muscle Shoals, and things got decidedly funky. Starting with "Heavy Makes You Happy (Sha-Na-Boom Boom)" and "I'll Take You There," the Staples counted 12 chart hits at Stax. When Stax encountered financial problems, Curtis Mayfield signed the Staples to his Curtom label and produced a #1 hit in "Let's Do It Again." The Staples went on to continued chart success, albeit less spectacularly, with Warner, through 1979. One more album followed on 20th Century Fox in 1981. After a three-year hiatus, they signed a two-album deal with Private I and hit the R&B charts five more times, once with an unlikely cover of Talking Heads' "Slippery People." The Staple Singers have not recorded since 1987. –RB

Make You Happy / EPIC
From Riverside, the Staples moved on to Columbia subsidiary Epic in 1964. With Epic, they delved further into the secular realm, hitting the pop charts twice with Pops Staples's plaintive "Why Am (I Treated So Bad)" and a cover of Stephen Stills's "For What It's Worth." Both are included on this two-disc anthology, as is a stunning side of live performance. Great stuff. –RB

Soul Folk in Action / STAX   1969
The Staples's debut Stax release included covers of Otis Redding's "(Sittin' On) The Dock of the Bay" and the Band's "The Weight." Steve Cropper produced and the Stax songwriting staff concocted a number of socially concious lyrics, the most notable being "Long Walk to D.C." –RB

We'll Get Over / STAX 1970
Their second Stax release was similar to *Soul Folk in Action*. The album's highlight, Randall Stewart's "When Will We Be Paid," remains one of my favorite Staples songs. –RB

The Staple Swingers / STAX / BB 117 1971
The Staples' first album produced by Al Bell and recorded in Muscle Shoals hit the winning formula. Other changes saw Pervis Staples departing just before the album was recorded and being replaced by sister Yvonne Staples. Everything was now in place for the Staples's golden years. Three songs, "Heavy Makes You Happy," "Love Is Plentiful," and "You've Got to Earn It," all charted. –RB

☆ **Beatitude: Respect Yourself / STAX / BB 19** 1972
The Staples's finest single album, containing three Top Ten R&B hits, "Respect Yourself," "I'll Take You There," and "This World." The first two also were pop Top 20s, "I'll Take You There" going all the way to #1. –RB

Be What You Are / STAX / BB 12 1973
Continuing in the same vein, *Be What You Are* contained three chart hits, the title song, "If You're Ready (Come Go with Me)," and "Touch a Hand, Make a Friend." The Stax songwriters, combined with Mavis Staples's unbelievably seductive vocals, were on a roll. –RB

City in the Sky / STAX / BB 125 1974
Stax was teetering on its last legs but the label still managed to squeeze two final chart hits out of the Staple Singers in the title cut and "My Main Man." A cut below the previous three albums. –RB

Great Day / FANTASY 1975
This two-album Fantasy reissue is an anthology of the material the Staples recorded for Riverside between 1960 and 1963. For Riverside, the Staples recorded mostly gospel but the shouting was toned down a bit. A few modern-day "message" songs make their way into their repertoire as well, including Bob Dylan's "Masters of War." Not quite as cataclysmic as their Vee Jay material but still essential. –RB

★ **The Best of the Staple Singers / STAX** 1975
Exactly what the title implies — seven monster soul hits plus three judiciously chosen album cuts. One chart hit, "Oh La De Dah" makes its only album appearance here. This disc is nearly too rich for one sitting. Early-70s soul simply does not get better. –RB

Let's Do It Again / CURTOM / BB 20 1975
As Stax neared bankruptcy, the Staples signed with Curtis Mayfield's Curtom label for this soundtrack album. The title track was a #1 hit and "New Orleans" reached #70, returning the Staples to the upper echelons of the charts for the last time. –RB

☆ **Pray On / CHARLY** 1990
The Staple Singers recorded ten 78s over a four-year period for Chicago's Vee Jay. These have been reissued countless times in various forms. The Charly CD is simply the most recent. For Vee Jay the Staples recorded a number of Pops Staples originals as well radical rearrangements of standards. Pops Staples and Mavis Staples shared the lead singing chores, with Pervis and Cleotha Staples moaning in the background. Superb gospel shouting. –RB

MAVIS STAPLES ♭ 1940

Soul. Born in 1940 in Chicago, most of Mavis Staples's career has been as lead singer for the Staple Singers. She first recorded solo for Stax subsidiary Volt in 1969. Subsequent efforts included a Curtis Mayfield-produced soundtrack on Curtom, a disappointing nod to disco for Warner in 1979, a misguided stab at electro-pop with Holland-Dozier-Holland in 1984, and, most recently, an uneven album for Paisley Park. Staples has a rich contralto voice that has neither the range of Aretha Franklin nor the power of Patti LaBelle. Her otherworldly power comes instead from a masterful command of phrasing and a deep-seated sensuality expressed through timbre manipulation. –RB

Only for the Lonely / STAX-VOLT 1970
A Muscle Shoals set of Southern-style soul ballads. –BC

○ **Don't Change Me Now / ACE** 1988
Mavis Staples' solo career has been largely undistinguished. *Don't Change Me Now* pulls together most of her better efforts, being a composite of Staples's two Volt solo albums, *Mavis Staples* and *Only for the Lonely*, recorded for Stax subsidiary Volt in 1969 and 1970, respectively. Ace has added a number of originally unreleased tracks to this collection. The liner notes are well written and the sound is fine. –RB

EDWIN STARR ♭ 1942

Soul. One of the best soul-shouters to come from the Motown stable, Starr's style was closer to James Brown than to any of the other male Motown artists. Best known for his 1970 hit "War," he made a brief comeback during the disco craze, but he now tours Europe and plays the oldies circuit. –RAB

Motown Superstar Series - Vol. 3 / MOTOWN
All the hits from this underrated singer. –RP

○ **Soulmaster / GORDY** 1968
A soul classic; includes his Ric Tic hits. –RP

25 Miles / MOTOWN 1969
An excellent value with this reissue of two solid albums. –RP

RINGO STARR ♭ 1940

Rock/pop. Ringo Starr, born Richard Starkey, was the drummer in the Beatles from 1962 to 1970 and thus one of the most famous musicians of the 60s. Though the least prominent member of the quartet, he distinguished himself as an occasional singer of good-natured material and as an actor. Upon the group's split, Starr went solo with two novelty projects: the first, an album called *Sentimental Journey*, found him covering pre-rock standards, and the second, *Beaucoups of Blues*, was a country music collection.
Starr then scored Top Ten hits with two nonalbum singles, "It Don't Come Easy" in 1971 and "Back off Boogaloo" in 1972. In 1973 he paired with producer Richard Perry and, with assistance from the three other ex-Beatles, made *Ringo*, which featured two #1 hits, "Photograph" and "You're Sixteen." "Oh My My," a Top Ten hit, was also included. Almost as successful was the 1974 followup, *Goodnight Vienna*, which featured the hits "Only You" and "No No Song."
Starr continued to release albums through 1981, though with diminishing success. His 1983 album *Old Wave* did not find a US distributor. Starr was also suffering from the excesses of his lifestyle, but by the late 80s he had cleaned up, and in 1989 he toured with his "All-Starr Band." In 1992, he signed to Private Music and released a new studio album, *Time Takes Time*. –WR

○ **Ringo / CAPITOL** 1973
One of the great Beatle solo albums, and the only one to feature a little help from all three ex-friends in the band. Starr's apex. –JT

● **Blast from Your Past / CAPITOL** 1975
A formidable collection, including a couple of the more venerable hits. –JT

All-Starr Band / RYKODISC 1990
"Soundtrack" from the 1989 tour, with contributions from not only Starr, but Joe Walsh, Billy Preston, and others. –JT

Time Takes Time / PRIVATE MUSIC 1992
A sober, reflective Ringo Starr returns, after a near-decade's absence, with a solid set of songs that could have been the work of, well, a Beatle. –JT

STEELY DAN

Rock/pop. If most art-rock bands borrowed from the European folk and classical-music traditions for their attempts at heightened hybrids of rock, Steely Dan (formed in 1972) drew inspiration from American jazz, big band, and R&B artists like Charlie Parker, Stan Kenton, and Ray Charles, as well as

Brill Building pop, to arrive at their sophisticated rock mutations. To say that Steely Dan was a rock band made about as much sense as saying Gentle Giant was a rock band. True, they employed rock instrumentation and various production values, but rock & roll was clearly not the bottom line in their artistic vision. Built around Donald Fagen (b Jan 10, 1948) and Walter Becker (b Feb 20, 1950), Steely Dan was more a studio vehicle for their songwriting and arrangement concepts than a real live touring unit. In fact, as Steely Dan shed members, Becker and Fagen merely plugged the holes by incorporating more session sidemen, as opposed to maintaining a band.

Thematically, Becker and Fagen relished exploring the fetishes, twisted logic, and misadventures of society's losers and misfits, with a blackly humorous, cryptic lyric style. Sonically, Steely Dan's albums have earned them raves from practically ever corner of the audiophile world. Their 1973 debut, *Can't Buy a Thrill* (#17), presented a six-piece band (with a handful of sidemen), sounding like a sophisticated alternative to fellow ABC labelmates Three Dog Night on tracks like "Midnight Cruiser," "Kings," and "Dirty Work." That album produced Steely Dan's first two hits, "Do it Again" (#6) and "Reeling in the Years" (#11).

By the time of their fifth album, the 1977 platinum *Aja* (#3), Becker and Fagen had fine-tuned their spare grooves, quirky melodies, and mildly dissonant jazz chordal clusters into a peculiarly seamless pop sound that was embraced by practically every radio format outside of country music. Sophisticated hits like "FM (No Static at All)" (#22), "Deacon Blues" (#19), "Peg" (#11), and "Josie" (#26) were among the many songs that became required soundtracks for every fern bar in the country. Becker and Fagen disengaged Steely Dan indefinitely after the 1981 release *Gaucho* (#9), which included the classy title cut and hits "Hey Nineteen" (#10) and "Time out of Mind" (#22).

Since then Becker has produced other artists, like China Crisis, and Fagen released a successful solo album, *The Nightfly* (#11), which produced a hit with "I.G.Y. (What a Beautiful World)" (#26). Fagen has also recorded "Century's End" for the movie *Bright Lights, Big City*. –RC

Can't Buy a Thrill / MCA / BB 17   1973
The Steely Dan that appeared on this debut was basically a sophisticated perversion of the sound forged by fellow ABC labelmates Three Dog Night. Check out "Dirty Work," "Kings," and "Midnight Cruiser," and say that it isn't true. It's certainly one of the best debuts by any group to emerge out of the 70s. *Can't Buy a Thrill* also produced two classic hits with the dirty Latin-influenced groove of "Do It Again" (#6) and the edgy shuffle "Reelin' In the Years" (#11). Of all the domestic MCA CDs, the remastering particularly shines on this one. –RC

Countdown to Ecstasy / MCA / BB 35   1973
Compared to their debut, *Countdown to Ecstasy* was a commercial failure (rocketing up and down the charts in three weeks) once it became apparent that this wasn't *Reelin' In the Years - Part II*. The melodies and arrangements were more subtle and the lyrics a little more inpenetrable. Nevertheless, this is the album that initially hooked many hardcore Dan fans. "Show Biz Kids" (#61) and "My Old School" (#63) became moderate hits. Other standouts include the jazzy rocker "Bodhisattva" and "King of the World." –RC

☆ **Pretzel Logic / MCA / BB 8**   1974
On *Pretzel Logic* Steely Dan most successfully synthesized their love for jazz into their dense pop-rock sound. The grooves were funky ("Night by Night," "Monkey in Your Soul") and the arrangements sophisticated ("Parker's Band," "Through with Buzz"). "Rikki Don't Lose That Number," featuring an incredibly lyrical guitar solo by Jeff Baxter, became Dan's biggest hit at #4. The title track (#57) and "Any Major Dude Will Tell You" are more highlights. –RC

Katy Lied / MCA / BB 13   1975
With its appealing melodies and oddball themes, this was a strong successor to *Pretzel Logic*. By this time, Steely Dan was

Becker and Fagen, aided by an army of Los Angeles's "A"-list session stars — Hugh McCracken, Larry Carlton, Jeff Porcaro, Hal Blaine, Michael McDonald, and more. Sonically, *Katy Lied*'s super-clean mix pointed the way to the elegantly shrink-wrapped sound of their later work. Among the standout tracks are "Black Friday" (#37), "Daddy Don't Live in That New York City No More," "Chain Lightning," and "Throw Back the Little Ones," featuring an expressive closing piano improvization by Michael Omartian. –RC

Royal Scam / ABC D-931 / BB 15   1976
With *The Royal Scam*, Steely Dan delivered a rather cluttered, abrasive-sounding collection of tracks, which were further undermined by weaker melodies. If fusion ever found a home in disco, "Kid Charlemagne" (#82) was it. Smugly humorous tracks like "Haitian Divorce," "Green Earrings," and the fetish sendup, "The Fez," are some of *Scam*'s highlights. –RC

☆ **Aja / MCA / BB 3**   1977
During the late 70s, *Aja* became required soundtrack music for fern bars throughout the country whose owners desired an upscale ambience. This was due to precision-crafted jazz-fusion pop/rock tracks like "Deacon Blues," "Josie," "Peg" (#11), and the title track, which featured a wonderfully musical drum solo by Steve Gadd. (By the time of this release, Steely Dan's albums had become favorite items for audiophiles. In that light, the Mobile Fidelity gold disc version is the way to hear this seamless production.) –RC

Gaucho / MCA / BB 9   1980
Three years after *Aja*, Becker and Fagen returned with the obsessively streamlined *Gaucho*. This impeccably recorded set contained two fine hits, "Hey Nineteen" (#10) and "Time Out of Mind" (#22). "Babylon Sisters" was another memorable highlight, while the title track sported one of the most entrancingly convoluted melodies of their career. However, "Glamour Profession," with its sophisticated disco feel, seemed tailor-made for the perpetual happy hour. (As with *Aja*, also available as a Mobile Fidelity gold-disc) –RC

● **A Decade of Steely Dan / MCA**   1985
This collection features many of Dan's high spots, but it's hardly definitive. Nevertheless, this is the place to go if you are only budgeting for a single disc. –CK

○ **Gold / MCA 5324**   1991
This companion to *Decade* features newly remastered versions of tracks like "FM (No Static at All)," Donald Fagen's "Century's End," and previously unreleased live work. –RC

STEPPENWOLF   ♭1944

Hard rock, psychedelic. Led by John Kay (b Joachim Krauledat, Apr 12, 1944), Steppenwolf's blazing biker anthem "Born to Be Wild" roared out of speakers everywhere in the fiery summer of 1968, John Kay's threatening rasp sounding a mesmerizing call to arms to the counterculture movement rapidly sprouting up nationwide. German immigrant Kay got his professional start in a bluesy Toronto band called Sparrow, recording for Columbia in 1966. After Sparrow disbanded, Kay relocated to the West Coast and formed Steppenwolf, named after the Herman Hesse novel. "Born to Be Wild," their third single on ABC-Dunhill, was immortalized on the soundtrack of Dennis Hopper's underground film classic *Easy Rider*. The song's reference to "heavy metal thunder" finally gave an assignable name to an emerging genre. Steppenwolf's second monster hit that year, the psychedelic "Magic Carpet Ride," and the followups "Rock Me," "Move Over," and "Hey Lawdy Mama" further established the band's credibility on the hard-rock circuit. By the early 70s, Steppenwolf ran out of steam and disbanded. Kay continued to record solo, as other members put together ersatz versions of the band for touring purposes. During the mid 80s Kay re-formed his own version of Steppenwolf, grinding out his hits (and some new songs) at oldies shows. Nevertheless, they'll be remembered for generations to come for creating one of the ultimate gas'n'go rock anthems of all time. –BD & CK

Early Steppenwolf / DUNHILL   1970
Early live recordings made when the band was still called
"Sparrow," working more out of a blues-band mold; features
a surprisingly great version of Junior Wells's "Messin' with the
Kid." (Out of print) –CK

○ **16 Greatest Hits / MCA**   1973
Just what the name implies; "Born to Be Wild," "Magic Carpet
Ride," "The Pusher," and "Rock Me" are just some of the
highlights. Everything you're going to want to hear in one neat
little package. –CK

CAT STEVENS   b1947

Singer/songwriter. Cat Stevens (b Steve Georgiou in London)
was the son of a Greek father and a Swedish mother. Stevens
became interested in folk and rock & roll in his teens and
scored his first UK hit, "I Love My Dog," before he turned 20.
Stevens reached the singles charts four more times, getting to
#2 with "Matthew and Son" and releasing the similarly titled
Top Ten album before he contracted tuberculosis in 1968 and
was forced to retire from music.

He reemerged with a new, mature style in 1970 with the
album *Mona Bone Jakon* and hit the UK Top Ten with "Lady
D'Arbanville." But it was his late 1970 followup, *Tea for the
Tillerman,* that made him an international success. The
album hit the Top Ten and went gold in the US, producing the
#11 hit "Wild World." *Teaser and the Firecat,* released in 1971,
did even better, getting to #2 and including the hits "Peace
Train" and "Morning Has Broken." Stevens became so
successful as an albums artist that, even though his next
couple of albums did not generate big hit singles, they were
still big sellers: *Catch Bull at Four* (1972) went to #1 and
Foreigner (1973) reached #3. Stevens's 1974 album *Buddha
and the Chocolate Box,* which included the #10 hit "Oh Very
Young," reached #2.

Stevens's records were gradually less successful during the
second half of the 70s. In 1979 he became a Muslim, adopted
the name Yusef Islam, and retired from music. He was not
heard from for another ten years, until he shocked admirers
at the end of the 80s by supporting the death sentence ordered
by the Ayatollah Khomeini against novelist Salman Rushdie
for writing the book *The Satanic Verses.* Some "classic rock"
radio stations discontinued playing him as a result, though his
music remains popular. –WR

Mona Bone Jakon / A&M   1970
Mona Bone Jakon was Stevens's first effort for A&M records,
unveiling him as a sensitive singer/songwriter, with gentle
tracks like "Trouble," "Katmandu," "Lady D'Arbanville," "Lily
White," and "I Wish I Wish." Fans of *Teaser and the Firecat* or
Tea for the Tillerman should check this one out. –RC

☆ **Tea for the Tillerman / A&M / BB 8**   1971
Tea for the Tillerman is like a musical collection of children's
tales by Stevens. The delicacy of the arrangements, Paul
Samwell-Smith's brilliant otherworldly production, and
Stevens's entrancing melodies and images easily make this his
best work. "Wild World" was a huge hit, but emotive tracks
like "Father and Son," "Where Do the Children Play," and the
haunting "Into White" and "Sad Lisa" make this a must-own
for fans of singer/songwriter pop. (Mobile Fidelity's reissue
should be on the Top Ten of any best-sounding CD list. Their
remastering job has made a home in many audiophile
listening salons with its wide range of dynamics, brilliant
highs, and warm full bass. This is Stevens' best album. (Also
available on Mobile Fidelity) –RC

Teaser and the Firecat / A&M / BB 2   1971
The followup to *Tea for the Tillerman* was almost as
impressive. Sonically, less energy was put into creating empty
real soundscapes, with more emphasis on tighter song
constructions and immediacy. The result paid off with three
international hits, "Peace Train," "Moonshadow," and
"Morning has Broken." Other highlights included "Tuesday's

Dead," "The Wind," "Bitter Blue," and "Ruby Love." After *Tea
for the Tillerman,* this is the one to get. –RC

Catch Bull at Four / A&M / BB 1   1972
Catch Bull at Four was Stevens' commercial peak, holding the
#1 spot for three weeks. Much of the reason for this was
probably public anticipation that this would be as smoothly
appealing as his previous two outings. With this album,
Stevens's melodies became more ornate and his delivery
became a little gruffer. Overall, it is one of his better albums
with "18th Avenue," "Sitting," and "Can't Keep It In" as
highlights. –RC

● **Greatest Hits / A&M / BB 6**   1975
This is the most popular best-of collection. It has his biggest
hits and a couple of important album tracks. The CD version
is just a straight reissue of the original LP release, therefore
utilizing only about half of the time available on disc. –RC

Greatest Hits - Vol. 2 / A&M / BB 165   1984
This is a spotty attempt to fill the holes left open from the first
Greatest Hits collection. Key tracks from *Mona Bone Jakon* and
Harold & Maude are here. Unfortunately, the remastering on
this disc is less than desirable. –RC

○ **Classics - Vol. 24 / A&M**   1987
After several collections, there has yet to be a definitive
representation of Stevens's work. Half of his Top 40 hits (like
"Wild World," "Another Saturday Night," "Two Fine People,"
"The Hurt," and "Ready") are missing. On the plus side, some
nice album cuts like "The Wind" and "18th Avenue" and
highlights from the movie *Harold & Maude* are here. –RC

AL STEWART   b1945

Singer/songwriter, folk/rock. Al Stewart has made a career out
of wistful pop odes obsessed with time and historical events,
all delivered with a slightly cosmic twist. During the early and
mid 60s, Stewart embraced the English folk scene and
released the albums *Bedsitter Images* and *Love Chronicles,*
which featured the guitar work of then-future Led Zeppelinite
Jimmy Page.

Stewart made his first dent on the US charts with *Past, Present
& Future* (#133), an album inspired by the works of the
ancient soothsayer Nostradamus. His followup, *Modern
Times,* did even better, reaching #30, but it was the Alan
Parsons-produced *Year of the Cat* (#5) that catapulted Stewart
into brief stardom. The title track went #8 and "On the
Border" rode to #42.

Stewart changed labels to Clive Davis's Arista in 1978,
releasing *Time Passages* (#10), also produced by Parsons. At
#7, the title cut became the highest charting hit of Stewart's
career. By this time, Stewart's sound possessed a sweeping
airy quality brought on in part by his light voice and Parsons'
cinematic production style. "Song on the Radio" (#29) and
"Midnight Rocks" (#24) were Stewart's remaining hits.
Stewart continues to play live and record. –RC

Love Chronicles / EPIC   1969
Notable for the 18-minute coming-of-age title cut, which
caused a stir at the time for its use of the word "f**cking."
Jimmy Page is featured on guitar. –RC

○ **Modern Times / RHINO / BB 30**   1975
Stewart's airy (sometimes sentimental) obsessions with the
passage of time take on a special resonance on this outing.
Highlights include "Carol," "Apple Cider Re-Constitution,"
"Dark and Rolling Sea," and "The Modern Times." –RC

○ **Year of the Cat / ARISTA**   1976
Stewart's calm delivery gives his songs a reserved, tasteful
sense of understatement, especially on the title track, one of
those "mysterious woman" songs, which captivated listeners
and turned the album into a million-seller. –WR

Time Passages / ARISTA   1978
A return to Stewart's historical themes lyrically, though it's
still the overall smoothness of his music that connected with
another million listeners. –WR

● **The Best of Al Stewart / ARISTA**   1988
All of Al Stewart's Stateside hits are available here, as well as
most of the best cuts from the hit albums *Year of the Cat* and
Time Passages. Not a comprehensive overview of his career,
but the best sampler available. –RC

BILLY STEWART   1937-1970

R&B, soul. Billy Stewart was one of the most distinctive vocal
stylists of the 60s. His stuttering, word-doubling attack owed
more to jazz scat singing than to the gospel influences of
many of his peers. A jovial, rotund piano player who toured
with Bo Diddley and, through him, gained entry to Chess
Records, Stewart scored biggest in 1966 with a smash Top Ten
version of George Gershwin and Dubose Heyward's
"Summertime," an atypically (for Chess) big-band
arrangement (featuring Earth, Wind & Fire's Maurice White
on drums) with Stewart in a vocal tour de force, masterfully
scatting around, stuttering through, and generally turning the
melody inside out. It was not your typical 60s soul music, but
Stewart's success opened the door for other jazz-influenced
singers like Georgie Fame to gain a place on radio playlists of
the day. Stewart died tragically at age 33 in a 1970 auto
accident. –CO
○ **One More Time - The Chess Years / MCA**   1985
Although a minor soul star of the 60s, Stewart possessed one
of the most unique and sweetest styles. His hits
"Summertime," "I Do Love You," and "Sitting in the Park" are
classics of the era. –JT

MARK STEWART

Alternative rock. A former member of the Pop Group.
Polemical, noise-funk with a hip-hop reggae feel. –JD
○ **Learning to Cope with Cowardice / PLEXUS**
Reggae-influenced; scary and powerful. Great! (Import) –JD
As the Veneer of Democracy ... / MUTE   1985
As the Veneer of Democracy Starts to Fade is a sleeker and less
powerful, but a fine record. (Import) –JD
Metatron / ENIGMA   1988
Stewart at his funkiest and most accessible; I wish it were
more confrontational. –JD

ROD STEWART   b 1945

Singer/songwriter, folk/rock, rock & roll, rock/pop. Before he
married models, before he cared if you thought he was sexy,
before he crooned pablum like "Forever Young," Rod Stewart
was a rock & roll singer/songwriter with a sharp eye for detail
and the ability to suck you into his world and make you feel
welcome, as if you were among friends. Stewart's boozy, good-
timey spirit allowed him to find humor in even the darkest
corners of life, and he had the heart of a born rocker. With that
in mind, the single albums listed here focus on his early- to
mid-70s work, when he was writing songs that overflowed
with self-deprecating humor and commitment anchored by a
rambunctious sound that remains one of the most communal
in all of rock. –JF
Rod Stewart Album / POLYGRAM   1969
An interesting if spotty hodgepodge of delicate folk ballads
and blazing rave-ups, highlighted by "An Old Overcoat Won't
Ever Let You Down." –JF
☆ **Gasoline Alley / POLYGRAM**   1970
A full-blown folk outing, conjuring the despair and humor of
Woody Guthrie and, on occasion, the wildcat appeal of
rockabilly. –JF
★ **Every Picture Tells a Story / POLYGRAM**   1971
Achieving the same variety as the debut, Stewart's title cut and
"Maggie May," plus his covers of vintage Temptations, Arthur
Crudup, and Tim Hardin material, flaunt the versatility and
savvy of his vision. A grand statement by a major player. (Also
available on Mobile Fidelity) –JF
Never a Dull Moment / POLYGRAM   1972

This repeats the formula of *Every Picture Tells a Story*, but the
originals, with the exception of the beautiful "Italian Girls,"
are just slightly below par. Still worthwhile though. –JF
Tonight I'm Yours / WARNER   1981
This lacks the muscle of the early stuff but remains Stewart's
last burst of creativity. This is the last time he sounds like he
cares. –JF
Storyteller - Complete Anthology / WARNER   1991
A 4-disc set containing most of the essentials (but not enough
material from the Faces) and all the late-70s and 80s hits for
those who care. Should've been better. –JF

STIFF LITTLE FINGERS

Punk. A brash, inflammatory Irish combo who released one of
punk's finest debuts, then made the mistake of sticking
around too long. –JF
○ **Inflammable Materials / ENIGMA**   1979
Despite the title, this is a scalding set that funnels the
influence of the Sex Pistols into a unique and riveting debut.
Includes "Alternative Ulster" and "Suspect Device." –JF

STEPHEN STILLS   b 1945

Singer/songwriter, rock/pop. Singer/songwriter and multi-
instrumentalist Stephen Stills first gained prominence with
the legendary late-60s group, Buffalo Springfield. Their first
hit was the Stills-penned "For What It's Worth" (#7), inspired
by Los Angeles police oppression of the youth community.
Another Springfield classic written by Stills was "Bluebird"
(#58), which featured his distinctive gutsy acoustic lead guitar
style and his mildly husky lower tenor voice. Stills left Buffalo
Springfield in 1968 to form the distinctively harmonic Crosby,
Stills & Nash.
As a solo artist, Stills has produced several successful albums
that mine a blend of acoustic/electric folk-rock with
occasional gospelish undertones. He recorded two albums
with his own group Manassas in 1972 and 1973.
His biggest hits were "Love the One You're With" (#14), "Sit
Yourself Down" (#37), "Change Partners" (#43), "Marianne"
(#42), and "It Doesn't Matter" (#61). –RC
Stephen Stills / ATLANTIC / BB 3   1970
Stephen Stills's self-titled debut started out his solo career
with much promise. The opening cut, "Love the One You're
With" (#14), was a huge hit. His warm, husky voice is used to
great effect on most of these tracks, and the album features a
cast of 1970 all-stars like Jimi Hendrix, Eric Clapton, David
Crosby, Graham Nash, John Sebastian, and Rita Coolidge.
Hendrix's lead contribution is occasionally buried by Stills's
overbearing organ work, and Clapton's guitar tone is too thin
and brittle, but the hit "Sit Yourself Down" (#37), with its
powerful piano introduction, is flawless in production and
performance. –RC
Manassas / ATLANTIC / BB 4   1972
After the uneven 1971 release *Stephen Stills 2*, Stills formed a
band around him of some solid players (Chris Hillman, Joe
Lala, Al Perkins, Fuzzy Samuels, Dallas Taylor, etc.) and called
it Manassas. Their first of two albums was a self-titled double-
record set. Many consider *Manassas* to be Stills' finest effort; it
would have made a grand single album. Atlantic has managed
to fit the whole thing on a single CD. Of Stills' albums reissued
on CD, this one sounds the best. –RC
○ **Still Stills - Best of Stephen Stills / ATLANTIC /**   1977
This is a decent sampling of his solo work up to this point. It
includes "Change Partners" from *Stephen Stills 2*, as well as
main tracks from the debut. –RC

STING   b 1951

Singer/songwriter, rock/pop. Sting launched his musical career
as the lead singer of the successful rock band the Police. After
the Police split in 1984, the English singer/songwriter and
bassist embarked upon a successful solo career.
Sting's solo works focus less on achieving pop success, instead
voicing his political views and concerns. His 1985 debut

album, *Dream of the Blue Turtles*, is heavily jazz-influenced and boasts a number of jazz musicians, including Branford Marsalis. This album, while it contained lyrical references to turbulent Soviet-American relations and the British coal-miners' strike, still managed to sell two million copies. The *Dream* tour resulted in a two-disc live album, *Bring on the Night,* which featured some new live renditions of Police songs. In 1987 Sting released a second solo album, *Nothing like the Sun* ..., which was very politically based as well. One of the most powerful songs on the album is "They Dance Alone," an outright criticism of the regime of Chilean General Augusto Pinochet. *The Soul Cages*, released in 1991, deals with the deaths of Sting's mother and father and veers away from political issues. It was a more introspective work, although rather gloomy, dealing with the ideas of death and loss.

In addition to his music, Sting also appeared in a number of movies and plays, including *The Bride* and *The Threepenny Opera*. Sting has used his status as a well-known performer to lend assistance to many worthy organizations, including Band Aid, Live Aid, Special Olympics, Greenpeace, Amnesty International, and the Rainforest Foundation. Sting has made a significant contribution, not only to the music world but to the rest of the world as well. –IME

○ **Dream of the Blue Turtles / A&M**   1985
Sting's early jazz experience was very evident on his solo debut album. Kenny Kirkland (piano), Omar Hakim (drums), Darryl Jones (bass), and Branford Marsalis (sax) contributed greatly to the jazz "feel" of the songs. This captures some of the energy and exuberance of the early Police, like *Regatta de Blanc*, but also maintains some of the somber, serious tone of *Synchronicity*. Sting's first album is his most impressive, boasting such songs as "Love Is the Seventh Wave," "Fortress around Your Heart," "Children's Crusade," and "Moon over Bourbon Steet." (Also available on Mobile Fidelity) –IME

Bring On the Night / A&M   1986
A terrific live-concert album, this contains songs dating back to Sting's years with the Police, as well as works from his first solo album, *Dream of the Blue Turtles*. In addition to performances of well-known songs, Sting performs the haunting "I Burn for You," a song written for the film *Brimstone and Treacle* (in which Sting had a role) but not included on any of Sting's own albums. This two-CD set features Branford Marsalis (sax), Omar Hakim (drums), Darryl Jones (bass), Kenny Kirkland (keyboards), and Janie Pendarvis and Dolette McDonald (vocals). –IME

● **Nothing like the Sun / A&M**   1987
This album is more somber than *Dream of the Blue Turtles* and light on the jazz influences, focusing more on Brazilian and Hispanic rhythms. Not as lively and concise as *Dream ...* due to the heavy, political lyrics (on such songs as "They Dance Alone" and "Fragile"), this is a good album, nevertheless. Along with Sting's own songs, the album includes a cover of Hendrix's "Little Wing." This album includes guests Mark Knopfler, Eric Clapton, the Gil Evans Band, former Police bandmember Andy Summers (who plays on "Lazarus Heart"), and, once again, Branford Marsalis featured on sax. (Also available as a Mobile Fidelity gold disc) –IME

The Soul Cages / A&M   1991
This long-awaited album followed the death of Sting's father, which may explain the melancholy, pained tone of these songs. The focus here is very much on death and dying, making the album a bit of a downer and hard to listen to at a single sitting. Although the material may not be as good overall as Sting's previous work, the song "All This Time" is definitely one of his best. –IME

STONE ROSES

Alternative rock. A super-hyped English band that got too big for its collective britches after only a few recordings, the Stone Roses play revved-up postmodern English pop that combines jaunty guitar with snotty, sardonic misery à la Morrissey. Could be a 90s flash in the pan. –JD

○ **Stone Roses / SILVERTONE**   1989
Ironically, other bands similar to Stone Roses (e.g., Happy Mondays) made crummier albums that got more press, but this energetic guitar pop shows off Stone Roses' legacy as a speedy guitar rock band without succumbing (at least not totally) to lame neo-hippie spirituality. –JD

THE STOOGES

Rock & roll. A Detroit rock & roll band formed in 1967 as the Psychedelic Stooges with lead singer Iggy Pop (born James Newell Osterberg, 1947; original stage name was Iggy Stooge, the Iggy appelation coming from his drumming tenure with local teen band the Iguanas). The group also comprised Ron Asheton (guitar), Scott Asheton (drums), and Dave Alexander (bass). If local favorites the MC5 were striking fear into the hearts of Motor City parents with their manifesto of sex, drugs, rock & roll, and politics, they looked normal in comparison to the stage antics of Iggy & the Stooges. Violent interaction with members of the audience (both verbal and physical), vomiting, and self-mutilation with beer bottles were some of the more predictable aspects of their live presentation, while the music itself was simplistic and angry one- to three-chord grunge-rock, with lyrics ranging from teenage disorientation to animal lust. Two excellent albums for Elektra followed (they were signed the same night as the MC5), but the drug lifestyle of the band caused its breakup in the early 70s. They re-formed with James Williamson on guitar and Asheton moving over to bass for the next album in 1973, but disbanded again a year later. Working with David Bowie, Iggy cut two good solo albums in the mid 70s, when bands like the Sex Pistols defined him as "The Godfather of Punk." He has kept recording and touring to his hardcore cult following up to the present time, with small acting roles in *The Color of Money* and *Cry Baby* as well. –CK

○ **The Stooges / ELEKTRA**   1969
Debut album; the true birth of punk-rock. –CK

○ **Fun House / ELEKTRA**   1970
Their second album, equally as great. –CK

★ **Raw Power / CBS**   1973
The title says it all. The blueprint for the Sex Pistols and the entire punk-rock movement. –CK

○ **Metallic K.O. / SKYDOG**   1976
The last Stooges live show;, scary as hell. Bootleg import. Worth the search. –CK

STORIES

Rock/pop. After the demise of the Left Banke, classically trained keyboardist and songwriter Michael Brown (b Apr 25, 1949) formed Stories in 1972 with singer Ian Lloyd. Their first two albums, *Stories* and (particularly) *About Us*, featured a brilliant collection of ultra-melodic pop-rock songs that were less baroque than those of Left Banke and (at times) harder-hitting than those of fellow pop-rockers like Badfinger.

Neither of these albums achieved any real success, and Stories would have (more than likely) sadly sunk without a trace had fate not intervened with the totally left-field hit (about an interracial encounter) titled "Brother Louie" (#1), written by Errol Brown of the British group Hot Chocolate. Their label, Kama Sutra, jammed the tune on *About Us*, and the album ended up charting at #29.

Brown left the group, and they released the spotty *Travelling Underground*, which produced the "Brother Louie" carbon-copy "Mammy Blue" (#50) and "If It Feels Good, Do It" (#88). Stories broke up shortly thereafter. –RC

○ **About Us / PAIR**   1973
The second Stories album melded ornate Anglo-pop with ever-so-slight art-pop tendencies. Loaded with great melodies and smart arrangements. Fans of Badfinger and Beatles-style rock/pop should love this outing. A commercial sleeper until

the band stuck their version of Hot Chocolate's "Brother Louie," which became a #1 hit. Unfortunately, the song didn't resemble anything else on the album. Highlights include "Darling," "Hey France," Please Please," "What Comes After," and "Top of the City." This disc may be hard to find, since their reissue label has historically done little to promote reissue product. –RC

STORMTROOPERS OF DEATH

Thrash. Stormtroopers of Death, formed in the summer of 1985 in New York City, involved members of Anthrax and Nuclear Assault for a one-album project, a project that helped spread the popularity of speed-metal and hardcore to a wider audience. –JB

○ **Speak English or Die / CAROLINE**   1985
The album that made the crossbreed of punk-rock and heavy metal official. It is essential and mandatory for students of thrash. –JB

STRAITJACKET FITS

Avant-garde. New Zealand's moody, ethereal pop band from the late 80s to the present. –ED

○ **Hail / ROUGH TRADE**   1990
Dissonant, dreamy, and hypnotic garage-rock with an aggressive edge from this New Zealand band. Highlights include "She Speeds" and "All That That Brings." The import CD contains additional tracks. –SWB

Melt / ARISTA   1991
Not as soaring as their first US album, but their musicianship and dark hypnotic energy make it worthwhile. –SWB

THE STRANGLERS

Alternative rock. The Stranglers — Hugh Cornwell (b Aug 28, 1949), guitarist/vocalist; Jean Jacques Burnel, bassist/vocalist; Dave Greenfield, keyboard player; and Jet Black, drummer — are one of the longest-lived bands associated with the British punk explosion of the 70s, but they were never really a punk group. Formed in Guildford in 1975, the group adopted a spare sound reminiscent of the Doors. They were categorized as punk because they came up at the same time as the punk originators and because their demeanor was angry and threatening.
The Stranglers broke through in 1977, scoring three Top Ten hits, "Peaches," "Something Better Change," and "No More Heroes," and two Top Ten albums, *IV Rattus Norvegicus* and *No More Heroes.* The group never achieved commercial success in the US but did well consistently in the UK. They gradually evolved from the hard-edged style of their early hits to a more mainstream rock sound. –WR

○ **Greatest Hits 1977-1990 / EPIC**   1991
This 15-track compilation takes the Strangers from the overtly sexist, tough-talking "Peaches" through more textured pop songs like "Always the Sun," to recent rock remakes like "96 Tears." –WR

THE STRAWBS

Folk/rock, prog-rock. Originally a folk and bluegrass trio formed by Dave Cousins, with Sandy Denny as lead singer, the Strawbs evolved into an acoustic folk quartet and later into a progressive rock quintet, complete with electric keyboards and an epic/classical orientation. The exits of bassist John Ford and drummer Richard Hudson in the early 70s led to a toughening of the group's sound but also a weaker songwriting contingent. Their return, and Cousins' hookup with guitarist Brian Willoughby, made them musically if not commercially viable again in the 80s and 90s. –BE

Sandy Denny & the Strawbs / HANNIBAL   1968
Acoustic folk and bluegrass. Mostly a showcase for Denny, plus a few clues to the group's future evolution. –BE

Strawbs / A&M   1969

Still an acoustic sound but with a much more expansive song structure and growing seriousness. (Import)–BE

○ **Bursting at the Seams / A&M**   1971
A magnum opus: romantic, mystical, electrifying, and it rocks with a defiant smile. "Down by the Sea" is as fine a piece of progressive rock as was ever produced. (German import) –BE

Grave New World / A&M   1972
Fulfillment! Singer/songwriter Dave Cousins finds a space somewhere between Bob Dylan and John Bunyan, Hudson and Ford come up with some superb hooks, and the electric sound is powerful and majestic. Powerful and sincere, if a little too serious and downbeat. (Japanese import) –BE

Hero and Heroine / A&M   1974
The group's last great album, filled with mysticism and sexuality but lacking melodic subtlety. Loud, but with less richness of expression. (Canada import) –BE

Strawbs by Choice / A&M   1974
A concise retrospective of some of the better moments from the first four A&M albums. (Import) –BE

STRAY CATS

Roots-rock. A neo-rockabilly trio consisting of Brian Setzer (b Apr 10, 1960), guitar and vocals; Slim Jim Phantom (b Jim McDonnell, 1961), drums; and Lee Rocker (b Lee Drucker, 1961), string bass. They formed in 1979 in Massapequa, Long Island, after the demise of Setzer's punk band, the Bloodless Pharoahs. The group moved to England in 1980 and broke through there, scoring Top Ten hits with "Rock This Town" and "Runaway Boys," as well as their debut album, *Stray Cats.* That album was not released in the US, nor was its followup, *Gonna Ball,* but EMI America combined tracks from the two albums to create their US debut, *Built for Speed.* It sold a milllion copies in 1982 and produced the US Top Ten hits "Rock This Town" and "Stray Cat Strut." *Rant N' Rave with the Stray Cats* (1983), featuring "(She's) Sexy + 17," was also successful. Setzer then split from Phantom and Rocker and went solo. (The rhythm section formed Phantom, Rocker, and Slim.) There was a contractual-obligation album, *Rock Therapy,* in 1986; they re-formed in 1988, and released *Blast Off* in 1989. –WR

○ **Best of Stray Cats ... / CAPITOL-EMI**   1982
Best of the Stray Cats - Rock This Town is a nice, solid compilation, featuring the title track, "Stray Cat Strut," and others. –CK

Built for Speed / EMI AMERICA   1982
The best tracks from the Stray Cats's two UK albums, the best produced by Dave Edmunds, as the group updates rockabilly and Brian Setzer comes on like a rock star. Infectious. –WR

NOLAN STRONG & THE DIABLOS   1934-1977

R&B, soul. Early Detroit R&B vocal group formed in 1950, which originally featured Nolan Strong, Juan Guiterriec, Willie Hunter, Quentin Eubanks, and Bob "Chico" Edwards on guitar. Strong was blessed with a beautiful high tenor voice (and even higher falsetto) and writing and arranging skills far surpassing those of most doo-wop groups of the era. What makes his recordings (with and without the Diablos) so special is that we're hearing the Motown sound in its embryonic form. Nolan was the original Smokey Robinson, the original Michael Jackson, years before either of them stood before a microphone at Motown. Recording his entire career for the tiny independent Fortune (Detroit's first Black R&B label), Strong's influence on Smokey and the early Motown stable of talent was unmistakable. As late as the early 60s, Berry Gordy tried to buy Nolan's contract from Fortune and install him as head arranger and producer but to no avail. (The job went instead to Robinson.) Incredibly handsome with a strong stage presence, Strong came close to the big time on several occasions (when his "Mind over Matter" started to break nationally, Gordy recruited the Temptations to cover it under the name the Pirates, the only time in the history of Motown that this was done), but his erratic temperament and lifestyle ensured that it was not to be. The genius of one of the greatest and yet most underappreciated artists in the history of pop music lives on in the 20-odd years of recordings Strong did in a tiny, crudely equipped studio situated in the back of a record shop. The original sound of the Motor City, indeed. –CK

Mind over Matter / FORTUNE
Early 60s. Very soulful. –CK

☆ **Fortune of Hits - Vol. 1 / FORTUNE**   1961
All the early hits, and the perfect place to start. –CK

Fortune of Hits - Vol. 2 / FORTUNE   1962
The companion piece to *Fortune of Hits - Vol. 1*. –CK

Daddy Rock / FORTUNE   1963
A great batch of rare and unreleased sides. –CK

THE STYLE COUNCIL

Alternative pop. After Paul Weller broke up the Jam in 1982, he formed the Style Council with pianist Mick Talbot. Together they elaborated on the slick soul music the Jam were perfecting, and, at their best, they maintained Weller's fierce liberal political agenda. Although they never hit it big in the US, the group was successful in Europe. –JF

○ **Introducing the Style Council / POLYGRAM**   1983
A solid EP collection of the band's initial British singles, including the ersatz soul of "Long Hot Summer," the bubbling pop of "Speak like a Child," and "Money-Go-Round," a fine British-funk manifesto. –JF

Singular Adventures of ... / POLYGRAM   1989
An adequate hits collection, which skims the cream from their otherwise disappointing albums. Includes "You're the Best Thing," the closest they've ever come to a US hit. –JF

STYLISTICS

Soul, R&B. One of the sweetest soul groups hailing from Philly, with an incredible run of soul smashes from 1971 to 1975. The fragile falsetto of Russell Thompkins Jr (b Mar 21, 1951) and sumptuous production of Thom Bell added up to serious long-term success for the Stylistics. The quintet debuted on the charts in 1971 with "You're a Big Girl Now" and proceeded to set the soul and pop markets ablaze with "You Are Everything," "Betcha by Golly Wow," "I'm Stone in Love with You," "Break Up to Make Up" — all ballads — and the untypical rocker "Rockin' Roll Baby" on Abco. Although they left the label in 1976, the hits rolled on for another decade, albeit not on so lofty a scale. –BD

○ **Best of the Stylistics / AMHERST**   1975
Any of their collections are good, but this one features their biggest and best hits, including "I'm Stone in Love with You," "Rockin' Roll Baby," "Betcha by Golly Wow," and "You Make Me Feel Brand New." –CK

STYX

Prog-rock, pop. This Chicago-based band was composed of Dennis DeYoung (keyboards), Tommy Shaw (lead guitar), James Young (guitar), John Panozzo (drums), and Chuck Panozzo (bass). Their mainstream rock sound flirted with art-rock at times. Between 1974 and 1984, they scored hits with sentimental ballads like "Babe" and "The Best of Times," as well as pop-rockers, "Too Much Time on My Hands" and "Mr. Roboto." –BC

○ **Classics - Vol. 15 / A&M**   1987
This best-of collection amply covers this group's primary radio hits and key album cuts. Included are "Babe," "Best of Times," "Too Much Time on My Hands," "Mr. Roboto," "Don't Let it End," "Blue Collar Man (Long Nights)," "Come Sail Away," "Crystal Ball," and "Grand Illusion." –RC

THE SUBDUDES

R&B. The Subdudes embrace New Orleans and Memphis soul

Music Map

Heavy Metal

Influences
Link Wray
The Who — The Yardbirds
The Kinks — Jimi Hendrix

British Metal - 70s
Judas Priest — Led Zeppelin
Black Sabbath — Deep Purple

European Metal - 70s
Scorpions — U.F.O.

Australian Metal - Mid 70s
AC/DC

American Metal - 70s
Van Halen — Kiss — Aerosmith

British Metal - Late 70s
Iron Maiden — Motörhead — Def Leppard

American Metal - Early 80s
Mötley Crüe — Dio

British Metal - Early 80s
Ozzy Osbourne — Diamond Head

Classical Metal
Yngwie Malmsteen

Thrash Metal - 90s
Anthrax — Metallica
Slayer — Megadeth

Heavy Metal - 90s
Skid Row — Guns N' Roses — Pantera
Forced Entry

Grindcore - 90s
Napalm Death — Carcass

Death Metal - 90s
Mercyful Fate — Venom — Death
Possessed — Morbid Angel

and filter it through an earthy acoustic/electric style, with rich, heartfelt harmonies. The fact that the Subdudes lack a drummer makes them unique in an idiom that traditionally is built on a foundation of solid drumming. They compensate with a percussionist who manages to make a tambourine sound like a trap set. –RC

○ **The Subdudes / ATLANTIC**   1990
Lovers of earthy soulful music, heavy in New Orleans spirit, should check out this impressive debut, produced by Don Gehman (John Mellencamp, of Treat Her Right). "Need Somebody," "Any Cure," "Got You on His Mind," and a version of the Crescent City standard "Big Chief" are among the highlights. –RC

Lucky / ATLANTIC   1991
This sophomore outing contains a nice version of Al Green's "Tired of Being Alone." Overall it's almost as consistent-sounding as their debut. –RC

SUGARCUBES

Alternative rock. To call them the greatest rock band from Iceland is like saying you know the greatest hockey player from Chile — it just doesn't mean much. Arty and pretentious, the Sugarcubes took the British pop press by storm with their artifice-laden pop. After a good first album, they've been trying to live up to their press clippings. –JD

○ **Life's Too Good / ELEKTRA**   1988
With strong songs built around Bjork Gudmusdottir's piercing, striking voice, this record lived up to all the advance hype. With songs like "Birthday" and "Motorcrash," this is the perfect introduction to the 'Cubes. –JD

Here Today Tomorrow Next Week / ELEKTRA   1989
A slip from the first album, but not so much that it's without merit. –JD

SUICIDAL TENDENCIES

Hardcore. This Los Angeles hardcore metal quintet (originally formed as a quartet in 1981) has earned a reputation for addressing unpleasant social topics. –JB

● **Suicidal Tendencies / FRONTIER**   1983
The album that started it for this band. Not heavy metal but hardcore punk. A lot of aggression, with some fun. Includes the classic song, "Institutionalized." –JB

How Will I Laugh Tomorrow ... / CBS   1988
The band is a bit more metal-oriented but still as aggressive as in their punk days. *How Will I Laugh Tomorrow When I Can't Even Smile Today* has lots of great songs, including "Trip to the Brain" and the title track. –JB

○ **Lights ... Camera ... Revolution! / CBS**   1990
Their strongest album since the debut, with great songs like "Send Me Your Money" and "You Can't Bring Me Down." –JB

SUICIDE

Alternative rock. This early punk duo featuring Alan Vega and Martin Rev brought punk dynamics to their minimalist synthesized art-rock. –JF

○ **Suicide / ENIGMA-RESTLESS**   1977
Harsh, demanding, relentless — the best place to start. –JD

Half Alive / ROIR   1981
Nasty live stuff. Singer Alan Vega is especially obnoxious. –JD

DONNA SUMMER   b 1948

Disco, pop. Summer starred in musicals across Europe in the early 70s. Along with Giorgio Moroder and Pete Bellotte, she created an awesome hit-making machine during the disco era. Though crowned the Queen of Disco, Summer quickly abandoned the throne and set about establishing herself as a serious pop-rock singer, which she has in fact done. –BC

Bad Girls / CASABLANCA   1979
A concept double album dealing with city life. The title tune, a scorching rock number with "Hot Stuff," and beautiful down tempos on "My Baby Understands," "On My Honor," and "There Will Always Be a You." –BC

○ **On the Radio ... / CASABLANCA**   1979
On the Radio - Greatest Hits I & II. If you want to be unadventurous and just go for the 70s hits, stop here;. however, you will still be missing some of Summer's finest work. Besides, in order to cram all the hits into a two-record set, many of them were abridged, including the stunning guitar solo on "Hot Stuff." –BC

She Works Hard for the Money / POLYGRAM   1983
Michael Omartian and Summer collaborated on this strong set of light keyboard funk, soft rock, and pop. –BC

THE SUN RHYTHM SECTION

Rock & roll. A congregation of Memphis rockabilly stalwarts, including Paul Burlison, Sonny Burgess, D. J. Fontana, Stan Kesler, Marcus Van Story, and Smoochie Smith. –JF

○ **Old Time Rock 'n Roll / FLYING FISH**   1988
Some of the originators have fun playing some of the originals, again. –RG

THE SUNDAYS

Alternative pop. A British alternative-pop band, the Sundays feature the airy vocal phrasing of Harriet Wheeler and the R.E.M.-meets-U2 ambient guitar jangle of David Gavurin. Their sound is simultaneously atmospheric and driving. –RC

○ **Reading Writing & Arithmetic / GEFFEN**   1990
The delicate vocals of lead singer Harriet Wheeler propel this top-notch collection of modern rock tracks. –DDC

SUPERTRAMP

Prog-rock, rock/pop. This British band included Roger Hodgson (guitars), Richard Davies (keyboards), Dougie Thomson (bass), John Anthony Helliwell (woodwinds), and Bob C. Benberg (percussion). Supertramp achieved their greatest success between 1974 and 1982, with an arty rock/pop sound that sported the band's distinctive keening tenor vocals. Their biggest hits were "The Logical Song" (#6), "Take the Long Way Home" (#10), "Goodbye Stranger" (#15), "It's Raining Again" (#11), "Give a Little Bit" (#15), "Dreamer" (#15), and "Bloody Well Right" (#35). They have a crisp, lucid 70s rock style. –BC

Crime of the Century / A&M   1974
This Ken Scott-produced concept album made it into the US Top 40. It includes the hits "Bloody Well Right," "Hide in your Shell," and "Dreamer." –BC

○ **Even in the Quietest Moments / A&M**   1977
The group produced this one without Ken Scott. The title track and "Give a Little Bit" are standouts. –ED

○ **Breakfast in America / A&M**   1979
Their radio breakthrough hit, "The Logical Song," and others. (Also available on Mobile Fidelity.) –ED

● **Classics - Vol. 9 / A&M**   1987
This is a fairly good sampler of this band's bigger radio tracks as well as key album numbers. Included are "Bloody Well Right," "Ain't Nobody but Me," "The Logical Song," "Give a Little Bit," "It's Raining Again," "Goodbye Stranger," "Take the Long Way Home," and "Dreamer." Unfortunately, "Even in the Quietest Moments" is curiously omitted. –ED

THE SUPREMES

Motown. The Supremes evolved from the Primettes to become the preeminent female group of their day, and Diana Ross emerged from the Supremes to become one of the all-time great pop divas. The Primettes were a local Detroit group that had recorded unsuccessfully for Lupine before they signed with Motown and changed their name to the Supremes — a name that seemed to create a self-fulfilling prophecy. After a few false starts, they broke through in 1964 with "Where Did Our Love Go?" From there, the roll call of hits is as familiar as Diana Ross's false eyelashes; they are part of the collective unconscious of anyone who lived through the 60s. The hits were the work of the production team of Holland-Dozier-Holland, which had been seconded from Martha & the Vandellas, a move that was later the font of considerable acrimony. Whether the hits were R&B or pop is a moot point. Certainly Diana Ross had pop aspirations aplenty, as her solo recordings showed, but it was a trend already evident on forlorn albums of standards that the Supremes cut at Motown. There is every indication that Motown founder Berry Gordy saw Diana Ross (with whom he had a close personal relationship) and the Supremes as his ticket into legitimate show business. Ross left in 1970, immediately after "Someday We'll Be Together," and although the Supremes soldiered on (even scoring another #1 R&B hit with "Stoned Love"), there is no doubt that to most people the Supremes will be forever associated with their former lead singer. –CE

Right On / MOTOWN 1970
The best of the post-Diana Ross group. Savvy Frank Wilson production. –RAB

☆ **Anthology / MOTOWN** 1973
A complete collection of their nonstop Motown hits. A must-have. –RAB

25th Anniversary / MOTOWN 1986
Includes all the biggies, and some excellent unreleased tracks for novelty. –RAB

SURVIVOR

Rock/pop. A Chicago group formed in 1978 by ex-Ides of March lead singer Jim Peterik and keyboardist and singer Dave Bickler, who first came into success with the #1 hit (and theme song to the Sylvester Stallone movie *Rocky III*), "Eye of the Tiger." In 1984, Bickler was replaced with ex-Target lead singer Jimmy Jamison of Memphis. This began a string of successful medium-tempo rockers and dramatic power ballads for the band, including "I Can't Hold Back" (#13), "High on You" (#8), "The Search Is Over" (#4), "Burning Heart" (#2), and "Is This Love" (#9). –RC

○ **Greatest Hits / SCOTTI BROS.** 1990
All of this mainstream AOR rock band's hits are here. –RC

SWAMP DOGG b 1942

Blues/rock. Swamp Dogg began life as Jerry Williams Jr, and it was as soul singer Little Jerry Williams that he recorded his first hit ("Baby, You're My Everything") in 1966. The eccentric and outrageous Swamp Dogg emerged in 1970, "an eclectic beast, crossed between 50s R&B and blues, Southern White rock & roll, and the New Breed ideas of Sly Stone and George Clinton," to quote R&B writer Cliff White. As Swamp Dogg, Williams immediately had another hit with one of his bluesiest singles, "Mama's Baby, Daddy's Maybe" (1970), but despite a number of major-label releases since then, he has become more of a cult figure to music insiders than a popular act with the public. His works have often been adventurous and topical but not, apparently, commercial. As a producer and songwriter, Williams/Swamp Dogg has been successful enough; his extensive credits include records by Irma Thomas, Z. Z. Hill, Solomon Burke, Patti LaBelle, and the Commodores. –JON

○ **Total Destruction to Your Mind / CANYON** 1970
His first and best. The title says it all. –RP

Cuffed, Collared & Tagged / EDSEL 1972
UK import. Part of a 2-fer. Great band, dynamite lyrics. –RP

I'm Not Selling Out, I'm Buying In / TAKOMA 1981
A fine collection, which includes a great duet with Esther Phillips. –RP

BETTYE SWANN b 1944

Soul, R&B. Los Angeles soul vocalist. Scored a #1 R&B hit in 1967 with her lilting mid-tempo "Make Me Yours." Swann began recording for the Money label in 1964 and found herself on the charts the next year with "Don't Wait Too Long." After "Make Me Yours" made her some money on Money, she stopped off at Capitol long enough to enjoy a hit with "Don't Touch Me" in 1969 and then settled in at Atlantic, where she notched several soul hits during the early 70s (including "Victim of a Foolish Heart"). –BD

Make Me Yours / COLLECTABLES
The Money label tracks 1964-1967, including her #1 R&B hit, "Make Me Yours." –RP

○ **The Soul View Now / CAPITOL** 1969
Haunting deep soul ballads. A gem. –RP

Don't You Ever Get Tired of Hurting Me / CAPITOL 1972
Classic country soul. –RP

KEITH SWEAT

Urban R&B. Keith Sweat is a Harlem-born R&B singer/songwriter who released his debut album, *Make It Last Forever*, at the end of 1987. The album sold over three million copies, spawning the hits "I Want Her" (#1 R&B, #5 pop), "Something Just Ain't Right" (#3 R&B), "Make It Last Forever" (#2 R&B), and "Don't Stop Your Love" (#9 R&B). It was followed in June 1990 by *I'll Give All My Love to You*, another million-seller, that featured the hits "Make You Sweat" (#1 R&B, #14 pop), "Merry Go Round" (#2 R&B), "I'll Give All My Love to You" (#1 R&B, #7 pop), and "Your Love - Part 2" (#4 R&B). Sweat's third album was *Keep It Comin'*, an R&B chart-topper at the end of 1991, whose title track was another #1 R&B hit. –WR

○ **I'll Give All My Love to You / ELEKTRA** 1990
Keith Sweat represents a new generation of R&B love men who combine the ballad strength of singers like Luther Vandross with percussion-heavy dance music, called new jack swing, that answers the needs of the current dance floor. His second album, with its four hit singles, is typical of his approach. –WR

SWEET

Power-pop. Mid-70s English glam-rock pioneers, the Sweet churned out Who-like Chapmann- and Chinn-composed teen raunch that, by the 90s, approached neoclassic status. With their chirpy harmonies and fuzzy (but never too dangerous) guitars, the Sweet's commercial grunge became far more influential than anyone had predicted. –JD

Desolation Boulevard / CAPITOL 1975
A surprisingly solid hard-rock record; features "Ballroom Blitz." –DH

○ **Sweet 16 / ANAGRAM** 1985
All of their cavity-inducing biggies, from "Little Willy" to "Love Is Like Oxygen." (Import) –DH

MATTHEW SWEET

Alternative pop. Matthew Sweet bopped around the mid-80s indie-rock scene with such groups as Oh-OK and Lloyd Cole. Sweet released two sinkers in 1986 and 1989, respectively, but his 1992 album, *Girlfriend* (recorded in 1990), brought his Big Star pop into the postmodern arena. –JF

○ **Girlfriend / ZOO** 1991
With crisp production and a band that includes the likes of Richard Lloyd and Robert Quine, Sweet's third album provides moments of Alex Chiltonian splendor that at times makes it easy to overlook what a romantic simp this guy really is. His whining on the title cut would be hard to swallow if the guitars weren't howling like horny dogs and if the riff wasn't good enough to make the cut on *Radio City*. –JF

RACHEL SWEET b 1963

Rock/pop. After a couple of failed singles as a teenage country singer, the diminutive Sweet plugged her big voice into the burgeoning punk movement after being signed to Stiff Records. Along with Lene Lovich, she was one of the early women recording for the label, with a succession of great records that garnered much critical acclaim but failed to catch on in the marketplace. She dropped out of sight for a few years, then came back working for director John Waters both on and off the screen (*Hairspray*, *Cry Baby*) and has recently turned up working on cable's Comedy Channel. –CK

○ **Protect the Innocent / STIFF** 1981
Sweet's second and most perfectly realized album features "Take Good Care of Me" and a slam-bang version of "Baby, Let's Play House." Out of print, but it's worth the search. –CK

● **Fool Around / RHINO** 1992
A solid best-of collection showcasing Sweet's dazzling vocal capabilities. –CK

SWELL MAPS

Alternative rock. Guitar-based British art-punks from the late 70s, overrated by their small cult. –JD

○ **Collision Time Revisited / ENIGMA**   1982
A terrific compilation, which touches on all phases of their
career without a lot of the dross. –JD

SWING OUT SISTER

Pop. This jazz-rock band features Corinne Drewery, Andy
Connell, and Martin Jackson. –BC
○ **It's Better to Travel / POLYGRAM**   1988
Includes their smash hit, "Break Out." –BC

SYLVESTER   1944-1989

Disco. Sylvester was raised by his grandmother, the 30s blues
singer Julia Morgan. He had a gospel career, then joined the
transvestite band the Cockettes. He went solo in the late 70s
with the backup of Two Tons of Fun. –BC
Greatest Hits: Non-Stop Dance Party / FANTASY
A falsetto whine on high-powered disco hits. –BC
○ **Original Hits / FANTASY**
Some of the same tunes as on the *Greatest Hits* album, plus
newer urban soul. –BC

DAVID SYLVIAN

Alternative rock. Alternative-rock vocal stylist from the band
Japan. His solo efforts include work with progressive sidemen
such as Robert Fripp (King Crimson), Bill Nelson (Be Bop
Deluxe), and Holger Czukay (Can). He draws his style
from 70s art-rock fixtures like Roxy Music and David Bowie,
with a spark from the experimental electronic movement of
the 80s. –ED
Gone to Earth / ATLANTIC   1986
Sylvian is joined by guitarists Robert Fripp and Bill Nelson on
this 68-minute CD, which features tracks of Sylvian's
trademark vocals and instrumentals. Dreamy, atmospheric
works, with nice musical support from Steve Nye, Kenny
Wheeler, and Mel Collins. –SWB
○ **Secrets of the Beehive / ATLANTIC**   1987
A consistent mood is sustained throughout this one. Sylvian is
joined by Ryuichi Sakamoto, David Torn, Mark Isham, ex-
Japan drummer Steve Jansen, and others. Includes a vocal
version of the Sylvian/Sakamoto cut "Forbidden Colours"
from the *Merry Christmas, Mr. Lawrence* soundtrack. –SWB
Flux and Mutability / CAROLINE   1989
A followup to *Plight and Premonition*, with Holger Czukay.
Two lengthy, dreamlike pieces. –MPD

SYREETA

Motown. Discovered by Brian Holland and developed by Stevie
Wonder (her first husband), Syreeta Wright has enjoyed
limited success, despite being one of the most exciting and
innovative vocalists at Motown. She still performs and records
in England. –RAB
○ **Set My Love in Motion / TAMLA**   1981
Her best work, a compilation of tracks by different producers.
(Out of print) –RAB

T. REX

Power-pop. Britain has a long history of championing style-
over-substance flavor-of-the-week artists. Former fashion
model Marc Bolan (b Marc Feld, Sep 30, 1947) was a
particularly fascinating self-promoter. Between 1970 and
1973, Bolan (operating under his group moniker, T. Rex) took
England by storm with his lightly funky, fantasy-heavy, glam-
rock songs, producing 11 Top Ten hits.
Stateside, T. Rex didn't quite catch on, generating a single hit
with the #10 "Bang a Gong (Get it On)," which came off of the
#32 album, *Electric Warrior*. His followup album, *The Slider*,
went to #17 on the wings of enormous hype. Nevertheless,
Bolan's quavering tenor, mutated Chuck Berry rhythm parts,
and plodding grooves generated some fine moments, thanks
in no small part to Tony Visconti's creative production input.

By late 1973, though, their success had waned. Bolan died
from injuries sustained in an automobile accident on
September 16, 1977. –RC
○ **Electric Warrior / REPRISE**   1971
Their greatest stateside success, featuring the hits "Jeepster"
and "Bang a Gong (Get It On)." –CK

TACKHEAD

Alternative rock. A reggae, dub, funk, noise-rock, politically
tinged collective, led by producer Adrian Sherwood. They
have created backing tracks for nine inch nails, Cabaret
Voltaire, and Bernard Fowler. –JD
○ **Friendly as a Hand Grenade / TVT**   1989
Not as jarring as you'd expect. Funky, slick, and soulful. –JD
Strange Things / SBIC   1990
More mainstream, but with many redeeming qualities. –JD

TAD

Heavy metal. A Northwest grunge outfit headed by
guitarist/vocalist Tad Doyle. In 1989 the band released its
debut on Seattle's influential Sub Pop label. –DS
○ **Salt Lick / SUB POP**   1990
Notable Seattle grunge for Soundgarden fans. The CD contains
most of the group's previous effort, *God's Balls*. –DS
8-Way Santa / SUB POP   1990
More noise from this grunge outfit. –DS

TAIL GATORS

Roots-rock. A rock & roll band from Austin, TX, featuring
former members of the Fabulous Thunderbirds and the LeRoi
Brothers, with strong emphasis on grungy, guitar-driven
blues-rock. –CK
Swamp Rock / WRESTLER   1985
A burning mixture of R&B and rockabilly, recommended to
all rockers. –DS
○ **Mumbo Jumbo / WRESTLER**   1986
A rave-up debut for these Austin roots rockers. –DS
Tore Up / WRESTLER   1987
A compilation of hot B-sides. –DS
Ok Let's Go / ENIGMA   1989
Another fine effort by the favorite band of ZZ Top guitarist
Billy Gibbons. –DS
Hide Your Eyes / ENIGMA   1990
More combustible 50s-style rock from the Gators. –DS

TALK TALK

Alternative pop. Synthesizer rock by Londoners Mark Hollis,
Paul Webb, and Lee Harris. Formed in 1981 and signed amid
the synth craze, Talk Talk released its debut and toured with
Duran Duran in 1982. –DS
○ **Natural History ... / CAPITOL**   1990
Natural History - The Very Best of Talk Talk is a collection of
the best material from their first four albums, plus two live
tracks. All their hits and highlights are here, like "It's My Life,"
"Such a Shame," and "Life's What You Make It." –SWB
Laughing Stock / POLYGRAM   1991
Hauntingly beautiful dissonance, almost like free-form jazz.
Not pop music, to be sure, but interesting atmospheric tracks.
This is the culmination of the direction they were taking on
their previous two albums. –SWB

TALKING HEADS

Alternative rock. With the exception of the Ramones, the Heads
are the only band from the CBGB days that has been able to
sustain an interesting and commercially successful career into
the 90s. David Byrne's clipped vocal style, art-school lyrics,
and dorky cool gave punks a new kind of hero, one who was
concerned with work, television, love, emotional crisis, and

mental imbalance. The crisp guitar funk of their early days has given way to everything from African trance rhythms and art-funk to bouncy guitar pop and slinky Caribbean jive. Byrne's lyrics are occasionally (okay, quite often) pretentious, and the band's experimentations sometimes fail, but their best albums remain contemporary benchmarks. –JF

Talking Heads '77 / SIRE   1977
An edgy set of weird, funk-like rockers, which introduced David Byrne's skewed world outlook. "Pull Me Up" and "New Feeling" are the standouts. –JF

More Songs about Buildings & Food / SIRE   1978
Producer Brian Eno added muscle and flair to the group's arty funk-rock, making this a dense and beautiful set. –JF

Fear of Music / SIRE   1979
A weird, dance-worthy album, made creepy by Byrne's paranoid vision and Eno's dense production. But "Life during Wartime" is one hell of a single. –JF

☆ **Remain in Light / SIRE**   1980
Song structure shimmies out the window as Eno and the band flex their Afro-funk muscles. Works as both brain music and dance music. –JF

The Name of the Band Is Talking Heads / SIRE   1982
A live double album that traces the band's progression, culminating in two sides of scalding material from *Remain in Light*. –JF

○ **Speaking in Tongues / SIRE**   1983
A pulsating mix of the heavy funk of *Remain in Light* and song structures that hark back to *More Songs about Buildings & Food*. Contains the hit "Burning Down the House" and the hypnotic "This Must Be the Place." –JF

○ **Little Creatures / SIRE**   1985
Musically, this is a return to spare production and simple melodies, but this is also Byrne's most coherent and mature set of songs. –JF

Naked / SIRE   1988
Another dense set of Third World funk, this time with some help from genuine African musicians and lyrics that talk loudly but mostly say nothing. –JF

TANKARD

Heavy metal. This German speed-metal band's primary theme revolved around extolling the virtues of alcohol. –JB

○ **Hair of the Dog / NOISE**   1990
A German speed-metal band who sang about beer, women, beer, food, and beer. Although not as good as their individual albums (*Zombie Attack*, *Chemical Invasion*, and *The Morning After*), this is a decent compilation of their best work. –JB

HOWARD TATE

Soul. A Georgia-born, Philadelphia-raised soul singer whose early work was guided by organist Bill Doggett. During the mid 60s, Tate teamed up with producer/songwriter Jerry Ragovoy on the Verve label. Tate's bluesy, plaintive falsetto and melismatic, gospel-influenced style were wedded to some fine Ragovoy/Shuman compositions. "Get It While You Can" was later a mega-hit for Janis Joplin; "Look at Granny Run Run" was covered by Ry Cooder. Tate went on to cut sides for Lloyd Price's NYC-based Turntable label. Sad to say, as of early 1992, the work of this fine singer is out of print. –CO

○ **Get It While You Can / VERVE**   1968
Fine Jerry Ragovoy production and soulful, wailing vocals from Tate. Includes original versions of "Get It While You Can" and "Look at Granny Run Run." (Out of print) –CO

TAVARES

Disco. This 70s soul quintet consisted of five brothers from Massachusetts. With the aid of producer Freddie Parren, they landed a 1976 disco hit with "Heaven Must Be Missing an Angel." –JF

○ **Best of Tavares / CAPITOL**   1982
A solid assortment of hits from the group best known for the great disco single "Heaven Must Be Missing an Angel." But there's more good stuff here besides the hit. –JF

JAMES TAYLOR   b 1948

Singer/songwriter, pop. When people use the term "singer/songwriter" (often by "sensitive"), in praise or in criticism, it's James Taylor that they're thinking of. Yet in a career now extending over a quarter-century, Taylor's biggest hits have come with his cover versions of other people's songs. Go figure.
Taylor grew up in Massachusetts and North Carolina, forming the band the Flying Machine with guitarist Danny Kortchmar in 1967. He was signed as a solo artist by Apple in 1968 and released his debut album, *James Taylor*, in 1969. But it was his 1970 album, *Sweet Baby James*, with its understated autobiographical hit, "Fire and Rain," that was his commercial breakthrough. *Mud Slide Slim and the Blue Horizon* went to #2 in 1971 and contained the #1 single, "You've Got a Friend," written by Carole King. Taylor scored his next big hit with a remake of Marvin Gaye's "How Sweet It Is (To Be Loved by You)" in 1975, and hit again in 1977 with Jimmy Jones's "Handy Man." He has recorded with Simon & Garfunkel, his ex-wife Carly Simon, and J. D. Souther, and he continues to release gold-selling albums every few years, the most recent of which is 1991's *New Moon Shine*. –WR

James Taylor / CAPITOL   1969
A lovely debut album, beautifully produced by Peter Asher. It features Taylor's sometimes dour sentiments sung in his compelling but quiet voice. "Something in the Way She Moves," "Carolina in My Mind," and "Rainy Day Man." –WR

☆ **Sweet Baby James / WARNER**   1970
The heart of James Taylor's appeal is that you can take him two ways. On the one hand, his music, including that warm voice, is soothing; its minor key melodies and restrained playing draw in the listener. On the other hand, his world view, especially on such songs as "Fire and Rain," reflects the pessimism and desperation of the 60s hangover that was the early 70s. Either way, this is impressive stuff. –WR

○ **Mud Slide Slim and the Blue Horizon / WARNER**   1971
The changeover here — and it's the big changeover in Taylor's work — is that he is trying to jettison the past ("Don't come to me with your sorrows anymore" is the album's opening line) and look to a hopeful future. That he doesn't quite succeed makes the album itself a success. You need a little darkness to make the light stand out. –WR

Gorilla / WARNER / BB 6   1975
After a three-year slump, Taylor made *Gorilla*, a comeback album of sorts. Its slick blend of light reflective originals and *Big Chill*-style song covers set the tone for many of his subsequent releases. Highlights included a remake of Marvin Gaye's "How Sweet It Is (To Be Loved by You)" (#5), "Mexico" (#49), the steamy "You Make It Easy," and "Sarah Maria," an ode to his daughter. All in all, *Gorilla* is one of Taylor's more enjoyable post-*Sweet Baby James* efforts. –RC

● **Greatest Hits / WARNER**   1976
Pretty great. Be warned, however, that the versions of "Something in the Way She Moves" and "Carolina in My Mind" are re-recordings. –WR

JT / CBS   1977
The bad news is that by the time he switched to Columbia, Taylor had made the transition to craftsmanlike pop music, abandoning the shadows of his earlier work. The good news is that the Columbia work *is* so well crafted, forcing you to acknowledge what a good singer Taylor is. If the songs are less thoughtful, they are no less appealing as music. This is the best of six Columbia albums so far, but they're all of a piece. Good, easy listening. –WR

JOHNNIE TAYLOR b 1938

Soul. Aptly dubbed the "Philosopher of Soul" by the Stax publicity department, Johnnie Taylor set the ladies' hearts aflutter during the early 70s with his tender brand of Memphis soul.

Taylor wasn't always the sincere crooner he developed into. A Sam Cooke protégé who took over with the Soul Stirrers when Cooke went secular, and who retained a hint of his mentor's mellifluous delivery, Taylor took the same pop route via Cooke's SAR label in 1961. Once he got on the Stax label in 1966, the vocalist forged a sublime blues/soul synthesis with a series of absolutely gorgeous efforts. But there was nothing subtle about Taylor's first #1 R&B hit in 1968: "Who's Making Love" was an uncompromising treatise on cheating lovers, with storming brass and slashing guitar. The followups "Take Care of Your Homework" and "Jody's Got Your Girl and Gone" pounded the same message home from different angles.

As the decade turned, though, Taylor perceptibly mellowed, turning increasingly to ballads for inspiration — "I Believe in You (You Believe in Me)," "We're Getting Careless with Our Love." By the time he went platinum with the horribly repetitive "Disco Lady" in 1976, the rough edges that made his early work so absorbing were smoothed away, although his recent Malaco output sometimes manages to suggest Taylor's glory years. —BD

○ **Chronicle - 20 Greatest Hits / STAX**
Taylor's finest Stax work on one album. —BC

Who's Making Love / STAX 1968
Mainstream soul with punch. —BC

Wanted One Soul Singer / ATLANTIC 1972
Deep, downhearted blues numbers. —BC

Eargasm / CBS 1976
An excellent album of sensual disco and well-produced ballads. —BC

Crazy 'Bout You / MALACO 1991
A return to blues roots and double entendres. —BC

TEARS FOR FEARS

Techno-pop, pop. Childhood friends Curt Smith (b Jun 24, 1961) and Roland Orzabal (b Aug 22, 1961) first worked together in 1980 with the ska/pop quintet Graduate, which produced an oddball British single "Elvis Should Play Ska." After the demise of Graduate, the twosome began recording demos of some of Orzabal's morose synth-pop tunes, "Suffer the Children" and "Pale Shelter," which eventually become part of *The Hurting*, their debut release as Tears for Fears (the name was inspired by primal scream therapy psychologist Arthur Janov).

Their 1985 sophomore release, *Songs from the Big Chair*, became a worldwide success, containing several huge hits in "Shout" (#1), "Everybody Wants to Rule the World" (#1), "Head over Heels" (#3), and "Mother's Talk" (#27).

Perfectionism delayed their overreaching third album, *The Seeds of Love*, by four years. One of the album's highlights was the addition of soulful American singer Oleta Adams, whom Orzabal and Smith discovered singing in a Kansas City hotel lounge. That album's hits included "Sowing the Seeds of Love" (#2), "Woman in Chains" (#36), and "Advice for the Young at Heart" (#89). —RC

The Hurting / POLYGRAM 1983
Roland Orzabal and Curt Smith's debut, featured the morose synth-pop hits "Pale Shelter" and "Mad World." —SWB

○ **Songs from the Big Chair / POLYGRAM** 1985
Their best album. A good mix of synthesizers and traditional instruments. Includes the hits "Shout," "Head over Heels," and "Everybody Wants to Rule the World." —KMC

The Seeds of Love / POLYGRAM 1989
Their third album, was an overreaching effort, that (in spite of itself) produced a couple of gems, particularly "Sowing the Seeds of Love" and "Woman in Chains." Oleta Adams's soulful voice added life to the proceedings. —RC

● **Tears Fall Down (The Hits 1982-1992) / FONTANA** 1992
All of this duo's hits, plus some other key tracks, from throughout their career. It's a perfect overview and (essentially) the only disc to have. This anthology includes "Pale Shelter," "Shout," "Everybody Wants to Rule the World," "Head over Heels," and "Sowing the Seeds of Love," among others. —RC

TECHNOTRONIC

Dance-pop. Technotronic is a dance-pop group masterminded by Thomas DeQuincy (Jo Bogaert), a Belgian DJ, and featuring rapper Ya Kid K (Manuella Komosi) from Zaire. —WR

○ **Pump Up the Jam / CAPITOL** 1989
Features the rap/dance hits "Pump Up the Jam" and "Get Up! (Before the Night Is Over)." —WR

TEENAGE FANCLUB

Alternative rock. This Glasgow pop-grunge quintet became the postmodern buzz band of 1992 with their plunderings of Big Star pop and Sonic Youth dissonance. —JF

○ **Catholic Education / MATADOR**
A grimy pop record that never loses its charm, even when it becomes nearly impenetrable. Filled to the brim with charm and ebullience (as well as a snotty attitude), this is a dazzling record. —JD

Bandwagonesque / GEFFEN 1991
Much cleaner than the debut, this is a slice of Big Star worship that never fails to deliver the goods. Although it gets bogged down in obviousness from time to time, Teenage Fanclub proves they are a fine pop band, loaded with ringing guitars and breathtaking choruses. —JD

TELEVISION

Punk. This four-piece vehicle for the expoundings of guitarist/vocalist Tom Verlaine was an enigma on the 70s CBGB scene: Verlaine's songs reflect the influence of punk in structure and content, but the guitar duels between Verlaine and Richard Lloyd harken back to the dense jams of old-school rockers. Despite their influence on 80s indie-rockers, their reputation is somewhat inflated. Their three releases, however, are more than worthwhile for both historians and guitar fiends. —JF

○ **Marquee Moon / ELEKTRA** 1977
It's hard to overrate this one, which features whiplash guitars, thrusting rhythms, and Verlaine's piercing vocals on his best set of songs. —JF

Adventure / ELEKTRA 1978
This is a subdued set in both sound and content, but the songs sport stronger melodies, and "Glory" anticipates R.E.M.'s sound. —JF

Blow Up / ROI 1982
Crappy fidelity mars this live set, but Verlaine and Lloyd conjure some scarifying and beautiful six-string magic. —JF

TEMPREES

Soul, R&B. A Memphis soul vocal trio. This polished group formed in 1970 and recorded for We Produce, a Stax offshoot. Bandmembers Harold "Scotty" Scott, Jasper "Jabbo" Phillips, and William Norvell Johnson rode a sumptuously produced remake of the often-covered Five Royales/Shirelles standard "Dedicated to the One I Love" onto R&B playlists in 1972. After "Love's Maze" made a little noise as a followup, the trio moved to Epic for their final hit in 1976, the entirely self-explanatory "I Found Love on a Disco Floor." —BD

○ **Best of the Temprees / STAX**
A great Memphis-based group whose style mirrored the sweet soul sound of the Delfonics and the Stylistics. —RW

THE TEMPTATIONS

Motown. The early history of the Temptations parallels that of the Supremes. The Tempts started as the Primes, the Supremes as the Primettes. They joined Motown at roughly the same time and broke through at the same time. The Temptations had a more thorough grounding in the R&B tradition, though, is a fact evident in their work. They employed the classic gospel-group formula: a light tenor against a gutbucket rasp, with flashes of falsetto for emphasis. The Temptations had the benefit of the writing and production skills of Norman Whitfield and Smokey Robinson, who crafted songs for them such as "The Way You Do the Things You Do" and "My Girl."

With a classic lineup that included David Ruffin and Eddie Kendricks, the Temptations were the hottest R&B group during the ten-year period between 1965 and 1975. Ruffin left in 1968, the year the group experimented with psychedelia ("Cloud Nine" and later "Psychedelic Shack"); Kendricks quit in 1971. Increasingly, they fell under the spell of Norman Whitfield's preoccupations and grandiose productions, although Whitfield rose to the occasion magnificently in 1972 with "Papa Was a Rolling Stone." It was the group's last #1 pop hit, and in 1976 the group left Motown for a brief stint with Atlantic before returning to the fold. They continue to record and score R&B hits, but most people associate them with their golden period. —CE

Temptin' Temptations / MOTOWN   1965
Their best album of the 60s. —RAB

Live / MOTOWN   1966
Their best live album. —RAB

I Wish It Would Rain / MOTOWN   1968
David Ruffin is outstanding throughout this set. —RAB

☆ **Anthology / MOTOWN**   1973
The best hit collection available. Exhausting! —RAB

Masterpiece / MOTOWN   1973
The best of the 70s Norman Whitfield productions. —RAB

Song for You / MOTOWN   1974
The group's best post-Norman Whitfield album. —RAB

Truly for You / MOTOWN   1985
This is their best 80s album. Ollie Woodson, especially, is excellent. —RAB

25th Anniversary / MOTOWN   1986
A good retrospective, containing some previously unreleased tracks. —RAB

10CC

Rock/pop. Formed in 1972, 10CC mixed pop craftsmanship with art-rock affectations. The band members already had quite a professional pedigree: Graham Gouldman (b May 10, 1945) had already penned hits for the Yardbirds ("For Your Love") and the Hollies ("Bus Stop," among others. While working in the Mindbenders, Gouldman met Eric Stewart (b Jan 20, 1945), Kevin Godley (b Oct 7, 1945) and Lol Creme (b Sep 9, 1947), both graphic arts students, had signed with ex-Yardbirds manager Giorgio Gomelsky's Marmalade label under the moniker of Frabjoy and Runcible. While they were recording their first single, "I'm Beside Myself," they met Gouldman and Stewart, sidemen for the band.

The foursome produced a number of records under a variety of fake band names, scoring a worldwide two-million-selling hit, "Neanderthal Man" (#22), using the name Hotlegs. Brit pop impresario Jonathon King heard the foursome's satirical 50s-style demos, "Donna" and "Waterfall," and signed them to his UK Records label, giving them the name 10CC along the way. "Donna" quickly became a huge English hit at #2. The bouncy "Rubber Bullets" went #1 in the UK. Subsequent albums became increasingly ambitious until the departure of Godley and Creme, who went on to pursue an idiosyncratic duo career and a very successful venture into video direction. Stewart and Gouldman continued with 10CC until 1983. —RC

○ **10CC/Sheet Music / DCC**   1973
This includes both of 10CC's first two albums on a single disc.

The self-titled debut featured material that spoofed lightweight late-50s/early-60s pop, with songs like "Donna" (which became a #2 UK hit) and "Johnny Don't Do It." "Rubber Bullets," off that album, became a #1 UK hit, reaching #73 stateside. On *Sheet Music,* 10CC took a more sophisticated arty direction. With that album, they became favorites of college-radio programmers, who liked the band's clever pretensions. Highlights on *Sheet Music* include "Wall Street Shuffle" (#103) and "The Worst Band in the World." Steve Hoffman mastered this CD for Dunhill, and the sound is quite good. Even though none of the band's major hits are here, this is probably the best starting place for the uninitiated. —RC

The Original Soundtrack / POLYGRAM / BB 15   1975
There are some very nice *sounding* songs here. The atmospheric "I'm Not in Love" was a worldwide hit. "Brand New Day" and "Second Sitting for the Last Supper" are highlights, but extended pieces like "Une Nuit à Paris" come off like art-pop for the terminally cute. —RC

How Dare You? / POLYGRAM / BB 47   1976
"Lazy Days" and the title cut are nice, and fans of the band champion tracks like "I'm Mandy, Fly Me" (#60), "Art for Art's Sake," and "I Want to Rule the World" as evidence of 10CC's smarts, but the end result is a little too smug at times. In terms of production, 10CC's ultra-clean production sound is impressive. —RC

Deceptive Bends / POLYGRAM / BB 31   1977
After *How Dare You,* Lol Creme and Kevin Godley left Eric Stewart and Graham Gouldman to their own devices. The result was *Deceptive Bends,* a poppier, at times McCartneyish album, which produced three hits: "People in Love" (#40), "Good Morning Judge" (#69), and the internationally successful "The Things We Do for Love," which hit #5. —RC

10,000 MANIACS

Alternative pop. 10,000 Maniacs (named after the low-budget horror movie *2,000 Maniacs*) was formed in Jamestown, NY, in 1981 by singer Natalie Merchant and guitarist John Lombardo. Other members of the sextet were Robert Buck (guitar), Steven Gustafson (bass), Dennis Drew (keyboards), and Jerry Ausugstyniak (drums). The group gigged extensively and recorded independently before signing with Elektra and making *The Wishing Chair* in 1985. Cofounder Lombardo left the band in 1986, and they continued as a quintet, releasing the second album, *In My Tribe,* in 1987. This album broke into the charts, where it stayed 77 weeks, peaking at #37. *Blind Man's Zoo,* the 1989 followup, hit #13 and went gold. —WR

The Wishing Chair / ELEKTRA   1985
Put simply, 10,000 Maniacs sound a lot like Fairport Convention with Sandy Denny, so it's appropriate that Fairport's original producer, Joe Boyd, was brought in to handle their major-label debut. The result is a gentle folk/rock record that highlights the haunting voice of Natalie Merchant. —WR

In My Tribe / ELEKTRA   1987
Guest vocal by Michael Stipe of R.E.M. Includes "Like the Weather" and their remake of "Peace Train." The album was produced by Peter Asher. —KMC

○ **Blind Man's Zoo / ELEKTRA**   1989
Natalie Merchant's lyrics have a subtle urgency on such tracks as "Eat for Two" and "Trouble Me," while the band contrives textured folk/rock backing and producer Peter Asher creates a well-articulated rock sound. —WR

Hope Chest - Fredonia Recordings / ELEKTRA   1990
A reissue of the band's first recordings. —KMC

TEN YEARS AFTER

Blues/rock. Ten Years After is a British blues-rock quartet consisting of Alvin Lee (b Dec 19, 1944), guitar and vocals; Chick Churchill (b Jan 2, 1949), keyboards; Leo Lyons (b Nov 30, 1944) bass; and Ric Lee (b Oct 20, 1945), drums. The group was formed in 1967 and signed to Decca in England. Its first album was not a success, but its second, the live *Undead* (1968) containing "I'm Going Home," a six-minute blues workout by the fleet-fingered Alvin hit the charts on both sides of the Atlantic. *Stonedhenge* (1969) hit the UK Top Ten in early 1969. Ten Years After's US breakthrough came as a result of its appearance at Woodstock, at which it played a nine-minute version of "I'm Going Home." Its next album, *Ssssh*, reached the US Top 20, and *Cricklewood Green*, containing the hit single "Love Like a Man," reached #14. *Watt* completed the group's Decca contract, after which it signed with Columbia and moved in a more mainstream pop direction, typified by the gold-selling 1971 album *A Space in Time* and its Top 40 single "I'd Love to Change the World." Subsequent efforts in that direction were less successful, however, and Ten Years After split up after the release of *Positive Vibrations* in 1974. They reunited in 1988 for concerts in Europe and recorded their first new album in 15 years, *About Time*, in 1989. –WR

Undead / POLYGRAM   1968
A live album from a group best experienced live, including some amazing guitar playing at phenomenal speeds from Alvin Lee. –WR

○ **Greatest Hits / POLYGRAM**   1977
The group's 1968-1970 best, including the hit "Love like a Man" and the Woodstock version of "I'm Going Home." –WR

TAMMI TERRELL   1946-1970

Motown. Signed to Motown in the mid 60s as a soloist, her greatest successes were duets with Marvin Gaye, including the original "Ain't No Mountain High Enough." Her solo successes were limited and her potential never fully realized, due to her illness and subsequent death from a brain tumor in 1970. –RAB

○ **Irresistible / MOTOWN**   1968
The title says it all. Irresistible! –RP

● **Greatest Hits / MOTOWN**   1970
Marvin Gaye & Tammi Terrell's Greatest Hits includes timeless love songs by Ashford and Simpson. Elegant performances. (Out of print) –RAB

TESLA

Hard rock. Tesla (from Sacramento) incorporates bluesy colorings into their mainstream hard-rock sound. –JB

Mechanical Resonance / GEFFEN   1987
Tesla's debut and one of their stronger albums. –JB

● **The Great Radio Controversy / GEFFEN**   1989
More use of acoustic instruments make this a treat. Features the Top Ten hit "Love Song," as well as "The Way It Is" and "Heaven's Trail (No Way Out)." –JB

○ **Five Man Acoustical Jam / GEFFEN**   1990
With the advent of "MTV Unplugged," it became popular for all types of groups to prove that they didn't have to rely on walls of amps and outboard gear to get their music across. *Five Man Acoustical Jam* was one of the most successful outings of that type, featuring versions of the Five Man Electrical Band's "Signs," Creedence's "Lodi," and a smattering of originals. –RC

Psychotic Supper / GEFFEN   1991
A solid followup to their breakthrough album, *The Great Radio Controversy.* –ED

TESTAMENT

Thrash. A sometimes-frightening thrash/speed-metal band, featuring guitarist Alex Skolnick. Their original name was Legacy, but the new name was suggested by Stormtroopers of Death/M.O.D. vocalist Billy Milano. –JB

○ **The Legacy / ATLANTIC**   1987
The Legacy is an essential listen for those who enjoy aggressive thrash-metal. Particularly impressive is the lead guitar work of Alex Skolnick. –JB

JOE TEX   1933-1982

Soul, R&B. Often pausing in the middle of a ballad for a brief but sincere secular sermon on the inherent value of true love or the hazards of cheating, Joe Tex was one of the Southern soul genre's most enduring performers — and one of its most versatile.

With a stage surname reflecting his home state, Tex first entered a recording studio in 1955 for King, singing some potent R&B before trying his luck in New Orleans with Ace. Tex joined forces with Nashville producer Buddy Killen (who formed the Dial logo to market the singer's output) and finally scaled the soul playlists in 1965 with his smash "Hold What You've Got." The intense gospel-tinged ballad proved the prototypal Tex track, loaded with sound advice and downhome homilies.

That's not to say that Tex didn't record some hard-driving uptempo soul during the mid 60s — "A Sweet Woman Like You," "S.Y.S.L.J.F.M. (The Letter Song)," and "Show Me" all sizzle, while the hilarious "Skinny Legs and All," another major R&B and pop hit, accurately testifies to Tex's live charisma.

With his microphone-stand acrobatics a longtime trademark, Tex's winning streak endured into the next decade with the grunting "I Gotcha," his biggest crossover success in 1972. He eked out another smash in the midst of disco fever with "Ain't Gonna Bump No More (With No Big Fat Woman)," his ebullient sense of humor still intact. Tex died in 1982. –BD

○ **Best of Joe Tex / RHINO**
Capturing the philosophical positivism and musical perfection of late-60s soul. Includes "I Believe I'm Gonna Make It" and his other 60s hits. –BLP

THE TEXAS TORNADOS

Tex-Mex. A Tex-Mex supergroup — Doug Sahm, Augie Meyers, Flaco Jimenez, and Freddy Fender — whose sound is a well-done rollicking version of country music in the Mexican style, accordion and all. The Tornados are good enough to have been twice nominated for a Grammy; they won with "Soy de San Luis." Play it at any party and forget about things being dull the rest of the night. –DV & JT

Texas Tornados - Spanish Versions / WARNER
Like it says. Their debut album, in español. –JT

○ **Zone of Our Own / WARNER**   1991
Not quite as jubilant as the first album, but these guys are incapable of not being fun. –JT

THEE HYPNOTICS

Psychedelic, alternative rock. British revivers of psychedelia for those who thought the Amboy Dukes were wimps. Thee Hypnotics blend period gimmicks with good old-fashioned crunch to make for a style of retro that keeps up with the times. A great live band. –DH

○ **Come Down Heavy / RCA**   1991
The title says it all. Dense, plodding, and quite intense. –DH

THEM

British Invasion. Unlike many of the squeaky-clean acts that were part of the British Invasion, the rough-and-tumble Them (formed 1963), fronted by the scruffy Van Morrison, delivered fiery blues-informed rock & roll. During their brief career, Them produced a handful of classics in songs like "Gloria" (#71), "Mystic Eyes" (#33), "Baby Please Don't Go," and "Here Comes the Night" (#24). In 1966 Them parted ways, with Morrison going on to a sucessful solo career and keyboardist Peter Bardens forming British art-rock band Camel. –RC

☆ **Featuring Van Morrison / POLYGRAM-LONDON**   1987
Remembered today as the starting point for Van Morrison, Them was a tough, bluesy Irish rock group that made two of the most compelling singles of the mid 60s: "Gloria" and

"Here Comes the Night." Both are here, along with the best of the rest of their small catalog. –WR

THESE IMMORTAL SOULS

Alternative rock. Another of the European bands bourbon-soaked in their conceptions of a gothic American South. This makes for sprawling, spacious, bluesy music. Features Rowland S. Howard of the Birthday Party and Epic soundtracks of the Swell Maps and the Jacobites. –BE

○ **Get Lost (Don't Lie) / SST**   1987
More Southern-Gothic landscapes as imagined by Aussies and Brits. –RG

THEY MIGHT BE GIANTS

Alternative pop. This Brooklyn-based duo, made up of John Flansburgh and John Linell, gives a new twist to pop music. Their lyrics (which are often funny and always offbeat) are accompanied by Flansburgh's guitar and Linell's accordion, giving their songs a unique sound. Full of puns, wisecracks, and thesaurus-dependent lyrics, TMBG's music is always entertaining. –IME

They Might Be Giants / ENIGMA   1986
TMBG's debut album. The album includes a few good songs, such as "Don't Let's Start," "Put Your Hand Inside the Puppet Head," and "I Hope That I Get Old Before I Die." Overall, the album is too rough and tedious, featuring TMBG's trademark "under three-minute" songs. –IME

○ **Lincoln / ENIGMA**   1988
TMBG's most entertaining album lets you have fun with the songs without trying to ferret out any deeper meaning in the bizarre lyrics. Here, TMBG reaches a good balance between goofy lyrics and listenable music. The songs won't spark any deep intellectual conversations, but you might just enjoy yourself. –IME

Flood / ELEKTRA   1990
Musically, this is their best album, but in their attempt to put meaning into their lyrics, they have lost sight of TMBG's most appealing quality — the fun. *Flood* features a cover of "Istanbul (Not Constantinople)," written by J. Kennedy and N. Simon. There are a few outstanding songs, such as "Birdhouse in Your Soul" and "Particle Man." –IME

THIN LIZZY

Hard rock. An Irish rock quartet led by Hendrix look-alike Phil Lynott (b 1951 - d 1986). Band members came and went over the years, but Lynott's rebel stance and intelligent, working-class lyrics won them a huge worldwide following. –CK

Jailbreak / POLYGRAM   1976
Their most perfectly realized album, featuring the title track and "The Boys Are Back in Town," a staple of classic-rock radio to this day. –CK

○ **Dedication - The Best of Thin Lizzy / POLYGRAM**   1991
A good, if somewhat brief look at all the high spots, featuring great guitar from fretmeisters Gary Moore, Eric Bell, John Sykes, and others. –CK

.38 SPECIAL

Southern rock, rock/pop. This hard-touring Jacksonville-based band (formed 1975) featured lead singer Donnie Van Zant, brother of Lynyrd Skynyrd's lead singer Ronnie Van Zant. .38 Special delivered a brand of Southern pop-rock that wasn't quite so hard-hitting as Skynyrd's, while showcasing an Allman Brothers-like lineup, with two lead guitarists and two drummers. They also charted more hits than either of those bands. Their most popular hits included "Caught up in You" (#10), "Hold on Loosely" (#27), "Back Where You Belong" (#20), "Like No Other Night" (#14), "Second Chance" (#6), "If I'd Been the One" (#19), and "Rockin' into the Night" (#43). –RC

Wild Eyed & Live / A&M   1978

A live album featuring an even balance of hits and smokin' crowd pleasers. –CK

○ **Flashback - Best of .38 Special / A&M**   1987
An excellent retrospective, featuring all the hits. The last commercial flowering of Southern rock. –CK

CARLA THOMAS   *b* 1942

Soul, R&B. In the glorious decade and a half of sound that was Stax in the 60s and early 70s, Carla Thomas was the Queen of Memphis Soul. She was born in Memphis in 1942, and 18 years later she recorded a duet with her father Rufus Thomas, giving the fledgling Satellite label its first taste of success with the regional hit "Cause I Love You." As her 18th birthday drew nigh, she cut her first solo single, the teen ballad "Gee Whiz (Look at His Eyes)." Written a few years earlier and rejected by Vee Jay in Chicago, it gave Satellite its first national hit, breaking the Top Ten mark on both the R&B and pop charts. Shortly thereafter Satellite became Stax, and Carla proceeded to claw her way onto the national charts another 22 times with such immortal slices of soul as her answer song to Sam Cooke, "I'll Bring It on Home to You," as well as "Let Me Be Good to You," "B-A-B-Y," "Tramp" (with Otis Redding), and "I Like What You're Doing to Me." Carla released six solo albums and, with Otis Redding, one duet album on Stax between 1961 and 1971. –RB

Gee Whiz / ATLANTIC   1961
Carla Thomas's first album was typical fare for the R&B market of the time, combining two chart entries (the title song and "A Love of My Own") with covers of recent chart hits (the Drifters's "Fools Fall in Love" and "Dance with Me," the Five Satins's "To the Aisle"), standards ("The Masquerade Is Over"), and a handful of originals. This was the first album produced by the then-fledgling Stax label and the unique Stax sound was not yet manifest. –RB

● **Carla / ATLANTIC / BB 130**   1966
Paired with Stax writing whiz-kids Isaac Hayes and David Porter, Thomas had her greatest chart run, beginning with the hit "B-A-B-Y" and continuing with "Let Me Be Good to You." Both of those appear here, alongside evocative slabs of country-soul in covers of Hank Williams's "I'm So Lonesome I Could Cry" and Patsy Cline's "I Fall to Pieces." For good measure, Thomas also tries her hand at the blues with covers of Howlin' Wolf's "Little Red Rooster" and Jimmy Reed's "Baby What You Want Me to Do." –RB

Comfort Me / ATLANTIC / BB 134   1966
A collection of twelve tracks recorded over a year and a half, *Comfort Me* showcases Thomas in the midst of the developed Stax sound. Backed by Booker T. and the MG's and the Mar-Key horns, Thomas turns in fine covers of Baby Washington's "Move on Drifter," the Marvelettes's "Forever," the Shirelles's "Will You Love Me Tomorrow," the Everly Brothers' "Let It Be Me," Jackie DeShannon's "What the World Needs Now," the Toys's "Lover's Concerto," and Barbara Mason's "Yes I'm Ready," coupled with a number of efforts by Thomas herself, Steve Cropper, and Eddie Floyd. The highlight is the Cropper-Floyd title cut, with utterly gorgeous backing by Gladys Knight and the Pips. –RB

○ **The Queen Alone / RHINO-ATLANTIC / BB 133**   1967
Another fine effort recorded during the Memphis-based Stax label's glory years. Two R&B hits, Isaac Hayes and David Porter's "Something Good (Is Going to Happen to You)" and Eddie Floyd and Al Bell's "I'll Always Have Faith in You," are included, as well as one of Thomas's finest ballad performances, Homer Banks's and Allen Jones's "Lie to Keep Me from Crying." –RB

Memphis Queen / STAX / BB 151   1969
Half recorded in Memphis with the usual stellar Stax crew and half recorded in New York with local session musicians (all overdubbed in Detroit), *Memphis Queen* finds Thomas and the Stax label in transition. Motown alumnus Don Davis handled production, draping many cuts in large,

lush orchestral settings. "I Like What You're Doing (To Me)" was a Top Ten R&B hit, and three other tracks had brief chart runs. −RB

○ **Hidden Gems / FANTASY-STAX**   1992
Twenty outtakes recorded for Stax between 1960 and 1968, a number of which are gems. In fact, it is really surprising just how good the unreleased Stax stuff was in the 60s. "Loneliness," "Sweet Sensation," and "It Ain't No Easy Thing" all could have been superb singles. −RB

CHRIS THOMAS

Blues/rock. Thomas's father is Tabby Thomas, a journeyman blues singer from Baton Rouge, LA. The younger Thomas has funneled his father's blues into a sound that makes nods to the old bluesmen, Prince-styled gospel, and Jimi Hendrix. −JF

○ **Cry of Prophets / WARNER**   1990
Thomas whipped up a fine debut, full of gospel urgency ("Dance to the Music") and hard-rock bite. −JF

IRMA THOMAS   b 1941

Soul, R&B. Radiating an outgoing joy that's inevitably at the heart of her infectious vocal delivery, Irma Thomas has no rivals as the Soul Queen of New Orleans. Working at a Crescent City nightery as a waitress in 1959, Thomas sat in one night with Tommy Ridgely's band and made such a favorable impression that the veteran bandleader hustled her into the studio shortly thereafter to wax her first hit for the Ron label, the driving "Don't Mess with My Man." She joined forces with producer Allen Toussaint to make some of her most moving outings for Minit Records during the early 60s, notably "It's Raining," "Ruler of My Heart," and "Cry On," before venturing to the West Coast, where she cut both her biggest seller, the lushly produced "Wish Someone Would Care," and her best-known song, the original "Time Is on My Side" — and she's still bitter enough about the Rolling Stones' cover stealing her thunder to discourage requests for the tune. The highly adaptable chanteuse also made some sizzling soul at Rich Hall's Muscle Shoals studio for Chess in the summer of 1967 before cooling off for a while during the 70s. But she's back now, as radiant as ever — and for convincing proof, listen to her buoyant 1990 concert performance on Rounder, *Live! Simply the Best.* Now that's truth in packaging! −BD

Wish Someone Would Care / IMPERIAL   1964
Her classic album. Includes the original version of "Time Is on My Side." −RP

New Rules / ROUNDER   1986
A great mix of old and new songs. −RP

Ruler of Hearts / CHARLY   1989
Twenty-four tracks; 16 studio from 1960 to 1962, 8 live from 1976. Excellent sound quality. (Import) −RP

☆ **Time Is on My Side - The Best of - Vol. 1 / EMI**   1992
Twenty-three sides representing the cream of Irma Thomas's brilliant Minit/Liberty years (1961-1966), when her reputation as "The Soul Queen of New Orleans" was built. Virtually all her best-known tunes are here — "Wish Someone Would Care," "Ruler of My Heart," "It's Raining," and "Time Is on My Side" (covered note-for-note by the Stones). Beautiful singing from one of the first ladies of soul music. Essential. −co

Live! Simply the Best / ROUNDER
Outstanding even among the great female voices of the 60s, and that's sayin' a lot. Her first "live" album ... shows her still commanding some mighty pipes, and her easy professionalism working a crowd is a joy to hear .... Emphasis is on gospel-drenched soul and New Orleans R&B. Irma makes a special delivery on these goods." −MARK A. HUMPHREY, ROCK & ROLL

Something Good - Muscle Shoals / MCA
Fourteen tracks recorded at Muscle Shoals in 1967. Soul music at its best. −RP

RUFUS THOMAS   b 1917

Soul, R&B. The self-proclaimed "world's oldest teenager" has been a staple on the Memphis music scene since the 20s. He recorded the first hit for Sun Records ("Bear Cat," from 1953); was a celebrity DJ on Memphis's WDIA; and, with his daughter Carla, he gave Stax their first hit (1960's "Cause I Love You"). He recorded an album for Alligator in 1988 but his best work was done for Sun and Stax. His Sun material is available on several various-artist collections. −JF

○ **Walking the Dog / ATLANTIC**   1964
Thomas's first album on Stax contains many of his best early hits, including the title track and several other dance- and novelty-oriented gems. −JF

RICHARD THOMPSON   b 1949

Singer/songwriter, folk/rock, rock & roll. Thompson's solo work presents something of a dilemma: he's still a masterful guitarist, and he continues to write incredible songs, full of pathos and venom, but he's not the singer ex-wife Linda Thompson was. But if his best solo albums lack the beauty and grace of vintage Richard and Linda, they're still highly personal and emotionally charged, which makes up for her absence. −JF

Guitar-Vocal / HANNIBAL-CARTHAGE   1976
A hodgepodge of rarities, including some Fairport Convention stuff and early cuts with wife Linda Thompson. Includes a beautiful alternate take of "A Heart Needs a Home." −JF

Hand of Kindness / HANNIBAL   1983
His first post-divorce release is an uncharacteristically bouncy set, shifting from 12-bar stompers to lilting folk ditties. −JF

Across a Crowded Room / POLYGRAM   1985
A somewhat predictable set of bitter love songs, accompanied by radio-ready production and, unfortunately, not enough guitar. −JF

● **Amnesia / CAPITOL**   1988
This dynamic and diverse set is his best, with loads of droll, biting rockers and broken-heart manifestos. −JF

○ **Rumor & Sigh / CAPITOL**   1991
Another creative triumph. Not quite so lashing as *Amnesia*, but here's the source of many future Thompson classics. −JF

RICHARD AND LINDA THOMPSON

Singer/songwriter, folk/rock, rock & roll. Over the course of a half-dozen albums, husband-and-wife team Richard and Linda Thompson produced some fine folk-rock albums. As a guitarist, Richard (formerly of Fairport Convention) displayed an ability for stunning, lyrical lead work. Vocally, his woody baritone had a manic undercurrent, while Linda possessed an entrancingly warm alto. Their most powerful artistic achievement was their final album *Shoot Out the Lights*, released in 1982. −RC

○ **I Want to See the Bright Lights ... / CARTHAGE**   1974
I Want to See the Bright Lights Tonight contains some of Richard Thompson's darkest songs and several beautiful vocal performances by Linda Thompson. "When I Get to the Border," "Calvary Cross," and "Withered and Died" define their early direction. −JF

★ **Shoot Out the Lights / HANNIBAL**   1982
One of the most mesmerizing recordings ever committed to tape by a husband/wife team, *Shoot Out the Lights* is the sound of a marriage falling apart — particularly Richard and Linda Thompson's. Linda's beautifully world-weary alto and Richard's indignant quaver deliver some monumental performances on tracks like "The Wall of Death," "Don't Renege on Our Love," "Did She Jump or Was She Pushed," "Walking on a Wire," and "Just the Motion." The title track features some incredible lead guitar playing by Richard. Indispensable for any comprehensive rock collection, particularly fans of folk-rock. −RC

THOMPSON TWINS

Dance-pop. This British trio, comprising Tom Bailey (b Jan 18, 1956), Alannah Currie (b Sep 28, 1957), and Joe Leeway (b Nov 15, 1957), specialized in accessible early-MTV-style synth/dance-pop. Among their hits were "Hold Me Now" (#3), "Lay Your Hands on Me" (#6), "King for a Day" (#8), "Doctor! Doctor!" (#11), and "Lies" (#30). –RC

○ **Greatest Mixes: Best of... / ARISTA** 1988
Greatest Mixes: The Best of the Thompson Twins. A collection of their best on Arista. It was downhill once they switched record labels. –KMC

GEORGE THOROGOOD & THE DESTROYERS

Blues/rock. A Delaware-based blues band formed in 1973 and led by guitarist/singer George Thorogood, who brings a rough-voiced enthusiasm to the music of John Lee Hooker, Elmore James, and others. The group scored five gold albums in 1980-1988. –WR

George Thorogood & the Destroyers / ROUNDER 1977
Contains Thorogood's crowd-pleasing rendition of John Lee Hooker's "One Bourbon, One Scotch, One Beer." Its basic approach — heavy on Thorogood's bluesy guitar playing — serves as the prototype for every Destroyers record that followed. –WR

○ **Bad to the Bone / CAPITOL** 1982
Though songs such as "Back to Wentzville" are credited to "G. Thorogood," he'd be the first to admit that they are proudly derivative of Chuck Berry and his other mentors. The title track, another Thorogood copyright, has become ubiquitous in *Terminator 2* and the *Problem Child* movies and elsewhere, but it's still terrific. –WR

THREE DEGREES

Soul. The Philadelphia trio (formed in 1965) was fashioned into a slick act, with the ability to do intense deep soul as well as smooth ballads. They will be forever known for the haunting 1974 hit "When Will I See You Again." They had a greater British impact than they had in America. –BC

○ **... And Holding! / ICHIBAN**
Their only album in print. A fine set of Southern blues/soul ballads and mid-tempo cuts. –BC

THREE DOG NIGHT

Rock/pop. At a time when rock elitists deemed Top 40 radio decidedly uncool, the slick multi-vocal blend of soulful pop-rock of Three Dog Night (formed 1968) made 21 trips to the charts from 1969 to 1975.
The centerpiece of Three Dog Night's sound was the band's trio of lead singers: Danny Hutton (b Sep 10, 1946), Chuck Negron (Jun 8, 1942), and Cory Wells (b Feb 5, 1944). Composed of seasoned players, the band displayed quite a bit of proficiency musically, even though their lurching, soulful dance rhythms occasionally sounded awkward.
Since the band lacked any real songwriting resource from within, they were smart enough to look outside for material and had the good taste to plug into some of the era's best songwriters. While Three Dog Night's versions of the material may not have been definitive, they opened the door to the mass market's awareness of talented writers like Steve Winwood, Harry Nilsson, Robbie Robertson, Randy Newman, Hoyt Axton, Neil Young, Laura Nyro, and many others. Elton John and Bernie Taupin had their first Stateside success with Three Dog Night's cover of "Lady Samantha." –RC

○ **Best of Three Dog Night / MCA** 1983
This collection contains all of Three Dog Night's hits, plus a few key album tracks. Among the tracks included are "One" (#5), "Easy to Be Hard" (#4), "Eli's Coming" (#10), "Mama Told Me Not to Come)" (#1), "Joy to the World" (#1), "Black & White" (#1), "Shambala" (#3), "An Old-Fashioned Love Song" (#4), "Never Been to Spain" (#5), and "Celebrate" (#15). –RC

THREE JOHNS

Alternative rock. Scratchy, amelodic guitar punk from a group of English left-wing intellectuals. Guitarist Jon Langford is also a Mekon. –JD

Atom Drum Bop / ABSTRACT 1984
Their debut album. Compelling, smart, literate — and rocks like crazy. (Import) –JD

○ **Demonocracy: The Singles 1982-1986 / ABSTRACT** 1986
Challenging, brutal, and very, very funny. This is an essential collection. (Out of print) –JD

World by Storm / ABSTRACT 1986
Fine followup to *Atom Drum Bop.* Ferocious. (Out-of-print import) –JD

Death of Everything & More / CAROLINE 1988
Perhaps not their best, but their funniest! –JD

THROBBING GRISTLE

Alternative rock. This is the group that defined the industrial sound, forging their distinctively dark outlook with sonic experimentation and dance beats at the dawn of the punk age. Although Throbbing Gristle followed no formulas — producing many unpredictable albums and hundreds of live tapes in just a few years — the pop aspects of industrial dance music became an identifiable mainstream genre. Consequently, TG split up into two entities, with members Chris and Cosey following the dance trend, while Genesis P. Orridge took the underground route in Psychic TV. –MB

2nd Annual Report / ELEKTRA 1977
Actually their first album, with singles and different live versions of two early pieces. –MB

○ **20 Jazz Funk Greats / ELEKTRA** 1979
As close as they got to the industrial-dance style of their many imitators. Fairly accessible. –MB

D.O.A. / ELEKTRA 1979
A dark lyrical content dominates these 15 tracks. –MB

Heathen Earth / ELEKTRA 1979
Live in the studio, combining the best of both harrowing worlds. –MB

● **Greatest Hits / ELEKTRA** 1980
Like the title says (with irony). An industrial primer with song sensibility. –MB

Mission of Dead Souls / ELEKTRA 1981
Their final and perhaps most extreme musical assault, live in San Francisco. –MB

JOHNNY THUNDERS 1941-1990

Punk, rock & roll. This ex-New York Doll guitarist recorded a slew of albums before a fatal 1990 heroin overdose. Unfortunately, most of them are garbage, consisting mostly of live shows that, more than anything, document the perils of heroin addiction and its effects on someone who should've remained a rock & roll contender well into the 90s. –JF

○ **So Alone / SIRE** 1978
Thunders's first solo shot enlisted members of the Sex Pistols, the Hot Rods, and the Only Ones, featuring a variety of material that showcased both his mangy vocals and his strangling guitar attack. –JF

Too Much Junkie Business / ROI 1983
The best of Thunders's live and outtake documents. For diehards only. –JF

TANITA TIKARAM

Singer/songwriter, pop. Tikaram, a singer/songwriter from the English town of Basingstoke, attracted much attention with her smoky conversational voice and her enigmatically mature-sounding debut, which was released while she was still in her teens. Tikaram's moody musical introspections and subtle new-age-like arrangements have an unusual sophistication. –RC

○ **Ancient Heart / WARNER**   1988
In spite of the fact that Tanita Tikaram was in her teens at the time of this debut, her smoky conversational vocal delivery, weighty open-ended lyrics, and moody introspective pieces portrayed an almost mystical level of maturity. Rod Argent and Peter Van Hooke's production is very clean and ambient, making this a fine marriage of sonic integrity and artistry. Highlights include "For All These Years," "Twist in My Sobriety," "He Likes the Sun," "Valentine Heart," and "World outside Your Window." –RC

SONNY TIL & THE ORIOLES

Doo-wop. A smooth, early-50s vocal group best known for the 1953 hit "Crying in the Chapel." –JF

○ **Greatest Hits / COLLECTABLES**
A good overview of this historic 50s-60s harmony group. One of the pioneering R&B vocal groups. A decent collection of their hits, marred by putrid sound. –RW

'TIL TUESDAY

Rock/pop. Aimee Mann was the lead singer and bass player in the Boston-based 'Til Tuesday, which scored a Top Ten hit with "Voices Carry" and a gold-selling album of the same name in 1985. The rest of the group was Michael Hausmann, drums; Robert Holmes, guitar; and Joey Pesce, keyboards. The group recorded two more albums but broke up after *Everything's Different Now* in 1988. –WR

○ **Voices Carry / EPIC**   1985
'Til Tuesday showed a lot of promise with this debut album, which focused on Aimee Mann's emotive singing, notably on the title track. –WR

TIMBUK 3

Singer/songwriter, alternative rock. Wry and dark, Timbuk 3 (Pat and Barbara MacDonald and a tape machine) specializes in politically tinged, folk-derived melodrama, which runs the gamut from spry pop to angst-ridden mellowness. –JD

○ **Greetings from Timbuk 3 / I.R.S.**   1986
Contains the hit single, "The Future's So Bright, I Gotta Wear Shades." But it's hardly a worthless album propping up a fluky hit: there's plenty of good stuff inside, especially the chilling "Life Is Hard" and the funny "Hairstyles and Attitudes." –HD

TIME

Dance, funk. From their origins as Prince's first pet project, to their self-produced funk-rock oeuvre, the Time has been a fascinating and outrageous congregation. Vocalist Morris Day infused his cocky, swaggering personality into dance hits that would make Rufus Thomas envious, and, unlike most of the competition, the band managed to do something unique with Prince's genre-busting innovations. Time broke up in the late 80s, with Day going on to a somewhat disastrous solo career, Jesse Johnson crafting two dazzling solo albums, and Jimmy Jam and Terry Lewis becoming one of the most successful production teams this side of Gamble-Huff, working with everyone from Full Force and Janet Jackson to the S.O.S. Band and Human League. The group re-formed in 1990 and released the excellent *Pandemonium*. –JF

○ **What Time Is It? / WARNER**   1982
After a tentative debut, the Time bounced back with one of 1982's best dance albums, full of hilarious stompers and braggadocio ballads. –JF

Ice Cream Castle / WARNER   1984
Ice Cream Castle finds the band stepping out of Prince's purple shadow and discovering their own personality. The relentless "Jungle Love" is their best song. –JF

● **Pandemonium / WARNER**   1990
Jam and Lewis bring their groundbreaking production techniques to a set that alternately demonstrates just how timeless the Time's boogie can be and just what the band members picked up during their sabbatical. –JF

TIN MACHINE

Alternative rock. To some ears, Tin Machine's sheets of guitar feedback and bash-ola drums may be overkill, but this quartet, fronted by pop chameleon David Bowie, takes aggressive, dissonant hard rock to bracing extremes, particularly on their exciting self-titled debut. –RC

○ **Tin Machine / EMI**   1989
For fans of wildly dissonant hard-rock, Tin Machine's debut effort (uneven as it is) is a gem. The band's chemistry, on tracks like "Heaven Is Here" (check the lead ride at the end), "I Can't Read," "Crack City," and "Baby Can Dance," is great. "Amazing" sports a nice descending guitar pattern and one of the album's more memorable melodies, but their version of Lennon's "Working Class Hero" rings hollow. Lyrically, most of this is Bowie at his most half-baked. –RC

TOM TOM CLUB

Alternative rock, dance-pop. Tom Tom Club began life as a side project for Talking Heads members Chris Frantz and Tina Weymouth, who adopted a light, tropical dance style that won them a gold album in *Tom Tom Club* in 1981 and a Top 40 single in "Genius of Love." They continued to make albums under this moniker between Heads production projects: *Close to the Bone* (1983) and *Boom Boom Chi Boom Boom* (1989). They even toured as Tom Tom Club in the summer of 1989. When the Heads broke up in late 1991, Tom Tom Club became Frantz and Weymouth's main outlet. They released *Dark Sneak Love Action* in 1992. –WR

○ **Tom Tom Club / SIRE**   1983
Frantz and Weymouth pulled off a surprising mixture of rap and dance music with light humor, expecially on "Genius of Love." Maybe it was a fluke: they never equaled the effervescence of this album, though they tried. –WR

TORNADOES

Rock/pop. Britain's premier instrumental group of the early 60s, the Tornadoes' fame rests principally on "Telstar," a haunting instrumental written by their producer, Joe Meek, which rocketed to the top of the charts in both England and the United States in early 1962. Although none of their subsequent work went so far (or deserved to), they achieved additional recognition after becoming Billy Fury's backup band — they played on his live album, *We Want Billy* — and their bass player, blond, German-born Heinz Burt (who went by the moniker "Heinz") later became a low-level chart success as a vocalist ("Just Like Eddie," etc.) –BE

○ **Roots of British Rock / SIRE**
"Telstar" is one of the good reasons (among many) for owning this out-of-print collection. –BE

Away from It All / DECCA   1963
An unfortunate collection of novelty tunes that fail to capture the excitement of "Telstar" or even of its lackluster followup "Globetrotter." For serious fans only. (Out of print.) –BE

TOTO

Rock/pop. Formed in 1978, Toto immediately became favorites on FM rock and pop formats with their million-selling mainstream rocker "Hold the Line" (#5), followed by the mildly funky "Georgy Porgy" (#48). Their sound, honed from years of session work, had a steely precision that, while sounding impressive, seemed bloodless. Nevertheless, their fourth album, *Toto IV* (1983), became the biggest album of their career, earning six Grammy awards. During this time, Toto continued doing session work for many artists, in a sense defining much of the sound of radio during the mid 80s. –RC

Toto IV / CBS   1982
This is the album that cleaned up at the 1982 Grammys. Most of *Toto IV* is a seamless collection of precision-crafted hard-rockers and power ballads. The album contains five hits, the biggest being "Africa," "Rosanna," and "I Won't Hold You Back." –RC

○ **Past to Present 1977-90 / CBS** 1990
Past to Present 1977-90 is a complete set of the biggest songs from this group of Los Angeles session pros, including "Africa" (#1), "Hold the Line" (#5), "Rosanna" (#2), "I Won't Hold You Back" (#10), "Stranger in Town" (#30), "99" (#26), "Make Believe" (#30), and "Georgy Porgy" (#48). –RC

THE TOURISTS

Rock/pop, psychedelic. In a brief career lasting from 1979 to 1980, the Tourists recorded three albums, *The Tourists*, *Reality Effect*, and *Luminous Basement*, all of which made the UK charts. They also scored five chart singles, two of which, "I Only Want to Be with You" and "So Good to Be Back Home Again," made the Top Ten. The band included singer Annie Lennox (b Dec 25, 1954), keyboardist/guitarist Dave Stewart (b Sep 9, 1952), vocalist/guitarist Pete Coombes (who wrote most of the songs), bassist Eddie Chin, and drummer Jim Toomey. After the split, Stewart and Lennox formed Eurythmics. –WR

○ **Should Have Been Greatest Hits / EPIC** 1984
A best-of released in the wake of Eurythmics's success, and therefore emphasizing Stewart and Lennox's contributions over Coombes's. Nevertheless, it's a well-chosen selection and includes four of their five UK hits, among them their sole US chart entry, a terrific remake of Dusty Springfield's "I Only Want to Be with You." –WR

ALLEN TOUSSAINT b 1938

R&B. His inherently funky piano work heavily influenced by his Crescent City forefathers — Professor Longhair, Huey "Piano" Smith, and Fats Domino — and with a heavy dose of Ray Charles, a young visionary named Allen Toussaint almost singlehandedly fashioned a fresh, vital New Orleans R&B sound for the early 60s.
Earning a vaunted reputation as a session pianist, Toussaint debuted on vinyl in 1958 with an obscure RCA album whimsically billed as "A. Tousan." When Joe Banashak inaugurated his Minit label in 1960, Toussaint joined the firm as A&R man and quickly proved himself the ultimate behind-the-scenes wizard on the New Orleans scene. During the early to mid 60s, Toussaint tirelessly wrote, arranged, produced, and played on hits by Ernie K-Doe, Irma Thomas, Jessie Hill, Chris Kenner, Barbara George, Lee Dorsey, Benny Spellman, the Showmen, and many more, his rolling keyboards vital to the charm of virtually all of them.
After unleashing the Meters on the world, Toussaint finally began to step out as a front man in 1970, although his low-key vocals have never achieved quite the same level of success as his previous productions for others. His brilliant compositions have been covered by everyone from Herb Alpert & the Tijuana Brass to Robert Palmer and Bonnie Raitt. Allen Toussaint's stature as a New Orleans musical giant endures. –BD

○ **Collection / WARNER**
A representative cross-section of the legendary New Orleans piano man's solo output — uneven but interesting. –BD

The Wild Sound of New Orleans / RCA 1958
His debut album, featuring a killer band, storming second-line instrumentals, and Toussaint's rolling 88s. –BD

TOWER OF POWER

Soul, pop. Studio session work has never lent itself to wide recognition except among other musicians, yet when not on the road as Tower of Power, the individuals who make up the critically acclaimed West Coast horn section might as well go by another name: "Backup for the World." Individually and in various incarnations, members of Tower of Power (fronted by Emilio Castillo) have recorded as sidemen for Elton John, Santana, Bonnie Raitt, Huey Lewis, Little Feat, David Sanborn, Michelle Shocked, Paula Abdul, Aaron Neville, and Riot. Tower of Power has had their share of personnel changes over

the years, but the core group members (including Castillo on saxes and vocals, Stephen "Doc" Kupka on baritone sax, Greg Adams on trumpet and vocals, and Rocco Prestia on bass) have remained, giving the band a percussive horn-based sound that is not rooted in any one genre. –RS

Tower of Power / WARNER 1972
Contains "So Very Hard to Go," "Soul Vaccination," and other trademark funk. –DH

○ **Back to Oakland / WARNER** 1976
A hard, tightly structured slice of funk; their best album. –DH

PETE TOWNSHEND b 1945

Singer/songwriter, rock & roll. Pete Townshend was the guitarist and songwriter for the Who from 1964 to 1982. Best-known for his conceptual works, he wrote *Tommy* and *Quadrophenia* for the group. Townshend made his first, tentative solo album, *Who Came First*, in 1972. Dedicated to his guru, Meher Baba, the album continued themes pursued in the previous Who album, *Who's Next*, and contained material from an abortive conceptual work, *Lifehouse*. The album sold modestly. In 1976, Townshend made a duo album, *Rough Mix*, with Ronnie Lane, formerly the bassist in the Small Faces.
Townshend's first full-fledged solo effort, however, was *Empty Glass* (1980), which sold half a million copies, reached the Top Five, and featured the Top Ten hit "Let My Love Open the Door," as well as the minor hits "A Little Is Enough" and "Rough Boys." Townshend followed this in 1982 with *All the Best Cowboys Have Chinese Eyes*.
Following the demise of the Who, Townshend released *Scoop*, a two-disc collection of demos, in 1983 (a second volume appeared in 1987). In 1985 he returned to thematic efforts with the album *White City - A Novel*, which included the Top 30 single "Face the Face." In the same year, Townshend published a book of short stories, *Horse's Neck*. As part of the *White City* project, Townshend appeared in an accompanying film, for which he organized a band called Pete Townshend's Deep End. The unit played only a few gigs, but one was videotaped and recorded, resulting in the 1986 album *Pete Townshend's Deep End Live!* In 1989 Townshend released an album based on Ted Hughes's children's story, *The Iron Man*. The record featured guest vocals by John Lee Hooker and Nina Simone, as well as two tracks featuring the three surviving members of the Who. Simultaneous with the album's release, Townshend embarked on a reunion tour with the Who. –WR

☆ **Empty Glass / ATLANTIC** 1980
A bright, energetic rock album, tightly played and sung in a manner equaling the best Who albums. –BE

Scoop / ATLANTIC 1983
Townshend's first batch of Who demos. Not viscerally exciting, but musically intriguing. –BE

Another Scoop / ATLANTIC 1987
The second batch of Who demos, with better songs than the first. Some surprises for the serious fan. –BE

PETE TOWNSHEND & RONNIE LANE

Rock & roll. Two British guitar heroes, ex-members of rival British mod bands, from the 60s and 70s team up. –ED

☆ **Rough Mix / ATLANTIC** 1977
Pete Townshend and Ronnie Lane rock it up, with some good melodies thrown in. Tops among Townshend's non-Who projects. –BE

TRAFFIC

Rock/pop, psychedelic. Among all the bands to emerge from England in the 60s, Traffic is one of the few who have aged gracefully.
At the time of Traffic's inception in 1967, former Spencer Davis bandmate Stevie Winwood (b May 12, 1948) was its most noted member, but with the release of their debut, *Mr. Fantasy*, it became clear that this was truly a band of four equally creative multi-instrumentalists. Their initial efforts

fused an ecumenical range of musical genres through a fairly psychedelic sensibility, most of it among the best examples of that approach to late-60s pop-rock. Guitarist and vocalist Dave Mason (b May 10, 1947) penned some particularly strong material on those first Traffic albums, especially "Feelin' Alright," a song that was later popularized by Joe Cocker, Three Dog Night, and many others.

After many instances of quitting the band over creative differences (the remaining three were resistant to his obvious pop tendencies), Mason left for good after 1971's *Welcome to the Canteen* (#26), a live album. By then, he had already earned a gold album for his 1970 debut, *Alone Together* (#22). After their second self-titled album, Traffic parted ways when Winwood joined the short-lived supergroup, Blind Faith. After Blind Faith's demise, Winwood began a solo effort, tentatively titled *Mad Shadows*. As the project developed, Winwood increasingly sought the input of Chris Wood and Jim Capaldi. The result was the funkier, earthier *John Barleycorn Must Die* (#5).

Traffic's studio followup, *The Low Spark of High Heeled Boys* (#7), incorporated a spacier improvisational sound. The title cut became an FM rock-radio standard. Several more albums followed, and the band parted ways in 1974.

Wood died on July 12, 1983, of liver failure. Capaldi and Dave Mason have experienced sporadically successful solo careers. Winwood, on the other hand, has had a phenomenally long and profitable string of releases. –RC

○ **Mr. Fantasy / ISLAND / BB 88**   1968
Produced by Jimmy Miller (other credits: the Rolling Stones, Spooky Tooth, Blind Faith), *Mr. Fantasy* is sonically decked out in *Sgt. Pepper*-period psychedelic splendor. Although much music of the period sounds quite dated, *Mr. Fantasy* and the self-titled followup have aged gracefully. This is in no small part due to Dave Mason's refined pop sensibilities. Even though he occasionally gets lost in a sea of sitars ("Utterly Simple"), Mason gives the material much of the form and restraint that the latter-period Traffic, at times, desperately needed. Even Winwood turns in some of the tightest pop-song constructions in his career, thanks to Jim Capaldi and Chris Wood's cowriting input. The band's almost whimsical approach to integrating its eclectic influences keeps the material sounding fresh too. Traffic's hodgepodge of psychedelia always sounds like the product of a band that really plays together rather than existing as a studio concoction. Check out "Coloured Rain" or the title cut for an example. –RC

☆ **Traffic / ISLAND / BB 17**   1968
It's songs like "Feelin' Alright," "Pearly Queen," "You Can All Join In," "Vagabond Virgin," and "40,000 Headmen" that make Traffic's self-titled second effort a classic. Although not quite as trippy as their debut, most of the sonic observations mentioned for *Mr. Fantasy* apply here. –RC

Last Exit / ISLAND / BB 19   1969
This collection of leftover studio tracks and live recordings from their 1968 tour was thrown together after Winwood jumped ship to go play with Blind Faith. It's a little spotty, but "Shanghai Noodle Factory" and the funky "Medicated Goo" are among their best early recorded work. –RC

John Barleycorn Must Die / ISLAND / BB 5   1970
Upon the demise of the short-lived supergroup project Blind Faith, Stevie Winwood began work on a solo album entitled *Mad Shadows*. As the project developed, it evolved into a Traffic reunion of sorts, as Winwood brought in Wood and Capaldi. The result, *John Barleycorn Must Die*, became an instant success, with its lengthy funky, R&B, jazz, and folk explorations. The playing is top-notch throughout, with Wood blowing some inspired sax, Capaldi laying down his trademark fluid percussion grooves, and Winwood's Hammond B3 and piano work in peak form. "Glad," "Freedom Rider," "Empty Pages" (#74), and the title cut are the highlights. –RC

Welcome to the Canteen / ISLAND / BB 26   1971
This fine live effort revealed Traffic as a seven-man touring unit, a precursor to their upcoming studio directions. On board for this outing were percussionist Reebop Kwaku Baah, drummer Jim Gordon, bassist Rick Grech, and Dave Mason, who briefly rejoined Winwood, Capaldi, and Wood for the tour. A revamped version of the Spencer Davis classic "Gimmie Some Lovin' (Part One)" became a moderate hit (#68). –RC

Low Spark of High Heeled Boys / ISLAND / BB 7   1971
Opening with the pastoral "Hidden Treasure," *Low Spark* flows effortlessly, almost lazily, to the last song, "Rainmaker." The band does shake things up a little with "Rock & Roll Stew" (#93) and "Light Up or Leave Me Alone." The title cut, at over 12 minutes of spacey jamming, is one of Traffic's most well known FM hits. –RC

Shoot Out at the Fantasy Factory / ISLAND / BB 6 1973
The title cut has its moments, but the augmentation of Muscle Shoals studio heavies Barry Beckett, Roger Hawkins, and David Hood ultimately turned down most of the remaining sparks in search of the eternal groove. –RC

Traffic - On the Road / ISLAND / BB 29   1973
This is another solid document of their live work. –RC

★ **Smiling Phases / ISLAND**   1991
Island remastered the tracks included in this double-CD anthology, and the difference is remarkable. Except for a few curious omissions, this is absolutely essential. –RC

THE TRAGICALLY HIP

Rock & roll. The Ontario band the Tragically Hip fuses a rough & tumble Stonesy ensemble guitar attack with more of a hard-rock rhythm drive. Their lyrics at times mix Delta folk-blues imagery with distinctly Canadian themes. –RC

The Tragically Hip / MCA   1987
This debut release revealed a band with a strong Canadian point of view, executing an edgy Heartland-rock sound. "Last American Exit" and "Small Town Bringdown" are two standout tracks. –RC

Up to Here / MCA   1989
Their first major Stateside release has a very dry, in-your-face, and unadorned sound. Blues influences are more evident here, melodically, and in the form of raw electric slide work. Highlights include "Blow at High Dough," "New Orleans Is Sinking," "38 Years Old," and "When the Weight Comes Down." –RC

○ **Road Apples / MCA**   1991
The Hip reunite with Don Smith, going down the river to Dan Lanois's studio in New Orleans for this batch. Smith continues to go for a lean, hard sound, this time with a few more embellishments. The melodies are a little stronger this time out. "The Luxury," "On the Verge," "Little Bones," and the acoustic "Fiddler's Green" are particularly strong. –RC

TRAMMPS

Disco. This powerhouse early-disco group created a dance-floor anthem with their 1977 hit "Disco Inferno." –JF

○ **Disco Inferno / ATLANTIC**   1983
Contains this seminal combo's incredible title hit and about three other pretty good dance scorchers. –JF

THE TRASHMEN

Rock & roll. A Minneapolis rock & roll band that evolved from a local group Jim Thaxter & the Travelers, recording one single under that name ("Sally Jo"/"Cyclone"). The group comprises Tony Andreason (lead guitar), Dan Winslow (guitar/ vocals), Bob Reed (bass), and Steve Wahrer (drums/vocals). Unfairly depicted as a novelty act, the Trashmen were in actuality a top-notch rock & roll combo, enormously popular on the teen-club circuit, playing primarily surf music to a landlocked Minnesota audience. Drummer Steve Wahrer combined two songs by the Rivingtons ("The Bird's the Word" and "Pa Pa

Ooh Mow Mow"), added freakish vocal effects and a pounding rhythm to the mix, and, by early 1964, the group was in the Top Ten nationwide with "Surfin' Bird." Though the group continued to release great followup singles and an excellent album, their moment in the sun had come and gone, the group disbanding by late 1967/early 1968. They re-formed in the mid 80s and continued to play locally until Wahrer's death. The Trashmen are revered by 60s collectors as one of the great American teen-band combos of all time, their lone hit exemplifying wild, unabashed rock & roll at its most demented, bare-bones-basic, lone-E-chord finest. –CK

Live Bird 65-67 / SUNDAZED
Storming unreleased live recordings. –CK

The Great Lost Trashmen Album! / SUNDAZED
Fine unreleased studio recordings. –CK

○ **Best of the Trashmen / SUNDAZED**
The original "Surfin' Bird" album, plus all the original Garrett singles from that period. The perfect primer set. –CK

THE TRAVELING WILBURYS

Rock/pop. Reversing the usual process by which groups break up and give way to solo careers, the Traveling Wilburys are a group made up of solo stars. The group was organized by former Beatle George Harrison (b Feb 25, 1943), former Electric Light Orchestra leader Jeff Lynne (b Dec 30, 1947), Bob Dylan (b May 24, 1941), Tom Petty (b Oct 20, 1953), and Roy Orbison (b Apr 23, 1936 - d Dec 6, 1988), thus representing three generations of rock stars. In 1988 the five (who had known each other for years) came together to record a Harrison B-side single and ended up writing and recording an album on which they shared lead vocals. It turned out to be a way to transcend the high expectations made of any of them as individuals, and a delighted public sent the album to #3, with two singles, "Handle with Care" and "End of the Line," hitting the charts. Unfortunately, Orbison died of a heart attack only a few weeks after the album's release. Two years later, the remaining quartet released a second album, inexplicably titled *Vol. 3*. It was another million-selling hit. –WR

● **Volume 1 / WARNER**   1988
The idea of Dylan, Orbison, Harrison, Lynne, Petty, and session drummer Jim Keltner getting together on a single album was pretty bizarre, inspiring curiosity and a little dread. Instead of trying to create something on a grand scale, these guys achieved much more by tossing together a refreshingly playful and unpretentious collection of homey pop-rock tunes. "Handle with Care" (#45) and "End of the Line" (#63) were the hits from this release. –RC

○ **Volume 3 / WARNER**   1990
Skipping over *Volume 2*, the Wilburys managed a more unified and harder-rocking sound. Party rave-ups like "Wilbury Twist," and "She's My Baby" indicate that these guys seem to enjoy how their fabricated identities have allowed them to ditch their living-legends status and possibly become more themselves in the process. –RC

PAT TRAVERS

Blues/rock, rock & roll. Known as the last of the red-hot boogie bashers, guitarist Travers is a staple of the club circuit, and continues to perform to appreciative audiences. –DH & CK

Crash and Burn / POLYGRAM   1980
Raw, amped-up blues-rock material, with loads of raucous guitar to recommend it. –CK

○ **Boom Boom ... The Best of Pat Travers / POLYDOR** 1983
Short on subtleties perhaps, but a solid collection of crowd pleasers, including his anthem, Little Walter's "Boom Boom - Out Go the Lights." –CK

TREAT HER RIGHT

Roots-rock. This Boston-based group has the same lineup as

the Cramps — two guitars, minimal drums, no bass — but adds the chromatic harmonica wailing of Jim Fitting to the formula. The results sound at times like a meeting of CCR swampadelics and Chicago blues, with the band's art-school snarl enhancing the mix. –JF

○ **Tied to the Tracks / RCA**   1989
Sounds just like their debut album, *Treat Her Right*, but "Hank" is their best song and "Junkyard" is a wonderful fetish rocker. –JF

THE TREMELOES

British Invasion. After splitting from Brian Poole (see Brian Poole & the Tremeloes), this quartet went off on their own in 1965. Their music altered from a relatively taut, R&B-inspired base to a softer, more upbeat and relaxed sound, which was subsequently replaced by a disastrous attempt to become a serious, progressive band. –BE

○ **Here Come the Tremeloes / CBS**   1967
A pleasant, upbeat collection with a jovial mood, but nothing as impressive as their Brian Poole-era "I Want Candy." (Out of print.) –BE

TRIP SHAKESPEARE

Alternative rock. If you couldn't guess by their name, this Minneapolis quartet plays arty, intoxicatingly melodic pop, with some of the most convoluted, arcane lyrics imaginable. They are also great singers, solid songwriters, and unusually cheery in a world full of dour artists. –JD

Are You Shakespearienced? / GARK   1989
The best of their early work. Features the great existential moving song "Two Wheeler, Four Wheeler" and the stupid "Toolmaster of Brainerd." –JD

○ **Across the Universe / POLYGRAM-A&M**   1990
There are those enamored of Trip Shakespeare's independent-label work, but I'd recommend starting here. This is their strongest collection of tunes and tightest, most assertive playing. –JD

THE TROGGS

British Invasion. A seminal British Invasion quartet led by vocalist/songwriter Reg Presley. "Wild Thing" was their masterpiece, but their catalog contains several pop gems, including "A Girl Like You" and "Love Is All Around." –JF

○ **Best of the Troggs / RHINO**
"Wild Thing" is the hit, but there's lots of good, raunchy rock here. –DH

TROUBLE

Heavy metal. British quartet (1980-1984) with a melodic upbeat pop-metal sound. Featuring Clive Gregson. –JB

○ **Psalm 9 / WARNER**   1984
This is the band's self-titled debut, now reissued on a major label and given the title *Psalm 9*. Although there are lots of Christian references, they're not a full-blown Christian metal band like Stryper. Very much in the spirit of Black Sabbath, Judas Priest, and Deep Purple. –JB

Trouble / WARNER   1990
The band's major-label album includes excellent heavy metal with positive lyrics and incredible guitar playing. –JB

TROUBLE FUNK

Funk. A pioneering early-80s go-go band from the Washington, DC, area, Trouble Funk plays deep, grooving funk. –ED

☆ **Drop the Bomb / SURGARHILL**   1982
Trouble Funk ushered in the go-go sound, a throbbing mix of heavy funk, rap, and hip-hop. This is their best album, but it's almost impossible to find. –JF

Trouble Over Here ... / POLYGRAM   1987
This Boosty Collins-produced set could use some better

songs, but fans will dig it. *Trouble Over Here, Trouble Over There* includes some vocals by Kurtis Blow. —JF

ROBIN TROWER   *b* 1945

Blues/rock, hard rock. Robin Trower's expressive lead guitar style possessed some of Clapton's lean blues sensibilities while embracing Hendrix's fascination with altered tonalities, sustain, and feedback. His lead work with the late-60s British band Procol Harum distinguished Trower as one of the finest players of that period. He left them in 1973 to pursue a highly successful solo career. During the 70s, Trower's albums were a staple of FM rock playlists. —RC

○ **Twice Removed from Yesterday / CHRYSALIS**   1973
The solo debut by this former Procol Harum guitarist. Moody Hendrix-inspired guitar, plus James Dewar's magnificent whiskey-throated vocals. A classic. —MPD

Bridge of Sighs / CHRYSALIS   1974
Trower's second album is another solid effort. —MPD

For Earth Below / CAPITOL   1975
His third album is less consistent than the previous two but still contains much excellent material. —MPD

Live / CHRYSALIS   1975
A truly fine live set, recorded in Sweden. —MPD

Long Misty Days / CHRYSALIS   1976
A good mix of down-and-dirty blues with Trower's ethereal ballads. —MPD

In City Dreams / CHRYSALIS   1977
Slightly funkier than the previous albums but highlighted by a delicate ballad, "Bluebird," and the majestic title track. —MPD

No Stopping Anytime / CHRYSALIS   1989
A compilation from Trower's two collaborations with Cream bassist Jack Bruce. —MPD

Essential / CHRYSALIS   1991
A well-chosen compilation. —MPD

THE TUBES

Alternative pop, rock/pop. A rock group fronted by vocalist Fee Waybill. Taking their cue from Frank Zappa's Mothers of Invention, the Tubes were one of the first to bring performance art (albeit with a satirical edge) to arena rock & roll. By the early 80s they had toned their image down to a more commercial, MTV-acceptable format. —CK

The Tubes / A&M   1975
The debut album for the Tubes, featuring the anthem "White Punks on Dope." —CK

○ **Young & Rich / A&M**   1976
Their breakthrough album and the best representation of the band's early days. —CK

What Do You Want from Life / A&M   1978
A great live album, featuring a good sampling from their mind-boggling 70s stage act. —CK

MAUREEN TUCKER

Alternative rock. An ex-Velvet Underground drummer turned wonderful primitive-pop performer. —JD

○ **Life in Exile after Abdication / WATTS**   1987
Fantastic! Straightforward, wonderfully succinct songs about life's assorted problems. —JD

THE TURBANS

Doo-wop. Decked out in their trademark headgear, the Turbans scorched the R&B charts in 1955 with "When You Dance." This teenage quartet from Philadelphia signed with Al Silver's Herald imprint. They debuted with the Latin-beat classic "When You Dance," with Al Banks's (b Jul 26, 1937) high-flying falsetto prominent. "Sister Sookey" was a worthy upbeat followup for the group in early 1956 but failed to chart, and three more fine 1956-1958 outings on Herald met the same undeserved fate. The Turbans went on to record for Imperial and Roulette, with no tangible results. Banks later

worked with one of the leading groups of Drifters populating the 70s lounge circuit before his death. —BD

○ **Best of the Turbans / COLLECTABLES**
Featuring "When You Dance" and other mid-50s doo-wop gems, with sax-led small-combo backing. A glimpse into a bygone era. —HD

IKE AND TINA TURNER

R&B, soul. There was a time when the Ike and Tina Turner Revue was one of the hottest, most durable, and potentially most explosive of all R&B ensembles. Fronted by Tina, with one of the rawest, most sensual and impossibly dynamic voices in Black music, the Ike and Tina Revue was an ensemble that dripped musical discipline while manifesting nearly unbearable tension, eventually giving way to wave upon wave of catharsis.

Their story is a long and convoluted one. Ike was born in 1931 in Clarksdale, MS; Tina was born Anna Mae Bullock in 1938 in Nutbush, TN. They met in 1959 in East St. Louis, where Ike's Kings of Rhythm were the reigning patriarchs of the local R&B scene. Up to that point, Ike had been a DJ on WROX in Clarksdale, a talent scout and producer for Modern Records (waxing sides for the likes of B. B. King, Rosco Gordon, Elmore James, and Junior Parker), and a recording artist, his Kings of Rhythm appearing in one guise or another on Chess, Modern, King, Cobra, Artistic, and Stevens. Their most famous record, *Rocket 88*, appeared under the moniker "Jackie Brenston with his Delta Cats" in 1951. It played an integral part in jump-starting the rock & roll revolution.

Once Tina joined the Kings of Rhythm, life changed for all concerned. They recording a demo of "A Fool in Love" in late 1959; by the autumn of 1960 the record was a #2 R&B hit on Sue Records. "I Idolize You," "It's Gonna Work Out Fine," "Poor Fool," and "Tra La La La La" all quickly followed, giving the Revue five Top Ten R&B hits in two and a half years. All told, from 1960 to 1975 Ike and Tina Turner placed 25 records on the R&B charts for nine separate record companies. Their most successful pop recording was a reworking of Creedence Clearwater Revival's "Proud Mary" in 1971. —RB

☆ **River Deep - Mountain High / A&M / BB 12**   1969
These sessions, recorded in 1966, were produced by Phil Spector. Spector's production chops and Tina's voice were a match made in heaven. Tina possesses one of the strongest voices ever committed to wax; Spector envelops it in the grandest version of his Wall of Sound that he ever conceived. Besides the title track, Spector cut the Turners redoing their first three chart hits, "A Fool in Love," "I Idolize You," and "It's Gonna Work Out Fine." Although it's a sacrilege to say so, I think I prefer these versions. Finally, Turner's performance of the obscure Holland-Dozier-Holland ditty "A Love like Yours" bowls me over with every listen. —RB

★ **Proud Mary ... / EMI**   1991
Proud Mary - The Best of Ike and Tina Turner is a fine 23-track collection that looks at the Turners' career at the beginning and the end. Their early-60s hits on Juggy Murray's Sue label are included, as are their early- and mid-70s successes on Liberty and United Artists. The mid- and late-60s recordings for Kent, Loma, Modern, Innis, Blue Thumb, and Minit are not here, unfortunately. Superior liner notes round out a fine package. —RB

SAMMY TURNER   *b* 1932

R&B, pop. The smooth R&B singer whose classy remakes of the standards "Lavender Blue" and "Always" lit up the pop charts in 1959. Signed to Big Top Records and given lush production by Jerry Leiber and Mike Stoller, Turner also hit with "Paradise" in 1960. He turned up on Motown later in the decade. —BD

○ **Lavender Blue / COLLECTABLES**
Lushly produced R&B-styled versions of venerable pop standards; from the late 50s/early 60s. —BD

TINA TURNER   ♭1938

R&B, soul, rock/pop. The woman who taught the world how to dance in high heels, Tina Turner has never been less than electrifying. Her full-throated rasp, full of low-note rumblings and soulful shrieks, is one of the most distinctive in any field of music, and her overtly sexual stage presence is nothing short of mesmerizing. The early part of her career, with then-husband Ike Turner, has been well documented (see entry for Ike and Tina Turner), but she really hit her stride and found a whole new audience with the coming of the MTV generation, her solo career bringing her the acclaim that had been long overdue. –CK

☆ **Private Dancer / CAPITOL**   1984
The one that won her a pile of awards, and rightly so, because it's simply her finest solo album. Using a multitude of producers and cut in a variety of locations, *Private Dancer* still sounds amazingly unified. Includes the title cut, "What's Love Got to Do with It," "Let's Stay Together," "Better Be Good to Me," and a blistering Jeff Beck solo on "Steel Claw." –CK

● **Simply the Best / CAPITOL**   1991
A solid greatest-hits collection culled from her solo Capitol albums. Includes "Typical Male," "Steamy Windows," written and produced by Tony Joe White, "I Can't Stand the Rain," and a duet with Rod Stewart on "It Takes Two." –CK

TITUS TURNER

R&B. This Atlanta, GA, native recorded sporadically during the R&B boom of the 50s, but he's best known as a songwriter, penning such hits as "All Around the World" (aka "Grits Ain't Groceries") and "Sticks and Stones." –JF

○ **Soulville / COLLECTABLES**
An underrated veteran R&B vocalist finally enjoying a reissue disc of his vintage efforts. BD

THE TURTLES

Folk/rock, rock/pop. The Turtles (formed in 1965) were one of the finest mid-60s West Coast pop-rock groups to respond to the British Invasion sound. Their initial hits were a lightweight approximation of the Byrds' folk-rock sound. That included the obligatory hip Dylan song cover (the #8 "It Ain't Me Babe"), as well as a handful of hits penned by the West Coast's pop-Dylan P. F. Sloan.
After their run of "serious" folk-rock calls to youthful individualism, the Turtles turned toward a more upbeat pop sound, which showcased their wonderful harmonies to fine effect. Their biggest hits include "Happy Together" (#1), "Elenore" (#6), "You Showed Me" (#6), and "She'd Rather Be with Me" (#3). During the 70s, vocalists Howard Kaylan (b Jun 22, 1947) and Mark Volman (b Apr 19, 1947) became in-demand sidemen for such artists as T. Rex and Frank Zappa. They also enjoyed a moderate following as the duo Flo and Eddie. The Turtles continue to perform regularly on various Oldies tours. –RC

It Ain't Me Babe / RHINO   1965
The Turtles's first album presents them as a folk-rock group covering a lot of Dylan and P. F. Sloan material. They also found "It Was a Very Good Year" on a Kingston Trio album and cut it. Frank Sinatra heard their version and had one of his bigger hits with it, but their version is good too. –WR

Happy Together / RHINO   1967
The Turtles's best studio album includes the title hit, "She'd Rather Be with Me," "Guide for the Married Man," and then-unknown Warren Zevon's "Like the Seasons," among other songs. –WR

○ **20 Greatest Hits / RHINO**   1983
A witty and underrated band, the Turtles compiled this fine set themselves. –DH

DWIGHT TWILLEY   ♭1951

Power-pop. Dwight Twilley fused rockabilly, mid-60s Anglo-pop, and Byrdsy jangle into a distinctly reverberant sound. In 1976 Twilley and his partner Phil Seymour released the exceptional #16 Anglo-rockabilly hit "I'm on Fire" on Denny Cordell's Shelter label. Unfortunately, Shelter's lack of organization delayed the release of Twilley's debut album, *Sincerely,* by over a year. In spite of glowing reviews concerning the album's rich melodicism and sparkling production, *Sincerely* sank without a trace.
After the followup, *Twilley Don't Mind,* Twilley jumped ship for Arista, releasing a self-titled album. In spite of some brilliant power-pop ("Alone in My Room," "It Takes a Lotta Love"), problems arose at the label, and Twilley jumped again to EMI, releasing *Scuba Divers.* It was on his next album that he scored his next hit, "Girls." –RC

○ **Sincerely / DCC**   1983
His debut album, containing his biggest hit and arguably his finest hour, "I'm on Fire." –CK

U.K.

Prog-rock. A progressive rock band featuring John Wetton, Allan Holdsworth, Bill Bruford, and Eddie Jobson. Bill Bruford was later replaced by drummer Terry Bozzio. –PK

○ **U.K. / CAROLINE**   1978
An impressive debut album featuring Allan Holdsworth, John Wetton, Bill Bruford, and Eddie Jobson. –PK

Danger Money / CAROLINE   1979
Followup album, with Terry Bozzio taking over the drumming. Exceptional synth work by Eddie Jobson and bass and vocals from John Wetton. –PK

Night after Night / CAROLINE   1979
A live album with the *Danger Money* lineup and songs from both studio recordings. A great show! –PK

U2

Alternative rock. In 1976, four Dublin schoolboys started the band that, under the name U2, would dominate rock music in the late 80s. Consisting of lead singer Bono (born Paul Hewson, May 10, 1960), guitarist the Edge (born David Evans, Aug 8, 1961), bassist Adam Clayton (b Mar 13, 1960), and percussionist Larry Mullen Jr (b Oct 31, 1961), U2 has helped to open up the doors for many other Irish bands.
U2 started out as a Dublin pub band and began earning recognition after the band won a talent contest sponsored by Guinness in 1979. This led to the Irish release of a three-track EP, *U2-3,* that topped the charts in Ireland and won them quite a following. They were signed by the Island label in 1980 and released their debut album, *Boy,* later that year. Unfortunately, *Boy* and the band's 1981 followup, *October,* did not gain much recognition outside of Ireland (where the band was playing soldout concerts). It was not until the 1983 release of the critically acclaimed album, *War,* that U2 began to get a taste of success. *War* was the band's major breakthrough in the US, going platinum although the first two albums had never made it into the Top 40. *Under a Blood Red Sky,* a live concert album from the *War* tour, was released in 1983, followed by *The Unforgettable Fire* in 1984; both went platinum in the States as well.
With the release of *The Joshua Tree* (1987), U2 became one of the world's leading rock bands. Entering at #1 on the UK charts, *The Joshua Tree* went platinum within 48 hours. The album also spent nine weeks at #1 on the US charts, and "With or Without You" became the band's first #1 single in America, followed by "I Still Haven't Found What I'm Looking For." As the new rock sensation, U2 appeared on the covers of *Time, Musician,* and *Rolling Stone* and won two awards at the 1988 Grammy Awards, including Album of the Year. In 1988 the band went on to release a full-length concert film, *Rattle and Hum,* and an album of the same name. Their latest album, *Achtung Baby,* released in late 1991, proved to be quite a departure from their previous work.
U2 could arguably be called the greatest rock band of the 80s. Out of sheer determination (or cockiness), they have avoided

the musical ruts that stardom can produce and have gone out of their way to experiment with new sounds and musical ideas. It is this musical growth and exploration that make U2 a truly great rock band. –IME

Boy / ISLAND   1980
The inexperience of the band, not yet at its musical peak, is compensated for by its raw power. The songs on *Boy* are full of teen angst and rebellion, a result of the influence of punk bands like the Virgin Prunes. In spite of the roughness of this album, its simplicity and directness are very appealing. Including "I Will Follow" and "Out of Control," this album is a good example of U2's early work; so far, the band has been unable to match the sheer energy of *Boy*. –IME

October / ISLAND   1981
U2's second album lost a lot of the fire and momentum that was in *Boy*. The band is better musically on this album, but it lacks spontaneity and seems a little too rehearsed. *October* incorporates Christian religious symbolism, apparent in songs like "Gloria" and "Rejoice." The album has some great songs (such as the minor UK hit "Gloria" and the melancholy "Tomorrow") but as a whole is a rather weak followup. –IME

☆ **War / ISLAND**   1983
This album was a major turning point for U2 — the band went from being a minor Irish band to being a world-renowned rock group. *War* retains some of the anger that is found on *Boy*, but it is more subtle and mature. This album features some of U2's best-known songs — "New Year's Day," "Sunday Bloody Sunday," "Seconds," and "Two Hearts Beat as One." In spite of all the protest, aggression, and outrage in these songs, the album ends with the optimistic "40," a song that sets the uplifting words of Psalm 40 to music. With such spectacular songs and emotion, *War* is a must for any fan of rock music. –IME

○ **Under a Blood Red Sky / ISLAND**   1983
This is a great concert album from U2's *War* tour, most of which was recorded during their concert at the Red Rocks Festival in Colorado. The album includes "11 O'Clock Tick Tock" and "Party Girl" (which previously were available only as singles) and intense performances of "New Year's Day" and "Sunday Bloody Sunday." *Under a Blood Red Sky* captures some of the power and charisma that make U2 such a great live band. –IME

The Unforgettable Fire / ISLAND   1984
After *War*, this was U2's second #1 album in the UK (#12 in the US) and it features two of the band's better-known songs, "Pride" and "Bad." Ironically, even in spite of its relative success, this remains one of U2's "forgotten" albums. The quality of the songs may play a part in this — either the songs are outstanding or they are not even worth mentioning. It is this kind of inconsistency that causes this album to be so frequently overlooked. –IME

Wide Awake in America / ISLAND   1985
This is a four-song EP that includes excellent live versions of "A Sort of a Homecoming" and "Bad," plus two largely forgettable songs, "Three Sunrises" and "Love Come Tumbling," that had previously only been released on singles. Unless you have to own the complete U2 collection, this album is not a necessity. –IME

★ **The Joshua Tree / ISLAND**   1987
Joshua Tree is the album that won the US (and the rest of the world) over. Before this release, the band had met with considerable success but nothing like what was to follow *Joshua Tree*. This album moved away from the loud anger of *War* and focused on a more subtle, refined sound. The wistful, searching quality of this album captures U2 at a transition, as the band attempts to rediscover themselves. Including such songs as "With or without You," "I Still Haven't Found What I'm Looking For," "Where the Streets Have No Name," "In God's Country," and "Running to Stand Still," this album is among U2's best works. –IME

Rattle and Hum / ISLAND   1988
U2's ego manifests itself. Billed as U2's "exploration of America," this album was a grave disappointment. There are, however, some excellent tracks, such as "When Love Comes to Town" (featuring B. B. King), "All I Want Is You," "Desire," and "Angel of Harlem." –IME

○ **Achtung Baby / ISLAND**   1991
This album was a big change in style for U2 — it's the band's only album to date that you can dance to. On this album, the group drops some of the pretentiousness of the last few albums and stops taking itself so seriously, and the result is very impressive. Although some of the lyrics are downright laughable, *Achtung Baby* is more direct and honest than some of the previous, preachier albums. Promoted as U2's "dark, trashy" album, this is, as far as I'm concerned, the most sophisticated work the band has yet created. The songs on this album (like the powerful "One" and "Love Is Blindness") revolve around human emotion instead of politics. I highly recommend *Achtung Baby* — it may be a shock the first time you hear it, but the more you listen, the better it gets. –IME

UB40

Rock/pop, reggae. Along with the 2-Tone groups that emerged during the late-70s ska revival that dominated the British charts, UB40 managed to insinuate their own personality into the conservative genre of reggae. Mixing leftist politics with pop-based melodies, the band scored many hits in England, but it was "Red Red Wine," a song recorded by the band in 1984 but rereleased in 1988, that broke them in America. –JF

Best of UB40 (1980-1983) / A&M   1983
This US compilation gathers the best of the early days of the UK's top White reggae band, displaying their love of dub and some of their best songs of the period, such as the caustic "One in Ten." –WR

○ **Labour of Love / A&M**   1983
Long stars in England, UB40 finally found Stateside success (and that belatedly) by recording an album of their favorite Jamaican cover tunes. One of these, "Red Red Wine," finally took off in the US in 1988 and went to #1. –WR

Little Baggaridim / A&M   1985
UB40 actually got their first US hit with a cover of Sonny and Cher's "I Got You Babe," set to a reggae beat and sung with the Pretenders' Chrissie Hynde, heard on this mini-album. –WR

Labour of Love II / VIRGIN   1989
UB40 repeats their formula for even more success, with reggae versions of "Here I Am (Come and Take Me)" and "The Way You Do the Things You Do." –WR

UFO

Hard rock. This English band was a big influence on newer English bands like Def Leppard. They have gotten back together, but with a new lineup. Michael Schenker was UFO's most noted guitarist. He also played with his brother on the first Scorpions album. –RDF

○ **Essential UFO / CHRYSALIS**   1992
UFO's best tracks, compiled on one smartly assembled single-disc collection. –STE

ULTRAVOX

Techno-pop. Ultravox (or Ultravox! — as it was called at first) had two separate identities and styles of music during its existence. Formed in London in 1974, it was originally intended as a platform for singer John Foxx (born Dennis Leigh) and included guitarist Stevie Shears, keyboardist and violinist Billy Currie, bassist Chris Cross, and drummer Warren Cann. With this lineup, the group recorded its debut album, *Ultravox!* (1977), produced by Brian Eno and Steve Lillywhite during the height of the punk/new-wave movement. A second album, *Ha! Ha! Ha!* (1977), was released only in the UK. A third, *Systems of Romance* (1978), marked the last appearance of Foxx, who went solo, and of guitarist Robin Simon, who had replaced Shears. The remaining trio enlisted singer/guitarist Midge Ure, formerly of the teenybop band ilk, and recorded *Vienna* (1980), which marked a sharp turn toward synthesizer pop and helped give birth to the British "new romantic" movement of the early 80s. The album was Ultravox's first to chart; the title track went to #2 and "All Stood Still" reached the Top Ten. There followed a series of successful albums in the UK: *Rage in Eden* (1981), *Quartet* (1982), *Monument - The Soundtrack* (1983), *Lament* (1984), and *U-Vox* (1986). *The Collection* (1984) was a hits album. Of these, only *Quartet* made any significant inroads in the US. Ultravox split in mid 1987, when Ure decided to turn his full attention to his solo career. –WR

○ **Ultravox / ISLAND**   1977
John Foxx proves to have an odd, Bowie-influenced vision, here aided and abetted by Brian Eno (then a Bowie crony) and Steve Lillywhite. "My Sex" and "I Want to Be a Machine" are standouts. –WR

Vienna / CAPITOL   1980
The new Ultravox, under Midge Ure, has a dreamy, ethereal sound heard at its best on its debut album, which features the title song, "All Stood Still," "Passing Strangers," and "Sleepwalk," all UK hits. –WR

Three into One / ANTILLES   1980
A compilation of Ultravox's three albums with John Foxx. –WR

● **Collection / CHRYSALIS**   1986
Ultravox's UK hit singles during the Midge Ure era. –WR

UNDISPUTED TRUTH

Motown. A pet project of Motown producer Norman Whitfield, this trio scored big in 1971 with "Smiling Faces Sometimes." Unfortunately, they remained overshadowed by the Temptations and never scored anther major hit. Members included Joe Harris, Billie Calvin, and Brenda Evans. –RAB

○ **Best of the Undisputed Truth / MOTOWN**   1991
"Smiling Faces Sometimes" is among the hits that are included on this album. –RAB

KING USZNIEWICZ & HIS USZNIEWICZTONES

Rock & roll. A hilariously inept Detroit bowling-alley/lounge band fronted by Ernie "King" Uszniewicz (b 1945) from 1969 to 1979. The crudest tenor saxophonist in the history of rock & roll, King Uszneiewicz (pronounced "you-snev-vitch") & the U-Tones had only one single, issued on a local label during the 70s. Dubbed by one critic as "the worst oldies band I ever heard in my life," they played with a bludgeoning energy, oblivious to the fact that they were woefully shy in the talent department. However, when the group's first album showed up on several college-radio playlists in 1989, they earned a minor cult following among both record collectors and young alternative-music fans. –STE

Teenage Dance Party / NORTOL
Their first album, featuring both sides of their original and lone 45 ("Surfin' School"/"Cry on My Shoulder") and insane versions of "Papa Ooh Mow Mow," "Little Latin Lupe Lu," and "This Should Go On Forever." Raw, crude, tuneless and wonderful. –STE

Twistin' and Bowlin' / NORTON
Subtitled "just when you thought it was safe to go back into the bowling alley," and more than living up to all that implies. Drunken, out-of-control versions of "Way Down Yonder in New Orleans," "Peppermint Twist," and Johnny Mathis's "Chances Are" are among the numerous highlights. Scary. –STE

○ **Doin' the Woo-Hoo / NORTON**
More oldies-band mayhem. "At the Hop," "G.T.O.," "Love Letters in the Sand," the title cut, and King Uszniewicz's wife Arlene belting out "It's My Party" are just a few of the standout tracks. Extremely potent stuff. –STE

UTOPIA

Prog-rock, rock/pop. Utopia is a rock quartet that theoretically features equal participation by its members, although singer and guitarist Todd Rundgren (b Jun 22, 1948), who formed the band, is a recognized solo star and frequently dominates the group. The first two albums found them billed as Todd Rundgren's Utopia, a six-piece unit. But as of the third album, *Ra*, Utopia was a four-piece unit, including Rundgren, Roger Powell, John Wilcox, and Kasim Sulton, and that lineup was still in place as of 1986, which is the last time they released new material. –WR

Deface the Music / RHINO   1980
This album ranks up there with the Rutles as a pastiche/parody of the Beatles, presenting a series of original songs in the evolving 60s styles of the Fab Four, from Merseybeat to *Sgt. Pepper* psychedelia. –WR

○ **Anthology (1974-1985) / RHINO**   1989
Some of Todd Rundgren's best pop-rock material is found among the 16 tracks of this well-chosen compilation, including the Top 30 hit "Set Me Free." –WR

STEVE VAI

Hard rock, fusion. A former "stunt guitarist" for Frank Zappa and student of Joe Satriani, Steve Vai has gained exposure with the bands he has played with in the past (Alcatrazz, David Lee Roth, Whitesnake), as well as for his flashy guitar style. A perfectionist who always gets what he wants and more, Vai is considered by many to be one of rock music's greatest musicians. –PK & JB

Flex-able / AKASHIC   1984
Self-released solo album from this former Zappa guitarist, featuring Zappa-influenced vocals. Recorded by Vai at home on an 8-track machine. The CD offers extra material from the *Flex-able* sessions originally released as a 10-inch EP. – PK

○ **Passion & Warfare / RELATIVITY**   1990
One of the most creative, musical, and mystical guitar albums ever made. Truly a musical genius. A must-have. –PK

RITCHIE VALENS   1941-1959

Rock & roll. A singer/guitarist of mixed Mexican-American and Native American descent, Valens was the first Hispanic rocker of any consequence. During an effective career of barely a year (until to his death in the same plane crash that killed Buddy Holly in 1959), Valens emerged with a basic high-energy rock sound that, at its most raucous, became an influence on performers up through the Kinks and Jonathan Richman. He delivered two classic songs, "Donna" and "La Bamba." –BE

In Concert at Pacioma Jr. High / RHINO   1960
A bizarre piece of work: a home-made tape of a high school concert. Possibly rock's earliest "official" live album, padded with narration and unfinished studio tracks. In shaky sound, but unique. –BE

○ **Best of Ritchie Valens / RHINO**   1981
The virtually complete recording legacy of an all-too-brief career. –BE

FRANKIE VALLI & THE FOUR SEASONS   b 1937

Rock/pop. The Four Seasons were the most successful male vocal group of the rock era. Although the personnel has changed through the years (especially after the 60s), the group has nearly always been a platform for the singing of Frankie Valli (b May 3, 1937). It was formed in Newark, NJ, in 1956, first as the Variatones and then as the Four Lovers, and featured Valli, brothers Tommy and Nick DeVito, and Hank Majewski. Under that name and with that lineup, they scored their first, minor hit, "You're the Apple of My Eye."
Over the next five years, the Four Lovers became the Four Seasons, songwriter Bob Gaudio replaced Nick DeVito, Nick

Massi replaced Hank Majewski, and the group began working with producer Bob Crewe. With this team — Valli singing lead, Gaudio and Crewe writing songs, and Crewe producing, plus Charlie Callelo arranging — the Four Seasons launched a series of teen-oriented hits in 1962 with the chart-topper "Sherry." The hits continued long into the Beatles era, totaling 13 Top Tens among 34 chart entries by the end of 1967. Valli also launched a solo career and had his own hits.

After more personnel changes, the group's career seemed to take a backseat to Valli's in the early 70s, though they came back in a multiple-lead-singer format for another series of hits in the mid 70s. –WR

Sing Big Hits / RHINO

How Bacharach/David and Bob Dylan ended up the subject of the same album is anyone's guess, but Valli and the boys pull it off with panache. –JT

Genuine Imitation Life Gazette / RHINO   1969

Frankie Valli & the Four Seasons go hippie in this concept album that stands out as one of the more bizarre entries in their catalog. –JT

☆ **25th Anniversary / RHINO**   1987

Frankie Valli and the Four Seasons scored hits from 1962 to 1978 under a variety of guises. Lead singer Valli started making solo records in 1965, and he had his own hits. They are all included in this long-overdue four-disc set, which runs from the Seasons's "Sherry" to Valli's "Grease." –WR

VAN DER GRAAF GENERATOR

Art-rock. An art-rock group principally centered around keyboardist, composer, and vocalist Peter Joseph Andrew Hammill (b 1948). With floating personnel, which changed from record to record, and "sound paintings" that varied from heavy-handed to somber, Van Der Graaf Generator was cited by British punk bands as a seminal influence. Hammill continued to release solo albums in a similar vein throughout the 80s. –CK

H to He, Who Am the Only One / CAROLINE   1970

A superb album, which includes the heavy metalish "Killer" and a guest appearance by guitarist Robert Fripp. –MPD

Least We Can Do Is Wave / CAROLINE   1970

Their ambitious second album. Bandleader Peter Hammill was already writing enduring songs. –MPD

○ **Pawn Hearts / CAROLINE**   1971

Lengthy prog-rock epics with Peter Hammill's intensely emotional lyrics. Robert Fripp guests on guitar. –MPD

Still Life / CAROLINE   1976

The second and best of the mid-70s comeback albums, highlighted by the incredible title track. Brilliant. –MPD

VAN HALEN

Hard rock. Van Halen was one of the most popular American hard-rock/heavy metal bands to emerge in the 70s, primarily distinguished by the fleet fingers of guitarist Eddie Van Halen. Actually, Eddie and his brother Alex, who played the drums, were born in the Netherlands, though they moved to California as children, as did bassist Michael Anthony and singer David Lee Roth. They formed the group in Pasadena in 1974 and worked their way up the Southern California club circuit, signing with Warner Brothers in 1977. Their debut album, *Van Halen*, released in 1978, went gold in three months, platinum in eight. Every album since has sold at least a million copies.

The group hit a popular peak in 1984 with *1984*, which sold four million copies in its first year of release, and its #1 single, "Jump," after which Roth left the band for a solo career. He was replaced by Sammy Hagar, and the success has continued, with three successive chart-topping albums to date. –WR

★ **Van Halen / WARNER**   1978

The prototype: Eddie Van Halen proves the hand is quicker than the ear, while David Lee Roth plays the role of outrageous frontman to perfection. Includes "You Really Got Me" and "Runnin' with the Devil." –WR

○ **1984 / WARNER**   1984

Adding synthesizers to the mix, Van Halen turned pop while retaining much of its hard-rock propulsion, resulting in a quantum leap in sales. Includes "Jump," "I'll Wait," "Panama," and "Hot for Teacher." –WR

5150 / WARNER   1986

Van Halen proves it can survive in the post-Roth era, as Eddie continues to burn up the fretboard and Sammy Hagar turns out to fit into the group's style just fine. Includes "Why Can't This Be Love," "Dreams," and "Love Walks In." –WR

JOHNNY VAN ZANT

Southern rock. The youngest of the singing Van Zant brothers (Donnie of .38 Special and Ronnie of Lynyrd Skynyrd), Johnny has mined similarly assertive Southern rock territory. More recently, Van Zant has been touring with Lynyrd Skynyrd, filling his late brother's frontman position. –RC

○ **Brickyard Road / ATLANTIC**

Accessible pop-rock, including the title track tribute to his brother, the late Ronnie Van Zant of Lynyrd Skynyrd. –DDC

LUTHER VANDROSS   b 1951

Urban R&B. In R&B music, Luther Vandross ranked with Prince, Stevie Wonder, and Michael Jackson as one of the most successful singer/songwriters and producers of the 80s. Amazingly, unlike those peers, Vandross for the most part did not cross over to widespread pop appeal, a situation that finally began to change at the end of the 80s and the start of the 90s. Born in New York City, Vandross has an elastic tenor that made him a natural for backup singing and commercial work in the 70s, when he became a top session vocalist. In 1975 Vandross worked with David Bowie on the latter's *Young Americans* album, even cowriting (with Bowie and John Lennon) the #1 hit "Fame." In the second half of the 70s, he recorded under a variety of guises, cutting two albums for Cotillion under the name "Luther," recording with the session groups Roundtree and Change, and singing on hits by Chic.

In 1981 Vandross signed with Epic and released his debut album *Never Too Much*, which topped the R&B chart and sold a million copies. The title track was also an R&B #1 hit single and reached the pop Top 40. Vandross went on to produce albums for Aretha Franklin and other female singers, while maintaining his own career through the 80s. His albums *Forever, For Always, For Love* (1982), *Busy Body* (1983), *The Night I Fell in Love* (1985), *Give Me the Reason* (1986), and *Any Love* (1988) were all million-sellers that spawned major R&B hits, but Vandross's pop success was spotty until 1989, when Epic released *The Best of Luther Vandross .... The Best of Love*, a double-pocket greatest-hits album containing the new track "Here and Now," which became Vandross's first Top Ten pop hit. That proved his breakthrough, and Vandross's next album, *Power of Love* (1991), another million-seller, featured two pop hits, "Power of Love/Love Power" and "Don't Want to be a Fool." –WR

Never Too Much / CBS   1981

The auspicious debut, demonstrating Vandross's gorgeous vocal arrangements and his lush, romantic singing on the #1 R&B smash "Never Too Much" and the Top Ten "Don't You Know That?," plus the tour de force version of "A House Is Not a Home." –WR

Busy Body / CBS   1983

An accurate title for a man who seemed to be producing all the divas in the business at this time, including Dionne Warwick, who turns up for a duet on "How Many More Times Can We Say Goodbye." It's one of three R&B Top Ten hits here, the others being "I'll Let You Slide" and the brilliant medley "Superstar/Until You Come Back to Me (That's What I'm Gonna Do)." –WR

The Night I Fell in Love / CBS 1985
A wonderful version of Stevie Wonder's "Creepin'" almost gets lost on another hit-filled collection, which includes the Top Five R&B smashes "'Til My Baby Comes Home" and "It's Over Now." –WR

☆ **The Best of Luther Vandross / EPIC** 1989
By the time this way-overdue double-record hits collection came out, Vandross had done many more R&B singles than could fit on it, so *The Best of Luther Vandross ... The Best of Love* is inadequate to encompass him. It does, however, contain "Here and Now," which broke Vandross through to the pop Top Ten long after most people had given up hope that he'd ever cross over. –WR

VANILLA FUDGE

Hard rock, psychedelic. Specializing in thundering psychedelia, Vanilla Fudge gave the Supremes hit "You Keep Me Hangin' On" an ultra-serious, somewhat indulgent arrangement and hit big in 1968. The quartet was introduced to Atco by veteran producer Shadow Morton and fronted by keyboardist Mark Stein. "You Keep Me Hangin' On" was only a minor seller in 1967. Reissued a year later, it proved far more potent its second time around. Bassist Tim Bogert and drummer Carmine Appice later played with Jeff Beck and Rod Stewart. –BD

○ **Best of Vanilla Fudge / ATLANTIC** 1982
Contains "You Keep Me Hangin' On" and other slow-motion catastrophes. –DH

GINO VANNELLI   b 1952

Pop, dance-pop. Vannelli played drums with the Cobra Band and later formed the Jacksonville Five, a Motown-style group. Discovered by an A&M executive in 1973, he cut his first album, *Crazy Life*, with his brothers, Joe and Ross. –BC

○ **The Best of Gino Vannelli / A&M / BB 172** 1981
Vannelli's most popular radio tracks from his years at A&M are here, like "I Just Wanna Stop" (#4), "People Gotta Move" (#22), "Wheels of Life" (#78), and "Love of My Life" (#64). "Living inside Myself" (#6) is not here, since it was later recorded on the Arista album *Nightwalker.* –RC

THE VAUGHAN BROTHERS

Blues/rock, rock & roll. Guitar-slinging brothers from Austin, TX, Jimmie Vaughan (of the Fabulous Thunderbirds) and Stevie Ray Vaughan. –RC

○ **Family Style / CBS / BB 7** 1990
Jimmie and Stevie Ray Vaughan team up for this relaxed one-off, produced by Nile Rodgers. In spite of a couple of throwaway songs, "Hard to Be," and "Good Texan" showcase their lean Austin-style electric blues/roadhouse R&B to good effect. "Tick Tock" became a poignant hit, released just as Stevie Ray died in a helicopter crash. –RC

STEVIE RAY VAUGHAN   1954-1990

Blues/rock, rock & roll. Stevie Ray Vaughan was the most impressive blues guitarist to appear in the 80s, which made his death in a helicopter crash at the start of the 90s all the more tragic. Vaughan grew up in Dallas, the younger brother of Jimmie Vaughan (cofounder of the Fabulous Thunderbirds). Stevie began playing in clubs at 12, and by 17 had dropped out of high school and moved to Austin. There followed years of struggling until April 23, 1982, when Vaughan and his group, Double Trouble, played a private audition for the Rolling Stones in New York. The gig led to an invitation to appear at the Montreux Jazz Festival, at which Vaughan was seen by David Bowie, who hired him to play guitar on his *Let's Dance* album, and Jackson Browne, who offered the free use of his recording studio. Vaughan took up that offer after being signed by legendary talent scout John Hammond to Epic, recording his debut album, *Texas Flood*, in the fall of 1982.

The release of the album led to a wave of recognition that included gold albums, Grammy awards, and other accolades over the next seven years. In 1987, Vaughan took time out to go through a rehabilitation program to overcome alcohol and drug addiction, and he wrote about the experience on his final studio album, *In Step* (1989). In the last year of his life, he embarked on a co-headlining tour with Jeff Beck and recorded a duo album with his brother. He had just finished a jam with Eric Clapton and Robert Cray at a show at Alpine Valley in East Troy, WI, when he was killed. In 1991 Epic released the posthumous *The Sky is Crying*, assembled by Jimmie Vaughan. –WR

○ **Texas Flood / CBS / BB 38** 1983
A late-arriving star, Vaughan did not make his first album until the age of 28. By that time he had become a seasoned player, so this doesn't really sound like a debut album; rather, it sounds like a blues guitar master at the top of his form. Highlights include "Pride & Joy," "Love Struck Baby," "Lenny," and the hard blues title cut. –WR

○ **Couldn't Stand the Weather / EPIC / BB 31** 1984
Vaughan does not ease up on this second set, even taking on Jimi Hendrix in a rendition of "Voodoo Chile (Slight Return)," and handling it beautifully. –WR

Live / CBS / BB 52 1987
Live not only covers many of Vaughan's most popular album tracks, but it also showcases a version of Stevie Wonder's "Superstition." Other standout tracks include "Look at Little Sister," "Willie the Wimp," and "Cold Shot." –RC

In Step / CBS / BB 33 1989
Vaughan sounds just as fierce sober as he did before, and he is beginning to bloom as a songwriter, a fact most notable on the driving "The House Is Rockin'" and the confessional "Wall of Denial." –WR

● **The Sky Is Crying / CBS** 1991
The posthumously released *The Sky Is Crying*, assembled out of tracks recorded between 1984 and 1989, is a lovingly assembled tribute to Vaughan's brilliance as a guitarist. Arguably this is Vaughan's finest album. The first-rate playing is unforced and natural in execution. On the songs, from his impeccable version of Hendrix's "Little Wing" to the hard blues shuffle of "Empty Arms," Vaughan's execution is unforced and his phrasing is relaxed. The release contains great liner notes and track information. Fans of hard blues-rock should check this one out. –RC

BEN VAUGHN

Rock & roll. Philadelphia native Ben Vaughn first gained notice in 1982, when the critically acclaimed Morells recorded his song "The Man Who Has Everything." In 1984 Vaughn formed the Ben Vaughn Combo, which became a Northeast favorite playing his quirky songs, one of which, "I'm Sorry (But So Is Brenda Lee)," appeared on Marshall Crenshaw's *Downtown* album in 1985. Vaughn recorded two albums with the combo in 1986 and 1987 and has since made two more solo albums. –WR

○ **The Many Moods of Ben Vaughn / RESTLESS** 1985
With a backing that includes bass, drums, and accordion, guitarist and singer Vaughn deadpans his way through a collection of his comic songs ("I Dig Your Wig," "Wrong Haircut"), most of which are played in a country/rockabilly style. –WR

Beautiful Thing / ENIGMA-RESTLESS 1987
"I feel like Jerry Lewis in France/When you hold me tight," sings Vaughn as the band re-creates a Bob Dylan-in-1965 sound. How can you not love a smart, funny guy like that? –WR

BOBBY VEE

Pop. Bobby Vee enjoyed his greatest success in the early 60s, with five Top Ten singles, including the classic, "Take Good Care of My Baby." Vee's vocal style was similar to that of his hero, Buddy Holly. Ironically, Vee's break came when he filled in for Holly the day after his death in a plane crash. Like those of many of his contemporaries, his career went into a tailspin with the arrival of the British Invasion in 1964. He did score one more Top Ten single in 1967 with "Come Back When You Grow Up." –KMC

Meets the Crickets / CAPITOL   1962
The reissue of this enjoyable album includes *ten* bonus tracks, including alternate takes, unreleased songs, and the "Buddy Holly Medley," a recent recording by Vee and the Crickets. –STE

I Remember Buddy Holly / EMI   1963
Vee's fun tribute to Buddy Holly has been beefed up on its CD reissue. Ten bonus tracks have been included and any songs that overlap with the *Meets the Crickets* album have been replaced with alternate versions. –STE

○ **Legendary Masters / EMI**   1990
The most complete collection of Vee's recordings, including "Take Good Care of My Baby," "Rubber Ball," and "The Night Has a Thousand Eyes." –KMC

SUZANNE VEGA   *b* 1959

Singer/songwriter. Vega was born in Santa Monica, CA, and moved to New York City at age two. She attended the High School of Performing Arts, then Barnard College. Vega was still at Barnard when she began attracting attention at Greenwich Village folk clubs and was featured on several issues of the songwriters' magazine/record album *The CooP* (later *The Fast Folk Musical Magazine*) in 1982. She was signed to A&M Records in 1984 and released her first album, *Suzanne Vega* in 1985. It was a critical success and a moderate seller. Vega's second album, *Solitude Standing*, featured "Luka," a song about child abuse that became a surprise hit single, reaching #3 in 1987. The album itself went gold. Vega took three years to release the followup, *Days of Open Hand* (1990), which was a commercial disappointment, though a few months later a couple of British DJs, under the name D.N.A., put out a dance version of her a cappella song "Tom's Diner" from the album *Solitude Standing*, and it became a #5 hit. –WR

○ **Suzanne Vega / A&M**   1985
Vega's most consistent collection of songs spotlights her hushed, restrained singing style and the spare, precise backup produced by Lenny Kaye. But it's those songs — "Small Blue Thing," "Undertow," "Marlene on the Wall" — with their brittle imagery (things are always frozen, flat, or cracking) and restraint — that let you know there's a big new talent here. –WR

Solitude Standing / A&M   1987
A more uneven but still striking album, featuring "Tom's Diner" (in its pre-disco version) and the hit "Luka." –WR

THE VELVET UNDERGROUND

Rock & roll, psychedelic. The Velvet Underground was one of the few bands of consequence to emerge from New York City in the 60s. They played their first gig near the end of 1965, and shortly thereafter they hooked up with pop artist Andy Warhol. Warhol in effect "sponsored" the band, allowing them to rehearse at his studio, known as the "Factory," and putting together a multimedia extravaganza featuring the Velvets, entitled *The Exploding Plastic Inevitable.* Warhol also grafted German chanteuse, model, actress, and would-be singer Nico onto the group's core: Lou Reed (vocals, guitar), John Cale (vocals, bass, viola), Sterling Morrison (guitar), and Maureen Tucker (drums).

Reed was the group's main songwriter. Via material such as "Heroin," "Sister Ray," "Candy Says," and "I'm Waiting for My Man," he chronicled a number of aspects of his community, as all folksingers have done. In Reed's case, the community was that of lower Manhattan: a mix of artists, junkies, homosexuals, and transvestites. Such being the case, the Velvets had problems even having radio ads for their first album. Their deliberate aesthetic of amateurish primitivism,

raw, distorted production, drones, and feedback did not help win them radio play. On top of all this, their stage presence (wearing wraparound shades and black clothes, making deadpan stage announcements, and at all times projecting ennui) appeared to be closed and hostile, flying directly in the face of the then-prevailing ethos of "love, peace, happiness, and the dawning of a new age." It is one of the great ironies of rock that they sold very few albums while together (1967-1970), yet in the 80s and early 90s their influence was pervasive, manifesting itself in the work of groups as disparate as R.E.M. and the Jesus & Mary Chain. The joke has always been that they didn't sell a lot of albums, but everyone who bought one started a band. One of the results of this is that everything they issued is still in print.

All told, the Velvets released four studio albums, one a year from 1967 through 1970. Nico left after the first, Cale after the second. Doug Yale took Cale's place for the final two studio albums. After Reed's departure in 1970, two live albums were issued, and in the 80s, Polygram released two albums of demos and outtakes. –RB

☆ **The Velvet Underground & Nico / VERVE**   1967
Nominally produced by Andy Warhol, *The Velvet Underground and Nico* is one of the most important and influential albums of all time. The only record the group recorded with Nico, the disc includes the seminal "Heroin," "I'm Waiting for the Man," and "Venus in Furs." As with the finest films and books, each song provides a window into a world that most will otherwise not have experienced. "Heroin" is probably the finest example of this, with the rush and subsequent down of the drug masterfully conveyed via Tucker's unorthodox drum style (simply involving padded beaters on a bass drum turned on its side), continuous changes in tempo, different musicians playing in different tempos at the same time, and Cale's shrieking viola-induced feedback at the end. In terms of sound the whole album is wide ranging, moving from the melodic beauty of "Femme Fatale" to the intense cacophony of "European Son." If you have not heard this at least one hundred times, you are missing an essential part of what life is all about. –RB

○ **White Light/White Heat / POLYGRAM**   1967
By the time of *White Light/White Heat*, Nico had departed to embark upon a solo career. The Velvets, now also minus Warhol, concocted an extraordinarily abrasive, tension-filled album, full of mind-numbing feedback and incessant drones. The playing and production on this album herald a punk aesthetic eight years ahead of the fact. Standout tracks include the sidelong improvisatory "Sister Ray" and the John Cale-narrated, Lou Reed-written "The Gift." –RB

☆ **The Velvet Underground / VERVE**   1969
By the time of the group's third release, John Cale had also left, replaced by Bostonian organist and bass player Doug Yule. The resulting album was much more melodic, minus the seemingly Cale-influenced aural onslaught that had marked part of the first and most of the second albums. *The Velvet Underground* also signaled a change in Lou Reed's writing, as he began to sympathetically address issues of human frailty ("Some Kinda Love" and "Pale Blue Eyes") and redemption ("Beginning to See the Light"). With the arrival of Yule, organ began to play a prominant role in the Velvet's sound. This is most evident on "The Murder Mystery," which is also intriguing for its dual set of lyrics, proclaimed simultaneously in the two separate stereo channels. –RB

☆ **Loaded / WARNER**   1970
Recorded in the summer of 1970 while the band was playing a summer-long residency at Max's Kansas City in New York. Feeling increasingly disaffected, Reed walked out after the last gig at Max's, never to return. The album was remixed and edited without him, much to his later chagrin. Whatever imperfections may have consequently occurred, *Loaded* remains an absolute must. The Velvets were now playing stripped-down rock & roll and Reed was writing such enduring classics as "Sweet Jane" and "Rock & Roll," as well

as the underrated "New Age," "Train round the Bend," and "Oh! Sweet Nuthin'." –RB

☆ **1969: Velvet Underground Live / MERCURY**   1974
Originally a double album and released in two volumes with added songs on CD, *1969: Velvet Underground Live* is a stunning document of the Reed, Yule, Morrison, Tucker edition of the Velvets at their pinnacle. Recorded privately in Texas and San Francisco, the Velvets play extended, intensely driven, out-and-out versions of songs from their first three albums as well as then-unreleased material such as "Ocean," "Real Good Time Together," and "Sweet Bonnie Brown." –RB

● **Best of the Velvet Underground / POLYGRAM**   1989
The Best of the Velvet Underground: Words and Music of Lou Reed is a 15-track summary of the Velvets' career, borrowing heavily from the debut (six tracks) and featuring "Sweet Jane" and "Rock & Roll," licensed from Atlantic. –WR

VELVETS

R&B, doo-wop. A Texas-based R&B vocal group, discovered by Roy Orbison in 1960. The Velvets tasted fleeting pop success with their violin-enriched "Tonight (Could Be the Night)." Lead singer Virgil Johnson was an Odessa, TX, high school teacher, and he recruited four of his students to form the Velvets. Orbison brought the quintet to Nashville-based Monument, but in spite of well-crafted material from the Big O (who also cut "Lana" himself at Monument) and the presence of Nashville's finest session players, only the up-tempo "Tonight (Could Be the Night)," penned by Johnson, and the spirited Orbison/Joe Melson tune "Laugh" graced the pop charts in 1961. –BD

○ **Tonight (Could Be The Night) / CSP**
This Texas R&B vocal quintet shares Orbison's trademark musical approach, with soaring lead vocals by Virgil Johnson and sumptuous string-drenched arrangements. –BD

VENOM

Thrash. A darkly humorous British thrash trio that combined deadly themes and stories of the netherworld. –JB

Possessed / RELATIVITY
A complete flip side to what Iron Maiden was doing with British heavy metal, Venom wanted attention and they got it with this classic album. –JB

○ **Black Metal / RELATIVITY**   1982
One of the first bands to do black-metal, heavy metal, and dark, Satanic lyrics. Not so tight as later albums but it is the origin of death-metal and black-metal. A power trio in all their glory. –JB

THE VENTURES

Rock & roll. Instrumental rock & roll group from Tacoma, WA, formed in 1959 originally named the Versatones. The early lineup consisted of Don Wilson (b 1937), rhythm guitar; Bob Bogle (b 1937), lead guitar; Nokie Edwards (b 1939), bass; and Howie Johnson, drums. They pressed a twangy, rocked-up version of Johnny Smith's "Walk Don't Run" on their own Blue Horizon label, which was later picked up by Dolton Records. It became a #2 hit in 1960. Bogle and Edwards switched instruments and Mel Taylor replaced Johnson on drums in 1963. More hit singles featuring their cleanly played but rockin' style followed, but the band wisely entered the album market early on, and it was there they found their true format — placing 37 chart entries and more than 50 albums between 1960 and the mid 70s.
The Ventures are the biggest-selling instrumental group of all time, but their influence extends far beyond mere record sales. With their solid-body Fender guitars (later switching to Mosrite Ventures models) and matching suits, their album covers defined what a rock & roll combo should look like. Likewise, their sound was so popular that they released several successful instructional albums in the *Play with the Ventures* series that many later rock stars cut their teeth on.

Because they played instrumentals, they were among the first American bands to break big in Japan (no language barrier), eventually honored as the first foreign members of that country's Conservatory of Music for selling over 40 million records. Edwards left and was replaced for a while by Jerry McGee, but he returned in 1972, restoring the early 60s lineup, which has endured to the present day. They continued to tour and record, sounding better than ever, their place in rock & roll guitar history assured. –CK

The Ventures on Stage / DOLTON   1965
Explosive live recordings from Japan, England, and the US, with a hot greatest-hits medley and a wild "Driving Guitars" being among the highlights. *The Ventures on Stage Around the World* is out of print but worth any search. –CK

○ **Walk - Don't Run - The Best of the Ventures / EMI**   1990
A perfect 29-track CD compilation, with great notes and superlative sound. All the hits, from "Walk Don't Run" to "Hawaii Five-O." Important album sides, plus interviews and radio spots. A perfect introduction. –CK

TOM VERLAINE   b 1949

Alternative rock. Ex-Television leader recorded numerous albums following TV's breakup. The best of them hint at what that group could've done, had they stuck it out for a few more albums. –JF

Tom Verlaine / ELEKTRA   1979
This, his solo debut, expands the musical vocabulary of Television, while elaborating on Verlaine's sometimes sketchy lyricism. –JF

○ **Dreamtime / WARNER**   1981
The closest he's come to crafting a solo masterpiece. Dense guitar structures and his best set of songs since Television's *Marquee Moon* hit the racks. –JF

Words from the Front / WARNER   1982
The material is patchy enough to make this one worthwhile only for devotees, who will no doubt scarf up the angst-ridden title cut. Others will groove on the picture-pop-perfect "Postcards from Waterloo." –JF

Cover / WARNER   1984
Dense, synth-heavy production notwithstanding, this 1984 set is a sharp and poignant set of desperate romantic gems. –JF

Flash Light / I.R.S.   1987
The guitars are brought back up front, but most of the songs are half-baked. Diehards will dig it, nonetheless. –JF

VIBRATORS

Punk. In 1977 British pub-rock veterans Knox and John Ellis made one punk rock classic, then became a relic of an era full of forgotten one-shotters. –JF

○ **Pure Mania / CBS**   1977
These early punks rock & roll with the energy of the new school, but the grooves are tighter and they have a genuinely creepy sense of humor. Not just for punk enthusiasts. –JF

GENE VINCENT   1935-1971

Rock & roll. Though his chart hits were few, no one defined the initial greasy-haired, leather-jacketed, hot-rods 'n' babes spark of rock & roll more than Gene Vincent. Far more influential as a live performer, Vincent, with his backing group the Blue Caps, defined the lifestyle and visual prowess of the music, as well as touring with a wild-ass stage show that usually left a sea of destroyed equipment, hotel rooms, deflowered schoolgirls, and musical converts in their wake. Dogged by tax problems and the emerging teen-idol trend in pop music, by the early 60s he emigrated to the UK, where he found himself revered as a founding father of the music. Several bids for a chart comeback failed, and by the late 60s, alcoholism had reduced his once-energetic stage prowess to a bloated self-parody. But a quick spin of his 50s Capitol sides dispels all that: the rebellious spirit of rock & roll's first flowering lives on in the supercharged recordings of Gene Vincent & the Blue Caps. Be-Bop-A-Lula, indeed. –CK

☆ **Capitol Collectors Series / CAPITOL** 1990
Breathless, unintelligible, and spirited rockabilly at its non-Sun best, this 21-track compilation covers Vincent's Capitol recordings (including "Be-Bop-A-Lula," "Race with the Devil," and "Lotta Lovin'") in admirable form. –HD & STE

VIOLENT FEMMES

Alternative rock. This entertaining folk-pop new-wave group features Gordon Gano (vocals, guitar, songwriter), Brian Ritchie (bass), and Victor DeLorenzo (drums). The Femmes formed in the early 80s in Milwaukee, WI. In 1982 they released their self-titled debut; their following albums were *Hallowed Ground* (1984), *The Blind Leading the Naked* (1986), *3* (1989), and *Why Do Birds Sing?* (1991). –MAE

○ **Violent Femmes / SLASH** 1982
One of the leading albums in alternative rock. On their first album (by far their best) the Violent Femmes began their professional career with a style that proves both entertaining and distinctive. Includes "Blister in the Sun," "Add It Up," and "Gone Daddy Gone." –MAE

Debacle: The First Decade / SLASH 1991
This album is a compilation of all their recordings. Even though it contains a variety of the Femmes's changes in style, it doesn't live up to the standards of their first release. Still, enough highlights are covered to make this album the only other Violent Femmes album you'll need. –MAE

VIRGIN PRUNES

Alternative rock. Irish proto-goth rock. The Prunes' arty approach to early/post-punk was alternately funny (albeit unintentionally) and harrowing. Not as aggressive as they were melodic, the Prunes are most definitely an acquired taste, as they were probably just slightly ahead of their time. –JD

○ **If I Die I Die / ROUGH TRADE** 1982
It has its slow moments (i.e., bad poetry, obtuse songwriting) but this is the most consistent Prunes on record. Gavan Friday sounds suitably gloomy, and the production by Wire's Colin Newman accents the groups artiness. For all those who value a sense of style more than substance. –JD

THE VOGUES

Rock/pop, pop. This Pittsburgh vocal group from the 60s was formed in 1960 and produced a series of wholesome lite-garage-pop hits, with "You're the One" (#4), "Five O'Clock World" (#4), "Magic Town" (#21), and "The Land of Milk and Honey" (#29), before transforming into a viable alternative for fans of the Lettermen with their hits "Turn Around, Look at Me" (#7) and "My Special Angel" (#7). –RC

○ **Greatest Hits / RHINO**
An essential overview of this Pennsylvania group, which contains all of the above-mentioned hits. –RC

VOIVOD

Thrash. Voivod was one of the first thrash bands out of Canada to gain popularity outside of their home country. From their beginning in the early 80s, their main goal was to be different from anyone else, and thus they incorporated odd musical tempos and futuristic story lines into their songs, often dealing with technology taking over the world. Voivod opened the way for other Canadian thrash bands and for metal bands with their unique styles of performing and writing. –JB

Rrroooaaarrr! / NOISE 1986
Techno-thrash with everchanging moods; musically challenging. –JB

Killing Technology / NOISE 1987
Innovators of techno-thrash; Canada's most influential band. Too loud and too strong. –JB

○ **Nothingface / MCA** 1989
Voivod's major-label debut includes an incredible version of Pink Floyd's "Astronomy Domine." –JB

THE VOLUMES

R&B, soul, doo-wop. Fronted by Ed Union, the Volumes cut their only hit in 1962, "I Love You," for the tiny Chex label. The Latin-beat R&B tune was written by bass singer Ernest Newsom and manager Willie Ewing. Followups on Chex and American Arts labels failed to click, despite their soulful grooves. –BD

○ **I Love You - Golden Classics / COLLECTABLES**
A nice collection of the group's early 60s Chex releases. –RP

WAITRESSES

Rock/pop. The Waitresses existed for the purpose of performing the witty, often female-oriented songs of guitarist Chris Butler, who had previously led a series of new-wave bands in Cleveland. The personnel of the band as of its 1982 debut album, *Wasn't Tomorrow Wonderful*, was, in addition to Butler, singer Patty Donahue, backup singer Ariel Warner, reed player Mars Williams, bassist David Horstra, drummer Billy Ficca (a once and future member of Television), and keyboardist Dan Klayman. The group recorded two albums and a mini-LP in the early 80s, stirring critical acclaim and international interest before both Donahue and Butler left. Ficca fronted the band for a while, then they broke up. –WR

○ **Wasn't Tomorrow Wonderful? / POLYDOR** 1982
"No Guilt," in which Donahue's matter-of-fact voice details what a spurned lover has found out since the breakup ("I learned the reason for a three-pronged outlet"), and "I Know What Boys Like" are the standouts among these clever songs, but the whole album has an attitude that won't quit. –WR

TOM WAITS ♭1949

Singer/songwriter. Singer/songwriter and actor Tom Waits has garnered considerable critical acclaim and a cult following during a 20-year singing career (he has also built up quite a résumé as a film actor since the late 70s), and his songs have been successfully covered by such mainstream artists as the Eagles and Rod Stewart, though he himself has never scored a notable commercial hit.

Born in Pomona, CA, Waits was heavily influenced by the Beat writers of the 50s and, by the early 70s, had developed a performing persona as a heavy-drinking, heavy-smoking street poet. He signed to Elektra/Asylum and released his debut album, *Closing Time*, a relatively conventional singer/songwriter album of the day, in 1973. One of its songs, "Ol' 55," turned up on an Eagles album. Waits followed it with *Heart of a Saturday Night*, which found him celebrating the same street life found in Bruce Springsteen's early albums. (Springsteen later recorded Waits's song "Jersey Girl.") *Nighthawks at the Diner*, a double live album, represented a peak in this material.

On his albums after the mid 70s, Waits's voice, already a raspy one, seemed to drop an octave, and his songs became less melodic. In the early 80s he switched to the Island label, and on albums such as *Swordfishtrombones*, his music became more experimental. He wrote and starred in a stage presentation called *Frank's Wild Years* in the mid 80s, and it was transferred to film under the title *Big Time*. –WR

Closing Time / ELEKTRA 1973
Bluesy cocktail jazz accompaniment underscores Waits's boozy, sentimental tales of life after hours. But songs like "Ol' 55" and "Martha" transcend the somewhat hackneyed form to be genuinely touching. –WR

The Heart of Saturday Night / ASYLUM 1974
The touchstone here isn't so much Charles Bukowski as it is Hoagy Carmichael, even if, in Waits's interpretation, it's a "bloodshot moon in that burgundy sky." –WR

Nighthawks at the Diner / ELEKTRA 1975
There are those who consider this two-record live set the culmination of Waits's nightlife persona, and others who worry that it's a comedy act in which the singer veers into self-parody. It's one of those tough questions, like, how drunk is *too* drunk? –WR

Small Change / ELEKTRA / BB 89 1976
On *Small Change*, Waits alternates between playing the sleezoid barker with "Step Right Up" and the sentimental bum on tracks like "Tom Traubert's Blues" and "I Wish I Was in New Orleans." This might not be one of Waits's best efforts, but fans of his drunken croak of a voice will find this enjoyable. Like many of his recordings from his Asylum period, *Small Change* was recorded live to two-track and produced by Bones Howe. Sonically, these albums are quite impressive. –RC

Foreign Affairs / ELEKTRA / BB 113 1977
Foreign Affairs continues Waits's immersion into orchestrated street short stories with tracks like "Burma-Shave," "A Sight for Sore Eyes," and "Muriel." Bette Midler duets with Waits on "I Never Talk to Strangers." –RC

Blue Valentine / ELEKTRA / BB 181 1978
With this effort, Waits continues the bum-fronting-an-orchestra approach he started on *Small Change*. Particularly striking is his interpretation of *West Side Story*'s "Somewhere." Other highlights include the bittersweet sentimentality of "Christmas Card from a Hooker in Minneapolis," the bluesy "$29.00," and "Romeo Is Bleeding." –RC

Swordfishtrombones / POLYGRAM 1983
On *Swordfishtrombones*, Waits (by now with a voice even deeper and more gravelly than ever) dropped Hoagy Carmichael as his chief influence and adopted Kurt Weill and Bertolt Brecht. Employing odd percussive instruments and horns, he turned to this imaginative, impressionistic approach, which is also followed on subsequent albums. –WR

○ **Anthology of Tom Waits / ELEKTRA** 1985
Anthology collects most of the key tracks from Waits's Asylum years, except for *Nighthawks at the Diner*. –RC

★ **Rain Dogs / POLYGRAM** 1985
From the New York streets to the Orient ("Singapore") and back, Waits continues his colorful survey, alternately challenging the listener (especially in Marc Ribot's guitar playing) and returning to the melodic style of the past ("Downtown Train"). Keith Richards guests on gritty "Big Black Mariah," while "Time" is one of his best ballads. –WR

Frank's Wild Years / ISLAND 1987
Frank's Wild Years continued Waits's weird blend of theatrical melodies and unusual production, which he began on *Swordfishtrombones*. "Rainville" and "Hang on St. Christopher" are highlights. Not as strong as *Rain Dogs*, this is still one of his better albums from this period. –RC

Big Time / POLYGRAM 1988
This is the soundtrack to Waits's in-concert film *Big Time*. It covers tracks from *Frank's Wild Years* and *Rain Dogs*, plus two new tracks, "Falling Down," and "Strange Weather." His careening version of "Big Black Mariah," with its dissonant guitar and roller rink organ, is even ruder than the original version. –RC

JUNIOR WALKER & THE ALL-STARS   b 1942

Motown. Of all the great musicians who played on scores of Motown records, none of them got label credit, much less a chance to bask in the spotlight. The lone exception was Junior Walker (born Audrey Dewalt), whose tenor sax wailings were made up of equal parts Illinois Jacquet high-note shrieks, Coleman Hawkins growls, and pure Midwest soul. Never much of a vocalist, Walker nonetheless scored hits with his rough-grained chops, though the sax solos remained the definite focal point. Highly influential on the Tom Scott/David Sanborn crowd. Walker should be close to the top of any list of rock & roll's great tenor saxophonists. –CK

○ **Greatest Hits / MOTOWN**
All the hits, including "Shotgun," "What Does It Take to Win Your Love," and "Roadrunner." The definitive package. –CK

Roadrunner / MOTOWN 1966
A good collection — mix of instrumentals and covers of Motown hits by other artists. –GB

Home Cookin' / SOUL 1969
A good late-60s offering with a great cover of "Come See about Me" that beats the original. –GB

Shotgun / MOTOWN 1973
All the early hits, including "Cleo's Mood," "Shake & Fingerpop," and "Road Runner" — along with King Curtis and Maceo Parker the soul sax man — and probably the most influential. –GB

WALL OF VOODOO

Alternative pop. Releasing its first effort in 1980, this Los Angeles punk dance band offers a serious version of Devo. Originally featured singer Stanard Ridgway, who was replaced in 1983 by Andy Prieboy. –DS

○ **Call of the West / I.R.S.** 1982
Tension-filled dance music with punk sensibilities. Includes "Mexican Radio." –DS

JOE WALSH   b 1947

Hard rock, singer/songwriter. After coming to national fame as the leader of the James Gang, Walsh's skewed humor and bluesy guitar chops have forged a nice solo career for him. Walsh briefly joined the Eagles for *Hotel California* and produced albums for Dan Fogelberg, Spirit's Jay Ferguson, and Ringo Starr (working as bandleader on Starr's late-80s/early-90s tours), and he continues to release solo albums. –CK

○ **Barnstorm / MOBILE FIDELITY / BB 79** 1972
Even though he had developed quite a rep as the lead guitarist for the James Gang, Joe Walsh's debut (under the band moniker Barnstorm) was an impressive showcase for his songwriting and arranging. Produced by Bill Szymczyk, *Barnstorm* exudes a thick, textured sound. Some of Walsh's most distinctive guitar sounds are found here. Sonically, *Barnstorm* is shown to fine effect on this Mobile Fidelity reissue. (Currently, there isn't a regular domestic disc available.) Highlights include "Here We Go," "Mother Says," and "Turn to Stone." –RC

● **The Smoker You Drink ... / MCA / BB 6** 1973
On *The Smoker You Drink, The Player You Get* Walsh fused the dynamics and textures of *Barnstorm*, mixed in a few well-crafted tunes, perfect for FM radio, and scored his highest charting album. *Smoker*'s centerpiece was the plodding "Rocky Mountain Way," a perfect vehicle for his soaring slidework and squirrelly tenor strangle. "Meadows" was also a substantial FM hit. Other highlights are "Days Gone By" and "Happy Ways." –RC

○ **Best of Joe Walsh / MCA** 1978
Featuring the biggest James Gang hits and early solo hits. –CK

But Seriously Folks / ELEKTRA 1978
This is his biggest solo success, featuring the hit "Life's Been Good." –CK

TRAVIS WAMMACK   b 1946

Rock & roll. A guitarist, singer, and young instrumental genius from Memphis who cut his first record at the tender age of twelve, Travis Wammack is one of the great unheralded guitarists of rock & roll. A contemporary of Lonnie Mack, Wammack was simply the fastest guitar player in a town bursting at the seams with great guitarists. By the time he was 17, he appeared on the national charts with "Scratchy," a speed-burner instrumental featuring incredible distortion and dazzling technique. Several incredible singles followed, but none charted. By the late 60s, Wammack had moved into session work at the FAME Studios in Muscle Shoals, AL, playing on countless hits. He continues recording and touring to the present day (recently working as musical director for Little Richard), his hot and speedy guitar chops intact. –CK

☆ **That Scratchy Guitar ... / BEAR FAMILY** 1987
That Scratchy Guitar from Memphis contains his Wammack's best instrumental and vocal sides, 1964-1967. Simply incredible. –CK

WAR

Funk, rock/pop. Freewheeling War mixed rock, jazz, and soul influences into a spicy stew throughout the 70s, resulting in a series of R&B and pop hits sporting funky melodies and politically aware messages. Born in Long Beach in 1969, the large combo initially served as rocker Eric Burdon's group, backing the ex-Animal on his 70-million-seller "Spill the Wine." Bidding Burdon adieu, the band signed with United Artists in 1971 and enjoyed its first smash the next year with "Slippin' into Darkness." Tapping into a sizzling, horn-fueled rock/soul synthesis, "The World Is a Ghetto," "The Cisco Kid," and "Why Can't We Be Friends?" all went gold during the mid 70s. Despite numerous personnel and label changes, War remained eminent throughout the 80s. –BD

☆ **Greatest Hits / UNITED ARTISTS / BB 6** 1976
If you can find this collection (only available on vinyl), get it. *Greatest Hits* truly lives up to the title, with tracks like "Summer," "All Day Music," "Cisco Kid," "Slippin' into Darkness," "The World Is a Ghetto," and more. –RC

Best of War & More / RHINO 1991
The "best of"? Hardly. But it covers most of this fine band's hits. That "The World Is a Ghetto" is missing defies common sense. Also includes a pointless remix of "Lowrider." –RC

JENNIFER WARNES

Singer/songwriter, country rock, pop. Over the last 25 years, Jennifer Warnes has enjoyed a widely varied career, including performing the lead female role in the Los Angeles production of *Hair*, appearing as a regular on the 60s hit show "The Smothers Brothers Comedy Hour," scoring hits as a country rock-pop singer ("Right Time of the Night" #6, "I Know a Heartache When I See One" #19), winning a Grammy for her duet with Joe Cocker on their version of "Up Where We Belong" (#1) from the movie *An Officer and a Gentleman*, and garnering critical acclaim for her solo interpretations of Leonard Cohen's songs on the album *Famous Blue Raincoat* (#72). In 1987 Warnes was featured on Roy Orbison's TV special, and she also landed a #1 hit duet with former Righteous Brother Bill Medley on "(I've Had) The Time of My Life" from the film *Dirty Dancing*. –RC

Best of Jennifer Warnes / ARISTA
This collection covers Warnes's earlier hits, like "Right Time of the Night" (#6), "I Know a Heartache When I See One" (#19), "When the Feeling Comes Around" (#45), and "Could It Be Love" (#47). The omission of her chart-topping duets with Bill Medley ("The Time of My Life") and Joe Cocker ("Up Where We Belong") as well as key *Famous Blue Raincoat* tracks keeps this from being definitive. –RC

☆ **Famous Blue Raincoat / PRIVATE MUSIC** 1986
Leonard Cohen's material never received a more elegant treatment than the one Jennifer Warnes gave him on *Famous Blue Raincoat*. Warnes is supported by an impressive cast of sidemen, including Stevie Ray Vaughan. The quality of this recording is first-rate. Among the many great songs found here is a powerful version of "Joan of Arc." "Song of Bernadette," "Coming Back to You," and "Came So Far for Beauty" are other highlights. –RC

DIONNE WARWICK   b1940

Pop. The magically melodic voice of Dionne Warwick and the sophisticated pop compositions of Burt Bacharach and Hal David were the proverbial match made in heaven. Warwick proved the prolific songwriting team's favorite interpreter,

scaling the pop and soul charts time and again with her soaring renditions of their memorable songs.
Warwick hailed from a musical brood with a strong gospel heritage, and her sister Dee Dee scored a few hits of her own. Dionne's sultry pipes stood out, even on the highly competitive background vocal scene in New York, and she got a chance to step out front in 1963, hitting big on Scepter with the uptown soul classic "Don't Make Me Over."
Under the expert tutelage of Bacharach and David, who doubled as her producers, Warwick's sound soon became smoother and more accessible to pop programming — a formula that resulted in the massive acceptance of her "Walk On By," "I Say a Little Prayer," "This Girl's in Love with You," and a slew of others.
Strangely, Warwick never made it to the top of the pop charts until she broke away from her mentors, traveling to Philadelphia to record the R&B-oriented "Then Came You" with the Spinners in 1974. As elegant and tasteful as ever, Dionne Warwick's breathy vocals still haven't gone out of style — she's managed to remain contemporary while never jeopardizing her appeal. –BD

○ **Collection - Greatest Hits / RHINO**
All of the 60s Bacharach/David piano classics. –BC

Dionne Warwick Greatest Hits (1979-1990) / ARISTA
Recent adult-contemporary and more R&B-styled hits. –BC

WAS (NOT WAS)

Dance-pop, alternative pop. Was (Not Was) plays contemporary R&B dance music, with lyrics that range from the satiric to the bizarre. The group is led by Detroit natives David Weiss (David Was), who plays flute and writes those lyrics, and Don Fagenson (Don Was), who plays bass and writes music, but the group is fronted by singers Harry Bowens and Sweet Pea Atkinson. Was (Not Was) first gained notice for a dance single called "Wheel Me Out" in 1980. Their first album, *Was (Not Was)* (1981), did not reach the charts, but its followup, *Born to Laugh at Tornados* (1983), did. Then little was heard from the group for five years. They returned in 1988 with *What Up, Dog?*, which featured the #16 hit "Spy in the House of Love" and the #7 hit "Walk the Dinosaur." (During this period, Don Was had become a prominent record producer, handling the board for Bonnie Raitt's Grammy-winning *Nick of Time*, among many other mainstream pop records.) The fourth Was (Not Was) album, *Are You Okay?*, appeared in 1990. –WR

Born to Laugh at Tornados / GEFFEN 1983
The Was brothers provide a strange bunch of songs with irresistible dance beats, plus an array of guest singers that is, well, unusual to say the least: Mitch Ryder, Dough Fieger (of the Knack), Ozzy Osbourne, and, on the ballad "Zaz Turned Blue," Mel Tormé. –WR

○ **What Up, Dog? / CHRYSALIS** 1988
The guests are fewer (though Frank Sinatra Jr sings one song), but the oddities go on, with "11 MPH," a review of the JFK assassination, and "Dad I'm in Jail," a proud rant by David Was. Also included: the hits "Spy in the House of Love" and "Walk the Dinosaur." –WR

Are You Okay? / CHRYSALIS 1990
The "hit" is a remake of "Papa Was a Rollin' Stone," but the album is more memorable for typically oddball tunes like "I Blew Up the United States" and "Elvis' Rolls Royce," which features a droll vocal by Leonard Cohen. –WR

BABY WASHINGTON   b1940

R&B, soul. Her sultry delivery earned Justine "Baby" Washington R&B chart bows in four different decades, most notably on the delectable uptown soul classic "That's How Heartaches Are Made" for Sue Records in 1963. Born in South Carolina but raised in Harlem, Washington was a member of the Hearts in 1956 before tallying her first R&B hit in 1959 with "The Time" for Neptune. Billed occasionally as Jeanette or Justine Washington, she scaled the soul charts into the mid

70s with hits still hot from the 60s, such as her nugget "Only Those in Love." –BD

○ **Best of Baby Washington / COLLECTABLES**
Neptune and Sue tracks from 1959 to 1963. –RP

That's How Heartaches ... / COLLECTABLES   1965
That's How Heartaches Are Made includes 12 Sue tracks from 1962 to 1965, nine of which are not on the *Best Of* album. –RP

THE WATERBOYS

Folk/rock, alternative rock. A critically acclaimed folk-rock band led by Scottish singer/songwriter and guitarist Mike Scott. The group's first recording was a five-track mini-album, *The Waterboys*, released in 1984, at which time the only other regular band member was sax player Anthony Thistlewaite. By the time their second album, *A Pagan Place*, was released, they had added keyboard player Karl Wallinger. They first gained extensive recognition for their third album, *This Is the Sea* (1985), which got to #37 in the UK charts and included the #26 single "The Whole of the Moon." Wallinger then left to form World Part, and Scott spent more than three years preparing *Fisherman's Blues*, which, when it appeared in late 1988, showed a distinct turn toward Irish folk music. It was followed two years later by *Room to Roam*. –WR

This Is the Sea / CAPITOL   1985
Mike Scott combines the forcefulness of rock with the earnestness of folk and adds a mystical poetic soul to this brilliant album, which also features notable musical contributions from saxophonist Anthony Thistlewaite and keyboardist Karl Wallinger. –WR

Fisherman's Blues / CAPITOL   1988
The Waterboys turn into a neo-traditional Irish folk band, complete with mandolins and fiddles, and Mike Scott's poetic muse just gets better. –WR

○ **Best of '81–'90 / CAPITOL**   1991
Sums up the story so far, tracing the band's evolution from rock to folk, the constant sensibility of Mike Scott remaining intact. –WR

ROGER WATERS   b 1944

Prog-rock. Roger Waters was the bassist for Pink Floyd from 1965 to 1983. Waters assumed an increasingly dominant position in the band, writing all lyrics in addition to some of the music as of *The Dark Side of the Moon* (1973) and singing most of the lead vocals on *The Wall* (1979). Waters issued his debut solo album, *The Pros and Cons of Hitch Hiking*, in 1984. In the mid 80s, he engaged in a protracted legal battle, arguing that the other members of Pink Floyd could not continue using the name without him in the band; he lost. In 1987 Waters released his second album, *Radio K.A.O.S.*, and in 1990 he staged a concert version of *The Wall* in Berlin. In 1992 he was said to be finishing his third album, *Amused to Death*. –WR

○ **Radio K.A.O.S. / CBS**   1987
There's more story than can be effectively told on this concept album dealing with radio, computers, and the threat of nuclear war, but many of the songs are up to Waters's Pink Floyd standard, and some rock out more than his former band ever did. –WR

The Wall in Berlin 1990 / POLYGRAM-MERCURY   1990
This is a gala two-disc live rendition of the Pink Floyd concept album, employing a raft of guest stars including Van Morrison, Sinéad O'Connor, Joni Mitchell, the Scorpions, and others. –WR

JODY WATLEY   b 1959

Dance-pop. Jody Watley got her start as a dancer on the TV show "Soul Train." From 1977 to 1984, she was a singer in the group Shalamar. Her debut solo album, *Jody Watley* (1987), sold a million copies and produced three Top Ten hits — "Looking for a New Love," "Don't You Want Me," and "Some Kind of Lover." As a result of its success, Watley won the

Grammy Award for Best New Artist of 1987. Her second album, *Larger Than Life* (1989), went gold and contained the #2 pop hit "Real Love" as well as the Top Tens "Friends" and "Everything." *You Wanna Dance With Me?*, released at the end of that year, contained dance remixes of her hits. Watley's third album, *Affairs of the Heart*, was released at the end of 1991. –WR

○ **Jody Watley / MCA**   1987
State-of-the-art R&B/dance pop, by a singer who was a veteran of the genre long before cutting her debut album. –WR

Jody Watley / MCA   1987
All high-energy R&B/dance songs. An Andre Cymone production. –BC

Larger Than Life / MCA   1989
Rock, R&B/dance, and soulful pop ballads. –BC

WEHRMACHT

Heavy metal. Formed in Portland, OR, in 1985, Wehrmacht plays superfast speed-metal that can only be described as "speedcore." –JB

○ **Shark Attack / NEW RENAISSANCE**
Not a Nazi band, as their name (pronounced VARE-MOCKT, meaning "war machine") suggests, this Portland, OR, quintet released one of the most energetic speed-metal albums of 1987, leaving many tagging them as "speedcore" for being the fastest band in speed-metal. –JB

BOB WEIR   b 1947

Rock & roll. Bob Weir is a guitarist and vocalist in the Grateful Dead. He was a founding member of the group in 1965 and has been with it throughout its history. Weir began making records under his own name and in other configurations in 1972 and has released solo albums as well as Kingfish and Bobby and the Midnites. Most recentl, Weir has toured in a duo with bassist Rob Wasserman, and they are said to be making an album together, perhaps under the name *Scaring the Children*. –WR

○ **Ace / GRATEFUL DEAD**   1972
Weir's debut solo album is really a Grateful Dead album in disguise and, at that, not a bad followup to the group's *American Beauty* album. While Weir handles lead vocals, the rest of the band is on the album, and the selections, including "Greatest Story Ever Told," "Playing in the Band," "One More Saturday Night," and "Cassidy," have entered the Dead's concert repertoire and the list of Dead Head favorites. –WR

Heaven Help the Fool / ARISTA   1978
A slickly produced pop-rock album, but one that demonstrates the range of Weir's abilities. –WR

Kingfish / GRATEFUL DEAD   1987
This side trip for Dead guitarist and friends is a rockin', satisfying record. Who says all Dead music has to be "cosmic"? This is rock & roll. –JT

MARY WELLS   1943-1990

Motown. Motown's first female star, Wells received international acclaim under the wing of Smokey Robinson. Her original recording of "My Guy" in 1964 is one of the most recorded songs from the Motown label. She was ill advised to leave the company in 1964, and future productions planned for her made Diana Ross a superstar. Wells never again scored a hit. Her voice was silenced by throat cancer in 1990. –RAB

Bye Bye Baby / MOTOWN   1962
Raw, early Motown soul featuring a gruffer Wells wailing the blues. –RAB

My Guy / MOTOWN   1964
A classic production by Wells with Smokey Robinson. –RAB

○ **Compact Command Performances / MOTOWN**   1985
"Lady Motown" is capsulized here with hit singles and album highlights from the 60s. –RAB

WENDY & LISA

Dance-pop. Wendy Melvoin and Lisa Coleman were one-time members of Prince's Revolution but left the fold in 1986 to record their own funky, Beatlesque art-soul. –JF

○ **Eroica / ATLANTIC**   1990
This duo successfully blends mood music with dance-pop. While they employ a softer approach, there are pop elements here that will appeal to Prince fans. –DDC

KIM WESTON

Motown. Kim Weston emerged as one of the most powerful vocalists on the Motown label but, like so many others, she was overlooked because of Diana Ross. Weston recorded the original version of "Take Me in Your Arms." Today she records in Europe. –RAB

○ **Greatest Hits & Rare Classics / MOTOWN**   1991
A good representation of pure Motown. Kim's excellent vocals are backed by the Funk Brothers. Includes the original "Take Me in Your Arms." –RAB

WET WILLIE

Southern rock, rock/pop. Originating out of Mobile, AL, this Southern pop-rock quintet was a popular touring unit who scored their first breakthrough with a live album. Their biggest hit was the reggae-meets-gospel-influenced "Keep On Smilin'" (#10). Other hits included "Street Corner Serenade" (#30) and "Weekend" (#29). –RC

○ **Greatest Hits / POLYGRAM**   1977
"Keep On Smilin'" and other pleasant Dixie rockers. –DH

WHAM!

Dance-pop. Wham! was a UK pop/dance duo formed in 1981 by George Michael (born Yorgos Panayiotou, Jun 26, 1963) and Andrew Ridgeley (b Jun 25, 1963). Combining light soul music with slow, romantic ballads, they first hit the UK charts in the fall of 1982 with "Young Guns (Go for It)." It hit #3, the first of ten UK Top Ten hits for the duo. The first Wham! album, *Fantastic*, topped the UK charts in 1983. The group broke through in the US the following year with "Wake Me Up Before You Go-Go," the first of three straight #1 hits. The second of those chart-toppers was "Careless Whisper," billed as "featuring George Michael," the first sign that Michael, who sang lead and wrote the songs, was emerging as a solo entity. Nevertheless, Wham! continued through 1986, finishing their career at Wembley Stadium in England, after which Michael went on to a successful solo career. –WR

○ **Make It Big / CBS**   1984
George Michael demonstrates a thorough knowledge of danceable pop, from the 60s-ish "Wake Me up Before You Go-Go" to the tear-jerking ballad "Careless Whisper." Also includes "Everything She Wants" and "Freedom." –WR

Music from the Edge of Heaven / CBS   1986
More of a hodgepodge of tracks than a coherent album, this still includes the Top Ten hits "I'm Your Man," "A Different Corner," and "The Edge of Heaven." –WR

THE WHISPERS

R&B, soul. The Whispers are a veteran R&B quintet with an impressive 23-year legacy of R&B hits. Formed in Los Angeles by twins Walter and Wallace Scott, Nicholas Caldwell, Marcus Hutson, and Gordy Harmon (who left in 1973), the Whispers turned up on the Dore label in 1964 with "I Was Born When You Kissed Me." In 1969 the quintet climbed the soul charts for the first time with "The Time Has Come" on Soul Clock, and they cracked the R&B Top Ten the next year with "Seems Like I Gotta Do Wrong." They've remained hitmakers ever since for the labels Janus, Soul Train, and Solar, with smashes like the solid gold chart-topper "And the Beat Goes On" in 1980 and another #1 urban contemporary hit, "Rock Steady," in 1987. –BD

○ **In the Mood / CBS**
Marvelous ballads and great contemporary dance hits. –RW

Just Gets Better with Time / CBS
A reissue of their landmark release. –RW

More of the Night / CAPITOL
A highly representative session. –RW

Somebody Loves You / QUICKSILVER
Soft, suave, and sentimental love sounds. –RW

Vintage Whispers / CBS
A reissue of their prime hits. –RW

BARRY WHITE   b 1944

Disco, pop. White had a long career as a behind-the-scenes producer, and other hits before making himself a featured attraction in the 70s with his salacious soul ballads and romantic disco hits. He led the elaborate Love Unlimited Orchestra. –BC

○ **Greatest Hits - Vol. 1 / POLYGRAM**   1979
The maestro's sweeping strings and orchestral overkill on fine love raps and 70s dance-floor hits. –BC

Greatest Hits - Vol. 2 / POLYGRAM   1981
More of the same as *Vol.1*, includes "Ecstasy." –BC

Put Me in Your Mix / A&M   1991
Back in the 90s, making the same big-sound love songs. With nostalgic horn arrangements and a duet with Isaac Hayes. –BC

KARYN WHITE

Dance-pop, urban R&B. This former Los Angeles session singer with Jeff Lorber had a solo career in the 90s, including the hits "The Way You Love Me" and "Facts of Love." –ED

○ **Karyn White / WARNER**   1988
Lush R&B produced mostly by L. A. Reid and Babyface. –DH

WHITESNAKE

Hard rock. Former Deep Purple vocalist David Coverdale formed his own band, which has featured a wide range of great musicians over the years. The group displays heaviness, with a love for the blues. –JB

○ **Whitesnake / GEFFEN**   1987
After slugging it out in the British hard-rock market for almost ten years, Whitesnake achieved platinum success with this highly crafted mainstream AOR. Includes the #1 "Here I Go Again," "Is This Love" (#2), and the Led Zeppelin rip "Still of the Night." –ED

BARRENCE WHITFIELD & THE SAVAGES

Rock & roll, blues/rock. A rock & roll band from Boston, centered around the hoarse, shouting vocals of frontman Whitfield. Adept at covering material from rockabilly to R&B, Whitfield & the Savages are best experienced live. –CK

Ow! Ow! Ow! / ROUNDER   1987
Little Richard vocals over 50s rock energy. –RG

○ **Let's Lose It / STONY PLAIN**   1990
More personality in each song — better playing, better sound. –RG

CHRIS WHITLEY

Singer/songwriter, blues/rock. Chris Whitley writes and sings provocatively dark folk/blues/pop. His debut featured an appropriately haunting production job by Daniel Lanois (U2, Bob Dylan). –RC

○ **Living with the Law / CBS**   1991
A stirring and classy debut of well-crafted blues, which was released to a flurry of critical praise. Whitley combines dreamy storytelling with commanding electric guitar work — all with the touch of a journeyman's blues. –DDC

THE WHO

British Invasion, hard rock. Founded in the early 60s by Pete Townshend, John Entwistle, and Roger Daltrey (with Keith

Moon coming along slightly later), the Who were originally a fairly conventional R&B-based outfit, with Townshend and Daltrey sharing guitar chores, Enwistle on bass, and Doug Sanden (later replaced by Keith Moon) on drums. Early on, however, they fell under the influence of Johnny Kidd & the Pirates, a British band that pioneered a lean, muscular sound built around a single guitar and a rhythm section of bass and drums (most British bands of the period also featured a rhythm guitar very prominently) behind a lone singer. Kidd had hit originally with "Shakin' All Over," a number that the Who would adopt into their repertoire. Daltrey gave up the guitar to concentrate on singing, Townshend turned his rhythm guitar into a lead instrument, and the band emerged with a powerful, sweaty brand of R&B, all very Memphis-influenced ("Green Onions" was long part of their stage act) and louder than anything that London audiences were used to. They quickly became favorites of the R&B-loving mods, and by 1964 were ready to cut their first single, a quickie rewrite of "Got Love If You Want It" entitled "I'm the Face" ("face" being a key part of mod slang) under the temporary name the High Numbers.

It was around this time that Pete Townshend discovered two key talents. As a songwriter, Townshend showed a remarkable capacity for writing anthem-like songs, which, if not exactly Top 40 material, were certainly memorable to their core audience and just different enough to get airplay. "My Generation" was the first and most important of these, and while his songwriting would broaden in coming years to embrace longer thematic canvases (including the so-called rock opera), it was songs like "My Generation," "The Magic Bus," and the epic-length "Won't Get Fooled Again" that would make the most lasting impact on rock & roll. Townsend's other major talent was in the area of destruction — by accident one night, he shattered the neck of his guitar during a performance and the crowd seemed to appreciate it. Gradually guitar smashing became a trademark of the band's sets, an effective but extremely expensive publicity vehicle.

Meanwhile, Roger Daltrey emerged as one of the most powerful singers of his generation, a soul-shouter whose voice could be heard even above Townshend's ringing power chords and Keith Moon's flamboyant drumming. They built their reputations gradually in the US during the mid 60s, emerging as one of the better acts at the Monterey Pop Festival (alongside Jimi Hendrix), but it was their rock opera, *Tommy*, that finally transformed the group into a major international rock act.

Tommy's pretensions aside, the passions and seemingly allegorical search for truth behind the story of the deaf, dumb, and blind boy seemed to strike a chord with an entire generation of teenagers and college students who were searching for something different and more genuine in their own lives — the opera's clear rejection of drugs (which echoed Townshend's own philosophy) was conveniently ignored, and the sky seemed to be the limit for the band for the ten years after *Tommy*'s release.

A live album followed, reminding audiences of the group's R&B roots, and after a false start on film project, in 1971 the Who released *Who's Next*, which was probably their strongest individual album. Very little that they did afterward was quite as successful artistically as this brilliant compendium of religious musings, idealism at high volume, and revolutionary anthems, but it didn't matter. *Quadrophenia* was too vague a subject for Americans who were unfamiliar with its mod-culture roots; *Who by Numbers* seemed slight after the records that had preceded it; and *Who Are You* showed a certain softening of the edges; but the audiences kept buying albums and, even more important, kept going to concerts. Then in 1978, shortly after the release of *Who Are You*, Keith Moon died, and that was pretty much it for the Who. Their work became softer and less urgent (a process that might have been hastened also by Pete Townshend's progressive hearing loss), and while the audiences still bought tickets, their music no longer seemed very important. What little musical capital the group still possessed in the late 80s was squandered on one-too-many farewell tours. —BE

○ **Sings My Generation / MCA** 1966
The group's debut album is more R&B-oriented than their subsequent records, but it's honest and direct. Includes covers of James Brown material and the Beatlesque originals such as "The Kids Are Alright." —BE

○ **The Who Sell Out / MCA** 1967
Arguably rock's first important concept album and infinitely more effective and humorous than *Tommy* or *Quadrophenia*, this is a full-length tribute to Britain's pirate radio stations, complete with commercials by the band. "I Can See for Miles" was the hit off of the record, but the material ranges from the ethereal "Sunrise" to the proto-*Tommy* mini-opera "Rael." Funny as well as scintillating. —BE

Tommy / MCA 1969
The original rock opera. The material hasn't worn well as a conceptual creation, but the individual songs still have an energy that is refreshing. Keith Moon's nasty sense of humor stands out. (MCA's edition of *Tommy* is spread over two CDs; Mobile Fidelity's gold-disc version is on one disc. Mobile Fidelity's reissue is drawn from the original master tape and sounds richer and fuller than the album ever did before. John Entwistle's bass stands out for the first time ever on this edition.) —BE

☆ **Live at Leeds / MCA** 1970
A loud, raunchy concert showcase for the group, with surprisingly little material from *Tommy*. The group's R&B roots are showcased here far better than on their post-*My Generation* studio albums, and the only problem for some listeners is the lack of the sophisticated studio sound they'd developed on previous releases. —RF

★ **Who's Next / MCA** 1971
The group's magnum opus, a rich, expressive, loud piece of hard rock that summed up the first six years of the band's history. "Won't Get Fooled Again" became a major radio anthem and "Behind Blue Eyes" unexpectedly became a favorite Pete Townshend song as well. Roger Daltrey never sang better, John Entwistle's bass achieved new heights of prominence, and Keith Moon turned in an explosive performance on drums. —BE

★ **Meaty, Beaty, Big & Bouncy / MCA** 1972
The first halfway decent retrospective on the group, covering their American singles as of 1972, including "I Can See for Miles," "My Generation," "The Magic Bus," "The Seeker," and a lot of other material that subsequently became staples of FM radio. —BE

○ **Quadrophenia / MCA** 1973
The group's second rock opera wasn't nearly the success that *Tommy* had been, but it proved more fertile in other media — "Love Reign o'er Me" was a moderate success as a single but precious little else seemed to register with the public. Ironically, this is a finely produced album, with a sound that is both hard and lush, and Roger Daltrey seemed to achieve a larger-than-life performance as the embattled mod Jimmy. (Mobile Fidelity's gold-disc reissue includes a beautiful, lavishly produced booklet reproducing the photos and liners from the original LP release in addition to improved sonics.) —BE

Odds & Sods / MCA 1974
Odds is right — a collection of outtakes and mistakes from the first eight years of the group's history, all of it listenable and half of it indispensable. "Long Live Rock" (which later turned up on the *Quadrophenia* soundtrack album) was the best song, but most of the rest is worth a listen. —BE

A Quick One (Happy Jack) / MCA 1974
The group's second album is a transitional work, containing a rudimentary rock opera ("A Quick One") and a bizarre collection of originals by Roger Daltrey and Keith Moon as well as the expected Pete Townshend and John Entwistle. The

flashes of brilliance make up for the defects in the writing, and Entwistle's "Boris the Spider" and "Whiskey Man" are among the best songs he has ever written. –BE

Who Are You / MCA 1978
The final worthwhile album by the band, a somewhat arch collection of pretentious rock anthems and failed concepts surrounding a powerful title track whose video clip marked Keith Moon's final public appearance with the band. (Mobile Fidelity has an Ultradisc version available which is worth the extra money.) –BE

○ **The Kids Are Alright / MCA** 1979
Soundtrack to a dazzling video portrait of the band, better in many ways than any of the hits collections out of the group for the surprises and odd takes that it contains. –BE

Who's Missing / MCA 1985
A collection of loose ends from the group's early years, mostly B-sides and some R&B covers. –BE

Two's Missing / MCA 1987
A followup to *Who's Missing*, with more obscure B-sides, little-known R&B covers, and other relics of the band's early history, of which the best part is their soulful rendition of "Anytime You Want Me." –BE

WEBB WILDER

Roots-rock. The Webb Wilder character was created for a short film about a backwoods private detective who fell out of the 50s and happened to also be a musician. As a group, Webb Wilder combined the surf guitar of the Ventures with the rock roots of Duane Eddy, drawing on the feel of both country music and film noir. Though sometimes bordering on the gimmicky, they are quite humorous and play serious music. *It Came from Nashville* featured a cover of Steve Earle's "Devil's Right Hand," appropriate because, like Earle, Wilder rocked too hard to be country but kept a twang that might put off mainstream rock fans. Their next two albums didn't necessarily forge new ground but refined their sound somewhat, making their R&B influence more apparent. In concert, Wilder often gives stream-of-consciousness recitations, that touch on motor homes, voodoo, television, and other somewhat kitschy subjects; usually they're funny enough to work. But if Webb Wilder intends to expand his audience, he will have to grow musically and steer away from too much camp. He has made another, longer film, indicating a potential career in that medium. –RG

It Came from Nashville / LANDSLIDE
Rock & roll at its heart, with gimmicks on its shoulder. Lots of fun. –RG

○ **Doo Dad / ZOO** 1991
Surf music meets country meets film noir. –RG

ANDRE WILLIAMS *b* 1936

R&B. Singer, songwriter, arranger, producer and one of the mightiest talents to emerge from Detroit's pre-Motown era, Andre Williams started recording in 1957 for the tiny Fortune label, with his group, the Five Dollars (aka the Don Juans), and as a solo artist. Employing his stop-time "wavy gravy" beat and hitting the charts with oddball spoken-word numbers like "Bacon Fat," "The Greasy Chicken," and "Jail Bait," Williams was the original rapper before there was ever a name for it. Moving to Chicago in the early 60s, he wrote "Shake a Tail Feather" for the 5 Du-Tones and "Twine Time" for Alvin Cash, produced albums for Bobby Blue Bland, and scored national hits of his own for Chess with "Cadillac Jack," "Girdle Up," and "Humpin', Bumpin' & Thumpin'." He continues to record and produce other artists sporadically, still keeping abreast of the times, still "Mr. Rhythm," the original rappin' man. –CK

○ **Jail Bait / FORTUNE**
Good (though not complete) overview of Andre's Fortune period. –CK

THE WILLIAMS BROTHERS

Rock/pop. Andrew and David Williams are guitar-toting brothers who began backing up artists such as Brian Setzer, the Plimsouls, Joe Ely, and the Cruzados in the early 80s. They then played in T-Bone Burnette's band during a European tour, before settling down and cutting their first album in 1987. Though in their 20s, they don't pander to the youth audience with their mature music, having opened shows for the late Roy Orbison and Suzanne Vega. –BC

Two Stories / WARNER
Tom Petty, Bob Dylan, and Stevie Nicks covers, as well as their own writings. Big electric-band backgrounds. –BC

○ **The Williams Brothers / WARNER** 1991
Acoustic guitar, light rock-based tunes featuring smooth harmonies, uncluttered instrumentation, and thought-provoking lyricism. "Can't Cry Hard Enough" and "The Family Room" stand out. –BC

LARRY WILLIAMS 1935-1980

R&B, rock & roll. Specialty groomed Williams to reinforce their rock & roll credentials after they lost Little Richard to religion in the late 50s. Williams recorded a few standards ("Bad Boy," "Dizzy, Miss Lizzy," "She Said Yeah"), which were covered by the Beatles and the Rolling Stones during their formative years. –JF

○ **Bad Boy / SPECIALTY**
Vintage (1957-1958) rock from this Little Richard soundalike, with backing from hot New Orleans and Los Angeles sidemen. Excellent 23-track collection with informative notes. –HD

Unreleased Larry Williams / SPECIALTY
A deeper look into the obscure and alternate takes of Williams's work. For collectors. –HD

LUCINDA WILLIAMS

Rock/pop. Born in Louisiana, Lucinda Williams recorded two albums for Folkways at the turn of the 80s, then spent a long time in the wilderness before cutting *Lucinda Williams* for Rough Trade in 1988, an album that was widely hailed for its passionate singing and eclectic music but not widely heard due to the limited resources of the record company (which has since gone bankrupt). Look for her on her new work on RCA/Chameleon. –WR

○ **Lucinda Williams / ROUGH TRADE** 1988
One of the most exciting recording artists to emerge in the second half of the 80s, Williams combined a recklessly passionate lyrical style with an exuberant, energetic performing approach to achieve this stunning result — an infectious album full of compelling songs like "Passionate Kisses" and "I Just Wanted to See You So Bad." Watch for her in the near future; meanwhile, try to find this album. –WR

MAURICE WILLIAMS & THE ZODIACS

Doo-wop. After recording one single for Excello as the Marigolds ("Little Darlin'," later covered by the Diamonds), Maurice Williams rechristened his group and scored a huge hit in 1960 with "Stay," which contains one of the greatest falsettos in the pantheon of soul. Later hits included "May I" and "Come Along." –JF

○ **Best of Maurice & the Zodiacs / RELIC**
Not much thought went into this set, but it'll do. –DH

VANESSA WILLIAMS *b* 1963

Dance-pop. She may've lost her Miss America crown, but Williams has become a soul-pop dance smash. –JF

○ **Right Stuff / POLYGRAM** 1988
Club dance music and soulful ballads. –BC

CHUCK WILLIS 1928-1958

R&B. Chuck Willis was one of the greatest R&B songwriters and vocalists, from his early-50s stint with Okeh up to his work with Atlantic. His best songs, "It's Too Late," "I Feel So Bad," and "What Am I Livin' For," focused on romantic pain and suffering, but he also produced one of rock's finest statements of longevity: "Hang Up My Rock and Roll Shoes." Willis died of peritonitis in 1958. –JF

☆ **My Story / CBS**
The best Okeh recordings by this brilliant R&B songwriter and vocalist, best known for his later work in the 50s on Atlantic. Great liner notes by Peter Guralnick. –JF

BRIAN WILSON   b1942

Rock/pop. Brian Wilson is arguably the greatest American composer of popular music in the rock era. Born and raised in Hawthorne, CA, Wilson formed the Beach Boys with his two younger brothers, cousin Mike Love, and school friend Alan Jardine, and they became the most successful American rock band in history by performing his songs, which initially combined the rock urgency of Chuck Berry with the harmonies of the Four Freshmen. Wilson's musical imagination expanded during the 60s to the point of such remarkable works as "Good Vibrations," a chart-topping Beach Boys single of 1966. Wilson retreated from his dominance of the Beach Boys after 1967, as their popularity declined. He made sporadic contributions to their records, returning briefly as a songwriter and producer in the mid 70s. Wilson issued a debut solo album in 1988, but his second one, *Sweet Insanity*, was rejected by Sire Records. Wilson was said to be preparing his next album. –WR

○ **Brian Wilson / WARNER**   1988
Any suggestion that Wilson's talents had waned was erased by this solo masterpiece, which found his sense of composition and arrangement — especially the gorgeous harmonies — intact, and even growing. –WR

DENNIS WILSON   1944-1983

Rock/pop. Dennis Wilson was the drummer in the Beach Boys. Like the other members of the group, he took a more active role in writing and producing the band's material after his older brother Brian ceased to dominate the group in 1967. Dennis cut a well-received solo album in 1977. He died of drowning. –WR

○ **Pacific Ocean Blue / CBS**   1977
This elaborately produced album demonstrates many of the qualities of the Beach Boys' music, especially the vocal harmonies, but also demonstrates an individual vision. It's a shame there wasn't more after this. –WR

JACKIE WILSON   b1934

R&B, soul. In terms of range, vocal gymnastics, and showmanship — not to mention the ability to simply belt out a song — nobody could match Jackie Wilson. Graduating from Billy Ward's Dominoes, he signed with the Brunswick label and began his career performing songs cowritten by fellow Detroiter Berry Gordy, later the founder of Motown. These included "To Be Loved," "Lonely Teardrops," and "Reet Petite." Wilson trod the line between R&B and pop, often favoring the latter, where he could use his astonishing range to good effect. His records were frequently characterized by a surfeit of brass and "Tonight Show" arrangements. Fans contend that Jackie Wilson was incapable of making a bad record but his output remains a mixed bag to most ears. The best is among the most thrilling music to emerge from the late 50s and early 60s. –CE

○ **Jackie Wilson Story / CBS**   1981
A loving look at the career of a brilliant talent. –DH

Jackie Wilson Story - Vol. 2 / CBS   1983
Lesser material, but that great tenor is still there. –DH

★ **Mr. Excitement / RHINO**   1992
A three-CD box from the experts of reissue at Rhino, *Mr. Excitement* takes Wilson's career from his first sides with Billy Ward and the Dominoes in 1956 through his final recordings

in the early 70s. The former Detroit boxer hit either the R&B or pop chart over 50 times, making him the 26th most successful R&B artist, in chart terms at least. Every one of those recordings is contained in this set, including such classics as "Reet Petite," "Lonely Teardrops," and "(Your Love Keeps Lifting Me) Higher and Higher." Wilson had an explosive falsetto and a downright weird sense of phrasing that made him utterly unique. Some of his productions were a little overwrought but even in the most extreme cases, that voice was a gift from God. Seminal. –RB

WILSON PHILLIPS

Rock/pop. A female vocal trio consisting of Carnie and Wendy Wilson (daughters of Beach Boy Brian Wilson) and Chynna Phillips (daughter of John and Michelle Phillips of the Mamas & the Papas). They broke through to enormous pop success with their debut album, which sold four million copies. The followup, *Shadows and Light*, got off to a fast start in the spring of 1992. –WR

○ **Wilson Phillips / CAPITOL**   1990
A pleasant, harmony-filled pop-rock album, featuring hits such as "Hold On," "Release Me," and "You're in Love." –WR

BEBE AND CECE WINANS

Soul, urban R&B. Detroit-born brother and sister BeBe (Benjamin) and CeCe (Priscilla) Winans are part of the gospel-singing Winans family that also includes the Winans, their four brothers. As a duo, BeBe and CeCe maintain the gospel message, although their records have the production values and style of contemporary R&B. They released their debut album, *BeBe & CeCe Winans*, in 1987 and scored a moderate hit (#49) in the R&B charts with the single "I.O.U. Me" scoring on the R&B and adult-contemporary charts. This earned them three Grammy nominations and one award (gospel). Their second album, *Heaven*, came in 1988 and found them scoring three R&B hits with the title track, "Lost without You," and "Celebrate Life." The album reached the R&B Top Ten (#95 in the pop chart) and went gold. 1991's *Different Lifestyles* was their biggest hit yet, topping the R&B album chart and featuring the R&B #1s "Addictive Love" and "I'll Take You There." –WR

○ **Heaven / CAPITOL**   1988
If you listen carefully, the songs *are* about Jesus rather than love sweet love, but even a casual hearing lets you know this is one of the most soulful duos to come along since Marvin Gaye and Tammi Terrell. Keith Thomas gives the production a contemporary R&B sheen. –WR

JESSE WINCHESTER   b1944

Singer/songwriter. The country folksinger/songwriter Jesse Winchester first gained notice for his debut album, *Jesse Wincheter* (1970), produced by the Band's Robbie Robertson. It featured such songs as "The Brand New Tennessee Waltz" and "Yankee Lady," which were covered by a wide range of performers. The subtext of his appeal, however, (and of songs like "Yankee Lady"), was that Winchester was an American living in Canada to avoid the draft. Born in Shreveport, LA, he had grown up in Memphis and attended Williams College, from which he graduated in 1966. While studying in Germany in 1967, he received his draft notice and moved to Montreal. Winchester's second album, *Third Down 110 to Go*, was released in 1972 and got into the charts briefly, but he was hindered by his inability to play in the US. In 1973 Winchester became a Canadian citizen. He released more records, but it wasn't until 1977, when President Jimmy Carter instituted an amnesty for draft resisters, that Winchester was able to appear in the US. His appearances made his next album, *Nothing but a Breeze*, his biggest-seller yet. *A Touch on the Rainy Side* (1978) was a more moderate success, while *Talk Memphis* (1981) featured the Top 40 hit "Say What." This was his last album for seven years, until the independent Sugar Hill label issued *Humour Me* (1988). Winchester continues to tour. –WR

Jesse Winchester / RHINO   1970
Robbie Robertson and Levon Helm lend a Bandlike sound to
these tracks, which, while not typical of Winchester's later
work, nevertheless have a pleasing rock feel. Some of
Winchester's best songs are here, and the album made him a
legend. –WR

Third Down, 110 to Go / RHINO   1972
Winchester's best album is full of songs about following your
desires and taking risks against high odds, though they're
sung and played buoyantly: "If we're treading on thin ice,"
Winchester sings, "then we might as well dance." –WR

Let the Rough Side Drag / BEARSVILLE   1976
A well-produced country-rock album with more songs
offering sage advice, from the title track to "Damned If You
Do" and "Blow On, Chilly Wind." –WR

○ **The Best of Jesse Winchester / RHINO**   1989
Not a perfect selection but good enough to give a reasonable
representation of Winchester's Bearsville years, 1970-1981.
Includes this transplanted Southerner's haunting "Mississippi
You're on My Mind," as well as "The Brand New Tennessee
Waltz," "Bowling Green," "Biloxi," and "Talk Memphis." –WR

COLIN WINSKI

Roots-rock. Former guitarist for Ray Campi, Winski delivers a
wild, uninhibited brand of rockabilly, which includes one of
the best recorded screams in rock. He released his one and
only album in 1980. –DS

○ **Rock Therapy / TAKOMA**   1980
Fiery 80s rockabilly by one of the greatest screamers. –DS

EDGAR WINTER   b 1946

R&B/rock. Johnny's younger brother. Multi-instrumentalist
and possessor of a vocal range of about a zillion octaves,
Edgar has zipped through so many styles he's simply not
worth pinning down. If you like unhinged blues-rock and
R&B, you'll like the early part of his career. If you like
commercial hard rock, there are songs like the mega-hit
"Frankenstein." Whatever you fancy, chances are Edgar's
recorded it. –JD

○ **Edgar Winter's White Trash / EPIC**   1971
A full R&B outfit with horns. Texas raunch. Only the ballad
sounds dated. –RG

They Only Come Out at Night / CBS   1973
Commercial hits, with "Free Ride" and "Frankenstein." –RG

WINTER HOURS

Folk/rock. 80s/90s quintet strongly influenced by the early
Buffalo Springfield, early Dylan, and the Gene Clark-era Byrds
but with a refreshingly aggressive, high-energy approach.
They specialized in what might best be called loud folk/rock
with a vengeance. Articulate, creative, and talented, they
didn't stand a chance in the 80s. –BE

Wait Till Tomorrow Comes / LIN
Compilation of two early EPs and some singles. It lacks the
punch of Chrysalis's release but is a very tuneful and engaging
record, with some pleasing rough edges. –BE

○ **Winter Hours / CHRYSALIS**   1985
Self-titled album resounds with echoes of Neil Young, Pete
Townshend, and Phil Ochs, haunting melodies, and dazzling
guitar by Mike Carlucci. A must-own for anyone who ever
cared about any of those three influences. –BE

JOHNNY WINTER   b 1944

Blues/rock. Blues guitarist Winter became a major star in the
late 60s and early 70s. Since that time he's confirmed his
reputation in the blues by working with Muddy Waters and
continuing to play in the style, despite musical fashion.
Born in Leland, MS, Winter formed his first band at 14 with
his brother Edgar at 14 in Beaumont, TX, and spent his youth
in recording studios cutting regional singles and in bars

playing the blues. His discovery on a national level came via
an article in *Rolling Stone* in 1968, which led to a management
contract with New York club owner Steve Paul and a record
deal with Columbia. His debut album (there are numerous
albums of juvenilia), *Johnny Winter*, reached #24 in 1969.
Starting out with a trio, Winter later formed a band with
former members of the McCoys, including second guitarist
Rick Derringer. It was called Johnny Winter And. He achieved
a sales peak in 1971 with the gold-selling *Live/Johnny Winter
And*.
He returned in 1973 with *Still Alive and Well*, his highest-
charting album. His albums became more overtly blues-
oriented in the late 70s and he also produced several albums
for Muddy Waters. In the 80s he switched to the blues label
Alligator for three albums, and has since recorded for the
labels MCA and Virgin. In 1992 he released *Scorchin' Blues* on
Columbia. –WR

Johnny Winter / CBS   1969
Winter's stunning debut features his fiery blues playing in
both electric and acoustic settings, with backup that includes
Willie Dixon. –WR

○ **Second Winter / CBS**   1969
Winter leans more toward mainstream rock & roll, though the
guitar playing remains fierce. Originally a *three*-sided LP, this
now makes a long CD. –WR

Johnny Winter And ... / CBS   1970
Winter puts together a new band and takes on the assistance
of Rick Derringer, who coproduces and provides such great
songs as "Rock and Roll, Hoochie Koo." –WR

● **Johnny Winter And ... Live / CBS**   1971
Winter and his new band turn out hard-rock versions of
"Jumpin' Jack Flash," "Johnny B. Goode," and other rock & roll
favorites. –WR

Nothin' but the Blues / CBS   1977
After a long period making rock records, Winter fronts the
Muddy Waters band (with Waters singing) on this Chicago
blues workout. He sounds happier than ever before. –WR

Guitar Slinger / ALLIGATOR   1984
The first of three blues albums recorded after a four-year
studio hiatus finds Winter as fleet-fingered as before and
sounding more vocally involved than in some of the later
Columbia material. –WR

STEVE WINWOOD   b 1948

Rock/pop. Singer/songwriter, keyboardist, and guitarist Steve
Winwood was a well-known musician long before he finally
embarked on a solo career in the second half of the 70s. Born
in Birmingham, England, Winwood joined the Spencer Davis
Group with his older brother Muff when he was only 15. His
was the soulful, Ray Charles-like voice on such hits as "Gimme
Some Lovin'" and "I'm a Man," songs he also cowrote. In 1967
he formed Traffic, which he led, with time off for the
supergroup Blind Faith in 1969, until 1974. Winwood finally
released his first solo album in 1977 and in 1981 had his first
million-seller with his second album, *Arc of a Diver*. *Talking
Back to the Night* (1982) was not as much of a success, and
Winwood spent four years preparing *Back in the High Life*
(1986), which sold three million copies. *Roll with It* (1988)
went to #1, but *Refugees of the Heart* (1990) was not up to his
usual standard. Winwood, who now lives in Nashville,
probably has many years of great music ahead of him. –WR

Winwood / UNITED ARTISTS   1971
A 2-disc compilation of Winwood's group activities, 1966-
1970, including work with the Spencer Davis Group,
Powerhouse, Traffic, and Blind Faith. –WR

○ **Arc of a Diver / POLYGRAM**   1980
Utterly unencumbered by the baggage of his long years in the
music business, Winwood reinvents himself as a completely
contemporary artist on this outstanding album, leading off
with his best solo song, "While You See a Chance." Winwood
also plays all the instruments. –WR

292

- **Back in the High Life / POLYGRAM** 1986
Turning to involved percussion tracks and horns, Winwood turns another musical corner on this sophisticated album, which contains echoes of everything from gospel to Caribbean music. Contains the #1 hit "Higher Love." –wr

Chronicles / POLYGRAM 1987
This isn't an adequate compilation of the years 1977-1986, but it does manage to gather some of the better songs of the period. –wr

Roll with It / VIRGIN 1988
Winwood manages to reintroduce some of the R&B elements of the Spencer Davis Group and some of the psychedelic effects of early Traffic here, though this is also an effective followup to the directions indicated on *Back in the High Life*. Contains the #1 title track and "Don't You Know What the Night Can Do?" –wr

THE WIPERS

Alternative rock. A loud and fast punk band from Portland, OR, that managed to dig a little deeper than most. Led by guitarist and vocalist Greg Sage, the Wipers played music that was raw and abrasive but retained an aspect of refinement, nonetheless. –ime

Youth of America / ENIGMA 1981
First EP. Set the stage for *Over the Edge*. –jd

○ **Over the Edge / RES** 1987
By far their best. Aggressive and direct, this burns! –jd

WIRE

Punk, alternative rock. Arty punks from the glory days of punk made a brilliant debut, then indulged their penchant for creative pomposity. They disappeared, and reappeared as an even artier bunch of pinheads. –jf

○ **Pink Flag / ENIGMA** 1977
Wire's debut effort, *Pink Flag*, was one of the strongest releases during the late-70s British punk scene, mixing the aggressive punch of the Sex Pistols with the humor and brevity of the Ramones. *Pink Flag* packed 22 tracks into the space of 37 minutes; twelve of the tracks were under a minute and a half. ("Field Day for the Sundays" clocked in at just 28 seconds.) Somehow none of these tracks felt short; Wire merely made their point and moved on to the next idea. –rc

Chairs Missing / ENIGMA-RESTLESS 1978
In *Chair's Missing*, Wire stretched out into longer pieces and artier production. Not as impressive as *Pink Flag*, *Chair's Missing* does contain some standout tracks with "Outdoor Miner," "French Film Blurred," "I Am the Fly," and "Question of Degree." –rc

154 / ENIGMA-RESTLESS 1979
154 integrated more keyboards and slowed the pace down a bit, but Wire didn't lose any of the eccentric edge. They just kept getting stranger. If *Ummagumma*-period Pink Floyd, early King Crimson, and Moody Blues, at their musically most cosmic, were filtered through the punk movement, you'd get an idea what a peculiar album *154* is. Call it psychedelic punk. Among the highlights are "Two People in a Room," "The 15th," "Map Ref. 41° N 93° W," "The Other Window," "Single K.O.," and "40 Versions." –rc

- **On Returning (1977-1979) / ENIGMA** 1989
A magnificent 31-song overview that collects highlights from *Pink Flag*, and many of the best songs from the two followups, plus some interesting rarities. –jf

BILL WITHERS   b 1938

Soul, urban R&B. It was a chance 1970 meeting with the legendary Booker T. Jones (of Stax's Booker T. & the MG's) that opened the door for Bill Withers into the world of pop success. At the time of their meeting, Withers was working in a factory that built toilet seats for jet airplanes. Jones, impressed with Withers's demos, helped secure a deal with Sussex Records.

Withers's Jones-produced debut, *Just As I Am*, was a classic of folky acoustic-guitar-driven soul, complemented by Withers's earthy vocal delivery and largely autobiographical tales. His next few albums capitalized on that sound, but as the late 70s came around, Withers gravitated toward a sophisticated urban R&B sound, sometimes collaborating with groups like the Crusaders. –rc

○ **Greatest Hits / CBS** 1981
A good sampler of Withers's hits, plus a few key album tracks, covering his transition from funky acoustic-guitar-rooted soul to smooth urban pop. Included are "Use Me" (#2), "Lean on Me" (#1), "Just the Two of Us" (#2), "Ain't No Sunshine" (#3), and "Who Is He and What Is He to You." Now if only Withers's early albums, like *Still Bill*, would see the light of day on CD ... –rc

PETER WOLF   b 1946

Rock/pop. Peter Wolf was the lead singer of the J. Geils Band from 1967 to 1983. After splitting from the band, he released three solo albums in 1984-1990, with varying success. –wr

○ **Lights Out / EMI-USA** 1984
On his own, Wolf achieves a more contemporary pop sound than that of the bluesy J. Geils Band and scores three chart hits: "Lights Out" (#12), "I Need You Tonight" (#36), and "Oo-Ee-Diddley-Bop!" (#61). –wr

Come As You Are / EMI-USA 1987
Wolf gets back in the Top 15 with the title track, but the best song is the leadoff, an R&B raveup ironically called "Can't Get Started." –wr

BOBBY WOMACK   b 1944

R&B, soul. Few careers in American popular music have been as consistently productive and influential as that of singer/songwriter and guitarist Bobby Womack. Sam Cooke, for whom Womack was playing guitar, financed his first recordings in the early 60s. With his brothers as the Valentinos, he cut two R&B classics, "It's All Over Now" (later a hit for the Stones) and "Lookin' for a Love" (a mega-hit for J. Geils). The Valentinos' combination of shouting lead vocals and blues/gospel harmonies predated late-60s soul music.
Womack knew and championed Jimi Hendrix early on, befriending him during a 1962 soul package tour. Womack's lean, groundbreaking guitar work, so similar in flavor to that of his contemporary Curtis Mayfield, influenced Hendrix. Later Hendrix would use it to chilling effect on Sly Stone's *There's a Riot Goin' On* album and its smash single "Family Affair" (he doubled here on bass). That's also Womack's guitar on Wilson Pickett's "Funky Broadway" and on Aretha Franklin's *Lady Soul* album.
In fact, Womack himself was one of the legendary "wild" soul men, friend and partying companion of Wilson Pickett, for whom he wrote "Midnight Mover" and "I'm in Love." He even scored a movie, *Across 110th Street*, which came out at the same time as the landmark blaxploitation film *Shaft*.
Womack's singing career resumed in the 70s; James Taylor covered his #1 R&B hit, "Woman's Got to Have It." He made a stunning 1981 comeback with the #1 R&B album *The Poet* and reunited with old Memphis studio friends and producer Chips Moman on 1986's *Womagic*.
Bobby Womack's career is far from over. Look for more greatness from this soulful, innovative musician and singer. P.S.: He belongs in the Rock & Roll Hall of Fame! –co

○ **Greatest Hits / LIBERTY** 1987
Includes his great remake of Valentinos' hit "Lookin' for a Love," as well as his other chart hits — "That's the Way I Feel about Cha," "Harry Hippy," and "Nobody Wants You When You're Down and Out." –co

WOMACK & WOMACK

R&B, soul. Cecil Womack (b 1947) and his wife Linda (b 1952) had a long history before the release of their first duo album in 1983. Cecil was one of the gospel-singing Womack brothers who became the Valentinos and toured with Sam Cooke in the early 60s; Linda was Cooke's daughter. Both Womacks were successful songwriters for such performers as Teddy Pendergrass, Wilson Pickett, and Aretha Franklin prior to hooking up as a performing team. The focus is on songwriting in their collaboration; they began with *Love Wars*, which featured the Top 40 R&B hit "Baby I'm Scared of You." *Radio M.U.S.I.C. Man* (1985) contains unfinished Sam Cooke songs completed by the duo. It was followed by *Conscience* in 1988 and *Family Spirit* in 1991. –WR

Conscience / POLYGRAM

This album didn't get airplay or a push, but it didn't lack quality. –RW

○ **Love Wars / ELEKTRA**   1983

Womack and Womack are steeped in the early-60s style of Cecil's Valentinos and Linda's father, Sam Cooke, but they have updated the style. Nevertheless, this is contemporary soul likely to be embraced by fans of Cooke, Otis Redding, and others of the genre. –WR

Radio M.U.S.I.C. Man / ELEKTRA   1985

Nice interaction and captivating lyrics. –RW

STEVIE WONDER   *b* 1950

Motown. Steveland Morris, blind at birth, came to Motown in 1962. He auditioned for Berry Gordy by playing every instrument in the studio. He was billed as "Little Stevie Wonder, the 12-year-old genius." His first #1 hit was "Fingertips" in 1963. As he matured, he collaborated with Motown producers Henry Cosby and Ron Miller for a string of memorable hits during the 60s. He fought Gordy for artistic independence and won. From that point he released an unparalleled string of hit albums and singles. He's been awarded more Grammy Awards (16) than any other Motown artist. His classic hits include "My Cherie Amour," "You Are the Sunshine of My Life," "Sir Duke," and "I Just Called to Say I Love You." –RAB

○ **Music of My Mind / MOTOWN-TAMLA / BB 21**   1972

When Wonder turned 21 he renegotiated his Motown contract; the key issue was control. Stevie Wonder had a vision that veered far away from that of the Motown hit-making machine. Influenced by the work of Isaac Hayes in 1969 and 1970 and labelmate Marvin Gaye in 1971, Wonder no longer was content with putting out albums that were a collection of two or three hit singles plus filler; he wanted to record full-length albums that had an integrity unto themselves. *Music of My Mind* was the first such effort. Wonder produced, wrote the songs, and played the majority of the instruments. At the time it was a revelation. Compared with Wonder's subsequent efforts, it pales just slightly. –RB

☆ **Talking Book / MOTOWN-TAMLA / BB 3**   1972

Talking Book is the album that crystallized Wonder as the self-contained singer/songwriter. "Superstition" and "You Are the Sunshine of My Life" were both #1 singles. The rest of the album maintains an equally torrid level. –RB

☆ **Innervisions / MOTOWN**   1973

For my money, Stevie Wonder's finest moment. Three massive hits, "Higher Ground," "Living for the City," and "Don't You Worry 'bout a Thing," were drawn from the album. "Golden Lady" and "He's Misstra Know-It-All" could have been equally successful. From the titles alone, one can see that Wonder had developed a social concience and, as were many other singer/songwriters of the time, he was politicizing his music. Intelligent lyrics that one can boogie to — what more could one want from popular music? (Mobile Fidelity's remastering is an improvement over Motown's standard version.) –RB

Fulfillingness' First Finale / MOTOWN / BB 1   1974

Two funky, clarinet-dominated singles, "Boogie On, Reggae Woman" and "You Haven't Done Nothin'," are the high points of this record. Much of the rest of the album is centered around the electric piano, a sound ubiquitous in Black music

in the early 70s. Wonder occasionally gets a little syrupy on the non-hit material, although his phrasing is so fine that one tends to be forgiving. –RB

Songs in the Key of Life / MOTOWN-TAMLA / BB 1   1976

Wonder the auteu, began to get out of hand with this sprawling double-album plus four-song-EP set. Much is maudlin, cloying, and pretentious, yet great songs, such as "Sir Duke," rear their heads at various junctures throughout the set. –RB

☆ **Looking Back / MOTOWN / BB 34**   1977

Between 1963 and the end of 1971, Little Stevie Wonder placed 25 songs on *Billboard's* charts. Twenty-four of those, including such radio staples as "Fingertips - Pt.2," "Uptight (Everything's Alright)," "I Was Made to Love Her," "For Once in My Life," "My Cherie Amour," and "Signed, Sealed, Delivered, I'm Yours" appear on *Looking Back*. Wonder's recordings in the 60s stand apart from most Motown acts partially because he was paired with producers and writers who very rarely worked with the Temptations, Supremes, et al. In the beginning Wonder was often produced by Clarence Paul and/or William Stevenson; during the golden years Henry Cosby was usually manning the controls. Then in 1970 Wonder started producing himself, beginning with "Signed, Sealed, Delivered." Most of Wonder's singles were written by Wonder himself in tandem with a variety of others, or by Ron Miller. The hits alternated between stomping barnburners and midtempo, understated ballads. –RB

★ **Original Musiquarium I / MOTOW/ BB 4**   1982

Most of Wonder's chart hits from 1972 through 1982 (although why "You Haven't Done Nothin'" is not here I will never know) are included on *Stevie Wonder's Original Musiquarium I*, plus three newly written and recorded tunes. Simply put, some of the finest Black music made in the 70s. Essential. –RB

BRENTON WOOD   *b* 1941

Soul. Wood's quirky rhythmic sense and happy-go-lucky vocal delivery clicked with R&B and pop audiences in 1967, when "The Oogum Boogum Song" and "Gimme Little Sign" both proved potent hits. Born in Shreveport, LA, Wood moved west to San Pedro and found inspiration in the mellifluous styles of Sam Cooke and Jesse Belvin. He formed a vocal group called the Quotations while attending college, before signing with Double Shot Records and hooking up with producers Joe Hooven and Hal Winn. After making it three hits in a row with "Baby You Got It," Wood only notched a couple more minor chart items for the label in 1968. –BD

○ **Best of Brenton Wood / RHINO**

The best, and much of the rest. –DH

RON WOOD   *b* 1947

Rock & roll. UK guitarist Ron Wood has spent most of his career in groups — the Jeff Beck Group, Faces, and, since 1976, the Rolling Stones — but he's found time to make a variety of non group albums, including duet albums with Ronnie Lane and with Bo Diddley, and even a few solo albums that serve as assemblages of his friends. –WR

○ **Gimme Some Neck / CBS**   1979

Wood leads a pickup band that includes, on various cuts, fellow Rolling Stones Charlie Watts, Mick Jagger, and Keith Richards, plus Mick Fleetwood, Dave Mason, and other notables. The highlight is a then-unreleased Bob Dylan song called "Seven Days," where the rough-voiced Wood sounds uncannily like Mr. D himself. –WR

WORLD PARTY

Rock/pop. Basically, World Party *is* singer/songwriter and multi-instrumentalist Karl Wallinger. Formerly of the popular British band the Waterboys, Wallinger's albums are fascinating, unapologetic exercises in pop self-referentialism. At times Wallinger's retro-60s obsessions and his vocal blend of Dylan and Jagger (less distinctive than either), coupled with his occasional forays into funk, make him sound like Prince fixated on classic rock. All in all, Wallinger manages to make the effect flow seamlessly. –RC

Private Revolution / CAPITOL   1986
This debut album from World Party is a solid release, even if it is a bit heavy on the synthesized sounds (what can you expect from a one-man band?). Wallinger's insightful songs deal primarily with the responsibility of the individual to recognize and cope with the problems of the world. Features mainly original songs like "Private Revolution," "World Party," and "It's All Mine," as well as a cover of Dylan's "All I Really Want to Do," which remains surprisingly true to the original version. –IME

○ **Goodbye Jumbo / CAPITOL**   1990
This excellent followup album from World Party is much tighter than the debut. Dealing with issues from the environment ("Take It Up," "Put the Message in the Box") to relationship woes ("And I Fell Back Alone"), these tracks manage to maintain a hopeful, positive mood without becoming trivial. In these songs, Wallinger has developed his own distinct style. A great album, worth checking out just for the uptempo groove of "Way Down Now." –IME

BERNIE WORRELL   b 1944

Funk. Raised in Plainfield, NJ, Worrell was a classically trained pianist at 3 and a half years old. Throughout his childhood he played with symphonies and orchestras, and even wrote his own concerto at the age of eight. Slowly, he listened to the radio and discovered sounds other than classical, and when he went to college, he played with a number of bar bands, including the Tavares (who were known as Chubby & the Turnpikes back then). It was also around this time that Worrell met George Clinton, who was the vocalist for a Motown-influenced group called the Parliaments. The Parliaments soon split up and moved to Detroit, where Clinton re-formed them into a new group, called Parliament. Clinton then formed another side band, called Funkadelic, several of whose members had been in Parliament but were now performing under the new name due to contractual glitches. Worrell joined Funkadelic in 1970, beginning with their album *Free Your Mind and Your Ass Will Follow.* He was an essential part of the P-Funk mob and continued to play with them right up until the early 80s. He then joined the Talking Heads as a session man and went on tour with them throughout the 80s, basically working with David Byrne and the band right up to their split in early 1992. Besides his solo career, Worrell continues to work with members of the P-Funk, including Bootsy Collins. His work on such songs as "Flashlight," "(Not Just) Knee Deep," and "Cosmic Slop" influenced not only other R&B/soul artists but also many rap groups, who continue to sample his work in their own songs. –JB

○ **Funk of Ages / RHINO**   1990
This solo album features some great funky songs as well as some leaning on the jazzy side. An amazing album by a musician that many know by ear but not by name. –JB

LINK WRAY   b 1930

Rock & roll. Up until Link Wray's groundbreaking instrumental "Rumble" (1958), White guitarists in the main either took the jazz route or tried their best to emulate some form of the Chet Atkins/Merle Travis style. Link changed all that. With the pioneering use of distortion, tremolo, and feedback, plus an unabashed attack that owed much to soul-blues, Wray created a style that was years ahead of its time. Creating one great instrumental after another on primarily chordal themes (making him the godfather of the now-common power chord), his music contained the groundbreaking roots of heavy metal, ten years before it came into being. A seminal influence on Pete Townshend, Jeff Beck, and others, Wray continues to record sporadically, sounding

wilder and crazier than ever, giving the lie to the cliché of being "too old to rock & roll." –CK

Missing Links - Vols. 1, 2, & 3 / NORTON
A brilliant three-volume set of rare recordings. –CK

Link Wray & the Waymen / EDSEL   1985
Sides from the 50s/early 60s; some of his best. –CK

☆ **The Original Rumble / ACE**   1989
A good cross-section of Link's best. –CK

BETTY WRIGHT   b 1953

Soul. A consistently strong presence on the Miami music scene throughout the 70s and 80s, Betty Wright was just 15 when she cut the Top 40 "Girls Can't Do What the Guys Do." A child gospel star who switched to R&B at age 13, she put the Miami scene on the map in 1971 with the #6 hit "Clean Up Woman," notable for its prominent guitar riff and Wright's swaggering lead vocal. She went on to win a Grammy in 1974 for "Where Is the Love?" (not to be confused with the Roberta Flack/Donny Hathaway tune of the same name). She collaborated with Stevie Wonder in 1981 on the Epic hit "What Are You Gonna Do with It?" Betty continues to live and work in the Miami area. –CO

○ **Clean Up Woman / CBS**
Her earliest Miami soul sides are also her most charming. –BD

Live / RHINO   1978
This may not be live, but it is an accurate record of Wright's energetic R&B approach in concert during the mid 70s. –BD

GARY WRIGHT   b 1943

Rock/pop. Gary Wright (born Apr 26, 1943) initially found success with the British hard-blues/rock band Spooky Tooth, from 1967 to 1970. He then pursued a solo career that peaked in 1975 with the atmospheric synth-pop hits "Dream Weaver" and "My Love Is Alive," both reaching #2. –RC

○ **Dream Weaver / WARNER / BB 7**   1975
During the fall of 1975, the title cut off of this album became an enormous hit, with its atmospheric synthesizer washes and spacey sentiments. The followup, "My Love Is Alive," did just as well. Most of the album trades on the same themes but with less success. –RC

O. V. WRIGHT   1939-1980

Soul. A truly incendiary deep-soul performer. O. V. Wright's melismatic vocals and Willie Mitchell's vaunted Hi Rhythm Section combined to make classic Memphis soul during the early 70s.
Overton Vertis Wright learned his trade on the gospel circuit with the Sunset Travelers before going secular in 1964 with the passionate ballad "That's How Strong My Love Is" for Goldwax in Memphis. Otis Redding liked the song so much that he covered it, killing any chance of Wright's version hitting.
Since Wright was already under contract to Houston-based Peacock as a gospel act, owner Don Robey demanded his return, and from then on, Wright appeared on Robey's Backbeat subsidiary. Wright's sanctified sound oozes sweet soul on the spine-chilling "You're Gonna Make Me Cry," a 1965 smash, but it took Memphis producer Willie Mitchell to wring the best consistently from Wright. Utilizing Mitchell's surging house rhythm section, Wright's early-70s Backbeat singles "Ace of Spades," "A Nickel and a Nail," and "I Can't Take It" rank among the very best Southern soul of their era.
No disco bandwagon for O. V. Wright — he kept right on pouring out his emotions through the 70s, convincing his faithful that "I'd Rather Be (Blind, Crippled & Crazy)," that he was "Into Something (Can't Shake Loose)." Unfortunately, he apparently was — drugs have often been cited as causing Wright's downfall; the soul great died at only 41 years of age in 1980. –BD

If It's Only for Tonight / BACK BEAT   1966
An earlier album by this Memphis soul great; includes the sublime "You're Gonna Make Me Cry." –BD

○ **A Nickle & a Nail & Ace of Spades / BACK BEAT** 1971
Since no domestic CDs yet exist on this gospel-drenched soul great, seek out this classic Memphis soul album which drips passion. −BD

Memphis Unlimited / BACKBEAT 1973
Hard-driving soul produced by Willie Mitchell. −BD

ROBERT WYATT

Prog-rock. The former Soft Machine drummer and vocalist has recorded a slew of albums in the British art-rock vein. −JF

○ **Rock Bottom / CAROLINE** 1974
A progressive rock-era masterpiece. Brilliantly simple songs, poems, and textures, with all-star support. −MB

Ruth Is Stranger Than Richard / CAROLINE 1975
Another enduring collaboration with Brian Eno, Fred Frith, and other 70s luminaries. On a par with *Rock Bottom*. −MB

Compilation / RHINO 1990
A reissue of his two strongest 80s albums, *Nothing Can Stop Us* and *Old Rottenhat*. Both are political and lyrical triumphs. −MB

X

Punk. X was a Los Angeles-based punk-rock band of the 80s. It was an outstanding critical success, especially in its first years of record making, but it never broke through to the kind of record sales necessary to sustain a band on a national level. X was formed in the winter of 1977-1978 by singer and bassist John Doe (b Feb 24, 1954), guitarist Billy Zoom (b Feb 20, late 1940s), singer Exene Cervenka (b Feb 1, 1956), and D. J. Bonebrake (b Dec 8, 1955). In 1988 they announced a hiatus, although Cervenka and Doe have made solo albums. A reunion is expected. −WR

○ **Los Angeles / WARNER** 1980
Although classified as punk because of their simple hard-rock sound and caustic lyrics ("The World's a Mess; It's in My Kiss"), X always had more of a rockabilly edge, courtesy of former Gene Vincent guitarist Billy Zoom, and were always funnier than the punk label implies, which may be why they were a cut above their competition. −WR

Wild Gift / WARNER 1981
As with many groups, X had more good songs in their repertoire than could fit on their debut, and their second album presents the rest. Appropriately, the two albums have been packaged together on a single CD. −WR

Under the Big Black Sun / ELEKTRA 1982
Unlike many groups, X responded to the pressure to write a new body of material after their initial burst of songs, by coming up with the goods, especially "The Hungry Wolf" and "Riding with Mary." −WR

See How We Are / ELEKTRA 1987
X had moved toward becoming more of a mainstream hard-rock act by the time of their last studio album, and, given how good the song "4th of July" is, it's a shame its writer, Dave Alvin, didn't stay with the band long enough to contribute more. −WR

X RAY SPEX

Punk. One of the first — and one of the artiest — British punk bands. −JF

○ **Germ Free Adolescents / CAROLINE** 1978
A squalling set of 1977-era art-punk. Poly Styrene is from the Yoko Ono school of irritating vocalists, but "Oh Bondage Up Yours!" is one for the time capsule. −JF

XTC

Alternative pop. England's XTC emerged during the late 70s, when new-wave and punk were informing rock with a renewed urgency. Their early recordings drew heavily from those movements, with arrangements that were edgy and

dissonant. Early on, though, it became evident that XTC had a spiritual affinity for post-*Revolver* Beatles and *Pet Sounds*-era Beach Boys. Their clever (often humorous) off-centered pop increasingly addressed adult topics (from whimsical takes on parenting to religion and class-structure divisions) that, by turns, exuded heady idealism, childlike wonder, or sober skepticism. All in all, XTC has produced some of the finest alternative pop-rock of the 80s and early 90s. −RC

○ **Drums and Wires / GEFFEN / BB 176** 1979
By the release of the Steve Lillywhite-produced *Drums and Wires*, XTC had developed a unique sound that integrated (and plundered) late-70s new-wave, 60s-style pop, and psychedelia. The album produced XTC's first big British hit with "Making Plans for Nigel" (#17 UK). −RC

○ **Black Sea / GEFFEN / BB 41** 1980
On *Black Sea*, again produced by Steve Lillywhite, XTC turned influences (like the Beatles and Beach Boys) inside out with agitated rhythms and mildly dissonant instrumental voicings. *Black Sea* generated four moderate British hit singles. One of them, "Towers of London," features a marvelously twisted Badfinger-style guitar hook set against a wonderfully galloping bass line. "Respectable Street" is another standout on this, one of their best albums. −RC

○ **Waxworks: Some Singles 1977-1982 / GEFFEN** 1982
A smartly assembled collection of the band's better early tracks. −RC

·· **English Settlement / EPIC / BB 48** 1982
English Settlement, a double-album set, heightened XTC's Stateside visibility with the track "Senses Working Overtime." Unfortunately, the album lacked the consistency of *Black Sea*, primarily because of the flat-sounding production, which seemed to steal the impact of the music. −RC

Mummer / GEFFEN 1983
With a couple of exceptions, *Mummer* is a relaxed, somewhat flat-sounding affair. Andy Partridge still manages to get a little venom out with the acidic "Funk Pop a Roll." Other highlights are Chris Mouldings's "Love on a Farmboy's Wages" (#50 UK), "Wonderland," and "Great Fire." −RC

The Big Express / GEFFEN 1984
Following up the relatively somnolent *Mummer*, *The Big Express* was a return to the playful upbeat pop/rock of some of XTC's previous works. "The Everyday Story of a Small Town" is a highlight, as well as "All You Pretty Girls." −RC

★ **Skylarking / GEFFEN / BB 70** 1986
With *Skylarking*, XTC addressed coming-of-age issues like marriage ("Big Day"), supporting a family ("Earn Enough for Us"), and the existence of a loving God ("Dear God"), while clothing them with performances that suggested XTC hadn't lost the capacity for childlike wonder. Todd Rundgren's production of *Skylarking* is one of his best, bathing the album in a pleasantly trippy soundstage. Other highlights include "The Meeting Place" and "Grass." −RC

Oranges & Lemons / GEFFEN 1989
Compared to their best work, *Oranges & Lemons* is a little uneven — a case of a double album that would have made a great single release if XTC had pared it down. *Oranges & Lemons* did produce two big alternative pop-rock hits with "The Mayor of Simpleton" and "King for a Day." Other highlights include the optimistic "The Loving" and "Pink Thing." −RC

Rag 'N' Bone Buffet / GEFFEN 1991
This is a collection of B-sides, live performances, and alternative versions culled from throughout their career. Among the oddities contained here is a cleaned-up-for-radio version of "Respectable Street," off of *Black Sea*. Among the live recordings is "Another Satellite," taken from a BBC broadcast, and a great version of "Scissor Man," originally on *Drums and Wires*. Also included are various solo recordings by bandmates Andy Partridge and Chris Moulding. All in all, *Rag 'N' Bone Buffet* is a desirable item for any XTC fan looking to round out their collection of this band's work. −RC

○ **Nonsuch / GEFFEN**   1992

Nonsuch, produced by Gus Dungeon (Elton John, Bowie), trims the excesses found on *Oranges and Lemons* and recalls the pastoral refinement of *Skylarking* and the rocky edge found on *The Big Express*. Andy Partridge's "The Ballad of Peter Pumkinhead," "The Disappointed," and "Crocodile" are highlights, as are Chris Moulding's "Books Are Burning" and "Bungalow." One of their better albums. –RC

THE YARDBIRDS

British Invasion, hard rock, psychedelic, blues/rock. Formed in 1963, the Yardbirds are one the most influential groups in the history of rock & roll. (The term "Yardbird" came from the designation given to hobos in a Jack Kerouac novel.) During the course of their career, the Yardbirds featured three of rock's greatest guitarists in Eric Clapton, Jeff Beck, and Jimmy Page. During their early period with Clapton, they pursued a highly charged style of electric blues, highlighted best on *Five Live Yardbirds*. Clapton split when he sensed the band was getting too pop with the release of their first single, "For Your Love."

Jeff Beck brought on phase two of the band's development with a highly experimental style that pioneered the application of feedback, fuzz, and unusual melodic scales. It was here that the Yardbirds achieved their creative peak, with songs like "I'm a Man," "Heart Full of Soul," "Evil Hearted You," "Lost Woman," and the masterly "Shapes of Things." Around the time Beck began unraveling at the seams, Jimmy Page came on board. For a very brief time, the Yardbirds had a dream twin-lead guitar lineup, best chronicled on the hits "Happenings Ten Years Time Ago" and "Stroll On," from the movie *Blow Up*.

After Beck left, Page hung on for a little over a year, recording the rather lightweight album *Little Games*. Shortly afterwards, the band feel apart, with Page going on to form Led Zeppelin. Lead singer Keith Relf helped form the art-rock group Renaissance and bassist Paul Samwell-Smith went on to a successful production career for artists like Cat Stevens and Carly Simon. Even though the Yardbirds weren't among the most commercially successful bands of the 60s British Invasion, their profound impact on rock laid the groundwork for hard blues-based rock and heavy metal.

Of particular note to those seeking out the best-sounding Yardbirds discs: none of their CD reissues utilize the original first-generation masters. EMI England has them but won't license them out, due to an unpaid studio bill dating back from the mid 60s. On the other hand, the Edsel import of *Roger the Engineer* sounds impeccable. The reason: The band owns the original masters. –RC

Five Live Yardbirds / RHINO   1964

Recorded live at London's Marquee Club, *Five Live Yardbirds* is the best document of Eric Clapton's work with the band. Tracks like "Too Much Monkey Business," "Got Love If You Want It," and "Smokestack Lightning" were good representations of the Yardbirds's "rave-ups," which were open-ended improvisations that helped lay the groundwork for groups like Cream and the Jimi Hendrix Experience. –RC

☆ **Roger the Engineer / EDSEL**   1966

Roger the Engineer is a classic Yardbirds studio album, thanks to tracks like "Lost Woman," "Over Under Sideways Down," "What Do You Want," "Psycho Daisies," and "Ever Since the World Began." Not available in the States, this British import (on Edsel) is the best-sounding Yardbirds CD by a long shot. A must-own for fans of this band. –RC

★ **Greatest Hits - Vol. 1 - 1964-1966 / RHINO**   1986

Sonically, these tracks fail to match the brilliance and warmth of the original vinyl pressings, but *Greatest Hits* has more punch. "For Your Love" is an exception, with the record version sounding extremely compressed. Of the various Yardbird collections that exist, this is still the most

intelligently chosen, even though it lacks key tracks from *Roger the Engineer*. –RC

○ **Vol. 1 - Smokestack Lightning / CBS**   1991

This double-disc set focuses on tracks from *For Your Love* and *Having a Rave-Up with the Yardbirds*. Included are live tracks recorded at the Crawdaddy Club while touring with Sonny Boy Williamson. Most of these tracks on *Smokestack Lightning* (as well as *Blues, Backtracks*) were mastered off of safety tapes, as opposed to the original masters, since EMI England has possession of them. Considering that EMI won't release the masters to anyone, this is a respectable sound — though not as good as the first vinyl pressings. –RC

Blues, Backtracks & Shapes of Things / CBS   1991

Vol. 2 - Blues, Backtracks & Shapes of Things, another double-disc set, covers some later hits (including the classic future-rock of "Shapes of Things"), *Roger the Engineer* outtakes, and various other oddities. The sound on some of the outtakes is pretty respectable, considering some of them were taken from the original acetates. –RC

The Yardbirds Little Games Sessions & More / EMI   1992

This digitally remastered 39-track, double-disc set covers Jimmy Page's tenure with the Yardbirds. This period didn't contain the band's best work, mainly because Mickie Most's poppish production reined in the band's experimental strengths. Nevertheless, tracks like "Little Games," "Puzzles," "Smile on Me," "Drinking Muddy Water," and a wonderful acoustic version of Jimmy Page's "White Summer" make this a good overview of the Yardbird's final stretch as a band. This set includes extensive liner notes and discography — a real treat for fans. –RC

YAZ

Techno-pop. Yaz was the American name taken by Yazoo, a British duo made up of former Depeche Mode synthesizer player Vince Clarke and singer Alison Moyet (b Jun 18, 1961). The two stayed together only about a year and a half (1982-1983), but that was long enough to score four British hit singles and two top-selling albums. Moyet then went solo and Clarke eventually formed another successful duo, Erasure. –WR

○ **Upstairs at Eric's / WARNER**   1982

Yaz's music is spare, striking electronic backup contrasted with full-throated, emotional singing, but one shouldn't discount some remarkable songwriting, especially the hits "Don't Go," "Only You," and "Situation." –WR

You & Me Both / WARNER   1983

Perhaps a more consistent collection overall than the first album, this one demonstrates that the duo was anything but played out. While both have gone on to successful careers, you can't help regretting that this is the end of Yaz. –WR

YELLO

Prog-rock, techno-pop. This group from Switzerland is a picture of professionalism, although none of the members are trained musicians. Boris Blank, Dieter Meier, and Carlos Peron do not go overboard trying to be innovative and original, but that is certainly the outcome. They have created a distinctive and bright listening style, unusual and very simplistic, not based on traditional harmony or pretensions. Their rich, unique sound and strong emphasis on modern synthesizer technology make this group one of the most significant in contemporary music history. –VB

○ **Stella / POLYGRAM**   1985

This is one of their disco-oriented albums. Includes "Desire" and "Sometimes." –VB

One Second / POLYGRAM   1987

This album offers a great variety of styles, effects, textures, and rhythms. Includes the songs "The Rhythm Divine" and "The Secret Fazida." –VB

Flag / POLYGRAM   1988

This is Yello's most dynamic album, with excellent

composition. Picking highlights would be difficult, since the songs segue, and the album just begs to be listened to as a whole. –VB

YES

Prog-rock. Yes is, without a doubt, the definitive English progressive-rock band, purveyors of cosmic lyrics, virtuoso playing, and vast musical tapestries topped off with heart-stoppingly gorgeous melodies and sealed with a rock & roll kick. Yes was formed in London in 1968 by singer Jon Anderson and bassist Chris Squire, both owners of high, clear tenor voices that blend seamlessly in the band's trademark harmonies. The history of Yes is one of constant changes in personnel, but the group's most celebrated lineup came about when founding members Anderson, Squire, and drummer Bill Bruford, plus guitarist Steve Howe (who had enlisted in 1970), were joined in 1971 by keyboard whiz Rick Wakeman. Thus constituted, the band cut its signature tune, "Roundabout" (from the fourth Yes album, *Fragile*), not to mention the sumptuously symphonic magnum opus *Close to the Edge*. A further series of comings and goings led to a disastrous 1980 lineup (documented on "Drama") in which Squire was the only remaining original member. After a three-year hiatus, a revamped Yes (Anderson, Squire, original keyboardist Tony Kaye, long-time drummer Alan White, and South African guitarist Trevor Rabin) emerged in 1983 with a streamlined, commercialized sound, topping the charts with the danceable "Owner of a Lonely Heart." Anderson split in 1988, teaming up with some old cohorts as Anderson Bruford Wakeman Howe — essentially a rival version of Yes! The two bands joined forces in 1991 as an eight-man "mega-Yes," combining their separately recorded efforts on *Union*. –MPD

★ **The Yes Album / ATLANTIC**   1971
This is the record that first shaped the established Yes sound, built around science-fiction concepts, folk melodies, and soaring organ, guitar, and vocal showpieces. "Your Move" actually got some airplay as a single, and "Starship Troopers" became a much-loved part of the band's set. –BE

○ **Fragile / ATLANTIC**   1972
The breakthrough album for the band, in which the science-fiction and fantasy elements of the songs became dominant and the addition of Rick Wakeman on organ added a larger-than-life element to the group's sound. Ironically, the album was a patchwork job, hastily assembled to help cover the cost of Wakeman's expanded array of instruments, but the short form of "Roundabout" clicked on AM radio, album buyers liked the long version, plus the rest of the material they found, and the band was made. –BE

☆ **Close to the Edge / ATLANTIC**   1972
The group's sound broke more boundaries here, as side-long suites allowed Jon Anderson even more opportunity for vocal acrobatics and Wakeman an even bigger canvas on which to paint his electronic-synthesizer swirls and organ arpeggios. The poetry also had a peculiarly hypnotic quality, which overcame its relatively obscure passages. –BE

Yessongs / ATLANTIC   1973
The best live album to emerge from the entire art-rock scene, a compendium of blazing performances covering the previous three studio albums by the group and the accompanying solo career of Rick Wakeman. Some of the performances are superior to their studio originals, although "And You and I" is something of a disappointment next to the version on *Close to the Edge*. –BE

Yesshows / ATLANTIC   1980
A double album chronicling the late-70s repertoire of the group, less interesting than *Yessongs* but probably the best compendium of this material that is likely to emerge. –BE

90125 / ATLANTIC   1983
A ridiculously successful "comeback" album with a slightly different membership. For completists. –BE

Yesyears / ATLANTIC   1991
This four-CD set is sonically so far superior to the individual

CDs by the group that on this basis alone it is worth owning. Unfortunately, there are important songs that didn't get the remastering treatment, and they are missed. –BE

YO LA TENGO

Alternative rock. Formed by music critic Ira Kaplan, Hoboken-based Yo La Tengo (Spanish for "I got it") appreciates a little America (the band) with their noise. Their music alternates and blends folky melodicism with postpunk aggression. Mostly, they sound as though they're enjoying what they're playing. –BE

Ride the Tiger / TWINTONE   198?
Basking in guitars. –RG

New Wave Hot Dogs / TWINTONE   1987
Heavy guitar; solid songs. They know that we know that they know it's too calculated, but it sounds good anyway. –RG

○ **President Yo La Tengo / TWINTONE**   1989
Features the 40-minute jam they've always wanted to do. –RG

Fakebook / ENIGMA   1990
A collection of mostly covers, Tengo-ized. –RG

THE YOUNG FRESH FELLOWS

Alternative rock. A quirky quartet from the Pacific Northwest, these guys evolved from a load of silliness (though it rocked) to a mature and tight band that allowed only enough juvenilia to keep their music from resembling the postpunk bozos who were becoming pedantic. Contenders. –BE

Men Who Loved Music / FRONTIER   1987
"Amy Grant" is a hilarious number. Good sense of melody throughout. –RG

This One's for the Ladies / FRONTIER   1989
They sound like the Replacements here, but goofily self-conscious. –RG

○ **Electric Bird Digest / FRONTIER**   1991
The quirky edge doesn't get in the way of their love of rock & roll. –RG

YOUNG GODS

Alternative rock. Swiss dance terrorists who sample everything and sing in French. Add to that gobs and gobs of attitude and you've got yourself one whale of a dance-floor concept. Painfully arty, the Gods offer enough primal lurch and scream to make up for their pretentiousness. –JD

○ **L'Eau Rouge / PLAY IT AGAIN SAM**
Thick, crushing percussive onslaught loaded with metallic riffing and extremely hoarse vocals. This is the future of dance rock loaded with attitude. –JD

Play Kurt Weill / PLAY IT AGAIN SAM   1987
Kurt Weill like you've never heard it before — or ever will again, for that matter! –JD

YOUNG MARBLE GIANTS

Alternative rock. A sadly missed and overlooked Welsh trio that played arty, airy pop/punk. –JD

Colossal Youth / ROUGH TRADE   1987
Bohemian and precious, and quietly commanding. –JD

NEIL YOUNG   b 1945

Singer/songwriter, rock & roll. With the exception only of Bob Dylan, Neil Young is the most acclaimed and accomplished singer/songwriter of his generation. Born in Toronto, Young learned to play ukelele and then guitar in his teens, and played in a variety of groups. He moved to Los Angeles with his friend, bassist Bruce Palmer, and hooked up with Stephen Stills, Richie Furay, and Dewey Martin to form Buffalo Springfield in 1966. After the Springfield split in 1968, Young went solo, releasing his first album, *Neil Young*, an acoustic effort with strings, in January 1969. Characteristically, Young followed it only four months later with the hard-rock *Everybody Knows This Is Nowhere*, backed by the electric three-piece band Crazy Horse; it became his first gold-selling album. Young joined Crosby, Stills & Nash in June 1969, and combined solo and group careers until the band split the following summer. His third solo album, *After the Gold Rush* (August 1970), reached the Top Ten and included his first Top 40 hit, "Only Love Can Break Your Heart." But Young's commercial peak came early in 1972, when he released the #1, three-million-selling album *Harvest*, which contained the chart-topping gold single "Heart of Gold."

Instead of following up such success, Young worked on the documentary film *Journey through the Past* (and its accompanying soundtrack album) for the rest of the year, then launched a concert tour in early 1973, by which time Crazy Horse's guitarist Danny Whitten had died of a heroin overdose. The tour was a ragged affair chronicled on the live album *Time Fades Away*. After it, Young recorded (but did not release) *Tonight's the Night*, which memorialized Whitten and Bruce Berry, a Young roadie who had also overdosed.

Young's first new studio album in 18 months, *On the Beach*, was released in the fall of 1974. Much of it was acoustic, and it expressed dire sentiments. He finally put out *Tonight's the Night* in the summer of 1975, and the hard-rocking *Zuma* the following autumn. In the spring of 1976, Young toured with Stephen Stills, and the two recorded the duo album *Long May You Run*. Young's next solo album was 1977's *American Stars 'n' Bars*, made up of studio tracks dating back three years. In the fall of 1977, he released *Decade*, a three-album (later two-CD) career retrospective. 1978 saw the release of *Comes a Time*, Young's most country-folk-oriented album since *Harvest*, and his first since *Harvest* to reach the Top Ten. In 1979 Young launched a tour with Crazy Horse under the banner *Rust Never Sleeps*, including a critically acclaimed album of the same name and, eventually, a tour film and a live album called *Live Rust*.

Young spent the better part of the 80s veering from one musical style to another, as his commercial fortunes declined. He turned to electronic music on *Trans*, to rockabilly on *Everybody's Rockin'*, to country on *Old Ways*, and to horn-backed R&B on *This Note's for You*. In 1989, however, Young returned to his more familiar folk and rock styles for *Freedom*, and was rewarded with critical hosannas and his first gold album in a decade. The hard-rocking *Ragged Glory* was even more rapturously received, topping the *Village Voice* critic's poll for Best Album of 1990. In late 1991 Young issued a double live album, *Weld*, as well as *Arc Weld*, an album of instrumental guitar feedback. He was said to be working on a boxed-set retrospective followup to *Decade*. –WR

☆ **Everybody Knows This Is Nowhere / WARNER**   1969
Young's breakthrough album is also the first one to feature the backup of Crazy Horse for a seminal rock session that produced the Young favorites "Cinnamon Girl," "Down by the River," and "Cowgirl in the Sand." –WR

☆ **After the Gold Rush / WARNER**   1970
The years have only been kind to what sounded like Young's best album when it was released. It's a mixture of his folkie ("Tell Me Why"), country ("Oh, Lonesome Me"), and hard-rocking ("Southern Man") selves, and there's also that mystical title track, which remains Neil Young's definitive statement of purpose. –WR

Harvest / WARNER   1972
Uneven, yes, perhaps due to the overambitiousness of the orchestral pieces, but this album, Young's biggest seller, still contains "Heart of Gold," the rocker "Alabama," and such telling ballads as "Old Man." –WR

Time Fades Away / REPRISE   1973
The beginning of Young's mid-70s descent into decadence, this is part of a trilogy including *Tonight's the Night* and *On the Beach* that explores drug addiction, desperation, and determination, and the subject matter isn't only expressed in the lyrics, it's in the roughly played music and the strained vocals. The most gripping music of Young's career. –WR

On the Beach / REPRISE   1974
Part three of the doom trilogy was actually the second to be released, as Young began to dig himself out of the depression of the previous year, noting that "Sooner or later, it all gets real" but also fearing that he's "just pissing in the wind." –WR

☆ **Tonight's the Night / REPRISE**   1975
This belatedly released masterpiece (part two of the trilogy) is one of the scariest records ever released. It names names and spares no one in its depiction of the druggy life of rock & roll. Least of all spared is the author, who often sounds like he's about to nod out himself. Probably the best album Neil Young will ever make, and not listed as his pick only because it's not the place to start. –WR

○ **Zuma / REPRISE**   1975
"Don't cry no tears around me," Young declares, trying for the second album in a row (after *On the Beach*) to put the past behind him and take on new topics and directions. And so he does, though by calling on other aspects of his past. Crazy Horse is back, with Frank Sampedro replacing Danny Whitten, and Young even includes "Through My Sails," a track from an abortive Crosby, Stills, Nash and Young session. But the highlight is "Cortez the Killer," Young's best guitar workout since *Everybody Knows This Is Nowhere*. –WR

★ **Decade / WARNER**   1977
A 3-LP/2-CD retrospective with material dating back to Buffalo Springfield (some of it unreleased) and including such previously non-LP gems as "Sugar Mountain." As a best-of, it's idiosyncratic, but as a rarities album, it's invaluable. –WR

○ **Comes a Time / REPRISE / BB 7**   1978
From the reflective opener "Goin' Back," to the airy remake of Ian & Sylvia's "Four Strong Winds," *Comes a Time* is Young's most delicately (and oddly) atmospheric album. The album's dreamy country/folk music frames Young's homey discourses on "Peace of Mind," the "Field of Opportunity," and the "Human Highway." The collective effect is a lulling optimism, even when his mind at times seems to be bangin' on one cylinder — merely dishing out alien-sounding toss-offs clothed in plain-speak. Overall, *Comes a Time* is a strangely entrancing high point in Young's willfully erratic carrer. –RC

☆ **Rust Never Sleeps / WARNER**   1979
Like the album that followed it, *Live Rust*, this is a live album. The difference is that this is a single disc containing all-new material. The songs are among Young's best ever, "My My, Hey Hey (Out of the Blue)," "Thrasher," and "Powderfinger," among them. –WR

☆ **Freedom / REPRISE**   1989
"Rockin' in the Free World" represents a renewal of Young's commitment to his artistic vision and to his audience, and, as with all his best work, it recognizes the worst while it hopes for the best. A stunning return to form for an artist who seemed to have wandered too far from his original promise ever to find his way back. –WR

☆ **Ragged Glory / REPRISE**   1990
Young is reunited with Crazy Horse for an album of noisy guitar rock that sounds perfect where played right after *Everybody Knows This Is Nowhere*, and that's a high recommendation. –WR

PAUL YOUNG   ♭1956

Pop, dance-pop. A soulful UK interpretive singer who gained fame in his native country in 1983 with a cover of Marvin Gaye's "Wherever I Lay My Hat (That's My Home)" and in the US with Daryl Hall's "Everytime You Go Away" in 1985. Young found less success writing his own songs, then returned to the US Top Ten with a cover of the Chi-Lites's "Oh Girl" in 1990. In 1992 he left Columbia and moved to MCA. –WR

○ **From Time to Time: The Singles Collection / CBS**   1991
All Young's UK and US hits, among them "Everytime You Go Away," "Come Back and Stay," "I'm Gonna Tear Your Playhouse Down," "Love of the Common People," "Wherever I Lay My Hat (That's My Home)," and "Oh Girl." –WR

THE YOUNGBLOODS

Folk/rock. The Youngbloods, formed in 1965, were led by singer/songwriter Jesse Colin Young (b Perry Miller, Nov 11, 1944). They incorporated bluegrass, folk, country, rock, and bits of psychedelia into their music. Their biggest hit was an up-with-people-style folk-rock anthem called "Get Together," which charted twice (#62 in 1967, #5 in 1969). Other hits included the jug band-influenced "Grizzly Bear" (#52); "Darkness, Darkness" (#86), a dramatic rocker that Mott the Hoople later recorded; and the gentle, acoustic "Sunlight" (#114 - 1969, #123 - 1971). –RC

The Youngbloods / EDSEL   1967
The debut from this folk-rocking, blues-loving quartet is a smile-inducing pleasure in a Lovin' Spoonful vein. (German import) –JT

○ **Elephant Mountain / MOBILE FIDELITY**   1969
The majestic beauty of the Northern California landscape and the idyllic lifestyle it inspires have never been as perfectly portrayed as on this free-flowing, easygoing 1969 album. –JT

Best of the Youngbloods / RCA   1970
It's a bit short at ten songs, but this collection offers a nice overview of this 60s band's growth from good-time ragtimers to laidback jammers. –JT

This Is the Youngbloods / RCA-VICTOR   1972
This out-of-print double-album collection is still the most comprehensive. –JT

Earth Music / EDSEL   1989
In a mood similar to their first, this followup presents an eclectic blend of pop-folk-jazz-blues. (German import) –JT

FRANK ZAPPA   b 1940

Prog-rock, fusion, psychedelic. Frank Zappa is one of the most accomplished composers of the rock era; his music combines an understanding of and appreciation for such contemporary classical figures as Stravinsky, Stockhausen, and Varese with an affection for late-50s doo-wop rock & roll and a facility for the guitar-heavy rock that dominated pop in the 70s. But Zappa is also a satirist whose reserves of scorn seem bottomless and whose wicked sense of humor and absurdity have delighted his numerous fans, even when his lyrics crossed over the broadest bounds of taste. Finally, Zappa is perhaps the most prolific record-maker of his time, turning out massive amounts of music on his own Barking Pumpkin label and through distribution deals with Rykodisc and Rhino after a long, unhappy association with industry giants like Warner Brothers and the now-defunct MGM.

Zappa became interested in music early and pursued his studies in school, up through a six-month stint at Chaffey College in Alta Loma, CA. He scored a couple of low-budget films and used the money to buy a low-budget recording studio. In 1964 he joined a local band called the Soul Giants, which, over the course of the next two years, evolved into the Mothers, who played songs written by Zappa. The band was signed to the Verve division of MGM by producer Tom Wilson in 1966 and recorded its first album, a two-LP set called *Freak Out!*, which introduced Zappa's interests in both serious music and pop as well as his scathing wit. (Verve insisted on adding "of Invention" to the band's name.)

Subsequent albums extended the musical and lyrical themes of the debut, and they came frequently. Three albums, for example, hit the charts in 1968: *We're Only in it for the Money*, a Mothers album that made fun of hippies and *Sgt. Pepper*; *Lumpy Gravy*, a Zappa solo album recorded with an orchestra; and *Cruising with Ruben & the Jets*, on which the Mothers played neo-doo-wop. Toward the end of the 60s, Zappa expanded the Mothers lineup, turning more toward instrumental jazz/rock, much of which displayed his technically accomplished guitar playing. But by the end of the decade, he had broken up the band.

In 1971, however, Zappa reassembled a new edition of the Mothers, featuring former Turtles lead singers Mark Volman

and Howard Kaylan as frontmen. The lineup moved the group more in the direction of X-rated comedy, notably on the album *Fillmore East June 1971*, but it was short-lived: during a performance at the Royal Albert Hall, Zappa was pushed from the stage by a demented fan and was seriously injured.

While he recovered, Zappa released several albums, then he re-formed the Mothers with himself as lead singer and made pop-rock albums, such as *Over-nite Sensation*, which were among his best-selling records ever. By the end of the 70s, Zappa was recording on his own labels, distributed in some cases by the majors, and he had attracted a consistent cult following for both his humor and his complex music. (Zappa's band, in fact, became a training ground for high-quality rock musicians, much as Miles Davis's was for jazz players.)

In the 80s Zappa gained the rights to his old albums and began to reissue them, at first on his own and then through the pioneering Rykodisc CD label. He published his autobiography and embarked on a world tour in 1988. That was the end of his live performing, except for such isolated appearances as one in Czechoslovakia at the invitation of its post-Communist president, Zappa fan Vaclav Havel.

In late 1991, it was confirmed that Zappa was seriously ill with cancer of the colon. Nevertheless, his schedule of album releases continued to be rapid, and he was reported to be preparing at least one classical music composition commissioned for the fall of 1992. –WR

☆ **Freak Out! / RYKODISC**   1966
Once a LP, now an hour-long CD, but still featuring the Mothers' opening salvo to the world, playing what is often melodic 60s pop-rock with doo-wop influences. But the lyrics in songs like "Who Are the Brain Police?" and "Trouble Every Day" mark composer Frank Zappa as having a social conscience and a wickedly satiric sense of humor. –WR

☆ **Absolutely Free / RYKODISC**   1967
The satire gets even sharper on such songs as "Plastic People" and "Status Back Baby," while the references are often only local to the band's Los Angeles environs (and, increasingly, part of a private, absurdist language), and the music gets increasingly complicated. –WR

★ **We're Only in It for the Money / VERVE**   1968
A simultaneous condemnation of the straights and the hippies, its songs segue as on *Sgt. Pepper* with verbal asides included, a sound collage that was the original Mothers' highest-charting album. (Note: Recommendation is for the original LP release, and not the CD reissue, which, available on one disc with *Lumpy Gravy*, has rerecorded rhythm tracks.) –WR

Uncle Meat / RYKODISC   1969
A sprawling, largely instrumental soundtrack to a movie that was never finished, including everything from the pop tune "The Air" to the extended "King Kong," complete with variations. –WR

Hot Rats / RYKODISC   1970
Zappa disbanded the original Mothers group in 1969 and cut this solo album, most of which consists of well-organized jazz-rock instrumentals such as "Peaches En Regalia," one of his most appealing compositions. Captain Beefheart provides a guest vocal on "Willie the Pimp," which also features violin by Jean-Luc Ponty. –WR

Weasels Ripped My Flesh / RYKODISC   1970
An album of live material recorded from 1967 to 1969 and featuring an expanded lineup with horn section. Highlights include Sugar Cane Harris's violin work on Little Richard's "Directly from My Heart to You" and Zappa's vocal on "My Guitar Wants to Kill Your Mama." –WR

Fillmore East June 1971 / RYKODISC   1971
A new Mothers lineup led by ex-Turtles singers Mark Volman and Howard Kaylan makes for a virtual comedy act based on the theme of life on the road. Very funny, and some of the playing is amazing too. –WR

100 Motels / UNITED ARTISTS 1971
The soundtrack to Zappa's crazed movie is full of great music
and is great fun. −CK

☆ **Apostrophe/Over-nite Sensation / RYKODISC** 1973
Over-nite Sensation was Zappa's first new studio album of
vocal music in three years, and it finds him with another
edition of Mothers (from this point, Mothers group albums
and Zappa solo albums become indistinguishable). This time
Zappa took the lead vocals himself and wrote a new set of
catchy, satiric rock-pop songs like "Camarillo Brillo" and
"Montana." *Apostrophe* is Zappa's only gold-selling Top Ten
album, featuring the satiric "Don't Eat the Yellow Snow," along
with other parodic songs in the same style as *Over-Nite
Sensation*. Rykodisc has combined the two 1973 albums onto
one CD. −WR

Bongo Fury / RYKODISC 1975
A live album recorded with Captain Beefheart on lead vocals,
which combines Zappa's provocative songs with Beefheart's
peculiar perspective. Contains the should-have-been-a-hit
"Carolina Hard-Core Ecstasy." −WR

Shut Up'n Play Yer Guitar / RYKODISC 1981
A compilation of crazed solo Zappa with the spotlight on his
guitar work. −CK

Tinsel Town Rebellion / RYKODISC 1981
From the mid-70s on, Frank Zappa's music divided ever more
extremely into complex instrumental passages and broadly
satiric songs, which stopped sounding clever and started
seeming smutty and sophomoric. There are elements of these
excesses on this live double album, but for the most part the
appeal of the music and the fine performances overcome
objections. There are also remakes of such old favorites as
"Brown Shoes Don't Make It." −WR

Ship Arriving Too Late ... / CAPITOL 1982
Ship Arriving Too Late To Save a Drowning Witch features the
novelty hit "Valley Girl," with vocals by Zappa's daughter,
Moon. (Steve Vai is featured on the appropriately credited
"impossible guitar.") −WR

Broadway the Hardway / RYKODISC 1988
A live album culled from Zappa's final world tour of 1988. It
features his comments on Elvis Presley ("Elvis Has Just Left
the Building"), televangelists ("Jesus Thinks You're a Jerk"),
and other objects of political scorn. −WR

You Can't Do That - Vol. 1 / RYKODISC 1988
In the late 80s, Frank Zappa, already the most prolific artist in
rock history, began releasing large amounts of archival
material. The *You Can't Do That on Stage Anymore* series was
to consist of six two-CD sets (the final two of which were
scheduled for release in 1992), on which Zappa mixed and
matched live recordings from throughout his career, editing
different versions of songs together (sometimes by different
bands). For an artist as inconsistent as Zappa, the results were
bound to be uneven, but for those willing to wade through the
hours of recordings, there are hidden gems. The first release is
typical of the series. −WR

Beat the Boots! Box / RHINO 1991
Frank Zappa frequently has been the victim of bootleggers,
and with this release he turns the tables on his tormentors.
This boxed eight-cassette set (also available as separate CDs)
presents a series of bootlegs as they appeared, without any
improvement. Nevertheless, the sound is often surprisingly
good, and especially the recordings by the original Mothers
(*The Ark*, RHI 70538, for instance) will be of interest to
Zappaphiles. (A second version of *Beat the Boots!*, available
only as a boxed set, appeared in 1992.) −WR

WARREN ZEVON b1947

Singer/songwriter, rock & roll. How did a guy with such a
wickedly black sense of humor and a love for tough rock & roll
get to be a 70s Los Angeles songwriting pro? By tempering
that dark streak with some evocative and personal ballads,

which surveyed the trappings of the Los Angeles lifestyle.
Even at his worst, Zevon was always better than the Eagles,
and with less sexism to boot. −JF

○ **Warren Zevon / ELEKTRA** 1976
A beautiful and ambitious debut that paints a gloomy and
cryptic portrait of Hollywood's casualties through gripping
songs like "Carmelita," "I'll Sleep When I'm Dead," and
"Mohammed's Radio." −JF

Excitable Boy / ELEKTRA 1978
A disappointing followup, in that Zevon's sensitivity is
sacrificed for mere weirdness. Nevertheless, there's some fine
music here. −JF

Stand in the Fire / ASYLUM 1981
This live set rocks harder than his studio discs and also works
as a career overview. −JF

Best Of - A Quiet Normal Life / ELEKTRA 1986
An adequate but skimpy best-of. −JF

Transverse City / VIRGIN 1989
Zevon's attempt to integrate the influence of Stravinsky makes
this album is a complex, dense but still absorbing blast of
jagged rock. −JF

Mr. Bad Example / GIANT 1991
For Zevon, this is a rather tranquil set of soul searchers, but
there's still some trenchant humor here. −JF

ZOMBIES

British Invasion. A British invasion band with a soulful but
sophisticated sound, whose hard-luck history ended with
their biggest hit topping the US charts and racking up two
million sales after they'd split up. Member Rod Argent later
formed the early-70s band Argent. −BE

○ **Greatest Hits / DCC**
The early sides. All well-chosen Brit-beat with a strong R&B
influence. −BE

Odessey and Oracle / DATE 1968
A psychedelic effort whose best song, "Time of the Season"
became a monster hit with a sultry, soulful sound not
replicated elsewhere on the album. −BE

ZZ TOP

Blues/rock. American blues-rock trio from Texas consisting of
Billy Gibbons (guitar), Dusty Hill (bass), and Frank Beard
(drums). Formed in 1970 in and around Houston from rival
bands, the Moving Sidewalks (Gibbons) and the American
Blues (Hill and Beard). Their first two albums reflected the
strong blues roots and Texas humor of the band. The third
album (*Tres Hombres*) gained them national attention with hit
"La Grange," a signature riff tune to this day. Their success
continued unabated throughout the 70s, culminating with the
year and a half-long Worldwide Texas Tour. Exhausted from
the overwhelming work load, they took a three-year break,
then switched labels and returned to form with *Deguello* and
El Loco, both harbingers of what was to come. By their next
album *Eliminator* and its worldwide smash followup
Afterburner, they had successfully harnessed the potential of
synthesizers to their patented grunge-groove, giving their
material a more contemporary edge while retaining their
patented Texas style. Now sporting long beards, golf hats, and
boiler suits, they met the emerging video age head-on,
reducing their "message" to simple iconography. Becoming
even more popular in the long run, they moved with the times
while simultaneously bucking every trend that crossed their
path. As genuine roots musicians, they have few peers;
Gibbons is one of America's finest blues guitarists working in
the arena of rock idiom, while Hill and Beard provide the
ultimate rhythm section support. The only rock & roll group
that's out there with its original members still aboard after 20-
plus years, ZZ Top's music is always instantly recognizable,
eminently powerful, profoundly soulful, and 100% American
in derivation. −CK

ZZ Top's First Album / WARNER 1970

This Texas trio's debut was a gritty exercise in bare-boned blues boogie. Tracks like "Brown Sugar," "Neighbor Neighbor," and "Shakin' Your Tree" helped establish them as a regionally successful act in the South. –RC

Rio Grande Mud / WARNER / BB 14 1972

Rio Grande Mud possessed a beefier sound than its predecessor. The "Brown Sugar"-style "Francene" became their first hit at #69. Other highlights included "Chevrolet" and "Just Got Paid." –RC

○ **Tres Hombres / WARNER / BB 8** 1973

Constant touring and favorable radio exposure made *Tres Hombres* ZZ's first hit album, thanks in no small part to "La Grange" (#41), an ode to a whorehouse. By this album, Billy Gibbons had practically perfected his distinctively dirty electric guitar sound. His riffs and chordal voicings were also more memorable. Highlights included "Beer Drinkers & Hell Raisers," "Precious & Grace," and the twosome "Waitin' For the Bus," and "Jesus Just Left Chicago." –RC

Fandango / WARNER / BB 10 1975

Fandango is a half-studio/half-live effort. The concert side is a fairly straightahead, no-nonsense affair, which includes a version of "Jailhouse Rock." The studio side featured their first Top 40 hit, "Tush" (#20). The hyper-boogie of "Heard It on the X" was another popular track off this release. –RC

★ **Best of ZZ Top / WARNER / BB 94** 1977

The sound may be a little muddy, but this anthology is still the best representation of ZZ's early work. Contains classic rude, riff-heavy blues rockers like "Just Got Paid," "Jesus Just Left Chicago," "Heard It on the X," "Tush," and "La Grange." –RC

☆ **Deguello / WARNER / BB 24** 1979

Deguello was ZZ's best album from their pre-robotic blues-rock period — the last reminder of what a tough ensemble this trio could be. It was the first time they infused their lunkhead approach to fast cars, kinky girls, and partying with some bizarre humor. Their version of Sam & Dave's "I Thank You" (#34) became their first Top 40 hit in five years. Other highlights included the oddball "Manic Mechanic," a rip-roaring version of Elmore James's "Dust My Broom," the funky boogie of "Cheap Sunglasses," and "Fool for Your Stockings," a down-and-dirty fetish blues. –RC

El Loco / WARNER 1981

Not as strong as *Deguello*, *El Loco* vacillates between half-baked ballads ("Leila") and novelty rockers ("Party on the Patio," "Groovy Little Hippie Pad," "Heaven, Hell or Houston"). "Pearl Necklace," with its not-too-subtle sexual double-entendre and Police-inspired groove, was a big AOR hit. –RC

☆ **Eliminator / WARNER / BB 9** 1983

Hardcore fans might have cried "sellout," but ZZ's introduction of a streamlined synth-heavy sound (and three slickly produced T&A videos) turned this trio from potential blues-rock has-beens to multi-platinum purveyors of space boogie. Most of this album became a staple on album rock radio, with "Gimmie All Your Lovin'" (#37), "Sharp Dressed Man" (#56), and "Legs" (#8) becoming the primary hits. –RC

Afterburner / WARNER / BB 4 1985

Basically a carbon-copy of *Eliminator*, *Afterburner* continued ZZ's winning streak, which includes four hit singles: "Sleeping Bag" (#8), "Stages" (#21), "Rough Boy" (#22), and "Velcro Fly" (#35). –RC

Six Pack / WARNER 1987

The idea of compiling albums one through five, plus their seventh effort, onto a three-CD set seemed like a good one. After all, there's a load of great playing on these discs. Unfortunately, the first five albums were hastily remixed from the original multi-tracks. The sound might have more definition and punch, but the effort to update the drum sounds with triggered samples, re-amped guitars, and cold digital reverbs gave some of the music a stiff, clinical quality. Why a band that touts the power of an organic genre like the

blues would so insensitively plunder the recordings they made when they really were a real live band, makes one wonder if the sequencers had finally gone to their brains. That ZZ's management and Warner allowed such a half-baked job on the market seems to support that assertion. –RC

Recycler / WARNER / BB 6 1990

ZZ seemed to be running low on good material as they cranked up the Fairlights for a third go-round. "My Head's in Mississippi," however, is a fine rocker, which synthesized the gritty virtues of their earlier sound with the hi-tech gloss of their later work. *Recycler* also includes "Doubleback," their hit from the movie *Back to the Future - Part III*. –RC

ROCK/POP COLLECTIONS

○ **20 Greatest Songs in Motown History / MOTOWN** 1986

A testimony to Motown's impact on pop music. –RAB

☆ **25 #1 Hits in 25 Years / MOTOWN** 1983

Excellent collection of the company's gems. –RAB

☆ **25 Hard to Find Motown Classics - Vol. 3 / MOTOWN**

The best of the *Hard to Find* series. –RAB

○ **All Star Funk / PRIORITY**

Good collection of 70s funk hits, including definitive cuts by Parliament, Funkadelic, and Bootsy Collins. –JF

Arista's Greatest Hits / ARISTA

Portrait of a Decade 1975-1985. Clive Davis's label and its many very soft-pop smashes. –DH

○ **At Death's Door: Brutal Death Metal / RDR**

A diverse selection of death-metal bands on the Roadracer label. –JB

☆ **Atlantic Rhythm & Blues - Vols. 1-7 / ATLANTIC** 1986

Vols. 1-7 (1947-1974). Along with Specialty, Aladdin, Chess, Sun, and a few other labels, Atlantic paved the way for rock & roll. Started by Ahmet Ertegun and Herb Abramson in 1947, Atlantic brought meticulous recording techniques — usually reserved only for jazz sessions — to R&B. They assembled a revolving cast of crack studio musicians. This seven-disc set (eight CDs on the boxed set) is a perfect collection of all the best singles from Atlantic Records. –JF

☆ **Atlantic Soul Classics / WARNER**

This was the first CD collection of Atlantic's greatest 60s soul burners. You can now find most of these on better collections, but this still isn't a bad place to start your education. –JF

○ **Back Seat Jams / DCC** 1987

A good oldies collection remastered by Steve Hoffman. –DH

○ **Baseball's Greatest Hits / RHINO**
Let's Play II / RHINO 1988

Two-CD set from Rhino entirely devoted to baseball-related tunes, ranging from odes to Jackie Robinson and a "duet" with Mickey Mantle and Teresa Brewer. An interesting glimpse at America's fascination with its favorite pastime and the music industry's anthologizing of it. –CK

○ **Beach Classics / GARLAND**

A brilliant collection of the best surf-rock hits. –DH

○ **Beachbeat Shaggin' / DCC**

A good overview of light 60s soul nuggets known on the Atlantic coast as beach music. –JF

○ **The Beat Generation / RHINO** 1992

This 3-CD boxed set is an ambitious musical and spoken portrayal of the early-50s and early/mid-60s Beat Generation, as well as later practitioners of that aesthetic. Among those represented are Jack Kerouac, Langston Hughes, Ken Nordine, William S. Burroughs, Lambert, Hendricks & Ross, Dizzy Gillespie, John Drew Barrymore, Lenny Bruce, Allen Ginsberg, and Tom Waits. –RC

Best of Chess Rhythm & Blues / MCA

A good various-artists collection from the great Chicago R&B label, including Fontella Bass's "Rescue Me," Billy Stewart's

"Summertime," Jan Bradley's "Mama Didn't Lie," and an early Smokey Robinson & the Miracles effort, "Bad Girl." –DH

Best of Chess Rock & Roll / MCA
Another great various-artists collection from the seminal Chicago label. This one features standard fare like "Johnny B. Goode" and "Bo Diddley," and left-field hits like "Book of Love" by the Monotones and "Rinky-Dink" by Dave "Baby" Cortez. –DH & STE

Best of Chess Vocal Groups / MCA
Rounding out the trilogy of Chess sampler albums, this one features "Long Lonely Nights" by Lee Andrews & the Hearts, the highly influential "Every Day of the Week" by the Students, and the Southern soul of the Knight Brothers "Temptation 'Bout to Get Me." –CK

○ **Best of Doo Wop Ballads / RHINO**   1989
○ **Best of Doo Wop Uptempo / RHINO**   1989
Rhino's *Best of Doo Wop* compilations are a glorious pair of discs that salute the finest doo-wop hits. Collectors already have this stuff, but novices would do well to start right here. –JF

○ **Best of House Music / PROFILE**   1988
Use this as an introduction into the frenetic world of house music. –RW

Best of Louie Louie - Vol. 1 / RHINO   1983
Superior cover versions of this classic rock & roll tune. –LL

☆ **Best of Malaco / MALACO**
Saucy R&B, funk, and some early tunes with leanings toward rap. –RW

○ **Best of Metal Blade - Vol. 1 / RES**   1988
The first best-of package from Metal Blade. Contains very early tracks from Bitch, Celtic Frost, Fates Warning, Hallow's Eve, Hirax, Lizzy Borden, Metal Church, Slayer, Trouble, and Voivod. –JB

Best of Metal Blade - Vol. 2 / ENIGMA   1988
A sampler of music from the excellent Metal Blade label, considered to be music for the "headbanging connoisseur." –JB

☆ **Best of New Orleans R&B - Vol. 1 / RHINO**   1988
Some of the greatest music ever, period — the Meters, Clarence Henry, Lloyd Price, etc. Endless groovin'. –JT

☆ **Best of New Orleans R&B - Vol. 2 / RHINO**   1988
More funky gumbo, from Smiley Lewis, Irma Thomas, Earl King, and others who know how to have a good time. –JT

☆ **Best of Nuggets / RHINO**
Punk and garage-rock from the 60s, raw and essential. Probably the best compilation ever done on the genre, featuring classics by the Seeds, the Syndicate of Sound, the Count Five, the Chocolate Watchband, and others. Part of a continuing series. –CK

○ **Best of Ric Records - Vol. 1: Carnival Time / ROUNDER**
One of two great 50s-vintage collections of music from the New Orleans Ric and Ron records. No hits, but plenty to keep you rocking. –JF

○ **Best of Ron Records - Vol. 1: We Got A Party / ROUNDER**
The second part of a collection of 50s vintage music on the New Orleans-based Ric and Ron records labels, including some rare Professor Longhair sides. –JF

○ **Best of Sue Records / COLLECTABLES**
Find out why Sue Records was one of New Orleans's greatest and most revered R&B/soul labels, and the early home to such artists as Aaron Neville and Ike & Tina Turner. –JF

The Big Itch / MR. MANNICOTTI
Insane compilation of extremely raw, crude, and obscure rock & roll tracks. Side 1 is all "Pa Pa Ooh Mow Mow" and "Surfin' Bird" related tunes, while Side 2 charts territory into the awesomely arcane, featuring the title track and offerings by King Uszniewicz and Trez Trezo. Not for the faint of heart. –CK

Volume 2 / MR. MANNICOTTI
More nutzo offerings on this memorial album for Joe E. Ross, which features Ross (of "Car 54 Where Are You?" fame) doing "Ooh-Ooh," Archie Pier's "Tamales & Rock 'n' Roll," and the best/worst version of "Heartbreak Hotel" you'll ever hear. –CK

Volume 3 / MR. MANNICOTTI
The third offering in an ongoing series, this time featuring the cast of "McHale's Navy" doing "Pa Pa Ooh Mow Mow," Terry Tene's "Curse of the Hearse," Jerry Coulston's "Cave Man Hop," and T. Valentine's "Hello Lucille, Are You a Lesbian?" as some of the crazed highlights. As insane as the first two volumes and then some. –CK

Billboard Top R&B Hits - 1955 / RHINO   1989
Ten pieces of primal git-down by Johnny Ace, Bo Diddley, Joe Turner, Little Walter, et al. –JT

Billboard Top R&B Hits - 1956 / RHINO   1989
No wonder R&B woke up teenage America, with Little Richard, the Cadillacs, Clyde McPhatter, and the Five Satins producing classics like these. –JT

Billboard Top R&B Hits - 1957 / RHINO   1989
A good year for good-time rockin'. Fats and Little Richard rule; the Dell-Vikings, Mickey & Sylvia, and Bobby "Blue" Bland bring it all home. –JT

Billboard Top R&B Hits - 1958 / RHINO   1989
Headed up by a handful of novelty sides — "Book of Love," "Rockin' Robin" — this is a blast. –JT

Billboard Top R&B Hits - 1959 / RHINO   1989
Fine R&B from the Falcons, Dee Clark, Jackie Wilson, and James Brown gives this set staying power. –JT

Billboard Top R&B Hits - 1960 / RHINO   1989
Headin' uptown with Brook Benton, Jerry Butler, and Dinah Washington — a classy collection. –JT

Billboard Top R&B Hits - 1961 / RHINO   1989
The roots of soul? The Miracles top the list; Ben E. King, Lee Dorsey, and the Jive Five round it out. –JT

Billboard Top R&B Hits - 1962 / RHINO   1989
Motown and Stax make their entries, while James Brown and a host of hot ladies give 'em a run. –JT

Billboard Top R&B Hits - 1963 / RHINO   1989
The Impressions, Jackie Wilson, Marvin Gaye, Mary Wells — we are talking fine. –JT

Billboard Top R&B Hits - 1964 / RHINO   1989
The complete Motown invasion — Four Tops, Temptations, Martha, and the Supremes. Non-Detroiters may as well have sat this one out. –JT

○ **Billboard Top R&B Hits - 1965 / RHINO**   1989
Put this on and even *try* to stop dancing. "Shotgun," "Rescue Me," "I Can't Help Myself," and — Yow! — "I Got You." –JT

Billboard Top R&B Hits - 1966 / RHINO   1989
The summit of soulsville — "Going to a Go-Go," Wilson Pickett, Joe Tex. –JT

Billboard Top R&B Hits - 1967 / RHINO   1989
Another batch of soul beauts. This one includes Aretha, Aaron Neville, and more Motown. –JT

Billboard Top R&B Hits - 1968 / RHINO   1989
Black pride anthems from James Brown and the Impressions; great love songs from the Delfonics and Smokey Robinson — plus six more. –JT

Billboard Top R&B Hits - 1969 / RHINO
Getting funky with the Isleys' "It's Your Thing" and Sly Stone's "Everyday People." Get ready for the change that's gonna come. –JT

Billboard Top R&B Hits - 1965-1969 (box set) / RHINO
The essential hits from the cream of the soul crop. –JT

Billboard Top R&B Hits - 1970 / RHINO   1990
The names were the same — Temptations, James Brown — but no doubt about it, a new decade was dawning. –JT

Billboard Top R&B Hits - 1971 / RHINO
JB said "Make It Funky" and Marvin wondered "What's Going On." And everyone was ready to do some dancing. –JT

Billboard Top R&B Hits - 1972 / RHINO   1990
Tougher times, tougher tunes. Al Green made it all sound sweeter, and Curtis Mayfield put out a warning. A good year for getting spiritual. –JT

Billboard Top R&B Hits - 1973 / RHINO   1990
The gospel-bred Staple Singers topped the charts, and Harold Melvin and the Isleys took it to the discos. –JT

Billboard Top R&B Hits - 1974 / RHINO   1990
Kool and the Gang, Tavares, and the perennial James Brown ushered in the disco era. Things were never gonna be the same. –JT

Billboard Top Rock & Roll Hits - 1955 / RHINO   1988
"Rock Around the Clock," "Earth Angel," the Moonglows, LaVern Baker ... as good a place to start as any. –JT

Billboard Top Rock & Roll Hits - 1956 / RHINO   1989
Rock & roll kicks into high gear — ten tracks of genius from Frankie Lymon, Elvis, Gene Vincent, Fats Domino, Carl Perkins, and ... Buchanan & Goodman? –JT

Billboard Top Rock & Roll Hits - 1957 / RHINO
One of the landmark years for rock & roll — Elvis, Chuck, Buddy, Jerry Lee. If you don't know the last names, you *deserve* Michael Bolton. –JT

Billboard Top Rock & Roll Hits - 1958 / RHINO
"At the Hop," "Tequila," and "Get a Job." Wow! Throw in Elvis, Jerry Lee, the Everlys, and Spector. Double wow!! –JT

Billboard Top Rock & Roll Hits - 1959 / RHINO
One of the sleeper years in rock history. The diversity of this collection is its strong suit — it had "Mack the Knife," Elvis, Lloyd Price's "Stagger Lee," doo-wop, and some cool instrumentals. –JT

Billboard Top Rock & Roll Hits - 1960 / RHINO
So this was gonna be the decade of change? Put on "The Twist" again and shut up & dance, will ya? –JT

Billboard Top Rock & Roll Hits - 1961 / RHINO
Look out 60s, here we come — "Runaway," "Mother-In-Law," "Blue Moon." –JT

Billboard Top Rock & Roll Hits - 1962 / RHINO
When rock & roll was fun — "The Loco-Motion," "The Wanderer," "Palisades Park." Have a beach party and bring this along. –JT

Billboard Top Rock & Roll Hits - 1963 / RHINO   1988
Who said pre-Beatles rock & roll was in bad shape? Like "Louie Louie," "Fingertips," and "Surfin' U.S.A." are losers? –JT

Billboard Top Rock & Roll Hits - 1964 / RHINO   1989
What, no Beatles?! Or Stones or Dave Clark Five? Sure, the Four Seasons and Beach Boys are ace, but let's get serious. –JT

○ **Billboard Top Rock & Roll Hits - 1965 / RHINO**   1989
Did one year really give us "Mr. Tambourine Man," "Wooly Bully," and "You've Lost That Lovin' Feelin'"? –JT

Billboard Top Rock & Roll Hits - 1966 / RHINO
Pop 'n' roll at its apex — "Good Vibrations," "Wild Thing," Nancy Sinatra, Lovin' Spoonful. Ten classic AM hits. –JT

Billboard Top Rock & Roll Hits - 1967 / RHINO
The Music Explosion at #1? The Turtles, Monkees, Raiders, etc.? You'd never know it was the year of Hendrix, Doors, and *Sgt. Pepper*. –JT

Billboard Top Rock & Roll Hits - 1968 / RHINO   1988
Marvin's Gaye's "Grapevine" and the Box Tops's "Cry Like a Baby" go a long way toward making up for Ohio Express and "Judy in Disguise." –JT

Billboard Top Rock & Roll Hits - 1969 / RHINO
So where is "Hey Jude," the year's true best-seller? Rhino couldn't license it, that's why. In its place — Tommy Roe, Steam, and ... the Archies?! You say you want a revolution?! –JT

Billboard Top Rock & Roll Hits - 1970 / RHINO
Did Three Dog Night, Shocking Blue, the Partridge Family, and Smokey really outsell the Jackson 5? And whatever happened to the Jaggerz? –JT

Billboard Top Rock & Roll Hits - 1971 / RHINO   1989
Funk (Sly) meets junk (Osmonds) and pop-rock (Tommy James) meets schlock (Cher, Dawn). –JT

Billboard Top Rock & Roll Hits - 1972 / RHINO
Get past #1, Gilbert O'Sullivan, and Chuck Berry's "My Ding-A-Ling," and America, and you might even find a few songs worth hearing again. –JT

Billboard Top Rock & Roll Hits - 1973 / RHINO   1989
Elton John, Jim Croce, and Edgar Winter — yeah, the 60s were over. –JT

Billboard Top Rock & Roll Hits - 1974 / RHINO   1989
Absolute proof that the Top Ten wasn't what it used to be — Grand Funk, David Essex, Steve Miller, etc. –JT

☆ **Black Rock Coalition ... / RYKODISC**   1990
Black Rock Coalition - History of Our Future is a fantastic collection of Black rock & roll from the organization formed by Living Colour's Vernon Reid. Diversity is the game here, with cuts by Blackasaurus Mex, Michael Hill's Bluesland, and Shock Council, mixing up funk, metal, and hip-hop as though they'd never heard of segregated radio playlists. –JF

Bridge - Tribute to Neil Young / CAROLINE   1989
Several alternative acts (Sonic Youth, Soul Asylum, Dinosaur Jr) take their 1989 shot at covering the enigmatic Young. –DH

☆ **British Invasion - History of British Rock / RHINO** 1991
Imagine nine CDs (available separately or in a box) of those classic AM radio hits of the 60s, all of them from England, most of them as fresh-sounding and exciting as they were more than two decades ago. Now imagine that these nine CDs are devoid of Beatles (except for one early track), Stones, Who, early Animals, Dave Clark Five, and Herman's Hermits (all due to licensing problems), but that you won't miss them, and you'll get an idea of just how much quality pop/rock & roll came out of the UK in those several years. Included are the Kinks, Zombies, Hollies, Small Faces, Yardbirds, Manfred Mann, Them, Donovan, Peter and Gordon, Bee Gees, Cream, and much more. –JT

Chunks / SST
Another worthwhile compilation of SST's enigmatic roster of artists. –JD

Classic Soul / MCA
A good blend of Stax, Chess, and even a bit of blues and Afro-pop from Hugh Masekela. –RW

○ **Club Columbia ... / CBS**   1990
Club Columbia - A Collection of Classic Dance Mixes contains extended versions of disco hits; SOS Band, Shalamar, and others. –RW

Club Epic - Classic Dance Mixes / CBS   1990
Extended versions of disco hits: SOS band, Shalamar, others. Cassette. –RW

Complete Death - Vol. 2 / RESTLESS
This album is a compilation of bands on the Death label. –ED

☆ **Complete Stax-Volt Singles 1959-1968 / ATLANTIC** 1991
This 244-track, 9-CD boxed set includes *all* of the 45 RPM A-sides ever released (as well as a few choice B-sides) on these legendary Memphis labels, during and preceding their association with Atlantic Records. Even though Stax/Volt continued to release more strong sides after 1968, with Isaac Hayes ("Shaft") and the Staple Singers, many consider that their classic sound is the one represented here. The consistently great songs and performances found on this collection, by artists like Otis Redding, Carla Thomas, Sam & Dave, Booker T. & the MG's, Eddie Floyd and many more, are a testament to Stax/Volt's vision. The tracks (remastered from the original mono masters on specially modified equipment) sound amazingly warm and full. Included is a booklet with extensively detailed liner notes and a generous selection of photos. For anyone who has the change to part with for a boxed set of this size, this is absolutely essential, provided you are a serious lover of gritty soul music. –RC

Concussion! / MR. MANNICOTTI
A rock-solid compilation of 18 stompin' instrumentals from the golden age of guitar combos, 1958-1965. No hits, no big names (unless you count Punk Carson & the Chucklers), just great, raw rockin'. –CK

Consider Yourself Housed / GREAT JONES
These are nonstop East Coast house cuts in pure dance-floor style. –RW

Cracks in the Sidewalk / SST   1971

Great compilation of early-80s California hardcore punk. –JD

○ **Dance Craze / CHRYSALIS** 1963
Finally on CD, this is a of collection of live tracks from the English Beat, the Specials, Bad Manners, Madness, and other 80s ska-revival bands. –SWB

Dance! Dance! Dance! / RCA
A first-rate compilation with tunes from 70s all-stars. –RW

Dance! Dance! Dance! - Vol. 2 / RCA
The 70s return. –RW

Dance Power / KTEL-QWIL
Up-to-date dance-floor cuts from radio-ready types like Paula Abdul, Johnny Kemp, and company. –RW

Dance to It / HEARTBEAT
More music to shake your rump, and other things. –RW

Dance Traxx - Vol. 2 / ATLANTIC
Rock, disco, domestic and international hits are showcased here. –RW

☆ **Dangerhouse - Vol. 1 / FRONTIER**
An essential punk compilation consisting of bands from the late 70s, many of which have influenced a lot of other groups. Some of the bands on the album include X, the Eyes (featuring Go-Go's guitarist Charlotte Caffey), the Weirdos, the Avengers, Rhino 39, and Black Randy & the Metrosquad. Many of the songs here are expensive to get on the original albums, making this a cost-effective collection. –JB

○ **Dangerous Doo Wop: Vols. 1-4 / DANGEROUS DOO WOP**
Obscure compilations of very rare vocal group records that really move and jive. Four volumes so far, which feature the Four Clippers, Baby Washington, the Selections, and the Rocketiers. No hits to speak of but everything here will ring the bells of doo-wop fetishes. –RM

Ddddance / PRIORITY
Standard contemporary dance-floor offerings. –RW

Deadicated - Grateful Dead Tribute / ARISTA 1991
This tribute record features everyone from Elvis Costello to Midnight Oil to Dr. John doin' the Dead. An attempt to showcase the Dead's songwriting. The rigid arrangements could have used more imagination, but the interpretations are mostly agreeable. –JT

Dealing with the Devil ... / CBS 1980
Dealing With the Devil - Immediate Blues Story - Vol. 2 is early British blues, featuring Eric Clapton, Jeff Beck, Jon Lord, Ron Wood, and other not-yet superstars in some rough, raw performances. –BE

Desperate Dallas Demos / NO HIT
Interesting collection of unissued demos and rare 45s from Dallas's teen combos of the 50s. No big names here but, as with most of the best rockabilly, it's the feel that counts. –CK

Disco Years - Vol. 1: Turn the Beat Around / RHINO 1990
Disco Years - Vol. 2: On the Beach / RHINO 1990
Disco Years - Vol. 3: Boogie Fever / RHINO 1992
Disco Years - Vol. 4: Lost in Music / RHINO 1992
Disco Years - Vol. 5: Must Be the Music / RHINO 1992

☆ **Doo Wop - 4 Funky Flashes from the 50s / SPECIALTY**
A good batch from the Specialty vaults, released in 1991; jump and vocal groups. –RW

Dope Guns & F*ing in the Streets - Vols. 1-3 / ANP**
Released in 1989, this is alienated, second-generation, post-hardcore guitar rant. –JD

Down & Dirty - Immediate Blues Story - Vol. 3 / CBS
Eric Clapton and Jimmy Page are the big names on this anthology, but the real value lies in songs by the late Jo Ann Kelly, who sounds utterly authentic. –BE

Elektra's 40th Anniversary: Rubaiyat / ELEKTRA 1990
The label's current artists cover its all-timers, e.g., the Cure meets the Doors. Interesting idea; sketchy results. –DH

EMI Legends of Rock N' Roll / CAPITOL 1991
EMI Legends of Rock N' Roll - 24 Greatest Hits of All Time samples one track from each of the volumes in EMI's *Legends of Rock N' Roll* series, giving a good taste of what the reissues

have to offer. Many big hits, such as "Blueberry Hill," "Summertime Blues," and "Walk Don't Run." –STE

Fillmore: The Last Days / CBS 1972
In the summer of 1971, Bill Graham closed the two halls that had redefined the way live rock music was heard. In San Francisco, the Fillmore Auditorium, and later the Fillmore West, had been home to virtually every major performing band of the era, a neighborhood meeting place and dance palace rolled into one. It was the place to see the Dead, the Airplane, Santana, and any visiting musical act with any hipness quotient at all. This 2-CD package features some of the recordings from the final week of shows at the fabled Fillmore West. Not all of the bands are remembered today (Lamb, anyone?) but with hot entries from Quicksilver Messenger Service, Tower of Power, Hot Tuna, Boz Scaggs, the Dead, Santana, etc., it's a tribute both to a time and place and to the inestimable contributions of the late Graham. The sound quality is lacking by today's standards, but the free 'n' easy Fillmore atmosphere comes through. –JT

☆ **Footstompin' Oldies / GARLAND**
Fine collection of early rock and soul hits, expertly remastered by Steve Hoffman. Includes the Rocky Fellers hit "Killer Joe" and 15 other cuts you should own. –JF

○ **Frat Rock / RHINO**
Frat Rock - Vol. 2 / RHINO
Frat Rock - Vol. 3 / RHINO
Frat Rock - Vol. 4 / RHINO
Son of Frat Rock / RHINO
Grandson of Frat Rock / RHINO
Rhino's *Frat Rock* series is an excellent overview of 60s rock & roll and R&B party anthems like the Kingsmen's "Louie Louie," "Double Shot of My Baby's Love" (Swinging Medallions), "La La La La La" (Blendells), "Shout" (Isley Brothers), "Do You Love Me" (The Contours), and "Mony Mony" (Tommy James & the Shondells). JF

From the Megavault / MGF 1986
A Megaforce Records sampler is an example of some of the thrash and heavy metal coming out of that time period. Features material from Anthrax, S.O.D., Overkill, Raven, Blue Cheer, Exciter, and more. –JB

From the Megavault - Vol. 2 / MGF
From the Vaults / MOTOWN 1978
Unreleased masters from several noteworthy Motown artists. Good quality. –RAB

Garage Sale! / ROIR 1985
In conjunction with record collectors' publication *Goldmine*, the cassette-only Reach Out International Records put out this compilation of 19 retro-rock garage bands, including the Mosquitos, the Vipers, the Fuzztones, and the Pandoras. Quality ranges from excellent to downright embarrassing. Any aficionado of the Seeds, the Strangeloves, or the Standells would love this; others should pass it by. –LL

☆ **Girl Groups - Story of a Sound / MOTOWN** 1983
This album chronicles the early-60s girl-group phenomenon, including the Supremes, Ronettes, Shirelles, etc. –RAB

☆ **Go Go Posse / HEADS UP** 1988
A vital collection depicting the mid- and late-70s premier Black sound. –RW

Go-Go Cranking / FOURTH & BROADWAY
Rhythm-heavy. This is soulful funk, pared down to just the necessities. –RG

God's Favorite Dog / TOUCH & GO
Notable for the two Hose tracks featuring Rick Rubin. Good noisy rock à la Big Black. –RG

○ **Golden Age of Black Music - 1960-1970 / ATLANTIC**
Golden Age of Black Music - 1970-1975 / ATLANTIC
Golden Age of Black Music - 1977-1988 / ATLANTIC
A three-volume anthology full of established, easy-to-find soul/pop hits. –RW

○ **Grindcrusher / RELATIVITY**

An excellent sampler of the Earache label in England, known for grindcore and alternative metal bands from Europe and America. Features music from Sore Throat, Napalm Death, Lawnmower Deth, Carcass, Morbid Angel, Naked City, and Spazztic Blurr. −JB

Groove N' Grind - 50s & 60s Dance Hits / RHINO
An 18-cut assemblage of 60s rock, soul, and R&B/dance tunes. Essential for strollers, peppermint twisters, hully-gulliers, monkey-timers, and cool-jerks. −JF

○ **Guitar Player Presents Rock - The 50s - Vol. 1 / RHINO**   1991
Nice collection of tracks featuring dazzling guitar work and classic sides from Chuck Berry, Bo Diddley, Les Paul, James Burton, Carl Perkins, and 12 others. −CK

○ **Guitar Player Presents Rock - The 50s - Vol. 2 / RHINO**   1991
Companion volume to the above, with dynamite tracks from Ike Turner, Joe Maphis, Ritchie Valens, Scotty Moore, Duane Eddy, Larry Collins, and 12 more. −CK

○ **Guitar Player Presents Rock - The 60s - Vol. 1 / RHINO**   1991
Excellent 18-track CD featuring dazzling guitar work by the Ventures, Steve Cropper, Dave Edmunds, the Byrds, Chet Atkins, Lonnie Mack, and others, showing the breadth of 60s guitar work. −CK

○ **Guitar Player Presents Rock - The 60s - Vol. 2 / RHINO**   1991
Companion volume to the above, featuring tracks by Jeff Beck, the Fendermen, Travis Wammack, Roy Buchanan, Eric Clapton, and other guitar giants of the 60s. −CK

○ **Guitar Player Presents Rock - The 70s - Vol. 1 / RHINO**   1991
Showcasing a selected sampling of the lesser-heralded guitarists of the era, this 18-track CD features selections by Rick Derringer, Brownsville Station's Cub Koda, the Outlaws, Ted Nugent, James Gang, and others. A nice selection with excellent sound. −DH

○ **Guitar Speak / MCA**   1988
Twelve-track CD with appearances by Eric Johnson, Steve Howe, Rick Derringer, and others. Great! −PK

Guitar Speak III / CIR   1991
Ten-track CD with ten rock players. Highlights include Steve Morse and Robert Fripp. −PK

○ **Guitar's Practicing Musicians / RELATIVITY**   1989
Thirteen-track CD featuring 13 rock guitarists and bassists, released through *Guitar for the Practicing Musician* magazine. A nice mixture of styles. Includes Steve Vai, Vinnie Moore, Billy Sheehan, Randy Coven, Paul Gilbert, and 8 others. −PK

Guitar's Practicing Musicians - Vol. 2 / RELATIVITY
This 16-track CD was released in 1991 and includes Steve Morse, Eric Johnson, Steve Lukather. Mostly rock material. −PK

Hard Rockin' 70s / PRIORITY
Good collection featuring the likes of Humble Pie, Free, and others. −DH

Hard-to-Find Motown Classics - Vol. 1 / MOTOWN   1986
Rare classics from the label's more obscure artists like the Elgins, Rare Earth, and others. −RAB

Hard-to-Find Motown Classics - Vol. 2 / MOTOWN
This second volume contains some not-so-rare tracks that remain ageless. −RAB

○ **Hard-Up Heroes / DECCA**
A surprisingly strong collection of mid-60s sides from British Decca, which was never perceived as that strong a label. Prepared by two experts from New Musical Express, this features the expected sides from Small Faces, Bowie, and the Zombies, but also all the blues (Alexis Korner, Cyril Davies), punk (Rocking Vickers) and psychedelic acts (Honeybus) that never made it here. (Out of print) −BE

○ **Harlem Shuffle - 60s Soul Classics / CHARLY**

A perfect selection (and disc order) of lesser-known but essential soul hits, including the Barbara Lewis hits "Hello Stranger," "Make Me Your Baby," and "Baby I'm Yours," plus "Oogum Boogum Song" and "Gimme a Little Sign" by Brenton Wood, and "Get On Up and Get Away" by the Esquires. Twenty-one classic sides in all, every one a delight. An import but worth the trouble to find. −JME

Have a Nice Day - Vol. 1 / RHINO   1990
Some of it's actually from the late 60s, but the 70s feel is in place -"Venus," "Smile a Little Smile for Me." The 60s were over. −JT

Have a Nice Day - Vol. 2 / RHINO   1990
This is where it gets silly — "My Baby Loves Lovin'," "Spirit in the Sky," "Everything Is Beautiful." Pass the smiley-face buttons, please. −JT

Have a Nice Day - Vol. 3 / RHINO   1990
What a weird decade — did we really buy all those Bobby Sherman and Melanie records? −JT

Have a Nice Day - Vol. 4 / RHINO   1990
Quick — name a song by the Glass Bottle or Christie. If you can, you need this. −JT

Have a Nice Day - Vol. 5 / RHINO   1990
"Chick a Boom," "Me and You and a Dog Named Boo," "When You're Hot You're Hot." And Nixon in the White House?! Say it was all a bad dream. −JT

Have a Nice Day - Vol. 6 / RHINO   1990
It just gets sillier, folks — By this time (1970-1971), "Signs" and "Gimme Dat Ding" were the best the Top 40 had to offer. No wonder Grand Funk got so huge! −JT

Have a Nice Day - Vol. 7 / RHINO   1990
Signs of funk in the distance — but signs of Jonathan Edwards too. −JT

Have a Nice Day - Vol. 8 / RHINO   1990
Did Gilbert O'Sullivan really exist? Did Sammy Davis Jr really sing "Candy Man?" Be a believer with this best of 1972. −JT

Have a Nice Day - Vol. 9 / RHINO   1990
"Brandy," "Popcorn," and "Frankenstein." And those were the good ones. −JT

Have a Nice Day - Vol. 10 / RHINO   1990
Even the 70s were realizing it was no 60s — "It Never Rains in Southern California," "Brother Louie," "Dead Skunk." Get a life, all of you. −JT

Have a Nice Day - Vol. 11 / RHINO   1990
Beyond camp, into kitsch — "The Morning After," "Dueling Banjos," etc. −JT

Have a Nice Day - Vol. 12 / RHINO   1990
A fun volume, featuring "The Streak," "Rock and Roll, Hoochie Koo," and "Jim Dandy," for starters. But then again, there's "Seasons in the Sun." −JT

Have a Nice Day - Vol. 13 / RHINO   1990
"Billy Don't Be a Hero," "The Night Chicago Died," "Beach Baby." If 1974 isn't a contender for rock's most inane year, I don't know what is. −JT

Have a Nice Day - Vol. 14 / RHINO   1990
Yes, "Kung Fu Fighting" really was a hit. So were "Chevy Van" and "Jackie Blue." Don't believe us? Here's proof. −JT

Have a Nice Day - Vol. 15 / RHINO   1990
Yeah, 1975-1976: "Convoy," "Rocky," "Run Joey Run," "I'm Not Lisa." No wonder punk rock was around the corner. −JT

☆ **Have a Nice Day - Vols. 1-4 (boxed set) / RHINO**   1990
The definitive collection of AM hits from an FM decade. −JT

Hear 'n' Aid / POLYGRAM   1986
Hear 'n' Aid was a metal version of USA for Africa, founded by Ronnie James Dio. The album featured songs by Dio, Kiss, Motörhead, and the Scorpions. The video and single "Stars" featured a motley crew of rock stars. −RDF

Heart of Soul / CBS   1989
Late-80s anthology; it's really disposable urban fluff mislabeled as soul. −RW

☆ **The Hi Records Story / HI**

306

Marvelous tribute to Willie Mitchell's Hi label, which, like Stax, revolutionized Memphis soul. A 24-song disc featuring the best of the two American volumes and a few different cuts. (British import) –JF

Hip House - Europe's Hottest Dance Mixes / QUA 1989
Worthwhile, due to the number of cuts that were previously hits only in Europe. –RW

○ **History of Hi Records R&B: Vol. 1 - Beginnings / MCA**
A terrific two-volume tribute to Willie Mitchell's Hi label, featuring a hodgepodge of rockabilly and soul from such artists as Mitchell and Ace Cannon. –JF

History of Hi Records R&B: Vol. 2 - Glory Years / MCA
The second volume contains the label's 70s hits, including prime movers Al Green, Ann Peebles, Otis Clay, and Syl Johnson. –JF

○ **History of Rock Instrumentals - Vol. 1 / RHINO**
The first part of an expertly compiled pair featuring rock's most atmospheric and raucous instrumental singles. Not much surf stuff, but both volumes provide an authoritarian overview of an overlooked subgenre. –JF

History of Rock Instrumentals - Vol. 2 / RHINO
The second volume of this instrumental compilation of an overlooked subgenre. –JF

Hit Singles 1980-1988 / ATLANTIC
Atlantic's 80s successes, most prominently Phil Collins. –DH

○ **Hits from the Legendary Vee Jay Records / MOTOWN**
A comprehensive survey of this seminal blues and soul label, including hits by the Dells, John Lee Hooker, and Jerry Butler. Plus Little Richard's obscure soul masterpiece, "I Don't Know What You Got." –JF

○ **Hot Power Mixes - Power Mix '87 / WARLOCK**
Great for remix fans; others approach with caution. –RW

House Hallucinates: Pump Up the World - #1 / A&M
Good introduction to acid-House and House sound. –RW

○ **Human Music / HOMESTEAD** 1988
Twenty-five diverse bands, all non-album tracks. A good taste of the mid-80s indie scene. –RG

○ **Immediate Singles Collection - Vol. 1 / CBS**
Interesting 20-song compilation of veddy British tunes by Small Faces, the Nice, and others, with an American or two thrown in. –JT

Immediate Singles Collection - Vol. 2 / CBS
For collectors of obscure 60s British rock only — includes Humble Pie, P. P. Arnold, Amen Corner, and more. –JT

Immediate Singles Collection - Vol. 3 / CBS 1991
Not much here to recommend to those who don't get excited about minor psychedelia. –JT

○ **In Loving Memory / MOTOWN** 1968
Gospel renditions by Motown's most popular artists. –RAB

○ **Island Story 1962-87 / POLYGRAM** 1987
A fine, if too brief look at the influential reggae/rock label. –DH

Jam Harder / A&M
Rock, dance, and the in-between. –RW

King Biscuit Live: Best Of - Vol. 1 / SAN FRANCISCO
Getting down with Tull, Rod Stewart, Skynyrd, and others, in concert. –JT

○ **King Biscuit Live: Best Of - Vol. 2 / SAN FRANCISCO**
An odd assortment including the Stray Cats, Elton John, Foghat, and Iggy Pop, all recorded live for vintage radio broadcasts. –JT

King Biscuit Live: Best Of - Vol. 3 / SAN FRANCISCO
More 70s and 80s live radio, this time with Lou Reed, Linda Ronstadt, the Allmans, and more. –JT

King Biscuit Live: Best Of - Vol. 4 / SAN FRANCISCO
Queen, Nugent, Thin Lizzy, and others, captured on this too-brief collection of radio tapes. –JT

Latin Beat / PRIORITY
An entertaining collection that shows the ties between Latin, dance, R&B, funk, and pop. –RW

○ **Let's Start the Dance - Vol. 1 / POLYGRAM**

Let's Start the Dance: Dance Classics - Vol. 1. A two-volume set of disco hits from Polygram ranks. –RW

Let's Start the Dance - Vol. 2 / POLYGRAM
This one includes Love Unlimited, Roy Ayers, and others. –RW

Lonely Is an Eyesore / NESAK
Rare tracks from the 4AD label, including the Cocteau Twins, Throwing Muses, Dead Can Dance, and This Mortal Coil. –MPD

Make a Difference Foundation: Stairway to Heaven /Highway to Hell / POLYGRAM
A charity album by modern metal acts, covering songs by bands who may have lost a member due to substance abuse. A wide range of bands featured. –JB

Marv-El Masters - Get with the Beat / RYKO 1989
The output of this obscure 50s rockabilly label is for genre fans only. –DH

Masters of the Beat / TOMMY BOY
A good overview of tunes from producers and artists on Tommy Boy. –RW

○ **Joe Meek - History of British Rock - Vol. 1 / SIRE**
This various-artist compilation containing "Telstar" and "Tribute to Buddy Holly" is worthwhile just for those two tracks. (Out of print) –BE

Joe Meek Story - Vol. 1 /
A superb 2-CD set (even without "Telstar" and "Tribute to Buddy Holly"). Meek's ear for hooks. His enjoyment of early-60s electronic keyboard sounds runs through all of this material. The Honeycomb's "Have I the Right" is the strongest, if not the most interesting. (Out of print import) –BE

Mega Hits Dance Classics - Volumes 1-14 / PRIORITY
A spotty but exhaustive series of 70s and 80s disco hits. The packaging is awful, with horrid graphics and no liner notes, but there are some rarities to be found on some of the sets. Every volume contains at least one treasure. –JF

○ **Memphis Soul Classics / WARNER** 1987
A skimpy but worthwhile sampler of various Memphis soul champions from the 60s, focusing on the biggest and best Stax and Atlantic hits. –JF

Mercury Rhythm & Blues: 1946-1962 / POLYGRAM 1990
Though it leaned more toward pop-flavored R&B like the Platters, Mercury had some fertile years. This set catches them well. –DH

○ **Metal Massacre - Vols. 2 & 3 / RES**
Features early tracks from Armored Saint, Bitch, Overkill, and Slayer. –JB

Metal Massacre - Vol. 4 / RES
Features early tracks from Lizzy Borden, Trouble, and Zoetrope. –JB

Metal Massacre - Vol. 8 / RES
Features early material from Viking and Sacred Reich. –JB

Metal Massacre - Vol. 11 / CAROLINE
Many promising bands here, including Epidemic, Chemikill, and Ministers of Anger. –JB

☆ **Monster Rock 'n Roll Show / DCC**
Hilarious and well-programmed collection of Halloween-geared blues, rock, and R&B cuts. Collectors will like the tunes by the Revels, the Hollywood Flames, and Johnny Fuller, while everyone will like the movie-trailer voiceovers that separate the songs. –JF

☆ **Monster Summer Hits - Drag City / CAPITOL**
★ **Monster Summer Hits - Wild Surf / CAPITOL**
The two-volume *Monster Summer Hits* (the above album, *Drag City,* and this one, *Wild Surf*) is surf and hot rod material culled from the Capitol archives. Lots of obvious cuts by the Beach Boys, Jan and Dean, and the Ventures, but there's plenty of rare stuff to keep you interested, with great sound quality too. –JF

Monterey Pop / RHINO 1992
The Monterey Pop Festival was one of the greatest of the late-60s music festivals. This 4-CD boxed set generously documents performances by artists as varied as the Byrds, the Association, Jimi Hendrix, Jefferson Airplane, Lou Rawls, Ravi

Shankar, Booker T & the MG's, the Who, Otis Redding, the Mamas & Papas, Eric Burdon & the Animals, Big Brother & the Holding Company, and more. −RC

Motor City Dance Party - Vol. 1 / QUALITY　　　　1991
Motor City Dance Party - Vol. 2 / QUALITY　　　　1991
Motor City Dance Party - Vol. 3 / QUALITY　　　　1991
Motor City Dance Party - Vol. 4 / QUALITY　　　　1991
Motor City Dance Party - Vol. 5 / QUALITY　　　　1991

All five volumes of *Motor City Dance Party* feature reunions from Motown's huge stable of artists. Particularly outstanding are Kim Weston, Scherrie Payne, and Billy Griffin. −RAB

☆ **Motortown Revue - Vol. 1 / MOTOWN**　　　　　　1964
The first live recordings of all the Motown greats, recorded at the Apollo. −RAB

Motortown Revue - Vol. 2 / MOTOWN　　　　　　　1963
Recorded in Detroit. Swing sets by Mary Wells, Martha Reeves, and the Miracles. −RAB

Motown around the World / MOTOWN　　　　　　　1987
A great novelty item — some of Motown's biggest hits sung in foreign languages. −RAB

○ **Motown Memories - Vol. 1 / MOTOWN**　　　　　　1987
Motown Memories - Vol. 2 / MOTOWN
Motown Memories - Vol. 3 / MOTOWN
Motown Memories - Vol. 4 / MOTOWN

The four-volume *Motown Memories* is one of the better compilations, featuring Motown hits over a 30-year period. −RAB

Motown Story: First 25 Years / MOTOWN　　　　　1984
The company's biggest hits. Spoken intros (that overlap the musical intros) by the artists who made them famous. −RAB

Motown's Brightest Stars / MOTOWN　　　　　　　1986
More unreleased tracks. The quality here is not as good as on *From the Vaults*, Motown 1978. −RAB

Mountain Stage: Best Of - Vol. 1 / BLUE PLATE
Dr. John and Jesse Winchester find a venue for themselves and other like players deserving one. −RG

○ **New Wave of British Heavy Metal / CAROLINE**
Many of today's thrash bands like Metallica and Anthrax were heavily influenced by British 80s bands, including Samson, Iron Maiden, Def Leppard, and Diamond Head. In the 70s, these bands offered something different from metal/hard rock, appealing to kids looking for a change. −JB

New York Eye & Ear Control / MATADOR　　　　　1991
A sampling of the progressive New York underground. Not especially melodic. −RG

○ **New York Thrash / ROI**
A classic collection of many hardcore bands from New York, who influenced a lot of metal bands to incorporate punk into their sound. Features music from Bad Brains, Beastie Boys, Adrenalin O.D., Nihilistics, and False Prophets. −JB

Nipper's #1 Hits: 1956-1986 / RCA
A good cross-section of RCA's pop hits, featuring everyone from Perry Como to Elvis and beyond. An interesting chronicle of pop music in general. −CK

Nipper's Greatest Hits: The 50s - Vol. 1 / RCA
Some truly lightweight fluff here, and a weird mix — Elvis, meet Mario Lanza — but it's an accurate reflection of the early 50s. −JT

☆ **Nipper's Greatest Hits: The 50s - Vol. 2 / RCA**
The label was on a roll — Elvis, Jim Reeves, Belafonte, even the Isley Brothers. A fascinating collection. −JT

Nipper's Greatest Hits: The 60s - Vol. 1 / RCA
Country and easy listening marked the early part of RCA's 60s, but by the end of the decade, the hippies had arrived. This is a fun study. −JT

☆ **Nipper's Greatest Hits: The 60s - Vol. 2 / RCA**　　1988
A nice collection running from the Tokens to Jefferson Airplane. Great songs. −JT

Nipper's Greatest Hits: The 70s / RCA　　　　　　1988

The Guess Who to Hall & Oates — and the King was still holding on. Not the greatest period, but some fine records. −JT

Nipper's Greatest Hits: The 80s / RCA
Ouch. If *Hooked on Classics*, Ronnie Milsap, and Mr. Mister are the best RCA had to offer in the 80s, they'd be better off hiding the fact. −JT

Nuggets - Vol. 1: Hits / RHINO　　　　　　　　　1986
A straightforward collection of garage/punk chart successes, including "Psychotic Reaction," "Dirty Water," "Nobody but Me," and "I Had Too Much to Dream Last Night." −BE

Nuggets - Vol. 2 / RHINO　　　　　　　　　　　1987
A top-notch collection of some of rock's spacier singles, B-sides, and odd tracks. −BE

Nuggets - Vol. 3: Psychedelic / RHINO
A good assembly of spaced-out works. −BE

○ **Oh Yeah! - Best of Dunwich Records / SUNDAZED**　1991
Dunwich Records was to 60s garage bands what Sun was to rockabilly. This CD features a generous sampling of the best of Chicago's teen scene of that period. Great sound and liner info too. −CK

Okeh Soul / CSP　　　　　　　　　　　　　　1982
Here's Chicago soul from Major Lance, the Vibrations, and other artists. −DH

○ **On the House: Best of Today's Hip House Music / KTEL**
A fine compilation continuing extensive set of dance hits by mixmasters and their protégés. −RW

One Hit Wonders: The 60s - Vol. 1 / RHINO
So what if Barry and the Tamerlanes and Jimmy Soul never had another hit? The dozen tracks here by them and others like them will hold up long after a bigger star's music has faded. −JT

○ **One Hit Wonders: The 60s - Vol. 2 / RHINO**
This stuff is too much fun! The Hombres, Soul Survivors, and more are a sure thing every time. −JT

○ **Package of 16 Big Hits / MOTOWN**　　　　　　　1991
This is the first volume of a ten-disc set also known as *A Collection of 16 Original Big Hits*. −RAB

☆ **Phil Spector - Back to Mono / ABKCO**　　　　　　1991
If you look hard enough, you can find decent one-album samplers of Phil Spector's greatest recordings, but this four-disc boxed set (three sets of singles and the entire *A Christmas Gift for You* on the fourth) is the jewel of Spector's legacy. Aside from his sporadic 70s productions, *Back to Mono* contains everything you'd ever want by rock's supreme romantic: early productions with Curtis Lee, Ben E. King, and Gene Pitney; the girl-group effervescence of the Ronettes, the Crystals, and Darlene Love; the soul innovations of the Righteous Brothers and the Checkmates; and his notorious sessions with Ike and Tina Turner. Throughout the set, Spector's artistic vision (which has influenced dozens of producers and hundreds of performers) shines like the smile on a lover's lips. One of the greatest and most fully realized boxed sets ever issued. −JF

○ **Place of General Happiness / EAST SIDE DIGITAL**
Hilarious and snappy settings for the poems of the octagenarian Ernest Noyes Brookings, with Brave Combo, Fred Frith, Birdsongs of the Mesozoic, Andy Partridge (XTC), the Splatter Trio, and more. −MB

Pops We Love You / MOTOWN　　　　　　　　　1978
The title cut features Diana Ross, Marvin Gaye, Smokey Robinson, and Stevie Wonder. −RAB

Power Jams - Today's Hottest Hits / KTEL-QWIL
Nice list of extended dance hits, aimed at the novice or general consumer. −RW

☆ **R&B (Funk) Collection / POLYGRAM**
A great package of seminal funk from Ohio Players, Gap Band, Parliament, James Brown. −RW

Radio Classics of the 50s / CBS　　　　　　　　1989
A very good collection of Columbia's pre-rock hits. −DH

Raging Harlem Hit Parade / RELIC

An eclectic mix of 50s and 60s blues nuggets from the vaults of Fire, Fury, and other minor labels. Includes hits by Lightnin' Hopkins, Buster Brown, King Curtis, and Wilbert Harrison. –JF

Red Hot & Blue / CHRYSALIS   1990
New recordings of Cole Porter songs (released in 1990) to benefit AIDS research. Artists include U2, the Neville Brothers, Fine Young Cannibals, k. d. lang, and Annie Lennox. The songs, recorded in a wide variety of styles, reaffirm what a great, timeless writer Porter was. –KMC

Remixed / DJ INTERNATIONAL
A nice selection of songs that were turned into hits through remixes. –RW

Rhythm Method / POLYGRAM
An excellent group of tunes previously unreleased but now turned into extended singles for the dance crowd. –RW

○ **Risque Rhythm: Nasty 50s R&B / RHINO**   1991
Would-be censors and PMRC fans take note: NWA and Guns N' Roses ain't got nothin' on the Dominoes or Dinah Washington. Double-entendre R&B at its most suggestively raw. –JT

Rock Classics of the 70s / CBS
A decent look at the label's FM-oriented (Mountain, Blue Oyster Cult) hits of the 70s. –DH

Rock Radio Vietnam / KTEL
An actual Armed Forces Radio broadcast from Saigon in 1970. This odd release features such hits of the day as Free's "All Right Now" and Aretha Franklin's "Don't Play That Song." –JT

Rock & Roll Dance Party / ROCK & ROLL   1990
Vols. 1-3. These obscure comps generally have Little Richard style — driving rock & roll. Vol. 3 features the Meloairs, Bobby Lester, and Masrie Adams. These are cool records. (Import) –RM

Rock & Roll - Early Days / RCA
Paltry but powerful collection of a dozen classics by Elvis, Haley, Waters, Berry, and more. –JT

○ **Rock This Town: Rockabilly Hits - Vol. 1 / RHINO**   1991
This devastating 50s rockabilly anthology expertly cuts across label and stylistic restraints. –BD

Rock This Town: Rockabilly Hits - Vol. 2 / RHINO   1991
The second volume of this anthology is just as satisfying through the first ten tracks, when it suddenly veers toward contemporary interpreters. –BD

Rockabilly Stars - Vol. 1 / CSP   1981
A patchy assortment of rockabilly and country-bop culled from Columbia's archives. Worthwhile mainly for Charlie Rich's solo reading of "I Feel like Going Home." –JF

☆ **Rockin' Again at the 2 I's / ACE**   1990
Easily the highest-quality multi-artist compilation of pre-Beatles British rock, although not the most comprehensive. The material features artists ranging from Bertice Reading to Janice Peters and styles ranging from R&B and rockabilly to proto-punk. All of it is high-grade, even if little of it saw huge chart action. (Import) –BE

☆ **Rockin' in the Farmhouse ... / HOLLOWBODY**   1992
Rockin' in the Farmhouse - Original Rockabilly and Chicken Bop - Vol. 2 is an excellent 20-track compilation featuring the best of the Roulette label's rarest rockabilly tracks. Highlights include Don "Red" Roberts's "Only One," Jimmy Isle's "Goin' Wild," Jimmy Lloyd's "Rocket in My Pocket," and five chaotic unissued tracks by the Rock-A-Teens. –CK

Romanian Angel Appeal - Nobody's Child / WARNER
Album compiled by George and Olivia Harrison and released in 1990 to benefit Romanian orphans. Contains previously unreleased tracks by, among others, Eric Clapton, Stevie Wonder, Elton John, and the Traveling Wilburys. –KMC

☆ **Roots of British Rock / SIRE**
Easily the most comprehensive rock collection ever assembled, and all the more amazing, since it is a US release.

From Tommy Steele in 1956 to the Tornadoes in 1962, there are few major stones left unturned on this jewel of a two-record set. An honest look at what was popular in Britain before the Beatles. A vital addition to any oldies collection. (Out of print) –BE

○ **Rumble / RELIC**
An excellent New York doo-wop anthology featuring mid-50s work by the Channels, the Bop Chords, the Love Notes, and the Continentals. Great sound quality from the original master tapes. –BD

Rutles Highway Revisited / SHIMMY   1990
A tribute album to a nonexistent band that was in itself a tribute to the Beatles?! Now we've heard everything. Includes Shonen Knife, Syd Straw, Galaxie 500, and others. –JT

Sam Dance Classics / SAM
This compilation is aimed at hardcore, but still has good hot dance cuts. –RW

○ **San Francisco Nights / RHINO**
Probably the most interesting and accessible collection of its kind ever to come from America, and more substantial than many European collections. Featuring the obvious and the weird, including the Beau Brummels, the Charlatans, the Vegetables, and the Mystery Trend. –BE

☆ **The Scepter Records Story / CAPRICORN-WARNER**
During the 50s and early 60s, NYC-based Scepter Records and its subsidiary Wand were part of a group of independents whose artists churned out hit after hit, defining the sound of the day and shaping the sound of the future. The Shirelles, Dionne Warwick, and the Isley Brothers all got their start there; if you love tough, pre-soul-era records like "Will You Still Love Me Tomorrow," "Twist and Shout," and "Walk On By," then this is for you. The label's roster also included singers Chuck Jackson, Maxine Brown, and Tommy Hunt; instrumentalist King Curtis; proto-pop-country artists B. J. Thomas and Ronnie Milsap; and punksters Kingsmen. That's right — "Louie Louie" is here, along with lots of other truly great music. I would have condensed the three discs down to a killer two, but on the whole this box gets high marks from me. –CO

Seven Inch Wonders of the World / SST
The best of SST's singles from the early 80s. –JD

Sex in the House / CONTEMPORARY
Showing off the steamy side of house music. –RW

Shut Down '66 / ERNIE DOUGLAS
Subtitled as *The World's Only 60s Punk Record*, this compilation features 18 garage-band rockers from the wimpier, "My Baby Shot Me Down" side of the equation. Plenty of 12-string guitars, Farfisa organ, and teenage angst — great fun all. –CK

Slash Early Sessions / WARNER
Decent overview of 80s cuts from the West Coast label that brought you Los Lobos, the Blasters, X, and the Gun Club. –JF

Slow Grooves / JCI
A collection that mixes sultry, steamy, and sappy-slow soul/pop acts. –RW

Songs of Protest / RHINO
A wide variety of topical songs from the 60s, ranging from the Kingston Trio's "Where Have All the Flowers Gone?" to Edwin Starr's "War." –KMC

Songs of the Civil War / CBS   1991
Actually an extension and improvement upon "White Mansions." Rock and folk stars doing Civil War songs, all well done. A good companion to the Dirt Band's *Will the Circle Be Unbroken.* –BE

☆ **Soul Hits of the 70s: Didn't it Blow Your Mind / RHINO**
This 15-volume set was released in 1991 and is a veritable Comstock Lode of overlooked hits from an era most rock fans have yet to discover. By offering the best recordings by the likes of the O'Jays, the Blue Notes, the Chi-Lites, and many others, *Soul Hits* gives the listener a feel for just how vital Black pop and disco was in an era when rock was starting to

sag. But the inclusion of dozens of forgotten one-shot hits makes each volume a history lesson in the continued innovation and sheer joy of R&B, proving that Blacks didn't stop making great music after Muddy Waters and Sly Stone bit the dust. –JF

Soul Shots - Vol. 1 - 60s Soul Classics / RHINO 1988
Soul Shots ... (Vols. 1-4) are CD compilations of *Soul Shots* collection albums. This volume features Johnnie taylor and J. J. Jackson. –LL

Soul Shots - Vol. 2 -"In" Crowd (Sweet Soul) / RHINO
This 1988 issue features Joe Jeffreys and the Intruders. –LL

Soul Shots - Vol. 3: Soul Twist / RHINO 1989
This one features Bobby & James Purify, and the Capitols. –LL

Soul Shots - Vol. 4: Urban Blues / RHINO 1989
Otis Rush and Lowell Fulson are featured here. –LL

○ **Speed Metal Hell - Vol. 3 / NEW RENAISSANCE**
Although hard to find, this compilation of then-unknown bands was released in 1987 and sold well within the underground. It featured some of the first songs by Prong, Wehrmacht, and Blood Feast, and some great songs from underground favorites like Papsmear, Regurgitation, and Metal Onslaught. –JB

○ **Stay Awake - Music from Disney Films / A&M** 1988
Cinematic, star-studded, highly inventive interpretations of the music of Disney, lovingly assembled by Hal Wilner. –SA

Street Buzz / NEXT PLATEAU 1988
A good collection of dance mixes and selections. –RW

Stroll On / CBS 1991
The Yardbirds, Eric Clapton, and a brace of early British bluesmen playing on what were intended as demos. Not profound, but entertaining. –BE

Sub-Pop-200 / SUB
A fine overview of the hottest new scene today, Seattle grunge rock. –JD

Sullivan Years: Born to Be Wild - Rock / TEEVEE TOONS
The Airplane, the Vanilla Fudge, Jams, and others bring classic rock to the masses in this 1991 release. –JT

○ **Sullivan Years: British Invasion / TEEVEE TOONS** 1990
No Beatles, but the Animals, Hermits, and others on this shriek-filled partytime disc. One "for the kiddies." –JT

Sullivan Years: Happy Together / TEEVEE TOONS 1991
60s hitmakers including the Turtles, the Lovin' Spoonful, and the Grass Roots, live (sometimes fake-live, though) on the legendary TV show. –JT

Sullivan Years: Mod Sound / TEEVEE TOONS 1990
The Mamas & the Papas, Dusty Springfield, the 5th Dimension, and others as they appeared on this "rilly big shoe." –JT

Summer & Sun / RHINO 1989
An entertaining roundup of summer-oriented hits from the 50s, 60s, and 70s. –DH

○ **The Sun Records Story / RHINO**
Nice, evenly balanced single-disc compilation of the best-known Sun sides — and the first to feature tracks by Elvis Presley as well. Great liners, wonderful sound, and the perfect place to start. Some of the greatest American rock & roll ever recorded. –CK

○ **Sun Records - The Rockabilly Years / CHARLY**
Gigantic 12-record import, 52-page book anthology of Sun's landmark contribution to the genre it virtually founded. Many classic sides by the better-known artists and even more great unissued sides by unknown rockers like Jimmy Wages and Tommy Blake, among others. Beyond classic. –CK

☆ **Sun Rockabilly - Classic Recordings / ROUNDER**
As the title suggests, Memphis rockabilly at its best. Featuring Carl Perkins, Warren Smith, Billy Riley, and a stellar cast of musical pioneers. –HD

○ **Surf & Drag - Vol. 1 / SUNDAZED** 1989
All the great surf and hot-rod sides from the Challenge label. Features Gary Usher, the Four Speeds, the Knickerbockers, Jan

and Dean, the Royal Coachmen, Donna Loren, and the Rhythm Rockers. Powerful genre material — this is as good as it gets. –CK

Surf Legends & Rumors / GARLAND
A superb assortment of rare surf instrumentals from 1961-1964. Not many hits but plenty of previously unreleased gems. –JF

Tamla Special - Number 1 / MOTOWN 1961
Includes extremely rare tracks from some obscure early Motown artists. –RAB

○ **Teenage Riot! / ATOMIC PASSION**
Insanely great rock & roll compilation centered around juvenile delinquent themes and featuring promo drop-ins from teen gang movies and anti-rock & roll sermons. Gene Maltais's "Gang War" is not to be missed. –CK

○ **Ten Years of Collectors Records / WHITE LABEL**
Highlights culled from a decade of issuing great rockabilly comps, this one features the Lonesome Drifters' hit "Eager Boy" and Charles Dean's "Train Whistle Boogie" and "Parking in the Dark" are just some of the highlights. –CK

○ **Texas Kat Music / GULF COAST**
A 15-track collection of rockabilly and rock & roll from the Texas-based Felco label. Billy Taylor ("Wombie Zombie"), Irwin Russ ("Crazy Alligator"), and the Twisters (the awesome "Bandstand Rocket") are featured. –CK

These People Are Nuts: 10th Anniversary / CIR 1989
A fine overview of the greatest hits of I.R.S. Records. –DH

○ **This Are Two Tone / CHRYSALIS** 1983
The best of the neo-ska label of the early 80s, featuring the Specials, English Beat, and others. –DH

☆ **This Is How It All Began - Vol. 1 / SPECIALTY**
A well-researched anthology of Black roots music, including gospel, country, city blues, R&B, and boogie. Barely pre-rock & roll. –HD

This Is How It All Began - Vol. 2 / SPECIALTY
The dawn of rock & roll, with Little Richard, Larry Williams, and Sam Cooke. –HD

Today's Greatest Love Songs - Heartbeat! / PRIORITY
Adequate collection of contemporary ballads. –RW

○ **Toga Rock / DCC** 1987
Toga Rock - Vol. 2 / DCC
The two-volume *Toga Rock* is an adequate collection of frat-party hits from the 60s. Not many surprises but the fidelity will knock you out. –JF

☆ **Top of the Stax - 20 Greatest Hits / STAX**
☆ **Top of the Stax - Vol. 2 / STAX**
Memphis Soul 101. *Top of the Stax* is the history of Stax in two concise volumes, tracing the music from the early hits of the Mar-Keys, Otis Redding, and Sam & Dave up to the major hits of the 70s. –JF

Treasure Chest of Musty Dusties - Vol. 1 / FORTUNE
Twelve-song compilation (originally issued in the early 60s) featuring the best-known sides of the lesser-known Fortune Records vocal groups. Some of the best of Detroit's pre-Motown R&B era is presented here, the Swans' "Wedding Bells" being a particular highlight. –CK

Treasure Chest of Musty Dusties - Vol. 2 / FORTUNE
Companion volume to the above (and no less essential), featuring more great Detroit doo-wop and R&B sounds from the pre-Motown era. Heavy emphasis on unissued tracks, bringing to light several gems that make this compilation live up to its title. –CK

○ **Tribute to Kurt Weill - Lost in the Stars / A&M**
Eclectic updates of Kurt Weill's distinctive German theater music, with Sting, Marianne Faithfull, John Zorn, Lou Reed, Carla Bley, Tom Waits, Charlie Haden, and more. –MB

Twelve X Twelve: Singles 1990-1991 / MEGATONE 1956
These songs had debatable value when aired on radio. –RW

Wailing - Ultimate / HOMESTEAD
Idiosyncratic post-punk with an attitude. Mostly hardcore and post-hardcore scum rockers. –JD

○ **Wattstax - Living Word / STAX**
The recorded account of the landmark Stax concept in Watts during the mid 70s. –RW

WCBS FM 101 - Doo-Wop Era, Pt. 1 / COLLECTABLES
WCBS FM 101 - Doo-Wop Era, Pt. 2 / COLLECTABLES
WCBS FM 101 - History Of Rock: Doo-Wop Era is a two-part anthology built around the old End, Gone, and Roulette catalogs, featuring Frankie Lymon and the Teenagers, the Chantels, etc. The songs are good but the sound quality is at times very rough — audiophiles beware. –BE

West Coast Doo-Wop / ACE
Nice collection of vocal group sides from the vaults of Modern Records. Arthur Lee Maye & the Crowns's "Loop-De-Loop-De-Loop" and "Oochie Pachie" are among the numerous highlights. –CK

○ **Where the Pyramid Meets the Eye / WARNER**   1990
Wherein Warner Brothers guys like R.E.M., Jesus and Mary Chain, ZZ Top, and Doug Sahm pay homage to Texas weirdo

Erickson, who's best known for his work with the 60s punk group the 13th Floor Elevators. Not great but you'll find a few nice surprises. –JF

○ **White Mansions - Tales from American Civil War / A&M**
A historical country/folk concept album featuring such diverse talents as Waylon Jennings, the Eagles' Bernie Leadon, and Eric Clapton. The result is a rather lovely blending of folk, blues, and country. Not central to a collection, but well made. See also *Songs of the Civil War.* –BE

○ **Wild Men Ride Wild Guitars / SUNDAZED**
Great rockabilly/hillbilly-boogie compilation of tracks from the vaults of Challenge Records. Highlights include Big Al Downing's "Down on the Farm," and Charlie Ryan's "Hot Rod Rocket." –CK

☆ **Wild Wild Young Women / ROULETTE**
Outstanding set of rare rockabilly recorded by female bop singers such as Janis Martin and Rose Maddox (but no Wanda Jackson), with informative liner notes to lead the way. –JF

VOCAL

If the human voice is the oldest musical instrument of all, then it's also the most recorded one in the history of the medium itself. In essence, this section reflects how that instrument has been part and parcel of the development of American pop music since recorded performances were being etched into cylinders in Thomas Edison's laboratories. What we now know as popular or "pop" music started right around the turn of the century. Song publishers were flourishing in a section of New York City known as "Tin Pan Alley," selling sheet music like crazy, while the recording industry was just getting off the ground. Once the sheet music publishers found they needed someone to sing or "plug" that song and make it popular, and the record companies realized that the singer in question could sell a lot of records for them by singing that song, we saw the birth of popular music and the pop singer.

As pop music, even before the advent of rock & roll, took many stylistic twists and turns, so it is with the artists profiled in this section. If one rule of thumb may be applied:

the pop music we're talking about predates rock & roll and is of the Tin Pan Alley variety, the artists profiled belonging to all the various offshoots that genre entails. We're covering nearly a century's worth of recordings from early vaudeville performers like Al Jolson to modern-day artists singing material that clearly falls outside of rock music's several subgenres, and pretty much everything in between. Vocal pop music embraces everything from Rudy Vallee to Barbara Streisand, the Andrews Sisters to Frank Sinatra, and Bette Midler to Tony Bennett. That's a lot of stylistic ground to cover, but the genre itself maps out the same territory, adding decided left-hand turns to include song-and-dance men like Fred Astaire and "international" favorites like Marlene Dietrich and Yma Sumac. Given the current climate of music, one can only wonder what will constitute an entry into this section by the 21st century. As long as people keep singing, the boundaries of vocal/pop music will keep expanding.

— Cub Koda

THE AMES BROTHERS

Brothers Ed, Vic, Joe, and Gene Ames formed a group in their native Malden, MA, going on to score 23 Top 40 hits between 1949 and 1960. When rock & roll made chart success more and more difficult to attain, they split up, Ed going on to a solo career of his own. –CK

☆ **The Best of the Ames Brothers / RCA**   1958
Though their early hits recorded for Coral (now MCA) will probably be anthologized at some point, this one features all their biggest and best: "You, You, You," "The Man with the Banjo," "Melodie d'Amour," "Tammy," and "The Naughty Lady of Shady Lane." Smooth as silk. –CK

THE ANDREWS SISTERS

This American vocal trio consisted of sisters Patty (b 1920), Maxine (b 1918), and LaVerne Andrews (b 1915 - d 1967). Their tight-knit harmonies were a direct descendant of the groundbreaking work done in the early 30s by the Boswell Sisters, but they soon developed their own successful strain. They went on to sell over 60 million records, cashing in on the boogie-woogie fad of the 40s and becoming wartime favorites with film appearances in *Buck Privates* and *Stage Door Canteen*, among others. They are still the biggest-selling girl-group ever. –CK

Capitol Collectors Series / CAPITOL   1991
Terrific overview of their mid-50s output for Capitol, including such songs as "Rum and Coca-Cola," "Boogie Woogie Bugle Boy," "Don't Sit under the Apple Tree (With Anyone Else but Me)," "Begin the Beguine," and "Beat Me Daddy, Eight to the Bar." –STE

○ **50th Anniversary - Vols. 1 & 2 / MCA**
A two-volume definitive overview, with their best and most interesting sides from a long and successful career. –CK

FRED ASTAIRE   1899-1987

Although best known for his dancing and acting, Astaire was a limited but extremely popular singer whose recordings of numerous pop standards have become the best-known versions. –BE

Irving Berlin Songbook / POLYGRAM
An unusual reconsideration of Astaire's best repertoire, with the singer fronting a jazz combo. Uneven but interesting. –BE

○ **Starring Fred Astaire / CBS**
The best of Astaire, featuring songs by Berlin, Gershwin, Kern, and others, which were written specifically for him. –BE

PEARL BAILEY   1918-1990

Bailey started in show business by winning an amateur contest at age 13. Her eventual move from Washington, DC, to New York City established her as the darling of the cabaret/night club circuit. Bailey's languid, bluesy style, with assorted humorous asides and dialogs, only improved with time as movies and Vegas beckoned. In the 40s and 50s, Bailey was one of the first women to bring salacious lyrics into the mainstream (witness her seduction of Hot Lips Page, "Baby, It's Cold Outside."). She was also the first female rapper (check "Tired"). In her rich, expressive alto, Bailey didn't just sing a song, she lived it and rhythmically talked you through it as few artists had done before or have done since. –CK & BC

The Intoxicating Pearl Bailey / MERCURY   1957
Spicy, sing-song storytelling. –BC

☆ **Pearl Bailey Sings for Adults Only / ROULETTE**   1959
Delightfully wicked set of standards done up in the inimitable Pearl Bailey manner, with immaculately swinging support from husband/drummer/bandleader Louis Bellson. –CK

312

☆ **The Best of Pearl Bailey / ROULETTE** 1961
Sassy and outlandish, this anthologizes most (but not all) of
Bailey's best sides, including "It Takes Two to Tango." –CK

○ **16 Most Requested Songs / CBS**
Her most memorable 40s/50s pop cuts. –BC

The Definitive Pearl Bailey / CSP
Her earliest "rapping" from 1946. –BC

Sings Porgy & Bess / FORUM
Backed by the Buddy Baker orchestra. –BC

JOSEPHINE BAKER 1906-1975

After drawing attention to herself with comic dancing in the
all-Black chorus line of *Shuffle Along*, Baker became the
sensation of Paris during the Jazz Age. Her silvery voice (said
to be strong enough in her prime to be able to fill a theater
without the use of a microphone), exotic good looks, and
energetic manner made her a legend for over a half-century
in France, with movies, musicals, revues, and hit records to
her credit; however, success eluded her in the US. She was still
active in a one-woman show (with a dozen costume changes)
in 1975 when she died in her sleep after giving 14 well-
received performances. –CK

○ **Josephine Baker / DCC**
One of a few examples of great Josephine Baker songs
available. Brassy, classy, and vital cuts; great sound. –RW

SHIRLEY BASSEY ♭1937

The Welsh belter supplied the strident theme song for one of
Sean Connery's action-packed James Bond films, *Goldfinger*,
in 1965. Bassey had scored a bundle of hits in Great Britain
prior to landing the movie theme. Among her later US chart
items for United Artists was the title song to another Bond
flick in 1972, *Diamonds Are Forever*. –BD

☆ **The Best of Shirley Bassey / CAPITOL**
CD release spotlights dynamic international showbiz star. –RW

HARRY BELAFONTE ♭1927

The Harlem-born vocalist spearheaded the mid-50s calypso
movement in America, although he started out as a more
conventional pop singer. Belafonte's clear diction, pure voice,
and strikingly handsome features made him a national
sensation when RCA released "Jamaica Farewell" in 1956 and
"Banana Boat (Day-O)" the next year. Although much of his
subsequent RCA output was calypso-oriented, Belafonte
dabbled in everything from blues to Gershwin over the next
few years. In addition to his music, Belafonte has starred in
several movies, including *Buck and the Preacher* in 1972 and
Uptown Saturday Night in 1974. His daughter Shari is a
successful actress. –BD

○ **Calypso / RCA** 1956
His third album, which made him a star. –RW

Belafonte at Carnegie Hall / RCA 1959
Landmark late-50s live set. –RW

☆ **Returns to Carnegie / MOBILE FIDELITY** 1960
A CD release of a wonderful concert from 1960. –RW

Day-O & Other Hits / RCA
A recent collection of past hits. –RW

○ **All Time Greatest Hits - Vols. 1-3 / RCA** 1987
The three-volume *All Time Greatest Hits* is the definitive
collection. –RW

Island in the Sun / PAIR
Most recent release. –RW

○ **Legendary Performer / RCA**
Good overview release. –RW

○ **Pure Gold / RCA**
Another overview/anthology. –RW

JESSE BELVIN

An influential, milky-voiced R&B crooner and songwriter

from the 50s, best known for his 1956 hit "Goodnight My
Love" and for writing the Penguins hit "Earth Angel." –JF

○ **Blues Balladeer / SPECIALTY** 1990
Loaded with previously unissued gems. Belvin's introspective,
subdued vocals are delightful. –BD

... But Not Forgotten / UNITED
Terrible sound quality, but this old LP features this balladeer's
best-known mid-50s work for Modern Records. –BD

TONY BENNETT ♭1926

One of the great pop singers of his generation, Tony Bennett
reached stardom with a series of hits starting with "Because of
You," a 10-week # 1 in 1951. Other chart-toppers were "Cold,
Cold Heart" (1951) and "Rags to Riches" (1953). Bennett
scored fewer hits in the second half of the 50s as popular
music turned toward the rock & roll style of Elvis Presley, but
he became more interested in jazz, recording albums with
Count Basie and other jazz musicians. He scored a major
popular comeback with "I Left My Heart in San Francisco" in
1962, a tune that won him a Grammy and became his
signature song. Through the rest of the 60s, Bennett's albums
were top-sellers, and he put his mark on a series of excellent
songs from old standards to new movie themes.
In the 70s, Bennett made a couple of outstanding albums with
jazz pianist Bill Evans, but he then stayed out of the recording
studio for many years, preferring to avoid commercial
pressures while performing for fans all over the world. He
made a triumphant return to recording in 1986 with *The Art
of Excellence* and was the subject of a four-CD boxed-set
retrospective of his career, *Forty Years: The Artistry of Tony
Bennett* in 1991.
With his ease of manner and warm vocal tone, Bennett has
always been a singer's singer, garnering high praise from such
peers as Frank Sinatra as well as from critics and fans, and he
shows every sign of continuing to please them for many more
years. –WR

☆ **Forty Years: The Artistry of Tony Bennett / CBS**
If there was one greatest-hits package that did the job
correctly, novices wouldn't have to spring for this four-disc
boxed set. However, this is where Bennett's genius and, as the
title says, his artistry proves itself most effectively. Buy this,
and you'll never need another Bennett disc. –JF

● **Art of Excellence / CBS**
Astoria: Portrait of the Artist / CBS
This represents some of Bennett's finest late-80s output. –JF

Bennett/Berlin / CBS
A fine Bennett release from the late 80s. –JF

Jazz / CBS
Here is more of Bennett's finest late-80s output. –JF

THE BOSWELL SISTERS

Vocal trio hailing from New Orleans with lead singer Connee
(b 1907 - d 1976) and sisters Helvetia and Martha Boswell.
Their purity of intonation and bluesy, infectious swing of
harmonies became the role model for the Andrews Sisters,
Ella Fitzgerald, the McGuire Sisters, and Bette Midler. Connee
went solo in the mid 30s, appearing in movies and radio. She
entertained the troops during WWII and remained active
through the mid 50s. The Boswell Sisters' jazz-like phrasing
and strong New Orleans roots made a transitional move away
from the stiff pop singing of the 20s. Their trailblazing style
lives on today in their numerous progeny. –CK

The Boswell Sisters / CBS
A truly comprehensive multi-record boxed set from Columbia.
Inspired programming and notes by Michael Brooks. –BE

○ **Everybody Loves My Baby / PRO ARTE**
It's sad that so far there's only one CD of this extraordinarily
gifted trio's work. The dexterous harmony singing and
unusual repertoire, anticipating the Andrews Sisters, shines
through. –BE

TERESA BREWER   b 1931

Specializing in bright, chirpy melodies, spunky Teresa Brewer was one of the top pop thrushes of the 50s. Raised in Toledo, OH, she was a regular on "The Major Bowes Amateur Hour" as a child. Brewer scored her first huge hit in 1950 at the tender age of 18 with "Music! Music! Music!" and followed it up with an impressive string of smashes for Coral Records that spanned the entire decade. Several of Brewer's mid-50s hits — Fats Domino's "Bo Weevil," Ivory Hunter's "Empty Arms" — were sanitized R&B covers. Brewer has pursued jazzier directions in recent years, still retaining her youthful vocal delivery. –BD

American Music Box - Vol. 1 / CBS
American Music Box - Vol. 1 - Songs of Irving Berlin has some wonderful selections. –RW

Memories of Louis / CBS
Nice tribute. Excellent production and arrangements. –RW

○ **Best of Teresa Brewer / MCA**   1989
This 1989 anthology is comprised of cuts from her Coral albums. –RW

Cotton Connection / CBS   1990
A fine 1990 session.

HOAGY CARMICHAEL   1899-1981

Lanky pianist and composer of the jazz and big-band era, who also became a popular and respected character actor in films. Some of his more popular songs include "Georgia on My Mind," "Heart and Soul," "In the Cool, Cool, Cool of the Evening," "Lazy River," and "Star Dust." –BE

Hoagy Carmichael Collection / SMITHSONIAN
A definitive, triple-volume set, mostly devoted to others' interpretations of his work, including recordings by Louis Armstrong and the Boswell Sisters. –BE

○ **Stardust & Much More / RCA**
A wide-ranging collection of recordings of his work by Carmichael and others, covering 1927-1960. A good starter on his work. –BE

VIKKI CARR   b 1941

After singing in various school functions, local groups, and Pepe Callahan's Mexican-Irish band, Carr began her solo career in earnest in the early 60s. Her solo debut was in Reno, supported by the Chuck Leonard Quartet, which led to a record contract with Liberty. While not gathering much attention in the US, her first single ("He's a Rebel") was a hit in Australia and led to numerous television appearances, a spell as a regular on the "Ray Anthony Show." In the late 60s, Carr scored three Top 40 hits, including the #3 "It Must Be Him." Her American sales dwindled in the beginning of the 70s. With the release of her 1980 album, *Vikki Carr y el Amor*, Carr gained enormous success in the Latin music world. In 1991 Carr won a Best Latin Pop Album Grammy for her *Cosas del Amor*. –STE

○ **It Must Be Him - The Best of Vikki Carr / EMI**   1992
A 23-track compilation of Carr's 60s singles, containing her three Top 40 hits, "It Must Be Him," "The Lesson," and "With Pen in Hand." Carr's overwrought reading of "He's a Rebel" (cut before the Crystals version) shows how out of touch she was with the pop sounds of her time. Her version of "A Bit of Love" (with the lyric "Tell him you're a slave and he's the king") helps explain why she's had devout followings in marketplaces where machismo still reins. Nevertheless, fans of her easy-listening style will appreciate the fine sound, detailed liner notes, and comprehensive discography that round out this collection. –STE

JUNE CHRISTY

After a mid-40s stint as Stan Kenton's vocalist, the "Misty Miss Christy" recorded a series of 50s albums that both jazz and pop fans could dig. The smoky-voiced singer managed to

project sexiness and sophistication without sacrificing a wholesome, girl-next-door quality. Damn, what a gorgeous voice! –RL

☆ **Something Cool / CAPITOL**   1954
Christy's classic first album, plus ten other 50s sides. The best introduction to Christy. –RL

Road Show / CAPITOL   1966
Fine live recording of June Christy with Stan Kenton & the Four Freshmen from 1959. Christy is a bit below par due to a cold on the day of the recording. –KMC

The Best Thing for You / AFFINITY   1986
A strong collection of 50s material, with Pete Rugolo arrangements and top West Coast jazzmen. An import and out-of-print. –RL

ROSEMARY CLOONEY   b 1928

Her imaginative choice of material made Rosemary Clooney a household word during the 50s. Clooney and her sister Betty sang over a Cincinnati radio station before joining Tony Pastor's orchestra. Signing with Columbia in 1949, Clooney hit with the inviting #1 smash "Come On-A My House," cowritten by Ross Bagdasarian (soon to unleash a trio of electronically created Chipmunks on the world as David Seville). Subsequent chart-toppers included "Half As Much" in 1952 and "Hey There" and the country-based "This Ole House" in 1954 (the same year she married actor Jose Ferrer). Clooney also starred in several movies, most notably Bing Crosby's *White Christmas* in 1954. Today Clooney sings in a jazzier vein, as alluring as ever. –BD

Blue Rose / MOBILE FIDELITY   1956
A moody 1956 collaboration with Duke Ellington; well worth seeking out. –CW

○ **16 Most Requested Songs / CBS**   1964
Vintage hits from the 50s, including a number of the novelty songs done with Mitch Miller. –CW

Sings Rodgers Hart & Hammerstein / CONCORD   1964
Sings Ira Gershwin / CONCORD JAZZ
First of a series of 80s albums in which Rosie, backed by a jazz combo, pays tribute to the great pop composers. The whole series is worth having. –CW

Sings Lyrics of Johnny Mercer / CONCORD JAZZ
Sings Harold Arlen / CONCORD JAZZ
Sings Jimmy Van Heusen / CONCORD JAZZ
Sings Ballads / CONCORD JAZZ   1985
With jazzman Scott Hamilton and his sextet. –CW

Sings Cole Porter / CONCORD JAZZ

NAT KING COLE TRIO   1919-1965

Nat King Cole formed an instrumental jazz trio with guitarist Oscar Moore (b Dec 25, 1912 - d Oct 8, 1981) and bassist Wesley Prince (later replaced by Johnny Miller) in 1939. The group established itself in jazz circles with a series of successful recordings. Then came a date in Hollywood when they were harrassed by a drunk asking Cole to sing "Sweet Lorraine," launching the pianist on a singing career that came to overshadow the trio and the jazz music it played.
The Cole Trio signed to the then-tiny Capitol label in Los Angeles and by 1944 was scoring such hits as "Straighten Up and Fly Right," "Get Your Kicks on Route 66," "(I Love You) For Sentimental Reasons," and "The Christmas Song." In 1948, Cole accompanied by an orchestra, recorded "Nature Boy" and saw it top the charts for eight weeks.
Cole maintained the trio until 1951, though his biggest successes came with more elaborate accompaniment. He then embarked on a career as a solo singer that made him one of the best-loved entertainers of the 50s and early 60s and found him a star on television and in the movies. (Another edition of the trio featuring guitarist John Collins and bassist Charlie Harris performed with Cole from 1952 to 1961.) Cole died of lung cancer in 1965. –WR

After Midnight / BLUE NOTE / BB 13	1956
Live 1957 Broadcast / RADIOLA	1957
○ Collectors Series / CAPITOL	1990

Most of Nat King Cole's biggest hits and best-known songs are here on this terrific 20-track compilation of his solo Capitol work. Includes "Mona Lisa," "The Christmas Song," "Send for Me," "Ramblin' Rose," and "Unforgettable." –STE

Straighten Up & Fly Right / PRO ARTE
Mid-40s sides. The jazz roots of Cole are in evidence here. –HD

● **Jumpin' at Capitol: Best of the Cole Trio / RHINO**
A similar vintage to *Straighten Up & Fly Right*, with a greater emphasis on mellow standards. Excellent West Coast trio sound. –HD

Hit That Jive Jack / MCA
Early 40s Decca sides. A hip, swinging 40s trio sound. –HD

☆ **Complete Capitol Trio Recordings / MOSAIC**
The definitive (18 full CDs!) collection. These are the trio recordings to listen to, with Nat playing and singing throughout. Lovely music for the jazz purist and everyone else as well. –JME

PERRY COMO   ♭1912

Starting out as a barber in his hometown of Cannonsburg, PA, Como gained national attention with the Ted Weems Orchestra in the mid 30s. After WWII, he signed with RCA Victor as a solo artist and started amassing hits, 42 of them in the Top 10 between 1944 and 1958. His laidback, laconic delivery and persona served him well when he became the most successful "band singer" in TV's early days, hosting his variety show for over eight years. Changing over to whimsical novelty material, he still had hits when rock & roll first started dominating the charts. After a 25-year layoff, Como started performing live again in 1970, to devoted audiences, and has maintained a modest touring schedule to this day. –CK

And I Love You So / RCA
Legendary Performer / RCA
Worth getting in album form for the booklet and photos. –CW

Today / RCA
80s recordings of favorites such as "Sing Along with Me." –CW

○ **Pure Gold / RCA**   1984
The essential greatest-hits package, with original masters dating from the 40s and 50s. –CW

HARRY CONNICK JR

If Harry Connick Jr is successful, he will spearhead a swing-era revival that will, in his words, "Put the big-band sound in everyone's ears." Given the power of a major label (CBS/SONY) behind him, his exhaustive performing schedule, not to mention two films to his credit, and his vibrant personality and youthful good looks, Connick just might succeed.

Much of Connick's music is rooted in the 40s and early 50s world of big-band swing. Like Mose Allison, another Southern jazz musician, Connick has given an increasingly prominent role to vocals in his repertoire. People come to his concerts expecting to hear him sing, and they are not disappointed. Connick's revival is working. His audiences are youthful and enthusiastic. He's got them laughing at his corny patter, watching his softshoe routines, and listening to sophisticated band arrangements instead of Mötley Crüe or Bon Jovi.

Connick has not paid dues on his multifaceted talent or broad interests. "You haven't heard me do my New Orleans funk stuff yet," he told columnist Stephen Holden. "Maybe a recording of Chopin Etudes. There are a million things." Just how much breadth Connick's audience will tolerate remains to be seen. Evidence of his stylistic wanderlust already exists. His 1990 all-instrumental piano album *Lofty's Roach Souffle* surprised many people and sounded for all the world like the reincarnation of Thelonious Monk. What Monk was doing in the body of a 23-year-old White kid from New Orleans was anybody's guess, but the album contained some moments of

brilliance. Its final track, "Bayou Maharajah," is worth the price of admission.

Connick's immense popularity is refreshing, even encouraging, despite the fact that he champions decidedly non-mainstream music. Connick had more albums on the *Billboard* best-seller list in November 1991 than any other artist. Moreover, his success will allow him the creative freedom to ensure his far-reaching musical goals. Connick's big-band swing, vocals, and trio work are antidotes to the corporate Top 40 product that has become the background noise in our daily lives. –HD

Harry Connick Jr / CBS   1988
A versatile, nervy pianist whose gift for rhythmic variation and countermelody is well displayed on this debut album, especially when he tackles such standards as "Love Is Here to Stay" and "Sunny Side of the Street." –WR

Twenty / COLUMBIA   1988
Even more confident and exuberant than his debut, Connick's second album (the title refers to his age) finds him pulling out the stops on Irving Berlin's "Blue Skies" and trying out his limited but earnest vocal style on a few tunes, notably "Do You Know What It Means to Miss New Orleans?" –WR

When Harry Met Sally ... / COLUMBIA   1989
The soundtrack that made Connick an MOR star. –RW

○ **We Are in Love / CBS**   1990
Sentimental, pre-rock pop-oriented music. Nicely done though quite mannered. –RW

Lofty's Roach Souffle / CBS   1990
Still in a pronounced jazz phase, this shows his debt to James Booker and New Orleans barrelhouse blues influences. –RW

Blue Light, Red Light / CBS   1991
His latest, with a slick, large-orchestra format. –RW

BARBARA COOK   ♭1927

A singer with a warm, light soprano, Barbara Cook became a successful Broadway musical performer in the 50s and 60s. By the 70s, she had moved largely into cabaret singing, at which she was equally successful. Born in Atlanta, she made her professional debut at the Blue Angel nightclub in New York in 1950 and her Broadway debut in *Flahooley* (1951), one of several flops in which she got good notices. Another of these was the original version of *Candide* (1956). Cook finally found a Broadway show with legs when she created the role of Marian the librarian in *The Music Man* (1957). The most successful of several shows in which she appeared in the 60s was *She Loves Me* (1963). By the mid 70s, she was popular enough to move up to concert halls, and this is reflected in her album *Barbara Cook and Carnegie Hall* (1975). Her more recent accomplishments include her appearance in the special recording *Follies in Concert* (1985), her inclusion in a new studio recording of *Carousel* (1987), and her delightful album of songs associated with Walt Disney children's films, *The Disney Album* (1988). –WR

It's Better with a Band / MOSS MUSIC   1981
A live recording from Carnegie Hall. Includes a wonderful Leonard Bernstein medley, as well as "The Ingenue," a song written for Cook by Wally Harper and David Zippel. –WR

○ **The Disney Album / MCA**   1988
A dream match: Barbara Cook's warm, optimistic voice singing songs taken from Disney films — "Some Day My Prince Will Come," "A Dream Is a Wish Your Heart Makes," and more. –WR

BING CROSBY   1903-1977

An American institution, Crosby started as part of the Rhythm Boys trio with bandleader Paul Whiteman, but he soon went on to major solo success. The first singer to truly understand the microphone (then a relatively new invention), he single-handedly revolutionized pop-music vocalizing by using it as if he were performing to an audience of one. Great success in both records and movies followed, with Crosby's laidback, easygoing style serving him well in both fields. With his roots in Louis Armstrong and Al Jolson, Crosby's laconic phrasing and uncanny ability to sing "in the pocket" have been matched by few singers before or since. –ck

★ **The Best of Bing Crosby / MCA**
No single package can hold all of Crosby's hits, but this is a start: original cuts from 30s and 40s, with many favorites. –cw

And Jazz Friends / MCA
Bing at his best; vintage 40s Decca sides with everyone from Louis Armstrong to Lionel Hampton. –cw

Crooner / CBS
Classic Columbia sides 1928-1934, with fine remastering and good notes. –cw

Radio Years 1 / GNP CRESCENDO
Radio air checks that contain some unusual songs and interesting duet partners. –cw

Bing & Basie / EMARCY
An excellent date with the Basie big band. –rw

○ **Bing Crosby 1927-1934 / BBC**
The best-sounding presentation of his formative 20s and 30s cuts. –rw

Bing's Hollywood / DECCA
A massive 15-disc collection of Crosby's film songs, long since deleted. –rw

When Irish Eyes Are Smiling / MCA   1952
One of the most popular of all Crosby collections, from his 40s Decca years. –cw

Story - Vol. 1 - Early Jazz Years / SONY   1984
More 20s Bing, some with Paul Whiteman and Bix Beiderbecke. –cw

SAMMY DAVIS JR   1925-1990

When Sammy Davis Jr died in 1990, the entertainment world lost one of its reigning superstars. The versatile Davis hailed from a showbiz family and started young, tap dancing up a storm in the 1933 featurette "Rufus Jones for President." His uncle headed the Will Mastin Trio along with Sammy and his dad, and they were a popular lounge act during the 40s. Davis signed with Decca as a singer in 1954, charting with "Hey There," but an auto accident that year cost him an eye. "Something's Gotta Give" was a major hit for Davis in 1955, but his recording career took a back seat for a time of cavorting with the Rat Pack, an all-star crew of Las Vegas swingers headed by Frank Sinatra and Dean Martin. They starred en masse in the films *Ocean's Eleven* (1960) and *Robin and the Seven Hoods* (1964). Moving to the Reprise label, Davis scored with the dramatic ballads "What Kind of Fool Am I?" in 1962, "The Shelter of Your Arms" in 1963, and "I've Gotta Be Me" in 1968, but his only #1 hit came on a very untypical 1972 effort — the saccharine "Candy Man," a million-seller on MGM. A superstar of Broadway, film, and recordings, Sammy Davis Jr earned his ranking as one of America's leading entertainers. –bd

● **The Decca Years / MCA**
Arguably his most popular period, the 70s. –rw

☆ **Collectors Series / CAPITOL**
Fine retrospective of pop- and jazz-flavored cuts. –rw

Hey There! It's Sammy Davis Jr / MCA
Another greatest-hits collection, this one a two-disc set. –rw

○ **With Laurindo Almeida / DCC**
Surprising but effective teamup. –rw

★ **Greatest Hits #1 & 2 / DCC**   1978
His best, most complete hits package. –rw

DORIS DAY   b 1922

Though better known for her film roles and All-American Girl image, Doris Day was a professional vocalist from her teens and enjoyed pop stardom as a lead singer with the Les Brown Orchestra. Critics still dispute whether she was truly a jazz singer. She was certainly no improviser, but she was effective on light novelty fare and innocent tunes of the 40s and 50s, as with her Oscar-winning hit "Que Sera, Sera (Whatever Will Be, Will Be)." –rw

The Best of the Big Bands / CBS
A good collection of Day's hit recordings with Les Brown. –rw

○ **Greatest Hits / CBS**   1958
Day at her most palatable, but not necessarily her best. –be

Hooray for Hollywood - Vol. 1 / CBS   1959
Soft, pop-oriented material that is well known but not her most inspired repertoire. –be

Hooray for Hollywood - Vol. 2 / CBS   1959
An acceptable followup to the first volume. –be

MARLENE DIETRICH   1901-1992

Probably Europe's most valued export of the late 20s, Dietrich rocketed to fame in the movie *The Blue Angel*. Her vamp blonde hair and corset-and-black-stockings look is still in use today (Madonna, Madeline Kahn's spoof of her in Mel Brooks's *Blazing Saddles*). Dietrich's deep, almost foghorn-like voice served her well into grandmotherhood, delighting audiences all around the world. –ck

○ **Her Complete Decca Recordings / MCA**
Though Dietrich recorded (and re-recorded) many of her best-known tunes for a variety of labels, this compilation catches her in fine form and features an excellent reading of her biggest hit, "Falling in Love Again." –ck

MICHAEL FEINSTEIN   b 1956

Michael Feinstein was born in Columbus, OH, and developed an interest in the piano and in show music at an early age. After moving with his family to Los Angeles in 1976, he met Oscar Levant's widow, who in turn introduced him to Ira Gershwin. He was hired by Gershwin in 1977 to help organize the Gershwin archives, and continued to work with the lyricist until Gershwin's death in 1983.

In 1984 Feinstein launched a career as a pianist and singer devoted to the music of the 30s and 40s, playing at private parties in the Los Angeles area. He had a seven-month residence at the Mondrian Hotel, during which Liza Minnelli threw a party in his honor (February 1985) that got his name around. In January 1986, he opened at the Algonquin Hotel in New York, where a six-week engagement stretched to 16 weeks.

Feinstein's debut album, *Live at the Algonquin*, mixed the songs of Irving Berlin and Oscar Levant with more current material by Stephen Sondheim and Gretchen Cryer. By 1988 he had been signed to Elektra Records, for whom he has recorded a series of albums spotlighting the work of specific composers, as well as a recent children's album. –wr

Live at the Algonquin / ELEKTRA   1986
Feinstein in his element. The limitations in his vocal range are made up for by an evident understanding of and enthusiasm for the material, starting with Ray Jessel's "Wanna Sing a Show Tune." –wr

○ **Pure Gershwin / ELEKTRA**   1987
Pure delight. Feinstein's reading of other composers is very, very good, but his feeling for Gershwin (as might be expected from a man who worked with Ira Gershwin for years) is near perfect. Feinstein's piano playing is excellent here, and he relishes every syllable of the words. 'S wonderful. –wr

Remember: Sings Irving Berlin / ELEKTRA   1987
The first of Feinstein's theme albums, and one of the best. He captures the simple (and at times deceptively clever) sentiment of Berlin with an unadorned approach that brings out the sturdiness of the melodies as well. –wr

JOSE FELICIANO   b 1945

Jose Feliciano's virtuoso guitar work and impassioned vocals have been spotlighted in numerous contexts, notably on his hit adaptation of the Doors hit "Light My Fire." Born in Puerto Rico and blind since birth, Feliciano was raised in New York City. He began his lengthy string of successes on RCA in 1968 with his intimate reworking of "Light My Fire," winning a Grammy for Best New Artist that year. He wrote the theme song for Freddie Prinze's acclaimed TV sitcom "Chico and the Man" and acted in numerous programs. Feliciano continues to perform frequently today. −BD

Jose Feliciano / MOTOWN
Nice set of pop/soul. Disco remakes of "I Second That Emotion" and "Ain't That Peculiar," plus a minor hit, "Everybody Loves Me," written by the late Doc Pomus. −BC

○ **All-Time Greatest Hits / RCA**   1965
Includes versions of "Light My Fire," "California Dreamin'," "Suzy Q," and "Walk Right In." −ED

EDDIE FISHER   ♭1928

A major pop star during the pre-rock 50s, Eddie Fisher's roller-coaster career includes seven million-sellers and two famous ex-wives (actresses Debbie Reynolds and Elizabeth Taylor). The Philadelphia-born Fisher sang with Buddy Morrow's orchestra before getting his big break on Eddie Cantor's radio show in 1949. He started his amazing string of hits for RCA Victor with "Thinking of You" in 1950, quickly developing into a teen heartthrob and peaking in 1953 with the chart-topping "I'm Walking behind You" and "Oh! My Pa-Pa." Fisher attempted to go with the rock & roll flow in 1955 with "Dungaree Doll," another big hit, but his style was unabashedly pop-oriented, and the rock revolt all but pushed him off the charts. Fisher continues to sing, and his daughter, Carrie Fisher, is a well-known actress and writer. −BD

○ **All-Time Greatest Hits #1 / RCA**   1991

FOUR FRESHMEN

With their highly advanced concepts of group harmony, the Four Freshmen scored a few hits during the 50s, while deeply influencing the vocal blend of the Beach Boys. Formed at an Indianapolis music conservatory, the Four Freshmen were brought to Capitol Records by jazz bandleader Stan Kenton, and the quartet (Bob Flanigan, brothers Ross and Don Barbour, and Ken Arrair) hit with "It's a Blue World" in 1952. Their top seller was "Graduation Day" in 1956, but six chart items in all by the Four Freshmen don't begin to indicate the influence of their breathtakingly close harmonies on subsequent vocal groups. −BD

○ **Capitol Collectors Series / CAPITOL**
An excellent and well-annotated collection of the best of this 60s harmony group. −CW

FOUR LADS

Soaring four-part harmonies were this Toronto group's stock in trade, and they parlayed their robust sound into a string of pop hits during the pre-rock era. Signed to Columbia Records as background vocalists in 1950, they harmonized behind Johnnie Ray on his 1951 smash "Cry" before making the most of their own shot in the spotlight with "The Mocking Bird" the next year for Okeh. Led by tenor Bernie Toorish, the Four Lads tallied numerous hits for Columbia, including "Skokiaan" in 1954, the powerful "Moments to Remember" in 1955, and "No, Not Much!" and "Standing on the Corner" in 1956. The Four Lads continued to chart frequently through 1959. −BD

○ **16 Most Requested Songs / CBS**
Features melodic early-50s pop hits by this Canadian quartet. Big-selling, extremely appealing harmonies. −HD

Moments to Remember / CBS
More of their melodic early-50s pop hits and harmonies. −HD

FOUR PREPS

While performing at a Hollywood High School talent show in 1956, the Four Preps impressed a Capitol Records producer enough to sign them to a long-term contract. By the end of the year, the wholesome, clean-cut group had their first chart

single, "Dreamy Eyes." From 1956 to 1964 the Four Preps (Bruce Belland, Ed Cobb, Marv Ingraham, and Glen Larson) charted 13 times on the Hot 100. As the British Invasion stormed US shores, their popularity withered away, although they continued to record until 1967. −STE

○ **Capitol Collectors Series / CAPITOL**   1989
All the Four Preps you'll ever need, in a superior 20-track compilation. Every one of their Top 40 hits is here, as are many smaller hits and unfamiliar songs, including their last chart hit, "A Letter to the Beatles," which alone is worth the price of the CD. −STE

JUDY GARLAND   1922-1969

Immortalized while a teenager in the 1939 film musical *The Wizard of Oz*, Judy Garland also recorded often. Of course, her classic rendition of "Over the Rainbow" from *Oz* was a smash that same year on Decca, and she scored numerous hits during the 40s. By 1954, Garland was recording for Columbia, and her rendition of "The Man That Got Away," from her hit movie *A Star is Born*, helped to define the Garland mystique. She hosted her own TV variety show in the early 60s and continued to belt out her classic material until her premature death. Daughters Liza Minnelli and Lorna Luft are very talented chips off Garland's brilliant block. −BD

● **Best of the Decca Years - Vol. 1 / MCA**
Prime early Garland, including the original "Over the Rainbow," as well as pieces from the 40s, like "The Trolley Song." −CW

Legendary / PAIR

Judy / CAPITOL   1956
Wonderful 1956 studio album recorded with Nelson Riddle's orchestra. −CW

Alone / CAPITOL   1957

○ **Judy Garland at Carnegie Hall / CAPITOL**   1961
The best of the later Garland, live at a 1961 concert. −CW

EYDIE GORME   ♭1931

Usually paired vocally with her husband, Steve Lawrence, Eydie Gorme cashed in on a Latin-flavored dance craze in 1963 with her bubbly "Blame It on the Bossa Nova" for Columbia Records. The Bronx, NY, product signed on as a regular on Steve Allen's "Tonight Show" in 1953, and the next year had her first chart hit with "Fini" on Coral. Moving to ABC-Paramount, Gorme's perky pipes rode the charts with the likes of "Love Me Forever" in 1957 and "You Need Hands" the next year. She married Lawrence, another "Tonight Show" regular, in 1957, and they're a popular TV and concert attraction to this day. −BD

Eydie Swings the Blues / ABC-PARAMOUNT   1957
Gorme spreading her jazz wings and digging into a nice selection of pop/jazz/blues-style material. −CK

○ **Eydie Gorme's Greatest Hits / CBS**   1967
Just what the title says, including "Blame It on the Bossa Nova" and her best pop material. −CK

Softly, As I Leave You / CBS   1967
One of Gorme's best ballad albums, nicely done. −CK

ROBERT GOULET   ♭1933

A robust vocalist whose handsome profile has turned up on countless TV variety programs, Goulet first made an impression while starring on Broadway in *Camelot*. He hit in 1962 on Columbia with "What Kind of Fool Am I?" and in 1964 with "My Love Forgive Me (Amore, Scusami)." Goulet still thrives as an actor and easy-listening crooner. −BD

○ **Greatest Hits / CBS**
"If Ever I Should Leave You" and all the rest. −BC

ANNETTE HANSHAW   1910-1985

If there's a female pop/jazz vocalist from the 20s whose recorded work deserves a much wider hearing, it's undoubtedly Annette Hanshaw. Discovered and recorded at the tender age of 15 during the height of the "flapper era," Hanshaw may have been the most talented and versatile of all. Dubbed "The Personality Girl," Hanshaw had a voice with a pronounced Virginian lilt, which could jump effortlessly from cute and bubbly on uptempo material to break-your-heart-in-two emotional on torch ballads. She was part of the early brigade of "radio stars" from the late 20s and early 30s (who made records back then only as an afterthought, most doing it for union scale and no royalties), but few could match her rhythmic bounce, instinctive reading of the lyric, or ability to adapt her voice to exactly what each song needed; certainly few could sing "in the pocket" as well as she. In her brief eight-year professional career, she sang everything with seemingly everyone backing her, from top-flight jazz musicians to Frank Ferera's Hawaiian Trio. Her remarkable versatility allowed her to tackle romantic ballads, comedy nonsense, and the uptempo pop material of the day, Hawaiian novelties, and dead-on Betty Boop impressions, all with consummate ease. The backing on all her records is equally superb, most featuring jazz legends like Benny Goodman, Eddie Lang, Red Nichols, Tommy Dorsey, Joe Venuti, and Jack Teagarden, to name a few.

Although she was quite popular on radio and records through the early 30s (even making a few short films for Paramount), she found show business not to her liking and retired in 1934 at the ripe old age of 23. Her unique voice and stylings only improved in the eight years she recorded. Her recordings have now become a lasting legacy not only of her superb work on them, but of a genre of pop music we most assuredly will never see the likes of again. –CK

☆ **It Was So Beautiful / HALCYON**
Superlative collection of Hanshaw's last recordings, with "Say It Isn't So," "Give Me Liberty or Give Me Love," and "I'm Sure of Everything but You" being particular standouts. Import. –CK

Benny Goodman Accompanies "The Girls" / SUNBEAM
Annette shares this compilation album with tracks by Ethel Waters and the Boswell Sisters, but her five tracks here (especially "I Hate Myself" and "Would You Like to Take a Walk") are major treasures and showcase her at her best. –CK

Sweetheart of the Twenties / HALCYON
Solid collection of Hanshaw's earliest sides, 1926-1928, with superb jazz backing. Import. –CK

The Rare BG 1927-29 / SUNBEAM
Features Benny Goodman backing Hanshaw on two Betty Boop-style sides originally issued in the 20s under the pseudonym "Dot Dare." –CK

RICHARD HARRIS   b 1932

Best known for his acting skills in such acclaimed movies as *The Guns of Navarone*, *This Sporting Life*, and *A Man Called Horse*, Irish thespian Richard Harris was a pop-music star for a brief moment in 1968 with his highly dramatic rendition of songwriter Jimmy Webb's "MacArthur Park." As utterly unlikely a hit as ever scaled US playlists, "MacArthur Park" was Harris's only major smash, although three followups also charted. Disco queen Donna Summer's version of "MacArthur Park" topped the pop charts a decade later. Harris remains busy in films and on stage. –BD

○ **Richard Harris: His Greatest Performances / MCA**
Harris performing songs — mostly by Jimmy Webb. Includes his two biggest hits, "MacArthur Park" and "Didn't We." –KMC

AL HIBBLER   b 1915

Blind vocalist who worked with Duke Ellington's orchestra for eight years before waxing a series of stately pop ballads in the mid 50s. Hibbler debuted in 1942 with Kansas City pianist Jay McShann's combo for Decca before joining Ellington the next year. Hibbler was on the R&B charts four times from 1948 to 1951 for major independent labels like Chess and Atlantic, but he signed with Decca and crossed over to the pop lists in 1955, battling Roy Hamilton for top honors on "Unchained Melody." The deep-voiced Hibbler encored with the inspirational "He"

and the blues-tinged "After the Lights Go Down Low," retaining his reputation as one of the jazz world's leading vocalists until his death. –BD

After the Lights Go Down Low / ATLANTIC   1957
Post-Decca period. The title track is a remake of the 1956 hit. The backing has a heavier backbeat than earlier efforts. –HD

○ **Best of Al Hibbler / MCA**
This contains all his mid-50s pop such as like "Unchained Melody" and "After the Lights Go Down Low," done in his compelling and at times bizarre vocal style, with a big-band backing. –HD

LENA HORNE   b 1917

A pop/jazz singer and a glamorous star of stage, screen, and TV, Lena Horne will forever be associated with the beautiful theme song of her 1943 hit movie *Stormy Weather*. Horne's immortal rendition was her first hit, although the pop charts don't do justice to her magnificent career. She appeared on Victor, MGM, RCA, and many other labels, but her striking presence in movies such as *Cabin in the Sky*, *Ziegfeld Follies*, and, more recently, *The Wiz*, remains her chief legacy. –BD

○ **Stormy Weather / RCA**   1956
A wonderful anthology covering her 40s and 50s show tunes, blues, and ballads. –RW

Lena Horne Sings Your Requests / CHARTER   1963
A double CD of two fine Horne albums from the 60s. –RW

Men in My Life / THREE CHERRIES   1967
A great session with Joe Williams and Sammy Davis Jr. –RW

THE INK SPOTS

The Ink Spots played a large role in pioneering the Black vocal group-harmony genre, helping to pave the way for the doo-wop explosion of the 50s. The quavering high tenor of Bill Kenny presaged hundreds of street-corner leads to come, and the sweet harmonies of Carlie Fuqua, Deek Watson, and bass Hoppy Jones (who died in 1944) backed him flawlessly.

Kenny's impeccable diction and Jones's deep drawl were both prominent on the Ink Spots' first smash on Decca in 1939, the sentimental "If I Didn't Care." From there through 1951, the group was seldom absent from the pop charts, topping the lists with "We Three (My Echo, My Shadow, and Me)" (1940), "I'm Making Believe" and "Into Each Life Some Rain Must Fall" (both in 1944), and "The Gypsy" and "To Each His Own" (both in 1946).

Watson eventually split to form his own group, the Brown Dots, and appeared in numerous low-budget film musicals, while Kenny attempted a solo career, notching a solo hit in 1951 with the uplifting "It Is No Secret." Countless groups masquerading as the Ink Spots have thrived across the nation since the 50s. –BD

○ **Greatest Hits 1939-46 / MCA**
The authentic Decca recordings showcase this seminal doo-wop vocal unit. –RW

AL JARREAU   b 1940

Jarreau, a onetime rehabilitation counselor with a Master's in psychology, used to sing at parties. He landed a deal with Reprise in the 70s and made an impact in 1975 with the album "We Got By." For a while, his passion, his ability to imitate instruments in the best Mills Brothers tradition, and his sense of swing overcame his showbiz tendencies. Later, as he became the darling of an upper-class/professional Black and urban audience, his albums grew more and more self-indulgent. At his best, he is reminiscent of early Johnny Mathis. –RW

Glow / WARNER   1976
A good session, though the gimmicks are kicking in. –RW

Look to the Rainbow / WARNER   1977
Live in Europe. Fine live sets, with Jarreau at his best. –RW

Breakin' Away / WARNER / BB 9   1981
Some nice R&B/pop cuts on this platinum album. –RW

Jarreau / WARNER / BB 13   1983
Pretty pop, R&B, and fusion on this gold album. –RW

All Fly Home/This Time / WARNER
A single-disc combination of two hit albums. –RW

○ **We Got By / WARNER**
Jarreau's best release, which shows him still improvising and interpreting. –RW

AL JOLSON   1888-1950

An entertainment dynamo who quickly established himself as Broadway's leading star by the dawn of the 20th century, Jolson was America's first superstar, years before the phrase was ever coined. A truly competitive and high-energy performer, Jolson left most of the competition in the dust with his impassioned singing, dancing, and jokes (borrowing much from Black ragtime music and early jazz and performing in the then-popular, now-taboo minstrel blackface style). His place in popular history was assured when he starred in the first successful talking picture, *The Jazz Singer*, in 1927. His tireless efforts performing for American troops during World War II (he almost single-handedly started the USO) won him a whole new audience who had never seen him perform in his halcyon days. When the film biography of his life became a major hit twenty years later, Jolson's popularity leapt to legendary status, making no one doubt his title of "The World's Greatest Entertainer." –CK

○ **Early Years / OLYMPIC**
Great single-disc compilation of the earliest Jolson material, which made him a sensation on Broadway. Essential sides and a fascinating glimpse into vaudeville's heyday. –CK

The Legendary Al Jolson / CBS
A three-disc set of Jolson's early Columbia recordings (1914-1923), with a sixth side devoted to early-30s Brunswick recordings from his movie days. Some duplication with the above-mentioned *Early Years* compilation, but essential nonetheless. –CK

ETTA JONES   b 1928

Often confused with Etta James, Jones is a nice jazz and popular-standards vocalist who was frequently a partner with tenor saxist Houston Person in the 70s and 80s. She is an understated, dynamic singer, who can express emotions without gimmicks or excessive animation. –RW

Don't Go to Strangers / OJC   1960
An overlooked, excellent set. Some of Jones's blues and strong leads. –RW

○ **Something Nice / OJC**   1960
An excellent reissue of some prime cuts with Oliver Nelson (reeds) and Roy Haynes (drums) from 1960 and 1961. –RW

Fine and Mellow / MUSE   1987
With fine sax from Houston Person. –RW

Fine & Mellow/Save Your Love for Me / MUSE   1987
A worthwhile combination of two good records (from 1987 and 1980) into one. –RW

I'll Be Seeing You / MUSE   1989
1989 release with good Houston Person tenor sax cuts. –RW

Sugar / MUSE   1989
Nice soul-jazz and light-swing cuts. –RW

DANNY KAYE   1913-1987

Kaye began his career in vaudeville and gained notice on Broadway in such shows as *Straw Hat Review* (1939). He became prominent in musical comedies on the stage and in film and, though never learning to read music, conducted several major orchestras. –DS

○ **The Best of Danny Kaye / MCA**
The best available overview of Kaye's work. –STE

GENE KELLY   b 1912

Showing an early aptitude in both gymnastics and dance,

Eugene Curran Kelly had devoured, by his early teens, everything he could about dance in general and ballet in particular. He was already a successful dance teacher in his hometown when he began his ascent in the original Broadway production of Rodgers and Hart's *Pal Joey*. This led to a film contract with David O. Selznick, which was sold to MGM before Kelly even reported to Hollywood.

The allegiance with MGM proved a godsend for both the studio and Kelly, who (with the help of producer Arthur Freed) came to energize the film company's musical output for the next 15 years. Kelly quickly revealed himself to be a quintuple threat: dancer, actor, singer, choreographer, and director. Beginning with his first film, *For Me and My Gal*, he showed an engaging personality on screen, and his voice, while never strong, was equally pleasing. As his influence at the studio grew, Kelly began proposing more ambitious projects as a director as well as a choreographer and performer. Kelly was never a popular singer, despite the fact that he acquitted himself onscreen alongside even the likes of Frank Sinatra in several films, but his on-screen geniality and overall popularity — as a younger, more masculine, and more conventionally handsome rival to Fred Astaire (who was at MGM at exactly the same time) — allowed him to effectively repopularize many songs by George Gershwin, Arthur Freed, Nacio Herb Brown, and others through his performances of them in films such as *An American in Paris* and *Singin' in the Rain*. His most popular and influential work as a singer can be found on the soundtracks for those films, plus *Brigadoon*, *It's Always Fair Weather*, *Summer Stock*, and the compilation soundtrack *That's Entertainment Part 2*.

As the 50s wore on and the public's taste for musicals waned, Kelly turned increasingly toward directing (*Gigot*, *Hello Dolly!*) and producing, allowing his acting — which he had never entirely forsaken but had never built into great prominence before the public either — to become the focus of his film work in movies such as *Marjorie Morningstar* and *Inherit the Wind*. He proved to be as adept at drama as he had been at dance. And in the 70s, spurred on by the growing interest in America's cinematic past that coalesced around MGM's compilation feature *That's Entertainment*, Kelly directed the equally fine followup, *That's Entertainment Part 2*. –BE

○ **Song & Dance Man / DRG**
Kelly's best output from feature film recordings early in his career. This collection pales next to the work on the soundtracks of *That's Entertainment Part 2* and *Singin' in the Rain*. –BE

MORGANA KING   b 1930

An accomplished actress, King has also made some albums in the jazz vein. She worked in several New York clubs during the late 50s and early 60s. Her 1964 album, *A Taste of Honey*, made some impact, although King didn't display strong jazz technique. Her late-70s albums for Muse had better material and more convincing performances but didn't match her appearances in the films *The Godfather* and *The Godfather Part II* for wide-ranging impact. King makes nice, occasionally arresting albums, and is a very good vocalist. –RW

○ **A Taste of Honey / MAINSTREAM / BB 118**   1964
Nice cuts; clean vocals. –RW

Everything Must Change / MUSE   1978
Good interpretations and arrangements from King. –RW

Simply Eloquent / MUSE   1986
Smooth and tasteful. –RW

EARTHA KITT

This alluring vocalist enjoyed a series of pop hits in 1953 and 1954, including the seductive Yuletide perennial "Santa Baby." Kitt's exotic style was first showcased in the Broadway production of *New Faces of 1952* (a film version was made in 1954), and she waxed the enticing "C'est Si Bon" in 1953 for RCA Victor. "Santa Baby" arrived in time for the 1953 holidays, and her 1954 output included "Somebody Bad Stole

De Wedding Bell (Who's Got De Ding Dong)." Kitt has remained active as an actress and singer; she was a convincing Catwoman on the campy mid-60s TV series "Batman," and she costarred in the recent movies *Pink Chiquitas* and *Erik the Viking*. –BD

○ **Best of Eartha Kitt / MCA**
Decent overview that concentrates on her pop-oriented material. –RW

At the Plaza / GNP
A live late-80s release. –RW

FRANKIE LAINE　　　　　　　　　　　　　　b 1913

Laine, one of the biggest recording stars of the late 40s and early 50s, is famous for his robust baritone. After working radio shows, dance marathons, and a brief stint replacing Perry Como in Freddy Carlone's band, Laine broke into the national spotlight in 1947 with his million-selling "That's My Desire." Nearly seventy Top 100 hits followed, with "Jezebel" and "I Believe" among the finest. (Note: Frankie Laine has re-recorded his Columbia hits numerous times; thus most Laine compilations contain later material with little warning. Check the label and select CBS if possible.) –STE & BC & HD

The Mercury Years / POLYGRAM
This starts with studio chatter and runs through 22 tracks, dated 1946-1950. Far more bluesy/jazzy than his later Columbia material. –HD

☆ **Greatest Hits / CBS**
The essential collection. Wild and energetic, with "Jezebel" and others. –HD

PEGGY LEE　　　　　　　　　　　　　　　　b 1920

Although she was one of the top pop singers of the 40s and 50s, Peggy Lee's love for jazz usually surfaced in her hip phrasing, and her cool cover of Little Willie John's "Fever" gave her a smash in the midst of rockmania in 1958. Lee was singing professionally by 1936, and she joined Benny Goodman's orchestra in 1941. Her tasty rendition of Lil Green's "Why Don't You Do Right?" gave Goodman a major hit in 1943, and by the end of the war, Lee was recording solo for Capitol. She and her husband Dave Barbour wrote "Mañana (Is Good Enough for Me)," a million-selling chart-topper in 1948, while "Lover" was one of her first big items for Decca in 1952. Lee had returned to Capitol by the time "Fever" emerged, and her anthemic "I'm a Woman," penned by Jerry Leiber and Mike Stoller, has proven an enduring favorite. The offbeat "Is That All There Is?" was Lee's final pop-chart bow in 1969. –BD

☆ **Capitol Series - Vol. 1: The Early Years / CAPITOL**
Capitol Collectors Series - Vol. 1: The Early Years is the best collection of Lee's jazz and blues hits. –RW

Miss Peggy Lee / CBS
Mirrors / A&M
Seductive / PAIR
There'll Be Another Spring / RCA-MUSICMASTERS
Recent jazzy pop. –RW

○ **Sings with Benny Goodman / CBS**
Her best songs that featured Benny Goodman. –RW

Close Enough for Love / DRG　　　　　　　1978
Vintage pop and swing material. –RW

Sings the Blues / MUSICMASTERS　　　　　1978
A late-70s date, with Lee updating her blues tracks. –RW

All-Time Greatest Hits / CAPITOL　　　　　1990
A decent collection of past triumphs. –RW

The Best of Peggy Lee / MCA
Another hits collection. –RW

THE LETTERMEN

Though styles changed drastically and frequently throughout the 60s, the Lettermen held still (for the most part), producing light pop songs full of easy harmonies. Tony Butala (b Nov 20, 1940), Jim Pike (b Nov 6, 1938), and Bob Engemann (b Feb 19, 1936) formed the trio in Los Angeles in 1960, cutting their first record a year later. The Lettermen charted 20 times on the Hot 100 from 1961 to 1971, a surprising rate of success considering the times. –STE

○ **Capitol Collectors Series / CAPITOL**　　　1992
All six of the Lettermen's Top 40 hits are here, along with a generous selection of lesser-known singles and album tracks. Informative liner notes and excellent sound help make this the definitive Lettermen collection. –STE

JULIE LONDON　　　　　　　　　　　　　　b 1926

Not only was Julie London absolutely gorgeous, she possessed one of the sultriest vocal deliveries around (perhaps best spotlighted on her smoky 1955 pop smash "Cry Me a River"). Born in Santa Rosa, CA, London landed roles in several films during the 40s and married tight-jawed "Dragnet" cop Jack Webb. London's singing ability was encouraged by her next hubby, Bobby Troup (the composer of "Route 66"). She signed with Liberty and hit big with "Cry Me a River," performing it in a memorable scene in the 1956 rock flick *The Girl Can't Help It*. Although that was her only pop hit, London's many Liberty albums were perfect mood music for late-night makeout sessions, and her acting resume includes a long stint during the 70s as a nurse in the Webb-produced TV hospital drama "Emergency." –BD

○ **Julie Is Her Name - Vols. 1 & 2 / LIBERTY-EMI**
A 50s album with Julie accompanied by bass and by Barney Kessel's guitar with hip chord voicings. This made a big splash in its day, with many guitarists working to decipher Kessel's work. –RL

○ **Time for Love - Best of Julie London / CAPITOL**
Often over-orchestrated but still effective, these are her best-known songs. –DH

TRINI LOPEZ　　　　　　　　　　　　　　　b 1937

Trini Lopez recorded a series of upbeat tunes for Reprise during the mid 60s, including a smash rendering of the folk standard "If I Had a Hammer" in 1963. The Dallas native cut some Ritchie Valens-influenced rockers for the King label prior to his discovery by producer Don Costa. Lopez's hits capture the excitement of his live performances, and his driving renditions of "Kansas City" (1963), "Lemon Tree" (1965), and "I'm Comin' Home, Cindy" (1966) were substantial sellers. Reportedly one of Dean Martin's favorite performers, Lopez hosted his own network TV variety program and co-starred as one of *The Dirty Dozen* in the popular 1967 movie. –BD

25th Anniversary Album / WEA LATINA
Remakes of hits plus new recordings, with a contemporary production that suits Lopez's style well. –JT

Trini Lopez / BELLA MUSICA
Original Reprise records hits and some remakes fill this hard-to-find import. –JT

○ **From the Original Master Tapes / REPRISE**
This Japanese import is an exquisite-sounding 20-song collection of the Mexican-American folk-rocker's 60s hits. It serves as evidence that the nearly forgotten Lopez deserves more credit as an interpretive artist. –JT

JON LUCIEN　　　　　　　　　　　　　　　b 1942

During the 70s, Jon Lucien became a popular figure as a jazz-tinged romantic song specialist. Lucien's deep, prominent baritone, his penchant for sentimental fare, and his suave, commanding personality and presence made him enormously popular on the cabaret/supper-club circuit as well as among fans of love ballads and similar material. After a long absence, Lucien returned in 1991 with a release that was very much what he'd done in his peak 70s years.

Unfortunately, the response wasn't anywhere near what it had been before. –RW

○ **Best of Jon Lucien / RCA**

DEAN MARTIN   ♭1917

Martin's boozy, easygoing vocal style doesn't feature Sinatra's dazzle or Bennett's kitsch, but it remains one of the friendliest in pop. He made his debut in 1948 with "That Certain Party," a duet with his then partner Jerry Lewis, but Martin's best work came in the early 50s, when he had scores of singles in the pop Top 40. His nonchalant way of twisting syllables and slurring notes played a major role in the development of Elvis Presley's ballad style; compare Martin's "I'd Cry Like a Baby" with Presley's "Love Me." He recorded a slew of albums, but his chart run was exhausted by the 60s. He's now a fixture in Las Vegas, where he rubs stage elbows with the likes of Frank Sinatra and Liza Minnelli. –JF

☆ **Capitol Collectors Series / CAPITOL**
Terrific 20-song overview of the Capitol years includes everything you need, from "That's Amore" and "Volare" to "Ain't That a Kick in the Head." –JF

AL MARTINO   ♭1927

Italian singer Al Martino had four hits from 1952 to 1953 and then vanished until the end of the decade — the result of being too young to handle his success and having various disreputable elements vying for control of his career. Martino tried to continue recording in England, to no avail, and returned to America in 1958. After re-signing to Capitol Records the following year, he launched a string of 34 Hot 100 singles that would last until 1977. During the 60s Martino blended country elements with pop songs, blurring the lines between the two genres. In 1972 he appeared in Francis Ford Coppola's masterpiece, *The Godfather*, as singer Johnny Fontaine. –STE

○ **Capitol Collectors Series / CAPITOL**   1992
All of Martino's major hits — "Here in My Heart," "Take My Heart," "I Love You Because," "I Love You More and More Every Day," and "Speak Softly Love," (the love theme from *The Godfather*) — are included on this comprehensive 25-track compilation, along with informative, lively liner notes and sparkling fidelity. The best Martino collection available. –STE

JOHNNY MATHIS   ♭1935

Mathis (b James Royce Mathis) made the smoothest makeout music ever recorded, and his rise to stardom in the mid 50s flew in the face of rock & roll's early domination. Staying almost exclusively with lushly orchestrated ballad material, Mathis racked up hit after hit and now has had albums in the charts for 30 years, an achievement few will better. –CK

☆ **Johnny's Greatest Hits / CBS**
The original greatest-hits package, which stayed on the charts for ten years; includes "Chances Are," "It's Not for Me to Say," "Wonderful! Wonderful!" and "The Twelfth of Never." It seldom gets more romantic than this. –CK

Open Fire, Two Guitars / CBS
A warm and intimate setting, with stellar guitar work from Al Caiola and Tony Mottola. –CK

AMANDA MCBROOM

This Los Angeles-based songwriter and cabaret singer is probably best known for her song "The Rose," a hit in 1979 for Bette Midler. McBroom has also appeared on stage in "Jacques Brel Is Alive and Well" and "See Saw," and also tours regularly. Her debut album, *Growing Up in Hollywood* with Lincoln Mayorga, was a best-seller for the prestigious Sheffield Labs label, as was her followup, *West of Oz*. –ED

Growing Up in Hollywood / SHEFFIELD LABS   1980
With the help of master pianist Lincoln Mayorga, McBroom sings her own world-weary songs of love and experiences and well-chosen oldies like "You've Lost That Lovin' Feelin'." –WR

○ **Dreaming / GECKO**   1986
Amanda McBroom remains best known for her composition "The Rose," the hit that served as the title song for the Bette Midler movie. McBroom's version of the song is included here, along with a collection of equally moving love songs. –WR

MAUREEN MCGOVERN   ♭1949

Maureen McGovern was a secretary when she was hired by Russ Regan to sing the theme from the movie *The Poseidon Adventure* in 1973. It was a #1 hit. The following year, McGovern sang the theme from *The Towering Inferno*, "We May Never Love like This Again," which was not a hit, though it did win an Academy Award. McGovern went on to other movie themes, then distanced herself from such work, appearing on Broadway in *The Pirates of Penzance*. She built a reputation as a sophisticated pop singer to the point that she was able to headline at Carnegie Hall by the 90s, singing show music and standards by George Gershwin and other songwriters. –WR

The Morning After / 20TH CENTURY   1973
Contains that big ballad, of course, though there is no album compiling all of McGovern's movie themes. –WR

○ **Naughty Baby / CBS**   1989
McGovern as sophisticated pop singer, effectively handling an album of Gershwin material. Includes "Of Thee I Sing," the theme from a show in which she starred in 1987. –WR

● **Greatest Hits / CAPITOL**
The best of her movie work and other hits, including "Different Worlds." –CK

JOHNNY MERCER   1909-1976

In the course of a remarkable career, Johnny Mercer wore many hats. He was one of the best and most prolific lyricists of his time ("One for My Baby," "Blues in the Night," "Ac-Cent-Tchu-Ate the Positive," "Moon River") and a fine composer ("Dream," "Something's Gotta Give"). He was also cofounder and president of Capitol Records, where he signed Nat King Cole and Peggy Lee, among others, and a cofounder and president of the Songwriters' Hall of Fame. He was a recording star in his own right in the 40s.

Mercer did not rely strictly on his own material nor did he possess a technically great voice, but he sang in an appealing, easygoing, swinging style, backed mainly by the Paul Weston Orchestra and the Pied Pipers on background vocals. Mercer's recordings are a bit reminiscent of the Sinatra swing albums of the 50s. His recording of "Ac-Cent-Tchu-Ate the Positive," one of his most popular, is currently enjoying renewed interest with its appearance in the movie *Bugsy* and its use as the theme of the TV show "Homefront." Mercer was one of those rare individuals who seemed able to achieve anything he put his mind to and do it well. –KMC

○ **Capitol Collectors Series / CAPITOL**
A collection of his best recordings from the 40s. –KMC

Uncollected Johnny Mercer (1944) / HINDSIGHT
A collection of radio transcripts, recorded in 1944 with the Paul Weston Orchestra. –KMC

Two of a Kind / ATCO   1963
An album of duets with Bobby Darin. –KMC

Too Marvelous for Words / CAPITOL   1991
Too Marvelous for Words: Johnny Mercer has Capitol recording artists, including Mercer himself, singing his songs. –KMC

Johnny Mercer Songbook / RCA
A collection of RCA recording artists singing the songs of Johnny Mercer. –KMC

MABEL MERCER   1900-1984

Mercer was a popular in cabaret singer, both in Paris and the US. Herstrong interpretive skills as a chanteuse and her penchant for popularizing obscure tunes such as "Fly Me to the Moon" brought her a loyal cult following. Her admirers included Lena Horne, Nat King Cole, and Frank Sinatra. –CK

○ **Mabel Mercer Sings Cole Porter / ATLANTIC**
A great song stylist working in a perfect lyric setting. –RW

ETHEL MERMAN   1908-1984

Merman developed her booming vocal style on her own. She attracted attention in Gershwin's *Girl Crazy* (1930), capping the show with her rendition of "I Got Rhythm." Dubbed the "Queen of Broadway," Merman starred in Cole Porter's *Anything Goes* (1934) and Irving Berlin's *Annie Get Your Gun* (1946) and *Call Me Madam* (1950). She also appeared in 14 movie musicals, including *There's No Business like Show Business*. –DS

○ **Musical Autobiography / DECCA**   1963
Two-album set that provides a solid introduction to Merman's distinctive style. –DS

BETTE MIDLER   ♭1945

Bette Midler counts singing as only one of her talents; at times, since 1972, when she first came to national recognition, it has seemed to be the least of her talents. Still, she has managed to score a number of major hits in a roller-coaster career as a recording artist. Born in Paterson, NJ, and raised in Hawaii, Midler early on showed an interest in singing and acting, and by the 60s she had moved to New York and gotten a role in the long-running Broadway hit *Fiddler on the Roof*. Midler developed a nightclub act that included comedy and singing of a variety of kinds of material, including show tunes, pop hits, and even a takeoff on the Andrews Sisters, and appeared with increasing frequency in New York with her accompanist, Barry Manilow. She was signed to Atlantic Records and released *The Divine Miss M* (1972), which went gold and included a Top Ten single cover of the Andrews Sisters' "Boogie Woogie Bugle Boy." *Bette Midler* (1973) was similarly successful.
Midler's album sales fell off during the rest of the 70s, though her records always reached the Top 100 in the album chart. But in 1979 she starred in the film *The Rose*, a fictional account of the life of Janis Joplin, and the title track became a Top Ten hit. 1980 saw the release of Midler's concert film, *Divine Madness*, and her best-selling book, *A View from a Broad*. Her next film, *Jinxed* (1982), however, was a major flop, and subsequent records didn't fare well. Midler made a cinematic comeback with *Down and Out in Beverly Hills* (1986), but it wasn't until 1989 that she had another pop hit, when her version of "Wind beneath My Wings" from her film *Beaches* became a #1 hit. This rejuvenated her singing career, and 1990's *Some People's Lives* became a Top Ten, million-selling album, with the song "From a Distance" hitting #2. Midler's soundtrack album to her 1991 film *For the Boys* was also a gold-selling hit. (Note that the albums below are sometimes recommended because of one or two cuts. Midler is desperately in need of a greatest-hits compilation.) –WR

○ **The Divine Miss M / ATLANTIC**   1972
Midler's early camp style is captured in this debut album, which features her torchy version of "Do You Want to Dance?," the bubbly remake of "Boogie Woogie Bugle Boy," and Buzzy Linhart's "Friends," all Top 40 hits.

Songs for the New Depression / ATLANTIC   1976
Notable for a duet with Bob Dylan on "Buckets of Rain" and an excellent version of Tom Waits's "Shiver Me Timbers." –WR

The Rose / ATLANTIC   1979
The soundtrack to Midler's successful film, with the title track written by Amanda McBroom. –WR

Beaches / ATLANTIC   1989
The soundtrack to Midler's musical comeback film, featuring her version of "Wind beneath My Wings." –WR

Some People's Lives / ATLANTIC   1990
Midler's most successful regular album release in some time, featuring "From a Distance." –WR

For the Boys / ATLANTIC   1991
A film placing Midler in the Andrews Sisters' milieu of WWII

was an inspired choice, and the soundtrack shows her abilities on period material as well as giving her a chance to sing a touching version of the Beatles' "In My Life." –WR

MILLS BROTHERS

Few Black vocal groups made the impact of the Mills Brothers, either commercially or musically, and their long-lasting reign as hitmakers stretched from the early 30s to the late 60s. John, Herbert, Harry, and Donald Mills were born in Piqua, OH. After polishing their harmonies around Cincinnati, they scored their first #1 hit in 1931 with the rousing "Tiger Rag." The group's enduring gimmick involved imitating various instruments vocally, with John providing guitar backing until his death in 1935 (his father, John Sr, replaced him). Major stars of records, radio, and film, the Mills Brothers were tremendously popular. "Paper Doll" and "You Always Hurt the One You Love" were wartime favorites on Decca. The group gently swung to the top of the charts with "Glow Worm" in 1952, and even took a tentative stab at rock & roll in 1958 with a cover of the Silhouettes' "Get a Job." As late as 1968, the group, by then a trio after their dad's retirement, registered a solid seller with "Cab Driver," and they remained a popular TV and nightclub attraction through 1982 (when Harry died). –BD

Close Harmony / RANWOOD   1969
○ **Best of Decca Years / MCA**
Most of the Mills Brothers' best-known hits, remastered well, with good notes. –CW

Four Boys & a Guitar / GNP-CRESCENDO
Our Golden Favorites / MCA

LIZA MINNELLI   ♭1946

The daughter of Judy Garland and movie director Vincente Minnelli, Liza started in show business early on, guest-dueting as a youngster with her mother, from whom she inherited much of her energetic singing and performing abilities. She scored on Broadway at age 20 with the original cast of *Cabaret*, later winning an Oscar for the movie version. Hollywood beckoned, as Minnelli is a fine actress, but her musical show and cabaret roots hold fast to this day. –CK

○ **Liza with a "Z" / CBS**   1972
An Emmy-winning TV concert performance. –LL

The Singer / CBS   1973
Early-70s contemporary music. A change of pace for her. –LL

Liza Minnelli at Carnegie Hall / TELARC   1981
Concert performances from 1979. –LL

Results / EPIC   1989
Produced by the Pet Shop Boys, this album has a more contemporary sound. –LL

MARILYN MONROE   1926-1962

Hollywood's most enduring legend (b Norma Jean Baker) was also a fine jazz-influenced singer, with a larger discography than one might expect. –CK

☆ **Some Like It Hot (Soundtrack) / UNITED ARTISTS**
Soundtrack of Billy Wilder's comedy features Monroe's breathy versions of several 20s jazz/pop classics, including a steamy "Running Wild." Out of print, but worth the search. –CK

Gentlemen Prefer Blondes / MGM
Another soundtrack album, her first, featuring "Diamonds Are a Girl's Best Friend" and duets with Jane Russell. In and out of print. –CK

VAUGHN MONROE   1911-1973

A big-voiced baritone who caught on at the tail end of the big-band era with his theme "Racing with the Moon." He followed this with over 20 Top Ten hits through the early 50s, among them "There! I've Said It Again," "The Trolley Song," "Cool Water," "Ghost Riders in the Sky," and "Red Roses for a Blue Lady." His pleasing delivery and deep voice worked well for him when he became a pitchman for parent company RCA in

1955, doing commercials to introduce America to the latest thing — color TV. –CK

○ **Best of Vaughn Monroe / MCA**
This big-band leader's original hits, including "Ghost Riders in the Sky," "Racing with the Moon," and "Ballerina." Until RCA reissues its collection, these versions will suffice. –HD

YVES MONTAND   1921-1991

Perhaps he's best known as a political revolutionary or as Marilyn Monroe's costar in *Let's Make Love*, but he was also a dynamic showman known for his almost somnambulistic style of crooning. –BC

○ **By Request / CBS**
C'est excellent. Montand crooning en français on such standards as "Les Feuilles Mortes" and "Planter Cafe." –BC

ELLA MAE MORSE   b 1924

One of the most talented and overlooked vocalists of the 40s, Ella Mae Morse blended jazz, country, pop, and R&B; at times she came remarkably close to what would be known as rock & roll. When she wasn't yet 14, Morse had her first taste of the big time, when Jimmy Dorsey's band came to Dallas for a stay at the Adolphus Hotel and she called for an audition. Unbeknownst to her, the band needed a new female vocalist. Believing that Morse was indeed 19, as she and her mother claimed, Dorsey hired her. When he received a letter from the school board declaring that he was responsible for the Morse's care, Dorsey fired her. Morse joined former Dorsey pianist Freddie Slack's band in 1942; she was only 17 when they cut "Cow Cow Boogie," which became Capitol Records' first gold single. The following year, Morse began recording solo. Although her recordings were consistently solid and sold fairly well (frequently charting better on the Black charts than on the pop charts), Morse never obtained a huge following. She retired from recording in 1957. –STE

☆ **Capitol Collectors Series / CAPITOL**   1992
After being out of print for many years, a well-chosen sampling of Morse's groundbreaking recordings are now available on this splendid compilation. Her ten charting solo singles are here, along with sides recorded with Freddie Slack and some obscure tracks. Morse blazes through every song, particularly "House of Blue Lights," "Milkman, Keep Those Bottles Quiet," "Pig Foot Pete," "The Blacksmith Blues," and her first recording, "Cow Cow Boogie." This is an album with terrific liners and superlative sound. Snatch up this disc and pray Capitol reissues more Morse material. –STE

NANA MOUSKOURI   b 1936

Born in Athens, Greece, Mouskouri grew up listening to American jazz and Black gospel music. She attended a classical music conservatory but was thrown out for playing jazz. Later she worked with Harry Belafonte and Quincy Jones. Mouskouri possesses an articulate, resonant soprano. –BC

Oh Happy Day / POLYGRAM   1969
This tribute to Black gospel has 14 soulful cuts done with an earthiness never shown on previous records. "In the Upper Room" and "Slow Train" stand out. –BC

Tu M'Oublies / POLYDOR   1986
French pop songs. "Parle-t-il de moi?" and "L'amour, qu'est-ce que c'est?" are the best cuts. –BC

○ **Only Love - The Best of Nana / POLYGRAM**   1991
Nana's English covers of 80s hits like Cyndi Lauper's "Time After Time." –BC

WAYNE NEWTON   b 1942

Though best known for his long-standing love affair with Las Vegas-style entertainment, Newton actually started in a country & western/rockabilly act with his brother Jerry, recording as the Newton Rascals. Wayne came to national prominence early in the 60s with regular appearances on the "Jackie Gleason Show." Though most effective with ballad

material and a Vegas-glitz style of performing, Newton is actually a fine guitarist whose voice packs more wallop than critics generally give him credit for. –CK

○ **Capitol Collectors Series / CAPITOL**
Thorough overview of his best sides for that label, with great fidelity and comprehensive notes. –CK

JANE OLIVOR   b 1947

A tender-voiced singer who made her mark in pre-WWII European cabaret-style music. Though influenced by Johnny Mathis and Simon & Garfunkel, Olivor is often compared to Edith Piaf. –BC

○ **Chasing Rainbows / CBS**   1977
Melancholy 40s Parisian cafe-style music. –BC

Stay the Night / CBS   1978
A subtle, sensitive try at the Top 40. –BC

Best Side of Goodbye / CBS   1980
Forlorn and moody — easy listening. –BC

In Concert / CBS   1982
Near riotous crowds feed this heartful cabaret act. –BC

PATTI PAGE   b 1927

Patti Page was one of pop music's leading singers during the early 50s. Her double-tracked vocals, highly innovative at the time, translated into gigantic commercial success. By the age of 19, Page was working as a singer at a Tulsa radio station, and she signed with Mercury in 1948. Page's use of multi-tracked vocals gave her a unique, full sound, and in 1950 her renditions of "All My Love" and "Tennessee Waltz" were both pop chart-toppers, the latter for a good three months. "Mockin' Bird Hill" (1951), "I Went to Your Wedding" (1952), and "Doggie in the Window" (1953) were only a few of her gold records for Mercury, and she persevered through the early rock era with "Allegheny Moon" in 1956 and "Old Cape Cod" the next year. Her last major pop smash in 1965, "Hush, Hush, Sweet Charlotte," was the theme song to a popular movie. –BD

● **The Mercury Years - Vol. 1 / MERCURY**   1991
Original hits from 1948-1952. Includes "Tennessee Waltz." Excellent package. –HD

○ **The Mercury Years - Vol. 2 / MERCURY**   1991
20 hits from 1952-1962. Includes "Old Cape Cod" and "Allegheny Moon." Informative packaging. –HD

MANDY PATINKIN   b 1947

Versatile stage and screen actor and singer, Patinkin first gained notice in the Broadway musical *Evita*. He has since made his mark in films (*Ragtime*, *The Princess Bride*) and most especially on Broadway in *Sunday in the Park with George*, *The Secret Garden*, and his own one-man show, *Dress Casual*. He began his recording career in 1989. –WR

○ **Mandy Patinkin / CBS**   1989
Patinkin has reserves of emotion that seem boundless on this tour de force collection mainly given over to show songs. Employing a vocal range that begins in a clear high tenor and plunges to a gruff baritone, Patinkin is able to act and sing duets with himself or sing beautifully alone. But feeling — sometimes overflowing feeling — is the core of his sense of interpretation. As a result, some very old songs sound newly written in his hands. –WR

Dress Casual / CBS   1990
An enormously ambitious collection of show and film music dominated by suites and medleys taken from Stephen Sondheim's obscure *Evening Primrose* (with guest Bernadette Peters) and *Pal Joey*. –WR

THE PIED PIPERS

Originally consisting of eight members, the Pied Pipers had their greatest success after nearly half of the members left the group. The remaining Pipers (Billy Wilson, Chuck Lowry, Jo Stafford, and her then-husband John Huddleston) joined the

Tommy Dorsey Band in 1939, backing Sinatra on many classic recordings. In 1942 the Pied Pipers broke away from Dorsey, and Huddleston joined the army, to be replaced by Hal Hopper, one of the original eight members. The group backed Johnny Mercer on several tracks during the early 40s, including "Candy" and "Blues in the Night." Their first single ("Deacon Jones"/"Pistol Packin' Mama") was released in 1943. Stafford had become quite busy with her solo career and left the group in 1944, to be replaced by June Hutton. Throughout the rest of the decade the Pied Pipers charted frequently, yet their popularity waned in the 50s. A group bearing the Pied Pipers' name still tours today. –STE

☆ **Capitol Collectors Series / CAPITOL**   1992
A terrific 20-track overview of this early vocal group. Features all of their best-known songs, including "The Trolley Song," "Dream," "Open the Door, Richard," "Mam'selle," and "My Happiness." The remastering is top-notch, and the liner notes contain many anecdotes and much information. –STE

LOUIS PRIMA   1911-1978

Though he started in his native New Orleans — heavily influenced by Louis Armstrong's playing and singing and composing the jazz anthem "Sing, Sing, Sing" — Prima really hit his stride in the mid 40s. Combining Armstrong's scat singing style with Neapolitan gibberish and an irresistible rhythm, Prima created a string of hits that presaged the coming of rock & roll by a good dozen years. He moved to Las Vegas by the early 50s, hooked up with his wife Keely Smith and saxophonist Sam Butera, and ruled the late-night scene there for almost 20 years. A manic performer with an unbelievable sense of rhythm and humor, Louis Prima remains a true American music original. –CK

☆ **Zooma Zooma: The Best of Louis Prima / RHINO**   1990
Eighteen Capitol recordings from 1956 to 1958, including the title track, "Just a Gigolo/I Ain't Got Nobody," "That Old Black Magic," and "I've Got You under My Skin." Great sound on tracks that rock like crazy. –CK

Capitol Collectors Series / CAPITOL   1991
An excellent way to fill in the gaps left by *Zooma Zooma*, even if this 26-track compilation duplicates a fair number of songs from the Rhino set. –STE

JOHNNIE RAY   1927-1990

Although practically deaf, Johnnie Ray's tear-inflected delivery tabbed him as an early-50s sensation. Leaving Oregon for Detroit, Ray found a gig at the Flame Club, an R&B and jazz institution. In 1951 Ray signed with Columbia's R&B subsidiary Okeh Records, although "Cry," his histrionic million-seller that year, was a pop entry all the way, with background vocals by the Four Lads. Produced by Mitch Miller, "Cry" remained perched atop the pop charts for nearly three months. Ray encored with "The Little White Cloud That Cried" before moving to the parent Columbia logo and enjoying a steady stream of pop hits, including "Walkin' My Baby Back Home" in 1952 and a cover of the Prisonaires' "Just Walking in the Rain" in 1956. Ray's frenzied antics set off riots among female admirers during his heyday, but the advent of rock soon dulled his hitmaking powers. By 1959, the hits were through. Guidelines: Stick with original Columbia recordings and select the most generous sample, such as *16 Most Requested Songs*. –BD

○ **16 Most Requested Songs / CBS**
The original 50s recordings of Ray's best, including "Cry" and "Just Walking in the Rain." –HD

Greatest Hits / CBS   1976
Best of Johnnie Ray / CBS

HELEN REDDY   b 1942

Reddy began performing at the age of four in her native Australia; by the early 60s she had her own television series. Between 1971 and 1978, Reddy hit the Top 40 fourteen times

with her smooth, airy light-pop singles, including #1s "Delta Dawn," "Angie Baby," and "I Am Woman." As her hits petered out toward the end of the 70s, her acting work increased, including roles in *Pete's Dragon*, *Sgt. Pepper's Lonely Hearts Club Band*, and *Airport 1975*. –STE

○ **Greatest Hits / CAPITOL**   1975
Reddy's biggest light-pop hits. –BC

DIANNE REEVES   b 1956

Reeves has found success working in both jazz and pop fields, but her background includes working as a teenager with Gene Harris and being discovered by Clark Terry. She later worked with the Colorado Symphony, studied at the University of Colorado, then moved to Los Angeles and worked with Sergio Mendes and Harry Belafonte. Her 1987 debut on Palo Alto, which followed rave reviews for her appearances at the Monterey Jazz Festival and recordings with Stanley Turrentine and George Duke, was in a mainstream/bop vein. She's shown versatility in doing anthems, scat, improvised works, pop, and originals. Reeves rankles traditionalists by going back and forth, but has displayed good potential as a straight jazz singer. –RW

Never Too Far / CAPITOL   1990
Well-sung pop/R&B release. –RW

○ **I Remember / CAPITOL**   1991
Her best and most complete jazz statement. Top-flight instrumental cast. –RW

Better Days / BLUE NOTE
Title track was a huge hit. Fluctuates from R&B to jazz. –RW

DEBBIE REYNOLDS   b 1932

Reynolds grew up in Burbank, CA, where she won a celebrity-impressions contest that led to a movie contract. Her biggest hit, "Tammy," a million-seller from 1957, pushed Buddy Holly's "That'll Be the Day" out of the #1 slot on the pop charts. Reynolds also starred in numerous films. –BC

○ **Best of Debbie Reynolds / CAPITOL**
Reynold's sweet voice against soft string arrangements and romantic lyrics. All of the material is from the 50s-60s. –BC

Best of Debbie Reynolds / CURB
Includes her hit "Tammy." –BC

DIANE SCHUUR

West Coast jazz and blues vocalist Diane Schuur burst into the national spotlight in the mid 80s with a number of critically acclaimed albums for GRP Records. Her recent album, *Pure Schuur*, consists of a range of songs that includes jazz, pop, and contemporary. Her appeal in performance and on record goes beyond a straight jazz audience, though, and she has been making inroads in the pop and contemporary music worlds of late. Schuur remains a singer with one foot firmly planted in the jazz world, but one who has great crossover potential. –RS

Schuur Thing / GRP
Excellent tenor sax from Stan Getz; some nice leads. –RW

○ **Timeless / GRP**   1986
Getz on tenor sax elevates things all around. –RW

○ **... And the Count Basie Orchestra / GRP**   1987
Her most traditional jazz album. Nice moments, good sound quality. –RW

Pure Schuur / GRP   1991
Contains some impressive and some uneven moments. –RW

● **Collection / GRP**
A good indicator of the artist's career on the label. –RW

DINAH SHORE   b 1917

Shore's public debut came at the age of four in Nashville. She sang at WSM there before moving in 1937 to New York, where she did radio shows with Eddie Cantor. Later she starred in

Hollywood musicals and her own TV talk show. During the 50s Shore was one of the top singers in the country. –BC

Bouquet of Blues / RCA 1942
This is a superb album of blues cuts in pop style. It includes "St. Louis Blues," among others. –BC

○ **16 Most Requested Songs / CBS**
Her best hits, including the peppy "Buttons & Bows." –BC

NINA SIMONE   ♭1933

An amazing performer and writer, Nina Simone's popularity endures even when her behavior could alienate the most faithful of her fans. Her parents were both involved in the Methodist Church. All seven of her brothers and sisters worked in the music industry, with her youngest brother at one time being her manager. Simone moved to Philadelphia at 17, and eventually went to New York, where she attended Juilliard. Her late 50s debut on Bethlehem was a major event, with the single "My Baby Just Cares for Me" having been an advertising staple for years. Simone has done every kind of song feasible, from jazz to folk to gospel to blues and covers of Beatles and Broadway tunes. She left America in the late 60s, initially going to Barbados and Liberia, then to France and England. Her 1969 composition "Young, Gifted & Black" is among the anthems of Black America. Many of her other albums are classics, while some of her protest work, especially "Mississippi Goddam" has earned her both plaudits and long stretches where employment opportunities have been limited. Simone unfortunately also has a long history of missed engagements, conflicts with promoters and fans, and periods when she'd announce her retirement. Her autobiography has just been released. –RW

My Baby Just Cares for Me / CHARLY 1959
Valuable reissue, under new title, of her debut album on Bethlehem. Title cut was a hit in England five years ago. –RW

At the Village Gate / CAPITOL 1961
1991 reissue of a killer concert. –RW

I Put a Spell on You / POLYGRAM 1965
Good (if rambling) set. –RW

In Concert / POLYGRAM / BB 12 1965
Fine, intimate set of Simone recordings. –RW

Wild Is the Wind / POLYGRAM / BB 110 1966
Rambles, but when focused she's commanding. –RW

☆ **High Priestess of Soul / POLYGRAM** 1967
Excellent, one of her best. –RW

A Very Rare Evening with Nina Simone / PM 1969
Extremely hard to find, but well worth the effort. –RW

Baltimore / CTI 1978
Includes an evocative rendition of the Randy Newman title composition. –RW

Let It Be Me / POLYGRAM 1987
This is a good live set, one of her few done recently. –RW

Don't Let Me Be Misunderstood / POLYGRAM 1989
A good bunch of her strongest cuts. –RW

Best of Nina Simone / RCA
Twelve late-60s RCA recordings. A mix of styles, with some nice blues. –RP

Let It All Hang Out / POLYGRAM
Erratic, but some powerful moments. –RW

Black Soul / RCA
From her peak performing and recording period. –RW

Blues / RCA
A 1991 reissue of some of Simone's most distinctive interpretations. –RW

Cry before I Go / MANHATTAN
Nice sessions, but the sales were sabotaged by feeble promotion. –RW

Here Comes the Sun / RCA VICTOR / BB 190
Magnificent title track, moving album. –RW

Pure Gold / RCA
Some dynamite performances. –RW

★ **The Best of Nina Simone / POLYGRAM / BB 187**
Twelve remastered tracks from Philips, 1964-1966. Her best period, worth missing a meal for. –RP

FRANK SINATRA   ♭1915

Frank Sinatra's public image as a boorish, Mafia-hobnobbing, wife-abusing, obnoxious right-wing lout is in direct conflict with the personality that dominates his finest music. From his ascent to pop stardom in the 40s up to his last moment of brilliance in the 60s, Sinatra was pop music's quintessential romantic, someone who could tell you how much love hurts and then jump and wail about how good it feels, with overwhelming amounts of conviction and sincerity. A character emerges from his best music: searching unflaggingly for the perfect lover; when he doesn't find it, he explores the bowels of abandon and heartbreak with an equally unflagging diligence.

This isn't the place to discuss the innovations Sinatra brought to pop vocalizing and album-making in the 20th century (buy the highlighted discs to discover that). Nor is this the place to discuss the vulgarity that has characterized his public life (check out Kitty Kelly's bio). The CDs highlighted below offer a biography of Frank Sinatra that is inarguably the most important. On record the guy was a sucker for love, and if you have a hard time relating to that, put this book back on the shelf and go browsing in the automotive section.

After cutting his teeth with the orchestras of Harry James and Tommy Dorsey in 1942, Sinatra pursued a career as a soloist. The rest, you could say, is history. Under the tutelage of producer Axel Stordahl, Sinatra developed a vocal style that stretched syllables with perfect amounts of subtlety and showmanship and gave millions of bobby-soxed girls their first sex symbol.

Sinatra left Columbia in 1953, disgusted by the shoddy material his label was tossing him. He hooked up with Capitol that same year and, with Nelson Riddle and producer Voyle Gilmore, took full advantage of the then-new long-play record by recording thematically linked albums. He also worked with arranger/conductors Billy May and Gordon Jenkins, who, along with Riddle, would embellish Sinatra's conceptual endeavors with perfectly suited accompaniment, adding new facets to his musical personality. For those keeping score, Riddle specialized in jazzy, sprite arrangements, while May favored splashy, pounding thumpers and Jenkins piled on thick gobs of orchestration, heavy on the strings.

Sinatra left Capitol in 1961 to form his own label, Reprise. Unfortunately, the magic that was so abundant during the first 20 years of his career had withered; his voice had lost most of its charms, becoming rougher and less dazzling in both emotion and technique. There's good stuff from this period but, sadly, not much. –JF

☆ **Songs for Young Lovers/Swing Easy / CAPITOL** 1954
This brings together Sinatra's first two 10-inch releases for Capitol, with zesty arrangements by Nelson Riddle and a new-found bounce and confidence in Sinatra's vocals. –JF

☆ **In the Wee Small Hours / CAPITOL** 1955
His first full-blown concept album (from 1955) is a gut-wrenching collection of maudlin ballads, including definitive readings of "I'll Be Around," "Ill Wind," and "Dancing on the Ceiling," with Nelson Riddle's most beautiful soundscapes. –JF

★ **Songs for Swingin' Lovers / MOBILE FIDELITY** 1956
The title says it all. Soaring big-band arrangements and the best set of songs Sinatra's ever sung make this release the best introduction to his swinging world. (Also available in a standard, non-audiophile issue from Capitol.) –JF

○ **The Frank Sinatra Story in Music / SONY SP** 1958
A stunning two-disc collection of Sinatra's early years. His nickname at the time was "The Voice," and you can hear why:

if you could "hear" velvet, it would sound like Sinatra's vocals on "I Concentrate on You" and "I've Got a Crush on You." –JF

No One Cares / CAPITOL   1959
Another Jenkins-conducted set of weepers. Essential cut: "I Can't Get Started." –JF

Sings for Only the Lonely / CAPITOL   1960
Gone is Nelson Riddle's trademarked light-swing jazz. Gone is the bounce in Sinatra's voice. This morose, almost gothic set of torch songs captures "The Voice" in the farthest regions of commiserative torment. –JF

Where Are You? / CAPITOL   1960
The first of Sinatra's three collaborations with Gordon Jenkins, who wraps his vocals in a lush, warm blanket of compassion and sympathy. The CD contains four Nelson Riddle-conducted bonus cuts. –JF

○ **Come Dance with Me! / CAPITOL**   1962
A bright, splashy set of hard-thumping dance-floor invitations. Sinatra's voice is showing signs of wear, but Billy May's arrangements make them easy to ignore. –JF

○ **September of My Years / REPRISE**   1965
After four years of duds on his own label, Sinatra and Gordon Jenkins bounced back with a set that examines the meaning of life, confronting both the ghosts of the past and the spectre of old age. –JF

Sinatra's Swingin' Session!!! (& More) / CAPITOL   1969
This decent collection of upbeat bouncers features the gorgeous "September in the Rain," one of Frankie's best moments. –JF

A Swingin' Affair / CAPITOL   1969
Features some fine Nelson Riddle swingers and a decent song selection but lacks the thematic wallop of *Swingin' Lovers*. Fanatics will enjoy it, though. –JF

Capitol Collectors Series / CAPITOL   1972
Rounding up the best material from otherwise mediocre albums like *This Is Sinatra*, *Nice and Easy*, and *All the Way*. –JF

Close to You (& More) / CAPITOL   1972
Another fine set of Nelson Riddle-arranged weepers, highlighted by the tear-jerking title cut and "I Couldn't Sleep a Wink Last Night." –JF

Come Swing with Me! / CAPITOL   1972
Once you've exhausted the other swingin' sets, check out this Billy May-powered set of dance-floor wailers, which was Sinatra's last album on Capitol. –JF

○ **Come Fly with Me! / CAPITOL**   1976
Sinatra's persona as a wanderlust romantic was introduced on this Billy May-arranged set of travel-oriented swingers and crooners that charts our hero all over the globe in his quest for the perfect love. –JF

○ **The Voice - The Columbia Years: 1943-1952 / CBS**   1986
An exhaustive six-disc presentation of his formative years, divided into six themes: saloon songs, standards, screen, love songs, swing, and stage. It might be too much for skeptical novices, but this is a marvelous set. –JF

Hello Young Lovers / CBS   1986
A 26-song grab bag that rounds up some choice leftovers from the Columbia years. –JF

Sinatra Rarities - The Columbia Years / CBS   1988
Don't let the title fool you; this batch of overlooked material (which includes a breathtaking version of "Why Shouldn't I?") is all grade-A Sinatra. –JF

Capitol Years / CAPITOL   1990
A well-selected three-disc set that contains the high marks of his Capitol era, but you really should hear them in their original contexts. –JF

The Reprise Collection / WARNER   1990
A lavishly packaged four-disc hodgepodge of later years. For fanatics it's essential, but it unintentionally documents the demise of Sinatra's talents. –JF

○ **The Very Good Years / REPRISE**   1991
This contains the worthwhile material from *The Reprise Collection* in a less cumbersome single-disc package. A necessary addition to your Sinatra collection. –JF

JO STAFFORD   b 1920
A pop vocalist with strong jazz leanings, excellent pitch, and flawless rhythm. Originally part of a trio with her sisters, Stafford joined Tommy Dorsey's Pied Pipers group, singing behind Frank Sinatra's tenure with the band. After going solo early in the 40s, she married bandleader Paul Weston and racked up over 80 hits between 1944 and 1957. Of particular interest are her comedy recordings with Weston (as Jonathan and Darlene Edwards), where Stafford deliberately sings off-key over Weston's terrible piano playing. Great fun, especially in light of their formidable talents. –CK

○ **Capitol Collectors Series / CAPITOL**   1991
Exquisite collection of Stafford's most memorable love songs from the 40s, complete with extensive liner notes and impressive sound. Includes "I Love You," "Long Ago (And Far Away)," and "Some Enchanted Evening." –STE & BC

KAY STARR   b 1922
Starr's torchy "Wheel of Fortune" was one of 1952's biggest sellers, holding down the #1 spot on *Billboard*'s pop list for ten weeks. She picked up early experience singing with the big bands of Glenn Miller and Charlie Barnet before racking up the first of many hits for Capitol in 1948. Starr blasted up the charts with "Bonaparte's Retreat," "Oh Babe!," "Side by Side," and plenty more during the early 50s, as well as enjoying a hit duet with Tennessee Ernie Ford in 1950, "I'll Never Be Free." After moving to RCA, Starr topped the pop charts once more in 1955 with the stately "Rock and Roll Waltz." She continued to tally chart hits into the early 60s. –BD

○ **In the 1940's / HINDSIGHT**   1947
1947 radio transcriptions. Kay at her jazziest, before "Wheel of Fortune" and pop stardom. –RL

● **Capitol Collectors Series / CAPITOL**   1991
A good collection of Starr's 50s pop material, including "Hoop Dee Doo," "If You Love Me (Really Love Me)," "Changing Partners," and "Wheel of Fortune." –RL

Kay Starr - Vol. 2 / HINDSIGHT
Swinging small-band sessions with Joe Venuti, Les Paul, and Billy Butterfield. –RL

Moon Beams and Steamy Dreams / STASH
Late-40s radio transcriptions. –RL

BARBRA STREISAND   b 1942
Despite having to compete with rock singers during what is known as the "rock era," Barbra Streisand has turned out to be one of the most successful recording artists since WWII. As of the end of 1989, she had collected more platinum records than any other person, and her gold albums were exceeded only by Elvis Presley's. Streisand is also a successful actress and film director.

She got her start in New York City nightclubs and in musical comedy, appearing in *I Can Get It for You Wholesale* on Broadway when she was signed to CBS Records (now Sony Music). She went on to a starring role in *Funny Girl* (she would also star in the film version), by which time she had released her first album, *The Barbra Streisand Album*. During the mid-60s, Streisand's albums were consistent sellers, though only her first single, "People," made the Top Ten. That meant she appealed primarily to adults and, as the 60s wore on, the music business became increasingly youth-oriented. In addition, Streisand turned more of her attention to Hollywood, resulting in a slight fall-off in her popularity as a singer.

She began to address this in the early 70s by singing more rock-oriented material, notably a Top Ten version of Laura Nyro's "Stoney End," but by the mid 70s she had found a niche as a singer of contemporary ballad material (for example, the theme song from her hit film *The Way We Were*). Streisand helped her own cause by cowriting the #1 hit "Evergreen" from her next film, *A Star Is Born*, and thereafter displayed a remarkable versatility that even found her at home in duets with disco diva Donna Summer and Bee Gee Barry Gibb. She was less active as a recording artist in the 80s, though in 1985 she scored an amazing success with *The Broadway Album*, probably her best-selling album ever. In 1991 she released a boxed-set retrospective, *Just for the Record ...*, and in 1992 was thought to be close to re-signing a lucrative deal with Sony, covering both her musical and film activities. –WR

The Barbra Streisand Album / CBS   1963
The birth of a legend, best exemplified by Streisand's slow ballad treatment of "Happy Days Are Here Again," which transforms it from a frothy celebration song into a far more complicated mixture of remorse and warmth. –WR

A Happening in Central Park / CBS   1968
Streisand's personality is on full display here, and her singing is mesmerizing. –WR

What about Today? / CBS   1969
Streisand's first, tentative attempt to try out the work of contemporary songwriters. –WR

● **Greatest Hits / CBS**   1970
Barbra's best of the 60s. –WR

Barbra Joan Streisand / CBS   1971
A confident Streisand takes on the songs of John Lennon and Carole King and even throws in an otherwise unheard tune by Steely Dan's Walter Becker and Donald Fagen. –WR

○ **Barbra Streisand's Greatest Hits - Vol. 2 / CBS**   1978
The best of Barbra in the 70s. –WR

Guilty / CBS   1980
A chart-topping collaboration with Barry Gibb, featuring three Top Ten hits.   WR

☆ **The Broadway Album / CBS**   1985
Streisand's abandonment of Broadway was the worst thing that happened to the theater in the 60s. This album, including masterful versions of the work of Stephen Sondheim along with some older classics, is some small recompense. It is also the best work of a very great career. –WR

○ **Greatest Hits ... and More / CBS**   1989
This is really the third volume of Barbra's greatest hits, her best from the 80s. –WR

YMA SUMAC   b1928

A singer with an amazing four-octave range, Sumac was said to have been a descendant of Inca kings. Her offbeat stylings became a phenomenon of early 50s pop music. While her album covers took advantage of her strange costumes and voluptuous figure, rumors abounded that she was, in actuality, a housewife named Amy Camus. It mattered little, since there has been no one like her before or since in the annals of popular music. –CK

○ **Enchantress / CAPITOL**
Early-50s recordings by a self-proclaimed Incan princess. Exotic music and a multi-octave vocal range. –HD

The Spell of Yma Sumac / PAIR

RUDY VALLEE   b1901

Rudy Vallee was an immensely popular vocalist in the late 20s and 30s. Singing into a megaphone became his vocal trademark. At the height of his popularity, he had his own national radio show. As his singing career faded with the arrival of Bing Crosby, he switched to a career on the stage and screen. The 1966 novelty hit "Winchester Cathedral" was inspired by Vallee. He attempted a brief, unsuccessful comeback, recording an album that included his own version of "Winchester Cathedral." –KMC

○ **Vagabond Lover / PRO ARTE**
The best of Vallee's recordings from the 20s and 30s. –KMC

BOBBY VINTON   b1941

As a child, Vinton played clarinet and was influenced by the big-band sound of Les Brown and Stan Kenton. He signed with Epic in 1960. He was renowned as the "King of Polka" for his Polish roots, but during the upbeat musical 60s he distinguished himself as an ultra-smooth, sentimental balladeer of the first order. –BC

○ **Greatest Hits / CBS**   1964
Some of the most beautiful ballads recorded, including "I Love How You Love Me" and "Blue Velvet." –BC

● **All-Time Greatest Hits / CBS**
A classy set of hits and other soft string ballads. –BC

ANDY WILLIAMS   b1928

Andy Williams parlayed his relaxed vocal delivery into massive pop success and TV stardom during the 60s. After starting out singing with his brothers over various midwestern radio stations as a youth, the Wall Lake, IA, native went solo in 1952 and became a regular on Steve Allen's "Tonight Show" through 1955. He signed with Archie Bleyer's Cadence Records the next year and hit with "Canadian Sunset," topping the charts with a cover of Charlie Gracie's rock-tinged "Butterfly" in 1957. "Are You Sincere" (1958) and "Lonely Street" (1959) preceded a move to Columbia in 1961 and the huge seller "Can't Get Used to Losing You" in 1963. Williams has long been one of America's top middle-of-the-road entertainers, hosting his own TV variety series throughout the 60s, and he remains a highly popular attraction. –BD

○ **Andy Williams' Best / CADENCE**   1962
A nice retrospective of Williams' early sides. –CK

Greatest Hits - Vol. 2 / CBS
Picks up where the Cadence compilation left off, including "Can't Get Used to Losing You," "Days of Wine and Roses," "Dear Heart," and others. –CK

Moon River & Other Great Movie Themes / CBS
The hit title song and lush interpretations of movie theme classics. –CK

NANCY WILSON   b1937

Wilson made her national debut in 1959, fronting the Billy May Orchestra. She has been a huge influence on a variety of singers, including Anita Baker and Regina Belle. Wilson's crisp, articulate, intricate jazz phrasing distinguishes her 53 albums, which encompass standards, Broadway, blues, jazz, pop, and contemporary soul. –BC

All in Love Is Fair / CAPITOL   1973
Urban-style R&B love songs. –BC

Life, Love and Harmony / CAPITOL   1979
The most sophisticated disco album ever cut. –BC

○ **Forbidden Lover / CBS**   1987
A jazz-flavored soul album. –BC

Lady with a Song / CBS   1990
Contemporary, relaxed R&B. –BC

● **Greatest Hits / CAPITOL**
Light jazz-style pop standards, and more. –BC

VOCAL COLLECTIONS

☆ **Irving Berlin: A Hundred Years / CBS**
Issued to commemorate Berlin's 100th birthday, this 21-track compilation of his songs is culled from recordings made primarily in the 30s, though there are a few from the 40s and 50s. The artists include Connee Boswell, Bing Crosby, Eddie Cantor, Fred Astaire, Benny Goodman, Dinah Shore, Tony Bennett, and Johnny Mathis. –WR

○ **Ertegun's New York / ATLANTIC**   1987
Ertegun's New York - New York Cabaret Music. Once upon a
time (roughly the early 50s), in a faraway land (Manhattan),
there lived a group of singers, piano players, and other
musicians with a fascinated audience that crowded into
dozens of little clubs to hear them sing and play some of the
best songs ever written. Most of them are gone now, but the
music lives on in this six-record boxed set that gathers the
work of Mel Tormé, Bobby Short, Mabel Mercer, Sylvia Sims,
Billy Taylor, and many other great nightclub performers. –WR

○ **Nipper's Greatest Hits: 1902-1920 / RCA**
Al Jolson, George M. Cohan, Enrico Caruso: RCA Victor was
there at the beginning, and this 20-song volume captures the
times nicely. –JT

Nipper'sGreatest Hits: The 20s - Vol. 1 / RCA
Many classic tracks, including "The Charleston," "Makin'
Whoopee," "My Blue Heaven," "Rhapsody in Blue," and Helen
Kane's "I Want to Be Loved by You." –SWB

○ **Nipper's Greatest Hits: The 30s - Vol. 1 / RCA**
A wonderful collection starring Duke Ellington, Bing Crosby,
Benny Goodman, Glenn Miller — all giants. –JT

○ **Nipper's Greatest Hits: The 30s - Vol. 2 / RCA**
As strong as the first volume. Louis Armstrong, Artie Shaw,
Gene Krupa — the big-band era begins here. –JT

○ **Nipper's Greatest Hits: The 40s - Vol. 1 / RCA**
With the likes of Frank Sinatra, Tommy Dorsey, Glenn Miller,
and Spike Jones, this is a solid set. –JT

○ **Nipper's Greatest Hits: The 40s - Vol. 2 / RCA**
A bit weaker than the early-40s collection, but you still can't
go wrong with Count Basie, Dizzy Gillespie, and even Desi
Arnaz. –JT

Cole Porter Collection / JASS
A delightful 25-song anthology of vintage (1928-1941)
recordings of obscure but equally arch Porter songs.
Performers include Ethel Waters, the Dorsey Brothers, the
Paul Whiteman Orchestra, and others. –MH

☆ **Cole Porter - A Centennial Celebration / RCA**
This master of the urban lyric and chic tune is himself heard
here singing demos of three of his standards. Includes 20
performances from the 30s to 80s, featuring Fred Astaire,
Artie Shaw, Lena Horne, and others. This is the cornerstone
of 20th-century music. –MH

○ **Songs That Got Us through WWII / RHINO**
An excellent collection of songs from the "War Years." The
Andrews Sisters, Frank Sinatra, the Dorsey Brothers, and
Harry James, among others. Great for the novice. –KMC

EASY LISTENING

Listening to music can have either a primary or a secondary focus. The musical genre we call easy listening clearly falls into the latter category. Its main function is usually as background music; for example, it can provide a pleasant backdrop for dinner, a romantic evening, or just relaxing. While one can't deny the musical contributions of artists such as Miles Davis, Jimi Hendrix, or Bob Dylan, they are not most people's idea of dinner music. In short, there is a time and place for everything. Not all music is meant to challenge or stimulate.

Easy listening is comprised of two elements: 1) soft string-laden arrangements of old familiar standards with some newer pop tunes and 2) the vocal stylings of such perennial favorites as Perry Como or Andy Williams and the lighter fare of artists such as Frank Sinatra, Tony Bennett, or Elvis Presley. Ironically, according to Joel Whitburn's *Top Easy-Listening Records 1961-1974* — which was compiled from *Billboard*'s Easy Listening Charts — the #1 artist on the chart during this period was Elvis Presley; however, you will not find Elvis listed in the Easy Listening section of this book, as his main musical contributions lie elsewhere. Also, for the sake of conformity, vocalists will be found in the Vocal section. Basically, this section consists of albums that are primarily instrumental, with some including an occasional vocal. Some of the most famous artists here are Liberace, Percy Faith, Lawrence Welk, and Mantovani, whose name is almost synonymous with the term easy listening. If there is

one common denominator for most of the artists in this section, it is that they have not created a body of work readily identified with them but have relied mostly on interpreting songs that were proven hits. Two notable exceptions to this are Henry Mancini and Leroy Anderson.

Newer artists in this field, such as Zamfir and Richard Clayderman, have relied heavily on TV advertising and mail-orders to sell their records and establish an identity. The two most likely reasons for this are: 1) most easy listening stations do not announce what they play, and 2) many fans of this music feel uncomfortable walking into the average record store, which clearly caters to the youth market.

The audience for easy listening can perhaps best be described as the parents of the baby-boomers, for they were the main buyers of the music when it was a much more dominant force in the marketplace, and they continue to support it today. But the times are changing. In 1979, *Billboard* changed the name of its Easy Listening Chart to Adult-Contemporary, acknowledging the shift in musical tastes of the baby-boomers themselves. Adult-contemporary, or soft-rock as it is sometimes called, features the familiar soft-rock hits of the last 30 years, and some stations sprinkle new-age instrumentals into the mix. It's a different name but the same concept for a younger generation. The more things change, the more they stay the same.

— Ken Cassidy

LEROY ANDERSON   1908-1975

Leroy Anderson was a light-classical pop composer, most popular in the 40s and 50s. He began his career in 1935, writing and arranging for Arthur Fiedler and the Boston Pops Orchestra. The sound effects he incorporated into many of his compositions became his musical signature. Among his most popular songs are the Christmas classic "Sleigh Ride," "The Syncopated Clock" (the old "Late Show" theme), "Blue Tango," and "Forgotten Dreams." Anderson's witty, melodic compositions gained wide acceptance in both pop and classical circles. –KMC

☆ **Leroy Anderson Collection / MCA**
His best, including "Sleigh Ride," "Blue Tango," "Syncopated Clock," and "Forgotten Dreams." –KMC

RICHARD CLAYDERMAN

Pianist Richard Clayderman is France's most internationally successful recording star. His grand style has earned him more than 114 gold albums. He offers a mix of classical standards and originals played in soft piano stylings and bathed in soothing strings. –JME

My Classic Collection / QUALITY
○ **Plays Love Songs of the World / CBS**   1987

RAY CONNIFF   *b* 1916

Conniff came up through the big-band ranks of the late 30s, eventually landing staff work on network TV by the early 50s. Arranging slick pop studio hits for singers Johnnie Ray, Don Cherry, Johnny Mathis, and others, he became most successful with a long series of chorus-laden easy-listening albums for the non-rock & roll market. –CK

○ **Conniff Meets Butterfield / CBS**
Showing off a jazzier side to Conniff that recalls his big-band work, this is a nice album with great trumpet work from Billy Butterfield. In and out of print. –CK

Somewhere My Love / CBS
The lushest of all Conniff albums, this one features the theme from *Dr. Zhivago*. –CK
'S Awful Nice / CBS   1977

FLOYD CRAMER   *b* 1933

Pianist Cramer gained attention playing backup for artists like Elvis Presley, Roy Orbison, and Loretta Lynn. He went on to become RCA's answer to easy listening by recording over 50 albums for them, many of which went gold. –JME

○ **The Best of Floyd Cramer / RCA**

PERCY FAITH   1908-1976

He started as a child piano prodigy, giving his first recital at Massey Hall at age 15, until an accident injuring his hands cut short his concert career. He broke into early radio, arranging for orchestras, developing a lush pop-instrumental style. Faith joined the Columbia staff in the early 50s after tenures at RCA Victor and Decca. He pioneered the "songs from Broadway shows" album format in the early 50s to great effect. He also wrote several film scores including hit songs like "Theme from *A Summer Place*," his first Grammy win. As rock & roll took over and his work became more schlocky in format (easy-listening arrangements of Beatle songs, etc.), the musical quotient remained high, thanks in large part to Faith's arranging skills and penchant for picking good material. –CK

Soft Lights and Sweet Music / RCA
Early-50s compilation of pre-Columbia work; lush and romantic. –CK

○ **All-Time Greatest Hits / CBS**   1978
Here it makes sense to stick with the tried and true. Much of the best of Faith's filmscore work (including "Theme from *A Summer Place*") is included here. –CK

FERRANTE & TEICHER

A piano duo, Arthur Ferrante and Louis Teicher met while both were studying at Juilliard in the late 40s. After years of being guests in front of large orchestras and cutting several cleverly arranged duo albums, they hit their stride in the early 60s with a string of lush orchestrated hit singles and albums based around their interlocking piano style. –CK

○ **Theme from *The Apartment* / UNITED ARTISTS**
Their breakthrough album, both in chart success and the establishment of the orchestrated formula that would carry them through the 60s. –CK

West Side Story & ... / UNITED ARTISTS
Despite the unwieldy title (*West Side Story & Other Broadway & Motion Picture Hits*), some of their best work. –CK

ARTHUR FIEDLER   1894-1979

Arthur Fiedler, the conductor of the internationally known Boston Pops Orchestra, has introduced much of America to classical music, if only on the lighter side. He has recorded dozens of albums over the years; most of them make excellent easy-listening music. –JME
○ **Popular Favorites / PAIR**

MYRON FLOREN

There is no doubt that Myron Floren is one of the finest accordion players in the world today. He first gained national attention on *The Lawrence Welk Show* and has recorded many albums, most of them polkas. –JME
World's Greatest Polkas / RANWOOD
With Lawrence Welk. –ED
○ **Polka King / RAN**

JACKIE GLEASON   1916-1987

Not only one of the finest comedians America has ever produced, Gleason applied his prodigious talents to music as well. With a strong jazz roots background (leaning to mesmerized idolatry when dealing with good trumpet players), Gleason developed a chart-topping series of mood music albums, citing his reason for their existence: "Every time I ever watched Clark Gable do a love scene in the movies, I'd hear this really pretty music, real romantic, come up behind him and help set the mood. So I'm figuring that if Clark Gable needs that kinda help, then a guy in Canarsie has gotta be dyin' for somethin' like this!" –CK

○ **Music to Make You Misty / CAPITOL**
Gleason's late-night-and-lonely album, lush and emotional, all the right feelings in place. Excellent, though out of print. –CK

Champagne, Candlelight and Kisses / CAPITOL
Not enough Os in smooth, to describe this one; everything the title implies and more. –CK
Movie Themes for Lovers Only / CAPITOL
Gleason conducting double string orchestra with jazz soloists Charlie Ventura and Pee Wee Irwin, interpreting a dozen film-score melodies with typically lush Gleason results. Uniformly excellent. –CK

ANDRE KOSTELANETZ   1901-1980

This music successfully straddles the borders between light classical and "highbrow" pop music. Kostelanetz was particularly effective at doing spectacular arrangements on Gershwin and Cole Porter material. –CK
○ **Meet Andre Kostelanetz / COLUMBIA**
Early-50s compilation of material, showcasing Kostelanetz's best arrangements of material by Gershwin, Porter, Jerome Kern, and Vincent Youmans. –CK

The Beautiful Music of Tchaikovsky / COLUMBIA
The classical side of Kostelanetz, and at the time of its 23-song production the most comprehensive Tchaikovsky album ever done. –CK

ALAN JAY LERNER   1918-1986

This Broadway musical lyricist, librettist, screenwriter, and author, usually paired with composer Frederick Loewe, is best known for the shows *Brigadoon*, *Paint Your Wagon*, *My Fair Lady*, and *Camelot*. Lerner also wrote the score for the film *Gigi* and an Oscar-winning screenplay for *An American in Paris*. –WR

○ **An Evening with Alan Jay Lerner / RELATIVITY**   1987
Star-studded two-disc live album taken from a benefit concert. The best of Lerner's songs and stories, sung, spoken, and played by a Broadway/West End Who's Who including Sally Ann Howes, Burton Lane, Marti Webb, Len Cariou, Tim Rice, Douglas Fairbanks, and others. –WR

LIBERACE   1919-1987

Born Wladziu Valentino Liberace on the outskirts of Milwaukee, Liberace learned piano from his father and received encouragement for a classical career from Paderewski. He opted for work in nightclubs and in 1940 moved to New York, where he became well known for his semi-classical repertoire. During the 50s he became famous through his involvement in television, known for the candelabrum on his piano (modeled after Chopin) and his flashy clothes. He published his autobiography in 1973. –DS
○ **The Best of Liberace / MCA**
This is an excellent sampler that showcases the flamboyant, semi-classical style of the pianist, including "Shubert's Serenade." –DS

GUY LOMBARDO   1902-1977

"The Sweetest Music This Side of Heaven" was the logo of Guy Lombardo & His Royal Canadians, who by 1930 had established themselves as America's top dance band. Unfairly lumped in with unswinging "mickey mouse" bands of the era, the music of Lombardo's outfit was actually top-notch, and they were constantly cited by Louis Armstrong as his favorite band for their purity of intonation. A cache of early sides for Gennett reveals that the band was capable of playing "hot" any time they wanted to, but sweet music and singing novelties featuring brother Carmen is what the public wanted, and Lombardo failed to disappoint. He became a national institution hosting televised New Year's Eve broadcasts from New York, making his rendition of "Auld Lang Syne" part of our national memory chest and his lasting legacy. –CK

Legendary Performer / RCA
A nice selection of middle-period material in straightahead mono. –CK

Guy Lombardo Medleys / CAPITOL
The first volume in a continuing series, featuring nice bandstand medleys done in the typical Lombardo fashion with nice fidelity. −CK
○ **The Best of Guy Lombardo / MCA**
All the hits, including the legendary "Boo Hoo." −CK

MAGIC ORGAN

No easy-listening collection would be complete without at least one Magic Organ album. And there are dozens of theater-organ album masterpieces: old-standards, carousel music, waltzes, and, most of all, polkas. −JME
○ **Magic Organ / RANWOOD**   1983
22 All Time Organ Favorites / RANWOOD   1984

HENRY MANCINI   b 1924

If the recognition of one's peers is the true measure of success, then few men are as successful as composer, arranger, and conductor Henry Mancini. In a career that has spanned 40 years, writing for film and television, Mancini has won four Oscars and twenty Grammys, the all-time record for a pop artist. For 1961's *Breakfast at Tiffany's* alone, Mancini won five Grammys and two Oscars. *Breakfast at Tiffany's* includes the classic "Moon River" (lyrics by Johnny Mercer), arguably one of the finest pop songs of the last 50 years. At last count, there were over 1000 recordings of it. His other notable songs include "Dear Heart," "Days of Wine and Roses" (one Oscar, two Grammys), and "Charade," the last two with lyrics by Mercer. He also had a #1 record and won a Grammy for Nino Rota's "Love Theme from *Romeo and Juliet*."
Among his other notable film scores are *The Pink Panther* (three Grammys), *Hatari!* (one Grammy), *Victor/Victoria* (an Oscar), *Two for the Road*, *Wait Until Dark*, and *10*. His television themes include "Peter Gunn" (two Grammys, recorded by many rock artists), "Mr. Lucky" (two Grammys), "Newhart," "Remington Steele," and the *Thorn Birds* television mini-series.
What has kept Mancini's work fresh is his ability to write in almost any style imaginable and his successful experimentations with unusual sounds and instruments. In his 1989 memoir *Did They Mention the Music*, Mancini's coauthor Gene Lees wrote that "More than any other person, he Americanized film scoring, and in time even European film composers followed in his path," and that Mancini wrote scores that "contained almost as many fully developed song melodies as a Broadway musical." Had he not remained true to his first love, film scoring, Mancini would have more than likely made as large an impact on the Broadway stage as he made on the silver screen. −KMC
Music from "Peter Gunn" / RCA
Soundtrack and incidental music from Mancini's early "Hollywood jazz" period. Great listening. −CK
○ **Best of Mancini / RCA**   1987
Mancini's most memorable scores, including "The Pink Panther," "Moon River," and others. The best overview of his voluminous work. −CK

MANTOVANI   1905-1980

Violinist, composer, and conductor Annunzio Paolo Mantovani was born in Venice, Italy. He started working in London at 16 and was conducting the Hotel Metropal Orchestra by 1925. Mantovani was a major pioneer in the heavy use of strings and one of the first to be almost exclusively interested in recorded rather than live music. He also was one of the first popular artists to concentrate on producing albums rather than singles. He had seven million-selling albums, including *Immortal Classics* (1954) and *Exodus and Other Great Themes* (1960). In 1935-1936 Mantovani had hits in the US with "Red Sails in the Sunset" and "Serenade to the Night." He was soon recognised as the undisputed king

undisputed king of easy listening, or mood music, as it was called then. He had 51 hit albums in the US alone. −JME
○ **Golden Hits / POLYGRAM**
Incomparable Mantovani / POLYGRAM

SERGIO MENDES   b 1941

An early proponent of his native Brazil's bossa-nova style, he formed the group, Brasil '65 (which later became Brasil '66 and was updated in semi-yearly increments) and scored hits with soothing, Latin-tinged pop throughout the 60s. −CK
○ **Greatest Hits of Brasil '66 / A&M**
Smooth-as-silk arrangements. His best sides and major hits such as "Fool on the Hill" and "The Look of Love." −CK

JERRY MURAD & HIS HARMONICATS

Murad & His Harmonicats perform easygoing 50s pop, all built around a harmonica orchestra. −DH
○ **Greatest Hits / CBS**   1990
Contains "Peg o' My Heart" and other hits. −DH

PETER NERO   b 1934

Nero is a pianist and New York native who started with Paul Whiteman, then moved up to symphony until the late 50s, when RCA Victor signed him and successfully promoted him into a pop music interpreter. He won the 1961 Grammy for Best New Artist. His lush orchestrated albums continued through the early 70s, when he returned to a harder jazz format, recording with a trio. −CK
○ **Hail the Conquering Nero / RCA**
The biggest of his early-60s successes. −CK
Nero Goes "Pops" / RCA
An interesting, largely successful album with Arthur Fiedler and the Boston Pops Orchestra. −CK
Peter Nero Now / CONCORD JAZZ
This is a smartly played set of standards interpreted in a trio setting. −CK

101 STRINGS ORCHESTRA

Published by Alshire International Inc., there are over 200 albums in this series of lush string-laden instrumentals designed for easy listening. −JME
○ **Best of the 101 Strings / ALSHIRE**

NELSON RIDDLE   1921-1985

While Nelson Riddle had experience as a trombonist and arranger for Charlie Spivak, Jerry Wald, and Tommy Dorsey in the 40s and was a staff arranger for NBC radio later in that era, he achieved his greatest success and notoriety during the 50s. Riddle was the arranger and conductor for Judy Garland, Jimmy Wakely, Betty Hutton, Ella Mae Morse, and many others in the early 50s, including Nat King Cole, but became the top arranger in Hollywood through his collaborations with Frank Sinatra during 1953. Riddle's orchestrations and careful, intelligent use of first-class jazz musicians accented Sinatra's voice perfectly, without obscuring, challenging, or threatening. No one was better at knowing when to increase the brass section's volume, how to support a singer, and what soloist to spotlight and for how long.
Riddle enjoyed some success on his own during the 50s, including a Grammy award in 1958 and a #1 pop hit in 1955. He later expanded his activities to work with Ella Fitzgerald, Oscar Peterson, Rosemary Clooney, and Johnny Mathis and became a busy film soundtrack arranger, composer, and conductor as well. He contributed to hit movies such as *The St. Louis Blues* and *Pajama Game* and did the theme music for the TV shows "Route 66" and "The Untouchables." He was musical director for the Julie Andrews variety show in the 70s and came back from health problems to arrange and conduct Grammy-winning albums for Linda Ronstadt in the 80s. His last work was a 1985 arrangement for opera singer Kiri Te Kanawa. −RW

Kiri Te Kanawa. –RW

○ **The Best of Nelson Riddle / CAPITOL**
Route 66 & Other Great TV Themes / CAPITOL   1980

BILLY VAUGHN   b 1919

Kentucky-born Vaughn began his career with the vocal group the Hilltoppers in 1952. He worked as music director for Dot Records, and as an arranger and conductor for Pat Boone, the Fontaine Sisters, Gale Storm, and other Dot artists. His 50s hits include "Melody of Love" and "The Shifting Whispering Sands." –ED

○ **Billy Vaughn & His Orchestra ... / RANWOOD**
Virtually any Vaughn collection will be acceptable to his fans. *Billy Vaughn & His Orchestra Play 22 of His Greatest Hits* contains numerous re-recordings of his hits (e.g., "Sail Along Silvery Moon," 1957), which retain his trademark close-harmony alto sax melodies and lilting rhythms. –HD

LAWRENCE WELK   1903-1992

Long a butt of comedians and music fans, Lawrence Welk survived into the 90s as America's most successful bandleader. From dirt-poor beginnings in rural North Dakota, the relatively uneducated and heavily accented Welk seemed an unlikely candidate to carve out a successful, 60-plus-year career in the music business, but through sheer dogged persistence and belief in himself, that's exactly what transpired. His "Champagne music" style (lighter and less rhythmic than Guy Lombardo's) remained remarkably unchanged over the years. Changes in music have been constant — the end of the big band era, rock & roll, country & western, the Beatles, disco — with Welk seemingly impervious to it all, and a built-in audience that felt the same way. While jazz legends like Coleman Hawkins were lucky to land a Timex jazz special once a year, Welk was on ABC-TV twice a week! After being dropped by that network, he was one of the first to successfully move into television syndication, ending up more visible than he had been on ABC at his peak. Expanding his musical family to include tap dancers, jazz musicians (notably Pete Fountain), and multitudes of singers (The Lennon Sisters, etc.), Welk made no pretense of being remotely "hip," merely delivering simple, well-played music and solid, family-oriented entertainment year after year. –CK

Calcutta! / RANWOOD-DOT
Welk's early-60s stab at pop/rock & roll instrumentals. Out of print. –CK

○ **In Concert / RANWOOD**
A two-record set. A nice sampling from the 70s version of Welk's burgeoning organization. –CK

Favorites / CORAL
A nice 12-song overview of Lawrence's 50s television band. No big hits, just nicely played and sequenced. Out of print. –CK

ROGER WHITTAKER   b 1936

British singer and whistler Roger Whittaker was born in Kenya. His first break came in 1970 with "Durham Town," a #12 hit on the UK charts. This was soon followed by a string of hits that became in time an avalanche of hit albums. *The Very Best of Roger Whittaker* reached #5 on the UK charts and logged an incredible 42 weeks on the British charts. With almost 100 albums in print, Whittaker has become one of the most popular of the easy-listening singers. –JME

○ **The Best of Roger Whittaker / RCA**

MASON WILLIAMS   b 1938

A talented guitarist and comedy writer who came into prominence on the late-60s TV show "The Smothers Brothers." Williams scored a major pop hit with the instrumental "Classical Gas," and he continues to write and perform interesting folk-based acoustic guitar pieces. –DS

○ **Handmade / WARNER**   1969
The best from this folk picker, who is sometimes moving, sometimes humorous. Includes the hit "Classical Gas." –DS

Music / WARNER   1969
A humorous collection from this underrated guitarist. –DS

ROGER WILLIAMS   b 1925

Juilliard-trained, Williams attained chart popularity with overwrought but cleanly played instrumentals like "Autumn Leaves" and the film theme "Born Free." He placed 38 albums in the Top 200 between 1956 and 1972. –CK

○ **The Best of Roger Williams / MCA**   1989
All the hits, with nice fidelity, in one neat package. The perfect place to start. –CK

GHEORGHE ZAMFIR

Romanian panpipe player Gheorghe Zamfir first reached #4 on the UK charts in 1976 with an ethereal hit called "Doina De Jale" — a traditional Eastern funeral piece. He has gone on to make dozens of albums and entrance millions of buyers with the other-worldly sound of the pan pipes. His repertoire includes Romanian folk music and classical melodies, but most of all popular film themes. –JME

○ **Lonely Shepherd / POLYGRAM**   1984

EASY LISTENING COLLECTIONS

○ **Hooked On Classics - Best of Hooked on Classics /**
KTEL-QWIL   1986
○ **Hooked On Classics - Vol. 1 / KTEL-QWIL**
Royal Philharmonic Orchestra conducted by Louis Clark. Medleys of famous classical pieces set to a disco beat. –KMC
Hooked On Swing - Best of Hooked on Swing / KTEL-
QWIL   1986
○ **Hooked On Swing - Vol. 1 / KTEL-QWIL**   1986
Medleys by big-band veteran Larry Elgart. The best of the *Hooked On* series. –KMC
Hooked On Themes / KTEL-QWIL   1977

RAP

No one who heard the Sugarhill Gang's "Rapper's Delight" when it was released in 1979 could have guessed that rap would become the most important and incendiary music of the 80s and 90s. Certainly there wasn't much in the song to suggest such grandiose notions: Over a bass groove borrowed from Chic's "Good Times," Big Bank Hank, Master Gee, and Wonder Mike offered a series of humorous boasts in a drawling fashion that wasn't quite spoken-word but definitely wasn't conventional singing. The pumping music was rooted in the house-party traditions of the Bronx, where DJs mixed throbbing funk records through massive sound systems. Although people snapped the record up, most critics thought the song was an intriguing novelty hit and left it at that.

But that silly novelty tune introduced the masses to a challenging new facet of R&B. By the time Grandmaster Flash and the Furious Five released "The Message" in 1982, rap had established itself as the next link in the chain that connects Delta and urban blues, R&B, soul, funk, and disco. "The Message" was a stark, shocking cry from the ghetto, centered around Melle Mel's warning, "Don't push me 'cause I'm close to the edge." By expanding the still-young genre's musical and lyrical boundaries, "The Message" opened the doors to a new form of expression. Coupled with the low-cost equipment needed to make the music — a couple of mikes, a PA, a turntable, and some source records — rap became accessible to anyone who had a way with words and a clever DJ who could cut records on the turntable.

By 1984 rap had exploded, with dozens of grassroots independent labels releasing bold new records (mostly singles) by the likes of Kurtis Blow, Run-D.M.C., the Fat Boys,

LL Cool J, and countless other young artists. Run-D.M.C.'s third album, *Raising Hell*, was a massive crossover hit in 1984, thanks in part to their collaboration with Aerosmith's Steven Tyler and Joe Perry on "Walk This Way." LL Cool J's 1985 debut (*Radio*) established him not only as one of the genre's greatest lyricists but also as rap's first sex symbol.

The contrast between "Rapper's Delight" and "The Message" continues today, with rap offering dance-floor novelties like Digital Underground's "Humpty Dance," explicit boasts of sexual potency à la Luke Campbell's 2 Live Crew, and the trenchant, militant wail of Public Enemy, N.W.A., and Ice Cube. Unlike punk rock, to which rap has always been compared, the genre has continually evolved, taking advantage of electronic innovations such as digital samplers (through which DJs can lift the riffs from old records and rework them around their own beats and soundscapes) and expanding and elaborating on the themes introduced in "The Message." There are nearly as many varieties of rap as there are of rock & roll.

Rap has come under constant attack from Black radio programmers, hostile White rock fans, and music censors. In the late 80s and 90s, the censors attacked everyone from N.W.A., Ice Cube, and 2 Live Crew to Public Enemy and the Geto Boys on the grounds that their music was vulgar and lewd. But the music has retained its vitality throughout these assaults, as suggested by new acts such as De La Soul, Brand Nubian, Arrested Development, and PM Dawn, who have taken the music farther than the Sugarhill Gang could have ever dreamed.

— John Floyd

ABOVE THE LAW

Los Angeles crew of the Cold 187um (Gregory Hutchinson), KM.G the Illustrator (Kevin Dulley), Go Mack (Authur Goodman), and Total K-oss (Anthony Stewart) mix hard-hitting tales of urban violence with explicit sex talk and/or commentary. They shared the mike for one cut with Eazy-E on their 1990 debut *Livin' Like Hustlers*; advance word on their upcoming new release *Black Maffia Life* is good. –RW

Livin' Like Hustlers / CBS   1990
Prototype gangsta rap. –RW
Vocally Pimpin' EP / CBS   1991
Improved production and studio techniques, and sharper quips. –RW

AFROS

A trio with a penchant for sight gags linked to huge bushy hairstyles from the same decade (two members, Hurricane and Koot Tee, were cleanshaven, while DJ Kippy-O had an extensive Afro). The group also has a good pedigree, with Hurricane being a former DJ for the Beastie Boys and a rapper for Davy D. Their material is more in a mode of parody and satire than

confrontation, with a couple of political-consciousness and cultural-awareness cuts added to spice the menu. –RW
○ **Kickin' Afrolistics / CBS**   1990
A wacky trio combine a love for 70s blaxploitation films and comedy with occasional inspired political commentary and witty repartee. –RW

ANTOINETTE

Introduced via hip-hop producer Hurby "Luv Bug" Azor's compilation disc *Hurby's Machine*, self-styled "gangstress of rap" and Queens native Antoinette has matured from essentially just a tough-talking mama into a more unpredictable, sometimes fresh, somtimes alluring, and sometimes defiant rapper whose musical surroundings are equally divided among funk, go-go, hip-house, and hardcore sampler and production snippets. –RW
Who's the Boss / NEXT PLATEAU   1989
Sturdy debut by the "gangstress of rap." –RW
○ **Burnin' at 20 Below / NEXT PLATEAU**   1990
A substantial improvement, venturing into hip-house, go-go, and funk. –RW

ARRESTED DEVELOPMENT

An innovative conglomeration from Brownsville, TN, fusing blues and Southern soul with the hip-hop innovations of De La Soul and PM Dawn. From group member Speech's intelligent, insightful lyrics and laidback delivery to the clever turntable techniques and prodigious self-production of their debut, Arrested Development is a band to watch in the 90s. –JF

☆ **Three Years, Five Months ... / CHRYSALIS**   1992
A crew that's become one of 1992's sensations by infusing hip-hop with blues sensibility on their debut, *Three Years, Five Months & Two Days in the Life of ...*, especially on the single "Tennessee." –RW

AUDIO TWO

Milk and Gizmo Dee (both of whom are sons of First Priority label president Nat Robinson and brothers of MC Lyte) are a Brooklyn-based duo who offer unflinching, sometimes repelling outlooks on inner-city living and hustling, sandwiched around often good studio and production efforts. Occasionally sexist and homophobic, they nonetheless have netted several minor hits. – JF & RW

○ **What More Can I Say / ATLANTIC**   1988
Contains their moment of glory, "Hickeys on My Neck." –DH
I Don't Care - The Album / ATLANTIC   1990
Crisper, tighter production, harder raps, with one hard-edged anti-drug tract "Get Your Mother off the Crack." Only a distasteful homophobic cut "Whatcha Lookin' At" keeps this from being a classic. –RW

AFRIKA BAMBAATAA

Some call him the godfather of rap; others put him in the category of genre creator. Bronx disc jockey Afrika Bambaataa's record "Planet Rock," cowritten by John Robie and produced by Arthur Baker, was the seminal presentation of scratching, electronic additions, high-tech beats, cutting rhythms, and highly processed vocals. The single, and its followers like "Looking for the Perfect Beat" and "Renegades of Funk" opened the door for the 80s electro-funk movement. Later his collaboration with James Brown on "Unity" and his joint vocals with John Lydon on "World Destruction" furthered the link between hip-hop, funk, soul, and rock. He's also done other work as a member of the group Shango, but it's as a producer, compositional force, rapper, influence and father figure that Africka Bambaataa rules within the hip-hop nation. –RW

★ **Planet Rock / TOMMY BOY**   1986
All the important early 12-inchers from 1982-1984 are here, including "Planet Rock" and "Looking for the Perfect Beat," plus three previously unreleased tracks. (Recorded with Soulsonic Force) –JF

○ **Beware (The Funk Is Everywhere) / TOMMY BOY**
Another stunning assortment of singles, with heavier beats, thicker rhythms, and a blistering cover of the MC5's "Kick Out the Jams." –JF

ROB BASE

A New York-based DJ who caused a stir with his clipped cadences and straightahead raps contrasted by choruses lifted from classic soul songs, notably Frankie Beverly and Maze's "Joy and Pain," which he neglected to credit. He had a partner, DJ E-Z Rock, on his first release It Takes Two. He did the second on his own, and continued the practice, this time using as his base (no pun intended) music from Edwin Starr, Marvin Gaye & Tammi Terrell, and Native American rockers Redbone. –RW

○ **It Takes Two / PROFILE**   1988
A wildly successful debut album from 1988 contains the excellent title cut and "Joy and Pain," which lifts from the Maze hit of the same name. Base is joined by DJ E-Z Rock. –JF

The Incredible Base / PROFILE   1989
On this good followup to his hit debut release, Base makes first-rate party raps and utilizes surging samples, rhythms, and grooves. He also makes a good plea for a resolution of rap rivalries on a reworking of the Edwin Starr/Temptations classic "War." –RW

THE BEASTIE BOYS   ♭1979

Obnoxious beyond all definitions of the word, the Beastie Boys are the first and most significant White rap group. Originally formed as a hardcore punk band at New York University in 1979, by 1983 the Beasties (MCA, born Adam Yauch; Mike D, born Michael Diamond; Ad-Rock, born Adam Horovitz) had begun experimenting with hip-hop. In 1986 the group released their first full-length album, *Licensed to Ill*, a brutal amalgam of hard-rock, hip-hop, and ridiculous macho posturing. *Ill* was produced by Def Jam cofounder Rick Rubin, who produced Run-D.M.C.'s *Raising Hell* the previous summer, another mixture of heavy metal and rap that gave hip-hop its first major crossover hit with "Walk This Way." However, nothing compared to the startling success of *Licensed to Ill*; the album rocketed to #1, selling four million copies, and scored a #7 single with "(You Gotta) Fight for Your Right (To Party)." After a terrifying tour, the group became embroiled in a vicious fight with Def Jam; they claimed the record label owed them some two million dollars in royalties, while Def Jam accused them of not recording their followup in sufficient time. In 1989 the Beasties reappeared on Capitol Records with *Paul's Boutique* (co-produced by the group and the Dust Brothers, who would go on to produce hits by Tone-Loc and Young MC), an album so different from the first that it hardly seemed like the same band. Although the most accessible song, "Hey Ladies," cracked the Top 40, *Paul's Boutique* could not measure up to the overwhelming success of *Licensed to Ill*. After another three-year absence, the Beastie Boys emerged with *Check Your Head*, an album that marked another stylistic change. –STE

☆ **Licensed to Ill / DEF JAM**   1986
Some of the album sounds dated, but its impact in 1987 was about as subtle as a brick through a window. It was the first #1 hip-hop album, selling four million copies and the first album from a White rap group. From the opening kick of John Bonham's drums (taken from "When the Levee Breaks"), the Beasties proceed to "steal" from every record they can get their hands on and "rhyme" about an absurd array of macho fantasies. Sure, it's obnoxious — but it's an act, and an insanely humorous one at that; no other rappers brag about being thrown out of White Castle, drinking Budweiser, or having "more rhymes than Phyllis Diller." Even if it sounds a tad dated today, the sheer force of the music and the whiny rhymes still make this worth hearing. –STE

★ **Paul's Boutique / CAPITOL**   1989
Complex, innovative, and brilliant, this is the Beasties' (and the Dust Brothers') tour de force. It's dense with samples from nearly every genre of music and clever, literate, absurd lyrics that drop references from Jack Kerouac to *Dragnet*; *Paul's Boutique* is a virtual catalog of pop culture, deeply rooted in the 70s. As rappers, the Beasties have grown immeasurably; now they can drop science without tripping over their tongues. Musically, *Paul's Boutique* is much richer than *Ill*, including a 12-minute suite at the end of the album. A few listens are needed before it all sinks in, but the rewards are great. –STE

Check Your Head / CAPITOL   1992
This time around, the Beasties concentrate on the grooves, producing some terrific jams. The group recorded with instruments, and while they are no pros, their playing is inspired. Two of the twenty tracks are instrumentals, and on about twelve, the raps seem nonexistent, quite a letdown after *Paul's Boutique*. While the lyrics are simplistic, the music is diverse, ranging from a punk rave-up to reggae-style grooves

to the funky 70s sounds that dominate the album. *Head* is impressive and very worthwhile, a solid followup to two influential albums. −STE

BIG DADDY KANE

Brooklynite Big Daddy Kane (born Antonio Hardy, KANE is an acronym for King Asiatic Nobody's Equal) has nicely been able to balance his image as the ultimate hipster with the requisite solemnity and air of indignation and anger necessary to creditably deliver messages of Afrocentric awareness and Muslim reverence. He's done alternately inspirational, prophetical, ridiculous, and scandalous raps over his career, and has also managed to include duets with the maestro of love Barry White and legendary comedian Rudy Ray Moore, aka Dolemite, who laid waste to Kane in a dozens (insult-swapping) classic. −RW

○ **Long Live the Kane / COLD CHILLIN'**   1988
Kane's debut was his hottest. −DH

It's a Big Daddy Thing / COLD CHILLIN'   1989
A good application of funk sentiments and influence within a hip-hop context, particularly "I Get the Job Done." But Kane also veers into homophobic and sexist territory, notably on "Pimpin' Ain't Easy." −RW

Taste of Chocolate / COLD CHILLIN'   1990
Worth the purchase price for the exchange between Kane and Rudy Ray Moore (*Dolemite*), longtime champion of the underground Black comic circuit. Moore lays waste to Kane with relish. −RW

KURTIS BLOW   b 1959

Arguably rap's first crossover star, at least from a chart standpoint. New Yorker Blow emerged in the early 80s doing both social protest/Afrocentric material and apolitical, boasting, and asexual postering material, though not to the degree that has since become commonplace. His landmark recording "The Breaks" was an eye-opener for its time in terms of pace, verbal dexterity, and rhythm track. Blow was also a big-time producer at one point, using the likes of Bob Dylan and George Clinton in guest stints and incorporating bits from television shows and cartoons in his production. Blow was finally overhauled by New School producers and rappers in the late 80s, and his early work now sounds quite dated by comparison. −RW

○ **The Breaks / MERCURY**   1980
New Jersey-style club rap. −BC

America / POLYGRAM   1985
Consistent rap beats with poignant social commentary. −BC

BOO-YAA T.R.I.B.E.

A 6-piece assemblage of Samoan-American brothers who boast a full-band live sound not unlike Stetsasonic, and augment their sound with surprisingly tasty horn charts. −JF

○ **New Funky Nation / 4TH & BROADWAY**   1990
Boo-Yaa T.R.I.B.E. came onto the scene in top form with *New Funky Nation*, a hard-bitten collection of surly, edgy raps delivered over music supplied by an equally animated live band. This is one of the more underpublicized fine album statements done in 1990. −RW

BOOGIE DOWN PRODUCTIONS

Formed in 1986 by Laurence Krisna Parker and Scott Sterling, Boogie Down Productions quickly became one of the most influential and important hip-hop groups. Parker adopted the name KRS-One (an acronym for Knowledge Reigns Supreme Over Almost Every One) and Sterling became DJ Scott LaRock, and they released an independent single, "Crack Attack," in 1986. BDP's stunning 1987 debut, *Criminal Minded*, full of blunt, matter-of-fact tales of life on the mean streets, was a prototype for gangsta-rap. As the album was building to a massive underground success, LaRock was shot to death in

the South Bronx as he tried to settle an argument. Instead of calling it quits, KRS-One continued BDP with his brother Kenny Parker and D-Nice as DJs and released *By All Means Necessary* the following year. KRS-One began calling himself "the Teacher," promoting self-awareness and education in his rhymes. KRS-One began touring colleges on the lecture circuit around 1989, and some of his writings appeared in the *New York Times*. It became evident that KRS-One had taken his role as the Teacher too far on 1990's *Edutainment*, where most tracks were lectures pasted over lackluster beats. KRS-One obliterated all concerns that he sold out on 1992's *Sex and Violence*, where he sounds angrier and stronger than he has in years. −STE

☆ **Criminal Minded / SUGARHILL-B BOY**   1987
Classic early "gangsta" rap work. *Criminal Minded* was the only time the contributions of DJ Scott LaRock (Scott Sterling) were featured on a Boogie Down Productions recording, as he was murdered shortly after this was issued. The toughest, hardest-hitting BDP effort. −RW

☆ **By All Means Necessary / JIVE**   1988
A spare, gloomy triumph. −DH

Ghetto Music: The Blueprint of Hip Hop / JIVE   1989
KRS keeps up the attack. −DH

○ **Live Hardcore Worldwide / JIVE**   1991
The Teacher sounds explosive on stage, tearing into BDP's greatest tracks and the myth that live hip-hop is bland and unnecessary. In fact, the pure energy of this album can be offputting at first — the group jumps around their catalog, playing fragments of their classics and complete tracks from their latest, *Edutainment*, and the audience sings along with almost every track. *Live Hardcore Worldwide - Paris, London & NYC!* may not be the first live hip-hop album (2 Live Crew released one a couple of months before BDP), but it is certainly the best. −STE

★ **Sex and Violence / JIVE**   1992
KRS-One demolishes any idea he's losing his clout or anger. *Sex and Violence* is his most chilling, slashing, and effective overall statement since *Criminal Minded*. −RW

BRAND NUBIAN

One of the better Islam-oriented groups that popped up in the early part of the 90s. Their religious fervor never dissipates into ranting, exclusionary dogma, and the beats are seriously funky. Watch these guys. −JF

○ **One for All / ELEKTRA**   1990
Post-De La Soul, daisy-age rappers here to wrap their Islamic-slanted lyrics around challenging, clever, and hard-hitting beats and samples. −JF

CASH MONEY & MARVELOUS

Philadelphia rappers Cash Money & Marvelous made only one album in the late 80s. The Joe "The Butcher" Nicolo-produced *Where's the Party At?* was undeservedly ignored. −STE

○ **Where's the Party At? / SLEEPING BAG**   1988
Undernoticed, undervalued work, boasting a nice mix of juvenile humor, funk-tinged hip-hop, and excellent production. −RW

NENEH CHERRY

A one-time member of Rip Rig + Panic and of the punk group, the Slits, she had a massive 1989 hit with "Buffalo Stance," which masterfully balanced hip-hop sensibilities with the crisp, accessible bounce of high-tech R&B. Cherry is also the stepdaughter of jazz trumpeter Don Cherry. −JF

☆ **Raw Like Sushi / VIRGIN**   1989
Cherry's wonderful debut, produced by British dance master Bomb the Bass, offers a brash, sassy portrait of a contemporary feminist, unwilling to take shit from a lip-flapping homeboy and confident enough to tackle thorny issues, both political and sexual. −JF

CHILL ROB G

Queens native Chill Rob G (born Rob Frazier) is an excellent rapper whose version of "The Power" was unfortunately obliterated by the hit rendition done by the duo Snap over the same music. Chill Rob G's original rap was done on a song called "Let the Words Flow." German producers Benito Benites and John Garrett II had taken it and added new musical trappings, renaming it "The Power." G's fine album *Ride the Rhythm* likewise didn't enjoy the commercial success it merited. −RW

☆ **Ride the Rhythm / WILD PITCH**   1990
Powerful raps with underrated percussion, production, and rhythm tracks. −RW

CHUBB ROCK

Weighing in at around 250 pounds, Chubb Rock (born Richard Simpson) often evokes images of a hip-hop Barry White (whom he dueted with on *And the Winner Is ...*). Chubb Rock had a group while he was a teenager in New York but started his career in earnest after he dropped out of college. After three singles from his first album went nowhere, his second album *And the Winner Is ...* was released to greater commercial and critical acclaim, thanks to a remixed single version of "Caught Up" that was released prior to the album. −STE

Featuring Hitman Howie Tee / SELECT   1988
Interesting, entertaining raps, witty quips, and good samples from disco and funk works. −RW

○ **And the Winner Is ... / SELECT**   1989
Sharp humor with first-rate samples and production, plus insightful commentary on ghetto violence and the ignorance of the National Academy of Recording Arts and Sciences. −RW

The One / SELECT   1991
Rock still raps hard, but uneven production and mixes sometime slow the momentum. −RW

COMPTON'S MOST WANTED

Interracial quartet who walk the same turf as 'hood mates N. W. A. and Ice Cube with similarly tough, swaggering grooves. Intricate production makes their best work stand out among the gangsta-rap pack. −JF

○ **It's a Compton Thang / CAPITOL**   1990
More tense, defiant, and obscene gangsta commentary. (Also available in a censored version) −RW

Straight Checkn 'Em / CBS   1991
Aggressive, hard-edged, but predictable. −RW

CYPRESS HILL

Named for their Los Angeles neighborhood, these rappers use some East Coast barbs in their production to push the edge of harrowing. −BE

○ **Cypress Hill / CBS**   1991
Hard gangsta rap done with brutal lyrics and a nonchalant delivery. −RG

THE D.O.C.

After the release of his debut album, the career of Texas-born rapper the D.O.C. was shattered by a car crash that almost took his life. −STE

○ **No One Can Do it Better / ATLANTIC**   1988
D.O.C. hooks up with Dr. Dre of N.W.A. fame to make an effective effort fusing funk, hip-hop, soul, and reggae, along with some tough, taut commentary and raps. Guest spots from Eazy-E, Miche'le, and MC Ren. −RW

D-NICE

D-Nice (born Derrick Jones), the former DJ for Boogie Down Productions, left the group in 1990, releasing his debut album *Call Me D-Nice.* −STE

○ **Call Me D-Nice / JIVE**   1990
D-Nice makes a strong impact with his first solo outing. −RW

DANA DANE

Though a New York rapper, Dana Dane forged an alternative style to the customary "hard" East Coast mode, spinning yarns and presenting his stories with a bemused British accent and often otherworldy tone. His songs "Nightmares" and the huge hit "Cinderella" took hip-hop through territory it seldom ventured into before (or since). Dane was also a rap fashion maven, opening a store to sell apparel long before it became almost mandatory for hip-hop artists to hawk clothing lines. −RW

○ **Dana Dane with Fame / PROFILE**   1987
Humorous, more pop-oriented rap, with a dose of reggae. −RW

Dana Dane 4 Ever / PROFILE   1990
Geared toward those who prefer hip-hop with a light touch. Good production. −RW

DAS EFX

A new rap crew currently making waves in the hip-hop world. Das Efx is an acronym for Dray (born Andre Weston) And Skoob (born Willie Hines; Skoob is "books" spelled backward) plus "effects." −ED

○ **Dead Serious / EAST-WEST**   1992
Their raps are often lightweight, but this album has made an immediate and substantial impact in the hip-hop community. −RW

DE LA SOUL

This trio of Long Island rappers consists of Posdnous ("sound sop" spelled backwards, born Kelvin Mercer), Trugoy (or "yogurt" backwards, born David Jolicoeur), and Mase. Their albums are lyrically keen and idiomatically diverse, sampling cuts from both the Coasters and the Turtles (the latter got them in some legal hot water), while espousing viewpoints that put them in the Afrocentric pocket yet don't wed them to any hard-and-fast religious or political position. Some have callled them hip-hop's first hippies; more to the point, they're among rap's sharpest and savviest performers. −RW

★ **Three Feet High & Rising / TOMMY BOY**   1989
A remarkable debut, with the hit "Me Myself and I," that runs the gamut from absurdity ("Jenifa Taught Me" and "Plug Tunin'") to hard-hitting social commentary ("Ghetto Thang" and "Say No Go"). De La Soul's inventiveness shines — not many rappers would be able to pull funky beats from Steely Dan and Turtles tracks. Throughout the album a mock game show is interspersed between the songs, giving the entire recording a bizarre, humorous feel. *Three Feet High & Rising* would be incoherent if it wasn't for the sizable rhyming and musical talents of the trio. The beginning of the D.A.I.S.Y. (Da Inner Sound Y'all) age. −STE

○ **De La Soul Is Dead / TOMMY BOY**   1991
The title and cover (a picture of a broken pot of daisies) illustrate the degree De La Soul wishes to debunk their myth and shed the attention their debut album earned them. For the most part, the songs on the album are considerably less lighthearted than the ones on the debut, yet they are no less impressive — "Millie Pulled a Pistol on Santa" is one of the most chilling tales of child abuse ever recorded. *De La Soul Is Dead* is not easy to assimilate on the first listen yet the rewards are great. −STE

DEF JEF

This California rapper entered 1989 with a strong debut that elaborated on the minimalism of hip-hop and highlighted both his quick-tongued delivery and his unique twists on Afrocentrisms. −JF

○ **Just a Poet with Soul / DELICIOUS VINYL** 1989
The title just about sums it up. −DH

DIGITAL UNDERGROUND

Nearly every rap posse from the 80s and 90s has borrowed from George Clinton's mountain of P-Funk, but this Bay Area conglomerate have mutated Clinton's boogie into the heaviest funk-fueled sound in rap. And their sense of humor is always dead on-target. –JF

○ **Sex Packets / TOMMY BOY** 1990
A pulsating and wiggy debut, powered by the two instant classics "The Humpty Dance" and "Doowutchyalike." It's sometimes spotty, but worthwhile for aficionados. –JF

This is an EP Release / TOMMY BOY 1990
Two decent remixes from their debut pad this half-hour mini opus. The new stuff ("Same Song," "Nuttin' Nis Funky") attests to the Underground's devotion to the funk and to their staying power. –JF

★ **Sons of the P / TOMMY BOY** 1991
Their devotion to brother George Clinton mutates into a full-blown sort-of concept album. No truly great singles, but as a whole, this is their best album. –JF

DJ JAZZY JEFF & THE FRESH PRINCE

If you're looking for bubble-gum rap, these guys are your best bet. The Prince spins his teen-suburban tales in a pleasant, if facile fashion, and Jeff isn't bad on the turntable. Don't look for anything gritty or street-smart: when Jeff boasts that he can beat Mike Tyson, that's about as menacing as it gets. The Fresh Prince starred in the early-90s TV sitcom, "The Prince of Bel Air." –JF

Rock the House / JIVE 1987
A 10-song work originally issued on Pop Art Records and later picked up by Jive. Containing the hit "Girls Ain't Nothing But Trouble," which launched them as the kings of teen/clean rap, it had maximum crossover appeal yet retained a large following among the core hip-hop audience. –RW

○ **He's the D.J. I'm the Rapper / JIVE** 1988
Their commercial breakthrough contains their #12 hit, "Parents Just Don't Understand," and other good-time raps. –DH

And in This Corner ... / JIVE 1989
More wit and whim from Jeff and the Prince, this time with assistance from saxes, flutes, and trumpets. Though not as commercially successful as its predecessors, it's actually a more faithful rap work. –RW

DREAM WARRIORS

New York rappers King Lou and Capital Q formed Dream Warriors, a crew that is pioneering the fusion of jazz and hip-hop. –STE

○ **And Now the Legacy Begins / 4TH & BROADWAY** 1991
A great example of the burgeoning jazz/hip-hop coalition, plus clever incorporation of TV themes and punk tidbits. –RW

EAZY-E

The whiny-voiced member of N.W.A. has also hit paydirt as a solo act. His 1988 debut, believe it or not, is even more caustic than the work of his Compton posse. –JF

○ **Eazy-Duz-It / RUTHLESS** 1988
N.W.A.'s mouthpiece should feel lucky that he hasn't been assassinated: his debut has something to offend just about everyone, regardless of leftist or rightist leanings or vehemence regarding issues of feminism. But at its best, *Eazy-Duz-It* is a fiery piece of hip-hop menace, marred only by E's incessant whine of a voice and his rampant sexism. Play at your own risk. –JF

EPMD

Long Island rappers Erick Sermon and Parrish Smith (EPMD stands for Erick & Parrish Making Dollars) have confounded some observers by achieving monumental success despite utilizing minimal production and rapping skills. The deadpan, almost mushmouth rapping style and simplistic insertion of samples and snippets throughout their three albums notwithstanding, such cuts as "You Gots to Chill" and "Rampage" have been hits. The duo are also accomplished producers and preside over the Hit Squad, a combination of rap acts including Redman, K-Solo, and Das Efx. Their brand new release *Business Never Personal* has gotten rave reviews in the hip-hop press. –RW

☆ **Strictly Business / PRIORITY** 1988
In reality a collection of singles, EPMD's debut turns some clever samples (Steve Miller, Kool & the Gang, Bob Marley, Otis Redding) into an overpowering funk assault. "You Gots to Chill" is a classic. –JF

Unfinished Business / PRIORITY 1989
Although this doesn't hit as hard as their debut, it does contain some good jabs at the quiet-storm, Black upwardly mobile crowd and also some slams at their doubters. –RW

Business as Usual / DEF JAM 1991
A little to the processed side production-wise, but it boasts one good collaboration with LL Cool J on "Rampage." –RW

ERIC B & RAKIM

The Queens, NY, duo has the distinction of being the first of dozens of ensembles to construct a sound around James Brown samples. The rapid-fire boasts of Rakim and Eric B's inventive turntable techniques make their entire catalog worth investigating. –JF

★ **Paid in Full / 4TH & BROADWAY** 1987
Their debut contains new mixes of early singles ("I Ain't No Joke," "Eric B. Is President") and adds some prime stuff, including the monumental "Paid in Full," which became a heavily sampled item in the late 80s. –JF

○ **Follow the Leader / MCA-UNI** 1988
No immediate standouts, but Rakim's tongue-twisting boasts are sharper, and Eric B. is still a monster at the turntable. –JF

Let the Rhythm Hit 'Em / MCA 1990
This subdued set works its magic more subtly, but the title is no joke. –JF

FAT BOYS

More a comedy troupe than a rap posse, the Fat Boys marketed their obesity and goofiness with true savvy during the early 80s. Most of the songs dealt with their prodigious food intake, and Buff the Human Beat Box was always good for at least one laugh. The music ain't bad and, in 1984, they made a novelty for the ages: "Jailhouse Rap." –JF

○ **The Best Part of the Fat Boys / SUTRA** 1987
Everything you need by rap's fattest trio can be found on this concise sample of their first three albums. Includes "All You Can Eat," "Jailhouse Rap," and "Stick 'Em." –JF

FATHER MC

Father MC straddles the line between hip-hop and new-jack-swing, which resulted in a #20 hit, "I'll Do 4 U," from his debut album *Father's Day*. –STE

○ **Father's Day / MCA** 1990
One of the better applications of vintage soul and romantic R&B to hip-hop formula, along with one bit of verbal warfare between Father MC and female rapper Lady Kazan. –RW

DOUG E. FRESH & THE GET FRESH CREW

New Yorker Doug E. Fresh (born Doug E. Davis), got his initial notoriety for being the "human beatbox," able to approximate and imitate a rhythm machine. He had a string of hit singles with his then partner Ricky Dee in the early and mid 80s, notably "The Show (Oh, My God)" in 1985, which included guest stints from jazz veteran trumpeter Jimmy Owens and synthesizer player Bernard Wright. Fresh had a long absence from the scene after 1988's *The World's Greatest Entertainer* and has just resurfaced with a new release on a small independent label. –RW

Oh My God! / REALITY   1985
Zany rhymes, slashing beats, with bits and pieces of everything from reggae to gospel to funk. –RW

○ **The World's Greatest Entertainer / REALITY**   1988
With the exception of the monster hit "Keep Rising to the Top," Fresh trimmed the religious zealotry and increased the lyrical and rhythmic potency. –RW

GANG STARR

Brooklyn rappers near the top among hip-hop artists influenced by and interested in jazz. In 1989 longtime jazz and Black-pop publicist Elliot Horne placed a poem he wrote with them, and the group used it as the foundation for the song "Jazz Music" on their debut *No More Mr. Nice Guy*. That track was later included on the soundtrack for Spike Lee's *Mo Better Blues*. The group has also used saxophonist and "Tonight Show" bandleader Branford Marsalis and included acoustic as well as electric instruments on their followup release *Step in the Arena*. They've also discussed the jazz/rap connection in such magazines as *The Source* and *The Wire*. They did make a big gaffe on one cut though, crediting Dizzy Gillespie with playing the saxophone rather than the trumpet. –RW

○ **Daily Operation / CHRYSALIS**   1992
Arguably the best example of the hip-hop/jazz coalition, Gang Starr's latest continues the trailblazing path. –RW

GANGSTA PAT

This hardhitting gangsta-rapper is the most notable artist to break nationally from Memphis's rap scene. She landed a 1990 hit with "The Gansta Walk," capitalizing on the hip-hop dance craze. –JF

○ **#1 Suspect / ATLANTIC**
Hip-hop with a Memphis tinge. –RW

GERARDO

A rap performer whose Latino-flavored macho posturings (he frequently performs barechested with his pants unzipped) have made him a minor sensation on both the dance and pop scene in 1988 with "Rico Suave" and "We Want the Funk." –CK

○ **Mo' Ritmo / ATLANTIC**   1991
A hard mix of soul and Latin music, with guest George Clinton. –BC

GETO BOYS

Houston rappers who've at times rivaled Public Enemy, 2 Live Crew, and Ice-T for their ability to generate controversial publicity. Among the most outrageous, outlandish, and frequently offensive gangsta-rap crews, they have released songs that include violent and perverse subject matter that some may find distasteful. They've also had problems with stores refusing to stock their albums, and in some cases even labels refusing to distribute them. The future of the group is now in doubt; Scarface's single album has been a big hit, Wille D. has split to do a solo release and the remaining Geto boys are working on their own projects. –RW

○ **We Can't Be Stopped / PRIORITY**   1991
Contains their best song, the disturbing "Mind Playing Tricks on Me." –DH

GRANDMASTER FLASH & THE FURIOUS FIVE

Grandmaster Flash (born Joseph Saddler, Jan 1, 1958) and the Furious Five (Cowboy, Keith Wiggins; Melle Mel, Melvin Glover; Kidd Creole, Danny Glover; Mr. Ness, Eddie Morris; and Rahiem, Guy Williams) were the most important group in the early days of rap music and, in fact, developed certain crucial aspects of the genre. Saddler was the DJ, providing the musical bed by manipulating records on turntables, scratching them, repeating particular instrumental sections,

and thus creating new music out of collages of existing recordings. The most important such work was the single "The Adventures of Grandmaster Flash on the Wheels of Steel," released in 1981.

Most of the group's records, however, featured the interlocking raps of the five rappers, and the most significant of these was "The Message" (1982), led primarily by Melle Mel, which turned away from the party subjects of many current rap records to focus on urban social issues. The group had split by 1984, with Melle Mel going off on his own. It later re-formed in 1987. –WR

☆ **Greatest Hits / SUGARHILL**   1987
Flash was the DJ and the Furious Five were the best multiple rappers around, moving from the music's low-rent dance origins (it was Flash who began cutting in repeated portions of other records) and party spirit to the "message" approach that took over in the mid 80s, prefigured in "The Message." Much of what came later, started here. –WR

HAMMER

Considered either the ultimate successs story or consummate fraud, Oakland's MC Hammer, a one-time jack-of-all-trades for the Oakland Athletics baseball team, dominated the charts in 1990 with *Please Hammer Don't Hurt 'Em*. The single "U Can't Touch This," despite a rather feeble rap and recycle job on Rick James's single "Superfreak," was a crossover smash. Hammer, live, puts on a fine show as far as dancing, sound, light effects, production, and such. But from a technical standpoint, everything, from his rhymes to his enunciation, qualifies as the ultimate in "wack" (weak) performance. He does have great taste in cover songs, picking choice items from Marvin Gaye, B. B. King, the Chi-Lites, and Prince, among others. He's since dropped the MC from his name. –RW

Let's Get It Started / CAPITOL   1988
His debut, with the hit "Turn This Mutha Out." –ED

● **Please Hammer Don't Hurt 'Em / CAPITOL**   1990
His breakthrough smash contains "U Can't Touch This" and other hits. –DH

○ **Too Legit to Quit / CAPITOL**   1991
Hammer's most recent offering was recorded with a live band, and includes the hit title track. –ED

HEAVY D & THE BOYZ

Jamaican-born Heavy D (born Dwight Myers) sports a 260-pound frame but can move and dance with agility and verve. He wisely chose sensitivity, rather than obesity or verbosity, as his framework, and many of his lyrics emphasize his search for a mate of similar qualities. He's also done good cover songs and penned cultural awareness tunes and tributes to Black women. –RW

Living Large / MCA   1987
This offers his first hit, a smartly done remake of "Mr. Big Stuff," plus charming romantic entries, though he sometimes overdoes the "overweight lover" routine. –RW

○ **Big Tyme / MCA**   1989
Heavy D's commercial breakthrough and best album. –DH

Peaceful Journey / MCA   1991
A continuation of the fine direction cemented in *Big Tyme*, this includes a first-rate rendition of the O'Jays/Third World hit "Now That We Found Love," plus strong message and romance cuts. –RW

ICE CUBE

Through his detailed, unflinching lyrical stance and his inventive phrasing, this former N.W.A. writer and rapper has become the finest mouthpiece gangsta-rap has produced. His posse, the Lynch Mob, construct sonic backdrops that kick with the force of the best Public Enemy. Ice Cube is a controversial but major figure in comtemporary pop, and has recently begun an acting career with films, including 1991's *Boyz 'n the Hood*. –JF

☆ **AmeriKKKa's Most Wanted / PRIORITY**   1990

Cube gets some production help from Public Enemy's Bomb Squad and comes up with a stark and gripping portrait of life in America's inner cities. If you can get past the sexism, you'll find this debut to be one of rap's most unflinching bursts of rhythmic and political fury. –JF

★ **Death Certificate / PRIORITY**   1991

His sexism is becoming even more repugnant, and his racism is sometimes misdirected, but this one perfectly articulates Cube's frustration and outrage at American injustice. –JF

○ **Kill at Will / PRIORITY**   1991

A few remixes from the debut bog this one down, but the title track, which examines the emotional facets of gangland murder with brutal nakedness and accuracy, is Cube's best moment. –JF

ICE-T

Los Angeles-based rapper and ex-con Ice-T was one of the first to establish the West Coast as a rival to the East Coast posses. Along the way he's become one of the genre's most intelligent (albeit sometimes sexist) gangsta-rap advocates. –JF

○ **Power / SIRE**   1988

His second release is a quantum-leap improvement over his debut — better samples, a more pronounced and developed rapping style, and smarter material. Ice-T does marvelous homage to Curtis Mayfield with an excellent adaption of "I'm Your Pusherman" from the vintage *Superfly* soundtrack. –RW

○ **The Iceberg / SIRE**   1989

The Iceberg: Freedom of Speech ... Just Watch What You Say is a brutal, occasionally brilliant condemnation of censorship, drug use, and societal injustice, marred only by a few conflicting ideals and his own sexism. –JF

★ **O.G. Original Gangster / SIRE**   1991

T's masterpiece. An ambitious, sprawling examination of gangsta-rap culture that confronts all the relevant issues and even offers a few alternatives and solutions. It's also Ice-T's most musically visceral outburst. –JF

Body Count / SIRE   1992

Recorded with his metal band, Body Count, the earliest pressings of this album contain the controversial "Cop Killer." –ED

INTELLIGENT HOODLUM

New York rapper Intelligent Hoodlum (born Percy Chapman) served 20 months on Riker's Island for robbery in 1988, using the experience to immerse himself in works on African-American culture and the theology of the Nation of Islam. That combination underscores all of his work and makes his songs radiate with righteousness, anger, indignation, and frustration. It doesn't hurt that ace producer Marley Marl supplies the undergirding as well. –RW

○ **Intelligent Hoodlum / A&M**   1990

A great social commentary. "Arrest the President" is a great rap. –RG

JIBRI WISE ONE

A new rapper with a street sense as well as a knack for songs with a pop touch. –JF

○ **Jibri Wise One / EAR CANDY**   1991

Good lyrics and a very promising talent. One of the first recordings on Nile Rodgers's new label. –JF

JUNGLE BROTHERS

An endlessly funky New York trio who've collaborated with like minds such as De La Soul and a Tribe Called Quest. Their love of James Brown goes deeper than mere sampling. –JF

Straight out the Jungle / WARLOCK   1988

The trio's debut is powered by muscular funk riffs underpinned by an Afrocentric sensibility and a sharp sense of humor. –JF

○ **Done by the Forces of Nature / WARNER**   1989

By injecting some vocal delicacy and some clever samples into their moderately militant message, they made a second album that elaborates on their own winning formula. –JF

KID FROST

Frost expanded rap's vocabulary by flaunting his Latin heritage and celebrating its culture. The fusion is fascinating, both lyrically and musically. –JF

○ **Hispanic Causing Panic / ATLANTIC**

Frost's debut brings his Latin heritage into the arena of rap, not just with the Spanish language but with his convincing and clever street dramas. A masterful and long overdue fusion of funk and salsa samples. –JF

KID 'N PLAY

They've recorded several decent albums with the aid of producer Hurby Luv Bug, but this duo is best known for their starring roles in the *House Party* film series. –JF

2 Hype / ELEKTRA   1988

A solid debut with snatches of house, dance, and go-go. Despite minimal rapping abilities, the duo quickly captured a chunk of the hip-hop audience. –RW

○ **Kid 'n Play's Fun House / SELECT**   1990

One of two releases from the twosome in 1990, this one has new cuts with funkier, looser foundations and more ambitious adult lyrics and rapping style. –RW

House Party (Soundtrack) / MOTOWN   1990

Not strictly, or even mainly, their album, it does contain the singles "Funhouse" and "Kid vs. Play (The Battle)." Its prime importance was as the soundtrack from an extremely successful film of the same name, which launched the duo into cinematic stardom. –RW

KING SUN

One of the first and most successful Afrocentric hip-hop prophets. –JF

○ **Xl / PROFILE**

A prominent player in the political rap movement. –RW

● **Righteous but Ruthless / PROFILE**

Noteworthy Afrocentric/Islamic rap. –RW

KOOL G RAP & DJ POLO

A young Big Apple duo chaperoned by production wiz Marley Marl. –JF

○ **Wanted: Dead Or Alive / WARNER**   1990

Their second album is a relevant and musically sumptuous collection. –JF

KOOL MOE DEE

One old-school rapper who's managed to thrive mixing it up with new-school types. Kool Moe Dee was a member of the Harlem trio the Treacherous Three in the early 80s, and was spotted by music veteran and producer Bobby Robinson. The trio eventually split from Robinson and joined rival Sugarhill Records, then disbanded when their contract there expired. Dee hooked up with producer Teddy Riley, now the king of new jack swing efforts, and hit instant gold with the single "Go See the Doctor," an amazing safe sex story that combines a cautionary message with a frenetic hypnotic beat. Since then, Dee has had a lengthy, disturbing sexist slant. He engaged fellow rapper LL Cool J, in a continuing battle of words which was interesting for a while but degenerated into a stock formula. –RW

Kool Moe Dee / JIVE   1986
A commanding debut, especially the smashing tune "Go See the Doctor," one of the best and most pointed cautionary sex songs ever. –RW

○ **How Ya Like Me Now / JIVE**   1987
The title track was a big smash, and it marked the beginning of the lengthy Kool Moe Dee vs LL Cool J rap war. The second hit "Wild, Wild West" was also a masterpiece; the album's greatness overcomes its forays into sexism on "Stupid." –RW

Knowledge Is King / JIVE   1989
Another brilliant hit with "They Want Money," though he expands a disturbing anti-female line. But it's balanced by a stirring anti-drug, Afrocentric philosophy and a rap methodology that puts him near the top among hip-hop purists. –RW

Funke Funke Wisdom / JIVE   1991
The single "Rise and Shine" was a summit meeting of rap theorists, with Dee joined by Chuck D from Public Enemy and KRS-One. Unfortunately, an overreliance on sexual posturing and macho imagery have begun to set in, weighing down an otherwise notable effort. –RW

KRIS KROSS

Rap successes come in the strangest packages. Kris Kross are two 13-year-olds from Atlanta who, with the help of 19-year-old producer Jermaine Dupri, released a gimmick-laden but fairly charming debut which promptly outsold nearly all of its competition in the summer of 1992. Whether they can turn their success story into a career remains to be seen. –JF

○ **Totally Krossed Out / RUFFHOUSE-COLUMBIA**   1992
The hottest rap duo of the summer, thanks to their penchant for wearing their clothes backward and the single "Jump," which crossed over to pop and R&B markets. –RW

KWAMÉ & A NEW BEGINNING

Kwamé's nice-guy personality — alternately humble and intelligent, outspoken and easy-stepping — offers a refreshing break from the usual bad-boy posturing of most of the rap pack. –JF

○ **Day in the Life ... / ATLANTIC**   1990
Day in the Life - A Pokadelick Adventure is a strange but fun hip-hop journey. –DH

THE LAST POETS

The Last Poets (Suliaman El Hadi, Alafia Pudim, Omar Ben Hassen, Abio Dun Oyewole, and Nilijah), arguably the first rap group. Formed in the early 70s, they have worked with producer Bill Laswell and recorded several albums before disbanding. –ED

○ **Right On! / COLLECTABLES**   1986
The foundation work for latter-day rappers — Afrocentric themes, improvisational vocal styles, obscenity, and a political slant. –RW

LATIN ALLIANCE

A one-off collaboration by Latino rappers Kid Frost, Mellow Man Ace, and M.C. A.L.T. –JF

○ **Latin Alliance / ATLANTIC**   1991
Hip-hop with an Afro-Latin/dance edge. –RW

LL COOL J

The importance of LL Cool J (born James Smith, his moniker stands for Ladies Love Cool James) in rap cannot be exaggerated. By fusing the beatbox minimalism of Run-D.M.C. with the b-boy snarl of his defiant lyrics, LL Cool J pushed the music into new terrain, opening the door for numerous hip-hop contenders and becoming a superstar in the process. –JF

☆ **Radio / DEF JAM**   1985
LL Cool J's debut, produced by Rick Rubin, is a brilliant mix of hardcore street anthems ("I Can't Live without My Radio,"

"Rock the Bells") and updated twists on the dozens ("That's a Lie"), with a couple of ballads thrown in. –JF

● **Walking with a Panther / DEF JAM**   1989
A sprawling followup to his stinko second album, and his most ambitious. LL Cool J not only regroups the strengths that made his debut a winner, but shows a musical expansion of his art that bodes well for the future. Includes "I'm That Type of Guy," "Going Back to Cali," and "Big Ole Butt." –JF

○ **Mama Said Knock You Out / DEF JAM**   1990
The future, Cool J 1990-style. He's mixing house and hip-hop into his minimalist backdrops, and he's finally come up with some decent love songs. With "The Boomin' System," he's created yet another essential rap anthem. Includes "Around the Way Girl," "6 Minutes of Pleasure," "Jingling Baby," and the title track. –JF

BIZ MARKIE

A productive member of Marley Marl's posse, Markie is a contemporary master of comedic rap. He doesn't have much to say, but songs such as "Picking Boogers" are worthy of the Fat Boys and "Spring Again" is a classic summer single. –JF

○ **Goin' Off / COLD CHILLIN'**   1988
Contains Markie's hit single "Pickin' Boogers." –DH

The Biz Never Sleeps / COLD CHILLIN'   1989
More silliness from the silliest. Contains "Spring Again." –DH

MARLEY MARL

Ace producer Marl has worked with the likes of Roxanne Shanté, Biz Markie, Big Daddy Kane, MC Shan, and Master Ace. His style maintains its roots in old-school hip-hop while pushing the music to new, oftentimes blatantly accessible levels. –JF

○ **In Control - Vol. 1 / WARNER**   1988
Marl shows off his greatest stars, including Roxanne Shanté and Big Daddy Kane. –DH

MASTER ACE

He's young, but Master Ace is a smart cookie. He expounds on such things as racial unity and the need for education, and Marly Marl fits him with thick grooves that suggest possible crossover appeal. –JF

○ **Take A Look Around / WARNER**   1990
Ace's throbbing Marley Marl-produced debut mixed the loopy humor of Biz Markie (who shares a cut here) with the urgency of the best LL Cool J. Best cut: "Music Man." –JF

MC 900 FT JESUS

This Dallas, TX, duo led by White rapper MC 900 Ft Jesus (born Mark Griffin), combines a collage of styles, including hip-hop/jazz industrial dance music. –ED

Welcome to My Dream / CIR
Mark Griffin continues his weird ways and records an album that is more personal and political than the debut. Although not credited, DJ Zero is still part of the group. Ethereal. –JB

○ **Hell with the Lid Off / CIR**   1990
Eccentric rap and hip-hop from White boy MC 900 Ft Jesus (Mark Griffin) and DJ Zero, a Texan who supplies some fierce cuts on the turntable. One of the few Caucasian rap artists that stays true to the traditions of rap. This album features "I'm Going Straight to Heaven," "Truth Is out of Style," and "Spaceman." –JB

MC LYTE

Though she's turned a bit in the pop direction on her latest release, Brooklyn rapper MC Lyte has done some inventive, distinctive material on her two prior releases. She's provided some of the better comebacks and putdowns aimed at out-of-control male egos and libidos, and she's also quite funny. It's to be hoped that the pop tinges on *Act Like You Know* are merely an alternative, rather than a primary direction. –RW

Lyte as a Rock / ATLANTIC   1988
The debut from this femme rapper thrusts a middle finger toward the sexism of the male-dominated rap turf, through clever rhymes and a sharp sense of humor, ensuring that her feminism never exhausts and always enlightens. –JF

○ **Eyes on This / ATLANTIC**   1989
This expands on the promise of her debut, both musically (the samples are more dense) and lyrically (witness "Shut the Eff Up! (Hoe)" and the winningly arty "Cuppucino"). –JF

MELLOW MAN ACE

The Los Angeles-based rapper from Havana works the same terrain as Kid Frost, throwing in a penchant for novelty numbers and the usual hip-hop boasts and bringing Hispanic culture to American hip-hop. –JF

☆ **Escape from Havana / CAPITOL**   1990
A landmark hip-hop/Afro-Latin merger. –RW

MONIE LOVE

This female hip-hoppist gained near-crossover success with her hook-laden, dance-oriented debut from 1990. –JF

○ **Down to Earth / WARNER**   1990
The mood moves through vibrant, concerned, bemused, and resigned. Nice samples and good production. –RW

MOVEMENT EX

Afrocentrism at its sharpest, from Lord Mustafa Hasan Ma'd and DJ King Born Khaaliq. The thick, intricate production of their 1990 debut expands on the Bomb Squad's work with Public Enemy; Ex's Five Percent Nation of Islam outlook is uncompromising and rightfully hostile. –JF

○ **Movement Ex / CBS**   1990
A forthright Islamic/Afrocentric outing, with tight studio production support. –RW

MS. MELODIE

A sassy rapper from the Boogie Down Productions stable, Ms. Melodie is the former wife of KRS-One. –JF

○ **Diva / JIVE**   1989
She turned some heads in the hip-hop nation with this excellent debut. –RW

N.W.A.

This Compton, CA, ensemble once held the title of "most controversial rap act," but in recent months others have surfaced to share some of the heat. The original posse, including Ice Cube, Eazy-E, Arabian Prince, MC Ren, and the D.O.C., made their first release in 1987. *N.W.A. and the Posse* was mainly a party/fun record but cuts like "Boyz N' the Hood" and "Dope Man" should have been a warning to alert ears of what was coming. Anyone who missed the debut was certainly caught by surprise when the 1988 followup *Straight Outta Compton* came along. The stark, brutal depictions of gang strife and urban warfare, the coarse, obscene language and the complete amoral tone, plus the anti-authority number "F**k Tha Police" earned N.W.A. scorn from middle-class types of all colors and also attempts from the FBI to get retailers not to stock it. Since that high point, N.W.A. has really become less an entity and more an amalgam of solo acts. Ice Cube, Eazy-E, Arabian Prince, D.O.C., and MC Ren have all done separate projects; Cube has not only left the group but has engaged in bitter, heated public feuds with them; and D.O.C. suffered a near-fatal car crash that took him out of circulation for quite some time. The EP *100 Miles and Runnin'* (1990) was half-hearted, and the group's 1991 release *Efil4zaggin* (Niggaz4Life backwards) elicited some controversy but nothing close to past albums. N.W.A.'s future is very much in question. –RW

○ **N.W.A. and the Posse / PRIORITY**   1987
A hodgepodge of early singles from N.W.A. and some of their Compton contemporaries (including D.O.C.). The highlights are N.W.A.'s "Boyz-N-the Hood" and "Dope Man." –JF

★ **Straight Outta Compton / PRIORITY**   1988
A scalding, relentless, and always jolting look at life in the ghettos of South Central Los Angeles. You may not agree with their relish for violence or the rampant sexism, but this series of inflammatory and bruising vignettes is a visceral landmark on a par with the MC5 or the Sex Pistols. –JF

NAUGHTY BY NATURE

One of the finest new rap posses received some help from Queen Latifah on their 1991 debut and landed a huge hit with the naggingly incessant "O.P.P." –JF

○ **Naughty by Nature / TOMMY BOY**   1991
This leering trio's first single, "O.P.P.," dominated the airwaves in the fall of 1991 on the strength of its home-truth bedroom message and its butt-hugging beat. Fans of the single will find plenty more in NBN's rollicking debut album. –JF

NO FACE

A ribald, often hilarious rap duo. –DH

○ **Wake Your Daughter Up / CBS**   1990
A raunchy, funny and not-too-misogynist debut. –DH

OAKTOWN'S 3-5-7

A female rap posse produced by MC Hammer. –JF

○ **Wild & Loose / CAPITOL**   1989
Some good moments, but erratic and rambling. –RW

Fully Loaded / CAPITOL   1991
The message is clear; the rest is chaotic. –RW

ORIGINAL CONCEPT

In 1986 this Long Island 4 piece released "Knowledge Me"/"Can You Feel It," a classic underground single that elaborated on the Art of Noise dance hit "Close to the Edit." That song has been sampled to death in the 90s, but the band has released only one album, 1988's *Straight from the Basement of Kooley High.* –JF

○ **Straight from the Basement ... / DEF JAM**   1988
Straight from the Basement of Kooley High is an entertaining, mainly comedic and dance-oriented album from a collection of Long Island rappers and disc jockeys. This is rap to amuse rather than inform, with the exception of a couple of anti-racism and anti-violence tracts. –RW

PM DAWN

The Cordes brothers put the daisy-age principles of De La Soul into sharper focus. –JF

☆ **Of the Heart ... / ISLAND**   1991
Of the Heart, of the Soul and of the Cross: The Utopian Experience is a standout release, sandwiching psychedelic tinges, political/social discourse, and invigorating raps and production. Includes the hit "Set Adrift on Memory Bliss." –RW

POOR RIGHTEOUS TEACHERS

This Trenton, NJ, trio bring their Islam Five Percent theories to ripping, inventive riffs and samples. –JF

○ **Holy Intellect / PROFILE**   1990
A sharp session, squarely in an Afrocentric groove. –RW

Pure Poverty / PROFILE   1991
An even tougher, harder lyric thrust, but not quite as strong or varied musically. –RW

PROFESSOR GRIFF

Professor Griff (born Richard Griffin), was the "minister of information" for Public Enemy until June of 1989. He gave a controversial interview to the *Washington Post* that included comments deemed anti-Semitic by many. In the ensuing furor, Chuck D eventually fired him from Public Enemy and even briefly disbanded the group, only to re-form them. Griff formed his own band, the Asiastic Disciples. The results have been mixed, the slant predictably Islamic and Afrocentric. –RW

○ **Pawns in the Game / LUKE** 1990
A respectable showing from Griff in the face of negative expectations. –DH

PUBLIC ENEMY

Without question the most talked about rap group ever and among the most controversial and publicized bands of its day in any genre. Carlton Ridenhour, a Long Island college student and former radio disc jockey, has parlayed a booming voice, congenial yet forceful personality, and the articulation skills necessary to cogently present often inflammatory viewpoints into a hugely successful performance, marketing, and proselytizing empire. As Chuck D, Ridenhour is Public Enemy's theorist, lyricist, and head rapper. He's quoted constantly, seen on television around the world, and idolized by legions of Black and White youth. Through three albums, Public Enemy has served as the hip-hop vanguard, rapping about issues of race, rage, and inequality without lapsing (too often) into vicious sexism or homophobia, though they've been tagged with charges of anti-Semitism. They did eventually cut loose former minister of information Professor Griff, following a flap about comments he made in an interview, but the group has been able to ride out storms over lyric content and maintain their popularity without any stylistic compromise. Hank Shockless, Terminator X, Flavor Flav, and the rest of the Bomb Squad and crew also deserve praise, especially Shockless and Terminator X, whose dynamite production keeps things anchored through hardhitting, rapid-fire snippets and impressive studio techniques. Flav's absurdist raps and on-stage antics provide some welcome levity and comic relief. –RW

☆ **Yo! Bum Rush the Show / DEF JAM** 1987
When their debut was released in 1987, very few rap groups even approached Public Enemy's musical or political stance. Listening to the first album now, it's surprising how few of the songs are actually political — the sheer force of the sound fools the listener into thinking Chuck D is saying more than he actually is. Still, "Megablast," "Public Enemy No. 1," and "Miuzi Weighs a Ton" carry a small amount of political rhetoric. Much sparer than later releases, the album is carried over the top by Chuck D's bulldozer roar. –STE

★ **It Takes a Nation of Millions / DEF JAM** 1988
Arguably the best hip-hop album ever made, *It Takes a Nation of Millions to Hold Us Back* was a huge leap forward not only for Public Enemy, but for all of hip-hop. PE's signature sound — a barrage of found sounds, densely woven samples, and noisy tape loops, — was evident for the first time, courtesy of the Bomb Squad. Chuck D's lyrics, full of revolutionary rhetoric yet managing to avoid being hysterical, matched the aural onslaught. The group's political stance would be meaningless if the music didn't put it over the top throughout, and on "Black Steel in the Hour of Chaos," "Night of the Living Baseheads," "Rebel Without a Pause," "Dont Believe the Hype," and "Bring the Noise" in particular. There's no time for relaxation on the album and there's not a weak moment. A landmark recording. –STE

☆ **Fear of a Black Planet / DEF JAM** 1990
Nothing could quite match the pure, concentrated fury of *It Takes a Nation of Millions* ... and Public Enemy wisely didn't try to replicate it on their third album. *Fear of a Black Planet* is much more experimental than its predecessor, boasting an impressive array of textures from pseudo-reggae to crushing hip-hop. Chuck D's phrasing and vocalization have matured; on "Pollywanacraka" he even sounds seductive. The basic theme of *Fear of a Black Planet* is an exploration of American racism, concentrating on interracial relationships and White injustice. The relative lack of heavy beats and the wall of rage caused some to cry sellout, but *Fear* is hardly a sellout. –STE

☆ **Apocalypse 91 / DEF JAM** 1991
In response to the accusations that *Fear of a Black Planet* was

a sellout, Public Enemy lashed back with *Apocalypse 91 ... The Enemy Strikes Black*, an album of hard, noisy funk, much closer to *Millions* than to *Fear*. Having dealt with White racism on their previous album, Public Enemy turns their sights on correcting the problems in the Black community. On "1 Million Bottlebags," "Nighttrain," "Shut 'Em Down," and "By the Time I Get to Arizona," Chuck D offers some of his hardest-hitting rhymes matched to equally hard rhythm tracks. Public Enemy offers solutions on a few tracks, a rarity in the rap world. Although the Imperial Grand Ministers of Funk have replaced the Bomb Squad (who are listed as executive producers) as the main production team, Public Enemy's sound has not changed drastically. –STE

QUEEN LATIFAH

The New Jersey-born Queen Latifah (born Dana Owens, Latifah is an Arabic word meaning sensitive and delicate) has almost singlehandedly opened the doors for female rappers in the 90s, belying the sexism that permeates the male side of the genre. Her versatility suggests she'll be around for a long while. –JF

★ **All Hail the Queen / TOMMY BOY** 1989
Her genius is two-fold. She preaches Afrocentrism through clever, versatile, and educated raps, and they're coming from a clever, versatile, and educated feminist. The whole shebang is funky beyond belief. –JF

○ **Nature of a Sista' / TOMMY BOY** 1991
Her feminism becomes even more focused on this followup. With an equally diverse and creative set list, Latifah is becoming the female voice in a male-dominated genre. –JF

RAHEEM

Raheem, a Geto Boys cohort from Houston, works within the confines of that group's direction, meaning there's something on his two albums that should offend almost everybody. –JF

○ **The Invincible / RAP-A-LOT** 1992
Tough-talking, hard-edged gangsta rap from the man that some are already calling the new Scarface. –RW

THE REAL ROXANNE

Not to be confused with the other rap Roxannes, this New York spitfire released one near-perfect album in 1988 (produced by Jam Master Jay and Hitman Howie Tee) but hasn't been heard from since. Too bad. –JF

○ **The Real Roxanne / ELEKTRA-SELECT** 1988
With the aid of Jam Master Jay, Howie Tee, and Full Force, this Puerto Rican whipped up a stunning debut that highlights her inimitable skills as a rapper and lyricist, as well as her band's way with the funk. –JF

REDHEAD KINGPIN & FBI

This carrot-top b-boy has scored numerous hits with his teen-geared raps which are sometimes vulgar and sometimes amusing. "Pump It Hottee" is his finest moment. –JF

○ **A Shade of Red / VIRGIN** 1989
Entertaining rap that's icy and confrontational at times. –RW

RUN-D.M.C.

The most famous exports from Hollis, Queens, NY, expanded the boundaries of rap in ways Grandmaster Flash could only imagine. Through their early singles they built up a devoted street following and, without ever diluting their music, managed to bust their grooves into the White pop mainstream. They've lost their edge in the 90s but their influence is still felt. –JF

☆ **Run-D.M.C. / PROFILE** 1984
Their album debut features all the early singles, including "It's Like That" and "Rock Box," which stripped rap down to the bare essentials and introduced slews of innovations, lyrically and musically. –JF

☆ **Raising Hell / PROFILE**   1986
The collaboration with Steven Tyler and Joe Perry on "Walk This Way" made this the most successful rap album of its time, but the blistering title track, the pulsating "You Be Illin'," kept it in the Top Ten. A masterful and important release, not just for rap but for modern music. –JF

● **Greatest Hits / PROFILE**   1991
A few necessary items are missing, but this provides a great introduction to the most influential posse in rap. –JF

SALT-N-PEPA

Queens, NY, rappers Sandy Denton, Cheryl James, and DJ Dee Dee Roper have been prime female stars since 1986, when *Hot, Cool & Vicious*, and this single smash "Push It" made them stars. The duo has been able to shift gears at will, sometimes being naughty, other times nice, letting the beat propel their rhymes on one song, and then slicing their exchanges off it on the next. They've done numbers that were feminist in their viewpoints, then turned around and echoed the conventional wisdom regarding male/female relationships in another number. But contradictions aside, they're among the tighter, most accomplished rap acts active, and their records have held up well. –RW

Hot Cool & Vicious / NEXT PLATEAU   1986
One of the earliest female rap groups, they hit the big leagues with this debut that includes the pulsating "Push It" and the salacious "Tramp." –JF

★ **A Salt with A Deadly Pepa / NEXT PLATEAU**   1988
A concept album musically, if not lyrically. This one fleshes out one terrific single, "Shake Your Thing," with a sharpening of the trio's sensibilities and talents. –JF

○ **Blacks' Magic / NEXT PLATEAU**   1990
Another concept album. This time the themes celebrate Black education and awareness, with some concise feminism included. –JF

SCHOOLLY D

The Baltimore-based D established himself in the mid 80s as an early voice on gangsta-rap with the shoot-em-up thriller "PSK What Does That Mean." –JF

○ **The Adventures of Schoolly D / RYKODISC**   1987
This collects his early singles, cut before his bad-ass rep subverted whatever creativity he had left. –JF

ROXANNE SHANTE

Roxanne Shante (born Lolita Goodeh) was walking outside a New York housing project called the Queensbridge when she heard three men talking about how the trio U.T.F.O. had cancelled their appearance at a show they were promoting. Gooden offered to make a rap record that would get back at U.T.F.O., who'd previously recorded "Roxanne, Roxanne," a song about a woman too stuck up to notice them. The three, Tyrone Williams, disc jockey Mister Magic, and producer Marley Marl, took her up on the idea, with Marl producing "Roxanne's Revenge." The song was confrontational, sneering, boastful, and even borderline obscene, and it spawned 102 additional answer records. Since then, she's had two albums. The original "Roxanne's Revenge" was issued by Pop Art. Eventually U.T.F.O. threatened to sue Shante for using their B-side as the musical foundation. She settled with them and recut the song with a different, though related track. –RW

○ **Bad Sister / COLD CHILLIN'**   1989
Her debut album doesn't quite live up to the promise of her early singles, which can be found on various rap compilations. –DH

SHINEHEAD

The Jamaican-born, Bronx-reared Edmund Carl Aiken is a major proponent in the combining of hip-hop and electronic dancehall reggae. While that merger is his specialty,

Shinehead's three albums also show his adeptness at contemporary soul and crossover savvy (e.g., his hit cover of Cat Stevens's "Wild World"). –JF

○ **Unity / ELEKTRA**   1989
A promising, original album. –DH

The Real Rock / ELEKTRA   1990
Fine followup to *Unity*, with Shinehead sandwiching together melodies from classic R&B with rock and reggae inflections, and adding his own wild originals as well. –RW

SLICK RICK

Born in London and raised in the Bronx, Ricky Walters carved himself a niche with his debut album *The Great Adventures of Slick Rick*, with a sly, drawling delivery and detailed and inventive storybook raps. The onetime partner of Doug E. Fresh, Slick Rick eventually wound up in jail following a shooting incident, and has been charged with attempted murder. –JF & RW

☆ **The Great Adventures of Slick Rick / DEF JAM**   1988
Superb slices and excellent rap technique on this fast-paced release. –RW

The Ruler's Back / DEF JAM   1991
A fine followup from a troubled soul. –RW

SON OF BAZERK

A blazing 5-piece posse recalls the late-60s sound of James Brown and combines it with the dense, intense caterwaul of Public Enemy. –JF

☆ **Bazerk Bazerk Bazerk / MCA**   1991
By enlisting Public Enemy's Bomb Squad for the musical muscle, this six-piece aggregation concocted an abrasive (but rhythmic) debut that stands as one of the genre's finest. –JF

SPECIAL ED

In 1989 this 16-year-old released a technically dazzling debut album that highlighted his rapid-fire delivery and the ace production of hip-hop mastermind Howie "Hitman" Tee. –JF

Youngest in Charge / PROFILE   1989
The debut from this hugely confident teenage rapper with a very adult, mature rapping style and boastful, though effective lyrics and themes. –RW

○ **Legal / PROFILE**   1990
Release number two by Special Ed marks his turning 18 and has a more varied, less excessive, production approach. Ed also moves smoothly between topical and romantic material, as well as serious and satirical tones. –RW

STETSASONIC

This Brooklyn-based rap group established a unique sound by using real instruments in addition to the twin-turntable techniques of Prince Paul and Wise. Prince Paul has become a formidable producer, working with the likes of 3rd Bass, De La Soul, and Queen Latifah, among others. –JF

○ **In Full Gear / TOMMY BOY**   1988
They're not "the world's only hip-hop band" anymore, but this seven-piece group (real drums even!) paved the way. Their second disc documents their innovative best, culminating in the anthemic "Talkin' All That Jazz." –JF

THE SUGARHILL GANG

The Sugarhill Gang — Master Gee (born Guy O'Brien, 1963), Wonder Mike (born Michael Wright, 1958), and Big Bank Hank (born Henry Jackson, 1958) — were the first group to record rap music, releasing the popular single "Rapper's Delight" in 1979. –WR

☆ **Rapper's Delight / SUGARHILL**
The Sugarhill Gang's 1979 hit "Rapper's Delight" is arguably the first true rap song to gain widespread recognition and, as such, the progenitor of one of the major musical genres of the 80s. No wonder it doesn't sound dated yet. –WR

SWEET TEE

A female rapper whose work has benefited from good production help. –DH

○ **It's Tee Time / PROFILE**   1988
Contains the excellent single "I Got Da Feelin'." –DH

TERMINATOR X

Terminator X (born Richard Griffin), Public Enemy's DJ extraordinaire, strikes out on a solo project in 1991. –JF

○ **Terminator X & the Valley of the Jeep Beats / CBS**   1991
Public Enemy's turntable whiz takes center stage on a debut that spans the gamut of contemporary Black pop, from scalding hip-hop to reggae. –JF

3RD BASS

Along with the Beastie Boys, 3rd Bass stand as the rare White hip-hop act that's actually won respect and credibility among the rap hardcore. Pete Nice, one-time English major at Columbia whose radio program "Top of the Hip-hop" was unceremoniously canceled by the purportedly progressive WKCR-FM, teamed with MC Serch to offer devastating putdowns of the hip-hop lifestyle and worldview. They have since disbanded, but their two albums were definitive, if at times uneven. –RW

○ **The Cactus Album / DEF JAM**   1989
White rappers MC Serch and Prime Minister Pete Nice wash out the taste of the Beastie Boys with their weird sense of humor, a commendable awareness, and some perspicacious samples. –JF

Derelicts of Dialect / DEF JAM   1991
After countless false starts and an EP/remix filler, 3rd Bass finally issued their second album. It was an impressive statement, with a devastating attack on Vanilla Ice via the cut "Pop Goes the Weasel." –RW

TONE-LOC

Tone-Loc (born Tony Smith) soared from obscurity into pop stardom in 1989 when his hoarse voice and unmistakable delivery made the song "Wild Thing" (using a sample from Van Halen's "Jamie's Cryin'") a massive hit. The song was cowritten by Marvin Young, better known as Young MC, as was the second single smash "Funky Cold Medina." The album *Loc-ed After Dark* became the second rap release to top the pop charts. –DH

○ **Loc-ed After Dark / DELICIOUS VINYL**   1988
An engaging debut that contains both "Wild Thing" and "Funky Cold Medina" –DH

TOO SHORT

Oakland rapper Todd Shaw has become a huge star without getting any pop airplay or crossover support. He's mined the mack (pimp) routine effectively, turning out albums routinely loaded with plenty of X-rated sexual escapades and commentary or variations on a day in the life of a player and pimp. He did score one classic sociopolitical number, his take on "The Ghetto," and has also done a good anti-censorship bit with Ice Cube on "Ain't Nothin' but a Word to Me." –RW

Born to Mack / JIVE   1988
A breakout release. –RW

Life Is ... Too Short / JIVE   1988
Essential, bawdy, and often offensive and troubling. –RW

○ **Short Dog's in the House / JIVE**   1990
A tremendous combination of outrage, anger, and morbid outlook. –RW

A TRIBE CALLED QUEST

The junior part of the Native Tongues — the prolific Afrocentric family from New York that also includes The Jungle Brothers and De La Soul — this foursome displayed intriguing subject variety on their debut, covering everything from social ills to the adventures of a shaggy dog and problems with lice. Their second effort, *The Low End Theory*, reflected through arrangements and sensibility the influence of an emerging jazz/rap stylistic coalition, and yielded a huge hit in "Scenario." –RW

○ **People's Instinctive Travels ... / JIVE**   1990
People's Instinctive Travels and the Paths of Rhythm is a brilliant concept with jazzy edges and tense, biting narratives. It's a visionary release blending the improvisatory force of jazz with the technological wizardry and verbal inventiveness of hip-hop. –RW

★ **The Low End Theory / JIVE**   1991
Excellent raps and production. –RW

TRUE MATHEMATICS

A mysterious rap act generally thought to be a collaboration between producers Hank Shockless and Carl Ryder, with vocals generally credited to Eric Sadler. –JF

☆ **Greatest Hits / ELEKTRA-SELECT**   1988
This overlooked rap masterpiece is a collaboration between Hank Shockless (Public Enemy), Eric Sadler, Carl Ryder, and someone credited as K. Houston. It leaps from pulsating, understated anthems ("For the Money") up to several Black-frat-party romps. –JF

2 LIVE CREW

This Florida rap band was organized, supervised, and conceived by Luther Campbell, a promoter, record label owner, and rapper, as an updated version of oldtime X-rated party performers. Campbell's production consists of heavy doses of booming synthesized bass, scratching effects, samples, and explicit sex raps and leers. From their beginnings in 1986, the notoriety of Campbell and the group grew in direct proportion to the lewdness of the material. As their songs attained more national prominence, Campbell has become part of a national controversy involving censorship and lyrics. He's issued two solo records. –RW

2 Live Crew Is What We Are / ATLANTIC   1986
The record that launched the whole phenomenon. If the puerile language and vulgarity had been allowed to run its course without censorship attempts, this lunacy might have ended right here. The production does provide good examples of Miami "bass" music. –RW

Move Somthin' / ATLANTIC   1987
Luther Campbell hits on the ingenious idea of issuing clean and dirty versions simultaneously in an ill-fated attempt to take censorship heat off. The clean version lacks guts; the dirty version lacks taste. –RW

○ **As Nasty As They Wanna Be / ATLANTIC**   1989
The one that caused all the fuss. It's good for a politically incorrect laugh. –DH

Banned in the USA / ATLANTIC   1990
This offers an interesting, if somewhat perverse version of Springsteen's "Born in the USA" as the title track and underlying theme. The rest is an erratic, meandering blend of X-rated sexual comments and quasi-political rhetoric. –RW

U.T.F.O.

Doctor Ice, the Kangol Kid, and the Educated Rapper (later joined by Mix-Master Ice); the Brooklyn group Untouchable Force Organization (U.T.F.O.) dreamed up a tune about a gorgeous woman oblivious to their charms and appeals. "Roxanne, Roxanne" dominated the airwaves for much of 1984 and 1985, yielding eventually over 100 answer versions. Their first albums included the hit single plus "Roxanne Part 2" and "The Real Roxanne." The group's popularity and influence waned as the Roxanne fad peaked, and subsequent releases had limited appeal. –RW

○ **Lethal / ELEKTRA**   1987
The title song is a collaboration with the speed-metal band Anthrax. –DH

URBAN DANCE SQUAD

An unlikely Dutch rock/rap aggregation, they won well-deserved raves for their debut album, *Mental Floss for the Globe*. –DH

○ **Mental Floss For The Globe / ARISTA** 1990
A heady brew of dense hip-hop, featuring the great hit single "Deeper Shade of Soul." –DH

VANILLA ICE

This White 1990 pop/rap sensation enjoyed his "15 minutes of fame" with "Ice, Ice Baby" (using a riff from the David Bowie/Queen song "Under Pressure"). –ED

○ **To the Extreme / CAPITOL** 1990
Contains the hit "Ice, Ice Baby." –DH

WHODINI

The influential Brooklyn, NY, rap group Whodini was one of the better groups to merge straight R&B with pop-fueled hip-hop. Whodini started recording in 1983 and broke up in 1988, scoring hits with "Magic's Wand" and "Freaks Come out at Night." –JF

Whodini / JIVE 1983
More singers than straight rappers, Jali Hutchins and Ecstasty made a successful conversion to hip-hop, scoring two hits on their debut with "Rap Attack" and "The Haunted House of Funk," a reworking of "The Monster Mash." –RW

○ **Escape / JIVE** 1984
Their best release, containing "Friends," "Freaks Come out at Night," and "Big Mouth." Memorable tunes and state-of-the-art (for that time) production. –RW

★ **Greatest Hits / JIVE** 1990
A worthwhile compilation that shows what all the fuss was about regarding this unit in the early 80s. –RW

X-CLAN

The most unflinching and militant of Afrocentric funkmeisters. –JF

○ **To the East, Blackwards / 4TH & WAY** 1990
An uncompromising Islamic session with frequently powerful raps. –RW

X Odus / POLYDOR 1992
Even more Afrocentric and Islamic-oriented than their previous effort, and better produced. –RW

YO-YO

Yolanda Whitaker has been among the most sophisticated and unpredictable female rappers around. She doesn't take an overtly feminist tack but urges young women to show sexual restraint and use their minds as well as their bodies. She's released two records as a leader. –RW

○ **Make Way for the Motherlode / ATLANTIC** 1991
Intelligent, forceful, and affirmative rap from a woman whose cadence, tone, and delivery are as hard as any man on either coast and anywhere in-between. –RW

YOUNG MC

Although his good looks and pop appeal would suggest he's beaten LL Cool J to the crossover punch, MC (Marvin) Young has pumped his own personality into some of rap's greatest across-the-board hits. "Bust a Move" and "Principal's Office," among others, hit harder than the similar work of Jazzy Jeff and the Fresh Prince, and the jokes last longer than the ones you'll find in the Fat Boys catalog. He also wrote Tone-Loc's smash single, "Funky Cold Medina" and cowrote "Wild Thing." –JF

○ **Stone Cold Rhymin' / POLYGRAM** 1989
Contains "Bust a Move" and "Principal's Office." –DH

RAP COLLECTIONS

○ **Rap's Greatest Hits - Vols. 1-3 / PRIORITY**
Well-known commonplace pop and crossover tunes. –RW
Bass That Ate Miami / PANDISC 1991
A collection spotlighting various artists performing in the Miami bottom-heavy bass hip-hop style. –RW

☆ **Bass Waves - Vol. 3 / ATLANTIC**
Bass Waves - Vol. 3: Rap's Biggest Hits of the 90s is a good collection of recent rap hits. –RW
Battle of the Boom / JAM CITY
A loose aggregation of contemporary rap/bass tunes. –RW
Best of B-More Nation / HOT PROD.
Routine rap filler. –RW

○ **Compton Compilation / KRU CUT**
An overview of the school from whence came N.W.A., Ice Cube, and P & 91. –RW
Cut-It-Up - Def Bass Jams / MAS-JAM
A collection of extended grooves and bass cuts, more of interest to rap completists. –RW

○ **Def Jam Classics - Vol. 1 / CBS**
A useful overview of the seminal rap label, including their best artists and some sumptuous rarities. –JF

○ **Detroit's Most Wanted - Tricks of the Trades / BRYANT**
A Midwest spin on the gangsta equation. –RW

☆ **East vs. West - Rap Battle Royale / KTEL-QWIL**
An entertaining contrast between hard-edged pop and gangsta crew: Run-D.M.C., Kool Moe, Dee, MC Lyte, and others. –RW

○ **Explicit Rap / PRIORITY** 1990
A caustic compilation directed to the PMRC and delivered by the likes of Ice Cube, 2 Live Crew, and the Geto Boys. –JF

○ **First Priority Music Family / ATLANTIC**
First Priority Music Family - Basement Flavor is a sampler aimed at new rap listeners. –RW

☆ **Fresh Rap / KTEL-QWIL**
This budget compliation does have a representative crop of recent hits and typical K-Tel sound. –RW

○ **Gangsta Rap / PRIORITY**
This sampler introduces proponents of urban fantasies and raw street chants. –RW

☆ **Great Hits of the Street / PRIORITY**
Great Hits of the Street - Rappin' & Scratchin' is a better-than-usual collection of uncut, non-pop rap. –RW

☆ **Greg Mack Compilation / MOTOWN**
Raps assembled by one-time major rap disc jockey Mack; *Greg Mack Compilation - What Does it All Mean?* gives a comprehensive portrait of songs he once aired. –RW

☆ **Hip Hop Heritage / JIVE** 1987
Pioneering cuts from Grandmaster Flash, Spoonie Gee, and others. –RW

☆ **Hip-Hop Greats: Classic Raps / RHINO**
A decent overview of rap's salad days, including the Sugarhill Gang's "Rapper's Delight," Grandmaster Flash's best singles ("White Lines," "The Message"), plus "Jam on It" from Newcleus. A nice place to start your education. –JF

○ **Kings of Rap / PRIORITY**
This entertaining anthology is loaded down with easily obtainable cuts. –RW

☆ **Miami Bass Express / PANDISC** 1986
The one to grab for an adequate portrait of bass music. –RW

☆ **Mixmasters / MCA**
A good collection of tricky, intricate arrangements. –RW

○ **Mr. Magic's Rap Attack / PROFILE**
Great series. Chronicles what is essentially a single genre. –DH
Power Rap / PRIORITY
Standard rap cuts with little unavailable elsewhere. –RW

○ **Pump That Bass / HOT PRODUCTIONS**
This has hearty sound and production. −RW

○ **Queens of Rap / PRIORITY**
The women get the spotlight. −RW

R-Rated Rap / PRIORITY
A cross-section of cuts, heavy on the four-letter words. −RW

☆ **Rap Beginnings - Vols. 1 & 2 / KTEL-QWIL**
Sound notwithstanding, these are a good look at early and tangential rap on a budget compilation. −RW

○ **Rap Miami Style / PANDISC**
Bass and Florida influences integrated into hip-hop. −RW

○ **Rap the Beat / PRIORITY**
A collection of pretty familiar rap cuts. −RW

☆ **Rap's Biggest Hits / KTEL-QWIL**   1990
Crossover rap by Tone-Loc, Run D.M.C., and others. Perfect for the casual listener. −RW

☆ **Rap's New Generation / PROFILE**
A good sampler showcasing up-and-coming stars. −RW

☆ **Rap's Next Generation - Hard As Hell / PROFILE**
Crisp, often compelling cuts from new-school rappers. −RW

☆ **Rapmasters - Vols. 1-15 / PRIORITY**
An ambitious and exhaustive historical survey of rap from the early days up to yesterday. The categorical divisions of each volume don't mean much, and each one contains at least four songs that are essential to any rap collection. Mix 'em, match

'em, or buy them all. *Vol. 1: The Best of the Jam, Vol. 2: The Best of the Rhyme, Vol. 3: The Best of the Cut, Vol. 4: The Best of Hip-Hop, Vol. 5: The Best of the Word, Vol. 6: The Best of the Beat, Vol. 7: The Best of the Laughs, Vol. 8: The Best of the Street, Vol. 9: The Best of the Hardcore, Vol. 10: The Best of Scratchin', Vol. 11: The Best of Hard Rockin' Rap, Vol. 12: The Best of the Mix, Vol. 13: The Best of the Bass, Vol. 14: The Best of the Hype,* and *Vol. 15: The Best of the Bad.* −JF

○ **Raps Street / PAR**
Recent hits from current and rising stars. −RW

○ **Straight from the Hood / PRIORITY**   1991
Street rap available with and without obscenities. −RW

☆ **This Is Bass / HOT PRODUCTIONS**
A good introduction to bottom-heavy bass music. −RW

☆ **This is Bass - Vol. 2 / HOT PRODUCTIONS**
A thorough followup to the initial volume. −RW

☆ **Tommy Boy's Greatest Beats / TOMMY BOY**
An excellent overview of 80s-era hits from the pioneering hip-hop label. Includes the finest work of Arthur Baker, Afrika Bambaataa, and many others. −JF

☆ **2 Nasty 4 Radio / WARNER**
A worthwhile collection of naughty and street raps that were left off the airwaves due to language. Solid content. −RW

Yo! MTV Raps! - Vol. 2 / JIVE   1991
Second collection of cuts culled from the television show. −RW

BLUES

To paraphrase the incomparable Delta blues performer Robert Johnson, "The blues is a low-down aching chill; if you ain't never had 'em, I hope you never will."

Blues is the most emotional, gut-wrenching style of 20th-century American secular music. It evolved in the deep South shortly before the turn of the century from the spirituals, work songs, and country-dance instrumentals sung or performed by African-Americans. This music has long exhibited strong regional as well as racial characteristics. Consider, for example, the light, easily understood ragtime-influenced music of Blind Boy Fuller in contrast to Texas Alexander's moaning, which sounds close to an old field holler. But not all blues are sorrowful and low-down — witness the "hokum" blues of Tampa Red and Georgia Tom, Frankie Jaxon, and others. They are laced with clever double-entendre as well as such salacious food metaphors as "hot nuts" and "jelly roll."

The blues have always kept up-to-date. The classic Chicago blues sound of Muddy Waters, Howlin' Wolf, and Little Walter is the perfect example of this. It is basically the Mississippi Delta blues sound, amplified and adapted for a Northern audience of southside Chicago immigrants who themselves had moved up from the mid South. When Charlie Christian, T-Bone Walker, and a handful of others began experimenting with electric guitars in the mid to late 30s, many of the popular blues singers like Big Bill Broonzy were right with them. Ultimately, this resulted in the commercial success of B. B. King and other similar urban blues legends, beginning in the early 50s.

In the 90s it is perfectly clear that this music and its 12-bar musical form have influenced not only most of our contemporary popular music but many musicians from outside the United States. This is particularly true in Europe and Great Britain, where rock stars ranging from Eric Clapton to U2 have long acknowledged their debt to the blues. In the middle of this latest blues boom, which has been partially fueled by the new wave of CDs, we are fortunate to have an immense range of blues. In 1968 I never thought I'd live to see a convenient way to have all of Sleepy John Estes's Victor and Decca 78s or a comprehensive retrospective of the Trumpet and Chess selections of Sonny Boy Williamson #2. With so much wonderful blues material around, the Hokum Boys summed it up well: "You can't get enough of that."

— Kip Lornell

JOHNNY ADAMS   b 1932

Electric R&B/soul blues. Though a lifelong New Orleans resident and a renowned R&B singer for more than 30 years, Adams is not a New Orleans R&B stylist in the traditional sense but more a modern soul singer — "perhaps America's greatest soul singer," in fact, according to Crescent City music historian Jeff Hannusch. In New Orleans, "Johnny is known as "The Tan Canary," ... esteemed by musicians for his unerring ear, taste, and imagination, loved by club and concert audiences for his always engaging performances." Adams sang in gospel quartets before cutting his first R&B record in 1959 (produced by Dr. John) and had a national Top Ten hit with "Reconsider Me" (SSS International) in 1969. His recent albums for Rounder have won him new acclaim among contemporary blues audiences. —JON

Heart & Soul / SSS INT   1970
Country soul. Contains all his hits from 1962-1968. Produced by Shelby Singleton. —RP

Stand by Me / CHELSEA   1976
A relaxed, live-in-the-studio recording of standards. —RP

○ **After Dark / ROUNDER**   1984
The first and best album of Adams's revival. —KL

LUTHER ALLISON   b 1939

Modern electric blues. Allison emerged as the fresh new face on the Chicago blues scene with his debut album in 1969 (Delmark) and soon put other notches on his guitar when he became the only outright blues artist on the Motown (Gordy) roster. A talented and expressive singer and guitarist from what has become known as the post-B. B. King school, Allison has veered between straight West Side blues, soul, and high-intensity blues/rock. His recordings range from raw live albums of blues standards to crossover-oriented European studio productions. —JON

Love Me Mama / DELMARK   1969
The uneven debut by this West Side Chicago guitarist. —BD

Luther's Blues / GORDY   1974
The most representative album showcasing his modern Chicago blues approach. —BD

○ **Serious / BLIND PIG**   1987
This album highlights Allison's contemporary rock-tinged approach. —BD

BILLY BOY ARNOLD   b 1935

Electric Chicago blues. Arnold is one of the last surviving original postwar Chicago bluesmen, and a great one at that. A major disciple of John Lee "Sonny Boy" Williamson, Arnold honed his craft on the streets of the Windy City, most often working with a young Bo Diddley. His best works are enlivened with witty, urbane lyrics and powerful harmonica playing, several of them going on to become certified classics of the idiom. —CK

○ **Crying and Pleading / CHARLY**
Collection of Billy Boy's complete Vee Jay output. Chicago blues at its best. Includes "I Wish You Would," "I Was Fooled," and the original "I Ain't Got You," later covered by the Yardbirds. (Import) —CK

KOKOMO ARNOLD   1901-1968

Delta blues, country blues. A popular recording artist of the 30s, James "Kokomo" Arnold was a left-handed bottleneck guitarist who usually recorded solo, occasionally with piano accompaniment. His first Chicago session (Decca, 1934) produced the widely covered "Milk Cow Blues" and "Old Original Kokomo Blues" (the model for Robert Johnson's "Sweet Home Chicago"), as well as the first appearance on record of the classic "I believe I'll dust my broom" line (in "Sagefield Woman Blues"). Critic Hugues Panassi wrote, "Arnold is one of the greatest blues singers ever recorded." Arnold continued to play for a few years in Chicago after his last session (1938) but later took a job in a steel mill, disillusioned with the music business. Interviewed by two Frenchmen in 1959, Arnold said, "I'm finished with music and that mad way of life." –JON

○ **Kokomo Arnold/Peetie Wheatstraw / BLUES CLASSICS**
Eight tracks each by Kokomo Arnold and Peetie Wheatstraw. Includes "Milk Cow Blues." –JME

ETTA BAKER   b 1913

Acoustic country blues. Etta Baker's first recordings appeared on a 1956 set called *Instrumental Music of the Southern Appalachians,* but only in recent years has her beautiful finger-picked acoustic blues been presented onstage and once again on record. Her traditional instrumental performances draw on old folk tunes such as "John Henry" and "Lost John" as well as on early blues, breakdowns, rags, and spirituals. *Blues & Rhythm's* Robert Tilling noted that most of her present-day repertoire is so timeless it "could have been recorded 80 years ago." –JON

○ **One-Dime Blues / ROUNDER**   1991
Gentle finger-picked Piedmont blues à la Libba Cotten. –MH

LONG JOHN BALDRY

Electric British blues. John was making music back in the 50s in England. He teamed up with the likes of Ramblin' Jack Elliott, Memphis Slim, Jack Dupree, and others. He was one of the people who brought the folk and blues artists together and then steered them toward rock music. –CR

○ **It Still Ain't Easy / STONY PLAIN**   1991
Baldry's deep, rough-edged vocals have not changed over the years. The band is tight, with Mike Kalanj's Hammond B-3 and Bill Rogers's sax standing out. There are no flaws on this one, just great music. –CR

BARBECUE BOB   1902-1931

Acoustic country blues. Barbecue Bob may be a familiar name to some blues fans today because at least two young White musicians have adopted the name, but back in the 20s the original Barbecue Bob (Robert Hicks) was a big name on the Black "race records" scene. Recording for Columbia from 1927 to 1930, Hicks was the most popular of the Atlanta blues guitarists of his time, and Columbia's best-selling bluesman. But Barbecue Bob died of pneumonia at the age of 29, and some of his contemporaries like Blind Willie McTell are much better known to modern-day audiences. Most of Bob's recordings were solo outings featuring rhythmic 12-string bottleneck-guitar work and original lyrical themes. In historian Stephen Calt's opinion, "For sheer musical verve and punch, Hicks easily rivals Charley Patton." –JON

Brownskin Gal / AGRAM
A boxed import set with a variety of blues, hokum, and comedy routines. Includes an 80-page bio and transcription book. Unfortunately, this compilation is marred by weak sound quality. –BLP

○ **Chocolate to the Bone / MAMLISH**
Fourteen selections from popular 20s Atlanta 12-string slide artist Robert Hicks, aka Barbecue Bob. A fine American collection, with good sound quality. –BLP

ROOSEVELT "BOOBA" BARNES   b 1936

Modern electric blues. Barnes and his Playboys band rocked the hardest of all the juke-joint combos in the Mississippi delta during the 80s, and after the release of his debut album (*The Heartbroken Man,* 1990), "Booba" took his act and his band north to Chicago, following the trail of his idols Howlin' Wolf and Little Milton. In a *Guitar Player* review, Jas Obrecht called Barnes "a wonderfully idiosyncratic guitar player and an extraordinary vocalist by any standard." –JON

○ **The Heartbroken Man / ROOSTER BLUES**   1990
No-frills recording of hair-raising modern Delta blues. –JO

CAREY BELL   b 1936

Electric Chicago blues. One of the reigning blues harp virtuosos, Bell was a protégé of Big Walter Horton and a former sideman with Muddy Waters and Willie Dixon. Head of one of the most talented blues families, Carey has often worked with his sons, including Lurrie (guitar) and Steve (harmonica), his adopted stepfather Lovie Lee (piano), and occasionally with famous cousins such as guitarist Eddy Clearwater. Bell first recorded as a bassist on a live Robert Nighthawk album in 1964. He cut his first album as a singer/harmonica player for Delmark in 1969. –JON

Carey Bell's Blues Harp / DELMARK   1969
An early effort by the underrated Chicago harp master. –BD

Son of a Gun / ROOSTER BLUES   1984
The raucous pairing of this harpist and his guitarist son Lurrie creates some sparks. –BD

○ **Mellow Down Easy / BLIND PIG**   1991
Bell's full-toned harp is showcased in a marvelous update of the original 50s Chicago sound. –BD

BIG MAYBELLE   1924-1972

Electric jump blues. Big Maybelle lived up to her billing in more ways than one. Her thundering voice was every bit as large as her physique, and she was one of R&B's leading belters during the mid 50s. After gaining early professional experience with the Sweethearts of Rhythm and Tiny Bradshaw's outfit, Maybelle Smith hooked up with producer Fred Mendelsohn, who negotiated her a contract with Columbia's R&B subsidiary Okeh. In 1953, she notched a trio of Top Ten R&B hits: "Gabbin' Blues," "Way Back Home," and "My Country Man." But her best-known Okeh release never made the charts, at least for her. Two full years before "Killer" Jerry Lee Lewis set the world on fire with his seismic rendition, Big Maybelle cut the first waxing of "Whole Lotta Shakin' Goin' On" with Leroy Kirkland's band in New York. Her version was much closer to rockabilly pianist and cowriter Roy Hall's original vision of the tune than the subsequent megahit reading by the Killer. Maybelle's jumping appearance in *Jazz on a Summer's Day,* the acclaimed documentary of the 1958 Newport Jazz Festival, affords us rare film footage of Maybelle's commanding stage presence. Heroin was allegedly a recurring problem for Maybelle. Although she later mounted a mini-comeback with a cover of Question Mark & the Mysterians' "96 Tears," she died much too soon in 1972. –BD

Blues, Candy & Big Maybelle / SAVOY   1958
Sixteen tracks of late 50s R&B from the Savoy label. Mickey Baker on guitar. –BD

Saga of the Good Life & Hard Times / ROJAC   1969
A mix of soul and blues from her last sessions, sung with despair. –RP

○ **The Okeh Sessions / EPIC**   1983
A mix of R&B and blues on 22 tracks, 1952-1955. With Sam "The Man" Taylor (ts) and Mickey Baker (g). –RP

BIG TWIST & THE MELLOW FELLOWS   1937-1990

Electric R&B/soul blues. Larry "Big Twist" Nolan & the Mellow Fellows developed their brassy, soul-influenced act in Southern Illinois and transported it to Chicago, where North Side and suburban White audiences of the 80s embraced their

Blues Styles

CLASSIC FEMALE BLUES — The earliest recorded form of the blues. This genre features female vocalists singing material with close connections to pop music of the period (mid 20s to early 30s) and primarily jazz backings. Main proponents: Mamie Smith, Bessie Smith, Ma Rainey, Lucille Bogan, and Victoria Spivey.

DELTA BLUES — Also known as Mississippi blues, this is the earliest guitar-dominated music to make it onto record. Consisting of performers working primarily in a solo, self-accompanied context, it also embraces the now-familiar string-band/small-combo format, both precursors to the modern-day blues band. Main proponents: Charlie Patton, Robert Johnson, and Son House.

COUNTRY-BLUES — A term that delineates the depth and breadth of the first flowering of guitar-driven blues, embracing all regional styles and variations (Piedmont, Atlanta, early Chicago, ragtime, folk, songster, etc.). Primarily acoustic guitarists, some country-blues performers later switched to electric guitars without changing their style. Major proponents: Henry Thomas, Skip James, Barbecue Bob, Leadbelly, Mississippi John Hurt, Lonnie Johnson, Blind Blake, and Tommy Johnson.

MEMPHIS BLUES — A strain of country-blues all its own, the Memphis style gives us the rise of two distinct forms, the jug band (humorous, jazz-style blues played on homemade instruments) and the beginnings of assigning parts to guitarists for solo (lead) and rhythm, a tradition that is now part-and-parcel of all modern-day blues bands. The later, post-WWII electric version of this genre featured explosive guitar work, thunderous drumming, and declamatory vocals. Main proponents: Cannon's Jug Stompers, Furry Lewis, Memphis Minnie, and the early recordings of B. B. King and Howlin' Wolf.

TEXAS BLUES — A subgenre earmarked by a more relaxed, swinging feel than other styles of blues. The earlier, acoustic version embraced both songster and country-blues traditions, while the post-war electric style featured jazzy, single-string soloing over predominantly horn-driven backing. Main proponents: Blind Lemon Jefferson, Lightnin' Hopkins, Clarence "Gatemouth" Brown, and T-Bone Walker.

CHICAGO BLUES — Delta blues fully amplified and put into a small-band context. Later permutations of the style took their cue from the lead guitar work of B. B. King and T-Bone Walker. Main proponents: Muddy Waters, Howlin' Wolf, Little Walter, Big Walter Horton, Jimmy Rogers, Elmore James, Jimmy Reed, Otis Rush, Magic Sam, and Buddy Guy.

JUMP BLUES — Uptempo, jazz-tinged blues, usually featuring a vocalist in front of a large, horn-driven orchestra with less reliance on guitar work than other styles. Main proponents: Amos Milburn, Johnny Otis, Roy Brown, Wynonie Harris, and Big Joe Turner.

NEW ORLEANS BLUES — Primarily (but not exclusively) piano- and horn-driven, this genre strain is enlivened by Caribbean rhythms, party atmosphere, and the "second-line" strut of the Dixieland music so indigenous to the area. Main proponents: Professor Longhair, Guitar Slim, and Snooks Eaglin.

WEST COAST BLUES — More piano-based and jazz-influenced than anything else, the West Coast style (California in particular) also embraces post-war Texas guitar expatriates and jump-blues practitioners. Main proponents: Charles Brown, Pee Wee Crayton, Lowell Fulson, and Percy Mayfield.

PIANO BLUES — A genre that runs through the entire history of the music itself, this embraces everything from ragtime, barrelhouse, boogie-woogie, and smooth West Coast jazz stylings to the hard-rocking rhythms of Chicago blues. Main proponents: Big Maceo Merriweather, Leroy Carr, Sunnyland Slim, Roosevelt Sykes, Albert Ammons, and Otis Spann.

LOUISIANA BLUES — A looser, more laidback and percussive version of the Jimmy Reed side of the Chicago style. Production techniques on most of the recordings utilize massive amounts of echo, giving the performances a "doomy" sound and feel. Main proponents: Slim Harpo, Lightnin' Slim, and Lazy Lester.

R&B/SOUL BLUES — A more modern form, this fuses elements of Black popular music (the rhythm and blues strain of the 50s and the Southern soul style of the mid 60s) to a wholly urban blues amalgam of its own.

MODERN ACOUSTIC BLUES — Newer artists reviving the older, more country-derived styles of blues. Main proponents: John Hammond, Rory Block, John Cephas, Taj Mahal, and the earlier recordings of Bonnie Raitt.

MODERN ELECTRIC BLUES — An eclectic mixture, this genre replicates older styles of urban blues while simultaneously recasting them in contemporary fashion. Main proponents: Stevie Ray Vaughan, the Fabulous Thunderbirds, Robert Cray, and Roomful of Blues.

BRITISH BLUES — More than a mere geographical distinction, the British style pays strict adherence to replicating American blues genres, with an admiration for its originators bordering on reverence. Main proponents: Alexis Korner, John Mayall, and the early recordings of Fleetwood Mac and the Rolling Stones.

— Cub Koda

---

style of R&B, a genre generally more popular with the Black audiences who support the music's originators like Little Milton and Bobby Bland. Big Twist was one of the first Chicago acts to do a blues video (*300 Pounds of Joy*, Alligator). The Mellow Fellows, now billed as the Chicago Rhythm & Blues Kings, have continued to tour and record since Nolan's death in 1990. –JON

Big Twist & the Mellow Fellows / FLYING FISH
This debut set proved accessible to even casual blues fans. –BD

○ **Playing for Keeps / ALLIGATOR**
Slickly produced soul-blues from this Chicago outfit. –BD

One Track Mind / FLYING FISH   1982
Very slick soul/blues/rock hybrid, with Twist's easygoing vocals as the prominent feature. –BD

Live from Chicago / ALLIGATOR   1987
An accurate live presentation of charismatic vocalist Twist and his polished group. –BD

SCRAPPER BLACKWELL   1903-1962

Acoustic Chicago blues. Best known for his duets with blues kingpin Leroy Carr, Blackwell was an exceptional instrumentalist who recorded several sessions on his own (usually unaccompanied) in 1928-1935 and again in 1958-1961. Blackwell's melodic single-note guitar work presaged much of the blues that was to follow. He had begun to record again, his talent reportedly undiminished, when he was shot to death in early 1962 in an Indianapolis alley. –JON

○ **Virtuoso Guitar 1925-1934 / YAZOO**
This early and influential guitarist is known for his work with his partner, pianist/singer Leroy Carr, two examples of which are found here among a collection of solo performances. His high-note, "string-snapping" solo style, developed to be heard over Carr's rolling piano, is echoed in the work of Johnny "Guitar" Watson, among others. –GB

African Roots

| Work Songs, Field Hollers | Church & Gospel Music
Standard Quartette (rec. 1894)
Dinwiddie Colored Quartet (rec. 1902)
Apollo Male Quartette (rec. 1912) | Black Entertainment
Minstrel, Ragtime, String Bands | Medicine Shows
Papa Charlie Jackson — Pink Anderson
Daddy Stovepipe |

Early Blues Recorders (ca. 1920)
● W. C. Handy (1873-1958) — Perry Bradford (1893-1970)
Clarence Williams (1898-1965)

Songsters
● Henry Thomas (1874-1950) — Frank Stokes (1888-1955)
Peg Leg Howell (1888-1966) — ● Leadbelly (1889-1949)
● Mance Lipscomb (1895-1976) — ● Mississippi John Hurt (1893-1966)

Classic Female Blues Singers
Mamie Smith (1883-1946) — ● Ma Rainey (1886-1939)
●Bessie Smith (1894-1937) — Lucille Bogan (1897-1948)
Sara Martin (1884-1955) — Clara Smith (1894-1935)
Ida Cox (1896-1967) — Sippie Wallace (1898-1986)
Victoria Spivey (1906-1976) — Chippie Hill (1905-1950)

Postwar Female Blues
Big Maybelle (1924-1972) — Big Mama Thornton (1926-1984   )
Little Esther Phillips (1935)

Religious Music That Influenced Blues
● Blind Willie Johnson (1900-1947)

Piano Blues

Origins – 1890s — Barrelhouses, Railroad & Lumber Camps

● Clarence "Pine Top" Smith (1904-1929)
Cow Cow Davenport (1894-1955) — George Thomas
Henry Townsend (1929-1971) — ● Roosevelt Sykes (1906-1983)
Albert Ammons (1907-1949) — Meade "Lux" Lewis (1905-1964)
●Big Maceo (1905-1953) — ● Sunnyland Slim (1907)
Peetie Wheatstraw (1902-1941) — Leroy Carr (1905-1935)
Johnnie Jones (1949-1964) — ● Otis Spann (1930-1970)
Pinetop Perkins (1913)

Major Influences
● Lonnie Johnson (1889-1970)
● Blind Lemon Jefferson (1897-1929)

Mississippi Blues

Delta-Style Blues
Charley Patton (1887-1934) — Willie Brown (1900-1952)
● Son House (1902-1971) — ● Robert Johnson (1911-1938)
●Fred McDowell (1904-1972) — Bukka White (1906-1977)
Big Joe Williams (1903-1982) — Arthur Crudup (1905-1974)
Tommy McClennan (1908-ca. 1962)
John Lee Hooker (1917)

Jackson-Style Blues
Rubin Lacy (1901-1972) — Ishmon Bracey (1901-1970)
Charles McCoy (1909-1950) — Tommy Johnson (1896-1956)

Bentonia-Blues
Henry Stuckey (1897-1966) — ● Skip James (1902-1969)
Jack Owens (1904)

Regional Down-Home Blues

Atlanta
● Barbecue Bob (Robert Hicks) (1902-1931)
Blind Willie McTell (1901-1959) — ●Curley Weaver (1906-1962)
Buddy Moss (1906)

Piedmont School
● Blind Blake (1890-1933) — Blind Boy Fuller (1908-1941)
● Sonny Terry (1911-1984) — ● Brownie McGhee (1915)
● Rev. Gary Davis (1896-1972)

Tennessee

Memphis Jug Bands
● Gus Cannon's (1885-1979) Jug Stompers — ● Memphis Jug Band
Will Shade (1898-1966) — ● Noah Lewis (1895-1961)

Memphis
Furry Lewis (1893-1981) — Frank Stokes (1888-1955)
Robert Wilkins (1896-1987) — ● Memphis Minnie (1897-1973)

Brownsville, Tennessee
Sleepy John Estes (1899-1977)
Yank Rachell (1910) — Sonny Boy Williamson (1914-1948)

The End of World War II — The Rise of Live Blues Radio — "King Biscuit Time" — KFFA — Helena, Arkansas 1941

● Sonny Boy Williamson II (Rice Miller) (1899-1965) — ● Robert Lockwood Jr (1915) — Willie Love (1906-1953)
Joe Willie Wilkins (1923-1979) — Houston Stackhouse (1910-1981) — Peck Curtis (1912-1970)
Doctor Isaiah Ross (1925) — ● Elmore James (1918-1963) — ● Hound Dog Taylor (1917-1975)

Chicago
The Bluebird Sound (mid 30s - late 40s)
Producer: Lester Melrose
Recorded:
- Big Bill Broonzy — Washboard Sam (1935-1964) — Jazz Gillum
  - Tampa Red — Memphis Minnie — Walter Davis
- Sonny Boy Williamson — Big Joe Williams — Arthur Crudup
Tommy McClennan — Henry Townsend (1909)

Chicago – Early Artists
- Big Bill Broonzy (1893-1958) — • Tampa Red (1900-1981)
Jazz Gillum (1904-1966) — Leroy Carr (1905-1935)
Big Maceo (1905-1953) — • Robert Nighthawk (1909-1967)
Scrapper Blackwell (1903-1962) — Kokomo Arnold (1901-1968)
  - Sonny Boy Williamson (1914-1948)

Chess Records
Producer: Leonard Chess
Recorded:
- Muddy Waters — Little Walter — Elmore James
Howlin' Wolf — Buddy Guy — Sonny Boy Williamson II
Jimmy Rogers

The Muddy Waters Band
- Muddy Waters (1915-1983) — • Little Walter (1930-1968)
  - Jimmy Rogers (1924) — • Otis Spann (1930-1970)

The Howlin' Wolf Band
Memphis ca. 1952
- Howlin' Wolf — Willie Johnson — Willie Steele

Chicago ca. 1954-1975
- Hubert Sumlin — Henry Gray — Eddie Shaw
Sam Lay — Detroit Jr — Jody Williams

2nd Generation Chicago Bands
- Buddy Guy (1936) — • Otis Rush (1934) — • Junior Wells (1934)
  - James Cotton (1935) — • Magic Sam (1937-1969)
- Hound Dog Taylor (1917-1975) & the Houserockers

Postwar Chicago Harmonica
- Little Walter — • Big Walter Horton — Snooky Pryor
  - Jimmy Reed — James Cotton — Billy Boy Arnold
Junior Wells — George "Harmonica" Smith
Sonny Boy Williamson II

- **Jimmy Reed** — • Eddie Taylor

Modern Postwar Blues Guitar
- T-Bone Walker (1910-1975)
- B. B. King — • Albert King — • Freddy King
Texas Guitar
- Clarence Gatemouth Brown (1924) — • Lowell Fulson (1921)
Albert Collins (1932) — Johnny Copeland (1937)

Chicago Guitar
Mississippi - influenced:
- Elmore James — • Eddie Taylor — Johnny Young
Johnny Shines — Homesick James — • Hound Dog Taylor
- Earl Hooker — Joe Carter — J. B. Hutto — Louis Myers
B. B. King - influenced (West Side School):
- Otis Rush — • Magic Sam — • Buddy Guy — • Hubert Sumlin
Magic Slim (1937) — Son Seals (1942) — Lonnie Brooks (1933)

Jump Blues
- Big Joe Turner (1911-1985) — • Amos Milburn (1927-1980)
Roy Brown (1920-1981) — Wynonie Harris (1915-1969)

Texas Bluesmen
Smokey Hogg (1908) — • Lightnin' Hopkins (1912-1982)
Lil Son Jackson (1915-1976) — Frankie Lee Sims (1917-1970)

West Coast
Jimmy McCracklin (1921) — Lowell Fulson (1921)
- Percy Mayfield (1920-1984) — • Jesse Fuller (1896-1976)
K. C. Douglas (1913-1975) — Floyd Dixon (1929)
Charles Brown (1920) — Johnny Otis (1921)
Jimmy Witherspoon (1923) — Pee Wee Crayton (1914)

Detroit
- John Lee Hooker (1917) — • Baby Boy Warren (1919-1977)
Bobo Jenkins (1916) — Eddie Burns (1928)
Eddie Kirkland (1928)

The Memphis Sound
Producer: Sam Phillips/Sun Records
Originally Recorded:
- B. B. King — • Howlin' Wolf — • Bobby Bland — • Junior Parker
  - Big Walter Horton — Joe Hill Louis — Willie Nix — Dr. Ross
Ike Turner — Roscoe Gordon

New Orleans
- Professor Longhair (1918-1980) — • Guitar Slim (1907-1975)

Zydeco
- Clifton Chenier (1925-1987) — Boozoo Chavis
Rockin' Dopsie — Fernest Arceneaux

Louisiana (Excello Records)
- Lightnin' Slim (1913-1974) — • Slim Harpo (1924-1970)
Lonesome Sundown (1928) — Lazy Lester (1933)
Silas Hogan (1911)

- Robert Pete Williams (1914-1980)

Modern Blues - Mid 60s to present:
Country Blues
John Hammond (1942) — Dave Van Ronk (1936)
John Koerner (1938) — Rory Block
Electric Blues
- Paul Butterfield (1942-1987) — • Michael Bloomfield (1944-1981)
Taj Mahal (1940) — Johnny Winter (1944)
Elvin Bishop (1942) — Roy Buchanan (1939-1988)
Lil' Ed and the Blues Imperials – Roomful of Blues
- Fabulous Thunderbirds — • Stevie Ray Vaughan (1956-1990)
Robert Cray (1953) — • William Clarke

Soul Blues
- Junior Parker — • Bobby Blue Bland (1930)
Little Milton (1934) — Little Johnny Taylor (1943) — Otis Clay
Z. Z. Hill (1940-1984)

BOBBY BLUE BLAND   b 1930

Electric R&B/soul blues. Bland's early years around Memphis were closely associated with Junior Parker, Johnny Ace, and B. B. King. His earliest recordings (Chess, Modern) are very rough, but beginning in the mid 50s on Duke Records, he became a distinctive blues/R&B voice. The Duke period produced a continuous stream of hit R&B singles. His work mellowed and became more album-oriented in the 70s. Two joint meetings with B. B. King are highlights of those ABC/MCA years. His work for Malaco (mid 80s to date) is formula blues and soul but quite satisfying in general. His Duke period is best represented by imports on the Ace label. *The Blues Years* (1952-1959) is a 25-song collection, while *The Voice* (1959-1969) contains 26 tunes. *Touch of the Blues* and *Spotlighting the Man* (a Mobile Fidelity collection of two complete Duke albums) are a little easier to find. The best of the Malaco discs would be *First Class Blues*, which has Bland's biggest single of the 80s, "Members Only." –BP

○ **Touch of the Blues/Spotlighting the Man / MOBILE FID.**

● **Blues Consolidated / DUKE**   1961
An album split between Bland and his Blues Consolidated touring partner Junior Parker, featuring great early 50s sides by these two Houston-based performers. –CK & HD

○ **Two Steps from the Blues / MCA**   1961
One of his classic early albums. –JME

○ **Here's the Man!!! / MCA / BB 55**   1962
Soulful vocals backed by superb jazzy arrangements by Joe Scott. –HD

Call on Me / MCA / BB 11   1963
A near-perfect collection of early 60s sides. The man at his best. –HD

Ain't Nothing You Can Do / MCA / BB 119   1964
Fine soulful mid-60s sides, including the title track, "Loneliness Hurts," and a cathartic reading of the soul classic "Blind Man." –CK & HD

○ **The Best of Bobby Blue Bland - Vol. 2 / MCA**   1967
Features the classics "It's My Life Baby," "Queen for a Day," and "Two Steps from the Blues." –CK

○ **Touch of the Blues / DUKE**   1967

★ **The Best of Bobby Blue Bland / MCA**   1973
Excellent compilation of the sides that made the legend. Includes "Call on Me," "Farther Up the Road," "I Pity the Fool," and "Turn On Your Love Light." –CK

○ **Woke Up Screaming / ACE**   1974
A 16-track import anthology of Bland's earliest Duke sides from 1952 to 1957, at which point the *Blues Consolidated* album takes over. –HD

BLIND BLAKE   ca. -ca.

Acoustic country blues. The high sales of Blind Lemon Jefferson 78s sent Paramount scouts scrambling to sign blues artists. In the fall of 1926, they recorded Arthur Blake, a swinging, sophisticated ragtime guitarist whose warm, relaxed voice was a far cry from harsh country blues. Paramount's newspaper ads boasted of Blind Blake's "famous piano-sounding guitar." Not much is known of Blind Blake, and the single surviving photograph only seems to deepen the mystery. He was a traveling man whose sponsors claimed he hailed from Jacksonville, FL. He worked in South Georgia and on the East Coast and spent at least part of the 20s living in a Chicago tenement. He made most of his 78s as a solo artist, although he sometimes featured sidemen and did some of his finest work as a sideman for women singers. "When he started to drink too much — you can hear it toward the end — it just doesn't work anymore," observes Ry Cooder. "He's physically past it, because you've got to be sharp to sound that good." After his final 1932 Paramount session, Blind Blake dropped out of sight and died in obscurity. For a while, though, his records sold almost as well as Blind Lemon's, and

he had a tremendous impact, setting the standard for ragtime-influenced blues fingerpicking. –JO

☆ **Ragtime Guitar's Foremost Fingerpicker / YAZOO** 1989
Brilliantly facile guitar playing, with great arrangements. –JO

Complete Recorded Works ... / DOCUMENT
Complete Recorded Works in Chronological Order, Vol. 1-4. Can't get enough of that stuff, yas, yas, yas! –JO

RORY BLOCK

Modern acoustic blues. Rory Block is one of the brightest stars among a galaxy of modern-day country blues interpreters. Rory's superb renderings of classic songs by Robert Johnson, Tommy Johnson, Charley Patton, and others display her deep passion and instinct for historic preservation, but seldom are her covers mere mimics. With its body-pounds, potent bass-string snaps, and precision rhythms, her fierce acoustic guitar attack recalls the great Willie Brown. Rory's originals are often as strong as her covers, a standout being the title track from *Mama's Blues.* Her urgent, soulful voice is in a class of its own. As Taj Mahal says, "She's very simply the best there is." –JO

Best Blues & Originals / ROUNDER
Sweet and tender, or down and dirty, but always uplifting. –JO

○ **High Heeled Blues / ROUNDER**   1982
A breathtaking, breakthrough CD of country-blues covers. –JO

Blue Horizon / ROUNDER   1983
A mixed bag. Emotionally powerful. –JO

Rhinestones & Steel Strings / ROUNDER   1984
Delta blues meets sweet, sweet soul. –JO

Mama's Blues / ROUNDER   1991
The woman's view. Highly recommended. –JO

MICHAEL BLOOMFIELD   1944-1981

Blues. Bloomfield was one of the first White players who got right into the Chicago blues scene and could actually play the music. As lead guitar for the Butterfield Blues Band, he exerted a powerful influence with far-reaching effect on young rock guitarists. He almost single-handedly pioneered the extended guitar solo, introducing many Western ears to the sounds of the Far East with his sitar-inspired solos. The Butterfield Blues Band album *East-West* (and the lovely title cut) broke new ground in the progressive rock scene — psychedelic rock was born. Bloomfield also backed Bob Dylan in his move into electric-land on *Highway 61 Revisited*, one of the landmarks of modern rock music. He went on to record albums with his own band, the Electric Flag, and with others (*Super Session* w/Al Kooper). These later efforts saw only limited success. He was best at blues, and those first two Butterfield albums mark a high point. Part of Bloomfield's enormous influence on younger rock guitar players was due to his very outgoing and generous spirit. Bloomfield was one of those rare performers who cared as much for sharing his vision with others as he did for the music he loved. –JME

○ **It's Not Killing Me / COLUMBIA**   1969

BLUES BOY WILLIE   b 1946

Modern electric blues. Willie McFalls, a native Memphian from Texas, not Tennessee, took the chitlin circuit by surprise in 1990 when the comical blues dialog of "Be-Who?" put his second album on the *Billboard* charts and his act on the road. Blues Boy Willie came to Ichiban Records courtesy of his boyhood friend from Texas, bluesman-producer Gary B. B. Coleman. Willie's three albums to date all bear the typical Coleman touch — competent but predictable blues tracks with a small studio band. It has been the spunky spoken repartee between Willie and his wife Miss Lee on the novelty numbers that has earned Willie an unexpected niche on the Southern soul/blues scene. –

○ **Strange Things Happening / ICHIBAN**   1989
A blues/R&B vocalist with a very contemporary Southern sound. –NJF

LUCILLE BOGAN   1897-1948

Classic female blues. The big-voiced Bogan made some important sides in the classic female blues tradition throughout the the mid 20s and early 30s. Unlike other women singers from the genre, she seldom strayed into pop-style music, remaining essentially a straightahead blues stylist. –CK

○ **1923-35 / BEST OF BLUES**
A solid 18-track compilation of Lucille's best sides from her peak period. (Import) –CK

SON BONDS   1909-1947

Acoustic country blues. An associate of Sleepy John Estes and Hammie Nixon, Bonds played very much in the same rural Brownsville style that the Estes-Nixon team popularized in the 20s and 30s. Curiously, either Estes or Nixon (but never both of them together) played on all of Bonds's recordings. The music to one of Bonds's songs, "Back and Side Blues" (1934), became a standard blues melody when John Lee "Sonny Boy" Williamson from nearby Jackson, TN, used it in his classic "Good Morning, (Little) School Girl" (1937). According to Nixon, Bonds was shot to death, while sitting on his front porch, by a nearsighted neighbor who mistook him for another man. –JON

○ **Complete Recorded Works in Chron. Order / WOLF**
Blues from Brownsville, 1934-1941, with Hammie Nixon and Sleepy John Estes. –JO

JUKE BOY BONNER   1932-1978

Electric Texas blues. A modern-day Texas blues poet with an insightful sense of lyricism, Bonner usually performed as a one-man band, playing basic rhythm on guitar accented by soulful bursts from the harp he wore in a rack around his neck. While his music was down-home and countrified, some of his most notable songs dealt with the urban ghetto life of Houston. Bonner's blues are of the calibre destined to bring him greater fame as a posthumous legend than he was ever able to enjoy during his alcohol-shortened life, when he was known mostly to local blues-bar patrons in Houston and to European fanatics. –JON

☆ **The Struggle / ARHOOLIE**
Recorded in extreme stereo, with drums on one channel and Bonner's guitar on the other, this is Juke Boy Bonner's most cohesive album. Great songwriting and performances throughout. –CK

1960-1967 / FLYRIGHT
A Lightnin' Hopkins-meets-Jimmy Reed sound on these delightfully funky guitar/harp-accompanied blues by this Houstonian, whose ironic lyrics are half the fun. –JO

BOOGIE WOOGIE RED   b1925

Piano blues. Though a Louisiana native, Vernon Harrison been associated with the Detroit blues sound as long as anyone. A Motor City resident since 1927, he began performing in the local clubs as a teenager. As a sideman he worked locally with Sonny Boy Williamson, Baby Boy Warren, and John Lee Hooker. Despite Red's renown for the blues and boogie-woogie style that earned him his nickname, he has recorded only a few times as a featured artist, and aside from a bit of European touring in the 70s, he has remained a local Detroit treasure, rarely appearing outside the area. –JON

○ **Red Hot / BLIND PIG**   1977
A crudely recorded but fun live album that captures the somewhat demented 80-proof charm of this Detroit pianist. Recorded in the basement of the Blind Pig in Ann Arbor, MI, this album features guest appearances by John Nicholas, Fran Christina, and Bill Heid. –GB

EDDIE BOYD   b1914

Piano blues. One of the most popular piano-playing bluesmen

around Chicago in the early 50s, Eddie Boyd contributed one certified classic to the idiom in the much-covered "Five Long Years." –CK

○ **Five Long Years / L + R**
Mid-60s session with superb backing reprising most of Boyd's 50s hits. (Import) –CK

ISHMON BRACEY   1901-1970

Acoustic Delta blues. One of the early giants of the Delta blues, Bracey's best work is marked by a tremulous vibrato to his largely nasal voice and simple but effective guitar work. –CK

○ **Ishmon Bracey & Charley Taylor / DOCUMENT**
Bracey's complete recorded works (1928-1929) in chronological order, with the bonus of four tracks by the elusive Charley Taylor. (Import) –CK

TINY BRADSHAW   1905-1958

Electric jump blues. Tiny Bradshaw was one of the most prominent bandleaders of the 30s and 40s who led groups of essentially jazz-trained musicians into the developing (and more commercial) field that came to be known as rhythm & blues. A vocalist with other bands early in his career, Bradshaw formed his own band in 1934 and kept it going through the early 50s, enjoying five *Billboard* hits (and also recording the original "Train Kept A-Rollin'") with King Records (where he was a labelmate to many of the other leading jump-blues performers of the era). Bradshaw's band produced such saxophone stars as Sonny Stitt, Red Prysock, and Sil Austin; among the vocalists to record with the group were Roy Brown, Arthur Prysock, Lonnie Johnson, and Tiny Kennedy. –JON

○ **Great Composer / KING**   1959
Jump-blues bandleader of the 40s & 50s rocks the house. –GB

LONNIE BROOKS   b1933

Modern electric blues. Lonnie Brooks has emerged as a standard-bearer of "genuine houserocking music" for Alligator Records over the past decade and a half, with a bright, energetic style that draws from blues, rock & roll, and Louisiana R&B. Brooks (real name Lee Baker, Jr) began his recording career in Lake Charles, LA, releasing "Family Rules," "The Crawl," and other 50s rhythm & blues sides under the name Guitar Jr. A move to Chicago put him in closer touch with hardcore blues (one of his first jobs in the city was with Jimmy Reed) and soon brought him a new stage name. Most of his singles continued to be in an R&B or soul vein until he adopted a bluesier approach when he began waxing albums for the blues market. –JON

● **Bayou Lightning / ALLIGATOR**   1979
One of the hottest good-time blues albums of the late 70s. –BD

Turn On the Night / ALLIGATOR   1981
The second Alligator album is enjoyable in its own right, though inconsistent. –BD

Hot Shot / ALLIGATOR   1983
A sizzler, with an impressive Brooks on guitar. –BD

○ **The Crawl / CHARLY**   1984
An import album of Southern Louisiana swamp-blues and rockers from Lonnie's late 50s formative years. It includes the often-covered title cut and "Family Rules." –BD

Wound Up Tight / ALLIGATOR   1986
Johnny Winter pays homage to Brooks (an early influence) by guesting on two tracks of this rocked-up set. –BD

Live from Chicago / ALLIGATOR   1988
On *Live from Chicago - Bayou Lightning Strikes*, Brooks shows he knows how to incite a packed nightclub. –BD

Satisfaction Guaranteed / ALLIGATOR   1991
The most rock-oriented album of this high-energy guitarist's career. Koko Taylor duets on one cut, and Lonnie's son on another. –BD

353

BIG BILL BROONZY   1893-1958

Acoustic country blues. Big Bill Broonzy's performing career spanned five decades, taking him from Mississippi to Chicago, and on to Europe — where he served as one of the first and finest spokespersons and role models for the blues. Over the course of his life he played multiple roles equally well: down-home country fiddler, "race records" recording star, Chicago studio sideman, and blues revival folksinger.

A songwriter, vocalist, and guitar hero, Broonzy recorded some 250 sides prior to WWII and hundreds more after for a dozen labels, wrote innumerable songs, and played on countless sessions other than his own. A terrifically influential artist, he played in several styles, including down-home finger-picking, ragtime, and single-string electric. Later on he effortlessly produced rich acoustic finger work targeted to the guitar-conscious folk-revival audience. During his later years he sang protest pieces and other "folk" material to a coffeehouse and cabaret crowd.

But most of his musical life, his repertoire of blues, ragtime, hokum, and pop was specifically directed to the "race market." Beyond his extensive recordings, he left an autobiography, *Big Bill Blues*, which shows him to be an engaging storyteller and a master of the spoken word as well as song. One of the first to become a star after moving from Mississippi to Chicago, Broonzy earned the love and respect of his fellow musicians. As the central character in the first generation of Chicago blues, his work bridged tradition and popular categories. He was known as a musician not just in the technical sense, but in the sense of a supportive co-worker and a friend who could be counted on to help others in need. Aside from his towering skills as a musician and his self-promoted predilection for whiskey, Broonzy was a venerated member of the blues community.

Slick enough to deal with shifts in musical taste, Broonzy changed styles in his younger days and changed audiences in his later days. One of the first artists to successfully work to Northern and European audiences, he shaped the way a generation thought about the blues. –BLP

Big Bill Broonzy & Washboard Sam / CHESS
This chronicles the last commercial hurrah (1953) for this pair of prewar blues greats. –BD

○ **The Young Big Bill Broonzy (1928-35) / YAZOO**   1968
Traditional as well as commercial material from a major bluesman. A must for those who only know Broonzy's later blues revival work. –BLP

★ **Big Bill Blues / CBS**   1969
Big Bill at his most representative. Includes "When I've Been Drinkin'," in which he supposedly takes several drinks on microphone as part of the cut. –BLP

○ **Do That Guitar Rag 1928-1935 / YAZOO**   1973
Great blues ragtime and hokum from a major singer, composer, guitarist, and sideman, whose recording career spanned four decades. –BLP

Good Time Tonight / CBS
Twenty cuts from the 30s Columbia, ARC, and Vocalion sessions with various sidemen, including Blind John Davis and Joshua Altheimer. –BLP

In Chronological Order / DOCUMENT   1991
Three CDs of Broonzy's earliest and best sides, 1932-1935. Includes "C-C Rider," "Milkcow Blues," and his finest instrumental, "House Rent Stomp." –CK

BUSTER BROWN   1911-1976

Modern electric blues. Brown was an obscure NY/NJ-based singer/harmonica player who came out of nowhere in late 1959 with the Fire Records issue of "Fannie Mae," which was a #1 R&B hit. Apart from one minor hit some years later and one album, *The New King of the Blues* (Fire 102), very little is known about this performer. The Fire album has been reissued on a variety of different labels. –BP

○ **The New King of the Blues / COLLECTABLES**   1987
Best of the Fire sessions, including #1 hit "Fannie Mae" and "Is You Is or Is You Ain't My Baby?" –BLP

CHARLES BROWN   b1922

Electric West Coast blues. The West Coast club-blues genre can be traced back directly to pianist Charles Brown, whose groundbreaking mid-40s work as part of guitarist Johnny Moore's Three Blazers deeply influenced a legion of younger wizards of the ivories — notably Floyd Dixon, Amos Milburn, and Ray Charles. Theirs was a quieter, more introspective brand of blues, with obvious pop and jazz overtones.

Influenced himself by the ultra-smooth stylings of Nat King Cole, Brown's cool vocals communicated a proper mood of isolation and heartbreak on the classic Blazers tune "Driftin' Blues" and the Yuletide perennial "Merry Christmas Baby." Brown broke out as a solo artist in 1948, signing with Aladdin and continuing his string of hits with the doomy "Trouble Blues" and "Black Night."

Best classified as a blues balladeer, the pianist saw his suave style fall out of favor as rock & roll swept the country, and he recorded only intermittently from the 60s on. But Brown never gave up hope, and he recently made the sort of miraculous comeback normally reserved for contrived Hollywood melodramas. His 1990 Bullseye Blues disc *All My Life* brilliantly spotlights Brown's timeless approach, and a three-month stint opening for Bonnie Raitt in stadiums nationwide exposed this venerated R&B pioneer to a fresh mob of potential fans. –BD

One More for the Road / ALLIGATOR   1986
Fine and mellow recordings. –MH

○ **All My Life / BULLSEYE BLUES**   1990
Fresh and triumphant performances from the year of Brown's celebrated "second coming." In the company of old pal Ruth Brown, incomparable saxman Clifford Solomon, Dr. John, and other top-drawer players, Brown sparkles. –MH

CLARENCE "GATEMOUTH" BROWN   b1924

Electric Texas blues. Labeling Clarence "Gatemouth" Brown a blues artist is an injustice. While it's an undeniable fact that he's one of the pioneers of the blistering Texas blues guitar style, he's as likely to whip out his fiddle and play country, jazz, or calypso as he is to lay down a smoldering Texas shuffle.

Brown fell under the spell of Lone Star blues legend T-Bone Walker early on, adopting his crisp single-string picking and turning up the heat. While Brown was playing at a Houston nightclub, owner Don Robey took an interest in his career, inaugurating Peacock Records to issue Brown's work. Although he only enjoyed two R&B chart items, Brown's 1949-1960 Peacock output was immensely influential on younger Texans such as Albert Collins and Johnny Copeland. With a torrid jazz-laced combo sizzling behind him, Brown dug in on the searing "Dirty Work at the Crossroads" and "Rock My Blues Away," setting nearly impossible standards for his protégés to duplicate on the incendiary instrumentals "Boogie Uproar" and "Okie Dokie Stomp." Brown left Peacock after a session showcasing his violin talent, later serving as house bandleader for the R&B TV variety program "The Beat."

With the resurgence of interest in Texas blues, Gatemouth was ready to answer the call. Three acclaimed Rounder albums (including the 1981 Grammy-winning *Alright Again!*) and three more Alligator discs proclaim that Gatemouth Brown is much more than a bluesman, although the genre will always be his inspiration. –BD

○ **Pressure Cooker / ALLIGATOR**
☆ **Original Peacock Recordings / ROUNDER**   1973
Brown's earliest recordings feature tons of smoldering guitar with brassy, high-powered arrangements. Those only familiar with his mellow later work will be startled by the gutsy wallop these tracks have to offer. Milestones in Texas blues. –CK

NAPPY BROWN   b 1929

Electric jump blues. Nappy Brown has, alternately and often simultaneously, devoted his considerable vocal talents to both blues and gospel music for most of his life. It was as a member of a gospel group that he went to record for Savoy Records, but the company fancied him as a blues singer. With Savoy he hit the national charts four times from 1955-1959, singing blues and novelty material that made use of his improvisational vocal phrasing. His modernized R&B version of "Night Time Is the Right Time," by Roosevelt Sykes, was not one of the big hits, but it did provide the model for Ray Charles's 1959 classic, and critics such as Peter Guralnick still cite Brown's rendition as the best. In the 60s Brown gave up the touring life and returned home to a renewed career in gospel, yet he would still heed the call of the blues on occasion, more and more so since 1984. He has since recorded several blues albums and enlivened many a blues stage with his energetic and humorous presence. –JON

○ **Tore Up (With the Heartfixers) / ALLIGATOR**   1984
A joyful noise: bright and brassy production with Brown in full belt. No mothballs here. The Heartfixers teaming up with the legendary singer Nappy Brown works very well. Tinsley Ellis plays guitar. Tunes are from Willie Dixon, Greg Allman, Hank Ballard, Bob Dylan, and others. –MH & MGN

Something Gonna Jump ... / BLACK TOP   1988
Something Gonna Jump out the Bushes is a second helping of recent Brown recordings. –MH

ROY BROWN   1925-1981

Electric jump blues. One of the premier shouters of the jump-blues era, Brown has been called "the first singer of soul" (in John Broven's *Walking to New Orleans*), "one of the great blues lyricists of all time" (in Jeff Hannusch's *I Hear You Knockin'*), and the artist responsible for the breakthrough of New Orleans rhythm & blues. An acknowledged and obvious influence on Bobby Bland, B. B. King, Junior Parker, Little Milton, James Brown, and Jackie Wilson in the blues and R&B fields, Brown also had followers on the rock & roll side by the names of Elvis Presley and Buddy Holly. He was a trendsetter both in his use of fervent gospel-style singing in Black secular music and in the infectious rhythms that helped pave the way for rock & roll in songs such as "Good Rockin' Tonight" and "Rockin' at Midnight." Though never again as commercially successful as he was in 1948-1951, when he had 15 records on the charts, Brown continued to perform and record now and again in later years, still boasting the magnificent voice that enthralled and inspired listeners when he was "the mighty, mighty man" of rhythm & blues. –JON

☆ **Hard Luck Blues / KING**   1971
Brown's highly influential crying vocal style is convincingly showcased on this two-record set of his late 40s and 50s material. (Out of print) –GB

GEORGE "MOJO" BUFORD   b 1929

Electric Chicago blues. An alumni of the Muddy Waters band, Buford moved to Minneapolis in the early 60s, where he recorded and worked as a solo artist, eventually heading back to Chicago to work again with Muddy and on his own. A good, solid harp player in the Chicago tradition. –CK

○ **Mojo Buford's Blues Summit / ROOSTER BLUES**
Buford in the company of guitarists Little Smokey Smothers, Pee Wee Madison, Sammy Lawhorn, and Sonny Rogers, with a rhythm section pounding it out like crazy. –CK

BUMBLE BEE SLIM   b 1905

Acoustic country blues. Popular and prolific, Bumble Bee Slim parlayed a familiar but rudimentary style into one of the earliest flowerings of the Chicago style. –CK

○ **1931-1937 / DOCUMENT**
A solid 18-track import compilation of all his best sides. –CK

EDDIE BURNS   b 1928

Modern electric blues. Primarily known for his early 50s work in support of singer and guitarist John Lee Hooker, Burns remains one of the finest Detroit bluesmen ever to step in front of a microphone. –CK

○ **Eddie Burns / BLUE SUITE**
His only solo album features solid, contemporary backing against Burns's impassioned vocals. –CK

GEORGE "WILD CHILD" BUTLER   b 1936

Electric Chicago blues. An alumni of the Muddy Waters band, with a strong style that owes a heavy debt to both Little Walter and Sonny Boy Williamson II. –CK

○ **Open Up Baby / CHARLY**
Solid collection of Butler's best sides for the Jewel label. (Import) –CK

PAUL BUTTERFIELD   1942-1987

Modern electric blues. Chicago born Paul Butterfield started out on classical flute before switching to amplified harmonica. He hung out and jammed with Chicago South Side blues players, starting his own band in 1963. The first Butterfield album (1965) had an enormous impact on young rock players who were used to getting their blues via groups like the Rolling Stones. This album was no deferential imitation of Black music by shy Whites, but a hard-driving blues album that rocked. It was a signal to White players to stop making respectful tributes to Black music and just play it. In a flash, the image of blues as old-time music was gone, and modern Chicago-style urban blues was out of the closet and introduced to mainstream White audiences.
The first two Butterfield Blues albums are essential from a historical perspective. While *East-West*, the second album, set the tone for psychedelic rockers with its Eastern influence and extended solos, it was that incredible first album (*The Paul Butterfield Blues Band*) that put the music scene on alert to what was coming. Later Butterfield material somehow misses the mark. Butterfield was one of the only White harmonica players to develop his own style — one respected by Black players (another is the brilliant William Clarke). Butterfield has no credible imitators. His harp playing was always understated, concise, and serious — only Big Walter Horton has a better sense of note selection. –JME

★ **Paul Butterfield Blues Band / ELEKTRA**   1965
Butterfield's unique amplified harmonica style is already present on his classic first album — a wakeup call for a generation of young White players wondering if they, too, could play the blues. Great guitar from Michael Bloomfield and Elvin Bishop. W/ Mark Naftalin (organ), Jerome Arnold (b), and Sam Lay (d). –JME

○ **East-West / ELEKTRA**   1966
These Chicago-based musicians took blues to a whole new level on this, their second album, paving the way for the experimentations that are still being explored today. –JT

The Resurrection of Pigboy Crabshaw / ELEKTRA   1968
A new direction was tried on this third album, stressing horn arrangements over guitar-fueled improvisations. –JT

CHRIS CAIN BAND

Modern electric blues. The San Jose, CA, native's crisp lead guitar and gravelly vocals have brought him national recognition, with a solid 1990 album on Blind Pig to his credit. Influenced by B. B. and Albert King as well as various jazz players, Cain has cooked up a jumping sound on the Bay Area circuit. –BD

Late Night City Blues / BLUE ROCKIT   1987
This debut album was rewarded with four Handy Award nominations. –BD

○ **Cuttin' Loose / BLIND PIG**   1990
A wonderful, big-voiced, contemporary West Coast bluesman

and superb guitar player. There are several horns in the band, giving it a great, huge sound. Even better things will be coming, I'm sure. —NJF

EDDIE C. CAMPBELL   b 1939

Modern electric blues. The self-styled "King of the Jungle" from Chicago's West Side, Campbell has employed a clever and often whimsical sense of humor in his songs to go along with a solid blues foundation built on the music of Magic Sam, Muddy Waters, and James Brown, among others. Campbell was a member of Willie Dixon's Chicago Blues All Stars when he cut his first album in 1977, backed by Dixon sidemen Carey Bell, Lafayette Leake, and Clifton James. Campbell, a man of many interests, maintained blues as only a part-time occupation, however, and did little to further his musical career until he moved to Europe in 1984. The receptive European blues climate has afforded him renewed opportunities to perform and record, and although he remains a refreshing entertainer, he also remains little known in his home country. —JON

○ **King of the Jungle / ROOSTER BLUES**   1977
Tough contemporary blues from Chicago's West Side. —BD

JOHN CAMPBELL

Modern electric blues. Contemporary Texas blues singer and guitarist, whose 1991 domestic debut on Elektra, "One Believer," is a gloomy, intense collection with lots of fiery guitar. Born in Shreveport, LA, and reared in Texas, Campbell cites Lightnin' Hopkins as a principal influence. He cut his first album, *A Man and His Blues*, for the German Crosscut imprint, and it earned a 1989 Handy Award nomination. —BD

○ **One Believer / ELEKTRA**   1991
A ten-tune program of mostly original compositions cowritten with Dennis Walker, who coproduced it. The Robert Cray Band rhythm section is on hand for half the album. A very impressive artist and album. —BP

CANNON'S JUG STOMPERS   1885-1979

Acoustic Memphis blues. Gus Cannon was the best known of all the jug band musicians and a seminal figure on the Memphis blues scene. His recollections have also provided us with much of our knowledge of the earliest days of the blues in the Mississippi Delta. Cannon led his Jug Stompers on banjo and jug in a historic series of dates for the Victor label in 1928-1930. The ensemble usually included a second banjoist or guitarist, one of whom often doubled on kazoo, and the legendary Noah Lewis on harmonica. The jug-band style enjoyed a revival during the folk boom of the 50s and 60s, resulting in an ultra-rare Gus Cannon album on Stax, of all labels, after his "Walk Right In" became the nation's best-selling record for the Rooftop Singers in 1963. Cannon's Victor output was also a favorite source of early blues material for the Grateful Dead. —JON

○ **Complete Works 1927-30 / YAZOO**
This innocent and exuberant Memphis good-time blues was the inspiration for 50s British skiffle and Greenwich Village folkies alike. —MH

LEROY CARR   1905-1935

Piano blues. The term "urban blues" is usually applied to post-WWII blues band music, but one of the forefathers of the genre in its pre-electric format was Leroy Carr. Teamed with the exemplary guitarist Scrapper Blackwell in Indianapolis, Carr became one of the top blues stars of his day, composing and recording almost 200 sides during his short lifetime, including such classics as "How Long, How Long," "Prison Bound Blues," "When the Sun Goes Down," and "Blues before Sunrise." His blues were expressive and evocative, recorded only with piano and guitar, yet as author Sam Charters has noted, Carr was "a city man" whose singing was never as rough or intense as the country bluesmen's; and as reissue producer Francis Smith put it, "He, perhaps more than any

other single artist, was responsible for transforming the rural blues patterns of the 20s into the more city-oriented blues of the 30s." —JON

Blues Before Sunrise / PORTRAIT
Originally issued in the 60s, this is a basic bare-bones introduction to Carr and Blackwell's sound. —CK

☆ **Naptown Blues 1929-1934 / YAZOO**
A seminal piano/guitar duo. Leroy Carr was among the most influential early blues singer/pianists, and Scrapper Blackwell was a remarkably fluid guitarist. —MH

BO CARTER   1893-1964

Acoustic Mississippi blues. Bo Carter (Armenter "Bo" Chatmon) had an unequaled capacity for creating sexual metaphors in his songs, specializing in such ribald imagery as "Banana in Your Fruit Basket," "Pin in Your Cushion," and "Your Biscuits Are Big Enough for Me." One of the most popular bluesmen of the 30s, he recorded enough material for several reissue albums, and he was quite an original guitar picker, or else three of those albums wouldn't have been released by Yazoo. (Carter employed a number of different keys and tunings on his records, most of which were solo vocal and guitar performances.) Carter's facility extended beyond the risqué business to more serious blues themes, and he was also the first to record the standard "Corrine Corrina" (1928). Bo and his brothers Lonnie and Sam Chatmon also recorded as members of the Mississippi Sheiks with singer-guitarist Walter Vinson. —JON

☆ **Bo Carter - 1930-1944 / YAZOO**   1968
Mostly solo selections by Bo, with a couple of Mississippi Sheiks songs included. Features very fine and distinctive country-blues guitar playing and singing. Most of the songs are of the double-entendre variety — a possible reason why he's not as well known as he deserves to be, since some blues researchers did not deem his material worthy. As with most Yazoo releases, the liner notes include various guitar tunings and chord progressions for each song — fascinating for guitarists. —GB

Banana in Your Fruit Basket / YAZOO   1973
Some of Carter's best double-entendre material, including the salacious "I Got Ants in My Pants." —CK

JOHN CEPHAS w/PHIL WIGGINS   b 1988

Modern acoustic blues. Products of the Washington, DC, area, Cephas and Wiggins have been working as an acoustic guitar and harmonica duet for over 15 years. Their music has its roots in the rural African-American dance music of Virginia and North Carolina and shows the influence of Blind Boy Fuller, Gary Davis, and Sonny Terry.
Their broad repertoire consists of Piedmont blues standards as well as an eclectic sampling of Delta stylings, R&B, ballads, ragtime, gospel, and country & western. Two of their best albums, *Dog Days of August* and *Guitar Man*, were voted the Best Traditional Blues Albums of the Year by the Handy Awards. In 1989 Cephas received a National Heritage Award in recognition of his efforts as a teacher and spokesperson for the traditional arts.
Cephas and Wiggins have literally toured the world, playing every major festival and winning new friends for their regional blues style. Their sound combines sophisticated traditional instrumentation and modern gospel-edged vocals, applied to traditional standards and their own hard-hitting compositions, offering a soulful acoustic option to electric blues. Today Cephas and Wiggins are the most visible exponents of Piedmont blues, gracefully carrying their tradition into the 90s. —BLP

Sweet Bitter Blues / L&R
A fine German import featuring several compositions by blues poet Otis Williams. —BLP

○ **Dog Days of August / FLYING FISH**   1986
Handy Award-winning acoustic guitar and harmonica

Piedmont blues. Includes ballads "John Henry," "Staggerlee," and ten original compositions. —BLP

Guitar Man / FLYING FISH   1987
Their second Handy Award winner includes slide guitar, Piedmont finger-picking, and wonderful harmonica. —BLP

Walking Blues / MARIMAC   1988
A fine assortment of Piedmont blues, ragtime, and country. Includes "Walking Blues." —BLP

SAM CHATMON   1897-1983

Acoustic country blues. A product of the prodigious Chatmon family that included not only Lonnie of the famous Mississippi Sheiks but also the prolific Bo Carter and several other blues-playing brothers, Sam Chatmon survived to be hailed as a modern-day blues guru when he began performing and recording again in the 60s. Sam continued brother Bo's tradition of sly double-entendre blues to entertain a new generation of aficionados, but he also showed a more serious side on songs like the title track of the early Arhoolie anthology *I Have to Paint My Face.* —JON

Chatmon & His Barbeque Boys / FLYING FISH   1987
An excellent set of trio recordings by this underrated performer. —RW

○ **Sam Chatmon's Advice / ROUNDER**   1988
Outstanding blues and double-entendre delights. —RW

RITA CHIARELLI

Modern electric blues. Chiarelli is a Canadian-born blues guitarist who can play blues guitar with the best of them. She has played with Ronnie Hawkins, Buddy Guy, and Spencer Davis. —CR

○ **Road Rockets / STONY PLAIN**   1992
"This Is My Life" and "Have You Seen My Shoes" are two of Rita's better songs on this release. This is a high-powered album. —CR

WILLIAM CLARKE

Modern electric blues. I had given up hope of ever seeing a new voice on amplified blues harp (harmonica) again in my life. It seemed that the best players out there couldn't even live up to classic harp players like Big Walter Horton or Little Walter, much less carry blues harmonica the next step. Then came William Clarke. Technically, Clarke is a master of both the cross and chromatic harps. He takes blues on the chromatic up to and beyond where Little Walter left it years ago. But far more important than the technique is the music. Clarke plays music to my ears, and it has been a long time since I have heard any really new sounds on a blues harp. Raised in the West Coast blues scene, Clarke studied with many players, in particular George "Harmonica" Smith — a veteran of the Muddy Waters band. Clarke (along with Big Walter Horton and Paul Butterfield) has an almost impeccable sense of which notes to play. Give him a listen. Harmonica recording artist Charlie Musselwhite says that Clarke is his "favorite living harp player — no doubt about it." I am in total agreement with Musselwhite. —JME

Can't You Hear Me Calling / RIVERA   1983
Clarke's debut album only gives a glimmer of what's to come from this new genius of the blues, but it is enjoyable nonetheless. —CK

Rockin' the Boat / RIVERA   1988
Recorded live in 1987, this features Clarke and his regular working band on a wide variety of material showcasing his formidable talents as a vocalist and harmonica man extraordinaire. —CK

★ **Blowin' Like Hell / ALLIGATOR**   1990
The title says it all. William Clarke cooks on this one. These are new sounds. —JME

○ **Serious Intentions / ALLIGATOR**   1992
Clarke's second album for the label burns with a ferocious intensity, particularly for his groundbreaking work on

chromatic harp and his ability to cover all styles with remarkable élan. —CK

EDDY CLEARWATER   b 1935

Modern electric blues. Eddy Clearwater was renowned as Chicago's duckwalking answer to Chuck Berry for years before he began to build an international following for the bluesier side of his wide-ranging repertoire. In his time, the genial blues rocker has played it all, from country to Motown to disco to gospel, and he remains one of the most versatile performers on the contemporary blues circuit. His albums usually feature his West Side brand of blues, heavily influenced by Otis Rush and Magic Sam, and his high-spirited 50s-style rockabilly and rock & roll numbers, along with a taste of his topical lyrics. —JON

○ **The Chief / ROOSTER BLUES**   1980
Clearwater's first domestic album is also his finest, with an all-star Chicago combo in driving support. —BD

Flimdoozie / ROOSTER BLUES   1986
The Chief's unique mixture of West Side guitar and Chuck Berry-style rhythm is high-energy fun! —BD

Real Good Time - Live! / ROOSTER BLUES   1990
Recorded at two Indiana college bars, this set showcases the rocking southpaw guitarist at his blistering best. —BD

GARY B. B. COLEMAN   b 1947

Modern electric blues. After a career as a local bluesman and blues promoter in Texas and Oklahoma, Gary Coleman found his niche when he signed over his first album, a self-produced outing originally issued on his own label, to the fledgling Ichiban company out of Atlanta in 1986. Since that time, both Coleman and Ichiban have made their marks in the blues field — not only has Coleman released half a dozen of his own albums, he has also overseen production of the bulk of Ichiban's hefty blues catalog, bringing to the studio a number of artists he'd booked or toured with in his previous career (Chick Willis, Buster Benton, and Blues Boy Willie, among others). A singer/guitarist onstage, Coleman has often taken on a multi-instrumentalist's role in the studio. His music remains true to the blues and to the King legacy saluted in his "B. B." moniker and in his acknowledged debt to fellow Texan Freddie King. —JON

Nothin' but the Blues / ICHIBAN   1986
Darker overall tone; sadder and more introspective. One of his more consistent records. Includes two very good slow blues, "Let Me Love You Baby" and "Shame On You." —NJF

○ **If You Can Beat Me Rockin'... / ICHIBAN**   1988
Highlights here are the title track and the Coleman-penned "Watch Where You Stoke." —NJF

Romance without Finance ... / ICHIBAN   1991
Romance without Finance Is a Nuisance is a little funkier and a little more naughty. —NJF

ALBERT COLLINS   b 1932

Electric Texas blues. One of the most influential guitarists in the post-WWII period, Collins was a prominent performer in the Houston area who began recording in the 50s but lingered in obscurity until discovered by members of the rock group Canned Heat in 1966. His early recordings for the Hall label were collected in *The Cool Sound of Albert Collins* (TCF Hall 8002), which featured primarily instrumentals with similar titles ("Frosty," "Sno-Cone," "Frost Bite"). Collins has kept this identity since. Three albums on Imperial are a mixed lot — gems mixed in with commercial dross. The 70s were largely uneventful for the guitarist until a 1978 relationship with Alligator Records. Here Collins began to blossom, and the Alligator albums, which continued to be released until 1986, are uniformly excellent and reveal a previously obscured ability as a blues singer. Still active and always a stimulating live performer, the "Master of the Telecaster" is going strong. His most recent album was on Charisma/Point Blank. —BP

○ **Truckin' with Albert Collins / MCA** 1969
Classic early-60s ice-laden instrumentals that established
Collins as "the Master of the Telecaster." –BD

★ **Ice Pickin' / ALLIGATOR** 1978
A killer album, with loads of icy guitar and Collins's
understated vocals. Classic contemporary blues! –BD

Frostbite / ALLIGATOR 1980
More searing Texas guitar. "Brick" just may be his hottest
shuffle to date! –BD

Frozen Alive! / ALLIGATOR 1981
This first legitimate live album is typically spellbinding. –BD

Live in Japan / ALLIGATOR 1984
Collins stretches out at this funky Tokyo concert. –BD

Showdown / ALLIGATOR 1985
A summit meeting between Texas guitar veterans Collins and
Johnny Copeland and newcomer Robert Cray. Scorching all
the way. –BD

Iceman / ATLANTIC 1991
His latest disc (and major-label debut) is solid. –BD

SAM COLLINS   1887-1949

Acoustic country blues. One of the earliest generation of blues
performers, Collins developed his style in South Mississippi
(as opposed to the Delta). His recording debut single ("The
Jail House Blues," 1927) predated those of legendary
Mississippians such as Charley Patton and Tommy Johnson
and was advertised as "Crying Sam Collins and his Git-
Fiddle." Collins did not become a major name in blues — in
fact his, later records appeared under several different
pseudonyms — but his rural bottleneck guitar pieces were
among the first to be compiled on LP when the country blues
reissue era was just beginning. Sam Charters wrote in *The
Bluesmen*: "Although Collins was not one of the stylistic
innovators within the Mississippi blues idiom, he was enough
part of it that, in blues like "Signifying Blues" and "Slow
Mama Slow," he had some of the intensity of the Mississippi
music at its most creative level." –JON

○ **Jailhouse Blues / YAZOO**
One of the 20s' most fascinating, eccentric obscurities,
although a little Collins goes a long way. –MH

JOANNA CONNOR

Modern electric blues. A Chicago-based blues singer and
guitarist who rapidly built a reputation as a strong slide
guitarist on the Chicago blues circuit. Connor's 1989 debut
album on Blind Pig (*Believe It!*) tabbed her as a talent to
watch. She was born in Worcester, MA, and migrated to the
Windy City in the mid 80s, joining Dion Payton and the 43rd
Street Band and backing Payton on Alligator's *New Bluebloods*
anthology in 1987. Connor went solo soon thereafter and
currently tours with her own band. –BD

○ **Believe It! / BLIND PIG** 1989
College bar-band blues/rock. –NJF

JOHNNY COPELAND   b 1938

Electric Texas blues. Copeland is associated with the Texas
blues and has been headquartered both in Houston and New
York for many years. A fine blues composer as well as guitarist
and vocalist, he is one of the most well rounded performers
of the genre. Early recordings on Home Cooking and Crazy
Cajun and two volumes on Mr. R&B are collections of singles
originally recorded for many labels from the early 60s to the
late 70s. Copeland's albums for Rounder Records begin in
1981, and it is here that the mature Copeland is to be found. A
total of six albums were issued (and two collections from the
earliest albums), and Copeland appears on the Grammy-
winning *Showdown* (Alligator 4743) with Robert Cray and
Albert Collins. Of the Rounder albums, all the US-recorded
studio sessions are fine, leaving one live album (*Ain't Nothin'
but a Party*, Rounder 2055) with a session recorded in Africa

("Bringin' It All Back Home," Rounder 2055) for specialists
only. –BP

○ **Copeland Special / ROUNDER** 1981
This immaculate collection put the veteran Houston axeman
among the blues elite. Features searing guitar and soulful
vocals. –BD

Make My Home Where I Hang My Hat / ROUNDER 1982
This second Rounder Records album has its share of
incendiary moments. –BD

Texas Twister / ROUNDER 1983
Some of Copeland's best contemporary work for Rounder
Records. –BD

Collection - Vol. 1 / HOMESTEAD 1988
Early 1960-1968 Houston sides. Obscure but satisfying. –BD

When the Rain Starts Fallin' / ROUNDER 1988
More highlights from his Rounder Records material. –BD

JAMES COTTON   b 1935

Electric Chicago blues. James Cotton learned blues harmonica
from Sonny Boy Williamson. He was playing in Howlin' Wolf's
Arkansas Band at the age of 13 and even recorded with Wolf
on his early Chess sessions. After Little Walter left, Cotton
went on to become Muddy Waters's main harp player and
worked with him for more than ten years before leaving to
form his own band in 1965. Along with Junior Wells, Cotton
is one of the two greatest Chicago harmonica players alive
today. Branching out from straight blues, Cotton's recent
albums show the influences of jazz, gospel, and pop music.
His singing is often in the style of Bobby Bland, and his harp
playing combines elements of amplified down-home harp
with the high-compression Chicago style. –JME

James Cotton Blues Band / VERVE / BB 194 1967
Upbeat, soul-influenced mid-60s work by Cotton's initial solo
aggregation. –BD

Cut You Loose! / VANGUARD 1968
One of Cotton's earlier solo efforts. –BD

100% Cotton / BUDDAH / BB 146 1974
Boogie burners from this searing harp master at his absolute
hottest. –BD

○ **High Compression / ALLIGATOR** 1984
Half low-down Chicago blues, half brassy, R&B-influenced
fare, this spotlights his high-energy harp and vocals. –BD

Take Me Back / BLIND PIG 1987
The harpist pays tribute to his roots with a tasty album of
covers done Chicago-style. –BD

Live at Antone's / ANTONE'S 1988
A relaxed club setting of Cotton picking some old favorites,
with Matt Murphy contributing blistering guitar. –BD

Mighty Long Time / ANTONE'S 1991
A classy contemporary collection of standards with crisp all-
star backing. –BD

ROBERT CRAY   b 1953

Modern electric blues. Cray is the man responsible for bringing
the blues into the pop charts at a time when synthesized
dance pop was the rage. He did it through songs that defined
blues themes but added modern and personal twists. He's also
a fine bandleader and a masterfully subtle guitarist. –JF

False Accusations / HIGHTONE 1985
Cray's most developed and consistent Hightone release, cut a
year before he signed with Polygram. –JF

☆ **Strong Persuader / POLYGRAM / BB 13** 1986
Cray's commercial breakthrough is a set of songs that work off
one another and sound great as singles. It is evocative enough
to have made him the most innovative bluesman of the last 20
years. –JF

Don't Be Afraid of the Dark / POLYGRAM 1988
A followup to *Strong Persuader*, this suffers from weak songs,
but is worthwhile for fans. –JF

PEE WEE CRAYTON   1914-1985

Electric West Coast blues. One of the preeminent West Coast bluesmen of the postwar era, Crayton was one of the first blues artists to scorch the charts with an electric guitar instrumental ("Blues after Hours," a #1 hit on Modern Records in 1948). A student of T-Bone Walker (and later his rival), Crayton did his most successful and influential work for Modern, but he maintained his stature as a blues guitar master throughout a career which found him still going strong until a heart attack felled him at the age of 70. In *Living Blues* magazine, Dick Shurman described Crayton's style as a mix of "jazzy single-note lines, wide bends, fancy picking, and some of the biggest, prettiest chords ever waxed by a blues player." –JON

★ **Pee Wee Crayton / CROWN**   1959
An ancient but indispensable collection of his Modern label output. It includes the instrumentals "Texas Hop" and "Blues after Hours." –BD

○ **The Things I Used to Do / VANGUARD**   1971
A later work by this influential Texas guitarist. The only domestic CD available. –BD

Rocking Down on Central Avenue / KENT   1985
Classic late-40s/early-50s on Modern that showcase Crayton's smooth, T-Bone Walker-influenced guitar work. –BD

ARTHUR "BIG BOY" CRUDUP   1905-1974

Electric country blues. Although a major contributor to American music history, Arthur "Big Boy" Crudup remains in relative obscurity, known more as a name associated with Elvis Presley than as a blues recording artist whose voice and songs are familiar. Presley, early in his career, credited Crudup with being a model. Asserting the juke-joint roots of his own style, Elvis claimed that if he could "feel" what Crudup felt, he'd have it made.
Crudup saw several of his songs transcend blues tradition and have an impact on pop music. These include "That's All Right Mama" and "Rock Me Mama," the first a hit for Elvis, the second a standard associated with B. B. King.
Crudup's recorded legacy shows an unusual consistency and dependence on tradition. A limited guitarist who learned to play late in life, he stuck with the key of *E*, reworking the same basic guitar figures time and again. His voice was high-pitched, keening, and strong enough to cut through to his juke-joint listeners. Above all else, he was a songwriter with a gift for reworking traditional poetry into memorable songs. His best works have become staples for blues players past and present. –BLP

Mean Ole Frisco / COLLECTABLES   1960
These are his 60s Fire sessions. It fits into the second stage of his recording career, with *Look on Yonder's Wall* and *Coal Black Mare.* –BLP

Look on Yonder's Wall / DELMARK   1969
This late-60s Delmark session represents the third stage of his career history. –BLP

☆ **The Father of Rock & Roll / RCA**   1971
The best collection of Crudup's seminal 40s and 50s Bluebird recordings, including the original version of "That's All Right Mama." –BLP

COW COW DAVENPORT   1894-1955

Piano blues. One of the great early exponents of boogie-woogie piano playing, Davenport is principally noted as the composer of his signature tune, "The Cow Cow Boogie." –CK

○ **Alabama Strut / MAGPIE**
Mostly solo instrumental, this is Davenport at his best. (Import) –CK

CYRIL DAVIES

Electric British blues. Balding, gnome-like Cyril Davies was, with Alexis Korner, the cofounder of the entire British blues scene, whence sprang the Rolling Stones, the Yardbirds, et al.

A virtuoso on harmonica, he split with Korner in 1963 over the latter's insistence on adding horns to their band, Blues Incorporated. Davies died of leukemia in early 1964. –BE

○ **R&B from the Marquee / DECCA**
The first British blues album ever to make the UK charts. The playing is more than competent, although not as flashy as anything by the Rolling Stones. –BE

Dealing with the Devil / CBS
Davies's "Someday Baby" is one of the superior tracks. (Out of print) –BE

The Legendary Cyril Davies / FOLKLORE
Acoustic blues, rougher and somewhat more persuasive than his Decca album. Recorded with Alexis Korner. –BE

BLIND JOHN DAVIS   1913-1985

Piano blues. The piano work of John Davis was featured on blues records by the score during the 30s and 40s. His accompaniments to Tampa Red, Sonny Boy Williamson, Big Bill Broonzy, and others brought him fame as a blues musician, but like his piano compatriot Little Brother Montgomery, Davis did not care to be typecast as such and often expressed a preference for the sweet, sentimental favorites he played in countless piano lounges. But as with Montgomery, most of Davis's own recording opportunities came from blues companies, and he never failed to acquit himself well when it came to blues and boogie-woogie. He was the first pianist to do a European blues tour (with Broonzy in 1952), returning to the continent frequently as a solo act during the 70s and 80s. With blues piano appreciation in Europe being what it is and has been, it's not surprising that most of the albums of Blind John Davis were recorded there and not in Chicago, his home from the age of two until his death. –JON

○ **Stompin' on a Saturday Night / ALLIGATOR**   1977
Solid blues piano. Excellent phrasing and rhythms. –RW

You Better Cut That Out / RED BEANS   1985
His final session, with hot piano licks and failing vocals. –RW

JAMES DAVIS   1938-1992

Modern electric blues. James "Thunderbird" Davis was an inspiring vocalist whose records were far better known than he himself was until he reappeared on the blues scene in 1988. The handful of Davis recordings in 1963-1964 for Houston's Duke Records produced such gems as "Bad Dream," "Your Turn to Cry," and the oft-covered "Blue Monday." He was presumed dead by many blues fans and fellow musicians until Black Top Records turned him up in Gray, LA, and brought him back to blues life via new recording sessions and personal appearances. Davis was on tour at the Blues Saloon in St. Paul when he collapsed and died as he ended the song "What Else Is There to Do?" –JON

○ **Check Out Time / BLACK TOP**   1989
After years of musical inactivity, Davis returns with a roaring set that expertly spotlights his melismatic vocal delivery. –BD

LARRY DAVIS   b 1936

Electric Texas blues. A fine guitarist and singer, Davis is principally noted for composing the classic "Texas Flood," covered in fine fashion by Stevie Ray Vaughan on his first album. –CK

○ **I Ain't Beggin' Nobody / PULSAR**
A solid collection from this Texas artist. –DH

MORGAN DAVIS

Modern electric blues. A blues guitarist who was born in Detroit, then moved to Canada in the 60s. He is known for his gritty vocals and covers of old blues classics. –CR

○ **Morgan Davis / STONY PLAIN**   1989
Morgan's songs have nice hooks, lots of energy, and are guaranteed to get you going. Great guitar work and catchy vocals. If you like electric blues, I recommend this one. –CR

REV. GARY DAVIS   1896-1972

Acoustic country blues. This blind South Carolina-born country-blues/gospel singer and guitarist was, after Blind Blake, the foremost exponent of the East Coast ragtime school of country-blues guitar. Davis recorded mostly gospel material, with an occasional ragtime or pop instrumental. His impassioned, gravelly vocals drew on his church and preaching experience. He recorded only a handful of sides in the 30s, but after a number of years spent singing on the streets of New York City, he became a fixture of the 50s & 60s folk revival, recording and performing extensively. Using finger-picking, Davis drew a tremendous sound from the jumbo Gibson guitars he favored. His guitar style (simplified and copied by his much-recorded protégé Blind Boy Fuller) enjoyed complex rhythms and countermelodies far more involved than the garden-variety alternating-bass style of finger-picking. To hear Davis perform his spectacular reworking of Blind Willie Johnson's "Samson and Delilah" is an electrifying experience, and humbling for aspiring guitar pickers. –RL

○ **Pure Religion & Bad Company / FOLKWAYS**   1957
A solid sampling of Davis's influential finger-picking and singing on this one. –KL

Say No to the Devil / ORIGINAL BLUES CLASSICS
A strong early-60s session. –RL

At Newport / VANGUARD
This live set includes instrumentals and novelty tunes, as well as gospel, and gives one a feel for the man. –RL

★ **1935-1949 / YAZOO**
Powerful stuff. Some of the finest East Coast country-blues guitar ever waxed. –RL

When I Die I'll Live Again / FANTASY   1972
This twofer offers Davis's best work of the 60s. –RL

At the Sign of the Sun / GOSPEL HERITAGE
Fine later performances are included on this CD. –RL

Blind Gary Davis / DOCUMENT
All of Davis's stunning early recordings (1935-1949). –KL

WALTER DAVIS   1912-1963

Piano blues. A solid, two-fisted piano player heavily influenced by Leroy Carr. One of the brightest stars from the 30s Bluebird period of the genre's development. Not to be confused with jazz pianist Walter Davis Jr.–CK

○ **The Bullet Sides / KRAZY KAT**
Simply the best collection available, including the incredible "Tears Came Rollin' Down," one of Davis's best. (Import) –CK

FLOYD DIXON   ♭1929

Electric West Coast blues. Though his name is not as recognizable as Charles Brown's or T-Bone Walker's, Dixon was also a major contributor to the West Coast blues sound that came to life in the 40s, and his contributions have continued over the years. In many ways an upbeat counterpart to the mellow Charles Brown style, Dixon's music incorporated jump, boogie, and humor. He sang the original versions of "Saturday Night Fish Fry" (known as a Louis Jordan standard) as well as the more recently revived "Hey Bartender." As with most of the leading jump-blues artists, Dixon had some hits in the late 40s and early 50s but none since, despite the quality of many of his later efforts. –JON

○ **Marshall Texas Is My Home / SPECIALTY**
A swinging 22-song collection of this influential jump-blues pianist's finest 50s sides, including the original "Hey Bartender." –JF

WILLIE DIXON   1915-1992

Acoustic & electric Chicago blues. The premier blues composer of the post-WWII era, Willie Dixon was also probably the single most influential figure in shaping the Chicago-blues sound of the Chess Records heyday in his role as writer,

arranger, producer, and bassist. The recordings of Muddy Waters, Howlin' Wolf, Koko Taylor, Otis Rush, and innumerable others bore the Dixon stamp. He frankly admitted that such artists could perform his songs better than he himself could; hence he did little recording on his own (apart from some early work with blues harmony groups like the Big Three Trio) until fairly late in the game. His growing renown for songs like "Little Red Rooster," "Seventh Son," and "Hoochie Coochie Man" enabled him to start touring and recording with his Chicago Blues All Stars from the late 60s through the 80s. Much of his important later writing was in a socially conscious vein, dedicated to world peace and to improving the human condition. Dixon founded the Blues Heaven Foundation to secure the blues its rightful respect, protection, and recognition and to educate present and future generations about what he liked to call "the facts of life" — the blues. –JON

Willie's Blues / ORIGINAL BLUES CLASSICS   1962
A tasty, understated 60s session with singer/pianist Memphis Slim and bassist/singer/songwriter Willie Dixon. –MH

☆ **The Chess Box / MCA**   1989
A 2-CD box of Dixon's best-known vintage compositions, performed by his Chess Records labelmates with a few by Dixon himself. –BD

Big Three Trio / CBS   1990
Smooth three-part harmonies and sizzling instrumentals from the late 40s and early 50s. –BD

GEORGIA TOM DORSEY   ♭1899

Acoustic country blues. Though he started out firmly entrenched in the vaudeville and hokum blues traditions of the 20s and 30s, Dorsey found his true calling as the composer of several enduring gospel classics. –CK

○ **Come On Mama, Do That Dance / YAZOO**
Hard to believe that America's greatest writer of gospel songs could come up with this solid a collection of risqué blues tunes in his earlier, "sinful" days. Believe it. –CK

K. C. DOUGLAS   1913-1975

Electric country blues. K. C. Douglas was a Mississippi bluesman who transplanted himself and his music not to Chicago but to the San Francisco Bay Area in 1945. He became one of the rare Californians with such a down-home rural style, as many of his recordings were remakes of old blues he knew from Mississippi. (His first album, an obscure item on the Cook label, was entitled *K. C. Douglas, a Dead Beat Guitar and the Mississippi Blues.*) His re-creations of Tommy Johnson's blues were of particular interest to fans of prewar blues, but his own compositions attracted attention as well (K.C.'s music was introduced to rock listeners when his "Mercury Boogie" was redone by the Steve Miller Band.) –JON

○ **K. C.'s Blues / ORIGINAL BLUES CLASSICS**   1961
Traditional Mississippi Delta blues. A 1990 CD reissue of 1961 recordings. –NJF

CHAMPION JACK DUPREE   1910-1992

Piano blues. One of the blues world's most colorful characters, Dupree was both a first-rate entertainer and a top-quality artist, whether he took the role of merry mirthmaker or down-and-out denizen of the gutters of life. The first of the American blues greats to emigrate to Europe, Dupree managed, perhaps better than any of the other expatriate bluesmen, to infuse his work on the continent (both live and on record) with a continuing sense of freshness and vitality. His recording career spanned 51 years, beginning with the 1940-1941 sessions for Okeh that produced, among other classics, "Junker Blues" (later rewritten by Fats Domino as "The Fat Man"). After having recorded in Europe since 1959, Dupree returned for triumphant US tours in 1990-1991, waxing his final sessions for Bullseye Blues. –JON

☆ **Blues from the Gutter / ATLANTIC**   1958

Dupree's masterpiece. His pounding piano contrasts with some very downbeat subject matter. –BD

Blues for Everybody / GUSTO   1969

Two records of mid-50s Dupree on King, cut in NYC and Cincinnati with top-flight support. –BD

Back Home in New Orleans / BULLSEYE BLUES   1990

His first New Orleans session in ages was a steamy success, with Dupree's rolling 88s and authoritative vocals remaining bedrock solid. –BD

Forever & Ever / BULLSEYE BLUES   1991

Dupree explores his Crescent City roots with sympathetic contemporary backing. –BD

SNOOKS EAGLIN   b 1936

Acoustic & electric New Orleans blues. The blind Crescent City guitar virtuoso was hailed in some circles as the hot new talent of the blues world during the folk-music boom of the early 60s, but the versatile Eaglin's eclecticism reportedly soon put him in disfavor with the tastemakers. Though absent from the studio for some time thereafter, Snooks continued to perform in New Orleans, evincing a talent for whatever funky, folky, or farfetched styles he chose. Since the 70s he has recorded several times, with and without backup bands, his wide-ranging repertoire often still in evidence. In recent years Eaglin has won a new following among fans of hot contemporary blues guitar for his electric axework. –JON

○ **Country Boy down in New Orleans / ARHOOLIE**   1958

An album of early works, including ancient blues ("Jack O'Diamond") and Crescent City R&B in an easygoing, understated mix. –MH

● **Baby, You Can Get Your Gun / BLACK TOP**   1987

A funky album showing Eaglin in a contemporary New Orleans R&B setting. MII

Out of Nowhere / BLACK TOP   1990

More sounds in the "Baby You Can Get It" groove. –MH

TINSLEY ELLIS

Modern electric blues. A blues-based guitarist from the Atlanta, GA, area, notable for his stage work and his recordings both with the Heartfixers and as a solo artist. –CK

Live at the Moon Shadow / LANDSLIDE   1983

Atlanta blues/rockers Tinsley Ellis and the Heartfixers hit in concert with vocalist Chicago Bob Nelson. –MGN

Cool on It / ALLIGATOR   1986

High-energy roadhouse-rock and blues/rock with the Heartfixers. –NJF

○ **Fanning the Flames / ALLIGATOR**   1989

Blues/rock in the Stevie Ray Vaughan tradition. –CK

SLEEPY JOHN ESTES   1899-1977

Acoustic country blues. Big Bill Broonzy called John Estes's style of singing "crying" the blues because of its overt emotional quality. Actually his vocal style harks back to his tenure as a work-gang leader for a railroad maintenance crew, where his vocal improvisations and keen, cutting voice set the pace for work activities. Nicknamed "Sleepy" John Estes, supposedly because of his ability to sleep standing up, he teamed with mandolinist Yank Rachell and harmonica player Hammie Nixon to play the houseparty circuit in and around Brownsville in the early 20s. Forty years later, the same team reunited to record for Delmark and play the festival circuit. Never an outstanding guitarist, Estes relied on his expressive voice to carry his music, and the recordings he made from 1929 on have enormous appeal and remain remarkably accessible today.

Despite the fact that he worked to mixed Black and White audiences in string band, jug band, or medicine show format, his music retains a distinct ethnicity and has a particularly plaintive sound. Astonishingly, he recorded during six

decades for Victor, Decca, Bluebird, Ora Nelle, Sun, Delmark, and others. Over the course of his career, his music remained simple yet powerful, and despite his sojourns to Memphis or Chicago he retained a traditional down-home sound. Some of his songs are deeply personal statements about his community and life, such as "Lawyer Clark" or "Floating Bridge." Other compositions have universal appeal ("Drop Down Mama" or "Someday Baby") and went on to become mainstays in the repertoires of countless musicians. One of the true masters of his idiom, he lived in poverty, yet was somehow capable of turning his experiences and the conditions of his life into compelling art. –BLP

Legend of Sleepy John Estes / DELMARK   1962

The best of his Delmark rediscovery recordings. –BLP

Deep South Blues / MCA

Part of an 80s MCA budget blues series, this album includes "Drop Down Mama" and "Someday Baby." With Hammie Nixon on harmonica. –BLP

☆ **Sleepy John Estes 1929-1940 / YAZOO**   1992

An influential collection of Estes classics, including "Diving Duck Blues." –BLP

FRANK FROST   b 1936

Electric Delta blues. A fine singer, guitarist, and harmonica player, Frost upholds the rich tradition of Delta blues. Responsible for some of the finest down-home blues records of the 60s, he holds the distinction of being the last bluesman to record for the Sun label in Memphis. –CK

○ **Ride with Your Daddy Tonight / CHARLY**

Frost's best sides for the Jewel label. Some of the most down-home 60s blues ever recorded. (Import) –CK

BLIND BOY FULLER   1908-1941

Acoustic country blues. Unlike blues artists like Big Bill or Memphis Minnie who recorded extensively over three or four decades, Blind Boy Fuller recorded his substantial body of work over a short, six-year span. Nevertheless, he was one of the most recorded artists of his time and by far the most popular and influential Piedmont blues player of all time. Fuller could play in multiple styles: slide, ragtime, pop, and blues were all enhanced by his National steel guitar. Fuller worked with some fine sidemen, including Davis, Sonny Terry, and washboard player Bull City Red. Initially discovered and promoted by Carolina entrepreneur H. B. Long, Fuller recorded for ARC and Decca. He also served as a conduit to recording sessions, steering fellow blues musicians to the studio.

In spite of Fuller's recorded output, most of his musical life was spent as a street musician and house party favorite, and he possessed the skills to reinterpret and cover the hits of other artists as well. In this sense, he was a synthesizer of styles, parallel in many ways to Robert Johnson, his contemporary who died three years earlier. Like Johnson, Fuller lived fast and died young in 1942, only 33 years old. Fuller was a fine, expressive vocalist and a masterful guitar player best remembered for his uptempo ragtime hits "Rag Mama Rag," "Trucking My Blues Away," and "Step It Up and Go." At the same time he was capable of deeper material, and his versions of "Lost Lover Blues" or "Mamie" are as deep as most Delta blues. Because of his popularity, he may have been overexposed on records, yet most of his songs remained close to tradition and much of his repertoire and style is kept alive by North Carolina and Virginia artists today. –BLP

☆ **Blind Boy Fuller / BLUES CLASSICS**

The finest collection ever of blues and ragtime. Fuller is here both solo and with Gary Davis, Sonny Terry, and Bull City Red. This is Piedmont blues at its best (1935-1940), a must for anyone interested in down-home blues. –BLP

East Coast Piedmont Style / CBS

A very good 20-cut roots and blues collection with Sonny Terry, Gary Davis, and Bull City Red. –BLP

Truckin' My Blues Away / YAZOO
Piedmont blues at its best, with fine guitar work from this popular and influential bluesman. –BLP

JESSE FULLER   1896-1976

Acoustic country blues. Equipped with a bandful of instruments operated by various parts of his anatomy, Bay Area legend Jesse Fuller was a folk music favorite in the 50s and 60s. His infectious rhythm and gentle charm graced old folk tunes, spirituals, and blues alike. One of his inventions was a homemade, foot-operated instrument called the "footdella" or "fotdella." Naturally, Fuller never needed other accompanists to back his one-man show. His best-known songs include "San Francisco Bay Blues" and "Beat It on Down the Line" (the first one covered by Janis Joplin, the second by the Grateful Dead). –JON

Favorites / ORIGINAL BLUES CLASSICS
Skiffle roots in full cry. –MH

○ **Frisco Bound / ARHOOLIE**
A one-man band with guitar, harmonica, kazoo, and "footdella" bass. Some of his first recordings, ca. 1955. Innocent echoes of turn-of-the-century rural America. –MH

Lone Cat / ORIGINAL BLUES CLASSICS
Fundamental roots, rags, blues, and more. –MH

San Francisco Bay Blues / ORIGINAL BLUES CLASSICS
Fuller's hit and more. No misses. –MH

LOWELL FULSON   b1921

Acoustic & electric West Coast blues. One of the great blues guitarists, singers, and composers of all time, Fulson began recording after WWII in California in a country-blues context but soon made a transition to a more urban sound. His recordings for Swingtime (1949-1952) have been collected on a variety of labels and are notable for Fulson's Texas guitar, slick piano (usually Lloyd Glenn), and subtle horns. Notable hits from the period include "Every Day I Have the Blues," "Blue Shadows," and "Low Society."

Fulson joined Chess Records in 1954 and had an immediate smash hit with "Reconsider Baby" on the Checker label. Though he had no other commercial successes for Checker, he continued to record for them until late 1963. By 1965, he began recording for Kent Records in Los Angeles (owned by the Bihari family of Modern/RPM/Flair fame). Once again he scored an enormous hit with "Tramp" and had other strong items with "Black Nights" and "Make a Little Love." Moving to Jewel in 1969, he began recording albums with some rock background. Since that time his recordings have been album projects with varying degrees of success. He has also recorded in France and Japan. Invariably Fulson's performances are fine — if the results are less than satisfactory as a whole, it is usually a failed concept or an inappropriate accompaniment that is at fault. –BP

River Blues / ARHOOLIE
Reissues of his 40s Swingtime material. –BLP

○ **Hung Down Head / MCA**   1970
A reissue of his 50s Chess recordings. –BLP

ANSON FUNDERBURGH & THE ROCKETS

Modern electric blues. This Texas-based blues guitarist is a mainstay of the Austin, TX, circuit. A master of Stratocaster-tinged, single-string-style blues, Funderburgh fronts his band, the Rockets, sometimes working with harmonica legend Sammy Myers as well. –CK

My Love Is Here to Stay / BLACK TOP   1986
First record where Sam Myers (who had been performing with Robert Jr Lockwood as the latest gig in a professional career that began in the mid 50s) joined Funderburgh's band. This successful coupling has here and since made some truly wonderful music. –NJF

Sins / BLACK TOP   1987
The best of old and new: straightforward, no-nonsense blues. A successful combination of Texas and Delta sounds. –NJF

Rack 'Em Up / BLACK TOP   1989
Gutsy, driving blues in a nice variety of tempos and moods. Classic sound. Great record! –NJF

○ **Tell Me What I Want to Hear / BLACK TOP**   1991
First-rate, contemporary Texas shuffle and blues with tasteful, biting guitar from Funderburgh and great vocals and harp from Mississippian Sam Myers. This is their most varied and ambitious release to date (the band seems to get better with each album). The title track was used in the movie *China Moon.* "Rent Man Blues" is a humorous dialog between Myers and guest vocalist Carol Fran. Myers also adds an "answer" song to the blues classic "Sloppy Drunk." –NJF

TERRY GARLAND

Modern acoustic blues. A country-blues interpreter who plays a National steel-body guitar, often with a slide, in the style of Bukka White and Fred McDowell. –NJF

○ **Trouble in Mind / RCA**   1991
Garland's National guitar sounds great on this CD. Mark Wenner backs him up on harmonica. Garland can sing the blues, and he chose some big-time blues artists' songs to cover (Willie Dixon, Willie McTell, Johnny Winter, Jimmy Reed). –CR

PAUL GAYTEN   1920-1991

Electric New Orleans blues. Paul Gayten, a seminal figure in New Orleans rhythm & blues, led a varied career in the music business as a bandleader, producer, label owner, and onetime overseer of the West Coast operation of Chess Records. A nephew of blues piano legend Little Brother Montgomery, Gayten once led one of the top bands of New Orleans, but he gave up the performing life in 1956 to turn his attention to production and eventually to his own California-based Pzazz label (which featured Louis Jordan, among others). Gayten wrote Larry Darnell's 1949 classic "For You My Love" and recorded a few Top Ten hits of his own for Regal and DeLuxe (1947-1950), some of them with vocalist Annie Laurie. –JON

○ **Regal Records in New Orleans / SPEED**   1991
Early 50s New Orleans jump-blues and ballads by pianist Paul Gayten and vocalist Annie Laurie are featured on this generous (27-track) disc. –BD

JAZZ GILLUM   1904-1966

Blues. Next to John Lee "Sonny Boy" Williamson, no harmonica player was as popular or as much in demand on recording sessions during the 30s as Jazz Gillum. His high, reedy sound meshed perfectly on dozens of hokum sides on the Bluebird label, both as a sideman and as a leader. –CK

○ **Roll Dem Bones 1938-49 / WOLF**
Best selection of Gillum sides available. Not a bad one in this bunch. (Import) –CK

LLOYD GLENN   1909-1985

Piano blues. An instrumental giant and pioneer figure in postwar California blues, Glenn was a prime contributor to recordings by Lowell Fulson, T-Bone Walker, B. B. King, and many more, as a pianist and sometime arranger or songwriter. In 1950-1951, when mellow blues instrumentals were in vogue, Glenn's own combo had two national R&B hits, "Old Time Shuffle" and "Chica Boo" (which displaced "Rocket 88" as *Billboard*'s #1 record). At the time, Glenn also teamed with Lowell Fulson on "Everyday I Have the Blues" and "Blue Shadows." Glenn's renown was such that when a young Ray Charles went on the road as Fulson's pianist, he reportedly had to pass himself off as Lloyd Glenn. A boogie-woogie devotee since his early years, Glenn continued to display his piano mastery throughout a long and distinguished career. –JON

Old Time Shuffle / BLACK & BLUE

European sessions from the late 70s. Swinging piano throughout, showing off Glenn's patented Texas-cum-West-Coast lope to good advantage. (Import) –CK

○ **After Hours / OLDIE BLUES**   1982
After Hours: Piano Blues & Boogie Woogie is a solid collection of instrumentals recorded in the mid 40s and 50s. –CK

GOOD ROCKIN' CHARLES   b1933

Electric Chicago blues. A masterful harmonica player in the rich Chicago tradition, Good Rockin' Charles Edwards has been very much an elusive mystery man for much of his career. If all the legendary sessions that Edwards supposedly bailed out on were strung together (for example, Jimmy Rogers's "Walkin' By Myself"), his discography would probably be the most voluminous in Chicago blues history. –CK

○ **Good Rockin' Charles / ROOSTER BLUES**
Solid-as-a-brick production and performance from this enigmatic performer. –CK

HENRY GRAY   b1925

Electric Chicago blues. Though a Louisiana native and current resident (since returning home in 1969), Gray is still known to many enthusiasts as a Chicago bluesman. His 20-plus years on the Chicago scene included an extensive stint as Howlin' Wolf's piano man, along with a few recordings on his own and countless club dates with various blues bands. He has come to prominence in his own right during his more recent years in the Baton Rouge area, playing in the company of swamp blues musicians who complement Gray's robust blues work in fine down-home style. Gray has also toured and recorded in Europe as a solo act. –JON

○ **Lucky Man / BLIND PIG**   1989
Gray's first solo album features the pounding piano work that earmarked his best work with Howlin' Wolf and others. –CK

CLARENCE GREEN & THE RHYTHMAIRES   b1937

Electric Texas blues. Though not one of the best known of the modern Texas blues guitarists, Clarence Green is regarded by his peers as one of the best. Green (not to be confused with the late Clarence "Candy" Green, a Texas blues pianist) did session work for Duke Records in the 60s with Junior Parker, Bobby Bland, and others, and performed with stars from Fats Domino to Johnny Nash. His own recordings have mostly been for small Houston labels. As Marcel Vos from Double Trouble Records wrote, "The Clarence Green of today plays a brand of Texas blues that is mixed with soul, jazz, and funk, not unlike the music of fellow Texans such as Roy Gaines, Cornell Dupree, and of course, his brother Cal Green." –JON

○ **Green's Blues / COLLECTABLES**   1991
A CD reissue of Texas blues, R&B, and pop. All very danceable and very enjoyable. Recordings from 1958 to 1965. –NJF

GUITAR SLIM   1926-1959

Electric New Orleans blues. A torrid guitarist, impassioned vocalist, and legendary showman who took electric blues guitar playing to savage new levels of intensity, Eddie "Guitar Slim" Jones inspired a whole generation of musicians from Buddy Guy to Earl King to Jimi Hendrix. He spent most of his professional career in New Orleans, yet his music owed little to the syncopated 50s R&B so popular in the area. Neither is he typically regarded as a Delta bluesman, although he was raised in the Mississippi Delta and performed in Hollandale, MS, and Lake Village, AR, in his early years. His slashing guitar work, though rooted in the Texas jump style of Gatemouth Brown, burst forth from his recordings as something uniquely and identifiably his. Slim's #1 hit of 1954, "Things That I Used to Do" (featuring Ray Charles on piano), has become a standard in the modern blues band repertoire. His son Guitar Slim Jr, who was just a boy when Guitar Slim died of pneumonia on a trip to New York, carries on his legacy in New Orleans today. –JON

Piedmont Blues

"Piedmont blues" refers to a regional substyle characteristic of African-American musicians of the southeastern United States. Geographically, the Piedmont means the foothills of the Appalachians west of the tidewater region and Atlantic coastal plain stretching roughly from Richmond, VA, to Atlanta, GA. Musically, Piedmont blues describes the shared style of musicians from Georgia, the Carolinas, and Virginia as well as others from as far afield as Florida, West Virginia, Maryland, and Delaware. It refers to a wide assortment of aesthetic values, performance techniques, and shared repertoire rooted in common geographical, historical, and sociological circumstances; to put it more simply, Piedmont blues means a constellation of musical preferences typical of the Piedmont region.

Piedmont artists include guitarists Blind Blake, Gary Davis, Josh White, Pink Anderson, Blind Boy Fuller, Buddy Moss, John Cephas, and John Jackson as well as harmonica players Sonny Terry and Phil Wiggins. The Piedmont guitar style employs a complex fingerpicking style in which a regular, alternating-thumb bass pattern supports a melody on treble strings. The guitar style is highly syncopated and connects closely with an earlier string-band tradition integrating ragtime, blues, and country dance songs. It's excellent party music with a full, rock-solid sound.

— Barry Lee Pearson

Atco Sessions / ATLANTIC
These later (1956-1958) sides seem slightly subdued, but still include highly rewarding material. –BD

☆ **Sufferin' Mind / SPECIALTY**   1991
Monumentally influential 1953-1955 tracks by this wild, charismatic axeman, including the R&B chart-topper "The Things That I Used To Do." –BD

GUITAR SLIM JR   b1951

Electric New Orleans blues. Despite the fact that his first and only album to date earned a Grammy nomination, Guitar Slim Jr remains a somewhat shadowy figure to the blues public. The son of Eddie "Guitar Slim" Jones, his real name is Rodney Armstrong. According to New Orleans historian Jeff Hannusch's notes on Slim's 1988 album, he "has been a fixture on the Black New Orleans club circuit for the better part of 20 years ... [but] doesn't get to play the posher uptown clubs." His Orleans album featured mostly covers of his father's inspirational blues, which he was loath to play earlier in life, but Slim is also known for his extensive soul repertoire. –JON

○ **Story of My Life / ORLEANS**   1988
Contemporary blues, blues/rock, and soul from the son of the late blues/R&B legend. Mostly credible covers of his father's tunes. Grammy nominee. –NJF

BUDDY GUY   b1936

Electric Chicago blues. The idol of many a blues and rock guitarist from the 60s on through the present, Buddy Guy has been called the world's best, although his performances in person and on record have been inconsistent. The moments of awe-inspiring guitar continue to set a blistering pace for the axemen who follow in his path.Some of Guy's tastiest work has come not as a pyrotechnician but as a sideman par excellence, particularly with Junior Wells. Buddy cut his teeth on the Baton Rouge blues scene, influenced by the guitar heroes of his youth, Guitar Slim and B. B. King, before moving to Chicago in 1957. Today Guy owns his own blues club in the city, appropriately named Legends. –JON

A Man & the Blues / VANGUARD 1968
From the late 60s, tasty but not as urgent as his Chess material. –MH

Left My Blues in San Francisco / MCA 1969
Some of Buddy's best from Chess. –MH

○ **I Was Walkin' through the Woods / CHESS** 1970
Searing guitar, tortured vocals — the best of Guy's early-60s Chess recordings. –MH

○ **Drinkin' TNT 'n' Smokin' Dynamite / BLIND PIG** 1982
Recorded live at Montreux 1974. Accurately represents the long-standing partnership of Guy and Junior Wells. –BD

Damn Right, I've Got the Blues / JIVE 1991
Guy's first album with the *Billboard* charts, with Eric Clapton, Jeff Beck, and Mark Knopfler. –MH

☆ **Complete Chess Studio Sessions / CHESS** 1992
A two-CD compilation of Guy's seminal work for the legendary Chicago label. Full of explosive guitar and impassioned vocals, these are some of Buddy's finest recordings. –CK

★ **The Very Best of Buddy Guy / RHINO** 1992
A single-disc overview of this highly influential guitarist's best work. –CK

TRAVIS HADDIX

Modern electric blues. A native of Walnut, MS, "Moonchild" Haddix was inspired in his early years by B. B. King's broadcasts on WDIA out of Memphis. In Cleveland, OH, where he has lived since 1959, Haddix developed into a fine modern bluesman and songwriter with an original and soulful touch. His albums for Ichiban contain some of the best blues material that label has released. –JON

Wrong Side Out / ICHIBAN 1988
Impressive debut for this Cleveland-based vocalist. –BD

○ **Winners Never Quit / ICHIBAN** 1991
An interesting contemporary-blues/soul synthesis. –BD

JOHN HAMMOND   *b* 1942

Modern acoustic blues. Now enjoying his 30th year of recording, Hammond remains one of the greatest White performers of traditional acoustic blues. Although he's also an excellent electric guitarist and knows how to work with a band, most of Hammond's shows these days are solo presentations, complete with harmonica, voice, slightly amplified guitar, and foot stomps. During the course of one of his performances, Hammond carefully arranges his song list to bring the listener to several peaks, during which he sings, plays guitar, stomps, and wails away on harmonica, all with an enthusiasm and energy that belies his age. Thirty years after he began performing professionally, John Hammond is one of the most intense and energy-filled performers on the scene. –RS

○ **Live / ROUNDER** 1983
A definitive live set featuring Hammond on guitar and harmonica. –MGN

● **Nobody but You / FLYING FISH** 1987
Hammond usually performs solo, but here he is backed by a five-piece band, including pianist Gene Taylor. It's good to hear him in this context. All the numbers are blues classics or standards written by John Lee Hooker, Muddy Waters, Arthur Crudup, Little Walter, and B. B. Fuller. –MGN

○ **Best of John Hammond / VANGUARD** 1989
The best early works of this folk-blues artist. Acoustic and essential. –MGN

SLIM HARPO   1924-1970

Electric Louisiana blues. Born James Moore, this popular Louisiana blues singer played both guitar and neck-rack harmonica in a more down-home approximation of Jimmy Reed, who plowed similar turf with a more pronounced Chicago edge to it. Slim's music was more laidback than Reed's

(if such a notion is possible) but the rhythm was insistent, and Harpo's material not only made the national charts from time to time but also was quite adaptable for white blues-rock bands, including the Rolling Stones, the Yardbirds, the Kinks, and the Fabulous Thunderbirds. –CK

○ **Rainin' in My Heart / EXCELLO** 1961
The original Excello album. –CK

★ **The Best of Slim Harpo / RHINO** 1989
All the hits, including the original "I'm a King Bee," "Baby, Scratch My Back," "I Got Love If You Want It," "Shake Your Hips," "Rainin' in My Heart," "Tip On In," and "Strange Love." A best-of that really is, with top-flight sound as a bonus. –CK

☆ **I'm a King Bee / FLYRIGHT**
Unissued sides and alternate takes, the perfect companion volume to *The Best of Slim Harpo.* –CK

PEPPERMINT HARRIS   *b* 1925

Electric jump blues. Harrison "Peppermint" Nelson's story is one of many hidden or mistaken identities. He acquired the name Harris when a producer couldn't remember the singer's name when his first hit single, "Raining in My Heart," was released in 1950. The following year Peppermint (retaining the Harris billing) recorded his biggest seller, "I Got Loaded" — one of a number of drinking songs waxed by a man who maintained that he wasn't even a drinker at the time. As a songwriter, he said he often sold his compositions outright, relinquishing both royalties and writer's credits on songs recorded by B. B. King, Bobby Bland, and others. As a youth he looked to Lightnin' Hopkins as his main inspiration, yet his own style was nothing like that of Hopkins. A smooth city stylist, the college-educated Harris had an urbane approach to the blues, singing with a deep, often mellow tone while employing the guitar sparingly. He has continued to compose and record blues over the years, and rates as one of the more interesting Texas blues tunesmiths, even based solely on the songs that do list his name. –JON

Being Black Twice / COLLECTABLES
These are 60s and 70s sides from the Jewel label. A good vocalist with some unusual material. –HD

○ **I Got Loaded / ROUTE 66**
An import collection of classic R&B sides by this deep-voiced Texas bluesman. Booze-related songs derived mostly from 50s Aladdin singles. –HD

WYNONIE HARRIS   1915-1969

Electric jump blues. One of the most popular and powerful singers to contribute to the birth of 40s rhythm & blues, Wynonie Harris achieved his greatest hits by rocking long and hard or by making his listeners laugh the same way. His two #1 hits were the Roy Brown-penned "Good Rockin' Tonight" and "All She Wants to Do Is Rock," while other chart records were often in a comic novelty vein. But his nickname was "Mr. Blues" and a blues powerhouse he was, as well as a humorist, showman, and "a profane and raucous individual," in the words of his lifelong friend Preston Love. Many of his 1946-1952 hits were recorded with top-flight jazz accompanists. Harris recorded sporadically afterwards but never again enjoyed the glory or success he'd known as one of the kings of jump-blues. –JON

○ **Battle of the Blues / KING**
Split between Harris and Roy Brown, another jump-blues shouter, these late-40s/early-50s efforts swing with gleeful abandon. –GB

Good Rockin' Blues / GUSTO 1970
This two-record set contains many of the blues shouter's raucous, often double-entendre-loaded jumpers of the late 40s and early 50s on the King label. –GB

★ **Mr. Blues Is Coming to Town / ROUTE 66**
The best available retrospective of Harris's career. –CK

TED HAWKINS   b 1936

Modern acoustic blues. The enigmatic, elusive Ted Hawkins may be more familiar to passersby on the streets and beaches of Southern California than he is to blues concert audiences. A street musician with a streetwise yet sweet delivery of highly original songs, usually performed with only strummed acoustic guitar accompaniment, Hawkins first recorded for producer Bruce Bromberg in 1971. Peter Guralnick described Hawkins's "strikingly personal" music as "neither the blues nor gospel [but] a combination of the two, a rural adaptation of contemporary soul music."–JON

○ **Watch Your Step / ROUNDER**   1982
His acoustic-based debut, recorded in 1971, was released while Hawkins was serving a prison sentence. This album runs the gamut from moody, tormented ballads to celebratory moments of release. –JF

Happy Hour / ROUNDER   1986
There's more full-band stuff on this one, but the songs are top-notch, especially "Bad Dog." –JF

JESSIE MAE HEMPHILL

Acoustic Delta blues. A Mississippi singer/guitarist who weaves strong Delta traditions into her idiosyncratic style. –CK

○ **Feelin' Good / HIGH WATER**
An excellent set from this idiosyncratic Delta blues artist. –CK

Z. Z. HILL   1935-1984

Electric R&B/soul blues. Arzell "Z. Z." Hill toiled for years as a second-line act on the chitlin circuit, recording soul, blues, and R&B in whatever vein was contemporary and for various labels both big and small, until he signed with Malaco Records in 1980. His early Malaco singles did fairly well, but neither Hill, Malaco, nor anyone else was prepared for the astonishing success of his second album for the label, *Down Home*, featuring the now-standard "Down Home Blues," which was quickly adapted into every blues or R&B band's repertoire. *Down Home* became one of the best-selling blues albums of all time and has been credited as a major force in reviving the blues in the 80s. The journeyman soul singer became the #1 blues man in Black America; there was little crossover to the White blues market. Hill's approach was designed to appeal both to the mature blues audience and to younger R&B listeners, and in trying to promote a youthful image he usually subtracted several years from his age (hence there are a number of published birthdates). The fruits of his success were tragically short-lived, as Z. Z. Hill died suddenly in 1984, just two years after *Down Home* had turned his career around.–JON

The Brand New Z. Z. Hill / EXCELLO   1972
A 70s Swamp Dogg-produced concept album. –RP

Down Home / MALACO   1982
Straight blues, not trendy but timeless. –RP

○ **Greatest Hits / MALACO**   1986
Faultless bluesy soul, 1980-1984. –RP

THE HOLMES BROTHERS

Modern electric blues. The Holmes Brothers Band (guitarists Sherman and Wendell, Gib Wharton and drummer Willie "Popsy" Dixon) has emerged as the most appealing "new" blues band of the 90s. What they do is actually far from new, and they have been doing it in New York for many years. They have created their own version of soul through the ultimate blending of the church and the juke, merging gospel, blues, rock, and hillbilly. Their vocalizing effectively erases the boundaries between sacred and secular songs. With the freshest, most welcome blues sound today, they remind us that good music is not confined to any single genre. –BLP

○ **In the Spirit / ROUNDER**
A distinct blend of gospel, R&B, and even C&W. The most exciting discovery of the 90s. –BLP

Where It's At / ROUNDER
An eclectic blend of musical styles, primarily blues, done with gospel harmony. –BLP

MIKI HONEYCUTT

Electric R&B/soul blues. This soul belter was based in Shreveport, LA. A onetime lounge singer and "hippie girl-singer," Honeycutt came late to blues and R&B after gigging on the "crawfish circuit" with a band called A-Train. –NJF

○ **Soul Deep / ROUNDER**   1989
A very nice version of Junior Wells's "Come On in the House." The rest of the album is more soul than blues. –NJF

EARL HOOKER   1930-1971

Electric Chicago blues. The blues artist and singer generally acknowledged by his peers as the finest all-around guitarist in Chicago blues circles, Earl Hooker brought much of a modern flavor to his music while never straying far from his Clarksdale, MS, roots. A cousin of John Lee Hooker and a major disciple of Robert Nighthawk, Hooker's slide guitar work was the most technically advanced of all bluesmen. Adept at a multitude of styles ranging from hillbilly to jazz, Hooker worked as a sideman and leader in more configurations than any other modern bluesman. While his lead guitar work graced the recordings of Muddy Waters ("You Shook Me"), Junior Wells, G. L. Crockett, and others, Hooker's solo career didn't really blossom until the late 60s, by which time the tuberculosis that dogged him throughout his life cut his career short. Perhaps the only traditional bluesman to successfully utilize electronic gimmicks like wah-wah pedals and distortion units without sounding ridiculous in the process, Earl Hooker remains one of the great listening surprises of the blues. –CK

○ **Two Bugs & a Roach / ARHOOLIE**   1969
A nice representative sample from Chicago's unsung master of the electric guitar. Includes the title track, "Anna Lee," and the atmospheric instrumental "Off the Hook." –BLP

JOHN LEE HOOKER   b 1917

Acoustic & electric Delta blues. By the time blues singer and guitarist John Lee Hooker made his recording debut in 1948 and had a national hit with "Boogie Chillen," he was already an anachronism. Except for his thunderous electric guitar, Hooker's one- and two-chord modal stylings sounded much like those of a Delta blues artist from the 20s. This was not surprising, since Delta legend Charley Patton was Hooker's childhood inspiration. But Hooker's music was altogether more fierce and rhythmic, solo for the most part, coupled with his dark, hypnotic voice on one end and his relentless foot-stomping on the other. Over the years he recorded with full band support, though he never really found one to keep up with his odd approach to meter and his violent bursts of solo guitar. Recording right up to the present time for seemingly every large and small blues label that's ever existed (and with little to no variation in his approach), Hooker's music is raw, riveting, doom-laden Mississippi blues which demands much from the listener. One of the great emotional listening experiences in the blues, John Lee Hooker stands alone as a true creative original, often imitated but never equaled. –CK

○ **Hooker 'n' Heat / EMI / BB 73**
Riveting solo recordings from 1970, plus full-band sides with Canned Heat in support. Some of his most cohesive work with a band. –CK

● **Boogie Awhile / KRAZY KAT**   1990
A double album chock-full of Hooker's earliest and rarest sides, arguably Hooker at his very best, a great companion piece to *The Ultimate Collection*. (It's also available as a CD, but with fewer cuts.) –CK

★ **The Ultimate Collection (1948-1990) / RHINO**   1991
A two-CD box-set overview of Hooker's best sides, more than living up to its title. Indispensable. –CK

LIGHTNIN' HOPKINS   1912-1982

Acoustic & electric Texas blues. A true giant in blues history, Lightnin' Hopkins cut an imposing figure on the Texas blues scene and set a standard for postwar down-home blues. His work influenced not only countless country bluesmen all across the land but also many of the younger urban blues stylists. His songs might hark back to Blind Lemon Jefferson or they might deal with the latest-breaking news. Whether traditional or topical, acoustic or electric, whether recording solo or with a small combo, Hopkins was a natural: a master musician, singer, and blues poet/storyteller. He recorded electric country blues and boogies for the Black R&B market as well as acoustic guitar albums for the folk market. Throughout a lengthy and prolific recording career that began in 1946, he was a consistent, engaging, and immediately identifiable artist who made many outstanding records and very few bad ones. –JON

Gold Star Sessions - Vol. 1 / ARHOOLIE
Whew! Serious stuff. –JO

How Many More Years I Got / FANTASY
A repackaging of three earlier albums: *Walkin' This Road by Myself*, *Lightnin' & Co.*, and *Smokes Like Lightnin'*. Lightnin' plays electric with small-band support on these sides, which probably come the closest to what he sounded like in the juke joints around Houston in the early 60s. –CK

Gold Star Sessions - Vol. 2 / ARHOOLIE
○ **Lightnin' Hopkins / SMITHSONIAN-FOLKWAYS** 1962
Recorded in a boarding house in 1959: the truth according to Lightnin'. –JO

New Orleans Jazz & Heritage Festival / RHINO   1976
Hopkins on three tracks, playing a Stratocaster, raw and distorted, dragging the rhythm section by the scruff of the neck. Worth it for these three tracks alone. –CK

★ **The Complete Aladdin Recordings / CAPITOL**   1991
A double-CD boxed set of Hopkins's first recordings, primarily solo and acoustic. Powerful and riveting. –CK

☆ **Complete Prestige/Bluesville / PRESTIGE**   1991
A 7-disc boxed set of Hopkins's complete Prestige/Bluesville recordings. Includes Sam Charter's brilliant liner notes. –JO

BIG WALTER HORTON   1917-1981

Electric Chicago blues. Raised in the South, Horton recorded with a Memphis jug band in 1927 before migrating to Chicago. He is without a doubt one of the all-time great blues harmonica players. Along with Little Walter (whom he claims to have taught), Horton defined modern amplified harp (harmonica). There is no harp player (and that includes Little Walter) with Horton's big tone and spacious sense of time. Although his early acoustic recordings in Memphis (1951) are excellent, it is his amplified harp work that will be most remembered. He plays just incredible backup harp (and solos) with both Muddy Waters and Jimmy Rogers; and his instumental "Easy" with guitarist Jimmy DeBerry is a classic. Horton recordings from the late 50s and mid 60s are unrivaled. In particular, the album *Chicago/The Blues/Today! Vol. 3* on Vanguard is a landmark recording — his contrapuntal backup harp seems to float behind the singer, loping along, always stretching and opening up the time. And Horton's taste in notes is unparalleled. Big Walter Horton is one of the high-water marks of modern Chicago-style blues. –JME

Mouth Harp Maestro / ACE   195?
Sixteen cuts from the early 50s. Classic acoustic harp! –JME

● **Soul of Blues Harmonica / MCA**   1964
A classic album with horton in great form — sort of a musical tour of the wide variety of musical styles that Horton has mastered. Includes a fine verion of "Hard Hearted Woman." The all-star band includes Buddy Guy (g), Jack Myers (b), Willie Dixon (v), and Willie Smith (d). –JME

★ **Chicago/The Blues/Today! - Vol. 3 / VANGUARD**   1967
Here is one of the all-time great blues albums. A classic! –JME

○ **Fine Cuts / BLIND PIG**   1978
Perhaps the best of later Horton. Contains re-recordings of some of his better early material. –JME

SON HOUSE   1902-1988

Acoustic Delta blues. His blues were intense, anguished, and powerful. Unlike his 30s playing partner Charley Patton — a "clowning man" with a guitar — Son House took his music mighty seriously. Sitting on a straight-back chair, he'd suddenly whip his head back, roll his eyes inside his skull, and slide a bottleneck up his guitar's neck. Veins bulging in his forehead, he'd moan, thump a bass note, and sing with the deep conviction of a sinner on judgment day. Seeing him in 1930 caused a teenage Robert Johnson to abandon harmonica for guitar. House cast a lifelong spell over Muddy Waters too. Eddie James "Son" House remained true to his Mississippi roots. His 1930 Paramount 78s captured unsurpassed Delta blues singing but brought him little money or recognition. He made superb field recordings — solo and with a band — in 1941 and 1942, and then followed a girlfriend to Rochester, NY, where he took a job on the New York Central Railroad. Blues researchers located House in 1964 and prompted him into playing again. The hard-drinking guitarist recorded passionately primitive albums for Columbia, Verve/Folkways, Vanguard, and other labels, giving concerts until deteriorating health forced his retirement in 1974. He lived with his family in Detroit until March 21, 1988, when the last great voice of first-generation Delta blues was finally stilled. –JO

Delta Blues / BIOGRAPH   1991
Digital transfers from the Library of Congress acetates, 1941-1942. –JO

★ **And the Great Delta Blues Singers / DOCUMENT**   1991
The complete 1930 session, with Willie Brown, Rube Lacy, and others. Stunning vocals. (Import) –JO

○ **The Complete 1965 Recordings / CBS**   1992
After being rediscovered by the folk-blues community in the early 60s, Son House rose to the occasion and recorded this magnificent set of performances. Allowed to stretch out past the shorter running time of the original 78s, House turns in wonderful, steaming performances of some of his best-known material. –CK

HOWLIN' WOLF   1910-1976

Electric Chicago blues. The Wolf was six-foot-six, weighed close to 300 pounds in his prime, and possessed a voice that could shake the city down to the last radio. There is no sound in the blues more primal and ferocious than the recordings of the Howlin' Wolf. A pupil of Charley Patton and a contemporary of Robert Johnson, Wolf didn't start recording until the early 50s (first in Memphis for Sam Phillips, then in Chicago for Leonard Chess), quickly racking up one classic after another, all of them precisely focused on Wolf's dominating personality. "How Many More Years," "Riding in the Moonlight," "Back Door Man," "Spoonful," and "I Ain't Superstitious" (all featuring the stinging guitar work of Willie Johnson or Hubert Sumlin, Wolf's two main musical partners throughout his career) are just a few of his tunes that have been covered again and again by rock groups and bluesmen alike. Though his sandpaper growl of a voice has been widely imitated from Wolfman Jack on down, and his disciples are many, there exists no real "school" of Wolf, since the man and his music were uniquely of one piece. Capable of simultaneously rocking the house while scaring its patrons out of their wits, the Howlin' Wolf stands alone in the annals of American music. –CK

★ **Moanin' in the Moonlight / CHESS**   1964
Wolf's first and second Chess albums on one CD. With all the early hits, it's the perfect introduction to his music. –CK

Ridin' in the Moonlight / ACE   1982
A great collection of the Memphis/RPM sides issued in the early 50s. A great companion piece to *Memphis Days*. –CK

● **Memphis Days ... / BEAR FAMILY**   1989
Memphis Days: The Definitive Edition comprises two volumes of Wolf's earliest and rarest sides at the Sun studios, featuring previously unissued material culled from long-lost acetates. Raw and explosive, this is Wolf at his most primitive. Highly recommended. –CK

○ **The Chess Box / CHESS**   1991
A 3-CD boxed set. The definitive overview of Wolf's career. Great booklet and mastering, with Wolf interview snippets interspersed throughout. –CK

JOE HUGHES   b 1937

Electric Texas blues. A T-Bone Walker devotee, Hughes grew up in Houston's Third Ward, "a breeding ground of tough Texas guitar," according to historian Alan Govenar. When he was a teenager, his neighborhood friends included Johnny "Guitar" Watson and Johnny Copeland (who learned guitar from Hughes). Until the 80s, Hughes spent most of his career gigging with local bands around Houston and recording a few hard-to-find 45s. Albums and concerts in the US and Europe and an appearance in the film *Battle of the Guitars* have helped bring Hughes's music to a wider audience, earning him belated recognition as a "Texas guitar master." –JON

○ **If You Want to See These Blues / BLACK TOP**   1989
Solid and tasty Texas blues. The best tracks feature Joe fronting Anson Funderburgh's band. –NJF

ALBERTA HUNTER   1895-1984

Classic female blues. The influence of the late legendary vocalist can be heard today in the singing styles of many of the current crop of women blues singers, including Carrie Smith and Ruth Brown. Hunter was the perfect example of how changing public tastes were able to make singers of her ilk fashionable again. In the early 80s, Hunter, then over 80 years old, began a series of weekly engagements at New York's Cookery, simultaneously rekindling the public's interest in blues as well as in the fire in her voice. Her most exceptional recordings were made in the early 80s for Columbia, with legendary impresario John Hammond at the helm. –RS

○ **Young Alberta Hunter / JASS**
1921-1940. 23 classic tracks, both small and large backup bands (Fletcher Henderson). Good sound. –JME

IVORY JOE HUNTER   1914-1974

Electric jump blues. Best known for his classic ballads "I Almost Lost My Mind" and "Since I Met You Baby" (both #1 hits), Ivory Joe Hunter was one of the major 50s R&B stars to cross over into the pop market. Prior to that, he'd been a popular blues singer/pianist in the urbane West Coast style of the 40s. In the beginning he was a Texas barrelhouse blues pianist who recorded for the Library of Congress in 1933, and in later years he did sessions as both a soul singer and a country & western artist. As a songwriter, Hunter claimed over 7000 compositions. His recorded output was so varied as to defy any overall categorization, but for the blues enthusiast the reissues of his 40s sides are of greatest interest. –JON

○ **I'm Coming Down with the Blues / COLLECTABLES**
Obscure later sides by this piano-playing balladeer. –BD

MISSISSIPPI JOHN HURT   1893-1966

Acoustic country blues. An exquisite country blues singer/guitarist with a subtle voice and refined fingerpicking guitar style, Hurt recorded in the 20s and again in the 60s. Both periods are well worth hearing: acoustic country blues with real technical clarity that is also comforting and easy to listen to. He never made a recording not worth hearing. With a gospel flavor in his blues, Mississippi John Hurt projects a sense of dignity and kindliness through all of his recordings. If you have trouble with the frequent heaviness of many blues players, you may find Hurt refreshing. He is one of a kind, and a kind one at that. –JME

Today / VANGUARD   1966
A fine 60s album. –JME

○ **Immortal Mississippi John Hurt / VANGUARD**   1967
The best of Hurt's 60s "rediscovery-era" recordings. –MH

The Best of Mississippi John Hurt / VANGUARD   1971
A great double-album collection of 60s Hurt. –JME

★ **1928 Sessions / YAZOO**   1988
Justifiably legendary, with gentle grace and power on these understated masterpieces of fingerpicked guitar and vocals. This is the one to get. These are the early (1928) recordings, which are very fine. –JME & MH

J. B. HUTTO   1926-1985

Electric Chicago blues. A contemporary Chicago blues singer and slide guitarist in an Elmore James mold, Hutto also developed a fierce, raw style of his own. Recording from the early 50s to the mid 80s, Hutto was also a dynamic live performer. His good-time approach to the music held sway on his recordings, giving a loose, barroom feel to almost all of them, regardless of who was backing him. –CK

★ **Chicago/The Blues/Today! - Vol. 1 / VANGUARD**   1967
Hutto only has five tracks on this album, sharing it with solo turns by Junior Wells and Otis Spann, but it's truly the place to start, because it doesn't get much better than this: "Too Much Alcohol," "Please Help," "Going Ahead," and "That's the Truth" are all classics. –CK

○ **Hawk Squat! (with the Hawks) / DELMARK**   1972
"Hip Shakin'" and the title track are the highlights. –CK

And the Houserockers Live 1977 / WOLF   1991
A live import recorded in 1977, featuring Hutto with Hound Dog Taylor's band in support, raw & steamy. –CK

BULLMOOSE JACKSON   1919-1989

Electric jump blues. Popular bandleader/saxophonist Jackson was a staple of the early R&B sound of the King label. –CK

○ **Big Fat Mamas Are Back in Style Again / ROUTE 66**
A solid reissue of Jackson's best sides from 1945-1956. –CK

JIM JACKSON   c189-1937

Acoustic Memphis blues. Coming from the rich medicine-show tradition of the Memphis area, Jackson's "Kansas City Blues" is one of the great classics of the idiom. –CK

○ **Kansas City Blues / AGRAM**
Sixteen tracks from Jackson's peak creative period. Includes many variations of the title track. –CK

JOHN JACKSON   b 1924

Acoustic country blues. For much of his life, John Jackson played for country houseparties in Virginia, or around the house for his own amusement. Then in the 60s he encountered the folk revival, and since that time he has been the Washington, DC, area's best-loved blues artist. Undoubtedly the finest traditional Piedmont guitarist active today, Jackson exemplifies the songster tradition at its best. His eclectic repertoire embraces the music of his guitar heroes Willie Walker (who once visited his father's house), Blind Boy Fuller, and — most notably — Blind Blake. Besides the blues, rags, and dance tunes associated with these masters, Jackson plays ballads, country songs, and what he terms "old folk songs," such as "The Midnight Special." His confident fingerpicking, down-home Virginia accent, and contagious good humor mark his performances, live or on record, as something special. A world-class storyteller and party-thrower as well as a National Heritage Award-winning musician, Jackson has recorded a half-dozen albums and toured the world as often as he has wanted to. Today he often performs with his son James. –BLP

○ **Step It Up & Go / ROUNDER**
Virginia ragtime, blues, and hillbilly from this amiable singer/guitarist. –MH

LIL SON JACKSON   1915-1976

Electric Texas blues. A Texas country-blues guitarist/singer who adapted his laconic rhythms to electric guitar, Jackson enjoyed brief fame in the late 40s and early 50s, resurfacing again in the early 60s. –CK

○ **Lil Son Jackson / ARHOOLIE**
One of the few 60s "rediscovery" recordings that really works. Highly recommended. –CK

PAPA CHARLIE JACKSON

Acoustic country blues. Jackson was the earliest of the bluesmen to record. His rich vein of material drew from vaudeville, minstrel show, and folk-song material. –CK

○ **Fat Mouth / YAZOO**
The best single-disc retrospective of this early country-blues artist. –CK

ELMORE JAMES   1918-1963

Electric Chicago blues. A major link between the traditional Mississippi Delta blues and the modern electric Chicago blues sound of today, Elmore James played throughout the Delta — often with his friend Sonny Boy Williamson II (Rice Miller). Elmore's brilliant singing and slide guitar playing helped define Chicago blues, along with Muddy Waters, Howlin' Wolf, and the other Southern bluesmen who had migrated from the Delta to Chicago. Heavily influenced by Robert Johnson, Elmore became well known after recording his own version of Robert's "Dust My Broom" in 1951. Elmore always played, and recorded, with the finest musicians — usually featuring harmonica, piano, or tenor sax as a complement to his passionate singing and slide playing.

Elmore and his band, the Broom Dusters, played an intense, emotional blues that drove the audience wild. Stories are told of patrons becoming so spellbound by Elmore's plaintive singing and sensual slide guitar work that they'd throw money at his feet as he played. The passion of Elmore's music comes through on any of his recordings — listen to "Something Inside of Me," "Look over Yonder Wall," "The Sky Is Crying," or "Standing at the Crossroads" for starters.

As a slide guitarist, Elmore was more accurately in tune than most others, and his full, rich tone — bordering on feedback with the amplifier — had a sound much like the human voice. This tone may well have inspired B. B. King to develop the voice-like string-bending technique for which he has become famous. Elmore's playing has certainly influenced all the modern blues guitarists — from J. B. Hutto and Earl Hooker to Jimi Hendrix, Duane Allman, Eric Clapton, and Johnny Winter. Elmore died of a heart attack in 1963 and was buried near Durant, MS. –RDE

Complete Fire & Enjoy Sessions / COLLECTABLES
Elmore's complete output for Bobby Robinson's labels in the early 60s. Though this material has been around in various packages before, this four-CD set includes some great alternate takes and three tracks newly issued to this set. The definitive package of the last four years of Elmore's recording career. Emotional and powerful. –CK

○ **Whose Muddy Shoes / CHESS**   1969
These Chess sides from the mid 50s to early 60s are chock-full of classics, including "Madison Blues," "I Can't Hold Out (Talk to Me Baby)," and Elmore's version of "Stormy Monday." Also features definitive tracks by Chicago bluesman John Brim. –CK

★ **The Original Meteor & Flair Sides / ACE**   1984
The best of Elmore's early 50s sides with stunning slide and driving band support. Elmore at the top of his form — a perfect introduction to his music. (Import) –CK

The Last Session / RELIC
Emotion-laden sides recorded in 1963, containing some of Elmore's finest moments. –CK

● **Rollin' & Tumblin' - The Best Of ... / RELIC**   1992
A great single-disc compilation containing the best of the Fire & Enjoy sessions, with Bobby Robinson producing. –CK

ETTA JAMES   b 1938

Electric R&B/soul blues. The redoubtable Etta James is presently embarked on her third or perhaps fourth career, having sunk into and risen from obscurity a number of times since topping the charts in 1955 with "Roll with Me Henry" and "Good Rockin' Daddy."

Born Jamesetta Hawkins, the precocious 14-year-old brazened her way into an audition with impresario Johnny Otis, achieving instantaneous success under his aegis with her throaty voice. Blessed with both power and subtlety, Hawkins can shout and growl with gospel fervor or deliver a ballad with silken, purring insinuation. Her gift of superb phrasing is beautifully illustrated by "Don't Cry, Baby," the B-side of her great Argo 45 (#5393) "Sunday Kind of Love"; it's a simple repetition of an 8-bar blues that crescendos and fades exquisitely — a small masterpiece.

James's mid-50s recordings were followed by a disappearance into personal problems. When she resumed recording for Argo in 1960, she was *Better Than Evah*, as one later album was titled. During the next three years, she whipped out tons of fabulous sides, then once more submerged until 1967, when she commenced her great *Tell Mama* period of recordings on Cadet, another Chess subsidiary.

A final emergence from oblivion came in the 80s, and her career seems to have resumed full steam ahead, with guest spots on widely viewed programs such as "The Tonight Show" as well as concert appearances nationwide. Her current material tends toward pop rather than traditional soul, but her powers are quite undiminished. It's a pleasure that this great artist has proven to also be a great survivor. –GB

At Last / MCA / BB 68   1961
Most of these are also on *Greatest Sides*. Those that are not, are well worth hearing. –GB

Etta James Sings / UNITED   1962
A collection of her 50s hits, including "Roll with Me, Henry" (the answer song to Hank Ballard's "Work with Me, Annie"). Out of print. –GB

○ **Etta James Rocks the House / CHESS**
James tears it up on this live 1964 recording. Highlights include incredible versions of Jimmy Reed's "Baby What You Want Me To Do" and B. B. King's "Sweet Little Angel." James at her scorching best. –CK

Tell Mama / CHESS / BB 82   1969
More fine 60s Chess sides. –GB

★ **Her Greatest Sides / MCA**   1987
This album contains most of James's greatest 60s Chess and Cadet singles. Soul with a vengeance. –GB

SKIP JAMES   1902-1969

Acoustic Delta blues. Among the earliest and most influential Delta bluesmen to record, Skip James was the best-known proponent of the so-called Bentonia school of blues players, a genre strain invested with as much fanciful scholarly "research" as any. Setting an oddball guitar tuning against eerie, falsetto vocals, James's early recordings could make the hair stand up on the back of your neck. It was even more surprising when blues scholars rediscovered him in the 60s and found his singing and playing skills intact. He influenced everyone from a young Robert Johnson (James's "Devil Got My Woman" became the basis of Johnson's "Hellhound on My Trail") to Eric Clapton (who recorded James's "I'm So Glad" on the first Cream album). Although James's music is from a commonly shared regional tradition, it remains infused with his own unique personal spirit. –CK

Devil Got My Woman / VANGUARD   1968
Fine blues-revival sides from a very influential artist. –BLP

☆ **Complete 1931 Session / YAZOO**   1983
A magnificent sampler of the 30s repertoire of a major Mississippi artist. Blues, ballads, and religious songs are included among the major songs from this idiosyncratic

musical genius who has influenced current artists such as John Cephas. –BLP

BLIND LEMON JEFFERSON   1897-1929

Acoustic Texas blues. One of the first blues guitar stars, Blind Lemon Jefferson went on to become the most famous bluesman of the Roaring Twenties. His 78s shattered racial barriers, becoming popular from coast to coast and influencing a generation of musicians. His best songs forged original, imagistic themes with inventive arrangements and brilliantly improvised solos. He was a serious showman, balancing a driving, unpredictable guitar style with a booming, two-octave voice. His guitar became a second voice that complemented rather than repeated his lyrics. He often halted rhythm at the end of vocal lines to launch into elaborate solo flourishes, and he could play in unusual meters with a great deal of drive and flash. A man well acquainted with booze, gambling, and heavy-hipped mamas, Blind Lemon lived the rough-and-tumble themes that dominate his songs. Portraits of Afro-American life during the early 1900s, his lyrics create a unique body of poetry — humorous and harrowing, jivey and risqué, a stunning view of society from the perspective of someone at the bottom. To this day, he ranks among the most gifted and individualistic artists in blues history. –JO

★ **King of the Country Blues / YAZOO**
Jefferson was the most popular male blues artist of the 20s, and here's why! Superior sound. –JO

○ **Complete Recorded Works / DOCUMENT**
A four-volume set of Jefferson's complete recordings, sequenced in chronological order. –JO

BIG JACK JOHNSON

Modern electric blues. A member of Frank Frost's Jelly Roll Kings. Johnson's powerful voice and biting guitar evokes comparisons with Magic Slim, but Johnson has a rougher flavor to his blues. –CK

☆ **The Oil Man / EARWIG**
A solid album from a fine, down-home artist, with "I'm Gonna Give Up Disco and Go Back to the Blues." –CK

JIMMY JOHNSON   b 1928

Modern electric blues. Jimmy Johnson grew up in a blues family, sang gospel in his early years, established himself in Chicago (playing soul and R&B), then switched back to the blues in the mid 70s. Now recognized as one of Chicago's finest blues singers and guitarists, Johnson performs with emotion and commitment that belie his claim that he only turned to the blues because he couldn't get jobs playing more "commercial" music. Johnson's blues are distinguished by high gospel-rooted vocals (not unlike his brother Syl Johnson) and string-bending guitar from the Otis Rush/Albert King school. –JON

Johnson's Whacks / DELMARK   1979
His ambitious domestic debut exhibits a witty, irreverent, lyrical approach. –BD

North/South / DELMARK   1982
Funkier than his Delmark debut. Johnson's soaring vocals stand out. –BD

○ **Bar Room Preacher / ALLIGATOR**   1985
This record contains mostly covers, but it's still the best representation of Johnson's slashing style. –BD

LONNIE JOHNSON   1889-1970

Acoustic & electric Chicago blues. A guitarist and vocalist with a career spanning over 40 years (born Alonzo). Working with everyone from Louis Armstrong to Duke Ellington, Johnson may have been the most durable of all bluesmen. Certainly, few could even come close to his versatility. With jazz orchestras, small groups, piano-guitar duos, and solo, he recorded everything from low-down blues and the then-

popular hokum style to duets with jazz guitarist Eddie Lang. Johnson's backup work behind vocalists or as part of a larger group (he soloed on one of the earliest versions of "Stardust") is as interesting as any of his better-known solo sides. His execution and knowledge of his instrument was a major influence on a young Robert Johnson (some of whose more obscure numbers are virtual homages to his namesake) and other Delta bluesmen, and he was lauded as a well-known recording star.

Lonnie Johnson was primarily noted for the cleanly picked, highly intricate patterns used on his turnarounds. Though his recording career goes as far back as 1925, Johnson had an R&B hit with the self-penned ballad "Tomorrow Night" in 1948. He recorded for folk labels in the 60s, mostly using an electric guitar, as durable and versatile as ever. –CK

● **Blues & Ballads (with Elmer Snowden) / OBC**   1960
Later Johnson, doing blues and ballads with jazz guitarist Elmer Snowden. Johnson's vocals are refined and sensitive. It is hard to hear him sing his own composition "I Found a Dream" and remain unmoved. Such a lovely album. –JME

Mr. Johnson's Blues / MAMLISH
Fourteen cuts from the late 20s to early 30s, with Eddie Lang, Victoria Spivey, Texas Alexander, Mooch Richardson, Katherine Baker, and Violet Green. Highlights include "Uncle Ned Don't Use Your Head" and "Winnie the Wailer." (Out of print) –BLP

★ **Steppin' on the Blues / CBS**
A fine collection of nineteen blues, ragtime, and pop songs from one of the best guitarists, vocalists, and composers around. –BLP

○ **Complete Recorded Works / DOCUMENT**   1991
A fantastic 7-CD collection of Johnson's earliest works. Includes "Bed of Sand," "Treat 'Em Right," "Woke Up with the Blues in My Fingers," "When a Man Is Treated like a Dog," "Have to Change Keys to Play These Blues," "Blues Is Only a Ghost," "Not the Chump I Used to Be," and the romantic "She's Making Whoopee in Hell Tonight." –CK

Complete 1937-1947 Recordings / DOCUMENT   1992
Two CDs from a full decade of Lonnie's best, featuring "Man Killing Broad," "I'm Nuts over You," and "Laplegged Drunk Again." –CK

LUTHER "GUITAR JR" JOHNSON   b 1939

Electric Chicago blues. A solid Chicago bluesman in the West Side tradition of Magic Sam, Johnson toured the world with the Muddy Waters band from 1973 to 1980. He parlayed his Chicago credentials into a new career as a bandleader and a popular act on the East Coast blues-bar circuit after moving to Boston. (Johnson should not be, but often has been, confused with another ex-Muddy Waters sideman named Luther Johnson [1934-1976] who also moved from Chicago to Boston; Luther "Houserocker" Johnson, from Atlanta, GA, is yet a different artist.) –JON

Doin' the Sugar Too / ROOSTER BLUES   1984
The group Roomful of Blues provides swinging support. –BD

○ **I Want to Groove with You / BULLSEYE BLUES**   1991
An excellent outing by this former Chicago guitarist. Full of blazing integrity. –BD

LUTHER "HOUSEROCKER" JOHNSON

Modern electric blues. The latest Luther Johnson to add his name to the blues directory is an adept singer/guitarist who is a current favorite on the Atlanta blues scene. Proficient in various shadings of the electric blues idiom, Johnson has recently extended his repertoire from covers of blues standards to his own material, performed with the same 50s/60s flavor. –JON

○ **Houserockin' Daddy / ICHIBAN**
Johnson is a traditional electric bluesman (now living and working in the Atlanta, GA, area) who was heavily influenced by Jimmy Reed. The album includes covers of Jimmy Reed,

Lightnin' Slim, Howlin' Wolf, and Guitar Slim tunes. Simple, driving, to the point, streamlined, no-frills blues. −NJF

Takin' a Bite outta the Blues / ICHIBAN
Tough, direct, small-group blues: sounds hardened by years in bars, "giving people what they want." Covers of B. B. King, Jimmy Reed, Ray Charles, Charles Brown. Real nice. −NJF

ROBERT JOHNSON   1911-1938

Acoustic Delta blues. Robert Johnson lived his blues, spending most of his life wandering the Depression-era South. An inveterate womanizer and drinker, he performed mostly at juke joints, levee camps, and street corners. While his slide- and finger-style playing drew from the work of Son House, Charley Patton, Willie Brown, Lonnie Johnson, Kokomo Arnold, and others, his amazing finesse made him the most sophisticated of the Delta bluesmen. (His former traveling partner Johnny Shines remembers him as something of a human jukebox, able to play almost anything after a single listening.) Robert could blend his guitar and lyrics into one inseparable voice, and the 29 songs he recorded form a uniquely passionate and poetic body of work. His playing had an immediate impact on his contemporaries and inspired generations of players ranging from Muddy Waters in the 40s to Eric Clapton in the 60s and Steve Vai in the 90s. A half-century after Johnson's murder, the emotion-charged voice, troubled lyrics, and superb guitarmanship of "Cross Road Blues," "Rambling on My Mind," "Kindhearted Woman Blues," "Sweet Home Chicago," and "I'll Believe I'll Dust My Broom" remain as fresh and potent as any blues ever recorded. −JO

☆ **Complete Recordings / CBS**   1990
Among the most impressive blues ever recorded. Absolutely essential! −JO

TOMMY JOHNSON   1896-1956

Acoustic Delta blues. One of the great Delta musicians of the late 20s and early 30s, Johnson was influenced by Charley Patton and Dick Bankston. But he soon developed his own style and became highly influential in his own right, with Howlin' Wolf, Floyd Jones, and Boogie Bill Webb among his many disciples. −CK

○ **Complete Recorded Works / DOCUMENT**
The complete Victor and Paramount sides from 1928-1929, sequenced in chronological order. −JO

CASEY JONES

Electric Chicago blues. Jones is one of Chicago's most solid and swinging drummers, his work on numerous sessions (particularly behind Albert Collins) showing him off to good effect. −CK

○ **Solid Blue / ROOSTER BLUES**
A great, loose, informal album by one of Chicago's best drummers. Includes the excellent "Tribute To the Boogie Men." −CK

CURTIS JONES   1906-1971

Electric Chicago blues. A fine piano player and singer, best known for his songs "Lonesome Bedroom Blues" and "Tin Pan Alley." −CK

○ **1937-40 / DOCUMENT**
A solid collection of Jones's earliest sides. (Import) −CK

FLOYD JONES   1917-1989

Electric Chicago blues. One of the earliest of the Chicago Maxwell Street gang to record, Jones's mournful voice and rudimentary guitar work in perfect tandem with harmonica man Snooky Pryor and guitarist cousin Moody Jones. −CK

○ **Masters of Modern Blues - Vol. 3 / TESTAMENT**
Don't be put off by the murky sound on this one, because it features Jones, guitarist Eddie Taylor, harmonica wizard Walter Horton, pianist Otis Spann, and drummer Fred Below playing their hearts out. −CK

LITTLE JOHNNY JONES   1924-1964

Piano blues. One of the great blues piano men of all time, Jones is well known for his striking work on a number of seminal sides by slide guitar legend Elmore James. He recorded very little as a solo artist, but what few recordings exist are all classics of the Chicago style. −CK

○ **Johnny Jones w/ Billy Boy Arnold / ALLIGATOR**
Beautiful but tough Chicago piano blues. Real good. −NJF

ALBERT KING   ♭1923

Modern electric blues. Albert King first played the guitar in his early teens — at times in a gospel quartet. Albert was in and out of music until the early 50s when, after playing drums for Jimmy Reed, he again took up the guitar and decided to go it on his own. His first single, "Bad Luck Blues"/"Be on Your Merry Way," was recorded for the Parrot label in the early 50s. In the years to follow — and into the 60s — King sang and played his way onto the blues charts with songs such as "Laundromat Blues" and "Don't Throw Your Love on Me So Strong." Then, during the so-called "blues revival" (the discovery of blues music by a White audience in the 60s), King's recordings of "Born under a Bad Sign" and "Personal Manager" caught the fancy of British blues guitarist Eric Clapton. In fact, Eric Clapton copied King's "Personal Manager" guitar solo note-for-note on the Cream's song "Strange Brew" (*Disraeli Gears* album) — thereby introducing King's style to a new audience. From that point on, King was more famous than ever and began getting more lucrative bookings, including many of the rock clubs of the day, such as the Filemore Auditorium in San Francisco.

Albert King is truly a "King of the Blues," although he doesn't hold that title (B. B. does). Along with B. B. and Freddie King, Albert King is one of the major influences on blues and rock guitar players. Without him, modern guitar music would not sound as it does, and his style has influenced both Black and White blues players from Otis Rush and Robert Cray to Eric Clapton and Stevie Ray Vaughan (Stevie Ray was especially influenced by King). It's important to note that while almost all modern blues guitarists seldom play for long without falling into a B. B. King guitar cliché, Albert King never does — he's had his own style and unique tone from the beginning.

Albert King plays guitar left-handed, without re-stringing the guitar from the right-handed setup; this "upside-down" playing accounts for his difference in tone, since he pulls down on the same strings that most players push up on when bending the blues notes. King's massive tone and totally unique way of squeezing bends out of a guitar string has had a major impact. Many young White guitarists — especially rock & rollers — have been influenced by King's playing without even knowing it. Many players who emulate his style may never have heard of Albert King, let alone heard his music. His style is immediately distinguishable from all other blues guitarists, and he's one of the most important blues guitarists to ever pick up the electric guitar. Albert King is a tough act to follow. −RDE

★ **Born under a Bad Sign / STAX**
King's original album for Stax features many of his classics, now part and parcel of the language of the blues. Includes the title cut and "Crosscut Saw." −BD

● **Live Wire/Blues Power / STAX / BB 150**   1968
Powerful 1968 live set at the Filemore West. −BD

○ **Years Gone By / STAX / BB 133**   1969
Typically inspired Stax work from the King of the Flying V. −BD

Albert King: King of the Blues Guitar / ATLANTIC   1969
No blues guitarist who emerged during the 60s wielded more influence. This incendiary collection contains his best 60s workouts for Stax. −BD

I'll Play the Blues for You / STAX / BB 140   1972
A moody, R&B-influenced set with plenty of intensity. −BD

Chronicle (With Little Milton) / STAX   1979
Half Albert King, half Little Milton. All early-70s soul/blues classics. –BD

I'm in a Phone Booth, Baby / STAX
King's most recent studio album. Still tough. –BD

Blues at Sunrise / STAX   1988
A searing live set from the 1973 Montreux Jazz Festival. –BD

Wednesday Night in San Francisco / STAX

Thursday Night in San Francisco / STAX
Wednesday and *Thursday* are outtakes from a 1968 Filemore show that are just as scorching as the *Live Wire* album. –BD

The Best of Albert King - Vol. 1 / STAX
Many of King's best post-1968 Stax classics, with blasting lead guitar and assured vocals. –BD

B. B. KING   b 1925

Modern electric blues. Born Riley B. King, B. B. King is perhaps the most important and influential electric guitarist ever. Inspired by Lonnie Johnson, Django Reinhardt, T-Bone Walker, Elmore James, and Blind Lemon Jefferson, B. B. studied their music and then took the electric guitar to new heights by developing a blues guitar "vibrato" — used primarily for soloing — that hadn't previously existed. B. B.'s vibrato (his method of trilling, slurring, or bending the string) has become the major lead guitar "tool" of every blues and rock guitarist since — White or Black. Now known as "The King of the Blues," B. B.'s roots are in the music of the Mississippi Delta and Southern church choirs. Within the Black community B. B. has been a famous recording artist and entertainer from the late 40s until the present, so when White audiences "discovered" the blues in the 60s, B. B. was already on top and was finally greeted by a worldwide audience. Since then, Mr. King has received more awards and honors in recognition of his music than could ever be listed here (Grammy, Best R&B Vocal by a Male in 1970 for "The Thrill Is Gone"; Honorary Doctor of Music, Yale University) and has toured the world many times over, playing for presidents, kings, and world leaders.
B. B. is as great a singer as he is a guitarist, his vocal artistry influencing the styles of the younger Texas bluesmen — from Freddie King and Magic Sam to Luther Allison and Mighty Joe Young. Fame has never changed B. B. King, either. He's a humble entertainer who names his audience as the reason for his greatness. B. B. lives for his music, and he still plays some 150+ engagements a year! –RDE

My Kind of Blues / CROWN
According to his biographer, Charles Sawyer, this is B.B.'s personal favorite among his recordings. Unlike most of his albums from this period (which are mostly collections of singles), this was recorded in one session and takes B.B. out of his usual big band setting, using only bass, drums, and piano for accompaniment. The result is a masterpiece: a sparse, uncluttered sound with nothing to mask B.B.'s beautiful guitar and voice. "You Done Lost Your Good Thing Now" (its unaccompanied guitar intro is a pure distillation of B.B.'s style), "Mr. Pawn Broker," "Someday Baby" (R&B Top Ten, 1961), "Walkin' Dr. Bill," and a great version of "Drivin' Wheel" are highlights. (Out of print) –GB

○ **Anthology of the Blues - B. B. King / KENT**
An out-of-print collection of King's earliest recordings (1949-1950), back in the days when he was known as the "Beale Street Blues Boy." Raw, jagged, distorted guitar with crude timing, both instrumentally and vocally. Long-time fans will find this work most compelling. –CK

★ **Live at the Regal / MCA**   1965
Full of some amazingly inspired moments, King's *Live at the Regal* (arguably his finest album) outdistances his usual rock-solid studio efforts. Recorded in November 1964, the album is nothing short of magical, one of the greatest live performances ever committed to tape, ranking with James Brown's classic *Live at the Apollo 1962.* King's rendering of

"How Blue Can You Get" is sure to convert anyone resistant to the power of the blues. (Mobile Fidelity's Ultradiscs are always a sonic treat, but *Live at the Regal* is one of their finest remasterings, and preferable to the standard issue.) –RC

○ **Live in Cook County Jail / MCA**   1971
A burning, intense performance from the master of modern blues, in front of a captive audience. The best live version King ever recorded of "The Thrill Is Gone." –CK

Best of B. B. King - Vol. 1 / VIRGIN ·   1991
Transferred off the original master tapes, this compilation of King's earlier work with the Kent, RPM, and Modern labels sounds surprisingly full, with fairly clean highs and a respectable bottom end. The performances shine through, with "Everyday I Have the Blues," "Sweet Little Angel," and "You Don't Know" being some of the highlights. –RC

Spotlight on Lucille / VIRGIN   1991
Fans of King's jazzy big-band synthesis with electric blues should be in heaven with this smartly compiled release (named after his guitar). A collection of instrumentals from King's work with the Kent, Modern, and RPM labels that feature plenty of his heartfelt guitar style. –RC

● **Singin' the Blues/The Blues / ACE**   1992
Two great original Crown albums from the 50s on one import CD, including most of King's Top Ten R&B hits from the period: "3 O'Clock Blues," "Please Love Me," "You Upset Me Baby," "You Know I Love You," "Woke Up This Morning," and "Sweet Little Angel," plus one of his best, "Crying Won't Help You." This is the stuff that was so hugely influential to other blues guitarists and singers in its original recorded version. Here is lots of the real early, gritty stuff: "That Ain't the Way to Do It," "When My Heart Beats like a Hammer," "Don't You Want a Man like Me." The guitar intro to "Early in the Morning" is one of the finest examples of King in a jazzy mode. Great guitar! –GB

EARL KING   b 1934

Electric New Orleans blues. One of the key figures in New Orleans blues and R&B, Earl King has been a constant presence either on or behind the scenes for more than 40 years. From powerful blues à la Guitar Slim (a huge influence on King's early work for Specialty) and South Louisiana-style ballads to classic New Orleans "second line" rhythms and contemporary R&B, King has proven his mastery time and again. He has produced or written songs for most of the major New Orleans artists, including Fats Domino and Professor Longhair, as well as recording hits of his own such as "Those Lonely, Lonely Nights" (Ace, 1955) and "Trick Bag" (Imperial, 1962). King also did the original version of "Come On," later repopularized by Jimi Hendrix. –JON

● **Trick Bag / EMI**   1983
Funky, irresistible early-60s R&B, with King's guitar brought to the fore. –BD

Glazed / BLACK TOP   1986
Less of an overt New Orleans second-line feel, and plenty of well-written originals. –BD

○ **Sexual Telepathy / BLACK TOP**   1990
King's piercing guitar and charming vocals are prominent on this exceptional modern New Orleans blues set. –BD

FREDDIE KING   1934-1976

Modern electric blues. An influential blues guitarist and singer who rode to early-60s fame with a spate of catchy instrumentals that became instant bandstand fodder for fellow bluesmen and White rock bands alike. Employing a more down-home (thumb- and finger-picks) approach to the B. B. King single-string style of playing, Freddie went on to late-60s/early-70s success. He recorded for a variety of labels and was one of the first bluesmen to employ a racially integrated group onstage behind him. Influenced by Eddie Taylor, Jimmy Rogers, and Robert Jr Lockwood, King influenced the likes of Eric Clapton, Mick Taylor, Stevie Ray Vaughan, and Lonnie Mack, among others. –CK

371

★ **Freddy King Sings / MODERN BLUES** 1961
This reissue of his massively influential first album for the
King label includes "I'm Tore Down," "Have You Ever Loved a
Woman," and "Lonesome Whistle Blues." A companion piece
to *Just Pickin'*. –CK

Getting Ready / DCC 1971
Later recordings in a more rock-oriented vein. –CK

○ **Just Pickin' / MODERN BLUES** 1986
Both of Freddie's all-instrumental albums for the King label
(*Let's Hide Away and Dance Away with Freddy King* and
Freddy King Gives You a Bonanza of Instrumentals) on one CD.
"Hide Away," "The Stumble," and "San-Ho-Zay" influenced
guitarists on both sides of the Atlantic. –CK

LITTLE JIMMY KING

Modern electric blues. Memphis blues singer/guitarist who was
born Manuel Gales (two other brothers, including his twin,
record for Elektra). Little Jimmy King renamed himself for his
two principal inspirations on guitar, Jimi Hendrix and Albert
King (Jimmy cut his blues teeth in King's band and called him
his adopted grandfather). The guitarist cut his self-titled
album for Bullseye Blues in 1991, a raucous affair that found
him mixing blues, soul, and rock influences. –BD

○ **And the Memphis Soul Survivors / BULLSEYE** 1991
Part Jimi Hendrix, part Albert King, this is soulful blues. –RG

BIG DADDY KINSEY   b 1927

Modern electric blues. Long before Lester "Big Daddy" Kinsey
and his clan hit the international blues circuit, he established
himself as the modern-day blues patriarch of Gary, IN, and as
the Steeltown's answer to Muddy Waters. A slide guitarist and
harp blower with roots in both the Mississippi Delta and
postwar Chicago styles, Kinsey worked with local bands only
long enough for his sons to mature into topflight musicians,
and since 1984 (when Big Daddy recorded his debut album,
Bad Situation) the family act has become one of the hottest
attractions in contemporary blues. Big Daddy's material
ranges from deep blues in the Muddy Waters vein to hard-
rocking blues with touches of funk and even reggae, courtesy
of sons Donald and Ralph (who venture even further afield in
their own outings as the Kinsey Report). –JON

○ **Can't Let Go / BLIND PIG** 1990
Fine patriarchal blues from this little-known Chicago artist,
backed by his sons (Kinsey Report). –CK

KINSEY REPORT

Modern electric blues. Donald Kinsey (b May 12, 1953, in Gary,
IN), (vocal, guitar); Ralph "Woody" Kinsey, (drums); Kenneth
Kinsey, (bass); Ronald Prince, (guitar). Solidly based in the
blues as a result of lifelong training in the Big Daddy Kinsey
household, the Kinsey scions are also versed in a broad range
of music. The older brothers Donald and Ralph had an early
blues-rock trio (White Lightnin') in the mid 70s, long before
they regrouped as the Kinsey Report and began to
launch new excursions into rock. Donald also recorded and
toured with Albert King and with Bob Marley, and the
influence of those giants (as well as that of Big Daddy Kinsey,
naturally) show through in the music of the Kinsey Report.
The band expertly covers all the bases from Chicago blues
through reggae, rock, funk, and soul, and their recordings are
also distinguished by the songwriting talents and self-
contained production approach of the Kinseys. –JON

○ **Edge of the City / ALLIGATOR** 1990
An engaging, original blues/rock album from this family
band. –NJF

Midnight Drive / ALLIGATOR 1990
More varied and ambitious, but ultimately less successful and
satisfying. Thin, strident production. –NJF

Powerhouse / ATLANTIC 1991
A hard-rock album spiced (lightly) with blues. –NJF

EDDIE KIRKLAND   b 1928

Modern electric blues. A multi-talented artist who was
performing essentially in a high-energy blues style years
before the genre (or even the term) came into vogue, Kirkland
has traversed the many byways of the blues, sometimes to
acclaim but often in obscurity. Jamaica-born but Alabama-
raised, Kirkland played a seminal role on the Detroit blues
scene, recording his first sides there (1952, RPM) in the
company of John Lee Hooker. Over the next decade, his style
evolved into one of burning intensity, and during the 60s and
70s he fused his blues with raw, hard-edged soul funk.
Onstage with a band he was (and is) a pulsating,
somersaulting live wire, yet he can also be convincing as an
acoustic rural blues act. His recordings find him in or between
all these moods and settings, while Kirkland himself might be
found living in Georgia, Florida, or the Hudson Valley. He and
his music may be off the beaten blues path, but they're well
worth the search. –JON

○ **Three Shades of the Blues / RELIC**
Kirkland's eight sides on this compilation are as hard-driving
and intense as you could possibly ask for. It also includes four
sides each from B. B. King disciple Mr. Bo and the Ohio
Untouchables, with dazzling guitar work from Robert Ward on
the latter. –CK

It's the Blues Man! / ORIGINAL BLUES 1961
Exuberant and eclectic album featuring King Curtis on sax
and Kirkland on guitar and harp. –BD

ALEXIS KORNER

Electric British blues. The cofounder of British blues (with Cyril
Davies), guitarist Alexis Korner never achieved anything like
the fame of the younger players who learned from him
(among them Charlie Watts, who played in Blues
Incorporated). Gifted though he was, Korner lacked the vocal
skills or the commercial edge needed for mass success. After
splitting up the last of his various incarnations of Blues
Incorporated, he began popularizing the blues as the host of a
children's TV show. He toured with the Rolling Stones in the
mid 70s, then formed his last (and best) band, Rocket 88, late
in the decade, prior to his sudden death in the early 80s. –BE

Rocket 88 / ATLANTIC 1981
Arguably the best record ever for an offshoot of the Rolling
Stones, with Korner on guitar, Ian Stewart on piano, Charlie
Watts on drums, and Jack Bruce on upright bass. This has
tight, rippling, rollicking interpretations of blues and jazz
standards and is a seminal part of any collection. –BE

○ **Bootleg Him! / WARNER** 1987
The best of all the Korner anthologies, boasting unreleased
tapes and a lot of interesting one-off recordings from the
various nooks and crannies of his career. –BE

THE SMOKIN' JOE KUBEK BAND

Modern electric blues. Another young Texas axeman from the
old school, Smokin' Joe Kubek issued his band's debut disc in
1991 on Bullseye Blues, *Steppin' Out Texas Style*. Kubek was
already playing his smokin' guitar on the Lone Star chitlin
circuit at age 14. The vocalist in his current crew, B'nois King,
hails from Monroe, LA, and plays rhythm guitar as well. –BD

○ **Steppin' Out Texas Style / BULLSEYE BLUES** 1991
Just like the title says. –NJF

LAZY LESTER   b 1933

Electric Louisiana blues. The definitive swamp-blues
harmonica player since the 50s, Lazy Lester has also become
the most active member of the original down-home Louisiana
blues circle on the national performing circuit today. Lester's
harp was once a trademark on Excello labelmate Lightnin'
Slim's records, often introduced by Slim's exhortations to
"Blow your harmonica, son." Lester's session discography
encompassed appearances on a number of recordings by
other Louisiana artists, playing harp, washboard, or

impromptu rhythm accompaniment on cardboard boxes or rolled-up newspapers. He also recorded regularly on his own, and both sides of his best-known single ("I'm a Lover, Not a Fighter/Sugar Coated Love," 1959) inspired rock cover versions. Long after Lester left Louisiana for Pontiac, MI, he recorded a new album on a 1987 tour of England, home to many an Excellophile. With that album, he bounced back into the spotlight and has continued to delight blues devotees with his harp, homespun humor, and high spirits. –JON

Lester's Stomp / FLYRIGHT
Primitive and rocking 50s sides by an overlooked harmonica genius who epitomized the ragged-but-right ethic of producer Jay Miller. –JF

○ **Rides Again / SUNJAY** 1988
Lester's original rediscovery album pairs him with English blues musicians, with surprisingly great results. (Import) –CK

★ **True Blues / EXCELLO** 1991
Lester's original album, collecting the best of his early Excello sides. Includes "Sugar Coated Love," "I Hear You Knockin'," and "I'm a Lover, Not a Fighter." –CK

LEADBELLY   1888-1949

Acoustic country blues. Huddie Ledbetter is one of the best-known 20th-century folk and blues singers. Leadbelly had begun putting together his wide repertoire of blues, gospel, dance tunes, pop songs, and ballads by about 1900. Leadbelly was primarily known as a 12-string guitar player, though he also played the piano and accordion. One-and-a-half years after being "discovered" by John and Alan Lomax at the Louisiana State Penitentiary in 1933, Ledbetter moved to New York City. Leadbelly's fame was spread through his personal appearances, radio work, recordings, and the legends that circulated about this "Sweet Singer of the Swamplands." "Goodnight, Irene" and "Midnight Special" are the two songs most closely associated with Leadbelly. His influence upon folk revival musicians like Woody Guthrie and Pete Seeger was immense. New York City remained Huddie's base of operation until his death in 1949. –KL

○ **Sings Folk Songs / SMITHSONIAN-FOLKWAYS**
Includes 40s Folkways recordings with Woody Guthrie, Cisco Houston, and Sonny Terry. –MH

○ **Alabama Bound / RCA**
Wonderful performances from the late 30s, some with the Golden Gate Quartet. –MH

☆ **King of the 12-String Guitar / CBS**
From 1935, his first and bluesiest commercial recordings. –MH

FRANKIE LEE   bc194

Electric R&B/soul blues. Lee, whose early records billed him as Little Frankie Lee, gained some degree of erroneous notoriety among blues collectors who assumed (and stated in print) that he was the son of Texas bluesman Frankie Lee Sims; however, the two were not related, nor is their music similar. Frankie Lee started as a gospel singer, and the flavor and fervor of the church has remained a part of his secular performing style. Influenced by such singers as Little Willie John and Bobby Bland, Lee has recorded sporadically since the early 60s, mostly in a soul or soul/blues style. A long-time fixture on the Oakland blues scene, Lee has recently taken his act East in hopes of hitting the big time that has eluded him despite his renown as a live performer. –JON

○ **Ladies & the Babies / HIGHTONE** 1984
On these soul-styled contemporary blues, Lee's vocals exhibit a strong gospel influence. –BD

LEGENDARY BLUES BAND

Electric Chicago blues. Calvin Jones (b 1926, Greenwood, MS; bass, violin); Willie Smith (1935, Helena, AR; drum); various others on vocals, guitar, harmonica, piano. When the Muddy Waters band quit the master en masse in 1980, most of the sidemen stuck together and formed their own group. The

Legendary Blues Band, as they were named, included Pinetop Perkins, Jerry Portnoy, Willie Smith, and Calvin Jones throughout its early years. Short-term member Louis Myers, another Muddy Waters alumnus, appeared as guitarist on the band's first album (Rounder, 1981). The band has since changed personnel with some regularity, and while its lineup has become progressively less "legendary" in name or historic associations, its music has remained solid and true to the mainstream Chicago style. In a later configuration, they even made the *Billboard* Black Music charts. Recent albums have featured guitarist Billy Flynn and harmonicist Madison Slim. The rhythm section of Jones and Smith has anchored the unit throughout the changes, never failing to deliver the Chicago blues with aplomb. –JON

○ **Keepin' the Blues Alive / ICHIBAN** 1990
Only bassist Calvin Jones and drummer Willie Smith remain from Muddy Waters's old crew, but guitarist John Duich helps keep the traditional Chicago sound in place. –BD

KERI LEIGH & THE BLUE DEVILS

Modern electric blues. Actually consisting of only two official members (vocalist and drummer Keri Leigh and guitarist, bassist, and harpist Mark Lyon), these Austin-based blues-rockers cut *Blue Devil Blues*, a rock-drenched collection of blues standards, in 1991 for Amazing Records. Together since 1988, the pair has relocated to Austin from Oklahoma. –BD

○ **Blue Devil Blues / AMAZING** 1991
Pleasant contemporary-blues interpreters. –NJF

J. B. LENOIR   1929-1967

Electric Chicago blues. Combining high-pitched vocals, driving boogie guitar, an unusual off-time drumbeat, and a riff-oriented sax section, Lenoir was one of the few Chicago bluesmen to constantly turn to topical themes in his music. A wild and popular stage performer, Lenoir was starting to inject African percussion and rhythms into his music at the time of his death. His best songs are still staples of the Chicago blues circuit. –CK

● **His J. O. B. Recordings 1951-54 / FLYRIGHT**
Lenoir's earliest sides, including "Let's Roll" and the classic "Mojo Boogie." (Import) –CK

★ **The Parrot Sessions (1954-55) / RELIC**
J. B. at his creative and performing best, including "Mama Talk to Your Daughter," "Eisenhower Blues," and "Give Me One More Shot." The lyrics are as metaphorically powerful as any in blues and are sung against grooves alternating between low-down blues and Lenoir's patented boogie. –CK

○ **Natural Man / CHESS**
Equally fine mid-50s recordings for Chess. –CK

RON LEVY

Modern electric blues. This Boston-based piano man honed his chops with the B. B. King orchestra, and now works on his own. –CK

○ **Wild Kingdom / BLACK TOP** 1986
This contemporary blues effort is part Who's Who, spiced by Jimmie Vaughan and Kim Wilson of Thunderbirds fame. –RW

Safari to New Orleans / BLACK TOP 1988
Well-played but average compositions. –RW

FURRY LEWIS   1893-1981

Acoustic Memphis blues. Furry Lewis became Memphis's favorite blues character late in life, famed for a bottle in one hand and a bottleneck on the other. His clowning nature sometimes overshadowed his considerable blues talents, but his best work (especially the early 1927-1928 sides) was moving and memorable. Furry's music was not only the Memphis blues, it was the music of early 20th-century medicine shows, country suppers, and riverboats. His lyrics were often colorful and sly, and few bluesmen have ever seemed to enjoy themselves as much as Furry, who became something of a TV/movie celebrity after his return to action in the 60s. –JON

In His Prime 1927-1928 / YAZOO
Lewis is the Memphis-based "songster" singer and guitarist whose gently rollicking early work flows from the same country font as John Hurt's. –MH

☆ **Complete Recorded Works / DOCUMENT**
A full plate (25 tracks in all) of early, great sides. Includes "Sweet Papa Moan," "Black Gypsy Blues," and two takes of the best version of "John Henry" you may ever hear. –CK

LIGHTNIN' SLIM   1913-1974

Electric Louisiana blues. The acknowledged kingpin of the Louisiana school of blues, Lightnin' Slim had a style built on his grainy but expressive voice and rudimentary guitar work, with generally nothing more than Lazy Lester's harmonica and drums (usually a cardboard box!) in support. This formula worked successfully, scoring him regional hits for the Excello label for over a decade. Combining the country ambience of a Lightnin' Hopkins with the plodding insistency of a Muddy Waters, Slim's music remained uniquely his own, even when reshaping others' material to his dark, somber style. Lazy, rolling and insistent, Lightnin' Slim (born Otis Hicks) is Louisiana blues at its finest. –CK

Rooster Blues / EXCELLO   1960
The original Excello album. Excellent from start to finish. –CK

★ **Rollin' Stone / FLYRIGHT**   1991
With all six sides from Lightnin''s earliest singles for the Feature label, plus excellent alternate takes of his best-known Excello numbers, this album is the perfect place to start. (Import) –CK

☆ **King of the Swamp Blues / FLYRIGHT**   1992
A perfect companion volume to the other Flyright CD, this collects more rare tracks from Lightnin' Slim. –CK

LIL' ED & THE BLUES IMPERIALS

Modern electric blues. Lil' Ed Williams (b Apr. 8, 1955, Chicago, IL; vocal, guitar); "Pookie" Young (bass); various others, guitar, drums. Lil' Ed Williams learned his trade as a teenager from his uncle, Chicago slide guitarist J. B. Hutto, and the resemblance to Hutto, vocally and instrumentally, continues to be no less amazing some 20 years later. If Ed, half-brother Pookie Young, and the latest members of the revamped Blues Imperials never do much to modernize their blues or develop a new sound, that will be just fine with the band's growing legion of followers ("Ed Heads," no less), to whom the raucous, rocking slide guitar heritage of Hutto, Hound Dog Taylor, and Elmore James is blues nirvana. –JON

Roughhousin' / ALLIGATOR   1986
Wild & greasy blues at its best. A two-song session for an anthology turned into an all-night, live-in-the-studio jam. Sounds like it was great fun. –NJF

○ **Chicken Gravy & Biscuits / ALLIGATOR** 1989
Wild, raw, rough-edged Chicago slide guitar blues, this is jumpin', partyin' music in the tradition of Hound Dog Taylor and J. B. Hutto (Lil' Ed's uncle). Recorded live in the studio with no overdubs. Includes nine original compositions plus covers of Hutto and Albert Collins tunes. –NJF

MANCE LIPSCOMB   1895-1976

Acoustic Texas blues. As with Leadbelly and Mississippi John Hurt, the designation as a strictly blues singer dwarfs the musical breadth of Mance Lipscomb. A sharecropper/tenant farmer all his life, Mance didn't record until 1960 and the term "songster" fits what he did best. A proud yet not boastful man, Lipscomb would point out that he was an educated musician. His ability to play everything (classic blues, ballads, pop songs, spirituals) in a multitude of styles and keys was his particular mark of originality. With a wide-ranging repertoire of over 90 songs, Lipscomb may have gotten a belated start in

recording but left a remarkable legacy (eight albums in 15 years) to be enjoyed. –CK

☆ **Texas Songster / ARHOOLIE**   1960
Includes 60s Texas blues, traditional songs, and jackknife slide by a country master. –JO

LITTLE CHARLIE & THE NIGHTCATS

Modern electric blues. This West Coast-based blues band features the jazz-tinged guitar work of Little Charlie Baty, plus off-kilter original material from vocalist and harmonica player Rick Estrin. –CK

All the Way Crazy / ALLIGATOR   1987
A very happening debut album — funny and danceable. –NJF

○ **Disturbing the Peace / ALLIGATOR**   1988
Jumpin' blues. Wild antics, a good sense of humor, tons of fun, often outrageous. Very, very good guitar from Charlie Baty and interesting harp from lead vocalist Rick Estrin. –NJF

Big Break / ALLIGATOR   1989
Here is another raucous, rollicking release. –NJF

Captured Live / ALLIGATOR   1991
This enjoyable live set captures the group's manic energy. –NJF

LITTLE MILTON   b 1934

Electric R&B/soul blues. One of the great blues guitarists, singers, and composers of all time, Milton began his recording career in Memphis with Sun Records in 1953. Small-label singles followed for Meteor and Bobbin before he landed at Chess records in Chicago in 1961. He became one of the best-selling blues artists of the 60s, with many hit singles, including a #1 R&B hit "We're Gonna Make It" and items such as "Feel So Bad," "If Walls Could Talk," and "Baby I Love You." There may be soap opera elements in much of Milton's work, but it is always done with flair and good humor. While the mold was pretty much established during his Checker period, it also worked with his later affiliations at Stax and Glades. His Malaco recordings (dating from 1984) bring the formula of strings, horns, and background vocals up to date, but the blues artistry of Milton still shines through. –BP

Grits Ain't Groceries / STAX / BB 159   1984
Hot and soulful early-70s live Stax performances. –MH

○ **His Greatest Sides / CHESS**   1984
Milton's 60s Chess performances are hot and bothered. –MH

Annie Mae's Cafe / MALACO   1986
The best of his Malaco recordings are on this 80s album. –MH

★ **Sun Masters / ROUNDER**   1990
Early-50s Sun label material with searing guitar and pleading vocals. This is Milton's moment. –MH

LITTLE WALTER   1930-1968

Electric Chicago blues. Little Walter was one of the two greatest Chicago-style amplified blues harp players, the other being Big Walter Horton. No one else can touch Little Walter. He pretty much defined modern amplified blues harp by virtue of his sheer genius, his extended recording career with Muddy Waters, and his own solo recordings. Perhaps the first to play amplified harmonica in the now classic Chicago style, Walter is the undisputed master of the blues shuffle. His jazz-influenced harmonica style did much to shape the direction of the Muddy Waters band, lending it a more modern sound. Walter was a fine songwriter, with 14 Top Ten R&B hits between 1952 and 1958. He also had great recording groups that included such players as Robert Jr Lockwood, Louis Myers, Fred Below, and Luther Tucker. –JME

★ **The Best of Little Walter / CHESS**   1958
A quarter-century after his death, Little Walter is still the standard that most harmonica players aspire to. This 12-track compilation of sides recorded in 1952-1955 shows exactly why. A cornerstone for any blues collection, this album features the classics "My Babe," "Sad Hours," "Blues with a Feeling," "You Better Watch Yourself," "Off the Wall," and "Juke," the national anthem of harp players. –CK

● **Hate to See You Go / CHESS** 1969
Another solid collection of tracks recorded between 1952 and 1960. Standout cuts abound anywhere the laser beam falls, but the set closer, "Blue and Lonesome," just may be the most emotionally terrifying masterpiece of Walter's illustrious career. –CK

Blues World of Little Walter / DELMARK
The title is a bit of a misnomer, because Walter is featured more as a sideman to Baby Face Leroy, Muddy Waters, and others on early Parkway, Regal, and Savoy sides. The explosive slide work from Waters on this pre-Chess version of "Rollin' & Tumblin'" is not to be missed. Many of these sides have appeared on previous compilations, but this one features superior sound, taken from the original lacquer masters. –CK

○ **The Best of Little Walter - Vol. 2 / CHESS** 1989
Vol. 2 continues the overview of Walter's enormous output for the Chess label, with more definitive tracks, including "It Ain't Right," the blistering instrumental "Boogie," and "Boom Boom (Out Go the Lights)." –CK

JOHNNY LITTLEJOHN b 1931

Electric Chicago blues. Recording only sporadically, Littlejohn remains one of Chicago's best slide guitarists. –CK

○ **And the Chicago Blues All Stars / ARHOOLIE** 1968
Tight and intense, this is Littlejohn's finest record to date. Great slide guitar work. –CK

PAULA LOCKHEART

Modern acoustic blues. Talented and interesting vocalist, songwriter, and interpreter of classic blues and jazz. Influences include Bessie Smith, Dinah Washington, Alberta Hunter, and Joe Williams. Paula's recordings generally feature topflight musicians backing her sexy, stylized, understated vocal mannerisms in a variety of settings from solo guitar accompaniment to horn-driven big band in full swing. She continues to perform regularly in and around New York City, along with festival appearances and tours of the US, Canada, and Europe. Paula has performed and recorded with, among others, John Hammond, David Bromberg, and Dr. John. She was nominated for a Handy Blues Award in 1982 and a New York City Music Award in 1986. –NJF

○ **Incomplete / FLYING FISH** 1980
This best-of collection features cuts from her other three Flying Fish releases and is the most effective showcase of her versatility and consistent quality. –NJF

ROBERT JR LOCKWOOD b 1915

Acoustic & electric Delta blues. Lockwood was actually christened after his father, but the junior part of his name has stuck with him to the present day because of his association with his "stepfather," Delta legend Robert Johnson. When he first started recording in 1941, it was with a heavy debt to Johnson (few play that style better than Lockwood, and for good reason), but playing with harmonica wizard Sonny Boy Williamson on the original "King Biscuit Time" radio show broadened his tastes. The resulting jazz-influenced tinges remain hallmarks of his later work and, in the process, influenced a young B. B. King. One of the main house musicians used by Chess Records in the 50s, Lockwood played behind Sonny Boy, Little Walter, and Chuck Berry, to name a few, but never appeared as a solo artist. Moving to Cleveland, OH, in the early 60s, Lockwood formed his own bands, exploring every strain of music that appealed to him in his typically stubborn and adventuresome manner. Not merely slavishly recycling or exploiting his connection to the Robert Johnson legend, Robert Jr Lockwood has remained his own man, with a fine brace of solo recordings from his later years to prove it. –CK

○ **Steady Rollin' Man / DELMARK**
A fine, low-key set from a major contributor to the Chicago blues sound, recorded with the Aces, Louis Myers, Davey Myers, and Freddy Below. –BLP

CRIPPLE CLARENCE LOFTON 1887-1957

Piano blues. A consummate entertainer, Lofton helped to spearhead the boogie-woogie movement in the Windy City, influencing everyone from Meade "Lux" Lewis to John Mayall in the bargain. –CK

○ **Cripple Clarence Lofton - Vol. 1 / RST**
Some of Lofton's best, with the selections "Strut That Thing," "Monkey Man Blues," and "Pitchin' Boogie" being particular standouts. (Import) –CK

LONESOME SUNDOWN b 1928

Electric Louisiana blues. Cornelius Green was renamed Lonesome Sundown when he made his first records for the Excello label in 1956, and it was Sundown and his similarly renamed counterparts Slim Harpo, Lightnin' Slim, and Lazy Lester who helped define the Louisiana blues sound. Sundown has been called the most versatile and urbane of the group, as his material extended beyond the down-home guitar-and-harmonica stylings most often associated with swamp blues. Though he made a number of fine singles, none of them hit it big, and a disillusioned Lonesome Sundown went back to being Cornelius Green again after his last Excello sessions in 1965. Producer Bruce Bromberg brought him out of retirement to record some solid new material in the 70s, some of it featuring Sundown's protégé Phillip Walker. Though he gave the blues life a brief shot again, Cornelius Green has since settled into the sunset back in Baton Rouge. –JON

○ **Lonesome Sundown / EXCELLO**
Classic Southern Louisiana swamp blues from the studios of producer J. D. Miller. –BD

Been Gone Too Long / ALLIGATOR 1977
A comeback effort for this veteran swamp-blues guitarist. –BD

LONNIE MACK b 1941

Modern electric blues. Blues/rock & roll guitarist, singer, and songwriter Mack took the organ-like tone of guitarist Robert Ward's Magnatone amp, added blinding speed and devastating-for-their-time whammy-bar techniques, and spot-welded them to the most bluesy and soulful of sources. He influenced numerous guitarists in the process, his most devoted disciple being the late Stevie Ray Vaughan. Not content to merely grind out his old hits and rest on his laurels, Mack continues to write, record, and tour to this day, sounding better than ever. –CK

★ **The Wham of That Memphis Man / ALLIGATOR** 1963
A reissue of Lonnie's first album — the one thousands of guitarists cut their teeth on. –CK

Strike like Lightning / ALLIGATOR 1985
On this album, coproduced by Stevie Ray Vaughan, the highlight is an inspired duet with Vaughan and Mack on "Wham (Double Whammy)." –CK

○ **Second Sight / ALLIGATOR** 1986
New recordings, with Lonnie in excellent form. –CK

Live - Attack of the Killer V / ALLIGATOR 1990
Live & cookin'. –CK

MAGIC SAM 1937-1969

Electric Chicago blues. From his collected Cobra sides to his Delmark masterpieces *West Side Soul* and *Black Magic*, Magic Sam's recordings prove that (with the possible exception of Otis Rush at his best) nobody captured the spirit and soul of the 60s Chicago blues like the late Sam Maghett. When Sam died, Chicago lost its brightest star, yet because of his deserved reputation for guitar techniques and vocal passion, most of his recorded sides are available in some format. Along with several other artists, Luther Allison and Jimmy Dawkins for example, Magic Sam was associated with the so-called West Side sound, a 60s shift away from the Chess Studio sound associated with Howlin' Wolf and Muddy Waters. According to West Side musicians, the innovations were economically motivated because the tough West Side clubs paid so little. In the stripped-down guitar/bass/drums format, the guitarist worked overtime filling lead and rhythm roles simultaneously. Moreover, the demanding West Side audiences, many of them recently up from the South, took their blues seriously, and musicians had to play full-tilt to win their approval. During the 60s, blues musicians also needed to cover the soul hits on the charts. Put it all together, and you have three-piece bands alternating between innovative hard treatments of blues classics and contemporary soul material reduced to bare-bones readings. It made for some of the very best high-energy blues ever created.

Vocally, Magic Sam drew on the church-based soul styling favored by B. B. King and Otis Rush. Instrumentally, he preferred the haunting minor-key phrases and upbeat rhythmic treatment of John Lee Hooker or J. B. Lenoir riffs. Add in Sam's songwriting skills and a heavy dose of charisma, and you come up with the embodiment of 60s Chicago blues at its best. There will never be another like him. –BLP

★ **West Side Soul / DELMARK**   1968
The best 60s West Side sound album, the best Magic Sam album, and probably the best blues album ever made. –BLP

Black Magic / DELMARK   1969
More West Side soul. –BLP

○ **Live at Ann Arbor & in Chicago / DELMARK**   1981
Don't let the homemade recording quality put you off for a second, because this is Magic Sam at his whiplash best. –CK

Magic Sam Legacy / DELMARK   1990
A compilation of leftovers, but it's still great music. –BLP

● **1957-1966 / PAULA**   1991
Excellent collection of Sam's earliest sides for the Cobra and Crash labels. –CK

Give Me Time / DELMARK   1991
Relaxed, loose, informal home recordings of Sam playing solo, interpreting a variety of soul and blues classics. –CK

MAGIC SLIM & THE TEARDROPS   ♭1937

Modern electric blues. Principally influenced by Magic Sam (whom he claims gave him his stage name), Slim's jagged guitar style and powerful voice are mainstays of today's Chicago blues sound. –CK

○ **Raw Magic / ALLIGATOR**
One of the best contemporary Chicago bands, unadorned and to the point. –BLP

Grand Slam / ROOSTER BLUES   1982
An interesting tribute to Florence's, one of Chicago's most famous blues bars and an old Magic Slim venue. –BLP

MARTIN BOGAN & ARMSTRONG

Acoustic country blues. Only violinist, storyteller, and philosopher Howard Armstrong remains to tell of the exploits of this remarkable African-American string band. Virginia-born guitar and mandolin blues artist Carl Martin died in 1979, and guitarist Ted Bogan passed away a few years ago. But in their prime, Martin, Bogan, and Armstrong enjoyed multiple incarnations, first (in the 30s) as "The Four Keys," "The Tennessee Chocolate Drops," and the "Wandering Troubadours." They played individually and collectively throughout the mid-South on radio, with medicine shows, and at country jukes before eventually making it to Chicago in the late 30s and 40s, where they made records but mostly supported themselves by what Armstrong calls "pulling doors." This meant going into different cafes and taverns and playing for tips if they weren't thrown out. Playing various ethnic neighborhoods, the group took advantage of Armstrong's gift with languages and learned to sing in a variety of tongues. Best described as an acoustic string band (violin, guitar, mandolin, bass), the group played blues, jazz, pop, country, and various non-English favorites. As skilled musicians eager to earn tips by playing whatever their audiences wanted, they built a necessarily large repertoire. After years of separation the group reunited as Martin, Bogan,

& Armstrong in the early 70s and enjoyed substantial blues revival acclaim. After Carl Martin died, Bogan and Armstrong continued. When I worked with them in 1986, Bogan and Armstrong were still the greatest living exponents of the African-American string-band style, equally at home playing blues, swing, jazz, ragtime, or older Black string-band material. Armstrong, who speaks seven languages and is a painter and a sculptor, was a National Heritage Award winner in 1990. What made their music so wonderful, besides its energy and flawless presentation and their personable good humor, was their ability to remind us that good music transcends classifications and a skilled artist can draw from many streams. –BLP

○ **Martin Bogan & Armstrong / FLYING FISH**
A fine Black string band. –BLP

That Old Gang of Mine / FLYING FISH
A mixed repertoire for all ethnic audiences. –BLP

SARA MARTIN   1884-1955

Classic female blues. Known in her heyday as "the blues sensation of the West," the big-voiced Martin was one of the best of the classic female blues singers of the 20s. –CK

○ **1922-1928 / BEST OF BLUES**
All of Martin's best, featuring fine support from Fats Waller and Clarence Williams. (Import) –CK

PERCY MAYFIELD   1920-1984

Electric West Coast blues. After his #1 R&B lament "Please Send Me Someone to Love" established him as a subtly moving singer in 1950, a disfiguring auto accident forced Percy Mayfield to accentuate his songwriting skills instead. It was lucky for Ray Charles that he-did, since the introspective composer penned some of Brother Ray's best material (notably "Hit the Road, Jack"). Based in Los Angeles, Mayfield proved to be one of his own best musical interpreters during the early 50s when he racked up seven Top Ten R&B sellers for Specialty Records. The despairing "Strange Things Happening," "The River's Invitation," and "Please Send Me Someone to Love" tabbed Mayfield as the poet laureate of R&B, a writer whose material has grown in stature with time (Johnny Adams recently cut a whole album of Mayfield tunes for Rounder). Although his own sound was based in sax and piano, Mayfield's recordings were apparently too gentle and troubling to weather the onslaught of early rock & roll. While under contract to Charles as a writer during the 60s, Mayfield cut a couple of nice albums for the Genius's own Tangerine logo, and he remained semi-active on the West Coast until his 1984 death. –BD

For Collectors Only / SPECIALTY
As the title suggests, this gives a deeper look at Mayfield's early career. Alternate takes and unissued material. –HD

☆ **Poet of the Blues / SPECIALTY**
The original 1950-1954 recordings by this influential songwriter and vocal stylist. The superb combo backing was led by Maxwell Davis. –HD

JERRY MCCAIN   ♭1930

Modern electric blues. McCain blows harp with a heavy debt to idol Little Walter, while bringing a raucous, almost rock & roll slant to his music. He has recorded prolifically from 1954 to the present day for Trumpet, Excello (arguably his best sides, available only as singles or stray tracks on compilation albums as of press time), Rex, Okeh, Jewel, and Ichiban, among others. –CK

☆ **Choo Choo Rock / WHITE LABEL**   1981
These demo recordings for Excello (ca. 1956) are wild and raucous, featuring overamplified guitars, crashing drums, and bizarre lyrics. What a rock & roll album by Little Walter might have sounded like. –CK

Strange Kind of Feelin' / ACOUSTIC ARCHIVES   1990

McCain's earliest sides (1954). Also includes tracks by Tiny Kennedy and Clayton Love. –CK

CASH MCCALL   b 1941

Modern electric blues. Morris Dollison Jr, a gospel quartet singer turned Chicago rhythm & blues artist, made the R&B charts with his first solo record in 1966 ("When You Wake Up," Thomas Records). With that record he assumed the name Cash McCall, but a number of his most famous works still came as M. Dollison, songwriter. "More and More," the Little Milton tune that became a Blood, Sweat & Tears smash, may be the best known, but there were plenty more, for Muddy Waters, Howlin' Wolf, Koko Taylor, Garland Green, Otis Clay, and various gospel groups. Dollison was also a valued session guitarist in the Chicago studios in the 60s. In recent years, following a move to California, he has rebuilt his Cash McCall act in the blues field, waxing new albums and working closely with the late Willie Dixon. –JON

No More Doggin' / L&R   1983
Pleasing blues, R&B, and soul, recorded in 1983. –NJF

○ **Cash Up Front / STONY PLAIN**   1987
An excellent, varied blues and R&B album, with ten original compositions. Top-notch session musicians give this the sheen of studio perfection rather than bar-band rawness. Yet McCall can still get down in the alley, as he does on the cheatin' story "Girlfriend, Women, and Wife." –NJF

TOMMY MCCLENNAN   1908-1962

Acoustic R&B/soul blues. A gravel-throated back-country blues growler from the Mississippi Delta, McClennan was part of the last wave of down-home blues guitarists to record for the major labels in Chicago. His rawboned 1939-1942 Bluebird recordings were no-frills excursions into the blues bottoms. He left a powerful legacy that included "Bottle It Up and Go," "Cross Cut Saw Blues," "Deep Blue Sea Blues" (aka "Catfish Blues"), and others whose lasting power has been evidenced through the repertoires and re-recordings of other artists. Admirers of McClennan's blues would do well to check out the 1941-1942 Bluebird sessions of Robert Petway, a McClennan associate who performed in a similar but somewhat more lyrical vein. McClennan never recorded again and reportedly died destitute in Chicago; blues researchers have yet to even trace the date or circumstances of his death. –JON

☆ **Travelin' Highway Man / TRAVELIN' MAN**
Paint-peelin' Delta blues, 1939-1942. –JO

DELBERT MCCLINTON   b 1940

Modern electric blues. A Texas music institution, McClinton honed his musical chops to razor sharpness as a teenage harmonica man, learning firsthand from blues legends traveling through the area. He got on the big-time circuit via his harp work on Bruce Channel's hit, "Hey Baby," making it over to tour England and eventually giving harmonica lessons to a young John Lennon. Much behind-the-scenes work throughout the 60s ensued, with McClinton fronting the Rondells, who hit the Hot 100 with "If You Really Want Me to, I'll Go." He hit the charts again in the 70s with Glen Clark as Delbert & Glen. Around this period, McClinton's songs started getting covered by country acts, Waylon Jennings and Emmylou Harris both having hits with his material. The Blues Brothers used his "B-Movie Box Car Blues" on their first album and in their hit movie. He has released idiosyncratic solo efforts and has guested on albums with everyone from Roy Buchanan to Bonnie Raitt. We've not heard the last of Delbert McClinton, a Texas music treasure. –CK

Victim of Life's Circumstances / ABC   1975
Genuine Cowhide / ABC   1976
Both *Victim of Life's Circumstances* and *Genuine Cowhide* contain a few strong originals and successfully capture Clinton's aggressive blend of country and R&B. –RC
Second Wind / CAPRICORN   1978

McClinton lays on the grease with two great originals, "'B' Movie" and "Maybe Someday Baby" (featuring a wailing support vocal by Clydie King). Also includes a decent collection of covers ("Spoonful" and "Big River"). –RC

Live from Austin / ALLIGATOR   1987
Rock-solid, gritty roadhouse R&B, performed with a no-nonsense spirit. –RC

○ **The Best of Delbert McClinton / CURB**   1989
This adequate overview contains mostly familiar material but lacks the cohesiveness of his best early albums. –RC

CHARLIE MCCOY   1909-1950

Acoustic country blues. McCoy was a Mississippi-born guitar/mandolin player whose best work (recorded in the 20s and 30s) shows an amazing versatility. –CK

○ **Complete 1928-1932 Recordings / RST**
An excellent 24-track collection, including "Times Ain't What They Used to Be," "Your Valves Need Grinding," and "It's Hot Like That." (Import) –CK

JIMMY MCCRACKLIN   b 1921

Electric West Coast blues. Along with Lowell Fulson and Johnny Otis, the most durable of the West Coast rhythm & blues pioneers, McCracklin is still going at it, keeping up with the times after making records for almost 50 years. McCracklin has enjoyed relatively few hits but has managed to record again and again, though now with less regularity than in earlier days. As tastes in blues have moved on since he first recorded with only piano accompaniment, McCracklin has also moved his music onward through small combos, bigger bands, and more current styles, yet has never strayed far from the blues. A distinctive singer and a gifted songwriter, McCracklin lists among his hits "The Walk" (1958), "Just Got to Know" (1961), "Every Night, Every Day" (1965), and "Think" (1965), as well as Lowell Fulson's "Tramp" (1967), a McCracklin-Fulson composition. –JON

○ **My Story / BULLSEYE BLUES**
A recent album by this great 50s and 60s R&B singer. –MH

LARRY MCCRAY   b 1960

Modern electric blues. Raised in Arkansas where his grandmother, father, and older sister all played the blues, McCray formed a band with his brothers Carl and Steve after the family moved to Saginaw, MI. While still in his 20s, McCray chalked up a wide range of experience on the Saginaw music scene, encompassing blues, jazz, country, R&B, and rock. From the combination of a deep blues background and fluency in a variety of styles, McCray has forged a hot blues sound for the 90s. –JON

○ **Ambition / ATLANTIC**   1990
Along with Joe Louis Walker, McCray is the best of the contemporary bluesmen. He's a superb, rock-influenced guitar player. This album includes good songs with blues, R&B, and Motown influences. –NJF

MISSISSIPPI FRED MCDOWELL   1905-1972

Acoustic country blues. A driving, propulsive bottleneck guitarist, McDowell hoboed around the South throughout the 20s and 30s, working as an itinerant musician. Eventually settling down to become a farmer in 1940, he was discovered and subsequently recorded by folklorist Alan Lomax in 1959. These recordings coincided with renewed interest in Delta blues during the folk-music boom of the 60s, and soon McDowell was recording for a variety of labels and touring the world to deserved acclaim. A major influence on Bonnie Raitt (whose slide work shows a major stylistic affinity to his), McDowell's "You Got to Move" brought him a small fortune in belated royalties when covered by the Rolling Stones. –CK

☆ **Mississippi Delta Blues / ARHOOLIE**

Nineteen great tracks (1964-1965) of bottleneck slide guitar. Excellent liner notes. –JO

Fred McDowell / FLYRIGHT
Another well-rounded collection. –JO

And Johnny Woods / ROUNDER   1971
A nice, laidback set from guitar legend McDowell and his old harmonica sidekick, Johnny Woods. –BLP

BROWNIE MCGHEE   b1915

Acoustic country blues. Probably the most underrated, or at least underappreciated, bluesman on the planet, Brownie McGhee is a master musician whose most familiar recordings have for some time been out of vogue with current tastes in blues. The same music that made Brownie and his partner Sonny Terry a hot item during the boom years of folk music now tends to be dismissed as too smooth and folksy for contemporary fans, not raw enough for country blues aficionados, and not hard-hitting enough for the more electric-oriented crowd. While perhaps the folk-blues routine was overdone, it is still a disservice to dismiss Brownie McGhee and his music, for he has written and recorded many fine blues in a variety of styles since his recording career began in 1940. For ears not attuned to the folk idiom, McGhee's 40s output as the Piedmont successor to Blind Boy Fuller, the early postwar electric guitar combo sides from New York, and various post-Sonny Terry albums with different bands will all provide different and sometimes surprising perspectives; for the folk/blues fan, the Terry-McGhee collaborations still set the standard. –JON

★ **Brownie McGhee & Sonny Terry Sing / FOLKWAYS**   1958
A great album by this influential folk/blues guitar-and-harmonica duo. –MH

○ **Folkways Years (1945-59) / SMITHSONIAN**   1991
A singer/guitarist from North Carolina whose best work is in the spirit of Blind Boy Fuller. –MH

BLIND WILLIE MCTELL   1901-1959

Acoustic country blues. A Depression-era recording star, Blind Willie McTell worked until just before his death in 1959. His repertoire was phenomenal, covering mellow blues, hillbilly music, spirituals, quick-fingered rags, minstrel show tunes, and even semi-pornographic ditties. He played with a light touch on a big-bodied Stella 12-string, specializing in shifting rhythms and resonant melodies that were as distinctive as his clear, somewhat nasal voice. His best-known song is "Statesboro Blues," a 1928 fingerpicking showpiece named after his Georgia hometown. (Four decades later, the Allman Brothers turned it into their signature song.) A shrewd, intelligent man, McTell is remembered as having extraordinary powers of perception and memory, as well as an uncanny sense of direction. A great improviser, he sometimes composed with great deliberation, while other tunes reflect a stream-of-consciousness approach bordering on poetry. He kept a large 78 collection and occasionally learned songs from Braille sheet music. During the Depression, he recorded as Georgia Bill for Okeh, Blind Willie for Vocalion, and Hot Shot Willie for Bluebird. He was often accompanied by a second guitarist, and his wife Kate McTell sometimes joined in on vocals. Folklorist John Lomax recorded McTell in 1940 for the Library of Congress's Archive of Folk Song, capturing a remarkable array of blues, ballads, rags, spirituals, and insightful monologs. McTell reactivated his recording career in 1949, cutting for Regal and Atlantic Records. By then, however, his solitary blues seemed a thing of the past. –JO

★ **Early Years 1927-33 / YAZOO**
A good sampler, emphasizing 12-string guitar. –JO

○ **Complete Library of Congress Recordings / RST**
Songs and autobiographical monologs. –JO

Complete Recorded Works / DOCUMENT   1990

A three-volume set of McTell's complete recordings from 1927-1935. Some of the most imaginative 12-string guitar work ever recorded. –JO

MEMPHIS JUG BAND

Acoustic Memphis blues. One of the definitive jug bands of the 20s and early 30s, this seminal group was comprised of Will Shade, Will Weldon, Hattie Hart, Charlie Polk, Walter Horton, and others, in various configurations. –CK

☆ **Complete Recorded Works - Vols. 1-3 / DOCUMENT**
A definitive three-CD set with all the issued material from this groundbreaking jug band. Includes "Cocaine Habit Blues," "Cave Man Blues," the original "He's in the Jailhouse Now," and the always wonderful "I Whipped My Woman with a Single Tree." –CK

MEMPHIS MINNIE   1897-1973

Acoustic Memphis blues. Tracking down the ultimate woman blues guitar hero is problematic because woman blues singers seldom recorded as guitar players and woman guitar players (such as Rosetta Tharpe and Sister O. M. Terrell) were seldom recorded playing blues. Excluding contemporary artists, the most notable exception to this pattern was Memphis Minnie. The most popular and prolific blueswoman outside the vaudeville tradition, she earned the respect of critics, the support of record-buying fans, and the unqualified praise of the blues artists she worked with throughout her long career. Despite her Southern roots and popularity, she was as much a Chicago blues artist as anyone in her day. Big Bill Broonzy recalls her beating both him and Tampa Red in a guitar contest and claims she was the best woman guitarist he had ever heard. Tough enough to endure in a hard business, she earned the respect of her peers with her solid musicianship and recorded good blues over four decades for Columbia, Vocalion, Bluebird, Okeh, Regal, Checker, and JOB. She also proved to have as good taste in musical husbands as music and sustained working marriages with guitarists Casey Bill Weldon, Joe McCoy, and Ernest Lawlers. Their guitar duets span the spectrum of African-American folk and popular music, including spirituals, comic dialogs, and old-time dance pieces, but Memphis Minnie's best work consisted of deep blues like "Moaning the Blues." More than a good woman blues guitarist and singer, Memphis Minnie holds her own against the best blues artists of her time, and her work has special resonance for today's aspiring guitarists. –BLP

○ **Complete Recorded Works / DOCUMENT**   1991
A five-volume CD set of Memphis Minnie's entire output from 1935-1941. Highlights include "Me and My Chauffeur Blues," "Good Biscuits," "You Can't Rule Me," "If You See My Rooster," and "Selling My Porkchops." An essential collection by the greatest female blues guitarist ever. –CK

★ **And Kansas Joe - 1929-1934 / DOCUMENT**   1991
Minnie's earliest recordings with first husband Kansas Joe McCoy. Includes "I Want That," "Bumble Bee," "Squat It," "I Don't Want That Junk outta You," and the original version of "When the Levee Breaks," later covered by (and re-credited to) Led Zeppelin. –CK

MEMPHIS SLIM   1915-1988

Piano blues. One of the most prolific of all blues recording artists, Memphis Slim was never away from the studio for too long after he cut his first records in 1940 (Okeh). Although a sophisticated vocalist with a suave approach, Slim seldom strayed from his deep blues roots when it came to piano playing. He recorded in various solo, band, and small combo settings, primarily in Chicago until he began touring abroad in 1960. In 1962 he moved to Paris and became the most successful of the transplanted American bluesmen in Europe. Recording album after album on the continent, he wore his licks and repertoire thin, but among the plethora of Memphis Slim releases are a number of prize blues items. –JON

Memphis Slim / CHESS   1961

Pounding Chicago piano blues and boogies from Slim's early 50s Chess Records stint. −BD

Real Folk Blues / CHESS   1966
More classics from the Chess Records vault. −BD

Memphis Slim - U.S.A. / PEARL   1978
Exceptional 1954 material from the United Records vaults, with Matt Murphy's blistering guitar. −BD

☆ **Rockin' the Blues / CHARLY**   1981
The immaculate late-50s Vee Jay sessions are collected on this one album. Thundering piano and authoritative vocals are by the prolific Slim. Matt Murphy is astonishing on guitar. This is *the* Memphis Slim album, with roaring saxes adding more power. (Import) −BD

All Kinds of Blues / ORIGINAL BLUES CLASSICS   1984
A typical solo effort from this prolific pianist. −BD

AMOS MILBURN

Blues. Important jump-blues pianist who scored numerous hits with Aladdin from the mid 40s to the 60s. A hard-drinking Texan, Milburn fashioned a slew of stomping, houseparty classics, including "Chicken Shack Boogie," "Let's Have a Party," "Good Good Whiskey," and its sequel, "Bad Bad Whiskey." −JF

○ **And His Aladdin Chicken Shackers / ROUTE 66**
Sixteen of their best, including the highly influential "Chicken Shack Boogie." Highly recommended. (Import) −CK

BIG MILLER & THE BLUES MACHINE   ♭1922

Electric jump blues. Big Miller was born in Sioux City, IA. After stays in the Midwest, Australia, and Hawaii he settled in Edmonton, Alberta. He plays a big-band style of blues with some jazz thrown in. −CR

○ **Live at Athabasca University / STONY PLAIN**
Big sings some great old blues numbers such as Willie Littlefield's "Kansas City," T-Bone Walker's "Stormy Monday Blues," his own boogie-woogie-style song "Big's Boogie," and Gertrude "Ma" Rainey's "See See Rider." A real nice big-band blues release, 51 minutes in length. −CR

MISSISSIPPI SHEIKS

Acoustic country blues. One of the classic string bands of the late 20s and early 30s, this group featured the talents of Walter Vinson, Bo Carter, and Lonnie Chatmon in various configurations. −CK

☆ **Mississippi Sheiks - Vols. 1-4 / DOCUMENT**
There's absolutely no way you can go wrong with this superlative four-CD import set of this seminal blues band. Covers everything they ever recorded from 1930 to 1936. −CK

LITTLE BROTHER MONTGOMERY   1906-1985

Piano blues. A virtual encyclopedia of blues piano styles, Eurreal "Little Brother" Montgomery was a consummate musician who often parlayed his sparkling memory of countless obscure piano men from Mississippi and Louisiana into recordings of his own, many decades later. Of course, Montgomery created plenty on his own, most notably the classic "Vicksburg Blues" (Paramount, 1930), which he claimed a collaborative effort with two of those forgotten piano greats. His 1936 recording of "The First Time I Met You" was transformed into a modern-day Chicago masterpiece when reworked by Buddy Guy as "First Time I Met the Blues." Montgomery was a perfectionist who could work solo, with a Dixieland group, or with a Chicago blues band. One of his biggest complaints was that record companies only wanted him to record blues and not the old popular songs and sentimental ballads he also loved; fortunately for the blues fan, the record companies persevered. −JON

○ **Chicago: The Living Legends (South Side Blues) / OBC**
Features 60s recordings by this venerable blues pianist. −MH

JOHN MOONEY

Modern acoustic blues. A pleasant, versatile blues interpreter with a believable blues voice. A solid guitarist (tasteful, not flashy), working primarily in a Delta acoustic style. Originally hailing from Rochester, NY, Mooney learned his craft firsthand from country blues legend Son House. Mooney later moved to New Orleans, switched to electric guitar, and began enlivening his music with second-line rhythms indigenous to the area. −CK & NJF

Comin' Your Way / BLIND PIG   1979
Original songs and covers of LeRoy Caw, Arthur Crudup, and Sleepy John Estes. Nice work on National steel guitar on several cuts. −NJF

○ **Late Last Night / BULLSEYE BLUES**
A mixture of solo (acoustic) and band (electric) tracks, this album is fun, but not too heavy or self-serious. −NJF

ALEX MOORE   1899-1989

Piano blues. One of the last of the old-time Texas barrelhouse pianists, Alex Moore was an institution in Dallas, his lifelong home. A colorful entertainer with a poetic gift for rambling improvisations, Moore had one of the longest recording careers in blues history (his first sides for Columbia were made in 1929; his final session was in 1988). Yet it was hardly one of the most prolific, as there were usually lengthy gaps between sessions. The spontaneous, autobiographical nature of his latter-day recordings imbue his albums with a special charm. −JON

○ **Wiggle Tail / ROUNDER**
Late recordings by this venerable Texas blues pianist. −MH

MIKE MORGAN & THE CRAWL

Modern electric blues. A Texas blues band, with twangy guitarist Mike Morgan and vocalist/harpist Lee McBee prominently spotlighted, this Dallas quartet is set squarely in the Lone Star blues tradition. Their 1990 debut for Black Top, *Raw & Ready*, was followed by the more polished *Mighty Fine Dancin'= the next year.* −BD

Raw and Ready / BLACK TOP   1990
Atmospheric but somewhat derivative contemporary Texas guitar blues. −BD

○ **Mighty Fine Dancin' / BLACK TOP**   1991
A more polished and varied set — their best to date. −BD

BUDDY MOSS   1906-1984

Acoustic country blues. Called "probably the finest of the North Carolina school of Piedmont blues artists" by blues author and reissue producer Bruce Bastin, Eugene "Buddy" Moss enjoyed only a brief period of real popularity on the blues scene (1933-19, when he was recording regularly for the American Record Company label group). In his later years, he was still an excellent musician by most accounts, yet for reasons of his own he did little to revive his career in the way of public performances or new recordings. (Bastin also described Moss as "moody" and "temperamental" in his 1971 book *Crying for the Carolinas*.) However, Moss left a substantial recorded legacy that included two-guitar sessions with such illustrious accompanists as Josh White, Curley Weaver, and Brownie McGhee. −JON

Rediscovery / BIOGRAPH
Piedmont blues master Buddy Moss featured in a good blues revival session. −BLP

○ **Buddy Moss 1933-35 / DOCUMENT**
A fine collection of blues from one of the major Piedmont guitarists and composers. −BLP

MATT MURPHY   ♭1927

Electric Chicago blues. Matt "Guitar" Murphy, once called the best guitar player in the blues by Willie Dixon, built a new, although not particularly illustrious career in the 80s based on his association with the Blues Brothers. (Not only was he a band member, he also had a memorable scene with Aretha Franklin in the movie.) Murphy, formerly a sideman extraordinaire with Memphis Slim, Bobby Bland, and others, subsequently put together a touring band of his own. He found ample nightclub work, but one noted blues club owner ostensibly hired the band, then told all of them except Murphy to stay in their hotel rooms, because it was only Murphy's legendary guitarmanship that the diehard blues fans wanted to hear, not another pseudo-blues revue. And it has only been in the role of blues guitar hero, not Blues Brothers bandsman, that Murphy has been able to record on his own in recent years, including his first full album (for the Austin-based Antone's label). His incendiary 50s work, most of which was with Memphis Slim, was revelatory for its time and sounds no less remarkable today. –JON

○ **Way Down South / ANTONE'S**   1990
Primarily an instrumental release, spotlighting Matt's fluid guitar playing. Matt's brother Floyd Murphy (who did session work for Sun Records in the early 50s) joins in on guitar. –NJF

CHARLIE MUSSELWHITE   b1944

Electric Chicago blues. One of the most heralded new harp players to emerge from the Chicago scene of the 60s, Musselwhite differed from the other White musicians on the circuit in that, like many Black bluesmen, he came from a working-class Mississippi family via Memphis to the Windy City. His early Chicago experience came at various South and West Side clubs with the city's blues veterans. In the late 60s he followed the westward movement to California, where he has lived since, but unlike some of the other transplanted Chicagoans, "Memphis Charlie" never attempted to become a pop-rock star and, over the years, has mellowed into a powerful, mature stylist with a continuing dedication to the roots of the blues. –JON

Stand Back! Here Comes Charley / VANGUARD   1967
Musselwhite's debut album is ambitious and self-consciously authentic. –MH

Memphis Charlie / ARHOOLIE
The rootsiest Musselwhite, but not the most fun. –MH

○ **Ace of Harps / ALLIGATOR**   1990
Musselwhite accompanied by a hot young band. Relaxed and real. –MH

LOUIS MYERS   b1929

Electric Chicago blues. A member of Little Walter's Jukes, Myers is one of the idiom's finest guitarists and an excellent harmonica player as well. –CK

○ **I'm a Southern Man / ADVENT**
Myers's debut album, with fine playing and singing throughout. –CK

KENNY NEAL   b1957

Modern electric blues. A versatile and dynamic new-generation bluesman, Kenny Neal grew up with the blues in Baton Rouge. He made his performing debut at the age of 6 with his father, harmonica player Raful Neal, and joined the family band at 13. After a late-70s apprenticeship as the bass man in Buddy Guy's Chicago band, Kenny struck out on his own with his brothers Larry, Raful Jr, and Ronnie in Toronto. Adept at playing soulful down-home blues as well as high-energy contemporary styles, Kenny Neal has recently taken his blues to the theatrical stages of New York City. –JON

Big News From Baton Rouge!! / ALLIGATOR   1987
A debut from this hot young Louisiana blues guitarist. –MH

Devil Child / ALLIGATOR
Hot chops and a mite slicker production than needed. –MH

○ **Walking on Fire / ALLIGATOR**   1991
This album includes a couple of neat acoustic blues numbers from the musical *Mule Bone*. –MH

RAFUL NEAL   b1936

Modern electric blues. The patriarch of the most prolific of Louisiana's blues families, Raful Neal performed for some 30 years around Baton Rouge before recording his first album. His first band included Buddy Guy and, at one point, bayou blues legend Lazy Lester, but Neal waxed only a handful of singles during the heyday of Louisiana blues recording. As his sons Kenny Neal and the Neal Brothers came to prominence on the international blues scene during the 80s, so did Dad, who has finally assumed a hard-earned position in the annals of swamp blues, carrying on the tradition of his old friend Slim Harpo. –JON

○ **Louisiana Legend / ALLIGATOR**   1990
An album that is grittier and nearer the swamp than his son Kenny's music. –MH

I Been Mistreated / ICHIBAN   1991
More fine Baton Rouge blues. –MH

ROBERT NIGHTHAWK   1909-1967

Acoustic & electric Chicago blues. Though he recorded from the 30s right up to his death, Nighthawk never achieved the success of his more celebrated pupil, Muddy Waters. Instead, he found himself being relegated to one-nighters in taverns and the Maxwell Street open market on Sundays. But his resonant voice and creamy-smooth slide guitar playing (played in standard tuning, unusual for a bluesman) would influence players for generations to come, and many of his songs would later become blues standards. –CK

○ **Drop Down Mama / CHESS-MCA**   1970
Nighthawk's early sides for Chess/Aristocrat, including "Sweet Black Angel," which later became a hit for B. B. King as "Sweet Little Angel." Also features tracks by Johnny Shines, Floyd Jones, and Honeyboy Edwards. –CK

Bricks in My Pillow / PEARL   1978
Superb Robert Nighthawk slide guitar, originally recorded in Chicago for the United label in the early 50s. –BLP

★ **Live on Maxwell Street / ROUNDER**   1982
Recorded live on the street (one can actually hear cars driving by!) in 1964 with minimal duo support. Nighthawk's slide playing (and single-string soloing, for that matter) are nothing short of elegant and explosive. One of the top three live blues albums of all time. –CK

THE NIGHTHAWKS

Modern electric blues. DC-based contemporary blues/rock combo. Hard-driving bar band with strong Chicago blues roots. Formed in 1972 by harpist and vocalist Mark Wenner and guitarist Jimmy Thackery, the band earned a reputation as a solid outfit through more than a decade of touring and recording projects with John Hammond and former members of the Muddy Waters Band. Thackery left in 1986, but Wenner regrouped around longtime members Jan Zukowski on bass and Pete Ragusa on drums. "Trouble," their recent release on Powerhouse, is a blend of blues, R&B, and rock influences, with a typically energetic sound born in thousands of one-night stands across the country. –DB

○ **Jacks & Kings / ADELPHI**   1977
Their best studio album. With guests Pinetop Perkins, Luther Johnson, Calvin Jones, and Bob Margolin, these Maryland hotshots do it right with the acclaimed masters. It's solid — a must to find. –MGN

Sidepocket Shot / ADELPHI   1977
Another solid album, recorded with the Rhythm Kings horn section. The bulk of the material was written by the band, with a couple of classics and Leo Kottke's "Vaseline Machine Gun #2" tossed in. –MGN

ST. LOUIS JIMMY ODEN   1903-1977

Piano blues. The piano-playing Oden contributed one certifiable classic, the much-recorded "Goin' Down Slow." –CK

☆ **1932-48 / BLUES DOCUMENT**
A solid sixteen-track import collection of Oden's earliest and best sides. –CK

JOHNNY OTIS   b1928

Electric West Coast blues. There was probably no one who played a greater role — or as many roles — in catalyzing rhythm & blues on the West Coast than Johnny Otis. Bandleader, club owner, producer, writer, DJ, and musician, Otis was responsible for recording such artists as Charles Brown, Little Esther, and Big Mama Thornton. Off and on since the 40s, he has led a revue that features both big names and new discoveries. Otis has sung on record, with "Willie and the Hand Jive" being his best-known vocal (Capitol, 1958), but he has usually preferred to put other singers out front, and the majority of his hits featured Little Esther and/or Mel Walker during the Otis aggregation's peak of popularity in 1950-1952. The Johnny Otis Show made a resurgence in the early 70s, with vocalists such as Big Joe Turner and Cleanhead Vinson heading an all-star cast that included Otis's son Shuggie on guitar. In varying configurations, the Otis crew has periodically regrouped to tour and record when the leader was not occupied with preaching or other new pursuits. –JON
New Johnny Otis Show / ALLIGATOR   1982
This features recent recordings with Shuggie Otis. Nice, but nonessential. –MH
○ **Capitol Years / CAPITOL**   1988
Big-band R&B, scaled down and jived up, from the early rock era. Includes his 1958 hit "Willie and the Hand Jive." –MH

JUNIOR PARKER   1932-1971

Electric Memphis R&B/soul blues. Though his creamy-smooth, Roy Brown–influenced voice stood him in good stead in later years in translating more soul-oriented material, Junior Parker contributed some of the best down-home blues recordings ever committed to wax. While Parker worked with Howlin' Wolf and B. B. King around Memphis, his initial recordings for the Sun label produced two enduring classics, "Feelin' Good" and "Mystery Train," later a hit for a young Elvis Presley. Moving to the Duke label, his sound became more urbane and polished, while still interpreting down-home material like Robert Johnson's "Sweet Home Chicago," Howlin' Wolf's "Riding in the Moonlight (Pretty Baby Blues)," and Roosevelt Sykes's "Driving Wheel," the latter a Top Ten R&B hit for him. Later recordings drifted further away from hard blues (no doubt influenced as much by constant touring with R&B stylist Bobby "Blue" Bland as by prevailing market trends), but Parker continued to work and record, having R&B chart hits up until his death from a brain tumor in 1971. –CK
★ **Driving Wheel / DUKE-MCA**   1962
One of the best historical recordings, featuring Memphis blues vocalists and harmonica players from the Duke recordings of the 60s. –BLP
The Best of Junior Parker / MCA
○ **Mystery Train / ROUNDER**   1990
A fine set of Parker's Sun recordings, including the cool original version of the title cut. It's great to compare with the hot Presley version. These classic uptown presentations also feature tracks by James Cotton and Pat Hare. –BLP

CHARLEY PATTON   1887-1934

Delta blues. If the Delta country blues had a convenient source point, it would probably be Charley Patton, its first great star. His hoarse, impassioned singing style, fluid guitar playing, and unrelenting beat made him the original "King of the Delta Blues." A major influence on Howlin' Wolf, Robert Johnson, and John Lee Hooker, Patton truly excelled as a live performer, making him tremendously popular throughout the Delta. The first blues guitarist to introduce the kind of flashy performing gymnastics modern audiences normally associate with artists like Jimi Hendrix, his music embraced everything from blues,

ballads, and ragtime to gospel. Recorded in the late 20s to early 30s on primitive equipment (no masters of any kind exist), Patton's music gives us the first flowering of the Delta blues form, before it became homogenized with turnarounds and 12-bar restrictions. –CK
☆ **Founder of the Delta Blues / YAZOO**   1969
A 24-track best-of compilation featuring all of Patton's best titles, this is a cornerstone of any blues collection. –CK
Complete Recorded Works / DOCUMENT   1990
A three-CD set of Patton's complete recorded works, sequenced in chronological order. Superior sound. –CK
○ **King of the Delta Blues / YAZOO**   1991
An excellent companion to *Founder of the Delta Blues.* –CK

PEG LEG SAM   1911-1977

Acoustic country blues. Peg Leg Sam was a performer to be treasured, a member of what may have been the last authentic traveling medicine show, a harmonica virtuoso, and an extraordinary entertainer. Born Arthur Jackson, he acquired his nickname after a hoboing accident in 1930. His medicine show career began in 1938, and his repertoire — finally recorded only in the early 70s — reflected the rustic nature of the traveling show. "Peg" delivered comedy routines, bawdy toasts, and monologs; performed tricks with his harps (often playing two at once); and served up some juicy Piedmont blues (sometimes with a guitar accompanist, but most often by himself). Peg Leg Sam gave his last medicine show performance in 1972 in North Carolina and was still in fine fettle when he started making the rounds of folk and blues festivals in his last years. –JON
○ **Joshua / TOMMY BOY**
Rootsy 70s performances by this southeastern country-blues harmonica player and singer. –MH

PINETOP PERKINS   b1913

Piano blues. Pinetop Perkins has been recognized by blues audiences as one of the world's top blues pianists ever since he replaced Otis Spann in the Muddy Waters Band in 1969. His talent had already been proven in his earlier years in the South with the King Biscuit Boys, Robert Nighthawk, Earl Hooker, and others, but his name never appeared on record until he settled in Chicago. (He had recorded "Pinetop's Boogie Woogie" for Sam Phillips in Memphis in 1953, but a British reissue label finally released the track more than 20 years later.) Perkins recorded one album and a few scattered tracks of his own during his 11-year stint with Muddy and has waxed several albums since his departure from the band, including two with the Legendary Blues Band. –JON
○ **After Hours / BLIND PIG**   1988
Easy-grooving blues and boogie, backed by the competent New York City-based blues band Little Mike and the Tornadoes. Though Perkins followed Otis Spann as the piano player in the Muddy Waters band, these are the first domestically available recordings under his own name. –NJF

JAMES PETERSON   b1937

Modern electric blues. James Peterson formed his first blues band in Buffalo, NY, where he also owned a blues club, the Governor's Inn, in the 60s and early 70s. The Inn featured acts such as Howlin' Wolf and Muddy Waters, as well as the James Peterson Blues Band, but Peterson and the club are best known today for nurturing the talents of young Lucky Peterson, James's son, who was on the bandstand before he was in grade school. It is Lucky who has carried on the family name in the blues world since those days, but his father is back on the scene, now based in Florida and still a soulful bluesman in his own right. –JON
○ **Rough and Ready / ICHIBAN**   1977
A pleasant album of original compositions by this Alabama-born bluesman. Features James's son Lucky Peterson (Alligator recording artist) on guitar and keyboards. –NJF

LUCKY PETERSON   b 1964

Modern electric blues. A former child prodigy who recorded his first album and appeared on the "Tonight Show" at the age of five, Lucky Peterson has continued to burn as one of the bright lights on the contemporary blues scene. As a teenager, Lucky toured with Little Milton, followed by a stint with Bobby Bland, and he now performs with his own unit in addition to doing session work with many of the top names in blues. A superb organist who has also become an excellent guitarist, Lucky was raised with the blues, and his musical instincts allow him to play down-home blues, funk, R&B, jazz, and up-to-the-minute original blues with equal ease. –JON

○ **Triple Play / ALLIGATOR**   1990
Very good, contemporary high-energy blues. Lucky sings and plays guitar and keyboards. –NJF

PIANO RED   1911-1985

Piano blues. An albino Black, this "Piano Red" was the cousin to another piano man, "Speckled Red." –CK

○ **Wildfire / MATCHBOX**
Dozen tracks of Red at his poundin' best. (Import) –CK

ROD PIAZZA & THE MIGHTY FLYERS

Modern electric blues. A California-based blues bandleader, harmonica, and singer, Piazza's stratospheric harmonica wailings owe a heavy debt to both Little Walter and George "Harmonica" Smith. –CK

○ **Blues in the Dark / BLACK TOP**   1991
A contemporary band, led by harmonica player/vocalist Piazza, with nice piano from Honey Alexander. –NJF

DAN PICKETT

Acoustic country blues. Reissuers have unearthed little information about Dan Pickett: he may have come from Alabama, he played a nice slide guitar in a Southeastern blues style, and he did one recording session for the Philadelphia-based Gotham label in 1949. That session produced five singles, all of which have now been compiled along with four previously unreleased sides on a reissue album that purports to contain Pickett's entire recorded output — unless, of course, as some reviewers have speculated, Dan Pickett happens also to be Charlie Pickett, the Tennessee guitarist who recorded for Decca in 1937. As Tony Russell observed in *Juke Blues*, both Picketts recorded blues about lemon-squeezing, and Dan uses the name Charlie twice in the lyrics to "Decoration Day." 'Tis from such mystery and speculation that the minds of blues collectors do dissolve. –JON

○ **1949 Country Blues / CBS**   1990
A CD reissue of beautiful, ragtime-esque acoustic blues. Generally very lighthearted. –NJF

PROFESSOR LONGHAIR   1918-1980

Acoustic New Orleans blues. Born Henry Roeland Byrd and known affectionately as "Fess" to most New Orleans residents, Professor Longhair began his musical career as a street entertainer in the early 30s. By the late 40s he was playing piano, leading small combos with arcane names such as the Four Hairs Combo and Professor Longhair & his Shuffling Hungarians. He worked as part of Dave Bartholomew's big band in 1949, then began a series of recordings for various labels, including Star Talent, Mercury, and Atlantic. For the next 20 years Professor Longhair continued to record for obscure labels but remained on the fringes of the New Orleans scene, forced to supplement his meager earnings from music with odd day jobs.

In 1971 he re-created the Four Hairs Combo for an appearance at the New Orleans Jazz & Heritage Festival. This inaugurated the comeback phase of his musical career and attracted the interest of a small but dedicated cadre of college students who undertook his rehabilitation as part of a burgeoning roots revival.

As he stated, "I'm a little rowdy with my playing," and the synthesis he developed of calypso and rhumba rhythms, boogie-woogie, and street-parade music became the basis for young groups like the Neville Brothers and the Radiators as they sought to translate their own respective musical visions of the New Orleans "good time" heritage. Despite his often unorthodox approach, Fess remained true to the essence of New Orleans music in never straying too far from the basic maxims of "feeling, freedom, and fun."

At the time of his death in 1980, he was the most popular and revered musician in New Orleans. His passing left a vacuum in the city's longstanding piano traditions, seemingly closing the book on an illustrious musical heritage. –BR

★ **New Orleans Piano / ATLANTIC** 1972
The ultimate Professor Longhair album (volume 2 of the *Blues Originals* series), featuring New Orleans legends Lee Allen and Earl Palmer. –BR

Rock 'n' Roll Gumbo / WINDHAM HILL 1974
Featuring great renditions of New Orleans standards such as "Junco Partner" and "Rockin' Pneumonia" with an all-star band that features Clarence "Gatemouth" Brown on guitar and violin. –BR

○ **Crawfish Fiesta / ALLIGATOR**   1979
Fess's revival-period band burns through a mixed bag of vintage favorites, complete with a horn section. The presence of Dr. John on guitar is a special treat. –BR

Mardi Gras in New Orleans / NIGHTHAWK 1982
A compendium of early Longhair classics (1949-1957) via the Shuffling Hungarians, the Blues Jumpers, and the Blues Scholars. –BR

Houseparty New Orleans Style / ROUNDER
A classic pairing of Professor Longhair with New Orleans guitar legend Snooks Eaglin and drummer "Zig" Modeliste of the Meters. –BR

SNOOKY PRYOR   b 1921

Electric Chicago blues. A staple of the Chicago scene from the mid 40s onward, Pryor contributed solid harp work to numerous early Chicago classics, as both a leader and a sideman. His signature instrumental, "Boogie," became the basis for Little Walter's hit "Juke," while his "Someone to Love" was later adapted by the Yardbirds. A true journeyman, Pryor worked with just about every major (and minor) bluesman at one time or another, and continues to record and perform today, his workmanlike skills intact. –CK

☆ **Snooky Pryor / FLYRIGHT**
These tracks from the JOB label, recorded from the early 50s to early 60s, include the classics "Boogie" and "Stockyard Blues" and the raucous, echo-laden stomp of "Boogie Twist." These are Pryor's finest moments on wax. –CK

YANK RACHELL   b 1910

Acoustic country blues. Best known for his down-home mandolin playing, guitarist, vocalist, and songwriter Yank Rachell played a central role in several of the most exciting chapters in blues history. Born in either Mississippi or Tennessee, he took up mandolin as a youngster and was soon making the rounds with the Brownsville, TN, blues crowd: John Estes, John Lee "Sonny Boy" Williamson, Jab Jones, and Homesick James Williamson. In the 30s he was part of the vibrant St. Louis blues community, working with Henry Townsend and Big Joe Williams before moving on to Chicago. For the past thirty years he has resided in Indianapolis, presiding over still another blues community, which once included Shirley Griffith, J. T. Adams, and guitarist Pete Franklin. When I met Rachell in the early 70s, he had put an electric band together with his son-in-law and some local R&B players. Although much of his recording career with Victor, ARC, Bluebird, and Delmark was spent accompanying others, he composed and sang powerful songs such as "Lake Michigan Blues" and "Gravel Road Woman." When he visited my classroom in 1976, he told the students he coauthored the classic "Schoolgirl" with his onetime partner Sonny Boy Williamson. Explaining his music, he said: "I learned it the hard way, out in the country all by myself — so far back in the woods my breath smelled like cord wood." Throughout his lengthy career, his music changed little, holding a country dance flavor. At the same time, he demonstrated a remarkable ability to play with other musicians — the mark of a seasoned string-band veteran. For 60 years Rachell worked in various ensemble formats, but his heart remained with his string-band roots. –BLP

Blues Mandolin Man / BLIND PIG
This contains fine material by one of the few great mandolin bluesmen. –BLP

○ **Chicago Style / DELMARK**   1987
Songwriter, vocalist, and mandolin master Rachell cut his teeth with Sleepy John Estes. Here are good contemporary recordings of a blues legend. –BLP

BOBBY RADCLIFF

Modern electric blues. Although blues guitarist and singer Bobby Radcliff has been honing his craft for the last 20 years around his native Washington, DC, the 40-year-old veteran only recently entered the national blues spotlight with a couple of stellar recordings for the Louisiana-based Black Top Records label.
Radcliff's fiery playing and strong, energetic vocals are sure to make him one of the guiding lights of blues music throughout the 90s. His two Black Top releases, "Dresses Too Short" and "Universal Blues," were received well by the critics, but were not big sellers. Perhaps the most exciting thing about Radcliff is knowing that he's only just begun. The best is yet to come. –RS

○ **Dresses Too Short / BLACK TOP**
A Magic Sam devotee who tastefully updates the Chicago sound. –RG

Universal Blues / BLACK TOP
Again, tasteful. Searing but not showy. –RG

MA RAINEY   1886-1939

Classic female blues. Ma Rainey wasn't the first blues singer to make records, but by all rights she probably should have been. In an era when women were the marquee names in blues, Ma Rainey was once the most celebrated of all — the "Mother of the Blues" had been singing the music for more than 20 years before she made her recording debut (Paramount, 1923). With the advent of blues records, she became even more influential, immortalizing such songs as "See See Rider," "Bo-Weavil Blues," and "Ma Rainey's Black Bottom." Like the other classic blues divas, she had a repertoire of pop and minstrel songs as well as blues, but she maintained a heavier, tougher vocal delivery than the cabaret blues singers who followed. Ma Rainey's records featured her with jug bands, guitar duos, and bluesmen such as Tampa Red and Blind Blake, in addition to the more customary horns-and-piano jazz-band accompaniment (occasionally including such luminaries as Louis Armstrong, Kid Ory, and Fletcher Henderson). –JON

☆ **Ma Rainey's Black Bottom / MILESTONE**
The archetypical "classic" blues femme belter on 1924-1928 recordings, with Fletcher Henderson on piano and Coleman Hawkins bass sax on two tracks. –MH

MOSES RASCOE   b 1917

Modern acoustic blues. Moses Rascoe got his first guitar in North Carolina at the age of 13 and turned professional in Pennsylvania some 50-odd years later. In between, he traveled the roads as a day laborer and truck driver, playing guitar only for "a dollar or a drink," as he told Jack Roberts in *Living Blues.* But he'd picked up plenty of songs over the years, from old Brownie McGhee Piedmont blues to Jimmy Reed's 50s jukebox hits, and when he retired from trucking at the age of 65, he gave his music a shot. The local folk-music community took notice, as did blues and folk festivals from Chicago to

Europe. Rascoe recorded his first album live at Godfrey Daniels, a Pennsylvania coffeehouse, in 1987. –JON

○ **Blues / FLYING FISH**   1987
A former truck driver turned touring bluesman, Rascoe primarily covers other people's tunes and classic blues themes. There is much Jimmy Reed and "traditional" material. –NJF

A. C. REED   b 1926

Electric Chicago blues. One of a handful of sax players to ever assume a featured role as singer/bandleader in Chicago blues, Aaron Corthen once based his act on a reputed relationship to Jimmy Reed, going so far as to assume the last name in addition to the musical posture. After years of sideman duty with Buddy Guy, Albert Collins, and others, recording occasional singles along the way, A. C. thrust his songwriting wit to the fore and came up with a successful new persona — that of the anti-blues bluesman. Co-producing his own albums with sidekick Casey Jones, Reed has become noted for titles such as "Take These Blues and Shove 'Em," "I Am Fed Up with This Music," and "I'm in the Wrong Business." Despite the comic-yet-sincere sentiments expressed, Reed has remained a bluesman through and through. –JON

Take These Blues ... / ROOSTER BLUES   1982
Take These Blues and Shove 'Em is a very nice record of seven of Reed's originals, plus a cover of Willie Dixon and Howlin' Wolf's "Howlin' for My Darling." –NJF

○ **I'm in the Wrong Business / ALLIGATOR**   1987
Solid, soulful blues, often with humorous, self-deprecating lyrics, from the well-respected vocalist, tenor player, composer, and veteran of the bands of Albert Collins, Buddy Guy, Magic Sam, and Son Seals. Reed has been called "the definitive Chicago blues sax player." This album features Reed's band, with guests Bonnie Raitt and Stevie Ray Vaughan. –NJF

JIMMY REED   1925-1976

Electric Chicago blues. Lazy, loping, and insistent, Reed's music revolved around his mush-mouthed vocals and countryish harmonica solos against the driving boogie guitar of long-time partner Eddie Taylor. The formula proved to be enormously successful, as Reed crossed over to the pop charts on many occasions, a rare feat for an unreconstructed bluesman. Songs like "Baby, What You Want Me to Do," "Bright Lights, Big City," "Going to New York," and "Big Boss Man" have become such an integral part of the standard blues repertoire, it's almost as if they had existed forever. Because Reed's style was simple and easily imitated, his songs were accessible to everyone from high school garage bands to Elvis Presley and the Rolling Stones, making him, in the long run, perhaps the most influential bluesman of all. –CK

○ **The Best of the Blues / VEE JAY**
○ **I'm Jimmy Reed / VEE JAY**
○ **Rockin' with Reed / VEE JAY**
○ **High & Lonesome / CHARLY**   1981
A great collection of Reed's earliest and rarest sides. –CK

● **Ride 'Em On Down / CHARLY**
A compilation shared with Eddie Taylor (with Reed in support on four tracks), this features a dozen tracks from Reed's early days. It's the perfect companion piece to *Big Boss Blues.* –CK

★ **Big Boss Blues / CHARLY**
Although many "best of Jimmy Reed" compilations exist on the market (most with variable sound quality and maddening duplication), this import features all the influential hits and is the perfect place to start. –CK

SONNY RHODES   b 1940

Modern electric blues. Sonny Rhodes is a bluesman who has found ways to set himself apart from the rest of the pack — visually with his trademark turban, musically with his tantalizing lap steel guitar playing, and philosophically with his "Disciple of the Blues" tag. The steel has been part of his act only since 1977, when he decided to carry on the Bay Area tradition of L. C. "Good Rockin'" Robinson; Rhodes is also a fine instrumentalist on the conventional electric guitar. As a songwriter of some note, Rhodes was a disciple of the legendary Percy Mayfield. With several European and American albums now to his credit, Rhodes is best known for his work in California during the 70s and 80s. He felt it was time for a change a few years ago and, always wanting to be different, now lives in New Jersey. —JON

○ **Disciple of the Blues / ICHIBAN**   1991
This be-turbaned bluesman plays lap steel guitar. This is a good one, but I know he's got an even better one in him. —NJF

TOMMY RIDGLEY   b 1925

Electric New Orleans blues. Tommy Ridgley has been right with the New Orleans rhythm & blues movement ever since the early Imperial recording era, achieving his share of local renown and regional success despite a lack of national hits. Influenced in his younger days by the blues shouting style of Roy Brown and Big Joe Turner, Ridgley eventually became known for his ballad singing; a similarity to Chuck Willis also earned him the title "The New King of the Stroll." After recording for Imperial, Atlantic, and Herald, Ridgley turned to local New Orleans labels in the 60s. After an ensuing lull, he has been recording again in recent years and is still a talent to be reckoned with. —JON

○ **New Orleans King of the Stroll / ROUNDER**
Atmospheric late-50s/early-60s New Orleans R&B by this veteran vocalist from the Ric/Ron vaults. —BD

FENTON ROBINSON   b 1935

Modern electric blues. "The Mellow Blues Genius," as his Japanese fans have dubbed him, is a widely praised and honored artist, yet Robinson has had to struggle financially throughout a career that has most often found him an undeniably distinctive and original stylist in search of a market. After recording in a Memphis-based blues style early in his career (Meteor, 1957, and Duke, 1959), Robinson moved from Arkansas to Chicago in 1961 and began staking out his own stylistic territory, one that made use of his extensive and growing knowledge of musical structures and progressions. His well-known "Somebody Loan Me a Dime" (Palos, 1967, later re-recorded for Alligator) was an early culmination of his blues vision. A thinking man of the blues, Robinson seems forever ready to explore something new, moving to a new city every few years and continually experimenting with his fluid, jazz-flavored blues, perhaps just too far ahead or too far removed for the rest of the blues world to catch up. —JON

○ **I Hear Some Blues Downstairs / ALLIGATOR**   1977
Mellow blues, featuring Robinson's jazz-inflected guitar work and smooth, soaring vocals. Very, very nice. —NJF

Special Road / BLACK MAGIC   1989
An import CD recorded April 1989 in the Netherlands. —NJF

JIMMY ROGERS   b 1924

Electric Chicago blues. Rogers was an original founding member of Chicago's first electric blues band with Muddy Waters and Little Walter, in a trio originally known as the Headhunters. He worked as a guitarist in Waters's band throughout the 50s, cutting solo sides for Chess at the tail end of Muddy's sessions. The first record issued in his name, "That's All Right," became a huge hit and a blues standard to this day. Further sessions throughout the 50s utilized the cream of Chicago blues players, making every side a gem of that genre. The most notable was Big Walter Horton's earth-shattering solo on Jimmy's "Walking by Myself." With his Mississippi roots fully intact, Jimmy Rogers stands as one of the last great Chicago blues artists actively performing and recording today. —CK

☆ **Chicago Bound / CHESS**   1970
Classic 50s Chess sessions with Little Walter and Muddy Waters, including the 1956 hit "Walking by Myself." —BLP

Ludella / ANTONE'S   1990
Representative of one of Chicago's most important artists. —BLP

DR. ISIAH ROSS   b 1925

Acoustic country blues. A triple-threat guitarist, harp blower, and vocalist, Dr. Ross decided to fire his sidemen over thirty years ago and carry on as a one-man band, a tradition that also includes Joe Hill Louis, Daddy Stovepipe, and Jesse Fuller. Ross's music does not depend on novelty effect, yet it has a distinctly recognizable sound, in part because he learned to play his own way and essentially plays everything backwards. His guitar is tuned to open *G* (like John Lee Hooker and other Delta artists), but Ross plays it left-handed and upside-down. He also plays harmonica in a rack, but it is turned around with the low notes to the right. As an instrumentalist, Ross has perfected the interplay between guitar and harmonica. Unlike other Delta artists who tune in *G*, Ross doesn't use slide, preferring a series of banjo-like strummed riffs, a percussive approach reminiscent of Atlanta twelve-string guitarist Barbecue Bob. A strong vocalist and excellent songwriter, Ross gained early experience playing Delta jukes and eventually landed radio shows in Clarksdale and Memphis, where he also recorded for Sam Phillips's Sun label. At the peak of Ross's career, he quit Sun, concerned that his royalties were being used to promote Elvis Presley's recordings. Relocating in Michigan, he recorded for his own label and for several Detroit labels, while working for General Motors. Returning to music as a recording artist, he recently worked the festival circuit. To the present day, Ross's music retains the spirit of his live radio and juke-joint work. I feel the sides he recorded with a band for Sun produced his best material, including classics like "Chicago Breakdown" and "Boogie Disease." As Dr. Ross put it in an interview ten years ago, "I'm kind of like the little boy from the West; I'm different from the rest." Different, yes, but very good. —BLP

I'd Rather Be an Old Woman's Baby / FORTUNE   1968
A wild, chaotic session, featuring the title cut, "Good Things Come to My Remind," and the original version of "Cat Squirrel." —CK

○ **Dr. Ross: His First Recording / ARHOOLIE**   1972
His best material, originally recorded for the Sun label in the 50s. Outstanding Delta blues in the unique Dr. Ross guitar-and-harmonica style. —BLP

OTIS RUSH   b 1934

Electric Chicago blues. Part of the celebrated West Side school of guitarists (the other two notables being Buddy Guy and Magic Sam), Rush quickly distanced himself from the pack by coming up with a style that was more broodingly intense and introspective than either of them. His early recordings combined Robert Johnson-like anguished vocals with sweet, stinging guitar solos in a B. B. King mode, both with a unique voice. Influencing countless young guitarists on both sides of the Atlantic (Jimmy Page, Eric Clapton, and Stevie Ray Vaughan being just the tip of the iceberg), Rush continues to record and tour to this day, still occasionally connecting with the private demons that make his brand of blues so compelling. —CK

● **Chicago/The Blues/Today! - Vol. 2 / VANGUARD**   1967
Features the version of "I Can't Quit You, Baby" that Led Zeppelin would later copy note-for-note on their first album. There are also featured tracks by James Cotton and Homesick James on this collection. —CK

○ **Door to Door (With Albert King) / CHESS**   1969
Rush's performance of "So Many Roads" here should not be missed at any cost. Also includes tracks by Albert King. —CK

★ **1956-1958 Cobra Recordings / PAULA**   1991
The songs that made the legend — "All Your Love," "Double

Trouble," "I Can't Quit You, Baby." All 16 Cobra sides plus the bonus of four alternate takes. These are milestone recordings in the history of blues. –CK

SAFFIRE

Modern acoustic blues. Saffire, a trio of women from Fredericksburg, VA, have been making fine acoustic blues together since 1984. They began pursuing blues as professionals in the mid 80s and have been delighting audiences around the country with their interpretations of the sassy blues tunes of Ma Rainey, Bessie Smith, and other blues divas from the 20s and 30s. But the three are also talented lyricists and arrangers, and their original tunes are firmly rooted in the blues tradition.

The group has released a couple of critically acclaimed albums for the Chicago-based Alligator Records label. Their mostly acoustic performances make theirs one of the freshest sounds on the contemporary blues scene. –RS

○ **Hot Flash / ALLIGATOR**   1991
A great place for blues beginners, but not for purists. Good variety. –RG

CURTIS SALGADO & THE STILETTOS

Modern electric blues. Reportedly a primary inspiration for John Belushi's "Joliet Jake" character in *The Blues Brothers*, Salgado was a prominent early member of Robert Cray's band during their formative years around Eugene, OR. Salgado has also worked with Roomful of Blues. He currently fronts his own group, the Stilettos. –BD

○ **Curtis Salgado & the Stilettos / RCA-JRS**   1988
The blues, spiked with 60s soul, delivered by West Coast singer Curtis Salgado. –DS

SATAN & ADAM

Modern acoustic blues. Sterling "Satan" Magee (b May 20, 1936, Mount Olive, MS; vocals, guitar, hi-hats); Adam Gussow (harmonica). Dubbed "a PR man's dream" by *Chicago Reader* critic David Whiteis, "this pairing of a grizzled veteran Harlem street singer and a young refugee from the Broadway theater" created something of a sensation after the release of their first album in 1991, following up on the buzz started by the inclusion of a Satan & Adam track in U2's *Rattle & Hum* (both on film and on record). Their material, while rarely falling within the typical guidelines of blues, is nonetheless spirited and moving, with enough of a blues base that the duo has now appeared at a number of major blues festivals. Adam, the Broadway refugee, never lets up on his harp, while Satan (who was an R&B session man before embarking on his New York street musician's career) stomps a hi-hat rig with both feet, as streams of rhythm flow from his guitar. Satan, who also recorded under his real name for the Ray Charles Tangerine label back in the 60s, is a Mississippi native who is as consumed by his music as the blues greats from his home state have been by theirs. –JON

○ **Harlem Blues / FLYING FISH**   1991
Satan (an outrageous and unique street musician/bluesman) meets Adam (a young harp player) with magic results! A wonderful album. –NJF

SON SEALS   b 1942

Electric Chicago blues. When Son Seals recorded his debut album in 1973, he quickly earned a reputation as the hottest new talent in blues. Not long up from Arkansas, he brought with him a searing, relentless guitar attack and a gruff vocal manner. His style was based mostly on Albert King but came across quite a bit more rough and urgent. (Seals had once been King's drummer.) Over the years, Seals acquired more of his mentor's musical polish, and although the fiery rawness has mellowed some, Seals remains one of Chicago's most highly regarded bluesmen. –JON

○ **Son Seals Blues Band / ALLIGATOR**   1973
The debut album from this fiery Chicago stringbender. –MH

Live & Burning / ALLIGATOR   1978
This lives up to its title! –MH

EDDIE SHAW

Electric Chicago blues. Once a saxophonist extraordinaire with Howlin' Wolf and Magic Sam, Shaw has successfully struck out on his own since the Wolf's death in 1976. –CK

○ **King of the Road / ROOSTER BLUES**
This former Howlin' Wolf sax man goes solo here, with nice results. –CK

JOHNNY SHINES   1915-1992

Acoustic & electric Delta blues. Johnny Shines's best material crackles with energy. In his prime, his slashing slide guitar carried more of the spirit of his onetime running mate Robert Johnson than any other traditional blues artist. Shines, however, was never a Johnson imitator. He had his own sound, his own guitar style, and a voice that can still take you on a roller coaster ride. (However, he did learn from Johnson and his classic recordings. "Ramblin'" and "Dynaflow Blues" feel like Johnson's best work.) Shines has too much personal magnetism to be confused with anyone else. Like many artists of his generation, he is also master of the spoken word, a gifted storyteller, a social critic, and a historian dedicated to telling the truth. On stage or off, he pulls no punches, and his independent spirit and readiness to fight for what he perceives to be fair have no doubt ruffled the feathers of the movers and shakers in Chicago's blues business.

Shine's distinctive style and songwriting skills should have brought him fame and fortune in music, but such was not the case. During the 40s and 50s, when he was at his peak, he only issued a handful of records. Although critically acclaimed today, these were not sufficient to keep him in the business at the time. Working outside of music in the 50s and over much of his career, he returned to the studio with Pete Welding in the 60s. These Chicago sessions showed his musical power had not diminished. Subsequent recordings, including his collaboration with Robert Jr Lockwood, have generally maintained a high quality. His later guitar work was hampered by a stroke, but he remained a powerful artist sustained by one of the all-time great blues voices. –BLP

○ **Traditional Delta Blues / BIOGRAPH**
Robert Johnson's pal pays homage on acoustic recordings from 1972-1974. –JO

Hey Ba-Ba-Re-Bop / ROUNDER   1978
One of the greatest voices in blues history. A good recent sampler. –BLP

★ **Johnny Shines & Robert Lockwood / FLYRIGHT**
Essential JOB sides, 1952-1953. –JO

FRANKIE LEE SIMS   1917-1970

Electric Texas blues. A Texas blues singer and guitarist who recorded in the late 40s and early 50s in a style similar to fellow Texas bluesman Lightnin' Hopkins, only much more percussive and electric. Sims had a better ability to work with full bands than Hopkins. Sims's lyrics borrow from traditional sources, with inventive twists of their own, while the music at times sounds like a strong precursor to rock & roll. –CK

○ **Lucy Mae Blues / SPECIALTY**   1974
Sims's only album, primarily in a drums-and-electric-guitar format. –CK

BESSIE SMITH   1894-1937

Classic female blues. Generally regarded as the greatest female blues vocalist ever, Bessie Smith — a protégé of Ma Rainey — surpassed her mentor to become the #1 blues act of the 20s. Smith's life and death were the stuff of legend, and no other blues singer has been so frequently memorialized in books and stage productions. Her music has been constantly revived over the years by leading jazz and blues vocalists. Among her most recognizable classics were "Tain't Nobody's Business if I

Do," "The St. Louis Blues," "Nobody Knows You When You're Down and Out," "Careless Love Blues," and "Empty Bed Blues." Altogether Smith recorded more than 200 sides in 1923-1933, many of them featuring her powerful, dramatic singing backed only by piano (Clarence Williams, Fletcher Henderson, James P. Johnson et al.), on others adding horns (Coleman Hawkins, Louis Armstrong, and Don Redman, to name just a few). –JON

★ **Collection / CBS**
Featuring her classics, from "Downhearted Blues" to "Gimme a Pigfoot." –JO

Complete Recordings - Vol. 1 (1923-1924) / CBS
Complete Recordings - Vol. 2 (1924-1925) / CBS
Excellent liner notes and state-of-the-art remastering of acetates on these companion boxed sets. –JO

BYTHER SMITH   b 1932
Modern electric blues. Byther Smith's cousin J. B. Lenoir was once Chicago's most intriguing lyricist, but these days Smith himself rates as a prime candidate for the honor. While Lenoir often wrote of political and social ills, Smith's most striking songs are disturbingly dark and deadly excursions into his own psyche. A former sideman with Junior Wells and others, Smith worked hard over the years at his musicianship, inspired especially by the guitar sound of Otis Rush. Although musically quite derivative (and usually quite a bit less dramatic) on past recordings, Smith arrived at a stylistic and emotional plane of his own, described by Chicago critic David Whiteis as one of "ominous, almost primal intensity." Though this kind of music seems not destined to win him a broad audience given current tastes in blues, Smitty's handful of releases have spawned a growing corps of true believers. –JON
○ **Tell Me How You Like It / GRITS**   1983
Fine guitar from this longtime Chicago bluesman, including four originals. –BLP

FUNNY PAPA SMITH   b 1890
Acoustic Texas blues. J. T. "Funny Papa" Smith acquired the name Howling Wolf from the title of his first record in 1930. Any influence on the more famous Chester "Howlin' Wolf" Burnett from Mississippi was probably in name only, but Smith was an influential musician within the Texas blues idiom. In fact, the liner notes of his Yazoo reissue album refer to his recordings as "practically definitive of what is known as Texas blues-playing." The notes also tout Smith's originality as a composer and his skill as an instrumentalist, "despite the fact that his guitar was chronically out of tune." Little biographical information has been published on Smith; blues guitarist Tom Shaw remembered him as the overseer of an Oklahoma plantation who was sent to prison for murder. He made his last recordings in 1935, presumably after his release. According to *Blues Who's Who*, Smith toured with Texas Alexander in 1939; "whereabouts unknown thereafter." –JON
○ **Howling Wolf 1930-1931 / YAZOO**   1971
Fine guitar-based Texas country blues by an artist completely unlike the later Howlin' Wolf. –MH

MAMIE SMITH   1883-1946
Classic female blues. A pillar in the classic female blues tradition, Mamie Smith is generally recognized as the first to record in the genre. Her version of "Crazy Blues" was the first major hit of the blues. –CK
☆ **In Chronological Order - Vol. 1 / DOCUMENT**
This first volume of a five-volume import set of her complete recordings features her earliest and best sides, including the classic "Crazy Blues." –CK

CHRIS SMITHER
Modern acoustic blues. Chris Smither has forged a blues/folk synthesis from his adopted hometown of Boston. Leaving the Crescent City in 1966, Smither wrote "Love You Like a Man" for Bonnie Raitt and recorded for Poppy during the 70s and

Adelphi in 1984. Smither's 1991 set for Flying Fish, *Another Way to Find You*, showcases his rough-hewn vocals and slide guitar work. –BD
○ **Another Way to Find You / FLYING FISH**   1991
Recorded live in the studio in Boston in 1989 with an audience of friends and guests. Smither is a very talented folk/blues singer/songwriter and a very good guitarist. He has an attractive low-key, introspective way about the blues. –NJF

OTIS SPANN   1930-1970
Electric Chicago blues. Otis Spann did more than anyone else to define the pianist's role in postwar Chicago blues. His rhythmic support of Muddy Waters throughout the 50s and 60s was superb, and during his last decade Spann recorded an impressive number of his own albums, convincingly showcasing the depth of his blues. Many of Spann's recordings were made with various configurations of the Muddy Waters band, but among his most memorable sessions were those pairing him with only a guitarist or a drummer. Spann's rumbling piano and ruminant vocals were sometimes reminiscent of the previous Chicago blues piano king, Big Maceo Merriweather. Ironically, Spann's only minor-hit single, "Hungry Country Girl," was released only after his death. –JON
○ **The Blues Never Die / OJC**
☆ **Walking the Blues / BARNABY**   1960
With guitarist Lockwood on many cuts. Haunting! A must-have for blues fans. –GB
○ **Complete Candid Recordings / MOSAIC**   1960
W/ Robert Lockwood Jr. Two classic Spann albums: *Otis Spann Is the Blues* and *Walkin' the Blues*. Early, potent Spann with flawless liner notes and a complete discography. Also included are the Candid sessions of Lightnin' Hopkins. –JME

DAVE SPECTER w/BILL SMITH
Modern electric blues. Guitarist Dave Specter has recently been kicking up noise around the Chicago blues club circuit with his band, fronted by longtime native Barkin' Bill Smith on vocals. –CK
○ **Bluebird Blues with Ronnie Earl / DELMARK**   1991
There's no generation gap with this Chicago retro-blues band. Young guitarist Dave Specter's T-Bone Walker-influenced sound blends smoothly with veteran West Side vocalist Barkin' Bill Smith on this set. –BD

VICTORIA SPIVEY   1906-1976
Classic female blues. A classic female blues singer who outlasted her competition by several decades, Spivey formed her own label in the early 70s, giving both young talent and forgotten artists a chance to reach a wider audience. –CK
○ **1926-31 / DOCUMENT**
Spivey is in marvelous form throughout. This album features the classics "Steady Grind," "Black Snake Blues," and "Blood Thirsty Blues." –CK

FRANK STOKES   1888-1955
Acoustic Memphis blues. Frank Stokes and partner Dan Sain recorded as the Beale Street Shieks, a Memphis answer to the musical Chatmon family string band, the Mississippi Shieks. According to local tradition, Stokes was already playing the streets of Memphis by the turn of the century, about the same time the blues began to flourish. As a street artist, he needed a broad repertoire of songs and patter palatable to Blacks and Whites. A medicine show and houseparty favorite, Stokes was remembered as a consummate entertainer who drew on songs from the 19th and 20th centuries with equal facility. Solo or with Sain and sometimes fiddler Will Batts, Stokes recorded 38 sides for Paramount and Victor. These treasures include blues as well as older pieces: "Chicken You Can't Roost Too High for Me," "Mr. Crump Don't Like It," an outstanding version of "You Shall" (commonly known as "You Shall Be Free"), and "Hey Mourner," a traditional comic anticlerical

piece. Stokes possessed a remarkable declamatory voice and was an adroit guitarist. His duets with Sain merit special attention because of their subtle interplay and propulsive rhythm. —BLP

☆ **The Victor Recordings / DOCUMENT**
Declamatory deep blues, Memphis style, recorded in 1928-1929. —JO

The Beale Street Sheiks / DOCUMENT
Contains his Paramount 1927-1929 sides with Dan Sain. —JO

ANGELA STREHLI

Modern electric blues. A strong-voiced blues singer from Austin, TX. A former mainstay of that city's Antone's Blues Mafia, Strehli sounds great on both blues and uptempo soul material. —CK

○ **Soul Shake / ANTONE'S**   1988
A 15-track program of great songs and gritty hard-rocking performances. —BP

SUGAR RAY & THE BLUETONES

Modern electric blues. An East Coast-based blues band fronted by singer and harmonica man Ray Norcia and featuring guitar work over the years by Ronnie Earl (Roomful of Blues, the Broadcasters) and Kid Bangham (the Fabulous Thunderbirds). —CK

○ **Knockout / VARRICK**   1989
A surprisingly tasteful and solidly swinging album. Sugar Ray is a powerhouse vocalist and a more-than-respectable harp player. There are some good songs, too, especially the slow blues "I'm Tortured." —NJF

Don't Stand in My Way / BULLSEYE BLUES
More swagger, less swing, and still quite good. —NJF

HUBERT SUMLIN   b 1931

Electric Chicago blues. Hubert Sumlin's lasting fame will likely remain with the slicing guitar work that emblazoned Howlin' Wolf's Chess singles of the late 50s and early 60s. The trademark sound of the longtime Wolf sideman earned him such renown that, even with virtually no experience as a bandleader or vocalist, he was seldom without an invitation to perform as a featured act or special guest on the blues club circuit after Wolf's death (1976). An early European release of Sumlin's recordings bore this quote from Jimi Hendrix on the jacket: "My favorite guitar player is Hubert Sumlin." His albums have been a varied and not always dynamic lot, but when Sumlin pulls out the stops, it's easy to understand why he's a guitar hero's hero. —JON

○ **Blues Party / BLACK TOP**   1987
A solo recording from the 80s by the former lead guitarist for Howlin' Wolf. —MH

SUNNYLAND SLIM   b 1907

Piano blues. A two-fisted barrelhouse piano man, armed with a voice that was once rumored to be capable of frying microphones in his prime. Sunnyland Slim has probably graced more recordings, both as sideman and leader, than any other blues piano player in history. —CK

☆ **Sunnyland Slim / FLYRIGHT**
Here is Slim at his indefatigable best, with great support from J. B. Lenoir and Snooky Pryor. (Import) —CK

ROOSEVELT SYKES   1906-1983

Piano blues. Sykes was a major contributor to the blues idiom, one of the most influential figures both as an artist and a composer from the time he made his first record, the classic "44 Blues," in 1929 (Okeh). Sykes did the original versions of such timeless staples of the blues as "Driving Wheel Blues" and "Night Time Is the Right Time," and as a pianist he exerted an impact in his day on younger men such as Memphis Slim and Otis Spann in much the way that B. B. King set the standard for upcoming guitarists in later years. Sykes

recorded nearly every year from 1929 through the early 50s, retaining his popularity through all the changes in music. He moved from solo piano to small combo to jump-blues band to electric postwar blues, and when the blues revival hit, Sykes was on his way again, recording robust and ribald albums for the new young audiences of the 60s and 70s. —JON

○ **The Honeydripper / BLUESVILLE**

○ **Country Blues Piano 1929-1932 / YAZOO**   1972
Featuring this Arkansas-born pianist/songster in some of his best early outings. —MH

☆ **Raining in My Heart / DELMARK**   1987
United recordings from the 50s by this enduring blues belter and pianist. —MH

TAJ MAHAL   b 1942

Modern acoustic blues. Taj Mahal emerged from the folk-rock era of the 60s with a spirited revivalist blues act that helped introduce rock audiences to the old country blues of Sleepy John Estes, Yank Rachell, and the like. Over the years, the basic blues-band format of his Columbia debut album gave way to an eclectic and sometimes bewildering array of stylistic configurations, ranging from Caribbean through old-timey to almost pop. Through it all, Taj Mahal has remained a spokesman for the blues, Black music, and civil rights, and his reworking of traditional blues continues to be a central theme in his performances (especially the solo personal appearances). —JON

○ **Taj Mahal / COLUMBIA**   1968
His debut, with Ry Cooder and Jesse Ed Davis. First and foremost. —MH

Shake Sugaree / MUSIC
A delightful album of stories and songs for kids. —MH

Mule Bone / RHINO   1991
Taj Mahal won a Grammy nomination with this music from the Broadway production of the Hurston/Hughes play. —MH

TAMPA RED   1904-1981

Acoustic & electric Chicago blues. Out of the dozens of fine slide guitarists who recorded blues, only a handful — Elmore James, Muddy Waters, and Robert Johnson, for example — left a clear imprint on tradition by creating a recognizable and widely imitated instrumental style. Tampa Red was another influential musical model. During his heyday in the 20s and 30s, he was billed as "The Guitar Wizard," and his stunning slide work on steel National or electric guitar shows why he earned the title. His 30-year recording career produced hundreds of sides: hokum, pop, and jive, but mostly blues (including classic compositions "Anna Lou Blues," "Black Angel Blues," "Crying Won't Help You," "It Hurts Me Too," and "Love Her with a Feeling"). Early in Red's career, he teamed up with pianist, songwriter, and latter-day gospel composer Georgia Tom Dorsey, collaborating on double entendre classics like "Tight Like That."

Listeners who only know Tampa Red's hokum material are missing the deeper side of one of the mainstays of Chicago blues. His peers included Big Bill Broonzy, with whom he shared a special friendship. Members of Lester Melrose's musical mafia and drinking buddies, they once managed to sleep through both games of a Chicago White Sox doubleheader. Eventually alcohol caught up with Red, and he blamed his latter-day health problems on an inability to refuse a drink.

During Red's prime, his musical venues ran the gamut of blues institutions: down-home jukes, the streets, the vaudeville theater circuit, and the Chicago club scene. Due to his polish and theater experience, he is often described as a city musician or urban artist in contrast to many of his more limited musical contemporaries. Furthermore, his house served as the blues community's rehearsal hall and an informal booking agency. According to the testimony of Broonzy and Big Joe Williams, Red cared for other musicians by offering them a meal and a place to stay and generally easing their transition from country to city life.

Today's listener will enjoy Tampa Red's expressive vocals and perhaps be taken aback by his kazoo solos. His songwriting has stood the test of time, and any serious slide guitar student had better be familiar with Red's guitar wizardry. –BLP

○ **Bottleneck Guitar 1928-1937 / YAZOO**   1974
Prime cuts from one of the greatest guitarists ever to strap on a slide. –CK

★ **Tampa Red: Guitar Wizard / BLUEBIRD**   1975
A 32-song collection of great slide guitar from 1934-1953, featuring sidemen Carl Martin, Black Bob, Blind John Davis, Johnnie Jones, and Walter Horton. Produced by Frank Driggs, this captures the full range of blues, hokum, and pop from a most popular and influential blues player. –BLP

It's Tight like That / STORY OF BLUES
Superb slide and suggestive hokum from 1928-1942. –JO

Bawdy Blues / BLUESVILLE
Latter-day Tampa, from the late 50s to early 60s, with Memphis Slim and Lonnie Johnson. –JO

EDDIE TAYLOR   1923-1985

Electric Chicago blues. Blues singer and guitarist. One of the cruel ironies of blues history is that the boogie lines on all the great Jimmy Reed records, always referred to as the "Jimmy Reed rhythm," were in fact played by Reed's long-time partner Eddie Taylor. But Taylor was no mere sideman, having started as a juke-joint performer in Mississippi back in the late 30s. When he finally got a chance to record in the mid 50s, his approach, though completely electric, drew its inspiration from his down-home roots, making every song a true gem of early Chicago blues. His playing on the Jimmy Reed sides may make him one of the most influential (if unheralded) guitarists in the history of the music. –CK

☆ **Ride 'Em On Down / CHARLY**
All the classic Vee Jay sides: "Bad Boy," "Big Town Playboy," "Find My Baby," the title track, and eight others, plus a dozen more early Jimmy Reed sides with Taylor in support. –CK

HOUND DOG TAYLOR   1917-1975

Electric Chicago blues. A truly great and influential slide guitarist, Taylor worked in a two-guitars-drums-no-bass format with guitarist Brewer Phillips and drummer Ted Harvey for well over a decade, putting his own raucous slant on the popular Elmore James style. His music was loud, raw, and totally infectious, with Phillips and Harvey driving the beat home like no one else. After seeing only two 45s issued locally in the 60s, Hound Dog became the first artist to record for Alligator Records in 1971, enjoying international success. One of his pupils, a young George Thorogood, would later co-opt Hound Dog's stage act and music with great success in the White teen market. –CK

★ **And the Houserockers / ALLIGATOR**   1971
Hound Dog's primitive, slashing bottleneck style gave Alligator Records its start, providing them with their first star and the model for their slogan of "houserocking music." Wild, raucous, crazy music straight out of the South Side clubs, this is the perfect place to start. Features "Give Me Back My Wig," "55th Street Boogie," "She's Gone," and "Taylor's Rock," the tune that became the basis for Freddie King's signature piece, "Hideaway." –CK

● **Natural Boogie / ALLIGATOR**   1973
A second album, just as wild as his debut. Features the high-octane kick of "Take Five" and "Hawaiian Boogie" and the throbbing boogie of "See Me in the Evening." –CK

○ **Beware of the Dog / ALLIGATOR**   1975
His first live album, perhaps even steamier than the first two studio efforts. Features driving versions of "Dust My Broom," "Kitchen Sink Boogie," and "Comin' 'round the Mountain." His unique take on soul music in "Let's Get Funky" is simmering in 100-proof lunacy. –CK

Genuine Houserockin' Music / ALLIGATOR   1982
Previously unissued tracks from the first two studio albums. "Crossroads," Brewer Phillips's version of "Kansas City," and a wild "What'd I Say" are the standouts on this one. –CK

○ **Live at Joe's Place / FAN CLUB**   1992
Live recordings with the Houserockers from 1972 in Boston. They're drunk, they're out of tune, but the whole shebang rocks like crazy, and the crowd goes nuts. I wouldn't be without it for a second, and neither should you. (Import) –CK

Have Some Fun / WOLF   1992
More 1972 live recordings from Boston, done with the Houserockers. Better fidelity, different song selection, and a much tighter performance make this one a nice addition to Taylor's meager discography. (Import) –CK

KOKO TAYLOR   b 1935

Electric Chicago blues. The reigning queen of the blues has been greatly influenced by Chicago blues artists like Howlin' Wolf. She's been recording professionally since the 60s and is renowned for her gospel-style ashy contralto and her contemporary blues repertoire. –BC

Koko Taylor / MCA   1972
A funky blues set. –BC

○ **I Got What It Takes / ALLIGATOR**   1975
This is 60s barrelhouse blues, featuring "Wang Dang Doodle." Produced by Willie Dixon. –BC

Live from Chicago / ALLIGATOR
Koko belts out soul songs with fury and feeds off a wild crowd. –BC

Jump for Joy / ALLIGATOR
Rocking blues, heartbreaking numbers, and duets with Lonnie Brooks. –BC

LITTLE JOHNNY TAYLOR   b 1943

Electric R&B/soul blues. Little Johnny Taylor (not to be confused with soul singer Johnnie Taylor of "Who's Makin' Love") came out of the Southern gospel scene to record for the Los Angeles-based Galaxy label where, from 1963-1968, he scored a string of hits, including his Top 20 version of "Part-Time Love." Taylor's style combines the smoothness and finesse of Bobby Bland and Little Milton with the anguish of Little Willie John and the intense, falsetto-gospel "preaching" style of Ted Taylor (no relation). Later, on the Shreveport-based Ronn label, Taylor kept alive the "cheatin' blues" tradition with songs such as "Open House at My House" and "Everybody Knows about My Good Thing," which were both covered by Z. Z. Hill. Ronn continues to issue material from this fine, underrated singer. –CO

○ **Greatest Hits / FANTASY**   1964
This singer's best 60s output, originally on Galaxy Records. Full of gospel-fired fervor. –BD

JOHNNIE "GEECHIE" TEMPLE   1906-1968

Acoustic Delta blues. Johnnie Temple is one of the great unsung heroes of the blues. A contemporary of Skip James, Son House, and other Delta legends, Temple was one of the very first to develop the now-standard bottom-string boogie bass figure, generally credited to Robert Johnson. –CK

○ **1935-39 / DOCUMENT**
A solid collection of Temple's earliest sides, including the killer "Lead Pencil Blues." (Import) –CK

SONNY TERRY   1911-1986

Acoustic country blues. Often cited as the greatest and certainly most famous of the acoustic blues harmonica players, Terry was also famed for the exuberant whoops and hollers he worked into his blues numbers, fox-chase imitations, and folk songs. Although much of his best work came with long-time partner Brownie McGhee, whom he met in 1939, Terry recorded with other accompanists, including Woody Guthrie, Lightnin' Hopkins, and Johnny Winter, in settings ranging from pure folk to rocking electric blues. Like Brownie, he went through an early-50s blues band period in the New York studios, followed by extensive albums in the folk-blues vein before the pair stopped speaking to one another and finally went their separate ways a few years before Terry's death. —JON

☆ **Folkways Years 1944-63 / SMITHSONIAN-FOLKWAYS**
Terry embodied country-blues harmonica whoops and train/hound imitations. The best of his Folkways performances are truly stunning. —MH

HENRY THOMAS   b 1874

Acoustic country blues. Texas songster Henry Thomas remains a relative stranger who made some great recordings, then returned to obscurity. Evidence suggests he was an itinerant street musician, a musical hobo who rode the rails across Texas and possibly to the World Fairs in St. Louis and Chicago just before and after the turn of the century. Most agree he was the oldest African-American folk artist to produce a significant body of recordings. His projected 1874 birthdate would predate Charley Patton by a good 17 years. Like Patton and a handful of other musicians generally termed songsters (including John Hurt, Jim Jackson, Mance Lipscomb, Furry Lewis, and Leadbelly), Thomas's repertoire bridged the 19th and 20th centuries, providing a compelling glimpse into a wide range of African-American musical genres. The 23 songs he cut for Vocalion between 1927 and 1929 include a spiritual, ballads, reels, dance songs, and eight selections titled blues. Obviously dance music, his songs were geared to older dance styles shared by Black and White audiences.

Thomas's sound, like his repertoire, is unique. He capoed his guitar high up the neck and strummed it in the manner of a banjo, favoring dance rhythm over complex fingerwork. On many of his pieces, he simultaneously played the quills or panpipes, a common but seldom-recorded African-American folk instrument indigenous to Mississippi, Louisiana, and Texas. Combining the quills, a limited-range melody instrument, with his banjo-like strummed guitar produced one of the most memorable sounds in American folk music. For example, his lead-in on "Bull Doze Blues" still worked as a hook when recycled 40 years later by blues/rockers Canned Heat in their version of "Going Up the Country." "Ragtime Texas," as Thomas was known, provides a welcome in-road to 19th-century dance music, but his music is neither obscure nor merely educational: it has a timeless quality — and while it may be an acquired taste, once you catch on to it, you're hooked. —BLP

☆ **Texas Worried Blues / YAZOO**
Songster Thomas plays a cross-section of blues and pre-blues with a unique guitar-and-panpipes instrumentation. Although it may sound archaic to the beginner, given time it will get your toes tapping and quickly become a favorite. —BLP

RON THOMPSON

Modern electric blues. After honing his chops behind Little Joe Blue and John Lee Hooker, guitarist Ron Thompson went solo in 1980, forming his own blues/roots-rock trio, the Resisters. *Just Like a Devil*, a 1990 release on pianist Mark Naftalin's Winner label, was culled from Thompson's appearances on Naftalin's "Blue Monday Party" radio program. Thompson had previously been a member of Hooker's Coast-to-Coast Blues Band for three years. Other solo recordings include a 1987 outing on Blind Pig, *Resister Twister*. —BD

○ **Resister Twister / BLIND PIG**   1987
Rockin' blues from a former John Lee Hooker sideman. —RG

BIG MAMA THORNTON   1926-1984

Electric West Coast blues. Despite her religious home environment, Willie Mae Thornton was working the Southern club circuit by the time she was fourteen. While appearing at Houston's Bronze Peacock, she caught the attention of Don Robey, the club's owner and a major African-American record producer, who signed her to his Peacock label, named in

honor of his club. Thornton's hard-edged blues voice contrasted with the sweeter, smoother style currently in vogue; nevertheless, her energy and showmanship allowed her to work with the best Southwestern and West Coast R&B bands, fronted by Johnny Otis, Roy Milton, Joe Liggins, and Gatemouth Brown. Along with fellow Duke/Peacock artists under contract to Robey (including Junior Parker, Johnny Ace, and Bobby Bland), she toured the Southern club and theater circuit. In 1953 she scored a #1 R&B hit with her grits-and-gravy version of "Hound Dog," later a hit for Elvis Presley. Continuous West Coast club work kept her active until the blues revival expanded her audience. In 1969, at the Ann Arbor Blues Festival, she proved to be the reigning woman artist, interacting as an equal with her peers Big Joe Williams, Howlin' Wolf, and Muddy Waters. Although she played several instruments, her voice was her strength, and she served as a model for female rock vocalists. Despite her bluff exterior, she was a warm, considerate person and a respected member of the blues community. During the 70s she was by far the premier down-home blueswoman in America. —BLP

○ **In Europe / ARHOOLIE**
Live sessions with the Muddy Waters Blues Band. —BLP

HENRY TOWNSEND   b 1909

Acoustic country blues. Influenced by Roosevelt Sykes and Lonnie Johnson, Townsend was a commanding musician, adept on both piano and guitar. —CK

○ **Henry Townsend & Henry Spaulding / WOLF**
Topflight country-blues from Townsend, with the bonus of two cuts from the seldom-heard Henry Spaulding. —CK

BIG JOE TURNER   1911-1985

Electric jump blues. This big-voiced blues shouter from Kansas City played a major role in the shaping of rock & roll vocalizing. The essentials are listed below, but everything he recorded is worth hearing. —JF

● **Boss of the Blues / ATLANTIC**   1956
A smoldering, jazz-based set from 1956 features pianist Pete Johnson and some of Turner's most confident vocals. —JF

Big Joe Rides Again / ATLANTIC   1959
More 50s sides in the vein of *Boss of the Blues*. —JF

★ **Greatest Hits / ATLANTIC**
These are Turner's finest early-rock-era recordings, including his best (and best-known) hits and some tasty obscurities. A must-have. —JF

Stormy Monday / PABLO
Sessions from 1974-1978 with Pee Wee Crayton, Dizzy Gillespie, and Blue Mitchell. Includes unreleased sides with a jazz jam-session feel. —HD

The Best of Big Joe Turner / PABLO
Mid-70s sessions with Roy Eldridge, Milt Jackson, and Sonny Stitt. Big Joe still sounds strong. —HD

○ **I've Been to Kansas City / MCA**
Sensational boogie piano and blues shouting on these 1940-1941 Decca sides. —HD

Memorial Album - Rhythm & Blues / ATLANTIC
Twenty-eight sensational 50s R&B tracks. —HD

MAURICE JOHN VAUGHN   b 1952

Modern electric blues. One of the sharp young guitarists to make his mark in 80s Chicago blues, Vaughn produced an impressive debut album and released it on his own Reecy label in 1984. The cleverly packaged *Generic Blues Album* and up-to-the-minute songs such as "Computer Took My Job" attracted a reissue deal with Alligator. Vaughn, whose previous experience included R&B, funk, and blues guitar work for A. C. Reed and Casey Jones, has done little to follow up this auspicious blues recording debut, but new releases are eagerly awaited by contemporary blues enthusiasts. —JON

○ **Generic Blues Album / ALLIGATOR**   1985
Anything but generic, actually this is powerful, contemporary,

funky Chicago blues. With excellent musicianship, Vaughn performs interesting songs focusing on the trials of modern urban life and work. Vaughn, a top session player, sings and plays guitar and sax. —NJF

JOE LOUIS WALKER   b 1949

Modern electric blues. By majority ruling of the music critics, the blues in its modern-day form has reached a peak in the work of San Francisco's Joe Louis Walker, whose individual creative vision has forged progressive musicianship and contemporary urban sensibilities with a blues/roots ethic. Gospel, funk, and soul flavor Walker's music, yet it remains identifiably and emotionally the blues (with strong Delta and Chicago elements). Perhaps for that very reason, Walker has not crossed over into the commercial market the way some of his more pop- or rock-oriented blues contemporaries have. Still, Walker has a strong following, especially in England, and regularly scores at or near the top in blues polls and awards — all this since he recorded his first album as a virtual unknown in 1986, having only recently returned to the blues life after turning to gospel in the 70s. —JON

Cold Is the Night / HIGHTONE   1986
A head-turning debut album of mostly original compositions. Walker's potential for greatness is in evidence. —NJF

○ **The Gift / HIGHTONE**   1987
Walker is an immensely talented and gifted songwriter, guitarist, and vocalist. *The Gift* is the bluesiest of his four releases to date. Walker plays blues, R&B, and funk, with a distinct and overriding gospel influence on his singing and songwriting. Still, he has been known to play a set of slide guitar pieces in concert and to rearrange band songs for solo guitar and voice. He is a bluesman in the best and broadest sense of the word, incorporating almost every aspect of 20th century African-American popular music into his unique and expressive style. —NJF

Blue Soul / HIGHTONE   1989
An appropriately titled and excellent showcase of Walker's soul- and gospel-influenced songwriting and singing. Highlights include the chilling slow blues of "City of Angels" and the solo "I'll Get to Heaven on My Own." —NJF

Live at Slim's - Vol. 1 / HIGHTONE   1991
A great live show, with guest appearances by Angela Strehli and Huey Lewis. A beautiful solo reworking of "Don't Play Games" from *Cold Is the Night.* —NJF

PHILLIP WALKER   b 1937

Modern electric blues. When *Playboy* magazine launched a record company in the early 70s, Phillip Walker was chosen to be the label's contemporary bluesman, and his first album (*Bottom of the Top,* now reissued on Hightone) was exemplary. Both the expectations and accolades for Walker have remained high, although he has never enjoyed a breakthrough beyond blues cult status. Raised in Port Arthur, TX, Walker was influenced by Lonesome Sundown (with whom he later recorded a reunion album), Lonnie Brooks, and Long John Hunter, and he spent three years as Clifton Chenier's guitarist before relocating to Los Angeles in 1959. Walker's smoky vocals and crackling guitar work are flavored by both his Louisiana/Texas background and his associations with such West Coast figures as Lowell Fulson and Percy Mayfield. —JON

Bottom of the Top / HIGHTONE   1973
Walker's first album. Los Angeles recordings done 1969-1972. Confident, tuneful, and resonant. —NJF

Someday You'll Have These Blues / HIGHTONE   1977
An exciting and eminently listenable second album. —NJF

From L.A. to L.A. / ROUNDER   1982
Walker's tunes from 1969, 1970, and 1976 sessions, produced by Bruce Bromberg and recorded with Lonesome Sundown. Very nice. —NJF

Tough As I Want to Be / ROUNDER   1984
Hotter and fiercer than other recordings. Originals and covers from Lowell Fulson and Jimmy McCracklin. —NJF

○ **Blues / HIGHTONE**   1988
These solid, no-nonsense blues are rooted in tradition, yet original and contemporary. The striking upper-register vocals cut right to the bone. Powerful, stately guitar. —NJF

T-BONE WALKER   1910-1975

Electric Texas blues. One of the great guitarists, vocalists, and composers of all time, Walker was the inventor of the Texas shuffle and a major influence on guitarists since the 40s. His recordings for Black & White (1945-1947), including his best-known hit "Call It Stormy Monday," were purchased by Capitol Records, who also won his Imperial recordings. These recordings were combined in a boxed set of six LPs/CDs by Mosaic Records (MD6-130), giving the best possible overview of Walker's distinguished career. The Imperial recordings (1950-1954) are available in a double CD on EMI. Also worth seeking is *T-Bone Blues* (1955-1957) on Atlantic. Walker's album projects in Europe (where he became a major star) included *Feeling the Blues* (Black & Blue), among his finest (available in the US on Delmark). Also worth finding is *Stormy Monday Blues* (Bluesway #6008), although Walker's later work does not generally compare with his magnificent work from the 40s and 50s. —BP

☆ **The Complete T-Bone Walker / MOSAIC**
1940-1954. A six-CD boxed set — an education in the lineage of urban blues. It appears that T-Bone Walker had a greater influence on urban blues players than any other single talent. His guitar, vocals, song selection, and sheer style live on today in nearly every blues performer. He is the master. —JME

● **T-Bone Blues / ATLANTIC**   1959
Walker's finest mid-period album. Classics abound any place you look, and T-Bone's guitar work is nothing short of extraordinary. —CK

Dirty Mistreater / MCA   1973
A reissue of a 1973 Bluesway album. T-Bone near the end. —HD

T-Bone Walker / BLUESBOY
A scholarly 17-track compilation with great photos and notes. Selections from 1929 to 1953. For the collector. —HD

★ **Complete Imperial Recordings / CAPITOL**
The 1950-1953 recordings by the man who virtually invented electric guitar blues. Performances range from soulful and mellow to jump blues. A double CD. —HD

○ **Original 1945-50 Performances / EMI**
A deep look into T-Bone's roots: 12 classic performances, including the original "Stormy Monday Blues." —HD

SIPPIE WALLACE   1898-1986

Classic female blues. A classic female blues singer from the 20s, who kept performing and recording until her death. She was a major influence on a young Bonnie Raitt, who recorded several of Wallace's songs and performed live with her. —CK

○ **1923-1929 / DOCUMENT**
Sippie's earliest and best sides, including "I'm a Mighty Tight Woman." (Import) —CK

ROBERT WARD

Electric R&B/soul blues. Robert Ward created a classic guitar sound on the 1962 hit "I Found a Love" by the Falcons (featuring lead vocalist Wilson Pickett). That same vibrato-drenched Magnatone amp sound has propelled Ward to guitar-hero status since his much-touted return to public performing and recording in 1990. This time around, Ward (who worked with the Ohio Untouchables, later known as the Ohio Players, and made the rounds backing various R&B singers before retreating to Dry Branch, GA, some years ago) is in the spotlight for his soulful vocals as well as his trademark guitar work (which retains more of a gospel-based R&B approach than a blues soloist's attack). —JON

☆ **Fear No Evil / BLACK TOP**   1991
Though recently recorded, this sounds like vintage soul. Ward is an exceptional individualist on the guitar. —RG

WASHBOARD SAM   1910-1966

Acoustic Chicago blues. A popular hokum blues artist, usually found in the company of singer/guitarist Big Bill Broonzy. –CK

○ **Washboard Sam - Vol. 1 / DOCUMENT**
Eighteen sides from the classic Bluebird period, with solid support from Big Bill Broonzy, Black Bob, and Blind John Davis. Includes "Who Pumped the Wind in My Doughnut" and "He's a Creepin' Man." –CK

WALTER WASHINGTON

Electric R&B/soul blues. Walter Washington became a local legend in the Black clubs of New Orleans in the 70s and 80s and worked his way up to national status with a series of well-received albums and appearances. His recording affiliations have likewise moved from local to national independent to major label. An innovative guitarist and fine singer who has also done some excellent work with vocalist Johnny Adams, Washington does not perform in the classic New Orleans R&B mold but incorporates soul, funk, jazz, and blues with fluency and power. –JON

Wolf Tracks / ROUNDER   1986
Washington's first nationally distributed album contains contemporary R&B filtered heavily through gospel and traditional New Orleans influences. –NJF

Out of the Dark / ROUNDER   1988
Truly soulful blues and R&B. Funky and inspired. –NJF

Sada / ATLANTIC   1991
Moving and tuneful, this album is more reflective and more inward. –NJF

○ **Wolf at the Door / ROUNDER**   1991
New Orleans blues and funk. Inventive, passionate, and irresistibly groovin', with very tasty guitar and snarly vocals. Walter writes great songs, along with creating unique versions of other people's compositions. This guy is undeservedly obscure, for he is a major talent. Highlights here are a slow blues called "At Night in the City," the rocking shuffle of "Tailspin," and Walter's eerie reading "Hello Stranger," penned by Doc Pomus and Dr. John. –NJF

MUDDY WATERS   1915-1983

Electric Chicago blues. Rolling his eyes toward heaven and shaking his head like a man possessed, Muddy Waters cast a powerful spell. He could easily work audiences into a frenzy, marrying the unmistakable sexual urgency of his lyrics to the vocal slide statements that for forty years were as much a part of his signature as his voice, which many claim was the best in electric blues. A native Mississippi Delta bluesman, Muddy instinctively understood the unpretentious beauty and power in simplicity. Time and again, he transformed basic patterns into blues masterpieces. Like the superstitions and voodoo images prominent in Waters's best-known lyrics, the primal earthiness of his rhythms contains a deep, almost subconscious appeal.

As a vocalist, Muddy Waters had few parallels. As a blues bandleader, he had none. More than any other performer, he was responsible for forging Delta acoustic music into the electrified, band-oriented urban blues of today. And some of his own bands were the stuff legends are made of. British groups copied his songs in the early 60s, one naming themselves after his "Rollin' Stone." Guitarists such as Buddy Guy, Mike Bloomfield, Eric Clapton, and Johnny Winter came to share his stage. By the end of his life, Muddy Waters was hailed as "Father of Electric Blues." Through the years and various sidemen, Muddy's music remained intensely his own. His vocals and playing patterns have often been imitated, but no one has ever quite captured his touch. –JO

★ **Best of Muddy Waters / CHESS**   1957
Twelve tightly compacted gems of seminal Chicago blues. Features the original versions of "I'm Your Hoochie-Coochie Man," "Long Distance Call," "I'm Ready," "Honey Bee," "I Just Wanna Make Love to You," "Still a Fool," and a song called

"Rollin' Stone," which provided the name inspiration for a hippie rock magazine and a group of British musicians. The perfect primer for those on a budget. –JO & CK

○ **Sings Big Bill Broonzy / MCA**   1960
Muddy's tribute album to the man who gave him his start on the Chicago circuit. Features "When I Get to Drinkin'," "The Mopper's Blues," and great harp from James Cotton as an added bonus. –CK

● **At Newport / CHESS**   1960
A sensational 1960 performance with crackerjack support from James Cotton, Otis Spann, and Pat Hare. This features Muddy delivering first-rate live renditions of "I Got My Mojo Workin'," "Baby Please Don't Go," "Tiger in Your Tank," and the brutally macho "I Got My Brand on You." –JO & CK

Folk Singer / CHESS   1964
Unadorned, down-home acoustic blues, with Buddy Guy on second guitar. –JO

Real Folk Blues / CHESS   1966
A mixed bag of early Chess sides from 1949-1954. Highlights include "Walkin' through the Park" and the "I'm a Man"-derived strut of "Mannish Boy." –JO & CK

More Real Folk Blues / CHESS   1967
More early Chess sides from 1948-1952. Features essential tracks not found on *The Chess Box*, with the bludgeoning stomp of "She's Alright" and the moody introspection of "My Life Is Ruined" among the numerous highlights. –JO & CK

○ **Down on Stovall's Plantation / TESTAMENT**   1971
Library of Congress field recordings done by Alan Lomax from 1941-1942, featuring Muddy with Percy Thomas on guitar, Louis Ford on mandolin, and Henry Sims on violin. Capturing Muddy in a string-band context playing his earliest repertoire, this is a major historical document. –BLP

They Call Me Muddy Waters / CHESS   1971
A Grammy winner for Best Ethnic/Traditional Recording. –JO

Muddy & the Wolf / MCA   1974
Contains six live Muddy tracks with Mike Bloomfield, Paul Butterfield, and Otis Spann. Also features tracks by Howlin' Wolf from his London sessions with Eric Clapton and Ringo Starr. –JO

Hard Again / CBS / BB 143   1977
Recorded in two days, this is absolutely brilliant. –JO

Muddy "Mississippi" Waters Live / CBS   1979
Fierce, declamatory vocals and an other worldly slide. A bluesman at the height of his powers. –JO

King Bee / CBS / BB 192   1981
Muddy's 1981 swan song, recorded with Johnny Winter. –JO

Rare & Unissued / CHESS   1984
Great but relatively obscure Chess sides from 1947-1954. –JO

☆ **The Chess Box / CHESS**   1989
The best of the best-ofs, it collects 72 classics from 1947 through the 70s. –JO

SYLVESTER WEAVER

Acoustic country blues. The pioneering guitarist from the early days of the blues who created the enduring classic "Guitar Rag," later popularized as "Steel Guitar Rag." Weaver was adept at everything from ragtime to slide guitar stylings, all performed with great technical skill and a marvelous sense of time. –CK

○ **Smoketown Strut / AGRAM**
Weaver's earliest and best sides, including "Guitar Rag." The sound is horrible in spots, but every note of the music is great. (Import) –CK

BOOGIE BILL WEBB   1926-1990

Electric country blues. Although he lived in New Orleans most of his life, and none other than Fats Domino brought him to Imperial Records for his recording debut in 1953, Boogie Bill Webb was never much a part of the New Orleans R&B scene. Webb's music grew out of the Jackson area country-blues tradition of Tommy Johnson and others, and he retained a down-home, idiosyncratic approach to a wide range of material from C&W to R&B and traditional jazz. Beginning in 1966, Webb recorded occasionally for folklorists and field researchers, finally recording his first full album in 1986 with funding from the Louisiana Endowment for the Humanities. Album producer Ben Sandmel, who also played drums with Webb for five years, described Boogie Bill's approach as "quirky, often anarchic," but it is appealing in its very unpredictability, humor, and warmth. –JON

○ **Drinkin' & Stinkin' / FLYING FISH**   1989
Houseparty, juke-joint blues. –NJF

KATIE WEBSTER   ♭1939

Electric New Orleans blues. Katie Webster, a music major in college, grew up playing gospel, classical, blues, boogie-woogie, and jazz. She was such an accomplished and in-demand pianist that discographers will probably never be able to count the number of recording sessions she played on, especially those from the 50s and 60s in Louisiana, where she accompanied everyone from Clifton Chenier to Slim Harpo. Although Webster recorded a number of early R&B singles of her own, it was not until the 80s that she really started hitting the touring circuit (especially in Europe) as a featured act. The momentum has carried over into a renewed career in the US, where Webster's saucy, energetic performances both on stage and on record have made her not only a favorite among contemporary blues fans but also a spokesperson for the female point of view in a typically male-dominated field. –JON

○ **Swamp Boogie Queen / ALLIGATOR**
Jay Miller's swamp-blues pianist of the 50s is unmuzzled in the 80s. A joyful noise. –MH

Two-Fisted Mama! / ALLIGATOR
More powerhouse piano and vocals. –MH

VALERIE WELLINGTON   ♭1959

Modern electric blues. Valerie Wellington took the Chicago blues scene by surprise in 1982, perhaps not forgoing her classical training as an opera singer as much as using it to enhance her work in the blues. As a blueswoman she fit right in, not only becoming a regular in the blues clubs but also compiling an impressive theatrical resume for her portrayals of Ma Rainey and Bessie Smith — women who, like opera singers, learned to project their voices without microphones. The influence of Koko Taylor has also been evident in Wellington's blues approach, which combines classic vaudeville-era blues with hard-driving Chicago sounds. Her power-packed voice has been heard on only a few record releases but has been featured frequently in TV and radio commercials. –JON

○ **Million Dollar Secret / ROOSTER BLUES**   1983
Wellington is a powerful yet subtle vocalist, backed by some of the best Chicago blues players, including Sunnyland Slim, Billy Branch, Casey Jones, and Magic Slim & the Teardrops. The CD reissue contains two bonus tracks. –NJF

JUNIOR WELLS   ♭1934

Electric Chicago blues. Wells started on the streets of Chicago, playing for tips as a teenager, and graduated to houseparties with the Aces, who became Little Walter's Jukes when Wells replaced him in Muddy Waters's band. Wells recorded on his own throughout the 50s and into the early 60s for a spate of smaller, Chicago-based labels, then came to national attention by teaming up with guitarist Buddy Guy in the mid 60s and recording a brilliant set of landmark recordings for collector-oriented labels like Delmark and Vanguard. Generally acknowledged as the last of the great Chicago harmonica players, Wells continues to record and perform to the present day, his skills honed to a fine edge, a perfect ambassador to the music he's represented for so long. –CK

★ **Hoodoo Man Blues / DELMARK**   1965
This is the album that started the collector blues label trend

of the late 60s — a simple, unadorned recording of a working Chicago blues band captured in all their unbridled glory. Features smoldering guitar from Buddy Guy and a crack rhythm section in support. –CK

It's My Life, Baby / VANGUARD   1966
Partly live from Pepper's Lounge in Chicago, with Buddy Guy and Freddy Below. Junior's first Vanguard album. –BLP

South Side Blues Jam / DELMARK   1970
Five Delmark cuts that capture the Theresa's Lounge feel. Includes Buddy Guy, Otis Spann, Louis Myers, and Freddy Below of the Aces. –BLP

On Tap / DELMARK   1974
A loose set of jams, including a powerful version of "Mystery Train." Phil Guy replaces Buddy Guy, while A. C. Reed and Charles Miles add saxes. –BLP

● **Blues Hit Big Town / DELMARK**   1977
A fine reissue set of Wells's early 50s States recordings. –BLP

○ **1957-1966 / PAULA**   1991
The best of Wells's output for Mel London's Chief and Profile labels, including the original "Messin' with the Kid." –CK

PEETIE WHEATSTRAW   1902-1941

Piano blues. A very popular bluesman in the 30s and early 40s, Wheatstraw's signature phrase, "Oh well well," was adapted by several bluesmen, Muddy Waters among them. –CK

○ **The Devil's Son-in-Law / BLUES DOCUMENT**
A 20-track import compilation of Wheatstraw's best. Includes "I Want Some Seafood" and "Fairasee Woman." –CK

ARTIE WHITE   ♭1937

Electric R&B/soul blues. As Artie White tells it, he was walking down the street one day during his Chicago gospel-singing days when "a guy drove up in a Cadillac and offered me ten grand to record some blues." It took years of dues-paying on Chicago's South Side club scene and the Southern and Midwestern chitlin circuit, but Artie White has proved his worth in the blues. A solid, hearty vocalist who has surrounded himself with a talented crew of musicians, White (at one time billed as Artie "Blues Boy" White) has most often performed squarely within the soul/blues territory staked out by Little Milton and Bobby Bland. If White's style is too close for comfort, Little Milton doesn't show it — he's even played guitar on some of Artie's recent tracks. –JON

○ **Thangs Got to Change / ICHIBAN**   1989
An excellent, varied mixture of tempos and tunes. –NJF

Dark End of the Street / ICHIBAN   1991
This album is less bluesy, with more soul/R&B feel. It's still very listenable and danceable. –NJF

BUKKA WHITE   1906-1977

Acoustic Delta blues. Achieving a distinctive musical voice is a highly prized blues value, yet few artists develop an easily recognizable vocal and instrumental style that is uniquely theirs. Bukka White was one of those remarkable artists with an overall approach and composition style that were unusual, yet he was a popular houseparty musician and a successful recording artist. Although he had a second career during the blues revival and remained a powerful performer, his best work was on his 1937 and 1940 Vocalion sides, reissued by Columbia. They feature down-home country-blues at its best, personal, moving, and instrumentally compelling. White's percussive approach to his open G-tuned steel National can be imitated but not duplicated. Like other Delta artists, White's sound was melodically simple but rhythmically complex. Sporting an attack vaguely reminiscent of Big Joe Williams, White worked his guitar like a drum, adding rhythmic nuances with his chording hand on the guitar neck. On his 40s session, he called for percussive rhythm. Many of White's pieces employ spoken or chanted passages, especially his train songs, which combined talking blues and train effects. His compositions generally either fall outside mainstream blues or bridge sacred and secular traditions, as in his classic "Fixing to Die." Moody and introspective, his songs let you into his life, detailing his experiences as a prisoner at Mississippi's notorious Parchman Farm or as a hobo riding the rails. His dance songs, such as "Bukka's Jitterbug Swing," aptly demonstrate his skills as a houseparty performer and bear out his reputation as a breakdown artist, which means people danced so hard to his beat that they literally broke the floors down at the jukes and plantation balls over which he reigned. –BLP

Mississippi Blues / TAKOMA   1969
The best of White's "rediscovery phase" recordings. –BLP

☆ **The Complete Sessions 1930-1940 / TRAVELIN' MAN**
Delta blues as propulsive as a runaway freight train. Not for the weakhearted! –JO

ROBERT WILKINS   1896-1987

Acoustic country blues. A superior guitarist, Robert Wilkins projected a relaxed ease on his exquisite country blues 78s. He was working as a Pullman porter in Memphis when he was hired by Victor to record in 1928. He was soon back in the studio for Brunswick and Vocalion. The 1929 "That's No Way to Get Along," the most famous of his prewar 78s, was covered by the Rolling Stones as "Prodigal Son."

Wilkins's great Mississippi vibrato was similar to that of Frank Stokes and Joe Callicott, and his records show considerable finesse with rag and blues guitar. Ungoverned by standard 12-bar conventions, Wilkins created his own structures and was especially strong in open *E*, as heard in "That's No Way to Get Along" and the spooky one-chord "Rollin' Stone." He crafted lyrics into coherent narratives, carefully avoiding any hint of the risqué. He showed up at the Chicago World's Fair but did most of his playing in Memphis and Hernando. Unnerving violence at a houseparty prompted him to quit the blues in 1936 and find Jesus. In 1964 a rediscovered Rev. Robert Wilkins, spiritual singer and minister of the Church of God in Christ, hit the folk circuit and made some deeply moving records. He refused to play blues but did recycle some old riffs. Near the end of his life, Rev. Wilkins was seen working as a root doctor on a Memphis side street. He lived to be 91. –JO

○ **The Original Rolling Stone / YAZOO**
Fourteen prewar tracks, with adequate liner notes. –JO

Memphis Blues 1928-1935 / DOCUMENT
Wilkins's complete works, plus sides by Tom Dickinson and Allen Shaw. –JO

BIG JOE WILLIAMS   1903-1982

Acoustic & electric Delta blues. Big Joe Williams may have been the most cantankerous human being who ever walked the earth with guitar in hand. At the same time, he was an incredible blues musician: a gifted songwriter, a powerhouse vocalist, and an exceptional idiosyncratic guitarist. Despite his deserved reputation as a fighter (documented in Michael Bloomfield's bizarre booklet *Me and Big Joe*), artists who knew him well treated him as a respected elder statesman. Even so, they may not have chosen to play with him, because — as with other old Delta artists — if you played with him you played by his rules.

As protégé David "Honeyboy" Edwards described him, Williams in his early Delta days was a walking musician who played work camps, jukes, store porches, streets, and alleys from New Orleans to Chicago. He recorded through five decades for Vocalion, Okeh, Paramount, Bluebird, Prestige, Delmark, and many others. As a youngster, I met him in Delmark owner Bob Koester's store, the Jazz Record Mart. At the time, Big Joe was living there when not on his constant travels. According to Charlie Musselwhite, he and Big Joe kicked off the blues revival in Chicago in the 60s.

When I saw him playing at Mike Bloomfield's "blues night" at the Fickle Pickle, Williams was playing an electric nine-string guitar through a small ramshackle amp with a pie plate nailed to it and a beer can dangling against that. When he played,

everything rattled but Big Joe himself. The total effect of this incredible apparatus produced the most buzzing, sizzling, African-sounding music I have ever heard.

Anyone who wants to learn Delta blues must one day come to grips with the idea that the guitar is a drum as well as a melody-producing instrument. A continuous, African-derived musical tradition emphasizing percussive techniques on stringed instruments from the banjo to the guitar can be heard in the music of Delta stalwarts Charley Patton, Fred McDowell, and Bukka White. Each employed decidedly percussive techniques, beating on his box, knocking on the neck, snapping the strings, or adding buzzing or sizzling effects to augment the instrument's percussive potential. However, Big Joe Williams, more than any other major recording artist, embodied the concept of guitar-as-drum, bashing out an incredible series of riffs on his *G*-tuned nine-string for over 60 years. –BLP

Piney Woods Blues / DELMARK
Fine Delmark cuts from the late-50s rediscovery phase of Big Joe's career. –BLP

★ **Back to the Country / TESTAMENT**   1964
Fellow Mississippians Jimmy Brown on fiddle and Willie Lee Harris on harmonica augment Big Joe's down-home Delta blues from the blues revival of the 70s. –BLP

● **Early Recordings 1935-41 / MAMLISH**
This blues legend and guitar wizard's best initial Bluebird recordings, including the best versions of "49 Highway" and "Baby Please Don't Go" from 1935. –BLP

○ **Stavin' Chain Blues / DELMARK**   1991
A CD reissue of 1958 recordings, including four previously unreleased tracks. Raw but beautiful country-blues, featuring the otherworldly sound of Big Joe's nine-string guitar. –NJF

ROBERT PETE WILLIAMS   1914-1980

Acoustic Louisiana blues. Discovered in the Louisiana State Penitentiary, Williams became one of the great blues discoveries during the folk boom of the early 60s. His disregard for conventional patterns, tunings, and structures kept him from a wider audience, but his music remains one of the great, intense treats of the blues. –CK

☆ **Angola's Prisoner's Blues / ARHOOLIE**
Not enough great things to say about this one, one of the finest field recordings ever done anywhere. If Robert Pete's "Prisoner's Talking Blues" doesn't move you, check your heart into your refrigerator's freezer section. –CK

SONNY BOY WILLIAMSON I   1914-1948

Acoustic & electric Chicago blues. John Lee Williamson, known to bluesologists as "the first Sonny Boy" or "Sonny Boy I" because he preceded another famed bluesman (Aleck "Rice" Miller) who also used the SBW moniker, can rightly be considered the forefather of the postwar Chicago blues style. It was he who brought the harmonica to prominence in the blues, and he who pioneered the harmonica-led small-combo format that defined the Chicago idiom in its 40s development. Williamson's records exuded charm and swing. His vocals and harp playing were widely imitated, and many of his songs survived in the repertoires of artists like Junior Wells, Snooky Pryor, and Little Walter. Before he died on a Chicago street, the victim of murder by icepick, Sonny Boy had contributed a wealth of memorable works to the discography of the blues, including "Good Morning (Little) School Girl," "Blue Bird Blues," and "Hoodoo Hoodoo" (the "Hoodoo Man Blues" of Junior Wells fame). –JON

☆ **Throw a Boogie Woogie (With Big Joe Williams) / RCA**
1930s Bluebird recordings from the influential harp-playing "Sonny Boy I" and the archetypical bluesman drifter Big Joe Williams, whose powerful vocals and percussive 9-string guitar epitomized the Delta. –MH

○ **Complete Recorded Works - Vols. 1-5 / DOCUMENT**
His complete works 1937-1947 in chronological order. Sonny Boy was a major influence (both harmonica and vocals) on

many of the younger Chicago bluesmen, in particular: Junior Wells. —JME

SONNY BOY WILLIAMSON II   1897-1965

Blues. One of the three greatest blues harmonica men who ever lived (Little Walter Jacobs and Big Walter Horton being the other two), Sonny Boy's style was 100% his own. A contemporary of Robert Johnson and other early Delta blues legends, Williamson worked under the name "Little Boy Blue." He began using the "Sonny Boy" tag when he started broadcasting over KFFA on the "King Biscuit Time" radio show in the early 40s. Williamson, however, didn't start recording until the early 50s. Early recorded success for the Mississippi-based Trumpet label brought him to Chicago's Chess label, where he remained for the rest of his career, having R&B chart hits into the early 60s. His appearance on European blues tours made him a direct influence on the then-burgeoning English R&B scene as well, and he recorded with the Yardbirds, the Animals, and Jimmy Page. Whether he worked solo or with a full band, Sonny Boy could keep any audience spellbound with his rhythmic bursts of harmonica, his sly singing of some of the best blues lyrics ever constructed, and a gift for entertaining that went back to his days of hoboing around the South. One of the true originals in the blues, Sonny Boy Williamson's recordings are classics of the genre. —CK

○ **Down and Out Blues / CHESS**
☆ **King Biscuit Time / ARHOOLIE**
Sonny Boy's early Trumpet sides from 1951. The original "Eyesight to the Blind," "Nine Below Zero," and "Mighty Long Time" are Sonny Boy at his very best. Added bonuses include Williamson backing Elmore James on his original recording of "Dust My Broom" and a live broadcast from 1965. —CK

○ **The Chess Years / CHARLY-CHESS**
This import multi-disc boxed set of Sonny Boy's Chess sides (1955-1964) is a definitive overview. —CK

Keep It to Ourselves / ALLIGATOR
Acoustic solo sides, recorded in Europe in 1963. Intimate and wonderful. —CK

CHICK WILLIS   ♭1934

Modern electric blues. Although he can play hard blues with the best of them, Willis is best known for his series of soft-core porno releases based on his initial hit, "Stoop Down Baby." —CK

○ **Stoop Down Baby / COLLECTABLES**
The original album, originally released on the LaVal party record label. Features the title track and other tracks just as raunchy. —CK

HOP WILSON   1927-1975

Electric Texas blues. Slide guitar blues with an Elmore James flavor, played on an eight-string table (non-pedal) steel guitar, was the trademark sound of Houston blues legend Hop Wilson. Strictly a local phenomenon, Wilson recorded fitfully and hated touring. Though he played fine down-home blues on conventional electric guitar, and was a powerful singer as well, it is Wilson's unique slide stylings that remain a signature influence on Johnny Winter and Jimmie Vaughan, to name a few. —CK

Blues with Friends at Goldband / GOLDBAND
The original trio sides, with King Ivory Lee Semiens on drums and Ice Water Jones on string bass. —CK

Steel Guitar Flash! / ACE   1988
Later sides for the Ivory label. —CK

☆ **Rockin' Blues Party / CHARLY-GOLDBAND**
Featuring a full side of Hop Wilson, with alternate (and superior) takes of all the classic Goldband sides on this import album. —CK

JIMMY WITHERSPOON   ♭1923

Electric jump blues. One of the great blues singers of the post-

WWII period, Witherspoon began recording with Jay McShann for Philo and Mercury in 1945 and 1946. His own first recordings, using McShann's band, resulted in a #1 R&B hit in 1949 with "Ain't Nobody's Business Parts 1 & 2" on Supreme Records. Live performances of "No Rollin' Blues" and "Big Fine Girl" provided Spoon with two more hits in 1950. Later singles were tried for Federal, Chess, Atco, Vee Jay, and others with little success. His album *Live at the Monterey Jazz Festival* (HiFi Jazz) from 1959 lifted him back into the limelight. Partnerships with Ben Webster (tenor sax) or Groove Holmes (organ) were recorded, and some memorable music resulted, but Jimmy's best 60s album is *Evening Blues* (Prestige), which features T-Bone Walker on guitar and Clifford Scott on saxophone.

Inactive for a time in the 70s due to throat cancer, Witherspoon has made a complete recovery and made one of his most memorable albums for Muse Records (*Midnight Lady Called the Blues*). Muse also released an album recorded in France, featuring Witherspoon with the Savoy Sultans. His newer records lack the spark of some of his earlier work, but given the proper circumstances Jimmy Witherspoon always delivers. —BP

○ **Spoon Concerts / FANTASY**   1959
A classic Monterey Jazz Festival date with Ben Webster, Roy Eldridge, and Coleman Hawkins. —HD

Baby Baby Baby / ORIGINAL BLUES CLASSICS   1963
A date with Leo Wright and Kenny Burrell. —HD

Blues around the Clock / PRESTIGE   1964
Moody, laidback after-hours set. —HD

Evenin' Blues / PRESTIGE   1964
Mellow 60s jazz/blues. —HD

● **Hey Mr. Landlord / ROUTE 66**
A thorough import survey of Witherspoon's earlier (1945-56) blues-shoutin' days. —HD

Rockin' L.A. / FANTASY   1988
Still shoutin' the blues. —HD

Spoon So Easy Chess Years / MCA
Chicago sides from 1945-1955 that are closer to R&B than jazz. —HD

MITCH WOODS & HIS ROCKET 88'S   ♭1951

Electric jump blues. Bay Area jump-blues singer/keyboardist. Dubbing his swinging approach "rock-a-boogie," Mitch Woods and his Rocket 88's have revived the jump-blues approach of the 40s and 50s on three Blind Pig albums. —BD

Mr. Boogie's Back in Town / BLIND PIG   1988
Jump-blues and boogie with a rockabilly edge. —NJF

○ **Solid Gold Cadillac / BLIND PIG**   1991
West Coast jump-blues and boogie-woogie piano. Tasty, if not particularly original. Charlie Musselwhite guests on harp. —NJF

JIMMY YANCEY   1898-1951

Piano blues. Yancey was a truly great stride and boogie-woogie piano man who influenced numerous players during his heyday in the 30s and 40s. —CK

☆ **Jimmy Yancey - Vol. 1 / DOCUMENT**
Yancey's earliest and best sides for the Solo Art label. Beautiful and sensitive performances. (Import) —CK

JOHNNY YOUNG   1918-1970

Electric Chicago blues. Although the mandolin is not an instrument commonly associated with Chicago blues, it has been used by Chicago-based string bands or on Chicago-made recordings by artists such as Carl Martin, Charles and Joe McCoy, and Yank Rachell. However, the only artist to use it successfully in the later electric blues format was Mississippi-born bluesman Johnny Young. An important figure in blues history, Young loved the rough-and-tumble string-band tradition of the Delta, a style that readily coexisted with blues. Young's initial 1947 Chicago classic, "Money Taking Women," exhibits the same exuberant down-home sound, fusing blues with the older country breakdown traditions. The string-band ensemble sound suited street performance as well, whether in Memphis or in Chicago's open-air Maxwell Street Market, where Young and his cronies were brought in off the streets to record. Over the years, Young's mandolin activity declined as Chicago's African-American blues audience demanded a more modern and urban sound. Since Young was also a skilled guitarist and a fine vocalist, he easily weathered the transition.

During the late 60s, an emerging White blues-revival audience proved eager for Young's mandolin styling. Unlike Yank Rachell, whose mandolin playing retained an older string-band feel, Young's style was firmly grounded in a more contemporary postwar blues idiom, and he interacted well with other electric blues artists. Through his life, he had worked with the major figures of blues history, including Sonny Boy Williamson, Muddy Waters, Walter Horton, and Otis Spann. He was, he insisted, born to be a musician. When I interviewed him shortly before he died, he told me how he had struggled all his life trying to make it in the music business. An emotional man, he hoped he would live long enough to make enough money to buy a house. He never made it. –BLP

○ **Chicago/The Blues/Today! - Vol. 3 / VANGUARD**   1967
○ **Chicago Blues / ARHOOLIE**   1968
Excellent 60s recordings by this down-home urban singer, guitarist, and mandolinist, accompanied by Otis Spann on piano and James Cotton and Big Walter Horton on harmonicas. –MH

BLUES COLLECTIONS

○ **20th Anniversary Collection / ALLIGATOR**   1991
A solid 2-disc compilation celebrating two decades of this label's existence. There are many worthwhile tracks but few surprises. –BD

○ **Alley Special / CBS**   1990
Blues of various styles and consistently high quality, released on the Gotham and 20th Century labels, with three previously unreleased cuts. Raw, early electric blues from the late 40s and early 50s. Includes Muddy Waters's first commercial recording. –NJF

○ **Angels in Houston / ROUNDER**
Great Duke recordings from the late 50s and 60s of Bobby Bland, James Davis, Larry Davis, and Fenton Robinson. Includes Bland's classic "Yield Not to Temptation." –BLP

○ **Antone's 10th Anniversary Anth. / ANTONE'S**   1986
Chicago blues living legends, recorded live at a popular Austin, TX, club in July 1985. Includes Buddy Guy, Jimmy Rogers, Eddie Taylor, James Cotton, Snooky Pryor, Otis Rush, Albert Collins, and more. The CD has 3 bonus cuts. Good sound and very good performances. –NJF

○ **Antone's Anniversary Anth. - Vol. 2 / ANTONE'S**   1991
This very consistent live package was cut at the Austin club. It includes incendiary tracks by Buddy Guy and Matt "Guitar" Murphy. –BD

☆ **Atlantic Blues - Boxed Set / ATLANTIC**   1986
If you've got the money, this is a worthwhile addition to any blues collection. –BD

○ **Beauty of the Blues / CBS**   1991
A beautiful 18-track collection from a sampling of Columbia/Legacy's *Roots 'N' Blues* series. The recordings, from 1929-1947, include a wide variety of traditional blues and blues-related styles. Excellent sound, with music from Robert Johnson, Big Bill Broonzy, and others. –NJF

○ **Best of Chicago Blues / VANGUARD**   1973
Mostly 60s recordings of tough Chicago blues, produced by Samuel Charters. Features James Cotton, Junior Wells, Otis

Spann, Buddy Guy, J. B. Hutto, Homesick James, Big Walter Horton, and Johnny Young. Very successful snapshots of what was happening in the Chicago blues bars at that time. Beautiful, powerful music. –NJF

○ **Black Top Blues Cocktail Party / BLACK TOP**   1991
This features non-album tracks from the label's roster. –RG

○ **Blow It till You Like It / CHARLY**
More blues and R&B harmonica on this generous 24-track import sampler. –HD

○ **Blue Flames - Sun Blues Collection / RHINO**   1990
A skimpy (18 songs) but tremendous set of Sam Phillips's gutbucket blues recordings, all of early-50s vintage and exquisitely remastered. Most of the big names are here. –JF

○ **Blues As Big As Texas - Vol. 1 / CBS**   1991
Previously unreleased Texas blues, digitally remastered from the original tapes. Various artists recorded between 1958 and 1971 in Houston (one cut in Beaumont, TX). Features Johnny Copeland, Gatemouth Brown, Percy Mayfield, and more. A good and varied set. –NJF

○ **Blues at Newport (1959-64) ... / VANGUARD**
Blues at Newport - Newport Folk Festival 1959-64 offers fine performances by John Hurt, Skip James, Rev. Gary Davis, Robert Wilkins, and others. –MH

○ **The Blues Came Down from Memphis / CHARLY**
A nice overview of Sun's early 50s blues recordings on a single-disc CD, primarily sticking to an issued-singles format. This is a perfect place to start. –CK

○ **Blues Deluxe / ALLIGATOR**   1989
A 1989 CD reissue. Recorded live at the 1980 Chicagofest. A budget CD with only 38 minutes of playing time. Muddy Waters, Koko Taylor, Willie Dixon, and three others. –NJF

○ **Blues Explosion / ATLANTIC**   1984
A very good collection of in-concert recordings from Stevie Ray Vaughan, Sugar Blue, and more. –NJF

○ **Blues from the Montreux Jazz Fest. / MALACO**   1991
Recorded at the Montreux Jazz Festival in Switzerland, during the Malaco Records European Tour in 1989. Features Bobby Bland, Denise LaSalle, Johnnie Taylor, and Mosley & Johnson. Anything LaSalle has done lately is worth listening to, and it's nice to have a snapshot of her in-concert style. –NJF

○ **Blues Is Killin' Me / PAULA**   1991
A 20-track, rock-solid collection of classic blues sides from Chicago's JOB label, primarily focusing on both sides of original-issue 78s by Floyd Jones, Memphis Minnie, Baby Face Leroy, and Little Hudson's Red Devil Trio, with a few unissued surprises rounding out the already excellent package. –CK

○ **Blues Piano Orgy / DELMARK**   1972
A sensational keyboard anthology with great cuts by Speckled Red, Roosevelt Sykes, and Little Brother Montgomery. –RW

○ **The Blues Vol. 6: 50s Rarities / MCA**   1991
Sixteen previously unissued tracks and obscure singles by Muddy Waters, Little Walter, and others. –HD

○ **Blues-A-Rama / BLACK TOP**   1990
A 21-track sampler of Black Top Records music. A very good example of contemporary blues, with a focus on Texas and Louisiana. –NJF

Blues-A-Rama - Vol. 1 / BLACK TOP   1988
Black Top Records blues recorded live at Tipitina's in New Orleans. The second volume is the most consistent from start to finish. Features Nappy Brown, Earl King, Ronnie Earl, and James "Thunderbird" Davis. –NJF

○ **Blues-A-Rama - Vol. 2 / BLACK TOP**   1988
Blues-A-Rama - Vol. 3 / BLACK TOP   1990
Blues-A-Rama - Vol. 4 / BLACK TOP   1990
Blues-A-Rama - Vol. 5 / BLACK TOP   1991

○ **Bringing You the Best in Blues / ANTONE'S**   1989
A sampler of artists on this Austin, TX, label. A variety of Texas blues and R&B, originally released 1987-1990. Includes Otis Rush, Angela Strehli, Doug Sahm, Matt "Guitar" Murphy, and several others. –NJF

○ **Chicago Ain't Nothin' but ... / DELMARK**   1972
Chicago Ain't Nothin' but a Blues Band is a solid collection of sides from Chicago's Atomic H label, with JoJo Williams, J. T. Brown, and Eddie Clearwater's earliest recordings among the highlights. –CK

○ **Chicago Blues Anthology / MCA**   1984
A wonderful 24-cut set of raw, early Chicago blues from the Chess label. Delta blues influences are evident in the work of Johnny Shines, Robert Nighthawk, and Floyd Jones. A more modern, urban style is shown by Buddy Guy and Otis Rush. A worthwhile collection. –NJF

○ **Chicago Boogie - 1947 / ST. GEORGE**   1983
All the earliest Maxwell Street acetate recordings from the short-lived Ora Nelle label. Debut sides of Little Walter, Jimmy Rogers, Johnny Young, and Othum Brown. A particular standout: Delta bluesman Johnny Temple's "Olds 98 Blues," done Robert Johnson-style on an electric guitar. –CK

○ **Chicago Boss Guitars / PAULA**   1991
Chicago's West Side blues guitar school, as recorded for Cobra/Artistic Records, with a rash of Otis Rush and Magic Sam alternate takes and Buddy Guy's very first recordings. Featuring impassioned vocals and bright, stinging lead work, this anthology succeeds on every level. –CK

☆ **Chicago/The Blues/Today! - Vol. 1 / VANGUARD**   1967
Includes 60s recordings of Junior Wells, J. B. Hutto and the Hawks, and Otis Spann. This is an outstanding historical document and contains great music. –BLP

☆ **Chicago/The Blues/Today! - Vol. 3 / VANGUARD**   1967
This is one of the all-time great blues series ever recorded. Aside from the classic Chess albums (Muddy Waters, Little Walter, Howlin' Wolf, etc.), there is no better introduction to Chicago-style blues than this three-volume set. Each one is incredible. This third album contains the Johnny Shines Blues Band, Johnny Young's South Side Blues Band, and Big Walter Horton's Blues Harp Band with Memphis Charlie Musselwhite. Here are the original Chicago artists who have grown up and played together for most of their lives, so the musical time is spacious — wide open. This is South Side Chicago blues with a trace of country at its best. Big Walter Horton plays some of the best harmonica of his career on this album. Listening to Horton on backup and solo harp is an education. This album is definitive. –JME

○ **Clownin' with the World / ACOUSTIC ARCHIVES**   1989
This wonderful CD from the vaults of Trumpet Records features unissued Sonny Boy Williamson sides and great tracks by his piano-playing buddy, Willie Love. –CK

☆ **The Copulatin' Blues Compact Disc / JASS**
Twenty-two risqué blues (1929-1940) by various artists. Great fun. –JO

☆ **Country Blues Bottleneck Guitar Classics / YAZOO**   1972
The first and possibly best anthology of prewar bottleneck guitar (1926-1937), this includes the singing slides of Robert Johnson, Bukka White, Memphis Minnie, and — although scarcely country blues — a stunning "St. Louis Blues" by Jim and Bob, the Genial Hawaiians! –MH

○ **Dark Muddy Bottom Blues / SPEED**
A country blues sampler from the Specialty label. Mostly early 50s recordings, this also includes rare material by Mercy Dee Walton. –HD

○ **Deep in the Soul of Texas / CBS**   1991
Texas soul from the 60s and 70s. Some previously unissued material. –NJF

○ **Delta Blues - 1951 / ACOUSTIC ARCHIVES**   1990
A great compilation from Trumpet Records (Jackson, MS) featuring early 50s sides by Big Joe Williams, wonderful acoustic duets by the Huff Brothers, and the first recordings by the original King Biscuit Boy, Willie Love. A wonderful document. –CK

○ **Don't Leave Me Here / YAZOO**
Don't Leave Me Here - Blues of Texas, Arkansas & Louisiana is a 14-track country-blues collection of recordings from 1927-1932. This contains a variety of traditional acoustic blues styles from the Gulf Coast area. Highlights include King Solomon Hill and Little Hat Jones. –NJF

○ **Drop Down Mama / MCA**   1970
A fine early-50s Chess blues anthology, with classic tracks by slide guitarists Robert Nighthawk and Johnny Shines, brooding Floyd Jones, Arthur Spires, and fleet-fingered Blue Smitty. –BD

☆ **East Coast Blues - 1926-1935 / YAZOO**
A fine assortment from Carl Martin, Willie Walker, William Moore, Blind Blake, Bayless Rose, and other East Coast guitarists. There are several very traditional blues like "Black Dog Blues" and "Crow Jane," plus lots of good ragtime guitar. For serious guitar players and Piedmont blues fans. –BLP

○ **Fathers & Sons / CHESS-MCA**   1969
Actually, this is a Muddy Waters album, recorded in 1969 and featuring members of Paul Butterfield's band (Paul Butterfield, Michael Bloomfield, Sam Lay), plus such other "sons" as the MGs bassist Donald "Duck" Dunn and drummer Buddy Miles. For over an hour, they back up the master beautifully, and Waters is in fine form, as usual. –WR

○ **Genuine Houserockin' Music - Vol. 1 / ALLIGATOR**
Virtually interchangeable samplers of good-time, high-energy, modern R&B produced by Chicago's Alligator label. Lonnie Brooks, Lonnie Mack, Koko Taylor, Fenton Robinson, Albert Collins, and others. Slick and well produced. –HD

○ **Going Away Blues / YAZOO**   1969
A fine prewar blues compilation. –MH

○ **Gonna Head For Home / FLYRIGHT**
A nice compendium of rare and unissued Excello sides by lesser-known names (Boogie Jake, Mr. Calhoun, Silas Hogan, and Jimmy Anderson) who recorded for the label. Excellent Louisiana swamp blues, crude and low-down. –CK

○ **Good Time Blues ... / CBS**   1991
Small-group acoustic blues, dance, and washboard band music recorded between 1930 and 1941. *Good Time Blues - Harmonicas, Kazoos, Washboards ...* is happy, generally uptempo party music. Lots of fun. Excellent sound. –NJF

○ **Got Harp if You Want It / BLUE ROCK'IT**
A decent overview of postwar blues harmonica, but hardly comprehensive. –RW

○ **Got My Mojo Working / FLYRIGHT**
A collection of blues sides recorded for New York's Baton label in the mid to late 50s, featuring Chris Kenner's first recording and Ann Cole's original, pre-Muddy Waters performance of the title track. –CK

○ **Gotham Series - House Party / CBS**
Hot R&B boogie and jump-blues 50s sides from the Philadelphia label. –HD

○ **Great Blues Guitarists - String Dazzlers / CBS**   1991
A high-quality survey of some of the finest blues guitar players, recorded 1924-1940. Includes, among others, Tampa Red, Blind Willie Johnson, and Big Bill Broonzy. Highlights include three instrumental duets featuring Lonnie Johnson and Eddie Lang. They take your breath away. –NJF

☆ **Great Bluesmen - Newport Festival / VANGUARD**
Performances from 1959-1965 by rediscovery legends Son House, Mississippi John Hurt, Skip James, Sleepy John Estes, and other compelling singers and guitarists such as Robert Pete Williams, John Lee Hooker, and Mississippi Fred McDowell. –MH

○ **Grinder Man Blues - Masters of Blues Piano / RCA**   1990
Six tracks each from Little Brother Montgomery (1935-1936), Memphis Slim (1940-1941) and Big Maceo Merriweather (1941-1945). Piano blues and boogie-woogie. Wonderful listening from beginning to end. –NJF

○ *Guitar Player* **Presents Electric Blues - Vol. 1 / RHINO**
An excellent 18-track CD compilation featuring definitive sides by Muddy Waters, Otis Rush, Hound Dog Taylor, Albert King, Eddie Taylor, and many more. –CK

○ *Guitar Player* **Presents Electric Blues - Vol. 2 / RHINO**
Companion volume to the above. Excellent selections from

B.B. King, Albert Collins, Eric Clapton, Michael Bloomfield, Magic Sam, Buddy Guy, and a dozen others. –CK

○ **Guitar Wizards - 1926-1935 / YAZOO**
An excellent collection of great prewar blues guitarists. –MH

○ **Gulf Coast Blues - Vol. 1 / BLACK TOP**   1990
Contemporary Texas and Louisiana blues from four artists deserving wider attention. Two cuts each from Carol Fran, Joe "Guitar" Hughes, and Grady Gaines, with four from Teddy Reynolds. Fran and Reynolds are the highlights, and each deserve their own full releases. –NJF

○ **Hand Me Down Blues / RELIC**   1990
Hand Me Down Blues - Various Chicago blues is one of the finest 50s Chicago blues compilations in existence, taken from the vaults of Parrot-Blue Lake Records. Unissued sides and rare singles create an incredible ambience here. Essential listening. –CK

○ **Harlem Rock 'N' Blues - Vol. 1 / CBS**
A decent collection of early East Coast blues and R&B. –RW

Harlem Rock 'N' Blues - Vol. 3 / CBS
This continues the theme. Material that either influenced or reflected evolutionary trends in blues and R&B. –RW

○ **Harmonica Blues / YAZOO**
A fine collection of prewar harp performances. –MH

○ **Harmonica Blues Kings / DELMARK**   1986
Featuring a side each of Big Walter Horton and Alfred "Blues King" Harris in primarily supporting roles behind various vocalists from the vaults of United/States Records. Featuring raw, lively harmonica, it's another missing piece of the early Chicago blues puzzle. –CK

○ **Harp Attack! / ALLIGATOR**   1990
An eleven-track CD spotlighting four Chicago harmonica players — Carey Bell, Billy Branch, James Cotton, and Junior Wells — in new recordings. All have played with Muddy Waters or Willie Dixon's Chicago Blues All-Stars (or both). Solid electric-band-style Chicago blues. –NJF

○ **If It Ain't a Hit ... / ZUZAZZ**
X-rated blues is the theme here, with selections ranging from totally raunchy to mildly titillating. Great listening and a full dollop of humor throughout. Features under-the-counter performances by Jackie Wilson, LaVern Baker, Chick Willis, The Clovers, and The Fred Wolff Combo. Blues with a nudge and wink to it. –CK

○ **In the Spirit - Vol. 1 / OJL**
The first of two albums that bring together 32 of the most striking prewar sacred commercial recordings by rural Black singers, including Charley Patton and Bukka White. –KL

○ **Jackson Blues - 1928-1938 / YAZOO**
Tommy Johnson and the school of Delta blues he inspired in Jackson, MS. –MH

○ **Legends of the Blues - Vol. 1 / CBS**
A first-rate, 20-track remastered collection of beautiful country blues and Black vaudeville blues from the 20s, 30s, and 40s. Volume 1 features Delta blues from Charley Patton, Robert Johnson, and Booker "Bukka" White. There's also one of the earliest recordings of Chicago blues king Muddy Waters (1946) and one of the last recordings of his teacher, Delta bluesman Son House (1965). Additionally, there's the full-throated roar of Texan Blind Willie Johnson and the powerful and lovely Bessie Smith. In stark contrast, this volume also includes John Hurt's gentle voice and rolling guitar figures, plus the ragtimey offerings of Blind Boy Fuller and Blind Willie McTell, and ten more. It's a varied yet consistently excellent collection. –NJF

○ **Legends of the Blues - Vol. 2 / CBS**
Volume 2 is just as diverse and entertaining as Volume 1, though the artists included are, in general, somewhat less well known. This collection (featuring recordings from 1929 to 1941, presented in chronological order) includes piano blues from Roosevelt Sykes, Charlie Spand, and Champion Jack Dupree; guitar greats Tampa Red, Buddy Boss, and Casey Bill Weldon; and "classic" blues from Lil' Johnson, Victoria Spivey,

and Bessie Jackson. Also here is one of T-Bone Walker's first-ever recordings (as "Oak Cliff T-Bone" from 1929) as well as 13 sides that were previously unissued by Columbia or are alternate takes of issued recordings. –NJF

○ **Living Chicago Blues - Vol. 1 / ALLIGATOR**   1978
Arguably the best entry in this pioneering anthology series, with excellent sides by guitarist Jimmy Johnson and saxophonist Eddie Shaw. –BD

Living Chicago Blues - Vol. 2 / ALLIGATOR   1978
Almost as incendiary as Vol. 1, thanks to four sides each from Magic Slim, Lonnie Brooks, and Pinetop Perkins. –BD

Living Chicago Blues - Vol. 3 / ALLIGATOR   1980
Laconic saxman A. C. Reed and crisp guitarist Lacy Gibson are standouts. –BD

Living Chicago Blues - Vol. 4 / ALLIGATOR   1980
Not quite as strong, although witty pianist Detroit Jr and guitarist Andrew Brown contribute strong tracks. –BD

○ **Lonesome Road Blues ... / YAZOO**
Tommy Johnson's influence is again here on *Lonesome Road Blues - 15 Years in the Mississippi Delta*, which includes other fine prewar Delta blues. –MH

○ **Louisiana Blues / ARHOOLIE**
Distinctive swamp blues by Henry Gray, Silas Hogan, Whispering Smith, and Guitar Kelley. –HD

○ **Low Blows / ROOSTER BLUES**
Low Blows - Anthology of Chicago Blues is a scatter-gun compilation of great early-70s recordings by Chicago's better-known (Walter Horton, Carey Bell) and lesser-known (Big John Wrencher, Good Rockin' Charles Edwards) harmonica men. A missing chapter in blues history. –CK

☆ **Mama Let Me Lay It on You - 1926-36 / YAZOO**
A fine collection of East Coast blues, including vintage Josh White, Pink Anderson, and guitarists Blind Blake and Willie Walker. –BLP

○ **Masters of the Delta Blues / YAZOO**   ·   1991
Subtitled *The Friends of Charley Patton*, this CD perfectly anthologizes some of the best and rarest tracks by early Delta blues legends like Son House, Tommy Johnson, and Bukka White. Sounds rough in spots, but it's indispensable nonetheless. –CK

○ **Memphis Jug Band / YAZOO**
Definitive 28-song collection by the city's finest jug band, spanning their output from 1927 to 1934. –JF

○ **Mississippi Blues - 1927-1941 / YAZOO**
Another well-programmed anthology. –MH

○ **Mississippi Moaners - 1927-42 / YAZOO**
More prewar Delta blues. –MH

○ **Mister Charlie's Blues - 1926-1938 / YAZOO**
A fascinating exploration of blues-drenched, prewar hillbilly recordings, including the great fingerpicked guitar of Sam McGee. –MH

○ **New Bluebloods / ALLIGATOR**   1987
An attempt to document "the next generation of Chicago blues." Generally a very exciting and successful collection, this includes the Kinsey Report, Lil' Ed and the Blues Imperials, Valerie Wellington, and several more. –NJF

○ **New Orleans Blues - Troubles Troubles / ROUNDER**
A sampler of late 50s and early 60s Ric and Ron label music by Edgar Blanchard, Mercy Baby, and Eddie Lang. –HD

☆ **News & the Blues - Telling It like It Is / CBS**
The best thematic Roots & Blues collection, including topical blues, gospel, and ballads from major artists Bessie Smith, Memphis Minnie, John Hurt, Charley Patton, Bukka White, Blind Boy Fuller, and Blind Willie Johnson. With interesting tributes to Joe Louis, Ma Rainey, and Leroy Carr. –BLP

○ **Orig. American Folk Blues Festival / POLYGRAM**   1962
Recorded live in a studio in Hamburg, Germany, in October 1962. Includes artists involved with that year's American Folk Blues Festival tour. With generally relaxed and reflective performances. The artists include T-Bone Walker, Sonny Terry, and John Lee Hooker. –CK

○ **Out of the Blue / RYKODISC** 1985
A 17-cut sampler of some of Rounder's blues and blues-related releases of the period. Features "straight" blues from J. B. Hutto, Phillip Walker, and Johnny Copeland; blues/rock from The Nighthawks and George Thorogood; soulful blues from Johnny Adams and Ted Hawkins; plus cuts from Buckwheat Zydeco, piano great James Booker, John Hammond, Solomon Burke, and several more. The Adams, Walker, and Copeland cuts are particularly nice, as is one entry from Marcia Ball and the Legendary Blues Band. –NJF

Out of the Blue - Anthology / ROUNDER 1985
Blues, blues/rock, zydeco, and R&B from Rounder and associated labels. Diverse, occasionally interesting, but very uneven. Highlights include the Legendary Blues Band, vocalist Johnny Adams, slide wizard J. B. Hutto, and piano man James Booker. –NJF

○ **Preachin' the Gospel - Holy Blues / CBS**
Serious inspiration from Blind Willie Johnson, Arizona Dranes, Josh White, Washington Phillips, and others on a digitally cleaned-up recording. –JO

○ **Prime Chops - Blind Pig Sampler / BLIND PIG** 1990
A 14-track sampler, with a variety of contemporary blues sounds. –NJF

○ **Raunchy Business - Hot Nuts & Lollypops / CBS**
A sampler of risqué blues. –MH

○ **The Real Blues Brothers / DCC** 1987
Ignore the meaningless, opportunistic title of this collection, and instead just listen to the music, an enjoyable collection of sides recorded between 1956 and 1962 by mostly well-known and successful artists. Included here are four performances by Jimmy Reed and five from John Lee Hooker, plus Pee Wee Crayton, Lightnin' Hopkins, Brownie McGee, Sonny Terry, Billy Boy Arnold, and others. These were mostly recorded for, and eventually released by, Vee Jay Records. Just over 60 minutes of playing time. –MH

☆ **Riot in Blues / MOBILE FIDELITY**
Excellent Lightnin' Hopkins, Sonny Terry, Brownie McGhee, James Wayne, and early Ray Charles scat singing. Partially field-recorded by Bob Shad in the early 50s. The best cuts include "Wayne's Junco Partner" and "Hopkins' Buck Dance Boogie." –BLP

Roots of Robert Johnson / YAZOO
Fourteen sides from various artists from whom Robert drew his inspiration. A good country-blues primer. –JO

○ **Saturday Night Blues / STONY PLAIN** 1991
A compilation album of Canadian blues artists who have been featured on "Saturday Night Blues" on the AM network of CBC Radio. It features Colin James, Dutch Mason, Amos Garrett, Rita Chiarelli & The Road Rockets, Paul James, and others. There are 20 songs in all — a great way to check out the great blues scene in Canada. –CR

○ **Shoutin' Swingin' & Makin' Love / MCA**
Jimmy Witherspoon, Al Hibbler, and other urbane blues/jazz belters in full cry on Chess. –MH

Sissy Man Blues / JASS
Twenty-five straight and gay blues, 1924-1941, by various artists. –JO

☆ **Slide Guitar - Bottles Knives & Steel / CBS**
A super collection of slide guitar pieces in such styles as blues, hokum, gospel, and dance songs from Blind Willie Johnson, Tampa Red, Bukka White, and other bottleneck masters. The Leadbelly cut, "Packing Trunk Blues," shows off his masterful slide style. For every blues guitarist. –BLP

The Soul of Texas Blues Women / CBS 1991
A very interesting, although uneven collection of female blues and soul vocalists recorded between 1961 and 1970. –NJF

○ **Sound of the Swamp - Vol. 1 / RHINO**
The Nashville-based Excello label specialized in obscure blues, R&B, and rock & roll from the 50s and early 60s. This first volume of *Sound of the Swamp (The Best of Excello Records)* covers the best from Crowley, LA, producer Jay Miller's blues, rockabilly, and swamp-pop sides. –JF

Southern Rhythm & Rock / RHINO
Southern Rhythm & Rock (The Best of Excello Records - Vol. 2) is the second volume of the Excello Records collection, with its companion *Sound of the Swamp*. This volume rounds up some wild and woolly R&B obscurities. –JF

St. Louis Blues - 1929-1935 / YAZOO
More fine prewar blues. –MH

○ **St. Louis Town - 1929-1933 / YAZOO**
Guitar and piano blues from this Mississippi River city. –MH

○ **Stax Blues Brothers / STAX** 1970
A decent collection of Stax blues artists of the 70s, including Albert King, Johnnie Taylor, and others. –DH

Stax Blues Masters - Blue Monday / STAX
A decent overview of Stax blues artists; inferior to individual records by Albert King and Little Milton. –RW

☆ **Story of the Blues / CBS**
An excellent blues sampler, ranging from prewar to the 60s, offering a broader palette of "shades of blue" than most. –MH

○ **Stroll On / CBS**
A various-artists compilation, of which Cyril Davies's "Not Fade Away" is a raw and honest highlight. –BE

○ **Sun Records Harmonica Classics / ROUNDER** 1990
A brilliant compilation of blues sides, cut at the Sun studios in the early 50s, featuring indispensable tracks by Walter Horton ("Easy" being one of the greatest harmonica instrumentals of all time), Joe Hill Louis, and Doctor Ross. –CK

○ **Sun Records - The Blues Years / CHARLY-SUNBOX**
Gigantic nine-record box with a 44-page booklet. This comes the closest to documenting the wide breadth of blues recordings done by Sam Phillips at the Sun studios in Memphis during the early 50s. A landmark achievement. –CK

Talkin' Trash / GREASY 1990
A very obscure R&B compilation with great irreverent jump and jivey blues from 1954-1963. The title cut is worth the price, but check out "Your Wire's Been Tapped" and "Roll Dem Bones." –RM

Texas Guitar Greats / CBS 1991
Texas blues, boogie, and blues/rock recorded 1962-1988. Includes several previously unreleased cuts, with Johnny Winter, Freddie King, Gatemouth Brown, and Johnny Copeland, among others. –NJF

○ **Voice of the Blues ... / YAZOO**
Voice of the Blues - Bottleneck Guitar Masterpieces contains an eclectic hodgepodge of prewar slide guitar styles, encompassing everything from blues and Hawaiian to ragtime and country. –JF

○ **Wrapped in My Baby / DELMARK** 1989
Basement rehearsal recordings from the early 50s for the United/States labels, featuring Morris Pejoe's raw & rockin' "Let's Get High" from a full unissued session, plus four amazing sides from Arthur "Big Boy" Spires. Another missing chapter of Chicago blues history brought to light — simply incredible. –CK

Cajun/Zydeco

Zydeco and Cajun are the premier cultural expressions of the spirited and hardy people of southwest Louisiana. While the two styles have some similarities, they are also quite different.

Cajun music as we know it today can be traced back to early Acadian, French, Creole, and Anglo-Saxon folk songs. These early ballads and lullabies — typically concerned with troubles and hard times — were often sung a cappella. For the most part, they were performed at home and passed down orally from generation to generation; however, the singers of these traditional songs were eventually accompanied by simple instrumentation.

Cajun music is of course meant for dancing — one-step, two-step, and waltzes. Traditionally, the Cajun dance ("Fais-do-do" in Cajun) was the major social function in Cajun society. The principal instrument in Cajun music is the diatonic accordion, preferably in the key of C. Although it is a German instrument, the Cajun people adopted it in the 1870s. To a lesser degree, the fiddle is also a favorite instrument in Cajun music. Early Cajun bands featured both of these instruments as well as a triangle to keep the rhythm. Acoustic guitars were added to the lineup by 1920, then, three decades later, steel, electric guitars, and sometimes drums. Although Cajun music has changed somewhat over the years and has been influenced by other styles of music — notably country and blues — it has remained a distinctive style.

The first Cajun record was Joe Falcon's "Allons à Lafayette" from 1928. Although the style was recorded only sporadically for several decades, Iry Le Jeune, Harry Choates, Nathan Abshire, Lawrence Walker, Leo Soileau, and Vin Bruce had become influential Cajun artists by the middle of the 20th century. While the music's popularity continued to grow within Louisiana, it didn't enter the spotlight nationally until the mid 80s, riding on the coattails of the Cajun food explosion. Today several traditional and contemporary Cajun artists — including Dewey Balfa, Zachary Richard, and Beausoleil — tour nationally and internationally.

Compared to Cajun music, zydeco music has a much shorter history. Like Cajun music, the dominant instrument is the accordion, but unlike Cajun music, zydeco adds electric bass, horns, and sometimes keyboards. In a nutshell, zydeco is creole (Black) dance music of southwest Louisiana that blends Cajun music with rhythm & blues and soul. The word "zydeco" is actually a bastardization of an early zydeco song, "L'Haricots Sont Pas Salés" (The Snap Beans Aren't Salted). The first Black-French recordings were made in 1928 by Amadé Ardoin, an accordion player who played in the Cajun style. However, the music we know as zydeco today didn't begin to evolve — at least on record — until the mid 50s, when Clifton Chenier and Boozoo Chavis made their initial recordings.

Like Cajun music, zydeco didn't achieve national popularity until 1980, buoyed somewhat by Rockin' Sidney's surprise hit "My Toot Toot." By the 90s, several zydeco artists were signed to major labels, including Terrance Simien, Boozoo Chavis, Buckwheat Zydeco, and Rockin' Dopsie.

— Jeff Hannusch

NATHAN ABSHIRE   1915-1981

Abshire, the best-known accordionist of the modern era, played more of a honky-tonk style of Cajun music, one often heard in the barrooms and dancehalls of Louisiana. Abshire's playing and singing were strongly rooted in the blues. Along with the legendary Iry LeJeune, Abshire is credited with restoring the accordion to its former prominence in Cajun Music following WWII. His 1949 O.T. label hit, "Pine Grove Blues," became his signature song, and its bluesy barroom bark epitomizes the best rough-edged Cajun honky-tonk. Abshire recorded extensively and often appeared at folk festivals with the Balfa Brothers. –JH & MH

○ **The Best of Nathan Abshire / SWALLOW**
With "The Good Times Are Killing Me" emblazoned on his accordion case, Abshire embodied the Cajun musician's ethos. There are 20 two-steps and waltzes here, some with the Balfa Brothers — includes a remake of the great "Pine Grove Blues" and a heartfelt "Tramp Sur La Rue" with wailing vocals from Nathan. –MH

AMADÉ ARDOIN   1896-1941

Although he recorded some of the purest early Cajun records, Amade Ardoin (his name has also been spelled Amadie or Amédée) was a French-speaking Black singer/accordionist who was popular with both Cajun and Creole audiences. His crying, high-pitched vocals were the model for much that came later in Cajun music, as was his empathetic squeezebox playing. Ardoin's recordings with fiddler Dennis McGee are noteworthy not only because they are among the first racially integrated folk recordings, but also for an emotional/artistic integrity which traditionalists like the Savoy-Doucet band continue to aspire to. –MH

○ **Louisiana Cajun Music - Vol. 6 / OLD TIMEY**
A stunning collection of 14 of his 30 recordings. (Ardoin also appears on several Cajun compilations, such as *J'Etais Au Bal - Vol. 1*). –MH

ARDOIN & FONTENOT

Accordionist Alphonse "Bois Sec" ("dry wood") Ardoin (b 1914) grew up idolizing his legendary uncle, Amadie

Ardoin, as did fiddler Canray Fontenot (b 1922). Ardoin and Fontenot began playing together in their youth, though they were unrecorded until the 70s. Their music is a still-strong reflection of the early Cajun/Creole traditions, with an added burst of bluesiness in Canray's fiddling. —MH

○ **Musique Creole / ARHOOLIE**
Haunting. The music on this album shaped modern Cajun/zydeco music. —JH

THE BALFA BROTHERS

The Balfas helped keep alive the traditional Cajun sound when it was disappearing in the 60s. Their style can be traced to the beginning of the century and is dominated by the fiddle. Unfortunately, Rodney and Will were killed in a car wreck in 1979, but Dewey continued to keep their sound alive until his death in 1992. —JH

○ **Let's Get Cajun / FLYING FISH**
Modern Cajun sounds played by young musicians. —JH

● **Play Trad. Cajun Music - Vols. 1 & 2 / SWALLOW**   1987
From the 60s recordings that helped launch the Cajun revival. Stirring performances still. —MH

○ **J'ai Vu le Loup, le Renard et la Belette / ROUNDER**   1988
Fine late recordings from one of Cajun music's greatest groups, the founding fathers of the Cajun folk revival. —JH & MH

DEWEY BALFA   1927-1992

The son and grandson of Cajun fiddlers, Dewey Balfa played fiddle in a relaxed yet spirited style, and inspired much of the best of the Cajun revival. A gentle and gracious man, he was passionate about his culture and was a father figure and guiding light for Cajun music. With his brothers, he helped introduce this music to the world at the Newport Folk Festivals of the 60s, and won renewed attention and support for Cajun music in Louisiana. He died in 1992, and is sorely missed. —MH

○ **Souvenirs / SWALLOW**   1987
A low-key but excellent effort from the late king of Cajun fiddle. —JH

BEAUSOLEIL

Led by Mike Doucet, Beausoleil is probably the best-known Cajun group in America today. Their early recordings were very traditional, but on recent efforts, strong hits of rock and R&B have influenced their music. Beausoleil is probably the most versatile group within the genre. —JH

Bayou Boogie / ROUNDER   1987
A fine modern Cajun collection, including "Cajun Dead" at full tilt. —JH & MH

Allons à Lafayette / ARHOOLIE   1988
A more traditional sound as compared with the group's other albums. —JH

● **Hot Chili Mama / ARHOOLIE**   1988
The perfect blend of Cajun, zydeco, and rock & roll. —JH

Bayou Cadillac / ROUNDER
Rock and Cajun/zydeco gumbo. —MH

Live from the Left Coast / ROUNDER
An excellent example of this popular group's live sound. —JH

Cajun Conja / RHINO   1991
A 1991 Grammy nominee. —MH

Déjà Vu / SWALLOW
Leader Michael Doucet's musical concoctions. —JH

Parlez-Nous à Boir & More / ARHOOLIE
Traditional Cajun, with a taste of the modern sound. The best of their Arhoolie albums. Cajun/zydeco zip with rock and ethno-synergistic overtones. —JH & MH

☆ **Cajun & Creole Music / MUSIC OF THE WORLD**
This recording combines the great masters of the Creole music tradition with the internationally acclaimed Cajun group, Beausoleil. This Library of Congress Award-winner belongs in every Cajun lover's collection. —MUSIC OF THE WORLD

VIN BRUCE

Known as the "King of Cajun Singers," this native of Cut Off, LA, (born Ervin Bruce), first recorded for Columbia in 1951, where he found some success with the ballad "Dans La Louisianne." A decade later this singer/guitarist was recording for Floyd Soileau's Swallow label, where he scored a hit with "Jole Blon" (at least the third go-round for "the Cajun national anthem"). Bruce currently resides in Galliano, LA, and is widely respected in Louisiana for his country-tinged Cajun traditionalism. —JH & MH

○ **Greatest Hits / SWALLOW**   1979
Recorded by one of the pioneers of Cajun music, these early 60s sides are a mix of traditional songs and French interpretations of country hits. —JH

Cajun Country / SWALLOW   1979
A good country-tinged album featuring "Dog" Guidry on fiddle, Harry Anselm on guitar, and Eldridge "Johnny" Comeaux on steel guitar. —CR

BUCKWHEAT ZYDECO

Currently one of the best-known zydeco artists, thanks to his work with Rounder and Island Records, Buckwheat Zydeco (Stanley Dural) got his first taste of zydeco working as a keyboardist with Clifton Chenier, and it was Chenier who inspired him to pick up the accordion. His style has a very modern edge. —JH

On a Night Like This / POLYGRAM   1979
Not bad, but not so good as his Black Top or Rounder label work. —JH

☆ **100% Fortified Zydeco / BLACK TOP**   1985
Currently the most visible zydeco artist nationally. This mid-80s effort is his best, as the material recorded is more inventive. The sound is great, and the song selection is superior. —JH

Turning Point / ROUNDER   1988
A good sampling of modern zydeco. —JH

Waitin' for My Ya-Ya / ROUNDER   1988
Contains his biggest hit, "Ya-Ya," and other gems. —JH

CHUBBY CARRIER & THE BAYOU SWAMP BAND

Louisiana-born Carrier got his training with Terrance Simien and the Mallet Playboys, going on to form his first band in 1990. Although his music is steeped in the tradition of the area, Carrier adds an original twist with a heavy reliance on rock & roll rhythms and electric guitar solos. —CK

☆ **Boogie Woogie Zydeco / FLYING FISH**   1991
One of the best new albums in the genre today, this is loaded to the brim with great songs and performances. Highlights include the title track, "Bernadette," "Good for the Goose," and "Young Creole Man." It's infectious beyond belief! —CK

BOOZOO CHAVIS

Chavis supplied the first-ever zydeco hit in 1954 with "Paper in My Shoe." Unfortunately, he was in musical semi-retirement for three decades, but he returned in the mid 80s with a bang. His many great albums underline his traditional but rocking zydeco style. —JH

○ **Louisiana Zydeco Music / MAISON DE SOUL**   1987
A zydeco masterpiece and a down-home foot-stomper. —JH

Zydeco Homebrew / MAISON DE SOUL

★ **Zydeco Trail Ride / MAISON DE SOUL**
This collects his best sides from the Maison de Soul label. Whoop-ti-yo cover and bootin' sounds to match. —JH & MH

Boozoo Chavis / ELEKTRA
Still bluesy and rockin' in the 90s. Part of the celebrated *American Explorer* series. —MH

Lake Charles Atomic Bomb / ROUNDER
Lake Charles Atomic Bomb (Orig. Goldband Recordings).

There's some spectacular stuff but also some dreadful things on this collection of early material from these rugged-and-ready 50s Goldband sides by a singer and accordionist who is among zydeco's still-active founders. –JH & MH

CLIFTON CHENIER   d 1987

There is no way to overstate the importance of this great artist. Known as the King of Zydeco, Chenier was responsible for nearly every stylistic innovation that zydeco has displayed since the mid 50s. Although Chenier died in 1987, his son C. J. and several other artists keep his style alive. –JH

Sings the Blues / ARHOOLIE   1969
Lots of great accordion and unique vocals from the blues side of the bayou. –JH & MH

○ **Bayou Blues / SPECIALTY**
Hotter than Tabasco! Rocking early zydeco by the King. –JH

Live at St. Mark's / ARHOOLIE
His best live al. Very entertaining. –JH

Louisiana Blues & Zydeco / ARHOOLIE   1981
Excellent small-combo zydeco. –JH

○ **Bon Ton Roulet / ARHOOLIE**   1981
Great rock'em-sock'em zydeco. –JH

I'm Here! / ALLIGATOR   1982
Although not so good as his Arhoolie albums, this one won Chenier a Grammy. –JH

The King of Zydeco Live at Montreux / ARHOOLIE   1984
A nice concert set. –MH

Bogalusa Boogie / ARHOOLIE   1987
Backed by a fuller band on this release, Clifton sounds great. Here's the hottest of the red-hot Louisiana bands, and they're feelin' frisky. –JH & MH

★ **60 Minutes with the King of Zydeco / ARHOOLIE**   1988
The singer/accordionist who brought R&B into zydeco and took zydeco to the world. A fine overview of his Arhoolie recordings. –MH

HARRY CHOATES   1922-1951

Choates's 1946 recording of "Jole Blon" (My Pretty Brunette) presented a simple traditional waltz, sung in Cajun French and played with few frills. Yet it became a national hit, was covered (in English) by Roy Acuff and others, and became as essential to any Cajun music performance as "The Star-Spangled Banner" is to a baseball game. "Jole Blon" was actually atypical of the frenetic Choates, whose Western-swing-tinged fiddling was jazzier than that of any Cajun before or since. Choates was also a passable singer who punctuated his songs with an energetic "Eh, hah hah!" in the manner of Bob Wills. Hard drink and fast living got the better of Choates, who died in an Austin jail in 1951. Disparaged by Cajun purists, he is the Acadian that Western swing enthusiasts find most approachable. –MH

His Original 1946-1949 Recordings / ARHOOLIE
Sixteen performances by the man dubbed "The Godfather of Cajun Music," including his swingin' takes on such standards as "Allons à Lafayette" and "Grand Mamou." –MH

○ **Jole Blon / D**   1979
The title cut "Jole Blon" has become the "Cajun national anthem," plus many other great fiddle-led Cajun tunes. –JH

Five-Time Lobster / KRAZY KAT   1990
A followup to "Jole Blon" and thirteen other performances, including the Hank Williams-inspired "Cat 'n Around." Rough sound but great music, blending Cajun, swing, and honky-tonk. –MH

CLARK & DUHON

Octa Clarke and Hector Duhon are a fiddle/accordion duo who still play the old-time Cajun houseparty music. –JH

○ **Old-Time Cajun Music / ARHOOLIE**
Old-time Cajun music played right. –JH

BRUCE DAIGREPONT   b 1959

An admitted child of the Cajun revival, Daigrepont only began regarding Cajun music as something other than the music of his grandparents' generation when he heard such young Turks as Michael Doucet and Zachary Richard in the 70s. Ironically, this singer and accordionist developed a style somewhat more traditional than that of his mentors. Writing his own material and fronting a tight band, Daigrepont has earned both the approval of his elders and the respect of his peers. –MH

Coeur Des Cajuns / ROUNDER
More fresh gumbo. –MH

○ **Stir up the Roux / ROUNDER**   1988
Heartfelt vocals and hot accordion. The best of the contemporary Cajun traditionalists. –MH

JOHN DELAFOSE   b 1939

Delafose's driving but down-home zydeco is indebted to Clifton Chenier but reaches back to African-tinged Creole roots. He played sporadically while farming, before committing to music with a family-based band that included sons Tony on drums (now bass) and John Jr on washboard. A fine singer and fiery accordionist, Delafose's unique traditionalism is a refreshing counterweight to the more R&B and funk-tinged zydeco bands. –MH

○ **Joe Pete's Got Two Women / ARHOOLIE**   1988
Delafose's best, containing his popular saga of Joe Pete. Zydeco fundamentalism from this singer/accordionist, who's so down-home, his music clearly echoes African hypnotic grooves. –JH & MH

Pere et Garcon Zydeco / ROUNDER   1992
Son Geno (20 years old) joins his father, singing and playing accordion in a typically spirited set of 14 zydeco stompers with the Eunice Playboys. –MH

DAVID DOUCET

The guitarist in the group Beausoleil, Doucet is adept at mixing traditional Cajun with more modern stylings. –JH

○ **Quand J'ai Parti / ROUNDER**
Cajun music meets acoustic guitar. An exciting hybrid of sound. –HD

MICHAEL DOUCET

Since the mid 70s, Doucet has been one of the dominant figures of the Cajun music revival, respected for his scholarship and admired for his showmanship. On the one hand Doucet dredges up ancient Cajun tunes with medieval French roots, and on the other plays flamboyant fiddle with Beausoleil. Aside from Beausoleil, singer and fiddler Doucet has performed and recorded with the more purely traditional Savoy-Doucet Cajun Band. He is as passionate about Cajun tradition as he is eager to drop-kick it into the 21st century, and for that reason Doucet has earned the applause of both purists and plebians who just wanna boogie. –MH

Beau Solo / ARHOOLIE
Fiddler/vocalist Doucet is up front. –MH

○ **And Cajun Brew / ROUNDER**   1988
Beausoleil leader Doucet's "gris-gris" solo outing — fun. –MH

JOSEPH FALCON   1900-1965

One of the pioneers of Cajun music, Falcon made the first commercial Cajun recording, "Lafayette" ("Allons à Lafayette") with his wife Cleoma in 1928. Cleoma's simple guitar and emotive singing, driven by Joe's crying accordion, was an instant hit in Cajun country, foisting a regional stardom on the team, who recorded for Columbia, Decca, Bluebird, and Okeh in the 30s. Cleoma's death in 1941 and changes in listeners' taste (the accordion was out, the fiddle in) led Falcon away from performing, though he and his second wife, Theresa, were fronting a band in the years before his death. Falcon's early recordings are among the enduring classics of the Cajun genre. –MH

☆ **Live at a Cajun Dance / ARHOOLIE**   1988
Perhaps the best live Cajun album of all time, this was recorded near the end of Falcon's career in the early 60s. –JH

FILÉ

A very good young Cajun dance band. –JH

○ **Two Left Feet / FLYING FISH**
Excellent dancehall music. –JH

● **Cajun Dance Band / FLYING FISH**   1988
The debut album by one of the more popular contemporary Cajun bands. –JH

WADE FRUGE   b 1916

This fiddler, popular in the 40s, learned much of his music from his grandfather, making him a link with 19th-century strains of Cajun tradition. –MH

○ **Old-Style Cajun Music / ARHOOLIE**
The title says it all. –JH

HACKBERRY RAMBLERS

Started by a group of teenagers in 1930, the Hackberry Ramblers went on to become the most popular and influential Cajun band of the 30s. Fiddler Luderin Darbone (b 1913) led this accordionless Cajun band with as many as three supporting guitarists. Their recordings featured songs in French but others in English, and their music was deeply influenced by the jazzy Western swing string-bands of Texas. In a sense, the Hackberry Ramblers were the first "hybrid" Cajun musicians, reflecting the impact of records and radio on an isolated regional culture. Despite long periods of inactivity, Darbone and a revived Hackberry Ramblers continue to appear at folk festivals across America. –MH

○ **Early Recordings - 1935-1948 / OT**   1988
No accordions here: this strain of Cajun music includes fiddles and guitars. –JH

JAMBALAYA

A young Cajun band that mixes the old with the new to good effect. –JH

○ **C'est Fun / SWALLOW**
An enjoyable mix of two-steps and waltzes from this four-piece group. –JH

DOUG KERSHAW   b 1936

Cajun country fiddler Kershaw emerged from the steamy South Louisiana swampland with his own wildly energetic approach on the violin. He is widely recognized as a Cajun music pioneer. Paired with his brother as Rusty & Doug, he first hit the country charts in 1955 for Hickory with "So Lovely Baby." In 1961 the pair issued the original "Louisiana Man" and "Diggy Liggy Lo," both solid country sellers and now the songs perhaps most vividly associated with the manic violinist. While Kershaw sawed his fiddle like a man possessed, his solo career took off during the 70s, although his popularity was never properly reflected by the charts. –BD

Cajun Way / WARNER
Kershaw's first calling card. Very good. –JH

Louisiana Man / WARNER
Contains the infamous title-track hit and several other goodies. –JH

☆ **The Best of Doug Kershaw / WARNER**
A compilation of Kershaw's 60s/70s Warner Bros. sides. The "Everly-Brothers-on-the-bayou" vocal harmonies, Doug Kershaw's fiddle, and crisp Nashville production make these a joy. –MH

SHORTY LEBLANC

LeBlanc is best remembered as the accordionist on the bluesy "Sugar Bee" by Cleveland Crochet and his Hillbilly Ramblers, which climbed to #80 in the *Billboard* Hot 100 in early 1961. LeBlanc's performance was Cajun accordion played to sounds such as amplified blues harmonica. Sidney Brown was an accordion maker and repairer who scored a regional hit with "Pestauche Ah Tante Nana" ("The Peanut Song"). –MH

○ **Best of Two Cajun Greats / SWALLOW**   1987
Shorty Le Blanc and Sidney Brown are two lesser-known but great Cajun artists. These are their best sides waxed for Swallow. –JH

EDDIE LEJEUNE

Eddie LeJeune is the youngest son of the legendary accordionist Iry LeJeune. He proudly plays accordion in the tradition of his influential father. –MH

○ **Cajun Soul / ROUNDER**   1988
A fine debut album. –JH

D. L. MENARD

One of the purest examples of Cajun music around today, the sound of D. L. Menard & the Louisiana Aces harks back to the genre's ground-floor days and has changed very little in style over the years. Menard's impassioned vocals (largely sung in French) have invited comparisons to country legend Hank Williams. –CK

○ **Cajun Saturday Night / ROUNDER**   1985
"The Cajun Hank Williams" in Nashville with Ricky Skaggs, Jerry Douglas, and others. No one can imitate Menard or the great sounds on this album. –JH & MH

No Matter Where You At ... / ROUNDER   1988
No Matter Where You At, There You Are is a traditional Cajun outing from this delightfully down-home singer/guitarist. Eddie LeJeune does accompaniment on accordion. –MH

QUEEN IDA

Ida Guillory is an inspiration to all latebloomers: she was over 40 when she left her job as a San Francisco school bus driver and moved to the button accordion and stardom as the first woman to front a zydeco band. Though a native of Lake Charles, LA, Ida has spent much of her adulthood on the West Coast, which may account for her music's being more breezy than swampy. An ebullient performer, Queen Ida won a 1982 Grammy (ethnic-folk category) for *Queen Ida and the Bon Temps Zydeco Band on Tour.* A festival favorite, Queen Ida maintains a busy road schedule. –MH

Caught in the Act / GNP-CRESCENDO   1985
Live from San Francisco, CA. Includes classics "Jole Blon," "Don't Mess with My Tu Tu," and Nick Lowe's "Half a Boy, Half a Man." Rollicking zydeco from the Queen. –MGN

○ **In San Francisco / GNP-CRESCENDO**   1988
A Grammy Award-winning, live, and potent album, with Al Rapone on accordion. –MGN

★ **Cookin' with Queen Ida / GNP-CRESCENDO**   1989
Her most recent album, which really does cook. –JH

BELTON RICHARD

Richard and the Musical Aces typify the successful melding in the 60s and 70s of Cajun roots with country and rock influences. Unlike Beausoleil, with an eclecticism appealing to "worldbeat" listeners, singer and accordionist Richard has opted for more mainstream ingredients for his gumbo. He was the biggest star to emerge from the generation midway between the postwar old guard of Nathan Abshire and children of the 70s Cajun revival, such as Bruce Daigrepont. Richard may not be known on the national festival circuit, but no Cajun jukebox is without his 45s — he is the Swallow label's biggest seller. –MH

○ **At His Best / SWALLOW**
Cajun honky-tonk music at its best. This is what Cajun barroom music is supposed to sound like. –JH

ZACHARY RICHARD

Like others of his generation, this native of Scott, LA, discovered his Cajun roots circuitously. Richard started out playing rock and country-rock in the 70s but found his way to Cajun music partly through his experiences in Quebec and France. The music he wound up creating was an aggressive, eclectic blend of rock, zydeco, and R&B, causing one scribe to dub the flamboyant Richard "the Mick Jagger of zydeco." –MH

Live / ARZED
An exciting live performer, Richard is at his best here. –JH

Allons Danser / ARZED
A foot-tapper all the way. –JH

★ **Looking Back / ARZED**
The greatest hits from this important artist. –JH

Zack's Bon Ton / ROUNDER   1990
Rock & roll meets Cajun music, with interesting results. –JH

☆ **Woman in the Room / A&M**   1990
Zach's writing comes together on this release with his most powerful songs to date. "No French, No More" is a sad tale about how teachers denied the Cajun people the use of their language. "Who Stole My Monkey" is a knock-you-out fun song. A very diverse release. Highly recommended. –CR

Bayou des Mystères / ARZED
Richard's traditional album. –JH

STEVE RILEY & THE MAMOU PLAYBOYS

Riley is a talented fiddler and accordionist whose mentor was the great Dewey Balfa. –MH

○ **Steve Riley & the Mamou Playboys / ROUNDER**
An exceptional debut from what is currently one of Louisiana's most popular contemporary Cajun groups. –JH

The Mamou Playboys / ROUNDER
Two-steps and waltzes. –JH

ROCKIN' DOPSIE

Rockin'' Dopsie enjoys an international reputation as one of zydeco's top exponents, thanks to a number of fine albums and numerous overseas tours. As you'd expect, Dopsie's early recordings are very bluesy, while his recent material tends to sound more contemporary. –MH

○ **Big Bad Zydeco / GNP-CRESCENDO**   1988
Hot Louisiana R&B/zydeco from one of its most popular modern practitioners. –HD

Good Rockin' / GNP-CRESCENDO   1988
Upbeat and spirited zydeco. –HD

ROCKIN' SIDNEY   b 1938

Sidney'Simien began playing guitar and harmonica before discovering accordion (he also played organ in Lake Charles lounges). He cut his first demo in 1958 and worked the zydeco circuit in Louisiana and Texas before the unlikely 1985 success of "My Toot Toot" (a'term of endearment, "my special one") made Rockin' Sidney a star and "Toot Toot" a Grammy winner which was the first zydeco record to get extensive pop, rock, and country air play. –MH

○ **My Toot Toot / MAISON DE SOUL**   1986
Rockin' Sidney had the biggest zydeco release of all time — "My Toot Toot" — and it enjoyed many subsequent covers. Some of this release is unfortunately unacceptable, as it includes updated covers, but Sidney rises above it most of the time. –JH

RODDIE ROMERO

Another up-and-comer, Romero has a distinctive, if somewhat samey sound. –JH

○ **New Kid in Town / SWALLOW**
Much of this music sounds alike, but Romero's definitely one to watch. –JH

MARC SAVOY   b 1940

Savoy labels himself a "crusader" for Cajun culture and, as such, is ranked at the top of the revivalists who followed the Balfa Brothers' example and championed pure Cajun music. Savoy's dedication to the music includes building Cajun accordions at his workship in Eunice, LA, as well as playing the music and discussing its background at festivals around the world. He and his wife, Ann (singer and guitarist with the Savoy-Doucet Cajun Band and author of the excellent *Cajun Music: A Reflection of a People*) were the subject of Les Blank's PBS documentary, "Marc and Ann." In September 1992, Savoy received the prestigious Heritage Award from the National Endowment for the Arts. –MH

○ **Oh What a Night / ARHOOLIE**   1988
Some excellent dance music. This album proves that not only is Savoy an accomplished accordion maker, but he can play one too. –JH

SAVOY-DOUCET CAJUN BAND

Accordionist Marc Savoy, guitarist/vocalist Ann Savoy, and fiddler Michael Doucet (Beausoleil) form this group's core. –ED

○ **Two Step D'Amadé / ARHOOLIE**
This is the kind of acoustic music you used to hear only at Cajun houseparties. Very spirited and a timepiece. A glorious tribute to Cajun pioneer Amadé Ardoin. –JH

TERRANCE SIMIEN

Simien's appearance in the movie *The Big Easy* made him a star, but unfortunately his recordings haven't lived up to his potential. –JH

○ **Zydeco on the Bayou / ENIGMA**   1992
A modern zydeco artist whose songs aren't yet in an essential category. More rock than zydeco, but lots of energy nonetheless. –RW & JH

RUFUS THIBODEAUX   b 1934

Thibodeaux is the consummate Cajun-fiddle session player and sideman. He worked at Jay Miller's Crowley studios in the 50s, playing various stringed instruments on everything from blues to rockabilly, and toured with Bob Wills and George Jones. But he is best known for a long association as sideman to Jimmy C. Newman: Thibodeaux's fiddle added Cajun spice to Newman's sometimes bland country fare. –MH

○ **The Cajun Country Fiddle of ... / LL**   1987
This album demonstrates the emotive style of one of the premier Cajun fiddlers. –JH

WAYNE TOUPS

A native of Crowley, LA, Toups began playing accordion at age 14. Like Zachary Richard, Toups is noted for his flamboyance and rock-derived rhythms. Not high on any purist's list of faves, Toups is nonetheless a great crowd pleaser. –MH

☆ **Zydecajun / POLYGRAM**
When rock meets Cajun, it must be Zydecajun. –JH

○ **Johnnie Can't Dance / POLYGRAM**
Uptown zydeco. Slick, with strong rock and Western-swing elements, and a touch of swamp-pop as well. –HD

JUSTIN WILSON

The best known Cajun comedian in Louisiana; the rest of the country probably knows him best as a chef, via his syndicated cooking show. –JH

○ **Ol' Favorites / GREAT SOUTHERN**   1987
From the top-rated Cajun comedian; this is Wilson's only CD, and it is very funny. –JH

CAJUN/ZYDECO COLLECTIONS

○ **101-Proof Zydeco / MAISON DE SOUL**
A good collection of contemporary zydeco from the Maison de Soul label. –JH

○ **14 Cajun Hits / SWALLOW**   1987
An exceptional sampling of modern Cajun music from the Swallow label. –JH

○ **Cajun Social Music / SMITHSONIAN-FOLKWAYS**   1987
Field recordings from various Cajun groups, recorded in the 60s. –JH

○ **Cajun Spice / ROUNDER**
A generous (over 60 minutes) sampling of great Cajun and zydeco music from artists who have recorded for the Rounder label during the last two decades. –JH

J'ai Ete Au Bal - Vol. 1 / ARHOOLIE   1992
Lively Cajun and zydeco music from the Les Blank documentary. –JH

J'ai Ete Au Bal - Vol. 2 / ARHOOLIE   1992

○ **Zydeco Blues N' Boogie / RYKODISC**   1990
A zesty collection of bayou boogie from the vaults of Lanor Records. –JF

○ **The Zydeco - Early Years - Vol. 1 / ARHOOLIE**
This exceptional collection includes very interesting early tracks from Clifton Chenier, Clarence Garlow, and Herbert Sam. –JH

○ **Zydeco Live! / ROUNDER**
Contains great material from two of South Louisiana's best zydeco artists: Boozoo Chavis and Nathan Williams. –JH

Zydeco Live! - Vol. 2 / ROUNDER
Not up to the caliber of the first album, but still pretty good. With John Delafose and Willis Prudhomme. –JH

GOSPEL

Religion has existed for thousands of years, but gospel music is just a few decades old. The term was coined by blues pianist Thomas A. Dorsey in 1920 soon after he wrote "If You See My Savior," his first religious song. After Dorsey established a firm that published his "Gospel" songs and those of others (the first such company), the name stuck.

Gospel music was born out of the blood, sweat, and tears of African slaves working on Southern plantations and in cotton fields. They attended segregated Protestant churches, where White ministers led them in worship. Over time, Blacks combined the Southern folk music, Protestant hymns, and European elements of the worship service with their African traditions and Negro spirituals (which were not religious songs but songs of vexation, e.g., "Nobody Knows the Trouble I've Seen"), and the distinct Black gospel sound was born.

In those early years, Gospel was segregated along racial lines: Southern gospel became a catchword for White gospel when Black gospel was equally Southern in its styling. Mahalia Jackson was the primary influence of her era, although the Swan Silvertones, the Clara Ward Singers, the Five Blind Boys, and others made significant contributions to early gospel. In Southern gospel, the Speers reigned "king of the charts," winning contracts on major labels such as Columbia and RCA, where they recorded such standards as "I'm Building a Bridge" and "I'll Meet You in the Morning."

As the 50s approached, there was a greater amalgamation of gospel, folk, and blues styles, which together were the foundation of rock & roll. Elvis Presley, Jerry Lee Lewis, and Little Richard were just a few of the singers with strong gospel backgrounds to make the leap into the secular arena. Groups like the Soul Stirrers and the Pilgrim Travelers supplied secular music with Sam Cooke, Johnnie Taylor, Lou Rawls, and others.

In the 70s, social movements began to influence what the White gospel young adults were recording. Artists such as Larry Norman pioneered "Jesus Rock." When a contemporary Christian music (CCM) magazine writer asked him if his 1969 *Upon This Rock* album was the first Christian rock album, Norman was cautious. "I can't really tell you if it was the first Christian rock album or not," he said. "I had never heard any. I was a Baptist, and the only Christian songs I had ever heard were the hymns and Negro spirituals .... So when Elvis Presley came along in 1956, and all those other boys, I thought, 'That's nothing new.' They were just stealing Black church music ... so I decided to steal it back."

A similar revolution was taking place among young Black musicians who had tired of the same old "church" beat. Edwin Hawkins has taken a lot of credit for sparking the contemporary Black gospel movement. Actually, Rance Allen was doing it better, and long before Hawkins.

Toward the very late 70s, Andrae Crouch did the unmentionable: he began making music that not only pleased his Black constituency and a progressive White audience but also touched mainstream pop. Amy Grant would later pick up on Crouch's theme and run with it.

During the 80s, gospel had its most lucrative decade to date. Many of the biggest hits were by women. Shirley Caesar and Tramaine Hawkins crisscrossed the traditional and contemporary Black audiences. Sandi Patti held down the inspirational arena as Amy Grant held the pop/rock youth market. Grant's success and subsequent influence in pop led to a lot of copycatting.

An area women did not get into was heavy metal, or heaven's metal as it's called in CCM. Bands that grew up on Aerosmith, Led Zeppelin, Black Sabbath, and other premier hard rock outfits, began to merge Christian lyrics with this type of music. Petra and Stryper are examples.

As the 90s kick in, the direction of the future is uncertain. Amy Grant has moved into the secular field, though she still commands a large gospel audience. Sandi Patti's records do well but don't strike gold as often. Now that the push for crossover success in the 80s has proven fruitless in most cases, gospel artists are returning to their music's roots and explicit message. After all, unadulterated gospel is the most intimate and emotional of all music forms. No matter what your usual music proclivity (be it country or rap), you'll find something in the following review that fits your musical tastes.

— Bil Carpenter

ABYSSINIAN BAPTIST GOSPEL CHOIR

Black gospel. Prof. Alex Bradford directed this choir, some of whose members recorded with the famous Back Home Choir of Newark. –OPLN

○ **Shakin' the Rafters / CBS**
An energetic choral release spotlighting one of the most popular, large (100-plus) vocal aggregations of the 60s. –RW

ACAPPELLA

Inspirational. An inspirational male quartet. –BC

○ **Better Than Life / CLIFTY**   1987
Soft, synchronized a cappella on original songs. –BC

RIC ALBA

CCM. As a former singer/guitarist, Alba worked with the Christian alternative bands the Choir and the Altar Boys. –BC

○ **Holes in the Floor of Heaven / GLASSHOUSE**   1991
An album with abstract lyrics and a rock guitar focus, with a British sound. –BC

RANCE ALLEN GROUP

Black gospel. This Detroit-based, traditionally trained Black gospel group formed in the 60s and were the first traditional gospel group to incorporate rock, jazz, and soul into their music. They were harbingers for the contemporary Christian music movement popularized in the late 70s by Andrae Crouch, Amy Grant, and the Winans. –BC

○ **Best of the Rance Allen Group / STAX**   1988
Creative, influential hits with a Memphis flavor. –BC
Phenomenon / CAPITOL   1991
Consistent with earlier recordings. –BC

THE ALLIES

CCM. This California-based melodic pop-style rock group, formed in the 80s, was influenced by blues/rockers and R&B groups. –BC

○ **Shoulder to Shoulder / DAYSPRING**   1988
Smooth, LA-style pop gospel. –BC
A Long Way from Paradise / DAYSPRING   1989
A hard, bluesy rock sound. –BC

MARGARET ALLISON

Spiritual. Margaret Allison and the Angelic Gospel Singers formed in 1944. Their "Touch Me Lord Jesus" (Gotham) hit was a #13 on R&B charts in August 1949. Traditional-style quartet music. Current line up: Allison, Darryl and John Richmond; Frances Leggett; and Theresa McDowell. –BC

My Sweet Home / NASHBORO
"Jesus Is All the World to Me" and "Goin' over Yonder" are outstanding. –BC
○ **Out of the Depths / MALACO**   1987
An album of traditional cuts featuring "It Could've Been the Other Way" and "Up above My Head." –BC
He's My Ever Present Help / MALACO   1992
An album of new traditional favorites, most notably the title song and "I'll Go." –BC

ALTAR BOYS

CCM. Punk trio formed by guitarist Mike Stand in 1981. They opened for the Jesus and Mary Chain in the late 80s. –BC
○ **Collection: Best of 1986-1991 / FRONTLINE**
Hard-edged rock music with introspective lyrics. –BC

THE AMAZING ZION TRAVELERS

Gospel. Spiritual. –BC
God Is Alive / CO-OP
Fine new recordings by this major postwar Los Angeles quartet led by the great L. C. Cohen. –OPLN

INEZ ANDREWS   b1935

Spiritual. Andrews became famous as a member of the Caravans in 1957. She later formed the Andrewettes before going solo. –BC
○ **Lord Don't Move the Mountain / ABC**   1972
This crossover pop album has a traditional mood. –BC
Raise Up a Nation / CBS   1991
Traditional Black arrangements with choir backing. –BC

VANESSA BELL ARMSTRONG   b1953

Black gospel. Born in Detroit, MI, Armstrong is a belting R&B singer toeing the line between traditional and contemporary Black gospel. –BC
○ **Peace Be Still / BENSON**   1984
Traditional hymns that are given "Holiness" treatment. –BC
Vanessa Bell Armstrong / JIVE   1987
Contemporary urban gospel, with traditional shouting style and vague lyrics for its gospel content. –BC

SUSAN ASHTON

CCM. Texas-born Ashton sang backup for Wayne Watson and Dallas Holm before going solo. *Wakened by the Wind* became one of CCM's most successful debut albums, garnering Ashton five hit singels and a Dove Award nomination for Best New Artist. Having Brown Bannister and Wayne Kirkpatrick, two people essential in Amy Grant's success, didn't hurt her, either. Her 1992 followup *Angels of Mercy* expanded both her musical and her emotional vocabularies. –BM

Wakened by the Wind / SPARROW   1991
Debut in the contemporary-folk vein, à la Shawn Colvin (whose voice Ashton's closely resembles). Ashton gets most of her material from producer Wayne Kirkpatrick, also one of CCM's top songwriters; she contributes to three, including the countryish "Ball and Chain." –BM
○ **Angels of Mercy / SPARROW**   1992
No sophomore slump here, as Ashton reaches for more and gets it. The topics are more complex — the devastating rumor mongering of "Started as a Whisper," the mysteries of salvation, and fallibility in "Alice in Wonderland" — and the music is more dramatic. –BM

JOHN AUSTIN   b1969

CCM. Born in Chicago, Austin began his career just after high school. He plays acoustic guitar and harmonica and writes most of his own material. He is one of the few rising voices in alternative Christian music. Based on his first effort alone, he's made a contribution to linking authentic gospel messages with uncommercial light-rock music/folk styles. His firm but mellow vocal style is reminiscent of 60s folk heroes such as the Byrds. –BC
○ **The Embarrassing Young / GLASSHOUSE**   1992
Austin's debut album contains 12 songs discussing relationships and Christianity in a nonproselytizing manner. Heavy guitar emphasis on mostly light-rock and alternative-style cuts. Musical support comes from Buddy Miller, Mark Heard, and a choir. Harmony vocals are supplied by Austin's singing partner, Erin Echo. –BC

WENDY BAGWELL

Southern gospel. This folksy country performer from Chamblee, GA, sings with the Sunliters duo. She is known for humorous story-songs. –BC
○ **This, That and the Other / HEARTWARMING**   1971
A classic album with "Here Come the Rattlesnakes." –BC
What's That Name / WORD   1988
Down-home, back-porch, Georgia pickin' is featured on this album. –BC

PHILIP BAILEY   b1951

CCM. Born in Denver, CO. Although Bailey was a singer and conga drummer with the rock/pop group Earth, Wind & Fire in the 70s, he became a solo artist in secular (a hit duet with Phil Collins on "Easy Lover") and gospel fields in the 80s. –BC
○ **Best of ... A Gospel Collection / MYRRH**   1990
Best of Philip Bailey: A Gospel Collection. Bailey's falsetto voice rips through inspiring R&B gospel. –BC

TAMMY FAYE BAKKER   b1942

Inspirational. Born in Minnesota. With former husband Jim Bakker, she was a tent revival preacher. Worked with the 700 Club; founded the PTL Club in 1978. Had gold albums in Southern-gospel/inspirational modes. –BC
You Can Make It / PTL   1982
Singalong battle cries for faith-weary souls. –BC
○ **Enough Is Enough / PTL**   1986
MOR, lively Southern numbers showing her warm chortle. –BC

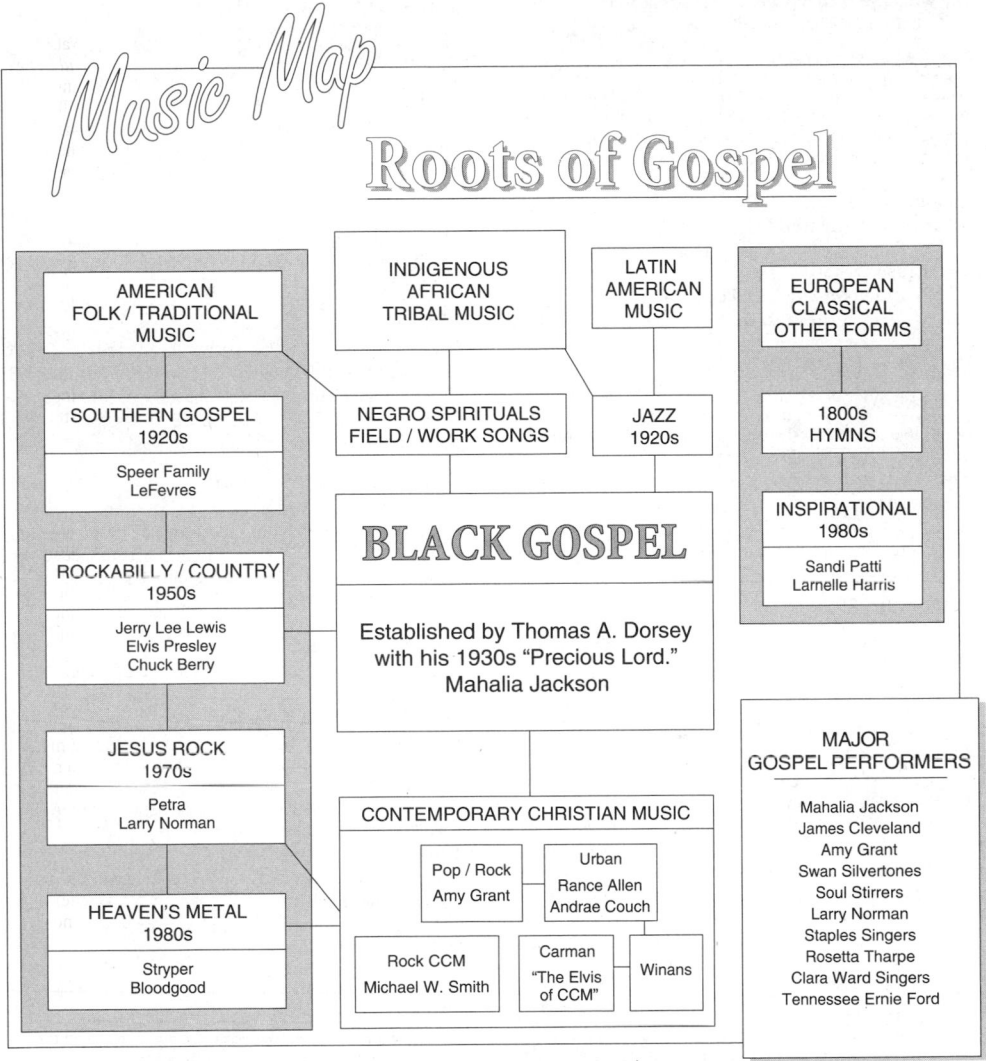

Music Map

Roots of Gospel

| AMERICAN FOLK / TRADITIONAL MUSIC | INDIGENOUS AFRICAN TRIBAL MUSIC | LATIN AMERICAN MUSIC | EUROPEAN CLASSICAL OTHER FORMS |

SOUTHERN GOSPEL 1920s
Speer Family
LeFevres

NEGRO SPIRITUALS FIELD / WORK SONGS

JAZZ 1920s

1800s HYMNS

ROCKABILLY / COUNTRY 1950s
Jerry Lee Lewis
Elvis Presley
Chuck Berry

INSPIRATIONAL 1980s
Sandi Patti
Larnelle Harris

BLACK GOSPEL

Established by Thomas A. Dorsey with his 1930s "Precious Lord."
Mahalia Jackson

JESUS ROCK 1970s
Petra
Larry Norman

CONTEMPORARY CHRISTIAN MUSIC

Pop / Rock
Amy Grant

Urban
Rance Allen
Andrae Couch

HEAVEN'S METAL 1980s
Stryper
Bloodgood

Rock CCM
Michael W. Smith

Carman
"The Elvis of CCM"

Winans

MAJOR GOSPEL PERFORMERS
Mahalia Jackson
James Cleveland
Amy Grant
Swan Silvertones
Soul Stirrers
Larry Norman
Staples Singers
Rosetta Tharpe
Clara Ward Singers
Tennessee Ernie Ford

TRACE BALIN   b1950

CCM. Balin started singing in Ohio bars and colleges, and has recorded gospel albums. –BC
○ **Here and Now / DAYSPRING**   1990
Crusty, blues-backed soft and hard rock. –BC
Out of the Blue / DAYSPRING   1991
Blues, hard rock, ballads, and ponderous lyrics. –BC

BISHOP JEFF BANKS

Black gospel. Banks is pastor of the Revival Temple Center of Deliverance, NJ. –BC
Love Lifted Me / SAVOY GOSPEL
Traditional Black gospel. –BC
○ **Caught Up in the Rapture / SAVOY GOSPEL**   1987
A traditional spiritual choir sound. Donald Malloy sings. –BC

WILLIE BANKS & THE MESSENGERS

Spiritual. Willie Banks is the ex-leader of the Jackson Southernaires. –OPLN

● **Heaven Must Be a Beautiful Place / MCA**
Very soulful early-70s sides. –HD
○ **Masterpiece / MALACO**
Engaging modern gospel with some deep harmony. –HD

BARNES & BROWN

Black gospel. Rev. F. C. Barnes and Janice Brown, both from North CA, where they are pastors at Red Budd Holy Church in Rocky Mountain, came together to record many traditional albums in the 80s. –BC
○ **Rough Side ... / ATLANTA INTNL**   1980
Rough Side of the Mountain. Mellow, bluesy, traditional Black gospel. –BC

LUTHER BARNES

Black gospel. The brother of F. C. Barnes (of Barnes & Brown), Luther Barnes combines traditional excitement with contemporary backbeats. He leads the Red Budd Choir. –BC

○ **See What the Lord Has Done / ATLANTA INTNL**   1987
Upbeat, testimonial-style traditional cuts. –BC

THE BARRETT SISTERS   ♭1926

Black gospel. Chicago-born Delois Barrett Campbell sang with the Robert Martin Singers for 18 years. In the 60s, she formed the Barrett Sisters with sisters Billie Greenbey and Rhodesa Porter. She is known for the cuts "Born Free" and "I'll Fly Away." –BC

○ **Nobody Does It Better / WORD**
What a Wonderful World / I AM
A more contemporary production, geared toward fans of a modern approach. –RW

● **What Will You Do with Your Life / SAVOY**
Classic "golden age" gospel, shouting vocals, and tight harmonies. –RW
I've Got a Feeling / WORD   1987

HELEN BAYLOR

CCM. Toured with *Hair.* Former backup for Aretha Franklin, Chaka Khan, B. B. King, and others. –BC

○ **Highly Recommended / CBS**   1990
Modern pop/soul with class. The title says it all. –BC
Look a Little Closer / CBS   1991
More Southern R&B-infused than her debut "Highly Recommended." –BC

MARGARET BECKER

CCM. The hardest female rocker/guitarist in CCM, she was influenced by a variety of styles that she incorporates into a unique sound, all built on guitar arrangements. Her hardy vocals cut through any style. –BC
Never for Nothing / SPARROW   1987
A debut with strident proselytizing. –BC
The Reckoning / SPARROW   1988
Spiritual renewal and thickly textured rock music. –BC

○ **Immigrant's Daughter / SPARROW**   1989
She sings' about degrees of holiness. Minimalist rock. –BC
Simple House / SPARROW   1991
British influences on the usual power rock. –BC

★ **Steps of Faith 1985-1992 / SPARROW**   1992
Becker's best, with a heavy emphasis on *Immigrant's Daughter* and *Simple House*, shows just what a talented pop stylist she is. The one new cut, "This Love," is essential Becker. –BM

MARGARET BELL

CCM. Younger sister of Vanessa Bell Armstrong. A former commercial jingle singer, she is married to Keith Byars of the Philadelphia Eagles. –BC

○ **Over & Over / WARNER**   1991
A strong voice on refined crossover pop/R&B. –BC

LISA BEVILL

CCM. Dance-pop diva who focuses on the teen audience with pumped-up tracks about chastity and clean living. Formerly sang backup for David Meece. –BM

○ **My Freedom / VIREO**   1992
A Christian record with an emphasis on dance. Heavily textured tracks like "My Freedom" and "Place in the Sun" dominated pop-oriented Christian radio during much of the spring and summer of 1992. –BM

ROBERT BLAIR & THE FANTASTIC VIOLINAIRES

Spiritual. Blair began his contemporary quartet group in the 60s and became known for his Julius-Cheeks-like falsetto shouting and raving. The group has recorded up to the present. While their recent AIR Records albums have been good, their best music was recorded in the 60s on the Chess and Checker labels. –BC

Sing with the Angels / MALACO
Strong material with passionate vocals. –HD

○ **Today Is the Day / MALACO**
Excellent modern gospel from an eight-man "quintet." –HD

● **Their Greatest Sides - Vol. 1 / MCA**
A collection of some of their best Chess album sides from the 50s and 60s, featuring Robert Blair. Includes "Mother Used to Hold Me," a song known to reduce entire audiences to tears. –BW

○ **The Pink Tornado / AIR**   1988
Smooth, old-style traditional gospel, with Blair's renowned panting on the title track. A younger member does falsetto on "People Get Ready." –BC

BLOODGOOD

Heaven's metal. Straightahead power metal band. –BC
Detonation / FRONTLINE   1987
Metal by rote. It's not innovative, but a good sound. –BC

○ **Rock in a Hard Place / FRONTLINE**   1988
Mainstream metal sound with strong melodies and lyrics. –BC

DEBBY BOONE   ♭1956

CCM. This light-voiced singer was born in Hackensack, NJ, and is especially known for the #1 pop hit, "You Light up My Life" (1979). She has done easy-listening albums followed by a string of CCM and inspirational albums. –BC
Best of Debby Boone / CAPITOL   1986
MOR pop hits from the late 70s. –BC

○ **Friends for Life / BENSON**   1987
This is an inspirational/pop offering, featuring "Every Generation." –BC

● **Reflections / BENSON**   1988
Her biggest gospel hits. –BC

KIM BOYCE   ♭1961

CCM. Born in Florida, Boyce rejected a network news position to go into the music ministry. –BC

○ **Time and Again / MYRRH**   1988
Christian dance music that would make Madonna jealous. –BC
This I Know / MYRRH   1991
There's an urban and rhythm focus on this Tim Miner production. –BC

PROF. ALEX BRADFORD   1926-1978

Black gospel. Born in Bessemer, AL, and influenced by the Blue Jays and Swan Silvertones, Bradford sang with groups such as the Protective Harmoneers, the Birdettes, and the Banks Family. He formed the Bradford Specials in 1954, an eight-man chorale, and appeared in "Black Nativity" and other musicals. Nicknamed "The Professor," he is known for the cuts "Let God Abide" and "Walking with the King." –BC

● **The Best of Alex Bradford / SPECIALTY**
A comprehensive selection of his fiery, stomping cuts with the Bradford Specials all-male quintet on Specialty Records. –RW
He Lifted Me / SPECIALTY
A good "hard gospel" outing, spiced with animated leads from Bradford. –RW

○ **Rainbow in the Sky / SPECIALTY**
A broad range of formats and self-penned songs by one of gospel's greatest writers, producers, and soloists. Some issued for the first time here (ca.1954-58). –OPLN

WILLMER BROADNAX   ♭1916

Black gospel. This bespectacled, dynamic lead tenor worked with various groups in Southern California before gaining a wider audience when he joined the Spirit of Memphis in 1950. Listed variously during his career as Willmer, Wilmer, Wilbur, and Willie "Little Ax" Broadnax, the "ringing tenor" led the

Southern Gospel Singers, the Golden Echoes, and later the Spirit of Memphis Quartet during the 50s. −BC & KL

○ **So Many Years / GOSPEL JUBILEE**
Broadnax's unique and influential voice in a variety of settings following World War II. −KL

BROOKLYN ALL-STARS

Gospel. A late 50s male quartet featuring Hardie Clifton on leads. They recorded several cuts for Peacock in 1959, including "Rest Awhile" and "Meet Me in Galilee." −BC

○ **Our Greatest Hits / NASHBORO**
Powerful material drawn from a variety of 60s and 70s Nashboro albums, led principally by the soaring tenor of the underrated Hardie Clifton. −OPLN

REV. MILTON BRUNSON

Black gospel. He founded the Chicago-based Thompson Community Singers in 1948 and is pastor of Christ Tabernacle Baptist Church in that city. −BC

○ **Available to You / CBS**
Traditional, Black mass choir music. −BC

Open Our Eyes / CBS
More of the same as *Available to You.* −BC

SHIRLEY CAESAR   b 1938

Spiritual. Born in Durham, NC, Caeser sang with the Caravans in the early 60s before going solo in 1966. A strict traditionalist known for her shouting style and evangelizing messages. −BC

○ **Her Very Best / CBS**
The passionate hits on this album include "Jesus." −BC

First Lady / CTC-SPECTOR   1977
Secular songs and Christian themes are mixed here. −BC

**Live in Chicago w/ Rev. Milton Brunson & the
Thompson Community Singers / CBS**   1988
Traditional Black gospel testifying, singing, and storytelling, recorded with the Thompson Community Singers and Albertina Walker. −BC

STEVE CAMP

CCM. A Bible intellectual and opinionated singer/songwriter, Camp infuses his scholarly knowledge and themes into his music. −BC

○ **Consider the Cost / SPARROW**   1991
Bible-based songs with pop and inspirational sounds. −BC

MICHAEL CARD   b 1957

Inspirational. Called the "Christian Dan Fogelberg" for his folk guitar style and Bible-based songs, Card learned the banjo from country legend Earl Scruggs and later picked up piano, dulcimer, guitar, and violin. He dropped out of a Ph.D. program to go into the music business. −BC

○ **The Final Word / SPARROW**   1987
Pensive, acoustic, and spiritually correct. −BC

The Way of Wisdom / SPARROW   1991
Superb, with mellow instrumentation and potent lyrics. −BC

CARMAN   b 1956

CCM. Born Dominic Licciardello. He was "saved" at an Andrae Crouch concert. After he was discovered by Bill Gaither, he started his own ministry with a recording arm. He sings in CCM and R&B formats, with a heavy evangelistic message. −BC

○ **Live ... Radically Saved / HEARTWARMING**   1988
A breakthrough album with Christian rap, R&B, and a little rock. −BC

Shakin' the House / HEARTWARMING   1991
A live Black gospel revival set with Commissioned and the Christ Church Choir. −BC

Southern White Gospel

Gospel songs from the beginning formed a large part of the country music repertoire. Two subgroups quickly formed. First came the traditional British ecclesiastical songs, reflecting a fundamental Protestant view of life as a vale of tears and suffering. But another form of gospel songs, one that tolerated joy in both worlds, became increasingly popular because of the upbeat, optimistic message of its lyrics and its fast-tempo melody. Whatever the mood of the musicians and audience, there was an appropriate gospel song: If you are feeling unreasonably good, "This World Is Not My Home" will bring you crashing back to earth; but if your daily life has so much real woe and suffering that a gospel dirge would be the last nail in your coffin, then request the band to play "I'll Fly Away" or "God Put a Rainbow in the Cloud." Southerners, Black and White alike, found gospel music a contrast to country music's standard fare of songs about family and home, good love and broken love, working men and failures, rambling and jail.

Most of country's great performers learned gospel music first, and a large number have returned to it after the pressures of the business drove them to self-destruction — in the old days with alcohol, but more recently with drugs. Thus, gospel songs often have saved not only the audience but the singers, who in the very act of singing "Amazing Grace" have found what the lyrics promise.

Because the church often offered the only opportunity for singing and musicmaking (fiddle and banjo music especially were thought to be the devil's music in the old days), country performers since the 50s have made it standard fare to record a gospel album after "making it" with mass-audience material. The Carter Family, Uncle Dave Macon, Roy Acuff, Bill Monroe, Hank Williams, Red Foley, Tennessee Ernie Ford, Elvis Presley, George Jones, Ricky Skaggs — these are only a few of the legions of country stars who have showcased gospel music in their careers. Bluegrass music, with its base of tradition, emphasizes gospel songs, often sung a cappella. The Lewis Family is the best example of a bluegrass/country group that has created a high reputation over many years by performing gospel and pretty much only gospel. Meanwhile, the Oak Ridge Boys, the epitome of country/rock in the 80s, began as a gospel group. So did the Statler Brothers, who toured as the Kingsmen with Johnny Cash in 1963. Southern gospel is now a subgenre of country music, with its own charts and awards and many groups who perform nothing but gospel. From the earliest country recordings through the most recent, gospel has permeated country music.

— David Vinopal

SISTER WYNONA CARR   d 1976

Gospel. Carr began her professional career in the 40s. Between 1949 and 1954, she infused traditional gospel with jazz and blues in a way that came across as too secular for gospel aficionados and too gospel for pop purists. One critic said that her music seemeed to be to the tune of "St. James' Infirmary." Her best-known cut was "The Ball Game" in 1952. Frustrated with the gospel industry, Carr tried to go completely secular in the 60s, but failed. She died in 1976. –BC

○ **Dragnet for Jesus / SPECIALTY**
This is a long-overlooked gospel writer, producer, and soloist is the. the "Billie Holiday" of gospel. The priceless material on this album is circa 1949-1954. –OPLN

THE CATHEDRALS

Southern gospel. Formed in 1965, this traditional Southern gospel group appeared regularly on Rex Humbard's "Cathedral of Tomorrow" broadcast in the 60s. The Cathedrals are led by George Younce and Glen Payne, who are known for their on-stage humorous exchanges. –BC

○ **Collection - Vol. 1 / HEARTWARMING**   1988
A fine collection of recent hits, styled in the manner of their old hits. –BC

STEVEN CURTIS CHAPMAN   b 1962

CCM. Born in Paducah, KY, this singer, songwriter, and guitarist is one of the best CCM songwriters. As a singer, his music is a cross between 70s-style light rock and orchestrated pop. –BC

First Hand / SPARROW   1987
Chapman's freshman debut is infused with country, soft rock, and pop. –BC

○ **Real Life Conversations / SPARROW**   1988
Harder-edged, elaborate, guitar-focused light rock. –BC

★ **For the Sake of the Call / SPARROW**   1990
Chapman's songwriting voice continues to mature, and the stirring title anthem helped make this his biggest album. –BM

The Great Adventure / SPARROW   1992
Chapman flirts with country, rap, and Springsteenian rock on his most ambitious project, both musically and lyrically. Includes guest appearances from Ricky Skaggs, DC Talk, and BeBe Winans. –BM

CHARIOTEERS

Black gospel. The group was led by the great high tenor Billy Williams, who later fronted the Billy Williams Quartet. –OPLN

○ **Jesus Is a Rock in the Weary Land / GOSPEL JUBILEE**
Some fine jubilee harmony singing from the early 40s. –KL

REV. JULIUS CHEEKS

Black gospel. Cheeks was the hardest-singing gospel lead in postwar quartet singing. –OPLN

At the Gate I Know / SAVOY
Family / SAVOY
Nice vocals and more mid-tempo song sermons. –RW

○ **Somebody Left on That Morning Train / SAVOY**
Marvelous leads and a good production. This is the best album Cheeks has made as a solo singer. –RW

We'll Lay Down Our Lives / SAVOY
Representative, but a cut below his best single sessions. –RW

THE CHOIR

CCM. This new-wave band, formed in 1985, is now on hiatus. Members include Derri Daugherty, Dan Michaels, Mike Sauerbrey, and Steve Hindalong. –BC

○ **Wide-Eyed Wonder / MYRRH**   1989
Moody music with subtle and challenging lyrics oriented to college-radio listeners. –BC

Circle Slide / MYRRH   1990
Strong poetic imagery and social commentary in a spiritual sense. –BC

CHOSEN GOSPEL SINGERS

Gospel. Among the original members were Lou Rawls, Joe

Hinton, and Joe Medwick, all of whom went on to successful secular careers. Largely an a cappella group, they later became the Gospel Keynotes with the shearing lead vocals of Paul Beasley. –BC

○ **The Lifeboat / SPECIALTY**   1954
Previously unreleased tracks, alternate takes, and long-out-of-print gems by this major gospel quartet, led at times by Lou Rawls. –OPLN

CHUCK WAGON GANG

Southern. A traditional-style country gospel quartet that's been singing with varying personnel since the early 40s. –BC

Greatist Hits - Vol. 1 / KTEL
Newer recordings by the reformed Chuck Wagon Gang — still simple, straightforward, plain country gospel. –CW

Old Time Hymns - Vol. 2 / KTEL-QWIL
Looking Away to Heaven / CBS   1976
One of the best of the more recent Columbia sets. –CW

☆ **Columbia Historic Edition / COLUMBIA**   1990
The best set of the group's vintage 30s and 40s sides, well-mastered, with excellent annotations. –CW

THE CLARK SISTERS

CCM. Formed in early 80s by the four daughters of Mattie Moss Clark. The contemporary Black style of this quartet is influenced by the Detroit gospel style of the Winans. "You Brought the Sunshine" hit the R&B charts in 1987, and the sisters later appeared in the Melba Moore video, "Lift Every Voice and Sing." Members: Dorinda, Twinkie, Karen, and Jackie Clark. –BC

○ **Heart and Soul / WORD**   1985
A caterwauling urban-funk set. –BC

REV. JAMES CLEVELAND   1932-1991

Black gospel. Born in Chicago, Cleveland was one of the pioneers of the trend toward mass choirs that developed in the 50s. He led this movement in Southern California but maintained his national reputation as a teacher, performer, and recording artist until his death in 1991. He played the piano behind the Roberta Martin Singers in the 50s and moonlighted with the Caravans during the same period. By the early 60s he had branched out on his own and gained a Savoy Records contract. He started the "traditional Black choir sound" with the 1962 *Peace Be Still* album and continued to promote the sound through the founding of the Gospel Music Workshop of America in 1968 to train mass choirs in the Cleveland sound. –BC

Called to Glory / COAST TO COAST

○ **Gospel Music Workshop of America / SAVOY GOSPEL**
A typically strong Cleveland performance with an all-star choir. –KL

○ **Live at Carnegie Hall / SAVOY**
A Grammy winner. –RW

★ **Peace Be Still / SAVOY**   1962
A set of original Cleveland tunes and traditional hymns done in the choir format he pioneered with the Angelic Choir of New Jersey. This live recording, done with crude technology, is helped somewhat by the high-fidelity pressing. It includes "I Had a Talk with God" and "I'll Wear a Crown." Cleveland's gruff vocals appear on most cuts. –BC

Victory Shall Be Mine / SAVOY   1991
This is among Cleveland's best later works. –KL

DOROTHY LOVE COATES   b 1930

Black gospel. Born in Birmingham, AL, Coates started singing in the 40s with the Original Gospel Harmonettes, who had the hits "I'm Sealed" and "Get Away." –BC

● **Best of Dorothy Love Coates - Vols. 1 & 2 / SPECIALTY**
A worthy sampling of her soulful work from the 50s,

highlighted by "Ninety-Nine and a Half" and "No Hiding Place."—KL

Original Gospel - Vols. 1 & 2 / SPECIALTY
Dynamic lead vocals from Coates, plus superb harmonizing and rollicking instrumental accompaniment. —RW

○ **Get On Board / SPECIALTY**
With the Original Gospel Harmonettes, here are 24 exciting songs supported by Herbert "Pee Wee" Pickard, gospel's organist supreme. Circa 1951-1956. —OPLN

DARYL COLEY   *b* 1955

Black gospel. Born in San Francisco, Coley grew up on jazz music and learned to play clarinet and piano. He played keyboards for the Hawkins Family from 1977 until he left to collaborate with James Cleveland in 1983. Later he did work with jazz artists Nancy Wilson and Rodney Franklin and pop singer Philip Bailey. —BC

I'll Be with You / LIGHT   1988
Coley shows his jazz technique on the heavily improvisational title cut, with breaks and gaps throughout. Further, the vocal arrangements are not in standard choir style. Otherwise, mostly upbeat Black gospel. —BC

○ **Live ... He's Right on Time / SPARROW**   1990
A live fusion of jazz, classical, and traditional gospel, wrapped up in Coley's zestful, upbeat arrangements. —BC

COMMISSIONED

CCM. An urban Black gospel band with crossover appeal. In concert they are an extremely evangelistic group who put on such a dramatic show that the altars are routinely packed with repenters following their performances. Members Fred Hammond and Keith Staten have done solo projects. —BC

Will You Be Ready? / LIGHT   1989
A mix of contemporary and traditional spirituals. —BC

○ **State of Mind / BENSON**   1991
An R&B/urban CCM spectacle with tight harmonies. —BC

LEE CONDRAN & CINDY

Southern gospel. Commercial jingle writers creating a gospel music community in Annville, PA. In an articulate style, they cover many idioms, principally Southern gospel and MOR. —BC

○ **Styles / CONDRAN**   1991
Crystal-clear production, from MOR to reggae to Southern gospel. —BC

ANDRAE CROUCH   *b* 1950

CCM. Born with twin sister Sandra in San Francisco, CA, he's a pianist, CCM artist, and esteemed songwriter and performer. —BC

☆ **Andrae Crouch & the Disciples / LIGHT**   1978
Andrae Crouch & the Disciples — Live in London has all the groundbreaking rock riffs, motifs, and crossover elements that had him labeled a "devil" by conservatives. —BC

SANDRA CROUCH   *b* 1950

Black gospel. Born in San Francisco, CA, with twin Andrae, she's an accomplished drummer and a Black gospel performer and songwriter of high esteem. —BC

○ **We Sing Praises / LIGHT**
More traditional than her brother Andrae on this fine set of worship pieces, including "Completely Yes." —BC

RICK CUA

Heaven's metal. This singer/pianist with the Outlaws turned down a Spyro Gyra post and turned to gospel in the 80s. —BC

You're My Road / REUNION   1985
Moderate rock; includes "Don't Say Suicide." —BC

○ **Can't Stand Too Tall / GEFFEN**   1988
Hard-rock message music, with a couple of ballads. —BC

Gospel Terms

BLACK GOSPEL — An art form that is essentially Black in tone. The term was coined around the popularity of Thomas Dorsey's "Precious Lord." Black gospel is usually traditional music, often choir-oriented. Mahalia Jackson, Clara Ward Singers, James Cleveland, etc.

CONTEMPORARY CHRISTIAN MUSIC — Picked up where Jesus rock left off, incorporating more funky and harder music elements, often soft-rock. Amy Grant, Michael W. Smith, and BeBe & CeCe Winans are such performers.

HEAVEN'S METAL — "Heavy metal meets gospel lyrics" is how this style is best defined. Strong bass lines, electric/amplified guitar riffs, and steel drumming. Stryper, Bloodgood, and the latter-day Petra coterie exemplify this form.

INSPIRATIONAL — Not unlike middle-of-the-road (MOR) music in the pop sphere, easy-listening, or adult contemporary. Heavy on strings and grandiose orchestrations. Sandi Patti, Dallas Holm, and Dino fall into this category.

JESUS ROCK — A contemporary "White" music style popularized in the late 60s and early 70s, coinciding with the Jesus movement. Pioneers of the form brought rhythm & blues, rock & roll, and folk elements into standard praise tunes. Larry Norman and Randy Stonehill were among the purveyors of the form.

QUARTET SINGING — Based on the old barbershop quartet styles, with gospel lyrics. Usually four-part harmony performed by traditional Black gospel or Southern gospel musicians. Usually performed by males.

SOUTHERN GOSPEL — A country music gospel art form with emphasis on steel and rhythm guitars as its foundation. Draws on bluegrass, blues, and hillbilly elements. Southern gospel groups tend to use four-part harmony with a high tenor and baritone. The Happy Goodmans, the Speers, and Gold City are examples.

SPIRITUAL — A Black gospel art form rising from the Negro spirituals and blues tradition. Characterized by wailing and guttural sounds. Inez Andrews and Shirley Caesar are examples.

STREET POETRY — Whether the term developed in Christian circles is uncertain; however, Christian rap musicians prefer this term to "rap." An urban, funk style of rap with, in this case, Christian lyrics.

— Bil Carpenter

DANIEL AMOS (DÄ)

CCM. Chameleonic Christian-rock band started out as a Gram Parsons-influenced country band. By the late 70s, the group had become an arena-size rock band before the collapse of its record label delayed the release of the landmark *Horrendous Disc.* During that time, frontman Terry Taylor discovered Elvis Costello and the Talking Heads. The few fans who stuck around during the band's three-year recording absence were shocked to hear the new-wave *Alarma!* released hot on the heels of the mainstream *Horrendous Disc.* The band (which eventually shortened its name to Dä) now follows its own music, with little concern for audiences and marketing. Taylor has become one of the most influential figures in Christian rock, as both a performer and a producer (Randy Stonehill, Jacob's Trouble, Scattered Few). —BM

○ **Daniel Amos / MARANATHA! MUSIC**   1976
Christian country-rock, along the lines of the Flying Burrito
Brothers, but hardly *Gilded Palace of Sin*. However, Gram
Parsons sideman Al Perkins does contribute pedal steel. –BM

○ **Shotgun Angel / MARANATHA! MUSIC**   1977
Country-rock album, tighter than *Daniel Amos*, with pop
harmonies, which made them Christian music's answer to the
Eagles. It also made *Shotgun Angel* one of the most popular
albums of its time. –BM

★ **Kalhoun / BRAINSTORM**   1991
"It's the magic word they claim came down from ancient
Babylon," Taylor sings by way of explaining the title word.
"Don't know exactly what it means, it's just a sacred kind of
thing." Satirical, often scathing, rock that brooks no
compromise. –BM

○ **Doppelganger / STUNT**   1992
The Alarma!! Chronicles - Vol. 2. After making (but before
releasing) *Horrendous Disc*, Terry Taylor discovered new-wave,
and Daniel Amos was never the same. *Alarma!!* stripped the
band down to bare bones, but *Doppelganger* returned the
production values that typified Daniel Amos records.
Doppelganger is the second of the four-part *Alarma!!* saga, but
it works just fine on its own. Stunt's 1992 reissue of the album
includes three live bonus tracks. –BM

○ **Horrendous Disc / SOLID ROCK**   1992
The country influences of *Daniel Amos* and *Shotgun Angel*
almost gone, *Horrendous Disc* established Daniel Amos as a
rock band with huge melodies and huge guitars, sweetened by
Beatles-influenced harmonies. –BM

THE DAVIS SISTERS

Black gospel. The group was founded by Ruth "Baby Sis" Davis
in Philadelphia. Other members included Alfreda, Audrey,
and Thelma Davis; Imogene Greene; Curtis Dublin on piano;
Jackie Verdell, lead vocalist. They recorded for the Savoy label
until 1962. Verdell recorded secular sides for Peacock 1961-
1964. Though a quintet, they sounded like a small choir with
their full sound. Four members died in separate but tragic
fashions. One was burned to death. Ruth died in 1970, while
still a young woman after fighting diabetes, liver disease, and
kidney disease. –BC

☆ **Best of the Davis Sisters / SAVOY**
Best of the Davis Sisters of Philidelphia. A remarkable family
gospel unit, plagued by personal tragedies. A nice anthology
of their Savoy songs. –RW

DC TALK

Street poetry. Trio of Washington, DC, area youth who met on
the campus of Rev. Jerry Falwell's Liberty Baptist College. –BC

○ **Nu Thang / HEARTWARMING**   1991
Crossover, pop-style Christian rap. –BC

DE GARMO & KEY

CCM. Eddie De Garmo & Dana Key are Memphis-reared
guitar rockers who started with the Globe band in early 1972.
Later they gave it up to create the Christian rock group called
the Christian Band, changing the name to De Garmo & Key
later in the decade. They were influenced by Elvis Presley, Al
Green, and similar Memphis-style performers. –BC

Feels Good to Be Forgiven / HEARTWARMING
A solo effort by Eddie De Garmo of bluesy Southern rock. –BC

The Journey / HEARTWARMING
A light, soft-rock solo effort by Dana Key. –BC

The Pledge / BENSON
Competent, keyboard-dominated arena-rock. Upside: "Aliens
and Strangers," an insightful (and amusing) U2 knock-off.
Downside: the labor-dispute metaphors of "Boycott Hell." –BM

○ **Straight On / LAMB & LION**   1979
Bluesy Southern rock that was ahead of its time. –BC

DIXIE HUMMINGBIRDS

Black gospel. Formed by James Davis in Greenville, SC, ca.
1928. Personnel: Davis (baritone), Ira Tucker (lead), Beachey
Thompson (tenor), and William Bobo (bass). Early on, they
sang hymns and jubilees with spare accompaniment and tight
harmonies. In the late 60s, they began to infuse jazz, blues,
and rock elements into their material. Notable cuts include
"Somebody Is Lying" and "You Don't Have Nothin' If You Don't
Have Jesus." They backed Paul Simon on "Loves Me Like a
Rock" in 1973, recorded at Muscle Shoals Studios. –BC

The Best of the Dixie Hummingbirds / MCA
A short (12 cuts) selection that is hardly their best, but still a
worthwhile collection of sides from the early 60s. –KL

○ **In the Storm Too Long / GOSPEL JUBILEE**
Their classic early recordings from 1939-1949. This is their
pre-Peacock Records material, from before lead singer James
Walker joined the quartet. –KL

Christian Testimonial / MCA-PEACOCK   1959
Includes "The Devil Can't Harm a Praying Man." –BC

☆ **Live / MOBILE FIDELITY**   1976
With these 75 minutes of fine performances, good sound
quality and a varied repertoire make this the one to buy. –KL

O'LANDA DRAPER & THE ASSOCIATES

Spiritual. Draper atMemphis State University, where he
formed a mass choir (the Associates) that later performed
with Shirley Caesar (on "Hold My Mule"), the Winans,
Nicholas, Timothy Wright, Myrna Summers, and others. They
currently record for Word/Epic. –BC

● **Above & Beyond / CBS**   1990
Contemporary Memphis-based choir; good singing, heavily
arranged. –RW

Do It Again / CBS   1990
This is the most recent release from this modern gospel
orchestra. –RW

PHIL DRISCOLL

Inspirational. This White trumpeter, with raspy vocals similar
to Ray Charles, performs soulful pop arrangements. –BC

○ **I Exalt Thee / SPARROW**   1983
Spiritual wailing and trumpet playing on old hymns. –BC

Classical Hymns - Vol. 1 / BENSON   1988
An orchestral, symphonic session featuring Driscoll's trumpet
solos. –BC

BRYAN DUNCAN

CCM. The former lead singer for Sweet Comfort Band, this
dry-voiced singer records in the pop/rock area with R&B
intensity and was the opening slot for BeBe & CeCe Winans on
their 1989 concert tour. –BC

Strong Medicine / DAYSPRING   1989
Reggae, rap, and the strong title-track ballad. –BC

○ **Anonymous Confessions of a Lunatic Friend / CBS**   1991
Quiet pop ballads and hard R&B/dance music. –BC

JEFF AND SHERI EASTER

Southern gospel. Both members of this husband/wife duo were
born into professional Southern gospel singing families. –BC

Picture-Perfect Love / HEARTWARMING   1989
Homey, folksy country music with bluegrass elements. –BC

○ **Brand New Love / HEARTWARMING**   1990
Peppy, guitar-driven country with story lyrics. –BC

MICHAEL ENGLISH

CCM. Michael English's roots are in Southern Gospel; he
performed with the Singing Americans, the Goodmans, the
Gaither Trio and the Gaither Vocal Band before going solo in
1991. English began drawing attention to his powerful tenor

when he recorded "I Bowed on My Knees and Cried Holy," first with the Singing Americans, then with the Brooklyn Tabernacle Choir. English is established as one of the top young names in the CCM field as he has won Dove Awards for Best New Artist and Best Male Vocalist. –BM

○ **Michael English / WARNER ALLIANCE**   1991
Wildly successful debut that rides the line between adult contemporary and dance-pop. But the real draw is English's eloquent voice, which is showcased to great effect on the likes of "Heaven" and "Solid As the Rock." –BM

EVIE (TORNQUIST)

Inspirational. This Norwegian singer made emphatic pop/inspirational albums in the 70s and 80s. She was the most popular woman in contemporary White gospel before the advent of Amy Grant and Sandi Patti. –BC

○ **When All Is Said and Done / WORD**   1986
Tornquist's light voice really rocks on these mid-tempo songs of joy. –BC

THE FAIRFIELD FOUR

Gospel. This group was created in the early 20s by the pastor of Fairfield Baptist Church in Nashville to occupy his sons, Harry and Rufus Carrethers. With John Battle, they became a gospel trio. The group was transformed into a quartet by the 30s and began the first of numerous personnel changes. They recorded for RCA Victor and Columbia during the decade and were known for their reinterpretation of standard hymns, employing staccato basslines and the ebbing soundwaves of their voices dropping from tenor to baritone. They continue to perform, though the original members are either deceased or retired. –BC

○ **Standing in the Safety Zone / WARNER**   1992
A recent recording by a riveting a cappella quartet in a down-home traditional fashion. Arrangements by stunning basso Isaac "Dickie" Freeman. –OPLN

FERNANDO

CCM. Born in Ecuador, raised in California, Fernando began his career in the late 80s. With a rather smooth singing voice, he tends to record pop-ish urban dance music and an occasional message rap tune. He's one of the first Hispanics to make a strong presence in gospel music; However, because of his outspoken pride in his Latin heritage, he's also become a visible role model to young Hispanics (mostly of a nontraditional Protestant bent) who are increasingly beginning to listen to gospel music. –BC

○ **True Love / MOVIN' UP**   1990
This is all-English, Top 40 pop-style gospel with catchy hooks, heavy use of background vocals, with sequenced instrumentation. –BC

Latin Perspective / MOVIN' UP   1992
His second album has a definite mix of urban Black music and traditional South American music styles, with a few English/Spanish cuts. –BC

FIRST CALL

Inspirational. Bonnie Keen, Marty McCall, and Melody Tunney (replaced by Marybeth Jordon). First Call is similar to Manhattan Transfer, with a Christian message. –BC

○ **Something Takes Over / DAYSPRING**
A range of styles, including Swahili, jazz, and a cappella. –BC

Human Song / DAYSPRING   1992
Michael Omartian-produced move for the secular adult-contemporary market. Breezy dance-pop includes a remake of Stevie Wonder's "Don't You Worry 'Bout a Thing." –BM

THE FIVE BLIND BOYS OF ALABAMA

Black gospel. Evolving out of the Happyland Jubilee Singers, this traditional Black gospel quartet was formed in 1937 at the Talladega Institute for the Deaf and Blind in Alabama. By the

40s they became "The Blind Boys" and recorded for Specialty, Vee Jay, Savoy, Elektra, and other labels. Their first hit was "I Can See Everybody's Mother but Mine" in 1949. Current lineup: Joe Watson, Jimmy Carter, Sam & Bobby Butler, Curtis Foster, Johnny Fields, and Clarence Fountain. They appeared on Broadway in *Gospel at Colonus.* –BC

○ **The Five Blind Boys of Alabama / GOSPEL HERITAGE**
An excellent 16-track anthology that predates their Specialty recordings by four years, with leads shared by Clarence Fountain and the legendary Paul Excano. With scholarly notes and photos, a must for collectors. –HD

● **Oh Lord Stand by Me/Marching Up to Zion / SPECIALTY**
Superb 50s Specialty sides. Hair-raising leads from Clarence Fountain, Rev. Samuel K. Lewis, and Rev. Percell Perkins. –HD

THE FIVE BLIND BOYS OF MISSISSIPPI

Black gospel. This traditional Black gospel quartet, formed in the 40s, included one of the most influential and sadly neglected figures in American music, the great Archie Brownlee. Without Archie, there would be no James Brown or Ray Charles. Brownlee's importance to the development of R&B and gospel can be compared to Lester Young's contribution to jazz saxophone.
The Mississippi group had a friendly rivalry with the "Five Blind Boys of Alabama" in which they appeared on the same bills and tried to outsing each other.
Later incarnations of the group, following the death of Brownlee, were not as historically important but produced good, solid gospel music. All of the original members are deceased. –BC & BW

★ **Best of the Five Blind Boys of Mississippi - Vol. 1 / MCA**
These Specialty recordings truly represent some of the best by this popular group. Arguably the greatest "quartet" ever. Featuring the wondrous Archie Brownlee. –KL & RW

Best of the Five Blind Boys of Mississippi - Vol. 2 / MCA
More gems from this seminal ensemble. –RW

Soon I'll Be Done / MCA
The Chess edition, with the first sighted member, Roscoe Robinson, who shares lead work with Wilmer "Little Ax" Broadnax. It doesn't quite equal its predecessors. –RW

My Desire/There's a God ... / MOBILE FIDELITY
My Desire/There's a God Somewhere combines two fine albums from the Peacock vaults. Also known as the Original Five Blind Boys and the Jackson Harmoneers. The lead vocals by Archie Brownlee have been known to slay souls and reduce grown men to tears. Powerful material! –HD

○ **You Done What the Doctor Couldn't Do / JUBILEE**
Quintessential "hard" gospel sifrom the late 40s and early 50s. Brownlee performs most of the lead chores, with vital dynamism and occasional lead singing from Rev. Percell Perkins and Vance "Tiny" Powell. –KL

FLORIDA BOYS

Gospel. This Southern gospel quintet was first formed in 1947 as the Gospel Melody Quartet. –BC

○ **Together / CANAAN**   1986
Foot-tapping Southern gospel quartet singing. –BC

TENNESSEE ERNIE FORD

Southern gospel. This traditional country star had roots in gospel hymn singing. His full biography can be found with his country listings. –ED

○ **16 Tons of Boogie - The Best of ... / RHINO**
The emphasis here is on the early country material. Lots of hot picking from Speedy West and Jimmy Bryant. –RL

● **All-Time Greatest Hymns / CURB**
His superb baritone on traditional hymns. –BC

Capitol Collectors Series / CAPITOL
Another good collection. Much duplication with the Rhino Records CD compilation. –RL

ARETHA FRANKLIN   b 1942

Soul/R&B. The Queen of Soul's roots are in gospel singing at her father's church. A more extensive biography can be found with her soul/R&B listings. —ED

★ **Aretha Gospel / MCA**   1956
Aretha sings solo and plays piano on these spectacular recordings made at father C. L. Franklin's church in 1956. —KL

○ **Amazing Grace / ATLANTIC**   1972
Traditional Black gospel with Rev. James Cleveland and the Southern California Community Choir. —BC

One Lord, One Faith, One Baptism / ARISTA   1987
Speeches by Jesse Jackson and Clarence Franklin. Guests include Mavis Staples on "Oh Happy Day" and Erma and Carolyn Franklin on "Packin' up Gettin' Ready to Go." —BC

REV. C. L. FRANKLIN

Black gospel. The pastor of Detroit's Bethel Baptist Church, confidant of Martin Luther King Jr., and father of Aretha Franklin, this charismatic preacher is known for "hair-raising" sermons. —BC

○ **Eagle Stirreth in Her Nest / MCA**
One wrenching, sweaty, hellfire sermon recorded for Joe Von Battle in the mid 50s. —BC

RODNEY FRIEND

CCM. Friend sang with the group Nicholas and did session work at the Command stable. —BC

○ **Don't Lose Sight / WORD**
Urban contemporary inspirational ballads. —BC

So Much to Celebrate / CBS

BILLY AND SARAH GAINES

CCM. A husband/wife duo who met while students on the Virginia Commonwealth University campus, they sang with the CCM group Living Sacrifice until 1980. Together they sing in CCM/inspirational style. Billy's is a mellow voice, while Sarah's is high-pitched. —BC

Billy & Sarah Gaines / HEARTWARMING   1986
Pop praise music, with stirring ballads. —BC

○ **He'll Find a Way / HEARTWARMING**   1988
An R&B, urban CCM collection of slow and uptempo cuts. —BC

BILL AND GLORIA GAITHER   b 1936

Inspirational. Aside from recording as a duo, they have recorded with other artists as the Gaither Vocal Band and the Bill Gaither Trio. The Gaithers are the most successful songwriters in Christian music. Their songs tend to be praise- and worship-oriented but often cross various music barriers stylistically; however, their most significant material is contemporary pop. —BC

○ **Live across America / WORD**   1980
A fine live double album of their 70s pop-gospel hits. —BC

MC GE GEE

Street poetry. First female rapper in Christian rap music. Born in the Bronx and raised in Dallas, where her parents run an inner-city youth outreach that was the subject of the film "The Cross and the Switchblade." In the middle of the rap fray, she's not a hard rapper, nor a pop one. She's picked up the serious issue-oriented street-poetry legacy of her late brother, D-Boy Rodriguez. —BC

○ **And Now the Mission Continues / FRONTLINE**   1991
A Tim Miner production of midrange rap that is not too hard and not too pop. The style is urban funk with spare sampling. Most of the album is message-oriented, such as "I Caught the Mike," a pickup of D-Boy's "I Dropped the Mike," which speaks to the continuance of his ministry to youth by Ge Gee. —BC

KATHIE LEE GIFFORD   b 1953

Inspirational. Born in Paris, France. After a twenty-year career doing game shows and night club acts, Gifford is currently a TV talk-show host on the successful "Live with Regis & Kathie Lee." —BC

○ **Finders Keepers / PETRA**   1978
Done during the disco craze, with Streisand-like ballads and Bee Gee-esque numbers. —BC

GLAD

Inspirational. They began in 1972 as the Fellowship, drawing upon jazz and pop-rock influences for their unique sound, which centers on tight, meticulous vocal harmonies. —BC

○ **The A Capella Project / HEARTWARMING**   1988
Old church hymns sans instrumentation. —BC

GOLD CITY

Southern gospel. Formed in the 70s, Gold City is a gospel quartet rife with excellent baritone and high tenor vocals This is kick-back Southern gospel. —BC

○ **Portrait / HEARTWARMING**   1989
Superb harmonies on this camp-meeting-style country music. —BC

THE GOLDEN EAGLE GOSPEL SINGERS

Gospel. An Alabamian a cappella outfit that later developed roots in Chicago, the Golden Eagles were formed in the 30s by Thelma Byrd. On a level with the Golden Gate Quartet, their popularity was strongest in the Midwest. Unlike other groups of the time, who were usually male and Baptist, this one was coed and Sanctified. Much of their music had a fast-paced blues feel, most notably on 1937's "Tone the Bell" and 1940's "He's My Rock," which showcased Hammie Nixon on blues harmonica. They recorded for the Decca label. —BC

○ **The Golden Eagle Gospel Singers / EDEN**
Gems from the three Chicago sessions (ca. 1937-1940) of this important mixed ten-member aggregation led by Thelma Byrd and supported at times by Hammie Nixon. —OPLN

THE GOLDEN GATE QUARTET

Black gospel. Pioneer Virginia gospel/pop quartet of the 30s and 40s. Calling their innovative approach to sacred hymns "jubilee" singing, the Golden Gate Quartet, propelled by Willie Johnson and William Langford, enjoyed massive acceptance far outside the church. Their smooth Mills Brothers-influenced harmonies made the Gates naturals for pop crossover success, and they began recording for Victor in 1937. National radio broadcasts and an appearance on John Hammond's 1938 "Spirituals to Swing" concert at Carnegie Hall made them coast-to-coast favorites. By 1941 the Gates were recording for Columbia minus Langford, and movie appearances were frequent: *Star Spangled Rhythm*, *Hollywood Canteen*, and *Hit Parade of 1943*, to name a few. Some experiments with R&B material didn't pan out during the late 40s, and Johnson defected to the Jubilaires in 1948. The group emigrated to France in 1959; led by veteran bass singer Orlando Wilson, the Golden Gate Quartet's vocal blend is as powerful as ever. —BD

★ **35 Historic Recordings / RCA**
Breathtaking sides from 1937-1939 — largely a cappella, with both gospel and pop music. The album also includes a landmark version of "Stormy Weather" that is at the root of doo-wop. —HD

○ **Nobody Knows / IBACH**
Another adequate recording by this once-mighty group. —KL

○ **Spirituals to Swing / JAZZ TIME**
An inspired effort, recorded between 1955 and 1969. —KL

☆ **Swing Down, Chariot / CBS**
The most influential "jubilee" quartet of the late 30s and 40s in inspired and deftly syncopated performances. An archetype. —MH

The Golden Gate Quartet / CARRERE
Okay, but nothing special. —KL

THE HAPPY GOODMAN FAMILY

Southern gospel. Founded in 1963, this Kentucky-based group dominated Southern gospel charts for years, picking up Dove and Grammy awards. They were associated with the PTL Club in the 80s. Members include Vestal, Howard, Rusty, and Sam Goodman, all legends in their own right. —BC

○ **Greatest Hits / CANAAN**   1985
A live recording of the Goodman Family's country gospel. —BC

THE GOSPEL HARMONETTES (DEMOPOLIS)

Spiritual. Not to be confused with the famous Dorothy Love Coates group, this convincing a cappella female quartet from Central Alabama recorded in 1991 and have strong roots in the Baptist church and Jefferson County singing tradition. —KL

○ **Gospel Harmonettes of Demopolis / GLOBAL VILLAGE**

AMY GRANT   b 1960

CCM. Born in Augusta, GA. No one has been a bigger influence on 80s gospel than Grant. Her girlish, smooth vocal style and fondness for a variety of contemporary rhythms and contemplative lyrics on more than celestial subjects has given her a wide audience and numerous less-talented imitators. She's married to secular country singer Gary Chapman. —BC

☆ **Age to Age / GEFFEN**   1984
Worshipful CCM in country, lullaby, and pop styles. —BC

The Collection / MYRRH   1986
An early gospel hits package, including "El Shaddai." —BC

Lead Me On / A&M   1989
A secular and sacred soft-rock album, with "Shadows." —BC

Heart in Motion / A&M   1991
Her first completely secular album, with urban R&B and light rock, featuring the hit "Baby Baby." —BC

AL GREEN

Black gospel. This Michigan soul singer has had many albums in both the gospel and soul genres. His full biography can be found with his soul album listings. —ED

○ **The Lord Will Make a Way Somehow / MYRRH**   1980
A hearty foray into Black gospel roots. —BC

Precious Lord / MYRRH   1983
Pop-ish R&B and traditional hand-clappers. —BC

Soul Survivor / A&M   1987
Urban funk with a gospel message. —BC

★ **One in a Million / WORD**   1991
A compilation from Green's gospel recordings, which reveals the emotional depth of his religious work. —BM

Love Is Reality / WORD   1992
After years of refusing to sing anything but gospel, Green decided the time had finally come to fuse the godly and the secular elements of his soul. *Love Is Reality* made an overt play for the mainstream R&B market. Unfortunately, Christian dance-pop producer Tim Miner works from formulas, while Green runs on inspiration. Green sounded great, but the final result paled in comparison to the rest of his catalog. —BM

KEITH GREEN   d 1982

Inspirational. Green founded Last Days Ministries with his wife Melody in the late 70s. A reformer trying to purge the church of unbiblical habits, Keith's music is lyrically a mix of Jesus Movement protest and 19th-century evangelistic writings. He died in a plane crash in July 1982. —BC

○ **The Ministry Years - Vol. 1 / SPARROW**   1987
1977-1979. Green makes the piano keys sing. —BC

The Ministry Years - Vol. 2 / SPARROW
1980-1982. Theological questioning and stirring MOR. —BC

STEVE GREEN

Inspirational. Green sang with White Heart and the Gaither Vocal Band before his solo outings. —BC

○ **For God and God Alone / SPARROW**   1986
A big symphonic sound and righteous lyrics. —BC

Tienen Que Saber / SPARROW   1987
A Spanish-language MOR set. —BC

THE HARMONIZING FOUR

Black gospel. Quartet based in Richmond, VA, comprising Tommy "Goat" Johnson (tenor), Lonnie Smith (baritone), "Gospel Joe" Williams, and Jimmy Jones. Recorded for Vee Jay and Nashboro labels in the 50s. —BC

The Best of the Harmonizing Four / CAPITOL
Featuring the bass voice of Ellis Johnson or the legendary Jimmy Jones. —OPLN

○ **Gospel in My Soul / CHAMELEON**
Featuring the bass voice of Jimmy Jones. —HD

Child of a King / PEACOCK
"Nobody Knows" and the original gospel cut of "Stand by Me," later popularized by Ben E. King. —BC

LARNELLE HARRIS

Inspirational. This singer, saxophonist, and percussionist was at one time a member of the Spurrlows, First Gear, and the Gaither Vocal Band gospel groups. —BC

From a Servant's Heart / HEARTWARMING   1987
MOR, inspirational best. —BC

○ **The Father Hath Provided / HEARTWARMING**   1988
Signs of pop progression with a little soul. —BC

● **The Best of 10 Years - Vol. 1 / BENSON**   1991
Few performers have powerful enough voices to overwhelm the psuedo-orchestral arrangements of modern inspirational music; Harris does. With *Volume 2*, this provides an excellent overview of the singer's work. —BM

○ **The Best of 10 Years - Vol. 2 / BENSON**   1991
Gets the edge over *Volume One* because it has the soulful "Friends in High Places" and "I Can Begin Again" from 1989's *I Can Begin Again* album. —BM

HARVEST

CCM. Ed Kerr and Jerry Williams split in 1990, then resurrected the following year, with Williams fronting a rock band. —BC

It's Alright Now / BENSON   1982
Contemporary pop. —BC

○ **Holy Fire / HEARTWARMING**   1988
Acoustic, light-rock worship songs. —BC

THE EDWIN HAWKINS SINGERS   b 1943

Black gospel. Through his mass choir worship seminars, Edwin Hawkins has kept traditional Black gospel styles in vogue, particularly among youth. —BC

Face to Face / POLYGRAM
Contemporary, with a spiritual mass choir sound. —BC

○ **Oh Happy Day / PAI-BUDDAH**
A classic traditional Black gospel recording from 1969. —BC

TRAMAINE HAWKINS

Black gospel. Briefly singing with the R&B group Honey Cones in the early 70s, she married Walter Hawkins and became a featured singer with the Hawkins Family. She is known for a hard, Black gospel singing style. —BC

The Search Is Over / WORD   1989
Urban-funk/R&B, crossover gospel. —BC

○ **Tramaine Hawkins Live / SPARROW**   1990
Traditional Black gospel belting. —BC

WALTER HAWKINS   b 1949

Black gospel. Born in Oakland, CA, Hawkins earned a Master of Divinity degree from UC at Berkeley. He is pastor of the Love Center Church. —BC

○ **Love Alive 1 / LIGHT**   1975
Walter and Tramaine Hawkins outsinging one another on this contemporary Black gospel recording. –BC

THE HIGHWAY QCS

Black gospel. This quartet was started in the 40s. Over the years, the lead singers have included Sam Cooke, Johnnie Taylor, Willie Rogers, and Spencer Taylor. –BC
○ **The Best of the Highway QCs / CAPITOL-CHAMELEON**
A respectable collection for the group that acted as a feeder for the Soul Stirrers and other first-echelon groups. Prior editions included Johnnie Taylor and the unrecorded Sam Cooke and O. V. Wright. –RW
The Lord Is Sweet / PEACOCK
Includes "Changes at the End" and "Rock Me." –BC

KIM HILL

CCM. This Mississippi guitarist with a folk-rock style akin to James Taylor and Suzanne Vega has a sturdy, low-alto vocal style. –BC
Talk about Life / REUNION
Honest looks at life crises in an acoustic setting. –BC
○ **Kim Hill / REUNION**   1988
Semi-philosophical mid-tempo worship songs. –BC
Brave Heart / REUNION   1991
A vocal Christian statement in a secular folk package. –BC

DALLAS HOLM

Inspirational. Holm is a singer and songwriter. In spite of a restrained, undistinctive, flat vocal style, Holm convincingly brings life to MOR ballads such as his signature song, "Rise Again," without attempting to. –BC
Early Works: Best of Dallas Holm / HEARTWARMING
Adult contemporary pop. –BC
○ **Beyond the Curtain / DAYSPRING**   1988
Inspirational MOR and a reworking of "Rise Again." –BC

LARRY HOWARD

Southern gospel. This blues guitarist played with the Allman Brothers and Marshall Tucker bands. –BC
Redeemed / HEARTWARMING
More blues-backed rockabilly. –BC
○ **Shout / SPECIALTY**   1988
Brassy blues and bluegrass gospel numbers. –BC

THE IMPERIALS

Inspirational. Formed in 1964, the Imperials have shifted back and forth between Southern gospel, MOR, and CCM styles. –BC
○ **The Very Best of the Imperials / DAYSPRING**
Contemporary pop from the 70s and 80s. –BC
Big God / STAR SONG   1991
Synthesizers and electric guitars - their hippest date yet. –BC

MAHALIA JACKSON   1911-1972

Black gospel. Born in New Orleans, Mahalia Jackson grew up in the Baptist Church, though she also admired blues singers such as Bessie Smith and Ma Rainey. Jackson made Chicago her home beginning in 1927, where she also began a lifelong association with gospel writer and performer Thomas A. Dorsey. She earned the title "Gospel Queen" with her 1947 version of "Move On Up a Little Higher." Tours of Europe and television appearances in the United States followed on the heels of this success. She remained one of gospel's most visible figures until her death. –KL
○ **Amazing Grace / COLUMBIA**
A nice sampling of Jackson's later recordings. –KL
Christmas with Mahalia Jackson / COLUMBIA
Although they lack the passion of her best work, these popular hymns will probably appeal to many. –KL

★ **Gospels, Spirituals & Hymns / CBS**
With a wonderful booklet, this is the best sampling of 50s to 60s work. –KL
Live in Antibes / FRENCH CONCERTS
A nice concert performance from late in her career. –KL
Silent Night (Songs for Christmas) / CBS
Once again, some of Jackson's best-known work. –KL
Sings America's Favorite Hymns / CBS
Another cross'of Jackson's 50s and 60s work. –KL

JIMMY A

CCM. Also known as Jimmy Abegg, he is a member of Vector and a sideman for Charlie Peacock. Abegg makes an unlikely guitar hero with his soul-dominated songs and his preference for textures over speed. –BM
○ **Entertaining Angels / SPARROW**   1991
Appealing guitar-pop record in the Charlie Peacock tradition. Peacock appears here, as does vocalist Vince Ebo, most notably on "Thin but Strong Cord," where the two share lead vocals with Abegg. But it's Abegg's show down the line, as he writes and produces the bulk of the material, showing real promise. –BM

BLIND WILLIE JOHNSON

Blues gospel. A guitar-playing evangelist with a scary, emotion-charged voice, Blind Willie Johnson played the most exquisite slide ever heard. Void of frivolity or uncertainty, his 78s were clearly the work of a pained believer seeking street-corner redemption with a guitar and a tin cup. He was gifted with an incomparable sense of timing and tone, using his pocket-knife slide to duplicate his vocal inflections or to produce an unforgettable phrase from a single strike of a string. With its wide, rough vibrato, his voice was as fierce as Charles Patton's or Son House's, but he's much easier to understand.
In 1927 Blind Willie Johnson became one of the first gospel guitarists on 78s. Among his 30 recorded songs is the landmark instrumental "Dark Was the Night, Cold Was the Ground," described by Ry Cooder as "the most transcendent piece in all American music." Blind Willie spent most of his life singing for the Baptist Church or playing for tips on the streets of Beaumont, TX. Decades later, his music echoed in the styles of Mississippi Fred McDowell and Mance Lipscomb. Still, he remains a slide guitarist without parallel, a player so perfect he's impossible to adequately imitate. –JO
★ **Praise God I'm Satisfied / YAZOO**
Pre-war gospel blues at its most harrowing and transcendental. Unsurpassed slide guitar! –JO
○ **Sweeter as the Years Go By / YAZOO**
The remaining selections by this superb, Texas-born slide guitarist, who is sometimes supported by his wife's haunting voice. –KL

BROTHER VERNARD JOHNSON

Spiritual. This saxophonist earned a doctorate in musicology from Southwestern Baptist Theological Seminary in 1982. Influenced by R&B sax man King Curtis, he played in a Kansas City jazz group. Now he plays only gospel-oriented music, touring with a 13-member combo. –BC
I'm Alive! / ELEKTRA
Contains some good sax solos, derivative arrangements, timid percussion. –RW
○ **Rocking the Gospel / ROIR**
Sanctified, hard-charging sax from gospel's best instrumental improviser since Ben Branch. –RW

WILLIE NEAL JOHNSON

Black gospel. Johnson has a hard country-blues approach to traditional Black gospel. He currently sings with the Gospel Keynotes. –BC
Just a Rehearsal / MALACO
Decent modern gospel. –RW

○ **Going Back with the Lord / MALACO**
Updated material featuring one-time quartet star Johnson with the Gospel Keynotes. –RW
I'm Yours Lord / MALACO
These are some fine songs and ordinary performances with the Gospel Keynotes. –RW

SHIRLEY JONES   b 1934

Inspirational. Jones was born in Smithton, PA. A broadway star and film actress, she played the matriarch on the "Partridge Family" sitcom in the 70s. –BC
○ **Silent Strength / DIADEM**   1990
Lightly operatic, inspirational. –BC

PHIL KEAGGY

CCM. This premier guitarist played with Glass Harp (which recorded for Decca) before going gospel in the 70s. He was influenced by the Beatles but has won respect for his authoritative plucking style. –BC
Love Broke Thru / MYRRH   1976
These are extended, McCartneyesque guitar solos. Stirring pop/rock. –BC
The Wind & the Wheat / HORIZON   1987
Several pieces of solo acoustic guitar, and the rest with a small group ensemble. Brilliant acoustic playing. –PK
● **Phil Keaggy & Sunday's Child / MYRRH**   1988
Fans of Anglo-rock/pop should love this outing, which has all the tuneful appeal of Crowded House or Jellyfish. Produced by Lynn Nichols (who later helped form Chagall Guevara), *Phil Keaggy and Sunday's Child* sparkles with a fine mix of chiming Rickenbacker guitars and soaring harmonies. Occasionally the Brit-pop focus gives way to a sturdy hard-rock sound, but it's still very well executed. Among the many highlights included are "Sunday's Child," "Tell Me How You Feel," and "I'm Gonna Get You Now."   RC
Town to Town/Ph'Lip Side/Play Thru Me / MYRRH 1990
Keaggy's early has dated rather badly, so while there's some impressive guitar work and some good songs on the two-CD reissue (material 1980-1982), there's a lot to wade through. –BM
○ **What a Day/Love Broke Thru / MYRRH**   1990
Keaggy's first two solo albums (from 1973 and 1976 reissued here on one CD) remain among his best. Keaggy was one of the first contemporary Christian musicians to bring an original melodic sense to his songs (indebted as it was to Paul McCartney), and his lyrical naivete comes across as refreshing rather than insipid. –BM
○ **Find Me in These Fields / MYRRH**   1990
His hooks are still firmly rooted in the 60s, but they're big ol' hooks, and a crack backing band makes this a power-pop classic interspersed with guitar instrumentals. –BM
Beyond Nature / CBS   1991
An album of solo acoustic guitar and small-group music. An excellent recording. –PK

THE KING'S MEN

Gospel. An old-time quarter, founded by Big Jim Hamill in 1955 and based in Ashland, NC. –BC
○ **Mississippi Live / RIVERSONG**   1987
Booming tenors and resounding baritones. Check out "Inside the Gates." –BC

CRISTY LANE   b 1940

Inspirational. Born Eleanor Johnston, this singer of country and pop standards was guided by husband Lee Stoller into a gospel career. She recorded her first record, "Janie Took My Place," on the K-Ark label in 1968. Though the majority of her records are of a secular nature, her biggest hit was "One Day at a Time" from 1979, which is one of the biggest-selling gospel songs of all time and sold several million copies. –BC

○ **One Day at a Time / KTEL-QWIL**   1978
A simplistic, soft-pop style of gospel from her gentle voice. –BC
All in His Hands / HEARTWARMING   1989
Lane's pristine sounds come through best on the 50s-style "He Loves Me Still." –BC

MYLON LEFEVRE & BROKEN HEART   b 1945

CCM. Mylon LeFevre sang with his family's Southern gospel group, the LeFevres, at the age of 12. Later he became a songwriter, with his songs recorded by Elvis and others. LeFevre formed the CCM band Broken Heart in 1981. –BC
Greatest Hits / CBS
Southern boogie/gospel rock and secular music from the early 70s. –BC
○ **Mylon / COTILLION**   1970
East Coast rock, with strong rhythm sections and Joe South guesting. –BC

THE ROBERTA MARTIN SINGERS   1907-1969

Black gospel. This talented pianist started a quartet with Theodore Frye in the 30s. This aggregation gradually evolved into the Roberta Martin Singers by the 50s. It is now known that she copied the piano style of blind pianist Arizona Dranes, who also influenced the Ward Singers. Martin's singers sang loudly and dramatically. She also wasn't concerned about a harmonious sound; when one member of the group was leading a song, whether male or female, you could easily identify the backing voices. This lack of synchronicity made the group's urgent sound a unique and welcome change amid the repetitive quartets of the time. Robert Anderson was one of Martin's principal singers. She herself was referred to as the Helen Hayes of the Gospel World. She died in 1969. –BC
Best of the Roberta Martin Singers / SAVOY
Twenty-one selections from their 1957-1961 period, with noted soloist Gloria Griffin. –OPLN
○ **The Roberta Martin Singers / SAVOY**
Most of Martin's best early work from the late 40s through the 50s is out of print, but this is a nice introduction to this dynamic singer and group leader. –KL

BROTHER JOE MAY

Black gospel. A bluesy tenor, May was a protégé of Willie Mae Ford Smith. When he began to record in the 50s, he copied her cuts "Search Me Lord" and "Old Ship of Zion" note by note. In the 60s he appeared in the play "*Black Nativity*." He was once called the "Thunderbolt of the Midwest." –BC
☆ **Thank You Lord for One More Day / SPECIALTY**   1967
Excellent hard gospel, with occasional support from Sister Wynona Carr and the Pilgrim Travelers. –RW
In Loving Memory ... / SPECIALTY   1974
In Loving Memory of Brother Joe May is a collection of May's finest shouts and duets on Specialty, supported on some cuts by the Pilgrim Travelers, the Sallie Martin Singers, or a live audience. –RW
○ **Search Me, Lord / SPECIALTY**   1974
Authoritative gospel and energized vocals with support from the Pilgrim Travelers and the Sallie Martin Singers. –RW

DEBBIE MCCLENDON   b 1960

CCM. Born in Pasadena, CA, McClendon sings gospel with a CCM/urban-Black style. –BC
○ **Count It All Joy / STAR SONG**   1987
Pop in an inspirational setting. –BC
Get a Grip / FRONTLINE   1989
A successful try at an urban sound. –BC

MARILYN MCCOO   b 1943

CCM. Born in Jersey City, NJ, McCoo was a featured singer with the Fifth Dimension in the 60s, doing smooth pop music.

In 1976 she and husband Billy Davis Jr split the group to form a duo and had three hit albums (two for ABC Records and one for CBS). By 1981 McCoo went solo, hosting the syndicated "Solid Gold" music series. –BC

○ **The Me Nobody Knows / WARNER**   1991
A soulful set with jazz and Caribbean overtones. Horns are featured. –BC

DAVID MEECE   ♭1952

CCM. This singer and pianist studied music at Peabody Conservatory in Baltimore. –BC

○ **Front Row / MYRRH**   1982
Humor, dazzling acoustic piano, and pop gospel. –BC

Learning to Trust / TWO-ONE-FOUR   1989
A cathartic grip on alcoholism and relationships. –BC

THE MIGHTY CLOUDS OF JOY

Black gospel. Formed in Los Angeles ca. 1959, the original members were Ermant and Elmer Franklin, Joe Ligon, Johnny Martin, Leon Polk, and Richard Wallace. They had some R&B hits in the 1974-1977 period with "Mighty High" and "Time." They have consistently adjusted their repertoire according to the current trends, having played everything from traditional Black gospel to light rock. –BC

○ **The Best of the Mighty Clouds of Joy / MCA**
The title is a bit misleading, but it's still a fair sample of the group's most popular performances. –KL

A Bright Side / MCA   1960
The title sermonette and other quartet-style cuts. –BC

★ **The Best of the Mighty Clouds of Joy - Vol. 1 / MCA** 1973
The titles get confusing, don't they? This time a collection of reissues from the group's best early Peacock albums. –KL

The Best of the Mighty Clouds of Joy - Vol. 2 / MCA 1973
A hodge podge of lesser material from their Peacock albums and singles. Vol. 2 includes some nice sides, but it's weaker than the first volume. –KL

THE MORNING STARS OF SAVANNAH

Spiritual. A notable quartet led by Mitchell Williams. –OPLN

○ **Mama's Old Dress / NASHBORO**
Impressive singing and sermonizing from the late 70s. –OPLN

RICH MULLINS   ♭1955

CCM. Mullins writes and records worship-style songs, merging the simpleness of folk with light CCM instrumentation. –BC

○ **Winds of Heaven, Stuff of Earth / REUNION**
Light, harmonious pop arrangements, yet full of sound. –BC

NICHOLAS   ♭1954

CCM. Now a husband/wife duo, Nicholas began as a quartet in the early 80s. As a duo they've been in the forefront of contemporary urban-style Black gospel. –BC

○ **Dedicated / A&M**   1985
The title cut and "Go Tell Somebody" are what modern Black gospel is all about. Their finest work. –BC

Nicholas Live in Memphis / WORD   1989
A spontaneous high-energy set. –BC

LARRY NORMAN

Jesus rock. One of the pioneers of the Jesus Rock Movement of the 60s and 70s, Norman combined Black gospel, the grit of rock & roll, and his own feelings on social issues into the folk rock of the time to aid in the creation of Jesus rock. –BC

☆ **Upon This Rock / IMPACT**   1970
Counterculture, psychedelic folk and blues. –BC

○ **Only Visiting This Planet / STREET LEVEL**   1972
Contains sociopolitical statements with hard-edged, Jesus rock zeal. –BC

DOROTHY NORWOOD

Black gospel. A belter with a harsh, gravelly voice, she's probably recorded more songs about wayward children than Shirley Caesar. Before going solo in the 60s, Norwood was a member of the Chimes and the Caravans. –BC

○ **Denied Mother / SAVOY**
Norwood's spectacular vocals are supported by the Combined Choir of Atlanta, GA. One of Norwood's greatest song sermons is the title track. –RW

Faithful Daughter / SAVOY
This has another classic single in the title track. –RW

Live / MALACO
An enthusiastic performance, but the energy level dips whenever Norwood stops singing. –RW

Look What They've Done to My Child / SAVOY
Wonderful anthvocals and a textbook selection that's a blueprint of gospel storytelling and lyric imagery. –RW

Wonderful Day — Live / I AM
Fine singing, but an overabundance of pop/contemporary devices and instrumentation. –RW

NU VISION

CCM. This Hispanic urban-contemporary vocal band was formed in 1990. Members: David, Pete, and Isaac Hernandez; Rick Olvera. –BC

○ **Forever Mine / CBS**   1991
Well-done urban rap/CCM with an obvious R&B influence. –BC

MICHAEL OMARTIAN

Gospel. Michael Omartian has enjoyed considerable success in the CCM and secular music fields, as a session sideman, songwriter, solo artist, and producer. During the 70s, Omartian's distinctive keyboard work graced projects by Loggins & Messina and Steely Dan. As a producer, Omartian worked with Christopher Cross (cleaning up at the 1981 Grammys with Cross's self-titled debut), as well as Donna Summer and Amy Grant (notably her platinum Heart in Motion album). During the mid 70s, Omartian's solo work helped set the standard for high-caliber pop statements that rivaled the best the secular world had to offer. Omartian continues to release solo efforts, the most recent being The Race. –RC

The Race / CBS   1991
On The Race, Omartian collaborates with singer/songwriter Michael Anderson and Bruce Sudano (formerly with Brooklyn Dreams). The style is contemporary keyboard-heavy pop, with several songs sporting strong melodic hooks (particularly "Faithful Forever" and "Heartbreak City"). –RC

☆ **White Horse/Adam Again / MYRRH**   1991
This CD combines Omartian's first two solo albums, White Horse (1974) and Adam Again (1975), both very important to CCM because they heralded the advent of advanced production techniques and sophisticated, multilayered lyrical imagery that went beyond standard gospel metaphors. Musically, these two albums are probably Omartian's most adventurous statements. Highlights include the reflective "Right from the Start" and "The Orphan," as well as the celebratory "Ain't You Glad" and the sweeping ballad "Annie the Poet." "White Horse," "Take Me Down," and "Silver Fish" showcase Omartian's fine arranging and keyboard chops. Nevertheless, certain tracks haven't aged very gracefully, particularly "Alive and Well," which instrumentally sounds like a clichéd 70s "Rockford Files"-style TV soundtrack. Both of these albums utilize the cream of Los Angeles's "A-list"

session sidemen, including Lee Ritenour, Leland Sklar, David Hungate, Larry Carlton, and Victor Feldman. –RC

ONE BAD PIG

CCM. A punk quartet that started as a lark for a youth rally in the band's Austin, TX, hometown. The positive reception led to a relatively long career, but the members of the band seemed to understand neither punk's culture nor its philosophy and ended up, depending on where you stood in the audience, as either a generic thrash band or a punk parody. –BM

○ **I Scream Sunday / MYRRH** 1991
These uninspired punk thrashings, produced by White Heart's Billy Smiley, quickly get tedious. But "Man in Black," a duet with (believe it or not) Johnny Cash, shows the exact spot where punk and Christianity intersect. And Cash comes off as a more committed punk than anybody in the band. –BM

SHUN PACE-RHODES

Gospel. Pace-Rhodes hails from a family of singers active in the Church of God in Christ (COGIC) music movement. She and her siblings formed the Anointed Pace Sisters of Atlanta in the mid 70s and were known for their contemporary R&B gospel sound. She sang "That Name" on one of Edwin Hawkins's Music and Arts seminal albums in 1987. It was he who personally went to the head of Savoy-Malaco Records and suggested they sign the belting singer as a solo artist, and they did. Rather than cutting her chops on modern styles, Pace-Rhodes sang music that recalls the days of Mahalia Jackson and the Ward Singers. –BC

○ **He Lives / SAVOY** 1992
The most astonishing traditional female gospel soloist in the church today. Her powerhouse pipes are supported by the Showers of Blessing Choir and the Voices of Power out of Atlanta, GA. –OPLN

TWILA PARIS ♭1958

Inspirational. Working with producer Johnathan David Brown, Paris created a distinguishable light pop sound in the early 80s on albums such as *Warrior Is a Child* and *Kingdom Seekers.* –BC

Cry for the Desert / JCI & ASSOCIATED
Intimate light praise/pop music, with Brown Bannister producing. –BC

○ **Sanctuary / STAR SONG** 1991
Complete inspirational worship, with Richard Souther producing. –BC

SQUIRE PARSONS

Southern gospel. Born in Newton, WV, Parsons began his gospel career singing with the Calvary Men. In 1975 he joined the Kingsmen as a baritone, but left in 1979 to pursue a solo career and has since recorded 25 Southern-gospel/MOR albums. Parsons won six *Singing News Magazine* awards, including the prestigious Marvin Norcross Award in 1990. "Sweet Beulah Land" was a #1 song on Southern gospel charts in 1981. –BC

○ **His Very Best / HEARTWARMING**
Includes "Hello Mama," "Jesus Is the Door," and "Sweet Beulah Land." –BC

JANET PASCHAL ♭1956

Southern gospel. Six years with the Nelons, a Southern gospel group. She sang with the Jimmy Swaggart Ministries before a solo career as a contemporary Southern gospel singer. –BC

○ **Janet Paschal / WORD** 1988
A set of pop country treats. –BC

SANDI PATTI ♭1957

Inspirational. Born in Oklahoma City, OK, Patti is an exquisite

pianist. Although she did commercial jingles for Wrigley's Gum, and others, she usually records light-pop or big-orchestra-style praise songs, which enhance her potent, high soprano delivery. Whereas Amy Grant dominated the 80s youth market, Patti sang for their parents. Her distinctive high notes defined 80s inspirational, string-orchestrated praise balladry and, like Grant, spurred a number of clones. –BC

Hymns Just for You / CBS
Traditional hymns given Patti's heartfelt imprint. –BC

Songs from the Heart / CBS
A mix of light CCM and pop-gospel. –BC

○ **A Morning like This / CBS** 1986
An inspirational tour de force featuring sweet string arrangements. –BC

Finest Moments / CBS 1990
Her greatest hits. –BC

Another Time ... Another Place / WORD 1991
A pop crossover setting. –BC

MICHAEL PEACE

Street poetry. Michael Peace is the reigning Christian rapper on the scene. He made his debut in 1987 with "Rrrock it Right." –BC

○ **Loud N' Clear / GEFFEN**
Live, salvation-maniacal, produced by Dez Dickerson (ex-guitarist with Prince). –BC

Rappin' Bold / REUNION

Rrrock It Right / REUNION
Easy rap lingo. Urban-styled, with fresh hooks. –BC

Vigilante of Hope / REUNION 1991
Direct, humorless rhymes and a slow groove style. –BC

CHARLIE PEACOCK

CCM. White-soul singer whose combination of Smokey Robinson-influenced falsetto vocals and cerebral lyrics have helped him develop one of CCM's most individual sounds. He cowrote Amy Grant's 1991 hit "Every Heartbeat." A sought-after producer, he was worked with Margaret Becker, the Choir, the 77's, and Jimmy A. –BM

The Secret of Time / SPARROW 1990
Because of their low-budget production, early Peacock projects classified him as "alternative." "Put the Love Back into Love," "Almost Threw It Away," and "Heaven Is a Real Place" suggested that he had more of an affinity for soul, but "Experience" showed that he still needed to learn that the best grooves are created by instinct, not academia. –BM

☆ **Love Life / SPARROW** 1991
Peacock's concept album about the correlation between a man's spiritual relationship with God and his physical relationship with his wife was the masterpiece that *The Secret of Time* pointed to. "After Loving You" made no bones about the object of its affections; it was an unabashed love song for Peacock's wife. But what really shook up the Christian audiences was the sensuous funk of "Kiss Me like a Woman," nothing less than the first Christian song about foreplay (and a scathing indictment of pop radio). –BM

West Coast Diaries - Vols. 1-3 / SPARROW 1991
Demos and live recordings Peacock released as individual albums between 1986 and 1988; Sparrow reissued them individually and as a boxed set. Peacock's the kind of artist who inspires a desire for completism, so even though these recordings show his tendency to overintellectualize his music, they're still worth having (especially *Volume Two,* which captures an acoustic concert with guitarist Jimmy A and vocalist Vince Ebo). –BM

Coram Deo: In the Presence of God / SPARROW 1992
This worship-oriented project featuring Michael Card, Michael English, and Susan Ashton reflects writer/producer Charlie Peacock's ongoing preoccupation with the relationship of the Christian life and the omnipresence of God. –BM

MAGGIE STATON PEEBLES

Black gospel. Peebles first sang with the Jewell Gospel Trio in the 50s with nine gold records on Nashboro label. Then she became a schoolteacher until returning to gospel in 1988. She has a melodious and sweetly powerful voice. –BC

Born Again / WINSTON-DEREK
Black gospel standards of the 50s redone in the 90s. –BC

○ **First Fruits / WINSTON-DEREK**
Recorded with a simple rhythm section and traditional arrangements. –BC

This Soul of Mine / WINSTON-DEREK
Piano-activated Black gospel. –BC

PETRA

CCM. Jesus rock band formed in 1972. In the 80s they drifted toward heavy metal without getting "heavy." –BC

Petra / WORD   1974
A musician's album in a blues/country-rock guitar style. –BC

○ **Unseen Power / CBS**   1992
This is a warm, crisp production, aside from its metal and bluesy-pop. –BC

LESLIE PHILLIPS

CCM. Gospel music's she-rebel, Phillips left the gospel industry in the late 80s because of its confining nature. She now records secular material on Virgin Records with producer and husband T-Bone Burnett, under the name of Sam Phillips. –BC

The Turning / MYRRH
Emotionally truthful CCM with eccentric instrumentation. –BC

○ **Recollection / MYRRH**   1987
A greatest-hits package. –BC

WINTLEY PHIPPS   *b* 1955

Inspirational. This Washington, DC, minister sings inspirational music in a booming baritone. –BC

○ **Sun Will Shine Again / CBS**   1990
Spirituals and inspirational numbers. –BC

THE PILGRIM JUBILEES

Black gospel. This Jackson, MS, quartet led by Clay and Cleve Graham used great guitar work and unique timing to make their mark in the 50s. –BC

The Old Ship of Zion / PEACOCK
This one includes "Pearly Gates" and "If You Don't Mind." –BC

Back to Basics / MALACO   1990
Another solid effort recorded by this label, which helped to bring good Southern gospel music into the 90s. –KL

○ **Gospel Roots / MALACO**   1990
This dynamic album shows why the Pilgrim Jubilees have remained one of the most respected "hard" gospel groups for so many years. –KL

THE PILGRIM TRAVELERS

Black gospel. This "walking rhythm" gospel quartet was extremely popular around 1950-1954. –OPLN

○ **Best of ... Vols. 1 & 2 / SPECIALTY**   1990
An aptly named sampler of early sides from the huge Specialty vaults, with the legendary Kylo Turner and Keith Barber on leads. –KL

SISTER LUCILLE POPE w/THE PEARLY GATES

Gospel. She has recorded for the Nashboro and AIR labels. –BC

○ **The Very Best of Sister Lucille Pope / NASHBORO**
Soulful and original 60s/70s gospel sung in the traditional way by this important Atlanta soloist, supported ably by the male members of her family — the Pearly Gates. –OPLN

DOTTIE RAMBO   *b* 1934

Southern gospel. Dottie was born in Madison, KY. (She is the wife of Buck Rambo, mother to Reba Rambo, and mother-in-law to Dony McGuire.) She is more influential for the 700 or more worshipful songs she's written over the years, which have inspired facsimiles and numerous covers, than for her own career as a Southern gospel singer or as one of the first female lead guitarists in gospel. –BC

○ **The Best of the Rambos - Vols. 1 & 2 / NK**
Dottie and Buck's country gospel. –BC

Soul of Me / HEARTWARMING
Late-60s soulful Southern gospel. –BC

Sunshine Shine on Me / HEARTWARMING
Mainstream Southern gospel from the 60s. –BC

This Is My Valley / HEARTWARMING
Rambo's warm voice on moody Southern gospel ballads. –BC

TROY RAMEY & THE SENSATIONAL SOUL SEARCHERS

Gospel. He has recorded for the Nashboro and AIR labels. –BC

○ **Troy Ramey / NASHBORO**
Troy Ramey & the Sensational Soul Searchers. Pew-scorching, sanctifying gospel from the 70s by this important Atlanta quartet. –OPLN

REV. D. C. RICE

Spiritual. Born in Alabama, Rev. Rice relocated to Chicago during WWI to join a Pentacostal church. A moving preacher, he was moved to record after witnessing the success of Bishop Fort Washington McGee on his sermonizing/singing records. Rice mimicked McGee's raucous singing and preaching style. He was a prolific recorder, but 1929's "I'm on the Battlefield for the Lord" on the Vocalion label stands out. –BC

○ **Rev. D. C. Rice / DOCUMENT**
Over twenty exemplary performances of jazz-accompanied, sanctified singing and preaching. –KL

PAUL ROBESON   1898-1976

Spiritual. This star football player at Rutgers held a law degree and starred in Hollywood films. A booming baritone, he specialized in Negro spirituals and folk songs. –BC

Golden Classics - Vol. 1 / COLLECTABLES
Golden Classics - Vol. 1 (American Balladeer). A great singer tries hard on established standards. –RW

☆ **Ballad for Americans / VANGUARD**
Superb songs, Americana, and more. –RW

○ **Essential / VANGUARD**
Some of his strongest and most defiant vocals. –RW

Golden Classics - Vol. 2 / COLLECTABLES
Golden Classics - Vol. 2 (A Man & His Beliefs). Political/topical material. –RW

○ **The Power & the Glory / CBS**
This is a retrospective of Robeson's best-known spirituals and folk music. –BC

Golden Classics - Vol. 3 / COLLECTABLES   1977
This erratic collection ranges from decent to marvelous. –RW

LULU ROMAN

Southern gospel. One of the "Hee-Haw" regulars, she's full of warmth and humor, with an incredible testimony of healing from drug addiction. –BC

○ **Take Me There / WORD**   1985
Smooth vocals on this pop-ish Southern gospel. –BC

2ND CHAPTER OF ACTS

CCM. A major Christian-rock act, which began in the early 70s, defined by the sibling harmonies of Annie Herring, Matthew Ward, and Nelly Greisen. Their music brought complex song structures to inspirational music. Their best-known song was 1974's "Easter Song," which achieved moderate mainstream radio airplay (and featured Michael Been, later founder of the Call, on bass). The group's self-deprecating attitudes may have kept them from achieving the renown of some contemporaries. Herring and Ward continued to record solo projects after the group disbanded in 1988. –BM

○ **20 / SPARROW**   1992
Twentieth-anniversary retrospective is a 41-track overview of the music of this influential group. Includes three early singles for MGM and two previously unreleased cuts.–BM

SENSATIONAL NIGHTINGALES

Black gospel. The Sensational Nightingales were assembled in the 40s. In 1957 they appeared on the Gospel Train tour with the Clara Ward Singers and five other big-name gospel acts. Members: Julius Cheeks (lead), Carl Coates (bass), JoJo Wallace (tenor), Howard Carroll (baritone), and Paul Gwens (tenor). Noted hit: "See How They Done My Lord." One of the earliest gospel quintets, they still record and tour today. Many of their 50s and 60s sides (found on MCA reissues) feature the stunning vocals of Rev. Julius Cheeks. As with Archie Brownlee, Cheeks reaches an intensity that distorts the actual recordings, and his style has been heavily "borrowed" by Bobby Bland, Wilson Pickett, and others. The later recordings by Charles Johnson are smoother and slicker, but still top-notch. –BC & BW

○ **Heart & Soul/You Know Not ... / MOBILE FIDELITY**
Heart & Soul/You Know Not the Hour. The CD remastering of these two early-70s albums by this fine harmony quintet is well worth owning. *Heart and Soul* is taken from the better pre-Paramount days (1970-1971), and *You Know Not the Hour* presents the group in a later, more hymnal song setting, both with Charles Johnson on lead. –KL

Songs of Praise / PEACOCK
Includes "I Want to Go." –BC

Glory Glory / PEACOCK
With "Behold God's Face." –BC

THE 77'S

CCM. Quintessential Christian rock band. Fronted by vocalist and guitarist Mike Roe, the band's always-anticipated but infrequent albums make few concessions for CCM compatibility. (Their live album, *88*, for instance, includes a rave-up of the Yardbird's "Over Sideways Down.") Drummer Aaron Smith previously played with Ray Charles and the Temptations, including the hit "Papa Was a Rollin' Stone." New band members — bassist Mark Harmon and keyboardist David Leonhardt — made their full-album debut with the band in late 1992, even though they've played live for four years, and promise a new direction for the group. –BM

The 77's / EXIT-ISLAND   1987
Promising debut shows a band equally influenced by Bob Dylan and blues/rock. Includes their concert favorite, "The Lust, the Flesh, the Eyes & the Pride of Life," and a killer anthem — "Do It for Love." –BM

☆ **Sticks and Stones / BRAINSTORM**
After the departure of keyboardist Mark Tootle, Mike Roe emerged as the dominant figure in the 77's. *Sticks and Stones* points the way to the 77's of the future: biting, guitar-dominated rock with provocative lyrics epitomized by "Perfect Blues." Also includes new recordings of the four best songs from *The 77's*. –BM

THE RICHARD SMALLWOOD SINGERS   ♭1948

CCM. Smallwood was born in Atlanta, GA. He formed the Richard Smallwood Singers in Washington, DC,in 1977. –BC

○ **Textures / WORD**   1987
Contemporary Black gospel styles, with "Center of My Joy." –BC

Portrait / CBS   1989
Piano-backed urban pop-gospel. –BC

MICHAEL W. SMITH

CCM. This singer, keyboardist, and songwriter who was born in Kenova, VA, has toured with Amy Grant and Gary Chapman. –BC

○ **The Big Picture / REUNION**
High-tech pop/rock on this John Potoker production. –BC

The Live Set / REUNION
A jammin' rock-concert aura. –BC

The Michael W. Smith Project / GEFFEN
Worshipful, inspirational pop. –BC

I 2 Eye / GEFFEN   1989
A mix of mature pop and soft rock. –BC

Michael W. Smith 2 / REUNION   1989
Still worshipful, but more rock-oriented. –BC

Go West Young Man / GEFFEN   1990
Adult contemporary music. –BC

MOTHER WILLIE MAE FORD SMITH   ♭1906

Black gospel. Born in Rolling Fort, MS, she was involved with Thomas Dorsey's National Convention of Gospel Choirs and Choruses and had a 1937 hit with "If You Just Keep Still." Smith had a blues-like contralto and was known for her dramatic vocal fits and improvisational skills on cuts like "Take Your Burdens to the Lord." She performed and recorded sparingly, but was influential by starting a tradition of opening a song with a sermonette. Currently living in Chicago, she was one of the most important gospel singers to emerge in the 30s. –BC & KL

● **Mother Willie Mae Ford Smith / SPIRIT FEEL**
Mother Willie Mae Ford Smith & Her Children is a compilation that highlights some of the best performances by Ms. Smith and her musical progeny. –KL

○ **Willie Mae Ford Smith / SAVOY**
Includes "I Must Tell Jesus" and "He Never Left Me Alone." –BC

Going On with the Spirit / NASHBORO
Of special note: "Give Me Wings" and "I've Got a Secret." –BC

REV. DAN SMITH   ♭1911

Blues gospel. Smith sang in church and played harmonica as a child. He didn't begin his professional career until the early 60s when he played behind folk legends Rev. Gary Davis and Pete Seeger. However, his musical style is overwhelmingly oriented to Chicago blues.

○ **Just Keep Goin' On / GLASSHOUSE**   1992
All original gospel material set to a twelve-bar blues backbeat. Harmonica is the instrumental focus, and the songs are separated by short testimonies by Smith in his folksy gravel of a voice. –BC

THE SOUL STIRRERS

Black gospel. A legendary gospel group known best for introducing Sam Cooke's mellifluous voice to the world, the Soul Stirrers were tremendously influential in the Black gospel scene from the mid 30s on. Formed in Texas in 1927, the group soon moved their base of operations to Chicago and recorded for the Library of Congress in 1936. A year later, they added lead tenor R. H. Harris, whose advanced concept of modern gospel harmony included alternating leads between two singers, and they became one of the nation's top gospel acts from the 40s on. Harris was replaced by Cooke in 1950, and the charismatic young singer led the group to new heights on Specialty Records through 1956. When Cooke left to go pop, he was succeeded by Jonnie Taylor, later to experience soul hitdom himself. Jimmy Outler and James Phelps also handled front work for a time, and by the mid 60s, when they were signed to Chess, Willie Rogers and Martin Jacox traded leads. A quarter-century later, Rogers and Jacox still lead the active group. –BD

● **The Gospel Soul of Sam Cooke - Vol. 2 / SPECIALTY**
The Gospel Soul of Sam Cooke & the Soul Stirrers - Vol. 2 is being promoted under Sam Cooke's name, but it's really the Stirrers' show with first-class titles like "Farther Along" and "I'm So Glad." Some of Cooke's greatest moments, ca. 1951-1955, with great second-lead support from Paul Foster Sr. Includes three previously unreleased cuts. –KL

○ **Shine on Me / SPECIALTY**
Contains 26 previously released tracks, alternate takes, and unissued tracks (ca. 1950) by this legendary quintet and features postwar gospel group's finest and most influential soloist, R. H. Harris. –OPLN

Sam Cooke with the Soul Stirrers / SPECIALTY   1992
This 1992 reissue features previously unreleased material. Sam Cooke incorporated the styles of Archie Brownlee, R. H. Harris, and Julius Cheeks (along with his own natural abilities) to become, as many say, the best all-around gospel and R&B singer ever. This recording gives 25 reasons why people might say that. –BW

SOUNDS OF BLACKNESS

CCM. This 30-piece choir and orchestra, formed in 1971 by Gary Hines at Macalester College in Minnesota, combine traditional African elements with contemporary R&B. –BC

○ **Evolution of Gospel / A&M**
Primitive, funky, secularized gospel. –BC

GREG AND REBECCA SPARKS

CCM. Husband-and-wife duo who left dance-rockers Bash-N-the-Code to concentrate on acoustic-based rock. They released two albums as Sparks (not to be confused with secular new-wave duo) before adding their first names for 1992's *Field of Your Soul.* –BM

○ **Through Flood and Fire / REUNION**   1990
Using the Memphis Horns and Russ Taff guitarist James Hollihan Jr, this duo (under the moniker Sparks) made a record that matches the power of its convictions. –BM

THE SPEER FAMILY   b 1921

Southern gospel. The Speers emerged when there were countless Southern gospel quartets and are noteworthy because of their longevity. Though personnel has changed over the years, their music in the 90s is true to the music they were making when the group was formed by patriarch G. T. in 1921. This group is an important reference point in the appreciation of traditional Southern gospel quartet singing. Current lineup: Brock, Ben, and Faye Speer; Robin Mew; Jane Green; Bill Itzel; and Martin Johnson. –BC

Hallelujah Time / HB   1990
○ **He's Still in the Fire / HB**   1990

SPIRIT OF MEMPHIS

Black gospel. This quartet includes Silas Steele (baritone), Jet Bledsoe, James Darling, and Wilmer Broadnax. –BC

○ **When Mother's Gone / GOSPEL JUBILEE**
First-class material from 1948-1958, this includes an enlightening 15-minute radio show. Great lead vocals by "Little Ax" Broadnax, Jet Bledsoe, and Silas Steele. –KL

THE STAPLES SINGERS

Soul/R&B. One of the genre's best-known family groups, they began making records for Vee Jay in 1955. Like many of their Chicago contemporaries, the Staples family has its roots in the mid-South, and "Pop" Staples began his career as a Delta bluesman. Though they are primarily known as gospel singers, the Staples have enjoyed commercial appeal and artistic integrity in the popular field as well. This has been particularly true since they began recording. –KL

Freedom Highway / CBS
A reissue of their first great Riverside collection, with "Daddy" Roebuck and the legendary Mavis Staples as leads. The Staples once again mix a positive political message with a dash of religion. –KL

○ **Greatest Hits / FANTASY**
A reissue of some of the fine Riverside sides (ca. 1962-1964) produced by Orrin Keepnews. This package actually does contain many of their best-known selections (like "Hammer and Nails") and is a good value for the money. –KL

Be Attitude: Respect Yourself / STAX   1978
An interesting diversion into the realm of popular music mixed with a spiritual message. –KL

Best of the Staples Singers / STAX   1990
A reasonable cross-section of their mid-period work. –KL

CANDI STATON   b 1940

Soul/R&B. Born in Hanceville, AL, Staton recorded at Fame Studios. She had disco hits on the Warner label in the late 70s and has done gospel work since 1982. Her weekly music show on the Trinity Broadcasting Network is "New Direction." Staton is one of the overlooked interpreters of Southern soul ballads in the Muscle Shoals sound. Serious listeners will appreciate her hoarsely coarse vocals on such sensual, sassy cuts as "That's How Strong My Love Is" and "I'd Rather Be an Old Man's Sweetheart (Than a Young One's Fool)." She brings equal passion to gospel recordings now that she's exited the secular industry. –BC

★ **I'm Just a Prisoner / ST**   1970
Rick Hall's horns, creeping piano, and Staton's grit. –BC

Young Hearts Run Free / WARNER   1976
Soul meets disco on this classy dance record with tender downbeats. –BC

○ **Love Lifted Me / BERACAH**   1988
Traditional gospel reflecting her deep-South roots. –BC

Stand Up & Be a Witness / BERACAH   1989
Urban, upbeat psalms and exhortations. –BC

RANDY STONEHILL

CCM. This singer and guitarist writes inspirational, humanitarian soft-rock cuts, often with an easy humor, that are on the fringes of Jesus rock. His appearance in the film *Son of Blob* in the 60s led to work with Billy Graham's World Wide Pictures and later to an introduction to Pat Boone. Boone produced Stonehill's first album, *Born Twice*, on One Way Records in 1971. –BC

○ **Welcome to Paradise / WORD**   1976
Shameless rock & roll. Catchy tunes. –BC

Wonderama / MYRRH   1991
A singer/songwriter album that comes off like pop music, not a confessional. Stonehill gets sarcastic when he writes with producer Terry Taylor ("Great Big Stupid World," "Barbie Nation"), but the sarcasm sounds humorous, not smug. The incredibly touching "Sing in Portuguese" is reason enough for the existence of CCM. –BM

STRYPER

Heaven's metal. A hard-rock/heavy metal CCM quartet founded in Orange County, CA, in 1983. At the time they signed to Enigma Records in 1984, the group consisted of lead singer Michael Sweet, guitarist Oz Fox, bassist Timothy Gaines, and drummer Robert Sweet. Their first recording was the mini-album *The Yellow and Black Attack*, followed by 1985's full-length album, *Soldiers Under Command*, which reached #84 on the charts. Engima remixed *The Yellow and Black Attack* and added two songs in 1986, and the new version hit #103. Stryper's second (or third) album *To Hell with the Devil* (1986) went gold and earned the band a Grammy nomination. *In God We Trust* (1988) repeated this success. *Against the Law* (1990) was somewhat less of a hit. –WR

○ **Can't Stop the Rock / HOLLYWOOD**
Can't Stop the Rock: The Stryper Collection 1984-1991 features thundering drums, wailing guitars, keening choruses, pseudo-castrati singing — all the accoutrements of metal, and here in the service of the Lord. This best-of selects from the group's five previous recordings. –WR
In God We Trust / HOLLYWOOD
Balanced soft-rock/metal guitar licks. –BC

THE SWAN SILVERTONES

Black gospel. The Swan Silvertones began their career in the late 30s as the Four Harmony Kings, a community quartet based in Charleston, WV. They were initially influenced by the Golden Gate Quartet and other jubilee-style a cappella groups. Their big break came around 1940 when the Swan Bread Company agreed to sponsor their daily fifteen-minute program on Knoxville's powerful WNOX. Part of the group's continued appeal has been a willingness to update their sound to meet changing trends; they were among the first quartets, for example, to add a rhythm section in the early 50s. –KL

○ **Get Your Soul Right / CHARLY**
A reissue of various 50s and 60s singles and album sides plus two unissued cuts. Lead vocal dynamics from Rev. Claude Jeter, Paul Owens, and Louis Johnson. This well-rounded and amply annotated cross-section deserves serious consideration. –KL

★ **My Rock/Love Lifted Me / SPECIALTY**
Some of the best hard-gospel harmonizing from the middle 50s, most notably "How I Got Over" and "My Rock." The group's toughest sides, with firm conviction from lead soloists Solomon Womack, Rev. Bob Crenshaw, Dewey Young, and Paul Owens. –KL

Day By Day / SAVOY　　　　　　　　　　　　　1972
An adequate set, but not thrilling. –KL

Get Right with the Swan Silvertones / RHINO　1982
A thoughtful compilation covering many years and several eras of their career. –KL

RUSS TAFF　　　　　　　　　　　　　　　b1953

CCM. Taff first gained recognition as lead vocalist for the Imperials, 1977-1981, but quickly gained a reputation as one of Christian music's most powerful and versatile artists, one whose music could hold its own against the best mainstream acts. His dynamic vocals reflect both the joys and the struggles of the Christian faith. –BM

Medals / HORIZON　　　　　　　　　　　　　1985
Feel-good music with hooks and Taff's soulful tenor. –BC

☆ **Russ Taff / MYRRH**　　　　　　　　　　　　1987
Pop soul, showcasing his somber lyrics and growth as a songwriter. –BC

The Way Home / WORD　　　　　　　　　　　1990
More rock-edged than his previous sides. –BC

★ **Under Their Influence - Vol. 1 / WORD**　　　1991
The musical roots of most CCM artists lie pretty close to the surface, but that's not the case with Taff, the son of a Pentecostal evangelist who preached in California migrant territory. Here Taff pays tribute to Blind Willie Johnson, Brother Joe May, and Mahalia Jackson, among others, with an album that provides the link between gut-level gospel and Southern rock. –BM

TAKE 6

CCM. A group of six men who formed their act on the campus of the Seventh Day Adventists' Oakwood College in Alabama. Their style is a modernized facsimile of the Mills Brothers and the like. –BC

○ **Take 6 / WARNER**　　　　　　　　　　　　　1989
Jazzy a cappella 40s nostalgia applied to gospel. –BC

So Much 2 Say / WARNER　　　　　　　　　　1990
Slightly more contemporary than their debut. –BC

STEVE TAYLOR

CCM. Sometimes referred to as the "clown prince of Christian music," Steve Taylor brought sarcasm and satire to Christian music. His acerbic lyrics engendered enough controversy to place him among the most visible Christian rockers of the mid 80s. Ultimately he felt stifled by the industry and quit recording for the Christian market, but resurfaced as the lead singer of Chagall Guevara in 1991. –BM

○ **I Predict 1990 / MYRRH**　　　　　　　　　　1987
It's small surprise the Christian community all but disowned Taylor after songs like "I Blew Up the Clinic Real Good" and "Since I Gave Up Hope I Feel a Lot Better." The songs on *I Predict 1990* don't look for easy answers — they rarely look for answers at all — and they're often unsettling. But half of Taylor's point is that life rarely gives easy answers. The other half is in the final song: "Harder to Believe Than Not To." –BM

★ **The Best We Could Find / SPARROW**　　　　1988
This compilation makes an excellent introduction to Taylor's iconoclastic songwriting, with music that frequently sounds like a new-wave Christian sideshow. Taylor gets his licks in on modern culture with "Meltdown (At Madame Tussaud's)," but he more often turns his gaze on the church with songs like "I Want to Be a Clone" and "This Disco (Used to Be a Cute Cathedral)." –BM

SISTER ROSETTA THARPE　　　　　　1921-1973

Black gospel. Born in Cotton Plant, AK, Sister Tharpe toured with P. W. McGhee's tent revivals as a child, singing and strumming guitar. She signed a record deal with Decca in 1938. In addition to her work with gospel artists, she performed folk/blues with Muddy Waters and Lucky Millinder and had R&B Top Ten hits with "Strange Things," "Up Above My Head," and "Silent Night." In a duo with Marie Knight in 1947-1954, their most-noted songs were "Didn't It Rain," "This Train," and "I Looked Down the Line." –BC

○ **Gospel Train / POLYGRAM**
These are great late-50s Mercury sides with Ernest Hayes on piano and Doc Bagby on organ, among others. The album contains good performances of some of Tharpe's most popular selections. –KL

Gospel Train - Vol. 2 / POLYGRAM
Recorded later than the material on Volume 1, some of Sister Rosetta's worst, most-overproduced recordings. –OPLN

Live in Paris — 1964 / FRENCH CONCERTS　1964
A nice, rather folk-like concert performance in front of an enthusiastic audience. –KL

KATHY TROCCOLI

CCM. Next to Amy Grant and Sandi Patti, New Yorker Kathy Troccoli was probably CCM's most popular female singer before leaving the business in 1986 when her record label, Reunion, couldn't produce the mainstream stardom she sought. Troccoli returned to Reunion when the label had mainstream possibilities (after signing a distribution pact with Geffen) to release hit *Pure Attraction* in 1991. –BM

○ **Pure Attraction / REUNION**　　　　　　　　1991
Troccoli's first recording after a five-year absence was her most commercial, with the Diane Warren-penned "Everything Changes" hitting Top Five on CHR radio. Troccoli had developed her songwriting during her time away; she wrote seven of *Pure Attraction's* cuts, emphasizing the torch-song style she loves. –BM

THE TRUMPETEERS

Black gospel. Influenced by the Golden Gate Quartet and led by the spectacular singing of Joe Johnson, this quartet hit the public's consciousness in the late 40s with "Milky White Way," which they recorded for Score Records. Other members included Raleigh Tunrage (tenor), Joseph Armstrong (baritone), and James Keels (bass). There were numerous personnel changes, and they disbanded upon Johnson's death in 1948. –BC & KL

☆ **Milky White Way / GOSPEL JUBILEE**
A wonderful sampling of the recordings made by this first-rate a cappella vocal group during the late 40s and early 50s. The title cut became one of this postwar quartet's heaviest-selling gospel 78s. Fine, smooth lead choruses from Joseph Johnson. –KL

THE TRUTHETTES

Spiritual. The Oklahoma City-based Morgan Sisters began recording in the late 80s. Personnel: Tiffanie and Tammy Morgan, Jennifer and Angela Tooley. –BC

Flowing / MALACO
Strong harmonies on this album of organ-dominated modern Black music. –KL

God Will Make Things Alright / MALACO
Half traditional, half contemporary. –BC

○ **Every Step of the Way / MALACO**   1987
Contemporary-style traditional gospel. –KL

THE TWELFTH TRIBE

Street poetry. The California duo of Dave Portillo and Eddie Sierra began rapping in 1985 under the name of Deity. Influenced by soul and heavy metal, they like the rap of Kool Mo Dee, Houdini, and the Fat Boys. They take their name from the twelfth tribe of Israel: the Benjamites, mighty warriors. They portray a tougher image than most Christian rap artists and have a hard street rap sound. –BC

○ **Knowledge Is the Tribe of Life / FRONTLINE**   1991
Produced, engineered, and mixed by master urban dance musician Scott Blackwell who easily moves into the hard, funky side of Christian rap here. There are 15 rhymes on war, peace, and knowing God. The sound is very Black, very hard, with a few metal elements; a good set though not overly original outside of the gospel music industry. –BC

GREG X. VOLZ

CCM. Former singer with "e" and Petra rock bands. –BC

○ **Come Out Fighting / WORD**   1988
Light vocals with mid range guitar backing. –BC

ALBERTINA WALKER   b 1930

Black gospel. Born in Chicago, Walker sang with the Pete Williams Singers and the Robert Anderson Singers before forming the Caravans in 1951. Among the Caravans' classics were "Mary Don't You Weep," "Soldiers in the Army," "The Solid Rock," and "The Blood Will Never Lose Its Power." Since 1960 Walker has been a solo singer, maintaining her ties to traditional gospel. –BC

○ **God Is Love / POLYGRAM**
A fine collection by this influential performer. –KL

Tell the Angels / SAVOY   1960
Her 1960 debut, after the Caravans. –BC

You Believed in Me / BENSON   1991
This recent album includes "Working on a Building." –BC

SHEILA WALSH

CCM. The co-hostess of the 700 Club came onto the scene as a punk-rock British expatriate. –BC

○ **Don't Hide Your Heart / SPARROW**   1985
This creative album, with pop overtones on the fringes of punk, makes good use of Walsh's high soprano. –BC

Say So / WORD   1988
Avant-garde rock gospel, with a reworking of "Love Is the Answer." –BC

CLARA WARD & THE WARD SINGERS   1924-1972

Black gospel. The Clara Ward Singers scored in the 50s with swinging traditional Black gospel songs like "Packing Up, Getting Ready to Go." In the 60s they became a mainstay, performing at Las Vegas hotels and drawing the wrath of the gospel music industry for "selling out." Ward died after suffering a stroke in 1972. The remaining members and new personnel continue to perform under the same name. –BC

The Clara Ward Singers / ROULETTE
Includes pleasant but not essential selections by this popular group. –KL

○ **The Clara Ward Singers / FORUM CIRCLE**
Recorded live at the Apollo, with traditional cuts like "Old Time Religion." –BC

ERNESTINE WASHINGTON

Gospel. Born in Arkansas, Madame Ernestine B. Washington grew up on the sanctified gospel of the 20s, singing primarily for her husband's church and denomination, Washington Temple C.O.G.I.C. Though inspired by the controlled Baptist style of the Roberta Martin Singers, she had a strident voice and was known to be a singing shouter in the mode of Mahalia Jackson. Her rare and most important recordings were executed from the late 40s through the 50s. –BC

○ **In Washington Temple / COLLECTORS ISSUE**
Gospel Singing in Washington Temple. Sensational solos supported rousingly by Brooklyn's Congregation of the Washington Temple C.O.G.I.C. Reissue of material recorded in 1958. –OPLN

WAYNE WATSON

CCM. Born in Wisner, LA, he is a meditative, cerebral performer known for gut-wrenching ballads early on, but now known for serious commentary on Christian living. –BC

Watercolour Ponies / WORD   1987
Children-inspired rock/pop ballads. –BC

○ **Fine Line / WORD**   1988
Sober, down-tempo reflections on life and faith. –BC

WHITE HEART

CCM. Band of "musician's musicians" with a revolving-door membership; their sound borders on hard-rock/prog-rock. Original vocalist Steve Green became a major inspirational act as a solo artist. Founder and guitarist Dann Huff became Los Angeles' premier studio guitarist in the late 80s before forming the arena rock group, Giant; bassist Tommy Sims joined Bruce Springsteen's road band in 1992. –BM

Freedom / SPARROW   1989
White Heart took the album's name to heart, allowing themselves more creative leeway on this than on any previous album. Most Christian arena-rock sounds derivative of its secular counterparts — not *Freedom*; even its weak spots are undeniably original. –BM

○ **Souvenirs / SPARROW**   1990
White Heart found its voice in 1986 with *Don't Wait for the Movie*, the first album with lead singer Rick Florian. *Souvenirs* collects the productive years that followed, including five tracks from *Freedom* and an unusual hard-rock remake of "The Little Drummer Boy." –BM

STEVE WIGGINS

CCM. Outspoken young singer/songwriter (and sometimes street evangelist) from Memphis by way of Arkansas. –BM

○ **Steve Wiggins / SPARROW**   1991
The bare-bones production of Wiggins's debut captures the direct, almost confrontational religious nature of his songwriting. He's got the soul of a street preacher and the heart of a Memphis rocker. –BM

STEPHEN WILEY

Street poetry. Wiley was the original gospel rapper, but his lightweight talents have been superseded by more skilled practitioners. −BC

○ **Rhythm and Poetry / STAR SONG**   1990
Hip-hop music. Sharper MC skills and a pop sound. −BC

THE WILLIAMS BROTHERS

Black gospel. The group was organized in 1960 by Leon "Pop" Williams, who is the founder and father of the Williams Brothers. They were then known as the Little Williams Brothers, but as the group grew in talent, experience, and performance, the name changed to the Sensational Williams Brothers. Today the group is simply called the Williams Brothers. All of the group members were born and reared in Mississippi in a little community called "Smithdale," about 100 miles south of Jackson, MS, where a road has been named in their honor. They have been writing and arranging most of their music since 1970 and producing since 1979.
The group recorded its first album in 1973 on the Songbird label, which included the instant hit, "Jesus Will Fix It." Since then they have recorded 16 albums listed as Top Ten in *Billboard* and *Cashbox* magazines, out of which came three #1 records and a Grammy nomination. Their repertoire of hits includes songs such as "Jesus Will Never Say No," "I Won't Let Go My Faith," "He'll Understand," "Sweep around Your Own Front Door," and "A Ship Like Mine," to name a few. They also performed on the Winans's grammy-winning song, "Ain't No Need to Worry," featuring Anita Baker. In April 1991 the group formed their own record label, Blackberry Records, which is the first Black-owned and-operated label in the state of Mississippi that has major distribution. Their first release on the label, "This Is Your Night," reached #4 on the *Billboard* gospel chart. −BW

Ain't Love Wonderful / MALACO
Strong material; solid production. −HD

○ **Blessed / MALACO**
Slick, well-crafted modern gospel, complete with synthesizer, strings, and percussion overdubs. −HD

DENIECE WILLIAMS   ♭1950

Soul/R&B. Born in Gary, IN, she sang with Wonderlove before signing with Columbia in 1976 and cutting sweet soul sides in high soprano. This singer/songwriter and backing singer with Stevie Wonder has had, from 1975 to the present, solo hits with "Let's Hear It for the Boy" and the duet "Too Much, Too Little, Too Late." −BC

○ **So Glad I Know / SPARROW**   1987
Her urban-pop gospel debut. −BC

DEWEY WILLIAMS

Black gospel. Born at the turn of the century, Williams has been the leader of the African-American shape-note movement in Southern Alabama for over 50 years. In the late 80s, he was honored with a Heritage Award from the National Endowment for the Arts/Folk Arts. −KL

☆ **Wiregrass Notes: Black Sacred Harp Singing from the South / WIREGRASS MUSIC**
This is a self-produced cassette of a rare Black religious tradition that is downhome and unique. −KL

MARION WILLIAMS   ♭1927

Black gospel. Born in Miami, Williams sang with a Florida gospel group before joining the Famous Ward Singers (later the Clara Ward Singers) in 1947. Upon leaving the group in 1959, she formed the Stars of Faith, which she left in 1965. She starred on Broadway and in a global tour of *Black Nativity* in the early 60s. She has been singing since the late 60s and is known for her sweet but muscular style of traditional Black gospel. −BC

Somebody Bigger Than You and I / SAVOY
Her first album after leaving the Ward Singers. Recorded in 1958, it includes "I Can't Forget." −BC

O Holy Night / SAVOY   1959
A Christmas album with the Stars of Faith. −BC

○ **Surely God Is Able / SPIRIT FEEL**   1989
A very strong soloist who reworked classic gospel material from the 30s and 40s into a wonderful 1989 album. −KL

★ **Strong Again / SPIRIT FEEL**   1991
Eclectic though satisfying 20-cut album by this major singer, her most impressive solo set in recent years. Sparse accompaniment; mainly traditional material. Excellent. −KL

BEBE AND CECE WINANS

Gospel. Born in Detroit, MI, they sang as the PTL Singers before launching a career as a duo in 1987. They have crossed over from gospel success to mainstream success in the secular market with their jazz-like, low-tempo style of R&B with inspirational lyrics. −BC

○ **Lord Lift Us Up / PTL**   1985
Pop/MOR-oriented praise tunes. −BC

Bebe & Cece Winans / CAPITOL   1987
R&B, urban-crossover CCM ballads. −BC

Addictive Love / SPARROW   1991
More of the same, with Mavis Staples and MC Hammer. −BC

THE WINANS

CCM. These four brothers hail from Detroit, MI. Their contemporary Black gospel style reflects traditional Black gospel roots. They sang gospel all their lives and began their professional careers in the 80s. Members: Marvin, Carvin, Ronald, and Michael Winan. They have performed several times with the likes of Michael McDonald, Anita Baker, and Vanessa Bell Armstrong. −BC

○ **Tomorrow / LIGHT**
The title track, a sparkling MOR-style ballad, is the hymn of the 80s. −BC

Live at Carnegie Hall / QWEST
A dynamic concert, with all the hits drawn out, on this double album. −BC

Let My People Go / QWEST   1985
Their distinctive, muddy, percussive, and jazzy sound. −BC

Decisions / QWEST   1987
Fine R&B with Anita Baker and Michael McDonald. −BC

Return / WARNER   1990
New jack swing and urban soul. −BC

GOSPEL COLLECTIONS

☆ **Ain't That Good News / SPECIALTY**
Super 50s gospel from the Specialty vaults, compiled by Barrett Hanson (aka Dr. Demento). Each cut is a true gem. Of special interest to audiophiles: the tracks carefully segue into each other, with no space between (which could be annoying to some). A spellbinding effect and a great album. −BLP

○ **All of My Appointed Time / STASH**
Some of the finest a cappella gospel performances from the fabulous Famous Blue Jay Singers and other greats can be found on this collection. −KL

Assassination / ZU-ZAZZ
Fine 60s quartet music. Primary features include Ollie Nightingale & the Dixie Nightingales, and the famous Memphis Gospel Writers. −OPLN

○ **Atlanta Gospel / GOSPEL HERITAGE**
A regionally focused compilation by very fine (but virtually unknown) groups like the Five Trumpets and the National Independent Gospel Singers. Drawn from rare 78 RPM sides ca. 1946-1951. −KL

○ **The Best of Gotham Gospel / GOSPEL HERITAGE**
This welcome CD covers the extensive Philadelphia-based Gotham label. Drawn from previously unreleased and rare sides from the 40s and 50s. –KL

○ **Black Religious Singers (1927-42) / HANS KLEMENT**
Extremely rare gospel soloist material by nine performers, notably Rev. D. C. Rice, Sister Clara Hudmon, Elder Curry, and Bozie Sturdivant. –OPLN

○ **Bless My Bones / ROUNDER**
Bless My Bones: Memphis Gospel Radio - 1950s highlights eight stellar ensembles in a stunning set of radio transcriptions from Memphis's WDIA. Includes "99 & 1/2 Won't Do" by the Song Birds of the South and "Milky White Way" by the Spirit of Memphis, as well as tracks by the Dixie Nightingales, Southern Wonders, and Sunset Travelers. –JF

○ **Chicago Gospel Pioneers / SPIRIT FEEL**
Fine contemporary recordings by Delois Barrett Campbell, Robert Anderson, and Little Lucy Smith. –KL

○ **Country Gospel Guitar Classics (1927-51) / WOLF**
Quintessential guitar rarities from A. C. and Blind Mamie Forehand, Dennis Crumpton, Robert Summers, Sister Mathews, Willie Mae Williams, and Sister O. M. Terrell. –OPLN

☆ **Early Negro Vocal Quartets (1894-1928) / DOCUMENT**
A strong collection of mostly religious sides by some pioneering a cappella groups, beginning with an 1894 cylinder by the Standard Quartet. –KL

○ **Get Right with God / GOSPEL HERITAGE**
An eclectic, exceptionally entertaining overview of African-American gospel solo and quartet material popular in the early, post-WWII era. –KL

○ **Glad I Found the Lord / GOSPEL HERITAGE**
Glad I Found the Lord - Chicago Gospel 1937-1957. Leading quartets, including the Famous Blue Jays, Pilgrim Jubilees, Norfolk Singers, and Kelly Brothers, spanning the years 1937 through 1957. –OPLN

○ **Go Devil Go - Modern/Kent Gospel Masters / P-VINE**
Distinguished postwar female aggregations plus the notable veteran Prof. James Earle Hines and Rev. G. W. Killens, from rare 78 RPM material. –OPLN

○ **Going on Home to Glory / P-VINE**
Going on Home to Glory - Trumpet Gospel Anthology. Priceless quartet music from the early 50s. Featuring the Blue Jay Gospel Singers, Carolina Kings of Harmony, Argo Gospel Singers, and others. –OPLN

○ **The Golden Age of Gospel Singing / FOLKLYRIC**
The Five Blind Boys, Zion Travelers, and others provide an invaluable overview of gospel quartet singing from the late 40s and early 50s. –KL

○ **Gospel Evangelists / GOSPEL HERITAGE**
Gospel Evangelists - Go's Mighty Hand. Various prewar and postwar soloists, most recorded with guitar accompaniment. Standouts include Rev. Utah Smith, Sister O. M. Terrell, Rev. Anderson Johnson, Mary De Loatch, and Joe Townsend. –OPLN

○ **Gospel Rarities (1926-1930) / EDEN**
Prime rare 78 RPM material focusing on five soloists, the most impressive being Rev. P. W. Williams and Homer Quincy Smith. –OPLN

○ **Gospel Stars in Concert / SPECIALTY**
Historically and spiritually important early-50s live performances by the Gospel Harmonettes with Dorothy Love Coates, Brother Joe May, and the Pilgrim Travelers. Side 2 features three riveting cuts by Sam Cooke and the Soul Stirrers. –JF

○ **The Gospel Tradition / COLUMBIA-LEGACY**   1991
The *Gospel Tradition: The Roots and the Branches - Vol. 1* is one of the few gospel collections that ignores the barriers between White and Black gospel music, *The Gospel Tradition* contrasts the blues of Bessie Smith and the Western swing of Bob Wills, the rough edge of Mitchell's Christian Singers and the smooth polish of the Sons of the Pioneers. Lots of obscure sides dating

back to 1927, and a wide range of styles from sanctified women to choral spirituals. –BM

☆ **Gospel Warriors / SPIRIT FEEL**
Gospel Warriors: 50s Years of Great Solo Performances is not misnamed and does include some of gospel's most moving soloists from the 40s to the present, most notably Bessie Griffin. –KL

○ **Gotham Gospel - Vols. 1 & 2 / COLLECTABLES**
A noteworthy two-volume anthology of obscure Black quartets from the "golden era" of a cappella gospel singing. Late-40s to early-50s recordings emphasize unissued and alternative takes. Very intense and emotional. –HD

☆ **Great Golden Gospel Hits - Vol. 4 / SAVOY GOSPEL**
A tremendous and far-reaching assortment of vintage gospel by such masters as the Ward Singers, the Davis Sisters, the Staples Singers, and the Gospel Harmonettes. –JF

○ **Greatest Gospel Gems / SPECIALTY**
An excellent 24-song sampling of 50s and 60s sacred testifying from the vaults of Specialty Records. Includes essential cuts from Dorothy Love Coates, the Swan Silvertones, and Sam Cooke and the Soul Stirrers. –JF

○ **I Hear the Music in the Air ... / RCA**   1990
I Hear the Music in the Air: A Treasury of Gospel Music offers great quartet-style singing (and three mini-sermons too!) for RCA Victor between 1926 and 1942. Features the likes of the Golden Gate Jubilee Quartet, the Morris Brown Quartet, and the Southern Sons. Also includes the first recording of Thomas Dorsey's "Precious Lord, Take My Hand," performed in 1937 by the Heavenly Gospel Singers. –BM

○ **In the Spirit - Vol. 2 / OJL**   1968
○ **'N-Effect / FRONTLINE**   1992
Christian rap compilation highlighted by cuts from the influential P.I.D. and the late D-Boy Rodriguez. MC Hammer guests on Jon Gibson's "The Wall." –BM

○ **Jesus Is Listening / P-VINE**
Jesus is Listening - Modern/Kent Gospel Masters. Treasure trove of postwar male quartets (late 40s/early 50s). The Echoes of Zion of Atlanta, Swanee River Quartet, and others. –OPLN

☆ **Jubilation - Vol. 1 - Black Gospel / RHINO**   1992
The Rhino *Jubilation: Great Gospel Performances* series is a terrific overview of Black gospel and country gospel. If you don't buy any other gospel CDs, or if you're looking for a good place to start, try this set. The first volume includes Mahalia Jackson, the Swan Silvertones, the Soul Stirrers, Aretha Franklin with James Cleveland, Shirley Caesar, the Trumpeteers, and many others. –BW

☆ **Jubilation - Vol. 2 - More Black Gospel / RHINO**   1992
Like the titles says, more of the same as the first volume, including the Staples Singers, the Original Gospel Harmonettes, Prof. Alex Bradford, the Harmonizing Four, Sam Cooke with the Soul Stirrers, and more. –ED

○ **Jubilation - Vol. 3 - Country Gospel / RHINO**   1992
Although slightly weaker than the the first two, this features tracks by Hank Williams, Kitty Wells, Patsy Cline, the Carter Family, the Louvin Brothers, Webb Pierce, Doyle Lawson & Quicksilver, Bill Monroe, and others. –ED

○ **Memphis Gospel Quartets / HIGH WATER**
Many of the interesting community-based groups on *Memphis Gospel Quartets - Happy in the Service of the Lord* make their recording debut here. –KL

○ **New York Grassroots Gospel / GLOBAL VILLAGE**
New York Grassroots Gospel - The Sacred Black Quartet contains strong recordings from the late 80s of contemporary but older-style quartets. –KL

○ **No Compromise ... / SPARROW**   1992
No Compromise: Remembering the Music of Keith Green. Petra, Steven Curtis Chapman, Russ Taff, and others cover songs by the late Keith Green, probably CCM's most influential early songwriter and performer. Most of the chosen material has worn fairly well over the years. –BM

○ **Preachin' the Gospel: Holy Blues / COLUMBIA**
This fascinating sampler encompasses all of the important forms of religious music expression from the 20s and 30s, except vocal groups. —KL

○ **Raisin' the Roof / MOBILE FIDELITY**
Indispensable early-60s Sunsets material with O. V. Wright, Rev. Julius Cheeks and the 4 Knights, plus great Swan Silvertones material led by Claude Jeter and Louis Johnson, from 60s Vee Jay sources. —OPLN

○ **Religious Recordings (1924-1931) / FIVE-O-FOUR**
Religious Recordings from Black New Orleans 1942-1931. A first-rate booklet and first-rate recordings make this a model for presenting historical recordings. —KL

○ **Rural Gospel Styles (1944-1951) / EDEN**
The two Gospel Keys plus gems by Rev. Utah Smith, Rev. Chas White, Sister Littlejohn, Prophet B. West, and Brother Willie Easton. Essential. —OPLN

○ **Sanctified Country Girls / WOLF**
A fascinating collection of pentecostal-style gospel performances by wonderful (though obscure) artists: Jessie Mae Hill, Cally Fancy, and Rev. Sister Mary Nelson. —KL

○ **Say Amen Somebody / DRG**
The soundtrack from the wonderful documentary film of the same name. —KL

○ **16 Golden Gospel Greats / TRIPINDICULAR**
Late 50s sides from the Vee Jay label. Prime work from the Harmonizing Four and others. —HD

○ **Something Got a Hold of Me / RCA**   1983
Country music has always had strong ties to Christianity, and this collection of RCA Victor country-gospel music from 1927-1941 demonstrates that heritage, starting with the Carter Family and continuing through the Monroe Brothers, Bill

Monroe, the Blue Sky Boys, Uncle Dave Macon, and others. The standouts are A. P. Carter's title track and Dorsey Dixon's "I Didn't Hear Nobody Pray," but there is an outpouring of fervor for "the old-time religion" through every one of these performances. —WR

○ **Stained Glass Hour / ROUNDER**   1992
Ricky Skaggs dominates this collection, both as a bandleader and as a member of Boone Creek and J. D. Crowe and the New South. Beyond that, *Stained Glass Hour: Bluegrass and Old-Timey Gospel Music* is an excellent sampler of religious-based bluegrass, past (the Blue Sky Boys, the Johnson Mountain Boys) and present (the Nashville Bluegrass Band, Dry Branch Fire Squad). —BM

○ **Ten Years of Black Country Religion / YAZOO**
A first-class overview of Southern rural religious music, including striking performances by Jaybird Coleman and Crumpton & Summers. —KL

○ **The Truth in the Gospel (1937-50) / EDEN**
Essential collection of gospel divas: the first sides of Mahalia Jackson (1937), Sister Goldia Hayes with the Joe Liggins Trio, plus Sister Ernestine Washington with and without the Dixie Hummingbirds and Heavenly Gospel Singers. —OPLN

☆ **White Gospel / COLLECTABLES**
An interesting presentation of jubilee-inspired White-gospel quartets. —MH

○ **White Spirituals from the Sacred Harp / NEW WORLD**
The polyphonic shape-note tradition provides what is surely some of the world's most beautiful folk choral singing. This continuously stunning collection, recorded by Alan Lomax at the Alabama Sacred Harp Convention in 1959, is enriched by his historical and musical notes. —JSR

COUNTRY

Country music is facts-of-life music. It's the music of experience. More so than with other music genres (with the possible exception of the blues), country music echoes and reflects the heights and depths of the collective lives of its audience, who up into the 70s were predominantly working class, White, and rural. Willie Nelson, Waylon Jennings, Dolly Parton, Kenny Rogers, Roy Clark, and other superstars in the 70s brought country music to a new and huge audience — the middle class, the educated, and the urban listeners — in the process forever changing the direction of the music. Yet this was only another step in what has been a continuous evolution in country music. In this American music form, the older styles are revered and retained rather than discarded, so that they remain dear to their listeners, while at the same time contemporary country heads off into new territory, thus attracting a new group of listeners. It's always been this way, since the day country music went commercial with its first record in the mid 20s. Though to a degree change-resistant because of its adherence to tradition, country in fact changes as the lives of its listeners change. And this is the common bond of all these styles from the 20s to the present: it's all facts-of-life music, from the hillbilly string-bands of the 20s through the cowboys and honky-tonkers and outlaws and even the creamy country-pop sounds up to Randy Travis, Dolly Parton, the Judds, and Ricky Skaggs. Country music's singers and musicians perform music they have lived. And now, because country music has become a major force in the record industry — in fact, *the* major force, with Garth Brooks and number of records sold — it has been given the respect and attention long lavished upon jazz, blues, and rock.

When the lines of distinction between country and other genres of music begin to blur, traditional country reasserts itself, thus preventing the country sound from evolving to the point of equivalence with pop. Judge George Hay, founder of the Grand Ole Opry, said it best in the mid 20s when he admonished performers with "Keep it close to the ground, boys," if they strayed from the country style that prevailed at the time. The essence of country music has remained pretty much intact ever since. Its repertory derives from folk, minstrel, medicine show, vaudeville, and gospel music. Country's subject matter falls into some general categories: home and family, working-man blues, death and sorrow, cheatin', good love gone bad, prison, trains and trucks and travelling, disasters, booze and sorrow-drowning, and gospel songs (which can uplift with promised redemption or depress with likely damnation). Sobering material, but true-to-life: to paraphrase Hank Williams, none of us will ever get out of this world alive. And enough country music tells us of the good love and fun possible on this earth before we pass over to Canaan's land, that we keep on the sunny side of life, at least occasionally.

Kris Kristofferson says that if a song *sounds* country, it is. Add to this a few generalizations about instrumentation (fiddle, banjo, dobro, steel guitar, guitar, harmonica, mandolin), about vocals (pure, often stark and rough-edged, highly emotional), and about country performers (revered by and loving of their fans), and we probably know enough to stop reading and start listening to the music.

— David Vinopal

ROY ACUFF
b 1903

Traditional country. Dizzy Dean, the famous pitcher and baseball announcer, called Roy Acuff the "King of Country Music," a title that's appropriate both because of his sheer longevity in the business and also because of his influence on country music for over half a century. In 1938 he became a regular on the Grand Ole Opry; as of this writing, he remains a weekly fixture on this most famous showcase of country performers, still balancing his violin bow on his nose, and still in very good voice on his signature songs. As the Opry's first singing star, in 1962 he became the first living musician to be elected to the Country Music Hall of Fame.

After singing popular music early in his career, when he toured with a medicine show, in 1936 Acuff recorded what became his two most requested songs, the Carter Family's "Wabash Cannonball" (the archetypal traveling song) and "The Great Speckled Bird" (probably the most famous country gospel song). Both feature Acuff's high, emotional, plaintive voice, which made him country's dominant performer during World War II. His band, the Smokey Mountain Boys, featuring the dobro guitar of Bashful Brother

Oswald, nationally became identified as the country sound up until Hank Williams made his debut on the Opry in 1949. No one, not even Williams, introduced more people to country music or influenced more future stars than did Acuff. For decades, throughout the South, Saturday night meant the crystal radio, the Opry, and — most important — Roy Acuff. Because Acuff's music is a bridge betweeen the earlier string-band sound of the 1920s and the later, more modern sound of Hank Williams, a listener can't get a better sense of country music's evolution than by listening to one of Acuff's many recordings. His band featured vestiges of the old vaudeville/medicine-show acts (Acuff's balancing act and his tricks with a yo-yo, corn-bred humor, clodhopper outfits) and at the same time, polished and refined, made the dobro and harmonica respectable instruments in mainstream country music. You're not going to know country music unless you know Roy Acuff. –DV

Songs of the Smokey Mountains / CAPITOL 1949
A nice assortment of Acuff hits, including "The Great Speckled Bird," "Wabash Cannonball," "Wreck on the Highway," and "Precious Jewel." –BLP

Sources of Country Music
Minstrel, Folk, Vaudeville, Gospel — all 19th century and earlier

1920s
Hillbilly/String Band Music
Gid Tanner and the Skillet Lickers

1922:
First Country Music Recording
Fiddlin' John Carson ("The Little Old Log Cabin in the Lane")

1924:
Country's First Million-Seller
Vernon Dalhart — ("The Wreck of the Old '97")

1927
RCA-Victor scout discovers country's first superstars
Jimmie Rodgers (Blue Yodels)
Carter Family ("Wildwood Flowers," "Wabash Cannonball")
Uncle Dave Macon (The Grand Ole Opry's first star)

1950s
Nashville Country Pop
Patsy Cline — Jim Reeves — Don Gibson

Honky-Tonkers
George Jones — Webb Pierce — Hank Thompson

Chet Atkins — Country's best-known guitarist

The Louvin Brothers
Charlie and Ira Louvin
influenced the Everly Brothers and Emmylou Harris

Eddy Arnold — Country's crooner ("Cattle Call")

Faron Young — The hillbilly heartthrob

Country Women
Kitty Wells — Country's first female superstar,
leads the way ("It Wasn't God Who Made Honky-Tonk Angels")

Hank Snow — The small Nova Scotian
with a huge voice ("I'm Moving On")

Bluegrass music's classical period
Bill Monroe and His Blue Grass Boys
Jim and Jesse McReynolds
Lester Flatt and Earl Scruggs
Reno and Smiley
The Osborne Brothers

1970s
Crossover Country
Charlie Rich ("The Most Beautiful Girl")
Anne Murray ("Snowbird")
Lynn Anderson ("Rose Garden")
John Denver — Dolly Parton — Barbara Mandrell
Crystal Gayle ("Don't It Make My Brown Eyes Blue")
Mac Davis ("Don't Get Hooked on Me")
Eddie Rabbit

The Outlaws
Waylon Jennings and Willy Nelson become superstars
individually and as a duet ("Luckenbach, Texas",
"Blue Eyes Crying in the Rain")

Hee Haw continues from the 60s,
Roy Clark and Buck Owens hosting

Country Rock
Charlie Daniels Band — Hank Williams Jr

Traditional Bluegrass
urbanized and modernized into "newgrass."

Country Groups
Alabama — Statler Brothers (continue from the 60s)
Oak Ridge Boys — Gatlin Brothers

1930s
The singing cowboy rides into town
Gene Autry — Sons of the Pioneer
(including Roy Rogers) — Tex Ritter — Patsy Montana

Decade of the duets
Blue Sky boys (Bill and Emel Bolick)
Delmore Brothers (Country boogie and blues)
Lulu Belle and Scotty — McGee Brothers

String band sound is refined
transition between hillbilly and bluegrass
Bill Monroe first appears in Grand Ole Opry in 1939

Solo stars
Jimmie Davis ("You Are My Sunshine")
Roy Acuff and the Smoky Mountain Boys (1930s to present)

Western swing
Bob Willis and His Texas Playboys
Bill Boyd and the Cowboy Ramblers
Space Cooley (West Coast)

1940s
Honky-Tonk Heroes
Hank Williams — (Country's most influential performer)
Ernest Tubb and His Texas Troubadours
Ray Price — Floyd Tillman — Lefty Frizzell

Bluegrass music
Invented by Bill Monroe,
whose classic band in the mid 40s included
Lester Flatt and Earl Scruggs
Merle Travis — a great composer ("Sixteen Tons")
and guitarist who influenced Chet Atkins
Grandpa Jones — Country's enduring comic/musician

1960s
The "Bakersfield Scene
Buck Owens ("Together Again," "Act Naturally")
and Merle Haggard ("Okie from Muskogee")
these two dominate the decade

The "Saga Song"
Johnny Horton ("The Battle of New Orleans")
and Jimmy Dean ("P. T. 109," "Big Bad John")

Roger Miller — country/pop genius ("King of the Road")

Johnny Cash — the "man in black,"
reaches superstardom through TV show

Tennessee Ernie Ford continues
as king of country gospel

Charley Pride — Country's Black superstar

Country/Pop Superstars
Kenny Rogers ("Lucille");
Roy Clark ("Yesterday, When I Was Young")
Glen Campbell ("By the Time I Get to Phoenix," "Wichita Lineman")

Tom T. Hall's "Harper Valley PTA" is a hit for Jeanne C. Riley

Country Women Come of Age
Loretta Lynn ("Coal Miner's Daughter");
Tammy Wynette ("D-I-V-O-R-C-E," "Stand By Your Man,"
a duet with husband George Jones)

1980s-early 1990s
Traditional Country rebounds
Randy Travis ("On the Other Hand"),
Ricky Skaggs ("Waitin' for the Sun to Shine"),
Emmylou Harris — George Straight — John Anderson
John Conlee ("Busted") — Vince Gill

Reba McEntire wins awards by the six-pack

The Judds
Mother Naomi and daughter Wynonna — sell billions and billions

Progressive Country explores new lands
Dwight Yoakam — k.d. lang — Lyle Lovett — Carlene Carter
Pam Tillis — Rosanne Cash — Garth Brooks

○ **The Essential / SONY** 1992
Acuff recorded for Columbia when he was the undisputed "King of Country Music," so these 40s gems are the ones to hear for a taste of what so inspired the young Hank Williams and George Jones. −MH

☆ **Steamboat Whistle Blues / ROUNDER**
Fine early (1936-1939) Roy Acuff band versions of blues, pop, and old-time country. −BLP

ALABAMA

Country rock. In 1989 this foursome with 21 straight #1 singles and nearly 80 major awards received the Artist of the Decade Award from the Academy of Country Music. As you might infer, this is the most popular country group in record history, in terms of records sold. Originally called Wildcountry, their country-pop material and delivery are showcased in two of their best-known hits, "My Home's in Alabama" and "Mountain Music." −DV

My Home's in Alabama / RCA 1980
The album that started it all for Alabama. Their Southern rock influences are obvious but encased in a country context. The title track's sentiment is overwhelming, whether you're from Alabama or Iowa. −TR

Feels So Right / RCA 1981
On their second album, Alabama's apparently more comfortable with the studio. The harmonies are tighter than in the debut, but the material selection — heavy on uptempo tunes — shows that the club mentality developed at the Bowery is still very much intact. Three hits — the title track, "Love in the First Degree," "Old Flame" — but nearly all the extra cuts are strong as well. −TR

○ **Mountain Music / RCA** 1982
Their best effort. The group hadn't quite fallen into any formulas, and as a result, they cover the stylistic gamut pretty well. The title track practically defined what country groups have strived to accomplish, and the group slides easily from sentiment, to social relevance, to out-and-out partying. −TR

● **Greatest Hits / RCA** 1986
The best of their early material, including "Mountain Music" and others. −CK

Southern Star / RCA 1989
After eight very successful years with record producer Harold Shedd, Alabama wisely opts for change. Half the album is recorded with Josh Leo and Larry Lee, the other half with Barry Beckett, and the guys from Fort Payne attack the project with a little more energy than in some of their prior efforts. Get it on CD — three of the four "bonus" tracks are substantial. −TR

Greatest Hits - II / RCA 1991
Companion piece to the above with more emphasis on ballad material. −CK

BILL ANDERSON b 1937

Traditional country. His nickname, "Whisperin' Bill," originated from his quiet vocal delivery and his numerous recitation songs, delivered in a low-key, hushed voice. Anderson came to fame with his self-penned "City Lights" was turned into a hit by Ray Price in 1958. In the 60s he wrote and recorded numerous hits, including "Mama Sang a Song" (a narration), "Still" (his signature tune), and "I Get the Fever." and in the 60s he had his own syndicated TV show. He remains an Opry regular. −DV

○ **Greatest Hits / MCA**
Budget CD package of the absolute essential best, including the classic "Still." −CK

JOHN ANDERSON b 1954

Country. Growing up in Apopka, FL, John Anderson was enamored with the Beatles and the Rolling Stones, like most of his peers. But, when he heard a Merle Haggard album at age 15, he found his true calling. Anderson headed for Nashville,

where he showed up unannounced on his sister's doorstep. He took low-paying club jobs in Music City's Printer's Alley for experience, and worked a variety of places for money in the early 70s. In one of those jobs, he actually helped do roofing on the Grand Ole Opry House, before its opening in 1974. Signed to Warner Brothers in the late 70s, Anderson's first album hit the streets in 1980, bringing with it critical acclaim for his attention to country tradition. Adding a vocal strain to the phrasing he picked up from Haggard and Lefty Frizzell, Anderson captured the Country Music Association's Horizon Award for 1983, given to an artist who makes the most career progress. "Swingin'," which, at 1.3 million in sales, is the best-selling single in Warner history, also reeled in the CMA's Single of the Year trophy. Unfortunately Anderson fell out of favor with country radio within two years and future albums failed to capitalize on his earlier momentum. With the help of producer James Stroud, Anderson's career was revitalized in 1992 with the release of his first BNA Records release, *Seminole Wind*, and the single "Straight Tequila Night." −TR

John Anderson 2 / WARNER 1981
His second album (obviously), this traditionally minded package contrasted with the bulk of the material released in the same *Urban Cowboy*-influenced time period. His cover of Lefty Frizzell's "I Love You a Thousand Ways" shows his roots nicely, and "I'm Just an Old Chunk of Coal (But I'm Gonna Be a Diamond Someday)" is simply classic. −TR

Wild & Blue / WARNER 1982
The occasional use of strings in this album was probably master-minded by former Don Law protégé Frank Jones, who coproduced it. Twin fiddles and steel guitar dominate, though, especially in a re-make of Ferlin Husky's "The Waltz You Saved for Me," featuring Emmylou Harris. Includes "Swingin'" and a new version of Lefty Frizzell's "Long Black Veil" — the very last track recorded in the legendary Columbia Studio B. −TR

○ **Greatest Hits / WARNER** 1984
Contains his biggest and best hit, "Swingin'." −DH

Greatest Hits - Vol. 2 / WARNER
Anderson keeps up the momentum. −DH

LYNN ANDERSON b 1947

Country-pop. This North Dakota native became a "Lawrence Welk Show" regular in 1967, but the best was yet to come. In 1971 her "Rose Garden" made it on both the pop and country charts and led to a Grammy. Other hits include "Top of the World" and "What a Man My Man Is." −DV

○ **Greatest Hits / CBS / BB 129** 1972
Big pipes, big production, and big hits from the mid to late 60s. Includes "Rose Garden." −MH

Country Spotlight / KTEL-QWIL
Anderson's early sides kick. Country purists prefer this to her slicker Columbia recordings. −MH

DAVE APOLLON b 1898

Instrumental: mandolin. On the mandolin, Dave Apollon was, in a word, a virtuoso. The late Jethro Burns (of Homer and Jethro) said that Dave Apollon was the best that he had ever heard, and he ought to know, for Burns himself was the best mandolin player of the last quarter-century. Born in Russia, Apollon made many recordings, the first in 1932, and became a celebrity through these and also through his movies. He was to the mandolin what Benny Goodman was to the clarinet. −DV

○ **Mandolin Virtuoso / YAZOO**
A ragtime/vaudeville mandolin maestro. −MH

EDDY ARNOLD b 1918

Traditional country. Once known as the Tennessee Plowboy, this Hall of Famer moved from hillbilly to the middle of the road, where through his talented voice and easy stage presence he became a highly successful crossover star. His many hits include "Bouquet of Roses," "Anytime," "Cattle Call," "Make the World Go Away," "Tennessee Stud," and "That's

What I Get for Loving You." Because of his continued popularity, Eddy Arnold has sold over 70 million records. –DV

○ **Anytime/Eddy Arnold and His Guitar / RCA**   1952
The fine, early country material ("Bouquet of Roses," "Molly Darling") featuring Little Roy Wiggins on steel guitar. –RL

The Best of Eddy Arnold / RCA / BB 34   1967
Mostly pop crossover material, not for hard country fans. –RL

ASLEEP AT THE WHEEL   b 1970

Western swing. Tall and bearded lead vocalist Ray Benson is the only original member. This group has kept Western swing alive and popular since the 70s, mixed with R&B, jazz, and hard country. The style works, producing a Grammy in 1978 for Count Basie's "One O'Clock Jump" and another in 1987 for "String of Pearls." "I See Miles and Miles of Texas" is their signature tune. –DV

Asleep at the Wheel / COLUMBIA   1974
Texas guitarist and singer Ray Benson started this band in the early 70s as a "longhair" tribute to Bob Wills, and they've been swinging ever since. Their first Columbia album. –MH

10 / CBS
Bodacious Western swing on their 10th Columbia album. –MH

○ **Western Standard Time / CBS**
Nicely done Western standards. –MH

Keepin' Me Up Nights / ARISTA
Still swinging in the 90s. –MH

CHET ATKINS   b 1924

Instrumental: guitar. "Mr. Nashville himself" is how Dale Evans referred to Chet Atkins at one of the awards shows in the late 60s. For two reasons is the nickname accurate: it pays great respect to the most famous and perhaps most influential guitar-picker the business has known, and it shows how much Atkins, among many others in the music business, changed the tastes in country music with the "Nashville sound," a middle-of-the-road style that ruled from the mid 50s through the 60s (a style that music writer Chet Flippo says would be called "Country Lite" if it were a beer). This much is sure: the "sound" proved commercial and drew to country music (or to country-pop) millions of listeners who otherwise would have stayed away.

There's no controversy about Atkins the guitar player. He transformed Travis-picking into a high art, playing hardcore country and jazz and blues and classical and whatever genre you want, as it had never been played before. He's played with them all, from Mother Maybelle Carter's band in the late 40s to a recent album with Jerry Reed, and a Who's Who of country giants in between. And along the way, he garnered Instrumentalist of the Year Awards as often as he changed guitar strings. As vice-president of RCA Records, a position he held until 1979 when he got back to his real love — music. Atkins discovered or guided the careers of Hank Locklin, Jerry Reed, Jim Reeves, Don Gibson, Waylon Jennings, Bobby Bare, the Everly Brothers, and scores of other stars.

The best thing to do with Mr. Chester Atkins is to listen to one of the more than 100 albums he's recorded over a long and artistically productive career. Everyone is bound to discover some bit of beauty among those 1000 or so tracks. He's one of the greatest ever to grace country music. –DV

☆ **C.G.P. / CBS**   1952
Great picking and guitar technique. –RW

Guitar for All Seasons / PAIR   1958
Good playing, but uneven material. –RW

☆ **Pickin' My Way / MOBILE FIDELITY**   1970
Superior sound. Two previous Atkins albums on CD. –RW

Work It Out with Chet Atkins C.G.P. / CBS   1983
A 1985 reissue of his 1983 Columbia album. –RW

★ **Best Selections / RCA**
A fine cross-section of the best work Atkins did on RCA; unfortunately, it is probably only available as a Japanese import. –RW

Beginnings: Hillbilly, Old-Time, andString-Band Music

If your experience of country music has consisted of playing the latest Garth Brooks or Barbara Mandrell CD, you'll be needing to set aside considerable time to listen to and appreciate the original country music — but it *will* be time well spent. Though this music from the 20s can be an acquired taste, depending on what you're accustomed to hearing, the enthusiasm, charm, and simplicity of the music and its performers will transport you back to a decade when country music was facts-of-life music, no more and no less.

The band names give a fair taste of the early performers and of their zest for playing: Gid Tanner and the Skillet Lickers, Al Hopkins and the Hill Billies, the Aristocratic Pigs, the Possum Hunters, the Fruit Jar Drinkers (Uncle Dave Macon's band), the Gully Jumpers, and the Dixie Clodhoppers, all string bands that flourished in the late 20s. The fiddle was the dominant instrument in the beginning; Texan Eck Robertson, who cut six songs for Victor in 1922 (including the classic "Sally Gooden"), is credited with the first recording in country music. The standard repertoire ranged from drinkin'-and-cuttin'-up songs to minstrel/medicine-show standards to gospel and spiritual numbers — something for everyone.

But by no means were hillbilly bands the only show in town in the 20s, nor the fiddle the only instrument: old-time music featured guitars (including the Hawaiian slide guitar), banjos, mandolins, and harmonicas, which soon backed up singers as diverse as Buell Kazee and Bradley Kincaid (folksingers) on one hand and Vernon Dalhart (a reformed opera singer) on the other. It was Dalhart who had the first country hit — "The Prisoner's Song," a 1924 million-seller. In the late 50s and early 60s, hillbilly/old-time/string-band music was rediscovered by the folkniks who, in listening to the New Lost City Ramblers, resurrected the popularity of country music's original genre.

— David Vinopal

Country Gems / PAIR
This ranges from maudlin to memorable. –RW

Pickin' on Country / PAIR
Fine solos, but below-par packaging and mastering. –RW

Picks on the Hits / SPECIAL MUSIC CO.
Decent starter/intro to the Atkins sound. –RW

○ **Stay Tuned / CBS**
This first-rate session teams Atkins with George Benson, Earl Klugh, Larry Carlton, and Mark Knopfler. –RW

Street Dreams / CBS
Country/fusion/countrypolitan with Tom Scott and Nancy Mason. –RW

GENE AUTRY   b 1907

Cowboy. In 1934, Gene Autry rode into Hollywood and became the prototypical singing cowboy — a handsome, gun-toting yodeler who came to town and set things right as he defeated the black-clad forces of evil, treated his clever horse kindly, married the prettiest girl, and found time to sing about it all. A country that was little interested in singing hillbillies flocked to the theaters to see the guitar-strumming embodiment of truth, justice, and the American way (the *western* American way) prevail over the baddies in the black hats. This romantic and fanciful image of the Golden West did much to help Americans forget the Depression and look beyond that sunset. This national fascination with that-which-never-was dominated country music in the 40s and has reappeared from Marty "El Paso" Robbins through Michael Martin Murphey and Riders in the Sky.

The cowboy song trail had been blazed before, by real or pretend cowboys such as Carl T. Sprague, Jules Verne Allen, Goebel Reeves, and even Jimmie Rodgers, but it was Gene Autry who caused the "country-western" term that for nearly fifty years has been commonly used (though inaccurately) to refer to country music in general. Hollywood studios discovered the goldmine in the sky, personifed by Ray Whitley, Eddie Dean, Jimmy Wakely, Rex Allen, Johnny Bond, Tex Ritter, and Roy Rogers, the latter being Autry's chief rival for the affection of every red-blooded American youth through the 40s.

Autry's bit-singing role in Ken Maynard's *In Old Santa Fe* led to the gun-and-guitar hero who lives on in country music, though ebbing and flowing with the times: the horse opera is out of style but the boots are in; yodeling is corny but sequined suits are hip (thanks perhaps to Porter Wagoner alone); six-shooters frighten too many people but not those clichéd cowboy hats, appendages to Garth Brooks, George Strait, Clint Black, and many contemporaries who hope the Look will lead them to that perfect happiness with which each cowboy movie ended. The Outlaw fad and *Urban Cowboy* fallout show that at least part of the country doesn't want to let go of what Gene Autry started. To sum up Autry's philosophy in one titled sentence, "After I get back in the saddle again, I'll be riding down the canyon to see that silver-haired daddy of mine who lives south of the border, near Mexicali Rose." America and Americana were never the same after Gene Autry. –DV

Columbia Historic Edition / COLUMBIA
Hollywood cowboy in full trot, circa 1940s. –MH

○ **Country Music Hall of Fame / COLUMBIA**
Country's first hat act, the inspiration to a generation crooning, smooth and sincere, in the Roosevelt era. –MH

Gene Autry's Western Classics / COLUMBIA

HOYT AXTON   b 1938

Country. Axton Hoyt has enjoyed an amazingly diverse career as a songwriter, recording artist and movie actor. While Axton is rooted equal parts in the folk and country traditions his pop smarts have enabled him to land substantial hits with numerous artists. Among the artists who have recorded Axton's songs are Three Dog Night ("Joy to the World," "Never Been to Spain"), the Kingston Trio ("Greenback Dollar"), Steppenwolf ("The Pusher," "Snowblind Friend"), and Ringo Starr ("No No Song"), as well as Waylon Jennings, Glen Campbell, Tanya Tucker, John Denver, and Commander Cody. As an artist, Axton has released a string of remarkably consistant albums that feature his warm baritone and wry earthy lyrical style. –RC

○ **Life Machine / A&M**   1974
Among Axton's many albums, *Life Machine* features some of his best writing. "When the Morning Comes" and "Boney Fingers" are highlights. –RC

Southbound / A&M   1975
Another solid effort. Includes "Pride of Man" and "Lion in the Winter." –RC

Fearless / A&M   1976
Includes "The Devil." –RC

Snowblind Friend / A&M   1977
This is the fourth in a series of enjoyable album releases. The title track is one of Axton's better-known songs, having been recorded by Steppenwolf. –RC

BAILLIE & THE BOYS

Country. Kathy Baillie, Alan LeBoeuf, and Michael Bonagura. Though originally from New Jersey, Kathy Baillie and Michael Bonagura met in Delaware through a friend who gave Bonagura a tape that featured Baillie's vocals. Fans of artists like the Four Tops, the Beatles, the Supremes, Linda Ronstadt, and James Taylor, they developed a strong harmony — both on stage and off: they were married in 1977. Bonagura's buddy, bass player Alan LeBoeuf, joined up, and after a number of years on the Garden State's nightclub circuit, yet another friend — a driver with Allied Van Lines — persuaded them to join him on a trip to Nashville. They stayed in Music City, and in 1982 they got their first chance to appear on a record, singing backup on Ed Bruce's *My First Taste of Texas.* Bonagura cowrote Marie Osmond's single "There's No Stopping Your Heart," and the trio sang backing vocals on a number of singles for Dan Seals and Randy Travis. Ultimately, they signed with RCA Records, making their debut in 1987. After completing their second album, LeBoeuf decided their touring schedule was too hectic and left. Baillie and Bonagura retained the original name, though Boys seems a bit misleading. –TR

○ **The Best of Baillie & the Boys / RCA**
Highlights the real strength of the act: tuneful melodies, pristine harmonies, and Kathy Baillie's infectious enunciations. Best cuts: "Oh Heart," "(Wish I Had A) Heart of Stone," "Long Shot," and "I Can't Turn the Tide." –TR

MOE BANDY   b 1944

Traditional country. This Mississippi native gave up rodeo riding for music. Traditionalist/honky-tonk singer Bandy has done well with "Bandy the Rodeo Clown," "Hank Williams, You Wrote My Life," and "It's a Cheatin' Situation." –DV

☆ **The Best of Moe Bandy - Vol. 1 / COLUMBIA**   1977
A Texas honky-tonker whose unabashed paeans to the bottle were among the greatest jukebox records of the 70s. Talk about wailin' and willin'! –MH

Many Mansions / CAPITOL   1989
A fine title song about homelessness, among others. –MH

Greatest Hits / CAPITOL
Allegedly George Bush's favorite country singer, but don't let that deter you. Bandy's 70s and 80s Columbia hits were among the great working-class anthems of their time. –MH

You Haven't Heard the Last of Me / CURB
Released nearly four years after his last previous Top Ten single, this album gave Bandy a brief return to the spotlight. Working with record producer Jerry Kennedy for the first time, Bandy maintains more command of his delivery than in any previous album. –TR

MOE BANDY & JOE STAMPLEY

Country. This short-lived pairing of two already-established solo artists occurred after a conversation at London's Hard Rock Cafe, where the performers joked that the moniker "Moe & Joe" sounded almost as musical as "Waylon & Willie." Back in the US, they went to work on a duet album, *Just Good Ol' Boys,* which hit the market in 1979. In a town full of songwriters who often take their jobs a little too seriously (not every song has to be as meaningful as "Help Me Make It through the Night"), their macho, male-bonding humor was a welcome relief. Unfortunately, the duo posed a problem for each artist's solo career. The tandem overshadowed their individual efforts, and they abandoned the Moe & Joe concept for good after 1984's send-up of Boy George, "Where's the Dress." –TR

○ **Greatest Hits / COLUMBIA**
Carousing, drinking, and dodging wives are the order of the day here. "Holding the Bag" and "Tell Ole I Ain't Here, He Better Get on Home" are particularly amusing, but the biggest laughs come with the transvestite storyline of "Honky Tonk Queen." –TR

THE BELLAMY BROTHERS

Country. Howard (b Feb 2, 1946) and David (b Sep 16, 1950) Bellamy. Growing up on a Florida farm that's been in the family since the Civil War, the Bellamys have an understandable interest in their roots — geographical, genealogical, and musical. The latter area is a mixed bag, evidenced in a line from "Kids of the Baby Boom": "We had sympathy for the devil and the Rolling Stones/Then we got a little older, we found Haggard & Jones." Entranced by the Beatles and Crosby, Stills, Nash & Young, the Bellamys also heard island rhythms and melodies from the migrant workers who labored in Florida. They performed as an opening act with a local R&B band that worked the same stage as Little Anthony & the Imperials and Percy Sledge, and signed up in the late 60s with Jericho, a Southern rock band that worked the same circuit as the Allman Brothers. Ultimately, David's song "Spiders and Snakes" was recorded by Jim Stafford, and the Brothers ended up in Los Angeles. Through happenstance, a producer heard Howard singing while working as a roadie for Neil Diamond, and in short order, they recorded "Let Your Love Flow," which hit #1 on the pop charts during 1976. Within a year, they were certified has-beens in the US, though they continued to find success in Europe. Finally, they found their niche in America on the country chart in 1979 with "If I Said You Have a Beautiful Body Would You Hold It Against Me," nominated for a Grammy. It began a series of double entendre songs that kept them from favor with the critics, but they quietly evolved through experimentation into one of country's most daring acts. With "You're My Favorite Star" and "Get into Reggae Cowboy," they melded country with Jamaican reggae, and they matched up country and another surprising genre with the self-explanatory title "country rap." The Bellamys also made great strides lyrically, particularly in their thirtysomething trilogy: "Old Hippie," "Kids of the Baby Boom," and "Rebels without a Clue."

The Bellamy Brothers have racked up more Top Ten country singles than any other duo in history, yet remain one of the format's most-underrated acts. –TR

Country Rap / CURB
"Kids of the Baby Boom," encapsulating images from JFK to Third World abusiveness, speaks out for an entire generation. But the album is dominated by experimental and infectious "fun stuff," including "D-D-D-D-Divorcee," "Country Rap," and their bopping group effort with the Forester Sisters, "Too Much Is Not Enough." –TR

○ **Greatest Hits / WARNER**
This ably documents the double-entendre period of the Bellamy Brothers' early country years — lots of silly, shallow lyrics in "Dancin' Cowboys," "Lovers Live Longer," and "Do You Love As Good As You Look." But it also demonstrates their trademark genetic harmony, and "Redneck Girl" and "You Ain't Just Whistlin' Dixie" show glimpses of the insightful songwriter that David Bellamy would become. –TR

Rebels without a Clue / CURB
David Bellamy shows the depth of his songwriting talents, particularly in "The Courthouse," "The Andy Griffith Show," and the autobiographical "When the Music Meant Everything." Firm images, lots of conviction. –TR

When We Were Boys / ELEKTRA
Michael Lloyd, probably best known as the producer on Shaun Cassidy's "Da Doo Ron Ron," oversaw the brothers' cute, early country years. In this album, they were given the reins for the first time, leading to a more serious, reflective and simple approach. Also for the first time, they recorded the album at their own home studio, located on their farm in Darby, FL. –TR

MATRACA BERG   b 1964

Contemporary country. Before cutting her successful first album, *Lying to the Moon*, Matraca Berg had written hit songs for other people, including "The Last One to Know," which Reba McEntire took to #1. Berg's debut album yielded singles

that did well, among them "I Must Have Been Crazy" and "Appalachian Rain." –DV

○ **Lying to the Moon / RCA**
A young Nashville singer/songwriter who takes a sultry photo and sometimes delivers with brio. –MH

CLINT BLACK   b 1962

Country. By appearing on the Roy Rogers *Tribute* album, Clint showed he has a feel for country tradition. Since bursting onto the scene in 1989, he has shot to the top: his debut album, *Killin' Time*, went platinum in eight months and yielded five singles that went to #1 in the charts. He won the Academy of Country Music's Awards for Best New Male Artist and Male Vocalist of the Year, the first time both awards had been given to the same artist. He married actress Lisa Hartman (*Knot's Landing*) in 1991. Black's first two albums sold more than two million copies each; his third album, *The Hard Way*, was released in July 1992. –DV & BM

☆ **Killin' Time / RCA / BB 31**   1989
The debut from this Texan who's the best of the Bush-era Haggard wannabees. Contemporary honky-tonk with more bite than you get from most members of the current class. –MH

Put Yourself in My Shoes / RCA   1990
A followup with more of Black's engaging Texas tonk. –MH

The Hard Way / RCA   1992
More kickers 'n cryers from this affable Texan. –MH

BLUE SKY BOYS

Old-time. In the 30s brother duets were common in country music: among the better known were the Monroes, the Delmores, the Dixons, and the Carlisles. Bill and Earl Bolick, who in 1936 were ready to make their first recording, followed their producer's suggestion that they should be "different" by avoiding the word *brother*. From "Blue Ridge Mountains, Land of the Sky" they took two words and named their act. But the Bolicks would have been different without the new name. Their intricate yet simple harmonics, their perfectly matching voices, and their unadorned mandolin and guitar instrumental backing set them off from the competition, so much so that two generations of subsequent duet singers echo them, some without realizing it. The Everly Brothers and the Louvin Brothers, themselves recognized as exceptional vocal duets, acknowledge the influence of the Blue Sky Boys.

In the 50s, when tastes in country music changed drastically, the Blue Sky Boys retired from music rather than forsake their love of old mountain ballads for the uptempo popularity of electric instruments, drums, and honky-tonk. In the 60s they were coaxed to come out of retirement, playing an occasional college date during the hootenanny phenomenon and recording albums in 1963, 1965, and 1976.

No one in country music has done vocal duets better than the Blue Sky Boys. If your taste runs more to Conway & Loretta, George & Tammy, Wynonna & Naomi, listen to the effortless, exquisite singing of Bill and Earl Bolick. See where it all started. –DV

○ **There'll Come a Time ... / BSR**   1936
There'll Come a Time/Can't You Hear That Nightbird — sacred songs, weepers, and hillbilly heart-singing at its best. –MH

In Concert '64 / ROUNDER
An excellent "rediscovery" concert of this legendary 30s brother duo. –MH

SUZY BOGGUSS

Country-pop. Winner of the Academy of Country Music's Top New Female Vocalist Award, Bogguss first became known as a headliner at Dolly Parton's Dollywood. "Hopelessly Yours," a duet with Lee Greenwood, did very well in the charts. She headlined a country show in Rio de Janeiro in front of thousands of cowboy-hatted Brazilians. –DV

Aces / CAPITOL   1991
Good'uns. –MH

○ **Moment of Truth / CAPITOL**
A pleasant Nashville thrush with a down-home cowgal twist beneath a yuppie gloss. —MH

BOXCAR WILLIE

Traditional country. Born Lecil Martin, this Texan has done as much as anyone to keep the hobo tradition alive in country music. Though he never had a Top Ten song, his *King of the Road* album sold over three million copies through TV advertising. Long a favorite in Europe, he received a standing ovation in his 1979 debut at the Opry, where he is now a regular. —DV

☆ **Boxcar Willie / MCA**
The best-recorded and best-produced of his numerous albums. —CW

BILL BOYD   b 1910

Western swing. If you love Western swing, listen to Bill Boyd and his Cowboy Ramblers, a band contemporary with the more famous one of Bob Wills, but with a different sound. The Wills band often used horns and recorded many types of songs, including jazz; the Cowboy Ramblers, though, stuck to string-band backing and featured Western songs. Aficionados of Western swing put Bill Boyd up there with Bob Wills. —DV

○ **Bill Boyd's Cowboy Ramblers / RCA**

BROOKS & DUNN

Country. Both Kix Brooks and Ronnie Dunn came from oil-pipeline families (Brooks in Louisiana, Dunn in Texas and New Mexico), so they come by at least part of their Western roughneck image honestly. Brooks moved to Nashville in 1981 and recorded a 1989 album for Capitol. Dunn began drawing Nashville attention after winning a national country music talent contest in 1989. Neither found much success until they joined forces for hits like "Brand New Man," "Neon Moon," and "My Next Broken Heart." —BM

○ **Brand New Man / ARISTA**   1991
The title tale of love and redemption was a classic single for all the same reasons that made this would-be modern cowboy duo's debut such a winner: tightly constructed choruses; a perfect balance between romance, macho swagger, and Wild West imagery; and bracing harmonies that'll clear the trail dust out of your throat quicker than a shot of good whiskey. —BM

GARTH BROOKS   b 1962

Contemporary country. In a word, phenomenal. After his first two albums went platinum (*Garth Brooks* and *No Fences*), Nashville knew that Garth was hot property. But no one would guess that this Oklahoma-born crooner with the big hat would sweep so many awards and end up the biggest crossover star in history. According to his press release (as of October 1991), his records were selling to the tune of 225,000 a week, making Tennessee Ernie Ford (and his smash "Sixteen Tons," in its time a huge crossover hit) look downright insignificant.
Brooks's 1991 *Ropin' the Wind* was the first country album to debut at the top of *Billboard*'s Pop Album chart. And that, country music fans, means money. When the pop fans think Brooks is one of theirs, and the country fans claim him as their own, he has the best of both worlds. His easy-to-listen-to style and content put him where Kenny Rogers was a decade earlier, though Brooks's fans are younger and in more of a record-buying mood. In the *Music City News* Top Albums chart of March 1992, Brooks's first three albums ranked one, two, and three, though in reverse order from when they were issued. The mind boggles when considering what he'll do for an encore. The good old days, when country fans would argue over whether a particular singer or song is *real* country, are just that — good old days. In the DSG (days since Garth), such questions are irrelevant. This is a phenomenon we're dealing with. —DV

Garth Brooks / CAPITOL   1989
Brooks's first, rather modestly produced album established his mortality/preciousness-of-loved-ones themes with "If Tomorrow Never Comes" and "The Dance," both substantial country hits. —RC

● **No Fences / CAPITOL**   1990
This was the album that took Brooks to the top of the charts, thanks to the playfully cocky hit "Friends in Low Places," as well as "Two of a Kind, Workin' on a Full House" and the sentimental ballad "Unanswered Prayers." "The Thunder Rolls" was a controversial track that also became a big country hit. —RC

○ **Ropin' the Wind / CAPITOL**   1991
Brooks expanded into more ambitious musical and thematic territory (for a country-based act) with the tracks "In Lonesome Dove" and "The River." He also covered Billy Joel's "Shameless" on this outing. —RC

○ **The Chase / LIBERTY**   1992
Brooks shows increasing maturity as a songwriter as he continues to mine his preciousness-of-love-and-life themes, and he again tackles a sensitive issue with "Face to Face," a song about date rape. He also includes a couple of covers, the rollicking version of the Little Feat classic "Dixie Chicken" and a swinging "Walkin' After Midnight." —RC

MARTY BROWN

Traditional country. Marty Brown, a native of the tobacco-farming community of Maceo, KY, is the kind of guy myths spring up around. He hitchhiked into Nashville with little more than his guitar, a cheap demo tape, and a knowledge of the music industry he'd picked up from TNN. (He's said to have accosted producer Barry Beckett at a music-biz function and said, "I know you! I saw you in a video.") Turned out that was enough. An unannounced visit to performing-rights organization BMI led to a mad scramble to sign Brown to a recording deal. His debut, for which he wrote all the songs, was one of the most universally praised country recordings of 1991. Brown's pinched voice is a throwback to an earlier time, sort of a Kentucky hill version of Jimmie Rodgers. —BM

☆ **High and Dry / MCA**   1991
If everything here were as pure a hillbilly distillation as the title track or the loopy "Old King Kong," Brown might come off like a simple hick with limited nostalgia appeal. But his range is surprisingly wide. Brown's ballads — "I'll Climb Any Mountain" and "Wildest Dreams" — though simple, build to stunning, emotional climaxes. "Every Now and Then" is the equal of many of the Everly Brothers' best. And "Nobody Knows" is surely one of the most lonesome wails in a long, long time. —BM

T. GRAHAM BROWN   b 1954

Country. Asked to describe his own music, "His T-Ness" calls it "Otis Redding meets George Jones." With the smoky timbre of rocker Chris Rea and the passionate energy of Joe Cocker, Brown possesses as much "blue-eyed soul" as Boz Scaggs or Hall & Oates. A former All-State baseball player in Georgia, Brown gave up the sport when he rode the bench on his college team. He put together a band for the Holiday Inn lounge, and in 1982 his wife Sheila convinced him it was time to head to Nashville. There, he became immersed in the world of jingles, working for McDonald's, Kraft, Coca Cola, and — once established — Taco Bell. He also sang the demo of "1982" that Randy Travis eventually recorded. His sound is a bit unusual for country music, and that's appropriate for Brown, who does nothing the same way as anyone else. Cases in point: he named his band the Rack of Spam and named his first child Acme. —TR

○ **I Tell It Like It Used to Be / CAPITOL**
With the sessions split between Nashville's Woodland Sound Studio and Muscle Shoals, T. Graham Brown's debut often sounds affectionately like the raw, impassioned work of a garage band. Shout it out! —TR

ED BRUCE   *b* 1939

Country. Born in Arkansas, raised in Memphis, Ed Bruce signed first with the rockabilly-heavy Sun Records, and later with the soul-oriented Septre label. But Bruce's deep resonance and laidback approach to life were more suited to country. He was able to move to Nashville with the help of Tommy Roe's pop hit "Sheila"; Bruce wrote the B-side, and collected enough royalties when it sold a million copies to swing a new home base. A jack-of-all-trades in the business, he's done some acting (the "Maverick" TV series); some radio work (on Nashville's WSM); some jingle-singing (United Airlines, Burger King, Tennessee Tourism, among many others); and some songwriting ("Mammas, Don't Let Your Babies Grow up to Be Cowboys," "Texas When I Die," and "See the Big Man Cry"). A journeyman recording artist, Bruce found brief success in the early 80s with a string of singles for MCA Records. –TR

○ **Greatest Hits / MCA**
An album that documents the most rewarding period of Ed Bruce's recording career. Easygoing, mid-tempo love songs dominate, particularly with "You're the Best Break This Old Heart Ever Had," "Ever, Never Lovin' You," and "You're Leavin' Here Tonight." The reflective "After All" is permanently haunting. –TR

JETHRO BURNS

Instrumental: mandolin. Behind the country hayseed garb, the hick patter, and the outrageous parodies of popular songs lay mandolin player Kenneth "Jethro" Burns and guitarist Henry "Homer" Haynes, expert jazz musicians who for nearly four decades were country comedy's most visible duo. Their exaggerated hillbilly appearance and zany send-ups of songs belie the cleverness of their comedy and the extraordinarily high quality of their music.
Both from Knoxville, they billed themselves first as the String Dusters but moved to comedy in 1936 when they created the Homer and Jethro characters that were intact until Haynes's death in 1971. And they made a good living from these rubes, winning a Grammy in 1959, starring in Las Vegas, and appearing regularly on TV, including "The Tonight Show." Although they canned the country corn occasionally (as in *Playing It Straight*, a 1962 album), their onstage wit and parodies of well-known songs ranging from the opera to the Opry made them famous. Regarding his "Jambalaya" being turned into "Jam Bowl Liar," Hank Williams said you know a song's good when it's been given the Homer and Jethro treatment. Other zingers include "She Was Bitten on the Udder by an Adder," "Mama, Get the Hammer (There's a Fly on Papa's Head)," and "I've Got Tears in My Ears from Lying on My Back in Bed While I Cry over You." What other act could put out a hit album titled *The Worst of Homer and Jethro*? Only they could be so creatively, zanily bad they were excellent. Shortly after Haynes's death, in a series of swing jazz albums, Burns showed why he's been considered the best mandolin player of a generation and, in the opinion of many, the best who has ever lived. –DV

Jethro Live / FLYING FISH   1990
Some laughs, and much "mando-marvelosity." –MH

● **Tea for One / KALEIDOSCOPE**
Known for cornball comedy as half of Homer & Jethro, Burns was also a deft swing-style mandolinist. This album features Jethro Burns and his mandolin and no one else. –MH

☆ **Back to Back / KALEIDOSCOPE**
The two modern giants of mandolin, Jethro Burns and Tiny Moore, are backed by guitar-great Eldon Shamblin of the Bob Wills Texas Playboys. –DV

GLEN CAMPBELL   *b* 1936

Country. Playing guitar on the Los Angeles session circuit, Glen Campbell got involved in such memorable releases as "Strangers in the Night," by Frank Sinatra; "I'm a Believer," by

the Monkees; "Viva Las Vegas," by Elvis Presley; and "The Legend of Bonnie & Clyde," by Merle Haggard. Campbell also toured as Brian Wilson's stand-in with the Beach Boys. But his own recording career was hardly rewarding at the start. After several albums, he was about to give it up when a song called "Gentle on my Mind" emerged with a smattering of success. Encouraged, he continued recording, and exploded with the release of "By the Time I Get to Phoenix." A string of hits followed — not to mention the network TV show "The Glen Campbell Goodtime Hour" — and in short order, he was selling more records than his labelmates, the Beatles. But his successes didn't sustain. He tailed off in the early 70s, re-emerged with the release of "Rhinestone Cowboy" in 1975, and continued through several more up-and-down periods. Campbell's vocal range, good looks, and sense of humor all combined to make him one of country music's best-recognized personalities, even when the music didn't work commercially. –TR

Glen Campbell's Greatest Hits / CAPITOL
Covers the most productive period of his recording career, the years in which Al De Lory's soaring string arrangements, Jimmy Webb's snapshot songs, and the identifiable low-tuned guitars vaulted Campbell to the upper strata of both the country and pop charts. You simply weren't alive if you didn't hear "Wichita Lineman," "Galveston," or "Try a Little Kindness." –TR

Greatest Country Hits / CAPITOL
A hodge podge of material from the mid 70s through 1989, this displays a variety of Glen Campbell approaches to country. "She's Gone, Gone, Gone" is twangy enough to do originator Lefty Frizzell justice. "Still within the Sound of My Voice" catches Campbell at his most sensitive, and "Southern Nights" is just plain fun. –TR

MARY-CHAPIN CARPENTER   *b* 1958

Contemporary country. Around her Washington, DC, home, Carpenter became quite a name in folk music, and she's brought this folk flavor to her country recordings. Her *State of the Heart* album was well received and produced two Top Five singles. Because of increased TV exposure and an avid audience for her country/folk style, Carpenter's star rose rapidly in 1992. –DV

○ **State of the Heart / CBS**   1990
Carpenter, a folkie, eventually turned to the country market, especially on her third album, *Shooting Straight in the Dark*. On this, her second, she's still in transition, which makes her more thoughtful than the average country singer and catchier than the average folkie, especially on her breakthrough country hit, "Never Had It So Good." –WR

Shooting Straight in the Dark / COLUMBIA   1991
Carpenter's third album expanded on the promise of her breakthrough, with the Searchers-style pop of "Going Out Tonight" and a guest spot from Beausoleil on the Cajun-rooted "Down at the Twist and Shout." It also held some of her most penetrating, introspective songs, with payoff lines that would impress Elvis Costello. –BM

Come On Come On / COLUMBIA   1992
The ultra-serious *Shooting Straight in the Dark* left Carpenter in need of a breather, which she takes by covering Dire Straits' "The Bug" and Lucinda Williams's "Passionate Kisses." On "I Feel Lucky," she wins the lottery and flirts with Lyle Lovett and Dwight Yoakam in a bar. It's tough to say which she enjoyed more. –BM

CARLENE CARTER

Country. Her musical pedigree (daughter of Carl Smith, a star singer and Opry standout in the 50s, and June Carter Cash, of the Carter Family and wife of Johnny Cash; and granddaughter of Mother Maybelle) made Carlene Carter the epitome of female country cool the minute she released her first record (*Carlene Carter*, Warner, 1978). She never really accepted Nashville's terms, preferring instead to record in places like London with musicians from the Rumour and Rockpile (Nick Lowe was Carter's third husband). She recorded sporadically through the 80s, with better press than sales, but she finally got it all together in 1990 with *I Fell in Love*, an across-the-board country hit. –BM & DV

○ **I Fell in Love / REPRISE**   1990
A comeback album with a perfect mix of old (A. P. Carter's "My Dixie Darlin'") and new (guest spots from Dave Edmunds, David Lindley, and Albert Lee). If Carter hasn't come to terms with her love for rock and her duty to heritage, she's at least learned to balance them. –BM

THE CARTER FAMILY

Traditional country. The most influential group in country music history, the Carter Family switched the emphasis from hillbilly instrumentals to vocals, made scores of their songs part of the standard country music canon, and made a style of guitar playing, "Carter-picking," the dominant technique for decades. For nearly 70 years the Carters's "Wildwood Flower" was the first victim of most young country people learning to play the guitar. In 1970 the Original Carter Family became the first group elected to the Country Music Hall of Fame.

In a remarkable coincidence, on Aug 1-4, 1927, the first two stars ("superstars" in today's inflation) were recorded in Bristol, TN, by an RCA scout looking for rural talent. One was the great Mississippi Blue Yodeler, Jimmie Rodgers; the other was a family group consisting of Alvin P. Carter, his wife Sara, and their sister-in-law Maybelle. These three — a gaunt, shy gospel quartet member and two reserved country girls — sang a pure, simple harmony that influenced not only the numerous other family groups of the 30s and the 40s, but Woody Guthrie and Bill Monroe and the Kingston Trio and Doc Watson and Bob Dylan and Emmylou Harris, to mention just a few. It's unlikely that bluegrass music would have existed without the Carter family.

A.P., the family patriarch, collected hundreds of British/Appalachian folk songs and, in arranging these for recording, both enhanced the pure beauty of these "facts-of-life tunes" and at the same time saved them for future generations. Those hundreds of songs the trio found around their Virginia and Tennessee homes, after being sung by A.P., Sara, and Maybelle, became *Carter* songs, even though these were folksongs and in the public domain. Among the more than 300 sides they recorded are "Worried Man Blues," "Wabash Cannonball," "Will the Circle Be Unbroken," "Wildwood Flower," and "Keep on the Sunny Side," their radio theme.

The Carter Family's instrumental backup, like their vocals, was unique. On her Gibson L-5 guitar, Maybelle played a bass-strings lead (the guitar being tuned down from the standard pitch) that is the mainstay of bluegrass guitarists to the present. Sara accompanied her on the autoharp or on a second guitar, while A.P. devoted his talent to singing a haunting though idiosyncratic bass or baritone. Although the Original Carter Family disbanded in 1943, enough of their recordings remained in the vaults to keep the group current through the 40s. Maybelle, through a Flatt and Scruggs album of Carter material, found a new and younger audience in the 60s; her work on the famous three-record album *Will the Circle Be Unbroken* (under the aegis of the Nitty Gritty Dirt Band), blended the old-guard country with the new, restoring to her the fame of 40 years earlier. This time, though, the audience was predominantly urban and educated. –DV

☆ **'Mid the Green Fields of Virginia / RCA**   1963
The Carter Family was the most important group in early country music, and this 16-track album selects some of their most notable initial recordings from the late 20s and early 30s, among them "My Clinch Mountain Home" and their theme song, "Keep on the Sunny Side." –WR

Diamonds in the Rough / COPPER CREEK   1990
Subtitled *Heart Songs, Hymns & Ballads as Featured on Border*

Radio in 1941, this radio-transcriptions reissue of the Carter Family's appearances on the legendary Del Rio border radio stations in 1938 is a fine representation of their repertoire of songs about home, hearth, and heartbreak. –MH

Country Music Hall of Fame / MCA   1991
After the Depression, the Carters (originally on RCA-Victor) recorded for Decca Records. Their music was little-changed from the earlier decade, though a slight Hispanic influence wafts through the lovely "You Are My Flower." This 16-track collection of 1936-1938 recordings is certainly quintessential Carter Family — simultaneously parlor delicate and oak-post solid. –MH

Country Music Hall of Fame Series / MCA   1991
After ending an eight-year association with Victor Records, the Carter Family recorded 60 sides for Decca between 1936 and 1938; 15 of those recordings are collected here. Decca wanted to emphasize new material; this posed no problem for A. P. Carter, who was long accustomed to taking copyright credit for minor rewrites of other people's songs. The Decca songs are less familiar than the recordings for Victor or, later, Okeh, but they're worth hearing. –BM

JOHNNY CASH   ♭1932

Traditional country. It is almost un-American not to like Johnny Cash. He sings songs about trains and God and farmers and Indians. And he's been around forever. Wasn't "I Walk the Line" in the 50s sometime? And wasn't he in jail for a while? No, he sang in jail — that's right! He's the guy who sang "Folsom Prison Blues." And he's still making records, right? How can you not like him?

The trick is to get past the myth and all the hype and just listen to some of the music.

Pick a period — there are lots to choose from! I'd recommend starting at the beginning, maybe with the aforementioned "I Walk the Line." Or you might go back several months to the original version of "Folsom Prison Blues." There are no convicts screaming in the background here, but it's a mighty fine record. In fact, many of Cash's early recordings for the Sun label are about as close to perfect as one can imagine. Things couldn't get much simpler. Perfectly simple, you might say.

Cash's early 45s, even his first album, feature just Johnny Cash and his two-man band, the Tennessee Two: a minimalist electric guitar and acoustic bass. You might think, "If there are just the two of them, they must do some mighty fancy picking, right?" Put it this way: the musical limitations of the Tennessee Two make Johnny Cash sound like Pavarotti. Rather than embellish Cash's strikingly sparse sound, Sun Label owner Sam Phillips let the band's "boom-chicka-boom" and Cash's lonely baritone vocals hang in an eerie sea of echo that, just months before, had swathed the vocals of Elvis Presley and Carl Perkins. These were friendly waters. The power of these early records (add "Train of Love" and "Big River" to the list) is unmistakable thirty-five years after they were made.

To his credit, Johnny Cash's recorded sound has remained almost unchanged across the decades. Like many survivors of the halcyon days at Sun Records, Cash has battled a host of demons, including substance abuse and personal tragedies. He has emerged strong and fit for battle. Considering the immense amount of material in his recorded legacy, there is little to be ashamed of. There are few artists with as instantly recognizable a sound and style as Johnny Cash, and few as worthy of the attention of a whole new generation of listeners.

·Johnny Cash should be approached chronologically. Stay away from his later (Polygram) work until you've digested his Columbia years (1958 through the mid 80s), and don't enter the Columbia years until you can pass a quiz on his Sun period. –HD

The Fabulous Johnny Cash / CBS / BB 19   1958
His first Columbia album. –HD

Ride This Train / CBS   1960
An early concept album detailing Cash's love of trains and Americana. –HD

At Folsom Prison & San Quentin / CBS / BB 13   1968
Here are all the prison songs on one disc. –HD

At Folsom Prison & San Quentin / COLUMBIA   1968
Originally released in two different double-album sets, these two different albums have been packaged together on CD. There's a certain tension inherent in the concept of playing live to a bunch of convicts, and the tension — as well as Cash's ability to cope with it — is very present. –TR

The Man in Black / BEAR FAMILY / BB 56   1971
For the serious Cash collector. Five CDs and a book detailing all of his Sun sessions, outtakes — warts and all — and his initial Columbia work. A unique behind-the-scenes glimpse. Superbly produced. –HD

☆ **The Sun Years / RHINO**   1984
An essential look at Cash's formative years, 1955-1958. Brooding and intense music. –HD

○ **Columbia Years 1958-1986 / COLUMBIA**   1987
An excellent overview of Cash's middle period with all the hits (like "Ring of Fire") as well as early lonesome tracks like "I Still Miss Someone." –HD

The Essential Johnny Cash 1955-1983 / COLUMBIA   1992
A three-CD set, this one traces his career from his Sun beginnings with "Hey Porter" and "Cry! Cry! Cry!" through the close of his Columbia association. It includes the obvious high points along the way ("Folsom Prison Blues," "Ring of Fire," etc.), but also packs in more obscure hits (like "Blistered" and "Singin' in Vietnam Talkin' Blues"), plus material from some of his later albums, and several appropriate gospel tracks. –TR

ROSANNE CASH   b 1955

Contemporary country. Reba McEntire sells more records, but Rosanne Cash, the daughter of Johnny Cash, may be the greatest woman currently working in country. Her brand of art, however, has never been confined to the cut-and-dried traditions of C&W, nor can she be pigeonholed as an "outlaw" upstart. Cash works within the context of country much as did Bob Wills: by bringing her unique perspectives to the genre, she has somehow eclipsed it, changing its patterns to suit her creative needs, tailoring it to encompass the complexities of her vision.

Her first hit, the self-penned "Seven Year Ache," was a crossover smash for several reasons: the sentiments of the song contradicted the roles enforced on female country artists, and the backbeat had more in common with Bonnie Raitt than Kitty Wells. Although many of her best personality-defining songs have come from outside writers, over the last few years Cash has blossomed into a clever and soul-searching songwriter. 1990's *Interiors*, produced and written entirely by Cash, uncompromisingly picked apart the disintegration of her marriage to Rodney Crowell. It remains a moody, unsettling masterpiece. At her best, Cash sounds like a meeting of Patsy Cline, Joni Mitchell, and Chrissie Hynde: she has a full-bodied vocal style reminiscent of Cline's; she manifests her emotions with the persistence of Mitchell; and she has the confidence and attitude of Hynde. –JF

★ **Seven Year Ache / CBS / BB 26**   1981
Cash was arguably the most important artist to emerge in country music in the early 80s, and this was her breakthrough album, which introduced a new, assertive, passionate stance to women in country and also helped foster the crossover between folk, rock, and country. Cash's songwriting (the title track and "Blue Moon with a Heartache") was first-rate, and her choices from others, notably Leroy Preston's "My Baby Thinks He's a Train," were equally strong. –WR

○ **Somewhere in the Stars / CBS / BB 76**   1982
A terrific collection, including Rodney Crowell's "Ain't No Money" and Tom T. Hall's "That's How I Got to Memphis." –WR

Rhythm & Romance / COLUMBIA   1985
Cash expected criticism for this album and got it but didn't deserve it. The orange hair and pink fingernails on the cover visually illustrate the musical risks she took in working with

---

Honky-Tonk

After the deification of mother, home, dead relatives, traveling, and the working man no longer bore a close-enough resemblance to reality for millions of country music listeners, a new form — honky-tonk — filled the void. This new genre didn't displace traditional country themes, but it certainly did add variety and spice by lamenting and more than occasionally celebrating the shady and seedy sides of life. When Prohibition brought booze and customers into the bars and taverns in the 30s, the patrons preferred to leave the glorification-of-home songs where they belonged, *at* home, and found a new form that better reflected a tavern's bar instead of a church's altar. And so songs about cheatin', lyin', thievin', fightin', and slippin' around — in other words, *real* life — proliferated. If something was illicit, but traditionally and conservatively illicit, there were good makings for a honky-tonk hit. The whine of a steel guitar and the beat of drums fit much better in a watering hole than in a church, and they lent themselves perfectly to this music. Whether the gin-mills' music imitated life or whether the patrons imitated the song lyrics is unclear. What is clear is that country music's love of honky-tonk themes continues unabated. Not much has changed in the forty years since Hank Thompson's complaint "I didn't know God made honky-tonk angels" (from "The Wild Side of Life") motivated Miss Kitty Wells to answer "It wasn't God who made honky-tonk angels." Then who's to blame? As Wells sings it, "From the start, most every heart that's ever broken/Was because there always was a man to blame." A classic case of both being right at the same time ... "Dim Light, Thick Smoke, and Loud, Loud Music" says it all. A good place to start your honky-tonk listening is Ernest Tubb; a representative sample should include Hank Williams, Floyd Tillman, Hank Thompson, Lefty Frizzell, Webb Pierce, the early Ray Price, George Jones, Tammy Wynette, Buck Owens, Merle Haggard, Willie Nelson, and Loretta Lynn.

— David Vinopal

Eddie Rabbitt's former producer, David Malloy, and the result is a scorcher. Best cuts: Grammy-winner "I Don't Know Why You Don't Want Me" and "Halfway House." –TR

King's Record Shop / CBS   1987
After writing most of 1985's *Rhythm & Romance*, Cash returned to largely interpretive work on this powerful collection highlighted by Eliza Gilkyson's feminist anthem "Rosie Strike Back" and her father Johnny Cash's "Tennessee Flat Top Box." –WR

☆ **Interiors / COLUMBIA**   1990
What makes *Interiors* brilliant isn't that Cash produced herself for the first time nor that she wrote all the songs. It's that *Interiors* — the last album Cash made for Columbia's Nashville division — meticulously chronicles the unraveling of a terribly dysfunctional relationship, namely Cash's marriage to Rodney Crowell. Cash gets at the psychology behind country's cheating and drinking themes — the emotional anesthetic of addictions, the desperate grasping for love in affairs. The arrangements are stripped as bare as Cash's soul, but *Interiors* is country at its core. –BM

CASH-JENNINGS-NELSON-KRISTOFFERSON

Country. Johnny Cash, Waylon Jennings, Willie Nelson, and Kris Kristofferson teamed for this country supergroup. –ED

○ **Highwayman / CBS**   1985
These old friends have appeared together in various

combinations, but never as effectively as on the epic title song here, written by Jimmy Webb. And the rest of the record, including Guy Clark's "Desperados Waiting for a Train" and Woody Guthrie's "Deportee," lives up to the leadoff hit. –WR

MARK CHESNUTT

Traditional country. The son of a country singer, Mark Chesnutt grew up in his father's footsteps. He started singing at Gilley's, the club *Urban Cowboy* made famous, when he was 17, and cut a number of independent singles before being signed to MCA. His debut album, 1990's *Too Cold at Home*, made him a dark-horse hat act, as he was overshadowed by the success of Garth Brooks and Clint Black. On his second album, the humor and personality in his delivery showed more, and Chesnutt began developing a name for himself. –BM

○ **Longnecks & Short Stories / MCA**   1992
Longnecks heralded the emergence of a Texas voice that contained both the knack for humor ("Old Flames Have New Names," "Bubba Shot the Jukebox"), and the depth for heartache ("I'll Think of Something"). –BM

CIRCUS MAXIMUS

Country. A precursor to the cosmic cowboy movement, this folk rock/outfit had more than a touch of psychedelia and plenty of country. Jerry Jeff Walker got his start here. "The Wind" was a minor hit for lthe band. –BE

○ **Circus Maximus w/ Jerry Jeff Walker / VANGUARD**
The psychedelic roots of progressive country music. –RG

GUY CLARK   b 1941

Country. Guy Clark was one of the founding fathers of the Texas singer/songwriter movement in Austin, TX, along with Waylon Jennings, Willie Nelson, Jerry Jeff Walker, and Townes Van Zandt. His musical influences have been strong, leading such musicians as Nanci Griffith, Robert Earl Keen Jr, Darden Smith, Lyle Lovett, and Hugh Moffatt to speak his praise. –CR

○ **Old #1 / SUGAR HILL**   1976
Every song is a classic. Clark is backed by Chip Young, Steve Gibson, Johnny Gimble, Rodney Crowell, Emmylou Harris, Steve Earle, and others. Start your collection here. –CR

Texas Cookin' / SUGAR HILL   1976
The songs here are more Nashville, hitting many emotions. "Texas Cookin'," "Virginia's Reel," and "Broken Hearted" are all great songs. What a way to finish the album, as Clark and Johnny Cash sing "The Last Gunfighter Ballad." –CR

Fool on the Roof / WARNER   1978
This very overlooked album is more country than his first two RCA albums. Just listen to the vocals (with the Whites, Rodney Crowell, Don Everly, Gordon Payne) and the words. You'll find this album grows on you. –CR

The South Coast of Texas / WARNER   1980
A good solid album. Check out Rosanne Cash's vocals on "Cystelle." Vince Gill, Ricky Skaggs, and Rodney Crowell give this album a real polished sound. –CR

Better Days / WARNER   1983
Produced by Rodney Crowell, this is a personal favorite containing some of Clark's trademark songs, like "The Carpenter," "Homegrown Tomatoes," and the tear-jerker "The Randal Knife." –CR

Old Friends / SUGAR HILL
Clark's finest moment. The production allows Clark to present his songs without any distractions. Sam Bush, Verlon Thompson, Michael Henderson, and Vince Gill blend with Clark perfectly, as do Rosanne Cash and Emmylou Harris. –CR

ROY CLARK   b 1933

Traditional country, country-pop. In the 70s Roy Clark symbolized country music in the US and abroad. Between guest-hosting for Johnny Carson on "The Tonight Show" and performing to packed houses in the Soviet Union on a tour that sold out all 18 concerts, he used his musical talent and

his entertaining personality to bring country music into homes across the world. As one of the hosts of TV's "Hee Haw" (Buck Owens was the other), for more than 20 years Clark picked and sang and offered kountry korn to 30 million people weekly. He is first and foremost an entertainer, drawing crowds at venues as different as Las Vegas, Atlantic City, and the Opry. His middle-of-the-road approach has filled a national void, with Clark offering music more country than Kenny Rogers but less country than Waylon Jennings. Among his numerous vocal hits are "Yesterday When I was Young" and "Thank God and Greyhound." Instrumentally he has won awards for both guitar and banjo. Multi-talented Clark co-starred on the silver screen with Mel Tillis in the comedy *Uphill All the Way.* Roy Clark's popularity will continue as long as he wants to stay in the business. Bob Hope refers to Clark as "the consummate entertainer." –DV

○ **The Best of Roy Clark / CAPITOL**   1971
Compilation of Clark's earlier (pre-"Hee Haw") hits, including "Yesterday When I Was Young" and "Tips of My Fingers." –CK

○ **In Concert / MCA**
Nice sampling of Clark's stage show with great guitar playing, corny jokes and all. –CK

PATSY CLINE   1932-1963

Country-pop. Before she died in an airplane crash in 1963, Patsy Cline had the best of both worlds, country and pop. By avoiding the country/western mold and appealing to fans more accustomed to middle-of-the-road music, she changed the course of country music and ushered in a new era for country female singers, one that dominates today. Cline's quality voice was perfect for torch songs — emotional yet distant and cool at the same time. In 1957 she won an Arthur Godfrey Talent Scout TV contest, singing "Walking after Midnight." The single became both a country and pop hit, creating a pattern Cline followed throughout her brief career. In 1960 she both joined the Opry and saw her first smash hit, "I Fall to Pieces," a song backed by many strings and voices. Her producers continued marketing her to the pop audience, and very successfully, with similar hits to follow, including "Crazy" (written by Willie Nelson), "She's Got You," and "Leavin' on Your Mind." Even after her death, the songs were hits, among them "Faded Love," "Sweet Dreams (of You)," and "Anytime" (1969).
Oddly enough, Cline entered the country-pop market against her wishes. She liked to yodel, wore cowgirl outfits into the early 60s, and detested some of her biggest hit songs. But she has become a legend and has influenced more modern female singers than all others combined. What a great voice ...–DV

Patsy Cline Showcase / MCA   1960
Pop and C&W standards plus three of her biggest hits: "I Fall to Pieces," "Crazy," and "Walkin' after Midnight." –GB

Sentimentally Yours / MCA   1962
Pop and C&W collection — several Hank Williams songs. Includes the great "She's Got You." –GB

A Portrait of Patsy Cline / MCA   1964
Country standards and some lesser-known material. Highlights: "Faded Love" and "Blue Moon of Kentucky." –GB

That's How a Heartache Begins / DECCA   1964
A few pop standards plus some of her best: "There He Goes," "Lovin' in Vain," "He Called Me Baby," "I'm Blue Again." Also a great "Lovesick Blues." –GB

★ **Patsy Cline's Greatest Hits / MCA**   1967
This is the standard collection of Patsy Cline's most successful singles, containing among its 12 tracks seven of her eight Top Ten country hits, 1957-1963. Since its release, the album has sold four million copies, and at this writing, it is enjoying its 66th consecutive week at #1 in *Billboard* magazine's Top Country Catalog Albums chart, a chart that has been in existence for 66 weeks. –WR

Patsy Cline Story / MCA   1969
Double-record set with many of her best — "Sweet Dreams,"

"I Fall to Pieces," "She's Got You," "Crazy," "Why Can't He Be You." −GB

☆ **The Patsy Cline Collection / MCA**   1991
With four hours and 25 minutes of music (104 cuts), this is pretty much the definitive Cline collection. It's got all the hits, 16 previously unreleased tracks (including some live radio transcriptions), even some silliness, like "Tra Le La La Le La Triangle." But in only ten years of recording, Cline became the most influential female vocalist in country music, so she's worth it. −BM

○ **20 Golden Pieces of Patsy Cline / BULLDOG**
In contention for the #1 pick — mainly because of the large number of songs included. This British collection may be difficult to find. It's heavy on the honky-tonk and rockabilly-ish numbers and leaves out the pop standards — a plus in my book. Unfortunately, it doesn't contain any of her big ballad hits. −GB

Country Great / VL
"Three Cigarettes in an Ashtray" and "Then You'll Know" are some highlights of this collection. −GB

Gotta Lot of Rhythm in My Soul / METRO (MGM)
How MGM got ahold of this stuff, I'll never know. Good collection, no pop — includes stuff from her early Coral years as well as later Decca sides. −GB

Live at the Opry / MCA
As everyone who listened to the Ryman opry knows, even a good singer can sound pretty bad live over the radio. Cline sounds simply great, with no studio effects and a sometimes pedestrian backup. −GB

Patsy Cline / EVEREST
Another good collection — "Walkin' after Midnight," "Never No More," "Just out of Reach," "There He Goes," no pop standards. −GB

Stop the World and Let Me Off / HILLTOP
Good collection that features stuff from her 1955 Coral sessions — "I Cried All the Way to the Altar," "Honky Tonk Merry Go Round" — through 1960 or so — "There He Goes," "Stop, Look & Listen." −GB

DAVID ALLAN COE   b 1939

Traditional country. If you want authenticity in your country singer, try David Allan Coe, who spent 20 years in reform schools and prison, gaining his release in 1967. His songwriting talent is obvious, having written "Would You Lay with Me (In a Field of Stone)" for Tanya Tucker and the workingman's anthem "Take This Job and Shove It" for Johnny Paycheck. Among his charting singles have been "Mona Lisa's Lost Her Smile" and "The Ride," which tells of an otherworldly meeting with Hank Williams. He operates a Willie Nelson and Family general store in Branson, MO. −DV

○ **Greatest Hits / COLUMBIA**   1978
All you need to know about this ex-con turned country con-man/songwriter. One of country's more intriguing egos from the 70s. −MH

For the Record - The First 10 Years / COLUMBIA   1985
An overview of Coe's Columbia sides. −MH

Biggest Hits / COLUMBIA
And then some! −MH

Just Divorced / COLUMBIA
A theme album (see title). −MH

Longhaired Redneck / COLUMBIA
This is 70s outlaw country at its most virulent. The tattoos and biker bravado thinly conceal Coe's sentimentality. −MH

MARK COLLIE

Traditional country. This Tennessee native moved to Nashville and worked as a songwriter before turning to singing in 1988. His current album, *Born and Raised in Black and White,* gives a good sense of his talents. −DV

Hardin County Line / MCA
This honky-tonk rebel's debut evokes the heart of 50s country,

with detailed and compassionate songwriting, wildcat vocals, and guitar by James Burton. −JF

○ **Born & Raised in Black & White / MCA**
This continues in the fine tradition set by this upstart's debut. He will be a major artist. −JF

JOHN CONLEE   b 1946

Country. Born and raised on a 200-acre farm in Versailles, KY, Conlee has continued to till the soil on his own farm in suburban Nashville, even since "hitting it big." Music was — and still is — a hobby as much as a career to him; he didn't even sign his first recording contract until age 30. Instead, he pursued work as a mortician (he still maintains his license) in Kentucky and worked as a disc jockey at a number of radio stations, including Nashville's WLAC, where he made numerous contacts on Music Row. One of his tapes attracted ABC Records, but Conlee's gruff, down-to-earth delivery wasn't an immediate success. It took a couple of years before "Rose Colored Glasses" — one of the few songs he's written himself — exploded in 1978. A self-avowed homebody, Conlee was never particularly enamored with touring and devoted most of his career time to the recording process instead, particularly his song selection. Noted for an astute sense of quality material (he was ably assisted through the bulk of his career by record producer and former Jim Reeves sideman Bud Logan), he made albums that rarely, if ever, contained "fluff." Even when they're not commercial, Conlee's songs are always interesting. −TR

○ **Greatest Hits / MCA**
Simple, slice-of-life statements about the real world, the songs cover infidelity ("She Can't Say That Anymore," "Baby, You're Something"), relationship issues ("Friday Night Blues"), and personal finance ("Busted," "Common Man"). The asylum piece, "I Don't Remember Loving You," is eternally vivid. −TR

With Love ... / MCA
Nine of the ten cuts in this package came from Tree Publishing, meaning that Conlee and producer Bud Logan limited themselves unnecessarily. But Conlee is extremely convincing on "Only Oklahoma Away" and "What's Forever For," not to mention the mysterious "Miss Emily's Picture." −TR

EARL THOMAS CONLEY   b 1941

Country. Early in his career, ETC's music picked up the label "thinking man's country." An accurate description — Conley looks into the heart and soul of his characters, finding the motivations for their actions and beliefs. In the process, the astute listener can find fragments of him/herself in nearly any Conley creation. Born into poverty in Portsmouth, OH, Conley struggled with the limits of his social class. He aspired to be a painter or actor but found that his aspirations for music lingered after the other interests died down. Influenced by everything from Hank Williams to the Eagles, Conley delved into the details of writing, trying to learn the craft by following the rules and regulations of the Music Row songwriting community. Eventually, torn by the limits of the "law," he found his own niche by breaking many of those same rules. His public self-analysis — in both his songs and his interviews — has proven inspirational to some, bothersome to others, but Conley has evolved stylistically, even though the thinking man label continues to follow him. He's admittedly chased a more commercial sound, with a certain degree of success, but the run for the dollars also put him into a financial bind. He spent part of the late 80s and early 90s overworking himself to pay off his debts. Although he has been a hitmaker for more than a decade, his contributions to country have often gone almost unnoticed. −TR

Blue Pearl / SUNBIRD
The album that earned Conley the thinking man label. "Middle-Age Madness" and "Blue and Green" stand out as classically written profiles of people in pain. "Silent Treatment," "Fire and Smoke," and "You Don't Have to Go Too

Far" possess a captivating, slick sheen that belies their raw approach. –TR

○ **Don't Make It Easy for Me / RCA**

Conley speaks of "programming" himself to write, and in setting the tone for this album — as well as the followup, *Treadin' Water* — he programmed "radio records" into his consciousness. The result: a driving, rock-inflected package that yielded four #1 singles — the first time an album did that in any format. The title track and "Your Love's on the Line" are particularly listenable, but there's not a bad cut on it. –TR

STONEY AND WILMA LEE COOPER

Traditional country. Stoney (b 1918) and Wilma Lee Cooper (b 1921), a husband-and-wife Opry act, were famed for their powerful stage presence and their authentic material that fell between mountain folk music and bluegrass. Since fiddler Stoney's death, Wilma has continued on the Opry. When she sings a song, it stays sung. –DV

○ **Wilma Lee & Stoney Cooper / COUNTY**

BILLY "CRASH" CRADDOCK   b 1939

Country. People often associate the "Crash" nickname with auto racing, but Craddock actually got it as a halfback in high school, crashing into linemen who were twice his size. Growing up in Greensboro, NC, he pantomimed Grand Ole Opry shows in the family's barn with a broomstick as a microphone, alternately pretending he was Hank Williams, Faron Young, or Carl Smith. But when he signed a recording contract in the late 50s, Columbia tried to mold him as a teen idol, much like Elvis Presley or Fabian. It didn't work in the US, but "Crash" did pick up a trio of hits in Australia. Fifteen years later, he finally got his chance in country music when record producer Ron Chancey signed him to his Cartwheel label. With a knack for making re-makes of pop hits like "Knock Three Times" and "Ruby Baby" — and for adding a certain energy to the country idiom — Craddock picked up the nickname "Mr. Country Rock." –TR

○ **Sings His Greatest Hits / ABC**

A good summation of his peak years, including the ballads "Easy As Pie" and "Broken Down in Tiny Pieces." But Craddock's at his best when he's "in the groove," as in "Ruby Baby," "Still Thinkin' 'bout You," and his staple, "Rub It In." –TR

RODNEY CROWELL   b 1950

Contemporary country. The consummate singer/songwriter, Crowell "grew up in Houston off of Wayside Drive" (as he says in the lyrics of Waylon Jennings's "I Ain't Living Long Like This"), latching onto everything from Hank Williams to Chuck Berry and Elvis Presley. He played as a kid in his dad's local band, and packed up with friend Donivan Cowart (now a successful engineer) to move to Nashville, lured by a "promoter's" promise of an opening slot on a major concert tour with a name entertainer. Once he got there, he realized he'd been taken, but Crowell decided to stay, and worked his way up from lounge singer to membership in Emmylou Harris's Hot Band. From there, he earned a reputation for his evaluation of material and for his arranging smarts, and picked up plenty of action as a songwriter and producer. His production credits include projects with now-ex-wife Rosanne Cash, Guy Clark, Bobby Bare, and Sissy Spacek, while his songwriting includes "Leaving Louisiana in the Broad Daylight," "Somewhere Tonight," "'Til I Gain Control Again," and "Shame on the Moon." Despite critical acclaim for his recording efforts, Crowell was unable to harness commercial success for a decade, but that problem ended with 1988's *Diamonds & Dirt* album. –TR

● **The Rodney Crowell Collection / WARNER**   1989

The best of Crowell's uneven but occasionally brilliant early recordings condensed into one neat little package. Includes "Shame on the Moon," which Bob Seger rightly turned into a pop hit. This isn't *Diamonds & Dirt*, but it's a good start. –BM

Keys to the Highway / COLUMBIA

Wide-ranging set, combining soul, blues, rock, and the country shuffle. Recorded shortly after the May 1989 death of Crowell's father, it's surprisingly upbeat and hopeful in its approach. Still, the two brooding songs most closely linked to James Crowell's passing — "Many a Long & Lonesome Highway" and "Things I Wish I'd Said" — stand out most. –TR

○ **Diamonds & Dirt / COLUMBIA**

Record producer Tony Brown convinced Crowell to do this one quickly and not second-guess himself; the advice paid off. Leaning hard on the country shuffle, Crowell broke through with this package — live, honest, and unassuming. It yielded five hits, including the Grammy-winning "After All This Time," but the best cut might be the tantalizing "I Know You're Married." –TR

Rodney Crowell / WARNER

Crowell plays down his performance on this album. Yes, he's a bit cool toward the material vocally on occasion, but the overall effect is raw, energetic, and natural, in the best garage-band tradition. A good mix of club rock & roll and country/rock with, incidentally, his own renditions of "'Til I Gain Control Again" and "Shame on the Moon." –TR

BILLY RAY CYRUS

Contemporary country. Enamored of baseball, Billy Ray Cyrus intended to become another Johnny Bench as he grew up in Flatlands, KY. While attending Georgetown College on a baseball scholarship, he bought a guitar and decided immediately that athletics wasn't the proper direction for his life. Instead, he formed a band called Sly Dog with his brother and gave himself a ten-month deadline for finding a place to play. One week prior to that cutoff date, the group went to work as the house band for a club in Ironton, OH, where they remained for two years.

When a 1984 fire destroyed the bar — and Cyrus's equipment — he moved to Los Angeles to pursue his career. Eventually, he decided to return to Kentucky and commuted regularly from there to Nashville in search of a record deal. Grand Ole Opry star Del Reeves got Mercury Records to take a look, and division head Harold Shedd signed him in the summer of 1990. When his first album came out in mid 1992, Cryus — with his good looks, sculpted body and the infectious "Achy, Breaky Heart" — became an instant groundbreaking sensation. –TR

○ **Some Gave All / MERCURY**   1992

Some Gave All became the first debut album by a country artist to enter the pop charts at #1 (it hit #1 on the country charts as well). The album's sales were fueled by the breakout single "Achy, Breaky Heart," which offered Southern-fried Rolling Stones rhythms and a goofy chorus with a hook so big it demanded a reaction. Not one to eschew the obvious, Cyrus pumped his songs full of as much rock & roll as the market would bear, so songs like "Could've Been Me" and "Never Thought I'd Fall in Love with You" appealed to young fans who had just discovered the possibilities (both musical and sexual) of country music. –BM

LACY J. DALTON

Contemporary country. Lacy J. Dalton, who has a voice one writer described as "honey laced with whiskey," took a circuitous route to Nashville. Born Jill Byrem in Bloomsburg, PA, she attended Brigham Young University but dropped out to become folk singer. She kicked around Utah, Minnesota, Pennsylvania, and New York before winding up in front of a psychedelic rock band in San Francisco in the late 60s. She married the group's manager, who died as the result of injuries sustained in a swimming-pool accident. Dalton kept performing, and a tape of her music eventually reached producer Billy Sherrill, who signed her to Columbia in 1979. The Academy of Country Music named her Best New Female Vocalist in 1979 on the strength of her debut, "Crazy Blue Eyes." Dalton's distinct sound and far-ranging musical interests may have kept her from being the star she could have been, but her records helped open doors for new sounds in country. –BM

○ **Greatest Hits / COLUMBIA**   1983
Dalton's best songs weren't always her hits, but *Greatest Hits* is still a good sampler, including "Crazy Blue Eyes," her first hit; "Hard Times"; remakes of "Tennessee Waltz" and "Dream Baby"; and the music-biz anthem "16th Avenue." –BM

Crazy Love / CAPITOL   1991
The title song is by Van Morrison, and if Dalton is not the vocalist Morrison is, she still may be the best female soul singer country offers, and she's a better one than Michael Bolton, whose "Walk Away" she also covers. *Crazy Love* is an appropriate title because Dalton seems genuinely bewildered by the vagaries of the emotion — why her lover loves her ("Crazy Love"), why he leaves her ("Forever in My Heart"), and why sometimes neither marriage nor divorce makes sense. But she's a great singer, not God. –BM

CHARLIE DANIELS BAND

Traditional country, country rock. Before there was "The Devil Went Down to Georgia," there was life for Charlie Daniels in bluegrass and as a session player in Nashville (he played on Bob Dylan's *Nashville Skyline* album). In fact, before his 1979 #1 hit, he had success in 1975 with "The South's Gonna Do It." The Charlie Daniels Band has built a strong bridge between rock and pure country, playing both with authority. His image symbolizes the good ol' boy who loves his music and his country. His annual Volunteer Jam brings together great musicians from country, rock, jazz, and blues, and has returned to Nashville. –DV

☆ **Fire on the Mountain / CBS / BB 38**   1974
A great slice of country-fried boogie. –DH

Million Mile Reflections / CBS / BB 5   1979
A commercial breakthrough for Daniels. –DH

● **Decade of Hits / CBS / BB 84**   1980
An all-too-brief summing-up. –DH

JIMMIE DAVIS   b 1902

Traditional country. This former two-time governor of Louisiana is best remembered for three country standards: "You Are My Sunshine," "It Makes No Difference Now," and "Nobody's Darlin' but Mine." He's been a Country Music Hall of Famer since 1972. –DV

○ **Country Music Hall of Fame / MCA**
1934-1953 sides by this hillbilly crooner with a penchant for blues include "You Are My Sunshine." –MH

SKEETER DAVIS   b 1931

Traditional country. Originally teamed with high school friend BJ (Betty Jack) Davis as the Davis Sisters, they scored mainstream C&W hits in a strong, emotive duo style. Both were involved in car crash (BJ was killed, Skeeter seriously injured) in mid 1954. Skeeter came back in 1958 as a solo artist, joined the Grand Ole Opry, and scored nearly 20 years worth of hits (over 40 in all), with many crossing over to the pop charts. –CK

○ **She Sings They Play / ROUNDER**   1983
Skeeter Davis, a prolific country singer since the 50s, teamed up with the versatile NRBQ for this delightful collaboration. Nashville with a kick. –JT

TONY DE LA ROSA

Tex-Mex. Norteno music veteran Tony de la Rosa was one of the first bandleaders to add drums and amplification to the tradition-bound conjunto style. After a long semi-retirement, he has emerged with his no-frills Tex-Mex sound intact, applying his accordion to the ever-popular polkas and rancheras of the Texas border. –MB

○ **Así Se Baila en Tejas / ROUNDER**
Straight from the heart, old-style Tex-Mex for Saturday night border dances. –MB

BILLY DEAN   b 1962

Contemporary country. Billy Dean received a basketball scholarship to attend East Central Junior College in Decatur, MS, where he majored in physical education, but instead of wearing a whistle around his neck, he opted for a guitar strap. Inspired by Merle Haggard, Marty Robbins, and Dean Martin, he played the club circuit along the Gulf Coast in Florida and used national talent contests as a vehicle for his music.
He made the finals of the Wrangler Country Star Search in 1982, then won as a Male Vocalist champ on Ed McMahon's "Star Search" program in 1988. Even before the release of his debut album, *Young Man*, he'd already gone on tour as an opening act for Mel Tillis, Gary Morris, and Ronnie Milsap. He's contributed to commercials for Valvoline, McDonald's, and Chevrolet, and had an acting role in the brief Elvis series on ABC-TV in 1990.
His good looks are undeniable but Dean has the talent to match, as proven when he won the Academy of Country Music's Song of the Year award for the enormously sensitive "Somewhere in My Broken Heart," cowritten with Richard ("Don't It Make My Brown Eyes Blue," "Come from the Heart") Leigh. –TR

○ **Young Man / SBK**   1991
Nashville launched so many new acts from 1989-1992 that many who deserved a shot went overlooked. Thanks in part to his own songwriting skills, and to signing with SBK Records, which had just one country act to push, Dean got a good listen and was able to capitalize with a strong debut. His vocals aren't unique, but he sings with strength and conviction, regardless of the style. You can't go wrong with "Somewhere in My Broken Heart." –TR

Billy Dean / CAPITOL   1991
Billy Dean's second album follows the same pattern that made his first so popular: a strong emphasis on the ballads on which his supple baritone thrives. The rollicking "Hammer Down" flies in the face of everything else, but even there the message remains the same: obvious but effective. –BM

JIMMY DEAN   b 1928

Traditional country. This Texan became famous for sausages long after he made a name for himself in music via his self-penned "Big Bad John" (1961), "PT 109," and "Dear Ivan." Dean's wit and quick humor make him a natural for T, and he had his own CBS show as well as one on ABC in the mid 60s. The syndicated "Jimmy Dean's Country Beat" did well in the 80s. Occasionally he's guest host on the Ralph Emery show, where he speaks his mind refreshingly often. –DV

○ **Jimmy Dean's Greatest Hits / COLUMBIA**   1980
This contains "Big Bad John" and "PT 109." –DH

THE DELMORE BROTHERS

Old-time, traditional country. Alton (b 1908 - d 1964) and Rabon (b 1910 - d 1954) in the late 30s and 40s were famed for their matchless vocal harmony and instrumental creativity. They differed greatly from other family duets of the time because of their prolific songwriting and their use of Black-inspired material. In the 30s their sound was country blues, while in the 40s the Delmores featured songs with a boogie beat. –DV

○ **The Best of the Delmore Brothers / STARDAY**   1987
Terrific nasal vocal harmonies, their brisk, bubblin' tenors, 6-string guitars, and Wayne Raney's wailin' locomotive harmonica make the Delmores' late-40s King label hits the most accessible of their early brother-duo material. Sounding a mite like the amiable smalltown uncles of Elvis and the Everly Brothers, the chooglin' "hillbilly boogie" of the Delmores was just a hairpin curve away from rockabilly. –MH

THE DESERT ROSE BAND

Country rock. Vocalist Chris Hillman is one of the founders of two Southern California bands, the Byrds and the Flying

Burrito Brothers. The country-rock tradition continues with the present band, which has produced five #1 singles, including "She Don't Love Nobody" and "He's Back and I'm Blue." –DV

○ **A Dozen Roses - Greatest Hits / MCA**   1991
A showcase for Hillman's pop-country vocals and the considerable chops of bandmembers such as Herb Pedersen. Together they made some of the best country singles of the late 80s, all collected here. –WR

The Desert Rose Band / CURB
For those concerned that California country might have disappeared, the mid-80s emergence of the Desert Rose Band, Southern Pacific, and Dwight Yoakam put those fears to rest. While S-Pac leaned toward country-rock, and Yoakam hits hard on the honky-tonk sound, TDRB offers just a tinge of bluegrass, lots of energy, and intriguing harmonies. The cuts "One Step Forward," "Love Reunited," and "Leave This Town" are simply stunning. –TR

DIAMOND RIO

Progressive bluegrass. A group that began playing bluegrass at Opryland USA as the Tennessee River Boys, Diamond Rio became one of the most sudden success stories of modern country music. Diamond Rio's initial release, "Meet in the Middle," topped the charts (the first debut single by a group to do so) in 1991; the band followed with more hits and an Academy of Country Music Group of the Year Award. The band's bluegrass pedigree (bassist Dana Williams is a nephew of the Osborne Brothers; other members have played for Vassar Clements and J. D. Crowe) helped establish the image of a new country band with traditional ties. The picking's hot, thanks to guitarist Jimmy Olander, and the group's tight harmonies complement Marty Roe's smooth tenor lead. –BM

○ **Diamond Rio / ARISTA**   1991
One of the most successful debut albums in country music, *Diamond Rio* sparked plenty of hits — "Meet in the Middle," "Mama Don't Forget to Pray for Me," "Nowhere Bound," "Norma Jean Riley" — by combining bluegrass harmonies, old-fashioned country virtues, and just enough rock to keep things moving. –BM

LITTLE JIMMY DICKENS   b 1925

Traditional country. At less than five feet tall (and looking much smaller with his huge Gibson guitar), Dickens's signature song is his first Top Ten single, "Take an Old Cold Tater and Wait" (1949). He's best known, though, for his crossover hit "May the Bird of Paradise Fly up Your Nose" from 1965. Since 1949 he's appeared weekly on the Opry, entertaining fans with his boundless energy and his many novelty tunes. –DV

○ **Columbia Historic Edition / COLUMBIA**
Some 40s-50s sides by this pint-sized hillbilly howler. One of the Opry's great characters. –MH

JOE DIFFIE   b 1958

Traditional country, progressive country. Joe Diffie combines musical diversity with straight country. His debut single, "Home," went to #1 on the charts, as did two other songs from *A Thousand Winding Roads*, his first album. Diffie can sing Hank Williams-style or progressive country with feeling. –DV

○ **A Thousand Winding Roads / EPIC**   1990
A likeable new country voice from Oklahoma who praises home and hearth. –MH

Regular Joe / EPIC   1992
Diffie's second album has all the clichés of country music and all the good stuff too. If "Ain't That Bad Enough" is a run-of-the-mill song, Diffie rescues it by tearing the melody loose from its mooring. He's also willing to push the line: of all Diffie's country heroes — and you'll be able to name them after one listen — maybe only Merle Haggard would rock out as hard as Diffie does on the title track. –BM

DAVE DUDLEY   b 1928

Traditional country, trucker country. Dudley (born David Pedruska) was one of country music's biggest troubadours of trucker songs. "Six Days on the Road," a #2 country hit in 1963, was the first of a string of classic songs in the idiom. Between 1961 and 1980, Dudley scored 41 hits. Currently there isn't an adequate domestically available collection on compact disc. –RC

○ **20 Great Truck Hits: Dave Dudley / EMI**   1983
This Swedish import collection includes a smattering of Dudley's hits like "Six Days on the Road," "Counterfeit Cowboy," and "Me and Ole C.B." –RC

HOLLY DUNN

Contemporary country. In 1991 her single "Maybe I Mean Yes" was removed from radio playlists, at her request, after some listeners claimed the song promoted date rape. She also was interviewed for TV's "Lifestyles of the Rich and Famous." But on a musical note, catch "Daddy's Hand," her best-known single and her signature tune. –DV

Blue Rose of Texas / WARNER   1989
A "nu-country/pop" belter with an occasional rock punch and a Western swing and sway. –MH

○ **Milestones - Greatest Hits / WARNER**   1991
A good overview of one of "nu-country"'s most amiable thrushes. –MH

Heart Full of Love / WARNER
More of Dunn's radio-friendly songs. –MH

BOBBY DURHAM

Traditional country. Bakersfield, CA, has become legendary as one of the alternatives to Nashville in country music, and Durham is one of the journeymen singers who has worked the bars there for three decades. He never attained the fame of Bakersfield'best-known sons, Buck Owens and Merle Haggard, but he did make a few good singles for Capitol in the 60s and, in the late 80s, a fine album for Hightone. –MH

○ **Where I Grew Up / HIGHTONE**   1987
Bakersfield in the late 80s, still kickin'! –MH

STEVE EARLE

Country rock. Sometimes singing rock, other times rockabilly, Steve Earle puts raw energy into whatever he sings. His *Guitar Town* album of 1986 caused a stir in Nashville. –DV

○ **Guitar Town / MCA**   1986
Steve Earle rode a suspiciously rocking band into Nashville and up to the top of the country charts with this album, after which it was decided he was just a little too extreme for the country market. Which means this record is "on the edge" in more ways than one. –WR

Copperhead Road / UNI   1988
Earle finally got around to re-recording his early classic, "The Devil's Right Hand," on an album that was heavily influenced by a hillbilly attitude and old Rolling Stones records. It was a potent combination. –WR

EXILE

Country rock, country-pop. For a while this quintet gave fellow country-pop rivals Alabama a run for their money. With their material, sound, and musical arrangements, they're closer to rock than to country roots. Their "Kiss You All Over" was a 1978 pop hit before they reconstituted themselves as a country band in the mid 80s. –DV

Greatest Hits / CBS   1986
Pop hits and the disco cut "Kiss You All Over." –BC

Complete Collection / CAPITOL
Their early-80s country hits. –BC

○ **Still Standing / ARISTA**
A fun, peppy country album. Their best. –BC

Shelter from the Night / EPIC
Almost a decade removed from "Kiss You All Over," the band

leans closer to Top 40 rock than country — don't read that as a complaint. The band commuted to Connecticut on off-days during a summer-long tour to record in Stamford with Bruce Hornsby producer Elliot Scheiner, and their effort is surprisingly inspired. If you can't dance to "I Can't Get Close Enough," "Just One Kiss," or "She's Already Gone," you can't dance. –TR

DONNA FARGO   b1949

Country-pop. This former teacher hit the top in 1972, when her self-penned "The Happiest Girl in the Whole USA" was chosen Country Music Association Single of the Year. Over the next eight years she had 15 Top Ten country-pop hits, among them "It Do Feel Good" and "That Was Yesterday." In 1979 she developed multiple sclerosis, but she continued with her career. –DV

○ **The Best of Donna Fargo / MCA**   1977
Contains "Funny Face" and "The Happiest Girl in the Whole USA." –DH

FREDDY FENDER   b1937

Traditional country, country-pop. With Johnny Rodriguez in the 70s, Freddy Fender popularized Tex-Mex music and helped to create a national interest in the genre. Born Baldemar Huerta, the son of Texas migrant farmers, Fender started in R&B, moving to country songs in which he alternated lyrics in Spanish and English. In 1975 he had three monster #1 hits, "Before the Next Teardrop Falls" and "Wasted Days and Wasted Nights," followed by "Secret Love." Further success eluded him for fifteen years, until he became part of the Texas Tornados. –DV

○ **Before the Next Teardrop Falls / MCA / BB 20**   1975
Textbook blend of Tex-Mex and country, spiced by Fender's immortal hit. –RW

★ **The Best of Freddie Fender / MCA / BB 155**   1977
This contains his other classics but stops at the mid '70s. –RW

RAY FLACKE

Instrumental: guitar. From England, Ray Flacke is a fingerpicking guitar whiz who is now much in demand in Nashville. He's been in Marty Stuart's touring band and is featured on a few cuts of Stuart's *Tempted* album. –DV

○ **Untitled Island / DPI**
This English country/rock guitarist is currently a Nashville session cat. –MH

FLATLANDERS

Country. This legendary band from Lubbock, TX, featured Joe Ely, Butch Hancock, and Jimmie Dale Gilmore. They released one record before going on their own. The record is a classic Texas singer/songwriter album. –CR

○ **More a Legend Than a Band / ROUNDER**   1989
When the material on this album was cut in 1972, it was for a release to be called *Jimmie Dale and the Flatlanders*, which should give ample indication of who dominates a session that matched Jimmie Dale Gilmore, Joe Ely, and Butch Hancock. Gilmore has an old-time country vocal sound, but his songs have a dark modern edge, especially "Dallas" and "Tonight I'm Gonna Go Downtown." This time the album lives up to the legend. –WR

ROSIE FLORES

Country. Flores came out of the late 80s Los Angeles Western Beat scene. A gifted singer/songwriter and guitarist, her music ranges from hard country to rockabilly. –CR

○ **After the Farm / HIGHTONE**   1992
From start to finish there is something special about this CD. Flores is a great guitarist, backed by Greg Leisz, David Lindley, Duane "DJ" Jarvis, and Dusty Wakeman. They rock, with some real killer slide-guitar work. If you like your country hard, you'll love it. –CR

Kitty Wells, Patsy Cline, and Country Women

In 1952, country music met its first bona fide woman star, Kitty Wells, the accepted Queen of Country Music. Patsy Montana had recorded the first million-seller by a woman ("I Want to Be a Cowboy's Sweetheart," 1935), but it was Miss Kitty who in release after release gave the male stars competition. Her first hit, "It Wasn't God Who Made Honky-Tonk Angels" (1952), an answer song to the anti-woman "Wild Side of Life," was in a sense the first women's rights song in country music; Wells and her song made it much easier for other women trying to make it in what had been a man's business. Songs sung from the woman's point of view were thereafter accepted in country music. *Billboard* voted Wells the Top Female Performer in country music from 1952 to 1965; this gives you a sense of how she dominated.

Wells's only real rival was Patsy Cline. Although only 13 years separated them in age (and Owen Bradley was producer for both of them at Decca), a gulf lay between them musically, in song content and in singing style. Wells's twang contrasts with Cline's smooth, un-rural delivery (later to be known as the "Nashville Sound"), and Kitty's honky-tonk content clashes with Cline's modern country crooning (for example, her famous version of "Crazy," a song written by Willie Nelson). Cline took the highly emotional, occasionally rough-sounding characteristics of previous female country singers and urbanized it, in the process losing much of the original soul but making country palatable to a much larger audience. Wells was at the end of the first group of country performers, the pioneers of traditional country, while Cline was at the beginning of what has proven to be modern country.

Few contemporary women singers represent Wells's group (Emmylou Harris often is true to the roots, and Reba McEntire is when she wants to be). The rest, a huge majority, have descended from Cline's camp, and distinguishing between them and pop singers is becoming increasingly difficult. Wells remains in the business she loves, as of this writing appearing frequently with her son and her husband Johnny Wright (of the Opry duet Johnny and Jack). Though Cline died in an airplane crash in 1963, her contemporary sound and two movies about her have kept her as popular now as ever, with a CD breaking the Top 20 album charts in 1992.

— David Vinopal

RED FOLEY   1910-1968

Traditional country, gospel. Hall of Fame member Clyde Julian "Red" Foley was graced with a rich baritone voice and a personality that made him a natural star. In 1950 he scored with three #1s, "Chattanoogie Shoe Shine Boy," "Steal Away," and "Just a Closer Walk with Thee," the latter two directing him toward religious material for the rest of his career, including his signature song, "Peace in the Valley." In 1954 he hosted the "Ozark Jubilee," one of the earliest country TV shows. He continued making appearances right up to his death. –DV

☆ **Country Music Hall of Fame / MCA**
A well-chosen sampling of 1944-1953 cuts. Foley is backed by some of the era's best country studio musicians. –RL

Tennessee Saturday Night / CHARLY
Another strong compilation, with the emphasis on Foley's boogie and uptempo material. –RL

BROWNIE FORD

Country. Ford was an Oklahoma-born cowboy who learned the old songs as a lad, spun a few of his own, told a few ribald tales, and offered to the world his wry take on life in a 1990 Flying Fish album, part field recording (Ford and guitar) and part recording session with an acoustic country band. Ford's wizened vocals and open spirit merited an unlikely nod from *People*, which said kind words over the sole recorded testament of an 80-something individualist. –MH

○ **Stories from ... / FLYING FISH**
Stories from Mountains, Swamps & Honky-Tonks. A delightful geezer who recalls skinny-dippin' in Oklahoma. He wails wizened folk and country to the guitar accompaniment of Dave Doucet and D. L. Menard. –MH

TENNESSEE ERNIE FORD   1919-1991

Traditional country, gospel. This radio announcer quickly changed careers when "Smokey Mountain Boogie," "The Cry of the Wild Goose," "Mule Train," and his self-penned rockabilly song "Shotgun Boogie" made him a star in 1950. The best was yet to come. In 1955 he recorded Merle Travis's superb "Sixteen Tons," a grimly real song about life in the coal mines that sold more than 4 million copies over the next ten years. Ernie's TV show on NBC lasted until he grew tired of it (six years), at which time he took his warm bass voice out of the business for a while; when he returned, it was mainly to gospel, on material that was beautifully suited to his exceptional voice. His *Hymns* album is considered the first country album to sell a million. This gentleman of country music died in 1991, shortly after a television special tribute to him. –DV

○ **16 Tons of Boogie / RHINO**   1990
16 Tons of Boogie: The Best of Tennessee Ernie Ford. In his later years, Ford's little pea-pickin' heart was closely associated with gospel and patriotic music, but in earlier years he knew how to — as the album title says — boogie. This includes all the essential material from that period: "Sixteen Tons," "The Shot Gun Boogie," "Mule Train," and "Blackberry Boogie," for starters. –TR

Ernie Sings & Glen Picks / CAPITOL
Country ballads in an intimate guitar/bass setting. Fine guitar from Glen Campbell. –RL

Collectors Series / CAPITOL
Another good collection. Much duplication with the Rhino Records CD compilation. –RL

THE FORESTER SISTERS

Traditional country, progressive country. These four — and they're actually sisters — still live in their home base of Lookout Mountain, GA, and are regularly seen on TV. They started singing in church and can cover many styles, from gospel to progressive country. –DV

The Forester Sisters / WARNER   1985
Rock music had the Go-Gos, Motown had the Supremes, and the standard pop era had the Andrews Sisters and the McGuire Sisters. Country music finally got an all-girl vocal group with the advent of the Foresters, and their debut is surprisingly uptempo and energetic. A first album that should have received more attention. –TR

○ **Sincerely / WARNER**   1988
Already the possessors of a wonderful vocal harmony style, the Foresters hit a peak when they hooked up with writer/producer Wendy Waldman for this album, cutting her "Letter Home" and other strong material (note especially the shoulda-been-a-single "You Love Me," cowritten by Matraca Berg). –WR

Greatest Hits / WARNER   1989
A good selection of Forester singles presents the various stylistic approaches they've taken with country material, which range from good to terrific. –WR

I Got a Date / WARNER   1992
Somewhere along the line, some executive got the idea that this Lookout Mountain group should concentrate primarily on ballads. As a result, their non-ballad material could've been better, but that's rectified in this collection, an excellent portrayal of the humor and heartaches faced by women in modern relationships. Wide-ranging stylistically, with a strong dose of wit, particularly in the title track and "Redneck Romeo." –TR

FOSTER & LLOYD

Country rock, contemporary country. Radney Foster and Bill Lloyd used their amalgam of rock, country, pop, and folk flavor to produce a few hits, including "Crazy over You," which charted in the Top Five in 1987. Since then, the group has broken up. –DV

Foster & Lloyd / RCA   1987
This self-titled debut effort contains the duo's most recognizable radio tracks, particularly "Crazy over You," a Top Five hit. Other hits included here are "Sure Thing" (#8), "What Do You Want from Me This Time" (#6), and "Texas in 1880" (#18). –RC

○ **Faster and Llouder / RCA**   1989
Foster & Lloyd's sophomore effort presented a harder, edgier collection of songs, which were even stronger than the ones found on their first album. Highlights include "Happy for Awhile," the roots-rocker "Fat Lady Sings," and the title track. Power pop artist Marshall Crenshaw guested on "She Knows What She Wants." –RC

Version of the Truth / RCA   1990
Foster & Lloyd's third album synthesized the energy of *Faster and Llouder* with the radio accessability of their first album. Two versions of the album exist, featuring different mixes. An instrumental, "Whoa," was nominated for a Grammy in 1990 and featured the guest artists Duane Eddy, Albert Lee, Felix Cavillere (of the Rascals), and Rusty Young (of Poco). –RC

GEORGE FOX

Contemporary country. Pleasant, easygoing Canadian country/folksinger. –RC

○ **With All My Might / WARNER**
Produced by Brian Ahern (Emmylou Harris), this album contains an affecting version of Dylan's "I Threw It All Away." There are good but unexceptional originals, the best being "Lonesome Avenue Goodbye" and "Angelina." –RC

SCOTT FREED

Country-rock. Scott Freed is a California singer/songwriter who plays country-flavored music with a Southern rock sound. –CR

○ **Indiana Moon / SCOTT FREED**   1990
An exceptional release! Freed's vocals are strong and deft. The production is clean, with just the right combination of pedal steel, dobro, mandolin (Jack Tuttle), and fiddle. Take notice — big things are in Freed's future. Guaranteed. –CR

JANIE FRICKIE   b1952

Country-pop. This versatile Indiana native made a good living writing jingles and singing backup until Nashville realized her talent as a solo star. In 1982 she had her first #1 with "Don't Worry About Me Baby," leading to her being named Country Music Association Female Vocalist of the Year two years running. –DV

It Ain't Easy / COLUMBIA   1982
The versatility that made Frickie a jingles success might have been a liability as a solo performer. She's so adaptable that her voice might not have been distinctive enough. Here she sounds like a strong woman who's very familiar with heartache, and producer Bob Montgomery gives her some rockin' material to shout on. –TR

○ **17 Greatest Hits / CBS**
Tenderly strident vocals on 80s country hits. –BC

LEFTY FRIZZELL   1928–1975

Traditional country. If a singer's greatness can be measured by those he's influenced, then Lefty Frizzell is at the top, his vocal style echoing in George Jones, Merle Haggard, Willie Nelson, John Anderson, Dwight Yoakam, Randy Travis, and others farther down from this summit. Frizzell took honky-tonk and vocally stretched the words and music, making them smoother and more ballad-like, wringing out the emotion in each phrase. He started out in the dance halls and honky-tonks of West Texas, scoring his first hit with "If You've Got the Money, I've Got the Time" in 1950, which stayed on the charts for 20 weeks. In 1951 he had four singles in the Top Ten at the same time: "I Want to Be with You Always," "Always Late," "Travelin' Blues," and "Mom and Dad's Waltz." Two later hits were "Long Black Veil" (1959) and "Saginaw, Michigan" (1964). After 22 years on the Columbia label, Frizzell joined ABC in 1973 and had three hits with them: "I Never Go around Mirrors" and "Lucky Arms" in 1974, and "Falling" in 1975, the year this ultimate honky-tonker died. –DV

Lefty Frizzell's Greatest Hits / COLUMBIA   1966
The title tells the tale. –MH

Goes to Nashville / ROUNDER   1988
More early (plus some later) Columbia recordings. –MH

☆ **Treasures Untold / ROUNDER**   1988
A wonderful selection of early performances. Rugged Texas honky-tonk delivered in a mellifluous drawl that Merle Haggard and others emulated. An archetype. –MH

American Originals / CBS
The hits. –MH

The Best of Lefty Frizzell / RHINO
A good overview of Frizzell's Columbia recordings. –MH

CHRIS GAFFNEY

Progressive country. Austrian-born Gaffney has been playing music for two decades, based in the American Southwest. A talented songwriter with the ability to make his song's characters and locales come alive, Gaffney handles the vocals, guitar, and accordion with the 5-piece Cold Hard Facts backing him up. Gaffney seamlessly blends country, conjunto, rockabilly, zydeco, and more. Ex-Blasters guitarist Dave Alvin adds a few guitar licks to Gaffney's two releases and cowrites two songs with Gaffney on *Mi Vida Loca*. –DMAC

○ **Mi Vida Loca / HIGHTONE**   1992
Gaffney infuses hard country with elements of Tex-Mex and pure rock & roll, coming off like a cross between Merle Haggard and the Blasters. Gaffney has a dusty voice with perfect country phrasing for ballads like "Quiet Desperation" and "Waltz for Minnie," but he's at his peak with rockers like "'68," a powerful song about a man who lost his best friend in Vietnam, and "Silent Partner," which sounds like souped-up George Jones. –BM

Chris Gaffney & Cold Hard Facts / ROM
Los Angeles dock-worker, singer, songwriter, and accordionist who reflects Hispanic influences and working-class themes in songs of steely poetry. –MH

HANK GARLAND   b 1930

Traditional country. Garland grew up outside Spartanburg, SC, listening to Arthur "Guitar Boogie" Smith and Mother Maybelle Carter on the radio as early inspirations. By his teens he had his own radio show, and his immense prowess on his instrument brought him to Nashville, where he signed as a solo artist in 1949 (as competition for the already established Merle Travis and Chet Atkins). But it was as a session player that Garland truly made his mark, playing on countless hits by Patsy Cline, Elvis Presley, the Everly Brothers, Brenda Lee, and others. Along with Ernest Tubb's guitarist, Jimmy Byrd, he co-designed the still-popular Byrdland model for Gibson

guitars in the early 50s. Garland's incredible talent was moving in a more jazz-oriented direction when an automobile accident in 1961 left his memory and coordination skills impaired, sadly putting his playing days to an end. –CK

☆ **And His Sugar Footers / BEAR FAMILY**   1992
The best of Garland's solo sides from the early 50s, featuring his signature tune, "Sugarfoot Rag," and 19 others equally abounding with hot guitar passages. Some of country's best guitar work is right here for the listening. –CK

LARRY GATLIN & THE GATLIN BROTHERS BAND

Country-pop, traditional country. With his brothers Rudy and Steve, strong-voiced Larry Gatlin sang gospel songs in childhood. His first break came when he worked with the Imperials in Las Vegas as part of Jimmy Dean's show. The late Dottie West gave him a hand by recording his compositions and Johnny Cash used some of his songs in his *Gospel Road* movie. Gatlin's first album, *The Pilgrim*, came out in 1974, and his "Broken Lady" single was a hit in 1975, leading to a Grammy. In the latter part of the 70s he had numerous #1 hits such as "I Wish You Were Someone I Love" and "All the Gold in California." In the 80s, Gatlin and his brothers were as hot as any in the business. Due to medical problems with Larry's vocal chords, the three brothers announced that at the end of 1992 they would disband. –DV

○ **Greatest Hits - Vol. 2 / CBS**   1991
Volume 2 features the best of the Gatlin Brothers. –ED

● **Greatest Hits / CBS**
Both of these packages feature the best of the Gatlins' work ("All the Gold in California" being a particular standout), with the first volume showcasing the best of Larry's solo sides. –CK

Help Yourself / COLUMBIA
Heavy on ballads that effectively show off the Gatlins' trademark genetic harmony. As always, all ten cuts are written by Larry; "Daytime Heroes," a nod to Prince Valium and the soaps, is most inspired. The Gatlin Brothers recorded "Songwriter's Trilogy" live — whether it's insightful or self-indulgent depends on the listener's viewpoint. –TR

○ **Straight Ahead / COLUMBIA**
Occasionally overstated but predominantly satisfying, a little jazz, a little gospel, a little pop, and a little country. Every country fan knows "All the Gold in California," but the best cuts are the controversial "Midnight Choir (Mogen David)" and a sweet little piece of ear candy: "Taking Somebody with Me When I Fall." –TR

CRYSTAL GAYLE   b 1951

Country-pop. Younger sister of Loretta Lynn, Crystal Gayle began her career when her debut single, "I Cried (The Blue Right out of My Eyes)," charted high in 1970. While Lynn became a superstar with traditional country material, Gayle reached the top of her profession with songs that are more pop-oriented, for example, "Don't It Make My Brown Eyes Blue" in 1979. She's scored many #1 hits and collected numerous awards. –DV

● **Classic Crystal / CAPITOL / BB 62**   1979
An early hits package. –BC

True Love / ELEKTRA   1982
When Gayle delivered the album to Elektra's then-division-head Jimmy Bowen, he complained that it rocked too much. Producer Allen Reynolds refused to make changes, so Bowen produced three new tracks that seem out of place. Yeah, the Reynolds tracks do rock. So what? Gayle gives some of her best performances ever on "Our Love Is on the Faultline" and "Deeper in the Fire." –TR

Greatest Hits / COLUMBIA   1983
Always greatly influenced by pop sounds, Gayle embraced that aspect of her musical heritage more in the late 70s and early 80s than any other period. This set covers it well ("Half the Way" is classic) and provides a nice cover photo too. –TR

Ain't Gonna Worry / CAPITOL   1990

An excellent set of country/pop. –BC
○ **What If We Fall in Love / WARNER**
Easy-listening and pop, with Gary Morris. –BC

THE GEEZINSLAWS

Country humor. With a guitar, mandolin, and clever comedy act, the Geezinslaws echo Homer and Jethro on one hand, Lonzo and Oscar on the other. While they pick and sing very well, their real talent is in country humor. Son Geezinslaw doesn't talk, doesn't smile, doesn't do nothing, but he does nothing very well. Check out their *World Tour* album. In a word, they're hilarious. –DV
○ **World Tour / STEP ONE**
Though the best of the Geezinslaws's earlier tracks have yet to be anthologized, this album comes the closest to capturing their peculiar brand of country mayhem. –CK

BOBBIE GENTRY   b 1944

Country-pop. Bobbie Gentry became an overnight star, moving from the Los AngelesSchool of Music to her smash single, "Ode to Billy Joe," a crossover hit in 1967 that led to three Grammy awards. Following this she did well on two duets with Glen Campbell, "Let It Be Me" and "All I Have to Do Is Dream." She hosted and starred on her own show for Britain's BBC in the late 60s and early 70s. –DV
○ **Greatest Hits / CAPITOL**
"Ode to Billy Joe" and duets with Glen Campbell. –BC

DON GIBSON   b 1928

Traditional country, country-pop. This talented singer and songwriter had numerous crossover hits in the 60s and 70s, without even trying to cross over into the pop charts. It was simply that his rich and mellow voice, combined with his exceptionally well-written songs, appealed to *many* listeners, not only those in country. After failing with four different record labels early in his career, Gibson was heard by Chet Atkins, who was then working as an executive for RCA. The two songs Atkins heard? "Oh, Lonesome Me" and "I Can't Stop Loving You," both of which are now country standards and which Gibson wrote in a single day in 1958 in a Nashville house trailer. Gibson immediately joined the Opry, giving him the regular exposure that helped his records reach the charts right into the 80s. In the 70s he had over 40 charted songs, including "Woman, Sensuous Woman," a #1 in 1972. His compositions have been recorded regularly by other stars, from Ray Charles ("I Can't Stop Loving You") and Ronnie Milsap ("Legend in My Time") to Emmylou Harris ("Sweet Dreams"), to mention just a few among dozens. –DV
18 Greatest Hits / CAPITOL
Some 50s-60s sides by one of Music City's greatest singer/songwriter. –MH
○ **All-Time Greatest Hits / RCA**
Hits from the man who wrote "Oh Lonesome Me," "Sea of Heartbreak," etc. A "countrypolitan" with soul. –MH

VINCE GILL   b 1957

Traditional country. This Oklahoman with the high and pure tenor voice performed with the Bluegrass Alliance (and in the late 70s) was lead singer of Pure Prairie League. He's quickly won numerous awards for his high, emotional voice and is renowned for his guitar playing. Gill's classy material shows respect for traditional country music. He excels in three areas: singing, instrumentals, and songwriting. –DV
When I Call Your Name / MCA   1989
The title hit and others, including a duet with Reba McEntire on "Oklahoma Swing." –MH
○ **Pocket Full of Gold / MCA**   1991
A hit album with high bluegrass vocals, traditional country arrangement, and contemporary production. –MH
The Best of Vince Gill / RCA
Some 80s RCA sides. –MH

STEVE GILLETTE & CINDY MANGSEN

Contemporary country. Steve Gillette is a singer/songwriter whose songs have been covered by Gordon Lightfoot, Garth Brooks, John Denver, Waylon Jennings, Tony Rice, Kenny Rogers, and others. His song "Darcy Farrow" is a classic. Cindy Mangsen plays guitar, banjo, English concertina, and mountain dulcimer. Her vocals are rich and beautiful. She has recorded with Anne Hills and Priscilla Herdman. –CR
○ **Live in Concert / COMPASS ROSE**   1991
This live recording was captured on DAT, giving it a nice sound quality. Over 60 minutes and 19 songs — I love it. Quantity and quality! Their vocals blend nicely and Gillette's guitar work is impressive. "Grapes on the Vine" is well done. They do a great cover of "Shake Sugaree." This album also has a stunning cover of "Annachie Gordon." Many stations have made this a Top Ten release, and I concur. This one is highly recommended. –CR

MICKEY GILLEY   b 1937

Traditional country. Like his cousin Jerry Lee Lewis, Mickey Gilley is a piano-playing singer who's at home with honky-tonk and country ballads alike. After considerable label-hopping early in his career, his remake of George Morgan's "Room Full of Roses" put him on the music map in 1974. From then to the mid 80s he scored seventeen #1s, including "I Overlooked an Orchid," "Don't the Girls Get Prettier at Closing Time," and "She's Pulling Me Back Again." When *Urban Cowboy* was filmed at Gilley's club in Pasadena, TX, his career got an extra boost and a pop hit in "Stand by Me." And for a couple of years, mechanical bulls stampeded across the country as far as the eye could see. In 1990 this famous club was eventually torched by a youth "to release anger." –DV
Live at Gilley's / EPIC   1978
A rough and rowdy roadhouse honky-tonk performance. –MH
That's All That Matters to Me / EPIC   1980
This is the album that benefited most from Gilley's *Urban Cowboy* associations, and there's a perfunctory backcover shot of some cowboy riding a mechanical bull at Gilley's night club. Though Gilley the Balladeer became pretty formulaic during the progression of the 80s, it was a new wrinkle with this album, and he delivers it convincingly. Gilley says the title track is his best performance ever; we agree. –TR
○ **Ten Years of Hits / CBS**   1984
This album makes a case for this journeyman country singer as more than an urban cowboy footnote. Gilley was a convincing honky-tonk howler on lust & suds soapers, and he had a sure way with smarmy ballads. The piano thunder stolen from Gilley's cousin Jerry Lee Lewis also rattles through his raveups. If nothing else, Gilley did a great job of effectively absorbing influences. –MH
Biggest Hits / CBS
A concise sampling of his 70s and 80s honky-tonk hits. –MH

JIMMIE DALE GILMORE

Contemporary country. Gilmore's music blends the traditional with the contemporary and adds a lot of unique Gilmore. His voice and vocal style have been compared to a cross between Willie Nelson's and Bob Dylan's. –DV
Jimmie Dale Gilmore / HIGHTONE   1989
More good songs from Austin. –MH
After Awhile / ELEKTRA   1991
From the celebrated "American Explorer" series. –MH
○ **Fair & Square / HIGHTONE**
If Willie Nelson were not so mellow and were still writing good songs, he would sound a lot like this soulful Texas singer/songwriter. –MH

JOHNNY GIMBLE   b 1926

Instrumental. Johnny Gimble is simply one of the greatest fiddlers who ever lived. After playing with the Bob Wills Band in the late 40s, he went back to barbering in Texas before becoming an outstanding studio fiddler, backing up Lefty Frizzell, Marty Robbins, Merle Haggard, Loretta Lynn, and Willie Nelson, to name just a few of hundreds. Name the music style and Gimble can play it on the fiddle. He's often seen on TV, looking young and playing country, swing, or jazz as well as it's played. −DV

● **Still Fiddlin' Around / MCA**
Gimble's amiable personality glows in the company of other top-drawer Nashville cats, along with the fleet bowing and pleasant vocals. −MH

○ **Still Swingin' / CMH**
Western style, that is. −MH

Texas Fiddle Collection / CMH
This Texas Playboy alumnus and first-call Nashville fiddler shows how it's done in the Lone Star State. −MH

Texas Honky-Tonk Hits / CMH
Swinging doors, hardwood floors, and some tunes by which to two-step. −MH

VERN GOSDIN   b 1934

Traditional country. One of the best vocalists in the business, for good reason is Gosdin called "The Voice." He's been in music a while, with the Gosdin Brothers in 1960 and then as a forming partner in the Hillmen. Gosdin is a country traditionalist and a subtle singer. If you like quality vocals, listen to his award-winning *Chiseled in Stone* album. −DV

If Jesus Comes Tomorrow ... / COMPLEAT   1984
If Jesus Comes Tomorrow (What Then) is part gospel standards, part complementary originals, all sung by a honky-tonk voice hoping for heaven. −BM

☆ **10 Years of Greatest Hits Newly Recorded / CBS**
Gosdin has George Jones's keening desperation in his vocals and an ironic wit in his writing. A fine overview of a great artist. −MH

Alone / CBS
Great performances. −MH

The Best of Vern Gosdin / WARNER
Some fine performances from the early and mid 80s, but a mite over-produced. Get his Columbia work first. −MH

Chiseled in Stone / CBS
The second coming of this veteran country balladeer during the late 80s. Righteous and wrenching. −MH

Out of My Heart / CBS
Bold bleating from "The Voice." −MH

JACK GREENE   b 1930

Country. Hailing from Maryville, TN, Greene got his start in the record business as a vocalist in Ernest Tubb's band, but he hardly had the same almost-on-key twang as his boss. In fact, Greene's smooth, pleasant sound contrasted a great deal with Tubb's blue-collar intonation.
Nicknamed the "Jolly Green Giant," Greene learned guitar and drums but mined his vocal chords for a solid string of hit records from 1966-1969, including one with Jeannie Seely, who joined his road show and recorded duets with him for several years.
A bit of trivia: In 1967 Greene became the first country artist ever to appear in the Macy's Thanksgiving Day Parade. −TR

○ **Greatest Hits / DECCA**
This basically sums up his peak years. Includes all the classics: "All the Time," "There Goes My Everything," and "Statue of a Fool." −TR

LEE GREENWOOD   b 1942

Country. Born with a good voice and a wide range, Greenwood turned it into a unique voice accidentally, by over-working it in a less-than-healthy setting. Hailing from Sacramento, he used his musical training on the casino circuit working in the

green-felt jungles of Reno and Las Vegas, where he dealt cards by day and sang in dark lounges by night.
The physical toll of two jobs, the vocal strain of performing six nights a week, and the damaging endeavor of singing in smoky nightclubs before the advent of smoking ordinances brought Greenwood a permanent hoarseness. He's used it to his advantage, becoming one of country music's premier balladeers.
Discovered by Mel Tillis's road manager, Larry McFaden, Greenwood paid for his own ticket to fly to Nashville and cut a few demos, and it took more than a year for that effort to pay off. When it finally did, Greenwood broke through in late 1981 with "It Turns Me Inside Out," in which his exaggerated vibrato brought frequent comparisons to Kenny Rogers.
In short order, Greenwood disposed of the "Kenny clone" image, but he continued to mine romantic material for the bulk of his hits. Occasional exceptions include "Touch and Go Crazy" and "Mornin' Ride," but the biggest exception is also his signature song, the self-written "God Bless the U.S.A.," which earned Song of the Year honors from the Country Music Association. −TR

○ **Greatest Hits / MCA**   1985
The extent to which Greenwood relies on ballads is fully evident here, although his departures — "Dixie Road" and "Ain't No Trick" — are most memorable. "God Bless the U.S.A." is the last track; if you're not inclined to ultra-patriotism, you can simply lift the needle or push "Stop." −TR

NANCI GRIFFITH   b 1953

Progressive country. Nanci Griffith emerged in the 80s as perhaps the most promising folk/country singer/songwriter of her day. Kathy Mattea had a 1986 hit with "Love at the Five & Dime," and Suzy Bogguss covered "Outbound Plane" in 1991; others, including Lynn Anderson, have recorded her songs as well. A former schoolteacher from near Austin, TX, Griffith first released *There's a Light Beyond These Woods,* on her own B.F. Deal label in 1978, followed by three more albums for the folk label Philo that displayed an ear for detail and times past. 1987's *Lone Star State of Mind* was her first for the country division of MCA and included Julie Gold's soon-to-be standard "From a Distance." After three country albums, Griffith switched to MCA's Los Angeles division, where she has moved toward pop with 1989's *Storms* and 1991's *Late Night Grande Hotel.* −BM & WR

Once in a Very Blue Moon / PHILO   1984
After two promising albums, Nanci Griffith finally perfected her mixture of singer/songwriter folk and Texas-based country on this lovely collection, which features her own story-songs such as "Mary & Omie" and well-chosen covers such as the Pat Alger/Eugene Levine title tune. −WR

★ **The Last of the True Believers / PHILO**   1986
Griffith hit her peak as a songwriter here with classics such as "Love at the Five & Dime" and "Banks of the Pontchartrain," while singing over an always-appropriate backup provided by the 80s new bluegrass specialists Bela Fleck, Mark O'Connor, and others. The album earned her a major-label contract with MCA and provided the basis of country singer Kathy Mattea's entire career, but it is also a pivotal 80s folk album. −WR

○ **Little Love Affairs / MCA**   1988
All of Griffith's albums have songs to recommend them; of her country/folk albums, this one has the most written by her, as well as good tunes by Harlan Howard and fellow Texan Robert Earl Keen Jr. The first half's prime Griffit, and the second suggests that, if she'd stuck with country, she might have started outselling her press — Suzy Bogguss later turned "Outbound Plane" into a hit, and there's probably at least one more of those tucked away here. −BM

Late Night Grande Hotel / MCA   1991
Two albums out of Nashville and Griffith doesn't even resemble the new-country/folkie role in which she was once cast. Britishers Rod Argent and Peter Van Hooke insulate Griffith with strings and moody atmospheres that

complement her wallflower fantasies. She's likely partial to "Power Lines" and "Down 'n' Outer," both tales of folks who fall through society's cracks — probably, come to think of it, because she identifies with them. –BM

MERLE HAGGARD   b 1937

Traditional country. A big difference between Merle Haggard and many other superstars is that while he's been wildly popular and the hottest performer in the business, he's won this acclaim on his own terms, maintaining his musical integrity and never pandering to musical whims, fads, or fancies. He doesn't know what middle-of-the-road is; he travels traditional country. His great voice and instrumental ability combine with superior songwriting productivity to make him one of the most significant personalities in country music this half-century. Like so many of the classic country singers, Haggard has first-hand knowledge of the music he writes and sings about. The son of Dust Bowl Okies, he was born in a converted boxcar in Bakersfield, CA. Haggard was only nine when his father died, a fact that probably led him into his many problems with the law, which included seven years in reform schools and three years at San Quentin for attempted burglary. After three years in prison, he played the honky-tonks around Bakersfield, debuting on the charts in 1963 with "Sing a Sad Song" and getting his first #1, "I'm a Lonesome Fugitive," three years later. Of his 31 other #1 hits, "Okie from Muskogee" may be the best remembered. Ironically, this song was taken up by the "silent majority" as an anti-hippie, pro-war anthem, though Haggard says he wrote it tongue-in-cheek. It's a country classic, in any case. With Merle Haggard, what you see (and hear) is what you get — in this case, a legendary figure in country music. Judging from the current crop of Haggard sound-alikes, he's surely one of the most influential. –DV

I'm a Lonesome Fugitive / CAPITOL / BB 165   1967
This early Capitol album contains the haunting "House of Memories." Haggard begins to really let his roots show on this one — see "Rough and Rowdy Ways," the Jimmie Rodgers classic. In this great early period Haggard, while seeming entirely contemporary, could evoke the Ghosts of Country Past in an absolutely convincing way without nostalgia or imitation. –GB

○ **Branded Man / CAPITOL / BB 174**   1968
An out-of-print classic album. –RL

Same Train, Different Time / CAPITOL / BB 67   1969
Haggard's loving 2-LP tribute to country pioneer Jimmie Rodgers. Lots of fine guitar from Roy Nichols and James Burton. –RL

○ **The Fightin' Side of Me / CAPITOL / BB 68**   1970
Electrifying live Philadelphia performance. Don't let the title put you off. –RL

Okie from Muskogee / SPECIAL MUSIC CO. / BB 46 1970
Another exciting live show. –RL

Tribute ... / CAPITOL / BB 58   1971
Tribute to the Best Damn Fiddle Player in the World, Haggard's salute to Bob Wills and His Texas Playboys, showcases many Playboy alumni along with Haggard's band, the Strangers. –RL

☆ **The Best of the Best / CAPITOL**   1973
Includes "Today I Started Loving You Again," "No Reason to Quit," "Every Fool Has a Rainbow," "Hungry Eyes" — some of his best ballads plus the jingoistic faves "Okie from Muskogee" and "Fightin' Side of Me." A few duds, though — some of the early Capitol albums are more consistent. –GB

Big City / EPIC   1981
Coming on the heels of a short-lived semi-retirement, Haggard's Epic debut is an appropriate group of songs that celebrates relaxation and expresses discontent with the situation forced on blue-collar America. Ironically, he puts plenty of energy into his work here. –TR

Going Where the Lonely Go / EPIC   1982
Dark, brooding package that includes some leftovers from the *Big City* sessions. Occasionally uplifting musically, but certainly a study in pain. Besides title track, check out "Someday You're Gonna Need Your Friends Again," "Shopping for Dresses," and the Willie Nelson-penned "Half a Man." –TR

A Taste of Yesterday's Wine / EPIC   1982
Merle Haggard and George Jones, the two most influential country stylists of the modern country era, hook up together. Occasionally disappointing in that respect, but a case study in music to down Jack Daniels by. They take a self-deprecating poke at George Jones's former reliability problem in "No Show Jones." –TR

Pancho & Lefty / EPIC   1983
This album with Willie Nelson is for those curious as to why younger artists try to imitate Haggard rather than Nelson. Funny thing — though it's a duet album, they very rarely sing in harmony. Some versions spell Pancho as Poncho and are supposedly collector's items. The title track is one of the best-produced country cuts in history. –TR

Best of Country Blues / CAPITOL
Includes his treatments of Bob Wills and Jimmie Rodgers, plus original material. From the Capitol Records period. –RL

★ **The Best of Merle Haggard (Shorter Version) / CAPITOL**
Great songs include "High on a Hilltop," the great "House of Memories," "I Threw Away the Rose" — a lot of Haggard's best weepers, plus his barroom classics "Swinging Doors" and "The Bottle Let Me Down." –GB

☆ **More of the Best / RHINO**
Includes some of his best Capitol Records and MCA material ("Branded Man," "Mama Tried," etc.). –RL

Strangers / CAPITOL
"Strangers," his first hit, plus some other early recordings. Reissued as *Sing a Sad Song*, CAP SN 16052. –GB

☆ **Swinging Doors / CAPITOL**
His two best honky-tonk songs, the title track and "The Bottle Let Me Down." Also Tommy Collins's haunting "High on a Hilltop." –GB

Capitol Country Classics / CAPITOL
A British compilation that covers much of his 70s material. Sixteen hits in all, and worth finding just to make sure you own "It's All in the Movies." –TR

TOM T. HALL   b 1936

Country-pop. Nashville's reigning storyteller, Hall started off as a DJ and a songwriter. In the 60s his songs were recorded by Dave Dudley, Roy Drusky, and Flatt and Scruggs, but the bigtime arrived in 1968 when Jeannie C. Riley cut "Harper Valley PTA," which sold 6 million copies and led first to a movie in 1978, then to a TV series in the early 80s. Hall was phenomenally popular in the 70s, charting with many "message" songs, among them "The Year That Clayton Delaney Died," "Old Dogs, Children, and Watermelon Wine," and "Ravishing Ruby." In the 80s he became host of "Pop Goes the Country," a syndicated TV show. With his low-key singing style and his unique songs, Hall is like no one else in the business. –DV

☆ **Essential Tom T. Hall / POLYGRAM**
Essential Tom T. Hall — 20th Anniversary Collection. Best known as an innovative songwriter, Hall did some splendid recordings for Mercury in the early 70s; this has the best of them, including most of the familiar hits. –CW

Greatest Hits - Vols. 1 & 2 / POLYGRAM
Greatest Hits - Vol. 3 / POLYGRAM

EMMYLOU HARRIS   b 1947

Traditional country, progressive country. It's difficult to label Emmylou Harris, except to say everyone agrees that her voice is exceptionally, achingly beautiful. Her career, now heading toward the quarter-century mark, spans many types of music and at the moment rests in traditional country — sort of. In fact, Harris, who came to country with a hip and rock image, is now one of the most vocal proponents of pure country. In a decade that has begun with a mania for singers with oversized Stetsons, she has the taste and the credentials to suggest that maybe George Jones and Merle Haggard ought to be given a good listen too.

Her career began with folk music in the late 60s in NYC and around the Washington, DC, area, where she met Gram Parsons, formerly of the Byrds. It was Parsons who fine-tuned her appreciation for country music, particularly songs that featured heart-tugging harmony work, a` la Louvin Brothers and Everly Brothers. During a brief spell Harris and Parsons worked together in his band the Fallen Angels. After his death in 1973, Harris went solo, pursuing a sound that melded strains of pure country with elements of singer/songwriter folk and acoustic-flavored rock into her sound.

It was with her second album, (*Elite Hotel*), that Harris achieved some real success. *Elite Hotel* blended country standards and country rock and yielded three #1 hits, including a remake of a Don Gibson song, "Sweet Dreams."

Later on in her career, the traditional *Blue Kentucky Girl* brought Harris a Grammy. Another album, *Roses in the Snow*, reinforced her reputation as a superb interpreter of traditional country. In the 80s, she teamed up with Dolly Parton and Linda Ronstadt on *Trio*, a great commercial success and the only country album of that decade to reach the pop Top Ten. As a live performer, Harris has enjoyed a reputation for assembling stellar road bands, which have included British guitar ace Albert Lee and bluegrass journeyman Ricky Skaggs.

Given her versatility and broad musical taste, it's difficult to predict what albums we'll see from Emmylou Harris through the 90s; but whether it's country-rock or blues, ballads or bluegrass, you can be sure it will be done right — memorably right. –DV

☆ **Elite Hotel / WARNER / BB 25**   1975
Picking up the torch from her late partner, Gram Parsons, Emmylou Harris defined the country-rock hybrid of the 70s and 80s. Here she presents her own versions of the Parsons classics "Sin City" and "Wheels," gives a boost to up-and-comer Rodney Crowell, and even covers the Beatles, all in her heartbreaking voice and backed by a group of session stars soon aptly named "The Hot Band." –WR

★ **A Quarter Moon ... / WARNER / BB 29**   1978
Harris's albums of the period are uniformly strong, and the choices made here are predicated more than usual on personal taste. *A Quarter Moon in a Ten Cent Town* gets the nod largely for its definitive versions of the Crowell songs "Leaving Louisiana in the Broad Daylight" and "I Ain't Living Long Like This." –WR

Roses in the Snow / WARNER   1980
The record label questioned Harris's decision to release an album featuring hybrid bluegrass — understandably, since it wasn't exactly in vogue. But Harris had Ricky Skaggs in her corner, and pulled it off with her usual flair. –TR

Evangeline / WARNER   1981
This rock-heavy package moves gracefully to bluegrass, folk, and jazz-inflected tracks as well. Thanks to contractual agreements, this is the only place you'll find the version of "Mister Sandman" that features Dolly Parton and Linda Ronstadt. –TR

☆ **The Ballad of Sally Rose / WARNER**   1985
Harris switched gears on this album, cowriting with Paul Kennerley a semi-autobiographical song cycle that makes you wonder why she had spent so much time interpreting the work of others. The album is unique in her catalog, but it's a successful attempt to try something different. –WR

○ **At the Ryman / REPRISE**   1992
The album debut of the Nashville Ramblers, her acoustic backing band featuring Sam Bush and Roy Huskey Jr, recorded over three nights in the former home of the Grand Ole Opry. Harris's choice of songs strikes a balance between hillbilly classics and folk-influenced rock, with Bill Monroe

Country Music Styles

Old-time — String-band/hillbilly music; country folk music from the 20s and 30s, including modern music in the old style (Doc Watson, Red Clay Ramblers, Uncle Dave Macon).

Traditional country — Sometimes called "hard country," as in hardcore; the main stream of country music from which these other catergories branch off; extends from Jimmie Rodgers and Roy Acuff in the 20s and 30s through George Jones, Merle Haggard, Randy Travis, George Strait, Loretta Lynn, Reba McEntire, and Ricky Skaggs.

Contemporary country — Traditional country that's been sanded and varnished, retaining most of its country soul and sound but appealing to a larger audience than its hardcore cousin (the Judds, Steve Wariner, Garth Brooks).

Progressive country — Performers who have taken country roads to new territory; highly innovative or idiosyncratic (Mark O'Connor, Willie Nelson, K. D. Lang, Lyle Lovett).

Country pop — Middle-of-the-road music with a country flavor (often imperceptible), sounding something like traditional country but modified and sweetened; crossover music — often crossing from the country to the pop charts (Kenny Rogers, Mandrell sisters, Gatlin brothers, Glen Campbell, Anne Murray).

Country rock — An amalgam — varying portions of rock and country (Charlie Daniels, Alabama, Travis Tritt, Hank Williams Jr).

Western swing — An often complex subcategory of country music; developed in the late 30s in the Southwest and incorporating many genres, including swing jazz, polkas, fiddle music, blues, cowboy songs, and what-have-you; rural rhythm's big-band sound (Bob Wills, Bill Boyd, Asleep at the Wheel).

Cowboy — Romantic songs of the Old West sung by cowboys and cowgirls dressed in rhinestones and Stetsons (Roy Rogers, Gene Autry, Patsy Montana, Sons of the Pioneers, Tex Ritter, and Riders in the Sky).

Instrumental — Self-explanatory — picking, plucking, bowing, harping, and tickling the 88s; the earliest country music featured fiddle and banjo, while contemporary country emphasizes the electric guitar and the pedal steel guitar.

Country humor — Self-explanatory; from the earliest days of country music through "Hee Haw," comedy was part of the act (Grandpa Jones, Roy Clark, Homer and Jethro, the Geezinslaws, Ray Stevens).

Gospel — Essential to country music; religious music predates other country genres and probably will outlive them all; traditionally a standard part of any performer's repertory (Tennessee Ernie Ford, the Whites, Lewis Family, bluegrass bands).

— David Vinopal

receiving heaviest tribute but sharing space with Tex Owens, Bruce Springsteen, and John Fogerty. –BM

JOHN HARTFORD

Traditional country, old-time, progressive country. "Gentle on My Mind," counterculture's think-I'll-be-movin'-along song, became Hartford's first hit when Glen Campbell covered it in 1967, leading to three Grammys and fame for its multi-talented composer. Soon Hartford appeared on TV's

"Smothers Brothers Comedy Hour" and then became a regular on the "Glen Campbell Goodtime Hour." After touring with his own band for a while, Hartford created a spellbinding solo act, which he continues to the present. His longtime love of riverboats is seen in many of his songs and was the basis of a TV special in the 1980s. With his fiddle and banjo, Hartford is first and foremost an exceptional entertainer and is famous for his riveting and memorable solo performances. –DV

Down on the River / FLYING FISH   1972
☆ **Gum Tree Canoe / FLYING FISH**   1984
The best rounded of all the Flying Fish albums — everything from bluegrass to Civil War songs. –CW

Me Oh My, How the Time Does Fly / FLYING FISH   1987
The CD version of *Me Oh My, How the Time Does Fly - A John Hartford Anthology* includes an additional ten tracks. –ED

Aereoplane / WARNER
Catalogue / FLYING FISH
A re-recording of some of the singer's hits from his days on RCA. –CW

Mark Twang / FLYING FISH
His first and one of his best, with Hartford as solo artist. –CW

Hartford & Hartford / FLYING FISH
Hartford's son Jamie is a fine mandolin player, and he joins his father for this album. –CW

HAWKSHAW HAWKINS   1921-1963

Country. Born Harold F. Hawkins, Hawkshaw is a country singer, guitarist, songwriter, and entertainer. A large man (6 ft 6 in) with a deep singing voice, Hawkins was an immensely popular performer in country music for many years without the benefit of big record success. He started on radio, becoming a regular on WWVA's "Wheeling Jamboree" by 1946 and making his first records for the King label around that time. By 1953 he signed with RCA Victor and became a regular member of the Grand Ole Opry by 1955. Described as "the man with eleven and a half yards of personality," Hawkins was a warm and engaging performer both onstage and on records, able to pull off a wide variety of material from maudlin weepers to uptempo novelties. His label-jumping from Columbia by the late 50s and back to King by the early 60s moved his material closer to commercial mainstream country, but his time in the spotlight ran out when he perished in the same plane crash as Cowboy Copas and Patsy Cline. –CK

○ **Hawk / BEAR FAMILY**
An excellent 3-CD boxed set. All the RCA-Victor and Columbia recordings,with superlative sound and liner notes. –CK

JIMMY HEAP & THE MELODY MASTERS

Country. Texas-born bandleader Heap put together the Melody Masters after WWII and quickly became an attraction on the roadhouse/dancehall circuit, mining similar turf to that of other Western swing bands of the area. Quite popular from the late 40s through early 50s, Heap & the Melody Masters are generally credited with one of the earliest versions of the country classic "Release Me," as well as several other hits, among them another country standard, "The Wild Side of Life." –CK

○ **Release Me / BEAR FAMILY**   1992
A great 30-track, single-disc compilation of Heap's earliest and best sides. Includes the title track, "Let's Do It Just Once," "It Takes a Heap of Lovin'," and "Ethyl in My Gas Tank (No Gal in My Arms)." This is great Western swing-style material in transition. –CK

DON HENRY

Progressive country. Don Henry came to prominence when Kathy Mattea's version of "Where've You Been" (cowritten with Mattea's husband Jon Vezner) won every award in sight in 1990 and 1991. Henry grew up in suburban San Jose, CA, and moved to Nashville in 1979, where he spent four years copying tapes for publisher Tree International (now Sony/Tree) and

then became a staff songwriter there. He wrote tunes for Mattea, John Conlee, T. G. Sheppard, and Conway Twitty and won Tree's Writer of the Year Award in 1990 before recording his first album. –BM

○ **Wild in the Backyard / COLUMBIA**   1991
Henry's debut album can only be classifed country because of its high moral sense (which it actually gets from folk) and from the styles of the session players. With its malls and Mercedes, *Wild in the Backyard* isn't country — it's suburban. Henry's a singer/songwriter capable of drama and humor within the same song. But his real strength is his ability to create honest humanity, a trait equally present in "Harley," about a boy named after a chopper, and "Half a Heart," a touching tale of unfulfilled promise. –BM

HIGHWAY 101

Country-pop, country rock. This country-pop quartet formed in Los Angeles in 1986 and a year later had a #4 hit with "The Bed You Made for Me." They won Group of the Year honors from two of the awards associations before lead singer Paulette Carson left for a solo career. –DV

○ **Highway 101 / WARNER**   1987
The main thing that this country-rock quartet had going for it was lead singer Paulette Carlson, who approximated the throaty, torn vocal style of Stevie Nicks but with a Southern accent. The group was heard best on its debut album, which included such characteristic hits as "Whiskey, If You Were a Woman" and "The Bed You Made for Me." –WR

HIGHWOODS STRING BAND

Old-time.

☆ **Fire on the Mountain / RO**
Old-time string-band music at its best, re-created from old 78s of the 20s and 30s. –CW

CHRIS HILLMAN   b 1942

Country rock, progressive country. This Californian has been perhaps the greatest influence on the country-rock/folk genre that's taken for granted today. He began as the mandolin player of the Scottsville Squirrel Barkers, a group which turned into the Hillmen, a bluegrass-oriented group based in California. Then came the Byrds, a legendary country-rock quintet that recorded Bob Dylan's "Mr. Tambourine Man" (in 1965) and the pioneer country-rock album *Sweetheart of the Rodeo*, with Gram Parsons. Hillman and Parsons then formed the Flying Burrito Brothers in 1969. In the 70s Hillman performed as a solo act. In the 80s Hillman formed the Desert Rose Band and has been touring with them. –DV

○ **Desert Rose / SUGAR HILL**   1984
Bluegrass, country, and country rock, Hillman played mandolin on this album, but his main instrument (with the Byrds and Desert Rose Band) is bass. –MH

TISH HINOJOSA

Folk. This wonderful, tender-voiced singer/songwriter from San Antonio writes and sings in English and Spanish. She paints telling portraits of Texas border life with music that hails from both sides of the Rio Grande, played by such experts as Flaco Jimenez and members of Los Lobos. –CR

○ **Homeland / A&M**   1989
Fans of Nanci Griffith and Linda Ronstadt's Mexican albums, take note. –WR

JOHNNY HORTON   1929-1960

Traditional country. Horton is remembered mainly for his popular historical "saga" songs such as "The Battle of New Orleans," "North to Alaska," and "Johnny Reb." However, during his brief career (he was killed in a car wreck in 1960 at the height of his popularity), he also produced a body of work that influences country singers today. Exemplified by songs like "Honky Tonk Man" (covered by Dwight Yoakam), "I'm Comin' Home," and "One Woman Man" (recently a hit for George Jones), this style bridged the gap between honky-tonk and rockabilly, with the chugging, twangy, picked-close-to-the-bridge guitar of Grady Martin perfectly complementing and answering Horton's vibrant and expressive singing. Horton has a fine voice with a huge range, versatile enough to adapt to almost any kind of song. On his (honkyabilly? rock-a-tonk?) sides he swoops effortlessly from low notes to high, adding just the right growling edge when needed, and the most effective use of the vocal "break" or "tear" since Hank Williams. −GB

☆ **1956-1960 / BEAR FAMILY**
From the first note recorded at Columbia, to the last hotel room demo, a superb in-depth look at Horton's later career. These four CDs are a collector's dream. −HD

Greatest Hits / CBS
This samples all the best, with breadth but little depth. It's heavy on historical epics, some country, and the memorable "Honky Tonk Man." −HD

DAVID HOUSTON   b 1938

Country. Houston apparently came from good stock: his lineage includes Sam Houston and Gen. Robert E. Lee. Born and raised in Bossier City, LA, Houston became a regular on the Louisiana Hayride as a teenager.
Apparently his soaring tenor voice wasn't totally appreciated; he found trouble getting work in the music business, and ended up as an insurance underwriter. But record producer Billy Sherrill brought Houston into the fold when Epic Records was still a young label (the early 60s), and Houston brought the company its first real hit with "Mountain of Love." In 1966 he broke through to major status with "Almost Persuaded," which netted a pair of Grammy Awards and brought pop recognition as well.
A member of the Grand Ole Opry since 1971, he racked up 28 hit records over a decade, including duets with Tammy Wynette and Barbara Mandrell. −TR

○ **American Originals / EPIC**   1989
Houston's soaring falsetto is well represented in this greatest-hits collection on CD. "Almost Persuaded," "Baby Baby (I Know You're a Lady)," "Mountain of Love," and "My Elusive Dreams" (duet with Tammy Wynette) are all here, though, sad to say, "Livin' in a House Full of Love" is missing. −TR

WALTER HYATT

Country. Walter Hyatt is a Texas singer, songwriter, and guitar player. He is the first vocalist to be included in the MCA Master Series. His music is unique, with original ideas built into a foundation of classic jazz and blues to create a tasteful, moving, highly individual sound. −CR

○ **King Tears / MCA**
Cocktail country, a must for Lyle Lovett fans. −RG

FRANK IFIELD

Country. This English-born, Australian-reared balladeer with a unique yodeling style was highly successful during the early 60s, with a string of pop/country hits, which includes "I Remember You," "I'm Confessing That I Love You" and "Lovesick Blues." −HD

The Best of Frank Ifield / CAPITOL   • 196?
Combines a hillbilly yodel with slick pop stylings. −HD

○ **The EMI Years / CAPITOL**
A generous 20-track sampler of his biggest hits (ca. 1960), including "I Remember You." −HD

ALAN JACKSON   b 1958

Traditional country. A traditional country singer and songwriter, Alan Jackson penned nine of the cuts on *Here in the Real World*, his debut album, which went platinum and made an instant name for him. Among his heroes is George "Possum" Jones, who duets with him on the *Don't Rock the Jukebox* album. If you love real country, give Alan Jackson a listen. −DV

Here in the Real World / ARISTA   1989
A debut of contemporary country heartthrob. −MH
○ **Don't Rock the Jukebox / ARISTA**   1991
A hit album of weepers, kickers, and keepers. −MH

STONEWALL JACKSON   b 1932

Traditional country. Stonewall Jackson (and this is his real name) probably thought he was doing well when his "Life to Go" was a big country hit in 1958. A year later, though, he had a career-maker in "Waterloo," a crossover that reached the top in country and pop charts. As a result, he starred on Dick Clark's "American Bandstand," the TV show that usually featured pop and only pop. He also had luck with his self-penned "I Washed My Hands in Muddy Water" and with "Stamp Out Loneliness." −DV

○ **The Dynamic / COLUMBIA**   1959
Collection of early hits — "Waterloo," "George Jones," "Life to Go," "Smoke along the Track," "Why I'm Walking" — almost all good songs, delivered in his powerful, homely but engaging voice. −GB

SONNY JAMES   b 1929

Country-pop. Known as the Southern Gentleman, he had 16 consecutive records between 1967 and 1971 that reached #1. His rich and mellow voice helped make him a crossover artist, starting with "Young Love," a pop hit in 1956. Even when his material was country, James presented it in a pop form acceptable to a large audience. Among his many hits are "Running Bear," "You're the Only World I Know," and "Take Good Care of Her." In the 60s he also appeared in the movies, including *Hillbilly in a Haunted House* with Lon Chaney, Jr and *Las Vegas Hillbillies* with Jayne Mansfield. −DV

American Originals / CBS
The best of James's Columbia hits. −MH
○ **Collectors Series / CAPITOL**
"Young Love" and other "countripolitan" hits. −MH

WAYLON JENNINGS   b 1937

Traditional country, progressive country. The ultimate Outlaw, Waylon Jennings squeezed a lot of recording and a lot more living into the years between touring as Buddy Holly's bass player and recording the *Highwayman II* album in 1991. And all the time he fought against the lush but sterile Nashville Sound and against the Nashville establishment record labels that produced this sameness of sound. With fellow Texan and close friend Willie Nelson, Jennings changed the way things were done in Music City, including insisting on recording with their own bands, rather than with homogenized studio musicians of the Nashville feudal system.
In the early 60s, Jennings and his band the Waylors were doing well out of Phoenix. Chet Atkins learned about the talented singer and offered him a contract. Jennings's first singles did well enough ("Anita You're Dreaming," for example), but the husky, powerful voice, the faded-jeans image, and the raw and emotional material delivered with a rock beat scared some people in Nashville. He enjoyed moderate success through the 60s, recording and touring and building up an enthusiastic audience (*cult* would be accurate) for this unique sound.
In spite of all the talent, Jennings wasn't to become a major star until the 70s brought such influential albums as *Good Hearted Woman* (1972) and *Honky Tonk Heroes* (1973). Then came the landmark album that sold millions, *Wanted: The Outlaws* (1976), that featured Jennings, Jessi Colter (his wife), Tompall Glaser, and Willie Nelson, performing eleven previously released songs. Jennings was a superstar and the outlaws had won. As further proof, in 1978 the *Waylon & Willie* album was a runaway hit, remaining on the country and pop charts for over a year. His singles did as well as the albums, with such hits as "Luckenbach, Texas," "The Wurlitzer Prize," "I've Always Been Crazy," and "Amanda."

Meanwhile, the outlaw clones proliferated, leading (thanks to the mechanical-bull movie) to the *Urban Cowboy* fad, and prompting Jennings to pen and record "Don't You Think This Outlaw Bit's Done Got Out of Hand." But Jennings had racked up eight consecutive gold albums while keeping his musical integrity, and the direction of country music had been changed.

With his superstar status intact, Jennings recorded regularly in the 80s, but his popularity slipped a notch or two, having in fact nowhere to go but down. In 1985, Jennings, Willie Nelson, Johnny Cash, and Kris Kristofferson produced their *Highwayman* album, a best-seller that spawned a #1 single of the same title. Jennings, having done his music his way, has earned the right to rest on his laurels, should he choose to. –DV

☆ **Greatest Hits / RCA / BB 28**   1979
Jennings's career dates back to his days as a Cricket in the 50s, but it wasn't until the 70s that he began to define a particular hard-edged subgenre of country music with his rock shuffles and his deep, sardonic voice on songs like "Lonesome, On'ry and Mean" and "Luckenbach, Texas," the best of which are included here. (A second volume, released in 1984, is also recommended.) –WR

Will the Wolf Survive / MCA   1986
Moving to MCA after a long stay at RCA brought Jennings a new producer in Jimmy Bowen and a fresh approach, resulting in one of his better albums, typified by his version of the Los Lobos title track and a cover of Steve Earle's tailor-made "The Devil's Right Hand." –WR

DOUG JERNIGAN w/BUCKY PIZZARELLI

○ **Doug & Bucky / FLYING FISH**   1989
A novel pairing of pedal-steel and electric guitars. Very creative duets, leaning toward jazz featuring standards and a Thelonious Monk tune. Delightfully under-produced. –HD

FLACO JIMENEZ

Tex-Mex. Flaco Jimenez is the best known of the talented Jimenez family of Tex-Mex accordionists. He has always been popular in the border region, and came to the attention of the wider pop-music-buying public with the help of roots-music enthusiast Ry Cooder. Since then Jimenez has toured internationally, made guest appearances on a number of recordings, teamed up with Doug Sahm and Freddy Fender in the Texas Tornados, and continued to record on small labels for the Texas Norteño community. –MB

Arriba el Norte / ROUNDER   1988
☆ **Ay Te Dejo en San Antonio / ARHOOLIE**
Two Arhoolie albums on this one. A generous helping of 22 Tex-Mex winners with lots of rancheras and polkas. –MB

Entre Humo y Botellas / ROUNDER
Mid-80s recordings for Texas labels. Real traditional stuff aimed at the Tex-Mex market. –MB

Flaco's Amigos / ARHOOLIE
His most eclectic album, with Ry Cooder and others. Some songs are in English to enhance his crossover appeal. –MB

San Antonio Soul / ROUNDER
Like *Entre Humo y Botellas*, more mid-80s recordings from this busy Tex-Mex star. –MB

SANTIAGO JIMENEZ JR

Tex-Mex. The namesake of one of the pioneers of Norteño music, this singer and accordionist takes a more traditional approach than that of his more celebrated brother, Flaco. Santiago favors the two-row button accordion, and many of his recordings offer the basic two voices, accordion, and guitar presentation of Tex-Mex music. In addition to recording extensively for local San Antonio labels, Santiago has recorded for Arhoolie and Rounder and has appeared in the documentary film, *Chulas Fronteras*. –MH

Familia y Tradición / ROUNDER   1989
Traditional Norteño and "You Are My Sunshine." –MH

El Gato Negro / ROUNDER
More rootsy grooves from San Antonio. –MH
○ **El Mero Mero de San Antonio / ARHOOLIE**
More traditional than his hermano Flaco, singer and accordionist Santiago plays Norteño music much the same as his celebrated father did in the 40s. –MH

MICHAEL JOHNSON   b1944

Progressive country. Pinpointing Michael Johnson on the musical scale of style is a difficult chore. As a teenage guitar player, he took notes from seminal rocker Chuck Berry and jazzman Charlie Byrd. At age 21, he spent a year in Barcelona, studying under classical guitarist Graciano Tarrago; once he'd returned to the US, he signed up for a one-year folk tour as a member of the Mitchell Trio, where his fellow musicians included John Denver. To complicate matters, when he first made inroads in the record business, he did it in pop, racking up hits with "Bluer Than Blue," "Almost Like Being in Love," and "This Night Won't Last Forever."

He hadn't yet covered polka music, or country, but he tackled the latter idiom after signing with RCA Records in the winter of 1985. His pleasant intonation, relaxed phrasing, and unusual pronunciations blend well with his usual acoustic arrangements, although Johnson's never quite earned the level of recognition his talents deserve. –TR

○ **Wings / RCA**   1986
Johnson's first country album didn't stray far from the formula that gave him pop hits. The band on *Wings* is essentially the same as on "Bluer Than Blue," but Johnson leaned toward songs by Nashville writers. And what songs they were. *Wings* yielded two #1 singles, "Give Me Wings" and the ultra-romantic "The Moon Is Still over Her Shoulder." Those are the hits, but the quality songwriting runs as deep as any country album of the time. –BM

DAVID LYNN JONES

Progressive country.

○ **Mixed Emotions / LIBERTY**   1992
After two albums for Mercury that left his promise unfulfilled, David Lynn Jones switched labels and recorded an album in his home studio in Bexar, AR. Like a saved man flirting with sin, Jones forsakes Nashville wisdom and takes his cues from renegade American rockers like Leon Russell and Robbie Robertson. In his heart he's still country, but he revs the tempos, cranks the guitars, and lays on the horns as he takes off screaming into the Arkansas Delta. –BM

GEORGE JONES   b1931

Traditional country. A singer's singer, George Jones is likely to appear on anybody's list of the top male singers in country music history, along with Hank Williams and Lefty Frizzell. Like the other two, Jones interprets the country archetypes — broken love, human failings, sweet dreams gone sour — through personal experience; unlike the other two, he has somehow managed to reach age sixty despite the excesses encountered over the decades in coping with the music business, the road, and life. And his unsurpassed voice remains unscathed after 40 years of artistic heights and the self-destructive depths that led to his nickname of "No-Show" Jones. By singing about what they have lived, he and Williams and Frizzell are the ultimate interpreters of honky-tonk.

In 1955 Jones made his first record on the Starday label, charting with the self-penned "Why Baby Why." From the start he showed his versatility by singing rockabilly and his trademark torch songs with equal ease. Immediately he signed with the Louisiana Hayride, moving on to the Opry in less than four months. More of his uptempo rollicking hits followed, among them "White Lightning" (his first #1) and "The Race Is On." In the 60s the hits kept coming, Jones scoring with the slow, emotion-draining sad songs that no one has done better, among them "Window up Above," "She Thinks I Still Care," and "We Must Have Been out of Our Minds," the latter recorded with Melba Montgomery, who travelled with Jones's show and whose voice blended with his perfectly. Though the heavy drinking was getting out of control, the hits continued in the mid 60s, with "Walk through This World with Me" and "If My Heart Had Windows," just two of those that charted.

In 1967 Jones met Tammy Wynette and they became the king and queen of country music, the two recording hits, both solo and together. Their duet "We're Gonna Hold On" (1973) brought Jones one half of a #1, the first he had since 1967. "Golden Ring" and "Near You" came out after the two had agreed on a divorce. In the 80s the awards came for Jones, including a Grammy for best country male vocalist. His life apparently had straightened out; Jones no longer was called "No-Show," and he was busy with collaborations (Merle Haggard and Ray Charles) and solo efforts, including "If Drinking Don't Kill Me Her Memory Will," "Yesterday's Wine," and "Who's Gonna Fill Their Shoes." As of this writing, this master singer is in perfect voice, bending notes and interpreting phrases in his inimitable way. His influence on other singers is obvious: when you listen to many of the contemporary singers, in a sense you're listening to Jones, for they graduated from his school, by listening to him in person or to one of the 100 albums he has recorded since 1956. The "legend in his own time" cliché seems much too weak to describe George Jones. –DV

Note: Since George Jones has over 100 albums in his catalog, it is important to keep in mind when considering the following list the many different record company affiliations he has had over the years and what labels have reissued his work. Jones recorded for Starday from 1954 to 1956, and this material also has been released on Mercury and on Ace (UK). He recorded for Mercury from 1957 to 1961, and this material also has been released on Ace (UK). He recorded for United Artists from 1962 to 1964. He recorded for Musicor from 1965 to 1971, and this material also has been released on Gusto and Rounder. He recorded for Epic from 1971 to 1990. He has recorded for MCA since 1991. –WR

★ **Burn the Honky-Tonk Down / ROUNDER** 1970
Good collection of songs from the Musicor era, including the beautiful and hard-to-find "Beneath Still Waters." The liner notes go to great length to carp about the overproduction of Jones's records over the years. Ironically, some of the more elaborate Musicor productions such as "Good Year for the Roses" are included here. A bit too much is made of this — fans of 60s mainstream country learn how to tune out sappy vocal choruses and such. In any case, this and the other Rounder selection, *Heartaches & Hangovers*, have the great advantage of being stuff from Jones's peak period that may actually be available for purchase. –GB

George Jones with Love / MUSICOR 1972
Includes a couple of big production numbers — "A Good Year for the Roses" and "A Day in the Life of a Fool." Also nice re-write of the gospel song "Never Grow Old," sung with Tammy Wynette and retitled "Never Grow Cold." –GB

Still the Same Ole Me / EPIC 1981
Recorded at the peak of his popularity, this album is sometimes restrained, and sometimes finds Jones at his uncontrollable best. Predominantly honky-tonk ballads; best cuts (besides the obvious hits) include: "Good Ones and Bad Ones," "Together Alone," and the raucous "You Can't Get the Hell out of Texas." –TR

○ **Encore - George Jones & Tammy Wynette / EPIC** 1981
One album in an entire series of greatest-hits releases for CBS artists, this package documents the very best singles by George Jones and Tammy Wynette, an act that was once country music's top running soap opera. The sad hitch in Wynette's voice and the greasy slides in the Possum's make for an interesting contrast. They sound just as good after their 1975 breakup ("Golden Ring," "Two Story House") as before ("We're Gonna Hold On," "Near You"). –TR

★ **Anniversary — Ten Years of Hits / EPIC** 1982

Covers the first ten years of Jones's two-decade association with Epic Records and, more importantly, record producer Billy Sherrill. Owing much to Sherrill's knack for locating quality material, the hits range from amusing ("Nothing Ever Hurt Me," "Her Name Is ...") to morbid ("He Stopped Loving Her Today") to classic ("The Grand Tour," "A Picture of Me without You"). Best cuts include "Bartender's Blues," "The Door," and "Still Doin' Time." –TR

☆ **The Ballad Side of George Jones / MERCURY** 1987
Good portrait of the later Mercury-era Jones. The title is something of a misnomer, as there are several uptempo songs. Includes several of his own compositions (notably "Glad to Let Her Go" and "The First One") and the incredible "Mr. Fool." –GB

One Woman Man / EPIC 1989
One of Jones's best Epic albums, despite two previously released songs being tagged on to fill it out. One of those is "Radio Lover," a bizarre cheating tale. Things get even stranger with "Ya Ba Da Ba Do (So Are You)," in which Jones gets drunk and talks to a Fred Flintstone glass and an Elvis Presley wine decanter (it also sparked legal action by Hanna-Barbera.) Beyond that, it's quality Jones honky-tonk and weepers, including a first-rate remake of "Just out of Reach (Of My Two Empty Arms)." –BM

And Along Came Jones / MCA 1991
Jones ended a long association with Epic and producer Billy Sherrill in 1990 when he jumped ship to MCA and Kyle Lehning. His MCA debut wasn't a masterpiece, but it was stronger than almost everything he'd done in the 80s. The abandoned house in "Where the Tall Grass Grows" is yet another symbol for the unchecked memories of Jones's mind, and the Post-it Notes in "You Couldn't Get the Picture" are the kind of trivial detail he loves. The Cajun remake of "You Done Me Wrong" (cowritten in 1960 with Ray Price) works, and the only moment of true silliness is "Heckel and Jeckel." –BM

The Best of George Jones / UNITED ARTISTS
Fine collection of songs all written or cowritten by Jones. Includes the Cajun-influenced "You Done Me Wrong," plus re-recordings of a couple of his old Starday tunes. Also two fine Jones Boys instrumentals. –GB

○ **The Best of George Jones / EPIC**
Most of the best mid-70s production numbers — "The Door," "The Grand Tour," and "These Days I Barely Got By," plus the all-time great performance "A Picture of Me without You." –GB

The Best of Sacred Music / MUSICOR
Country gospel classics like "I'll Fly Away" plus a great song cowritten by Jones, "Small Time Laboring Man." Also "Family Bible." Highly recommended. –GB

Country & Western #1 Male Singer / MERCURY
Fine collection of Mercury stuff, with the emphasis on honky-tonk. Includes "Out of Control (What Goes Wrong with the Mind of a Man in a Bar?)" and the classic "You're Still on My Mind." –GB

○ **George Jones' Golden Hits - Vol. 1 / UNITED ARTS.**
The 12 best-selling singles from his United Artists period. "The Race Is On," "She Thinks I Still Care," "A Girl I Used to Know," "Your Heart Turned Left," and more. –GB

George Jones & Melba Montgomery / MUSICOR
Great duets with Tennessee beauty Melba Montgomery — her voice suits Jones's better than Wynette's. Includes the eerie "Long as We're Dreaming" and "Long Walk off a Tall Rock." Lots of dobro. Not for the countrypolitan. –GB

George Jones Salutes Hank Williams / MERCURY
Country's greatest singer performs the songs of country's greatest writer. Liner notes by Elvis Costello. (The 1984 release is a 10-song abridged version of a longer, earlier set, Mercury SR 60257.) –WR

George Jones Sings from the Heart / MERCURY-WING
Great collection — all the songs except "Tender Years" have "heart" in the title. –GB

○ **George Jones Sings His Greatest Hits / STARDAY**

All Starday singles reissued by Starday/Gusto in 1975. –GB

○ **Greatest Hits / MERCURY**
A 10-song compilation of Jones's Mercury years including the Top Ten hits "Treasure of Love," "White Lightning," "Who Shot Sam," "The Window up Above," "Tender Years," plus the song that started it all, "Why Baby Why." –WR

☆ **Heartaches & Hangovers / ROUNDER**
Excellent collection of some of his best Musicor sides, and some of the best country singing ever recorded by anyone. The liner notes do an excellent job of describing Jones's style and importance (in fact, they'd make a good sidebar for Jones). An absolute must for anyone interested in country music, or American music in general. –GB

I'm a People / MUSICOR
One of the more consistent Musicor offerings, with a good mix of uptempo honky-tonk and novelty ("I'm a People," "Ship of Love," and "Blindfold of Love"), ballads (the eerie "The Lonely Know My Secret"), and sacred songs ("If You Believe" and "Old Brush Arbors"). –GB

★ **The Lone Star Legend / ACE**
Mostly Mercury material, with a couple of Starday cuts. Emphasis is on the ballads, including previously unissued songs. Includes the great "Hearts in My Dreams" and the incredible "Mr. Fool," one of the most masterful pieces of country singing ever recorded. Along with *White Lightnin'*, a good portrait of the 50s Jones. –GB

Long Live King George / STARDAY
A lot of the best Starday stuff — "Nothin' Can Stop My Love," "Why Baby Why" (his first hit), and "I Gotta Talk to Your Heart." –GB

Love Bug / MUSICOR
A couple of Jones's hits — the title song and "Things Have Gone to Pieces" — plus Jones's versions of hits by other artists — "Six Days on the Road" (Dave Dudley), "Strangers" (Merle Haggard), and more. Highlights: "Blue Side of Lonesome" and "Unfaithful Man." –GB

Mr. Country & Western Music / MUSICOR
Early Musicor offering features "Don't You Ever Get Tired" (a great version of the Hank Cochran song) and a couple of gems written by Joe Poovey, "How Proud I Would Have Been" and the good-sport "Worst of Luck." Also "Flowers for Mama." It may be maudlin, but it'll get ya. –GB

My Very Special Guests / EPIC
Jones duets with some expected country contemporaries (Tammy Wynette, Johnny Paycheck), some outlaws (Waylon Jennings, Willie Nelson), and, most interestingly, some up-and-coming and pop-oriented guests (Emmylou Harris, Linda Ronstadt, Elvis Costello), often to beneficial effect for both. –WR

New Country Hits / MUSICOR
Includes the early Musicor hits "Love Bug" and "Things Have Gone to Pieces" plus some little-known gems like "Till I Hear from You" and "Memory Is," both cowritten by Jones. Cover features the 1965 version of the Jones Boys featuring Johnny Paycheck (Donny Young) on bass and harmony vocals. –GB

The Race Is On / UNITED ARTS.
Lots of good stuff — "World's Worst Loser," "Ain't It Funny What a Fool Will Do," covers of "Take Me As I Am," and "Don't Let the Stars Get in Your Eyes." –GB

Rockin' the Country / MERCURY
Uptempo stuff from the late-50s Mercury era. Includes "White Lightnin'," "Little Boy Blue," and the great and obscure "Slave Lover." –GB

★ **Trouble in Mind / UNITED ARTS.**
One of his best albums. There are sappy vocal choruses on some of the tunes, but they can't diminish George. A few that don't — "You Done Me Wrong" (written by George) and "It's a Sin" — are among the best things he's ever recorded. Also included are great versions of a couple of Hank Williams songs and a couple of truly definitive songs: "My Tears Are Overdue" and "Sometimes You Just Can't Win." Essential for anyone

interested in Jones, country music, or American folk-based popular music in general. –GB

Walk through This World with Me / MUSICOR
Hit title song plus Jones's versions of hits by others including "Almost Persuaded" and a great version of "Lonely Street." –GB

Where Grass Won't Grow / MUSICOR
The title song's a big production number about the wretchedness of unsuccessful dirt farming. Other depressing highlights — "Old Blue Tomorrow" about approaching death, and "For Better or for Worse (But Not for Long)" (self-explanatory). –GB

☆ **White Lightnin' / ACE**
Uptempo material from the Starday and Mercury eras — includes the rockabilly experiments from Starday. –GB

The Young George Jones / UNITED ARTS.
Includes re-recordings of some of his old Starday tunes, a couple of great Hank Williams covers, a great version of Ted Daffan's "Worried Mind." –GB

We Found Heaven Right Here on Earth / MUSICOR
Includes the haunting "From Here to the Door" and "Developing My Pictures." –GB

GRANDPA JONES   ♭1913

Country humor, old-time. Louis Marshall "Grandpa" Jones is one person who has aged right into his makeup. His nickname reportedly was given to him by hillbilly crooner Bradley Kincaid when Jones was about 23 years old. His geezer image has thus been with him for over 55 years. In the early 40s, Jones, Merle Travis, and the Delmore Brothers formed the Brown's Ferry Four, an influential group. After the war, Jones joined the Opry, where he has appeared regularly ever since, often with his wife Ramona. Jones is among the last of the Uncle Dave Macon school of banjo picking and all-round entertaining. His years on "Hee Haw" made him even more famous; he was elected to the Country Music Hall of Fame in 1978. –DV

Country Music Hall of Fame Series / MCA   1992
The banjo player's entire recorded output for Decca Records between 1956 and 1959, including a live performance and previously unreleased tracks. Jones sings about dogs and trains, re-records some previous hits for King Records, and parodies Johnny Cash's "Don't Take Your Guns to Town." –BM

○ **Grandpa Jones Story / CMH**
The "Hee Haw" banjo comic in a pleasant folksy setting with Ramona. –MH

STEVE JORDAN

Tex-Mex. Esteban Jordan bears the moniker "El Parche" for his trademark eyepatch, and admirers have also called him the "Jimi Hendrix of the accordion" for his aggressive rock attack and use of such effects as phase shifters. His music, however, is firmly rooted in the Norteño tradition and simply reflects the influences an adroit musician like Jordan naturally absorbs into a traditional core repertoire. His wonderful 60s rock-meets-Norteño singles for regional labels have been reissued on Arhoolie, while more recent recordings have appeared on sundry Texas labels, Rounder, and RCA. Jordan appeared in David Byrne's 1986 film *True Stories* and was featured in the soundtrack of *Born in East LA*. –MH

Many Sounds of Steve Jordan / ARHOOLIE   1985
Some of his earliest and greatest traditional Norteño accordion music; not much of his trademark lunacy. –MB

☆ **Return of El Parche / ROUNDER**   1986
Prime late-70s and early-80s material. A wild mix of Norteño, salsa, rock, and psychedelic accordion. –MB

El Hurracane / ROUNDER
From the same period as *Return of El Parche* comes more of Jordan's eclectic fare. –MB

WYNONNA JUDD

Contemporary country. See the entry for the Judds. –ED

☆ **Wynonna / CURB-MCA**   1992
Daughter Judd stakes out her own territory. It's probably safe to say Wynonna has more in her than most people guessed. From the tender "She Is His Only Need" to the Southern rock 'n' soul of "No One Else on Earth," she sings with a smoldering sensuality that pulsed beneath the surface of the duo's best records — even "Live with Jesus" sounds sexy. After a few more albums like this, folks may not even remember the Judds. –BM

THE JUDDS

Contemporary country. Between their first single, "Had a Dream," in 1983 and their farewell concert in Murfreesboro, TN, in December of 1991, mother Naomi and daughter Wynonna had quite a ride. They had dozens of hits, including "Mama He's Crazy," "Change of Heart," "Grandpa," and "Guardian Angels," and won numerous awards along the way, including two Grammys in 1992, one for vocal duo/group and another for "Love Can Build a Bridge" as the best country song of the year.
Because of incurable hepatitis, Naomi retired from the business. Wynonna continues solo. The Judds were *the* dominant duet in the 80s. –DV

The Judds (Wynonna & Naomi) / RCA   1983
The debut for this mother/daughter duo who became one of country's leading lights in the 80s. –MH

Why Not Me? / RCA / BB 71   1985
Their second album. Wynonna establishes herself as a fearsome and sultry belter. The production is built around an essentially acoustic base. –MH

☆ **Rockin' with the Rhythm / RCA / BB 66**
On the third album, "Have Mercy" and the title track (among others) kick with a funky glee that makes this the most plainly joyous Judds album. –MH

Judds Greatest Hits / RCA / BB 76   1988
Overview of their chart successes, although the non-singles from their early albums were delights. –MH

Love Can Build a Bridge / RCA   1990
Their final album together. –MH

Greatest Hits - Vol. 2 / RCA   1991
More chartbusters. –MH

THE KENDALLS

Traditional country. When father Royce and daughter Jeannie saw their "Leavin' on a Jet Plane" reach the charts in 1970, Royce put his barber's clippers away and left Missouri for Nashville. Not until 1977 did they find real success, with the B-side "Heaven's Just a Sin Away," which climbed to #1 and brought awards to the father and daughter. Another chart-topper came in 1984, "Thank God for the Radio." –DV

16 Greatest Hits / DELUXE   1986
This represents the bulk of their best work, with those cut-to-the-quick harmonies fully omnipresent. One sad note: Royce and Jeannie claim they don't receive a dime for this stuff, thanks to legal wranglings when the original label, Ovation, went under. –TR

○ **20 Favorites / CBS**
Jeannie Kendall had a winsome hillbilly soprano. Daddy Royce sang hand-in-glove harmony. Here daddy and daughter delivered some of the best cheatin' anthems of the late 70s and early 80s. –MH

KENNEDY-ROSE

Contemporary country. Pam Rose and Mary Ann Kennedy, otherwise known as Kennedy Rose, have provided back-up singing support for artists like Emmy Lou Harris, Dan Fogelberg and Sting. Their songs have been covered by Garfunkel and Restless Heart. As artists, this Nashville-based duo has fashioned a distinctive hard acoustic pop/rock sound that has showcased their fine vocal sound to great effect. –RC

○ **Hai-Ku / PANGAEA**   1989

Songwriters Mary Ann Kennedy and Pam Rose decided to turn to performing, and the result is this debut album, which reprises familiar songs of theirs, such as "Love Like This" and "The Only Chain." The production is deep and echoey, with sharply recorded acoustic instruments, and the swinging is as forceful as the writing. –WR

KENTUCKY HEADHUNTERS

Country. You won't confuse this group with any others, not in sound, not in image. These two brothers and a cousin from Kentucky and two brothers from Missouri have been making music for over 20 years, yet their debut, *Pickin' on Nashville*, turned some heads — and some ears — by adding Southern metal boogie to the likes of "Walk Softly on This Heart of Mine." When appearing at the Grammy show to pick up their Best Country Vocal Group award in 1990, they dressed in their normal outfits, but the overalls didn't fit in so well among all the tuxedos. The group split in 1992 when lead singer Ricky Lee Phelps and his brother Doug decided to pursue a more mainstream country direction; they were replaced by Anthony Kenney and Mark Orr, who had previously played with the three remaining HeadHunters. –DV & BM

○ **Pickin' on Nashville / MERCURY**   1989
As their album title suggests, the Headhunters aren't entirely comfortable with the country tag, which is appropriate when you hear their guitar-heavy, rambunctious music. The vocals have that twang, but these good old boys are often closer to Lynyrd Skynyrd than they are to Merle Haggard, and all the better for it. –WR

CLARK KESSINGER

Instrumental. One of the greatest of old-time fiddlers, Kessinger and his nephew Luches were billed as the Kessinger Brothers and recorded for the Brunswick company in the late 20s, producing records that greatly influenced other fiddle players around the South. When Kessinger was "rediscovered" during the folk revival of 1960, he appeared on the Opry, giving two encores because of audience demand. He entered many of the better-known fiddle contests, winning first place and the title as World's Champion Fiddler at the 47th Annual Union Grove, when he was in his mid-eighties. –DV

☆ **Clark Kessinger - Fiddler / FOLKWAYS**   1966
Tunes played with incredible drive. (Like all Folkways albums, now available on tape from Smithsonian/Folkways.) –CW

★ **Old-Time Music w/ Fiddle & Guitar / ROUNDER**   1984
A West Virginian who began recording in 1928, Kessinger was rediscovered in the 60s and made several "comeback" albums, of which this is one of the best. –CW

HAL KETCHUM

Country-pop. This country-pop singer was raised in upstate New York and started off in rock. His "Small Town Saturday Night" debut single went to #1 on the charts. –DV

○ **Past the Point of Rescue / CURB**   1991
An unassuming album that doesn't try to pass plain-guy Ketchum off as a country hunk or honky-tonk hero. "Small Town Saturday Night" introduced him to the masses, but Ketchum's voice carries more weight when dealing with matters of the heart in "Past the Point of Rescue" and "Somebody's Love." Ketchum worked up a cover of the Vogue's 1965 hit "Five O'Clock World" to surprise producer Allen Reynolds, who wrote the song; it turned out to be such a gem they recorded it. –BM

CLAUDE KING   b 1932

Traditional country. Although "The Burning of Atlanta" and "Big River" made everyone in the business think that Claude King was the next big star, this wasn't to be. Tastes changed, and the Louisiana native with the big voice had one more hit in him, but it was a *huge* hit: "Wolverton Mountain," which told the story of Clifton Clowers and his unfriendly welcome toward any and all suitors who came a-courtin' his daughter. In one of the great songs of the 60s is the memorable line, "Her tender lips were sweeter than haw-nee." –DV

○ **American Originals / CBS**
"Wolverton Mountain" and other 60s hits from Johnny Horton's pal. –MH

FRED KOLLER

Country. Fred Koller is a Nashville songwriter whose songs have been covered by Kathy Mattea (three #1 hits), the Jeff Healey Band, Nanci Griffith, Peter Rowan, New Grass Revival, the Forester Sisters, Lacy J. Dalton. Koller has collaborated with such artists as John Prine, Tom Paxton, John Hiatt, Shel Silverstein, John Gorka, Bill Staines, and others. He is the author of a book on songwriting, *How to Pitch and Promote Your Songs.* Koller has developed a cult following who appreciate his deep rough-edged vocals and powerful, often humorous songwriting. A class act! –CR

○ **Where the Fast Lane Ends / ALL CITY**   1990
Koller's versions of his songs "Goin' Gone" and "Lone Star State of Mind" are here, but he has a deep, bluesy voice that puts a very different spin on these familiar tunes. –WR

KRIS KRISTOFFERSON   b 1937

Traditional country, progressive country. The 70s was a decade ripe and waiting for rebels. The Nashville establishment, though, which had sold a lot of records with the bland "Nashville Sound," wasn't quite ready for this songwriting former soldier who, with long beard and dressed in jeans, in 1970 walked on stage at the Country Music Association awards and got his award for "Sunday Morning Coming Down," a song that friend Johnny Cash had made a hit. When in the next year Janis Joplin sold a million with "Me and Bobby McGee," he was on his way, anti-establishment or not. Then Sammi Smith's version of "Help Me Make It through the Night" was a hit on both the country and the pop charts, also in 1971; suddenly Kristofferson's creative lyrics and memorable music made the establishment forget about his image and created a cult following.

In 1973, the year he and singer Rita Coolidge married, *The Silver Tongued Devil and I* went gold. Meanwhile, his duets with Coolidge sold well and produced two Grammys for them. It was at about this time that his record sales began to dip, so he stepped up a film acting career. Role followed role, among them *Cisco Pike, Pat Garrett and Billy the Kid* (costarring Bob Dylan), *Alice Doesn't Live Here Anymore, Blume in Love, Rollover.* Critics liked his work on the silver screen, writing that Kristofferson had real talent, that he wasn't only a singer who might sell tickets. He charted again, right into the 80s, but nothing like his phenomenal sales of the previous decade, though his collaboration with Johnny Cash, Willie Nelson, and Waylon Jennings on *Highwayman* (1985) produced another #1 album. This gifted songwriter, performer, and actor made success easier for subsequent musicians who, like him, don't fit into the mold. –WR

☆ **Me and Bobby McGee / MONUMENT / BB 43**   1971
In the late 60s and early 70s, Kris Kristofferson's adult, reality-based songs were the most shocking thing to hit Nashville in a long time, and what's more, they were hits. This album contains his own versions of some of the best, including the title song, "Help Me Make It through the Night," and "Sunday Mornin' Comin' Down." –WR

K. D. LANG

Progressive country. Katherine Dawn, from Alberta, Canada, won a Grammy for Best Vocal Collaboration in her duet with Roy Orbison on his hit "Crying." She's famous for her unisex look and her powerful voice. –DV

Angel with a Lariat / SIRE   1987
On her debut album, big-voiced K. D. Lang took a rockabilly approach, with Dave Edmunds as her perfect producer choice.

Edmunds brought out the sharp, rhythmic aspects of her band the Reclines, and Lang wailed over them. The record, which was underappreciated at the time of its release, was an amazingly confident first effort. –WR

Shadowland / WARNER   1988
Rebuffed commercially, Lang turned to veteran Nashville producer Owen Bradley for this genre exercise, which recreates the kind of country-diva style of Patsy Cline. It was an accomplished, if puzzling, effort that broke Lang through to the country market, at least temporarily. –WR

○ **Absolute Torch and Twang / SIRE**   1989
As the title suggests, Lang's third (and last country) album combines the best qualities of the first two — the affected-but-original country songwriting of *Angel with a Lariat* and the soaring, Patsy Cline-influenced vocals of *Shadowland*. –BM

JIM LAUDERDALE

Country. North Carolina-born Jim Lauderdale is a Nashville-based songwriter whoses big influences were Gram Parsons, George Jones, Buck Owens, Hank Williams, and Merle Haggard. He considers himself a country artist with rock, soul, and blues influences thrown in. –CR

○ **Planet of Love / WARNER**   1991
Jim Leventhal and Rodney Crowell produced and helped out on this release and Shawn Colvin and Emmylou Harris provide great vocal support. Great debut — an example of the new singer/songwriter "traditionalist" coming out in country music today. –CR

CHRIS LEDOUX

Cowboy. This cowboy-and-western singer knows what he's singing about, having been a champion bronc-rider. –DV

Radio & Rodeo Hits / CAPITOL
Contemporary cowboy singer/songwriter. –MH

○ **Rodeo Songs "Old & New" / CAPITOL**
The title tells the tale. –MH

BRENDA LEE   b 1944

Country. This country, rockabilly, and rock & roll singer was born Brenda Mae Tarpley. One of the most popular female vocalists of her time, with fifty Hot 100 entries between 1957 and 1973. The classic little girl with the big voice, Lee started as a child prodigy on the radio in her native Georgia at the age of five and began recording and appearing on television by 1955. Few can jump from rockabilly to country to novelty rockers to world-weary ballads as well as she. Lee went back to recording country by the early 70s, with consistent hits in that marketplace ever since. The voice and style of Brenda Lee continue to be an American music treasure. –CK

Brenda Lee / DECCA / BB 5   1960
Brenda Lee at 15 — her nickname was "Miss Dynamite" and it's no lie. Some of her early hits — "Sweet Nothin's," "That's All You Gotta Do," plus "I'm Sorry," a great rocking reworking of "Weep No More My Lady," the bluesy "Be My Love Again," and "Just Let Me Dream." –GB

☆ **Anthology 1956-1980 / MCA**   1991
A 40-song, two-CD collection that proves Lee was the best wWite female rock singer of the pre-Beatles 60s. By the time she turned 18, Lee had hit the pop Top Ten 11 times. All those cuts are here, from the innocently salacious "Sweet Nothin's" to the string-laden "I'm Sorry" to her remake of Earl "Fatha" Hines's "You Can Depend on Me." Her best country singles — "Johnny One Time" and "Big Four Poster Bed" — are also included. The compilers wisely passed over some minor hits in favor of obscure sides like the odd rockabilly "Let's Jump the Broomstick," a cover of Edith Piaf's "If You Love Me (Really Love Me)," and "Is It True?," a middling hit from 1964 that features guitarist Jimmy Page (who is 11 months older than Lee). *Anthology* thoroughly traces Lee's development as a vocalist, from early childish exuberance to mature, graceful phrasing. –BM

JOHNNY LEE   b 1946

Country. Like many his age, Johnny Lee grew up on the music of Chuck Berry, Elvis Presley, and Jerry Lee Lewis. Raised on a dairy farm in Alta Loma, TX, he formed his first band, Johnny Lee & the Road Runners, during high school. He tricked his way into playing on stage with Mickey Gilley at a Houston club called the Nesadel, and that shot brought him a long-term run at Gilley's clubs. When *Urban Cowboy* was shot at Gilley's, record executive Irving Azoff offered Lee an opportunity to sing in the picture, and he ended up with a song that more than 20 artists had previously rejected. In his hands, that song — "Lookin' for Love" — became a million-seller and the musical centerpiece of the movie.

Stardom occurred practically overnight for Lee, but it was a mixed bag. He and Gilley toured steadily; Lee got a substantial string of hits for about three years and ended up marrying Dallas starlet Charlene Tilton. But the marriage soured, he found his name constantly in the tabloids, and he was forced to record a large amount of same-sounding material. Nevertheless, Johnny Lee had an important role in a huge era for country music, and his easygoing vocal style still makes him very listenable. –TR

○ **Greatest Hits / WARNER**   1983
Lots of midtempo love songs, much in the vein of "Lookin' for Love." Too bad Lee couldn't break out of that mold a little sooner — "Sounds like Love" and "Hey Bartender" show some real teeth. –TR

HANK LOCKLIN   b 1918

Traditional country. When you hear Hank Locklin's high, sweet tenor, you'll know why he has been popular in Ireland for so many years. He's recorded two country classics: his self-penned "Send Me the Pillow That You Dream On" (1959) and "Please Help Me I'm Falling," a blockbuster #1 in 1960. Though his hits slowed down, Locklin toured internationally in the 70s and played to packed houses. –DV

● **Hank Locklin / WRANGLER**
One of the most perfect early country albums ever recorded; heart-wrenching songs sung in Locklin's perfect tenor — before the hits. It does not get any better than this. Hard-to-find album, but quintessential. –JME

○ **The Best of Hank Locklin / RCA**

VALERIO LONGORIA SR

Tex-Mex. Valerio is a Tex-Mex accordion veteran, one of the first to update the conjunto sound by adding drums. His music retains a strong "old school" sound and is always danceable, particularly when he breaks into a polka or Colombian cumbia rhythm. –MB

○ **Caballo Viejo / ARHOOLIE**
Roots-conscious border music from a pioneer of the genre, excelling here on the catchy "cumbia" rhythm. –MB

THE LOUVIN BROTHERS

Traditional country. From the close-harmony brother acts of the 30s evolved Charlie (b 1927) and Ira (Loudermilk) Louvin (b 1924 - d 1965), ranking among the top duos in country music history. With Ira's incredibly high, pure tenor and Charlie's emotional and smooth melody tenor, they learned well from the Bolick brothers (the Blue Sky Boys), the Monroe Brothers, the Delmore Brothers, and other major family duos of the previous generation, preserving the old-time flavor, while bringing this genre into the 50s, when country music moved to a newer sound. Whatever type of songs they recorded — gospel, folk, hillbilly, or 50s pop — those songs became the Louvins. Add to the list the many Louvin compositions (for example, "If I Could Only Win Your Love," Emmylou Harris's first hit), and you have an act that is outstanding in country music history. Their career took a while to get going, partly because of interruptions from WW II and the Korean War. In the early 50s, after making a reputation for unexceled gospel singing, the Louvins broadened their repertoire, recording "The Get Acquainted Waltz" (with Chet Atkins adding another guitar to Charlie's and to Ira's mandolin), a fair hit that showed success was reachable with non-religious music. The electric guitar, with the duo's unique harmony and Ira's exceptional tenor, created a sound that fans asked for in increasing numbers. In 1955, after ten unsuccessful auditions, they finally joined the Opry, where they performed to great acclaim until 1963, when they broke up. They had a number of hits, including the much-covered "When I Stop Dreaming." Ira continued on with a solo career. Charlie has remained with the Opry to this day, where his excellent voice has only improved with the years, scoring a major hit with "See the Big Man Cry, Mama." Driving home from a performance one night in 1965, Ira's car was struck in a head-on collision, killing probably the most exceptional high tenor country music has ever known. –DV

☆ **The Family Who Prays / CAPITOL**   1990
All-sacred album, all songs written by the brothers themselves, with one exception ("Swing Low Sweet Chariot"). Country duos just don't come any better. –GB

The Louvin Brothers / ROUNDER
Mostly sacred songs from three MGM recording sessions. This includes the original recording of "Weapon of Prayer," their first successful record. A fine example of their early work. –GB

★ **The Louvin Brothers / JS**
The best of their later non-sacred recordings, including "When I Stop Dreaming" and "My Baby's Gone." Probably the ultimate expression of country music's brother-duet tradition. Essential, not only for country fans, but for anyone interested in American music. Previously released on Capitol. –GB

My Baby's Gone / CAPITOL
Same general era and backing as *The Louvin Brothers*, with some overlap of songs. (Also a British reissue on Longhorn #3028.) –GB

Satan Is Real / CAPITOL
Great fire and brimstone songs, including the original "The Christmas Life," which was covered by the Byrds on their *Sweetheart of the Rodeo* album. –GB

Songs That Tell a Story / ROUNDER
Live on-the-radio performance from 1952. –GB

☆ **Tragic Songs of Life / ROUNDER**
A reissue of their first Capitol album. A sort of tribute album to the country duos that preceded them, it's the Louvins at their best. –GB

Weapon of Prayer / CAPITOL
A re-recording for Capitol of the title song and "The Great Atomic Power," plus "Searching for a Soldier's Grave" and other mostly sacred "songs of those who serve God and country." –GB

PATTY LOVELESS

Country rock. Loveless came to Nashville from Pikeville, KY, at age 14 and was eventually signed by the Wilburn Brothers to replace her cousin Loretta Lynn as the band's singer. Her sound ranges from rock to progressive country sound. She sings with emotion. –DV

○ **If My Heart Had Windows / MCA**   1988
Fine songs by Steve Earle, Dallas Frazier, and others. –DH

Honky Tonk Angel / MCA   1988
The song subjects hardly classify Loveless as a honky-tonk angel, at least by Hank Thompson's definition. But this was the album that established Loveless as a major presence, and it includes two of her biggest singles — "Chains," "Timber I'm Falling in Love" — and two of her best — "Blue Side of Town" and "Don't Toss Us Away," a duet with Rodney Crowell. –BM

Up against My Heart / MCA   1991
Loveless gets a little more adventurous with each album, though she never forgets to include sure-fire hits like "Hurt Me Bad (In a Real Good Way)" and "Jealous Bone." This time she invites comparisons to Patsy Cline with "Can't Stop Myself

from Loving You" and implies that God is female by switching the pronouns in Lyle Lovett's "God Will." –BM

BOB LUMAN   1937-1978

Country rock. Bob Luman started out as a rockabilly in the Elvis Presley mold. His first break came when he replaced Johnny Cash on Shreveport's Louisiana Hayride. Then came Las Vegas bookings and soon after a national name resulting from "Let's Talk about Living," a crossover hit in 1960. After some success in following years, he recorded *Alive and Well*, an album produced by friend Johnny Cash. He died a year later. –DV

○ **American Originals / CBS**
A likable 60s country/pop singer. –MH

LORETTA LYNN   b 1935

Traditional country. Because of her 1980 biographical movie, *Coal Miner's Daughter*, this native of Butcher's Hollow, KY, is country music's most famous rags-to-riches story. In the late 60s and early 70s, her country voice, quality material (much of which she wrote), and winsome personality combined to make her Nashville's most prolific female star. Most of her singles reached the charts, including "Don't Come Home A-Drinkin'," "Coal Miner's Daughter," and the controversial "The Pill." With Conway Twitty she recorded numerous duet hits; "Louisiana Woman, Mississippi Man" was probably the best-known. Paying a compliment to two country woman greats who preceded her, Lynn says that Kitty Wells's singing and Patsy Cline's personality have been her biggest influences. –DV

Country Music Hall of Fame / MCA   1962
Few greatest-hits packages pack the wallop of these 16 performances (1961-1976). This album includes duets with Ernest Tubb and Conway Twitty, men who knew to stand clear when Lynn wailed "Your Squaw Is on the Warpath" or "Fist City." –MH

Loretta Lynn's Greatest Hits / DECCA   1968
Lynn had a big hand in raising Nashville's perception of women as capable and competent (although the city still has a way to go). "Don't Come Home A-Drinkin'" and "You Ain't Woman Enough" are particularly representative: sassy, honest, and aggressive. –TR

Loretta Lynn's Greatest Hits - Vol. 2 / MCA   1974
In the liner notes, Pete Axthelm cites "the range of her personality," and that range is in evidence here: reflective ("Coal Miner's Daughter"), feisty ("Fist City"), humorous ("One's on the Way"), and sentimental ("Love Is the Foundation"). –TR

○ **Here's Loretta Lynn / CB**
A collection of her earliest recordings, made for the Zero label (unfortunately not including "Honky Tonk Girl," her first hit). Good, bluesy honky-tonk, with Lynn already in top form and a very swinging band. –GB

SHELBY LYNNE   b 1969

Country. This country balladeer with the powerful voice is young and talented. The day after she appeared on Ralph Emery's "Nashville Now" in 1987, she received four contract offers. Her *Soft Talk* album showcases her talent. –DV

○ **Soft Talk / CBS**   1976
Defiant, emotionally drenching country., as on "Stop Me." –BC
Sunrise / CBS   1976
"The Hurtin' Side." Her debut album. –BC
Tough All Over / CBS   1989
Throaty, sensual covers in country and bluesy formats. –BC

UNCLE DAVE MACON   1870-1952

Traditional country, old-time. David Harrison Macon, born in Smartt Station, TN, didn't performprofessionally until he was past 50, but he became one of the first superstars of country music. A talented banjoist and comic (and sometimes preacher and farmer), Uncle Dave Macon was the Grand Ole

Opry's first major star and an audience favorite from 1925 until his death in 1952. He derived much of his repertoire and stage patter from vaudeville and minstrel shows, but his songs reflected on a wide variety of subjects from political corruption to current events like the advent of the automobile. His presence affected country music like none before it; even today a three-day festival, Uncle Dave Macon Days, is held in Murfreesboro, TN, the site of the National Old-Time Banjo Championship. –BM

○ **Country Music Hall of Fame Series / MCA**   1992
"Shout if you are happy!" Uncle Dave Macon exclaims during "Tom and Jerry" as Mazy Todd saws away at her fiddle. "Kill yo'self!" That's the kind of enthusiasm Macon brings to these 16 fine examples of string-band music, recorded between 1926 and 1934 for the Vocalion, Brunswick, and Champion labels. Macon, who was 55 at the first of these recording sessions, frequently starts the songs with a spoken anecdote (including a plug for his Macon Midway Mule and Wagon Transportation Company). This collection is essentially an expanded version of *Uncle Dave Macon: First Featured Star of the Grand Ole Opry*, a retrospective issued in 1966 after his posthumous election to the Country Music Hall of Fame. –BM

THE MADDOX BROTHERS & ROSE MADDOX

Traditional country. If you were to see a photo of the Maddox Brothers & Rose ca. 1950, you'd know why they were billed as "The Most Colorful Hillbilly Band in the Land." The music of these four brothers and Rose was as colorful as their embroidered and sequined costumes, blending uptempo and highly emotional gospel with tinges of rockabilly. These native Alabamans first established their reputation in California, where they had moved during the Depression. (The whole Maddox family hopped a freight in Meridian, MS, and ended up in the San Joaquin Valley.) After numerous hits and a stint on the Opry, the group disbanded at the start of the 60s, with Rose going it alone. This singer with the powerful voice had numerous hits, including a double-sider with Buck Owens in 1961, *Loose Talk/Mental Cruelty*. Through the 70s she recorded albums for Starday. –DV

The Maddox Brothers & Rose / FORUM-AVON
Bluehonkabilly madness from this raucous and irrepressible combo. Highlights: "That'll Learn Ya, Durn Ya" and their amazing version of "Honky Tonkin'." –GB
Go Honky Tonkin' / HILLTOP
More of the same — "Mama Says It's Naughty," "Water Baby Blues," "Shimmy Shakin' Daddy." –GB
○ **Rockin' Rollin' / BFX**
This German import contains a fair cross-section of their bizarre bluegrass/honky-tonk/rockabilly madness. Includes "Ugly and Sloughy (That's the Way I Like 'Em)" and "The Death of Rock & Roll." –GB

BARBARA MANDRELL   b 1948

Country-pop. A show-biz veteran of over thirty years, this country-pop superstar is the first artist to win the Country Music Association Entertainer of the Year Award two consecutive years. She started early, touring with Johnny Cash when she was thirteen. Her first hit was with Otis Redding's "I've Been Loving You Too Long" in 1969. Among her many #1 records are "Sleepin' Single in a Double Bed," "I Was Country When Country Wasn't Cool," "Years," and "One of a Kind Pair of Fools." She and her sisters Louise and Irlene have received much TV play through their national show, on which each shows her versatility on lots and lots of instruments. Her biography, *Get to the Heart: My Story*, recounts how her near-fatal auto accident of 1984 changed her life. –DV

Moods / MCA / BB 132   1978
Includes "Sleepin' Single in a Double Bed." –BC
The Best of Barbara Mandrell / MCA / BB 170   1979
Classic Southern twists on 60s R&B. –BC
Live / MCA / BB 86   1981

A lively atmosphere, with an appearance by George Jones. –BC
He Set My Life to Music / MCA   1982
A contemporary gospel album. –BC
○ **Greatest Hits / MCA**   1985
Late-70s Nashville tunes and slick pop. –BC
Key's in the Mailbox / CAPITOL   1991
Heartful soul and contemporary country. –BC

JOE MAPHIS

Instrumental. Joe and Rose Maphis were a popular husband-and-wife act in the late 40s and early 50s, singing traditional material backed by the amazing instrumental talent of Joe, who played everything with strings on it, especially the twin-neck guitar. The honky-tonk anthem "Dim Lights, Thick Smoke (And Loud, Loud Music)" was their big hit. Until his death in 1986, Joe was a sessions instrumentalist, backing such stars as Rick Nelson, Tex Ritter, and Wanda Jackson. –DV
○ **Flat-Picking Spectacular / CM**
These are later recordings made by this 40s-era sessionman and singer. –CW

KATHY MATTEA   b 1959

Country-pop. A former tour guide at Nashville's Country Music Museum, Kathy Mattea scored her first #1 country hit with "Eighteen Wheels and a Dozen Roses." Another hit was "Where've You Been," which brought awards her way. Give a listen to *Time Passes By*, country with a folk flavor. –DV
○ **A Collection of Hits / POLYGRAM**   1990
Kathy Mattea has risen to near the top of the Nashville ranks because of a haunting, soulful voice, well-produced recordings that have a simple, folkie directness, and, most especially, an amazing talent for picking the best songs being written for the country market, among them "Eighteen Wheels and a Dozen Roses," "Goin' Gone," and the heartbreaking "Where've You Been." –WR
Time Passes By / MERCURY   1991
On her most ambitious album, Mattea gets impeccably chosen songs (as usual) and strong supporting performances (from Emmylou Harris, Dougie MacLean, and the Roches). She doesn't write her own stuff, so she may not be the romantic dreamer of "Asking Us to Dance," but she sure sounds like it. Songs like "Time Passes By," cowritten by husband Jon Vezner, suggest there's more honesty here than image. She can even make the half-baked "From a Distance" convincing. –BM

THE MAVERICKS

Country-rock. Miami quartet that cut its teeth playing country music in Florida rock clubs. Lead singer and main songwriter Raul Malo is of Cuban descent and has a serious jones for rockabilly; he's also got a haunting tenor that promises to become one of country's most distinctive voices. –BM
○ **The Mavericks / MCA**   1992
In spite of Malo's Cuban heritage and the band's Miami roots — *because* of them, as a matter of fact — the Mavericks understand outsiders like Buck Owens and Hank Williams (both of whom they cover) better than most of country's recent comers. And originals like "I Got You" and the scathing title track, about Malo's aunt's escape from Cuban oppression, are so good the covers don't really matter. –BM

CHARLY MCCLAIN   b 1956

Country. Originally named Charlotte, Charly McClain was given her masculine moniker by neighborhood friends in Memphis, and she also used it when she started playing hotel lounges. Epic Records decided it was more "catchy" than Charlotte, and it became a permanent professional banner.
Her father had tuberculosis when she was eight, and, since she was under age for visitation rights at the hospital, she had to communicate with him through a tape recorder. That inspired her interest in recording, and by age 17 she was a regular on the club circuit.

Signed to her first recording contract in 1976, McClain's distinct vocal sound provided an edge in recognizability — as did her appearance. She hit country's Top Ten fairly regularly from 1978-1985, both as a solo artist and in duets with Mickey Gilley and former soap star Wayne Massey, whom she married in 1984. –TR
○ **Greatest Hits / EPIC**   1982
McClain's Southern heritage is very much in evidence in her vocal style. No other woman sounds as simultaneously tough and feminine as she does; this is simply McClain at her best — "Men," "Sleepin' with the Radio On," "Who's Cheatin' Who," and "The Very Best Is You." –TR

MEL MCDANIEL   b 1942

Country. McDaniel collects tools for a hobby and collects hits for a living. Born in Checotah, OK, he decided at age 14 that he had to pursue music, inspired by seeing Elvis Presley on TV. After establishing himself on the Tulsa club circuit, he moved briefly to Nashville, then headed off to Anchorage, AK, where he refined his stage skills.
Once he returned to Music City, he signed his first recording deal in 1976 with Capitol Records, but it took five years for him to first hit the Top Ten. He had sporadic success thereafter, but his signature song, "Baby's Got Her Blue Jeans On," invited a bevy of recognition, including multiple nominations for Grammy and Country Music Association Awards. –TR
○ **Greatest Hits / CAPITOL**   1987
He is gravelly-voiced and has a limited range, but McDaniel gets the most out of his talents by concentrating on songs with the proper "groove." "Louisiana Saturday Night" and "Baby's Got Her Blue Jeans On" are staples; "Stand Up" and "Big Ole Brew" are pretty damn good. –TR

SKEETS MCDONALD

☆ **Skeets McDonald's Tattooed ... / FORTUNE**   1959
Skeets McDonald's Tattooed Lady Plus Eleven Other Sizzlers. McDonald checks in here with the risqué title track and "Birthday Cake Boogie," while the rest of the album features equally naughty fare by the York Brothers, Tommy Odim, Johnny Bucket, Roy Hall, and Rufus Shoffner. Great fun all. –CK

RONNIE MCDOWELL   b 1950

Country. Raised in rural Portland, TN, north of Nashville, McDowell didn't take performing seriously until he was stationed in the Philippines with the navy. The first song he performed in public: "It's Now or Never," appropriate since Elvis Presley has had a huge impact on his career.
McDowell wrote his first hit, "The King Is Gone," the day that Elvis died. Enough people shared his grief that a reported three million copies were sold. McDowell did all the Elvis vocal imitations for a 1979 Elvis TV movie, starring Kurt Russell, and he began to take on the image of an Elvis imitator.
McDowell consciously distanced himself from those comparisons, which became easier when record producer Buddy Killen took over the reins of his career, bringing in solid uptempo material that consistently showcased McDowell's strong (though a bit nondescript) vocal talents.Now comfortable with his reputation, he's returned on occasion to more "Elvis" work, providing the vocal parts for the short-lived ABC series "Elvis" in 1990. –TR
○ **Older Women and Other Greatest Hits / EPIC**   1987
McDowell fell into this "clone" thing for a couple of years where he re-made his own hits; and all three soundalikes ("Older Women," "Wandering Eyes," "Watchin' Girls Go By") are curiously placed back-to-back. His later material is the most emotive, especially "I Dream of Women Like You," "In a New York Minute," and "Love Talks," recorded with Exile. –TR

REBA MCENTIRE
b 1954

Traditional country, contemporary country. With her powerful, versatile voice, this Chockie, OK, native can sing traditional country as well as it's sung. Like Dolly Parton before her, talented Reba McEntire has moved sideways out of hard country into songs that appeal to a broader, more popular palate, following the path of so many contemporary country performers. And again like Parton, McEntire is on the silver screen. She ably plays a desert girl in the sci-fi comedy *Tremors*, in which the sub-sand critters are lured to their death by vibrations of the non-musical kind. Before moving toward the middle of the road, she cut *My Kind of Country*, a traditionalist's delight, and from this album came the hit single "How Blue," which led to the Country Music Association's Female Vocalist of the Year Award in 1984. McEntire's awards haven't stopped since. She's a natural talent who can sing country or pop or anything in-between with power and beauty. In 1990 seven of her band members and her road manager died in a plane crash on a California mountain. –DV

My Kind of Country / MCA   1984
McEntire's celebration of the back-to-basics movement in country. Many country shuffles here. Her purest country performances and most straightforward production. –MH

The Best of Reba McEntire / POLYGRAM   1985
A compilation of her late 70s and early 80s Polygram hits. Reflections of future triumphs on MCA. –MH

● **Whoever's in New England / MCA**   1986
The album that elevated McEntire from pretty-good-country-singer to megastar. A number of the melodies have pop sensibilities, but the production is decidedly country. –TR

The Last One to Know / MCA   1987
Recorded as McEntire went through the process of divorce from first husband Charlie Battles. Understandably heavy on songs about breakups and the uncertainty of the future, "The Stairs" — about domestic violence — is particularly moving. Despite her personal pain, she still holds out hope in "Love Will Find Its Way to You." –TR

☆ **For My Broken Heart / MCA**   1991
Only the quietly moving "If I Had Only Known" might be considered a tribute to the members of McEntire's band who died in a 1990 plane crash, but the tragedy creeps into McEntire's voice and her song selection. Throughout the album, McEntire dwells on regrets, unvoiced feelings, and missed chances. The best songs aren't the hits "For My Broken Heart" and "Is There Life out There" but a group of evocative story-songs which unfold slowly, leaving loose threads and developing complex emotional undercurrents. *For My Broken Heart* may be the strongest album of McEntire's career; it's certainly her most heartbreaking. –BM

Greatest Hits / MCA / BB 139
Overview of her late 80s MCA hits. Powerful pipes. –MH

FRANKIE MILLER

○ **Rockin' Rollin' Frankie Miller / BEAR FAMILY**   1983
A stunning 18-track selection of tracks cut for the Nashville Starday label between 1959 and 1963. Distinctive and haunting music. –HD

Hey! Where You Going? / BEAR FAMILY   1984
A complete collection of this country "groaner's" early 1954-1956 Columbia sides. –HD

ROGER MILLER
b 1937

Country-pop, progressive country. One of the most gifted and original songwriters ever, at the peak of his popularity in the 60s he won an unprecedented 11 Grammys in two years. He began by writing songs, lots of songs for lots of stars, including Ray Price, George Jones, and Ernest Tubb. His first country-pop hits were "Chug-a-Lug" and "Dang Me"(1964); a year later came "King of the Road," and Miller was a crossover

superstar. Other hits that did well on both the country and pop charts are "Kansas City Star," "England Swings," and "Little Green Apples." When his songs started doing less well, versatile Miller took his *Big River* musical, based on Mark Twain, to Broadway (1985), where he won a Tony for his musical score. –DV

☆ **Golden Hits / SMASH / BB 6**   1965
A good gathering from his 1964-1965 peak. –DH

○ **Country Spotlight / KTEL-QWIL**
All the hits, and a few other favorites. –DH

More Golden Hits / SMASH
Miller's lesser late-60s hits. –DH

RONNIE MILSAP
b 1944

Country-pop. Born blind, Milsap formed his first band at the State School for the Blind in North Carolina. His first release was R&B, and he was able to sing blues and jazz with equal ease. In the early 70s he changed to country-pop and since has had many Top Ten hits, including "A Legend in My Time," "Daydreams about Night Things," "No Gettin' Over Me," and "Still Losing You." He has won many awards, including the Country Music Association Entertainer of the Year. –DV

● **Greatest Hits / RCA**   1980
A solid, albeit random assessment of Milsap's first seven years in country music. Mainstream country, with "Pure Love" and "(I'm A) Stand by My Woman Man," but Milsap really shines on the elaborate and challenging arrangements of "(I'd Be) A Legend in My Time," "It Was Almost like a Song," and "Let's Take the Long Way around the World." One previously unreleased track: "Smoky Mountain Rain." –TR

One More Try for Love / RCA   1984
In his effort to expand the boundaries of country, Milsap pushes the edge harder here than in any other album. The electronically altered vocals in the tracks "She Loves My Car" and "Suburbia" have a winning effect — tasteful, not overdone. –TR

○ **Greatest Hits - Vol. 2 / RCA**   1985
Juxtaposed to the first *Greatest Hits* package, this one nicely displays the evolution of a motivated risk-taker. Milsap redefines the outer limits of the commercial country format with his soul- and/or rock-inflected singles "(There's) No Gettin' over Me," "Lost in the Fifties Tonight," and (most dramatically) "Stranger in My House." –TR

PATSY MONTANA
b 1914

Cowboy. Born Rubye Blevins in Arkansas, Patsy Montana is the first woman in country music to have a million-seller, "I Want to Be a Cowboy's Sweetheart," in 1935. For more than 25 years she was a mainstay on Chicago's WLS National Barn Dance. In the 30s and 40s she was the sweetheart of many a cowpoke, appearing in numerous Westerns on the silver screen. Boy, could she yodel. –DV

○ **Cowboy's Sweetheart / FLYING FISH**
Late recordings by this Western radio star. The title track, from 1935, was the first million-selling female country vocal performance. –MH

TINY MOORE

Instrumental. Three of the greatest mandolin players of all time (and probably the greatest) only obliquely played country music, devoting their time instead to swing and jazz. Dave Apollon and Jethro Burns are covered elsewhere in this book, and Tiny Moore is the third. Tiny played lead mandolin with Bob Wills's Texas Playboys in the 40s. In the 50s he invented a five-string electric mandolin that he has played while touring with Merle Haggard's band, the Strangers, a group famed for its instrumental excellence. Moore's virtuosity is a joy to listen to. –DV

○ **Tiny Moore Music / KALEIDOSCOPE**   1972
Tiny Moore's electric mandolin carries you through some

great jazz/swing music. Merle Haggard, David Grisman, and Jethro Burns guest on the album. –CR

★ **Back to Back / KALEIDOSCOPE**
Tiny Moore and Jethro Burns and Eldon Shamblin play country jazz magnificently. –DV

LORRIE MORGAN   ♭1960

Traditional country, contemporary country. Loretta Lynn Morgan, daughter of Opry star George Morgan ("Candy Kisses") and widow of bluegrass and country star Keith Whitley, appeared on the Opry at 13, becoming its youngest member in 1984. Her white-blonde hair and striking good looks are appropriate for her country/pop and torch delivery. Her 1991 album *Something in Red* yielded her biggest hit, "A Picture of Me without You," the video of which got considerable TV play. –DV

○ **Leave the Light On / RCA**
"Trainwreck of Emotion" and other belters. Hailed by some as the "new Tammy Wynette." –MH

Something in Red / RCA   1991
Morgan's second RCA album. More sultry contemporary country/pop. –MH

GARY MORRIS   ♭1948

Country. An artist who refuses to be categorized, Morris has explored a variety of country sounds — acoustic folk, rock-edged commercial songs, romantic ballads — but also accepted a couple of roles on Broadway, including the physically demanding part of Jean Valjean in *Les Miserables.* Born and raised in Texas, Morris got his break by working on Jimmy Carter's 1976 election campaign. For his efforts, he got a chance to play for some influential members of the Country Music Association at a Presidential function, and when his demo tape crossed the desk of Warner's executive Norro Wilson, Wilson remembered him immediately and signed him to a recording deal.
Frustrated by the restrictions inherent in the marketing of modern music, Morris refuses to compromise his musical integrity, and some of his work has thus fallen between the cracks. But few country artists — if any — have been able to match Morris for his vocal strength and clarity. –TR

○ **Hits / WARNER**   1987
Morris may have the best "pipes" in country music, but he works so hard at showcasing them that most of his studio albums are bogged down by ballads. This collection includes the best of those ballads ("The Love She Found in Me," "100% Chance of Rain") plus his best overall material ("I'll Never Stop Loving You," "Baby Bye Bye," "Velvet Chains"), which he seemingly undervalues. For those who appreciate such things, it also includes a sampling of his Broadway work, with a song from *La Boheme.* –TR

MOON MULLICAN   1909-1967

Traditional country, instrumental. Jerry Lee Lewis, who knows something about country piano, lists Moon Mullican as a primary influence, especially in the two-finger style. Among his hits is "I'll Sail My Ship Alone," a million-seller and his signature tune. From the mid 40s to the 60s, he was a major solo attraction. –DV

○ **Moon Mullican Sings His All-Time Greatest Hits / KING**

MICHAEL MARTIN MURPHEY   ♭194?

Traditional country, cowboy. Murphey has done country and the country a favor with his West Fest, an annual celebration of the music, culture, and history of the American West. This Texan is one contemporary singer who has earned the right to wear his cowboy hat. He's active in environmental issues and Native American causes. And he loves the Golden West. Try his *Cowboy Songs* album. –DV

Blue Sky-Night Thunder / CBS / BB 18   1975

His best record of the 70s. Includes "Wildfire" and "Carolina in the Pines." –KMC

Best of Michael Martin Murphey / CAPITOL
A collection of his best from the early 80s. –KMC

○ **River of Time / WARNER**   1987
Murphey's best. Includes "From the Word Go," "I'm Gonna Miss You Girl," "Talking to the Wrong Man," and "What Am I Doing Hanging Around," a song Murphey originally wrote for the Monkees. –KMC

Cowboy Songs / WARNER   1990
A collection of mostly cowboy standards, including "Tumbling Tumbleweeds" and "Happy Trails," with some new tunes. Murphey shines throughout. –KMC

ANNE MURRAY   ♭1945

Country. Nova Scotia-born Anne Murray built her musical influences from the pop sounds that her parents listened to (Rosemary Clooney, Perry Como) and the Top 40 sounds that AM New York radio stations piped into Canada (Buddy Holly, Elvis Presley, Brenda Lee).
Originally she intended to work as a physical-education instructor, but she continued to pursue an interest in music. Turned down for a spot on a national TV show called "Singalong Jubilee," she received a call from the show's producer two years later. He offered her a chance to make records, and when she agreed, she found herself with a million-selling crossover single in 1970, "Snowbird."
Murray was frequently at odds with the trappings of success — she even performed barefoot in Las Vegas — and when she got married in 1975, she seemingly dropped out of the business. With her family established, she started working in 1978 with a new producer, Jim Ed Norman, who returned her to prominence with "Walk Right Back" and the million-selling followup "You Needed Me."
Throughout the late 70s and early 80s, Murray successfully walked the line between country and pop with a rich alto voice and a knack for romantic material. Admirably, she continues to insist that no matter how high or low her career goes, her family in Toronto is her top priority. –TR

○ **Greatest Hits / CAPITOL**   1980
Covers Murray's first decade in the international limelight, beginning with "Snowbird" and concluding with "Could I Have This Dance," a track from the 1980 movie *Urban Cowboy.* Ranges from the folky "Danny's Song" to her cover of the Beatles' "You Won't See Me," but the middle-of-the-road approach is quite obvious. –TR

Greatest Hits - Vol. 2 / CAPITOL   1989
With her country base firmly established, Murray grew restless in the early and mid 80s, very much desirous of conquering the pop market. It never quite happened, though she made a nice stab at it in her duet with Dave Loggins, "Nobody Loves Me Like You Do." She may not be country in the classic sense, but good music is good music and it's hard not to like "Time Don't Run Out on Me" or "Now and Forever (You and Me)." –TR

WILLIE NELSON   ♭1933

Traditional country, progressive country. A lot of people, including lovers of country music, hadn't heard of Willie Nelson until 1975, the year that an old Roy Acuff song titled "Blues Eyes Crying in the Rain" made him famous to the multitudes and led to the first of his five Grammy awards. During the two previous decades, though, he had written hundreds of quality songs, played thousands of honky-tonks, and perfected his vocal style, which many think ranks among the best of any kind of popular American music. His "outlaw" and anti-establishment image, which now seems old hat, less than twenty years after its creation, was not an act but the real thing. His abundance of talent allowed him to back up this image; there's only one Willie Nelson.
After a stint as a country DJ on a Fort Worth radio station,

Nelson played bass with the Ray Price band, and Price recorded his "Night Life," now a country standard. Faron Young then cut "Hello Walls" and Patsy Clin, "Crazy" and "Funny How Time Slips Away": Nelson had made his reputation as a premier songwriter. (Though he never sang them as such, many of his songs are natural crossovers. Frank Sinatra, Perry Como, Stevie Wonder, and Bing Crosby are a few of the stars who have recorded his songs.) He then borrowed members of Price's band and started on the road. Despite reasonable success, only when he moved back to Texas from Nashville did his singing start getting the attention it deserved. In this period before "Blue Eyes Crying in the Rain," he recorded three albums, including *Shotgun Willie* and *Phases and Stages*, a concept album about a broken marriage, telling the point of view of both the husband and the wife. Nelson had ignored the prevalent "Nashville Sound" lushness and had succeeded.

Starting in 1975, Nelson reached the top, in the process melding country and "hip" music while turning millions of younger listeners into fans. His *Red-Headed Stranger*, a concept album about the Old West, hit #1, as did *Wanted: The Outlaws*, with Waylon Jennings, Jessi Colter, and Tompall Glaser. The Outlaws' national tour following this album created an explosion of interest in country music. Nelson, now a superstar, recorded a number of hit singles ("Remember Me," "Good-Hearted Woman," and others) before joining with Waylon Jennings in 1978 for *Waylon and Willie*, an album that quickly sold a million and locked both singers into the outlaw image for years. *Stardust*, a hit album of popular songs, showcased Nelson's versatility.

In 1979, Nelson showed his acting talent in the well-received movie, *Electric Horseman* (with Robert Redford and Jane Fonda); *Honeysuckle Rose* was released a year later, drawing praise for Nelson's acting. The film's soundtrack album was another hit. The early 80s brought more superstardom, with "On the Road Again" and "Angel Flying Too Close to the Ground."

Nelson's contributions to country music are enormous. His unsurpassed vocal style, his tasteful and subtle guitar playing, his introduction of country music to millions of new listeners, his sophisticated yet real song compositions: these all show us what a unique and incomparable talent is Willie Nelson. And his Farm Aid benefits show us that his heart is where his music is. –DV

★ **Red Headed Stranger / CBS / BB 28**　　　　　1975
A country classic, a song cycle about the Old West. –DH

To Lefty from Willie / CBS / BB 91　　　　　　1975
A fine tribute to Lefty Frizzell. –DH

The Troublemaker / COLUMBIA / BB 60　　　　1977
An interesting biblical allegory. –DH

Stardust / COLUMBIA　　　　　　　　　　　　1978
The record label didn't want Nelson to do this project, inspired partially by the death of pop crooner Bing Crosby. Standard material — "Moonlight in Vermont," "All of Me," "Don't Get Around Much Anymore" — arranged by Booker T. Jones (of "Green Onions" fame) and recorded in Nelson's inimitable style in Emmylou Harris's house. –TR

○ **Greatest Hits / CAPITOL / BB 27**　　　　　　1981
The cream of Nelson's crossover success. –DH

Greatest Hits ... / COLUMBIA　　　　　　　　1981
Greatest Hits (And Some That Will Be). Capsulizes Nelson's first five years in the spotlight, with lots of classics: "On the Road Again," "Blue Eyes Crying in the Rain," "Heartbreak Hotel" (a duet with Leon Russell), as well as the smartly produced "My Heroes Have Always Been Cowboys." –TR

Half Nelson / COLUMBIA　　　　　　　　　　1985
An appropriate collection, since Nelson has recorded more duets with more fellow performers than any other country singer in history. This runs the gamut from traditional country singers Merle Haggard and George Jones to soulman Ray Charles, Latin lover Julio Iglesias, and the rock band

Santana. Even has a duet with the late Hank Williams, arranged through modern studio recording technology. –TR

Nite Life ... / RHINO　　　　　　　　　　　　1989
Nite Life - Greatest Hits & Rare Tracks (1959-1971). The best of Nelson, the Nashville songwriter. –DH

MICKEY NEWBURY　　　　　　　　　　　　b 1940

Progressive country. This talented songwriter moved to Nashville in the mid 60s, with Elvis Presley, Ray Charles, and Jerry Lee Lewis recording some of his emotional songs. He wrote "Just Dropped In (To See What Condition My Condition Was In)," which was covered by Kenny Rogers and the First Edition. In his "American Trilogy" (1972), Newbury combined three Civil War songs, creating an international hit. His songs are intricate and well crafted. –DV

○ **'Frisco Mabel Joy / ELEKTRA**　　　　　　　1971
Elvis Presley took Newbury's "American Trilogy" as his own, but the deeply felt original is here, along with some other excellent songs by a songwriter who has long deserved far more recognition than he has received, and who turns out to be an affecting singer as well. –WR

JIMMY C. NEWMAN　　　　　　　　　　　　b 1927

Traditional country. This native of Big Mamou left Cajun country for Shreveport's "Louisiana Hayride," proving ground of many country greats, and graduated to the Grand Ole Opry in 1956 after the success of "Cry, Cry Darling" and other Dot label hits. The "C" in his name stands for Cajun, his stage suit is covered in rhinestone alligators, and the cry in his voice comes from his Cajun background, but Newman's material is essentially 50s Nashville. A notable exception was a fine 1963 Decca album, *Folk Songs of the Bayou Country.* –MH

○ **The Alligator Man / ROUNDER**　　　　　　　1991
○ **Jimmy Newman & Cajun Country / MCA**
A collection of Newman's country/Cajun hits. –JH

JUICE NEWTON　　　　　　　　　　　　　　b 1952

Country rock. This country-rocker moved from Virginia to Northern California in the late 60s, when she formed Dixie Peach with Otha Young, an electric band. In the mid 70s she moved to Los Angeles and formed the Silver Spur Band, which mixed rock and pop with country. Her *Juice* album yielded two #1 singles, "Angel of the Morning" and "Queen of Hearts" (1981). Throughout the 80s she moved closer to rock and farther from country. –DV

○ **Greatest Hits / CAPITOL / BB 178**　　　　　1984
Her countrified pop hits of the 80s. –BC

THE NITTY GRITTY DIRT BAND

Country-rock. In their 25 years together, the Nitty Gritty Dirt Band has recorded music that ranges from rock to pop to country. Under their aegis the 3-disc *Will the Circle Be Unbroken* album in 1972 brought together many country music greats (including Earl Scruggs, Doc Watson, Roy Acuff, and Jimmy Martin) and brought national recognition to the NGDB. Their *WTCBU Vol. 2* (1989) won a Grammy. Through their music they have introduced country to millions of city and suburban listeners. –DV

☆ **Will the Circle Be Unbroken / EMI-USA / BB 68**　1972
The influence of this two-disc set, which brought the previously pop-oriented Dirt Band together with some of the seminal names in country music, is incalculable. Mother Maybelle Carter, Earl Scruggs, Doc Watson, Roy Acuff, and others sat down with a bunch of longhairs, found common ground on the best of old-time country music, and changed the direction of popular music. Two decades on, it still sounds great. –WR

20 Years of Dirt ... / WARNER　　　　　　　1986
20 Years of Dirt - The Best of the Nitty Gritty Dirt Band. This album traces the development of the Nitty Gritty Dirt Band from a pop outfit with folk and country edges into a

contemporary country band. Their version of "Mr. Bojangles" remains memorable, as does "American Dream." The other tracks are sturdy, middle-of-the-road 80s Nashville. –WR

More Great Dirt - Best of - Vol. 2 / WARNER   1989
Tight harmonies and infectious arrangements are the staple of this compilation. "I've Been Lookin'," "Fishin' in the Dark," and "Baby's Got a Hold on Me" are the musical equivalent of a good book — you can't put 'em down. –TR

Will the Circle Be Unbroken - Vol. 2 / UNIVERSAL   1989
Easily won the Country Music Association's Album of the Year Award, thanks to a stellar cast that includes John Denver, Johnny Cash, the Carter Family, Bruce Hornsby, Ricky Skaggs, Chris Hillman, Roger McGuinn, Rosanne Cash, Steve Wariner, Roy Acuff, Chet Atkins ... you get the message. Tracks were all recorded in one "take" with no overdubs, making the outstanding musicianship particularly noteworthy. Atheists beware, there's a lot of gospel! –TR

THE OAK RIDGE BOYS

Country-pop, gospel. The Oaks (as they prefer to be called) started out as an award-winning gospel quartet, and each of the four singers worked for other gospel groups before forming the present band composed of Duane Allen, lead singer; Joe Bonsall, tenor; Richard Sterban, bass; and Steve Sanders, guitarist. In the mid 70s they swung toward country-pop, where they have remained. A break came when Johnny Cash asked them to open for him in Las Vegas. Subsequent country-pop groups such as Alabama owe a lot to the Oaks. Among their many hits are "Elvira" and "Y'All Come Back Saloon." William Lee Golden, who has country's longest (and grayest) beard, left the group after singing baritone for two decades, because of an "image problem." –DV

○ **Greatest Hits / MCA**   1980
Their earliest package of hits, with gospel roots showing on material like "Y'all Come Back Saloon." –CK

Fancy Free / MCA   1981
Their best-selling album, thanks to the presence of "Elvira." Each of the Oaks gets a turn at the lead part, although Duane Allen is easily best suited to that role. Includes some quasi-folk and straightahead country, but the best track is the obligatory gospel tune "I Would Crawl All the Way (To the River)." –TR

Greatest Hits 2 / MCA   1984
Covers the Oaks at their peak, with repetitive, singalong choruses predominating in "American Made," "Love Song," and "Everyday." The delicate "I Guess It Never Hurts to Hurt Sometimes" is a nice change of pace, but why did MCA hold out "Bobbie Sue" until *Greatest Hits 3*? –TR

Sensational Oak Ridge Boys / STARDAY   1987
Solid collection of their early gospel recordings. Interesting to compare to their secular success. –CK

Monongahela / MCA   1988
Though *Heartbeat* was recorded after the dismissal of William Lee Golden, this is the first album in which replacement Steve Sanders was involved from beginning to end in the recording process. Harmonies are understandably more soulful — and more in tune — and the project is generally more uplifting. Includes "Gonna Take a Lot of River." –TR

MARK O'CONNOR   b 1961

Country. Born and raised in Seattle, O'Connor was always a bit out of sync with his teenage peers. Understandably — he was winning fiddle contests and had even mapped out a sketchy career path. O'Connor moved to Nashville in 1983, already a former sideman for jazz violinist Stephane Grappelli, a job that allowed him to play on the stage at Carnegie Hall.
At the time O'Connor arrived in Music City the post-*Urban Cowboy* era — fiddle was hardly in vogue, and it took a couple of years for him to make his mark. Finally, in 1985, the Nitty Gritty Dirt Band used him in its single "High Horse"; and thanks to that work, O'Connor's phone number became a popular one with country record producers. Over the next five

years, he played on 450 albums, including such stellar projects as *Trio*, by Dolly Parton, Linda Ronstadt, and Emmylou Harris; *Always & Forever*, by Randy Travis; *Killin' Time*, by Clint Black; and *Loving Proof*, by Ricky Van Shelton.
Despite his success, O'Connor gave up session work to concentrate on his own solo career as an artist, in the process providing a new focus on Nashville's studio players, while simultaneously building a reputation for himself with the general public. –TR

○ **The New Nashville Cats / WARNER**   1991
Incredible lineup of Nashville's very best musicians. This mostly instrumental package covers a wide range of musical territory, from bluegrass to the blues, with plenty of stellar "pickin'." Ironically, this instrumental album won a vocal Grammy when Vince Gill, Ricky Skaggs, and Steve Wariner teamed with O'Connor on "Restless." –TR

THE O'KANES

Country. During their relatively brief time together, Kieran Kane and Jamie O'Hara, otherwise known as the O'Kanes, produced three albums of absolutely superb country music. The self-titled, first, and arguably strongest effort contains everything that is best about the O'Kanes' sound. It is rich in country music's finest traditions, yet it is by no means a nostalgia album. It is sparse in instrumentation, yet richly textured. Most of all, it contains direct, honest music, whose emotional intensity stays with the listener long after the sound waves have stopped vibrating.
The O'Kanes' vocals recall the best of country harmony. Some critics liken them to the Louvin Brothers. Others, because of the more driving sound of their backing, compare them to the Everlys. The instrumental sound ranges from bluegrass (prominent mandolin) to the tense drive of Sun rockabilly (their hit "O Darlin'" is evidence of this). The addition of an accordion adds both Tex-Mex and unmistakably bluesy feels to the proceedings. This is truly hybrid music.
Kane and O'Hara's best songs ("O Darlin'," "Can't Stop My Heart," and "This Isn't Love") explore the lonely, desperate, and occasionally obsessive side of love. Whether they continue to record or not, the O'Kanes reflect and contribute to the renaissance of solid, unaffected country music that has spawned the success of stars like Dwight Yoakam and Randy Travis and heralds a welcome return to basics. –HD

The O'Kanes / CBS   1987
Introspective lyrics and occasional guitar/mandolin jams make an interesting concept from Music City before the "hat" proliferation of 1990. –MH

○ **Tired of the Runnin' / CBS**   1988
A strong title song, austerely folkish, represented this short-lived duo at its best. –MH

K. T. OSLIN   b 1942

Country-pop. As a veteran of a 60s folk trio, commercials, and successful songwriting, Kay Toinette Oslin was in her mid-forties when her debut album, *80s Ladies*, sold platinum and led to many awards in 1987-1988. Her country-pop flavor found a receptive audience of middle-aged single women. –DV

○ **80s Ladies / RCA / BB 68**   1988
A pop-turned-country belter with anthems meant for thirtysomething women. –MH

Love in a Small Town / RCA   1990
More ballads from this pop/country hitmaker. –MH

MARIE OSMOND   b 1959

Country-pop. Recorded with her singing brothers, Marie Osmond's debut single, "Paper Roses," hit the country charts in 1973. While most of her career has been spent on pop and rock, she occasionally swings back into a country flavor. In 1975 she and brother Donny Osmond did well with the country standard "Make the World Go Away." In the mid 80s Osmond relocated to Nashville and had success with "There's No Stopping Your Heart" and "Meet Me in Montana," the latter a duet with Dan Seals. She was Utah Woman of the Year in 1989. –DV

This Is the Way I Feel / POLYGRAM   1977
Rick Hall-produced pop music. –BC

There's No Stopping Your Heart / CAPITOL   1985
An exciting country-pop album. –BC

○ **Best of Marie Osmond / CAPITOL**
Light arrangements. Osmond's finest country moments. –BC

Stepping Stone / CAPITOL
Her most mature set to date. –BC

PAUL OVERSTREET   b 1929

Contemporary country, gospel. This songwriter-turned-performer has helped pen "On the Other Hand" and "Forever and Ever, Amen," both huge hits for Randy Travis. A born-again Christian, he emphasizes basic values in his music and is also found on the gospel charts. His hits include "Heroes" and "Ball and Chain." –DV

○ **Sowin' Love / RCA**
A pleasant nonregional mix of country and gospel. –BC

BUCK OWENS   b 1929

Traditional country. In 1992 Alvis Edgar "Buck" Owens retired from performing after 26 consecutive #1 hits in the 1960s and the creation of the "Bakersfield sound" that continues to influence contemporary honky-tonk singers, including Dwight Yoakam. With the Buckaroos, his band of exceptional musicians, Owens sang his gritty, real-life songs, which changed the direction of country music.

When Route 66 led Owens from his Texas home to Arizona and finally to Bakersfield, he began as a guitar player, singing (against his own wishes) only when the band's usual lead singer lit out for Hollywood. The crowds in the honky-tonks kept asking for more Owens, so Owens the guitarist became Owens the singer. His first chart song was "Second Fiddle" (1959), followed by "Under Your Spell Again," "Excuse Me (I Think I've Got a Heartache)," and "Fooling Around"; and he was a star. Duets with Rose Maddox brought him more fame. Throughout the 60s he scored hit after hit, including "Act Naturally" (covered by the Beatles), "I've Got a Tiger by the Tail," "Waiting in the Welfare Line," "Love's Gonna Live Here," "Tall Dark Stranger," and "Together Again."

In the early 70s, the hits continued with "I Wouldn't Live in New York City" and "Ruby (Are You Mad?)." His glory days came to an end after years at the top, except for a "Play Together Again, Again" duet with Emmylou Harris and his appearance on Dwight Yoakam's *Streets of Bakersfield* album more than ten years later. As co-host (with Roy Clark) of "Hee Haw," TV's long-running country-music/country-corn series, Owens kept in the public eye until 1986, after having spent 17 years on the program. Owens has left us with years of beautiful music and a honky-tonk/rockabilly influence that remains. –DV

The Best of Buck Owens / CAPITOL / BB 46   1964
Late 50s and early 60s hits including "Above and Beyond," "Love's Gonna Live Here," "Act Naturally," and "Under Your Spell Again" — mostly written by Owens. A classic. –GB

☆ **The Best of Buck Owens - Vol. 2 / CAPITOL**   1964
"I've Got a Tiger by the Tail," "Together Again," "My Heart Skips a Beat" — all classic Owens from his mid-60s peak. Features the Fabulous Buckaroos, including Don Rich on lead guitar and harmonies and Tom Brumley on steel. A must for any serious country & western fan. –GB

I Don't Care / CAPITOL / BB 135   1964
Studio album version of Owens and the Buckaroos' mid-60s stage show — Owens plays "Buck's Polka." Doyle Holly and Don Rich are featured — also "Loose Talk," a duet with Owens and Rose Maddox. –GB

Together Again/My Heart Skips a Beat / CAPITOL 1964
Includes his covers of "Truck Drivin' Man," "A-11," and "Hello Trouble." –GB

I've Got a Tiger by the Tail / CAPITOL / BB 43 1965

The title track, plus some great ballads including "Cryin' Time." These 60s Capitol albums are not just mish-mashes like many C&W albums of the period — they're well thought-out, usually including a vocal or two by Don Rich (one of C&W's unsung heroes) or the deep-voiced bass player Doyle Holly and a fiddle or steel guitar instrumental by Don or Tom Brumley, respectively. –GB

Roll Out the Red Carpet / CAPITOL / BB 16   1966
Mostly written or cowritten by Owens, this is Owens and the boys at their peak. –GB

○ **Country Hit Maker #1 / STARDAY**
Pre-Capitol material, half of this album consists of Owens's very early recordings like "Sweethearts in Heaven" and "There Goes My Love" (covered later by Highway 101), which show his developing vocal style. A little more down-home than his later stuff. The other half consists of covers of Owens's later material by other artists. –GB

LEE ROY PARNELL

Country/rock. Texas country-rocker with strong R&B roots, who wrote songs for Johnny Lee, Marcia Ball, and others before getting his own recording deal. He was the second artist, behind Alan Jackson, signed to Arista's Nashville division when the label opened shop in the late 80s. –BM

Lee Roy Parnell / ARISTA   1990
Hard-rocking country-soul, complete with horn section. Produced by Barry Beckett, whose experiences at Muscle Shoals mean he knows how to make this kind of record. –BM

○ **Love without Mercy / ARISTA**   1992
For his second album, Lee Roy Parnell drops the horns and gives his slide guitar a bigger role. He's still a Texas rocker disguised by a pedal steel. –BM

GRAM PARSONS   1946-1973

Progressive country. Country-rock pioneer as member of the Byrds, the Flying Burrito Brothers, and on his own. Born Cecil Ingram Connor in Winterhaven, FL, Parsons began playing guitar at age 13. He briefly attended Harvard as a divinity student in 1965 but dropped out to concentrate on music and LSD. He joined the Byrds in 1968, just long enough to make the classic *Sweetheart of the Rodeo*; he and Chris Hillman left to form the Flying Burrito Brothers. Parson's recordings with these bands and on his own are considered the birth of the country-rock movement, and his influence is incalculable; he covered artists as diverse as Emmylou Harris (who sang backup for him), Tom Petty, Dwight Yoakam, and the Rolling Stones. Parsons died September 19, 1973, in Joshua Tree, CA, from heart failure, the result of years of substance abuse. –BM

☆ **GP/Grievous Angel 1973/1974 / REPRISE**   1990
Parson's two best albums on one compact disc. Seeking to synthesize his own ideas with those of classic country and rock, Parsons hired Merle Haggard's recording engineer (he had approached Haggard himself about producing) and members of Elvis Presley's band, including pianist Glen D. Hardin and guitarist James Burton. The result had its roots in everything but sounded like nothing else. Parson's songs were the musings of a wounded soul, and his taste in others' material ran from Harlan Howard to the J. Geils Band. On *Grievous Angel*, Emmylou Harris emerges from the background to provide an angelic foil for Parsons's lost folkie voice. –BM

DOLLY PARTON   b 1946

Traditional country, contemporary country. It's difficult to find a country performer (except, of course, for Elvis Presley) who has moved from country roots to international fame more successfully than Dolly Parton. Her autobiographical single "Coat of Many Colors" shows the poverty of growing up one of 12 children on a run-down farm in Locust Ridge, TN. At 12 years old she was appearing on Knoxville television; at 13 she was recording on a small label and appearing on the Grand

Ole Opry; at present she has to her credit hit albums, hit singles, hit movies, and a TV variety show.

Her 1967 hit "Dumb Blonde" (and she's not) caught Porter Wagoner's ear, and he hired Parton to appear on his television show, where their duet numbers became famous. By the time her "Joshua" reached #1 in 1970, Parton's fame had overshadowed the boss's, and she had struck out on her own, though still recording duets with him. Between those duets and her recent one with Ricky Van Shelton came a lot of stardom.

Parton's debut on the silver screen was in the 1980 hit *9 to 5* with costars Lily Tomlin and Jane Fonda; Parton's *9 to 5 and Odd Jobs* album was released with the film. *The Best Little Whorehouse in Texas* brought further fame, or notoriety, two years later; in 1984 she and Sylvester Stallone starred (and in fact sang a duet) in *Rhinestone*. "Tennessee Homesick Blues," from the film's soundtrack, earned Parton another Grammy nomination. Since then she has appeared in *Steel Magnolias* and in *Wild Texas Wind*, a made-for-TV thriller-melodrama costarring Ray Benson, leader of Asleep at the Wheel, a Western-swing band.

The critics have told us that she can act, but can Parton sing? Yes, and very well, in spite of her reputation created by her movies, her cheesecake image, and her many forays into pop music. She can still be pure country when she wants, all tinsel aside. Try listening to "Coat of Many Colors," "Jolene," "But You Know I Love You," and "Tennessee Homesick Blues." Parton is a woman of considerable talents, country singing chief among them. –DV

The Best of Dolly Parton / RCA   1975
Dolly projects an admirable childlike sense of hope and positivism, which is matched to some degree by her thin, girlish vocal quality. It translates well in her pre-Hollywood, unencumbered productions, notably "Coat of Many Colors," "Love Is Like a Butterfly," and "The Bargain Store." –TR

9 to 5 and Odd Jobs / RCA / BB 11   1980
Dolly Parton has never been an albums artist, and RCA has always been adept at shoving poorly organized products onto the market (look how they've treated Elvis Presley). Hence, though she is an important country figure, most of Parton's albums are hard to recommend. This one contains the title hit, plus a few other Parton originals and a version of Woody Guthrie's "Deportee" among its eight tracks. But that's enough to put it a notch above most of Parton's RCA catalog. –WR

Greatest Hits / RCA   1982
A good sampling of Parton's work in the first few years that she deliberately chased a crossover career in Hollywood. The country-pop stuff might offend purists, but it still gets the toe tappin'. "Hard Candy Christmas" and her updated version of "I Will Always Love You" (both from *The Best Little Whorehouse in Texas*) show her growth as an interpreter. –TR

☆ **Collector's Series / RCA**   1985
This is a well-programmed selection of Parton's RCA hits, among them "Jolene," "Coat of Many Colors," and "Me and Little Andy." –WR

Real Love / RCA   1985
A lot of critics would push this one aside, perhaps with good reason since she turned over much of the creative control on the project to David Malloy. But Malloy set out to highlight the bright, bubbly facet of her personality, and he succeeded. –TR

Trio / WARNER   1987
Dolly Parton, Linda Ronstadt, and Emmylou Harris tried to make this album in 1978, but contractual problems (they all recorded for different labels), a lack of specific direction, and a shortage of time (they tried to make the album in 10 days), kept it from occurring, although occasional tracks did emerge on Harris's solo albums. The wait was worth it — shimmering harmonies in a traditional acoustic package that emphasizes their very different vocal styles. –TR

White Limozeen / CBS   1989
Parton moved to Columbia in the late 80s and started paying

more attention to her recordings, the best of which is this album. It's produced by Ricky Skaggs, who brought in such fast-picking cronies as Bela Fleck and Jerry Douglas and used more of Parton's own songs than usual. The result is an unusual consistency and a musical revitalization for the singer. –WR

JOHNNY PAYCHECK   b1941

Traditional country, country rock. If knowing what you're singing about is a requirement for country singers, then Johnny Paycheck is the real thing. Released last year after serving time for shooting a man in a bar, he has lived up to his image of a renegade.

After playing guitar of steel in some well-known bands (George Jones, Ray Price, Faron Young) and fighting alcoholism through the 60s, he got himself together and in 1977 had a #1 hit with "She's All I Got," followed by "Slide off Your Satin Sheets" and "I'm the Only Hell Mama Ever Raised." Then came his signature song, "Take This Job and Shove It," written by fellow anti-establishment musician David Allan Coe, who also knows something of prison life. Plenty of Americans who never listen to country music connect with this workingman's anthem.

When the Governor of Ohio commuted Paycheck's sentence, country fans waited to welcome him home. Within a week of his release he appeared on the Ralph Emery TV show, looking rested and healthy and in excellent voice. When Paycheck sings about life's troubles, we should listen. –DV

Take This Job & Shove It / CBS / BB 72   1977
His big 70s novelty hit and an uneven selection of tunes, but worth having for "Colorado Kool-Aid" — a sort of Red Sovine-from-hell recitation on the subject of barroom etiquette. –GB

☆ **The Lovin' Machine / LITTLE DARLIN'**   1986
The "Bad News Buckeye" at his mid-60s peak. Three, count 'em, *three* murder songs, plus heartbreak too. Lloyd Green plays on steel guitar. –GP

Jukebox Charlie / LITTLE DARLIN'
One of the all-time great honky-tonk singers before his bad habits got the better of him. Includes two of the greatest country songs ever — "Apartment #9" and "Touch My Heart," both written by Paycheck. –GB

WEBB PIERCE   1926-1991

Traditional country. A Louisiana native, Webb Pierce first found fame on Shreveport's KWKH, home of the Louisiana Hayride, where he quickly became a popular performer, recording two hits during this period, "Wondering" and "Back Street Affair," the latter prompting an answer song from Miss Kitty Wells, "Paying for That Back Street Affair." Quickly he moved on to the Opry, where (with his high and nasal tenor) he gained fame for singing honky-tonk songs that stayed sung. "Slowly," a 1954 hit, is the first to feature a pedal guitar (played by Buddy Isaacs). In 1955 he had three #1s, and a year later "Why Baby Why," a duet with Red Sovine, charted high. Though Pierce charted in 1982 in a duet with Willie Nelson that covered "In the Jailhouse Now" (by Jimmie Rodgers), changes in music taste left a lot of lean years after the heights he reached in the 50s. When he died in 1991, he left a legacy of authentic, well-done honky-tonk music, many of the songs having been written by Pierce himself.

Though Pierce never quite managed to be what people expected — the next Hank Williams — he had enough success (32 hits from his debut record to 1960) to be fondly remembered by fans who like their music gritty and sparse in instrumentation. His "There Stands the Glass" of 1952 remains the beer-drinker's anthem. And he really did have a guitar-shaped swimming pool, with bridge, sound hole, and strings visible on the bottom. –DV

☆ **The Wondering Boy (1951-1958) / BEAR FAMILY**   1990
For the devout, Germany's Bear Family offers a 4-CD boxed set of Pierce's primal honky-tonk. A total of 113 songs by one of

the seminal post-War country artists, including duets with Kitty Wells, Red Sovine, and the Wilburn Brothers. The best sound quality and presentation available of this influential music. –MH

Walking the Streets / DECCA
Good weepers, including "Drinkin' My Blues Away." –GB

Webb with a Beat! / DECCA
Includes "I Ain't Never" (cowritten by Mel Tillis) and "In the Jailhouse Now." The title is a bit misleading, but "I Ain't Never" definitely rocks. –GB

○ **That Wondering Boy / DECCA**
Includes "Slowly," "There Stands the Glass," and "Back Street Affair." –GB

PINKARD & BOWDEN

Country humor. Sandy Pinkard and Richard Bowden are in the Lonzo-and-Oscar/Homer-and-Jethro tradition of spoofing hit songs. Two of their parodies are "Driving My Wife Away" (a sendup of "Driving My Life Away") and "Blue Hair's Driving in My Lane" ("Blue Eyes Crying in the Rain"). Bowden is a former member of Emmylou Harris's Hot Band. –DV

○ **Live in Front of a Bunch of Dickheads / WARNER** 1990
Nashville's wiseacres and country parodists in their element, such as it is. –DH

RAY PRICE   ♭1926

Traditional country, country-pop. Ray Price has always seen music trends ahead of other people and has changed to keep up with current tastes. When he started in 1948, he wore suits of sequins and spangles, and to his credit he could easily back up this image with his great voice. When Hank Williams died, many of his Drifting Cowboys joined Price's Cherokee Cowboys, and Price for a while sang honky-tonk in the Williams vein, and sang it beautifully.
In 1952 Price joined the Opry with "Don't Let the Stars Get in Your Eyes," a recent charter. 1954 began a string of major hits stretching into the 70s — a few are "Crazy Arms," "City Lights," "Release Me," "My Shoes Keep Walking Back to You," "Night Life," and "Heartaches by the Number." All of these are now country standards. In the 60s he set a trend by adding lush orchestration and millions of strings behind his great voice. The hits continued, among them "Make the World Go Away" (1963) and "Burning Memories" a year later. Price recorded Kris Kristofferson's "For the Good Times," a hit on both the country and pop charts as well as internationally. Whether dressed in a cowboy suit or a business suit, Price made hits. Through the 80s he recorded with good success. Now into the 90s, Price is still in excellent voice, appearing occasionally on TV. –DV

The Best of Ray Price / COLUMBIA 1976
This compilation presents the highlights of Price's string-laden years. "For the Good Times" is simply one of the most mature singles ever recorded. "She's Got to Be a Saint" has somehow gotten lost over the years. –TR

☆ **Essential Ray Price (1951-1962) / COLUMBIA** 1991
A not-completely-accurate title, as this 20-track compilation excludes a few later necessities like "Night Life" and "For the Good Times," but the important stuff from Price's hard-country heyday is all here, from the teetering rise-and-fall of "Crazy Arms" (the first of a thousand country songs to employ a walking bassline and modified swing beat that became known as the "Ray Price shuffle") to Harlan Howard's "Heartaches by the Number." The fake stereo that marred earlier reissues of his 50s material is happily absent here. Essential country music. –BM & MH

Night Life / COLUMBIA
Probably the first country & western "concept" album. Willie Nelson penned the title track plus other 3 AM classics — tied together by the masterful steel guitar of Buddy Emmons. –GB

Talk to Your Heart / CL
Great collection of "weepers," honky-tonk, and Western

swingy numbers from the 50s. Several songs by Floyd Tillman. Features "I'll Keep On Loving You," "Deep Water," "I Gotta Have My Baby Back," and "I'm Tired." A real "Texas-flavored" record by a honky-tonk master. –GB

CHARLEY PRIDE   ♭1938

Traditional country. Being the first Black star in country music has been no advantage to Country Charley Pride, who with 36 #1 hits has a great voice that knows no color distinction. Things weren't always so reasonable, though: his first single, "Snakes Crawl at Night," was released without publicity photos, letting the voice rather than color do the talking. Since then, according to the *Book of Lists*, Pride's 12 gold albums in the US, combined with 30 gold and 4 platinum internationally, place him in the top 15 all-time record sellers. His easygoing singing style and easy-to-listen-to voice show why these honors have come his way.
From picking cotton in his native Mississippi, Pride ended up working in a smelting plant in Montana after a stint as a semi-pro baseball player. At the suggestion of Red Sovine, Pride moved to Nashville, where he was signed by Chet Atkins of RCA. In 1966 "Just Between You and Me" brought Pride a Grammy nomination and national fame. At the end of the 60s and the early part of the 70s, he had five #1s in a row, including "All I Have to Offer Is Me" and "Is Anybody Goin' to San Antone?" Numerous awards came in 1971 and 1972, with many more hits following, among them "She's Too Good to Be True," "Kiss an Angel Good Mornin'," and "Night Games." Pride's warm baritone voice and relaxed style made him the highest-selling act for RCA since Elvis Presley. His #1 album in 1980, *There's a Little Bit of Hank in Me*, showed why he is called Country Charley. –DV

○ **The Best of Charley Pride / CAPITOL / BB 24** 1969
Pride sang in a Hank Williams-influenced voice that yielded some of the best country performances of the late 60s and early 70s. –MH

The Best of Charley Pride - Vol. 2 / RCA 1972
Perhaps because RCA wanted to leave no doubts about Pride's country heritage, his early career mined the standard three-chord structure almost exclusively. As with the first volume, this set does that, but in "Kiss an Angel Good Mornin'" and "Is Anybody Goin' to San Antone?," his performance is a notch or two above the previous package. –TR

The Best of Charley Pride - Vol. 3 / RCA 1975
To be honest, Pride sounds a bit bored with some of this material. But "Mississippi Cotton Pickin' Delta Town" is practically a page out of his life. By the way, the cover art, with its rope script and blue-jeans-and-patches sports suit, is so 70s it's camp. –TR

Greatest Hits / RCA 1981
Another good compilation of Pride's best. –MH

Greatest Hits / RCA 1981
Pride seems a little uninvolved with some of the material, but when he lets loose — as in "When I Stop Leaving (I'll Be Gone)" or "A Whole Lotta Things to Sing About" — he's absolutely convincing. –TR

Charley Sings Everybody's Choice / RCA 1982
Dumb title, but an excellent album. Producer Norro Wilson revitalized Pride's career by bringing out the Memphis soul that rests in the shadows of his country veneer. –TR

EDDIE RABBITT   ♭1941

Country. One of country music's most innovative artists during the late 70s and early 80s, Rabbitt has made contributions to the format that have often gone overlooked. Especially in songs like the R&B-inflected "Suspicions" and the rockin' "Someone Could Lose a Heart Tonight," Rabbitt challenged the commonly recognized creative boundaries of the idiom.
Hailing from Brooklyn and New Jersey, Rabbitt moved to Nashville in 1968. Though it took a few years to get his

recording career off the ground, he paid the rent through songwriting, authoring Elvis Presley's "Kentucky Rain" and Ronnie Milsap's "Pure Love."

Signing with Elektra Records' newly established country division in 1975, Rabbitt made recordings that were decidedly country — mostly uptempo material, like "Two Dollars in the Jukebox" and "Drinkin' My Baby (Off My Mind)" — with thick, inimitable harmonies, most of them overdubbed by Rabbitt himself.

Driven in part by then-associates David Malloy and Even Stevens, Rabbitt's records became "progressively progressive" well into the late 80s. At that time, his country shuffle "On Second Thought" demonstrated a return to more traditional sounds. –TR

○ **The Best of Eddie Rabbitt / ELEKTRA**   1979
Strong melodies enhanced by Rabbitt's searing harmonies. The instruments are "hotter" in the final mix than in other productions from the same period, so even the mainstream country fare is a little different from that of his mid-70s contemporaries. –TR

Loveline / ELEKTRA   1979
Fellow reviewers will cringe at this choice, but it displays Rabbitt at his most daring. Lots of R&B influence — even a bit of a "disco" feel on a couple of tracks — inspired melodies and unusual chord progressions throughout. Lyrically lightweight, but hey, this is music not poetry. –TR

Horizon / ELEKTRA   1980
Rabbitt's rockabilly release. "I Love a Rainy Night" and "Drivin' My Life Away" set the pace for Side 1: Sun-inspired, guitar-based productions, heavy on the echo. Side 2 is a bit ballad-heavy, though most of the tracks stand up well individually. "That's Just the Way It Is" is something of a forerunner for "Someone Could Lose a Heart Tonight." –TR

RADIO FLYER

○ **Old Strings New Strings / TURQUOIS**
This CD has the kind of bluegrass sound that makes you want to hear more. Their contemporary sounding vocals help fill the void left by the New Grass Revival and Hot Rize. –CR

Radio Flyer / TURQUOIS
Good album. If you are looking for an unknown bluegrass band to watch mature, this is it. Great potential. –CR

BOOTS RANDOLPH   b1925

Instrumental, country-pop. Tenor saxophonist Randolph has been a very influential instrumentalist within the country field, with his peak years in the 60s. Randolph switched from trombone to tenor sax in high school, and played in local combos in Evansville in the 40s and 50s. He scored with "Yakety Sax," a novelty work cowritten by James Rich, and was signed to RCA by Chet Atkins. His playing was and is quite simple; pleasant melodies, catchy themes, and occasional use of vocal effects have made up his signature style. He became a featured session musician and did many "countrypolitan" (country MOR) dates, placing 13 albums on the charts in the 60s and 70s. –RW

Greatest Hits / CBS   1988
This country saxman shows his versatility. –BD

Sunday Sax / CBS   1988
Tasty, fun, and more country than jazz. –RW

○ **Yakety Sax! / MONUMENT**   1988
Nashville session tenor saxman doing what he does best. A rocking set. –BD

Country Boots / CBS
Randolph is a fine country saxist. –RW

Sentimental Journey / CBS
Nice stuff. More jazz-influenced country than country-tinged jazz. –RW

EDDY RAVEN   b1945

Country. Born Edward Garvin Futch, it's no wonder that his name was changed by a record executive to Raven on his very first single, released on tiny Cosmos Records in the the late 60s. Numerous influences have made his music almost indescribable: the Cajun sounds of his native Louisiana, the blues influence from working with Johnny Winter, the rock and roll of his idol Elvis Presley, and the pure country of the Grand Ole Opry.

Befriended by Jimmy C. Newman, Raven made the first of many trips to Nashville in 1970, though he didn't move permanently for a couple of years. Signed to a publishing deal with Acuff-Rose (the same company that owns the Hank Williams songwriting catalog), he wrote songs for Don Gibson and Roy Acuff, among others, and started making records himself in 1974.

Despite the acclaim of his peers, Raven didn't actually earn a hit record as a recording artist until 1981, with the release of his *Desperate Dreams* album. After he lost his recording contract in a 1983 consolidation involving Elektra and Warner, Raven took the next year to realign his business. The Oak Ridge Boys earned a hit at that time with his song "Thank God for Kids" and Raven came out of his forced vacation strong, signing with RCA and gaining his first #1 single with "I Got Mexico." For the next half-dozen years, Raven remained a consistent staple of country radio: frequently adventurous, always listenable. –TR

Desperate Dreams / ELEKTRA   1981
Raven had more creative control than in previous efforts and developed a tough-sounding album. Heavy on rhythm guitar, long on bravado. –TR

○ **The Best of Eddy Raven / RCA**   1988
After his 1983 layoff, Raven put together a string of some of the best "in-the-groove" records Nashville had to offer. Many of them — "I Got Mexico," "Shine, Shine, Shine," "Sometimes a Lady," among others — are here, plus his refried Cajun effort, "I'm Gonna Get You." –TR

Temporary Sanity / UNIVERSAL   1989
Successfully merges elements of the Cajun sound into the mainstream country format. Snaps, crackles, and pops! –TR

RED CLAY RAMBLERS

Old-time. One of the most authentic of the string-band revival groups, the RCR perform traditional Appalachian folk music, contemporary compositions, and mixed genres with considerable talent and authority. For years they have been considered among the best of the modern revivalists of string-band music. –DV

Stolen Love / FLYING FISH   1976
The Ramblers hit on all cylinders: old-timey, jazz, country, fiddle tunes, and blues. –CR

Twisted Laurel / FLYING FISH   1977
Good old-timey music. A good cover of "Mississippi Delta Blues." –CR

Chuckin' the Frizz / FLYING FISH   1979
A good, funny album. One of my favorites. –CR

Hard Times / FLYING FISH   1981
A good collection of music: 13 songs. Guest Triona Ni Dhomhnail. –CR

It Ain't Right / FLYING FISH   1986
A good mix of music. –CR

A Lie of the Mind / RYKODISC   1986
The soundtrack for Sam Shepard's screenplay. Very clean sound. Highly recommended. –CR

Far North / SUGAR HILL   1989
From Sam Shepard's film *Far North*, this is a very good soundtrack album. –CR

○ **Merchant's Lunch / FLYING FISH**
One of their top three albums. Flying Fish features *Merchant's Lunch* and *Twisted Laurel* on one CD. –CR

JERRY REED   b1937

Progressive country, instrumental. Before there were *Smokey*

and the Bandit I & II, Gator, W. W. and the Dixie Dance Kings, and *BAT 21*, there was Jerry Reed — a guitarist and singer/songwriter whose musical talents have now been overshadowed by his roles on the silver screen. Reed first made his reputation as a hot studio guitarist. More fame came when Elvis Presley made hits of two Reed compositions, "Guitar Man" and "US Male." In 1970 his "Amos Moses" reached #1, resulting in a Grammy. Three other Reed singles reached #1: "When You're Hot, You're Hot," "Lord, Mr. Ford," and "She Got the Goldmine (I Got the Shaft)." His fast-playing, fast-talking performances have shown Reed to be a man of many talents. –DV

○ **When You're Hot You're Hot / RCA / BB 45**   1971
Wild and loose, this is Reed's best album. –DH

East Bound & Down / RCA   1977
The title song was Reed's last sizable hit. –DH

JIM REEVES   1924-1964

Country-pop. Gentleman Jim Reeves was perhaps the biggest male star to emerge from the Nashville Sound. His mellow baritone voice and muted velvet orchestration combined to create a sound that echoed around his world and has lasted to this day. Detractors will call the sound country-pop (or plain pop), but none can argue against the large audience that loves this music.

Reeves was capable of singing hard country ("Mexican Joe" went to #1 in 1953). From 1955 ("Bimbo") through 1969, Reeves was without exception in the charts, country and/or pop — an amazing fact in light of his untimely death in an airplane accident in 1964.

"Four Walls" (1957) and especially "He'll Have to Go" in 1957 solidified the reputation of Reeves as the Crooner of Country. After his death a near cult develope, and songs of his released after his death actually outsold his previous hits, with six #1s coming in a three-year period following his burial. (These include "I Guess I'm Crazy," "Is It Really Over?," and "Blue Side of Lonesome.") In the 70s, hits continued with "Angels Don't Lie" and "Don't Let Me Cross Over." Through technical wizardry he had duet hits in the early 80s: "Take Me in Your Arms and Hold Me" with Deborah Allen and "Have You Ever Been Lonely?" with his smooth-singing female counterpart of the plush Nashville Sound, Patsy Cline, who also perished in an airplane crash, in 1963. –DV

☆ **He'll Have to Go & Other Hits / RCA / BB 18**   1960
There may have been other country crooners as smooth, but no one else in his era had the hand-in-glove marriage of great songs and appropriate "countrypolitan" production. –MH

The Best of Jim Reeves / RCA / BB 9   1964
And very good! –MH

Live at the Opry / COUNTRY MUSIC FND.   1977
Here's a fascinating glimpse of Gentleman Jim Reeves in performance. –MH

Collector's Series / RCA
A fine overview of RCA hits by Reeves. –MH

Four Walls (The Legend Begins) / RCA
A golden throat and melifluous moroseness. –MH

Pure Gold Volume 1 / RCA
Enduring faves. –MH

RESTLESS HEART

Country. John Dittrich (b Apr 7 1951), Dave Innis (b Apr 9, 1959), Greg Jennings (b Oct 2, 1954), and Paul Gregg (b Dec 3, 1954). The origins for Restless Heart are a bit unusual. Songwriter Tim DuBois couldn't find an outlet for some of his material — "too pop" for many Nashville acts, "too country" for Los Angeles — and he sought out some of his friends to help work up the songs for demo tapes.

He pulled in five musicians he already knew, and as fate would have it, the combination worked better than anyone expected. The group pursued a recording deal, and signed with RCA Records in 1983. Just as they started to work on the first

album, lead vocalist Verlon Thompson had second thoughts, and Larry Stewart was brought in as his replacement.

Often compared to the Eagles in their early days, Restless Heart displayed a strong reliance on tenor harmonies, working country/rock territory. Despite a resurgence in traditional country, the band was able to consistently place its hybrid sound on country radio. At the end of 1991, Stewart left the group for a solo career. –TR

○ **Wheels / RCA**   1986
The guys found their niche with this project. Big, overpowering sound, heavy backbeats, and very tight harmonies. In contrast, the ballads "I'll Still Be Loving You" and "New York (Hold Her Tight)" are incredibly sensitive. –TR

CHARLIE RICH   ♭1932

Progressive country, country-pop. It is doubtful that any artist in the *All-Music Guide* presents more of a challenge to pigeonhole than Charlie Rich. Rich, who would have initially been happy arranging and playing piano for Stan Kenton's band, spent his first professional years in the late 50s as a singer, songwriter, and session pianist at Sun Records. His gospel-rock hit "Lonely Weekends" (1960) remains a classic of the genre.

Following Sun, Rich moved to RCA where he recorded persuasively in a variety of styles ranging from country to blues and pop/jazz. If you can survive "River Stay Away from My Door," you're probably immune to Rich's brand of hybrid soul. He next recorded two highly acclaimed R&B albums for Smash, which included the hit single "Mohair Sam" (1965). A brief tenure with the Memphis Hi label yielded, among other things, some startlingly good White soul music.

It wasn't until Rich joined forces with Sun alumnus Billy Sherrill at Epic Records that country hits like "Behind Closed Doors" (1973) started to occur. But a procession of albums for Epic and UA became increasingly formulaic and tepid, until Rich was virtually phoning in his vocals and all but his bedrock fans had departed.

Charlie Rich currently lives in semi-obscurity in Memphis. Periodic rumors surface about a definitive Charlie Rich album worthy of his talent. The man has never been captured at his soulful, hybrid best for an entire album, although there are glimpses here and there, and they are stunning to say the least.

Charlie Rich epitomizes Memphis music. His roots stretch across racial boundaries and genres in a totally unselfconscious way. When his voice and piano are on, there is no finer and more impassioned Memphis artist. Whether the music is country, soul, R&B, or jazz is strictly academic. The listener who has never sampled beyond Rich's slick country hits is strongly encouraged to dig more deeply into the early roots of this formidable and reclusive talent. –HD

○ **Behind Closed Doors / CBS / BB 8**   1973
Classic early-70s country schmaltz. Laidback vocals and great chintzy production by Billy Sherrill. –MH

I'll Shed No Tears / HI
Stunning and surprising soul music from the early 60s Memphis sessions. –HD

Original Hits & Midnight Demos / CHARLY
All the Sun singles plus rare glimpses of informal jam sessions on this import CD. Country, blues, jazz, and boogie demos from the multitalented Rich. Do not confuse this with *Rebound*, also on Charly (CD-52), which is missing virtually all the "midnight demos." –HD

RIDERS IN THE SKY

Cowboy. Since 1979 this trio (who named themselves after a classic Vaughan Monroe/Sons of the Pioneers song) has been mildly satirizing the standard Roy Rogers-Gene Autry "B" Westerns from the 40s and 50s, in the process creating a mini-cult among young urbanites. Their act is part yodel, part genuine love of the material, and a larger part good-natured spoof. Their short-lived Saturday-morning CBS show appeared in 1991. –DV

Best of the West / ROUNDER
Western cowboy song standards. –MH

Best of the West Rides Again / ROUNDER
More faves. –MH

Live / ROUNDER
Square-but-hip comedy with songs crooned in lush Sons of the Pioneers-style Western harmony. –MH

○ **Riders Radio Theater / MCA**
A recording of the syndicated sendup (now on video) of an old-time Western radio serial. –MH

Saddle Pals / ROUNDER
Performances for young wranglers. –MH

JEANNIE C. RILEY   b 1945

Country-pop, gospel. Tom T. Hall's song about small-town hypocrisy did a lot for his reputation, but it absolutely made Jeannie C. Riley a star. "Harper Valley P.T.A." sold 6 million copies, went gold as far away as Australia, and in 1968 brought a Grammy to its singer. Other hits followed, including "The Girl Most Likely," but nothing was going to match her initial success. Riley eventually moved to gospel. –DV

○ **Harper Valley PTA & Other Hits / RHINO / BB 12**
Late-60s hot pants and go-go country. –MH

TEX RITTER   1906-1974

Traditional country, cowboy. Father of TV's John Ritter ("Three's Company"), Woodward Maurice "Tex" Ritter was a college-educated Broadway performer long before he rode into the sunset as a singing cowboy of the silver screen. *Song of the Gringo* in 1936 started a movie career that was to last through nearly 60 horse operas. As one of the first artists to sign with the newly created Capitol label, in 1942 Ritter recorded enough hits ("There's a New Moon over My Shoulder," "Deck of Cards," "Boll Weevil") to make him one of the better-selling country singers in the 40s. Nothing before or after matched the theme song of *High Noon*, starring Gary Cooper. This movie did what all the "B" Westerns couldn't — it made Ritter a national star. –DV

☆ **Country Music Hall of Fame / MCA**
Pure Texan, Ritter was grittier than most of Hollywood's singing cowboys and nearer the roots of western song. His 1935-1939 sides are here. –MH

Greatest Hits / CAPITOL
Ritter's Capitol recordings, including "High Noon." –MH

MARTY ROBBINS   1925-1982

Country. No artist in the history of country music has had a more stylistically diverse career than Marty Robbins. Never content to remain just a country singer, Robbins performed successfully in a dazzling array of styles during more than thirty years in the business. To his credit, Robbins rarely followed trends, but often took off in directions that stunned both his peers and fans.

Plainly Robbins was not hemmed in by anyone's definition of country music. Although his earliest recordings were unremarkable weepers, by the mid 50s Robbins was making forays into rock music, adding fiddles to the works of Chuck Berry and Little Richard. By the late 50s, Robbins had pop hits of his own with teen fare like "A White Sport Coat." Almost simultaneously, he completed work on his *Hawaiian Songs of the Islands* album. In 1959 Robbins stretched even further with the hit single "El Paso," thus heralding a pattern of "gunfighter ballads" that lasted the balance of his career. Robbins also enjoyed bluesy hits like "Don't Worry," which introduced a pop audience to fuzztone guitar in 1961. Barely a year later, Marty Robbins scored a calypso hit with "Devil Woman." Marty Robbins also left a legacy of gospel music and a string of sentimental ballads, showing that he would croon with nary a touch of hillbilly twang.

Although it is fashionable to criticize such diversity, Robbins was not simply a dabbler. The truth is he was possessed of a superb voice and the ability to adapt it to an unprecedented range of styles. It also didn't hurt that most of Robbins's biggest hits were his own compositions. Robbins literally established trends, then, while others swarmed in to capitalize, he moved on to other pursuits. If you already know some of Robbins's music, choose a different phase to sample. There is bound to be some aspect you haven't heard. If you are unfamiliar with any of it, the new CBS sampler covers more than a quarter of a century of his career and can be used as a smorgasbord to help define your preferences. There is a lot to enjoy here. –HD

Gunfighter Ballads & Trail Songs / CBS / BB 6   1959
This landmark 1959 collection featuring "El Paso," was a trendsetter. –HD

Hawaii's Calling Me / BEAR FAMILY   1963
Take a complete look at Robbins's Hawaiian period on these 28 tracks. –HD

○ **Marty Robbins Country (1951-1958) / BEAR**   1991
Listeners charmed by his pre-*El Paso* country have a motherlode to explore in this 5-CD boxed set filled with dewy-eyed weepers (his earliest recordings), his rockabilly (he cut the first cover of "Maybellene"), ancient country/folk accompanied solely by acoustic guitar ("The Dream of the Miner's Chill"), Hawaiiana ("Aloha Oe"), and a handful of his country-pop outings arranged by Ray Conniff. –MH

○ **The Essential Marty Robbins: 1951-1982 / CBS**
Beware of greatest-hits compilations by Marty Robbins. He had a long and unusually varied career. There are certain phases that might not be to everyone's taste (e.g., early hillbilly 1951-1954; pop/rock & roll 1954-58; gunfighter ballads; calypso; sentimental ballads). –HD

Ruby Ann / BEAR FAMILY
The best of his bluesy rockers from the early 60s. –HD

JIMMIE RODGERS   1897-1933

Traditional country. In 1927 Ralph Peer, an RCA talent scout, placed an ad offering auditions for local hillbilly talent. The results exceeded his wildest expectations: on August 1 and 2 he recorded the Carter Family, and two days later a gaunt, ex-railroad man, Jimmie Rodgers. His brass plaque in the Country Music Hall of Fame reads, "Jimmie Rodgers' name stands foremost in the country music field as *the man who started it all*." This is a fair assessment. The "Singing Brakeman" and the "Mississippi Blue Yodeler," whose six-year career was cut short by tuberculosis, became the first nationally known star of country music and the direct influence of many later performers from Hank Snow and Ernest Tubb and Hank Williams to Lefty Frizzell and Merle Haggard.

Rodgers sang about rounders and gamblers, bounders and ramblers — and he knew what he sang about. At age 14 he went to work as a railroad brakeman, and on the rails he stayed until a pulmonary hemorrhage sidetracked him to the medicine-show circuit in 1925. The years with the trains harmed his health but helped his music. In an era when Rodgers's contemporaries were singing only mountain and mountain/folk music, he fused country (hillbilly), gospel, jazz, Black blues, Appalachian soul, pop, cowboy, and folk; and many of his best songs were his compositions, including "TB Blues," "Waiting for a Train," "Travelin' Blues," "Train Whistle Blues," and his 13 blue yodels. He was the first musician inducted into the Hall of Fame, in 1961.

Although Rodgers wasn't the first to yodel on records, his style was distinct from all the others. His yodel wasn't merely sugarcoating on the song, it was as important as the lyric, mournful and plaintive or happy and carefree, depending on a song's emotional content. His instrumental accompaniment consisted sometimes of his guitar only, while at other times a full jazz band (horns and all) backed him up. Country fans could have asked for no better hero/star — someone who thought what they thought, felt what they felt, and sang about the common person honestly and beautifully. In his last recording session, Rodgers was so racked and ravaged by TB that a cot had to be set up in the studio so he could rest before attempting that one song more. No wonder Jimmie Rodgers is to this day loved by country music fans. —DV

First Sessions 1927-28 / ROUNDER
Mississippi's hillbilly/pop/blues synthesist, blue yodeler, and proto-rockabilly on occasion. —MH

Early Years 1928-29 / ROUNDER
More seminal sides from "the father of country music." —MH

On the Way Up 1929 / ROUNDER
Rodgers flowering into the first country star. —MH

Riding High 1929-1930 / ROUNDER
More excellent recordings with Hawaiian guitarists. —MH

☆ **America's Blue Yodeler 1930-31 / ROUNDER**
A best-of-show, including "Blue Yodel #9" with Louis Armstrong, and other great hillbilly/blues/pop graftings. —MH

Down the Old Road 1931-32 / ROUNDER
More fine yodeling and yearning. —MH

Country Legacy / PAIR
A collection of the "Singing Brakeman's" recordings. —MH

JOHNNY RODRIGUEZ   b1952

Traditional country, country-pop. Johnny Rodriguez was a singing stagecoach driver at the Alamo Village when Bobby Bare and Tom T. Hall heard him, brought him to Nashville, and made him one of Hall's Storytellers. His "Pass Me By" (1972) entered the chart Top Ten, and he followed up with 20 consecutive #1s, including "You Always Come Back (To Hurting Me)," "Riding My Thumb to Mexico," and "That's the Way Love Goes." With his good looks and easy-to-listen-to voice, he has done well enough right through the 80s, after solving a drug problem. With Freddy Fender, he blended English and Spanish lyrics, creating a Tex-Mex craze. —DV

☆ **Introducing / MERCURY / BB 156**   1973
Stunning mid-70s debut; probably out-of-print. —RW

Greatest Hits / POLYGRAM   1976
A comprehensive overview of a Latino country singer who never achieved the stardom he merited. —RW

KENNY ROGERS   b1940

Country-pop. Kenny Rogers was a star before he was Kenny Rogers. As a member of the First Edition (and the New Christy Minstrels before that), he shared in some million-sellers, among them "Reuben James" and "Ruby, Don't Take Your Love to Town," an excellent Mel Tillis song about a disabled veteran. But superstardom lay ahead for this Texan with the rasp of mellow. If superstardom can be counted, then count 48 major music awards, one at a time, and he's still not done.

His experience with the two previous pop groups had prepared him well: he knew the easy-listening audience was out there, and he supplied them with well-done middle-of-the-road songs with a country flavor. Having gone solo, in 1976 Rogers charted with "Love Lifted Me." But it was with an outstanding song by writer Don Schlitz, "Lucille," that his star shot upward. The rest (as they say) is history: award-winning duets with Dottie West and Dolly Parton, 12 TV specials, another song-of-the-year with "The Gambler," "Daytime Friends," "Coward of the County," "We've Got Tonight," "Crazy," "Lady" (his first pop #1), etc., etc., etc.

And that's just the *music* side of Kenny Rogers. In 1980 the made-for-TV movie *The Gambler* blasted the competition, followed quickly by *Coward of the County*, then enough sequels to *The Gambler* to get him to Roman numeral IV. In music and television and in movies, Kenny Rogers puts the *super* back in superstar, enough so as to have his own private 18-hole golf course on his spread outside Nashville. —DV

Every Time Two Fools Collide / LIBERTY / BB 186   1978

Country-pop with Dottie West. —BC

○ **The Gambler / CAPITOL / BB 12**   1979
Plaintive Southern storytelling. —BC

Love Lifted Me / EMI-USA   1980
Traditional Southern gospel. —BC

20 Greatest Hits / CAPITOL / BB 22   1983
Southern pop hits. —BC

Eyes That See in the Dark / RCA / BB 6   1983
Contemporary pop, with Bee Gees production. —BC

Duets / CAPITOL / BB 85   1984
Duets Kim Carnes, Sheena Easton, and others. —BC

Greatest Hits / MCA / BB 57
His First Edition hits and more. —BC

Something Inside So Strong / WARNER
Adult-contemporary, inspirational music, with guest Gladys Knight. —BC

ROY ROGERS & THE SONS OF THE PIONEERS

Cowboy. Roy Rogers (born Leonard Slye in southern Ohio, 1912) eventually outdrew Gene Autry, his fellow Republic Studio star, at least at the box office. Autry won the battle of the records (his *Silver-Haired Daddy of Mine* alone sold over five million copies). Rogers, in spite of his excellent voice and superior yodel, is perhaps best known musically as the founder of what's generally considered to be among the best, if not the best vocal group ever to grace country music — the Sons of the Pioneers. Rogers, Bob Nolan, and Tim Spencer began as a trio (The Pioneers) in 1933, changing to their more famous name a year later, when Hugh Farr, with his swing-style fiddle and bass voice, joined. When Rogers, who was to become known as "King of the Cowboys," left for the silver screen in 1938, the six-piece group in a sense went with him, appearing in scores of his movies through 1949.

Over the years the Sons of the Pioneers recorded hundreds of Western-flavored songs, many of which other Western groups also recorded (for example, "Ghost Riders in the Sky," "Empty Saddles"), but two classic songs written by Bob Nolan, "Cool Water" and "Tumblin' Tumbleweeds," elevated the Sons above the competition. In addition, because of the sophisticated musical arrangements, the intricate instrumentals, and the complicated vocal harmonies, the Sons of the Pioneers have for the past 60 years remained at the top of the scale, against which all subsequent country vocal groups must measure themselves. Happy trails to you, Dale and Roy. —DV

○ **The Best of Roy Rogers / CAPITOL**
The singing cowboy crooning his hits. —MH

Tribute / RCA   1991
A well-received recent solo album on which Rogers is joined by Clint Black and other young "hats." —MH

Country Music Hall of Fame Series / MCA   1992
When Gene Autry got into a contract dispute with Republic Pictures in 1937, the studio replaced him with Sons of the Pioneers member Len Slye, whose name they changed to Roy Rogers. These Decca tracks, which range from 1934 to 1942, cover Rogers's output just before he became "King of the Cowboys" with the release of *Ridin' Down the Canyon*. Two of these cuts were recorded with the Sons of the Pioneers; the rest are solo. —BM

BILLY JOE ROYAL   b1945

Country-pop. It's been a varied career for Billy Joe Royal. He started as pure pop: "Down in the Boondocks" was a huge hit in 1965, and as a teen idol he toured with Dick Clark's "Cavalcade." He's jumped from pop to country and back ever since, along the way hitting 12 consecutive Top 25 singles. "A Ring Where a Ring Used to Be" was his sixth consecutive #1 video. —DV

○ **Greatest Hits / CBS**   1964
Can't go wrong with this one, featuring his two biggies, "Down in the Boondocks" and "Cherry Hill Park." —CK

DAN SEALS   b 1948

Country-pop. Country-pop singer/songwriter Dan Seals was half of England Dan & John Ford Coley. Some of their hits during the 70s include "We'll Never Have to Say Goodbye Again" and "Nights Are Forever without You." The first of nine consecutive #1s was "Meet Me in Montana," a duet with Marie Osmond. –DV

Rage On / CAPITOL   1988
On *Rage On*, Seals tells stories woven around traditional country themes while rarely resorting to country clichés. "Addicted," "They Rage On," "Five Generations of Rock County Wilsons" — these are tales of quiet desperation, and the empathy in Seals's voice makes their impact devastating. Almost as good as his *Best*. –BM

On Arrival / CAPITOL   1990
This is the product of a man very much in touch with his emotions. In "Bordertown," "A Heart in Search of Love" and "Wood," he works the listener's heart with the skill of a surgeon. At the same time, "Good Times" and "Love on Arrival" are incredibly celebratory. –TR

○ **Best of Dan Seals / CAPITOL**
All the hits ("Bop," "Big Wheels in the Moonlight," etc.) collected up in one nice, solid package. –CK

RICKY VAN SHELTON   b 1952

Contemporary country. This talented baritone's debut album, *Wild-Eyed Dreams*, yielded three #1 songs, making him an instant star and producing a ton of awards in 1988-1989. Subsequent hits have included "I Am a Simple Man," from his *Backroads* album. He and Marie Osmond cohosted the "Music City News Country Songwriters Awards" in 1992. –DV

○ **Loving Proof / COLUMBIA / BB 78**
Here are stabs at rockabilly alongside the ballads at which Shelton excels. –MH

Wild-Eyed Dream / COLUMBIA / BB 76
The debut from this country hunk balladeer, with occasional thumpin' at the hop. –MH

RVS 3 / CBS   1990
The third album puts out more sounds in the winning Shelton formula. –MH

SHENANDOAH

Country. The five founding members of Shenandoah (Mike McGuire, Ralph Ezell, Marty Raybon, Jim Seales, and Stan Thorn) were all associated in some way with the small-but-mighty musical community in Muscle Shoals, Al. They performed locally on occasion, calling themselves the MGM Band, simply for the chance to play live. But songwriter Robert Byrne caught their act one night and persuaded producer Rick Hall to let him work up some demo tapes with the group. Shortly thereafter, they signed with Columbia Records, which gave them the name Shenandoah.
By their third single, in 1987, they hit the Top Ten with "She Doesn't Cry Anymore," and their next, "Mama Knows," became a signature song. Strong lead vocals by Marty Raybon and a high level of musicianship have propelled Shenandoah, alternating between sensitive ballads and often-inspired uptempo singles.
The group's name came under dispute in the courts, and they filed for bankruptcy while still signed to Columbia. They re-emerged in 1992 with RCA. –TR

The Road Not Taken / COLUMBIA   1989
Blue-collar romance. The songs mix the day-to-day struggles of an Everyday Joe with a steady respect for love, personal roots, and family. It doesn't hurt to have six bona fide hits on it, either. –TR

T. G. SHEPPARD   b 1944

Country. A native of Humboldt, TN, Bill Browder (his name at birth) headed off to Memphis after high school, getting involved in the record business on several different levels. He tried recording as a pop artist, and even signed with Atlantic Records under the name Brian Stacy, opening shows for the Beach Boys.
A few years later, he took a job with a Memphis record distributor, then ended up in record promotion, where the job entailed calling radio stations and trying to persuade them to play his company's records. In that capacity for RCA, he helped break Elvis Presley's "Suspicious Minds," Perry Como's "It's Impossible," and John Denver's "Take Me Home Country Roads."
After "going independent," he came across a demo tape of "Devil in the Bottle." He tried to talk a number of artists into doing the song, and when no one was interested, he decided to do it himself. Then a number of record labels said no as well, although Motown's fledgling country division, Hitsville Records, said yes. Primarily a recitation, "Devil" went to #1 in 1975, but within three years the company folded, and Sheppard's career was in limbo. Connecting with record producer Buddy Killen, he signed with Warner, and starting in 1979, the two churned out some of country's best-crafted singles over a four-year period.
Sheppard gradually moved away from recitations and grew significantly as a vocalist, though the press often ignored his achievements. He changed producers several times in the mid 80s and, after a divorce in 1987, took a couple of years off for personal reflection. When he returned, Sheppard found it difficult to regain his earlier momentum. –TR

● **The Best of T. G. Sheppard / WARNER**   1981
You'll have to look for this one at used-record stores. A sampler released only to radio, it covers the half-dozen years up to and including "I Loved 'Em Every One." Some of the performances are a little stiff but it lends appreciation for his improved, later work. –TR

Slow Burn / WARNER   1983
This album has its weak moments, but Sheppard's performance is stronger than in previous albums. He's more confident, probably understands the craft of singing a little better, and — this being his first outing with record producer Jim Ed Norman — the arrangements don't bury T. G. –TR

RICKY SKAGGS   b 1954

Traditional country, progressive country, traditional bluegrass, progressive. For someone still in his 30s, Kentuckian Ricky Skaggs has already produced a career's worth of music. At age seven he appeared on TV with Flatt and Scruggs; at 15 he was a member of legendary Ralph Stanley's bluegrass band (with fellow teenage, the late Keith Whitley). None of the contemporary stars, male or female, has better credentials than Skaggs. The term "multitalented" lacks the power to characterize this extraordinary singer and instrumentalist. Not only can he sing and pick with the best in progressive country, his broad and deep experience in traditional music separates him from the crowd. In the estimation of many, he is without peer as a combination vocalist and intrumentalist (guitar, mandolin, fiddle, banjo).
After playing with Ralph Stanley for three years, Skaggs moved on to progressive bluegrass bands the Country Gentlemen and J. D. Crowe and the New South. With his own band, Boone Creek, he mixed the old and the new, adding the influence of French jazz guitarist Django Reinhardt. He took Rodney Crowell's place in Emmylou Harris's Hot Band in 1977, and the band's excellent *Roses in the Snow* album showcased his versatility. Two #1s came out of his *Waitin' for the Sun to Shine* self-produced album (1981), and the awards started arriving.
Skaggs is largely responsible for a back-to-basics movement in country music. He showed many that a bluegrass tenor with impeccable taste and enormous talent can sell traditional country, at a time when pop music has invaded the land of rural rhythm. His remake of Bill Monroe's "Uncle Pen," for example, was the first bluegrass song since Flatt and

Scruggs's the "Ballad of Jed Clampett" to reach #1 in the charts. –DV

Waitin' for the Sun to Shine / EPIC   1981
His first album after signing with Epic Records, this one took Skaggs into the mainstream, in effect beginning the new-traditionalist movement. Simple, mountain approach, with lots of remakes and Skaggs's mournful vocal tones. The best cut is the plaintive title track. –TR

Highways & Heartaches / EPIC   1982
Long a sideman or supporting vocalist in previous situations, Skaggs wasn't totally comfortable with his role as a lead vocalist when he signed with Epic Records. Thanks to a year of touring and greater support from his record label (when Epic signed him, the company honestly didn't think he'd sell more than 100,000 copies of his debut for the company), he had greater confidence vocally the second time around. And the material's more upbeat. –TR

Country Boy / CBS / BB 180   1984
Every one of Ricky Skaggs's albums is a pickin' festival and a country delight. Not only is this one no exception, but it also includes Bill Monroe's "Wheel Hoss" with Monroe himself picking along on mandolin, which earns it a listing here. If you like this album, you'll probably like every other one Skaggs has made. –WR

○ **Live in London / CBS**   1985
This is the one Skaggs album to own if you can only have one. Because it's a live recording, the picking is just that much more exciting, and the album serves as an unofficial best-of, its highlights including "Heartbroke," "Uncle Pen," and a version of "Don't Get Above Your Raising" that features noted country fan Elvis Costello. –WR

Family & Friends / ROUNDER   1985
Skaggs's last breath of pure bluegrass, recorded with help from the Whites, guitarist Peter Rowan, dobroist Jerry Douglas, and others. Two songs by Carter Stanley, one by Bill Monroe, and some fine examples of Appalachian gospel, including a stunning a cappella trio vocal on "Talk About Sufferin'." –BM

My Father's Son / EPIC   1991
A concept album about families, *My Father's Son* is the Skaggs album that owes the least to bluegrass. Skaggs is concerned with the legacies fathers leave their sons, both the wisdom ("Father Knows Best") and the limitations ("My Father's Son"). He also sees materialism for the distracting, destructive force it is. His duet with Waylon Jennings on "Only Daddy That'll Walk the Line" fits neatly, though perhaps not the way the writer intended. And because Skaggs's background is bluegrass rather than honky-tonk, every father image is inextricably bound to God. –BM

CARL SMITH   b 1927
Traditional country. For the first five years of the 50s, this Opry headliner was perhaps country's biggest star, going on to rack up nearly three dozen hits in the decade. Although he could sing great honky-tonk, Smith discovered that his country ballads sold so well he soon specialized in them. His second release for Columbia, "Let's Live a Little," was a huge hit, followed by "If Teardrops Were Pennies" and "Mr. Moon." In 1953 three singles reached #1: "Hey Joe," "Satisfaction Guaranteed," and "Trademark." He branched out from Nashville with two movies, and his "Country Music Hall" TV program was broadcast coast-to-coast in Canada in the mid 60s. In his quarter-century with the Columbia label, Smith sold over 15 million records. Both he and his wife Goldie Hill (also an Opry star) retired early to their horse farm in Tennessee. Smith was "Mr. Country" in the 50s. –DV

☆ **The Essential Carl Smith (1950-1956) / CBS**
Twenty tracks, including his early hits, from this smooth and soulful country vocalist who was popular in the 50s. If you like Hank Williams and Lefty Frizzell and the 50s fiddle and steel sound, give this a try. –RL

DARDEN SMITH
Contemporary country. Named for a local rodeo rider, Darden Smith grew up in Austin, TX, and placed two singles, "Little Maggie" and "Day after Tomorrow," on the country charts in 1988. In 1989 he teamed up with British songwriter Boo Hewerdine of the Bible rock band to record *Evidence*, which expanded his following beyond the country market. –WR

Native Soul / REDI MIX   1986
A fine debut album, temporarily out of print. Nanci Griffith sings harmony vocal on "Two Dollar Novels." Lyle Lovett sings harmony on five songs. This one's a gem. Smith is just breaking out and developing his style. –CR

○ **Darden Smith / CBS**   1988
Darden's big-label debut that features three cuts off of his *Native Soul* album. This time the production is better, with strings and extra vocals. Nanci Griffith and Lyle Lovett back him, along with Roland Denney and Paul Pearcy. All of his songs are strong and the playing is dead-on. It's a keeper. –CR

Trouble No More / CBS   1990
A strong album, not as diverse as *Darden Smith*, but as good. Contains "Midnight Train," "Frankie & Sue," "Trouble No More," "Fall Apart at the Seams," and the list goes on. With two songs cowritten with buddy Boo Hewerdine. –CR

HANK SNOW   b 1914
Traditional country. Canada's greatest contribution to country music, for over 40 years Hank Snow has been famous for his "traveling" songs. It's no wonder. At age 12 he ran away from his Nova Scotia home and joined the Merchant Marines, working as a cabin boy and laborer for four years. Once back on shore, he listened to Jimmie Rodgers records and started playing in public, building up a following in Halifax. His original nickname, the Yodeling Ranger, was modified to the Singing Ranger when his high voice changed to the great baritone it is today. And great his voice is — great enough for him to record on the same label, RCA, for 45 years. In 1950, the year he became an Opry regular, his self-penned "I'm Moving On" (the first of his many great traveling songs) became a smash hit, reaching #1 and remaining on the charts for 40 weeks. "Golden Rocket" (also 1950) and "I've Been Everywhere" (1962), two other hits, show his lifelong love for trains and travel. But he was as much at home with two other styles, the ballad and the rhumba/boogie. Among his many great ballads are "Bluebird Island" (with Anita Carter, of the Carter Family), "Fool Such As I," and "Hello, Love" a hit when Snow was 60 years old.

Still appearing regularly on the Opry, Snow shows that his incredible voice has suffered no loss of quality over the last half-century. And he still proves what a tasteful, understated guitar stylist he is. To show you his impact on the business, in 1963 the nation's disk jockeys voted *I'm Moving On* their favorite all-time country record. With small stature and huge voice, Snow is a country traditionalist who has given much more to the business than he's taken. Hit output of over 100 albums gives a sense of his importance to country music history. –DV

Collector's Series / RCA
A nasal Canadian crooner, a crisp flat-top picker, and one of the most influential country artists of the early 50s. Snow is relaxed and driving at the same time. –MH

I'm Moving On / PAIR
Another nice RCA hits package. –MH

☆ **I'm Movin' On & Other Country Hits / RCA**
Rockabilly couldn't have happened without him. Train songs with hillbilly rumbas and more. –MH

JO-EL SONNIER
Progressive country, Cajun. In the late 80s, when the folks in Nashville realized country consisted of more than the Tennessee-Texas axis, they started looking for new sounds.

One of the best was that of Cajun accordionist Jo-el Sonnier, who had kicked around for a number of years, gaining a reputation as a "musician's musician." Sonnier initially caused a major fuss in Nashville and a minor one elsewhere, though his songs — a blend of Cajun music, twangy guitars, and New Orleans R&B — briefly added a touch of spice to country radio. –BM

Cajun Life / ROUNDER
Recorded in the mid 70s. Sonnier proves himself a master of the accordion, with passionate performances of authentic Cajun music. –JH & MH

● **Come On Joe / RCA**   1987
Sonnier's French-Cajun accent brings new life to songs by Randy Newman, Richard Thompson, Moon Martin, and Dave Alvin. Steve Winwood takes an organ solo on a cover of Slim Harpo's "Raining in My Heart." Cajun-tinged contemporary country with a rock edge and intelligent songs. The best of Sonnier's Nashville work. –BM & MH

Have a Little Faith / RCA   1990
The emphasis here lies more heavily on ballads, as Sonnier discovers John Hiatt and delivers penetrating versions of his "Have a Little Faith" and "I'll Never Get Over You." Also includes a remake of Iry LeJeune's 1945 "Evangeline Special" and a straight-country single in "If Your Heart Should Ever Roll This Way Again." –BM

Tears of Joy / CAPITOL   1991
In the Cajun/pop/country mold of his RCA albums. –MH

○ **The Complete Mercury Sessions / MERCURY**   1992
Fifteen fine 70s country songs, including the aching "Blue Is Not a Word." –MH

THE SONS OF THE PIONEERS

Cowboy. See the biography under Roy Rogers. –ED

Cool Water / RCA   1960
Later 50s material, but still smooth and fine. –MH

Columbia Historic Edition / CBS   1989
This group wrote the book on dreamy, close-harmony crooning to panoramic vistas. Leader Bob Nolan supplies poetic lyrics, and Hugh and Karl Farr provide the Django Reinhardt/Stephane Grappelli-inspired accompaniment. Archetypal sounds from the 30s. –MH

Country Music Hall of Fame / MCA
Decca recordings from the 30s to early 50s. –MH

☆ **Empty Saddles / MCA**
All of the Pioneers 30s-era compilations are fine, but this includes Bob Nolan's darkest and most beautiful song, "Blue Prairie." –MH

Tumbleweed Trails / MCA
The Sons had their biggest and earliest hits on Decca, and many appear here. –MH

SOUTHERN PACIFIC

Country. Stu Cook, John McFee, Tim Goodman, David Jenkins, and Kurt Howell formed this group in mid 1983. Southern Pacific's rock & roll past constantly dogged the group's reputation. Keith Knudsen and John McFee were former members of the Doobie Brothers (McFee had also played alongside Huey Lewis in a band called Clover), original lead vocalist Tim Goodman had recorded a solo album, and Stu Cook performed in Creedence Clearwater Revival. Even when Goodman left the band, they replaced him with another ex-rocker, former Pablo Cruise vocalist David Jenkins. They did have one member with strong country roots: Kurt Howell played keyboards for Crystal Gayle.
Southern Pacific signed with Warner, and released a strong debut album in 1985, though the media continually questioned the band's commitment to country. The group plied a very danceable brand of country, and hit a high point with their 1988 album *Zuma*, which included their biggest single, "New Shade of Blue."

Eventually, Southern Pacific left country music, intending to pursue a pop career. –TR

○ **Greatest Hits / WARNER**   1991
Why this group never quite made "the big time" remains a mystery. The material's sometimes two-step-able, sometimes kick-ass, and in "New Shade of Blue," they out-Eagled the Eagles. –TR

RED SOVINE   1918-1980

Traditional country, trucker country. Sovine is regarded as the king of truck-driving songs. Between 1955 and 1980, Sovine scored 31 country hits, including "Phantom 309," a song about a truck-driving ghost. "Teddy Bear," a maudlin story about a crippled boy who talked to friendly truckers with his CB radio, was a #1 hit. Other chart successes included "Giddyup Go" (#1) and several duets with Webb Pierce on "Why Baby Why" (#1), "Little Rosa" (#5), and "Hold Everthing" (#5). Sovine died in an automobile accident in 1980. –RC

○ **The Best of Red Sovine / STARDAY**
This set includes some of Sovine's big hits but a definitive collection still isn't available domestically. Among the tracks present are "Phantom 309," "Giddyup Go," and "I Know You Are Married, But I Love You Still." –RC

BUDDY SPICHER

Instrumental. Since playing with the progressive country band Area Code 615 in the late 60s, Buddy has been a much-in-demand session fiddler. He has recorded with the Pointer Sisters and Henry Mancini, along with making albums of his own. –DV

American Sampler / FLYING FISH   1988
Varied dates with fine playing by Spicher. –RW

☆ **Fiddle Classics / FLYING FISH**   1988
A high-caliber acoustic session by Spicher, showcasing country, folk, and blues influences. –RW

Me & My Heroes / FLYING FISH   1990
A nice folk/jazz/country mixture. –RW

THE STATLER BROTHERS

Traditional country. Brothers Harold and Don Reid (Phil Balsey and Jimmy Fortune round out the present quartet) have been the kings of country groups since the mid 60s. The brothers, who began as a gospel quartet in 1955, made it big in 1965 with "Flowers on the Wall," a pop and country hit. In spite of competition from other groups over the years (the Oak Ridge Boys, Alabama, the Judds), the Statler Brothers have pretty much remained in the traditional country mold while winning every award in sight, over 400 in all. Their distinct sound is unmistakable, nostalgic, and unique. Hits include "You Can't Have Your Kate and Edith Too," "Elizabeth," "Class of '57," and "I'll Go to My Grave Loving You." In 1991 their television show quickly became the highest-rated weekly series on TNN. –DV

○ **Holy Bible - Old & New Testament / MERCURY**   1956
CD twin disc of great single country gospel albums. –RW

○ **Big Hits / CBS**   1967
This gathers all their 60s Columbia hits. –RW

○ **Oh Happy Day / CBS**   1969
Another "roots" effort, this one from the 60s. –RW

☆ **Bed of Roses / POLYGRAM / BB 126**   1970
Their first Mercury album. –RW

Radio Gospel Favorites / POLYGRAM   1970
This harks back to their roots as a spiritual ensemble. Heated vocals. –RW

Best of the Statler Brothers / POLYGRAM / BB 121   1975
Gathers past hits for the label. –RW

Best of the Statler Brothers - Vol. 2 / POLYGRAM   1975
A followup to their prior greatest-hits release. –RW

★ **10th Anniversary / POLYGRAM**   1980
Celebratory session. –RW

○ **Today / POLYGRAM / BB 193**   1983
An excellent prototypical session. –RW
○ **Atlanta Blue / POLYGRAM / BB 177**   1984
A tremendous title track, with marvelous singing. –RW
○ **Maple Street Memories / POLYGRAM**   1987
Nice autobiographical touches. –RW
○ **Country Music Then & Now / POLYGRAM**
From the early 70s. A bit rougher and less slick than some 80s
dates. –RW
Country Music Then & Now/Bed of Roses / POLYGRAM
A twin release pairing two solid albums. –RW
Greatest Hits / POLYGRAM
A recycled greatest/best-of. –RW
○ **Holy Bible - New Testament / MERCURY**
A companion to the previous release. –RW
○ **Holy Bible - Old Testament / MERCURY**
Fine country/gospel; the first of two. –RW
○ **Pardners in Rhyme / POLYGRAM**
Sparkling leads and harmonies. –RW
○ **Short Stories / POLYGRAM**
Nice songs, better-than-usual lyrics. –RW

GARY STEWART   b 1944

Country rock, traditional country. Gary Stewart's versatility
allows him to cover rockabilly and honky-tonk material
equally well. After playing piano for Charley Pride's band, he
had a 1974 hit with "Drinking Thing," a honky-tonker's
delight. –DV
☆ **Gary's Greatest / HIGHTONE**   1991
An excellent collection of Stewart's hits from 1973-1990. –DH

DOUG STONE

Traditional country. Doug Stone's sensitive Deep South
baritone has made him one of country's premier romantic
balladeers. This Georgian can sing hard traditional country
and easy country with equal ease. For years diesel mechanics
was his day job, and he hated it. This dissatisfaction carries
over into his music and his stage presence, which presents
him as distant and alone; he knows what he's singing about.
With the release of his first album, his record company
announced the dawning of a new "Stone Age." They weren't
far off, as acceptance from country's female-dominated
audience was almost immediate; his second album, 1991's *I
Thought It Was You*, overdid the self-pity but yielded a couple
of hits, including the title cut. "I'd Be Better Off (In a Pine
Box)" was his breakthrough song. Shortly before the release
of his third album, *From the Heart*, in 1992, 35 years of
Southern-fried food sent Stone under the surgeon's knife for
quadruple bypass surgery. –BM & DV
○ **Doug Stone / EPIC**   1990
"I'd Be Better Off (In a Pine Box)" is a towering expression of
self-pity that most singers could spend a career trying to top.
If Stone never bested his performance on his debut, he came
close with ballads like "In a Different Light" and "My Hat's off
to Him," becoming a genuine heartthrob in the process. –BM
I Thought It Was You / CBS   1991
From the Heart / EPIC   1992

THE STONEMAN FAMILY

Old-time, traditional country. The Stonemans are literally the
first family of country music. Patriarch E.V. "Pop" Stoneman
recorded "The Sinking of the Titanic" in 1925 and watched it
become one of the biggest-selling country records of the
decade. With fiddler Hattie Stoneman, his wife, he toured
widely until the Depression cut into recording and personal
appearances. In the 50s, when the 13 kids had taught
themselves the family music, the Stonemans became a
popular act, appearing on the Opry in 1962 and at numerous
folk festivals. The spots on national TV, combined with their
albums for Starday and Folkways, gave them coast-to-coast

exposure. When "Pop" died in 1966, the family kept going,
making them the longest continuous act in country music.
–DV
○ **First Family of Country Music / CMH**   1928
New recordings by members of this classic group whose
patriarch began recording in 1924. Bluegrass-flavored old-
time country. –CW

GEORGE STRAIT   b 1952

Traditional country, western swing. The fact that *People*
magazine named George Strait one of the 50 most beautiful
people in the world might mislead you: he can still sing pure
country, as witnessed by his 22 #1 singles, ten gold albums,
and four platinum. On the debit side, he may have unwittingly
started the "hat act" fad, singers with Stetsons as big as (and
sometimes bigger than) their voices. But from his *Strait
Country* debut album in 1981, country listeners have found
pleasure in his rich, unadorned voice and his straightahead
delivery.
Neither his songs nor his style is varnished or gussied-up, a
breath of fresh air in modern country. He reintroduced twin
fiddles and a tasteful steel guitar accompaniment, perfectly
matching his voice and his Western-swing style. He's earned
his rewards, including Vocalist of the Year and Album of the
Year (1985) for *Does Fort Worth Ever Cross Your Mind*. If you
like listening to Merle Haggard, and you ought to, give George
Strait a serious listen. –DV
Strait Country / MCA   1981
First and still fine. –MH
If You Ain't Lovin' (You Ain't Livin') / MCA / BB 87
A great cover of the old Faron Young title song, and other
swingin' tonkers. –MH
Strait Country/Strait from the Heart / MCA
Two early albums in one. The first and arguably the best of the
80s crop of Haggard-indebted hats, Strait has never much
wavered from a Western-swing-tinged, honky-tonk base. –MH
☆ **Does Fort Worth Ever Cross Your Mind / MCA** 1984
Hardcore country shuffles, sudsy weepers, and swinging
stompers. This is 80s "nu-traditional" country at its finest and
most heartfelt. –MH
Right or Wrong / MCA / BB 163   1984
The title track is vintage Bob Wills, and much here draws
from similar swinging Southwestern roots. –MH
Greatest Hits / MCA   1985
A good overview of Strait's early MCA chartbusters. –MH
#7 / MCA / BB 126   1986
No frills 'n' fine. –MH
Greatest Hits - Vol. 2 / MCA / BB 68   1987
More chartbusters from the Texan in the white hat. –MH
Chill of an Early Fall / MCA   1991
A hit album. Strait holds his own despite a plethora of new
hats in the decade since his debut. –MH

MARTY STUART

Traditional country. Mississippi-born Stuart began his career on the
road with Lester Flatt and later Johnny Cash. An in-demand sideman,
he has played with Willie Nelson, Bob Dylan, and lately Wynonna
Judd and Travis Tritt. His style pays homage to early country and
bluegrass masters with his twangy, neo-hillbilly sound. –ED
○ **Tempted / MCA**   1991
Upbeat contemporary country with rockabilly roots. –MH
This One's Gonna Hurt You / MCA   1992
Stuart starts by relating how he received Hank Williams Sr's
blessing in a dream. With covers of Charlie Pride's "Just
Between You and Me" and Ola Mae Belle's "High on a
Mountain Top," he makes you believe. But the most retro stuff
gets too hamfisted to keep *This One's Gonna Hurt You* on the
same level as *Tempted*. –BM
Hillbilly Rock / MCA
Like the title says, contemporary rockabilly from this
singer/guitarist. –MH

SWEETHEARTS OF THE RODEO

Contemporary country. By winning the Wrangler Country Showdown with "Gotta Get Away," California sisters Kristine Arnold and Janis Gill (wife of singer Vince Gill) received a Columbia contract. They've done well with "Blue to the Bone" and "Midnight Girl" and have been nominated for Best Vocal Duo Awards. –DV

○ **Sweethearts of the Rodeo / CBS**
Californian sisters gone to Music City. Good vocal harmony on contemporary, rock-tinged country. –MH

SYLVIA   b 1956

Country. Growing up in Kokomo, IN, Sylvia moved to Nashville around Christmas of 1975 with a definite game plan: get a job as a secretary, get to know influential people in town, and build a career as a recording artist.

The plan worked. She picked up a job as the receptionist for Pi-Gem Music, headed by record producer Tom Collins. She started singing on demo sessions, and Collins helped her secure a recording contract with RCA. Since she'd never performed live before, Sylvia ended up learning to do concerts at the same time she was making hit records.

With an engaging voice, a bubbly personality, and a beautiful appearance, Sylvia was practically a marketing dream, and Collins built her sound around catchy melodies and strong backbeats. The material was often lyrically shallow, however, and Sylvia grew increasingly frustrated. She left Collins and recorded a pair of albums with record producer Brent Maher. The second was never released. Sylvia, instead, was dropped by RCA in 1987.

She used the opportunity for personal growth (she toured almost constantly during the height of her career and was emotionally drained) and to develop as a songwriter. In 1992 she re-emerged as a touring artist and pursued a recording deal with self-penned material that was inner-directed and uplifting. –TR

Just Sylvia / RCA   1982
Producer Tom Collins plays around with Sylvia's vocals a lot, altering them electronically for effects that range from ever-so-slight to overbearing. But the material's predominantly sassy and as catchy as a virus. The honesty in "You Can't Go Back Home" really hurts. –TR

GID TANNER & HIS SKILLET LICKERS   1885-1960

Old-time. This influential string band of the 20s and 30s featured three major figures of early country music: Gideon "Gid" Tanner, fiddler Clayton McMichen (b 1900 - d 1970), and Blind Riley Pucket (b 1894 - d 1946) on guitar. Tanner's band, the Skillet Lickers, featured fiddle breakdowns, folk material, and comedy skits dealing with moonshine. This high-spirited band broke up in 1934. –DV

○ **Kickapoo Medicine Show / ROUNDER**   1988
A 20s string band plays raucous and rippin' old-time music on this album –MH

B. J. THOMAS   b 1942

Country/rock, country-pop, gospel. Billy Joe Thomas began as a rocker but had his first Top Ten with Hank Williams's "I'm So Lonesome I Could Cry" in 1966. In 1969 "Raindrops Keep Fallin' on My Head," the theme song from the movie *Butch Cassidy and the Sundance Kid*, made a country-pop star of him. After years of substance abuse he found Christianity and rose again to the top with gospel albums, with *Home Where I Belong* winning him a Grammy. He now mixes gospel and secular country-pop with equal success. –DV

○ **Greatest Hits / RHINO**   1969
His country-pop and easy-listening cuts. –BC

HANK THOMPSON   b 1925

Traditional country, western swing. Country Hall of Famer Hank Thompson has had chart hits in five different decades.

Between Bob Wills and Asleep at the Wheel, there was Thompson with his Brazos Valley Boys, keeping the sound of Western swing alive. His swing music and well-written honky-tonk songs produced 21 Top 20 charters from 1949 and 1958. His signature song, "The Wild Side of Life" (1952), was his biggest hit, prompting Miss Kitty Wells to defend bar-life females in "It Wasn't God Who Made Honky Tonk Angels." Much of his best music was set in the dim lights and thick smoke of the honky-tonk, with such hits as "Hangover Tavern," "On Tap, in the Can, or in the Bottle," "Smokey the Bar," "A Six-Pack to Go," and "Honky-Tonk Girl." While music tastes changed during his career, he kept on touring worldwide with his band, keeping true honky-tonk and Western swing in the public's ear. He's often seen on Ralph Emery's "Nashville Now" TV show. –DV

Country Music Hall of Fame Series / MCA   1992
1968-1978 recordings from Dot Records, when Thompson was past his prime but still capable of turning out good singles when the Nashville Sound didn't smother him. –BM

○ **A Six Pack to Go / CAPITOL**
Beer-drinkin' music and honky-tonk from the 50s. Great band, including Merle Travis on guitar on some cuts. –GB

The Best of Hank Thompson / CAPITOL
Several of his best beer-drinkin' tunes and novelty songs, many done with his Bob Wills-style big band at a time when Thompson was pretty much carrying the torch of western swing alone. –GB

MARSHA THORNTON

Country. Thornton is one of the new Nashville thrushes. Her two MCA albums are 1989's *Marsha Thornton*, produced by the legendary Owen Bradley, and 1991's *Maybe the Moon Will Shine*. Like many of her contemporaries, Thornton is labelled a "new traditionalist" and is stylistically indebted to Emmylou Harris. –MH

○ **Maybe the Moon Will Shine / MCA**
Pleasant pipes and Emmylou Harris-style production. –MH

MEL TILLIS   b 1932

Traditional country. Though he stutters when he speaks, Mel Tillis is downright eloquent in his singing and superb songwriting ("Ruby, Don't Take Your Love to Town" and "Detroit City," a huge hit for Bobby Bare). Over 500 of his songs have been covered by the likes of Faron Young, Kenny Rogers, folksinger Burl Ives, and Webb Pierce. Among his recordings that hit #1 are "Good Woman Blues," "Heart Healer," "Coca-Cola Cowboy," and "Southern Rains." As an actor he's appeared in *W. W. and the Dixie Dance Kings* and *Uphill All the Way* (1986), with Roy Clark. His winning personality and sense of humor lead him to regular TV appearances. –DV

○ **American Originals / CBS**
Good 60s shuffles in a Ray Price vein. –MH

Best of Mel Tillis / MCA
Fine 60s hard-country singer/songwriter with Ray Price shuffles, etc. –MH

M-M-Mel Live / MCA
Tillis the showman heard working a crowd. –MH

PAM TILLIS   b 1957

Contemporary country. Daughter of country singer and actor Mel Tillis, she appeared with dad at the old Ryman Auditorium when she was eight. She sings pop, rock, R&B, and country. Her compositions have been recorded by Ricky Van Shelton and Conway Twitty. Her hard-country "Don't Tell Me What to Do" was the first debut record to top the country charts in 17 years. –DV

○ **Put Yourself in My Place / ARISTA**   1991
The album that established Tillis as a performer in her own right has a traditional country base, cut with bluegrass, folk, and rock. It all creates the same sort of mixed breed she sang about in "Melancholy Child": "You take a black Irish temper,

some solemn Cherokee, a Southern sense of humor, and you got someone like me." Her characters are the awkward dancers of "I've Seen Enough to Know": bruised, tentative, and needing to be cajoled back to love. Even the throwaway songs are of a high standard; the best ones ("Maybe It Was Memphis," "Don't Tell Me What to Do") are truly enticing. –BM

FLOYD TILLMAN   b 1914

Traditional country. This Hall of Famer is probably best known for writing "It Makes No Difference Now," a country classic that he sold to Jimmie Davis for $300 in 1938, only to watch it become a hit for Davis, Bob Wills, Bing Crosby, Gene Autry, and others. In the late 40s he had recording hits with his self-penned "Slippin' Around" and "I Love You So Much It Hurts." His Western swing/honky-tonk mixture and his easy vocal delivery have made him a much-imitated performer, and for good reason. –DV

Country Music Hall of Fame Series / MCA   1991
Tillman had his biggest hits in the late 40s while recording for Columbia, but these WWII-era sides for Decca show him as a leader of a Texas dance band that's not afraid to mix it up with some jazz playing. Moon Mullican plays piano on a number of these sides. –BM

☆ **The Best of Floyd Tillman / CBS**
Contains his classics, such as "Slippin' Around" and "Gotta Have My Baby Back." Wait for this one; with Columbia reissuing much of its vintage country material, this stuff has got to appear on CD in some form. (Come on guys!) –RL

AARON TIPPIN   b 1958

Traditional country. This South Carolina singer can sing traditional country and hillbilly blues when he wants to. His *Read between the Lines* and *You've Got to Stand for Something* albums give a good flavor of this sound-different talent. –DV

○ **You've Got to Stand for Something / RCA**   1991
A debut album by a solid singer/songwriter from South Carolina. –MH

Read between the Lines / RCA   1992
A good followup by this popular hatless hillbilly. –MH

KAREN TOBIN

Country. Tobin worked in the Los Angeles-area country bars in the late 80s as half of the country duo Crazy Hearts (cf. Enigma's *A Town South of Bakersfield II* anthology) before signing a solo deal with Atlantic in 1991. Her debut album offers contemporary traditional country tunes. –MH

○ **Carolina Smokey Moon / ATLANTIC**   1991
An impressive debut from this California-based traditional country singer. –MH

MERLE TRAVIS   1917-1983

Instrumental. As satisfying as it must have been for Merle Travis to be voted into the Country Music Hall of Fame, doubly satisfying it must have been for him to see both Doc Watson and Chet Atkins (a couple of pretty fair guitar pickers) name sons after him. As a guitarist and songwriter, Travis is unsurpassed in the business; he's one of the few to have an instrumental style named after him — "Travis picking" — putting him in the elite company of Earl Scruggs and the Carter Family. Travis learned his distinctive 3-finger-style guitar from fellow Kentuckians Mose Rager and Ike Everly (father of Phil and Don), and he transferred the banjo roll to the guitar. Travis style uses the thumb to play the bottom notes of a chord individually, while playing the melody on the higher strings with the index finger and occasionally the third finger. The result is a constant motion and flow of the lower notes, while the melody floats on the top. The influence of this style can't be overstated: super-picker Chet Atkins has acknowledged his debt to Travis.
Before the war, Travis was a member of two important bands: the Georgia Wildcats and the influential Browns Ferry Four, with Grandpa Jones and the Delmore brothers, Alton and

Rabon. After his discharge from the Marine Corps, he had numerous hits, self-written or with others, including "Divorce Me C.O.D.," "So Round, So Firm, So Fully Packed," "Smoke, Smoke, Smoke That Cigarette," "Dark As a Dungeon," and "Sweet Temptation." In 1947 he wrote and recorded "Sixteen Tons" and watched Tennessee Ernie Ford eight years later make it perhaps the blockbuster hit in the history of country music. Country music is so much richer thanks to multi-talented Merle Travis. –DV

☆ **Walkin' the Strings / CAPITOL**   1960
Mostly instrumental. A classic of finger-style guitar. –RL

★ **The Best of Merle Travis / RHINO**   1983
The emphasis here is on Travis's novelty vocals and songwriting, rather than his guitar. –RL

Travis Pickin' / CMH
Until his Capitol Records instrumental recordings become available again, this is one for guitar buffs to go for. –RL

RANDY TRAVIS   b 1959

Traditional country. Contemporary superstar Randy Travis is a neo-traditionalist swimming against the tide. In a time when the distinction between country and pop has all but disappeared, this man with the expressive and smooth baritone provides a link with country music tradition. Polite, unhip, and respectful, he merely records beautiful songs, some of which ("On the Other Hand," "Forever and Ever, Amen," and the exquisite "He Walked on Water") should become classics. Enough fans apparently revere the traditional style: Travis's *Storms of Life* went gold faster than any other debut album in country history. His *Heroes and Friends* album (featuring duets with George Jones, Merle Haggard, Tammy Wynette, and Roy Rogers) shows us clearly Travis's taste and reverence for the past. He is an oasis to fans of the traditional country sound. –DV

☆ **Storms of Life / WARNER / BB 85**   1986
His first and best album. Astonishing Frizzell-style pipes, excellent material, and sympathetic production. Easily the most impressive country debut of the 80s. –MH

Always & Forever / WARNER   1987
This one stayed at the top of the country charts for 10 *months*. Well, of course he was huge. If you got songs as good as "Forever and Ever, Amen" you'd be a star too. –BM

Old 8x10 / WARNER   1988
On a par with *Storms of Life*, *Old 8x10* lacks the monster hits of his debut but wears just as well. When Travis sings of love, he doesn't mean romance; there's a permanence in his voice that sounds like settling down. –BM

Heroes and Friends / WARNER   1990
Singing with George Jones and others. –MH

High Lonesome / WARNER   1991
With young whippersnappers like Clint Black and Garth Brooks breathing down his neck, Travis realized he needed to be more than just a pretty voice. On *High Lonesome* he proved he could write, too, helping pen five of the album's ten songs, including "Forever Together" for his manager-turned-wife Lib Hatcher, and the country-gospel "I'm Gonna Have a Little Talk," sung a cappella with Take 6. –BM

TRAVIS TRITT   b 1963

Traditional country. This Marietta, GA, native's first album, *Country Club*, did well, with the title song reaching the top ten on the charts. His *It's All About to Change* album sold a million copies and resulted in a Grammy nomination. He's had consecutive #1 singles, "Drift Off to Dream" and "Here's a Quarter." –DV

Country Club / WARNER
The debut for this singer, with a rougher and more soulful edge than most graduates of the current country class. –MH

○ **It's All About to Change / WARNER**   1991
Tritt's highly acclaimed second album. –MH

ERNEST TUBB   1914-1984

Traditional country. The incomparable Ernest Tubb ("E. T." to all who knew him) became a legend as much for what he was personally as for the half-century career that stretched from his first radio date in 1932 to his death in 1984. Though other singers with better voices and more raw musical talent have come and gone, none has inspired greater love of the fans over six decades. Along with such performers as Jimmie Rodgers, Roy Acuff, Bill Monroe, Hank Williams, Lefty Frizzell, and George Jones, E.T. is country music personified. Tubb was among the first of the honky-tonk singers and the first to achieve national recognition. His first recording was "The Passing of Jimmie Rodgers," a tribute to his hero. His long association with Decca began with "Blue Eyed Elaine" in 1940. Three years later his self-penned "Walkin' the Floor over You," a country classic, was a hit, leading to the Opry, movie roles, and stardom. In 1947 he opened his Nashville record store and began the "Midnight Jamboree," which followed the Opry on WSM and advertised the shop while showcasing stars and those on the rise.

Over the years, Tubb toured widely with his Texas Troubadours, pressing the flesh with fans after shows that featured his many hits, including "Slippin' Around," "Two Glasses Joe," "Tomorrow Never Comes," "Drivin' Nails in My Coffin," "Rainbow at Midnight," "Let's Say Goodbye Like We Said Hello," and "Driftwood on the River." In 1975, after 35 years with Decca/MCA, he was let go, the allegiance of company executives not matching that of his multitude of fans. Because of a lung disease Ernest Tubb had to rest in pain on a cot between takes, ending his career just as his hero Jimmie Rodgers had 50 years earlier. Quoting one of his album titles, Tubb left a legend and a legacy. –DV

Collection with Guests: Pt. 1 / STEP ONE   1987
A late-70s all-star tribute, whose guests include Marty Robbins, Loretta Lynn, Merle Haggard, Willie Nelson, and Conway Twitty, features the lean and likable Tubb's final strong vocal performance. –MH

The Ernest Tubb Story / MCA   1987
Honky Tonk Classics / ROUNDER   1987
A nicely varied selection of early Tubb recordings (not necessarily hits) from 1940-1954. –MH

☆ **Country Hall of Fame / CDL**
A great chronological retrospective that includes the original 1941 "Walkin' the Floor over You" and Tubb's Jimmie Rodgers imitation on "Mean Mama Blues," then moves up through the 40s and 50s. Great bands, featuring (among others) Billy Byrd and Leon Rhodes on guitar and Buddy Charlton on steel. –GB

Golden Favorites / MCA
Re-recordings of older material. Well done, but it would be better to have the original stuff. –GB

The Importance of Being Ernest / DL
A good album, representative of his later (50s and 60s) sound. Above-average song selections. –GB

Let's Say Goodbye Like We Said Hello / BEAR FAMILY
This 5-CD boxed set of Tubb's 1947-1953 recordings (all 115 of them) is arguably "most of the best" of E. T., including his hillbilly jive exchanges with Red Foley. –MH

TANYA TUCKER   ♭1958

Country rock, contemporary country. In 1972 thirteen-year-old Tanya Tucker had a hit with "Delta Dawn"; more than 20 years later this woman with the husky voice is a veteran of country, rock, and all that lies in between. With over 30 Top Ten hits and a few movie roles (*Jeremiah Johnson* and *Hard Country*), she sings with conviction and great experience. From the start, a renegade/bad-girl label was pinned on her, reinforced by her controversial material — "Would You Lay with Me (In a Field of Stone)" is an example — and her brush with rock music. Fans welcomed her return to mainstream country, where her unique voice and powerful stage presence have led to albums and singles that regularly reach the charts. –DV

Greatest Hits / CBS   1975
A teenager at the time of her first Billy Sherrill-produced Columbia hits (ca. 1975), Tucker aleady had a maturity and presence beyond her years. –MH

T.N.T. / MCA / BB 54   1978
Tucker rocks out on this steamy album. –MH

Tennessee Woman / CAPITOL   1990
Here's one Tennessee singer who is more fiery than most Nashville divas. –MH

What Do I Do with Me / CAPITOL   1991
Ballads belted by the best female country singer of her generation. –MH

The Best of Tanya Tucker / MCA
Later 70s material for the blooming of a belter, honky-tonk style. –MH

Girls Like Me / CAPITOL
A bad girl tries to go good in the 80s on a new label. –MH

Greatest Hits / CAPITOL
Tanya's second coming as commercial country queen, here with her 1986-1991 hits. –MH

Love Me Like You Used To / CAPITOL
A fully mature artist, uncompromisingly gritty in the sanitized new Nashville. –MH

Strong Enough to Bend / CAPITOL
More pop/country, but still Tanya. –MH

Greatest Hits / MCA
Strong charters from 1975-1980. –MH

CONWAY TWITTY   ♭1933

Traditional country. This fact says a lot: With over 50 #1 singles, Conway Twitty is at the top of the list, outselling all other artists in any genre. Starting in the rock & roll Elvis Presley mold, he charted high with "I Need Your Lovin'" and his self-penned "It's Only Make Believe" (1958). He appeared on major TV shows, including "American Bandstand" and the "Ed Sullivan Show." To give you an idea of his audience at that time, he appeared in six movies ("B" is too high a letter to describe them), including *Sex Kittens Go to College.* When his pop career waned in the mid 60s, he moved to country, gaining fame through appearances on the Opry and on TV shows, including "Hee Haw" and "Johnny Cash." In 1970 his signature tune, "Hello Darlin'," was a smash, and Twitty was a national star. His hit singles during the 70s are far too numerous to list, but they include "You've Never Been This Far Before," "Linda on My Mind," "This Time I've Hurt Her More Than She Loves Me," "I May Never Get to Heaven," and "Tight Fittin' Jeans." His duets with label-mate Loretta Lynn were also hits, among them "Lead Me On" and "Louisiana Woman, Mississippi Man." His #1 hits continued into the 80s, with "Ain't She Something Else" and "Between Blue Eyes and Jeans."

Twitty's done as well in his business interests, owning Twitty Bird Music and Twitty City, a sort of theme park that contains Twitty family homes. Not a bad dual career for the Mississippi native who was born Harold Lloyd Jenkins and who chose his professional name from Conway, AR, and Twitty, TX. Country fans are lucky that once he came over from pop, he stayed with us. –DV

☆ **Conway Twitty / MGM**   1965
One of early rock & roll's most soulful and dramatic singers — inspired by Elvis Presley, but with a country/gospel edge all his own. This includes his biggest hits, the self-penned "It's Only Make Believe," along with "Lonely Blue Boy" and the great gospel-tinged "I'll Try." –GB

Look into My Teardrops / DECCA   1966
A great version of "Almost Persuaded" that beats David Houston's #1 hit version all to hell. Twitty also cuts Webb Pierce with a searing "There Stands the Glass." Good covers of some George Jones songs too. –GB

☆ **Hello Darlin' / MCA / BB 65**   1970

Twitty's finest hour as a country singer and songwriter. The great title track, plus "Up Comes the Bottle" and "I'm So Used to Loving You." He's at his C&W vocal peak on this one, and almost all of the material is good — even forgive the inclusion of "Rocky Top." −GB

The Very Best of Conway Twitty / MCA   1978
Includes "Hello Darlin'" and "Linda on My Mind." −GB

Number Ones / MCA   1982
After moving from rock & roll to country, Twitty remained sensitive to criticism he might not be serious, rarely deviating from the standard three-chord country song for about his first decade in the format. This package, which selects material almost randomly from 1975-1981, does a good job of showing a Twitty more willing to experiment, particularly with the soulful "Don't Take It Away" and the dramatic "I May Never Get to Heaven." −TR

Conway Twitty's #1's ... / WARNER   1988
Conway Twitty's #1's: The Warner Years. This greatest-hits set shows (with the exception of "The Rose") an artist in command of his own performance, with a clear grasp on quality material and a strong sense of powerful arrangements. Diverse and engaging. −TR

Making Believe / MCA   1989
A reunion of early 70s hitmakers (Twitty and Loretta Lynn), still in fine form. −MH

Conway Twitty Sings / DECCA
Includes his first country hit, Liz Anderson's "Guess My Eyes Were Bigger Than My Heart," and a version of "Truck Drivin' Man" that could duke it out with Buck Owens's and win. −GB

★ **The Very Best of Conway & Loretta / MCA**
Lust and guilt, and stunning soulful harmonizing by Twitty and Loretta Lynn from the early to mid 70s. Stupendous country vocalizing in a honky-tonk vein. −MH

UNCLE WALT'S BAND

Progressive country. An eclectic acoustic band from Austin, this group features tight harmony and fine original songs. −CW

○ **An American in Texas Revisited / SUGAR HILL**
Compilation of *An American in Texas* (1980), and *Live* (1982). The band members are well suited to one another. Walter's vocals are great. −CR

The Girl on the Sunny Shore / SUGAR HILL
This is a compilation of a 1975 release (*Uncle Walt's Band*) and a 1988 release (*6-26-79*). Very good. Features some great vocals and Champs's great fiddle. −CR

FRANK WAKEFIELD

Instrumental. One of the chief experimenters with the mandolin, Frank Wakefield played straight bluegrass with a number of well-known bands, including Red Allen and the Greenbriar Boys. Based in Saratoga Springs, NY, he remains one of the all-time innovators on the mandolin. −DV

Frank Wakefield / FLYING FISH
Top-notch bluegrass with the Good Ol' Boys. −CR

○ **Frank Wakefield with Country Cooking / ROUNDER**
A fine bluegrass album. Wakefield is backed by Country Cooking, featuring Peter Wernick, Tony Trischka, Russ Barenberg, and Kenny Kosek. Hear them before they became known. −CR

JERRY JEFF WALKER   b 1942

Progressive country. Born Paul Crosby in upstate New York, Walker travelled the country in the 60s, playing folk music, and finally settled in Austin. In 1966 he formed Circus Maximus, a rock group. He went solo, writing "Mr. Bojangles," a song that hit the Top Ten for the Nitty Gritty Dirt Band in 1970. His good-natured approach to country-style music has created a loyal following. −DV

● **Driftin' Way of Life / VANGUARD**   1969
A beautifully simple album of country-flavored original songs, mostly from the point of view of the sentimental roustabout. This great record sounds as though the players just went in,

knocked it off, and hit the road. Classic. Re-released last year on CD. −RM

Jerry Jeff Walker / ELEKTRA   1972
Kind of folksy, featuring David Bromberg. −RG

Viva Terlingua / MCA / BB 160   1973
The Lost Gonzo spirit settles in. −RG

○ **Ridin' High / MCA / BB 119**   1975
Progressive country at its most fun. −RG

A Man Must Carry On / MCA   1977
An interesting mix of live material, spoken word, studio recordings, and stereo chickens. −RG

Live from Gruene Hall / RYKODISC   1989
A solid comeback, more mainstream country-ish. −RG

STEVE WARINER   b 1954

Contemporary country. One of country's most versatile performers, Wariner has gone seemingly unnoticed for each of his skills: as a vocalist, guitarist, and songwriter.
Wariner grew up in suburban Indianapolis, interested in the Beatles on the radio and Chet Atkins and George Jones, the artists his father listened to most frequently. He started playing music in his dad's band, and by his high school years, he was playing local clubs. At age 17, Wariner caught the ear of Dottie West, who persuaded him to join her band, and in that position he ended up playing bass on her classic "Country Sunshine."
Wariner moved on to work as a sideman for Bob Luman and signed with RCA Records in 1976. His career developed slowly — he didn't put out an album until 1982 — and in the beginning, the low-tuned guitars and wide range of his singles brought frequent comparisons to the early Glen Campbell hits.
Gradually, Wariner took more personal direction in his recording career, and his albums became progressively more guitar-oriented as well as both more adventurous musically and more insightful lyrically. −TR

Steve Wariner / RCA   1982
RCA waited until they had a veritable greatest-hits package before releasing Wariner's first album. Bright arrangements with lots of dovetailing instruments. And Wariner shows off a substantial vocal range. −TR

It's a Crazy World / MCA   1987
Wariner's in charge vocally and seems to glide through the album effortlessly. He's received more responsibility for his own direction and — with one or two exceptions — has upgraded every aspect of his record, particularly in song selection and musicianship. −TR

○ **I Am Ready / ARISTA**   1991
Wariner, a master of the subtle touch, builds this album's impact quietly and methodically, with songs like Bill Anderson's "The Tips of My Fingers" and Wariner's own "Like a River to the Sea." "Leave Him out of This" is a masterpiece of smoldering intensity, its raging anger and pain barely held in check. The only time Wariner lets it loose is at the end, where he locks his guitar in mortal combat with Mark O'Connor's fiddle in the cathartic "Crash Course in the Blues." −BM

DOC WATSON   b 1923

Old-time, traditional country. In this half of our century there have been three preeminently influential guitar players: Merle Travis, Chet Atkins, and Arthel "Doc" Watson, a flat-picking genius from Deep Gap, NC. Unlike the other two, Watson was in middle age before gaining any attention. Since 1960, though, when Watson was recorded with his family and friends in Folkways' *Old Time Music at Clarence Ashley's*, people have remained in awe of this gentle blind man who sings and picks with a pure and emotional authenticity. The present generation, folkies and country pickers alike, including Ricky Skaggs, Vince Gill, the late Clarence White, Emmylou Harris, and literally hundreds of others, acknowledge their great debt to Watson. Watson has provided a further service to country/folk by his encyclopedic knowledge of many American traditional songs.

While Merle Travis and Chet Atkins started on acoustic guitars and moved to electric, before Watson's "discovery" during the folk revival in the early 60s, he played electric in a local all-purpose band that played current rock, swing, country, and of course folk music. He gained recognition gradually, first from the *Clarence Ashley* album, which led to a rave performance at the Newport Folk Festival in 1963. Folkways soon recorded an album of Watson, followed in 1964 by a series of albums by Vanguard, nearly one a year through the decade. No sooner had interest in folk music waned than Watson was back in great demand because of the three-disc *Will the Circle Be Unbroken*, a watershed album in 1972 that was created by the Nitty Gritty Dirt Band. It featured Watson, Merle Travis, Roy Acuff, and a Who's Who of country greats.

Merle, Watson's son and a talent in his own right, began appearing with his father regularly. The result was good enough for them to win two Grammys for traditional music, in 1973 and 1974. Father and son played beautiful music together for over fifteen years, until Merle died on the family farm in 1985, the victim of a tractor accident.

Watson continues with his appearances, showcasing his beautiful voice, his great instrumental talent, and his mastery of traditional material. He is an American treasure. –DV

★ **The Doc Watson Family / FOLKWAYS**   1963
The most traditional performances of Watson and such family members as fiddler Gaither Carlton. This is as authentic as country music gets. –MH & DV

☆ **Doc Watson / VANGUARD**   1964
His first Vanguard album, ca. 1964. Warm vocals, influential guitar, harmonica, and old-time banjo. –MH

Southbound / VANGUARD   1966
Watson's second Vanguard album and the debut of son Merle on second guitar. –MH

○ **Treasures Untold / VANGUARD**
Newport Festival performances, including four guitar duets with Clarence White. –MH

On Stage (Featuring Merle Watson) / VANGUARD   1971
A fine live album with Watson's son Merle. –MH

Essential Doc Watson / VANGUARD   1973
Fine 60s Newport Festival performances. –MH

Riding the Midnight Train / SUGAR HILL
A bluegrass album with Nashville super-pickers Sam Bush, Mark O'Connor, and Bela Fleck. These are the last recordings of Merle Watson. –MH

On Praying Ground / SUGAR HILL   1990
Down-home gospel. –MH

My Dear Old Southern Home / SUGAR HILL   1991
A Grammy nominee with sentimental songs. –MH

Ballads from Deep Gap / VANGUARD
Fine traditional songs, old ballads, and more. –MH

Sings Songs for Little Pickers / SUGAR HILL
Children's songs. –MH

Down South / RYKODISC
More fine Vanguard tracks. –MH

Guitar Album / FLYING FISH
Instrumentals. –MH

Old-Timey Concert / VANGUARD
Wonderful performances w/ Fred Price and Clint Howard. –MH

○ **Watson Family Tradition / ROUNDER**
Austere beauty, ancient ballads, and rough string-band sounds. Joining in are mother Annie Watson, wife Rosa Lee Watson, father-in-law Gaither Carlton, brother Arnold Watson, and son Merle Watson. The unpolished roots of Doc Watson. –MH

GENE WATSON   b1943

Traditional country. Though he can sing honky-tonk, Gene

Watson has made a reputation for soulful ballads in the classical country tradition. After working as an auto-body man, he finally had success with "Love in the Hot Afternoon," which as a single and as his debut album did well in 1975. His hits have been steady since then, with "Farewell Party," "Got No Reason Now for Going Home," "Nothing Sure Looked Good on You," and "Memories to Burn." Watson is a vocal stylist of considerable talent. –DV

Back in the Fire / WARNER   1989
His comeback album, rife with Watson's trademark hard balladeering. –MH

○ **Greatest Hits / CAPITOL**
In the 70s, Watson (along with Moe Bandy) tended the honky-tonk flame whilst others emulated Kenny Rogers. –MH

Honky Tonk Crazy / CBS
Fine as always. –MH

Old Loves Never Die / MCA
Sudsy weepers and plangent pipes. –MH

KEVIN WELCH

Country. Singer/songwriter from Oklahoma who made his name as a writer of hits for the Judds, Ricky Skaggs, Gary Morris, Moe Bandy, Don Williams, and others before bringing the fully realized characters of his songs to his own recordings in 1990. Though based in Nashville, Welch's music claims kinship with the songwriting style of Texans like Joe Ely and Butch Hancock. –BM

○ **Kevin Welch / REPRISE**   1990
Welch's songs sprawl out like great open flatlands, mixing elements of folk, country, and rock in a captivating way. Welch himself — half-singing, half-speaking songs such as "Hello, I'm Gone" and "Some Kind of Paradise" — comes off as a cross between a renegade storyteller and a heartland romantic. –BM

KITTY WELLS   b1919

Traditional Country. One of the few country stars born in Nashville, Kitty Wells (born Muriel Deason) had a string of hits from the 50s to the early 70s that earned her the title "Queen of Country Music." She made her radio debut on Nashville's WSIX, where she met her future husband, Johnnie Wright of Johnnie and Jack. She began touring as part of Johnnie and Jack's show; Wright gave her the stage name, taken from a folk song called "I'm A-Goin' to Marry Kitty Wells." Wells recorded unsuccessfully for RCA before switching to Decca, where she hit with 1952's "It Wasn't God Who Made Honky Tonk Angels," a response to Hank Thompson's "The Wild Side of Life." Its controversial pre-feminist lyrics, which blamed unfaithful men for creating unfaithful women, paved the way for Loretta Lynn and Tammy Wynette and established Wells as the first major female country star. Wells recorded a number of answer songs and remakes, but she got top-notch original material as well, including some of Harlan Howard's earliest hits. She joined the Grand Ole Opry in 1952 and was elected to the Country Music Hall of Fame in 1976. –BM

☆ **Country Music Hall of Fame Series / MCA**   1991
This 16-track overview is hardly complete (Wells issued more than 400 singles for MCA between 1952 and 1973), but it's got the essentials: "It Wasn't God Who Made Honky Tonk Angels," "I Can't Stop Loving You," "Heartbreak U.S.A.," etc., all sung with the thin Tennessee vibrato that made Wells famous. –BM

PETER WERNICK

Instrumental. Pete Wernick is a founding member and banjo player for Hot Rize, a progressive bluegrass group from Colorado. –DV

○ **Dr. Banjo Steps Out / FLYING FISH**
Wernick steps out on this one and explores new ground. Not a Hot Rize album. –CR

DOTTIE WEST   1932-1991

Country-pop. Dottie West had a successful career singing music that ranged from traditional to country-pop to TV commercials. "Here Comes My Baby" was a huge hit for her in 1964 and led to a Grammy. She appeared in movies, wrote more than 400 songs, made commercials, recorded hit duets with Jim Reeves, Don Gibson, and Kenny Rogers ("A Lesson in Leaving"), and was a country beauty queen. In 1991, while en route to the Opry, where she was a member of the regular cast, she was killed in an auto accident. For the two previous years, she had gone through personal bankruptcy and had seen her personal belongings auctioned off by the IRS. A happier end should have come to this veteran performer. She is missed. –DV

○ **A Legend in My Time / RCA**
Sparse instrumentation on a 1970 reissue of sad ballads: "Don't You Ever Get Tired of Hurting Me" and "There Goes My Everything." –BC

Special Delivery / UNITED ARTISTS   1979
With her career revitalized by the duets with Kenny Rogers, West takes a new tack. Her "Country Sunshine" is replaced with country-funk and a touch of melancholy. –TR

THE WHITES

Traditional country, gospel. Originally a traditional country/bluegrass group known as the Down Home Folks, this family band consists of father Buck and daughters Cheryl and Sharon. Close harmony and exceptional instrumentation (Buck is an extraordinary mandolin player) are their trademark. In recent years, gospel has dominated their material. Sharon and her husband Ricky Skaggs won a Country Music Association Award for the duet "Love Can't Ever Get Better Than This." The Whites were the Gospel Group of the Year in 1989. –DV

○ **Greatest Hits / CURB**
Early 80s sweet harmony from dad and his daughters. –MH

KEITH WHITLEY   1955-1989

Traditional country, progressive country. Keith Whitley and Ricky Skaggs started at the top in show business when, as teenagers, they went on the road with Ralph Stanley's bluegrass band. Whitley could sing pure country and honky-tonk. He lived the fast life and died young. Wife Lorrie Morgan and he sang together. "Till a Tear Becomes a Rose" was a posthumous creation, with Whitley's voice layered over Morgan's. –DV

☆ **A Hard Act to Follow / RCA**
The last album released during Whitley's life. Some stunning White soul balladeering and an ironic album title, given the plethora of Whitley wannabees recently adrift on country radio. –MH

Don't Close Your Eyes / RCA / BB 121 /   1989
More heartfelt. Artist and producer focus on good songs and piquant performances. –MH

I Wonder Do You Think of Me / RCA   1989
Recorded shortly before his death, the bounty of drinking songs provides a morbid weight to a generally excellent collection. –MH

Greatest Hits / RCA   1990
Whitley started singing bluegrass with Ralph Stanley, drew great inspiration from Lefty Frizzell and Merle Haggard, and developed an incomparably smooth, melismatic vocal style. The best balladeer of his generation. –MH

Kentucky Bluebird / RCA   1991
A posthumous collection of previously unreleased performances. –MH

SLIM WHITMAN   ♭1924

Traditional country. Otis Dewey "Slim" Whitman became popular nationwide in the early 80s with his cable TV ads

featuring his remarkable voice. Extraordinarily popular in England ("Rose Marie" was #1 for eight straight weeks in 1955), he specializes in slow, romantic songs showcasing his flexible voice that changes easily to falsetto. He may be the only contemporary yodeler who sells scads of records. –DV

○ **Best of Slim Whitman (1952-1972) / RHINO**

THE WHITSTEIN BROTHERS

Traditional country.

☆ **Old Time Duets / ROUNDER**
Here the brothers return to their pure classic duet sound, with only mandolin and guitar. –CW

★ **Rose of My Heart / ROUNDER**
First album, heavily influenced by the Louvin Brothers. –CW

Trouble Ain't Nothin' but the Blues / ROUNDER
Second set — more modern sound. –CW

THE WILBURN BROTHERS

Traditional country. As members of the larger Wilburn Family group (mother, father, elder brothers, sister), nine-year-old Teddy (b 1931) and ten-year-old Doyle (b 1930 - d 1982) appeared on the Opry in 1940; thirteen years later, when they had grown up, they became part of the Opry's regular cast. With Jim and Jesse McReynolds and Bobby and Sonny Osborne, the Wilburns continue the tradition of brother duets in country music. Their wide choice of material is shown by the traditional "Knoxville Girl," a hit in 1959, and the more modern sound of "Hurt Her Once for Me" (1966). –DV

Carefree Moments / VL
Their sometimes slick "Nashville Sound" recordings and tendency to double-track the vocals sometimes obscure the fact that these guys are one of the great brother duets in C&W. When they keep it straight, as in the rockabilly-esque "Cry Baby Cry" here, they can hold their own with anyone. –GB

Retrospective / MCA
A nice overview of the Wilburn Brothers' smooth Decca hits of the 50s and 60s. –MH

DON WILLIAMS   ♭1939

Traditional country. Known as the "gentle giant," Don Williams is known for the trademark rolled-brim hat that was a prop he used when appearing in *W. W. and the Dixie Dance Kings* (1975). His easygoing personality and laidback baritone vocals have produced many hits, among them "You're My Best Friend," "'Til the Rivers All Run Dry," "Amanda," "Some Broken Hearts Never Mend," and "I Believe in You," the last becoming a hit on the pop charts. His songs are among the prettiest and easiest-to-listen-to in country music. –DV

I Believe in You/Especially for You / MCA   1981
Two early (1980-1981) collections for the price of one. Contains the gem "Lord, I Hope This Day Is Good." –HD

Cafe Carolina / MCA   1984
Williams has a very identifiable core sound, but occasional subtle differences can seem like major alterations. Here he recruits sax player Jim Horn, and while Horn doesn't play on every track, his mere presence provides a fresh change. –TR

○ **20 Greatest Hits / MCA**
A good overview of hits by this gentle, mellow stylist. Contains "Say It Again" and "I Believe in You." –HD

Prime Cuts / CAPITOL   1989
Williams released four greatest-hits albums for MCA, so this is the fifth of his career. The R&B flavor of "Heartbeat in the Darkness" shakes up his approach. Much of the remainder is a thing of sparsely scored beauty. –TR

HANK WILLIAMS JR   ♭1949

Country rock, traditional country. Hank Williams Jr's 1966 recording of "Standing in the Shadows (Of a Very Famous Man)" told us how tough it is to be the son of country music's greatest legend. Up to this point, this enormous talent in his own right had made something of a career doing his father's old songs, and doing them well. When in the mid 70s he embarked on his own musical journey, with his own sound of country, country/rock, and rockabilly, he attracted a following that would have astonished even his famous father. In 1975 he left Nashville for Alabama to prepare the *Hank Williams Jr and Friends* album, the first of his unique Southern-rock albums. In spite of a terrible climbing accident in Montana, Williams went on to bigger and more frequent hits. When "My Rowdy Friends" reached #1 in 1981, it was his sixth chart-topper. In the late 80s he was the biggest draw of any country music star or act, packing them in coast to coast, to the degree that he had eight albums on the *Billboard* charts simultaneously. Like his father, Williams is a cult figure, enjoying the limelight created by his own talent and opening for Monday Night Football over the past three years. –DV

Hank Williams Jr & Friends / POLYGRAM   1975
The breakthrough record of Williams's career. On his first mature record (made in his mid 20s), Williams teamed with Southern rockers Charlie Daniels, Toy Caldwell (Marshall Tucker Band), and Chuck Leavell (Allman Brothers Band), among others, for a session that opened his musical vistas to folk, blues, and rock, and incidentally introduced his mature persona in songs like "Stoned at the Jukebox" and "Living Proof." –WR

14 Greatest Hits / POLYDOR   1976
Williams was a good, if conventional, country singer during the early years covered in this anthology (1966-1974). It includes 11 of his first 12 Top Ten hits, among them the #1s "Eleven Roses" and "All for the Love of Someone." –WR

Family Tradition / WARNER   1979
Williams returned to the upper reaches of the country charts with this album, his "outlaw" image, and songs like the title track, a #4 hit. –WR

Rowdy / WARNER / BB 82   1981
In 1981 Hank Williams Jr was one of the hottest acts in country music, starting the year with this album, which spawned the #1 hits "Texas Women" and "Dixie on My Mind" and the striking "Are You Sure Hank Done It This Way." –WR

○ **Greatest Hits / WARNER / BB 10**   1982
The biggest hits of Hank Williams Jr, 1979-1982, are among the best country music of the time: hard, tough, and (in the manner of one of country's great eccentrics) weird. –WR

Major Moves / WARNER / BB 10   1984
Williams topped the country charts with this album, largely on the strength of the raucous "All My Rowdy Friends Are Coming Over Tonight," though the title track and the caustic "Attitude Adjustment" were also hits. –WR

Greatest Hits - Vol. 2 / WARNER / BB 183   1985
A well-chosen collection covering 1983 to 1985. –WR

Greatest Hits - Vol. 3 / WARNER   1989
This chronicles Williams's ongoing 80s success, 1985-1989, featuring the #1 hits "I'm for Love," "Ain't Misbehavin'," "Mind Your Own Business," and "Born to Boogie." –WR

HANK WILLIAMS SR   1923-1953

Traditional country. It is impossible to overstate the importance of Hank Williams to country music. Incredibly, that statement is as true today as it was during the peak of his career more than 40 years ago.
Both as a composer and a recording artist, Hank Williams has few peers. This is doubly impressive when one realizes that Williams was dead before his 13th birthday and his entire recording career spanned barely six years. It is easy to lose sight of this in terms of the sheer number of greatest-hits left in his wake. Virtually every noteworthy country artist for the past 40 years has recorded an album of Hank Williams songs, while tunes like "Your Cheatin' Heart" and "Cold Cold Heart" have frequently crossed musical boundaries and enriched the careers of distinctively non-hillbilly artists such as Tony Bennett and Ray Charles.
Hank Williams's music is noteworthy for the quality of his

songs and the emotional intensity of his performances. Both are truly timeless. Throughout the years, owners of the Hank Williams catalog have subjected it to a variety of indignities, such as vocal and instrumental overdubbing, to tart up the recordings for the marketplace. Undoubtedly, Williams's records work best just as they were made, which, after many years, is how they are again being released. It is perhaps in Hank Williams's midnight home recordings, which feature only vocal and acoustic guitar, that one best hears the harrowing emotional intensity of his work. Williams came by it honestly. His short life was filled with physical pain, substance abuse, and enough backwoods pathos to fuel a dozen TV movies.
There is perhaps no greater indication of Hank Williams's appeal to new audiences than that 40 years after his death virtually every song he recorded remains in Polygram's active catalog. The label continues to spend as much time repackaging and promoting his music as it does their hottest country acts, whose names will be lost in the mists of time while the Hank Williams catalog is being transferred to DAT, or whatever format changes the 21st century brings. –HD

☆ **40 Greatest Hits / POLYGRAM**   1978
The ideal starting place; the title says it all. –HD

On the Air / POLYGRAM   1985
Collectors only. Radio show performances 1949-1952. –HD

Just Me & My Guitar / COUNTRY MUSIC FND.   1985
Passionate, unaccompanied, and intense. Listen to these after you are familiar with the hit versions. –HD

○ **I Ain't Got Nothin' but Time / POLYGRAM**   1985
The first volume of an in-depth chronological look (1946-1947), warts and undubbed demos and all. –HD

○ **Lovesick Blues / POLYGRAM**   1985
The second volume (1947-1948). –HD

First Recordings / COUNTRY MUSIC FND.   1986
The underside of the Hank Williams legend. An eye-opener, but get to know the hits first. –HD

○ **Lost Highway - Vol. 3 / POLYGRAM**   1986
The third in this series, with his 1948-1949 material. –HD

○ **I'm So Lonesome I Could Cry / POLYGRAM**   1986
Volume four, 1949. –HD

○ **Long Gone Lonesome Blues / POLYGRAM**   1987
Volume five, 1949-1950 –HD

○ **Hey Good Lookin' / POLYGRAM**   1987
Volume six, 1950-1951. –HD

○ **Let's Turn Back the Years / POLYGRAM**   1987
Volume seven, 1951-52. –HD

○ **I Won't Be Home No More / POLYGRAM**   1987
Volume 8. Hank Williams's life and music to its end on January 1, 1953. Contains "Your Cheatin' Heart." –HD

★ **Original Singles Collection ... Plus / POLYGRAM**   1990
A three-CD collection of all original singles as issued during his lifetime. Plus an undubbed solo version of "Tears in My Beer" without Hank Williams Jr's voice. –HD

KELLY WILLIS

Progressive country. Kelly Willis was heard in Austin by singer Nanci Griffith, leading to her debut album for MCA, *Well Travelled Love.* She visited 24 military bases nationwide as part of the Marlboro Music Military Tour. –DV

Well Travelled Love / MCA   1990
On her debut, this Austin country-rocker sings Texas-steel tunes and roisterous rockers with spirited assurance, but there's a natural tremble in her voice that makes her sound dangerous yet vulnerable. Willis is one of the few country singers with the disarming beauty to become a true sex symbol, and if she's the feminine response to all the hat acts, that's just fine. –BM

○ **Bang Bang / MCA**   1991
A young, lean country voice with an occasional rock edge. –RG

BOB WILLS & HIS TEXAS PLAYBOYS   1905-1975

Western swing. While he may not have invented Western swing (Milton Brown, Leon Selph, Ted Daffan, and Bill Boyd deserve some credit), Bob Wills defined the genre. Take fiddle-based old-time string-band music from the 20s and 30s, move it to a city such as Tulsa or Fort Worth, add jazz and blues and pop and sacred music, back it with strings and horns played by a dozen or so musicians, add an electric steel guitar along the way, and you have Western swing; and when you talk Western swing, you start with Bob Wills. Though the sound began in the 30s, the 40s were its heyday, with Bob Wills and his Texas Playboys filling dancehalls across the South. Wills picked his musicians carefully: bluesy crooner Tommy Duncan was the vocal lead, Leon McAuliffe played electric steel guitar (doing much to popularize it countrywide), and the great Eldon Shamblin played lead guitar. Wills, a fiddler himself, always featured one or two of the hottest around, including the incredible Johnny Gimble. One of country's best-known songs, "San Antonio Rose," was written by Wills and sold a million in 1940.

Wills and his Texas Playboys sold so well that they appeared in eight movies, Westerns in which the solitary singing cowboy was replaced by a hot-playing swing band. Superstardom was brief. The mania for Western swing ended by the 50s, and though Wills played dates (including Las Vegas) right through the 60s, and recorded occasionally, the heights of the 40s were never again reached.

In 1973 Wills called together a group of his best Playboys (plus Merle Haggard, one of his greatest fans) for one last recording session. In a wheelchair, Wills was present for the first day only, suffering a stroke and never regaining consciousness. This final album was titled *For the Last Time.* –DV

Tiffany Transcriptions - Vol. 1 / KALEIDOSCOPE
A series of radio transcriptions from post-WWII San Francisco. Looser than their studio recordings and presenting the hottest-ever Playboys in full gallop. All volumes of this series are uniformly excellent. Wills enthusiasts will want them all. –MH

Vol. 2 (Best of the Tiffany) / KALEIDOSCOPE
Vol. 3 (Basin St. Blues) / KALEIDOSCOPE
Vol. 4 (You're from Texas) / KALEIDOSCOPE
Vol. 5 (It's Fun Dancing To) / KALEIDOSCOPE
Vol. 6 (Sally Goodin) / KALEIDOSCOPE
The bluesy stuff is here. It's a good place to start with this series for an understanding of their range. –MH

Vol. 7 (Keep Knockin') / KALEIDOSCOPE
Vol. 8 (More of the Best) / KALEIDOSCOPE
Vol. 9 (In the Mood) / KALEIDOSCOPE   1991
☆ **Anthology / CBS**
These 24 essential songs from the 30s and 40s, in chronological order, show the evolution of one of American pop's most eclectic and adventuresome dancebands, the Texas Playboys. A cornerstone of any inclusive pop collection. –MH

Columbia Historic Edition / COLUMBIA
Fun and funky 30s sides. –MH

Fiddle / COUNTRY MUSIC FND.
A fascinating document of a range of fiddle styles, from Celtic-inspired "frontier" tunes to the genuinely swingin' stuff. –MH

Anthology (1935-73) / RHINO
A good overview of several decades of Wills's music. –MH

The Best of Bob Wills / MCA
A collection of post-Columbia sides. –MH

Bob Wills & Tommy Duncan / UNITED ARTISTS
Volume 5 of the United Artists *Legendary Masters Series,* perhaps the best of the pre-CD albums. –DV

JOHNNIE LEE WILLS

Western swing. Johnnie Lee Wills was younger brother to legendary Bob Wills and a member of the original Texas Playboys, the most famous Western-swing band in history.

Wills was a talent in his own right, playing tenor banjo in the Light Crust Doughboys, which became the Playboys and finally the Texas Playboys. When business was good, Bob Wills started a satellite band called Johnnie Lee Wills and his Boys. They had two hits, "Rag Mop" and "Peter Cottontail." And when business got bad, Johnnie Lee Wills retired and operated Tulsa's Stampede as well as a popular Western clothing shop. –DV

○ **Reunion / FLYING FISH**
Bob Wills's brother remained in Tulsa in the 30s and led a band that became a training ground for dozens of Western swing sidemen; many of the best are reunited here, in what were to be Wills's last recordings. –CW

TAMMY WYNETTE   b 1942

Traditional country. One of the major voices in country history, male or female, Tammy Wynette has had eleven #1 albums and thirty-five #1 singles (21 in a row) in a career that has produced at least two country standards: "Stand by Your Man" and "D-I-V-O-R-C-E," both from 1968. She and the great Loretta Lynn alternated in the 60s and early 70s as country music's most popular female singer. Along the way Wynette married George Jones, the singer's singer, resulting in duets as great as have been sung, including "We're Gonna Hold On," "Near You," and "Golden Ring." In spite of these song titles, Mr. and Mrs. Country Music labored through a turbulent relationship, beautiful harmony coming in the songs only, and were divorced in 1975. (A 1982 film, *Stand by Your Man*, tells of Wynette's heartaches.) Wynette remains in demand: she appears on a 1991 album by the British rap duo KLF. Her exceptional voice is as good as it's ever been. –DV

☆ **Your Good Girl's Gonna Go Bad / CBS**   1967
Her unmatched first album proves why she's the greatest female C&W "heart" singer. –GB

★ **Greatest Hits / CBS / BB 37**   1969
Her best and best-known hits from the 60s, including "Stand by Your Man" and "D-I-V-O-R-C-E." –GB

Greatest Hits - Vol. 3 / EPIC   1975
The best reason to include this package is to simply say that one greatest-hits album from Wynette just isn't enough. The lyrical and musical themes here are much the same as in the first package, but the quiet determination of "'Til I Get It Right" and the pure celebration of "My Man (Understands)" help broaden the picture of Wynette just a little. –TR

TRISHA YEARWOOD

Contemporary country. One of the first artists to benefit by association with Garth Brooks, not that she wouldn't have made it big on her own anyway. The product of Monticello, GA (the self-proclaimed deer capital of the world), Yearwood came to Nashville to study the music business at a local college before graduating to record-company receptionist, demo singer, and backup singer (for Brooks, among others). Her first single, "She's in Love with the Boy," went straight to #1, her first album went platinum, and she's hardly slowed down since. –BM

○ **Trisha Yearwood / MCA**   1991
An impressive debut that brought everybody to lend a hand: Vince Gill, Mac McAnally, keyboardist Al Kooper, and more. Garth Brooks cowrote two songs and helped sing one, the tentatively tender "Like We Never Had a Broken Heart." Yearwood's more at home with blue-collar romance than sweltering Texas nightlife, but her big Georgia range lets her sing just about anything, from the ballad "When Goodbye Was a Word" to Pat McLaughlin's saucy "That's What I Like About You." –BM

DWIGHT YOAKAM   b 1956

Traditional country, country rock. His highly successful debut album, *Guitars, Cadillacs Etc., Etc.,* a repackaging (with four new cuts) of a 1984 Oak album, showed the listening public that somebody different had arrived. Outspoken and self-assured, Yoakam mixes country oldies ("Ring of Fire" and a reprise of Johnny Horton's "Honky Tonk Man," his first Top Ten single) with his own country/rock and hard-country compositions. Platinums and golds and numerous chart-toppers later, he's still marching to his own drum while paying respect to his heroes along the way. He and Buck Owens collaborated on "Streets of Bakersfield," a song that gives you an accurate sense of what Dwight Yoakam's all about. –DV

Guitars, Cadillacs Etc., Etc. / WARNER / BB 61   1986
Who would have guessed when this album was released, with its uncompromisingly basic, honky-tonk approach, that it would not only be a success but would help move the country music industry back from its crossover ways of the early 80s to a new renaissance based on its most traditional sounds? Maybe Yoakam, who doggedly stuck to that approach and wrote a bunch of songs that fit in with covers like "Honky Tonk Man." –WR

Buenos Noches from a Lonely Room / REPRISE   1988
The first five cuts constitute a cold-blooded cycle that runs from possessive love to murderous rage with alarming quickness. The rest is subsequently a letdown but still gave Yoakam a couple of big hits in "I Sang Dixie" and "Streets of Bakersfield," a duet with Buck Owens. –BM

○ **Just Lookin' for a Hit / WARNER**   1989
A strong singles collection with a typically sarcastic title, paced by the duets with k. d. lang on "Sin City" and with Buck Owens (a match made in heaven) on "Streets of Bakersfield." –WR

If There Was a Way / REPRISE   1990
Yoakam's strongest studio album to date, with 14 songs (rare for Nashville). Includes the classic Yoakam/Roger Miller collaboration "It Only Hurts When I Cry." –BM

FARON YOUNG   b 1932

Traditional country. Versatile Faron Young is. In his younger days known as "the Hillbilly Heartthrob," he has managed to remain in the public eye for nearly 40 years, due to his musical talent, his entertaining personality, his numerous TV appearances (especially on Ralph Emery's "Nashville Now" show), and his many side interests, which have included movie acting and publishing. Young began *Music City News*, country music's dominant monthly magazine.
In 1951 Young signed with Capitol, and because of two quick hits ("Have I Waited Too Long" and "Tattle Tale Eyes") he became an Opry regular within the year. The next two years he spent in the army, entertaining the troops at home and abroad. His first major success came with "I've Got Five Dollars and It's Saturday Night" (1956), rounding out the 50s with "Sweet Dreams" and "Country Girl" (1959). In 1961 "Hello Walls," a Willie Nelson composition, became Young's best-known hit. He continued to sell well, singles and albums alike, through the 60s and 70s, with "Wine Me Up," "Another You," and "Crutches."
Young's strong, clear voice has been a perfect vehicle for his up-beat, let's-have-some-fun material. He's in the same league with Jimmy Dean in wit, candor, and downright entertainment as a guest on TV talk shows. The audience gets the feeling that in his life Young has followed the suggestion of "Live Fast, Love Hard, and Die Young" (a 1955 hit for him), except for the dying part, though no doubt he'd come up with some pun about even that, too. –DV

○ **The All-Time Great Hits ... / CAPITOL**   1966
The All-Time Great Hits of Faron Young. An interesting chronological retrospective that illustrates Young's transformation from a Hank Williams-inspired honky-tonk singer into a "sophisticated balladeer." The two find a happy medium in "Hello Walls," a great song (written by Willie Nelson). A fine performance by Young and one of the best country records ever. The earlier stuff, like "Live Fast, Love Hard," is fun too. –GB

STEVE YOUNG   b 1942

Progressive country, contemporary country. Alabama-raised singer/songwriter Young is best known as the writer of "Seven Bridges Road," a pop success for the Eagles in 1980. Since his acclaimed 1972 A&M debut, *Rock Salt & Nails*, Young has recorded a meager handful of albums, which garnered him cult status (Waylon Jennings called him "the second-best country singer, after George Jones"). "Lonesome, On'ry, and Mean" was the title track of a 1973 Waylon Jennings album, and writer Young was one of the leading poetic spirits of the "outlaw" alternative folk/country movement of the 70s. –MH

Rock Salt & Nails / CANYON   1969
A Japanese import worth looking for. Showcases Young's lonesome vocals on tunes by Hank Williams and Johnny Horton, plus memorable originals. Features Gram Parsons, Chris Hillman, and Gene Clark. –HD & CR

Seven Bridges Road / ROUNDER   1971
The title tune is this folkie's best work. –HD

Honky Tonk Man / MOUNTAIN RAILROAD   1975
Early sides by this Colorado folkie, surrounded by stellar, largely acoustic backing. A good album — a four-year layoff helped him hone his trade. –HD & CR

○ **Renegade Picker / RCA**   1976
A partially successful attempt by a major label to package Young. With Tracy Nelson, Buddy Emmons, and Johnny Gimble. "I Can't Be Myself" is a standout track. –HD

No Place to Fall / RCA   1978
Critically acclaimed album — this one and *Renegade Picker* were forerunners of the progressive country movement. –CR

Steve Young Live / WATERMELON   1991
A good collection of Young's music. The sound is rich and the audience is into the show. –CR

COUNTRY COLLECTIONS

☆ **Bristol Sessions/COUNTRY MUSIC**
These sessions launched the careers of the Carter Family and Jimmie Rodgers, and 21 other acts, including the Stoneman Family and Blind Alfred Reed. An amazing display of rural talent and the birth of country music. –WR

○ **Cowboy Songs on Folkways / FOLKWAYS**
Fifteen performers singing, bragging, and reciting poetry about the cowboy life. –RM

○ **Hillbilly Music - Thank God! - Vol. 1 / CAPITOL**   1989
An excellent double-disc compilation of country music from the late 40s to the mid 50s, featuring Buck Owens, Merle Travis, Faron Young, Tennessee Ernie Ford, and more. –WR

○ **Legends of Guitar - Country - Vol. 1 / RHINO**
Part one of an astutely compiled pair that showcases the kings of country guitar from the 30s to the 70s. Includes work from Jimmy Bryant, Speedy West, Chet Atkins, and Joe Maphis. Good liner notes on both sets. –JF

○ **Legends of Guitar - Country - Vol. 2 / RHINO**
Part two of this well-done collection. –JF

○ **Sixty Years of Grand Ole Opry / RCA**
A carefully selected collection of vintage RCA cuts by many key Opry stars from 1928 to the present. –CW

○ **Stars of the Grand Ole Opry - Vol. 1 / RCA**
Mediocre RCA cuts, emphasizing post-1950 stars. –CW
o Rose" by Bob Wills and "I Want to Be a Cowboy's Sweetheart" by Patsy Montana, among others. –MH

Urban Cowboy (Soundtrack) / ASYLUM   1980
Includes Joe Walsh, Bob Seger, Boz Scaggs, and Dan Fogelberg. Im portant soundtrack -- ED

When I Was a Cowboy / MORNINGSTAR
A compilation of classic original cowboy songs. –RM

BLUEGRASS

Of all the sub-styles within country music, bluegrass is the most distinctly different. The average country music fan who might listen to five average country songs — one each from honky-tonk, country rock, Western swing, country pop, and bluegrass — most likely would label the first four generically as "country" while specifying the last as "bluegrass." Despite common roots, bluegrass and mainstream country diverged during WWII, bluegrass following a path of tradition that has changed relatively little in the last half-century, in sharp contrast to country music's many paths that over the years have continually led into numerous and often far-from-home musical territories.

In the early 40s, country and bluegrass parted company, country moving on to honky-tonk, Western swing, rockabilly, and electrified instruments, with bluegrass remaining closer to its roots, especially to the string-band music of the 20s and 30s. Among these traditional string bands (at the time called "hillbilly") were Gid Tanner and the Skillet Lickers, the Possum Hunters, the Georgia Wildcats, and many others, most of which played traditional music in bands of three to six performing on guitars, fiddles, banjos, mandolins, and unamplified steel guitars (dobros) — instruments that were eventually adopted as the standard bluegrass configuration. While it's clear that bluegrass evolved from these bands, it remained for the great Bill Monroe (accurately called the "Father of Bluegrass"), with his band the Blue Grass Boys, to refine the old sound . The music itself does a much better job than words in showing how Monroe transformed this old music from a Model T to the bluegrass Cadillac V-8, with overdrive: no listener can mistake Mainer's Mountaineers, Roy Hall and His Blue Ridge Entertainers, or any other early 40s string band with Bill Monroe's Blue Grass Boys of the same period.

In 1945 Monroe formed the classic bluegrass band: Lester Flatt, guitar and vocal lead; Earl Scruggs, instrumental lead with the reinvented banjo; Chubby Wise, fiddler and cowriter of "Orange Blossom Special"; Cedric Rainwater, standup bass; and Bill. "Kentucky Waltz" and "Footprints in the Snow" were hits, and Monroe and his Boys were wildly popular. Though the term bluegrass wasn't commonly used until ten years later, the bluegrass sound attracted enough attention among country musicians to create numerous competitors to the Blue Grass Boys, by 1950 including Flatt & Scruggs (they had left Monroe after three years), Reno and Smiley, the Stanley brothers, Jim & Jesse, the Osborne brothers, and the Lilly brothers, to name only the prominent bluegrass bands from the "classical" period. Though none of these bands were Monroe soundalikes, they shared characteristics that have come to define bluegrass: the standard instruments (listed above) played acoustically, with the five-string banjo dominating; alternating instrumental solos (as in jazz bands); close harmony, whether with two, three, or four parts; and a tempo generally much faster than mainstream country's. These are only general characteristics, though, not rules, and they often have been ignored, even by the most conservative of traditional bluegrass bands; Bill Monroe allowed an accordion in early recordings, and that music was still bluegrass. Further, it's difficult to specify a characteristic content of bluegrass songs. To cite two extreme examples, Jim and Jesse in 1965 recorded an album of Chuck Berry songs (*Berry Pickin'*), while the Boston-based Charles River Boys bluegrassed the Fab Four in *Beatles Country*, also in the 60s. And both albums sound bluegrass — not classical bluegrass, but bluegrass nonetheless. Bluegrass and country often have shared the same song repertory, though bluegrass bands have shown more reticence at accepting the latest musical fads than have many of their country cousins.

But like mainstream country, bluegrass itself has evolved into sub-styles. These changes were all but assured when urban audiences discovered bluegrass during the urban folk-revival of the late 50s and early 60s. The nation may not have been prepared for Jethro Bodine, Granny, Ellie May, and TV's "Beverly Hillbillies," but they positively embraced the Flatt & Scruggs background music, as witnessed by "The Ballad of Jed Clampett" in 1963 becoming the first bluegrass song to hit #1 in the country charts. Then followed "Foggy Mountain Breakdown" by Earl Scruggs in the popular *Bonnie and Clyde* movie and "Dueling Banjos" in *Deliverance*. Bluegrass music, and especially the five-string banjo, had become so popular with a new and huge and urban audience that traditional bluegrass had to make way for variations. Bluegrass was divided: traditional bluegrass remained, for the lovers of the pure, original sound; and progressive bluegrass (often called "newgrass") was created. The rules for newgrass were more relaxed, allowing electric instruments, rock songs, and whatever else creatively fit within the confines of this new and malleable term. Newgrass doesn't mean worse, it just means different. The top-notch newgrass bands (Seldom Scene, Country Gentlemen, J. D. Crowe and the New South, New Grass Revival) by and large are vocally and instrumentally on the same plane as the traditional bluegrass bands. There's room for both.

— David Vinopal

EDDIE ADCOCK

Traditional, progressive bluegrass. Among the major-league

talent that emerged from the folk music scare of the late 50s were the Country Gentlemen, a DC-based quartet that introduced bluegrass to a generation of city folks and college

484

students, people who had never heard of Flatt and Scruggs or Bill Monroe or the Stanley Brothers. The Gentlemen, in playing the old bluegrass standards but playing them "different," were in a sense the first newgrass group. Adcock became their banjo player in 1959, and a player of distinction, whose style was as innovative as Don Reno's. Adcock's considerable talent spread to other country instruments when he left the Gentlemen in 1970. He has continued to perform his unique music to the present day, in the II Generation and other groups. –DV

And His Guitar / CMH   1975
Just Eddie and his guitar, no backup, and a very clean sound. Chet Atkins and Merle Travis-influenced. –CR

○ **Talk of the Town / CMH**
Backed by four women, Eddie is at his best here. The album features nice vocals. –CR

PAUL ADKINS & THE BORDERLINE BAND

Traditional bluegrass. They are a top-notch bluegrass band featuring Paul Adkins (guitar, vocals), Ron Pennington (mandolin, guitar), Ned Luberecki (banjo, guitar, bass, vocals), Fred Travers (dobro, vocals), and Robin Smith (bass vocals). They are fine musicians and deliver strong harmonies. –CR

○ **Reflections of Love / REBEL**
Everything on this CD is first-class. Fourteen songs dealing with all aspects of love. –CR

MIKE AULDRIDGE

Instrumental bluegrass. Formerly of Cliff Waldron's New Shades of Grass, Mike Auldridge has earned a well-deserved reputation as one of the great contemporary dobro players. In addition to cutting albums under his own name, he was featured in the Seldom Scene, a newgrass/traditional supergroup formed in 1971 by former Country Gentlemen mandolin player John Duffy. –DV

Mike Auldridge / FLYING FISH   1976
On this one, the bluegrass dobroist is joined by apt accompanists. –MH

○ **High Time / SUGAR HILL**
This great dobro picker plays here with Lou Reid and Michael Coleman. –MH

Treasures Untold / SUGAR HILL
More bluesy barrin'. –MH

AUSTIN LOUNGE LIZARDS

Progressive bluegrass. The Austin Lounge Lizards are a country bluegrass band out of Austin. The Lizards are Hank Card (guitar, vocals), Conrad Deisler (guitar, mandolin), Tom Pittman (banjo, pedal steel, vocals), Michael Stevens (bass, vocals), and Tim Wilson (mandolin, fiddle, vocals). After the first album, Paul "Tex" Sweeney (mandolin) and Kirk Williams (bass, vocals) replaced Stevens and Wilson. They are known for the humor in their songs and live shows. –CR

○ **Creatures from the Black Saloon / WATERMELON**   1984
This good, humorous record features "The Car Hank Died In" and "Anahuac," with Jerry Jeff Walker singing some vocals. The band plays a good blend of country and bluegrass. –CR

Highway Cafe of the Damned / WATERMELON   1988
Another good, solid, humor-packed CD featuring "The Highway Cafe of the Damned," "Industrial Strength Tranquilizer," "Ballad of Ronald Reagan," and more. –CR

Lizard Vision / FLYING FISH   1991
This very funny album was a Grammy nominee. It features the hit, "Jesus Loves Me." –CR

BUTCH BALDASSARI

Traditional bluegrass. Butch Baldassari is a member of the bluegrass band Weary Hearts. He is one of the better mandolin players in his field. –CR

○ **Old Town / REBEL**   1990
One of the finer bluegrass albums of 1990 — Butch Baldassari has five originals on the CD, plus strong material by Alison Krauss and Bill Monroe. Tom Adams (banjo) and Stuart Duncan (fiddle) are very good in support. –CR

E. C. AND ORNA BALL

Old-time, gospel. This fine old-time gospel singer and guitarist, Estil C. Ball (b 1913 - d 1978) hailed from Rugby, VA and performed with his wife Orna (b 1907) and the Friendly Gospel Singers. First recorded for the Library of Congress in 1938, Ball was recorded extensively in his later years by the County and Rounder labels. His lively, Travis-style guitar was an unusual element in traditional gospel singing. –MH

○ **E. C. Ball / ROUNDER**
This is old-time mountain gospel as good as it gets. Estil's guitar virtuosity and powerful baritone blend beautifully. –DV

BANJO DAN & THE MID-NITE PLOWBOYS

Traditional bluegrass. Traditional bluegrass band featuring Alan Davis (guitar, vocals), David Gusakov (fiddle, vocals), Dan Lindner (banjo, lead guitar, vocals), Peter Riley (bass vocals), and Andy Sacher (mandolin). –CR

○ **Banjo Dan ... / GREENER PASTURES**   1990
Banjo Dan & the Mid-Nite Plowboys is a good traditional bluegrass CD recorded in one take: 19 songs all solid and well played. This band might be unknown, but they're well worth checking out. –CR

RUSS BARENBERG

Progressive bluegrass. Russ Barenberg is a guitarist who played with the bluegrass band Country Cooking. He later went solo, playing a blend of jazz, funk, Latin, and bluegrass. –CR

Behind the Melodies / ROUNDER   1983
A very good cast: Tony Trischka, Andy Statman. –CR

○ **Halloween Rehearsal / ROUNDER**   1987
Combines his *Cowboy Calypso* and *Behind the Melodies*. –CR

Moving Pictures / ROUNDER   1988
The second choice, after *Halloween Rehearsal*. –CR

Cowboy Calypso / ROUNDER
A good album w/ Andy Statman and Jerry Douglas. –CR

BASHFUL BROTHER OSWALD

Instrumental bluegrass. Since 1938, Beecher Kirby's dobro has added the special sound that makes Roy Acuff's music unique, at the same time adding comedy through the Bashful Brother Oswald rube. Beecher Kirby has done much to popularize the dobro (unamplified resonator Hawaiian guitar) in mainstream country and bluegrass. –DV

○ **Brother Oswald / ROUNDER**
Roy Acuff's dobroist since the 30s, in a pleasant set of Hawaiian-inspired old-time country songs. –MH

BYRON BERLINE   b 194?

Instrumental bluegrass. This prodigy won his first fiddle contest at age ten. A much-in-demand session man, he appeared on the Dillards's *Pickin' and Fiddlin'* in 1964, an album that brought bluegrass to a new, urban audience. Byron Berline cofounded the Los Angeles-based Country Gazette, an influential bluegrass band, in the early 70s. He left the Gazette to form another group, Sundance. –DV

● **... And the L.A. Fiddle Band / SUGAR HILL**   1980
Put together three fiddles and some great acoustic bluegrass music and you have *Byron Berline & the L.A. Fiddle Band*, a great album. Guests are Vince Gill and John Hickman. –CR

Outrageous / FLYING FISH   1980
Berline has a strong cast featuring Dan Crary, Albert Lee, James Burton, and John Hickman. –CR

○ **Berline, Hickman, Crary / SUGAR HILL**   1981
Nice songs: "Bonapart's Retreat," "Turkey in the Straw." –cr
Night Run / SUGAR HILL   1984
Fine bluegrass. Pistol Pete, Forked River, Berline, Dan Crary, and John Hickman will knock you out. –cr
B-C-H / SUGAR HILL   1986
Eclectic. This one's my favorite. –cr
○ **Double Trouble / SUGAR HILL**   1986
Berline and John Hickman feed off each other's talents. Very smooth. –cr
Now They Are Four / SUGAR HILL   1989
You'll love "Kodak 1955." A must-have for Berline fans. –cr

NANCY BLAKE

Old-time. Nancy Blake has released albums with husband Norman Blake and solo. She is an accomplished musician whose musical styles include bluegrass, traditional, and classical. –cr
Blind Dog / ROUNDER   1988
Nancy and Norman Blake on traditional songs like "Wreck of the Old 197," "Black Mountain Rag," and a good cover of Woody Guthrie's "Grand Coulee Dam." –cr
Just Gimme Somethin' I'm Used To / SHANACHIE   1992
More pleasant parlottunes by Norman and Nancy Blake. Fine guitar from both, plus Norman's fiddle and Nancy's cello. –mh
○ **Grand Junction / ROUNDER**
A good debut album featuring Nancy Blake and her many instruments. –cr

NORMAN BLAKE   b1938

Old-time. Tennessee-born and Georgia-raised, Norman Blake is an unassuming vocalist, but an impressive multi-instrumentalist (guitar, mandolin, fiddle, dobro) who came to prominence in the 70s as one of the outstanding acoustic flatpickers of the Doc Watson school.
Beginning at the age of 16 with the Dixie Drifters, he quickly established a reputation for his instrumental skills and has worked with the banjoist Bob Johnson as the Lonesome Travelers, as a member of June Carter's touring band, as session player on Bob Dylan's *Nashville Skyline* (1969), in Kris Kristofferson's 70s road group, with John Hartford, and with the Nitty Gritty Dirt Band on *Will the Circle Be Unbroken* (1973). Norman also performs with wife Nancy. –mh & ed
Back Home in Sulphur Springs / ROUNDER   1972
Norman Blake and Tut Taylor (dobro), basic and pure. –cr
Blackberry Blossom / FLYING FISH   1974
Norman and Nancy Blake. A little less bluegrass with the addition of Nancy Blake's cello. –cr
○ **Fields of November / FLYING FISH**   1974
A first-class album. Tut Taylor, Charlie Collins, and Nancy Short come up strong. Features "Greycoat Soldiers," "Last Train to Poor Valley," and "The Fields of November." –cr
Live at McCabe's / TAKOMA   1976
Very good recofeatures "Nine Pound Hammer" and "Arkansas Traveler." Good sound. –cr
Whiskey Before Breakfast / ROUNDER   1976
Blake's best. He and Charlie Collins let their guitars do the talking. Perfect. –cr
Norman Blake and Red Rector / COUNTY   1976
On these 12 cuts, Blake and Red Rector (on mandolin) are backed by Charlie Collins and Roy Huskie Jr. –cr
Full Moon on the Farm / ROUNDER   1981
This album features Norman Blake and the Rising Fawn String Ensemble — James Bryan, Charlie Collins, and Nancy Blake. It has a nice, well-rounded feeling. –cr
Nashville Blues / ROUNDER   1984
Blake's vocals give this one more of an old-timey bluegrass feel. –hd

Bluegrass Music

Traditional — Partly a refinement of traditional string-band music and partly pure invention. Defined by Bill Monroe and his Blue Grass Boys in the 40s, it characteristically features banjo, guitar, mandolin, dobro, fiddle, and bass (Bill Monroe, Stanley Brothers, Lilly Brothers, Jimmy Martin).

Progressive — Often called "newgrass," these groups use the instrumentation of traditional bluegrass but with huge differences in new material and nontraditional style (Seldom Scene, Hot Rize, New Grass Revival).

— David Vinopal

Lighthouse on the Shore / ROUNDER   1985
Norman teams up with Nancy Blake, James Bryan, and Tom Jackson. Features "Hello Stranger," "President's Garfield's Hornpipe," and "Wildwood Flower." –cr
● **Original Underground Music / ROUNDER**
Original Underground Music from the Mysterious South includes deceptively simple acoustic string music featuring multiple mandolins, mandolas, cellos, fiddles, and guitars for a hauntingly beautiful yet old-timey feel. –hd & cr
Rising Fawn String Ensemble / ROUNDER
More memorable acoustic instrumental work. –hd
Slow Train through Georgia / ROUNDER
Modern and soulful bluegrass sound. –hd

NORMAN BLAKE w/TONY RICE

Traditional bluegrass. This duo represents two of the most important influences in the bluegrass revival of the 70s. Both Blake (b 1938) and Rice have been in-demand session players and represent near-perfection on their instruments — Rice on flat-top guitar and Blake on the guitar, mandolin, dobro, and fiddle. Blake's Rising Faun String Ensemble shows a love and refined taste for the old-time music. –dv
○ **Blake & Rice / ROUNDER**   1987
Underrated but sprightly. Two fleet-fingered acoustic guitar flatpickers flex their chops in these 14 cuts. –mh
Blake & Rice #2 / ROUNDER
More hot licks and backporch singing. –mh

BLUE ROSE

Traditional bluegrass. This band features the talents of Laurie Lewis, Cathy Fink, Marcy Marxer, Molly Mason, and Sally Van Meter. –cr
○ **Blue Rose / SUGAR HILL**   1972
This is the women's bluegrass version of Blind Faith. Cathy Fink, Laurie Lewis, Marcy Marxer, Molly Mason, and Sally Van Meter combine for a fantastic sound. This was a supergroup. Highly recommended! –cr

THE BLUEGRASS ALBUM BAND

Traditional bluegrass. This group features an all-star lineup including Tony Rice (guitar), J. D. Crowe (banjo), Doyle Lawson (mandolin), Bobby Hicks (fiddle), Todd Phillips (bass), and Jerry Douglas (dobro). –ed
○ **Bluegrass Album - Vol. 1 / ROUNDER**
The debut from this superstar bluegrass band. –cr
Bluegrass Album - Vol. 2 / ROUNDER   1973
A good followup. Perfection. –cr
Bluegrass Album - Vol. 3 / ROUNDER
They just do not put out a bad album. –cr
Bluegrass Album - Vol. 4 / ROUNDER
They get tighter as they go along. Any one of these records is gonna get you movin'. –cr

Bluegrass Compact Disc / ROUNDER
A full, classic bluegrass album. –CR
Bluegrass Compact Disc - Vol. 2 / ROUNDER
A collection of the group's first four releases. There are 21 songs in all. –CR

BLUEGRASS CARDINALS

Traditional bluegrass. Before founding the Cardinals, Kentucky banjo player Don Parmalee played with a California band, the Hillmen, and for nine years played background banjo for the "Beverly Hillbillies" TV show. The Bluegrass Cardinals are noted for their intricate harmonies and for Parmalee's exceptional picking. –DV

Livin' in the Good Old Days / CMH	1978

Twelve solid songs. –CR

Cardinal Soul / CMH	1979

Early sound. Good. –CR

○ **Live & on Stage / CMH**	1980

The double album has 29 songs. –CR

Sunday Mornin' Singin' / CMH	1980

One of your better gospel albums. –CR

Cardinal Class / SUGAR HILL	1983

A very good, solid, tight album. The Cardinals at their best. Highly recommended. –CR

Home Is Where the Heart Is / SUGAR HILL	1984

A good mix of music. Jerry Douglas guests. –CR

Shining Path / SUGAR HILL	1986

My favorite of their gospel releases. –CR
Welcome to Virginia / ROUNDER
Great vocals. –CR

GINGER BOATWRIGHT

Progressive bluegrass. Ginger Boatwright is a singer/songwriter and guitar player. Her musical style leans toward bluegrass with a country-rock influence. She was an original member of the Red, White & Blue(grass) band. –CR
○ **Fertile Ground / FLYING FISH**
An excellent album. Ginger Boatwright brings her great vocals from the Red, White & Blue(grass) band. She gets better with age. –CR

BOONE CREEK

Traditional bluegrass, progressive bluegrass. After playing with bluegrass bands that varied from ultraconservative (Ralph Stanley's) to more progressive (Country Gentlemen, J. D. Crowe & the New South), instrumental wizard Ricky Skaggs formed Boone Creek in 1977, a band that blended the traditional with the new. –DV
Boone Creek / ROUNDER
A fine album with great picking. –CR
○ **One Way Track / SUGAR HILL**
Jerry Douglas and Ricky Skaggs are outstanding. Tight, well-played bluegrass, including "In the Pines." –CR

ALISON BROWN

Bluegrass. Alison Brown is a fine picker of the banjo. She plays for Alison Krauss and Union Station, and she has released a record with Stuart Duncan. –CR

○ **Simple Pleasures / VANGUARD**	1990

A fine, well-produced CD featuring David Grisman, Mike Marshall, and Alison Krauss, plus some great banjo from Brown on this all-instrumental album. –CR

JAMES BRYAN

Traditional bluegrass. Bryan, from north Alabama, is considered to be the best traditional Southern fiddler playing today. –CW

☆ **First of May / ROUNDER**
This set includes a variety of unusual local tunes and old favorites. –CW

PAT BURTON & THE BRAY BROTHERS

Traditional bluegrass. Pat is a guitar player who teamed up with Nate and Harley Bray to play a country/bluegrass brand of music. –CR
○ **We've Been Waiting for This / FLYING FISH**
Burton teams with John Hartford, Vassar Clements, Harley Bray, and Frances Bray for some great bluegrass sounds. Pat tries for a "hit" on this album. –CR

CACHE VALLEY DRIFTERS

Progressive bluegrass. The Cache Valley Drifters are an eclectic bunch who are comfortable playing boogie, bluegrass, country, Grateful Dead, folk, and old timey music. Cyrus Clarke (guitar, vocals), Bill Griffin (mandolin, vocals), Tom Lee (string bass), and David West (guitar, vocals) are the members. –CR
New Cache Valley Drifters / FLYING FISH
Their debut album combines bluegrass with rock for a great sound. –CR

○ **Step Up to Big Pay / FLYING FISH**	1980

A great sophomore album. Good vocals and playing, with nice covers of John Prine's "Hello in There" and the Grateful Dead's "Cumberland Blues." –CR
Tools of the Trade / FLYING FISH
There is a lot of energy on this live album from McCabe's Guitar Shop. Very good! –CR

THE CHICKEN CHOKERS

Progressive bluegrass. The Chicken Chokers are a highly energetic band that plays music from string band to synthesizer. Chad Crumm (fiddle, synthesizer), Jim Reidy (banjo, ukelele, mandolin), Stefan Senders (banjo, guitar), Chip Taylor Smith (guitar, steel guitar), and Paul Strother (bass) make up this band. –CR

○ **Shoot Your Radio / ROUNDER**	1987

Old-time instrumentation, a pseudo-punk bad attitude, and a hilarious title-track rap from this short-lived but fun band from Boston. –MH
Old Time Music / ROUNDER
On this album, two avant-garde/old-time bands, the Chicken Chokers and the Horseflies, pushed the envelope of the new/old-time styles. –MH

VASSAR CLEMENTS   ♭1928

Instrumental bluegrass. In the company of Johnny Gimble and Mark O'Connor, Vassar Clements has been among the elite of contemporary sidemen fiddlers. He started in mainstream country and bluegrass, playing for Bill Monroe, Faron Young, and Jim and Jesse. With his virtuosity, he moved occasionally to progressive country, including a stint with the Earl Scruggs Revue. His technique and versatility are astounding. –DV

Crossing the Catskills / ROUNDER	1987

Tasty fiddling from one of the finest. –MH

○ **Hillbilly Jazz / FLYING FISH**	1987

Wonderful 70s swing (western and otherwise). W/ Vassar Clements, David Bromberg on guitar, and D. J. Fontana on drums, plus many more on this loose session. –MH

Grass Routes / ROUNDER	1991

This recent album shows why Clements is one of the greatest fiddlers in modern country music. –MH
The Bluegrass Session / FLYING FISH
The title tells the truth. –MH

BILL CLIFTON   ♭1931

Traditional bluegrass, traditional country. A pioneer in

bluegrass and traditional music, Bill Clifton was a prime mover in starting the Newport Folk Festival and the bluegrass festival phenomenon. Since the mid 50s he has assembled the best musicians on album after album. His sound over four decades has remained pretty much the same, uniquely and beautifully Clifton. –DV

○ **Bill Clifton & the Dixie Mountain Boys / COUNTY**

THE COUNTRY GAZETTE

Progressive bluegrass. In 1972, when the Flying Burrito Brothers broke up, the bluegrass segment of the band reformed, creating the influential Country Gazette. At their many festival shows, this California group performed a blend of traditional bluegrass and newgrass, gaining a reputation for vocal harmonies and instrumental excellence. Their *Traitor in Our Midst* album, their first, remains perhaps their best. –DV

Keep on Pushing / FLYING FISH
Fourteen great bluegrass cuts with Alan Munde. The Country Gazette's 20th year. –CR

THE COUNTRY GENTLEMEN

Traditional bluegrass, progressive bluegrass. In 1957, when the Country Gentlemen formed in the Washington, DC, area, their sound expanded the definition of "bluegrass"; they were progressive bluegrass before the term existed. The Gentlemen came along with the first wave of the folk-music revival and quickly made a name for themselves as a band who could not only play traditional material straight but who also brought Bob Dylan and contemporary country material into the genre. Because of their exceptional singing and virtuoso instrumentals, the Gentlemen attracted a broad audience, ranging from traditional country/bluegrass fans to folk and soft-rock lovers. Their earlier albums featured the remarkable quartet of Charlie Waller, guitar and lead vocal; Eddie Adcock, banjo; John Duffey, mandolin; and Tom Gray, bass. –DV

★ **Country Songs Old & New / FOLKWAYS**   1960
This is a reissue of the 1960 Folkways album that launched their career. Includes "The Little Sparrow," "The Long Black Veil," "Under the Double Eagle," and 13 other classic cuts. A magic album. –JME

One Wide River / RB   1987
Nice, but not so energetic or ambitious as other releases. –RW

○ **Folk Songs & Bluegrass / FOLKWAYS**   1988
Another essential 60s release. –RW

☆ **Sit Down Young Stranger / SUGAR HILL**   1988
A tremendous date; brilliant playing by Mike Aulridge. –RW

○ **River Bottom / SUGAR HILL**   1989
Great solos and harmonies, excellent compositions. –RW

○ **Award Winning / RB**
Outstanding session. –RW

Sound Off / RB
Good, with a more contemporary sound. –RW

DAN CRARY

Progressive bluegrass. Crary is among the "sons of Doc" who emerged in the 70s, taking Doc Watson's flatpicked guitar style a step further. The Kansas native was among the founders of the Bluegrass Alliance, and subsequently pursued a solo career while teaching speech communications in California. Recording for Sugar Hill and similar labels, Crary has carved a niche for himself as a distinctive interpreter of traditional material for acoustic 6- and 12-string guitars. He also records original compositions. He may be best known for his work with "Fiddler" Byron Berline and "Banjoist" John Hickman, who combined with Crary in a bluegrass-and-beyond trio that has been active for more than a decade. –MH

○ **Guitar / SUGAR HILL**   1983
The title leaves the erroneous impression that this is a solo set. Instead, it's an exciting blowing session featuring the cream

of the new generation of bluegrass players who emerged in the 80s — Sam Bush, Mark O'Connor, and Bela Fleck. But on selections ranging from a "Bill Monroe Medley" to a transcribed Mozart piano sonata, Crary and his guitar more than hold their own. –WR

J. D. CROWE & THE NEW SOUTH

Progressive bluegrass. In the late 50s, bluegrasser Jimmy Martin attracted a number of highly talented musicians to his Sunnysiders. One is J. D. Crowe, a Kentucky native who quickly made a reputation on the five-string banjo, initially as a first-rate interpreter of traditional bluegrass and then, with his band the New South, as a highly respected proponent of progressive — a blend of the old with modern country and rock, sometimes with electrified instruments. Rounder's 1975 album *J. D. Crowe and the New South* greatly influenced other progressive bluegrass groups. The band's personnel, in addition to the stellar picking of Crowe, included guitarist Tony Rice, Ricky Skaggs on mandolin and fiddle, and dobro player Jerry Douglas, all of whom went on to make big names in the business. –DV

☆ **J. D. Crowe & the New South / ROUNDER**   1975
A trailblazing album of "young blood" in bluegrass, with Ricky Skaggs and Tony Rice. Very influential. –MH

My Home Ain't in the Hall of Fame / ROUNDER   1978
Crowe, on banjo and baritone, moves closer to country in the company of Keith Whitley and Doug Jernigan. –MH

Somewhere Between / ROUNDER   1981
A hard-country album. Lovely ballads, with Lefty Frizzell-style vocals from Keith Whitley. –MH

Live in Japan / ROUNDER   1982
Spirited performances with Keith Whitley and the great mandolinist Jimmy Gaudreau. –MH

Straight Ahead / ROUNDER   1986
More or less traditional bluegrass, with Sam Bush on mandolin and Jerry Douglas on dobro. –MH

CROWE-RICE-LAWSON-HICKS-PHILLIPS

Traditional bluegrass. J. D. Crowe, Tony Rice, Doyle Lawson, Bobby Hicks, and Todd Phillips, along with Jerry Douglas, have teamed up to produce several bluegrass albums that are of the highest caliber. All members of the band are considered the tops in their field. –CR

○ **Bluegrass Album / ROUNDER**   1986
A good, straightforward bluegrass album. –CR

DILLARD & CLARK

Traditional bluegrass. This duo consisted of ex-Byrd Gene Clark and Doug Dillard of the Dillards. –KMC

☆ **Expedition/Through the Morning / MOBILE FIDELITY**
Good writing, singing, and playing on one CD containing two of their albums. These songs have been covered by Linda Ronstadt, the Eagles, and others. –KMC

DOUG DILLARD   b 1937

Traditional bluegrass. See the listing for the Dillards. –ED

What's That? / FLYING FISH   1974
A solid album. –CR

○ **Jackrabbit / FLYING FISH**   1979
A live album from the Telluride Bluegrass Festival, with guests Sam Bush and Byron Berline. –CR

Heaven / FLYING FISH   1979
A gospel album featuring Dan Crary, Byron Berline, John Hartford, Herb Pedersen. It includes an excellent cover of "Turn Your Radio On." –CR

RODNEY DILLARD   b 1942

Progressive bluegrass. See the listing for the Dillards. –ED

○ **At Silver Dollar City / FLYING FISH** 1988
A very Dillard-like album. It must be those trademark vocals. Includes a good cover of "Caney Creek." –CR

THE DILLARDS

Progressive bluegrass. Remember the Darling family, the hillbillies who now and again came down to Mayberry to visit sheriff Andy Griffith? The Darlings were the Dillards, a progressive West Coast bluegrass band with brothers Doug and Rodney as the nucleus. The band regrouped in 1987 for the TV movie *Return to Mayberry*. The brothers are still making music, though separately, with Doug heading up his own band. –DV

Homecoming & Family Reunion / FLYING FISH 1979
A pleasant album of several Dillard generations live at a picnic. –MH

Let It Fly / VANGUARD 1990
Recordings produced by Herb Pedersen of the Desert Rose Band. –MH

○ **There Is a Time / VANGUARD**
A 29-track retrospective of their 1963-1970 Elektra recordings. Influential urban bluegrass. –MH

JERRY DOUGLAS

Traditional bluegrass. Jerry Douglas is considered the premier dobro player on the Nashville music scene. He plays on most sessions and often teams up with Sam Bush, Mark O'Connor, Bela Fleck, and Edgar Meyer to form the group Strength in Numbers. –CR

Fluxology / ROUNDER 1979
A good bluegrass album with Tony Rice, Darol Anger, Todd Phillips, and Ricky Skaggs. –CR

Fluxedo / ROUNDER 1982
A smoother sound, which has become his trademark with Strength in Numbers. Featuring Sam Bush, Bela Fleck, the Whites, Mark Shatz, and Russ Barenberg. –CR

Under the Wire / MCA 1986
MCA gave Douglas total control on this album featuring Sam Bush, Bela Fleck, Russ Barenberg, Edgar Meyer, and Mark O'Connor. It's a shame they could only fit ten songs on the CD. Buy it! –CR

○ **Everything Is Gonna Work Out Fine / ROUNDER** 1987
Fluxology and *Fluxedo* on one CD — a great value from the master of the dobro. –CR

● **Slide Rule / SUGAR HILL** 1992
His finest release hits the jackpot. Featuring Sam Bush, Alison Krauss, Tim O'Brien, Maura O'Connell, Stuart Duncan, Artie McGlynn, and others, this album is produced to perfection. Highly recommended. –CR

Plant Early / MCA

DRY BRANCH FIRE SQUAD

Traditional bluegrass. This southern Ohio bluegrass group is fronted by Ron Thomason, a mandolin player, comic, and philosopher who says that "*Lonesome* (the essential word in bluegrass music) is a car up on blocks." Now that's a traditional value country fans can appreciate ... –DV

Antiques & Inventions / ROUNDER 1966
Kenny Baker and Hazel Dickens give this a nice flavor. –CR

Long Journey / ROUNDER 1972
Old timey — in a modern way. Very good. –CR

Born to Lonesome / ROUNDER 1979
Good. Featuring Kenny Baker, Bobby Osborne. A nice cover of "Brand New Tennessee Waltz." –CR

Fannin' the Flames / ROUNDER 1982
Very nice album. –CR

Fertile Ground / ROUNDER 1983
Very good. "Devil Take the Farmer" and "Bonaparte Crossing the Rhine." –CR

Good Neighbors / ROUNDER 1985
Tight mountain harmonies on 14 cuts. A must-have. –CR

Golgotha / ROUNDER 1986
A nice gospel album. –CR

BUDDY EMMONS

Instrumental bluegrass. A much-in-demand session man, Buddy Emmons is credited with bringing the pedal steel guitar to prominence and great popularity, so much so that the instrument is no longer considered "country" only, having been accepted by rock and nearly every other form of popular music. Earlier in his career he played in the road bands of Little Jimmy Dickens, Roger Miller, Ernest Tubb, and others. He and fellow steel player Shot Jackson founded the Sho-Bud steel guitar company, which made numerous innovations in the instrument. –DV

○ **Buddy & Lenny / FLYING FISH**
Country meets jazz as two super-pickers, Buddy Emmons and Lenny Breau (pedal steel and electric guitar), collide. A very creative and innovative album. –HD

GLENDA FAYE

Traditional bluegrass. Glenda Faye is one of the top guitar (flatpicker) players in the bluegrass field. –CR

○ **Flat Pickin' Favorites / FLYING FISH**
Faye shines on her debut album. Bill Monroe and Jesse McReynolds give the album a nice sound. –CR

LESTER FLATT   1914-1979

Traditional bluegrass. After Lester Flatt and Earl Scruggs parted ways in 1969, Flatt reassembled many of the Foggy Mountain Boys, renamed the group Nashville Grass, and toured very successfully until his death in 1979. Unlike Scruggs, who with his sons moved on to music that was only marginally country, Flatt and the Grass stuck to traditional bluegrass material. Even without Scruggs, the band shone, and Flatt's vocals, musical direction, and taste received the credit they had so long deserved. –DV

Live - Bluegrass Festival / CM 1986
A bluegrass veteran in concert in the 70s. –MH

○ **Vol. 1 - Greatest Bluegrass Hits / CM**
A good overview of Flatt's post-Scruggs recordings with Nashville Grass, a band that included a young Marty Stuart on mandolin. –MH

FLATT & SCRUGGS

Traditional bluegrass. Probably the most famous bluegrass band of all time was Flatt and Scruggs and the Foggy Mountain Boys. They made the genre famous in ways that not even Bill Monroe, who pretty much invented the sound, ever could. Because of a guitar player and vocalist from Tennessee named Lester Flatt and an extraordinary banjo player from North Carolina named Earl Scruggs, bluegrass music has become popular the world over and has entered the mainstream in the world of music.

Like so many other bluegrass legends, Flatt and Scruggs were graduates of Bill Monroe's Blue Grass Boys. Because of the unique sound they added ("overdrive," one critic called it), Monroe felt let down after Flatt's quality vocals and Scruggs's banjo leads left in 1948. Quickly the two assembled a band that in the opinion of many was among the best ever, with Chubby Wise on fiddle and Cedric Rainwater on bass; a later band, with Paul Warren on fiddle and Josh Graves on dobro, was equally superb. With so many extraordinary musicians and the solid, controlled vocals of Flatt, it's no wonder the Foggy Mountain Boys was the band that brought bluegrass to international prominence. From 1948 until 1969, when Flatt and Scruggs split up to pursue different musical directions, they were *the* bluegrass band, due to their Martha White Flour segment at the Opry and, especially, their tremendous exposure from TV and movies.

TV's preeminent hillbilly sitcom, "The Beverly Hillbillies," helped Flatt and Scruggs (and bluegrass) immensely. In the early 60s this top-rated show not only featured Flatt and Scruggs singing and playing "The Ballad of Jed Clampett," the show's theme song and the first bluegrass song to reach #1 in the country charts, it occasionally presented the two in cameo appearances, year after year. Further, in the early 60s the folk revival, then in its glory, made Flatt and Scruggs popular to a different audience, one that was educated and urban. In 1967 the movie *Bonnie and Clyde* was a huge hit, and with it came even more exposure for Flatt and Scruggs, whose "Foggy Mountain Breakdown" was the chief background music, making that song the most well known of all bluegrass instrumentals. Listeners who never had warmed up to straight country music grew hot for bluegrass, and festivals proliferated nationwide.

What made Flatt and Scruggs so famous, when numerous other excellent bluegrass groups of high quality (Jim and Jesse, the Stanley Brothers, the Osborne Brothers, Reno and Smiley, the Lilly Brothers) remained relatively unknown? One reason is that they always attracted the talent and their 1948 sound was way ahead of the others. More important, the Foggy Mountain Boys had Earl Scruggs, who reinvented the banjo with his three-finger picking (forever after known as "Scruggs picking") of mile-a-minute syncopated notes. The banjo was never the same after Earl Scruggs, whose presence at that time would have made *any* country band unique. They were elected to the Country Music Hall of Fame in 1985. –DV

Mercury Sessions #1 / RS 1948
1948-1950 recordings by the banjo whiz and baleful vocalist who took Bill Monroe's music a step further. –MH

At Carnegie Hall / CBS 1962
A highly influential "folk-boom" concert album . –MH

☆ **20 All-Time Great Recordings / CBS** 1983
Three-part gospel-style harmonies, breakneck banjo, flinty Americana, and "a bubblin' crude" are the cornerstone collection of bluegrass at its best. –MH

Columbia Historic Edition / COLUMBIA
Wonderful 50s recordings, including some rarities. –MH

Don't Get Above Your Raisin' / RS
Flatt's song became a back-anthem when Ricky Skaggs waxed it ca. 1981. The original is here, along with other greats from the 50s. –MH

Golden Era 1950-55 / ROUNDER
Classic Columbia performances. –MH

Greatest Hits / CBS
A concise sampler for those who don't want their *20 All-Time Great Recordings* album. –MH

Mercury Sessions #2 / RS
More great 1948-1950 recordings, including the original "Foggy Mountain Breakdown." –MH

Songs of the Famous Carter Family / CBS
Depression-era country/folk performed bluegrass style. –MH

The World of Flatt & Scruggs / CBS
Another good Columbia sampler. –MH

BELA FLECK & THE FLECKTONES

Progressive bluegrass. A highly original banjo stylist, Fleck has played traditional bluegrass, newgrass (with the New Grass Revival), and his own innovative material. He has been in high demand as a session player. –DV

○ **Bela Fleck & the Flecktones / WARNER** 1990
After disbanding New Grass Revival, Bela Fleck began recreating the role of the banjo in the same way Charlie Parker redefined the role of the saxophone. But Fleck may be the least innovative member of this quartet: Howard Levy gets chromatics from his blues harp, Victor Wooten picks banjo rolls on his bass, and Roy "Future Man" Wooten plays a Frankenstein-monster drum machine/guitar synthesizer. For all the Flecktones's flash, there's little pretense; the group's

astonishing musicianship keeps an "aw-shucks" accessibility that lets everybody follow the melody while they marvel. –BM

Flight of the Cosmic Hippo / WARNER 1991
The Flecktones owe more to bebop than bluegrass, and here the group finally names its style "blu-bop." Which is why *Cosmic Hippo* topped the jazz, not the country, chart. The Flecktones continue to make it look easy, adding banjo power chords to "Turtle Rock" and reworking Lennon/McCartney's "Michelle." –BM

TONY FURTADO

Progressive bluegrass. Tony Furtado is a highly regarded banjo player who hits all styles of banjo music: bluegrass, old-timey, swing, and jazz style. –CR

○ **Swamped / ROUNDER**
A very good album, featuring Laurie Lewis, Darol Anger, and Todd Phillips. –CR

JOSH GRAVES

Traditional bluegrass. Burkett "Josh" Graves has been probably the most influential dobro player in history, with Pete Kirby (Brother Oswald of Roy Acuff's band) in the running. Graves at least is responsible for making the dobro so popular in bluegrass music. He played for years with the Flatt & Scruggs band, his energetic playing beautifully complementing Scruggs on the banjo. In the 70s he played with the Earl Scruggs Revue and since then has has been active in recording work and on TV. Graves did much to bring the dobro out of the hillbilly and into the mainstream. –DV

○ **The Puritan Sessions / REBEL**
Longtime fiddler Kenny Baker appears in an uncharacteristic role as a fingerstyle guitarist in a delightfully low-key set of tunes and songs with dobroist (and sometime-singer) Josh Graves. –MH

○ **King of the Dobro / CMH**
The man who created bluegrass-style dobro with his bluesy hound-dog slide playing. –MH

DAVID GRIER

Traditional bluegrass. David Grier is a top-notch guitar player who has played with some of the best bluegrass musicians in the business. –CR

○ **Freewheeling / ROUNDER**
David Grier is backed here by Stuart Duncan, Roland White, Sam Bush, Wyatt Rice, and Mark Shatz. –CR

DAVID GRISMAN
b 1945

Instrumental bluegrass. Grisman began as a bluegrass mandolin player, working with Red Allen, Don Stover, and others. Greatly influenced by mandolin superplayer Jethro Burns, Grisman played briefly in Earth Opera, a rock band, and in the non-country Great American Music Band, while continuing to experiment with new approaches for the mandolin. This new sound, which echos the past but includes many other music genres, has become known as "dawg." –DV

Rounder Album / ROUNDER 1976
○ **The David Grisman Quintet / ROUNDER** 1976
Creative and adventurous sessions by this jazz/bluegrass group. –HD

Hot Dawg / MOBILE FIDELITY 1979
W/ Stephane Grappelli and a Django-esque sound. –HD

Early Dawg / SUGAR HILL 1985
Bluegrass meets jazz. –HD

Hot Dawg 90 / A&M 1987
Here Today / ROUNDER 1988
Hot mandolin-led newgrass with guests Pedersen, Gill, and Buchanan. –HD

Home Is Where the Heart Is / ROUNDER 1988
Mandolin Abstractions / ROUNDER 1988
Modern mandolin playing in a variety of acoustic settings. At

times hot and driving, other times melodic and haunting, and occasionally abstract and eerie. This is challenging yet pleasant music with guest Andy Statman. –HD

Svingin' with Svend / ZEBRA
A Django-esque sound, with Svend Asmussen on violin. –HD

THE HILLMEN

Progressive bluegrass. An early 60s, West Coast bluegrass band with Chris Hillman, Vern and Rex Gosdin, and Dan Parmley (later a Bluegrass Cardinal), which evolved from the Scottsville Squirrell Barkers. –MH

○ **The Hillmen / SUGAR HILL**   1970
Traditional bluegrass plus Dylan covers. –MH

HOT RIZE

Traditional bluegrass, progressive bluegrass. This Colorado progressive bluegrass band can also play traditional, jazz, and rock. As part of their stage act they become Red Knuckles and the Trail Blazers and, in good fun, parody hardcore 50s country music. –DV

Hot Rize / FLYING FISH
Debut album. Very good. Featuring Tim O'Brien and Pete Wernick. –CR

Radio Boogie / FLYING FISH
No sophomore high jinks on this release. Solid album, highly recommended. –CR

○ **Untold Stories / SUGAR HILL**
It all comes together on this CD. Tim O'Brien's swan song. –CR

JIM & JESSE (MCREYNOLDS)

Traditional bluegrass. One of the great bluegrass bands in history, brothers Jim (b 1927) and Jesse (b 1929) and their Virginia Boys have remained at the top by changing with the times. Starting as a traditional brothers duet, Jim on guitar and Jesse on mandolin showed their versatility by following country's changing tastes, moving to country/folk when necessary to keep a road band going. Whatever style they played (including *Berry Pickin' in the Country*, an album of bluegrass versions of Chuck Berry tunes), they retained a pure country core, due in no small part to Jim's pure, high tenor and Jesse's virtuoso mandolin playing. Opry regulars since 1964, they have recorded hit singles over the years, among them "Johnny B. Goode," "Diesel on My Tail," "Better Times A-Comin'," Jesse's "Cotton Mill Man," and a well-known version of John Prine's "Paradise." Jim's exquisite voice and Jesse's innovative cross-picking style of mandolin are well worth the price of admission. –DV

○ **Music among Friends / ROUNDER**   1991
A celebration of this bluegrass duo's 25 years on the Grand Ole Opry, with guest appearances by Bill Monroe, Emmylou Harris, Porter Wagoner, and others. –MH

Jim & Jesse: 1952-1955 / BEAR FAMILY   1992
Twenty stunning performances for the Capitol label (their first label) featuring hand-in-glove harmonies and Jesse's unique banjo-influenced mandolin. –MH

★ **Bluegrass Special / EPIC**
A bluegrass classic. Many of their most popular songs. –RL

Jim & Jesse Saluting the Louvin Brothers / EPIC
The best of the duo's recordings, with electric country rather than bluegrass accompaniment. –RL

Jim & Jesse Story / CMH
Remakes of some of their best-known tunes. –RL

JOHNSON MOUNTAIN BOYS

Traditional bluegrass. From the band's formation in 1978 until its breakup in 1988, the Johnson Mountain Boys were the salvation of bluegrass traditionalists, the hardcore who prefer the pure to progressive bluegrass and newgrass. Led by guitarist/vocalist Dudley Connell, the Washington, DC-based

band echoed the classic bands of the 50s, instrumentally and vocally. They left a void. –DV

Let the Whole World Talk / ROUNDER   1987
More great wailin'! –MH

Requests / ROUNDER   1987
An eclectic album by this short-lived but brilliant quintet. –MH

At the Old School House / ROUNDER   1988
Wonderful live and traditional bluegrass from their farewell tour. –MH

☆ **Working Close / ROUNDER**
Dudley Connell's chilling, high-lonesome lead vocals were only one of the delights of this militantly traditional, young bluegrass band. Any of their albums are among the best bluegrass of recent decades. –MH

BILL KEITH

Instrumental bluegrass. Boston-born Bill Keith is a highly innovative five-string banjo player who first mastered the Scruggs style and then invented his own. His chromatic style departed from the Scruggs approach, which lay down right-sounding notes around the melody, but with only some of those notes carrying the melody. Keith's system allows the picker to play intricate melody lines, note for note, fiddle-like. Bill Keith has played with numerous major league bands, including Bill Monroe and the Blue Grass Boys and Red Allen. Just as Scruggs reinvented the banjo, Bill Keith reinvented it again. –DV

○ **Something Bluegrass / ROUNDER**   1976
Catch Tony Rice, David Grisman, Jim Rooney, Tom Grey, Vassar Clements, Ken Kasek, and Al Jones on this album. The bluegrass is top-notch, and Bill Keith struts his stuff. –CR

THE KENTUCKY COLONELS

Traditional bluegrass. Evolving from the Country Boys in 1962, the California-based Kentucky Colonels quickly garnered a national following. Members Clarence White (guitar), his brother Roland (mandolin), Billy Ray Latham (banjo), Roger Bush (bass), and Leroy Mack (dobro) brought their traditional/progressive sound to a young urban audience. –DV

☆ **Appalachian Swing / WORLD PACIFIC**   1964
With bluegrass guitarist Clarence White. –RL

★ **Long Journey Home / VANGUARD**   1964
Fiercesome recordings from a 1964 live performance at the Newport Folk Festival, with Clarence White and many others, including duets with Doc Watson. –RL & MH

ALISON KRAUSS

Traditional bluegrass, progressive bluegrass. With a Grammy in her hand, this excellent fiddler with the high, fragile voice has made it, after years of small jobs on the road, paying her dues. With all the TV coverage she's had at the beginning of the 90s, this folk/bluegrass traditionalist should continue her great success with Union Station, her band. –DV

Two Highways / ROUNDER   1989
Earlier recordings of a fine young singer and fiddler, this time with Union Station. –MH

○ **I've Got That Old Feeling / ROUNDER**   1990
A sweet voice, fine fiddling, and a tight plaintive band on this breakthrough bluegrass/country/pop album that produced the first music video for bluegrass. –MH

DOYLE LAWSON & QUICKSILVER

Traditional bluegrass. After first making a name as a mandolin player and guitarist for J. D. Crowe's band, in 1971 Doyle Lawson moved to the Country Gentlemen, another well-known band that played traditional bluegrass with a progressive touch. In the late 70s he formed his own band, Quicksilver, which quickly drew raves for its inspired gospel singing. –DV

● **Gospel Collection #1 / SUGAR HILL**   1987
The best way to have their gospel music is with this collection.
Highly recommended. –CR
○ **Rock My Soul / SUGAR HILL**   1991
Not a flaw on the album. –CR
○ **My Heart Is Yours / SUGAR HILL**
As good as *Rock My Soul*. First-class bluegrass. –CR

LAURIE LEWIS

Progressive bluegrass. Laurie Lewis is a fine violinist and
vocalist in bluegrass music and is the leader of the Grant
Street String Band. She also performs with Blue Rose and
Lewis & Kallick. –CR
Love Chooses You / FLYING FISH   1989
A followup in the spirit of the first, with a good choice of
material. –MH
○ **Together - Lewis & Kallick / KALEIDOSCOPE** 1990
Laurie Lewis and Kathy Kallick perform some really fine duets
on this long-awaited collaboration. Lewis's violin playing is
first-rate and her vocals are always a joy to listen to. Kallick's
songwriting is spotlighted, along with her strong rhythm
guitar work. –CR
● **Restless Rambling Heart / FLYING FISH**
The first solo album from this Bay Area singer and fiddler.
Sweet but not saccharine, this is a mix of old-time, bluegrass,
and rootsy contemporary folk. –MH

THE LILLY BROTHERS

Traditional bluegrass. Starting in 1962, for 18 years West
Virginians Everett (b 1923) and Bea Lilly (b 1921) turned
downtown Boston into an oasis for music lovers in New
England. With their extraordinary banjo player, Don Stover,
they played nightly at the Hillbilly Ranch, a watering hole in
Boston's "Combat Zone," bringing their pure and traditional
mountain bluegrass to an audience of sailors, sailors'
companions, other denizens of the night, and many lovers of
the real thing. For whatever reason (and in spite of recording a
number of albums), the Lilly Brothers and Don Stover never
got the acclaim they deserved. –DV
☆ **Early Recordings / RB**
Driving, late-50s performances with breathtaking banjo from
Don Stover and hand-in-glove vocal harmonies. One of the
best bluegrass albums ever. –MH
Bluegrass Breakdown / ROUNDER
Great 1964 performances. –MH

JOEL MABUS

Traditional bluegrass. Based in Michigan, Mabus has released
albums over the years on his Fossil Record label and on Flying
Fish. –RM
Fairies and Fools / FLYING FISH
Firelake / FOSSIL
Settin' the Woods on Fire / FLYING FISH
○ **Fortunes / FOSSIL**

JIMMY MARTIN

Traditional bluegrass. Blessed with a great tenor voice, this
traditional bluegrass singer and guitarist mastered his craft
as lead vocalist for Bill Monroe's Blue Grass Boys for much of
1949-1951 and again in 1952-1953. Martin's vocals and his
dynamic guitar playing both complemented Monroe perfectly,
and in the opinion of many, he was the finest lead singer and
guitarist Bill Monroe ever had. In 1951, between stints with
Monroe's band, Martin joined with the Osborne Brothers,
forming the Sunny Mountain Boys. Though this association
lasted only until 1955, Martin has used this band name up to
the present. In keeping up such high standards over the years,
Martin has hired numerous major-league musicians,
including banjo players J. D. Crowe, Bill Emerson, Vic Jordan,
and Alan Munde, and mandolin player Paul Williams, all of

The Banjo

With the possible exception of pedal steel guitar, the banjo is
that one instrument most identified with country music,
especially bluegrass music. Beginning as a four-stringed
fretless instrument, the banjo became much more versatile
with an added fifth string (the shorter "drone" string). In the
South after the Civil War, banjos of many configurations —
some with four strings (the tenor and plecctrum banjo),
others with five strings (since the 20s *the* country banjo) —
were plentiful; in fact, in the 20s the banjo/fiddle combination
formed the basis of country music instrumentals.

Uncle Dave Macon, the first real star of the Opry, in the 20s
played five-string in the old style, often called frailing,
clawhammer, or simply "thumping." In this style, the backs
of the fingernails pick out the melody, while the thumb
catches the drone string, thus creating a regular beat and
rhythm. (Grandpa Jones is no doubt the most famous living
player of the frailing banjo.)

Although the banjo didn't die out in the 30s, the many
guitar/mandolin duets put it on the back burner for the
decade. String bands, precursors to Bob Wills and other
Western swing bands of the 40s, used the tenor banjo for
volume and rhythm. Meanwhile, a banjo picker from North
Carolina, Charlie Poole, had developed his own style of
playing, three-finger picking instead of frailing; he was in fact
paving the way for another North Carolinian, Earl Scruggs,
who may not have invented the banjo but certainly reinvented
it. Bill Monroe's Blue Grass Boys, formed in 1939, were
without a five-string banjo until 1942, when Dave
"Stringbean" Akeman added his frailing style to the band. But
it wasn't until 1945, when Earl Scruggs joined the Blue Grass
Boys, that what is now known as bluegrass banjo was
invented.

It's nearly impossible to overstate the effect of Earl Scruggs on
banjo playing. Live audiences gaped and gasped in disbelief
when hearing the flood of careful notes that rolled off Earl's
fingers. Many banjo pickers who rose to prominence admit to
giving up the old style the same night they heard the new
"Scruggspicking" style on the Grand Ole Opry. This new
sound absolutely dominated, in large part because of
Scruggs's signature songs "Foggy Mountain Breakdown"
(recorded with Flatt and the Foggy Mountain Boys around
1951 and later the chase music for the movie *Bonnie and
Clyde*) and "The Ballad of Jed Clampett" (on TV's "Beverly
Hillbillies"). Further reinforcement came in the form of
"Dueling Banjos" in the weirdly memorable version from the
1973 film *Deliverance*.

Though Earl Scruggs will rightly be remembered as the
reinventor of the banjo, other musicians, all beholden to Earl,
have taken the instrument in yet different directions: Buck
Trent electrified it; Bill Keith invented the chromatic/melodic
style; and Bela Fleck adds jazz, classical, and other difficult-
to-label influences.

— David Vinopal

whom subsequently made it big in bluegrass. Jimmy Martin
is required listening for anyone with more than a passing
interest in bluegrass. –DV
☆ **You Don't Know My Mind (1956-1966) / ROUNDER**
A Monroe band veteran with astonishing high pipes and a
penchant for blending bluegrass and honky-tonk. Great
bands, great songs, and classic 1956-1966 Decca sides. –MH

THE MCCOURY BROTHERS

Traditional bluegrass. Del and Jerry McCoury pursued individual careers in bluegrass before the Pennsylvania-born siblings teamed up for the 1987 Rounder album, *The McCoury Brothers.* Older brother Del had played banjo before switching to guitar and singing lead with Bill Monroe's Blue Grass Boys in 1963-1964. He subsequently led his Dixie Pals and recorded for both Rounder and Rebel. Jerry sang and played bass with Red Allen and the Kentuckians, as well as with Don Reno and Bill Harrell. The McCoury Brothers' sole album together to date is a wonderful close-harmony exposition of bluegrass, rooted in the "brother duo" tradition. –MH

○ **The McCoury Brothers / ROUNDER**
Jerry and Del McCoury fit together like hand-in-glove on these fine performances. –MH

DEL MCCOURY

Traditional bluegrass. Del McCoury was guitarist and lead singer in one of Bill Monroe's great bands in the early 60s. He went on to form high-quality traditional bluegrass bands, including the Dixie Pals, a band he organized with his brother Jerry in 1969. Del McCoury is well known for his exceptional vocal leads. –DV

Don't Stop the Music / ROUNDER   1990
The title track is a George Jones song. The album includes diverse and often bluesy material and fine performances. –MH

○ **Classic Bluegrass / RB**
Rebel label recordings from the 70s by the man who sometimes sounds more like Bill Monroe than Monroe himself. Stunning, pure, high lonesome pipes and mountain bluesy songs. Beautiful. –MH

High on a Mountain / ROUNDER
More grand bluegrass. –MH

BILL MONROE   ♭1911

Traditional bluegrass. Bill Monroe invented bluegrass music and reinvented the mandolin, two of the many reasons he's in the Country Music Hall of Fame. He has for decades been a tower in country music, as influential as the Carter Family, Jimmie Rodgers, and Hank Williams. His band, the Blue Grass Boys, has yielded graduates who make up a Who's Who in bluegrass history, including Flatt and Scruggs, Reno and Smiley, Mac Wiseman, and Carter Stanley. No one has shown greater love for the music, nor done more to promote it, than Bill Monroe. From 1927, when he and his brothers got a band together, up to the present, Bill Monroe has toured and played in schools and cellars and tents and auditoriums and in the open; as of this writing, he has been on the road for over 55 years. And he obviously loves what he does at least as much now as when he started. He'll perform his beloved bluegrass until he dies. It's difficult to imagine any type of music having a stronger advocate.

With Bill on mandolin, Charlie on guitar, and Birch on fiddle, in 1934 the Monroe Brothers played on a Chicago radio station, then moved to the Carolinas, where Bill and Charlie cut some records in 1936. The duo's sound was much closer to the prevailing duet sounds at the time than to what evolved into bluegrass. Two years later the band separated, with Bill moving on to an Atlanta radio station and forming the first of his many Blue Grass Boys configurations. By October 1939, when he debuted on the Opry with "Mule Skinner Blues" (a Jimmie Rodgers song), he had already established his trademarks — the high, pure tenor and the powerful instrumental leads on the mandolin. In 1945 Earl Scruggs and his banjo entered the band, and the bluegrass sound was complete. When Earl Scruggs left three years later, Bill Monroe replaced him with the first of a long succession of Scruggs-style banjo pickers. As band members came and went, the Monroe sound stayed intact.

As country music tastes have changed over the last half-century, so have most of the acts, with performers understandably trying to make a better living from prevailing musical fads. But not Bill Monroe and his Blue Grass Boys. In feast or famine, Bill's sound has remained the same — that high and lonesome tenor, the mastery of the mandolin, and that unyielding determination to protect and preserve the bluegrass music he so loves. –DV

○ **Bill Monroe - Bluegrass / BEAR FAMILY**
1950-1958. This superb 4-CD boxed set from Bear Family (import) offers the most comprehensive collection of Bill Monroe ever assembled. The liner notes are beautifully done — pictures, discography, the works. A second box covering the period from 1959 on is also available. –JME

Mule Skinner Blues / RC   1940
On these 1940-1941 recordings of the earliest and loosest bluegrass band, Monroe is wearing his blues, old-time, and even swing influences on his sleeve. –MH

☆ **The Essential Bill Monroe (1945-1949) / SONY**   1992
A 2-CD set of all the "classic" Blue Grass Boys material (the band with Flatt and Scruggs). This is the music that defined bluegrass. –MH

★ **Country Music Hall of Fame / MCA**
A brilliant overview of one of the great originators and synthesists of 20th-century music on these 16 selections from 1950-1988. Classic music with a consistent vision and varied accompanists. –MH

LYNN MORRIS BAND

Traditional bluegrass. Lynn Morris is a well-respected vocalist and guitar player. Her band consists of Tom Adams (banjo), David McLaughlin (mandolin), Stuart Duncan (fiddle), and Marshall Wilborn (bass and vocals). They play a blend of bluegrass, folk, and country music. –CR

The Bramble and the Rose / ROUNDER   1992
A solid release, with great vocals and a good cover of "Blue Skies and Teardrops." Another fine effort. Lynn Morris and Marshall Wilborn's harmonies are very good. Stuart Duncan stands out on fiddle. –CR

○ **Lynn Morris Band / ROUNDER**
Great sound, great vocals, and outstanding bluegrass. It includes "Enjoy Black Pony" and "Come Early Morning." –CR

THE NASHVILLE BLUEGRASS BAND   ♭1984

Traditional bluegrass, progressive bluegrass. This veteran group got together in 1984 and plays traditional bluegrass, sometimes in a more progressive style. Guitarist Pat Enright is the bandleader. Their video received considerable airplay in 1992, unusual for a bluegrass band. –DV

My Native Home / ROUNDER   1985
A flawless album. One of their best. –CR

Idletime / ROUNDER   1986
This hits on all cylinders with 12 tight songs. Has the classic "The Train Carryin' Jimmie Rodgers Home." –CR

To Be His Child / ROUNDER   1987
A gospel album. Good. –CR

○ **The Boys Are Back in Town / SUGAR HILL**   1990
Very well performed, highly recommended. These vocals are on the mark. Produced by Jerry Douglas. –CR

NEW GRASS REVIVAL

Progressive bluegrass. The Revival, formed in 1972 by four former members of the Bluegrass Alliance, was named by leader Sam Bush and flourished in the decade when numerous groups took traditional bluegrass and changed it to varying degrees. Bush's group was successful enough to have the group's name become a generic label: "newgrass." The band's image, with long hair and occasionally electrified instruments, as well as its musical material, contrasted greatly with standard (traditional) bluegrass like that played by Bill Monroe, Ralph Stanley, the Lilly Brothers, and Lester Flatt's band. In terms of longevity, popularity, and exposure, the

Revival, with its hip reputation, was perhaps the most successful in competition against II Generation, Seldom Scene, the Country Gentlemen, and others. In personnel, the Revival's best-known band includes Bush, John Cowan, Bela Fleck, and Pat Flynn. They have covered material from Leon Russell, Bob Marley, and Curtis Mayfield. –DV

Fly through the Country / FLYING FISH   1975
This first version of New Grass was not so polished as their second era, but they had good chemistry. You've gotta love "These Days," "Skippin'," "All Night Train," and "Fly through the Country." –CR

Too Late to Turn Back Now / FLYING FISH   1977
Recorded live at Telluride, CO, with guests J. Hartford and Peter Rowan, this one has a good-time feel. –CR

Barren County / FLYING FISH   1979
The first incarnation of this band was never better than on this one. Strong songs and vocals. –CR

○ **Commonwealth / FLYING FISH**   1981
The best of their newer era, with guests Leon Russell, Sharon White, and Kenny Malone. The cover of Hartford's "Steam Powered Aereo Plane" is great. –CR

Live / SUGAR HILL   1984
Includes a 19-minute version of "Sapporo." Buy this one after checking the rest of their material. –CR

New Grass Revival / EMI-USA   1986
A solid release, and a great cover of Peter Rowan's "Revival." Pat Flynn shows some good songwriting on "In the Middle of the Night," "Lonely Rider," "Sweet Release," and "How Many Hearts." Sam Busit and John Cowan come together well on T. Moore's "Saw You Runnin'." –CR

Hold to a Dream / CAPITOL   1987
A good use of drums on this one. It worked. Standout tracks include "Looking Past You," "Unconditional Love," "Metric Lips," and the title track. –CR

On the Boulevard / SUGAR HILL   1988
An overlooked CD with a couple of standout tracks. Played beginning to end, this one will leave you fulfilled. –CR

Friday Night in America / CAPITOL   1989
Their last album covers John Hiatt's "Angel Eyes," Jesse Winchester's "Let's Make a Baby King," and Bela Fleck's "Big Foot." Hot! These guys will be missed. –CR

MARK O'CONNOR

Progressive country, instrumental bluegrass. Even the fiddling contests Mark O'Connor was winning while still a kid didn't prepare listeners for how good he would become, and he's barely into his thirties now. He started out playing pure country, but the fact that he has been a sideman on over 400 albums tells us that he's incredibly versatile. Lots of fiddlers are more "pure country," but only a handful (if that) can match his technique. He's a virtuoso. His *New Nashville Cats* album (with 53 guest musicians and a variety of music styles) won a Grammy in 1992 and made him famous. He's also the music director of TNN's "American Music Shop." –DV

○ **The New Nashville Cats / WARNER**   1991
A fine collection of friends on this CD. Slick country featuring Sam Bush, Jerry Douglas, Bela Fleck, Vince Gill, John Cowan, Ricky Skaggs. This CD won two Grammy Awards. As good as they come! –CR

Championship Years / COUNTRY MUSIC FOUNDATION
These are good-quality early recordings from his championship days. –CR

Elysian Forest / WARNER
More in the new-age frontier. Mark O'Connor's fiddle turns into a violin right in front of your ears, if you know what I mean. –CR

False Dawn / ROUNDER
New-age acoustic music. A turning-point album in which O'Connor comes of age. –CR

Mark O'Connor / ROUNDER
An early album. Raw. –CR

Markology / ROUNDER
An acoustic-guitar album. –CR

On the Mark / WARNER
Featuring James Taylor, Jerry Douglas, and Michael Brecker (one of my favorites). Great sax on "Get Set, Go." A must-have for O'Connor fans. –CR

On the Rampage / ROUNDER
New-age. –CR

Pickin' in the Wind / ROUNDER
Bluegrass, newgrass. –CR

Retrospective / ROUNDER
A good all-around sampler of O'Connor's Rounder catalog. –CR

Soppin' the Gravy / ROUNDER
Good Texas fiddle music. –CR

Stone from Which the Arch Was Made / WARNER
R&B featuring Bela Fleck, Jerry Douglas, John McCutheon, and Maura O'Connell. Very nice; more rock and electric. –CR

OLD & IN THE WAY

Progressive bluegrass. Jerry Garcia (banjo and vocals), Peter Rowan (guitar and vocals), David Grisman (mandolin and vocals), Vassar Clements (fiddle), and John Kahn (acoustic bass). –CR

○ **Old & in the Way / RYKODISC**   1975
This release was one of the greatest things to happen to bluegrass music, in that it exposed a whole new audience to bluegrass music and acoustic music. –CR

THE OSBORNE BROTHERS

Traditional bluegrass, progressive bluegrass. From Hyden, KY, Bobby (b 1931) and Sonny (b 1937) Osborne for the last 40 years have been one of country music's most successful bluegrass bands. As music tastes changed, so did the Osbornes, remaining true to Bobby's mandolin and Sonny's five-string banjo, though modifying traditional music to make it more palatable to current tastes and adding songs from other genres. Their swings into and out of progressive bluegrass and electrified instruments worked — the Osbornes have not only survived but thrived over all these years, maintaining their insistence on quality and their unique sound.
In 1956 they became regulars on WWVA's Wheeling Jamboree (the Opry's chief competitor) and developed, with guitarist Benny Birchfield, their trademark trio-singing which was intricate and modern and traditional at the same time. In 1959, in the heat of the folk revival, they became the first bluegrass band to play a college date (at Antioch College in Ohio). In 1964 the brothers joined the Opry, where their progressive sound alienated some purists; but even the detractors admitted that, with musical tastes aside, the Osbornes were vocally and instrumentally unsurpassed. Bobby's highest-of-the-high tenor and his exceptional mandolin playing combined beautifully with Sonny's vocal harmony and dynamic banjo playing.
In 1968 the Osbornes had a hit with the song that has become their signature tune, "Rocky Top." Their many albums offer material from traditional bluegrass to newgrass, and the many variations in between. –DV

Singing Shouting Praises / SUGAR HILL   1988
Nice bluegrass gospel. –MH

Bobby & His Mandolin / CMH
An album featuring sprightly mandolin renditions of traditional fiddle tunes. Nice. –MH

Greatest Bluegrass Hits / CM
A good "favorites" collection. –MH

☆ **The Osborne Brothers / RS**
Great vocal harmonies and tightly woven banjo-mandolin conversations. The best early material from 1959-1963. –MH

Best of the Osborne Brothers / MCA
Their 1963-1967 Decca hits blend smooth bluegrass with then-contemporary country production. A unique sound, radical for its time. —MH

PETER ROWAN

Progressive bluegrass. Rowan has been a high-profile figure in American popular music since the 60s, among a group of Bostonians (including Jim Rooney and Bill Keith) who helped bluegrass grow big in northern cities. After a stint as a Blue Grass Boy, Rowan played with various progressive country bands, and with David Grisman and Bill Monroe. He has been a founding member of the bands Seatrain, Earth Opera, and Old & in the Way. —DV & RM

Walls of Time / SUGAR HILL 1982
This release is hard to put a finger on. The music takes on a feel more like that of the Old & in the Way band, yet seems to be missing the "something special" that project had. —CR

Red Hot Pickers / SUGAR HILL 1984
Peter Rowan is backed by Richard Greene (fiddle), Tony Trischka (banjo), Andy Statman (mandolin), and Roger Mason (bass). This is a lively, well-played album. —CR

First Whippoorwill / SUGAR HILL 1985
A good album. Rowan stacks the deck with Sam Bush, Bill Keith, Richard Greene, Buddy Spicher, and Roy Huskey Jr. —CR

○ **New Moon Rising / SUGAR HILL** 1988
Tight album. Rowan is backed by the Nashville Bluegrass Band. Maura O'Connell sings harmony vocals on "Meadow Green" and Jerry Douglas is featured on dobro. This release set the tune for some real good music. —CR

Dust Bowl Children / SUGAR HILL 1990
A very good album. It is all acoustic featuring Peter Rowan alone on guitar, mandola, and vocals. This grows on you. —CR

All on a Rising Day / SUGAR HILL 1991
An all-around fine release. Rowan picks up where he left off on *Dust Bowl* but improves on the idea with some great backup musicians — Stuart Duncan, Sam Bush, Jerry Douglas, Alison Krauss, Roy Husky Jr, Alan O'Bryant, Edgar Meyer. Twelve solid songs. Highly recommended! —CR

THE ROWANS

Progressive bluegrass. Formed in the mid 70s, the group consists of brothers Peter, Chris, and Lorin Rowan. The Rowans produced three albums of original songs and rich harmonies. This was a turning point for Peter Rowan away from his more rock efforts. —CR

○ **The Rowans / ASYLUM** 1975
The Rowans put out a strong album featuring killer songs of Peter's — "Midnight Moonlight," "Thunder on the Mountain," and "Beggar in Bluejeans." The album also features Lorin's "On the Ground" and Chris's "Here Today and Gone Tomorrow." First-class album. —CR

Jubilations / ASYLUM 1977
The final Rowans album. Peter steps back, only producing three songs. —CR

Sibling Rivalry / ASYLUM 1978
Not so good as their debut album. Includes Peter and Lorin's "Tired Hands" and "Mongolian Swamp/Kings Men." —CR

EARL SCRUGGS b 1924

Traditional bluegrass. Earl Scruggs is to the five-string banjo what Paganini was to the violin. After more than twenty years with the Foggy Mountain Boys, forming the most famous band in bluegrass history, Scruggs and Lester Flatt parted company in 1969 because of artistic differences, with Flatt pursuing more traditional sounds and Scruggs forming the Earl Scruggs Revue with his two sons. The Revue appealed more to a young and urban audience and, with dobro player Josh Graves, played rock and other non-country music. Scruggs has made many albums since his parting with Flatt

(including *The Storyteller and the Banjoman* with Tom T. Hall in 1982) and is seen on TV, often for reunion appearances. —DV

○ **Dueling Banjos / COLUMBIA** 1984
A classic album. Scruggs shines on this one. —CR

Family Portrait / COLUMBIA
Scruggs and family put out a nice, well-crafted album. —CR

Live from Austin City Limits / COLUMBIA
The crowd enjoys this live show — you will too. —CR

SELDOM SCENE

Progressive bluegrass. Mandolin-great John Duffey, formerly of the Country Gentlemen, formed the Seldom Scene newgrass band in 1971 in the Washington, DC, area. He surrounded himself with major-leaguers, including Mike Auldridge on dobro, Ben Eldridge on banjo, John Starling as guitarist/lead singer, and Tom Gray (another Country Gentleman alumnus) as bass player. They are at (or near) the top of newgrass bands. —DV

Act Two / RB 1973
They cover some good songs by Gene Clark and B. Lead on "Train Leaves Here," Norman Blake's "Last Train," and Hank Williams's "House of Gold." —CR

Old Train / RB 1974
Catch this album featuring Duffy, Starling, Eldridge, Auldridge, and Gray, plus Linda Ronstadt, Ricky Skaggs, Paul Craft, and Bob Williams. Includes a good cover of "Pan American." —CR

Live at the Cellar Door / RB 1975
A two-record set of a very good live show, with covers of "City of New Orleans," "Raw Hide," and "If I Were a Carpenter." —CR

○ **New Seldom Scene Album / RB** 1976
Duffey, Starling, Auldridge, Eldridge, and Gray put out one of the best bluegrass albums ever. Linda Ronstadt sings with them on one song. It doesn't get much better than this. —CR

Act Four / SUGAR HILL 1978
Features a good cover of Bob Wills's "San Antonio Rose." —CR

Baptizing / RB 1978
An enjoyable gospel album, with guest Ricky Skaggs. —CR

After Midnight / SUGAR HILL 1981
Good vocals, with covers of Eric Clapton's "Lay Down Sally" and J. J. Cale's "After Midnight." —CR

15th Anniversary Celebration / SUGAR HILL 1981
A 20-song live CD with Duffey, Auldridge, Mike Reid, Eldridge, and Gray. A must for fans, with special guests galore — Emmylou Harris, Ricky Skaggs, Linda Ronstadt, John Starling, Tony Rice, Jonathan Edwards, and others. —CR

Change of Scenery / SUGAR HILL 1988
Their vocal sound is changed here, but this is a first-class CD. Check out "West Texas Wind." —CR

○ **Blue Ridge / SUGAR HILL**
Songwriter and vocalist Jonathan Edwards ("Sunshine") teams with the Seldom Scene's flawless playing. Featuring Edwards, John Duffey, Mike Auldridge, Phil Rosenthal, Ben Eldridge, Tom Gray, Robbie Magruder, and Kenny White. —CR

Best of Seldom Scene - Vol. 1 / RB
A good collection from the Rebel label. —CR

SHADY GROVE BAND

Traditional bluegrass. This band plays traditional bluegrass with an old-timey feel. —CR

Mulberry Moon / FLYING FISH
Same level as *On the Line.* —CR

○ **On the Line / FLYING FISH**
A good, solid bluegrass album. —CR

SIDESADDLE

Progressive bluegrass. Sidesaddle is a bluegrass band that has country, Western, Irish, and folk influences. The band features Kim Elking (mandolin), Lee Anne Caswell (fiddle), Sheila

McCormick (guitar), Jackie Miller (guitar), and Sonia Shell (banjo). –CR

○ **Daylight Train / TURQUOISE**
Sidesaddle's unique sound sets it apart from other bluegass bands. The vocals blend nicely, with an Irish feel at times. These are also first-class musicians. An exciting album. –CR

The Red Rose Saloon / TURQUOISE
A very good record — nominated for Best Bluegrass Album (NAIRD). –CR

SKYLINE

Progressive bluegrass. Featuring banjoist Tony Trischka, Skyline helped pioneer the newgrass sound in the 80s, combining a bluegrass/country blend with strong songs and tight harmonies. –CR

Skyline Drive / FLYING FISH
A strong project with great harmonies. –CR

Late to Work / FLYING FISH   1979
Skyline's debut album. Strong songs. Trischka's band blends vocals to perfection. –CR

Fire of Grace / FLYING FISH   1979
Rachel Kalen replaced DeDe Wyland on this record. –CR

○ **Stranded in the Moonlight / FLYING FISH**
The band hits its stride on this very rich album. Tight harmonies and great original compositions. –CR

SOUTHERN RAIL

Traditional bluegrass. Southern Rail is a bluegrass band that plays traditional and original material. They consist of Jim Muller (guitar, vocals), Jim Rohrer (mandolin, bass vocals), Sharon Horovitch (bass, tenor vocals), and Dave Dick (banjo, baritone vocals). –CR

○ **Drive by Night / TURQUOISE**
Good solid bluegrass. Clean, with rich vocals and first-class playing. –CR

LARRY SPARKS

Traditional bluegrass. One of the finer lead singers in contemporary bluegrass, Sparks filled in with Ralph Stanley's band after the great Carter Stanley died in 1966. He went on to head the Lonesome Ramblers, an excellent traditional band popular on albums and at festivals right through the 80s. –DV

The Best of Larry Sparks / REBEL
A fine traditional bluegrass singer. –MH

○ **Larry Sparks Sings Hank Williams / REBEL**
A minor classic. Honky-tonk meets bluegrass. –MH

THE SPECIAL CONSENSUS

Traditional bluegrass. The current band features Greg Cahill (banjo), Dallas Wayne (bass), Marty Marrone (guitar), and Al Murphy (fiddle). They are a highly respected bluegrass band that also plays gospel, covers, and original material. –CR

○ **Hey, Y'All / TURQUOISE**
This great album features Elvis Presley's "Viva Las Vegas," "When the Walls Come Tumblin' Down," "I Can't Sit Down," and others. Some of the better bluegrass music around. –CR

THE STANLEY BROTHERS

Traditional bluegrass. If you even *think* you know bluegrass, you have to know Ralph (b 1927)and Carter Stanley (b 1925), the Stanley Brothers. Parallel to Flatt and Scruggs and Bill Monroe's Blue Grass Boys, though not with their renown, were Virginians Ralph and Carter, mountain boys who took those mountains and their traditions and their songs and wove them into a traditional bluegrass sound of utter purity, simplicity, and astonishing beauty. Their first band, formed around 1947, played more of a mountain/folk music reminiscent of the old string bands, changing to their style of ultra-traditional bluegrass when Bill Monroe's band became popular. Even on their recordings in the early 50s, the

Stanleys' unmistakable sound is there, with guitarist Carter singing lead and banjo player Ralph singing tenor harmony. In the opinion of many, Carter possessed the best lead voice in bluegrass history — rich, emotional, and (in the best sense of the word) lonely. He took a happy song and sang it sad; he took a sad song and sang it sadder. And Ralph's unworldly mountain tenor matched his brother's voice perfectly, soaring above and often lightening the emotional load of the lyrics, creating a duet unsurpassed in country history.

The great Carter Stanley died in 1966. In spite of numerous personnel changes over the last quarter-century, Ralph Stanley has retained the original sound with the Clinch Mountain Boys, his high tenor and tasteful banjo playing preserving the legacy of the inimitable Stanley Brothers. –DV

Stanley Series - Vol. 2 #1 / COPPER CREEK   1956
Live recordings and wonderful performances of several Stanley standards. –MH

Stanley Series - Vol. 3 #3 / COPPER CREEK
More fine live performances. –MH

Hymns and Sacred Songs / KING   1960
King-label sacred sides. Lovely. –MH

Long Journey Home / REBEL
From the 60s, and great as always. –MH

☆ **Columbia Sessions 1949-1950 #1 / ROUNDER**
Beautiful vocal harmonies and piquant songs. Bluegrass poetry at its purest. –MH

Columbia Sessions #2 / ROUNDER
More wonderful early performances. –MH

★ **The Stanley Brothers (1949-1952) / BEAR FAMILY**
All 22 of the their Columbia recordings, superbly remastered, including the issued and alternate takes of two classics, "The Fields Have Turned Brown" and "Little Glass of Wine." Carter Stanley's dramatic story songs are underpinned by chilling vocal harmonies and an ensemble sound that bore their unique signature. –MH

RALPH STANLEY

Traditional bluegrass. After brother Carter died in 1966, Ralph Stanley was quick in hiring talented Larry Sparks (to handle Carter's leads) and fiddler Curly Ray Cline. In the years since, the Clinch Mountain Boys have undergone numerous changes in band personnel, but Stanley has kept his standards high, over the years hiring Ricky Skaggs, Keith Whitley, Roy Lee Centers, Jack Cooke, and others. As of this writing, the band is still much in demand, with a full schedule year-round. –DV

Pray for the Boys / REBEL   1990
Sacred performances with the Clinch Mountain Boys. –MH

☆ **Bound to Ride / REBEL**
This legendary singer and banjoist's most atavistic performances, with claw-hammer banjo and terrific wailing Baptist banshee vocals on old-time songs. –MH

STAR-SPANGLED WASHBOARD BAND

Progressive bluegrass. A hilarious washboard band that features humor and high-energy bluegrass in their shows. –CR

○ **Collector's Item / FLYING FISH**   1978
A very funny, oddball bluegrass band. This album brings out the best of their live show, "Radarbeems." –CR

JOHN STARLING

Progressive bluegrass. A US Army surgeon, guitarist, and singer, Starling played with the Seldom Scene progressive bluegrass band from 1971 until 1977. After playing with various other groups in the 80s, he recently rejoined Seldom Scene. –DV

○ **Long Time Gone / SUGAR HILL**
This is the kind of album you play over and over again. Featuring Lowell George, Emmylou Harris, Tony Rice, and Ricky Skaggs. Highly recommended. –CR

Waitin' on a Southern Train / SUGAR HILL
Another strong effort. Mike Auldridge, Sam Bush, and John Cowan back up John. Good selection of songs; "New Delhi Freight Train" stands out. –CR

ANDY STATMAN

Progressive bluegrass. Andy Statman is a talented mandolin player who plays all styles of mandolin music. –CR

Flatbush Waltz / ROUNDER
A good album featuring Kenny Kosak, Russ Barenberg, Matt Glaser, and others. –CR

○ **Nashville Mornings, New York Nights / ROUNDER**
An excellent display of mandolin artistry, featuring Bela Fleck, Tony Trischka, Jerry Douglas, Vassar Clements, Russ Barenberg, and Kenny Kosek. –CR

CARL STORY   ♭1916

Traditional bluegrass, gospel. Carl Story could rightly be called the father of bluegrass gospel. Though from the late 30s he has recorded much secular material, it's with the sacred-quartet material with bluegrass instrumentation that he's gained his reputation. His falsetto voice is his trademark. –DV

○ **Mighty Close to Heaven / STARDAY**

STRENGTH IN NUMBERS

Progressive bluegrass. Strength in Numbers consists of Sam Bush (fiddle and mandolin), Jerry Douglas (dobro), Bela Fleck (guitar and banjo), Mark O'Connor (guitar and mandolin), and Edgar Meyer (bass). Each is recognized as a highly influential master of his instrument. After working together in various combinations through the 80s on each other's solo albums, they became known as the Telluride All Stars for their outstanding performances at the Telluride Bluegrass Festival in Telluride, CO. All the members are involved in other endeavors and consider this a fun project. –CR

○ **Telluride Sessions / MCA**
Bush, Fleck, Douglas, O'Connor, and Meyer. Each song is a collaboration by two members of the group. These guys just don't put out a bad record. Bluegrass to newgrass to jazz-grass! –CR

TONY TRISCHKA

Progressive bluegrass. An influential banjo player with Country Cooking (a Syracuse University-based band that recorded progressive bluegrass for Rounder Records in the 70s), Trischka has moved further from bluegrass into jazz and other non-traditional styles. –DV

Hill Country / ROUNDER   1991
A traditional bluegrass album. –CR

○ **Dust on the Needle / ROUNDER**
A good collection of Trischka's six Rounder albums, featuring Sam Bush, Marc O'Connor, and David Grisman. –CR

Robot Plane Flies over Arkansas / ROUNDER
An early release that spotlights Trischka's banjo skills. A progressive album. –CR

SALLY VAN METER

Traditional bluegrass. Sally Van Meter is one of the top dobro players in the bluegrass field. She has played with Blue Rose and the Good Ol' Persons. –CR

○ **All in Good Time / SUGAR HILL**
Sally Van Meter's debut album is a chance for her dobro to stand out, and it does. She gets help from Mike Marshall, Todd Phillips, Tony Furtado, and John Pederson. –CR

RHONDA VINCENT

Progressive bluegrass. Rhonda Vincent is one of the finest vocalists in bluegrass today. Her voice is clear and rich. She is also a respectable fiddler and mandolinist. –CR

○ **Timeless and True Love / REBEL**   1991
Rhonda Vincent's vocals shine on this release, cementing her place as one of the finest vocalists in bluegrass. This CD features 12 solid cuts, and she is backed by Darrin Vincent, Bela Fleck, Alison Brown, Randy Kohrs, Scott Sanders, Kenny Malone, Sonny Louvin, and Hargus "Pig" Robbins. –CR

CLARENCE WHITE   1944-1973

Traditional bluegrass. With his brother Roland, guitar'Clarence White began his career in bluegrass and first gained fame with the influential Kentucky Colonels on the West Coast in the early 60s. In 1965, after the Colonels had recorded two albums, White left to become a much-in-demand session guitaris, working with Ricky Nelson, the Everly Brothers, and others. White joined the Byrds full-time in 1968, becoming famous as a country-rock guitarist, before he died accidently in 1973. –DV

○ **And the Kentucky Colonels / ROUNDER**   1964
Clarence White & the Kentucky Colonels includes 1964-1967 live performances that are musts for bluegrass guitar enthusiasts. White was a member of the Byrds and a session player for Linda Ronstadt and the Everly Brothers. –RL

Live in Sweden 1973 / ROUNDER
A good live show. Clarence White is at his best, performing with the White Brothers. –CR

MAC WISEMAN   ♭1925

Traditional bluegrass. If a poll were conducted to find the most popular bluegrass artists, on the list would be a number of groups but only one name unassociated with a particular band. And that would be Mac Wiseman, who over the years has been famous for his clear and mellow tenor voice. Though Wiseman has with many of the great bands, including those of mountain singer Molly O'Day, Flatt and Scruggs, Bill Monroe, and the Osborne Brothers, his great voice has always kept a separate identity of its own. His material has ranged from the old ("Jimmy Brown the Newsboy," "I'll Be All Smiles Tonight") to the new ("You're the Best of All the Leading Brands," "A Million Million Girls," "If I Had Johnny's Cash and Charley's Pride"). Wiseman's command of traditional material makes him much in demand by bluegrass and folk fans alike. –DV

Essential Bluegrass Album / CM   1969
Classics on a double album. These old salts play like spring chickens. Highly recommended. –CR

Songs that Made the Jukebox Play / CM   1974
A nice album. –CR

Mac Wiseman Sings Gordon Lightfoot / CM   1979
Well done. Belongs in the collection of any Gordon Lightfoot fan. –CR

Classic Bluegrass / RB   1987
Very good. Bluegrass at its best. –CR

Greatest Bluegrass Hits / CM   1989
A good collection. –CR

Country Music Memories / CMH
This has a slightly different sound than other albums; more country than bluegrass. –CR

Grassroots to Bluegrass / CMH
Grammy finalist with 22 songs. –CR

○ **The Mac Wiseman Story / CM**
The best of Mac Wiseman. A good place to start. –CR

BLUEGRASS
COLLECTIONS

○ **Bluegrass Class of 1990 / ROUNDER**   1990
An excellent sampler, featuring Ricky Skaggs, Tony Rice,

Alison Krauss, Lynn Morris, Sam Bush, and J. D. Crowe. A good way to start your bluegrass collection. –CR

○ **Country Cooking: 14 Instrumentals / ROUNDER**
Country Cooking: 14 Bluegrass Instrumentals is a good collection of instrumentals. –CR

○ **Country Cooking: 26 Instrumentals / ROUNDER**
The best place to start. *Country Cooking: 26 Bluegrass Instrumentals* is packed with music. –CR

○ **Early Mandolin Classics - Vol. 1 / ROUNDER**
A fascinating glimpse into multi-ethnic mandolin music in the 20s and 30s. Recordings from ragtime and blues to Ukrainian bands and, of course, hillbillies. –MH

○ **Flatpicking Guitar Festival / SHANACHIE**   1989
A very clean, traditional flatpicking album featuring David Bromberg, Richard Lieberson, Dick Fegy, Tom Gilfellon, and others. –CR

○ **Mountain Music - Bluegrass Style / FOLKWAYS**
This classic reissue features performances by Don Stover, Earl Taylor, Chubby Anthony, Tex Logan, and others. –RM

○ **Rounder Banjo / ROUNDER**
An extensive catalog of banjo music featuring Snuffy Jenkens, J. D. Crowe, Bela Fleck, Tony Trischka, and many more. –CR

○ **Rounder Bluegrass - Vol. 1 / ROUNDER**
Highly recommended. The best bluegrass money can buy! –CR

Rounder Bluegrass - Vol. 2 / ROUNDER
A collection of fine music. –CR

○ **Rounder Fiddle / ROUNDER**
A loaded album featuring a wide range of fiddle music by Ricky Skaggs, Eddie Stubbs, Alison Krauss, Vassar Clements, and Byron Berline. More than 60 minutes of music. –CR

○ **Rounder Guitar - Acoustic Guitar / ROUNDER**
Rounder Guitar - Collection of Acoustic Guitar is a fine compilation of flat- and finger-pickin' acoustic guitar featuring Tony Rice, Mark O'Connor, Norman Blake, Dan Crary, and others. –CR

○ **Rounder Sampler - Traditional Music / ROUNDER**
A good collection of traditional music. Start your collection here and discover some new artists. –CR

☆ **Twenty-Four Greatest Bluegrass Hits / CMH**
The bluegrass greats, ranging from Bill Monroe to Flatt and Scruggs and the Osborne Brothers. –DV

FOLK

In its widest possible application, "folk music" refers to music composed and performed by amateurs and passed down in an oral tradition devoid of formal training. In this sense, folk music is not only the ballads that derive from the Scots and the Irish and have descended from the Appalachian Mountains, it is also the rural blues of the Mississippi Delta and the drum-heavy music of northwestern Africa, not to mention any other tribal or traditional genres.

In the 20th century in the US, however, the definition of folk music has tended to narrow over time, as other musical styles have encroached on it. Thus, though the Carter Family was an obvious influence on Woody Guthrie, and though they played their traditional music on acoustic instruments and sang it with untrained voices, we think of them as country musicians, not folk ones. Woody Guthrie, however, is resolutely categorized as folk, even though he introduced two main innovations to the form: first, he moved to the city, and second, he wrote his own songs.

It is probably the second factor that's the most important. By the early post-WWII era, Guthrie's songs were getting pop treatments in the hands of the Weavers, and by the mid 50s, two distinct camps had grown up, both of whom benefited from the boomlet of popular interest in folk music that lasted roughly from the 1955 Weavers comeback concert at Carnegie Hall (after years of blacklisting) to the summer day in 1965 when Bob Dylan turned up on stage at the Newport Folk Festival with an electric guitar in his hands.

The first camp followed in Guthrie's footsteps, writing their own songs and singing them in some approximation of Guthrie's Oklahoma accent. This camp tended to be more political and artistic, and most of them were individuals. Dylan was the most prominent of them, though Phil Ochs, Tom Paxton, Dave Van Ronk, and many others were included.

The second camp followed in the footsteps of the Weavers, singing the songs of others (including many of the Child ballads, but also songs written by those in the first camp) in sweet harmonies and clearly enunciated phrases. This camp tended to be apolitical and entertainment-oriented, and most of them were singing groups. Peter, Paul, and Mary were preeminent in this camp, along with the Kingston Trio, the Limeliters, and others. Joan Baez started in the second camp and gradually moved to the first.

After 1965, the first camp merged with pop and rock & roll, especially the "sensitive singer/songwriter" school of the early 70s, and the second camp retreated into a nostalgic past. By the end of the 70s the folk boom was over, but folk music remained healthy, continuing to flourish in the places it always had — in hundreds of small clubs spread across the US and Europe and at dozens of summer festivals. A new crop of singer/songwriters was emerging, and if they didn't have the clear road to national recognition enjoyed by their 60s forebears, they were nevertheless gradually able to build up reputations on a viable circuit, record their own tapes, and even eventually move up to independent labels like Flying Fish and Rounder.

You will find in the listings that follow, therefore, records by the old hands (many of them reissued on CD in recent years) and a healthy sampling of those younger artists operating in what is now, as perhaps it always should have been, a highly decentralized field. It's likely that many of those names will be unfamiliar, but the reader is encouraged to try out a recording or two by the new folk acts and to keep an eye out for their appearances in local venues. That's where folk music lives today.

— William Ruhlmann

PAT ALGER

Pat Alger, who is among the most successful country songwriters of the late 80s and early 90s, comes from a folk background, and that colors the unusually thoughtful, articulated songs he writes. He first turned up on record himself playing guitar and singing with the loosely constructed Woodstock Mountains Revue on the album *More Music from Mud Acres* in 1977. He was a coauthor of the song "Ocracoke Time," which appeared on the Revue's third album, *Pretty Lucky*, in 1978, as well as "Old Time Music" on its fourth album, *Back to Mud Acres*, in 1981, and the sole author of "Southern Crescent Line" on the same album.

But Alger really began to gain recognition as a songwriter with the release of Nanci Griffith's third album, *Once in a Very Blue Moon* in 1985. Alger cowrote the title song, which reached the country charts in 1986. He was also heard from on Griffith's fourth album, *The Last of the True Believers*, in

1986, for which he cowrote the song "Goin' Gone." (He also played guitar on the album and did its graphics.) Alger was coauthor of the title song on Griffith's 1987 album, *Lone Star State of Mind*, and that song became a Top 40 country hit. In 1988, Kathy Mattea's version of "Goin' Gone" hit the top of the country charts. In 1990 Mattea took Alger and Fred Koller's "She Came from Fort Worth" to #2.

It's no surprise, then, that when Alger came to record his debut album, *True Love & Other Short Stories*, in 1991, he was able to call on the help of the cream of the young Nashville writers and performers. Trisha Yearwood, Nanci Griffith, Mary Black, Ashley Cleveland, Kathy Mattea, and Lyle Lovett all turn up, though Alger himself is the focus, singing his best-known songs. "No one sings or plays Pat Alger like Pat Alger himself," Griffith writes. –WR

○ **True Love & Other Short Stories / SUGAR HILL**   1991
This country/folk songwriter sings his own versions of such hits as "Lone Star State of Mind" and "Goin' Gone." Guests include Nanci Griffith and Kathy Mattea. –WR

AMY & LESLIE

Amy Fradon and Leslie Ritter are Woodstock-based composers and vocalists. −CR

○ **Amy & Leslie / ALCAZAR** — 1990
Vocals are strong — these women were meant to sing together. Artie Traum plays and coproduced; Rory Block plays some sweet slide guitar. −CR

ERIC ANDERSEN   b 1943

Eric Andersen has maintained a career as a folk-based singer/songwriter for 30 years. In contrast to such peers as Tom Paxton and Phil Ochs, Andersen's writing has had a romantic/philosophical/poetic bent for the most part, rather than a socially conscious one, though one of his best-known songs, "Thirsty Boots," has as its background the Freedom Rides of the early 60s. (The song has been recorded by Judy Collins and others.)

After emerging from the Northeast folk-club circuit, Andersen began to record in 1965 with *Today Is the Highway*. His second album, *'Bout Changes & Things*, contained some of his most accomplished writing, including the highly poetic "Violets of Dawn," "Thirsty Boots," and "I Shall Go Unbounded." All were sung in Andersen's flexible tenor (he shaded toward a baritone later), backed by rapid, intricate fingerpicking. In the late 60s and early 70s, Andersen experimented with country, pop, and rock music, settling on an amalgamation by the time of his masterpiece *Blue River* in 1972. This was also his most commercially successful album, but Andersen, like friends Leonard Cohen and Townes Van Zandt, was always too serious-minded for the mainstream. In the 70s and 80s, he recorded sporadically while playing folk clubs around the US and especially in Europe, where he took up residence. His newest recording is the remarkable *Ghosts upon the Road*, in which he reflects ruefully on the 60s. −WR

○ **'Bout Changes & Things / VANGUARD** — 1966
The best early Andersen. Includes "Violets of Dawn" and "Thirsty Boots." −WR

○ **Tin Can Alley / VANGUARD** — 1968
This record, which contains "Hello Sun" and "Rollin' Home," is one of his most solid early albums. It begins and ends with the title cut played by a great junkyard band. −RM

★ **Blue River / CBS / BB# 169** — 1972
One of the best folk/rock singer/songwriter albums of the early 70s. −WR

Be True to You / ARISTA / BB# 113 — 1975
Includes the tender title track and the epic "Time Run Like a Freight Train." −WR

Ghosts upon the Road / CAPITOL — 1989
Evocative songs that reflect on Andersen's past and current concerns. −WR

JOAN BAEZ   b 1941

The most accomplished interpretive folksinger of the 60s, Joan Baez has influenced nearly every aspect of popular music in a career still going strong after more than 30 years. Baez is possessed of a once-in-a-lifetime soprano, which, since the late 50s, she has put in the service of folk and pop music as well as a variety of political causes. Starting out in Boston, Baez first gained recognition at the 1959 Newport Folk Festival, then cut her debut album, *Joan Baez*, released in December 1960. The record was made up of 13 traditional songs, some of them Child ballads, given near-definitive treatment. A moderate success on release, the album took off after the breakthrough of *Joan Baez - Vol. 2*, released a year later, and both albums became huge hits, as did Baez's third album, *Joan Baez in Concert*. Each album went gold and stayed in the bestseller charts more than two years.

From 1962 to 1964, Baez was the popular face of folk music, headlining festivals and concert tours and singing at a variety of political rallies, including the August 1963 March on Washington led by Dr. Martin Luther King Jr. During this period, she began to champion the work of folk songwriter Bob Dylan, and gradually her repertoire moved from traditional material toward the socially conscious work of the emerging generation of 60s artists like him.

In the late 60s and early 70s, Baez moved toward country and rock music and also began to write her own songs, culminating in the gold-selling *Diamonds & Rust* in 1975. Since then, while her recording career has gradually declined, she has maintained her status on the concert circuit and her commitment to social issues. −WR

☆ **Joan Baez / VANGUARD** — 1960
Revelatory first album features Baez singing traditional folk songs. −WR

Joan Baez - Vol. 2 / VANGUARD / BB# 13 — 1961
In Concert - Part 1 / VANGUARD / BB# 10 — 1962
A vibrant concert recording with a radiant sound, humor, and topicality. −BE

In Concert - Part 2 / VANGUARD / BB# 7 — 1963
A superb followup to *Part 1*, with some more interesting material. −BE

5 / VANGUARD / BB# 12 — 1964
A good folk set, from a variety of sources. −BE

Farewell, Angelina / VANGUARD / BB# 10 — 1965
Baez moves toward contemporary work, with songs by Donovan and Woody Guthrie. She sings four songs by Bob Dylan, including the title track. −WR

Joan / VANGUARD / BB# 38 — 1967
Ornate, heavily orchestrated versions of other people's songs. Overproduced, but quite beautiful. −BE

Any Day Now / VANGUARD / BB# 30 — 1968
All-Dylan album includes definitive performance of "Love Is Just a Four-Letter Word." −WR

● **First 10 Years / VANGUARD / BB# 73** — 1970
A nearly perfect cross-section of her most enduring work, both traditional and contemporary. −BE

Come from the Shadows / A&M — 1972
After recording for the folk label Vanguard for more than a decade, Baez moved to A&M. On this label debut, she maintained her interest in country music, recording in Nashville with some of the city's session aces. She also continued to dedicate herself to radical politics, from her set opener "Prison Trilogy," which pledged, "We're gonna raze the prisons to the ground," to the closer, John Lennon's "Imagine." In between were her call on Bob Dylan to return to protest music ("To Bobby") and her sister Mimi Farina's touching tribute to Janis Joplin, "In the Quiet Morning." −WR

Hits/Greatest & Others / VANGUARD / BB# 163 — 1973
An alternate cross-section of Baez's Vanguard music, including her monster hit "The Night They Drove Old Dixie Down." −BE

Where Are You Now, My Son? / A&M — 1973
This isn't only *not* the place to start listening to Joan Baez, it's the album that separates the true fans from the, um, fellow travelers. Side 2 is taken up by the title song, a musical account of Baez's trip to Hanoi over Christmas of 1972, complete with the sound of US bombs falling on the city. Side 1, on the other hand, contains one of Baez's best original songs, "A Young Gypsy," and two by her sister, "Mary Call" and "Best of Friends." −WR

★ **Diamonds & Rust / A&M / BB# 11** — 1975
Baez's peak as a songwriter (title track) and folk/rock interpreter, singing songs of Jackson Browne, John Prine, and Bob Dylan. −WR

○ **The Best of Joan C. Baez / A&M** — 1977
Emotionally charged songs from her 70s albums on A&M. Not early Baez, this album of touching songs is probably too commercial for diehard folk fans. Excellent. −JME

Honest Lullaby / CBS — 1979
On her second album for CBS's Portrait label (and her last new album issued in the US for eight years), Baez was given a full-

scale pop-rock production by veteran Barry Beckett and the studio band in Muscle Shoals, AL. The result, on songs that range from "Let Your Love Flow" to "Before the Deluge," is accessible but not particularly memorable 70s-style pop. If you always wanted to know what the words to "No Woman, No Cry" are, however, this is the place to find out. –WR

Very Early Joan Baez / VANGUARD   1982
A masterful raid on the vault, recapturing the purity and simplicity of her debut recording. –BE

○ **Live Europe 83 - Children of the Eighties / ARIOLA**   1983
While Baez declined to record again in the US unless she could get on a major label, she did make several live albums in Europe in the interim. This is the best of them, mixing old favorites like "Farewell, Angelina" with originals like her heartfelt "For the Children of the Eighties. (Import) –WR

○ **Recently / CAPITOL-GOLD CASTLE**   1987
Baez returned to US record shops with a vengeance here, delivering her interpretations of songs by Dire Straits, Johnny Clegg, U2, and Peter Gabriel, performers whose political consciousness had been formed by listening to old Joan Baez albums. And on the title track, a stunning original, she boldly answered ex-husband David Harris's downbeat memoir of the 60s, *Dreams Die Hard*. –WR

GEOFF BARTLEY

A longtime resident of Cambridge, MA, Bartley is the three-time national finger-picking champion and a contributor to *The Fast Folk Musical Magazine*. –RM

○ **Blues Beneath the Surface / MAGIC CROW**   1986
The title track here is an extraordinary example of Bartley's guitar work. His lyric songs are also quite fine. –RM

CINDY LEE BERRYHILL

A savvy, witty singer/songwriter in what has been called the "anti-folk" style of the mid 80s, she has released two albums on Rhino Records. –WR

○ **Naked Movie Star / RHINO**   1989
This quirky, Los Angeles-based folkie, aided by a folk/rock production courtesy of Lenny Kaye, comments on life in Hollywood, Donald Trump, and other subjects with a sometimes flip, sometimes self-deprecating attitude. –WR

PETER AND LOU BERRYMAN

This Wisconsin duo writes and performs humorous suburban songs. –RM

○ **So Comfortable / CORNBELT**

SOHIPA BILIDES

A Massachussetts artist who performs traditional Greek music. –RM

○ **Greek Legacy / E. THOMAS**   1991

MILO BINDER

This Los Angeles-based singer/songwriter is sly, romantic, and childlike. He is a contributor to *The Fast Folk Musical Magazine* and Windham Hill's *Legacy*. –RM

☆ **Milo Binder / ALIAS**   1991
"Effigy," "New Toys," and "Donald Thorn" are gems. –RM

DAVID BLUE   1941-1982

Born in Providence, RI, as S. David Cohen (a name he returned to for one of his albums), David Blue was a member of the folk singer/songwriter community of Greenwich Village in the 60s and a close friend of Bob Dylan's (he recounts this period of his life in Dylan's movie *Renaldo & Clara*). Blue made several albums for Elektra, Reprise, and Asylum in the 60s and 70s, and is best remembered for his songs "I Like to Sleep Late in the Morning" and "Wanted Man" (recorded by the Eagles). –WR

○ **David Blue / ELEKTRA**   1966
Blue's debut album features the first recording of his remarkable "Grand Hotel" and other well-written folk/rock songs. –WR

Nice Baby and the Angel / ASYLUM   1973
Blue is joined by an all-star California cast (Dave Mason, Graham Nash, David Lindley, and Glenn Frey) for this excellent 70s singer/songwriter collection, which includes his "Outlaw Man." –WR

Com'n Back for More / ASYLUM   1975
Blue takes a more jazz/rock approach here, using members of the crony group the Los Angeles Express, whose employer, Joni Mitchell, makes an appearance, as does Blue's old crony, Bob Dylan. –WR

HUGH BLUMENFELD   b1958

A Connecticut-based poet, songwriter, and teacher. Blumenfeld has been associate editor and contributor to *The Fast Folk Musical Magazine*. –RM

○ **The Strong in Spirit / GRACE AVENUE**   1987
Contains many of his signature songs. –RM

Barehanded / GRACE AVENUE   1991
A recent all-acoustic collection. –RM

ERIC BOGLE   b1944

An Australian singer/songwriter best known for "... And the Band Played 'Waltzing Matilda'." –RM

○ **Scraps of Paper / FLYING FISH**
When the Wind Blows / FLYING FISH
Singing in the Spirit House / FLYING FISH

OSCAR BRAND

A fixture on the American folk scene since the 40s, Oscar Brand has over 70 albums of political, humorous, and bawdy songs. He hosts the radio show "Folk Song Almanac" in New York City. –RM

○ **The Wild Blue Yonder / ELEKTRA-SPECIALTY**

ANDY BRECKMAN

A New York singer/songwriter, guitarist, and writer for both "Saturday Night Live" and David Letterman, Breckman has written many sly, comedic "folk" songs. –CR & RM

○ **Don't Get Killed / GADFLY**   1990
A collection of 14 live songs that are guaranteed to make you laugh. The audience is into Breckman's songs. It makes for an enjoyable experience! This contains the surrealist revisionist folksong "Railroad Bill." –CR & RM

DAVID BROMBERG

Often referred to as a musician's musician, throughout his career Bromberg has spent almost as much time being a sideman to people like Bob Dylan and Jerry Jeff Walker as he has fronting his own band. Session credits for albums by Tom Paxton and Jerry Jeff Walker started getting Bromberg attention in the mid 60s, and he began making the transition from sideman to frontman in the early 70s, when he got signed to record for Columbia Records.
The key to appreciating Bromberg is to realize he has equal passion for blues, folk, country and western, bluegrass, and rock & roll. This diverse range of influences is reflected on all his recordings for Columbia, Fantasy, and Rounder, and in his performances as well. His musical eclecticism over the years may have cost him some fans, but a typical Bromberg concert can be a musical education. –RS

○ **David Bromberg / CBS**   1972
David Bromberg was already a well-known folk instrumentalist before this album proved he was also a top-notch songwriter and an appealing vocalist as well. The styles

mix folk, blues, rock, and jug-band music, and the songs alternate from the painfully sensitive ("Sammy's Song") to the rib-tickling ("The Holdup," which was cowritten by George Harrison). –WR

How Late'll Ya Play 'Til? / FANTASY 1976

Bromberg's band, with two horns and a fiddle player, is capable of playing just about any style of popular music, and most of them are here on a double album, half recorded in the studio and half live. (Fantasy has also issued the two discs separately.) The standout inclusion is Bromberg's "Will Not Be Your Fool," which became his onstage showstopper from here on out. –WR

SAUL BROUDY

This New Jersey-based folksinger primarily interprets others' songs. –RM

○ **Travels with Broudy / ARISTA** 1977

GREG BROWN

Greg Brown is from southwestern Iowa, and he brings a rural Midwestern sensibility to his songs that is alternately homey, tender, and witty. Gaining recognition on the "Prairie Home Companion" radio show, Brown has made a series of albums for Minnesota-based Red House Records. –WR

In the Dark with You / RED HOUSE 1985

Humorous and sardonic reflections on domestic life and aging, from a journeyman folksinger. –WR

○ **One More Goodnight Kiss / RED HOUSE** 1986

Brown's best collection of touching, funny, small-town songwriting. –WR

One Big Town / RED HOUSE 1989

Brown turns his eye outward and views the world cynically on "America Will Eat You." –WR

SANDY BULL ♭1941

Sandy Bull was a teenage guitar prodigy and later a multi-instrumentalist who made a series of instrumental albums in the 60s that embraced Eastern music styles along with classical, folk, country, and jazz. His career was interrupted by a drug habit in the 70s, although he resumed recording in the late 80s. –CR

○ **Sandy Bull / VANGUARD**

Good solid album. –CR

JANE BYAELA

New York-based singer/songwriter of the 80s and 90s, with a sound that crosses between the purity and perfection of Judy Collins and the quirkiness and drama of Suzanne Vega, without ever imitating either. Byaela is a classically trained guitarist, and her songs are all characterized by a virtuoso's command of her instrument and rich tonal colorations amid their intimacy. –BE

○ **On the Edge / SPARK**

An especially pleasing all-acoustic record, soaring artfully and plunging bluesily along on a beguiling and stylized roller-coaster ride that is twice as interesting and three times more honest than Suzanne Vega's best work. –BE

ANDREW CALHOUN

A Chicago-based singer/songwriter with a sly but deeply reverent view of life. –RM

○ **The Gates of Love / FLYING FISH**

Walk Me to the War / FLYING FISH

HAMILTON CAMP

An early-60s city folksinger, Camp was an early interpreter of otherwise-unrecorded Bob Dylan songs. Best known for his song "Pride of Man," popularized by Quicksilver Messenger Service. –RM

○ **At the Gate of Horn / ELEKTRA** 1963

Bob Gibson and Hamilton Camp both play on this album. –ED

Paths of Victory / ELEKTRA 1964

SARAH ELIZABETH CAMPBELL

Sarah Elizabeth Campbell is a Texas singer/songwriter who also resides in California. She was part of the popular California bluegrass band Fiddlestix. Her songs have been covered by Jim Messina, Rick Danko and Levon Helm (of the Band), Blue Rose, and others. –CR

○ **Little Tenderness / KALEIDOSCOPE** 1986

This CD is a collection of slow-paced, bluesy folk ballads that almost remind you of songs that could have been written 50 years ago. Her songs are from the heart. She is backed by Nina Gerber on guitar (producer of the CD), and three members of the Good Ol' Persons: John Reischman, mandolin; Sally Van Meter, lap steel and dobro; and Kathy Kallick, harmony vocals; along with Barbra Higbie, Sam Page, Jake Lampert, Joe Craven, Ed Johnson, Joe Goldmark, Sharon O'Connor, and Joe Weed. –CR

GUY CARAWAN ♭1927

Guy Carawan is a hammer dulcimer, guitar, and banjo player from Tennessee. He plays traditional Appalachian music. –CR

Green Rocky Road / JUNE APPAL 1976

Songs from Appalachia and the British Isles. Features "Soldiers Joy," "Green Rocky Road," and "St. Anne's Reel." –CR

Jubilee / JUNE APPAL 1979

Covers of David Mallet's "Inch by Inch" and "Road to Lisdoonvarna," plus 14 more. –CR

Songs of Struggle & Celebration / FLYING FISH 1982

Fifteen songs recorded at workshops. Good backup. –CR

○ **Hammer Dulcimer Music / FLYING FISH** 1984

Guy Carawan and his son Evan play great traditional music on this release. –CR

DOYLE CARVER

A Houston-based singer/songwriter who writes mostly about local issues and conditions. –RM

○ **Live at the Circle K / CARVER MUSIC**

Carver's first album is a fine collection and includes the beautifully balanced "Deer Hunter," which is about hunting, coming of age, and love of family tradition, all in three minutes without one extra syllable. –RM

High Ground / CARVER MUSIC

"Red Iron Rain" and the title song are particularly fine songs on this album. –RM

CENTRAL PARK SHIEKS

An important mid-70s NY band that gave an urban slant to country swing. –RM

○ **Honeysuckle Rose / FLYING FISH**

Great playing and arrangements throughout. –RM

THE CHENILLE SISTERS

The Chenille Sisters feature Cheryl Dawdy, Connie Huber, and Grace Morand. They sing songs on the humorous side, with tight harmonies. –CR

The Chenille Sisters / RED HOUSE

First album. Good, humorous songs. –CR

○ **At Home with the Chenille Sisters / RED HOUSE** 1988

A good record, featuring "Girl Shoes," "Crazy People," and "Bad Habits." –CR

Mama, I Wanna Make Rhythm / RED HOUSE

Very strong. –CR

FRANK CHRISTIAN

An exceptional guitarist and songwriter, Christian released one album in addition to his participation on the Italian Song Project record and various cuts on the *The Fast Folk Musical Magazine*. –RM

○ **Somebody's Got to Do It / GREAT DIVIDE**   1982
W/ his signature song, "Where Were You Last Night." –RM

CHRYSALIS

A folk/rock band based in Ithaca, NY, in the late 60s. Their leader, Spider Barbour, went on with solo work and with the Mothers of Invention. –RM

○ **Definition / MGM**   1967
Key songs are "Cynthia Jerome," "Lacewing," "30 Poplar," and "Lake Hope." The writing has a particularly sophisticated sense of psychology for this style in this era. –RM

SHEILA CLARK

Sheila Clark collects murder ballads and performs them with guitar and banjo. –RM

○ **The Legend of Tom Dula / FOLKWAYS**   1986
The Legend of Tom Dula and Other Tragic Love Ballads is a group of her finds. –ED

PAUL CLAYTON

A 60s folk song collector and writer. –RM

○ **Folk Ballads ... / FOLKWAYS**
Folk Ballads of the English Speaking World is a good example of Clayton's work. –ED

LEONARD COHEN   ♭1934

Although he played music during his college years, Canadian poet, novelist, and singer/songwriter Leonard Cohen did not turn professional until he was in his 30s. A graduate of McGill University, he published several books of poetry starting in the 50s and two novels, *The Favorite Game* and *Beautiful Losers*, in the 60s. After his songs had been recorded by Judy Collins, Cohen turned to singing and released his debut album, *Songs of Leonard Cohen*, in 1968. It contained such typical material as the highly poetic "Suzanne," which had been a singles hit for Noel Harrison. Cohen continued to write and record albums (though less and less frequently) throughout the 70s and 80s, all of them featuring his deepening voice and lyrics that were by turns depressing, comic, and erotic. His 1977 album, *Death of a Ladies Man*, was a collaborative effort with eccentric producer Phil Spector. By the 80s, Cohen's music was being celebrated by the school of doom-rock performers led by Nick Cave and others (resulting in the tribute album *I'm Your Fan*, 1991), but Jennifer Warnes's all-Cohen album *Famous Blue Raincoat* (1987) was a more accessible sampler. The artist himself made one of the best albums of 1988 in *I'm Your Man*. –WR

★ **The Songs of Leonard Cohen / CBS / BB# 83**   1968
His debut album features such standards as "Suzanne," "Sisters of Mercy," and "So Long Marianne." Many of these were featured in the 1971 Warren Beatty film, *McCabe and Mrs. Miller*. –WR

Songs from a Room / CBS / BB# 63   1969
Includes his versions of his classics, "Bird on a Wire" and "Story of Isaac." –WR

Songs of Love and Hate / CBS / BB# 145   1971
"Famous Blue Raincoat," "Joan of Arc," and more great Cohen songs. –WR

○ **I'm Your Man / CBS**   1988
Pessimism, humor, and poetry add up to a profound world view in Cohen's most recent collection. –WR

JUDY COLLINS   ♭1939

Judy Collins was one of the major interpretive folksingers of the 60s. A child prodigy at classical piano, she turned to folk music at the age of 15 and released her first album, *A Maid of Constant Sorrow*, in 1961 when she was 22. That album and its followup, *The Golden Apples of the Sun*, consisted of traditional folk material, with Collins's pure, sweet soprano accompanied by her acoustic guitar playing. By the time of

Judy Collins #3, she had begun to turn to contemporary material and to add other musicians. (Jim, later Roger, McGuinn tried out his first arrangements of "The Bells of Rhymney" and "Turn, Turn, Turn" on this album, before using them with the Byrds.)

Collins's musical horizons were expanded further by 1966 and the release of *In My Life*, which added theater music to her repertoire and introduced her audience to the writing of Leonard Cohen; it was one of her six albums to go gold. Her first gold-seller, however, was 1967's *Wildflowers*, which contained her hit version of "Both Sides Now" by the then-little-known songwriter Joni Mitchell.

By the 70s, Collins had come to be identified as much as an art song singer as a folksinger and had also begun to make a mark with her original compositions. Her best-known performances cover a wide stylistic range: the traditional gospel song "Amazing Grace," the Stephen Sondheim Broadway ballad "Send in the Clowns," and such songs of her own as "My Father" and "Born to the Breed."

Collins recorded less frequently after the end of her 23-year association with Elektra Records in 1984, though she made two albums for Gold Castle. In 1990, she signed to Columbia Records and released *Fires of Eden*, her 23rd album. –WR

○ **In My Life / ELEKTRA**   1966
Collins, who by this point has moved from the acoustic renderings of traditional folk ballads to more extensive instrumentation and the work of contemporary folk writers, takes another step here, turning to tasteful string arrangements by Joshua Rifkin and adding theater music from *Threepenny Opera* and *Marat/Sade* to the Bob Dylan covers. She also starts covering Leonard Cohen ("Suzanne," "Dress Rehearsal Rag"). –WR

Wildflowers / ELEKTRA   1967
Passionate and filled with memorable passages. Includes her hit "Both Sides Now" and her first major original composition "Since You Asked." Leonard Cohen's "Priests" has not appeared elsewhere. –BE & WR

Who Knows Where the Time Goes / ELEKTRA   1968
Rock and country leanings are found on this album featuring guitarists James Burton and Stephen Stills. Includes the hit "Someday Soon" and Collins's own brilliant "My Father." –WR

● **Colors of the Day - Best of Judy Collins / ELEKTRA**   1972
The biggest hits of her early career, well chosen. –BE

True Stories and Other Dreams / ELEKTRA   1973
Collins at her most political, saluting Che Guevara, among others. Elaborately produced and well sung. –BE

Judith / ELEKTRA   1975
A soaring collection of songs from the Depression, 70s Broadway ("Send in the Clowns"), and modern C&W. –BE & WR

☆ **So Early in the Spring ... / ELEKTRA**   1977
So Early in the Spring, the First 15 Years. Double-album best-of covering the years 1961 to 1976; the place to start and also some of the best singing in contemporary folk music. –WR

○ **Fires of Eden / CBS**   1990
A graceful, personal, and finely crafted work that crosses between art song and folk music. –BE

LUI COLLINS

A Connecticut singer/songwriter and interpreter of songs by Jack Hardy and Julie Snow. –RM

Made in New England / GREEN LINNET

○ **Baptism of Fire / GREEN LINNET**
The title song is lush. Jack Hardy's "Tinker's Coin" is another highlight. –RM

There's a Light / GREEN LINNET

SHAWN COLVIN   ♭1958

Singer and songwriter Shawn Colvin was born in South Dakota and has lived in London (Ontario) and in Carbondale, Illinois, where she graduated from high school. She dropped out of Southern Illinois University to join a hard-rock group, later playing with the Dixie Diesels, a Western swing band in Austin. After a sojourn in San Francisco, she moved to New York City in 1980 and gradually worked her way up to the folk circuit, also appearing in such off-Broadway shows as *Pump Boys and Dinettes, Diamond Studs,* and *Lie of the Mind.* Her work appeared in *The Fast Folk Musical Magazine,* and she got her first real break in 1987, singing backup on a Suzanne Vega tour. Recruited by Vega's management, she signed to Columbia Records in 1988 and released her debut album, *Steady On,* in 1989. –WR

○ **Steady On / COLUMBIA**   1989

Sharp production, surprising arrangements, and Shawn Colvin's alternately breathy and ringing vocals give the best possible forum to her astute reflections on life and love. The album won a Grammy Award for Best Folk Album, but its roots go into rock and country as well. –WR

ELIZABETH COTTEN   1893-1987

Elizabeth Cotten has influenced the finger-picking style of every guitarist who tried it since she began performing publicly in the 50s. Cotten worked as a domestic for the Charles Seeger family (whose children included Pete, Peggy, and Mike) in Washington, DC, and was persuaded by Mike Seeger to take up performing at the age of 60. The song "Freight Train," which she wrote when she was 12, became a Top 5 hit in the UK and is now a standard. She recorded several albums for Folkways in the 50s and 60s, displaying her remarkable dexterous style, which (like stride piano playing) mixed a strong rhythmic backing with precisely yet delicately picked melody work. She continued to perform until shortly before her death in her mid 90s. –WR

★ **Folksongs & Instrumentals ... / FOLKWAYS**   1958

Folksongs & Instrumentals with Guitar. This first LP collection by a widely influential guitarist includes her classic "Freight Train." –WR

○ **Freight Train / FOLKWAYS**

Reissue of initial recordings of this National Heritage Award-winning Piedmont guitarist. A major model for finger-pickers. –BLP

MIKE CROSS

Mike Cross is a gifted musician (guitar and fiddle), who started playing late in his life. He is known for his high-energy live shows. His songwriting styles lean toward folk, country, and Gaelic. –CR

○ **Live & Kickin' / SUGAR HILL**

Cross mixes country, folk, bluegrass, and Scots/Irish music, playing fiddle and guitar and singing on material ranging from spirited dance tunes to off-the-wall novelties. He is thus best heard in a live setting, especially one that includes the infectious "Whiskey 'Fore Breakfast." –WR

CATIE CURTIS

Catie Curtis is a singer/songwriter from Maine who has won recognition and numerous awards in the folk community. –CR

○ **Dandelion / MONGOOSE**   1989

Curtis's debut cassette, featuring 12 songs, is not as polished as her *From Years to Hours* CD. Her acoustic guitar work is good, and she uses just enough backup to add to her music without overpowering it. Good effort. –CR

● **From Years to Hours / MONGOOSE**   1991

Curtis shines on her second release, really maturing as a songwriter. Her music is well produced (Darleen Wilson), and her songwriting is intelligent and thought-provoking. "Hole in the Bucket" is the key song on this collection. –CR & RM

ERIK DARLING   b 1933

Singer/guitarist/banjoist briefly attended New York University and then backed folkster Ed McCurdy. In 1956, Darling formed the Tarriers who scored a hit with "The Banana Boat Song" (1956). He subsequently headed the Folk Singers who

hit with "Run Come Here" (1958), recorded a solo LP, joined the Weavers in 1958, and four years later formed the Rooftop Singers. –DS

The Possible Dream / ELEKTRA   1975

Featuring guest Patricia Street. –JME

○ **True Religion / ELEKTRA**

THE DEIGHTON FAMILY

A six-piece band that plays a combination of bluegrass, blues, Celtic folk, and Cajun music. –CR

Rolling Home / GREEN LINNET

The Deighton Family have developed a unique brand of music. They're a traditionalist's dream. –CR

○ **Mama Was Right / PHILO**

More fun performances with squeezebox, tin whistles, and mandolin. Includes a wiggy take on George Harrison's "Tax Man." –MH

★ **Acoustic Music to Suit Most Occasions / PHILO**   1989

A delightful British folkabilly band that defies easy pigeon-holing. National Public Radio named this its Album of the Year. –MH

IRIS DEMENT

A very lyrical singer/songwriter from Arkansas who plays country-edged folk music and whose view of the world is relaxed and filled with lovely irony. –RM & CR

○ **Infamous Angel / PHILO**   1992

"Hotter Than Mojave" and "Our Town" stand out. –RM

SANDY DENNY   1941-1978

From her debut with Fairport Convention in 1968, one of England's most important folk stylists and a major influence in rock as well, with a striking alto voice and daunting compositional style. Prior to her accidental death a decade later, Denny recorded a brace of superb solo albums with her former Fairport stablemate, guitarist Richard Thompson, and her husband Trevor Lucas (d 1990). She left behind one classic song ("Who Knows Where the Time Goes"). Major influence: Isla Cameron. –BE

North Star Grassman & the Ravens / CARTHAGE   1971

Some second thoughts and reapproaches to older work. –BE

Sandy / A&M   1972

Those seeking initiation into the ranks of Denny fans may consult listings for Fairport Convention and Fotheringay. Also, try this solo album, which features many of the same players (Richard Thompson, Dave Swarbrick, etc.) and contains a good collection of Denny originals along with her rendition of Dylan's "Tomorrow Is a Long Time." –WR

Rendezvous / CARTHAGE   1973

Stylistically varied, if not so fresh as her album *Sandy.* –BE

Sandy Denny & the Strawbs / CARTHAGE   1985

Denny with a British bluegrass band that later moved into progressive rock (without her). Her voice and a moody rendition of her classic "Who Knows Where the Time Goes" make it worthwhile. –BE

○ **Who Knows Where the Time Goes / HANNIBAL**   1985

This magnificently produced multi-disc boxed set presents a complete portrait of Sandy Denny, the haunting singer, the melodic, mournful songwriter, and the mesmerizing bandleader of Fairport Convention and Fotheringay. Much of the material is previously unheard, but it's all of a piece with Denny's accomplished work on her solo albums and in her groups. The album makes the case for Denny as a major folk artist. –WR

● **The Best of Sandy Denny / HANNIBAL**   1989

Concise collection of key tracks. Excellent introduction. –BE

DEVONSQUARE

Devonsquare is a New England-based folk trio featuring Alana MacDonald (vocals, violin), Herb Ludwig (vocals), and

Tom Dean (vocals, guitar, and percussion). They were voted "Act of the Year" by WNEW-FM of New York City. Tight harmonies and solid songwriting are their trademark. –CR

Walking on Ice / ATLANTIC   1987
A very rich album. Folk with a pop flavor. "Black Africa" and "Walking on Ice" are very strong songs. –CR

○ **Bye Bye Route 66 / ATLANTIC**   1991
It's hard to believe this is the same band. It has a Fleetwood Mac sound: more rock. Highly recommended. –CR

HAZEL DICKENS

One of 11 children of a West Virginia preacher, Hazel Dickens has recorded self-penned songs of deep conviction delivered with rough-edged passion. A country singer too raw for Nashville, Dickens is generally pegged a folksinger, albeit one without a dulcet warble. She's more akin to Sara Carter than to Joan Baez. Dickens also has been placed in the bluegrass camp, though one suspects her labor activism and feminism make much of her company there uneasy. Twenty years ago, her album with Alice Gerrard, *Hazel & Alice* (Rounder), was a cult classic that inspired, among others, Emmylou Harris. Her anthem "They'll Never Keep Us Down" appeared in the award-winning documentary *Harlan County, USA*. Dickens's solo albums for Rounder are uniformly excellent, the title of one (borrowed from Woody Guthrie) neatly summarizing her work: *Hard Hitting Songs for Hard Hit People*. This is a woman Guthrie would've loved as a kindred spirit. –MH

Hard Hitting Songs / ROUNDER   1980
Hard Hitting Songs for Hard Hit People is a very good record that deals with the out-of-work, down-on-his-luck, average American. It features Nancy & Norman Blake, Tony Trischka, Ross Barenberg, James Bryan, Matt Glaser, Barry Mitterhoff, and Buddy Spicher. –CR

★ **By the Sweat of My Brow / ROUNDER**   1983
A great record, which features "By the Sweat of My Brow," "Old & in the Way," "The Ballad of Ira Hayes," and "Your Greedy Heart." –CR

○ **Hard to Tell the Singer from the Song / ROUNDER**   1987
Dickens covers Dylan's "Only a Hobo" and Dallas Frazier's "California Cottonfields." Jerry Douglas, Pat Enright, Roy Husky, Ross Barenberg, and Mike Compton back her up. –CR

A Few Old Memories / ROUNDER
Good songs. –MH

KITTY DONOHOE

A Michigan singer and songwriter. –RM
○ **Farmer in Florida / ROHEEN**

BARRY DOW

Barry Dow is a California singer and songwriter, a winner at the 1991 Kerrville Folk Festival (Emerging Songwriting Award). Dow's music combines contemporary folk with occasional ventures around the edges of ragtime and blues, all finger-picked in an easy, rolling style. –CR

○ **Barry Dow's Urban Folk Tales / BARRY DOW MUSIC**
Dow's album is full of imagery dealing with love — love of whiskey, love of the West Coast and Pacific Ocean, and love of memories. His vocals are a cross between Jim Croce and Phil Ochs. Dow is an artist to watch for. –CR

NICK DRAKE   1948-1974

Mention the name Nick Drake and it's likely that Van Morrison or Tim Buckley will be mentioned as well. If you asked fans to provide a one-word description of Drake's music, "haunting" would surface most frequently. While his works were known to only a cultish few in his lifetime, the legacy of Nick Drake looms ever larger as the years have passed.
In discovering the music, most people gravitate to Drake's second album, *Bryter Layter*, a seemingly cheery and agreeable work that stands in sharp contast to the stark and desperate *Pink Moon*. Not even the lush, baroque

orchestrations of *Five Leaves Left* can mask the real-life gloom, not a studied pose, that Drake was unable to escape from. All three of Drake's actual albums remain astonishingly valuable, with Joe Boyd's production of *Bryter Layter* being a particularly standout effort. That Drake's music has sold increasingly well in recent years comes as little surprise, since Nick Drake has become a most trendy namedrop among contemporary artists. It is safe to say that the sad but beautiful music of Nick Drake will continue to inspire for years to come. –SA

○ **Fruit Tree / HANNIBAL**   1986
Multi-disc album contains the complete works of this enigmatic British singer/songwriter. –WR

JUDY DUNAWAY

From rural Mississippi, Dunaway uses balloons, bottle brushes, and standard instruments for songs about monsters, nudity, death, and immigration. Her songs range in style from rock to salsa to country to blues to noise, suspended over irregular rhythms and forms that often incorporate free improvisation. This is experimental but not at all self-indulgent. –RM

○ **Judy Dunaway / LOST RECORDS**
Remarkable variety, "Missionary Kid" and "El Norte." –RM

RICHARD DYER-BENNETT

Dyer-Bennet began his performing career in 1934 and became one of the preeminent "concert folksingers" of his generation. His genteel interpretations did much to popularize old English and American ballads. –RM

Ballads / STINSON
The key song is "Spanish Is the Loving Tongue." –RM

Twentieth Century Minstrel / DECCA
Includes "The Devil and the Farmer's Wife," "Swapping Song," and "Eggs and Marrowbone." –RM

○ **Richard Dyer-Bennett - Vols. 1 - 7 / DYB**
These comprehensive collections of Dyer-Bennett form the most complete collection of his work. Recorded in the mid-to-late 50s. –RM

CLIFF EBERHARDT

New York-based singer/songwriter Cliff Eberhardt combines a hoarse, expressive voice with a dynamic guitar style for some of the most moving music to be heard in the "new folk" music of the 80s and 90s. Though his debut album released in 1990, *The Long Road*, shows how stirring he can be, *The Songwriters Exchange*, a compilation made ten years earlier, shows he's been that good for a long time. –WR

○ **Long Road / WINDHAM HILL**   1990
The debut from one of the best of the new crop of folksinger/songwriters. –WR

ED'S REDEEMING QUALITIES

Quirky contemporary folk trio. Singing of distributor caps, lawn darts, and guys named Bob, Ed's Redeeming Qualities is responsible for two cleverly amusing albums that transcend genre limitations. Sharing vocals are violinist and guitarist Carrie Bradley, uace Dan Leone, and bongos and clarinet man Neno Perrotta (who also shakes a mean jar of rice). The San Francisco-based ERQ made its debut on Flying Fish Records with *More Bad Times* in 1990 (the set is dedicated to Dom Leone, writer of "Buck Tempo," who died before its release), and encored with *It's All Good News*, another delightfully off-the-wall 1991 collection. –BD

○ **More Bad Times / FLYING FISH**   1990
Creative, low-fi folk with a silliness that is almost, but not quite, cloying. Humorous lyrics, with instruments like xylophones, ukeleles, and a coffee can. –RG

RAMBLIN' JACK ELLIOTT   b 1931

Ramblin' Jack El, who has been playing folk music since the

40s, is an important link between Woody Guthrie (Elliot's dominant influence) and the folk artists of the 60s and after. A repository of folk/blues, cowboy songs, and early country, an archivist and an excellent performer. –WR

☆ **The Essential Ramblin' Jack Elliott / VANGUARD** 1970
Elliott was the complete folksinger of the 60s, singing and yodeling traditional material derived from folk, country, and blues sources and (especially) carrying on the tradition of Woody Guthrie. This two-pocket set, some of which is taken from a 1965 concert, provides a representative sampling of his repertoire and style. –WR

Sings Woody Guthrie & Jimmie Rodgers / MONITOR
Elliott devotes one side each to his two chief influences, re-creating Guthrie standards such as "Grand Coulee Dam" and "I Ain't Got No Home" as well as Rodgers favorites like "T for Texas" and "Waitin' for a Train." Not coincidentally, he brings out the similarities between them. –WR

PETER ELMAN

Elman was born in Washington, DC, and moved to California. He is a talented piano and guitar player. He has played with Roy Buchanan, Mike Marshall, Darol Anger, Lacy J. Dalton, and others. His music falls between folk and new-age. –CR

○ **Durango Saloon / ACORN MUSIC** 1990
There is a nice balance between Elman's piano and guitar playing and his brother Tony's hammer dulcimer. Flaco Jimenez's accordion and Pete Grant's pedal steel add nicely to the recording. Todd Phillips (bass), John Blakeley (guitar and dobro), Darol Anger (violin), and J. Eriksen (harmonica and percussion) are all skilled musicians. This release has a real Western feel to it. –CR

TONY ELMAN

Elman is one of better hammer dulcimer players around. He has sold over 400,000 copies of his recordings. His music is a combination of folk and new-age. –CR

○ **Winter Creek / ACORN MUSIC** 1991
This is a beautiful album featuring traditional Christmas carols and winter tunes; however, it's one to enjoy all year round. Elman is a skilled hammer dulcimer player and is backed by his brother Peter (piano, guitar, and synthesizer), along with Mike Marshall (guitar and violin), Todd Phillips (string bass), Pete Grant (pedal steel, dobro, autoharp), Jon Eriksen (percussion, harmonica), Barry Phillips (cello), and the Arlekin String Quartet. All solid and well-crafted, it's a good buy for the money. –CR

MICHAEL ELWOOD

Michael Elwood ia Texas-based singer/songwriter and a fine lyricist. –RM

○ **Scarecrow's Prayer / AGUA AZUL**
"Scarecrow's Blues" and "White Gold and Rubies" are outstanding tracks. –RM

MARVIN ETZIONI

Cofounder of the'band Lone Justice. A key figure in the 80s Los Angeles songwriters' scene. –RM

○ **Mandolin Man / RESTLESS** 1992
This is an album of quiet grace framed by the tracks "How Great Is the Ocean" and "My Ultimate Home." –RM

JOHN FAHEY   b1939

One of the great and certainly among the most influential acoustic guitarists in folk and popular music, Fahey started his own record label, Takoma, in 1959, to release his debut album, *The Transfiguration of Blind Joe Death*. He has since recorded 40 or more albums. A student of rural blues music, Fahey did a Ph.D. thesis on Charley Patton and incorporated the Delta blues into his increasingly eclectic style. Also important as a record-company executive, Fahey recorded what he liked, resurrecting the career of Bukka White and

taking on young protégé Leo Kottke, who has never really escaped his influence. Nor have the army of new-age guitarists of the 70s and beyond, many of whom sound like Fahey in isolated moments, though none can keep up with his musical ability and. By now there are elements of almost all genres in his music, yet his playing remains his own. –WR

○ **The Transfiguration of Blind Joe Death / TAKOMA** 1980
This is the definitive work by this influential acoustic guitar master. –WR

MIMI FARINA   b1945

Mimi Farina, Joan Baez's younger sister, first got into performing professionally in partnership with her husband, novelist and songwriter Richard Farina, whom she married in 1963. Singing harmony, the couple released two remarkable albums on Vanguard, *Celebrations for a Grey Day* in 1965 and *Reflections in a Crystal Wind* (1966), before Richard was killed in a motorcycle accident. Mimi Farina was 21.

She subsequently released an album of the duo's outtakes, *Memories*. (The two albums made during Richard's lifetime were reissued as a best-of twofer.) In the late 60s, Farina, based in California, worked with a satiric improvisational acting group and began to write her own songs. She re-emerged on record in 1971 on *Take Heart*, a duo album with Tom Jans that included her tribute song to Janis Joplin, "In the Quiet Morning." (This and other songs of hers were also recorded by her sister.)

In the 70s, Farina founded Bread & Roses, a charity organization devoted to putting on musical performances in hospitals and prisons. Some of the organization's annual benefit concerts, featuring some of the biggest names in folk and popular music, have been recorded and released. In 1985, Farina finally released a solo album, appropriately entitled *Solo*, and undertook a national tour. –WR

☆ **Best of Mimi and Richard Farina / VANGUARD**
The brilliant novelist, singer, and songwriter Richard Farina died young, but not before recording two great albums with his wife, Mimi, that are combined on this compilation. –WR

Solo / PHILO 1985

FICTION BROTHERS

Alan Senauke (guitar) and Howie Tarnower (guitar, banjo, and mandolin) play a blend of bluegrass to blues. –CR

○ **Things Are Coming My Way / FLYING FISH** 1984
Very good old-time music with a new-time freshness. Featuring Tony Trischka, Kenny Kasek, and Matt Glaser. –CR

FIVE CHINESE BROTHERS

The Five Chinese Brothers are not Chinese or brothers. What they are is a five-piece band that plays a combination of folk, rock, and country. The New York-based band is made up of Tom Meltzer (lead vocals, acoustic guitar), Paul Foglino (bass), Charlie Shaw (drums), Neil Thomas (accordion, piano, vocals), and Kevin Trainor (lead guitar, vocals). –CR

○ **Singer, Songwriter, Beggarman, Thief /**
(INDEPENDENT) 1992
A real enjoyable 14-song cassette featuring "Paul Cezanne," "If I Ain't Falling," and "Baltimore." Meltzer's vocals are very easy to listen to, making you want to hear more. Thomas's accordion-playing helps give the band a definitive sound. Trainor's guitar work is flawless. Foglino and Thomas share the writing (Trainor wrote one song on the tape). Somebody sign these guys! –CR

FOLK LIKE US

A traditional band featuring Debra Bagwell (flute, piccolo, pennywhistle, recorder, piano), Johnny Carlisle (guitar, five-string banjo), Doug Reid (fiddle), David Shaw (string bass, tenor banjo), Mark Shelton (hammer dulcimer, bodhran, bones, snare drum, spoons), Dave Yonley (fiddle), and special guest Beth Shelton on oboe. –CR

○ **Spring Dance / NORTH STAR**

A fine collection of reels, polkas, jigs, and traditional standards. If you enjoy traditional instruments played to perfection, pick up this CD. −CR

FOTHERINGAY

A short-lived offshoot of Fairport Convention, featuring key member and leader Sandy Denny. A second album was planned but never completed; tracks from it turn up on the triple-CD Denny anthology *Who Knows Where the Time Goes*. This is far more interesting and beguiling than their work with Fairport Convention, especially the Bob Dylan songs, but it lacks Fairport's precision and focus. −BE & WR

○ **Fotheringay / CARTHAGE**   1970

Also featured are Trevor Lucas and Jerry Donahue, both of whom eventually joined Fairport when Denny rejoined. The album is a close relative of Denny's other solo and group work and features several of her flowing ballads, showcasing her lovely voice. A footnote, but a pleasing one. −BE & WR

KINKY FRIEDMAN   b1944

Texas-born Richard "Kinky" Friedman operated on the outer fringe of the "outlaw" country movement of the 70s, forming a band called the Texas Jewboys and performing highly satiric country/rock material. He has since written successful detective novels. −WR

○ **Sold American / VANGUARD**   1973

A renegade figure who often stresses the outrageous. The title song is a gem. Part of the 70s country/folk/rock wave. −HD

● **Lasso from El Paso / EPIC**   1976

Of the many albums that grew out of Bob Dylan's *Rolling Thunder Revue*, this must be the strangest. Friedman has a husky voice and an off-kilter sense of humor best captured on the live-from-the-revue track, "Sold American." Also notable for a version of the Bob Dylan outtake, "Catfish." −WR

PAUL GEREMIA

A bluesy acoustic guitarist with a new-age sound. −CR

○ **I Really Don't Mind Livin' / FLYING FISH**   1982

A good selection of blues songs, all written by Geremia. Highly recommended. −CR

My Kinda Place / FLYING FISH   1986

Geremia covers Leadbelly, Blind Willie McTell, Lonnie Johnson, and Blind Lemon Jefferson. Some fine playing. −CR

BOB GIBSON   b1931

Bob Gibson is a singer, songwriter, and music collector. He plays guitar and banjo. He was popular in the 60s. −CR

○ **Homemade Music / MOON. RAIL.**   1978

Bob and Hamilton Camp — featuring several Shel Silverstein songs and a Steve Goodman cover "Lookin' for Trouble." −CR

Perfect High / MOUNTAIN RAILROAD   1980

Bob cowrites with Shel Silverstein and Tom Paxton. −CR

Uptown Saturday Night / HOGEYE   1984

A good record, featuring "Tequila Sheila" and the title track, "Uptown Saturday Night." −CR

ELIZA GILKYSON

Daughter of singer and songwriter Terry Gilkyson (who hit with "Marianne" in 1957), Eliza Gilkyson has made three albums; the first, *Love from the Heart*, was under the name Lisa Gilkyson. −WR

○ **Pilgrims / CAPITOL**   1987

Said to be concerned with "Jungian archetypes," this album can be enjoyed for the impassioned singing, song structures that sometimes recall Joni Mitchell at her most accessible, and the ethereal instrumental backgrounds that got the album tagged "new-age" upon release. −WR

Legends of Rainmaker / CAPITOL   1989

More directly autobiographical and issue-oriented material

(including Gilkyson's version of her song "Rosie Strike Back," done earlier by Rosanne Cash) played with more of a back beat characterizes this striking followup to *Pilgrims*. −WR

JANE GILLMAN

Gillman is a DC-based singer/songwriter who performs nationally in a play about Woody Guthrie. She plays guitar, harmonica, and dulcimer and is known for her well-crafted songwriting. −RM & CR

Pick It Up / GREEN LINNET

A great debut album. Gilman plays some good cross-picking guitar and is backed by Lyle Lovett and Mark O'Connor. −CR

○ **Jane Gillman / GREEN LINNET**   1980

A beautifully produced album. Mary Chapin Carpenter, Marcy Marxer, Lucy Kaplansky, John Gorka, Nina Gerber, and Seamus Egan back Gillman up. There is something about her vocals that catches you. Gillman's songwriting is topnotch, especially on songs such as "Listen to the Thunder," "Three Quarters," and the 90s folk view of romance in the pop 60s, "Song on the Radio." −CR

NEAL GLADSTONE

Gladstone is a singer/songwriter from Oregon who uses humor in his brand of folk/rock. −CR

○ **Sleep Neat / KALEIDOSCOPE**   1988

Gladstone likes to use humor in his songs to get you thinking. "Get Cloned" is about the uses of personal clones, "Country Cliché" hits the old country music industry for its songwriting clichés, and "Dodge Dart" is about that old indestructible car — all great songs. The music style is more rock/pop. −CR

CYNTHIA GOODING

A major interpreter of folk songs from around the world in their original language and translation. −RM

○ **Best of Cynthia Gooding / PRESTIGE**

Early English Folk Songs / ELEKTRA

STEVE GOODMAN   1948-1984

Chicago-based singer/songwriter Steve Goodman made a number of excellent albums on Buddah, Asylum, and his own Red Pajamas Records before his premature death from leukemia. His best-known song was "The City of New Orleans," which was a hit for Arlo Guthrie and was recorded by many others. −WR

Steve Goodman / BUDDAH   1971

The debut of a great new songwriter. −WR

○ **Artistic Hair / RED PAJAMAS**   1983

Goodman achieved artistic control with this album, featuring his "City of New Orleans" and other classics. −WR

Affordable Art / RED PAJAMAS

This one features "A Dying Cub Fan's Last Request" and "Watchin' Joey Glow." −WR

JOHN GORKA

This perceptive, husky-voiced singer/songwriter spent the early 80s hustling around the Northeast folk circuit, then won the Kerrville Folk Festival's New Folk award in 1984. He has since recorded four albums. −WR

● **I Know / RED HOUSE**   1987

Still some of his best work, including "Blues Palace," Downtown Tonight," and "Down in the Milltown." −RM

○ **Land of the Bottom Line / WINDHAM HILL**   1990

Keen observations and an earnest performance style mark Gorka as a major new folk talent. −WR

Jack's Crows / HIGH STREET   1992

GREEN GRASS CLOGGERS

A mountain dance troup. −CW

○ **Through the Ears / ROUNDER**   1988

A splendid collection of never-before-released tracks by many of the old-time country groups who toured with or performed with the Cloggers. –CW

ROBIN GREENSTEIN

A New York singer/songwriter and interpreter with a light jazz sensibility. –RM

○ **Slow Burn / WINDY**
Her beautiful song "When You Leave Amsterdam" is here. –RM

STEFAN GROSSMAN   ♭1945

Stefan Grossman is a student of the folk, blues, and ragtime styles of the Reverend Gary Davis (with whom he studied) and a variety of other performers. He has become a virtuoso guitarist, as is demonstrated by numerous recordings and concert appearances. –WR

○ **Shining Shadows / SHANACHIE**   1985
Stirring guitar instrumentals. –WR

ARLO GUTHRIE   ♭1947

Like his father Woody Guthrie, Arlo Guthrie has carved out a career as a folksinger and songwriter with a social conscience who leavens political messages with humor. Though Woody Guthrie was hospitalized for much of Arlo's youth, the youngster nevertheless grew up in a musical community that included Pete Seeger, Leadbelly, and Cisco Houston. He learned to play the guitar at age six and was performing in coffeehouses by his late teens.

Guthrie's early fame was based on his anti-Establishment shaggy-dog story in song, "Alice's Restaurant," actually a comic monolog about the singer's troubles with the police and the draft board that was extremely timely when it appeared on record in 1967. The *Alice's Restaurant* album became Guthrie's only gold record, but he made a series of folk/rock records through the 70s, filling them with his own songs and those of his contemporaries, notably Steve Goodman's "The City of New Orleans," which became Guthrie's sole hit single in 1972.

Guthrie's commercial fortunes, like those of most folkies, declined by the end of the 70s, and he made his last album for Warner Bros. in 1981. Since then, he has launched his own label, Rising Son, which has reissued his Warner's albums and released his new recordings. He continues to tour extensively and to work for such causes as environmentalism. –WR

○ **Together in Concert / WARNER**   1975
Separately and together, Arlo Guthrie and Pete Seeger delight in a live setting. –WR

○ **Amigo / RISING SON**   1976
An excellent, rocking collection including Guthrie's adaptation of "Guabi, Guabi," a song about Victor Jara, and a knockabout cover of the Rolling Stones song "Connection." –WR

● **Precious Friend / WARNER**   1982
A second excellent collection by Pete Seeger and Arlo Guthrie, veterans of two generations. –WR

○ **Best of Arlo Guthrie / WARNER**   1987
This includes "Alice's Restaurant," the equally comic "Motorcycle Song," "Coming into Los Angeles," and "City of New Orleans." –WR

WOODY GUTHRIE   1912-1967

Woody Guthrie was the most important American folk music artist of the first half of the 20th century. Coming out of Oklahoma, Guthrie had firsthand knowledge of the dustbowl diaspora chronicled in John Steinbeck's novel, *The Grapes of Wrath*. In fact, Guthrie wrote his own version of the story in a song called "Tom Joad." By the time he gained recognition in the 40s, Guthrie had written hundreds of songs, many of which remain folk standards to this day. When he was interviewed by Alan Lomax for the Library of Congress in March 1940, Guthrie punctuated his reminiscences by singing "So Long, It's Been Good to Know You," "Dust Bowl Blues," "Do-Re-Mi," "Pretty Boy Floyd," "I Ain't Got No Home," and

other songs. He later wrote "Pastures of Plenty," "The Grand Coulee Dam," and his masterpiece, "This Land Is Your Land." He was also an author (*Bound for Glory*) and a newspaper columnist.

Guthrie made some recordings for RCA in 1940, but much of his work was issued on the small Folkways label. Meanwhile, in the late 40s and early 50s, versions of his songs became hits for such artists as the Weavers. By then, Guthrie himself was in physical decline, suffering from a hereditary paralytic disease. But during his long illness, Guthrie's influence spread to the next generation, fostering the folk boom of the late 50s and early 60s. Not only is Bob Dylan unimaginable without him, but large segments of popular music are permanently affected by his concerns as a songwriter and his approach to the form. Guthrie also composed a body of children's music toward the end of his performing career in the early 50s, when he was raising a family with his wife Marjorie. The songs, many sung from a child's point of view, have been covered and performed extensively since. –WR

○ **Sings Folk Songs / SMITHSONIAN-FOLKWAYS**   1962
Guthrie sings traditional material here, with Leadbelly and others. –WR

○ **Dust Bowl Ballads / ROUNDER**   1964
His classic Okie songs, "Talking Dust Bowl Blues," "Do-Re-Mi," and more. –WR

○ **Library of Congress Recordings / ROUNDER**   1964
A multi-disc set of songs and conversations from 1940. –WR

★ **This Land Is Your Land / FOLKWAYS**   1967
The title track and some of the Columbia River songs. –WR

Struggle / SMITHSON-FOLKWAYS   1976
A powerful collection of songs about American labor. –MH

Columbia River Collection / ROUNDER   1987
An intelligent reconstruction of Guthrie's Columbia River songs, including "Grand Coulee Dam" and "Pastures of Plenty." –WR

CHUCK HALL

A Boston-area writer of quite graceful, direct songs about day-to-day life. –RM

○ **One Night in a Cheap Hotel / CHEAP HOTEL MUSIC**
"Dollmaker's Secret" is a key cut. –RM

BUTCH HANCOCK   ♭1945

An obscure, legendary Texas songwriter whose work has been covered by Jerry Jeff Walker and Joe Ely, Hancock has a gift for wordplay and nuance. The songs become gradually more accessible, as the tentative voice-and-guitar approach is replaced by surprisingly full folk/rock settings and assured singing. –WR

● **Own & Own / SUGAR HILL**   1989
This compilation is culled from Hancock's many albums on his own Rainlight label from 1978 to 1987 (plus four tracks from 1989). –WR

○ **No Two Alike / RAINLIGHT**
This 14-tape series (available by subscription only) is a document of six nights at the Cactus Cafe, where Butch performed with a host of great guests and never repeated a single one of his songs. –RM

TIM HARDIN   1941-1980

Tim Hardin brought a trance-like personal touch to the songs he wrote, though in the hands of others they became more accessible pop hits, notably "If I Were a Carpenter" and "Reason to Believe." Hardin's own music spanned folk and jazz, and his talent belied his uneven career. –WR

○ **3-Live in Concert / LINE**   1968
A great live recording that captures Hardin at his peak as a performer. –KMC

● **Reason to Believe (Best Of) / POLYGRAM**   1970
The early work of a top-flight 60s singer/songwriter includes

the title track, "If I Were a Carpenter," and "Misty Roses." Great stuff. –KMC & WR

Bird on a Wire / CBS / BB# 189   1971
His last new American release, and a good one. –KMC

○ **The Shock of Grace / CBS**   1981
His best from the 70s, including "Bird on a Wire" and "First Love Song." –WR

JACK HARDY   b 1948

Jack Hardy has been a central figure in folk music since his arrival in tGreenwich Village in 1978. Instrumental in founding The Songwriter's Exchange, The SpeakEasy Musician's co-op, and *The Fast Folk Musical Magazine*, Hardy has released nine albums domestically on his Great Divide label. Considered a writer's writer, he is known for politics in his songs, Americanized Irish influences, and a preoccupation with mythological imagery, mixed up with standard New York folk & roll. –RM

○ **Mirror of My Madness / GREAT DIVIDE**   1976
New York urban folk/rock period. Includes "The Tailor" and "Go Tell the Savior." –RM

The Nameless One / GREAT DIVIDE   1978
Landmark / GREAT DIVIDE   1980
These two albums (*The Nameless One, Landmark*) show Hardy's Irish influence and some of his best work, including "The Tinker's Coin," "Orphan from Madrid," and "The Inner Man." –RM

● **White Shoes / GREAT DIVIDE**   1982
A brilliant collection of songs by this husky-voiced founder of New York's "Fast Folk" movement. –WR

The Cauldron / GREAT DIVIDE   1984
Politically charged and neo-traditional originals, adeptly performed. –WR

The Hunter / GREAT DIVIDE   1986
An excellent example of Hardy's various lyric preoccupations. Includes "Dublin Farewell" and "The Changing Wind." –RM

Retrospective / BRAMBUS   1990
Through / BRAMBUS   1991

RICHIE HAVENS   b 1941

Born in the Bedford-Stuyvesant section of Brooklyn, Richie Havens moved to Greenwich Village in 1961 in time to get in on the folk boom then taking place. Havens had a distinctive style as a folksinger, appearing in such clubs as the Cafe Wha? His guitar set to an opening tuned, he would strum it while barring chords with his thumb, using it essentially as percussion while singing rhythmically in a gruff voice for a mesmerizing effect.

Havens was signed to Douglas Records in 1965 and recorded two albums that gained him a local following. In 1967, the Verve division of MGM Records formed a folk section (Verve Forecast) and signed Havens and other folk-based performers. The result was Havens's third album, *Mixed Bag*. It wasn't until 1968 and the *Something Else Again* album, however, that Havens began to hit the charts — actually, Havens's fourth, third, and second albums charted that year, in that order. In 1969 came the double album *Richard P. Havens 1983*.

Havens's career benefited enormously from his appearance at the Woodstock festival in 1969 and his subsequent featured role in the movie and album made from the concert in 1970. His first album after that exposure, *Alarm Clock*, made the Top 30 and produced a Top 20 single in "Here Comes the Sun." These recordings were Havens's commercial high-water mark, but by this time he had become an international touring success. By the end of the 70s, he had abandoned recording and turned entirely to live work.

Havens came back to records with a flurry of releases in 1987: a new album, *Simple Things*; an album of Bob Dylan and Beatles covers; and a compilation. In 1991, Havens signed his

first major-label deal in 15 years when he moved to Sony Music and released *Now*. –WR

○ **Mixed Bag / POLYGRAM**   1967
Havens's first major-label album, and his best, featuring his distinctive interpretations of such songs as Dylan's "Just Like a Woman" and the scathing anti-war anthem "Handsome Johnny." (It should be noted that, while it is his best overall collection, *Mixed Bag* is a also characteristic album: If you like it, you'll probably like other Havens records, which adopt much the same style.) –WR

Collection / RYKODISC   1987
A compilation of Havens's 60s and early 70s material. It leaves out some of his signature material, but is the only means of getting hold of this music at present. It does include his version of "Here Comes the Sun." (A reissue program announced by Five Star in 1990 had not begun as of spring 1992.) –WR

MARK HEARD

A California-based singer/songwriter with strong ties to the Christian-music world, though his songs are universal. Heard has released 14 albums in as many years. –RM

● **Dry Bones Dance / FINGERPRINT**   1990
Includes the great "House of Broken Dreams," "Rise from the Ruins," and "Lonely Road." –RM

○ **Second Hand / FINGERPRINT**   1991
A more contemporary pop production style. "Lonely Moon" and "I Just Wanna Get Warm" are two key tracks here. –RM

WAYNE HENDERSON

Henderson was born in the community of Rugby, in the Blue Ridge Mountains of Virginia. He has played guitar since the age of five; he plays a finger-picking style. Henderson is also well-known for making some of the most sought-after guitars and mandolins. –CR

○ **Rugby Guitar / FLYING FISH**   ·
This is a fine guitar album featuring Henderson and Gerald Anderson along with local Virginia musicians. The guitar work is clean and clear, backed by fiddle, banjo, mandolin, and bass at times. A must for you acoustic guitar fans. –CR

JUDY HENSKE

A West Coast folksinger, Judy Henske started out working with ex-Kingston Trio member Dave Guard in 1962 as part of the Whiskeyhill singers. A fine folksinger who was very popular in the early 60s, Henske has never achieved real commercial success. –JME

○ **Judy Henske / ELEKTRA**

PRISCILLA HERDMAN

A folksinger and guitarist from New York, she has released five albums since 1976, including *Stardreamer, Nightsongs*, and *Lullabies*, which is a collection of songs for children. –MH

○ **Seasons of Change / FLYING FISH**   1983
Herdman presents a compelling rural landscape, singing in a clear, reassuring voice of struggling farmers, family ties, and feminist consciousness. She continues the interpretive folksinging tradition of Joan Baez and Judy Collins, updating it for the 80s and 90s. –WR

● **The Water Lily / PHILO**   1987
Herdman presents a more traditional set of songs on this collection, which was recorded in 1976. Accompanied by fiddle, mandolin, and cello, along with her own guitar, she is remarkably affecting on such emotional selections as "The Drover's Sweetheart" and, especially, "The Band Played Waltzing Matilda," which is all but guaranteed to provoke tears. –WR

CAROLYN HESTOR   b 1937

Singing songs from her Southwestern roots as well as

standard folk items, Carolyn Hestor was a mainstay of the folk scene in the 60s. Her first album for Columbia, *Carolyn Hestor*, received rave reviews. She graduated to a more contemporary folk music and in the early 80s was still providing rare appearances on the folk circuit. –JME

○ **That's My Song / DOT**   1965

CHRIS HICKEY

A Los Angeles-based singer/songwriter. He is a member of the band Show of Hands (with one album on IRS). –RM

● **Frames of Mind, Boundaries of Time / CNC**
○ **Looking for Anything / CNC**

HOBO JIM

Hobo Jim is a Nashville-based singer/songwriter whose songs depict life in the Northwest. –CR

○ **Thunderfoot / FLYING FISH**
Debut album. Hard to find, easy to listen to. –CR

Lost & Dyin' Breed / FLYING FISH
A good folk/bluegrass album. Not so mature as his followup record, but worth checking out. –CR

● **Where Legends Are / FLYING FISH**
Solid songs. Hobo Jim stacks the deck with some fine musicians, including Sam Bush, Bela Fleck, Pat Flynn, and Kenny Malone. Short in length, but long on quality. –CR

ROBIN HOLCOMB   b 1954

This Georgia-born singer/songwriter, composer, pianist, and poet incorporates elements of gospel, blues, R&B, and rock into her music. Holcomb has had a varied background in chamber music, ethnomusicology (including performing in a Javanese gamelan ensemble), musical theater, and work with her husband, Wayne Horvitz of the New York downtown avant-garde experimental scene. After attending the University of California at Santa Cruz, she and Horvitz moved to New York, before settling in Seattle in 1988. –ED

○ **Robin Holcomb / ELEKTRA**   1990
The songs are arty, piano-based, spooky, and very sensual. "Deliver Me" is particularly fine. –RM

BOB HOLMES

A Boston-based singer/songwriter of bluesy-style contemporary folk music. –RM

Railroad / NOVEMBER   1980
○ **Hard Times in the Flood / NOVEMBER**   1982

DAVID HOLT

Holt is a banjo player and storyteller based in Nashville. He has hosted *The American Music Shop* and other specials on TNN. –CR

○ **Reel & Rock / FLYING FISH**   1986
Holt plays some great banjo. This album is all music, featuring Doc and Merle Watson and Jerry Douglas. –CR

THE HOLY MODAL ROUNDERS

Peter Stampfel (b 1939) and Steve Weber (b 1944) formed one of the strangest groups to come out of Greenwich Village in the 60s, mixing traditional music with novelties and off-kilter originals. They had added more instruments by the end of the 60s, by which time their recordings had become infrequent. They have reunited occasionally since. –WR

○ **Indian War Whoop / ESP**   1969
Comic, absurdist folk with Peter Stampfel as ringleader. –WR

Last Round / ADELPHI   1978
More madness, with "Pink Underwear" and "Romping through the Swamp." –WR

HOT MUD FAMILY

This excellent young old-time string band from Ohio specialized in tight vocals and a diverse repertoire. –CW

Live as We Know It / FLYING FISH   1989
○ **Meat & Potatoes (& Stuff Like That) / FLYING FISH**

CISCO HOUSTON   1918-1961

An associate of Woody Guthrie, with whom he made many recordings, Houston scored a hit single with "Rose, Rose, I Love You" in 1951. He was a popular folk interpreter until his death from cancer. –WR

○ **Sings Songs of the Open Road / FOLKWAYS**   1968
This Woody Guthrie sidekick sings Guthrie's songs and traditional tunes. –WR

SONYA HUNTER

This San Francisco-based singer/songwriter has a sound like vintage English folk/rock combined with a hip urban-American sensibility. –RM

Railroad / NOVEMBER   1980
○ **Favorite Short Stories / HEYDAY**   1992
"Foggy Moon" and "Wedding" are great cuts. –RM

IAN & SYLVIA

The 60s duo of Canadians Ian Tyson (b 1933) and Sylvia Fricker (b 1940) was notable for its combination of contemporary folk with the countryish music of rural Canada, once described as "country and Northwestern." Both singers wrote original songs that became standards (Tyson's "Four Strong Winds" and "Someday Soon," Fricker's "You Were on My Mind"), and they championed the work of then-little-known writers such as fellow-Canadians Gordon Lightfoot and Joni Mitchell. –WR

○ **Greatest Hits / VANGUARD**   1989
This compilation (CVSD 5/6) captures much of their best work. Do not confuse it with the identically titled Vanguard album 73114, which includes only half the material found on this set. –WR

THE INCREDIBLE STRING BAND

Scotland-born Mike Heron (b 1941) and Robin Williamson (b 1943) led one of the most eclectic folk groups of the 1960s, starting as a duo and later expanding and electrifying into a folk/rock group. –WR

Wee Tam / ELEKTRA / BB# 174   1969
Mixing English and American folk with what we now call "world music," the multi-instrumental Scottish duo of Robin Williamson and Mike Heron achieve a whimsical, delicate style that has never been duplicated. It reaches a peak here with such songs as "You Get Brighter." (*Wee Tam* is sometimes packaged with the simultaneously released *The Big Huge*, which is also recommended.) –WR

○ **Relics of the Incredible String Band / ELEKTRA**   1971
The ISB's prolific output makes a compilation a virtual necessity, and this two-record set selects wisely from the seven albums the group released in the US between 1967 and 1970. From Robin Williamson's "First Girl I Loved" (covered by Judy Collins) and "Way Back in the 1960s" (recorded in 1967), to Mike Heron's "Air," and "This Moment," the ISB's eclectic, fanciful acoustic style is well portrayed. –WR

No Ruinous Feud / REPRISE   1973
The ISB began to change its approach in 1971, cutting back on its sometimes open-ended song structures and adding a rock rhythm section to selected tracks. But it wasn't until this album that everything came together, resulting in a delightful collection of songs that range from reggae to light pop, along with the traditional folk styles that had always been the group's strong suit. –WR

TOM INTONDI

Originally based in Greenwich Village and now residing in the Northwest, Intondi has toured throughout the US and internationally, alone and as a member of the Song Project. He has three albums on his own and various cuts on *The Fast Folk Musical Magazine*. –RM

City Dancer / CITY DANCER 1976
○ House of Water / CITY DANCER 1983
Exuberant folk/pop with jazzy overtones makes up the musical base for this earnest New York singer, whose songs carry a warmth and depth of feeling rare even in the singer/songwriter genre and a melodic sense welcome in any musical style. The title song and "High Times" are highlights on this self-produced album. –WR & RM
Bringin' Up the Sun / CITY DANCER 1992
Includes a guest appearance by Nanci Griffith. –RM

ANDY IRVINE

A principal songwriter with the Irish folk groups Planxty and Patrick Street. –RM
○ **Rude Awakening / GREEN LINNET**

BURL IVES   b 1909

Ives traveled as an itinerant handyman throughout the United States after a brief stay at New York University. He became a working actor and performed concerts of folk ballads. He has published several songbooks and an autobiography, *Wayfaring Stranger*. –DS
☆ **Wayfaring Stranger / CBS**
This is traditional folk from the smooth-sounding Ives. Includes "On Top of Old Smokey," "Roving Gambler," and "Green Broom." –DS

BERT JANSCH   b 1943

Born in Scotland, Jansch moved to England and popularized the "folk baroque" movement. His style is a combination of jazz-flavored folk, traditional, and blues. –CR
○ **Early Bert - Vol. 2 / XTRA MUSIC** 1966
This was originally titled *Jack Orion*. More folk than his other releases. –CR
Moonshine / REPRISE 1973
Jansch covers a Ewan MacColl song, "The First Time Ever I Saw Your Face." –CR
Avocet / KICKING MULE 1984
The jazz side of Jansch's music is very strong. Mandocellist Martin Jenkins takes front stage on this album, along with Jansch. –CR
Sketches / TEMPLE 1990
With 13 cuts, this is very good. –CR
● **Ornament Tree / CAPITOL** 1990
An influential British folksinger/guitarist of the 60s on recent recordings. –MH

VICTOR JARA   d 1973

Victor Jara was the main proponent of the Chilean New Song movement, which brought a political consciousness to native folk music in Chile much as the "protest" singers of the 60s did to US folk music. A national figure, he was closely associated with the Allende government of the early 70s and was brutally murdered by the military junta that took over Chile in 1973. –WR
○ **An Unfinished Song / REDWOOD** 1990
Jara's expressive, vibrant singing shows why he was the leading light of the South American New Song movement as well as a significant political figure. This compilation includes not only original political songs but also traditional Chilean folksongs and even an adaptation of Malvina Reynolds's "Little Boxes." The album's 23 tracks, taken from various sources, provide a thorough view of Jara's broad talent. (Also recommended: Monitor Records' four-volume series of Jara recordings.) –WR

MICHAEL JERLING

A Chicago native, Jerling has developed an urban style with the feel of country blues. He is an excellent guitar player and singer/songwriter and his songs are full of strong imagery.

"The Long Black Wall" has become one of his signature pieces. –RM & CR
Blue Heartland / MOONLIGHT MAGIC
Includes "The Long Black Wall" and "Road House." –RM
On Top of Fool's Hill / MOONLIGHT MAGIC
○ **My Evil Twin / SHANACHIE** 1992
Jerling has a way with words that can paint a picture in your mind's eye. "Take Me to Juarez" is a classic tale; also worthwhile are "Breakdown," and the title cut. "Before the Country Moved to Town" features Robin and Linda Williams singing nice background vocals. All in all, this is a good label-debut album, with great songs and great production. –CR

JOSH JOFFEN

Brooklyn-born Josh Joffen has recorded often for *The Fast Folk Musical Magazine* (1982 to the present). He released an album with songwriter David Roth (they each have one side). Joffen won the Kerrville New Folk Competition in 1987. –RM
○ **Josh Joffen w/ David Roth / 6 OF 1** 1987
Joffen highlights are "Video Arcade" and "Chain of Love." David Roth faves are "Rising in Love" and "Fireflies." –RM

CROW JOHNSON

Based in Gravette, AR, Johnson is a popular songwriter in the South and West. She edits the magazine *Zassafrass Music News*. –RM
○ **As the Crow Flies / ZASSAFRASS**

PRUDENCE JOHNSON

Primarily an interpreter, Minnesota-based Prudence Johnson has recorded songs for children as well as adults. –RM
○ **Sings the Songs of Greg Brown / RHR** 1991
A beautifully presented set of interpretations of the work of a fine Midwest songwriter. –RM

BRENDA KAHN

This New Jersey singer/songwriter plays punk, thrash, blues, and folk on her maple Martin acoustic guitar. –CR
○ **Goldfish Don't Talk Back / COMMUNITY**
A high-energy album — part folk, part punk. The lyrics would gray the hairs on a nun's head. –CR

SI KAHN

A Southern activist and political songwriter, Kahn is known for his direct community work and also for his articulate writing. –RM
○ **Home / FLYING FISH**
● **Doing My Job / FLYING FISH**
I'll Be There / FLYING FISH

CONNIE KALDOR

She is from Alberta and is one of the main figures of the contemporary Canadian singer/songwriter community. –RM
○ **Moonlight Grocery / REDWOOD**
One of These Days / COYOTE

CINDY KALLET

Cindy Kallet is a singer/songwriter and guitarist whose songwriting mirrors her love for the New England coast. She is a fine guitarist whose musical styles vary from folk, fiddle tunes, traditional, and sea chanties. Her voice is smooth and deep, reminiscent of Joni Mitchell. She is not consumed by her music career, which could explain the reason she is not so well known as she so richly deserves. –CR
Working on Wings to Fly / FOLK LEGACY 1981
Kallet's debut album is a nice collection of songs performed acoustically, dealing mainly with the New England sea. This 1981 release is exactly what the rest of the folk community is doing in the 90s. –CR

○ **Cindy Kallet 2 / FOLK LEGACY**   1983
Start out with this release. The songwriting is a little more
expressive, and she plays some fine instrumentals. The music
is well crafted and the songs are from the heart. −CR

Angels in Daring / OVERALL MUSIC   1988
The trio of Kallet, Ellen Epstein, and Michael Cicone performs
a variety of songs a cappella and accompanied by guitar and
dulcimer. It is a collection of contemporary and traditional
music of the British Isles and America. Dougie MacLean's
"Ready for the Storm" is powerful. 14 songs in all. −CR

Dreaming Down Quiet Line / STONES THROW   1989
All her writing and musical talent fit together on this one. The
songs are varied in content, dealing with war, politics, love,
and family. The music and vocals are balanced so as not to
take away from each other. −CR

PAUL KAMM w/ELEANORE MACDONALD

A Nevada City, CA, duo whose songs are incisive and gentle
and beautifully performed. −RM

Unbroken Chain / FREEWHEEL
○ **Into the Clouds / FREEWHEEL**

PAUL KAPLAN

Chicago native, now resides in Amherst, MA, with his two
daughters. In addition to appearing on various Folkways
records and contributing songs to *Fast Folk*, Kaplan has
compiled three Phil Ochs albums for that company, and edited
the 1982 *Fast Folk* songbook. −RM

○ **Life on This Planet / HUMMINGBIRD**   1982
Contains his signatures, "Call Me the Whale" and "Henry the
Accountant." −RM

The King of Hearts / HUMMINGBIRD   1985
A concert of new material recorded live at the SpeakEasy club
in Greenwich Village in 1985. Features his beautiful song "The
King of Hearts" as well as some great audience participation
on "I Had an Old Coat." This album really captures the
atmosphere of a more traditional NY singer/songwriter in the
mid 80s. −RM

PETER KEANE

Keane is a guitarist and folksinger from Boston. He plays
traditional country, blues, and folk. −CR

○ **Goodnight Blues / NORTHEASTERN POP. ARTS**   1992
Keane steps out on his blues originals and is backed by Matt
Leavenworth (fiddle and mandolin) and Darrell Scott on
dobro. This release is very enjoyable. Keane's song "Jimmy
Yancey" is wonderful and relaxed, as are his versions of John
Hurt blues and the 60s chestnut, "Ruby Baby." −CR & RM

ROBERT EARL KEEN JR

Keen is a Texas singer/songwriter whose songs have been
covered by Nanci Griffith, and he has cowritten with Lyle
Lovett. −CR

● **No Kinda Dancer / PHILO**   1984
A well-crafted debut, not one bad song. "Armadillo Jackal &
This Old Porch," cowritten by Lyle Lovett, features Lovett and
Nanci Griffith singing harmony. −CR

○ **Live Album / SUGAR HILL**   1988
Good sound, new material, good stories, plus audience
interaction make this worthwhile. Featuring great mandolin
and fiddle by Johnathan Yadkin and a nice cut of "I Would
Change My Life." −CR

West Textures / SUGAR HILL   1989
Solid and well-produced, his storytelling has never been
better. This album is as good as *No Kinda Dancer*, with Jerry
Douglas on dobro and a cover of the Koller/Silverstein song
"Jennifer Johnson & Me." −CR

KIRK KELLY

Part of the New York anti-folk movement, this highly political

songwriter was inspired by Phil Ochs. Kelly is a contributor to
The Fast Folk Musical Magazine. −RM

○ **Go Man, Go / KIRK - SST**   1990
The title song is hard driving and great, typical of Kelly. −RM

STEVE KEY

Key was born in Brooklyn, NY, and raised in San Francisco,
CA. He later returned to New York City and joined the *Fast
Folk* crowd. He hosted a radio show on WFUV-FM in New
York. He now resides in Washington, DC, has issued the DC
compilation *Capitol Acoustics*, and is involved in the
Washington folk community. Key is a polished performer
whose songs are well crafted. They are also full of deep
imagery and emotion. −CR

Between Trains / LOCAL FOLKEL
Key's debut album is a rich collection of well-written stories
that were greatly influenced by his NYC lifestyle. −CR

○ **Record Time / LOCAL FOLKEL**
Key's songs represent the best of the suburban homespun
genre in contemporary folk. The title cut of this CD is a
recommended example. −RM

● **New Hope / LOCAL FOLKEL**   1990
This release is more upbeat than his first release. Every song is
strong. The title song could be an anthem for the 60s
generation. −CR

THE KINGSTON TRIO

Bob Shane (b 1934), Nick Reynolds (b 1933), and Dave Guard
(b 1934, d 1991) formed the Kingston Trio in California in
1957. For the next ten years the group was perhaps the most
popular in folk music, starting with their hit version of the
traditional song "Tom Dooley," which topped the charts in
1958. The Trio adapted traditional songs and novelties to their
exuberant style, which filled nightclubs and then concert
halls. Critics, especially in folk music, objected to the
inauthenticity of their approach, but the Trio popularized folk
music to millions who might never have heard it otherwise.
They racked up seven gold albums by 1964 and paving the
way for Joan Baez; Peter, Paul & Mary; Bob Dylan; and others.
Guard left the Trio in 1961 and was replaced by John Stewart;
and the Trio disbanded completely in 1967, its music in
popular decline. But Shane put together a new Kingston Trio
in 1973, which has performed and recorded sporadically
since. Recently, much of the group's Capitol Records output
from the early 60s was been reissued on CD. −WR

The Kingston Trio / CAPITOL   1958
The debut album of the most popular act in the folk boom of
the late 50s. This contains their #1 hit "Tom Dooley," Dave
Guard's "Scotch and Soda," "Wreck of the 'John B'," and others.
A massive hit, it spent almost four years in the best-seller
charts. −WR

The Kingston Trio at Large / CAPITOL   1959
Perhaps the Trio's best-selling album (15 weeks at #1), this
contains their hilarious "M.T.A.," the lovely "Scarlet Ribbons,"
and several Dave Guard originals. −WR

☆ **Capitol Collectors Series / CAPITOL**   1990
Here's a well-chosen 20-track compilation containing all 17 of
the Trio's hit singles. −WR

PETER KNIGHT

Knight is a Celtic musician who plays mandolin, banjo, and
fiddle. He was a member of Steeleye Span in the 60s. −CR

○ **An Ancient Cause / SHANACHIE**   1991
A strong Celtic album with traces of his classical background.
Bordering on new-age but steeped in Celtic tradition. −CR

SPIDER JOHN KORNER

Korner was a major force in the 60s folk community around
Minneapolis. His Vanguard album *Running, Jumping,
Standing Still*, recorded with Tony Glover and David Ray, was a

seminal album of American folk and blues played by urban players. –RM

Nobody Knows the Trouble I've Been / RED HOUSE
A truly great album. The joyous playing and arrangements of these songs, including "Leatherwing Bat," "Froggy Went A-Courtin'," and others, are positive proof of the life that can be brought to the great American folk-song catalog in the hands of a master. –RM

○ **Raised by Humans / RED HOUSE**
Produced in the same style as *Trouble*, this includes some new Koerner originals and great driving, jubilant versions of "Titanic," and "The Fox and the Boll Weevil." –RM

LEO KOTTKE   b 1945

Kottke is considered (along with John Fahey) one of the finest virtuoso finger-picking guitarists on the music scene. The two worked closely in the 70s, playing and producing some of the most innovative solo guitar playing of that period. Kottke and Fahey influenced Preston Reed and Michael Hedges, both of whom have carried on their vision in the years since. –CR

Circle Round the Sun / SYMPOSIUM-BAY STREET   1970
This is a good, hard-to-find record. –CR

Dreams & All That Stuff / CAPITOL / BB# 45   1974
Very early sound. –CR

Ice Water / CAPITOL / BB# 69   1974
Kottke adds vocals, drums, bass, dobro, and steel guitar for a unique Kottke sound. –CR

Leo Kottke / CHRYSALIS / BB# 17   1976
Very good guitar playing. –CR

Did You Hear Me? / CAPITOL / BB# 153   1976
This album contains early and influential acoustic hot licks from this fleet guitarist. –MH

Balance / CAPITOL   1979
Good guitar work, featuring "Embryonic Journey" and Buddy Holly's "Learning the Game." –CR

Guitar Music / CAPITOL   1981
Twelve solid guitar instrumentals. –CR

My Father's Face / PRIVATE MUSIC   1989
Funky songs and staccato picking make this a very good album. –MH

○ **Great Big Boy / PRIVATE MUSIC**
Kottke sings on this record to good effect. Features Lyle Lovett and Margo Timmons. –CR

JIM KWESKIN & HIS JUG BAND   b 1940

Jim Kweskin's Jug Band, including Bill Keith, Geoff Muldaur, Maria D'Amato (later Muldaur), and others, came out of Cambridge, MA, in 1963 with a combination of old-timey country music, bluegrass, and ragtime, and became the major 60s proponents of jug-band style. It never caught on in a big way, but it was fun while it lasted. –WR

○ **Greatest Hits / VANGUARD**   1970
Washboards, kazoos, novelty songs, and general hilarity combine to make some of the most delightful, foolish music of the 60s. The jug-band craze was small and short-lived, but Kweskin and his band, which included Maria D'Amato, soon to marry bandmember Geoff Muldaur, were its premier act, and this double-disc set captures much of their whimsical style. –WR

PETER LAFARGE   1931-1965

Singer/songwriter Peter LaFarge was the son of Pulitzer Prize-winning author Oliver LaFarge and like his father, a spokesman for Indian rights. His involvement in the Korean War, where he was decorated five times, served as the inspiration for his best-known song, "Ballad of Ira Hayes," about a Pima Indian who was at the battle of Iwo Jima in World War II but suffered in the post-war world. After a career as a rodeo cowboy, LaFarge turned to folksinging in the late 50s and was part of the *Broadside* magazine/Folkways Records

community in New York in the early 60s, recording several albums devoted to cowboy songs and Native American concerns. Johnny Cash took "Ira Hayes" to #3 in the country charts in 1964. LaFarge died of a stroke the following year. –WR

○ **As Long as the Grass Shall Grow / FOLKWAYS**   1963
Surprisingly, this collection of songs about what we now call Native Americans does not include LaFarge's best-known song, "The Ballad of Ira Hayes." But the singer/songwriter, who was a Native American himself, still manages to turn in one of the most thorough and moving examinations of the sorry history of White deception and aggression ever recorded. He gives his songs a dramatic, near-spoken delivery, making the messages all the more convincing. –WR

PATTY LARKIN

Larkin is a Boston-based singer/songwriter. After studying jazz, she went into the acoustic folk style she is currently playing. Her guitar work is highly respected, as is her songwriting. –CR

○ **Step into the Light / PHILO**   1985
Fine debut album. –CR

○ **I'm Fine / PHILO**   1987
Powerful CD featuring songs such as "If I Was Made of Metal" that leave you wanting more. –CR

In the Square - Live / PHILO
Any way you cut it, you will enjoy this album. It is better than most live albums. –CR

● **Tango / WINDHAM HILL**   1991
Most polished of her releases — backed by John Gorka and Darol Anger. Very mature. –CR

LAST FAIR DEAL

Connecticut-based bluegrass band with original songs and clean, simple arrangements. –RM

○ **Last Fair Deal / BREAD AND BUTTER**   1989
Be sure to check out "Spend a Little Time" and "Your Heart and Mine." –RM

CHRISTINE LAVIN

Christine Lavin emerged out of the crowded New York City songwriter scene of the 80s with a style that distinguished her from her peers. First of all, her songs were overwhelmingly concerned with contemporary romantic mores (that scary, uncertain world of "relationships" and "commitments" and "biological clocks"). Second, while her takes on this subject could sometimes be sentimental or maudlin, more often they were humorous: "If You Need Space, Go to Utah" was the first track on her first recording, a 1983 EP called *Husbands and Wives*, later reissued as *Another Man's Woman*. By 1984, Lavin had managed to release her first full-length album, *Future Fossils*, which included both her serious and comic numbers, notably "Damaged Goods" (what people start to feel like after enough failed relationships) and "Don't Ever Call Your Sweetheart by His Name" (how difficult it is to remember people's names after enough failed relationships). In 1986, Lavin signed to Rounder's Philo label, and since then she has recorded regularly, also touring extensively and building up a wide following.
Lavin has also made a particular point of promoting the work of her contemporaries, notably on such collections as *When October Goes* and *Buy Me, Bring Me, Take Me, Don't Mess My Hair!!! (Life According to Four Bitchin' Babes)*. –WR

○ **Future Fossils / PHILO**   1986
A bright, wry, and earthy collection of her early songs. A great introduction. –BE

LAVIN-LARKIN-MCDONOUGH-FINGERETT

Solo artists Christine Lavin, Patty Larkin, Megon McDonough, and Sally Fingerett teamed for this one-time outing of some of contemporary folk's best singer/songwriters. –ED

○ **Buy Me, Bring Me, Take Me ... / PHILO**   1991
Buy Me, Bring Me, Take Me: Don't Mess My Hair is more than just a best-of sampler of four of the best contemporary folksinger/songwriters. This live album presents a cohesive group as well as soloists performing material that ranges in subject matter from romance to vacation troubles, and in mood from heartbreaking to sidesplitting. It will make you want to hear each of the singers on her own, but it will also make you hope they tour together more often. –WR

DEBORAH LAVOY

Deborah is a California singer/songwriter whose vocal style is similar to Patty Larkin's. Her songwriting style is serious, dealing with many of today's problems. –CR

○ **Hungry City / LILOLA**   1991
Her deep rich vocals will win you over after one listen to this CD. This is mostly Lavoy and her guitar with little distraction from her songs. A talent to watch. Highly recommended. –CR

EDDY LAWRENCE

This Alabama-born, New Jersey-based songwriter creates wry and insightful songs with an urban but Southern sensibility. He has three self-produced albums and is represented on the *The Fast Folk Musical Magazine*. –RM

★ **Walker County / SNOWPLOW**   1987
This is Lawrence's song cycle of his home county and contains some of his most arresting songs, including "Cecil's Gone," "Say It in Southern," and "Mary Lee." –RM

○ **Up the Road / SNOWPLOW**   1988
  Whiskers & Scales / SNOWPLOW   1990
  Used Parts / SNOWPLOW   1992
Great songs with great humor, including the title cut and "Luthor." –RM

ANNE LEDERMANN

Ledermann is a Canadian musician who plays fiddle, five-string violin, mandolin, piano, banjo, and jaw harp. She has played with the Ontario folk group Muddy York & the Flying Bulgar Klezmer Band. –CR

○ **Not a Mark in This World / AURAL TRADITIONS**   1991
This album is a collection of Canadian traditional music. Ledermann plays logging songs, Nova Scotia abolition songs, Ukrainian music, Yiddish folksongs, and backwoods music — a great collection. If you like old-timey, traditional folk music, you will enjoy this release. –CR

MARK LEVY

Levy is a California singer/songwriter who uses humor and irony to show the listener how crazy life is. –CR

○ **Sheroes Heroes / NEW-CLEAR**
Very funny CD featuring fine guitar playing and singing. "Send a Man to Mars" is just what Bush needs. With 16 songs, it's a very nice CD. –CR

  Take Off Your Clothes / NEW-CLEAR
Another political, humor-filled album, with "Between Iraq and a Hard Place," "Ramb. O," and "Take Off Your Clothes." –CR

TOM LEWIS

Belfast-born and a British submarine officer for 24- years, Lewis is now based in Canada. –RP

○ **Surfacing / SELF-PROPELLED**   1990
A good collection of sea shanties and naval songs. –RP

  Sea Dog See Dog / FLYING FISH   1991
More songs and tales of the sea from this former British submarine officer. –RP

GORDON LIGHTFOOT   ♭1938

Canadian Gordon Lightfoot first began to gain recognition in the mid 60s as a songwriter when his compositions "For

Lovin' Me" and "Early Morning Rain" became hits for Peter, Paul & Mary, and Marty Robbins topped the country charts with "Ribbon of Darkness." Lightfoot's own style was understated, his tasteful folk arrangements topped by a gentle burr of a voice. His albums began to appear in 1966, but it was not until the start of the 70s that he became a big success as a performer, scoring in 1970 with *Sit Down Young Stranger*, which contained his hit "If You Could Read My Mind," a song with a typically flowing melodic line and gently poetic lyrics. Thereafter, the first half of the 70s were his. Lightfoot hit a peak in 1974 with *Sundown*, which went to #1, as did the title song when released on a single. Though he had developed a timeless style, Lightfoot was caught by the popular decline of folk-based music in the latter half of the 1970s, and has performed and recorded less frequently since, sometimes trying to conform to perceived commercial trends without success. But concert appearances in the early 90s confirmed that he remains an engaging performer and that his catalog of original songs is hard to match. –WR

Sit Down Young Stranger / REPRISE   1970
Lightfoot's Reprise albums are always tastefully constructed, with their careful finger-picking, restrained rhythm sections, and subtle string arrangements serving as a bed for the singer's sturdy baritone. What distinguishes the albums is the quality of Lightfoot's songwriting, and this one, featuring the title track as well as "Approaching Lavender" and "If You Could Read My Mind" has the best overall selection. –WR

Summer Side of Life / REPRISE   1971
This extraordinary release doesn't have big hits on it but contains some of his finest songwriting, from the political song "Miguel," to the wistful songs about divorce, "Same Old Loverman" and "Talking in Your Sleep," to the joyous "Cotton Jenny." This is highly recommended. –RM

○ **Sundown / REPRISE**   1974
Lightfoot's commercial peak came with this album, which topped the US charts, containing both the #1 title song and the Top 10 hit "Carefree Highway." But songs like "Somewhere U.S.A." and "High and Dry" are textured, catchy folk/rock on a par with the better known tunes. –WR

Summertime Dream / REPRISE   1976
Due to Lightfoot's tendency to re-record his hits when preparing compilations (the warning "caveat emptor" applies to the two volumes of *Gord's Gold*), this is the only place to find the original version of his #2 "Wreck of the Edmond Fitzgerald." –WR

● **The Best of Gordon Lightfoot / CAPITOL**   1980
A compilation of material Lightfoot recorded for United Artists in the 60s, and this features the best of that period, including Lightfoot standards such as "For Lovin' Me," "Early Morning Rain," and "Canadian Railroad Trilogy." –WR

LIMELIGHTERS

A folk group formed in 1959 by Louis Gottlieb (bass), Alex Hassilev (baritone, guitar, banjo), and Glenn Yarbrough (tenor, guitar). They played in concert and at folk houses like San Francisco's Hungry I. After their Top-40 hit "Baby, the Rain Must Fall" in 1965, they appeared on TV and radio nationwide. They disbanded in the mid 60s. –JME

○ **Tonight In Person / RCA**   1961
Live concert at the Ash Grove. One of their best sellers. –JME

  The Slightly Fabulous Limelighters / ELECTRA 1961
This album reached #8 on the charts in 1961. –JME

LARRY LONG w/CHILDREN OF OKEMAH

Contemporary singer and songwriter Larry Long had a mission: to take Woody Guthrie's music back to the Dust Bowl balladeer's hometown. Okemah, OK, had spent about 40 years with its jaw set against its most famous native son. Decent folk there called him a Communist and said a decided "NO" when the Guthrie family proposed a kind of museum at the decaying homeplace back in the 70s. "It would just attract hippies," said the decent folk who knew this Woody was just trouble. Long's gentle subversion was to teach Guthrie's songs to the kids of Okemah and encourage them to make up their own songs in Guthrie's kid-friendly idiom. The results were recorded at a local theater by the Flying Fish label, and now Okemah's water tower proudly proclaims the town as "Home of Woody Guthrie." –MH

○ **It Takes a Lot of People ... / FLYING FISH**   1988
It Takes a Lot of People (Tribute to Woody Guthrie) was recorded by Long and his young friends at the Crystal Theater in Okemah, OK, Guthrie's hometown. When they are singing Guthrie songs or reading from Guthrie's works, the tribute works beautifully. Long's own children's material is somewhat less successful. –WR

KIMBERLY M'CARVER

M'Carver is a Texas singer, songwriter, and guitarist who was greatly influenced by Guy Clark, Nanci Griffith, and Bev Doolittle. –CR

○ **Breathe the Moonlight / PHILO**
M'Carver uses Stuart Duncan, Jeff White, Jerry Douglas, Roy Huskey Jr, and Dennis M'Carver as backup. "Whistle Down the Wind" and "My Way Back Home to You" are exceptional. Highly recommended. –CR

ROD MACDONALD   b1949

Connecticut-born MacDonald has performed internationally and many of his songs have been adapted as standards by the contemporary folk/songwriter community. With his pure emotive tenor and stirring, catchy tunes, MacDonald is one of the most appealing singer/songwriters to emerge in the 90s. Add to that thoughtful lyrics that touch on a variety of political and social issues, and you have a remarkable artist deserving a much wider public. MacDonald has contributed over 20 songs to *The Fast Folk Musical Magazine*, in addition to his solo releases. –RM

○ **No Commercial Traffic / CINEMAGIC**   1984
"On the Road to NY Town" should not be missed. –RM

● **White Buffalo / MOUNTAIN RAILROAD**
This, MacDonald's second album, is something of a best-of, covering much of his work in the late 70s and early 80s. –WR

Highway to Nowhere / SHANACHIE   1992

MALICORNE

Malicorne founder Gabriel Yacoub, taking his inspiration from the French/Celtic explorations of Alan Stivell and Dan Ar Braz as well as the British folk/rock of Steeleye Span, led his crew in producing rich, haunting arrangements of the folk music of France, Brittany, and francophone Canada. The band's later recordings feature original compositions and more contemporary instrumentation while retaining a traditional flavor. –MPD

○ **Legende: DeuxiÉme Epoque / HANNIBAL**   1991
This is a superb compilation from France's answer to Steeleye Span. –MPD

DAVE MALLETT

Mallett is a singer/songwriter whose songs often deal with New England and the working man. His "Garden Song" is a well-known standard. –CR

○ **Vital Signs / FLYING FISH**   1986
On this, the best of several quite good albums, Mallett provides a feeling examination of the state of a generation now too old to die young. Putting aside "Midnight Madness" and "that whole James Dean thing," he embraces "solid wood and aging wine" among other long-lasting items and finds a way to look bravely into middle age. –WR

CINDY MANGSEN

Mangsen plays guitar, banjo, English concertina, and

mountain dulcimer. Her vocals are rich and beautiful. She has recorded with Anne Hills and Priscilla Herdman. –CR

○ **Long Time Traveling / HOG EYE**
Settledown / FRONT HALL

ROGER MANNING

Manning is a NYC-based singer/songwriter who began his career playing in the New York streets and subways. He plays a flat-picked, thrash acoustic guitar and writes with poetic optimism about subjects from real life, such as poverty and sex. –CR

Roger Manning / SST   1988
"Pearly Blues" and "Airport Blues" are the hip songs on this debut. –RM

HIRTH MARTINEZ

This East Los Angeles-born singer/songwriter released two albums, one produced by Robbie Robertson and the other by John Simon. –RM

○ **Big Bright Street / WARNER**   1977
If you find this great album, don't pass it up. Especially great are the following cuts: "The Driver," "Valley of the Music," and "Nuthin' is New." –RM

JOHN MARTYN

Scottish folksinger with a jazzy-blues style whose career dates from the late 60s. –ED

The Road to Ruin / WARNER   1970
Martyn's wife Beverley is the vocalist. South African saxophonist Dudu Pukwana is on three tracks. This is folk mixed with new-age musings. Excellent musicianship. By now it is rare, both musically and as a collector's item. –MGN

○ **One World / ISLAND**   1977
This virtuoso British guitarist and innovator mixes the music world of folk, blues, and fusion with some surprising results. Guests include Jamaican trombonist Rico, Steve Winwood, and fusioneers Hansford Rowe and Morris Pert. String arrangements are by Harry Robinson. For aficionados, a must-buy; for novices, it's a good one to try. –MGN

DAVID MASSENGILL

Massengill is a New York-based singer/songwriter. He is a member of the New York *Fast Folk* community. His songwriting is brilliant, and his guitar and dulcimer playing are excellent. He has just signed with the Flying Fish label. –CR

★ **Great American Bootleg Tape / BOWSER WOWSER** 1986
Massengill assembled this tape himself, using tracks recorded for the Stash Records *Cornelia Street* collection, *The Fast Folk Musical Magazine*, and the video of the Folk City 25th-Anniversary concert. The result is the single most impressive folk-based song collection of the decade. Massengill's lyrical facility is the most astounding to appear since that of Elvis Costello — he can be wickedly funny and deeply touching in the same line, and his imagination seems unlimited. By rights, this should be on all lists of the best albums of the 80s. (Write to David Massengill, 179 E. 3rd St., Apt. 20, NY, NY 10009.) –WR

The Kitchen Tape / BOWSER WOWSER   1987
More varied and novelty-oriented than *The Great American Bootleg Tape*, this collection of demos (recorded on a Sony Walkman) nevertheless shows the range in Massengill's mastery of the English language even more extensively than the earlier tape. His guitar, dulcimer, and harmonica are clean (except for an occasional fire engine or street noise caught on the tape). (See above address to order.) –WR & CR

○ **Coming Up for Air / FLYING FISH**   1992
Massengill's first studio album. He does a great job on several old songs like "Fairfax," "My Name Joe," and some new material. Producer Steve Addabbo, who has produced Suzanne Vega, manages to bring out the best in the music. Long overdue, but well worth it! –CR

IAIN MATTHEWS   b 1946

Iain Matthews was the first lead singer in Fairport Convention, with which he stayed from 1967 to 1969, leaving to form his own band, Matthews Southern Comfort, which scored a #1 British hit with "Woodstock." He has made many solo albums since, the latest being *Pure and Crooked*. –WR

○ **Pure & Crooked / GOLD CASTLE**   1990
It's amazing, but in a career dating back to the late 60s and filled with valuable work, Matthews waited until 1990 to produce that first consistently brilliant solo album. Maybe it took all that time to develop the instrumental, lyrical, and recording mastery demonstrated on this disc, which has a thoroughly modern pop sheen (fans of Peter Gabriel and Sting will feel right at home) but at the same time maintains a folkish directness and depth of feeling. –WR

JAMES MCCANDLESS

McCandless is based in Chicago and performs across the northern US and Canada. –RM
We Had a Big Back Yard / ST. CHRISTOPHER   1989
○ **Out West Somewhere / ST. CHRISTOPHER**   1991

CORMAC MCCARTHY

Boston-based singer/songwriter. –RM
○ **Troubled Sleep / GREEN LINNET**   1990
McCarthy delivers rich, strong vocals and is backed by Patty Larkin, Peter Gallway, Devonsquare, Rich Watson, Bob Thompson, Teg Glendon. His songs are well written in a folk/pop style. If you like the classic folksinger with rich production, you will enjoy what this CD has to offer. –CR

CAROL MCCOMB

McComb is a California singer/songwriter whose music ranges from country to folk. –CR
○ **Tears into Laughter / KALEIDOSCOPE**   1989
McComb's album is very compelling. The sad "Faded Dresden Blues," about the effects of Alzheimer's disease on her grandmother, touches the soul. She is backed by Nina Gerber on acoustic guitar (Kate Wolf's guitar player), Sally Van Meter on dobro (Good Ol' Persons), Laurie Lewis on vocals, and Barbra Higbie on piano. Catch onto McComb's music now and say you heard her when no one knew her — she's good! –CR

ED MCCURDY   b 1919

Singer/songwriter Ed McCurdy dropped out of college to make a career as a folksinger. In the late 40s, he learned guitar, put together a folk repetoire, and began performing on radio and TV in Canada. By the early 50s he was known in the US and made NYC his home in 1954. Throughout the 60s, McCurdy was a mainstay of the folk scene and a pacesetter for the younger 60s folksingers. –JME
Ballad Singer's Choice / TRADITION
○ **The Best of Ed McCurdy / TRADITION**

MEGON MCDONOUGH

McDonough is a singer/songwriter out of Des Plaines, IL, who also plays guitar and piano. Her voice is beautiful and she can sing folk, rock, and country — all with style. –CR
○ **American Girl / SINGING FLOWER**   1990
This release starts out strong with "American Girl," a country song, and a great cover of Lennon and McCartney's "I'm Looking through You." She covers two Michael Smith songs. All in all, this is a musically diverse album, well worth adding to your collection. –CR

KATE AND ANNA MCGARRIGLE

Kate (b 1946) and Anna (b 1944) McGarrigle are Canadian songwriting sisters whose work first came to international recognition in 1974 when Linda Ronstadt recorded Anna's "Heart Like a Wheel" as the title song to one of her albums.

The sisters were signed to Warner Brothers and recorded *Kate & Anna McGarrigle*, an album of deeply felt (sometimes deeply funny) songs with a homey, eclectic folk backing and tart, striking vocals. It was widely hailed. Its two followups seemed rushed, though they contained some good songs. In 1981, the sisters (having left Warner) recorded *French Record* for Joe Boyd's Hannibal label, and it showed considerable charm. *Love Over and Over*, in 1982, marked a move toward rock that cheered fans but also turned out to be their last album for almost a decade.
In the meantime, they raised families and ventured out every now and then to play a few rapturously received dates, especially in the Northeast. At one of these in the late 80s, they said they'd been working on a musical with producer Roma Baran. That project never came to fruition, but in 1990 they finally returned to the record racks with *Heartbeats Accelerating*. –WR

☆ **Kate & Anna McGarrigle / HANNIBAL**   1975
This album was *Melody Maker's* pick for Best Record of 1975, and it's hard to argue with that choice when you listen to the tart harmonies and solo singing on one of the best songwriting collections ever. From Anna's famous "Heart Like a Wheel" to Kate's bouncy "Kiss and Say Goodbye," the songs paint a deeply felt, highly detailed portrait of life and romance. A revelation when it was released and a classic today. –WR

French Record / HANNIBAL-CARTHAGE   1981
Many McGarrigle fans cite this as their favorite, even if they don't speak French. The Canadian-based sisters are expressively at home in the country's other language, and this may be the most musical of their albums. –WR

Love Over and Over / POLYDOR   1982
The first English-language record the sisters had done in several years found them rocking harder (Mark Knopfler of Dire Straits was a prominent guest star), but the layoff had also given them time to write a strong set of songs that found new things to say about love and motherhood. –WR

Heartbeats Accelerating / PRIVATE MUSIC   1990
Eight years later, the McGarrigles have adopted a more new-age sound, with extensive synthesizer programming. The sound may be lush and modern, but the sentiments are still deeply felt and the observations remain laser-sharp. –WR

ELLEN MCILWAINE

A gutsy, raw, energized purveyor of jazz, blues, rock, pop, folk, Jimi Hendrix, and Jack Bruce. Her wonderful voice commands with authority. –MGN
Honky Tonk Angel / POLYDOR   1972
An album of songs by McIlwaine, Hendrix, Jack Bruce, Steve Winwood, Isaac Hayes, and Bobbie Gentry. A sweet date. One side is live, the other is a studio recording. –MGN
● **The Real / KOT'AI**   1975
Her best. McIlwaine sings and plays slide guitar in a blues/rock vein and composes prolifically. This album also includes music by Stevie Wonder, Jack Bruce, John Lee Hooker, Booker T., and Tracy Nelson. Dedicated to Jimi Hendrix. –MGN
○ **Everybody Needs Somebody / BLIND PIG**
This early-80s recording with Jack Bruce is dedicated to Professor Longhair and Tim Hardin. One half of the album features McIlwaine's own compositions. –MGN

EL MCMEEN

This Connecticut-based guitarist has impeccable technique and is a sensitive interpreter of solo guitar material. –RM
○ **Of Soul & Spirit / SHANACHIE**   1974
Irish Guitar Encores / SHANACHIE   1992

RALPH MCTELL   b 1944

British singer/songwriter Ralph McTell is one of those artists whose career has been defined by the success of a single song. That song is "Streets of London," in which the narrator takes a companion complaining of loneliness through London's backstreets, pointing out the army of poor and wretched who are truly lonely. McTell recorded the song on his second album, *Spiral Staircase*, in 1969, but it wasn't until he re-recorded it in 1974 that it became a #2 UK hit. He has continued to make albums, has become associated with the Fairport Convention family of musicians, and has appeared on British TV, especially on children's shows. –WR

○ **You Well-Meaning Brought ... / PARAMOUNT**   1971
You Well-Meaning Brought Me Here includes McTell's "Streets of London," which has by now become a genuine folk song — lots of people don't know he wrote it. Sadly, its portrait of what we now call the homeless is even more relevant in these times than it was in the early 70s. Happily, this album, gorgeously but simply produced by Gus Dudgeon, almost lives up to its most memorable track. –WR

RICHARD MEYER

Meyer is a New York-based singer/songwriter and former editor of *The Fast Folk Musical Magazine*. –CR

Laughing/Scared / OLD FORGE   1987
Meyer's folk/rock debut sometimes has an almost-rockabilly exuberance, even when he's dealing with the "scared" side of his lyrical dichotomy. And then there are those songs, such as "All My Ex-Girlfriends (Are Married)," in which singer and listener are laughing and shivering at the same time. Still, Meyer remains able to assure us there's "No Reason to Cry" with a song that's one of those hit-single shoulda-beens. A fine, varied collection. –WR

○ **The Good Life! / SHANACHIE**   1992
Meyer's second release is solid throughout. He has a very good group helping out — Rex Fowler, Mark Dann, Lucy Kaplansky, Andrew Hardin, Lisa Gutkin, Margo Hennebach, and Barry Mitterhoff. This is not the kind of CD that jumps out at you, it just grows on you. –CR

WALT MICHAEL

Walt Michael is one of the premier hammer dulcimer players in the bluegrass/folk field. He is equally accomplished at guitar, mandolin, and harmonica. He is backed by Frank Orsini (fiddle), John Kirk (fiddle, guitar, banjo, mandolin, and vocals), and Mark Murphy (cello, string bass, and vocals). –CR

Music for Hammer Dulcimer /   1983
Early work. One of the finest hammer dulcimer players out there. –CR

○ **The Good Old Way / FH**   1985
Highly recommended. –CR

● **Step Stone / FLYING FISH**   1986
Twelve solid songs. His best work. –CR

HUGH MOFFATT

After leaving the Austin and Washington, DC, music scene, Moffat moved to Nashville, where he has become a respected singer/songwriter. His songs have been covered by Ronnie Milsap, Dolly Parton, Bobby Bare, Lacy J. Dalton, Jerry Lee Lewis, Alabama, and more. –CR

○ **Loving You / PHILO**
A very good album. Solid songwriting. Russ Barrenberg and Jerry Douglas back up Moffatt. –CR

● **Troubadour / PHILO**
Hghly recommended. Moffatt's songwriting is at its best. –CR

KATY MOFFATT

Moffatt is a singer/songwriter who has released three albums. She has cowritten with Tom Russell and released an acoustic album with Andrew Hardin (of the Tom Russell Band). –CR

○ **Walkin' on the Moon / PHILO**   1976
Moffatt's album is not overproduced. It features her on vocals

and acoustic guitar and Andrew Harden on vocals and guitar. Moffatt cowrote with Tom Russell and covers three of her brother Hugh Moffatt's songs. Nice job on "Walkin' on the Moon." –CR

Kissin' in the California Sun / CBS   1978
Nice a. Features Dickie Betts, Chuck Leavell (Sea Level), the Allman Brothers rhythm section, and the Muscle Shoals horn section. –CR

Child Bride / PHILO   1990
Fine release. More production than *Walkin' on the Moon*. –CR

BUDDY MONDLOCK

Chicago born and now based in Nashville where he is busy as a writer and collaborating songwriter with artists such as Janis Ian. –RM

○ **On the Line / SPARKING GAP**
A beautiful self-produced album. Highlights are "Aunt Anna" and "Fire of Change." –RM

DAVE MOORE

Dave Moore is a Midwestern singer/songwriter who plays guitar, harmonica, and button accordion. He has appeared on many of Greg Brown's albums and on "A Prairie Home Companion." –CR

○ **Jukejoints & Cantinas / RED HOUSE**   1956
A fine collection of blues, standards, and Norteno dance music. This was not originally meant to be released as an album. –CR

Over My Shoulder / RED HOUSE   1956
Moore's debut as a songwriter; an outstanding release, featuring Peter Ostroushko and Radislav Lorkovic. Dave steps out with "Just a Dog," (heavy Greg Brown sound), "Over My Shoulder," and "God Moves on the Water." Highly recommended. –CR

NANCY MORAN

Moran is a Maryland-based singer/songwriter. Her songs are intelligent and deal with love, doubts, homelessness, and the "good old days." –CR

○ **A Little Off Balance / AZALEA**   1991
Moran's debut album is a collection of music that goes from bluesy saxophone to rock to delicate acoustic-guitar work. The songs are very personal, and Moran lets you know it. –CR

GEOF MORGAN

Morgan is a Washington State singer/songwriter who is known for his sensitive songs dealing with birth, AIDS, and the male-female relationship. His songs are intelligent and well crafted. –CR

It Comes with the Plumbing / NEXUS
An independent debut release. Shows the promise of a great career. –CR

Finally Letting It Go / FLYING FISH   1981
This album is ripe with promise. Good vocals and guitar playing. –CR

○ **At the Edge / FLYING FISH**   1984
A fine collection of music, including "Five Months into a Miracle," "Glad to Be a Man," "Goodbye John Wayne," and "Anna's Dance." One of my favorite singer/songwriters. –CR

Talk It Over / FLYING FISH   1987
His most adventurous; moves into bolder material. –CR

BILL MORRISSEY

Since 1984 Bill Morrissey has released four albums of original songs that have startled and delighted the following he's built up in touring around the Northeast. By the second one, *North*, he'd been picked up by the Philo division of Rounder. Morrissey sings in a surprisingly flexible deep voice (somewhat reminiscent of Leon Redbone's croak, but more supple). His songs are full of humor and pathos, expressed in keenly observed details. This is small-town life, sometimes desperate, sometimes hopeful, but always presented in new, unexpected ways. –WR

○ **North / PHILO** 1986

Morrissey's New England country accent and self-deprecating humor make it easy to miss the bite in many of his songs, which have a Hemingwayesque understatement both in their sly, sidelong observations and their matter-of-fact presentation. In fact, Morrissey is a taste well worth acquiring for anyone seeking perceptive songwriting and the occasional dry laugh. –WR

Inside / PHILO

Great production, great arrangements, and perfectly honed lyrics bring a timeless sense to these short stories of rootlessness and love. "Long Gone," "Robert Johnson," and "The Man from Out of Town" are key songs. Morrissey has matured so that these songs sound as if they have always been with us. –RM

MOVING HEARTS

This Irish folk/rock group of the first half of the 80s had a lineup including Brian Calnan, Keith Donald, Donal Lunny, Christy Moore, Eoghan O'Neill, and Davy Spillane. It was the forerunner of such followers as the Pogues, the Mekons, and the Oyster Band and mixed a traditional approach (they played acoustic instruments, such as bodhran and Uilleann pipes, as well as electric ones) with a contemporary repertoire, some of it socially conscious material. For example, *Moving Hearts* in 1981 included "Hiroshima, Nagasaki, Russian Roulette." The second album, *Dark End of the Street*, was internationally hailed.

The band's talented lineup had trouble staying together, and *Live Hearts* in 1983 was their last real album, though *The Storm* in 1985 was an interesting instrumental collection. The band's influence has been extensive, and Christy Moore has gone on to a successful solo career. –WR

○ **Moving Hearts / GREEN LINNET** 1986

This compilation album features Hearts standards such as "Hiroshima, Nagasaki, Russian Roulette" and "McBrides," as well as a version of Jackson Browne's "Before the Deluge" that turns it into an Irish folk song. –WR

GEOFF MULDAUR

Muldaur grew up just outside NYC in Pelham, NY. He plays country-blues guitar. Muldaur was a member of Jim Kweskin's Jug Band. –CR

○ **Sleepy Man Blues / BIG BEAT** 1965

Great covers of Blind Willie Johnson's "The Rain Don't Fall on Me," Bukka White's "Good Gin Blues," and Sleepy John Estes's "Drop Down Mama." –CR

HEIDI MULLER

Muller is a Washington State singer/songwriter who has been a part of the Victory Music project. Her style is reminiscent of Kate Wolf. Her music has dealt with the Pacific Northwest and her social concerns. –CR

Between the Water & the Wind / CASCADIA

Muller's songwriting is strong ("Honey in My Tea," "Paradise in Puget Sound"), and her choice of cover material (Guy Clark, Bill Staines, Bob Blue) is well done. A pleasure to listen to. –CR

○ **Matters of the Heart / MULLER MUSIC**

A more mature release of 13 songs. Her song "Good Road" is a great traveler's song. "Matters of the Heart" is one of Muller's finest songs. A very good production. –CR

DAVID MUNYON

David is a hard-driving guitarist and blues-based singer/songwriter. –RM

○ **Code Name: Jumper / LOS HERMANOS**

MUSTARD'S RETREAT

The Micduo of Dave Tamuelevich and Michael Hough sings primarily original songs. –RM

Home by the Morning / RED HOUSE

Look for "Great Lakes Fishing Trade." –RM

○ **Midwinter's Night / RED HOUSE**

The key song is "Jeremy Brown." –RM

THE NEW CHRISTY MINSTRELS   b1961

A ten-member choral group organized by Randy Sparks in 1961, the New Christy Minstrels were among the most popular performers on the clean-cut, fresh-faced, earnest, fun-loving side of the folk music boom. If all those clichés don't sound like what 60s folk music was all about, it's because the scruffy, "authentic," critical, politically oriented side of the folk music boom turned out to be more influential. But the Christys' side was initially more successful: Between 1962 and 1965, the group placed eight albums on the Top 100 best-seller charts by cheerily singing songs like "That Big Rock Candy Mountain." After that, times changed, and such original members as Barry ("Eve of Destruction") McGuire left, but the group continued till the end of the decade. Other members of the troupe at one time or another included Gene Clark and Kenny Rogers. –WR

☆ **Presenting: / COLUMBIA / BB# 19** 1962

Presenting: The New Christy Minstrels, the Christys' first album, was also the closest founder Randy Sparks came to his conception of a modern folk chorus singing such American standards as "Nine Hundred Miles" and "That Big Rock Candy Mountain." The original group contained some excellent solo and ensemble singers, and the overall impact is of full, warm harmony with an unabashedly sunny outlook. –WR

★ **Ramblin' / COLUMBIA / BB# 15** 1963

Featuring "Green, Green." The Christys scored their biggest seller with their fourth album, which also contained their biggest hit single, Barry McGuire's "Green, Green." The album was also their artistic high-water mark. Their arrangements were never more stirring and their singing never lustier, as Barry Kane and McGuire made their marks as soloists. –WR

○ **Greatest Hits / CBS / BB# 76**

Decent folk/pop like "Green, Green" (sung by Barry McGuire), grouped with pure-pop choir versions of "Downtown." An honest anthology. –BE

NEW COON CREEK GIRLS

An all-female band that plays contemporary bluegrass with striking vocals. –CR

○ **So I'll Ride / TURQUOISE**

This well-crafted album features a high energy level. Jesse McReynolds, Dempsey Young, Mike Stevens, Edgar Meyer, and Raymond McLain were guests on the album. –CR

THE NEW LOST CITY RAMBLERS

During the folk boom of the late 50s and early 60s, the NLCR introduced the authentic string-band sound of the 1920s and 1930s, in the process educating a generation that had never heard this uniquely American sound of old-time music. While maintaining music with a social conscience, they added guts and reality to the folk movement, performing with humor and obvious reverence for the music.

Mike Seeger, John Cohen, and Tom Paley in 1958 modeled their band after groups like the Skillet Lickers, the Fruit Jar Drinkers, and the Aristocratic Pigs, choosing a name in keeping with the past. When Tracy Schwarz replaced Paley in 1962, the Ramblers added solo songs from the Appalachian folk repertoire, religious and secular, educating a large segment of the American population about traditional music. Folkways recorded the NLCR on five albums in the early 60s, making the Ramblers famous and leading to TV appearances, successful tours, and appearances at the Newport Folk Festival. A songbook with 125 of their songs came out in 1964 and sold well.

The NLCR served at least three important purposes: They brought real folk music to a huge audience, they entertained us well with their highly entertaining acts, and they led us to rediscover the original music on which they had based their band. In the early 70s, after a long career, the group broke up. Tracy Schwarz went on the road with his wife and then his son, gradually leaning toward Cajun squeezebox music; Mike Seeger toured with his wife, Alice, and did many solo spots; and John Cohen continued playing in another string band, while making award-winning documentaries about the old music. –DV

20 Years of Concert Performances / FLYING FISH   1979
Live Ramblers. –MH

20th Anniversary Concert / FLYING FISH   1987
A nicely spirited celebration of a band that was longer-lived than many of its old-time role models. –MH

☆ **Early Years (1958-1962) / FOLKWAYS**
These influential revivalists of old-time string-band music played it straight, but with spirit and a keen ear for the music's inherent humor. –MH

PENNY NICHOLS   b 1947

Penny Nichols, with a background as a composer and vocal arranger, has worked as a backup singer for a wide variety of R&B and rock acts, including Jimmy Buffett, Arlo Guthrie, Art Garfunkel, Susie Quatro, and Donna Summer. She received a platinum record with Jimmy Buffett and a Grammy nomination. Nichols is one of the new lights in the modern folk scene and her songs are living proof that all the great folk songs were not written 60 years ago. "Pioneer Woman" and "New Moon Refugees" are on their way to becoming modern folk classics. You can catch her live at any number of folk festivals, and her most recent album, *All Life Is One*, is mandatory listening for all folk-music fans. –JME

Penny's Arcade / BUDDAH   1968
This debut album sold over 50,000 copies. Hard to find. –JME

○ **All Life Is One / PENNY NICHOLS' MUSIC**   1992
Includes "Pioneer Woman" and "New Moon Refugees." –JME

JOHN JACOB NILES   1892-1980

Singer/songwriter, instrumentalist (dulcimer, lute, piano), and song collector John Jacob Niles was a major force in folk music for over five decades. His nontraditional countertenor vocals and dulcimer accompaniment, plus his extensive publication of song collections, had a major impact on the development of the folk music scene in the early 50s. He was most active from the late 40s through the 60s. –JME

○ **John Jacob Niles: Folk Balladeer / RCA**   1965

NORTHERN LIGHTS

Northern Lights is a New England-based bluegrass band known for their creative and distinct sound. The band consists of Taylor Armerding (mandolin and vocals), Billy Henry (guitar and vocals), Oz Barron (bass), and Mike Kropp (banjo). –CR

○ **Take You to the Sky / FLYING FISH**
One of the best bluegrass albums you can buy; a nice blend of old and new sounds. Featuring guests Peter Rowan, Matt Glasen, and Alison Krauss, it's worth the price of the CD just to hear the vocal on "T for Texas." Highly recommended. –CR

TIM AND MOLLIE O'BRIEN

○ **Take Me Back / SUGAR HILL**   1988
Mollie and Tim O'Brien's vocals blend perfectly. A masterpiece. –CR

PHIL OCHS   1940-1976

Depending on your point of view, you might find Phil Ochs to be an idealistic American hero or the ultimate 60s casualty. Relocating to New York City from Ohio with a college journalism background and already well versed in the emerging political left, Ochs found his niche as a topical singer/songwriter and quickly became a favorite in the Village's blossoming folk scene of the early 60s. When Bob Dylan eventually moved into the rock arena, Ochs became the folk protest movement's de facto king.

By 1967 Ochs had realigned his management and record company and his music as well. He responded to the musical changes of the day with a trilogy of three heavily arranged albums that were far from the simplicity of the earlier three. These albums also graphically documented a deeply troubled singer, in terms of both his personal life and the now full-blown radical politics of the period. When the left-wing movement died, evidently so did much of Ochs's muse.

Ochs could never grasp why his status in the rock world never'matched what he achieved in folk music. His final studio album, with the self-deprecating title, *Phil Ochs's Greatest Hits*, proved to be a harrowing look back at his life and a clairvoyant pointer to his short-lived future. While some elements of his music carry a dated air about them, many of the same causes ring true today, and Ochs remains one of the 60s's most fascinating characters. –SA

All the News / HANNIBAL-CARTHAGE   1964
All the News That's Fit to Sing is his bittersweet debut and is a vital and topical album of its time. –BE & WR

I Ain't Marching Anymore / HANNIBAL   1965
A strident, searching, and haunting echo of the 60s. –BE

★ **Pleasures of the Harbor / A&M**   1967
Moving from his acoustic base to elaborate musical arrangements, Ochs also turns largely away from his topical material to more lyrical and poetic songs, though the caustic "Outside a Small Circle of Friends" and the apocalyptic "The Crucifixion" clearly retain his social and political focus. (Out of print) –WR

Phil Ochs's Greatest Hits / EDSEL / BB# 194   1970
Not really his greatest hits (the title was intended as irony). This is his final, troubled studio album, and a good companion to *Gunfight at Carnegie Hall*. –BE

○ **Gunfight at Carnegie Hall / MOBILE FIDELITY**   1974
Most unusual. Ochs does Elvis and Buddy Holly songs exceptionally to an angry audience and plays out his own internal conflicts at the same time. –BE

○ **Chords of Fame / A&M**   1976
A fine collection on vinyl only, but worth having for the liner notes. Note that this out-of-print double LP is the only album to combine Ochs's Elektra work (1964-1966) with his A&M work (1967-1970). The two CD samplers cover the same ground separately. –BE & WR

The War Is Over: The Best of Phil Ochs / A&M   1988
Not his best by a longshot, but a cross-section of his better A&M recordings. –BE

There but for Fortune / ELEKTRA   1989
The best of his early sides, covering his first three albums, though weighted heavily toward the third, *Phil Ochs in Concert*, probably because it's the only one not reissued by Hannibal-Cathage. –BE & WR

○ **There and Now - Live in Vancouver / RHINO**   1990
Definitive Ochs (along with *Gunfight at Carnegie Hall*). A "lost" 1968 concert featuring his most beloved songs. The real "best of." –BE

MAURA O'CONNELL

Irish singer, formerly associated with the traditional group De Danann, who has turned to more of a contemporary folk/rock approach as a solo artist, interpreting the songs of Nanci Griffith, John Hiatt, and other literate songwriters on a series of albums Warner Bros. –WR

○ **Helpless Heart / WARNER**   1989
Irish interpretive singer O'Connell has suffered from the inability of her record company to figure out whether she's a folkie, a country singer, or a pop artist. Meanwhile, she keeps singing her heart out, cherrypicking the work of such writers as Paul Brady, Nanci Griffith, Linda Thompson, and others. If you already own the albums those writers have made, maybe she's redundant. However, great songs still benefit greatly from being performed by great singers, and if you're looking for a sympathetic sampler of the best of today's songwriters, here it is. –WR

ODETTA   ♭1930

Starting out in classical voice training, Odetta crossed over to folk just before she turned 20. Teaching herself to play the guitar, she began singing in coffee houses in the early 50s. Her appearances with Pete Seeger and Harry Belefonte helped establish her as a major talent. She began recording solo albums in the late 50s and has been active ever since. She sings in a deep, husky voice with great control and clarity. –JME

At Town Hall / VANGUARD   1962
○ **Essential / VANGUARD**   1989

DON OJA-DUNAWAY

Florida-based singer/songwriter whose original historical ballads have a very strong sense of humanity. –RM

○ **Kennesaw / DUNAWAY**
This album is a song cycle of the Civil War. The song "Paducah" is an extraordinary extended ballad. (Write to Oja-Dunaway to obtain this recording, at: 15 South Comares, St. Augustine, FL 32084.) –RM

TOM OVANS

Tom Ovans is a Nashville-based, Boston-raised street rocker and song poet who is comfortable playing folk, blues, and hard-driving rock. His vocal style is eerily similar to that of Bob Dylan, with the power of Joe Ely. –CR

○ **Industrial Days / NEBULA**   1991
From the slow-paced "Crazy" to the hard paces of "Wild Wind Blowing" to the jazzy "Early One Morning," this CD is guaranteed to keep you interested. With Woody Guthrie lyrics and Bob Dylan-like vocals, Tom Ovans is a force to be reckoned with. –CR

TOM PAXTON   ♭1937

Though he has never achieved widespread popular success, Tom Paxton has proven to be one of the most talented and certainly the funniest of the topical folksinger/songwriters who emerged in the 60s. Born in Chicago, Paxton moved to Oklahoma when he was ten. After earning a BFA at the University of Oklahoma in 1959, he joined the army, which gave him the experiences recounted in one of his best early satiric songs, "The Willing Conscript." After leaving the service, he moved to New York City and worked his way up the local Gaslight Club. His first national release was *Ramblin' Boy* on Elektra in 1965. In addition to his own renditions, his songs were recorded by a variety of fellow performers, including Peter, Paul & Mary and Judy Collins. Paxton recorded seven albums for Elektra through 1971, two of which, *The Things I Notice Now* and *Tom Paxton 6*, sold well enough to reach the charts. He then switched to Reprise Records for three albums, two of which, *How Come the Sun* and *Peace Will Come*, also made the charts. Since then he has recorded for Private Stock, Vanguard, Flying Fish, Mountain Railroad, and his own Pax label. Paxton has continued to write satiric topical material over the years, from "I'm Changing My Name to Chrysler" (an attack on the government bailout of the auto giant) to "Little Bitty Gun," which mocked Nancy Reagan. But his songs can also be scathingly serious, such as his account of "The Death of Stephen Biko," and romantically touching, such as "The Last Thing on My Mind."

Recently Paxton has recorded more children's music and penned books for children as well. –WR

Tom Paxton 6 / ELEKTRA   1970
The best of Paxton's Elektra albums came toward the end of his tenure with the label and featured an above-average collection of trenchant originals. "Whose Garden Was This" remains a masterpiece on ecology, while "Forest Lawn" is one of Paxton's funniest songs ever. –WR

The Paxton Report / MOUNTAIN RAILROAD   1980
An unusually high quotient of comic/political material makes this one of his most scathing collections. "I Am Changing My Name to Chrysler" nails its subject perfectly. –WR

○ **Even a Grey Day / FLYING FISH**   1983
This collection is filled with Paxton's more serious, romantic, and thoughtful songs, some of them re-recordings of 60s favorites. The overall mood is unusually somber, but the album is unusually moving, too. –WR

A Paxton Primer / PAX   1986
One of the frustrating things about Tom Paxton is his tendency to scatter his best material across his many albums, a couple of gems per record. This makes him a prime candidate for a "Best of," and though these are re-recordings, they are the artist's own choices, issued on his own label. This is the compilation that covers the most ground and therefore the one to look for. (74 East Park Place, East Hampton, NY 11937) –WR

HERB PEDERSON   ♭1944

Pederson is a member of the Desert Rose Band. He is a skilled studio musician equally adept at the guitar and banjo. He has released several solo albums and appeared on countless musical projects. –CR

○ **Lonesome Feeling / SUGAR HILL**   1964
A very fine blend of bluegrass and country. Sugar Hill lets Pederson shine. –CR

Southwest / EPIC   1976
A solid album featuring David Lindley, Mike Post, Larry Carlton, Josh Graves, Al Perkins, Jim Gordon, and some fine backing vocals by Linda Ronstadt and Emmylou Harris. (Out of print.) –CR

Sandman / EPIC   1977
The same backups as on the *Southwest* album, with the additions of Lowell George and Dolly Parton. This album is out of print, but worth the search. –CR

PENTANGLE   ♭1968

A major British folk group of the late 60s and early 70s led by master guitarists John Renbourn and Bert Jansch and featuring singer Jacqui McShee, Pentangle combined traditional folk styles with contemporary songs and arrangements. –WR

○ **A Maid That's Deep in Love / SHANACHIE**   1987
Currently, only this 9-track compilation is available to remind listeners of this British traditional folk/rock quintet, which provided Fairport Convention's main competition in the late 60s and early 70s. Much of it is lovely, notably McShee's haunting singing and Jansch's finger-picking. But a more complete picture is provided by the two volumes of *Essential Pentagle* on Transatlantic in the UK, which may be found in US record racks. –WR

PETER PAUL & MARY

Peter, Paul & Mary were the most popular folk group of the 60s. Put together by manager Albert Grossman in 1961, Peter Yarrow (b 1938), Paul Stookey (b 1937), and Mary Travers (b 1937) carried on in the tradition of the Weavers, mixing old folk songs with newly written ones, especially those of the new crop of socially committed songwriters of the early 60s. Though their musical approach embraced clear enunciation and carefully shaded harmonies over the more "authentic" approach of other singers of the time, they were distinguished from such competitors as the Kingston Trio, the Limeliters, and the Chad Mitchell Trio by their seriousness and their ties to political causes.

They were also enormously popular, scoring 19 hit singles (6 of which hit the Top 10) and 11 hit albums (8 of which went gold) between 1962 and 1970. Most of their songs were written by others, their biggest hits including "Leaving on a Jet Plane" (a John Denver composition that helped establish him as a solo artist), "Blowin' in the Wind," and "If I Had a Hammer" (a song written by Weavers Pete Seeger and Lee Hays), but they could also write their own, as proven by Yarrow's "Puff the Magic Dragon" and Stookey's co-composition "I Dig Rock and Roll Music." The latter was a satire that accurately described their musical dilemma as the 60s wore on (popular music was becoming much more rock-oriented than they felt comfortable with).

The group split in 1970, leading to three moderately successful solo careers. But they reformed in 1978 and have maintained a steady performing and recording schedule since. –WR

Peter, Paul & Mary / WARNER / BB# 1   1962
Their debut, and their purest studio album. –BE

○ **In Concert / WARNER / BB# 4**   1965
This definitive collection highlights Paul Stookey's comedic talents and features the expected hits plus "Single Girl," a surprisingly early feminist song. –BE

10 Years Together ... / WARNER   1970
10 Years Together - The Best of Peter, Paul & Mary. Exactly what it says, and no more. This is a good companion to *In Concert*. –BE

Reunion / WARNER / BB# 16   1978
Much underrated, with a hauntingly beautiful version of Bob Dylan's "Forever Young." –BE

FAITH PETRIC

A leader in the folk and political communities of San Francisco for many, many years. –RM

Faith Petric / BAY   1988
○ **As We Were / CENTER**

PIERCE PETTIS

An excellent songwriter who was probably first heard by most people when Joan Baez covered his "Song at the End of the Movie" on her *Blowin' Away* album in 1979. Pierce Pettis put out his independent album, *Moments*, in 1984, and has since been releasing albums on Windham Hill, the most recent of which is *Tinseltown*. –WR

○ **Moments / SMALL WORLD**   1987
Containing the title cut, "Grandmother's Song," and "St. Paul's Song," this is his first album, and still his best. –RM

● **While the Serpent ... / WINDHAM HILL**   1989
While the Serpent Lies Sleeping. The keen observations in Pettis's songwriting gain force from the caught-in-the-throat emotionalism of his singing. As befits this record label, the instrumental settings are somewhat busy in a new-age way. But where the drum and keyboard programming leave off, a strong contemporary folk album remains, especially on "Legacy," in which Pettis confronts the conflicts of his Southern heritage. –WR

Tinseltown / HIGH STREET   1991

UTAH PHILLIPS

Phillips is an entertaining (and just plain fun) singer/songwriter and guitarist in the traditional style. Famous for his jokes, hobo and railroad songs, and sound effects, he is a well-known and popluar performer on the folk and concert circuit. –JME

El Capitan / PHILO   1979
○ **Good Through / PHILO**   1988

CLIVE PIG

A Londoner and member of the Rogue Folk movement. –RM

○ **One Night in Greece / PIG**   1985
One Night in Greece with an American Tourist is acoustic punk, most notable for the title cut. –RM

TOM PIROZZOLI

Based in Sunapee, NH, Pirozzoli is a very strong impressionistic acoustic guitarist and singer/songwriter. –RM

Tom Pirozzoli / NOUMENON   1983
Ashiata and the Owl / NOUMENON   1985
○ **Eyes and Footprints / NOUMENON**   1987
Travels / GREAT NORTHERN ARTS   1991

POLKA DOGS

The band consists of John Millard (banjo, vocals), Tiina Kiik (accordion), Colin Couch (tuba), Ambrose Pottie (drums), and Tom Walsh (trombone). The band was formed in 1987 as the pit band for a Toronto musical (Kensington Sons et Lumières). They play a type of polka music with a banjo. –CR

○ **Polka Dogs / AURAL TRADITIONS**   1991
A strange record: it starts out as polka, and ends like rock & roll — Alabama-Starspangled-Washboard Band meets the Red Clay Ramblers. Unique release. –CR

DANNY QUINN

Quinn is a singer/songwriter who plays Celtic and folk music. He is an accomplished guitarist who sings with a warm baritone voice. –CR

For Family and Friends / BLACK WATER
A fine debut album, featuring Eric Bogle's "... And the Band Played "Waltzing Matilda" and Don McLean's "Vincent." The vocals are outstanding. A well-rounded album. –CR

○ **Overnight Success / BLACK WATER**
Quinn's music and songwriting matured on this release. It is more commercial than his debut, but is not compromised. The title track is a good look at being an overnight success (after all the years he has put into his craft). He borrows songs from Stan Rogers, Eric Bogle, and Liam Reilly. –CR

● **Time for a Change / BLACK WATER**
Quinn uses more of his originals on this release. He and Tom Chapin do a fine version of the traditional song "The Water Is Wide." "Ordinary Man" is included, and Eric Bogle's "Leaving the Land" finishes the release. Great job! –CR

DAVID REA

David Rea is a singer/songwriter whose music has been covered by Ian & Sylvia and Mountain, and he has played with Gordon Lightfoot. –CR

○ **Feelin' Good / CANADIAN RIVER MUSIC**   1985
Rea is a very good guitar picker who goes easily from ballad to flatpicking. It's a laidback album that grows on you. Not commercial. –CR

BLIND ALFRED REED

This West Virginia singer/songwriter and fiddler was one of Ralph Peer's discoveries on the legendary 1927 Bristol field trip that unearthed the Carter Family and Jimmie Rodgers. Reed was one of those uniquely Southern contradictions, both reactionary and progressive in his songs. "How Can a Poor Man Stand Such Times and Live?" echoed the sentiments of the rural poor, who tasted none of the Roaring Twenties prosperity (a myth for all but a privileged few). "Why Do You Bob Your Hair, Girls?" invoked Biblical sanctions against flappers. Topical commentary of this sort was rare in early hillbilly recordings: Reed's contemporaries usually pruned a branch from the folk tree or swiped a page from Mom's Victorian songbook. Incongruously, Reed was a protest singer/songwriter out of time and place. Ry Cooder revived a couple of his songs in the 70s, the decade of Rounder's reissue of several Reed performances, *How Can a Poor Man Stand Such Times and Live?* –MH

○ **How Can a Poor Man ... / ROUNDER**   1920
How Can a Poor Man Stand Such Times and Live is 20s hillbilly social commentary, both reactionary ("Why Do You Bob Your Hair, Girls?") and progressive ("How Can a Poor Man Stand Such Times and Live") from this West Virginia singer and fiddler. Austere and engaging. –MH

JOHN RENBOURN

Renbourn was a founding member of Pentangle with Bert Jansch, and like Jansch, he is one of the most influential acoustic guitarists in Great Britain. Although Pentangle is best known for its revivals of traditional English folk songs, Renbourn is equally at home in blues, ragtime, jazz, and pre-classical idioms. –MPD

Faro Annie / REPRISE   1972
A bit of blues mixed in. –CR

The Hermit / SHANACHIE   1976
Solo guitar album — exceptional! One of his best. –CR

○ **A Maid in Bedlam / SHANACHIE**   1977
A superb collection of traditional songs and Renaissance dances. Features the sublime voice of his Pentangle mate Jacqui McShee. –MPD

The Enchanted Garden / FLYING FISH   1980
His followup to *Maid in Bedlam*, with multi-instrumentalist John Molineux replacing fiddler Sue Draheim. –MPD

Live in America / FLYING FISH   1981
An excellent double album on one CD, featuring the *Enchanted Garden* lineup. –MPD

The Nine Maidens / FLYING FISH   1985
Solo album. –MPD

○ **Live in Concert / SHANACHIE**   1985
Live solos and duos with Stefan Grossman, including a couple of Charles Mingus compositions. –MPD

Ship of Fools / FLYING FISH   1988
Featuring flutist Tony Roberts, guitarist Steve Tilston, and singer Maggie Boyle. –MPD

Three Kingdoms / SHANACHIE   1988
A ragtime/jazz/folk collaboration. A very mellow guitar album. –CR & MPD

The Black Balloon / SHANACHIE   1989
Features Renbourn's extended guitar fantasies. –MPD

Snap a Little Owl / SHANACHIE
More ragtime-laced duets. –MPD

MALVINA REYNOLDS   1900-1978

A topical songwriter who came to prominence in the 60s when she was at an age at which most people retire, Malvina Reynolds is best known as the author of the satirical song "Little Boxes," which was Pete Seeger's only pop singles hit in 1964. She also wrote "What Have They Done to the Rain," a hit for the Searchers in 1965. Her songs also have been covered by Joan Baez, Judy Collins, and others. Reynolds herself recorded for Columbia (*Malvina Reynolds Sings the Truth*), Folkways (*Another Country Heard From*), and her own Cassandra label. She also wrote children's songs and material for the TV show *Sesame Street*. –WR

○ **Malvina / CASSANDRA**
Reynolds is best known for Pete Seeger's versions of her compositions, songs like "Little Boxes" and "What Have They Done to the Rain." The first is included on this collection, along with 11 other uncompromisingly political songs that mark Reynolds as one of the great topical songwriters of the 60s. She has other excellent albums (including a long out-of-print Columbia LP), but this is a good place to start. –WR

JEAN RITCHIE   b 1922

Singer, songwriter, song collector, dulcimer player, and author.

Jean Ritchie, who was born in the heart of the Cumberland Mountains of Kentucky, was raised in the folk music of that area. She has been active in preserving and performing traditional mountain ballads and songs. She eventually moved to the New York City area and achieved a national reputation throughout the 50s and 60 singing solo voice, or with the mountain dulcimer. A number of Ritchie albums are still available from Smithsonian/Folkways recordings. (The address can be found in the back of the book. –JME

○ **High Hills and ... / GRH**
This album is still available today. –JME

GAMBLE ROGERS   1937-1991

Gamble Rogers was a singer/songwriter who was influenced by Merle Travis, Chet Atkins, Josh White, Earl Scruggs, and Doc Watson. He died trying to save a drowning person in 1991. –CR

○ **Sorry Is As Sorry Does / FLYING FISH**   1989
Rogers was a master storyteller. His songs are witty and worth a listen. –CR

STAN ROGERS   1949-1983

Stan Rogers came from Hamilton, Ontario, a six-foot-four poet who started out as a rock bassist before turning to folk music. With his rich voice, he used his music to call to life all of the wonder and mysticism of his native Canada. His singing is occasionally mistaken for that of Gordon Lightfoot, but it's huskier and earthier than Lightfoot's, and his repertoire — made up of song cycles drawn from throughout Canada — is also more tradition-oriented and more mystical. Rogers died in a fire aboard an Air Canada flight in Cincinnati, OH, in June 1983, leaving behind a half-dozen albums. –BE

○ **Fogarty's Cove / FCM**   1977
A dozen songs of and about Nova Scotia, mostly about the sea and all but one written by Rogers. They successfully capture not only a people but their sense of time and beauty, with the Rogers baritone tastefully and effectively moving through the spaces and ages of his subject, and with traditional acoustic backing (guitar, violin, flute, etc.) –BE

From Fresh Waters / FOC
The final Stan Rogers album, mixed and mastered after his death, is a dazzling array of songs devoted to the Great Lakes region and the rest of inland Canada. Some of the environmental sensibilities are bitter, and the politics, as with all his work, are defiantly Canadian. –BE

Northwest Passage / FCM   1981
Precisely what its title indicates — a collection of material from and about the vast western expanse of Canada, all filled with robust singing and melodies that are practically part of the landscape. –BE

Between the Breaks - Live! / FCM
A superb concert album, without a weak moment in any of its nine songs. The highlight is Rogers's rendition of Archie Fisher's "The Witch of Westmoreland," which opens the disc, although it is hard to get past Rogers's own "The Flowers of Bermuda" without having it run through your head for days afterward as well. The upbeat, ebullient mood of the performances is also rather infectious. –BE

ROOFTOP SINGERS

Founded by Weaver alumnus and banjo player Erik Darling in 1962, the Rooftop Singers included guitarist Bill Svanoe and vocalist Lynne Taylor. The group, active in concerts and festivals in the early 60s, was most known for their 1963 nationwide hit "Walk Right In." –JME

○ **Best of Rooftop Singers / VANGUARD**

BETSY ROSE

Betsy Rose is a California-based singer/songwriter whose songs often deal with social action or protest and the environment. –CR

○ **Sacred Ground / KALEIDOSCOPE**
A first-class release of acoustic music. Features Nina Gerber on guitar and producer. "Kneeling at the Trains," inspired by Vietnam veteran Brian Willson, is strong. "Read My Lips" deals with a rebellion at Gallaudet University by deaf students. All in all, it is her finest record. –CR

DICK ROSMINI

This guitarist from the late-50s/early-60s folk scene made two albums before pursuing a career of professional photography. –RM

○ **Adventures for 6 & 12 String Guitar / ELEKTRA**
This album predates much of John Fahey's work and certainly that of Leo Kottke and the other "American primitive" guitarists. Hard to find but well worth the search. –RM

TOM RUSH   b1941

Tom Rush came up in the Cambridge folk scene of the early 60s, playing folk-blues on a series of albums for Prestige Records, then moved to Elektra, and by the late 60s was interpreting the work of such upcoming writers as Joni Mitchell and James Taylor. By the early 70s, he was mixing his own songs on albums for Columbia. In recent years, Rush has become something of a folk packager, putting together road shows that include some of the newer folk performers. –WR

● **The Circle Game / ELEKTRA / BB# 68**   1968
Rush managed an undistinguished career in the early 60s as a folkie who performed old blues and rock & roll tunes until he changed gears on this album and turned to the songs of a group of then-unknown contemporary songwriters: Joni Mitchell, James Taylor, and Jackson Browne. That was impressive in 1968, but even today Rush's versions of songs like "Something in the Way She Moves" and the title track hold up well against those of their now-famous composers. And Rush's own songs, among them "No Regrets," are up to their standard. –WR

○ **Wrong End of the Rainbow / COLUMBIA / BB# 110**   1970
Fellow songwriters, such as James Taylor and Jesse Winchester, continue to be represented here, but the focus is on Rush's own compositions, notably the title track and "Merrimac County," and the result is one of the strongest albums in the style of the early-70s soft-rock singer/songwriters. –WR

TOM RUSSELL BAND

Tom Russell is a NY-based singer/songwriter who has cowritten songs with Nanci Griffith, Peter Case, Ian Tyson, Sylvia Tyson, Katy Moffatt, and Dave Alvin. His band features Andrew Hardin (guitar), Fats Kaplin (pedal steel, fiddle, and accordion), Billy Troiani (bass), and Charles Caldarola (percussion). The sound varies from country to Tex-Mex to rock. –CR

○ **Road to Bayamon / PHILO**   1988
A great CD, with songs full of images. Songwriters do not get much better. This contains a great cover of Tom Waits's "Downtown Train." –CR

Hurricane Season / PHILO
A solid performance, and the band clicks. Features a great song about Bill Haley's demise, plus Russell cowrites with Peter Case, Bob Neuwirth, Sylvia Tyson, and Dave Alvin. –CR

Poor Man's Dream / DARK ANGEL   1990
This CD is as good as *Road to Bayamon*. The songs might even be more polished. "Blue Wing," "Veterans Day," and "Navajo Rag" are all classics. Russell cowrites with Nanci Griffith, Kathy Moffatt, and Ian Tyson. –CR

Cowboy Real / STONEY PLAIN   1992
A real nice cowboy/western release featuring new and old Tom Russell favorites. Russell scales down the production on "Navajo Rug," "Gallo Del Cielo," and an old Hardin and Russell song, "Zane Grey." –CR

BUFFY SAINTE-MARIE   b1941

A Canadian-born, part-Native American pop/folksinger, she began in the 60s with a series of albums in which she sang bitterly about the treatment of Native Americans. Her later albums branched out into country and pop. –WR

☆ **It's My Way / VANGUARD**   1964
This is one of the most scathing topical folk albums ever made. Sainte-Marie sings in an emotional, vibrato-laden voice of war ("The Universal Soldier," later a hit for Donovan), drugs ("Cod'ine"), sex ("The Incest Song"), and most telling, the mistreatment of Native Americans, of which Sainte-Marie is one ("Now That the Buffalo's Gone"). Even decades later, the album's power is moving and disturbing. –WR

The Best of Buffy Saint-Marie / VANGUARD   1988
Sainte-Marie pursued a variety of musical styles, from folk to country to experimental rock, and all are represented on this wide-ranging double-record compilation. It doesn't all work, but there are some terrific songs, among them the Native American lament "My Country 'Tis of Thy People You're Dying," the romantic "Until It's Time for You to Go," and a musical adaptation of a passage from a Leonard Cohen novel, "God Is Alive, Magic Is Afoot." (Beware of the abbreviated version, Vanguard 73113.) –WR

CARL SANDBURG   1878-1967

Not only a great poet, Carl Sandburg is an interesting singer and guitarist who continued to perform and record traditional folk music throughout his life. –JME

○ **Flat Rock Ballads / COLUMBIA**

CLAUDIA SCHMIDT

A folksinger with an impressive vocal range, Schmidt has recorded both as a solo artist and with Sally Rogers. –MH

○ **Claudia Schmidt and Sally Rogers / RED HOUSE**   1991
This CD features some fine dulcimer and guitar work, along with vocals that will thrill you. Many of the songs deal with social problems facing today's generation. –CR

DAVID SCHNAUFER

David Schnaufer is a transplanted Texan now residing in Nashville, TN. His mountain dulcimer playing is legendary, making him one of the premier dulcimer session men in Nashville. He has joined up with Paul Kirby, John Golemon, Will Goleman, Dave Kennedy, and Sam Polano in the band the Cactus Brothers. –CR

○ **Dulcimer Player / SMITHSONIAN-FOLKWAYS**   1989
This is one of the finest mountain dulcimer albums you will ever find. Schnaufer goes all out with the help of Mark O'Connor and the Cactus Brothers. This album is more polished and uptempo than *Dulcimer Deluxe*. –CR

● **Dulcimer Player Deluxe / SMITHSONIAN-FOLKWAYS**
This is a combination of his first two releases, *Dulcimer Deluxe* and *Dulcimer Player*. –CR

○ **Dulcimer Deluxe / SMITHSONIAN-FOLKWAYS**
A fine collection of old standards and traditional music. –CR

SCHOONER FARE

Schooner Fare is a New England folk trio featuring Steve Romanoff, Chuck Romanoff, and Tom Rowe. Their music often reflects New England life and the sea. –CR

Alive / OUTER GREEN
Recorded live at the Chocolate Factory Church. The band and audience are into the show, featuring "Rattlin' Bog" and "Mary Ellen Carter" (by Stan Rogers). –CR

First 10 Years / OUTER GREEN
Schooner Fare recorded this double album live at the Birchmere in Washington, DC. –CR

Day of the Clipper / OUTER GREEN   1977
This album features Ralph McTell's "Streets of London." –CR

Classic Schooner Fare / OUTER GREEN
A collection of Schooner Fare's favorite songs, recorded with the Atlantic Chamber Orchestra. −CR
Closer to the Wind / OUTER GREEN   1981
An essential Schooner Fare album, with "The King Fisher," "John Cook," and "The Ballad of Mad Jack." −CR
○ **We the People / OUTER GREEN**   1985
This is the best collection, featuring "Portland Town," "We the People," "Make a Friend." The music is strong and the vocals blend to perfection. −CR
Signs of Home / OUTER GREEN
Features "Sweet Tennessee," "Golden Golden," and "Hills of Isle Au Haut." −CR

STEVE SCHUCH

Schuch is a singer/songwriter, storyteller, and multi-instrumentalist from New Hampshire. He is a three-time winner of the New Hampshire fiddle contest. −CR
○ **Circle of Days / RARE EARTH**   1988
Schuch's debut album is rich in both music and vision. It features well-crafted original songs and Celtic instrumentals. His guitar and fiddle playing are flawless, with folk, classical, and Celtic flavor. A very mature release. −CR
Fields of Summer / RARE EARTH   1991
Schuch uses 18 musicians to back him up. This is produced with a fuller sound than his debut CD, yet his playing is not overpowered. −CR

CARLA SCIACY

Colorado-based traditionally styled singer/songwriter whose lovely interpretations have an inviting and lightly swinging feel. −RM
○ **In Between / PROPINQUITY**
Under the Quarter Moon / PROPINQUITY

MIKE SEEGER   b 1933

Singer, multi-instrumentalist, and folklorist. Seeger played a central role in the revival of old-time country and related traditional music through his work with the New Lost City Ramblers and on his own. The son of composer and folklorist Charles Louis Seeger and Ruth Crawford Seeger, he heard field recordings as a child, and the fascination continued into adulthood. The New Lost City Ramblers (ca. 1958-1979) were the first urban folk-revival band to attempt to perform "old-time" country in the manner heard on 20s-vintage 78s. The Ramblers were also the major inspiration for the Hot Mud Family, the Red Clay Ramblers, and other string bands of the back-to-the-earth 70s. Seeger made a couple of fine albums for Mercury with his disciples (Ry Cooder, Maria Muldaur) in the 70s, and in his varied roles as performer, lecturer, collector, and engineer and producer, he has been a tireless advocate for old-time American roots music for nearly 40 years. −MH
○ **Oldtime Country Music / ROUNDER**
Solo material from this multi-instrumentalist and founder of the New Lost City Ramblers. −MH

PEGGY SEEGER   b 1935

The half-sister of Pete Seeger and widow of Ewan MacColl, Peggy Seeger has carved a niche for herself writing and singing folk ballads, especially with a feminist slant. Many of her albums are collaborations with her husband and other British folk artists. −WR
○ **At the Present Moment / ROUNDER**   1987
This album collects some of Seeger's best topical material, some of which she sings with her husband, Ewan MacColl. The most striking song remains "I'm Gonna Be an Engineer," which encapsulates most of what the women's movement has been saying for the past 20 years. −WR

PETE SEEGER   b 1919

Pete Seeger probably has had a greater influence on the development of modern folk music than any other single individual. The son of musicologist Charles Seeger, he began playing the banjo in his teens, soon turning to the five-string version that would become his trademark. He hooked up with Woody Guthrie in the late 30s, and the two formed the politically oriented Almanac Singers with several other folksingers to promote unions and condemn fascism. He was a cofounder of such organizations as People's Songs and People's Artists. In 1948 he formed the folk group the Weavers, which scored massive hits with "Tzena, Tzena, Tzena," Leadbelly's "Goodnight Irene," and "On Top of Old Smokey" before losing its record contract and bookings during the Communist witchhunts of the 50s. Seeger refused to testify before the House Committee on Unamerican Activities and was charged with contempt of Congress, winning his case in 1962. By that time, he had made numerous solo albums for Folkways and more Weavers albums for Vanguard. In 1961 he signed to Columbia Records, staying with the label until the end of the decade.

Seeger was a major force at the Newport Folk Festivals and a promoter of upcoming talent. His marathon-length concerts included Spanish songs, African songs, Negro worksongs, new protest songs, and old folk songs, sometimes with rewritten lyrics. And he got everyone singing along, often in multi-part harmony. Seeger's own songs, sometimes adaptations from other sources, became hits for others: "If I Had a Hammer" for Trini Lopez and Peter, Paul, & Mary; "Turn!Turn!Turn!" for the Byrds — but he was also known for his hit version of Malvina Reynolds's "Little Boxes," for "We Shall Overcome," for "Guantanamera," and for dozens more. In 1969, Seeger launched the sloop Clearwater and formed a group to help clean up the Hudson River. He maintained a busy appearance schedule, much of it given over to benefits for a variety of causes. The last time I saw him (at a shad festival in Sparkhill, NY, a few days after his 73rd birthday), Seeger didn't appear to have slowed down a bit. And when he took the makeshift stage in front of a Baptist church, he noted that the Hudson River was a lot cleaner than it had been 20 years before. −WR
○ **Broadsides / FOLKWAYS**   1964
Pete Seeger's fearless, clearly articulated voice and spare, accurate guitar and banjo playing are presented here in the service of a collection of songs published in early editions of *Broadside*, the topical song magazine, among them Malvina Reynolds's "From Way Up Here" and the civil rights anthem "We Shall Overcome." −WR
○ **Broadsides Ballads - Vol. 2 / FOLKWAYS**   1964
Seeger turns to the work of the new generation of topical folksingers on this followup to the first *Broadsides* collection, leading off with Malvina Reynolds's best-known song, "Little Boxes," and including the work of Bob Dylan, Tom Paxton, Peter LaFarge, and Phil Ochs. −WR
○ **Rainbow Race / COLUMBIA**   1971
For once, Pete Seeger went into the studio to make an album of mostly original songs with a few more instruments than his own accompaniment. The result is a stunning singer/songwriter collection, ranging from the topical "Last Train to Nuremberg" to the pastoral "Snow Snow" and Seeger's own wise words for the world, "My Rainbow Race." The record is a masterpiece and remains Seeger's most personal and accomplished original statement. −WR
★ **World of Pete Seeger / CBS**   1973
An excellent two-disc compilation of Seeger's Columbia years, this album contains 20 songs, most of which will be familiar to Seeger fans and folk enthusiasts in general. There's far more valuable Seeger on Columbia, but it's good to have "Turn! Turn! Turn!" as sung by its adapter and "If I Had a Hammer" as sung by its coauthor, not to mention such Seeger

concert staples as "Guantanamera" and "Last Night I Had the Strangest Dream." –WR

○ **Singalong Demonstration Concert / FOLKWAYS**   1980
Having reached his 60s, Seeger asked Folkways to document a typical concert "before my voice, memory, and sense of rhythm and pitch were too far gone." What they got is this 25-track, two-record boxed set containing the amazing variety and depth of Seeger's repertoire, from the traditional "John Henry" to the African lullaby/story "Abiyoyo" to Charlie King's anti-nuke tune "Acres of Clams." But what most impresses is Seeger's rapport with an audience that is willing and able to sing along on every song. – WR

☆ **We Shall Overcome ... / COLUMBIA**   1989
We Shall Overcome: The Complete Carnegie Hall Concert shows that Pete Seeger was at his apex as a performer and as an influential figure in the surging folk movement when John Hammond turned on the Columbia Records tape machine to capture this performance. Out flowed stories, traditional songs, covers of songs by new songwriters like Bob Dylan, and lots more. Seeger was perfectly in tune with his audience as well, and in the acoustic wonder of the hall, the harmonies were well captured. Columbia cut the tape down to a single disc in 1963, but this reissue, running over two hours on compact discs, presents the full concert for the first time. Anyone wondering what it is that has put Seeger at the forefront of folk music for the better part of his life need only hear this to understand.–WR

THE SEEKERS

A vocal group from Melbourne, Australia, the Seekers made an impact on the US folk scene in the mid 60s. The group included Athol Guy (bass), Keith Potger (guitar), Bruce Woodley (guitar), and Judith Durham (vocal). They made several worldwide tours, performing a wide range of folk music — from Black spirituals to Woody Guthrie. –JME

○ **The Best of Seekers / CAPITOL**

PAUL SEIBEL

In addition to *Live at McCabes*, this reclusive 60s singer/songwriter only made two studio albums, and they are both essential. –RM

Jack Knife Gypsy / ELEKTRA
Wood Smoke and Oranges / ELEKTRA
○ **Live at McCabes / RAG BABY**

RICHARD SHINDELL

Born in Lakehurst, NJ, Shindell began his musical career in college in Bethlehem, PA, where he was the lead guitar player in the infamous Razzy Dazzy Spasm Band (which also included John Gorka). Shindell began writing songs in earnest in 1986. In addition to his debut album, *Sparrows Point*, he has been recorded extensively by *The Fast Folk Musical Magazine*. He was also featured on Christine Lavin's 1991 compilation *When October Goes* (Rounder). Shindell earned an MA in theology from Union Theological Seminary in 1991 but says he has no intention of joining the priesthood. –WR

○ **Sparrows Point / SHANACHIE**   1992
A strong debut release "à la Eric Andersen." Shindell's songwriting is intense at times ("Sparrows Point," "The Courier," "On the Sea of Fleur de Lis"). His "Kenworth of My Dreams" is the classic blue-collar truck-driver song, and the title song should not be missed, either. "Are You Happy Now" is the most commercial song — very strong. This is an up-and-coming artist you should check out. –CR & RM

DICK SIEGEL

Born in New Jersey, Siegel relocated to the southern Michigan area. He is a well-known local artist who plays folk music laced with R&B, rock, and humor. He was a winner at the 1991 Kerrville Folk Festival. –CR

Snap / SCHOOL KIDS   1980
Siegel did a nice job on this release. The songs are strong and the music well played. "When the Sumac Is on Fire," and "What Would Brando Do" are very good. –CR

○ **Live / BOO-KAY**   1990
This live release is loaded with Siegel's humor. The audience is into the show and the sound quality is good, with more solo and low backup. Folky. –CR

SHEL SILVERSTEIN   ♭1932

Silverstein is a man of many talents. His cartoons have graced the pages of *Playboy*, *Stars & Stripes*, and *Time*. Silverstein is also a poet and one of the most prolific songwriters in the music scene. He teamed up with the country-rock band Dr. Hook & the Medicine Show in the early 70s. He was responsible for most of the songs on the early albums, such as "Sylvia's Mother," "Cover of the Rolling Stone," and "Sing Me a Rainbow."
Silverstein later worked with Bobby Bare in the mid-to-late 70s. They collaborated on the first country concept album, *Bobby Bare Sings Lullabies, Legends, & Lies.* –CR

Inside Folk / CBS   1961
Features his hit, "The Unicorn Song." –CR

Shel Silverstein / CADET   1967
A very strong album. –CR

Freakers Ball / CBS / BB# 155   1972
A very humorous and satirical collection of music. –CR

○ **The Great Conch Train Robbery / FLYING FISH**   1980
Silverstein is joined by Sam Bush, Josh Graves, John Hartford, Roy Husky, Benny Martin, Pig Robbins, Joe Stuart, and Amos Garrett. A great, funny album. –CR

PATRICK SKY

Patrick Sky is a singer/songwriter whose musical style ranges from folk to blues. –CR

Patrick Sky / VANGUARD   1965
A great album. "Ballad of Ira Hayes," "Wreck of the 97," and "Separation Blues." –CR

Harvest of Gentle Clang / VANGUARD   1966
A good album. –CR

Reality Is Bad Enough / VERVE   1968
The change of label to Verve helps Sky on this release. Excellent songwriting. –CR

Photographs / VERVE   1969
Good cover of "I Like to Sleep Late in the Morning." –CR

Two Steps Forward One Step Back / VANGUARD   1975
A tribute to the late John Hurt. Very good. –CR

○ **Through a Window / SHANACHIE**   1985
Twelve of Sky's most influential songs. All classics. –CR

MICHAEL SMITH

Smith lives in Chicago and is best known for writing "The Dutchman," popularized by Steve Goodman. Recent work has included the score for the Steppenwolf Theater Company's Broadway production of *The Grapes of Wrath*. Other recordings include a live coffeehouse album, the long out-of-print *Juarez*, which, strictly speaking, is not a Michael Smith album, but an electric band performing his songs with other singers — interesting. –RM

○ **Michael Smith & Love Stories / FLYING FISH**
This CD compiles Smith's two solo albums for the Flying Fish label on one disc. It has all his signature tunes, including "Three Monkies" and "Dead Egyptian Blues." A writer's writer, highly recommended. –RM

KILBY SNOW

New and traditional songs performed on the autoharp. –RM
○ **Country Songs and Tunes with Autoharp / FOLKWAYS**

THE SONG PROJECT

The Song Project was a group formed in the late 70s/early 80s in Greenwich Village, with various lineups through the years. During an Italian tour in 1985, the current members Lucy Kapbinsky, Tom Intondi, Martha Hogen, and Frank Christian recorded an album. They covered the work of Village writers as well as their own. –RM

○ **The Song Project / FOLKSTUDIO PRODUCTIONS**   1985
The sonic quality is not state of the art here, but the performances are, and the fact that this is the only Song Project material aside from the few *Fast Folk* cuts makes this an important record. Good liner notes by Dave Van Ronk. –RM

ROSALIE SORRELLS

An important voice in American folk for the last 30 years. Sorrells is a writer and interpreter whose material has a strong political but humanistic tone. –RM

Then Came the Children / GREEN LINNET
Be Careful ... / GREEN LINNET
Be Careful, There's a Baby in the House is another worthwhile album from Sorrells. –RM

○ **Report from Grimes Creek / GREEN LINNET**

PETER SPENCER

An excellent jazz/blues-based singer/songwriter. –RM
○ **Paradise Loft / REGULAR ROUNDER**   1980

SPIRIT OF THE WEST

Geoffrey Kelly, J. Knutson, and John Mann comprise this Vancouver, BC band. They play Celtic music mixed with strong rock & roll. –CR

Tripping Up the Stairs / STONY PLAIN   1988
Reels and jigs, topical songs, Celtic rock — what an album! This music has to be heard to be believed. Outstanding. –CR

Go Figure / WARNER   1992
This release is a slight departure from their other records. The band is going in a more commercial, alternative-rock direction. The addition of Vince Ditrich to the band is partly responsible. –CR

○ **Labour Day / STONY PLAIN**
Their finest release features high energy and well-crafted songs. "Profiteers" is a biting commentary on the people who turned out tenants to make a buck on the Vancouver World Fair. "Take It from the Source" is a great heckler song. Highly recommended. –CR

PETER STAMPFEL & THE BOTTLE CAPS   ♭1938

Former Holy Modal Rounder Peter Stampfel founded the Bottle Caps in 1981 to provide a folk/rock backup to his zany collection of novelty songs. They have recorded several albums for Rounder. –WR

Peter Stampfel & the Bottle Caps / ROUNDER   1986
Peter Stampfel remains a folkie eccentric, and the main difference between his 80s band and his 60s one (the Holy Modal Rounders) is that the later one rocks harder and that more of the material is original. But much of the act still consists of novelties ("Surfer Angel" and "Funny the First Time," to name only two), and it's never quite clear whether Stampfel is celebrating or parodying his sources. Not that it matters. –WR

○ **People's Republic of Rock 'n' Roll / HOMESTEAD**   1989
Stampfel hasn't quite turned pro on this album, but the band is a lot tighter than usual, which only makes the result funnier in songs such as "Bridge and Tunnel Girls" and "Bigfoot Stole My Wife." –WR

STAMPFEL & WEBER

Peter Stampfel and Steve Weber are the founding members of the Holy Modal Rounders. Some of their albums together have been billed as "Stampfel & Weber," however, perhaps for

contractual reasons, perhaps to distinguish them from the Rounders albums that featured a larger band. –WR

○ **Going Nowhere Fast / ROUNDER**   1981
Properly speaking, this is a reunion album by the Holy Modal Rounders, which is the name Peter Stampfel and Steve Weber used for their folk duo when they formed it in the early 60s. The group eventually expanded and went electric, then disbanded. This album is a return to form in more ways than one, restricted to Weber's guitar and Stampfel's banjo and fiddle, plus their squeaky, enthusiastic vocals. It blends folk standards and novelty tunes as the early Rounder albums did and, like them, is an off-the-wall gem. –WR

STEELEYE SPAN

The brainchild of Fairport Convention's Ashley Hutchings, Steeleye Span came about as a furthering vehicle for his infatuation with traditional British folk music. Hutchings succeeded in landing no less a folk deity than Martin Carthy; however, both would be gone by the time Steeleye found its great success.
In 1974, "Gaudette" (a track from their album *Below the Salt*) became a huge Christmas hit in England. Now launched into the pop charts, Steeleye discovered the volume knobs on their amps, cranking out reels with a tenacious bite. Suddenly, they sported a full rock rhythm section and David Bowie was producing their records. The results were often spectacular, with Maddy Prior's pristine vocals riding on top. But by the late 70s, a realignment in the group (including a return by Carthy) saw the group slowly return to a more traditional approach and quickly lose its pop audience. Still, there's rarely been a bad Steeleye Span record through the group's many phases, and they remain most excellent listening. –SA

Hark the Village Wait / SHANACHIE   1970
Their debut, with a smoother and more traditional sound than later albums. The only album to feature the original lineup. –BE & SW

Ten Man Mop / SHANACHIE   1971
Ten Man Mop or Mr. Reservoir Butler Rides Again features the same lineup, with a more traditional folk sound. –SW

Please to See the King / SHANACHIE   1971
The group solidifies its lineup and sharpens its sound. Fiddler Peter Knight and the well-known singer and guitarist Martin Carthy joined the band on this album. –BE & SW

○ **Below the Salt / SHANACHIE**   1972
Fine renditions of traditional ballads, songs, and tunes. –SW

Parcel of Rogues / SHANACHIE   1973
Increasingly tinged with hard-rock sounds. –SW

● **Now We Are Six / SHANACHIE**   1974
High-energy folk that rocks hard despite three throwaway numbers. Their best. –BE

All Around My Hat / SHANACHIE   1975
More rock & roll versions of folk songs. –SW

Commoner's Crown / CHRYSALIS   1975
Live at Last / CHRYSALIS   1978
Steeleye's only live album, recorded at their farewell concert. This one features Martin Carthy and John Kirkpatrick. –SW

Tempted & Tried / SHANACHIE   1989
The reformed group's most recent work. An impressive return, complete with videos; their best album since reforming in the mid 80s. –BE & SW

JOHN STEWART   ♭1939

John Stewart first gained recognition as a songwriter when his songs were recorded by the Kingston Trio. In 1960 he formed the Cumberland Three, which recorded three albums for Roulette. The following year, he joined the Kingston Trio, replacing Dave Guard, and stayed with them until 1967. His song "Daydream Believer" was a #1 hit for the Monkees at the end of that year. Stewart traveled with Senator Robert Kennedy on his 1968 Presidential campaign, an experience that affected him deeply. In 1969 he released his classic album *California Bloodlines*, the first of seven solo albums to reach the charts through 1980. Stewart found his biggest commercial success with the Top Ten album *Bombs Away Dream Babies* and its single "Gold" in 1979. He released several of his albums and albums by others on his own Homecoming label starting in the 1980s. −WR

○ **Calif. Bloodlines/Willard Minus 2 / BEAR FAMILY** / 1969
This German import contains some of Stewart's most powerful work. *California Bloodlines* offers 12 original tunes backed by Nashville's finest studio musicians. *Willard Minus 2*, though not so powerful as *Bloodlines*, still features many great songs (two tracks missing from the original) and a good cast of musicians. Highly recommended. −CR

Lonesome Picker Rides Again / WARNER 1971
Good collection of music, with more energy than his first two records. −CR

Sunstorm Live 1972 / BEAR FAMILY 1972
Featuring Russ Kunkel, James Burton, Buddy Emmons, and brother Michael Stewart. Contains the song "Kansas Rain." A good, solid release. −CR

Cannons in the Rain ... / BEAR FAMILY 1973
In this twofer (*Cannons in the Rain/Wingless Angels*) the *Wingless Angels* release is the stronger collection of music, featuring Robert "Waddy" Wachtel on guitar and a guest appearance by John Denver. *Cannons ...* is a nice collection of ballads and folk/rock. −CR

The Complete Phoenix Concert / BEAR FAMILY 1974
A great collection of live music covering Stewart's first five albums. −CR

Trancas / AFFORDABLE DREAMS 1984
Stewart's electric guitar is nicely backed by touches of strings, drums, keyboards, and synthesized sounds. This album is positive in content and easy listening. −CR

Secret Tapes '86 / HOMECOMING 1986
An 80-minute featuring songs recorded in Stewart's studio. Includes "California Bloodlines," "Chilly Winds," "Cheyenne," "The River." A must for any serious collector. −CR

Secret Tapes II / HOMECOMING
Another collection, featuring "A Grace of Rain," "Seven Angels," "Tears of the Sun," "Quarter Moon on the Golden Gate," and "Irresistable Targets." Another must-have for the serious collector. −CR

Punch the Big Guy / A&M 1987
An exceptional release. Stewart stands out on his electric guitar with minimal backup. Bela Fleck, Sam Bush, and Pat Flynn (New Grass Revival), along with Rosanne Cash, Edgar Meyers, Brent Rowan, and others add just enough, but do not take away from Stewart's sound. Great job on "Runaway Trains." A classic. −CR

Neon Beach Live 1990 / LINE 1990
Over 60 minutes of great live music, featuring some old and new favorites: "Angels with Guns," "Lady Came from Baltimore," "Seven Angels," "Gold Medley," and "Bad Rats," to name a few. Stewart's talking between songs is insightful. −CR

Deep in the Neon / HOMECOMING 1991
Deep in the Neon - Live at McCabe's features just Stewart and Dave Batti and 16 well-performed songs. The audience is into the show, and Stewart plays an easy and relaxed quiet set. −CR

Last Campaign / HOMECOMING
Influenced by Robert Kennedy's campaign for president, the songs paint a tapestry of America. Very good. −CR

JUNE TABOR   b 1947

Known primarily as an English folksinger, Tabor has sung jazz ballads and is serenely competent and convincing. She's best known for her collaboration with Maddy Prior on their Silly Sisters album. −MGN

○ **Some Other Time / HANNIBAL** 1989
English folksinger sings American popular ballads. A lovely album from a lovely vocalist. −MGN

ERIC TAYLOR

Eric Taylor is a Texas-based singer/songwriter. −CR

○ **Shameless Love / FEATHERBED**
Every song is good on this album. The acoustic guitar blends well with Taylor's voice, and Nanci Griffith sings nice harmony on several songs. This is a highly recommended album for the Texas singer/songwriter's fans. −CR

AILEEN AND ELKIN THOMAS

A Texas-based duo who bid fair to become the South's answer to Ian and Sylvia, with a robust mix of folk and country sounds and a pair of clean, pleasing voices that meld together beautifully. −BE

○ **Arise, We Must Be Growing / SHANTIH**
A gorgeous collection of material, alternately upbeat, sentimental, and serious, with Charlie Daniels sitting in on guitar and bass. A sweet and low-keyed mid-80s folk/country gem. −BE

ARTIE TRAUM   b 1943

Artie Traum is a singer-songwriter based in Woodstock, New York. Born in the Bronx, he followed his brother Happy into folk music in the early 1960s in the New York area, taking guitar lessons from jazz artists. He and his brother formed the folk/rock group the Children of Paradise in the mid 60s and, after Happy's departure, they changed their name to Bear and recorded an album for Verve/Forecast. Traum moved to Woodstock in 1967 and has worked as a record producer and written film soundtracks. He has also recorded albums with his brother and with the Woodstock Mountains Revue. −WR

● **Life on Earth / ROUNDER** 1977
A fine album with Pat Alger, featuring "Is There Life on Earth," "Girls of Montreal," and "Riptide." −CR

○ **From the Heart / ROUNDER** 1980
Traum and Pat Alger are two guys who were meant to play together. Highlights include "Gambling Man," "City Lights," and "Screwin' It Up." −CR

○ **Cayenne / ROUNDER** 1986
Traum shows off his very tasteful guitar work. More jazzy than country, this album features Jay Ungar, Vinnie Martucci, Rick Derringer, Happy Traum, and Nick Parker. They called this "new acoustic music"; I just call it a class album. −CR

HAPPY TRAUM   b 1939

Happy Traum is a singer/songwriter based in Woodstock, New York who served as editor of *Sing Out!* magazine for three years and currently runs Homespun Tapes, a company that sells instructional tapes narrated by well-known folk and rock musicians for aspiring musicians. Born in the Bronx, Traum attended the High School of Music and Art, where he took up music and was drawn into the folk music boom of the late 1950s in the New York area. He was a member of the New World Singers and formed a folk/rock band in the mid 60s called the Children of Paradise with his brother Artie, Eric Kaz, and others. He moved to Woodstock in 1967. Traum conducted one of the first interviews Bob Dylan granted after the 1966 motorcycle accident and, in October 1971, he recorded several tracks with Dylan that appeared on *Bob Dylan's Greatest Hits, Volume II*. He has made solo albums, records with his brother, and recordings with the Woodstock Mountain Revue. −WR

Double Back / CAPITOL 1971
A nice album featuring Artie Traum, Bill Keith, Amos Garrett, Eric Kaz, Billy Sanford, and Buddy Spicher. −CR

Relax Your Mind / KM 1975
Traditional fingerpicking guitar styles. Good covers of "John Henry" and "Worried Blues." −CR

○ **Hard Times in the Country / ROUNDER**   1975
Artie Traum, Paul Butterfield, Roly Salley, Arlen Roth, Pat Alger, and Jim Rooney blend nicely. Great covers of "Blow Your Whistle," "Freight Train," and "Penny's Farm." –CR

● **Bright Morning Stars / GR**   1980
A fine collection of music and friends make this a special album. With Pat Alger, Merle Watson, John Sebastian, Richard Manuel, Maria Muldaur, and Artie Traum. –CR

DAVE VAN RONK

One of the most important veterans of the New York folk community, Van Ronk has been active since recording his first album in the late 50s. Van Ronk began as a traditional jazz performer. His distinctive raw vocal style and his ability to incorporate elements of the blues, jazz, jug-band music, and show music allowed him to build a loyal international audience for his eclectic but still traditionally based finger-picking guitar style. While he has composed some songs, Dave Van Ronk is known primarily as an interpreter. His recent compilation, *The Folkways Years - 1959-61*, finds him covering Gary Davis's "Twelve Gates to the City," "Willie the Weeper," and "Come Back Baby." He is a knowledgeable performer with a fine sense of humor who never lets clinical traditionalism get in the way of great interpretations. Van Ronk is an active participant in the folk scene in the US and around the world. As friend, guitar teacher, and touring artist of the highest order, he has lent his support to many up-and-coming songwriters and performers, including Bob Dylan, David Massengill, and Christine Lavin. –RM

☆ **Folkways Years 1959-61 / SMITHSON-FOLKWAYS**
Van Ronk's earliest recordings for Moses Asch. The coffeehouse-folksinger period captured perfectly. –CK

TOWNES VAN ZANDT   b 1940

Townes Van Zandt is among the most widely admired country and folk songwriters of the last quarter century. Texas-born, Van Zandt has a dry, witty, allusive writing style that looks desolation in the eye and chuckles. Starting with Guy Clark, who became a songwriter after hearing him, Van Zandt has influenced an entire generation of artists, up to and including such current leading lights as Lyle Lovett. Van Zandt's own career has suffered from neglect, however. He began putting out albums on the tiny Poppy label in the late 60s and made one remarkable album after another until 1973, then switched to the equally obscure Tomato label. In the early 80s, his songs began to become country hits, including Emmylou Harris's version of "If I Needed You" and Willie Nelson and Merle Haggard's rendition of "Pancho and Lefty." His *At My Window* album in 1987 was his first new effort in nearly a decade. By the 90s, Van Zandt was working on an ambitious boxed set of his songs, to be issued by a newly resuscitated Tomato. –WR

★ **Live at the Old Quarter / TOMATO**   1977
Townes Van Zandt is one of the most impressive songwriters to emerge in the 70s, and his extensive catalog is sufficiently consistent to be recommended in its entirety, once the listener has acquired a taste for his spare, dry delivery and gallows humor. The place to get that taste is on this live disc (originally a two-LP set), which features the best of Van Zandt's early songs, including "If I Needed You" and "Pancho and Lefty." –WR

○ **At My Window / SUGAR HILL**   1987
Van Zandt's first album after a long layoff found him in a more accessible musical setting, courtesy of producers Jack Clement and Jim Rooney, with his striking lyrical observations intact. Van Zandt's qualities are sometimes subtle, and this is an album that gets better every time it's listened to. –WR

LOUDON WAINWRIGHT III   b 1946

Loudon Wainwright III is a singer/songwriter with a humorous, confessional style that has made him a concert favorite and moderately successful recording artist, with

almost a dozen albums to his credit. He had a fluke pop hit with "Dead Skunk" in 1973. –WR

Album III / COLUMBIA / BB# 12   1972
Wainwright's directly autobiographical songs are both brutally honest and extremely funny. Usually he plays alone, but here he gets a full folk/rock backup, which brings out the pop implications of his music. His fluke hit "Dead Skunk" is here, and so is "Red Guitar," about the destruction of one. –WR

○ **A Live One / ROUNDER**   1980
Wainwright is well served by this collection of samples of his live work, which also doubles as the best of his 70s material, with songs like "Whatever Happened to Us," "Nocturnal Stumblebutt," and "Clockwork Chartreuse." –WR

Fame & Wealth / ROUNDER   1983
Bitterness and regret become bigger factors in Wainwright's albums in the 80s. The best of these (also recommended: *I'm Alright* and *More Love Songs*), this collection shows tremendous personal insight, continuing passion for children (Wainwright may have written more about children than any contemporary singer/songwriter), and a brave humor, holding out against the little defeats of middle age. –WR

KIM WALLACH

Wallach is now based in New Hampshire and has released solo and group albums with the Short Sisters. –RM

Two Dozen Favorite Children's Songs / BLACK SOX   1982
Coldest Winter in Living Memory / BLACK SOX   1983
○ **A Little Gracefulness / BLACK SOX**   1987
With the Short Sisters. –RM

T. E. KELLISON WARREN

Warren is a west Texas singer/songwriter who plays a 1920 electric steel-bodied dobro, string guitar, national dobro, and banjo. He plays a blend of blues, bluegrass, country, and rock & roll. –CR

Wind Blown Blues / CANADIAN RIVER   1990
A very good mix of blues, bluegrass, and country, with a dose of rock & roll to boot. "Death Drives a DeSoto" is a great song (and title), and the combination of guitar and mandolin on this album is also great. –CR

○ **Hazardous Cargo / CANADIAN RIVER**   1991
Terry Warren and sister Deborah handle all the instruments on this release, playing socially conscious ballads that are reminiscent of Woody Guthrie's music. –CR

Auggie the Doggie / CANADIAN RIVER
A great collection of guitar instrumentals in the finest tradition. The songs are rich, well played, and a joy to hear. Highly recommended for guitar fans. –CR

THE WASHINGTON SQUARES

New York-based folk trio formed in 1983 by Tom Goodkind, Bruce Paskow, and Lauren Agnelli, specializing in neo-Peter, Paul & Mary harmonies and song styles and (especially in concert) parodies of contemporary pop music. They broke up at the start of the 90s after two albums. –WR

○ **The Washington Squares / GOLD CASTLE**   1987
The Squares resurrect boldly sung 60s folk/pop harmonies and try to reinvoke the political spirit that went with them on such songs as "New Generation" and "You Are Not Alone." Such an ambition can't really be realized 20 years later, but in the meantime, the music is stirring. –WR

THE WATERSONS

Superstardom seems a far cry from the cupped-ear school of a cappella folksinging, yet the Watersons were once called "the Beatles of folk music." Originally composed of sisters Lal and Norma, brother Mike Waterson, and their cousin John Harrison, the English quartet caused a stir in the folk world with their 1965 debut, *Frost & Fire*, which featured ceremonial folk songs (one, "John Barleycorn Must Die," was picked up by the band Traffic). The Watersons have produced only a handful of albums, many of the songs joined by a thematic thread. Martin Carthy replaced John Harrison in 1972, and the distinctive English country harmonies of the group have appeared in British film and television soundtracks. The Watersons guested on the acclaimed Richard and Linda Thompson album *Shoot Out the Lights. Four Pence and Spicy Ale* (1975) is one of their best-received efforts to date. –MH

○ **For Pence & Spicey Ale / SHANACHIE**   1975
A British a cappella family group exploring British folk traditions. –MH

THE WEAVERS

Pete Seeger, Lee Hays, Fred Hellerman, and Ronnie Gilbert formed the Weavers in 1948 to sing folk music in harmony. The group got its big break at a two-week gig at the Village Vanguard in New York City at Christmas, 1949; the gig lasted six months. The Weavers were signed to Decca and scored a double-sided hit in the summer of 1950 with "Tzena, Tzena, Tzena," which went to #2, and "Goodnight Irene," which topped the charts for 13 weeks, one of the biggest hits of the first half of the century. More hits followed through 1952, but then the Weavers fell afoul of the Communist Red scare of that decade, and their career declined precipitously. They came back, however, at a Carnegie Hall concert in 1955 that is remembered as the birth of the late-50s/early-60s folk boom. They then toured and recorded (for Vanguard) more successfully. Seeger left in 1958, replaced by a succession of good musicians: Frank Hamilton, Bernie Krause, and Erik Darling. In 1963, the Weavers (with Seeger and his replacements onstage) staged a reunion and farewell at Carnegie Hall. There was a final reunion and farewell of the original four at the hall in 1980. In addition to their considerable musical accomplishments, the Weavers are remembered as popularizers of folk music and as the inspiration for a whole generation of folk performers. –WR

☆ **At Carnegie Hall / VANGUARD / BB# 24**   1969
The Weavers made a dramatic comeback from the McCarthy era at their 1955 Christmas Eve Carnegie Hall concert, immortalized here. Many of the songs were the same ones from the pop-star days — "Kisses Sweeter than Wine," "Goodnight Irene" — but backed only by guitar and banjo, they were fresh and stirring. –WR

Greatest Hits / VANGUARD   1971
This is an excellent double-disc compilation of this group's more directly folk-related work from the mid 50s to the mid 60s. Note, however, that these are not the original Weavers recordings of their hits. –WR

Together Again / LOOM   1981
After years apart, the Weavers played together one last time at — where else? — Carnegie Hall in November 1980. Lee Hays was ailing (he would die the following year), but the show still transcended nostalgia, demonstrating their individual and collective talents and proving they still were a seminal folk ensemble. –WR

The Best of the Weavers / MCA   1987
The recording career of the Weavers falls into two categories: pre-blacklist and post-blacklist. In their pre-blacklist days, they recorded for Decca (now MCA), and their adaptations of folk songs were backed by orchestras and choruses. Frequently, these songs (notably "Goodnight Irene"), were giant pop hits. This two-album set captures 24 examples of this quasi-folk pop style, and though the group's singing is excellent, the arrangements, intended to modernize the material, now sound quaintly dated. –WR

ILENE WEISS   ♭1953

Weiss is from Philadelphia and now resides in New York City. A very perceptive writer of songs about romantic irony, which have been covered by Anne Hills, Deidre McCalla, Robin Flowers, Marcy Marxer, Cathy Fink, and others, she has been nominated for a BMI Songwriters Award and two New York Music Awards. A contributor to *The Fast Folk Musical Magazine.* –CR & RM

○ **Outside and Curious / GADFLY**   1992
This CD is just Weiss singing and playing guitar. Her vocals as well as her guitar playing are very good. What stands out is her songwriting. Her songs are often filled with humor, yet they can make you think. A very good release. –CR

WELLSPRING

Features Steve Schuch (guitar, fiddle, vocals), and Odds Boskin (Celtic harp, guitar, piano, and recorder). –CR

Live at Folkway / WISDOM TREE-RARE EARTH   1991
Both Steve Schuch and Odds Boskin are masters of their instruments. The duo trade off on songs (24 in all), mixing well together. Schuch's "Wale Trilogy" is wonderful, as are Boskin's "Troubadour" and "Dragon's Tales." –CR

CHERYL WHEELER

Wheeler is a gifted songwriter and singer. Her song "Addicted" was a hit by Dan Seals. –CR

● **Cheryl Wheeler / NORTH STAR**   1986
Her debut album features her hit "Addicted," and is more rock & roll than her other albums. If you like the rest, you should add this to the collection. –CR

○ **Circles & Arrows / CAPITOL**   1990
Wheeler shines on this CD. Guests include Mark O'Connor, Jerry Douglas, Jonathan Edwards, and Billy Joe Walker. Every song is a winner, especially "Northern Girl," "Aces," and "I Know This Town." –CR

Half a Book / NORTH STAR   1991
With guest Jonathan Edwards, this features a clean sound and "Emotional Response." –CR

JOSH WHITE   1908-1969

Most blues enthusiasts think of Josh White as a folk revival artist.It's true that the second half of his music career found him based in New York playing to the coffeehouse and cabaret set and hanging out with Burl Ives, Woody Guthrie, and fellow transplanted blues artists Sonny Terry and Brownie McGhee. When I saw him in Chicago in the 1960s his shirt was unbuttoned to à la Harry Belefonte and his repertoire consisted of folk revival standards such as "Scarlet Ribbons." He was a show business personality — a star renowned for his sexual magnetism and his dramatic vocal presentations. What many people don't know is that Josh White was a major figure in the Piedmont blues tradition. The first part of his career saw him as apprentice and lead boy to some of the greatest blues and religious artists ever, including Willie Walker, Blind Blake, Blind Joe Taggert (with whom he recorded), and allegedly even Blind Lemon Jefferson. On his own, he recorded both blues and religious songs, including a classic version of "Blood Red River." A fine guitar technician with an appealing voice, he became progressively more sophisticated in his presentation. Like many other Carolinians and Virginians who moved north to urban areas, he took up city ways, remaining a fine musician if no longer a down-home artist. Like several other canny blues players, he used his roots music to broaden and enhance his life experience, and his talent was such that he could choose the musical idiom that was most lucrative at the time. –BLP

○ **The Legendary Josh White / MCA**
This is a two-record set that has a good sampling of White's major songs. –JME

JOSH WHITE JR   ♭1940

Josh White Jr got his inspiration and start from his famous father, folk/blues singer Josh White Sr. In the late 40s and early 50s, White worked on Broadway, performing in various plays. He also did extensive work on TV from the 50s through the 70s. After his father's death, he recreated Josh White Sr's folk act in concerts across the country. He has recorded for Vanguard and is very active at major folk festivals. —JME

○ **Ballads & Blues / RYKODISC** 1987
This is a tribute to Josh White Sr. —JME

DAVID WILCOX

Wilcox is an up-and-coming singer/songwriter who is known for his deep, personal, well-crafted songs and smooth, rich vocals. —CR

Nightshift Watchman / SONG OF THE WOOD 1987
This debut release shows his earliest work. Worth a listen. —CR

○ **How Did You Find Me Here / A&M**
Nice songs that, although sometimes sad, are all solid on this sophomore release. —CR

Home Again / A&M
A little more mature and better produced. Great songs. —CR

JEFF WILKINSON

Detroit native Wilkinson now is a member of the NY folk scene. —RM

○ **Pitchin' Pennies / BLACKBIRD** 1987
This record is full of great songs — Wilkinson's songs create images that you keep long after the record is over. "C'mon Down" is a good ol' fishin' song. Wilkinson uses a nice array of mandolin, accordion, fiddle, pennywhistle, and harmonica, along with his guitar. —CR

Ballads in Plain Talk / BRAMBUS
Seventeen songs, seven from his *Pitchin' Pennies* album. What an experience! Wilkinson guides you from the Triple-A ballfields of Toledo to Hoboken to Detroit. His songs are vivid and well crafted. Anyone who is into the new acoustic folk style should enjoy this CD. It's worth the import price. —CR

Brave and True / BRAMBUS
A more electric album then his previous ones. Wilkinson is backed by the Navigators (at times they sound like a cross between Blue Rodeo and the Kinks). "When the River Was King" and "Henry Villard's Great Train Ride" are just two of a great collection of songs. —CR

BROOKS WILLIAMS

Based in central Massachusetts, a great guitarist and spiritual writer. —RM

○ **North from Statesboro / RED GUITAR**
"On the Rollin' Sea" and "Big Blue Wonder" are outstanding tracks. —RM

How the Nighttime Sings / RED GUITAR
"Jubilee" is a joyous lush song, and "Hard Love" is also excellent. —RM

ROBIN AND LINDA WILLIAMS

Singers-songwriters Robin and Linda Williams were regulars on Garrison Keillor's "A Prairie Home Companion" radio show. Some of their songs have been recorded by Emmylou Harris, Kathy Mattea, and Michael Martin Murphey. Their harmonies are smooth and well matched. Their musicianship is tight and well crafted. —CR

Harmony / JUNE APPAL 1981
Very hard to find, but it should be in your collection. —CR

Close As We Can Get / FLYING FISH 1984
Perfect in all ways. "The Leaving Train" is one of their best songs. As good as *All Broken Hearts*. —CR

Nine 'Til Midnight / FLYING FISH 1985
A very good live album featuring gospel, traditional country, and contemporary songs. One of your finer live albums. —CR

○ **All Broken Hearts Are the Same / SUGAR HILL** 1988
With top-notch songwriting and smooth vocals, this features Jerry Douglas, Stuart Duncan, and T. Michael Coleman. —CR

Rhythm of Love / SUGAR HILL 1990
These 12 songs are all good. Features guests Jerry Douglas and Stuart Duncan. —CR

ROBIN WILLIAMSON & HIS MERRY BAND   b 1943

Robin Williamson was one half of the Incredible String Band from 1966 to 1974, then went on to form His Merry Band to back up his playing of traditional Scottish music and originals in a folk style. He has released many albums on Flying Fish, including some devoted to harp music. —WR

○ **American Stonehenge / FLYING FISH** 1978
This album is perhaps Williamson's most generally accessible, featuring his late-70s touring band on a variety of humorous and pastoral Williamson originals. —WR

KATE WOLF   1942-1986

Wolf was born in San Francisco, CA, as Kathryn Louise Allen. She started playing piano at age four, stopping at age sixteen due to shyness. In 1969, Wolf got together with the Big Sur music community, where her music blossomed. She was a gifted guitarist and songwriter. After releasing seven records, Wolf died of acute leukemia at the age of 44. Wolf was inducted into the NAIRD Independent Music Hall of Fame in 1987. According to her wishes, material from her unreleased recordings continues to be brought to life. —CR

Close to You / KALEIDOSCOPE 1963
Good. Features Tony Rice, Norton Buffalo, Nina Gerber. —CR

Poet's Heart / KALEIDOSCOPE 1964
One of my favorites. Wolf at her best. —CR

Back Roads / KALEIDOSCOPE 1976
A nice album, mostly recorded on one take. Few overdubs. —CR

Lines on the Paper / KALEIDOSCOPE 1977
This album shows her early songwriting. —CR

Safe at Anchor / KALEIDOSCOPE 1980
A good album. Wolf's first record with Nina Gerber and first studio production. —CR

○ **Give Yourself to Love / KALEIDOSCOPE** 1983
Two-album set recorded live. Voted Best Folk Album of 1983 by NAIRD. The sound is clear and the audience is receptive. Highly recommended. —CR

The Wind Blows Wild / KALEIDOSCOPE 1988
Solid, well produced, and well put together by Nina Gerber after Wolf's death. —CR

Gold in California / KALEIDOSCOPE 1988
Two retrospective albums. A good way to get a feel for Wolf's music. —CR

An Evening in Austin / KALEIDOSCOPE 1990
A very good live show, recorded on "Austin City Limits." There are 70+ minutes. —CR

WOODSTOCK MOUNTAIN REVUE

Woodstock Mountain Revue is a loose, informal affiliation of folk-based musicians who live in the area of Woodstock, New York, and record occasionally for Rounder Records. Their first album (at which time they had not yet adopted their name) was *Mud Acres-Music among Friends*. It was recorded in 1972 and featured Happy Traum, Artie Traum, Maria Muldaur, John Herald, Eric Kaz, Jim Rooney, Bill Keith, Tony Brown, and Lee Berg. Their second album, 1977's *More Music from Mud Acres*, was credited to "Woodstock Mountains," and featured the Traums, Herald, Rooney, Keith, and Berg, plus Pat Alger, Eric Andersen, Rory Block, Paul Butterfield, Roly Salley, John Sebastian, and Paul Siebel. Their third album, 1978's *Pretty Lucky*, was the first to be credited to Woodstock Mountain Revue, which was defined as an eight-member group consisting of the Traums, Herald, Rooney, Keith, Alger, Solley, Larry Campbell, and Caroline Dutton, with special guest Cyndi Cashdollar. —WR

Mud Acres - Music among Friends / ROUNDER 1972
With Happy and Artie Traum, Bill Keith, Maria Muldaur, Eric Kaz, Jim Rooney, John Herald, Tony Brown, and Lee Berg. Their first release, just sittin' and pickin'. Very informal. —CR

○ **Woodstock Mountains / ROUNDER** 1977
Woodstock Mountains (More Music from Mud Acres) features

Pat Alger, Happy and Artie Traum, Eric Andersen, Lee Berg, Rory Block, Paul Butterfield, John Herald, Bill Keith, Jim Rooney, Roly Salley, John Sebastian, and Paul Siebel. This album brought it all together! Their peak. –CR

FOLK COLLECTIONS

○ **Adventures in Music - Folk Sampler #7 / AIM**
A 15-cut sampler, some good, some strange. Dan Berggren plays nice Adirondack traditional music. David Schnaufer is one of the finest mountain dulcimer players you'll ever hear. Andy Wilkenson (Texas singer/songwriter), James Mee (singer/songwriter), Savoy Doucet (Cajun), Lee Murdock (folk), Peter Leman (folk, country, bluegrass), and others make this a good way to find some new music. –CR

Linda Allen's Washington Notebook / VMR   1991
This album is a collection of songs written by Linda Allen and performed by 33 Northwest musicians. Allen has a way of transporting you to the Northwest when you listen to her songs. The album has a real community feel to it. After several plays, you have the feeling you know the musicians. They go to church, recycle, don't eat meat, and would not be caught dead in a McDonald's. –CR

○ **Atomic Cafe / ROUNDER**
A fine and varied compilation of 50s songs reacting to life in the atomic age. –MH

○ **Been in the Storm So Long / SMITHSONIAN-FOLKWAYS**
A truly wonderful collection of spirituals, folk tales, and children's stories recorded in the early 60s on Johns Island, SC. How much the Gullah culture of the islands is an ante-bellum US survival and just how it links with its Caribbean cousins isn't clear. What is clear is the beauty and importance of this recompilation of two old Folkways albumss (3841 and 3842), with new notes. –JSR

○ **Ben & Jerry's Newport Folk Festival / RED HOUSE**
Sixteen live cuts on a nice collection featuring Robert Earl Keen Jr, the Indigo Girls, Shawn Colvin, Luka Bloom, Richard Thompson, Greg Brown, Michelle Shocked, Cheryl Wheeler, and more. Highly recommended. –CR

○ **Ben & Jerry's Newport Folk Festival - Vol. 2 / ALACAZAR**
Featuring Bill Morrissey doing "Grizzly Bear," Doc Watson's "St. James Infirmary," and Richard Thompson's "Two Left Feet" and "Stands Out." Cheryl Wheeler's "I Know This Town" is also great. –CR

○ **Ben & Jerry's Newport Folk Festival 88 / ALACAZAR**
Richard Thompson does a great version of "Turning of the Tide." Shawn Colvin and Patty Larkin are solid. Bill Morrissey's "Married Man" hits home. This very diverse album also features Doc Watson, Taj Mahal, Dr. John, Nashville Bluegrass Band, Tom Paxton, Cheryl Wheeler, Queen Ida, Holly Near, and Moses Roscoe. –CR

Best of Mountain Stage Live / BLUE PLATE
Recordings taken from the "Mountain Stage" live performance radio program. Featuring Richard Thompson, Danko and Hudson, Gregson and Collister, Loudon Wainwright III, and others. Very wide range of music. –CR

○ **Best of Mountain Stage - Vol. 2 / BLUE PLATE**
Features John Prine, Billy Bragg, Maura O'Connell, Michelle Shocked, Kathy Mattea, Jimmie Dale Gillmore, and others. Very good. –CR

☆ **Bleecker & Macdougal / ELEKTRA**   1984
Bleecker & Macdougal - Folk Scene of the 60s proves that along with Vanguard, Jac Holzman's Elektra Records was one of the two major folk record labels of the 60s, its most popular artists being Judy Collins, Tom Paxton, and Phil Ochs. Sprawling across four albums on this boxed set, programmer and annotator Lenny Kaye presents the big names and quite a few of the small but interesting ones: Fred Neil, Dave Van Ronk, Patrick Sky, Oscar Brand, and many more. This is an in-depth compilation, more than the casual listener may want, but it yields surprising pleasures. –WR

○ **Bread & Roses Festival 1977 / FANTASY**   1979
This two-record set chronicles the October 1977 benefit concert for Mimi Farina's Bread & Roses organization, which brings music into prisons and hospitals. A broad range of folk-related artists, including Joan Baez, Jackson Browne, Pete Seeger, and Arlo Guthrie, among many others, turns this into a brilliant songwriting showcase. –WR

○ **Bread & Roses Festival 1979 / FANTASY**   1980
The lineup for the 1979 festival was even broader than the 1977 one, including the Chambers Brothers and Chick Corea, plus the Roches, Graham Nash and David Crosby, and many more. But the folk theme still runs through all the wonderful music. –WR

○ **Broome Closet Anti-Folk Sessions / 109 RECORDS**
Compilation by members of the New York "anti-folk" East Village scene, including Roger Manning, Kirk Kelly, Cindy Lee Berryhill, and others. –RM

○ **Camp Cuisine Tapes / AGUA AZUL**   1991
These recordings of *Music from the Kerrville Campgrounds* were made at the 1989 festival on a portable DAT machine. Most of the artists are not well-known, but they should be. Jon Ims does his song "She's in Love with the Boy" (#1 for Trisha Yearwood). "Here Comes the Water," by Chuck Pyle, is very strong. Bob Franke has the crowd join in on "Invasion of the Money Snatchers." This record is hard to get. Write to Agua Azul, PO Box 161556, Austin, TX 78716. The crickets in the background on the CD will lull you into a trance — so will the music. –CR

○ **Capitol Acoustics / CAPITOL ACOUSTICS**
Contemporary and traditional music from the area around Washington, DC. –RM

○ **Capitol Acoustics - Vol. 2 / IMPACT**
A less well known group that on Vol. 1, but this CD has some great music. Shady Grove and Tony Furtado play some good bluegrass. The Jon Henrys, featuring Jonathan Edwards, Henry Gross, Henry Paul, and Toulouse le Trac, are great. Cathy Fink and March Marxer also play on the CD. Here's folk, traditional, bluegrass, and contemporary on one CD. Can't wait to hear the third volume (how about Mary-Chapin Carpenter, guys?). –CR

○ **Capitol Acoustics - 17 Song Collection / IMPACT**   1991
Featuring Magpie, Jane Gillman, Steve Key, Anne Louise White (formerly of Trapezoid), Hazelwood (real nice female duo), and others. The Washington area is rich in talent — traditional folk and bluegrass. This is a good way to hear some of it. –CR

○ **Circle Dance ... / GARLAND**
Circle Dance - Hokey Pokey Charity Compilation is a well-done collection featuring the cream of British folk/rock. Many rarities. Includes Richard Thompson, Sandy Denny, June Tabor, Fairport Convention, and others. –MPD

○ **15 Years of Stony Plain Music / STONY PLAIN**   1991
A two-CD collection of Canada's Stony Plain artists; 2 1/2 hours, 45 artists, and 46 tunes. CD #1 features blues, Cajun, and a touch of folk with Zachary Richard, John Hammond, Robert Gray, Aaron Neville, Jo-El Sonnier, Walter Shakey Horton, and others. CD #2 is country, folk, bluegrass, Irish, rock, and singer/songwriters with Alison Krauss, Guy Clark, Doc Watson, Ricky Skaggs, John Prine, Bonnie Raitt, Steve Goodman, Ian Tyson, Roy Rogers, Jonathan Richman, Spirit of the West, the Tom Russell Band, and others. You do not often find collections so full of talent as this. Buy it! You'll find music you never even knew existed. –CR

○ **The CooP - February 1982 / COOP**   1982
The CooP's debut issue combined the work of established folk figures such as Ed McCurdy and Dave Van Ronk (who contributed the hilarious "Jersey State Stomp") with up-and-coming performers like folk-blues guitarist Frank Christian, Ilene Weiss, David Massengill (whose "Fairfax County"

turned up on a Roches album later in the year), and Suzanne Vega (whose "Cracking" would be recorded three years later for her debut album). –WR

○ **The CooP - April 1982 / COOP**   1982
Highlights of this issue include "Small Town on the River," by Bill Morrissey, who later recorded four albums on Rounder Records; "I'm Talking to You," by Shawn Colvin, later a Grammy-winning folk artist on Columbia Records; and perhaps the most impressive song of the new folk movement of the time, David Massengill's epic "The Great American Dream." –WR

○ **CooP - May 1982 ... / COOP**   1982
The CooP - May 1982, The Political Song Revisited. A thematic album featuring Matt Jones's version of *CooP* editor Jack Hardy's Civil War story, "Incident at Ebenezer Creek," Sherwood Ross's humorous "I Sliced Pastrami for the CIA and Found God," and a duet between Steve Forbert and Jack Hardy on Woody Guthrie's "This Land Is Your Land." –WR

○ **The CooP - June 1982 ... / COOP**   1982
The CooP - June 1982, Traditional Music Revisited. Actually, humorous music revisited is more like it, what with the first appearance of future Philo recording artist Christine Lavin on her "Regretting What I Said ...," and David Massengill's "The Eunuch's Lament." Also included is Suzanne Vega's "Gypsy," later to appear on her second A&M album, five years hence. –WR

○ **The CooP - September 1982 / COOP**   1982
An especially strong collection recorded live at SpeakEasy and including Suzanne Vega's "Knight Moves," Rod MacDonald's "Sailor's Prayer," George Gerdes's "The Policeman Is My Friend," and Jack Hardy's "The Children." –WR

○ **The CooP - February 1983 ... / COOP**   1983
The CooP - February 1983, 1st Anniversary! Standouts here are Tom Paxton performing his Nancy Reagan parody, "Little Bitty Gun," Suzanne Vega's "The Queen and the Soldier," future editor and Shanachie recording artist Richard Meyer's "Jive Town," and then-editor Jack Hardy's Central American topical song "Porto Limon." –WR

○ **The CooP - May 1983: The Political Songs / COOP**   1983
Appropriately, this album contains a contribution from *Broadside* magazine founder Sis Cunningham, and the other highlights include Michael Jerling's Vietnam vets song "Long Black Wall" and Fred Small's "Everything Possible." –WR

○ **The CooP - June 1983: Love Songs / COOP**   1983
Suzanne Vega (who seems to have recorded much of her first two albums for *The CooP*) contributes "Some Journey," while Richard Meyer presents what will be the title track of his debut album, "Laughing/Scared." John Gorka, who now records for Windham Hill, makes his first appearance with "Downtown Tonight." –WR

○ **Cornelia Street - Songwriter's Exchange / STASH**   1980
Re-released in 1991 with addtracks on CD. From the late 70s on, there was a weekly meeting of the many contemporary Greenwich Village songwriters. This compilation album spotlights some of the fine work from that time. A precursor to *The Fast Folk Musical Magazine*. –RM

○ **Country Hicks - Vols. 1 & 2 / BARK LOG**
A compilation of obscure humorous country songs, apparently from the late 50s and 60s. –RM

○ **Cowboy Songs from Folkways / FOLKWAYS**
Richly varied set, from Leadbelly to Woody Guthrie, drawn from the vast Folkways archives and dating from the early 40s to the 60s. Excellent annotations. –CW

○ **Cowboy Songs on Folkways / FOLKWAYS**
Various artists — a compilation of obscure humorous country songs, apparently from the late 50s and early 60s. –RM

○ **Don't Mourn - Organize! / FOLKWAYS**
A compilation of songs by and about labor songwriter Joe Hill (turn-of-the-century labor organizer). –RM

○ **Fast Folk Magazine - Vol. 1 #1 / FAST FOLK**   1984
This first issue of the renamed record/magazine features Eric

Andersen's "The Girls of Denmark," Suzanne Vega's future Top 10 hit "Tom's Diner," John Gorka's "I Saw a Stranger with Your Hair," and Christine Lavin's "Don't Ever Call Your Sweetheart by His Name." –WR

○ **Fast Folk Magazine - Vol. 1 #2 / FAST FOLK**   1984
Pete Seeger turns up on this edition, as do such other folk veterans as Oscar Brand, Sammy Walker, and Jim Glover (of Jim and Jean). Among the new generation, Shawn Colvin contributes "I Don't Know Why," and Rod MacDonald sings the anthem-like "Every Living Thing." –WR

○ **Fast Folk Magazine - Vol. 1 #4 / FAST FOLK**   1984
Subtitled: *Live at the Bottom Line.* On January 28, 1984, The Fast Folk cooperative staged the first of what would be an annual concert series presenting the best of the songs that had appeared so far on the records. The result is an essential greatest-hits album that makes the case for a folk-music renaissance in the early 80s. –WR

○ **Fast Folk Magazine - Vol. 1 #6 / FAST FOLK**   1984
Subtitled: *The Blues.* "Traditional" is the author of the majority of these folk-blues cuts, which are performed by the likes of John Hammond, Dave Van Ronk, and some less illustrious but equally talented musicians. –WR

○ **Fast Folk Magazine - Vol. 1 #8 / FAST FOLK**   1984
Subtitled: *Women in Song.* This exceptional album leads off with Nanci Griffith and also includes Shawn Colvin and Christine Lavin. Among the less well known names, the duo Palmer and Bragg turn in the impressive "Bayonne" and Megan McDonough contributes "A Lesson in Every Good-Bye." –WR

○ **Fast Folk Magazine - Vol. 2 #10 / FAST FOLK**   1985
Tom Paxton returns in this album, along with a large number of folksingers who have gone on to greater recognition, among them Pierce Pettis, David Mallett, Greg Brown, Bob Franke, Schooner Fare, and Cliff Eberhardt. All of them recorded at SpeakEasy. –WR

○ **Fast Folk Magazine - Vol. 2 #8 / FAST FOLK**   1985
A new batch of singer/songwriters gets their first exposure in this release, among them Lyle Lovett, Buddy Mondlock, and Cindy Lee Berryhill. –WR

○ **Fast Folk Magazine - Vol. 3 #10 / FAST FOLK**   1986
Richie Havens is here in this release, as is Michelle Shocked (that's right, another debut). Buddy Mondlock and Fred Small return, too. –WR

○ **Fast Folk Magazine - Vol. 3 #3 / FAST FOLK**   1986
Lyle Lovett, Aztec Two Step, Steve Gillette, and Tom Russell are the stars of this issue, but also note Tom Intondi's stirring "Straight from the Heart" and the Folkano version of Pierce Pettis's "Moments." –WR

○ **Fast Folk Magazine - Vol. 3 #4 / FAST FOLK**   1986
Subtitled: *Boston One.* This issue is notable for the first recorded appearance anywhere of Tracy Chapman (singing "For My Lover"), but also as a representative sampling of Boston folk music, much of it on a par with the New York scene *Fast Folk* usually chronicles. –WR

○ **Fast Folk Magazine - Vol. 3 #6/7 / FAST FOLK**   1986
Subtitled: *Live at the Bottom Line.* Double-pocket souvenir of the third annual Fast Folk Revue show, recorded May 10, 1986, it is once again a best-of, containing the most impressive songs from *Fast Folk* over the previous year, highlights including the heartbreaking Irish emigration ballad "Kilkelly" and the sidesplitting "Railroad Bill," written and sung by Andy Breckman, whose day job is head writer for "Late Night with David Letterman." –WR

○ **Fast Folk Magazine - Vol. 4 #5/6 / FAST FOLK**   1988
Subtitled: *The 6th Anniversary Issue.* Nicknamed "the flag album" for its cover, this double-album features such *Fast Folk* regulars as David Massengill, Jack Hardy, Rod MacDonald, and Richard Meyer, plus old friends like Dave Van Ronk and Eric Andersen, new stars like Christine Lavin and Michelle Shocked, and guest Suzanne Vega, whose "The Marching Dream" is unavailable elsewhere. –WR

○ **Fast Folk Magazine - Vol. 4 #9 / FAST FOLK**   1989
Subtitled: *Los Angeles. Fast Folk* goes bicoastal for an album featuring Peter Case, Victoria Williams, and Milo Binder. –WR

○ **Folk Classics / COLUMBIA**   1989
Though one thinks of Elektra and Vanguard as the main record labels of the folk revival, the giant Columbia Records also made some inroads into the field, signing up not only Bob Dylan but also a wide range of folkies, from Pete Seeger to the New Christy Minstrels. This 15-track compilation delves deeper into the Columbia vault for tracks by Leadbelly and Burl Ives, but its focus is on 60s performers — the Brothers Four, Carolyn Hester, Malvina Reynolds. Many of them, like Dylan, are John Hammond signings. The focus of the album is scattered, but the selection is excellent, and Columbia was long overdue to examine its folk archives. –WR

○ **Fresh Oldtime String Band Music / ROUNDER**
A Mike Seeger-compiled anthology of contemporary groups playing with the hillbilly string-band tradition. –MH

○ **From the New World ... / STRANGE THINGS**
From the New World - Folk Rock of the 1960s is a compilation of obscure-but-cool 60s folk/rock bands. –RM

☆ **Greatest Folksingers of 60s / VANGUARD**   1972
Not only was Maynard Solomon's Vanguard Records one of the major folk labels of the 60s (having the prescience to pick up Joan Baez early on, and then recording the cream of the singer/songwriters thereafter), but it also had the rights to record and release material from the Newport Folk Festival, giving it access to several artists who were not signed to the label. As a result, this double-packet compilation features songs by nearly every major folk figure of the decade, from the Weavers to José Feliciano, with Vanguard artists such as Buffy Sainte-Marie, Eric Andersen, and Odetta sharing space with Elektra's Phil Ochs and Judy Collins and Columbia's Bob Dylan. Listen to this one record and you'll know what the 60s folk revival sounded like. –WR

○ **Greatest Songs of Woody Guthrie / VANGUARD**   1972
This 23-track, 70-minute disc, assembled from recordings dating from the 50s and the 60s, is by now a historical document tracing the kinds of interpretations offered by the first generation of folksingers to be influenced by Guthrie, some of whom were his contemporaries. For the most part, the singers, who include the Weavers, Odetta, Ramblin' Jack Elliot, Cisco Huston, and Joan Baez, offer covers of Guthrie favorites that are sweeter and more conventional than the originals. Thankfully, they are interspersed with a handful of tunes featuring Guthrie himself. –WR

○ **Greenwich Village Folk Festival / GADFLY**   1991
Both the up-and-coming and the well-established perform on this CD. Five Chinese Brothers do a nice version of "My Dad's Face." Cliff Eberhardt's "When the Circus Comes to Town" is great. Tom Paxton, Jack Hardy, Guy Davis, Ilene Weiss, Dave Van Ronk, Frank Christian, Andy Breckman, Mark Johnson, and Erik Frandsen also are on this. A good collection. –CR

○ **Woody Guthrie/Leadbelly ... / FOLKWAYS**
Woody Guthrie/Leadbelly - Folkways Original Vision. This collection of recordings made between 1940 and 1947 was assembled as a complement to the album *A Tribute to Guthrie and Leadbelly: A Vision Shared* (Columbia OC 44034), on which various country, folk, and rock stars covered the Guthrie and Leadbelly songs. The result is an excellent sampler, made all the more potent when heard in contrast with the Columbia album. –WR

○ **Hard Cash / GRL**
A talent-packed album featuring Richard Thompson, Clive Gregson and Christine Collister, Martin Carthy, June Tabor, and others. The album was for a BBC series on the theme of exploited workers. –CR

○ **Have Moicy! / ROUNDER**   1976
The various members of the Holy Modal Rounders are a sneaky bunch of folks with a tendency to turn up on record in

The Fast Folk Musical Magazine

At the beginning of the 80s, it would have been easy to suppose that the spark that had ignited the folk boom of the 60s was long since extinguished. The artists who abetted and benefited from that boom had gone in various directions, most of them dropped from record labels by the mid 70s, and only such minor commercial entities as the Roches and Steve Forbert had made any noise at all while using New York's Greenwich Village as a base in the late 70s. But, in fact, a whole new generation of performers was coming up, and if the record labels were going to ignore them, they were nevertheless determined to support their own community and foster songwriting themselves. Performers such as Jack Hardy, David Massengill, and Rod MacDonald set up the Songwriters' Exchange so writers would have a forum where their work could be heard by their peers. This resulted in an album released in 1980 on Stash Records. In 1981, the group formed a cooperative, which took over the booking of SpeakEasy, a Village club. And in February 1982, the cooperative launched The CooP, a combination magazine and record album featuring the work of new songwriters. A decade later, The CooP, now renamed The Fast Folk Musical Magazine, was a nonprofit corporation that had published over 70 issues and served as the springboard for such nationally recognized performers as Suzanne Vega and Tracy Chapman. The selected albums listed in this section may or may not be in print at the present time. To order any of them, write to The Fast Folk Musical Magazine, Inc., P.O. Box 938, Village Station, New York, NY 10014.

— William Ruhlmann

a variety of guises, which is only a partial explanation of why, with three artists credited on the cover, this album is really the brainchild of one who is unmentioned: Rounder cofounder Peter Stampfel. And as with his other manifestations (see the Holy Modal Rounders, Stampfel & Weber, and Peter Stampfel & the Bottle Caps), this is a collection of folk, blues, country, and rock novelties, some of which are ridiculously funny. A Rounder by any other name is still a hoot. –WR

○ **The Jupiter Book of Ballads / FOLKWAYS**
Includes tracks from Isla Cameron, Jill Balcon, Pauline Letts, John Laurie, and others. –RM

Kerrville Festival 1972-1976 / ADELPHI
Kerrville Festival 1972-1976 (Texas Folk & Outlaw Music) is a first-class sampling of Kerrville featuring Guy Clark, Willie Nelson, Jerry Jeff Walker, Townes Van Zandt, Steve Fromholz, and others. Two-record set. –CR

○ **Kerrville Folk Festival / KERRVILLE**
A great collection of music from the campfires of Kerrville, featuring David Wilcox, Bob Franke, Rachel Polisher, and many more. The CD has three extra cuts. –CR

Kerrville Folk Festival - First 15 Years / KERRVILLE
Roger Allen Polson pieced together this album, featuring some fine performances by Butch Hancock, Guy Clark, Nancy Griffith, Kate Wolf, Garry P. Nunn, and Tom Paxton. If you enjoy Kerrville, pick this one up — it's obscure. –CR

Kerrville Folk Festival - 1976 / KERRVILLE   1976
All 13 Kerrville Folk Festival tapes are available by contacting the Kerrville Folk Fest in Kerrville, TX. Very rare, featuring Bill Staines, Carolyn Hestor, Hardin and Russell, Hondo Crouch. –CR

Kerrville Folk Festival - 1977 / KERRVILLE   1977
A good album featuring Steven Fromholz, Townes Van Zandt,
Hardin and Russell, Mike Williams, Butch Hancock. –CR
Kerrville Folk Festival - 1978 / KERRVILLE   1978
A real Texas feel, featuring Joe Ely and Butch Hancock, Guy
Clark, Eric Taylor and Nanci Griffith, Rusty Weir, and Alvin
Crowe. –CR
Kerrville Folk Festival - 1979 / KERRVILLE   1979
Featuring Peter Rowan and Nanci Griffith. –CR
Kerrville Folk Festival - 1980 / KERRVILLE   1980
Featuring Garry P. Nunn, Spider John Koerner, and Uncle
Walt's Band. –CR
Kerrville Folk Festival - 1981 - A / KERRVILLE   1981
Guy Clark, Bob Gibson, Peter Rowan, and Riders in the Sky.
The sound quality is not so good as it could be. –CR
Kerrville Folk Festival - 1981 - B / KERRVILLE   1981
Steve Young, Jimmie Dale Gillmore and Butch Hancock, and
Bob Gibson. The sound quality could be better. –CR
Kerrville Folk Festival - 1984 / KERRVILLE   1984
Featuring Bill Staines, Anne Hills, Guy Clark, Billy Joe Shavers,
Steve Gillette and Courtney Campbell, Artie and Happy
Traum. The first year out on cassette — quality music. –CR
Kerrville Folk Festival - 1985 / KERRVILLE   1985
One of my favorite shows — John Gorka, Jane Gillman, Tish
Hinojosa, Garry P. Nunn, Kate Wolf, Peter Rowan, and Lyle
Lovett. A 20-song cassette. –CR
Kerrville Folk Festival - 1987 / KERRVILLE   1987
Steven Fromhultz, Trapezoid, Garry P. Nunn, and Austin
Lounge Lizards. A 22-song cassette. –CR
○ **Kerrville Folk Festival - 1988 / KERRVILLE**   1988
Another good one, featuring Laurie Lewis, Valdy, Michelle
Shocked, Fred Koller, Butch Hancock & Marce Lacouture,
Robert Earle Keen Jr, Eddie Adcock, Red Clay Ramblers. –CR
Kerrville Folk Festival - 1989 / KERRVILLE   1989
One of my top three favorites, featuring Robert Earl Keen Jr,
Laurie Lewis, Steven Fromholz, Valdy, Tish Hinojosa, Hobo
Jim, John Stewart, Rod MacDonald, Steve Gillette, Austin
Lounge Lizards. A 23-song cassette, 80 minutes of music. –CR
Kerrville Folk Festival - 1990 / KERRVILLE   1990
A wide range of music — Tony Bird, Cheryl Wheeler, Peppino
D'Agostino, Patty Larkin, David Wilcox, Tish Hinojosa, Peter
Rowan & the Rowans, Rosie Flores, Sparky Rucker, Celtic
Elvis, and Poi Dog Pondering. –CR
○ **Legacy - A Collection ... / WINDHAM**   1989
Legacy - A Collection of New Folk Music. Although only a few
of them managed to break through to national attention, a
generation of important folk talents appeared during the 80s,
playing clubs and festivals and recording for *The Fast Folk
Musical Magazine* and self-financed records sold at gigs. In
1989, Windham Hill noticed and copied the *Fast Folk* formula,
presenting some of the best — David Massengill, Cliff
Eberhardt, Bill Morrissey, John Gorka, and others — on this
15-track disc and even signing a few of them to contracts. The
result is a stunning showcase of talent that will shock anyone
who thinks good folk music disappeared around 1970. –WR
Legends of Folk / RED HOUSE
An excellent concert recording by Utah Philips, Spider John
Koerner, and Ramblin' Jack Elliott. –RM
Masters of the Folk Violin / ARHOOLIE   1989
Six premier American fiddlers appear on this release —
Alison Krauss, Seamus Connolly, Michael Doucet, Kenny
Baker, Claude Williams, and Joe Cormier. The release features
Texas long-bow (Alison), Irish (Seamus), Cajun (Michael),
bluegrass (Kenny), jazz (Claude), and Scottish (Joe) styles of
music. –CR
Mountain Music / FOLKWAYS
This classic Folkways reissue features performances by Don

Stover, Earl Taylor, Chubby Anthony, Tex Logan, and other
artists. –RM
○ **On a Winter's Night / NORTH STAR**
Christine Lavin's compilation album, with each guest artist
performing a song dealing with the theme "on a winter's
night." Featuring David Wilcox, Cheryl Wheeler, Rod
MacDonald, Ferron, Electric Bonsai Band, Anne Hills, Sally
Fingerett, and many others. A good collection, worth looking
into. –CR
One Wide River ... / AMERICAN MELODY   1988
One Wide River: Songs & Stories. A nice collection of folk
ballads, songs, and stories that can be enjoyed by adults and
children. Jonathan Edwards and Dave Mallett offer up their
usual strong performances. Tom Callinan, Phil Rosenthal, and
Phil Bloch do a great version of "The Rattlin' Bog." Not the
kind of music that will wind up your children at bedtime. –CR
○ **Out of the Darkness: ... / KALEIDOSCOPE**
Out of the Darkness: Songs for Survival. A fine collection of
songs written and sung in the cause of peace and
environmental sanity. Featuring Kate Wolf, Pete Seeger, Holly
Near, Don Lange, Chris Williamson, Jesse Colin Young, Charlie
King, Dick Gaughan, and Sweet Honey in the Rock. –CR
Resume Speed ... / END CONSTRUCTION   1990
Brian Doser, Jim Infantino, John Svetkey, and Ellis Paul
perform together and with other musicians on *Resume Speed -
A New Artist Compilation*, this fine CD of Boston-based
acoustic singer/songwriters. This is a good look at Boston's
folk/acoustic scene. –CR
Spirit of the West: ... / STONY PLAIN
Spirit of the West: Old Material 1984-1986. A compilation of
early music, featuring Dougie MacLean. Both live and studio
recordings. –CR
○ **Strength of Strings / FORESHORTENED ARM**   1990
Strength of Strings - An Acoustical Fringe Collection is a 12-cut
collection of acoustic songs from fringe artists — not folk, not
rock — alternative, maybe? It's hard to classify but worth
checking out if you are an alternative-music fan. –CR
○ **Threadgills Super Session / BUDDY**   1991
Every Wednesday they get together and put out some of the
best music in Austin. This cassette features Jimmie Dale
Gilmore, Sarah Elizabeth Campbell, Champ Hood, Butch
Hancock, Christine Albert, Marvin Denton, and the Threadgill
Troubadors. A good selection for the Austin diehard. –CR
○ **Tribute to Guthrie/Leadbelly: ... / CBS-FOLKWAYS** 1988
Tribute to Guthrie and Leadbelly: A Vision Shared. This album
was organized as a benefit to help the Smithsonian buy the
Folkways Records catalog. The performers, mostly rock-based
pop stars influenced by folk music, present their
interpretations of Guthrie and Leadbelly songs, with varying
results. The best, however, is very good, and that includes Bob
Dylan doing "Pretty Boy Floyd," Willie Nelson's "Philadelphia
Lawyer," and Taj Mahal's "The Bourgeois Blues." –WR
○ **Tribute to Woody Guthrie / WARNER**   1972
Woody Guthrie died on Oct 3, 1967. Tribute concerts to him
were organized at Carnegie Hall in New York in January 1968
and at the Hollywood Bowl in Los Angeles in September 1970.
This double-record set presents highlights from both shows
and is notable for a rare Bob Dylan performance and a
collection of Guthrie songs sung by others of his children
(literally and figuratively): Arlo Guthrie, Judy Collins, Odetta,
Richie Havens, Tom Paxton, Pete Seeger, and more. –WR
Vancouver Folk Music Festival ... /   1980
Vancouver Folk Musical Festival - July 1980. A real nice
collection — Ferron's "Ain't Life a Brook" is good. Jim Post
does a Bob Dylan soundalike ("Brain Damage"). Features
Berline, Crary & Hicks, Leon Rosselson, Holly Near, the
Tannahill Weavers, and Bryan Bowers. Good sound. –CR
○ **Victory Music: ... / VICTORY MUSIC**   1989
Victory Music: 20th Anniversary Year. This is a wide-open CD

featuring 21 cuts by Northwest musicians. The music ranges from singer/songwriter ballads, traditional instrumentals, blues, and back again. A strong and diverse CD done up the typical classy Victory Music way. –CR

Victory Sings at Sea / VICTORY MUSIC   1989

This album ranges from traditional working chanties to contemporary ballads. The tight harmonies intermesh with the simple acoustic accompaniment. This collection of 19 songs is a great value. –CR

When I Was a Cowboy / MORNINGSTAR

A compilation of original classic cowboy songs. –RM

When October Goes / PHILO

A compilation of outstanding singer/songwriters, assembled by Christine Lavin. –RM

○ **Wind in the Rigging: ... / NORTH STAR**   1988

A Wind in the Rigging: New England Voyage. A rich collection of sea chanties — 23 songs that transport the listener to the salty brine. This album grows on you — shiver me timbers! –CR

CONTEMPORARY INSTRUMENTAL
(INCLUDES NEW-AGE)

As the Beatles took the United States by storm, jazz artist Tony Scott took a deep breath and uttered the first notes of *Music for Zen Meditation*. Back then, no one really knew what to do with an exotic set of interactions between clarinet, Japanese koto, and shakuhachi flute. Released on Verve in 1964, *Music for Zen Meditation* remained an anomaly in the jazz label's bebop and swing catalog until this subtle cross-cultural venture was hailed as the first "new-age" album some 20 years later. If Scott had come up with the same American-Japanese collaboration in the 90s, he might just have easily found himself under the "world music" banner.

Scott's story is not unusual among contemporary instrumental artists. If these musicians have anything in common at all, it's their ability and intention to defy categorization. Of course, this sort of attitude tends to confound everyone else: from record labels, distributors, critics, and retailers to listeners trying to find the music in stores.

After a few frustrating decades trying to force innovative, instrumental releases into jazz and classical markets, some members of the record industry thought they had come across a handy new term. In the mid 80s, new-age music became the catchall designation for recordings that didn't seem to fit anywhere else. This phrase arose from the music's success in alternative outlets like health food stores, bookstores, and occult-oriented stores, as well as massage and meditation centers associated with the new-age movement. However, while a small number of artists openly supported new-age lifestyles and concepts through their music, most instrumentalists resented the association. As the 80s came to a close, cynical members of the media were having a field day allying the new-age music-marketing category with crystal gazers and trance channelers, in the process ignoring the merits of serious artists with highly original ideas. The whole thing left a bad taste in everyone's mouth, and much effort has been made in the early 90s to wipe out the stigma of this unfortunate development.

Back when the phrase "new-age" was being thrown around as a possibility, some people lobbied for the more general designation "contemporary instrumental." It wasn't short or catchy enough for most marketing executives, but increasing numbers of artists, record companies, critics, and radio producers have been using it. Contemporary instrumental (or CI for short, if you wish) is one of the few terms broad enough to encompass the myriad approaches and innovations taking place daily in this field. We've also come up with a list of subgenres to distinguish certain trends that have arisen in recent years; however, most artists regularly cross, combine, and recombine these tendencies as well. It's just the nature of CI musicians to create new fusions based on fusions of fusions.

— Linda Kohanov

PHILIP AABERG

Solo instrumental, adult alternative, chamber jazz. This Montana-born keyboardist and composer studied music at Harvard on a Leonard Bernstein scholarship before paying his dues on the San Francisco blues scene. Aaberg's wide range of abilities led to guest appearances on over 80 albums. He also toured with artists as varied as Peter Gabriel, John Hiatt, Kenny Rogers, and the Doobie Brothers. Upon signing with Windham Hill in 1985, Aaberg made his eclectic background pay off through a series of solo albums that show off his rigorous keyboard technique, diverse influences, and colorful compositional style. –LK

High Plains / WINDHAM HILL
Aaberg's Windham Hill debut. Solo piano pieces with folk and impressionistic elements that evoke the wide-open spaces of the American West. –LK

○ **Out of the Frame / WINDHAM HILL** 1979
Lush yet pensive instrumental pieces masterfully combining acoustic and electronic sounds. –LK

Cinema / WINDHAM HILL 1992
Aaberg pays tribute to several contemporary film composers with a collection of piano solos. Movements of scores from *Cinema Paradiso*, *Diva*, *My Brilliant Career*, and *Awakenings*, among other films, are elegantly performed and nicely sequenced. –LK

WILLIAM ACKERMAN b 1949

Adult alternative, solo instrumental, chamber jazz. William Ackerman has gained prominence both as a musician and a businessman, and at least one of those occupations seems to have been unintentional. Though Ackerman has played guitar since the age of 12, when he dropped out of college it was to become a carpenter, and his first company was called Windham Hill Builders. But Ackerman composed guitar music for Stanford University theater productions, and the encouragement of friends led him to record an album of his tunes, *The Search for the Turtle's Navel*, in 1976. The album was surprisingly successful, and Ackerman found himself in the music business.

Since then, Ackerman has continued to record his own albums, producing Windham Hill albums for such other artists as George Winston, Alex de Grassi, and Liz Story, and to serve in various capacities in the record company. (He stepped down as CEO in 1986; his function now primarily concerns A&R, the liaison between a record company and its artists.) Though Ackerman has long since sickened of the new-age tag, threatening physical violence against anyone categorizing Windham Hill's music with the term, he has had more to do with the rise of acoustic-based instrumental music as a popular form in the 70s and 80s than anyone else. –WR

☆ **Search for the Turtle's Navel / WINDHAM HILL**   1976
For many people, this is the album that invented new-age music. Ackerman's acoustic guitar improvisations, full of shifting moods and tempos, evocative and stirring, transformed him from a carpenter to a record company executive and charmed a surprisingly large audience. The music retains its power to move listeners today. –WR

Past Light / WINDHAM HILL   1983
For his fifth album, Ackerman added new instrumental colors to his guitar work. Especially notable are Michael Manring's bass playing and the one-track "Garden," featuring the Kronos Quartet. The added instrumentation serves only to accentuate Ackerman's typically inventive playing. –WR

ANCIENT FUTURE

Adult alternative, ethnic fusion. Ancient Future was formed in 1978 by guitarist Matthew Montfort, who was interested in combining ancient musical traditions with modern technology. The band's inviting melodies, exotic instruments, and ethnic textures helped popularize world-music fusion. –LK

Quiet Fire / MCA
A more subtle approach to the mix of new-age lyricism and world-music rhythms. –LK

○ **World without Walls / MCA**   1990
An upbeat, skillful fusion of ethnic beats and cosmopolitan melodies. –LK

DAROL ANGER

New-acoustic, chamber jazz. Fiddler extraordinaire Anger was one of the early proponents of new-acoustic music, a virtuosic blend of folk, bluegrass, and jazz. –LK

Live at Montreux '84 / WINDHAM HILL   1984
This recording is a precursor to a series of albums released by the band Montreux on Windham Hill. Barbara Higbie's gift for highly melodic piano improvisation mixes well with Darol Anger and Mike Marshall's new acoustic tirades and Andy Narell's Caribbean-flavored steel drums. –LK

○ **Chiaroscuro / WINDHAM HILL**   1985
This 1985 release is still one of the finest examples of new-acoustic music's appeal. Some fiery ensemble pieces are balanced by a few slower, moodier works and even some down-home versions of melodies by J. S. Bach. –LK

Tideline / WINDHAM HILL   1986
Anger plays various stringed instruments, accompanied by Barbara Higbie on piano. Mike Marshall joins in on a couple of tunes. –LK

The Duo / ROUNDER   1988
Anger and Mike Marshall were snatched up by Windham Hill soon after this early Rounder release, which offers a look at the duo's stylistic development. –LK

DAVID ARKENSTONE

Adult alternative. Southern California-based Arkenstone honed his chops as a guitarist and keyboardist in various local bands and touring groups before the music of Kitaro inspired him to create a lavish synthesizer-based sound of his own. Most of his albums have enjoyed lengthy runs on the *Billboard* new-age sales chart due to a combination of accessible melodies, pop sensibilities, and cinematic textures. –LK

○ **Valley in the Clouds / NARADA**   1987
Arkenstone's finest album of electronic soundscapes is also his least commercial effort. Nicely designed atmospheres and warm, flowing melodies characterize Arkenstone's first album for Narada. –LK

Citizen of Time / NARADA
A sonic odyssey telling the story of a traveler who visits earth's past and present civilizations. This album has some nice moments but generally the concept is more ambitious than the music. –LK

In the Wake of the Wind / NARADA   1991
One of the better examples of pop electronic music. –LK

ASHRA

Progressive electronic, adult alternative, minimalist. Formed in the late 60s by guitarist and synthesist Manuel Gottsching, this German group was highly influential in the field of contemporary electronic music. Ashra's album *New Age of Earth* (1977) is a classic in that it foreshadows the serene atmospherics used by subsequent "space music" composers. Gottsching continues to record to this day, though the results have been uneven. His rock-based albums are generally uninspiring, while his more recent work, which tends toward a form of trance-inducing electronic minimalism, is interesting though not particularly original. –LK

○ **New Age of Earth / CAROLINE**   1977
The last great Ashra disc — all spacey, floating guitars and synthesizers. –MPD

WILLIAM AURA

New-age, adult alternative. Before signing with Higher Octave Records in the late 80s, Aura composed music for the healing arts based on research into psycho-acoustic audio production. He mixed zithers and other acoustic instruments with synthesizers to create a warm, relaxing bath of sounds. Aura has picked up the tempo on his latest albums with pleasant results. –LK

Half Moon Bay / HIGHER OCTAVE   1987
Aura's first recording for Higher Octave was recorded at a seaside studio in Half Moon Bay, CA. It has lots of ocean ambience and silky synthesizer washes. –LK

○ **Timepiece / HIGHER OCTAVE**   1988
Timepiece (A Ten Year Perspective) is a good introduction to Aura's style and appeal. The album is a compilation of selected works from the first 10 years of his career. –LK

Paradise / HIGHER OCTAVE   1991
Some remixes of Aura's early music for healing, complete with 3-D nature sounds. –LK

Every Act of Love / HIGHER OCTAVE   1992
Though the album is billed as "global fusion for the contemporary mainstream," it really has more to do with pop and light jazz than anything ethnic. Aura's characteristic synthesizer timbres are enhanced by saxophone, piano, drums, and flute. –LK

PAUL AVGERINOS

Progressive electronic, ambient, ethnic fusion. Avgerinos is a classically trained composer who served as principal bassist with the Hong Kong Philharmonic and performed with numerous other orchestras. He has also toured with popular music and jazz acts and has done some scoring for films and television commercials. His true calling, however, seems to be as an electronic-music composer. The three albums he has released so far are all gems. –LK

Balancing Spheres / WORLD ROOM   1988
Softly unfolding sequencer patterns, whispered synthesizer harmonies, and evocative electronic effects that shimmer and melt characterize this two-part journey through "Day Dreams" and "Night Illusions." –LK

Maya the Great Katun / WORLD ROOM   1988
A powerful portrayal of an ancient Mayan ritual, this deliciously cryptic music consists of sacred words chanted over ceremonial percussion and atmospheric electronic sounds that draw forth shadows from other realms. –LK

○ **Muse of the Round Sky / HEARTS OF SPACE**   1992
Richly impressionistic soundscapes inspired by Avgerinos's ancestral homeland of Greece. Guest artists include guitarist Brian Keane and Omar Faruk Tekbilek, who plays Middle Eastern flutes. The composer's dense synthesizer textures and dreamy electronic effects make the album feel like one long, luscious mirage. –LK

JAY AZZOLINA

Adult alternative. Azzolina is a guitarist with the jazz-fusion group Spyro Gyra. –PK

○ **Never Too Late / POLYGRAM** 1988
This tasty jazz-fusion debut album from the current Spyro Gyra guitarist was influenced by Mike Stern. –PK

WALLY BADAROU b 1955

Adult alternative. Badarou was born in Paris, where his physician parents were educated and his father later served as ambassador from their West African homeland of Cotonon Benin (formerly Dahomey). Although he planned a career as a pilot, he was seduced by synthesizers and rock & roll, eventually becoming a well-known session keyboardist in England and his own Nassau, Bahamas, studio. Badarou's early career included work with M (on the hit "Pop Music"), Joe Cocker, Herbie Hancock, and Island Records artists like Grace Jones, Black Uhuru, and the British funk band Level 42. In addition to his production and keyboard work for Level 42, he has done several film scores, most notably *Kiss of the Spider Woman.* You can hear both the rhythmic sensitivity of his African heritage and the harmonic sensibility of his classical training in his music. His expressive and sophisticated synthesizer textures are full of life, especially on his more dance-oriented *Echoes* album. –SWB

○ **Echoes / ISLAND** 1984
You can actually feel Caribbean sunshine with this music. Badarou breathes real life into his synthesizers on this album of happy, upbeat, and danceable music. –SWB

Words of a Mountain / ISLAND 1989
This album has a more contemplative mood than his last, and a distinctly classical feel, although the atmospheres are no less vivid. –SWB

PATRICK BALL

Solo instrumental. With a vast knowledge of folklore and music from the British Isles, Celtic harp player Patrick Ball calls forth the music of a simpler, more magical time. His scintillating performances on the traditional wire-strung harp are by far the best-selling titles on the Fortuna label. –LK

Celtic Harp 1 - Music of O'Carolan / FORTUNA 1983
Celtic Harp 1 - Music of Turlough O'Carolan. All of Ball's recordings that feature traditional tunes from the British Isles are great. –LK

Celtic Harp 2 - From a Distant Time / FORTUNA 1983
Celtic Harp 3 - Secret Isles / FORTUNA 1990
○ **Celtic Harp 4 - O'Carolan's Dream / FORTUNA** 1991
A gentle, yet masterful collection of music by the renowned late 17th-century Irish harper Turlough O'Carolan. –LK

TOM BARABAS

Adult alternative. Before developing a taste for rock and jazz, Barabas studied classical music at the Caracas Conservatory in Venezuela. His skills as a pianist are admirable; Barabas's use of synthesizers is not quite so sophisticated but shows some promise. –LK

○ **Sedona Suite / SOUNDINGS OF THE PLANET**
This new-age pop jaunt through Southwestern scenes has some nice moments. –LK

PETE BARDENS

Adult alternative. Best known for his work with the 70s progressive rock band Camel, Bardens has played with a number of rock legends over the years. His solo instrumental music is catchy and well produced, yet rarely ventures beyond the tenets of pop music and tends to suffer as a result. –LK

Seen One Earth / CAPITOL 1987
A concept album based on the space exploration and astronaut book *The Right Stuff.* –LK

○ **Water Colors / MIRAMAR** 1991
This soundtrack to a video by the same title is a mixed bag. Some simplistic and superficial selections are balanced by some well-produced, thoughtful keyboard work. –LK

BAREFOOT

Ethnic fusion, adult alternative. Percussionist Henry Clay and violinist Steve Kindler came up with the concept of Barefoot, an ensemble inspired by the dance traditions of many different cultures. The band tends to compose collectively, often featuring ethnic dancers on stage to add to the excitement of the music. –LK

○ **Barefoot / GLOBAL PACIFIC** 1990
Earthy world/fusion/dance music featuring a multicultural ensemble led by violinist Steve Kindler. Kindler is best known for his work with Kitaro and the Mahavishnu Orchestra. –LK

BRUCE BECVAR

Adult alternative. This California guitarist and synthesist writes highly melodic, commercially accessible ensemble music. Though he plays most of the instruments himself, his technique on acoustic guitar is most admirable. He's also a well-known luthier — one of his hand-crafted guitars is on display at the New York Metropolitan Museum of Art. –LK

○ **Forever Blue Sky / SHINING STAR** 1989
A good example of Becvar's style. –LK

PIERRE BENSUSAN

Solo instrumental, ethnic fusion, chamber jazz. This French guitarist was actually born in Algeria and has long been fascinated with his North African roots as well as the Celtic folk traditions of western Europe. After making a name for himself as a folk musician in the late 70s, Bensusan began to incorporate jazz and classical elements into his music, creating a virtuosic, highly original style on the acoustic guitar. –LK

○ **Solilai / ROUNDER** 1982
This incredible album mixes jazz riffs and gentle impressionistic improvisations, with some expressive vocals on a few of the cuts. –LK

Pres de Paris / ROUNDER
An acoustic guitar tour de force. –LK

DANIEL BLANCHET

Neo-classical, progressive electronic, ambient. A classically trained guitarist, Montreal-based Blanchet is part of a growing electronic music contingent in Canada. He began experimenting with synthesizers in 1985, intrigued by their endless possibilities of sound color and spatial enhancement. Blanchet's early fascination with Bach's oratorios is reflected in his use of electronic reverb to create cathedral-like dimensions for his thoughtful compositions. –LK

Le Chemin de l'Ermite / RUBICON 1987
Blanchet's first album features lyrical pieces that suggest imaginary environments with an innocence reminiscent of Kitaro. –LK

○ **L'Harmonie des Mondes / RUBICON** 1991
An homage to the famous *Harmony of the Spheres* treatise by the 16th-century astronomer Johannes Kepler, this collection explores a variety of musical moods and settings with the same poetic theme of order and beauty that Kepler believed ruled the universe. –LK

BOTANICA

Progressive electronic. Led by synthesist Sanford Ponder, this group creates music generated by fractal mathematics. The computer programs are connected to numerous synthesizers. The musicians then interact with the resulting soundtracks by overdubbing percussion, sax, flute, and piano. For something created by the seemingly impartial mathematics of "chaos"

Contemporary Instrumental Music Types

SOLO INSTRUMENTAL — Solo instrumental recordings launched successful labels like Windham Hill and Narada, ushering in a whole movement oriented toward impressionistic, often folk-inspired originals for piano, guitar, celtic harp, even hammered dulcimer. Though some of these releases offer innovative, emotionally moving performances, enough second-rate opportunists have jumped on the bandwagon to give the genre its "aural wallpaper" reputation. Still, some fine musicians continue to battle this stigma.

ADULT ALTERNATIVE — This genre attracts a wide cross-section of listeners who are looking for something a little different without straying too far from the mainstream. It's actually hard to say whether new adult contemporary radio formats were created to play this music or whether the music was created for radio airplay. Adult alternative styles — whether acoustic, electronic, or electro-acoustic — are heavily influenced by pop, rock, and jazz fusion elements. (Some albums feature a few vocal selections with lyrics, although the main orientation remains instrumental.) The best artists have a flair for melodic invention, colorful instrumentation, and rhythmic vitality while retaining a strong level of accessibility. At worst, adult alternative releases sound like trite pop songs without words.

PROGRESSIVE ELECTRONIC & ELECTRO-ACOUSTIC — This music thrives in more unfamiliar territory. The styles that emerge are often dictated by the technology itself. Rather than sampling or synthesizing acoustic sounds to electronically replicate them, these composers tend to mutate the original timbres, sometimes to an unrecognizable state. True artists in the genre also create their own sounds (as opposed to using the preset sounds that come with modern synthesizers).

In progressive electro-acoustic music, the electronics play an equal if not greater part in the overall concept. Acoustic instruments performed in real time are usually processed through reverb, harmonizing, etc., which adds an entirely new dimension to the player's technique.

At best, this music opens up new worlds of listening, thinking, and feeling. At worst, progressive electronic artists worship technology for its own sake, relinquishing the heart and soul of true artistic expression.

NEW AGE — Born from an aesthetic that aims to induce a sense of inner calm, new-age music emerged from the meditational and holistic fields. Generally these are harmonious and nonthreatening albums that are allied with new-age philosophies encouraging spiritual transcendence and physical healing. Some of these albums are artistically satisfying as well as therapeutic. Lesser musicians, however, often make ridiculous claims in the liner notes as to their ability to catapult listeners into advanced spiritual states through specially designed sonic vibrations and "immaculately conceived" musical ideas.

AMBIENT — A term popularized by Brian Eno but used here in a broader sense. Ambient composers use echo, electronic reverb, and other spatial techniques as important musical elements in creating atmospheric pieces and sonic environments.

The best artists have developed the ability to manipulate the listener's sense of space and time in highly sophisticated ways. Many ambient recordings involve extended compositions that change subtly in content and timbre over a long period of time. Though some musicians use ambient techniques for their meditative benefits (and can thus be allied with the new-age movement), other ambient composers create ethereal, alien environments that are more mysterious and confrontational than comforting.

NEO-CLASSICAL — Many contemporary instrumentalists are conservatory trained, yet don't subscribe to the modern classical world's emphasis on intellectual, atonal forms of composition. As these artists follow their own vision, however, classical music may continue to be an important inspiration. In the context of CI music, the neoclassical distinction refers to any style influenced by classical music, whether the performer is offering updated arrangements of actual works by an established composer (Bach, Pachelbel, and Debussy seem to be popular in this respect) or weaving elements from the baroque, classical, romantic, impressionistic, and/or more challenging 20th-century styles into a more original approach.

NEW-ACOUSTIC — An exhilarating mix of bluegrass and jazz. Folk instruments like the mandolin, fiddle, banjo, and acoustic guitar play lead roles on new-acoustic albums. Virtuosity is the name of the game as the musicians stretch the boundaries of their traditional roles with heated improvisations and complex jazz harmonies.

ETHNIC FUSION — One of the major trends among all contemporary instrumental subgenres is the fusion of ethnic instruments, modes, and rhythms with Western styles. The possibilities are as wide-ranging as the world's vast musical cultures.

TECHNO-TRIBAL — A more specific variation on the ethnic fusion theme, techno-tribal music is becoming more prominent among progressive electro-acoustic artists who are fascinated by the idea of combining man's most primeval musical expressions with his most technologically advanced inventions. Tribal rhythms and instruments from the aboriginal cultures of Africa, Australia, and North and South America are mixed with sophisticated electronics. Though successful efforts are immensely powerful, it takes great skill and sensitivity to keep the music from sounding like cheap parodies of the cultures from which these artists are borrowing.

CHAMBER JAZZ — This style is distinguished by small, acoustic-based ensembles in which improvisation is a major factor. Though some groups are more jazz-based than others, they all tend to employ neo-classical aesthetics, particularly from the Impressionistic period and later 20th-century movements. Ethnic elements are also an important factor. These world-music leanings, however, are usually oriented toward the classical traditions of other cultures (Indian, Middle Eastern, and Oriental), although South American styles also figure prominently in a lot of these recordings.

MINIMALISM — One of the main innovations in the contemporary classical field, minimalism has also influenced many CI composers, particularly in progressive electronic styles where sequencers play an important role. Generally this music is characterized by a strong and relentless pulse, the insistent repetition of short melodic fragments, and harmonies that change over long periods of time.

— Linda Kohanov

theories, this music is surprisingly beautiful and emotionally stimulating. –LK

○ **A Garden of Earthly Delights / DEEP MUSIC**   1989
Though both Botanica releases are well worth owning, the band's first fractal effort is more serene and melodious, thus more accessible. –LK

Strange Attractor / DEEP MUSIC   1991
The album's title is probably the best description of this music. Sometimes mysterious and floating, other times aggressively beat-oriented, *Strange Attractor* sounds like something you might encounter in outer space. –LK

KEVIN BRAHENY

Progressive electronic, ambient. This Los Angeles-based synthesist builds much of his own equipment, including the 3-D binaural recording technology he uses on his *Secret Rooms* album. His sounds and special effects are sophisticated and highly evocative, but Braheny's music is not all technique. His graceful improvisations on electronic wind instruments bring a lyrical dimension to his music. –LK

○ **The Way Home / HEARTS OF SPACE**   1978
This lush, romantic space music has an overall feeling of longing. –LK

Galaxies / HEARTS OF SPACE   1988
Braheny's score for a planetarium soundtrack is filled with slowly evolving, synthesized atmospheres that are appropriately spacey. –LK

Secret Rooms / HEARTS OF SPACE   1991
A varied album, with a few uneven tracks. Overall, the album showcases Braheny's meticulous production standards and virtuosity on the electronic wind instrument. –LK

SPENCER BREWER

Adult alternative. This Northern California-based pianist has released a half-dozen records on the Narada label. His pleasant, pop-flavored style and strong melodic sense make for nice easy-listening music that often suffers under the scrutiny of concentrated listening. His collaborations with other artists on the Narada label are stronger. –LK

Emerald / NARADA   1985
A collaboration with guitarist Eric Tingstad and wind player Nancy Rumble that puts Brewer in a more substantial musical setting than his own albums. –LK

○ **Dorian's Legacy / NARADA**
An optimistic jaunt through contemporary instrumental textures. –LK

Piper's Rhythm / NARADA
More of Brewer's light, yet technically proficient style. –LK

MICHAEL BROOK

Techno-tribal. This innovative guitarist and producer received early recognition as an engineer and performer on projects with Brian Eno, Daniel Lanois, and Jon Hassell. Brook went on to produce albums on Peter Gabriel's Real World label by African artist Youssou N'Dour and Pakistani singer Nusrat Fateh Ali Khan. Brook also did some fine guitar work on the latter release. His style as a composer is characterized by a unique "infinite guitar" sound (created through heavy signal processing), mixed with Eno-style ambience and Hassell-influenced "fourth world" rhythms. –LK

○ **Hybrid / CAROLINE**   1985
An album by which all world-music fusions should be judged. This has incredible musicianship, production, compositional ideas, and voodoo percussion. –LK

HAROLD BUDD

Ambient, neo-classical. Budd is America's sovereign slow-motion composer. You could practically drive a truck through the spaces between each note on many of his compositions — that is, if you weren't so tempted to ease on the brakes and linger in the expansiveness of the sound.

A principal figure in the California avant-garde of the 60s, Budd developed a talent for composing lyrical, liquid music that unfolded at rarefied speeds. His solo albums and collaborations with Brian Eno have since become classics for their depth of expression and masterful execution. With every tone reverberating into a translucent silence, Budd always manages to sustain a keen sense of emotional intensity and anticipation. The effect is that of romantic yearnings and perilous undercurrents turned loose among wide open spaces. –LK

Ambient 2 - Plateaux of Mirror / CAROLINE   1980
A collaboration with Brian Eno on this installment of the *Ambient* series. Meditative solo piano with Eno touch. –SWB

The Serpent/Abandoned Cities / OPAL   1981
The Serpent (In Quicksilver)/Abandoned Cities is mostly piano, some electric and pedal steel guitar. –MGN

☆ **The Pearl / CAROLINE**   1984
A collaboration with Brian Eno. One of the finest ambient albums of all time and a beautiful, highly emotional work of art. –LK

Lovely Thunder / CAROLINE   1986
White Arcades / WARNER   1988
Beautiful texture music. –MGN

By the Dawn's Early Light / WARNER   1991
Contemporary chamber music in slow motion, filled with a delicious sense of yearning. –LK

PETER BUFFETT

Adult alternative, ethnic fusion. Buffett's full-bodied electronic sound and rock-influenced accessibility make his music a congenial transition between the lighter pop instrumentals that have flooded the market and artists who are pushing the boundaries of modern electronic music with more challenging fare. The Nebraska-born pianist went to Stanford University, where he converted his Bay Area apartment into an efficient recording studio that provides soundtracks for numerous advertising, television, and film companies. Upon hearing of Kevin Costner's plans to create the movie *Dances with Wolves*, Buffett sent the actor a copy of his album *One by One*, which featured several cuts inspired by the plight of Native Americans. Costner was impressed enough to use some of Buffett's music in the film. Buffett's four Narada recordings combine a flair for drama and cinematic-style electronic orchestrations with his interest in Native American cultures. His later albums feature a progressively more prominent use of acoustic timbres, both sampled and authentic. –LK

The Waiting / NARADA   1987
Buffett's first album is characterized by grand sweeps of sound and dramatic themes that are a bit on the trite side at times. –LK

One by One / NARADA   1989
The composer's interest in orchestral grandeur is further refined as he routes various acoustic sources — cellos and guitars to owls and basketball sounds — through his samplers and keyboards to create thick timbral tapestries. His Native American interests emerge on several cuts. –LK

○ **Lost Frontier / NARADA**   1991
A collection of sonic essays inspired by the American West and its original inhabitants. Buffett's keyboards are enhanced by an ensemble of strings, woodwinds, and guitar. –LK

Yonnondio / NARADA   1992
Buffett's most recent effort is breezy and lighthearted while maintaining a certain level of instrumental intricacy and imaginative sound construction. –LK

RICHARD BURMER

Progressive electronic, adult alternative, ambient. Burmer is a gifted melodist and a meticulous electronic craftsman. His style grew out of a love for East Indian and European folk music, as well as an interest in the progressive rock of the 70s à la Moody Blues and Pink Floyd. Adept in sophisticated studio techniques, Burmer honed his craft in the Southern California electronic scene of the mid 80s before returning to his Michigan homeland at the end of the decade. –LK

Mosaic / AMERICAN GRAMAPHONE   1984
An early collection of electronic vignettes that showcase an already original style. –LK

○ **Bhakti Point / FORTUNA**   1987
A well-balanced collection of Burmer's style. Imaginative, often luxurious electronic textures and themes. –LK

On the Third Extreme / AM. GRAMAPHONE   1990
Burmer in a more commercial setting. Well constructed and interesting, yet lacking the soul of his earlier works. –LK

DOUG CAMERON

Adult alternative, ethnic fusion. The Ohio-born, classically trained violinist developed an interest in jazz early on. He later toured with Gregg Allman, moved to Southern California, and became a popular session man. His albums as a leader subsist on urban beats and spicy Latin rhythms that provide exhilarating settings for his violin improvisations, yet the compositions themselves often lack the substance to support repeated listenings. –LK

○ **Journey to You / MCA**
A few insubstantial compositions grow tiresome after a while, but Cameron's jazz-tinged improvisations show that he has talent. –LK

JIM CHAPPELL

Solo instrumental, adult alternative, chamber jazz. While trying to make it as a country/pop star in Nashville, Chappell accidentally hit upon a formula for success. At night, he'd noodle around on the piano to help himself unwind from the frustrations of the music business. A friend suggested he should release some of these piano vignettes instead of struggling in the pop world. Chappell followed the advice, and his first two albums (*Tender Ritual* and *Dusk*) were enthusiastically received by fans of solo piano music. On later albums, he composed and arranged works for various ensemble settings, gaining considerable exposure on the New Adult Contemporary charts. Chappell's strength lies in his ability to create memorable themes with lyrical, impressionistic accompaniments. Though his large-ensemble music leans toward a contemporary easy-listening style, its moodiness saves it from banality. He remains most expressive in the solo piano and small-ensemble realms. –LK

Tender Ritual / MUSIC WEST   1979
Impressionistic solo piano music from a sensitive composer and performer. –LK

Dusk / MUSIC WEST   1987
More piano vignettes. –LK

Living the Northern Summer / MUSIC WEST   1989
Chappell's first ensemble efforts show his promise as an arranger. –LK

Saturday's Rhapsody / MUSIC WEST   1990
The full-string orchestrations really don't help the music other than to bring Chappell's style firmly into the easy-listening realm. –LK

○ **Nightsongs and Lullabies / MUSIC WEST**   1991
Although his solo piano efforts are arguably his best, this album (which offers a cross-section of solo piano pieces and works for small ensemble) is a good all-around introduction to Chappell's style. –LK

CHI

Adult alternative, ethnic fusion. Taking its name from the Chinese word for energy, this instrumental duo composes the kinds of animated, well-performed, yet sometimes frivolous tunes that new adult-contemporary radio tends to eat up. With its heavy pop/jazz orientation, this is fun music for

listeners interested in taking an upbeat aural vacation from the pressures of everyday life. –LK

○ **Jet Stream / SONIC ATMOSPHERES**   1990
Chi core members Tom Chase on guitars and Steve Rucker on keyboards are joined by consummate percussionist Luis Conte and several other guest artists, including the West African Goun ensemble. A colorful, multicultural romp. –LK

Pacific Rim / SONIC ATMOSPHERES   1990
Chi's debut. –LK

Sun Lake / SONIC ATMOSPHERES   1991
A little more upbeat and acoustically oriented than the *Jet Stream* album. –LK

COLIN CHIN

Adult alternative. This San Francisco native got his start hanging out and eventually touring with the members of Group 87, a late-70s instrumental ensemble that featured Mark Isham and Patrick O'Hearn. With Isham, Chin attended a seminar conducted by Brian Eno on applying advanced technology to music. The event was a revelation for the young guitarist, who was motivated to expand his horizons into the field of electronic music. –LK

○ **Intruding on a Silence / MCA**   1988
Chin's debut as a leader, though not particularly adventurous, features some well-designed electronic atmospheres with rock influences. Isham and O'Hearn add some characteristic solos as guest artists, giving the entire album a Group 87 reunion feel without the band's original edge. Overall, however, it's a promising beginning for Chin. –LK

SUZANNE CIANI

Adult alternative. One of the first and finest woman artists to make a name for herself in the electronic music world, Ciani earned a Masters degree in composition from the University of California at Berkeley, where she studied with electronic pioneers Max Matthews, John Chowning, and Don Buchla. In 1975 she moved to New York, where she got involved in the Soho art scene, and also worked with minimalist Philip Glass. She began to hit the big time with the establishment of Ciani Musica, Inc., one of the foremost commercial production companies in the country. Ciani later expanded into film scoring and gained recognition for her work on Lily Tomlin's *The Incredible Shrinking Woman* as well as the award-winning feature documentary *Mother Teresa*. Ciani's career as a recording artist, however, took a more indirect route. Her 1982 Japanese release *Seven Waves* became an underground hit, prompting its American release in 1984. Then *Velocity of Love* came along, which, with its intriguing synthesizer work balanced by strong melodies and pop sensibilities, helped define various contemporary instrumental radio formats, including the Wave. –LK

○ **Neverland / PRIVATE MUSIC**   1988
Ciani is a master at constructing complex compositions using electronic keyboard instruments that nevertheless retain the ability to speak to listeners emotionally. On her most accomplished work, Ciani explores a broad musical range, from majestic landscapes to humorous percussive patterns, always retaining a strong sense of melody and overall structure. –WR

Pianissimo / PRIVATE MUSIC   1990
After 20 years of perfecting her abilities with electronic music, Ciani turned back to the acoustic piano for this live recording of material largely taken from *Neverland* and its excellent followup, *History of My Heart*. Demonstrates that Ciani is not dependent on electricity to produce vital music. –WR

TIM CLARK

Progressive electronic, ambient, ethnic fusion. You'd expect high-quality electronics from a musician who has clocked in a good 20,000 hours composing soundtracks for Toronto's McLaughlin Planetarium and writing scores for numerous other planetarium programs, award-winning radio dramas, films, and theater productions. Clark's graduate studies in composition also seem to come in handy. Though he only has one solo album out so far, *Tales of the Sun People* is impressive because he refuses to settle for the exciting sounds and few engaging melodies many electronic players work hard to attain. Clark's engaging music is filled with unexpected turns and inventive new twists on old ideas. –LK

○ **Tales of the Sun People / HEARTS OF SPACE**   1990
A clever, richly evocative album of electronic music. It deserved more attention when it was first released. –LK

TIM CLEMENT

Progressive electronic, ethnic fusion, ambient. Best known for the electronic environments he created as half of the Canadian duo Danna & Clement, this Toronto-based composer has also written music for theater, dance, and film. His early work with Danna explored ways of translating the serenity of Canada's Ontario wilderness into music through ambient compositions that combine synthesizers with recordings of natural sounds. Clement's first major album as a leader, however, is more tuneful and rhythmic as it successfully incorporates ethnic influences into an engaging electro-acoustic context. –LK

○ **Waterstation / CHACRA ALTERNATIVE MUSIC**   1990
One of the most creative and eclectic contemporary instrumental albums of 1990. *Waterstation* features everything from an atmospheric take on country music with liquid pedal-steel guitar musings by Kim Deschamps (of Cowboy Junkies fame) to extended pieces fueled by relentless yet almost translucent ethnic rhythms. Other compositions involve highland bagpipes, Egyptian reed flute, and zither. One selection even features a bizarre union of electronics, glassy trance rhythms, and spoken word tracks. –LK

JESSIE ALLEN COOPER

Adult alternative. This self-taught saxophonist has long had an interest in mixing environmental sounds with his contemporary-jazz-influenced compositions to create relaxing, highly melodic musical vignettes that convey an appreciation for nature. –LK

○ **Soft Wave / MCA**
Cooper's first (and so far only) major release uses the sounds of ocean waves and dolphin cries to accompany his tranquil soprano sax solos. Synthesists Mark Cohen and Rusty Hamilton are also featured. –LK

SCOTT COSSU

Adult alternative, neo-classical, chamber jazz. Scott Cossu's ensemble works have the heart, soul, and skill that come from an artist motivated by personal vision rather than industry trends. His 1980 debut album *Still Moments* featured harp, cello, and vibes as foils for his own pianistic improvisations, at a time when solo instrumentals were the rage. His style has evolved and become more sophisticated over the years. Yet because each stage in his development was carried out with the utmost sincerity and expressive intent, each album he has recorded continues to have a life of its own. –LK

Islands / WINDHAM HILL   1984
Cossu began to expand his musical vocabulary with larger arrangements featuring horns, bass, and drums. The more impressionistic leanings of his previous releases are also expanded upon through the album's fusion of blues, jazz, Latin, and classical elements. *Islands* features some major contemporary jazz names like flutist Dave Valentin, bassist Mark Egan, drummer Danny Gottlieb, and violinist Michal Urbaniak. –LK

Wind Dance / WINDHAM HILL   1984
The pianist's first original release for Windham Hill features duets with Alex de Grassi and Dan Reiter. –LK

○ **She Describes Infinity / WINDHAM HILL**   1989

An artistically satisfying summation of Cossu's previous styles, this album includes lyrical duet and trio performances as well as arrangements for an expanded rhythm section. It's a thoughtful and mature collection of pieces. –LK

Switchback / WINDHAM HILL   1989
Cossu's forays into rock and blues were coproduced with jazz flutist Dave Valentin. –LK

COYOTE OLDMAN

Ambient, ethnic fusion. This duo creates highly reverberant soundscapes featuring Native American flutes. Michael Graham Allen began visiting museums to research ancient musical instruments over 20 years ago. He went on to construct and play many kinds of flutes and panpipes, later naming his own flute-building company Coyote Oldman. In 1986 Allen was selling his handcrafted instruments at an Oklahoma arts fair when he met Barry Stramp, an accomplished studio engineer who played flute, keyboards, and guitar. Using synthesizers and other digital processors to manipulate the "physics of echoes," Stramp helped define the Coyote Oldman sound by electronically enhancing and multi-tracking Allen's haunting flute melodies. –LK

Tear of the Moon / COYOTE OLDMAN MUSIC   1987
Though there is an earlier Coyote Oldman release available on cassette only, *Tear of the Moon* is really the first in which Stramp's special engineering techniques are as important to the music as the flutes themselves. A sophisticated use of reverb augments the effects of primal flute sounds to create an otherworldly, almost aquatic atmosphere. –LK

Landscape / COYOTE OLDMAN MUSIC   1988
Native American flutes with Incan, Peruvian, and bass panpipes as well as Aztec log drum, bells, and Chapman stick are used in original compositions with plaintive melodies that echo through meditative atmospheres. –LK

○ **Thunder Chord / HEARTS OF SPACE**   1990
Allen and Stramp's most masterful execution of the sound that had begun to mature on previous albums. It took 18 months of patient work to record these timeless flute melodies elegantly enveloped in a lush, 3-D digital ambience. –LK

RUSTY CRUTCHER

Ambient, progressive electronic. A former Los Angeles saxophone studio musician, Crutcher performed with pop stars like Lionel Ritchie and the Commodores before moving to Santa Fe, NM, and developing his own introspective style of music. Crutcher's main body of work falls under his *Sacred Sites* series, a set of concept albums that convey his musical impressions of historic locations. As part of the compositional process, Crutcher visits these ancient areas to record environmental sounds that he weaves into his synthesized soundscapes. Crutcher is producing a new *Sacred Sites* project dealing with the Serpent Mound built by Ohio's prehistoric Hopewell Indian culture. –LK

Machu Picchu Impressions / EMERALD GREEN   1988
One of Crutcher's earliest *Sacred Sites* projects, this album features synthesized atmospheres and subtle melodies with sounds recorded at Machu Picchu. –LK

○ **Chaco Canyon / EMERALD GREEN**   1990
Crutcher went to New Mexico's Chaco Canyon to record environmental sounds primarily during solstices and equinoxes. This prehistoric archeological site is thought to have been the trading and spiritual center for the Anasazi, one of the earliest-known Native American cultures in the Southwest. Crutcher's music, often performed on wind synthesizer, is reminiscent of Native American styles. –LK

CUSCO

Adult alternative, ethnic fusion. Two German keyboardists lead this band: Michael Holm had a long string of Top Ten vocal records in Germany during the 60s and 70s; Kristian Schultze, is one of Europe's busiest studio musicians. They share an interest in South America's prehistoric musical heritage, yet their albums are far from traditional. Cusco combines catchy melodies and steady rock/funk beats with just enough ethnic percussion and electronically generated panpipe sounds to give a South American flavor. –LK

○ **Apurimac / HIGHER OCTAVE**   1988
Cusco's first US release is the band's celebration of the Amazon River, with plenty of Peruvian rhythms and panpipe sounds to set the mood. Their subsequent albums are variations on this theme. –LK

Mystic Island / HIGHER OCTAVE   1989
Water Stories / HIGHER OCTAVE   1990

DANNA & CLEMENT

Ambient. Though both artists have released satisfying solo albums (see the separate listings), these Canadian electronic musicians first became widely known as a team. Their music together is an organic synthesis of sounds from nature and softly unfolding electronic ambiences. –LK

A Gradual Awakening / FORTUNA   1982
The duo's first release is a haunting collection of tone poems inspired by Canada's untamed landscapes. Synthesizers, guitars, harps, and flutes are enhanced by natural sounds like rushing water and the cries of timber wolves. –LK

○ **Summerland / FORTUNA**   1984
This gentle collection of pieces evoking the essence of the summer season combines lush electronics with sounds of surf, gulls, songbirds, and cathedral bells. –LK

MYCHAEL DANNA

Ambient, progressive alternative, neo-classical. Danna is one of Canada's busiest composers. With a degree in composition from the University of Toronto, he has won numerous prizes for his music, including the prestigious Glenn Gould Award. In addition to his classically oriented work, Danna has long had an interest in electronic music. Since the 80s, he has released several albums of synthesized soundscapes in collaboration with Tim Clement (see Danna & Clement). He also serves as composer-in-residence at Toronto's McLaughlin Planetarium, where his electronic music skills are widely appreciated. –LK

○ **Sirens / HEARTS OF SPACE**   1991
Danna's first widely available album as a leader is sensual and spacey, with episodes of melting pedal-steel guitar solos and sighing female vocals that symbolize his fascination with the mysteriously compelling qualities of feminine archetypes. –LK

ALEX DE GRASSI

Solo instrumental, ethnic fusion, chamber jazz, adult alternative. Music has long been a family affair for de Grassi. Though he's primarily self-taught as a guitarist, his grandfather played violin with the San Francisco Symphony and his father was a classical pianist. Even more significant are de Grassi's ties to one of contemporary instrumental music's most influential labels: Windham Hill. In addition to his status as one of the company's finest and most consistently intriguing artists, de Grassi is literally a member of the Windham Hill clan. After earning a degree in urban geography from U. C. Berkeley and performing as a street musician in London, he made ends meet by learning the carpentry trade from his cousin Will Ackerman, who was just starting a small instrumental record label. De Grassi was encouraged to record his first album, *Turning: Turning Back*, for the fledgling Windham Hill company. As it turns out, he had more going for him than good connections. Over the years, de Grassi has proven to be an innovative guitarist and composer whose mastery of acoustic finger-picking styles has grown to include a variety of other techniques and ethnic influences. Though he left briefly to record with RCA Novus, de Grassi has since returned to the Windham Hill fold. In the mid 80s, his travels to Bolivia became a major inspiration. He made numerous field recordings during his visits and first incorporated indigenous

influences from the culture on his 1987 RCA Novus release *Altiplano*. His contacts with Bolivia's Contemporary Orchestra of Native Instruments also set in motion the ensemble's first American release *Arawl* on the New Albion label. –LK

○ **Turning: Turning Back / WINDHAM HILL**   1978
An excellent technician, de Grassi is able to vary his effects on the acoustic guitar from textured chording to involved picking, evoking folk and madrigal styles and alternating his approaches at will. He somehow seems to have absorbed all the important guitar styles of the previous 20 years and can mix and recreate them at will. –WR

Altiplano / RCA   1987
He branched out from his solo guitar albums on Windham Hill to this ambitious effort, which finds him in a variety of band settings that underscore his acoustic flights, bringing out previously unheard aspects of his music. –WR

CONSTANCE DEMBY

Progressive electronic, neo-classical, new-age. Demby is one of the few representatives of the new-age movement (in both her music and her personal philosophies) who consistently creates artistic, highly expressive compositions. She was a member of an East Coast experimental group in the early 70s and began releasing her own music on cassette in 1978, shortly after moving to California. Her early recordings consist primarily of extended pieces for hammer dulcimer, atmospheric compositions featuring instruments of her own design, and (increasingly) original works based on her love of sacred classical music from the Baroque period. She really came into her own, however, when digital sampling synthesizers arrived on the scene. Recording in her own 16-track studio, Demby integrated electronically sampled sounds of orchestral instruments into her ambitious, two-part masterpiece *Novus Magnificat*, released in 1986. It has since been acknowledged as a classic in the realms of new-age and progressive electronic music. Though subsequent recordings have not matched the scope and emotional power of this work, Demby continues to evolve as an artist in some promising new directions. –LK

☆ **Novus Magnificat / HEARTS OF SPACE**   1986
Novus Magnificat (Through the Stargate) is an electronic masterpiece. Demby's extended, classically influenced composition is also a deeply moving work. –LK

Sacred Space Music / HEARTS OF SPACE   1988
An early precursor to *Novus*, this classically influenced, yet meditative album was re-released on CD in 1988. –LK

Set Free / HEARTS OF SPACE   1989
Demby's first release since her landmark recording *Novus Magnificat* features some selections reminiscent of that work, as well as shorter pieces heading in new directions, including some selections influenced by Balinese music and some other tunes more on the pop side. –LK

DEUTER

Ethnic fusion, ambient, new-age. Like many artists in the contemporary instrumental realm, Deuter mixes acoustic and electronic instruments, ethnic influences, and sounds from nature — only he's been doing it since the early 70s. Born in the German village of Falkenhagen, Deuter learned flute and taught himself to play guitar but was discouraged from pursuing music as a career. The trauma of a nearly fatal auto accident in 1970, however, motivated him to pursue his dreams. His first recording, *D*, was released on Kuckuck in 1971. (He still records for this label.) Over the years, Deuter's spiritual search has taken him around the world, most notably to India, where he lived in an ashram, studied Indian music, and recorded several albums. In the mid 80s he moved to the US, eventually settling in Santa Fe, NM. Deuter's style is characterized by gentle melodies and joyful rhythms that render his music accessible even as he presents an intriguing blend of Eastern and Western styles. –LK

Land of Enchantment / KUCKUCK   1978
Call of the Unknown 1972-1986 / KUCKUCK   1986
This compilation features selections from eight releases as well as two works recorded especially for the project. –LK

Celebration / CELESTIAL HARMONIES   1989
○ **Sands of Time / KUCKUCK**   1991
Deuter has so much material available that it's best to start with one of several compilations of his work. Although *Call of the Unknown* is also a fine introduction to his music, the double CD *Sands of Time* is really the best choice for several reasons; first because it features some of his most recent compositions (including a selection taken from his video soundtrack to *The Petrified Forest*) that you won't find on any other recording. The first disc also offers a balanced presentation of music from some of his best albums. The second disc, however, is the real treat because it features never-before-released improvisations and extended compositions recorded live in performance. –LK

Henon / KUCKUCK   1992
Deuter's latest album is consistent with the style he established twenty years ago. The music here, while taking advantage of the latest in recording technology, hasn't evolved much over the last decade, yet it retains its expressive integrity and uplifting, celebratory qualities. –LK

DJAM KARET

Progressive electronic, ambient, techno-tribal. This eclectic Los Angeles band is equally adept at writing aggressive, rock-influenced electro-acoustic music and sophisticated, ambient pieces that suggest dark, ethereal landscapes. –LK

○ **Reflections from the Firepool / HC PRODUCTIONS**   1989
Although the group's subsequent albums are equally good, this well-rounded disc represents the prowess these musicians have developed during their ten years together in the instrumental rock field, and features some intriguing ethno-ambient passages and urban soundscapes. –LK

Burning the Hard City / HC PRODUCTIONS   1991
This guitar-attack album was released simultaneously with *Suspension and Displacement* as a statement of total contrast. A cathartic experience. –LK

Suspension and Displacement / HC PROD.   1991
The Djam Karet ambient album. However, with titles like "Dark Clouds, No Rain," "8:15-No Safe Place" and "Angels without Wings," you know you're in for more than a pleasant walk in the park. –LK

DO'AH

Ethnic fusion, adult alternative. Two New Hampshire residents, Randy Armstrong and Ken LaRoche, are the ringleaders of this long-standing ensemble founded in 1974. The name, which was spelled "Do'a" on the band's first few recordings, comes from an Arabic word signifying a call to prayer and meditation; but the music is often upbeat and festive. The members of Do'ah play somewhere in the neighborhood of 75 instruments from various ethnic persuasions, yet the overall feeling owes much to Western music. Some of their compositions seem a little too good-natured and naive at times; however, you have to admire their virtuosic playing and vision, especially since Do'ah was creating world-music fusions a good 10 or 15 years before the idea hit the mainstream. –LK

Light upon Light / PHILO   1979
Do'ah's first album was recorded back when Armstrong and LaRoche were working as a duo. –LK

Ornament of Hope / PHILO
Do'ah's second album is significant in that Armstrong and LaRoche were beginning to hear larger orchestrations in their compositions. On this release, they brought in other musicians to perform on various pieces. –LK

Companions of the Crimson Coloured Ark / PHILO
Do'ah finally decided on a quintet instrumentation, and that's how the band has operated since. –LK

The Early Years / ROUNDER   1988
This is a collection of selected tunes from the band's first two albums and, as such, is a document of Do'ah's early development. –LK

○ **World Dance / GLOBAL PACIFIC**   1988
A mature example of a group that has been working for nearly two decades to dissolve the barriers between various ethnic musical styles and build bridges between cultures in the process. –LK

JOHN DOAN

Neo-classical, chamber jazz. Though Doan is a master of renaissance lute as well as classical and contemporary guitar styles, he's one of the few artists around who has explored the possibilities of the harp guitar. The instrument was popular in America around the turn of the century, yet today has been all but forgotten. The way Doan plays it, you have to wonder how this intriguing medium could ever have slipped into obscurity. In addition to the standard six strings of regular guitars, the harp guitar features five bass strings that add a special warmth and richness, as well as several treble strings that create a translucent sense of delicacy. The Oregon-based artist and guitar professor has so far released only one recording, *Departures*, on the Narada label. –LK

○ **Departures / NARADA**   1988
Doan's ensemble settings for harp guitar take full advantage of the instrument's expressive range and rich timbral palette. This is contemporary instrumental music at its finest; however, its thoughtful, often sublime lyricism and subtle classical music influences didn't add up to commercial success when the album was first released. It's still available, and definitely worth going out of your way to find. –LK

BILL DOUGLAS

Ethnic fusion, neo-classical, chamber jazz. This Canadian-born artist couldn't have a much more varied musical background. His first band did Elvis covers in the 50s, yet Douglas went on to gain a music degree and spent several years as a classical bassoonist with the Toronto Symphony. Over the years he has also worked as a jazz improviser, an avant-garde composer, and a college professor. He finally settled in Boulder, CO, where he remains music director at the Naropa Institute. For the last seven years, he has toured and recorded with classical clarinetist Richard Stoltzman, as well as writing much of the material for Stoltzman's popular crossover albums *Begin Sweet World* and *New York Counterpoint*. Those who've enjoyed these recordings will find Douglas's own releases for the Hearts of Space label similar in conception. There's no mistaking his sweet, lyrical melodies; his combination of Western, folk, and classical styles; his virtuosity on several instruments; and the poignant sense of innocence in much of his music. –LK

Jewel Lake / HEARTS OF SPACE   1988
Douglas's debut as a leader was a surprise hit in Spain, of all places. The composer's style on this release, however, may be a little too sweet for some tastes. –LK

○ **Cantilena / HEARTS OF SPACE**   1990
This is his most masterly and well-balanced effort so far. Most of the selections are smooth, melodious songs-without-words inspired by everything from spirited-yet-flowing Celtic dances and modal folk songs to some deeply emotional music that conveys a near religious profundity. –LK

WILLIAM EATON

Ambient, chamber jazz, ethnic fusion. Eaton designs and builds many of the stringed instruments he plays, and he's come up with some unique hybrids like the "koto harp guitar," the "o'ele 'n strings" (a double-necked instrument), and even a 26-string guitar. The Phoenix-based artist performs and records most often with Native American flutist R. Carlos Nakai. Together they create haunting, highly resonant, original pieces inspired by places and cultures of the Southwest. (See also albums listed under Nakai.) –LK

○ **Tracks We Leave / CANYON**   1989
An evocative collection of highly impressionistic compositions on which Eaton plays some of his most intriguing instruments (including the lyre and the koto harp guitar) in sparse ensemble settings that feature special guests like Nakai on Native American flutes, Rich Rogers on the Japanese shakuhachi flute and percussion, as well as Udi Arouh on guitar and tablas. –LK

WILLIAM ELLWOOD

Solo instrumental, neo-classical, chamber jazz. As the story goes, Ellwood cajoled his parents into buying him a cheap, nearly unplayable guitar when he was 12 years old. The instrument was too warped to play chords, so he came up with the right-handed picking style he uses to this day. The Canadian-born artist later developed an interest in renaissance and baroque music, taught himself to play the lute, and eventually designed a 7-string guitar so he could transcribe lute pieces without sacrificing any voicings. Ellwood's classical music leanings are apparent on his Narada recordings, although his music has a gentle, contemporary feel to it as well. –LK

Openings / NARADA   1986
Like many contemporary instrumentalists, Ellwood began his recording career as a solo artist. His debut for Narada is a collection of pieces for guitar. –LK

○ **Renaissance / NARADA**   1987
Ellwood expands his scope a bit on this album, with subtle ensemble works that elegantly express his love for renaissance and baroque music in an updated context. Keyboards, percussion, flute, and bassoon are used sparingly and effectively in arrangements that feature several guest artists (including fellow Canadian Bill Douglas). A delicate, well-balanced effort. –LK

Vista / NARADA   1989
Ellwood dives further into ensemble music on his third Narada release. Violinist Billy Oskay of Nightnoise, keyboardist Robert O'Hearn (Patrick O'Hearn's brother), and keyboardist George Mitchell (who performs with Diana Ross) are among the musicians who thicken the sound and provide some nice moments, at the cost of the intimacy of Ellwood's previous albums. –LK

EMERALD WEB

Progressive electronic, ambient. In addition to releasing a dozen albums on various independent labels, husband-and-wife team Bob Stohl and Kat Epple have scored and produced music for numerous film and TV projects at the state-of-the-art recording studio in their Florida home. These projects have gained them numerous awards, including several Emmy and Addy awards and a 1986 Grammy nomination. In 1990 their close creative partnership ended when Stohl tragically drowned. *Manatee Dreams of Neptune*, one of the finest albums Emerald Web ever made, was recorded shortly before his death. Though many of their releases are difficult to find, the evocative, mood-altering compositions on the releases listed here are exemplary of the Emerald Web sound. –LK

Nocturne/Lights of Ivory Plain / FORTUNA   1989
This CD-only release brings together selections from two albums recorded in 1983 and 1984. Haunting bass flute and Celtic harp melodies flow into the rhythmic permutations of digital synthesizers and the colorful sounds of the Lyricon wind synthesizer. –LK

○ **Manatee Dreams of Neptune / SCARLET**   1990
Emerald Web's last album is arguably the duo's best. The inspiration comes from an unusual juxtaposition of experiences. Several of the selections were inspired by Voyager's photographs of Neptune and its moons (Emerald Web provided music for a network of television programs on the space probe's rendezvous with Neptune). At the time this

album was made, the composers were also spending a lot of time watching manatees swim in the waterways near their home, enjoying the graceful movements of these endangered marine mammals. The resulting music is mysterious and otherworldly while conveying a deep appreciation for life on this planet. –LK

BRIAN ENO

Ambient, progressive electronic. One of the most important figures in the realm of contemporary electronic music, this highly respected English producer and former underground pop hero began creating what he called "ambient music" in the late 70s through a series of influential solo albums and ethereal collaborations with Laraaji, Jon Hassell, and Harold Budd.

Trained as a visual artist, Eno rose through the ranks of glam-rock group Roxy Music as an engineer and behind-the-scenes synthesizer player who eventually came up with enough weird sounds to warrant appearances on stage with the band. The recording studio remained his instrument after he left the group in 1973. It was among those early synthesizers, mixing boards, and reverb units that he began to hear new sonic possibilities bubbling to the surface. His interest in creating "sound landscapes" with sophisticated manipulations of echo and timbre led to the establishment of his "ambient music" ideal in the late 70s. He unwittingly became one of the fathers of new-age music, a genre he was quick to criticize for not encompassing enough "evil and doubt." The intention and effect of Eno's style, however, is markedly different from the soothing sound-baths associated with many new-age and contemporary electronic recordings, notoriously one-dimensional in their approach to sound construction.

Eno himself best describes the intricacies involved in creating good ambient music: "In the past, timbre was a very limited question for a composer. Clarinet, violin, viola, piccolo, oboe, these all meant a certain range of possibilities. With recording studios and synthesizers, you can make any sound you want, and you can extend any aspect of something's sound out of all proportion. It's no longer a question of writing melodies and words and rhythms; it's a question of devising a sound landscape as well." According to Eno, this also involves an imaginative use of echo: "Generally recordings are done in fairly dry places, and you add the ambience you want. You can do this realistically; you can make it sound like a room or a club or Albert Hall. Or you can do it entirely whimsically. You can say, "I want it to sound like the biggest intergalactic space you ever heard." Or you can do very weird combinations like "I want this sound to be in a tiny concrete box down there, but I want that sound to be in a tub of oil 200 meters across, and I want this other sound to be floating by on the wind." Rather than create their own sounds, however, most keyboardists use the sounds that come with commercial synthesizers, and their concept of echo is pedestrian as well. All of this adds to the mediocrity associated with many contemporary electronic recordings. "These people who are using stock sounds," Eno says, "are pretending sound is the whole issue, and they're not working it at all."

In recent years, Eno has created increasingly sophisticated ambient soundtracks for his own multi-media installations, which have graced galleries in Venice, Milan, and Tokyo. Eno is also one of rock's most sought-after producers, a miracle worker whose resume includes recordings with Devo, the Talking Heads, and U2. Eno continues to release albums in both pop and CI genres and is currently working on his first ambient recording in nearly a decade. –LK

Discreet Music / CAROLINE   1975
Eno's experimental precursor to his ambient series explores his fascination with the element of "chance" in composition. The title cut was created by setting the parameters for a series of synthesizers, equalizers, echo units, and tape players to interact with each other. He then sat back and let the piece follow its own course. The second work, which is comprised of

three variations on Pachelbel's famous "Canon in D," involved giving live players fragments of the original score with instructions that caused them to overlay their parts in unusual and unpredictable ways. Both pieces are intriguing and surprisingly musical. −LK

Ambient 1 - Music for Airports / CAROLINE   1978
Four subtle, slowly evolving pieces grace Eno's first conscious effort at creating ambient music. The composer was in part striving to create music that approximated the effect of visual art. Like a fine painting, these evolving soundscapes don't require constant involvement on the part of the listener. They can hang in the background and add to the atmosphere of the room, yet the music also rewards close attention with a sonic richness absent in standard types of background or easy-listening music. −LK

☆ **My Life in the Bush of Ghosts / WARNER**   1980
Talking Heads singer David Byrne teams with art-rock guru Brian Eno to create this unique techno-tribal music by combining tapes of Third World vocalizations with African-like rhythm tracks. Dense and hypnotic, the recording of an exorcism is downright spooky. −SWB

○ **Ambient 4 - On Land / CAROLINE**   1982
Eno's most masterful ambient effort to date was created as a musical antidote to the confusion of life in New York City. An earthy sense of repose underlies intricate sonic essays. −LK

ROGER ENO

Ambient, neo-classical. Brian Eno's brother plays romantic, heavily processed piano music that sounds like a cross between Harold Budd's poignant minimal phrasing and the classical miniatures of French composer Erik Satie. −LK

○ **Voices / CAROLINE**   1985
Lilting atmospheric piano music in slow motion. −LK

Between Tides / WARNER   1988

ESTEBAN

Solo instrumental, neo-classical, ethnic fusion. Guitarist Stephen Paul was affectionately called "Esteban" by his teacher, the legendary classical virtuoso Andres Segovia. Though Esteban has released only one album of original music so far, he shows much promise as both a composer and a performer. −LK

○ **Duende / SOUND DESIGN OF ARIZONA**   1991
Esteban calls his style "new-world guitar music," an accurate moniker for *Duende*'s combination of classical, flamenco, and ethnic influences from various cultures. Estaban's touch is expressive and his technique impressive — the album was all recorded without editing or overdubbing. −LK

DEAN EVENSON

Ambient, new-age. In the 70s, Evenson and his wife Dudley traveled across the country with early portable video equipment to document "the awakening consciousness as it was manifesting in people's lives." The couple eventually settled in Tucson, AZ, and built a small empire with their Soundings of the Planet record company. Their stated purpose was to help people "experience the healing energies of music and natural sounds and get in touch with a more peaceful place inside themselves." Soundings of the Planet has had amazing success in creating and distributing recordings that communicate this goal. Evenson produces many of the label's artists. He also has several albums of his own that combine natural sounds with his softly flowing flute melodies and various other acoustic and electronic instruments. −LK

Ocean Dreams / SOUNDINGS OF THE PLANET   1989
Ocean waves and whale sounds weave in and out of music that is highly atmospheric and melodic. Though the motivation is sincere, it's all been done better before, most notably by Paul Winter. −LK

○ **Desert Moon Song / SOUNDINGS OF THE PLANET**   1991
An environmentally inspired thematic album, more accomplished than *Ocean Dreams*. −LK

CHRISTOPHER FRANKE

Adult alternative, progressive electronic, minimalist. After nearly two decades as one of the main pillars of the legendary electronic group Tangerine Dream, this German keyboardist struck out on his own in the late 80s. Before he left, his mastery of sequencer-driven synthesizer techniques defined much of the trademark TD sound with pulsing, multilayered mosaics of precise yet exhilarating note patterns. −LK

○ **Pacific Coast Highway / VIRGIN**   1991
Franke's first solo album is surprisingly melodic, highly accessible, and immaculately produced. As the title suggests, this music would make the perfect soundtrack for a drive up the California coast. The innovative sequencer work of his Tangerine Dream years has given way on this album to more predictable pop electronic orchestrations that would easily fit into new adult contemporary radio formats. −LK

FRIEDEMANN

Adult alternative, ethnic fusion. West German guitarist Friedemann Witecka is a popular arranger, producer, and studio musician in his homeland. His US releases for Narada prove he's also one of the most imaginative composers of instrumental music influenced by rock and jazz fusion styles. This catchy, spirited music gracefully sidesteps most pop clichés. −LK

○ **Indian Summer / NARADA**   1987
The guitarist's North American debut is an engaging mix of styles and instrumental colors. Standard guitars and keyboards are enhanced by Chinese hammer dulcimer, harp, vibes, marimba, and lots of percussion. −LK

Aquamarine / NARADA   1990
Friedemann is working with an even larger palette of colors here (12 guest musicians). −LK

EUGENE FRIESEN

Chamber jazz, neo-classical. Best known for his work with the Paul Winter Consort, this classically trained cellist was inspired by equal parts sacred orchestral music and mid-60s pop styles. (The innovative use of the cello by the Beatles in some of their arrangements was a strong influence on young Friesen.) His work with a diverse roster of artists over the years has further expanded his scope. He has recorded and performed with everyone from Dave Brubeck and Anthony Davis to Scott Cossu and Steven Halpern. −LK

○ **Arms around You / LIVING MUSIC**
Friesen's lyrical cello solos are the highlight of this romantic contemporary instrumental album. −LK

EDGAR FROESE

Progressive electronic, adult alternative. A founding member of the pioneering German synthesizer group Tangerine Dream, Froese proved to be the most ambitious in releasing solo albums alongside the voluminous output of the band. He was also considered a master of the Mellotron, an early keyboard device (made famous by the rock group Moody Blues) that produced its sound through key-activated tape loops of actual recordings of orchestras, choirs, and other acoustic sounds. Froese's individual style has a more direct and personal quality, while still drawing from TD's trademark sequencer sound. These albums also feature his penchant for rock-style guitar work. −LK

Aqua / CAROLINE   1974
The solo debut from Tangerine Dream's leader. −MPD

○ **Epsilon in Malaysian Pale / CAROLINE**   1975
Lush, entrancing electronic pieces. −MPD

Stuntman / CAROLINE   1979
A less otherworldly version of Froese's sound. −MPD

Kamikaze 1989 / CAROLINE   1982
A patchy soundtrack effort. −MPD

GANDALF

New-age, ambient, progressive electronic, adult alternative.
Austrian musician Hein Strobl took his stage name from the goodhearted magician in J. R. Tolkien's trilogy *Lord of the Rings*. As such, the composer's goal is to create music that magically inspires positive thoughts and feelings in his listeners as an antidote to the negative forces of modern life. From his early spatial electronic and guitar soundscapes to his more recent symphonic compositions, Gandalf's work conveys his love of nature and commitment to preserving the environment. –LK

More Than Just a Seagull / EUROCK   1988
Gandalf's USA debut was originally composed as the soundtrack for a multimedia performance of Richard Bach's book *Jonathan Livingston Seagull*. Sounds of the sea mix with bird calls, bells, guitars, synthesizers, Mellotron, and grand piano to create wistful music that floats and soars. –LK

○ **Labyrinth / EUROCK**   1990
This music was composed as the soundtrack to an Austrian experimental film screened at the Berlin and Cannes Film Festivals in 1989. A refreshing departure from Gandalf's eternally optimistic style, *Labyrinth* explores the deeper psychological realms of sound through dense, darkly evocative melodies, minimalist rhythmic patterns and contemplative soundscapes. –LK

Reflection / EUROCK
A collection of essential pieces recorded between 1986 and 1990, chosen by Gandalf himself to represent various aspects of his style. Influences range from classical and symphonic music to rock, pop, new age, and oriental. –LK

T. K. GARDNER

Adult alternative. New-age? Light jazz? Adult-contemporary? The 8-string guitar work of T. K. Gardner may be hard to classify, but it makes for great listening. Too much of so-called space music is just that — vacuous. Although Gardner's music has that new spacious sound, it also has definition and real substance — integrity. This is how new-age music should sound. You may have trouble finding his one album, *8 X 10*, in stores, so here is the address: Wildcard Records, P.O. Box 4565, Anaheim, CA 92803. –JME

○ **8 X 10 / WILDCARD (*.*)**   1990

MICHAEL GARRISON

Progressive electronic. A longstanding American exponent of sequencer-based music, Garrison has released over a half-dozen albums of high-energy electronics. Strongly influenced by European innovators like Klaus Schulze and Tangerine Dream, this Oregon-based artist enjoys propelling listeners into rhythmic travels along the space-time continuum. –LK

○ **Eclipse / WINDSPELL**   1983
One of Garrison's finest sequencer scorchers, with some quiet, impressionistic moments to balance things out. –LK

An Earth-Star Trilogy / WINDSPELL   1988
Not quite as frenetic and hard-edged as many of Garrison's previous releases. –LK

The Rhythm of Life / WINDSPELL   1991
This recent release accelerates into the breathless sequencer work Garrison is known for, though his style is rather predictable at this point. –LK

ROBERT GASS

New-age, ambient, neo-classical. A nationally known lecturer, Gass holds a doctorate in clinical psychology from Harvard and has received classical training in music at the New England Conservatory and Tanglewood. As director of the 30-person performing group On Wings of Song, he has produced a number of recordings under his *Extended Chant* series that feature uplifting, updated versions of sacred choral traditions from around the world. Though many of these works are based on authentic spiritual texts and melodies, Gass's

primary goal seems to be oriented toward making the music as comforting and as accessible as possible to modern audiences. However, listeners who enjoy Middle Eastern chanting, American Indian music, and medieval plain-chant singing in their purest, most traditional forms will likely find Gass's interpretations a little too sweet and Westernized. –LK

From the Goddess / SPRING HILL MUSIC   1989
This celebration of the feminine spirit features a weaving of three well-known goddess chants sung by the 24 women of On Wings of Song, with delicate instrumental accompaniments involving harp, guitar, and percussion. –LK

○ **Heart of Perfect Wisdom / SPRING HILL MUSIC**   1990
Gass's finest recording to date is his adaptation of the Buddhist heart sutra. Striking a delicate balance between Eastern and Western sensibilities, the album features full chorus, Tibetan bells, Nepalese wooden flutes, and some overtone singing, with a subtle use of acoustic guitar and Celtic harp. This presentation retains a sense of mystery and reverence for Eastern tradition that is lost to various degrees on some of Gass's other recordings, which lean toward the sentimental at the expense of the mystical. –LK

Kalama / SPRING HILL MUSIC   1990
On *Kalama: A Sufi Song of Love*, the members of On Wings of Song sing ancient Sufi lyrics in Arabic to contemporary melodies and arrangements featuring guitars, violin, tabla, and sarod, among other instruments. –LK

MICHAEL GETTEL

Adult alternative. This Seattle-based composer and music teacher writes contemporary piano-based ensemble works inspired by family, friends, and the beauty of the Pacific Northwest. Though his uptempo pieces are on the trite side, he is at his best when he creates flowing, impressionistic music involving acoustic piano and melodic instruments like oboe, French horn, and flugelhorn. –LK

Intricate Balance / MIRAMAR
Return / NARADA   1990
○ **Places in Time / NARADA**   1992
A finely produced album, *Places in Time* features a wide variety of guest artists including violinist Billy Oskay, oboists Nancy Rumbel and Russel Walder, and synthesist David Arkenstone, among others. –LK

JERRY GOODMAN

Progressive electronic, adult alternative. As a member of John McLaughlin's influential jazz/rock fusion band Mahavishnu Orchestra in the early 70s, Goodman used his violin to create phrasings and sonorities previously associated with the electric guitar. His subsequent albums as a leader for Private Music expand on these experiences to create a dynamic and aggressive style that fuses rock textures through tightly arranged compositions. –LK

Ariel / PRIVATE MUSIC   1985
Vivid fusion textures and combustible fiddle playing. –LK

○ **On the Future of Aviation / PRIVATE MUSIC**   1989
Goodman's debut as a leader features his abilities on guitar, mandolin, synthesizers, and percussion, in addition to violin solos that subsist on his characteristic screaming, electronically distorted sound. –LK

GOVI

New-age, ethnic fusion. This California-based artist was born in Germany. His inspiration and style are similar to that of another German immigrant, Deuter, who co-produced and performed on Govi's debut album *Sky High*. Like Deuter, Govi spent a number of years living and studying in India, where he added sitar to his vocabulary of acoustic and electric guitars, mandola, and cello. His music is a gentle, melodious combination of influences from around the world. –LK

○ **Sky High / REAL MUSIC**
Heart of a Gypsy / REAL MUSIC

WAYNE GRATZ

Adult alternative, chamber jazz. Gratz spent over a decade playing keyboards in a Florida-based pop band before he sent a tape of some of his more reflective solo piano pieces to Narada. The label was immediately intrigued by his songwriting skills and signed him up. Though he's primarily self-taught, Gratz possesses a natural talent for creating lush, impressionistic music that somehow sidesteps the cliches many of his labelmates lapse into. Though he's not as well known as David Lanz or Spencer Brewer, Gratz is in many ways more successful at creating subtle, artistically satisfying compositions. –LK

○ **Reminiscence / NARADA**   1989
Gratz's debut for Narada is primarily devoted to solo piano music with a few guest performances by Scottish fiddler Alasdair Fraser and oboist Nancy Rumbel. This is evocative, understated music with an innate sense of elegance. –LK

Panorama / NARADA   1990
Gratz plays keyboards and guitar as well as piano on this collection of ensemble pieces produced by violinist Billy Oskay. Though the composer has managed to keep the subtleties of his own style intact for the most part, the Gratz sound occasionally gets mired in thick arrangements that threaten to obscure his delicate insights. –LK

GREEN ISAC

Progressive electronic, ethnic fusion. Green Isac is a Norwegian-based duo featuring Morten Lund on keyboards, guitar, and flute. His partner Andreas Eriksen is an imaginative percussionist well versed in African and Arabic styles. Their first and only album available so far is astounding in its creative manipulation of a wide range of influences. –LK

○ **Strings and Pottery / EUROCK**   1991
From the intricate minimalist patterns of Steve Reich, the techno-tribal mystery of Jon Hassell, and the tango seductions of Astor Piazzola to the rhythmic vitality of rock and the percussive ecstasy of third-world traditions, Green Isac seems to have summed up the major innovations of the late 20th century in a single well-crafted album. –LK

CHUCK GREENBERG

Ethnic fusion, progressive electronic, adult alternative. One of the founding members of the influential world-music/fusion band Shadowfax, Greenberg plays flutes, saxophones, and keyboards. The California-based artist is also well known for his use of the Lyricon, an electronic wind instrument he helped develop. The Lyricon adds an ethereal dimension to his masterful melodic improvisations. As a composer, Greenberg combines rock, pop, and jazz elements into his music while retaining a progressive edge. –LK

○ **From a Blue Planet / CAPITOL**   1991
Greenberg's first album as a leader allows him to shine as a soloist, though he is accompanied by some first-class artists like guitarist Alex de Grassi, as well as fellow Shadowfax bandmates Charles Bisharat on violin and Phil Maggini on bass. An impressive album. –LK

SYLVAN GREY

Solo instrumental, neo-classical, ethnic fusion. Grey works wonders with the 36-string Finnish folk zither known as the kantele, which she discovered during a trip to England and studied briefly with Finland's highly regarded teacher Ulla Katajavuori. Back in the United States, Grey devoted herself to composing music for the kantele and honed her chops performing in coffeehouses. She recorded her first album, *Ice Flowers Melting*, for Fortuna Records in 1981. (It was re-released in 1988.) Her finest effort, however, is her rhapsodic followup recording *Recurring Dream.* –LK

Ice Flowers Melting / FORTUNA   1981
○ **Recurring Dream / FORTUNA**   1989

Without the use of electronic processing of any kind, Grey produces a lush, scintillating sound from the kantele through her skillful use of bell-like accents, ringing harmonics, arpeggios, and delicate ostinatos. The music is both stirring and intimate. –LK

PAUL HALLEY

Solo instrumental, neo-classical, chamber jazz. Though he's best known as a member of the Paul Winter Consort, this English-born pianist has an impressive career of his own. After receiving a Masters degree from Cambridge, with prizes in composition and harpsichord playing, Halley was named Musical Director at New York's Cathedral of St. John the Divine. There he expanded its music program to include a rich combination of contemporary as well as classical styles. He also wrote choral works and Broadway scores. Winter, whom Halley met in 1980, was the first to recognize the keyboardist's talent for improvisation and invited him to join the Paul Winter Consort. Halley has since been a featured performer on many of the Consort's finest albums. –LK

New Friend / LIVING MUSIC
This is an imaginative collection with Eugene Friesen of improvisations for cello and piano, featuring two of the Paul Winter Consort's long-standing members. –LK

○ **Pianosong / LIVING MUSIC**
Halley's first solo album for Winter's Living Music label consists of rich and varied solo piano improvisations, augmented on three cuts by the sonorous sounds of the Cathedral of St. John the Divine's pipe organ. –LK

STEVEN HALPERN

New-age, neo-classical, ethnic fusion. Halpern is the original new-age artist, in the most accurate sense of the term. In 1975 he released *Spectrum Suite*, his first album of music specifically designed for relaxation and healing. Before that, Halpern had been immersed in the New York City jazz scene as a trumpeter and guitarist. His disgust at the adverse effects of life in the fast lane were accentuated by a move to California, where he perfected his idea of "anti-frantic alternative" music. Based partly on his metaphysical beliefs and partly on more solid scientific research into the effects of sound on the human body, he came to the conclusion that the Western foundation of tension and release in music couldn't by nature provide listeners with relief from stress. He decided the answer was to create music that "didn't go anywhere" in the traditional sense but instead immersed the listener in a positive atmosphere conducive to recuperative and transcendental experiences. Halpern created music that was centered largely around cascades of major-key arpeggios improvised at the electric piano, and he added generous helpings of reverb to create a spacey, other-worldly feeling. He took a certain amount of inspiration from oriental classical music and looked into the ceremonial, magical, and healing aspects of sound used by ancient cultures. While some of his ideas take on the pseudo-science pallor of new-age mysticism, Halpern's importance as one of the true fathers of modern meditational and healing forms of music cannot be overemphasized. He has released over 50 instrumental and guided-meditation recordings, some of which are better than others. He has also written two books on his theories: *Tuning the Human Instrument* and *Sound Health.* –LK

☆ **Spectrum Suite / SOUND RX**   1975
Halpern's first release is a cornerstone of the new-age genre and one of the best examples of the comforting electric-piano reverberations that have continued to dominate his style over the years. –LK

Connections / SOUND RX   1984
This collaboration with flutist Paul Horn is appropriately soothing, yet delightful on a purely musical level as well. –LK

Higher Ground / SOUND RX   1991
Arguably Halpern's most artistically accomplished album, *Higher Ground* mixes his trademark sounds of the past with

some new directions, particularly a more skillful use of synthesizers. For those interested in Halpern's latest therapeutic developments, there's an added benefit: the composer has included what he calls "binaural beat phrasing" to the music, which he says "sonically entrains your brain to an immediate 8-cycles per second response" that locks you "into phase with the natural harmonics of the Earth." −LK

PETER MICHAEL HAMEL   b 1947

Neo-classical, ethnic fusion, minimalist. As a young man, Hamel studied music, psychology, and sociology in his native Germany. He then spent three extensive periods in Asia, where his studies of Eastern musical traditions (particularly Tibetan and Indian) had a profound effect not only on his compositional style but on his views concerning Western music as a whole. Hamel shared his unconventional insights on music and its place in society in his influential book *Through Music to the Self.* First published in 1976, the treatise discusses the transformational effects of music through the ages and calls for a more spiritual approach to composition in 20th century Western music. While many of his concepts fueled the American new-age movement, Hamel's music is a far cry from the good-natured doodling often associated with that genre. Though some of his works are more successful than others, they all exhibit the grace and intelligence of classical music, the spontaneity of jazz, the hypnotic qualities of Far Eastern styles, and (quite often) the relentless drive of American minimalist techniques. −LK

○ **Transition / KUCKUCK**   1983
All of Hamel's albums have their moments, but *Transition* presents some of the composer's most beautiful and most emotionally arresting music. Hamel performs several extended works on piano that combine rhapsodic melodies with rich harmonic flourishes. There's also an ambitious essay for pipe organ, PPG wave computer, and synthesizer that takes listeners out of the realm of everyday experience. The real gem, however, is a 25-minute masterpiece for prepared piano that transforms the standard 88 keys into a sort of mini percussion ensemble. The music on this clever, yet highly expressive work sounds like everything from an Indonesian gamelan to an African bamboo orchestra. −LK

Let It Play / KUCKUCK   1984
Hamel in various moods 1979 to 1983. Samples taken from *Transition, Colours of Time, Bardo,* and a few previously unreleased selections. This is a fine introduction to his varied style. −LK

Organum / KUCKUCK   1986
Hamel's contemporary interpretation of the medieval musical concept known as "organum," which involved an intricate interplay of modal melodies. Four extended works on pipe organ culminate in acutely intense barrages of sound and sensation. A challenging album. −LK

MICHAEL HARRISON

Ethnic fusion, minimalist. A protégé of minimalist godfather La Monte Young, this conservatory-trained pianist and composer successfully mixes classical, jazz, and ethnic influences into his music. Harrison also works extensively with alternate tuning systems and invented what he calls the "harmonic piano." This instrument is capable of playing 24 notes per octave (not the standard 12). The strings are also designed to resonate sympathetically like those of a sitar. −LK

In Flight / FORTUNA   1987
A most unusual album of piano solos that combine lyrical melodies and impressionistic harmonies with some Indian and Oriental influences. A couple of the pieces were also performed in "just intonation." Unfortunately, the passionate and sublime flights of fancy featured on this recording never got the attention they deserved. −LK

DON HARRISS

Adult alternative. This keyboardist and computer whiz has derived his unique sound from a diverse background that includes classical training, 60s Haight-Ashbury psychedelia, stints of touring and recording with rock idol Pat Travers, and jobs composing corporate film soundtracks. Though he lapses into glitzy pop triteness on occasion, he is light-years ahead of most adult contemporary synthesists in his sophisticated use of texture and sound. He has several albums on the market that did well on new adult contemporary radio, including *Shell Game, Vanishing Point,* and *Elevations,* but his best release by far is *Abacus Moon.* −LK

○ **Abacus Moon / SONIC ATMOSPHERES**   1989
A brilliant combination of pop sensibilities and playful, imaginative sound designs. −LK

JON HASSELL

Ethnic fusion, techno-tribal, minimalist. Hassell is the original techno-tribal musician. One of the most important innovators in ethnic-based instrumental music, Hassell studied at the Eastman School of Music and the University of Rochester before working in Europe with electronic-music pioneer Karlheinz Stockhausen. He also explored the world of minimalism through performances with Terry Riley and La Monte Young in the 60s and studied with Indian musical guru Pandit Pran Nath in the 70s. Toward the middle of that decade, Hassell came up with a concept he called "Fourth World music" to describe his ideal of uniting past and present, Eastern and Western, Third World and First, and acoustic and electronic influences into a new form of artistic expression for members of an emerging global village. The trumpeter, synthesist, and composer has since recorded with and influenced a wide variety of artists, including Brian Eno, Peter Gabriel, David Sylvian, and Daniel Lanois. −LK

Earthquake Island / TOMATO   1978
"Miles Davis meets the Bermuda Triangle" on Hassell's first album with Miroslav Vitous, Nana, Dom Um Romao, and Badal Roy. Stunning music and cover art. −MGN

☆ **Fourth World: Vol.1 ... / CAROLINE**   1979
Fourth World - Vol 1: Possible Musics. Brian Eno's most satisfying and captivating set of mood music came through this collaboration with Jon Hassell. Evocative, eerie, and druggy. Jungle music on Venus — is an apt description of *Fourth World - Vol. 1: Possible Musics.* With percussionists Nana Vasconcelos and Ayibe Dieng, and bassists Percy Jones and Jerome Harris. Essential. −JF & MGN

Dream Theory in Malaya / CAROLINE   1981
An academic feel proceeds from the subject matter, a meditation on the inspirational seed of artistic composition. It takes its lead from the dream-telling of Malaysian aborigines, the Senoi, whose environment, beliefs, and music shape Hassell's approach. −LK

Aka Darbari Java / CAROLINE   1983
A wild combination of Pygmy voices, Indian ragas, Senegalese drumming, Javanese gamelan styles, and computer-enhanced trumpet choruses. −LK

Power Spot / ECM   1984
An unexpectedly hot raga approach and rock sensibility contribute to the most accessible of Hassell's solo recordings, which proves he can manipulate Asian and African rhythms in the service of the body as well as the mind. −BT

City: Works of Fiction / OPAL   1990
Hassell's "Fourth World" explorations move into a futuristic metropolis. Tribal sensibilities combine with hip-hop rhythms to create a *Blade Runner* atmosphere. −LK

STEVE HAUN

Adult alternative. With his gift for catchy melodies and vibrant keyboard textures, this Colorado-based artist has consistently placed well on both *Billboard* and major NAC/adult-alternative radio charts. Tight musicianship is an important feature of Haun's contemporary jazz- and pop-based ensemble recordings, although his compositional style is not particularly original. −LK

Inside the Sky / SILVER WAVE   1988

Midnight Echoes / SILVER WAVE   1989
○ **Collage / SILVER WAVE**   1991
A nice fusion-flavored mixture of acoustic and electronic sounds. –LK

MICHAEL HEDGES

Solo instrumental, new acoustic. A virtuoso acoustic guitarist on the Windham Hill label. On his first two albums, *Breakfast in the Field* and *Aerial Boundaries*, his playing style combined two-handed tapping ostinatos with percussive slides and slaps to produce rhythmic intensity and hypnotic melodies. This is compositional guitar, with Hedges coaxing a full ensemble of sounds from his guitar. His acoustic sound is treated with reverb and delays, producing a spacious atmosphere that is warm and inviting. His third album, *Watching My Life Go By*, is a change of pace, on which Hedges adds his voice to the music and interprets Bob Dylan's "All Along the Watchtower." Following a double live album, he returned with the *Taproot* album, on which he again did vocals and, for the first time, included other musicians. –SWB

Breakfast in the Field / WINDHAM HILL   1981
Debut album featuring extraordinary guitar work with alternate tunings and his two-handed tapping technique. –PK
☆ **Aerial Boundaries / WINDHAM HILL**   1984
Hedges shines on his second album, producing an amazing variety of sounds with just his acoustic guitar and ample reverberation. One track features extensive electronic processing. Very melodic and musical. –SWB
Watching My Life Go By / WINDHAM HILL   1985
Hedges adds his vocals to the mix, with a cover of Bob Dylan's "All Along the Watchtower" and his own well-crafted originals. –SWB
○ **Live on the Double Planet / WINDHAM HILL**   1987
This exceptional live release features both vocal and instrumental pieces. Superb recording! –PK
Taproot / WINDHAM HILL   1990
Acoustic guitar with a small group, including two tracks of Hedges on electric guitar! –PK

DANNY HEINES

Solo instrumental, chamber jazz, adult alternative. The Colorado-based guitarist seems inspired by equal parts jazz, rock, and contemporary acoustic guitar styles exemplified by Windham Hill artists like Alex de Grassi and Michael Hedges. Heines, however, has transcended his influences to create a spirited style of his own. –LK
Aqua Touch / SILVER WAVE   1986
Debut features solo and ensemble pieces, with guest appearances by woodwind player Paul McCandless and cellist Eugene Friesen. –LK
One Heart Wild / SILVER WAVE   1987
Another finely crafted collection of Heines's work. –LK
○ **Every Island / SILVER WAVE**   1988
The richly-hued guitar stylings of Heines are enhanced by the lyricism of soprano saxophonist and oboist Paul McCandless and the spicy Latin rhythms of Brazilian percussionist Cafe. –LK

MAX HIGHSTEIN

Adult alternative, new-age. With a BA in music, a Masters degree in psychotherapy, and a license to practice massage therapy, this keyboardist began his recording career creating guided relaxation tapes. His later instrumental albums combine gentle pop rhythms with optimistic melodies designed for the new-age-lifestyle market already familiar with his narrated work. –LK
○ **Stars / SERENITY**   1988
New-age pop music featuring Highstein on acoustic piano and synthesizers accompanied by some top studio musicians on flute, oboe, violin, cello, trumpet, electric bass, and drums, among other instruments. –LK

HIMEKAMI

Adult alternative, ethnic fusion. This Japanese synthesist creates lush, pop-influenced music that's almost symphonic in conception. A composer of film and television scores in his native country, Himekami is also well known for his multimedia events at historic shrines and temples throughout Japan. His recorded music, however, is inconsistent in quality. Even his "best of" collections released in the United States feature sweet, easy-listening fluff alongside his more masterful musical journeys. –LK
○ **Moonwater / HIGHER OCTAVE**   1989
Himekami's first release in the US is actually a collection of some of the better selections from his numerous Japanese recordings. Oriental influences are couched in thick synthetic textures and Western harmonies. –LK
Snow Goddess / HIGHER OCTAVE   1991
A followup to his successful US debut release, *Moonwater*. –LK

MICHAEL HOENIG

Progressive electronic, minimalist. Hoenig was one of many German composers to emerge from the innovative, electronic underground scene thriving in that country during the 60s and 70s. He first came to recognition in the progressive rock group Agitation Free in the 70s. After a short stint with Tangerine Dream, Hoenig went on to produce what is considered by many to be one of the most important albums to come out of the German electronic school. He has since moved to Los Angeles, where he currently pursues a career as a film composer. –LK
☆ **Departure From ... / KUCKUCK**   1978
Departure from the Northern Wasteland, a classic of the progressive electronic genre, contains four pieces that are almost perfect in their realization of the sequencer as a compositional tool. Hoenig took the concept of repetitive music further than most anyone in his homeland and claimed his inspiration was drawn from American minimalist composers Philip Glass, Steve Reich, and Terry Riley. The title track is a sublime 20-minute journey through ever-changing melodic and rhythmic phase relationships, creating the vivid sensation of a train ride through misty Northern European landscapes. –LK

WALTER HOLLAND

Progressive electronic, adult alternative. This California-based synthesist and guitarist honed his chops in the progressive rock band Amber Route. His solo albums firmly state his love of powerful, rock-anthem-style electronic pieces inspired in part by Tangerine Dream and Pink Floyd. Holland has also been instrumental in supporting the vital underground electronic scene that continues to develop outside the mainstream music industry. Toward this end, he established his independent Coriolis record label and distribution company, which released the critically acclaimed, multi-artist concept album *Dali: the Endless Enigma* (see entry under the collections and compilations of various artists at the end of this chapter). –LK
○ **Relativity / CORIOLIS**   1986
Urgent sequencer-driven pieces mixed with searing electric guitar solos and rock-influenced acoustic drums. –LK
Transience of Love / CORIOLIS   1989
Ambitious but inconsistent example of his style. –LK

ROBERT JULIAN HORKY

New-age, ambient, neo-classical, ethnic fusion, minimalist. Horky received both classical and modern music training in some of the best music schools in Vienna, Austria. Though he plays keyboards and percussion, his main instrument is the flute. This includes bass, alto, soprano, bamboo, and glass flutes, as well as others of exotic origin. His style is characterized by traces of minimalist, ambient, ethnic, and ritual music. Horky is also closely allied with the new-age movement in his desire to create deeply spiritual, uplifting music. –LK

○ **Voyager / EUROCK**
Horky's first US release ranges from free-flowing meditative pieces to a 30-minute new-age symphony. One of the most intriguing sections, however, is based on ancient Greek scales played on instruments from that period. This is a good cross-section of Horky's varied approaches, with some uneven moments. –LK

Ios / EUROCK
A flute concert recorded live at the Greek island of Ios. –LK

Apolys / EUROCK
An intriguing collection of music for clavichord tuned to an ancient Greek scale. –LK

PAUL HORN

New-age, ambient, chamber jazz. This classically trained flutist went on to become a respected jazz artist. After honing his chops in Chico Hamilton's famous band, Horn made numerous recordings with his own jazz groups and received two Grammy Awards in the 60s for his "Jazz Suite on Mass Texts." He also played with the NBC Hollywood Staff Orchestra but soon became dissatisfied with commercial music and the Los Angeles lifestyle. In the mid 60s, Horn flew to India, where he studied Transcendental Meditation with Maharishi Mahesh Yogi (who was to become the Beatles's famous guru). During his stay, Horn recorded *Inside the Taj Mahal*, the album that became one of the cornerstones of the new-age music movement. It was also one of the first albums to explore the creation of a sense of space and ambience in music, years before sophisticated electronic reverb units hit the market. Horn went on to record in such architectural wonders as Egypt's Great Pyramid and the majestic cathedrals of the former Soviet Union. His cross-cultural collaborations with musicians from China, India, and the Middle East gained critical accolades, as did his highly refined works for more conventional Western ensembles. The British Columbia-based artist continues to record and perform throughout the world. –LK

☆ **Inside the Taj Mahal / KUCKUCK**   1969
Horn's most influential album was captured when Horn slipped into the Taj Mahal one night with his flute and a tape recorder. The resulting set of spontaneous solo flute improvisations took full advantage of the magical resonances of India's famous monument. Each tone Horn plays hangs suspended in space for 28 seconds, and the acoustics are so perfect you can't tell when the original sound stops and the echo takes over. –LK

Inside the Great Pyramid / KUCKUCK   1976
The flutist continues his travels, arriving in Egypt to record in the Great Pyramid of Giza. The double-CD set features a powerful introspective suite of 40 spontaneously composed "psalms" created by Horn on piccolo, alto, and C flutes. –LK

China / KUCKUCK   1983
An exquisite collaboration between Horn and Chinese multi-instrumentalist David Mingyue Liang that captures the timeless elegance of oriental music. –LK

○ **Traveler / KUCKUCK**   1989
Originally released in 1987, this album is a striking summation of Horn's many talents. Reverberant solo instrumental episodes are complemented by evocative original compositions involving synthesizers, string quartet, and even a boys' choir. –LK

Nomad / KUCKUCK   1990
A collection of pieces from eight of his albums, including *Inside the Cathedral*, *The Peace Album*, *In Concert*, *China*, and *Traveler*, among others. –LK

LUCIA HWONG

Progressive electronic, ambient, ethnic fusion. Hwong has a degree in ethnomusicology, experience in writing for New

York dance companies and multimedia artists, and a stamp of approval from minimalist innovator Philip Glass, who has acted as her mentor to a certain extent. Her masterfully produced, electro-acoustic albums on the Private Music label are filled with ethereal yet sensual dreamscapes and breathless, rhythmic journeys through fantastic worlds. Unfortunately, Hwong disappeared from the recording scene after the release of her second album, *Secret Luminescence*. –LK

○ **House of Sleeping Beauties / PRIVATE MUSIC**   1985
Though both of her Private Music releases are excellent, this particular collection of colorful, Oriental-inspired music is stunning. –LK

Secret Luminescence / PRIVATE MUSIC   1987
More ethereal and moody than her first release, this is also downright erotic at times. –LK

IASOS

New-age. One of the original new-age musicians, this California synthesist creates expansive, uplifting music that floats and shimmers. Iasos has always been sincere in his desire to induce higher states of consciousness through his music. Sometimes his lofty aims get bogged down in an overly sweet presentation, but at other times he succeeds in creating transcendent and artistically satisfying music. –LK

Angelic Music / INTER-DIMENSIONAL MUSIC   1978
An earlier dose of Iasos's cosmic aspirations. –LK

Elixir / SOUND   1983
The quintessential Iasos recording. Whether the album has the potential to carry people to Nirvana on wings of song is up to the personal experience of each listener. In any case, the music is beautiful and deeply inspired. –LK

RALF ILLENBERGER

Adult alternative. Inspired by the Beatles and the Rolling Stones, this German guitarist essentially taught himself to play from records, later adding Leo Kottke, J. S. Bach, and Keith Jarrett to his list of influences. Honing his chops in local dance bands, Illenberger graduated to concert dates and eventually released seven albums in Europe before signing with Narada Records in the US. His style is an intelligent mix of pop and jazz, making him one of the better adult-alternative instrumentalists on the market. –LK

○ **Circle / MCA**   1989
Illenberger's American debut mixes colorful instrumentals with some introspective moods. –LK

Heart & Beat / MCA   1990
This more energetic and lighthearted album features a number of prominent European sidemen. –LK

INKUYO

Ethnic fusion. Inkuyo comprises four musicians who bring the ancient instruments and songs of their South American Incan heritage firmly into the 20th century. Their name and inspiration are taken from a remote mountain village high in the heart of the Andes where the people retain many of the customs their ancestors followed centuries ago. In addition to performing their own arrangements of traditional tunes, the members of Inkuyo present modern compositions inspired by the Chilean "new song" movement, as well as a number of spirited folk-inspired originals. –LK

○ **Land of the Incas / FORTUNA**   1988
Although both of Inkuyo's albums are equal in artistic merit, this is perhaps the best place to start. This festive collage of tradition and innovation features a wide variety of intriguing South American instruments: cane flutes, panpipes of all sizes, and traditional drums and percussion, as well as acoustic guitar, violin, and harp. –LK

Temple of the Sun / FORTUNA   1992
More crisp, evocative performances from these masterful performers. This time the music is inspired by the legends surrounding Coricancha, the famous fallen temple of the sun

located in the Incan capital city of Cusco. With its exterior walls covered in gold, the building was mercilessly plundered by the Spanish in the 1500s. Inkuyo succeeds in capturing the mystery, majesty, and tragedy of this historical wonder. −LK

MARK ISHAM

Progressive electronic, chamber jazz. This multi-instrumentalist and composer, born in New York but now based in San Francisco, made his reputation early in the 70s while playing with progressive rock bands and jazz groups like Art Lande's Rubisa Patrol. He has performed or recorded with such artists as Van Morrison, Was (Not Was), and David Sylvian. His trumpet sound is reminiscent of Miles Davis with his use of a mute and his sparse phrasing, but his great talent as a composer lies in his ability to combine synthesizer and acoustic instruments into evocative music and he is in demand for film scores. Isham's stately and often dreamy music belies his classical training while inventively exploring the sonic possibilities of electronic instruments. −SWB

☆ **Vapor Drawings / WINDHAM HILL**   1983
Crystalline synthesizer textures form the perfect atmosphere for his melodic trumpet solos. His talent for blending electronic and acoustic sounds produces beautiful and organic music. This first album for the Windham Hill label cemented his reputation. The percussion is from his Group 87 bandmate Peter Van Hooke. −SWB

○ **Film Music / WINDHAM HILL**   1985
His scores for *Never Cry Wolf*, the Academy Award-winning documentary *The Times of Harvey Milk*, and the Mel Gibson/Diane Keaton film *Mrs. Soffel* showcase his musical depth and dreamy style. On the *Mrs. Soffel* score, Isham's blend of acoustic and synthesizer textures are haunting and deeply moving. −SWB

Castalia / VIRGIN   1988
More jazz-oriented music on this ensemble recording featuring Isham's muted trumpet over a dense and percussive backdrop from longtime Isham sidemen David Torn, Peter Maunu and Patrick O'Hearn, plus Paul McCandless, Terry Bozzio, and Mick Karn. The sweeping strings and classical guitar on "My Wife with Champagne Shoulders" and the evocative "A Dream of Three Acrobats" are highlights. −SWB

Mark Isham / ATLANTIC   1991
Isham continues his ensemble-style collaborations with guests Tanita Tikaram, Chick Corea, John Patitucci, and John Novello, and the contributions of sidemen David Torn, Peter Maunu, and Peter Van Hooke. Pleasing group work that provides a nice complement to the two vocal tracks. If you like these, try Isham's soundtrack recording for *Trouble in Mind* with Marianne Faithfull. −SWB

Songs My Children Taught Me / WINDHAM HILL 1991
Over 70 minutes of Isham's musical accompaniment to the Windham Hill children's story series minus the voice-over. Quite nice as background music. −SWB

JEAN MICHEL JARRE

Progressive electronic, adult alternative. Son of film composer Maurice Jarre, Jean Michel Jarre became France's most famous electronic musician in the 70s, when two of his finest albums, *Oxygene* and *Equinoxe*, were released. He has since had an interesting, if uneven, career. His later rock-oriented work seems a bit heavy on the testosterone as well as the ego, a development no doubt influenced by the impact of playing for hundreds of thousands of people in settings such as his giant outdoor concert in Houston during the mid 80s. −LK

☆ **Oxygene / NTI**   1976
This album conveys the excitement and freshness you'd expect from a talented young man embarking on a career in what was still a relatively unknown and unjaded electronic music scene. Sometimes innocent and introspective, other times ambitious and even a little spooky, this is a must for anyone interested in electronic music. −LK

Equinoxe / NTI   1978
Progressive, multilayered electronic music with glistening sequencer patterns, flowing melodies, and futuristic special effects that sound like you're blasting off into outer space. After all these years, most of it holds up. −LK

Zoolook / NTI   1984
Jarre went off in an unexpected and intriguing direction on this album. Taped voices in a number of languages are juiced up through electronic processing and then combined with synthesizers and live musicians. Guitarist Adrian Belew and vocal wizard Laurie Anderson add some interesting angles of their own. For adventurous listeners. −LK

Rendezvous / NTI   1988
Jarre explores more conventional rock ground, much of it already hoed by other artists. −LK

EDDIE JOBSON

Progressive electronic, adult alternative. This dynamic rock violinist has played with everyone from UK, Roxy Music, and Frank Zappa to Jethro Tull. Jobson's recordings as a leader showed much promise in their use of keyboards, computer-generated sounds, and wailing electric-violin solos. Too bad he hasn't released more of his own music. −LK

Zinc / CBS   1983
Jobson's solo debut is mostly instrumental, with a few vocals tracks −PK

○ **Theme of Secrets / PRIVATE MUSIC**   1985
A masterpiece of soundscapes created by using the Synclavier computer. A brilliant album from start to finish. −PK

MARNIE JONES

New-age, neo-classical. Jones came to a professional recording career late in life — after 15 years of working in the industrial design field. Though she had sung and played guitar as an avocation since childhood, Jones later taught herself to play the harp and began releasing albums of improvised music for that instrument. Her more recent recordings show a steady growth in her abilities as a performer and composer of tender, contemplative music that Jones herself says is great for meditation, relaxation, or massage. −LK

○ **Journeys / THRIVAL**   1988
Jones's harp music is enhanced by guest artists playing flute, clarinet, bells, percussion, synthesizers, and Indian drum. −LK

Golden Wave / THRIVAL   1989
Another album of tender ensemble settings. −LK

MICHAEL JONES

Solo instrumental, neo-classical. A native of Ontario, Canada, Jones studied classical piano and kept up his chops throughout his college courses in psychology. During seminars he conducted as part of his own business-management consulting practice, he began including interludes of piano improvisations. Finally, after years of encouragement from friends and clients, he released *Pianoscapes* in 1983. It was the first album ever released on the Narada record label. Over the years, Jones has recorded a number of solo piano and small-ensemble albums. Especially nice is his 1987 duo with cellist David Darling. −LK

Pianoscapes / NARADA   1985
His solo piano debut. −LK

Solstice / NARADA   1985
Seasonal piano pieces from two of Narada's best-selling artists, Michael Jones and David Lanz. −LK

○ **Amber / NARADA**   1987
Jones teams up with cellist David Darling for a delicate set of improvisational pieces. −LK

After the Rain / NARADA   1988
Impressionistic pieces in small ensemble settings. −LK

Magical Child / NARADA   1989

○ **Michael's Music / NARADA**   1990
A retrospective of Jones's subtle solo piano and ensemble pieces. –LK

PETER KATER

New-age. This German-born pianist and composer currently lives in rural Virginia. Since 1983, he has released over a dozen albums spanning solo piano music to contemporary jazz ensemble projects. Though some of his music comes from more predictable light-jazz molds, his finest work in recent years is featured on two inspired collaborations with Native American flutist R. Carlos Nakai. –LK

Spirit / OPTIMISM   1983
This is Kater's 1983 debut. –LK

The Fool & the Hummingbird / SILVER WAVE   1987
Gateway / SILVER WAVE   1988
Moments, Dreams & Visions / SILVER WAVE   1989
Natives / SILVER WAVE   1990
Kater and R. Carlos Nakai's first collaboration got excellent reviews for good reason. –LK

○ **Collection 1983-1990 / SILVER WAVE**   1991
A summation of Kater's varied style taken from his numerous albums as a leader. –LK

Rooftops / SILVER WAVE   1991
○ **Migration / SILVER WAVE**   1992
A quiet, thoughtful album inspired by a desire to "create and experience ritual in one's life." Contemporary melodies coalesce with subtle Native American themes and liturgical-style wordless choral passages. R. Carlos Nakai chants and plays flutes and eagle-bone whistles, trading lines with Kater's piano and synthesizers. Guest artists include cellist David Darling and saxophonists Mark Miller and Bob Read. –LK

BRIAN KEANE

Progressive electronic, ethnic fusion. This virtuoso guitarist and sought-after producer has performed with some of the biggest names in jazz, including Bobby McFerrin, Larry Coryell, and Paco de Lucia. In addition to his own contemporary jazz albums, Keane is an accomplished composer and arranger who has written soundtracks for award-winning films. His score to the documentary *Suleyman the Magnificent* caught the ear of Celestial Harmonies owner Eckart Rahn, who eventually released the soundtrack. The label has since commissioned several other albums of Middle East-inspired instrumentals from Keane, with Turkish multi-instrumentalist Omar Faruk Tekbilek. These exotic recordings are among Keane's finest work. –LK

Suleyman ... / CELESTIAL HARM.   1988
Suleyman the Magnificent, Keane's imaginative soundtrack to the documentary and traveling art exhibit on the Ottoman Empire, also features Tekbilek and several other Middle Eastern musical experts. –LK

○ **Fire Dance / CELESTIAL HARMONIES**   1990
This masterful collection of music mixes traditional Turkish, Egyptian, and North African folk melodies and dances with synthesized atmospheres that sound like hot desert winds blowing over the Sahara. An artful union of Eastern and Western sensibilities, with Omar Faruk Tekbilek. –LK

Beyond the Sky / CELESTIAL HARMONIES   1992
This latest Middle Eastern venture by Brian Keane and Omar Faruk Tekbilek is a continuation of their previous work for Celestial Harmonies. –LK

GEORGIA KELLY

Solo instrumental, new-age, neo-classical. Kelly was a major force in popularizing the harp in contemporary instrumental music. Years before American audiences had even heard of Andreas Vollenweider, this West Coast musician was gaining considerable attention for her albums of solo harp performances, which she initially released through her own recording and distribution company. The relaxing and inspirational qualities of her music attracted the attention of hospitals, cancer clinics, and drug-abuse programs, which regularly used her recordings for therapeutic purposes. A sensitive and skillful musician, Kelly has made several noteworthy recordings for Global Pacific, some of which being highly recommended collaborations with other artists. –LK

☆ **Seapeace / GLOBAL PACIFIC**
Originally released in the 70s, Kelly's influential recording of solo harp music is now considered a classic in the CI and new-age realms. –LK

Harp and Soul / GLOBAL PACIFIC   1983
Kelly mixes her own originals with arrangements of Barbra Streisand's "Evergreen" and "Trois Gymnopèdies" by Satie. Wind player Richard Hardy joins the her on several cuts. –LK

Fresh Impressions / GLOBAL PACIFIC   1987
This set of classical duos with violinist Steven Kindler offers arrangements of some of the most famous impressionist pieces by Gabriel Fauré, Erik Satie, and Claude Debussy, plus two originals in the French style by Kelly and Kindler. –LK

○ **A Journey Home / GLOBAL PACIFIC**   1989
This elegant, heartfelt collaboration with Yugoslavian guitarist Dusan Bogdanovich was inspired by Kelly's quest to connect with her own Yugoslavian roots. Traditional folk songs from the region come to life in contemporary arrangements. Sprinkled between are original compositions inspired by the beauty and spirit of the duo's shared heritage. –LK

AL GROMER KHAN

Ambient, ethnic fusion. German composer Alois Gromer decided to dedicate himself to playing the sitar after he attended a 1969 recital in London given by Indian classical-music master Vilayat Khan. During a 1975 ceremony conducted by respected teacher Imrat Khan, Gromer became the first European to be inducted into the legendary Khan dynasty of sitar players, which dates back to Moghul India. Adding the Khan surname to his professional identity, he created a number of albums that skillfully combined his adopted Eastern heritage with his Western classical birthright. –LK

Divan I Khas / BEYOND
Khan's pop instrumentals with Middle Eastern and Indian influences are interesting, but not entirely successful. –LK

Mahogany Nights / HEARTS OF SPACE   1990
This album of "night music" is a collection of exotic, highly atmospheric soundscapes with subdued sitar occasionally wafting out of Khan's lush synthesizer tapestries like a fine incense. Although the composer's sitar talents are better represented on other albums, this is a good, all-around introduction to his style, especially for those who normally shy away from Indian music. –LK

BOB KINDLER

Chamber jazz, ethnic fusion, neo-classical. This classically trained cellist performed with the Honolulu Symphony for 14 years, played jazz with Dave Brubeck's son Darius, and formed a guild that organized cross-cultural events involving dancers, poets, artists, and musicians from around the world. All of these influences and experiences are apparent in his contemporary instrumental albums, which are eclectic to say the least. –LK

Waters of Life / GLOBAL PACIFIC
Complete title is *Waters of Life - Music from the Matrix III.* –ED

○ **Tiger's Paw / GLOBAL PACIFIC**   1990
An exceptional album of contemporary, ethnic-inspired instrumentals. In addition to cello, autoharp, and flutes, the album features an extended range of tablas (an Indian drum) used in creative settings. –LK

STEVE KINDLER

Chamber jazz, ethnic fusion, neo-classical. Like his brother Bob, violinist Steve Kindler played in the Honolulu Symphony, but he cut his jazz chops as a member of John McLaughlin's fusion band, Mahavishnu Orchestra. Kindler has also toured and recorded with Jan Hammer, Jeff Beck, and Kitaro. Kindler's smooth yet impassioned violin improvisations are the perfect vehicle for his own highly melodic compositions, combining classical, jazz, rock, and ethnic influences. In addition, Kindler is a member of Barefoot, a co-op world-music dance group. –LK

Across a Rainbow Sea / GLOBAL PACIFIC
Kindler's melodic gifts are topped off by some sophisticated keyboard work and lively Latin grooves. –LK

○ **Dolphin Smiles / GLOBAL PACIFIC**   1987
A series of duets with synthesist Teja Bell, featuring lush, fluid textures and flowing melodies. –LK

BEN TAVERA KING

Ethnic fusion, chamber jazz. A Texas-born master of the nylon-string guitar, King likes to call his music "Southwestern Hispanic jazz." Not only does he combine flamenco with jazz and Native American styles, he throws in influences from Mexico and the Caribbean as well. Acknowledged as a leader in the renaissance of Hispanic music, King has been the subject of a PBS television special and has performed at Lincoln Center. –LK

Desert Dreams / GLOBAL PACIFIC   1984
Though not as well produced as *Coyote Moon*, King's debut for Global Pacific is a gem, with lively, more straightforward pieces for guitar, sax, bass, and percussion. –LK

○ **Coyote Moon / GLOBAL PACIFIC**   1990
An infectious mix of impassioned flamenco guitar stylings with all kinds of Hispanic references — everything from Tex-Mex grooves to mariachi rhythms with a jazz twist. –LK

KITARO

New-age, progressive electronic, ethnic fusion. Kitaro's style is the epitome of the contemplative, highly melodic synthesizer music often associated with the new-age movement. Interestingly enough, this famous Japanese composer taught himself to play electric guitar in high school — inspired by the R&B music of Otis Redding. In the early 70s, Kitaro formed the Far East Family Band, which released two albums of progressive rock. In 1972, however, he met the innovative German synthesist Klaus Schulze during a trip to Europe. Kitaro was hooked. He built his first synthesizer and began experimenting with all kinds of unusual sounds. His first solo album, *Astral Voyage*, appeared in 1978 and quickly gained a cult following. Two years later, he produced the first of several soundtracks for "Silk Road," a Japanese television documentary series that ran for five years. Several albums of music from "Silk Road" were released to a growing international contingent of fans who admired his combination of lush, majestic textures and gentle, almost naive, melodies. Kitaro, however, was still considered an underground artist in America until he signed with Geffen Records in 1986, which re-released seven of his earlier albums and gave him the support to expand his scope in many ways. For instance, after years of creating albums in the privacy of his home studio near Japan's Mt. Fuji, Kitaro produced his 1987 release, *The Light of the Spirit*, with the help of Mickey Hart. The album featured an array of American musicians and was nominated for a Grammy Award in the Best New-Age Performance category. That same year, Kitaro also made his first live tour of North America and sold two million albums in the US alone. Kitaro's style had changed as well, becoming more theatrical and assertive while retaining a certain level of innocence and purity. His more recent recordings also show a renewed interest in the rock and pop elements that originally attracted him to music in the late 60s. –LK

My Best / GRAMAVISION   1986
Kitaro's synthesizer-based compositions are extended aural landscapes full of dramatic peaks of intensity and valleys of emotional calm. He is fond of loud, tympani-like drums, sweeps of sound that approximate electronic winds, and

majestic melodies played in singing, upper-register tones. And his music is quite consistent. If you like this, you'll probably like every record he's made. –WR

☆ **Silk Road I & II / CELESTIAL HARMONIES**   1986
Kitaro's masterwork remains this two-record score for a Japanese TV series. His most ambitious themes and involved playing are found here. –WR

The Light of the Spirit / GEFFEN   1987
With the help of Grateful Dead drummer Mickey Hart, Kitaro made this album using American musicians, which gives it slightly more of an ensemble feeling than his usual one-man productions. –WR

Live in America / GEFFEN   1991
Kitaro's already dramatic music is given even greater force when played before a live audience, as this 1990 show from Atlanta's Fox Theatre demonstrates. –WR

GARY LAMB

Solo instrumental, adult alternative. Lamb's music is exemplary of his early musical interests. The Northern California native grew up listening to R&B and was playing drums in Bay Area rock bands before the age of 20. Along the way, he dabbled in piano and actually took some time off from the club scene to concentrate on building his chops on that instrument. He recorded a couple of solo piano albums in the mid 80s, eventually adding electronic keyboards to the mix on his 1989 release *Watching the Night Fall*, his first album to get national radio airplay. His subsequent recordings mix his love of catchy, generally cheerful, pop melodies with his penchant for rock & roll backbeats. –LK

Walk in the Garden / GOGA   1987
An early album of piano vignettes. –LK

Watching the Night Fall / GOGA   1989
Lamb's first blend of acoustic piano with synthesizers and percussion was inspired by California's Big Sur coastline. –LK

○ **Distant Fields / GOGA**   1990
Lamb's all-electronic album retains the sounds of acoustic piano and percussion through the use of sophisticated sampling programs. Though he expands his palette with a few unusual tone colors here and there, the sounds remain fairly conventional. Generally, these are lively tunes with a subtle use of backbeats. –LK

DAVID LANZ

Solo instrumental, adult alternative. One of the most popular artists in the solo instrumental and adult-alternative spheres, Lanz played in several rock bands during his teens, then began developing his style as a solo pianist in a small Seattle nightclub. He introduced some of his originals into the bar's required mix of standards and pop tunes, receiving such a positive response from patrons that, before long, he was playing his own material almost exclusively. His early albums of solo piano works are still among the Narada label's best-sellers. His two collaborative efforts with guitarist Paul Speer also hit the *Billboard* Top 200 Albums chart; yet as Lanz's national popularity grew, he began to experiment with works for larger and larger ensembles, culminating in full orchestral accompaniments on *Skyline Firedance* (1990). His most recent album is a refreshing return to his solo piano roots. –LK

☆ **Cristofori's Dream / NARADA**   1988
Among the most popular new-age recordings ever made, this is an album of instrumental piano music (with other instruments, especially strings and string-like synthesizers, added). Its selections have a calm elegance, as Lanz spends most of his time in the upper register of the piano, delivering precise, articulated melodies, culminating in a recreation of Procol Harum's "A Whiter Shade of Pale" that features original organist Matthew Fisher. –WR

Skyline Firedance / NARADA   1990
On his popular followup to *Cristofori's Dream*, Lanz turns in two discs of the same music, one scored for orchestra and the

other played solo on the piano. The alternate approaches to the music bring out Lanz's talents as a composer. –WR

○ **Return to the Heart / NARADA**   1991
Return to the Heart is a return to Lanz's roots as a solo pianist, yet his new compositions for this medium show a remarkable sense of maturity, elegance, and taste. –LK

LARAAJI

Ambient, progressive electronic, ethnic fusion. This multi-instrumentalist creates shimmering, meditative tapestries using electronically enhanced zither, autoharp, and other acoustic instruments. He was first brought to wider audiences through his association with Brian Eno. –LK

○ **Day of Radiance / CAROLINE**   1980
An enchanting recording divided into two moods. The first part is buoyant with folk-like jigs that move toward a more hazy zither-in-space sound exemplary of Eno, who produced this album as part of his *Ambient* series. –LK

MAX LASSER

Adult alternative, ethnic fusion, chamber jazz. The Swiss guitarist was best known for his association with boyhood chum Andreas Vollenweider. Lasser's tours and recordings with the harpist culminated in Vollenweider's Grammy-winning album *Down to the Moon.* A year later, the guitarist formed Max Lasser's Ark and made several colorful, versatile albums. –LK

○ **Earthwalk / COLUMBIA**   1988
Max Lasser's Ark combines a wide variety of influences on this release — everything from classical, jazz, and folk to touches of ethnic styles. A thoroughly enjoyable romp though a variety of moods and textures. –LK

Timejump / SONA GAIA   1990
Lasser's release on the Sona Gaia label is slickly produced with some intriguing approaches to the guitar, from sparkling classical miniatures and powerful electric solos to Indian raga-style melodies played on slide guitar, among other things. The album also features Lasser's abilities on keyboards. –LK

ADRIAN LEGG

Solo instrumental, chamber jazz, new-acoustic. An acoustic guitarist from England, Adrian has played in many country-based bands. His current work showcases his solo acoustic guitar playing. –PK

Technopicker / SPINDRIFT   1983
Debut from this acoustic guitarist. If you enjoy great guitarists, do yourself a favor and check this album out. –PK

Fretmelt / SPINDRIFT   1985
This release features Legg with a small group. Brilliant, with Legg sounding like three guitarists playing at once! –PK

Lost for Words / MAKING WAVES   1986
This album from the British acoustic guitar wizard features jaw-dropping playing. –PK

○ **Guitars & Other Cathedrals / RELATIVITY**   1988
Using an acoustic guitar modified with banjo tuners, Legg takes his guitar where no one has gone before. Essential listening. –PK

ANDREAS LEIFELD

Progressive electronic, adult alternative, ethnic fusion. This brilliant, yet little-known, German artist has a flair for combining refined ambiences with driving funk bass lines and rock beats. His well-constructed melodies and improvisations are often quite catchy, while his song titles and symbolic sonic imagery are lined with social commentary. Classically trained, Leifeld makes a living as a music teacher in Paderborn, Germany, and his modest apartment is overrun with all manner of electronic gadgetry. He is truly a living, breathing example of the cyberpunk mentality — you get the feeling he would gladly leave earthly concerns behind if he

could download the essence of his mind, body, and soul onto a hard disk. –LK

Mysterious Messages / MUSIQUE INTEMPORELLE
1990
Though not as polished as *Discoveries*, this album is another fine example of Leifeld's style. Most of the pieces are upbeat with ethereal underpinnings and some disco grooves. On "Tokio" he also hints at the Japanese mentality of technological supremacy by mutating oriental melodies through heavy-handed electronics. –LK

○ **Discoveries / MUSIQUE INTEMPORELLE**   1991
Futuristic in conception and execution, this album still harkens back to the sequencer-driven sound of the German electronic school. Yet unlike Tangerine Dream, Leifeld has managed to add rock and pop influences without losing his progressive edge. His two-part suite "African Dreams" delves into the techno-tribal realm. He also adds some amusing political cynicism on the final selection, "Same Old Game," by layering recorded voice fragments of George Bush's most banal catchphrases over combat sounds and a brooding, almost sinister electronic score. –LK

OTTMAR LIEBERT

Ethnic fusion, adult alternative. Liebert has said that "flamenco is a music both romantic and dangerous; it is an attitude as much as it is a musical genre." Therein lies the philosophy that catapulted him to fame at the end of the 80s with an engaging mix of subdued flamenco guitar and South American percussion, rock, jazz, and pop influences. Liebert's "attitude" actually suppresses the more challenging and "dangerous" aspects of flamenco in favor of the romantic — and the stylish. He's not a technical wizard on the guitar, but he has a feel for the music's innate sensuality and a gift for creating memorable melodies.

Born in Cologne, Germany, to a Chinese-German father and a Hungarian mother, Liebert traveled throughout Russia and Asia before moving to Boston and eventually settling in Santa Fe, NM. After years of trying to hit the big time in various jazz-funk bands, he began playing acoustic guitar in Santa Fe restaurants. His first (self-produced) cassette, *Nouveau Flamenco*, was basically recorded for friends, but the album received heavy radio airplay on WAVE in Los Angeles. Higher Octave Records re-released it nationally in 1990. After his subsequent album *Borrasca* quickly climbed the charts, Liebert was picked up by a major label, Epic. With his exotic good looks and enigmatic stage presence, Liebert has brought flamenco to mainstream America with a certain level of class and accessibility. His prowess as a composer and instrumentalist has steadily improved over the years. –LK

Nouveau Flamenco / HIGHER OCTAVE   1990
Originally released in 1988, this independently produced album went on to top *Billboard*'s new-age chart and sell a half-million copies. The music, however, lacks the craftsmanship of later releases. In fact, almost all of the short selections end in mediocre fadeouts. –LK

Borrasca / HIGHER OCTAVE   1991
This is another nicely produced, flamenco-influenced chart-climber. –LK

○ **Solo Para Ti / EPIC**   1992
Liebert's first recording for Epic is his finest effort to date. Along with his group Luna Negra (bassist Jon Gagan and percussionist Dave Bryant), the album also features a guest appearance by rock guitarist Carlos Santana on a couple of cuts and some subtle vocals by Santa Fe artist Joe Bradley. A few of Liebert's originals also add strings, horns, and piano, although acoustic guitar remains the prominent voice throughout. –LK

LIGHTWAVE

Progressive electronic, ambient. A leading French electronic band, Lightwave creates extended works that can best be described as "sonic architecture" in their use of slowly unfolding blocks of synthesized sound and sensation. –LK

○ **Nachtmusik / ERDENKLANG**   1990
After releasing four independently produced cassettes
through the European underground, Lightwave has released
its first CD on the pioneering German electronic label
Erdenklang. The title, translated as "night music," is the
perfect description of the dark, delightfully ambiguous
compositions. –LK

JOAQUIN LLEVANO

Adult alternative. Llevano gained early recognition for his
work with jazz violinist Jean-Luc Ponty before starting his
own recording career with Global Pacific. –LK

○ **One Mind / GLOBAL PACIFIC**   1987
Llevano's debut as a leader is a combination of new-age, jazz,
and rock styles. Includes A. West on bass. –PK

RAY LYNCH

Adult alternative, new-age, neo-classical. Though he's one of the
most influential artists in "new-age pop" and adult-alternative
circles, Lynch has extensive formal music training. Inspired
by Andres Segovia's classical guitar recordings, Lynch studied
the instrument in Barcelona, Spain, in the early 60s. He later
attended the University of Texas as a composition student.
Toward the end of the decade, Lynch moved to New York and
became a fixture in the city's "early music" scene as a lutenist
with the Renaissance Quartet. A period of personal and
spiritual crisis, however, led him to retreat from his career in
conventional classical music. He moved to California, spent
some time investigating various spiritual traditions and
philosophies, and started experimenting with electronic
music. His 1983 debut album, *The Sky of Mind*, artfully
meshed his early classical music leanings with spatial,
synthesized orchestrations and became an underground
success with virtually no promotional support. Two years
later, he released his most famous album, *Deep Breakfast*.
While much of the album continued in a neoclassical vein
(with some lyrical duets for viola and keyboards, among other
things), Lynch's catchy tune, "Celestial Soda Pop," became a
hit in the newly emerging WAVE radio formats. The album
was one of the first new-age releases to sell over 500,000
copies. While Lynch's later albums have their moments, his
increasingly pop-oriented style seems to have lost the
expressive intensity of his earlier work. Still, growing numbers
of listeners seem attracted to his vibrant electronic textures
and heartrending melodies. –LK

☆ **Deep Breakfast / RAY LYNCH PROD.**   1986
Ray Lynch's synthesizer playing sometimes approximates
keyboard instruments and sometimes sounds like
individually plucked strings on electrified string instruments,
but always has a deeply textured melodic structure and a
buoyant rhythmic underpinning. Isolated notes in series and
patterns make a pointillistic mosaic of sound that alternately
soothes and stimulates. No wonder this is one of the best-
selling new-age albums of all time. –WR
Music of Ray Lynch / RAY LYNCH PROD.
A boxed set. –LK

MANNHEIM STEAMROLLER

Adult alternative, neo-classical, progressive electronic. This
Omaha-based group has sold a lot of albums over the years
with its high production standards and accessible pop
orchestral sound. Best known for their extensive *Fresh Aire*
series of albums, the members of Mannheim Steamroller mix
a certain level of classical inspiration with piano, synthesizers,
guitar, bass, drums, and sometimes full symphony orchestra.
The resulting music is sometimes fascinating, yet often no
better than muzak on amphetamines. In fact, it's extremely
difficult to recommend one album over the next: they all offer
a few arresting moments next to forgettable music that, at its
worst, can be downright embarrassing. (Some of the albums
are even accompanied by pretentious liner notes analyzing the

music's form and inspiration, yet the compositions inside
don't begin to live up to these classical references.) –LK

Fresh Aire 1 / AMERICAN GRAMAPHONE   1975
The first in composer Chip Davis's ongoing series of
instrumental new-age albums is, as the album cover says, "a
collection of original music set in a hybrid musical style,
combining the long-lived forms of the classics, performed on
both old-world and contemporary instruments," to which we
might add that Davis also mixes in the sounds of nature,
especially rain, on an album meant to evoke spring. –WR

Fresh Aire 2 / AMERICAN GRAMAPHONE   1977
Davis's "fall" collection is also a recasting of madrigal and
Renaissance musical styles — harpsichord and flute sounds
in stately cadences. With typical eclecticism he mixes in
drums and rhythms that would not be out of place on a rock
stage. –WR

Fresh Aire 3 / AMERICAN GRAMAPHONE   1979
The "summer" album is dominated by a version of a 16th-
century toccata, played rapidly and evoking the energy and
life of the season. –WR

Fresh Aire 4 / AMERICAN GRAMAPHONE   1981
Bach is the touchstone for this 18th-century tribute that
constitutes the "winter" selection in the *Fresh Aire* series,
appropriately filled with organ-like sounds. –WR

○ **Fresh Aire 5 / AMERICAN GRAMAPHONE**   1983
Accompanied by the London Symphony and the Cambridge
Singers, Mannheim Steamroller journeys back in time to
1609, then takes off for the moon. It's all a dream, but makes
for some of the liveliest music of the series. –WR

Fresh Aire 6 / AMERICAN GRAMAPHONE   1986
Siren-like sounds and stately melodies dominate on an album
whose theme is "impressions of Greek mythology." –WR

Classical Gas / AMERICAN GRAMAPHONE   1987
Guitarist Mason Williams teams up with the Steamroller for
an orchestrated, synthesized version of his 1968 instrumental
hit, plus more in the same vein. –WR

MICHAEL MANRING

Chamber jazz, adult alternative. Inspired by his teacher Jaco
Pastorius, Manring has taken the electric bass into new
territory. A native of the Washington, DC, area, he played
classical bass in high school chamber groups and orchestra
while also working in local Top 40 bands. From 1979 to 1982,
he honed his chops in the DC fusion group Natural Bridge and
also started performing with guitarist Michael Hedges.
Manring played on Hedges's Windham Hill debut *Breakfast in
the Fields*. Since then, the bassist has become *the* Windham
Hill session man, recording on albums by Will Ackerman, Ira
Stein, and Russel Walder in addition to his frequent tours with
Hedges. Manring is a also a key member in the label's all-star
band, Montreux. –LK

Unusual Weather / WINDHAM HILL   1986
Manring's debut as a leader is a striking combination of
ethereal atmospheres and stormy solos. –LK

Toward the Center of the Night / WINDHAM HILL 1989
Another finely crafted bass exploration. –LK

○ **Drastic Measures / WINDHAM HILL**   1991
Manring takes drastic measures in his continuing crusade to
push the bass out of the rhythm section and into the spotlight.
Lyrical solos, bass overdubs, some virtuosic arpeggios, and
breathless passage work illuminate ensemble-oriented
originals as well as updated versions of Jimi Hendrix's "Purple
Haze" and Chick Corea's "500 Miles High." –LK

JON MARK

Ambient, progressive electronic. A top English session musician
in the 60s, Mark played with everyone from the Rolling Stones
and Marianne Faithfull to blues sensation John Mayall. As the
decade came to a close, the vocalist, composer, and guitarist
began exploring the potential of jazz/rock fusion as coleader
of the highly influential Mark-Almond Band. After the group

dispersed in the late 70s, Mark moved to New Zealand, where he has so far produced two albums of impressionistic synthesizer pieces. –LK

○ **Standing Stones ... / CELEST. HARM.**   1988
Standing Stones of Callanish, Mark's tribute to his Celtic roots, is a set of elegant synthesizer sketches that capture the mystery and the simple beauty of the British Isles. –LK

Land of Merlin / CELESTIAL HARMONIES   1992
Mark's most recent album is almost a seamless continuation of the softly melodic synthesizer style he established on *Standing Stones*. *Land of Merlin* was inspired by Mark's childhood experiences traveling through the enchanted landscapes of Cornwall, the legendary birthplace of King Arthur and home to his fabled Knights of the Round Table. –LK

GERALD JAY MARKOE

New-age, ambient. Since the early 60s, this composer and astrologer has been fascinated by the relationships among music, meditation, sacred geometry, and spiritual teachings. Boasting Bachelor and Masters degrees from Juilliard and the Manhattan School of Music, respectively, Markoe has also received ASCAP awards for his scores to theatrical productions. Though he's obviously a knowledgeable musician, his potential as an electronic composer is inhibited by his blatantly new-age ideas. –LK

○ **Music from the Pleiades / ASTRO MUSIC**   1989
Eleven synthesizer pieces designed to create the sensation of an otherworldly voyage to the Pleiades, a star cluster in the constellation of Taurus often cited as the origin of extraterrestrial visitors to Earth. Markoe recorded the album in a studio filled with crystals, which he says gives the music a very special vibration. One reviewer called *Music from the Pleiades* "a good tape for out-of-body projection." However, the spacey, orchestra-inspired compositions themselves don't necessarily stand up to concentrated listening. –LK

Sacred Music from Seven Stars / ASTRO MUSIC   1991
This album is more on the neo-classical side, with thick layers of synthesized sound suggesting celestial orchestras. –LK

JUAN MARTIN

Neo-classical. Classical guitarist. –ED

○ **Painter in Sound / NOVUS**   1986
Light and tranquil, this is Spanish-flavored classical guitar with synthesizer and trumpet support from Mark Isham. Each piece is meant as a companion to a famous painting. –SWB

PETER MAUNU

Adult alternative, progressive electronic. Though he's not publicly well known, this veteran guitarist is highly respected in the inner music circles of Los Angeles for session work ranging from Claus Ogerman, Jean-Luc Ponty, and Mark Isham to Bobby McFerrin, the Commodores, and the Pointer Sisters. Together with Isham and Patrick O'Hearn, Maunu performed in the short-lived but still-talked-about Group 87, an early 80s progressive band. Maunu's single release as a leader is one of the finest albums on the Narada label. –LK

○ **Warm Sound in a Gray Field / MCA**
An exceptional album of electronically based ensemble music. From atmospheric country-blues numbers to inventive reworkings of Gregorian chants and Sufi whirling-dervish influences, Maunu's music is filled with well-designed synthetic textures, compelling melodies and absorbing solos. Guest appearances by O'Hearn and Isham also give the album a Group 87 reunion feel. –LK

PAUL MCCANDLESS

Neo-classical, ethnic fusion, chamber jazz. McCandless was a finalist in the 1971 English-horn auditions for the New York Philharmonic. Lucky for the rest of us, he didn't get the job. As a member of the Paul Winter Consort for three years in the early 70s, McCandless played on five of the group's finest albums. Since 1970, he has also been a member of the

innovative chamber-jazz ensemble Oregon, one of the first and finest groups to blur the boundaries between classical, jazz, and ethnic influences. Over the years, this versatile woodwind player has appeared on albums by everyone from Pat Metheny, Mark Isham, and Carla Bley to Jaco Pastorius, Eberhard Weber, and Wynton and Branford Marsalis. –LK

○ **Heresay / WINDHAM HILL**   1988
McCandless's first album as a leader for Windham Hill is an impressive summation of his style to date. Essentially contemporary chamber music with jazz improvisation and world influences, his elegant instrumental arrangements leave plenty of room for the woodwind player to show off his soaring, lyrical solos. –LK

WIM MERTENS

Neo-classical, minimalist, progressive electronic. This Belgian composer is not well known among US audiences, although he has made several highly regarded appearances at the New Music America festivals. In Spain, however, where he was the subject of a major television special, he is a new-music celebrity. Mertens's style employs mesmerizing minimalist techniques with a sense of the romantic that appeals to both serious music aficionados and more mainstream listeners. The keyboardist uses a certain amount of electronics along with some acoustic instruments like violin, flute, and saxophone. –LK

○ **Close Cover / WINDHAM HILL**
Compiled from Mertens's solo and group projects recorded during the early to mid 80s, this Windham Hill collection offers an overview of his textural, multilayered style of minimalist composition. –LK

METAMORA

New acoustic, ethnic fusion, chamber jazz. This trio excels at instrumentals that combine traditional Northern European folksongs, jigs, hornpipes, and reels with modern improvisational techniques. Malcolm Dalglish, Grey Larsen, and Pete Sutherland are all multi-instrumentalists who tackle a virtual bandstand of acoustic and electric sounds. All of their albums provide fresh perspectives on folk music played with grace, humor, and a sense of adventure. –LK

○ **Morning Walk / WINDHAM HILL**
Though it's difficult to choose among the group's albums based on musical reasons, this Windham Hill release holds the highest production standards. –LK

STEPHAN MICUS

Neo-classical, ethnic fusion. This respected German composer and multi-instrumentalist made his first journey to the Orient at the age of 16. He has since traveled around the world. He spent extensive periods of time studying ancient musical techniques in India and Japan and collected a number of ethnic instruments previously unknown in the West. His recordings for the ECM label are essentially solo efforts in which the illusion of an ensemble is created by the composer's extensive overdubs. Micus's intention is not to play these instruments according to tradition, but to combine modes of expression from around the world in exciting new ways. Though he sometimes creates sounds you'd swear were the result of electronic keyboards, Micus is an acoustic purist who often develops unconventional performance techniques on ethnic instruments. –LK

○ **Implosions / ECM**   1977
These pieces for various ethnic instruments are all played by Micus. –MPD

Wings over Water / ECM   1982
He even coaxes beautiful music from ordinary items like tuned flowerpots! –MPD

Ocean / ECM   1986
A four-part suite, similar to *Implosions* but recorded nine years later. –MPD

Darkness & Light / ECM   1986
This features his latest find, an elongated wind instrument from Russia. –MPD

East of the Night / POLYGRAM   1986
Two long fantasias for guitars and Japanese flutes. –MPD

Twilight Fields / POLYGRAM   1987
Like all of his albums, this one is haunting and serene. –MPD

Music of Stones / ECM   1989
Micus is joined by three other musicians playing sculpted, resonant stone blocks. –MPD

RADHIKA MILLER

Neo-classical, ethnic fusion. Though she studied classical piano as a child, Miller took up the flute in college after reading some passages about the instrument in a yoga book. It turned out to be more than a whim. By the end of her first year, she was studying in France with famed classical virtuoso Jean-Pierre Rampal. Three years later, Miller graduated from San Francisco State University with a degree in music. Inspired by her love of sacred vocal music, she developed a style she calls "the singing flute."

Over the years, Miller has arranged and transcribed sacred classical scores, choral works, and spirituals for her own performances, involving flute, harp, piano, and cello to create prayerful, uplifting works. In 1983 she launched the independent record label Radhika Miller Music (RRM) and has since released over a half-dozen high-quality albums that include soulful interpretations of Gregorian chant, Palestrina, Bach, Debussy, Telemann, Vaughan Williams, American spirituals, and Irish folk music in addition to her own compositions and improvisations. –LK

○ **Gems of Grace / RRM**
Though all of Miller's recordings could be considered gems, this collection of lullaby-like serenades is particularly satisfying in conception and execution. It helps that she has some top-notch musicians with her: cellist David Darling, pianist Allaudin Mathieu, harpist Michelle Sell, and French horn player Alicia Telford. –LK

MODERN MANDOLIN QUARTET

Neo-classical. This ensemble was formed in the mid 80s as the brainchild of Mike Marshall, an internationally acclaimed mandolin player best known for his work with David Grisman and Montreux. Marshall was looking for a way to bring respectability to an instrument primarily known for bluegrass and quaint folk tunes. Toward this end, he established a string-quartet-style group featuring the extended family of mandolin instruments. Marshall and Dana Rath play standard mandolins (which take the place of violins), John Imholz plays mandocello (with a range similar to the cello), and Paul Binkley holds up the middle with his mandola (the alto counterpart to the viola). Together they interpret well-known classical works and premiere newly commissioned compositions of "serious mandolin music." –LK

Modern Mandolin Quartet / WINDHAM HILL   1988
A fine debut for Windham Hill, yet not quite as sophisticated as *Intermezzo*. –LK

○ **Intermezzo / WINDHAM HILL**   1990
Selections by Haydn, Ravel, Debussy, Copland, Brahms, and Shostakovich take on new levels of scintillating intensity and charm at the hands of the Modern Mandolin Quartet. –LK

MONTREUX

New-acoustic, chamber jazz. This Windham Hill "all-star" band features Mike Marshall, Darol Anger, Barbara Higbie, and Michael Manring. All of the musicians involved come from eclectic musical backgrounds. Their work in this band mixes folk, bluegrass, and new acoustic elements with more subtle traces of jazz improvisation. –LK

○ **Sign Language / WINDHAM HILL**   1987
Montreux's debut adds selected percussion and some vocal harmonies to an uplifting, shape-shifting conglomeration of acoustic-oriented styles. –LK

Let Them Say / WINDHAM HILL   1989
The quartet expands to quintet with drummer Tom Miller. –LK

R. CARLOS NAKAI

Neo-classical, ethnic fusion, chamber jazz. Tucson-based multi-instrumentalist R. Carlos Nakai is a Native American musician and cultural anthropologist of Navajo-Ute descent. Though he received classical training on the trumpet, his numerous recordings consist primarily of resonant solo performances of Native American flute improvisations with a judicious use of synthesizers, chanting, and nature sounds. Nakai only occasionally features arrangements of traditional melodies from various tribes; instead, he is primarily concerned with creating original compositions that capture the essence of his heritage in highly personalized ways. In addition to his solo recordings, Nakai has had the opportunity to create new avenues of expression for the Native American flute through collaborations with various artists over the years, including the ethnic jazz band Jackalope, keyboardist Peter Kater, contemporary classical composer James DeMars, and multi-instrumentalist William Eaton. –LK

○ **Earth Spirit / CANYON**   1987
At times criticized for modernizing the spirit of Native Americans, Nakai crystallizes these melodies and rhythms into an accessible and enjoyable palette of wonderful meditational music. All his work is very worthwhile, but this is his best. He plays North American flute and is an expert visual artist as well. Go see him if he's in town! –MGN

Sundance Season / CELESTIAL HARMONIES   1987
Native American themes combined with contemporary and classical motifs. Nakai's use of Tibetan bells is intriguing. –MGN

NIGHTNOISE

Neo-classical, ethnic fusion, chamber jazz. The brainchild of American violinist Billy Oskay and Irish guitarist Michael O'Domhnill, Nightnoise has evolved from a studio-oriented duo to a high-energy performing band. The music has been described as "classical Celtic pop" and "Irish-flavored, jazzy chamber music." Whatever you call it, the band's style is infectious, fun, and technically impressive. –LK

At the End of the Evening / WINDHAM HILL   1988
Something of Time / WINDHAM HILL   1989
○ **The Parting Tide / WINDHAM HILL**   1990
The band's most sophisticated album to date uses computer-triggered synthesizers to expand the palette of colors beyond the already impressive acoustic talents of the quartet. The album also includes originals by O Domhnill's sister, Triona, whose abilities on keyboards, whistle, and accordion are second only to her expressive vocals. –LK

PATRICK O'HEARN

Progressive electronic, adult alternative. In the early 80s, this bassist and synthesist was mired in the glitz and grind of pop music as a member of the group Missing Persons. Then friend Peter Baumann, best known for his work with Tangerine Dream, made O'Hearn an offer he couldn't refuse. Baumann had visions of starting a record label catering to his first love, contemporary electronic music, and he wanted O'Hearn to become a charter member of the new company. Nearly a decade and a half-dozen albums later, O'Hearn is still amazed at the success of *Ancient Dreams*, the richly hued debut release that established his career as a solo artist and helped launch the Private Music label.

Born in Los Angeles and raised in Oregon, O'Hearn was exposed to a wide variety of music by his parents, who were both working musicians. Though he studied cello, violin, and flute, he gained early experience playing bass with his parents' lounge act. As his musicianship began to excel, he found himself accompanying jazz greats like Joe Henderson, Joe Pass, Tony Williams, and Charles Lloyd. While living in San Francisco in the mid 70s, he played with Frank Zappa and co-founded the visionary progressive band Group 87 with Mark Isham and Peter Maunu before joining Missing Persons. O'Hearn's style reflects all of these experiences within the context of a highly personal electronic sound. During the late 80s, however, his innovative vision seemed to blur under the strain of the commercialism infiltrating the new-age and contemporary instrumental realms. Urged on by increasingly conservative, pop-oriented executives at Private Music, O'Hearn conformed to more conventional song forms on albums like *Between Two Worlds* and *Rivers Gonna Rise*. His music suffered from excessive predictability as a result. The record label even released some crass disco mixes of the composer's most tuneful selections on the embarrassing *Mix Up*. Fortunately, O'Hearn's good musical sense prevailed in the long run. His more recent releases *El Dorado* and *Indigo* are both admirable, highly satisfying albums. He is, however, the last remnant of the Private Music label's original roster of innovative, electronic-based instrumentalists. –LK

○ **Ancient Dreams / PRIVATE MUSIC**　　　　1985
Though *El Dorado* and *Indigo* are certainly among O'Hearn's finest albums, his startling debut *Ancient Dreams* remains the purest example of his innovative style. The keyboardist creates a sense of understated drama through a starkly elegant interplay of synthesized melodies and pseudo-pop rhythms. This unpredictable manipulation of the composer's rock and jazz roots suggests the wide open spaces of surreal landscapes. An all-time classic in the contemporary electronic field. –LK

Between Two Worlds / PRIVATE MUSIC　　　1987
Rivers Gonna Rise / PRIVATE MUSIC　　　　1988
Two watered-down, yet technically proficient, examples of O'Hearn's sound. –LK

El Dorado / PRIVATE MUSIC　　　　　　　1989
A marvelous experiment in contemporary, Middle-Eastern-flavored electro-acoustic music. O'Hearn seemed to be embarking on a new direction in his musical career with this thoughtful yet sensuous blending of ancient and modern modes of expression. The album features two prominent Iranian artists — singer Shahla Sarshar and violinist Farid Farjad — though the music was obviously ahead of its time in the notoriously conservative world of adult alternative music. Hopefully, O'Hearn will someday be able to return to the exotic world he touched on in *El Dorado* and create more music from the Fertile Crescent. –LK

Indigo / PRIVATE MUSIC　　　　　　　　1991
O'Hearn's most recent release is an unabashed return to the style he pioneered on *Ancient Dreams*. His characteristically expansive textures are anchored by booming bass drums that feel simultaneously primeval and futuristic. Lush electronics with a hefty dose of rhythmic testosterone. –LK

MIKE OLDFIELD　　　　　　　　　　　　b 1953

Progressive electronic. Multi-instrumentalist Mike Oldfield's musical roots were in English folk and experimental pop. In one early stint, Mike played bass on the Kevin Ayers (Soft Machine) album *Shoot at the Moon*. His claim to fame primarily rests on his 1974 instrumental opus *Tubular Bells*. The track became the theme for the movie *The Exorcist* and the album rose to #3 on the charts. Even though he has not charted in the US, he has enjoyed a successful career in England, including a royal celebration concert on the eve of Prince Charles's wedding, for which he received a Freedom of the City of London Award in 1982. His many solo albums feature orchestra arrangements as well as synthesizer instrumentation. –RC

☆ **Tubular Bells / VIRGIN**　　　　　　　　1974
The then-newly-formed Virgin Records allowed Oldfield a year to complete this 49-minute conceptual effort, which required him to record eighty tracks of himself playing 28

different instruments. *Tubular Bells* achieved Top Ten chart success in the US when it was used in the soundtrack for the film *The Exorcist*, selling over 10 million copies. –SWB

Orchestral Tubular Bells / ATLANTIC　　　1975
A nice idea that comes out rather silly — the original record was livelier and fresher, although this version of *Tubular Bells* does offer some distinct timbral differences for those who care enough. –BE

DAVID PARSONS

Progressive electronic, ambient, ethnic fusion. Since 1975, this New Zealand artist has made numerous trips to India to absorb the culture, study the music, and record performances by indigenous artists. In addition to producing two albums of traditional Tibetan ritual music by the monks of the Dip Tse Chok Ling Monastery (for the Fortuna Records *Sacred Ceremonies* series), Parsons has translated the essence of his oriental journeys through the lush yet profound soundscapes he has created for a number of highly regarded solo albums. Originally a jazz-rock drummer, he became interested in the music of India when he heard a performance by sitar master Ravi Shankar over two decades ago. Parsons bought a sitar and explored the instrument on his own for several years before studying with Krishna Chakravarty, one of Shankar's most accomplished disciples. After several trips to the East, Parsons composed almost exclusively for Indian instruments until 1979 when he purchased his first synthesizer. He now owns one of the largest electronic recording studios in New Zealand, where he composes for radio, TV, and film. His devotion to both Western technology and Eastern music makes for a potent and highly imaginative style of composition. –LK

Himalaya / FORTUNA　　　　　　　　　1989
An artfully austere sonic ascent of the legendary mountain range. –LK

○ **Yatra / FORTUNA**　　　　　　　　　　1990
Though all of the albums recorded by Parsons are highly recommended, this double CD (which includes 35 minutes of material not featured on the cassette versions) offers a balance of shorter, more uptempo pieces and longer, more contemplative works. *Yatra* (which means "journey" in Sanskrit) is a musical travelog through the Indian countryside, with its busy open-air markets and joyful folk melodies. Gradually, the composer moves into the ethereal realm of Tibet, a landscape imbued with secret ceremonies and hidden knowledge. –LK

Tibetan Plateau/Sounds of the ... / FORTUNA　　1991
Tibetan Plateau/Sounds of the Mothership is a CD collection from the first two Fortuna releases recorded by Parsons in 1980-1982. Deep spatial compositions for synthesizer, enhanced by classical Indian instruments. –LK

Dorje Ling / FORTUNA　　　　　　　　　1992
Parsons's latest release was inspired by his recent return to Dharamsala, India, the seat of Tibetan Buddhism in exile. Samples of traditional Tibetan music (taken from his recordings for the *Sacred Ceremonies* series) are mixed into these gently evolving electronic compositions. –LK

PENGUIN CAFE ORCHESTRA

Adult alternative, neo-classical, minimalist. The Penguin Cafe Orchestra creates dreamlike music. It is beautiful, yet illogical, unpredictable, and often bizarre. Lush violins swirl between classical melodies and country hoedowns. Is that Beethoven or "Walk, Don't Run" they're playing? Is that a touch-tone telephone playing the melody? Yes to all the above, and much more. And don't forget the repetition. Things go on just a little longer than you think they should. Remember Supersax, the jazz group that fully orchestrated Charlie Parker's sax solos and gave them a fuller and richer sound? Well, it's almost as if the Pengies have taken the two-note picking of Luther Perkins (Johnny Cash's guitarist) and taught his repetitive, minimalist picking to a string quartet. The incredible thing is that these are beautiful, compelling records. You may feel as if you dreamed the whole thing, but it is not a nightmare. Probably because no one knows how to classify their music, Penguin Cafe Orchestra is often described as new-age. Until a better label comes along, don't let that put you off. Instead, find a copy of the album called *Penguin Cafe Orchestra* — great cover! — and see what the subconscious mind sounds like when it's given some stringed instruments to play with. –HD

Music from the Penguin Cafe / CAROLINE   1976
In many ways this release is virtually interchangeable with *Broadcasting from Home*. Haunting melodies are played over hypnotically repeated string patterns. –HD

○ **Penguin Cafe Orchestra / CAROLINE**   1981
Stunning and inventive string music. –HD

Broadcasting from Home / CAROLINE   1984

Signs of Life / CAROLINE   1991
"Southern Jukebox Music" is beautiful. This is a superb collection. –HD

FRANK PERRY

New-age, ambient, ethnic fusion. Frank Perry is a modern musical mystic who takes his inspiration from ancient ideas concerning the power of sound to transform consciousness. Buddhist traditions, the writings of Plato, and Pythagoras's famous treatise *Music of the Spheres* are all seriously taken into consideration by this percussionist. Perry has rejected the rhythmic qualities of drums, woodblocks, etc., in favor of instruments like Chinese Buddha gongs and Tibetan bells, producing ethereal, elongated resonances. His albums feature extended compositions that are quiet and delicate, yet abstract in nature, and his liner notes are filled with lengthy discussions of the philosophies behind the music. His work is likely to be fascinating to many listeners, especially those who also enjoy the Celestial Harmonies *Tibetan Bells* series of releases by Henry Wolff and Nancy Hennings. However, people with more conventional musical and religious tastes may find Perry's style and ideas disturbing. –LK

○ **Deep Peace ... / CELEST. HARM.**   1983
Deep Peace/New Atlantis, a double-CD collection, features two albums originally recorded in 1980 and 1983. The four extended works featured are exemplary of Perry's mystical, meditative style. They also illustrate his skill in composing for a variety of ancient instruments that are by nature extremely difficult to manipulate artistically. –LK

Zodiac / CELESTIAL HARMONIES   1986
As the title suggests, this album offers a suite of pieces symbolizing the 12 zodiac signs. Due to the appeal of this programmatic element and the shorter selections involved, you would expect this album to be the most accessible introduction to Perry's style. However, with music as abstract and unfamiliar as this, it doesn't really matter. Perry's vision just seems most effective in the long-form mode. –LK

MICHAEL PLUZNICK

Adult alternative, ethnic fusion. This New Jersey native has been fascinated with percussion since childhood. Like Mickey Hart, Pluznick has gone beyond Western traditions in his lifelong pursuit of the magic of rhythm. His music weaves electronic drums and synthesized melodies with a vast collection of ethnic instruments and rhythms hailing primarily from Africa, South America, and the Caribbean. –LK

Where the Rain Is Born / MCA   1989
Pluznick's debut is a tasteful mix of synthetic imagery and ethnic percussion. –LK

○ **Cradle of the Sun / MCA**   1990
There are 17 artists and what seems to be nearly a hundred different instruments scattered throughout this album, but the effect is never overpowering. In fact, there's a strong emphasis on Western pop beats and fusion-style synthesizer melodies with some jazzy trumpet solos. The ethnic influences are primarily rhythmic in nature and often quite subtle, making this music accessible to a wide variety of

listeners. Some nice keyboard textures add to the appeal of these familiar-sounding yet well-crafted originals. –LK

SANFORD PONDER

Progressive electronic, minimalist. This California-based synthesist recorded two albums in the early 80s during the initial years of the Private Music label. He dropped out of sight for a while, then went on to establish the group Botanica, which has so far released two fascinating albums of music created by fractal mathematics programs. (See albums listed under Botanica.) –LK

○ **Etosha / PRIVATE MUSIC**   1985
Serene, unpretentious synthesizer music with minimalist underpinnings characterize Ponder's debut album. –LK

Tigers Are Brave / PRIVATE MUSIC   1986
Ponder's second release is more varied in conception and instrumentation with traces of violin and other acoustic instruments. –LK

POPOL VUH

Progressive electronic, neo-classical, ethnic fusion. One of Germany's premiere progressive electronic bands, Popol Vuh was founded in 1969 by keyboardist Florian Fricke. The band took its name from the Mayan Indian bible, and, in fact, the group's first album *Affenstunde* (*The Time of the Monkey King*) was a strong reflection of Fricke's interest in Mayan lore. Over the course of nearly 20 albums, Popol Vuh combined sacred musical traditions and instruments from around the world with classical, jazz, and rock elements. It also created quite a stir as one of the first bands to use the Moog synthesizer in the early 70s. As such, the band influenced several generations of electronic and contemplative artists. Popol Vuh also gained considerable attention for its scores to films by the celebrated German director Werner Herzog, including *Nosferatu* and *Aguirre, the Wrath of God.* –LK

○ **Tantric Songs ... / CELESTIAL HARMONIES**   1991
Tantric Songs/Hosianna Mantra is new-age devotional-rock chamber music that is spacey and spacious on this pairing of two early albums (from 1973 and 1978) on one CD. –MPD

RAPHAEL

New-age, neo-classical, ethnic fusion. Raised by Benedictine nuns in Tulsa, OK, Raphael learned classical music and Gregorian chants during his solitary childhood. From the age of 13, he felt a strong connection to baroque music, particularly the works of Antonio Vivaldi, the 18th-century violinist and composer who was himself a Catholic monk. In reaction to his strict upbringing, however, Raphael plunged wholeheartedly into the late-60s San Francisco scene. Yet even as he explored rock & roll and tribal music, he never lost his love of his classical roots and occasionally admitted to feeling like a reincarnation of Vivaldi. After a period playing gypsy violin on the streets of the city, dressed like a European count, Raphael completed piano and composition studies at the San Francisco Conservatory. A 12-year stint as staff musician at the Esalen Institute at Big Sur helped him consolidate his ideas on the role of music in healing and relaxation. His two resonant albums of neo-romantic music make perfect sense considering his background. Sweeping grand piano, ethereal violin solos, sparkling synthesizer textures, and floating chorals sound like Rachmaninoff and Paganini reeling through space with a chorus of liberated nuns (conducted from the great beyond, no doubt, by Vivaldi himself). It's an irresistible formula — Raphael's music has attracted a broad following of enthusiastic fans. –LK

Music to Disappear In / HEARTS OF SPACE   1988
The original best-seller. –LK

○ **Music to Disappear in II / HEARTS OF SPACE**   1991
The albums in this series are closely related and practically interchangeable. *Music to Disappear in II*, however, was able to take advantage of finer production techniques. It also seems a bit more refined on a musical level. Passionate

episodes of gypsy violin coalesce with floating synthesizers, subtle hand-drum rhythms, eerie bamboo flute solos, and sensuous female choral passages. –LK

GILES REAVES

Progressive electronic, ambient. Though his music is of the progressive electronic variety, this keyboardist and percussionist got his start through country music channels. While living in Nashville in the 80s, Reaves hooked up with producer Marshall Montgomery and ended up working as his assistant engineer. Eventually Reaves's own music caught the ear of MCA producer Tony Brown, who signed the synthesist up to the company's Master Series label. Reaves recorded two solo albums and one collaboration with Jon Goin before a tightening in the music market forced MCA to let go of artists on its instrumental sub-label. Reaves's latest album for Hearts of Space is a finely produced, technically accomplished evolution of his textural electronic style. –LK

Wunjo / MCA   1986
Reaves's debut is arguably his best effort for MCA in its subtle yet refined use of space and electronics. –LK

Nothing Is Lost / MCA   1988
○ **Sea of Glass / HEARTS OF SPACE**   1992
Subdued drums and percussion, liquid soundscapes, and slowly shifting layers of melting electric guitars are among the evocative sounds Reaves uses on this sensitively designed electro-acoustic album. –LK

JORGE REYES

Progressive electronic, ethnic fusion, techno-tribal. This enigmatic multi-instrumentalist draws from the diverse culture and history of his Mexican homeland, as well as his early experiences playing in progressive rock bands south of the border. Currently based in Mexico City, Reyes combines flute, pre-Columbian instruments, and percussion with synthesizers and voice to cast a spell of ritualistic intensity. Like shadows from Mexico's sultry and savage past, his music has a dark quality to it that sometimes scares off the unprepared, but adventurous listeners will find plenty to admire in his evocation of jungles, jaguars, and Aztec rites. Though his albums are often difficult to find, most of his imported releases are well worth the extra effort and expense involved. –LK

Comala / MUNDO MUSIC   1989
If the Aztecs and Mayans had been able to play synthesizers and electric guitars along with their flutes and drums, it might have sounded something like this. –LK

○ **Bajo El Sol Jaguar / PARAISO**   1991
Techno-tribal music to raise the dead, rip the hearts out of your sacrifices, or dance to under the full moon. Reyes's latest album as a leader also features the innovative sounds of Spanish electric guitarist Suso Saiz. Some booming Peter Gabriel-style beats can be found among mysterious atmospheres and virtuosic percussion. –LK

ROBERT RICH

Progressive electronic, ambient, ethnic fusion, techno-tribal. Building his first synthesizers at the age of 13, Rich spent his teen years hiding out in his unique sound environments. While gaining a degree in psychology from Stanford University, he became more adept at translating his interests in dreams and trance states into music. (After graduation, he remained a part of the lucid-dream-research team headed by pioneer Stephen LaBerge.) Rich's all-night Sleep Concerts and all-evening Trance Concerts introduced his style to audiences in the San Francisco Bay Area. At the same time, he was developing his chops by diligently practicing baroque keyboard music, experimenting with ethnic influences, and delving into alternate tuning systems and sacred geometry. Though still in his late 20s, Rich's music has been appreciated throughout the new-music underground in Europe and North

America for years, though his three *Hearts of Space* albums have since brought his music to wider audiences. Besides a wide array of synthesizers, Rich plays flutes, steel guitar, and acoustic percussion, which not only add depth to his music, but allow him to explore his obsession with microtonality and tunings based on non-Western scales. Ranging from latticelike polyrhythms and pieces with a strong Indonesian feel, to deep, time-suspended studies of stasis and slow motion, his compositions are meticulous in detail and subtlety. In 1990 Rich also teamed up with longtime friend Steve Roach to create the critically acclaimed *Strata*, which successfully merged their individual sounds into a shared musical vision. Rich and Roach will release their second collaboration, *Soma*, in the fall of 1992. –LK

○ **Rainforest / HEARTS OF SPACE**   1989
Robert's debut for Hearts of Space is a finely wrought collection of lush, textural pieces and engaging uptempo works inspired by the intricacies of baroque counterpoint exemplified by Bach and the fluid melodies of Indonesian gamelan music. –LK

○ **Strata / HEARTS OF SPACE**   1990
This highly regarded collaboration between Rich and Steve Roach uses layers of the earth as a metaphor for exploring layers of the psyche. With a wide variety of acoustic and electronic instruments, the two create surreal landscapes of throbbing world-music rhythms, broad synthesizer washes, and ethereal sounds. –LK

Gaudí / HEARTS OF SPACE   1991
Like the melting, three-dimensional visions of the album's namesake — early 20th-century Spanish architect Antonín Gaudí — Rich's musical structures are geometrical yet organic. Throughout the recording, his offbeat timbres flow in swirls of mutating patterns, their subtle sense of strangeness resulting from Rich's extensive use of just intonation. –LK

Geometry / SPALAX MUSIC   1991
Originally recorded in 1986-1987, *Geometry* is an early example of the delicate, synthesized latticework Rich creates by mapping various mathematical relationships directly into shimmering, intertwining musical structures. –LK

STEVE ROACH

Progressive electronic, ambient, techno-tribal. Roach's major longstanding influences are not necessarily musical; rather he draws inspiration from empowered geological places, particularly the Mojave and Sonoran deserts and the aboriginal rock-art sites of the Australian outback. In the early years of his career, however, this former adrenaline addict and motocross racer cited the European electronic scene of the 70s as an important impetus in his fascination with sequencer-based music. Yet by the release of his 1983 album, *Structures from Silence*, it was clear Roach was developing his own style. His thick, breathing waves of sound were initially embraced by listeners, meditators, and therapists in the holistic fields; however, Roach's music was far from angelic or superficially comforting. His inspiration grew from the expansive landscapes of the Southwest, complete with the feelings of danger and mystery he associated with these places. A chance to score music for a PBS documentary on the rock art of the Dreamtime (a system of aboriginal mythology) gave Roach the opportunity to visit a number of sites deep in the Australian outback. He also met up with aboriginal didjeridu master David Hudson, who taught Roach how to play the ancient wind instrument and helped him build his own didjeridu. These experiences fueled his landmark double album *Dreamtime Return*. Now considered a classic in the progressive electronic field, it marked the synthesis of Roach's earlier sequencer-based sound with his expansive, chordal atmospheres and his growing infusion of tribal aesthetics. In the late 80s, Roach moved from his base in Los Angeles to the Sonoran desert outside of Tucson, Arizona. There he has produced a number of projects that continue to blur the lines between ancient ritual and modern technology. His numerous collaborations include albums with Michael Stearns, Kevin Braheny, Robert Rich, and Michael Shrieve. In addition, he has recently been working with Mexican multi-instrumentalist Jorge Reyes and Spanish guitarist Suso Saiz. Their album *Suspended Memories, Forgotten Gods* is set for release in the spring of 1993. –LK

Structures from Silence / FORTUNA   1984
This influential album of extended works marked the emergence of his serene, yet haunting synthesizer breaths. –LK

☆ **Dreamtime Return / FORTUNA**   1988
Roach's sojourn into the mythological mind of the Australian aborigines demonstrates that electronic music's greatest potential may lie in bringing our most elusive dreams and ancient memories into focus through potent, highly imaginative soundscapes. Altered chords that breathe ever so slowly, floating textures, digitally sampled aboriginal instruments, primitive trance rhythms, and arresting abstract sounds lead you through an unfolding maze of sonic dimensions that depict a sense of mystery and confrontation with the unknown. Double CD has 38 minutes of music not in the cassette version. –LK

Quiet Music / FORTUNA   1988
A subtle collection of ambient pieces with subdued melodies, *Quiet Music* evokes images of shimmering desert mirages. –LK

Desert Solitaire / FORTUNA   1989
The second of two collaborations with Kevin Braheny inspired by the desert, this album pays homage to the Edward Abbey book of the same title. It inadvertently became a memorial to that Southwestern nature writer when Abbey died shortly after the music was recorded. Featuring some powerful work by Michael Stearns, this album taps into the psychological depths of stark Southwestern landscapes through a subtle set of soundscapes depicting the hidden dangers, unseen gifts, and intoxication that the desert promises. –LK

Western Spaces / FORTUNA   1990
This reissue of Roach and Kevin Braheny's first evocation of the American Southwest features several selections not included on the original 1987 version. This album is considered by many to be a classic in the progressive electronic and ambient genres. –LK

Australia: Sound of the Earth / FORTUNA   1990
After the success of *Dreamtime Return*, which was inspired by Australian aboriginal mythology, Roach returned to Australia. He traveled the continent with a tape recorder collecting natural sounds and capturing performances by native musicians, which he then wove into a sonic journey through the outback. The album is significant in that it features high-quality recordings of aboriginal didjeridu master David Hudson, who does some startling things with this ancient wind instrument. There are also some powerful performances by a group of five didjeridu players, as well as some intriguing contemporary compositions by Australian composer Sarah Hopkins. –LK

World's Edge / FORTUNA   1992
Roach's first solo release since *Dreamtime Return* is another double CD. With shorter pieces on the first disc and a single 67-minute work on the second, *World's Edge* explores the paradoxical relationships between sound and silence, space and rhythm, ancient ritual and modern technology. An accomplished album. –LK

Now/Traveler / FORTUNA   1992
This CD reissue features music from Roach's first two albums, originally recorded in the early 80s. A good example of his early, high-energy, sequencer-based style, with some hints at his developing ambient and tribal leanings. –LK

GABRIELLE ROTH

Techno-tribal, minimalist. Roth doesn't actually play the ritualistic, heavily percussive music featured on her recordings. Instead, the style emerged from her dance performances and movement workshops in which she strives

to unite spiritual and sexual energies into what is often referred to as the "dance of ecstasy." Her book, *Maps to Ecstasy: Teachings of an Urban Shaman*, explains the philosophy behind the music she requisitions for her performances and ultimately her albums. She has her own New-York-based label, Raven Recording, which has expanded its scope in recent years to release other artists as well. Listed as "musical director" in the liner notes to her five albums, Roth often "composes" by dancing along with a musician's improvisations to communicate her vision, relying on her husband, percussionist Robert Ansell, to lead their ensemble, the Mirrors. –LK

Initiation / RAVEN   1984
The albums *Initiation, Bones, Ritual,* and *Waves* feature techno-tribal trance music of various tempos and moods, designed for everything from meditation and massage to ecstatic dancing. –LK

Bones / RAVEN   1989
Ritual / RAVEN   1990
○ **Waves / RAVEN**   1991
Roth's most aggressive and accomplished recording features some respected percussionists, including Mino Cinelu. Driving tribal rhythms are the basis for six compositions, several of which also make effective use of wailing female vocals. Some synthesizers and electronic guitars add to the sense of mystery Roth craves in her music. –LK

BERNARDO RUBAJA

Adult alternative, ethnic fusion. Raised in Argentina, Rubaja studied piano formally as a child, performed in local pop groups during his teens, and advanced to Argentina's National Academy of Fine Arts. Several years spent studying music in the multicultural climate of Paris added to his skills as a performer and composer. Rubaja, who now lives in Southern California, released his first album as a leader on the Narada label. –LK

High Plateaux / WINDHAM HILL   1987
High Plateaux, a collaboration with Cesar Hernandez, was Rubaja's recording debut. The album was produced in 1987 by Mark Isham. –LK

○ **New Land / NARADA**   1990
Amidst his rich synthesized sounds, pop textures, and spicy Latin rhythms, Rubaja also performs on such exotic South American instruments as the charango (a guitarlike instrument made from an armadillo shell) and the bandoneon (a button accordion made famous by fellow Argentinian Astor Piazzola). Guest artists include trumpeter Mark Isham and percussionist Alex Acuna, among others. –LK

RYUICHI SAKAMOTO

Progressive electronic, ethnic fusion. Electronic keyboard whiz who received his training at the University of Tokyo. He released his first solo effort in 1978 and shortly thereafter formed the techno-pop band Yellow Magic Orchestra. Sakamoto has successfully combined electronics and world music. He has written the scores for several soundtracks, including half of *The Last Emperor* soundtrack, which won an Oscar. –DS

Neo Geo / EPIC   1988
An interesting combination of Japanese and funk rhythms with such notable guests as jazz drummer Tony Williams, reggae star Sly Dunbar, and Iggy Pop. –DS

○ **Beauty / ATLANTIC**   1990
A world-music tapestry featuring a mixture of Eastern, Western, and African elements and such musicians as Robbie Robertson, Sly Dunbar, and even Brian Wilson. –DS

EBERHARD SCHOENER

Progressive electronic, ambient. German composer Schoener is a sonic explorer who has not only stepped outside European traditions for inspiration, but has created breathtaking music from the most unlikely sources, both natural and electronic.

After an extended journey through the Far East, in which he studied religious as well as musical practices, he came to the conclusion that artists need to come to terms with their own cultural heritages to be truly effective. His 1973 release *Meditation*, for instance, expressed the ideal of spiritual contemplation often associated with the East, through synthesized music rooted in Western experience. –LK

○ **Meditation/Sky Music ... / KUCKUCK**   1973
This double-CD reissue features music originally contained on two albums of extended pieces recorded in 1973 and 1983 respectively. *Meditation* consists of two reflective works for synthesizers. On *Sky Music - Mountain Music*, however, he creates delicate, transparent soundscapes from more natural sources, though it was actually created by attaching tuned whistles to carrier pigeons and allowing the birds to fly through air currents generated by BMW's wind tunnel. –LK

SCHONHERZ & SCOTT

Adult alternative, progressive electronic, ambient. This duo features Vienna-born keyboardist Richard Schonherz, who has written music for full orchestra as well as soundtracks for Austrian films and television projects. A native of San Francisco, Peter Scott studied guitar privately, then enrolled in the Musicians Institute of Technology, where he concentrated on composing and arranging. Both artists have played a wide variety of styles over the years, from classical and jazz to rock and blues. Shortly after the two musicians met, they began producing a series of pop demos as well as a series of instrumental selections. The latter became the basis for the duo's 1987 Windham Hill debut, *One Night in Vienna*. Their pop demos provided the impetus for a second release, *Under a Big Sky*, which includes vocal tunes as well as more pop-oriented instrumentals. –LK

○ **One Night in Vienna / WINDHAM HILL**   1987
Dazzling electronic-based music with romantic underpinnings. These warm, atmospheric pieces are best listened to by candlelight. –LK

Under a Big Sky / WINDHAM HILL   1991
While the duo have a flair for sensual yet subdued instrumentals, the vocal selections that tend to dominate this album are completely pedestrian. –LK

KLAUS SCHULZE

Progressive electronic, minimalist. One of the cornerstone figures in the German electronic scene, this pioneering synthesist has recorded nearly two dozen solo albums over the past 20 years. His music has grown and changed with the evolution of technology, but his concept of long-form, highly rhythmic sequencer music pulsing under soaring melodies has remained constant. Though he established his own identity years ago, Schulze was briefly a member of Tangerine Dream, appearing on one album, *Electronic Meditation*, in 1970. He did not, however, cave in to convention or engage in cheap pop-electronic exploits, as did his former TD colleagues in the mid 80s and beyond. Still, Schulze's collaborations with former Santana drummer Michael Shrieve brought a new level of percussive intensity to his music, as well as a wider audience from the progressive rock world. The availability of Schulze's music has always been inconsistent in the US, and many Americans have no idea how strong his influence has been on electronic music worldwide. (He was, for instance, the inspiration behind Kitaro's initial investigations of synthesizer music.) Schulze continues to perform throughout Europe and is tireless in releasing new recordings, some of which are better than others. When Schulze does hit the nail on the head, his music is immensely powerful. –LK

Timewind / VIRGIN   1975
Two masterful sequencer essays that make effective use of minimalistic patterns to suspend and ultimately erase all sense of objective "clock-time" experience. –LK

☆ **X / METRONOME MUSIK**   1978
Schulze's 10th solo release marks the peak of his most influential period of work. Presented with a classic sense of

German drama, this double-CD artfully combines the composer's synthesizers and sequencer patterns with live drums and full orchestra. Intense, driving, long-form pieces frame surreal, abstract sounds. Each of six pieces is named for a historical figure Schulze admires, beginning with a 24-minute selection titled "Friedrich Nietzsche." –LK

Mirage / ISLAND   1986
Mirage gives the listener impressionistic sequencer work depicting winter landscapes. –LK

Beyond Recall / CAROLINE   1991
Schulze in a more sedate and reflective mood, with acoustic guitar samples creating lyrical melodies. –LK

TONY SCOTT

Ethnic fusion, chamber jazz. Jazz clarinetist Tony Scott is best known among contemporary instrumental artists for creating what is generally considered to be the first album in the genre. The impact was so strong, in fact, that in the 80s Verve searched its vaults for the original 1964 recording and reissued it on CD. Curiously enough, other than *Music for Zen Meditation*, Scott's influence has not been felt in contemporary instrumental music. –LK

○ **Music for Zen Meditation / VERVE**   1964
This elegant, contemplative set of pieces was conceived during one of the jazz artist's trips to Japan when Scott had the opportunity to record with a shakuhachi flutist and a koto player. Though ears unaccustomed to oriental styles might assume it's a performance of traditional Japanese music, the album is actually a set of finely wrought improvisations merging Eastern and Western sensibilities. –LK

JOHN SERRIE

Adult alternative, progressive electronic, ambient. Leading planetarium composer Serrie has been looking to the heavens for inspiration for over a decade. Coming from a family ensconced in the aviation field, Serrie now soars and glides with his hands on the controls of analog and digital synthesizers. His rhythmic outings often have an understated heroic feel, although he has also done some more pop-oriented instrumentals on his 1990 release *Tingri*. However, he seems most at home in the longer-form space-music journeys for which he initially became known. –LK

And the Stars Go with You / MIRAMAR   1988
Serrie's debut release on CD captures the development of 10 years of planetarium work. Lush romantic pieces with episodes of subtle sequencer patterns maintain a consistently peaceful yet wondrous mood, perfect for stargazing. –LK

○ **Flightpath / MIRAMAR**   1989
This album offers the best of both worlds in terms of Serrie's style, from sequencer patterns that sail through hyperspace to enigmatic, ambient textures that sparkle like star clusters or float with shrouded density through black holes and other cosmic wonders. –LK

Tingri / MIRAMAR   1990
The first few cuts have more of a superficial, adult-alternative feel to them. The latter part of the album opens up into beautifully produced spaces that drift and hover. –LK

○ **Planetary Chronicles - Vol. 1 / MIRAMAR**   1992
Serrie's most recent effort is a continuation of the liquid stargazing music pioneered on his 1988 debut *And the Stars Go with You*. –LK

SHADOWFAX

Chamber jazz, ethnic fusion, adult alternative. Originally a blues band from the south side of Chicago, Shadowfax was formed in the early 70s by saxophonist and Lyricon player Chuck Greenberg, bassist Phil Maggini, and guitarist G. E. Stinson. The musicians soon began experimenting with other forms of electronic music in combination with various world-music styles. Critics and listeners alike immediately began responding to the group's hybrid of styles and textures, which was quite unusual at the time. After releasing their first album, *Watercourse Way*, on Passport/ABC, the members of the band went on to record four albums for Windham Hill before moving to Virgin Records and winning the Grammy for Best New-Age Album in 1988. Though there have been several label and personnel changes over the years, Greenberg has remained devoted to keeping the Shadowfax vision alive. Plans are under way for a new album by the end of 1992. –LK

○ **Shadowfax / WINDHAM HILL** 1982
On its debut album, Shadowfax was a contemporary instrumental quartet led by guitarist G. E. Stinson and Lyricon/sax player Chuck Greenberg, its mostly calm pieces full of carefully placed riffs played by clearly delineated instruments. A true ensemble, Shadowfax can be listened to with pleasure for its individual players and its group sound on this and several subsequent Windham Hill albums. –WR

The Odd Get Even / PRIVATE MUSIC 1990
By the release of this album, Shadowfax had expanded into a sextet with a strong reliance on drum programming and synthesizers. The sound was far more powerful and dramatic, and worth hearing for that, although early listeners had some adjusting to do. –WR

MICHAEL SHRIEVE

Progressive electronic, adult alternative. Shrieve has had a long and interesting career as a rock drummer, percussionist, and progressive electronic composer. Gaining early recognition as the powerhouse drummer for Santana, the teenage Shrieve was launched into the popular culture maelstrom when he performed an extended drum solo during Santana's appearance at the legendary Woodstock festival. Over the years, Shrieve has continued to strive for innovative approaches to percussion-based music. His numerous collaborations include work with Stomu Yamash'ta, Klaus Schulze, Steve Roach, David Beal, David Torn, and Andy Summers, to name a few. –LK

The Leaving Time / RCA 1988
Virtuoso percussionist Shrieve teams with synthesist Roach to create some highly atmospheric soundscapes, replete with unusual sounds and stray melodies. –WR

○ **Stiletto / NOVUS** 1989
Always a team player (witness his long stint in Santana), Shrieve puts together an unusual ensemble for his first "solo" album, including trumpeter Mark Isham and former Police guitarist Andy Summers. The tracks (combining elements of rock, jazz, and industrial noise) are dominated by percussion elements, and even the guitar and trumpet playing are handled more rhythmically than melodically. But this extraordinarily inventive album yields subtle pleasures. –WR

The Big Picture / FORTUNA 1989
This collaboration between Shrieve and the talented young drummer David Beal is an electronic percussion tour de force with epic rhythms, powerful melodies, and broad textural brushstrokes. Amazingly enough, this innovative album fell through the cracks when it was first released and didn't get nearly the attention or distribution it deserved. –LK

SOFTWARE

Adult alternative, progressive electronic. Formed in 1983, this German electronic duo owes much to electronic pioneer Klaus Schulze. Software's music usually builds on sequencer patterns and simple melodies, creating a lighter version of the Schulze style. Their later work is woven into concept albums, yet the music rarely lives up to their poetic aspirations. Software's earlier recordings with Peter Mergener are generally more satisfying. –LK

○ **Past, Present, Future - Vol. 2 / INNOV. COMM.** 1987
An efficient collection of music from five of the group's mid-80s recordings. Vol. 1 is also nice. –LK

SOLITAIRE

Progressive electronic, ambient, techno-tribal. The brainchild of German keyboardist Elmar Schulte, this recording entity is based in the small town of Paderborn, yet draws inspiration from foreign landscapes, particularly the wide open spaces of the American Southwest, Scotland, and Norway. Schulte named the group, in fact, after his admiration for the music on *Desert Solitaire*, an album by American synthesists Steve Roach, Kevin Braheny, and Michael Stearns (see listing under Roach). Solitaire's dark, textural pieces and occasional ethnic rhythms are a marked contrast to the sequencer-dominated heritage of the 70s German electronic school popularized by Tangerine Dream and Klaus Schulze. –LK

Altered States / MUSIQUE INTEMPORELLE 1990
A commendable debut. "Heart of the Desert," a long, hypnotic dirge, is particularly well done. –LK

○ **Plains and Skies / MUSIQUE INTEMPORELLE** 1992
Schulte's slowly emerging compositional voice is urged along by the obvious influences of his favorite artists, particularly Steve Roach, Jon Hassell, and Michael Brook. –LK

RICHARD SOUTHER

Adult alternative, ethnic fusion. As a promising session keyboardist in Los Angeles, Souther began landing work in recording studios while still in his teens, eventually performing with such artists as Barry McGuire, Debby Boone, the Mothers of Invention, and Phil Keaggy. In 1980, however, a near-fatal bout with food poisoning suspended Souther's career for several years. Following his recovery, he began to focus on developing a solo career that would involve more personal themes, including his Christian perspective on life. Strong, hopeful melodies are his trademark, yet his albums for the Narada label also reflect his pop background as well as his early classical training, his feeling for contemporary jazz, and his subsequent interests in ethnic music. –LK

Cross Currents / NARADA 1989
Optimistic melodies in a pop-jazz ensemble setting. –LK

○ **Twelve Tribes / NARADA** 1990
Souther's second release shows a marked evolution in style from his first album, recorded just a year earlier. Not only are his keyboard parts based on more original timbres, Souther also abandons customary drum sounds for a stronger emphasis on live and sampled percussion. Rather than a standard kick drum, for instance, he uses an African log drum. In place of cymbals, he uses samples of someone breathing. The emphasis is still on catchy melodies and contemporary jazz textures, yet Souther's creative use of ethnic rhythms and instruments adds a new level of sophistication to his accessibility. –LK

HILARY STAGG

Adult alternative. Stagg was working as an electrician when he heard Swiss harp sensation Andreas Vollenweider in concert. At that moment, the Northern California native was inspired to learn all he could about the electro-acoustic harp. A few years later, he was releasing his own albums, using his knowledge as an electrician to amplify his instrument to suit the soft, dreamy music he was developing. Stagg also credits the sweet melodic stylings of Loggins & Messina, the Doobie Brothers, and the Moody Blues as influences. Over the course of three recordings, Stagg has grown increasingly accomplished as a performer and composer. –LK

Beyond the Horizon / REAL MUSIC 1987
Feather Light / REAL MUSIC 1987
Beyond the Horizon / REAL MUSIC 1988
Stagg's debut release. –LK
Feather Light / REAL MUSIC 1989
○ **Dream Spiral / REAL MUSIC** 1991
Though Stagg is backed by an ensemble featuring synthesizer, electric bass, percussion, acoustic guitar, and violin, his custom-electrified Troubadour harp remains the focus of eight originals that take on a silky, dreamlike quality through the composer's resonant techniques. –LK

BRUCE STARK

Solo instrumental, neo-classical. As a physics major in college, Stark found himself spending more time in the dormitory lounge playing piano than doing his homework. Inspired by Keith Jarrett's extended improvisations, the self-taught musician abandoned his scientific studies and just barely managed to get accepted into the music department of California State University at the age of 22. He went on to gain a Masters degree in composition from Juilliard, studying with heavies like Roger Sessions and Vincent Persichetti. Yet along the way, Stark never lost his interest in the tonal, highly improvisational styles that attracted him to music in the first place. Unlike the George Winston clones who gave solo piano music a bad name in the 1980s, this Tokyo-based artist starts out with strong compositional ideas and actually develops them in intelligent and emotionally charged ways. –LK

○ **Song of Hope / HEARTS OF SPACE**   1991
One of the finest solo piano releases in recent years, *Song of Hope* strikes a rare balance between musical literacy and pure emotion. –LK

MICHAEL STEARNS

Progressive electronic, ambient. An accomplished sound sculptor, Stearns developed an appetite for psychedelic music from listening to Jimi Hendrix and Cream in the 60s while playing in his own rock bands. In 1974, a fortuitous meeting with dance/movement icon Emilie Conrad provided Stearns with the impetus to move to Los Angeles from his hometown of Tucson, AZ, leaving behind plans to become a Sufi mystic in the process. During the next dozen years, Stearns worked in close association with Conrad's Continuum dance collective, creating spontaneous live accompaniment for the group's explorations of movement and sound. In the process, he developed an electronic-based style that mixed environmental recordings with synthesizers and exotic instruments including "the beam," a 12-foot aluminum shaft strung with piano wire that produced extremely low tones. In 1983, Stearns was selected to score the IMAX film, *Chronos,* an opportunity that allowed the composer to further develop his interests in sophisticated multi-channel techniques and mind-expanding soundscapes. Over the last decade, Stearns has scored numerous IMAX and OMNIMAX films and has been able to build and refine a state-of-the-art studio to continue his search for new sounds. –LK

○ **Planetary Unfolding / SONIC ATMOSPHERES**   1985
A masterful electronic symphony based on the idea that the universe is made of sound rather than solid matter (a notion that has its roots in Oriental philosophy as well as in some modern theoretical physics circles). Stearns's performances on the Serge synthesizer actually give the feeling that atoms, cells, planets, and other celestial bodies are creating a complex orchestration that is unfolding on itself and expanding into deep space. –LK

Chronos / SONIC ATMOSPHERES   1985
This soundtrack for the IMAX film by Ron Fricke stands on its own. Stearns's interests in sound design and innovative recording techniques take an equal seat with the music, which captures the drama of large-format film and inspires majestic visuals in the mind of the listener. –LK

Encounter / HEARTS OF SPACE   1988
A musical science-fiction fantasy, *Encounter* is "space music" in the most obvious sense of the word. Stearns's ten-piece suite depicts contact with a UFO, culminating in a journey to the stars. The imagery is so effective that it's probably not advisable to listen to this album alone in the desert. –LK

STEIN & WALDER

Neo-classical, chamber jazz. Keyboardist Ira Stein and oboist Russel Walder met in 1981 at a series of master classes taught at the Naropa Institute by two of their major influences, Ralph Towner and Paul McCandless. Shortly thereafter, Stein and Walder produced a demo and were signed to Windham Hill. Over the years, their sound has expanded from the acoustic duets of their 1982 debut, *Elements,* to a satisfying blend of electronic keyboards, drums, bass, and intricate studio enhancements. –LK

Elements / WINDHAM HILL   1982
A choice collection of duets for acoustic piano and oboe with impressionistic, neo-classical leanings. –LK

Transit / WINDHAM HILL   1986
Produced by Mark Isham, this album added lush electronics and a number of talented sidemen to the mix, including bassist Michael Manring. –LK

○ **Under the Eye / SONA GAIA**   1990
An invigorating display of the duo's diversity, maturity, and inventiveness, *Under the Eye* features ensemble settings with guitarist Tom Vatlin, bassist Shido, drummers Robbie Bean and Gene Refkin, and percussionist Marc Anderson. –LK

LIZ STORY

Solo instrumental, neo-classical, adult alternative. Story studied classical piano while growing up in Southern California and even thought about becoming a music librarian or theorist for a while. Then she heard jazz pianist Bill Evans at a New York club, and the experience changed her perspective on music overnight. Story, who had studied at Juilliard and was enrolled at Hunter College at the time, abandoned her academic program in favor of jazz lessons with Sanford Gold, a teacher Evans had recommended. Back in Los Angeles, she continued her musical education at UCLA and the Dick Grove Music Workshops, but it was a job playing piano at a French restaurant that sparked her major breakthrough as a composer. Since the front casing of the piano was missing, Story had no place to put her sheet music and was forced to improvise freely. Eventually, she put some of her spontaneous compositions on tape and sent them to Windham Hill. Within four days, Will Ackerman had called her back and the contract was signed for her first release, *Solid Colors,* an album of impressionistic piano miniatures. Over the course of five recordings — including a two-album stint with RCA Novus —Story's style has expanded to include electronic duets with Mark Isham and works for various types of ensembles, yet the piano remains the prominent voice in her finely crafted compositions. –LK

☆ **Solid Colors / WINDHAM HILL**
With remarkable technical facility, tremendous feel, and a playful sense of musical progression, Liz Story proves a moving and fascinating pianist on her debut album. Intuitive yet intellectual, Story nevertheless has a strong sense of structure, and her quick, light playing always keeps things moving. –WR

Unaccountable Effect / WINDHAM HILL   1985
A particularly striking album of rhapsodic piano solos and gorgeous collaborations with synthesist Mark Isham. –LK

Part of Fortune / NOVUS   1986
On several tracks of this label debut, Story experiments with added instrumentation — percussion, a cello, strings, a choir — giving her music a more formal cast that does not reduce its attraction. –WR

Speechless / NOVUS   1988
Story's second and final recording for RCA Novus is a return to the solo piano realm after her forays into arrangements involving other instruments on her previous two releases. –LK

○ **Escape of the Circus Ponies / WINDHAM HILL**   1990
It's actually difficult to recommend one of Story's albums over all the rest, because they all offer different sides of her musical personality, complete with brilliant moments and less successful ideas. Her 1990 return to Windham Hill, however, shows a level of maturity in her ability to compose for solo piano, especially in her creative use of altered harmonies and her mastery of the thoughtful lyricism associated with her greatest inspiration, Bill Evans. –LK

TIM STORY

Progressive electronic, ambient, neo-classical. Though he also recorded for Windham Hill at one time, this Ohio-based keyboardist is not related to Liz Story. His intimate style thrives on cavernous spaces, an element that eventually caught the attention of Hearts of Space Records, which released his most recent (and in many ways his best) album, *Beguiled*. Other than some early guitar lessons, Tim Story is self-taught. With experience as a recording engineer and a studio musician under his belt, he turned his attention to composing and released his first albums on a tiny Norwegian label called Uniton in 1982. His music attracted the attention of Windham Hill's Will Ackerman, who released two of his albums in the late 80s and included several of Story's pieces on some of the label's samplers. Though his melodic voice is often expressed with uncommon delicacy on grand piano, Story sets the contours of his pieces with broad synthesized brushstrokes in hazy, enigmatic veils of color. Like Harold Budd, he also injects a profound sense of ambiguity into his compositions, suggesting emotions for which there are no words. –LK

Glass Green / WINDHAM HILL   1987
More upbeat selections are included in the midst of Story's characteristically elegant, open-ended lyricism. –LK

○ **Beguiled / HEARTS OF SPACE**   1991
Story's most subtle and masterful work to date can best be described as graceful, visceral chamber music for 21st-century romantics. His miniatures for Steinway grand piano and synthesizers, sometimes enhanced by the velvet richness of Martha Reikow's cello, embody passion at a whisper. –LK

TANGERINE DREAM

Adult alternative, progressive electronic, minimalist. Formed as a rock group in 1967 by Edgar Froese, Tangerine Dream is one of the most important entities to shape contemporary instrumental music over the last 20 years. The turbulent 60s, Froese's association with surrealist painter Salvador Dali, and the arrival of the Moog synthesizer were just a few of the forces that helped to fuel this German electronic group through a barrage of constant change in style and personnel. Core members over the years have included Froese and Chris Franke as well as Peter Baumann, who went on to start the Private Music label. Curiously enough, the band's most recent addition is Jerome Froese, Edgar's son, whose enigmatic photos as a baby can be found in the artwork to TD's early albums. Over the past 25 years or so, the TD sound has moved from the droning nightmares of *Zeit*, to the mesmerizing sequencer-based masterpieces of *Rubycon* and *Ricochet* in the 70s, to the sparkling high-tech rock of the 80s. A cult phenomenon for decades, Tangerine Dream gained wider recognition when the group's highly evocative music attracted the interest of William Friedkin. This resulted in the score to the film *Sorcerer* and the beginning of a large number of soundtracks. (TD's music for the Tom Cruise scorcher, *Risky Business*, probably attracted the most attention.) In recent years, Tangerine Dream has moved toward shorter, song-based pieces that seem superficial and predictable compared to the group's pioneering work, yet Froese and company must be admired for TD's continuous output and place in electronic music history. –LK

Rubycon / VIRGIN   1975
Classic, uncompromising Tangerine Dream. A must for any serious collector of electronic music. –LK

○ **Logos Live / VIRGIN**   1982
This live recording captures the Dream at a high point that occurred midway through the band's career. Longer, more intricate pieces are present, yet the action takes place at a brisk pace, moving through many of the trademark TD motifs and soundscapes. The recording's studio quality and engrossing performances are clearly inspired. –LK

Le Parc / RELATIVITY   1985
A selection of different moods, all of a consistently high quality. Each track takes its name and inspiration from a different park in the world, like Central, or Yellowstone for example. –VB

Canyon Dreams / MIRAMAR   1987
TD received its first Grammy nomination with this album. The music was originally composed for a scenic video on the Grand Canyon, released under the same title. The style is a rather ingenious combination of the group's progressive style and current commercial leanings, and, as such, is Tangerine Dream's finest album of recent years. –LK

Melrose / PRIVATE MUSIC   1990
Quite a contrast from *Logos Live*, this album is one of the better examples of the band's recent immersion in adult-alternative electronic pop. –LK

Rockoon / MIRAMAR   1992
Though the music has its moments, TD's most recent album is listed mostly as a reference. –LK

TINGSTAD & RUMBEL

Neo-classical, chamber jazz. Guitarist Eric Tingstad and oboist Nancy Rumbel create music directly inspired by the chamber-jazz styles of Oregon and the Paul Winter Consort. After studying at Northwestern University, San Antonio-born Rumbel moved to New York. There she met oboist Paul McCandless (who played with the Winter Consort before helping to establish Oregon with guitarist Ralph Towner). McCandless put her in contact with Winter, and before she knew it, Rumbel herself was touring and recording with the Paul Winter Consort. After a five-year stint with the group, Rumbel dropped out to start a family when she met Eric Tingstad at an outdoor festival. The Seattle-based guitarist had been influenced by Oregon's Ralph Towner. Tingstad studied classical guitar in college and spent the better part of the 70s playing lead guitar in a Seattle progressive-rock band. In the 80s, however, he returned to the acoustic guitar and released two solo albums that established his popularity as a regional musician known for creating "Northwest Impressionism." When Rumbel moved to Washington, she and Tingstad agreed to collaborate. They have since recorded a number of contemporary chamber-music-style albums for the Narada label. The musicians, who have a long history of environmental activism, often create albums with outdoor themes and have been known to give away tree seedlings at their live performances. –LK

Woodlands / MCA   1987
An early collaboration with pianist David Lanz. –LK

○ **Homeland / MCA**   1990
Tingstad and Rumbel's pastoral sound is a bit more aggressive on this album, due to a stronger rhythmic emphasis and the appearance of over a dozen guest artists. The overall effect, however, remains subtle, with snatches of Oriental and South American influences mixed with the duo's usual fusion of classical and North American folk influences. –LK

In the Garden / MCA   1991
The duo created this album based on their mutual interests in gardening and to promote responsible land stewardship concepts. Some of the proceeds were donated to national gardening organizations. –LK

TRI ATMA

Adult alternative, ethnic fusion. Founded in 1977 by German guitarist Jens Fischer and Indian tabla player Asim Saha, Tri Atma specializes in fusing Eastern musical elements with Western electronic pop. In 1982, the duo met Klaus Netzle, a veteran German record and television producer who brought the space-age sounds of the Fairlight and Synclavier computer synthesizers to their music. –LK

○ **Yearning & Harmony / FORTUNA** 1982
Buoyant Eastern rhythms and Western grooves support some intricate acoustic guitar work and compelling electronic keyboard solos. –LK

Essential Tri Atma / HIGHER OCTAVE 1990
A collection of digitally remastered pieces from three of Tri Atma's previous recordings with an emphasis on their more pop-oriented fusions. –LK

NIK TYNDALL

Progressive electronic, ambient. As a designer of sound units and amplifiers in the 70s, this German artist made a natural progression into composing for electronic instruments at the end of the decade when he formed the avant-garde duo Tycoon with Rudolf Lager. In the mid 80s, he struck out on his own and released a number of recordings on the German Sky label, in addition to composing soundtracks for film and television. His style combines primarily lush environmental soundscapes with the delicate percussive textures of bamboo, gongs, and windchimes. –LK

○ **Lagoon / HEARTS OF SPACE** 1990
Tyndall's first American release concentrates on shorter pieces with each selection exploring a single mood through finely-crafted, primarily computer-generated sounds. –LK

DAVID VAN TIEGHEM

Progressive electronic, techno-tribal. Drummer and percussionist Van Tieghem first remembers making music with pots and pans when he was five years old. During his entertaining and innovative solo shows in the 80s, he was still banging on kitchen utensils, toys, and other found objects, in addition to illustrating his obvious mastery of more conventional percussion instruments. Over the years, Van Tieghem has worked with everyone from Steve Reich, Laurie Anderson, Brian Eno, and choreographer Twyla Tharp to the Talking Heads, Nona Hendrix, and Jerry Harrison. –LK

○ **These Things Happen / WARNER** 1984
David Van Tieghem is a percussionist, nominally speaking, but as far as he's concerned, everything on earth is a percussion instrument. On this album, which features a variety of found sounds (including radio transmissions) mixed in with more conventional instruments, Van Tieghem plays a wine bottle, a hair comb, metal ashtrays, and balloons, among other things. But this musically arranged junk heap is often amazingly musical. If you like it, try Van Tieghem's three albums on Private Music, especially *Strange Cargo*. –WR

Strange Cargo / PRIVATE MUSIC 1989

VANGELIS

Progressive electronic, ambient, neo-classical,. With his lush synthesizer textures, sweeping romantic melodies, and undeniable flair for the dramatic, Vangelis has been called "the electronic Tchaikovsky." This self-taught artist grew up in Athens, Greece, where he shunned piano lessons at an early age in favor of conducting his own musical experiments by playing with radio interference and stuffing the family piano with nails and other foreign objects. After achieving considerable success in Greece with his early-60s rock group, Vangelis moved to Paris at the age of 25 and formed the progressive band Aphrodite's Child. He was even invited to replace Rick Wakeman in Yes, but turned the position down as his interests floated away from rock and into soundtrack work. His early scores to Frederic Roussif's *Apocalypse des Animaux* and *Opera Sauvage* were released as albums. Nearly 20 years later, this music stands on its own as some of Vangelis's finest work. In the mid 70s, the composer moved to London where he set up an extensive electronic music studio. There he recorded some of his most popular solo albums while continuing to create masterful soundtracks for film and television projects, including the theme to Carl Sagan's *Cosmos* and the ethereal, futuristic music for *Blade Runner*. He is best

known, however, for his Academy Award-winning score to *Chariots of Fire*. Though many electronic composers have fallen in and out of fashion over the years, Vangelis's music possesses the kind of originality and quality that makes it seem timeless. His sophisticated use of texture and atmosphere is balanced by highly expressive melodies and swells of emotional intensity. It's hard not to be moved by this music. –LK

Opera Sauvage / POLYGRAM 1979
An early film score with a delicious sense of romanticism. –LK

China / POLYGRAM 1979
One of the composer's least-known albums is also one of his best. Exalted invocations of Oriental majesty frame playful, folk-like melodies and mystical rites of passage. –LK

○ **Chariots of Fire / POLYGRAM** 1982
Vangelis's Academy Award-winning score to the movie continues to be his most famous album, probably because the theme is immediately recognizable yet quickly lures listeners into a musical world that stands on its own. –LK

☆ **Antarctica / POLYGRAM** 1983
Originally composed for a forgettable Japanese film on the South Pole, this album is a masterpiece of sonic sensations depicting vast plains of ice, sunlight glittering across the snow, and the sting of Antarctic winds. Expansive melodies are punctuated by the lashing sounds of whips urging dog sleds into mysterious and forbidden landscapes. –LK

Soil Festivities / POLYGRAM 1984
A five-movement suite that emerges from a thunderstorm into a celebration of nature's savage beauty. –LK

Mask / POLYGRAM 1985
Primal rituals in a futuristic setting. –LK

Themes / POLYGRAM 1989
Selections from his most famous soundtracks, including many themes never before available on a recording (such as those from *Blade Runner, The Bounty*, and *Missing*). –LK

ANDREAS VOLLENWEIDER

Adult alternative, ethnic fusion. Vollenweider was one of the few musicians to gain superstar status as a "new-age artist" back when the term was first used as a marketing category in the mid 80s. The Swiss harpist, however, quickly transcended the need for alternative record sales when his albums simultaneously broached *Billboard*'s pop, jazz, and classical charts in 1986. Born in Zurich in 1953, Vollenweider was ensconced in the city's fine art scene, courtesy of his father, one of Europe's leading organists. After becoming proficient on guitar, flute, and other instruments, the young Vollenweider developed a passion for the harp, which he modified to suit his needs. Not only did he construct a damper to expedite more rhythmic playing, he broadened the harp's tonal range by electrifying it. His buoyant funk beats, exotic pan-cultural influences, and colorful harp improvisations began to sweep Europe in the early 80s as Vollenweider was signing with CBS Records to release *Behind the Gardens ... Behind the Wall*. Three albums later, he won his first Grammy for 1987's *Down to the Moon*. Over the years, Vollenweider has managed to maintain his artistic integrity and vision despite increasing commercial success. The harpist's 1991 album *Book of Roses* is a testament to his ability to expand his scope as a composer while keeping his trademark sound intact. –LK

Behind the Gardens / CBS 1981
Vollenweider's debut album featured electric harp music. Beautiful sounds. –PK

Caverna Magica / CBS 1983
A followup album featuring harp in a small group ensemble. Very nice. –PK

White Winds / CBS 1984
A fantastic album of intricate compositions and moods. –PK

Trilogy / CBS
Excellent 2-CD compilation. Contains the first three albums plus *Pace Verde* and half of *Eine Art Suite in 13 Teilen*. –PK

○ **Down to the Moon / CBS** 1986
A masterpiece of beautiful melodies and rhythms from Vollenweider's electric harp. –PK

Dancing with the Lion / CBS 1989
A recent release of Vollenweider's new-age/jazz harp music in a large group setting. –PK

Book of Roses / CBS 1991
A multicultural tapestry combining symphonic, flamenco, African, and Eastern European elements with Vollenweider's characteristic "otherworldly" atmospheres and spirited pop rhythms. –LK

Eine Art Suite in 13 Teilen / (SWISS IMPORT)
A rare import-CD from Switzerland, featuring early material not found on any other release. Worth looking for. –PK

KIT WATKINS

Progressive electronic, ethnic fusion, adult alternative. The Virginia-based keyboardist creates finely crafted music that always seems to straddle a handful of genres with ease. He was a founding member of the short-lived, yet highly original, progressive 70s band, Happy the Man. In the early 80s, Watkins began building his own home studio and produced consistently inviting music that draws on his first-rate keyboard skills and his keen ear for sonic detail. He has recently been exploring a darker, more ambient side with the release of his two *Thought Tones* albums, both of which are highly recommended. –LK

Azure / EAST SIDE DIGITAL 1990
A truly eclectic brew of progressive rock, classical, jazz, world, and ambient music. –MPD

○ **Sunstruck / EAST SIDE DIGITAL** 1990
Watkins is at his best on the lengthy ambient synthesizer excursions. –MPD

WIND MACHINE

Adult alternative, new acoustic, chamber jazz. Since its inception in 1986, Wind Machine has excelled at creating guitar-based music that dabbles in styles ranging from blues and bluegrass to jazz, rock, and new-age atmospherics. Core members Steve Mesple, Joe Scott, and Blake Eberhard utilize a vast arsenal of instruments ranging from mandolin, dobro, banjo, and some of their own guitar-hybrid inventions to trombone, harmonica, and fretless bass. –LK

Rain Maiden / SILVER WIND 1989
Another fine album of contemporary instrumental music. –LK

○ **Voices in the Wind / SILVER WIND** 1991
Breezy instrumentals with an emphasis on contemporary jazz and folk influences. The production is crystal clear and as smooth as silk, which gives the group's upbeat originals a soothing quality. –LK

GEORGE WINSTON

Solo instrumental, neo-classical. Though George Winston is one of the most popular solo pianists in the history of contemporary instrumental music, he didn't start playing until after high school. Inspired by blues, rock, and R&B styles, he initially gravitated toward the organ and electric piano. Then in 1971 he heard the records of legendary stride pianist Fats Waller, which motivated him to concentrate on the acoustic piano and develop his own style. After recording his first solo album, *Ballads and Blues*, in 1972, he stopped playing for several years. He eventually was encouraged to delve into the instrument again when he discovered the music of New Orleans R&B pianist Professor Longhair. In 1980 he released the first of four solo piano albums for the Windham Hill label. These became amazingly successful and helped create industry support for more pastoral forms of the instrumental music subsequently referred to as "new age." Winston's recording style combines his gift for impressionistic melodies with American folk influences, yet his live

performances continue to reflect his longstanding interests in stride and blues piano styles as well. –LK

Autumn / WINDHAM HILL 1980
Winston's impressions of the fall season are full of slow chording and sudden melodic runs on his acoustic piano. He captures the mixed feelings of the season, both its final flaring of life and its gradual retreat. –WR

☆ **December / WINDHAM HILL** 1982
The mother of all solo instrumental albums, and with good reason. Mixing traditional carols with Pachelbel's Canon and a few originals, Winston produces a solo piano album of unparalleled — and undeniable — beauty. How can music be simultaneously stirring and soothing, relaxed yet exalted? Millions have found the answer here, and an industry has spent more than a decade trying to duplicate it. –WR

Winter into Spring / WINDHAM HILL 1982
In a sense, this second seasonal album follows an opposite direction from *Autumn*, its hard, isolated notes and stop-and-start style gradually giving way from the stasis of winter to the growth and movement of spring. It's a good album for beginning your day. –WR

PAUL WINTER CONSORT

New-age. For the past 30 years, Paul Winter has been following a steady path toward his ideal of creating what he calls "Earth Music," a vital celebration of the creatures and cultures of the planet. Much of that time has been spent touring the world with his influential Paul Winter Consort, which combines jazz, classical, Brazilian, and other ethnic influences with sounds from nature. Best known for his attempts to weave humpback whale songs and wolf cries into his music, Winter's desire to awaken listeners to the plight of endangered species has won him the World Wildlife Fund Award and the United Nations Global 500 Award, among other distinctions. *Earthbeat*, his collaboration with Moscow's Dmitri Pokrovsky Singers, became the first album to feature original music by Russians and Americans together. This project brought Winter international attention as a musical peacemaker and gained him the 1991 Peace Abbey "Courage of Conscience" Award. Musically, Winter's most admirable features include his soaring lyricism as a soprano saxophone soloist, his ability to surround himself with top-notch musicians, and his gift for weaving natural sounds and atmospheres into his music while retaining the spontaneous spirit associated with jazz. –LK

☆ **Icarus / CBS** 1972
This, a reissue of saxophonist Paul Winter's finest album, marks a transitional point in his career from jazz to his own brand of contemporary instrumental. But one can simply revel in the lovely melodies, the contemplative sounds, and the tasteful production of George Martin, especially on the justly famous title track by Ralph Towner. –WR

Common Ground / A&M 1978
This is a good example of Winter's nature-conscious music, as he has incorporated the sounds of birds, wolves, and humpback whales into his ensemble. It's surprising how close such wild animals come to playing pop music. –WR

Sun Singer / LIVING MUSIC 1983
Striking example of Winter's lyricism. Paul Halley on keyboards and Glen Velez playing frame drum and percussion. –LK

Earthbeat / LIVING MUSIC 1987
Billed as the album of original music created by Americans and Russians together, this album features Halley, Velez, guitarist Oscar Castro-Neves, and cellist Eugene Friesen collaborating on some selections with the Dmitri Pokrovsky Singers, a vocal ensemble rooted in the tradition of Russian village music. Traditional music from throughout Russia is mixed with Winter's Brazilian-influenced sound. There are also some beautiful instrumentals and, true to Winter's style, some natural sounds, most notably the calls of the Alaskan tundra wolf and Russian loon. –LK

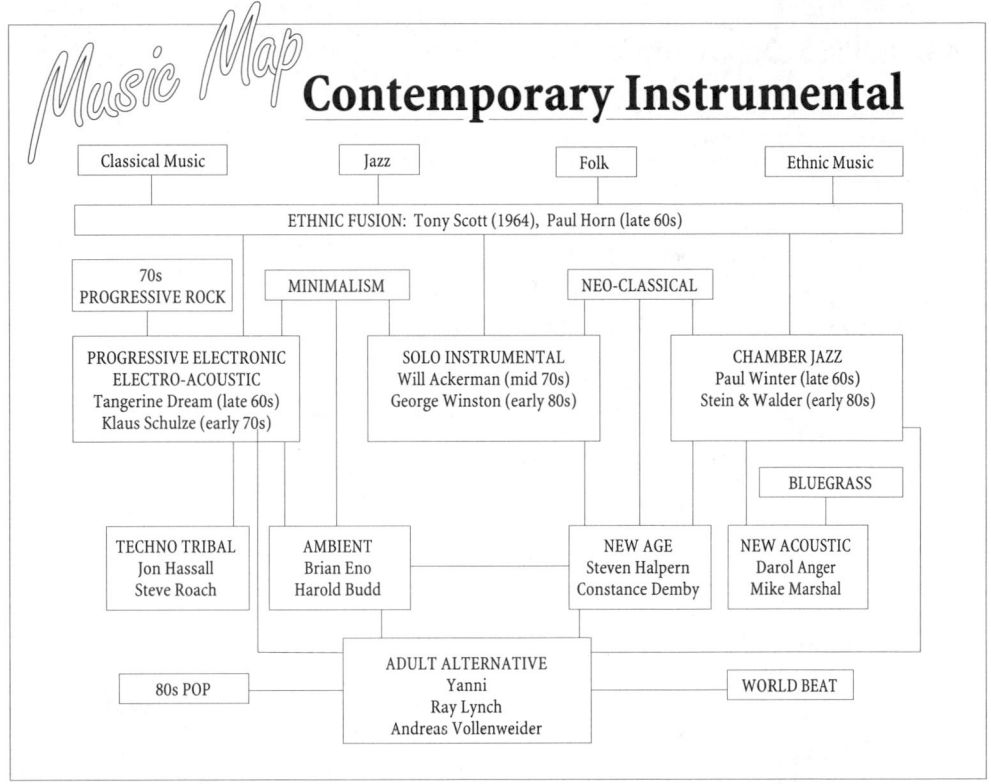

Contemporary Instrumental

Music Map

| Classical Music | Jazz | Folk | Ethnic Music |

ETHNIC FUSION: Tony Scott (1964), Paul Horn (late 60s)

70s PROGRESSIVE ROCK   **MINIMALISM**   **NEO-CLASSICAL**

PROGRESSIVE ELECTRONIC ELECTRO-ACOUSTIC
Tangerine Dream (late 60s)
Klaus Schulze (early 70s)

SOLO INSTRUMENTAL
Will Ackerman (mid 70s)
George Winston (early 80s)

CHAMBER JAZZ
Paul Winter (late 60s)
Stein & Walder (early 80s)

BLUEGRASS

TECHNO TRIBAL
Jon Hassall
Steve Roach

AMBIENT
Brian Eno
Harold Budd

NEW AGE
Steven Halpern
Constance Demby

NEW ACOUSTIC
Darol Anger
Mike Marshal

80s POP

ADULT ALTERNATIVE
Yanni
Ray Lynch
Andreas Vollenweider

WORLD BEAT

Earth: Voices of a Planet / LIVING MUSIC   1990
Winter regulars and some special guest artists have put together a musical journey that starts in North America and travels through Africa, Antarctica, South America, Australia, Asia, and Europe. Selections feature indigenous nature sounds and traditional influences from various regions. –LK

WOLFF & HENNINGS

Ambient, ethnic fusion. The mystical sounds of Tibetan bells and singing bowls have been used for centuries in Buddhist meditation and religious rites. Henry Wolff and Nancy Hennings first encountered these instruments during a 1969 trip to India and Nepal where they studied with the Kagyu branch of Tibetan Buddhism. Since 1971, the duo has been releasing a subtle, haunting series of recordings featuring Tibetan bells, including a collaboration with Grateful Dead percussionist Mickey Hart called *Yamantaka*. Wolff and Hennings also contributed their skills to the Philip Glass soundtrack for the film *Koyaanisqatsi*, which brought the transcendent sound of the bells to wider audiences. The uncanny resonances of these acoustic instruments produce music that often sounds electronically generated. –LK

Tibetan Bells II / CELESTIAL HARMONIES   1978
While the duo creates its own compositions, this early album is closer in concept to the way these instruments are traditionally used. –LK

Tibetan Bells III / CELESTIAL HARMONIES   1988
Tibetan Bells III: The Empty Mirror is another compelling album of purely acoustic Tibetan bell music. –LK

○ **Bells of Sh'ang Sh'ung / CELESTIAL HARM.**   1991
This album is actually a 14-part sound poem depicting a journey to the mythic precincts of Sh'ang Sh'ung, the fabled lost kingdom where the most precious teachings of Buddhism

originated. While the purity of the Tibetan bells remains central to the vision of the artists, this recording also makes use of other instruments, both Eastern and Western. The synthesizer, long considered the electronic counterpart to the magic resonances of the bells, adds additional depth and atmosphere to this ambitious venture. Consistent with previous Tibetan bells recordings, the studio itself is exploited as an instrument in its own right. –LK

Yamantaka / CELESTIAL HARMONIES
Grateful Dead drummer and world musicologist Mickey Hart's most ethereal work is on this collaboration with Wolff & Jennings. (See the Worldbeat section of the World Music chapter for more Mickey Hart recordings.)–LK

ERIC WOLLO

Progressive electronic, ambient, ethnic fusion. Norwegian composer Erik Wollo started out as a jazz guitarist and dabbled in jazz-rock fusion on his early recordings. In 1984, however, he came out with *Traces*, an electronic album of startling originality. His most recent release is equally impressive. While there's always a sense of warmth to his atmospheric pieces, his music resounds with the stark beauty of Norway's wintry landscapes. Through his subtle minimalist patterns and nebulous breaths of sound, you can easily imagine the composer staring through windows splayed with ice crystals as Arctic winds whisper across the snow fields and ethereal northern lights pulse steadily in the distance. –LK

○ **Traces / BADLAND**   1984
Expansive synthesizer textures float over the slowly churning, hypnotic drives of sequencer patterns and primal rhythms on this collection of richly hued electronic dreamscapes. –LK

Images of Light / EUROCK   1990
Another sublime set of Northern visions with a few darker, more experimental pieces. On "Urban Space," for instance,

Samplers & Collections

The field of contemporary instrumental music has probably inspired more artist collections than any other musical genre. Established CI record companies generally release at least one sampler every year or so, giving listeners a taste of the most engaging and accessible cuts from upcoming albums. As it turns out, these compilations are often the label's best-selling title, a fact that has led several of the companies to produce a number of fine thematic collections as well. The following list distinguishes up to three samplers for each label (though most have released many more), as well as a miscellaneous section for the best collections released through smaller companies.

— Linda Kohanov

some gritty sampled saxophone undulations and long melodic lines successfully romanticize the cold, hard imagery of mechanized life. –LK

YANNI

Progressive electronic, adult alternative. Yanni's grandiose keyboard style is both accessible and exciting, two elements that have led to his success in the realm of adult-alternative radio. His explosive, pop-influenced instrumentals and romantic pianistic ballads have also made him a popular touring and recording artist for the Private Music label. In addition to his original television, commercial, and film scores, Yanni's music has been used extensively on programs like *Wide World of Sports* and coverage of the Olympic Games. This aspect of his career seems especially appropriate when you consider that he achieved early success not as a musician, but as a member of the Greek National Swimming Team. (He broke the national freestyle record at age 14.) Born in Kalamata, Greece, Yanni arrived in the US after high school and obtained a degree in psychology from the University of Minnesota before diving headfirst into music. It didn't take long for the self-taught keyboardist and composer to establish himself as a studio musician, jingles composer, and producer. After gaining an impressive cult-following for his first independently released album, Yanni was picked up by Private Music and has become one of the label's best-selling artists. One of the most visible artists in the contemporary instrumental realm, Yanni's rise to fame was expedited in the early 90s by his romantic relationship with actress Linda Evans, which gained him coverage on mainstream programs like "Lifestyles of the Rich and Famous" as well as appearances on the daytime talk show circuit. –LK

○ **Out of Silence / PRIVATE MUSIC**   1987
Yanni's second album, like his first (*Keys to Imagination*) was recorded entirely on synthesizers at his home studio. The composer/performer makes extensive use of the orchestral possibilities of electronics, creating big themes to play across elaborate, echoing rhythm tracks. Unlike much adult alternative music, it's constantly stimulating foreground music with an extremely modern sound. –WR

Niki Nana / PRIVATE MUSIC   1989
Yanni takes a more overtly pop approach here, adding other musicians and vocalists (on the title track) and even playing in dance rhythms, so what was always an engaging style of music becomes more accessible to a wider audience. –WR

YAS-KAZ

Progressive electronic, ethnic fusion. A university-trained percussionist, Japanese artist Yasukazu Sato gained attention for his international tours as composer for the innovative dance group Sankaijuku. His unusual combination of ancient Oriental forms, spacious musical atmospheres, and

ceremonial percussion provided perfect accompaniment to the ritualistic movements and slowly unfolding acrobatic feats of this modern Japanese dance company. He has also scored several award-winning Japanese films, performed with American jazz saxophonist Wayne Shorter and Japanese synthesist Himekami, and recorded a number of imaginative solo albums. –LK

○ **Darkness in Dreams / KUCKUCK**   1991
Compiled from six of his finest recordings, these selections illustrate the composer's gift for translating fantasy into sonic reality. Each cut is a world in itself, in which luminous zither cascades and tribal percussion tracks alternate with joyous folk dances and Oriental melodies for full string orchestra that soar over waves of synthesized sequencer patterns. A good introduction to the varied moods of Yas-Kaz (most of his recordings are rare Japanese imports). –LK

NEW-AGE COLLECTIONS

○ **Amer. Gramaphone Sampler #1 / AMER. GRAM.**   1987
American Gramaphone Samplers #1 & #2 feature a number of selections from Mannheim Steamroller's *Fresh Aire* series as well as pieces by other American Gramaphone mainstays like Eric Hansen, Ron Cooley, and Checkfield. –LK
○ **Amer. Gramaphone Sampler #2 / AMER. GRAM.**
○ **Anthems / LIVING MUSIC**   1992
In celebration of the label's tenth anniversary, Living Music has brought together music from 18 of the 22 albums in its catalog, featuring Eugene Friesen, Oscar Castro Neves, Glen Velez, Paul Halley, Russia's Dmitri Pokrovsky Singers, and of course, the label's founder Paul Winter. Though Living Music has two other samplers on the market, *Anthems: Ten Years of Living Music* is by far the most comprehensive. –LK
○ **Dali: The Endless Enigma / CORIOLIS**   1990
In homage to the late Salvador Dali, some of the world's top electronic musicians were commissioned to create surrealistic sound interpretations of their favorite Dali paintings. Selections by American musicians Michael Stearns, Djam Karet, Robert Rich and Steve Roach, Walter Holland, Loren Nerell, and Bo Tomlyn sit side-by-side with pieces by German synthesist Klaus Schulze and Spanish electronic artist Michel Huygen. (Coriolis Records, Box 3528, Orange, CA 92665.) –LK
○ **A Door in the Air / ECHODISCS**   1991
Like the Hearts of Space record label, Echodiscs is the offshoot of a widely syndicated contemporary instrumental radio program — in this case, "Echoes" (Box 224, Eagle, PA 19480). The company's first release is a collection of noteworthy recordings made especially for broadcast. These "Living Room Concerts" are captured in the homes of the artists by Echoes producer and host John Diliberto. *A Door in the Air* offers a sampling of his favorites by Robert Rich, Stein & Walder, Arco Iris, Michael Brook, David Torn, and Steve Roach. –LK
○ **Erdenklang - Magic Age II / ERDENKLANG**   1992
This German label has an extensive roster of European contemporary instrumental artists with an emphasis on electronic music (both pop-oriented and progressive). *Magic Age II* is the second in a series that features evocative pieces of a more ambient nature, including some previously unreleased material from Peeter Vahi, Hector Zazou, Blue Chip Orchestra, and Lightwave, among others. –LK
○ **The Fruits of Our Labor / GLOBAL PACIFIC**   1986
The Global Pacific label's first sampler, *Global Pacific - The Fruits of Our Labor*, features the early work of artists like Steve Kindler, Ben Tavera King, Paul Greaver, and Bob Kindler, among others. –LK
○ **Global Pacific - Global Voyage / GLOBAL PACIFIC**   1988
Selections from popular Global Pacific recordings by Paul Horn, David Friesen, Georgia Kelly, Bob Kindler, Do'ah, Steve Kindler, and Teje Bell. –LK

○ **Hearts of Space - Starflight 1 / HEARTS OF SPACE**   1986
This album's also originally produced for the popular weekly
radio show. Overall feeling is quite different than *Cruisers 1.0*.
The ten lush, ambient pieces featured are taken from albums
by Michael Amerlan, Tim Clark, and Steve Roach. −LK

○ **Hearts of Space - Cruisers 1.0 / HEARTS OF SPACE**   1988
Produced in the tradition of the "Music from the Hearts of
Space" syndicated radio show, *Cruisers 1.0* is a tightly
programmed musical journey in which selections by various
artists flow in and out of each other almost seamlessly over
the course of an hour — an effect more akin to a "soundtrack
for the mind" than a label sampler. Pieces by Don Harriss,
Gershon Kingsley, Klaus Schonning, Michael Stearns, and Ken
Stover are featured on these gently rhythmic pieces. −LK

○ **Hearts of Space - Sampler '90 / HEARTS OF SPACE**   1990
While the previous *Hearts of Space* collections featured music
from other labels, the *Universe Sampler '90* is the first
compilation of artists signed to the Hearts of Space record
company (which grew out of the radio program). Music is by
Kevin Braheny, Bill Douglas, Constance Demby, Raphael, and
others. −LK

○ **Inner Landscapes / CLEAR PRODUCTIONS**   1991
The best and most recent Clear Productions venture includes
selections by Kit Watkins, John Serrie, Laraaji, and Steve
Roach, among others. −LK

○ **Looking East - Hungary / ERDENKLANG**   1991
The unexpected opening of the Iron Curtain has recently given
birth to Erdenklang's collections of synthesizer music from
Eastern European countries. This album offers an evocative
cross-section of pop, cross-cultural, and avant-garde
electronic composers who have never before been heard in the
West. A noteworthy achievement. −LK

○ **Looking East - Poland / ERDENKLANG**   1990

○ **Narada - A Childhood Remembered / NARADA**
Twelve Narada artists were commissioned to compose pieces
inspired by favorite works of children's literature, each
colorfully illustrated in storybook fashion included with the
CD booklet. −LK

☆ **Narada - Alma Del Sur / NARADA**   1992
One of Narada's classiest packages yet, *Alma Del Sur* is a
showcase for contemporary South American music by
Argentinian multi-instrumentalist Bernardo Rubaja, Brazilian
flutist and percussionist Junior Homrich, Bolivian panpipe
virtuoso Gonzalo Vargas (accompanied by the North
American band Ancient Future), Paraguayan harpist Roberto
Perera, and the Bolivian ensemble Rumillajta, among others.
Liner notes include exquisite photos of traditional artwork
and overviews of South American history and music, as well
as biographies of the artists. Don't be misled into thinking this
is a collection of traditional music, however. It is instead a
survey of modern styles palatable to a wide variety of
listeners. −LK

☆ **Narada Wilderness Collection / NARADA**
Although Narada has released numerous samplers over the
years, this Wisconsin-based label has become the leader in
producing engaging thematic albums. The *Narada Wilderness
Collection* features impressionistic works by company staples
like David Arkenstone, Spencer Brewer, Tingstad and Rumbel,
Peter Buffett, David Lanz, and others. The extensive CD

booklet includes a statement from each artist about the
specific landscape that inspired his or her piece, as well as
stunning nature photography to go along with it. −LK

○ **Private Music - Polar Shift / PRIVATE MUSIC**   1991
This project was created to raise awareness and money to aid
in the preservation of Antarctica, with a portion of the
proceeds going to the Cousteau Society and other
environmental organizations working toward that goal.
Opening appropriately with the main theme to Vangelis's
famous album, *Antarctica*, Polar Shift also features selections
by Constance Demby, Yanni, Chris Spheeris/Paul Voudouris,
Enya, John Tesh, Suzanne Ciani, and Kitaro, among others. −LK

○ **Private Music Sampler 5 / PRIVATE MUSIC**   1990
A more recent sampler with selections by artists like Yanni,
Tangerine Dream, Andy Summers, and Patrick O'Hearn. −LK

○ **Raven: A Sampler / RAVEN RECORDING**   1991
An eclectic sampling of the recordings released on the small
New Jersey-based company, Raven Recording, including
music by the label's founder and main artist Gabrielle Roth as
well as pieces by Matt Balitsaris, Nicholas, and Raphael. −LK

○ **Visionaries / CLEAR PRODUCTIONS**   1989
Clear Productions (1489 Coddington Rd., Brooktondale, NY
14817) occasionally puts out admirable collections of work by
independent artists. Often these pieces are commissioned
especially for the project rather than taken from previously
released albums. This particular recording features new-age
synthesist Iasos, hammered-dulcimer virtuoso Dan Duggan,
and pianist Richard Shulman, among others. −LK

☆ **Windham Hill - First Ten Years / WINDHAM HILL**   1990
Windham Hill has put out so many samplers that it can be
confounding to choose one over another. This double CD,
however, features a selection or two from just about everyone
who has ever recorded for the *main* label (not the Windham
Hill jazz or singer/songwriter divisions). A comprehensive
overview of the contemporary instrumental sound for which
the company is most famous. −LK

○ **Windham Hill - Sampler '92 / WINDHAM HILL**   1992
A taste of the most recent work from label mainstays like
Michael Manring, Alex de Grassi, Nightnoise, Michael Hedges,
Mark Isham, Montreux, David Torn, Liz Story, Modern
Mandolin Quartet, Phil Aaberg, and Will Ackerman. −LK

○ **Windham Hill - Soul of ... / WINDHAM HILL**   1987
Windham Hill's *Soul of the Machine* collection of
contemporary electronic and electro-acoustic music primarily
features little-known artists, many of whom are not signed to
the label, including Michael Foreman, Fred Simon, Michael
Whiteley, Schoenherz and Scott, Colin Chin, Philippe Saisse,
Mark Darnell, Tim Story, Roy Finch, Ted Greenwald, and Scott
Hiltzik. −LK

☆ **World of Private Music - Vol. I / PRIVATE MUSIC**   1986
Private Music's first sampler is arguably its most interesting,
since many of the artists featured are now considered
pioneers in the contemporary electronic field. This recording
is also historical in the sense that it illustrates the admirable
aesthetics on which the company was founded, before
commercial concerns took over. Selections from early albums
by Yanni, Patrick O'Hearn, Lucia Hwong, Sanford Ponder,
Eddie Jobson, Leo Kottke, and Jerry Goodman. −LK

SOUNDTRACKS

The motion picture soundtrack as we know it today dates from the early 40s, although film music itself goes back much farther than synchronized sound. Piano and organ accompaniments were played live in theaters from the beginning of the century, and it was during 1916 that Victor Schertzinger wrote the first full orchestral and choral score for a motion picture.

During the 30s, it became customary for record companies to release official recorded versions of songs heard in musical films. Hence, much of the musical history of Fred Astaire's RKO work, in films such as *Top Hat* and *Swing Time*, was captured simultaneously on the Brunswick label (now reissued by Columbia Records). And certain orchestral scores by recognized composers, such as Arthur Bliss's music for Alexander Korda's 1936 science-fiction epic *Things to Come*, found a separate life in the concert hall.

But it wasn't until 1942 that a record company fixed on the notion of recording and releasing the major parts of a full orchestra score. The film was *The Jungle Book*, produced by Alexander Korda and scored by Miklos Rozsa. One piece of Rozsa's, the waltz from his score for the 1942 film *Lydia*, had previously been recorded on a single 78 RPM disc by RCA Records with some success. Shortly after *The Jungle Book*'s release, RCA brought Rozsa to New York to record a suite of the key movements from his new score with the NBC Symphony Orchestra, with a narration of the story provided by Sabu, the star of the film. This set of 78 RPM records, which has since been issued many times, marked the start of the movie soundtrack as a record genre.

The next major development took place in 1945, when MGM established its record label, MGM Records. The studio had originally planned to start the label in 1941, with Tommy Dorsey heading it, but the war intervened with a five-year delay. The first "musical biography" was *Till the Clouds Roll By*, inspired by the life and songs of Jerome Kern. It seemed logical to release eight of the musical highlights from the film in a set of four 78 RPM records, which was precisely what was done, with some modifications to make the songs suitable for release on record. These included the removal of lengthy instrumental breaks and sound effects that were germane to the screen presentation but not to the record.

Till the Clouds Roll By was a success, if not a raging best-seller, but it established the pattern for musical soundtracks. Its release ahead of the film secured radio play for the songs, thus promoting the film, and also made the record-buying public aware of the release of the movie in a way that print advertising alone would not have. Subsequently, with the advent of the long-playing record two years later, studios would release their musicals in reasonably complete form, either on their own labels or under contract to other record companies.

Looking at this history more than 40 years later, one must bear in mind just how important the soundtrack album was to the public. In the days before home video (and the boom in movie memorabilia shops), the soundtrack album was the only piece of a movie a fan could actually own, take home, and enjoy at will, without having to depend on the movie studio or the local theater or, in later years, the television station. Additionally, the early soundtrack albums appeared in the era of radio, before the visual medium completely overwhelmed popular culture, and their impact and importance were that much greater at the time.

For the film studios, the soundtrack album (whether devoted to dramatic film scores or musicals) became a major marketing tool, promoting the film by its release weeks ahead of the opening date, securing radio play for the major songs, and promoting the studio's own music-publishing interests. This often led to peculiarities in song and musical lineups. Most movie musical albums, for example, failed to include dance numbers, incidental music, and choral pieces, since these were not hooked to specific singing personalities. Additionally, the running-time restrictions on 78s and early long-playing records required the cutting of extended instrumental breaks, however pleasant.

Finally, there were the peculiarities of the music and movie businesses themselves: Frank Sinatra, who was under contract to MGM Studios for a period of five years and turned in at least one major musical performance on screen during that time (*On the Town*), never appeared on an MGM soundtrack album because he was under exclusive contract to Columbia Records in the 40s. However, the soundtrack album to MGM's 1956 *High Society*, featuring Sinatra, Bing Crosby, and Louis Armstrong, did appear on Capitol Records, where Sinatra was recording in the 50s.

The soundtrack business went along as an adjunct to the movie business until the 60s, when changes began occurring, most notably a splintering of the market. Swept up by the boom in pop and rock music and a decline in traditional entertainment and subjects, studios stopped making musicals (except for major, multi-million-dollar blockbusters) and began demanding a lighter touch in the scoring of their dramatic films. At the same time, two generations of listeners and fans — one that had grown up when the older films were originally in the theaters, and one that had grown up with them on television — began expressing an interest in the music that had filled their lives. The business of reissuing soundtracks had existed, particularly where musicals were concerned, since the switch from 78s to long-playing records. But in the early 60s, various labels (most notably Capitol, Decca/London, and Warner Bros.) began commissioning new recordings that made use of the dramatic improvements that had been made in record fidelity and stereo sound. *Gone with the Wind* by Max Steiner, *Ben Hur*, *El Cid*, and *King of Kings* by Miklos Rozsa, and the *Adventures of Robin Hood* by Erich Wolfgang Korngold were just a few of the scores represented in new recordings, often done under the supervision of their original composers.

By the beginning of the 70s, with the recognition of film's cultural importance (it even became a field of academic study), re-recordings had become common. Producers Peter Munves and George Korngold and conductor Charles Gerhardt brought the first successful extended series of such efforts to RCA Records in the form of the *Classic Film Scores* series, with each volume devoted to a specific composer (e.g., *The Classic Film Scores of Alfred Newman*). The Gerhardt series was ideal for the serious listener and the novice just getting started. Careful attention was paid to the details and nuances of the music itself, and the material was assembled in suites of easily absorbed length.

Meanwhile, on a more intensive level, Elmer Bernstein (himself a major movie composer) had begun a concerted effort to preserve scores and secure rights for the original composers and their estates. As an adjunct to this effort, he made a monumental series of re-recordings in England of vintage film scores in their entirety, through his Film Music Society label.

The 70s and 80s saw a veritable explosion in the field of film music, as a second generation of major screen composers — Elmer Bernstein, Jerry Goldsmith, Leonard Rosenman, Ennio Morricone (whose music for the Clint Eastwood/Sergio Leone "man with no name" Westerns virtually revolutionized that genre) — achieved wide recognition and major composer status. Along with new soundtrack albums, which now seem to accompany virtually every film release, even of the lowest-budgeted picture, re-recordings became still more common using various European orchestras, which work under far less restrictive union rules and for far less money than their American counterparts.

The 80s also saw the establishment of a new kind of soundtrack album, which actually had its roots in the 70s: the rock & roll soundtrack. Films built around rock groups and personalities had been common from the 50s onward (most notably the relatively well-made early films showing the young, lean Elvis Presley; the early British films of Cliff Richard and the Shadows; and the one great work in the genre, the Beatles in *A Hard Day's Night*), but the 70s saw the emergence of the rock soundtrack as a separate screen entity. It began with George Lucas's *American Graffiti*, the soundtrack which, filled with a superbly selected body of rock oldies, was nearly as prominent in the film as any of the actors. The accompanying double album also became a massive seller.

Francis Ford Coppola's *Apocalypse Now*, with its use of 60s hits, moved the formula up a decade and a notch in dramatic intensity, even if its most famous scene involved Wagner's "Ride of the Valkyries" and a helicopter attack. But it was *Fast Times at Ridgemont High*, another film about adolescent life, that brought the formula first used in *American Graffiti* into a contemporary time frame, with an enviable assembly of catchy singles and FM-style hits by contemporary rock artists. From there on, the die was cast: producers saw the path to success with otherwise flawed and conceptually weak movies was simply to license the right rock tracks, and many movies of the 80s and 90s acquired the feel of a jukebox in operation. With varying degrees of success, the specific music involved everything from post-new-wave (*I Was a Teenage Zombie*) to such vintage music-and-myth-mixing efforts as Oliver Stone's *The Doors*, where the songs structured the film and occasionally the soundtracks outperformed and outlasted the movies themselves.

— Bruce Eder

SOUNDTRACKS

○ **The Adventures of Robin Hood / VARESE**
A surprisingly dull score (from the 1938 movie) by Erich Wolfgang Korngold — one that he reportedly had a lot of trouble finishing — well and rousingly re-recorded and elevated by its moments of inspiration, which are fewer in number than typical for this composer. –BE

Against All Odds - Orig. Soundtrack / ATLANTIC   1984
The soundtrack to this remake of *Out of the Past* is highlighted by the title song, "Against All Odds (Take a Look at Me Now)," a dramatic ballad sung by Phil Collins that topped the charts for three weeks. It also contains songs by Stevie Nicks, Peter Gabriel, Big Country, and Kid Creole & the Coconuts, plus selections from the score by Michel Colombier and Larry Carlton. –WR

Alamo Bay / WARNER   1985
One of Ry Cooder's more impressive scores ties in with the Texas location of the film with some Tex-Mex mood music. Most of Cooder's usual session friends are present, including Van Dyke Parks, David Lindley, Jim Keltner, and John Hiatt. Lee Ving of Fear makes a guest appearance, and Cesar Rosas and David Hidalgo of Los Lobos sing on one track. –WR

○ **The Alamo - Soundtrack / VARESE / BB# 7**   1960
A famous Dimitri Tiomkin score, which suffers from a lack of melodic invention and extended flat passages broken by a few memorable moments. It has its fans, however. –BE

☆ **Alien / SILVA SCREEN / BB# 113**   1980
Jerry Goldsmith's music, recorded under the baton of Lionel Newman, holds up nearly as well as Ridley Scott's 1979 movie, with long, lyrical passages broken up by genuinely unsettling timbral effects. –BE

American Gigolo - Orig. Soundtrack / POLYGRAM   1980
Danceable electronic score by Eurodisc master Giorgio Moroder, including "Call Me" by Blondie, which was #1 for six weeks. –WR

☆ **American Graffiti - Vol. 1 / MCA / BB# 10**   1973
A stunner of an oldies soundtrack, which revolutionized the licensing and use of classic rock songs in movies. One of the great rock oldies collections. It's enjoyable on every level. –BE

☆ **An American in Paris - Original Soundtrack / CBS**
An expanded edition of the George Gershwin showcase soundtrack from the 1951 movie, with good sound (especially on the title ballet, re-scored by Saul Chaplin). –BE

☆ **Animal House - Orig. Soundtrack / MCA / BB# 71**   1978
A superb reinterpretation of the oldies soundtrack format, with new renditions of classics like "Louie Louie" that work as well as the originals. An enjoyable souvenir from the movie, one that holds up on its own. –BE

Back to the Future - Original Soundtrack / MCA   1985
Huey Lewis and the News scored a #1 hit with the typically bouncy "The Power of Love" from this album. Completists will also want to note the appearance of otherwise unavailable tracks by Lindsey Buckingham and Eric Clapton. –WR

○ **Back to the Future - Part 2 / MCA**   1989
This is mostly "effect" or "mood" music, without much that would draw your attention during the movie. Of course, there is a healthy sprinkling of variations on the theme that Alan Silvestri uses in all the *Back to the Future* movies. –TEH

○ **Back to the Future - Part 3 / VARESE SARABANDE**   1990
More of the same from Silvestri, with perhaps a bit more thematic material. It also includes ZZ Top's "Doubleback," arranged (by Silvestri) for banjo, fiddle, and bass. –TEH

○ **The Film Music of John Barry / CBS**
An interesting if predictable compilation, touching most of the key parts of the composer's 1960 output. –BE

☆ **Batman - Original Soundtrack / WARNER**   1989
The best of all the Danny Elfman soundtracks. The "Batman Theme" is familiar to all who've seen the film, but anyone who hasn't listened to the "Finale" is in for a real treat. Without a doubt Elfman has a flair for writing for brass. –TEH

Batman Returns / WARNER   1992
As anyone would expect, this is more of the same thematic material as in the first movie. However, Elfman does use more of the choral effects of which he seems to have become so fond. Includes "Face to Face," performed by Siouxsie and the Banshees and cowritten by the group and Elfman. –TEH

Beauty and the Beast / DISNEY   1991
This music by Alan Menken and lyrics by Howard Ashman are positively delightful. While not as good as the *Little Mermaid* score, this album has its moments, such as "Be Our Guest" (in an *A Chorus Line* style). Includes both orchestral and vocal selections, featuring the talents of Robby Benson, Paige O'Hara, and Angela Lansbury, among others. Album also includes "Beauty and the Beast" as a duet between Celine Dion and Peabo Bryson. –TEH

○ **Beetlejuice / GEFFEN**   1989
Danny Elfman's score for this 1988 Tim Burton film is dark, rollicking fun. It includes Harry Belafonte's hits "Day-O (The Banana Boat Song)," and "Jump in Line (Shake, Shake Senora)." –TEH

○ **Belle of New York / CBS**   1991
A deliberate period music collection from the 1952 movie, lacking in topflight songs but a good showcase for Fred Astaire's voice. –BE

○ **Ben-Hur / POLYGRAM / BB# 6**
Miklos Rozsa conducting the Royal Philharmonic Orchestra. This 70s re-recording by the composer of the 1959 movie has a very bright sound and most of the highlights, but lacks the weight of the original recordings. –BE

☆ **Ben-Hur / COLUMBIA**
A monumental double CD of Miklos Rozsa's music, assembled from the complete two original albums plus the original film tracks, all cleaned up and properly re-sequenced. –BE

Beverly Hills Cop / MCA   1984
Two million copies of this album were sold within a year of release, which is no surprise, given that it contained such hits as Patti LaBelle's "New Attitude," Glenn Frey's "The Heat Is On," and Harold Faltermeyer's "Axel F." Another notable aspect of the recording is the small-print admission "Contains additional songs that are not in the film." In other words, this is more of a compilation than a soundtrack album *per se*. It didn't bother anybody, though. –WR

○ **The Big Chill / MOTOWN**   1983
Motown scored big with this album, which contains ten 60s hits, from Marvin Gaye's "I Heard It through the Grapevine" to Procol Harum's "A Whiter Shade of Pale," just the sort of thing the yuppie thirtysomethings in the movie loved, and music rediscovered by the audience that saw the film. –WR

The Big Country / SILVA SCREEN
A good idea not brought off well. Jerome Moross's sweeping score for the 1958 movie *The Big Country* (re-recorded digitally) has been performed much too flaccidly, with none of the verve the music demands, despite some fine attention to detail by Tony Bremer and the Philharmonic Orchestra. –BE

○ **Blade Runner / WARNER**   1982
A somewhat unsatisfying orchestral re-recording of Vangelis's original electronic score, but acceptable in the absence of the Vangelis music on record. –BE

Border Radio / CAPITOL-ENIGMA   1987
Former Blasters and X songwriter/guitarist Dave Alvin scored this film and brought in his friends — the cream of the early 80s Los Angeles rock scene — to help. Various tracks feature

Alvin, fellow X member John Doe, Green on Red, Steve Berlin of the Blasters, and Los Lobos, among others. –WR

○ **Born on the Fourth of July / MCA**   1989
The first eight tracks on this disc are rock and pop, including songs from Edie Brickell & the New Bohemians, Don McLean, and the Temptations. The last six are from the pen of John Williams. When I saw the movie, I was haunted by the music that is on these tracks. It's just as effective here. –TEH

The Breakfast Club / A&M   1985
Anchored by the Simple Minds hit "Don't You (Forget About Me)," this also features tracks by Wang Chung and Jesse Johnson and several inviting instrumentals by producer Keith Forsey (producer of Billy Idol, Psychedelic Furs). –SWB

Bright Lights, Big City / WARNER   1988
Excellent contemporary dance music on this album, including Prince, New Order, Bryan Ferry, and Depeche Mode, plus a rare song by Steely Dan's Donald Fagen. –WR

Brimstone and Treacle / A&M   1982
The better part of this album is given over to songs by the Police and by Sting (who starred in the film), though IRS labelmates the Go-Go's and Squeeze also turn up. –WR

○ **Buccaneer / VARESE SARABANDE**   1958
A rousing Elmer Bernstein score, written for a larger-than-life swashbuckler. –BE

○ **The Buddy Holly Story / CBS / BB# 86**   1978
In the movie, these performances hold up well, but on record Gary Busey's performances of Holly's originals are pale and flawed and have been supplanted by MCA's definitive Holly collection. –BE

☆ **The Carl Stalling Project / WARNER**   1990
The Carl Stalling Project - Music from Warner Brothers Cartoons is music almost everyone will recognize. Generations of children and adults know Carl Stalling's music, whether consciously or not. This CD collects nearly 80 minutes of Stalling's music from 1936 to 1958. He was a master of making the music fit the animation, using every style of music from the time, including jazz, classical (Wagner, Mendelssohn, and Mozart), big band, children's songs, and Christmas music. An excellent collection of highly innovative soundtrack music. Guaranteed to spark all of your cartoon memories. –TEH

○ **Casualties of War / CBS**   1989
A dark, brooding, and surprisingly restrained work by Ennio Morricone, also more sentimental than his usual standard, and very operatic — parts of it sound like music for a Broadway extravaganza waiting to happen. –BE

○ **Cat People / MCA / BB# 47**   1986
David Bowie's featured "Putting Out Fire (With Gasoline)" is the best part of this otherwise predictable electronic score from the 1982 movie. –BE

Christine - Original Soundtrack / MCA   1983
An exuberant collection of late-50s pop and rock songs, plus George Thorogood's "Bad to the Bone." Put it on and have a sock hop. –WR

☆ **Classic British Film Music / SILVA SCREEN**
An essential import recording of several long-neglected English film scores, most notably Ralph Vaughan Williams's "Coastal Command"; the playing is competent if not always inspired. Kenneth Alwyn and the Philharmonic Orchestra. –BE

○ **Close Encounters of the 3rd Kind / VARESE**   1977
John Williams's score draws too much from Ravel for its own good, but the sound is impressive and the effects are entertaining. –BE

Club Paradise / CBS   1986
For all intents and purposes, this is a Jimmy Cliff album, which means some high-quality, pop-oriented reggae. On one track, "Seven-Day Weekend," Cliff duets with Elvis Costello (they also wrote the song together), along with the Attractions. –WR

Cocktail / ELEKTRA   1988
The four-million-selling summer party album of 1988,

featuring the #1 hits "Don't Worry, Be Happy" by Bobby McFerrin and "Kokomo" by the Beach Boys, plus radio hits by Starship, the Fabulous Thunderbirds, the Georgia Satellites, and John Cougar Mellencamp. –WR

○ **Cocoon / POLYGRAM**   1985
This James Horner score includes music ranging from ethereal to big band. One can't help but be touched by the plaintive oboe theme found throughout the album. It also includes "Gravity" by Michael Sembello. –TEH

The Color of Money / MCA   1986
Ex-Band songwriter/guitarist Robbie Robertson put together this soundtrack, which allowed him to collaborate with blues master Willie Dixon and jazz master Gil Evans, though it was his collaboration with Eric Clapton that produced the album's hit song, "It's in the Way That You Use It." Also featured: Don Henley, Robert Palmer (three tracks), and B. B. King. –WR

○ **Coma - Original Soundtrack / BAY CITIES**
A pure thriller score from the 1978 by Jerry Goldsmith, filled with eerie musical effects that anticipated his soundtrack for *Alien*. It transferred well to CD. –BE

Country - Original Soundtrack / WINDHAM HILL 1984
Charles Gross composed and conducted this score, but it's played by several of the new-age artists from Windham Hill Records, notably piantist George Winston, whose distinctive piano playing actually dominates the proceedings. –WR

Crossover Dreams / ELEKTRA   1986
An album of salsa music prominently featuring the work of Ruben Blades, who also starred in the 1985 film. –WR

Crossroads - Original Soundtrack / WARNER   1986
The ersatz blues story of the film gives Ry Cooder leeway to turn in an impressive blues-derived soundtrack featuring Sonny Terry along with his usual collaborators Van Dyke Parks, Jim Keltner, Nathan East, and others. But it's Cooder's guitar playing that highlights the album. –WR

☆ **Dances with Wolves - Original Soundtrack / CBS** 1990
This majestic John Barry score is slightly underrecorded but very rewarding despite its occasional overreliance on material all too familiar from the James Bond movies. –BE

Darkman - Soundtrack / MCA   1990
The music is dark, like the title suggests. Danny Elfman definitely achieves a sinister quality. Not something to listen to alone at night! –TEH

Erich Wolfgang Korngold

A composer and performer prodigy from an early age, Erich Wolfgang Korngold (born in 1897) was already an established and respected author of operatic and orchestral works by his twenties. He bid fair to be a successor to Richard Strauss when a chance offer to go to Hollywood to supervise the scoring of *A Midsummer Night's Dream* brought him to America. He stayed for over a decade, bringing his skills to bear on some of the most celebrated movies of that period. Beginning with *Captain Blood* in 1935, he was inextricably associated with the intense and rousing music for Errol Flynn's swashbucklers, but he also wrote the landmark dramatic scores to such serious films as *Kings Row* and *Between Two Worlds*. He returned to Europe during the period after WWII and attempted to resume his career in serious music, but he found that tastes and styles had altered too radically and that his work was regarded as archaic. He died in 1957.

— Bruce Eder

Danny Elfman

Since 1980 Danny Elfman has enjoyed modest success as frontman for the eccentric alternative band Oingo Boingo, but an opportunity to score Tim Burton's 1985 film *Pee Wee's Big Adventure* opened up a lucrative career as a composer of TV and film soundtracks. Since then, his credits have included *Batman*, *Dick Tracy*, *The Simpsons*, *Edward Scissorhands*, *Scrooged*, *Beetlejuice*, *Big Top Pee Wee*, and too many more to mention.

— Rick Clark

○ **Deep in My Heart / CBS / BB# 4**
The Sigmund Romberg material is generally extremely well performed, even by Jose Ferrer, and this collection, from the 1954 movie, is unique in terms of content. –BE

○ **Diamonds Are Forever / CAPITOL / BB# 74**
John Barry wrote a big, impressive-sounding score for this 1971 film, which on record comes off as a good followup to "You Only Live Twice." –BE

Dick Tracy - Original Soundtrack / WARNER
This is the original score from the 1990 movie, composed by Danny Elfman. It is considerably jazzier and more upbeat than much of his work. Of course, it still has a decidedly Elfman flavor to it. –TEH

○ **Dirty Dancing / RCA**   1987
This album includes songs from the hit movie — both old favorites (Bruce Channel's "Hey Baby," "In the Still of the Night," from the Five Satins, and Mickey & Sylvia's "Love Is Strange") and recent ones (Eric Carmen's "Hungry Eyes" and "(I've Had) The Time of My Life," performed by Bill Medley and Jennifer Warnes). "She's Like the Wind" is performed by Patrick Swayze, who played the male lead in the movie. While this may not be "the time of your life," as the album cover advertises, it is a fun collection. –TEH

☆ **Diva / RYKODISC**   1982
A spellbinding mix of opera and new-age music, haunting and memorable. –BE

☆ **Doctor Zhivago / CBS / BB# 1**   1990
A lush, beautiful score for an epic film. "Lara's Theme" was the biggest hit from the 1965 movie, but there were enough secondary tunes to turn it into one of the biggest-selling soundtrack albums in history. Glittering and gorgeous. –BF

○ **Dr. No / CAPITOL / BB# 82**   1963
John Barry's "James Bond Theme" from the 1962 movie is the best part of this weakest of the James Bond soundtracks, which otherwise boasts pseudo-Jamaican melodies and a couple of guitar instrumentals. –BE

○ **Easter Parade / CBS / BB# 185**   1989
The sound of these 1947 movies is old, but the assembly of Irving Berlin tunes sung by Fred Astaire, Judy Garland, and Ann Miller is one of the best — especially "Drum Crazy." –BE

Eddie & the Cruisers / SCOTTI BROS.   1983
There was a year's delay before this film, which concerns the mysterious death of a fictional 60s rock star, took off via video and cable TV; but when it did, the soundtrack album, featuring such songs as "On the Dark Side" and "Tender Years," by John Cafferty and the Beaver Brown Band, took off with it. To most, the music sounded like Bruce Springsteen clones, but it was appealing nonetheless. –WR

Edward Scissorhands - Orig. Soundtrack / MCA   1990
This Danny Elfman soundtrack uses a considerable amount of choral effects, including both an adult chorus and a boys choir. The result is a pleasant (albeit occasionally dark) and ethereal score. Includes "With These Hands" as performed by Tom Jones. –TEH

El Cid / SONY   1977

Rozsa and most listeners agree that *El Cid*, from the 1961 movie, was his last great score. Overall, it is a surprisingly lyrical and sensitive body of music for what was essentially an epic-scale action film — much of the material has been most inventively derived from medieval Spanish and Arab sources, and while the recording has an unfortunate softness to modern ears, the playing is exceptionally polished and the 1962-vintage stereo separation still holds some surprises. –BE

○ **Music for a Darkened Theatre / MCA**   1990

A very representative collection of some of Elfman's best work for films and television. It includes music from *Batman*, *Dick Tracy*, *Midnight Run*, even the theme from "The Simpsons," among others. –TEH

○ **The Empire Strikes Back / VARESE SARABANDE**   1980

Here is an album that includes what are probably some of the most overplayed, overused themes in the history of film scores. However, if you can get past the familiarity and actually *listen* to what's there, you'll find another well-written score from John Williams. –TEH

○ **Exodus - Original Soundtrack / RCA / BB# 1**

A grand-scale orchestral soundtrack. Contains the hit title theme from the 1960 movie and a brace of accompanying material done in the best grand style of the era. –BE

○ **The Falcon and the Snowman / EMI**   1985

Pat Metheny and Lyle Mays lent their trademark sound to the sweeping (occasionally orchestral) score of this original soundtrack. Featuring vocals by David Bowie on "This Is Not America." –SWB

☆ **Fame / RSO**   1980

The film's setting in the New York High School of the Performing Arts provided a frame for one of the most inspiring soundtracks of a film in the 80s. Film star Irene Cara scored with the chart-topping title track and the Top-20 "Out Here on My Own." This soundtrack, most of it by Michael Gore, is a knockout. –WR

☆ **Fantasia / DISNEY**   1991

One of the best and one of the earliest full orchestral scores available (it was recorded for the 1940 film), featuring Leopold Stokowski and the Philadelphia Orchestra in top form. Avoid the digital re-recording from the 80s at all costs. –BE

○ **Far and Away / MCA**   1992

A fine score (as is to be expected from John Williams), although parts of it are reminiscent of his scores from *Hook* and *JFK*. The Chieftains are featured on three tracks, and the album includes Enya's "Book of Days." One thing is puzzling, however. Why, when "Book of Days" is in Gaelic on Enya's *Shepherd Moons* album, is it translated into English for a movie about people from Ireland? –TEH

☆ **Far from the Madding Crowd / CBS**   1985

Possibly the best score written for any English picture since

Ennio Morricone

Morricone (an Italian composer born in 1928) came out of a mixed jazz and classical background and first started scoring low-budget action/adventure films in the early 60s. His music for Sergio Leone's three Clint Eastwood "man with no name" Westerns brought him to the attention of moviegoers around the world, who appreciated his mix of refined, elaborate scoring (often with chorus as well as full orchestra) and witty, clever humor — all rather like serious comic opera, and eminently listenable. In addition to his work with Leone, Morricone is famous for his music for such films as *The Mission* and has, by his own estimate, scored 600 or more films.

— Bruce Eder

Irving Berlin

Irving Berlin (1888-1989) was the most successful songwriter of the 20th century. Though, like his contemporaries, he spent the better part of his career writing songs (usually both words and music) to be used in Broadway musicals, he is better remembered for the songs themselves than for the shows (and sometimes films) in which they were introduced. This is because Berlin was a master at the kind of music that flourished from the turn of the century until World War II, shows that were really just collections of production numbers, scenes, and novelty acts (organized vaudeville presentations, really) rather than the story musicals that became prevalent starting with Rodgers and Hammerstein's *Oklahoma!* in 1943. It is also because Berlin, who did not read music and could play the piano in only one key and only on the black notes (he used a special piano with a lever that changed keys for him and employed a musical secretary to notate his compositions), wrote songs, not scores.

But what songs! Out of more than a thousand, a short list would include "Alexander's Ragtime Band" (his first major hit, in 1911), "God Bless America," "A Pretty Girl is Like a Melody," "Always," "Blue Skies," "Puttin' on the Ritz," "How Deep is the Ocean?," "Cheek to Cheek," "Let's Face the Music and Dance," "White Christmas," "There's no Business Like Show Business," "I Love a Piano," "What'll I Do?," "Easter Parade," and "Oh, How I Hate to Get Up in the Morning." The last came from one of the two shows Berlin organized and performed in during the two world wars (he can be seen in the film version of the second one, *This is the Army*).

Berlin became his own song publisher and built and owned a Broadway theater, the Music Box, to house his shows. Perhaps his greatest and his last hit came with the musical *Annie Get Your Gun* in 1946, though he did write three more before retiring in 1962.

— Bruce Eder

the 40s heyday of Vaughan Williams and William Walton's film work — Richard Rodney Bennett has composed a haunting, melodic yet atonal score for this 1967 movie, built on English folk melodies, that lingers long in the listener's memory. James Galway's flute playing is a bonus. –BE

☆ **Fast Times at Ridgemont High / ELEKTRA**   1982

The first great rock & roll compilation soundtrack of the 80s, which sold in the millions (justifiably) and gave Jackson Browne a Top Ten hit with "Somebody's Baby." –BE

○ **Fastest Guitar Alive / CBS**   1985

The soundtrack to this 1968 Roy Orbison movie is better than the film (based on a leftover Elvis Presley script), with two good tunes and the rest quite enjoyable. –BE

☆ **Jerry Fielding - Film Music / BAY CITIES**

A very imposing and worthwhile volume of amazingly good music from surprisingly lackluster movies. Each one stands on its own. The music is a worthy memorial to an underrated composer. –BE

○ **Jerry Fielding - Film Music 2 / BAY CITIES**

○ **55 Days at Peking / VARESE SARABANDE**   1963

One of Dimitri Tiomkin's better 60s scores, with more interesting material than usual and fewer sluggish spots — one to get. –BE

Flashdance - Soundtrack / POLYGRAM   1983

Giorgio Moroder's score for this dance fantasy album turned into a blockbuster (five million copies and counting) due to the title track, sung by Irene Cara, Michael Sembello's "Maniac," and a bunch of other modern dance tracks. —WR

☆ **Forbidden Planet - Original Soundtrack / PLANET** 1978
This startling and overpowering score from the 1956 movie is based on electronic tonalities rather than orchestral performance. A real wonder, and years ahead of its time. —BE

☆ **From Russia with Love / CAPITOL / BB# 27** 1975
Probably the best of the James Bond scores, with radiant music for strings and startling percussion passages punctuating this recording from the 1963 film. —BE

○ **Get Yourself a College Girl / COLUMBIA** 1964
A pretty cool soundtrack for a pretty lousy movie. Featured here are the Dave Clark Five, the Standells, the Animals, and Stan Getz. —TEH

☆ **The Ghost and Mrs. Muir / VARESE SARABANDE** 1975
Elmer Bernstein conducting the Royal Philharmonic Orchestra. An excellent re-recording, from the 1947 movie, of one of Bernard Herrmann's finest scores, a dark, brooding, romantic work that is lovely and haunting. —BE

☆ **Giant / CAPITOL / BB# 16**
The best of Dimitri Tiomkin's original soundtrack albums, in a crisp, dense mono that is extremely impressive on CD. This album, from the 1956 movie, is a treat for the ears, and well worth owning. —BE

☆ **Goldfinger / CAPITOL / BB# 1** 1964
The first of the hit James Bond albums, driven by Shirley Bassey's inimitable performance of the title track. —RF

☆ **Gone with the Wind / CBS**
An expanded and remastered edition of the original 1939 track, with much of the echo and distortion removed. —BE

○ **Gone with the Wind / POLYGRAM**
A satisfying CD transcription of the original 1939 Max Steiner tracks, but marred by many imperfections in the original sources and too much echo. —BE

☆ **The Good, the Bad & the Ugly / CAPITOL / BB# 4** 1968
Probably Ennio Morricone's most appealing and enduring Western score — funny, intense, dramatic, and filled with haunting melodies. The CD's stereo separation adds to the fun of this 1967 soundtrack. —BE

○ **The Graduate / CBS / BB# 1** 1968
An okay release from the 1967 movie, featuring some of Simon & Garfunkel's tunes alternating with instrumentals by Dave Grusin. —BE

○ **Grand Canyon - Soundtrack / RCA** 1992
A very diverse score by James Newton Howard. It uses everything from rock styles and jazz to delicate orchestral tracks and a huge brass fanfare. It also includes "Searching for a Heart," by Warren Zevon. —TEH

☆ **The Great Escape / INTRADA / BB# 50** 1963
An impressively remastered recording, with a very rich sound, despite a little more hiss than one might like. —BE

○ **Hang 'Em High/Guns for San Sebastian / CBS / BB# 193**
Dominic Frontiere's Hang 'Em High, from the 1968 film, is a spare, clever score, but Ennio Morricone's Guns for San Sebastian (1968) is practically an opera without words — intense, draining, and magnificent. —TEH

☆ **A Hard Day's Night / CAPITOL / BB# 1**
The first great rock & roll soundtrack album from the 1964 movie, equal in quality to the best non-film-related albums by the Beatles. Filled with jewels. —BE

☆ **The Great Hitchcock Movie Thrillers / LONDON**
Bernard Herrmann - Music from the Great Hitchcock Movie Thrillers is a well-programmed and well-performed overview of Herrmann's work in association with Hitchcock. None of the scores is anywhere near complete, but all of the famous movie selections from Psycho, North by Northwest, Vertigo, and The Trouble with Harry are represented. —BE

☆ **Film Fantasy: Cinema Gala / LONDON**
Bernard Herrmann - Film Fantasy: Cinema Gala is an extraordinarily fine collection of some of Herrmann's most

Bernard Herrmann

The dean of film composers, Bernard Herrmann was probably the most gifted musician ever to work in films, with barely a note of music to his credit that is not worthwhile. A classically trained composer, Herrmann worked for Orson Welles's Mercury Theatre and the CBS radio network before he went to Hollywood with Welles in 1940. His first two film scores, Citizen Kane and The Devil and Daniel Webster, were both nominated for Oscars in the same year (Webster won), and he was established from then on. Herrmann worked principally for 20th Century-Fox from the mid 40s until the end of the 50s, and did brilliant work on such films as The Ghost and Mrs. Muir, The Day the Earth Stood Still, Beneath the 12-Mile Reef, and Journey to the Center of the Earth. In the 50s and 60s, Herrmann also contributed notably to the success of Alfred Hitchcock's films and wrote inspired scores for early films by Brian De Palma and Martin Scorsese. He died the night he finished work on Taxi Driver.

— Bruce Eder

famous film music, originally well recorded by the composer during the 60s and remixed for a bright sound today. Worth owning just for the suite from The Day the Earth Stood Still, but it's all first-rate. —BE

☆ **Citizen Kane: Cinema Gala / LONDON**
Performed by the London Philharmonic Orchestra and National Philharmonic Orchestra. The Citizen Kane material isn't as interesting as that on Charles Gerhardt's RCA collection, but the material from The Devil and Daniel Webster and Jason and the Argonauts is a necessary part of any collection. (Unicorn Records has a still-better rendition of the former that simply has never turned up on CD.) —BE

☆ **Citizen Kane / RCA**
Citizen Kane: The Classic Film Scores of Bernard Herrmann is probably the best of the entire series by conductor Charles Gerhardt and the National Philharmonic Orchestra. Every track is worthwhile and memorably played, especially Beneath the 12-Mile Reef and the suite from Citizen Kane, the latter highlighted by Kiri Te Kanawa's performance of the Strauss-like aria from Salammbo. —BE

☆ **Bernard Herrmann - Classic Fastasy Film Scores /**
Four of Bernard Herrmann's fantasy film scores written for the movies of Ray Harryhausen (Seventh Voyage of Sinbad, etc.) and taken from the original film recordings. The sound is a little soft and compressed, which is understandable given its origins, and the representation of Jason and the Argonauts here is a bit of a cheat, but the rest of the material has never been excerpted as fully. —BE

○ **Hollywood Screen Classics / CHESKY**
Charles Gerhardt conducting the National Philharmonic Orchestra. Chesky has done unexpectedly well with these mostly 1968-vintage recordings. Although the sound is a little compressed compared with Gerhardt's later work, the detail is all there, and the work does have a youthful freshness. Highlights include perhaps the best of all Gone with the Wind suites, plus oddities such as the music from Rashomon. —BE

○ **Home Alone / CBS** 1990
In this score, John Williams manages to cleverly interweave traditional Christmas music with his own Christmas themes. It also includes "O Holy Night" and "Carol of the Bells," both performed by a children's chorus, and Mel Tormé's rendition of "Have Yourself a Merry Little Christmas." —TEH

○ **Hook - Original Soundtrack / CBS** 1991
A John Williams masterpiece. The emotion that he evokes through this music is incredible: it can make you experience

577

what the characters in the movie are feeling — see the menace of Captain Hook, or find your happy thought and fly. I could sit and listen to it for hours without finding all the little nuances in the music. It includes the vocal selections "We Don't Wanna Grow Up" and "When You're Alone." –TEH

The Hot Spot - Soundtrack / POLYGRAM   1990

This score is credited to "The Ultimate Blues Band," and you can't argue with the name when the personnel includes John Lee Hooker and Miles Davis. A moody, slinky, bluesy, jazzy, improvised score that's full of treats. –WR

☆ **How the West Was Won / CBS / BB# 4**   1985

This soundtrack, from the 1962 movie, was the most successful Western film album ever issued, and justifiably so — spacious, poignant, and inspired. –BE

☆ **I Was a Teenage Zombie / ENIGMA**   1987

An excellent compilation album featuring a Who's Who of the premier roots-rock bands of the 80s: the Fleshtones, the Del Fuegos, the dB's, Dream Syndicate, the Violent Femmes, the Smithereens, Los Lobos, Alex Chilton, the Ben Vaughn Group, and Bob Pfeifer. Want to know what 80s alternative rock sounded like? Just put this album on. –WR

○ **It's Always Fair Weather / CBS**   1955

This curious Comden/Green/Previn score is generally downbeat, but highlighted by two killer numbers featuring Dolores Grey and released in stereo for the first time. –BE

☆ **James Bond 13 Original Themes / CAPITOL**   1977

A greatest-hits album of sorts, overall very impressive, especially for its diversity of styles. –BE

Jaws - Original Soundtrack / MCA   1975

This is an outstanding John Williams score. Almost everyone is familiar with the driving and repetitive main theme, but few would recognize anything else from this score. There's some really good stuff here, and it's worth investigating. –TEH

○ **JFK / ELEKTRA**   1992

This is a very diverse soundtrack album. It includes tracks by John Williams, a performance of the Royal Scots Dragoon Guards (drummers), jazz from Tony Bennett, the first movement of a Mozart horn concerto, and more. –TEH

☆ **The Jungle Book / ENTR'ACTE / BB# 19**   1990

A surprisingly crisp 1942 recording of the Miklos Rozsa score, with Sabu narrating. A rich, expressive score. –BE

○ **Kings Row / VARESE SARABANDE**   1979

Charles Gerhardt conducting the National Philharmonic Orchestra. A well-produced, early digital recording of Erich Wolfgang Korngold's 1942 score for the classic melodrama, capturing the original's majesty. –BE

Music by Erich Wolfgang Korngold / STANYAN

The granddaddy of all film score re-recordings, this 1962 vintage collection is also one of the best, presenting Korngold's most popular film work in well-chosen excerpts

Ennio Morricone

Morricone (an Italian composer born in 1928) came out of a mixed jazz and classical background and first started scoring low-budget action/adventure films in the early 60s. His music for Sergio Leone's three Clint Eastwood "man with no name" Westerns brought him to the attention of moviegoers around the world, who appreciated his mix of refined, elaborate scoring (often with chorus as well as full orchestra) and witty, clever humor — all rather like serious comic opera, and eminently listenable. In addition to his work with Leone, Morricone is famous for his music for such films as *The Mission* and has, by his own estimate, scored 600 or more films.

— Bruce Eder

Jerry Goldsmith

Jerry Goldsmith (born in Los Angeles in 1929) is the leading figure in film music of his generation. After starting out in radio, he moved to television and into motion pictures in the early 60s, where his instrumental inventiveness and superb melodic sense quickly moved him to the top of his profession. His scores are seldom less than inspired and are always absorbing, whether they are written for thrillers (*The Prize*, "The Twilight Zone" TV series), science fiction (*Logan's Run*), military subjects (*Patton*, *The Blue Max*), or serious drama (*A Patch of Blue*).

— Bruce Eder

performed by the Warner Brothers Orchestra, conducted by Lionel Newman. Steve Hoffman has done an exceptionally fine job remixing the CD, and even the original insert booklet is re-created. Probably the best recorded version of Korngold's *Adventures of Robin Hood* music too. –BE

○ **The Last Emperor - Soundtrack / ATLANTIC**   1987

Ex-Talking Head David Byrne and actor/composer Ryuichi Sakamoto (who co-starred in the film) each get a side of this beautiful score to Bernardo Bertolucci's Academy Award-winning film, and each took home Oscars and Grammys for their efforts. –WR

☆ **Laura, and Other Soundtracks ... / RCA**

Laura, and Other Soundtracks by David Raskin and the New Philharmonic Orchestra, is a colorful collection of Raskin's film music, from the haunting dark strains of "Laura" and "The Bad and the Beautiful" to his inventive historical setting for "Forever Amber," all well performed. –BE

Less Than Zero / CBS   1987

Rap/metal producer Rick Rubin put together this hard-edged soundtrack, which features rockers Aerosmith, Poison, and Slayer, plus rappers L L Cool J and Public Enemy, though the hit from the album was a remake of Simon & Garfunkel's "Hazy Shade of Winter," performed by the Bangles. –WR

Light of Day / CBS   1987

Ian Hunter and the Fabulous Thunderbirds turn up on this mainstream rock soundtrack, though it's dominated by the film band, the Barbusters, led by Joan Jett and Michael J. Fox, notably on the Bruce Springsteen title tune. –WR

○ **The Lion in Winter / VARESE / BB# 182**   1968

An unusually stark and serious John Barry score, nicely remastered. –BE

○ **The Little Mermaid - Orig. Soundtrack / DISNEY**   1989

A delightful soundtrack by Howard Ashman and Alan Menken, creators of *Little Shop of Horrors*. The first half is vocal numbers, the last ten are instrumental, with styles that range from English to French, Caribbean to Broadway. This may be the best music from a Disney movie yet. –TEH

☆ **Logan's Run - Original Soundtrack / BAY CITIES**

Jerry Goldsmith's brilliant, witty, often very touching score for this 1976 big-budget science-fiction thriller was easily the best part of the movie, and it has been cleaned up and polished up considerably for this CD reissue. It's the first time this music — a mix of hauntingly lyrical orchestral passages and electronic tonalities — has been properly treated. –BE

○ **The Man Who Would Be King / BAY CITIES**

This soundtrack, from the 1975 film, was probably Maurice Jarre's best movie music of the 70s, lyrical and powerful. –BE

☆ **Manhattan / CBS / BB# 94**   1978

A brisk rescoring of George Gershwin's music for the 1979 Woody Allen film — very pleasant. –BE

Married to the Mob / WARNER   1988

Director Jonathan Demme has a talent for compiling terrific

soundtrack albums, and this is a good example, featuring Sinéad O'Connor, New Order, Chris Isaak, Debbie Harry, Ziggy Marley and the Melody Makers, Tom Tom Club, the Feelies, and Brian Eno. Quite a mixture, but it all works. –WR

○ **Medicine Man / VARESE SARABANDE**   1992
Jerry Goldsmith score uses a great many ethnic styles and drums, as well as some emotional themes. At times it's reminiscent of Cusco's new-age compositions. –TEH

Metropolis / CBS / BB# 110   1984
As an album, *Metropolis* is an interesting if unexceptional rock collection. It was notable on screen for its dubious taste, although it made a bundle. –BE

☆ **Legendary Italian Westerns / RCA**
This rousing and entertaining collection contains highlights from Morricone's most famous scores and provides quite a few surprises. –BE

○ **The Natural / WARNER**   1984
This Randy Newman score is spectacular! The main theme is such that one feels that something wonderful has happened, even without knowing anything about the film. It includes some big-band-style tracks and a fragment of "Take Me Out to the Ball Game," which should come as no surprise in a baseball movie score. –TEH

☆ **North by Northwest / VARESE SARABANDE**   1980
Laurie Johnson conducting the London Studio Symphony Orchestra. A fair account of the classic Bernard Herrmann 1959 score, suffering only fro

Miklos Rozsa

Born in Hungary in 1907, Miklos Rozsa is the last surviving veteran of moviemaking's "golden age," having scored his first film in 1936 and his latest in 1984. His early success as a serious composer, working in an idiom inspired by the work of Bartók and Kodaly, gave Rozsa the foundation for his dual career in motion pictures. A post-romantic who never accepted atonalism, his best work — and there is much of it — is derived from the texture of native Hungarian folk songs. He began collecting these as a child, giving him a unique command of orchestral timbre and the most distinctive approach of any composer of his generation.

After working for Alexander Korda's London Films, where he provided the memorable and brilliant scores for *The Four Feathers*, *The Thief of Baghdad*, and *The Jungle Book*, Rozsa took up residence in Hollywood in the early 40s, and by mid-decade had made his mark in the area of film noir. The rhythmic nature of his music and his facility with dark melodic lines gave a brooding savagery to films like *The Killers* and *The Naked City*. In the 50s he became the master of the religious epic. His sweeping scores for *Quo Vadis*, *Ben Hur*, *King of Kings*, and *El Cid* found favor among serious choral groups as well as the public, who devoured his albums (originally on the MGM Records label) including two complete albums of music from *Ben-Hur*.

The end of the studio system, the increasing demand for pop tunes in movie soundtracks, and the general coarsening of film subjects in the 60s didn't serve Rozsa well, and his activity in films declined steeply after 1963. Fortunately, he had his career as a serious classical composer to keep him occupied, and by the 70s, filmmakers such as Alain Resnais (*Providence*), Nicholas Meyer (*Time after Time*), and Carl Reiner (*Dead Men Don't Wear Plaid*) gave him a chance for a satisfying "Indian summer" prior to his retirement in the mid 80s.

— Bruce Eder

George Gershwin

In a career tragically cut short in mid-stride by a brain tumor, George Gershwin (1898-1937) proved himself to be not only one of the great songwriters of his extremely rich era, but also a gifted "serious" composer who might bridge the worlds of classical and popular music. The latter is all the more striking, given that, of his contemporaries, Gershwin was the most influenced by such styles as jazz and blues.

Gershwin's first major hit, interpolated into the show *Sinbad* in 1919, was "Swanee," sung by Al Jolson. Gershwin wrote both complete scores and songs for such variety shows as George White's *Scandals* (whose annual editions thus were able to introduce such songs s "I'll Build a Stairway to Paradise" and "Somebody Loves Me").

After 1924, Gershwin worked primarily with his brother Ira as his lyricist. The two scored a series of Broadway hits in the 20s and early 30s, starting with *Lady be Good* (1924), which included the song "Fascinatin' Rhythm." 1924 was also the year Gershwin composed his first classical piece, "Rhapsody in Blue," and he would continue to work in the classical field until his death.

By the 30s, the Gershwins had turned to political topics and satire in response to the onset of the Depression, and their *Of Thee I Sing* became the first musical to win a Pulitzer Prize. In the mid 30s, Gershwin ambitiously worked to meld his show music and classical leanings in the creation of the folk opera *Porgy and Bess*, with lyrics by Ira and by Dubose Heyward. The Gershwins had moved to Hollywood and were engaged in several movie projects at the time of George Gershwin's death.

— Bruce Eder

1959 score, suffering only from poor dynamics as one of the earlier digital recordings. –BE

○ **Odds Against Tomorrow / CBS**   1959
This superb jazz score by John Lewis was later turned into a hit by the Modern Jazz Quartet. It's dark and dynamic, and a classic. –BE

☆ **On Her Majesty's Secret Service / CAPITOL / BB# 13**
A complex, lyrical John Barry score from the 1969 movie, featuring his greatest song ("We Have All the Time in the World") amid its brilliant instrumentals. –BE

One from the Heart / CBS   1982
A series of romantic duets by the seemingly unlikely couple of Tom Waits and Crystal Gayle in fact works surprisingly well, bringing out the ballad side of each. The score is heavily integrated into the film and tells its story of love and loss in Las Vegas. –WR

○ **110 in the Shade / RCA**
Based on an N. Richard Nash play that also became the Katharine Hepburn/Burt Lancaster film *The Rainmaker*, this film was a moderate success in 1963. The Harvey Schmidt/Tom Jones score is not their best but shouldn't be overlooked. Stephen Douglass singing the opening number "Gonna Be Another Hot Day" evokes *Oklahoma!*, clearly an inspiration to this production. –MER

One Trick Pony - Soundtrack / WARNER   1980
This is usually categorized as a regular Paul Simon album, although its songs were featured in the Simon-written-and-starring film of the same name. Featuring New York session aces like Steve Gadd, Richard Tee, Tony Levin, and Eric Gale, the music has a contemporary jazz feel, and typical of a Simon album there are some extraordinary lyrics. "Late in the Evening" was the hit, but that's only the beginning. –WR

Paris, Texas / WARNER   1985
This Ry Cooder score has a spare, evocative sound created by the guitarist, with partners Jim Dickinson and David Lindley. Star Harry Dean Stanton is also heard, providing some of the dialog from the 1984 film. –WR

○ **Patton / POLYGRAM / BB# 117**   1970
A stunning, haunting martial score by Jerry Goldsmith. This is possibly the finest military film score ever written. –BE

○ **Pennies from Heaven / WARNER**   1981
Original recordings from the 20s and 30s by Bing Crosby, Helen Kane, Fred Astaire, Rudy Vallee, and others formed the soundtrack to this Steve Martin/Bernadette Peters film. A collection of timeless show tunes, this album is sadly out of print. –SWB

Performance - Soundtrack / WARNER   1970
Future soundtrack composers Randy Newman and Ry Cooder contributed heavily to this score, most of which was written by veteran Jack Nitzsche. Singers include Merry Clayton, Newman, and Buffy Sainte-Marie, though the most memorable song is "Memo from Turner," the film's star, Mick Jagger's only recorded solo performance until his first album in 1985. –WR

○ **Plan 9 from Outer Space / PERFORMANCE**
A silly and sublime sound recording from one of the most enjoyably silly sci-fi films ever made. The music cues from this 1959 movie are fine familiar fun; the dialog is a hoot. –BE

☆ **Porky's Revenge! - Soundtrack / MOBILE FIDELITY**
Dave Edmunds produced this album of rockin' tunes featuring a couple of his own, though it's really an album of high-profile ringers: George Harrison, Jeff Beck, Willie Nelson, Robert Plant, and Phil Collins all make appearances, and the result is a rollicking set of songs from the 1985 film that are far above the usual soundtrack effort. –WR

☆ **Pretty in Pink / A&M**   1986
The Psychedelic Furs achieved stardom with their re-recorded version of the title track, an old song of theirs, but the soundtrack album also makes a good modern rock sampler, featuring tracks by Orchestral Manoeuvres in the Dark, New Order, Echo and the Bunnymen, and the Smiths, plus the Suzanne Vega/Joe Jackson collaboration "Left of Center." –WR

The Princess Bride - Soundtrack / WARNER   1987
A charming, low-key instrumental score, appropriate to the funny, wistful tone of the film, by Dire Straits leader Mark Knopfler. –WR

○ **Providence / DRG**   1980
A lyrical, subtle score by Miklos Rozsa from the 1977 movie. One of his most accomplished pieces of music, and most enjoyable. –BE

☆ **Quo Vadis / LONDON**
A well-produced re-recording of the classic 1951 score by Miklos Rozsa and the Royal Philharmonic Orchestra, with a bright but not too brittle sound and excellent stereo balances. The music itself sounds hokey, but only for having been imitated so many times since 1951. –BE

Ragtime / ELEKTRA   1981
It's probably not necessary to describe the style of music on this album, though it is worth noting that the music was written and largely performed by Randy Newman, and that the record contains more music than is heard in the film. –WR

○ **The Rescuers Down Under / DISNEY**   1990
A charming soundtrack by Bruce Boughton. It is in Australian-outback style, using aboriginal drumbeats. It also includes "R-E-S-C-U-E, Rescue Aid Society" from the original 1975 Rescuers movie. –TEH

○ **Robin Hood - Prince of Thieves / MORGAN CREEK**   1991
Eight fantastic tracks of instrumentals plus the Bryan Adams hit "(Everything I Do) I Do It for You" and Jeff Lynne's "Wild Times." –TEH

○ **Rock Goes to the Movies - Vols. 1-4/ CBS**
A wide-ranging, four-album collection of rock tracks,

Cole Porter

Cole Porter (1891-1964) has been described as the greatest songwriter of the century; he was unquestionably the wittiest. A child of enormous wealth, Porter did not turn his complete attention to songwriting until the 1920s, but from then until the end of the 40s, he turned out nearly a show a year, and he even managed three more in the 50s, not to mention a fair amount of work for motion pictures.

Porter, who wrote both words and music, had a flair for melody, but his gift for lyrics was unparalleled. Like Irving Berlin, his work of the 30s is better remembered for individual song hits than complete scores, and those songs included "Let's Do It," "You do Something to Me," "What Is This Thing Called Love?," "Night and Day," "Begin the Beguine," and "Just One of Those Things." An exception to this rule was *Anything Goes* (1934), which, in addition to the title song, included "You're the Top" and "I Get a Kick out of You." The entire score is brilliant, and the show has been revived on stage and in films frequently.

Porter was severely injured in a riding accident in 1937 and lived in pain for the rest of his life. His work, however, continued largely without interruption. His greatest success came with an adaptation of Shakespeare's *Taming of the Shrew* called *Kiss Me, Kate* in 1948, after which he worked less frequently, though *Can-Can* (1953) and *Silk Stockings* (1955) were notable later hits.

— Bruce Eder

covering various styles and periods. It is all movie-related and most of it hard to find. –BE

○ **Royal Wedding / CBS**
This witty Alan Jay Lerner and Burton Lane score from the 1951 film is sparked by one great novelty number and the personalities of Fred Astaire and Jane Powell. –BE

○ **Classic Rozsa / DRG**
Some of Miklos Rozsa's most endearing folk-based classical material. Not in a league with his most heavyweight pieces, but enjoyable and very direct expressions of his love of native Hungarian music. –BE

☆ **Saturday Night Fever / RSO**   1977
One of the biggest-selling albums of all time, this double-disc soundtrack features the Bee Gees hits "Stayin' Alive," "Night Fever," and "How Deep Is Your Love"; Yvonne Elliman's "If I Can't Have You"; and a selection of popular disco hits by Tavares, K. C. & the Sunshine Band, and others. This wasn't only the soundtrack to a film, it was the soundtrack to an era; that era is over, but it's evoked by the music. –WR

☆ **Sea Hawk - Soundtrack / VARESE SARABANDE**   1987
With the Utah Symphony Orchestra. A lush, spirited re-recording (from the 1940 movie) of Erich Wolfgang Korngold's best action score, including all of the choruses. A great achievement. –BE

☆ **The Secret Policeman's Third Ball / ATLANTIC**
Above-average rock-performance soundtrack, sparked by a superb duet between Kate Bush and David Gilmour. –BE

☆ **She's Having a Baby / MCA**   1988
A charming collection of modern rock songs based on the themes of marriage and family, including Dave Wakeling's title song (the best thing that came from his brief solo career), XTC's "Happy Families," Kate Bush's "This Woman's Work," and especially the infectious "Apron Strings" by Everything but the Girl. –WR

☆ **David Shire - At the Movies / BAY CITIES**
A too-often-overlooked composer gets to play some of his best

movie music at the piano, with help from Maureen McGovern. The album includes material from *Norma Rae, Farewell My Lovely, The Conversation*, and *Return to Oz*. −BE

○ **Singin' in the Rain / CBS / BB# 185**
A towering film score from the 1952 movie made up of some grand tunes of the 30s, climaxing with the extended "Broadway Ballet." −BE

○ **Sleeping with the Enemy / CBS**
A lyrical, moving Jerry Goldsmith score, which soars to elegant heights of wistfulness and menace. −BE

Something Wild / MCA   1986
Another brilliant compilation of unusual music handled by director Jonathan Demme. The hit was "Ever Fallen in Love," by Fine Young Cannibals, but the album also includes tracks by David Byrne (one of his earliest Latin American outings), Oingo Boingo, Jimmy Cliff, Jerry Harrison, and New Order, among others. −WR

○ **A Star Is Born (Judy Garland) / CBS / BB# 1**
This album, from the 1954 movie, was Judy Garland's last musical soundtrack of any note, sounding a little compressed but not severely marred by age. Garland is in fine voice and spirits on the songs themselves, and the notes are about as full and informative as they get. −BE

○ **Star Trek: The Motion Picture / CBS / BB# 50**   1979
Jerry Goldsmith's music, alternately eerie and savage, was the best part of the movie. It still holds up. −BE

○ **Star Wars / POLYGRAM / BB# 2**   1977
John Williams at his most ostentatious, a grand Wagnerian-scale soundtrack that deserves credit at least for reviving interest in the classic Hollywood film score. −BE

Staying Alive - Soundtrack / POLYGRAM   1983
This sequel to *Saturday Night Fever* lacked the box office clout of the original, and the soundtrack album was likewise a disappointing seller, but it actually contains some of the better Bee Gees work of the 80s, notably the sad ballad "Someone Belonging to Someone." WR

Straight to Hell / ENIGMA   1987
This soundtrack to Alex Cox's bizarre Western features British new-wave graduates the Pogues, Joe Strummer, and the MacManus Band (i.e., Elvis Costello). They also appeared in the film. −WR

Streets of Fire - Soundtrack / MCA   1984
Jim Steinman (the melodramatic writer behind Meat Loaf's *Bat out of Hell*) is the author of many of the tracks here, and they have his typical rock & roll *Sturm und Drang*, especially when the backup group consists of members of Bruce Springsteen's E Street Band. Also on hand are the Blasters, Maria McKee, and Ry Cooder. The album's hit single turned out to be Dan Hartman's "I Can Dream about You." −WR

○ **Subterraneans / CBS**   1960
A very effective, moody jazz score by Andre Previn, featuring Gerry Mulligan and Carmen McRae, which holds up better than the movie for which it was written. −BE

○ **Summer Stock / CBS**   1950
Judy Garland's final MGM outing, sparked by her rendition of "Get Happy" and some good Gene Kelly numbers. −BE

○ **That's Entertainment Part 2 / CBS / BB# 128**   1974
The 43 tracks on both volumes represent complete versions of pieces either abridged or left off entirely from the original album. Covering song and dance numbers by everyone from Cole Porter to Arthur Freed, this is a magnificent panorama of musical gems from Hollywood. −BE

☆ **Themes by Hollywood's Great Composers / CBS** 1988
A truly different collection, covering celebrated rarities and many of the best renditions of key hit themes. −BE

The Three Musketeers / BAY CITIES   1974
This is Michel Legrand's lush soundtrack to Richard Lester's comic version of the Alexandre Dumas novel. It's some of the most romantic and stirring instrumental music to turn up in a film in years. −WR

Lerner and Loewe

Alan Jay Lerner (1918-1986) and Frederick Loewe (1901-1988) wrote some of the most stylish, sophisticated theater music of the 20th century. The collaboration didn't come until relatively late in the career of each. New York-born, Harvard-educated Lerner wrote material for radio and for individual performers in the 30s. Loewe, born in Berlin, came to the US in 1924 and gradually worked his way into theater music. The two were introduced in 1942. They scored their first hit, the fantasy *Brigadoon*, in 1947.

The Lerner-Loewe formula was to combine Loewe's lush, melodic music, redolent of Viennese waltz, with Lerner's witty, literate lyrics. This they did in some of the most popular and best-remembered musicals of the 40s, 50s, and 60s, notably *Paint Your Wagon, My Fair Lady*, and *Camelot* (plus the film musical *Gigi*). After Loewe's retirement, Lerner wrote with other composers, most successfully with Burton Lane (*On a Clear Day You Can See Forever*).

— Bruce Eder

○ **Thunderball / CAPITOL / BB# 10**   1978
John Barry's fourth James Bond score from the 1965 movie shows a little weariness, as some material is repeated and the new stuff isn't always memorable. −BE

○ **The Western Film World of Dimitri Tiomkin / UNICORN**
Laurie Johnson conducting the London Studio Symphony Orchestra and the John McCarthy Singers. A brace of long-overdue modern recordings of Tiomkin's best Western music, including a good (but not complete) accounting of his score for *Red River*. −BE

Dimitri Tiomkin - Lost Horizon ... / RCA
Lost Horizon: The Classic Film Scores of Dimitri Tiomkin. Tiomkin was arguably the least talented of the major composers associated with Hollywood, and a surprising amount of the material here simply doesn't hold up. On the other hand, the 23-minute suite from *Lost Horizon* does, and then some — a radiant pastiche of largely Russian influences that surges and soars brilliantly. Charles Gerhardt conducts the National Philharmonic Orchestra. −BE

○ **Tonite Let's All Make Love in London / CBS**   1968
A dazzlingly trippy, psychedelic look at swinging London through the music and dialog of this documentary film. Featuring Pink Floyd (in their first recording), the Small Faces, and a host of less-well-known acts, as well as an interview with Mick Jagger. −BE

Trouble in Mind / ISLAND   1986
Mark Isham provides the brooding instrumental texture and Marianne Faithfull adds her gravelly chanteuse vocals to the score of this Alan Rudolph film. −SWB

Warsaw Concerto: Cinema Gala / LONDON
A handy if unexceptional collection of mostly 60s-vintage recordings from the Decca Records vaults by various conductors and orchestras. It is notable for Bernard Herrmann's slow but powerful renditions of Arthur Bliss's "Things to Come" and the prelude from Ralph Vaughan Williams's "49th Parallel." −BE

☆ **The Way West, Scalphunters ... / EMI**   1967
The Way West/Scalphunters/Hang 'Em High. Bronislav Kaper's moody, lyrical music from *The Way West* gets its well-deserved first-class treatment with surprisingly good sound. *The Scalphunters* is adequately represented, as is *Hang 'Em High*. −BE

☆ **John Williams - Tribute to Spielberg / CBS**
This is a must-have for any John Williams fan who hasn't started a collection yet, as some of the scores from which

these tracks were taken may be difficult to find. Includes music from the Indiana Jones movies, *Empire of the Sun*, *E.T.*, *Always*, *Jaws*, *1941*, *Sugarland Express*, and *Close Encounters of the Third Kind*. A great representation of some of his finest scores. −TEH

○ **Willow - Soundtrack / ATLANTIC**   1988
This James Horner score goes along with the landscape in the movie — lush, sweeping, and absolutely breathtaking. Of course, it has its share of bad-guy themes too. As a whole, you could hardly ask for a more beautiful score. −TEH

○ **Wizard of Oz / CBS**
What else can one say about this bright, tuneful 1939 score — it's a treasure! −BE

Woodstock / ATLANTIC / BB# 7   1970
The wrong notes are jarring and the recording flaws seem obvious, but the energy and enthusiasm compensate. −BE

☆ **Woodstock Two / ATLANTIC / BB# 7**   1971
This is actually more interesting than *Woodstock*, in terms of repertoire and artists. −BE

☆ **Zabriskie Point / COLUMBIA**   1970
This a classic psychedelic rock soundtrack, with three otherwise hard-to-find Pink Floyd songs and a Jerry Garcia solo piece. −BE

CAST RECORDINGS

○ **Annie - Original Cast / CBS**   1977
One of the biggest Broadway hits of the 70s, this Charles Strouse and Martin Charnin musical based on the *Little Orphan Annie* comic strip charmed audiences with its Depression-era nostalgia and a score that is highlighted by the standard "Tomorrow." −WR

○ **Annie Get Your Gun - Original Cast / MCA**   1955
Although this recording does not quite represent the "original Broadway cast" of the 1946 Irving Berlin musical, it's the next best thing, starring Ethel Merman, Ray Middleton, "and members of the original cast, chorus, and orchestra, under the direction of Jay Blackton." Merman is in fine voice, and the score remains one of Broadway's best collections of songs, from "Doin' What Comes Naturally" to "They Say It's Wonderful" and "Anything You Can Do," not to mention "I Got Lost in His Arms," "The Girl That I Marry," and the showstopping standard "There's No Business like Show Business." −WR

○ **Annie Get Your Gun / RCA VICTOR**   1966
This revival of the Irving Berlin show once again stars Ethel Merman and also features Jerry Orbach. It includes the newly written "An Old-Fashioned Wedding." −WR

○ **Anyone Can Whistle / COLUMBIA**   1964
Stephen Sondheim's second complete Broadway score, with a book by Arthur Laurents, was not a success onstage, running only nine performances. But the cast album has kept the show alive, due to such outstanding songs as "There Won't Be Trumpets," "With So Little to Be Sure Of," and the title tune, plus a cast led by Lee Remick and Angela Lansbury. −WR

○ **Anything Goes / RCA**   1987
This classy 1987 revival features Patti LuPone's spirited interpretations of Cole Porter classics, including the title song, "I Get a Kick out of You," "You're the Top," and "Blow, Gabriel, Blow." −MER

Anything Goes / EMI   1989
This is a re-creation of the original 1934 score, not a cast album, put together by John McGlinn and featuring such opera singers as Kim Criswell, Cris Goenendaal, and Frederica Von Stade, along with the London Symphony Orchestra. It is most notable for containing the show's incidental music as well as its famous songs. −WR

Assassins / RCA   1991
Stephen Sondheim's show about presidential assassins is unusual to say the least — which may be why it never got

beyond an off-Broadway showcase — but it's filled with brilliant songs. −WR

○ **The Band Wagon / CBS**   1991
Fred Astaire's personality dominates this collection of songs from the musical, and that's a plus. The classic "That's Entertainment" is the best number by far, and Fred carries the rest well. −BE

○ **Barnum / COLUMBIA**   1980
This musical about the life of the great promoter, with music by Cy Coleman and lyrics by Michael Stewart, is dominated by Jim Dale's bravura performance in the title role, although Glenn Close, in one of her few musical-comedy appearances, is also featured. −WR

○ **Bells Are Ringing - Original Cast / CBS**   1956
Book and lyrics by Betty Comden and Adolph Green, music by Jule Style. The recording documents Judy Holliday's genius for musical comedy. "The Party's Over" and "Just in Time" are the most memorable numbers in a clever score. −MER

○ **The Best Little Whorehouse in Texas / MCA**   1978
Tommy Tune staged this rip-roaring, country-style musical, and while you can't see the dance steps on record, Carol Hall's songs accurately express the show's down-home vitality. −WR

○ **The Boyfriend / RCA VICTOR**   1955
A tribute to the frivolous musicals of the 20s, this tongue-in-cheek entertainment was one of the few successful musicals of its time to originate in Great Britain. It's notable for introducing a 19-year-old Julie Andrews to Broadway. −WR

○ **Brigadoon / RCA VICTOR**   1947
The tale of an 18th-century Scottish village that travels through time and its romantic encounter with two 20th-century visitors became the first major hit written by the team of Alan Jay Lerner and Frederick Loewe. It features "Almost Like Being in Love." −WR

○ **Brigadoon / CBS**   1988
This pleasant Lerner and Loewe soundtrack is sung with sincerity, if not great power, by Gene Kelly, and features a couple of near-hits. −BE

Broadway Classics - Vol. 1 / MCA   1991
The choice seems nearly random but this sampler of Broadway songs from Broadway shows originally released on Decca includes everything from "The Impossible Dream" to "Don't Cry for Me, Argentina." Listen, and then seek out the complete show. −WR

○ **Bubbling Brown Sugar / AMHERST**   1976
A musical revue featuring some of the most memorable jazz-age tunes of Black 30s composers such as Duke Ellington, Eubie Blake, and Fats Waller: "Sophisticated Lady," "Honeysuckle Rose," and more. On record, the show becomes essentially a sampler of that music, and it's effective for that, though the listener should also check out the original versions. −WR

○ **Buddy (London Cast) / RELATIVITY**   1989
Buddy - The Buddy Holly Story is the London cast recording of a biographical musical about the rock & roll legend. It contains Holly's greatest hits enthusiastically performed by Paul Hipp, who also performed the role on Broadway. −WR

☆ **Bye Bye Birdie - Original Cast / CBS**   1960
The original Broadway cast album of the Charles Strouse/Lee Adams musical that fictionalizes the impact Elvis Presley's departure for the army had on American teenagers. The authors deftly satirize teen life and early rock & roll and provide a typical Broadway musical love story involving Dick Van Dyke and Chita Rivera. Paul Lynde is also a standout, singing "Kids." The other hit of the show is "Put On a Happy Face." −WR

○ **Cabaret - Original Cast / COLUMBIA**   1966
With a malevolent grin and the words "Willkommen, bienvenue, welcome," actor Joel Grey established his future as well as the dark tone of this 1966 Tony Award-winning musical. This recording includes a number of songs not in the film version, several performed by the remarkable Lotte

Lenya (widow of composer Kurt Weill, whose work clearly influenced the Kander and Ebb score). –MER

Cabaret - Soundtrack / MCA   1972
Liza Minnelli hit a career peak in this film musical, and she dominates the soundtrack, lending personal meaning to such songs as the title track (in which she almost seems to be singing about her mother, Judy Garland). Joel Grey is equally impressive. –WR

○ **Camelot / WARNER / BB# 11**
The Lerner and Loewe music in this film version is sung with passion, if not great control, by Richard Harris and Vanessa Redgrave, and is livelier than the movie. –BE

○ **Camelot / COLUMBIA**   1960
One of the great Lerner & Loewe musicals, based on the King Arthur legend, starring Richard Burton and Julie Andrews. The music is both a Broadway landmark and a delight. Highlights include the title song, "How to Handle a Woman," and "If Ever I Would Leave You" (sung by Robert Goulet). –WR

Camelot - London Cast / VARESE SARABANDE   1982
Richard Harris took over the stage role of King Arthur (he played the part in the film) and played it on the road and in revivals. Here he appears in a London revival and brings great presence to the part. The album is well recorded and includes some music not found on other recordings. –WR

○ **Can-Can / CAPITOL**   1974
A Cole Porter dalliance set in Paris and featuring a young Gwen Verdon, plus such memorable songs as "I Love Paris" and "It's All Right with Me." –WR

○ **Candide / COLUMBIA**   1974
A complete recording of the revised version of the Bernstein musical (containing some additions to the lyrics by Stephen Sondheim), taken from its most successful theatrical run. Some of Leonard Bernstein's best show music. –WR

Candide / NEW WORLD   1986
A recording by the New York City Opera, based on its 1982 revival of the show, once again with revised music. –WR

Carnival - Original Cast / POLYGRAM   1961
Bob Merrill produced his best-loved score for this delicate musical based on the 1953 French film *Lili* about an orphan taken in by a traveling carnival. Michael Stewart was the lyricist, and the stars included Anna Maria Alberghetti and Jerry Orbach. The title song, "Theme from Carnival (Love Makes the World Go 'Round)," became a standard. –WR

☆ **Carousel - Original Cast / DECCA MCA**
This was Rodgers and Hammerstein's 1945 followup to their landmark hit *Oklahoma*. It includes such chestnuts as "If I Loved You" and "You'll Never Walk Alone," as well as John Raitt's soaring vocals. –MER

○ **Carousel / RCA VICTOR**   1965
The Twentieth Anniversary Lincoln Center revival of the Rodgers and Hammerstein classic, with John Raitt re-creating his original portrayal of Billy Bigelow. He's still in good voice, and the stereo recording is superb. –WR

○ **Cats / GEFFEN**   1981
The original London cast album of Andrew Lloyd Webber's musical revue celebrating T. S. Eliot's *Old Possum's Book of Practical Cats*. It contains Elaine Paige's UK Top Ten recording of "Memory." –WR

○ **Cats - Original Cast / GEFFEN**   1983
This is the original Broadway cast album, containing slight musical alterations from the earlier London version and, of course, different singers, though it is not very different. Geffen 2031 is a two-disc complete version of the show. There is also an abridged, one-disc version, Geffen 2026. –WR

○ **Chess / RCA**   1984
This is a studio recording made prior to any staged version of the musical, with music by former ABBA members Benny Andersson and Bjorn Ulvaeus and lyrics by Tim Rice about an international chess tournament. A UK Top Ten hit, it includes Murray Head's hit version of "One Night in Bangkok." –WR

Stephen Sondheim

According to most critics and theater historians, Stephen Sondheim (b. 1930) stands among Broadway show composers and lyricists not only as the greatest of his generation but as the *only* great one of his generation. There may be many reasons why Broadway has failed to produce consistently great writers to follow the Rodgers and Hammersteins and Lerner and Loewes of the 40s and 50s, but the fact remains that, though he operates without serious competition, Sondheim clearly ranks with such masters, as well as with the Jerome Kerns and Irving Berlins of an even earlier generation.

Sondheim became a mentor of Hammerstein's after befriending the lyricist's son in school, but he got his first big break when he was hired to write lyrics to Leonard Bernstein's score for *West Side Story* (1957), which turned out to be one of the biggest hits and most memorable works of its time. This led to a lot of lyric-writing work, though Sondheim always wanted to write music as well. Nevertheless, he worked with Jule Styne on *Gypsy* (1959), another enormous hit, and would later agree to do the same with Richard Rodgers for the unsuccessful *Do I Hear a Waltz?* (1965).

Before that, however, Sondheim scored his first success as composer and lyricist with *A Funny Thing Happened on the Way to the Forum* (1962). It was his last hit until *Company* (1970), a show about contemporary life and mores that did much to revolutionize the Broadway musical and, as Hammerstein's 50s shows had, move it more toward serious and exotic subjects. Since that time, Sondheim's shows have been amazingly daring in terms of subject matter, with unusual musical ideas and stunningly original lyrics. But they have not always been big hits and have marked a time in the theater when Broadway show music became a marginalized art form in terms of popular culture.

Nevertheless, Sondheim's shows of the 70s and 80s are benchmarks of the genre: *Follies* (1971) brought together aging follies girls for a look at middle-aged American life; *A Little Night Music* (1973) is based on Ingmar Bergman's film *Smiles of a Summer Night* and contains Sondheim's sole hit song, "Send in the Clowns"; *Pacific Overtures* (1976) ambitiously took on the subject of Japanese-American relations; *Sweeney Todd* (1979) was an operetta based on the British grand guignol tale of a murderous barber; *Sunday in the Park with George* (1984) was a biography of impressionist painter Georges Seurat; and *Into the Woods* (1987) wove together children's fairy tales with the theories of psychologist Bruno Bettelheim. At this writing, Sondheim's latest show is *Assassins* (1991), a short piece about presidential killers. In recent years, he has turned more to films (he wrote a score for Stavinsky in the 70s), writing songs for Madonna in *Dick Tracy* in 1990 and reportedly currently working on an original movie musical.

— Bruce Eder

☆ **A Chorus Line - Original Cast / COLUMBIA**   1975
Michael Bennett's 1975 valentine to "gypsies," the dancers who are often treated as so much mobile scenery in Broadway musicals, is sometimes considered to have broken new ground with its frank portraits of talented but frustrated performers. The score by Marvin Hamlisch and Edward Kleban is a favorite of "theater people" everywhere, but was

designed to showcase the abilities of dancers rather than singers. Consequently, only the ballad "What I Did for Love" has had a life outside of the show's context. –MER

○ **City of Angels / COLUMBIA**   1990
The original Broadway cast version of a musical set in Hollywood in the 40s, exploring the interaction between a writer of hard-boiled detective novels and his gumshoe hero. Cy Coleman has turned in some low-key, jazzy period music, and David Zippel's witty lyrics are a match for the book, which was written by Larry Gelbart, the man who brought you the TV series M*A*S*H. –WR

○ **Closer Than Ever / RCA**   1990
A followup to Richard Maltby Jr and David Shire's previous off-Broadway revue, *Starting Here, Starting Now*, featuring two discs' worth of smart songs about the ups and downs of modern life, especially, romance. –WR

○ **Company - Original Cast / CBS**   1970
Winner of both the Drama Critics Circle and Tony Awards in 1970, this show established composer Stephen Sondheim as a demigod of the contemporary musical theater. The story of a bachelor afloat in a sea of the very married was certainly of its time, but it has proven to have enduring appeal, as has Sondheim's deliciously tongue-twisting libretto. –MER

○ **Crazy for You / ANGEL**   1992
Broadway's 1992 Tony winner for Best Musical is a newly written show that borrows Gershwin songs primarily from *Girl Crazy*, but also from some of the Hollywood musicals of the 30s. You've heard the songs before, but they're freshly, enthusiastically presented here, and there's enough of the show's book in the lengthy CD to get a sense of the new context. Harry Groener and, especially, Jodi Benson shine in the starring roles. –WR

○ **Damn Yankees / RCA VICTOR**   1955
The Faust legend is retold in sports terms, as a baseball fan sells his soul so his team can win the pennant. Stars Gwen Verdon and Ray Walston. Score by Richard Adle and Jerry Ross. Highlights: "Whatever Lola Wants," "Heart." –WR

○ **Do I Hear a Waltz? / COLUMBIA**   1965
With music by Richard Rodgers and lyrics by Stephen Sondheim, based on the Arthur Laurents play *The Time of the Cuckoo* (which also served as the basis for the Katharine Hepburn movie *Summertime*). It was not a big success, though some of the songs do reflect the talent that created them, especially the humorous "What Do We Do? We Fly!" –WR

○ **Dreamgirls - Original Cast / GEFFEN**   1981
This rags-to-riches story of a Black 60s girl group was a 1981 success for director/choreographer Michael Bennett, in part due to speculation about its possible similarity to the real-life rise of the Supremes. The score by Henry Krieger and Tom Eyen deliberately evokes the pop and R&B sounds that are the play's subject matter. Jennifer Holliday's rendition of "And I Am Telling You I'm Not Going" stopped the show and began her musical career. –MER

○ **Evita / MCA**   1976
The two-disc pre-stage studio recording by Andrew Lloyd Webber and Tim Rice, billed as "an opera" about Argentine political figure Eva Peron, was a massive UK hit, reaching #4, with Julie Covington's "Don't Cry for Me, Argentina" hitting #1 and Barbara Dickson's "Another Suitcase in Another Hall" reaching the Top 20. –WR

○ **Evita - London Cast / MCA**   1978
A single-disc recording of the original London cast features UK pop star David Essex and Elaine Paige. –WR

○ **Evita / MCA**   1979
This two-disc American cast recording, featuring Patti LuPone and Mandy Patinkin, was the first cast album to go gold in four years. It's now a million-seller. –WR

○ **Falsettoland / DRG**   1990
Original off-Broadway cast album from William Finn's sequel to his previous off-Broadway show, *March of the Falsettos*, and one of the most impressive musical scores in years, a fact

Rodgers and Hammerstein

Composer Richard Rodgers (1902-1979) and lyricist Oscar Hammerstein II (1895-1960) had both had extensive careers in Broadway theater music before they scored their first hit together with Oklahoma! in 1943. Rodgers first teamed with Lorenz Hart (1895-1943), with whom he scored a series of Broadway successes that began when the team's song "Manhattan" was interpolated into *The Garrick Gaities of 1925*. Rodgers and Hart's shows included *Present Arms* (1928), *On Your Toes* (1936), *Babes in Arms* (1937), and *Pal Joey* (1940), among others, and they are responsible for a slew of song standards including "You Took Advantage of Me," "Dancing on the Ceiling," "There's a Small Hotel," "Where or When," "The Lady Is a Tramp," "My Funny Valentine," "I Wish I Were in Love Again," "Isn't It Romantic," and "Bewitched, Bothered and Bewildered." But Hart's health declined, and Rodgers had sought out Hammerstein prior to his partner's death from pneumonia.

Hammerstein, scion of a theatrical family (his grandfather owned several theaters and wrote shows and his father and brother were also involved in the theater), attended Columbia University, where he wrote college shows with Rodgers. He was a considerable success in the 1920s, collaborating with Jerome Kern on *Show Boat* (1927) and also working with Sigmund Romberg, but he went for a long stretch in the 30s without having a hit.

The Rodgers and Hammerstein team returned to the plot-oriented, socially conscious style of *Show Boat* for a series of landmark musicals in the 40s and 50s, notably *Carousel* (1945), *South Pacific* (1949), *The King and I* (1951), and *The Sound of Music* (1959), among others.

Rodgers, who had the luck to work with two of the most gifted lyricists of the century, continued after Hammerstein's death, though without lucking into a third major partner. He wrote music and lyrics to *No Strings* in 1962, and tried working with Stephen Sondheim on *Do I Hear a Waltz?* (1965), but his later work was less successful.

— Bruce Eder

confirmed when the combined shows came to Broadway under the title *Falsettos* and won a Tony for best score. –WR

☆ **The Fantasticks - Original Cast / POLYGRAM**   1960
Overwhelmingly the world's longest-running musical, it debuted May 3, 1960, at the Sullivan Street Playhouse in Greenwich Village, where it remains ensconced at this writing. Boy meets girl, boy loses girl, boy gets girl in the end. The simple and utterly charming score by Tom Jones and Harvey Schmidt includes "Try to Remember," "Soon It's Gonna Rain," and "They Were You." –MER

○ **Fiddler on the Roof / RCA**   1964
Original Broadway cast recording of Sheldon Harnick and Jerry Bock's massively successful musical based on Sholem Aleichem's stories about poor Russian Jews at the turn of the century, starring Zero Mostel, who gets to sing such songs as "Tradition," "If I Were a Rich Man," and "To Life." One of the great musicals of all time, this album was a Top Ten, gold-selling hit. (Note: This edition is a 1986 CD reissue containing two previously unreleased tracks. The still-in-print cassette version, RCA 1005, does not contain these new songs.) –WR

Fiddler on the Roof - Original London Cast / CBS   1984
This is the original London cast recording and features Israeli

actor/singer Topol in the starring role of Tevye. Topol has since gone on to play the part on film and in a Broadway revival, which means his version is by now more familiar than that of the role's originator, Zero Mostel. Topol's Tevye is notably less comic than Mostel's, but he brings great warmth to his performance, and this, not the film soundtrack, is his definitive rendition. –WR

○ **Finian's Rainbow / CBS**   1948
Ella Logan, Donald Richards, and David Wayne starred in this mixture of Southern politics and Irish blarney, which was the most successful of Burton Lane's musicals. –WR

Finian's Rainbow / RCA VICTOR   1960
Revival of the 1947 musical by E. Y. Harburg and Burton Lane. The story is too complicated by half, but that doesn't matter on record, and the music is some of Lane's best. The songs include "How Are Things in Glocca Morra?," "Look to the Rainbow," "Old Devil Moon," and "If This Isn't Love." –WR

Fiorello! - Broadway Cast / CAPITOL   1989
Based on the life and times of New York City's most beloved mayor, Fiorello La Guardia. This show won the 1959 Pulitzer Prize for drama, a rare feat for a musical. It was the first success for the composer/lyricist team of Jerry Bock/Sheldon Harnick, and was Tom Bosley's Broadway debut in the title role. –MER

○ **Flower Drum Song - Original Cast / CBS**
Rodgers and Hammerstein return to a theme that had served them well in both *The King and I* and *South Pacific*: misunderstanding and reconciliation between individuals of differing cultural backgrounds. This 1958 musical revolved around the meeting of old and new worlds in San Francisco's Chinatown. The score is a serviceable score but not the team's most exciting. The novelty "I Enjoy Being a Girl" is more often excerpted than the lovely and overlooked "Love Look Away." –MER

Follies / CAPITOL   1971
Stephen Sondheim's show about aging follies girls remains one of his greatest scores. This Broadway cast recording is somewhat abbreviated, even though the 1989 CD reissue includes previously unreleased material. –WR

○ **Follies - In Concert - Studio Cast / RCA**   1985
This performance, recorded live at New York's Avery Fisher Hall, features a dream cast singing Stephen Sondheim's ambitious and fascinating score. With Barbara Cook, George Hearn, Mandy Patinkin, Lee Remick, Betty Comden, Adolph Green, Liliane Montevecchi, Elaine Stritch, Phyllis Newman, and Carol Burnett, among others. –MER

Follies / ENCORE   1987
A two-disc London cast recording of the complete score as revised by Sondheim for a West End production. This includes newly written songs. –WR

42nd Street - Original Cast / RCA   1977
In a reversal of usual practice, producer David Merrick turned to the 1933 movie musical for this stage musical, which uses Harry Warren and Al Dubin's venerable songs — such as "You're Getting to Be a Habit with Me," "We're in the Money," "Lullaby of Broadway" — and the chorus-girl-becomes-a-star storyline. The result was new and exciting, almost 50 years later. Stars Tammy Grimes and Jerry Orbach. –WR

○ **Funny Face / SMITHSONIAN**   1980
A reconstruction of the 1927 George and Ira Gershwin musical, using period recordings by Fred and Adele Astaire, various orchestras, and even a couple of piano recordings by George Gershwin himself. –WR

Funny Girl / CAPITOL   1964
The Jule Styne/Bob Merrill musical about Ziegfeld Follies comedienne Fanny Brice became a star vehicle for Barbra Streisand — her first and last starring role on Broadway. It also provided her with some of the best material of her early repertoire: "I'm the Greatest Star," "People," and "Don't Rain on My Parade." This album went gold and reached #2. –WR

Andrew Lloyd Webber

Andrew Lloyd Webber (b. 1948) is the most successful composer of musicals of his generation and also a breaker of molds for the type. His predecessors were for the most part American: New York-based songwriters steeped in Broadway tradition. Lloyd Webber saw his share of shows as a child, too, but he was born in London, the son of William Lloyd Webber, director of the London College of Music, and was trained at the Royal Academy of Music, hardly the sort of place where you'd be likely to hear *Oklahoma!*

Nevertheless, Lloyd Webber hooked up with lyricist Tim Rice, and the two began work on what would be a typical project for them, a musical based on the Biblical story of Joseph and his coat of many colors. Titled *Joseph and the Amazing Technicolor Dreamcoat*, it brought in a strong rock & roll influence. After writing a second unproduced musical, the two hit on the idea of writing a musical based on the life of Jesus Christ from the point of view of Judas (not the sort of idea likely to occur to a Broadway composer) and, again, imbued with rock. Unable to finance a stage version, Lloyd Webber and Rice did manage to record their show, and *Jesus Christ Superstar* went on to sales in the millions all over the world. The hit musical version followed.

Lloyd Webber and Rice then split, with the composer writing film scores and working on an abortive musical with playwright Alan Ayckbourne (*Jeeves*), after which Rice returned with another audacious idea: a musical based on the life of Argentine dictator (or dictator's wife, depending on how you look at it) Eva Peron. *Evita* (1976) repeated the pattern of *Jesus Christ Superstar*, with its hit record album followed by a successful theatrical run in the West End and then on Broadway.

The Lloyd Webber-Rice partnership having proved itself again, it was severed (Rice went on to write *Chess*), and Lloyd Webber next wrote a musical revue based on T. S. Eliot's whimsical poems about *Cats* (1981). This time the show came before the album, and it's still running. By this time, Lloyd Webber had largely abandoned the rock elements of his work in favor of what critics found a pastiche style largely borrowed from classical and opera sources. He had also become a brand name (and a corporation, the Really Useful Company) that assured at least a modest success for subsequent shows, though critics were often unimpressed with his efforts.

Downgrading the status of his lyricists, Lloyd Webber went on to a series of successful shows (*Song and Dance, Starlight Express*) before scoring another long- (and still-) running hit in 1987 (1988 in New York) with a musical adaptation of *The Phantom of the Opera*. *Aspects of Love* (1989-1990) was less successful, however. Lloyd Webber is presently working on a musical based on the Billy Wilder film *Sunset Boulevard*.

— Bruce Eder

○ **A Funny Thing Happened ... /**   1962
A Funny Thing Happened on the Way to the Forum, Stephen Sondheim's first musical as both composer and lyricist, was a delightful comedy hit set in ancient Rome and starring Zero Mostel. It included "Comedy Tonight," one of the great opening numbers in Broadway history. This is a reissue of the original Broadway cast recording. –WR

A Funny Thing Happened ... / DRG 1963
A Funny Thing Happened on the Way to the Forum. This is the original London cast recording, featuring British comedian Frankie Howard. –WR

George M! - Original Cast / CBS 1968
Joel Grey's second triumph on Broadway (after *Cabaret*) was this musical biography of George M. Cohan, who ruled the Great White Way at the turn of the century. Unlike the Jimmy Cagney movie, the show pulled no punches, but what really mattered were the Cohan songs, including his biggest hits, "Over There" and "Give My Regards to Broadway." A young Bernadette Peters played Cohan's sister. –WR

○ **Gigi / COLUMBIA / BB# 1** 1958
One of the finest musical scores ever recorded. A warm, witty, romantic confection highlighted by Andre Previn's spirited conducting, Betty Wand's delectable singing, and Lerner and Loewe's greatest film score. –BE

☆ **Gigi - Original Cast / RCA** 1974
A Broadway version of the film musical by Alan Jay Lerner and Frederick Loewe, this recording is notable for a cast that includes Alfred Drake and Agnes Moorehead and introduces four new songs, including the cynical and witty "The Contract." –WR

Girl Crazy / ELEKTRA 1990
A non-stage restoration of the original 1930 show by George and Ira Gershwin, conducted by John Mauceri and featuring Lorna Luft, Judy Blazer, and Frank Gorshin. –WR

☆ **Godspell - Soundtrack / ARISTA** 1973
A stirring rock/pop score by Stephen Schwartz and a strong lead performance by Victor Garber make a success of this film version of the stage hit emphasizing the religious nature of Christ (as opposed to the secular *Jesus Christ Superstar*). Robin Lamont's rendition of "Day by Day" was a Top 15 hit. –WR

Godspell - Original Cast / ARISTA 1974
Stephen Schwartz's reverent musical based on the St. Matthew gospel actually opened off-Broadway (which is where it stayed) before the Broadway version of *Jesus Christ Superstar*, to which it was a kind of response. As a piece of theater, *Godspell* was much more successful, running more than five years. This cast album appeared several years into the run, but it effectively captures the show's rock/pop score and Schwartz's re-reading of the Bible into the American vernacular (he had done much the same with Leonard Bernstein on *Mass*). –WR

The Gospel at Colonus / WARNER 1984
The original cast recording of the Bob Telson/Lee Breuer musical based on Sophocles's *Oedipus at Colonus* has music written in gospel style and sung by the Five Blind Boys of Alabama and other gospel groups. It is beautifully produced by Telson, Daniel Lazerus, and the Steely Dan team of Donald Fagen and Gary Katz. –WR

The Gospel at Colonus - Original Cast / ELEKTRA 1988
This is a little complicated. Bob Telson and Lee Breuer's musical, which mixes gospel music sung by gospel singers with Sophocles's *Oedipus at Colonus*, was originally performed off-Broadway, and a cast album was released. A year later, it was videotaped for the PBS series "Great Performances," and that is the version heard on the album reviewed here. Then three years later, it opened on Broadway. But there's no Broadway cast album. Got that? Okay. This version is similar to the one above (in fact, one track is taken from that recording), but it is a little looser, and in gospel music that's all to the good. –WR

Grand Hotel / RCA 1992
It took years for this Tommy Tune musical to reach disc, during which time one of the leads, David Carroll, died (he is remembered in a club performance of one of the songs, included as a bonus track). But most of the rest of the principals — Liliane Montevecchi, Karen Akers, Michael Jeter — are here, making the most of this musical adaptation of the famous movie about a hotel in Berlin in the 20s. The score, by

---

Jerome Kern

Jerome Kern (1885-1945) is arguably the father of the modern American musical theater. Born in New York of German heritage, he attended the New York College of Music and began to break into Broadway theater during the first decade of the century by having songs of his interpolated into shows. An Anglophile and friend of P. G. Wodehouse, Kern scored his first success with songs inserted into *The Girl From Utah*, a British import, in 1914, including the ballad "They Didn't Believe Me." Breaking away from the European model of waltz music, Kern proved adept at adapting contemporary dance music into his songs as well as producing subtle, inventive ballads. He collaborated with Guy Bolton and, later, Wodehouse on a series of shows presented at the Princess Theater in the middle of the decade, notably *Very Good Eddie*, and continued to score successes into the 20s.

But Kern really entered the history books with *Show Boat* (1927), the first truly modern American musical, with an integrated story and such memorable songs as "Ol' Man River" and "Can't Help Lovin' Dat Man." Like many of his contemporaries, Kern divided his time between Broadway and Hollywood in the 30s, after sound came to the movies, and his movie hits included the Fred Astaire-Ginger Rogers film *Swing Time*, which such songs as "A Fine Romance" and "The Way You Look Tonight" (with lyrics by Dorothy Fields). Kern worked steadily — he wrote or contributed to 37 shows during his career — and was beginning work on *Annie Get Your Gun* when he died suddenly in 1945. He left behind one of the richest catalogs of show music in history.

— Bruce Eder

Robert Wright and George Forrest, with significant additions by Maury Yeston, is not the show's strong point (the staging and choreography were what made it a hit), but it gives a good sense of the story and is true to the original source. –WR

○ **The Grass Harp / PAINTED SMILES** 1971
This Kenward Elmslie/Claire Richardson musical, based on a novel by Truman Capote, was a flop, but it is notable for Barbara Cook's outstanding starring role performance. –WR

○ **Greenwillow / COLUMBIA** 1960
The original Broadway cast recording of the Frank Loesser musical (perhaps his least well known, but still imbued with his musical talent), starring Anthony Hopkins. –WR

☆ **Guys & Dolls / MCA** 1951
Frank Loesser's brilliant musical version of the stories of Damon Runyon was a massive hit, running 1200 performances, and this original Broadway cast album shows why, with songs like "The Oldest Established," "A Bushel and a Peck," "Luck Be a Lady," and "Sit Down You're Rockin' the Boat," sung by a cast including Stubby Kaye, Sam Levene, Robert Alda, and Vivian Blaine. –WR

○ **Gypsy - Original Cast / COLUMBIA**
This tribute to burlesque was a star vehicle for Ethel Merman. The score by Jule Styne and Stephen Sondheim includes the Merman standard "Everything's Coming Up Roses," and the song that is invariably used to introduce anything having to do with the strip tease, "Let Me Entertain You." –MER

☆ **Hair - Original Cast / RCA**
The appearance of "The American Tribal Love Rock Musical" on Broadway in April of 1968 had an effect not unlike the arrival of the motion picture *Woodstock* two years later. *Hair* helped to popularize and, ultimately, to trivialize the "counterculture" it sought to celebrate. But the Gerome

Cast Recordings

The truth is that the Broadway musical does not travel well. Conceived as a combination of comedy, drama, song, and dance for one of those thousand-seat theaters that sit on a handful of streets in midtown Manhattan, the Broadway musical, if it is successful, immediately gets translated into a variety of forms into which it doesn't really fit. A road version may travel the country, playing before abbreviated sets in much larger theaters. A film version may appear that, even if it doesn't alter the work in other ways, somehow looks less impressive on film than it does when you're in the theater. Why is it easy to accept that a person onstage may just burst into song, when it looks silly on celluloid? Maybe the stages are the real dream factories — in movies, things are just too realistic. And then, of course, there are the cast albums, which, in a sense, are the farthest-removed translations of Broadway musicals. Here are a few songs, but no story, no dance. The volatile chemistry of opposing art forms that gives birth to the musical simply isn't present. A cast album is a souvenir, but no more to be confused with the real thing than a three-inch model of the Statue of Liberty you can buy at Battery Park.

And yet Broadway musicals have been the spawning ground for some of the most important popular music of the 20th century. In the first few decades of this century, when most people heard new songs by obtaining the sheet music and playing them themselves, Broadway introduced America to most of its new music. Musicals then were often what we would now call revues, developed out of vaudeville and really just collections of individual scenes and songs. But the country's best songwriters — George M. Cohan, Irving Berlin, George Gershwin — were devoting their efforts to the Broadway stage. Despite this dominance, only occasionally was anything resembling an "original Broadway cast" recording made. Recordings had limited popularity, especially after the start of the Depression when record sales fell precipitously, and while Broadway served as a source for pop songs, usually they were recorded by other singers. One reason for this, of course, was that the record industry's main format — the 78 RPM single — allowed for two songs, each no more than about 3 minutes in length. "Albums" (bound collections of several 78s) were rarities, though *Show Boat*, for example, appeared in this form a year after it hit Broadway in 1927. But *Show Boat* was different in many ways. For one thing, it told a single, unified story, and the songs were mostly integrated into the plot.

By the 40s, the style set by *Show Boat* became the norm for most shows, especially after *Oklahoma*. At the same time, CBS developed the 33 1/3 RPM, long-playing record, and CBS president Goddard Lieberson recognized the Broadway cast album to be ideal for the new medium. As a result, cast albums frequently became big hits. From 1945 to 1965, *Song of Norway* (1945), *Carousel* (1945), *Kiss Me, Kate* (1949), *South Pacific* (1949), *Three Little Words* (1950), *Guys and Dolls* (1951), *The Music Man* (1958), *My Fair Lady* (1958),

Flower Drum Song (1959), *The Sound of Music* (1959), *Camelot* (1961), *Carnival* (1961), and *Hello Dolly!* (1964) all hit #1 on the *Billboard* album charts. The peak of popularity came in the late 50s and early 60s. Then came the rock & roll era, and Broadway show music (like many other pre-rock styles) was swept into a marginalized pop category. Only *Hair* (1968), a rock pastiche, got to the top of the charts, and most cast albums sold modestly.

Stephen Sondheim, the acknowledged master of the Broadway musical in the 70s and 80s, has enjoyed no genuinely successful cast albums, though his song "Send In the Clowns (from *A Little Night Music*) has become a standard. Andrew Lloyd Webber, on the other hand, has largely bucked the trend, starting with his *Jesus Christ Superstar*, of which the pre-stage studio version went to #1 in 1970. Webber has gone on to enjoy million-selling hit cast albums for *Evita*, *Cats*, and *Phantom of the Opera*. Alain Boublil and Claude-Michel Shonberg have also sold a respectable number of copies of *Les Miserables*. These are the exceptions, however. For the most part, not only is the Broadway cast album no longer a commercial sure shot, it may not even get made. Used to be, the week after a show opened and good reviews indicated a hit, the cast would be in a recording studio to get the album out fast. Today, it may be six months before a cast album appears. Recent cases in point include *The Will Rogers Follies* and *The Secret Garden*, both of which opened in the spring of 1991, with their cast albums not available until December. And *Grand Hotel* was at the conclusion of its two-year run before a cast album appeared, by which time it was impossible to append the word "original," since one of the principal actors had died. If this is what happens with big hits, you can imagine how things are for less successful shows.

In spite of all this, there is probably more recording of show music going on now than at any time in the past. Archivists such as John McGlinn, John Mauceri, and Thomas Z. Shepard are hard at work restoring full scores of vintage shows and presenting them in new studio recordings with classically trained singers, further blurring a line between musical and opera already grown fuzzy enough as opera companies have incorporated musicals like *Sweeney Todd* and *South Pacific* into their repertoires. In addition, a plethora of small labels — First Night, Bay Cities, DRG — have taken up the task of recording shows with limited popular appeal, while the majors are digging into their vaults and reissuing long-out-of-print cast albums on compact disc. And then, of course, people keep writing musicals, and audiences keep going to them. How much worry can we have for the musical when we look to the 1992-1993 Broadway season and see on the horizon a version of *Jekyll and Hyde* that already has a cast album out, as well as a new Lloyd Webber musical, *Sunset Boulevard*? Even if the original Broadway cast album is the souvenir of a great evening (as it's always been) and no longer the blockbuster seller it was 30 years ago, it's still the repository of some of the best music of yesterday and today.

— William Ruhlmann

Ragni/James Rado/Galt MacDermot score remains one of the most appealing artifacts of the "Age of Aquarius." —MER

Hello Dolly! - Original Cast / RCA   1964
Jerry Herman's musical (with book by Michael Stewart) based on Thornton Wilder's *The Matchmaker* was one of the last great old-style musicals and a massive hit. Even today, its

songs (including the title track, "Before the Parade Passes By," and "So Long Dearie") are so memorable most people can hum them. Herman used a turn-of-the-century, major-chord, big-melody approach, effectively kidded and overcome by Carol Channing in the title role. It's precisely because Channing doesn't quite have the range for these melodies that she's able to express the character so well (an effect lost in the Barbra Streisand movie version, though Streisand has no trouble expressing character in other ways). And the supporting cast, including Charles Nelson Reilly, Eileen Brennan, and David Burns, is ideal. –WR

Hello Dolly! - Black Broadway Cast / RCA   1967
This is the recording of the all-Black cast that took over the show more than three years into its run, with Pearl Bailey and Cab Calloway in the lead roles. Though less accomplished than the original, it is notable for Bailey's individual interpretation of Dolly. Bailey was sadly underrecorded during her career, and this is a highlight of what little there is. –WR

☆ **House of Flowers / CSP**   1955
With a score by Truman Capote and Harold Arlen and a cast that included Pearl Bailey and Diahann Carroll (in her stage debut), this had the elements of a great show. They're best heard on this cast album in such songs as "A Sleepin' Bee" and "Two Ladies in de Shade of de Banana Tree," which bring out the show's Caribbean flavor. It was a flop onstage for reasons too complicated to explain here, but the soundtrack is very much a hit. –WR

○ **How to Succeed in Business ... / RCA**   1961
Frank Loesser's satire on the business world, *How to Succeed in Business without Really Trying*, is as meaningful today as ever. Starring Robert Morse and Rudy Vallee, it features such highlights as "The Company Way" and "I Believe in You." It's overdue for a revival, but this original cast album is probably unbeatable. –WR

○ **I Do! I Do! / RCA**   1966
The main draws to this two-character musical are the two stars: Mary Martin and Robert Preston. *I Do! I Do!* traces 50 years of a marriage, and the show's relative banality is overcome by the strong performances of the principals, as well as the quality of the Tom Jones score which includes the standard, "My Cup Runneth Over." –WR

○ **Into the Woods / RCA**   1987
Stephen Sondheim and James Lapine's re-telling of children's stories is an intricate, moving show that works on many levels. The music and lyrics are among Sondheim's best (which is to say, the best there are), and the performances, especially those of Bernadette Peters and Chip Zien, are outstanding in this original Broadway cast recording. –WR

Into the Woods - London Cast / RCA   1991
An excellent recording of the Sondheim classic. –WR

Jacques Brel Is Alive and Well ... / ATLANTIC   1974
This film version of the musical revue of the songs of Belgian singer and songwriter Jacques Brel retains the pleasure of the stage version of *Jacques Brel Is Alive and Well and Living in Paris* and adds to it by including the author himself on the moving "Ne Me Quitte Pas" (known in English as "If You Go Away"). But the standout performer is Mort Shuman, who, with Eric Blau, also provides the English translations. –WR

☆ **Jacques Brel Is Alive and Well - Original Cast / CBS** 1987
This 1968 off-Broadway revue of *Jacques Brel Is Alive and Well and Living in Paris* established an "in concert" style of presentation for dramatic music that has often been used since. The poetic lyrics of Jacques Brel, expertly translated by Mort Shuman and Eric Blau, lend themselves to this bookless format. Its best-remembered numbers include "Marathon (Les Flamandes)," "Amsterdam," "Carousel (La Valse a Mille Temps)," and "If We Only Have Love (Quand On A Que L'Amour)." –MER

☆ **Jerome Robbins' Broadway / RCA**   1989
A two-disc cast album from Robbins's anthology show, which includes his re-creations of production numbers excerpted from such shows as *On the Town*, *West Side Story*, *The King and I*, *Gypsy*, and *Fiddler on the Roof*. Onstage it was breathtaking; on record it makes for a sort of Broadway's-greatest-hits album, albeit with re-recorded versions. –WR

☆ **Jesus Christ Superstar / MCA**   1970
Writers Andrew Lloyd Webber and Tim Rice set several

precedents with this album. First, it is a pre-stage studio version, and it topped the US charts upon release. Second, it is the first show to successfully put rock music in a theatrical context (*Hair* is really a pop/show-music pastiche, not rock). Third, it is a "sung-through" musical without spoken dialog, technically an operetta. Fourth, though musicals had turned more serious at this point, writing a show about Jesus Christ from the point of view of Judas was about as daring as you could get. It succeeds in all ways. In addition to the title song (a #14 hit sung by Murray Head), it includes "I Don't Know How to Love Him" by Yvonne Elliman. –WR

○ **The King & I - Original Cast / DECCA**   1955
This 1951 Rodgers and Hammerstein triumph is one of those few musical comedies that gives definition to the art form. This original cast recording stars Gertrude Lawrence, for whom the show was written, as well as Yul Brynner. "I Whistle a Happy Tune," "Getting to Know You," and "Shall We Dance?" are among the classics that grace the score. –MER

☆ **Kismet / CBS**   1953
This adaptation of Edward Knoblock's play about a Baghdad beggar who rises to the rank of Emir in one magical day is notable for its score, adapted by Robert Wright and George Forrest from the music of classical composer Alexander Borodin (Borodin even won a Tony!) and for the lead performance by Alfred Drake. This cast album was a big hit, reaching #4 in the charts, and "Stranger in Paradise" got to #2 in a contemporary recording by Tony Bennett. Onstage, the song was a duet between Doretta Morrow and a young Richard Kiley. –WR

Kismet / CBS / BB# 134   1961
The Wright/Forrest movie score, released for the first time in stereo, and chock-full of fine singing and those Borodin melodies. –BE

☆ **Kiss Me Kate - Original Cast / CBS**   1961
Cole Porter's most successful show and his most popular score came with this adaptation of Shakespeare's *The Taming of the Shrew*, updated by the addition of a contemporary backstage subplot. Songs such as "I Hate Men," "Too Darn Hot," "Where Is the Life That Late I Led?," and "Always True to You (In My Fashion)" shows that Porter had lost none of his lyrical wit or compositional skill, especially when heard in the voices of a cast led by Alfred Drake and including Lisa Kirk. This cast album spent 10 weeks at the top of the album charts in 1949 and stayed in the best-seller lists over a year. The show ran more than a thousand performances. –WR

Kiss Me Kate / RELATIVITY   1987
It's scandalous that there hasn't been a Broadway revival of this Porter masterpiece, but at least the Royal Shakespeare Company in England tried it, and here's the result: a cast led by Paul Jones and Nicola McAuliffe enthusiastically enunciating every delicious bit of wordplay, while a full orchestra plays the music beautifully. –WR

☆ **Kiss Me Kate / EMI**   1990
A two-disc, non-stage, orchestral version of the score of the Cole Porter show, conducted by John McGlinn and featuring the London Sinfonietta. It contains large, instrumental parts of the score not previously recorded. –WR

○ **La Cage aux Folles / RCA**   1983
Composer Jerry Herman finds much greater depth in this French farce about a club for transvestites in St. Tropez than did the original play or the film, turning it into a virtual proclamation of gay pride ("I Am What I Am"). The score has his typically catchy tunes and slangy lyrics, and it remains touching, perhaps even more so in the age of AIDS. George Hearn is outstanding in the lead role. –WR

○ **Lady Be Good! / SMITHSONIAN**   1977
A reconstruction of the 1924 George and Ira Gershwin musical featuring period recordings by Fred and Adele Astaire, George Gershwin himself, and others. The songs include "Fascinating Rhythm" and "The Man I Love." –WR

○ **Lenny / BLUE THUMB**
A two-disc version of the Broadway play based on the comedy routines of Lenny Bruce, starring Cliff Gorman. Funny and heartbreaking, the play served as the basis for a film directed by Bob Fosse and starring Dustin Hoffman. –WR

☆ **Les Miserables / RELATIVITY**   1985
This is the original London cast recording of the musical by Alain Boublil and Claude-Michel Shonberg and starring Colm Wilkinson. A riveting theatrical experience, the show is somewhat less impressive in a merely aural version, but it remains an excellent souvenir for the millions who have seen this show all over the world. –WR

○ **Les Miserables - Complete Sym. / RELATIVITY**   1990
This is quite easily the most impressive complete symphonic recording of Les Miserables on the market. The three-disc set is the entire production, not just the major numbers. The company is an all-star cast taken from productions around the world. The singers hail from New York, Los Angeles, London, Sydney, and Tokyo. Perhaps the most remarkable performance is from Kaho Shimada of Tokyo in the role of Eponine. Shimada herself speaks virtually no English, but you wouldn't be able to tell by listening to this recording. A simply outstanding set. –TEH

○ **Let's Face It / SMITHSONIAN**   1979
A reconstruction of the 1941 Cole Porter musical featuring performances by Danny Kaye and Hildegard. Also included on the album are five selections from Red, Hot, and Blue!, a 1936 Porter show with Ethel Merman, and three from Leave It to Me!, the 1938 show that introduced Mary Martin. –WR

○ **Li'l Abner / COLUMBIA**   1956
The Johnny Mercer/Gene de Paul musical captures the arch, sometimes cynical tone of Al Capp's comic strip and contains all those hayseed characters. Songs like "Jubilation T. Cornpone" and "The Country's in the Very Best of Hands" are much more satiric than anything one normally associates with the 50s, but they certainly don't sound dated today. The cast includes Edith Adams, Stubby Kaye, Tina Louise, and Julie Newmar. –WR

○ **A Little Night Music - Orig. Broadway Cast / CBS**   1973
This recording of Stephen Sondheim's musical based on the Ingmar Bergman film Smiles of a Summer Night is at least as charming as its source material. Sondheim sets the romantic roundelay of the story to a series of waltzes with lyrics that bring out the ups and downs of "Liaisons," to borrow one song title. "Send In the Clowns" is the show's hit, but it is no more impressive than "The Glamorous Life," "You Must Meet My Wife," or "The Miller's Son." The score is effectively handled by a cast led by Len Cariou, Glynis Johns, Hermione Gingold, and Beth Fowler. –WR

○ **A Little Night Music - Original London Cast / RCA**   1975
A London production of the Broadway hit with Jean Simmons and Joss Ackland, as well as Hermione Gingold reprising her role in the original. –MER

○ **Lost in the Stars - Original Cast / MCA**   1985
A 1949 musical with a Black cast, dealing with racial unrest in South Africa. Music by Kurt Weill, words by Pulitzer Prize-winning playwright Maxwell Anderson. Based on Alan Paton's condescending novel Cry, the Beloved Country. The score is lovely but not very African. –MER

○ **Lovely to Look At / CBS**   1988
This film version of Jerome Kern's Roberta is updated, with some humorous bits added on and some pleasing new arrangements. –BE

☆ **Mame / COLUMBIA**   1966
Jerry Herman's score hasn't a weak song, and it has some very strong ones, starting with the title tune and including "We Need a Little Christmas" and "If He Walked into My Life." Add a cast headed by Angela Lansbury and a book by Jerome Lawrence and Robert E. Lee (based on the Patrick Dennis novel about a boy and his zany aunt), and you have a big Broadway hit. –WR

○ **Man of La Mancha - Original Cast / MCA**   1965
The musical version of Cervantes's Don Quixote, Man of La Mancha opened inauspiciously in an off-Broadway house in the fall of 1965, moved to Broadway, and became the hit of the 1965-1966 season. The original cast recording, with Richard Kiley in the title role, was a gold-selling hit that stayed on the best-seller charts more than three years, and no wonder, with a Mitch Leigh/Joe Darion score that included the stirring title song and the anthemic "The Impossible Dream." –WR

○ **March of the Falsettos - Original Cast / DRG**   1981
A complex exploration of love, selfishness, and the post-modern family. William Finn's 1981 tour de force is entirely sung but not at all reminiscent of conventional operetta. The story is of a man, his wife, his son, the man's male lover, and his shrink. Outstanding cast with Michael Rupert and Chip Zien. –MER

○ **Marry Me a Little / RCA**   1981
Craig Lucas and Norman Rene cobbled together a show based on Stephen Sondheim songs dropped from other shows, on the accurate theory that Sondheim discards are better than most people's best. On record, it's more like a Sondheim rarities album, but that's pretty great too. –WR

○ **Me and My Girl / MCA**   1986
A revival/revision of Noel Gay's 30s musical comedy about a Cockney who is heir to an earldom, this Broadway cast album has plenty going for it: Robert Lindsay, who gives a delightful star turn in the main role, and a score including such favorites as "The Lambeth Walk" and "Leaning on a Lamppost." –WR

☆ **Merrily We Roll Along / RCA**   1982
Stephen Sondheim wrote one of his typically outstanding scores for this show, tracing the lives of a composer and lyricist — backwards. It was a complete flop onstage, but the album proves its quality. RCA 5840 is a 1986 CD reissue of the LP version (RCA 4197), containing one song that previously didn't fit. The cassette version does not have the added song. –WR

○ **Miss Saigon - Original London Cast / GEFFEN**   1990
Alain Boublil and Claude-Michel Schonberg's followup to Les Miserables is another sung-through operetta with a serious theme and a classic source: They have placed Madame Butterfly in the waning days of the Vietnam War. Jonathan Pryce stands out as a pimp named the Engineer in this London cast recording, and the score has the same rock feel as Schonberg's Les Miserables music. –WR

○ **Mister Wonderful / MCA**   1956
This Jerry Bock/Larry Holofcener/George Weiss show is remembered today for boosting Sammy Davis Jr to stardom. It also featured a young Chita Rivera. –WR

☆ **The Most Happy Fella / COLUMBIA**   1956
A three-LP (now two-CD) complete score of the Frank Loesser operetta about a California grapegrower and his mail-order bride. It's one of the most heartwarming shows ever, and this original Broadway cast features Robert Weede and Loesser's future wife Jo Sullivan. –WR

○ **The Most Happy Fella / RCA**   1992
A new Broadway cast recording led by opera singer Spiro Malas. The two-piano arrangement lacks the sweep of the classic original orchestrations but brings out the material in a relatively unadorned fashion that probably works better onstage in the more naturalistic 90s than the original score might. –WR

○ **The Music Man - Orig. Broadway Cast / CAPITOL**   1958
The original Broadway cast of Meredith Willson's most successful musical was headed by Robert Preston, who played the part of Harold Hill, a conman who breezes into an Iowa town and tries to sell the inhabitants on non-existent boys band equipment. Willson concentrates on percussive effects and rapid-fire spiels for Preston, though the musical standout is Barbara Cook as Marian the Librarian. Highlights of this perennial hit show include "Seventy-Six Trombones" and "Till There Was You." –WR

The Music Man - Studio Recording / TELARC   1991
Erich Kunzel leads the Cincinnati Pops Orchestra in this concert version of the score, which features more incidental music than previous albums. Timothy Noble is only adequate in the lead role, but Doc Severinsen proves a surprisingly effective Marcellus Washburn on his featured number, "Shipoopi." –WR

☆ **My Fair Lady - Orig. Broadway Cast / COLUMBIA**   1956
The original Broadway cast recording of Alan Jay Lerner and Frederick Loewe's musical, based on George Bernard Shaw's *Pygmalion*, about the relationship between an elocutionist and a flower girl. This is one of the great musical scores, including "Wouldn't It Be Lovely," "I Could Have Danced All Night," and "On the Street Where You Live," sung by a cast that includes Rex Harrison, Julie Andrews, and Stanley Holloway. The album spent 15 weeks at #1 in the charts. –WR

○ **My Fair Lady - Original London Cast / CBS**
This mega-hit moved into the Drury Lane Theatre in London in April of 1958 with the British stars of the Broadway version intact; hence the original London cast recording is very similar to its more familiar American counterpart. At present this album in CD form is often rather less expensive than the original Broadway cast CD, and it is far better to have this *My Fair Lady* than none at all. –MER

○ **My One & Only - Orig. Broadway Cast / ATLANTIC**   1983
"The New Gershwin Musical" was the subtitle given this musical, but most people knew it as the new Tommy Tune musical, since he starred in it (with Twiggy) and staged and choreographed it (with Thommie Walsh). On record, Tune's personality comes across even if his long legs aren't visible, and the mostly understated arrangements of Gershwin favorites sound newly minted. –WR

New York, New York - Orig. Soundtrack / CAPITOL   1977
A movie musical with songs by John Kander and Fred Ebb. They tell the story of the evolution of popular music from the swing era to the singer era and bebop, with reference to the lavish movie musicals of the late 40s. Liza Minnelli sings brilliantly, especially on the title song and on "But the World Goes 'Round," while big-band sax player Georgie Auld handles the music for Robert De Niro. –WR

○ **No, No, Nanette - Broadway Cast / COLUMBIA**   1971
A revival of a 1925 musical by Vincent Youmans, Irving Caesar, and Otto Harbach, mounted in an essentially faithful style 41 years later with a cast featuring Ruby Keeler and a production supervised by Busby Berkeley. A romantic roundelay with a flapper at its center, it proved a success all over again in the 70s, probably because it still had a score featuring such songs as "I Want to Be Happy" and "Tea for Two." –WR

○ **Of Thee I Sing/Let 'Em Eat Cake / CBS**   1987
The Brooklyn Academy of Music staged concert versions of these two Gershwin political musicals of the 30s, one a sequel of the other, with Michael Tilson Thomas as music director and conductor and a cast including Maureen McGovern, Larry Kert, and Jack Gilford. The result is an exquisite recording that restores valuable Gershwin material to the record racks. –WR

○ **Oh, Kay! / SMITHSONIAN**   1978
A reconstruction of the 1926 George and Ira Gershwin musical, featuring recordings by Gertrude Lawrence, with George Gershwin playing many of the piano parts. Songs include "Clap Yo' Hands," "Do, Do, Do," and "Someone to Watch over Me." –WR

☆ **Oklahoma! - Original Cast / DECCA-MCA**
Rodgers and Hammerstein's first collaboration in 1943 created the mold from which most musicals were made for the next twenty-five years. The combination of a serious book, with score and ballet truly subservient to the plot, proved a successful formula, particularly in the hands of this team. Alfred Drake's dreamy "Oh, What a Beautiful Mornin'" and Celeste Holm's "I Cain't Say No" are irresistible. –MER

Oklahoma! - Broadway Revival / RCA   1980
An excellent Broadway revival of the 1943 Rodgers and Hammerstein show that still ranks among their greatest works, and which gets a hi-fidelity workout here. –WR

○ **Oliver! - Original Broadway Cast / RCA**   1962
Lionel Bart's musical version of *Oliver Twist*, Charles Dickens's novel of Industrial Revolution London in the late 19th century, was far more entertaining than the subject matter would suggest. The show has Dickens's sad story of poverty and crime, but also one of the strongest scores heard on Broadway in the 60s — "I'd Do Anything," "Be Back Soon," "Oom-Pah-Pah," "As Long As He Needs Me" — in fact, it's one hit after another (no wonder this reached #4 in the charts and went gold). And it has the incomparable Georgia Brown too. –WR

○ **On the Town - Studio Recording / COLUMBIA**   1960
This is a studio re-creation of the 1944 show about three sailors on leave for a day in New York City, featuring original cast members Nancy Walker, Betty Comden, and Adolph Green, plus John Reardon. Comden and Green provided lyrics to this delightful work, and the music is by Leonard Bernstein, who conducts here. In addition to such standards as "New York, New York" and "I Can Cook Too," this version includes a great deal of instrumental dance music. –WR

○ **Once on This Island / RCA**   1990
A wonderful Caribbean-influenced musical by Lynn Ahrens and Stephen Flaherty. You can't see the fluid staging of Graciela Daniele on this disc, but the music almost makes up for it. –WR

○ **Pacific Overtures / RCA**   1976
One of Stephen Sondheim's most ambitious works, treating the relations between Japan and the West and, in retrospect, containing some of Sondheim's best songs, among them "Pretty Lady" and "Someone in a Tree." Mako leads a distinguished Asian-American cast. –WR

Pacific Overtures / TER   1988
Edited version of the English National Opera production. –WR

○ **Paint Your Wagon / RCA**   1951
Alan Jay Lerner and Frederick Loewe turn their attention to the American West and come up with a story that anticipates the romantic triangle of *Camelot*. On the way, they present one of their best scores, featuring such songs as "They Call the Wind Maria" and "Wand'rin' Star." James Barton stars. –WR

○ **Pajama Game - Original Cast / CBS**   1954
This 1954 comedy about organized labor launched Bob Fosse's Broadway career. The jazzy score by Richard Adler and Jerry Ross includes "Steam Heat," "Hernando's Hideaway," and "Hey There." This recording features John Raitt, one of the era's most popular actor/singers. –MER

○ **Pal Joey - Studio Recording / COLUMBIA**   1951
Rodgers and Hart's *Pal Joey*, with a book by John O'Hara, was a sophisticated, downbeat tale about a gigolo. It may have been a bit too dark for audiences in 1940, when it had a moderate run on Broadway. More than a decade later, Columbia Records' Goddard Lieberson decided to make a studio recording of the show, which included such classic songs as "I Could Write a Book" and "Bewitched, Bothered and Bewildered," with Harold Lang and Vivienne Segal in the main roles. It is *not*, as the album jacket suggests, a "Broadway cast," although, just to confuse matters, the success of this album led to a Broadway revival starring Lang and Segal. –WR

○ **Pal Joey: Froman, Beavers & B'way Cast / CAPITOL**   1952
One of the biggest hits of the 1951-1952 Broadway season was the revival of *Pal Joey*. Capitol got the rights to the cast album, but couldn't use the stars, who had already recorded the score for Columbia, so they substituted with Jane Froman and Dick Beavers, plus the revival cast. They sing wonderfully, however, and with a score this good, how could they miss? –WR

☆ **Peter Pan - Original Cast / COLUMBIA**
This 1950 version of J. M. Barrie's children's classic predates

the more familiar Mary Martin production by four years. Words as well as music are by Leonard Bernstein in one of his earliest Broadway efforts. It stars Jean Arthur and Boris Karloff. –MER

○ **Peter Pan / RCA**   1054
A minor success in 1954, this show owes its persistence in the American consciousness to two television broadcasts. The second (in 1960) was taped for posterity and re-run religiously in the 60s, so the whole baby-boom generation can sing "Tender Shepherd," "I've Gotta Crow," "Never Never Land," "I'm Flying," and "I Won't Grow Up" in a giant chorus. Mary Martin stars as the little boy traditionally played by adult actresses. Betty Comden, Adolph Green, and Jule Styne are among those who contributed to the score. –MER

○ **Phantom of the Opera - Orig. Cast / POLYGRAM**   1987
This is one of Andrew Lloyd Webber's most highly acclaimed productions. The two-disc set comes with a booklet that has not only the lyrics, but also the dialog and stage directions. Sarah Brightman as Christine Daae (the heroine) and Michael Crawford as the Phantom. Also available in a one-disc "highlights" version. –TEH

○ **Pippin - Original Broadway Cast / MOTOWN**   1972
The biggest hit of the 1972-1973 season on Broadway, *Pippin* is perhaps better remembered for Ben Vereen's performance and for the choreography by Bob Fosse than for the songs by Stephen Schwartz. The score is not as good as Schwartz's masterpiece, *Godspell*, but nevertheless has an appealing pop style, especially on such songs as "Corner of the Sky" and "Spread a Little Sunshine." –WR

☆ **Pirate / CBS**   1990
An interesting fantasy score by Cole Porter, not quite successful but featuring one classic ("Be a Clown"). –BE

○ **Porgy & Bess - Original Cast / MCA**   1989
According to Alan Jay Lerner, "It was the first of its kind and remains to this day the greatest triumph of the modern musical theater." According to noted Black theater historian Loften Mitchell, it was "a work generally hailed by Whites and disliked by many Negroes." George Gershwin's 1935 "folk opera," with lyrics by Ira Gershwin and Du Bose Heyward, based on Heyward's novel, introduced "Summertime," "I Got Plenty o' Nuttin'," and "It Ain't Necessarily So." Even if, as Mitchell says, the characters are stereotypical and the story "not as moving as its source," the musical importance of *Porgy and Bess* is undeniable. –MER

○ **Pump Boys & Dinettes - Original Cast / COLUMBIA**
An ensemble piece written and performed by John Foley, Mark Hardwick, Debra Monk, Cass Morgan, John Schimmel, and Jim Wann. This was quickly promoted from supper club to off-Broadway, and then to Broadway in 1982. It's a warm, small-scale, country-style celebration of life among the denizens of the Double Cupp Diner and the filling station across the highway, somewhere in the contemporary American South. –MER

○ **Purlie - Original Broadway Cast / RCA**   1970
This musical comedy adaptation of Ossie Davis's play about a Black preacher who returns to his Southern hometown has a boisterous gospel score written by Gary Geld and Peter Udell and also boasts a cast including Cleavon Little, Melba Moore, Linda Hopkins, and Sherman Hemsley. –WR

○ **Return to the Forbidden Planet / RHINO**   1991
What a jumble of sources! This is the original London cast recording of a musical based on the sci-fi movie *Forbidden Planet* and Shakespeare's *The Tempest*, employing pop songs of the 50s and 60s. On record, it's just a bunch of rock oldies, but it's still fun. –WR

○ **Roar of the Greasepaint - Orig. B'way Cast / RCA**   1965
Roar of the Greasepaint, the Smell of the Crowd. A sequel to Anthony Newly and Leslie Bricusse's previous show, *Stop the World — I Want to Get Off*, and almost as winning a score, largely sung by Newly and Cyril Ritchard. Featuring "Who Can I Turn To (When Nobody Needs Me)." –WR

☆ **The Rocky Horror Picture Show / RHINO**   1975
It took almost six years for this soundtrack of the all-time midnight movie favorite to go gold, but it is one of the most memorable film scores (and show scores, for that matter) of the 70s, combining old-time rock & roll with campy horror movie clichés. Tim Curry and Meat Loaf star. –WR

The Rocky Horror Picture Show / RHINO   1990
This 15th Anniversary four-CD boxed set contains the film soundtrack, the Roxy cast album, a disc of international performances, and a disc of rare tracks by such film principals as Tim Curry and Little Nell. There's also a booklet of photos and such. Pricey, but essential for Rocky fans. –WR

The Rocky Horror Show / RHINO   1974
The first American production of this sci-fi/rock & roll pastiche from Britain, presented at the Roxy in Los Angeles and featuring Tim Curry, who originated the starring role of Dr. Frank N. Furter in London. Richard O'Brien's score has passed into legend, but it's still fresh here. –WR

○ **Rodgers & Hart Songbook /**   1988
A twenty-track compilation album of show songs by Richard Rodgers and Lorenz Hart, recorded by a variety of pop singers in the 50s and 60s, among them Perry Como, Jack Jones, and Ann-Margret. –WR

○ **Runaways / COLUMBIA**   1978
Elizabeth Swados conducted this show about teenage runaways, which features a child cast who turn in outstanding performances on some terrific pop-rock material. It's the kind of thing Broadway needs more of. –WR

Sarafina! / SHANACHIE   1987
An abbreviated version of the Mbongeni Ngema musical about South African school children. It was recorded in South Africa prior to the show's arrival in New York. Cheaply made, but stirring. –WR

○ **Sarafina! / RCA**   1988
This is the more complete Broadway cast version of this show, which by November 1988 had turned into the most moving evening in a Broadway theater. Ngema's music captures the newly popular mbaqanga sound of the homelands, and the story paints apartheid in its most glaring colors. –WR

○ **Seven Brides for Seven Brothers / COLUMBIA**   1954
An engaging folk-like musical, this soundtrack was remastered into stereo for the first time and sounds quite crisp. –BE

She Loves Me - Orig. Broadway Cast / POLYDOR   1976
Sheldon Harnick and Jerry Bock's musical version of *The Shop Around the Corner* was not a stage success (unlike their *Fiddler on the Roof* the following year), but the score has been well remembered in this near-complete recording (originally on two LPs), especially for Barbara Cook's performance. –WR

○ **Shenandoah / RCA VICTOR**   1975
It's no coincidence that this antiwar musical, set during the Civil War, became a big Broadway hit around the time Vietnam fell, but that doesn't mean the Gary Geld/Peter Udell work isn't a profound and tuneful meditation on war and peace: it is. It has John Cullum's Tony-winning performance at its center. –WR

☆ **Show Boat - Broadway Score / COLUMBIA**   1928
This album, originally issued on 78s, presents eight selections recorded by members of the original 1927 Broadway production of the landmark musical, plus Paul Robeson's rendition of "Ol' Man River." (Robeson was in the original London production and the first Broadway revival.) *Show Boat* is the crowning achievement of Jerome Kern's career. It is the prototype for the unified story musicals that followed it, especially after World War II. It begins lyricist Oscar Hammerstein II's series of socially conscious musicals. And its songs, especially in these versions, are unforgettable. Here you also get Helen Morgan singing "Bill" and "Can't Help Lovin' Dat Man." –WR

○ **Show Boat - Original Cast / CBS / BB# 184**   1951
An extravagant, dressed-up 1951 film score, nicely sung. –BE

Show Boat - Original Cast / CBS   1962
Non-stage studio recording featuring John Raitt, Barbara Cook, William Warfield, Anita Darian, Fay De Witt, Louise Parker, and the Merrill Staton Choir, conducted by Franz Allers. Cook is especially impressive (she went on to a stage revival of the show four years later). –WR

Show Boat - Original Cast / RCA   1966
This is the cast recording of the 1966 City Center revival of *Show Boat* starring Barbara Cook, Constance Towers, Stephen Douglass, and David Wayne. –WR

Show Boat - London Cast / STANYAN   1972
This is a well-recorded 1971 London revival, starring Cleo Laine. –WR

Show Boat - A Collector's Show Boat / RCA   1976
Performances culled from various recordings of *Show Boat*. It leans heavily on a 1956 version featuring Robert Merrill and Patrice Munsel, but also includes 1928 recordings by Paul Robeson and Helen Morgan. –WR

☆ **Show Boat / EMI**   1988
This lavish three-CD studio reconstruction of the original score is more than complete: it includes outtake material cut from the show before the opening and also restores controversial lyrics. This was lovingly and thoroughly put together by John McGlinn, who brought in such opera singers as Frederica von Stade and Jerry Hadley, backed by the London Sinfonietta, and is the most exhaustive rendering of perhaps the most important American musical of the 20th century. –WR

○ **Showstoppers / RCA**   1989
A collection of 20 songs from Broadway show recordings made between 1909 and 1941. Features such stars as Fanny Brice, Al Jolson, George M. Cohan, Beatrice Lillie, Helen Morgan, Paul Robeson, Eddie Cantor, Ethel Merman, Fred Astaire, Noel Coward, Cole Porter, and Gertrude Lawrence. –WR

Side by Side by Sondheim - London Cast / RCA   1976
A two-disc London cast recording of a revue culled from songs written by Stephen Sondheim for such musicals as *A Funny Thing Happened on the Way to the Forum*, *Company*, *A Little Night Music*, *Follies*, *Anyone Can Whistle*, *Pacific Overtures*, *Do I Hear a Waltz?*, *West Side Story*, and *Gypsy*, and more obscure works such as "Evening Primrose" (a TV show), *The 7% Solution*, and *The Mad Show*. In anthology and presented starkly, the songs are (if possible) even more impressive than when heard in the shows for which they were written. If there was any doubt that Stephen Sondheim was the greatest talent writing contemporary musicals, this show erases it. –WR

Silk Stockings - Original Broadway Cast / RCA   1955
Cole Porter based this charming musical on the movie *Ninotchka*, about a Russian official tempted by the romantic and capitalistic elements of Paris. Hildegarde Neff inhabits the Greta Garbo role, while Don Ameche plays Melvyn Douglas's film part. It isn't one of the great Porter scores, but with lyrics like "Siberia" and "It's a Chemical Reaction, That's All," it is full of Porter's typical wit. –WR

Sondheim: A Musical Tribute / RCA   1973
A two-disc recording of a special benefit show held Mar 11, 1973, featuring many of the original performers from Stephen Sondheim musicals, reprising their performances of his songs. Thus, the album is a kind of "Sondheim's Greatest Hits," with the added excitement of being a one-time event. Originally isssued as a two-LP set by Warner in 1973, it was reissued by RCA on CD/cassette with previously unreleased tracks. –WR

A Collector's Sondheim / RCA   1985
A four-LP boxed-set compilation that gathers material from a variety of Stephen Sondheim scores over the 30 years 1954-1984 (those for which he only provided lyrics are excluded). This is an outstanding, if pricey sampler that features many rarities and is a must for Sondheim fans. –WR

Sondheim / BOOK-OF-THE-MONTH   1985
A three-LP boxed set of newly recorded Sondheim songs, featuring such singers as Cris Groenendaal, Bob Gunton, and Debbie Shapiro and conducted by frequent Sondheim orchestrator Paul Gemignani. The album presents Sondheim's songs outside a theatrical context, in renditions by great singers. A welcome addendum to the Sondheim library.. –WR

○ **The Sound of Music - Original Cast / CBS**
The Sound of Music was a huge hit in 1959 for Rodgers and Hammerstein, and a highlight in the remarkable career of Mary Martin. The book by Howard Lindsay and Russel Crouse was based on Maria von Trapp's autobiography. It's a rather cloying story that involves nuns, Nazis, and seven cute kids, but it has pleased audiences for years. The title song, "Climb Every Mountain," "My Favorite Things," "Do-Re-Mi," "Sixteen Going on Seventeen," and "Edelweiss" all entered the culture through this score. The cast album features Theodore Bikel in the romantic lead, which unfortunately became a non-singing role in the subsequent film. –MER

○ **South Pacific - Original Cast / COLUMBIA**
Adapted from James A. Michener's *Tales of the South Pacific*. Starring Mary Martin and opera star Ezio Pinza, with music and lyrics by Rodgers and Hammerstein, it enjoyed the largest advance ticket sale ever recorded on Broadway when it opened in 1949. The book intertwines two wartime love stories complicated by American prejudices against Asians. The brilliant score includes "A Cockeyed Optimist," "Some Enchanted Evening," "There Is Nothin' Like a Dame," "I'm Gonna Wash That Man Right Outa My Hair," and "Younger Than Springtime." –MER

South Pacific / CBS   1986
A studio recording featuring a combination of opera singers (Kiri Te Kanawa, José Carreras), jazz singers (Sarah Vaughan), and Broadway singers (Mandy Patinkin), with the London Symphony Orchestra, directed by Jonathan Tunick. –WR

○ **Starting Here, Starting Now / RCA VICTOR**   1977
This celebrated off-Broadway revue serves as a retrospective of the work of Richard Maltby Jr and David Shire, a songwriting team that has done just about everything *except* write a successful Broadway musical. Contemporary mores are examined in a series of songs including the title tune and "What About Today," both previously recorded by Barbra Streisand. –WR

○ **Stop the World ... - Original Cast / POLYDOR**   1962
Stop the World, I Want To Get Off, Anthony Newley and Leslie Bricusse's innovative show, holds up very well after 30 years, due as much to the score as to Newley's singing on such standards as "Gonna Build a Mountain" and "What Kind of Fool Am I?" –WR

Sunday in the Park with George - Orig. Cast / RCA   1984
Stephen Sondheim's musical, imaginatively based on the life of French painter Georges Seurat, is a meditation on life and the creative process, brilliantly realized by Mandy Patinkin and Bernadette Peters. –WR

☆ **Sweeney Todd - Original Cast / RCA**   1979
A complete, two-disc recording of Stephen Sondheim's *grand guignol* operetta about a barber who cuts things close. This show is a masterpiece full of stirring music and witty, intricate lyrics, lustily delivered by a cast led by Angela Lansbury and Len Cariou. Don't confuse this complete score with a single-disc "highlights" album also in print. –WR

○ **Sweet Charity - Broadway Cast / CBS**   1966
Gwen Verdon is the standout performer in this recording of the Cy Coleman/Dorothy Fields score, but consider that the songs she has to sing include "Big Spender," "If My Friends Could See Me Now," and "Where Am I Going?" –WR

Sweet Charity / CAPITOL   1986
This revival stars Debbie Allen in the title role and features Michael Rupert. The score is somewhat modified from the original, so it conforms more to the movie version. –MER

○ **They're Playing Our Song / CASABLANCA**   1979
A successful musical with a book by Neil Simon and songs by Marvin Hamlish and Carole Bayer Sager. It concerns the on-again, off-again relationship between a composer and lyricist. *They're Playing Our Song* has a pop music score characteristic of its time, even to the point of the disco style of some of its songs. Robert Klein and Lucie Arnaz are the principals. –WR

Threepenny Opera / COLUMBIA   1976
A marvelous staging of the Brecht/Weill musical by the New York Shakespeare Festival and a cast headed by Raul Julia. The new translation by Ralph Manheim and John Willett is fresh and highly singable. –WR

○ **Threepenny Opera - Original Cast / POLYDOR**   1954
Marc Blitzstein's translation of the Kurt Weill/Bertolt Brecht musical ran for six years off-Broadway and established the work as a major theater piece in the US. This excellent recording not only presents Blitzstein's terrific versions of the songs but also a cast led by Jo Sullivan, Beatrice Arthur, and Lotte Lenya. –WR

○ **Till the Clouds Roll By / COLUMBIA**
This soundtrack is an all-star tribute to Jerome Kern, without the climactic Frank Sinatra "Ol' Man River" but filled with worthwhile performances. –BE

○ **The Unsinkable Molly Brown / CAPITOL**   1960
Meredith Willson's followup to *The Music Man*, about a *nouveau riche* Colorado mine owner's wife who survives the sinking of the Titanic, is not quite as impressive as its predecessor, but the irrepressible Tammy Grimes does much to make it a success on record. The original Broadway cast recording. –WR

○ **The Unsinkable Molly Brown / CBS / BB# 11**   1981
Debbie Reynolds sparks this homespun early-60s movie musical version that has proved a favorite over the years. She can be a bit overbearing, but it works, and Harve Presnell sings well. –BE

○ **West Side Story - Original Cast / COLUMBIA**
A fabulous collaboration of Jerome Robbins (concept, direction, choreography), Arthur Laurents (book), Leonard Bernstein (music), and Stephen Sondheim (lyrics). This modern retelling of the *Romeo and Juliet* story debuted on Broadway in 1957. Larry Kert and Carol Lawrence sing leads magnificently. Bernstein's instrumental ballet music for this show is probably as familiar as its many standout songs: "Maria," "Tonight," "I Feel Pretty," and "Somewhere," among others. –MER

☆ **West Side Story / COLUMBIA**   1962
This film version of the Leonard Bernstein/Stephen Sondheim score of a modern, urban *Romeo and Juliet* spent more weeks at #1 in the charts (54) than any other album in history. It is an effective rendition of the score, featuring Natalie Wood, Richard Beymer, Russ Tamblyn, Rita Moreno, and George Chakiris, and features all of the show's important songs, among them "Something's Coming," "Maria," "Tonight," and "Somewhere." –WR

West Side Story / DEUTSCHE GRAMMOPHON   1985
Leonard Bernstein conducts his own score on this studio recording, which features opera singers Kiri Te Kanawa and José Carreras. The singers somewhat overwhelm the material (and it's more than a little odd that the only person with a Spanish accent is Carreras, who plays Tony, the American Romeo), but the music is magnificent. –WR

○ **The Will Rogers Follies - Original Cast / CBS**   1991
Original Broadway cast recording of the musical by Cy Coleman, Betty Comden, and Adolph Green (book by Peter Stone), which tells the story of the humorist and Ziegfeld

Follies star — "a life in revue." Directed and choreographed by Tommy Tune, it won the 1991 Tony Award for Best Musical. On disc, the show's charm comes across, especially when star Keith Carradine is before a microphone. –WR

○ **Wonderful Town - Original Broadway Cast / MCA**   1953
Leonard Bernstein brings a typical sense of invention and musical ambition to this score, and Betty Comden and Adolph Green their usual street-smart New York lyrics, for a show based on the play *My Sister Eileen* about two siblings struggling in 30s Greenwich Village. Rosalind Russell leads a strong cast. –WR

○ **Wonderful Town — Television Soundtrack / SONY**   1958
This is a studio recording employing the cast (most of it from the original Broadway production) of a TV telecast made five years after the stage version. Since there is no film version of *Wonderful Town*, this expensively mounted album, which is a match for the cast album above, stands as the only other recording. Rosalind Russell is again the leading figure. –WR

○ **Words & Music / CBS**
An all-star (or nearly so) tribute to Rodgers and Hart, and worthwhile for the Judy Garland and Mel Tormé numbers. –BE

○ **Zorba - Original Broadway Cast / CAPITOL**   1968
John Kander and Fred Ebb's score to this musical adaptation of *Zorba the Greek* was less accomplished than their last show, *Cabaret* and clearly under the influence of *Fiddler on the Roof*, but it is performed in a spirited manner by a cast led by Herschel Bernardi and Maria Karnilova. –WR

TELEVISION SOUNDTRACKS

Cinderella / COLUMBIA   1957
Perhaps Rodgers and Hammerstein's most seen but least performed musical, *Cinderella* was written for and played on television, for only one, non-taped time. The typically lovely music and affecting lyrics softened some of the harder aspects of the fairy tale, and Julie Andrews gave a wonderful performance in the title role. This recording features the TV cast and was made a couple of weeks before the broadcast. The score features memorable songs such as "Do I Love You Because You're Beautiful." –WR

☆ **Great Western Themes (w/Geoff Love & Orch.) / EMI**
Twenty-four tracks done with verve but not much insight, highlighted by "The Big Country," "The Big Valley," "Wagon Train," and a creditable version of "The Virginian." –BE

○ **Mr. Lucky - TV Soundtrack / RCA / BB# 2**
Henry Mancini tried for something similar to Peter Gunn in his music for this Blake Edwards-produced series, but didn't quite succeed. This music is moody and occasionally interesting, but nowhere near as driving as the other. –BE

○ **Peter Gunn - TV Soundtrack / RCA / BB# 1**   1989
This was televison's first big hit music track. The title theme from this series produced by Blake Edwards is one of the finest things Henry Mancini ever wrote. Here is driving, popular jazz, with a beat and style. –BE

○ **Secret Agent File / GNP CRESCENDO**
An all-right compilation, highlighted by lots of 60s TV themes, including the title music from "The Prisoner." –BE

○ **Star Trek - Vol. 1 / GNP CRESCENDO**   1990
The first "Star Trek" TV soundtrack includes some of the finest music written for television during the 60s — moody, atmospheric, and very striking, all broken into relatively short cues. Unfortunately, the source tapes haven't held up well, and the quality leaves a lot to be desired. –BE

○ **Star Trek - Vol. 2 / GNP CRESCENDO**
Far more impressive sonically than *Vol. 1*, this consists of cues

from two second-season episodes, "Amok Time" and "The Doomsday Machine." It is unexpectedly rewarding. −BE

○ **Sullivan Years: Best of Broadway - Orig. Cast / TVT** 1992
This two-disc set collects TV performances of some of Broadway's biggest hits as they were done with original cast members on Broadway. Among the priceless material from shows like *Camelot*, *West Side Story*, and *My Fair Lady* is a bonus interview with Richard Rodgers and Oscar Hammerstein II (not on the cassette version). −WR

☆ **Television's Greatest Hits - Vol. 1 / TEEVEE TOONS**
An uneven but enjoyable compilation of the good, the bad, and the forgettable among TV music themes from the 50s and 60s, with variable sound quality to boot. But it's unique. −BE

☆ **Twilight Zone - Vol. 1 / VARESE SARABANDE** 1983
Ignore the slightly compressed sound and take in the eerie, beautifully wrought compositions, every one of them memorable not only from the series but from lots of subsequent use. −BE

VIDEO

The music video, along with the compact disc, was a major marketing innovation in the performing arts of the 80s, but performance clips of musicians — fortunately for all of us — go back virtually to the dawn of talking pictures. As early as 1929, Bessie Smith, Louis Armstrong, and Cab Calloway were appearing on film clips of varying lengths and quality, either in live performance or mimed to pre-recorded tracks. By the 40s, short clips called "soundies" were an established part of the music business and were frequently designed in a conceptual fashion, anticipating the modern rock video. In 1951 Michael Powell and Emeric Pressburger directed and produced *The Tales of Hoffman*, a complete 127-minute movie shot to a recording of the opera and designed as a vast conceptual creation. Rock videos in their earliest form grew out of similar mimed sequences in feature films of the late 50s and early 60s.

The difference in the 80s was that the videos themselves were sold as commercial releases instead of being created to promote the records featured (although they did this, too, so the difference wasn't that great, just the availability). Consequently, a critical analysis of rock videos on aesthetic grounds is difficult and often pointless — if prospective viewers are fans of a particular artist and inclined to own and watch videos in the first place, the chances are they will appreciate the key elements of a release by that artist. The exceptions are the handful of blatant rip-off titles, usually incorporating old newsreel footage (sometimes not even associated with the particular act being featured) with vintage songs dubbed over it.

Some series are of note. Rhino's *Shindig* videos frequently feature live performances by artists who didn't leave full-length concerts behind (Jackie Wilson is the best of the series). EMI's *Ready, Steady, Go* releases from England capture the milieu of the pop/rock world of mid-60s Britain, even though most of the songs are lip-synched (the big exceptions are the Otis Redding and Motown volumes, which are live performances). Among full-length films, *A Hard Day's Night*, *The Kids Are Alright*, *Quadrophenia*, *Gimme Shelter*, *Monterey Pop*, *Woodstock*, and *Woodstock: The Lost Performances* are obvious examples of excellence, and Media Home Entertainment's *That Was Rock* is less well known but equally rewarding. New Line Cinema's *Jazz on a Summer Night* is also a key item for rock fans, featuring a superb Chuck Berry clip — all of which points up the problem in picking and choosing movies on video: sometimes only one clip is any good, but all it takes is one clip.

In the 90s, both picture and sound quality have improved. Another factor to watch for is remastering; a lot of older video releases, on linear as opposed to hi-fi stereo formats and mastered before the introduction of digital, audio, and video, do not hold up under scrutiny, but can when (and if) they are remastered. For example, Kate Bush's *Whole Story* is a great video collection, and even better on laserdisc, but has not been remastered at its source to take full advantage of the latter format.

Listed here is only a fraction of the worthwhile releases available, as space permits.

— Bruce Eder

A.R.M.S.

○ **Concert: 1 & 2 / RHINO**
A memorable concert collection, with a first-rate repertoire (for a change). –BE

ABBA

ABBA in Concert / PIONEER
Live "greatest hits." It's visually grainy, but fun. –BE

KING SUNNY ADE

Juju Music / KINO ON VIDEO
One of the best live performers around (and most energetic — his average concert lasts over three hours), this makes a great souvenir for fans and an introduction for those unfamiliar with this Nigerian juju artist. –SWB

AEROSMITH

Live Texas Jam '78 / CBS   1988
This concert video caught Aerosmith on a fairly hot set. The 12-song performance includes "Toys in the Attic," "Sweet Emotion," "Draw the Line," "Walk This Way," and "Lick and a Promise." Running time: 50 minutes. –RC

The Making of Pump / CBS   1990
The package states that this is "110 minutes of video that your mother doesn't want you to see." In spite of the implications, *The Making of Pump* is merely a document of a band slogging through the writing and recording (and re-writing and re-recording) process of making an album. Some of it is fascinating, particularly the squabbles among the band members, and the scenes in which producer Bruce Fairburn and A&R man John Koladner are giving guidance. At close to two hours, *The Making of Pump* might get a little long, but studio junkies and hardcore fans of the band will like it. Videos of "The Other Side" and "What It Takes" are included, but this is not a collection of their videos. –RC

ALABAMA

○ **In Concert / BRENTWOOD**
Now *this* is the real stuff, showing the group at its musical best and its most outgoing. –BE

ALLMAN BROTHERS

Brothers of the Road / PIONEER
Alas, the only full-length video by this legendary band comes

from its post-legendary era — Dickie Betts is just fine, but the later group can't hold a candle to the energetic and inspired classic band, and the wraparound footage adds nothing. –BE

LAURIE ANDERSON

Home of the Brave / WARNER
The kind of rock/performance-art fun you've come to expect from Laurie Anderson — well organized and well photographed — with guests Adrian Belew and William S. Burroughs. A good companion to *Stop Making Sense* by the Talking Heads. –SWB

LOUIS ARMSTRONG

☆ **Satchmo / CBS**   1989
Anyone wanting a great documentary on Armstrong should definitely check out *Satchmo*. This 86-minute video contains over a dozen great performances, including his appearances on films like *Pennies from Heaven*, *Atlantic City*, *New Orleans* (with Billie Holiday), *High Society* (with Bing Crosby), and *Hello Dolly* (with Barbra Streisand). Also included is footage from a 1935 Chicago nightclub gig. Great interviews and digitally remastered sound make this a must. –RC

THE BAND

☆ **The Last Waltz / MGM**   1978
Martin Scorsese's documentary of The Band's final concert on Thanksgiving Day, 1976, is one of the greatest films ever made about rock & roll. Throughout the movie, Scorsese's fascinating interviews with Band members illuminate the reasons why the group could not stay together any longer. Yet the performances from the group and their musical guests are what make this really special. (Dr. John, Ronnie Hawkins, Muddy Waters, Neil Young, Van Morrison, and the show-stopping finale by Bob Dylan are quite outstanding.) –STE

THE BATTLEFIELD BAND

The Battlefield Band's Hi-Light / TONN MOR   1991
A good set from the new lineup, caught live in the Scottish Highlands. –SW

THE BEACH BOYS

○ **An American Band / VESTRON**
A thoroughly detailed and enjoyable documentary, with dozens of rare vintage clips. –BE

THE BEATLES

○ **The First US Visit / MPI**
This newly released documentary is an enjoyable chronicle supported by excellent concert clips. –BE
☆ **Hard Day's Night / MPI**
It's still the best rock & roll movie ever made, without a single frame wasted and some of the band's best music. –BE
○ **Help! / MPI**
Richard Lester returned to direct the encore feature in 1965, and it's in color to boot. The Fab Four are on the lam once again, attempting to safeguard Ringo's precious ring, and the sight gags and classic songs come fast and furious. –BD
☆ **The Compleat Beatles / MGM**
This is perhaps the best documentary of the Beatles phenomenon. –SWB
○ **Let It Be / MAGNETIC VIDEO**
A spellbinding fadeout for the band, climaxing with their legendary rooftop concert. (Out of print) –BE
○ **Live: Ready Steady Go Special Edition / EMI-PIONEER**
A good, short, lip-synched appearance by the Beatles on Britain's top rock & roll showcase, from early in their careers. The energy is there despite the miming. This video is worthwhile owning just for their unique performance of "Shout" by the Isley Brothers. –BE

TONY BENNETT

○ **Tony Bennett Live: Watch What Happens / SONY**   1991
Bennett covers the highlights of his 40-year career with this elegant 29-song, 83-minute concert video collection, recorded in London's Prince Edward Theater with the Ralph Sharon Trio and the UK Symphony Orchestra. The set includes "The Shadow of Your Smile," "'S Wonderful," "On the Sunny Side of the Street," "I Left My Heart in San Francisco," "The Good Life," "Fly Me to the Moon," and "It Don't Mean a Thing If It Ain't Got That Swing." –RC

BLONDIE

○ **Best of Blondie / POLYGRAM**
The longevity of Blondie's videos, in terms of their value, is still astonishing, as this collection proves — erotic, scintillating, and emotionally isolated music, translated to the screen about as well as anything from this period. –BE

BOARDING HOUSE BLUES

Boarding House Blues /
Gravel-voiced comedian Jackie "Moms" Mabley stars in this 1948 all-Black feature. Musical guests include Lucky Millinder's orchestra (with singer Bullmoose Jackson) and elegant cabaret pianist Una Carlisle. –BD

MARC BOLAN

○ **Marc / POLYGRAM**
The definitive Marc Bolan/T. Rex collection, which recalls the best and most regrettable excesses of the glitter-rock era. A colorful, fascinating trip through the past for anyone who remembers 70s rock television. –BE

DAVID BOWIE

○ **Love You Til Tuesday / MEDIA**
Startling early Bowie material, from the tail-end of his psychedelic period, with the original "Space Oddity." –BE

ERIC BURDON w/THE ANIMALS

○ **Finally ... / ATLANTIC**
A genuinely detailed and lively history of the group from 1963 through the mid-80s reunion, featuring not only Eric Burdon but interviews with guitarist Hilton Valentine and other key players in the band. The only problem is that the video cuts off prior to the two IRS reunion albums and the 1983 tour. –BE

KATE BUSH

Live at Hammersmith / EMI
Sexy, provocative, and maddeningly stylized — the same attributes that apply to Bush's music apply to her only concert video, from her only British tour. The sound isn't as controlled as her studio material, but the solutions she came up with to do her music live are always interesting. –BE

CARNIVAL ROCK

Carnival Rock / RHINO
This 1957 effort by legendary B-movie director Roger Corman sports a more involved plot than most early rock films, but there's still room for sizzling rockabillies David Houston and Bob Luman, whose combo includes young guitar whiz James Burton (just before he jumped to Ricky Nelson's camp). The Platters also drop in for a quick number. –BD

THE CARPENTERS

Yesterday Once More / A&M
Really a memorial tribute to Karen Carpenter as much as anything else, this collection of vintage promotion film clips does tend to tug at the heartstrings, even of non-fans. The early music holds up surprisingly well, and the unabashedly

middle-brow sensibilities now seem to have a refreshing hint of self-parody about them, especially on numbers like "Top of the World" and "Beechwood 4-5789." –BE

CASEY KASEM'S ROCK & ROLL GOLDMINE

The British Invasion / VESTRON
If you can deal with Kasem's lengthy intros (sometimes running over the front of the clips), there's some rare footage to be found here. The English beat bands include Gerry & the Pacemakers, Manfred Mann, the Troggs, and the Hollies. –BD

The Soul Years / VESTRON
A few rare clips — Ben E. King in an annoyingly edited segment, Sam and Dave, James Brown — mixed with more common footage in this tribute to 60s soul superstars. –BD

ROSANNE CASH

○ **Retrospective / SONY**
Good cross-section of Cash's work on video. –BE

Interiors Live / CBS   1991
Filmed in black & white, *Interiors Live* is a wonderfully intimate performance of Cash (backed up by an excellent guitar/bass duo) delivering an overview of her career, with emphasis on her *Interiors* album. Included in this 19-song set are "Real Me," "On the Inside," "Seven Year Ache," "Tennessee Flat Top Box," and "Real Woman." The sound quality is particularly fine. Running time: 80 minutes. –RC

CHEAP TRICK

Every Trick in the Book / CBS   1990
Every Trick in the Book is an end-to-beginning career glance at this Midwestern hard-rock/pop quartet's body of videos. That means the highest-quality video work is at the front (with their worst songs), and the cheesy footage, during the last half, is where the fun and the best songs begin. Running time: 72 minutes. –RC

CHICAGO BLUES

Chicago Blues / RHAPSODY
Enlightening 1971 documentary on the Chicago blues scene (see how it used to be before yuppification!). Muddy Waters, Junior Wells, Buddy Guy, J. B. Hutto, and Floyd Jones provide some of the musical highlights. –BD

THE CHIEFTAINS

○ **The Bells of Dublin / BMG**
Joined by Nancy Griffith, the Irish group presents a superb concert, blending folk and country music. Well recorded and well photographed. –BE

THE CLANCY BROTHERS

Reunion Concert / SHANACHIE   1991
Recorded at the Royal Ulster Hall in Belfast, this is an example of what the lads can do for an audience. –SW

ERIC CLAPTON

○ **The Cream of Eric Clapton / POLYGRAM**
This is easily the best of the various concert and retrospective videos on Clapton, covering 1964 through the late 80s. –BE

DICK CLARK

The Best of Bandstand / VESTRON
The venerable host of "American Bandstand" opens his vaults just long enough to unearth priceless footage of Jerry Lee Lewis, the Silhouettes, the Big Bopper, Sam Cooke, Chubby Checker, and Buddy Holly (from the "Arthur Murray Show"; Holly's "Bandstand" clips are apparently long gone). All clips are full-length and in black & white, taken from "Bandstand," "Where the Action Is," and Clark's prime-time "Beechnut" program. –BD

○ **The Best of Bandstand — Superstars / VESTRON**
More highlights from Clark's incredible run as the world's oldest teenager. Soul greats Sam Cooke and Jackie Wilson are both showcased, along with the Supremes, the Beach Boys, the Four Seasons, and Roy Orbison. Worthwhile just for the Buddy Holly segment (which really is live) and the Jackson Five material, which is outstanding and the only color clip. The Dion & the Belmonts clip isn't bad either. –BD & BE

HARRY CONNICK

Singin' & Swingin' / CBS   1990
Connick's stylish piano and vocal performances are given a nice overview in this 45-minute collection, which features the live tracks and video clips "It Had to Be You," "Don't Get Around Much Anymore," "Stompin' at the Savoy," and many others. –RC

○ **Swinging Out Live / SONY**   1991
Connick has developed quite a reputation as a live performer, and *Swinging Out Live*, with his 16-piece big band, is ample testament to that. This 15-song, 77-minute concert video features "Don't Get Around Much Anymore," "Avalon," "Do You Know What It Means to Miss New Orleans," "It Had to Be You," and "When the Saints Go Marching In." –RC

ALICE COOPER

Trashes the World / CBS   1990
Cooper's legendary live horror-rock show is featured on this 20-song video. All of Cooper's big 70s hits are here, plus some of his more recent stuff. Running time: 90 minutes. –RC

REV. GARY DAVIS w/SONNY TERRY

Rev. Gary Davis w/ Sonny Terry / SHANACHIE
This black & white 60s footage, which the Seattle Folk Society was fortunate to capture, focuses on two North Carolina blues greats — Rev. Gary Davis, who's remarkable on guitar, and whooping harpist Sonny Terry. Both blues legends perform solo. –BD

DECLINE OF THE WESTERN CIVILIZATION

☆ **The Metal Years / RCA**
Penelope Spheeris's followup to the first *Decline* documentary shows the dark side of *Spinal Tap*. A close-up look at the 80s Los Angeles metal-music scene and its bands. Since the video's completion, a couple of these acts have gotten deals and gone somewhere else, but the interviews (more like interrogations) of rock star wannabes, as well as those who had "made it," are pretty sobering. All in all, this is a provocative piece of work, well worth seeing for those fascinated by hard rock and the culture around it. –RC

DEJA VIEW

Deja View / WARNER
This busted pilot to an unsold TV series is a good idea, presenting new performances of classic 60s artists like John Sebastian. It needs livelier treatment and footage to make it work, but the whole production is an interesting post-60s artifact and a look back at what was not successful in the early rock-video era. –BE

DIRE STRAITS

○ **Alchemy Live / POLYGRAM**
For a change, here's a live video better than the album it's attached to. –BE

THOMAS DOLBY

○ **Live Wireless / EMI VIDEO**   1983
A semi-live concert performance from his first album tour, interspersed with a running subplot and images from his

videos. Lene Lovich guests on "New Toy," a song Dolby wrote for her. Includes three non-album songs. –SWB

THE DOORS

Live: Europe '68 / ATLANTIC
Slow starting but ultimately a fascinating video documentary, with some astounding footage. –BE

○ **The Soft Parade / MCA**
An excellent collection of clips from the group's only extended US TV appearance. –BE

○ **A Tribute to Jim Morrison / WARNER**
A broad overview video on the Doors, contrived but filled with vital footage. –BE

BOB DYLAN

☆ **Don't Look Back / WARNER**
The best documentary movie ever made about a single rock artist (although Dylan wasn't really a rocker when much of it was shot). It's all about Dylan's 1964 British tour and the frantic scene that surrounded him. A minor flaw: it doesn't get any better than the opening conceptual video of "Subterranean Homesick Blues." –BE

FAIRPORT CONVENTION

○ **It All Comes Round Again / FAIRPORT ASSOC.**
One of the best-produced and best-directed documentaries ever made on any band. –BE

FISHBONE

○ **The Reality of My Surroundings / CBS**   1991
Unlike most bands, Fishbone doesn't rely on glamorous models or exotic fantasies to make them interesting on video; their energetic presence is all that's required. *Reality* is a great compilation of Fishbone's videos from 1985 to 1991. Included are "It's a Wonderful Life," "Everyday Sunshine," and their great reading of Curtis Mayfield's "Freddie's Dead." The band's between-song commentary is fairly interesting, even though it's rather dim-witted at times. Running time: 50 minutes. –RC

DAN FOGELBERG

○ **Greetings from the West / SONY**   1991
Fans of this singer/songwriter should love this concert video with material spanning his career. The performances are strong and the band is first-rate. Included in this 18-song, 100-minute video are "Leader of the Band," "Heart Hotels," "Part of the Plan," "Same Old Lang Syne," "There's a Place in the World for a Gambler," and "Run for the Roses." –RC

MARVIN GAYE

○ **Greatest Hits: Live / CBS**   1990
Gaye performs his biggest numbers at this 1978 concert in Holland. Included are "What's Going On," "I Heard It through the Grapevine," "Let's Get It On," "How Sweet It Is (to Be Loved by You)," and many others. Running time: 55 minutes. –RC

GENESIS

○ **A History of Genesis / POLYGRAM**
A thorough, entertaining, and detailed history of the band. –BE

DIZZY GILLESPIE

Jivin' in Be-Bop / JCV
Presented concert style, this all-Black 1947 stageshow stars a young Dizzy Gillespie, who leads his innovative big band through several bop classics. Ex-Basie chanteuse Helen Humes is also featured. –BD

THE GIRL CAN'T HELP IT

The Girl Can't Help It / KEY
Director Frank Tashlin stocked this big-budget 1956 Technicolor classic with crazy sight gags, a funny script, and a fine cast — and there's plenty of indispensable first-generation rock by Little Richard, Fats Domino, the Platters, Eddie Cochran, Gene Vincent and the Blue Caps, Eddie Fontaine, Johnny Olenn, and then-unknown Nino Tempo (with a wild sax workout) played for laughs. –BD

GO GO BIG BEAT

Go Go Big Beat / RHINO
Also known as "British Big Beat," this marginally interesting 60s compilation video is in rough shape, all redded out and faded. But amid dross like Migil Five, it does contain Millie Small ("My Boy Lollipop," the first ska hit and the single that started Island Records) and early appearances by the Hollies, the Merseybeats (Johnny Gustavson on bass), and Lulu. –BE

GO JOHNNY GO!

Go, Johnny, Go! / VIDEO TREASURES
Stellar musical lineup, including Eddie Cochran, Jackie Wilson, the Cadillacs, the Flamingos (choreographed to perfection on the blistering "Jump Children"), ex-Moonglows lead Harvey Fuqua, Chuck Berry (who costars with Alan Freed), and Ritchie Valens (in his only film appearance), all sharing the screen with teen heartthrob Jimmy Clanton in one of the last great 50s rock musicals. Watch for Joe Flynn of "McHale's Navy," uncredited as an usher. –BD

☆ **Go, Johnny, Go! / HAL ROACH VIDEO**
Disc jockey Alan Freed made several rock & roll movies in the 50s, all featuring great music, neglible plots, and wooden acting. This one features the best of all three, with top-notch performances from Chuck Berry, the Flamingos, Eddie Cochran, and Ritchie Valens, corny dialog from all the participants, and just enough of a plot not to get in the way of what's really important. This is some of the best rock & roll ever committed to nitrate film stock. –CK

GOODTIMES VIDEO COLLECTIONS

○ **Fabulous 50s / GOOD TIMES**
A surprisingly solid series of extremely inexpensive tapes, with first-rate clips. Only the tape stock leaves something to be desired. –BE

○ **60s American Rock / GOOD TIMES**
○ **60s English Rock / GOOD TIMES**
○ **60s Soul / GOOD TIMES**

GRATEFUL DEAD

○ **The Movie / MONTEREY VIDEO**
Classic concept and concert film, with some dazzling animation. –BE

BILL HALEY & THE COMETS

Rock around the Clock /
Daddy of all the rock flicks, this black & white 1956 groundbreaker introduced Bill Haley & the Comets to the world, and there's plenty of lip-sync footage — practically their entire first Decca album. Seems the Comets are tearing up the hinterlands when a disillusioned agent stumbles across them. Alan Freed makes the first of many cameos in such quickie films, while the Platters and Las Vegas rockers Freddie Bell and the Bell Boys provide more excitement. –BD

JOHN HAMMOND

☆ **From Bessie Smith ... / SONY MUSIC VIDEO**   1990
John Hammond may not have been a household name, but as the man at Columbia Records who "discovered" talent for the label, he signed some of the most important artists of the century, particularly Bessie Smith, Billie Holiday, Benny Goodman, Pete Seeger, Bob Dylan, Aretha Franklin, Bruce Springsteen, and Stevie Ray Vaughan. *From Bessie Smith to Bruce Springsteen* is a lovingly compiled tribute to Hammond

and the artists with whom he was affiliated. Running time: 60 minutes. −RC

THE HARDER THEY COME

○ **The Harder They Come / POLYGRAM**
A classic reggae video that is basically a day in the life of Jimmy Cliff. The music is one of the most essential reggae soundtracks and a one-of-a-kind video experience. −ED

JIMI HENDRIX

○ **Live: Monterey / HBO**
Arguably Hendrix's greatest concert video, all brilliantly shot by D. A. Pennebaker and padded out slightly with some earlier footage and commentary by John Phillips (of the Mamas & Papas). −BE
Rainbow Bridge / RHINO
Near the end of his career, Hendrix plays some superb music in the concert sequence that concludes this documentary — the rest is all devoted to pre-new-age mumbo-jumbo at a Hawaiian retreat, which may also be interesting to those with overfond memories of the 60s. −BE

HIGH SCHOOL CONFIDENTIAL

High School Confidential / REPUBLIC
Rock fans can safely rewind this 1958 black & white juvenile-delinquent period-piece right after its opening credits, since that's when blond-tressed Jerry Lee Lewis pounds out the title song (from the back of a moving flatbed truck, no less). You'll be rewarded if you stick with it, though — Mamie Van Doren at her sleaziest, and Russ Tamblyn is amusingly tough as an undercover cop infiltrating the high school drug trade. −BD

HILLBILLIES IN A HAUNTED HOUSE

Hillbillies in a Haunted House / GOODTIMES
This 1967 sequel to *Las Vegas Hillbillies* is even weirder, as horror vets Basil Rathbone, Lon Chaney Jr, and John Carradine rub elbows with Ferlin Husky, Sonny James, and Merle Haggard (who redeem themselves by singing a few then-current hits). −BD

SON HOUSE w/BUKKA WHITE

Son House w/ Bukka White / SHANACHIE
Mississippi Delta blues giants Son House and Bukka White play stunning solo slide guitar on these rare 60s black & white films from the Seattle Folk Society. White switches to piano at one point, but it's his slashing guitar and gruff vocals that satisfy. House sermonizes a little too much, but his "Death Letter Blues" is chilling. −BD

HULLABALOO

○ **Hullabaloo / VIDEO YESTERYEAR**
Two back-to-back half-hour episodes of the NBC-TV rock program from the autumn of 1965, with fascinating footage of the Animals, Brenda Lee, the Byrds, Peter & Gordon, the Beau Brummels, and Paul Revere and the Raiders. −BD

INDIGO GIRLS

○ **Live at the Uptown Lounge / CBS**   1990
This singer/songwriter duo returns to its hometown roots and plays at the Athens, GA, Uptown Lounge. As a performance-and-interview video, it has a nice warm vibe to it, and the performances are wonderfully heartfelt and spirited. Running time: 68 minutes. −RC

MICHAEL JACKSON

○ **Moonwalker / CBS**   1988
For those wanting to immerse themselves in Jackson's bizarre fantasy world, *Moonwalker* might just do the trick. This 94-minute collection of conceptual videos portrays Jackson as the misunderstood (relentlessly pursued) star who's really a down-to-earth guy who loves kids. In fact, Jackson cares about them so much that in "Smooth Criminal" (*Moonwalker*'s centerpiece), he becomes a Terminator-style superhero and blows up the evil Mr. Big, who is intent on hooking kids on drugs. Jackson's montage of his evolution from Jackson 5 to solo artist is nice. "Leave Me Alone" is in parts a playful depiction of Jackson as a tortured media icon, which would be an absolute whine-fest if it weren't for the dazzling effects. −RC

JETHRO TULL

○ **20 Years of Jethro Tull / ATLANTIC**   1989
Fans of Tull should enjoy this collection that amply documents the band's entire career. There are loads of live performances, TV appearances, and good interviews. The sound quality is quite good. −RC

BILLY JOEL

Live at Yankee Stadium / CBS   1990
Joel delivers a strong 12-song performance at the famous baseball stadium. Included are "Piano Man," "New York State of Mind," "Pressure," "A Matter of Trust," "Scenes from an Italian Restaurant," and more. Running time: 85 minutes. −RC
A Matter of Trust / CBS   1991
A Matter of Trust is more than a document of Billy Joel's tour of the Soviet Union in 1987; it's a Joel's-eye discourse on the Russian people and their love for music, including his. At one hour and twenty minutes, you would think there would be ample performance footage of songs in their entirety. Actually, much of the time is spent covering the backstage mechanics of the shows and Joel's interactions with the Russian public. It wouldn't be a far stretch to put this on PBS. When Joel does get down to performing, he does it with the zeal of a missionary. The fidelity of this film is quite good. −RC

ELTON JOHN

○ **Live: Australia / J2 COMM.**
One of the two best-looking and best-sounding of the numerous Elton John videos out there. −BE
○ **Two Rooms / POLYGRAM**
A well-crafted portrait of Elton John and Bernie Taupin, joined by various guest performers. −BE

SPIKE JONES

☆ **The Best of Spike Jones - Vol. 1 / PARAMOUNT**
The Spike Jones brand of musical mayhem is perfectly captured on this compilation of performances taken from his early 50s television show. Highlights include "I'm in the Mood for Love," "It's Tough to Be a Girl Musician," and a greatest-hits medley that must be seen to be believed. −CK
☆ **The Best of Spike Jones - Vol. 2 / PARAMOUNT**
This second volume of highlights culled from Spike's early 50s television show is every bit as potent as the first volume. Includes "Cry," "South," and "Life's Not So Bad in Prison." −CK

LOUIS JORDAN

Look Out Sister /
Louis Jordan checks into a sanitarium for a rest, then dreams himself out West to a dude ranch in this all-Black 1948 musical. Like all of Jordan's low-budget features, there's plenty of hot music by the alto saxman. −BD
Reet, Petite, and Gone / VIDEO YESTERYEAR
One of alto saxist Louis Jordan's most entertaining features, this 1947 black & white film spotlights the R&B pioneer and his swinging combo, the Tympany Five, with a load of their best numbers, including "Let the Good Times Roll" and the title theme. −BD
Louis Jordan and Friends / JCV
This compilation of 40s soundies includes several incendiary tunes by R&B pioneer Jordan and two more by thundering boogie pianist Maurice Rocco. Also included is Jordan's 1945 featurette "Caldonia." −BD

Louis Jordan and the Tympany Five / BMG
Ostensibly compiled to tie in with the success of the Broadway hit *Five Guys Named Moe*, this collection of 40s soundies by the pioneering alto saxist also includes "Honey Chile," "Fuzzy Wuzzy," and others. –BD

KILLER DILLER

Killer Diller /
Most of the musical highlights in this 1948 all-Black film are conveniently arranged at the end in a stage-show format, including three swinging numbers by the incomparable·King Cole Trio. Moms Mabley also puts in an appearance. –BD

B. B. KING

B. B. King in Africa / HBO
This is some of the best concert footage of B. B. King available on home video. Dating from the 70s, the Blues Boy and his trusty partner Lucille wow the African crowd with his classic hits. –BD

FREDDIE KING

The Best of the Freddie King Blues Band / MSC
Powerful blues guitarist Freddie King in strong 70s concert footage from an outdoor festival sponsored by Leon Russell. King's tight band backs him with solid contemporary grooves, and Freddie's in typically fine form. –BD

LAS VEGAS HILLBILLIES

Las Vegas Hillbillies / GOODTIMES
Country crooner Ferlin Husky inherits a broken-down Las Vegas nightclub and attempts to rehab it in this 1966 musical. Ferlin encounters a few Nashville buddies along the way, including Roy Drusky, Del Reeves, Sonny James, Connie Smith, and Whispering Bill Anderson. Also features Mamie Van Doren and Jayne Mansfield. –BD

THE LAST OF THE BLUE DEVILS

The Last of the Blue Devils / RHAPSODY
The greatest Kansas City jazz and blues names appear in this heartwarming feature documenting their heyday and subsequent activities. Director Bruce Ricker rounded up the KC legends still surviving in the 70s for his film: Count Basie, Jay McShann, Big Joe Turner, Jimmy "Night Train" Forrest, and many more, and their hearty reminiscences form the backbone of the movie. –BD

JOHN LENNON

Imagine / PIONEER
The long-delayed release of this film, originally intended to accompany the album of the same name, proved somewhat disappointing — the film isn't nearly so engaging as the album, and the overall effect is of a gift for people with an excessive fondness for Lennon's politically active and idealistic period. –BE

Imagine (Documentary) / WARNER   1988
An excellent look at Lennon's Beatles and post-Beatles life and career. –SWB

LEVEL 42

Live at Wembley / POLYGRAM
For fans not able to catch the band live, this concert should suffice. Well photographed and well recorded. –SWB

JERRY LEE LEWIS

☆ **I Am What I Am / J2 COMM.**
One of the best documentaries of one of rock & roll's all-time greats, featuring essential live performances from all phases of Lewis's lengthy career. The performance of "Whole Lot of Shakin' Goin' On," from his network debut on the "Steve Allen Show," must be seen to be believed. –CK

MANCE LIPSCOMB w/LIGHTNIN' HOPKINS

Mance Lipscomb w/ Lightnin' Hopkins / SHANACHIE
Texas songster Mance Lipscomb and legendary Houston guitarist Lightnin' Hopkins are dazzlingly spotlighted in this black & white video, taken from 1960s Seattle Folk Society films that were done solo with no frills. Hopkins alone is worth the price of admission, with a rocking "Mojo Hand." –BD

LIVING COLOUR

Primer / CBS   1989
Primer covers this hard-rock fusion band's video output from their first album. Included are the hits "Cult of Personality" and "Open Letter to a Landlord." The band provides some observations as well. Running time: 30 minutes. –RC

○ **Time Tunnel / CBS**   1990
Fans of the band should enjoy this 59-minute overview of Living Colour, covering their early days as well as concert footage, and interviews. "Cult of Personality," "Pride," "Fight the Fight," and "It's Only Rock 'N' Roll" are among the songs included. –RC

MADONNA

○ **Truth or Dare / INTL. VIDEO ENTERPRISES**
Madonna's controversial tour documentary, with the onstage footage in color and the behind-the-scenes shots in black & white. As always, Madonna shows the audience exactly what she wants them to see, even though this film was promoted as a peek behind the facade. –ED

NELSON MANDELA 70TH BIRTHDAY TRIBUTE

Nelson Mandela 70th Birthday Tribute / CBS   1988
This is a documentary of the Artists Against Apartheid tribute to Nelson Mandela at Wembley Stadium in London, England, June 1988. The artists included are George Michael, Simple Minds, Whitney Houston, Dire Straits, Peter Gabriel, Eric Clapton, Stevie Wonder, Eurythmics, Sly & Robbie, Sting, Aswad, and more. The sound quality is good and the camera angles do a good job of capturing the spirit of the event. Running time: 117 minutes. –RC

BRANFORD MARSALIS

Steep / CBS   1988
Steep is a combination of live and interview footage with Branford Marsalis and his quartet, containing Kenny Kirkland (piano), Delbert Felix (bass), and Lewis Nash (drums). Tracks included are "Swingin' at the Haven," "Crescent City," "Giant Steps," and more. Running time: 90 minutes. –RC

WYNTON MARSALIS

○ **Blues & Swing / CBS**   1988
Blues & Swing is a great collection of Marsalis performances. The digital recording is excellent and the camera work captures the spirit of the performances quite well. This ten-song set includes "J Mood," "Caravan," "Goodbye," "(Do You Know What It Means to Miss) New Orleans," and "Cherokee." Running time: 79 minutes. –RC

MARTY ROBBINS w/ERNEST TUBB

Marty Robbins w/ Ernest Tubb / SHANACHIE
Allegedly a shy TV performer, Marty Robbins seems to be having a great time on his dozen priceless clips here (even a rocking "Pretty Mama"), filmed in bright color for TV during the mid 50s. Ernest Tubb is every inch the country gentleman, his 14 tunes sparked by the guitar work of Billy Byrd (who winks at the camera at every available opportunity). Wonderfully done. –BD

GEORGE MICHAEL

○ **George Michael / CBS**   1990
This is basically a one-hour documentary on Michael's career

from his early projects — such as Wham! — through his *Listen without Predjudice* solo effort. Includes footage of Michael working in the studio and talking about his songwriting process and artistic self-image. –RC

MIDNIGHT OIL

Black Rain Falls / CBS   1990
During the aftermath of the Exxon Valdez oilspill, Midnight Oil took it upon themselves to set up a lunch-hour protest concert, across the street from the oil company's headquarters in New York. What this performance lacks in technical perfection, it more than makes up for in passion. Included in this six-song set are versions of "Dreamworld," "Blue Sky Mine," and an impromptu sendup of John Lennon's "Instant Karma." Running time: 45 minutes. –RC

CHARLES MINGUS

☆ **Mingus 1968 / RHAPSODY FILMS**
Incredible document. An oddly relaxed interview of Mingus during a 24-hour period when he is being evicted from his New York City apartment. Very loose, up close, and filled with brilliant Mingus remarks and antics. This, plus shots of Mingus playing with a small group, make this one-of-a-kind video — a must for fans of Mingus and for jazz lovers in general. –JME

THELONIOUS MONK

☆ **Straight No Chaser / WARNER**
Most revealing. A chance to see Monk on stage, and off. The title of this video says it all. A classic. –JME

MONTEREY POP

Monterey Pop / SONY
Director D. A. Pennebaker's remarkable documentary of the 1967 festival, with irreplaceable performances by Otis Redding, Jimi Hendrix, Simon and Garfunkel, the Mamas and the Papas, the Animals, and more. –BD

MOODY BLUES

Legend of a Band / POLYGRAM
A somewhat superficial but enjoyable video history, too short on vintage clips but containing just enough new and old footage to make it worth a look. The later repertoire (post 1986) is weak. –BE

MOTÖRHEAD

Everything Louder Than Everything Else / SONY   1991
This 12-song, 66-minute video is a straightahead live concert video that also includes band interviews and occasional touring antics. The film work and sound do a good job of capturing the band's power. Included are "Orgasmatron," "Killed by Death," "Traitor," "I'm So Bad (Baby I Don't Care)," and "Ace of Spades." –RC

ROY ORBISON

○ **Black and White / HBO-PIONEER**
An all-star concert from the cable special, featuring Orbison in a last great flash of glory. –BE

The Fastest Guitar Alive / UNITED ARTISTS
Roy Orbison's only starring movie role, and after you see him blasting away at the bad guys with his gun-rigged guitar, you'll know why. The shadeless Big O does brighten this goofy 1967 Western with a few tunes, and MGM stablemate Sam the Sham cameos but doesn't sing. –BD

CARL PERKINS

○ **Blue Suede Shoes / MCA**
Perkins in some first-rate live renditions of his and others' hits, with George Harrison, Dave Edmunds, Ringo Starr, Roseanne Cash, and more. –BE

PET SHOP BOYS

Highlights on Tour / EMI   1990
This 33-minute video of the Pet Shop Boys covers their live shows, which feature many dancers, costume changes, and film backdrops, to entertaining effect. "It's a Sin" is a particularly showy presentation. The Spanish-style choreography of "Domino Dancing" is another highlight. –RC

TOM PETTY & THE HEARTBREAKERS

○ **Take the Highway / MCA**   1992
Take the Highway is a no-nonsense document of Petty and the Heartbreakers in top concert form. The video captures performances of favorites like "Free Fallin'," "Refugee," "Here Comes My Girl," "Don't Come Around Here No More," as well as a version of Count Five's "Psychotic Reaction," and Van Morrison's "I'm Tired Joey Boy." Directed by Julien Temple, *Take the Highway* features first-rate camera work and sound. Running time: 92 minutes. –RC

WEBB PIERCE w/CHET ATKINS

Webb Pierce w/ Chet Atkins / RHINO
Taken from mid-50s TV shows shot in Nashville on brilliant 35mm color film, these wonderful videos present country great Webb Pierce and guitar virtuoso Chet Atkins live in a set constructed to look like a barn (complete with hay bales). If you've viewed the syndicated *Classic Country* series, then you know how great these clips are — and thanks to Shanachie's precise editing, you don't have to sit through the square dances and cornball comedy. –BD

ELVIS PRESLEY

Jailhouse Rock / MGM-UA
One of Elvis Presley's best film outings (his third), this 1957 classic includes "Treat Me Nice," "(You're So Square) Baby I Don't Care," and the immortal title track in crisp black & white, as hot-tempered Elvis exits jail to become a fickle singing sensation. –BD

King Creole / FOX
The most convincing dramatic role in Presley's long (and frequently undistinguished) film career, this 1958 black & white epic boasts one of the best casts (Walter Matthau and Vic Morrow costar) and some of the hottest tunes, rendered with a touch of New Orleans jazz. Tunes include "Trouble," "Dixieland Rock," "New Orleans," and the title cut. –BD

Loving You / WARNER
Shot in 1957 in blazing Technicolor, Elvis Presley's second starring film role was a rough approximation of his own career — country boy becomes a star, singing rock & roll. Songs include "Teddy Bear," "Hot Dog," "Party," "Got a Lot of Livin' to Do," and the title tune. –BD

○ **One Night with You / MEDIA-IMAGE**
The King, in the uncut rock & roll portion of his 1968 comeback special, is shown rocking with his buddies from Memphis. –BE

PUBLIC ENEMY

Fight the Power: Live / CBS   1989
Fight the Power: Live captures 13 Public Enemy performances, in concert and conceptual video form, including "Countdown to Armageddon," "Bring the Noise," "Rebel without a Pause," "Prophets of Rage," and "Night of the Living Baseheads." Running time: 60 minutes. –RC

Tour of a Black Planet / CBS   1991
This video is a 13-song, 65-minute collection of this rap act's stage show, plus extra video footage of the band. Includes "Can't Truss It," "911 Is a Joke," "Brothers Gonna Work It Out," "Bring the Noise" (Anthrax with Public Enemy), and "Burn Hollywood Burn." –RC

QUEENSRŸCHE

Video: Mindcrime / EMI   1989
The Wall meets George Orwell on this series of conceptual videos off Queensrÿche's *Operation: Mindcrime* album. The provocative imagery and high-quality direction elevate this release above many rock-video collections. The audio is pretty impressive too. Running time: 40 minutes. –RC

RAINBOW QUEST

Rainbow Quest /
At least nine episodes of this 60s black & white folk TV show, hosted by Pete Seeger, are available on video. Notable entries include shows starring Sonny Terry and Brownie McGhee, Donovan and Rev. Gary Davis, Judy Collins, the New Lost City Ramblers, the Stanley Brothers, and a folk jam that includes Mississippi John Hurt. –BD

THE RAMONES

Rock & Roll High School / WARNER
Not just for Ramones fans, this 1979 feature-length, low-budget comedy was a punk-era tribute to the 50s rock & roll B-movies and a celebration of the Ramones as a cultural icon. Starring Vince Van Patten, P. J. Soles (*Stripes*), Clint Howard (Ron's brother), and (husband and wife) Paul Bartel and Mary Woronov (*Eating Raoul, Scenes from the Class Struggle in Beverly Hills*). –SWB

READY STEADY GO

Ready Steady Go - Vol. 2 / PIONEER
This one-hour tape also dazzles, although it is less interesting than Volume One. Features the Beatles and the Stones (doing comedy, not music), Jerry Lee Lewis, and the Beach Boys. –BE

○ **Ready Steady Go - Vol. 1 / EMI-PIONEER**
This one-hour tape is a dazzling look back on the mid-60s British pop scene. Volume One is easily the best of the three, featuring the best songs and artists (including the Beatles, Them, the Animals, the Rolling Stones, and others). –BE

○ **The Sound of Motown / HBO-PIONEER**
Ready Steady Go - The Sound of Motown is the finest of all vintage Motown videos, all played and sung live and quite brilliantly, featuring the Miracles, Martha and the Vandellas, and more. From 1965. –BE

Ready Steady Go - Vol. 3 / PIONEER
Volume Three is easily overlooked except by British humor buffs, who will appreciate the period commercials featuring comic legends Tony Hancock and Benny Hill. Features the Beatles and Denny Laine-era Moody Blues. –BE

RED HOT CHILI PEPPERS

Psychedelic Sexfunk Live from Heaven / EMI   1990
This is a decent concert video that includes the Peppers blasting through numbers like "Magic Johnson," "Sexy Mexican Maid," "Subway to Venus," and "Star Spangled Banner." Running time: 40 minutes. –RC

OTIS REDDING

○ **Live: Monterey / HBO**
Otis's live set from this show probably would have been his greatest video but for two problems — he went on too near to curfew, so his set was cut short, and he kept moving between the cameras and the lights, so a lot of the film was unusable. But he was in brilliant form for the 20 minutes of this show, and the producers have done an excellent job of assembling the material. –BE

Live: Ready, Steady, Go / HBO-PIONEER
A live 1966 TV special. Too short, but incomparable. –BE

JIM REEVES & RAY PRICE WITH ERNEST TUBB

Jim Reeves & Ray Price with Ernest Tubb / SHANACHIE
Three mid-50s country legends at their peak in eye-popping

color! Edited down from TV programs later syndicated as "Classic Country," the country classics come at you one after another, with an unaffected charm that makes these videos a collector's dream. –BD

ROCK BABY ROCK IT!

☆ **Rock, Baby, Rock It! / RHINO**
The best and worst 50s rock & roll movie ever made. It was shot on location in Dallas, TX, on a shoestring budget utilizing local rockabilly talent. No plot, no big name musical talent, and crappy acting abounds throughout, but this film perfectly encapsulates the driving spirit of rock & roll's earliest days. –CK

ROCK ROCK ROCK

Rock, Rock, Rock / GOODTIMES
Excruciating plot involving young Tuesday Weld's insatiable desire for a prom dress interrupts priceless clips by Chuck Berry, the Johnny Burnette Trio, LaVern Baker, Frankie Lymon and the Teenagers, the Flamingos, the Moonglows, and emcee Alan Freed's all-star band in this 1956 black & white rock musical. Connie Francis dubbed Weld's singing voice; love interest Teddy Randazzo croons his own vocals. –BD

ROCKIN' THE BLUES

Rockin' the Blues /
Terrific 1955 all-R&B lineup includes performances by the Harptones, Linda Hopkins, the Hurricanes, Pearl Woods, Connie Carroll, and the Wanderers in this brisk black & white feature, which clocks in at just over an hour. Lame comedy bits are provided by the ubiquitous F. E. Miller and Mantan Moreland, stars of countless Black films during the 40s. –BD

ROLLING STONES

○ **25 x 5 / SONY**
An overlong but rewarding portrait of the band from 1963 through 1989. The Sullivan videos are the best part. –BE

○ **Gimme Shelter / ABKCO**
Anatomy of a murder and a great but disastrous 1969 concert, preserved in a spellbinding documentary. –BE

THE RUTLES

○ **The Rutles / PACIFIC ARTS**   1978
A hilarious spoof of the Beatles and Beatlemania with Eric Idle and the original Saturday Night Live troupe, with cameos by Mick Jagger, George Harrison, and Paul Simon. –SWB

SEAL

Seal / WARNER   1992
Although the song order and packaging is similar to the CD, this video is a live-in-the-studio, all-acoustic performance. Recorded at Church Studios, the arrangements are sparse and much less polished, but the emphasis on Seal's raw voice and songs is more moving. Three video clips (his hit "Crazy" and two others) are tacked on at the end. –SWB

SEASIDE SWINGERS

Seaside Swingers / CHARTER
Tough-to-locate 1964 British import that served as a vehicle for the zany rock sounds of Freddie and the Dreamers. Everybody stops long enough to tune into a storming number by Jerry Lee Lewis, then in the midst of his triumphant comeback. –BD

THE SECRET POLICEMAN

○ **The Secret Policeman's Other Ball / MGM**
One of the best multi-artist concerts available, featuring acoustic performances by Sting on "Roxanne" and "Message in a Bottle," Pete Townshend on "Won't Get Fooled Again" and

"Behind Blue Eyes," comedy from the Monty Python crew, and countless other delights. –BE

The Secret Policeman's Private Parts / MEDIA-PIONEER
A disjointed, solackluster followup, featuring Bob Geldoff, Donovan, and various Monty Python alumni, and others. –BE

PETE SEEGER

○ **Family Concert / SONY**   1992
Pete Seeger's gently enthusiastic way of teaching a love for great folk music is very successfully conveyed in this intimate 12-song video. Typical of Seeger, his song choices have instructive origins, and are delivered with heart. *Family Concert* will entertain not only children but adults as well. Running time: 45 minutes. –RC

SHINDIG!

Shindig! Presents: Frat Party / RHINO
Wide variety of mid-60s acts on this one — the Kingsmen with "Louie Louie," naturally, and the Isley Brothers with "Shout," but also the Olympics, Dobie Gray, the McCoys, the Sir Douglas Quintet, and an amazing clip of Roy Head singing "Treat Her Right" while cutting loose with bizarre yoga moves on his head! –BD

Shindig! Presents: Groovy Gals / RHINO
The grooviness quotient fluctuates — everyone from the Shangri-Las and Fontella Bass to Lesley Gore and Petula Clark. The Toys, Ketty Lester, and a fired-up Aretha Franklin are also standouts, while Jackie DeShannon and the show's resident R&B trio, the Blossoms, add their charms. –BD

Shindig! Presents: Jerry Lee Lewis / RHINO
The Killer on the mid-60s comeback trail, and insane as ever, pounding his piano and looking evil on "Whole Lotta Shakin' Goin' On" (with Jackie Wilson and the Righteous Brothers), "Mean Woman Blues," "High School Confidential," "I Believe in You," "Rockin' Pneumonia" (a rare foray into electric piano), and a lowdown duet on "Take Me out to the Ballgame" that finds Neil Sedaka perched on top of Jerry Lee's 88s. –BD

Shindig! Presents: Motor City Magic / RHINO
Brief but electrifying, this collection features mid-60s black & white footage taken from ABC-TV's "Shindig!" series, including the Supremes, the Four Tops, the Temptations, Junior Walker, and Marvin Gaye. –BD

Shindig! Presents: 60s Superstars / RHINO
A particularly potent selection of mid-60s rockers — the Turtles, the Yardbirds, the Byrds, the Gentrys, the Beau Brummels, the Mamas and Papas, and Donovan, captured on black & white video tape instead of the kinescope norm of the series. –BD

Shindig! Presents: Soul / RHINO
A cross-section of the soul greats who performed on "Shindig!" Clips of Joe Tex, Major Lance, Tina Turner, Aretha Franklin, Booker T. & the MGs, and James Brown. It only scratches the surface, but it's very enjoyable nonetheless. –BD

Shindig! Presents: The Righteous Brothers / PIONEER
Regulars on the mid-60s series, Bill Medley and Bobby Hatfield were at their commercial peak, harmonizing soulfully on "You've Lost That Lovin' Feeling," "Koko Joe," and more, while Hatfield croons an "Unchained Melody" solo. –BD

○ **Shindig! Presents: Jackie Wilson / ATLANTIC**
Jackie Wilson at his prime — animated, sexy, and brilliant — and the best of the "Shindig!" tapes to date. –BE

○ **Shindig! Presents: British Invasion Vol. 1 / RHINO** 1992
Brit Invasion fans should enjoy this collection that features Gerry & the Pacemakers ("Don't Let the Sun Catch You Crying"), Herman's Hermits ("I'm into Something Good"), Manfred Mann ("Doo Wah Diddy"), Searchers ("Needles & Pins"), Peter & Gordon ("World without Love"), and more. Running time: 30 minutes. –RC

○ **Shindig! Presents: The Kinks / RHINO**   1992
This 30-minute collection (in black & white) features tracks

such as "You Really Got Me," "All Day and All of the Night," "Tired of Waiting for You," "Set Me Free," "Who'll Be the Next in Line," and more. –RC

PAUL SIMON

○ **The Special / PACIFIC ARTS**
A network-TV appearance by this singer/songwriter from the late 70s. He's in top form, but again not nearly as animated or animating as one would hope for on a full-length video. –BE

FRANK SINATRA

○ **#1: Reprise Collection / WARNER**
A fine and fitting set of video anthologies, covering Sinatra through the years from the early 60s onward, in various TV specials. Volume One is the best, showing him as a still-youngish song stylist in the early 60s, in color and with a top-flight band, beginning in the days before rock music redefined popular music. Watching and listening to Sinatra is like watching a young, magnificent god playing in his domain. –BE

SOUL TO SOUL

Soul to Soul / ATLANTIC
Filmed live during a 1971 tour of Ghana, this feature-length film is equal parts travelog and concert footage, but the music is solid — Wilson Pickett, Ike & Tina Turner, the Staple Singers, Roberta Flack, Santana, Les McCann, and Eddie Harris. –BD

SPINAL TAP

☆ **This Is Spinal Tap / EMBASSY**
The definitive heavy-metal video production, and a total goof on the field. *This Is Spinal Tap* is the funniest full-length rock video this side of the Rutles, and in many ways even more effective — it led to the current Spinal Tap tour and the release of an album by this group of rock satirists, here directed by Rob Reiner in inimitably humorous style on sendups of MTV, heavy metal, and the fans of both. –BE

SPLIT ENZ

History Never Repeats / A&M
Here are all the video clips (1975-1985), from their experimental art-rock days to their classic MTV hits "I Got You," "History Never Repeats," and "Dirty Creature." Witness the transformation. –SWB

BRUCE SPRINGSTEEN

○ **Video Anthology 1978-1988 / CBS**   1989
Video Anthology is just that, covering primarily the singles Springsteen released after the beginning of the MTV age. As an overview of his body of music, this collection falls short; nevertheless, all of his main conceptual videos are here, as well as some great concert performances. Highlights included are "Rosalita," "Brilliant Disguise," "One Step Up," "Dancing in the Dark," and a great version of Edwin Starr's classic "War." Running time: 100 minutes. –RC

ALAN STIVELL

Alan Stivell in Concert / SHANACHIE
Stivell is backed by acoustic guitarist Bernard Coutelan and performs a beautiful program of tunes and songs. –SW

TALKING HEADS

○ **Stop Making Sense / WARNER**   1984
Jonathan Demme's creative direction and this group's brilliance make for an unusual live performance event. Starting solo with David Byrne, each song brings another band member to the stage until the full band kicks in. With Bernie Worrell on keyboards and a strong hit-filled set from the *Speaking in Tongues* tour, this is definitely worth checking out. –SWB

THAT WAS ROCK

☆ **That Was Rock / MEDIA-IMAGE**
Bar none, the greatest vintage concert video available, featuring Smokey Robinson & the Miracles, the Rolling Stones, Chuck Berry, Bo Diddley, the Ronettes, the Supremes, Jan & Dean, and James Brown, all at the top of their form, doing their hits. It was taped in two concerts, one in 1964 and the other in 1965, before an audience of hysterical teenage fans — and then transferred to film. The sound and picture quality of these shows is somewhat deficient by modern standards but the energy of the acts just spills off the screen. The only regret is that the producers didn't use the Lovin' Spoonful and Byrds sets from the same shows. –BE

U2

○ **Live at Red Rocks / COLUMBIA-PIONEER**
Live at Red Rocks: Under a Blood-Red Sky showcases U2 in a somewhat abbreviated concert video doing "Sunday Bloody Sunday," "Gloria," and others, all rather loud, but exciting and in a magnificent setting. –BE

Rattle & Hum / PARAMOUNT
A documentary done about U2 in their post-*Joshua Tree* period of mega-stardom, with excerpts of numerous songs. A fair portrait of the band and part of its history. –BE

LUTHER VANDROSS

○ **Live at Wembley / CBS**   1989
As far as videos go, this release dispenses with dazzling effects and camera angles and focuses on the singing of Vandross. Since the portly singer does very little moving, some viewers might find this no-nonsense presentation somewhat taxing. Nevertheless, if merely seeing this amazing urban-R&B stylist at work is enough, then *Live at Wembley* should be very satisfying. Running time: 90 minutes. –RC

VILLAGE OF THE GIANTS

Village of the Giants /
Science fiction and rock collide in this 1965 feature built around a miracle growth potion concocted by little Ronny Howard. Stars Tommy Kirk and Beau Bridges check out the Beau Brummels (who play to a pair of gigantic geese forced to dance by someone yanking on less-than-invisible ropes around their necks), Freddy "Boom Boom" Cannon, and crooner Mike Clifford. –BD

A VISION SHARED

A Vision Shared / CBS   1988
This video presents Bruce Springsteen, Little Richard, Willie Nelson, Emmy Lou Harris, Arlo Guthrie, Pete Seeger, Taj Mahal, John Mellencamp, Sweet Honey in the Rock, and others doing versions of Woody Guthrie and Leadbelly songs. Interviews with those acquainted with Guthrie and Leadbelly are also included. A distinctly uncomfortable Robbie Robertson narrates this tribute. Some might rather have heard the original artists' versions, but most of the performances here are quite good, with the highlights going to Springsteen, Mellencamp, Harris, Guthrie, and Seeger. Little Richard puts on his usual schtick (sans piano) but fails to do justice to "Rock Island Line." All in all, this is an enjoyable intro to the great folk legends. Running time: 72 minutes. –RC

WASHINGTON-LONGHAIR-TOUSSAINT

Piano Players Rarely Ever Play Together / STEVENSON
A moving feature-length account of a historic multi-generational meeting of three New Orleans piano masters: Tuts Washington, Professor Longhair, and Allen Toussaint. Sad to say, Longhair died during filming; his Crescent City-style funeral was made part of the documentary. –BD

THE WHO

☆ **The Kids Are Alright / HBO**
Funny, poignant, nasty, and exciting documentary of the band's history. –BE

WOODSTOCK

○ **Woodstock / WARNER**
This classic document of the rock festival, where 60s ideals seemed to run their highest, captured a wide variety of performances (ranging from brilliant to listless) from artists as diverse as Sha Na Na, Country Joe & the Fish, Santana, Ten Years After, The Who, and Crosby, Stills & Nash. –RC

YARDBIRDS

○ **Yardbirds / A*VISION**
A too-short but enlightening video portrait covering all three eras of this band's development, and their major songs, with some dazzling live clips from American and English television. A fine companion to the various Yardbirds CDs now circulating. –BE

YES

Yessongs / VIDAMERICA-IMAGE
This 1973 concert is typically grainy-looking but otherwise nicely constructed. Steve Howe's guitar gets as much screen time as Rick Waterman's synthesizers. –BE

○ **Yesyears: A Retrospective / ATLANTIC**
A too-long but very enlightening portrait of the band, well filled out with rare concert footage. –BE

WOMEN'S

There is no more controversial category of modern music than women's music. The very name itself, referring to a perspective rather than a style, is often disputed among participants as excessively limiting and not sufficiently defining. In essence, women's music is written and performed by women, principally for women. Although it started out in a folk vein, it has embraced pop, jazz, classical, R & B, and hard rock.

Women's music had its origins in the late 60s as an offshoot of early organized feminism, and its early examples drew from leftist/separatist/activist influences — this was radical stuff, created by rebels who were alienated not only from mainstream society but from the 60s left and its inattention to women's issues. The women making this music were breaking fresh ground socially as much as musically — they frequently attempted to reinvent various music forms in a distinctly woman-centered manner — and they found a core of support, mostly among politically aware, college-age women. Unfortunately, a lot of what they did was more inspired for its message than its music, although some statements linger for their sheer cleverness: for example, Alix Dobkin's "Talking Lesbian," from the groundbreaking 1974 album *Lavender Jane Loves Women*, was a knowing adaptation of Woody Guthrie's "Talking Union."

During the early and mid 70s, there were also some attempts at mainstreaming the music. The all-woman rock band Fanny, led by Jean and June Millington, got serious attention from the rock press and recorded for Warner Bros., and the Deadly Nightshade trio recorded two albums on RCA and toured as the opening act for Billy Joel. Neither ever amounted to much more than a curiosity in terms of their cultural or commercial impact, however. In the mid 70s,

when labels such as Olivia, Redwood, and Ladyslipper were established behind the work of artists like Cris Williamson, Meg Christian, and — later — Holly Near, the music began finding favor with a wider audience. Williamson in particular is to women's music what Joan Baez was to the folk-protest movement of the 60s: a vibrant, powerful singer and songwriter who evolved out of her folk roots into a rocker (and social/historical critic) of no small measure and lured a bigger audience, including a cadre of respectful males. Holly Near, by contrast, is practically a mainstream artist, at least in terms of name recognition, whose songs have embraced such wider political issues as nuclear disarmament.

Women's music has expanded as a category in recent years to embrace a wide range of performers, working from vastly different starting points and purposes: Tret Fure, a guitarist's guitarist, who rocks better than anyone else in the field; Sweet Honey in the Rock, a quintet whose gospel roots make them unique on the scene; Kay Gardner, a multi-instrumentalist with a strong mystical bent; Alix Dobkin, a veteran folkie with a wickedly knowing sense of humor; Teresa Trull and Barbara Higbie, who come from pop and jazz backgrounds (Higbie has also recorded for the new-age jazz label Windham Hill); Dianne Davidson, a blues guitarist with a Nashville background; Linda Tillery, whose roots are in R&B; folkies like Ferron and Lucie Blue Tremblay, who come at this material from a pop music background; and Ronnie Gilbert, cofounder of the Weavers in the 40s, whose voice is still strong 50 years later.

–Bruce Eder.

HEATHER BISHOP

Folk. This strong-voiced Californian singer, songwriter, and guitarist draws from the blues tradition, performing classic blues as well as original songs. –ED
Celebration / MOTHER OF PEARL
Classic blues covers "Cry Me a River" and "Fever" and feminist-themed originals. –ED
I Love Women ... Who Laugh / MOTHER OF PEARL
Synthesizers, saxophone, and congas yield a funky and rock-oriented sound to this collection of mostly originals. –ED
○ **A Taste of the Blues / MOTHER OF PEARL**
Bluesy covers of Joan Armatrading, Leslie Gore, and Carolyn Brady. Great production and Heather's wonderful voice. –ED

MEG CHRISTIAN

Folk. Meg Christian recorded Olivia's first album and, along with Cris Williamson, brought the whole field of women's

music into its golden age. A singer/songwriter with a folk and classical bent, her music tends to be impassioned and filled with intense feelings, and her sound very elegant and restrained. Although she retired from performing during the 80s, her work still looms large among older listeners, and she is revered within the field. –BE
○ **The Best of Meg Christian / OLIVIA**
Here are all of the landmark songs from this remarkable singer/songwriter and her decade-long career. Probably the best introduction to her work. –BE
Face the Music / OLIVIA
The poignant and reflective lyrics are balanced against an opulent sound. Featuring the supporting talents of Holly Near and Sweet Honey in the Rock. –BE
I Know You Know / OLIVIA
The first "produced" women's music record, this has held up with its humor and poignancy, although it may seem dated to some modern ears and sensibilities. –BE

DIANNE DAVIDSON

Folk. A veteran country and blues guitarist and singer, Dianne Davidson burst on the scene in the late 80s as a songwriter and interpreter of Willie Dixon, among other established composers. An imposing figure on stage, she is also one of the music's best instrumentalists. –BE

○ **Breaking All the Rules! / OLIVIA**
An excellent showcase for Davidson's powerful voice and guitar, highlighted by her loud, raunchy version of Willie Dixon's "Built for Comfort" –BE

ALIX DOBKIN

Folk. Alix Dobkin came out of the New York folk scene of the late 60s before "coming out" for real. Her 1974 debut record with Kay Gardner, *Lavender Jane Loves Women*, broke a lot of ground, and she's still singing away in the 90s, with a tough, no-nonsense sound and a cutting sense of humor. –BE

○ **Lavender Jane Loves Women / LADYSLIPPER**
A pioneering lesbian-oriented record with a clever collection of material, such as an interpretation of Dusty Springfield's "I Only Want to Be with You," that holds up well today. –BE
Living with Lesbians / LADYSLIPPER
A surprisingly lively followup with earthy, powerful material featuring basic guitar and all-woman backup singing. –BE
Yahoo Australia! / LADYSLIPPER   1990
A *Live from Sydney* concert featuring Dobkin at her best and having fun with her subjects, even as she stridently sings out on any number of political issues. –BE

FERRON

Folk. One of several Canadian singer/songwriters (others include Lucie Blue Tremblay and Heather Bishop) to emerge during the 80s, Ferron has a talent for lyrics that has gotten her compared to Bob Dylan. Her music is a pastiche of rock, folk, and jazz. –BE
Testimony / REDWOOD   1982
Considered her best record, this is a collection of song-poems that run the gamut of deep and intense emotions. –WR
○ **Shadows on a Dime / REDWOOD**   1984
Literate songs by one of the best singer/songwriters, on an elaborate followup album courtesy of producer Terry Garthwaite, with a special instrumental luster. –BE & WR

SUE FINK

Rock/pop. A popular jazzy vocalist and songwriter, Fink's music includes a wide range of styles, including ballads, new-wave, and rock. –ED

☆ **Big Promise / LADYSLIPPER**
From new-wave dance tunes to ballads to rock, Sue's polished debut makes her strong political statements in a fun and enjoyable manner. –ED
True Life Adventure / FROST-FIRE   1989
A strong and long-awaited followup with a jazzy torch style. Sophisticated and polished. –ED

TRET FURE

Rock/pop. The loudest rocking guitarist/singer in the field, Tret Fure (pronounced "Fury") formerly wrote songs and played with Spencer Davis, and did an album in a soft, Bonnie Raitt-like vein in the early 70s. Since the early 80s, she's become virtually the Bruce Springsteen of feminist music, with an emphatic, crunchy Stratocaster sound and an aggressive vocal approach. –BE
Edges of the Heart / SECOND WAVE
Not as strong as "Terminal Hold," but with one seriously sexy number ("Tight Black Jeans"); well worth owning. –BE
Terminal Hold / SECOND WAVE
Half of this record (mostly one side) rocks beautifully hard and breaks a lot of new ground, with help from Dave Davies of the Kinks and Lou Reed alumnus Steve Hunter. –BE

☆ **Time Turns the Moon / OLIVIA**   1991
One of the best women's music records ever, and one of the finer rock albums of 1991. Assertive and sensitive, tough and reflective, with a sense of humor nearly as prominent as its beat. –BE

KAY GARDNER

New-age. An early 60s feminist veteran, flutist Kay Gardner started out with Alix Dobkin, working in a folk-based idiom before moving into realms of classical and Eastern-based music. Since the 70s, she has been responsible for some of the most ambitious, complex, and accomplished work in the whole field of women's music. –BE
Fishersdaughter / LADYSLIPPER
Some of Gardner's most fascinating work outside of classical/new-age. She re-creates folk music in a distinctly woman-centered mode. Not to all tastes, but resounding with a lot of heart. –BE
Garden of Ecstasy / LADYSLIPPER
Her followup to *A Rainbow Path* is just as lush and surprising, although the medieval and mystical ideas may be over the heads of some listeners. –BE
Mooncircles / LADYSLIPPER
Her earliest instrumental album is a mellow, luscious collection of compositions for her instrument, the flute, with piano and guitar accompaniment. –BE
○ **A Rainbow Path / LADYSLIPPER**
A multi-year project that embraces medieval and Eastern influences, yet is almost new-age in its ambience. The closest that any record has gotten to the feel of Van Dyke Parks's classic "Song Cycle." –BE

RONNIE GILBERT

Folk. One of the cofounders of the Weavers, Gilbert had a surprisingly sporadic recording career during the period following that premier folk quartet's breakup, that is, until Holly Near (with whom she has toured several times) and Redwood Records came along and provided a new outlet for this big-voiced contralto who paved the way for Judy Henske, Judy Collins, and a host of other female folk stars. Gilbert's music is melodic, sincere, idealistic, and utterly current, yet also timeless, delving into long-neglected subjects of special interest to female listeners. –BE
Lifeline / REDWOOD
A fresh and vibrant concert album with Holly Near, and a repertoire ranging from current topical songs like "Biko" to romantic classics like "Stormy Weather" Followed up by the album *Singing with You*. –BE
Love Will Find a Way / REDWOOD
A very honest and representative live album consisting of a dozen numbers drawn from her current repertoire. –BE
○ **Spirit Is Free / REDWOOD**   1985
Gilbert retains a strong vocal presence on standards and feminist-oriented originals. A rousing mix of old standards like "The Midnight Special" with the new like 'Mothers, Daughters, Wives.' A good startup album. –BE

HOLLY NEAR

Folk. Originally a folkie, and before that a pretty straightlaced football princess and actress, Holly Near emerged in the early 70s as a pacifist (her first album, *Hang in There*, was an anti-war work) and feminist singer/songwriter. Near formed her own Redwood Records label, which began with selling albums at her shows and has grown into a full-fledged company. Less of a separatist in her leanings than most of the other recording pioneers in the field, she has always attracted a fair degree of respect from mainstream critics, also owing to the strength of her melodies and lyrics, which edify and energize without overwhelming the listener. For more on Holly, look for her autobiography *Fire in the Rain ... Singer in the Storm*. –BE & WR

○ **Don't Hold Back / REDWOOD**
Near's party album, a thoroughly pleasing collection of love songs, with guest appearances by Bonnie Raitt and Kenny Loggins. –BE
Singer in the Storm / CHAMELEON
This live recording defines what Near is about. Divided between love songs and political statements, it is spirited and well executed. –BE
Imagine My Surprise! / REDWOOD   1979
A playful, quirky feminist record with elements of jazz, country, and even a little bit of Broadway. –BE
Speed of Light / REDWOOD   1982
A lively, snappy followup to *Imagine My Surprise!*, with extra pop wrinkles. –BE
Journeys / REDWOOD   1983
A handy retrospective, covering Near's first six albums. –BE

PHRANC

Folk-pop. A Californian singer/songwriter whose experience in punk bands like Nervous Gender and Catholic Discipline adds an irreverent edge to her righteously political folk-pop, rooted in the guitar/harmonica music of 60s icons Phil Ochs, Tom Paxton, and Joan Baez. Despite the humor and irony of her music, Phranc pulls no punches. Her bold acknowledgment that she is a "Jewish lesbian" has made her a popular voice of modern women's music. –ED
Folksinger / POLYGRAM   1985
Her debut of modern acoustic folk with a rock edge. Voice, guitar, and harmonica. –ED
☆ **I Enjoy Being a Girl / POLYGRAM**   1989
Her pop breakthrough, with songs like "Take off Your Swastiska." She doesn't mince words, and as with the great folk singers of the past, her music is just as good as the message. Politics infused with humor and irony. A great album cover! –ED
Positively Phranc / POLYGRAM   1991
Harder and more electric, with a song about Billy Tipton and a wonderful a cappella cover of the Beach Boys classic "Surfer Girl." –ED

RHIANNON

Jazz. Former lead singer with Alive! and member of Bobby McFerrin's Voicestra vocal group, Rhiannon is involved in music education and has released several cassettes describing techniques to improve the singing voice. –ED
○ **Toward Home / LADYSLIPPER**   1991
With material by Betsy Rose, Janet Small, and Carolyn Brady, Rhiannon shows her stuff. Accompanied by Nina Gerber and Barbara Borden, she displays her range and diversity. –ED

SWEET HONEY IN THE ROCK   ♭1973

A cappella. A dynamic group of Black female singers, with gospel roots, who work a cappella and have carved out a niche for themselves with mainstream as well as feminist audiences. –BE
☆ **Breaths / FLYING FISH**
A CD-only compilation of their best tracks from the Flying Fish label. Over an hour of music. –ED
Good News / FLYING FISH
Sweet Honey in the Rock / FLYING FISH
○ **Live at Carnegie Hall / FLYING FISH**   1981
Probably the group's best showcase, playing to their audience in high spirits and with excellent sound. –BE

LINDA TILLERY

Blues-rock. A gutsy, soulful singer, Linda Tillery first emerged from obscurity in the late 60s as part of the San Francisco psychedelic/soul outfit Loading Zone. Since then, she has emerged as a definitive feminist interpreter of R&B. –BE
○ **Secrets / REDWOOD**
A powerful collection of sultry, potent rock and R&B driven by Tillery's forceful voice and personality. –BE

LUCIE BLUE TREMBLAY

Folk. A French-Canadian singer/songwriter who sings her love songs in both French and English. –ED
○ **Tremblay, Lucie Blue / OLIVIA**
Her debut features sweetly sung material in both French and English, although the listener should have no trouble following the emotional content of either. One live side and one studio-recorded side, featuring backing vocals by Cris Williamson, Teresa Trull, Tret Fure, and Deirdre McCalla. –ED
Tendresse/Tenderness / OLIVIA
Beautiful love songs, political statements, and traditional folk music show her diversity. Poignant stories in both French and English. –ED

TERESA TRULL

Country-pop. Vocalist Trull was raised in Durham, SC, and has performed solo and in a duo with pianist Barbara Higbie. –ED
○ **A Step Away / REDWOOD**
Her best. A high-quality work of hope and joy from this vocalist/keyboardist. –ED
Unexpected / SECOND WIND
A duo recording with Barbara Higbie that covers gospel, country, and ballad styles. Higbie, an accomplished pianist, can also be found in the Contemporary Instrumental chapter. –ED

CRIS WILLIAMSON

Rock/pop. One of the founding mothers of women's music, and its most long-lived and enduring talent, Williamson is a major singer/songwriter whose music incorporates sensitivity, passion, and a great deal of power and dignity. Originally inspired by folk and country, her albums veer between folk and rock, although the latter tend to be less well regarded by the fans. She has also produced one album of holiday music, *Snow Angel.* –BE
The Best of Cris Williamson / OLIVIA
It's not quite what the title says. The folk material dominates, leaving out some cool and hot rock numbers. –BE
Country Blessed / OLIVIA
Recorded as a duo with Olivia Records ace producer Teresa Trull in a somewhat country-fied vein. An especially unusual record that showcases Williamson doing songs of other writers. –BE
○ **Prairie Fire / OLIVIA**
Her hardest rocker ever, and her cleverest, most pointed collection of songs, covering concerns that range from Native Americans to new-age vacuousness. –BE
Cris Williamson / OLIVIA   1971
A remastered reissue of her first album. Very basic and raw, with veiled hints of things to come. –BE
The Changer and the Changed / OLIVIA   1975
The record that set a new standard in the field. Soulful, passionate, and poignant. –BE
Blue Rider / OLIVIA   1982
Bonnie Raitt guests on this, Williamson's most highly regarded rock album, which successfully mixes electric guitars and topical concerns with some very personal lyrics. –BE
Meg and Cris at Carnegie Hall / OLIVIA   1983
This live album of Williamson and Meg Christian consists of a surprising amount of new material. It pretty much sums up their own and Olivia Records's first decade. –BE

GAY

The work of openly gay songwriters is a small genre with a devoted and growing audience. Many would argue that it wasn't until the Stonewall rebellion in New York in June 1969 that the new political activism of lesbians and gay men brought with it a language of liberation that made "gay songs" possible.

Still, there is little agreement on what constitutes gay music. If it were enough that the composer be gay or lesbian, the genre would be huge! But by my definition, and for purposes of this essay, the composer must be gay-identified and the songs must relate in some way to the gay experience. Further, since the chapter on women's music in this book includes much work by openly lesbian musicians, this chapter will deal with gay men only.

Probably the first post-Stonewall album in this category is Michael Cohen's *What Did You Expect?* on the Folkways label (1973). This was followed shortly by Steven Grossman's *Caravan Tonight* (Mercury, 1974). Grossman, who died of AIDS in 1990, was a poetic lyricist with a captivating, smokey voice. He toured to promote the album, apparently without much support from his label, playing in coffeehouses and cabarets.

Like many gay people, Grossman fought the battle against invisibility. He found it hard to get booked, hard to get the album played on the air, and hard to get it distributed. He remains part of a venerable tradition in gay music: a fine, single-album artist.

In the late 70s, Charlie Murphy released *Catch the Fire*. Folkways also released *Walls to Roses*, an anthology of songs by gay and non-gay writers and performers. Blackberri's *Finally* appeared at about this time, as did Tom Wilson's *Gay Name Game*, (Aboveground Records, 1979) and *All-American Boy* (same label, 1982).

Through the graces of the women's distribution network, these albums found an audience. Women's companies such as Ladyslipper, Midwest Music, and Horizon included gay men's music in their catalogs. The best outlets were (and continue to be) gay/feminist bookstores such as Giovanni's Room (Philadelphia), Oscar Wilde (New York), Lambda Rising (Washington and Baltimore), Glad Day (Boston and Toronto), A Different Light (New York, Los Angeles, and San Francisco), A Brother's Touch (Minneapolis), and many others.

The British rock scene has included many fine openly gay musicians such as Jimmy Sommerville, Boy George, Tom Robinson, and the groups Bronski Beat, the Communards, and the Smiths. On the American side of the Atlantic some would include the Village People and the late Sylvester, more for their presentation of themselves than for the lyrical content of their music.

Current stars on the scene are Romanovsky and Phillips, the Flirtations, Michael Callen, and the many fine gay men's choruses, which primarily perform and record classical choral music and Broadway show songs. Though the genre is still small, these artists are finding larger audiences, more airplay, and wider distribution.

— Tom Wilson Weinberg

JOE BRACCO

Vocal. Joe was working on his first album when he died of AIDS in 1991, at the age of 30. A New Yorker through and through, his music is street-smart and rhythmic. Still at the beginning of his career, Joe Bracco opened concerts for Romanovsky & Phillips and Lynn Lavner and played at ACT-UP and PWA Coalition benefits. –TW

○ **True to Myself / FRESH FRUIT**
This album is a fitting memorial to a proud young man. Bracco had recorded vocal and guitar/piano tracks for 15 songs before he became too ill to continue the project. Paul Phillips took that tape into the studio and produced a professional cassette, including "Friend in My Pocket," "Cruiser's Blues," "South Shore Boy," and "With Our Voices." –TW

MICHAEL CALLEN

Vocal. Michael is a well-known AIDS activist and writer, having battled the disease himself since 1981. He's also a singer with the a cappella group, the Flirtations. His soaring soprano is truly a one-of-a kind voice, with or without the high heels he sometimes dons in concert. He continues to tour with the Flirts and is at work on a second solo album. –TW

○ **Purple Heart / SIGNIFICANT OTHER**
This album is one of the best gay-themed albums ever. The fine choice of material includes the definitive cover of "Where the Boys Are" and several of Callen's own songs, which cover territory as diverse as AIDS politics, father-son relationships, safe sex, and hot dancing. –TW

THE FLIRTATIONS

Vocal. Five gay men who put on a funny, uplifting show on stage and on record. In just a few years, the Flirts have become a favorite of the gay community nationwide. –TW

○ **The Flirtations / SIGNIFICANT OTHER**
This is their debut album, which includes a fine cover of Cris Williamson's "Shooting Star," a campy "Why Do Fools Fall in Love?," "Lida Rose" from *The Music Man*, Sweet Honey in the Rock's "Breaths," and a wide variety of serious and outrageous songs. –TW

Out on the Road /
This live album, was recorded in Vancouver. Songs include

"Everything Possible," Michael Callen's "Living in Wartime," "Johnny Angel," and "The Boy from New York City." –TW

ELLIOT PILSHAW

Vocal. Elliot has been on the scene making gay music for about ten years. His collaboration with Lorin Sklamberg resulted in a cassette, *Bending the Rules.* Elliot also recorded a cassette of songs by contemporary Israeli songwriters. –TW

○ **Feels Like Home / EDPC**
This is Elliot's solo album, issued on the now-defunct Icebergg label and recently reissued on his own label. This is a vocal-and-piano-only album, but with Elliot's voice and John Bucchino's accompaniments, nothing more is needed. There are songs by Holly Near, Jeff Langley, Willie Sordill, and Gary Lapow, among others. –TW

ROMANOVSKY & PHILLIPS

Vocal. Perhaps the busiest and best-known gay troubadors in the business, Ron Romanovsky and Paul Phillips have been writing, singing, traveling, loving, and breaking up with each other for more than a decade. In performance, R & P are funny, campy, poignant, and political. With a devoted and growing audience coast to coast, they've paved the way for a lot of local openly gay musicians. –TW

I Thought You'd Be Taller / FRESH FRUIT
This is R & P's debut album. Some of the songs celebrate their personal relationship in a funny, off-beat way. Tunes include "The Prince Charming Tango," "Outfield Blues," "Womb Envy," and "Paint by Numbers." –TW

Trouble in Paradise / FRESH FRUIT
This album was produced by Teresa Trull and includes some terrific backup musicians. Highlights are "What Kind of Self-Respecting Faggot Am I?," "Wimp," "Guilt Trip," "Homophobia," and "Don't Use Your Penis for a Brain." –TW

Emotional Rollercoaster / FRESH FRUIT
This album has lush horn and string arrangements and includes "My Mother's Clothes," "Living with AIDS," and "Straightening up the House." –TW

○ **Be Political, Not Polite / FRESH FRUIT**
This is their best and most recent album. With 15 songs and backup support from Holly Near, Phranc, Alix Dobkin, and Michael Callen, as well as keyboard work and arrangements by John Bucchino. Titles include, "Oh, No... I'm in Love (With My Therapist)," "When Heterosexism Strikes," "Queers in the Closet," and "Hymn." A good introduction to R & P. –TW

○ **Hopeful Romantic / FRESH FRUIT**
This is Ron Romanovsky's first solo album. Again produced by Teresa Trull, this album is less political and more love-song oriented, with lots of comic relief. –TW

TOM WILSON WEINBERG

Show music. As Tom Wilson, before reclaiming the name Weinberg in 1983, he released two albums of original songs, *Gay Name Game* and *All-American Boy.* Wilson Weinberg has traveled and performed extensively, and continues to do so, but in recent years his writing has been focused on musical theatre. His new show *Get Used to It* played off-Broadway in 1992, and Wilson Weinberg is now at work on a book musical. –TW

○ **Ten Percent Revue / ABOVEGROUND**
This album is a studio cast recording of the musical revue that had a long run off-Broadway in 1988 and has played in more than two dozen cities. Two men and two women sing such songs as "Flaunting It," "Safe Sex Slut," "The Supremes" (a spoof on our highest court), "Turkey Baster Baby," and "Before Stonewall." –TW

CHRISTMAS

Once upon a time, Christmas music lovers could look forward to a holiday helping of brand new sounds of the season every year around Christmas. Radio stations would begin playing Christmas music on Thanksgiving Day and continue past Christmas all the way through New Year's. It seemed every popular artist of the day could be counted on to present us with a special album or 45 RPM single just in time for the holidays. *Billboard* magazine tabulated these tunes with annual charts of best-selling Christmas records, along with their legendary "Top 100," "Easy-Listening," "Country & Western," and "Soul/Rhythm & Blues/Urban Contemporary" charts. Then in the late 70s, Christmas music suddenly began to do a disappearing act.

By 1980, radio programmers for the most part x-ed out "Xmas" music from their playlists until almost Christmas Eve. And while we were putting our gifts away after Christmas Day, radio stations were returning their Noel records to their record libraries for another year. As 45s began to disappear in general, there were fewer and fewer artists putting out those wonderful Christmas singles. Meanwhile, the major record companies were cutting back on their catalogs. Many of the holiday music albums from the 50s, 60s, and 70s were out of print, and except for a few big sellers by big names, or anthologies grouping various acts, Christmas music lovers were generally out of luck. (Except for Rhino, which began a wonderful series of Christmas music reissues in the mid 80s.) *Billboard* even discontinued its "Christmas Hits" charts for lack of interest.

Then came the 90s, the CD, and the great Christmas comeback! The record companies have re-disc-covered Christmas. Now you can stuff your stocking with many previously out-of-print musical presents from Yuletides Past. Santa and his musical elves began to have also taken note of wider contemporary musical tastes such as new-age and the increasing popularity of light jazz and classical artists. That's why there are more super sounds of the season for you to choose from than ever before. We'd like to help you fill your home and car stereo with those special memories that can only be created through the magic of Christmas music. These are our reviews of the best Christmas music this side of the North Pole. We think "Yule" enjoy them this Christmas and for many holidays to come.

— David Milberg

AIR SUPPLY

○ **Christmas Album / ARISTA**
The adult-contemporary sounds of the season, from light-rock radio's favorite group from Australia. –DAM

ALABAMA

○ **Alabama Christmas / RCA**
A must for your C&W Christmas, it contains the classic "Christmas in Dixie." –DAM

HERB ALPERT & THE TIJUANA BRASS

☆ **Christmas Album / A&M**
A million-seller from 1968. This is an essential part of any Christmas collection, especially their hit version of "The Christmas Song." –DAM

JULIE ANDREWS w/ANDRE PREVIN

○ **Christmas Treasure / RCA**
Orchestra with Andre Previn arrangements that feature Andrews. –ED

EDDY ARNOLD

○ **Christmas with Eddy Arnold / RCA**
The classic Christmas album from the immortal "Tennessee Plowboy." First released in 1962, it still sounds great. –DAM

JOAN BAEZ

☆ **Noel / VANGUARD**
This is the classic Joan Baez folk sound of 1966. It includes her hit rendition of "Little D

her hit rendition of "Little Drummer Boy." An essential sound of the season.–DAM

THE BEACH BOYS

☆ **Christmas Album / CAPITOL**
What more can you say about this all-time classic? A million-seller from 1964, featuring "Little Saint Nick" and "Man with All the Toys." –DAM

HARRY BELAFONTE

☆ **To Wish You a Merry Christmas / RCA**
This is the Belafonte sound of 1958, including his famous rendition of "I Heard the Bells on Christmas Day." –DAM

TONY BENNETT

☆ **Snowfall: The Tony Bennett Christmas Album / CBS**
Tony Bennett at his peak in 1968, adding his uncommon style to the common standards of the day. –DAM

DAVID BENOIT

○ **Christmastime / RHINO**
Pleasant piano stylings. Perfect for meetings under the mistletoe. –DAM

KURT BESTOR

○ **An Airus Christmas / AIRS**
Instrumental variations on standard Christmas carols for the new age. Bright, clean, and easy to listen to. –ED

BOOKER T. & THE MGS

☆ **In the Christmas Spirit / ATLANTIC**
Essential instrumental sounds of the season from the legendary band behind many 60s and 70s hits on Stax Records. –DAM

BOSTON CAMERATA

○ **Noel! Noel! / ERATO**
Joel Cohen conducts medieval/renaissance French Christmas music with the Boston Shawn and Sackbut Ensemble. Very fine traditional music. –JME

LIONA BOYD

○ **A Guitar for Christmas / CBS**
Classical guitarist extraordinaire manages to shine once in a while, even when the Muzak production is smothering her in a morass of holiday Velveeta cheese — Richard Clayderman for classical guitar music. –RICK CLARK, ROCK & ROLL DISC

JACK BROKENSHA w/LENORE PAXTON

○ **Holiday Inventions / US STEEL-CBS**   1968
One side has vibist Brokensha with Bess Bonnier on piano; one side has pianist Paxton and vocalist Robert Chambers. Crystalline chamber Christmas jazz. The album was subsidized by US Steel. –MGN

JAMES BROWN

☆ **Santa's Got a Brand New Bag / RHINO**
How can anyone resist James Brown's music? To listen to him get down on "Let's Make Christmas Mean Something This Year" or "Santa Claus Santa Claus" is to be baptized in pure holiday soul. Essential for R&B lovers. –RC

KENNY BURRELL

☆ **Have Yourself a Soulful ... / MCA-CADET**   1966
Have Yourself a Soulful Little Christmas is recently back in print after its original release on Cadet Records in 1966. Pensive, meditative, precise playing. A must-have, with a definitive jazz hit version of "Little Drummer Boy." –DAM & MGN

THE CALIFORNIA RAISINS

○ **Christmas with the California Raisins / PRR**
From their 1988 claymation CBS-TV special. The cut "Hark" is especially worth hearing. –DAM

THE CAMBRIDGE SINGERS

○ **Christmas Night - Carols of the Nativity / COLLEGIUM**
The lovely Cambridge Singers as conducted by John Rutter — one of the most brilliant living composers. If you yearn for an elegant Christmas album in the traditional style, this is it. Includes 22 carols. –JME

GLEN CAMPBELL

○ **Merry Christmas / CAPITOL**
A great combination of easy-listening and C&W treatments of Christmas standards. –DAM

LARRY CARLTON

○ **Christmas at My House / MCA**
One of the greatest jazz/rock guitarists of the 80s/90s provides this classic Christmas guitar album. –DAM

THE CARPENTERS

★ **Christmas Portrait / A&M**
An essential album for your fireside Christmas. It sold a million in 1978 and contains the classics "Merry Christmas, Darling" and "Have Yourself a Merry Little Christmas." –DAM

○ **Old-Fashioned Christmas / A&M**
Their second Christmas album. More of the soft sounds of the season. Made for mistletoe and someone you love. –DAM

RAY CHARLES

○ **Spirit of Christmas / CBS**
Ray's capable of better than this, but it ain't half bad either. Freddie Hubbard knocks off a fine solo during the hard-swinging break on "What Child Is This" and Ray almost gets down on "Santa Claus Is Coming to Town." "All I Want for Christmas" is another highlight. However, for every good cut, there's a throwaway track. But some Ray is a lot better than no Ray at all. –RICK CLARK, ROCK & ROLL DISC

THE CHIPMUNKS

○ **Christmas with the Chipmunks / CAPITOL**
Their first Christmas album, with the classic "Chipmunk Song." Great for kids of all ages. –DAM

CHRISTMAS COMEDY CLASSICS

☆ **Christmas Comedy Classics / PARROTT**
Collectibles by Dancer, Prancer & Nervous — the Singing Reindeer (Stan Freberg, Mel Blanc, and Yogi Yogesson). –DAM

CHRISTMAS WITH THE CANADIAN BRASS

○ **Christmas with the Canadian Brass / RCA**
Christmas favorites performed by this popular brass choir plus the great organ of St. Patrick's Cathedral. The combination works. Fine traditional arrangements with some modern flavor. –JME

NAT KING COLE

★ **Christmas Song / CAPITOL**
Originally released as *The Magic of Christmas* in 1960, it's a must for any Christmas collection. It includes one of his three different versions of the title track classic. –DAM

☆ **Cole, Christmas & Kids / CAPITOL**
More Christmas magic with touching tunes like "The Little Boy That Santa Forgot." –DAM

MITZIE COLLINS w/ROXANNE ZIEGLER

○ **Nowell / SAMPLER**
Hammer dulcimer, with harp and flute accompaniment. Lesser-known, but lovely works done in a creative and bright way. –JME

PERRY COMO

★ **Christmas Album / RCA**   1968
A million-seller with an updated version of his 1950 classic "There's No Christmas Like a Home Christmas." –DAM

○ **I Wish It Could Be Christmas Forever / RCA**   1982
His fans will delight to this Christmas present. His most recent recording of the sounds of the season. –DAM

RAY CONNIFF SINGERS

★ **We Wish You a Merry Christmas / CBS**   1959
This is a million-selling album, and includes their hit version of "Silver Bells." –DAM

○ **Christmas Album / CBS**   1962
This album, also known as *Merry Christmas to All*, was a million-seller in 1962 and a top-seller for ten years. A good 60s sound-of-the-season timepiece. –DAM

○ **Here We Come-A-Caroling / CBS**   1965
More classics with the Conniff touch, from 1965. His second-most-popular Christmas album collection. –DAM

FLOYD CRAMER

○ **We Wish You a Merry Christmas / STEP ONE**
Nashville's most famous pianist recorded and released this in 1967. Great C&W easy-listening. –DAM

BING CROSBY

★ **Bing Crosby Sings Christmas Songs / MCA**
Includes his definitive "White Christmas." –JME

○ **Christmas Classics / CAPITOL**   1962
This is a reissue of Crosby's 1962 album *I Wish You a Merry Christmas*. Above-standard renditions of famous Christmas standards. –DAM

BOBBY DARIN

☆ **25th Day of Christmas / ATLANTIC**
This tribute to the tremendous talent of the late Bobby Darin includes hit seasonal legacies "Christmas Auld Lang Syne" and "Child of God." –DAM

DANNY DAVIS & THE NASHVILLE BRASS

○ **Christmas with Danny Davis ... / RCA**
This album was a Christmas hit in 1970, and the smooth C&W stylings of Christmas standards still sound great after 20 years. –DAM

DORIS DAY

○ **Christmas Album / CBS**
The Doris Day sound of the 60s. Includes a notable new (at that time) Christmas number, "Christmas Present." –DAM

JOHN DENVER

★ **Rocky Mountain Christmas / RCA**
This million-seller is a must! It contains the classics "Aspen Glow" and "Christmas for Cowboys." –DAM

○ **Christmas Together / WINDSTAR**
John Denver and the Muppets. The most fun since David Seville & the Chipmunks. Moving renditions of "Have Yourself a Merry Little Christmas" and "We Wish You a Merry Christmas." –DAM

PLACIDO DOMINGO

○ **Christmas with Placido Domingo / CBS**
A perennial favorite. Christmas standards in the great tradition of legendary operatic tenors. –DAM

ELMO & PATSY

○ **Grandma Got Run Over by a Reindeer / CBS**
Worth buying, if only for the classic title tune. –DAM

JOHN FAHEY

○ **Christmas Guitar / VARRICK**
Fahey's studious acoustic guitar explorations of traditional music won him a lot of notoriety in folk circles during the 50s and 60s. *Christmas Guitar* features cuts previously available on other Fahey Christmas albums. Fahey's style is a distinctive blend of blues, folk, and ragtime. Even though his playing sometimes sounds a little too stiff and academic, all of the songs on this collection are wonderfully rendered. –RC

PERCY FAITH

● **Christmas Is / CBS**
This one debuted at Christmastime 1954. It's a great "time peace" of the decade's sounds of the season. –DAM

○ **Music of Christmas / CBS**   1966
Hit album with a notable rendition of "Silver Bells." –DAM

ARTHUR FIEDLER

○ **A Christmas Festival / RCA**
Fiedler and the Boston Pops are in good form on this holiday album. –DAM

● **Pops Christmas Party / RCA**   1959
This album is most famous for the classic version of "Sleigh Ride." –DAM

ELLA FITZGERALD

● **Ella Fitzgerald's Christmas / CAPITOL**
1968 hit album representing a change in Ella's style after her switch to the Capitol. Re-released in 1978 as *Ella Fitzgerald Sings Christmas*. –DAM

○ **Wishes You a Swinging Christmas / POLYDOR**
Originally released in 1960 as *A Swinging Christmas*, this album is representative of Ella Fitzgerald's Verve label career. –DAM

RITA FORD

○ **Joyous Music Box Christmas / MUSICMASTERS**
Christmas music played on old music boxes. –JME

● **Music Box Christmas / CBS**
This one has been part of the Christmas record scene continuously since 1961. Warm and pleasant sounds for a fireside Christmas. –DAM

TENNESSEE ERNIE FORD

○ **Star Carol / CAPITOL**
A best-seller for ten years; the sacred sounds of the season never sounded better! –DAM

THE FOUR SEASONS

☆ **Christmas Album / RHINO**
A reissue of their 1966 best-selling Christmas classic on the Philips label. "Santa Claus Is Coming to Town" is a great rocker. "Joy to the World Medley" is a surprise treat. –DAM

CONNIE FRANCIS

○ **Christmas in My Heart / POLYDOR**   1959
Originally released in 1959. Vintage Connie Francis. –DAM

JAMES GALWAY

○ **Christmas Carol / RCA**
Galway's magic flute is perfect for a fireside Christmas Eve with the entire family. –DAM

ART GARFUNKEL w/AMY GRANT

☆ **Animal's Christmas / CBS**
One of the best Christmas albums of the 80s, featuring "Carol of the Birds." –DAM

JACKIE GLEASON

○ **Merry Christmas / CAPITOL**   1956
Originally released in 1956, this is the album for Christmas cuddling, in the great tradition of Jackie Gleason instrumental arrangements. –DAM

AMY GRANT

○ **A Christmas Album / GEFFEN**
One of the better Christmas albums of the 80s. Great music for the fireside and families. –DAM

DAVID GRISMAN

○ **Acoustic Christmas / ROUNDER**
Fans of the mandolin should seek out this collection, which covers a range from straight classical readings of Respighi to

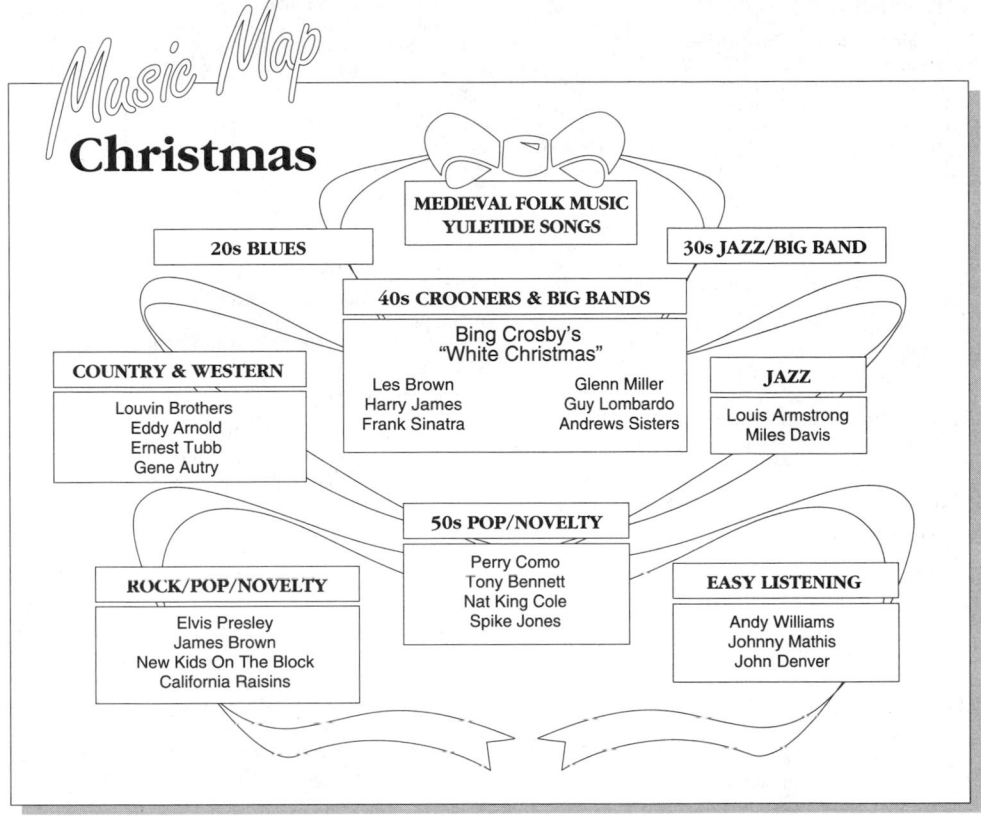

Music Map

Christmas

MEDIEVAL FOLK MUSIC YULETIDE SONGS

20s BLUES

30s JAZZ/BIG BAND

40s CROONERS & BIG BANDS

Bing Crosby's "White Christmas"

Les Brown	Glenn Miller
Harry James	Guy Lombardo
Frank Sinatra	Andrews Sisters

COUNTRY & WESTERN

Louvin Brothers
Eddy Arnold
Ernest Tubb
Gene Autry

JAZZ

Louis Armstrong
Miles Davis

50s POP/NOVELTY

Perry Como
Tony Bennett
Nat King Cole
Spike Jones

ROCK/POP/NOVELTY

Elvis Presley
James Brown
New Kids On The Block
California Raisins

EASY LISTENING

Andy Williams
Johnny Mathis
John Denver

Stephane Grappelli-style jazz raveups. Dock this a notch for an utterly pointless version of "Silent Night" and Donald Duck vocals on "We Wish You a Merry Christmas." It's nothing that a programmable player can't remedy. –RICK CLARK, ROCK & ROLL DISC

VINCE GUARALDI

☆ **Charlie Brown Christmas / FANTASY**
Anyone who has seen the Charlie Brown specials can't help but notice the distinctive jazzy piano trio work on the soundtracks. The artist, the late Vince Guaraldi, specialized in a very expressive direct style of playing, not unlike Bill Evans. On this disc, Guaraldi applies his signature to an assortment of holiday standards and originals, one of them being the famous Peanuts theme "Linus and Lucy." That song, as well as everything else here, sounds great. This is a special addition to any Christmas CD collection. –RICK CLARK, ROCK & ROLL DISC

MERLE HAGGARD

○ **Christmas Present / CURB**   1973
While Hag keeps the mood light with selections such as "Santa Claus and Popcorn" and more traditional fare, he also has some bite with the high and lonesome "Daddy Won't Be Home for Christmas." His matter-of-fact tale about layoffs at the factory, "If We Make It through December," has become timeless in tough times. –DMAC

EMMYLOU HARRIS

☆ **Light of the Stable / WARNER**
An album of soaring beauty, as if from angels on high. Neil

Young, Dolly Parton, and Linda Ronstadt add harmony vocals to the moving title track, aided by James Burton's electric guitar and Hank DeVito's pedal steel. Beauty beyond belief. Sadly, this release is (as we go to press) available only on cassette. –DMAC

MICHAEL HEDGES w/KELLY MCGILLIS

○ **Santabear's First Christmas / WINDHAM HILL**
A story disc. Kelly McGillis narrates a Christmas tale over the lovely acoustic guitar of Hedges. –ED

PAUL HORN

○ **Peace Album / KUCKUCK**
Contemporary instrumental. Fifteen holiday-oriented compositions with the soft, soothing flute of Paul Horn. –ED

ENGELBERT HUMPERDINCK

○ **Merry Christmas / CBS**
This was a hit album in 1980. All the romance of a typical Humperdinck album. –DAM

MAHALIA JACKSON

○ **Christmas with Mahalia Jackson / CBS**
This was the second of her two legendary gospel Christmas albums for Columbia. A worthy companion to her earlier *Silent Night* album. –DAM

Silent Night / CBS
What an inspirational voice! The album loses points for the organ and choir sounding too Presbyterian. Nevertheless, Mahalia transcends all that by singing these Christmas songs as if she's lived them every day of her life. –RC

EVAN JOHNS & THE H-BOMBS

☆ **Please, Mr. Santa Claus / RYKODISC**
Put this nine-song mini-album CD in the Christmas stocking of any rock & roll fan. The "crash and burn" guitar style of Johns recalls Santo and Johnny ("Snowed In") and Jimmy Bryant ("Santa's Little Helper"), while his snarly vocals on the title track bring new meaning to "cool yule." Spiced with original instrumentals and a cover of "Telstar," this is a must for Evan Johns fans and those who want a little bite in their yuletide listening. –DMAC

SPIKE JONES

☆ **It's a Spike Jones Christmas / RHINO**
A collection of Spike Jones Christmas classics, including his hit versions of "My Two Front Teeth" and "I Saw Mommy Kissing Santa Claus." –DAM

THE JUDDS

○ **Christmas Time with the Judds / RCA**
Country Christmas with Wynonna and Naomi Judd. Strong performances. –ED

PETER KATER

○ **For Christmas / SILVER WAVE**
Supper-club piano stylings of familiar holiday songs. Very fine pianist. It works. –JME

STAN KENTON

☆ **Merry Christmas! / CAPITOL**   1961
A hit album from 1961. A definite Kenton collectible. –DAM

KING'S COLLEGE CHOIR

○ **O Come All Ye Faithful / LONDON**
Sixteen traditional carols done by this classic Christmas choir. This is what carols were meant to sound like. –JME

THE KINGSTON TRIO

☆ **The Last Month of the Year / CAPITOL**
An essential part of any Christmas album collection. True Christmas folk songs, from spirituals to Old English rounds. A must! –DAM

GLADYS KNIGHT & THE PIPS

○ **That Special Time of Year / CBS**
Their second Christmas album, with their updated sound of the 80s. Features a great version of "Santa Claus Is Coming to Town." –DAM

ERICH KUNZEL

○ **Christmas with the Pops / TELARC**
Trim your tree with the full orchestral delights of holiday standards with a true maestro. –DAM

PEGGY LEE

○ **Christmas Carousel / CAPITOL**
This is the classic Christmas sound of Peggy Lee during her peak recording years. –DAM

THE LETTERMEN

○ **For Christmas This Year / CAPITOL**
Here is the early Lettermen sound of 1966. Put a log on the fire, sit back, and enjoy. –DAM

RAMSEY LEWIS TRIO

Sounds of Christmas / MCA-CHESS
If the whole album were as cool as the first half of this disc, it would rate a lot higher, but the strings on the last half are overbearingly sweet and pointless. ... This disc contains less than 30 minutes of music, a letdown of sorts when you consider how much CDs cost. –RICK CLARK, ROCK & ROLL DISC

○ **More Sounds of Christmas / MCA**
The fabulous followup to *Sounds of Christmas*, containing the trio's hit-single version of "Jingle Bells." –DAM

NORMAN LUBOFF CHOIR

○ **Christmas with the Norman Luboff Choir / RCA**
This one debuted in 1964 and made the *Billboard* charts. If you like the choral group sound of the early 60s, you'll love this one. –ED

MADELINE MACNEIL

○ **Christmas Comes Anew / KICKING MULE**
European and American Christmas songs with the bright voice of MacNeil backed by acoustic guitar, dulcimer, and strings. –JME

HENRY MANCINI

○ **Merry Mancini Christmas / RCA**
Mancini magic at its best, for the holidays. Perfect background music for holiday family get-togethers. –DAM

BARRY MANILOW

○ **Because It's Christmas / ARISTA**
Christmas classics in the Manilow style. Nestle under the mistletoe with this one. –DAM

MANNHEIM STEAMROLLER

★ **Christmas Album / AMERICAN GRAMOPHONE**
Classical Christmas music, so well produced that many hi-fi shops used the album to demonstrate high-end equipment and speakers. –DAM

○ **Fresh Aire Christmas / AMERICAN GRAMOPHONE**
A worthy successor to their first *Christmas Album*. –DAM

MANTOVANI

○ **All-Time Xmas Favorites - Vol. 1 & 2 / POLYGRAM**
Great music to wake up to on Christmas morning. Many cuts taken from his 1953 million-selling album. –DAM

WYNTON MARSALIS

☆ **Crescent City Christmas Card / CBS**
Unless you happen to be a hardcore Wyntonphile, skip over the long-winded liner notes (typical of his albums) and let the music do the talking. This elegant album swings with heart and soul and is sure to be a jazz standard for the season. –RC

THE MARTIN BEST MEDIEVAL ENSEMBLE

○ **Thys Yool — A Medieval Christmas / NIMBUS**
Elegant music. Early Christmas celebrations on original instruments. –JME

JOHNNY MATHIS

Christmas Eve with Johnny Mathis / CBS
More romantic sounds of the season, 70s-style, featuring "Christmas Is." –DAM

☆ **Merry Christmas / CBS**   1958
A classic million-seller from 1958. The original Mitch Miller arrangements that made Mathis a superstar. –DAM

Give Me Your Love for Christmas / CBS   1969
A million-seller featuring the Mathis sound after he returned to Columbia Records from the Mercury label. –DAM

JOHN MCCUTCHEON

Winter Solstice / ROUNDER
This is a blend of Christmas, Chanukkah, and New Year's music performed around the hammer dulcimer and other acoustic instruments. McCutcheon, the Washington Bach

Consort, and members of Trapezoid focus on fairly traditional folk arrangements of these songs. —RICK CLARK, ROCK & ROLL DISC

MAUREEN MCGOVERN

○ **Christmas with Maureen McGovern / CBS**
Velvety smooth. Great for Christmas cuddling. —DAM

MITCH MILLER

● **Christmas Sing-Along with Mitch Miller / CBS**
The first *Sing Along with Mitch* Christmas album. The MOR sound of the 50s. —DAM

○ **Holiday Sing-Along with Mitch Miller / CBS**
A Christmas timepiece of the 60s. —DAM

MORMON TABERNACLE CHOIR

☆ **Mormon Tabernacle Choir Sings Christmas Carols / CBS**
This was the first of a dozen Christmas albums by this choir, which dates back to 1957. It's an essential part of any comprehensive collection of Christmas music. —DAM

Spirit of Christmas / CBS   1959
This album was recorded and originally released in 1959. It still sounds good a generation later. —DAM

JIM NABORS

○ **Christmas Album / CBS**
An easy-listening treat that includes one of the best versions of "White Christmas" ever. —DAM

Merry Christmas / CBS
More Christmas classics ... G-O-L-L-Y ! —DAM

WILLIE NELSON

○ **Pretty Paper / CBS**
Worth the price just for the title song. —DAM

NEW EDITION

○ **Christmas all over the World / MCA**
A musical Christmas party, featuring the title tune. —DAM

NEW KIDS ON THE BLOCK

○ **Merry Merry Christmas / CBS**
"This One's for the Children" opens things up with a surprisingly thoughtful note, but the following song, "Last Night I Saw Santa Claus," makes the Osmond Brothers sound like soul incarnate. Same goes for the embarrassingly inept "Funky, Funky Xmas." Still, there are a couple of decent blue-eyed pop/soul moments when producer Maurice Starr keeps things silky and smooth, particularly on "The Christmas Song." —RICK CLARK, ROCK & ROLL DISC

NRBQ

○ **Christmas Wish / ROUNDER**
NRBQ bring a sense of goofy fun to this eight-song mini-album, covering standards in their wacky style and contributing a few originals — Terry Adams's "Electric Train" and Joey Spampinato's "Christmas Wish." The cover photo of NRBQ decked out in their winter pajamas is a real hoot. —DMAC

ALEXANDER O'NEAL

○ **My Gift to You / TABU**
So good I want to play it year 'round. Decent contemporary holiday discs are hard to come by, but Minneapolis's finest soul singer and producers Jimmy Jam and Terry Lewis created a disc that nearly rivals Spector's in concept (all the originals are brilliant) and Elvis' in performance. "Sleigh Ride" is the hardest piece of Xmas funk James Brown never cut, and the brassy treatment given to "Winter Wonderland" would make Sinatra proud. —JOHN FLOYD, ROCK & ROLL DISC

ODETTA

○ **Christmas Spirituals / ALCAZAR**
Odetta's husky voice is often stunning, both in her a cappella performances and her songs with accompaniment. Odetta says these songs are traditional spirituals, neither purely African nor American, but songs that emerged from the sufferings of slavery. Powerful stuff. —DMAC

EUGENE ORMANDY

○ **Glorious Sound of Christmas / CBS**
Although they're not credited in the title, this album also features the Mormon Tabernacle Choir. It was a million-seller when it was first released in 1962. —DAM

Greatest Christmas Hits / CBS
This album also includes the Temple University Choir, combined with the Philadelphia Orchestra for a truly classical Christmas. —DAM

OSMOND FAMILY CHRISTMAS

○ **Osmond Family Christmas / CURB**
Donny and his brothers singing smooth harmonies for the holidays. —DAM

BUCK OWENS

○ **Christmas with Buck Owens / CURB**
Buck adds fun to the season's festivities when dishing out country corn such as "Santa Looked a Lot like Daddy." The Buckaroos turn in a romping instrumental of "Jingle Bells," and Buck contributes a honky-tonk Christmas classic with "Blue Christmas Lights." —DMAC

PATTI PAGE

○ **Christmas with Patti Page / POLYGRAM**
Holiday standards and sacred sounds, as with the hit "Happy Birthday, Jesus." —DAM

STEVAN PASERO

○ **Christmas Classics for Guitar / SUGO**
Guitar transcriptions and arrangements of a variety of traditional Christmas fare, folk tunes, and classical compositions. —JME

LUCIANO PAVAROTTI

○ **O Holy Night / POLYGRAM**
A million-seller originally released in 1976. This album is a worthy successor to previous recordings by the great Italian tenors Caruso and Lanza. —DAM

PETER, PAUL & MARY

○ **Holiday Celebration / GOLD CASTLE**
Contains both Christmas and Chanukkah songs. Some nice and new versions of their older recordings. —DAM

MICHAEL PETRI

○ **Noel! Noel! Noel! / RCA**
Christmas music from one of the world's finest recorder players. Backed by the Westminster Abbey Choir and the National Philharmonic with Martin Neary. —JME

THE PLATTERS

○ **Christmas with the Platters / POLYGRAM**
Christmas standards with the Platters touch, plus a couple of Buck Ram originals: "Come Home for Christmas" and "Merry Christmas, Baby." —DAM

ELVIS PRESLEY

★ **Elvis' Christmas Album / RCA**
Contains most of his most famous Christmas songs, including

including "Blue Christmas" and "If Every Day Was Like Christmas." –DAM

○ **Memories of Christmas / RCA**
A worthwhile re-packaging of Elvis Christmas classics. –DAM

○ **Sings the Wonderful World of Xmas / RCA**
The later (70s) sound of the King. Includes a great rendition of "Merry Christmas, Baby." –DAM

LEONTYNE PRICE

○ **Christmas Offering / POLYGRAM**
This is a time-tested classic from 1961, with one of the most talented sopranos of the 50s and 60s. –DAM

CHARLEY PRIDE

○ **Christmas in My Home Town / RCA**
The title tune was a great Christmas hit. Mellow C&W for the holidays. –DAM

RAFFI

☆ **Christmas Album / MCA**
This is an essential collection that's perfect for kids and still enjoyable for adults. –DAM

LOU RAWLS

○ **Merry Christmas Ho! Ho! Ho! / CAPITOL**
Early Lou Rawls at his best, including his hit version of "Little Drummer Boy." –DAM

LEON REDBONE

○ **Christmas Island / AUGUST**
The enigmatic Leon Redbone gives his time-warp treatment to a predictable bunch of Christmas standards. Fans of Redbone's low-key camp style will enjoy this, particularly the duet with Dr. John on "Frosty the Snowman." –RC

JIM REEVES

○ **Twelve Songs of Xmas / RCA**
The 60s C&W sound is still great in the 90s. –DAM

PAUL REVERE & THE RAIDERS

☆ **Christmas Present & Past / CBS**
A rocking-great trip back to the 60s with Mark Lindsay and Paul Revere. An essential oldie-but-goodie. –DAM

BOB RIVERS

☆ **Twisted Christmas / ATLANTIC**
This is one of the funniest Christmas albums of all time! Essential! Includes the classic "Message from the King." –DAM

ROCK & ROLL CHRISTMAS

☆ **Rock & Roll Christmas / ACE**
Reissue of Huey "Piano" Smith and the Clowns' *Twas the Night before Christmas* album on Ace, with six added tracks from other New Orleans artists. Oddly, the tracks are not identified by artist, but that won't spoil your yule dance party. Prepare to do the mambo to Smith's "Almost Time for Santa" and the Popeye on "All I Want for Christmas (Is a Little Bit of Music)." A nutty but danceable party platter. –DMAC

KENNY ROGERS

○ **Christmas / CAPITOL**
Kenny Rogers does his thing with old and new Christmas tunes. Just what you would expect. –ED

ROTARY CONNECTION

○ **Peace / MCA**
A great Christmas present from the 60s, featuring the late Minnie Riperton. –DAM

ROYAL COLLEGE OF MUSIC CHOIR & BRASS ENSEMBLE

☆ **Carols for Christmas / RYKODISC**
This is as pure as it comes. Unpretentious. No sentimental slop, just an excellent choir doing the obvious and not so obvious with subtlety and class. Sonically, this collection is a real treat. Perfect. –RC

ROYAL PHILHARMONIC w/DAVID NEWMAN

○ **It's a Wonderful Life; A Christmas Carol ... / TELARC**
Royal Philharmonic with David Newman. Original scores for three of the greatest Christmas films of all time, *It's a Wonderful Life*, *A Christmas Carol*, and *Miracle on 34th Street*. Restored and recorded in pristine digital sound. –JME

THE SACKVILLE ALL-STARS

○ **Christmas Record / SACKVILLE**
Jazz improvisations on standard Christmas tunes. With Milt Hinton on bass, Gus Johnson on drums, Ralph Sutton on piano, and Jim Galloway on soprano saxophone. –JME

MIKE, PEGGY, AND PENNY SEEGER

○ **American Folk Songs for Christmas / ROUNDER**
Lovers of traditional serious folk music will enjoy this double CD set, which features everything from earnestly untrained a cappella performances to a whole array of acoustic instrumentation, including mandolin, dulcimer, guitar, psaltery, autoharp, banjo, and so forth. –RC

DOC SEVERINSEN

○ **Merry Christmas / AMHERST**
"Tonight Show" band treatment of Christmas classics. –DAM

ROBERT SHAW CHORALE

○ **Many Moods of Christmas / TELARC**   1962
This is one of the later, and better, Christmas offerings from these performers. –DAM

HARRY SIMEONE CHORALE

☆ **Little Drummer Boy / POLYGRAM**
Contains the definitive version of the title song and similar performances of other sounds of the season. Essential. –DAM

FRANK SINATRA

☆ **Sinatra Christmas Album / CAPITOL**
Essential Sinatra Christmas sounds of his Capitol era, with "Christmas Waltz" and "Have Yourself a Merry Little Christmas." –DAM

Christmas Dreaming / CBS
A collection of Sinatra sides cut between 1944 and 1950 to commemorate the season. The refinement of his phrasing and vocal timbre during those years is stunning. Even though his best work was yet to come, this is a worthwhile CD for Sinatra lovers. –RICK CLARK, ROCK & ROLL DISC

THE STATLER BROTHERS

○ **Christmas Card / POLYGRAM**
Wonderful stuff, with "I Believe in Santa Claus." –DAM

Christmas Present / POLYGRAM
Lots of C&W Christmas originals like "I Never Spend a Christmas That I Don't Think of You." –DAM

BARBRA STREISAND

☆ **Christmas Album / CBS**
An essential collection including "Sleep in Heavenly Peace (Silent Night)" and "Jingle Bells." –DAM

THE SUPREMES w/STEVIE WONDER

○ **Merry Christmas/Someday at Christmas / MOTOWN**

Contains the classics "Twinkle, Twinkle Little Me" and "Someday at Christmas." Truly supreme wonders. –DAM

TAKE 6

○ **He Is Christmas / WARNER**
Interesting and slick arrangements of Christmas classics and sacred sounds. –DAM

THE TEMPTATIONS

★ **Christmas Card / MOTOWN**
The Christmas sound for the "Big Chill Generation," including a great rendition of "Rudolph the Red-Nosed Reindeer." –DAM

☆ **Give Love at Christmas / MOTOWN**
A more mellow Christmas sound from the Temptations, especially the title tune. –DAM

● **Christmas Card/Give Love at Christmas / MOTOWN**
This two-album CD contains all of their Christmas hits, including "Rudolph the Red-Nosed Reindeer," "Give Love at Christmas," and "Silent Night." –DAM

DYLAN THOMAS

○ **A Child's Christmas in Wales / CAEDMON**
Everyone should hear Dylan Thomas read this lovely prose piece. Enchanting, in the true sense of the word. Also included are Thomas poems such as "Do Not Go Gentle into That Good Night." –JME

ERIC TINGSTAD & NANCY RUMBEL

○ **The Gift / SONIA GAIA**
Tingstad and Rumbel, who have a couple of the best cuts on the *Narada Christmas Collection*, blend a spatial new-age sensibility with straight melodic readings of traditional Christmas music, performed on acoustic string and wind instruments. Sometimes the exquisite technique is a little bloodless but, all in all, very well done.
—RICK CLARK, ROCK & ROLL DISC

RANDY TRAVIS

○ **An Old-Time Christmas / WARNER**
Ten Christmas songs by Travis. "God Rest Ye Merry Gentlemen" is outstanding. –ED

TRINITY COLLEGE CHOIR

○ **Carols from Trinity / CONIFER**
Twenty-seven carols (old and new) from renowned Trinity College Choir, with Richard Marlow. Classic and elegant. –JME

BOBBY VEE

○ **Merry Christmas / CAPITOL**
Not just the standards, but some tasty originals like "A Not So Merry Christmas" in this 60s Christmas time capsule. –DAM

THE VENTURES

☆ **Christmas Album / CAPITOL**
Originally issued on Dolton, this instrumental classic was reissued briefly in 1990 on CD by EMI and curiously is out of print as we go to press. The Ventures have a blast with unique covers of secular Christmas songs: each instrumental borrows riffs from popular mid-60s hits, incorporating them into their twangy guitar yule melodies. "Sleigh Ride" uses the Ventures' own hit, "Walk, Don't Run," while other selections borrow from hits of other artists. It's a gas to hear "Frosty the Snowman" set to the Champs' "Tequila." I don't want to spoil the party by telling you any more of the revamped riffs, but do not rest until you find a copy of this release. –DMAC

THE WHISPERS

○ **Happy Holidays to You / CBS**   1978
A hit when it was first released, the title tune is especially good. –DAM

SLIM WHITMAN

○ **Christmas Album / CAPITOL**   1969
This is a reissue of an album originally released in 1969. Vintage Slim Whitman for the holidays. –DAM

ROGER WHITTAKER

○ **Christmas Album / RCA**   1978
This is the sound of Roger Whittaker at the peak of his career. A worthwhile stocking-stuffer. –DAM

ANDY WILLIAMS

☆ **Christmas Album / CBS**
An essential Christmas classic! A million-seller in 1963, and a perennial hit ever since. –DAM

Merry Christmas / CBS
Andy's voice is custom-made for Christmas. Here are 17 tunes crooned by an expert. –ED

Christmas Present / CBS   1965
This was Andy Williams's second million-selling Christmas album, and with good reason. Here is Andy's sound at its peak. –DAM

JACKIE WILSON

☆ **Merry Christmas from Jackie Wilson / RHINO**   1963
After being out of print for years, this gem from one of the most exciting R&B entertainers of all time is finally available. Essential. –DAM

GEORGE WINSTON

○ **December / WINDHAM HILL**
Although you won't hear any standard holiday tunes, Winston's lovely *December* album has become the new-age holiday recording of choice. –JME

FRANK YANKOVIC

☆ **Christmas Memories / POLYGRAM**
This one won a Christmas-music Grammy, and with good reason. You'll love this version of "Blue Christmas." –DAM

CHRISTMAS COLLECTIONS

An Austin R&B Christmas / EPIC
Christmas music for those who like roadhouse raunch and cool jazzy swing. Despite a couple of lapses into lounge-lizard land (Paul Ray), the Fabulous Thunderbirds' "Merry Christmas Darling," Angela Strehli's "Boogie Woogie Santa Claus," or Lou Ann Barton's "Please Come Home for Christmas" are certain to have you reaching for some yule longnecks. –RICK CLARK, ROCK & ROLL DISC

○ **Big Band Christmas / CBS**
Noel nostalgia the big-band way: Les Brown, Doris Day, Russ Morgan, Artie Shaw, Sammy Kaye, Harry James, and others. Great stuff! –DAM

○ **Billboard Greatest Christmas Hits: 1935-1954 / RHINO**
Some of the biggest seasonal classics are represented on these two discs. *Vol. 1* opens with Bing singing (guess what?) "White Christmas" and runs through Gene Autry's "Rudolph the Red-Nosed Reindeer," "The Christmas Song" (Nat King Cole), "Let It Snow, Let It Snow, Let It Snow" (Vaughn Monroe), the annoying "All I Want for Christmas (Is My Two Front Teeth)" by Spike Jones, and more. –RC

○ **Billboard Greatest Christmas Hits: 1955 ... / RHINO**
Billboard Greatest Christmas Hits: 1955 - Present / Vol. 2 features Elvis on "Blue Christmas," Bobby Helms ("Jingle Bell Rock"), and Brenda Lee ("Rockin' around the Christmas

Tree"). On the novelty side, this disc has "Grandma Got Run over by a Reindeer," "The Chipmunk Song," and others. While these collections are packed with the biggies, it's questionable how many times one can enjoy hearing David Seville & the Chipmunks or Elmo & Patsy. −RC

☆ **Billboard Greatest Christmas Hits - Country / RHINO**
Primarily late 40s and late 50s hits, many more novelty than C&W. The Texas Troubadour, Ernest Tubb, hit the charts twice with his 1949 A-side, "Blue Christmas," and then the B-side, "White Christmas" (both are here). Country corn from Tex Ritter, Buck Owens, Eddy Arnold, and others, alongside Johnny Cash's solemn "The Little Drummer Boy." −DMAC

☆ **Billboard Greatest Christmas Hits - R&B / RHINO**
Includes the original version (1947) of "Merry Christmas, Baby" by Johnny Moore's Three Blazers, featuring Charles Brown's smoother-than-brandy vocals; jump-blues from Mabel Scott on "Boogie-Woogie Santa Claus"; vocal group contributions from the Orioles and the Cadillacs; Chuck Berry's "Run Rudolph, Run"; and five more. −DMAC

○ **Blue Yule / RHINO**
Great Christmas classics from Lightnin' Hopkins, Canned Heat, Charles Brown, John Lee Hooker, and others. Essential for a hip holiday. −DAM

☆ **Blue Yule - Christmas Blues and R&B Classics / RHINO**
A stellar 18-song compilation with most tracks not duplicated on other in-print collections. Treasures abound here: rare tracks from John Lee Hooker and Lightnin' Hopkins, Hop Wilson's original "Merry Christmas, Darling" (covered by the Fabulous Thunderbirds on *An Austin Rhythm & Blues Christmas*), Louis Jordan's last recording (1968, "Santa Claus, Santa Claus"), and more. −DMAC

☆ **Bummed-Out Christmas! / RHINO**
This compilation ranges from the humorous (Sherwin Linton, "Santa Got a D.W.I.") to the mournful (George Jones, "Lonely Christmas Call"), with rare gems like "Christmas Eve Can Kill You" by the Everly Brothers and the powerful call-and-response deep soul from Johnny & Jon on "Christmas in Vietnam." −DMAC

○ **Christmas Album / CBS**
A wonderful holiday sampler. Includes Tony Bennett, Frank Sinatra, Andy Williams, Johnny Mathis, and others. −DAM

☆ **Christmas Cheers from Motown / MOTOWN**
A hit album from 1973 with great Christmas presents from the Temptations, Diana Ross & the Supremes, Stevie Wonder, and Smokey Robinson & the Miracles. −DAM

☆ **Christmas Classics / RHINO**
A well-rounded compilation of R&B, rock & roll, pop, and rocking instrumentals (the Ventures and Santo & Johnny). Aretha Franklin is elegant on "Winter Wonderland," while Stevie Wonder and the Supremes represent "The Motown Sound." Roy Orbison is in top form on "Pretty Paper," and Bobby "Boris" Pickett would make the Grinch smile with "Monsters' Holiday." −DMAC

☆ **The Christmas Collection / PRESTIGE**
Devotees of acoustic combo jazz will love *The Christmas Collection*. Every song is a highlight on this who's who of jazz giants, featuring Dexter Gordon, Paul Bley, Art Blakey, Charles Mingus, Gene Ammons, Bobby Timmons, Eddie "Lockjaw" Davis, Bill Smith, Don Patterson, and more. There is a continuity from beginning to end that makes this a very playable collection. A must! −RICK CLARK, ROCK & ROLL DISC

☆ **Christmas Gift Set / CAPITOL**
With tracks from Bing Crosby, Nat King Cole, and Frank Sinatra, essential stuff for a nostalgic Noel. Cuddle under the mistletoe or by a warm fireplace with this one. −DAM

☆ **Christmas Kisses / CAPITOL**
An outstanding 22-track compilation from Capitol's vaults, 1944-1963, covering many styles, from the folk blues of Leadbelly to the entrancing pop vocals of Nancy Wilson. Doo-wop, honky-tonk, piano boogie, and the playful girl group Pop of the Bookends on "Christmas Kisses" all fit in with Les

Paul's dazzling display of guitar virtuosity on "Jingle Bells" and the irresistible "Rudolph the Red-Nosed Reindeer Mambo" from Billy May and his orchestra. −DMAC

○ **Christmas Memories / RCA**
Relive the Christmas sounds of pop singers and artists of the 40s and 50s. −DAM

☆ **Christmas Party with Eddie G. / CBS**
If there is a more entertaining Christmas compilation than this CD, I have not heard it. This is a party platter that includes international Christmas greetings and amusing comedy bits from old radio in between 17 tracks of R&B, blues, country, exotica, rock, novelty, and more. Most tracks are unavailable elsewhere on CD. From the surf sounds of Untamed Youth to the strains of Monty & Marsha Brown's "Cajun Christmas," this is a nonstop Christmas party. −DMAC

☆ **A Christmas Present for You from Phil Spector / RHINO**
There is no doubt that Phil Spector's production vision was brilliant. This Christmas album was one of his greatest achievements (which is saying a lot). Features Darlene Love, the Ronettes, Bob B. Soxx & the Blue Jeans, and the Crystals. Spector focuses Christmas through the attitude of early 60s pop magic the way Crosby did for music of the 40s. −RC

○ **Christmas Rap / PROFILE**
Early rap-masters from the early 80s, including Run D.M.C., Sweet Tee, Surf MCs, Derek B, Dana Dane, Spyder-D, and others! −DAM

○ **Christmas Rock Album / PARROTT**
Great Christmas hits from Elton John, Foghat, Queen, Beach Boys, Elvin Bishop, Waitresses, and others. Super stuff! −DAM

☆ **Cool Yule - Best of Cool Yule / RHINO**
Eighteen tracks culled from two out-of-print "Cool Yule" albums, this includes "Santa Claus" by the 60s garage band the Sonics (set to the tune of "Farmer John"); the hilarious R&B novelty "Christmas in the Congo" from the Mar-Keys; Tina Turner's wailing on "Merry Christmas, Baby"; and more essential offerings from James Brown, Solomon Burke, and others. −DMAC

☆ **Cool Yule - Vol. 2 / RHINO**
Great Christmas rock from the 50s and 60s. Essential songs from the Marcels, Chuck Berry, Gary U.S. Bonds, Brenda Lee, Johnny Preston, Jack Scott, and others. −DAM

○ **Country Christmas - Vol. 1 / RCA**
Great stuff from the 70s and 80s by Alabama, Charley Pride, Willie Nelson, Razzy Bailey, and others. −DAM

○ **A Creole Christmas / CBS**   1990
Featuring some of the finest singers of New Orleans, including Aaron Neville, Johnny Adams, Irma Thomas, and more. −DMAC

○ **December's Eve / RCA**
Fireside Christmas sounds from RCA's popular (not rock & roll) artists of the 50s. −DAM

☆ **Dr. Demento Presents ... / RHINO**
Dr. Demento Presents: Greatest Novelty Records - Vol. 6 (Xmas) Dr. Demento's novelty collections are usually in synch with those folks who think *Mad* magazine is essential reading. Nothing wrong with that, even though this collection is at times overbearingly cute and the humor often too dated to be meaningful or funny for those who didn't remember the songs the first time around. Nevertheless, where else can you find "Grandma Got Run over by a Reindeer," Bob & Doug McKenzie's (of SCTV) "Twelve Days of Christmas," the Barking Dogs, Wild Man Fischer, Weird Al Yankovic, Cheech & Chong, and Stan Freberg on one disc? If Handel's *Messiah* represents the loftier aspects of Christmas, then this album the season's whoopee cushion. −RICK CLARK, ROCK & ROLL DISC

○ **God Rest Ye Merry Jazzmen / CBS**   1981
A compilation of tracks not on any other albums. With Dexter Gordon Quartet, McCoy Tyner (solo), Arthur Blythe Quartet, Heath Brothers, Paquito D'Rivera Duo, Wynton Marsalis Quintet in modern and modal settings. −MGN

○ **A GRP Christmas Collection / GRP**
Chick Corea's Elektric Band, Special EFX, Lee Ritenour, David Benoit, Tom Scott, Gary Burton, Mark Egan and a host of others run through a batch of standards with an inhumanly high level of virtuosity. As with many GRP releases, the state-of-the-art sound tends to take precedence over sparks. Gary Burton's mathematically precise "God Rest Ye Merry Gentlemen" does for jazz what "Gentle Giant" did for rock. Dave Grusin, Szakcsi, and Lee Ritenour turn in emotive solo performances, and the unique Kevin Eubanks arrangement of "Silver Bells" works well. –RC

○ **GRP Christmas Collection - Vol. 2 / GRP**
If you loved the first one, you'll love this too. –DAM

○ **Have a Merry Chess Christmas / MCA-CHESS**
This fine collection focuses on Chess's R&B, pop, and rock catalog, with Chuck Berry, the O'Jays, the Ramsey Lewis Trio, Rotary Connection, the Moonglows, the Soul Stirrers, and others. There aren't any wasted tracks here and the liner notes, by Amy McKaie, are concise and informative. –RC

○ **Have Yourself a Jazzy Little Christmas / POLYGRAM**
A terrific sampler of classic jazz artists and their Christmas improvisations, with Billie Holiday, Jimmy Smith, Ella Fitzgerald, Oscar Peterson, Bill Evans, and more. –DAM

Have Yourself a Merry Little Christmas / RHINO
This is a well-intentioned effort with a portion of the proceeds going to some unspecified charity. The Roches open things up with a cappella versions of "Adeste Fidelis" and "Angels We Have Heard on High," while Eastern Bloc blasts through a garage band trashing of "Jingle Bells." Dr. John sleepwalks through "Silent Night" and Eugene Ruffolo does a good approximation of early Livingston Taylor on "Have Yourself a Merry Little Christmas." Eclectic, but too uneven to make this ecumenical effort a satisfying listen. –RICK CLARK, ROCK & ROLL DISC

☆ **Hillbilly Holiday / RHINO**
Music from the 50s and 60s, complete with holiday cheating and drinking laments. Bill Monroe, Tex Ritter, Ernest Tubb, Hank Snow, Loretta Lynn, George Jones, Buck Owens, and more country greats fill this solid collection. True to most great country, the music included gets to the heart of things, avoiding the sentimental goop embraced by most modern seasonal "country" efforts. –RICK CLARK, ROCK & ROLL DISC

☆ **Hipster's Holiday - Vocal Jazz & R&B Classics / RHINO**
Typical of Rhino releases, *Hipster's Holiday* has very well laid-out annotation and pictures. This collection covers tracks from 1946 to 1988. Eartha Kitt's "material girl" ode, "Santa Baby," as well as its antithesis in the Miles Davis "Blue Xmas (To Whom It May Concern)," are here, as well as the hyper-scat singing of Leo Watson in Lambert, Hendricks & Ross. Both of the former are also on the CBS *Jingle Bell Jazz* collection, but they sound better here. As with the Jass and Savoy discs, Rhino has drawn from some performances of off-vinyl sources. All in all, this disc sounds cleaner and more detailed than those two releases, primarily due to the more recent vintage of recordings. –RC

In a Christmas Mood: Swing Era Big Band Celebration / MOBILE FIDELITY
Christmas big-band-style, performed by the Starlight Orchestra. The playing is very tight, professional, and true to style, but like Glenn Miller (to whom this collection tips its hat), *In a Christmas Mood* might be too much white bread for certain lovers of jazz. As with all Mobile Fidelity discs, the sound is impeccable. –RC

○ **It's Christmas Time Again / STAX**
Only the *Soul Christmas* collection of Atlantic beats this compilation of Christmas soul and blues. Rufus Thomas, Mack Rice, and Albert King sound downright salacious, while the Rance Allen Group sanctify "White Christmas" in a way Bing Crosby never could. The Emotions joyously set the record straight with "Black Christmas," and the Staples Singers sermonize in their special fashion with "Who Took

the Merry out of Christmas?" Isaac Hayes, the Temprees, and Little Johnny Taylor are also in great form here. –DMAC & RC

☆ **Jingle Bell Jazz / CBS**
Jingle Bell Jazz is a single-CD compilation of two previously released CBS holiday jazz albums, *Jingle Bell Jazz* (1974) and *God Rest Ye Merry Jazzmen* (1985). This disc is loaded with strong performances by Herbie Hancock, McCoy Tyner, Dexter Gordon, Wynton Marsalis, Duke Ellington, Lionel Hampton, Miles Davis, and more. –RICK CLARK, ROCK & ROLL DISC

○ **Lump of Coal / FIRST STRING**
These are old holiday standards performed in a punk/new-wave style. Fun and nicely done. –DAM

☆ **Merry Christmas Baby (King) / KING**
The original issue of this classic was subtitled *Intimate Christmas Music for Lovers*, and with five of the dozen tracks featuring the smoothest of the smooth vocalists, Charles Brown, that subtitle is appropriate. Other King artists represented here are bluesmen Lowell Fulson and Jimmy Witherspoon and Lloyd Glenn on "Sleighride" doing a swinging piano workout. Mabel Scott's original jumping "Boogie-Woogie Santa Claus" can be found here. –DMAC

☆ **Merry Christmas Baby (Paula) / PAULA**
R&B and blues from 15 artists on 23 songs including some re-recordings by Charles Brown and Lowell Fulson. Includes the riveting "Christmas in Vietnam" by deep-soul duo Johnny and Jon. –DMAC

☆ **Merry Christmas Baby: Romance & Reindeer / CAPITOL**
For that beneath-the-mistletoe mood-setter, this compilation of crooners and pop singers is hard to beat. You'll be put under the spell of sultry sounds from Julie London and Nancy Wilson or the silky soul of Nat King Cole. Dean Martin's dreamy "Winter Romance" is here, along with the seductive pairing of Johnny Mercer and Margaret Whiting on "Baby, It's Cold Outside." Twenty-five tracks from 1946-1968. –DMAC

○ **Mr. Santa's Boogie (Santa's Secret) / SAVOY JAZZ**
Jazz, blues, and early R&B: the Ravens, Johnny Otis, Little Esther Phillips, and Big Maybelle. Charlie Parker turns in a great "White Christmas," and Jimmy Butler dispenses with subtlety on "Trim Your Tree." –RICK CLARK, ROCK & ROLL DISC

Narada Christmas Collection / NARADA
Even though Narada is known as a new-age label, this collection maintains the musical attitude of that genre, while embracing the classier pieces of the Christmas holiday, i.e., "What Child Is This," "It Came Upon a Midnight Clear," "O Holy Night," and so forth. Nice, unobtrusive, polite — ultimately the kind of stuff that may teeter a little too close to easy listening for some listeners. –RC

Nipper's Greatest Christmas Hits / RCA
Nipper's Greatest Christmas Hits is a time-warp escape into the 50s world of the Ames Brothers, Roger Whittaker, Dinah Shore, Perry Como, and Arthur Fiedler. –RC

○ **Reggae Christmas / RAS**
Here are all your favorite carols with a Rastafarian twist. –ED

☆ **Rhythm & Blues Christmas / HOLLYWOOD**
Twenty tracks from the King vaults, duplicating much of *Merry Christmas Baby*. Two tracks that don't appear on that album, but found here, are scorchers by Hank Ballard and the Midnighters, "Santa Claus Is Coming," and "Christmas Time for Everybody But Me." The latter rivals the most testifying pleas of Ballard's King labelmate, James Brown. –DMAC

☆ **Rockin' Little Christmas / MCA**
A dozen sides of rock & roll, R&B, girl group (the 1964 "Love for Christmas" by the Gems), and more. "Mambo Santa Mambo" by the Enchanters and "Hey, Santa Claus" by the Moonglows are unbeatable fun. –DMAC

○ **Santa Claus Blues / JASS**
Santa Claus Blues, covering almost 50 years of jazz, blues, and swing, will appeal to archivists of those forms. Victoria Spivey wails on the "Christmas Morning Blues," and Duke Ellington's Hot Five (with Ozie Ware) get down with "Santa Claus, Bring My Man Back." Some of the other artists that shine on *Santa Claus Blues* are Fats Waller, Count Basie,

Woody Herman, Ella Fitzgerald, and Lionel Hampton. Many of these tracks have been taken from vinyl sources, but the transfers are generally very good. Nevertheless, the Louis Armstrong tracks can be found in much better shape on Rhino's *Hipster's Holiday* and MCA's *Traditional Classics*. Unfortunately, this compilation lacks decent liner notes, a feature that should be standard on releases like this. –RC

☆ **Soul Christmas / ATLANTIC**

This 1991 reissue includes eight of the original 11 tracks included on the Atco 1968 release (a rare album still worth seeking), with 11 more tracks added from the Atlantic vaults. Few, if any, Christmas compilations are more essential than this. Otis Redding's performances of "White Christmas" and "Merry Christmas, Baby" are alone worth the price of admission. Clarence Carter's funky "Back Door Santa" and Joe Tex's ballad "I'll Make Every Day Christmas (For My Woman)" are only two more tracks that make this collection an absolute must-have CD. –DMAC

○ **Traditional Christmas Classics / MCA**

Why the artists performing on this disc aren't listed on the outside of the package is a mystery. Mel Torme does "The Christmas Song," and there's Bing Crosby's "White Christmas."

Christmas." "Christmas in New Orleans" by Louis Armstrong is easily the highlight on this outing. Easy-listening kingpins Billy Vaughn, LeRoy Anderson, and Roger Williams are here doing their most famous Christmas music contributions. –RC

A Very Special Christmas / MOBILE FIDELITY

Many of the biggest artists over the last few years are given gold disc treatment on this very worthwhile endeavor, which helps fill the coffers of the Special Olympics with its proceeds. U2, the Pretenders, Bob Seger, Whitney Houston, Springsteen, Mellencamp, Run-D.M.C., Bon Jovi, Madonna, Sting, and more show their hearts are in the right place in performance and spirit on this excellent-sounding disc. –RC

☆ **Windham Hill - A Winter's Solstice / WINDHAM HILL**

Windham Hill has put out its successful *Winter Solstice Vols. 1 & 2* in a two-disc gift package. The atmospheric instrumental performances by Michael Hedges, Phillip Aaberg, William Ackerman, Mark Isham, Turtle Island String Quartet, and more of Windham Hill's best are quietly emotive meditations on the spirit of the season. Excellent sound and performances make this a disc worth having if you don't want the predictable menu of Christmas standards. –RICK CLARK, ROCK & ROLL DISC

CLASSICAL

Classical music is probably the most misunderstood of all musical categories, a result of its seeming remoteness — it is, after all, far older than any of the other major musical fields, dating back to the fifth and sixth centuries. But it is also easy to understand — even for the listener utterly unschooled in its forms — on its own terms, because it is the most formalistic of music. It is a music of precision and allows the listener a very clear look at both the intent and design of the composer.

Most of us were not raised in a "classical" environment of elegance, clarity, and symmetry. Thus classical music seems to run against the grain of the turmoil and randomness of 20th-century living. To appreciate classical music, you must first understand that most of the people for whom it was written — whether through the medieval church, the royal courts of Europe during the baroque era, or the concert halls of the 19th and early 20th centuries — had a good deal less sense of understanding of their world and the forces that shaped it (whether in science or history) than most of the people reading this page. This may even have been an advantage of sorts, for it allowed them to think of the world

as a relatively tight-knit, ordered place, in which their positions were secure . The music of the church, the court, and the concert hall served as affirmation or, at its best, both a challenge to and an exaltation of this order.

The classical repertoire can serve as a springboard to joying in the very act of being a thinking, sentient creature. Through the music, we gain a compelling perception of the world, much as through a great novel. The literary comparison is very apt, because many classical works contain literary, cultural, and biographical subtexts. Unlike a novel, however, classical music in performance has the virtue of motion and activity — it moves in real time, like a play or film.

If you're just starting out, you should be aware that you have a vast advantage over any previous generation in the availability of recordings (especially digital recordings and compact discs) and annotations for them. You have a better start at appreciating and understanding classical music, which can raise you to new heights of awareness about the magnificence of the creative mind.

— Bruce Eder

ISAAC ALBÉNIZ   1860-1909

Romantic. An important Spanish pianist and composer of solo piano music (*Suite Iberia,* 1906) and opera music (*Pepita Jimenez,* 1896). Albéniz was a precocious, self-taught, and instinctive musician, a stowaway who toured the world in his youth. He wrote with Moorish rhythms, an Andalusian sense of harmony, and the poetic height of southern Spanish music and dance forms. –BGT

☆ **Iberia (Suite for Piano - 4 books) / LONDON**
de Larrocha.

TOMASO ALBINONI   1671-1750

Baroque. Albinoni was a famed Italian violinist and prolific composer in all forms, including opera (*Rodrigo in Algeri,* 1702) and secular instrumental works (*Adagio for Organ & Strings*). His output includes more than 50 operas, most of which were produced in his native Venice. The ubiquitous "Adagio in g" was arranged, or rather reconstructed, for organ and strings by Remo Giazotto in the late 1940s from a six-bar fragment of music by Albinoni along principles the composer would have employed. –BGT

☆ **Adagio for Organ & Strings in g**
  (arranged by Remo Giazotto) / KOCH-SCHWANN
Werther/I Fiamminghi. Werther has interesting and radical ideas about this music and he is not afraid to express them, especially in the companion Vivaldi pieces. –PM

HUGO ALFVÉN   1872-1960

20th century. A Swedish composer of symphonic and choral program music, including *Midsummer Vigil* (1903) and *Shepherd-Girl's Dance* (1923), whose symphonies are among the earliest of the great modern Swedish symphonies and are renowned for their virtuosic orchestral writing and color. The second symphony and the *Midsommarvaka, "Swedish Rhapsody" no. 1,* established his reputation; the symphony is a serious academic work, but both pieces have great Nordic flavor and scene-painting. –BGT

○ **Midsommarvaka, "Swedish Rhapsody" no. 1 / BIS**
○ **The Mountain King / MUSICA SVECIAE**
Svetlanov/Swedish Royal SO. Three-act pantomime ballet. If you like *Peer Gynt,* chances are you'll like this very romantic and fantastic 78-minute ballet, filled with haunting and mysterious folk-like tunes and lush, bizarre orchestration. –PM

○ **Symphony no. 1 / BIS**
Järvi/Stockholm PO. Nature, especially the sea, inspires Alfvén's evocative (even erotic) tone poems and symphonies. If you're not in the mood, they can sound too much like wandering movie music. The technicolor performances by Järvi are a bit too bombastic, but they're all we have, and they have good sound. –PM

☆ **Symphony no. 2 / BIS**
Järvi/Stockholm PO.

○ **Symphony no. 3 / BIS**
Järvi/Stockholm PO.

○ **Symphony no. 4, op. 39;**
Legend of the Skerries, op. 20 / BIS
Järvi/Stockholm PO.

CHARLES-HENRI ALKAN   1813-1888

Romantic. A French composer of unusual piano music. –ED
○ **Preludes (25) for Piano, op. 31 / LONDON**
Mustonen (piano). Easily the best Alkan disc I have ever
heard! –PM
Preludes (25) for Piano, op. 31; Esquisses (6);
Barcarolle, op. 65; Toccatina, op. 75 / VALOIS
Sermet (piano). A more gentle and lyrical approach to these
preludes and the other pieces as well. –PM
○ **Various Chamber & Piano Works - Vol. 1 / ADDA**
Bou (piano), Mefano/Ensemble 2E 2M. Curious and unusual
doings by one of music's most enigmatic composers. Finally a
chance to hear something besides just his solo keyboard
works. –PM

GREGORIO ALLEGRI   1582-1652

Baroque, sacred choral. Allegri's *Miserere Mei, Deus* is a chant
for five-part a cappella choir in nine sections in the
falsobordone style, in which four of the voices sing highly
embellished and decorative passages, improvised by the
original choir and later written down to be preserved. Allegri
probably wrote only the basic chant. This work has been sung
in the Sistine Chapel during Holy Week every year since it was
composed, and the ornamentation was kept secret until
historian Charles Burney discovered the original manuscript
and reconstructed the complete work. *Miserere Mei, Deus* is
the work that Mozart transcribed from memory at age 14 — a
legendary feat in music history. –BGT
☆ **Miserere / GIMELL**
Phillips/The Tallis Scholars. This is a haunting piece, as good a
place as any to start with early vocal music. –PM

ANTON STEPANOVICH ARENSKY   1861-1906

Romantic. A Russian composer, prolific in many genres and
most successful in smaller forms, whose lyric style is akin to
Tchaikovsky's. His four suites for two pianos, subsequently
orchestrated, are his most popular works. –MKS
○ **Trio for Violin, Cello & Piano in d, op. 32 / CHANDOS**
Dubinsky, Turovsky, Edlina.

THOMAS AUGUSTINE ARNE   1710-1778

Baroque. This important British contemporary of Handel
composed songs and ballad operas such as *Dido and Aeneas*
(1734) and *Alfred* (1740) (which featured the song "Rule,
Brittania"). –MKS
○ **Songs / HYPERION**
Kirkby, Morton, Goodman/The Parley of Instruments.

JUAN CRISOSTOMO ARRIAGA   1806-1826

Classical. A Spanish composer who studied in Paris; an early
death prevented him from being a true rival to Mozart. –PM
○ **Quartets (3) for Strings / CRD**
Chilingirian Quartet.
○ **Symphony in d / ENSAYO**
Lopez-Cobos/English CO. May be hard to find but is worth
searching out. –PM

KURT ATTERBERG   1887-1974

Neo-classical. Extremely prolific and skilled Swedish
composer; also a music critic and one of the founders of the
Swedish Society of Composers (1924). Atterberg deserves to
be heard outside his native country more frequently. –MKS
○ **Symphony no. 1 in b, op. 3 (1912) / STERLING**
Westerberg/Swedish Royal SO.

○ **Symphony no. 4 in g, op. 14, "Sinfonia Piccola" (1919) /**
STERLING
Frykberg/Norrkoping SO.
○ **Symphony no. 6 in C, op. 31 / BIS**
Hirokami/Norrkoping SO. This isn't really going to rival the
Beecham and the Toscanini (they have better orchestras right
off), but it's a very lyrical performance of a very intersting
symphony in a very mellow sound. –PM

CARL PHILIPP EMANUEL BACH   1714-1788

Classical. The second son of J. S. Bach was a keyboardist, a
composer of keyboard sonatas, and author of the *Essay on the
True Art of Keyboard Playing*, whose output includes chamber
music, songs, and oratorios. His music marks the transition
from the baroque to the classical style and features minute
attention to the details of expression in the beautiful
"empfindsamer Stil" (sensitive style), which led toward a
more romantic style of music. –BGT
Cello Concertos nos. 1-3, H, 431, 435, 439,
WQ. 160, 167, 172 / HUNGAROTON
Mate (cello), Szuts/Concerto Armonico. A worthy rival to the
Bylsma. –PM
☆ **Concertos (3) for Cello & Orchestra / VIRGIN**
Bylsma, Leonhardt/Orchestra of the Age of Enlightenment.
○ **Concerto doppio for 2 Harpsichords & Orchestra in F /**
DGG
Staier, Hill, Goebel/Musica Antiqua Köln.
○ **Concerto for Harpsichord & Strings in A / PHILIPS**
Koopman/Amsterdam Baroque Orchestra.
○ **Flute & Piano Duets, Trios & Sonatas /**
CHANNEL CLASSICS
Hazelzet/Ogg.
○ **La Folia / HYPERION**
Purcell Quartet. One of the best of the *La Folia* series of
chamber works. –PM
○ **Orchestral Symphonies (5), "Berlin" / CAPRICCIO**
Haenchen/C. P. E. Bach CO.
○ **Orchestral Symphonies (6), "Hamburg Symphonies" /**
DGG
Pinnock/English Concert.
Orchestral Symphonies (6), "Hamburg Symphonies" /
OISEAU-LYRE
Hogwood/Academy of Ancient Music.
Orchestral Symphonies (6), "Hamburg Symphonies" /
DHM
Hangelbrock/Freiburg Baroque Orchestra.
○ **Quartets (3) for Flute, Viola, Harpsichord & Cello /**
EDITO CLASSICA
Les Adieux.
○ **Sonata for Flute unaccompanied in a, WQ. 132 / MD&G**
Meisen (flute). The most hauntingly played and recorded solo
flute recital I have ever heard. –PM

JOHANN CHRISTIAN BACH   1735-1782

Classical, gallant. The youngest son of J. S. Bach, a composer
of many symphonies, operas, chamber music, and solo
keyboard pieces in the gallant style. –ED
○ **Overtures / OISEAU-LYRE**
Hogwood/Academy of Ancient Music.
○ **Quintet for Flute, Oboe, Violin, Cello & Harpsichord, no.**
1, op. 22 / DGG
English Concert members.
○ **Symphonies (5) op. 3, nos. 1 & 2; op. 6, nos. 1 & 6;**
op. 9, no. 2 / HUNGAROTON
Concerto Armonico. Lively, well-proportioned, and reasonably
well-in-tune performances on original instruments of hard-
to-come-by music. –PM

JOHANN SEBASTIAN BACH   1685-1750

Baroque. The major works of this German composer and organist encompass every form save opera and oratorio and include the *Brandenburg Concertos* (1721), the *Musical Offering* (1747), and the *St. Matthew Passion* (1727). Bach was the perfecter of several centuries of the polyphonic style. He wedded an ironic sense of humor ("Coffee" and "Peasant" cantatas; English, Italian, and French suites) to a search for God in which his music transcended the harshness of life (the religious cantatas) — all expressed either through the most brilliantly flowing and complex cyclic compositional technique or through the heartfelt directness of the solo sustained line "Air on a G string" and the unaccompanied sonatas). –BGT

☆ **The Art of Fugue, BWV. 1080 / DGG**
Gilbert (harpsichord).

The Art of Fugue, BWV. 1080 / ARCHIV GALLERIA
Goebel/Musica Antiqua Köln. The only really convincing instrumental version of this piece I have heard yet. –PM

The Art of Fugue, BWV. 1080 / EDITO CLASSICA
Leonhardt, van Asperen (harpsichords).

☆ **Brandenburg Concerti / DGG**
Goebel/Musica Antiqua Köln. These are terrifically virtuosic performances at hair-raising tempos, and this is my personal version of choice. The CD also includes the best triple concerto I have ever heard. If you feel adventurous, go for it; if conservative, pick the Pinnock. Either way add Hogwood, and if possible, get all three. You'll then have the original-instrument bases all covered. –PM

Brandenburg Concertos / OISEAU-LYRE
Hogwood/Academy of Ancient Music. Hogwood uses Bach's first versions, and a lot of the movements are considerably shorter, resulting in a first CD of just 35 minutes. On the other hand, they are soulful and supremely well recorded, with plenty of bite. Highly recommended as a supplement. –PM

Brandenburg Concertos (1-3) / DGG
Pinnock/English Concert. A bit glib, mechanical, and uninspired, and sounds as if a mike were on every instrument, but still the standard performance. –PM

Brandenburg Concertos (4-6) / DGG
Pinnock/English Concert.

○ **Canons, BWV. 1072-1078, 1086 / DGG**
Musica Antiqua Köln.

○ **Cantata no. 1, "Wie schön leuchtet der Morgenstern" / TELDEC**
Esswood, Equiluz, Egmond, Harncourt/Vienna Concertus Musicus & Boys Choir.

○ **Cantata no. 51, "Jauchzet Gott in allen Landen" / KOCH-SCHWANN**
Baird (soprano), Thomas/American Bach Soloists. Compare this recording to the famous Kirkby performance and see what you think! –PM

○ **Cantata no. 54, "Widerstehe doch der Sünde" & other compositions / MERIDIAN**
Bowman, King/The King's Consort.

Cantata no. 54, "Widerstehe doch der Sünde" / HYPERION
Bowman, King/The King's Consort.

Cantata no. 54, "Widerstehe doch der Sünde" / KOCH-SCHWANN
Minter (counter-tenor), Thomas/American Bach Soloists. Fast but expressive original-instrument performance. –PM

○ **Cantata no. 55, "Ich armer Mensch, ich Sündenknecht" / KOCH-SCHWANN**
Thomas (tenor)/American Bach Soloists.

○ **Cantata no. 78, "Jesu, der du meine Seele" / HARMONIA MUNDI**
Herreweghe/La Chapelle Royale.

○ **Cantata no. 80, "Ein feste Burg ist unser Gott" / HARMONIA MUNDI**
Schlick, Lasna, Crook, Herreweghe/La Chapelle Royale.

○ **Cantata no. 82, "Ich habe genug" / KOCH-SCHWANN**
Sharp (bass), Thomas/American Bach Soloists.

○ **Cantata no. 106, "Gottes Zeit ist die allerbeste Zeit" / RICERCAR**
Bowman (alto), Ricercar Consort, etc.

○ **Cantata no. 110, "Unser Mund sei voll Lachens" / TELDEC**
Vienna Concentus Musicus, Tölz Boys' Choir. Thie recording also includes cantatas 107, 108, and 109. *Cantata no. 110* is one of the most beautiful of all. –JME

○ **Cantata no. 211, "Schweigt stille, plaudert nicht" / MERIDIAN**
Dawson, Robertson, Adler/The Friends of Apollo.

○ **Chorale Preludes (46), BWV. 599-644 / PHILIPS**
Chorzempa (organ).

○ **Christmas Oratorio, BWV. 248 / VIRGIN**
Schlick, Chance, Crook, Kooy, Herreweghe/Ghent Collegium Vocale Orchestra & Chorus.

☆ **Chromatic Fantasy and Fugue for Harpsichord in d, BWV. 903 / SUPRAPHON**
Moravec (piano). This is a classic on piano. –PM

Chromatic Fantasy and Fugue for Harpsichord in d, BWV. 903 / VIRGIN
Cole (harpsichord).

Chromatic Fantasy and Fugue for Harpsichord in d, BWV. 903 / DGG
Pinnock (harpsichord).

○ **Concerto for Flute, Violin, Harpsichords & Strings in a, BWV. 1044 / DGG**
Goebel/Musica Antiqua Köln.

○ **Concertos (16) for Harpsichord, BWV. 972-987 / PIERRE VERANY**
Brosse (organ - BWV. 972). Terrific organ and sound; fine playing. –PM

○ **Concertos for Harpsichord & Orchestra no. 1 in D / JECKLIN**
Lipatti.

Concertos for Harpsichord & Orchestra no. 1 in D / MELODRAM
Richter (piano), Talich/Czech PO.

○ **Concertos for Harpsichord & Orchestra nos. 2-7 / TELDEC**
Leonhardt (harpsichord and conductor)/Leonhardt Consort.

○ **Concertos (2) for Three Harpsichords & Strings, BWV. 1063, 1064; Concerto for Four Harpsichords & Strings in a, BWV. 1065 / OISEAU-LYRE**
Moroney, Rousset, Tilney (harpsichords), Hogwood/Academy of Ancient Music. Vibrant performances, less uptight and mechanical than the Pinnock recording. –PM

○ **Concertos for Oboe, BWV. 1052, 1055, 1059; Sinfonias BWV. 12, 21, 249 / NOVALIS**
Indermuehle (oboe), Preston/English CO. One terrific oboe CD, with plenty of ornamentation and accompaniments to set your feet tapping. This one has soul! –PM

○ **Concertos (7) for Piano & Orchestra, S. 1052-1058 / LONDON**
Schiff (piano)/Chamber Orchestra of Europe. If you want the seven solo concertos played on piano, you can't do better than this set, which is imaginatively played and well recorded. One of Schiff's best. –PM

○ **Concertos for solo Organ nos. 1-5, BWV. 592-597 / DGG**
Preston (organ).

☆ **Concertos (2) for Violin & Orchestra, BWV. 1041-1042 / DGG**
Standage (violin), Pinnock/English Consort.

Concertos (2) for Violin & Orchestra, BWV. 1041-1042 / OISEAU-LYRE
Schröder (violin), Hogwood/Academy of Ancient Music.

○ **Concertos (3) for Two Harpsichords & Orchestra, BWV. 1060-1062 / TELDEC**
Leonhardt/Leonhardt Consort.

○ **English Suites for Harpsichord nos. 1-6, BWV. 806-811 / HARMONIA MUNDI**
Gilbert (harpsichord). Not one of Gilbert's best efforts (the harpsichord and/or sound is a bit jangly), but it's all we have right now. –PM

English Suites for Harpsichord nos. 1-6, BWV. 806-811 / LONDON
Schiff (piano). To me these performances are very mannered, but they are well played and well recorded. If you must have them on piano, go for them. –PM

English Suites for Harpsichord nos. 2 & 3, BWV. 807-808 DGG
Pogorelich (piano). What is one to say about the self-proclaimed "Greatest Piano Player in the World?" Grin and bear it, I guess, because he *is* very good, and he reveals something new about every piece he plays. –PM

○ **Fantasias for Harpsichord, BWV. 904 / DGG**
Gilbert.

○ **French Suites for Harpsichord nos. 1-6, BWV. 812-817 / OISEAU-LYRE**
Hogwood (harpsichord). Why doesn't Hogwood make more harpsichord recordings? In fact, why is this his only one? –PM

French Suites for Harpsichord nos. 1-6, BWV. 812-817 / FHM
Gilbert (harpsichord). Man, this is a tough choice: Hogwood is more rugged and "masculine," Gilbert more sensual and beautiful. –PM

☆ **Goldberg Variations for Harpsichord, BWV. 988 / VIRGIN**
Cole (harpsichord). Combines the drive of Pinnock, the elegance of Leonhardt, and the sensuality of Jarrett with terrific ornamentation to give us possibly the best *Goldberg* ever and my current first choice. Beautiful sound. –PM

Goldberg Variations for Harpsichord, BWV. 988 / TELDEC
Leonhardt (harpsichord). His earlier version is all askew, his later one too bland. The sound is a bit dated and the harpsichord a bit out of tune at times, but this is the most interesting harpsichord version ever recorded. –PM

Goldberg Variations for Harpsichord, BWV. 988 / DGG
Pinnock (harpsichord). Less elegant than Leonhardt, Pinnock is more fiery and down-to-earth. –PM

Goldberg Variations for Harpsichord, BWV. 988 / ECM
Jarrett (harpsichord). Slow but very hypnotic, with beautiful sound. –PM

Goldberg Variations for Harpsichord, BWV. 988 / ERATO
Barenboim (piano). The best piano version yet. Very imaginative, spontaneous, and technically secure, especially for a live performance. –PM

☆ **Inventions (2- & 3-Part) for Harpsichord, BWV. 772-801 / DGG**
Gilbert.

☆ **Lute Works, BWV. 995-1000, 1006 (complete) / DHM**
Junghänel (lute). A clear first choice on CD because of the remarkable poise and line and because of the striking beauty and sensuality of the sound. –PM

☆ **Magnificat in D, BWV. 243 / ANGEL**
Marriner/ASFM with choir and soloists. Mainly because of its superior solo singing, I'll have to give the new Marriner the nod, but I do miss the old instruments of the other four. –PM

Magnificat in D, BWV. 243 / CHANDOS
Kirkby, Bonner, Chance, Ainsley, Varcoe, Hickox/Collegium Musicum 90. Hickox is used to conducting larger forces,

which shows in the tightness not quite achieved in the other original instrument performances. –PM

Magnificat in D, BWV. 243 / VIRGIN
Reyghere, Jacobs, Pregardien, Lika, Kuijken/La Petite Band. A lot of interesting moments but without the command of the Hickox, and not quite such good singing. –PM

Magnificat in D, BWV. 243 / OISEAU-LYRE
Nelson, Kirkby, Watkinson, Elliott, Thomas, Preston/Academy of Ancient Music.

☆ **Mass in b, BWV. 232 / PHILIPS**
Smith, Chance, van der Meel, van der Kamp, Brüggen/Orchestra of the 18th Century, Netherlands Chamber Choir. A tougher, more aggressive live performance than the smoother, more religious, and more conservative Leonhardt approach. –PM

Mass in b, BWV. 232 / EDITO CLASSICA
Leonhardt/La Petite Band.

○ **Masses (4), "Lutheran Masses," BWV. 233-236 / VIRGIN**
Herreweghe/Ghent Collegium Vocale Orchestra & Choir. Very smooth and rounded (and very beautiful) French-style performances. Not quite aggressive enough for my taste and not very rhythmic, but the beauty of the singing carries it through, and it's by far the best version we have. –PM

○ **Motets (6) / TELDEC**
Harnoncourt/Stockholm Bach Choir, Concentus Musicus Wien. No need for instruments to double the voices as they do here, but this is such a wonderful choir (which seldom records) that these albums just have to be recommended. –PM

Motets (6) / DHM
Kammler/Augsburg Cathedral Boys Choir. These joyous works, almost lost to us forever, show Bach's polyphonic techniques in the most exposed and direct manner. –BGT

Motets (6) nos. 1, 3, 4, 6 / ASV
Grier/Christ Church Cathedral Choir. These motets are very pure and ethereal. –PM

Music Transcribed for Lute / DHM
Smith (lute). A more beautiful and elegantly played lute CD you are not likely to find. The sound is as good as it gets for the lute. –PM

☆ **A Musical Offering, BWV. 1079 / DGG**
Musica Antiqua Köln. One of Bach's last works — profound and beautiful beyond words. Ranks with the *Art of the Fugue*. –JME

A Musical Offering, BWV. 1079 / PHILIPS
Marriner/ASMF.

○ **Organ Works / MOTETTE**
Böhme (organ). Very impressive sound. Böhme is not quite in the league of the other Bach organists mentioned here, but he plays in a style I very much like and one I would call "informed baroque romantic." If only his fingers and feet were just a bit fleeter. –PM

○ **Organ Works (complete) - Vol. 5 / NOVALIS**
Koopman (organ). Koopman uses more radical, more "authentic" accentuation and phrasing than Preston (or anyone else for that matter), and his organ performances are very dramatic but not at all romanticized. –PM

○ **Organ Works (including Toccata & Fugue in d, BWV. 565) / NOVALIS**
Koopman (organ). This is highly vigorous, nonsentimental playing. –PM

○ **Organ Works (various) / NOVALIS**
Koopman.

○ **Organ Works - Vol. 1 / DHM**
Vogel (organ). Outstanding fingerwork and registration but a little too laid back and lacking in brilliance for an ultimate recommendation. –PM

○ **Partita for Flute unaccompanied in a, BWV. 1013 / MD&G**
Meisen.

Partita for Flute unaccompanied in a, BWV. 1013 / DHM
Kuijken.

○ **Partitas (6) for Harpsichord, BWV. 825-830 / DGG**
Pinnock (harpsichord). Nonpareil. It's a shame Pinnock (and Hogwood too) doesn't record more solo harpsichord literature. –PM

Partita for Harpsichord no. 4, BWV. 828; Toccatas 1 & 3, BWV. 910 & 912; Sonata for Harpsichord in d, BWV. 964 / KOCH-SCHWANN
Mattax.

○ **Sonatas (7) for Flute & Harpsichord, BWV. 1030, 1032, 1034, 1035 / DHM**
B. Kuijken, W. Kuijken, Leonhardt.

Sonatas (7) for Flute & Harpsichord, BWV. 1030-1035, 1020 / HARMONIA MUNDI
See (baroque flute), Moroney (harpsichord), Springfels (viola da gamba). A bit new-agey and "pretty," this is still a fine set. A little more guts might have helped –PM

○ **Sonatas for Piano, BWV. 963, 964, 966; Capriccio, BWV. 993; 4 Duets, BWV. 802-805; Italian Concerto for Harpsichord in f, BVW. 971 / STRADIVARIUS**
Richter (piano). Clean and relaxed piano playing. Richter's latest CD. –PM

○ **Sonatas (3) for Viola da Gamba & Harpsichord, BWV. 1027-1029 / EDITO CLASSICA**
Kuijken, Leonhardt

Sonatas (3) for Viola da Gamba & Organ, BWV. 1027-1029 / SONY
Bylsma, van Asperen. The use of the organ instead of harpsichord gives these wonderful works a very different feel, the legato of the organ having a much more soothing effect than the staccato harpsichord, which has a more dynamic effect. Both these versions are superlative, with Bylsma ever the virtuoso and Kuijken possibly a bit more soulful. –PM

○ **Sonatas (6) for Violin & Harpsichord, BWV. 1014-1019 / VIRGIN**
Csaba, Kocsis (pianos), Holloway, Moroney, Sheppard (cellos). The choice here is very tough: I love the stylishness of Kuijken/Leonhardt (they were the standard-bearers for years), the incisiveness of Huggett/Koopman, and the more laidback, sensual approach of Holloway/Moroney. But be warned: Holloway's less-than-perfect intonation has been known to drive listeners up a wall. –PM

Sonatas (6) for Violin & Harpsichord, BWV. 1014-1019 / PHILIPS
Huggett, Koopman (period instruments).

Sonatas (6) for Violin & Harpsichord, BWV. 1014-1019 / EDITO CLASSICA
Kuijken, Leonhardt.

☆ **Sonatas (3) & Partitas (3) for Violin unaccompanied, BWV. 1001-1006 / DHM**
Kuijken (violin). The premiere "baroque violin" performance, this is easily the finest recording I have ever heard of these pieces: it stands up to repeated hearings as well as to some of my favorite recordings of other works (like the recording of Vivaldi's *Four Seasons* by the Drottningholm Ensemble). The rhythmic verve and the special sonorities of the violin, helped by superb recording, are outstanding. –PM

Sonatas (3) & Partitas (3) for Violin unaccompanied, BWV. 1001-1006 / CAMERATA
Shiokawa (violin). Playing with a good deal of reticence and a lot less vibrato than usual, Shiokaw produces a pure, soaring tone on her beautiful Stradivari Emperor violin. More and more I am drawn to her non-show-off approach. This has the best sound of any of the current sets and is now my preferred non-baroque performance. –PM

Sonatas (3) & Partitas (3) for Violin unaccompanied, BWV. 1001-1006 / EDELWEISS
Chumachenco (violin). Plain and unadorned but with passion and a lot less vibrato, not so "interpreted" as Milstein. –PM

Sonatas (3) & Partitas (3) for Violin unaccompanied, BWV. 1001-1006 / DGG
Milstein (violin). Probably the best of the "older" school of violin playing. –PM

Sonatas for Violin unaccompanied nos. 1 & 3; Suite for Cello no. 6 / DHM
Leonhardt (harpsichord). Convincing arrangements brilliantly recorded. –PM

○ **St. John Passion / EDITO CLASSICA**
Kuijken/La Petite Bande. From the opening chorus, this piece is just what its title promises — a passion. A great work. –JME

○ **St. Matthew Passion / EDITO CLASSICA**
Leonhardt/La Petite Bande, Tolz Boys Choir. One of Bach's great vocal statements. –JME

☆ **St. Matthew Passion / PHILIPS**
Jochum/Royal Concertgebouw Orchestra, Netherlands Radio Choir, Boys Choir of St. Willibord's Church. Like the "Crucifixus" of the *Mass in b*, this *Passion* shares a technique invented by Bach — slowly amassing dissonances, which create emotional tension through small chromatic movements (a sound not explored again until the second half of the 20th century). –BGT

☆ **Suites (4) for Orchestra, BWV. 1066-1069 / HYPERION**
Goodman/The Brandenburg Consort. New group, old conductor. These are happy performances and well played, with nice sound and ornamentation. The added sinfonias are tasty fillers. –PM

Suites (4) for Orchestra, BWV. 1066-1069 / OISEAU-LYRE
Hogwood/Academy of Ancient Music.

☆ **Suites (6) for unaccompanied Cello, BWV. 1007-1012 / CHANNEL CLASSICS**
Wispelway (cello). With its big sound, this is haunting and very sensual. –PM

Suites (6) for unaccompanied Cello, BWV. 1007-1012 / PRO ARTE
Bylsma (cello). More "intellectual" than Wispelway, with bite to match the approach. –PM

Suites (6) for unaccompanied Cello, BWV. 1007-1012 / CBS
Ma (cello). Seamless and beautiful, but he doesn't dig into the music as much as Schiff or Bylsma or Wispelway. –PM

Suites (6) for unaccompanied Cello, BWV. 1007-1012 / ANGEL
Casals (cello). The sentiment is there, but the sound and old-fashioned performances are decided drawbacks. –PM

○ **Toccatas (7) for Harpsichord, BWV. 912-914, 916 / DGG**
Gilbert.

○ **Toccata & Fugue for Organ in d, BWV. 565 / DGG**
Preston (organ). These are fast and virtuosic, nonromantic performances on a now-modern tracker organ, with some very imaginative and no-nonsense phrasing. I find them very exciting, the way Bach should be played on nonhistorical instruments, but I have to admit they are a bit breathless. –PM

Toccata & Fugue for Organ in d, BWV. 565 / NOVALIS
Koopman.

Toccata & Fugue for Organ in d, BWV. 565 / DGG
Koopman.

☆ **Trio Sonatas (6) for Organ, BWV. 525-530 / PHILIPS**
Chorzempa. These are some of the most sublime of Bach's keyboard works. –JME

Trio Sonatas (6) for Organ, BWV. 525-530 / FHM
Butt (organ). A very jazzy version, all on one 75-minute CD, and one that will appeal to many; ultimately, however, I find it a bit too jazzy and wearing, and a bit superficial. Stick with

the more traditional Chorzempa, in beautiful sound and with a great organ. –PM

○ **Various Harpsichord Works / PHILIPS**
Leonhardt.

☆ **The Well-Tempered Clavier [2 books], BWV. 846-893 / DGG**
Gilbert (harpsichord). If you like the sound of harpsichord, no need to look further. –PM

The Well-Tempered Clavier (Book 1) / ECM
Jarrett (piano). Jarrett is terrific in Book 1 on piano, but he obviously came to like the sound of the harpsichord and felt it more appropriate when doing Book 2 and the *Goldbergs*. I agree but have to admit having a piano version of Book 2 as good as his Book 1 would have been something. –PM

The Well-Tempered Clavier (Book 1) / LONDON
Schiff (piano).

The Well-Tempered Clavier (Book 2) / ECM
Jarrett (harpsichord). Most listeners would have preferred that he stick with the piano, but you have to respect Jarrett's decision. –PM

○ **The Well-Tempered Clavier (complete) / CBS**
Gould (piano). Gould's performances, for all their idiosyncrasies, show a thoughtful presentation that is at all times cognizant of the structure and tonal implications of each piece. A great scholar and musician at work. –MKS

MILY BALAKIREV   1837-1910

Romantic, nationalist. A Russian composer of vocal, piano, and orchestral music, and mentor to many important Russian composers of the time. Balakirev was one of the group of Russian nationalist composers known as "The Mighty Five." –BGT

○ **Symphony no. 1 in C / ANGEL**
Beecham/Royal PO. The classic early-stereo account. –PM
Symphony no. 1 in C / HYPERION
Evgeni Svetlanov/USSR SO. Not quite up to the Beecham, but a very good modern alternative and a more sensitive performance than we are used to from Svetlanov. –PM

CLAUDE BALLIF   bb 19

Modern. A French avant-garde composer of metatonal music who studied with Messiaen. –ED

○ **A Cor et a Cri, for Orchestra, op. 39 (1962); String Quartet no. 3, op. 30 (1959); Concerto "Haut les Reves," for Violin, op. 49 / ADDA**
Bonaldi (violin), Vis/Orchestre National, Kronos Quartet. Ballif's music isn't particularly original but it is very representative of the French avant-garde, and this is a nice selection of it. –PM

SAMUEL BARBER   1910-1981

Neo-romantic. An American singer and composer of modern, accessible, neo-romantic symphonies and chamber music, including *The School for Scandal* (1933), *String Quartet* (1936), and *Adagio for Strings* (1936). Barber's music has integrity, retaining a noble and lyrical sound of its own through changing fashions and never sounding dated. –BGT

☆ **Adagio for Strings (arranged from the *String Quartet, op. 11*) / DGG**
Bernstein/LAPO.

Adagio for Strings (arranged from the *String Quartet, op. 11*) / TELDEC
Slatkin/St. Louis SO.

○ **Concerto for Piano & Orchestra, op. 38 / RCA**
An excellent performance of this important modern piano concerto. –MKS

○ **Hermit Songs / SONY**
Price, Barber. An important reissue of this significant song cycle, this is all the more interesting because the beauty of

Price's voice is enhanced by the accompaniment of the composer. –MKS

○ **Knoxville, Summer of 1915 (words by James Agee) / SONY**
Steber, Strickland/Dumbarton Oaks CO. A lyrical work for soprano and orchestra. The recording also contains *Dover Beach*, *Hermit Songs*, and *Andromache's Farewell*. –BGT

○ **Symphony no. 1 in One Movement, op. 9 / CHANDOS**
Järvi/Detroit SO.

○ **Three Essays for Orchestra / CHANDOS**
Järvi/Detroit SO.

BÉLA BARTOK   1881-1945

20th century, nationalist. An Hungarian composer and musicologist who transcribed Hungarian folk melodies and composed ballet, opera, orchestral, and chamber music, including *Dance Suite* (1923), *Music for Two Pianos & Percussion* 1937), *Mikrokosmos, 6 Books* (1926-39), and *Concerto for Orchestra* (1943). Bartók was a 20th-century original who showed how superb intellectual effort (he invented a composition system using Golden Sections, the Fibonnacci series, and quasi-serial techniques) and great passion (as can be seen in his in-depth studies of the Hungarian folk music, the "night music" expressionist social tension between the wars, and his own life as a forced émigré) can combine to make great art. –BGT

○ **Allegro Barbaro, for Piano / HUNGARATON**
Ranki.

○ **Bluebeard's Castle (1-act opera), op. 11 / LONDON**
Ludwig, Berry, Kertesz/London SO. His stunning opera. –JME

☆ **Concerto for Orchestra / CBS**
Boulez/NYPO. The classic more modern performance (i.e., since Reiner). The NYPO never sounded this good again. –PM

Concerto for Orchestra / RCA
Reiner/Chicago SO. The classic one. Rivaled (by Boulez especially), but never surpassed and unlikely to be so. –PM

Concerto for Orchestra / MERCURY
Dorati/London SO. A special feeling for Bartók's rhythms and tone color. This just sounds more Hungarian to me than the others. –PM

Concerto for Orchestra / VIRGIN
Iwaki/Melbourne SO. A real sleeper. This recording has plenty of profile and is very well played and recorded. –PM

○ **Concerto for Piano no. 1 / SONY**
Serkin (piano), Szell/Columbia SO. Cutting and demonic, this piece is performed by the two razor-sharp intellects of Serkin and Szell — what a match. –PM

○ **Concerto for Piano no. 3 / HUNGARATON**
Ranki, Ferencik/Hungarian State Orchestra.

Concerto for Piano no. 3 / DGG
Anda/Fricasy.

○ **Concerto for Piano & Orchestra no. 1 / DGG**
Pollini, Abbado/Chicago SO. Better played than the classic Serkin/Szell (now back in limited-edition circulation) but not nearly so demonic, especially in the slow "night music" movement. –PM

☆ **Concerto for Piano & Orchestra no. 2 / DGG**
Anda, Fricsay/Berlin RSO. Not so virtuosic as it might be, but the authentic Hungarian sound is there in spades. –PM

○ **Divertimento / HUNGARATON**
Rolla/Liszt CO.

○ **Divertimento for String Orchestra / CAPRICCIO**
Végh/Camerta Academica des Mozarteums Salzburg. Big, warmhearted, and very romantic. It wouldn't be my first choice but may be just the ticket for those wanting to get into Bartók. A unique approach. –PM

Divertimento for String Orchestra / DGG
Orpheus CO.

Divertimento for String Orchestra / HUNGARATON

Middle Ages 1100 – 1450

Monophonic music (i.e., music in which only one tune, or line, is being played by all the musicians), polyphonic music (many lines being played at once, independent but equal), primarily vocal and sacred.

Forms:
Motet, solo song, mass

Major works:
de Machaut's *Messe de Nostre Dame*, Dufay's chansons

Composers:
Perotin (ca. 1155-1250)
Guillaume de Machaut (ca. 1300-1377)
John Dunstable (ca. 1380-1453)
Guillaume Dufay (ca. 1400-1474)
Johannes Okeghem(1410-1497)

Renaissance 1450 – 1600

Polyphonic music, primarily vocal and sacred, although instrumental and secular music start to become important.

Forms:
Madrigal, mass, chanson, dance, anthem, fantasia, variations

Major works:
Palestrina's *Missa Papae Marcelli*, Dowland's lute music, Lassus's motets, Morley's madrigals

Composers:
Josquin des Prez (ca. 1440-1521)
Andrea Gabrieli (ca. 1510-1586)
Giovanni Palestrina (ca. 1525-1594)
Orlandus Lassus (1532-1584)
William Byrd (1543-1623)
Tomas Luis de Victoria (ca. 1549-1611)
Giovanni Gabrieli (ca. 1554-1612)
Don Carlo Gesualdo (ca. 1560-1613)
John Dowland (1563-1626)
Orlando Gibbons (1583-1625)

Baroque 1600 – 1750

Strong, rhythmic, highly ornamental instrumental and vocal music, both sacred and secular. Primarily polyphonic, but also the start of music in which one line is more important than the others played at the same time, which accompany it rather than being played independently. First appearance of opera as a form.

Forms:
Opera, cantata, oratorio, concerto grosso, solo concerto, fugue, trio sonata, suite, prelude, chorale

Major works:
Monteverdi's *Orfeo*; J. S. Bach's *Brandenburg Concertos*, *St. Matthew Passion*, *Well-Tempered Clavier*; Handel's *Messiah* and concerti grossi; Vivaldi's concertos

Composers:
Claudio Monteverdi (1567-1643)
Heinrich Schütz (1585-1672)
Dietrich Buxtehude (1637-1707)
Arcangelo Corelli (1653-1713)
Henry Purcell (1659-1695)
Alessandro Scarlatti (1660-1725)
François Couperin ("The Great") (1668-1733)
Antonio Vivaldi (1678-1741)
Jean Phillipe Rameau (1683-1764)
J. S. Bach (1685-1750)
George Frideric Handel (1685-1760)
Domenico Scarlatti (1685-1757)
Johann Pachelbel (1653-1706)
Giovanni Battista Pergolesi (1710-1736)

Classical era 1750 – 1827

Music, primarily instrumental (although opera begins to come into its own), of many types (dominated by the sonata form) and textures, marked by clarity, balance, and restraint. Melody with harmonic accompaniment becomes predominant.

Forms:
Sonata, concerto, symphony, string quartet, opera

Major works:
Mozart's *Don Giovanni*, "Jupiter" symphony, "Prussian" string quartets; Haydn's symphony no. 88, *Creation*

Composers:
C. P. E. Bach (1714-1788)
Franz Joseph Haydn (1732-1809)
Wolfgang Amadeus Mozart (1756-1791)
Ludwig van Beethoven (1770-1729)

Romantic era 1827 – 1890

Very expressive music (primarily instrumental, with opera becoming very important) in which melody is the dominant feature, with full-bodied harmonies.

Forms:
Lieder, sonata, symphony, symphonic tone poem, opera, short forms such as nocturne and intermezzo

Major works:
Wagner's *Tristan und Isolde*, Beethoven's ninth symphony, Schubert's lieder, Tchaikovsky's "Pathétique" symphony, Bizet's *Carmen*, Verdi's *Otello*

Composers:
Franz Schubert (1797-1828)
Hector Berlioz (1803-1869)
Fredric Chopin (1810-1849)
Robert Schumann (1810-1856)
Franz Liszt (1811-1886)
Giuseppe Verdi (1813-1901)
Richard Wagner (1813-1883)
Johannes Brahms (1833-1897)
Piotr Ilyich Tchaikovsky (1840-1893)
Antonín Dvorák (1841-1904)
Edvard Grieg (1843-1907)
Giacomo Puccini (1858-1924)
Gustav Mahler (1860-1911)

Contemporary era 1890 – present

Highly eclectic music of various forms and types (melodic and otherwise), such as impressionism, nationalism, neo-classicism. Traditional structures and forms are broken up and recast using influences from non-Western music, technology, and abstract ideas.

Forms:
Symphony, concerto, sonata, opera, many others.

Major works:
Stravinsky's *Sacre du Printemps*, Bartók's quartets, Berg's *Lulu*, Webern's *Five Pieces for Orchestra*

Composers:
Claude Debussy (1862-1918)
Arnold Schoenberg 1874-1951)
Maurice Ravel (1875-1937)
Béla Bartók (1881-1945)
Igor Stravinsky (1882-1971)
Anton Webern (1883-1945)
Alban Berg (1885-1935)
Sergei Prokofiev (1891-1953)
Aaron Copland (1900-1990)
John Cage (b. 1912-1992)
Benjamin Britten (1913-1976)

Rolla/Liszt CO.

○ **Elegies (2) for Piano, op. 8b / SAPHIR**
Keller (piano). I love the depth of Keller's playing and his ability to make the pieces seem avant-garde and traditional at the same time. –PM

○ **Hungarian Sketches; Romanian Dances / MERCURY**
Dorati/Minneapolis SO.

☆ **The Miraculous Mandarin (ballet) / DGG**
Abbado/London SO. Although a bit too elegant and toned-down and not so primitive as some, this is nevertheless a very well organized, powerful, and well played performance of one of the most barbaric and fascinating scores of the century. I once knew a mental patient who listened to this piece over and over again — up to 20 times — nothing else. –PM

The Miraculous Mandarin (ballet) / VIRGIN
Iwaki/Melbourne SO. Not so sophisticated as Abbado, but rawer in emotion. –PM

The Miraculous Mandarin (ballet) / LONDON
Dorati/Detroit SO. As always, a special feel for Hungarian rhythms and tone coloring. –PM

○ **Music for Strings, Percussion & Celesta (1936) / LONDON**
Dorati/Detroit SO. The first movement is a completely new idea about the fugue form. It slowly and mysteriously winds along new tonal principles until a place of revelation is reached with the entrance of the strange harp figure. A breakthrough composition. It is on the same CD as *The Miraculous Mandarin*. –BGT

○ **Out of Doors (suite); Improvisations; Sonata (1926) / CBS**
Perahia.

☆ **Quartets (6) for Strings / DGG**
Emerson Quartet. Wins by default, since all the great performances of these classics (Juilliard, Eder, Hungarian) are out of print. –PM

○ **Sonata for Violin & Piano no. 1 in E / DGG**
Kremer, Argerich. Better played than the Smirnov below, but not with quite the same intensity –PM

○ **Sonata for Violin & Piano no. 2 in D; Sonata for Violin & Piano no. 1 in E / HUNGARATON**
Kremer, Smirnov. This has both sonatas on one CD and is the only performance that has the harshness and brutality these works deserve and need. –PM

○ **Sonata for 2 Pianos & Percussion / HUNGARATON**
Kocsis, Ranki, Cser, Racz. Very spontaneous and Hungarian-sounding, and with terrific live sound. –PM

ARNOLD BAX   1883-1953

20th century. British composer of modern classical music, characterized by chromatic harmonies, whose works encompass all forms except opera and theatre music; known for tone poems (*Tintagel* (1919)) and *Sonata for Piano no. 2* (1919). –ED

○ **The Garden of Fand (symphonic poem) / CHANDOS**
Thomson/Ulster Orchestra. Lush English countryside romanticism. –PM

LUDWIG VAN BEETHOVEN   1770-1827

Classical/romantic. Beethoven's symphonies, quartets, concertos, and piano sonatas are significant advances in their respective genres, revealing a passion marking the move from the classical to the romantic period. Naturally democratic, Beethoven strove to express his ideal of a world of freedom and equality. He rose from an adverse childhood in Germany, making his way on charm and self-education (especially shown in his opera *Fidelio* and the famous *Symphony no. 9*), sometimes masking frustration with angry behavior. Beethoven was destined to become the "inventor" of "modern music," composing from a "seed" or "germ" idea rather than a

full melody and treating rhythm in new ways (for example, the phase variations in the third symphony). –BGT

○ **Ah! Perfido (scene & aria), for Soprano & Orchestra, op. 65 / DGG**
Studer (soprano), Abbado/Berlin PO. Brilliant! With some beautiful clarinet playing. –PM

○ **Bagatelle, "Für Elise" / PHILIPS**
Brendel.

○ **Bagatelles for Piano, op. 119 / CBS**
Serkin.

○ **Bagatelles for Piano, op. 126 / VICTORIA LTD**
Smebye.

○ **Concertos (5) for Piano & Orchestra (complete) / DGG**
Pollini, Jochum, Böhm/Vienna PO.

Concertos (5) for Piano & Orchestra (complete) / SONY
Fleisher, Szell/Cleveland Orchestra. This is powerful, classical, and romantic all at once: The American standard-bearer for years. –PM

Concertos (5) for Piano & Orchestra (complete) / ANGEL
Tan (fortepiano), Norrington/London Classical Players.

○ **Concerto for Piano & Orchestra no. 1 in C, op. 15 / DGG**
Kempff, Leitner/Berlin PO. Kempff was the thinking person's pianist, and all five of his concertos from the early 60s can be highly recommended. –PM

Concerto for Piano & Orchestra no. 1 in C, op. 15 / DGG
Michelangeli, Giulini/Vienna SO.

Concerto for Piano & Orchestra no. 1 in C, op. 15 / RCA
Richter, Munch/Boston SO.

○ **Concerto for Piano & Orchestra no. 2 in B-flat, op. 19 / DGG**
Kempff, Leitner/Berlin PO.

○ **Concerto for Piano & Orchestra no. 3 in c, op. 37 / ANGEL**
Richter, Muti/PO.

Concerto for Piano & Orchestra no. 3 in c, op. 37 / DGG
Kempff, Leitner/Berlin PO.

○ **Concerto for Piano & Orchestra no. 4 in G, op. 58 / DGG**
Kempff, Leitner/Berlin PO.

☆ **Concerto for Piano & Orchestra no. 5 in E-flat, op. 73, "Emperor" / DGG**
Michelangeli, Giulini/Vienna SO.

Concerto for Piano & Orchestra no. 5 in E-flat, op. 73, "Emperor" / DGG
Kempff, Leitner/Berlin PO.

○ **Concerto for Violin, Cello, Piano & Orchestra in C, op. 56 / ANGEL**
Oistrakh, Rostropovich, Richter, Karajan/Berlin PO. With giants like these, all at the top of their powers, no one's likely to touch this performance ever. –PM

☆ **Concerto for Violin & Orchestra in D, op. 61 / PHILIPS**
Grumiaux, Galliera/New Philharmonia Orchestra. Much less romanticized than Kreisler and Menuhin. *The* classical performance. –PM

Concerto for Violin & Orchestra in D, op. 61 / MUSIC & ARTS
Kreisler, Blech/Berlin State Opera Orchestra. If sound quality were not a consideration, this would be my first choice. –PM

Concerto for Violin & Orchestra in D, op. 61 / ANGEL
Menuhin, Furtwängler/New Philharmonia Orchestra.

Concerto for Violin & Orchestra in D, op. 61 / PHILIPS
Grumiaux, Davis/Royal Concertgebouw Orchestra. Better sound than Grumiaux's earlier performance but not so fresh a performance, and a bit heavier and more romantic in concept from both the orchestra and the conductor. –PM

○ **The Creatures of Prometheus (ballet), op. 43 / DIGITAL CONCERTO**
Pantelli/Philharmonia Slavonica. The scale is just right, and this is a nicely played chambe

this is a nicely played chamber orchestra budget version, where the winds shine through in just the proper balance. –PM

The Creatures of Prometheus (ballet), op. 43 / DGG
Orpheus CO. Much more virtuosic than the budget version but perhaps with a bit less charm. –PM

○ **Egmont: Incidental Music / DGG**
Studer (soprano), Ganz (speaker), Abbado/Berlin PO.

○ **Fantasia for Piano, Chorus & Orchestra in c, op. 80 / DGG**
Kissin, Abbado/RIAS Chorus.

Fantasia for Piano, Chorus & Orchestra in c, op. 80 / ANGEL
Tan (fortepiano), Norrington/London Classical Players, Shuetz Choir. Terrific fire from all parties. But like so many other things by Norrington, it all seems to wear thin and be a bit superficial with repeated hearings. Or is it just me? –PM

Fantasia for Piano, Chorus & Orchestra in c, op. 80 / DGG
Pollini, Abbado/Vienna PO & Vienna State Opera Chorus.

○ **Fidelio (2-act opera), op. 72 / ANGEL**
Hallstein, Ludwig, Vickers, et al., Klemperer/Philharmonia Orchestra & Choir. This recording is not so scintillating as it might be, but is noble, powerful, and dramatic. –PM

☆ **Missa Solemnis in D, op. 123 / ANGEL**
Klemperer. The classic performance: not bettered in my lifetime so far and not likely to be with today's crop of conductors. –PM

○ **Overtures (complete) / DGG**
Karajan/Berlin PO.

Overtures (various) / CBS
Davis/Bavarian RSO. These are heavy (but not stodgy) performances that have a depth, resonance, and Beethoven sound unmatched by any other modern performance — and at the low/mid-price, they are a true bargain. Highly recommended. –PM

☆ **Quartets (16) for Strings (complete) / VALOIS**
Végh Quartet. The quintessential Beethoven quartet performances. They are sometimes a bit out of tune, and the cello is recorded too heavily, but they are unmatched for depth, profundity, and spirituality. The performers do better in the later ones where they have no real rivals — this is one of my most treasured sets. The quartets are also available individually so you can sample and see just how good they are. This was one terrific quartet, which stayed together for roughly 40 years. They made few recordings, of which this is by far their best and a fitting tribute. Sandor Végh is now a conductor of note (especially in Mozart). –PM

○ **Quintet for Piano & Winds in E-flat, op. 16 / PHILIPS**
Brendel, Holliger, Brunner, Thunemann, Baumann.

Quintet for Piano & Winds in E-flat, op. 16 / DGG
Levine/Ensemble Wien-Berlin.

○ **Septet for Strings & Winds in E-flat, op. 20 / HUNGARATON**
Adria Ensemble. This may not be better than the Swiss Soloists, but the sound is so superb and the fillers so interesting. –PM

Septet for Strings & Winds in E-flat, op. 20 / NOVALIS
Swiss Soloists.

Septet for Strings & Winds in E-flat, op. 20 / LONDON
Vienna Octet members. A classic — and with remarkably good early analog sound. –PM

○ **Sonatas (5) for Cello & Piano / PHILIPS**
Rostropovich, Richter. Amazing drama and tension. Is there any point in even listing another performance? –PM

○ **Sonatas for Violin & Piano (10) / GLOBE**
Leertouwer (baroque violin), Reynolds (fortepiano). A beautiful sound, and more sensual, laidback performances than on the Schröder, but it's only fair to point out the full-price cost disparity on four CDs. –PM

Sonatas for Violin & Piano (10) / EDITO CLASSICA
Schröder, van Immerseel. A dramatic and "intellectual" approach. The standard for years, it is now rivaled by the Globe performances. Mid-pricing on three CDs helps, but older sound pushes this to second choice. –PM

○ **Sonatas for Violin & Piano no. 1 in D, op. 12; no. 2 in A, op. 12; no. 3 in E-flat, op. 12 / LONDON**
Perlman, Ashkenazy. I miss the last bit of incisiveness from these artists, but in every other way these are captivating and outstanding performances, in ideal sound. –PM

○ **Sonatas for Violin & Piano no. 4 in A, op. 23; no. 6 in A, op. 30; no. 8 in G, op. 30 / LONDON**
Perlman, Ashkenazy.

○ **Sonatas for Violin & Piano no. 5 in F, op. 24, "Spring"; no. 9 in A, op. 47, "Kreutzer" / LONDON**
Perlman, Ashkenazy.

○ **Sonatas for Violin & Piano no. 7 in c, op. 30 & no. 10 in G, op. 96 / LONDON**
Perlman, Ashkenazy.

☆ **Sonata for Violin & Piano no. 9 in A, op. 47, "Kreutzer" / LONDON**
Perlman, Ashkenazy.

○ **Sonata for Piano no. 3 / MELODRAM**
Michelangeli.

○ **Sonatas for Piano nos. 3, 5, 8, 20 / DENON**
Gelber.

○ **Sonatas for Piano nos. 6, 7, 17, 18 / PYRAMID**
Richter.

○ **Sonatas for Piano nos. 8, 14, 15 / DGG**
Gilels.

☆ **Sonatas for Piano nos. 8, 13, 23 / VICTORIA LTD**
Steen, Nokleberg.

○ **Sonatas for Piano nos. 13-15 / DENON**
Gelber.

Sonatas for Piano nos. 13-15 / DGG
Pollini (piano). Not so warm as Gelber but with more of a sense of architecture and momentum. Pollini makes you rethink all three sonatas. –PM

○ **Sonata for Piano no. 17 in d, op. 31, "Tempest" / ANGEL**
Richter (piano). A classic: no one gets that cumulative, hypnotic feeling in the last movement like Richter. –PM

☆ **Sonata for Piano nos. 18, 23, 26 / DENON**
Gelber.

☆ **Sonata for Piano no. 21, "Appassionata" / RCA**
Richter.

Sonata for Piano nos. 21, 23, 26 / DGG
Gilels.

Sonata for Piano nos. 21, 25, 26 / DGG
Pollini (piano). A bit dry, but technically impressive and intense. –PM

○ **Sonata for Piano no. 29 / VICTORIA LTD**
Smebye (piano). Meticulous, very well prepared and organized, and with very good sound, this is a very musical and technically secure performance — now my version of choice not just on CD. It doesn't quite scale the ultimate heights, but how refreshing to hear the music without all the hype. –PM

○ **Sonata for Piano no. 32 / DGG**
Pogorelich (piano). The best performance, with the best sound. –PM

Sonata for Piano no. 32 / MEMORIES
Michelangeli.

☆ **Symphonies nos. 1-9 (complete) / EMI**
Furtwängler/Vienna PO. The sound is not very good and the performances are too slow at times, but this set has a depth and intensity unrivaled by any others. –PM

Symphonies nos. 1-9 (complete) / DGG

Karajan/Berlin PO. The sound of the classic 1963 set is not so smooth as on LP, but has more bite. This is many people's favorite set, a steal at $39.99. –PM

Symphonies nos. 1-9 (complete) / DGG
Karajan/Berlin PO. More intense than the 1963 set, but a bit hard-driven for most people. If you must have digital and a set, this is the best overall. –PM

Symphonies nos. 1-9 (complete) / ANGEL
Norrington/London Classical Players. Toscanini-like on old instruments. Surprisingly well played and, for the most part, extremely well recorded. May not hold up so well as first expected. –PM

○ **Symphony no. 1 in C, op. 21 / PHILIPS**
Brüggen/Orchestra of the 18th Century.

○ **Symphony no. 2 in D, op. 36 / PHILIPS**
Brüggen/Orchestra of the 18th Century.

Symphony no. 2 in D, op. 36 / ANGEL
Norrington/London Classical Players.

☆ **Symphony no. 3 in E-flat, op. 55 / ARKADIA**
Furtwängler/Berlin PO. You won't hear intensity like this on anything short of Furtwängler's 1942 *Ninth*! –PM

Symphony no. 3 in E-flat, op. 55 / PHILIPS
Brüggen/Orchestra of the 18th Century. Brüggen changes tempos and is more flexible about rubato than other conductors of this type of music. This is the best period-instrument *Third* and one of the best examples of Brüggen's style. –PM

○ **Symphony no. 4 in B-flat, op. 60 / ORFEO**
Kleiber/Bavarian State Orchestra. Controversial, especially for the very fast last movement. I find this the best stereo *Fourth* ever. –PM

Symphony no. 4 in B-flat, op. 60 / PHILIPS
Brüggen/Orchestra of the 18th Century.

☆ **Symphony no. 5 in c, op. 67 / DGG**
Kleiber/Vienna PO. As good a *Fifth* as has ever been recorded, this performance is lean and mean, without an ounce of fat anywhere. –PM

○ **Symphony no. 6 in F, op. 68, "Pastorale" / PHILIPS**
Brüggen/Orchestra of the 18th Century.

☆ **Symphony no. 7 in A, op. 92 / DGG**
Kleiber/Vienna PO. Arguably the best *Seventh* ever, certainly in the top three or four. –PM

☆ **Symphonies nos. 7 & 8 / PHILIPS**
Brüggen/Orchestra of the 18th Century. *Symphony no. 7* is so good, it is probably the best period-instrument performance of any Beethoven symphony I have ever heard; the *Eighth* is not far behind. –PM

Symphonies nos. 7 & 8 (versions for wind ensemble) / EMI
Sabine Meyer Wind Ensemble. Intriguing version for nine winds, led by the indomitable Sabine Meyer. –PM

☆ **Symphony no. 9 in d, op. 125 / HUNT**
Furtwängler/Berlin PO, Kittelcher Choir. The most intense and passionate performance ever made of the *Ninth*. Best to be in the proper mood, or the tempo changes and frequent lapses from unanimity can and will drive you crazy. –PM

Symphony no. 9 in d, op. 125 / PHILIPS
Davis/Bavarian RSO & Choir. My current "standard" *Ninth*: a bit slow and stodgy for some tastes, but it has soul. –PM

Symphony no. 9 in d, op. 125 / DENON
Inbal/Vienna SO, et al. A very underrated *Ninth* but not one to die for. Inbal does everything right. His and Davis's are the two to live with, Inbal's being more straightforward and intense. –PM

Symphony no. 9 in d, op. 125 / PEARL
Fried/Berlin State Opera Orchestra, Bruno Kittel Choir. One of the greatest *Ninths* ever by this spontaneous and almost-forgotten conductor. –PM

○ **Trios for Piano, Violin & Cello (complete) / INTERCORD**

Abegg Trio. The first two volumes are better than the last two, but all are superior to the competition. –PM

○ **Variations (33) on a waltz by Diabelli, for Piano, op. 120 PHILIPS**
Richter (piano). Live recording, but in many ways this is the best. –PM

Variations (33) on a waltz by Diabelli, for Piano, op. 120 PHILIPS
Bishop (piano). Concert classics. –PM

Variations (33) on a waltz by Diabelli, for Piano, op. 120 UNICORN-KANCHANA
Hill (piano). What a piece to make your recording debut with! But Hill can compete: for those just getting to know this fascinating piece, it could be as good as any because it does not over-interpret. I like it a lot but am not quite so moved as with other performances. –PM

Variations (33) on a waltz by Diabelli, for Piano, op. 120 PHILIPS
Arrau.

○ **"Wellington's Victory," op. 91 / CBS**
Maazel/Vienna PO. With the orchestra in top form and seeming to enjoy themselves immensely, this is an exciting and musical performance. –PM

○ **Wind Music - Vol I / RICERCAR**
Rondino [octet] in E-flat, WoO. 25; Trio for 2 Oboes & English Horn, op. 87; Sextet for 2 Clarinets, 2 Horns & 2 Bassoons in E-flat, op. 71; Variations on Mozart's "La ci darem," for 2 Oboes & English Horn; Quintet in E-flat for Oboe, 3 Horns & Bassoon.
Despite some later opus numbers, this is all early Beethoven, piquantly and rustically played on early instruments. –PM

VINCENZO BELLINI   1801-1835

Romantic. Italian composer noted for skill in writing long, flowing, graceful, and inventive melodies. Bellini influenced Chopin and many other composers of the early 1800s. He had a pronounced effect on the opera of that time, advocating simplicity over showmanship as a way to touch the heart. –BGT

☆ **Norma (4-act opera) / LONDON**
Sutherland, et al. /Welsh National Opera

○ **I Puritani / LONDON**
Sutherland, Pavarotti, et al./London SO.

I Puritani / ANGEL
Callas, di Stefano, Panerai, Rossi-Lemeni, Sarafin/La Scala. Although the vigor, energy, and orchestral richness of *Norma* make it Bellini's masterpiece, the constant inventiveness, expressive development, and perfection of his method of "sung declamation" shown in *I Puritani* forged a new pathway of almost stream-of-consciousness or natural-speech expressiveness. –BGT

○ **La Sonnambula (2-act opera) / LONDON**
Sutherland, Pavarotti, et al./National Philharmonic.

JIRI ANTONIN BENDA   1722-1795

Classical. Benda's works are distinguised by the rapid mood changes that have become characteristic of the northern German school of music. He was also very influential in the development of the opera and ballad forms in Germany, especially with his innovative use of spoken recitative accompanied by orchestra. –MKS

○ **Symphonies nos. 1-12 (complete) / CHANT DU MONDE**
Támas Pál/Salieri CO. Quirky and spritely symphonies by a Bohemian forerunner to Haydn. –PM

ALBAN BERG   1885-1935

Modern. An Austrian composer primarily of atonal music in many genres, including opera; known for *Wozzeck* (1925) and *Three Orchestral Pieces* (1915). Webern, Berg, and Schoenberg (Berg's teacher) made up the Viennese School, Berg being the romantically impassioned point of this composer-triangle — highly original and lyrical, with a brilliant sense of orchestral color. Information about his life and love affairs is encoded in many of his works (especially the *Lyric Suite* and the *Violin Concerto*), which are the subjects of controversy. –BGT

☆ **Concerto for Violin & Orchestra / DGG**
Perlman, Ozawa/Boston SO. Not so soul-searching as Kremer, but not so cloying either. –PM

Concerto for Violin & Orchestra / PHILIPS
Kremer, Davis/Bavarian RSO. Many beautiful and heartfelt moments, but too self-indulgent to be a first choice. –PM

○ **Lulu: Suite for Soprano & Orchestra; Three Pieces for Orchestra, op. 6 / MERCURY**
Pilarczyk, Dorati/London SO. The most elegantly sweeping of all performances. –BGT

○ **Lyric Suite for String Orchestra / CAPRICCIO**
Végh/Camerata Academica des Mozarteums Salzburg. Heartfelt and romantic. –PM

Lyric Suite for String Quartet or Orchestra / SONY
Boulez/NYPO. Clear and analytical. –PM

○ **Quartet for Strings, op. 3 / DGG**
LaSalle Quartet.

☆ **Three Pieces for Orchestra, op. 6 / DGG**
Levine/Berlin PO. These are big, romantic interpretations that may not convince fans of this music but should produce some converts. Dynamite dynamic range — this will test your stereo. –PM

Three Pieces for Orchestra, op. 6 / DGG
Abbado/London SO. A bit more analytical than Levine, but also highly romanticized. –PM

Three Pieces for Orchestra, op. 6 / PHILIPS
Davis/Bavarian RSO. More soulful than the Abbado but not so analytical. –PM

○ **Wozzeck / LONDON**
Silja, Jahn, et al./Vienna PO.

HECTOR BERLIOZ   1803-1869

Romantic. A renowned French orchestrator and composer of *Symphonie fantastique* (1830) and opera, vocal, and choral music. Berlioz continued to influence romantics through the late 19th and early 20th centuries with monumental yet graceful orchestrations. He was the embodiment of the romantic sensibility — idealism, a tendency toward pastoral reverie and the macabre, infatuation with the ideal lover (as reflected in the recurrent "theme of the beloved" in the *Symphonie fantastique*), and a wild, Byronesque lifestyle (the *Symphonie* is built around a program based on DeQuincey's *Confessions of an English Opium Eater*). A great love of nature infuses *Harold in Italy*, and great terror and grandeur is expressed in his *Te Deum*. He revived pure modal tonalities from French folk music, combining them with the turbulence of chromaticism to express the spirit of his revolutionary age. One of the greatest of all melodies, "D'amour l'ardente flamme" ("The ardent flame of love"), occurs within a landscape of dramatic gesture in *La Damnation de Faust.* –BGT

○ **Beatrice et Benedict / PHILIPS**
Eda-Pierre, Baker, Watts, Tear, Allen, Lloyd, Bastin, Davis/London SO.

○ **La Damnation de Faust, op. 24 / PHILIPS**
Veasey, Gedda, Bastin, Davis/London SO, Ambrosian Singers.

☆ **Harold in Italy, for Viola & Orchestra, op. 16 / SUPRAPHON**
Suk, Fischer-Dieskau/Czech PO. This is a leaner, less romantic approach, with outstandingly sensitive conducting. I wish Dieskau had continued as a conductor, but there's still time. –PM

Harold in Italy, for Viola & Orchestra, op. 16 / PHILIPS
Imai, Davis/London SO. Warm, rich sound ideally suited to this French romantic viola concerto. –PM

○ **Romeo et Juliette, op. 17 / PHILIPS**
Kern, Tear, Shirley-Quirk, Davis/London SO & Choir.

☆ **Symphonie fantastique, op. 14 / PHILIPS**
Davis/London SO.

☆ **Symphonie fantastique, op. 14 / PHILIPS**
Davis/Royal Concertgebouw Orchestra.

Symphonie fantastique, op. 14 / PHILIPS
Davis/Vienna PO. Interesting choices: I have always preferred the fire and sense of discovery of Davis's first *Fantastique* with the London SO. Others disagree and feel that the power and precision of the Concertgebouw (together with smoother recorded sound) make that the version of choice. I have to admit that the Concertgebouw is subtler and was a first choice for years. But now comes yet a third to muddy the waters — I like this one just as well, and it is for those who need and want digital sound. I feel the sanity and again the subtlety of Davis's reading, which makes this a first choice. –PM

Symphonie fantastique, op. 14 / DENON
Inbal/Frankfurt RSO. Tremendously well-thought-out, held together, and controlled, this super-analytical performance is probably more for those who like interesting conducting but don't like the *Fantastique* all that well. –PM

Symphonie fantastique, op. 14 / EMI
Norrington/London Classical Players. Very interesting, on original instruments. For some (especially jaded listeners like me), this could well be a first choice, with good sound and interesting new sonorities. –PM

☆ **Te Deum, op. 22 / DGG**
Araiza, Abbado/European Community Youth Orchestra & Chorus.

Te Deum, op. 22 / PHILIPS
Tagliavini, Davis/London SO & Chorus, Wandsworth School Boys Choir.

○ **Les Troyans (opera) / PHILIPS**
Lindholm, Veasey, Vickers, Glossop, Soyer, Davis/Royal Opera.

LEONARD BERNSTEIN   1918-1990

20th century. An American composer and pianist who conducted the Boston Symphony and New York Philharmonic Orchestras and wrote music in many forms, including musicals (*West Side Story* ,1957). –ED

○ **Chichester Psalms, for Chorus & Orchestra / HYPERION**
Best, Corydon Singers.

○ **Symphony no. 2, "The Age of Anxiety" / DGG**
Foss, Bernstein/Israel PO.

○ **Symphony no. 3, "Kaddish" / DGG**
Caballé, Wager, Bernstein/Israel PO, et al.

○ **West Side Story (complete) / DGG**
Te Kanawa, Troyanos, Carreras, Ollmann, Bernstein/Studio Orchestra & Choir.

FRANZ BERWALD   1796-1868

Romantic. A Swedish composer of symphonic and chamber works. At various times an orthopedist, manager of a glass works, and part-owner of a sawmill, Berwald is recognized as a great symphonist and the greatest Swedish composer of the 19th century. His four symphonies (*Serieuse*, *Capricieuse*, *Sinfonie singulière*, and the *Symphony no. 4 in E-flat*) are his best works — fine examples of his audacious sense of modulation combined with a strong classic melodic line. –BGT

☆ **Symphonies (4) / DGG**
Järvi/Gothenburg. The performances are a bit gimmicky but exciting, and this is one of Järvi's better efforts. –PM

○ **Symphonies nos. 3 & 4 / MUSICA SVECIAE**
Salonen/Swedish RSO. Fresh. –PM

HEINRICH VON BIBER   1664-1704

Baroque. An Austrian violinist and composer who became the most celebrated violin virtuoso of the 17th century. Biber wrote many sonatas for violin that employ both normal tuning and *scordatura*, where the strings are tuned to a chord instead of in perfect fifths. He also composed many sacred and secular pieces. The *Mystery* (or "Rosary") *Sonatas*, for solo violin and various continuo instruments, are musical metaphors, even allegories, of religious mysteries. –BGT

☆ **The Mystery Sonatas (15) for Violin & Continuo / VIRGIN**
Holloway (violin), Moroney (chamber organ and harpsichord). The out-of-tune playing drives me crazy, but these are such stylish and sensitive performances. –PM

The Mystery Sonatas (15) for Violin & Continuo / ARCHIV GALLERIA
Goebel (violin), et al. More virtuosic and rhythmic by far than Holloway and Maier, who are much more sensual and laidback, with sound to match. –PM

The Mystery Sonatas (15) for Violin & Continuo / EDITO CLASSICA
Maier (violin), Lehrndorfer (organ), Engel (cello), Junghänel (theorbo).

○ **Sonatas (12) for Trumpets, Strings, Timpani & Continuo (1976) / HYPERION**
Goodman/The Parley of Instruments.

GEORGES BIZET   1838-1875

Romantic. A French composer of piano, vocal, and dramatic music known for the opera *Carmen* (1875). Torn between his gift for evocation of narrative imagery with an extraordinary musicality, and a respect and love for simple classic form, Bizet achieved a powerful synthesis of the two in the *L'Arlésienne Suites* and the famous *Carmen* shortly before he died in his mid 30s. –BGT

☆ **L'Arlésienne: Suites nos. 1 & 2 / DGG**
Abbado/London SO.

L'Arlésienne: Suites nos. 1 & 2 / ANGEL
Beecham/Royal PO.

☆ **Carmen (4-act opera) / ANGEL**
Freni, Bumbry, Vickers, Paskalis, Frühbeck de Brugos/Paris Opera Orchestra & Chorus. A passionate and rousing French performance with exciting singing. –PM

Carmen (4-act opera) / DGG
Cotrubas, Berganza, Domingo, Milnes, Abbado/London SO, Ambrosian Opera Chorus. Overall superb performance, but lacking the last ounce of flair, especially from the singers. –PM

Carmen (4-act opera) / DGG
Riccarelli, Baltsa, Carreras, van Dam, Karajan/Berlin PO, Paris Opera Chorus. Superbly realized but still a bit too Germanic for my sensibilities. –PM

☆ **Jeux d'enfants, op. 22 / PHILIPS**
K. and M. Labeque (piano).

○ **Les pêcheurs de perles (3-act opera) / ANGEL**
Hendricks, Aler, Quilico, Plasson/Toulouse Capitole Orchestra & Choir.

○ **Symphony no. 1 in C / CHANDOS**
Bychkov/Orchestre de Paris. Taste and delicacy — a real classical feel for the Bizet. –PM

Symphony no. 1 in C / LONDON
Marriner/ASMF.

ARTHUR BLISS   1891-1975

Modern. The most successful of the English modernist composers emerging after WWI. Bliss wrote in a variety of genres, including film scores, and in 1953 succeeded Sir Arnold Bax as Master of the Queen's Musick. –MKS

○ **Checkmate (ballet suite): 5 Dances / CHANDOS**
Handley/Ulster Orchestra.

○ **A Colour Symphony / CHANDOS**
Handley/Ulster Orchestra.

ERNEST BLOCH   1880-1959

Modern. A Polish composer who moved to noise-based

composition from neo-classical beginnings. Bloch was a composer of psychologically profound works who was greatly influenced by world music (Hebrew melody, Southeast Asian music, and Tibetan music) in creating a totally original music with a traditional fluidity of inflection. His later works, like the *Sinfonia Breve* (1952), written when he was 72, developed a bold, energetic dissonance. –BGT

○ **Concerto for Violin & Orchestra / MUSIC & ARTS**
Szigeti (violin), Mengelberg/Royal Concertgebouw Orchestra. Recorded live in 1939, this is one of Bloch's greatest works of creative splendor. –BGT

○ **Concertos Grosso nos. 1 & 2 / MERCURY**
Hanson/Eastman-Rochester SO.

☆ **Schelomo - Hebrew Rhapsody for Cello & Orchestra / MD&G**
Schmid, Roggan/Herford PO. Dedicated — a real sleeper of a performance. –PM

Schelomo - Hebrew Rhapsody for Cello & Orchestra / DGG
Fournier, Wallenstein/Berlin PO.

KARL-BIRGER BLOMDAHL   1916-1968

Modern. A Swedish composer and one of the organizers of the "Monday Group" in Stockholm (composers who worked in an abstract, objective idiom rather than the prevailing Scandinavian romantic style). Blomdahl's late works incorporate electronic sounds and musique concrète styles, as well as synthetic speech. –MKS

○ **Aniara, "Space Opera" (1957-58) / CAPRICE**
Westerverg/Swedish RSO & Chorus.

○ **Symphony no. 2; Preludio & Allegro; Concerto Grosso; Violin Concerto / MAP**
Westerberg, Rudner (violin), Rudner/Helsingborg SO.

○ **Symphony no. 3 / CAPRICE**
Ehrling/Stockholm Philharmonic.

JOHN BLOW   1649-1708

Baroque. A British organist and composer of sacred and secular vocal music as well as instrumental pieces for organ, harpsichord, and strings. –ED

○ **Ode on the Death of Mr. Henry Purcell / HYPERION**
Bowman, Chance, King/The King's Consort.

LUIGI BOCCHERINI   1743-1805

Classical. An Italian composer who specialized almost entirely in chamber music and wrote chamber symphonies, numerous violin and cello sonatas, and guitar music. His profound admiration for Haydn gave rise to the saying "Boccherini is the wife of Haydn." –MKS

○ **Concertos for Cello in E-flat, G. 474; B-flat, G. 482; G, G. 480 / EMI**
Moeller (baroque cello), Linde/Linde Consort. Not quite the virtuoso that Bylsma is, Moeller (at least as recorded here) has a much more laidback, warmer, richer, and more sensual tone, and his shaping and coloring of the pieces are every bit as valid and interesting. May be hard to find. –PM

○ **Concertos for Cello in G, G. 480 & D, G. 483 / DHM**
Bylsma (cello), Lamon/Tafelmusik. The sound is a bit strange on this one (too electronic and processed), but Bylsma gives an outstandingly virtuoso performance. –PM

○ **Stabat Mater for Soprano & String Quintet; String Quintet, op. 31/4 / FHM**
Mellon (soprano), Banchini/Ensemble 415. Heartfelt and moving old-instrument performance. The *Stabat Mater* is not your usual frivolous Boccherini. –PM

○ **Symphonies (29), G. 506 / FONE**
Orizio, Brescia/Bergamo Festival CO. Old-fashioned but very Italian and soulful, and worth seeking out for this most interesting of Boccherini's symphonies. –PM

Symphonies (29), G. 490, 506, 511, 512 / HARMONIA MUNDI
Banchini/Ensemble 415. Fiery and quirky original-instrument performances. This one is a bit eccentric, but well worth seeking out. –PM

○ **Trios (6) for Violin, Viola & Cello, op. 47 / OPUS 111**
Trio L'Europa Galante. A lot of style, energy, and soul. Exceptionally fine recording. –PM

JOSEPH BODIN DE BOISMORTIER   1689-1755

Baroque. A prolific French composer of instrumental music, much of it intended for amateurs and published with descriptive titles like *Gentillesses*. –MKS

○ **Motets avec Symphonies / ADDA**
Niquet/Le Concert Spirituel Choeur et Orchestra. Boismortier has a terrific gift for the theatrical and the melodic, and these are infectious and inspiring pieces. –PM

ARRIGO BOITO   1842-1918

Romantic. The Italian librettist for Verdi's *Falstaff* and *Otello* and the composer of *Mefistofele* (1868). –ED

○ **Mefistofele (4-act opera) / LONDON**
Freni, Caballé, Pavarotti, Ghiaurov, de Fabritiis/National PO.

ALEXANDER BORODIN   1833-1887

Romantic, nationalist. A Russian composer in many forms, including opera (*Prince Igor*, 1887). Borodin was one of "The Mighty Five" Russians who wrote nationalist music. The illegitimate son of a prince and a civil servant, he became an important research chemist and physical scientist. He wrote music of great originality and beauty — bold orchestral tone poems on exotic lands and subjects, as well as Russian nationalist works influenced by folk melodies and featuring astonishing harmonic and rhythmic innovation (chords in fourths, harmonies with nonharmonic "added tones," quasi-jazz syncopation). –BGT

☆ **In the Steppes of Central Asia / SUPRAPHON**
Ancerl/Czech PO. This whole disc features passionate and committed musicmaking by one of the most underrated conductors of all time. One is readily able to overlook the early-60s sound, which is nevertheless clear and razor sharp. –PM

☆ **Prince Igor: Polovtsian Dances / ANGEL**
Beecham/Royal PO. A classic! No one finds the music Beecham finds in this potboiler: he makes it vibrant and completely exciting. –PM

○ **Quartet for Strings no. 1 in A / ANGEL**
Borodin Quartet. I'm not a big fan of the Borodin Quartet, which plays consistently too out-of-tune and heart-on-sleeve for my taste. Others, however, will disagree, and this is one of their best recordings. –PM

☆ **Quartet for Strings no. 2 in D / ANGEL**
Borodin Quartet.

○ **Symphony no. 2 in b; Symphony no. 3 in a (unfinished); Polovetsian Dances / LONDON**
Ansermet/L'Orchestre de la Suisse Romande. Back at budget price and worth the wait, all three performances are consistently inspired. –PM

Symphony no. 2 in b / PHILIPS
Gergiev/Rotterdam PO.

WILLIAM BOYCE   1711-1779

Baroque. A British composer of instrumental and sacred vocal works and one of the early symphonists. Boyce was the son of a London cabinetmaker. He became hard-of-hearing at an early age but nevertheless attained popular success, writing joyous and lyrical music of classic design, like the collection of overtures and his eight symphonies rediscovered in the 1930s by Constant Lambert. –BGT

○ **Select Anthems & Organ Voluntaries / CRD**

Cooper (organ), Higginbottom/The Choir of New College, Oxford. 76 minutes of some of the most sublime, inspired, and heartfelt all-male British choral singing you are ever likely to hear. –PM

○ **Solomon: A Serenata for Soprano, Tenor, Choir & Orchestra / HYPERION**
Mills (soprano), Crook (tenor), Goodman/The Parley of Instruments Orchestra & Chorus. Somewhere between a cantata and an opera, *Solomon* has all the delicious tunes Boyce is so noted for. –PM

☆ **Symphonies (8) / DGG**
Pinnock/English Consort. The classic confrontation between original instruments and the superb "modern" chamber orchestra. –PM

Symphonies (8) / ARGO
Marriner/ASMF. The choice is difficult, but overall I prefer the piquancy of the old instruments and Pinnock's stylish and dramatic conducting. –PM

JOHANNES BRAHMS   1833-1897

Romantic. A German composer of major works in all forms except opera, including symphonies, lieder, and solo piano music. Playing in rough taverns down by the docks as a teenager in order to supplement his family's humble income, Brahms persevered to become a renowned conductor of Bach, Beethoven, Schubert, and Schumann and a great composer, faithful to the traditional architecture and logic of classical forms but a romantic in love with German folksong. He eschewed chromaticism and told a personal and non-programmatic story in every composition. –BGT

○ **Ballades (4) for Piano, op. 10; Scherzo, op. 4; Intermezzi, op. 117; Klavierstücke, op. 199 / GLOBE**
Janssen (piano). Passionate and dramatic playing. May be a bit too objective for some tastes, but the clarity shines through like a beacon. –PM

Ballades (4) for Piano, op. 10 / DGG
Michelangeli.

Ballades (4) for Piano, op. 10 / PHILIPS
Brendel (piano). Very soulful and "meaningful" playing but not so virtuosic as Michelangeli or Janssen. –PM

Ballades (4) for Piano, op. 10; Sonatas for Piano nos. 2 & 3; Scherzo, opp. 4; Variations, opp. 24 & 35 / PHILIPS
Arrau (piano). All of Arrau's solo Brahms recordings are on an important three-CD Philips set at mid-price. Arrau always lets us in on an alternative sound world. Outstanding here is his recording of the Paganini *Variations* — truly original and passionate, taking this piece right out of the realm of just a show-off virtuoso vehicle. Heartfelt and sensitive, especially in the fourth ballade, but without the control and clarity of Michelangeli, or Janssen. –PM

○ **Chorale Preludes (11) for Organ, op. 122 / MD&G**
Innig.

☆ **Concerto for Piano & Orchestra no. 1 in d, op. 15 / CBS**
Serkin (piano), Szell/Cleveland Orchestra. Intensity and concentration that just never let up. –PM

Concerto for Piano & Orchestra no. 1 in d, op. 15 / LONDON
Curzon, Szell/London SO.

Concerto for Piano & Orchestra no. 1 in d, op. 15 / PHILIPS
Arrau (piano), Haitink/Royal Concertgebouw Orchestra. Worth it for the grand passion and commitment of the slow movement alone; more mystical, intense, and ethereal than any other performance, ever. –PM

Concerto for Piano & Orchestra no. 1 in d, op. 15 / DGG
Pollini (piano), Böhm/Vienna PO.

☆ **Concerto for Piano & Orchestra no. 2 in B-flat, op. 83 / RCA**
Richter (piano), Leinsdorf/Chicago SO. One of Richter's greatest performances and a classic of the gramophone. –PM

Concerto for Piano & Orchestra no. 2 in B-flat, op. 83 / DGG
Pollini, Abbado/Vienna PO.

○ **Concerto for Violin & Orchestra in D, op. 77 / ACANTA**
Neveu, Schmidt-Isserstedt/North German RSO. Too bad her EMI performance (coupled with the Sibelius) isn't available in America, but this flamboyant performance by the much-lamented Neveu will do almost as well. –PM

Concerto for Violin & Orchestra in D, op. 77 / ANGEL
Perlman (violin), Giulini/Chicago SO. A bit too ponderous for an ultimate recommendation. –PM

○ **Concerto for Violin, Cello & Orchestra in a, op. 102 / SUPRAPHON**
Suk, Nevarra, Ancerl/Czech Philharmonic. This recording has that perfect combination of clarity and passion, plus a raw and engaging sound from the early 60s that is surprisingly good. –PM

Concerto for Violin, Cello & Orchestra in a, op. 102 / PHILIPS
Krebbers, Haitink/Royal Concertgebouw Orchestra.

Concerto for Violin, Cello & Orchestra in a, op. 102 / ANGEL
Boskovsky, Brabec, Furtwängler/Vienna PO.

Concerto for Violin, Cello & Orchestra in a, op. 102 / AS DISC
Schneiderhan (violin), Mainardi (cello), Furtwängler/Lucerne Festival Orchestra. Tremendous passion, but the pirate sound is not all it should be. –PM

○ **Ein deutsches Requiem, op. 45 / ANGEL**
Schwarzkopf, Fischer-Dieskau, Klemperer/Philharmonia Chorus & Orchestra. Very monumental and contrapuntal, with the best playing and (especially) singing of any performance, ever. –PM

Ein deutsches Requiem, op. 45 / DGG
Hendricks, van Dam, Karajan/Vienna PO. The best modern alternative to Klemperer, with Karajan in a spiritual and less-phlegmatic mood. Fine solo singing, although not nearly so individual as on the Klemperer. –PM

Ein deutsches Requiem, op. 45 / CBS
Walter/New York Philharmonic, Westminster Choir. A work of universal vision, and Brahms's first public success. –BGT

○ **Ernste Gesänge, for Voice & Piano, op. 121 / DGG**
Fischer-Dieskau.

Ernste Gesänge, for Voice & Piano, op. 121 / ONDINE
Hynninen, Gothoni.

○ **Gesang der Parzen ("Song of the Fates"), for Chorus & Orchestra, op. 89 / DGG**
Abbado/Berlin Radio Choir, Berlin PO. Although turgid and not top-drawer Brahms, perhaps this is nonetheless welcome as a filler to Abbado's fine Brahms's *Symphony no. 1*. –PM

○ **Hungarian Dances (21) for 2 Pianos / PHILIPS**
K. and M. Labeque (pianos). These twins can really play — this is a fiery performance, the best one I have ever heard on piano, with great sound. –PM

Hungarian Dances (21) for Orchestra / HUNGARATON
Fischer/Budapest Festival Orchestra. Much more Hungarian-sounding than any of the rival orchestral recordings, with a lot of verve. –PM

Hungarian Dances (21) for Orchestra / PHILIPS
Masur/Leipzig Gewandhaus Orchestra. A heavier, more Germanic approach than Fischer's, but with a lot of soul. –PM

○ **Piano Music (8 pieces), op. 76 / PHILIPS**
Bishop-Kovacevich.

○ **Piano Music, opp. 116, 117, 119 (complete) / PHILIPS**
Bishop-Kovacevich.

○ **Piano Music, op. 118 / PHILIPS**
Bishop-Kovacevich.

○ **Quartets for Strings nos. 1 & 2, op. 51 / ADDA**

Muir Quartet. A bit stiff, but at least they don't exaggerate the music as much as Takacs. Outstanding sound. –PM

☆ **Quintet for Clarinet & Strings in b, op. 115 / EMI**
Meyer (clarinet), Members of the Vienna String Sextet. For the extraordinary sensitivity and shading of Meyer's playing, my current favorite. –PM

Quintet for Clarinet & Strings in b, op. 115 / HYPERION
King (clarinet)/Gabrieli Quartet.

☆ **Quintet for Piano & Strings in f, op. 34 / HUNGARATON**
Ranki/Bartók Quartet.

Quintet for Piano & Strings in f, op. 34 / DGG
Pollini/Quartetto Italiano. Pollini plays well (albeit as if he were playing a concerto), but the Italians don't give him the greatest support, playing too heavily and with a bit too much vibrato for my taste. –PM

Quintet for Piano & Strings in f, op. 34 / BALKANTON
Eynden (piano). "Dimov" Bulgarian String Quintet. A very musical sleeper from Bulgaria. I like this performance as much as the other two, though it doesn't have quite as high a profile. –PM

○ **Scherzo for Piano in e-flat, op. 4 / GLOBE**
Janssen. Very "objective" and powerful piano playing. –PM

Scherzo for Piano in e-flat, op. 4 / PHILIPS
Bishop-Kovacevich.

○ **Die schöne Magelone / AS DISC**
Richter/Fischer-Dieskau. Although Dieskau's Angel recording from about the same time has better sound, it is not available on CD, but this "pirate" disc from the 1965 Aldeburgh Festival is fine. –PM

Die schöne Magelone / ONDINE
Gothoni (piano), Hynninen (baritone). Hynninen's voice is dark and expressive. He sings with more vibrato than Dieskau and isn't quite so suave, but this is a fine modern alternative. Gothoni's accompaniments are nearly in Richter's class. But Richter just has that grace and subtlety! –PM

○ **Serenades for Orchestra nos. 1 & 2 / LONDON**
Kertesz, Istvan/London SO. The freshest performance at the cheapest price: a real bargain.

Serenade for Orchestra no. 1 in D, op. 11 / PHILIPS
Nonet version. ASMF. Terrific playing and recording of an interesting alternative version. –PM

Serenade for Orchestra no. 1 in D, op. 11 / DGG
Abbado/Berlin PO.

○ **Sextet for Strings in G, opp. 38 & 18 / INTERCORD**
Stuttgart Soloists. The Germans have more depth and soul, the English more air and light. –PM

Sextets nos. 1 & 2 / HYPERION
Raphael Ensemble.

☆ **Sonatas (2) for Cello & Piano in e & F, opp. 38 & 99 / DGG**
Rostropovich, Serkin. The combination of the passionate, rhapsodic Rostropovich and the intellectual, controlled Serkin proves to be a good one. This is the only time these two recorded together. –PM

Sonata for Cello & Piano no. 1 in e, op. 38 / MUSIC & ARTS
Rostropovich, Richter. And now yet a third label: Italian pirate AS Disc #349. Also now on the Italian pirate label Intaglio (#705), in somewhat richer sound. –PM

○ **Sonatas (2) for Clarinet & Piano, op. 120 / CHANDOS**
de Peyer (clarinet), Pryor (piano). De Peyer isn't the player he once was, but he still exhibits beautiful tone color and shadings. –PM

Sonatas (2) for Clarinet & Piano, op. 120 / HYPERION
King (clarinet), Benson (piano).

Sonatas (2) for Clarinet & Piano, op. 120 / VIRGIN
Collins (clarinet), Pletnev (piano).

○ **Sonata for Piano no. 2 in f#, op. 2 / DENON**
Grimaud.

○ **Sonata for Piano no. 3 in f, op. 5 / AULOS**
Lahusen (piano). This is a very commanding, intelligent, and no-nonsense performance, especially by one so young; a very welcome disk debut. –PM

Sonata for Piano no. 3 in f, op. 5 / EBS
Joeres.

○ **Sonatas (3) for Violin & Piano, opp. 78, 100, 108 / PHILIPS**
Grumiaux, Sebok. More elegant and introverted than the Suk/Katchen, which is more "beery" and flamboyant but a bit on the wild side for such inward music. Sebok is a bit too reticent, Katchen a bit too aggressive. –PM

Sonatas (3) for Violin & Piano, opp. 78, 100, 108 / LONDON
Suk, Katchen.

○ **Violin Sonatas plus Scherzo from FAE Sonata / LONDON**
Amoyal (violin), Roge (piano). This is a surprisingly effective performance by these two Frenchmen (Roge was a student of Katchen). Too bad there wasn't room for the full FAE sonata, but it is nice to have all of Brahms's violin music on one CD. –PM

○ **Songs (10) / KOCH-SCHWANN**
Blegen, Katz. A studio recording made in 1987 and including some of Brahms's more familiar songs such as "Botschaft" and "Weigenlied no. 4, op. 49." –MKS

Songs (17) / ERNSTE
Fischer-Dieskau, Moorc. Recorded live at the Salzburg Festival in 1958. A masterful collaboration. –MKS

○ **Symphony no. 1 in c, op. 68 / DGG**
Karajan/Berlin PO. Pretty much the ultimate on CD, combining ruggedness with beautiful tone colorings. –PM

Symphony no. 1 in c, op. 68 / DGG
Abbado/Berlin PO. Very lyrical, plush, and sumptuous; not so troubled or dramatic as most, but with such a rich sound that it can be highly recommended. –PM

☆ **Symphony no. 2 in D, op. 73 / DGG**
Abbado/Berlin PO. The most sheerly beautiful Brahms *Second* I have ever heard! Sumptuous in every way. –PM

Symphony no. 2 in D, op. 73 / DGG
Karajan/Berlin PO.

○ **Symphony no. 3 in F, op. 90 / DGG**
Karajan/Berlin PO.

Symphony no. 3 in F, op. 90 / DGG
Abbado/Berlin PO.

Symphony no. 3 in F, op. 90 / RCA
Davis/Bavarian RSO.

○ **Symphony no. 4 in e, op. 98 / DGG**
Kleiber/Vienna PO. Lean and mean — a bit too unyielding for some tastes, and not terrifically well recorded. –PM

Symphony no. 4 in e, op. 98 / DGG
Karajan/Berlin PO. One of his most probing, least smooth, and least mannered performances. To my taste, he was rejuvenated in his last years. –PM

Symphony no. 4 in e, op. 98 / RCA
Davis/Bavarian RSO. Moments of ineffable beauty, but maybe not quite the command of a Kleiber or a Karajan, and not a great orchestra. –PM

Symphony no. 4 in e, op. 98 / LASER LIGHT
Haenchen/Netherlands PO. Immediately, you're in the presence of a special Brahmsian sound world — and all for $5.99 or less. –PM

○ **Trio for Clarinet, Cello & Piano in a, op. 114 / HYPERION**
King (clarinet), Georgian (cello), Benson (piano).

○ **Trio for Horn, Violin & Piano in E-flat, op. 40 / LONDON**
Tuckwell, Perlman, Ashkenazy.

○ **Trios (3) for Piano, Violin & Cello, op. 8 (first version) / AULOS**

Arcadia Trio. You'd think the Abegg trio's performance of the early (1854) version of Brahms's first trio would be the one to have, but theirs is a bit too uptight and pedantic. The Arcadia Trio version is effusive, very lyrical and rhapsodic, and warm and rich, but not sentimental. And it has great detail and spacious sound. Could it be because it isn't digital? The disc is filled out by some very interesting and highly romantic novelettes by Theodor Kirchner (1823-1903). –PM

Trios (3) for Piano, Violin & Cello, opp. 8, 87, 101 / INTERCORD
Abegg Trio.

○ **Variations on a Theme by Haydn, for Orchestra, op. 56a / DGG**
Karajan/Berlin PO.

Variations on a Theme by Haydn, for Orchestra, op. 56a / HUNT
Mitropoulos/NYPO. Also contains *Academic Festival Overture* and *Concerto for Piano no. 1.* –BGT

○ **Variations on a Theme by Paganini, for Piano, op. 35 / ELAN**
Rodrigues (piano). Fiery and poetic by turns, with a lot of technique and flamboyance. –PM

Variations on a Theme by Paganini, for Piano, op. 35 / ONDINE
Raekallio (piano). This man thinks about what he plays before playing it, which makes him special, especially in this age. –PM

○ **Zigeunerlieder (8), op. 103 & 7 miscellaneous songs / ARS VIVENDI**
Lang (mezzo), Arens (piano). I still prefer these as vocal quartets or with choir, but these mezzo readings are quite interesting and will do just fine. –PM

BENJAMIN BRITTEN   1913-1976

Neo-romantic. A popular British composer of operas, such as *Peter Grimes* (1941), and most other musical forms, including choral and orchestral music and solo vocal music. Several of Britten's works, including *A Ceremony of Carols*, are performed on a seasonal schedule. Britten has also achieved renown as an opera composer, using themes from American, Japanese, and British cultures. He is equally famous for his vocal music, whose aesthetics of matching word and music showed the influences of Auden and Isherwood. As a conscientious objector, he spoke eloquently against militarism in his *War Requiem*. –BGT

○ **Albert Herring, op. 39 / LONDON**
Fisher, Cantelo, Rex, Brannigan, et al., Britten/English CO.

○ **Billy Budd, op. 50 / LONDON**
Pears, Glossop, Shirley-Quirk, Luxon, Langdon, Brannigan, Britten/London SO, Ambrosian Singers.

○ **Concerto for Piano & Orchestra in D, op. 13 / LONDON**
Richter, Britten/English CO.

○ **Death in Venice (opera), op. 88 / LONDON**
Pears, Bowman, Shirley-Quirk, Bedford/English CO, English Opera Group Choir.

○ **Gloriana: Choral Dances / HYPERION**
Hill, Wetton/Holst Orchestra & Singers.

○ **Les Illuminations (song cycle), op. 18 / LONDON**
Pears, Britten/English CO.

○ **A Midsummer Night's Dream (opera), op. 64 / LONDON**
Harwood, Veasey, Watts, Pears, Deller, Shirley-Quirk, Britten/London SO & Chorus.

○ **Nocturne, for Tenor, 7 Obbligato Instruments & Strings, op. 60 / LONDON**
Pears, Britten/London SO.

○ **Paul Bunyan (operetta), op. 17 / VIRGIN**
Brunelle/English CO, London Philharmonic Choir.

○ **Serenade for Tenor, Horn & Strings, op. 31 / LONDON**
Pears (tenor), Tuckwell (horn), Britten/London SO. Given this

combination of artists, are we likely ever to have a better performance? –PM

☆ **Simple Symphony for Strings, op. 4 / DGG**
Orpheus CO.

○ **Sonata in C for Cello & Piano, op. 65; Suites nos. 1 & 2, opp. 72 & 80 / LONDON**
Rostropovich, Britten.

○ **Suites (3) for solo Cello, opp. 72, 80, 87 / GLOBE**
Wispelway (cello). Not quite Rostropovich, but he's working on it. –PM

○ **Symphony for Cello & Orchestra, op. 68 / CBS**
Ma (cello), Zinman/Baltimore SO.

☆ **Variations on a Theme of Frank Bridge, for String Orchestra, op. 10 (1937) / ANGEL**
Karajan/Philharmonia Orchestra. Karajan has more character and finds more music in this fascinating piece than any other conductor; however, he is limited by the mono sound and the performance is available only as part of a four-CD set. –PM

Variations on a Theme of Frank Bridge, for String Orchestra, op. 10 / LONDON
Marriner/ASMF. Scintillating chamber-orchestra alternative to the Karajan. One of Marriner's best. –PM

☆ **War Requiem, op. 66 / LONDON**
Vishnevskaya, Pears, Fisher-Dieskau, Britten/London SO & Choir. Still the definitive one. With a cast like this, how could it be anything else? –PM

○ **The Young Person's Guide to the Orchestra, op. 34 / LONDON**
Britten/London SO. Completely musical. –PM

MAX BRUCH   1838-1920

Romantic. A German composer of operas, cantatas, and choral works known for his violin concertos and *Kol Nidrei, for Cello & Orchestra.* Such works as his *Concerto for Violin & Orchestra no. 1 in g* exhibit a Mendelssohnian melodic warmth in a flowing, beautifully varied texture. –BGT

○ **Concerto for Clarinet, Viola & Orchestra, op. 88 (1911) / KOCH-SCHWANN**
Brunner, Zagrosek/Bamberg SO.

Concerto for Clarinet, Viola & Orchestra, op. 88 (1911) / HYPERION
King, Imai, Francis/London SO.

☆ **Concerto for Violin & Orchestra no. 1 in g / DGG**
Shaham (violin), Sinopoli/Philharmonia Orchestra. It may not match Kreisler's (to name one of the best old performances), but it is the best of the current batch, with good sound. As usual, Sinopoli finds a depth and resonance in the orchestral part that few contemporary conductors can match. Shaham (along with van Keulen) is one of the best of the young violinists. –PM

Concerto for Violin & Orchestra no. 1 in g / ANGEL
Little, Handley/Royal Liverpool PO. Fresh and exciting. –PM

○ **Kol Nidrei, for Cello & Orchestra, op. 47 / LONDON**
Harrel, Ashkenazy/Philharmonia Orchestra.

○ **Swedish Dances for Clarinet & Piano, op. 63 / BEYER**
Kloecker (clarinet), Genuit (piano).

○ **Trios (8) for Clarinet, Viola & Piano, op. 83 / BEYER**
Kloecker (clarinet), Sebastian (viola), Genuit (piano).

ANTON BRUCKNER   1824-1896

Romantic. An Austrian composer of orchestral, chamber, keyboard, sacred vocal music, and several symphonies, who was influenced by Wagner. Bruckner was a deeply religious man. Often misunderstood and under-programmed in his lifetime, this mysteriously retiring, reticent composer of simple, rustic tastes amazed audiences with his improvisatory skill on the organ. He created nine symphonies of absolutely unique form and expression that speak of an awe of nature. Their flowing sense of development leads into the most

unexpected imaginary zones, with thematic material (often drawn from the dances and folk tunes of his homeland) sometimes suddenly reappearing in disguised and metamorphosed visage. –BGT

○ **Mass for Chorus & Brass no. 2 in e / DGG**
An exquisitely beautiful combination of Renaissance idioms and feel, with 19th-century techniques, like the motets. –BGT

Mass for Chorus & Brass no. 2 in e; 4 Motets / SONY
Bernius/German Wind Philharmonic, and featuring the Stuttgart Chamber Choir.

○ **Mass no. 3 in f / DGG**
Stader, Hellmann, et. al, Jochum/Bavarian RSO & Choir.

☆ **Motets / HYPERION**
Best, Corydon Singers.

○ **Organ Music / NOVALIS**
Horn.

○ **Quintet for Strings in F / GLOBE**
Raphael Quartet. Their intonation is not the greatest, but this is a dynamic and exciting version of one of the great romantic quintets, and it is very well recorded. –PM

Quintet for Strings in F / CLAVES
Sonare Quartet. Tighter and more straightforward than the Raphael but lacking their dynamism and charisma. –PM

Quintet for Strings in F / LONDON
Vienna Philharmonia Quintet. Used to be the front-runner, but with the sound quality a bit dated and an overly *gemuetlich* approach, this version can now be relegated to third place. –PM

○ **Requiem in d (1849) / HYPERION**
Rodgers, Denley, et al., Best/English CO, Corydon Singers.

○ **Symphony in f, "Study Symphony" (1863) / TELDEC**
Inbal/Frankfurt RSO. Finally a first-class recording of the *Study Symphony* by someone who really understands the idiom. –PM

○ **Symphony no. 0 in d / TELDEC**
Inbal/Frankfurt RSO. Much more inward, spiritual, and "Brucknerian"-sounding than Chailly's extroverted, bombastic, and ultimately more superficial reading. –PM

Symphony no. 0 in d / LONDON
Chailly/Berlin RSO.

○ **Symphonies (9) / DGG**
Jochum/Berlin PO (nos. 1, 4, 7, 8, 9), Bavarian RSO (nos. 2, 3, 5, 6). The Deutsche Grammophon (DGG) set is such a mystical experience that I can't imagine some critics preferring the Angel box, which, for the most part, is peasanty, at times sloppy and uninspired. Go for the DGG: it's an experience and in the long run will be much more rewarding. –PM

Symphonies (9) / TELDEC
Inbal/Frankfurt RSO. Different (original) editions on performances of most of the symphonies make this set a must for any committed Brucknerian. –PM

Symphonies (9) / DGG
Karajan/Berlin PO. Better played than Jochum's DGG set, and more "objective" in approach, but missing some of the latter's inwardness and mysticism. This is a tough choice, especially since Karajan is so good (and better than Jochum) on some of the later symphonies. –PM

○ **Symphony no. 1 in c (Linz version) / MELODIYA (KOCH-SCHWANN)**
Rozhdestvensky/USSR Ministry of Culture SO. Heartfelt, tender, and more traditional Russian-style performance in good late-analog sound with some AAD tape hiss. With many terrific moments, this is a fine supplement to Inbal's more traditionally Germanic and dry-eyed approach. –PM

Symphony no. 1 in c (Linz version) / TELDEC
Inbal/Frankfurt RSO.

○ **Symphony no. 2 in c / DGG**

Karajan/Berlin PO. A good, generic Bruckner *Second*. Nothing special but so much better played than the Jochum. –PM

○ **Symphony no. 3 in d (1889 version) / LASER LIGHT**
Haenchen/Netherlands PO. An amazing bargain at $5.99 or less, this has the right sound world for Bruckner. It has plenty of energy and is simply more engagingly done than are most performances of Bruckner symphonies, which tend to be too serious in an awestruck way. –PM

Symphony no. 3 in d, "Wagner Symphony" (1877 version) / DGG
Sinopoli/Dresden State Orchestra. Very impressive, easily the best version of the so-called "Wagner" version from 1877. –PM

☆ **Symphony no. 4 in E-flat, "Romantic" / VIRGIN**
Janowski/Orchestra Philharmonia de Radio France. An unlikely source for a real underdog contender. –PM

Symphony no. 4 in E-flat, "Romantic" / DGG
Jochum/Berlin PO. A classic wayward and "romantic" approach, ultimately a bit too fragmented but special nonetheless. –PM

Symphony no. 4 in E-flat, "Romantic" / LONDON
Chailly/Royal Concertgebouw Orchestra. This won't cause you sleepless nights, but it is a well-played and well-recorded solid contender. –PM

Symphony no. 4 in E-flat, "Romantic" / DGG
Abbado/Vienna PO. "Stranger speaks with forked tongue," yet there's so much to admire here. This is not "Germanic" Bruckner, but it is consistently beautiful and musical, although it can be a bit bombastic, especially in the brass. –PM

○ **Symphony no. 5 in B-flat / MUSICA CLASSICA**
Schuricht/Vienna PO. Could be the best Bruckner I have ever heard, with passionate and committed playing from the VPO. A lot of tempo changes, but they all work for me. This *Fifth* is just making its appearance as part of a 12-CD 150th anniversary set of the VPO and will probably appear as a single at some point. PM

Symphony no. 5 in B-flat / ORFEO
Karajan/Vienna SO. Not so fiery or dramatic as other Bruckner *Fifths*, this one is more tender, lyrical, and mystical, with an amazing sense of inevitability. It also has very good playing and sound, especially considering the complexity of the work and the age (1954) of the recording. –PM

Symphony no. 5 in B-flat / DGG
Karajan/Berlin PO.

Symphony no. 5 in B-flat / MUSIC & ARTS
Horenstein/BBC SO (live, Sep 15, 1971, Royal Albert Hall). There's some tape hiss but very good live sound. It's tough to choose between Karajan's more mystical, sensual approach (especially in his live Vienna SO performance) and Horenstein's dramatic, architectural command. –PM

○ **Symphony no. 6 in A / ANGEL**
Klemperer/New Philharmonia Orchestra. Craggy and monolithic, this is one of the few convincing statements of this tough nut. –PM

☆ **Symphony no. 7 in E / ARKADIA**
Stuttgart RSO. Pirate or no pirate, this is one of the most luminous, poised, and shapely performances of my favorite symphony. The sound is stereo and not bad for 1971, but the playing, while obviously well rehearsed, suffers from many imperfections. Still a performance to treasure. –PM

Symphony no. 7 in E / DGG
Karajan/Vienna PO. The greatest of the (digital) studio performances. –PM

Symphony no. 7 in E / LONDON
Chailly/Berlin RSO. This won't blow you away, but it is a very well done standard performance, with good playing and fine sound. –PM

○ **Symphony no. 8 in c / SEVEN SEAS**
Knappertsbusch/Berlin PO. Jan 7-8, 1951. So many details on this disk are as good or better than on any other performance,

and they all add up to a soulful and well-argued whole. My current favorite *Eighth*. –PM

Symphony no. 8 in c / DGG
Karajan/Vienna PO.

Symphony no. 8 in c / STRADIVARIUS
Nanut/Ljubljana SO. A very straightforward and dramatic super-budget performance, surprisingly well played and well recorded. A real deal! –PM

○ **Symphony no. 9 in d / SUPRAPHON**
Von Matacic/Czech PO. Anything Matacic does with Bruckner is worth hearing. I list only the *Ninth* because it has a special sweep, grandeur, and depth and a sense of inevitability. But it also has a buoyancy, so the symphony isn't quite so depressing as usual. The keystone of the work is nostalgia and longing, and there's plenty of that. –PM

Symphony no. 9 in d / DGG
Karajan/Berlin PO.

Symphony no. 9 in d / PHILIPS
Haitink/Royal Concertgebouw Orchestra. This is the best of the more "objective" style performances, with great playing and sound. –PM

Symphony no. 9 in d / DGG
Giulini/Vienna PO. Giulini's *Ninth* is a slow, power-packed, highly charged, emotionally draining live performance from 1989 (exact date not given), with superb, highly committed, and responsive playing by the VPO in top form. It's not for everyday use and not for everyone — safer standard readings remain Haitink's and Karajan's. Giulini's *Seventh* and *Eighth* are also good, but not like this. –PM

FERRUCCIO BUSONI   1866-1924

20th century. An Italian/German pianist and composer of chamber pieces whose later works imply a rethinking of his distinct compositional style. An accomplished concert pianist and visionary musical theorist, Busoni wrote with great subtlety and invention and created a strange tonal world entirely his own. –BGT

○ **Doktor Faust (opera) / DGG**
Hillebrecht, Cochran, Fischer-Dieskau, Kohn, Leitner/Bavarian RSO & Chorus. Busoni's masterpiece, which he worked on for 15 years. His original text is extremely interesting in its imagery and conceptually unlike any libretto form. The opening symphonia "Pax, Pax, Pax" for chorus and orchestra is one of the most transcendent and beautiful introductions ever written, and the fight between religious factions in the beerhall is one of the most telling scenes ever staged. –BGT

○ **Fantasia Contrappuntistica (solo piano) / CENTAUR**
O'Riley.

DIETRICH BUXTEHUDE   1637-1707

Baroque. A Danish (or German) organist and composer of vocal and organ music, sacred cantatas, and chorales. Buxtehude was the famed organist and composer whom J. S. Bach made a 200-mile journey on foot to hear. His organ music (toccatas, preludes and fugues, passacaglias, ciacconas, and chorale preludes) greatly influenced Bach with their clarity of line, nobility, and often daring harmonic invention. His chorale music contains innovations such as the exchange of the normal roles of the orchestra and chorus in *Gott hilf mir* ("God help me"): the orchestra plays the straight chorale tune while the singers provide elaborate ornamentations. –BGT

○ **Cantata Cycle in 7 parts / ARCHIV GALLERIA**
English Baroque Soloists, London Monteverdi Choir.

○ **Organ Music / CHANDOS**
Kee (organ). Various pieces played by Piet Kee on the newly restored 17th-century Grote Kerk organ in Alkmaar, Holland. A wonderful cross-section of work, this disc is well recorded and also contains works by Sweelinck. –BGT

○ **Sonatas for Violin, Viola da Gamba & Continuo /**
HARMONIA MUNDI
Boston Museum Trio.
Sonatas for Violin, Viola da Gamba & Continuo / DGG
Goebel/Musica Antiqua Köln.

WILLIAM BYRD   1543-1623

Renaissance, sacred choral. An extremely prolific British
organist and composer of sacred (Catholic and Anglican) and
secular vocal music and instrumental works, including
virginal music designed to be played at home. Byrd is
considered the "father of British music" and one of England's
greatest composers, highly praised both by his
contemporaries and by people today. –BGT
○ **Consort Music-Fretwork / VIRGIN**
○ **The Great Service / GIMELL**
Phillips/The Tallis Scholars.
☆ **Keyboard Musick / CLAVES**
Duetschler (harpsichord).
Keyboard Musick / KOCH-SCHWANN
Thornburgh.
☆ **Masses for 3, 4 & 5 voices / GIMELL**
Phillips/The Tallis Scholars.

ANDRÉ CAMPRA   1660-1744

Baroque, vocal. A French composer of sacred vocal works,
operas, and opera-ballets such as *Tancrède* (1702) and "*Les
fêtes venitiennes*" (1710). –ED
○ **L'Europe Galante (opera-ballet) / EDITO CLASSICA**
Yakar, Kweksilber (sopranos), Jacobs (countertenor),
Nimsgern (baritone), Leonhardt/La Petite Bande.
○ **Motet: Benedictus Dominus; Requiem - Vol. 2 / ADDA**
Niquet/Le Concert Spirituel. This is somehow not nearly so
good as Vol. 1 in either sound or performance, but I can still
recommend it to those interested in French baroque religious
music. –PM
○ **Te Deum; Deus in Nomine Tuo; Notus in Judea Deus /**
ADDA
Niquet/Le Concert Spirituel.

JOSEPH CANTELOUBE   1879-1957

20th century, nationalist. A French composer who arranged
and collected local French folk songs and produced four
volumes of *Chants d'Auvergne* for voice and orchestra (1923-
1930). He produced works in many other forms, including
opera. –ED
☆ **Songs of Auvergne / VANGUARD CLASSICS**
Davrath (soprano), de la Roche/Studio Orchestra. Probably
because Davrath is no opera star and has a lighter voice, she
leaves all later performers in the shade. –PM

MANUEL CARDOSA   1566-1650

Renaissance, sacred vocal. This Carmelite monk was an active
organist and choirmaster who wrote masses in the style of
Palestrina. He wrote a quantity of sacred music, most of it lost
in the Lisbon earthquake and fire of 1756. –MKS
○ **Requiem; Magnificat; Motets / GIMELL**
Phillips/The Tallis Scholars. This is late-Renaissance
Portuguese religious music performed with Peter Phillips's
usual purity. –PM

MARIO CASTELNUOVO-TEDESCO   1895-1968

20th century. An Italian-born American composer of
orchestral, chamber, and film music who wrote many songs
and pieces for guitar, including two guitar concertos and 24
preludes and fugues for two guitars. –MKS
○ **Concerto for Guitar & Orchestra no. 1 in D, op. 99 /**
LONDON
Fernandez, Gomez, Martinez/English CO.

Concerto for Guitar & Orchestra no. 1 in D, op. 99 /
PHILIPS
Romero, Marriner/ASMF.
○ **The Well-Tempered Guitar (24 preludes & fugues),**
op. 199 / TELDEC
Hill, Wiltschinsky. Also contains other guitar repertoire. –MKS

MARC-ANTOINE CHARPENTIER   1645-1704

Baroque. A French composer known mainly for church music
and motets and as a collaborator with Molière for theater
music. –ED
○ **Te Deum; Magnificat / ANGEL**
Marriner/ASMF Orchestra & Chorus.

ERNEST CHAUSSON   1855-1899

Romantic. A French composer of opera, chamber music, and
the symphonic poem *Viviane* (1882). The influences of
Wagner and Franck are evident in Chausson's music, although
he developed an intense individual style. –MKS
○ **Poème de l'amour et de la mer, for Voice & Piano**
(or Orchestra), op. 19 / COLLINS CLASSICS
Caballé, Morris/Symphonica of London.
○ **Poème for Violin & Orchestra, op. 25 / DGG**
Perlman, Mehta/NYPO.
○ **Symphony in B-flat, op. 20 / ASV**
D'Avalos/Philharmonia. D'Avalos is tough but tender —
this performance is powerful and yields plenty of new
insights. –PM

FRÉDÉRIC CHOPIN   1810-1849

Romantic. Except for some Polish songs and a few works for
cello and piano trio, Chopin devoted his life to the creation of
a richly melodic and harmonically original literature for the
keyboard. From dances of his Polish homeland (such as the
polonaise and the mazurka) to original "free" forms (such as
the ballade), his music is still loved today and studied by both
composition and keyboard students. –BGT
○ **Ballades (4) for Piano (complete), opp. 23, 38, 47, 52 /**
DGG
Zimerman (piano). This has beautiful sound and I like it a lot,
but I think it's fair to point out that some have found it
unacceptably mannered. –PM
Ballades (4) for Piano no. 1, op. 23 / DENON
Grimaud.
☆ **Concerto for Piano & Orchestra no. 1 in e, op. 11 /**
ANGEL
Pollini (piano), Kletzki/Philharmonia Orchestra.
Concerto for Piano & Orchestra no. 1 in e, op. 11 /
JECKLIN
Lipatti (piano), Ackerman/Zürich Tonhalle Orchestra.
Concerto for Piano & Orchestra no. 1 in e, op. 11 /
ANGEL
Lipatti (piano), Ackerman/Zürich Tonhalle Orchestra.
○ **Concertos for Piano & Orchestra nos. 1 & 2 /**
MELODIYA (KOCH)
Kissin (piano), Kitaenko/Moscow Philharmonic SO. Kissin
was all of 12-and-a-half when he made his debut concert
appearance on March 27, 1984, in the Grand Hall of the
Moscow Conservatory, playing and recording both Chopin
concertos. These performances are no "better" than a lot of
others, but there won't be any other 12-year-olds in the next
few centuries coming along to rival this. Kissin has everything
you need: technique, poetry, a sense of wonder and fantasy. In
addition, he has imagination and thinks about the notes he
plays. Amazing! –PM
Concertos for Piano & Orchestra nos. 1 & 2 / HUNT
Pollini, Kletzki/Orchestre National de l'ORTF. Recorded in
Paris just after he won the 1960 Chopin Competition, this is
Pollini's finest recording of the Chopin *First* in terms of
technical brilliance, spontaneity, and fire, and his only

recording of *Concerto no. 2* (featuring Milan Rai and Mario Rossie), which is a lot more ragged but still worth having. Acceptable pirate sound. –PM

○ **Concerto for Piano & Orchestra no. 2 in f, op. 21 / DGG**
Pogorelich (piano), Abbado/Chicago SO.

○ **Etudes (24) for Piano, opp. 10 & 25 / SAPHIR**
Varsi (piano). A terrific supplement to Pollini's, with very interesting phrasing and a good balance between poetry and passion. No mincing here, and a unique outlook. –PM

Etudes (24) for Piano, opp. 10 & 25 / DGG
Pollini (piano). A bit too hard-driven for me and stressing technique too much at the expense of poetry, but nothing's perfect, and this is the set (with good sound) by which all others are judged. –PM

☆ **Mazurkas (10) for Piano; Ballade no. 1; Scherzo no. 2; Prelude, op. 45 / DGG**
Michelangeli (piano). Michelangeli was at the height of his powers when he made this Chopin recital in 1964. If I were starting a Chopin collection, this is where I would begin. Outstanding sound, although the performance is a bit shallower on CD than LP. –PM

Mazurkas (10) for Piano / RCA
Rubinstein (piano). I've always felt Rubinstein to be a bit too bland in most music, including Chopin, but here his subtle sense of rhythm really stands him in good stead. If only he hadn't played with such a narrow and restricted dynamic range! –PM

○ **Nocturnes (21) for Piano / NONESUCH**
Moravec (piano). These were the best noctures ever as a set on LP; if only Nonesuch hadn't ruined the sound on CD — it's a shallow, thin-toned shell of its former self. But the control is still there, just not the resonance. –PM

Nocturnes (21) for Piano / PHILIPS
Arrau (piano). A bit choppy, the legato not all it should be. But the depth of tone is there, and the sound is gorgeous. –PM

○ **Piano Music (miscellaneous) / PEARL**
Koczalski (piano). First the bad news: The sound from 1923-1939 is not very good; especially in the louder parts, there is heavy 78-rpm noise and some ragged playing and missed notes. Now for the good: these are beautifully phrased and shaded performances, and the pure sound (allowing for such old recordings) Koczalski draws from his piano shines through remarkably well. You simply won't hear trills like this again, and the freedom and naturalness of his playing are remarkable, especially from one so unknown today. I mean, why wasn't he rediscovered sooner? –PM

○ **Polonaises for Piano nos. 1-7 / FORLANE**
Clidat (piano). Much more "human" and poetic than Pollini's. I like her phrasing, and the use of a Yamaha piano is interesting — very resonant bass but otherwise good sound. This one's a sleeper. –PM

Polonaises for Piano nos. 1-7 / DGG
Pollini (piano). A bit "objective" but with fearsome technique; sets the standard again. –PM

☆ **Preludes (24) for Piano, op. 28 / GLOBE**
Janssen (piano). My current favorite. This guy has it all: poetry and passion, a great technique, and taste. Plus he's got a splendid version of Ravel's *Tombeau* as makeweight. –PM

Preludes (24) for Piano, op. 28 / SUPRAPHON
Moravec (piano). Moravec's earlier set for Connoisseur Society was a bit more poetic and dynamic and had better sound, but this is still among the leaders. –PM

Preludes (24) for Piano, op. 28 / HUNGARATON
Ranki (piano). Another favorite. Ranki has a brilliant technique and is too straightforward and "cold" for some, but this is a thinking person's Chopin that also has depth and passion with not an ounce of sentimentality. –PM

Preludes (24) for Piano, op. 28 / DGG
Pogorelich (piano). Controversially slow in the slow ones and

fast in the fast, these are nevertheless performances that are always challenging and grow on you. Pollini takes 35 minutes, Pogorelich 45. That will give you some idea. –PM

○ **Scherzos (4) for Piano, opp. 20, 31, 39, 54 / DGG**
Pollini (piano). More rugged and intense than Moravec and certainly Arrau but possibly without quite the shading and individualism, especially of Arrau. A little bit too uptight. The recorded sound is sharp and thin, stressing brilliance at the expense of depth and soul. –PM

Scherzos (4) for Piano, opp. 20, 31, 39, 54 / DORIAN
Moravec (piano). Moravec's is a bit too mellow, but these are still good performances, with lifelike sound. –PM

Scherzos (4) for Piano, opp. 20, 31, 39, 54 / PHILIPS
Arrau (piano). Too slow, and the technique could be a bit better, but Arrau knows how to make a piano sound, and no one ever accused him of being superficial. These show-off pieces receive a decidedly "un-show-offish" approach. –PM

○ **Sonata for Cello & Piano in g, op. 65 / CLAVES**
Starck, Requejo. This recording has beautiful sound and very sensual playing. –PM

○ **Sonatas for Piano no. 1 in c, op. 4; no. 2 in b-flat, op. 35; no. 3 in b, op. 58 / ADDA**
Rodrigues (piano). With playing that is considerably warmer and more rhapsodic than Pollini's, this is a very nice foil to the latter's more dramatic and upfront approach. I love the sound. –PM

☆ **Sonata for Piano no. 2 in b-flat, op. 35 / DGG**
Pollini (piano). Possibly Pollini's greatest studio recording. Everything is just so "right" about this one. –PM

Sonata for Piano no. 2 in b-flat, op. 35 / DGG
Pogorelich (piano). One of my favorite Chopin recitals. As always, Pogorelich makes you rethink old pieces. –PM

○ **Sonata for Piano no. 3 in b, op. 58 / DGG**
Pollini.

○ **Waltzes (19) for Piano / ODYSSEY**
Lipatti (piano). No one's bettered it in 40 years; only Arrau and Pires have come close. –PM

Waltzes (19) for Piano / ERATO
Pires (piano). My favorite "modern" performance. She doesn't try to do too much with them. –PM

Waltzes (19) for Piano / PHILIPS
Arrau (piano). In Arrau's hands, miniature tone poems. –PM

DOMENICO CIMAROSA   1747-1801

Classical. An Italian composer of various concertos, chamber music, and operas, especially in the buffa style, whose vocal writing and orchestration make him an important predecessor to Rossini. –MKS

○ **Il Maestro di Cappella (intermezzo) for Bass & Chamber Orchestra / HUNGARATON**
Gregor, Pál/Corelli CO.

○ **Sonatas (32) for Keyboard (complete) / ASTORIA**
Mamou (piano).

JACOBUS CLEMENS NON PAPA   1510-1555

Renaissance, vocal. A French/Flemish composer of sacred vocal music, chansons, and drinking songs. –ED

○ **Missa & Motet, "Pastores Quidnam Vidistis" / GIMELL**
Phillips/The Tallis Scholars. One of Peter Phillips's greatest strengths is giving us completely unknown music in "definitive" performances. This one's a beauty and one of his best. –PM

MUZIO CLEMENTI   1752-1832

Classical. An Italian keyboardist and composer of keyboard sonatas, exercises, and symphonies. –ED

○ **Monferrinas (12) for Piano / AMON RA**
Burnett.

○ **Sonatas for Piano / ACCENT**
Immerseel (fortepiano). Clementi has suffered the slings and arrows of a fickle public over the years, but these fine fortepiano performances by Immerseel (and the ones above by Richard Burnett) could go some way toward restoring his tarnished reputation. –PM

LOUIS-NICOLAS CLÉRAMBAULT   1676-1749

Baroque. A successful French court composer of theatrical pieces and solo cantatas who also wrote for the organ. –MKS
○ **Medée: Cantata pour Soprano et Symphonie / KOCH-SCHWANN**
Baird (soprano), Schultz, Stephen/American Baroque. Stylishly sung and beautifully recorded French baroque cantatas. –PM

AARON COPLAND   1900-1990

20th century, nationalist. An American composer of film scores, opera, piano, chamber music, and other forms. Copland is best known for his ballet music (*Appalachian Spring*, 1944; *Rodeo*, 1942) and his orchestral works (*Lincoln Portrait*, 1942; *Fanfare for the Common Man*, 1942). Sincerely concerned about relating to a wide public without compromising his music, Copland succeeded brilliantly both with more complex works like the *Piano Variations* and *Twelve Poems of Emily Dickinson* (1949-1950) and the subtle simplicity of his highly popular ballet music suites. He was the quintessential American nationalist composer. –BGT
☆ **Appalachian Spring (complete ballet); Rodeo (four dance episodes); El salón México / LONDON**
Dorati/Detroit SO. The bright, positive sound that Copland is best known for. –BGT
○ **Appalachian Spring: Suite / DGG**
Bernstein/LAPO.
Appalachian Spring: Suite / CBS
Bernstein/NYPO.
Appalachian Spring: Suite / CBS
Copland/London SO.
☆ **Billy the Kid: Suite / CBS**
Bernstein/NYPO.
○ **Concerto for Clarinet & String Orchestra / CHANDOS**
Hilton (clarinet), Bamert/Scottish National Orchestra.
○ **Fanfare for the Common Man / CBS**
Bernstein/NYPO.
○ **Lincoln Portrait, for Speaker & Orchestra / TELARC**
Hepburn, Kunzel/Cincinnati Pops.
○ **Nonet for Strings; Appalachian Spring Suite; Two Pieces for String Orchestra / MUSIC MASTERS**
Davies/St. Luke's Chamber Ensemble. The nonet is a lovely, meditative work of somber tonality. –BGT
○ **Piano Variations / DELOS**
Fiero (piano). Also includes the *Passacaglia* and *Piano Fantasy*. –MKS
○ **Symphony no. 2 (Short Symphony) / PRO ARTE**
Davies/St. Paul CO. The *Short Symphony* is one of Aaron Copland's finest works — extremely interesting rhythmic complexity. –BGT
○ **Symphony no. 3 / DGG**
Bernstein/NYPO.
○ **The Tender Land (opera in 3 acts) / VIRGIN**
Brunelle/The Plymouth Music Series.
○ **Tribute to Aaron Copland / ANGEL**
Slatkin/St. Louis SO. Good collection and performance. Includes *Old American Songs*, *Quiet City*, and *Symphony no. 3 (finale)*. –MKS

ARCANGELO CORELLI   1653-1713

Baroque. An Italian violinist and composer of trio sonatas and concerti grossi who distinguished himself solely in

instrumental music and whose style typified the baroque period. Corelli created some of the most popular compositions of the 18th century — richly spirited music with a refined and touching melodic sense. –BGT
☆ **Concerti grossi (12), op. 6 / EDITO CLASSICA**
Kuijken/La Petite Bande. This performance is much more expressive and sensual than Pinnock's more dramatic and straightforward approach. –PM
Concerti grossi (12), op. 6 / DGG
Pinnock/English Consort. This is dramatic and lacks the Italian sun. –PM
Concerti grossi (12), op. 6 / HARMONIA MUNDI
McGegan/Philharmonia Baroque Orchestra. McGegan is very cute and mannered at times, but these are still unique and outstanding performances. –PM
○ **Concerto Grosso no. 8, op. 6, "Christmas" / KOCH-SCHWANN**
Werther/I Fiamminghi.
○ **La Folia & other sonatas / HYPERION**
Purcell Quartet.
○ **Sonatas after Concerti grossi, op. VI: Arrangements for 2 Recorders, Bassoon / OPUS 111**
Le Concert Français.
○ **Sonatas for 2 Violins & Continuo Instruments, opp. 1-4 (selections) / HYPERION**
Purcell Quartet.
○ **Sonatas (12) for Violin & Continuo Instruments, op. 5 / VERITAS**
Trio Sonnerie.
Sonatas (12) for Violin & Continuo Instruments, op. 5 / HYPERION
The Locatelli Trio.
○ **Trio Sonatas / DGG**
Pinnock/English Concert.
Trio Sonatas / PHILIPS
Huggett.
Trio Sonatas / ANGEL
Medlam/London Baroque.

WILLIAM CORNYSH   d1523

Renaissance. A British composer of sacred vocal works. –ED
○ **Complete Sacred Music Including Stabat Mater / GIMELL**
Phillips/The Tallis Scholars

FRANÇOIS COUPERIN   1668-1733

Baroque. A French harpsichordist and composer known for his boldly harmonized and highly ornamented harpsichord works of dance suites as well as organ, chamber, and sacred music. Possessed of a lively, curious mind and a refined, ironic sense of humor, Couperin (known as "The Great") wrote the *Pièces de Clavecin* as character portraits, both of general types and of specific people of his day, which are studied even today for their deliberate fantasy and innovativeness ("The Player," "The Courteous One," "The Little Nothing," and many others). He was also a master of the Italian and French vocal styles of the period, demonstrated in his profoundly lyrical church motets (*Legions de ténèbres*, for Ash Wednesday; a *Magnificat*). Couperin's music leads from the baroque to the early classical periods. –BGT
○ **Les Nations / ARCHIV GALLERIA**
Musica Antiqua Köln. I passed on this as an early digital album, but must admit it is a lot more stylish than I had remembered and easily the best *Nations* in the catalog, with fine early-digital sound. It simply doesn't sound quite French enough to these ears. –PM
○ **Pièces d'orgue consistantes en deux Messes no. 1 / HARMONIA MUNDI**
Chapuis.

☆ **Pièces de Clavecin (Books 1-4) / HARMONIA MUNDI**
Gilbert. This is one of the monumental Gramophone undertakings; stylish readings with beautiful sound — and it's complete. –PM

Pièces de Clavecin (selections) / DHM
Sempe (harpsichord). A very representative cross-section of 27 pieces, stylishly played and well recorded. –PM

LOUIS COUPERIN   1626-1661

Baroque. A French organist and composer of organ fugues, harpsichord, and plainchant music. Louis Couperin established the model of the French keyboard suite and wrote a famous treatise, *L'art de toucher le clavecin* ("The Art of Playing the Harpsichord"), which was studied by the young J. S. Bach. –BGT

Pièces de Clavecin (selections) / ASTREE
Verlet.

Pièces de Clavecin (selections) / EDITO CLASSICA
Leonhardt.

Pièces de Clavecin (selections) / GLOBE
Ogg.

BERNHARD HENRIK CRUSELL   1775-1838

Classical. A Finnish clarinetist and composer of clarinet concertos, quartets, and an opera. –ED

○ **Concertos (3) for Clarinet / ASV**
Johnson (clarinet), Herbig/RPO, Groves/English CO, Schwartz/English CO. Now Emma Johnson's three Crusell concertos have all been recoupled and placed on one CD, making choices even more difficult. –PM

○ **Concerto for Clarinet no. 1 in E-flat, op. 1 / HYPERION**
King, Francis/London SO.

○ **Concerto for Clarinet no. 2 in f, op. 5 / HYPERION**
King, Francis/London SO.

Concerto for Clarinet no. 2 in f, op. 5 / ASV
Johnson, Groves/English CO.

Concerto for Clarinet no. 2 in f, op. 5 / BIS
Leister (clarinet), Vanska/Lahti SO. Leister's got all three clarinet concertos on one CD, making his the better buy, but King has slightly better performances, especially from the orchestra. –PM

○ **Concerto for Clarinet no. 3 in B-flat, op. 11 / HYPERION**
King, Francis/London SO.

JEAN-HENRI D'ANGLEBERT   1635-1691

Baroque. French keyboardist, composer, and harpsichordist to Louis XIV whose works include organ fugues and dance suites; known for *Pièces de Clavecin* (1689). –ED

○ **Keyboard Works (selections) / GLOBE**
Ogg (harpsichord).

SIGISMONDO D'INDIA   1582-1629

Baroque. In his lifetime, this Italian composer was considered second only to Monteverdi. –MKS

○ **Lamento d'Olimpia & other laments / HYPERION**
Kirkby (soprano), Rooley (chitarrone).

PETER MAXWELL DAVIES   ♭1934

20th century. One of the most influential contemporary British composers, whose works combine seemingly disparate elements: evocations of medieval hymnody, surrealistic depictions of historic figures, and dramatic theatrical effects. He is also a political activist and an avid environmentalist. –MKS

○ **Concerto for Violin & Orchestra (1985) / CBS**
Stern, Previn/Royal PO.

○ **Eight Songs for a Mad King, for Baritone & Ensemble (1969) / UNICORN-KANCHANA**

Eastman, Davies/The Fires of London.

○ **Sinfonia; Sinfonia Concertante for 5 Solo Winds, Timpani & Strings / UNICORN-KANCHANA**
Davies/Scottish CO.

CLAUDE DEBUSSY   1862-1918

Impressionist. A French composer of piano music, opera, cantatas, ballets, and orchestral and chamber works. His most notable pieces are *Prélude à l'après-midi d'un faune (Prelude to the Afternoon of a Faun)* (1894) and *Nocturnes* (1899). Inspired often by pictorial subjects (Monet's water impressions became "reflections in the water" for piano) and by the elusive and unnameable in nature (footsteps in the snow, still leaves, and the hypnotic, overwhelming sensations of his rare visits to the French coastline), Debussy's music develops chords, melodies, and orchestration that are connected more by a single surreal observation than by an overriding logic. For example, one note is similar to another in a distantly related, enharmonic chord, but this brief tie is enough to follow, or a single gesture will soon evolve, spreading outward in all directions until a whole orchestral piece is made from a single falling line (*Afternoon of a Faun*; *Jeux*). Not bad for a kid born over his parents' china shop, who loved Lassus and Palestrina as much as ragtime and Javanese music. –BGT

○ **Arabesques (2) for Piano / DGG**
Vásary.

○ **Children's Corner Suite, for Piano / DGG**
Michelangeli.

○ **La damoiselle élue / DGG**
Ewing, Balleys, Abbado/London SO & Chorus. I never hope to hear a better performance. –PM

La damoiselle élue / COLLINS CLASSICS
Caballé, Coster, Morris/Symphonica of London.

○ **En blanc et noir, for 2 Pianos / LDR**
Coombs, Scott.

○ **Estampes (3) for Piano / DGG**
Richter.

Estampes (3) for Piano / FONE
Husson (piano). Beautiful touch and tone — Husson can hold her own with Richter. –PM

○ **Iberia (no. 2 from *Images pour Orchestre*) / DGG**
Abbado/London SO.

☆ **Images (6) for Piano (Books 1 & 2) / DGG**
Michelangeli (piano). Michelangeli hasn't made many studio recordings over the years, and each one should be savored. This and his Chopin on Deutsche Grammophon (DGG) are two of his best. –PM

Images (6) for Piano (Books 1 & 2) / PHILIPS
Arrau.

○ **Jeux-Poème Danse / PHILIPS**
Haitink/Royal Concertgebouw Orchestra. This performance has the best combination of sound, virtuoso performance, and atmosphere, but I certainly wouldn't want to be without the versions of Boulez and Celibidache, who provide unique touches. –PM

Jeux-Poème Danse / HUNT
Celibidache/Berlin PO. More sensual and free than Boulez and Haitink but just as well controlled and disciplined in its own way. –PM

Jeux-Poème Danse / CBS
Boulez/New Philharmonia Orchestra. The most "intellectual" of the three readings. –PM

☆ **La Mer / DGG**
Sinopoli/Philharmonia Orchestra. My current favorite: it combines passion with drama and is flamboyant but well held together. –PM

La Mer / DGG

Karajan/Berlin PO. Beautiful sonorities (Karajan is such a tone-meister), but it doesn't sound French enough for me. −PM

La Mer / PHILIPS
Haitink/Royal Concertgebouw Orchestra. Superbly played and recorded but a bit too controlled and objective for higher recommendation. −PM

La Mer / NUOVA ERA
Celibidache/Milan Italian Radio & TV SO. A pirate supplement to any of the brilliantly played and recorded ones listed. Combines intellect and emotion as only Celibidache can do — I just wish it had better sound, so the more general public could see just what a great musician this man is. −PM

☆ **Nocturnes (Nuages, Fêtes, Sirènes) for Orchestra & Chorus / PHILIPS**
Haitink/Royal Concertgebouw Orchestra. Along with his *Jeux*, the best Debussy Haitink has given us. −PM

Nocturnes (Nuages, Fêtes, Sirènes) for Orchestra & Chorus / DGG
Abbado/Boston SO.

○ **Pelléas et Mélisande (opera in 4 acts) (1892-1902) / ANGEL**
von Stade, Denize, Stilwell, van Dam, Raimondi, Karajan/Berlin PO.

○ **La plus que lente (waltz), for Piano / DGG**
Vásary.

○ **Prélude à l'apres-midi d'un faune / DGG**
Abbado/London SO.

Prélude à l'apres-midi d'un faune / DGG
Karajan/Berlin PO.

○ **Préludes for Piano (Books 1 & 2) / DGG**
Michelangeli (piano). This is the finest set of complete *Préludes* ever recorded (I still prefer either of Richter's recordings of Book 2, but neither is available on CD at the moment). When the going gets tough, Michelangeli is the man: no blurring of the notes, no excess pedaling for impressionistic effects — Michelangeli's up there on Mt. Olympus. He has what I call the "three tees" — taste, technique, and temperament, although many consider him cold and abstract. −PM

Préludes for Piano (Books 1 & 2) / PHILIPS
Arrau (piano). Much warmer piano sound than Michelangeli and not quite so commanding, but Arrau is very subtle, especially in chord voicing. I certainly wouldn't want to be without his preludes, especially since the sound is so rich compared to Michelangeli's sharp, dryer digital sound. −PM

Préludes for Piano (Books 1 & 2) / FINLANDIA
Tateno (piano). This won't rival any of my first choices in terms of finger dexterity or subtlety, but it is nice to have all these preludes on one CD in good sound. −PM

Préludes for Piano (Books 1 & 2) / ANGEL
Gieseking (piano). A major interpretation of these works. The use of pedal and the tone colors achieved are singular. −MKS

Préludes for Piano nos. 2, 3, 5 (Book 1) / DGG
Richter.

☆ **Quartet for Strings in g, op. 10 / WHITE LABEL**
Bartók Quartet. A terrific sleeper. Who would think a Hungarian quartet could play French music this well? A real bargain with the Ravel and the Dvořák American all on one disc. −PM

Quartet for Strings in g, op. 10 / DENON
Nuovo Quartetto. See the review of Ravel. −PM

○ **Sonata for Cello & Piano no. 1 in d / LONDON**
Rostropovich (cello), Britten (piano). Although not so piquant and French-sounding as it might be, this is still a rhapsodic and hypnotic performance by the greatest cellist who ever lived. Why did he ever take up conducting? −PM

Sonata for Cello & Piano no. 1 in d / PHILIPS
Gendron (cello), Françaix (piano). There are many good performances of this piece, but I'll take this one for its French stylishness. −PM

○ **Sonata for Flute, Viola & Harp no. 2 / PHILIPS**
Bourdin (flute), Lequien (viola), Challan (harp).

○ **Sonata for Violin & Piano no. 3 / PHILIPS**
Grumiaux (violin), Hajdu (piano).

○ **Songs / EMI**
Teyte, Cortot (piano). A reissue of a historic recording done in 1936. A wonderful collection of some of the composer's most effective songs. −MKS

Songs / NIMBUS
Cuenod, Isepp.

Songs / CLAVES
Fischer-Dieskau, Höll.

○ **Suite bergamasque, for Piano / DGG**
Vásry.

○ **Trio in G for Piano, Violin & Cello / INTERCORD**
Abegg Trio. An early piece but one worth getting to know, especially in this, the best performance yet issued. It is better played and moves with more forward momentum. −PM

○ **The Unknown Debussy: Little-Known Piano Works by Claude Debussy / UNICORN-KANCHANA**
Sharon (piano). 77 minutes worth of piano rarities, played with style, a delightful sense of whimsy. This album has some of the best piano sound I have ever heard. Moody, late-night listening. −PM

FREDERICK DELIUS   1862-1934

Romantic. A British composer of opera, vocal, choral, orchestral, and chamber music. The ear of the young Delius was engaged, one summer night in Florida, by the sound of close-harmony Afro-American singing gently wafting over the St. John River (he had been sent to manage an orange plantation). Delius suddenly realized that his vocation was to be a musician. A romantic with the musical vocabulary of the impressionists, he wrote often-imitated but never-matched tone poems of great subtlety and beauty in a very personal style that is not reducible to a formula. −BGT

○ **The Complete Stereo Orchestral Recordings / EMI**
Beecham/RPO. Nonpareil! −PM

○ **Hassan: Intermezzo and Serenade; A Song before Sunrise / LONDON**
Marriner/ASMF. With sensual and well-held-together readings, this is the place to start with Delius. If you like it, by all means move on to the extraordinary Beecham. −PM

○ **Irmelin Prelude / CHANDOS**
del Mar/Bournemouth Sinfonietta.

○ **Late Swallows, for String Orchestra; On Hearing the First Cuckoo in Spring / CHANDOS**
del Mar/Bournemouth Sinfonietta.

○ **Quartet for Strings / ASV**
Brodsky Quartet.

○ **Sea Drift, for Baritone, Orchestra & Chorus (poem by Walt Whitman); Florida Suite / ARGO**
Hampson, Mackerras/Welsh National Opera, Orchestra & Chorus.

JOSQUIN DES PREZ   1440-1521

Renaissance. A greatly regarded and influential French composer of the High Renaissance who wrote sacred music and secular chansons. Des Prez was one of the most innovative of the later 15th-century contrapuntalists, balancing unequal phrases into an eventual unity and employing unusual modes with great purity, grace, and depth of emotion. −BGT

○ **Benedicta es / GIMELL**
Phillips/The Tallis Scholars.

○ **Missa, "Hercules Dux Ferrariae"; Motets / ANGEL**
Hiller/Hilliard Ensemble.

☆ Missa, "La sol fa re mi"; Missa, "Pange lingua" /
GIMELL
Phillips/The Tallis Scholars.
○ Motets / HARMONIA MUNDI
Herreweghe/La Chapelle Royale Chorus.

ANDRÉ CARDINAL DESTOUCHES   1672-1749

Baroque. A seminal composer in the transition from
mythological musical drama to early opera. −BGT
○ Les Eléménts (opera-ballet) / OISEAU-LYRE
Hogwood/Academy of Ancient Music.

ERNST VON DOHNÁNYI   1877-1960

Romantic. A widely respected Hungarian pianist, melodist,
and composer of orchestral and chamber music with a
stylistic mix of Brahms (who admired his earlier chamber and
pieces) and Liszt; known for *Variations on a Nursery Song*
(1914). −BGT
○ Serenade for String Trio in C, op. 10 (1902) / CALIG
Vienna String Trio.
○ Variations on a Nursery Song, for Piano & Orchestra,
op. 25; Ruralia hungarica / WHITE LABEL
Lantos, Lehel/Budapest SO.

GAETANO DONIZETTI   1797-1848

Romantic, opera. A leading Italian opera composer of the
1830s and 40s who also wrote sacred and instrumental
chamber music; known for *Don Pasquale* (1843), *Maria di
Rohan* (1843), *L'elisir d'amore* (1832), and *Lucia di
Lammermoor* (1835). As an important exponent of the bel
canto style, Donizetti wrote more than 70 operas in his life,
which are noted for their fluent melodies, brilliant
orchestration, and the individuality and believability of the
characters as supported in the music. −BGT
○ Anna Bolena (opera) / LONDON
Sutherland, Mentzer, Manca di Nissa, Hadley, Ramey,
Bonynge/Welsh National Opera.
☆ L'elisir d'amore (opera) / LONDON
Sutherland, Pavarotti, Malas, Cossa, Bonynge/English CO.
○ La fille du regiment (opera) / LONDON
Sutherland, Sinclair, Pavarotti, Malas, Bonynge/Royal Opera
House.
○ Lucia di Lammermoor (3-act opera) / ANGEL
Callas, di Stefano, Gobbi, Arie, Serafin/Maggio Musicale
Fiorentino.
Lucia di Lammermoor (3-act opera) / LONDON
Sutherland, Pavarotti, Milnes, Ghiaurov, Bonynge/Royal
Opera.
○ Lucrezia Borgia (3-act opera) / LONDON
Sutherland, Horne, Aragall, Wixell, Bonynge/National
Philharmonic.
Lucrezia Borgia (3-act opera) / LONDON
Sutherland, Tourangeau, Pavarotti, Morris, Soyer,
Bonynge/Bologna Teatro Community Orchestra & Chorus.

JOHN DOWLAND   1563-1626

Renaissance. A British composer of melancholy songs, lute
music, and sacred and secular vocal music. Dowland was one
of the greatest and most insightful songwriters who ever lived.
His instrumental works demonstrate a mastery of
contrapuntal complexity and a feeling for rhythmic liveliness.
His famous *Lachrimae*, or *Seaven Teares*, was also acclaimed
in literary circles. −BGT
○ Ayres (songs for voice & lute in 3 books) / VIRGIN
Kirkby (soprano), Rooley (lute and orpharion).
☆ Lachrimae (Seaven Teares) / VIRGIN
Fretwork (viols & lute consort).

Lachrimae (Seaven Teares) / BIS
Lindberg/Dowland Consort.
○ A Pilgrim's Solace (songs for voice & lute) / VIRGIN
Kirkby (soprano), Rooley (lute and orpharion).
○ Songs / VIRGIN
Chance (countertenor), Wilson (lute), Fretwork.

GUILLAUME DUFAY   1398-1474

Medieval, sacred choral. The French composer of the motet
Nuper Rosarum Flores (1436) and many masses and sacred
vocal works; considered the leading composer of his time.
Skilled in the *fauxbourdon* style (vocal imitation of an
instrumental drone), Dufay created fascinating religious
music based on folk tunes and notable for its rhythmic twists
and turns, beauty of its pure melodic line, and moments of
startling harmonic cadences. His music opens an auditory
time-window into pre-codified musical sensibilities. −BGT
○ Missa & Chanson, "Se la face ay pale"; Chansons
"Resvelons nous" & "Bon jour, bon mois" / NUOVA ERA
Chiaroscuro Ensemble.
☆ Missa, "L'Homme Arme" / ANGEL
Hillier Ensemble.

PAUL DUKAS   1865-1935

Romantic. A French composer of symphonies, opera, ballet
music (*La Peri*, 1912), and a piano sonata (*Sonata in e-flat
minor*); known for *The Sorcerer's Apprentice* (1897). −ED
○ The Sorcerer's Apprentice / DGG
Levine/Berlin PO.
○ Symphony in C / CLAVES
Foster/Monte Carlo PO.

MARCEL DUPRÉ   1886-1971

20th century. A French organist and composer of virtuoso and
modal organ pieces and religious symphonic works. −ED
○ Symphonie-Passion for Organ, op. 23; Symphony for
Organ no. 2, op. 26 / ADDA
Mathieu (organ). This seethes with an underlying current of
passion. −PM

FRANCESCO DURANTE   1684-1755

Baroque. An Italian composer of sacred masses, dramas,
cantatas, and instrumental works. −ED
○ Concerto for Organ & Strings in g / CLAVES
Noda (double bass), Meyer/Sonare Quartet Frankfurt. I have a
very soft spot in my heart for this recording. −PM
○ Concertos for Strings nos. 1-5, 8 / CAPRICCIO
Camerata Köln. The playing could have a bit more Italian
warmth, but I like the slight astringency and roughness too,
and these concertos are well worth getting to know. −PM

MAURICE DURUFLÉ   1902-1986

20th century. A French organist and composer in a modal style
who is known for his *Requiem* (1947). −ED
○ Requiem, op. 9 / HYPERION
Murray, Allen, Best/English CO.

HENRI DUTILLEUX   b1916

Modern. A French composer of instrumental, orchestral,
chamber, and piano works. −ED
○ Choral, Cadence & Fugato for Trombone & Piano /
ADDA
Sluchin, P. Aimard, L. Aimard.
○ Quartet for Strings / ADDA
Rosamonde Quartet. A challenging but relatively lyrical and
gentle string quartet from 1977. −PM
○ Symphony no. 1 / HARMONIA MUNDI
Baudo/Lyon Orchestra National.

ANTONIN DVORÁK   1841-1904

Romantic. The dean of Czech composers and a violist and composer with a major output of orchestral and chamber music, including *Symphony no. 9, "From the New World"* (1893); *String Sextet in A, op. 48* (1878); and *Trio for Violin, Cello, & Piano no. 3 in f, op. 65* (1883). Dvorák is noted for his symphonies and symphonic poems, which have the emotional energy and scope of conception found in Schubert and Beethoven. –BGT

○ **Carnival Overture, op. 92 / LONDON**
Chailly/Royal Concertgebouw Orchestra. Easily the best-played and best-recorded performance I have ever heard. It misses only a few of the insights to be found in the more rustic performances of the Czech Philharmonic. –PM
Carnival Overture, op. 92; Overtures opp. 62, 67, 91, 93 / SUPRAPHON
Ancerl/Czech PO. Ancerl ranks right up there as one of the most underrated conductors of all time, and despite many slight orchestral imperfections, these are the most natural, outdoorsy, and sensual recordings of the major Dvorák overtures ever made. You won't hear this kind of tenderness and warm-hearted playing these days, not even from the proud and glorious Czech Philharmonic. –PM
☆ **Concerto for Cello & Orchestra in b, op. 104 / DGG**
Rostropovich (cello), Karajan/Berlin PO. Combining passion and drama in equal parts, this is still Rostropovich's best recording among the six he made of this work. –PM
Concerto for Cello & Orchestra in b, op. 104 / LONDON
Harrell (cello), Ashkenazy/Philharmonia Orchestra.
Concerto for Cello & Orchestra in b, op. 104 / DGG
Fournier (cello), Szell/Berlin PO.
○ **Concerto for Piano & Orchestra in g, op. 33 / MELODRAM**
Richter (piano), Smetácek/Czech PO. Richter's studio performance with Kleiber is out of print, but this one with Smetácek is even more spontaneous and dramatic, although not so note-perfect. –PM
Concerto for Piano & Orchestra in g, op. 33 / VOX BOX
Firkusny (piano), Neumann/Czech PO. This fourth recording of Firkusny's, recorded live in a triumphal return to Prague after four decades, is spectacular. The quality of recording is excellent, and the playing is full of warmth and vitality. –MKS
☆ **Concerto for Violin & Orchestra in a, op. 53 / FIDELIO**
Suk, Ancerl/Czech PO. This classic earlier performance has more purity and intense poetry than the later remake with Neumann. –PM
Concerto for Violin & Orchestra in a, op. 53 / ANGEL
Little (violin), Handley/Royal Liverpool PO. Remarkably fresh and spontaneous performance by this young violinist. –PM
Concerto for Violin & Orchestra in a, op. 53 / VOX BOX
Ricci (violin), Susskind/St. Louis SO. Ricci is an original and interesting violinist. In this age of copycats, it's nice to know he's still around to give us a glimpse of past violin glories. –PM
○ **Cypresses, for String Quartet / DGG**
Hagen Quartet.
○ **My Home (concert overture), op. 62 / SUPRAPHON**
Ancerl/Czech PO.
○ **Othello (concert overture) / SUPRAPHON**
Ancerl/Czech PO.
○ **Piano Music (4-hand piano works) / OLYMPIA**
Thorson, Thurber.
○ **Quartets for Piano & Strings in D, op. 23 & E-flat, op. 87 / HYPERION**
Domus Ensemble.
Quartets for Piano & Strings in D, op. 23 & E-flat, op. 87 / ODYSSEY
Firkusny/Members of the Juilliard String Quartet.

☆ **Quartet for Strings no. 12 in F, op. 96, "American" / SUPRAPHON**
Panocha Quartet. The Panocha have plenty of energy and great recorded sound. They really sound authentically Czech. –PM
Quartet for Strings no. 12 in F, op. 96, "American" / LONDON
Janácek Quartet.
Quartet for Strings no. 12 in F, op. 96, "American" / WHITE LABEL
Bartók Quartet.
Quartet for Strings no. 12 in F, op. 96, "American" / DGG
Hagen Quartet.
○ **Quartet for Strings no. 13 in G, op. 106 / SUPRAPHON**
Panocha Quartet.
○ **Quartet for Strings no. 14 in A-flat, op. 105 / SUPRAPHON**
Panocha Quartet.
○ **Quintet for Piano & Strings in A, op. 81 / ODYSSEY**
Firkusny (piano)/Members of the Juilliard String Quartet. Dramatic but also very rustic and Czech-sounding. –PM
○ **Quintet for Strings in E-flat, op. 97 / HYPERION**
Raphael Ensemble.
○ **Serenade for String Orchestra in E, op. 22 / PHILIPS**
Marriner/ASMF.
Serenade for String Orchestra in E, op. 22 / DGG
Orpheus CO.
Serenade for String Orchestra in E, op. 22 / LONDON
Hogwood/London PO.
Serenade for String Orchestra in E, op. 22 / TELDEC
Wolff/St. Paul CO. A wonderful, lyrical performance with excellent playing by the St. Paul Orchestra. –MKS
○ **Serenade for Winds in D, op. 44 / LONDON**
Hogwood/London PO.
Serenade for Winds in D, op. 44 / PHILIPS
Marriner/ASMF.
Serenade for Winds in D, op. 44 / DGG
Orpheus CO.
○ **Sextet for Strings in A, op. 48 / HYPERION**
Raphael Ensemble.
○ **Slavonic Dances for Orchestra, opp. 46 & 72 / BIS**
Segerstam/Rheinland-Pfalz State PO.
Slavonic Dances for Piano Duet, op. 46 & 72 / OLYMPIA
Thorson, Thurber.
○ **Stabat Mater, op. 58 / CHANDOS**
Bélohlávek/Czech PO, Prague Philharmonic Chorus.
Stabat Mater, op. 58 / SUPRAPHON
Sawallisch/Czech PO & Chorus.
Stabat Mater, op. 58 / SUPRAPHON
Benácková, Wenkel, Dvorsky, Rootering, Sawallisch/Czech PO.
○ **Symphonic Variations, op. 78 / LONDON**
Kertesz/London SO.
○ **Symphonies (9) (complete) / LONDON**
Kertesz/London SO.
Symphonies (9) (complete) / DGG
Kubelik/Berlin PO.
Symphonies (9) (complete) / PHILIPS
Rowicki/London SO. Rowicki is more structured and architectural than Kertesz, who is looser and a good deal more outdoorsy and woodsy. Kubelik is somewhere in between. –PM
Symphony no. 4 in d, op. 13 / LONDON
Kertesz/London SO.
○ **Symphony no. 5 in F, op. 76 / MULTISONIC**
Kulinsky/Prague PO. Don't be misled by the obscure conductor and orchestra. These are fine, genuinely Czech

performances with oodles of charm and enough drama and momentum to keep things from sagging. –PM

Symphony no. 5 in F, op. 76 / LONDON
Kertesz/London SO.

○ **Symphony no. 6 in D, op. 60 / LONDON**
Kertesz/London SO.

☆ **Symphony no. 7 in d, op. 70 / PHILIPS**
Davis/Royal Concertgebouw Orchestra. It isn't digital, but it's by far the best *Seventh* around, and a good *Eighth* too. –PM

Symphony no. 7 in d, op. 70 / LODIA
Paita/Philharmonic SO.

☆ **Symphony no. 8 in G, op. 88 / LODIA**
Paita/Royal PO.

Symphony no. 8 in G, op. 88 / MAP
Welser-Möst/Norrkoping SO. Welser-Möst has so much energy and subtlety that this is a real collector's item. The orchestra plays way above their heads, there is plenty of tension and rustic feeling, and the sound is as good as there is. Now for the downside: There is a good deal of tape-hiss in this 1986 ADD recording. –PM

Symphony no. 8 in G, op. 88 / DGG
Karajan/Vienna PO. This is more together and unified than Karajan's earlier performance, but I miss the special touches. With great sound and funky playing, it gets the safest overall recommendation. –PM

☆ **Symphony no. 9 in e, op. 95, "From the New World" / SUPRAPHON**
Ancerl/Czech Philharmonic. Reticent and vulnerable in the quiet parts, slashing and powerful in the dramatic, this very Czech-sounding performance has always been a special favorite of mine. –PM

Symphony no. 9 in e, op. 95, "From the New World" / DGG
Karajan/Vienna PO. The best international, generic performance. Everything sounds "right," but I miss the special Czech sound of the Ancerl. –PM

Symphony no. 9 in e, op. 95, "From the New World" / PHILIPS
Davis/Royal Concertgebouw Orchestra. All of Davis's Dvorák has a special funky, rustic, outdoorsy quality that is hard to resist. –PM

GOTTFRIED VON EINEM   b1918

Modern. An Austrian composer-in-residence at the Dresden State Opera, whose harmonic idiom is terse, his melodies often bordering on the atonal. –MKS

○ **String Trio in E-flat, op. 74 / CALIG**
Vienna String Trio.

HANNS EISLER   1898-1962

20th century, serial. A German composer of songs, film scores, and incidental music that reflects socialist politics. Eisler is widely known for his political works, which beautifully adapt modern techniques (such as 12-tone harmonies) to generally accessible but noncompromised song forms that honestly state our current relations with each other and express hope for a more humane future. He also wrote extended forms and tone poems in a personal and unique style of vivid melody and color. –BGT

○ **Deutsche Sinfonie (German Symphony) / ARS VIVENDI**
Pommer/Berlin RSO & Chorus. Text by Bertolt Brecht.

○ **Divertimento for Wind Quintet, op. 4 / ARS VIVENDI**
Danzi Wind Quintet, Berlin.

○ **Variations for Flute, Clarinet, Violin, Viola, Cello & Piano, op. 70 / ARS VIVENDI**
Deutsche Staatsoper, Friedrich-Carl Erben/Berlin.

○ **Vierzehnte Arten den Regen zu beschreiben (Fourteen Ways of Describing the Rain) / MD&G**
Ensemble "des neuen werk" Hamburg.

EDWARD ELGAR   1857-1934

Romantic. A British composer of choral, orchestral, chamber, and instrumental music known for the oratorio *The Dream of Gerontius* (1900) and the tone poem *Enigma Variations* (1899). A chronological list of Elgar's works is like an autobiography of his interior life within English society, from the early choral works about the "hero" bringing new vision and even a childlike sense of wonder (*The Black Night, op. 25*, 1889), to the mysterious tone poems that, while they lack a specific program, often contain musical portraits of friends and family in the process of self-discovery (*Enigma Variations*), and finally to the stark landscape and lone-survivor solos of the *Concerto for Cello & Orchestra in e* (1919). He is known for developing a unique variation technique for symphonic writing and for the popular *Pomp and Circumstance March no. 1, op. 39.* –BGT

○ **Chanson de Nuit, no. 1, op. 15 / CHANDOS**
del Mar/Bournemouth Sinfonietta.

☆ **Concerto for Cello & Orchestra in e, op. 85 / PHILIPS**
Schiff, Marriner/Dresden State Orchestra. Least depressing and most sensitive of all the many versions. –PM

○ **Concerto for Violin & Orchestra in b, op. 61 / DGG**
Perlman (violin), Barenboim/Chicago SO. Perlman has such utter command of the violin part. –PM

○ **Elegy for Strings, op. 58 / LONDON**
Marriner/ASMF.

☆ **Enigma Variations, op. 36 / LONDON**
Monteux/London SO. Another one of those terrific bargains. The sound is a little dated, but this is the most natural *Enigma* ever recorded. –PM

Enigma Variations, op. 36 / DGG
Sinopoli/Philharmonia Orchestra. Although Sinopoli doesn't have quite the control or wonderful naturalness of Monteux, he is more serious and moving, without being depressing or oppressive. PM

Enigma Variations, op. 36 / VIRGIN
Litton/Royal PO.

○ **Falstaff (symphonic study), op. 68 / EMI**
Mackerras/London PO. If the Boult becomes available, snatch it up. In the meantime, this will have to do. But Boult "owns" *Falstaff.* –PM

○ **Introduction and Allegro for Strings, op. 47 / LONDON**
Marriner/ASMF.

○ **Quartet for Strings in e, op. 83 / ASV**
Brodsky Quartet.

Quartet for Strings in e, op. 83 / CHANDOS
Gabrieli Quartet.

○ **Quintet for Piano & Strings in a, op. 84 / ASV**
Schiller/Coull String Quartet.

☆ **Symphony no. 1 in A-flat, op. 55 / ANGEL**
Boult/London PO. No one touches Boult, who recorded the symphonies five times. –PM

Symphony no. 1 in A-flat, op. 55 / ARGO
Mackerras/London SO.

☆ **Symphony no. 2 in E-flat, op. 63 / ANGEL**
Boult/London PO.

Symphony no. 2 in E-flat, op. 63 / DGG
Sinopoli/Philharmonia Orchestra. Very broad and exquisitely detailed in a much more international, less English performance that goes a long way toward making Elgar a bit more universal. –PM

GEORGES ENESCU   1881-1955

20th century. A Romanian violinist and composer known for rhapsodic, poetic orchestral music (such as *Rhapsodies Roumanains,* 1901) that speaks with an original elegance and a flow of melodic invention, showing a different feeling for this part of Europe than has been expressed by other composers. −BGT

○ **Roumanian Rhapsody no. 1 / MERCURY**
Dorati/London SO.

○ **Sonatas for Violin & Piano no. 2, op. 6 & no. 3, op. 25 / HYPERION**
A. Oprean (violin), J. Oprean (piano). Rhapsodic pieces and performances in very fine digital sound. −PM

MANUEL DE FALLA   1876-1946

Romantic. An important Spanish composer of opera, oratorio, piano, and ballet music such as *El amor brujo* ("Love, the Magician") and *El sombrero de tres picos* ("The Three-Cornered Hat"). De Falla wrote bold, passionate, and colorful Andalusian gypsy dance forms with folk-style original melodies (*Fantasia betica*); operas and zarzuelas (a Spanish operetta form) about magic: *El amor brujo* ("Love, the Magician") contains the famous "Ritual Fire Dance" to ward off evil spirits while pots and pans are being forged); and mirthful pieces (*El sombrero de tres picos*, a ballet about a miller's wife and a presuming town official). −BGT

☆ **El amor brujo (ballet), for Mezzo-Soprano & Orchestra / LONDON**
Tourangeau, Dutoit/Montreal SO.

○ **Fantasia betica, for Piano / LONDON**
de Larrocha.

☆ **Nights in the Gardens of Spain, for Piano & Orchestra / LONDON**
de Larrocha, de Burgos/London PO. To me, the earlier one is fresher and more Spanish-sounding, but the later one does have better sound. −PM

Nights in the Gardens of Spain, for Piano & Orchestra / LONDON
de Larrocha (piano), Dutoit/Montreal SO.

○ **The Three-Cornered Hat (ballet), for Soprano & Orchestra / LONDON**
Berganza (soprano), Ansermet/Suisse Romande.

The Three-Cornered Hat (excerpts) / LONDON
de Larrocha (piano).

GILES FARNABY   1563-1640

Renaissance. An important English composer of sacred and secular vocal music and keyboard pieces. −MKS

○ **Keyboard Works (selections - fantasias, etc.) / ADDA**
Hantai (harpsichord).

GABRIEL FAURÉ   1845-1924

Romantic, vocal. A French organist and composer of orchestral, piano, chamber, vocal, and dramatic music, such as the opera *Penelope* (1913). Fauré wedded the chromatic freedom of the Wagnerian palette with his strong French sensibility for melodic line and transparent timbres, retaining his own compositional voice to create pieces of great beauty. His songs (over 100) establish a new relation of music to words — by never reacting directly to the meaning of the words, Fauré uses the music to change and/or expand them, making the piano more than a mere accompaniment: it is an integral part of the composition. −BGT

○ **Dolly (4-hand piano suite), op. 56 / PHILIPS**
K. and M. Labeque.

○ **Elégie for Cello & Orchestra / LONDON**
Harrell (cello), Chailly/Berlin RSO.

○ **Fantasie for Flute & Piano, op. 79 / ARGO**
Bennett, Marriner/ASMF.

○ **Fantasie for Piano & Orchestra in G, op. 111 / LONDON**
de Larrocha, Foster/London PO. Also contains Franck symphony and Ravel concertos in D and G −BGT

○ **Nocturnes nos. 1, 6, 7, 12, 13; Barcarolles; Impromptus; Theme & Variations for Piano in c#, op. 73 / NIMBUS**

Perlmuter.

○ **Quartets (2) for Piano & Strings, opp. 15 & 45 / HYPERION**
Domus.

☆ **Requiem, op. 48 / HYPERION**
Best/Corydon Singers. Ethereal. −PM

Requiem, op. 48 / COLLEGIUM
Ashton, Varcoe, Rutter/The Cambridge Singers & City of London Sinfonia members. Rutter reconstructed it, and his recording remains one of the best. −PM

○ **Sonata for Cello & Piano in g, op. 117 / HYPERION**
Isserlis, Devoyon.

○ **Sonata for Violin & Piano in A, op. 13 / DGG**
Mintz (violin), Bronfman (piano).

○ **Songs / PHILIPS**
Souzay, Baldwin. "Minor" masterpieces of lyric subtlety with texts by Hugo, Baudelaire, Gautier, Verlaine, and so forth. −BGT

BRIAN FERNEYHOUGH   b 1943

20th century. Ferneyhough studied in England and the Netherlands, has taught in Germany and the US, and is considered one of the most important younger English composers. −MKS

○ **Miscellaneous Chamber Works / ET CETERA**
Spanjaard/Nieuw Ensemble. Extremely modern and dissonant British composer living in Switzerland. Only for the very adventurous. −PM

○ **Sonatas for String Quartet; Quartets nos. 2 & 3; Adagissimo / DISQUES MONTAIGNE (HMD)**
Arditti Quartet.

JOHN FIELD   1782-1837

Romantic. An Irish pianist and composer of delicate and expressive piano pieces. Field was the inventor of the nocturne, a new concept in romantic music and a precursor to Chopin's work in that form (Chopin taught his pupils Field's work). Field, the proverbially incurable romantic, was on the move all his life — from Ireland to Paris to Vienna to St. Petersburg to Moscow. His lovely piano concertos have the grace and subtle line of his nocturnes. Many of his other piano works remain unplayed. −BGT

○ **Nocturnes nos. 1, 2, 4, 5, 6, 8-16, 18 / TELARC**
O'Connor (piano).

○ **Rondo for Piano & Strings in A-flat / EDITO CLASSICA**
Selheim/Collegium Aureum. Also contains Boccherini concerto with Schobert (piano). −BGT

GERALD FINZI   1901-1956

20th century. A British composer primarily of neo-romantic and folk-influenced songs and some chamber pieces, influenced by Elgar and Vaughan Williams. Like Britten, Finzi was a conscientious objector; his *Farewell to Arms, for Tenor & String Orchestra, op. 9* (1926-1945) expresses the futility of destruction. *Concerto for Clarinet & Strings* (1949), with its energetic and extroverted style, shows a happier side of the composer and is Finzi's most popular work. Even in this work there are moments of introspection, but they are more pastoral and lyrical, and the work ends with a burst of impetuous energy. −BGT

☆ **Concerto for Clarinet & String in c, op. 31 / HYPERION**
King, Francis/Philharmonia Orchestra. One of Finzi's best pieces, in a great performance. −PM

○ **Song Cycles for Baritone & Piano (poems of Hardy) / HYPERION**
Varcoe, Benson.

○ **Song Cycles for Tenor & Piano (poems by Hardy) / HYPERION**
Hill, Benson.

ANTOINE FORQUERAY   1671-1745

Baroque. A French viola da gambist and court composer to Louis XIV. –MKS

○ **Livre de Clavecin de Madame Forqueray / ERATO**
Koopman (harpsichord). Probably a bit too much ornamentation for most people's taste, but these are major additions to the harpsichord literature. Exciting, highly charged, aggressive performances. –PM

○ **Suites in D & g (transcribed from *Viola da Gamba Pieces* by Jean-Baptiste Forqueray) / SONY**
Leonhardt (harpsichord). Leonhardt can be recommended, especially since there's no overlap with the Koopman disc, but his playing on this occasion seems a bit heavy-handed, and I definitely prefer the harpsichord and sound quality on Koopman's, making his the clear first choice among Forqueray harpsichord discs. –PM

CÉSAR FRANCK   1822-1890

Romantic. A noted French organist and composer of chamber, symphonic, keyboard, and sacred choral music, whose major works include *Six Pièces* (1862) and *Les Béatitudes* (1879). In the late 1800s, when France was still in shock from war and warring factions, Franck and his pupils (d'Indy, Chausson, and others, often called "la bande à Franck") steered French composition toward symphonic and chamber music and away from the more conservative opera. Franck incorporated organ-like textures, timbres, and immense sonorities of highly chromatic adoration and idealism into his symphonic compositions, with which his graceful chamber works stand in constrast (*Sonata for Violin & Piano in a, Variations symphoniques for Piano & Orchestra* — his masterpiece). –BGT

☆ **Sonata for Violin & Piano in A / MOBILE FIDELITY**
Oistrakh (violin), Richter (piano). This is the classic but may be hard to find. –PM

Sonata for Violin & Piano in A / DGG
Shaham (violin), Oppitz (piano). I just love the intensity and lack of sentimentality in Shaham's playing. Oppitz's accompaniments are just fine and much better than his somewhat unimaginative solo playing. –PM

Sonata for Violin & Piano in A / DGG
Mintz, Bronfman.

Sonata for Violin & Piano in A / LONDON
Perlman (violin), Ashkenazy (piano).

○ **Symphonic Variations for Piano & Orchestra / RICERCAR**
Ciccolini (piano), Strauss/Liege PO. This recording also contains *Le chasseur maudit, Les djinns, Les éolides, Psyche*, and the *Symphony in d*. –BGT

☆ **Symphony in d / PHILIPS**
Bychkov/Orchestre de Paris. Passionate but restrained, with more dignity than usual. –PM

Symphony in d / LONDON
Ashkenazy/Berlin RSO. Ashkenazy lets you hear everything (his counterpoint is very clear), and he's a bit faster and more dramatic in the last two movements. –PM

Symphony in d / ASV
D'Avalos/Philharmonia Orchestra. D'Avalos is more sensuous, "mystical," and "romantic," but he still manages to hold it all together, really making you love this much-maligned work. –PM

Symphony in d / DGG
Giulini/Berlin PO. Molded in the intense Giulini style. –PM

GIROLAMO FRESCOBALDI   1583-1643

Baroque. An Italian organist and composer primarily of keyboard music and some sacred and secular vocal music who is said to have had a beautiful singing voice and been an accomplished lute and organ player. Frescobaldi's keyboard pieces transformed the toccata into a much more dramatic

form and were used as instrumental breaks during the mass (for instance, when the host was elevated). He introduced the variation technique into the canzone, brilliant chromatic counterpoint in the fugal ricercare, and was one of the few composers whose work J. S. Bach, while learning the craft of music, copied out in full by hand. –BGT

○ **Harpsichord Works (selections) / PHILIPS**
Leonhardt.

○ **Il primo libro di capricci (12 harpsichord works) / EDITO CLASSICA**
Leonhardt.

○ **Toccate, Canzona, Partite, Capricci for Harpsichord / GLOBE**
Egarr (harpsichord). Add another outstanding Frescobaldi collection to the two by Leonhardt. –PM

JOHANN JAKOB FROBERGER   1616-1667

Baroque. A German organist and composer of keyboard music credited with contributing to the standardization of the baroque suites. –MKS

○ **Harpsichord Works (various) / FHM**
Rousset (harpsichord). The best young harpsichordist I've heard in years. He simply seems to capture the moods of most pieces better. There's a depth and resonance here you won't find in most other players. –PM

Harpsichord Works (various) / KONTRAPUNKT
Mortensen.

Harpsichord Works (various) / ASTREE
Verlet.

Harpsichord Works (various) / DHM
Leonhardt (harpsichord). All four of the listings of Froberger's music currently in the catalog are absolutely outstanding. –PM

GIOVANNI GABRIELI   1553-1612

Baroque. An Italian composer of sacred and secular vocal music and some instrumental keyboard, string, and wind ensemble pieces. Gabrielli's music is considered the epitome of the High Renaissance Venetian school. He was the perfecter of the impressive and lively ceremonial style of *cori spezzati* ("broken-up choirs or groups"), in which the musicians are located in widely separated spaces; he also wrote strangely chromatic motets about hell and damnation, promoted the music of Monteverdi, and influenced the young Heinrich Schütz. –BGT

○ **Canzoni (7) for Brass Choirs; 7 Intonazioni d'organo; 7 Motets; 3 Mass Movements; Sonata in the 9th tone for 8 parts / CBS**
Biggs (organ), Gregg Smith Singers, Texas Boys Choir, Edward Tarr Bass Ensemble. Recorded 1967 at St. Mark's Basilica, Venice. –BGT

○ **Sacrae Symphoniae / ADDA**
Uyama-Bouvard, A Sei Voci & Les Saqueboutiers de Toulouse.

NIELS WILHELM GADE   1817-1890

Romantic. An influential Danish composer, conductor, teacher, and admirer of Mendelssohn and Schumann who adopted the German romantic style in his own works. –MKS

○ **Piano Works - Vol. 1 / KONTRAPUNKT**
Westenholz (piano). Solid playing of some fascinating and beautiful Danish romantic piano pieces, including the sonata and "Aquarelles." –PM

○ **Quartets (3) for Strings in D, e, & f, op. 63 / BIS**
Kontra Quartet. Dripping with drawing-room sentiment. –PM

DENIS GAULTIER   1603-1672

Baroque. A Parisian lutenist and a major influence on the keyboard music of Froberger. –MKS

○ **La rhétorique des dieux (solo lute suites) / ASTREE**
Smith. Always something new to find: my single favorite lute recording of all time. –PM

ENNEMOND GAULTIER   1575-1651

Renaissance. A lutenist, cousin of Denis Gaultier, and valet de chambre to Henri IV's queen. –MKS
○ **Selections for Solo Lute / ASTREE**
Smith.

FRANCESCO GEMINIANI   1687-1762

Baroque. An Italian violinist and composer of instrumental, orchestral, chamber, and some harpsichord music. –ED
○ **Concerti grossi, op. 3 / OISEAU-LYRE**
Schröder (violin), Hogwood/Academy of Ancient Music. One of Hogwood's earliest and best Florilegium recordings, just restored to the catalog on CD. –PM
○ **Concerti grossi, opp. 2, 3, 7 (selections) / EDITO CLASSICA**
La Petite Bande. This has more depth and soul than the other two English Geminianis listed, without quite the incisiveness. –PM
○ **La Folia & other concertos & sonatas / HYPERION**
The Purcell Band, Purcell Quartet. This is a good all-around selection, spiritedly and incisively played, with brilliant sound. –PM

GEORGE GERSHWIN   1898-1937

20th century, popular. An American composer primarily of musicals and songs (with lyricist and brother Ira Gershwin), famous for "Rhapsody in Blue" (1924); other notable works include the folk opera *Porgy and Bess* (1935) and the *Piano Concerto in F* (1925).
Gershwin was probably the first composer of extended musical forms, aside from Scott Joplin in his operas, to embrace fully African-American creative music as a fundamental source of inspiration. Certain works, such as the *I Got Rhythm Variations*, scenes in *Porgy and Bess*, and the *Preludes for Piano*, have a sophistication of variation technique and orchestration comparable to the best of modern French melodists, like Poulenc. (Gershwin applied to study with Ravel and then with Nadia Boulanger, but was turned down by each, who did not want to cramp his natural style.) Gershwin's influence on jazz has been enormous (his harmonic sense studied by bebop composers) and his music continues to have freshness and warmth. –BGT
☆ **An American in Paris & Rhapsody in Blue / CBS**
Bernstein/NYPO. An American classic: could be the best thing Bernstein ever did. –PM
○ **Complete Works for Orchestra & Piano / VOX BOX**
Siegal, Slatkin/ St. Louis SO. Contains *Concerto in F, An American in Paris, Cuban Overture, I Got Rhythm Variations, Lullaby for String Quartet, Porgy and Bess, Catfish Row Suite, Promenade, Rhapsody in Blue, Second Rhapsody.* –BGT
○ **Three Preludes for Piano; The G. Gershwin Songbook / TRAX CLASIQUE**
Ratusinski.

DON CARLO GESUALDO   1561-1613

Renaissance, vocal. An Italian composer of motets (settings for sacred texts) and madrigals (settings for secular texts). As Ernst Krenek once said, "If Gesualdo had been taken seriously in his time as he is now, music history would have taken an entirely different course." From the amazing works of Gesualdo's contemporary Lassus, back to the strange smoking songs of Johannes Symonis and Solage in the 1300s (*Ars Magis Subtiliter*, Ensemble PAN, New Albion Records NA 021), extreme chromaticism has always been around, and perhaps it's more realistic to view it as a means of expression for some of our more unusual experiences. But the austere, graceful, often slowly developing and surprisingly changing

interior feeling of Gesualdo's work exerts the unnameable fascination of an unknown world. Gesualdo's music and bizarre life are still being admired and debated. Even Igor Stravinsky became a Gesualdo fan and wrote a *Monumentum pro Gesualdo.* –BGT
○ **Madrigals (17) for 5 Voices / GIMELL**
The Tallis Scholars. Completely ethereal as this group always seems to be but not so red-blooded as the Italian group. –PM
Madrigals (17) for 5 Voices / FHM
Christie/Les Arts Florissants.
○ **Responsoria & Sacrae Cantiones / ARGO**
Picottii/Centro Musica Antica di Padova. Except for sibilant emphasis (which sometimes drives me up a wall) this is a sensitively sung and beautifully recorded production. Technically not quite in the same class as the Tallis Scholars, but the trade-off is that it sounds quite a bit more Italian. –PM
○ **Sabbato Sancto Responsoria / FHM**
Herreweghe/La Chapelle Royale.
○ **Tenebrae (The Complete Responsoria) / ECM**

ORLANDO GIBBONS   1583-1625

Renaissance. A Tudor English master of smaller musical forms (madrigals and keyboard music) and the declamatory solo voice style; known for his tuneful church music. Gibbons was a masterful contrapuntalist imbued with lively spirit of a decidedly English flavor. His madrigals include "The Silver Swan," "What Is Our Life," "Dainty Fine Bird That Art Encaged," and "Now Each Flowry Bank." His *Short Service* retained popularity because of its melodiousness. –BGT
○ **Instrumental and Vocal Works / ADDA**
Includes "The Cries of London and other Musicke Apt for Viols and Voyces" (a delightful setting of actual street cries), consort anthems, songs, odes, and so forth. –BGT
○ **Second Service & Anthems / CRD**
The Choir of New College, Oxford.

ALBERTO GINASTERA   1916-1983

20th century. An Argentine composer of energetic and even ecstatic music in various forms — opera (*Don Rodrigo*, 1964), ballet, chamber, vocal, and choral. Ginastera exhibits a Bartókian sense of harmony, bright orchestral colors, and gripping melodic and rhythmic gestures. –BGT
○ **Concerto for Piano & Orchestra / PHOENIX**
Somer, Marzendorfer/Vienna PO.
○ **Concerto for Violin (1963) / PROMPT**
Ricci (violin), de la Fuente/Orquestra de las Americas. This fascinating concerto starts with a virtuoso cadenza and never lets up. It was written for Ricci, and he "owns" it. –PM
○ **Danzas argentinas, for Piano, op. 2 / FONE**
Husson (piano). If this is the only record Suzanne Husson has made, it is a crime — she certainly deserves more. Husson plays with the luminosity of a Michelangeli and the taste of a Pollini. –PM
○ **Milena (Cantata no. 3 for Soprano & Orchestra) / PHOENIX**
Curtin (soprano), Priestman/Denver SO. Text adapted from Kafka's *Letters to Milena.* Also contains Peter Mennin's *Symphony no. 4.* –BGT
○ **Piano Music (various) / ELAN**
Rodriguez (piano). He understands the Spanish idiom and conveys it with brilliant pianism. –PM

UMBERTO GIORDANO   1867-1948

Romantic. A modest, genial man who once threatened his librettist with a toy pistol (they both burst out laughing), Giordano is now chiefly known for the marvelous opera *Andrea Chenier* (about the French poet who was both a champion and a victim of the French Revolution) and

the opera *Fedora* (about a Russian princess in love with a nihilist). –BGT
○ **Andrea Chenier (4-act opera) / LONDON**
Caballé, Pavarotti, Nucci, Chailly/National Philharmonic.

MAURO GIULIANI   1781-1829

Romantic. An Italian guitarist and composer of duets, quartets, concertos, sonatas, and études for guitar. –ED
○ **Concerto for Guitar & String Orchestra no. 1 in A, op. 30 / PHILIPS**
Romero, Marriner/ASMF.
○ **Concerto for Guitar & Strings Orchestra no. 3 in F, op. 70 / PHILIPS**
Romero, Marriner/ASMF.

ALEXANDER GLAZUNOV   1865-1936

Romantic, nationalist. A Russian composer of symphonies, ballet (*Raymonda*, 1897), orchestral, and chamber music; one of the group of Russian nationalist composers known as "The Mighty Five." The end of *Symphony no. 4* and the beginning of *Symphony no. 5* are genuine emotional experiences, as is the lovely *Concerto for Violin & Orchestra in a* (1904), but despite having tremendous popularity in his day, much of Glazunov's music now sounds formulistic. He is perhaps best seen as a late Russian romantic in the tradition of Glinka and early Tchaikovsky. –BGT
☆ **Concerto for Violin & Orchestra in a, op. 82 / ANGEL**
Perlman (violin), Mehta/Israel PO.

MIKHAIL GLINKA   1804-1857

Romantic. A Russian composer of orchestral pieces (*Kamarinskaya*, 1848), instrumental works, and opera (*A Life for the Tsar*, 1836); influenced "The Mighty Five." –MKS
○ **Grand Sextet in E-flat for Piano, String Quartet & Double Bass / HYPERION**
Capricorn. This tuneful and engaging piece for piano and string quintet is sprightfully played and well recorded. –PM
○ **Ruslan and Ludmilla: Overture / URANIA**
Mravinski/Leningrad PO.
○ **Trio pathétique (version for violin, cello & piano) / CHANDOS**
Dubinsky, Turovsky, Edlina. This is not the original version but passionate and high-profile playing of a very interesting piece. –PM

KARL GOLDMARK   1830-1915

Romantic. An Hungarian composer of opera (*Die Königin von Saba*, 1875) and various string and piano pieces. –ED
○ **Concerto for Violin & Orchestra no. 1 in a, op. 28 / ANGEL**
Perlman, Previn/Pittsburgh SO.
○ **Overtures (various) / HUNGARATON**
Korodi/Budapest PO.

LOUIS GOTTSCHALK   1829-1869

Romantic. Born and raised in Haiti and an immigrant to New Orleans, this American champion of native Cuban and South American music would stage massive concerts in Rio de Janiero and Havana, perhaps inspired by the love his friend and mentor Hector Berlioz had for monstrous orchestral forces. His pieces, like *Night in the Tropics* for orchestra or two pianos (refer to the out-of-print disc on New World Records NW 208), contain no Americanisms but introduce rhythms and tunes unheard of in the late 19th century. –BGT
○ **Piano Music (various) / AMON RA**
Burnett.

PERCY GRAINGER   1882-1961

20th century. An Australian/American composer in various forms whose style was influenced by folk music. –ED

○ **Music of Percy Grainger (various) / CHANDOS**
Montgomery/Bournemouth Sinfonietta.

ENRIQUÉ GRANADOS   1867-1916

Romantic. A Spanish composer of opera, orchestral, and piano music who wrote in the romantic style but incorporated Spanish rhythms and melodic instrumental patterns into his music. "Goyescas" was inspired by the paintings and etchings of Goya. –MKS
○ **Allegro di Concierto, for Piano in C / RCA**
de Larrocha.
○ **Goyescas (suite of six piano pieces) / LONDON**
de Larrocha.
Goyescas (suite of six piano pieces) / RCA
de Larrocha.
○ **Piezas sobre cantos populares espanolas (6) / LONDON**
de Larrocha (piano).
○ **Spanish Dances (12), op. 37 / LONDON**
de Larrocha (piano).

MAURICE GREENE

Baroque, vocal. An English organist and composer to the Chapel Royal and Master of the King's Musick. Greene was one of the most important vocal composers of his day, in both sacred and secular forms. –MKS
○ **Select Anthems & Organ Voluntaries / CRD**
Cooper (organ), Higginbottom/Choir of New College, Oxford. I had never been particularly impressed with Higginbottom's choir, but this and the Boyce *Anthem* CD have changed all that: these are heartfelt, emotional performances tempered by real dignity, restraint, and a sense of reticence. –PM

EDVARD GRIEG   1843-1907

Romantic, nationalist. A Norwegian composer of folk-inspired works, including incidental music for *Peer Gynt* (1875). Grieg wrote for orchestra, solo piano, and string quartet and composed the *Concerto for Piano & Orchestra in a, op. 16*. Norway's most famous composer, actually of Scottish descent on his father's side, Grieg studied the folk tunes of his country in his youth (although he only actually quoted them once in his works) and studied with Robert Schumann in Leipzig. The clear mountain beauty of a Scandinavian landscape can be felt in the pure modal harmonies of pieces like the famous *Concerto for Piano in a*, with its melodies varied in inflection but not modulated in pitch. Sustained transparent textures combine with the warmth of a Schumannesque melodic sensibility. –BGT
○ **Complete Piano Music / VICTORIA LTD**
Braaten (piano). Only Vol. 1 has been issued so far, but this looks like the best bet for the most authoritative performance of this lightweight but tuneful corpus. –PM
☆ **Concerto for Piano & Orchestra in a, op. 16 / ANGEL**
Lipatti (piano), Galliera/Philharmonia Orchestra. One of the classics of the Gramophone. –PM
Concerto for Piano & Orchestra in a, op. 16 / TROLD
Kayser (piano), Andersen/Bergen SO. Not so bland as your everyday performance, this performance is very Nordic in temperament. –PM
Concerto for Piano & Orchestra in a, op. 16 / AURORA
Smebye (piano), Andersen/Norwegian Youth Orchestra. A labor of love by all concerned. –PM
Concerto for Piano & Orchestra in a, op. 16 / SWEDISH SOCIETY
Waldeland (piano), Westerberg/Danish RSO. This has an authentic Nordic sound and feel. Any of these three Scandinavian performances is a valuable supplement to the Lipatti. –PM

☆ **Holberg Suite, op. 40 / BIS**
Tonnensan/Norwegian CO. The phrasing is so sensitive and well thought out, the feeling so Nordic, that despite the fact that this isn't so good an orchestra as the other two, it has to be a first recommendation; moreover, it includes seldom-played Grieg string pieces as filler. –PM

Holberg Suite, op. 40 / ARGO
Marriner/ASMF. Stay away from Marriner's remake on Philips: this performance is much more vital, committed, and full of character. –PM

Holberg Suite, op. 40 / DGG
Orpheus CO. More generic in approach, with probably the best playing overall, but lacking a bit of the temperament and sense of direction of the other two. –PM

Holberg Suite, op. 40 / AUDIOFON
Davis, Ivan (piano). It's great to have a good performance in the piano version with a special feel all its own. –PM

○ **In Autumn (concert overture), op. 11 / ANGEL**
Beecham/Royal PO.

○ **Lyric Pieces for Piano (20 selections) / DGG**
Gilels (piano). The best single issue ever of Grieg's piano music. –PM

○ **Lyric Suite, op. 54 / DGG**
Järvi/Gothenburg SO.

☆ **Peer Gynt (complete incidental music), op. 23 / PHILIPS**
Ameling, de Waart/SFSO & Chorus. Beecham has a special feeling for this score and gives character to each section, but his playing, singing, and recording are a bit rough, and I like de Waart's sophistication and great sound just as much. –PM

Peer Gynt (complete incidental music), op. 23 / ANGEL
Hollweg, Beecham/Royal PO, Beecham Choral Society.

Peer Gynt (complete incidental music), op. 23 / ANGEL
Popp, Marriner/ASMF, Ambrosian Singers.

Peer Gynt (complete incidental music), op. 23 / DGG
Bonney, Sandve, Malmberg, Järvi/Gothenburg SO & Chorus. If you want it complete with all the dialog and a good filler, "*Sigurd Jorsalfar*," go for this very theatrical performance, one of Järvi's most committed. –PM

○ **Quartet for Strings, op. 27; Incomplete Quartet in F; Fugue in F / VICTORIA LTD**
Norwegian String Quartet. Outstanding sound and Nordic feeling. –PM

○ **Sonata for Cello & Piano in a, op. 36 / MUSIC & ARTS**
Rostropovich, Richter. Recorded at the Aldeburgh Festival in 1964, this and its companion piece, the Brahms *Cello Sonata*, are two of the most thrilling performances ever put on CD. Don't be put off by the sound: it's not that bad, and the aliveness of the event more than makes up for it, anyway. –PM

Sonata for Cello & Piano in a, op. 36 / CLAVES
Starck, Requejo. If you must have this piece in modern sound, this is the one to get. Very rhapsodic, but doesn't have the passion or subtlety of the Rostropovich/Richter. –PM

☆ **Sonatas (3) for Violin & Piano, opp. 8, 13, 45 / AURORA**
Veselka, Dratvova. Czech emigrants who have a special feeling for the rhythms in this gypsy-like music. –PM

Sonatas (3) for Violin & Piano, opp. 8, 13, 45 / ADDA
Milosi, Lee.

Sonatas (3) for Violin & Piano, opp. 8, 13, 45 / CLAVES
Turban, Dunki.

Sonatas (3) for Violin & Piano, opp. 8, 13, 45 / EDELWEISS
Chumachenco (violin), Levy (piano). These get off to a bit of a rocky start with too many ritards and too much swooning, but I like Chumachenco's and Levy's rhapsodic and soulful playing. Afterwards I think a bit more straightforward might have been even better, though. –PM

○ **Symphonic Dances, op. 64 / TROLD**
Andersen/Bergen SO.

○ **Symphony in c / DGG**
Järvi/Gothenburg SO.

Symphony in c / BIS
Kamu/Gothenburg SO.

○ **Two Elegiac Melodies for String Orchestra, op. 34 / ARGO**
Marriner/ASMF.

CHARLES TOMLINSON GRIFFES   1884-1920

20th century, impressionist. The foremost American impressionist composer, whose early works were influenced by studies in Germany. Upon returning to the US, Griffes experimented with exoticism and Oriental scales. The music of Debussy and Mussorgsky provided models for his brilliant orchestration. –MKS

○ **The Pleasure Dome of Kubla Khan, for Piano (1912; orchestrated 1917 as op. 8) / NEW WORLD**
Ozawa/Boston SO.

○ **Sonata for Piano in F (1917-18) / GASPARO**
Tocco.

FERDE GROFÉ   1892-1972

20th century, nationlist. An American composer and arranger best known for *Grand Canyon Suite* (1931); also made arrangements for Gershwin and Paul Whiteman. –ED

○ **Grand Canyon Suite / LONDON**
Dorati/Detroit SO.

Grand Canyon Suite / TELARC
Kunzel/Cincinnati Pops.

REYNALDO HAHN   1875-1947

20th century, vocal. A Venezuelan-born French conductor, critic, and composer, who studied with Massanet. Hahn was an excellent singer, which may have influenced his facile, melodic style. He was well known in literary circles for his wit and was a friend of Proust. –MKS

○ **Le bal de Béatrice d'Este, for Small Orchestra / HYPERION**
Corp/The New London Orchestra. A lot of French fun. –PM

○ **Complete Piano Music - Vol. 1 / VALOIS**
Sermet, Paik (pianos). Have time to explore some jolly French pianistic backwaters? You'll find the sound and playing on this release outstandingly natural. –PM

○ **Songs / ADDA**
Miraille, Boulanger. Collection of 19 songs. –MKS

Songs / VIRGIN
12 Hahn songs, along with others by Bizet and Chabrier. –MKS

GEORGE FRIDERIC HANDEL   1685-1759

Baroque. A German/British composer of operas and oratorios as well as most other forms, known for his orchestral work *Water Music* (1717), his oratorio *Messiah* (1742), and various pieces of chamber music. Often working under breakneck pressure for English patrons, Handel wrote music that achieved a wide emotional range through the most direct and superb technical mastery. His melodies are unforgettable and his works are so beloved that they are part of the popular culture, as witnessed by the thousands of *Messiah* performances every year at Christmas and Easter. –BGT

○ **Belshazzar (Oratorio) / ARCHIV GALLERIA**
Johnson, Auger, Bowman, et al., Pinnock/English Concert & Choir.

☆ **Concerti grossi (12), op. 3 / OISEAU-LYRE**
Hogwood/Handel & Haydn Society.

Concerti grossi (12), op. 3 / DGG
Pinnock/English Consort.

☆ **Concerti grossi (12), op. 6 / CAPRICCIO**
Pommer/Leipzig New Bach Collegium Musicum. A three-CD set, containing four concertos per disc. –PM

○ **Concerto for Harp no. 6, op. 4 / KOCH-SCHWANN**
Antonelli (harp), Hirsch/Innsbruck CO. Rich and resonant sound combined with stylishly ornamented and rhythmically alive harp playing make this an outstandingly successful harp CD, even though the slow movements are a bit over romanticized and heavy. –PM

○ **Concertos (3) for Oboe & Strings / DGG**
Reichenberg (oboe), Pinnock/English Concert.

○ **Coronation Anthems / HYPERION**
King/The King's Consort, Choir of New College, Oxford. Marriner and Pinnock both sound like they're trying too hard. I prefer King's more relaxed and soulful approach. –PM

○ **Dettingen and Te Deum; Dettingen Anthem / DGG**
Preston/Westminster Abbey Orchestra & Chorus.

○ **Dixit Dominus, for 5 Vocal Soloists, Orchestra & Chorus DGG**
Auger, Dawson, Montague, Nixon, Birchall, Preston/Westminster Abbey Orchestra & Chorus.

○ **Jubilate in D, "Utrecht" / OISEAU-LYRE**
Kirkby, Nelson, Brett, Covey-Crump, Elliott, Thomas, Preston/Acadamy of Ancient Music.

☆ **Messiah (oratorio) / TELDEC**
Harnoncourt/Concentus Wien. Quirky live performance, with by far the best choral singing ever from the renowned Stockholm chamber choir under Eric Ericson. –PM

Messiah (oratorio) / CHANDOS
Hickox/Collegium Musicum 90. Without top-drawer sopranos, this is still a stylish and very well recorded *Messiah*: it deserves a top recommendation. –PM

Messiah (oratorio) / DGG
Auger, von Otter, Chance, Crook, Tomlinson, Pinnock/English Concert & Choir. Although not quite so stylish or well recorded as the Hickox, it has better female soloists and in many ways is the most consistent overall. –PM

Messiah (oratorio) / LONDON
Te Kanawa, Gjevang, Lewis, Howell, Solti/Chicago SO & Chorus. The best star-studded, traditional, non-original-instrumental performance. –PM

○ **Ode for St. Cecilia's Day / DGG**
Lotte, Rolfe, Johnson, Pinnock/English Concert & Chorus.

○ **Royal Fireworks Music & Coronation Anthems (4) / HYPERION**
King/King's Consort & Choir of New College, Oxford. What a glorious noise! The first-ever recording on period instruments of the original 1749 scoring for 24 oboes, 12 bassoons, 9 trumpets, 9 horns, and 4 sets of timpani. –PM

○ **Sonatas for Recorder / FINLANDIA**
Adams (recorder), et al. Piers Adams is a real virtuoso (some of the tempos are very fast and he negotiates his runs and ornamentations very cleanly) and plays reasonably well in tune, and the ornamentation is tasteful and exciting, adding up to the best CD recording of these much-played (especially in the LP era) and always challenging pieces. –PM

○ **Sonatas (7) for Transverse Flute & Continuo / RICERCAR**
Beukels (transverse flute)/Ricercar Consort. The playing displays an extraordinary delicacy and winning reticence and atmosphere everywhere. The flute playing itself has a breathy quality. –PM

○ **Suites for Harpsichord nos. 1-8 / HARMONIA MUNDI**
Gilbert.

Suites for Harpsichord nos. 1, 3, 5, 8; Chaconne in g / DGG
Pinnock.

○ **Trio Sonatas, HWV. 361, 386, 388, 393, 397, 399 / DGG**
Pinnock/English Concert.

○ **Trio Sonatas for 2 Violins, Cello & Harpsichord, op. 2 / FHM**
London Baroque. London Baroque is loosening up, and their

playing is developing a much-needed and gorgeous sensuousness. This is their best CD so far and sweeps the competition. –PM

○ **Trio Sonatas for 2 Violins & Continuo, op. 5 / FHM**
London Baroque.

○ **The Triumph of Time and Truth (oratorio) / HYPERION**
Fisher, Kirkby, Brett, Partridge, Varcoe, Goodman, Darlow/London Handel Orchestra & Chorus. A bit austere and controlled at times, this is nonetheless a major contribution to the Handel discography. –PM

○ **"Utrecht" Te Deum in D / OISEAU-LYRE**
Kirkby, Nelson, Brett, Covey-Crump, Elliott, Thomas, Preston/Academy of Ancient Music.

☆ **Water Music (complete) / WHITE LABEL**
Sandor/Franz Liszt CO. Long one of my favorites on LP, this features some very fine ornamentation, although it's a bit dated in terms of both sound and performance practice. I don't find Rolla's digital remake, at a third more the price, any better than this older one. In any case, it's still the best on "modern" instruments. –PM

Water Music (complete) / OISEAU-LYRE
Hogwood/Academy of Ancient Music.

Water Music (complete) / DGG
Pinnock/English Concert. I wasn't a big fan of this performance when it first came out on LP in 1983; perhaps I was expecting more from the first period-instrument *Water Music*. In any case, I've just listened to it again and this is among the best ever, with much better sound than I had remembered. –PM

Water Music (complete) / HARMONIA MUNDI
McGegan/Philharmonia Baroque Orchestra. Like so many of McGegan's CDs, this is a clear yuppie favorite (like the Corelli *Concerti grossi, op. 6*) with all sorts of cute effects and little baroque tricks. In other words, it's pretentious and not very straightforward. But it can't be dismissed and is very interesting in many ways, with significantly better sound than any of the others. –PM

HOWARD HANSON   1896-1981

Neo-romantic, nationalistic. An American composer who wrote in various forms, including choral, solo piano, and symphonic pieces. Hanson's sweeping orchestrations are among the best of the 30s nationalist style. –BGT

☆ **Symphony no. 2, op. 30, "Romantic" / MERCURY**
Hanson/Eastman-Rochester Orchestra.

JOHN HARBISON   b1938

20th century. An American composer primarily of opera and large-scale choral works, also of solo piano and chamber pieces; studied with Roger Sessions and Earl Kim. –MKS

○ **Quartets for Strings nos. 1 & 2; November 19, 1828 for Piano & String Trio / FHM**
Wyner/Lydian String Quartet.

ROY HARRIS   1898-1979

20th century. An American composer of orchestral and choral music with typically American melody and rhythm. His instrumental music is particularly effective. –MKS

○ **Symphony no. 3 / DGG**
Bernstein/NYPO.

KARL AMADEUS HARTMANN   1905-1963

Modern. An important student of Webern who developed a chromatic, atonal idiom and a "variable meter" approach to rhythm while writing within the structural confines defined as classical. Hartmann wrote nine symphonies and in a variety of musical genres. –MKS

○ **Piano Music / VIRGIN**
Mauser (piano). Dissonant and percussive; much more interesting than his orchestral music. –PM

FRANZ JOSEPH HAYDN   1732-1809

Classical. A renowned and prolific German composer, famous for his many symphonies. Not only are Haydn's works vitally important in the evolution of musical form, they are delightful and inspirational. Haydn was directly responsible for establishing the form of the string quartet and he perfected the classical symphony, synthesizing a range of emotions and anticipating by many years the work of composers from Beethoven through Schumann. His keyboard sonatas are marvels of invention and surprise and the church masses are joyous and full of energy and rhythmic counterpoint. To quote his friend and admirer Mozart, "There is no one who can do it all — to joke and to terrify, to evoke laughter and profound sentiment — and all equally well, except Joseph Haydn." –BGT

☆ **Concerto for Cello & Orchestra no. 1 in C & no. 2 in D /**
OISEAU-LYRE
Coin (cello), Hogwood/Academy of Ancient Music.
Concerto for Cello & Orchestra no. 1 in C & no. 2 in D /
DHM
Bylsma (cello), Lamon/Tafelmusik Orchestra. Ever the thinker, Bylsma delivers a virtuoso performance that would have been at the top of the list if the sound and orchestra had been as good as Hogwood's. –PM
Concerto for Cello & Orchestra no. 1 in C & no. 2 in D /
PHILIPS
Schiff (cello), Marriner/ASMF. As much as I normally like Schiff (and I think he is the best cellist around right now), these performances seem a bit glib to me. –PM

○ **Concertos (3) for Clavier & Orchestra / ADDA**
Mouzalas, Duczmal/Amadeus CO. Cautious and careful, adding to a sense of seriousness and purpose that eludes most performers. –PM
☆ **Concerto for Clavier & Orchestra no. 11 in D / PREISER**
Brendel (piano), Angerer/Vienna CO. Scintillating. –PM
Concerto for Clavier & Orchestra no. 11 in D / DGG
Pinnock/English Concert. A completely different feeling when played on the harpsichord and period instruments. –PM
Concerto for Clavier & Orchestra no. 11 in D / FONE
Magaloff (piano), Brescia/Bergamo Festival CO. An old-fashioned, more romantic approach. –PM
Concerto for Clavier & Orchestra no. 11 in D / ONDINE
Gothoni/Finlandia Sinfonietta. A tad on the dry side but still highly enjoyable. –PM
○ **Concertos (6) for Organ & Orchestra / PHILIPS**
Koopman/Amsterdam Baroque Orchestra.
○ **Concerto for Trumpet & Orchestra in E-flat / PHILIPS**
Hardenberger (trumpet), Marriner/ASMF. If this isn't the best recording ever of this piece, I'd like to hear what is. –PM
○ **Concerto for Violin & String Orchestra no. 1 in C /**
PHILIPS
van Keulen (violin), Ros-Marba/Netherlands CO. Still a teenager when she made her first CD, von Keulen is a sweet-toned and beautifully in-tune violinist in the Grumiaux mold, and my favorite young player. –PM
Concerto for Violin & String Orchestra no. 1 in C / DGG
Pinnock/English Concert.
Concerto for Violin & String Orchestra no. 1 in C /
CLAVES
Lysy/Camerata Lysy of Gstaad.
○ **Mass no. 9 in d, "Nelson Mass," HOB. XXII/11 / DGG**
English Concert. With Lott, Watkins, Davies, Wilson-Johnson, and Pinnock. –BGT
○ **Mass no. 14 in B-flat, "Harmoniemesse"; Missa Brevis,**
"Kleine Orgelmesse" / HYPERION
Hill/The Brandenburg Orchestra, soloists, Winchester Cathedral Choir. A bit on the tame and lyrical side, but well done, nonetheless. –PM
Mass no. 9 in d, "Nelson Mass," HOB. XXII/11 / DGG

Lott, Watkinson, Davies, et al., Pinnock/English Concert.
○ **Music for Lute & Strings (complete) / BIS**
Lindberg (lute), Drottningholm Baroque Ensemble .
○ **Quartets (6) for Strings nos. 1, 2, 4, 6, op. 2 /**
HUNGARATON
Tátrai Quartet.
○ **Quartets (6) for Strings, op. 9 / HUNGARATON**
Tátrai Quartet.
○ **Quartets (6) for Strings, op. 17 / HUNGARATON**
Tátrai Quartet.
○ **Quartets (6) for Strings, op. 20 / HUNGARATON**
Tátrai Quartet.
○ **Quartets (6) for Strings, op. 33, "Russian" /**
HUNGARATON
Tátrai Quartet. These quartets were a shock to Mozart and affected much of his work. –BGT
○ **Quartets (6) for Strings nos. 1-4, op. 33 / SUPRAPHON**
Panocha Quartet. Outstanding! Warmer and richer than the Tátrai but just as much in tune and together. –PM
Quartets (6) for Strings nos. 1-4, op. 33 / ASTREE
Mosaiques Quartet. A whole new sensitivity and subtlety in string quartet playing on period instruments. –PM
○ **Quartet for Strings in d, op. 42 / HUNGARATON**
Tátrai Quartet.
Quartets (6) for Strings, op. 50, "Prussian" /
HUNGARATON
Tátrai Quartet.
○ **Quartets (3) for Strings, op. 54 / VIRGIN**
Endellion Quartet. I have to admit that I prefer the vibrancy of the Endellion to the more ascerbic sound of the Tátrai. This is one of the best performances ever given of any Haydn quartets. –PM
Quartets (3) for Strings, op. 54; Quartets (3), op. 55 /
HUNGARATON
Tátrai Quartet.
○ **Quartets (6) for Strings, op. 64 / HUNGARATON**
Tátrai Quartet.
○ **Quartet for Strings no. 5 in D, op. 64, "The Lark" / DGG**
Hagen Quartet.
○ **Quartets (3) for Strings, op. 71 / HUNGARATON**
Tátrai Quartet.
○ **Quartets for Strings nos. 1 & 2, op. 71 / HYPERION**
Salomon String Quartet.
○ **Quartet for Strings no. 3, op. 71 / HYPERION**
Salomon String Quartet.
○ **Quartets (3) for Strings, op. 74 / HYPERION**
Salomon Quartet.
Quartets (3) for Strings, op. 74 / VIRGIN
Endellion Quartet.
Quartets (3) for Strings, op. 74 / HUNGARATON
Tátrai Quartet.
○ **Quartets (3) for Strings nos. 2 & 3, op. 74 / HYPERION**
Salomon Quartet.
○ **Quartet for Strings no. 3, op. 74 / DGG**
Hagen Quartet.
☆ **Quartets (6) for Strings, op. 76 (complete) /**
HUNGARATON
Tátrai Quartet. The Tátrai may be a bit dry for some tastes (they certainly don't use much vibrato), but they are peerless in matters of style. It sounds as if they've lived with this music for centuries. –PM
○ **Quartets (6) for Strings nos. 2, 3, 4, op. 76 / TELDEC**
Eder Quartet.
○ **Quartets (6) for Strings nos. 4-6, op. 76 / SUPRAPHON**
Panocha Quartet. A clear rival to the Tátrai; but where's their nos. 1-3? –PM
Quartets (2) for Strings, op. 77 / HYPERION

Salomon Quartet.

Quartets (2) for Strings, op. 77 / HUNGARATON
Tátrai Quartet.

Quartets (2) for Strings, op. 77; Quartet, op. 103 / QUINTANA
Quatour Festetics. On period instruments. A bit more ragged and out-of-tune than the others but with very interesting sonorities and great sound. –PM

○ **The Seasons (oratorio) / DGG**
Janowitz, Schreier, Talvela, Böhm/Vienna SO. One of Böhm's greatest recordings, the other being the Deutsche Grammophon (DGG) *Magic Flute*. –PM

○ **The Seven Last Words of Christ on the Cross, for Orchestra / ASTREE**
Savall/Le Concert des Nations. The emphasis is on sensuality, sonority, and finesse in this beautifully recorded (if slightly too resonant) CD, which now becomes a clear first choice for orchestral versions despite some less-than-perfect intonation. Let me repeat: This is a beautiful performance, although you may want to program out the Latin text spoken between movements. –PM

The Seven Last Words of Christ on the Cross (version for string quartet) / QUINTANA
Quatour Festetics. A sonorous period-instrument string-quartet performance. –PM

The Seven Last Words of Christ on the Cross (string quartet version) / HUNGARATON
Tátrai Quartet. The last word in standard string-quartet performances. –PM

○ **Sinfonia Concertante for Oboe, Bassoon, Violin, Cello & Orchestra in B-flat, op. 84 / DGG**
Abbado/Chamber Orchestra of Europe. Abbado's Haydn is always perky, infectious, subtle, and beautifully played. I hope he'll do all the late symphonies and then move on to the middle ones, because his versions will probably be the standard-bearers for years to come. –PM

○ **Sonatas for Piano nos. 20, 32, 34, 37, 40, 42, 48, 49, 50, 51, 52; Adagio; Fantasia in C / PHILIPS**
Brendel (piano). Haydn's piano sonatas need more "help" than those of most composers, and Brendel gives it to them in spades with some of his best performances ever. Here his thoughtfulness, overintellectualizing, and tendency to underline really make this music come alive. –PM

○ **Sonatas for Piano nos. 34, 48, 40, 32, 50 / CENTAUR**
Meister (piano). Very lucid and beautiful performances of five of Haydn's best piano sonatas, played on a Baldwin SD-10 piano. Outstanding, natural sound. –PM

○ **Sonatas for Piano nos. 36, 40, 41, 49, 50 / NONESUCH**
Kalish. Very fine performance. –JME

○ **Sonatas for Piano nos. 48, 49, 58, 59 / GLOBE**
Van Immerseel (fortepiano). Stylish and thoughtful. –PM

○ **Songs (15) for Tenor & Piano / ARS VIVENDI**
Schreier (tenor), Demus (piano). Schreier still had a lot of voice left when he made these touching and beautifully recorded performances in 1981. –PM

○ **Stabat Mater in g / DGG**
Pinnock/English Concert & Choir.

○ **Named Symphonies: Overture: The World on the Moon; Armida / COLLINS CLASSICS**
Clark/Consort of London. These are stylish and rhythmically alert performances in fine sound, and competitive with any: less regimented than Pinnock but more biting than Hogwood and with more traditional tempos than Goodman. These may be a first choice for many people, although, since they are available only in a four-CD set, most people will be discouraged from purchasing them. –PM

○ **Symphonies "A" & "B"; Symphonies nos. 1-3 / MELODIYA (KOCH)**
Ermler/USSR Bolshoi Theater Chamber Music Ensemble. In the notes to this release, Melodiya says they are going to record all the Haydn Symphonies, and in *Opus, Symphonies "A" & "B"* are called numbers 107 & 108; interesting. Be that as it may, these are functional performances, which use a harpsichord and are reasonably well played, although sounding a bit old-fashioned by today's standards. But at least they don't try to hype up the music, and they're sane and enjoyable. –PM

○ **Symphony no. 12 in E / FHM**
Entremont/Vienna CO.

○ **Symphony no. 22 in E-flat, "Der Philosoph" / SONY**
Salonen/Stockholm CO.
Symphony no. 22 in E-flat, "Der Philosoph" / DGG
Orpheus CO.

○ **Symphony no. 26 in d, "Lamentatione" / VIRGIN**
Kuijken/La Petite Bande.

○ **Symphony no. 31 in D, "Hornsignal" / TELARC**
Mackerras/Orchestra of St. Luke's.
Symphony no. 34 in D / FHM
Entremont/Vienna CO.

○ **Symphony no. 35 in B-flat / ALBANY**
Bolle/Monadnock Festival Orchestra. These are not so together or in tune as the best of the competition, but I just love the sound of the orchestra and the sense of exploration and discovery. –PM

○ **Symphony no. 41 in C / DGG**
Pinnock/English Concert.

○ **Symphonies nos. 43, 28, 34 / IMP**
Aadland/European Community CO. Rather plain, but solid modern-instrument performance of three of Haydn's better-known earlier symphonies in good sound. Has a good-enough Haydn style but could be more dramatic and "interpreted"; still, these performances are likely to wear well. –PM

☆ **Symphony no. 45 in f#, "Farewell" / TELARC**
Mackerras/Orchestra of St. Luke's.
Symphony no. 45; M. Haydn: Symphony in G with Mozart's introduction, K. 444; Overture to Idome / MELODIYA (KOCH)
Barshai/Moscow CO. These are very warmhearted but clean, non-schmalzy performances. Don't be misled by the recording dates (1967 for Joseph Haydn, 1976 for all else): this is ideally warm and rich analog sound. –PM

○ **Symphony no. 48 in C, "Maria Theresia" / DGG**
Orpheus CO. The music just leaps out of the speakers. One of the OCO's best. –PM

○ **Symphony no. 59 in A, "Fire" / DGG**
Pinnock/English Concert.

○ **Symphonies nos. 60, 70, 90 / ANGEL**
Rattle/City of Birmingham SO. Although a bit cutesy (isn't Rattle always?), these are still eminently musical and listenable performances, and it is nice to have *Symphonies nos. 60 & 70* back in the catalog. I prefer Brüggen and Kuijken in *Symphony no. 90*. Why does Rattle always have to over-interpret (cf. "Andante" of *Symphony no. 70*)? If the music were allowed to speak more for itself, wouldn't it have more lasting value? –PM

○ **Symphony no. 80 in d / EBS**
Jöres/West German Orchestra.

○ **Symphony no. 82 in C, "Bear" / SONY**
Salonen/Stockholm CO.
Symphony no. 84 in E-flat, "In Nomine Domini"; Symphonies nos. 82 & 83 / VIRGIN
Kuijken/Orchestra of the Age of Enlightenment.

○ **Symphony no. 85 in B-flat, "La Reine de France"; Symphonies nos. 86 & 87 / VIRGIN**
Kuijken/Orchestra of the Age of Enlightenment.
Symphony no. 85 in B-flat / FHM
Entremont/Vienna CO.

○ **Symphony no. 88 in G / DGG**

Böhm/Vienna PO.

○ **Symphony no. 88 in G / DGG**
Furtwängler/Berlin PO. Here, as always, Furtwängler reveals depths in Haydn that no one before or since had thought were there. –PM

○ **Symphony no. 88 in G / AS DISC**
Furtwängler/RAI Turin Orchestra.

○ **Symphonies nos. 90 & 93 / PHILIPS**
Brüggen/Orchestra of the 18th Century. Quirky and unique readings with many felicitous details. As always, Brüggen is dynamic and subtle. –PM

○ **Symphony no. 90 in C / VIRGIN**
Kuijken/La Petite Bande.

○ **Symphony no. 91 in E-flat / VIRGIN**
Kuijken/La Petite Bande.

○ **Symphonies nos. 92 & 44 / FHM**
Entremont/Vienna CO. From the opening "Adagio" of *Symphony no. 92*, I feared these would be a bit too sweet, but not so, and these stylish Haydn performances, with woodwind detail prominent and excellent Harmonia Mundi sound overall, can be confidently recommended. –PM

☆ **Symphonies nos. 93-104 / PHILIPS**
Davis/Royal Concertgebouw Orchestra. I continue to have mixed feelings about Davis's Haydn and probably always will. The playing is lively, brilliant, funky even; but it's just oh-so-cutesy at times. Leave Haydn alone already: he's a good enough composer to speak for himself, he doesn't need this much help. Still, as a mid-priced set of four CDs, this is a terrific bargain; as a set we have none better. But I'm waiting. Abbado's *Symphony no. 96* is terrific, or could Salonen be the main man? As much as I normally admire Davis as a conductor, I'm afraid this set merely perpetuates the myth of the genial Papa Hadyn. We need more guts and passion here. These readings are a bit too complacent. –PM

☆ **Symphonies nos. 93 & 101 / DGG**
Abbado/Chamber Orchestra of Europe. More terrific Haydn from Abbado. As in *Symphony no. 96* and *Sinfonia Concertante*, he's got the scale and the rhythm down right and his orchestra is very responsive. If he decided to do all the London symphonies, they would probably lead the field. –PM

○ **Symphony no. 96 in D, "Miracle" / DGG**
Abbado/Chamber Orchestra of Europe.

☆ **Symphonies nos. 99 & 102 / PHILIPS**
Marriner/ASMF. Except for a perfunctory (and too fast) slow movement in *Symphony no. 99* (one of the most moving and haunting movements Haydn ever wrote), these are spirited and very well played and well recorded, and deserve top recommendation. –PM

○ **Symphonies nos. 100 & 103 / TELARC**
Mackerras/The Orchestra of St. Luke's.

○ **Symphonies nos. 102 & 104 / MELODIYA (KOCH)**
Barshai/Moscow CO. This 1973 recording sounds better than virtually any digital recording being made nowadays, in terms of dynamic accuracy and timbral realism. I guess the degree of tape hiss is just too off-putting for those who listen for such things over the music. There's a lot more warmth on this disc from the conductor and the orchestra than on most current digital recordings. As for the sound, as far as I am concerned, the scale is correct. –PM

○ **Symphony no. 103 in E-flat, "Drum Roll" / PHILIPS**
Brüggen/Orchestra of the 18th Century.

○ **Symphony no. 104 in D, "London" / PHILIPS**
Davis/Royal Concertgebouw Orchestra.

Symphony no. 104 in D, "London" / DGG
Furtwängler/Berlin PO.

HILDEGARD OF BINGEN   1098-1179

Medieval, sacred choral. A German mystic and abbess and composer of monophonic settings of lyric and dramatic

poetry. Hildegard was one of the most creative and celebrated personalities of the Middle Ages: a visionary, naturalist (she wrote two books on natural history and medicine), playwright (her morality play *Ordo Virtutum* predates other works in that genre by a century), poet, and composer — her *Symphonia Armonie Celestium Revelationum* ("Symphony of the Harmony of Celestial Revelations") contains some of the finest and most elaborate songs written in that time and are conceived on a massive, synaesthetic scale ("of writing, seeing, hearing, and knowing, all in one manner"). She was called the "Sybil of the Rhine" and was deeply involved in politics and diplomacy. Her poetry is Byzantine, lyrical, erotic, and transcendent, and the music is likewise of the whole spirit and body. –BGT

○ **Hymns and Sequences / HYPERION**
Gothic Voices. Ethereal. –PM

○ **Ordo Virtutum / EDITO CLASSICA**
Sequentia (Ensemble for Early Music, Cologne).

○ **Symphoniae (spiritual songs) / EDITO CLASSICA**
Sequentia (Ensemble for Early Music, Cologne).

PAUL HINDEMITH   1895-1963

Neo-classical, modern. A German composer whose style combined neo-classicism with modern harmonic conventions and jazz elements. Hindemith's works include opera (*Mathis der Maler*, 1935), ballet, orchestral, choral, and chamber music. Although idealizing an aesthetic of use over beauty (*Gebrauchsmusik*) as a younger man, Hindemith's best-known works are appreciated for their warmth, rich, even opulent orchestral colors and gestures, a unique multi-rhythmic sense, and flowing, rapid polyphony. –BGT

○ **Concerto for Cello & Orchestra / ET CETERA**
De Machula, Kondrashin/Royal Concertgebouw Orchestra.

○ **Concerto for Clarinet & Orchestra / ET CETERA**
Pieterson (clarinet), Kondrashin/Royal Concertgebouw Orchestra.

○ **Concerto for Horn & Orchestra / ANGEL**
Brain, Hindemith/Philharmonia Orchestra.

○ **Ludus Tonalis (a cycle of 24 preludes & fugues) / PYRAMID**
Richter. Richter has the crotchetiness and individuality, Janssen the beautiful sound and straightforward delineation of the score. Both are superb. –PM

Ludus Tonalis (a cycle of 24 preludes & fugues) / GLOBE
Janssen.

☆ **Mathis der Maler (symphony) / CHANDOS**
Horenstein/London SO. Stern and serious, and much better held together than any other performance. –PM

○ **String Quartet no. 1 in C, op. 2; Quartet no. 5, op. 32 (complete) / CAPRICCIO**
Sonare Quartet. This is a good group, which plays modern music well because it has the right balance between spikiness and lyricism. This promises to be a very worthwhile series of interesting quartets. –PM

☆ **Symphonic Metamorphosis on Themes of Carl Maria von Weber / PHILIPS**
Davis/Bavarian RSO. You just knew Davis would play things close to the vest. He finds more music and less bombast than most in this score. –PM

GUSTAV HOLST   1874-1934

Romantic. Of Swedish descent, Holst was one of the best of the English "colorists" (Bliss, Vaughan Williams, and others). He was inspired by world religions (*Rig Veda* of 1908-1912, the beautiful opera *Savitri* of 1908, and *Hymn of Jesus* of 1917), English folk melody (*Somerset Rhapsody for Orchestra*), and transcendental poetry (*Ode to Death on Whitman's Words*, the *Choral Symphony* on a text by Keats, and *Egdon Heath* — one of his best pieces — on an excerpt from a Hardy novel).

The Planets is his best-known work — dramatic and atmospheric. –BGT

☆ **The Planets, op. 32 / ANGEL**
Boult/London PO. If you want the English style (as opposed to a more international approach), this is the clear first choice on CD. –PM

The Planets, op. 32 / LONDON
Karajan/Vienna PO. This earlier version is less uptight and aggressive and more musical sounding. –PM

The Planets, op. 32 / DGG
Levine/Chicago SO & Chorus. For those who must have the latest in everything. –PM

The Planets, op. 32 / DGG
Karajan/Berlin PO. A bit bombastic and pretentious but nonetheless impressive. –PM

ARTHUR HONEGGER   1892-1955

Modern. A Swiss composer of operas, chamber music, and orchestral music who was influenced in his early work by the impressionists and Stravinski's modernism. Honegger used a personal style in his main work that is densely bitonal, classically polyphonic, and emotionally austere. This is especially apparent in the beautiful *Symphony for String Orchestra no. 2*, with a mysteriously emerging trumpet solo in the last movement — a work written in occupied Paris of WWII. His oratorio *Jeanne d'Arc au bucher* is a significant work told in a series of episodic "flashbacks," a form that fits well with the music. –BGT

○ **Pacific 231 (Movement symphonique no. 1) (1923) / VANGUARD**
Abravanel/Utah SO.

○ **Le Roi David / CASCAVELLE**
Corboz/Gulbenkian Choir & Orchestra, plus soloists.

○ **Sonatina for Violin & Cello / HUNGARATON**
Duo Ongarese.

☆ **Symphony for String Orchestra no. 2 / DGG**
Karajan/Berlin PO. A bit too smooth and sophisticated but still very powerful, and so much better played than the competition. –PM

○ **Symphony no. 3, "Liturgique" / DGG**
Karajan/Berlin PO.

JOHANN NEPOMUK HUMMEL   1778-1837

Classical. An Austrian pianist and composer of piano, chamber, and vocal music as well as opera and ballet music. A contemporary of Beethoven. –ED

○ **Concerto for Bassoon in F / PHILIPS**
Thunemann, Marriner/ASMF. Brilliant performances by the reigning bassoon virtuoso. –PM

○ **Concerto for Piano & Orchestra in a, op. 85 / CHANDOS**
Hough, Thomson/English CO. Virtuosic performances not likely to be bettered for years to come. –PM

○ **Concerto for Piano & Orchestra in b, op. 89 / CHANDOS**
Hough, Thomson/English CO.

○ **Concerto for Trumpet & Orchestra in E-flat / PHILIPS**
Hardenberger, Marriner/ASMF.

○ **Mass in B flat, op. 77; Tantum Ergo (after Gluck) / KOCH-SCHWANN**
Crowell, Floreen/New Brunswick CO, Westminster Oratorio Choir. A beautiful performance of an undervalued piece, but at 36:32 total playing time, it's hard to justify purchase. –PM

○ **Piano Septet no. 1 in d, op. 74 & no. 2 in C, op. 114 / HYPERION**
Capricorn. Hummel may be a sort of poor man's Beethoven, but these are charming, large-scale chamber works and are sprightfully played, well balanced, and well recorded. –PM

JACQUES IBERT   1890-1962

20th century. A French composer of songs, operas, chamber music, and ballet music, also *Concerto for Flute & Orchestra* (1934). Ibert's music is full of humor and color and exhibits elements of both impressionism and classicism. –MKS

○ **Divertissement; Concertino da Camera / KOCH-SCHWANN**
Donald Barra/San Diego CO. Vivacious and infectious performances. –PM

○ **Escales for Piano, "Ports of Call" / GALLO**
Mueller (piano). I can imagine more virtuosic playing, but not more idiomatic. –PM

○ **Escales, "Ports of Call" / MERCURY**
Paray/Detroit SO.

JOHN IRELAND   1879-1962

20th century. A British composer of chamber, piano, and orchestral music who wrote in a modal style influenced by chant and Tudor music. Ireland incorporated many impressionist traits into his music. –MKS

○ **Concerto for Piano & Orchestra in E-flat / CHANDOS**
Parkin, Thomson/London PO.

○ **Legend for Piano & Orchestra / CHANDOS**
Parkin, Thomson/London PO.

○ **These Things Shall Be, for Baritone, Orchestra & Chorus / CHANDOS**
Terfel, Hickox/London SO & Chorus.

CHARLES IVES

20th century. See 20th Century Avant-Garde for a biography on Ives. –ED

☆ **Central Park in the Dark / CBS**
Thomas/Chicago SO.

○ **Sonata for Piano no. 2, "Concord, Mass., 1840-1860" / ELEKTRA**
Kalish.

○ **Songs (26 songs) / ETCETERA**
Alexander, Crone.

Songs - Vol. 2 (28 songs) / ETCETERA
Alexander, Crone.

○ **Symphony, "Holidays" / CBS**
Thomas/Chicago SO & Chorus.

○ **Symphony no. 1 / SONY**
Thomas/Chicago SO & Chorus.

Symphony no. 1 / CHANDOS
Järvi/Detroit SO. It won't please purists (it's way too romanticized), and it doesn't even sound like Ives, but it's a good performance nonetheless. –PM

○ **Symphony no. 2 / SONY**
Thomas/Royal Concertgebouw Orchestra.

Symphony no. 2 / CBS
Bernstein/NYPO.

○ **Symphony no. 3 / SONY**
Thomas/Royal Concertgebouw Orchestra.

Symphony no. 3 / CBS
Thomas/Royal Concertgebouw Orchestra.

○ **Symphony no. 4 / SONY**
Thomas/Chicago SO & Chorus.

○ **Three Places in New England / DGG**
Thomas/Boston SO.

○ **The Unanswered Question / MERCURY**
Hanson/Eastman Rochester Orchestra. Also includes *Symphony no. 3.* –MKS

ELISABETH JACQUET DE LA GUERRE   1666-1729

Baroque. A child prodigy who appeared at the court of Louis XIV and so astonished her audience that the king undertook her education, which was supervised by his mistress,

Madame de Montespan. A prolific composer of cantatas, operas, string and harpsichord music, she was the most famous woman composer of the baroque. –MKS

○ **Cantatas françoises (6) sur des sujets tirés de l'écriture (Book 1) (1708) / ARION**
Boulin, Poulenard, Robert/Instrumental Ensemble.

○ **Pièces de clavecin (14) qui peuvent se jouer sur le violin (selections) / ARION**
Charbonnier, Guillard.

LEOS JANÁCEK   1854-1928

Romantic, nationalist. A Czech composer of opera (*Jenufa*, 1904) and orchestral, instrumental, and sacred vocal music utilizing folk elements; employed his own "speech melody" concept based on the Czech language. From an early age, Janácek believed that music should follow the natural rhythms of human speech, animals, and birds. He went on to produce works of a completely original sound that are romantic, delight in the natural, and have an "angular" and even ascetic quality and a rhythmic vitality, all at the same time. His best-known piece is probably the *Sinfonietta*, with its wonderfully tuneful brass writing. Among his many popular and masterly operas are the first, *Jenufa*; *Katya Kabanova* (1919), with its snow scenes sounding amazingly like contemporary pattern or minimalist music; and *The Makropoulos Affair*, about a 300-year-old woman spurning lovers. His string quartets seem to have no precedents in harmonic sense and development and are astonishing. The profound, even terrifying religiosity of the *Slavonic Mass* is almost indescribable. –BGT

○ **Concerto for Piano, 2 Violins, Viola, Clarinet, Horn & Bassoon / FHM**
Ensemble Walter Boeykens.

○ **The Diary of One Who Disappeared (song cycle) / DGG**
Balleys, Langridge, Abbado/Berlin PO, RIAS Chamber Chorus. Mostly I won't go for orchestrations or arrangements, but this is so well done that I feel it supersedes all of the voice/piano versions. –PM

○ **In the Mists (4 pieces for piano) / RCA**
Firkusny.

In the Mists (4 pieces for piano) / DGG
Firkusny.

○ **Jenufa (3-act opera) / LONDON**
Soderstrom, Popp, Randova, Dvorsky, Ochman, Mackerras/Vienna PO.

○ **Mladi (Youth) for Wind Sextet / FHM**
Ensemble Walter Boeykens. Beautifully in-tune, chipper, and idiomatic-sounding performances in natural sound. –PM

☆ **Quartet for Strings no. 1, "Kreutzer" / DGG**
Hagen Quartet. Intense and impassioned! –PM

Quartet for Strings no. 1, "Kreutzer" / SUPRAPHON
Smetana Quartet. More laidback than the Hagen and sounding even more Czech, making a choice between the two virtually impossible except that the sound on Deutsche Grammophon (DGG) is better. –PM

Quartet for Strings no. 1, "Kreutzer" / BEYER
Stamitz Quartet.

Quartet for Strings no. 1, "Kreutzer" / LONDON
Gabrieli String Quartet. More urban-style and sophisticated; less primitive performance. –PM

○ **Quartet for Strings no. 2, "Intimate Pages" / DGG**
Hagen Quartet. Brilliant and impassioned and remarkable technically for a group with such young players. –PM

Quartet for Strings no. 2, "Intimate Pages" / SUPRAPHON
Smetana Quartet. Smoother than the other two but just as Czech-sounding, if not more so for being subtler. –PM

Quartet for Strings no. 2, "Intimate Pages" / BEYER
Stamitz Quartet. Rough and very dramatic and in some ways

more appropriate to the works than the Smetana and Hagen, but they're just not so good a quartet. –PM

Quartet for Strings no. 2, "Intimate Pages" / LONDON
Gabrieli Quartet.

☆ **Sinfonietta / DGG**
Abbado/Berlin PO. The choice is difficult here: The newer one is more burnished and sophisticated; the older performance, by London SO, is more fiery. –PM

Sinfonietta / LONDON
Abbado/London SO.

☆ **Slavonic Mass / FIDELIO**
Ancerl/Czech PO & Chorus.

Slavonic Mass / SUPRAPHON
Soderstrom, Drobkova, Livora, Novak, Mackerras/Czech PO & Chorus.

Slavonic Mass / LONDON
Kubiak, Collins, Tear, Schone, Kempe/Royal PO & Chorus.

○ **Sonata for Piano, "October 1, 1905" / DGG**
Firkusny.

○ **Sonata for Violin & Piano / DGG**
Kremer, Argerich.

○ **Taras Bulba / URANIA**
Ancerl/Czech PO. No one before or since has given this such a right-sounding performance. It just doesn't sound as disjointed as always, and the playing is superbly focused and atmospheric. –PM

JOHN JENKINS   1592-1678

Renaissance. A lute and lyra viol player and the foremost consort musician of his day. Jenkins composed over 800 instrumental pieces, as well as sacred and secular vocal music. –MKS

○ **Consort Music for Viols in 6 Parts / ASTREE**
Savall/Hesperion. Even the happier pieces have a mournful tinge. How could it be any other way with six viols and an organ? –PM

DMITRI KABALEVSKY   1904-1987

20th century. A prolific composer in all genres who wrote music that represents a model of the Russian school of composition during the Soviet period. His melodies are broad and diatonic and have a beautiful lyricism. He could also express incredible rhythmic vitality and was influential as both a composer and a teacher. He was especially active in music education. –MKS

○ **Colas Bruegnon: Overture (1938) / DELL'ARTE**
Toscanini/NBC Symphony.

○ **The Comedians (symphonic suite), op. 26 / ANGEL**
Sawallisch/Bavarian State Orchestra.

○ **Concerto for Cello & Orchestra no. 1 in g, op. 49 / CBS**
Ma, Ormandy/Philadelphia Orchestra.

○ **Concerto for Cello & Orchestra no. 2 in c, op. 77 / VIRGIN**
Isserlis, Litton/London PO.

○ **Concerto for Violin & Orchestra no. 3 in C, op. 48 / CHANDOS**
Mordkovitch, Järvi/Scottish National Orchestra.

VASILY SERGEYEVICH KALLINIKOV   1866-1901

Romantic. A Russian composer of orchestral works, especially his first symphony, and the incidental music for *Tsar Boris*, 1899. –ED

○ **Symphony no. 2 in A / CHANDOS**
Järvi/Scottish National Orchestra.

KEYBOARD WORKS

Classical.

○ **Bach and Handel: Chaconnes for Piano / PAVANE**

Akl (piano). This isn't the most flamboyant playing I've ever heard, but at least it's serious, and it's just great to have all five of these on a single CD. –PM

ARAM KHACHATURIAN   1903-1978

20th century. A Russian composer of orchestral, chamber, choral, piano, and ballet music in the tradition of Russian Orientalism. These recording feature folk idioms and colorful orchestrations. –MKS

○ **Armenian Dances / MERCURY**
Fennell/Eastman Wind Ensemble.

○ **Concerto for Piano & Orchestra / CHANDOS**
Orbelian, Järvi/Scottish National Orchestra.

○ **Concerto for Violin & Orchestra (1940) / CHANDOS**
Mordkovitch, Järvi/Scottish National Orchestra.

○ **Gayane (ballet) (exerpts) / CHANDOS**
Järvi/Scottish National Orchestra.

○ **Sparticus (ballet suites nos. 1-3) / CHANDOS**
Järvi/Scottish National Orchestra.

○ **Symphony no. 2 / CHANDOS**
Järvi/Scottish National Orchestra.

ZOLTÁN KODÁLY   1882-1967

20th century, nationalist. An Hungarian composer and associate of Bartók who incorporated folk music into his operas, chamber, orchestral, and choral music. Kodály was a kind of "national hero" of Hungarian music — a bearded, quiet man who guided musicians through WWII after years of being famous for his *Psalmus Hungariscus*, a large-scale religious work. His style was informed by folk music and traditional church music, heard abundantly in the suite from his opera *Háry János*. –BGT

○ **Duo for Violin & Cello, op. 7 / HUNGARATON**
Duo Ongarese. Not quite so well played or well recorded as some versions from the past, this is nevertheless a very authentically Hungarian-sounding performance. –PM
Duo for Violin & Cello, op. 7 / DELOS
Gingold, Starker.

○ **Galanta Dances; Háry János Suite; Marosszek Dances / MERCURY**
Dorati/Minneapolis SO.

☆ **Háry János: Suite / CBS**
Szell/Cleveland Orchestra.

○ **Sonata for Cello unaccompanied, op. 8 / DELOS**
Starker.

JOSEPH MARTIN KRAUS   1756-1792

Classical. A German-born Swedish composer whose works were praised by Gluck and Haydn and who was almost an exact contemporary of Mozart. His music will remind you of "Sturm und Drang" Haydn. An early death cut short a promising career. –PM & MKS

○ **Symphonies (4) in c, E-flat, C, D / CAPRICCIO**
Camerata Köln. Expressive and gutsy original-instrument performances of his four symphonies. –PM

○ **Symphony in c; Concerto for Violin in C; Symphonie funebre in c / ORFEO**
Peinemann (violin), Martin Sieghart/Stuttgart CO. Well-shaped and -scaled performances in good sound, and you get your money's worth with 72:23 playing time. Get this disc if you're at all curious as to what was going on then. –PM

FRITZ KREISLER   1875-1962

20th century. An Austrian-born American violinist whose mastery of the instrument is reflected in the brilliant pieces he wrote and arranged for it. –MKS

○ **Violin Pieces & Arrangements / ANGEL**
Perlman, Sanders.

ERNST KRENEK   ♭1900

20th century. An influential Austrian/American composer whose compositional style mirrors many of the important developments of the 20th century. His highly intellectual and eclectic style may be the reason his works are not heard more often. –MKS

○ **String Quartets no. 1, op. 6 & no. 2 / MD&G**
Sonare Quartet.

○ **String Quartets no. 3, op. 20 & no. 7 / MD&G**
Sonare Quartet.

○ **Quartets nos. 5 & 8 / MD&G**
Sonare Quartet.

○ **Trio for Strings, op. 118 / CALIG**
Vienna String Trio. This group is just so polished, with such Viennese soul. –PM

FRANZ KROMMER   1759-1831

Classical. A Moravian violinist, conductor, and composer, known for his fine solo concertos for wind instruments. –MKS

○ **Concertino in C for Flute, Oboe & Strings, op. 65 / CLAVES**
Graf, Holliger/English CO.

○ **Concerto in E-flat for Clarinet & Orchestra, op. 36 / CLAVES**
Friedli, Pay/English CO.

MEYER KUPFERMAN   ♭1926

20th century, neo-classical. An American composer, clarinetist, and teacher with a vast list of works for stage, film, and concert use. His eclectic style incorporates neo-classicism, electronic music, and jazz. –MKS

○ **Images of Chagall, for Chamber Ensemble; Summer Music, for Flute, Cello, & 2 Guitars / SOUNDSPELL PRODUCTIONS**
Mauk (soprano sax), Stout (percussion), Kupferman/Bronx Arts Ensemble, Cygnus Ensemble. There's a lot of humor and jazz influence in this accessible modern music by an interesting composer. –PM

ROBERT KURKA   1921-1957

20th century. An American composer whose untimely death cut short a promising career. Kurka's opera *Good Soldier Schweik* is one of the important 20th-century works in this genre. His style is reminiscent of those of Prokofiev and Shostakovitch. –MKS

○ **The Good Soldier Schweik Suite, op. 22 (1956-57) / KOCH-SCHWANN**
Schenk/The Atlantic Sinfonietta. A sort of a poor man's anti-war *Lieutenant Kije*, with more underlying bitterness and pessimism. –PM

EDOUARD LALO   1823-1892

Romantic. A French composer of chamber and orchestral music, opera, and ballet. Lalo is most famous for his *Symphonie espagnole* (1875), the brilliant and colorful prototype of French impressionism, which used Spain as its subject in such pieces as Chabrier's *España* and Debussy's *Iberia*. But the real genius of Lalo lies both in his extraordinary, wholly original orchestration — which anticipated many of the most beautiful scores of the impressionists (the teenage Debussy was in fact among the audience for the ballet *Namouna* and had to be ejected from the house for defending it to a partially hostile audience) — and in his synthesis of Wagnerian harmony and French melodic grace in such works as his masterpiece, the opera *Le Roi d'Ys* (based on an ancient Breton story), and in *Namouna*. –BGT

☆ **Concerto for Cello & Orchestra in d / LONDON**
Harrell, Chailly/Berlin RSO.

Concerto for Cello & Orchestra in d / MERCURY
Starker, Skrowaczewski/London SO.
○ **Symphonie espagnole for Violin & Orchestra, op. 21 /
DGG**
Perlman, Barenboim/Orchestre de Paris.

LARS-ERIK LARSSON   1908-1986

Serial, neo-classical. A student of Berg who was instrumental in introducing elements of the dodecaphonic style into the music of his native country, Sweden. –MKS
○ **Concertinos (12) for Solo Instruments & String
Orchestra, op. 45 / BIS**
Various soloists/Stockholm Chamber Ensemble & Orchestra.
○ **Forkladd Gud (God in Disguise) / BIS**
Nordin, Hegegard, Jonsson, Frykberg/Helsingborg Symphony & Chorus.
○ **Quartets (3) for Strings, opp. 31, 44, 65 / BIG BEN**
Helsingborg String Quartet.
○ **Symphony no. 1 in D, op. 2 / BIS**
H. Frank, P. Frank/Helsingborg Symphony.
○ **Symphony no. 3 in c, op. 34 / BIS**
Frykberg/Heksingborg Symphony.

ORLANDUS LASSUS   1530-1594

Renaissance, vocal. Prolific Franco-Flemish composer of sacred works in most forms as well as much secular music. His *Prophetiae Sibyllarum*, one of the most unusual and innovative works of the 15th century, is one of those trailblazing compositions that could, potentially, have changed the course of music, had it been better known in his lifetime. It was discovered only after his death (by his sons, who were settling his estate). As the titles of the pieces indicate (*Missa Osculetur Me, Salve Regina,* and *Regina Coeli*) these are choral settings of prophetic statements (often parenthetical, in abbreviated sentences with definite pronouns). The music captures the tone of the sybil/oracle through devices like the graphic musical arrangement of the text words, unusual connections accomplished through the musical arrangements of the words, and extremely strange chromaticism within a predominantly chordal context, which was a totally new form for that time. By contrast, his *Moresken,* or morescas (Moorish dances), were the popular music of the day — humorous, with word plays and mixtures of languages, including gibberish. They are still very entertaining and funny, even today. –BGT
○ **Missa Osculetur Me; Salve Regina; Regina Coeli /
GIMELL**
Phillips/The Tallis Scholars.

JEAN-MARIE LECLAIR   1697-1764

Baroque. An important French violinist (founder of the French violin school), who fused the best of the Italian and French styles. –MKS
○ **Concertos (6) for Violin & Strings, op. 7 / ADDA**
Culler/Stradivari Ensemble.
○ **Sonatas (5) for Violin & Continuo, opp. 1/4, 2/3, 5/4, 7/9,
7/10 / ADDA**
Schröder (baroque violin), Foulon (gamba), Haugsand (harpsichord).

RUGGERO LEONCAVALLO   1857-1919

Romantic, opera. Leoncavallo, an Italian, started as a staunch Wagnerite, his style gradually evolving to the Italian verismo (realism) movement in opera. He wrote many operas, but was never able to duplicate the success of *Pagliacci.* –MKS
○ **Pagliacci / DGG**
Carlyle, Bergonzi, Benelli, Panerai, Taddei, Karajan/La Scala.
Pagliacci / PHILIPS

Stratas, Domingo, Pons, Pretre/La Scala.

ANATOLY LIADOV   1855-1914

Romantic. The teacher of Prokofiev and a Russian composer who was fascinated by variation techniques. Many of his works capture the imaginative quality of the fairy tales of his homeland. –MKS
○ **Baba-Yaga, op. 56 / URANIA**
Mravinsky/Leningrad PO.

FRANZ LISZT   1811-1886

Romantic. An Hungarian composer and virtuoso pianist. A major musical sensation of his time, Liszt was influential as a composer of difficult music, primarily for the keyboard, but also of orchestral, chamber, operatic, and vocal music; known for the *Hungarian Rhapsodies.* Liszt was not only the greatest pianist of his age — revolutionizing piano technique (in such works as the two *Concertos for Piano & Orchestra,* the *Sonata for Piano in b,* and the *Transcendental Etudes*) and giving the first complete "piano recital" in a full evening — but he also created the one-movement symphonic form (*A Faust Symphony, for Tenor, Orchestra & Chorus,* 1857) and an advanced harmonic palette that anticipated by many years the harmonic language of Debussy, Bartók, and Schoenberg (*Les Preludes, Années de pèlerinage,* and his late music for organ). In addition, he invented the compositional technique of the "transformation of themes," in which all the motifs in a work are derived from a single idea — anticipating Wagner's "leitmotiv" and Schoenberg's use of one tone-row for an entire piece (as in *Moses und Aaron.*) –BGT
○ **Années de pèlerinage: 1st Year (9 works for piano) /
PHILIPS**
Brendel.
○ **Années de pèlerinage: 2nd Year no. 7, "Dante Sonata" /
DENON**
Grimaud (piano).
○ **Concert Paraphrases, etc., for Piano / GLOBE**
Orlowetsky (piano). Beautiful sound from this 1889 Erard concert grand. Orlowetsky has plenty of technique, even on this old piano, to carry his 70-minute recital off in style. This is a beautiful disc. –PM
○ **Concerto for Piano no. 3; Lieder Book - Vol. 2 for Piano;
Schubert, Marches for Piano / HUNGARATON**
Jandó (piano), Gardelli/Hungarian State Orchestra. This gets off to a bit of a rocky start in the orchestra, with the wind chords not at all precise. The orchestra is tentative all the way through, but Jeno Jandó's playing really is very poetic and Hungarian-sounding. He saves the day on this interesting curiosity of the recently discovered third concerto. Interesting solo fillers. –PM
**Concerto for Piano no. 3 in E-flat; De Profundis;
Totentanz (1853 version) / ASV**
Mayer (piano), Vásary/London SO. The orchestra is much better here, but the playing isn't so poetic; again, interesting fillers. –PM
☆ **Concertos (2) for Piano & Orchestra nos. 1 & 2 /
PHILIPS**
Richter (piano), Kondrashin/London SO. The classic 1961 performance, sounding better than ever. –PM
Concertos (2) for Piano & Orchestra nos. 1 & 2 / DGG
Zimerman (piano), Ozawa/Boston SO. Serious, not superficial bombast. This recording is the standard performance, in good sound. –PM
**Concertos (2) for Piano & Orchestra nos. 1 & 2; Haydn,
Clavier Concerto in D, HOB. XVIII / PREISER**
Brendel (piano), Gielen/Vienna SO. An oldie but goodie. There's a bravura and risk-taking about this early one that is missing from the later versions with Haitink. One of Brendel's

first and best, with very fine old sound. The same applies to the Haydn concerto — it's the best one ever on that. –PM

Concertos (2) for Piano & Orchestra nos. 1 & 2 / HUNGARATON
Ranki, Kovacs/Hungarian State Orchestra.

○ **Harmonies poetiques et religieuses; Consolations / ASTREE**
Bonatta (fortepiano). Sensitively and poetically played on the Eduard Steingraeber 1873 Liszt grand piano, this is the only current complete recording of this fascinating piece. –PM

○ **Hungarian Rhapsodies for Orchestra nos. 1-6 (complete) / MERCURY**
Dorati/London SO. If you must have these potboilers orchestrated, this old Dorati (1960-1963) is still the one to go for. Don't be put off by the age of the recording; it still sounds great. And the playing has that Hungarian feeling that is so hard to describe in words. –PM

○ **Mephisto-Waltz (orchestral version) / LONDON**
Solti/Orchestre de Paris.

○ **Organ Music / PIERRE VERANY**
de Zeeuw.

○ **Organ Music ("Late Organ Works" - Vols. 1 & 2)/ ADDA**
Bousseau (organ). Supplementary to Liszt's major output, these are moody and interesting arrangements of (mostly) late piano pieces. –PM

○ **Organ Music, "Late Organ Works" - Vol. 2 / ADDA**
Bousseau.

○ **Piano Music: Dante Sonata, Ballade, Funerailles, La Leggierezza, Fantasy & Fugue on B-A-C-H / HUNGARATON**
Mocsari (piano). A passionate and poetic (and more Hungarian-sounding than usual) Liszt recital by this young Hungarian now living in Paris. I believe this is just his second disc. –PM

☆ **Les Préludes (symphonic poem no. 3) / SUPRAPHON**
Ancerl/Czech PO. This old performance is still the most musical around, avoiding the bombast, superficiality, and turgidity of most contemporary performances. –PM

Les Préludes (symphonic poem no. 3) / LONDON
Solti/London PO.

Les Préludes (symphonic poem no. 3) / DGG
Karajan/Berlin PO.

○ **De Profundis; Wanderer Fantasy, for Piano & Orchestra (arranged by Liszt); Fantasy on Themes from Beethoven's _Ruin of Athens_ / HUNGARATON**
Thomson (piano), Stratton/Hungarian State Orchestra. It's nice to have the curiously orchestrated version of the _Wanderer Fantasy_ back on CD. Some may prefer more intensity, but I like the nice, gentle approach displayed by Thomson (he is a very lyrical player), because it downplays a lot of the Lisztian bombast. –PM

○ **Sacred Piano Music (8 Pieces) / CHRISTOPHORUS**
Betz (piano). 75 minutes of some of the most poetic and deeply felt music Liszt ever wrote, played in a sensitive and tasteful manner that avoids the hype and lets the music shine through. –PM

☆ **Sonata for Piano in b / MUSIC & ARTS**
Richter (piano). Eccentric, free, and passionate: Richter sees clear to the end of the score, so details are more telling in the scope and architecture of the whole. –PM

Sonata for Piano in b / DGG
Zimerman (piano) draws a beautiful, rich sound from his piano, and there's an underlying ominousness I quite like. Furthermore, he displays a bigger and more solid technique than usual, but I am still put off by his tendency to milk every phrase in his attempt to draw extra meaning from this already quite "meaningful" score — if only he would let Liszt speak a little bit more for himself. I just don't quite find the seriousness of purpose in this reading that I find in the very best, but there certainly are some terrific touches here.

Zimerman's concentration tends to wander on the shorter pieces, and they are not quite so unified or convincing as his sonata. –PM

Sonata for Piano in b; Danta Sonata; Scherzo & March, S. 177 / IMP
Cohen (piano). Stresses beauty of tone and sensuality, but there's plenty of virtuosity, too, in one of my favorite underdog performances. I mean, who ever heard of Arnaldo Cohen? –PM

Sonata for Piano in b / VICTORIA LTD
Bratlie (piano). Straightforward and dramatic, with a minimum of "interpretation." –PM

○ **Totentanz for Piano & Orchestra / DGG**
Zimerman (piano), Ozawa/Boston SO. The finest recording Zimerman has yet done. Ozawa and the Boston SO seem more at home with all the delivery. –PM

○ **Transcendental Etudes (12) for Piano / NUOVA ERA**
Campanella (piano). All the virtuosity is there, but also a lot of musicality. –PM

Transcendental Etudes (12) for Piano / PICKWICK
Weber (piano). The very different 1828 version, spectacularly played by Janice Weber. –PM

Transcendental Etudes (12) for Piano / HYPERION
Howard. Leslie Howard is in the process of recording the complete Liszt piano music. While this is a most laudable endeavor, it must be said that the playing is not of the very highest caliber and that a lot of the performances are on the utilitarian rather than inspired side. Still, these _Transcendental Etudes_ are very dramatic, just missing the sweep and passion of some of the best individual performances; as a set, this is the best one currently available. Howard's playing is plenty demented and demonic where that's called for, but it's not always very subtle or poetic and not reposeful enough. –PM

○ **Transcendental Etudes (6) after Paganini for Piano / ONDINE**
Raekallio. A bit too much pedal for my taste but a lot more musical and less bombastic than the way in which these pieces are usually played. –PM

○ **Transcriptions & Paraphrases for Piano / TIMPANI**
Mocsari (piano). The sound is a bit on the drab side, but Moscari has a real flair for making the more superficial side of Liszt sound less so. –PM

○ **Variations on "Weinen, Klagen, Sorgen, Zagen," S. 179 / NOVALIS**
Kaunzinger.

PIETRO LOCATELLI   1695-1764

Baroque. An important Italian composer of violin sonatas and concertos. As a violinist, his feats in double stops and changes in tunings are said to have influenced Paganini. –MKS

○ **Sonatas for Flute & Continuo, op. 2 / PHILIPS**
Hazelzet, van der Meer.

○ **Sonatas for Violin / HYPERION**
The Locatelli Trio.

CHARLES MARTIN LOEFFLER   1861-1935

Romantic. A Berlin-born violinist and composer who settled in the US as a member of the Boston Symphony Orchestra. He was influential in introducing French stylistic elements into the German-dominated musical circles in which he traveled. His careful orchestration and opulent harmonies show exceptional refinement. –MKS

○ **Five Irish Fantasies (song cycle) for Tenor & Orchestra (1934-1935) / NEW WORLD**
Rosenskein, Nelson/Indianapolis SO.

○ **La Mort de Tintagiles for Viola d'amore & Orchestra (1897) / NEW WORLD**
Hansen, Nelson/Indianapolis SO.

JEAN BAPTISTE LULLY   1632-1687

Baroque. A French composer of opera, ballet, and some religious music. Lully established the *tragedie lyrique* style of opera. –ED

○ **Atys (opera) / HARMONIA MUNDI**
Mey, Laurens, Mellon, Gardeil, Christie/"Les Arts florissants" Orchestra & Chorus.

○ **Le bourgeois gentilhomme (comédie-ballet) / EDITO CLASSICA**
Yakar, Kweksilber (sopranos), Jacobs (countertenor), Nimsgern (baritone), Leonhardt/La Petite Bande.

EDWARD MACDOWELL   1860-1908

Romantic. America's best-known 19th-century composer and pianist and the first to achieve international recognition. Macdowell's compositional style is strongly rooted in the German romantic tradition. –MKS

○ **Concerto for Piano & Orchestra no. 2 in d / RCA**
Cliburn, Hendl/Chicago SO.

GUILLAUME DE MACHAUT   1300-1377

Medieval, vocal. A French composer and important figure in the French Ars Nova whose works include sacred and secular vocal music, notably *Messe de Notre Dame.* As the great synthesizer and inventor of contrapuntal techniques in the 1300s, Machaut composed works that are wonders of technique and lyricism. Especially notable: the lovely isorhythmic motets (*De bon espoir; Puisque la douce rousée; Speravi*), where all three texts are sung at the same time; the glorious rhythmic inventions of the *Messe de Notre Dame*; and the rondeau *Ma fin est mon commencement* ("My end is my beginning"). –BGT

☆ **Le lai de la Fonteinne; Rondeau, "Ma fin est mon commencement" / HYPERION**
Hillier/The Hilliard Ensemble. On the same album as *Messe de Notre Dame.* –BGT

○ **The Mirror of Narcissus / HYPERION**
Page/Gothic Voices.

GUSTAV MAHLER   1860-1911

Romantic. An Austrian conductor and composer of symphonies, opera, and lieder cycles whose most notable works include *Das Lied von der Erde* (1909) and *Symphony no. 9* (1909). Mahler was known for the length, depth, and painful emotions of his works. He loved nature and life and, based on early childhood experiences, feared death (family deaths, a suicide, and a brutal rape he witnessed). This duality appears in almost all his compositions, especially in the *Kindertotenlieder* ("Songs on the Deaths of Children"), which are actually about the loss of an innocent view of life. Mahler's orchestral music is clear, complex, and full of musical imagery, from the heavenly to the banal (the family lived near a military barracks, so march tunes sometimes appear; an argument was associated with the sound of a hurdy-gurdy outside the window). The "program" in the incredible symphonies is therefore that of personal tragedy and hope projected onto a universal scale. The traumas of the 20th century are expressed in the *Symphony no. 9* (especially the "Adagio"); the elusiveness of beauty and its loss among harshness and modern tragedies are the subjects of the first and fifth symphonies. Mahler discovered the verbal expression of this auditory imagery in poems translated from the Chinese of the T'ang dynasty; *Das Lied von der Erde* ("The Song of the Earth") was the musical result, expressing the transience of all things in a mixture of warmth and severe beauty. –BGT

☆ **Kindentotenlieder (5 songs for voice & orchestra) / ANGEL**
Fischer-Dieskau, Kempe/Berlin PO.

Kindentotenlieder (5 songs for voice & orchestra) / DGG
Fischer-Dieskau, Böhm/Berlin PO.

Kindentotenlieder (5 songs for voice & orchestra) / DGG
Ludwig, Karajan/Berlin PO.

Kindentotenlieder (5 songs for voice & orchestra) / ANGEL
Baker, Barbirolli/Halle Orchestra.

○ **Kindentotenlieder, for Alto & Piano / CAPRICCIO**
Schreckenback (alto), Moll (piano). Good supplementary alto and piano account. –PM

○ **Das klagende Lied / LONDON**
◦ Chailly/Berlin RSO, etc.

○ **Des Knaben Wunderhorn / ANGEL**
Schwarzkopf, Fischer-Dieskau, Szell/London SO. With singers like these, this is head and shoulders above all the other performances in the catalog. –PM

☆ **Das Lied von der Erde / ANGEL**
Ludwig, Wunderlich, Klemperer/Philharmonia Orchestra. Slow and contemplative but dramatic in the craggy Klemperer style, with by far the best singing. –PM

Das Lied von der Erde / CBS
Miller, Haefliger, Walter/NYPO. The very moving later performance. –PM

Das Lied von der Erde / PEARL
Thorborg, Kullman, Walter/Vienna PO. The sound will be a negative factor on this recording, but the performance is as good as it gets — more heroic than Walter's more valedictory later effort. –PM

○ **Songs / HYPERION**
Baker, Parsons.

○ **Songs from Rückert (set of 5) / DGG**
Fischer-Dieskau, Böhm/Berlin PO.

Songs from Rückert (set of 5) / ANGEL
Baker, Barbirolli/New Philharmonia Orchestra.

Songs from Rückert (set of 5) / ANGEL
Fischer-Dieskau, Barenboim.

Songs from Rückert (set of 5) / CAPRICCIO
Schreckenbach (alto), Moll (piano).

☆ **Songs of a Wayfarer (set of 4) / ANGEL**
Fischer-Dieskau, Furtwängler/Philharmonia Orchestra.

Songs of a Wayfarer (set of 4) / HYPERION
Baker, Parsons.

Songs of a Wayfarer (set of 4) / VIRGIN
Murray, Litton/Royal PO.

Songs of a Wayfarer (set of 4) / ANGEL
Baker, Barbirolli/Halle Orchestra.

☆ **Symphony no. 1 in D / PHILIPS**
Haitink/Berlin PO. This recording, still the first choice for me, features outstanding playing and recording. –PM

Symphony no. 1 in D / DGG
Sinopoli/Philharmonia Orchestra. With a wider emotional response than most, Sinopoli is still always in control. He combines the architecture of Haitink with the drama of Litton and the poetry of Kubelik and Davis. –PM

Symphony no. 1 in D / VIRGIN
Litton/Royal PO. A very fresh and dramatic but well-controlled performance, featuring outstanding playing from London's lesser orchestra. Plus Litton has a very fine *Songs of a Wayfarer* filler. –PM

Symphony no. 1 in D / CBS
Walter/Columbia Symphony. A classic, albeit a bit heart-on-sleeve, but vibrant, spontaneous, and full of feeling. –PM

○ **Symphony for Mezzo-Soprano, Orchestra & Chorus no. 2 in c, "Resurrection" / ANGEL**
Schwarzkopf, Rössi-Majdan, Klemperer/Philharmonia Orchestra & Chorus.

Symphony for Mezzo-Soprano, Orchestra & Chorus no. 2 in c, "Resurrection" / DGG
Plowright, Fassbaender, Sinopòli/Philharmonia Orchestra & Chorus.

Symphony for Mezzo-Soprano, Orchestra & Chorus no. 2 in c, "Resurrection" / ODYSSEY
Cundari, Forrester, Walter/NYPO.

○ **Symphony for Mezzo-Soprano, Orchestra & Chorus no. 3 in d / UNICORN-KANCHANA**
Procter, Horenstein/London SO, Ambrosian Singers, Wandsworth School Boys Choir. The best *Third* I have heard and possibly the best recording of any Mahler symphony ever made. –PM

○ **Symphony for Mezzo-Soprano, Orchestra & Chorus no. 4 in G / DENON**
Donath, Inbal/Frankfurt RSO. With such warm, radiant sound and natural boy-like singing from the wonderful Helen Donath, the choice for the *Fourth* is easy. –PM

Symphony for Mezzo-Soprano, Orchestra & Chorus no. 4 in G / EMI
Lott, Welser-Möst/London PO. A fresh, contrapuntal approach with every line given full weight. Mastery like this from one so young is extraordinary: Welser-Möst is a conductor to be watched. –PM

Symphony for Mezzo-Soprano, Orchestra & Chorus no. 4 in G / SONY
Szell, Raskin/Cleveland Orchestra. Szell is certainly on top of everything, but he sounds a bit too well ordered and a bit too "objective" for my taste. –PM

○ **Symphony no. 5 in c# / DIGITAL CONCERTO**
Nanut/Ljubljana RSO. Not quite so good as his *Sixth*, but a remarkable value. –PM

Symphony no. 5 in c# / PHILIPS
Haitink/Berlin PO. May not have quite the angst of Sinopoli or some of the others, but it is an "objective" performance that holds up well, with an "Adagietto" that is reserved, chaste, and reticent. –PM

Symphony no. 5 in c# / DGG
Sinopoli/Philharmonia Orchestra. The excesses, turmoil, and tragedy are certainly conveyed in this highly expressive performance. –PM

Symphony no. 5 in c# / DENON
Inbal/Frankfurt RSO. With many telling details in rich and atmospheric sound, this is one of Inbal's best recordings. –PM

○ **Symphony no. 6 in a / DGG**
Karajan/Berlin PO. An intensely beautiful slow movement, with orchestral perfection unrivaled by any other version. –PM

Symphony no. 6 in a / DIGITAL CONCERTO
Haenchen/Philharmonic Slavonica. The Steal of the Century: as good a performance as anyone's, with great sound and surprisingly adept playing — on one CD for $5.99! –PM

Symphony no. 6 in a / LONDON
Chailly/Royal Concertgebouw Orchestra. Despite an inordinately slow first movement, this is a performance full of character, fine detail, and wonderful playing, with the best sound ever on the *Sixth*. If the whole doesn't quite add up and the architecture seems a bit lacking in a symphony that needs plenty of control, still all those details are just tellingly beautiful, and I certainly wouldn't want to be without this performance. Nice filler too: Zemlinsky's *Maeterlinck Songs (6), op. 13*. –PM

Symphony no. 6 in a / DENON
Inbal/Frankfurt RSO.

○ **Symphony no. 7 in e (1905) / DENON**
Inbal/Frankfurt RSO.

Symphony no. 7 in e (1905) / DGG
Abbado/Chicago SO.

○ **Symphony no. 8 in E-flat, "Symphony of a Thousand" / LONDON**
Solti/Chicago SO. Dramatic to the nth degree — and the piece can stand it. –PM

Symphony no. 8 in E-flat, "Symphony of a Thousand" / DENON
Inbal/Frankfurt RSO, various choruses. With fabulous sound, its the only real rival to Solti but without the intensity. –PM

☆ **Symphony no. 9 in D / DISQUES MONTAIGNE (HMD)**
Horenstein/French National Orchestra. This is an amazing performance, especially considering that it was recorded in 1967 with an orchestra that was obviously unused to playing Mahler and especially the complicated *Ninth*. It makes the piece come alive in a special and less depressing way than usual. –PM

Symphony no. 9 in D / CBS
Walter/Columbia SO. Walter's heartbreaking and soul-searching remake. He wears his heart on his sleeve and tends a bit toward the maudlin, but there's such commitment that for once I don't mind. –PM

Symphony no. 9 in D / MUSIC & ARTS
Horenstein/London SO. This is the most committed, intense, and well-held-together *Ninth* I have ever heard, but, unfortunately, the pirate sound will be more than a bit of a drawback for most buyers. –PM

Symphony no. 9 in D / DGG
Karajan/Berlin PO. Powerful and epic, but I don't sense the hand of a true Mahlerian behind it. –PM

☆ **Symphony no. 10 ("Adagio" only) / DGG**
Sinopoli/Philharmonia Orchestra.

Symphony no. 10 ("Adagio" only) / DENON
Inbal/Frankfurt RSO.

Symphony no. 10 ("Adagio" only) / LONDON
Chailly/Berlin RSO. A sadness and longing combined with a reticence and vulnerability that I find quite compelling. Movingly played and beautifully recorded. –PM

MARIN MARAIS   1656-1728

Baroque. A French bass violist and composer who is known primarily for works for three bass viols that are considered the prototype of the French trio sonata. Marais also wrote four operas and various dance pieces. –ED

○ **La Folia & other gamba pieces / HYPERION**
Hunt (viola da gamba)/The Purcell Quintet.

○ **Pièces de Viole, Book 2 (selections) / SIMAX**
Dreyfus, Haugsand. Tremendously soulful, mellow, late-night listening. This is the best gamba playing I have ever heard. Not so subtle as Jordi Savall, who always sounds too world-weary for me, Dreyfus is more in tune and, on the whole, considerably livelier. –PM

○ **Pièces en Trio for 2 Recorders, Harpsichord, Basse de Violon & Theorbe / VALOIS**
Ensemble Fitzwilliam. You want those wine-and-cheese parties to be a real success? Whip on some of this and you've got the authentic thing, because this is Marin Marais, probably as good a composer imaginable for a cheese soiree. Nobody will have ever heard of him, but he's as French as it gets, and he's played by five Frenchmen. His very name just rolls off the tongue. You can program out the somber parts and just stick to the gay ones. –PM

○ **Suites in d & G; Le Tombeau de M. Meliton, for 2 Gambas & Lute / DHM**
Slowick, ter Linden (bass viols), Junghänel (theorbo)/Smithsonian Chamber Players.

LOUIS MARCHAND   1669-1732

Baroque. A French organist and composer of harpsichord suites, organ works, cantatas, and an opera. –ED

○ **Pièces de Clavecin (2 books) / SIMAX**
Haugsand (harpsichord). Norwegian harpsichordist Ketil

Haugsand has an outstanding feel for French baroque style and plays these pieces wonderfully. –PM

FRANK MARTIN   1890-1974

20th century. A Swiss composer whose compositional style can be described as shifting tonality: the chords are regular, but the center is always moving. Similarly, the *Petite Symphonie concertante* utilizes a traditional classical setup of strings and a continuo made up of piano, harp, and harpsichord. The continuo gradually become solo instruments while the sonata-allegro form expands with free, spontaneous development. –BGT

○ **Ballade for Cello & Piano / JECKLIN**
Honegger, Martin.

○ **Ballade for Flute & Piano / JECKLIN**
Willoughby, Martin.

○ **Ballade for Piano & Orchestra / CLAVES**
Antonioli, Viotti/Torino PO.

Ballade for Piano & Orchestra / JECKLIN
Benda, Martin/Lausanne CO.

○ **Ballade for Trombone & Orchestra / JECKLIN**
Rosin, Martin/Lausanne CO.

○ **Concerto for Cello & Orchestra / PRELUDIO**
Decroos (cello), Haitink/Royal Concertgebouw Orchestra. An honest, direct account of two of Frank Martin's most under recorded and under-appreciated pieces. –PM

○ **Concerto for Harpsichord & Orchestra / JECKLIN**
Jaccottet, Martin/Lausanne CO.

○ **Concerto for Piano & Orchestra no. 1 / CLAVES**
Antonioli, Viotti/Torino PO.

○ **Concerto for Piano & Orchestra no. 2 / CLAVES**
Antonioli, Viotti/Torino PO.

Concerto for Piano & Orchestra no. 2 / JECKLIN
Badura-Skoda, Martin/Luxembourg RSO.

○ **Concerto for Violin & Orchestra / JECKLIN**
Schneiderhan, Martin/Luxembourg RSO.

○ **The Four Elements, for Orchestra / PRELUDIO**
Haitink/Royal Concertgebouw Orchestra.

○ **Maria Triptychon, for Soprano, Violin & Orchestra / JECKLIN**
Seefried, Martin, et al./L'Orchestre de la Suisse Romande.

○ **Passacaille / JECKLIN**
Martin/Berlin PO.

☆ **Petite Symphonie Concertante / JECKLIN**
Martin/L'Orchestre de la Suisse Romande.

○ **Preludes (8) for Piano / JECKLIN**
Martin.

○ **Quintet for Piano & Strings / JECKLIN**
Schmid-Wyss/Die Kammermusiker Zürich Ensemble.

○ **Requiem for SATB Soloists & Orchestra / JECKLIN**
Speiser, Bollen, Tappy, Lagger, Martin/L'Orchestre de la Suisse Romande.

○ **Trio for Strings / JECKLIN**
Die Kammermusiker Zürich Ensemble.

○ **Trio sur les melodies populaires irlandaises / JECKLIN**
Schmid-Wyss/Die Kammermusiker Zürich Ensemble.

○ **Trois chants de Nöel, for Soprano, Flute & Piano / JECKLIN**
Ameling, Ode, Martin.

○ **Le Vin Herbe (oratorio) / JECKLIN**
Martin, Desarzens/Members of the Winterhur State Orchestra.

BOHUSLAV MARTINU   1890-1959

20th century. A Czech composer of opera, orchestral, and chamber music in a 20th-century style that includes elements of jazz. Influenced early in his life by the French "Les Six," Martinu (a rough contemporary of Janácek but a composer of

very different music) wrote the ballad "Who Is the Most Powerful Man in the World?"; *La Revue de Cuisine* (about kitchen utensils coming to life); and *The Tumult* (to celebrate Lindbergh's flight). Martinu's best works, which combine French lyricism with Czech drive, are *Quartet for Strings no. 1* (rediscovered in 1953) and *Double Concerto* for piano and two string orchestras (1938), the latter similar to Frank Martin's *Petite Symphonie Concertante* and Bartók's *Music for Strings, Percussion & Celesta* — a highly emotional work written in 1938 at the start of the war. Martinu's *Tre Ricerari*, written the same year, seems to share this feeling. Leaving Paris in 1940 for America, Martinu created the energetic *Sinfonia Giacosa* for piano and orchestra and the powerful and charged *Field Mass*. In the 50s he turned to religious themes and commentaries on the past, producing an opera in 1959, *The Greek Passion*, based on the novel *Christ Recrucified* by Kazantzakis (English libretto by Martinu), and the wonderful *Les Fresques de Piero della Francesca* for orchestra (1955). –BGT

○ **Concertos (2) for Cello & Orchestra / SUPRAPHON**
May, Neumann/Czech PO.

○ **Concerto for Piano & Orchestra no. 3 / SUPRAPHON**
Palenicek, Neumann/Czech PO.

○ **Concerto for Piano & Orchestra no. 4, "Incantation" / URANIA**
Palenicek, Pinkas/Brno State PO.

○ **Concertos (2) for Violin & Orchestra / SUPRAPHON**
Suk, Neumann/Czech PO.

☆ **Double Concerto for 2 String Orchestras, Piano & Timpani / URANIA**
Sejna/Czech PO.

Double Concerto for 2 String Orchestra, Piano & Timpani / CHANDOS
Bélohlávek/Czech PO.

☆ **Les Fresques de Piero della Francesca, for Orchestra / URANIA**
Ancerl/Czech PO.

○ **Nonet for Winds & Strings / DGG**
Ensemble Wien-Berlin.

Nonet for Winds & Strings / HYPERION
Dartington Ensemble.

○ **Parables for Orchestra; Les Fresques de Piero della Francesca; Symphony no. 6 / SUPRAPHON**
Ancerl/Czech PO. Don't be put off by the mono sound (which is very good) from 1961, 1959, and 1956, respectively: these performances have a commitment, command of detail, and sense of inevitability not displayed by any of the current performances (or performers). –PM

Parables for Orchestra / SUPRAPHON
Bélohlávek/Czech PO.

○ **Piano Music (selections) / RCA**
Firkusny.

○ **Quartets (7) for Strings (complete) / BEYER**
Stamitz Quartet.

○ **Rhapsody-Concerto for Viola & Orchestra / SUPRAPHON**
Suk (viola), Neumann/Czech PO.

○ **Sonata for Piano (1954) / RCA**
Firkusny.

○ **Sonata for Violin & Piano no. 2 (1943) / SUPRAPHON**
Suk (violin), Hala (piano).

○ **Sonata for Violin & Piano no. 3 (1944) / SUPRAPHON**
Suk (violin), Hala (piano).

○ **String Trio no. 2 (1934) / BEYER**
Members of the Stamitz Quartet.

○ **Symphony no. 1 (1942) / CHANDOS**
Bélohlávek/Czech PO.

☆ **Tre Ricerari (1938) / URANIA**
Turnovsky/Czech PO.

PIETRO MASCAGNI   1863-1945

Romantic. Mascagni's masterpiece, *Cavalleria Rusticana*, must have been a breath of fresh air at the turn of the century to opera-goers who for years had heard only impressionism, romanticism, and Wagnerian-ism. Its realistic portrayal of a Sicilian love tryst and murder is compact, direct, and underscored with music of great warmth and scenic orchestration. –BGT

○ **Cavalleria Rusticana (1889) / DGG**
Baltsa, Mentzer, Domingo, Pons, Sinopoli/Philharmonia Orchestra.

Cavalleria Rusticana (1889) / DGG
Cossotto, Bergonzi, Guelfi, Karajan/La Scala Orchestra & Chorus.

JULES MASSENET   1842-1912

Romantic. A French composer of opera, ballet, and other dramatic music, plus choral, vocal, and instrumental music. Fluid melodies, bright and rich orchestration, and lightly emotional aesthetics characterize much of Massenet's appealing output, such as the highly enjoyable and tuneful ballet *Le Cid* and the portrait of the "amoureuse" in the opera *Manon*. Massenet's harmonic writing influenced the young Debussy. In a way, Massenet is like Mascagni in presenting what is imagined to be basic in the "internal life" of a national character (at least for those times). –BGT

○ **Le Cid (ballet suite) (1885) / ANGEL**
Fremaux/City of Birmingham SO.

○ **Manon (4-act opera) (1884) / ANGEL**
Cotrubas, Kraus, Quilico, van Dam, Plasson/Toulouse Capitole Orchestra & Choir.

NIKOLAI MEDTNER   1880-1951

Neo-classical, neo-romantic. A Russian pianist and composer who wrote almost entirely for piano and voice. His style, never capitulating to the strong nationalism around him, was an attempt to fuse classical and romantic traits. He was most successful in pieces inspired by fairy tales. –MKS

○ **Concertos for Piano nos. 1-3; Sonata - Ballade for Piano in F#, op. 27 / CHANDOS**
Tozer (piano), Järvi/London PO. Turgid and somber Russian piano concertos with plenty of beautiful moments. –PM

○ **Forgotten Melodies (Book 1) for Piano, op. 38 (selections) / CEDILLE**
Paperno (piano). Exquisite playing by this Russian pianist, who now resides in the US. The rest of the album contains worthwhile selections by Lisdov, Rachmaninoff, Scriabin, and Tchaikovsky. –MKS

FELIX MENDELSSOHN   1809-1847

Romantic. Known in his time as a great conductor, Mendelssohn helped promote the works of Bach, which were largely forgotten by this time. Such respect for the beauties of musical form carried over into *Songs without Words*, each an individual gem (often studied by composition students) and lovely to hear for their lyricism and surprising alternatives to the expected melodic and harmonic turns. The works that have endured of this natural talent are primarily his orchestral pieces: the fresh lyricism and invention of the *Midsummer Night's Dream* overture and incidental music; the youthful energy and tone-painting of the *"Scottish"* and *"Italian"* symphonies; the brilliant *Concerto for Violin & Orchestra in e,* which has a noteworthy and appealing balance of classical and romantic writing; the thrilling, operatically dramatic oratorio *Elijah, op. 70;* also the skillfully written *Octet for Strings in E-flat,* which is light and floating on the strings. All these survive. I hope more of his solo piano music, which has great depth of feeling (for example, the *Variations serieuses, op. 54*), will someday be equally appreciated. –BGT

○ **Capriccio brillant for Piano & Orchestra / CBS**

Serkin, Ormandy/Columbia SO.

○ **Concert Pieces (2) for Clarinet & Bassett Horn (and Piano or Orchestra), opp. 113 & 114 / HYPERION**
King, Dobree.

Concert Pieces (2) for Clarinet & Bassett Horn (and Piano or Orchestra), opp. 113 & 114 / AMON RA
Hacker, Schatzberger, Burnett (period instruments).

○ **Concertos (2) for Piano & Orchestra; Capriccio brillant, op. 22 / CBS**
Serkin (piano), Ormandy/Columbia SO. These are the classics: Serkin digs beneath the surface more than anyone else, and Ormandy provides terrific support. –PM

○ **Concerto for Piano & Orchestra no. 1 in g, op. 25 / CBS**
Serkin, Ormandy/Columbia SO.

Concerto for Piano & Orchestra no. 1 in g, op. 25 / NIMBUS
Kite, Goodman/The Hanover Band.

○ **Concerto for Piano & Orchestra no. 2 in d, op. 40 / CBS**
Serkin, Ormandy/Columbia SO.

☆ **Concerto for Violin & Orchestra in e, op. 64 / DGG**
Shaham, Sinopoli/Philharmonia Orchestra. The freshest, least hyped-up performance currently before the public, in good sound. –PM

Concerto for Violin & Orchestra in e, op. 64 / ANGEL
Menuhin, Furtwängler/Berlin PO. This may be the best recording Menuhin ever made. –PM

Concerto for Violin & Orchestra in e, op. 64 / NIMBUS
Hudson, Goodman/The Hanover Band. Challenging original-instrument performance with a lot of new insights. –PM

Concerto for Violin & Orchestra in e, op. 64 / ANGEL
Perlman, Haitink/Royal Concertgebouw Orchestra. Very sweet from Perlman, but Haitink keeps the caloric intake down to an acceptable level. –PM

○ **Elijah (oratorio), op. 70 / PHILIPS**
Ameling, Burmeister, Schreier, Adam, Sawallisch/Leipzig Gewandhaus Orchestra, Leipzig Radio Chorus. German version. –ED

Elijah (oratorio), op. 70 / CHANDOS
Plowright, Finnie, Davies, White, Hickox/London SO & Chorus. The best version in English, but the German one has fresher singing and a more knowing conductor. –PM

A Midsummer Night's Dream (overture) / ORFEO
Davis/Bavarian RSO.

☆ **A Midsummer Night's Dream (overture/incidental) / PHILIPS**
Auger, Murray, Marriner/Philharmonia Orchestra, Ambrosian Singers.

A Midsummer Night's Dream (selected incidental) / PHILIPS
Davis/Boston SO.

A Midsummer Night's Dream (selected incidental) / VIRGIN
Mackerras/Orchestra of the Age of Enlightenment.

☆ **Octet for Strings in E-flat, op. 20 / SUPRAPHON**
Smetana & Janácek Quartets. The best performance I have ever heard, but not in very good sound on CD. –PM

Octet for Strings in E-flat, op. 20 / LONDON
Vienna Octet.

○ **Preludes & Fugues (3) for Organ, op. 37; Sonatas (6) for Organ, nos. 2 & 6, op. 65 / ARS VIVENDI**
Buschnakowski (organ). Beautiful organ, sumptuous late-analog sound, and fine, rhythmically alert (no sogginess here) playing of these "Victorian" works. Short measure, though, at 51:42. –PM

○ **Quartets (complete) / ACCORD**
Artis Quartet.

Quartets no. 1 in E-flat, op. 12 & no. 2 in a, op. 13; Andante and Scherzo, / HYPERION

Coull Quartet. Tasteful, lyrical, and soulful! Not so dry as many British performances of string quartets. Artis Quartet is more dramatic and forceful but may be hard to find. –PM

○ **Sonata for Cello & Piano no. 1 in B-flat, op. 45 / CLAVES**
Starck, Eschenbach. This recording has rich, resonant performance and sound. –PM

○ **Sonata for Cello & Piano no. 2 in D, op. 58 / CLAVES**
Starck, Eschenbach.

○ **Sonata for Clarinet & Piano in E-flat / AMON RA**
Hacker, Burnett.

○ **Sonatas (6) for Organ, op. 65 / ARKAY**
Beck (organ). Easily the better of the two performances of all six in the catalog. –PM

○ **Sonata for Violin & Piano in f, op. 4 / DGG**
Mintz, Ostrovsky.

○ **Songs without Words / DGG**
Barenboim.

Songs without Words / CHANDOS
Edlina (piano). A bit too new-agey (i. e., undramatic and laid-back) a performance but very beautiful and soulful at times, especially compared with Barenboim's more "masculine" playing. –PM

○ **Symphony no. 1 in c, op. 11 / UNICORN-KANCHANA**
Wetton/Milton Keynes CO. A bracing chamber orchestra version of a delightful symphony. –PM

○ **Symphony no. 3 in a, op. 56, "Scottish" / LONDON**
Magg/London SO. One of the most inspired recordings ever made: it's nice to have it back in a budget price range. Maag is one of the five most underrated conductors ever. –PM

Symphony no. 3 in a, op. 56, "Scottish" / ARS VIVENDI
Haenchen, Hartmut/Staatskapelle Berlin. There's a reticence and a vulnerability about this performance that I find quite appropriate and appealing. And then there's the sumptuous playing and the amazingly detailed nondigital sound. All in all, an effort, from an unlikely source, that is worthy to stand by the more tempestuous Bychkov and the fiery Maag. –PM

Symphony no. 3 in a, op. 56, "Scottish" / PHILIPS
Bychkov/London PO. Warmhearted and rhapsodic, with beautiful sound and melting phrasing. Bychkov always gets such a radiant sound out of his orchestras. –PM

Symphony no. 3 in a, op. 56, "Scottish" / ORFEO
Davis/Bavarian RSO.

☆ **Symphony no. 4 in A, op. 90, "Italian" / DGG**
Sinopoli/Philharmonia Orchestra. See the review of Sinopoli's *Symphony no. 8* by Schubert. –PM

Symphony no. 4 in A, op. 90, "Italian" / PHILIPS
Brüggen/Orchestra of the 18th Century. You'd have to be a hardcore hater of period instruments not to respond to these scintillating and incisive performances. They have all the flexibility of traditional performances, together with very fine sound in which every instrument can be clearly heard in perspective. This is one of Brüggen's two or three best performances. –PM

Symphony no. 4 in A, op. 90, "Italian" / PHILIPS
Bychkov/London PO.

Symphony no. 4 in A, op. 90, "Italian" / VIRGIN
Mackerras/Orchestra of the Age of Enlightenment.

○ **Symphony no. 5 in d, op. 107, "Reformation" / HUNGAROTON**
Fischer/Hungarian State Orchestra. More musical and less bombastic than most. –PM

Symphony no. 5 in d, op. 107, "Reformation" / UNICORN-KANCHANA
Wetton/Milton Keynes CO. A fine chamber-orchestra version, as opposed to the larger-scale Fischer above. –PM

○ **Trio for Violin, Cello & Piano no. 1 in d, op. 49 / CAMERATA**
Beethoven Trio of Vienna. A more dynamic performance here

than on the Grieg *Trio* (which is a bit more muddily recorded), but it has a somewhat better blend and soul. –PM

○ **Trio for Violin, Cello & Piano no. 2 in c, op. 66 / CAMERATA**
Beethoven Trio of Vienna.

Trios for Piano, Violin & Cello nos. 1 & 2 / SIMAX
Grieg Trio. These young Norwegian musicians play with plenty of soul and passion. You have to crank this one up to get the mud out of the sound. –PM

○ **Variations sérieuses, for Piano, op. 54 / DENON**
Magaloff.

NIKOLAI MIASKOVSKY   1881-1950

20th century. Miakovsky was a prolific, facile composer, cosmopolitan in approach. He never wrote in an extremely modern style, instead expanding traditional tonality. His 27 symphonies, chamber and piano pieces, and songs are structurally cohesive and full of emotional intensity. –MKS

○ **Sonatas for Piano nos. 1-9 / OLYMPIA**
MacLachlan.

DARIUS MILHAUD   1892-1974

20th century. A French composer of dramatic, orchestral, vocal, chamber, and instrumental music. Milhaud was a member of "Les Six," whose works were influenced by Erik Satie and Jean Cocteau, and was one of the first composers to use bitonality (playing in two keys at once). In the 20s and 30s he incorporated jazz and Latin rhythms into his music, especially beautifully done in the soulful *La création du monde* (1923), also notable in *Saudades do Brasil* (1921) and *Le boeuf sur le toit* (1919) (named for the avant-garde artists' cafe). Milhaud's fine and prolific sense of melody, which is both modern and pure like the modes of folk music, can be appreciated in works like the *Scaramouche Suite* and the *Sonatina for Oboe & Piano.* –BGT

○ **La création du monde (1923) / KOCH-SCHWANN**
Schenk/The Atlantic Sinfonietta. Plenty jazzy and idiomatic, with very good music. –PM

La création du monde (1923) / ELEKTRA
Weisberg/Contemporary Chamber Ensemble. Also contains Kurt Weill: "Little Threepenny Suite." –BGT

○ **Scaramouche Suite for 2 Pianos, op. 165b / PHILIPS**
K. and M. Lebeque (pianos). As always from these twins, A brilliant performance. –PM

○ **Sonatina for Oboe & Piano, op. 337 / ORFEO**
Holliger, Maisenberg.

○ **String Quartets (complete) / CYBELIA**
Chambre d'Aquitaine String Quartet, Arcana Quartet. For very adventurous listeners, it may be worth the time and effort to get to know these interesting pieces. –PM

○ **Suite pour le Piano (1913) / GALLO**
Mueller (piano). Thoughtful late-night listening. –PM

FEDERICO MOMPOU   1893-1987

Modern. A Spanish composer of songs and piano minatures whose music shares a great deal stylistically with Satie's, but with a deep Andalusian feel and more complex harmonies, especially in the moving *Paisajes* (1942-1960). Mompou also revived the use of notation without bar lines, reaching back to the style of mensural notation in pre-Renaissance music. –BGT

○ **Piano Music (selections) / GAILY**
Huybregts.

CLAUDIO MONTEVERDI   1567-1643

Baroque, vocal. An Italian composer of opera (*Orfeo*, 1607) as well as sacred and secular vocal music. Monteverdi was a significant early composer in the operatic genre. Basing his music on his interpretations of ancient texts by Greek theorists (who were greatly respected by Renaissance intellectuals), Monteverdi produced original music from the material of the prevailing Venetian styles. His music is of almost unsurpassable beauty, especially the *Vespro della Beata Vergine*. Monteverdo's theorizing and experimentation in developing theater-music forms led to the fundamentals of opera in the next century, his most notable work in this genre being *Combattimento di Tancredi et Clorinda* (1624). −BGT

○ **Combattimento di Tancredi et Clorinda (1624) / VIRGIN**
Kirkby, Agnew, King, Rooley/The Consort of Musicke.

Combattimento di Tancredi et Clorinda & 3 other madrigals / HYPERION
Byrd/The Parley of Instruments.

○ **Lamento d'Arianna / DGG**
Watkinson, Goebel/Musica Antiqua Köln.

○ **Lamento d'Olimpia (and other laments) / HYPERION**
Kirkby (soprano), Rooley (chitarrone).

○ **Madrigals / OISEAU-LYRE**
Kirkby, Nelson, Holden (sopranos), Elliott, King (tenors), Wistreich (baritone), Thomas (bass), Rooley/The Consort of Musicke.

○ **L'Orfeo (1607) / DGG**
Gardiner/English Baroque Soloists, Monteverdi Choir.

○ **Sacred Music / HYPERION**
Kirkby (soprano), Partridge (tenor), Thomas (bass), Goodman/The Parley of Instruments.

○ **Vespri di San Giovanni Battista / PHILIPS**
Leonhardt/Monteverdi Ensemble Amsterdam (period instruments), Netherlands Chamber Choir.

○ **Vespro della Beata Vergine (1610) / OISEAU-LYRE**
Pickett/New London Consort.

○ **Volgendo il ciel (ballet) (1636) / VIRGIN**
Kirkby, LeBlanc, Nichols, Agnew, Ewing, Rooley/The Consort of Musicke.

ENNIO MORRICONE   *b* 1928

20th century. An Italian composer of film scores, chamber music, and instrumental pieces who is famous for his scores for *The Good, the Bad, and the Ugly* and *Once upon a Time in the West.* −ED

○ **Chamber Music / VENTURE**
No personnel given. If you want to know what the writer of film music writes when he isn't writing film music, listen to this. Sounds a lot like lyrical Italian Webern to me, and I like it. −PM

WOLFGANG AMADEUS MOZART   1756-1791

Classical. This Austrian composer and child prodigy was a major figure in the classical period who wrote in most musical forms of the time, especially opera, symphony, concertos, and chamber music; his notable works are too numerous to mention. Mozart had a great and lively mind, which he engaged in such experiments as deciding progressions by playing dice and billiards, placing players in adjacent rooms echoing each other (*Notturno for Four Orchestras, K. 269*), and the encoding of Masonic rituals in *The Magic Flute*. Mozart was capable of the most earthshaking and profound works (*Requiem, K. 626*, written as he lay on his deathbed), the sweetest of arias in his many operas, and the most beautiful of melodic invention and variation (the piano concertos, *Eine Kleine Nachtmusik*, and much more). His feeling for the balance of lines that have separate functions (melody, accompaniment, sostenuto, and melisma) is revealed in the quintets, the *Sinfonia Concertante in E-flat*, and the string quartets. Many structures in his symphonies are copies of innovations by Haydn, in some ways more conservative, but their drive, surprising modulations, and memorable melodies are purely Mozart. −BGT

○ **Church Sonatas (14) for Strings & Organ; Church Sonatas (3) for Strings, Wind, Brass & Organ / HYPERION**

Watson (organ), King/King's Consort. A bit too dry and British, but at least it's complete, and it's all we have for the moment. −PM

○ **Concerto for Bassoon & Orchestra in B-flat, K. 191 / PHILIPS**
Thunemann (bassoon), Marriner/ASMF. Thunemann leads the field in both, but the orchestral support is better from Marriner. −PM

Concerto for Bassoon & Orchestra in B-flat, K. 191 / CLAVES
Thunemann, Stoutz/Zürich CO.

☆ **Concerto for Clarinet & Orchestra in A, K. 622 / PHILIPS**
Hoeprich (basset clarinet), Brüggen/Orchestra of the 18th Century.

Concerto for Clarinet & Orchestra in A, K. 622 / LONDON
de Peyer, Maag/London SO.

Concerto for Clarinet & Orchestra in A, K. 622 / NIMBUS
Lawson (clarinet), Goodman/The Hanover Band. Very alert performance with some terrific ornamentation. Not so good in the orchestra, though, as the Brüggen. −PM

Concerto for Clarinet & Orchestra in A, K. 622 / PHILIPS
Leister, Marriner/ASMF.

Concerto for Clarinet & Orchestra in A, K. 622 / HYPERION
King (clarinet), Tate/English CO. A bit schmaltzy and heavy in the orchestra, but with beautiful playing on the basset-clarinet by Thea King. −PM

○ **Concerto for Flute & Harp in C, K. 299 / NOVALIS**
Holliger, Nicolet, Holliger/English CO.

Concerto for Flute & Harp in C, K. 299 / PHILIPS
Grafenauer, Graf, Marriner/ASMF.

○ **Concertos (2) for Flute & Orchestra, K. 313, 314 / CLAVES**
Graf, Leppard/English CO.

Concerto for Flute & Orchestra no. 1 in G, K. 313 / PHILIPS
Grafenauer, Marriner/ASMF.

☆ **Concertos (4) for Horn & Orchestra, K. 412 / LONDON**
Tuckwell, Maag/London SO.

Concertos (4) for Horn & Orchestra, K. 412 / HARMONIA MUNDI
Greer, McGegan/Philharmonia Baroque Orchestra.

Concertos (4) for Horn & Orchestra, K. 412 / DGG
Jolley, Purvis/Orpheus CO.

Concerto for Oboe, K. 314 / ASV
Boyd, Berglund/The Chamber Orchestra of Europe.

○ **Concerto for Oboe & Orchestra in C, K. 285 / PHILIPS**
Holliger (oboe), Marriner/ASMF. Has anyone ever played the oboe as well as Holliger? −PM

○ **Concertos (3) for Piano & Orchestra, K. 107 / OPUS 111**
Hantai (harpsichord)/Le Concert Français.

○ **Concerto for Piano & Orchestra no. 9 in E-flat, K. 271 / HUNGARATON**
Ranki, Rolla/Liszt CO.

Concerto for Piano & Orchestra no. 9 in E-flat, K. 271 / OMEGA
Meyer, Brown/Norwegian CO.

Concerto for Piano & Orchestra no. 9 in E-flat, K. 271 / LONDON
Schiff, Végh/Salzburg Camerata Academica.

○ **Concerto for Piano & Orchestra no. 11, K. 413 / CLAVES**
Studer (piano), Muller-Bruhl/Cologne CO. Sturdy, with some subtle and forceful piano playing. The orchestra is a bit too plain and plainly recorded. −PM

Concerto for Piano & Orchestra no. 11, K. 413 / LONDON
Schiff, Végh/Salzberg Camerata Academica.

Concerto for Piano & Orchestra no. 11, K. 413 / PHILIPS

Brendel (piano), Marriner/ASMF. Christian Zacharias has done most of the Mozart piano concertos with American conductor David Zinman and various orchestras. These performances are on EMI but are hard to find. Sometimes EMI copies them from LPs and brings them into America on CD; some are available at exorbitant prices from Allegro Imports. These performances have the "three t's" in adundance — taste, technique, and temperament. Zimerman is gutsy and delicate by turns and has a beautiful tone, plus he isn't so willful as Brendel and follows the printed page a bit better; in general, these would be my first choices for Mozart piano concertos. Zacharias is even more "Mozartean" than Végh, although not quite so insightful or passionate at times. EMI should bring this set out as a budget in the US as well as Zacharias's Mozart sonatas, which are available in Germany but which no one I know has seen here. –PM

Concerto for Piano & Orchestra no. 11, K. 413 / CLAVES
Studer, Muller-Bruhl/Cologne CO.

○ **Concerto for Piano & Orchestra no. 12 in A, K. 414 / ASV**
Rutman (piano), Stamp/Academy of London. This is a romanticized but stylish reading with simply beautiful liquid piano tone. –PM

Concerto for Piano & Orchestra no. 12 in A, K. 414 / KOCH-SCHWANN
Entremont (piano and conductor)/Vienna CO.

○ **Concerto for Piano & Orchestra no. 13, K. 387b / LONDON**
Schiff, Végh/Salzburg Camerata Academica.

Concerto for Piano & Orchestra no. 13, K. 387b / HUNGARATON
Ranki, Rolla/Liszt CO.

Concerto for Piano & Orchestra no. 13, K. 387b / DGG
Michelangeli, Garben/North German Radio Orchestra.

Concerto for Piano & Orchestra no. 13 in C, K. 387b / EMI
Zacharias, Zinman/English CO.

○ **Concerto for Piano & Orchestra no. 14, K. 449 / LONDON**
Schiff, Végh/Salzburg Camerata Academica.

Concerto for Piano & Orchestra no. 14 in E-flat, K. 449 / KOCH-SCHWANN
Entremont (piano and conductor)/Vienna CO. Stylish performance but without quite the character of Schiff's. –PM

○ **Concerto for Piano & Orchestra no. 15 in B-flat, K. 450 / EMI**
Zacharias, Zinman/English CO.

Concerto for Piano & Orchestra no. 15, K. 450 / PHILIPS
Brendel, Marriner/ASMF.

Concerto for Piano & Orchestra no. 15, K. 450 / DGG
Michelangeli, Garben/North German Radio Orchestra.

○ **Concerto for Piano & Orchestra no. 16 in D, K. 451 / ANGEL**
Zacharias (piano), Marriner/Stuttgart RSO. An aggressive and exciting performance with very good orchestral support and sound. –PM

Concerto for Piano & Orchestra no. 16, K. 451 / PHILIPS
Brendel (piano), Marriner/ASMF. Brendel is just a little bit too quirky here and on many of his other Mozart concertos to be given a top recommendation. –PM

○ **Concerto for Piano & Orchestra no. 17, K. 453 / HUNGARATON**
Ranki, Rolla/Liszt CO.

Concerto for Piano & Orchestra no. 17, K. 453 / LONDON
Schiff, Végh/Salzburg Mozarteum Camerata Academica.

○ **Concerto for Piano & Orchestra no. 18, K. 456 / LONDON**
Schiff, Végh/Salzburg Mozarteum Camerata Academica.

○ **Concerto for Piano & Orchestra no. 19, K. 459 / ANGEL**
Zacharias, Marriner/Stuttgart RSO.

Concerto for Piano & Orchestra no. 19, K. 459 / DGG

Pollini (piano), Böhm/Vienna PO. Big-band Mozart, with plenty of heft and power, but not sloppy. A true bargain. –PM

Concerto for Piano & Orchestra no. 19, K. 459 / LONDON
Schiff, Végh/Salzburg Mozarteum Camerata Academica.

○ **Concerto for Piano & Orchestra no. 20 in d, K. 466 / NIMBUS**
Kite (fortepiano), Goodman/The Hanover Band. Could be the best recording of a Mozart concerto I've ever heard on fortepiano. Combines lyricism with incisiveness and wonderful ornamentation to create a most winning performance. –PM

Concerto for Piano & Orchestra no. 20, K. 466 / BIS
Westenholz (piano), Sconwandt/Copenhagen Collegium Musicum. Nothing extraordinary here, but this is a completely recommendable *Concertos nos. 20 & 23*: good sound, good playing, and the proper scale in the orchestra. –PM

Concerto for Piano & Orchestra no. 20, K. 466 / AS DISC
Lefebure (piano), Furtwängler/Berlin PO. Tragic and profound, especially from the orchestra. –PM

○ **Concerto for Piano & Orchestra no. 21, K. 467 / PHILIPS**
Brendel (piano), Marriner/ASMF. Brendel has moments of rare insight, but I don't always find that he sustains that level throughout a complete performance, and that's true in his Mozart in general. Orchestral accompaniment is a bit dry (especially compared with the hot-blooded Végh), but there's that unusual Academy and Marriner perfection that's hard to deny. –PM

Concerto for Piano & Orchestra no. 21 in C, K. 467 / VIRGIN
Ambache (piano)/Ambache CO. Straightforward, perfectly scaled performances; quite a deal at a bargain price. –PM

○ **Concerto for Piano & Orchestra no. 22, K. 482 / LONDON**
Schiff (piano), Végh/Salzburg Mozarteum Camerata Academica. Sprightly and delicate piano playing, combined with a tougher orchestral approach, make this a safer recommendation than the Richter, I suppose. Schiff really plays with a lot of fantasy and whimsy in Mozart, and he isn't so wimpy as he is in Bach. All of his concertos are highly recommended. Too bad he reverts again to wimpiness in his Mozart sonatas. –PM

Concerto for Piano & Orchestra no. 22, K. 482 / ANGEL
Richter (piano), Muti/Philharmonia Orchestra. A bit heavy at times but with the usual Richter insights. Does any piano player make you think, the way Richter does? –PM

Concerto for Piano & Orchestra no. 22 in E-flat, K. 482 / ASV
Rutman, Stamp/Academy of London.

☆ **Concerto for Piano & Orchestra no. 23, K. 488 / LONDON**
Schiff (piano), Végh/Salzburg Mozarteum Camerata Academica. Helped a tremendous amount by the insightful and incisive orchestral contributions from Végh, these are now overall my standard Mozart concerto performances. The only real competition is Zacharias, but his set is too hard to obtain, at least for now. –PM

Concerto for Piano & Orchestra no. 23, K. 488 / ANGEL
Zacharias (piano), Zinman/Dresden State Orchestra. Serious and very fine Mozart. –PM

Concerto for Piano & Orchestra no. 23, K. 488 / DGG
Pollini (piano), Böhm/Vienna PO. Larger than life, with excellent, big-boned support from Böhm and the orchestra. –PM

Concerto for Piano & Orchestra no. 23, K. 488 / SUPRAPHON
Moravec (piano), Vlach/Czech PO. The piano playing is as good as anybody's, but the orchestra and sound are a bit of a drawback. –PM

○ **Concerto for Piano & Orchestra no. 24, K. 491 / DGG**
Kempff (piano), Leitner/Bamberg SO. Profound, from the old German school. This piece has fallen on hard discographic

times, and until Zacharias or Brendel makes a reappearance in the catalog, the Kempff will have to do. –PM

○ **Concerto for Piano & Orchestra no. 25, K. 503 / SUPRAPHON**
Moravec (piano), Vlach/Czech PO. The orchestra and sound on this recording are a bit of a letdown, but Moravec is just such a stylish Mozartean. –PM

Concerto for Piano & Orchestra no. 25 in C, K. 503 / VIRGIN
Ambache/Ambache CO.

○ **Concerto for Piano & Orchestra no. 26, K. 537 / ANGEL**
Zacharias (piano), Zinman/Bavarian RSO. The only really recommendable *Concerto no. 26* around. –PM

○ **Concerto for Piano & Orchestra no. 27, K. 595 / LONDON**
Schiff, Végh/Salzburg Mozarteum Camerata Academica.

Concerto for Piano & Orchestra no. 27 in B-flat, K. 595 / HUNGARATON
Ranki, Rolla/Liszt CO.

○ **Concerto for Violin & Orchestra no. 1 in B-flat, K. 207 / PHILIPS**
Kremer (violin), Harnoncourt/Vienna PO. A lot of temperament from both conductor and violinist in all five concertos and the *Sinfonia Concertante*. –PM

○ **Concertos for Violin & Orchestra nos. 1 & 2; Adagio, K. 261; Rondos, K. 269, 373 / CAPRICCIO**
Schmid (violin), Graf/Salzburg Mozarteum Orchestra. What a find, plus a real sleeper! The scale is right, the orchestra responsive, and the violinist has some profile and panache, without going overboard, a beautiful tone in all registers. In other words, this is playing that cuts straight to Mozart and avoids the rhetoric and self-glorification. Made me appreciate these works completely anew. –PM

○ **Concertos for Violin & Orchestra nos. 1-5 / OISEAU-LYRE**
Standage (violin), Hogwood/Academy of Ancient Music. On the first recording to include all of Mozart's authenticated music for violin and orchestra on authentic instruments, Standage is in fine form. This is a self-recommending and obligatory purchase for anyone curious to hear how these perennial favorites might have sounded in Mozart's time. –PM

○ **Concerto for Violin & Orchestra no. 2 in D, K. 211 / DGG**
Kremer, Harnoncourt/Vienna PO.

Concerto for Violin & Orchestra no. 2 in D, K. 211 / PHILIPS
Van Keulen (violin), Ros-Marba/Netherlands CO. I believe van Keulen was 13 when she made this, and she is amazingly poised and pure. –PM

○ **Concerto for Violin & Orchestra no. 3 in G, K. 216 / PHILIPS**
Grumiaux, Davis/London SO.

Concerto for Violin & Orchestra no. 3 in G, K. 216 / DGG
Kremer, Harnoncourt/Vienna PO.

Concerto for Violin & Orchestra no. 3 in G, K. 216 / DGG
Mutter, Karajan/Berlin PO.

○ **Concertos for Violin & Orchestra nos. 3 & 5 / PHILIPS**
Van Keulen (violin), Concertgebouw CO. Van Keulen is fresh and elegant, and this is the best Mozart-concerto playing since Grumiaux's. –PM

○ **Concerto for Violin & Orchestra no. 4 in D, K. 218 / DGG**
Kremer, Harnoncourt/Vienna PO.

☆ **Concerto for Violin & Orchestra no. 5 in A, K. 219 / PHILIPS**
Van Keulen (violin), Royal Concertgebouw Orchestra.

Concerto for Violin & Orchestra no. 5 in A, K. 219 / PHILIPS
Grumiaux (violin), Davis/London SO. Grumiaux is just so elegant and emotional underneath his restraint. All five of his concertos and his *Sinfonia Concertante* will always be treasured collector's items. –PM

Concerto for Violin & Orchestra no. 5 in A, K. 219 / DGG
Kremer, Harnoncourt/Vienna PO.

Concerto for Violin & Orchestra no. 5 in A, K. 219 / DGG
Mutter (violin), Karajan/Berlin PO. Mutter's first CD. This is all a bit heavy for my taste, but it is quite a bargain as a budget reissue. –PM

☆ **Così Fan Tutte (two-act opera), K. 588 / ANGEL**
Schwarzkopf, Otto, Merriman, Simoneau, Panerai, Bruscantini, Karajan/Philharmonia Orchestra & Chorus. This is as good as Karajan ever got in Mozart, with singing to match. –PM

Così Fan Tutte (two-act opera), K. 588 / ANGEL
Schwarzkopf, Steffek, Ludwig, Kraus, Taddei, Berry, Böhm/Philharmonia Orchestra & Chorus.

Così Fan Tutte (two-act opera), K. 588 / PHILIPS
Mattila, Szmytka, von Otter, Araiza, Allen, van Dam, Marriner/ASMF & Ambrosian Opera Chorus. With a sparkling, lighter orchestral approach, and singing to match, this becomes the digital version of choice for the 90s. –PM

Così Fan Tutte (two-act opera), K. 588 / PHILIPS
Caballé, Baker, Gedda, Ganzarolli, Davis/Royal Opera Orchestra & Chorus.

○ **Davidde Penitente (cantata), K. 469 / PHILIPS**
Margar, Marshall, Marriner/Stuttgart RSO.

Davidde Penitente (cantata), K. 469 / EDITO CLASSICA
Laki, Fallien, Blochwitz, Kuijken/La Petite Bande. This is the classic confrontation between authentic instruments and one of the best baroque conductors, using a not-really-top-of-the-line orchestra on "modern" instruments. The choice is tough, but the more in-tune Marriner, with the inclusion of a very fine *Exsultate, Jubilate*, will probably sway most folks toward him. –PM

○ **Divertimento in E-flat, K. 113 / PHILIPS**
ASMF Chamber Ensemble.

○ **Divertimento in D, K. 131 / PHILIPS**
Marriner/ASMF.

○ **Divertimentos (3) in D, B-flat & F, K. 136-138 / BIS**
Drottningholm Baroque Ensemble. These are outstanding baroque-style performances; they even add ornamentation at times. –PM

Divertimentos (3) in D, B-flat & F, K. 136-138 / LONDON
Marriner/ASMF.

○ **Divertimentos (6), K. 439b; Duos (12) for 2 Basset-horns, K. 487 / DGG**
Prinz (clarinet), Schmidl (basset-horn); Zeman (bassoon). Almost two hours of Mozart on the clarinet: even in "minor" works, a real treat! –PM

○ **Divertimentos for 6 winds, K. 213, 240, 252, 253, 270 / OISEAU-LYRE**
Amadeus Winds. For the piquancy of the period winds, I'll take this one over the Berlin PO winds. Others will feel just the opposite! –PM

Divertimentos for 6 winds, K. 213, 240, 252, 253, 270 / ORFEO
Berlin Philharmonic Winds.

○ **Divertimentos for Strings in D, K. 136 / PHILIPS**
Marriner/ASMF Chamber Ensemble.

☆ **Divertimento for String Trio in E-flat, K. 563 / CALIG**
Vienna String Trio.

Divertimento for String Trio in E-flat, K. 563 / INTERCORD
Deutsches String Trio. The choice is really tough here, with the German string trio predictably tighter and more urgent, and the Viennese trio a bit more gemuetlich. –PM

Divertimento for String Trio in E-flat, K. 563 / PHILIPS
Grumiaux Trio. Very stylish and well recorded for its age, but probably now superseded by both other versions which, being permanent string trios, are more tightly organized. –PM

○ **Divertimento no. 7 in D, K. 205 / PHILIPS**
ASMF Chamber Ensemble.

○ **Divertimento no. 10 in F, K. 247 / PHILIPS**
ASMF Chamber Ensemble.

Divertimento no. 10 in F, K. 247 / LONDON
Vienna Octet members.

○ **Divertimento no. 11 in D for, K. 251 / PHILIPS**
Holliger, Baumann/Orlando Quartet.

Divertimento no. 11 in D, K. 251 / ERATO
Koopman/Amsterdam Baroque Orchestra.

Divertimento no. 11 in D, K. 251 / PHILIPS
ASMF Chamber Ensemble.

Divertimento no. 11 in D, K. 251 / DGG
Orpheus CO.

○ **Divertimento no. 17 in D, K. 334 / ANGEL**
Welser-Möst/Stockholm CO. Tremendously stylish and inspired; one of the greatest Mozart records ever made. –PM

Divertimento no. 17 in D, K. 334 / BEYER
Egger/Bozen String Academy. You know, this isn't bad at all, proving once again the great (Welser-Möst) is truly the enemy of the good. –PM

Divertimento no. 17 in D, K. 334 / LONDON
Vienna Octet Members. One player to a part, and gemuetlich all the way. –PM

☆ **Don Giovanni (two-act opera), K. 527 / HUNT**
Grümmer, della Casa, Streich, Simoneau, Siepi, Frick, Berry, Corena, Mitropoulos/Vienna PO & State Opera Chorus. More serious than Giulini, and, if possible, even better sung all the way around. Giulini sees it as a comedy; with Mitropoulos, it is more life and death. The problem is Mitropoulos has some erratic tempos and is hampered by pirate sound. –PM

Don Giovanni (two-act opera), K. 527 / ANGEL
Sutherland, Schwarzkopf, Sciutti, Alva, Wächter, Cappuccili, Taddei, Frick, Giulini/Philharmonia Orchestra & Chorus. The classic, still sounding good after 30 years. –PM

Don Giovanni (two-act opera), K. 527 / PHILIPS
Marriner/ASMF. Good men, conducting, orchestra, scale, and sound. (Five out of six isn't so bad, especially these days; the women aren't so hot.) –PM

○ **Die Entführung aus dem Serail, K. 384 / DGG**
Auger, Grist, Schreier, Neukirch, Moll, Böhm/Dresden State Orchestra, Leipzig Radio Chorus.

○ **Exsultate Jubilate (motet for soprano & orchestra), K. 165 / OISEAU-LYRE**
Kirkby/Hogwood Academy of Ancient Music, Westminster Cathedral Boys Choir.

○ **Fantasia for Piano in d, K. 397 / DGG**
Gilels (piano). Outstanding Mozart playing, more rugged and incisive than usual and one of Gilels's best. –PM

Fantasia for Piano in d, K. 397 / DGG
Pires.

○ **Fantasia for Piano in c, K. 475 / DGG**
Pires (piano). It could be a bit more flamboyant, but it does have beautiful tone and control. –PM

○ **Idomeneo Re di Creta (three-act opera), K. 366 / DGG**
Böhm/Dresden State Orchestra.

Idomeneo Re di Creta (three-act opera), K. 366 / LONDON
Popp, Gruberova, Baltsa, Pavaroti, Nucci, Pritchard/Vienna PO & State Opera Choir.

Idomeneo Re di Creta (three-act opera), K. 366 / PHILIPS
Rinaldi, Tinsley, Shirley, Davies, Tear, Dean, Davis/BBC SO & Chorus.

☆ **The Magic Flute (two-act opera), K. 620 / DGG**
Lear, Peters, Otto, Wunderlich, Fischer-Dieskau, Böhm/Berlin PO, RIAS Chamber Chorus. The classic 60s recording, still in great sound. OK women, great men, and great conducting.

Unfortunately, it's now available only on a five-CD mid-priced set with a not-quite-so-fine *Entführung*. –PM

The Magic Flute (two-act opera), K. 620 / PHILIPS
Te Kanawa, Studer, Lind, Araiza, Van Dam, Ramey, Marriner/ASMF, Ambrosian Opera Chorus.

The Magic Flute (two-act opera), K. 620 / ANGEL
Seefried, Lipp, Loose, Dermota, Kunz, Weber, Karajan/Vienna PO, Musikfreunde Chorus.

The Magic Flute (two-act opera), K. 620 / EMI
Upshaw, Johnson, Schmidt, Hoch, Hauptmann, Norrington/London Classical Players. A striking new performance that emphasizes light, quick tempos. The small orchestra and excellent singers phrase and ornament gracefully and skillfully. –MKS

☆ **The Marriage of Figaro, K. 492 / ANGEL**
Schwarzkopf, Seefried, Jurinac, Hongen, London, Kunz, Karajan/Vienna PO, State Opera & Chorus.

The Marriage of Figaro, K. 492 / PHILIPS
Popp, Hendricks, Baltsa, Raimondi, van Dam, Marriner/ASMF, Ambrosian Opera Chorus.

The Marriage of Figaro, K. 492 / ANGEL
Schwarzkopf, Moffo, Cossotto, Wächter, Taddei, Vinco, Guilini/Philharmonia Orchestra & Chorus.

The Marriage of Figaro, K. 492 / LONDON
Te Kanawa, Popp, von Stade, Ramey, et al., Solti/London PO.

○ **Masonic Funeral Music, K. 477 / DGG**
Böhm/Vienna PO.

○ **Mass in C, "In Honorem SSmae Trinitatis," K. 167 / PHILIPS**
Kegel/Leipzig RSO & Chorus.

○ **Mass in C, "Coronation," K. 317 / ARGO**
Marshall, Murray, Covey-Crump, Wilson-Johnson, Cleobury/English CO, King's Collegium Chorus. A bit on the heavy side but the best we have at the moment. –PM

○ **Mass in C, "Missa Solemnis," K. 337 / ARGO**
Marshall, Murray, Covey-Crump, Wilson-Johnson, Cleobury/English CO, King's Collegium Chorus.

☆ **Mass in c, "Great," K. 427 / PHILIPS**
Hendricks, Schreier. Barbara Hendricks is in better voice here than on her other recording of this work, and Schreier has a good choir, too. Schreier keeps a consistently balanced view between the classical and romantic elements in this great work, and overall his is the finest performance yet. The sound from Philips is top drawer. –PM

Mass in c, "Great," K. 427 / HUNT
Giebel, Lear, Munteanu, Guthrie, Celibidache/Rome Radio Orchestra & Chorus. An ethereal performance; one of Celibidache's best pirates. –PM

Mass in c, "Great," K. 427 / FHM
Herreweghe/Orchestre des Champs, soloists. As mannered as he always is, but at least a lot more forceful. –PM

○ **Missa Brevis in G, K. 140 / PHILIPS**
Kegel/Leipzig RSO & Chorus.

○ **Missa Brevis in C, K. 258 / PHILIPS**
Kegel/Dresden PO, Leipzig Radio Chorus. Kegel is a veteran East German choral conductor. All of his Mozart performances, while not scaling any heights or uncovering any new epiphanies, can be highly recommended for their straightforward dedication. –PM

○ **Missa Brevis in G, K. 47d / PHILIPS**
Kegel/Leipzig RSO & Chorus.

○ **Missa Brevis in d, K. 61a / PHILIPS**
Kegel/Leipzig RSO & Chorus.

○ **Missa in c, "Waisenhausmesse," K. 47a / DHM**
Henning/Collegium Aureum, soloists & Hanover Boys Choir. The piquancy of the old instruments and the boys choir gives this performance a special flavor, but it's hard to ignore the more together and in-tune Abbado, who is certainly more

"professional." Here we have a great contrast between modern- and original-instrument performances, both of which can be appreciated about equally. –PM

Missa in c, "Waisenhausmesse," K. 47a / DGG
Janowitz, von Stade, Ochman, Moll, Abbado/Vienna PO & State Opera Chorus.

○ **Missa, "Dominicus Mass," K. 66 / PHILIPS**
Kegel/Leipzig RSO & Chorus.

○ **Missa [longa] in C, K. 262 / PHILIPS**
Kegel/Dresden PO, Leipzig Radio Chorus.

○ **A Musical Joke, K. 522 / PHILIPS**
Marriner/ASMF Chamber Ensemble.

A Musical Joke, K. 522 / DGG
Orpheus CO.

A Musical Joke, K. 522 / BEYER
Egger/Bolzano String Academy. The Egger may not be so well played as the Academy or the Orpheus, but it has more soul and is funnier. –PM

○ **Organ Works / MOTETTE**
Weinberger (organ). Once you get the melodies in your head, these are some of Mozart's most charming and endearing pieces, some of them written for mechanical clocks and transcribed for organ. –PM

Organ Works / NOVALIS
Haselbock.

Organ Works / GLOBE
van Doeselaar.

○ **Overture (*Clemenza di Tito*) / PHILIPS**
Brüggen/Orchestra of the 18th Century.

○ **Overture (*The Marriage of Figaro*) / PHILIPS**
Brüggen/Orchestra of the 18th Century.

○ **Piano Music for Four Hands (complete) / PAVANE**
O. and D. Ouziel (piano). The sound could be a bit richer and fuller and the playing a bit more flamboyant. However, these are still highly recommended because of the direct, clean, no-nonsense approach and because of the inclusion of the wonderful smaller pieces. –PM

○ **Quartets (23) for Strings nos. 1-13 / DGG**
Hagen Quartet. This is easily the finest set on CD of the early quartets,and the thrown-in K. 136-138 divertimentos played as string quartets are one of the best things to come out of the much-hyped Mozart bicentennial. The Hagen's performances are alert, vibrant, and vital, just about perfectly recorded with the right blend of presence and warmth. If this is not the best quartet in the world right now, they are rapidly getting there. –PM

○ **Quartet for Strings no. 14 in G, K. 387 / WHITE LABEL**
Bartók Quartet.

○ **Quartets (23) for Strings nos. 14-17 / NUOVA ERA**
Prazak Quartet.

○ **Quartets (23) for Strings nos. 14 & 16 / HYPERION**
Salomon Quartet.

○ **Quartets (23) for Strings nos. 14-19, "Haydn Quartets" / ASTREE**
Quatour Mosaiques.

☆ **Quartet for Strings no. 15 in d, K. 421 / WHITE LABEL**
Bartók Quartet.

Quartet for Strings no. 15 in d, K. 421 / HYPERION
Salomon String Quartet. The Esterházy was the first original-instruments quartet to tackle the six dedicated to Haydn, and it is good to see theirs back at mid-price; however, I think for the final ten quartets, I would have to go with the somewhat better-balanced and more natural-sounding Salomon. This is really splendid playing, a bit less intellectual-sounding than the Jaap Schröder-led Esterházy. Both groups play in a dry style, with every part completely and perfectly clear. But wait, there's a new original-instruments group on the scene, the Quartour Mosaiques, and they are formidable rivals. They

have a much richer, agogic style and are recorded in a more reverberant acoustic. Four of their Haydn quartets are out. –PM

○ **Quartet for Strings no. 16 in E-flat, K. 428 / WHITE LABEL**
Bartók Quartet.

○ **Quartet for Strings no. 17 in B-flat, K. 458 / WHITE LABEL**
Bartók Quartet.

○ **Quartets (23) for Strings nos. 17 & 18 / HYPERION**
Salomon Quartet.

○ **Quartet for Strings no. 18 in A, K. 464 / WHITE LABEL**
Bartók Quartet.

○ **Quartets (23) for Strings nos. 18 & 19 / NUOVA ERA**
Prazak Quartet.

○ **Quartet for Strings no. 19 in C, "Dissonant," K. 465 / WHITE LABEL**
Bartók Quartet.

Quartet for Strings no. 19 in C, "Dissonant," K. 465 / HYPERION
Salomon Quartet.

○ **Quartets (23) for Strings nos. 20 & 22 / HYPERION**
Salomon Quartet.

○ **Quartet for Strings no. 21 in D, K. 575 / PHILIPS**
Orlando Quartet. To my way of thinking, this is the best recording the Orlando Quartet ever made. It's one of my treasured Mozart recordings. –PM

○ **Quartet for Strings no. 22 in B-flat, K. 589 / DGG**
Hagen Quartet. Likewise Hagen: this young quartet moves from strength to strength, and will, I hope, be around for a long time to come. –PM

Quartet for Strings no. 22 in B-flat, K. 589 / PHILIPS
Orlando Quartet. There is an added depth and pungency to go along with their usual sweetness, most appropriate to Mozart's late quartets. –PM

☆ **Quartet for Strings no. 23 in F, K. 590 / DGG**
Hagen Quartet.

○ **Quartets (4) for Flute & Strings / CHANNEL CLASSICS**
Schönbrunn Ensemble Amsterdam. Played on period instruments, this is the first recording I have ever heard that makes the flute quartets sound like truly inspired Mozart music. –PM

○ **Quartet for Oboe & Strings in F, K. 370 / PHILIPS**
Holliger/Orlando Quartet.

Quartet for Oboe & Strings in F, K. 370 / DENON
Schellenberger/Members of the Berlin Philharmonia Quartet.

☆ **Quartets (2) for Piano & Strings, K. 478 & 493 / FHM**
Mozartean Players. The most dramatic performance I have ever heard of these pieces. The timbres are quite striking on original instruments, with great sound quality. –PM

Quartets (2) for Piano & Strings, K. 478 & 493 / DGG
Bilson, Wilcock, Sclapp, Mason.

Quartets (2) for Piano & Strings, K. 478 & 493 / CALIG
Gothoni/Munich String Trio. Despite some rhythmic insecurities and less-than-perfect intonation, these are heartfelt and passionate Mozart performances that steer a near-perfect line between the "romantic" and "classical" Mozart. –PM

Quartets (2) for Piano & Strings, K. 478 & 493 / WHITE LABEL
Kiss/Tátrai Trio.

○ **Quintets (2) for Clarinet, Basset Horn & String Trio, K. 516c & 580b / AMON RA**
Hacker, Schatzberger/Members of the Salomon Quartet. Important movements that are similar in style to the clarinet quintet. –PM

☆ **Quintet for Clarinet & Strings in A, K. 581 / DENON**

Meyer/Berlin Philharmonia Quintet. Beautiful tone and control and simply ethereal playing, with such taste. –PM

Quintet for Clarinet & Strings in A, K. 581 / PHILIPS
Hoeprich/Members of the Orchestra of the 18th Century.

Quintet for Clarinet & Strings in A, K. 581 / DGG
Brunner (clarinet)/Hagen Quartet. A bit smooth and bland but with virtually "perfect" playing. A bit more profile might have been in order. –PM

○ **Quintet for Horn & Strings in E-flat, K. 407 / DENON**
Hauptmann/Berlin Philharmonia Quintet.

○ **Quintet for Piano & Winds in E-flat, K. 452 / PHILIPS**
Brendel, Holliger, Brunner, Thunemann, Baumann. How could you go wrong with players of this caliber? Taste, technique, and temperament — this has the "three tees" in abundance. –PM

Quintet for Piano & Winds in E-flat, K. 452 / DGG
Levine/Ensemble Wien-Berlin. This performance is an outstanding alternative — not so well played individually but outstanding collectively. –PM

○ **Quintets (6) for Strings, K. 515, 516, 593, 614 / PHILIPS**
Grumiaux Quartet.

Quintets (6) for Strings, K. 515, 516, 593, 614 / HYPERION
Salomon Quartet.

☆ **Requiem, K. 626 / PHILIPS**
Price, Schmidt, Araiza, Adam, Schreier/Dresden State Orchestra & Leipzig Radio Chorus. Overall the best of the more traditional *Requiems*. A bit cautious but with as good a choir and soloists as any. –PM

Requiem, K. 626 / ERATO
Schlick, Watkinson, Pregardien, van der Kamp, Koopman/Amsterdam Baroque Orchestra, Netherlands Bach Choir. Fire and brimstone, and the current leader among authentic performances. Terrific sound (live); among the best digitals I have ever heard. –PM

Requiem, K. 626 / ACCENT
Kuijken/La Petite Bande, Netherlands Chamber Choir & soloists. The soloists are not first-class, but this is the most introverted and ethereal *Requiem* ever recorded. –PM

Requiem, K. 626 / HUNT
Giebel, Hoffge, Trazel, Arie, Celibidache/Milan Radio Orchestra & Chorus. One of Celibidache's most profound and moving performances, but the sound is not very good, even for a "pirate," and neither is the singing. –PM

○ **Rondo for Horn & Orchestra in E-flat, K. 371 / HARMONIA MUNDI**
Greer, McGegan/Philharmonia Baroque Orchestra.

○ **Serenade no. 1 in D, K. 62a / PHILIPS**
Marriner/ASMF.

○ **Serenade no. 3 in D, K. 167a / PHILIPS**
Marriner/ASMF.

○ **Serenade no. 4 in D, K. 189b / PHILIPS**
Marriner/ASMF.

○ **Serenade no. 6 in D, "Serenata Notturna," K. 239 / PHILIPS**
Marriner/ASMF.

Serenade no. 6 in D, "Serenata Notturna," K. 239 / LONDON
Marriner/ASMF.

○ **Serenade no. 7 in D, "Haffner," K. 250 / PHILIPS**
Marriner/ASMF.

Serenade no. 7 in D, "Haffner," K. 250 / NOVALIS
Davis/Bavarian RSO.

○ **Serenade no. 9 in D, "Posthorn Serenade," K. 320 / PHILIPS**
Marriner/ASMF.

☆ **Serenade for 13 Wind Instruments no. 10 in B-flat, K. 361 / PHILIPS**
Brüggen/Orchestra of the 18th Century. The playing may not be quite ideally in tune, but this has style and panache in abundance. –PM

Serenade for 13 Wind Instruments no. 10 in B-flat, K. 361 / OISEAU-LYRE
Hogwood/Amadeus Winds. More together and symphonic than the other period-instruments performances, but not so stylish as the Brüggen. –PM

Serenade for 13 Wind Instruments no. 10 in B-flat, K. 361 / DGG
Berlin Philharmonic Winds.

Serenade for 13 Wind Instruments no. 10 in B-flat, K. 361 / ANGEL
Furtwängler/Vienna PO Winds.

○ **Serenades for 8 Wind Instruments nos. 11 in E-flat & 12 in C, K. 375 & 388 / PHILIPS**
Holliger, Pellerin, Brunner, Schmid, Thunemann, Wilkie, et al. When stars of this magnitude get together, they usually try to outdo each other, and I run for cover. Well, I need not have worried here — this is individually and collectively the finest recording ever likely to be made of these wonderful pieces. –PM

Serenade for Wind Instruments no. 11 in E-flat, K. 375 / OISEAU-LYRE
Amadeus Winds.

Serenade for Wind Instruments no. 11 in E-flat, K. 375 / CHANDOS
Järvi/Scottish National Orchestra Wind Ensemble. A sleeper of the first magnitude, by the young Järvi. –PM

Serenade for Wind Instruments no. 11 in E-flat, K. 375 / ORFEO
Berlin PO Winds.

○ **Serenade for Wind Instruments no. 12 in c, K. 388 / OISEAU-LYRE**
Amadeus Winds.

Serenade for Wind Instruments no. 12 in c, K. 388 / CHANDOS
Järvi/Scottish National Orchestra Wind Ensemble.

Serenade for Wind Instruments no. 12 in c, K. 388 / ORFEO
Berlin PO Winds.

☆ **Serenade in G, "Eine Kleine Nachtmusik," K. 525 / PHILIPS**
Marriner/ASMF. Virtually flawless in ensemble, balance, and sound quality. Some may find this too "objective" a performance, but I find it near perfect and a model of modern Mozart playing. Now why can't Marriner be this convincing with the symphonies? –PM

Serenade in G, "Eine Kleine Nachtmusik," K. 525 / NIMBUS
Goodman/The Hanover Band. Featuring the fifth movement, which Mozart later removed. The warm, rich sound gives an interesting tone quality to the period strings. –PM

Serenade in G, "Eine Kleine Nachtmusik," K. 525 / DGG
Furtwängler/Berlin PO. The grace, beauty, and even tenderness of this performance make it something so special that not even the minor flaws in ensemble and tempo can detract from it. This performance really gets beneath the surface of an always challenging piece. –PM

Serenade in G, "Eine Kleine Nachtmusik," K. 525 / ANGEL
Furtwängler/Vienna PO.

☆ **Sinfonia Concertante for Oboe, Clarinet, Bassoon, Horn & Strings in E-flat, K. 297B / PHILIPS**
Marriner/ASMF.

☆ **Sinfonia Concertante for Violin, Viola & Orchestra in E-flat, K. 364 / DGG**

Kremer, Kashkashian, Harnoncourt/Vienna PO. More incisive but also more "romantic" than the classic Grumiaux. Harnoncourt is stylish and dramatic (even angry at times); Kremer is incisive and committed to getting underneath the surface beauty of one of Mozart's most profound pieces. –PM

○ **Sonatas for Piano (17) (complete) / DGG**
Pires (piano). Outstanding in style and accuracy, with very fine piano sound. –PM

○ **Sonata for Piano no. 3 in B-flat, K. 281 / DGG**
Gilels.

○ **Sonatas for Piano no. 4, 10, 15 / PHILIPS**
Richter (piano). Eccentric readings that really make you rethink these much-played works. Recorded live at London's Barbican Centre, March 29, 1989, an example of Richter's most recent playing. –PM

○ **Sonata for Piano no. 8 in a, K. 310 / DGG**
Gilels (piano). Stylish and intense, one of Gilel's greatest recordings. –PM
Sonata for Piano no. 8 in a, K. 310 / DGG
Pires.

○ **Sonata for Piano no. 11 in A, K. 331 / DGG**
Pires.

○ **Sonata for Piano no. 12 in F, K. 332 / MERIDIAN**
Kite.

○ **Sonata for Piano no. 13 in B-flat, K. 333 / SUPRAPHON**
Moravec (piano). No one plays Mozart with more depth and style. Why doesn't Moravec do them all? –PM
Sonata for Piano no. 13 in B-flat, K. 333 / MERIDIAN
Kite (fortepiano). What a gem! This has all the bite and piquancy lacking in the Mozart by Uchida and Perahia. Kite is scholarly but not pedantic, and he has a very good technique. Meridian is not an easy-to-find label, but this one is worth searching out. –PM

○ **Sonata for Piano no. 14 in c, K. 457 / DGG**
Pires.
Sonata for Piano no. 14 in c, K. 457 / MERIDIAN
Kite.

○ **Sonatas for Piano no. 15 & 16 / OISEAU-LYRE**
Schiff (fortepiano). Mozart's last two piano sonatas and six other mostly late works "performed on Mozart's own [Anton Walter] piano, in the room where he was born." How much authenticity can you take? –PM

○ **Sonatas (42) for Violin & Piano, K. 296, 301, 378, 304, 454 PHILIPS**
Grumiaux (violin), Klien (piano). Grumiaux's last recording: he and Klien do the mature Mozart sonatas. –PM
Sonatas (42) for Violin & Piano, K. 296, 301, 378, 304, 454 PAVANE
Rubinstein (violin), Ouziel (piano). A very straightforward and well-integrated duo. –PM

○ **Sonatas (42) for Violin & Piano, K. 301, 304, 378, 379 / DGG**
Dumay (violin), Pires (piano). The violin playing is a bit whiney and out of tune, but Pires's playing is so heavenly that this is a must for these works. –PM

○ **Sonatas (42) for Violin & Piano, K. 301-304 / DGG**
Perlman, Barenboim.

○ **Sonatas (42) for Violin & Piano, K. 306 & 378 / ANGEL**
Kagan, Richter.

○ **Sonatas (42) for Violin & Piano, K. 378-380 / DGG**
Perlman, Barenboim.

○ **Sonatinas for Piano, K. 439b / PARTRIDGE**
Kooiker.

○ **Symphonies nos. 1-41 (complete) / PHILIPS**
Marriner/ASMF. This 12-disc set of recordings is clean, incisive, and stylish. –PM
Symphony no. 25 in g, K. 183 / ORFEO
Kubelik/Bavarian RSO.

○ **Symphonies nos. 25-27, 29, 32 / LONDON**
Marriner/ASMF. These fine old Argo performances are still better than Marriner's been able to do since, and at mid-price and 70:08 playing time, they're a deal. –PM

○ **Symphony no. 28 in C, K. 200 / PHILIPS**
Brüggen/Orchestra of the 18th Century. Not one of his very best efforts, but significantly above those of the competition. A bit too fast and perfunctory, without enough shading. –PM
Symphony no. 29 in A, K. 201 / PHILIPS
Marriner/ASMF.

○ **Symphony no. 29 in A, K. 201 / DGG**
Böhm/Vienna PO.

○ **Symphony no. 32 in G, K. 318 / PHILIPS**
Marriner/ASMF.
Symphony no. 32 in G, K. 318 / NOVALIS
Davis/Bavarian RSO.

○ **Symphony no. 34 in C, K. 338 / HUNGARATON**
Fischer/Budapest Festival Orchestra.

○ **Symphony no. 35 in D, K. 385 / PHILIPS**
Marriner/ASMF.
Symphony no. 35 in D, K. 385 / PHILIPS
Brüggen/Orchestra of the 18th Century.
Symphony no. 35 in D, K. 385 / DGG
Böhm/Vienna PO.

○ **Symphony no. 36 in C, K. 425, "Linz" / PHILIPS**
Brüggen/Orchestra of the 18th Century. See note to his *Symphony no. 28.* –PM

☆ **Symphony no. 38 in C, K. 504, "Prague" / PHILIPS**
Brüggen/Orchestra of the 18th Century. Short measure, but original instruments or no original instruments, this is the best *38th* since Maag's. No matter how well you think you know this symphony, you'll hear new things and different relationships in this one — guaranteed. With all the repeats in place (the first movement lasts 18:44), Brüggen takes us on a grand metaphysical journey. This is Mozart with depth, the way he should always be played. –PM
Symphony no. 38 in C, K. 504, "Prague" / ORFEO
Kubelik/Bavarian RSO.

☆ **Symphony no. 39 in E-flat, K. 543 / PHILIPS**
Brüggen/Orchestra of the 18th Century.
Symphony no. 39 in E-flat, K. 543 / DGG
Furtwängler/Berlin PO. This doesn't have the greatest sound (even for 1942-1943), but it's a very mellow, natural, and moving performance. –PM
Symphony no. 39 in E-flat, K. 543 / DGG
Böhm/Vienna PO.

☆ **Symphony no. 40 in g, K. 550 / NIMBUS**
Goodman/The Hanover Band. A revelation that forced me to reevaluate the music. –PM
Symphony no. 40 in g, K. 550 / PHILIPS
Marriner/ASMF.
Symphony no. 40 in g, K. 550 / PHILIPS
Brüggen/Orchestra of the 18th Century. A good, standard original-instruments performance. –PM
Symphony no. 40 in g, K. 550 / DGG
Böhm/Vienna PO.

☆ **Symphony no. 41, "Jupiter," K. 551 / NIMBUS**
Goodman/The Hanover Band. Even more of a revelation. I wouldn't like the harpsichord in this music always, but I love it here: it is subtle and tastefully employed. –PM
Symphony no. 41, "Jupiter," K. 551 / PHILIPS
Brüggen/Orchestra of the 18th Century.
Symphony no. 41, "Jupiter," K. 551 / PHILIPS
Marriner/ASMF.
Symphony no. 41, "Jupiter," K. 551 / HUNGARATON
Fischer/Budapest Festival Orchestra.

○ **Tenor Arias from Operas / PHILIPS**
Schreier (conductor & tenor)/Dresden State Orchestra.
○ **Trios (7) for Violin, Cello & Piano (complete) / HARMONIA MUNDI**
Mozartean Players. Very dramatic, a worthy followup to their Mozart piano quartets. –PM
Trios (7) for Violin, Cello & Piano (complete) / BIS
Arion Trio.
○ **Variations (6) on Paisiello's "Salve tu, Domine," for Piano, K. 398 / DGG**
Gilels.

ALONSO MUDARRA   1510-1580

Renaissance. A Spanish cleric and composer who served at the cathedral in Seville. –MKS
○ **Pieces for Guitar & Vihuela / ASTREE**
Smith.

WILLIAM MUNDY   1529-1591

Renaissance, sacred vocal. A contemporary of Thomas Tallis and William Byrd who wrote florid church music for both the Catholic and the then-new Anglican liturgies. –MKS
○ **Vox Patris Caelestis, for 6 Voices / GIMELL**
Phillips/The Tallis Scholars.

MODEST MUSSORGSKY   1839-1881

Romantic, nationalist. A member of the group of Russian nationalist composers known as "The Mighty Five," Mussorgsky wrote opera (*Boris Godounov* (1868)), songs, and incidental music (*Pictures at an Exhibition* for piano (1874)), and *A Night on Bare Mountain*). Leading a very difficult life (nearly impoverished at times, working at the dreary job of a civil clerk, and suffering from alcoholism), Mussorgsky nevertheless produced some of the most original and remarkable songs from Russia, which are now part of the standard repertoire. The beauty, strength, and emotion of Russian folk songs and tales inspired him and fellow composers who were looking for a true Russian sound and voice. This is achieved with great coloristic effect in the famous *Night on Bare Mountain* (usually presented in the reorchestrated version by Rimsky-Korsakov) and with intimately stirring feeling (like that evoked by a good storyteller) in the song cycles *Songs and Dances of Death* and *Bez solntsa* (Sunless, or Without Sun), not to mention the popular *Pictures at an Exhibition*, with its many moods and memorable melodies. The operas *Boris Godounov*, *Kovanschina*, and *Sorochintsy Fair* should be heard in their original versions whenever possible for an experience of the spirit that was to change Russian music in the next century. –BGT
○ **Boris Godounov (four-act opera, Rimsky-Korsakov version) / LONDON**
Vishnevskaya, Spiess, Maslennikov, Ghiaurov, Diakov, Karajan/Vienna PO, State Opera Chorus, Sofia Radio Chorus. Karajan's *Boris* is a bit old-fashioned and romanticized, but it sure is hard to argue with the singing and the sumptuous sound and orchestral playing. –PM
Boris Godounov (four-act opera, original version) / PHILIPS
Arkhipova, Masurok, Vedernikov, Fedoseyev/USSR Radio & TV Orchestra & Chorus.
○ **Khovanshchina: Prelude (orchestrated by Rimsky-Korsakov) / URANIA**
Mravinsky/Leningrad PO.
☆ **A Night on Bare Mountain (reorchestrated by Rimsky-Korsakov) / DGG**
Sinopoli/NYPO.
A Night on Bare Mountain (reorchestrated by Rimsky-Korsakov) / PHILIPS
Haitink/London PO.

☆ **Pictures at an Exhibition, for Piano / URANIA**
Richter (piano). At least five versions of Richter's *Pictures* have been available, and any of them is preferable to anyone else's on piano. –PM
Pictures at an Exhibition, for Piano (orchestrated by Ravel) / DGG
Sinopoli/NYPO. The individual variations are well characterized, and he sees the whole in commanding fashion. My current favorite version. –PM
Pictures at an Exhibition, for Piano (orchestrated by Ravel) / DGG
Abbado/London SO.
Pictures at an Exhibition, for Piano (orchestrated by Ravel) / DGG
Karajan/Berlin PO.
○ **Songs (selected) / PYRAMID**
Milcheva (mezzo-soprano), Protich (piano). From the song cycles "Songs and Dances of Death" and "Nursery Cycle." –JME

CARL NIELSEN   1865-1931

Romantic, nationalist. A Danish composer of many musical forms whose finest achievements are his symphonies. Nielson's music is characterized by its direct expression, clarity like that of a mountain spring, and deep humanity and warmth. In the second movement of his *Third Symphony*, a soprano and baritone sing wordless songs to each other across the expanse of the gently murmuring orchestra — after the listeners have been swept away by a first movement that combines a glorious waltz-like theme and punctuations reminiscent of Beethoven's *Symphony no. 3* (also partly in 3/4 time). There is humor and lyricism in the *Concerto for Clarinet* and a variety of moods and inventive sonorities that is unlike anyone else's in the piano music. –BGT
○ **Aladdin (incidental music), op. 34 / BIS**
Chung/Gothenburg SO.
○ **Commotio for Organ, op. 58 / BIS**
Westenholz.
○ **Concerto for Clarinet & Orchestra, op. 57 / BIS**
Schill, Chung/Gothenburg SO.
Concerto for Clarinet & Orchestra, op. 57 / CHANDOS
Hilton, Bamert/Scottish National Orchestra.
○ **Concerto for Flute & Orchestra / BIS**
Gallois, Chung/Gothenburg SO.
○ **Concerto for Violin & Orchestra, op. 33 / BIS**
Kang, Chung/Gothenburg SO.
○ **A Fantastic Voyage to Faeroerne (rhapsodic overture) / BIG BEN**
Veto/Odense SO.
○ **An Imaginary Trip to the Faroe Islands (rhapsodic overture) / BIS**
Chung/Gothenburg SO.
○ **Little Suite for Strings, op. 1 / BIG BEN**
Veto/Odense SO.
○ **Maskarade (opera - orchestral excerpts) / BIS**
Chung/Gothenburg SO.
Maskarade (opera - orchestral excerpts) / BIG BEN
Veto/Odense SO.
○ **Motets (3) for Mixed Chorus a cappella, op. 55 / BIS**
Enevold/Camerata Chamber Choir.
○ **Organ Works (complete) / BIS**
Westenholz.
○ **Pan and Syrinx (nature scene for orchestra), op. 49 / BIG BEN**
Veto/Odense SO.
○ **Piano Music (complete solo works) / BIS**
Westenholz.
○ **Preludes (29) for Organ, op. 51 / BIS**
Westenholz.

○ **Quartets (4) for Strings, opp. 5, 13, 14, 44 / DGG**
Carl Nielsen String Quartet.

○ **Quintet for Winds, op. 43 / BIS**
Bergen Wind Quintet.

○ **Saga-drøm, op. 39 / BIG BEN**
Veto/Odense SO.

Saga-drøm, op. 39; Symphony no. 5, op. 50 / UNICORN-KANCHANA
Horenstein/New Philharmonia Orchestra. Incandescent. Despite some orchestral imperfections, this is one of the greatest recordings ever made. –PM

○ **Symphony no. 1 in g, op. 7 / BIS**
Chung/Gothenburg SO.

○ **Symphony no. 2, op. 16, "The Four Temperaments" / BIS**
Chung/Gothenburg SO.

○ **Symphony no. 3, op. 27 "Sinfonia Espansiva" / AUDIOFON**
Sixten Ehrling/Danish National Orchestra. Recorded live at the Kennedy Center, May 19, 1984, in very good sound. This is one of those cumulative and definitive performances that carry all before it. Easily the best Nielsen *Third* ever. –PM

Symphony no. 3, op. 27 "Sinfonia Espansiva" / BIS
Chung/Gothenburg SO.

○ **Symphony no. 4, op. 29, "Inextinguishable" / VIRGIN**
Karajan/Berlin PO. A tough choice here: Karajan of course has the better orchestra, but he doesn't have the Nordic feel that Andersen does. –PM

Symphony no. 4, op. 29, "Inextinguishable" / AURORA
Andersen/Norwegian Youth Orchestra. A labor of love and an amazing performance for a youth orchestra. –PM

○ **Symphony no. 5, op. 50 / UNICORN-KANCHANA**
Horenstein/NYPO. Incandescent. Terrific snare-drum playing. Some orchestral imperfections but one of the greatest recordings ever. –PM

Symphony no. 5, op. 50 / BIS
Chung/Gothenburg SO.

○ **Wind Chamber Music (complete) / BIS**
Bergen Wind Quintet, et al.

Wind Quintet, op. 43 / DGG
Vestjysk Chamber Ensemble.

JOHANNES OCKEGHEM   1410-1497

Renaissance, sacred choral. A French-Flemish composer of sacred and secular vocal music featuring contrapuntal techniques that influenced later composers like Josquin des Prez. Appreciated by his peers as the greatest composer of the 15th century, Ockeghem was a master of the contrapuntal language, expanding harmony through stepwise descent in the bottom voice creating surprising combinations. He wrote melodic lines so fluid they seem to be improvised and spontaneously invented, using the rule of "musica ficta" — the same passages sung again may freely (almost) include added sharps and flats, throwing the mood into an altogether new feel ... "the same thing only different." His *Missa Prolationum* ranks with J. S. Bach's *The Art of the Fugue* as the highest point of contrapuntal achievement. –BGT

○ **Requiem (Missa pro Defunctis) / DGG**
Turner/Pro Cantione Antiqua, Hamburger Bläserkreis für alte Musik.

○ **Missa Prolationum; Marian Motets / EMI**
Hillier/The Hilliard Ensemble.

JACQUES OFFENBACH   1819-1880

Romantic, operetta. A German/French composer of dramatic music, vocal, and instrumental works, the progenitor of the operetta form. His music influenced Gilbert and Sullivan. One doesn't want everything to be romantic or serious in a collection of symphonic music, and the lovely tunes and variations in *Gaité Parisienne* and in his one try at grand

opera, *Les contes d'Hoffman* ("The Tales of Hoffman"), are well worth hearing from time to time. His ballet *Le papillon* ("The Butterfly") is also delightful, especially its lovely waltz. The libretti of his operettas contain much satire and humor (which don't always come off in English translation). –BGT

○ **Les contes d'Hoffmann / LONDON**
Sutherland, Tourangeau, Domingo, Cuenod, Bacquier, Bonynge/Suisse Romande Orchestra. A classic, with all the participants near or at the top of their form. –PM

○ **Gaité Parisienne (arrangement by Rosenthal) / PHILIPS**
Previn/Pittsburgh SO.

○ **Overtures / ANGEL**
Fremaux/City of Birmingham SO. Filled with French insouciance, long my favorite recording of these pieces. –PM

Overtures / PHILIPS
Marriner/Philharmonia Orchestra. Superbly scaled and styled. –PM

Overtures / DGG
Karajan/Berlin PO. The large-scale, less French, and more serious approach. –PM

CARL ORFF   1895-1982

20th century. A German composer primarily of dramatic music with primal rhythms and raw emotional effects; known for *Carmina Burana* (1937). His early works were influenced by Richard Strauss and Schoenberg; around 1930 he began writing "Schulwerk" — teaching methods for schools — which allowed him to delve into his obsession with "primitive" rhythms and turn back to Monteverdi for melodies. The result was the *Catulli Carmina* (1931), seven settings of "gutter Latin" texts from medieval monasteries for a cappella choir. His study of Bach and Schütz led to his setting some of their works and inspired *Carmina Burana*, Orff's most popular work. The opera *Antigonae* (which uses *Steinspiel* or tuned rocks among its many percussive devices) and *Trionfo di Afrodite* (1950-1951) are particularly interesting for their orchestral effects. –BGT

☆ **Carmina Burana (scenic cantata) / ANGEL**
Popp, Unger, Wolansky, Noble, Frühbeck de Burgos/New Philharmonia Orchestra & Chorus. The most elemental version, with great precision too. This would easily top the list except that the sound is really showing its age and the sibilants drive me crazy, on CD especially. Too bad: this is a performance not likely to be bettered in my lifetime. –PM

Carmina Burana (scenic cantata) / DGG
Janowitz, Stolze, Fischer-Dieskau, Jochum/Deutsche Oper Orchestra & Choir. Composer-approved! What would Orff think of the current proliferation? –PM

Carmina Burana (scenic cantata) / ANGEL
Hendricks, Chance, Black, Welser-Möst/London PO & Chorus, St. Alban' s Cathedral Choristers. It all sounds very serious to me, but I like that in this most hedonistic of all pieces. –PM

Carmina Burana (scenic cantata) / ANGEL
Anderson, Creech, Weikl, Levine/Chicago SO & Chorus. A very strong all-around choice but not so characterized or so full of character as some of the others. –PM

JOHANN PACHELBEL   1653-1706

Baroque. A German organist, important predecessor of Bach, and composer of organ, sacred vocal, and chamber music. Pachelbel was a gifted vocal composer and a pioneer in "word printing" — correspondences in notational symbolism to the meaning of the words, such as in his motet *Durch Adams Fall* ("Through Adam's Fall"), which contains a falling figure in the bassline. –MKS

○ **Canon in D / PHILIPS**
Marriner/ASMF. One of the most dignified and moving *Canons*. –PM

Canon in D / DGG

Musica Antiqua Köln. How cleansed and interesting it sounds on original instruments! –PM

Canon in D / KOCH-SCHWANN
Werther/I Fiamminghi. Soulful and sorrowful. –PM

Canon in D / RCA
Paillard/Paillard CO. It's actually his earlier performance that is in most of the movies, but that one has been deleted in favor of a somewhat tighter and less heavy approach. If you want those strings that sound more like harps, you'll have to go to the original. –PM

IGNACE JAN PADEREWSKI   1860-1941

Romantic. A legendary virtuoso pianist in the great romantic tradition; also a philanthropist and Polish patriot. Several times Paderewski interrupted his concert career to serve Poland, first in 1919 to serve as Prime Minister, then in 1940 to serve as President of the Polish Parliament in exile in Paris. His piano compositions give insight into the last vestiges of the virtuoso who composed music for his own use. –MKS

O **Piano Works / ADDA**
Malicki (piano). These pieces are a lot better and more serious than you might think, and this is a very dedicated performance. –PM

NICCOLO PAGANINI   1782-1840

Romantic. An Italian virtuoso violinist, guitarist, and composer of chamber and orchestral music featuring violin and guitar music. Paganini revolutionized the art of violin playing (his *Concerto no. 1 in D* gives some idea of his incredible technique), even as he was surrounded by gossip, often self-promoted, about amorous affairs in Napoleon's court; being supported in his teens by an older mistress (her identity still unknown), who saved him from self-destructive drinking brought on by quick fame; a pact made with the devil that gave him superhuman ability to play his instrument; and so on. –BGT

O **Caprices (24) for Unaccompanied Violin, op. 1 (complete) / ANGEL**
Perlman (violin). I have a lot of mixed feelings about these pieces, which I've been unable to resolve. As much as I admire Perlman's tone and technique, I just think they're not so inventive and diabolical as they should be. Perhaps that's asking a bit too much from one man. –PM

O **Concerto for Violin & Orchestra no. 1 in D, op. 6 / DGG**
Accardo (violin), Dutoit/London PO. Accardo and Dutoit are reliable throughout this performance, but they never really scale the heights. –PM

☆ **Concerto for Violin & Orchestra no. 1 in D, op. 6 / PROMPT**
Ricci (violin), de la Fuenta/Orquesta de las Americas. This is the performance that really captures my imagination. With a breathtaking combination of virtuosity and histrionics, nobody does it better. –PM

Concerto for Violin & Orchestra no. 1 in D, op. 6 / DGG
Shaham (violin), Sinopoli/NYPO. Sinopoli and Shaham find more music in Paganini than anyone since Grumiaux, and they also add a certain sense of fun that I don't find in the other versions. –PM

Concerto for Violin & Orchestra no. 1 in D, op. 6 / ANGEL
Perlman, Foster/Royal PO.

Concerto for Violin & Orchestra no. 1 in D, op. 6 / DGG
Ashkenasi, Esser/Vienna SO.

O **Concerto for Violin & Orchestra no. 2 in b, op. 7 / DGG**
Ashkenasi, Esser/Vienna SO.

O **Concerto for Violin & Orchestra no. 3 in E / DGG**
Accardo, Dutoit/London PO.

O **Concerto for Violin & Orchestra no. 4 in d / DGG**
Accardo, Dutoit/London PO.

GIOVANNI PALESTRINA   1526-1594

Renaissance, sacred choral. An Italian composer of sacred music who was an important musical figure of the Renaissance; known for his "seamless texture" of polyphony. Palestrina composed over 100 settings of the mass (in Richard Wagner's words, with "indescribable depth of expression"), including the *Missa Papae Marcelli*, composed after an edict by Pope Marcellus that the vocal music for the mass "must be sung in a fitting manner, with properly modulated voices, so that everything may be heard and understood." Palestrina succeeded in doing this with remarkable clarity of line, beauty of modal harmony, and a festive rhythmic sense. The *Assumpta est Maria* is probably his best mass, with the voices moving more like orchestra parts than block harmony or contrapuntal choirs. –BGT

☆ **Missa Assumpta est Maria; Missa Sicut Lilium / GIMELL**
Phillips/The Tallis Scholars.

O **Missa Benedicta es / GIMELL**
Phillips/The Tallis Scholars.

O **Missa brevis; Missa, "Nasce la gioia mia" / GIMELL**
Phillips/The Tallis Scholars. As stunning here (if not more so) as they are on anything else. –PM

O **Missa, "Nigra Sum" / GIMELL**
Phillips/The Tallis Scholars.

☆ **Missa Papae Marcelli / GIMELL**
Phillips/The Tallis Scholars.

SELIM PALMGREN   1878-1951

Impressionist. An important Finnish composer excelling in piano composition, many of whose works contain impressionistic elements such as whole-tone scales and parallel-chord constructions. –MKS

O **Concerto for Piano & Orchestra no. 2, op. 33, "The River" / FINLANDIA**
Lagerspetz, Mercier/Turku PO.

O **Concerto for Piano & Orchestra no. 3, op. 41, "Metamorphoses" / FINLANDIA**
Raekallio, Mercier/Turku PO.

O **Concerto for Piano & Orchestra no. 5 in A, op. 99 / FINLANDIA**
Kerppo, Mercier/Turku PO.

ANDRZEJ PANUFNIK   b1914

20th century. An important Polish composer, highly innovative and experimental in his early works (using quarter-tones and blank spaces instead of rests), and in his later years adopting a more expressive, direct style suitable for large audiences. Most of his pre-1944 compositions were destroyed during the Warsaw uprising. –MKS

O **Symphony no. 8, "Sinfonia Votiva" / HYPERION**
Ozawa/Boston SO.

O **Symphony no. 9; Concerto for Piano / CONIFER**
Poblocka (piano), Panufnik/London SO. The opinion is divided over this controversial composer, but to those who care, this last recording of his is a must. –PM

PIETRO DOMENICO PARADIES   1707-1791

Classical. An Italian composer of operas, cantatas, symphonies, overtures, and keyboard music who lived for a time in London earning a living as a harpsichordist. –MKS

O **Concerto for Organ & Strings in B-flat / CLAVES**
Noda (double bass), Meyer/Sonare Quartet Frankfurt.

GIOVANNI BATTISTA PERGOLESI   1710-1736

Baroque, vocal. An Italian composer known for comic opera as well as sacred and secular vocal music. In his short life, Pergolesi managed to establish a style of beautiful melodies accompanied by a clear orchestra of harmonic tensions, as in the breathtaking *Stabat Mater*, with its slow build of emotion accomplished apparently by the simplest means (in the centuries following Pergolesi's death, some composers attempted to beef up his lovely music by adding huge, pretentious orchestras). The *Stabat Mater* is essentially a vocal chamber-music work inspired by religion, rather than a work for the church. It was composed on Pergolesi's deathbed and he was paid ten ducats for it — one less than it took to bury him. His lovely and lively *Concertinos*, the *Concerto for Flute, Strings & Cembalo in D*, and his opera *La Serva Padrona* are necessary listening for appreciating the natural talent of this wonderful composer. –BGT

○ **Salve Regina, for Countertenor & Strings in f / OISEAU-LYRE**
Bowman, Hogwood/Academy of Ancient Music.

○ **La serva padrona (opera buffa) for Soprano, Bass-Baritone & Orchestra (1733) / HUNGARATON**
Farkas, Gregor, Németh/Capella Savaria.

○ **Sinfonia for Cello & Continuo in F / LONDON**
Hogwood/St. Paul CO.

☆ **Stabat Mater for Soprano, Contralto, String Orchestra, Female Chorus & Organ / ADDA**
Zaepffel, Dietschy, Colleaux/Stradavaria Ensemble. This one is not so technically adept as the Hogwood, but I like its soul and its sound, which is much less dry. –PM

Stabat Mater for Soprano, Contralto, String Orchestra, Female Chorus & Organ / OISEAU-LYRE
Kirkby (soprano), Bowman (alto), Hogwood/Academy of Ancient Music.

HANS PFITZNER   1869-1949

Romantic. A German composer, conservative in style and harmony, who is nonetheless considered part of the modern school typified by Richard Strauss. Pfitzner's opera *Palestrina* made use of that composer's themes and was tremendously popular. His staunch support of the Nazi regime contributed to his fall from favor as a composer. –MKS

○ **Concerto for Piano & Orchestra in E-flat, op. 31 / CAPRICCIO**
Banfield, Albert/Munich PO.

○ **Concerto for Violin & Orchestra in b, op. 34 / CAPRICCIO**
Gawriloff, Albert/Bamberg SO.

○ **Duo for Violin, Cello & Small Orchestra, op. 43 / CAPRICCIO**
Gawriloff, Berger, Albert/Bamberg SO.

Duo for Violin, Cello & Small Orchestra, op. 43 / PREISER
Strub, Hoelscher, Pfitzner/Berlin State Opera Orchestra.

○ **Das Fest auf Solhag (incidental music for Ibsen play) / CAPRICCIO**
Albert/Bamberg SO.

○ **Das Kathchen von Heilbronn (overture) & others / ORFEO**
Sawallisch/Bavarian RSO.

○ **Palestrina (opera) / DGG**
Donath, Fassbaender, Gedda, Weikl, Fischer-Dieskau, Prey, Ridderbusch, Kubelik/Bavarian RSO & Chorus.

○ **Sonata for Cello & Piano in f#, op. 1 / PREISER**
Hornstein, Jakab.

○ **Songs / PREISER**
Husch, Pfitzner.

○ **Symphony, op. 44, "Kleine Sinfonia" / CAPRICCIO**
Albert/Bamberg SO.

○ **Symphony in C, op. 46 / CAPRICCIO**
Albert/Bamberg SO.

Symphony in C, op. 46 / PREISER
Pfitzner/Berlin PO.

WALTER PISTON   1894-1976

Neo-classical. An American composer with an unique tonalist style and a teacher whose book on music theory, *Harmony*, became an American standard. Piston wrote compositions primarily in an orchestral, tonal style, neo-classical and nationalist in character. We may hear a tune that starts out something like folk music, but soon it stretches off into the eeriest of dark universes, as in *Symphony no. 2*, or into breadth and lyricism and a blaze of major-key glory, as in *Symphony no. 6*. Piston's sound is fresh, sometimes on a big landscape and sometimes evoking a feeling of being lost in the woods, much like traveling across the US. –BGT

○ **Sinfoniette / DELOS**
Schwartz/NY Chamber Symphony.

○ **Symphony no. 2 / DGG**
Thomas/Boston SO. Better orchestra and conducting give this performance the edge. –PM

Symphony no. 2; Symphony no. 6 / DELOS
Schwarz/Seattle SO. Walter Piston's music is making a comeback. I would leave it to listeners more sympathetic than I to decide if it is successful. –PM

AMILCARE PONCHIELLI   1834-1886

Classical. An Italian composer whose fame is based upon one work, *La Gioconda*, an opera that contains the famous "Dance of the Hours." Ponchielli also wrote band pieces, vocal chamber pieces, and music for voice and piano. –MKS

○ **La Gioconda (opera) / LONDON**
Caballé, Baltsa, Pavarotti, Milnes, Ghiaurov, Bartoletti/National PO.

FRANCIS POULENC   1899-1963

20th century. A French composer of many forms, including choral and vocal music, opera, piano, and orchestral works. Poulenc was described by one of his friends as "moitié moine, moitié voyou" (half monk, half guttersnipe), which seems to fit his distinct type of musical composition. The *Concerto for Organ, Strings & Tympani in g* and the *Gloria for Soprano, Orchestra & Chorus in G* are heroic and often lovely; together with his famous opera, *Dialog of the Carmélites*, they reflect his religious bent with dramatic gestures and clear French melodic lines. The ballet music *Les biches* is an example of his humor, which verges on triviality but never really falls into it. And there are works that fall somewhere in the middle, like the wonderful *Sonata for Two Pianos* and the *Concert champêtre* (1929), written for harpsichordist Wanda Landowska. –BGT

○ **Aubade, for Piano & 18 Instruments / HYPERION**
Corp/The New London Orchestra.

○ **Concert champêtre for Harpsichord & Orchestra / VIRGIN**
Cole, Hickox/City of London Sinfonia.

○ **Concerto for two Pianos & Orchestra in d / PHILIPS**
K. and M. Labeque, Ozawa/Boston SO. Impressive energy and savoir-faire. –PM

☆ **Concerto for Organ, Strings & Timpani in g / LONDON**
Malcolm, Brown/ASMF.

Concerto for Organ, Strings & Timpani in g / VIRGIN
Weir, Hickox/City of London Sinfonia.

☆ **Gloria for Soprano, Orchestra & Chorus in G / COLLEGIUM**
Deam, Rutter/City of London Sinfonia, The Cambridge Singers.

○ **Litanies à la Vierge Noire / HARMONIA MUNDI**
Baudo/Lyons Orchestra National & Chorus.

○ **Piano Music (selections) / LONDON**
Roge.

○ **Salve Regina / HARMONIA MUNDI**
Baudo/Lyon Chorus.

○ **Sinfonietta / KOCH-SCHWANN**
Barra/San Diego CO. This is a real find. –PM
Sinfonietta / HYPERION
Corp/The New London Orchestra.
○ **Sonata for Clarinet & Piano (1962) / CALIG**
Brunner (clarinet), Hoehenrieder (piano). Less spiky and concentrating more on lyricism and beauty of tone, this is a very winning performance. –PM
Sonata for Clarinet & Piano (1962) / CHANDOS
de Peyer, Pryor.
Sonata for Clarinet & Piano; Sonata for Clarinet & Bassoon; Trio for Oboe, Bassoon & Piano / ADDA
Paik (piano); di Donato (clarinet)/Trio d'anches OZI. Idiomatic and well-recorded French-style performances. –PM
○ **Stabat Mater / HARMONIA MUNDI**
Lagrange, Baudo/Lyon Orchestra.

MICHAEL PRAETORIUS   1571-1621

Renaissance. One of the most significant German composers of his time, whose *Musae Sioniae*, a collection of over 1200 settings of Lutheran chorales, is a valuable source for hymnology. A three-volume treatise by Praetorius, *Syntagma Musicum*, has significant information about the compositional style and instruments of his day. –MKS
○ **Magnificat & other choral works / SONY**
van Nevel/Huelgas Ensemble. Rather stylized, involving performances of some very interesting choral music. –PM
○ **Terpsichore (instrumental dances) / OISEAU-LYRE**
Pickett/New London Consort.
Terpsichore (instrumental dances) / ANGEL
Munrow/London Early Music Consort.

SERGEI PROKOFIEV   1891-1953

20th century. A Russian composer whose modernity seems to be inherent in him rather than something artificial or over-intellectualized. His natural feeling for melody and rhythm — by turns humorous (*Peter and the Wolf*), lyrical (*Concerto for Piano & Orchestra no. 3*), elegiac (*Visions fugitives*), aggressive (*Scythian Suite*), or all of the above (*Lieutenant Kije Suite*) — is wedded to a desire for direct communication with the listener and a quality of continually interesting invention. From the piano sonatas, we can see that his style was established at an early age and flowed from his character. It is strange, then, that he should have been criticized by Soviet authorities for "formalistic deviations and anti-democratic musical tendencies" and by American critics on his 1921 tour for expressing Bolshevism through music. He was guilty of neither, and now we can appreciate his wonderful pieces for what they are. –BGT
○ **Alexander Nevsky (cantata) / RCA**
Elias, Reiner/Chicago SO & Chorus. The classic performance, although, in stunning sound, Abbado is not far behind. –PM
Alexander Nevsky (cantata) / DGG
Obraztsova, Abbado/London SO & Chorus.
○ **Autumn (symphonic sketch), op. 8 (1911) / ONDINE**
Grin/Tampere PO.
○ **Chout [The Tale of the Buffoon] (ballet suite), op. 21a / LONDON**
Abbado/London SO. Raw but elegant. –PM
Chout [The Tale of the Buffoon] (ballet suite), op. 21a / MELODIYA (KOCH)
Rozhdestvensky/The USSR Ministry of Culture SO. Raw and rawer still, and very Russian! –PM
○ **Concerto for Piano Left Hand & Orchestra no. 4, op. 53 / SONY**
Serkin, Ormandy/Philadelphia Orchestra. Sometimes Serkin just clicks right in — and if there's one thing Ormandy does best, it's Prokofiev. –PM
○ **Concertos (5) for Piano & Orchestra / LONDON**
Ashkenazy, Previn/London SO.

○ **Concerto for Piano & Orchestra no. 1 in D-flat, op. 10 / CBS**
Graffman, Szell/Cleveland Orchestra.
☆ **Concerto for Piano & Orchestra no. 3 in C, op. 26 / SIMAX**
Andsnes, Ruud/Bergen PO. A real sleeper. No point in looking any further or listening to any others. This has guts, drive, soul, and an original point of view. –PM
Concerto for Piano & Orchestra no. 3 in C, op. 26 / CBS
Graffman, Szell/Cleveland Orchestra. Graffman's best recording, and one of Szell's too. –PM
○ **Concerto for Piano & Orchestra no. 5 in G, op. 55 / DGG**
Richter, Rowicki/Warsaw PO. Despite the less-than-great sound and orchestral support, no one's going to better this performance. –PM
○ **Concertos (2) for Violin & Orchestra, opp. 19, 63 / ANGEL**
Perlman, Rozhdestvensky/BBC SO. This would be such a "perfect" CD if only the orchestra weren't so far in the background. –PM
Concertos (2) for Violin & Orchestra, opp. 19, 63 / DGG
Mintz, Abbado/Chicago SO.
☆ **Lieutenant Kije Suite, op. 60 / RCA**
Reiner/Chicago SO.
Lieutenant Kije Suite, op. 60 / DGG
Abbado/Chicago SO. Again, Abbado and Reiner! –PM
Lieutenant Kije Suite, op. 60 / CBS
Szell/Cleveland Orchestra.
○ **The Love for Three Oranges (ballet suite), op. 33a / MERCURY**
Dorati/Minneapolis SO.
○ **The Love for Three Oranges (opera - complete) / VIRGIN**
Dubos, Bacquier, Bastin, Gautier, Biala, Nagano/L'Opéra de Lyons Orchestra & Chorus.
○ **Mélodies (5) for Violin & Piano, op. 35b / ADDA**
Pasquier, Roge.
○ **Ode to the End of the War, for Orchestra, op. 105 / MELODIYA (KOCH)**
Rozhdestvensky/USSR Ministry of Culture SO.
○ **Le Pas d'acier [The Steel Step] (ballet suite), op. 41a / MELODIYA (KOCH)**
Rozhdestvensky/USSR Ministry of Culture SO. Man, is this Russian-sounding! –PM
☆ **Peter and the Wolf, op. 67 / VIRGIN**
Gielgud, Stamp/Academy of London. Gielgud is even better than I thought he would be. –PM
○ **Quartets for Strings no. 2 in b, op. 92 & no. 1 in b, op. 50 / NONESUCH**
Sequoia Quartet.
○ **Quintet for Oboe, Clarinet, Violin, Viola & Double-bass, op. 39 / MD&G**
Ensemble Villa Musica. A very unknown and interesting Prokofiev chamber piece for a unique combination of instruments, well played and well recorded. –PM
○ **Romeo and Juliet (complete ballet) / LONDON**
Maazel/Cleveland Orchestra.
Romeo and Juliet (excerpts) / URANIA
Ancerl/Czech PO. There's just something so heady about this performance. –PM
Romeo and Juliet (excerpts) / PHILIPS
Mravinski/Leningrad PO. Drilled to the last degree, but a bit charmless, as Mravinsky always is. –PM
○ **Russian Overture, op. 72 / MELODIYA (KOCH)**
Rozhdestvensky/USSR Ministry of Culture SO.
☆ **Scythian Suite, op. 20 / DGG**
Abbado/Chicago SO. More elegant and not so brutal as other performances, but it has plenty of fire and drama and a lot of poetry too, where called for. –PM
Scythian Suite, op. 20 / MERCURY

Dorati/Minneapolis SO.
○ **Sonata for Cello & Piano, op. 119 / LONDON**
Harrell, Ashkenazy.
Sonatas for Piano nos. 1-3; Visions fugitives for Piano, op. 22 / ONDINE
Raekallio (piano). With new and interesting things to say about the sonatas and with a terrific technique and intellect, Raekallio (who reminds me of Richter) moves right to or near the top of the list in every single piece. No matter how tough the part gets, he remains intensely musical and never gets bombastic. –PM
○ **Sonata for Piano no. 2 in d, op. 14 / GLOBE**
Janssen.
Sonata for Piano no. 3 in a, op. 28 / CBS
Graffman.
○ **Sonata for Piano no. 4 in c, op. 29 / ONDINE**
Raekallio.
○ **Sonata for Piano no. 5 in C, op. 38 / ONDINE**
Raekallio.
○ **Sonata for Piano no. 6 in A, op. 82 / DGG**
Pogorelich.
Sonata for Piano no. 6 in A, op. 82 / SONY
Kissin.
Sonata for Piano no. 6 in A, op. 82 / ONDINE
Raekallio.
Sonatas for Piano nos. 7, 8, 9 / ONDINE
Raekallio.
○ **Sonata for Piano no. 7 in B-flat, op. 83 / DGG**
Pollini.
○ **Sonata for Piano no. 8 in B-flat, op. 84 / DGG**
Richter.
○ **Sonata for Violin & Piano no. 1 in f, op. 80 / DGG**
Mintz, Bronfman.
Sonata for Violin & Piano no. 1 in f, op. 80 / ADDA
Pasquier, Roge.
○ **Sonata for Violin & Piano no. 2 in A, op. 94a / DGG**
Mintz, Bronfman.
Sonata for Violin & Piano no. 2 in A, op. 94a / ADDA
Pasquier, Roge.
○ **Summer Day (Children's Suite for Small Orchestra), op. 65a; Pushkin Waltzes / ONDINE**
Grin/Tampere PO. Beautiful Russian nostalgia, with heartfelt playing and clear but atmospheric sound. –PM
○ **Summer Night, for Orchestra / ONDINE**
Grin/Tampere PO.
○ **Symphony no. 1 in D, op. 25, "Classical" / LONDON**
Marriner/ASMF.
○ **Symphony no. 2 in d, op. 40 / ONDINE**
Grin/Tampere PO. So much better sound than the competition's, and such a dedicated performance. –PM
○ **Symphonies nos. 3 & 4 / CHANDOS**
Järvi/Scottish National Orchestra.
○ **Symphony no. 5 / LONDON**
Ashkenazy/Royal Concertgebouw Orchestra. All the usual Ashkenazy attributes in Russian music: raw, committed, and with plenty of details. –PM
○ **Symphony no. 6 in e-flat, op. 111 / URANIA**
Mravinski/Leningrad PO. Forget anybody else: This is the most intense and together performance of the piece ever. –PM
○ **Symphony no. 7 in c#, op. 131 / SIMAX**
Ruud/Bergen PO. Everything about this performance makes me like this piece much better than I ever did before. –PM
○ **Visions fugitives for Piano nos. 3, 6, 9, op. 22 / DGG**
Richter (piano). Completely authoritative: too bad he didn't do them all, but overall this is one of the best discs Richter ever made. –PM

○ **Waltz Suite, op. 110 (1946) / ONDINE**
Grin/Tampere PO. A lot of this is in Prokofiev's more humorous "kookie" mood, and Grin handles the eccentricities perfectly: never condescending and with just the right amount of nostalgia and subtlety. This is a terrific, much more low-key performance than Järvi's hyperkinetic one. –PM

GIACOMO PUCCINI   1858-1924

Romantic, opera. An Italian composer of opera in the "verismo" (truth and reality) style, which was a reaction against heavy symbolism. Speaking in a harmonic language that is a mixture of Wagner, Debussy, and early Stravinsky, Puccini adds his gift for the liquescent melodic line that speaks and sighs and builds slowly to a beautiful sostenuto, seeming to evoke rather than be accompanied by the orchestra. Puccini's brave heroines are true, fully developed characters, sometimes straight from the real world, who meet tragic ends (the consumptive in *La Bohème*; the shocking suicide in *Tosca*; *Madame Butterfly*, based on a magazine story by John Luther Long). –BGT

☆ **La Bohème (four-act opera) / ANGEL**
de los Angeles, Bjoerling, Merrill, Beecham/RCA Victor Orchestra. Overall the finest *Bohème* ever. The orchestra sounds a bit thin in this mono recording from 1955, but the voices come shining through in fine form. –PM
La Bohème (four-act opera) / LONDON
Freni, Harwood, Pavarotti, Panerai, Karajan/Berlin PO, Deutsche Opera Chorus. This is a bit too heavy and Teutonic-sounding, but with such perfection in the orchestral execution and such beautiful singing even in the smallest roles, it is hard to deny this one — if only there had been a little more fire and temperament. But such perfection does not come easily, especially in opera, and Karajan can be a master perfectionist. –PM
La Bohème (four-act opera) / RCA
Caballé, Blegen, Domingo, Milnes, Raimondi, Solti/London PO. Caballé is glorious, but Solti's reading is a bit hard-driven and inflexible. –PM
○ **La fanciulla del West (three-act opera) / LONDON**
Capuana, Tebaldi, del Monaco, MacNeil, Tozzi/St Cecelia. The classic 1958 performance, still in good sound, and featuring the radiant Renata Tebaldi. –PM
La fanciulla del West (three-act opera) / DGG
Neblett, Domingo, Milnes, Mehta/Royal Opera. Neblett is a bit of a drawback, but this is one of Mehta's best. –PM
☆ **Madame Butterfly (two-act opera) / DGG**
Freni, Berganza, Carreras, Pons, Sinopoli/Philharmonia Orchestra, Ambrosian Opera Chorus. Very slow but very beautiful, with outstanding shadings and subtlety. Very well held together despite slow speeds, with great cumulative impact. –PM
Madame Butterfly (two-act opera) / LONDON
Freni, Ludwig, Pavarotti, Kerns, Karajan/Vienna PO. This was the standard for 25 years before Sinopoli arrived. It features the same sort of approach, with even better singing, and Karajan had a better feel for Italian opera in his younger days. The choice is tough. –PM
○ **Manon Lescaut (four-act opera)/ DGG**
Freni, Bruson, Domingo, Sinopoli/Philharmonic Orchestra. Once again Sinopoli's love of clarity and sensuality stands him in good stead in a Puccini opera. –PM
○ **Tosca (three-act opera) / LONDON**
Price, di Stefano, Taddei, Karajan/Vienna PO & State Opera Chorus. Karajan pretty much rules in *Tosca*. As usual, his earlier performance is more Italian-sounding, a bit more flexible, lighter, less austere, and better sung (what a cast!). –PM
Tosca (three-act opera) / PHILIPS
Caballé, Carreras, Wixell, Davis/Royal Opera. Davis is not a

conductor we readily associate with Puccini theater, but he is completely idiomatic here and he has Caballé. –PM

Tosca (three-act opera) / DGG
Ricciarelli, Carreras, Raimondi, Karajan/Berlin PO, Deutsche Opera Chorus. There's a power and intensity and seriousness in this later performance, which I suppose is better recorded than Karajan's earlier version. –PM

○ **Turandot (three-act opera) / LONDON**
Sutherland, Caballé, Pavarotti, Ghiaurov, Mehta/London PO, Alldis Chorus. With these soloists, and with Mehta conducting with the fire and concentration that used to be his hallmark, this is the *Turandot* to own. –PM

Turandot (three-act opera) / DGG
Ricciarelli, Hendricks, et al., Karajan/Vienna PO.

HENRY PURCELL   1659-1695

Baroque. An English composer in every category and form of music practiced in his time, remembered today for lively trumpet voluntaries and sweet vocal airs. *Dido and Aeneas* has plenty of both. Writing it on commission for the head of a boarding school for "gentlewomen" in Chelsea, Purcell included 17 different dances for the girls amidst the lovely arias of the mythological libretto, a type of "masque" — important in the development of opera and a curiously interesting form of theater today. –BGT

○ **Anthems / DGG**
Preston/English Concert, Christ Church Cathedral Choir.

☆ **Dido and Aeneas (opera) / CHANDOS**
Kirkby, Nelson, Thomas, Parrott/Taverner Players & Chorus. Until the Janet Baker-Thurston Dart/Anthony Lewis performance returns to the catalog, this rather small-scale and dry reading will have to do. –PM

Dido and Aeneas (piano) / ARCHIV GALLERIA
Dawson, von Otter, Pinnock/English Concert & Choir. Outstanding women, but all a bit dry and musicological. –PM

Dido and Aeneas (opera) / ANGEL
Flagstad, Schwarzkopf, Hemsley, Jones/Mermaid Orchestra & Singers. Old-fashioned but notable for Flagstad's noble singing. –PM

○ **The Fairy Queen / DGG**
Gardiner/English Baroque Soloists, Monteverdi Chorus.

○ **The Indian Queen (selections) / HARMONIA MUNDI**
Deller/The King's Musick & Deller Choir. One of Deller's best recordings. –PM

○ **King Arthur (dramatic five-act opera) / HARMONIA MUNDI**
Sheppard, Knibbs, Hardy, A. and M. Deller, Elliott, Nixon, Bevan, Beavan, Deller/King's Musick & Deller Choir.

○ **Ode for St. Cecilia's Day, "Hail Bright Cecilia" / DGG**
Woolf (treble); Esswood, Tatnell (countertenors); Young (tenor); Shirley-Quirk (baritone); Rippon (bass); Mackerras/English CO, Ambrosian Singers.

○ **Odes and Welcome Songs (complete) / HYPERION**
King/The King's Consort. On the whole, outstanding singing, if not quite such a good instrumental backup. –PM

○ **Odes: Come, Ye Sons of Art, Away; Welcome to All the Pleasures / ARCHIV GALLERIA**
Soloists, Pinnock/The English Concert & Choir. Pinnock has a real talent for directing choral works. He tends to loosen up and become less dry, and these are infectious and exuberant performances in some of the best sound ever on Archiv. –PM

☆ **Songs / HYPERION**
Bowman, Chance, King/The King's Consort.

Songs / HYPERION
Esswood, Sonnleitner, Medlam.

Songs / HYPERION
Kirkby, Thomas, Rooley.

○ **Te Deum and Jubilate in D / DGG**
Preston/English Concert, Christ Church Cathedral Choir. Another outstanding CD from the English Concert, this time directed by Simon Preston. –PM

○ **Trio Sonatas (22) for 2 Violins, Viola da Gamba & Continuo Instruments, Z. 790-811 / CHANDOS**
Purcell Quartet. 22 sonatas in three volumes.

SERGEI RACHMANINOFF   1873-1943

Romantic. A Russian virtuoso pianist and composer in the Russian romantic style of piano and orchestral works; known for *Rhapsody on a Theme of Paganini, for Piano & Orchestra, op. 43* (1934). Strange as it may seem, Rachmaninoff's popularity overshadows his contribution to music, which was the continuation of the traditions in sound of two other composers: Tchaikovsky (cf. *Concerto no. 2 in c*) and Grieg (the op. 43 *Rhapsody*). His symphonies (especially the *Symphony no. 3*, 1936), his tone poem *The Isle of the Dead* (1907), the *Symphonic Dances* (1940), and several choral works, including *The Bells* (1913) and *Vespers* (1915), can still be appreciated as innovations within these traditions — as expansive in imagery and timbre as is the brilliance of his melodic sense for the piano. –BGT

○ **Aleko: Intermezzo & Women's Dance / ANGEL**
Previn/London SO.

○ **The Bells (choral symphony), op. 35 / LONDON**
Troitskaya, Karczykowski, Krause, Ashkenazy/Royal Concertgebouw Orchestra & Chorus.

○ **Concertos for Piano & Orchestra nos. 1-4 / CHANDOS**
Wild (piano), Horenstein/Royal PO. This performance features the virtuosity and flamboyance of Wild and the backbone and control of Horenstein. –PM

Concertos for Piano & Orchestra nos. 1-4 / LONDON
Ashkenazy, Haitink/Royal Concertgebouw Orchestra.

○ **Concerto for Piano & Orchestra no. 1 in f#, op. 1 / CHESKY**
Wild, Horenstein/Royal PO.

☆ **Concerto for Piano & Orchestra no. 2 in c, op. 18 / DGG**
Richter (piano), Wislocki/Warsaw PO. After 30 years, Richter still reigns supreme. –PM

Concerto for Piano & Orchestra no. 2 in c, op. 18 / RCA
Cliburn, Reiner/Chicago SO.

Concerto for Piano & Orchestra no. 2 in c, op. 18 / CHANDOS
Wild, Horenstein/Royal PO.

Concerto for Piano & Orchestra no. 2 in c, op. 18 / LONDON
Ashkenazy, Haitink/Royal Concertgebouw Orchestra.

○ **Concerto for Piano & Orchestra no. 3 in d, op. 30 / CHANDOS**
Wild, Horenstein/Royal PO.

○ **Concerto for Piano & Orchestra no. 4 in g, op. 40 / LONDON**
Ashkenazy, Haitink/Royal Concertgebouw Orchestra.

○ **Études-Tableaux for Piano, op. 33 / DENON**
Grimaud.

Études-Tableaux for Piano, opp. 33 & 39 / LONDON
Ashkenazy.

Études-Tableaux for Piano, opp. 33/6, 39/1-4, 9, 7 / MELODIYA (KOCH)
Richter (piano). He only plays nine of them, but no one plays them better. –PM

○ **The Isle of the Dead, op. 29 / LONDON**
Ashkenazy/Royal Concertgebouw Orchestra.

The Isle of the Dead, op. 29 / CHESKY
Horenstein/Royal PO.

The Isle of the Dead, op. 29 / ANGEL
Previn/London SO.

○ **Prelude for Piano no. 2 in c#, op. 3 / LONDON**
Ashkenazy.

○ **Preludes (23) for Piano, opp. 23 & 32 (complete) / LONDON**
Ashkenazy.

○ **Preludes (23) for Piano nos. 2 & 12, op. 32 / DENON**
Grimaud.

Preludes (23) for Piano opp. 23 & 32 (selections) / DGG
Richter.

☆ **Rhapsody on a Theme of Paganini, for Piano & Orchestra / CHANDOS**
Wild, Horenstein/Royal PO.

Rhapsody on a Theme of Paganini, for Piano & Orchestra / RCA
Cliburn, Ormandy/Philadelphia Orchestra.

Rhapsody on a Theme of Paganini, for Piano & Orchestra / LONDON
Ashkenazy, Haitink/Philharmonia Orchestra.

○ **Sonata for Cello & Piano in g, op. 19 / PHILIPS**
Schiff, Leonskaja.

○ **Sonata for Piano no. 1 in d, op. 28 / KINGDOM**
Fergus-Thompson.

○ **Sonata for Piano no. 2 in b-flat, op. 36 / DENON**
Grimaud.

Sonata for Piano no. 2 in b-flat, op. 36 / KINGDOM
Fergus-Thompson.

Sonata for Piano no. 2 in b-flat, op. 36 / LONDON
Ashkenazy.

○ **Symphonic Dances (for orchestra), op. 45 / LONDON**
Ashkenazy/Royal Concertgebouw Orchestra.

Symphonic Dances (for orchestra), op. 45 / VIRGIN
Litton/Royal PO.

Symphonic Dances (for orchestra), op. 45 / ANGEL
Previn/London SO.

○ **Symphony no. 1 in d, op. 13 / VIRGIN**
Litton/Royal PO.

Symphony no. 1 in d, op. 13 / LONDON
Ashkenazy/Royal Concertgebouw Orchestra.

○ **Symphony no. 2 in e, op. 27 / PHILIPS**
Bychkov/Orchestre de Paris.

Symphony no. 2 in e, op. 27 / VIRGIN
Litton/Royal PO.

Symphony no. 2 in e, op. 27 / LONDON
Ashkenazy/Royal Concertgebouw Orchestra.

○ **Symphony no. 3 in a, op. 44 / VIRGIN**
Litton/Royal PO.

Symphony no. 3 in a, op. 44 / LONDON
Ashkenazy/Royal Concertgebouw Orchestra.

○ **Trio for Violin, Cello & Piano no. 1 in g / PHILIPS**
Beaux Arts Trio.

○ **Trio for Violin, Cello & Piano no. 2 in d, op. 9 / PHILIPS**
Beaux Arts Trio.

○ **Variations on a Theme by Corelli, for Piano, op. 42 / LONDON**
Ashkenazy.

JEAN PHILIPPE RAMEAU   1683-1764

Baroque. The great French theoretician who synthesized the current rules of harmonic practice and suggested others in *Traité de l'Harmonie* ("Treatise on Harmony") (1723) and *Nouveau Système de Musique Théorique* ("New System of Musical Theory") (1726) — works that are studied by composers to this day. Rameau was a bold experimenter in harmony and a master of orchestration who introduced new effects (e.g., storm scenes), especially in the choruses of his

"operas" (heroic pastorales, allegoric ballet, fêtes — not opera as we think of it now). The finest of these are *Les Indes galantes* (1739) and *Zoroastre* (1749). His harpsichord pieces are exquisite miniature studies in harmonic and evocative invention. –BGT

○ **Anacreon (ballet) / HARMONIA MUNDI**
Christie/Ensemble Les Arts Florissants.

☆ **Harpsichord Works / OISEAU-LYRE**
Rousset (harpsichord). This new entry sweeps the board in every way. –PM

Harpsichord Works / ADDA
Baumont. The complete works for solo harpsichord in three volumes. –ED

○ **Hippolyte et Aricie (orchestral suite from 5-act drama) / EDITO CLASSICA**
Kuijken/La Petite Bande.

○ **Les Indes galantes / HARMONIA MUNDI**
McFadden, et al./Ensemble Les Arts Florissants. This is an opera-ballet in four acts. –ED

Les Indes galantes: Symphonies / HARMONIA MUNDI
Herreweghe/Chapelle Royale Orchestra.

○ **Motets: In Convertendo; Quam Dilecta; Laboravi / HARMONIA MUNDI**
Herreweghe/Chapelle Royale Orchestra & Chorus.

○ **Les Paladins: Orchestral Suite / PHILIPS**
Leonhardt/Orchestra of the Age of Enlightenment. Self-recommending. A conductor who understands French baroque style and is able to communicate his understanding to British orchestras. This is an expressive performance. –PM

○ **Pièces de clavecin en concert / VIRGIN**
Trio Sonnerie.

○ **Pygmalion (acte de ballet) / EDITO CLASSICA**
Yakar, van der Sluis, et al., Leonhardt/La Petite Bande.

○ **Zoroastre (tragédie lyrique in 5 acts) / EDITO CLASSICA**
Mellon, de Reyghere, et al., Kuijken/La Petite Bande.

MAURICE RAVEL   1875-1937

20th century, impressionist. A French composer known for melodic and tonal invention. Giving the lie to the idea that turn-of-the-century musical trends were necessarily elite impressionism or "decadent" (whatever that may mean), Ravel's music always speaks directly to the heart in a subtle rhythmic sense through great melody, harmonic richness, and iridescent orchestration. (The art of stacking partials in Ravel's *Boléro* and in the work of Ives predate harmonic synthesis in electronic music by half a century.) Ravel's ballet *Daphnis et Chloé*, with its gently sustained, wordless vocal chorus amidst heaven-on-earth sound-painting, is probably the finest synthesis of his aesthetic. Ravel's melodic abilities and method of making subtle timbre changes by harmonic shift (rather than loud/soft articulation) are beautifully amplified in his piano works, including the famous *Sonatine*, *Gaspard de la Nuit*, and in each *Concerto for Piano Lefthand* in D and G), which also contain some of his most advanced harmonic writing. The expansive *La valse* shows a more extroverted Ravel, with much of the same fine orchestral composition. The *Quartet in F*, with its rich, earthy melodies, shows perhaps a more intimate side of Ravel. –BGT

○ **Alborada del gracioso / DGG**
Abbado/London SO. Ravel is one of my favorite composers and my favorite French composer. Roughly, this is the score. There have been three great Ravel conductors recently: Boulez in the 70s, Haitink in the 80s, and Abbado in the 90s. Karajan and others have, of course, made good recordings of certain pieces, but these three have done most of the Ravel orchestral music and they have been terrific in all of it, not just in a few isolated pieces. Let me mention one other conductor too — Inbal: his Ravel is convincingly thought through and he has the best sound quality. What he lacks is a great orchestra; but he is always worth hearing, especially in *Daphnis et Chloé*. He

makes you *think*. Boulez is an intellectual — he has clarity. Haitink is terrifically well organized and he has a sensuality and humanity not normally associated with him. Abbado is more "romantic" and he too is very sensual in a more Italian way. But you should make no mistake — he also has clarity in abundance. –PM

Alborada del gracioso / DENON
Inbal/Orchestre National de France.

○ **Une barque sur l'océan (from *Miroirs*, orchestrated by Ravel) / DGG**
Abbado/London SO.

○ **Berceuse sur le nom de Fauré, for Violin & Piano / ADDA**
Bonaldi, Lee.

Berceuse sur le nom de Fauré, for Violin & Piano / CYBELIA
Wacheux, Penven.

☆ **Boléro / DGG**
Sinopoli/Philharmonia Orchestra. Ravel called it "orchestration without music." Sinopoli has a good handle on the irony and delivers the fastest (at 14:11) performance since Ravel's, and one of the tautest and quirkiest. It's elegant as well as dynamic, all at once. –PM

Boléro / DGG
Abbado/London SO.

Boléro / DGG
Barenboim/Orchestre de Paris.

Boléro / PHILIPS
Haitink/Royal Concertgebouw Orchestra.

○ **Concerto for Piano (left hand) & Orchestra in D / DGG**
Beroff, Abbado/London SO.

○ **Concerto for Piano & Orchestra in G / DGG**
Argerich, Abbado/London SO.

☆ **Daphnis et Chloé (complete ballet) / DGG**
Abbado/London SO. Abbado has the passion and the sensuality, and this is the most orgiastic *Daphnis* since Munch. Abbado milks the score, with pronounced tempo changes, but he is quite elegant and in complete control. –PM

Daphnis et Chloé (complete ballet) / LONDON
Monteux/London SO, Royal Opera Chorus. So natural — nothing is forced; the piece just unfolds. –PM

Daphnis et Chloé (complete ballet) / PHILIPS
Haitink/Boston SO. Maybe a bit too dry and analytical for most tastes but still a fascinating reading. –PM

Daphnis et Chloé (complete ballet) / DGG
Inbal/Orchestre National de France & Chorus. A very interesting alternative. –PM

○ **Daphnis et Chloé: Suite no. 2 / DGG**
Abbado/Boston SO.

Daphnis et Chloé: Suite no. 2 / DGG
Sinopoli/Philharmonia Orchestra.

Daphnis et Chloé: Suite no. 2 / DGG
Karajan/Berlin PO.

Daphnis et Chloé: Suite no. 2 / PHILIPS
Haitink/Royal Concertgebouw Orchestra.

○ **L'enfant et les sortilèges "fantasie lyrique" / DGG**
Ogeas, Gilma, Berbie, Herzog, Senechal, Maurane, Rehfuss, Maazel/Orchestre National de France & Chorus.

○ **Fanfare (for ballet *L'éventail de Jeanne*) / DGG**
Abbado/London SO.

Fanfare (for ballet *L'éventail de Jeanne*) / DENON
Inbal/Orchestre National de France.

☆ **Gaspard de la nuit, for Piano / FONE**
Husson.

Gaspard de la nuit, for Piano / HUNGARATON
Ranki.

Gaspard de la nuit, for Piano / DGG

Pogorelich.

○ **L'heure espagnole (comedie musicale) / DGG**
Berbie, Giraudeau, Senchal, Bacquier, van Dam, Maazel/Orchestre National de France.

○ **Introduction and Allegro for Harp, Flute, Clarinet & String Quartet (arrangement for 2 pianos) / OLYMPIA**
Thorson, Thurber.

Introduction and Allegro for Harp, Flute, Clarinet & String Quartet / DGG
Ensemble Wien-Berlin.

○ **Jeux d'eau, for Piano / FONE**
Husson.

○ **Ma Mère l'Oye / DGG**
Abbado/London SO.

Ma Mère l'Oye (4-hand piano suite) / PHILIPS
K. and M. Labeque.

Ma Mère l'Oye (4-hand piano suite) / OLYMPIA
Thorson, Thurber.

Ma Mère l'Oye (ballet) / DENON
Inbal/Orchestre National de France.

Ma Mère l'Oye (ballet) / PHILIPS
Previn/Pittsburgh SO.

○ **Menuet antique (orchestral version) / DGG**
Abbado/London SO.

Menuet antique (piano version) / THESIS
Kanno.

○ **Menuet sur le nom d'Haydn: Prélude / HUNGARATON**
Ranki.

○ **Orchestral Works / DGG**
Abbado/London SO.

☆ **Pavane pour une infante défunte / DGG**
Barenboim/Orchestre de Paris.

Pavane pour une infante défunte / DGG
Abbado/London SO.

Pavane pour une infante défunte / PHILIPS
Haitink/Royal Concertgebouw Orchestra.

Pavane pour une infante défunte / CBS
Boulez/NYPO.

○ **Piano Music (complete 4-hand piano works) / OLYMPIA**
Thorson, Thurber.

○ **Piano Music (complete solo piano works) / CIRCE**
Merlet (piano). This sounds more like authentic Ravel than any of the other sets around right now, which tend too much toward virtuoso display and not enough toward Ravel and poetry. –PM

☆ **Quartet for Strings in F / DENON**
Nuovo Quartetto. A bit too slow and Italian-sounding to be completely ideal, but boy, are they hypnotic and subtle, and do they ever have great sound. A lot of details are revealed anew in these fascinating connoisseur pieces. –PM

Quartet for Strings in F / WHITE LABEL
Bartók Quartet.

☆ **Rapsodie espagnole / DGG**
Abbado/London SO.

Rapsodie espagnole / DGG
Karajan/Berlin PO.

Rapsodie espagnole / DENON
Inbal/Orchestre National de France.

Rapsodie espagnole; Ma Mère l'Oye; Valse nobles et sentimentales; La valse / LONDON
Ashkenazy/Cleveland Orchestra. It is hard not to respond to such virtuoso playing, especially when so many new details are revealed in such new light. This is Ashkenazy's best French CD — it rivals my big three, and in some ways, surpasses them. What a great orchestra this is: the best in America. Chicago, Boston — even they can't rival this, at least not in French playing. –PM

☆ **Schéhérazade, for Mezzo-Soprano & Orchestra / DGG**
Price, Abbado/London SO.
Schéhérazade, for Mezzo-Soprano & Orchestra / PHILIPS
Ameling, de Waart/SFSO.
Schéhérazade, for Mezzo-Soprano & Orchestra / LONDON
Crespin, Ansermet/Suisse Romande.
Schéhérazade, for Mezzo-Soprano & Orchestra / LONDON
Danco, Ansermet/Suisse Romande.
○ **Sonata for Violin & Cello / ADDA**
Bonaldi, Chiffoleau.
Sonata for Violin & Cello / DGG
Ensemble Wien-Berlin.
Sonata for Violin & Cello / HUNGARATON
Duo Ongarese.
○ **Sonata for Violin & Piano / ADDA**
Bonaldi, Lee (piano). Sounds a lot more French than Mintz and Bronfman, but theirs is the higher-profile playing. –PM
Sonata for Violin & Piano / DGG
Mintz, Bronfman.
☆ **Sonatine for Piano / HUNGARATON**
Ranki.
Sonatine for Piano / THESIS
Kanno.
○ **Le tombeau de Couperin / DGG**
Abbado/London SO.
Le tombeau de Couperin / GLOBE
Janssen (piano).
Le tombeau de Couperin / DENON
Inbal/Orchestre National de France.
Le tombeau de Couperin / DENON
Magaloff.
○ **Trio for Violin, Cello & Piano / INTERCORD**
Abegg Trio. Makes up in power and sensitivity what it lacks in French delicacy. –PM
Trio for Violin, Cello & Piano / COLLINS CLASSICS
Trio Zingara. More delicate and ephemeral than Abegg's, but not so powerful. –PM
○ **Tzigane for Violin & Orchestra / DGG**
Accardo, Abbado/London SO.
☆ **La valse (poème choréographique) / OLYMPIA**
Thorson, Thurber (piano).
La valse (poème choréographique) / DGG
Abbado/London SO.
La valse (poème choréographique) / DGG
Barenboim/Orchestre de Paris.
La valse (poème choréographique) / DENON
Inbal/Orchestre National de France.
○ **Valses nobles et sentimentales / HUNGARATON**
Ranki (piano).
Valses nobles et sentimentales / DENON
Magaloff (piano).
Valses nobles et sentimentales / DGG
Sinopoli/NYPO.
Valses nobles et sentimentales / DGG
Abbado/London SO.

MAX REGER   1873-1916

Romantic. A widely respected German composer, pianist, organist, conductor, teacher, and master of polyphonic techniques, applied within the framework of a romantic harmonic vocabulary; known for his organ music. –MKS
○ **Chorale Fantasia for Organ, op. 40 / HYPERION**

Barber.
○ **Concerto for Piano & Orchestra in f, op. 114 / SONY**
Serkin (piano), Ormandy/Philadelphia Orchestra. A Reger classic! –PM
○ **Organ Works (complete) / MD**
Haas (organ). Vols. 1-6 of a projected 12-disc series have been completed. –MKS
○ **Quintet for Clarinet & Strings in A, op. 146 / CAMERATA**
Leister/Philharmonia Quartet.
○ **Sextet for Strings in F, op. 118 / JECKLIN**
Zürich Chamber Players.
○ **String Trios, opp. 77b & 141b / CALIG**
Wiener Streichtrio. Is Reger the least-loved (Germanic) composer? Well, there's still a lot of tedium here, but these performances are so good that they just have to be recommended, and the pieces are very representative of Reger's style. –PM
○ **Suite for Violin & Orchestra in a, op. 103a / KOCH-SCHWANN**
Maile, Lajovic/Berlin RSO.
○ **Variations & Fugue on a Theme by Mozart, op. 132 / PHILIPS**
Davis/Bavarian RSO. All Davis's loving attention to detail and phrasing doesn't quite save Reger's turgid piece, but it comes close. –PM
○ **Variations & Fugue on a Theme of Johann Hiller, op. 100 ORFEO**
Davis/Bavarian RSO. Everything I said for the Mozart variations (above) is true for this Davis performance, too. –PM

OTTORINO RESPIGHI   1879-1936

Neo-romantic. An Italian composer of orchestral works, vocal music, and operas who based his music on church modes and plainchant; known for his orchestral arrangements. Respighi's music may perhaps be best described as romantic-impressionist, because the melodies are extended and fully developed and the orchestral sound has the richness of an impressionist landscape. His two best-known (and probably his best) works are the orchestral arrangements *The Fountains of Rome* and *The Pines of Rome.* Less known but very rewarding to hear are the works in which he reset older music, such as the fine *Ancient Airs and Dances* (three sets), 1917, 1924, 1932), or those in which he used a rather poetic interpretation of ancient Greek and Gregorian modality (*Concerto Gregoriano for Violin & Orchestra,* 1921, and the interesting *Concerto in Modo Misolidio for Piano & Orchestra,* 1925). A fan of *Pines* and *Fountains* may also wish to check out Respighi's *Roman Festivals, Brazilian Impressions,* and *Church Windows.* –BGT
○ **Ancient Airs and Dances (3 sets) / MERCURY**
Dorati/Philharmonia Hungarica. Marriner's new performance is a bit slick. These are still the ones to own. –PM
Ancient Airs and Dances (3 sets) / PHILIPS
Marriner/ASMF.
○ **La boutique fantastique (ballet after Rossini) / PHILIPS**
Marriner/ASMF.
○ **Feste Romane (Roman Festivals) / KOCH-SCHWANN**
de Sabate/Berlin PO. This and the Toscanini sweep the competition so badly that it's hardly worth metioning the modern Ozawa version. –PM
Feste Romane (Roman Festivals) / DGG
Ozawa/Boston SO.
○ **The Fountains of Rome / RCA**
Reiner/Chicago SO.
The Fountains of Rome / DGG
Karajan/Berlin PO.
The Fountains of Rome; The Pines of Rome; The Birds / LONDON
Kertesz.

○ Gli Uccelli [The Birds] (suite for small orchestra) /
PHILIPS
Marriner/ASMF.

☆ **The Pines of Rome; The Fountains of Rome; Feste
Romane / RCA**
Toscanini/NBC SO.
The Pines of Rome / RCA
Reiner/Chicago SO.
The Pines of Rome / DGG
Karajan/Berlin PO.

SILVESTRE REVUELTAS   1899-1940

20th century. An outstanding Mexican composer whose
knowledge of his native music produced works of great
originality, melodic charm, and rhythmic vitality. –MKS

○ Ocho x Radio (1933); Sensemaya (1938) / O. M.
Herrera de la Fuente/Kalpa SO. *Sensemaya* is a spectacular
piece that epitomizes Revueltas's ability to create spectacular
rhythmic drive and momentum. –MKS

○ String Quartets nos. 2 & 4 / ELAN
Cuarteto Latinoamericano.

JOSEPH RHEINBERGER   1839-1901

Romantic. A German composer, one of the most famous organ
teachers of his day,whose organ sonatas are among the most
important works in that genre for the instrument. –MKS

○ Sonatas (20) for Organ / PREZIOSO
This seven-disc series, available separately, contains all 20 of
the sonatas. Eden, Munns, Farrell, and Fisher are the
performers. –MKS

○ Sonatas for Violin & Piano no. 1 in E-flat, op. 77; no. 2 in
e, op. 105 / CHRISTOPHORUS
Besig (violin), Brembeck (piano). Worthwhile romantic
byways, well-played and -recorded. –PM

NIKOLAI RIMSKY-KORSAKOV   1844-1908

Romantic, nationalist. A renowned Russian theoretician whose
book on orchestration (*Principles of Orchestration,* 1913) is
still widely studied; part of "The Mighty Five," who revived the
Russian musical spirit and sound in the second half of the
19th century. His *Scheherazade,* with its exotic imagery,
flowing melodies, and balletic rhythms, is his most famous
piece, but Rimsky-Korsakov regarded his operas as his best
achievement. In fact, two of the eight operas — *The Invisible
City of Kitezh* and *The Golden Cockerel* — are unappreciated
masterpieces, and the opera *Mlada* is notable for its
Wagnerian influences. The *Russian Easter Overture* is a fine
example of his mastery of orchestral timbres. –BGT

○ The Legend of the Invisible City of Kitezh (suite) /
CHANDOS
Järvi/Scottish National Orchestra. This recording also
contains: "Christmas Eve" (suite), "Le coq d'or" (suite), "May
Night" (overture), "Mlada" (suite), "The Snow Maiden"
(suite), and "Tsar Sultan" (suite). –ED

○ Quintet for Piano, Flute, Clarinet, Bassoon & Horn in B-
flat / HYPERION
Capricorn. This is a thoroughly entertaining piece of Russian
chamber music, which is well played and well recorded. –PM

☆ Russian Easter Overture, op. 36 / DGG
Järvi/Gothenburg SO.

☆ Scheherazade, op. 35 / PHILIPS
Haitink/London Philharmonic. More serious and more
symphonic than the others, with the emphasis on power and
drama rather than strictly on color. –PM
Scheherazade, op. 35 / LONDON
Ansermet/L'Orchestra de la Suisse Romande. Long a very
colorful favorite, now at bargain price. Ansermet has the
pizzazz, but he also has a thorough grasp of every detail. –PM
Scheherazade, op. 35 / ANGEL

Beecham/Royal Philharmonic. The classic performance. –PM
Scheherazade, op. 35 / LONDON
Stokowski/London SO. Very fiery and Stokowskiized, with
great drama and impact. It's exceptionally tough to choose
among these four performances. –PM

○ Symphony no. 1 in b / DGG
Järvi/Gothenburg SO.

JOAQUIN RODRIGO   b 1901

Romantic, impressionist. The Spanish romantic-impressionist
composer of *Concierto de Aranjuez,* which is often heard in
the setting by Gil Evans for Miles Davis on *Sketches of Spain.*
The original has many more charms and beauty of
orchestration; it and its companion piece, *Fantasia para un
gentilhombre for Guitar & Orchestra,* each have elegant, warm,
and memorable melodies. –BGT

○ Concierto Andaluz, for 4 Guitars & Orchestra / PHILIPS
Romeros, Marriner/ASMF.

☆ Concierto de Aranjuez, for Guitar & Orchestra /
PHILIPS
Romero, Marriner/ASMF.
**Concierto de Aranjuez, for Guitar & Orchestra /
LONDON**
Bonell, Dutoit/Montreal SO.

○ Concierto Madrigal for 2 Guitars & Orchestra / PHILIPS
P. Romero, A. Romero, Marriner/ASMF.

○ Fantasia para un gentilhombre for Guitar & Orchestra /
LONDON
Bonell, Dutoit/Montreal SO.

○ Piano Music (complete) / BRIDGE
Allen.

JOHAN HELMICH ROMAN   1694-1758

Baroque. Called the "father of Swedish music" for being the
first to write instrumental and choral works that could be
favorably compared to German and Italian pieces, Roman
wrote at least 400 works, in most instrumental and vocal
genres. His music shows the influence of Handel. He is known
for his orchestral suite *Drottningholmsmusiquen* (1744). –MKS

○ Concertos (3) for Violin & Orchestra / BIS
Sparf/Orpheus Chamber Ensemble of Stockholm.

○ Golovinmusiken (orchestral suite - selections) /
CAPRICE
Drottningholm Baroque Ensemble.

○ Sinfonie (3) nos. 14, 17, 26 / BIS
Orpheus Chamber Ensemble of Stockholm.

○ Sinfonie (8) nos. 3, 9, 10, 11, 15, 22, 24, 30 / MUSICA
SVECIAE
Schröder/Drottningholm Baroque Ensemble.

GIOACCHINO ROSSINI   1792-1868

Romantic, opera. A celebrated Italian composer of opera,
considered among the greatest masters of the genre. The
extroverted style of Rossini's characterization and orchestral
writing is still uplifting today. He is known for *The Barber of
Seville* (1816), but his operas written for the Paris stage are
perhaps his best, especially the very original and powerful
William Tell. –BGT

☆ Il barbiere di Siviglia ("The Barber of Seville") /
PHILIPS
Baltsa, Araiza, Allen, Lloyd, Marriner/ASMF. The lightest and
liveliest of *Barber*s. Marriner's very first opera recording. –PM
Il barbiere di Siviglia ("The Barber of Seville") / DGG
Berganza, Alva, Prey, Motarsolo, Abbado/London SO &
Chorus.

○ La Cenerentola (two-act opera) / DGG
Marriner/ASMF.
La Cenerentola (two-act opera) / DGG

Berganza, Alva, Capecchi, Trama, Abbado/London SO & Chorus.

○ **Le Comte Ory (opéra comique) / PHILIPS**
Jo, Montague, Aler, Quilico, Cachemaille, Cardiner/Lyon Opera Orchestra & Chorus.

○ **La donna del lago (two-act opera) / CBS**
Ricciarelli, Valentini-Terrani, et al., Pollini/Chamber Orchestra of Europe, Prague Philharmonic Chorus.

○ **L'Italiana in Algeri (two-act opera) / DGG**
Baltsa, Lopardo, Dara, Raimondi, Abbado/Vienna Philharmonic & State Opera Chorus.

☆ **Overtures (various) / COLLINS CLASSICS**
Solomons/The Authentic Orchestra. If you want soul and high comedy, give these a try. –PM

Overtures (various) / RCA
Reiner/Chicago SO. Who said Reiner couldn't relax? –PM

Overtures (various) / PHILIPS
Marriner/ASMF.

Overtures (various) / DGG
Orpheus CO. Stylish, but I still miss a firm command. –PM

○ **Semiramide (two-act opera) / LONDON**
Sutherland, Horne, Serge, Rouleau, Malas, Bonynge/London SO, Ambrosian Singers.

♭ **Stabat Mater / PHILIPS**
Vaness, Bartoli, Ariaza, Furlanetto, Bychkov/Bavarian RSO. I don't know why Bychkov should have any special affinity for this piece, but he certainly seems to, and he has instilled it into his soloists, chorus, and orchestra. Another triumph for this somehow controversial conductor. –PM

○ **Il viaggio a Reims / DGG**
Ricciarelli, Gasdia, Cuberli, Valentini, et al., Abbado/Chamber Orchestra of Europe, Prague Philharmonic Chorus.

☆ **William Tell (four-act opera) / LONDON**
Freni, Pavarotti, Milnes, Ghiaurov, Chaily/National PO.

William Tell (four-act opera) / PHILIPS
Studer, Merritt, Zancanaro, Muti/La Scala Orchestra & Chorus. Recorded live. –BGT

ALBERT ROUSSEL   1869-1937

Impressionist. A French composer of ballet, orchestral, chamber, and piano music. Much of Roussel's work begins with detailed, intimate imagery and experiences, like the humor of an insect ballet in *Le Festin d'Araignée* or ancient dances in the tuneful and rhythmic *Suite in F;* but then he expands the music to vast seascapes or dramatic encounters. Roussel, like his fellow impressionists Debussy and Ravel, is able to build rich orchestrations from seed fragments that seem to grow and occupy intersecting planes of sound, as in the *Symphony no. 3* and the *Rapsodie flamande.* However, his writing is of a simpler line by choice, with "added note" harmonies and a different, attractive impressionist character. –BGT

○ **Rapsodie flamande, op. 56; Resurrection, op. 4 / CYBELIA**
Stoll/Rhenish Philharmonic.

○ **Suite in F, op. 33; Symphonies no. 3 in g, op. 42 & no. 4 in A, op. 53 / ASTREE**
Baden-Baden, Bour/South German Radio Orchestra. Spiky, aggressive, even abrasive, with tons of energy: this is the way Roussel was meant to be played. Upfront sound too clear (from 1965, 1977, 1967), with every instrument clear. –PM

○ **Symphony no. 1 in d, op. 7 / CYBELIA**
Segerstam/Swedish RSO.

○ **Various Pieces / ADDA**
The Sandman for Harp, Clarinet, Flute, Horn & String Quartet, op. 13 (1908); *Impromptu for Harp, op. 21* (1919); *Trio for Flute, Viola & Cello no. 2, op. 40* (1929); *Ronsard Poems (2), for Flute & Soprano, op. 26* (1924); *Elpenor, for Flute & String Quartet, op. 59* (1937); *Divertissement for Wind Quintet &*

Piano, op. 6 (1906). A full 67 minutes of chamber music: chips off the Roussel musical block. –PM

EDMUND RUBBRA   1901-1986

20th century, neo-romantic. An English composer and student of Vaughan Williams whose output consists of one opera, one ballet, and a variety of instrumental and vocal works. His style can best be described as neo-romantic, with occasional polytonal passages. –MKS

○ **Amoretti (5 Spenser sonnets), for Tenor & String Quartet / VIRGIN**
Hill/Endellion String Quartet.

○ **Four Medieval Latin Lyrics, for Baritone & String Orchestra / VIRGIN**
Wilson-Johnson, Schönzeler/City of London Sinfonia.

○ **Improvisations on Virginal Pieces by Giles Farnaby / CHANDOS**
Schönzeler/Bournemouth Sinfonietta.

○ **Resurgam (concert overture), op. 149 / LYRITA**
del Mar/Philharmonia Orchestra.

○ **Sinfonietta for Large String Orchestra, op. 163 / VIRGIN**
Schönzeler/City of London Sinfonia. A real find. Schönzeler is committed to Rubbra's music, and it shows. –PM

○ **Symphony no. 3, op. 49 / LYRITA**
del Mar/Philharmonia Orchestra.

○ **Symphony no. 4, op. 53 / LYRITA**
del Mar/Philharmonia Orchestra.

○ **Symphony no. 5 in B-flat, op. 63 / CHANDOS**
Schönzeler/Melbourne SO.

○ **Symphony no. 10, op. 145 / CHANDOS**
Schönzeler/Bournemouth Sinfonietta.

○ **A Tribute [for Vaughan Williams on his 70th birthday], op. 56 / LYRITA**
del Mar/Philharmonia Orchestra.

A Tribute [for Vaughan Williams on his 70th birthday], op. 56 / CHANDOS
Schönzeler/Bournemouth Sinfonietta.

NEIDHART VON RÜNTAL   dd. c

Medieval. A Medieval German composer of songs in the Minnesinger tradition. –ED

○ **Fourteen Songs for Various Groups / CHRISTOPHORUS**
Augsburg Ensemble for Early Music. Probably the most important and popular German Minnesinger. Verses intoned in Sprechgesang-style and featuring "songs that are virtuoso and expressive, funny, boastful, erotic, obscene, brutal, complaining, nagging, imploring — most of them with very catchy melodies that, after numerous repetitions of numerous verses, creep into the ear and become haunting tunes." –PM

JOHN RUTTER   ♭1945

20th century. An important contemporary English composer and conductor whose affinity for choral music has stemmed from his study and editorial collaborations with David Willcocks. His choral compositions are numerous and accessible. –MKS

○ **Gloria / COLLEGIUM**
Rutter/Cambridge Singers, Philip Jones Brass Ensemble.

○ **Requiem / COLLEGIUM**
Ashton, Deam, Rutter/The Cambridge Singers & City of London Sinfonia.

CAMILLE SAINT-SAËNS   1835-1921

Romantic. A French composer and melodist of the Liszt school. Although Saint-Saëns is appreciated for the mix of Parisian wit and academic seriousness found in *Carnival of the Animals* and the tone painting in his famous *Danse Macabre,* his work is more beautifully developed in his *Concerto for Piano no. 4, Symphony no. 3 in c,* and *Concerto for*

Violin no. 3 in b, which contain harmonically advanced writing (à la César Franck) and some of his most beautiful and fluid melody lines. —BGT

☆ **Carnival of the Animals, for 2 Pianos & Orchestra / ADDA**
Devoyon, Rouvier (pianos), Pettitgirard/Orchestre Symphonique Français. Quirky, rambunctious, and very French in sprit. —PM

Carnival of the Animals, for 2 Pianos & Orchestra / VIRGIN
Nel, Snell (pianos), Stamp/Academy of London.

Carnival of the Animals, for 2 Pianos & Orchestra / PHILIPS
V. and P. Jennings (pianos), Previn/Pittsburgh SO.

Carnival of the Animals, for 2 Pianos & Orchestra / BIG BEN
Frantz, Eschenbach (pianos), Eschenbach/NDRSO.

○ **Concertos for Piano nos. 2 & 4; La Muse et la Poète, for Violin, Cello & Orchestra / ADDA**
Devoyon (piano), Rouger (violin), Bantigny (cello). Another sleeper! A little brittle in the piano sound, but I like its French style and its sense of "tragedy" and nostalgia. The pieces don't sound so superficial as usual. —PM

○ **Concertos (5) for Piano & Orchestra / LONDON**
Roge, Dutoit/Royal Philharmonic.

○ **Concerto for Piano & Orchestra no. 4 in c, op. 44 / ADDA**
Devoyon, Pettigard/Orchestre Symphonique Français.

○ **Concerto for Violin & Orchestra no. 3 in b, op. 61 / PHILIPS**
van Keulen (violin), Colin Davis/London SO. Man, this would be a tough choice, since I like this soloist and conductor about as much as in the version below. Van Keulen plays with more sweetness and tenderness; Shaham more "romantically" and with power. —PM

Concerto for Violin & Orchestra no. 3 in b, op. 61 / DGG
Shaham, Sinopoli/NYPO.

○ **Fantasie for Violin & Harp, op. 124 / AUVIDIS VALOIS**
Poulet (violin), Moretti (harp). I'm not certain this is "better" than the competition, but it is more vulnerable and more French-sounding, two worthwhile characteristics in this music. —PM

○ **Quartet for Piano, Violin, Viola & Cello in B-flat, op. 41 / AVVIDIS VALOIS**
R. Pasquier (violin), B. Pasquier (viola), Pidoux (cello), Sermet (piano). Saint-Saëns is a highly underrated composer, as this formidable piano quartet (beautifully, passionately, and idiomatically played by these veteran French string players and a fine unknown piano player) will readily attest. This is a real find. —PM

○ **Samson et Dalila / PHILIPS**
Baltsa, Carrerras, et al., Davis/Bavarian RSO & Chorus.

○ **Sonata for Clarinet & Piano, op. 167 / CALIG**
Brunner (clarinet), Höhenrieder (piano). Happy and joyous performance; light and elegant. —PM

○ **Sonata for Violin & Piano no. 1 in d, op. 75 / PHILIPS**
Zukerman (violin), Neikrug (piano). Elegant, beautiful reading of this virtuoso semi-fluff. —PM

Sonata for Violin & Piano no. 1 in d, op. 75 / DGG
Shaham (violin), Oppitz (piano). A more hot-blooded performance than Zukerman's, but it misses some of the elegance and delicacy. —PM

○ **Suite for Cello & Piano, op. 16 / AVVIDIS VALOIS**
Henkel (cello), Sermet (piano). Interesting early Saint-Saëns and a welcome addition to the cello repertoire on CD. —PM

○ **Symphonies nos. 1 & 2 / ERATO**
Pretre/Vienna SO. Sprightly: This is a worthy successor to Martinon. —PM

○ **Symphony no. 3 in c, op. 48, "Organ Symphony" / DGG**
Preston (organ), Levine/Berlin PO. It's hard not to like the

large-scale approach used here, with playing and recording as good as this. —PM

Symphony no. 3 in c, op. 48, "Organ Symphony" / ERATO
Alain, Pretre/Vienna SO.

Symphony no. 3 in c, op. 48, "Organ Symphony" / IMP
Chorzempa (organ), Maag/Bern SO. Maag presents a fresh and dancing performance of this score, which is pleasingly lighter in weight than usual. —PM

GIOVANNI BATTISTA SAMMARTINI   1701-1775

Classical. An Italian composer of orchestral, chamber, and vocal music who helped establish the classical style, especially through his symphonies and concertos. Sammartini made extensive use of thematic development and contributed to the evolution of the sonata form. —MKS

○ **Quintet in G; Sinfonias in D & G / HARMONIA MUNDI**
Banchini/Ensemble 415.

ALESSANDRO SCARLATTI   1660-1725

Baroque, vocal. An Italian composer of opera, sacred and secular vocal music, and some instrumental works. Scarlatti's operas, oratorios, and cantatas made him one of the foremost Neopolitan composers of the day. —MKS

○ **Dixit Dominus / DGG**
Pinnock/English Concert & Choir.

○ **Variations on *La Folia* & 2 Cantatas / HYPERION**
Dawson (soprano)/Purcell Quartet.

DOMENICO SCARLATTI   1685-1757

Baroque. The sixth son of composer Alessandro Scarlatti. His 555 known harpsichord sonatas, more than half of which were written during the final six years of his life, show him to be the most original innovator of harmony in the 18th century. Some, with their wonderful Italian, Portuguese, and Spanish dance rhythms, combined with lively, surprising harmonic turns, make for very uplifting listening; others are more lyrically sombre and quiet in mood. Scarlatti wrote in many other genres (operas, cantatas, church music). *Salve Regina* (1757), his last work, is beautiful. —BGT

☆ **Sonatas for Keyboard, "Essercizi," K. 1-30 / NUOVA ERA**
Alvini (harpsichord).

Sonatas for Keyboard (selections) / AMON RA
Cole (harpsichord). Aggressive but elegant, with extremely rich, full sound and startling detail. —PM

Sonatas for Keyboard (selections) / CLAVES
Dutscheler (harpsichord).

Sonatas for Keyboard (selections) / PMG
Tomsic (piano). Probably the best single piano CD of Scarlatti. Tomsic may not be so flamboyant as some, but she sure gives you Scarlatti and not Tomsic. —PM

Sonatas for Keyboard (selections) / FONE
Husson (piano). Husson is tasteful and elegant, and with fleet fingers. —PM

Sonatas for Keyboard (selections) / WILD BOAR
Parmentier (harpsichord). An outstanding sense of phrasing and rubato. —PM

Sonatas for Keyboard (selections) / KOCH-SCHWANN
Thornburgh (harpsichord).

ALFRED SCHNITTKE   b 1934

20th century. One of the boldest musical innovators in modern Russia, Schnittke has written five symphonies, chamber music, concertos, and vocal and piano music. —MKS

○ **Canon in Memoriam Igor Stravinsky, for String Quartet / DGG**
Hagen Quartet.

○ **Concerto for Oboe, Harp & String Orchestra / BIS**

Jahren, Lier, Markiz/Stockholm CO.
○ **Concerto for Viola & Orchestra / BIS**
Imai, Markiz/Malmo SO.
○ **Concerto for Violin & Chamber Orchestra no. 3 / BIS**
Krysa, Klas/Malmo SO.
○ **Concerto for Violin & Chamber Orchestra no. 4 / BIS**
Krysa, Klas/Malmo SO.
○ **Concerto Grosso for 2 Violins, Harpsichord, Piano & Strings no. 1 / BIS**
Bergqvist, Swedrup (violins), Pontinen (piano), Markiz/Stockholm CO.
Concerto Grosso for 2 Violins, Harpsichord, Piano & Strings no. 1 / DGG
Kremer, Grindenko (violins), Smirnov (piano, harpsichord), Schiff/Chamber Orchestra of Europe.
○ **Concerto Grosso for Violin, Cello & Orchestra no. 2 / BIS**
Thedeen, et al./Danish National RSO.
○ **Faust Cantata, for Contralto, Countertenor, Tenor, Bass, Orchestra & Chorus / BIS**
Blom, Bellini, Devos, Cold, DePreist/Malmo SO & Chorus.
○ **In Memoriam (orchestral version of piano quintet) / BIS**
Markiz/Malmo SO.
○ **Klingende Buchstaben, for Solo Cello / BIS**
Thedeen.
○ **Passacaglia; Ritualein Sommernachtstraum für Orchestra / BIS**
Segerstam/Malmo SO.
○ **Pianissimo, for Large Orchestra / BIS**
Järvi/Gothenburg SO.
○ **Quasi una Sonata; Moz-Art à la Haydn / DGG**
Kremer (violin), Schiff/Chamber Orchestra of Europe.
○ **Quintet for Piano & String Quartet; Canon in Memoriam Igor Stravinsky / ET CETERA**
Oldenburg/Mondrian String Quartet.
○ **Requiem for 3 Sopranos, Contralto, Tenor, Chorus & Chamber Orchestra / BIS**
Salomonsson, Sjoberg, Lindholm, Eker, Hogman, Parkman/Stockholm Sinfonietta & Uppsala Academic Chamber Choir.
○ **String Quartets nos. 1-3 / BIS**
Tale Quartet.
○ **Symphony no. 3 / BIS**
Klas/Stockholm.
○ **Symphony no. 4 / BIS**
Parkman, Bellini, Kamu/Stockholm Sinfonietta & Uppsala Academic Chamber Choir.
○ **Symphony no. 5 (Concerto Grosso no. 4) / BIS**
Järvi/Gothenburg SO.

JOHANN SCHOBERT   1735-1767

Classical. An Austrian composer whose style is highly reminiscent of the Mannheim school, though he never actually worked there. Mozart, who was significantly influenced by Schobert, incorporated movements of this composer's scores into his sonatas and piano concertos. –MKS
○ **Concerto for Piano & Orchestra in G / EDITO CLASSICA**
Selheim/Collegium Aureum.

OTHMAR SCHOECK   1886-1957

Classical. One of the most significant Swiss composers of his era, whose greatest achievements were in opera, choral music, and songs, of which he wrote more than 400. Schoeck also wrote instrumental music and was a noted accompanist and conductor. –MKS
○ **Concerto for Cello & String Orchestra, op. 61 / CLAVES**
Goritzki/German Chamber Academy of Neuss.

○ **Concerto for Violin & Orchestra in B-flat, op. 21 / NOVALIS**
Hölscher, Griffiths/English CO.
○ **Lebendig Begraben (song cycle), for Baritone & Orchestra / CLAVES**
Fischer-Dieskau, Rieger/Berlin RSO.
○ **Serenade for Orchestra, op. 1 / NOVALIS**
Griffiths/English CO.
○ **Sommernacht, for String Orchestra / CLAVES**
Goritzki/German Chamber Academy of Neuss.
○ **Das stille Leuchten (song cycle), for Baritone & Piano / CLAVES**
Fischer-Dieskau, Holl.
○ **Suite for Orchestra in A-flat, op. 59 / NOVALIS**
Griffiths/English CO.
○ **Unter Sternen (song cycle), op. 55 / CLAVES**
Fischer-Dieskau, Holl.

ARNOLD SCHOENBERG   1874-1951

20th century, serial, atonal. Schoenberg, who taught Webern and Berg, is the well-known inventor of the 12-tone system (Josef Hauer independently invented one on separate principles about the same time). Schoenberg was, amazingly, a self-taught musician, whose *Harmonienlehre* ("Theory of Harmony") is still studied for the breadth of its understanding of the deepest meaning of structure in music. For all its theoretical underpinning, Schoenberg's music is most often dramatic in a romantic way, at the same time leaping to the horizons of pitch in its melodies and, through fragmentation and "Klangfarbenmelodie" (sound-color-melody), creating an angular, "modern" sound in its rhythm and unique orchestration.

Schoenberg's earlier and more romantic scores are *Verklärte Nacht* ("Transfigured Night") for string sextet or orchestra; *Pelleas und Melisande* (no relation to Debussy's work); and *Gurre-lieder* ("The Anticipation"), which is Mahleresque in texture; all are conceived on a sweeping scale of interior emotion. The early *Chamber Symphony* combines this style with the angular style that would appear in Schoenberg's violin and piano concertos of the 30s.

The first of Schoenberg's works in which tonality is completely absent is the song "Du lehnst wider eine Silberweide" ("You Lean against a White Willow") from *The Book of the Hanging Gardens* (1907). Following this came the first 12-tone pieces, most notably the brilliant *Five Pieces for Orchestra, op. 16* (1909), with its entirely new approach to orchestration (the suspended chords and color-melody of "Summer Morning by a Lake"); the *Piano Music, opp. 11 & 19*; and *Pierrot Lunaire*, all of which completely changed the sound of symphonic, chamber, and piano music. The later expressionistic pieces followed — *Variations for Orchestra, Quartets for Strings nos. 3-5, Von Heute auf Morgen* ("From Today until Tomorrow"), and *Die glückliche Hand* ("The Fortunate Hand"). The culmination of these efforts was his masterpiece, the opera *Moses und Aaron,* which shares with the early work *Friede auf Erden* ("Peace on Earth") the idea of music being a vehicle for the expression of philosophy. His pleas for humanity during and following the horrors of WWII are contained in *A Survivor from Warsaw* and the *Ode to Napoleon Bonaparte.* –BGT

☆ **Chamber Symphony in E, op. 9 / DGG**
Sinopoli/Berlin PO. This selection is sensual but plenty modern-sounding. –PM
Chamber Symphony in E, op. 9 / DGG
Orpheus CO. Less romantic than Sinopoli and without his subtlety, but a very fine performance: I can see people preferring its drier approach. –PM
○ **Chamber Symphony no. 2, op. 38 / DGG**
Orpheus CO.
○ **Erwartung, for Soprano & Orchestra, op. 17 / LONDON**

Silja, von Dohnányi/Vienna Philharmonic.

○ **Fantasy for Violin & Piano, op. 47 / SIMAX**
Veselka (violin), Dratvova (piano). They have a way with this music: Could being a husband-and-wife team have something to do with it? –PM

○ **Five Pieces for Orchestra, op. 16 / DGG**
Levine/Berlin PO. Overly romanticized but completely compelling. Some of the best sound ever on CD. –PM

○ **Gurre-Lieder / PHILIPS**
Norman, Troyanos, McCracken, Klemperer, Ozawa/Boston SO & Tanglewood Chorus.

○ **Moses und Aron / LONDON**
Bonney, Zakai, Langridge, Mazura, Haugland, Solti/Chicago SO & Chorus.

○ **Pelleas und Melisande (symphonic poem), op. 5 / DGG**
Karajan/Berlin PO. Performances of this complex piece come and go, but Karajan's remains supreme. –PM

○ **Piano Music, opp. 11, 19, 23, 25, 33a, 33b / DGG**
Pollini (piano). Not likely to be touched any time in this century or in my lifetime. –PM

○ **Pierrot Lunaire, op. 21 (1912) / CAPRICE**
Hoglind (mezzo); Risberg (sonanza). I don't know about the "best," but this is probably the most musical, least gimmicky performance in the catalog. It is not too romanticized, and it has the best sound. –PM

○ **Quartets (5) for Strings / DGG**
LaSalle Quartet.

○ **Quintet for Flute, Oboe, Clarinet, Horn & Bassoon, op. 26 / ARS VIVENDI**
Danzi Quintet.

○ **Trio for Strings, op. 45 / CALIG**
Vienna String Trio.

Trio for Strings, op. 45 / DGG
Members of the LaSalle Quartet.

○ **Variations for Orchestra, op. 31 / DGG**
Karajan/Berlin PO. Because of sound quality and orchestra, I'll have to give the nod to Karajan, but Rosbaud's is the more uncompromising, honest, and intellectual performance. –PM

Variations for Orchestra, op. 31 / MUSIC & ARTS
Rosbaud/Southwest German RSO.

☆ **Verklärte Nacht, for Orchestra, op. 4 / LONDON**
Chailly/Berlin RSO. A wrenching, emotionally distraught performance that causes me a lot of turmoil. –PM

Verklärte Nacht, for Orchestra, op. 4 / DGG
Karajan/Berlin PO. This recording, part of a box of Karajan goodies from the Second Viennese school, should be approached with caution and sampled first, since the other performances included are big, beefy, and fatty, though nonetheless extraordinarily beautiful and sensual. –PM

Verklärte Nacht, for Orchestra, op. 4 / DGG
Orpheus CO. Very well played, but lacks the sense of direction of Chailly and Karajan. –PM

Verklärte Nacht, for Orchestra, op. 4 / DGG
LaSalle Quartet. The best sextet version by far: very committed. –PM

FRANZ SCHUBERT
1797-1828

Romantic. A short-lived, astonishingly prolific German composer of songs, symphonies, piano and chamber music who is perhaps the true link in the tradition from Beethoven and Mozart to Liszt and Wagner. Schubert's splendid sense of melody and drama testify to the developing romantic ideals in his music; his harmonic palette is essentially that of Beethoven. *Winterreise*, completed on his deathbed, is regarded as his best song cycle. The quartets, octets, and quintets incorporate many elements of his songwriting styles (and even some of the music, as in his *Quartet in d*: the variations movement on "Der Tod und das Mädchen" ("Death

and the Maiden"). The piano music (sonatas, impromptus) and especially the symphonies show Beethoven's influence, the melodic line becoming longer, perhaps more graceful, in the romantic style. –BGT

○ **Allegretto for Piano in c, D. 915 / DGG**
Pollini.

○ **Deutsche Messe, D. 872 / ANGEL**
Sawallisch/Bavarian RSO & Chorus.

○ **Fierrabras (3-act romantic opera), D. 796 / DGG**
Mattila, Studer, Gambil, Hampson, Holl, Polgar, Abbado/Chamber Orchestra of Europe, Arnold Schoenberg Choir. The only really good performance of any Schubert opera on CD. –PM

○ **Der Hirt auf dem Felsen, for Soprano, Clarinet & Piano, D. 965 / ORFEO**
Price, Schoneberger, Sawallisch. Price is in gorgeous voice, and I like Sawallisch's simple accompaniments. –PM

Der Hirt auf dem Felsen, for Soprano, Clarinet & Piano, D. 965 / DHM
Ameling (soprano), Demus (fortepiano), Deinzer (clarinet). This is charming, with the young Ameling and original instruments. –PM

○ **Impromptus (8) for Piano, D. 899 & 935 / DGG**
Zimerman. A bit mannered and precious — but in case you hadn't noticed, there's not much to choose from out there these days. Piano music just isn't what it used to be. –PM

☆ **Impromptus (8) for Piano nos. 2 & 3, op. 90 / DENON**
Ranki.

☆ **Impromptus (8) for Piano opp. 90, 142 / PHILIPS**
Brendel.

○ **Mass for SATB, Chorus, Orchestra & Organ no. 4 in C / ANGEL**
Donath, Fassbaender, Araiza, Fischer-Dieskau, Sawallisch/Bavarian RSO & Chorus.

○ **Mass for Soprano, Tenor, Chorus & Strings no. 2 in G / ANGEL**
Popp, Dallapozza, Fischer-Dieskau, Sawallisch/Bavarian RSO & Chorus.

○ **Mass no. 5 in A-flat, D. 678 / ANGEL**
Popp, Fassbaender, Dallapozza, Fischer-Dieskau, Sawallisch/Bavarian RSO & Chorus.

○ **Mass no. 6 in E-flat, D. 950 / DGG**
Mattila, Lipovsek, Hadley, Holl, Abbado/Vienna PO, State Opera Chorus.

Mass no. 6 in E-flat, D. 950 / ANGEL
Donath, Fassbaender, Araiza, Fischer-Dieskau, Sawallisch/Bavarian RSO & Chorus.

○ **Moments Musicaux (6) for Piano, D. 780 / DGG**
Pires.

☆ **Octet for Strings & Wind in F, D. 803 / ANGEL**
Hausmusik. The playing is very sensitive and lyrical. I find this group's sense of reticence captivating. –PM

Octet for Strings & Wind in F, D. 803 / OISEAU-LYRE
Academy of Ancient Music Chamber Ensemble. The most together of all the performances. –PM

Octet for Strings & Wind in F, D. 803 / VIRGIN
Atlantis Ensemble. A more forceful and dramatic approach, with many fine details, but it doesn't convey the overall picture so well as Hausmusik or Hogwood. –PM

Octet for Strings & Wind in F, D. 803 / DGG
Kremer, van Keulen, Zimerman, Geringas, Posch, Brunner, Vlatkovic, Thunemann. Terrific individually, though not so good collectively; but if you must have modern instruments, this is the best available. –PM

○ **Quartet for Strings no. 9 in g, D. 173 / ORFEO**
Brandis Quartet.

○ **Quartet for Strings no. 10 in E-flat, D. 87 / DGG**
Hagen Quartet. Fresh and natural. –PM

Quartet for Strings no. 10 in E-flat, D. 87 / ORFEO
Brandis Quartet. A heavier, more vibrato-laden approach than Hagen's. –PM

○ **Quartet for Strings no. 12 in c, D. 703 / DGG**
Hagen Quartet.

○ **Quartets for Strings nos. 12-15 / ODYSSEY**
Juilliard String Quartet.

○ **Quartet for Strings no. 13 in a, D. 804 / DGG**
Hagen Quartet.

Quartet for Strings no. 13 in a, D. 804 / COLLINS CLASSICS
Vanbrugh String Quartet.

○ **Quartet for Strings no. 14 in d, D. 810 / ANGEL**
Busch Quartet. One of the greatest string-quartet recordings ever made. –PM

Quartet for Strings no. 14 in d, D. 810 / PHILIPS
Orlando Quartet.

Quartet for Strings no. 14 in d, D. 810 / CAMERATA
Vienna String Quartet.

Quartet for Strings no. 14 in d, D. 810 / LONDON
Vienna Philharmonic String Quartet.

○ **Quartet for Strings no. 15 in G, D. 887 / ANGEL**
Busch Quartet.

Quartet for Strings no. 15 in G, D. 887 / GM RECORDINGS
Franz Schubert Quartet.

☆ **Quintet for 2 Violins & Cellos in C, D. 956 / ANGEL**
Schiff/Berg Quartet. Tough competition in this, one of the greatest pieces ever written. There has never been a completely standout performance. –PM

Quintet for 2 Violins & Cellos in C, D. 956 / INTERCORD
Stuttgart Soloists.

Quintet for 2 Violins & Cellos in C, D. 956 / CBS
Greenhouse/Juilliard String Quartet.

☆ **Quintet for Piano & Strings in A, D. 667, "Trout Quartet" ANGEL**
Leonskaja/Berg Quartet. All around, I like this combination of heft and sensitivity. –PM

Quintet for Piano & Strings in A, D. 667, "Trout Quartet" ONDINE
Gothoni/Munich String Trio. A bit severe, but I like its straightforward approach. –PM

Quintet for Piano & Strings in A, D. 667, "Trout Quartet" LONDON
Schiff/Hagen Quartet. Gemuetlich in a more modern way. –PM

Quintet for Piano & Strings in A, D. 667, "Trout Quartet" LONDON
Curzon/Vienna Octet members. *Gemütlich* in a more old-fashioned way. –PM

Rosamunde (incidental music), D. 797 (complete) / PHILIPS
Ameling (soprano), Masur/Leipzig Gewandhaus Orchestra & Radio Chorus. This has all the longing and nostalgia, and the singing is radiant. –PM

Rosamunde (incidental music), D. 797 (excerpts) / PHILIPS
Davis/Boston SO.

Rosamunde (incidental music), D. 797 (complete) / DGG
Abbado, et al./Chamber Orchestra of Europe, et al. Could have been a bit more tender and less objective, but it's nice to have a chamber-scale performance in the catalog. –PM

Rosamunde: Overture, Ballet Music no. 2; Entr'acte no. 3 / KOCH-SCHWANN
Furtwängler/Berlin PO. Unfortunatly Furtwängler's later, even better performance is not available at the moment; but to get some good idea of the tenderness and ethereal quality he finds in this haunting music, this early performance will have to do. –PM

○ **Scherzi (2) for Piano, D. 593 / DGG**
Pires.

☆ **Die schöne Müllerin (song cycle) / DGG**
Fischer-Dieskau, Moore.

Die schöne Müllerin (song cycle) / ONDINE
Hynninen, Gothoni. A heavier, darker, deeper voice, more suited to tragic situations. –PM

○ **Schwanengesang, D. 957 / PHILIPS**
Fischer-Dieskau, Brendel. Because of Brendel's extra authority and beauty of tone and Dieskau's deeply communicative singing, I prefer this latest version, in digital sound. –PM

Schwanengesang, D. 957 / DGG
Fischer-Dieskau, Moore.

Schwanengesang, D. 957 / ANGEL
Fischer-Dieskau, Moore.

○ **Sonata for Arpeggione & Piano in a, D. 821 / LONDON**
Rostropovich (cello), Britten (piano). Way too romanticized for this music, but I love it anyway. –PM

○ **Sonata for Piano in a, D. 537 / DGG**
Michelangeli.

Sonata for Piano in a, D. 537 / BRIDGE
Crow (piano). A labor of love. –PM

Sonata for Piano in a, D. 537 / DGG
Pires.

Sonata for Piano in a, D. 537 / AMON RA
Shelley (fortepiano).

○ **Sonata for Piano in e, D. 566 / MUSIC & ARTS**
Richter.

○ **Sonata for Piano in A, D. 574 / ONDINE**
Chumachenco.

○ **Sonata for Piano in B, D. 575 / MUSIC & ARTS**
Richter.

○ **Sonata for Piano in C, D. 840, "Unfinished" / PHILIPS**
Richter (piano). Uncommonly slow and thoughtful, maybe a bit too much so. But playing like this simply does not exist except from Richter. –PM

○ **Sonata for Piano in a, D. 845 / DGG**
Pollini.

○ **Sonata for Piano in G, D. 894 / AMON RA**
Shelley.

○ **Sonata for Piano in c, D. 958 (posthumous) / DGG**
Pollini.

○ **Sonata for Piano in A, D. 959 (posthumous) / BRIDGE**
Crow (piano). Likewise a labor of love. –PM

Sonata for Piano in A, D. 959 (posthumous) / DGG
Pollini (piano). Pollini's technique is formidable and he projects the architecture better than anyone, but he's also a bit too dry and aloof for me. –PM

☆ **Sonata for Piano in B-flat, D. 960 (posthumous) / MUSIC & ARTS**
Richter (piano). The starkest, deepest, most profound reading I have ever heard of Schubert's most resigned sonata. Slow tempos and pirate sound will unfortunately militate against purchase for most, but they will be missing one of the great recorded experiences. –PM

Sonata for Piano in B-flat, D. 960 (posthumous) / HYPERION
Bishop-Kovacevich.

Sonata for Piano in B-flat, D. 960 (posthumous) / PHILIPS
Brendel.

Sonata for Piano in B-flat, D. 960 (posthumous) / DENON
Ranki.

○ **Sonatinas (3) for Violin & Piano, D. 384, 385, 408 (complete) / ONDINE**
Chumachenco, Gothoni. You don't need a ton of vibrato to do justice to these deceptively "naive" and "simple" pieces. What

you do need is simplicity, tenderness, grace, and concentration, and Chumacheno and Gothoni provide these qualities in spades. –PM

○ **Songs (selections) / PHILIPS**
Ameling (soprano), Baldwin (piano).
Songs (selections) / PHILIPS
Ameling (soprano), Jansen (piano).
Songs (selections) / PHILIPS
Fischer-Dieskau (baritone), Brendel (piano).
Songs (selections) / ORFEO
Price (soprano), Sawallisch (piano).

○ **Symphony no. 1 in D, D. 82 / NIMBUS**
Goodman/The Hanover Band.

○ **Symphony no. 2 in B-flat, D. 125 / EBS**
Jöres/Westdeutsche Sinfonia.

○ **Symphony no. 3 in D, D. 200 / DGG**
Kleiber/Vienna PO.
Symphony no. 3 in D, D. 200 / HUNGARATON
Fischer/Budapest Festival Orchestra. Kleiber is nonpareil, but Fischer gives close chase. –PM

○ **Symphony no. 4 in c, D. 417, "Tragic" / NIMBUS**
Goodman/The Hanover Band.

○ **Symphony no. 5 in B-flat, D. 485 / PHILIPS**
Brüggen/Orchestra of the 18th Century. A probing original-instrument performance. –PM
Symphony no. 5 in B-flat, D. 485 / HUNGARATON
Fischer/Budapest Festival Orchestra.
Symphony no. 5 in B-flat, D. 485 / EBS
Jöres. Very straightforward and architectural. Misses some of the sensualness of the piece, but at least it is not bloated like many other versions. –PM

☆ **Symphony no. 8 in b, D. 759, "Unfinished" / DGG**
Sinopoli/Philharmonia Orchestra. There's a combination of tension and beauty here, unmatched in any rival. –PM
Symphony no. 8 in b, D. 759, "Unfinished" / DGG
Kleiber/Vienna PO. Kleiber had the best *Eighth* in the stereo age, but Sinopoli's is even "better" in the digital. Kleiber is lean and intense, Sinopoli more relaxed and meltingly beautiful. Kleiber is pure tragedy; Sinopoli enlightened psychology. Both are must recordings. –PM
Symphony no. 8 in b, D. 759, "Unfinished" / HUNGARATON
Fischer/Budapest Festival Orchestra.
Symphony no. 8 in b, D. 759, "Unfinished" / PHILIPS
Davis/Boston SO.

☆ **Symphony no. 9 in C, D. 944, "The Great" (1953) / DGG**
Furtwängler/Berlin PO. The classic studio *Ninth*; less radical and a safer recommendation than either the 1953 Hunt or the 1942. All the intensity is there, with better control of the tempos. –PM
Symphony no. 9 in C, D. 944, "The Great" / VIRGIN
Mackerras/Orchestra of the Age of Enlightenment. This has most of the virtuosity and polish of a modern symphony orchestra and is one of the finest original-instrument performances of anything ever made. A lot of orchestral texture is clarified here, and relationships are brought home in a new and different way. Mackerras should conduct with period instruments more often. –PM
Symphony no. 9 in C, D. 944, "The Great" / LONDON
Krips/London SO. Long my favorite stereo performance and still one of the best. –PM
Symphony no. 9 in C, D. 944, "The Great" / LODIA
Paita/Royal PO. I have a soft spot in my heart for this emotional and intense conductor, who refuses to join the establishment. This is a powerful and dramatic performance, and many details are cast in a new and interesting light. –PM

○ **Tantum Ergo in E-flat, D. 962 / ANGEL**

Popp, Fassbaender, Dallapozza, Fischer-Dieskau, Sawallisch/ Bavarian RSO & Chorus.

○ **Trio for Piano, Violin & Cello no. 1 in B-flat, D. 898 / PHILIPS**
Beaux Arts Trio.

○ **Trio for Piano, Violin & Cello no. 2 in E-flat, D. 929 / PHILIPS**
Beaux Arts Trio.

○ **Wanderer Fantasie for Piano, D. 760 / DGG**
Pollini (piano). Richter has the best recording ever of the *Wanderer Fantasie*, but his is not on CD. Pollini's is much more straightforward and uptight but is probably the best of those available on CD. –PM
Wanderer Fantasie for Piano, D. 760 / DGG
Kissin (piano). A bit blustery and "immature" at times, but some gorgeous and dramatic playing by this (then) 19-year-old phenomenon. Good, up-to-date digital sound. –PM
Wanderer Fantasie for Piano, D. 760 / PHILIPS
Brendel.

☆ **Winterreise (song cycle) / PHILIPS**
Schreier, Richter. Very slow and emotionally overwrought and draining. This is the classic tenor performance and one of the greatest lieder recordings ever made. –PM
Winterreise (song cycle) / PHILIPS
Fischer-Dieskau, Brendel. Possibly not so well-sung as his earlier five or so versions, this one, however, is bleaker, darker, and deeper, with the extra-added advantage of Brendel and better sound than the others. –PM
Winterreise (song cycle) / ONDINE
Hynninen (baritone), Gothoni (piano). Heavy and intense, with Hynninen using a bit too much vibrato for my taste, but Gothoni contributes a straightforward and concentrated reading of the piano part. –PM
Winterreise (song cycle) / GLOBE
Reinemann, Jansen.

ERWIN SCHULHOFF   1894-1942

Modern. A Czech pianist and composer (and a student of Reger) who was influenced by jazz, dadaism, and the quarter-tone music of Hába. Schulhoff died in a concentration camp. –ED

○ **Sextet for Strings / EMI**
Vienna String Sextet. This is an impressively moving piece in the style of Schoenberg and Berg, the equal of anything written at the time (the first years of this century). Outstanding sound and performance on this import. –PM

WILLIAM SCHUMAN   b1910

20th century. An American composer of vocal music, chamber works, orchestral and film music, as well as several ballets and operas. Schuman's cosmopolitan style of composition shows a command of contemporary techniques within a largely tonal framework. Musical allusions to America occasionally appear, as in the *Triptych*. –MKS

○ **American Festival Overture / DGG**
Bernstein/LAPO.

○ **Concerto for Violin & Orchestra / DGG**
Zukofsky, Thomas/Boston SO.

○ **New England Triptych / MERCURY**
Hanson/Eastman-Rochester Orchestra.

○ **Symphony no. 3 / DGG**
Bernstein/NYPO.

CLARA SCHUMANN   1819-1896

Romantic. Clara Schumann, wife of Robert, was a child prodigy who, after her husband's death, became one of the most famous performers and teachers in the 19th century. Her compositions are extremely well crafted and show great individuality, as well as the influence of her husband Robert and friend Johannes Brahms. –MKS

○ **Complete Piano Music / PARTRIDGE**
De Beenhouwer.
○ **Trio for Violin, Cello & Piano in g, op. 17 / BEYER**
Clara Wieck Trio.
Trio for Violin, Cello & Piano in g, op. 17 / HYPERION
Dartington Trio.

ROBERT SCHUMANN   1810-1856

Romantic. A German composer of romantic music in many
forms, including piano pieces, orchestral music, and lieder.
Among his notable works are the *Davisbündlertänze* (1837),
Dichterliebe (1840), and the *Quintet in E-flat for Piano &
Strings.* From his early years, Schumann spoke of the piano as
a diary for his thoughts and feelings. Later, while establishing
the fundamentals for the journalistic criticism of music in his
Neue Zeitschrift für Musik ("New Journal for Music"), he
seems to have continued that relationship with all the forms
in which he composed. Many of his songs, song cycles, and
piano works are collections of musical characterizations,
which, like the *Kinderszenen* ("Scenes from Childhood") and
Waldszenen ("Scenes from the Woods"), are often humorous.
In his more dramatic works, the meaning is often personal
and elusive, with a hidden "program," although often
passionately beautiful. Schumann's symphonies, neglected for
a long time, are now appreciated for the many innovative
qualities of their melody and form. –BGT
○ **Arabeske for Piano, op. 18 / ANGEL**
Egorov. Warm and soulful. –PM
Arabeske for Piano, op. 18 / DGG
Pollini. Dry and elegant. –PM
Arabeske for Piano, op. 18 / DGG
Bunin. More impetuous. –PM
Arabeske for Piano, op. 18 / LONDON
Ashkenazy. Simple and affecting. –PM
○ **Blumenstück for Piano in D-flat, op. 19 / LONDON**
Ashkenazy.
○ **Bunte Blätter, for Piano, op. 99 / AS DISC**
Richter. It's a pirate, but the sound is good, and the tenderness
and simplicity of his playing is extraordinary. –PM
Bunte Blätter, for Piano, op. 99 / ANGEL
Egorov. More warmhearted than Richter, but without the
same sort of inwardness and intimacy. –PM
☆ **Carnaval, for Piano, op. 9 / ANGEL**
Egorov.
Carnaval, for Piano, op. 9 / LONDON
Ashkenazy.
○ **Concerto for Cello & Orchestra in a, op. 129 / DGG**
De Machula (cello), Furtwängler/Berlin PO. Furtwängler
brings the orchestral part alive in a way no other conductor
does. –PM
Concerto for Cello & Orchestra in a, op. 129 / LONDON
Harrell, Marriner/Cleveland Orchestra.
Concerto for Cello & Orchestra in a, op. 129 / MERCURY
Starker, Skrowaczewski/London SO.
☆ **Concerto for Piano & Orchestra in a, op. 54 / ODYSSEY**
Lipatti, Karajan/Philharmonia Orchestra. Nowadays pianists,
conductors, and orchestras play the concerto much too
objectively and perfunctorily, which is why you won't see
any modern performances on my list. In any case, Lipatti's
elegant and aristocratic pianism is completely timeless, and
this is as good as any recording ever made of one of my
favorite pieces. –PM
Concerto for Piano & Orchestra in a, op. 54 / DGG
Richter, Rowicki/Warsaw National PO.
Concerto for Piano & Orchestra in a, op. 54 / DGG
Gieseking, Furtwängler/Berlin PO.
Concerto for Piano & Orchestra in a, op. 54 / ARKADIA
Gieseking, Wand/Cologne RSO.

○ **Davidsbündlertänze for Piano, op. 6 / KOCH-SCHWANN**
Riche. Very thoughtful. –PM
Davidsbündlertänze for Piano, op. 6 / LONDON
Ashkenazy.
☆ **Dichterliebe, op. 48 / PHILIPS**
Fischer-Dieskau, Brendel. Again Brendel's playing is
captivating and Dieskau's singing rich and subtle. You simply
hang onto every breath. –PM
Dichterliebe, op. 48 / PHILIPS
Schreier, Sawallisch. Live performance with some slips, but
easily my favorite tenor performance. –PM
Dichterliebe, op. 48 / DGG
Fischer-Dieskau, Eschenbach.
Dichterliebe, op. 48 / HUNGARATON
Esswood, McGegan. New insights from this "authentic"
version for alto and fortepiano. –PM
☆ **Fantasia for Piano in C, op. 17 / GLOBE**
Egorov. Spontaneous and intense, with plenty of foward
motion. –PM
Fantasia for Piano in C, op. 17 / VANGUARD CLASSICS
Brendel. If Richter's performance on Angel were around,
it would sweep the board clean. It has a sweep and grandeur
lacking in all the others, but every detail is firmly in place.
It will be back out some day, and that's why I mention it
here. –PM
Fantasia for Piano in C, op. 17 / PHILIPS
Brendel. This is much more full of character than his earlier
performance, though I miss the power and swagger of that
one. –PM
Fantasia for Piano in C, op. 17 / CLAVES
Studer. An outstanding sleeper here, though hard to rank
above the other performances. But I've always liked
underdogs. –PM
○ **Fantasiestücke (4) for Violin, Cello & Piano, op. 88 /
INTERCORD**
Abegg Trio.
○ **Fantasiestücke for Clarinet & Piano, op. 73 / CHANDOS**
de Peyer, Pryor.
Fantasiestücke for Clarinet & Piano, op. 73 / CLAVES
Friedli, Requejo.
○ **Fantasiestücke for Piano, op. 12 / AS DISC**
Richter. Titanic, as only Richter can be. –PM
Fantasiestücke for Piano, op. 12 / PHILIPS
Brendel. Molded and soulful, this has beautiful piano
sound. –PM
Fantasiestücke for Piano, op. 12 / LONDON
Ashkenazy.
Fantasiestücke for Piano, op. 12 / PAVANE
Carbonel. A lot of interesting details and phrasing. If it weren't
for the opaque heaviness of the recording, this would be a lot
more pleasurable. –PM
○ **Faschingsschwank aus Wien, for Piano, op. 26 / DGG**
Bunin.
**Faschingsschwank aus Wien, for Piano, op. 26 / MK
(MEZHDUNARODNAYA KNIGA)**
Kuleshov. Valeri Kuleshov is a phenomenon in this day and
age of programmed pianists: a virtuoso with taste, who has
imagination and makes the piano sing. –PM
○ **Frauenliebe und -leben, op. 42 / ORFEO**
Price, Lockhart. It's a shame Margaret Price didn't have more
of a career. –PM
Frauenliebe und -leben, op. 42 / DGG
Fassbaender, Gage.
**Frauenliebe und -leben, op. 42; four miscellaneous
songs / ARS VIVENDI**
Lang (mezzo), Arens (piano). This is a bit stolid and doesn't
always have the soaring lyricism needed, especially in the

Schumann songs. But it has a lot of soul, which counts for a lot, in the *Frauenliebe* especially. –PM

○ **Humoreske for Piano, op. 20 / HUNGARATON**
Ranki. The only remote challenge to the Richter (out of print) I have ever heard. –PM

Humoreske for Piano, op. 20 / LONDON
Ashkenazy.

Humoreske for Piano, op. 20 / PAVANE
Carbonel.

○ **Impromptus (10) on a Theme by Clara Wieck, for Piano, op. 5 / KOCH-SCHWANN**
Riche.

○ **Introduction & Allegro appassionata (Concertstück) for Piano & Orchestra in G, op. 92 / AS DISC**
Richter, Britten/English CO. Surging and passionate from both the orchestra and pianist. –PM

Introduction & Allegro appassionata (Concertstück) for Piano & Orchestra in G, op. 92 / ODYSSEY
Serkin, Ormandy/Philadelphia Orchestra. Not quite so passionate and seething as Richter, but more "intellectual" in a good way. –PM

○ **Introduction & Allegro for Piano & Orchestra in d & D, op. 134 / ODYSSEY**
Serkin, Ormandy/Philadelphia Orchestra.

○ **Kinderscenen, for Piano, op. 15 / SUPRAPHON**
Moravec. Moravec is the most poetic and sensitive of the three. –PM

Kinderscenen, for Piano, op. 15 / DGG
Bunin. Quirky and more dramatic than the usual approach, with new shadings and plenty of details put in new light. –PM

Kinderscenen, for Piano, op. 15 / LONDON
Ashkenazy. Very poetic, but again a bit low-key for me. –PM

○ **Kreisleriana, for Piano, op. 16 / DENON**
Grimaud. In absolute terms, the profile could be a bit higher, but in every other way this is a major performance, especially from one so young. –PM

Kreisleriana, for Piano, op. 16 / EMI
Egorov. Robust, intense, dramatic playing. –PM

☆ **Liederkreis (12-song cycle), op. 39 / PHILIPS**
Fischer-Dieskau, Brendel. Late Dieskau is darker and more intense and has its own very personal rewards, especially with the inspired and subtle accompaniment of Brendel. –PM

Liederkreis (12-song cycle), op. 39 / DGG
Fischer-Dieskau, Eschenbach.

Liederkreis (12-song cycle), op. 39 / HUNGARATON
Esswood, McGegan. With the high male voice and original fortepiano, this is very interesting. –PM

Liederkreis (9 song cycle, poems by Heine), op. 24 / DGG
Fassbaender, Gage.

○ **Manfred Overture, op. 115 / DGG**
Sinopoli/Vienna PO.

○ **Märchenbilder (4) for Viola & Piano, op. 113 / CLAVES**
Fukai, Requejo.

○ **Märchenerzählungen for Clarinet, Viola & Piano, op. 132 / CLAVES**
Friedli, Fukai, Requejo.

○ **Novelettes for Piano nos. 1 & 2, op. 21 / LONDON**
Ashkenazy.

○ **Organ Music (complete solo works for pedal organ) / MOTETTE**
Mechler.

○ **Overture, Scherzo & Finale, op. 52 / CAPRICCIO**
Marriner/Stuttgart RSO.

○ **Papillons, for Piano, op. 2 / CLAVES**
Studer. Full of character. –PM

Papillons, for Piano, op. 2 / LONDON
Ashkenazy.

○ **Quartet for Piano & Strings in E-flat, op. 47 / CBS**
Gould/Juilliard Quartet.

Quartet for Piano & Strings in E-flat, op. 47 / PHILIPS
Rhodes (viola)/Beaux Arts Trio. A bit on the old-fashioned and schmaltzy side, but it will have to do for now. –PM

Quartet for Piano & Strings in E-flat, op. 47 / AMON RA
Burnett (fortepiano)/Fitzwilliam String Quartet. Interesting original-instrument recording. –PM

○ **Quartets for Strings nos. 1 & 3, op. 41 / ADDA**
Muir String Quartet. I can imagine better, but these are the most dedicated we have, and they have good sound, so they'll have to do for now. –PM

○ **Quintet for Piano & String Quartet in E-flat, op. 44 / BALKANTON**
Eynden (piano)/"Dimov" Bulgarian String Quartet.

Quintet for Piano & String Quartet in E-flat, op. 44 / PHILIPS
Bettelheim, Rhodes/Beaux Arts Trio.

Quintet for Piano & String Quartet in E-flat, op. 44 / CBS
Gould/Juilliard Quartet.

Quintet for Piano & String Quartet in E-flat, op. 44 / AMON RA
Burnett (fortepiano)/Fitzwilliam String Quartet on original instruments.

○ **Requiems (2) for SATB, Orchestra & Chorus, op. 148 & 98b / EURODISC**
Donath, Lipovsek, Moser, Rootering, Sawallisch/Bavarian RSO & Chorus.

○ **Romances (3) for Oboe & Piano, op. 94 / CLAVES**
Goritzki, Requejo.

○ **Der Rose Pilgerfahrt (oratorio), op. 112 / EMI**
Donath, Hamari, Altmeyer, Sotin, Frühbeck de Burgos/Düsseldorf SO & Chorus.

○ **Sonata for Piano in f sharp; Kinderscenen; Waldscenen / LONDON**
Ashkenazy.

○ **Sonata for Piano in f sharp, op. 11 / DENON**
Grimaud. This teenager can really play. She's not so dry or "technical" as Pollini and not so warm and rich as Ashkenazy, but she has a more beautiful tone than either (at least as recorded here) and amazing musicality. –PM

Sonata for Piano in f sharp, op. 11 / DGG
Pollini. As usual with Pollini, a technical tour de force, but not so warm and gracious as Grimaud. –PM

○ **Sonata for Piano in g, op. 22 / HUNGARATON**
Ranki.

○ **Sonatas (2) for Violin & Piano, opp. 105 in a & 121 in d / EDELWEISS**
Chumachenco (violin), Levy (piano). These have the soul, but lack brilliance. I guess you can't have it both ways. –PM

Sonatas (2) for Violin & Piano, opp. 105 in a & 121 in d / DGG
Kremer (violin), Argerich (piano). These are brilliant but a bit too technical and lacking in soul. –PM

○ **Songs / ORFEO**
Price, Lockhart.

○ **Stücke im Volkston (5 pieces for cello & piano), op. 102 / LONDON**
Rostropovich, Britten.

☆ **Symphonic Etudes for Piano, op. 13 / AS DISC**
Richter. Incandescent — hair-raising from start to finish. He just never lets up. –PM

Symphonic Etudes for Piano, op. 13 / DGG
Pogorelich. Despite an extremely slow reading of the opening theme, this is a remarkable performance of remarkably beautiful moments. –PM

Symphonic Etudes for Piano, op. 13 / DGG

Pollini. A bit dry as always, but with playing of the first magnitude. –PM

Symphonic Etudes for Piano, op. 13 / VANGUARD CLASSICS
Brendel. One of Brendel's best early recordings. –PM

○ **Symphonies nos. 1-4 (complete) / TELDEC**
Masur/London PO. Masur's new London PO set has the drive missing from his old Leipzig performances; with lots of splendid details shown in new light, this is clearly a rival to the Marriner and Sawallisch performances. –PM

Symphonies nos. 1-4 (complete) / CAPRICCIO
Marriner/Stuttgart RSO. Marriner may not have the passion of some, but at least he has clarity and a sense of scale, and these qualities count for a lot in Schumann. –PM

○ **Symphony in g, "Zwickau" / CAPRICCIO**
Marriner/Stuttgart RSO.

○ **Symphony no. 1 in B-flat, op. 38, "Spring" / ANGEL**
Sawallisch/Dresden State Orchestra.

Symphony no. 1 in B-flat, op. 38, "Spring" / COLLINS CLASSICS
Solomons/The Authentic Orchestra (period instruments). These performances are really soulful, and the delineation of the instruments and instrumental choirs is remarkable. No need for the usual re-orchestrations here! These are the cleanest Schumann symphonies I have ever heard. –PM

Symphony no. 1 in B-flat, op. 38, "Spring" / CAPRICCIO
Marriner/Stuttgart RSO.

○ **Symphony no. 2 in C, op. 61 / DGG**
Sinopoli/Vienna PO. Almost in the same league as Furtwängler's *Fourth*, with the same kind of control and seething passion and superb playing from Vienna. –PM

Symphony no. 2 in C, op. 61 / ANGEL
Sawallisch/Dresden State Orchestra. Sawallisch is a bit grim and doesn't take wing and probe the way Sinopoli does. –PM

Symphony no. 2 in C, op. 61 / CAPRICCIO
Marriner/Stuttgart RSO. Carefully considered: every detail is in its proper place. –PM

○ **Symphony no. 3 in E-flat, op. 97, "Rhenish" / ANGEL**
Sawallisch/Dresden State Orchestra. For the guts, charisma, and spontaneity of the playing, this has always been my favorite *Third*. –PM

Symphony no. 3 in E-flat, op. 97, "Rhenish" / DGG
Giulini/LAPO. Despite orchestral retouchings I frown on in principle, this is such a warmly spontaneous and deeply felt performance that it will always have a special place in my heart and my collection. –PM

Symphony no. 3 in E-flat, op. 97, "Rhenish" / CAPRICCIO
Marriner/Stuttgart RSO. The usual Marriner sense of scale and perfection are here. –PM

☆ **Symphony no. 4 in d, op. 120 / DGG**
Furtwängler/Berlin PO. The finest recording of any Schumann symphony ever made — an utter classic. –PM

Symphony no. 4 in d, op. 120 / ANGEL
Sawallisch/Dresden State Orchestra.

Symphony no. 4 in d, op. 120 / COLLINS CLASSICS
Solomons/The Authentic Orchestra (period instruments).

○ **Toccata for Piano, op. 7 / AS DISC**
Richter.

Toccata for Piano, op. 7 / ANGEL
Egorov.

Toccata for Piano, op. 7 / KOCH-SCHWANN
Rische.

○ **Trios for Violin, Cello & Piano no. 1, op. 63 / INTERCORD**
Abegg Trio. I miss a bit of warmth, but this is top-drawer playing in every other way. –PM

○ **Trios for Violin, Cello & Piano no. 2 & 3, opp. 80 & 110 / INTERCORD**
Abegg Trio.

○ **Variations on A-B-E-G-G, for Piano, op. 1 / CLAVES**
Studer. It won't rival the Richter, but what a fresh and poetic account. –PM

○ **Waldscenen (6 pieces for piano), op. 82 / LONDON**
Ashkenazy. Needs more oomph and solidity, but it has very poetic playing. –PM

HEINRICH SCHÜTZ   1585-1672

Baroque, sacred choral. Schütz synthesized Italian multichordal and rhythmic styles with the German dramatic and melodic sensibility to construct a powerfully moving and emotional music with a classical restraint that serves to accent these emotional qualities rather than inhibit them. This is especially evident in the marvelous *Symphoniae Sacrae; Saul, Saul Was verfolgst du mich?* ("Saul, Why Persecutest Thou Me?"); the heartbreaking *Fili Mi, Absalon* ("Absalom, My Son"); the multiple-chorus splendor and tone-painting of the *Psalms of David*; and the funeral mass *Musicalische Exequien.* In his older age, Schütz aimed at a more spare style, as shown in the *Christmas Oratorio* (1664), in which all the characters are accompanied by their own scoring and the evangelist/narrator is accompanied only by the continuo part. –BGT

☆ **Christmas Oratorio / SONY**
Bernius/Stuttgart Baroque Orchestra & Chamber Choir.

Christmas Oratorio / ANGEL
Parrott/Taverner Choir & Taverner Players.

Christmas Oratorio / HARMONIA MUNDI
Jacobs/Concerto Vocale & Instrumental Ensemble.

○ **Easter Oratorio / SONY**
Bernius/Stuttgart Baroque Orchestra & Chamber Choir.

○ **Heute ist Christus geboren, for Double Chorus & Ensemble / HARMONIA MUNDI**
Jacobs/Concerto Vocale & Instrumental Ensemble.

○ **Kleine geistliche Konzerte à nos. 1-5 (selections) / HARMONIA MUNDI**
Concerto Vocale.

Kleine geistliche Konzerte à nos. 1-5 (selections) / HARMONIA MUNDI
Herreweghe/La Chapelle Royale.

Kleine geistliche Konzerte à nos. 1-5 (selections) / HARMONIA MUNDI
Jacobs/Concerto Vocale & Instrumental Ensemble.

○ **Magnificat anima mea / HARMONIA MUNDI**
Clément Janequin Vocal Ensemble, Toulouse Saqueboutiers.

○ **Motets / DGG**
Gardiner/English Baroque Soloists, Monteverdi Choir.

○ **Music of Schütz (selections) / HARMONIA MUNDI**
Clément Janequin Vocal Ensemble, Toulouse Saqueboutiers.

○ **Musicalische Exequien / DGG**
Gardiner/English Baroque Soloists, Monteverdi Choir.

Musicalische Exequien ("Music for the Dead") / HARMONIA MUNDI
Herreweghe/La Chapelle Royale.

○ **Psalms of David / BELLAPHON**
Beringer/Windsbach Boys' Choir. Also contains motets. –BGT

☆ **The Seven Words of Jesus / HARMONIA MUNDI**
Clément Janequin Vocal Ensemble, Toulouse Saqueboutiers.

○ **Symphoniae Sacrae / HARMONIA MUNDI**
Concerto Vocale.

ALEXANDER SCRIABIN   1872-1915

20th century. A Russian composer known for visionary symphonies and piano music, which grew out of his experience with theosophical mysticism in Switzerland in

1903. Driven to express a vision of the future transformation of the world (in a moment of grand, collective ecstasy, not so different from the rapturists of today, though not apocalyptic), Scriabin began to write wholly original piano music and symphonies (no. 3, *The Divine Poem*, no. 4, *The Poem of Ecstasy*, and no. 5, *Prometheus, the Poem of Fire*). Scriabin invented many musical devices (like the octatonic scale and the "mystic" chord) that remained tonal in nature and yet produced a new sound that, while characterized both by the transparency of impressionism and the chromaticism of late romanticism, was a wholly new and strange sensation. –BGT

○ **Concerto for Piano & Orchestra in f#, op. 20 / LONDON**
Ashkenazy, Maazel/London PO.

○ **Late Piano Works, opp. 61-63, 65, 67, 69, 71-74 / ET CETERA**
Woodward (piano). Woodward specializes in ultramodern music, and he makes Scriabin sound like the phantasmagorical modernist he really is. –PM

○ **Morceaux (2) for Piano, op. 57 / PHILIPS**
Steuerman.

○ **Poèmes (2) for Piano, op. 32 / PHILIPS**
Steuerman.

○ **Poèmes (2) for Piano, op. 44 / PHILIPS**
Steuerman.

○ **Poèmes (2) for Piano, op. 63 / CALLIOPE**
Rudy.

○ **Preludes for Piano, opp. 67 & 74 / CALLIOPE**
Rudy.

○ **Sonatas (10) for Piano (complete) / LONDON**
Ashkenazy.

○ **Sonata for Piano no. 1 in f, op. 6 / LONDON**
Ashkenazy.

○ **Sonata for Piano no. 3 in f sharp, op. 23 / PHILIPS**
Steuerman.

○ **Sonata for Piano no. 4 in F sharp, op. 30 / PHILIPS**
Steuerman.

○ **Sonata for Piano no. 5 in F sharp, op. 53 / DGG**
Richter (piano). Richter is Scriabin's best advocate, and this is one of his best recital discs from the 60s. If you want to get to know Richter's art, this is as good a place to start as any. –PM
Sonata for Piano no. 5 in F sharp, op. 53 / PHILIPS
Steuerman.

○ **Sonata for Piano no. 6, op. 62 / LONDON**
Ashkenazy.
Sonata for Piano no. 6, op. 62 / CALLIOPE
Rudy.

○ **Sonata for Piano no. 7 in F sharp, op. 64, "White Mass" / BIS**
Pontinen.
Sonata for Piano no. 7 in F sharp, op. 64, "White Mass" / CALLIOPE
Rudy.

○ **Sonata for Piano no. 8, op. 66 / LONDON**
Ashkenazy.
Sonata for Piano no. 8, op. 66 / CALLIOPE
Rudy.

○ **Sonata for Piano no. 9 in F, op. 68, "Black Mass" / CALLIOPE**
Rudy.

○ **Sonata for Piano no. 10, op. 70 / CALLIOPE**
Rudy.

○ **Symphonies (5) (complete) / MELODIYA (KOCH)**
Svetlanov. Russian hothouse performances. –PM

○ **Symphony no. 5, op. 60, "Prometheus the Poem of Fire" LONDON**
Maazel/London PO.

Symphony no. 5, op. 60, "Prometheus the Poem of Fire" BIS
Derwinger (piano), Segerstam/Stockholm PO.

○ **Symphony no. 1 / BIS**
Segerstam/Stockholm Philharmonic Choir & Orchestra. You're always waiting for something meaningful to happen in Scriabin; as with Reger, it seldom does, and you're left with this vast expanse of turgidity. Still, Segerstam conducts a much more sensitive performance of the *First* than usual, and things actually come closer to happening. –PM

○ **Symphony no. 2 in c, op. 29 / BIS**
Segerstam/Royal Stockholm PO. We're still looking for the *perfect* performance of the second symphony, the one that supplies the proper proportions of ecstasy and clarity. This new Segerstam comes close and has a lot of good details, but the recorded sound becomes hard and congested in loud tuttis. –PM

○ **Symphonies nos. 3 & 4; Reverie / LONDON**
Ashkenazy/Berlin RSO. All the passion, voluptuousness, and ecstasy is there. With outstandingly committed playing from the RSO and detailed and wide-ranging digital sound, this now becomes the version of choice for all three works. –PM
Symphony no. 3, op. 43, "Divine Poem" / DGG
Sinopoli/NYPO.

☆ **Symphony no. 4, op. 54, "Poem of Ecstasy" / DGG**
Abbado/Boston SO.
Symphony no. 4, op. 54, "Poem of Ecstasy" / LONDON
Maazel/Cleveland Orchestra.
Symphony no. 4, op. 54, "Poem of Ecstasy" / DGG
Sinopoli/NYPO.

○ **Vers la flamme, for Piano, op. 72 / CALLIOPE**
Rudy.

ROGER SESSIONS   1896-1985

20th century. An American composer of music in many forms, including orchestral music, opera, and piano pieces. –ED

○ **Concerto for Orchestra / HYPERION**
Ozawa/Boston SO.

○ **When Lilacs Last in the Dooryard Bloom'd (cantata) for Soprano, Mezzo, Baritone, Orchestra & Chorus (1970) / NEW WORLD**
Hinde, Quiver, Cossa, Ozawa/Boston SO & Tanglewood Chorus.

DMITRI SHOSTAKOVICH   1906-1975

20th century. A Russian composer of orchestral-choral, opera, chamber, symphonies, and vocal and piano music. Like Prokofiev a generation later, Shostakovich was a highly visible and harshly criticized composer. Often in peril from the Stalinist regime and the advancing German armies in WWII, he nevertheless became the last (for now) great symphonist, producing a style that expressed ironic humor (his ninth symphony), or had vast epic qualities (the fifth, seventh, and eleventh symphonies), or had a tragic and desolate visage (the tenth symphony). His melodic sense developed from the warm, rich, and even sweet qualities of the *Preludes (24) for Piano* — which skillfully employ Russian folk song modality and magnificent characterization, updating classical techniques — to the bare, large-interval skips of the later works. At times, Shostakovich was able to reach the public with the most modern of his works (the tragic opera *Lady Macbeth of Mtsensk* (1934), widely popular in the Soviet Union and Europe until the press came down on it.) He was one of the most courageous of composers. –BGT

○ **The Age of Gold (ballet suite), op. 22 / LONDON**
Haitink/London PO.
The Age of Gold (ballet suite), op. 22 / DGG

Järvi/Gothenburg SO.
○ **Ballet Suites nos. 1-3 / CHANDOS**
Järvi/Scottish National Orchestra.
○ **Chamber Symphony for String Orchestra, op. 110a / DGG**
Barshai/Chamber Orchestra of Europe.
Chamber Symphony for String Orchestra, op. 110a / CHANDOS
Turovsky/I Musici de Montreal.
○ **Concertino for 2 Pianos, op. 94 / SWEDISH SOCIETY**
Wikstrom (piano). This recording is a terrific all-Shostakovich recital. –PM
○ **Concerto for Cello & Orchestra no. 1 in E-flat, op. 107 / PHILIPS**
Schiff, Shostakovich/Bavarian RSO. Because of the coupling of the second concerto and the superb recorded sound, this simply has to be ranked #1. –PM
Concerto for Cello & Orchestra no. 1 in E-flat, op. 107 / CBS
Rostropovich, Ormandy/Philadelphia SO.
Concerto for Cello & Orchestra no. 1 in E-flat, op. 107 / CBS
Ma, Ormandy/Philadelphia SO.
○ **Concerto for Cello & Orchestra no. 2, op. 126 / PHILIPS**
Schiff, Shostakovich/Bavarian RSO.
○ **Concerto for Piano & Orchestra no. 2, op. 102 / CHANDOS**
D. Shostakovich Jr, M. Shostakovich/I Musici de Montreal.
Concerto for Piano & Orchestra no. 2, op. 102 / CBS
Bernstein (piano and conductor)/NYPO.
○ **Concerto for Piano, Trumpet & Orchestra no. 1, op. 35 / RCA**
Kissin, Kan, Spivakov/The Moscow Virtuosi. A virtuoso performance. –PM
Concerto for Piano, Trumpet & Orchestra no. 1, op. 35 / CHANDOS
D. Shostakovich Jr, M. Shostakovich/I Musici de Montreal.
Concerto for Piano, Trumpet & Orchestra no. 1, op. 35 / CBS
Previn, Bernstein/NYPO.
○ **Concerto for Violin & Orchestra no. 1 in a, op. 99 / ANGEL**
Perlman, Mehta/Israel PO.
○ **Fantastic Dances (3) for Piano, op. 5 / SWEDISH SOCIETY**
Wikstrom.
○ **The Flea (incidental music), op. 19 / SWEDISH SOCIETY**
Wikstrom.
○ **Fragments (5) for Orchestra, op. 42 / LONDON**
Ashkenazy/Royal PO.
○ **From Jewish Folk Poetry, op. 79 / LONDON**
Soderstrom, Wenkel, Karczykowski, Haitink/Royal Concertgebouw Orchestra.
○ **Hamlet (incidental music), op. 32 / DGG**
Järvi/Gothenburg SO.
○ **Lady Macbeth of Mtsensk, op. 29 / ANGEL**
Vishnevskaya,   Finnila,   Gedda,   Haugland, Rostropovich/London PO, Ambrosian Opera Chorus.
○ **Moderato for Cello & Piano (discovered in 1986) / LONDON**
Harrell, Ashkenazy.
○ **October (symphonic poem), op. 131 / DGG**
Järvi/Gothenburg SO.
○ **Overture on Russian and Khirgiz Folk Themes / DGG**
Järvi/Gothenburg SO.
○ **Preludes (24) for Piano, op. 34 / LONDON**
Mustonen (piano). A superior debut of welcome, offbeat

material by this young artist, who is one to watch. This has very good sound and is percussive without being harsh in any way. –PM
Preludes (24) for Piano, op. 34 / SWEDISH SOCIETY
Wikstrom.
○ **Quartet for Strings no. 1 in C, op. 49 / ANGEL**
Borodin Quartet.
○ **Quartet for Strings no. 2 in A, op. 68 / ANGEL**
Borodin Quartet.
○ **Quartet for Strings no. 3 in F, op. 73 / ANGEL**
Borodin Quartet.
○ **Quartet for Strings no. 4 in D, op. 83 / ANGEL**
Borodin Quartet.
○ **Quartet for Strings no. 5 in B-flat, op. 92 / ANGEL**
Borodin Quartet.
○ **Quartet for Strings no. 6 in G, op. 101 / ANGEL**
Borodin Quartet.
○ **Quartet for Strings no. 7 in f sharp, op. 108 / ANGEL**
Borodin Quartet.
☆ **Quartet for Strings no. 8 in c, op. 110 / ANGEL**
Borodin Quartet.
○ **Quartet for Strings no. 9 in E-flat, op. 117 / ANGEL**
Borodin Quartet.
○ **Quartet for Strings no. 10 in A-flat, op. 118 / ANGEL**
Borodin Quartet.
○ **Quartet for Strings no. 11 in f, op. 122 / ANGEL**
Borodin Quartet.
○ **Quartet for Strings no. 12 in D-flat, op. 133 / ANGEL**
Borodin Quartet.
○ **Quartet for Strings no. 13 in b-flat, op. 138 / ANGEL**
Borodin Quartet.
○ **Quartet for Strings no. 14 in F sharp, op. 142 / ANGEL**
Borodin Quartet.
○ **Quartet for Strings no. 15 in e-flat, op. 144 / ANGEL**
Borodin Quartet.
○ **Quintet for Piano & Strings in g, op. 57 / LONDON**
Ashkenazy/Fitzwilliam Quartet.
Quintet for Piano & Strings in g, op. 57 / ANGEL
Richter/Borodin Quartet.
○ **Sonata for Cello & Piano in d, op. 40 / LONDON**
Harrell, Ashkenazy.
○ **Sonata for Piano no. 2, op. 61 (aka op. 64) / SWEDISH SOCIETY**
Wikstrom.
○ **Symphony no. 1 in F, op. 10 / MELODIYA (KOCH)**
Rozhdestvensky/The USSR Ministry of Culture SO. Rozhdestvensky finds details and relationships that no one knew existed in this music. But his consistently quirky approach toward all the symphonies wears a bit thin on this listener; and Ashkenazy, Haitink, and others may wear a bit better on most listeners. –PM
Symphony no. 1 in F, op. 10 / LONDON
Ashkenazy/Royal PO. A good combination of passion, commitment, and objectivity. –PM
Symphony no. 1 in F, op. 10 / LONDON
Haitink/London PO. A bit faceless but so well controlled, played, and recorded. –PM
○ **Symphony no. 2, op. 14, "To October" / LONDON**
Haitink/London PO.
○ **Symphony no. 3 in E-flat, op. 20, "May Day" / MELODIYA (KOCH)**
Rozhdestvensky/USSR Ministry of Culture SO.
Symphony no. 3 in E-flat, op. 20, "May Day" / LONDON
Haitink/London PO.
○ **Symphony no. 4 in c, op. 43 / LONDON**
Ashkenazy/Royal PO.

Symphony no. 4 in c, op. 43 / CHANDOS
Järvi/Scottish National Orchestra.

☆ **Symphony no. 5 in d, op. 47 / PHILIPS**
Bychkov/Berlin PO. The ideal combination of power and passion. If for no other reason, Bychkov's orchestra puts him into first place. –PM

Symphony no. 5 in d, op. 47 / LONDON
Haitink/Royal Concertgebouw Orchestra. One of the most dramatic and "perfect" performances, every detail right in place in relation to all the others. –PM

Symphony no. 5 in d, op. 47 / HUNT
Mravinsky/Leningrad PO. There's more sadness and terror in this performance from 1968 and more insidiousness, too, but sound quality will be a limiting factor. –PM

Symphony no. 5 in d, op. 47 / ERATO
Mravinsky/Leningrad PO. Mravinsky finds more of everything in this symphony than any other conductor, and the live sound from April 4, 1984, isn't at all bad. –PM

○ **Symphony no. 6, op. 54 / LONDON**
Haitink/Royal Concertgebouw Orchestra. A bit too objective and impersonal. –PM

Symphony no. 6, op. 54 / LONDON
Ashkenazy/Royal PO. A bit too unrefined. –PM

Symphony no. 6, op. 54 / ANGEL
Previn/London SO. A bit too warm and romanticized. –PM

○ **Symphony no. 7 in C, op. 60, "Leningrad" / CHANDOS**
Järvi/Scottish National Orchestra.

○ **Symphony no. 8 in c, op. 65 / PHILIPS**
Mravinsky/Leningrad PO. No conductor quite combines power and drama with depth of emotion like Mravinsky; with his firm grasp of detail and of the overall picture, he remains the finest conductor of Shostakovich ever. –PM

Symphony no. 8 in c, op. 65 / LONDON
Haitink/Royal Concertgebouw Orchestra.

○ **Symphony no. 9 in c, op. 70 / MELODIYA (KOCH)**
Rozhdestvensky/USSR Ministry of Culture SO. Rozhdestvensky wins me over in this, the lightest and quirkiest of Shostakovich's symphonies after the *First*. He simply finds more fantasy and whimsy than anyone else. –PM

Symphony no. 9 in c, op. 70 / LONDON
Haitink/London PO. A good alternative straighter reading. –PM

○ **Symphony no. 10 in e, op. 93 / LONDON**
Ashkenazy/Royal PO. Working with a less-than-top-drawer orchestra, Ashkenazy nevertheless continues to impress, and when finished, his will be one of the top cycles. He simply understands the sound world and the angst, but he doesn't wear his heart on his sleeve and he doesn't overdo things. Despite some less-than-great playing, this *Tenth* hangs together and doesn't ramble. –PM

○ **Symphony no. 10 in e, op. 93 / PHILIPS**
Bychkov/Berlin PO.

Symphony no. 10 in e, op. 93 / DGG
Karajan/Berlin PO. This later digital Karajan is a bit more inclusive, but it suffers from digital brightness. –PM

Symphony no. 10 in e, op. 93 / DGG
Karajan/Berlin PO. Despite being a bit too bland and round, à la Karajan, this performance has a power and precision matched only by Mravinsky, who in turn has much more passion. –PM

○ **Symphony no. 11 in g, op. 103, "The Year 1905" / PHILIPS**
Bychkov/Berlin PO. Superb playing and sound. The orchestra sounds a bit more Russian, and the playing is more idiomatic under a Russian conductor. –PM

Symphony no. 11 in g, op. 103, "The Year 1905" / LONDON
Haitink/Royal Concertgebouw Orchestra.

○ **Symphony no. 12, op. 112, "The Year 1917" / URANIA**
Mravinsky/Leningrad PO. No one's going to touch this! –PM

Symphony no. 12, op. 112, "The Year 1917" / DGG
Järvi/Gothenburg SO.

○ **Symphony no. 13, op. 113, "Babi Yar" / CHANDOS**
Storjev, Kamu/City of Birmingham SO & Chorus.

○ **Symphony no. 14 for Soprano, Bass, Orchestra & Chorus, op. 135 / MELODIYA (KOCH)**
Rozhdestvensky/USSR Ministry of Culture SO.

○ **Symphony no. 15 in A, op. 141 / MELODIYA (KOCH)**
Mravinsky/Leningrad PO.

Symphony no. 15 in A, op. 141 / MELODIYA (KOCH)
Rozhdestvensky/USSR Ministry of Culture SO.

Symphony no. 15 in A, op. 141 / DGG
Järvi/Gothenburg SO.

○ **Symphony for Strings, op. 188a / DGG**
Barshai/Chamber Orchestra of Europe.

Symphony for Strings, op. 188a / CHANDOS
Turovsky/Montreal SO.

○ **Trio for Piano, Violin & Cello no. 2 in e, op. 8 / COLLINS CLASSICS**
Trio Zingara.

○ **Two Pieces for String Octet / LONDON**
Fitzwilliam Quartet.

JEAN SIBELIUS   1865-1957

Romantic, nationalist. A Finnish composer identified with the Finnish nationalism movement before 1918 who is popularly known for the romantic, nationalist works he produced at that time, including *Finlandia* (written for the Press Celebrations of 1899) and the *Valse Triste*. His last work in this style, written a few years later, was *Symphony no. 2*, with its Scandinavian flavor of open spaces. Sibelius continually sought new techniques and sounds, from the neo-classicism of the third symphony to the almost nontonal-based *Symphony no. 4* (1911). The symphonic poem *Tapiola, op. 112* of 1925 is a good example of his later style. Sibelius also wrote piano music, mostly bagatelle-style pieces but also some that are more serious, like the three *Sonatine, op. 67* and *Kyllikki, Three Lyric Pieces for Piano, op. 41*, based on the Finnish epic *Kalevala*.–BGT

○ **The Bard (tone poem), op. 64 / RCA**
Saraste/Finnish RSO.

The Bard (tone poem), op. 64 / KOCH-SCHWANN
Beecham/London PO.

○ **Belshazzar's Feast: Suite, op. 51 / BIS**
Järvi/Gothenburg.

☆ **Concerto for Violin & Orchestra in d, op. 47 / FINLANDIA**
Ignatius (violin), Jarm/Berlin State Orchestra. The sound (from 1943) is pretty poor on this, but the heartfelt performance comes shining through. –PM

Concerto for Violin & Orchestra in d, op. 47 / FINLANDIA
Fried (violin), Kamu/Helsinki PO. This has more of a Nordic feel than other performances and probes deeper beneath the surface of the notes. –PM

Concerto for Violin & Orchestra in d, op. 47 / ANGEL
Perlman (violin), Previn/Pittsburgh SO. Generic, but very good. –PM

Concerto for Violin & Orchestra in d, op. 47 (original 1903-1904 version) / BIS
Kavakos (violin), Vanska/Lahti SO. The original version is longer and has some interesting ideas, but the tighter, published version is more satisfying overall. –PM

○ **En Saga, op. 9 / ANGEL**
Karajan/Berlin PO. Very cumulative and powerful. –PM

En Saga, op. 9 / CHANDOS
Segerstam/Danish National RSO.

En Saga, op. 9 / RCA
Saraste/Finnish RSO.

En Saga, op. 9 / LONDON
Ashkenazy/Philharmonia Orchestra.

☆ **Finlandia, op. 26 / FINLANDIA**
Kamu/Helsinki PO. Makes it sound like a national anthem instead of a potboiler. A Nordic performance of tremendous power and dignity. –PM

Finlandia, op. 26 / ANGEL
Beecham/London PO.

Finlandia, op. 26 / RCA
Saraste/Finnish RSO.

Finlandia, op. 26 / DGG
Karajan/Berlin PO.

○ **Four Legends from the Kalevala, op. 22 / RCA**
Saraste/Finnish RSO. This won't replace Okko Kamu's version in my affections, but it has its moments, and Saraste always conducts with power, dedication, and conviction. –PM

○ **Humoresques (6) for Piano, Violin & Orchestra, opp. 87 & 89 / BIS**
Kang, Järvi/Gothenburg SO.

○ **Impromptu for String Orchestra (arrangement of piano impromptus) / FINLANDIA**
Helasvuo/Finlandia Sinfonietta.

○ **In Memoriam (funeral march for orchestra), op. 59 / KOCH-SCHWANN**
Beecham/London PO.

○ **Jungfrun i tornet (The Maid in the Tower - opera) / BIS**
Haggander, Hagegard, Hynninen, Kruse, Järvi/Gothenburg SO & Chorus.

☆ **Karelia Suite, op. 11 / FINLANDIA**
Kamu/Helsinki PO. One of the few "light" pieces I really like. Kamu's performance reveals depths and subtleties no one but Saraste even thinks about. –PM

Karelia Suite, op. 11 / RCA
Saraste/Finnish RSO.

Karelia Suite, op. 11 / DGG
Kamu/Helsinki RSO.

Karelia Suite nos. 1 & 3, op. 11 / ANGEL
Beecham/BBC SO, Royal PO.

○ **Koskenlaskijan Morsiamet, for Baritone & Orchestra, op. 33 / BIS**
Hynninen, Panula/Gothenburg SO.

○ **"Kullervo" Symphony, for Soprano, Baritone, Orchestra & Male Chorus, op. 7 / BIS**
Järvi/Gothenburg SO.

○ **Kuolema (incidental music), opp. 44 & 62 / FINLANDIA**
Helasvuo/Finlandia Sinfonietta.

○ **Lemminkainen's Return, op. 22 / KOCH-SCHWANN**
Beecham/London PO.

○ **Luonnotar, op. 70 / LONDON**
Soderstrom, Ashkenazy/Philharmonia Orchestra.

Luonnotar, op. 70 / BIS
Haggander, Panula/Gothenburg SO.

○ **Malinconia, for Cello & Piano, op. 20 / PHILIPS**
Schiff, Leonskaja/Philharmonia Orchestra.

○ **Music for Cello & Piano / FINLANDIA**
Sariola, Liu.

○ **Music for Violin & Orchestra / KOCH-SCHWANN**
Holmes, Handley/Berlin RSO.

○ **Music for Violin & Piano - Vol. 1 / BIS**
Sparf, Forsberg.

Music for Violin & Piano - Vol. 1 & 2 (complete) / ONDINE
Arai, Heinonen.

○ **Night Ride and Sunrise, op. 55 (symphonic poem) / RCA**
Saraste/Finnish RSO.

○ **The Oceanides (tone poem), op. 73 / RCA**

Saraste/Finnish RSO.

The Oceanides (tone poem), op. 73 / ANGEL
Beecham/Royal PO.

○ **Pelleas et Melisande (incidental music), op. 46 / ANGEL**
Beecham/Royal PO. Beecham has more character and atmosphere. –PM

Pelleas et Melisande (incidental music), op. 46 / DGG
Karajan/Berlin PO. Karajan has more finesse. He's smooth and beautiful. –PM

○ **Pohjola's Daughter, op. 49 / CHANDOS**
Segerstam/Danish National RSO. A lot of terrific details that add up to a convincing whole. –PM

Pohjola's Daughter, op. 49 / RCA
Saraste/Finnish RSO.

Pohjola's Daughter, op. 49 / SAPHIR
Rozhdestvensky/London SO.

○ **Presto, for String Orchestra (based on movement 4 of op. 4) / FINLANDIA**
Helasvuo/Finlandia Sinfonietta.

○ **Quartet for Strings in a (1889) / FINLANDIA**
Sibelius Academy Quartet.

Quartet for Strings in a (1889) / ONDINE
Jean Sibelius Quartet.

○ **Quartet for Strings in B-flat, op. 4 / FINLANDIA**
Sibelius Academy Quartet.

○ **Quartet for Strings in d, op. 56, "Voces Intimae" / ONDINE**
Jean Sibelius Quartet. A more Nordic-sounding performance than the Gabrieli, which is in turn a bit more polished and sophisticated. –PM

Quartet for Strings in d, op. 56, "Voces Intimae" / CHANDOS
Gabrieli String Quartet.

○ **Quartet for Strings in E-flat / FINLANDIA**
Sibelius Academy Quartet.

○ **Quintet for Piano & Strings in g / FINLANDIA**
Tawaststjerna/Sibelius Academy String Quartet.

Quintet for Piano & Strings in g / CHANDOS
Gladstone/Gabrieli String Quartet.

○ **Rakastava, for Strings & Percussion, op. 14 / ARGO**
Marriner/ASMF.

Rakastava, for Strings & Percussion, op. 14 / CHANDOS
Gibson/Scottish National Orchestra.

○ **Romance for Strings in C, op. 42 / FINLANDIA**
Helasvuo/Finlandia Sinfonietta.

○ **Scene with Cranes (from Kuolema, op. 44) / RCA**
Saraste/Finnish RSO.

○ **Scènes Historiques, op. 25 & 66 / RCA**
Saraste/Finnish RSO.

Scènes Historiques, op. 25 & 66 / BIS
Järvi/Gothenburg SO.

Scènes Historiques, op. 25 & 66 / ANGEL
Beecham/Royal PO.

○ **Songs / ONDINE**
Auvinen, Djupsjobacks.

Songs / FINLANDIA
Hynninen, Gothoni.

Songs / BIS
Von Otter, Forsberg.

○ **Songs for Male Voice Choir (complete) / FINLANDIA**
Helsinki University Chorus.

○ **Songs (for solo voice & orchestra) / BIS**
Haggander, Hynninen, Panula/Gothenburg SO.

○ **Suite mignonne for Flute & Strings, op. 98 & more / FINLANDIA**
Helasvuo/Finlandia Sinfonietta.

☆ **The Swan of Tuonela (from *Four Legends*, op. 22) / DGG**
Karajan/Berlin PO. Seamless, hypnotic, and mysterious. –PM

The Swan of Tuonela (from *Four Legends*, op. 22) / DGG
Kamu/Helsinki RSO.

The Swan of Tuonela (from *Four Legends*, op. 22) / SAPHIR
Rozhdestvensky/London SO.

○ **Swanwhite: Suite, op. 54 / BIS**
Järvi/Gothenburg SO.

○ **Symphonies nos. 1, 2, 3, 5; Belshazzar's Feast, op. 51; Pohjola's Daughter, op. 49 / FINLANDIA**
Kajanus/London SO. A historical document of tremendous importance, in carefully prepared and surprisingly good sound, considering the 1930 and 1932 originals. –PM

○ **Symphonies nos. 2, 5, 7; Swanwhite; Tapiola; Pohjola's Daughter / PEARL**
Koussevitzky/Berlin SO, BBC SO. More dramatic than Kajanus, if not quite the authentic Nordic sound. –PM

○ **Symphony no. 1 in e, op. 39 / ANGEL**
Karajan/Berlin PO. A big, lush, romanticized reading that is powerful and impressive. –PM

Symphony no. 1 in e, op. 39 / RCA
Saraste/Finnish RSO. For once the symphony sounds like Sibelius instead of warmed-over Tchaikovsky. –PM

Symphony no. 1 in e, op. 39 / LONDON
Ashkenazy/Philharmonia Orchestra. Ashkenazy's whole series can be highly recommended. –PM

Symphony no. 1 in e, op. 39 / DGG
Kamu/Helsinki RSO. Not so good as his *Third*, but a warmhearted performance. –PM

☆ **Symphony no. 2 in D, op. 43 / PHILIPS**
Szell/Royal Concertgebouw Orchestra. Despite sound that is inevitably somewhat dated, this remains one of the three premier performances (along with Barbirolli and Monteux) of the *Second* ever made. –PM

Symphony no. 2 in D, op. 43 / MENUET
Barbirolli/Royal PO. Big, warmhearted: many people's favorite version, ever! –PM

Symphony no. 2 in D, op. 43 / ANGEL
Karajan/Berlin PO. This performance is powerful, romantic, and larger than life. –PM

Symphony no. 2 in D, op. 43 / RCA
Saraste/Finnish RSO. Razor-sharp at times, incisive and keenly intelligent. –PM

○ **Symphony no. 3 in C, op. 52 / DGG**
Kamu/Helsinki RSO. This is as good as any version at full price; at budget price, it's a steal. –PM

Symphony no. 3 in C, op. 52 / LONDON
Ashkenazy/Philharmonia Orchestra.

○ **Symphony no. 4 in a, op. 63 / CHANDOS**
Segerstam/Danish National RSO. One of the bleakest pieces ever written, but this is the quirkiest and most optimistic reading I've ever heard, and it works. –PM

Symphony no. 4 in a, op. 63 / RCA
Saraste/Finnish RSO.

Symphony no. 4 in a, op. 63 / ANGEL
Karajan/Berlin PO.

Symphony no. 4 in a, op. 63 / DGG
Karajan/Berlin PO.

○ **Symphony no. 5 in E-flat, op. 82 / RCA**
Saraste/Finnish RSO. This is a performance of real mastery and true stature and moves right to the top of the all-time Sibelius *Fifths*. Hundreds of details in tempo and phrasing are slightly different than usual; everything is unique and fresh-sounding, without in any way seeming or sounding perverse. And there's that Saraste seriousness coupled with a luminosity that elevates the symphony to more than it usually is. *En Saga* and *Tapiola* make heavyweight fillers. –PM

Symphony no. 5 in E-flat, op. 82 / FINLANDIA

Panula/Helsinki PO. There is a complete naturalness to the conducting of this most underrated musician. –PM

Symphony no. 5 in E-flat, op. 82 / LONDON
Ashkenazy/Philharmonia Orchestra.

Symphony no. 5 in E-flat, op. 82 / DGG
Karajan/Berlin PO.

○ **Symphony no. 6 in d, op. 104 / DGG**
Karajan/Berlin PO. This is smooth but oh-so-hypnotic and cumulative. –PM

Symphony no. 6 in d, op. 104 / ANGEL
Karajan/Philharmonia Orchestra.

Symphony no. 6 in d, op. 104 / RCA
Saraste/Finnish RSO. Karajan is smooth and hypnotic (especially on the Deutsche Grammophon (DGG) performance); Saraste is chiseled. His *Sixth* doesn't really come completely alive until the fourth movement, which features some volcanic playing. But elsewhere the performance is filled with such character and features such unique phrasing, tempo changes, and tone color that it can be firmly recommended. And does he ever make the most of his filler — this *Scène historique* buries the erstwhile competition. –PM

Symphony no. 6 in d, op. 104 / FINLANDIA
Schneevoigt/Helsinki PO. I've always admired this gentle performance from 1933, even if the orchestral playing leaves a lot to be desired. It's like a vision of paradise. –PM

Symphony no. 6 in d, op. 104 / ANGEL
Karajan/Berlin PO. Not so smooth or "Karajanized" as the Deutsche Grammophon (DGG) performance and not such a unique statement, but much more powerful (helped by large sound) and craggy, with a lot of telling new details. –PM

○ **Symphony no. 7 in d, op. 105 / LONDON**
Ashkenazy/Philharmonia Orchestra. Original issue, coupled with a very powerful and well recorded *Tapiola*. A more straightforward and true-to-the-score performance than Karajan's or Beecham's, which are much more unique. –PM

○ **Symphony no. 7 in d, op. 105 / LONDON**
Ashkenazy/Philharmonia Orchestra. Same performance as above, coupled with Sibelius's *First*. –PM

Symphony no. 7 in d, op. 105 / ANGEL
Beecham/Royal PO. Chiseled and quirky but undeniably powerful and unique. –PM

Symphony no. 7 in d, op. 105 / DGG
Karajan/Berlin PO. Not quite rugged enough but a beautifully textured performance. –PM

Symphony no. 7 in d, op. 105 / RCA
Saraste/Finnish RSO. The conception is there, craggy and rugged, but neither the orchestra nor the sound is all it should be. It does have many noble, beautiful, and individual touches. –PM

☆ **Tapiola, op. 112 / RCA**
Saraste/Finnish RSO.

Tapiola, op. 112 / DGG
Karajan/Berlin PO.

Tapiola, op. 112 / LONDON
Ashkenazy/Philharmonia Orchestra.

○ **The Tempest (incidental music for the play) / ANGEL**
Beecham/Royal PO.

The Tempest (incidental music for the play) / CHANDOS
Segerstam/Danish National RSO.

○ **Tone Poems (complete) / CHANDOS**
Gibson/Scottish National Orchestra. Straightforward and dramatic performances, but a bit lacking in poetry and subtlety. –PM

○ **Trio for Piano, Violin & Cello in c / FINLANDIA**
Tapiola Trio.

○ **Two Pieces (Serious Melodies) for Violin & Orchestra / BIS**
Kang, Järvi/Gothenburg SO.

○ **Two Pieces (Serious Melodies) for Violin & Orchestra / KOCH-SCHWANN**
Holmes, Handley.

○ **Two Serenades for Violin & Orchestra, op. 69 / BIS**
Kang, Järvi/Gothenburg SO.

○ **Valse triste (from *Kuolema, op. 44*) / RCA**
Saraste/Finnish RSO.

Valse triste (from *Kuolema, op. 44*) / ARGO
Marriner/ASMF.

Valse triste (from *Kuolema, op. 44*) / DGG
Karajan/Berlin PO.

Valse triste (from *Kuolema, op. 44*) / KOCH-SCHWANN
Beecham/London PO.

ROBERT SIMPSON   b 1921

20th century. An important modern British composer. –ED

○ **Brass Band Music Complete / HYPERION**
Watson/Desford Colliery Caterpillar Band. This is serious and challenging music, brilliantly played and recorded, with a lot of overwhelming details. –PM

○ **Symphony no. 9 / HYPERION**
Handley/Bournemouth SO. This is the place to start with Simpson. –PM

BEDRICH SMETANA   1824-1884

Romantic, nationalist. The "father of Czech music" suffered through the revolt of June 1848 in Prague, continuing to support Czech nationalism in all of his music. Smetana was strongly influenced by Liszt, who praised him, and his symphonic writing shows a pronounced feeling for scene setting and drama, even containing some of the "Leitmotiv" technique of Wagner. Smetana's masterpiece is considered to be the symphonic tone-"poem cycle *Má Vlast* ("My Country"), from which "Vltava" ("The Moldau") and "From Bohemian Fields and Groves" are the most popular sections. –BGT

○ **The Bartered Bride (3-act opera) / ANGEL**
Lorengar, Wunderlich, Frick, Kempe/Bamberg SO & RAIS Chorus.

○ **Hakon Jarl (symphonic poem) / SUPRAPHON**
Neumann/Czech PO.

☆ **Má Vlast (My Fatherland - symphonic poem cycle) / DGG**
Levine/Vienna PO. Levine has splendid sweep and thrust, with bold, dramatic, and very colorful playing from the Vienna PO. –PM

Má Vlast (My Fatherland - symphonic poem cycle) / HUNT
Maag/Turin Radio Orchestra. This would be my performance of choice, free of bombast and superficiality, save for two minor details: poor pirate sound and a less-than-first-rate orchestra, which nevertheless tries its hardest. Conducting: A+; orchestra: C-; sound: D+. –PM

Má Vlast (My Fatherland - symphonic poem cycle) / KOCH-SCHWANN
Talich/Czech PO. *The* classic performance — but of course sound is a definite drawback. –PM

Má Vlast (My Fatherland - symphonic poem cycle) / DGG
Kubelik/Boston SO. No one knows this piece better than Kubelik, who recorded it five or six times. I still feel, however, that his performance is a bit too mellow and avuncular. –PM

○ **March for the Shakespeare Festival / SUPRAPHON**
Neumann/Czech PO.

☆ **The Moldau (Vltava - symphonic poem from *Má Vlast*) / DGG**
Karajan/Vienna PO.

○ **Quartets for Strings nos. 1 & 2 / BEYER**
Stamitz Quartet. Powerful and intense readings that reveal a lot of new details. –PM

Quartet for Strings no. 1 in e / LONDON
Gabrieli Quartet. More controlled and sophisticated readings than the Stamitz Quartet's, but less powerful and intense. –PM

○ **Richard III (symphonic poem) / SUPRAPHON**
Neumann/Czech PO.

○ **Wallenstein's Camp (symphonic poem) / SUPRAPHON**
Neumann/Czech PO.

ANTONIO SOLER   1729-1783

Classical. A Catalan monk, organist, and prolific composer of sacred and secular music who studied with Domenico Scarlatti and is known today for his keyboard works, which show Scarlatti's influence in their idiomatic keyboard treatment, structure, and affinity for Spanish harmonic and rhythmic inflections. –MKS

○ **Fandango / VIRGIN**
Cole (harpsichord).

○ **Sonatas for Harpsichord (selected) / VIRGIN**
Cole (harpsichord and fortepiano). The choice here, especially between Ogg and Cole, is very difficult, but since Cole has the extra variety of a beautifully recorded fortepiano, I'll give her a slight edge. –PM

Sonatas for Harpsichord (selected) / GLOBE
Ogg.

Sonatas for Harpsichord (selected) / CRD
Black.

Complete Works for Harpsichord - Vols. 1-6 / ASTREE
Van Asperen (harpsichord). And now along comes Bob van Asperen with a projected complete set to cloud the waters further. –PM

FERNANDO SOR   1778-1839

Classical. A Spanish guitarist and composer known mainly for guitar pieces. Sor also wrote opera, ballet, chamber music, and songs. –ED

○ **Sonata for Guitar, op. 25 / DGG**
Sollscher.

○ **Variations on a Theme of Mozart, for Guitar, op. 9 / DGG**
Sollscher.

JOHN PHILIP SOUSA   1854-1932

Romantic, martial. An American composer known for his march music, including "The Stars and Stripes Forever" (1897). The sousaphone instrument was named for him. –ED

○ **Marches & Dances - Vol. 1, "Stars & Stripes Forever" / ANGEL**
Hoskins/Royal Marines Band.

○ **Marches & Dances - Vol. 2, "Hands Across the Sea" / ANGEL**
Hoskins/Royal Marines Band.

LUDWIG (LOUIS) SPOHR   1784-1859

Classical/romantic. A celebrated German violinist and composer whose compositional style is typical of the transition period between classicism and romanticism. Besides writing extensively for the violin, Spohr composed several operas and symphonies, which were were extremely well received in his lifetime and continue to be performed. –MKS

○ **Concertante for Harp, Violin & Orchestra no. 1 in G / CLAVES**
Holliger, Schneeberger, Graf/English CO.

○ **Concertante for Harp, Violin & Orchestra no. 2 in E / NOVALIS**
Poppen, Holliger/English CO.

○ **Sonatas concertantes for Harp & Violin, opp. 113 & 114 / JECKLIN**
Holliger, Furi.

○ **Symphony no. 3 in c, op. 78 / KOCH-SCHWANN**
Albrecht/Berlin RSO.

○ **Symphony no. 4 in F, op. 86, "Die Weihe der Tone" / MARCO POLO**
Walter/Budapest SO.

○ **Symphonies nos. 6 & 9, opp. 116 & 143 / ORFEO**
Rickenbacker/Bavarian RSO.

○ **Variations sur l'air "Je suis encore dans mon printemps" for solo Harp, op. 36 / JECKLIN**
Holliger.

CARL STAMITZ   1745-1801

Baroque. A German composer, one of the major architects of the classical period; he wrote many concertos and other instrumental pieces. –ED

○ **Concerto for Clarinet & Orchestra in E-flat / HUNGARATON**
Horvath, Rolla/Liszt CO.

○ **Concerto for Trumpet & Orchestra in D / PHILIPS**
Hardenberger, Marriner/ASMF.

JOHANN WENZEL ANTON STAMITZ   1717-1757

Classical. A Bohemian violinist, conductor, and composer who became the Director of Instrumental Music at the Mannheim court in 1750. Under his direction the orchestra became known throughout Europe and provided the model for what was to become the standard classical orchestra. His 56 extant symphonies are among his most important works. –MKS

○ **Concerto for Clarinet & Orchestra in B-flat / HUNGARATON**
Horvath, Rolla/Liszt CO.

CHARLES VILLIERS STANFORD   1852-1924

Romantic. A distinguished Irish composer of the romantic style infused with English and Irish folk elements. He wrote operas, chamber music, piano pieces, and seven symphonies. –MKS

○ **Concerto for Clarinet & Orchestra in a, op. 80 / HYPERION**
King, Francis/Philharmonia Orchestra.

○ **Symphony no. 3 in f, op. 28, "Irish" / CHANDOS**
Handley/Ulster Orchestra.

○ **Symphony no. 4 in F, op. 31 / CHANDOS**
Handley/Ulster Orchestra.

○ **Symphony no. 5 in D, op. 56 / CHANDOS**
Handley/Ulster Orchestra.

○ **Symphony no. 6 in E-flat, op. 94 / CHANDOS**
Handley/Ulster Orchestra.

○ **Symphony no. 7 in d, op. 124 / CHANDOS**
Handley/Ulster Orchestra.

JOHN STANLEY   1712-1786

Baroque. An English organist and composer whose cantatas and keyboard works are especially important. Stanley was a friend and associate of Handel. –MKS

○ **Organ Concertos (6), op. 2 / NUOVA ERA**
Frige (organ)/Ensemble "Pian & Forte." These are such quirky and interesting pieces and the performances are so alive and sonorous that it's a shame to have to report that the intonation leaves a lot to be desired. I still love it, but you've been warned. –PM

Organ Concertos (6), op. 2 / HYPERION
Goodman/The Parley of Instruments. This is better played than the "Pian & Forte," but without some of the endearing quirkiness. –PM

WILLIAM GRANT STILL   1895-1978

Classical. The "dean of American Black composers," who developed a Black symphonic style (*Afro-American Symphony*, 1930). Still occasionally used original Black themes but for the most part created his own melodic materials. Text-related pieces reveal his heritage; his wife Verna Arvey, a writer, was his frequent collaborator. –MKS

○ **Ennanga for String Quartet, Harp & Piano (1956) / NEW WORLD**

○ **Piano Pieces / KOCH-SCHWANN**
Oldham (piano). Short, atmospheric, and moody piano pieces by this interesting American composer, who was born in Mississippi and grew up in Little Rock, AR. –PM

JOHANN STRAUSS II   1825-1899

Romantic. An Austrian composer of Viennese waltzes; known as "the Waltz King." His almost 500-dance pieces are his crowning achievement, while his *Die Fledermaus* is the epitome of operetta. –MKS

○ **Die Fledermaus (three-act operetta) / ANGEL**
Schwarzkopf, Streich, Gedda, Krebs, Christ, Kunz, Donch, Karajan/Philharmonia Orchestra & Chorus.

Die Fledermaus with Gala Sequence / LONDON
Gueden, Koth, Resnik, Kmentt, Zampieri, Wächter, Berry, Kunz, Karajan/Vienna PO & State Opera Chorus.

Die Fledermaus (three-act operetta) / ANGEL
Rothenberger, Holm, Fassbaender, Gedda, Dallpozza, Berry, Fischer-Dieskau, Boskovsky/Vienna SO, Volksoper Chorus.

Die Fledermaus (three-act operetta) / DGG
Varady, Popp, Kollo, et al., Kleiber/Bavarian State Opera.

○ **Music of Johann Strauss / LONDON**
Boskovsky/Vienna PO.

○ **Eine Nacht in Venedig (operetta) / ANGEL**
Schwarzkopf, Loose, Gedda, Kunz, Donch, Ackermann/ Philharmonia Orchestra & Chorus.

○ **Waltzes / LONDON**
Boskovsky/Vienna PO.

○ **Waltzes & Overtures / ANGEL**
Welser-Möst/London PO. If he doesn't stumble (as so many others recently have), Welser-Möst will be the next great conductor. These aren't just waltzes but miniature tone poems lovingly shaped and phrased. He elevates and makes fresh whatever he touches, from Mozart to Orff. –PM

○ **Wiener Blut (operetta) / ANGEL**
Schwarzkopf, Koth, Loose, Gedda, Kunz, Ackermann/ Philharmonia Orchestra & Chorus.

○ **Der Zigeunerbaron (operetta) / ANGEL**
Schwarzkopf, Koth, Gedda, Kunz, Prey, Ackermann/ Philharmonia Orchestra & Chorus.

RICHARD STRAUSS   1864-1949

Romantic, 20th century. A German composer, one of the great "late romantics," known primarily for his great tone poems and innovative operas (*Elektra*, *Salome*, and *Der Rosenkavalier*, controversial both for their music and their extra-musical subject matter). *Don Juan* and *Aus Italien* ("From Italy," 1886); Stauss's first symphonic poem) are good examples of his earlier tone poems, which draw almost operatic pictures and use references to national music. *Also Sprach Zarathustra* (1896) describes the different worlds of consciousness and being (more than Kubrick's *2001* movie would lead you to believe) and thus marks the other trend in Strauss's musical thought. The texts from Oscar Wilde, Stefan Zweig, and Josef Gregor for various operas got Strauss into hot water with the moralists in Boston and with the Nazis. His later, post-WWII works are more refined and energetic. –BGT

○ **Eine Alpensinfonie / VIRGIN**
de Waart/Minnesota Orchestra. Doesn't quite scale the heights, but doesn't take itself too seriously either, with a simplicity and sense of purpose that I really admire in this

turgid work. Not as virtuosic as Haitink or Ashkenazy, let alone Karajan, de Waart still makes more "music" out of this problematic piece. He is very lyrical, even tender. –PM

Eine Alpensinfonie / PHILIPS
Haitink/Royal Concertgebouw Orchestra. In technicolor, but not bombastic. Much more structured and controlled than usual and all the more exciting for that, with terrific sound and playing. Very well sculpted and held together. –PM

Eine Alpensinfonie / LONDON
Ashkenazy/Cleveland Orchestra. Very dramatic, with more telling details than the other two. For me, all three of these are must-haves and bury the rest of the competition. –PM

☆ **Also Sprach Zarathustra, op. 30 / RCA**
Reiner/Chicago SO. One of the first stereo recordings (1954) ever made, and a classic. The later (1962) version doesn't quite have the fire, control, and spontaneity of the earlier. –PM

Also Sprach Zarathustra, op. 30 / PHILIPS
Haitink/Royal Concertgebouw Orchestra.

Also Sprach Zarathustra, op. 30 / DGG
Karajan/Berlin PO. Powerful, all-digital, more Hollywood-style version. But not superficial. –PM

Also Sprach Zarathustra, op. 30 / PHILIPS
Bychkov/Philharmonia Orchestra.

○ **Arabella, op. 79 / LONDON**
Te Kanawa, Fontana, Tate, Dernesch, et al., Tate/Royal PO.

Arabella, op. 79 (excerpts) / ANGEL
Schwarzkopf, Loose, et al., Matacic/Philharmonia Orchestra.

○ **Ariadne auf Naxos, op. 60 / ANGEL**
Schwarzkopf, Seefried, Streich, Otto, Hoffman, Schock, Unger, Cuenod, Prey, Ollendorff, Karajan/Philharmonia Orchestra.

Ariadne auf Naxos, op. 60 / PHILIPS
Norman, Varady, Gruberova, Frey, Bar, Fischer-Dieskau, Masur/Leipzig Gewandhaus Orchestra.

Ariadne auf Naxos, op. 60 / DGG
Tomowa-Sintow, Battle, Baltsa, Lakes, Prey, Levine/Vienna PO.

○ **Aus Italien, op. 16 / LONDON**
Ashkenazy/Cleveland Orchestra. With an orchestra and sound as good as this and a Straussian as careful and meticulous as Ashkenazy, it's going to be hard to rival this one. –PM

Aus Italien, op. 16 / ASV
del Mar/Aarhus SO, Denmark. Considering the orchestra, this is a very interesting and competitive performance. –PM

○ **Le bourgeois gentilhomme (orchestral suite), op. 60 / RCA**
Reiner/Chicago SO. Forget anyone else: this is the only one to bestow a sense of dignity on this potboiler. –PM

○ **Burleske for Piano & Orchestra in d / ELECTRECORD**
Richter, Georgescu/Bucharest "George Enescu" PO. The orchestra is very spotty and the sound fuzzy, but Richter is awe-inspiring and makes this fluff into a whole new and more serious piece of music. –PM

Burleske for Piano & Orchestra in d / RCA
Janis, Reiner/Chicago SO. The classic studio performance, but the piano part is still bettered by Richter. –PM

○ **Capriccio, op. 85 / ANGEL**
Schwarzkopf, Moffo, Ludwig, Gedda, Fischer-Dieskau, Wächter, Hotter, Sawallisch/Philharmonia Orchestra. This is the classic recording, with Schwartzkopf completely unequaled. –PM

Capriccio, op. 85 / DGG
Janowitz, Troyanos, Schreier, Prey, Fischer-Dieskau, Ridderbusch, Böhm/Bavarian RSO. Böhm was our most devoted Strauss-opera conductor, and this is a beautifully sung and prepared performance. It's just too bad Schwarzkopf wasn't the Countess. –PM

Capriccio: Closing Scene / ANGEL
Schwarzkopf, Ackermann/Philharmonia Orchestra.

○ **Concertos for Horn & Orchestra no. 1 in E-flat, op. 11, & no. 2 in E-flat (1942) / ANGEL**
Brain, Sawallisch/Philharmonia Orchestra.

Concertos for Horn & Orchestra op. 11, no. 1 in E-flat & no. 2 in E-flat (1942) / PHILIPS
Baumann, Masur/Leipzig Gewandhaus Orchestra.

○ **Concerto for Oboe & Orchestra in D / ASV**
Boyd, Berglund, Paavo/Chamber Orchestra of Europe.

○ **Daphne, op. 82 / DGG**
Gueden, Little, King, Wunderlich, Schoffler, Böhm/Vienna SO & State Opera Chorus.

○ **Death and Transfiguration, op. 24 / CHANDOS**
Horenstein/London SO. The toughest performance ever. It's scary. –PM

Death and Transfiguration, op. 24 / PHILIPS
Haitink/Royal Concertgebouw Orchestra.

Death and Transfiguration, op. 24 / RCA
Reiner/RCA Victor SO.

Death and Transfiguration, op. 24 / DGG
Karajan/Berlin PO.

☆ **Don Juan, op. 20 / DGG**
Furtwängler/Berlin PO. An amazing combination of grace, nobility, and Teutonic fun. –PM

Don Juan, op. 20 / PHILIPS
Haitink/Royal Concertgebouw Orchestra.

Don Juan, op. 20 / RCA
Reiner/Chicago SO.

Don Juan, op. 20 / DGG
Karajan/Berlin PO.

○ **Don Quixote, for Cello & Orchestra, op. 35 / PHILIPS**
Schiff (cello), Masur/Leipzig Gewandhaus Orchestra. Terrific sound. Schiff, the finest cellist since Rostropovich, turns in a really soulful performance, and Masur is really colorful while managing to hold together this rambling work. –PM

Don Quixote, for Cello & Orchestra, op. 35 / RCA
Janigro (cello), Reiner/Chicago SO.

Don Quixote, for Cello & Orchestra, op. 35 / LONDON
Harrell (cello), Ashkenazy/Cleveland Orchestra.

Don Quixote, for Cello & Orchestra, op. 35 / DGG
Fournier (cello), Karajan/Berlin PO.

○ **Elektra, op. 58 / LONDON**
Nilsson, Collier, Resnik, Stolze, Krause, Solti/Vienna PO.

☆ **Four Last Songs / ANGEL**
Schwarzkopf, Ackermann/Philharmonia Orchestra. More objective and less self-indulgent than we're used to nowadays. Speeds are faster, and Schwarzkopf is in radiant voice. –PM

Four Last Songs / ANGEL
Schwarzkopf, Szell/Berlin RSO. A more mature, probing, and intense performance, but a bit tired and not so well sung as her earlier version above. –PM

Four Last Songs / PHILIPS
Norman, Masur/Leipzig Gewandhaus Orchestra. No version can touch this one for opulence. –PM

○ **Die Frau ohne Schatten (3-act opera) / DGG**
Nilsson, Rysanek, Hesse, King, Berry, Böhm/Vienna PO & State Opera Chorus.

○ **Ein Heldenleben, op. 40 / RCA**
Reiner/Chicago SO.

Ein Heldenleben, op. 40 / DGG
Karajan/Berlin PO. The sumptuousness, sweep, and grandeur of this performance are hard to deny, but sometimes a bit of ruggedness might have been in order. –PM

Ein Heldenleben, op. 40 / LONDON
Ashkenazy/Cleveland Orchestra.

○ **Metamorphosen, for 23 Solo Strings / ANGEL**
Klemperer/Philharmonia Orchestra. Stark and powerful. –PM

Metamorphosen, for 23 Solo Strings / DGG

Karajan/Berlin PO. Ultimately too sumptuous for my taste and for such tragic music. –PM

○ **Piano Pieces (5), op. 3 / CBS**
Gould.

○ **Romanze for Cello & Orchestra in F / PHILIPS**
Schiff, Masur/Leipzig Gewandhaus Orchestra.

○ **Der Rosenkavalier (three-act opera), op. 59 / ANGEL**
Schwarzkopf, Stich-Randall, Ludwig, Edelmann, Karajan/ Philharmonia Orchestra.
Der Rosenkavalier (three-act opera), op. 59 / DGG
Tomowa-Sintow, Karajan/Vienna PO & State Opera Chorus.
Der Rosenkavalier (three-act opera), op. 59 / LONDON
Crespin, Donath, Minton, Jungwirth, Solti/Vienna PO.

○ **Salome, op. 54 / LONDON**
Nilsson, Hoffman, Stolze, Kmentt, Wächter, Solti/Vienna PO.

○ **Serenade for 13 Wind Instruments in E-flat / VIRGIN**
de Waart/Minnesota Orchestra.

○ **Sonata for Cello & Piano, op. 6 / ADDA**
Drobinsky, Buokoff.
Sonata for Cello & Piano, op. 6 / ONDINE
Rousi, Lagerspetz.

○ **Sonata for Piano in b, op. 5 / ADDA**
Boukoff.
Sonata for Piano in b, op. 5 / CBS
Gould.

○ **Sonata for Violin & Piano in E-flat, op. 18 / ADDA**
Lielmane, Boukoff.
Sonata for Violin & Piano in E-flat, op. 18 / DGG
Shaham, de Silva.

○ **Songs / PHILIPS**
Norman, Masur/Leipzig Gewandhaus Orchestra.

○ **Suite for 13 Winds, op. 4 / VIRGIN**
de Waart/Minnesota Orchestra.

○ **Symphonia Domestica, op. 53 / RCA**
Reiner/Chicago SO. One of Reiner's five best recordings. –PM
Symphonia Domestica, op. 53 / DGG
Furtwängler/Berlin PO. Many magical moments but without quite the same flow and thrust of Reiner. –PM
Symphonia Domestica, op. 53 / VIRGIN
de Waart/Minnesota Orchestra. De Waart's conducting of the late romantics always has a special nostalgia. And combined with great clarity and more simplicity than usual, this is the outstanding recording of the *Domestica*, with good sound. –PM

○ **Symphony in d / KOCH-SCHWANN**
Rickenbacher/Bavarian RSO.

☆ **Till Eulenspiegels lustige Streiche, op. 28 / PHILIPS**
Masur/Leipzig Gewandhaus Orchestra. Masur can be so good sometimes; I just wish he were more consistent. –PM
Till Eulenspiegels lustige Streiche, op. 28 / SUPRAPHON
Ancerl/Czech PO. What a sense of fun, but what a sense of purpose too. –PM
Till Eulenspiegels lustige Streiche, op. 28 / DGG
Furtwängler/Berlin PO.
Till Eulenspiegels lustige Streiche, op. 28 / PHILIPS
Haitink/Royal Concertgebouw Orchestra.

IGOR STRAVINSKY   1882-1971

20th century, neo-classical. An important Russian composer of totally original and exciting music in many forms. Stravinsky's ballet *The Rite of Spring* (1913), a work of exotic and primal character, marked a shift in modern Western music. In early pieces such as *Fireworks* (1908) and the marvelous *King of the Stars* for chorus and orchestra (1911), Stravinsky exhibits a love of orchestral color that seems like a combination of Debussy, Scriabin, and Wagner. The wood-flute song and plainchant intervals from one layer of his music. Other layers are the added harmonic dissonances, either in a rhythmic pattern (like the famous sacrificial dance

in *The Rite of Spring*) or in sparkling arpeggios of violin harmonics and woodwinds. Stravinsky wedded the primitive, ancient, and neo-classical to the scale of the present. There seems to be a progression from *Petrouchka* and *The Firebird* for the Ballets-Russes, to the neo-jazz *Ebony Concerto*, to the purity of religious feeling shown in the *Symphony of Psalms* and *Agon*, which begins to use the 12-tone technique in a limited way — but maybe it's more an unfolding of a personality that was there from the start. –BGT

○ **Abraham and Isaac; Babel (from the Genesis Suite) / ORFEO**
Fischer-Dieskau, Bertini/Stuttgart RSO.

○ **Agon (ballet) / MELODIYA (KOCH)**
Mravinsky/Leningrad PO.
Agon (ballet) / VIRGIN
Iwaki/Melbourne SO.

○ **Apollo [Apollon Mausagete] (ballet) / CAPRICCIO**
Végh/Camerata Academica des Mozarteums. Too lush, but full of deep character. –PM
Apollo [Apollon Mausagete] (ballet) / DGG
Karajan/Berlin PO. Too lush and not so good as the best on LP (i.e., Mravinsky), but very beautiful and at times haunting. –PM

○ **Le baiser de la fée / PHILIPS**
Bychkov/Orchestre de Paris. This is an utterly innocent and charming performance. –PM
Le baiser de la fée / FONIT-CETERA
Furtwängler/Berlin PO. A uniquely Teutonic view. –PM
Le baiser de la fée / RCA
Reiner/Chicago SO.
Le baiser de la fée / LONDON
Chailly/London Sinfonietta.

○ **Concerto for Two Solo Pianos / PHILIPS**
K. and M. Labeque.

○ **Concerto for Violin & Orchestra in D / DGG**
Mutter (violin), Sacher/Philharmonia Orchestra. Mutter tones down her vibrato and her romantic excesses. I hope she will be doing more modern music, because this is absolutely outstanding playing and the best thing she has ever done. –PM
Concerto for Violin & Orchestra in D / DGG
Perlman (violin), Ozawa/Boston SO.

○ **Concerto in E-flat, "Dumbarton Oaks" / LONDON**
Hogwood/St. Paul CO. I'm impressed! There's a special care with the phrasing and attention to details; who says period-instrument conductors can't do later music? –PM
Concerto in E-flat, "Dumbarton Oaks" / DGG
Orpheus CO.

○ **Ebony Concerto / CBS**
Goodman (clarinet), Stravinsky/Columbia Jazz Combo.

○ **Elegy for J. F. K. / ORFEO**
Fischer-Dieskau, Gruber, Adler, Berger.

○ **Fanfare for a New Theatre; three Pieces for Clarinet / LONDON**
Chailly/London Sinfonietta.

○ **The Firebird (complete ballet) / PHILIPS**
Haitink/Berlin PO. Beautifully shaded and controlled performance, but may be on the cool side for some tastes. Interesting shimmering, digital electronic-type sound. –PM
The Firebird (complete ballet) / MERCURY
Dorati/London SO.
The Firebird (complete ballet) / CBS
Boulez/NYPO.

☆ **The Firebird: Suite / DGG**
Abbado/London SO.
The Firebird: Suite / HUNGARATON
Fischer/Budapest Festival Orchestra. The emphasis is on soul and substance rather than just sheer brilliance. –PM

○ **Fireworks, for Orchestra, op. 4 / LONDON**

Chailly/Berlin RSO.

○ **Five Easy Pieces for Piano (four hands); Three Easy Pieces / PHILIPS**
K. and M. Labeque.

○ **Four Norwegian Moods / LONDON**
Chailly/Cleveland Orchestra.

○ **L'Histoire du soldat: Suite in Nine Sections for Instrumental Ensemble / REFERENCE**
Chicago Pro Musica.

○ **Jeu de cartes / DGG**
Abbado/London SO.

○ **King of the Stars / LONDON**
Chailly/Berlin RSO.

○ **Mass / DGG**
Bernstein/English Bach Festival Orchestra.

○ **The Nightingale / ERATO**
Boulez/BBC SO, BBC Singers (choir), various singers. Boulez makes a triumphant return to the recording studio with this early "opera-ballet" that is very much in the mold of *Firebird* and authoritatively performed by Boulez. –PM

○ **Les noces, for Vocalists, Four Pianos, Percussion Ensemble & Chorus / DGG**
Mory, Parker, Mitchinson, Hudson (vocalists), Argerich, Francesch, Zimerman, Katsaris (pianos), Bernstein/English Bach Festival Orchestra.

○ **Octet for Wind Instruments / LONDON**
Chailly/London Sinfonietta.

○ **Oedipus Rex (two-act opera/oratorio) / ORFEO**
Norman, Moser, Nimsgern, Bracht, Davis/Bavarian RSO & Bonn Opera Chorus.

☆ **Petrouchka (complete ballet) / PHILIPS**
Bychkov/Orchestre de Paris. Exciting and charismatic performance. Russian with a French accent: The perfect combination for Stravinsky. –PM

Petrouchka (complete ballet) / HUNGARATON
Fischer/Budapest Festival Orchestra. Relies less on brilliance and more on soul and solidity. The momentum is there, and there are many original touches of rhythm and color, with fine recorded sound. –PM

Petrouchka (complete ballet) / DGG
Abbado/London SO.

Petrouchka (complete ballet) / VIRGIN
Iwaki/Melbourne SO. This is a flamboyant and exciting performance. –PM

○ **Petrouchka: Three Scenes for Piano / PHILIPS**
K. and M. Labeque.

Petrouchka: Three Scenes for Piano / DGG
Pollini.

○ **Pulcinella (ballet), for Soprano, Tenor, Bass & Orchestra DGG**
Berganza, Davies, Shirley-Quirk, Abbado/London SO. A tough choice here: I like the charm and small-scale intimacy of Hogwood, but Abbado has more flair and charisma — and he has the LSO in top form –PM

Pulcinella (ballet), for Soprano, Tenor, Bass & Orchestra LONDON
Hogwood/St. Paul CO.

○ **Pulcinella: Suite / LONDON**
Marriner/ASMF. My favorite performance ever of the suite, by virtue of its lightness of touch and terrific sense of humor, not to mention brilliant playing. –PM

Pulcinella: Suite / DGG
Orpheus CO. A very brilliant first album, but it doesn't achieve the sense of direction Marriner achieves. –PM

○ **The Rake's Progress / LONDON**
Pope, Walker, Langridge, Dean, Ramey, Chailly/London Sinfonietta & Chorus.

○ **Renard / LONDON**

Langridge, Jenkins, Hammond-Stroud, Lloyd, Chailly/London Sinfonietta. Brilliant, but lacks the Russian soul of earlier (LP) performances like Ansermet's. –PM

☆ **Le sacre du printemps ("The Rite of Spring") / LONDON**
Chailly/Cleveland Orchestra. I collect *Rites*, and this is probably the finest one I have ever heard. With terrific drama and precision, it is among the best, if not THE best played, and it is elegant and primitive to boot. What a combination! –PM

Le sacre du printemps ("The Rite of Spring") / DGG
Abbado/London SO.

Le sacre du printemps ("The Rite of Spring") / SUPRAPHON
Ancerl/Czech Philharmonic. Yes, it isn't so well played or well recorded as the Chailly, but it has a sense of urgency and inevitability, and the details are fully integrated into the whole. It is quirky, and it has a unique sound and a lot of singular details. –PM

Le sacre du printemps ("The Rite of Spring") / DGG
Karajan/Berlin PO.

○ **Scherzo à la russe / MERCURY**
Dorati/London SO.

○ **Scherzo fantastique, op. 3 / LONDON**
Dorati/Detroit SO.

○ **Song of the Nightingale / CBS**
Boulez/NYPO. Four outstanding and completely competitive performances: It's a shame to have to rank them. –PM

Song of the Nightingale / RCA
Reiner/Chicago SO.

Song of the Nightingale / MERCURY
Dorati/London SO.

Song of the Nightingale / LONDON
Chailly/Berlin RSO.

○ **Songs / ORFEO**
Bertini, Fischer-Dieskau/Berlin Stuttgart RSO.

○ **Suites for Small Orchestra nos. 1 & 2 / LONDON**
Chailly/London Sinfonietta.

○ **Symphony in C / PHILIPS**
Davis/Bavarian RSO. Davis has always had a way with Stravinsky rhythms. He can clarify, but he makes Stravinsky sound "romantic" at the same time. –PM

○ **Symphony in Three Movements / FONIT-CETERA**
Furtwängler/Vienna PO. Every note "tells" in this uniquely Furtwänglerian reading. But is it Stravinsky? –PM

Symphony in Three Movements / PHILIPS
Davis/Bavarian RSO.

○ **Symphony no. 1 in E-flat, op. 1 / LONDON**
Dorati/Detroit SO.

○ **Symphony of Psalms / ORFEO**
Bertini/Stuttgart RSO & Chorus. Bertini is an underrated conductor, and this is a sleeper of a disc. –PM

Symphony of Psalms / LONDON
Chailly/Berlin RSO.

○ **Violin & Piano Works (complete) / PHILIPS**
van Keulen (violin), Mustonen (piano). Just the right spikiness and sense of style for these tricky and frivolous works. –PM

JOSEF SUK   1874-1935

Romantic. A Czech composer of quartets, piano music, and orchestral tone poems who was Dvořák's favorite student. –ED

○ **Asrael (symphony for large orchestra), op. 27 / CHANDOS**
Bělohlávek/Czech PO. Pesek has his moments, but Bělohlávek is a better conductor, and his version is more mysterious and better held together plus he has a better orchestra and more atmospheric sound. –PM

Asrael (symphony for large orchestra), op. 27 / VIRGIN

Pesek/Royal Liverpool PO.

○ **Serenade for String Orchestra in E-flat, op. 6 / KOCH-SCHWANN**
Talich/Czech PO.

FRANZ VON SUPPÉ   1819-1895

Romantic. An Austrian conductor and composer of opera, operetta, and incidental music who is famous for overtures to such works as *Poet and Peasant* and *Morning, Noon, and Night in Vienna.* –ED

○ **Overtures / LONDON**
Dutoit/Montreal SO.

Overtures / DGG
Karajan/Berlin PO. A bit too Germanic-sounding, but the usual Karajan virtues. –PM

KAROL SZYMANOWSKI   1882-1937

Romantic, nationalist. An eminent Polish composer whose early style was influenced by German romanticism. About 1917, his music began to show an awareness of Scriabin and impressionism and a new style began to emerge. As a director of the Warsaw Conservatory, his compositions and teaching had a strong impact on Polish music. His ballet *Harnasie* (based on a folk legend) and his *Stabat Mater* are among his most important works. –MKS

○ **Harnasie (ballet-pantomime in three scenes) / KOCH-SCHWANN**
Stepien, Satanowski/Polish National Opera Warsaw Orchestra & Chorus.

○ **Piano Music: Studies (4), op. 4; Metopes, op. 29; Fantasy, op. 14; Masques, op. 34 / HYPERION**
Lee (piano). Could be a bit more flamboyant and less on the dry British side, but it still gives a good idea of this enigmatic composer. –PM

○ **Quartet for Strings no. 1 in C, op. 37 / OLYMPIA**
Varsovia Quartet.

○ **Quartet for Strings no. 2, op. 56 / OLYMPIA**
Varsovia Quartet.

○ **Sonata for Violin & Piano in d, op. 9 / ONDINE**
Koskinen, Lagerspetz.

○ **Stabat Mater for Soprano, Contralto, Baritone, Orchestra & Chorus, op. 53 (1926) / MUZA**
Woytowicz, Szczepanska, Hiolski, Rowicki/Warsaw National PO & Chorus.

○ **Symphony no. 2 in B-flat, op. 19 / LONDON**
Dorati/Detroit SO.

○ **Symphony no. 3, op. 27, "Song of the Night" / LONDON**
Karczykowski, Dorati/Detroit SO.

THOMAS TALLIS   1505-1585

Renaissance, sacred vocal. The "father of English cathedral music" is primarily known for his vocal music, mainly the motets of the collection *Cantiones Sacrae* (published jointly with William Byrd in 1575 and dedicated to Queen Elizabeth, a collection intended to show the skill of English composers in handling dramatic styles cultivated in continental Europe but rare in English music). Tallis and Byrd couldn't have succeeded better — there are many antiphonal motets in striking harmonic style, such as *In Ieiunio et Fletu*, but the most overwhelming work, which has never been matched in conception or sonority, is the motet *Spem in Alium Nunquam Habui* for 40 voices divided into eight antiphonal choirs. The voices enter successively in imitation, then sing antiphonally to each other, alternating contrapuntal phrases with chordal responses and creating daring dissonances — for example, successively minor seconds (F-natural, F-sharp, G) that resolve and overlap from choir to choir. Suddenly there is silence, and then the choirs build up again to a magical moment when, on the word "respice," all 40 voices change

harmony together (to the minor of the fifth) for a spine-tingling effect. –BGT

○ **Church Music / GIMELL**
Phillips/The Tallis Scholars.

○ **The English Anthems (complete) / GIMELL**
Phillips/The Tallis Scholars. As always with the Tallis Scholars, their singing is extraordinarily pure and vibrant, and this is one of their best CDs. In fact, if you want an introduction to their art, go for this one or the *Allegri Miserere.* –PM

☆ **Spem in alium (40-part motet) / GIMELL**
Phillips/The Tallis Scholars.

GIUSEPPE TARTINI   1692-1770

Baroque. An Italian violinist, composer, and music theorist who made several important acoustical discoveries (resulting in treatises) and wrote numerous violin pieces, the most famous of which is *The Devil's Trill* sonata. –MKS

○ **The "Four Tasso Sonatas," for Violin alone & Violin with Basso Continuo / KOCH-SCHWANN**
Accademia Claudio Monteverdi. Very interesting supplement to the Locatelli Trio CD. –PM

○ **Sonatas for Violin - Vol. 1 / HYPERION**
The Locatelli Trio. The best Tartini CD I have ever heard, and the only one that really makes sense. –PM

Sonatas for Violin - Vol. 2 / HYPERION
The Locatelli Trio.

JOHN TAVERNER   1490-1545

Renaissance. An important English church musician and composer who wrote a large number of sacred pieces, including masses, motets, Magnificats, and part-songs. –MKS

○ **Choral Works / GIMELL**
Phillips/The Tallis Scholars.

○ **Gloria tibi Trinitas (mass); Leroy Kyrie & more / GIMELL**
Phillips/The Tallis Scholars.

PIOTR ILYICH TCHAIKOVSKY   1840-1893

Romantic. A Russian composer of major importance who composed many notable works in most forms, including the *Nutcracker Suite* (1892), *Swan Lake* (1877), *Symphony no. 4* (1878), and *Symphony no. 6* ("Pathétique"). In the background of the sweeping, rich, romantic themes, the vitality of the dance scores, and the expressive arias, there is a mind at work thinking about life — about childhood visions of good and evil (*Nutcracker Suite*), about the despair caused by aristocratic class-based societies (*The Queen of Spades*, *Eugen Onegin*), about hope even when we feel alienated from the contemporary world (the emotional program of the great "Pathétique" symphony). Tchaikovsky has made us feel wonderful with vigorous, lovely works like the *Concerto for Violin & Orchestra in D* and the famous *Concerto for Piano & Orchestra no. 1 in b-flat*; but within them we also find the soul searching for enlightenment. –BGT

○ **1812 Overture, op. 49 / SUPRAPHON**
Ancerl/London SO.

1812 Overture, op. 49 / CBS
Maazel/Vienna PO & State Opera Chorus.

1812 Overture, op. 49 / DGG
Karajan/Berlin PO, Don Cossack Chorus.

○ **Arrangement of String Quartet no. 3, movement 3, op. 30 for Violin & Piano / ONDINE**
Kagan, Lobranov.

○ **Capriccio italien, op. 45 / SUPRAPHON**
Ancerl/Czech PO.

Capriccio italien, op. 45 / DGG
Karajan/Berlin PO.

Capriccio italien, op. 45 / LONDON
Ashkenazy/Royal PO.

☆ **Concerto for Piano & Orchestra no. 1 in b-flat, op. 23 /
DGG**
Kremer (piano), Maazel/Berlin PO. Everything just seems to
come together on this one: Maazel is less glib than usual and
Kremer less eccentric. –PM
**Concerto for Piano & Orchestra no. 1 in b-flat, op. 23 /
URANIA**
Richter (piano), Mravinsky/Leningrad PO. The ultimate in
virtuosity, fantasy, and subtle poetry. But the sound is a bit
limiting: clear enough, but not very hi-fi. –PM
**Concerto for Piano & Orchestra no. 1 in b-flat, op. 23 /
DGG**
Richter (piano), Karajan/Vienna SO. A more languid, sensual
approach, as befits the conductor. –PM
**Concerto for Piano & Orchestra no. 1 in b-flat, op. 23 /
RCA**
Horowitz (piano), Toscanini/NBC SO. Hell bent for leather.
One of Horowitz's best. –PM
**Concerto for Piano & Orchestra no. 1 in b-flat, op. 23 /
DGG**
Pogorelich, Abbado/London SO.
**Concerto for Piano & Orchestra no. 1 in b-flat, op. 23 /
DGG**
Kissin (piano), Karajan/Berlin PO. This is one maddening CD
(how easy it would be just to dismiss it!), but it is hypnotic,
and when your mood is aligned with their vision, it is
overwhelming. At nearly 40 minutes, this has to be the slowest
version ever made, but how rhapsodic and what poetry! And
it was Karajan's last recording. Approach this album with
caution. It will be your only chance to hear a legend with a
legend-in-the-making! –PM
○ **Elegy for Strings / LONDON**
Ashkenazy/Royal PO.
○ **Eugen Onegin (three-act opera), op. 24 / LONDON**
Kubiak, Hamari, Burrows, Senechal, Weikl, Ghiaurov,
Solti/Royal Opera.
**Eugen Onegin, op. 24: Introduction, Waltz & Polonaise /
PHILIPS**
Bychkov/Berlin PO.
Eugen Onegin, op. 24: Waltz & Polonaise / DGG
Karajan/Berlin PO.
○ **Francesca da Rimini, op. 32 / PHILIPS**
Gergiev/London PO. An exciting new recording, with plenty of
Russian temperament. –PM
Francesca da Rimini, op. 32 / LONDON
Ashkenazy/Royal PO.
○ **Humoresque for Violin & Piano no. 2, op. 10 / ONDINE**
Kagan, Lobranov.
○ **Manfred (symphony), op. 58 / LONDON**
Ashkenazy/Philharmonia Orchestra.
Manfred (symphony), op. 58 / LONDON
Chailly/Royal Concertgebouw Orchestra.
○ **Marche slave, op. 31 / DGG**
Karajan/Berlin PO.
○ **The Nutcracker, op. 71 (complete ballet) / PHILIPS**
Bychkov/Berlin PO. Until Rozhdestvensky's innocent and
sparkling account with the Bolshoi Theatre Orchestra makes it
back to the catalog, this well-played performance will have to
do. It just doesn't have the charisma I normally associate with
Bychkov. –PM
The Nutcracker, op. 71 (complete ballet) / TELARC
Mackerras/London SO.
**The Nutcracker, op. 71 (excerpts from CD-80137) /
TELARC**
Mackerras/London SO.
☆ **The Nutcracker Suite, op. 71a / LONDON**
Celibidache/London PO. This performance is serious and it
communicates. –PM

The Nutcracker Suite, op. 71a / PHILIPS
Mravinsky/Leningrad PO.
The Nutcracker Suite, op. 71a / PHILIPS
Dorati/Royal Concertgebouw Orchestra. Great orchestra, great
ballet conductor, and great budget price: what more could you
want? –PM
The Nutcracker Suite, op. 71a / PHILIPS
Marriner/ASMF.
○ **Piano Music (Nocturne in F; Valse-Scherzo in A) /
MELODIYA (KOCH)**
Richter.
○ **Romeo and Juliet (fantasy overture) / DGG**
Abbado/Boston SO.
Romeo and Juliet (fantasy overture) / LONDON
Ashkenazy/Royal PO.
○ **Serenade for String Orchestra in C, op. 48 / PHILIPS**
Davis/Bavarian RSO.
Serenade for String Orchestra in C, op. 48 / PHILIPS
Marriner/ASMF.
Serenade for String Orchestra in C, op. 48 / DGG
Orpheus CO.
○ **Sérénade mélancolique for Violin & Orchestra, op. 26 /
ONDINE**
Kagan, Lobanov.
○ **Sleeping Beauty, op. 66 (complete ballet) / PHILIPS**
Dorati/Royal Concertgebouw Orchestra.
Sleeping Beauty, op. 66 (excerpts) / TELARC
Mackerras/Royal PO.
○ **Souvenir d'un lieu cher, for Violin & Piano, op. 42 /
ONDINE**
Kagan, Lobanov.
○ **Suites for Orchestra nos. 1-4 / CAPRICCIO**
Marriner/Stuttgart RSO.
○ **Swan Lake (excerpts) / TELARC**
Mackerras/Royal PO.
○ **Symphonies nos. 1-6 (complete) / DGG**
Karajan/Berlin PO.
○ **Symphony no. 1 in g, op. 13, "Winter Dreams" /
CAPRICCIO**
Marriner/ASMF. Conducted with the force and clarity of a
Haydn symphony, this is a welcome change from the normal
inflated and overly romanticized accounts of this and all other
Tchaikovsky symphonies. It reminds me of the classic Dorati
LP recording. –PM
Symphony no. 1 in g, op. 13, "Winter Dreams" / DGG
Karajan/Berlin PO. Impressive, but a bit too bloated for my
taste. –PM
○ **Symphony no. 2 in c, op. 17, "Little Russian" /
CAPRICCIO**
Marriner/ASMF. Like *Symphony no. 1*, this is a very forthright
and clear-eyed account, with beautiful, delicate sound
to match, and striking for its rhythmic precision and
alertness. –PM
Symphony no. 2 in c, op. 17, "Little Russian" / DGG
Abbado/New Philharmonia Orchestra.
Symphony no. 2 in c, op. 17, "Little Russian" / DGG
Karajan/Berlin PO.
○ **Symphony no. 3 in D, op. 29, "Polish" / DGG**
Karajan/Berlin PO.
○ **Symphony no. 4 in f, op. 36 / DGG**
Mravinsky/Leningrad PO.
Symphony no. 4 in f, op. 36 / DENON
Inbal. A soberingly different look at this potboiler, which
turns it into a dignified tragedy. A very distinctive reading,
with outstanding sound. –PM
Symphony no. 4 in f, op. 36 / DGG
Abbado/Vienna PO.

Symphony no. 4 in f, op. 36 / LONDON
Ashkenazy/Philharmonia Orchestra.

○ **Symphony no. 5 in e, op. 64 / LONDON**
Ashkenazy/Philharmonia Orchestra.

○ **Symphony no. 5 in e, op. 64; The Nutcracker Suite / LONDON**
Celibidache. Recorded in July 1948 when Celibidache was 36, these are two of the only three currently surviving studio recordings this controversial Romanian conductor has made (fortunately, many pirate performances have been issued over the last 40 years). For my money, Celibidache is the greatest living conductor, if not the greatest ever, and the booklet to this CD helps explain why. Suffice it to say that he combines raw and sensual emotion with an uplifting mysticism that I find goes straight to the heart of virtually everything he conducts, from Bach to Hindemith. –PM

Symphony no. 5 in e, op. 64 / AS DISC
Furtwängler/RAI Turin Orchestra. Emotionally overwrought at times, but outstanding. –PM

Symphony no. 5 in e, op. 64 / DGG
Mravinsky/Leningrad PO.

Symphony no. 5 in e, op. 64 / DENON
Inbal/Frankfurt RSO.

☆ **Symphony no. 6 in b, op. 74, "Pathétique" / PHILIPS**
Bychkov/Royal Concertgebouw Orchestra. My current favorite *Sixth*! Bychkov's performance is romantic, but at the same time sane, sober, and serious, and very well held together. Details are prevalent and to the fore but blend in with the whole and count in its context. It has tension and dignity, with a remarkable sustained line. It also is one of the best played and well recorded. An outstanding achievement. –PM

Symphony no. 6 in b, op. 74, "Pathétique" / DGG
Sinopoli/Philharmonia Orchestra.

Symphony no. 6 in b, op. 74, "Pathétique" / DGG
Mravinsky/Leningrad PO.

Symphony no. 6 in b, op. 74, "Pathétique" / DGG
Abbado/Berlin PO.

○ **Trio for Violin, Cello & Piano in a, op. 50 / PHILIPS**
Beaux Arts Trio.

Trio for Violin, Cello & Piano in a, op. 50 / ANGEL
Perlman, Harrell, Ashkenazy.

○ **Valse-Scherzo for Violin & Piano, op. 34 / ONDINE**
Kagan, Lobanov.

○ **Variations on a Rococo Theme, for Cello & Orchestra, op. 33 / DGG**
Rostropovich, Karajan/Berlin PO. No one has touched the beauty and subtlety of this performance for 20 years, and it will likely be another 20 before someone does. –PM

GEORG PHILIPP TELEMANN   1681-1767

Baroque. A remarkably prolific, skillful, and forward-thinking German composer, one of the foremost of his day, who wrote a great many sacred and secular vocal works as well as orchestral, chamber, and keyboard music. A contemporary of Bach and Handel, Telemann shared many of their musical techniques and wrote for many of the same genres; and though his music is overshadowed by theirs, it has many charms, perhaps more evident in Telemann's modest instrumental works (of which the *Suite for Flute & Strings in a* is a good choice) than in his 40 operas, 600 overtures, 44 liturgical passions, and other large works. Handel said Telemann could write an eight-part motet with the ease that someone else would write a letter. –BGT

○ **La Changeante (orchestral suite in g) / CHANDOS**
Standage/Collegium Musicum.

○ **Concerto for Four Violins & Orchestra in A; Concerto in G for Four Violins unaccompanied / CHANDOS**
Comberti, Golding & Manze (violins), Standage (solo violin & conductor)/Collegium Musicum.

○ **Concerto for 2 Chalumeaux & Orchestra in d / DGG**
Goebel/Musica Antiqua Köln.

○ **Concertos for Flute & Orchestra / DGG**
Goebel/Musica Antiqua Köln. Aggressive and committed playing, with utmost vitality and rhythmic displacement, in startlingly clear digital sound. This is the most challenging Telemann CD I have ever heard. –PM

○ **Concerto for Flute, Strings & Continuo in D / DHM**
Camerata Köln.

○ **Concerto for Flute, Violin & Orchestra in e / CHANDOS**
Brown, Standage/Collegium Music.

○ **Concerto for Oboe, Strings & Continuo in e / DHM**
Camerata Köln.

○ **Concerto for 3 Oboes & Orchestra in B-flat / DGG**
Goebel/Musica Antiqua Köln.

○ **Concerto for Recorder, Bass Viol & Strings in F / RICERCAR**
de Roos, Beeuckels/Ricercar Consort.

○ **Concerto for Recorder, Bassoon & Strings in F / BIS**
Pehrsson, McCraw/Drottningholm Baroque Ensemble.

○ **Concerto for Recorder, Flute & Strings in e / DGG**
Goebel/Musica Antiqua Köln.

○ **Concerto for Recorder, Flute & Strings in F / RICERCAR**
de Roos, Beeuckels/Ricercar Consort.

○ **Concerto for Recorder, Strings & Continuo in F; Concerto for Recorder, Strings, Viola da Gamba & Continuo / DHM**
Camerata Köln.

○ **Concerto for Recorder & Strings in C / BIS**
Pehrsson/Drottningholm Baroque Ensemble.

○ **Concertos for 2 Recorders, Bassoon & Strings in B-flat, F, a / DGG**
Musica Antiqua Köln.

○ **Concertos for Trumpet, Two Oboes & Continuo in D and Four other Telemann trumpet concertos / PHILIPS**
Brown, Harvenberger/ASFM. As always, brilliant! –PM

○ **Concerto for Trumpet & Strings in D / DGG**
Goebel/Musica Antiqua Köln.

○ **Concerto for Trumpet, Violin & Orchestra in D / DGG**
Goebel/Musica Antiqua Köln.

○ **Concertos for Violin & Orchestra in a & E / CHANDOS**
Standage/Collegium Musicum.

○ **Darmstadt Overtures / TELDEC**
Harnoncourt/Concentus Musicus Wien.

○ **Duos, Sonatas & Miscellaneous Pieces for Recorder / BIS**
Pehrsson, Laurin (recorders); Larsson (cello); Kamata (harpsichord).

○ **Fantasies (12) for Violin / INTERCORD**
Kalafusz.

☆ **Musique de Table (18 instrumental compositions) / TELDEC**
Brüggen/Concerto Amsterdam.

Musique de Table (Book Two - excerpts); Two Trumpet Concertos / NUOVA ERA
Cassone (natural trumpet)/Ensemble "Pian & Forte." Intonation isn't the best, and it doesn't have much tonal allure (which is not helped by the dry but honest recording), but I sure like the style of these Italian players. –PM

Musique de Table (complete) / DGG
Goebel/Musica Antiqua Köln. Fast, aggressive performances, a bit on the charmless side but with much great playing and togetherness to admire. –PM

Musique de Table (selections) / TELDEC
Brüggen/Concerto Amsterdam. Selections from the complete recording listed above.

○ **Suite for Flute & Strings; Sinfonia in F; Concertos for Recorder / HYPERION**
Holtslag (recorder), Holman, Goodman/The Parley of Instruments.

☆ **Suite for Flute & Strings in a / BIS**
Pehrsson (recorder)/Drottningholm Baroque Ensemble. Fascinating for the sonorities and ornamentation and great rhythmic style but disconcertingly out of tune and world-weary at times. Lighter and more imaginative than Roos, who in turn is more compact and weighty in a good way. –PM

Suite for Flute & Strings in a / RICERCAR
de Roos/Ricercar Consort.

○ **Volume 3: Domestic Music / CHANDOS**
Standage, et al./Collegium Musicum. 78:35 minutes of fascinating Telemann byways: Sonatas, cantatas, suites, quartets, trios, and more. –PM

○ **Water Music (overture in C, "Hamburg's Tides") / DGG**
Musica Antiqua Köln. Outstanding performance of one of Telemann's best pieces. –PM

MICHAEL TIPPETT   ♭1905

20th century, neo-romantic. An important English composer in the neo-romantic style who excels in large-scale vocal and instrumental forms and, though incorporating dissonance, operates within a largely tonal framework. Not adverse to unusual effects, he interjects several instances of "heavy glottal aspiration" in his fourth symphony. –MKS

○ **Concerto for Double String Orchestra / LONDON**
Marriner/ASMF.

○ **Concerto for Orchestra / PHILIPS**
Davis/London SO.

○ **Concerto for Violin, Viola, Cello & Orchestra / PHILIPS**
Pauk, Imai, Kirshbaum, Davis/London SO.

○ **Fantasia Concertante for String Orchestra / LONDON**
Marriner/ASMF.

○ **King Priam (opera) / LONDON**
Harper, Palmer, Minton, Murray, Tear, Langridge, Bailey, Roberts, Atherton/London Sinfonietta & Chorus.

○ **Little Music for String Orchestra / LONDON**
Marriner/ASMF.

○ **Quartets for Strings nos. 1-3 / LONDON**
Lindsay String Quartet.

Quartets for Strings nos. 1-4 / COLLINS CLASSICS
Britten Quartet.

○ **Sonatas (4) for Piano (complete) / CRD**
Crossley.

○ **Symphonies (complete) / LONDON**
Davis/London SO; Solti/Chicago SO.

EDUARD TUBIN   1905-1982

20th century. An Estonian composer of concertos, dance and ballet suites, and ten symphonies. –ED

○ **Ballade for Violin & Orchestra / BIS**
Garcia, Järvi/Gothenbyrg SO.

○ **Concertino for Piano & Orchestra / BIS**
Pontinen, Järvi/Gothenburg SO.

○ **Concerto for Balalaika & Orchestra / BIS**
Sheynkman, Järvi/Swedish RSO.

○ **Concerto for Double Bass & Orchestra / BIS**
Ehren, Järvi/Gothenburg SO.

○ **Concerto for Violin & Orchestra no. 1; Estonian Dance Suite / BIS**
Lubotsky, Järvi/Gothenburg SO.

○ **Concerto for Violin & Orchestra no. 2 / BIS**
Garcia, Järvi/Gothenburg SO.

○ **Estonian Dance Suite / BIG BEN**
Frank, Frank/Helsingborg SO.

Estonian Dance Suite / BIS
Järvi/Gothenburg SO.

○ **Kratt (ballet suite) / BIS**
Järvi/Bamberg SO.

○ **Music for Strings / BIG BEN**
Frank/Helsingborg SO.

Music for Strings / BIS
Järvi/Swedish RSO.

○ **Piano Music (complete) / BIS**
Rumessen.

○ **Prélude solennel, for Orchestra / BIS**
Järvi/Gothenburg SO.

○ **Requiem for Fallen Soldiers; Ave Maria & more / BIS**
Järvi/Lund's Student Choral Society, instrumental ensemble.

○ **Sinfonietta on Estonian Motifs / BIS**
Järvi/Gothenburg SO.

○ **Symphony no. 1 in c / BIS**
Järvi/Swedish RSO.

○ **Symphony no. 2, "Legendaire" / BIS**
Järvi/Swedish RSO.

○ **Symphony no. 3 / BIS**
Järvi/Swedish RSO.

○ **Symphony no. 4, "Sinfonia Ilirica" / BIS**
Järvi/Bergen Philharmonic Society Orchestra.

○ **Symphony no. 5 in b / BIS**
Järvi/Bamberg SO.

○ **Symphony no. 6 / BIS**
Järvi/Swedish RSO.

○ **Symphony no. 7 / BIG BEN**
Frank/Helsingborg SO.

Symphony no. 7 / BIS
Järvi/Gothenburg SO.

○ **Symphony no. 8 / BIS**
Järvi/Swedish RSO.

○ **Valse triste / BIS**
Järvi/Gothenburg SO.

FRANZ TUNDER   1614-1667

Baroque. A celebrated German organist who held a prestigious position at the Marienkirche in Lübeck. His successor, Buxtehude, married Tunder's daughter (presumably one of the conditions for employment). –MKS

○ **Organ Works (complete surviving works) / MOTETTE**
Syre.

JOAQUIN TURINA   1882-1949

20th century, impressionist. Spanish composer of songs, opera, symphony, chamber music, and instrumental works (guitar and piano) in the style of Spanish impressionism. –MKS

○ **Gypsy Dances (5) for Piano, op. 55; Gypsy Dances (5) for Piano, op. 84 / GALLO**
Mueller.

○ **Rapsodia sinfónica for Piano & Strings / LONDON**
de Larrocha, de Burgos/London PO.

○ **Trios for Piano & Strings nos. 1 & 2 / CALIG**
Munich Trio. Man, this is interesting music. –PM

CHRISTOPHER TYE   1505-1572

Renaissance. A British composer of church music and instrumental consort pieces. –ED

○ **Church Music: Anthems, Antiphons, Motets / CRD**
Oxford New College Choir.

○ **Mass "Cathedral Music" / HYPERION**
Hill/Winchester Cathedral Choir.

○ **Mass "The Western Wind" / CRD**
Oxford New College Choir.

RALPH VAUGHAN WILLIAMS   1872-1958

20th century, nationalist. An important modern British composer of songs, opera, orchestral, church, and chamber music. Vaughan Williams is of the British nationalist school in the sense that he used English folk and music-hall-type tunes as well as other scene-describing devices in serious works (the *Pastoral* and *London* symphonies). But going beyond mere nationalism, he exalts life around him, approaching the expression of his roots with a magnificent and touching sense of melody (the beautiful *Fantasia on a Theme of Thomas Tallis* and *The Lark Ascending*) and an exploration of visionary projections of spirit (*The Pilgrim's Progress, Symphonies nos. 5 & 6*). −BGT

○ **Concerto accademico for Violin & Orchestra / RCA**
Buswell, Previn/London SO.

○ **Concerto for Bass Tuba & Orchestra / RCA**
Fletcher, Previn/London SO.

○ **Concerto for Oboe & Strings / DGG**
Black, Barenboim/English CO.

☆ **Fantasia on a Theme by Thomas Tallis / ARGO**
Marriner/ASMF.

Fantasia on a Theme by Thomas Tallis / DGG
Orpheus CO.

Fantasia on a Theme by Thomas Tallis / ANGEL
Haitink/London PO.

○ **Fantasia on "Greensleeves" / ARGO**
Marriner/ASMF.

Fantasia on "Greensleeves" / DGG
Orpheus CO.

○ **Job (A Masque for Dancing) / ANGEL**
Boult/London SO.

☆ **The Lark Ascending (romance for violin & orchestra) / ARGO**
Brown, Marriner/ASMF.

○ **Mass in g / HYPERION**
Best/Corydon Singers.

○ **Partita for Double String Orchestra / ANGEL**
Boult/London PO.

○ **Serenade to Music / VOX UNIQUE**
Vocal soloists, Klein/New York Virtuosi Chamber Symphony.

˙○ **Symphony no. 1 / EMI**
Armstrong, Case, Boult/London PO. Boult's London PO and New Philharmonia Orchestra performances of Vaughan William's nine symphonies are finally out on mid-price EMI. While not for those who must have digital sound, Boult pretty much sweeps the board on all symphonies, although Previn is a very interesting alternative, as is Haitink on the ones he has done. −PM

Symphony for Orchestra & Chorus no. 1, "Sea" / ANGEL
Lott, Summers, Haitink/London PO & Chorus.

Symphony for Orchestra & Chorus no. 1, "Sea" / RCA
Harper, Shirley-Quirk, Previn/London SO.

○ **Symphony no. 2, "London" / EMI**
Boult/London PO.

Symphony no. 2, "London" / ANGEL
Haitink/London PO.

Symphony no. 2, "London" / RCA
Previn/London SO.

○ **Symphony no. 3, "Pastoral" / EMI**
Price, Boult/New Philharmonia Orchestra.

Symphony no. 3, "Pastoral"; Symphony no. 4 in f / RCA
Harper, Previn/London SO.

○ **Symphony no. 4 in f / EMI**
Boult/NPO.

☆ **Symphony no. 5 in D / EMI**
Boult/London PO.

Symphony no. 5 in D / RCA
Previn/London SO.

Symphony no. 5 in D; Symphony no. 6 in e / RCA
Slatkin/Philharmonia. An atmospheric, virtuosic performance of both works, with flawless playing and sonic excellence. −MKS

○ **Symphony no. 6 in e / EMI**
Boult/NPO.

Symphony no. 6 in e / RCA
Previn/London SO.

○ **Symphony no. 7, "Sinfonia antartica" / RCA**
Harper, Previn/London SO.

○ **Symphony no. 8 in d / EMI**
Boult/London PO.

Symphony no. 8 in d / RCA
Previn/London SO.

○ **Symphony no. 9 in e / EMI**
Boult/London PO.

Symphony no. 9 in e / RCA
Previn/London SO.

○ **Te Deum in G / HYPERION**
Best/Corydon Singers.

○ **Variants (5) of *Dives and Lazarus* / ARGO**
Marriner/ASMF.

GIUSEPPE VERDI   1813-1901

Romantic, opera. Considered Italy's greatest composer of operas. Verdi's works are remarkable for their melodic beauty, superb dramatic construction, and rich orchestration — evoking worlds that lived more in Verdi's mind than, for instance in *Aida*, in the actual Egypt of ancient times. His ability to balance the subjective, intimate lives of his characters with the objective world in which they are set is another wonder of his operas, as in the contrast in *Aida* between the profound, despairing quality of the love duet in the tomb and the marches and grandeur of the earlier scenes. Verdi's dramatic, operatic sensibilities are carried over directly to the *Requiem Mass*, which in its drive and terror is unlike any liturgical music that came before. −BGT

☆ **Aida (four-act opera) / ANGEL**
Freni, Ricciarelli, Baltsa, Carreras, Cappuccili, Raimondi, Van Dam, Karajan/Vienna PO & State Opera Chorus.

Aida (four-act opera) / VICTROLA
Milanov, Barbieri, Bjoerling, Warren, Christoff, Perlea/Rome Opera Orchestra & Chorus.

Aida (four-act opera) / LONDON
Tebaldi, Karajan/Vienna PO & State Opera Chorus.

Aida (four-act opera) / LONDON
Price, Gorr, Vickers, Merrill, Tozzi, Solti/Rome Opera.

○ **Attila / PHILIPS**
Deutekom, Bergonzi, Milnes, Raimondi, Gardelli/Royal PO, Ambrosian Chorus.

○ **Ballet Music (excerpts from various operas) / LONDON**
Chailly/Bologna Teatro Comunale Orchestra.

○ **Choruses / DGG**
Abbado/La Scala.

○ **Il corsaro (three-act opera) / PHILIPS**
Caballé, Norman, Carreras, Gardelli/New Philharmonic Orchestra, et al.

○ **Don Carlos (five-act opera - Italian version) / ANGEL**
Caballé, Verrett, Domingo, Milnes, Raimondi, Giulini/Royal Opera.

Don Carlos (five-act opera - Italian version) / LONDON
Tebaldi, Bumbry, Bergonzi, Fischer-Dieskau, Ghiaurov, Solti/Royal Opera.

Don Carlos (opera - revised Italian version) / ANGEL
Freni, Baltsa, Gruberova, Carreras, Cappuccilli, Ghiaurov, Raimondi, van Dam, Karajan/Berlin PO, Deutsche Opera Chorus.

**Don Carlos (opera - complete original French version) /
DGG**
Ricciarelli, Valentini-Terrani, Domingo, Nucci, Raimondi,
Abbado/La Scala.
○ **Ernani (four-act opera) / ANGEL**
Freni, Domingo, Bruson, Ghiaurov, Muti/La Scala.
Ernani (four-act opera) / RCA
Price, Bergonzi, Sereni, Flagello, Schippers/RCA Italian Opera.
☆ **Falstaff (three-act opera) / DGG**
Ricciarelli, Hendricks, Valentini, Gonzalez, Bruson, Nucci,
Giulini/LA PO & Chorus.
Falstaff (three-act opera) / ANGEL
Schwarzkopf, Moffo, Merriman, Barbieri, Alva, Gobbi,
Panerai, Zaccaria, Karajan/Philharmonic Orchestra & Chorus.
Falstaff (three-act opera) / PHILIPS
Kabaivanska, Schmidt, Ludwig, Araiza, Taddei, Panerai,
Karajan/Vienna PO, State Opera Chorus.
○ **La forza del destino / DGG**
Plowright, Baltsa, Carreras, Bruson, Burchuladze,
Sinopoli/Philharmonic Orchestra, Ambrosian Opera Chorus.
La forza del destino / RCA
Price, Cossotto, Domingo, Milnes, Giaiotti, Bacquier,
Levine/London SO.
La forza del destino / RCA
Price, Tucker, Merrill, Tozzi, Schippers/RCA Italiana Opera.
○ **I masnadieri (four-act opera) / PHILIPS**
Caballé, Bergonzi, Cappuccilli, Raimondi, Gardelli/New
Philharmonic Orchestra, Ambrosian Singers.
○ **I lombardi alla prima crociata (4-act opera) /
HUNGARATON**
Sass, Lamberti, Kovats, Gardelli/Hungarian State Opera
Orchestra & Chorus.
○ **Luisa Miller (three-act opera) / LONDON**
Caballé, Reynolds, Pavarotti, Milnes, Maag/National PO.
Luisa Miller (three-act opera) / DGG
Ricciarelli, Obraztsova, Domingo, Bruson, Maazel/Royal
Opera, Covent Garden.
○ **MacBeth / PHILIPS**
Zampieri, Shicoff, Bruson, Lloyd, Sinopoli/Deutsche Opera.
MacBeth / DGG
Verrett, Domingo, Cappuccilli, Ghiaurov, Abbado/La Scala.
○ **Nabucco / DGG**
Dimitrova, Terrani, Domingo, Cappuccilli, Nesterenko,
Sinopoli/Deutsche Opera.
○ **Oberto, Conte di San Bonifacio / ORFEO**
Dimitrova, Baldani, Browner, Bergonzi, Panerai,
Gardelli/Munich Radio Orchestra & Chorus.
☆ **Otello (4-act opera) / RCA**
Scotto, Domingo, Milnes, Levine/National PO.
Otello (4-act opera) / RCA
Rysanek, Vickers, Gobbi, Serafin/Rome Opera.
Otello (four-act opera) / LONDON
Tebaldi, del Monaco, Protti, Karajan/Vienna PO.
Otello (four-act opera) / LONDON
Solti/Chicago SO. Intense, powerful and a bit bombastic. High-
voltage in the typical Solti style and sure to be controversial.
Terrific sound. –PM
○ **Overtures and Preludes (from various operas) /
PHILIPS**
Sinopoli/Vienna PO.
**Overtures and Preludes (from various operas) /
LONDON**
Chailly/National PO.
○ **Quattro Pezzi Sacri (Four Sacred Pieces) / ANGEL**
Baker, Giulini/Philharmonia Orchestra & Chorus.
☆ **Requiem Mass (in memory of Manzoni) / ANGEL**

Schwarzkopf, Ludwig, Gedda, Ghiaurov, Giulini/Philharmonia
Orchestra & Chorus. The combination of a terrific British
chorus and orchestra, four of the best continental singers ever
assembled for this work, and an Italian conductor who hadn't
yet developed the slowness and idiosyncrasies of his later
years produced the best *Requiem* from the 60s; only the sound
is now a bit of a drawback. –PM
Requiem Mass (In memory of Manzoni) / LONDON
Sutherland, Horne, Pavarotti, Talvela, Solti/Vienna PO & State
Opera Chorus. Passionate and intense, highly theatrical and
dramatic. I miss a bit of Italian warmth and sunlight, but has
there ever been a better group of soloists? –PM
Requiem Mass (In memory of Manzoni) / DGG
Ricciarelli, Verrett, Domingo, Ghiaurov, Abbado/La Scala.
Overall not such good singers as some of the others, but
Abbado avoids the hype and bombast and is intensely musical
and beautiful. –PM
Requiem Mass (In memory of Manzoni) / TELARC
Dunn, Curry, Hadley, Plishka, Shaw/Atlanta SO & Chorus.
Outstanding choral singing and better soloists than you might
expect; sound is the best ever in this work, but as always I find
Shaw just a bit too "American" and utilitarian-sounding. –PM
○ **Rigoletto (three-act opera) / PHILIPS**
Gruberova, Fassbaender, Schicoff, Bruson, Lloyd, Sinopoli/St.
Cecilia Orchestra & Chorus.
Rigoletto (three-act opera) / DGG
Cotrubas, Obraztsova, Domingo, Cappuccilli, Giulini/Vienna
PO & State Opera Chorus.
Rigoletto (three-act opera) / LONDON
Sutherland, Tourangeau, Pavarotti, Milnes, Talvela,
Bonynge/London SO & Chorus.
Rigoletto (three-act opera) / ANGEL
Callas, di Stefano, Gobbi, Zaccaria, Serafin/La Scala.
○ **Simon Boccanegra (three-act opera) / LONDON**
Te Kanawa, Aragall, Nucci, Burchuladze, Solti/La Scala
Orchestra & Chorus.
○ **Stiffelio (aka Aroldo) / PHILIPS**
Sass, Carreras, Manuguerra, et al., Gardelli/ORFSO & Chorus.
☆ **La traviata (three-act opera) / LONDON**
Sutherland, Pavarotti, Manuguerra, Bonynge/London Opera
& Chorus.
○ **Il trovatore (four-act opera) / RCA**
Price, Cossotto, Domingo, Milnes, Mehta/New Philharmonia
Orchestra & Chorus.
Il trovatore (four-act opera) / ANGEL
Callas, Barbieri, di Stefano, Panerai, Zaccaria, Karajan/La
Scala Orchestra & Chorus.
Il trovatore (four-act opera) / DGG
Plowright, Fassbaender, Domingo, Zancanaro, Giulini/St.
Cecilia Orchestra & Chorus.
○ **Un ballo in maschera (three-act opera) / DGG**
Ricciarelli, Abbado/La Scala.
Un ballo in maschera (three-act opera) / LONDON
Price, Ludwig, Pavarotti, et al., Solti/National PO & Chorus.
Un ballo in maschera (three-act opera) / PHILIPS
Caballé, Payne, Carreras, Wixell, Davis/Royal Opera.

TOMÁS LUIS DE VICTORIA   1548-1611

Renaissance, sacred vocal. An outstanding Spanish composer
who combined ardor with mysticism. His religious music is
some of the most important written during this period. –MKS
○ **Missa, "Ave Maris Stella"; Missa, "O Quam Gloriosum" /
HYPERION**
Hill/Westminster Cathedral Choir.
○ **Missa & Motet, "Ascendens Christum in Altum" & more
HYPERION**
Hill/Westminster Cathedral Choir.
○ **Missa & Motet, "Vedi Speciosam" / HYPERION**

Hill, O'Donnell/Westminster Cathedral Choir.
○ **Motet, "Nigra Sum" / GIMELL**
Phillips/The Tallis Scholars.
○ **Officium defunctorum, for 6-part choir / GIMELL**
Phillips/The Tallis Scholars. Not quite so sensual as it should be, but otherwise as good as all his others. –PM
Officium defunctorum, for 6-part choir / HYPERION
Hill, O'Donnell/Westminster Cathedral Choir.
○ **Sacred Choral Music / HYPERION**
Hill, O'Donnell/Westminster Cathedral Choir.
○ **Tenebrae Responsories / GIMELL**
Phillips/The Tallis Scholars.

LOUIS VIERNE   1870-1937

Romantic. Eminent French organist and composer who became Widor's assistant at St. Sulpice (1892), and subsequently, in 1900, the organist at Notre-Dame, where he remained until he died. Among his pupils were Nadia Boulanger and Marcel Dupré. –MKS
○ **Carillon de Westminster, for Organ no. 6, op. 54 / DGG**
Preston.
○ **Messe solennelle, for Chorus & 2 Organs, op. 16 / FY**
Notre Dame de Paris Cathedral Choir.
○ **Pièces (24) en style libre for Organ, op. 31 / KOCH-SCHWANN**
Kaunzinger.
○ **Pièces de fantasie for Organ, op. 53: Suite no. 2 / PIERRE VERANY**
Houbart.
○ **Pièces de fantasie for Organ, op. 53: Suite no. 3 / PHILIPS**
Chorzempa.
○ **Symphony for Organ no. 1 in d, op. 14 / PHILIPS**
Chorzempa.
○ **Symphony for Organ no. 1 in d, op. 14 / PIERRE VERANY**
F. Houbart, H. Houbart.
○ **Symphony for Organ no. 3 in f#, op. 28 / FY**
Cochereau.
○ **Triptyque for Organ, op. 58 / FY**
Cochereau.
○ **Various Organ Works / KOCH-SCHWANN**
Long.

HEITOR VILLA-LOBOS   1887-1959

20th century. Brazil's best-known composer. Villa-Lobos studied his homeland's Afro-Brazilian music as a young man. After travels in Europe, he returned to form his own symphony orchestra and to play many of the classics in Brazil for the first time. The beautiful *Bachianas brasileiras* for various instrumental and vocal combinations are well known and are of course inspired by Bach's music, which Villa-Lobos very much admired (he gave the first performance in Brazil of Bach's *Mass in b*). Villa-Lobos also ventured into certain experiments, such as the "New York Skyline Melody," written graphically to a photograph of the city. –BGT
○ **Bachiana brasileira for 8 Celli no. 1 / ANGEL**
Villa-Lobos/Orchestre National de France.
Bachiana brasileira for 8 Celli no. 1 / HYPERION
Pleeth Cello Octet.
Bachiana brasileira for 8 Celli no. 1 / ANGEL
Batiz/Royal PO.
○ **Bachiana brasileira for Flute & Bassoon no. 6 / ANGEL**
Capolongo/Orchestre de Paris.
○ **Bachiana brasileira for Orchestra no. 2 / ANGEL**
Capolongo/Orchestre de Paris.
Bachiana brasileira for Orchestra no. 2 / ANGEL

Villa-Lobos/Orchestre National de France.
○ **Bachiana brasileira for Orchestra no. 7 / ANGEL**
Batiz/Royal PO.
☆ **Bachiana brasileira for Soprano & 8 Celli no. 5 / ANGEL**
De los Angeles, Villa-Lobos/Orchestre National de France.
Bachiana brasileira for Soprano & 8 Celli no. 5 / RCA
Moffo, Stokowski/American SO.
Bachiana brasileira for Soprano & 8 Celli no. 5 / ANGEL
Mesplé, Capolongo/Orchestre de Paris.
Bachiana brasileira for Soprano & 8 Celli no. 5 / ANGEL
Hendricks, Batiz/Royal PO.
○ **Bachiana brasileira for Strings no. 9 / ANGEL**
Villa-Lobos/Orchestre National de France.
Bachiana brasileira for Strings no. 9 / ANGEL
Capolongo/Orchestre de Paris.
○ **Bachianas brasileiras nos. 1-9 (complete) / SIGLA**
Karabtchewsky/Brazil SO.
○ **Concerto for Guitar & Orchestra / PHILIPS**
Romero (guitar), Marriner/ASMF.
○ **Etudes (12) for Guitar / LONDON**
Fernandez.
○ **Preludes (5) for Guitar / LONDON**
Fernandez.
○ **Quartets for Strings nos. 4-6 / CHANT DU MONDE**
Bessler-Reiss Quartet. Spiky and dissonant, but melodic all the same. A very interesting and unique set of 17. –PM
Quartets for Strings nos. 12-14 / CHANT DU MONDE
Bessler-Reiss Quartet.
Quartets for Strings nos. 15-17 / CHANT DU MONDE
Bessler-Reiss Quartet.
○ **Quartet for Strings no. 17 / ELAN**
Cuarteto Latinoamericano.

ROBERT DE VISÉE   ca. 1650

Baroque. A French guitarist as well as a theorbo and viol player who became a court musician and taught guitar to Louis XIV from 1695-1719. –MKS
○ **Lute Works / ASTREE**
Smith.

ANTONIO VIVALDI   1678-1741

Baroque. A prolific Italian composer of over 750 works discovered so far, renowned in his time as a violinist and known for solo violin concertos, including the famous *L'Estro armonico, op. 3.* In tone-painting works, such as *I Quattri Stagioni* ("The Four Seasons"), Vivaldi established the essential drama and strong rhythms applied to basic harmonies that would prepare the way for the symphonic sonata-allegro form and the 18th-century "sound." He invented the idea that the soloist and orchestra should be in conflict with each other, holding a dialog that was essentially developmental, with effects like swift scales, arpeggios, and tremoli adding to the drama. –BGT
○ **La Cetra (12 concertos), op. 9 / OISEAU-LYRE**
Standage, Mackintosh, Hogwood/Academy of Ancient Music.
○ **Il Cimento dell'armonia e dell'inventione, for Violin & Orchestra nos. 1-12, op. 8 / CRD**
Standage, Pinnock/English Concert.
Il Cimento dell'armonia e dell'inventione, for Violin & Orchestra nos. 1-12, op. 8 / VERITAS
Huggett, Kraemer/Raglan Baroque Players.
○ **Concertos for Bassoon & Orchestra / PHILIPS**
Thunemann/I Musici. Easily the finest Vivaldi bassoon collection ever made. –PM
Concertos for Bassoon & Orchestra - Vol. 2 / PHILIPS
Thunemann/I Musici. Finally a followup, and this is just as good. –PM

Concerto for Bassoon & Orchestra, R. 485 only / BIS
McCraw/Drottningham Baroque Ensemble.
Concerto for Bassoon & Orchestra, R. 485 only / DGG
Pinnock/English Concert.
○ **Concertos (6) for Cello / OISEAU-LYRE**
Coin (baroque cello), Hogwood/Academy of Ancient Music.
○ **Concertos (5) for Cello & Orchestra / OISEAU-LYRE**
Coin, Hogwood/Academy of Ancient Music.
Concertos (5) for Cello & Orchestra / PHILIPS
Brown/ASMF.
○ **Concertos for Diverse Instruments / DGG**
Pinnock/English Concert.
○ **Concerto for Flute, Bassoon & Strings, R. 104 / BIS**
Pehrsson, McCraw/Drottningholm Baroque Ensemble.
Concertos for Flute & Orchestra (miscellaneous) / DGG
Pinnock/English Concert.
Concertos for Flute & Orchestra (miscellaneous) / HARMONIA MUNDI
See (flute), McGegan/Philharmonia Baroque Orchestra. High-class yuppie dinner music: sensual and relaxing. A bit too low-key, but very nicely played and recorded. –PM
☆ **Concertos (6) for Flute & Orchestra, op. 10 / TELDEC**
Il Giardino Armonico. Using the Venetian version of these ever-challenging and delightful pieces (recorder instead of transverse flute), Il Giardino Armonico (in what I believe is their recording debut) have come up with one of the most bizarre and radical performances since Harnoncourt's infamous *Water Music*. This is one wild ride and not for the faint of heart, with altered rhythms and a ton of ornamentation. The sound is a bit Teldec-harsh in the tuttis, but we've come to expect that on virtually all original-instrument recordings. –PM
Concertos (6) for Flute & Orchestra, op. 10 / DENON
Arita (transverse flute) Bach-Mozart Ensemble, Toyko. A beautifully recorded, standard original-instrument performance, lively and well ornamented. –PM
Concertos (6) for Flute & Orchestra, op. 10 / DGG
Beznosiuk, Pinnock/English Concert.
Concertos (6) for Flute & Orchestra, op. 10 / OISEAU-LYRE
Preston, Hogwood/Academy of Ancient Music.
○ **Concerto for 2 Flutes & Orchestra, R. 533 / HARMONIA MUNDI**
See, Schultz (flutes), McGegan/Philharmonia Baroque Orchestra.
○ **Concertos for Guitar / DGG**
Sollscher (guitar), Camerata, Bern/Fueri.
○ **Concertos for Lute / BIS**
Lindberg (lute). Drottningholm Baroque Ensemble. Haunting and sensual music played that way, and with imagination. –PM
○ **Concertos for Mandolin & Lute / HYPERION**
The Parley of Instruments.
○ **Concerto for 2 Mandolins & Orchestra in G, R. 532 / DGG**
Tyler, Jeffrey (mandolins), Pinnock/English Concert.
☆ **Concertos for Orchestra / OISEAU-LYRE**
Hogwood/Academy of Ancient Music.
Concertos for Orchestra / HYPERION
Lamon/Tafelmusik Baroque Orchestra.
Concertos for Orchestra / DGG
Pinnock/English Concert.
Concertos for Orchestra / OPUS 111
Biondi (violin and conductor)/L'Europa Galante. Very rich, soulful, and creative performances on period instruments. Outstanding sound. –PM
○ **Concertos for Recorder / HYPERION**
Holtslag (recorder), Holman/The Parley of Instruments. Outstanding recorder playing,

Outstanding recorder playing, with subtlety and drive, plenty of ornamentation, and a great sense of style. Fine sound. –PM
☆ **L'Estro armonico, for Violin & Orchestra nos. 1-12, op. 3 DGG**
Standage, Pinnock/The English Concert.
L'Estro armonico, for Violin & Orchestra nos. 1-12, op. 3 OISEAU-LYRE
Hogwood/Academy of Ancient Music.
☆ **The Four Seasons nos. 1-4, op. 8 / BIS**
Sparf/Drottningholm Baroque Ensemble. The finest period-instrument performance ever made of this overrecorded classic, in my top five of all time. I've played this more than any CD, and probably more even than any of my treasured LPs (which go back 30 years) — it's that fascinating and good! It's a bit bright in sound, and very good for testing stereo equipment. –PM
The Four Seasons nos. 1-4, op. 8 / OPUS 111
Biondi/L'Europa Galante. The most radical *Four Seasons* yet: it makes the Drottningholm look traditional. –PM
The Four Seasons nos. 1-4, op. 8 / ARGO
Loveday, Marriner/ASMF. The standard chamber performance on "modern" instruments. –PM
The Four Seasons nos. 1-4, op. 8 / OISEAU-LYRE
Hogwood/Academy of Ancient Music. Four different violinists, one for each season! –PM
○ **Gloria in D / ANGEL**
Marriner/ASFM & Chorus & Soloists. This is a tough choice, but the overall superiority of Marriner's soloists carries the day. –PM
Gloria in D / CHANDOS
Kirkby, Bonner, Chance, Hickox/Collegium Musicum 90.
Gloria in D / DGG
Pinnock/English Concert.
Gloria in D / OISEAU-LYRE
Preston/Academy of Ancient Music, Christ Church Cathedral Choir.
○ **Motets (various) / HYPERION**
Kirkby, Lamon/Tafelmusik Baroque Orchestra & Chamber Choir.
Motets (various) / OISEAU-LYRE
Preston/Academy of Ancient Music.
○ **Nisi Dominus (Psalm 126), R. 608 / OISEAU-LYRE**
Bowman, Hogwood/Academy of Ancient Music.
○ **Salve Regina, R. 616 / ARION**
Bowman, Audolini/Audolini Instrumental Ensemble.
○ **Salve Regina, R. 619 / MERIDIAN**
Bowman, King/The King's Consort.
○ **Sonatas (6) for Cello & Continuo Instruments / DHM**
Bylsma, Suzuki, Ogg. Too close to call, although I'll give·the nod to Bylsma. But you really should own the Coin, especially since he uses the baroque guitar and archlute in some of the pieces. Bylsma, however, has the better sound. –PM
Sonatas (6) for Cello & Continuo Instruments / OISEAU-LYRE
Coin, Hogwood.
Sonatas for Cello & Continuo Instruments - Vols. 1 & 2 / CRD
L'Ecole d'Orphée.
○ **Stabat Mater, for Contralto & Orchestra, R. 621 / OISEAU-LYRE**
Bowman (contralto), Hogwood/Academy of Ancient Music. This performance is very moving and ethereal in an authentic-instruments way. –PM
○ **La Stravaganza nos. 1-12, op. 4 / DGG**
Standage, Pinnock/English Consert.
La Stravaganza nos. 1-12, op. 4 / OISEAU-LYRE
Huggett, Hogwood/Academy of Ancient Music.

JAN VÁCLAV VORISEK   1791-1825

Romantic. A Bohemian pianist and composer noted for piano pieces; his impromptus influenced Schubert. –MKS

○ **Sonata for Violin & Piano in G, op. 5; Rondo for Violin & Piano, op. 8 / SUPRAPHON**
Pavlik (violin), Jerie (cello), Klansky (piano). The performances aren't the greatest, but this music is not likely to be recorded again in the near future, and these are early romantic pieces in the style of Schubert and Beethoven that are definitely worth getting to know. –PM

○ **Symphony in D, op. 24 / EBS**
Jöres/Westdeutsche Sinfonia.

RICHARD WAGNER   1813-1883

Romantic, opera. An important German composer of opera and vocal music, with some orchestral and piano works, who used chromatic and dissonant harmonies and conceived all aspects of a performance as a *Gesamtkunstwerk* or total art work. He composed many notable operas, including *The Flying Dutchman* (1843), *Tristan and Isolde* (1865), and a four-opera cycle *The Ring of the Nibelung* en (1876).
The trouble surrounding Wagner's works seems to grow out of the lyrics and his attitudes, and their appeal stems from the hypnotic beauty of music that exists in its own time-suspended world. His anti-Semitic attitudes are well known, though his actual father was the actor Ludwig Geyer, who was Jewish. Wagner makes embarrassingly chauvinistic national appeals at the end of *Die Meistersinger*, but most of the rest is a series of lovely choruses and airs, the whole supposedly conceived as a light comedy. Generations of people have been swept away by the marvelous effects in his works, from the "Ride of the Valkyrie" to the "Love Duet" (with the duo floating away into the cosmos). They were also drawn to the beauty of the gently unfolding revolutionary harmonies, complex transformations, and intertwinings of the "Leitmotivs." Well, art isn't supposed to be easy all the time, and working out one's relation to Wagner's aesthetic is certainly good for the spirit. –BGT

○ **Der fliegende Holländer (three-act opera) / LONDON**
Martin, Kollo, Bailey, Talvela, Solti/Chicago SO & Chorus.

Der fliegende Holländer (opera - excerpts) / LONDON
Nilsson, et al., Solti/Vienna PO.

○ **Lohengrin / ANGEL**
Grümmer, Ludwig, Thomas, Fischer-Dieskau, Frick, Kempe/Vienna PO & State Opera Chorus.

Lohengrin / LONDON
Norman, Randova, Domingo, Nimsgern, Fischer-Dieskau, Sotin, Solti/Vienna PO & State Opera Chorus.

☆ **Die Meistersinger von Nürnberg / ANGEL**
Schwarzkopf, Malaniuk, Hopf, Unger, Edelmann, Kunz, Dalberg, Karajan/Bayreuth Festival Orchestra & Chorus.

Die Meistersinger von Nürnberg / ANGEL
Donath, Hesse, Kollo, Schreier, Adam, Evans, Ridderbusch, Karajan/Dresden State Orchestra & Chorus.

☆ **Overtures and Preludes (for various operas) / CHESKY**
Horenstein/Royal PO.

Overtures and Preludes (for various operas) / ANGEL
Karajan/Berlin PO.

Overtures and Preludes (for various operas) / DGG
Karajan/Berlin PO.

Overtures and Preludes (for various operas) / ANGEL
Tennstedt/Berlin PO.

○ **Parsifal (three-act opera) / PHILIPS**
Dalis, Thomas, London, Hotter, Neidlinger, Knappertsbusch/Bayreuth Festival Orchestra & Chorus.

Parsifal (three-act opera) / DGG
Vejzovic, Karajan/Berlin PO, Deutsche Oper Chorus.

○ **Das Rheingold (part I of the *Ring* opera cycle) / LONDON**

Flagstad, Madeira, Svanholm, London, Neidlinger, Böhme, Solti/Vienna PO.

○ **Der Ring des Nibelungen (cycle of four operas) / HUNT**
Flagstad, Furtwängler/La Scala Chorus and Orchestra. For meaning and characterization (not to speak of a hundred other reasons), the ultimate *Ring*. –PM

Der Ring des Nibelungen (cycle of four operas) / LONDON
Nilsson, Flagstad, Crespin, Watson, Ludwig, Madeira, Windgassen, Svanholm, King, Stolze, London, Fischer-Dieskau, Hotter, Neidlinger, Frick, Solti/Vienna PO. Next to Furtwängler's version, the best *Ring*, and in the best sound. –PM

Der Ring des Nibelungen (cycle of four operas) / ANGEL
Mödl, Konetzni, Jurinac, Grümmer, Cavelti, Malaniuk, Klose, Furtwängler/Rome Radio Italiana Orchestra & Chorus.

○ **Der Ring des Nibelungen (orchestral excerpts) / LONDON**
Solti/Vienna PO.

Der Ring des Nibelungen (orchestral excerpts) / CBS
Szell/Cleveland Orchestra.

Der Ring des Nibelungen (orchestral excerpts) / ANGEL
Tennstedt/Berlin PO.

○ **Siegfried Idyll; Brahms, Serenade no. 1 / PHILIPS**
ASMF Chamber Ensemble. Exquisite: that's the word that comes to mind when hearing these two beauties. Talk about being able to hear every note! And what delicacy! Hearing the nonet version of Brahms's first serenade is a real eye-opener, and this is easily the best CD version of the Wagner. –PM

Siegfried Idyll / DGG
Karajan/Vienna PO.

Siegfried Idyll / CHESKY
Horenstein/Royal PO.

Siegfried Idyll / LONDON
Solti/Vienna PO.

Siegfried (part III of the *Ring* opera cycle) / LONDON
Nilsson, Wundgassen, Stolze, Hotter, Neidlinger, Solti/Vienna PO.

○ **Tannhäuser / DGG**
Studer, Sinopoli/Philharmonia Orchestra.

Tannhäuser (Paris revision) / LONDON
Dernesch, Ludwig, Kollo, Braun, Sotin, Solti/Vienna PO.

Tannhäuser (Dresden version with Paris Venusberg) / PHILIPS
Silja, Bumbry, Windgassen, Wächter, Greindl, Sawallisch/Bayreuth Festival Orchestra.

○ **Tristan und Isolde (three-act opera) / ANGEL**
Flagstad, Thebom, Suthaus, Fischer-Dieskau, Greindl, Furtwängler/Philharmonic Orchestra, Royal Opera Chorus. The classic recording. –PM

Tristan und Isolde (three-act opera) / DGG
Price, Fassbaender, Kollo, Fischer-Dieskau, Moll, Kleiber/Dresden State Opera. A noble modern alternative. –PM

Tristan und Isolde: Prelude & Liebestod / DGG
Karajan/Berlin PO.

Tristan und Isolde: Prelude & Liebestod / ANGEL
Karajan/Berlin PO.

○ **Die Walküre (part II of the *Ring* opera cycle) / LONDON**
Nilsson, et al., Solti/Vienna PO.

WILLIAM WALTON   1902-1983

20th century. A British composer in most forms, especially orchestral music and including film scores, who has aptly described himself as a lyrical classical composer. His *Symphony no. 1* (1935) and the Vaughan Williams *Symphony no. 4 in f* (1934) are the most important British symphonies of the period between the wars — extroverted, with high symphonic color, magnificence, and a bittersweet lyricism. –BGT

○ **As You Like It (orchestra arrangement of Walton's film score) / CHANDOS**
Bott, Marriner/ASMF.

○ **Battle of Britian (1969 film score suite) / CHANDOS**
Marriner/ASMF.

○ **Belshazzar's Feast, for Baritone, Orchestra & Chorus / CHANDOS**
Howell, Wilcocks/Philharmonia Orchestra, Bach Choir.

○ **Concerto for Cello & Orchestra / CBS**
Ma (cello), Previn/London SO.

○ **Concerto for Viola & Orchestra / ANGEL**
Kennedy (viola), Previn/Royal PO.

○ **Façade (with spoken poems by Edith Sitwell) / LONDON**
Ashcroft, Irons, Chailly/London Sinfonietta.

○ **Hamlet (orchestral arrangement of Walton's 1948 film score) / CHANDOS**
Gielgud, Marriner/ASMF.

○ **Henry V (orchestral arrangement of Walton's 1944 film score) / CHANDOS**
Plummer, Marriner/ASMF Orchestra & Chorus.

○ **Partita for Orchestra / SONY**
Szell/Cleveland Orchestra.

○ **Quartet for Piano & Strings / MERIDIAN**
McCabe/English String Quartet.

○ **Quartet for Strings in a / MERIDIAN**
English String Quartet.

☆ **Symphony no. 1 in b-flat / ANGEL**
Mackerras/London PO.

○ **Symphony no. 2 / SONY**
Szell/Cleveland Orchestra.

Symphony no. 2 / ANGEL
Mackerras/London SO.

CARL MARIA VON WEBER   1786-1826

Classical/romantic. Weber, a German composer, almost single-handedly established the romantic movement in music, or at least paved the way for it. His operas, especially *Der Freischütz* — with its simple human characters surrounded by a wild, mysterious nature imbued with the supernatural in eerie, atmospheric scenes (the casting of the magic bullets, for instance) — paved the way for Wagner, just as his piano music inspired Liszt, Schumann, and Chopin. He was equally an innovator in harmony and orchestral timbre, and his lovely concertos feature the soloist as a character who "speaks" rather than plays an objective, instrumental role. –BGT

○ **Concertino for Clarinet & Orchestra in E-flat, op. 26 / ASV**
Johnson, Gorves/English CO.

Concertino for Clarinet & Orchestra in E-flat, op. 26 / CHANDOS
Hilton, Järvi/City of Birmingham SO.

Concertino for Clarinet & Orchestra in E-flat, op. 26 / VIRGIN
Pay/Orchestra of the Age of Enlightenment.

○ **Concerto for Bassoon in F, op. 75; Andante & Rondo for Bassoon & Orchestra in F / PHILIPS**
Thunemann (bassoon), Marriner/ASMF.

☆ **Concerto for Clarinet & Orchestra no. 1 in f, op. 73 / ANGEL**
Meyer (clarinet), Blomstedt/Dresden State Orchestra. As good as the competition is (and it is very good), no one touches Sabine Meyer for her vibrancy and grace under pressure. This is clarinet playing as good as you will ever hear. –PM

Concerto for Clarinet & Orchestra no. 1 in f, op. 73 / CHANDOS

Hilton, Järvi/City of Birmingham SO.

Concerto for Clarinet & Orchestra no. 1 in f, op. 73 / VIRGIN
Pay/Orchestra of the Age of Enlightenment.

○ **Concerto for Clarinet & Orchestra no. 2 in E-flat, op. 74 / ANGEL**
Meyer, Blomstedt/Dresden State Orchestra.

Concerto for Clarinet & Orchestra no. 2 in E-flat, op. 74 / CHANDOS
Hilton, Järvi/City of Birmingham SO.

Concertos for Clarinet & Orchestra nos. 1 & 2; Concertino / PHILIPS
A. Marriner (clarinet), N. Marriner/ASMF. Andrew Marriner is not a truly major clarinetist, but he and his dad probe the latent sadness and bittersweet qualities of these works and explore their vulnerability and fragility better than anyone else, and I wouldn't be without their performance. –PM

○ **Concerto for Piano & Orchestra no. 1 in C / ANGEL**
Rosel, Blomstedt/Dresden State Orchestra.

○ **Concerto for Piano & Orchestra no. 2 in E-flat / ANGEL**
Rosel, Blomstedt/Dresden State Orchestra.

☆ **Der Freischütz / DGG**
Janowitz, Mathis, Schreier, Weikl, Adam, Crass, C. Kleiber/Dresden State Orchestra.

Der Freischütz / EURODISC
Watson, Schadle, Schock, Frick, von Matacic/Deutsche Opera.

Der Freischütz / HUNT
Grümmer, Streich, Hopf, Pröbstle, E. Kleiber/Cologne Radio Orchestra & Chorus. Not very good (pirate) sound, but such an interesting performance. –PM

○ **Introduction, Theme & Variations for Clarinet & String Quartet in B-flat / DENON**
Meyer/Philharmonia Quartet Berlin.

○ **Invitation to the Dance, op. 65 / SUPRAPHON**
Ancerl/Czech PO.

Invitation to the Dance, op. 65 / NIMBUS
Goodman/The Hanover Band.

○ **Overtures / NIMBUS**
Goodman/The Hanover Band.

○ **Quintet for Clarinet & Strings in B-flat, op. 34 / DGG**
Brunner/Hagen Quartet.

Quintet for Clarinet & Strings in B-flat, op. 34 / CHANDOS
Hilton/Lindsay String Quartet.

○ **Rondo brillante, for Piano in E-flat, "La Gaite" / ARABESQUE**
Ohlsson.

○ **Sonatas (4) for Piano / ARABESQUE**
Ohlsson (piano). This is very virtuosic but a little cold and objective. –PM

○ **Sonata for Piano no. 2 / PHILIPS**
Brendel (piano). Makes sense out of a difficult piece with a lot of filigree. –PM

Sonata for Piano no. 2 & other piano pieces / CENTAUR
Moss (piano). I like her straightforward, rugged approach, but she's not quite the artist Brendel is. –PM

○ **Sonatas ("Six sonates progressives") for Flute & Piano / AMON RA**
Preston, Burnett.

○ **Sonatas ("Six sonates progressives") for Violin & Piano / KOCH-SCHWANN**
Dansczowska, Malicki.

○ **Symphonies nos. 1 & 2 in C / NIMBUS**
Goodman/The Hanover Band.

Symphonies nos. 1 & 2 in C / ORFEO
Sawallisch/Bavarian RSO.

○ **Trio for Flute, Cello & Piano in g, op. 63 / AMON RA**

Preston, Clarke, Burnett.
○ **Variations (7) on a Theme from *Silvana*, for Clarinet & Piano / CHANDOS**
De Peyer, Pryor.

KURT WEILL   1900-1950

Modern. A German composer. Searching for music and words that would directly affect and address their contemporaries, Weill and Bertolt Brecht had a big hit with the *Mahagonny-Songspiel* (1927) in Berlin (it was expanded to a full stagework in 1930). Representing the surrounding society on stage and mirroring it back on itself, Brecht and Weill invented what has been called the "educational opera." Others in the genre: *Happy End, Der Jasager* ("The Yes-man"), *Der Lindberghflug* ("The Lindbergh Flight"), and *The Ballad of Magna Carta* (with the famous line "Resistance unto tyrants is obedience to God"). The music was based on the style of the cabaret-theater (an old format for political satire) and developed to a richness never heard before, with modern harmonies, progressions having more to do with the freedom of bebop decades later than the normal song of the Bierhalle, and wonderful melodies ("Alabama Song," "Mäckie Messer" ("Mack the Knife"), and many others) connected by scene-developing music of a refined imagination. Weill eventually had to flee Germany when the Nazis burned his music and attacked his publishing house. Amazingly, he managed to become one of the most popular composers on the Broadway stage (*Street Scene; Lady in the Dark; Knickerbocker Holiday; Love Life*), but he always kept up his love for music that fulfilled a responsibility by addressing the real world (*Lost in the Stars*, based on Alon Paton's *Cry the Beloved Country*, about racial conflict in South Africa), paving the way for a kind of American "verismo" in musical theater, such as Bernstein's *West Side Story*. For a full understanding of Weill's musical vision, it is important to hear one of his extended instrumental works. –BGT

○ **American and Berlin Theatre Songs / CBS**
Lenya.
○ **Aufstieg und Fall der Stadt Mahagonny / CBS**
Lenya, Bruckner-Ruggenberg/North Germany Radio Orchestra & Chorus.
○ **Berlin im Licht & 10 other songs & instrumental pieces / LARGO**
Gruber/Ensemble Modern. Has there ever been a better Weill record? It has the decadence and it has the nastiness and it has a great mixture of obscure vocal and instrumental, with interesting, echoey sound, fitting for the cabaret-style music. Oh, and don't forget the 200-page booklet that comes with it. Documentation as it was meant to be! –PM
○ **Berlin Requiem (1928) / KOCH-SCHWANN**
Schmidt/Düsseldorf SO Wind Instruments, soloists, choruses. I love the extra degree of authenticity of this one, but you can't go wrong with either. –PM
Berlin Requiem / POLYDOR
Langridge, Luxon, Rippon, Atherton/London Sinfonietta. This is well rehearsed, well played, and well recorded, but the Koch CD sounds authentically German and more like Weill. –PM
○ **Concerto for Violin & Wind Orchestra, op. 12 / ONDINE**
Wächter (violin), Pommer/Leipzig RSO.
Concerto for Violin & Wind Orchestra, op. 12 / POLYDOR
Ajemian, Solomon/MGM Wind Orchestra.
○ **Happy End (3-act comedy with music) / CBS**
Lenya, Bruckner-Ruggenberg/Orchestra & Chorus.
○ **Der Jasager / POLYDOR**
Kohler/Düsseldorf CO.
○ **Kleine Dreigroschenmusik, for Wind Ensemble / KOCH-SCHWANN**
Schenk/The Atlantic Sinfonietta. A bit tamer and not so sarcastic as usual, this is nevertheless a well-played and well-

recorded performance, and isn't so sleazy as the Max Pommer. –PM
Kleine Dreigroschenmusik, for Wind Ensemble / ONDINE
Pommer/Leipzig RSO. The sound and the playing cut like a stiletto, and the irony and sarcasm are all there, more forcefull than in most of the watered-down Weill performances. –PM
Kleine Dreigroschenmusik, for Wind Ensemble / DGG
Atherton/London Sinfonietta.
○ **Mahagonny-Songspiel / DGG**
Dickinson, Thomas, Langridge, Partridge, Luxon, Rippon, Atherton/London Sinfonietta.
○ **Recordare, for Choir, op. 11 (1923) / KOCH-SCHWANN**
Schmidt, various choirs.
○ **The Seven Deadly Sins (ballet in song) / POLYDOR**
May, Kegel/Leipzig RSO.
○ **The Threepenny Opera / CBS**
Lenya, Bruckner-Rüggeberg/Orchestra & Chorus.
The Threepenny Opera / PHILIPS
Rennert/Frankfurt Opera Choir & Orchestra & soloist. Authentic and very German-style performance, with very fine 1966 sound. –PM
○ **Walt Whitman Songs (4), for Baritone & Chamber Orchestra / KOCH-SCHWANN**
Holzmair (baritone), Schlingensiepen/Robert Schumann CO. Holzmair has a fresh and charming voice, even if his English isn't the greatest. –PM

SAMUEL WESLEY   1766-1837

Classical. An important British composer of Latin and Anglican church music. –MKS
○ **Symphonies nos. 3, 4, 5, 6 / UNICORN-KANCHANA**
Wetton/Milton Keynes CO. Interesting English symphonies in the mold of J. C. Bach, Haydn, and Mozart. The performances are a bit too sweet and rounded for my taste and could have used a bit more staccato and attack, but they have a nice, transparent sound. –PM

CHARLES MARIE WIDOR   1844-1937

Romantic. A French organist, composer, and creator of the organ-symphony form, for which he is mainly known, though he composed for other instruments as well. –MKS
○ **Symphony for Organ no. 1 in c, op. 13 no. 1 / BIS**
Fagius.
○ **Symphony for Organ no. 3 in e, op. 13 no. 3 / BIS**
Fagius.
○ **Symphony for Organ no. 5 in f, op. 42 no. 1 / PHILIPS**
Chorzempa.
Symphony for Organ no. 5 in f, op. 42 no. 1 / DGG
Preston.
○ **Symphony for Organ no. 6 in g, op. 42 no. 2 / BIS**
Fagius.
○ **Symphony for Organ no. 9 in c, op. 70, "Gothique" / NOVALIS**
Kaunzinger.
○ **Symphony for Organ no. 10 in D, op. 73, "Romane" / NOVALIS**
Kaunzinger.
Symphony for Organ no. 10 in D, op. 73, "Romane" / PHILIPS
Chorzempa.

HENRYK WIENIAWSKI   1835-1880

Romantic. A Polish violinist and composer whose violin pieces reflect his formidable skill as a performer. –MKS
○ **Concerto for Violin & Orchestra no. 2 in d, op. 22 / DGG**
Perlman, Barenboim/Orchestre de Paris.

HUGO WOLF   1860-1903

Romantic, vocal. One of the finest and most innovative songwriters of the late romantic period, this Austrian composer wrote an astonishing flow of 174 songs in a blast of creative energy over a 33-month period. He was also a gifted lyricist, with a musical and literary talent for bringing characters in a poem to life and expressing psychological depths. Both voice and piano sing in his music, working toward conveying a whole impression. Aside from the songs, his best-known work is the beautiful *Italian Serenade* of 1887 for string quartet, later orchestrated in 1892. His only finished orchestral work was *Penthesilea* (1883-1885). Like many artists who consciously (or subconsciously) sacrifice their well-being for their art, Wolf experienced a breakdown due to mental stress and was institutionalized from 1898 to 1903. —BGT

○ **Der Corregidor (opera): Prelude & Intermezzo / ERATO**
Barenboim/Orchestre de Paris.

○ **Goethe-Lieder (selections) / DGG**
Fischer-Dieskau, Barenboim.

☆ **Italian Serenade, for String Quartet or Orchestra / ERATO**
Barenboim/Orchestre de Paris.

Italian Serenade, for String Quartet or Orchestra / DGG
Hagen Quartet.

○ **Michelangelo-Lieder (3) / ANGEL**
Fischer-Dieskau, Moore.

○ **Mörike-Lieder (selections) / DGG**
Fischer-Dieskau, Barenboim.

Mörike-Lieder (selections) / ANGEL
Fischer-Dieskau, Moore.

○ **Penthesilea (symphonic poem) / ERATO**
Barenboim/Orchestre de Paris.

○ **Scherzo & Rondo Finale [2 symphonic movements] / ERATO**
Barenboim/Orchestre de Paris.

○ **Songs (miscellaneous) / DGG**
Von Otter, Gothoni.

☆ **Spanisches Liederbuch / DGG**
Schwarzkopf, Fischer-Dieskau, Moore.

CLASSICAL COLLECTIONS

BAROQUE MUSIC

Classical.

○ **Purcell's London / HYPERION**
Goodman/The Parley of Instruments. Instrumental works by Keller, Matteis, Baltzar, Blow, Eccles, Anonymous.

BASS VIOL MUSIC

Baroque.

○ **Play this Passionate: Music for Solo Viol / VIRGIN**
Cunningham (bass viol). Soulful and very well-in-tune performances of pieces by Hume, Demachy, Schenk, Kuehnel, and Telemann. —PM

CLARINET RECITAL

Romantic, 20th-Centruy.

○ **Poulenc, Stravinsky, Eklund, Pierne, Milhaud, Brahms / MALMO AUDIO**
Lofving (clarinet), Ernst (piano), etc.

○ **Saint-Saëns, Messiaen, Roussel, Ravel, Debussy, Chausson, Françaix, Messager / CALIG**
Brunner (clarinet), Hoehenrieder (piano).

DOUBLE BASS MUSIC

Classical.

○ **Pieces by Fauré, Saint-Saëns, Vivaldi, Mozart, Koussevitzky, etc. / LARGO**
Kawahara (double bass), Hoffmann (piano). Nicely played and recorded potpourri of classical pops for double bass and piano duo. —PM

○ **Solo Bass Works by Am, Dallapiccola, Françaix, et al. / SIMAX**
Ianke.

EARLY MUSIC

Medieval, renaissance.

○ **Cantigas de Santa Maria / BIS**
Spanish vocal and instrumentals works performed by the Joculatores Upsalienses (Upsala Jesters). —ED

○ **Carmina Burana - Vol. 1 / OISEAU-LYRE**
Pickett/New London Consort. The original 13th-century Latin secular songs in imaginative and exciting performances, with a good combination of the authentic and the entertaining. —PM

Carmina Burana - Vol. 2 / OISEAU-LYRE
New London Consort.

Carmina Burana - Vols. 3 & 4 / OISEAU-LYRE
New London Consort.

○ **The Castle Fair Welcome (various composers) / HYPERION**
The Gothic Voices.

○ **Early Music at Wik / BIS**
Joculatores Upsalienses (Upsala Jesters).

○ **The Four Seasons / BIS**
Joculatores Upsalienses (Upsala Jesters). 13th- through 17th-century secular songs and dances. —PM

○ **The Garden of Zephirus (various composers) / HYPERION**
The Gothic Voices.

○ **The Marriage of Heaven and Hell / HYPERION**
The Gothic Voices. 13th-century motets. —PM

○ **Music From the Time of Christopher Columbus / PHILIPS**
Morrow, Beckett/Musica Reservata.

○ **Music of the Crusades / LONDON**
Munrow/Early Music Consort of London.

○ **Musique de la Grèce Antique / HARMONIA MUNDI**
Madrid Atrium Musicae.

○ **Mysterium Passionis et Resurrectionis Festum Sanctissimae Paschae / NUOVA ERA**
Réné Clemencic/Clemencic Consort. 14th-century. —PM

○ **La Spagna / BIS**
Madrid Atrium Musicae.

○ **Woods, Women & Wine / BIS**
Joculatores Upsalienses (Upsala Jesters). Rambunctious, like all their recordings. —PM

○ **Works of Pachelbel, Gluck & Handel / OISEAU-LYRE**
Academy of Ancient Music.

EUROPEAN LUTE MUSIC

Baroque.

○ **European Lute Music - Vol. 1: 17th Century, Suites by Ennemond Gaultier, Mouto / DHM**
Junghänel (lute). 17th-century France. —PM

FLUTE COLLECTION

20th century.

○ **Music by Olsen, Kvandal, Jolivet, Böhm, Windor & Moszkowski / SIMAX**
Gulbransen (flute) with various orchestras, conductors, and piano and flute players.

○ **20-Century French Pieces, for Flute & Piano / ADDA**
Beaucoudray (flute), Henry (piano). Stimulating collection of flute works by Martin, Roussel, Sancan, Enescu, Ibert, and Dutilleux. –PM

GREGORIAN & LITURGICAL CHANT

Midieval.
○ **Advent and Christmas / CHRISTOPHORUS**
Joppich/Choir of the Scholars of the Benedictine Abbey; Munsterschwarzach. Not the greatest singing I've ever heard, but a nice selection with very atmospheric and palpable sound. –PM
○ **Ave Maris Stella - Life of the Virgin Mary in Plainsong / SONY**
Ruhland/Niederaltaich Scholars. 75 minutes of chant spanning 1700 years sung by a mixed choir of 26 at full strength in beautifully atmospheric and scholarly performances, with sound to match. –PM
○ **The Ecclesiastical Year in Gregorian Chant / SONY**
van Gerven/Schola Cantorum of Amsterdam Students. Recorded in 1966 and 1968, with a bit of tape hiss, this still has remarkably good sound; and at a budget price, it is easily recommendable. –PM
○ **Gregorian Chants for Easter / HARMONIA MUNDI**
Ruhland/Munich Capella Antiqua. This is haunting sound combined with scholarly and sensual performance. Very atmospheric. –PM

GUITAR & LUTE MUSIC

Baroque, classical.
○ **Baroque Lute Recital - Works by J. S. Bach / CHANNEL CLASSICS**
Satoh.
○ **Eighteenth Century Lute Music (various composers) / TITANIC**
Schneiderman.
○ **The Lute in Dance and Dream: Three Centuries of Lute Masterpieces / SONY**
Kirchhof (Renaissance & baroque lute). Sort of a greatest-hits of the lute but none the worse for that when played as well as this. –PM

HARP MUSIC

Classical.
○ **Harp Collection - Early Music on Period Harps / AMON RA**
Kelly.
○ **Harp Music of the Italian Renaissance / HYPERION**
Lawrence-King.
○ **The Harp of Ludovico - Fantasias, Arias & Toccatas by Frescobaldi / HYPERION**
Lawrence-King (baroque harp). Andrew Lawrence-King is a virtuoso stylist of the early harp, and both CDs contain very convincing performances that might just change your conception of the harp. –PM

HARPSICHORD/CLAVICHORD MUSIC

Baroque.
○ **Clavichord Recital - Works by Bach, Ritter / PHILIPS**
Leonhardt.
○ **German Harpsichord Music before Bach (various composers) / GLOBE**
Ogg.
○ **Harpsichord Recital - Works by Louis Couperin, Purcell, Croft, Kuhnau, Bach, etc. / PHILIPS**
Leonhardt.

○ **Pieces by Froberger, Louis Couperin, Chambonières & d'Anglebert / WILD BOAR**
Parmentier (harpsichord). Very elegant playing on a beautiful Keith Hill harpsichord. Tuning and notes by the very modest Joseph Spencer and beautiful, natural recording by Michael Lynn. –PM

HISTORICAL ORCHESTRA

Classical.
○ **Wilhelm Furtwängler: The Early Recordings, 1926-37 / KOCH-SCHWANN**
Furtwängler, Berlin PO. Contains Bach: *Brandenburg Concerto no. 3*; *Air on a G String*; Mozart: Overtures to *Figaro* and *Entführung*; *Eine Kleine Nachtmusik*; Schubert: *Rosamunde* (3 pieces); Beethoven: "Egmont Overture"; *Symphony no. 5*; Weber: "Freischütz Overture"; Rossini: Overtures: *La gazza ladra* and *The Barber of Seville*.
○ **Wilhelm Furtwängler: The Early Recordings, 1926-37 - Vol. 2 / KOCH-SCHWANN**
Furtwängler/Berlin PO. Contains Weber: "Freischütz Overture" and "Entr'acte"; *Invitation to the Dance*; Mendelssohn: "A Midsummer Night's Dream Overture" and "Hebrides"; Berlioz: "Damnation of Faust March"; Wagner: *Lohengrin*: "Prelude to Act 1"; *Tristan and Isolde*: "Prelude" and "Liebestod"; Brahms: *Hungarian Dances nos. 1 & 3*; Johann Strauss Jr: *Die Fledermaus*: "Overture"; Richard Strauss: *Till Eulenspiegel*.
These outstanding early issues of Furtwängler prove he had most of the soul of his late years but was relatively free of the annoying mannerisms (e.g., constant wide tempo changes). In other words, he was a lot more straightforward in those earlier years but did not always have the richness and depth achieved in later performances of the same pieces. –PM

KEYBOARD WORKS

Baroque, classical.
○ **A. B. Michelangeli: Bach/Busoni: *Chaconne*; Beethoven: *Sonata for Piano no. 3, op. 2/3* / MELODRAM**
Michelangeli (piano). When Michelangeli had been in semi-retirement for some years and was in Warsaw (in March of 1955) judging the Chopin piano competition, he agreed to give a series of impromptu concerts. And despite veiled and distorted sound, especially in loud passages, this is a document of rare importance, with clarity, luminosity, and amazing perfection (does anyone use pedal like this man?) that shines through in every bar. For misunderstood and misrepresented artists like Furtwängler, Knappertsbusch, Celibidache, Michelangeli, and Richter, "pirate" issues and reissues are invaluable. –PM

ORGAN MUSIC

Various.
○ **European Organ Music of the 17th & 18th Centuries / RENE GAILLY**
Bastiaens (organ). An outstanding representation of 17 short works by Storace, Walther, Kerckhoven, Bach, Muffat, Reincken, Burney, Handel, Martini, Ruppe, Gheyn, and Mozart, played on two beautiful Flemish organs. –PM
○ **Organ History: German Classicism / KOCH-SCHWANN**
Sacchetti (organ). A well-recorded recital of mostly obscure short pieces by W. F. Bach, Krebs, C. P. E. Bach, Kittel, Albrechtsberger, Michael and Joseph Haydn, J. C. Bach, Mozart, Beethoven, and Rinck. And at a playing time of 73:18, you get your money's worth. –PM
○ **Pamela Decker "Performs" / ARKAY**
Decker.

○ **Swiss Organ Music of the 18th & 19th Centuries /
KOCH-SCHWANN**
Hulliger (organ). Here is a very interesting organ CD,
beautifully recorded, with sprightly playing. These are fairly
but not completely unknown composers (Stalder, Sidler,
Sulzer, Neukomm, Jucker, and the ever-popular Anonymous);
the styles are firmly in the mold of Haydn, Mozart, and
Mendelssohn; and all the works are very tuneful — just the
CD for a Sunday afternoon. –PM

○ **Toccata / ARKAY**
Decker.

PIANO MUSIC

Various.
○ **Horowitz at Home - Works by Mozart, Schubert & Liszt /
DGG**
Horowitz.

○ **In Moscow - Works by Scarlatti, Mozart, et al. / DGG**
Horowitz.

○ **The Last Recording - Works by Haydn, et al. (1989) /
SONY**
Horowitz.

○ **Recital - Works by Schumann, Scriabin, Liszt, et al. /
DGG**
Horowitz.

○ **Studio Recordings (various composers) / DGG**
Horowitz.

RECORDER MUSIC

Baroque.
○ **Canzoni, Fantasie e Sonate - 3 works each by
Frescobaldi, Selma, Fontana, etc. / NUOVA ERA**
Tripla Concordia. 17th-century Italian recorder, performed in
a very seductive style. –PM

○ **Various works by Handel, Couperin, et al. / VNP**
Thorsen, et al.

ROMANTIC CHORAL MUSIC

Romantic.
○ **Works by Schubert, Schumann, Mendelssohn, Brahms,
Hauptmann & Reger / NOVALIS**
Jürgens/Hamburg Monteverdi Choir.

SACRUM CHANT

Midieval.
○ **Missa in Gallicantu / GIMELL**
Phillips/The Tallis Scholars.

TRUMPET CONCERTOS

Classical.
○ **Concertos by Richter, L. Mozart, Hertel, Molter &
Michael Haydn / PHILIPS**
Hardenberger (trumpet), Howarth/London PO. Brilliant and
musical — the best (young) trumpet player in the world. –PM

Classical Rating System

This section uses a different star rating system than elsewhere
in the book, since with classical music we have individual
compostions that are performed by many different goups.

The empty circle or bullet (○) marks the beginning of an
individual composition. Additional performances of that piece
are listed underneath, but are not bulleted. It is important to
note that multiple performances of a classical piece are listed
in order of preference by the reviewers. In other words, the
first performance listed is the pick, the second the next best
pick, and so on.

Stars (☆) in this section indicate the most representative
compositions for the composer and should be part of any
comprehensive collection of classical music.

Major/Minor Keys— Listings in major keys are indicated with
a capital letter (A, B, C, etc.), minor pieces in lower case letters
(a, b, c, etc.). Thus Mozart's "Great" mass in c minor would be
listed as *Mass in c.*

20TH CENTURY AVANT-GARDE

Categories are at best relative, and this is especially true in avant-garde music. In this section, you'll find music made with stones and symphony orchestras, home-built computers, and the unadorned human voice. The subjects are diverse — from personal political concerns to meditations on natural phenomena. What these pieces have in common are composers who pursued unique visions intertwined with their lives. These works go beyond any recognized categories and help enhance our sensitivity to the physical and imaginary worlds (both of which are "real," because we do the imagining).

There is a wide range of musical invention in this section —

1. Pattern music that gradually evolves over a steady pulse into complex and changing forms in the way of many natural processes such as the "divine proportion" of the chambered nautilus or the splitting of the amoeba. Examples: the pieces of Riley, Reich, Tom Johnson.

2. Music that takes single sounds and other elements out of pop music's usual song forms, formally expanding on them to make music of universal vision. Examples: Branca, the Residents, Chatham.

3. Music employing chance procedures (sometimes called "aleatory," which is actually a limited special case of chance operations) that produce the unexpected at every moment for performer, listener, and even composer. The compositions are often described as indeterminate of their "realization" (a one-time performance like sand paintings erased after a particular ceremony, with the basic tradition or score remaining until the next realization). This music gives the performer both greater responsibility and greater freedom, while encouraging us to experience the myriad events of every moment outside and inside ourselves — a sort of "ecology of the mind." In a very real sense, this music is not "about" something but is that "something" itself. Examples: Cage, Brown, Wolff, Feldman.

4. Music based on psychoacoustic illusions and other natural phenomena — brainwaves, sonic blasts from sand dunes, chaotic vibrations, a plant's apparent response to emotional or even telepathic stimuli. Examples: The Backster effect used in "Plant Music," an unrecorded piece by Tom Zahuranec (1972); Lucier; Amacher.

5. Compositions for home-built and composer-built instruments. Examples: Partch, Behrman.

6. Sound installations and other pieces designed to happen in places other than the usual concert halls. Examples: Kuivila, Hunt.

7. Music in alternate tunings, creating new sensations of hearing (Johnston, Wyschnegradsky), and music that explores new ways of playing traditional instruments (Goldstein, Lkucevsek, Celli).

8. Unique approaches to melody, harmony, and rhythm, as well as to traditional music (Hovhaness, Thomson, Garland, Hosokawa), including what could be called "the downtown sound," where pop, world, techno, folk, and concert sounds have all become part of the general vocabulary, not "collaged" in some artificial way but as a result of the musicians having grown up hearing and playing this music (Pickett, Gordon, Zorn).

9. New narrative forms and text/sound pieces. Examples: Ashley, Atchley, Anderson.

10. Deeply meditative music of an altered and expanded time sense. Examples: Vierk, Niblock, Radique.

11. Unique "crossover" pieces from jazz, rock, etc. Examples: Ornette Coleman's "Skies of America," Lou Reed's "The Amino ß Ring."

12. Super-formalist pieces, by academics who are seen, even by their fellows, as somewhat out of the fold. Examples: Wolpe, Barraque.

13. The whole array of electronic and tape music: generated by digital computers or by analog synthesizers; "musique concrete" made with manipulation of tape speed and editing (also sound accumulation by covering the erase head, delay by multiple tape loops, etc.); "live electronic" performance and interactive performance with acoustic instruments and voices; sampling of acoustic and electronic sounds and modulating them with wave-shaping synthesis, etc.; computer-controlled installations and acoustic instruments; electronically amplified instruments and environmental sounds; and much more.

14. Collective improvisation and group "process/procedure" work. Examples: Deep Listening Band, Cardew and the Scratch Orchestra, Yankees.

And of course,

15. Composer/performers and any of their pieces that can be described as employing several of the techniques, aesthetics, and influences mentioned above.

— "Blue" Gene Tyranny

MUHAL RICHARD ABRAHMS   b 1930

See the Jazz section for his biography.

☆ **Muhal Richard Abrams / BLACK SAINT**   1991

Muhal Richard Abrahms has had an important musical, spiritual, and social influence as president of the AACM (Association for the Advancement of Creative Musicians),

founded in Chicago in 1965 by members of his earlier group, The Experimental Band. *Blu Blu Blu* gives a good overview of the current range of his music, from the title piece, a wonderfully drafted polytonal Chicago shuffle-blues with perfectly placed and wry guitar licks from David Fiuczynski, to the chromatic and angular contrapuntal lyricism of "Cycles Five" and "Septone," the multilayered tone poem

"Petsrof," and "Stretch Time," which is literally that: an etude for band, over a steady walking bass, of an eternally winding main tune ("head") followed by consecutive solos, each of which starts *in time* with the pulse and slowly *stretches out* into rhythms of extremely complex ratios that float *outside* the pulse. All of the excellent performances on this CD reach out to the listener. Abrams's recent and daring work, the masterpiece "Duet for Pianos no. 1" and his string quartets, have yet to be recorded. Performed by the Muhal Richard Abrams Orchestra. —BGT

JOHN ADAMS   b 1947

An American minimalist composer who is known for *Nixon in China.* —ED

Shaker Loops (1978) / VIRGIN   1990
From the collection *LCO 8, Minimalist* (reviewed in 20th-Century Collections in this same section). An exceptionally good performance: rushing, trembling sounds represent the practices of the utopian religious group the Shakers and also the musical "shake." The two lovely inner movements, "Hymning Slews" and "Loops and Verses," are Adams's best harmonic writing — a lot of activity for so-called "minimal" music. Directed by Christopher Warren-Green. —BGT

Pat's Aria from *Nixon in China* (1987); Gradus (1968) for solo saxophone / POINT MUSIC   1992
Jon Gibson performs this pattern music with a lyrical feeling and makes "Pat's Aria" from *Nixon in China (Act II/I)*, for saxophone, piano, and synthesizer the best it has ever sounded. (See *Portraits* in 20th-Century Collections in this same section.) —BGT

MARYANNE AMACHER

○ **Stain - The Music Rooms / NONESUCH**   1989
From the collection *Imaginary Landscapes*. Amacher has created some of the finest pieces and sound-installations based on psychoacoustic illusions. Until the advent of CDs, most of her work was unrecordable, partly because of the extreme ranges of pitch and dynamics, the duration of the piece necessary to create some illusions, and the stability of the medium. The "music rooms" are just that — installed on floors of a house or in adjacent rooms that the audience walks through to create its own mix from enormously amplified environmental and electronic sounds. —BGT

BETH ANDERSON   b 1950

Very original composer in a variety of forms and musical styles, including textsound and tape pieces; known for her opera about Queen Christina. —BGT

● **Torero Piece (1973) ... / 1750 ARCH STREET**   1974
Torero Piece, in 10 + 2 Equals 12 American Text Sound Pieces (1973) is an imaginative and drolly humorous piece — a duet for the composer and her mother in which the mother describes her relationship to her daughter while the daughter makes unrelated phonemic sounds decoded from a paint-by-number picture she found in a junk antique store. —BGT

○ **I Can't Stand It (1975) / DIAL-A-POEM POETS**   1980
From the album *Sugar, Alcohol & Meat*, a textsound piece for speaker and drummer. —BGT

Poetry Music Quilt / WIDEMOUTH TAPES   1982
Works from 1975 to 1981: textsound pieces, tape works, flute solos, and instrumental combinations. —BGT

Revel (1981/1984) / OPUS ONE   1984
New romantic music that combines rock harmony and an interest in world music. Performed by the Richmond Symphony, conducted by Jacques Houtman. —BGT

AREA

Arbeit Macht Frei / CRAMPS
One of five incredible reissues (1990-1991) by this rock-influenced Italian communist new-music group; compo-

sitions are by several of Italy's leading avant-garde artists. The other four albums are listed below. —BGT

ARe(A)zione / CRAMPS
Caution: Radiation Area / CRAMPS
Crack! / CRAMPS
Maleditti (maudits) / CRAMPS

ROBERT ASHLEY   b 1930

Robert Ashley, influential for several decades as both a composer and writer, has created a series of operas-for-TV that speak on many levels of the lives of the people that constitute present-day America. —BGT

She Was a Visitor / ODYSSEY   1968
From the collection *Extended Voices*. The Brandeis University Chamber Chorus, conducted by Alvin Lucier. Ashley describes musically how "rumor" is spread among people, with leaders of a group selecting phonemes of the chanted line "She was a visitor" and the group sustaining each individual sound. The amassed sound, a "surface" of normalized disturbances in which an audience can participate, resembles airplanes, cars, trains — or perhaps the subatomic world. —BGT

The Wolfman for Amplified Voice & Tape / SOURCE MAGAZINE   1968
Part of the legendary theater piece *The Wolfman Motorcity Revue* (10-inch disc, out of print). —BGT

Purposeful Lady Slow Afternoon / MAINSTREAM   1970
From the collection *Sonic Arts Union*. One of two pieces that make up the legendary theater piece *The Wolfman Motorcity Revue*, which is about the melodrama of the love/sex/violence songs of the nightclub scene and an examination in minute, 2000-watt, enormously amplified phonemic detail of the physical changes in the language of an individual in a repressive society. —BGT

○ **Automatic Writing / LOVELY MUSIC**   1979
A close and intimate recording based on spontaneous speech. "My mind is censoring my own mind." —BGT

Music Word Fire and I Would Do It Again (Coo Coo): The Lessons from *Perfect Lives* / LOVELY MUSIC   1981
Robert Ashley, Jill Kroesen, and David Van Tiegham (vocals), with prepared piano solos improvised by "Blue" Gene Tyranny, and instrumental and vocal percussion by Van Tiegham. "This may be the first — dazzling — use of variation form in rock & roll" (Gregory Sandow, *The Village Voice*). —BGT

Yellow Man ... / LOVELY MUSIC   1990
Yellow Man with Heart with Wings (1978) is an inspired prose-poem in Spanish and English. It's about agriculture and the perspectives and feelings that occur to people in who live both inside and outside of cities. Heart-lifting. —BGT

● **In Sara Mencken Christ and Beethoven There Were Men and Women / CRAMPS**
A long-awaited reissue of this wonderful work. The text is by the legendary John Barton Walgamot and the voice activates beautiful and humorous electronic sounds designed by Paul DeMarinis. —BGT

★ **Perfect Lives / LOVELY MUSIC**   1991
This three-CD recording is part of a trilogy of operas-for-TV including *Atalanta (Acts of God)*, *Now Eleanor's Idea* (a total of 39 half-hour episodes), and *Perfect Lives* (realized for Channel Four of British Television). In this epic work, set in the American Midwest, the rhythms of the music, the geometry of the scenes, and the relations of the characters all seem to be from the same cloth, as if being described by the martyred first natural scientist Giordano Bruno, a "background" character who never appears in this work. For the characters that do appear, this is the basic plot: Raoul de Noget (No-zhay), a singer, and his friend Buddy, "The World's Greatest Piano Player," have come to a small town in the Midwest to entertain at the Perfect Lives Lounge. For some

unexplained reason, they have fallen in with two people from the town, Isolde ("nearing 30 and not yet eager for") and her brother "D," just out of high school and known as "The Captain of the Football Team" (his parents call him Donnie), with whom they plan to commit the perfect crime (a metaphor for something philosophical): in this case, to remove a sizable amount of money from the bank for one day (one day only) and "let the whole world know it was missing." The seven episodes are "The Park (Privacy Rules)," "The Supermarket (Famous People)," "The Bank (Victimless Crime)," "The Bar (Differences)," "The Living Room (The Solutions)," "The Church (After the Fact)," and "The Backyard (T'Be Continued)." –BGT

☆ **Don Leaves Linda (Improvement) / NONESUCH**   1992
Don Leaves Linda, in a completely new sound for voices and an electronic orchestra, recalls the Spanish influence in America and the problem of the separation of beauty ("Linda") from truth. Through touching and genuinely humorous metaphorical incidents and characters, and a music that is equally intimate and dramatically universal, we are presented with a driving sense of the "eternal present." A masterpiece. –BGT

KENNETH ATCHLEY   b 1954

○ **Don Giovanni / LEONARDO MUSIC JOURNAL**   1991
Don Giovanni, Act I, Scenes 1-4, from volume one of the collection *Anthology of Music for the 21st Century*, is a musical conversation with the characters of Da Ponte's libretto for Mozart's opera about the cultural myth of Don Juan and the history of our attitudes about sexuality (and "going to hell" for sharing sensual feeling). A subtle, surreal evocation for voices and electronics, with a highly poetic and intelligent text by the composer. –BGT

MILTON BABBITT   b 1916

American composer of 12-tone serial music; known for *Partitions* (1957) and *Three Compositions for Piano* (1947). –ED
Ensembles for Synthesizer / COLUMBIA
From the collection *New Electronic Music*. Non-narrative electronic sound organized with strict serialist procedures usually applied only to instrumental pitch, rhythm, and/or articulation. –BGT
Piano Music (complete) / HARMONIA MUNDI
Taub (piano). Dedicated. –PM
All Set for Jazz Ensemble / NONESUCH   1990
Formal writing for a jazz group, like experiments for other "progressive jazz" ensembles of the late 40s and 50s — the Sauter-Finegan Orchestra, the Stan Kenton Orchestra, and so forth. Written in 1957, this is a piece of its decade, but still interesting. Other works on this CD are by other well-known formalist composers George Rochberg (1918), Lalo Schifrin (1932), Richard Wernick (1934), and Stefan Wolpe. –BGT

TADEUSZ BAIRD   1928-1981

Psychodrama (1972) / OLYMPIA   1990
An interesting blend of Schoenbergian romanticism, serial pointillism, and orchestral color writing by a composer who went from a rather bland style of what was then imagined to be "people's music" to a radical change in the 60s. (See *New Music from Poland* in 20th-Century Collections in this section.) –BGT

JEAN BARRAQUÉ   1928-1973

French composer of chamber music; a contemporary of Messiaen; one of the first serialists. His unique style combined a rich impressionism with extremely formal pointillism. The use of jazz instrumentalists in classical ensembles playing his serial music led to social stigmatization in the late 50s. The pieces *...au delà du hasard* and *Chant après Chant* (1966) for six percussionists, voice, and piano were inspired by *The Death of Virgil*, by Hermann Broch. These pieces do not

merely set the text but reflect upon it, as shown in "Unable to evolve or regress," "Before the quotation," and "On a thought without night." –BGT
... au delà du hasard (beyond mere luck), for Four Intrumental Formats (1959) / ASTREE   1981
○ **Le Temps Restitué (1968), excerpt from** *La Mort de Virgile* **(The Death of Virgil) / HARMONIA MUNDI** 1987
A work similar in many aspects to *... au delà du hasard ...*, although more in the pointillisitic serial style. Beautiful performance by mezzo-soprano Anne Bartelloni. On the same CD is the virtuosic "Concerto" (1962-1968) for alternating trios of instruments (violin-bassoon-trumpet, violoncello-flute-tenor saxophone, and others). Performed by 2E2M and directed by Paul Mefano. –BGT

LOUIS AND BEBE BARRON

Wrote electronic music for film. The Barrons also assisted John Cage in making "Williams Mix." –BGT
Forbidden Planet (filmscore) (1954) / PLANET   1988
Forbidden Planet was the first Hollywood filmscore to use electronic music (the first all-electronic soundtrack was for Anaïs Nin's *The Bells of Atlantis* in 1952). The sound results from cybernetic (controlled feedback) circuitry, especially designed by the Barrons, producing Krells and monsters from the Id. –BGT

DAVID BEHRMAN   b 1937

○ **On the Other Ocean; Figure in a Clearing / LOVELY MUSIC**   1977
Subtle, sustained, and serene electronics with flute, bassoon, and cello soloists. Innovative, interactive performance setup and a beautiful listening experience. –BGT
Leapday Night / LOVELY MUSIC   1990
Several pieces with computer-aided interactive electronics and improvising musicians on mutatrumpet, trumpets, keyboards, violin. With Takehisa Kosugi, Ben Neill, and Rhys Chatham. Warm, beautiful, and gently humorous. –BGT
☆ **Unforeseen Events / EXPERIMENTAL INTERMEDIA FOUNDATION XI** 1992
Beautiful interactive computer music with Ben Neill, mutatrumpet. Contains *Unforeseen Events* with four sections: "View Finder," a canon with gradually more ornate responses to what the trumpeter is playing; "Fishing for Complements," a trio for computer, mutatrumpet, and a listener to the interchange who enters changes into the computer on a silent keyboard as the music progresses from simple repeating figures to hundreds of rapidly cascading sounds; "Witch Grass," more complex figures with sustained computer chords gradually slipping away from their tonal centers; "Canyon," a cerebral canyon with shadowy trains of pitch-shifted chords. It also contains "Refractive Light," in which tonal changes occur as "deflections" at the on-and-off edges of overlapping events. It has three sections: "Harbinger," "Crisscrossed Eights," and "Ein Glaesele Warems." –BGT

JACQUES BEKAERT

Summer Music 1970 / LOVELY MUSIC   1977
Twelve musical portraits — vignettes in sound with various instrumentalists performing verbal-instruction sources. Varied and charming. At the time of this recording, Bekaert was the voice of the legendary "King Kong" new-music radio show for Radio Belgium. –BGT

LUCIANO BERIO   b 1925

Italian composer of 12-tone and electronic music in most genres, including ballet, vocal, and piano music. –ED
Coro, for 40 Voices & 40 Instruments / DGG
Berio/Cologne RSO & Chorus.
Sequenza V, for Solo Trombone / BIS
Lindberg (trombone).

Momenti; Omaggio a James Joyce /
MERCURY LIMELIGHT   1968
From the collection *Images Fantastiques*. Wonderful early
musique concrète works. (See also *Cathy Berberian, Voice*;
Electronic Music; *Severino Gazzelloni, Flute*; *Images
Fantastiques*; *Music from Mills*; and *Neue Chormusik* (vol. 1)
in 20th-Century Collections in this section.) –BGT

JOHANNA MAGDELENA BEYER   b 1888

☆ **IV, for Percussion (1935) / AERIAL**   1991
From *The Aerial #3* (reviewed under 20th-Century Collections
in this section). Performed by Essential Music. Percussion
music for nine unspecified (!) instruments, completely unique
but appealing to a fundamental feeling. Beyer was involved in
much new-music activity, but her personal life remains a
mystery, her music still largely unperformed. (See *New Music
for Electronic and Recorded Media* in 20th-Century Collections
in this section.) –BGT

JOHN BISCHOFF   b 1949

Rendezvous (1978) / LOVELY MUSIC   1979
From *Just for the Record* (reviewed under 20th-Century
Collections in this section). Melodic phrases that "sometimes
... go their separate ways, sometimes drifting apart and at
other times coordinating together." Multitimbral synthesizer
sounds suggest an underlying surreal story. With "Blue" Gene
Tyranny (synthesizers). –BGT

○ **Artificial Horizon / ARTIFACT RECORDINGS**   1989
Wonderful collaborative and individual compositions for
personal computer systems. Includes "Touch Typing," "Next
Tone, Please," "Engagement," "Dovetail," "Artificial Horizon,"
"Clicks," "Clavitron 6000," "Audio Wave," and "Happy Trails."
With Tim Perkis. (See also The Hub in this section.) –BGT

CARLA BLEY   b 1938

See the Jazz section for her biography.
Escalator over the Hill /
JAZZ COMPOSERS ORCHESTRA ASSOC.   1967
Labeled a "chronotransduction" by composer Bley and
librettist Paul Haines, this unusual extended work for many
singers and instrumentalists is another opera that isn't an
"opera" in the European mold. Sections have titles like "Song
to Anything That Moves," "Small Town Agonist," "Like
Animals," "A.I.R. (All-India Radio)," "Rawalpindi Blues,"
"Holiday in Risk," and "... And It's Again." Characters are
Phantoms, Mindsweepers, Mutants I and II, Bullfrogs,
Ancient Roomer, the Hotel Lobby Band, Lion, the Desert
Band, Yodeling Ventriloquist, Sand Shepherd, and others. The
performers are from advanced jazz and rock fields — Gato
Barbieri (sax), Charlie Haden (bass), Roswell Rudd
(trombone), Michael Mantler (trumpet), Perry Robinson
(clarinet), Don Preston (well known for playing keyboard with
Zappa's Mothers of Invention), Paul Motian (drums), Don
Cherry (trumpet), Bob Stewart (tuba), John McLaughlin
(guitar), Leroy Jenkins (violin), Ron McClure (bass), Calo
Scott (cello), Sam Brown (guitar) — with many other
orchestra members and vocals by Jack Bruce, Viva (Warhol's
superstar), Linda Ronstadt, Howard Johnson, opera singer
Rosalind Hupp, and with many of the instrumentalists also
performing spoken and sung vocals on this three-CD set. Like
many jazz and rock records of the 60s, there is a willingness in
this work to find new sounds through unusual processing and
mixing, with the piece technically never-ending because of an
engineered loop at the end of Side 6 that keeps the universal
humming sound going for as long as you want the record to
continue. –BGT

BOB AND BOB

Across America (1981) / M.I.T.B.
A wonderful record, as well as a "document" of a performance
art piece: poetry and comments and stories from a cross-

country journey. You may also want to follow up with their
band record *We Know You're Alone* (backed with *We've Been
Seeing Things*) on Polygram/Polydor (New York, 12-inch EP
disc, 1983). And one of them, the Dark Bob, has also made
One Bob Job (includes "Outside of Moab," "The List," and
"Interstate" on a one-sided 12-inch album) and
Kabbalamobile (cassette, from soundtrack of theater work),
all available from M.I.T.B. –BGT

LARS-GUNNAR BODIN   b 1935

For Jon (Fragments of a Time to Come) (1977) /
FOLKWAYS   1978
A "surrealistic science fiction," even cyberpunk (the term
wasn't in wide usage at the time) cantata for narrator,
chamber choir, and electronics, with the text processed
through and triggering the electronics. Reflects Bodin's
continuing concern with concepts relating to modern science,
technology, and the role of art in a post-revolutionary
(Marcusean sense) society. –BGT

○ **Anima (1984) / WERGO**   1990
From the collection *Computer Music Currents 7*. A brief work
perfectly depicting a profound psychic process — the
unification of consciousness with the higher self. The human
voice (soprano) hears its counterpart in the computer voice
and the two merge in the course of the piece. Beautiful — a
good direction for new-music to take. –BGT

DAVID BORDEN

The Continuing Story of Counterpoint, Parts 9-12 (1976-
1987) / CUNEIFORM RUNE   1988
Influenced by other pattern-music composers (Glass, Reich,
Riley), Borden's music nevertheless has its own character
made from rich layers of free-wheeling solos over the
patterns, with some very lovely textures. The structure of the
music is built on composer and performer names and
birthdates in an elevated soap-opera structure. Performed by
Mother Mallard. –BGT

ANDRÉ BOUCOURECHLIEV

Ombres (Shades) (Hommage à Beethoven) / EMI
Recordings of Boucourechliev's music are difficult to find but
well worth the effort. This is an "hommage" to the father of
modern music. Beethoven's Third Symphony, *Eroica*, and
sometimes other works are often credited with being the first
modernist compositions, partly because they were built from
small "kernels" of ideas rather than being variations on full
melodies, and also because the music did not need outside
references to justify it. Instead of falling for the obvious idea of
"collaging" Beethoven's works, Boucourechliev creates an
impression of the "interior" nature of Beethoven's democratic
and universal pieces. This is difficult to put into words, but it
is something like the "feeling" you have left after the music
has ended. This is a transcendental and sustained piece,
unique in character. Performed by the National CO of
Toulouse, directed by Louis Auriacombe. –BGT

Texte I / MERCURY LIMELIGHT   1968
From the collection *Panorama Électronique*. Lovely musique
concrète piece. –BGT

PIERRE BOULEZ   b 1925

French composer and conductor whose music includes
elements of serialism and the aleatoric. Boulez conducted the
New York Symphony Orchestra from 1971 to 1978. –ED

○ **Improvisations sur Mallarmé / HUNGAROTON**
Improvisations sur Mallarmé I & II ("Improvisations on
Mallarmé," for symphony), with "Le marteau sans maître
(The Hammer without a Master)," established the particular
sound of Boulez's approach to serialist composition, a poetic
pointillism with a Debussyian sense of timbres that has
characterized most of his works and is more interesting than
most of the later, rather arid pieces that followed it. This CD

also contains two lovely classics of 12-tone music (upon which serialism is based): Schoenberg's *Pierrot Lunaire, op. 21* (1912) and Webern's *5 Canons on Latin Texts, for Soprano & Instrumental Ensemble, op. 16* (1923-1924), plus two of Webern's songs. –BGT

Éclat for 15 Instruments / SONY CLASSICAL
Boulez/Ensemble InterContemporain. Boulez is the most "intellectual" of contemporary composers and one of the most challenging. Any of his own music conducted by him can be considered a "definitive" statement. –PM

Figures, Doubles, Prismes / ERATO
Boulez/BBC SO.

Sonata for Piano no. 2 (1948) / DGG
Pollini (piano). Brilliant. –PM

Sonatas for Piano nos. 1, 2, 3 / WERGO
Henck (piano). Dedicated, but doesn't have the swagger or musicality of Pollini in the second sonata. –PM

Sonatina for Flute & Piano (1946) / ERATO
Boulez, Cherrier, Aimard.

PAUL BOWLES   b 1910

○ **The Voices of Paul Bowles / TELLUS**
Audio portrait of the author and composer with stories, selected works, early compositions (*Music for a Farce* and *Interlude and Prelude no. 2*, long unavailable), and environmental recordings made near his Moroccan home. In a private collection you may still find his wonderful pieces *A Picnic Cantata* (1955) for four women's voices, two pianos, and percussion, including a milk bottle and cigar box (Columbia album with pianists Gold and Fizdale); and *The Wind Remains* (1943), an opera based on an abstraction of the third act of Garcia Lorca's *Así que pasen cinco anos* (MGM disc E3549; also contains composer Peggy Glanville-Hick's "Letters from Morocco," which are settings of texts by Bowles). –BGT

GLENN BRANCA

○ **Symphony no. 1 (Tonal Plexus) / ROIR**
Recommended studies in gradually denser sonorities ("resultant masses") with a rock-steady pulse — this music digs deep into the mind/feeling to elicit bardo-like sensations often approached by the profoundest Buddhist chant. (See note below for *Symphony no. 6*.) –BGT

**Music for ... *The Belly of an Architect* /
LES DISQUES DU CRÉPESCULE**   1987
Music for Peter Greenaway's Film "The Belly of an Architect" (1987). A different light-music for string orchestra, with the gradually sliding tone-densities of the guitar music transferred to orchestral strings for some of the best moments in this score. –BGT

Symphony no. 6 (Devil Choirs at the Gates of Heaven), for 10 Guitars, Keyboard / BLAST FIRST   1989
(See note above for *Symphony no. 1*.) John Cage and Glenn Branca once had a disagreement about whether Branca's music is "fascist." Cage argued that densities that create a "sustained climax" restrict the mind from opening up. I doubt that fascists would like these symphonies. –BGT

HENRY BRANT   b 1913

Orbits, A Spatial Symphonic Ritual ... / CRI   1979
Orbits, A Spatial Symphonic Ritual for 80 Trombones, Organ & Sopranino (1979) is one of Brant's most ambitious spatial pieces: sounds accelerate in a circular motion as they ascend the cupola of St. Mary's Cathedral in San Francisco. His enormous multispatial work *Meteor Farm* (1982), which requires a symphony orchestra, two choruses, a jazz band, a Javanese gamelan, West African drummers and singers, Western percussion groups, and two sopranos, has not yet been recorded. Performed by the Bay Bones Trombone Choir, Brant (organ), Amy Snyder (voice), and conducted by Gerhard Samuel. –BGT

Solar Moth, for Solo Violin, Voice, String & Wind Ensemble / 1750 ARCH STREET   1979
A curious, funny little piece, with the violin wildly slipping and sliding as the "moth" that brings solar energy to all in one of its cycles, and in the other "races defenseless and suicidal toward its ... immolation." Daniel Kolbialka (violin). –BGT

☆ **Angels and Devils, for Flute & Flute Orchestra (1932, revised 1947) / CENTAUR**   1991
A "spatial music" piece for 14 flutes, with the performers standing on ladders or on different levels. Performed by the Eastman Wind Ensemble. –BGT

ANTHONY BRAXTON   b 1945

See the Jazz section for his biography.

Four Compositions (1982-1988) / HAT ART   1990
Excellent solo and ensemble pieces. –BGT

Composition 98 / HAT ART   1991
More of the same. –BGT

☆ **Composition no. 107 (excerpt, 1982), from *The Virtuoso in the Computer Age - Vol. 1*, CDCM Computer Music Series, Vol. 10 / CENTAUR**   1991
A "dry and glass-like sound universe," punctuated with high-energy improvisation. The performances are excellent. Braxton has taken the "graph score" to a new level for his compositions, which involve a combination of spontaneous and charted playing, and has extended his imagination into the future with pieces to be played from planet to planet — like Charles Ives in *Universe Symphony*, to be played from mountaintops. –BGT

EARLE BROWN   b 1926

☆ **Four Systems / EDITION**
Fundamental work that uses "indeterminate" procedures and graph scores. –BGT

○ **Times Five (1963); Octet 1 (1953); December (1952); Novara (1962) / CRI**
Kaleidoscopic mobiles. Elegant pieces by one of the composers who radically altered our concept of the freedom that is possible in music. Enthusiasts may also want to check out his *Four Systems for Four Amplified Cymbals* (1964) in the collection *Electronics and Percussion*, with Max Neuhaus on percussion (Columbia MS 7139 disc, currently out of print). Max Neuhaus currently makes sound-installation pieces. –BGT

Morton Feldman, Earle Brown / TIME   1965
Contains well-played performances of Brown's "Music for Violin, Cello & Piano" (1952), "Music for Cello & Piano" (1955), and "Hodograph" (1959), for ensemble, as well as Morton Feldman's serene "Durations" (1960-1961), for chamber ensembles. –BGT

Available Forms II / RCA VICTROLA   1968
Ethereally beautiful performance conducted by Bruno Maderna. The score is constructed in blocks of music ("available forms") that the conductor cues and guides with various signals, like an engineer with tracks of recorded material to mix. A combination of spontaneous music making and pre-composed intentions that works well. –BGT

LEIF BRUSH

Terrain Instruments Are Activated (1990) / AER   1992
From the collection *The Aerial #4*. Since 1968 Leif Brush has made sound installations and performances in galleries and public places around the world using his "terrain" instruments: Minnesota Permanent Forest Terrain, Signal Disc, Whistler, Wind Ribbons, Rainpattern Tree Filters, Treeharps Networking, Modified Treeways — and an array of transducers (solar-powered sensor amplifiers connected to microprocessors controlled and updated by telephone) and speaker-environments that amplify and articulate natural phenomena. Mysterious and beautiful. –BGT

GAVIN BRYARS   b 1943

First Viennese Dance (M. H.) (1985-1986), from *Three Viennese Dancers* / ECM   1986
This work by Gavin Bryars, scored for French horn and percussion — ethereal and slowly unfolding music — is different from his other "sound" (which he shares with Michael Nyman) of jauntingly repeating, minimally changing chords. The time-sense of this work reminds me of his famous "Jesus' Blood Never Failed Me Yet" (for string orchestra and pre-recorded older man's voice singing the repeated tune), although this "dance" (M. H. is Mata Hari, one of three famous dancers in Vienna in late 1906) is more transparent in texture. –BGT

WARREN BURT w/CHRIS MANN

Of Course; Anyway You Can Always Put Your Language Down to Experience / NMA
Of Course ... is a 77-minute piece that comes on a cassette accompanied by a plastic glove and a red rock from Australia, but no liner notes. Needless to say, a strange electronic piece, with the natural voice as a "trigger." –BGT

SYLVANO BUSSOTTI   b 1931

Coeur pour Batteur - Positively Yes / COLUMBIA
From the collection *Electronics and Percussion*. As a talented graphic artist, Bussotti has made some of the most amazing-looking graph scores, like the famous "Five Pieces for David Tudor," a score made in 1959 from a drawing made in 1949. Lines run in every direction and there are wild squiggles and vortices, small icons of imaginary characters, laconic word phrases of the same import as the other symbols, formless dark areas. Likewise, the score for *Coeur pour Batteur* is as defined as it is open (synaesthesically) to subjective readings by the performer. In this recording, Neuhaus divides the score into spatial directions for unusual body movements that result in sounds; other inadvertent body movements and voice sounds are also amplified and recorded. There are additional instruments that are not played but are set up to vibrate sympathetically out of the control of the performer. Max Neuhaus (percussion). –BGT

Bergkristall (1973) / DGG   1978
Bergkristall ("Crystal Mountain") is a ballet in one act and seven scenes based on a tale by Adalbert Stifter. A young boy and girl get lost in a snowstorm on Christmas Day on the way home from the valley where their grandparents live in the dyeworks. Following the spirit of a baker's boy who had once become lost, they wander off toward the "regions of eternal ice." Nature takes on supernatural forms — snow spirits and comets, which dance with the children to keep them awake (together with their mouthfuls of coffee) — and in the morning the children are rescued as the sun "burns like fire over the vast expanses of snow ... and glittering quartz ... as though a mass of roses were shining." The music is presented often in brief "illustrations" as dense (in a good sense) as multicolored drawings in a children's book — the Christmas tree decorations, the dancing spirits, the icy dissonance. If Charles Ives had decided to write with serialistic gestures and sounds, the result would probably be close to this unusual and exciting score. Bussotti has also composed several erotic monodramas — "La Passion selon Sade" ("Passion According to De Sade," 1966), "Il nudo" (The Nude), and "Ancora odone i colli" (Anchor Your Teeth in Their Necks). Performed by the Symphony of the North German Radio, Hamburg, directed by Giuseppe Sinopoli. –BGT

MICHAEL BYRON

○ **Marimbas in the Dorian Mode / COLD BLUE**
From the collection *Cold Blue Anthology*. Unusual fluttering sounds from four marimbas played in a sustained and very quiet manner — absolutely peaceful. If you run across one,

grab a copy of these lovely orchestral pieces on *Tidal* on the defunct Neutral Records. –BGT

GEORGE CACIOPPO

☆ **Time on Time in Miracles / ADVANCE**   1966
From the collection *Music from the ONCE Festival*. There will eventually be an issue of Cacioppo's work on Mode, but in the meantime all that is available is this live performance from the legendary ONCE Festival. Cacioppo produced some remarkably original ensemble music — the graph score based directly on the form of the constellation "Cassiopeia;" "Two Worlds" (1962), which contrasts the worlds of instrumental and vocal sounds; "Advance of the Fungi," based on ideas in the book by E. C. Large, which describes various plagues that overwhelm plants and animals from time to time; and "Bestiary 1 Eingang." Several of his works generated pitches, and the overall form is based on Markov chains. –BGT

JOHN CAGE   1912-1992

American composer of avant-garde music based on non-Western philosophy and employing aleatoric, electronic, and prepared instruments. Known for "4'33"" (1952), "HPSCHD" (1969), and "Imaginary Landscape no. 1" (1939). –ED

☆ **Empty Words (complete recording, Parts I - IV) / LOVELY MUSIC**
A gradually fragmenting text based on Thoreau's "Walden Pond," this heartwarming piece shows how Cage's structural procedures serve to enhance, rather than distance, human feeling and attention. Part III of *Empty Words* was performed live at the Teatro Lyrico di Milano on December 2, 1977 (Cramps CRSCD 037/038, 1991). John Cage (voice). –BGT

Solo for Sliding Trombone / BIS
Lindberg (trombone).

○ **Sonatas and Interludes for Prepared Piano / ET CETERA**
Fremy (prepared piano).

○ **String Quartet in Four Parts / DGG**   1950
The movements of *String Quartet in Four Parts* are "quietly flowing along," "slowly rocking," "nearly stationary," and "quodlibet." A beautiful score, all in natural tones (no sharps or flats) — a transition piece. This CD also contains quartets by Lutoslawski, Penderecki, and Mayuzumi. Performed by the LaSalle Quartet. –BGT

Music for Merce Cunningham: Five Stone Wind (with David Tudor and Takehisa Kosugi) / CARTRIDGE MUSIC   1960
Amplified violin, bamboo flute, nine clay pots, tapes, and live electronics. The spirit of gentle indeterminancy. "Cartridge Music" is a classic of graph music for phonograph cartridges and amplified small objects. A 1988 realization of this music by David Tudor is available on the Mode label, number 24 (1991 issue). –BGT

HPSCHD / NONESUCH   1967
Composed in collaboration with Lejaren Hiller for 51 computer-generated sound tapes and 7 solo harpsichord compositions, with each record containing a unique KNOBS computer printout for playback control of volume and equalization. –BGT

Études Boréales (1978); Ryoanji (1983) / MODE   1985
Composer-supervised recordings. One of the most beautiful albums of Cage's music: wonderful silences, no sense of pulse, perfectly played gestures on piano and cello with mezzo-soprano vocal. Peaceful, eternal. –BGT

○ **Thirty Pieces ... ; Music for Piano / HUNGAROTON**   1986
Five conductors for groups of the Savari SO. There is excellent spatial separation in *Thirty Pieces for Five Orchestras* (1981); *Music for Piano* (1952-1956) also includes mysterious sounds from the total-surround space. –BGT

Cheap Imitation / CRAMPS   1991
A recent reissue of a lovely performance of melodies that are fragments and transformations of melodies from Erik Satie's

opera *Socrate*, on the death of Socrates. Cage had to produce "cheap imitations" of these melodies for a performance when the rights to the Satie score could not be obtained. John Cage (piano). –BGT

☆ **John Cage: Music for Marcel Duchamp (1947); Music for Amplified Toy Pianos / CRAMPS** 1991
A reissue of wonderful performances by composers Hidalgo, Marchetti, Simonetti, and Stratos of these well-known pieces, including the famous "silent" piece "4'33"" (four minutes and thirty-three seconds of silence, for any instrument), in three parts. –BGT

★ **Singing Through / NEW ALBION** 1991
Beautifully performed pieces from 1942 to 1985. Contains "A Flower" (1950), "Mirakus" (1984), "Eight Whiskus" (1984), "The Wonderful Widow of 18 Springs" (1942), for voice and closed piano, "Nowth upon Nacht" (1984), "Sonnekus" (1985), "Forever and Sunsmell" (1942), "Solos for Voice" (from *Song Books*) nos. 49, 52, 67 (1970), "Music for Two (by One)" (1984). John Cage, Joan LaBarbara (voice), with piano and percussion. –BGT

● **One; In a Landscape ... / MUSICWORKS** 1992
One (1988); *In a Landscape* (1948); *Atlas Eclipticalis* (1961-1962); and *Winter* is music by and for John Cage in fabulous performances. Also has Udo Kasemets's "Hexagram no. 14 for John Cage: a Yi Jing Jitterbug Vococtet" (1991); Linda Catlin Smith's "Music for John Cage" (1990); "C(ag)elebration Messagemix" (1977), performed by callers from around the world and organized by Udo Kasemets and Peter Anson. –BGT

CORNELIUS CARDEW

☆ **Memorial Concert 16th May 1982: First Movement for String Quartet; Octet '71; Treatise; The Great Learning No. 1 and Other Pieces / GELBE MUSIK** 1982
A retrospective of this musically and morally influential British composer's work played by his composer friends Bryars, Nyman, Dave Smith, John White, John Tilbury, Rzewski, Tom Philips, Christopher Hobbs, Balanescu, Janos Negyesy, and members of the "Scratch Orchestra," a performing collective for musicians and non-musicians that Cardew cofounded in 1969. In their constitution draft they stated that "the word music ... is here not understood to refer exclusively to sound ... (but) is flexible and depends entirely on the members." (See *Scratch Music*, ed. by Cornelius Cardew, M.I.T. Press, MIT 239, paperback, 1974.) –BGT

WENDY CARLOS   b 1939

Carlos stirred popular interest in synthesizer music with her *Switched-On Bach* recordings, and continues to explore the possibilities of electronic music. –ED

Secrets of Synthesis / CBS
More than just a demonstration disc on electronic music, the examples are original creations from her own works, from the best-selling "Switched-On Bach" to "Digital Moonscapes," and contain extremely interesting theories and a new procedure for harmonic synthesis that result in sounds never heard before. (There's an interesting article on this with a floppy-disc demo in *Keyboard*, November 1986.) –BGT

ELLIOTT CARTER   b 1908

American composer influenced by Hindemith, Stravinsky, and Varèse. His compositions include ballets, chamber pieces (*First Quartet*, 1951), and symphonic works (*A Symphony of Three Orchestras*, 1976). –ED

Concerto for Oboe & Orchestra / EDITO CLASSICA
Holliger (oboe), Boulez/Ensemble InterContemporain.

Concerto for Piano & Orchestra / NEW WORLD
Oppens (piano), Gielen/Cincinnati SO.

Quartets for Strings nos. 1 & 4 / ET CETERA
Arditti String Orchestra.

Quartets for Strings nos. 2 & 3 / ET CETERA
Arditti String Orchestra.

Quintet for Woodwinds; Eight Études & a Fantasy for Woodwind Quartet / STRADIVARIUS
Arnold Wind Quintet.

○ **String Quartet no. 3 (1971); Elegy (1943) / ET CETERA** 1988
From the collection *Music for String Quartet - Vol. 2*. Pieces that illustrate the best of his early and later styles. Particularly noteworthy are the dense "abstract expressionist" complexities of the third quartet — instrumental conversations — and the unpredictable but warm, advanced-Coplandesque harmonies of the "Elegy." Incredible perfomances by the Arditti. –BGT

JOSEPH CELLI   b 1944

No World Improvisations / O. O. DISCS 1992
Virtuoso solo and duo improvisations with Jin Hi Kim (Korean komungo, changgo, and electric komungo) and Celli (Indian Mukha Veena, English horn without reeds, and Yamaha WX-7 MIDI-breath controller). Wonderful. –BGT

Sky: S for J, for 5 English Horns without Reeds (1976) / O. O. DISCS 1992
From the collection *Organic Oboe*. New and startling techniques for the English horn. –BGT

JOEL CHADABE   b 1938

Modalities / CENTAUR 1990
From the collection *The CDCM Computer Music Series - Vol. 7*. Gamelan-like, peaceful. –BGT

RHYS CHATHAM

Die Donnergötter (The Thundergods), for 6 Electric Guitars & Bass (1984-1986) / HOMESTEAD
Rhys merges both pattern-rock-influenced riffs (like Peter Gordon) and dense sonorities (like Glenn Branca) to produce music of an extended time sense — with the imagery of thundergods, Waterloo (complete with the requisite drums and massed trumpets), and the 60s-style rock trio. –BGT

JOHN CHOWNING   b 1934

An American composer of computer music at Stanford University. –ED

☆ **Phone; Turenas; Stria; Sabelithe / WERGO** 1988
Phone (1980-1981); *Turenas* (1972); *Stria* (1977); *Sabelithe* (1971) includes lyrical and sophisticated FM-synthesis computer music with psychoacoustic illusions (especially found in "Turenas," the first piece to create the impression of sound sources moving in a 360-degree space.) –BGT

HENNING CHRISTIANSEN   b 1932

A composer who uses normal instruments and noises and who also makes art objects in the Fluxus tradition: e.g., his "Betrayal, op. 144," a carton filled with various small objects and an EP, signed and numbered (available from Gelbe Musik). –BGT

Abschiedssymphonie (Farewell Symphony) (1985) / EDITION BLOCK 1985
The *Farewell Symphony* was composed for the opening of the Friedensbiennale (Freedom Biennial) in Hamburg, 1985, and is played by artists Joseph Beuys, Nam June Paik, and Henning Christansen. For further listening, try the albums *Fluxid: Höhlenmonat* ("A Month in a Hole"), *Concerto for Flute and Noises*; *Fressmonat* ("A Month of Devouring"), *Concerto for Sax, Cello, and Noises*; *Fluxyl: König Frost* ("King Frost"), *Concerto for Oboe and Noises*; and *Maskenmonat* ("A Month of Disguises"), *Concerto for Trumpet, Tuba, and Noises* (available from Gelbe Musik). –BGT

ORNETTE COLEMAN   b 1930

See the Jazz section for his biography.

☆ **Forms and Sounds / BLUEBIRD**
Includes "Forms and Sounds" (played by the Philadelphia

Woodwind Quartet): densities of melodies alternately free-floating or played to an automaton-pulse with trumpet interludes played by Coleman that are commentary-like to bluesy to celebratory — calls to reconsider life; "Saints and Soldiers": repression by the religious and political (contrasted with saintly) discernment; "Space Flight": flashes of unidentified fluttering things that suddenly disappear (performed by the Chamber Symphony of Philadelphia String Quartet). Coleman is legendary as the performer/composer who freed jazz from the harmony and songforms of Tin Pan Alley ballads. These pieces show more of Coleman's path since his densely chromatic orchestral piece *Skies of America* (movements are "Holiday for Heroes," "Place in Space," "Foreigner in a Free Land," "Sunday in America," among others). –BGT

Trinity / WHAT NEXT?
From the collection *Sounding the New Violin*. Fragments of melodies that range from joyous to contemplative to spontaneously explorative. Malcolm Goldstein (violin). –BGT

NICOLAS COLLINS   ♭1954

Going Out with Slow Smoke / LOVELY MUSIC   1982
With Ron Kuivila. Four compositions by Collins: "Killed in a Bar When He Was Only Three," "Little Spiders," "Second State," and "Is She/He Really Going Out with Him/Her/Them?" Also three by Kuivila. Fascinating electronic music, with a sense of humor. –BGT

Let the State Make the Selection / LOVELY MUSIC   1984
Contains "A Letter from My Uncle," "Vaya Con Dios (Go with God)" and "A Clearing of Deadness at One Horse Pool," with homemade electronics designed, built, and programmed by Nicolas Collins. –BGT

100 of the World's Most Beautiful Melodies /
TRACE ELEMENTS   1989
A tongue-in-cheek title, perhaps, depending on your idea of a "beautiful melody." Played by an all-star downtown group: Nicholas Collins, Pippin Barnett, Anthony Coleman, Tom Cora, Peter Cusack, Shelley Hirsch, George Lewis, Christian Marclay, Ben Neill, Zeena Parkins, Robert Poss, Ned Rothenberg, Elliott Sharp, Davey Williams, John Zorn, and Peter Zummo. The music ranges from electronically and physically modified instruments with a definite edge, to the barely perceptible: it awakens the ear. Collins is also part of the Impossible Music group (with David Weinstein, David Shea, Ted Greenwald, and Tim Spelios), not yet available on recordings. Performing live, they strangely manipulate CD players in the spirit of Plunderphonics and rap-scratch style to create a new style of electronic ensemble. Works include the spatial and surreal "Simulcatastrophy"; "In CD" by Collins, which often humorously re-thinks the cadences and forms of Beethoven and Mozart (he has made some recent work with Ben Neill along this same line); and the dense work "Salvador Dali's Digital Cinema." –BGT

PHILIP CORNER

Pictures of Pictures, from *Pictures of Pictures* /
EDITION BLOCK
A terrific instrumental work. –BGT

The Gold Stone (1985) / WHAT NEXT?
From the collection *Sounding the New Violin*. Sighing, sliding tones of rough to sweet texture, like a "folk" violinist, restrained to pleading. Malcolm Goldstein (violin). –BGT

HENRY COWELL   1897-1965

○ **Quartet Euphometric (1916-1919) / NEW WORLD   1977**
Like the "Quartet Romantic" (1915-1917) and the "Concerto for Rhythmicon & Orchestra," this brief, two-minute work is built on yet another of Cowell's groundbreaking "resources," converting pitch intervals into rhythms (all tones vibrate in rhythmic cycles, but you can hear the separate beats only on very low notes). Although these works were too difficult for

players of the 1910s, they are quite playable now. Cowell was the prime mover of the so-called "ultramodernist" music scene in the early part of the century, which established the vitally important New Music Editions (publishing some modern classics) and produced many concerts of new-music (see Rita Mead's *Henry Cowell's New Music 1925-1936 — The Society, the New Music Editions, and the Recordings*, University Microfilms International, Ann Arbor, Michigan, Research Press, 1981). Cowell invented many technical musical devices (see his book *New Music Resources*, 1930), such as playing inside the piano (in his famous work "Banshee"), producing artificial harmonics. Like Charles Ives, he was writing atonally before the similar technique reached America from Europe (Schoenberg, Berg, Webern, Hauer). His interest in the musical techniques of other cultures led to attempts to synthesize a "world music" and greatly influenced his later, more conservative works (his writing seemed to change after the sad episode of his undeserved imprisonment — see an article by Michael Hicks, "The Imprisonment of Henry Cowell," in the *Journal of the American Musicological Society*). Nevertheless, he made the best of the situation, organizing and inspiring prison bands and continuing his editing and correspondence with the help of friends. A recording of his piano works is essential to any new-music collection, but at the moment of this writing there are (amazingly) none available. Performed by the Emerson String Quartet. –BGT

Piece for Piano ... / FINNADAR   1979
Piece for Piano (Puris, 1924), in *Doris Hays: Adoration of the Clash* is a piece that uses a variety of the piano techniques that Cowell pioneered — strumming, plucking, damping with the hand and hitting the strings, and playing tone clusters on the keys with fist, forearm, and palm. This recital album also contains pieces by Morton Feldman, Doris Hays, Leo Ornstein, Russell Peck, and Ilhan Mimaroglu. –BGT

RUTH CRAWFORD (SEEGER)   1901-1953

○ **Quartet (1931) / GRAMAVISION**
From the collection *Arditti String Quartet*. A highly expressive piece and an innovative breakthrough in its use of harmonics and extended tones. Crawford invented structural techniques that have had a great influence on avant-garde music. –BGT

ALVIN CURRAN   ♭1938

American composer and student of Elliott Carter who has written small- and large-scale pieces that make use of environmental sounds. –ED

○ **Electric Rags II / NEW ALBION   1990**
Rova Saxophone Quartet with Curran (electronics) and Scot Gresham-Lancaster (Oberheim expander). Playing lots of tuneful and rhythmic material ("Z-Train," "Corny Island," "Scusami, I Walk Alone," "Continental Shelf-Dance," etc.), the computer spontaneously structures the concert while the sax players control synthesizers, and all is constantly transformed in real time. –BGT

ZULEMA DE LA CRUZ   ♭1958

Pulsares (1990) / RTVE   1991
From the collection *Compositoras Madrileñas*. A study for piano and taped electronics, "creating points of sound in space of major and minor intensity." –BGT

THE DEEP LISTENING BAND

○ **Troglodyte's Delight (1989) / WHAT NEXT?   1990**
Exploring the sound properties of the Tarpaper Cave in Rosendale, NY, this group of renowned improvisers includes Stuart Dempster on trombone and didjeridu, Pauline Oliveros on accordion with voice and whistles, the vocals of Panaiotis and Julie Lyon Balliett, and the percussion of Fritz Hauser. Satisfying natural and meditative beauty, with two cuts featuring just cave water ("Cave Water"). My favorite cut is "After Dinner with the Trogs." –BGT

The Ready Made Boomerang / NEW ALBION 1991
This time our intrepid new-music crew is found mucking around in an enchanting manner underground in the Cistern Chapel, Fort Worden Cistern, Olympic Peninsula, Washington, exploding a balloon ("Balloon Payment") to demonstrate the natural reverberation time of the space, making suspended vocal ("CCCC" or Cistern Chapel Chance Chants) and unusual instrumental sounds, and dropping percussive stuff. Lovely and mysterious. −BGT

PAUL DEMARINIS ♭1948

I Want You; Kokole / MUSIC AND ARTS 1988
From the collection *Another Coast*. Inventive and charming interactive vocals with electronics. −BGT

☆ **Music as a Second Language / LOVELY MUSIC** 1991
Interactive electronics outlining voices with computer-shadowing melodies, beautiful sustains, gentle humor, and humanity. Contains "Fonetica Francese," a take-off on language lessons; "Odd Evening," about a Chinese radio play; "An Appeal," "a fit of legal dictation plagued by spurious vocal melodies"; "The Sand Clock"; "Cincinnati 1830-1850"; "The Power of Suggestion," based on the voices of hypnotists, evangelists, and salesmen; and "Beneath the Numbered Sky," based on an Indonesian folksong. It's all marvelously imaginative. −BGT

STUART DEMPSTER ♭1936

○ **In the Great Abbey of Clement VI / NEW ALBION** 1987
Mellow solo-trombone calls, earth-energy drones, and cries of a didjerido invoke the resonate standing waves built into the harmonic geometry of the architecture. −BGT

ROBERT DICK

Venturi Shadows / O. O. DISCS 1992
Music of flute revolutionary Robert Dick in performances by Neil Rolnick, Steve Gorn, Ned Rothenberg, and Mary Kay Fink. −BGT

DIE TÖDLICHE DORIS (DEADLY DORIS)

Naturkatastrophen / GELBE MUSIK
Naturkatastrophen ("Natural Catastrophes," 1985) is a 7-inch disc, with instructions in German and English on how to produce do-it-yourself disasters — a way of dealing with "the dread generated by State, society and nature," as kids do by means of fairy tales and others do by forms of resistance. This record is one of the group's milder productions, but be warned: playing this album will definitely not endear you to the neighbors. −BGT

HERBERT DISTEL

Die Reise (The Journey) / HAT ART 1990
A dazzling four-part work designed for radio broadcast. −BGT
La Stazione (The Train Station) / HAT ART 1990
A very different kind of opera in two acts. −BGT

LUCIA DLUGOSZEWSKI ♭1931

○ **Angels of the Inmost Heaven / FOLKWAYS** 1975
Music for a dance by Erick Hawkins. The "Angels" are described by transformations called Novae (bursts of energy), Coronae (transparent densities), and Clear Core (tiny distinctions in static walls, a nervous surface of extremely quick pulses). Extraordinary variations of glissandos, fast lip and finger trills, and constant shifting of mutes are the ingredient techniques of a unique style that flows with high energy and the eloquence of a Debussy-like orchestral brass section. Brass ensemble conducted by Gerard Schwarz. −BGT
Tender Theater Flight Nageire (1971/1978) / CRI 1978
A "series of musical rituals involved ... with the poetic roots of erotic experience. Nageire is an oriental aesthetic principle of nondevelopment, of nonlinear ... leap. It uses constant and

extreme surprise ... leaping into unknown material ... for the flexibility of the mind. One drop of water can unhinge my throat into miracles of swallowing. The sudden shiver of a delicate paper rattle or an unusually sensitive tonguing on a brass instrument becomes transparency utterly alive" (from notes by the composer). For brass ensemble with the composer playing on many of her one hundred percussion instruments: lovely silence, surprising sounds. May be reissued on CD. −BGT

Fire Fragile Flight / CANDIDE 1979
This gorgeous piece is totally unique in sound and conception. A chamber orchestra with an unusual percussion section (four players on slide whistles, hanging bells, playing inside the piano, and so forth) re-create the physical phenomenon of falling leaves in early March in the Great Lakes country. The music has 65 freely chosen, musically dangerous "leap-points," which trigger whirling "startle-juxtapositions" of varying speed, in the way that the reflected light on turning and falling leaves will sometimes appear to set them on fire. Performed by the Orchestra of Our Time, and conducted by Joel Thome. −BGT

TOD DOCKSTADER

Drone; Two Fragments from *Apocalypse*; Water Music / OWL 1966
Luna Park; Traveling Music; Apocalypse / OWL 1966
In 1966 Dockstader, working in his independent studio to record sounds made by ordinary objects, produced this prolific blast of musique concrète compositions, which he referred to as "organized sound." Very curious and sometimes quite beautiful. −BGT
Quartermass / OWL 1966
See note above.

CHARLES DODGE ♭1942

An American composer of computer music and the director of the Center for Computer Music at Brooklyn College. −ED
Earth's Magnetic Field (1970) / NONESUCH 1971
Realized at the Columbia University Computer Center, this piece is built from directly translating a record of the magnetic changes (Kp indices) for planet Earth in 1970. Values are read daily from graphic charts that look so much like music they are popularly known as Julius Bartel's "musical diagrams." An interesting experiment. −BGT
In Celebration ... / CRI 1990
Includes *In Celebration*; *Speech Songs*; and *Story of Our Lives*: poetry readings that are digitized and restructured in the computer to modify the vocal and other sounds. −BGT

PAUL DOLDEN

Threshold of Deafening Silence / TRONIA DISC 1992
Exhibits wonderfully uninhibited and compact densities of amassed acoustic sounds, like the 400 tracks of "Below the Walls of Jericho" or the modulated galactic racket of "In the Natural Doorway I Crouch," for alternately tuned balalaikas. Highly recommended. −BGT

PAUL DRESHER ♭1951

Other Fire (1984) / MUSIC AND ARTS 1988
From the collection *Another Coast*. A rich mix of naturally occurring rhythmic and cycling environmental sounds (birds, temple bells, and more) from tape recordings made during Asian and Southeast Asian travels; the mix gives the illusion of electronic synthesis of all these disparate elements. −BGT

MARCEL DUCHAMP

○ **Erratum Musical ... / EDITION BLOCK** 1990
Includes *Erratum Musical*, for three voices (1913); *Sculpture Musicale*, realized as Mesostic by John Cage and a version for music-boxes; *La Mariée mise à nu par ses cèlibataires même*

("The Bride Stripped Bare Even by Her Bachelors," 1913), pianola version and realization for alto flute, trumpet, trombone, celeste, and marimbaphone. The S.E.M. Ensemble, directed by Petr Kotik, realizes these early pieces using chance operations for "any instrument in which the virtuoso intermediary is suppressed." Another interesting realization is by percussionist Donald Knaack, who used a large funnel, five open-connected wagons, and numbered balls (Finnadar SR-9017, 1977, out of print). –BGT

WILLIAM E. DUCKWORTH   b 1943

○ **Thirty-One Days ... / LOVELY MUSIC**   1990
Thirty-One Days, for Alto Saxophone (1987) includes singing and wailing sax, solo and multitracked in ensemble. Great playing by Michael Swartz, who uses movement in the stereo space to change presence and "throw" sounds. –BGT

The Time Curve Preludes (1982): Books I and II, Preludes I-XXIV / LOVELY MUSIC   1990
Accurately described by a reviewer as a "new-age *Well-Tempered Clavier*," the *Time Curve Preludes* are elegantly played by pianist Neely Bruce. –BGT

☆ **Southern Harmony (1980-81) / LOVELY MUSIC**   1992
The first complete recording of this exceptionally fascinating and moving choral work. By concentrating and sampling only certain aspects — such as rhythm and a single gesture — of shape-note ("sacred harp") singing (a style of the rural South), the interior nature of these hymns is brought to the surface — a very different idea from merely setting the hymns with new harmonies. Performed by the Gregg Smith Singers, assisted by Rooke Chapel Choir of Bucknell University, and conducted by Gregg Smith. –BGT

DAVID DUNN

Chaos and the Emergent Mind of the Pond / AER   1990
From the collection *The Aerial #2*. An assembly of bio-acoustical underwater recordings that lets us listen to a burgeoning level of life we do not normally hear. –BGT

DUKE ELLINGTON   1899-1974

See the Jazz section for his biography.
○ **The Clothed Woman / NEW WORLD**   1977
Much will be said about the magnificent compositions and career of Duke Ellington in the jazz section of this guide, but this piece, *The Clothed Woman, from Mirage: Avant-Garde and Third Stream Jazz*, recorded on December 30, 1947 (originally issued on Columbia 38236), deserves special attention as a precursor of the pointillistic style in both advanced Afro-American and Eurocentric music. The opening and closing statements of this short work are in free or open time (no pulse or rhythm) and are made from chordal forms abstracted from Ellington's piano "punctuation" accompaniment style (developed over 20 years at the time of this recording). The resulting sound is several years in advance of a similar sound in serialist music and free-jazz. Avoiding the usual idea of the bridge of a song, Ellington gave the midsection of this composition a steady pulse that he built by placing these gestures over a chromatic boogie-bass figure that serves as a non-modulating, suspended-in-time nervous drone. –BGT

JEAN-CLAUDE ELOYS   b 1938

Equivalences (1963) / EVEREST   1967
A wonderful pointillist experiment in which typical wind (sustained tones) and typical percussion (brief, attacked) sounds gradually metamorphose into each other while arcs are formed that transverse the orchestral landscape. Eloys has turned to world music and improvisation for his current works. Performed by Domaine Musicale, directed by Pierre Boulez. –BGT

BRIAN ENO   b 1948

See the Contemporary Instrumental section for his biography.
Discreet Music / OBSCURE   1975
Taking a cue from Satie's idea of "musique d'ameublement" (furniture music), music that just exists, like furnishings in an apartment, and is played so as not to draw attention to itself (not really Muzak, a company that seeks to produce a more intentional work-product effect), Eno created several albums of what he termed "ambient music," which combined a softer style of pattern music (influenced by Bryars, Nyman, Harold Budd) with environmental noises. This album is probably the best of these, using Pauline Oliveros-style tape-delay to slowly change patterns of repeating sounds. –BGT

ROBERT ERICKSON   b 1917

Ricercar à 3 for Contrabass Solo (1967); Sierra, for Baritone & Ensemble (198 / CRI   1991
The "Ricercar" is a bass solo with an improvised quality played sensitively by Bertram Turetzky. "Sierra," with text by Erickson and sung here by Philip Larson with the SONOR Ensemble, is a very peculiar recitative, with instrumental colors about the California environs, interspersed with greetings to friends. Erickson's writing is built from "academic" elements, but is always personal, unique, and lively. –BGT

MARIA ESCRIBANO   b 1954

Jondo ... / RTVE   1991
Jondo, for Sax Ensemble, Piano & Percussion is from the collection *Compositoras Madrileñas*. A piece built of dance-like rhythm patterns that describe the beating of a heart at rest, or rushing forward, or waiting in anticipation. –BGT

JOHN FAHEY

○ **The Singing Bridge of Memphis, Tennessee; March! For Martin Luther King / VANGUARD**
John Fahey, like Moondog, has often used environmental sound, not as background, but integrally with his modern folk-style guitar music — like the mournful train sounds in the distance on his "Raga for Pat" (Takoma Records, out of print). –BGT

MORTON FELDMAN   1926-1986

American composer of quietly textured music, sometimes of extreme length; notable works are *Viola in My Life* (1970-1971) and *Rothko Chapel* (1971). –ED

Pieces for More than Two Pianos / SUB ROSA
Sublime, slowly evolving chordal textures. Contains "Four Pianos," in which the four players all read from the same material but play at their own speed, gradually creating a landscape of indeterminate delays. Performed by Le Bureau des Pianistes. –BGT

Intersection 3 / DEUTSCHE GRAMMAPHON   1969
Intersection 3 (1953), from the collection *Gerd Zacher, Organ*, is one of the earliest graph scores, originally intended for piano. Zacher produces a unique realization by distributing notes that are difficult to play on one keyboard, and by selectively stopping the organ's wind supply — an eerie, dissolving sound. –BGT

○ **Viola in My Life ... ; False Relationships ... / CRI**   1971
False Relationships and the Extended Ending alternates between exact proportions and "free time" in the vertical style (slowly changing chords, common-tone suspensions) in pieces such as "Atlantis," 1958, and "The Swallows of Salangan," which came after the counterpoint style of the early-50s graph pieces. *Viola in My Life, for Viola & Six Instruments* (1970-1971) was the next development, adding melody-like gestures. –BGT

For Samuel Beckett / CLASSIC   1991
Mobiles for chamber orchestra, similar to his last orchestral

work, "Coptic Light." Performed by the San Francisco Contemporary Players, directed by Stephen Mosko. –BGT

☆ **Rothko Chapel; Why Patterns? / NEW ALBION**   1991
After inventing graph notation ("Projection I" for solo cello in 1950), Feldman began to write works that used long tones and wordless singing and were played very quietly (allowing sounds that could not otherwise be heard), creating a changing but unbroken "surface." In the 70s he began to work with gently pulsing mobile-like rhythmic figures, of which *Why Patterns?* (1978) is a good example. *Rothko Chapel, for Chorus, Viola and Percussion* (1971) was first recorded by the Gregg Smith Singers (Odyssey Y-34138, out of print), with the lovely instrumental "For Frank O'Hara." –BGT

LUC FERRARI   b 1929

○ **Brise-Glace ... / ADDA**
Brise-Glace, et si toute entière maintenant ... ("Icebreaker, Supposing Now I Were To ...") was the winner of the Prix Italia 1987. Surreal, poetic interior monolog of passenger on shipboard near the Arctic Circle. Beautiful and original blend of orchestral writing, with natural and electronic sounds. French text by Colette Fellous. –BGT

FLUXUS (GROUP/MOVEMENT)

☆ **FluxTellus / TELLUS AUDIO CASSETTE MAGAZINE**
Soundworks by the legendary East Coast artists group who, together with other 60s performers such as the ONCE Group in Michigan, radically accepted all activity of art and life in their work. Contributions from George Brecht (organizer of the New Jersey-based Yamday Festivals), Dick Higgins (writer and publisher of the famous *Something Else Press*), Alison Knowles, George Maciunas, Emmet Williams, La Monte Young, Takaka Saito, Jackson MacLow, Joe Jones, Tomas Schmit, James Tenney, Robert Watts, and Larry Miller. –BGT

BILL FONTANA   b 1947

Australian Sound Sculptures / EDITION BLOCK
Fascinating sounds by one of the pioneers of sound-installation pieces. This work was made while Fontana was a producer for the Australian Broadcasting Commission (1975-1978). Based on eight-channel field recordings (made for a tape archive) of Australian environmental sounds, it was presented as an exhibition called "Sound Sculpture" at the National Gallery of Victoria in Melbourne. –BGT

○ **Landscape Sculpture with Fog Horns / KQED-FM**   1982
Landscape Sculpture with Fog Horns (Installation Version, 1981; Live Radio Version), created for the San Francisco New Music America 1981 Festival, involved eight loudspeakers, each playing a broadcast of ambient sound from distant locations in the Bay Area as listeners walked along the 600-foot pier (East Wall of Pier 2, Fort Mason Center) on a trajectory towards Angel Island three miles away. A changing and drifting configuration of echo and delay patterns was created by the uncoordinated pulses of the horns and the wide spatial placement of the microphones at Point Blunt, West Garrison, Treasure Island, Yacht Harbor, Fort Point, China Beach, the Legion of Honor, and the Cliff House. Four locations were used for the live radio version. The sound of a fog horn can travel about five miles. Under certain atomspheric conditions, the fog will mask certain pitches (on the radio version, the horns form a mysteriously beckoning major chord with a flat second added, plus seagulls and some brief unintelligible conversation by passerbys). Certain horns are louder at a distance than at close proximity. These variations make for a beautiful listening experience. –BGT

FAST FORWARD   b 1954

○ **Panhandling / LOVELY MUSIC**   1990
Not your usual percussion music. Sometimes studies of a single sound: a bullroarer (Africa, Australia) in "Bullroarer"; a metal ball rolled about a water-filled, tuned oil drum,

producing beautiful harmonics, in "Waterball"; assemblies of metals from life — a bathtub, metal snake, and two temple bells in "Precious Metals." Sometimes there's the bright emotion of steel pan solos in "Red Dance," "The Big Wind," and "Stix," exploring closely placed tones moving on a steady rhythm figure, like some guitar picking, a Bach prelude, or African marimba music. –BGT

FRED FRITH

The only ex-Henry Cow member who has been active in the US, Frith has attained a global reputation as a composer, improviser, multi-instrumentalist, instrument builder, and eclectic collaborator of the first rank. His myriad activities freely cross over the boundaries of rock, world music, improvisation, and the avant-garde; he is one of the few new pioneers to be the subject of a feature-length film (*Step Across the Border*). His work in Henry Cow and related groups (including those of Brian Eno and Soft Machine founder Robert Wyatt) is based on the folk and blues sonic discoveries of British guitarists Derek Bailey, Keith Rowe, and John McLaughlin (among others), yet his originality and self-critical nature have prevented him from being derivative. –MB

Skeleton Crew Learn to Talk / RIFT
A brilliant band album with Tom Cora and additional voices, far beyond the normal idea of what the music industry tries to sell us as "progressive rock," with a constant and highly imaginative variety of complex political collage and biting humor, accompanied by triggered noise, riffs in 5/4 time, and distorted Sousa marches gated by the guitars. –BGT

Guitar Solos / EAST SIDE DIGITAL   1974
Made in four days; improvised, some to a roughly preconceived idea. "Glass c/w Steel": "four layers of sound in an eerie haze out of which bounds a rubbery, animal-like line" (Cole Gagne in the book *Sonic Transports*); "Ghosts": distorted chords appearing and disappearing; "Out of Their Heads (On Locoweed)": "like being harangued by an automobile accident" (Gagne); "Hello Music," a cheery welcome; "No Birds": a tour through imaginary landscapes. A remarkable album, it predated so much radical guitar playing of the following decades and still has a lot of originality to offer. –BGT

○ **Gravity / EAST SIDE DIGITAL**   1979
With members of the Muffins and fellow Art Bears/Henry Cow-mates, improvised rock of the most inventive kind. –MGN

Speechless / RALPH   1980
Sessions with Etron Fou Le Loublan Quartet and Bill Laswell's material and guests Mars Williams and George Cartwright. Powerful rock extensions with lots of improvisation. –MGN

☆ **The Technology of Tears ... / SST**   1988
The Technology of Tears and Other Music for Dance and Theater (1987) includes "Sadness, Its Bleached Bones Behind Us" and "You Are What You Eat," which are unrelenting slices of hard-edged sounds over a pulse. "The Palace of Laughter, the Technology of Tears" is an imaginative, intense, varied suite that compares the best "frozen tears" of sadness — displayed by the media as images before us — with the "hot tears" of the moment, which cannot be absorbed by technology. "Jigsaw" and "Jigsaw Code" (1986) create patterns with constantly shifting accents and subdivisions — uneven pieces to be fit together. "Propaganda" (1987), music for a theater production, is a series of brilliantly evocative soundpieces with electronics, guitar, and sound effects: feedback and explosions in the distance, tantric harmonizing in the desert. –BGT

JAMES FULKERSON   b 1945

Co-Ordinative Systems no. 10 ... / IRIDA   1980
Co-Ordinative Systems no. 10, for Trombone and Tape Delay (1976); *Music for Brass Instruments II* (1975); *Antiphonies and Streams* (1978); *Suite for Solo 'Cello, Amplified* (1978-1979). James Fulkerson is a talented composer and trombonist who uses alternate mouthpieces to create electronic-like tones,

which are fed into a delay network in the piece "Co-Ordinative Systems no. 10." In "Music for Brass Instruments II," the bass trombone player follows an "aural score" of two other trombones on tape and attempts to follow and blend with them. "We play and think differently when we follow only our ears." –BGT

ELLEN FULLMAN

Staggered Stasis / AER
From the collection *The Aerial #3*. Rich acoustic waves of sound from the Long String Instrument (Fullman's own invention), featuring harmonics and ancient Pythagorean intervals. Originally this was the music for "The Navigator," a dance by Deborah Hay's company. –BGT

DIAMANDA GALÁS

☆ **Plague Mass (1984 - End of the Epidemic) / MUTE**   1991
Galás, who has been known for both her own work and as a singer of extremely demanding modern scores, has created this heart-wrenching cry about the suffering of persons with AIDS, compounded by the shameful arrogance of self-appointed moralists. Maintaining an incredible intensity and depth for over an hour's solo vocal (recorded live at the Cathedral of St. John the Divine, NYC, with suitably minimal band and electronics backup), Galás proceeds from Mahalia Jackson-influenced spiritual singing, breaking at points into high saxophone-like wails, to dramatic dialogs in many dialects and languages illustrating the callousness of "voyeurs" ("There are no more tickets to the funeral") and people who cannot deal with the reality of other people's suffering. She goes into totally engrossing Portuguese "fado" singing for a setting of the "Cris D'Aveugle" (Blind Man's Cry), a text by Tristan Corbière (1873) that is similar in form to her combination of biblical quotations and dialog from life experiences. In order to challenge the concept of a vengeful deity (and society), she compares the ordeal of people with AIDS to Christ on the cross by taking on the attributes of Satan (in "Sono L'Antichristo," I Am the Anti-Christ), much as Nina Simone did in her controversial song "God Is a Killer" in the 60s. The Mass ends with the lyrics "I go to sleep each evening now dreaming of the grave and see the friends I used to know calling out my name. O Lord Jesus, do you think I've served my time?" Despite her articulate compassion, she has been accused of blasphemy by the Italian church and arrested as an activist in the US. Her recent piece "Vena Cava" (1992) compares the speech of dying AIDS patients with the indifferent banalities of their surroundings (hospital and TV sounds, and so forth), somewhat like the quieter work of Brenda Hutchinson, who uses recordings made in an insane asylum for one performance piece (and pig calls for another piece — see *The Aerial #4* in Collections). –BGT

GE GAN-RU   b 1954

○ **Yi Feng (Ancient Wind); Gu Yue / TELLUS #19**
From the collections *New Music China* and *Sonic Encounters*. China's first avant-garde composer. After receiving degrees in violin and composition from the Shanghai Conservatory of Music, he was forbidden to play anything but scales during the Cultural Revolution and was later incarcerated and tortured. In 1983 he was awarded a fellowship to Columbia University, where he studied with Chou Wen-chung and Mario Davidovsky and received his Doctor of Musical Arts degree. He has composed concert music as well as music for dance, theater, and several films: *Tang Dynasty*, *Who Killed Vincent Chin* (1988 Oscar nominee for Best Documentary Film), and *A Great Wall*, the first Chinese-American feature collaboration. His dramatic and effective music combines "contemporary Western compositional techniques with my Chinese feeling and experience, along with Chinese musical characteristics inherited from thousands of years ago, so as to set up a universal music world expressing natural and primitive

beauty." Watch for a future recording of "Wu (Rising to Height)" for piano and chamber orchestra (1986). –BGT

ORLANDO JACINTO GARCIA

○ **La Belleza del Silencio / O. O. DISCS**   1992
La Belleza del Silencio ("The Beauty of Silence") is characterized by beautiful groups of sounds and soft, sharp, sustained dissonances in constantly varying permutations. This Cuban-American composer studied with Morton Feldman, and these performances — by Joan LaBarbara (voice), the Gregg Smith Singers, Jan Williams (percussion), and others — are perfect –BGT

PETER GARLAND

○ **Matachin Dances / COLD BLUE**
A work in six movements for two violins and gourd rattles, inspired by Native American music. –BGT

Three Strange Angels (1972-1973) / COLD BLUE   1984
From the collection *Cold Blue Anthology*. A piano cluster, drum, and bullroarer are the sounds of the angels, and their alternation seems to provide a kind of blessing. –BGT

Border Music / WHAT NEXT?   1992
Early percussion pieces and works for solo harp, as well as a newer piece for harp, violin, and percussion, influenced by Yaqui Indian pascola dances. Peter Garland is the publisher of Soundings Press, which for years has been an invaluable source of scores and information about new-music. –BGT

PETER GENA

Mother Jones / LOVELY MUSIC   1991
From the collection *Full Spectrum Voice*. A new approach to political song: a complex vocalise gradually gains momentum, breaking into a ballad, "The Death of Mother Jones," and then, returning to the vocalise, brings the music into another dimension. T. Buckner (vocal). –BGT

JON GIBSON

Two Solo Pieces / CHATHAM SQUARE   1977
Contains "Cycles" (1973) and "Untitled" (1974). Using seven notes in very slow four-part harmony, Gibson builds an organ texture of exquisite presence. Improvising on a simple, long melody with dedicated sweetness, he constantly varies with innate musicianship the piece "Untitled," which closes this album of two classics of music truly built on "minimal" means. Gibson (pipe organ, alto flute). –BGT

Rainforest/Brazil (He Was Not Disappointed) / LOVELY MUSIC   1991
From the collection *Full Spectrum Voice* and the theater work "The Voyage of the Beagle," with text by Charles Darwin: rainforest sounds, the melismatic wanderings of wood flute and synthesizer, and gorgeous vocals by T. Bruckner. –BGT

★ **Jon Gibson / POINT MUSIC**   1992
The essential collection for understanding the variety of expressions possible in pattern or phrase music (sometimes rather misleadingly called "minimal" music). Amazingly gorgeous saxophone playing by Jon Gibson. Includes "Tread the Trail" (1964-1965) by Terry Riley; "Reed Phase" (1967) by Steve Reich; "Bed" from *Einstein on the Beach*, Act IV/2 (1976); "Gradus for Jon Gibson" (1968) by Philip Glass; "Pat's Aria from Nixon in China (Act II/I)" (1987) by John Adams; "Waltz" (1981), "Song Three" (1976), and "Extensions II" (1981-1982) for sound environment and saxophone, by Jon Gibson; "Terry's G Dorian 12-Bar Blues (9x5) + 3" (June 1962) by Terry Jennings; and "Any Integer (to Henry Flynt)" (April 1960) by LaMonte Young. –BGT

☆ **Waltz, for Saxophone and Piano (1981); Song Three (1976); Extensions II (1981) / POINT MUSIC**   1992
The beautiful "waltz" seems to become suspended and lead to another dimension of mind. All three pieces are subtle combinations of melody with conceptual patterning. –BGT

MICHAEL WILLIAM GILBERT

○ **Moving Pictures (1978) / GIBEX**   1978
Heavenly electronic music from this Massachusetts composer. Echoes of Far East folk music combined with synthesizers, flutes, voice, and percussion. –BGT

PHILIP GLASS   ♭1937

American composer primarily of minimalist music for film, ballet, and opera using an ensemble of electronic and amplified acoustic instruments. Glass also has a body of instrumental works for acoustic instruments. –ED

Songs from Liquid Days / CBS   1986
Glass commissioned several "artsy" singer/songwriters (Paul Simon, Suzanne Vega, David Byrne, and Laurie Anderson) to write lyrics for these pieces, then used such performers as Linda Ronstadt, the Roches, and the Kronos Quartet to perform them. What came out sounds much more like Glass than it does like any of the other contributors, but the mixture is an intriguing one. –WR

☆ **Music in 12 Parts / VIRGIN**   1990
Glass is renowned for his pattern-music style, presented in its most developed form in this early work, still one of his best. He has developed a method of writing that retains the sense of the timeless "present" while bringing a new possibility of rethinking melody and harmony in a non-virtuoso sense. At times this is very elegant and profound, as with this CD and in the opera *Akhnaten* (CBS-2/M2K-42457), and at times this verges on the direct appeal of a movie-music sensibility, as in *1000 Airplanes on the Roof* (Virgin 91065-2); for having this range, he remains a very controversial composer. –BGT

VINKO GLOBOKAR   ♭1934

Les Emigrés (The Emigrants) (1982-1986) /
HARMONIA MUNDI   1991
A music-theater work by this Yugoslavian composer/jazz trombonist, who lives in Paris and whose works are nearly impossible to classify — in his words: "Any model of organization existing in nature or in culture can become music." Five narrators singing, shouting, and speaking in many languages "give the impression of sitting in a court that is in the process of judging the public," with the listener also placed in a similar situation. We are dealing with people who left their countries in order to survive or improve their way of life. The first part, "Miserere," is a historical allegory: letters from Italians who had emigrated to Brazil and also from Turkish emigrants, interviews with women who follow their husbands, and so on. The second part, "Réalitiés/ Augenblicke" (Realities/Flashes), contrasts images of hope, represented by dance music, with projected images of potential misery. The third part, "Sternbild der Grenze" (Border Constellation), with a text by Peter Handke, is a series of nine tableaux performed by giant puppets contriving to cross "a hermetically sealed border" in a clandestine way. At various points the singers cross the "border" of the stage and go into the audience. There are also parts for an orchestra, a small choir, two vocal soloists, and a jazz trio. Performed by the Ensemble Musique Vivante, directed by Diego Masson and V. Globokar. –BGT

ANTHONY GNAZZO   ♭1936

Asparagas / MUSIC FROM MILLS
From the collection *Music from Mills*. A gradual "process piece" using drum-set outtakes from a recording session re-edited, to emphasize the rhythmic irregularities, into a wild cluster of drum beats. –BGT

MALCOLM GOLDSTEIN

Soweto Stomp (1985) / MUSICWORKS
Freely accessed sax and wind riff patterns with African 6/4 rhythms. Gradually mutating dense to simple textures suggest some incredible celebration of simultaneous emotions. Performed by the Malcolm Goldstein Workshop Ensemble in Montreal. –BGT

A Summoning of Focus (1977) / O. O. DISCS   1992
From the collection *Organic Oboe*. A framework for improvisation, a ritual of sorts, a richness of sound textures, a depth of intensity, and a presence sustained to the end. J. Celli (oboe). –BGT

DANIEL GOODE

Circular Thoughts for Clarinet Unaccompanied (1974);
Selected Chambers (1977) / FROG PEAK MUSIC
This album of Daniel Goode's music contains skillfully played solo and ensemble pieces with tape collage. –BGT

PETER GORDON

○ **Star Jaws / LOVELY MUSIC**   1977
Imaginative polytonal rock songs, including "I'm Dreaming in the Sun and Dreaming in the Moon" and "Life is Boring" (texts by Kathy Acker), mixed with multiple ensemble pattern-phase music ("Machomusic" and "Intervallic Expansion"), performed by the Love of Life Orchestra — bold, beautiful, genuine lyricism and humor. Some of this music appeared on one of the first art-rock shows, "Trust in Rock," which Gordon organized in 1976. A portion of the material will be found in new performances on *Peter Gordon and the Love of Life Orchestra: Geneva and Extended Niceties* (New Tone Records CD NT 6706, reissued 1992). –BGT

○ **Otello (1983) / ROIR**   1987
A radical rethinking of the opera, which takes extractions from the original Verdi score and reworks these with electronic sounds, new polyrhythmic music, electronically processed recordings, entirely new scenes and sections, and rhythmic vocal phrases that are "intended to pass through actions without explaining them." This creates "a new version of *Otello* with contemporary emotional language and sensitivity .... The accuracy of the atmosphere was extremely important to me, the musicological accuracy entirely unimportant." –BGT

● **Leningrad-Xpress / NEWTONE**   1990
Music from dance and theater productions in a musical language equally informed by world music, tough New York City rock, pattern music, Albert Ayler jazz, and electronic music. Gordon makes it all work in these highly original tone poems — from the almost Weillian "Leningrad-Xpress" and "Warsaw," to the disco-Italian folk music of "Toscana," to the electronic and dissonant "In the Fields," "Trinity Site," and "Inside the Nuclear Power Plant" (text by Kathy Acker), the sublime atonal chamber music of "Inside Marie," the Chopinesque-Tibetan "Woyzeck's Dream," the 1920s Berlin-style "Der Kindertotentanz," and the unabashedly pretty "Pastis" acoustic guitar solo. –BGT

GERARD GRISEY

Partiels for 16 or 18 Musicians; Derives for two
Orchestral Groups / ERATO
Ensemble Ars Nova, directed by Boris de Vinogradov; Orchestre National de France, directed by Jacques Mercier. Extremely quiet washes of harmonic colors over the orchestral surface, with other unusual timbres. –BGT

TOM HAMILTON   ♭1946

Pieces for Kohn / SOMNATH   1976
Four electronic pieces that are musical responses to four paintings by artist Bill Kohn, large geometrics of mythical cities. –BGT

○ **Formal and Informal Music / SOMNATH**   1981
Contains "Formal and Informal Music" (1980) and "Crimson Sterling" (1973), for electronics, winds, and percussion. Rich O'Donnell (percussion) and J. D. Parran (woodwinds and saxophones). –BGT

PHIL HARMONIC

○ **Timing (1978) / LOVELY MUSIC**   1979
From the collection *Just for the Record*. Improvised sustained synthesizer chords are changed on a spontaneous verbal cue from the composer, a simple but surprisingly engaging experience for the listener, forming the externalization of a musical sense that the public normally never hears. Harmonic has also created many art installations in the form of walk-in store fronts called "Art while You Wait." (See *Lovely Little Records* in Collections.) –BGT

LOU HARRISON   b 1917

American composer whose style has been influenced by Asian music, including the Javanese gamelan. His ensembles rely on Asian folk instruments, especially the percussion. –ED
Double Music, for 4 Percussionists (collaboration with John Cage) (1941) / NEW WORLD   1990
A wild and wacky, by-now classic percussion piece. Using a small range of pitches, it begins as a modest melody and winds up as a heated and joyous village celebration for many unusual instruments. An excellent example of a successful collaboration in composition. This CD is especially recommended as a good collection of percussion music. With the New Music Consort. –BGT

☆ **Music for Guitar & Percussion / ETCETERA**   1990
A good overview of Harrison's work, especially the alternately pastoral and crashingly celebratory "Canticle no. 3, for Ocarina, Guitar & Percussion" (1941). The ocarina suggests Native American and Japanese folk melodies; the guitar is used as a percussion instrument along with gamelan-like suspended brake drums and shaker. Also contains the more melodic "Suite no. 1" (1976) (though it's still in unusual Pythagorean, just-tuning, Babylonian/Arabic, and artificial scales); "Plaint and Variations on Song of Palestine"; "Serenado por Gitaro" (1952), with the strange chromatic "Infinite Canon" and Usul movements; "Serenade for Guitar with a Percussion Player" (1978); and "Waltz for Evelyn Hinrichsen" (1977). Excellent performances by the Cal Arts Percussion Ensemble, conducted by John Bergamo, with John Schneider (well-tempered guitar). –BGT

PIERRE HENRY   b 1927

French composer of electronic musique concrète pieces for ballet and on religious themes. –ED
○ **Le Voyage / PHILIPS**   1964
Le Voyage, like the two works below, is a hauntingly beautiful album drawn from this composer's over forty years of work in electronic and musique concrète forms and collaborations with Pierre Schaeffer. –BGT
Variations pour une porte et un soupir ("Variations for a Door and a Sigh") / PHILIPS   1964
See note above.
Futuriste / PHILIPS   1980
See note above.

JUAN HIDALGO

☆ **Tamaran ... / CRAMPS**   1990
Tamaran - Gocce di Sperma per dodici pianoforti ("Tamaran - Sperm Drops for 12 Pianos"). A brilliant conceptual work by a leading figure in Spanish avant-garde music. –BGT

LEJAREN HILLER   b 1924

Illiac Suite (excerpt) / BELL LABS   1960
From the collection *The Voice of the IBM 7090 Computer*. The *Illiac Suite*, composed with engineer L. M. Issacson, was the first instrumental score composed with a computer. It demonstrated possibilities for complex rhythms and transpositions of melody, and it suggested a spectrum of controlled to quasi-random systems for composition. The

IBM 7090, with the computing ability now possessed by a modest personal computer, occupied two rooms. Included on this disc are brief experiments by Drs. J. R. Pierce, M. V. Mathews, Newman Guttman, M. E. Shannon, David Slepian, David Lewin. (See *New Music for Guitars* in Collections.) –BGT
Algorithms, Versions I and IV (1968) / DGG   1969
An interesting ensemble piece for acoustic instruments and magnetic tape, composed using the IBM 7094 computer. Titles of the three sections reflect some of the mathematical constructs represented: "The Decay of Information," "Icosahedron," and "The Incorporation of Constraints." –BGT

TOSHIO HOSOKAWA   b 1955

Seeds of Contemplation ... / FONTEC   1990
Includes *Seeds of Contemplation (Mandara), for Shomyo & Gagaku Ensemble* (1986) and *Fragmente I, for Shakuhachi, Koto, and Snagen* (1988) — two exquisitely spare compositions combining ancient court-music gestures with matrix-combinatory European compositional techniques. Beautifully paced performances in the "breath" tempo of traditional Gagaku ensembles. Hosokawa studied with Isang Yun and Witold Szaloneck in West Berlin and has received commissions and prizes in Japan, Europe, and the United States. His pure use of the Gagaku ensemble is different from Takemitsu's somewhat more romantic approach. For comparison with the tradition, listen to the still-excellent *Gagaku: The Imperial Court Music of Japan*, by the Kyoto Imperial Court Music Orchestra, reissued on CD on Lyrichord (LYRCD 7126). –BGT

ALAN HOVHANESS   b 1911

American composer with a variety of stylistic traits, including non-Western, Renaissance, and his own personal compositional ideals. He composes in many forms (opera, choral, solo piano/vocal, and orchestral). –ED
☆ **Lousadzak, for Piano & Orchestra, op. 48 (1945);** **Symphony / MUSICMASTERS**
Informed by the highly melismatic, floated melodic sense of Armenian song, with simple, refined orchestration, *Lousadzak* ("Dawn of Light") is a lovely work that nearly caused a riot at its New York premiere, when it innocently stepped on the mental toes of the academic chromaticists and the American nationalists in the audience. The *Mysterious Mountain* symphony combines many of the elements of Hovhaness's later style: parallel chordal passages of universal religious feeling (similar to Eastern Orthodox Church chanting), the treatment of canon and fugue in an entirely original manner (more of a variation form), quasi-random pizzicatos and strange transparent bells on odd harmonics that suggest landscapes at long distances from civilization. Hovhaness is a prolific composer of nearly 500 compositions to date, but these two pieces will give the listener a good idea of his general instrumental approach. Keith Jarrett (piano), American Composers Orchestra with Dennis Russell Davies, conductor. –BGT
Wind Music of Alan Hovhaness ... / MACE
Includes *Wind Music of Alan Hovhaness: Return and Rebuild the Desolate Places (Concert for Trumpet)*; *Symphony no. 7* ("Nanga Parvat," 1959); *Hymn to Yerevan*; and *Symphony no. 14 "Ararat"* show another side of Hovhaness's: dissonant clusters, fury and devastation, wild improvised village marches, a mountain frozen forever in treeless snow, the fierceness of volcanic earthquakes, rocks sculptured by tornados. Visions from Armenia, Hovhaness in the church of nature. Performed by the North Jersey Wind Symphony with percussion, conducted by Keith Brion, with Gerald Schwartz (trumpet). –BGT
○ **Shalimar / FORTUNA**   1988
Fortuna Records convinced Hovhaness himself, at age 76, to record some of his most engaging piano works. Even at this age, the composer is facile-of-hand, cascading up and down the piano during many of the lush, oriental-inspired pieces

featured in this collection. *Shalimar* is a must for anyone interested in the roots of solo instrumental, new-age, and world music styles. Hovhaness has been perfecting these ideals for over 50 years. −LK

And God Created Great Whales, for Orchestra; Concerto for Orchestra no. 8 / CRYSTAL 1989

And God Created Great Whales, for Orchestra; Concerto for Orchestra no. 8; Elibris (Dawn God of the Urardu); Alleluia and Fugue (1942); *Anahid* (1944). This is a magnificently beautiful recording of an orchestra in an old abbey and a good overview of the composer's work. Performed by the Philharmonia Orchestra, conducted by David Amos. −BGT

Lady of Light, op. 227 (1968) / CRYSTAL 1991

Simple elegiac chant and solo song, with and without text and mixed with sudden and random rushings of voices, harmonizations on non-European scales, a protest against war based on the Swiss "Chalabala" legend. Includes "Dancing to the Stars over Bridges of Thread," "I Am Dancing in Heaven," "No More Serve Your Brutal War Lords." Patricia Clark (soprano), Leslie Fyson (baritone), the Ambrosian Singers and Royal PO conducted by Hovhaness, and the Crystal CO conducted by Ernest Gold. −BGT

○ **Visionary Landscapes / HEARTS OF SPACE** 1991

This set of piano works was released in the US by Hearts of Space Records in celebration of the 80th birthday of Alan Hovhaness in 1991. (The album was originally recorded in 1986 for the Positively Armenian label.) Armenian virtuoso Sahan Arzruni presents a fluid, magical performance of the music of Hovhaness. −LK

THE HUB

☆ **Hub — Computer Network Music / ARTIFACT RECORDINGS** 1989

A totally new idea in live electronic music. The six composers of the Hub play computer music live by interacting with musically sensitive responses to each other's programs, the computers often physically connected through complex networks that make many aspects of their performances spontaneous. Contains John Bischoff's terrific "Perry Mason in East Germany"; "Farabi" and "The Minister of Pitch" by Tim Perkis; "Roll 'Em" by Chris Brown; "Borrowing and Stealing" by Phil Stone; "Whackers" by Scot Gresham-Lancaster; "Simple Degradation" by Mark Trayle; "Hot Pig" by Perkis, Brown, and Stone; and "Dovetail" by Bischoff, Perkis, and Trayle. −BGT

JERRY HUNT

Transform; Cantegral; Transphalba / IRIDA 1979

For various mechanical and electronic instruments and systems. In *Transform (Stream)* (1977), *Transphalba*, and *Cantegral Segment 18, 17* (1977-1976), Hunt investigates the relation of nerve bonding in the human body and its descriptive, analogous patterning in electronic systems. −BGT

☆ **Fluud, for Dual Synclaviers (1988) / CENTAUR** 1988

From the collection *The CDCM Computer Music Series - Vol. 1.* Ceremonial moves based on Robert Fluud's *monochordum mundi syphiphoniacum* (1622). Otherworldly. One of the most original composers of our time, Hunt often creates scores of complex physical moves in space, making a concert into an occasion that re-creates music's divinatory role in all countries and ages; for example, his "Sur John Dee" (1966) in John Cage's thought-provoking compilation *Notations* (1969, Something Else Press). Hunt is also an innovative computer-systems designer and creates mysterious alliances of computers and primal energy in his installation pieces (one a voodoo hut with computerized proximity detectors triggering electronic sounds for the New Music America festival in Houston). −BGT

Babalon (string) / AER 1990

From the collection *The Aerial #1.* Mysterious, hermetic

evocations with shamanic rattles and bells and an interactive computer-retrieval system of many sounds. −BGT

DAVID HYKES w/THE HARMONIC CHOIR

Hearing Solar Winds / OCORA 1983

An extended choral work made from the Hoomi singing of Western Mongolia and the overtone chanting of Tantric Buddhism — spectacular shimmering surfaces (overtones from clusters of fundamentals beating against each other). Some titles are "Multiplying Voices at the Heart of the Body of Sound," "Gravity Waves," and "Rainbow Voice." −BGT

TOSHI ICHIYANAGI   ♭1933

Extended Voices, for Voices & Synthesizers / ODYSSEY

From the collection *Extended Voices.* An interesting collage of peculiar vocal sounds. −BGT

Solo Compositions / CAMERATA 1991

Includes "Cloud Figures" for solo oboe, "Hoshi-No-Wa" for sho, "Scenes III" for solo violin, and "Time Sequence" for piano — lovely pieces by the composer who introduced much of new-music to Japan by organizing concerts and exhibitions of graph music. Some of his early pieces are classics — "Kaiki" (1960), for sho, organ, koto, harmonica, and saxophone; *Sapporo* (1963), theater music. −BGT

CHARLES IVES   1874-1954

Highly original American composer of orchestral, chamber, and solo vocal and piano music who used and anticipated polytonality, atonality, and polymeter/polytone clusters. A unique quality of his music is the combination of well-known hymns and popular tunes with a complex dissonant accompaniment. Notable works include *Three Places in New England* (1914) and the *Sonata for Piano no. 2, "Concord, Mass"* (1920). −MKS

Charles Ives: The Complete Works for Piano / DESTO

Wonderful performances. Contains the "First Sonata," the "Piano Sonata no. 2 (Concord)," the complete "Studies" from published and unpublished archival material (still being sifted through), the bi-tonal "Waltz-Rondo," the "March in G and D, Here's to Good Old Yale," "The Celestial Railroad, a Phantasie for Piano Solo," "The Seen and Unseen," and "Bad Resolutions and Good" ("bad" are academic harmony exercises and "good" are rushing dissonances). This recording of Ives also contains contrasting dichotomies, such as those in the renowned orchestral work *The Unanswered Question*: "Anthem-Processional"; "Storm and Distress"; "Allegretto (Invention)"; "Baseball Take-Off"; "Varied Air and Variations"; "Three-Page Sonata"; "Song without (Good) Words"; "Rough and Ready"; and "Scene Episode." Four discs, out of print. With Alan Mandel (piano). −BGT

○ **Three Quarter-Tone Pieces, in *New Music in Quarter-Tones* / ODYSSEY**

Three beautiful pieces — "Largo," "Allegro," and "Chorale" — for two pianos tuned quarter-tones apart from each other. This is a fine recording and performance, but these pieces should really be heard live. As with much of Ives, additional transparent "ghost" sounds occur in the performance space, caused by the strange combinations of harmonics and tunings, which can be heard by listeners but not recorded. This is especially true of these pieces. As a child, Charles Ives sang tunes in quarter-tones, along with other children in the family, inspired by their bandleader father, George E. Ives, who also staged such experimental spectacles as bands playing different tunes marching from opposite ends of town and crossing in the middle. That event is re-created in "Three Places in New England." With George C. Pappastravrou and Stuart Warren Lanning (pianos). −BGT

☆ **The Unanswered Question ... / CBS**

The Unanswered Question (1908); *Central Park in the Dark* (1898-1907); *Holidays Symphony* (1904-1913). This recording is particularly interesting because both the original and revised versions of *The Unanswered Question* are performed. The dissonant flute-clusters and trumpet theme are played completely free of the consonant, serene chords of the strings in the original version, another innovation by Charles Ives. Performed by the Chicago Symphony and conducted by Michael Tilson Thomas. –BGT

○ **Sonata for Piano no. 2, "Concord, Mass., 1840-1860" / ELEKTRA**
Kalish.

○ **Songs (26 songs) / ETCETERA**
Alexander, Crone.

Songs - Vol. 2 (28 songs) / ETCETERA
Alexander, Crone.

○ **Symphony no. 1 / SONY**
Thomas/Chicago SO & Chorus.

Symphony no. 1 / CHANDOS
Järvi/Detroit SO. It won't please purists (it's way too romanticized), and it doesn't even sound like Ives, but it's a good performance nonetheless. –PM

○ **Symphony no. 2 / SONY**
Thomas/Royal Concertgebouw Orchestra.

Symphony no. 2 / CBS
Bernstein/NYPO.

○ **Symphony no. 3 / SONY**
Thomas/Royal Concertgebouw Orchestra.

○ **Three Places in New England / DGG**
Thomas/Boston SO.

○ **The Unanswered Question / MERCURY**
Hanson/Eastman Rochester Orchestra. Also includes *Symphony no. 3.* –MKS

Ives Plays Ives (record no. 4 in Charles Ives, the 100th Anniversary) / CBS   1974
Ives playing spontaneously (improvising) on published and unpublished material/ideas. Reveals the creative process in its searching mode (apart from the necessary structural work), with Ives enthusiastically letting his hands discover what cannot be preconceived. Especially remarkable are the so-called "X,Y,Z Improvisations." (Five discs, issued 1974, out of print.) –BGT

The Orchestral Music of Charles Ives / KOCH   1990
Includes "Calcium Night Light," "Country Band March," "Largo Cantabile," "Postlude in F," "Set for Theater Orchestra," "Set of Four Ragtime Dances," "Three Places in New England," and "The Yale-Princeton Football Game." Great performances. The collection does not include other orchestral works, such as the *Orchestral Set no. 2* (probably the best performance of this was Stokowski conducting the London SO on the out-of-print disc London SPC 21060), or the visionary "Tone Roads," a twelve-tone piece written many years before that technique found its way from Europe to the States. Performed by Orchestra New England, conducted by J. Sinclair. –BGT

● **Symphony no. 4; Robert Browning Overture; Songs: "An Election" / SONY CLASSICAL MASTERWORKS**   1991
A magnificent, transcendental vision of life performed with full spirit by Stokowski's orchestra (the American SO), with attention paid to the polyrhythms, transparent "memory" textures, and harmonic layerings of this completely innovative music. The songs (especially "Lincoln, the Great Commoner," with its amazing tone-cluster glissandos for voices and strings) are perfect complements to the symphony. Songs performed by the Gregg Smith Singers. –BGT

TERRY JENNINGS

☆ **Terry's G Dorian 12-Bar Blues ... / POINT MUSIC**   1992
Terry's G Dorian 12-Bar Blues (9x5) + 3 (1962) is from the collection *Jon Gibson* (see listing under Gibson in this section). Terry Jennings was one of the first players on any wind instrument to play multiphonic chords, which are produced by a combination of unusual fingering and overblowing. Yet to be recorded are his classics of extended

time-sense music, ethereally beautiful piano music, and the remarkable "String Quartet" (September 1960; see score in La Monte Young's *An Anthology*). Performers are Jon Gibson (saxophone), La Monte Young and Michael Riesman (synthesizer), and Bill Ruyle (percussion). –BGT

SCOTT JOHNSON   ♭1952

○ **John Somebody; No Memory ... / NONESUCH**   1986
"Remember that guy ... John Somebody? He was a ... sort of a b ..." asks a woman's voice on the repeating master tape loop, as other smaller loops join in; then pop-jazz instrumental figures imitate the rhythm and add funky melodies and cross-rhythms (built on the smaller samples of the loop) in accumulating levels, which suddenly break and start again with interpretations of the loops. We find ourselves tapping our feet and wanting to dance. An original and appealing album, in which Johnson clearly demonstrates the relation between ordinary speech and musical rhythms. Speech in this case also includes the laughter of "Involuntary Songs." *No Memory, for Electric Guitar, Woodwinds, Percussion, and Electronics* (1981-1983) is also built on this speech sampling idea but is more complex in its modulation of both the loop sounds and the layering of the more chromatic instrumental phrases. –BGT

TOM JOHNSON

Nine Bells / INDIA NAVIGATION   1982
A lovely, hypnotic ceremonial composition directed by a steady sequence of changing geometric formations that guide the steps of the performer. All sounds, including the shuffling footsteps of the performer, are considered part of the piece. A beautiful process, performed elegantly by the composer. (See also the collection *Bang on a Can Live - Vol. 1.*) –DGT

BEN JOHNSTON

☆ **Amazing Grace (String Quartet no. 4) (1973) / NONESUCH**
Also called *String Quartet no. 4* on out-of-print vinyl (Gaspano GS-205), where it is played in more accurate tuning by the Fine Arts Quartet. Heart-rendingly beautiful microtonal setting and variations on this traditional melody. –BGT

MAURICIO KAGEL   ♭1931

○ **Atem (Breath), for Solo Wind & Tape / BIS**
Lindberg.

Der Tribun (10 Marches to Miss the Victory) / AULOS
Kagel/Military Band.

"Rrrrrrr......." (8 organ pieces) / AULOS
Zacher.

☆ **String Quartets nos. 1, 2 & 3; Pan ... / DISQUES MONTAIGNE**
String Quartets nos. 1 and 2 (1965-1967); *String Quartet no. 3* (1986-1987), and *Pan, for Piccolo and String Quartet* (1985) are played with great sensitivity by the Arditti String Quartet. The marvelous first and second quartets take late-Bartók string techniques to new levels: snap string, tremolos of bow wood (col legno), rebounding off strings, non-vibrato glassy textures, maximum bow "crunch," random pizzicato, playing on the wood of the instrument. The quartet is treated like electronic music in terms of composition — at turns mysterious, dramatic, and lyrical. With scale-like fragments and operatic "bird" figures, *Pan* seems to reset *The Magic Flute*. The third quartet, like *Pan*, contains elements of past musical gestures treated for their sound value (not as quotes or satire), combined with techniques from the first quartets. All this makes for very original music. –BGT

Staats Theater / DGG   1967
Kagel takes apart the apparatus of the State Theater of operas, plays, and other spectacles and examines in detail the images and sounds apart from plot, libretto, and subject matter with which we are presented. Not a satire, but a surreal

concentration. Many of Kagel's original instruments and sound-making devices are used (listen to *Akustica*, 1968-1970, a two-disc set on Deutsche Grammaphon — hard to find), both for their sound and their symbolic value. A steel strip partially strapped to the player's feet (he is part of the circuit) is in the form of a Möbius strip, which is associated with getting from one side, the *real*, to the other side, the *figurative*, without going over the edge. Likewise, tape music, choral and operatic ensembles, stage sets (Wagnerian to pop-art large soda bottles), stock characters (the Barber, the Imaginary Invalid, Amor, and the Knight/Troubadour), stock themes (Concern, Virginity, Iron Curtain, Investigation, Nighttime), movement (Contradance), the players in the pit, calisthenics done by the performers to keep in shape, and even the resultant waste paper of programs and notices — all are presented in their physical and imaginary contexts. –BGT

JIN HI KIM   b 1956

Komungo Permutations / AER   1990
From the collection *The Aerial #2*. Electronic exploration of this ancient Korean instrument, bamboo on silk. –BGT

GUY KLUCEVSEK   b 1948

○ **Flying Vegetables of the Apocalypse / EXPERIMENTAL INTERMEDIA FOUND. XI**   1991
Dance music for accordion solo and top-notch combos of winds, strings, saxes, percussion. Unique transitions between the new-music, downtown style, tango, blues, polka, and more — poetic, even hum-a-long. My favorite cuts: "Waltzing Above Ground," "Fez Up." (See also *Manhattan Cascade* in 20th-Century Collections in this section). –BGT

ALISON KNOWLES

Mantra for Jesse ... / FINNADAR   1985
Mantra for Jesse (Some Help in Sleeping) is from the collection *Sleepers*. It is a lullaby for speaker, with gentle shaker accompaniment. –BGT

Frijoles Canyon / WHAT NEXT?   1992
An extended work weaving together text and field recordings of the New Mexico landscape by this former member of the Fluxus group. Mixed sounds of rocks, sticks, trees, cacti, and of course beans. –BGT

GOTTFRIED MICHAEL KOENIG

○ **Klangfiguren ... ; Essay; Terminus 1 & 2; Output; Funktionen / BVHAAST**
Includes *Klangfiguren II* ("Sound Figures II," 1955-1956); *Essay* (1957-1958); *Terminus I* (1962); *Terminus II* (1966-1967); *Output* (1979); *Funktionen: Rot, Grau, Violett, Blau, Indigo* ("Functions: Red, Gray, Violet, Blue, Indigo," 1968-1969). Classic pointillistic electronic music in a two-CD set called *Acousmatrix I & II*. –BGT

TAKEHISA KOSUGI   b 1938

Violin Improvisations New York, September 1989 / LOVELY MUSIC
Warm melodic phrases, sometimes almost romantic, sometimes slipping away like a bird heavenward. Always unpredictable and unanalyzable. –BGT

PETR KOTIK

○ **Explorations ... ; Solos and Incidental Harmonies ... / EAR-RATIONAL**   1992
Excerpts from the recent, magnificent "Explorations in the Geometry of Thinking," a four-hour-long setting of the "Numerology" section of F. Buckminster Fuller's brilliant *Synergetics*, scored for three drummers, woodwinds, trombones, and vocal soloists. Also included is the melodic *Solos and Incidental Harmonies*, for flute, brass, and tambourine. Petr Kotik's music is a very personal blend of

austere, often strange rhythmic feelings and a Gregorian-chant-like simple melodic sensibility, with sudden startling chromatic and other tonal shifts. Hypnotic and compelling music, including his now-legendary setting of Gertrude Stein's "Many Many Women" (out-of-print disc set). –BGT

JILL KROESEN   b 1949

Stop Vicious Cycles / LOVELY MUSIC   1982
Like the albums of Ned Sublette and Laurie Anderson, this disc presents only the songs that make up part of her extended and inventive performance pieces. Jill Kroesen has made stage works, including a ballet *The Lou and Walter Story*, that reduce historical and social icons, like Alexander the Great and even the History of the World (as an icon in itself), to the personal and emotional, thereby stripping away much of the pomposity and abstraction that often accompanies the cant of the historical imperative. One European fan said to her, "You try to make everything so simple, whereas we try to make everything complex." These songs with a beat also make use of electronic and acoustic noise, free-style brass playing, bizarre percussion and mixing, and a totally new approach to the idea of pitched/non-pitched singing. Some of the pieces are "I'm Sorry I'm Such a Weenie"; "I Am Not Seeing That You Are Here"; "I'm Just a Human Being" ("I'm just a human being who can hardly keep her own house clean. And I lie in bed and think how the president is just a human being, and it scares me to think about the life he leads"); "Alexander the Great" ("I want to travel all around and get lost conquering everybody's ground. And send plunder to my mother and kill my threatening brother. I'm Alexander and I'm pretty and I ain't in no hurry to get home"); and the legendary "Fay Shism Blues." –BGT

PHILIP KRUMM

○ **Sound Machine / IRIDA**   1979
"Sound Machine" is from *Texas Music* (1986). It is a lovely short piece from a composer of much innovative music, here featuring an electronic but somehow living being with a gently insistent pulse (or is it a purr?) who sometimes emits quasi-random tiny beeps and sighs. Other pieces include *Music for Clocks* (for multiple clock/metronomes and orchestra, composed several years before Ligeti's *Poème Symphonique* for 100 metronomes, 1965, and Ichiyanagi's *Music for Electronic Metronome*, 1961); *Piano Variations* (all on one C-chord; the variations consist of fingering changes affecting the pressure and consequently the timbre of the chord); the outer-space *Formations (Score of Heavenly Lattices)*, and much more. –BGT

RON KUIVILA

○ **Blurred Genres / SLOWSCAN - VOL. 6**
Electronic music by a composer renowned for his evocative and beautiful sound-installation pieces based on subtle concepts and realized with self-designed and self-built electronics. Kuivila's latest work — not yet recorded — is a high-voltage arcing sound sculpture entitled *Dolci Mura* ("Sweet Walls"). –BGT

Going Out with Slow Smoke / LOVELY MUSIC   1982
Four compositions by Nicolas Collins and three by Kuivila — "Fast Feet, Slow Smoke," "In Appreciation," and "Alphabet." Fascinating electronic music with a sense of humor. –BGT

JOAN LA BARBARA

○ **Sound Paintings / LOVELY MUSIC**
Extended vocal techniques (circular breathing, multiphonics like that in Buddhist chant, imitation of environmental sounds, speech just on the edge of comprehensibility) multitracked into some beautiful pieces. I especially like "Erin," on a photograph of an Irish child with his father's coffin, and "Klee Alee," inspired by the imagery of Paul Klee's

paintings and the squiggles and brushstrokes when viewed up-close. –BGT

GEORGE LEWIS   b 1948

The Solo Trombone Record / SACKVILLE   1977
The extended and overdubbed work "Piece for Three Trombones Simultaneously" shows just about everything that can be done with a trombone, at least in the hands of George Lewis — a wonderful alternatively humorous and pensive work. "Phenomenology" is an intricately structured and improvised solo inspired by the bebop style, in which the compositions tend to have nominally similar points of departure ("Anthropology" and "Ornithology" by Charles Parker and "Pithecanthropus Erectus" by Charles Mingus). "Untitled Dream Sequence" is a lyrical and touchingly funny solo, full of the little critters of your dreams. The disc concludes with a rendition of the Billy Strayhorn classic "Lush Life," which is played like a person singing a beloved tune to himself sans harmonic accompaniment, sometimes "sitting" on part of it, repeating a favorite phrase or two. For many years now George Lewis has been developing interactive work with computer and acoustic instruments that has not yet been recorded, but watch for his magnificent composition "Voyager," an interactive piece for computer and trombone, scheduled for release in the near future. –BGT

George Lewis / BLACK SAINT   1978
Contains "Monads" for an ensemble, with Anthony Davis (piano), Douglas Ewart (bass clarinet), Leroy Jenkins (violin), George Lewis (alto and tenor trombones), Roscoe Mitchell (soprano sax), and Abdul Wadud (cello) — fleeting melodic fragments amidst pointillistic (but not abstract!) textures, constantly redefined and varied; "Triple Slow Mix," a trio for two pianos and sousaphone — a steady and slowly varied bass passacaglia surrounded by either extremely fast pointillistic playing or banal quote-like figures as if from music "literature," like a blasé music student in the practice room just trying to make it through the day (every once in a while someone shouts "Hey!"); "Cycle" (with Lewis on Moog synthesizer) — humorous and touching solos of mid-range sounds that make you smile without knowing why; "Shadowgraph, 5 (Sextet)" for the large ensemble mentioned above, and also with Muhal Richard Abrams on piano and George Lewis on sound-tube — someone near us is explaining something but we don't quite get it (perhaps it's something "foreign"): a tapestry of gestures, quick shadows of the initial event. –BGT

☆ **Homage to Charles Parker / BLACK SAINT**   1979
Both of Lewis's compositions on this album are for an ensemble with Anthony Davis (piano), Douglas Ewart (bass clarinet), George Lewis (tenor trombone and electronics), and Richard Teitelbaum (Polymoog, Multimoog, and Micromoog synthesizers). "Blues" (1977) is a "collective orchestration" that builds in a fragmentary style of changing timbres, with a spirit that ranges from happy to that of Tibetan meditation, taken from material arranged in four basically diatonic choruses, using the essential harmonic sequence of the classic blues form as a starting point — but don't expect to hear a traditional "blues," because this music goes to the spirit behind the tune, rather than playing the tune. In the "Homage to Charles Parker" (1978), "the iconography [of the first section] ... represents the life of Charles Parker — what is known, what is thought to be known, what is dreamed, heard and said — and his 'reality', i.e., birth and death." The second part is based on the form of traditional solo with chordal accompaniment that Charles Parker "brought to a rare level of perfection" and making "loving inferences as to Parker's afterlife," pointing "to a new appraisal of world music after his life — one in which Afro-American creative music decisively affirms its place as a living, growing, vital part of world culture." –BGT

☆ **Chicago Slow Dance (1977) / LOVELY MUSIC**   1981
An elegantly slow, evolving, introspective portrait of Chicago

life. There is the sound of shakers like the clacking of overhead subway rails, solos that range in attitude from resignation to spontaneous joy (Douglas Ewart on musette, bassoon, tenor sax, flute, bass, clarinet, percussion; George Lewis on electronics, alto and tenor trombones; J. D. Parran on nagaswaram, baritone sax, piccolo; Richard Teitelbaum on Moog synthesizer). There are gentle, surreal dream sounds and melodies evoking many images, perhaps a bird lost in the city, kids playing in vacant lots, night sounds on the edge of town, a passing police car, boats on the lake, the noises of your neighbors heard through the walls of an apartment house — an exquisite and beautifully played work. –BGT

GYÖRGY LIGETI   b 1923

Austrian composer of keyboard, electronic, orchestral, chamber, opera, and choral works. –ED

○ **Lux Aeterna, for 16-Voice Mixed Chorus (1966) / DGG**
The famed "sound of the monolith" in Stanley Kubrick's film *2001* was lifted from *Lux Aeterna*, in a lovely performance here. There's a surface of sustained and overlapping clusters of multi-timbral quality that suggests universality without bigness. Performed by the North German Radio Chorus, conducted by H. Franz. –BGT

Adventures for Three Singers & Seven Instrumentalists / DGG
Manning, Thomas, Pearson, and Boulez/Ensemble InterContemporain.

Adventures; Nouvelles Aventures / WERGO
Cahn, Charlent, Pearson, Maderna/Darmstadt International Chamber Ensemble.

Continuum, for Harpsichord / WERGO
Vischer.

Drel Stucke, for Two Pianos / WERGO
Ballista, Canino.

Quartet for Strings no. 1, "Metamorphoses Nocturnes" / DGG
It's always nice when an established international quartet plays modern music (as opposed to the Arditti, who specialize in modern music), especially when they play it as naturally and knowingly as here. Nothing smoothed over or made more presentable — the mystery in the piece is brought out as in no other recording. Hagen Quartet. –PM

Quartet for Strings no. 1, 'Metamorphoses Nocturnes' / WERGO
Arditti Quartet.

Quartet for Strings no. 1, "Metamorphoses Nocturnes" / BIS
Voces Intimae Quartet.

Quartet for Strings no. 2 / DGG
LaSalle Quartet.

Quartet for Strings no. 2 / WERGO
Arditti Quartet.

Requiem / WERGO
Gielen/Hession RSO & Choir, soloists.

Six Bagatelles for Wind Quintet / NONESUCH
Tuckwell Wind Quintet (cassette tape).

Trio for Horn, Violin & Piano, "Hommage à Brahms" / BRIDGE
Purvis, Schulte, Feinberg. More old-fashioned and traditional-sounding, but in this piece I actually like it better. –PM

Trio for Horn, Violin & Piano, "Hommage à Brahms" / WERGO
Performed by Gawriloff, Baumann, Besch. Dissonant and uncompromisingly modern, partly because of the clear and dry recording. –PM

☆ **Atmospheres ...; Lontano ... / DGG**   1990
Atmospheres, for Large Orchestra (1961), also with *Lontano, for Large Orchestra* (1967). Transparent washes of neo-impressionistic colors; inter-dimensional landscapes. Perfect

companion pieces; beautiful. The Vienna Philharmonic under Claudio Abbado. –BGT

ANNEA LOCKWOOD   b 1939

Sound Map of the Hudson River / LOVELY MUSIC   1990
This is listening to nature in heightened detail, beautiful for the ear and mind. –BGT

ALVIN LUCIER   b 1931

North American Time Capsule (1967) / ODYSSEY   1968
From the collection *Extended Voices*. Choral members prepared individual stories about "beings far from our environment, either in space or in time, the physical, spiritual, social, scientific or any other situation in which we currently find ourselves." The stories were then fed into a Sylvania Electronics Systems vocoder (a device that digitizes sound for transmission over long transmission lines, used to scramble codes for secrecy), both as programs and modulating controls. Very mysterious broadcasts from afar, an electronic Akashic Record in the ether. –BGT
Vespers (1968) / MAINSTREAM   1970
From the collection *The Sonic Arts Union*. Performing in darkness, the performers find their way by "echolocation" by using electronic click devices. An homage to dolphins, bats, and nocturnal birds — nocturnal sound photographs. –BGT
○ **Music for Solo Performer / LOVELY MUSIC**   1982
Music for Solo Performer, for Enormously Amplified Brain Waves and Percussion (1964-1965) is the first musical work to use brain waves to generate sound. World instruments, a cardboard box, and a trash can are vibrated by loudspeakers placed near and under them, as bursts and trains of the amplified alpha waves disturb the cones of the speakers. –BGT
Still and Moving Lines of Silence in Families of Hyperbolas (1973) / LOVELY MUSIC   1983
Based on interference phenomena between two or more sound waves. If the sound of the differently pitched waves are separated, their resultant beats spin in elliptical patterns through space from the higher source to the lower one. In various versions of the work, musicians play against these patterns, dancers move among them, and passive instruments are vibrated by them. –BGT
☆ **I Am Sitting in a Room / LOVELY MUSIC**   1990
A new-music classic — the magical transformation of a sense of person and place into a sense of universal presence. Lucier is the dean of psychoacoustic music. –BGT
● **In Memoriam Jon Higgins (1984); Septet for Three Winds, Four Strings, and Pure / LOVELY MUSIC**   1991
Pure, profound, and classic. Complex ideas realized simply. Recommended. –BGT
Music on a Long Thin Wire / LOVELY MUSIC   1992
A recording of an installation made on May 10, 1979, in the rotunda of the US Customs House, Bowling Green, New York City. The wire was extended 80 feet through the oval of the rotunda and was driven by one pure-wave oscillator. The wire played itself, registering all changes in volume, timbre, harmonic structure, rhythmic and cyclic patterning, and other sonic phenomena. –BGT

WITOLD LUTOSLAWSKI   b 1913

Polish pianist and composer of orchestral, chamber, and piano music. –ED
Postlude I ... ; Paroles Tissées ... ; Livre pour Orchestra; Cello Concerto / POLSKIE NAGRANIA
Album contains *Postlude I, for orchestra* (1958); *Paroles Tissées* ("Weaving Songs"), for tenor, strings, harp, piano, and percussion, 1965; *Livre pour orchestra* (1968); and *Cello Concerto* (1968-1970). These pieces, especially the beautiful *Livre* and the highly original *Cello Concerto*, are strikingly different in their tone-colors and organization from

Lutoslawski's pre-1960 works, which are almost 19th-century in their gestures and development. –BGT
Chain 2, for Violin & Orchestra / DGG
Sophie Mutter (violin), Lutoslawski/BBC SO. Mutter proves she can play modern music. By toning down her vibrato and playing more incisively, she outdoes herself. We can only hope she does much more 20th-century music. –PM
Concerto for Cello & Orchestra / PHILIPS
Schiff (cello), Lutoslawski/Bavarian RSO. Definitive on all counts. I can't imagine the music being done any better. –PM
Concerto for Oboe, Harp & Chamber Orchestra / PHILIPS
H. Holliger, U. Holliger, Lutoslawski/Bavarian RSO.
Concerto for Orchestra / MUZA
Rowicki/Warsaw National PO.
Dance Preludes (5) for Clarinet, Harp, Piano, Percussion & Strings (1955) / PHILIPS
Brunner, Lutoslawski/Bavarian RSO.
Dance Preludes (5) for Clarinet, Harp, Piano, Percussion & Strings (1955) / CHANDOS
Hilton, Bamert/Scottish National Orchestra. A bit too British and without the underlying soul and subtlety of the Brunner/Lutoslawski. –PM
Les espaces du sommeil, for Baritone & Orchestra (1975) / PHILIPS
Fischer-Dieskau (baritone), Lutoslawski/Berlin PO.
Partita for Violin, Orchestra & Obbligato Piano / DGG
Mutter, Moll, Lutoslawski/BBC SO.
String Quartet / DGG
Hagen Quartet.
String Quartet / DGG
LaSalle Quartet.
Symphony no. 1 / MUZA
Krenz/Polish Radio National Symphony.
Symphony no. 2 / MUZA
Lutoslawski/Warsaw National PO.
Symphony no. 3 / PHILIPS
Lutoslawski/Berlin PO.
Venetian Games, for Chamber Orchestra / MUZA
Rowicki/Warsaw National PO.
☆ **Mi-Parti ... ; Novelette; Preludes and Fugue ... / POLSKIE NAGRANIA**   1989
Preludes and Fugue, for 13 Solo Strings (1972) totally redefines preludes as mysterious sound-pieces with a "fugue" of brilliant, aleatoric, sliding, perpendicular lines. *Mi-Parti for Orchestra* (French for a whole with two unequal parts) and the *Novelette* imply nonspecified narratives. Performed by the National Chamber Orchestra in Warsaw and the Polish Radio National SO, conducted by Lutoslawski and Hollinger. –BGT

BRUNO MADERNA   1920-1973

In Memoriam Bruno Maderna / BV HAAST
Contains *Concerto for Oboe and Chamber Ensemble no. 1* (1962); *Concerto for Oboe and Orchestra no. 3* (1973); *Concerto for Violin and Orchestra* (1969); and *The Juilliard Serenade* for 22 instruments (1971). Various orchestras and conductors (available from Gelbe Musik). –BGT
☆ **A Quadrivium / DGG**   1980
A Quadrivium ("Crossroads"), *for four Percussionists & four Orchestral Groups* (1969) includes the expressive, shimmering neo-impressionism of "Aura" and "Biogramma," and the ever-changing landscape (guided by the conductor's choices, different for each performance) of "Quadrivium," by the poet of the serialist composers. Performed by the North German Radio SO, directed by Giuseppe Sinopoli. –BGT

WALTER MARCHETTI

☆ **Natura Morta (Still Life) / CRAMPS**   1991
The legendary piano recording, finally reissued. –BGT

Vandalia; Per la sete del orecchio / CRAMPS   1991
Vandalia and *Per la sete del orecchio* ("For the Thirst of the Ear") were both reissued in 1991.

CHRISTIAN MARCLAY

○ **Black Stucco / ELEKTRA-NONESUCH**   1989
From the collection *Imaginary Landscapes*. Marclay plays turntables — the clicks of vinyl discs, scratching, back-and-forth manual rotation, mixing, varispeed — using recordings as "artifacts" of our society. He has also created art objects with the same records: *Footsteps* is a one-sided record containing the sounds of footsteps. Thirty-five hundred copies were spread on the floor of the Shedhalle Galleries in Zürich and people were invited to walk on them over the course of six weeks; a thousand of the records with dirt and scratches are available from Gelbe Musik. Marclay has also made *Record without Grooves*, with a gold label housed in a black velour cover with golden writing, signed and numbered. –BGT

INGRAM MARSHALL   *b* 1942

○ **Fog Tropes; Gradual Requiem; Gambuh I / NEW ALBION**
Atmospheric and subtle, with almost new-age transparency but more ideas: one of Marshall's best albums. *Fog Tropes* creates the beautiful landscape suggested by the title, with gently phasing orchestral brass and taped ocean sounds. –BGT

RICHARD MAXFIELD   1927-1969

○ **Night Music / ODYSSEY**
Part of the album *New Sounds in Electronic Music*. Like his pieces *Sine Music* (1959) and *Trinity Piece* (1960), this exquisite pre-synthesizer electronic music is made with only the supersonic bias signal of a tape recorder and a supersonic sawtooth waveform from an oscilloscope producing audio-range difference-tone "ghosts." Identical in feeling to a response to the sound of birds and insects on a summer night in a city park. –BGT

☆ **Richard Maxfield: Electronic Music / ADVANCE RECORDINGS**   1969
This album contains some of the most beautiful and imaginative electronic and live-electronic music ever made, using pre-synthesizer Army surplus-store electronics. *Pastoral Symphony* (1960) for three channels — one behind the audience — is a lovely work, as is *Night Music* and "Swarm of Butterflies Encountered on the Ocean" (unissued). "Bacchanale" (1963) is made from a noise-improv-collage ensemble with poetry by Edward Fields, folk-music recordings (many from Henry Cowell), jazz hang-outs, scraping violin noises, underwater clarinet, drum, typewriter, and parts of Maxfield's *African Symphony* and the poetic *Wind*. The latter is made of events separated from each other by beautifully timed silences. The sounds are composed of wind and the sounds of things that wind moves, like squeaking rusty gates. Maxfield turns it all into an intriguing piece. Other pieces on this recording include *Piano Concerto for David Tudor* (1961), for piano and tapes made from the performer's improvisations; *Amazing Grace* (1960), a mass of tape loops cut to a score (like Maxfield's *Cough Music* (1959-1961) and *Italian Folk Music*); humorous samples from a religious revival; and part of the sketches for Maxfield's opera *Stacked Deck*. "Composers, Performance, and Publication," a very interesting essay, appears in *An Anthology* by LaMonte Young. The disc is out of print, but a cassette is available from MELA Foundation, 275 Church Street, NYC. –BGT

TOSHIRO MAYUZUMI   *b* 1929

Mandala Symphony (1960) / ODYSSEY
Although bordering on a large contemporary romantic work, this symphony attempts to express a "Japanese Buddhist view of the omnipotent universe," and uses only collections of sounds to achieve this aim. The two parts of the mandala are expressed in the two parts of the symphony: "Kongokai-Mandala symbolizes spiritual awakening through contemplation and oneness with eternity; Taizokai-Mandala represents the world of Sokushin Jyobutsu, which is made up of the phases of life, such as Gakido (a place of hunger and thirst where sinners go in the afterlife) or Shurado (passage of pandemonium, the world of the immature until they attain spiritual awakening)." (See also *String Quartets*, LaSalle Quartet in Collections.) –BGT

BARTON MCLEAN

Little Night Music ... / CENTAUR   1990
Little Night Music; Demons of the Night is from the collection *The CDCM Computer Music Series - Vol. 7*. Nocturnal tone poems, beautifully formed computer sounds that express different night sensations. –BGT

OLIVIER MESSIAEN   1908-1992
French organist and composer of music that is mostly religious in nature. Messiaen composed in most forms, especially keyboard (organ, piano) and orchestral. –ED

☆ **Des canyons aux étoiles; Oiseaux exotiques; Couleurs ... / CBS**
A terrific two-CD showing the best of Messiaen's later style: *Des Canyons aux étoiles* ("From the Canyons to the Stars," 1971-1974); *Oiseaux exotiques* ("Exotic Birds," 1956); and *Couleurs de la cité céleste* ("Colors of the Celestial City," 1963). These pointillistic tone paintings are performed by the London Sinfonietta, directed by Esa-Pekka Salonen. Good performances, but I prefer the Erato STU 70974/975 (discs out of print) with Marius Constant conducting. –BGT

L'Ascension / KOCH SCHWANN
These four symphonic meditations for orchestra (1933) are performed by the Bavarian Radio Orchestra, directed by Karl Anton Rickenbacher. Compassionate and sacramental, similar to *Les Offrandes oubliées* ("The Forgotten Offerings," 1930); unlike the severe religious works of his later style. CD includes *Chronochromie* (1959-1960). –BGT

O Sacrum Convivium / ARION
O Sacrum Convivium, Motet for Mixed Chorus (1937) is a warm, hopeful religious work in Messiaen's early style. This subtle performance is by the Groupe Vocal de France. CD includes *Cinq Rechants* and *Nuits* by Iannis Xenakis. –BGT

Trois Petites Liturgies / ERATO
Trois Petites Liturgies ("Three Brief Liturgies," for women's chorus, 1943-1944) is a very curious, Byzantine work with a poetic and controversial text by the composer on gems and colors, with reflections on the presence of the Creator in us, in others, and in things. With Ondes Martenot. –BGT

La nativité du Seigneur / UNICORN-KANCHANA
La nativité du Seigneur ("The Nativity of the Lord," 1935) is nine meditations for organ, performed by Bate. –PM

Organ Works - Vol. 1-4 (complete) / BIS
Ericsson (organ).

Quatuor pour la fin de temps, for Clarinet, Violin, Cello & Piano (1941) / DGG
Quartet for the End of Time is performed by Yordanoff, Tetard, Desurmont, Barenboim.

Theme and Variations, for Violin & Piano / DGG
Kremer (violin), Argerich (piano).

Turangalilia - Symphonie for Ondes Martenot, Piano & Orchestra (1949) / CBS
Salonen/Philharmonia Orchestra.

ROSCOE MITCHELL

☆ **Four Compositions / LOVELY MUSIC**
Fleeting chromatic gestures; bizarre multiphonicacoustics and unusual instruments (triple contrabass, viol, and contrabass

sarrusophone); touching, brief melodies; and humor combine to create unique music. Excellent performances, highly recommended. –BGT

DARY JOHN MIZELLE

Polyphonies; Spectra; Primavera ... / IRIDA   1981
Polyphonies, for Shakuhachi and Electronic Sounds (1975); *Spectra, for Bass and Computer Tape* (1975-1979); and *Primavera-Heterophony, for 24 Celli* (1977) contains polyphonies of earth, air, fire, and water sounds; dualities of musical gesture (such as slow/fast); and varieties of musical organization (drone, pointillistic, gestural, polyphonic, stochastic, and cyclic) all in a strange duet. Unique dramatic sounds from massed strings. –BGT

GORDON MONAHAN

○ **The Long Aeolian Piano (Sound Sculpture with Thaddeus Holownia) / MUSICWORKS**   1990
From *Sound Symposium* (see 20th-Century Collections). A lovely "aeolian harp" resonated by the wind, activating piano strings attached to an upright piano and stretched down a hill. (Incidentally, another lovely "aeolian harp" with metal resonators lives as a permanent installation atop the Exploratorium in San Francisco — built by Doug Hollis. See *Soundviews* in Collections.) See also Monahan's "Speaker Swinging" (excerpt) in the collection *Imaginary Landscapes* and watch for a future recording of his piano playing, intense and full of new sounds. –BGT

MEREDITH MONK

Key / LOVELY MUSIC
Monk's modern folk music from her beautiful and noble performance-ceremonies, which recall former times and a lineage of human understanding beyond the present state of things. Songs include "Porch," "Under Street," "What Does It Mean?," "Vision," "Fat Stream," "Do You Be?," "Vision" (reprise), "Change," and "Dungeon." With Meredith Monk (voice, organ, jaw harp), Daniel Ira Sverdlik, Dick Higgins, Colin Walcott, Lanny Harrison, and Mark Monstermaker (voices). –BGT

MOONDOG (LOUIS HARDIN)   ♭1916

More Moondog; The Story of Moondog / PRESTIGE
Reissues of Prestige LP 7069 (1956) and Prestige LP 7099 (1956-1957). Moondog is on the street and everywhere else. The sources are from everyday life, with music and life blending as a whole: a soundtrack to spur the imagination. Contains "Softshoe and Hard-shoe (7/4)," "A Duet with the Queen Elizabeth Whistle and Bamboo Pipe," "Ostrich Feathers Played on Drums," "All Is Loneliness," "5/8 in Two Shades," "Violetta's Barefoot Dance," "A Portrait of Niñon, a Cocker Spaniel," and others. –BGT

☆ **The Music of Moondog / CBS**   1990
A reissue of two albums recorded in 1969 and 1972 — rounds, canons, and other pieces that are the precursors of much pattern music. (Incidentally, John Fahey has made a wonderful arrangement of Moondog's *Theme and Variations* (1952) for guitars, percussion, and synthesizer on *John Fahey: Rain Forests, Oceans, and Other Themes*, Varrick CD 019.) –BGT

○ **Elpmas / KOPF**   1991
This album contains "Wind River Powwow"; "Westward Ho!"; "Suite Equestria"; "Marimba Mondo 1 - the Rain Forest"; "Fujiyama 1"; "Marimba Mondo 2 - Seascape of the Whales"; "Fujiyama 2"; "Bird of Paradise"; "The Message"; "Introduction and Overtone Continuum"; and "Cosmic Meditation" — environmental sounds, gently rocking marimbas, lovely counterpoint for winds, sweetly sung wisdom, "a protest against our treatment of aboriginal people ... and nature, plants, and animals...." –BGT

ROBERT MORAN   ♭1937

The works listed below have been unavailable in the US for a long time; or they have just been newly recorded by this highly original and often lyrical composer. Robert Moran collaborated with Phillip Glass in the creation of the opera *The Juniper Tree*. –BGT

Desert of Roses; 10 Miles High ... ; Open Veins / DECCA
Contains five excerpts from *Desert of Roses*; *Ten Miles High Over Albania, for Eight Harps*; and *Open Veins, for Orchestra* (soon to be issued). –BGT

Hagoromo; Enantiodromia / MUSIC FACTORY
To be reissued.

Music from the Towers of the Moon, for String Quartet / MUSIC FACTORY
To be reissued.

CHARLES MORROW   ♭1942

The Birth of the War God (1973); The Cloud Will Break; The Canticle for Brot / LAUREL
These and the following are unique works by a composer who has an abiding interest in world music and has produced some fine compositions with minimal orchestration. –BGT

BP for bp / MUSICWORKS
See note above. –BGT

DAVID MOSS

Language Linkage (1988) / AER   1990
From the collection *The Aerial #1*. Energetic setting of Italo Calvino's text for many processed voices, electronic sounds, percussion. The music gives the impression of a parallel universe — a very different sound. –BGT

RAPHAEL MOSTEL WITH THE TIBETAN SINGING BOWL ENSEMBLE

Nightsongs / SCARLET-INFINITY   1992
Not a new-age group, this ensemble is described on their first CD cover as creating "new music for old instruments," and that's what they do. Raphael Mostel resonates Tibetan brass meditation bowls, gradually introducing sharp and startling sounds that will awaken the chakras. "Jacob's Ladder" combines didjeridus, water, and breaking sounds with wailing thighbone trumpets. John Charles Thomas produces a solo on the ancient lyzarden with jazz-line inflections in "Nightsong." The brilliant singer and instrumentalist Mieczyslaw Litwinski is featured throughout (watch for future recordings of his music). –BGT

GORDON MUMMA   ♭1935

Gordon Mumma is a cofounder, with Robert Ashley, of the Cooperative Studio for Electronic Music in Ann Arbor, MI, which has been in existence since the early 60s. –ED

○ **The Dresden Interleaf ... ; Venezia Space Theater; Megaton ... / LOVELY MUSIC**
Contains *The Dresden Interleaf 13 February 1945*; *Music from the Venezia Space Theatre*; and *Megaton for William Burroughs*.

Hornpipe (1967) / MAINSTREAM   1970
From the collection *The Sonic Arts Union*. A piece for French horn played with unusual reed mouthpieces, cybersonic circuits, and other devices. We hear the sound of the processing circuits balancing and unbalancing themselves, as the horn player's chosen responses gradually build an "orchestra" of accumulated decisions. A mysterious live performance. –BGT

☆ **Mesa; Pointpoint; Fwyyn / LOVELY MUSIC**   1986
Performed by the composer, with Pauline Oliveros and David Tudor. *Fwyyn* is a lament that tries to bring back to life a dancing princess who had been enchanted — beautiful, slowly evolving textures. *Mesa* describes expansive, eroded mesa landscapes, and *Pointpoint* interprets a bridge in a rural French village through an analogous bridging movement in the acoustical space. Pure electronic music. –BGT

CONLON NANCARROW   b1912

An American composer residing in Mexico since 1940. His works involve manipulation of the workings of player pianos, producing sounds and gestures not possible for human performers. –ED

☆ **Studies for Player Piano - Vol. I-II / WERGO**

Secluded in a quiet suburban district of Mexico City, Conlon Nancarrow spent three decades composing these incomparable pieces, punching the player-piano rolls himself and designing a pneumatically operated percussion ensemble. Unparalleled rhythmic complexity and fascinating energy — boogie-woogie as you've never heard it before. –BGT

☆ **Studies for Player Piano - Vol. III-IV / WERGO**

☆ **Studies for Player Piano - Vol. V / WERGO**

Study no. 15 / MUSICMASTERS

Transcribed for piano four-hands by Yvar Mikhashoff and containing the same wonderful rhythmic complexities and drive as the piano rolls. Live performance. –BGT

BEN NEILL

☆ **Collapse of the Illusory One-Tribe Nation / TELLUS**

Excerpt from *Site-less Sounds* by ITSOFOMO (In the Shadow of Forward Motion) with David Wojnarowicz. Shows the raw truth of a personal experience of anti-gay violence. The energetically telegraphing style of the music is superbly imagined and performed. Extraordinarily moving. The entire composition will be released on New Tone in late 1992 or early 1993. –BGT

○ **Mainspring / EAR-RATIONAL**

Pieces featuring the mutatrumpet (Neill's invention), a combination of three trumpets plus slide that facilitates rapid change between a variety of sonorities. An electronic processing system by Robert Moog and a computer program by David Behrman have been designed to work with the mutatrumpet. This CD exemplifies the idea of "unified multi-sidedness" in the sounds and compositional style: for example, "Mainspring" (1985), which, after an intro in the style of a fanfare, goes into a riff-steady march tune over a half-stepping accompaniment with steel-guitar country-music slides and, later, a solo for the bridge — really delightful and peculiar. "Dis-solution 2" (1986) is for mutatrumpet and percussion with pitch-sensing electronics (David Behrman), providing a lovely treble shadow. "No More People" (1988), for soprano and band (with text by Stevie Smith), is a classic aria over constantly intense telegraphic figures. Wow ... –BGT

PHIL NIBLOCK   b1933

● **Nothin' to Look At ... / INDIA NAVIGATION**   1982

Nothin' to Look At Just a Record contains "A Trombone Piece" for bass trombone (multitracked), played by James Fulkerson, and "A Third Trombone," played by Jon English. Slow changes in tuning and harmonics. Pure and hypnotic. –BGT

○ **Four Full Flutes / EXPERIMENTAL INTERMEDIA FOUNDATION XI**   1991

Meditative, sustained, divine; slowly changing clusters. –BGT

NO WORLD (TRIO)

No World Improvisations / O. O. DISCS   1992

Highly imaginative group improvs by Joseph Celli (double reeds) and Jin Hi Kim (komungo and electric komungo) in trio format with different guest soloists, including Alvin Curran (electronics), Shelley Hirsch (voice), and Malcolm Goldstein (violin). –BGT

LUIGI NONO   1924-1990

Italian composer in the 12-tone or atonal style, whose work encompasses many forms, including opera and electronic music. Many fundamental works by Nono are out of print — "y su sangre ya viene cantando (And Even Your Blood Comes

Singing)," for flute, strings, and percussion, from *Epitaffio per Garcia Lorca* ("Epitaph for Garcia Lorca," RCA Victrola VICS 1313, 1968); the choral settings of texts by Cesare Pavese; and the operas *Intolleranze* ("Intolerance," 1960, which attacks segregation, the bomb, and Nazism); *Al Gran Sole Carico d'Amore* ("To the Great Sun Charged with Love," 1975, about the Paris Commune of 1871). –BGT

☆ **Das atmende Klarsein ... / KOCH**

A fragment of "Das atmende Klarsein (The Breathing Clarity), for Bass Flute and Magnetic Tape," from *Flute XX*. Breath and the clarity of being — "pneuma moving through metal": mysterious, dramatic, and beautiful. With Roberto Fabbriciani (flute). –BGT

Il Canto Sospeso (1956) / STRADIVARIUS

From the collection *La Nuova Musica - Vol. 1*. This piece, based on letters of WW II resistance fighters, introduced new choral-writing techniques of word fragmentation and suspension. Soloists, choir, and orchestra directed by Bruno Maderna. –BGT

Como una ola de fuerza y luz / DGG

Como una ola de fuerza y luz ("Like a Wave of Strength and Light"), *for Tape, Piano, Orchestra, and Soprano*. Taskova, Pollini, Abbado/Bavarian RSO.

Contrappunto dialettico alla mente ... / DGG

Contrappunto dialettico alla mente ("Dialectic Counterpoint in the Mind"), *for Voice and Tape*. Poli (soprano), Bove, Mazzoni, Vicini, Troni (voices), Antonelli/RAI Chamber Chorus.

a floresta e jovem e cheja de vida   1979

a floresta e jovem e cheja de vida ("In the Forest and Youth and Flood of Life"), for soprano, voices, and clarinet, is a good example of Nono's pieces — such as "Non Consumiamo Marx (Don't Wear Out Marx)" and "La Fabrica Illuminata (The Lit-Up Factory)," both for voices and tape — that call for attention to immediate situations, in this case the escalation of the Vietnam War by American forces. Nono uses tapes that mix multiphonics played on the clarinet with various electronic sounds produced at the national radio RAI studios, as well as texts from pro- and anti-war groups and individuals, a Vietnamese partisan, American workers and students, vocalized by the legendary New York-based group the Living Theater. In live performance with this tape, a soprano and others sing a lament and deliver other texts, accompanied by five suspended copper-metal plates of various thicknesses (ancient sounds of the call to war). –BGT

Fragmente - Stille ... / DISQUES MONTAIGNE   1992

Fragmente - Stille, an Diotima ("Fragments - Stillness, to Diotima," 1980) is played by the Arditti String Quartet. According to Nono, seeking to "externalize as fully as possible that which has been internalized ... that is what matters today." Nono is guided by lines from Hölderlin's famous poem; Diotima, teacher of Socrates, is associated with the concept "Time." The poem is present only as an unspoken meditation. With guideposts written into the score in 52 places, Nono poses the fundamental question "Where am I, and who am I?" by examining old music and distant memories as catalysts of both pain and hope. This quartet was written for the Beethoven Festival in Bonn and uses Beethoven's piano-sonata instruction "mit innigster Empfindung" (roughly, "with innermost searching of the heart") to imply a readiness to break out of the habitual and "into the open air." *Fragmente* produces a positive sensation that has been used as an instruction in several John Cage works — "play until you feel the presence of silence ...." (There is also a lovely 1986 performance by the LaSalle Quartet on DGG 415 513-2. –BGT

○ **La lontananza nostalgica utopica futura / NONO**   1992

La lontananza nostalgica utopica futura (The Future Nostalgic Utopian Remoteness), for violin and taped electronics, will be issued on *Nono 2* with Irvine Arditti (violin).

MICHAEL NYMAN   b1944

A Zed and Two Noughts ... / VIRGIN   1990

A Zed and Two Noughts is a score for the film by Peter

Greenaway that effectively makes use of baroque (Pergolesi, Vivaldi, Purcell, often in the traditional technique called the "chain of suspensions") and Philip Glass-style harmonies (Wagnerian thirds mixed with modal scales), combined with obsessive patterns in the British minimalist style, to make a sound all his own. Excellent production by composer David Cunningham. –BGT

PAULINE OLIVEROS   b 1932

○ **I of IV (1966) / COLUMBIA ODYSSEY**   1968
From the collection *New Sounds in Electronic Music*. This is a good example of the earlier electronic music of Oliveros. It uses a configuration of tape recorders patched into each other with magnetic tape spliced in loops in such a way that a form of "automatic generation" system is created by feedback. Like Richard Maxfield, Oliveros used bias frequencies of tape recorders and lower "ghost tones" produced by the interference of very high frequencies. –BGT
Lullaby for Daisy Pauline / FINNADAR   1985
From the collection *Sleepers*. Lovely choral work. –BGT
☆ **The Roots of the Moment / HAT HUT**   1988
An amazing hour-long live creation (improvisation) with Oliveros on accordion in just intonation within an interactive electronic environment created by Peter Ward. Images of valleys, other universes, whatever comes to mind — an exercise in true "deep listening" reminiscent of the concerts her Foundation presents in upstate New York. –BGT

BOB OSTERTAG

○ **Sooner or Later ... / RECREC MUSIC**   1991
Ostertag was known for his technique of live-performance sampling before there were samplers (by recording a performance, cutting the tape and making a loop, then playing it back on a tape recorder with the tape guards held up by balloons). In *Sooner or Later (Tarde o Temprano)*, he has created a stark and moving work based on the recorded voice of a young Salvadoran boy burying his father who has been killed by El Salvador's National Guard. "There is the sound of the boy's voice, a fly buzzing nearby, and the shovel digging the grave." Ostertag has spent the last ten years working in or around El Salvador. "I saw a lot of death. In that culture, which is both Catholic and highly politicized, death gets surrounded with all kinds of trappings that are intended to make it heroic and purposeful. Death is God's will, or else it is irrelevant, since the victims 'live on in the struggle.' It's all glorious and heroic ... but some 70,000 people have died there ... most ... because they were in the wrong place at the wrong time. They didn't want to. There was no plan. There was no glory. Even for the heroes, there is a starker, more immediate side to their death ... sooner or later. No angels sang and no one was better. If there is a beauty, we must find it in what is really there ... the boy, the shovel, the fly. If we look closely, despite the unbearable sadness, we will discover it." –BGT

JOHN OSWALD

○ **Nine Examples of Plunderphonic Techniques / MUSICWORKS**
These are techniques used to make the legendary not-for-sale but nevertheless illegal-to-possess CD "Plunderphonics." Free speech, anyone? So distorted by creative sampling that no one would mistake them for the real thing, Canadian composer Oswald comments hilariously and surrealistically on sound material that has become the archtypical if not the downright kitsch *geck* of civilization — a procedure is reminiscent of pre-samplers James Tenney ("Collage #1: Blue Suede," 1961) and Richard Maxfield (*Amazing Grace*; *Cough Music*). –BGT

ARVO PÄRT   b 1935

Estonian composer of choral and orchestral music. –ED
Fratres ... ; Cantus; Tabula Rasa / ECM
Pärt uses medieval modal harmonies and lines with modern

techniques to create a sound that has been referred to as "the new religiosity." In *Fratres, for Violin, Piano, and Cello Ensemble, Cantus*, and *Tabula Rasa* the "religiosity" is specifically that of the European churches. Some clustering, patterning, and other techniques are used that make these works more interesting than the rather more arid, specifically religious ones (the *Miserere*, for example), which really don't have the clarity of actual, simple, pre-Renaissance music. Pärt does maintain a lovely sound, however, and the works have a well-formed structural integrity. –BGT
Arbos ... / ECM
Arbos (chamber works for diverse instruments) is performed by the Kremer/Stuttgart Brass Ensemble and the Hilliard Ensemble. The performance and sound on all the ECM recordings is impressive, but the music still seems derivative and gimmicky to me — modern classical music for people who don't really like (modern) classical music. –PM
Miserere; Festa Lenta; Sarah Was Ninety Years Old / ECM
Hilliard Ensemble & Beethovenorchester.
Passio Domini nostri Jesu Christi secundum Joannem / ECM
"The Passion of Our Lord Jesus Christ according to John." Dawson, James, Potter, Covey-Crump, Jones, George, Hillier/The Hilliard Ensemble & Western Wind Chamber Chorus.

HARRY PARTCH   1901-1974

American composer of music featuring micro-tonality using self-made instruments. Harry Partch was the most original thinker on tuning theory in centuries (see his *Genesis of a Music*, Da Capo Press), as well as an instrument designer and builder extraordinaire. –BGT
☆ **And on the Seventh Day ... ; The Bewitched ... ; Castor and Pollux; The Letter ... ; Cloud Chamber Music ... / CRI**
"And on the Seventh Day, Petals Fell on Petaluma" (1964); "The Bewitched: Final Scene and Epilogue" (1952-1955); "Castor and Pollux" (from *Plectra and Percussion Dances*, 1952); "The Letter, for Narrator and Instrumental Ensemble" (1943); and "Cloud Chamber Music" (1950). This album also contains "Of the Chromelodeon" (1945-1949); "The Blo-Boy" (1958); "The Cloud-Chamber Bowls" (1950-1951); "The Boo" (1955-1957); "The Spoils of War" (1950-55); "The Marimba Eroica" (1951-1955); "The Crychord" (1960-61); "The Eucal Blossom" (1964-1967); "The Xymo-Xyl" (1963); "The Mazda Marimba" (1963); "The Quadrangularis Reversum" (1965); and "The Harmonic Canon III" ("Blue Rainbow," 1965) — just for starters. Wonderful humor. "The Letter" is from a fellow hobo traveling the rails in the 30s. Sophisticated canonic writing in "Petals ..."; sublime mystery in "Cloud Chamber Music." –BGT
Delusion of the Fury / COLUMBIA
A ritual of voices, mime, original instruments, dance, lighting, and staging in which instrumentalists sometimes sing and act — théâtre complète as ancient as it is new. Titles of some scenes: "A Son in Search of His Father's Face," "The Quiet Hobo Meal," and "Pray for Me Again." (Two discs, out of print). –BGT

MAGGI PAYNE

○ **Airwaves (realities) (1987) / MUSIC AND ARTS**   1988
From the collection *Another Coast*. A comparison of consensual reality in desert and urban cultures by slow sound-imaging. Wonderful recording. –BGT
☆ **Crystal / LOVELY MUSIC**   1991
Some of the most beautiful and well-crafted electronic music ever, suggesting vast interior and exterior dimensions. Some titles are "Subterranean Network," "White Night" (a French expression for a sleepless night of repeating thoughts), and "SolarWind" (based on shock-wave interactions of Saturn and Venus with the solar wind). –BGT

KRZYSZTOF PENDERECKI   b1933

Polish composer of choral and orchestral music, opera, and chamber music in modern harmonic setting. –ED

Polish Requiem, for SATB, Orchestra & Chorus / DGG
Haubold, Winogrodska, Terzakis, Smith, Penderecki/North German RSO & Chorus.

String Quartet no. 1 (1960) / DGG
LaSalle Quartet.

String Quartet no. 2 (1968) / OLYMPIA
Varsovia Quartet.

Jutrznia/Utrenya, for Two Mixed Choirs / POLSKIE NAGRANIA   1989
Although there are references in the program notes to sections of the orthodox mass, *Jutrznia/Utrenya (The Entombment and Resurrection of Christ)*, they are rarely heard in this deeply felt music that speaks to the naked soul before the appearance of the various churches — it could just as well be Buddhist as Christian. The elegant choral and orchestral material is made of tone clusters, chants, and percussive punctuation, and takes us into an inter-dimensional world of boundless interior and exterior. Performed by the Warsaw National Philharmonic Orchestra and Choir. –BGT

☆ **Vol. 1: Threnody for the Victims of Hiroshima, for 52 Strings / POLSKIE NAGRANIA**   1989
This three-CD collection is a good overview of Penderecki's early work, including the famous *Threnody* (1959) for solo strings making sound masses that had never been heard before. Sensitive performances and great pieces. Set also includes *Polymorphy for 48 Strings* (1961); *String Quartet no. 1* (1960); *Psalms of David, for Mixed Choir and Percussion* (1958); *Dimensions of Time and Silence, for 40-Voice Choir, Percussion, and Strings* (1959); and *St. Luke's Passion* (1963-1965). Performers are the LaSalle Quartet and the Warsaw and Cracow Philharmonic Orchestras and Choirs. –BGT

PHILIP PERKINS

Neighborhood with a Sky (1982) / FUN MUSIC   1982
A beautiful album of compositions where the electronic and natural sounds are barely distinguishable. Significantly, Perkins does not try to simulate natural sounds, but lets their dynamic form and movement influence his electronic sounds (somewhat in the way that Cage, using chance methods, tries to imitate nature, not in its appearance but in its manner of working). For Perkins, the "neighborhood" is that of the disc itself, where the natural and the artificial co-exist successfully. Contains "Bird Variations," "The Black and White Cat," "Este's Request," "The Fountain," "Equinox Weather," "Rico in the Birdhouse" for trombone solo in an environment, and "Retreat." –BGT

The Flame of Ambition / FUN MUSIC   1986
A collection of pieces about people "burning literally with ambition ... the root of both mankind's greatest triumphs and worst self-made calamities," with scenes from a corporate skyscraper, the company fort: "Taking the Stairs," "Worrisome Fanfare/Weekend with the Kids," "At the Bar," "Talk/Exit (for Corazon Aquino)." A good blend of electronic and natural sound, plus tuneful mixes. –BGT

☆ **The Remotes (I) / FUN MUSIC**   1990
A mix of nine live-radio broadcasts of *The Remotes*, a live-performance work for interactive electronic system and various guest musicians, in which spontaneous playing and processing allows for all sorts of interesting, communal, and intuitive music-making. –BGT

LENNY PICKETT

○ **Lenny Pickett ... / CARTHAGE**   1987
Lenny Pickett with the Borneo Horns. Pickett, seen nationally every week as the wailing tenor-sax soloist with the "Saturday Night Live" TV show band, is also an original and talented composer. This album contains delightful and highly contrapuntal dance music (pattern riffs sometimes suggest Latino music as well as James Brown) and a suite, a septet, and a solo for sax and tape. Top-notch musicians and one of the best of the downtown-sound mix of popular styles with new-music techniques. –BGT

LARRY POLANSKY

Movement for Andrea Smith (My Funny Valentine, for Just String Quartet) / TELLUS
From the collection *Just Intonation*. An extremely slowed-down, angular ballad. How can I possibly describe the pleading feeling? –BGT

○ **The Theory of Impossible Melody / ARTIFACT**   1989
Fascinating formal (transformational) logic programs that generate electronic and acoustic pieces using the HMSL (Hierarchical Music Specification Language, designed by Phil Burk, Polansky, and David Rosenboom). A feeling of the Cabalistic mysteries. Contains "B'rey'sheet (In the Beginning)," computer-aided melodic transformations of traditional Hebrew tropes and melodies used for singing the *Torah*; "Cantillation Study no. 1 for Jody Diamond," for voice and electronics; "Four Voice Canons nos. 3-6" (#3 for computer, #4 for marimbas, #5 for percussion, #6 for computer); "Simple Actions - Rules of Compossibility for Voice and Live Computer"; "Psaltery for Lou Harrison." –BGT

HENRI POUSSEUR   b1929

○ **Scambi / BV HAAST**
The pure evolving electronic masses of *Scambi* ("Exchanges," 1954) a portrait of Liège, the city of Pousseur's youth (and commissioned by the city of Liège), is a semi-improvised, live, electro-acoustic mixture changed every performance. The CD also contains *Trois visages de Liège* ("Three faces of Liège," 1961); *Paraboles-mix* (1972); "Love Duet"; "Viva Cuba"; "Hymn to the Ornithological Zeus"; and "Aerial View of Haiphong, Massachusetts"). Pousseur is a wonderfully poetic composer. From the collection *Acousmatrix 4*. –BGT

ELIANE RADIGUE   b1932

☆ **Kyema, Intermediate States / EXPERIMENTAL INTERMEDIA FOUNDATION. XI**
Profound and serenely meditative electronic music inspired by the *Bardo Thodol* (*The Tibetan Book of the Dead*) and covering six states: Kyene (Birth), Milam (Dream), Samten (Contemplation), Chikai (Death), Chönyi (Clear Light), Sipai (Becoming). This is the real thing. –BGT

Mila's Journey Inspired by a Dream / LOVELY MUSIC
Wonderful images and stories from the *100,000 Songs of Milarepa*, Radigue's lifelong project. With Lama Kunga Rinpoche (Tibetan singing) and Robert Ashley (English singing). –BGT

STEVE REICH   b1936

American percussionist and composer of minimalist ostinato-based music, whose notable works include *Music for 18 Musicians* (1976) and *Drumming* (1970). –ED

○ **Music for 18 Musicians / POLYGRAM**   1978
His best. One composition and 60 minutes of wonder-filled music. –MGN

Music for a Large Ensemble ... / POLYGRAM   1981
Music for a Large Ensemble, Violin Phase features Reich's "phase music" techniques. –MPD

Tehillim / POLYGRAM   1983
A mesmerizing devotional work for female voices and chamber ensemble. –MPD

○ **Different Trains, for String Quartet and Tape (1988) / NONESUCH**   1989
A more interesting use of the rather mechanistic edge of Reich's pattern music. In an acoustic equivalent to interactive electronics, Reich creates a rhythmic tape of train whistles of

the 30s and 40s and of speakers recalling train rides of the past in the US and in Nazi-occupied lands. The natural pitch inflections of the voices are then transferred to pitches for the instruments. A rich emotional experience akin to his earlier pieces: "It's Gonna Rain" (1965) and the shocking "Come Out" (1966), both on Elektra/Nonesuch 79169-2. The Kronos Quartet performs. –BGT

BRIAN REINBOLT   b 1955

It's Not That Simple / ARTIFACT RECORDINGS   1990
Interesting microcomputer music, especially "Black Noise" and the three-dance set "Simple Dance," containing "Simple Dance on the Plain of a Dream," "IVO, the Patron Saint of Lawyers," and "Cones - Made of Ever-Increasing and -Decreasing Circles." –BGT

THE RESIDENTS

The Residents are one of rock's oddest and most mysterious groups. Their identity has been a closely guarded secret for two decades. In rare public appearances, they are typically disguised as giant eyeballs decked out in tuxes and top hats. But behind all the weirdness is … more weirdness — primitive mutations of popular songs by the likes of Elvis, James Brown, and Hank Williams, frightening nursery rhymes, elaborate mythological epics that span several albums, and pure sonic explorations. Like the most adventurous modern composers, the Residents understand the emotive power of sound; early works like *Eskimo* are unforgettably evocative. Their later projects contain subtle social commentary. Even when the parody verges on self-parody, the music retains shock value and sophistication. –MB

Meet the Residents / EAST SIDE DIGITAL   1974
The very first Residents album. Unbelievably primitive genius. Bonus tracks on the CD. –MB

Third Reich & Roll / EAST SIDE DIGITAL   1975
Another document of early primitivism — the first to explore the art of nightmarish cover versions. –MB

Fingerprince / EAST SIDE DIGITAL   1976
Outtakes from "Third Reich & Roll," including a 15-minute ballet. –MB

Duck Stab / EAST SIDE DIGITAL   1978
More weird covers from the Residents, including the unforgettable "Constantinople." –MB

Not Available / EAST SIDE DIGITAL   1978
This early record shows the Residents hitting their stride. Unforgettable "songs" and creepy vocals abound. The CD contains additional material from a collaboration with Renaldo and the Loaf. –MB

● **Eskimo / RALPH-ESD**   1979
A wild vision of what original polar Eskimo life was like before government housing came along in the late 60s. Contains "The Walrus Hunt," "Birth," "Arctic Hysteria," "The Angry Angakok," "A Spirit Steals a Child," "The Festival of Death." A totally engaging tone-poem filled with humor, pathos, and shamanism, with skillful electronic sound-painting and always the right touch. –BGT

○ **Commercial Album / RALPH-ESD**   1980
Forty brief stories, homilies, instrumentals, and slices of life, each exactly 60 seconds long — "The Coming of the Crow," "Nice Old Man," "My Work Is So Behind," "Die in Terror," "Floyd," "Act of Being Polite," and more, each unique in vocals and instrumentation, and each weirdly humorous or momentarily stunning. –BGT

Mark of the Mole / EAST SIDE DIGITAL   1981
The first installment of the "Mole Trilogy," an extensive mythological work. –MB

Tunes of Two Cities / EAST SIDE DIGITAL   1982
Part two in the "Mole Trilogy."

Mole Show / EAST SIDE DIGITAL   1983
The third installment of the "Mole Trilogy."

The Big Bubble / EAST SIDE DIGITAL   1985
Part four in the "Mole Trilogy."

Heaven? / RYKODISC   1986
Part of a two-CD sampler. This one highlights the more appealing sounds of the Residents. –MB

Hell! / RYKODISC   1986
Part of a two-CD sampler. This collection is based on a general theme of "ugly" music. –MB

☆ **God in Three Persons / RYKODISC**   1988
Employing the same stress-scheme as Poe's "The Raven" throughout its 62 minutes, *God in Three Persons* is an extended work in talking-blues style for narrator, electronic instruments, and a chorus providing comments not to be found in the libretto. They sing production credits at the beginning and lines such as "Something's coming, but not real soon," and "This is a sad part, oh, such a sad part." This surreal and yet directly delivered work is as lovingly human as it is comic, with profound experience simply expressed — in short, an original masterpiece of American music, directly in the tradition of the Thomson-Stein and Robert Ashley operas. As in all Residents pieces, the voices are modified electronically and the musical elements are deceptively minimal: most of its 14 episodes have only two chords, which, however, still manage to produce the correct atmosphere instantly (Phillip Glass-like Wagnerian thirds for mythic import, tonic-dominant in triplets for a 50s teenage love story). There are only passing riffs, which are more like comments, and the only melody in the whole piece is a wheezy organ quote of the standard doxology hymn "Holy, Holy, Holy" (God in Three Persons). The subject matter is, in part, the derivation of religious and other symbolic images from the naturally erotic — but that's only part of it. Please give this one a listen. –BGT

King & Eye / RESTLESS   1989
A warped Elvis tribute, in typical Residents style. –MB

Cube-E Live in Holland / ENIGMA-RESTLESS   1990
A live version of their American music retrospective. Cowboy songs, Black music, and Elvis revisited. –MB

ROGER REYNOLDS   b 1934

○ **Voicespace: Still; A Merciful Coincidence; Eclipse; The Palace / LOVELY MUSIC**   1992
The Voicespace: Still (1975); *A Merciful Coincidence* (1976); *Eclipse* (1979); and *The Palace* (1980) are pieces for computer electronics and voices, which amplify (to an extreme degree) the components and expressive qualities of the voice. *Still*, with a text from Samuel Taylor Coleridge's "The Wanderings of Cain" (1798), moves extremely slowly in a "vocal fry" across the aspirate clicks and wind of the performer; *A Merciful Coincidence*, based on a text from Samuel Beckett's *Watt* (1953), uses the aggressive-passive inflections of the frog-performers croaking, which seem to have intent, if not syntactical meaning; *Eclipse*, with a combined text from Jorge Luis Borges, Gabriel Marquez, Issa, James Joyce, Herman Melville, and Wallace Stevens, eclipses strains of modulated texts into each other; *The Palace* (1980), on a translated text by Borges, is a dramatic monodrama about how the Self imagines its confines in the space of the Mind — a pre-recorded modified voice is added to the singer onstage, yielding an enormous, supra-human quality. –BGT

TERRY RILEY   b 1935

An American composer of minimalist electronic keyboard music, whose works are influenced by his studies of East Indian music. –ED

☆ **Rainbow in Curved Air; Poppy Nogood and the Phantom Band / CBS**
After several graph compositions and early pattern-pieces with jazz ensembles in the late 50s and early 60s (see "Concert for Two Pianists and Tape Recorders" and "Ear Piece" in La Monte Young's book *An Anthology*), Riley invented a whole

new music, which has since gone under many names — minimal music (a category often applied to sustained pieces), pattern music, phase music, and others — set forth in its purest form in the famous *In C* (for saxophone and ensemble, reviewed below). *Rainbow in Curved Air* demonstrates the straightforward pattern technique and also has Riley improvising with the patterns, making gorgeous timbre changes on the synthesizers and organs, and presenting contrasting sections that have become the basic structuring of such current works of his as the following: *Cadenza on the Night Plain* (Kronos Quartet, Gramavision R22Z-79444, two CDs), *Salomé Dances for Peace* (1989) (Kronos Quartet, Elektra/Nonesuch 79217-2, two CDs), and the recently premiered *The Jade Palace* (1991), commissioned and played by the St. Louis Symphony (unrecorded at present), which was scored for large orchestra with extra percussion and electronics. Some of this work's seven movements are "Star Night," "Blue Lotus," "The Earth Below" and "Island of the Rhumba King." –BGT

○ **In C / CELESTIAL HARMONIES**   1968
Riley's first album, a 42-minute piece that introduced his vision. With John Hassel, David Rosenbloom, and Stuart Dempster as members of SUNY/Center of Creative Arts Ensemble. –MGN

Persian Surgery Dervishes / SHANTI   1972
Another important document from the early 70s. –MGN

Shai Camel / CBS   1980
Stunning and soothing, from a minimalist master. Some great music here! –MGN

Tread on the Trail ... / POINT MUSIC   1992
Tread on the Trail, for Sax and Synthesizer (1964-1965) is from the collection *Jon Gibson* (see listing under Gibson in this section). Gibson's exquisite tone shines. –BGT

JEAN-CLAUDE RISSET   ♭1938

Songes; Passages ... ; Sud / WERGO   1988
Contains *Songes* ("Dreams," 1979); *Passages, for Flute and Tape* (1982); *Computer Suite* (from *Little Boy*, 1968); and *Sud* ("South," 1985). Jean-Claude Risset was one of the early developers of computer music with Max Matthews at Bell Laboratories (see *Voice of the Computer* in Collections) and at IRCAM in Paris. Exquisite textures in an aural space that constantly changes its dimensions; soft velvet, to digital glacier edges, to the ringing of huge bells. *Sud* is filled with electronic tropical sounds and washes, such as extended raindrops and wind chimes. A delight to the ear. –BGT

NEIL B. ROLNICK

Electricity / O. O. DISCS   1992
Great performances of Rolnick's music by George Lewis (trombone), the New York Contemporary Music Ensemble, and Robert Dick (flute). –BGT

Macedonian Air Drumming / BRIDGE   1992
Contains "Sanctus," a computer-generated tape; the complete "Balkanization" (see also *Imaginary Landscapes* in 20th-Century Collections in this section); "ReRebong," for the gamelon Son of Lion; and the title piece, "Macedonian Air Drumming," for MIDI-controlled instruments. –BGT

DAVID ROSENBOOM   ♭1947

● **Roundup - Vol. 7 / SLOWSCAN**
A live electro-acoustic retrospective of unpublished works from 1968 to 1984. –BGT

Systems of Judgment (1987) / CENTAUR   1990
A many-timbred computer-music composition, sweeping in scope. Dynamic sonic illusions of natural sound, the meeting of mythical and philosophical worlds. –BGT

○ **A Precipice in Time (1966) / CENTAUR**   1991
From the 20th-century collection *CDCM Computer Music Series - Vol. 1*. A unique blend of free-jazz, live "phantom

doubles" (computer resynthesis of acoustic instruments), and graphed structure. From high energy to quiet anticipations with interior tension. Terrific playing. –BGT

CARL RUGGLES   1876-1971

○ **Vox Clamans in Deserto / CBS**
Vox Clamans in Deserto ("A Voice Crying in the Wilderness," 1923). Part of a two-disc, out-of-print set *The Complete Works of Carl Ruggles*. This is a magnificent work, years ahead of its time, with texts by Robert Browning, C. H. Meltzer, and Walt Whitman in a sweeping performance by Speculum Musicae, conducted by Michael Tilson Thomas, with Beverly Morgan (mezzo-soprano). –BGT

☆ **Sun-Treader / DGG**   1991
Ruggles shared the Emersonian transcendentalist vision of society and the soul's possibilities, and this work, written from 1926 to 1931, is his most eloquent expression of that. Ruggles would work by placing enormous scores on the floor and craft every note and passage in detail. Performed by the Boston SO, conducted by Michael Tilson Thomas. (An earlier recording of the orchestral "Lilacs" and "Portals," played by the Julliard String Orchestra, conducted by Frederick Prausnitz, is also recommended.) –BGT

ARTHUR RUSSELL   1951-1992

○ **Tower of Meaning / CHATHAM SQUARE**   1983
An almost medievally pure music in which tone combinations of two or three notes tuned to modal/raga scales are played by various instrumental groups. There is a love of listening to the pure combinations per se, as they are delivered at a regular, moderate pace ... then, unpredictably, rich or dissonant chords will be held, which open your mind's ear and take your breath away. The sudden ceasing of the music at certain points also has a similar effect. With Julius Eastman conducting. –BGT

JOEL RYAN   ♭1945

☆ **The Number Readers / OR LTD (LONDON)**   1992
One of our most original writers on the aesthetics of new music, Ryan also has been associated with the S.T.E.I.M. studios in Amsterdam as a software designer. This elegant work for live computer-driven electronics, video, and spoken text is based on shortwave radio transmissions heard in the evenings, of women's voices reading numbers with great precision in German, and sometimes Spanish and Czech, sometimes preceded by electronic chime patterns. "No nation or agency has claimed authorship of these broadcasts." Ryan observed a middle-aged woman in Amsterdam sitting at the front window of a well-kept old house, who sat with pad and pencil in semi-darkness by an old-style model radio; he soon began to realize that there was a "synchrony of the number of readers broadcasts with the woman's vigils." Ryan weaves a variety of musical imagery using this central "coding" idea as a stepping-stone: "Codes to protect property," "Julius Caesar's code to confuse the Gauls equals c + 3Mod24," "Code as reason contradicting itself," "The Language of Flowers," "Codes you can eat," and many others. Fascinating, innovative work. –BGT

FREDERIC RZEWSKI   ♭1938

The People United Will Never Be Defeated / HAT NOW
A thrilling, virtuoso, political classic for piano — 36 variations on "¬El Pueblo Unido Jamas Será Vencido!" here played brilliantly by the composer. –BGT

☆ **Winnsboro Cotton Mill Blues (1980) / CRI**
Played by the Double Edge piano duo. The whirring and clanging of the factory, mixed with the rhythmic blues of the workers — very exciting music played with a lot of heart by this astonishingly talented duo. –BGT

Coming Together - Attica, for Narrator and Instruments (1972) / HUNGAROTON   1990
A new-music classic, in a fine performance. –BGT

CARLOS SANTOS ♭1940

Voicetracks / LITERNA MUSICA
Available from P. A. Taylor. Santos is a self-described "romantic structuralist" — outrageous humor, vocal virtuosity, sharply contrasting emotions. –BGT

ERIK SATIE 1866-1925

Satie's music, in sound and aesthetics, was fundamentally different from the prevailing 19th-century German school that prized ideals of continuity and development. It is music as sound per se (*Musique d'ameublement*, i.e., "Furniture Music" or "Music for Furnishing," 1920). In *Musiques intimes et secrètes* ("Intimate and Secret Music") and the famous "Vexations" from *Pages mystiques*, 1892-1895), Satie describes the conceptual nature of human mental activity and then requires the performers to experience and scrutinize, simultaneously, the exact moments of shifting psychological states. "Vexations" is a short musical passage of neutral feeling (augmented and diminished chords) repeated 840 times very slowly. Satie emphasizes natural and spontaneous mentation apart from "ideas" in *The Dreaming Fish*, *Heures séculaires et instantanées* ("Ordinary and Snapshot Times"), and *Véritables préludes flasquers - pour un chien* ("Authentic Flabby Preludes - for a Dog"). Ironic titles and commentaries poke fun at pomposity, as in *Le duc de Connaught et le President aux manoeuvers* ("The Duke of Connaught and the President on Manouvers") and *Enfantines* ("Infantile Pieces," 1913 which go by such titles as "The Bean-King's War Chant"; "Importune Peccadillos, I"; "Being Jealous of His Comrade with the Big Head, II"; "Him Eat His Cookie, III"; and "Taking Advantage of His Corns to Steal His Hoop"). Satie's religious feeling was of a mystical, pre-clerical kind, expressed in works such as *Première pensée rosée + croix* ("First Rosey Thought + Cross," 1891, French word play on "Rosicrucians"); the beautiful and compassionate *Messe des Pauvres* ("Mass for the Poor," 1893-1895); and the moving *Socrate* (1918) on the death of Socrates and based on texts by Plato. Satie invented many musical techniques — the use of whole-tone scales, chords built in fourths, pattern melodies, unresolved "dissonances" used for their value as sounds, "open" large forms without contrasting or developing sections, and others. Perhaps more important, he was the first conceptual composer. –BGT

★ **Trois Gymnopédies; Parade / HYPERION**
If you're buying only one orchestral Satie CD, make it this one. Includes *Trois Gymnopédies*; *Parade*; *Mercure*; *Trois Gnossiennes*; *Relâche* — his best pieces on one carefully prepared, well-recorded album. –PM

☆ **Trois Gymnopédies / BIS**
Music for ancient Greek gymnastic exercises, written in old modal scales. Pontinen (piano). –BGT

Trois Gymnopédies; Gnossiennes; Miscellaneous Piano Pieces / MOUNTAIN APPLE COMPANY
You can't tell a book by its cover — or maybe you can. Olof Hojer (piano) looks like the proverbial, disheveled starving artist, and he plays to the manner born. Here is all the simplicity, fragility, and quirkiness you just know is in Satie's music, which all of the other, more sophisticated pianists miss. I still like Pontinen, Queffelec, and Roge but this is a unique and classic CD with simply beautiful sound that cuts straight to the heart of the composer. –PM

Piano Works for Four Hands / ADDA
I really like the subtle blend of sophistication and simplicity from Campion and Vachon on piano. –PM

☆ **Piano Works - Vol. 1 (First & Last Works) / ANGEL** 1989
Aldo Ciccolini plays with clarity, lightness, and the appropriate humor, but never with the rubato sweetness that some performers slip in. –BGT

☆ **Piano Works - Vol. 2 (Mystical Works) / ANGEL** 1989
Ciccolini (piano).

☆ **Piano Works - Vol. 3 (Études) / ANGEL** 1989
Ciccolini (piano).

☆ **Piano Works - Vol. 4 (Whimsical Works) / ANGEL** 1989
Ciccolini (piano).

☆ **Piano Works - Vol. 5 (Music for Dance) / ANGEL** 1989
Ciccolini (piano).

The Complete Ballets / VANGUARD CLASSICS 1990
Wonderful performances and recording, recently reissued. Contains *Parade* (1917, realist ballet after Jean Cocteau); *Mercure* ("Mercury," 1924, plastic poses in 13 scenes, designed by Pablo Picasso), *Relâche* ("Respite," 1924, instantaneous ballet in two acts, a cinematic intermission, and a dog's tail, designed by Francis Picabia, film by René Clair); *Jack in the Box* (pantomime, 1899, orchestrated by Milhaud in 1923); "Gymnopédies" 1 and 3 (orchestrated by Debussy, 1888); "Trois morceaux en forme de poire" ("Three Pieces in the Form of a Pear," 1903, orchestrated by Desormiére); "Cinq Grimaces pour *Le Songe d'une Nuit d'Été*" ("Five Grimaces" for [Cocteau's production of] *A Midsummer Night's Dream*," 1914); and "The grand ritournelle" from *La belle excentrique* ("The Beautiful Eccentric," 1920). Performed by the Utah Symphony Orchestra, with Maurice Abravanel. –BGT

GIACINTO SCELSI 1905-1988

Five String Quartets; Trio for Strings; Khoom, for Soprano, Horn, and Percussion / SALABERT-ACTUELS
Arditti Quartet. Committed performances in outstanding sound. –PM

Tre pezzi ("Three Pieces"), for Soprano Saxophone / ADDA
Kientzy (saxophone).

Tre pezzi ("Three Pieces"), for Trombone / ADDA
Sluchin (trombone).

Various Chamber Music / ADDA
The Accord CDs of Scelsi's music are temporarily unavailable in the US, but they are all outstanding, especially the orchestral. This CD is the place to start, along with Scelsi's string quartets. –PM

○ **Anahit (1965) / CP 2 RECORDINGS** 1976
From the 20th-century collection *Paul Zukofsky, Violin*. Built from one central tone and gesture — a primary compositional procedure for Scelsi — this slowly evolving and intense piece for a violin tuned to a G-chord (scordatura) and small orchestra is passionately played. Anahit is the ancient Egyptian name for Venus. –BGT

Pfhat, for Chorus and Orchestra (1974) / ACCORD 1988
Without the heaviness with which Scelsi sometimes depicts the mythologies of Buddhist, Egyptian, Latin, and other ancient cultures (in a ponderous style sometimes called "the new religiosity"), *Pfhat* employs a concentrated palette of sounds and compositional ideas: breathing sounds from the chorus, imitation of a single giant ringing bell, and a lovely finale by two flutes holding a dissonance surrounded by about a hundred small, tinkling bells. For contrast, this CD also contains "Aion" (1961) and "Konx-om-pax" (1969). Performed by the Orchestra and Choir of the Polish Radio-Television of Cracow, directed by Jörg Wyttenbach. –BGT

PIERRE SCHAEFFER ♭1910

Erotica Symphonie ... / DISQUES INA.GRM 1984
Erotica Symphonie pour un homme seul ("Erotic Symphony for a Lonely Man"), *Collaboration with Pierre Henry* is from the 20th-century collection *Concert Imaginaire*. A short and sweetly humorous feuilleton (or bonbon, as the case may be). Schaeffer was at the vanguard of the early French composition with environmental and extra-musical sounds or musique concrète. His work resulted in *Concert de bruits* ("Concert of noises," 1948), the establishment in 1951 of the Groupe de Recherches de Musique Concrète, and in 1958 the Group for

Musical Research of the Office of French Radio-Television (O.R.T.F.). Musique concrète now also includes electronic and world music. –BGT

STEPHEN SCOTT   b 1944

○ **Minerva's Web (1985); The Tears of Niobe (1986) / NEW ALBION**   1990
Ten musicians of the Colorado College New Music Ensemble play one piano by plucking and bowing the strings. Appealing, slowly developing music with surprising celestial and rhythmic textures. –BGT

RAMON SENDER

Audition (excerpt) / MUSIC FROM MILLS   1986
One of my favorite composers since I heard, at a ONCE Festival in the mid 60s, both his electronic tape *Kore* (1962) and "Information." The score of "Information" is a huge roll of transparent material giving improvised "information" to the performer(s), a few receiving instructions on headphones while performing on accordion with Sender's wonderful electronic tape *Desert Ambulance*. –BGT

ELLIOTT SHARP   b 1951

See the Rock section for his biography.

● **Hammer, Anvil, Stirrup / SST**   1989
An excellent rendering of some of Sharp's best music — visceral patterns with searing harmonic content and new string techniques. The unique title piece, present in two takes that are interesting to contrast, first seems to be partly a gritty and humorous take-off on hoedown/cowboy horseback-riding music (as depicted in movies), and then wanders into some strange slithery tuning zones traversed by squiggly melodies. Using the Fibonacci series to generate tunings, rhythms, and forms, the next selection, "Tessalation Row," delivers an electrifyingly gorgeous image as geometric and scintillating as the Zapotec design from Oaxaca, Mexico, on the CD's cover. "Digital" is a toe-tapping rhythmic study, in which a strip of spring steel is woven into the strings near the bridge, the instruments then played with a two-handed hammering technique. "Diurnal" and "Ringtoss" study massed- and unison-melodic gestures through the use of looping and deconstruction techniques. "Re/Iterations" is for string orchestra (made here by overdubbing the Quartet), with contact microphones attached to the instruments to pick up the subtle "ghost" tones produced by the combinations of high harmonics — dense masses of swirling frequency/rhythm patterns that are lovely in their rawness. Performed by the Soldier String Quartet. –BGT

○ **Twistmap / EAR-RATIONAL**   1991
Four works performed by the Soldier String Quartet. Like the first Mauricio Kagel quartets, these pieces introduce new playing techniques and sounds, some stimulating the ear and mind with the aural equivalent of painting with gravel. Raw and beautiful, especially "Shapeshifter." –BGT

LAETITIA SONAMI

○ **Pie Jesu - Sounds from Empty Spaces no. 3 / MUSIC AND ART**   1988
From the 20th-century collection *Another Coast*. We hear Moslem song, sweet synthesizer tones, CB radio, the beginnings of an anxious explanation, a dog's bark, and other environmental sounds, which depict an imaginary world built from the drama of "unforeseen change." –BGT

LAURIE SPIEGEL

○ **Unseen Worlds / SCARLET-INFINITY SERIES**   1991
This album gives a good overview of Spiegel's approaches to digital synthesis, from folk-music-like steady sequences of single sounds to the stately, galactic "Sound Zones," a beautiful and original piece using sweeps of clusters, sounds-within-sounds, images-within-images, and tunings never

before experienced. A truly moving experience. A similar mix can be heard in her currently out-of-print CD *The Expanding Universe* on Philo PH 9003. –BGT

JIM STALEY   b 1950

Don Giovanni / EINSTEIN   1992
A reconstructed montage of improvisations: pointillistic pop, primal nonverbal vocals, lyric synchronicity, "a hyper-suite of Mozartean dogfights [by] master virtuosos of the proto-form [who] stir up the red soup." Produced by Fred Frith, this is a terrific downtown album. With Ikue Mori (drums and electric drums), Zeena Parkins (electric and acoustic harps), Jim Staley (the "kinesthetic trombonist" and on didjeridu), Tenko Ueno (the Tokyo vocalist), and Davy Williams (the power guitarist) — a great world mix. –BGT

KARLHEINZ STOCKHAUSEN   b 1928

German composer in electronic and acoustic media who is concerned with abstract processes in composition. Stockhausen composed for many forms, including opera, orchestral, chamber, and vocal works. –ED

☆ **Konkrete und Elektronische Musik ... / STOCKHAUSEN**
Contains *Konkrete und Elektronische Musik - Etude*; *Studie I u. II*; *Gesang der Jünglinge* ("Song of the Youths"); and *Kontakte*. Classic and well-developed electronic music, some pieces, such as "Song of the Youths," with specific images — in this case, a fiery biblical furnace — and others without extra-musical images. –BGT

Kurzwellen (Shortwaves) / STOCKHAUSEN GESAMTAUSGABE
Mysterious transmissions from the ether, the romance of sounds broadcast through and emitted from the universal night. Later works in this series will include "Mikrophonie" for choirs and electronics, "Hymnen (National Anthems)," and the "Klavierstücke (Piano Pieces)," all highly recommended. Stockhausen's work in the 60s inspired "Revolution Number Nine," the musique concrète cut from the famous *White Album* of the Beatles. –BGT

Donnerstag ("Thursday") / DGG
From the piece *Licht* ("Light"). Stockhausen/Cologne Radio & Hilversum Radio Ensemble.

In Freundschaft (solo saxophone) / ADDA
In Freundschaft ("In Friendship"). Kientzy.

In Freundschaft (solo trombone) / BIS
Lindberg.

Klaverstücke I-VIII for Piano / KOCH-SCHWANN
Wambach.

Klaverstücke I-XI for Piano / WERGO
Henck.

Klaverstücke IX, X, XI for Piano / KOCH-SCHWANN
Wambach.

Klaverstücke XII, XIII, XIV for Piano / KOCH-SCHWANN
Wambach (piano). Wambach's performances tend to be more gentle and lyrical; Henck's are more aggressive and percussive, with sound to match. –PM

Oberlippentanz, for solo Trumpet / ACANTA
"Upper Lip Dance." Stockhausen.

Samstag ("Saturday") / DGG
From the piece *Licht* ("Light"). Vocal soloists, Stockhausen/ University of Michigan Symphony Band, Kolberg Percussion Ensemble.

Stimmung, for Six Vocalists / HYPERION
Flowers, Walmsey-Clark, Long, Covey-Crump, Rose, Hillier. A tour-de-force. –PM

Tierkreis (Zodiac) Suite, for Clarinet, Flute, Trumpet & Piano / ACANTA
Stephens, Pasveer, Stockhausen. Includes *Oberlippentanz*.

Tierkreis (Zodiac) Suite, for solo Double Bass / SIMAX
Ianke.

CARL STONE

○ **Woo Lae Oak (1981) / WIZARD**   1983
Lovely, sustained, and slowly changing music made by classic musique concrète means: sounds such as a rubbed string, blowing in a bottle, and more are made into tape loops and changed by means of precise tape-speed change, layering, and other techniques. –BGT

NED SUBLETTE

See his biography in the About the Editors section in the front of the book.
Western Classics / LOVELY MUSIC   1980
This CD, recorded in Albuquerque, NM, is the traditional straight-roots music from which Sublette created a unique and eccentric cowboy/downtown music with impossibly great words (the infamous cattle mutilation song and many others) of interest to both Country & Western and new-music fans. The music has been evolving through Texas-Mexican border music and Cuban influences. Sublette recently traveled to Cuba to study the remaining authentic bands and musicians outside the cities. In the late 70s and early 80s, he produced many unusual new-music programs of other composers commissioned especially for National Public Radio in the Southwest (single compositions lasting most of the day). He recently produced a score for Chinese instruments written in both European and Chinese notations for an opera with text by Lawrence Weiner. New Tones Records will be issuing a solo album, *Guitar Solo*, in 1992. Sublette will also be featured on several albums to be released in Cuba in 1992, with the Southwesterners. –BGT
○ **Cowboys Are Frequently Secretly / GIORNO POETRY SYSTEMS**   1982
The famous gay-cowboy song from the collection *Life Is a Killer.* –BGT

MORTON SUBOTNICK   ♭1933

American composer of primarily electronic music. –ED
○ **The Key to Songs (1985); Return (1985-1986) / NEW ALBION**   1986
Subotnick's music has always been descriptive of poetic, lyrical imagery, as in the electronic-music classics *Silver Apples of the Moon* and *The Wild Bull*. Similarly, "The Key to Songs" is based on Max Ernst's collage novel *Une Semaine de Bonté* ("A Week of Kindness, or the Seven Deadly Elements"); and "Return - A Triumph of Reason" refers to the changes that Edmond Halley experienced upon explaining the circuit of the well-known comet — from dread to foreboding to reason. A good example of modern tone-poem electronic music. –BGT

SUN RA   ♭1918

See the Jazz section for a biography of Sun Ra.
☆ **Heliocentric Worlds of Sun Ra - Vol. 1 / ESP-DISK**   1965
Re-pressed and available from BASE Record. The first of the series by Sun Ra and the Solar Arkestra. –BGT
☆ **Cosmic Equation ... / ESP-DISK**   1966
Cosmic Equation (a retitled reissue of *The Heliocentric Worlds of Sun Ra, Vol. 2*; Magic Music 30011-CD, 1990; ESP-Disk 1017, 1966). The astonishing sessions that went light-years beyond free-jazz improvisation to create a music of deeply felt explosive and gentle gesture, made from sound itself without reference to previous notions of melody or harmony. –BGT
nothing is ... / ESP-DISK   1966
Re-pressed and available from BASE Records. More of the *Heliocentric Worlds* expanded to include vocals about the future ... "Next Stop Mars!" –BGT
★ **Voice of the Eternal Tomorrow; The Rose Hue Mansions of the Sun / SATURN**   1980
This album has all the spectacular excitement of a live Sun Ra event. "Voice of the Eternal Tomorrow" is a sequence of astonishing solos by members of the Arkestra; the end solo by

Sun Ra is so "out there" that the audience sits in stunned silence before applauding respectfully. "The Rose Hue Mansions of the Sun" begins with a high-energy loose chordal hymn by the group and then launches into another incredible 20-minute solo by Sun Ra punctuated by the band. Sun Ra demonstrates a mastery of electronic modulation, and the alternation between solo and the various Arkestra entrances leads unceasingly into the most unpredictable zones. –BGT
The Cosmic Explorer / RECOMMENDED   1981
Sun Ra was one of the first instrumentalists to use a Moog synthesizer in live performance. *The Cosmic Explorer* (1970), from *Nuits de la Fondation Maeght*, is a 20-minute solo improvisation (with minimal extra sounds from the ensemble); it ranges between high-energy clusters and the lyrical and shows his ability to create an astonishing range of sound and emotion, inspiring a truly cosmic conclusion from the Arkestra. –BGT
John Cage Meets Sun Ra (June 8, 1986 at Sideshows by the Seashore, Coney Island) / MELTDOWN   1987
Two aesthetic approaches on the same stage; it worked, as everyone became "attuned to the next moment, the next sound." –BGT

AKIO SUZUKI

Soundsphere / HET APOLLOHUIS   1990
This CD features two instruments, an echo instrument created by Suzuki in 1970 called the "Analapos" and his version of a glass harmonica, which was used in the installation piece "Space in the Sun." CD with 36-page booklet in English and Japanese. –BGT

TORU TAKEMITSU   ♭1930

Japanese composer in Western media and forms, guided by Oriental aesthetics and occasionally making use of Oriental instruments. –ED
☆ **Works of Toru Takemitsu IV / JVC**   1988
Includes "Music of Tree" (1961); "Coral Island" (1962), for soprano and orchestra; "Kaidan" (1966), for magnetic tape; "Water Music" (1960), for magnetic tape; and "Vocalism A-I" (1956), for tape. Stunningly beautiful tone poems that combine pointillistic writing with a Debussy-like harmonic sense. The tape composition "Vocalism A-I" ("ai" means "love" in Japanese) is already a classic. –BGT
Riverrun ... / VIRGIN CLASSICS   1991
Includes *Riverrun, for Piano and Orchestra* (1984); *Waterways* (1977); *Rain Coming, for Chamber Orchestra* (1982); *Rain Spell* (1982); and *Tree Line, for Chamber Orchestra* (1982). Pointillistic, colorful tone poems for various instrumental ensembles with many new orchestral techniques, especially in the elegant "Rain Coming" for chamber orchestra. Played by the London Sinfonetta, conducted by Paul Crossley. –BGT

CECIL TAYLOR   ♭1929

See the Jazz section for his biography.
Alms/Tiergarten (Spree), from *Cecil Taylor in Berlin 88* / FREE MUSIC PRODUCTION   1989
Two CDs from a large set with an extensive booklet analyzing in detail the pieces and the workshop sessions that led to the final concert, with pictures galore. This set is interesting primarily to hear European musicians interpret Taylor's kinesthetic directing: mostly an intense density of "free playing" (actually following specific internalized instructions and images), with almost everyone going on different gestures at once, slow unison melodies emerging from the environment. The most interesting series is "Weight-Breath-Sounding Trees." Cecil Taylor European Orchestra. –BGT

RICHARD TEITELBAUM   ♭1939

○ **Blends (1977) / LUMINA LTD.**   1985
As the title promises, one of the most perfect blends of world

music, with Katsuya Yokoyama on shakuhachi, Trilok Gurtu on tabla and other percussion, and Teitelbaum on synthesizer. The score is written in different notations based on Japanese, Indian, and American practices. –BGT

JAMES TENNEY
♭1934

Koan (1971) / WHAT NEXT?
"Koan" (1971), from *Sounding the New Violin* is hypnotic process music containing slowly detuning pulses. With Malcolm Goldstein. –BGT

★ **Music of James Tenney / MUSICWORKS**
The Music of James Tenney: Selected Works 1963-1984 includes "Three Indigenous Songs no. 3: Hey When I Sing These 4 Songs Hey Look What Happens" (1979), a computer-generated tape composition with words based on an Iroquois chant coded into instrumental music; "Phases" (1963); "Quiet Fan for Erik Satie" (1970-1971), for an ensemble of 13 instruments — lyrical, hypnotically phase-modulated, Satie-like pastoral melodies; "For Ann (Rising)" (1969), tape composition, a vertical version of the persistence of motion illusion — tones rising but getting nowhere until the final ascension; "Spectral CANON for CONLON Nancarrow" (1974) for harmonic player-piano; "Bridge" (1982-1984, excerpt) for two pianos eight-hands; "Voice(s)" (1982-1984) for instrumental ensemble, voice(s), tape, and tape delay — like a field of supernatural rainbows. Watch for a future recording of Tenney's wonderful "Tableaux Vivante" (1989), which creates a new perspective on harmony without the traditional meanings. Another interesting ensemble work for similar instruments is "Critical Band," played by the Relache Ensemble of Philadelphia on Mode 22. –BGT

Septet for Electric Guitars / TELLUS
From the collection *Just Intonation*. A universe of spinning harmonically based pulses. Beautiful. –BGT

☆ **Computer Music 1963-1968 / FROG PEAK MUSIC** 1992
Some of the earliest and most beautiful computer music. Tenney was one of the first composers to use Max Mathew's computer-music-synthesis system at Bell Labs. –BGT

VIRGIL THOMSON
1896-1989

Highly original American composer who exerted considerable influence as music critic of the *New York Herald Tribune* and whose compositions reflect a universal approach embracing many idioms and styles. Thomson's score to the film *Louisiana Story* won the Pulitzer Prize in Music in 1948. –MKS

★ **Four Saints in Three Acts (1934) / ELEKTRA-NONESUCH**
A setting of the magnificent text by Gertrude Stein (1874-1946), on two CDs. For this opera, Thomson employed her writing technique of having characters and images just appear on the landscape of the stage — no linear plotline, only a real/historical/imaginary connection to a specified subject. This frees the creative process to attempt great character and language combinations to stimulate insight, which makes for a completely modern opera where melodies and moods follow in surprising sequences, but always with a sense of the whole in the background, or what Stein called "the eternal present." There are humorous choruses about "pigeons on the grass, alas," "Lucy Lily," "the garden inside and outside of the wall" (subtle lines about perception), St. Ignatius predicting the Last Judgment, and St. Teresa painting flowers on very large eggs. An all-African-American cast gave the first productions of this opera because Thomson wanted clear American speech. Thomson had set three songs on Stein's texts before attempting this opera. Performed by the Orchestra of Our Time. –BGT

○ **The Mother of Us All (1947) / NEW WORLD** 1990
The text is again by Stein, but the organization is somewhat more narrative, even with a semblance of plot. The theme is the life and struggles of suffragist Susan B. Anthony: the weariness of leading a totally public life and the seemingly

endless fight for rights — deep reflections about the meaning of family and humanity as opposed to laws. Beautiful, atmospheric, musical writing. Much of Thomson's other writing is very lyrical and always has a sound of its own, while being conventional in structure. If you love these operas, try the "Sonata da Chiesa" (Church Sonata, 1926), and the award-winning film scores for *The River* (1937), *The Plow That Broke the Plains* (1936), and *Louisiana Story* (1948). *A Portrait Album* (Elektra/Nonesuch D4-79024) contains selections from Thomson's 147 musical portraits of friends, similar to Stein's many portraits in writing. Two-CD set, performed by the Santa Fe Opera. –BGT

ERNST TOCH
1887-1964

Der Fuge aus Geographie / THOROFON
"Der Fuge aus Geographie (Geographical Fugue), for Spoken Chorus" (1930, from *Music between the Wars*). A different kind of work for Toch, a moment of "Spielmusik" (music for fun and play) in this otherwise contemporary romantic's music. An enjoyable and sophisticated sort of German rap on world place names. –BGT

DAVID TUDOR

☆ **Rainforest IV (1973) / EDITION BLOCK** 1981
A purely electronic piece designed for Merce Cunningham's dance of the same name. –BGT

Pulsers (1970); Untitled (1972) / LOVELY MUSIC 1984
Starting out like a castenet player on amphetamines, the "Pulsers" are gradually transformed by "home-brewed electronics" into many sounds, describable only by analogy: like a Latin percussion section; a forest of creatures cackling and whistling; a band with harmonica, guitar, and a crazed drummer; and a steel drum with a wire-beaters section. *Untitled*, with improvised vocals by Takehisa Kosugi, has a lot more "squiggles," is jolly and varied, but otherwise defies description. –BGT

★ **Microphone (1975) / CRAMPS** 1991
One of the great, wild, live-electronic pieces (recently reissued), with sounds that range from dinosaur-like howls echoing in prehistoric caves to timid, sweet calls of unidentifiable creatures. Original circuitry designed by Tudor and Gordon Mumma. –BGT

"BLUE" GENE TYRANNY
♭1945

See his biography in the About the Editors section in the front of the book.

Real Life and the Movies / FUN MUSIC 1981
A retrospective of electro-acoustic pieces from 1958-1980, including some hi- and low-fi soundtracks for independent movies: "Closed Transmission" (1966), realized on the IBM 7090 computer (at the Logic of Computers Group in Ann Arbor, Michigan); a gay/lesbian-rights piece, "The White Night Riot"; a parapsychological experiment, "Pals"; and "Remembering" (inspired by Robert Ashley's "Automatic Writing"). –ED

○ **The Intermediary / LOVELY MUSIC** 1982
This spontaneously performed piano piece is shadowed interactively with beautiful computer voicings designed by Joel Ryan. The feedback creates an illusion — the inspirational message seeming to occur sometimes before and sometimes after the performer plays material of similar shape. "A genuine delight ..." (*Recordings of Experimental Music*). –ED

○ **Free Delivery / LOVELY MUSIC** 1990
Live keyboard performances from 1983 to1989. Includes "Five Takes on the Nocturne with and without Memory" (1989), for solo piano; "The Country Boy Country Dog Intro" (1984), for piano and tape; "The Intermediary Following Traces of the Song" (1988), for acoustic piano and live sampling keyboard; "Intermediary with a Rendition of Stardust" (1983), for solo

piano and electronics; and "Sunrise or Sunset in Texas" (1983), from a film soundtrack." "'Blue' Gene Tyranny is the Mozart of his generation" (Kyle Gann, *The Village Voice*). –ED

★ **CBCD (1967-1992) / LOVELY MUSIC**   1992
Before there was "Twin Peaks," the "Country Boy Country Dog" series revealed an unscripted sub-rosa level of codes and events in a small Midwestern town. Based on the procedural score for musicians and nonmusicians, "How to Make Music from the Sound of Your Daily Life" (1967), environmental sounds, including voices, are recorded following a formal plan of movement. These sounds are then analyzed electronically in "transforms," which enable built-in melodies, rhythms, and surreal connections to be heard for the first time. These transforms are presented by themselves as meditative pieces for voice and piano with electronics; they also provide the material for an orchestra work, "The CBCD Variations for Soloist and Orchestra," performed by the Arch Ensemble for New Music. Like Tyranny's audio-storyboard "The Driver's Son," this piece is about the physical illusions that make up reality, the "waking dream" that is co-dependent on both the "inside" — intuitive decision, spontaneous mental image, feeling — and the "outside." –ED

VLADIMIR USSACHEVSKY   1911-1990

○ **Suite from *No Exit* (1962); Line of Apogee (1967) / NEW WORLD**
Two lyric, eerie, and innovative filmscores for the film of Jean-Paul Sartre's play and Lloyd William's avant-garde film by the master of the Columbia-Princeton electronic-music sound. Also employs vocal, animal, and environmental sounds. (See *Pioneers of Electronic Music* in 20th-Century Collections.) –BGT

PETER VAN RIPER

Sound to Movement / VRBLU   1979
Sound to Movement (New Music for Saxophones) has a lovely live performance at the Museum of Modern Art in Oxford, England, on Side 1 and concise conceptual pieces on Side 2. Contains "Circle Song," "Double Sound," "Doppler Piece," and more. –BGT

Heart (from *Acoustic Metal Music*) / AER   1992
From the collection *The Aerial #4*. Playing on a twirling metal strip about eight feet long that a sculptor used to make interlocking heart constructions, Van Riper makes a transparently beautiful and almost electronic effect. –BGT

DAVID VAN TIEGHAM

Safety in Numbers / PRIVATE MUSIC   1987
Not comfortably labeled new-age, or percussion, or pop, or electronic music, Van Tiegham's music has that downtown mix of all these and yet is distinctly his own, from the lush "Crystals" to the droll and rhythm-steady "Night of the Cold Noses." This is twisted easy listening. –BGT

EDGARD VARÈSE   1883-1965
French-American composer of music for orchestra, percussion ensemble, and electronic music, using theremin, Ondes Martenot, tape, and early electronic devices; his whose works emphasize dissonance, intricate rhythms, and the exploration of sound. –ED

★ **Offrandes (1921); Integrales (1925); Octandre (1923); Ecuatorial (1934) / ELEKTRA-NONESUCH**
The best performances of Varèse's acoustic and vocal works by the Contemporary Chamber Ensemble, Arthur Weisberg, conductor. Ancient forests, Queen of the Polar Dawns, the sacred Mayan texts — musical and verbal imagery par excellence. –BGT

Amériques / SONY CLASSICAL
Boulez/NYPO.

Amériques / VANGUARD CLASSICS
Abravanel/Utah SO.

Arcana / SONY CLASSICAL
Boulez/NYPO.

Density 21.5, for Solo Flute / SONY CLASSICAL
Ensemble InterContemporain.

Equatorial / VANGUARD CLASSICS
Abravanel/Utah SO.

Ionisation, for 13 Percussionists / SONY CLASSICAL
Boulez/Ensemble InterContemporain.

Nocturnal / VANGUARD CLASSICS
Bybee, Abravanel/Utah SO.

Nocturnal / VANGUARD CLASSICS
Bybee, Abravanel/Utah SO.

Integrales; Amériques / SONY CLASSICAL   1990
Integrales for 11 Winds and Percussionists (1924-1925); *Amériques* (1918-1922) is wonderful orchestral music. Not the best performances but passable, and the only one of *Arcana* currently available. *Amériques* is played beautifully on Vanguard Classics OVC 4031 by the Utah Orchestra, conducted by Maurice Abravanel. Watch for future recordings of *Deserts* with the original tape interpolations (once available on the out-of-print disc *The Varèse Record* on Finnadar SR 9018, issued 1977, with notes by Frank Zappa). Directed by Pierre Boulez. –BGT

☆ **Poème Électronique (1958) / NEUMA**   1990
From the collection *Electro-Acoustic Music: Classics*. A visionary piece, "opacities and rarefactions," the jungle, outer space, the Golden Section, strange ceremonies .... The CD booklet includes a spectrogram score of the music. –BGT

LOIS VIERK   ♭1951

Manhattan Cascade / CRI   1992
From the collection *Manhattan Cascade*. A beautiful work that gradually develops from repeating single tones to masses of swirling clusters. More of a horizontal cascade between harmonic dimensions than a vertical waterfall. With Guy Klucevsek (accordion). –BGT

○ **Simoom / EXPERIMENTAL INTERMEDIA FOUNDATION XI**   1992
Cuts include "Go Guitars" for five electric guitars, "Cirrus" for six trumpets, and "Simoom" for eight cellos. Sighing, sliding tones, rhythmic pulse, and strange harmonics reach an indescribable state, like music from an unknown culture. This piece is influenced by Japanese-Buddhist chant. Seriously meditative. –BGT

LARRY WENDT

Bring Your Mom Too / FROG PEAK MUSIC
"Sadness without Brains" is a sound-assembly cassette of small hand-tools, amplified auto parts, shortwave radios, stories, and junk. The tape is packaged in a metal case opened with a Phillips screwdriver. Other Wendt cassettes are available from the same distributor (*Guided Missile Favorites*, *Slowscan vol. 3* with Nicolas Collins, *Upper and Lower California*, *Live from Bakersfield*). –BGT

HILDEGARD WESTERKAMP

Cricket Voice (1987) / AER   1990
From the collection *The Aerial #2*. The score is for electronically modified environmental sounds made by "playing" the desert (plucking on cactus spikes, dried roots, and palm leaves — the resonance of an old water reservoir). Beautifully assembled. –BGT

RUTH WHITE

Seven Trumps from the Tarot Cards / MERCURY LIMELIGHT   1968
Ruth White was one of the early users of Moog synthesizer equipment. She produced some quite original and beautiful

music in her independent studio. This and the other Ruth White albums listed are now out of print.) –BGT

Flowers of Evil / MERCURY LIMELIGHT   1969
Short Circuits / ANGEL   1971

CHRISTIAN WOLFF

Summer (1961), for String Quartet / VOX BOX
From the collection *The Avant-Garde String Quartet in the USA*. A sensitive performance of this graph score in the composer's early style. (*See 20th Century Collections*.) –BGT

☆ **Mayday Materials / CENTAUR**   1990
From the collection *CDCM Computer Music Series - Vol. 6*. A "mix of abstraction, lightheartedness and perhaps political suggestiveness," an interesting combination of Wolff's earlier new-music sensibilities and his later use of folk songs as guiding lines rather than direct quotes. Nine out of twenty pieces were made for a dance by Lucinda Childs. –BGT

STEFAN WOLPE

○ **String Quartet (1968-1969) / CRI**   1991
Although writing in a strict atonal style, Wolpe composed clear, angular music that weaved gestures directly appealing to the body senses, sometimes with a sense of humor; a nonabstract academic composer (not always recognized as one by contemporary academics). This quartet, one of Wolpe's finest works, stands out from the other two works on this CD (by Roger Sessions and Milton Babbitt). Also recommended are "Enactments for 3 pianos" (1950-1953) on Elektra/Nonesuch 78024-4 (cassette tape), and the "Passacaglia" from *Four Studies of Basic Rows* (1936) on New World NW-344-2. Juilliard String Quartet. –BGT

THE WORD

The Word / TELLUS
Spoken works with music, processed voices, and many other combinations by novelists and poets. –BGT

IVAN WYSCHNEGRADSKY

Compositions for String Quartet and String Trio / EDITION BLOCK   1990
Performed by the Arditti String Quartet. Includes the three microintervallic string quartets, a "Composition" (op. 43), and a "Trio" (op. 53). A pioneer (with Willy Möllendorf, Jörg Mager, Alois Haba, and Fredrich Trautwein) in quarter-tone and ultrachromatic music. The "Trio," with its tone leaps that collapse into each other, and the first quartet are probably the most distinctive. –BGT

IANNIS XENAKIS   b 1922

Greek-born French composer whose mathematical compositional techniques and electronic media in orchestral, chamber, choral, vocal, ballet, and acoustic works have considerably influenced the development of composition in Europe and America. –MKS

○ **Medea / ERATO**   1969
Medea, for male choir, hand-held stones, and orchestra. A good combination of Xenakis's more spare abstract music and ancient Greek chant, which is more involving than his often-violent themes or the forced humor of his music based on stochastic procedures, transformation groups, Poisson's law of probabilities, and so forth, where structure is the only content. This record also includes "Syrmos" for 18 strings, and "Polytope, for 4 Orchestras Disseminated in the Audience." Performed by the Orchestra and Choir of the French Radio-Television, directed by Marius Constant. –BGT

Mycenae-Alpha (1978) / NEUMA   1990
From the collection *Electro-Acoustic Music: Classics*. Images of natural phenomena digitized directly into dense and intense computer music. –BGT

YANKEES

○ **Yankees / CELLULOID CELL**   1983
A collective improvisation by Derek Bailey (acoustic and electric guitars), George Lewis (trombone), John Zorn (alto and soprano sax, clarinets, game calls). Subtle, droll, hilarious takes on the trivia of baseball sounds — Lewis says "ball one, ball one ..." through the trombone; there are snippets of a slipping and sliding version of "Take Me Out to the Ball Game," and more. Sections are titled "City City City"; "The Legend of Enos Slaughter"; "Who's On First"; "On Golden Pond" (a tongue-in-cheek tone poem of the flora and fauna and mosquitos); and "The Warning Track," about a very tiny railroad system. –BGT

LA MONTE YOUNG   b 1935

89 VI 8 c. 1:42-1:52 AM ... / TELLUS
"89 VI 8 c. 1:42-1:52 AM Paris Encore," from "Poem for Chairs, Tables, Benches, etc." (1960) in the piece *FluxTellus*. A piece with a verbal instruction score (what we used to call "music without notes," "procedural music," and "events") — the floor sounds of precisely moved furniture in a resonant space. Young's early style. –BGT

☆ **90 XII 9c. 9:35-10:52 PM NYC / GRAMAVISION**
The Melodic Version of the Second Dream of the High-Tension Line Stepdown Transformer" (1984), from *The Four Dreams of China* (1984), performed by the Theater of Eternal Music Brass Ensemble, led by Ben Neill. Eight trumpets with Harmon mutes play a meditative re-creation of the experience of listening to the harmonics of public electrical-power-transformer lines on telephone poles, which Young remembers from childhood next to his grandfather's Conoco gas station; tuning as a function of events compared over time, and vice-versa. –BGT

The Well-Tuned Piano (1964-81) / GRAMAVISION
The legendary just-intonation work. The booklet goes on a bit much, trying to justify Young's place in history, so just listen to the music, which is pleasant and non-virtuosic in the usual sense. This five-CD set is also available on cassettes and albums. –BGT

Any Integer ... / POINT MUSIC   1992
Any Integer (to Henry Flynt), for Multilayered Saxophones (April 1960). From the collection *Jon Gibson* (see this section). Henry Flynt is known for pieces similar to the Fluxus group output (for example, his "Work Such That No One Knows What's Going On" and "Concerto for Kitchen Sink and Monkey Chorus"). As a meta-aesthetician and protestor against Serious Art, he produced complex essays on conceptual art (see his writing in La Monte Young's *An Anthology*). –BGT

FRANK ZAPPA   b 1940

See the Rock section for his biography.

Freak Out! / VERVE   1966
An early art-rock album with a unified program throughout (concept album), characterized by unusual rhythmic meters and a wide use of sound-processing techniques available at that time (speed changes, tape delay, multi-tracking, echo, and flanging). The final piece, "The Return of the Son of Monster Magnet," is pure musique concrète. The albums *Lumpy Gravy* (1967) on Verve V6-8741 and *Uncle Meat* (1969) on Bizarre 2Ms-2024 are also recommended for these techniques and for orchestral sections mostly written in a Varèse-wannabe style. Double-disc set. –BGT

○ **The Black Page (1977) / KEYBOARD MAGAZINE**   1987
Floppy vinyl-disc insert in *Keyboard Magazine*. An extremely interesting one-line solo programmed on a Synclavier. The solo is notated in complex polyrhythmic ratios (à la Stockhausen) but has the effect of the "stretch-rhythm" used in the most sensitive jazz solos. A score is included in the text of the magazine. –BGT

JOHN ZORN   b 1953

See the Jazz section for his biography.

The Classic Guide to Strategy / LUMINA   1985
Solo woodwind improvisations with game calls, parts of saxes and clarinets. Eccentric, pure Zorn. –BGT

The Classic Guide to Strategy - Vol. 2 / LUMINA 1986
Beautifully intense solo pieces with inflections like those in ancient Japanese music. The sections are named after various Japanese artists — Aoyama Michi, Enoken, Kazumi Shigeru, Kondo Toshinori, Yano Akiko, Togawa Jun, and Mori Ikue. The cover art is calligraphy of the character for "water." –BGT

Cobra / HAT ART   1990
A studio- and live-performance recording on two CDs with many of New York City's downtown improvisers: Anthony Coleman, Bill Frisell, Wayne Horwitz, Bob James, Guy Klucesvek, Arto Lindsay, Christian Marclay, Zeena Parkins, Bobby Previte, Elliott Sharp, Jim Staley, David Weinstein, J. A. Deane, and Carol Emanuel. –BGT

PETER ZUMMO   b 1948

○ **Zummo with an X / LORIS BEND FOUNDATION**   1985
Also contains "Instruments" (1980) and "Song IV" (1985) from the suite *Six Songs* (commissioned for Trisha Brown's dance *Lateral Pass*). "Instruments" is a pure, spare study of musical intervals with a gently humorous quality, using phase (mobile) techniques to produce variations. The *Six Songs* are all played over the same peacefully persuasive tabla pulse from Bill Ruyle. Arthur Russell's singing and cello playing (harmonics, counter-rhythms) together create one warm voice, and Peter Zummo's open and muted trombone statements (simple riffs, sweet pleas, and sometimes snores) combine to make an irresistible mental dance. Highly recommended. Watch for his forthcoming CD, *Experimenting with Household Chemicals.* –BGT

20TH-CENTURY COLLECTIONS

The Aerial #1 - A Journal in Sound / AERIAL   1990
David Moss, "Language Linkage"; Terry Setter, "Aphorism III: Like a Coat or Mask"; Christine Baczewska, "Day of the Dead"; Richard Kostelanetz, "Murdoch and the Sufi from Invocations"; Rich Jensen, "Folly"; Loren Mazzacane and Suzanne Langille, "Haunted House"; Lost Souls, "Idumea"; Malcolm Goldstein, "qerneraq; our breath as bones"; Floating Concrete Octopus, "Burial Song"; Jerry Hunt, "Babalon (string)"; Stuart Sherman, "Four Sound Pieces: Doors, Water, Click, Pinball"; Bern Porter, "The Last Acts of St. Fuckyou."

○ **The Aerial #2 - A Journal in Sound / AERIAL** 1990
Bob Davis and Jon Raskin, "Poison Hotel"; David Dunn, "Chaos and the Emergent Mind of the Pond"; Jin Hi Kim, "Komungo Permutations"; Jeff Greinke, "Road to Solo"; Christopher Shultis, "motion/less"; Chris Cochrane, "Santiago Penando Estas"; Sue Ann Harkey, "In This Year of the Snake"; Annea Lockwood, "Nautilus"; LaDonna Smith and Davey Williams, "Green Song"; Hildegard Westerkamp, "Cricket Voice." This is an interesting collection from all over the US, which shows that avant-garde music is not restricted to cultural centers. –BGT

The Aerial #4 - A Journal in Sound / AERIAL   1992
Another terrific anthology of the latest. Contains Brenda Hutchinson, "Eeeyah!"; Peter Van Riper, "Heart"; Erik Belgum, "Dick Tracy All over His Body"; Leif Brush, "Terrain Instruments Are Activated"; Elodie Lauten, "Music for the Trine, Part IV"; Elise Kermani, "Spiral"; Anna Homler and Steve Mosher, "Sirens"; Joseph Weber, "Transformation of the Brothers into the Sun and Moon"; Patsy Rahn, "Trojan Horse"; and N. Sean William, "Come Window Golds Coming." –BGT

All Guitars / TELLUS
All the weirdest guitarists on the New York scene. Includes contributions from Lee Ranaldo, Bob Mould, Arto Lindsay, the Butthole Surfers, Blixa Bargeld, Tim Schellenbaum, Elliott Sharp, David Linton, and others. –BGT

☆ **Another Coast (New Works from the West) / MUSIC & ARTS**   1988
Contains Carl Stone, "Wall Me Do" and "Hop Ken"; Paul Dresher, "Other Fire" and "Water Dreams"; Maggi Payne, "Airwaves (realities)"; Paul DeMarinis, "I Want You" and "Kokole"; and Laetitia Sonami, "Pie Jesu - Sounds from Empty Places no. 3." –BGT

Anthology of Music for the 21st Century / LEONARDO MUSIC JOURNAL - VOL. 1, NO. 1   1991
Music by Marc Battier, Sarah Hopkins, Larry Austin, Ed Osborn, Daniel Goode, I. Wayan Sadra (gamelan), Craig Harris, Amnon Wolman, Graeme Gerrard, Steven Paxton with Paula Claire, David Rothenberg, Simon Running, Erling Wood, and Kenneth Atchley (see Atchley listing).

Audio Works by Visual Artists / TELLUS
Visual artists from the Futurists to the present. Includes pieces by Joseph Beuys, A. Russolo, Kurt Schwitters, Lawrence Weiner, Richard Huelsenbeck, Joan Jonas, Terry Allen, Marcel Duchamp, Y Pants, Magdalena Abakanowicz, and many others. –BGT

Austral Voices / NEW ALBION   1990
Avant-garde music by Australian composers: Alan Lamb (b 1944), "Journeys on the Winds of Time I" (1987-1988), which uses sounds made by three miles of abandoned telegraph wires singing in the wind, a sort of giant Aeolian harp in the Great Southern Hinterland of Western Australia; Alistair Riddell (b 1955), "Fantasie," for computer-driven piano; Sarah Hopkins (b 1958), "Cello Chi" (1986), which uses extended vocal and cello techniques such as harmonic singing, bowed harmonics, and circular didjeridu bowing; Warren Burt (b 1949), "Three Inverse Genera" (1989), for four musicians on tuning forks tuned to a 19-tone system, recorded in a barn with sounds of the Australian bush country filtering in; Ross Bandt (b 1951), "Genesis" (1983), for medieval psaltery, recorded in a large, hollow, concrete cylinder five floors underground in Melbourne's Collins Place Car Park; Jeff Pressing (b 1946), "Butterfly's Dream," for synthesizers; Ross Bolleter (b 1946), "Nallan Void" (1987), for a ruined piano that was found at the Nallan sheep station near Cue, 700 km north of Perth (this piano had once graced the bar at the Big Bell Hotel in the 30s and 40s and was now slowly returning to nature). –BGT

○ **Bang on a Can Live - Vol. 1 / CRI**   1992
A collection of live performances from the annual new-music festival in Manhattan. Includes Alison Cameron, "Two Bits"; Bill Doerfeld, "Evening Chant"; Michael Gordon, "Strange Quiet"; Tom Johnson, "Failing"; Scott Lindroth, "Relations to Rigor"; Julia Wolfe, "The Vermeer Room"; Evan Ziporyn, "Luv Time." –BGT

Cassette Mythos Audio Alchemy / WHAT NEXT?   1991
So much of the newest music is just in cassettes and computer discs freely exchanged through the mail, contacts made by word-of-mouth, small publications soliciting contributions. (I'm reminded of Frankie Mann's remark that some of the best music in the country is made by "12-year-olds in their attics with cassettes.") *Casette Mythos Audio Alchemy CD/K7* contains some of the most inspired samplings of the cassette culture (also some gawd-awful stuff, but always unique) ... maybe more in-the-air than underground. Twenty-one selections: Heather Perkins, "What You Think Will Happen Will"; Ric E. Braden, "Columbus Ave. 10 PM"; Jim Steele, "Splatter Experience of the Green Gods"; Daniel Johnston, "Grievances"; John Wiggins, "Timbre Melody"; Yximalloo, "China-Pong"; Qubais Ghazala, "The Delphian Oracle"; Frederick Lonberg-Holm, "The Second Minuet"; Costes, "Oh Fortuna"; Kitchen Table Ensemble, "Exploded Views"; Solomonoff and Von Hoffmanstahl, "Banzai Noir"; Vosch,

"Tunnel at Dawn"; Philip Perkins, "Remoting (excerpt from Berkeley Remote)"; Minÿy, "Sspress"; Triptic of a Pastel Fern, "Shiny Things"; Gregory Whitehead, "It makes me blush ..."; Mystery Laboratory, "Excerpt from V.T."; Bat Lenny, "Delphi (Δ ø)"; Collapse/Relapse, "Webs"; Hope Organ, "Sneaky"; (no composer given) "Tentatively, a Convenience Drying Clothes Made Entirely from Zippers (Partial Cycle)." –BGT

Cathy Berberian, Voice / MAINSTREAM
Astonishing mid-60s performance by one of new music's first vocal-sound experimenters. Berberian had many pieces written especially for her. Includes Luciano Berio's "Circles" (text by e. e. cummings), Bussotti's "Frammento," and an especially noteworthy presentation of the John Cage "Aria with Fontina Mix." You may also wish to hear her "Stripsody for solo Voice" (1966) on Wergo WER 60054-50. –BGT

CDCM Computer Music Series - Vol. 1 / CENTAUR   1988
CDCM Computer Music Series - Vol. 1: CEMI: Center for Experimental Music and Intermedia (1988) at the University of North Texas, Denton. Contains Larry Austin, "Sinfonia Concertante: A Mozartean Episode"; Thomas Clark, "Peninsula," for piano and computer; Jerry Hunt, "Fluud," for dual synthesizers; and Phil Winsor, "Dulcimer Dream," for amplified piano. –BGT

○ **CDCM Computer Music Series - Vol. 10 / CENTAUR**   1991
CDCM Computer Music Series - Vol. 10: The Virtuoso in the Computer Age - I. Contains Paul Lansky, "As If," for string trio and computer-synthesized sound; Larry Austin, "Montage: Themes and Variations for Violin and Computer Music on Tape" (1985); John Melby, "Concerto no. 1 for Flute and Computer-Synthesized Tape" (1984); David Rosenboom, "A Precipice in Time" (1966); Anthony Braxton, "Composition no. 107" (excerpt, 1982). –BGT

CDCM Computer Music Series - Vol. 2 / CENTAUR   1988
CDCM Computer Music Series - Vol. 2: EAR Studios (1988) at Rensselaer Polytechnic Institute, Troy, NY. Contains Richard Teitelbaum, "Golem 1" (1987); Martin Bresnick, "Lady Neil's Dumpe" (1987); Neil B. Rolnick, "What is the use?" (1985); Rick Baitz, "Kaleidocycles" (1985); Scott Lindroth, "Syntax" (1985). –BGT

CDCM Computer Music Series - Vol. 3 / CENTAUR   1989
CDCM Computer Music - Vol. 3: Experimental Music Studies and Computer Music Project at the University of Illinois, Urbana-Champaign. Contains Salvatore Martirano, "Everything Goes when the Whistle Blows for Zeta Violin & MIDI Orchestra" (1985); John Melby, "Chor der Waisen (Chorus of the Orphans)," 1985, for computer-generated tape; Sever Tipei, "Cunculi" (1986), for five tubas — mostly quietly played clusters with complex beat patterns, pleasant to hear; Scott A. Wyatt, "Still Hidden Laughs" (1988), for Synclavier and Yahama systems; Herbert Bruen, "Project SAWDUST Nr. 6: i toLD You sol" (1981) — speech-like gestures made from filtered-spectrum noise sources for computer-generated tape; Carla Scaletti, "sunSurgeAutomata" (1987) — a mysterious short work (realized using the Platypus Digital Processor) built from clicks that are collected to resemble pitch and rhythm, and expressive of the proposal by Lewis Thomas that the development of life on Earth may have been "thermodynamically inevitable," given the steady stream of energy from the sun to the unfillable sink of space by way of the Earth. Thomas suggests that the "urge to make music" may be a desire to recapitulate this transformation of inanimate random matter in chaos into the improbable ordered dance of living forms. –BGT

CDCM Computer Music Series - Vol. 6 / CENTAUR   1990
CDCM Computer Music Series - Vol. 6: Bregman Electronic Music Studio at Dartmouth College in Hanover, NH. Contains Jon Appleton, "Brush Canyon" (1983), a wonderful short tone poem using the Synclavier; Paul Moravec, "Devices and Desires" for Synclavier, a musique concrète work about social mores and strictures; David Evan Jones, "Still Life in Wood and Metal" and "Still Life Dancing," for percussion ensemble

and tape; Jon Appleton, "Degitaru Ongaku" (1983), for Synclavier; Christian Wolff, "Mayday Materials." –BGT

CDCM Computer Music Series - Vol. 7 / CENTAUR   1990
CDCM Computer Music Series - Vol. 7: Ear Studios at Rensselaer Polytechnic Institute, Troy, NY. This CD contains Neil B. Rolnick, "Vocal Chords" (1988), for voice and digital processors; "A Robert Johnson Sampler" (1987); Pauline Oliveros, "Lion's Tale" (1989), for digital sampler; Julie Kabat, "Child and the Moon-Tree" (1989), for vocalist and electronics; Barton McLean, "Visions of a Summer Night" (1989), for MIDI-based computer system; and Joel Chadabe, "Modalities" (1989), for an interactive computer-music system. –BGT

Chicago 82 / LES DISQUES DU CREPESCULE
Chicago 82 - A Dip in the Lake is music from New Music America 1982, including Branca's "Indeterminate Activity of Resultant Masses" and a Cage interview and pieces. A terrific overview. –BGT

○ **Cold Blue Anthology / COLD BLUE**   1984
When you listen to the pieces on this record in succession, an unnameable, evocative narrative seems to underlie the whole. Includes Charles Smith, "Beatrix"; Ingram Marshall, "Gradual Siciliano (for Gus)"; Peter Garland, "The Three Strange Angels" (1972-1973), for piano, drum, and bullroarer; Daniel Lentz, "You Can't See the Forest... Music, 1971"; Michael Byron, "Marimbas in the Dorian Mode" (May Day, 1976); Jim Fox, "Appearance of Red"; Read Miller, "Weddings, Funerals, and Children Who Cannot Sleep"; John Kuhlmann, "In This Light"; Rick Cox, "Necessity"; Michael Jon Fink, "Celesta Solo" (1981); Eugene Bowen and Harold Budd, "Wonder's Edge"; James Tenney, "Spectral CANON for CONLON Nancarrow," for player piano. –BGT

Compositoras Madrileñas / RTVE   1991
Compositoras Madrileñas ("Women Composers of Madrid") contains Alicia Santos, "Sonata para flauta y piano" (1958); Marisa Manchado, "Obertura" (1956); Consuelo Diez, "Naggareth" (1958), for percussion ensemble; Zulema de la Cruz, "Pulsares" (1958), for piano and taped electronics; Maria Escribano, "Jondo" (1954), for sax ensemble, piano, and percussion. –BGT

Computer Music / FOLKWAYS   1983
Interesting collection. Contains Larry Austin, "Canadian Coastlines"; John Celona, "Music in Circular Motions"; Charles Dodge, "Any Resemblance"; Stanley Haynes, "Prisms"; Bruce Pennycook, "Speeches for Dr. Frankenstein." –BGT

Computer Music Currents 7 / WERGO   1990
Contains Richard Karpen (b 1957), "Il Nome (The Name)," 1987; Jean-Claude Risset, "L'autre face (The Other Side)"; Lars-Gunnar Bodin, "Anima (Spirit)," 1984); Tracy L. Petersen, "Digital Tantra I" (1978); Frances White (b 1960), "Ogni pensiero vola (Every Thought Flies)," 1985; and Joji Yuasa, "A Study in White" (1987). –BGT

Computer Music from the Outside In / FOLKWAYS 1983
Demonstrations of the components and compositions of computer music in the early 80s: Barton McLean, "Etunytude" and "The Last Ten Minutes"; Karl Korte, "The Whistling Wind"; and Reed Holmes, "Moire." –BGT

Concert Imaginaire, GRM / INA   1984
Concert Imaginaire, GRM ("Imaginary Concert") is a good collection of musique concrète pieces by the GRM, or Groupe de Recherches Musicales (Group for Musical Research). It contains J. Schwarz, "And Around"; Bernard Parmegiani, "La roue Ferris (Ferris Wheel)"; Pierre Schaeffer and Pierre Henry, *Erotica symphonie pour un homme seul* ("Erotic Symphony for a Lonely Man"); Michel Chion, "La Ronde (The Ring)"; Jacques Lejeune, "L'invitation au départ (Invitation to the Departure)"; Ivo Malec, "Reflets (Reflections)"; Jean Schwarz, "Suite N"; Christian Zanesi, "D'un jardin à l'autre (From one Garden to the Other)"; Denis Dufour, "Vocalises"; Philippe Mion, "Puzzlasept"; François Bayle, "Erosphère." –BGT

○ **A Confederacy of Dances - Vol. 1 / EINSTEIN** 1992
These concert recordings from the Roulette Experimental
Music Series come with a 32-page booklet containing essays
on Roulette and the "downtown scene" by Mark Dery, Tim
Page, Kevin Whitehead, and David Weinstein. It contains Bill
Frisell, "April 16, 1988"; Christian Marclay, "Untitled"; Tohban
Djan (Ikue Mori and Luli Shioi), "Blue Seed"; Zeena Parkins,
"Scruples"; Billy Bang, "One for Albert"; Anthony Coleman,
"Acid Jazz Burnout"; David Weinstein, "Icetralia"; Chris
Cochrane, "To Disenfranchise (Repatriation)"; Ron Kuivila,
"Canon Y"; John Zorn, "Sebastopol"; Guy Klucevsek, "Sylvan
Steps"; David Weinstein, "Poland"; Hirsch-Mori-Shea-Staley
Quartet, "Ulula Zone"; and Jeanne Lee and Wadada Leo
Smith, "Beauty Is a Rarity." –BGT

☆ **Les Magistères ... / HARMONIA MUNDI** 1991
*Les Magistères du 19e Concours International de Musique
Électroacoustique* ("Magisterium of the Nineteenth Electro-
acoustic Competition," 1991). An excellent compilation of
elegant, subtle, and poetic electronic works, including
Bernard Parmegiani (b 1927), "Exercisme 3" ("Exercise/
Exorcism 3," 1986); Barry Truax (b 1947), "Riverrun" (1986);
Wilhelm Zobl (b. 1950), "Ändere die Welt, sie braucht es"
("Change the World, It Needs Changing," 1973); and James
Dashow (b 1944), "Whispers Out of Time" (1976). –BGT

○ **Prix Quadrivium / HARMONIA MUNDI** 1991
Prix Quadrivium (Bourges 1992) is another interesting
collection of prize-winning electro-acoustic pieces.
Sometimes the overall tastefulness makes them seem
somewhat similar, but especially distinctive are Andrew Lewis
(b 1963, UK), "Time and Fire"; Mike Vaughan (b 1954, UK),
"Ensphered," for soprano sax and tape; Ake Parmerud (b
1953, Sweden), "Alias"; Justice Olsson (France, b
Johannesburg, South Africa, 1949), "Up!"; Alicyn Warren
(b 1955, US), "Longing for the Light." Other compositions are
by Cort Lippe (b 1953, US), "Music for Harp and Tape"; David
Arzouman (b 1955, US), "Precipitation"; Jon Appleton (b 1939,
US), "Stereopticon"; Roderik De Man (Pays Bas, b 1941,
Indonesia), "Chordis Canam"; Georg Katzer (b 1935,
Germany), "Rondo." –BGT

Double Edge / CRI 1992
A brilliantly played collection of works, mostly recorded for
the first time, by the legendary piano duo Double Edge.
Includes Frederic Rzewski, "Winnsboro Cotton Mill Blues"
(1980); David Borden, "Double Portrait" (1987); "Blue" Gene
Tyranny, "The Decertified Highway of Dreams" (1991); James
Tenney, "Chromatic Canon" (1983); Paul Bowles, "Night
Waltz" (1949); Duke Ellington and Billy Strayhorn, "Tonk"
(1940); Meredith Monk, "Phantom Waltz" (1989) and "Ellis
Island" (1981); Mel Powell, "A Setting for Two Pianos" (1987);
and Morton Feldman, "Two Pianos" (1957). –BGT

☆ **Electro-Acoustic Music: Classics / NEUMA** 1990
Some of the best of the European academic style: Verèse,
"Poème Electronique"; Milton Babbitt, "Phenomena" and
"Philomel," both with soprano Judith Bettina; Roger Reynolds,
"Transfigured Wind IV," with Harvey Sollberger (flute); and
Iannis Xenakis, "Mycenae-Alpha." –BGT

Electronic Music / VOX TURNABOUT 1965
Early compositions utilizing the RCA Mark II synthesizer at
Columbia-Princeton: Andres Lewin-Richter, "Study no. 1";
Ilhan Miraroglu, "Le tombeau d'Edgar Poe" (The Tomb of
Edgar Allan Poe), "Intermezzo," and "Bowery Bum"; Tzvi
Avni, "Vocalise"; and Walter Carlos, "Variations for Flute and
Electronic Sound" and "Dialogues for Piano and Two
Loudspeakers." –BGT

Electronic Music / FOLKWAYS 1966
Early works from independent composers in Canada, the US,
and Australia. Includes Victor Grauer, "Inferno"; Jean Ivey,
"Pinball"; John Robb, "Collage"; Hugh Le Caine, "Dripsody"
(one of the first Canadian tape pieces); Walter Olnick-
Schaeffer, "Summer Idyl Noesis"; Myron Schaeffer, "Dance R
43"; and Val Stephen, "Fireworks" and "Orgasmic Opus." –BGT

Electronic Music / VOX TURNABOUT 1967
Ilhan Mimaroglu, "Agony" (1965); John Cage, "Fontana Mix"
(1958); and Luciano Berio, "Visage" (1961, based on the
fabulous vocal sounds of Cathy Berberian). –BGT

Elektroakustische Musik aus Finnland / EDITION
"Electro-acoustic Music from Finland." Rarely heard music by
Patrick Kosk, Petri Hiidenkari, Harri Nouri, and Tapio
Nevanlinna. –BGT

Experimental Theater / TELLUS
Sound from performance-art presentations. Includes
Spalding Gray, "Sex and Death to the Age 14 (excerpt)";
Vulcan Death Grip with Ann Magnuson, "Get It Up or Get Out"
(1986), vocals with band; Mike Kelley with Sonic Youth,
"Plato's Cave, Rothko's Chapel, Lincoln's Profile" (1986); Jerri
Allyn, "Queer Revolution" (1984); Ann Magnuson, "Arachnae
X. Pudenda" (1987); and Lydia Lunch, "The Cancer Has
Finally Become Contagious" (1987). –BGT

Exquisite Corpses from P. S. 122 / WHAT NEXT? 1990
Not actually a collection but a collective improvisation by 30
performer/composers. Each participant was given only a hint
of the contributions of other participants. The whole of the
improvisations was then collected together unedited, without
overdubbing or retakes. A panorama of approaches to the
meaning of improvisation. –BGT

☆ **Extended Voices / ODYSSEY** 1968
New pieces for chorus and voices altered electronically; some
of the best performances and recordings of new-music, ever.
Includes Pauline Oliveros, "Sound Patterns"; Alvin Lucier,
"North American Time Capsule 1967," for voices and Sylvania
Electronic Systems Vocoder; John Cage, "Solos for Voice 2";
Toshi Ichiyanagi, "Extended Voices"; Morton Feldman,
"Chorus and Instruments (II)" and "Christian Wolff in
Cambridge." –BGT

False Phonemes / TELLUS
A wonderful anthology of works for computer-generated
voice. Includes Remko Scha, "French Recitatif" and
"katadeedo daynatadoh (restored to youth according to
beauty I walk)," from *Impressions of Africa*; Larry Wendt,
"Galaxy Love"; Brian Reinbolt, "Brain Monkey"; Mark
Rudolph, "Beautiful but marred by the blemish of a perpetual
dissatisfaction"; Alice Shields, "Mass for the Dead"; Paul
DeMarinis, "Mind Power"; Paul Lansky, "Not Just More Idle
Chatter"; Jon English and Jim Pomeroy, "The Hartford
Address"; Ron Kuivila, "Linear Predictive Zoo"; John Cage,
"Writings through the Essay: On the Duty of Civil
Disobedience" (excerpt). –BGT

Funnel Zone / DOSSIER 1991
Music by Vivante Tableaux, Setrakian, Slap, TVD, Marilyn
Manson, Quayle, Rivet Ecks, Vociferous Mutes, Happiness
Boys, Chameleon Circus, King Felix. Wonderful grass-roots
new-music and some industrial-rock mostly from the Miami
area. I especially like "Second Nature" and "Haides" by King
Felix. –BGT

Futura 1 - (Soundtext Poetry) / CRAMPS
Fascinating historical re-creations and new insights into this
unique branch of inter-art activity, soundtext poetry. Includes
"La declamazione futurista (The Futurist Declamation)" and
"Lo Zaum, linguaggio trasmentale (Zaum, the Transmental
Language)." –BGT

Futura 2 - (Soundtext Poetry) / CRAMPS
"Simultaneismo francese (French Simultaneism)" and
"Precursori e dadaisti in Germania (Forerunners and Dadists
in Germany)."

Futura 3 - (Soundtext Poetry) / CRAMPS
"L'urlo: Antonin Artaud (The Howl)" and "La poesia sonora
oggi (Sound Poetry Today)."

Futura 4 - (Soundtext Poetry) / CRAMPS
"La poesia sonora oggi (Sound Poetry Today)."

Futura 5 - (Soundtext Poetry) / CRAMPS
"La poesia sonora oggi (Sound Poetry Today)."

○ **Images Fantastiques / MERCURY LIMELIGHT**   1968
A great collection of musique concrète pieces: Luciano Berio, "Momenti (Moments)" and "Omaggio a James Joyce (Homage to James Joyce)"; Bruno Maderna, "Continuo"; Luc Ferrari, "Visage V"; Iannis Xenakis, "Orient-Occident"; and Jean Baronnet and François Dufrene, "U 47." –BGT

☆ **Imaginary Landscapes / NONESUCH**   1989
Ron Kuivila, "Loose Canons" (excerpt); Shelley Hirsch and David Weinstein, "On the Swing" (an excerpt from *Pomp and Circumstance*); Neil B. Rolnick, "Balkanization" (excerpt); Mark Trayle, "Simple Degradation (Border)"; Gordon Monahan, "Speaker Swinging" (excerpt); Laetitia Sonami, "What Happened"; Maryanne Amacher, "Stain - The Music Rooms" (excerpt); Alvin Lucier, "Music for Alpha Waves, Assorted Percussion, and Automated Code Relays"; David Tudor, "Dialects" (excerpt); Nicolas Collins, "Real Electronic Music"; Voice Crack, "A Spoonful of Tea in a Barrel Full of Honey" (excerpt); Christian Marclay, "Black Stucco"; "Blue" Gene Tyranny, "Somewhere in Arizona 1970," for baritone and electronics. Seventy minutes of some of the best and most innovative of new electronic music of varied idiosyncratic approaches. –ED

○ **Island of Sanity ... / REVIEW (NO MAN'S LAND)**   1991
Island of Sanity - New Music from New York City contains David Linton, "Lumbago"; Mofungo, "Slimeball Necktie"; Christian Marclay, "1930"; Fish and Roses, "Checkered Past"; Details at Eleven, "Music for Secretaries"; Skeleton Crew, "The Sparrow Song" (Frith); Mark Dery, "Banging Khruschev's Shoe"; Charles K. Noyes, "Mouse and Ermine"; Locus Solus, "Wrap Backwards and the Usual Snowflakes/Beda Fomm"; David Fulton, "Border Patrol"; David Garland, "The Golden Years"; Bump, "Spies in Space/Beer in My Bed"; Chris Vine, "Alignment"; Carbon, "Cormorant"; Bosho, "Boy Yaca"; The Scene Is Now, "Lullaby Stomp/Cool Pool"; H/M/D, "Runner"; Robert Previte, "Requiem for Vincent." Edited by Elliott Sharp, this collection clearly shows the spillover of people and styles from "New Music" to new-music and art-rock and no-wave bands in what may be called the downtown style: composer/performers who play gigs at bars and also at new-music festivals in academia. This has been happening with the American avant-garde since Ives played ragtime in East Village bars, or with any composer who is familiar with dance and song and wants to express the conceptual and meditative flashes that occur in life. –BGT

○ **Just for the Record / LOVELY MUSIC**   1979
"Blue" Gene Tyranny plays multi-keyboard works by Robert Ashley, "Sonata" and "Trio: Christopher Columbus Crosses to the New World in the Nina, the Pinta, and the Santa Maria Using Only Dead Reckoning and a Crude Astrolabe"; John Bischoff, "Rendezvous"; Phil Harmonic, "Timing"; and Paul DeMarinis, "Great Masters of Melody."–BGT

○ **Just Intonation / TELLUS**
Just intonation is any tuning system in which all of the intervals can be represented by whole-number ratios, with a strong preference for simple ratios. This album contains pieces radically different from each other but all aiming for this "maximum clarity" tuning: Harry Partch, "O Frabjous Day! (The Jabberwock)" (1954); Ralph David Hill, "Malachite"; Carola B. Anderson, "Shibboleth" (1985); David Hykes, "Opening Kyrie"; Lou Harrison, "A Phrase for Arion's Leap" (1974); Jon Catler, "Sleeping Beauty (excerpt) Queen of the Ogres"; David Canright, "Rosier Sands," using Partch instruments; David B. Doty, "Fake Greek Music" (1985); John Bischoff, Jim Horton, and Tim Perkis, "The League of Automatic Music Composers" (1980); Ben Johnston, "Toccata for Violoncello"; Erling Wold, "Tune for Lynn Murdock #2"; Susan Norris, "Medley: Untitled Irish Jig, Untitled Swedish Waltz"; James Tenney, "Septet for Electric Guitars"; Larry Polansky, "Movement for Andrea Smith (My Funny Valentine for Just String Quartet)"; Alexis Alrich, "Didymus Set (Tango)," for troubadour harp; Jody Diamond, "In That Bright World." –BGT

○ **LCO 8 (London Chamber Orchestra) "Minimalist" / VIRGIN**   1990
A very well played, good overview of some of the better-known pattern ("minimalist") composers. Includes John Adams, "Shaker Loops"; Philip Glass, "Facades" and "Company"; Steve Reich, "Eight Lines"; and Dave Heath, "The Frontier" (1956). –BGT

Les Ondes Martenots (50th Anniversary) / PRODUCTIONS DISQUES ADES   1980
Les Ondes Martenots (50th anniversary of the Ondes Martenot electronic keyboard). Includes classic and newer works for one to six Ondes Martenots, sometimes with piano. The Ondes Martenot (the "Martenot Waves"), somewhat patterned after the Russian Theremin, was an early electronic-music instrument that was first presented publicly in May 1928 at the Parisian Opera House by its inventor, Maurice Martenot. This two-CD collection contains "Fête des belles eaux (Holiday of the Beautiful Waters)," 1937; Darius Milhaud, "Suite for Ondes Martenot and Piano" (1933); André Jolivet, "3 Poèmes" (1935); and Roger Tessier, "Hexade" (1973). –BGT

○ **Life Is a Killer / GIORNO POETRY SYSTEMS**   1982
A Dial-A-Poem Poets life-centering collection of different ensembles of speakers with and without instrumental music; works by Amiri Baraka, William S. Burroughs, Jim Carroll, Jayne Cortez, the Four Horsemen (Nichol, Steve McCaffery, Paul Dutton, Rafael Barreto Rivera), John Giorno, Brion Gysin, Rose Lesniak, and Ned Sublette. –BGT

Live Electronic Music Improvised / MAINSTREAM
Two influential, late-60s, European-based, live-electronic bands. Includes M.E.V. (Musica Electronica Viva), based in Rome with members Alan Bryant, Alvin Curran, Frederic Rzewski, Richard Titelbaum, and Ivan Vandoor; and A.M.M., based in London, with members Cornelius Cardew, Lou Gare, Christopher Hobbs, Eddie Prevost, and Keith Rowe. –BGT

○ **Lovely Little Records / LOVELY MUSIC**   1980
Box of six 7-inch discs with booklet. Includes John Bischoff, "Silhouette" (1979) and "The League of Automatic Music Composers: Recording, December 17, 1978"; Paul DeMarinis, "If God Were Alive (And He Is) You Could Reach Him by Telephone" and "Forest Booties"; Phil Harmonic, "Phil Harmonic's Greatest Hits" and "WPA/Composite Mix: John Bischoff and Phil Harmonic"; Frankie Mann, "I Was a Hero (from the Mayan Debutante Revue)" and "How to Be Very Very Popular"; Maggi Payne, "Lunar Disk" and "Lunar Earthrise"; "Blue" Gene Tyranny, "Harvey Milk (Portrait) Part I: The Action; Part II: The Feeling." –BGT

Mallets Hands Sticks and Drums / O. O. DISCS   1992
With Brian Johnson, Jan Williams, and drummers from Africa, Cuba, and Brazil. "Channeled violence ... perceptual minimalism full of uncontrollable variations" (*Village Voice*). Features the cut "Snare for Camus." Recorded in Studio B (the Toscanini studio) at Radio City Music Hall. Wild! –BGT

○ **Guy Klucevsek (accordion) / CRI**   1992
A marvelous, uplifting concert of twisted tunes and new uses for the "free bass accordion": Mary Ellen Childs, "Oa Poa Polka," charming and Pygmy-music-like; Anthony Coleman, "Below 14th Street, Above 125th Street," plaintive; Rolf Groesbeck, "Polka 1," full of tone-clustering and conjuring; Aaron Kernis, "Phantom Polka," a cinematic joke (Kernis is also a composer of some brilliant orchestral music; watch for future recordings); John King, "All Together Now" (hymn-based); Guy Klucevsek, "Samba D Hiccup" and the lovely "An Air of Gathering Pipers"; Christian Marclay, "Ping Pong Polka," with wildly modulated record collage; Lois Vierk, "Manhattan Cascade"; John Zorn, the humorous "Road Runner." –BGT

○ **Music from Mills / MILLS COLLEGE**   1986
A three-CD centennial anthology produced and compiled at the Center for Contemporary Music at Mills College: Lou Harrison, "Sonata no. 2," for cembalo; Terry Riley, "The Ethereal Time Shadow (excerpt)"; Luciano Berio, "Chamber Music"; Dave Brubeck, "Summer Song"; David Rosenboom,

"In the Beginning: Étude 1 (Trombones)"; Robert Ashley, "Flying Saucer Dialogue from the Opera *Atalanta* (Acts of God)"; Anthony Braxton, "Composition no. 62 (+30 +96)"; David Behrman, "Interspecies Smalltalk, Part 2 (excerpt)"; Elinor Armer, "Thaw"; Steve Reich, "Melodica"; Maggi Payne, "Subterranean Network (excerpt)"; Darius Milhaud, "Segoviana"; Pauline Oliveros, "Alien Bog (excerpt)"; Anthony Gnazzo, "Asparagas"; Katrina Krimsky, "Apparitions"; Larry Polansky, "Four Voice Cannon #3"; Pandit Pran Nath, "Dira Dira Ta Na in Raga Bhairavi (excerpt)"; Janice Giteck, "Breathing Songs from a Turning Sky (excerpt)"; "Blue" Gene Tyranny, "Remembering"; Ramon Sender, "Audition (excerpt)"; and an excerpt from Morton Subotnick's "The Key to Songs." –BGT

○ **Music from the ONCE Festival / ADVANCE**   1966
The only recording of compositions from this legendary festival, which presented the newest in avant-garde music, film, and dance from 1961 to 1968. Includes Gordon Mumma, "Music from the Venezia Space Theater"; Robert Ashley, "Crazy Horse Symphony"; George Cacioppo, "Time on Time in Miracles"; Donald Scarvarda, "Landscape Journey." –BGT

○ **Music with Memory / TELLUS**
A collection of works by composers whose instruments are microcomputers. Includes Nicolas Collins, "Devil's Music" (1985); John Driscoll, "Stall" (1981, excerpt), with Phil Edelstein and Peter Labiak's rotating robotic loudspeaker system; Brenda Hutchison, "Interlude from Voices of Reason" (1984); Ron Kuivila, "Parodicals" and "Cannon Y for C.N." (1985); and Paul DeMarinis, "Eenie Meenie Chillie Beenie" (1983) and "Yellow Yankee" (1983). –BGT

Musica Futurista / CRAMPS   1991
A terrific two-CD collection of early soundtext, piano, radio, and noise pieces from the Italian futurists (1913-1933), with Italian and English liner notes. Includes works by Luigi Russolo, Filippo Marinetti, A. Casella, Virgilio Mortari, Franco Casavola, Francesco Pratella, and Daniele Napoletano. –BGT

Musik um dem Futurismas (Akademie der Künste) / ACADEMY OF THE ARTS, BERLIN
More futuristic music — *Music at the Time of Futurism* — from 1915 to 1925, including Russian, French, and German composers influenced by this Italian movement: Arthur V. Lourie, "Formes en l'air - à Pablo Picasso (Formes in the Air, to Pablo Picasso)," 1915; Nicholas Obouchove, "Le temple est mesuré - l'espirit est incarné (The Temple is Measured - The Spirit Is Incarnate)," "Je t'attendrai (I Will Wait for You)," 1913, and "Le Sang! (The Blood!)," 1918; Hans-Jürgen von der Wense, "Musik für Klavier, op. 1" (1916), "Ich hatt einen Kameraden - Groteske (I Had a Comrade - A Grotesque)," 1919, and "Musik für Klarinette, Klavier, und freihangendes Blechsieb (Music for Clarinet, Piano, and Free-Hanging Perforated Sheet Metal)," 1919; Ivan Wyschnegradsky, "Streichquartett, op. 13 in Vierteltoenen (String Quartet, op. 13 in Quarter-Tones)," 1925); Francesco Baililla Pratella, "Fragmente aus der Oper *L'aviatore Dro* (Fragments from the Opera *Dro the Aviator*)," 1914; Antonio Russolo, "La Pioggia (The Rain)." –BGT

○ **Musique Expérimentale / DISQUES**
Musique Expérimentale - Groupe de Recherches Musicales de la R.T.F. ("Experimental Musics from the Musical Research Group of the French Radio-Television"). An exquisite collection of musique concrète pieces: François-Bernard Maché, "Volumes" (1960), for 12-track tape and a chamber orchestra consisting of seven trombones, two pianos, and two percussionists (cosmic sounds of great import on the distant horizon slowly approaching and suddenly disappearing, large rattlings and small ones like crickets, breaking, impacting percussion); Romuald Vandelle, "Crucifixion" (excerpts; based on a poem by Poe spoken by a fragmented voice — gloomy and terrifying); Michel Philippot, "The surreal, elegant Ambiance II (Toast Funèbre)," for woman's spoken voice and tape, based on a Mallarmé text; Luc Ferrari, "Tautologos II," one of the best musique concrète compositions, masses of

speech-inflected, tape-manipulated sounds like conversations among alien beings, bizarre glass-like drones caused by rotating metal resonators on piano strings, humorous mobiles of sounds combining and re-combining, a soundtrack to stimulate the imagination; André Boucourechliev, "Texte II" (1953), described as "a form in movement" employing "controlled chance" and recorded on two tapes to be played simultaneously on two tape recorders so that coincidences of the mono tracks are always variable from performance to performance — an astonishingly rich palette of sounds for such an early piece. –BGT

Neue Chormusik / WERGO   1985
Neue Chormusik - Vol. 3 ("New Music for Chorus") is performed by the Schola Cantorum Stuttgart and conducted by Cytus Gottwald. Includes Brian Ferneyhough (b 1943), "Time and Motion Study III" (1974-1975), for 16 voices, percussion, and electronics; and excellent performances of compositions by Mahler, Aribert Reimann (b 1963), Messiaen, Ligeti, Alban Berg, and Maurice Ravel. Vol. 1 in this series contains works by Dieter Schnebel (composer of "Für Stimmen ... Missa Est" ["For Voices ... Missa Est]," 1956-1958, 1964-1968, with movements entitled "dt 31," "AMN," and "! (Madrasha II)"; and "Atemzüge (Respirations)" for voices; also works by Hans Otte, Bussotti, Ligeti, Pousseur, Webern, and Nono. Vol. II includes works by Hans Holliger, Schnebel, Pendrecki, and Cerha. –BGT

New American Music - vol. 4 / FOLKWAYS   1975
An interesting collection of new compositions using a variety of compositional techniques and sound sources: Gordon Mumma, "Cybersonic Cantilevers," live electro-acoustic performance; Joel Chadabe, "Echoes," interactive computer music with percussionist; V. Ussachevsky, "Conflict," for voice plus electronics; Noa Ain, "Used to Call Me Sadness," a text-sound piece with violin accompaniment; Ann McMillan, "Carrefours," and "Whale" (modified whale sounds). –BGT

New Music Articles Magazine - Cassette 1 / FROG PEAK
Another great source for emerging new composers and music. Improvised work and computer-controlled piano pieces by Warren Burt, Brian Parish, David Hurst, Graeme Gerrard, John Jenkins, Jon Rose, Alistair Riddell, and Essendon Airport. –BGT

New Music Articles Magazine - Cassette 2 / FROG PEAK
Vocal, electronic, and chamber music by Chris Mann, Ron Nagorcka, Anti Music, Mark Pollard, John Gillies, Ernie Althoff, Les Gilbert, and Rainer Linz. –BGT

New Music Articles Magazine - Cassette 3 / FROG PEAK
Jon Rose and Martin Wesley-Smith, Richard Vella, Rik Rue, John Oswald, Makers of the Dead, Travel Fast, Japanese Coke Ads, and the Australian Bicentennial Authority. –BGT

New Music Articles Magazine - Cassette 4 / FROG PEAK
Music by women composers, including solo and chamber compositions, electronic and computer music, installations, and improvised works by Jennifer Fowler, Ros Bandt, Sarah Hopkins, Annea Lockwood, Caroline Wilkins, Vineta Lagazdina, and others. –BGT

New Music Articles Magazine - Cassette 5 / FROG PEAK
Vocal, instrumental, and electronic work by Chris Mann, Rainer Light, SWSW THRGHT, Syd Clayton, Amanda Stewart, Ernie Althoff, Daniel Kahans, Caroline Wilkins, John Gillies and Greg Hooper, and Densil Cabrera. –BGT

New Music Articles Magazine - Cassette 6 / FROG PEAK
Computer and computer-assisted music by Greg Schiemer, David Hurst, Alistair Riddell, Warren Burt, Mark Randolph, Cindy John, Amanda Baker, and Graeme Gerrard. –BGT

New Music Articles Magazine - Cassette 7 / FROG PEAK
Music accompanying the "history" issue. Performance and radio pieces, environmental composition, music theater, and more by Greg Schiemer, Jon Rose, Ron Nagorcka, Helen Gifford, Ernie Gallagher, Percy Grainger. –BGT

New Music China / TELLUS
Contains new popular music, folk music, and new-music: Fred Houn, "I Wor Kuen" (The Boxers), from *Bamboo That*

Snaps Back; Chen Yi, "Xie Zi'/Ge Gan-Ru" (Yi Feng, Ancient Wind), for solo cello; Zhou Long, "Kong Gu Liu Shui (Valley Stream)," for traditional ensemble; Wu Wen Guang, "Liu Shui (Flowing Water)," for guqin (ancient seven-string zither); Tan Dun, "Plucking Instruments Suite" (excerpt); R. I. P. Hayman, "Nightsongs," a score from a film about immigrant life in Chinatown; Jing Jing Luo, "Monologue Part 1" (Jing Jing Luo also writes for large orchestra and traditional Chinese ensembles). –BGT

○ **New Music for Media / 1750 ARCH STREET** 1977
New Music for Electronic and Recorded Media is a great collection of music by contemporary women composers writing from 1938 to 1977. Includes a realization of Johanna Beyer's "Music of the Spheres" (1938); Annea Lockwood, "World Rhythms"; Pauline Oliveros, "Bye Bye Butterfly" (1965); Laurie Spiegel, "Appalachian Grove I"; Megan Roberts, "I Could Sit Here All Day"; Ruth Anderson, "Points"; Laurie Anderson, "New York Social Life," "Time to Go," and "For Diego." –BGT

New Music from South America for Chamber Orchestra / MAINSTREAM 1973
Music by Oscar Bazan (b 1936, Argentina), Marlos Nobre (b 1939, Brazil), Cesar Bolanos (Peru), Gerardo Gandini (b 1936, Argentina), Manuel Enriquez (b 1926, Mexico), and Alcides Lanza (b 1929, Argentina). –BGT

☆ **New Sounds ... / COLUMBIA ODYSSEY** 1968
New Sounds in Electronic Music is one of the most beautifully pressed vinyls of electronic music. It contains three important works: Steve Reich, "Come Out"; Richard Maxfield, "Night Music"; Pauline Oliveros, "I of IV." –BGT

Organic Oboe / O. O. DISCS 1992
Wonderful performances by Joseph Celli in this historic recording reissued on CD. Includes the only American release of Stockhausen's "Spiral" (1968) for soloist on shortwave radio and other instruments. Other pieces: Celli, "Sky: S for J" (1976); Elliott Schwartz, "Extended Oboe" (1973-1974), for oboe and electronic tape; Malcolm Goldstein, "A Summoning of Focus" (1977), for wind instrument. –BGT

○ **Panorama Électronique / MERCURY LIMELIGHT** 1968
Classic pure electronic and musique concrète compositions from studios in Paris and Cologne. Includes Pierre Henry, "Entite"; György Ligeti, "Artikulation"; Herbert Eimert, "Selection I"; Mauricio Kagel, "Transition I"; André Boucourechliev, "Texte I"; and Henri Pousseur, "Scambi." –BGT

○ **Paul Zukofsky, Violin / CP 2 RECORDINGS**
Four beautifully played works: Giacinto Scelsi, "Anahit"; Iannis Xenakis, "Mikka" (1972) and "Mikka 'S'" (1975); and Philip Glass, "Strung Out" (1967). –BGT

Pioneers of Electronic Music / CRI 1991
Contains material originally released on Desto DC-6466, CRI 612, and SD 268 — the Columbia/Princeton sound from 1952 to 1971 in compositions by Vladimir Ussachevsky, Otto Luening (b 1900), Pril Smiley, Bulent Arel, Mario Davidovsky, Alice Shields. Recommended cuts: "Incantation" by Luening and Ussachevsky, "Stereo Electronic Music" by Arel. –BGT

Portraits / NEW ALBION 1986
A good sampler. Excerpts from Ingram Marshall, "Fog Tropes"; Somei Satoh, "Birds in Warped Time"; Paul Dresher, "Channels Passing"; Stephen Scott, "Rainbows"; Daniel Lentz, "O-KE-WA"; John Adams, "Light over Water." –BGT

Pulse: The New Music Consort / NEW WORLD 1990
A great collection, with some classic percussion music: John Cage and Lou Harrison, "Double Music" (1941); John Cage's rhythmically sophisticated "Second Construction" (1940) and jazzy "Third Construction" (1941); Henry Cowell, "Pulse" (1939), for six percussionists; Harvey Sollberger, "The Two and the One" (1972); and Lukas Foss, "Percussion Quartet" (1983). –BGT

Response: Electronic Music from Norway / MERCURY LIMELIGHT 1967
A mid-60s collection: Arne Nordheim, "Epitaffio for Orchestra

and Tape" and "Response I"; Alfred Janson, "Canon for Chamber Orchestra and Tape"; and the outstanding "Galaxy for Three Electric Guitars in Quarter-Tones," by Björn Fongaard. –BGT

Severino Gazzelloni with Aloys Kontarsky / TIME 196?
Lovely performances of solo-flute pieces: Franco Evangelisti, "Proporzioni"; Luciano Berio, "Sequenza"; Yoritsune Matsudaira, "Somaksah," for flute and piano; Niccolo Castiglioni, "Gymel"; Olivier Messiaen, "Merles Noir"; and Bruno Maderna, "Honeyreves." –BGT

○ **Site-Less Sounds / TELLUS**
Powerful personal and political visions: Shelley Hirsch, "#39"; Gregory Whitehead, "How to Pronounce 'Prosthesis'," "M is for the Million Things," and "This Is Not a Test"; David Moss, "Conjure"; Jacki Apple, Keith Antar Mason, Linda Albertano, Akilah Nayo Oliver, "Redefining Democracy in America: Episodes in Black and White"; David Wojnarowicz and Ben Neill, "The Collapse of the Illusory One-Tribe Nation from ITSOFOMO (In the Shadow of Forward Motion)"; Constance DeJong with Brenda Hutchinson, "Vanishing Act." Highly recommended. –BGT

Sleepers / FINNADAR 1985
Available from Deep Listening Publications, eight takes on the lullaby: Doris Hays, "Hush"; Annea Lockwood, "Malolo"; Ilhan Mimaroglu, "Sleepsong for Sleepers"; Daniel Goode, "The Red and White Cows"; Tom Johnson "Lullaby"; Pauline Oliveros, "Lullaby for Daisy Pauline" (a choral piece); Alison Knowles, "Mantra for Jessie (Some Help in Sleeping)," for speaker with shaker; Ann Silsbee, "Go Gentle," for three flutes. –BGT

○ **The Sonic Arts Union / MAINSTREAM** 1970
The famous American new-music group; performances of Alvin Lucier, "Vespers" (1968), for echolocation devices; Robert Ashley, "Purposeful Lady Slow Afternoon"; David Behrman, "Runthrough"; Gordon Mumma, "Hornpipe" (1967). –BGT

○ **Sonic Encounters / MODE** 1990
An interesting collection demonstrating the mutual effects of Asian and American aesthetics; contains first recordings of two John Cage pieces: "Primitive" (1942) and "In the Name of the Holocaust" (1942), for prepared piano. Also contains Alan Hovhaness, "Orbit #2" (1952) and "Jhala" (1952); George Crumb, "Five Pieces for Piano" (1962); Somei Satoh, "Cosmic Womb" (1975), for two pianos with digital delay; Ge Gan-Ru, "Gu Yue" (1986, premiere recording). With Margaret Leng Tan (piano). –BGT

○ **Soundviews - Vol. 1 (Sources) / WHAT NEXT?** 1990
An audio magazine with cassette and booklet, containing excerpts from Annea Lockwood, "A Sound Map of the Hudson River" and "Interview"; Mary and Bill Buchen, "Harmonic Compass"; Stephan Von Huene, "Totem Tone #2"; Karen McPherson, "A Pond at Dusk"; Julius, "Music in the Air"; Hildegard Westerkamp, "Interview" and "A Walk through the City"; Andrej Zdravic, "Cicadas Head Dance"; Bill Fontana, "Landscape Sculpture with Foghorns"; Richard Lerman, "Interview" and "Brass Screen and Bronze Screen"; Brigitta Bertoia, "Interview"; Harry Bertoia, "Energizing"; Jim Pomeroy, "Mozart's Moog"; Doug Hollis, "Interview" and "A Sound Garden"; Dr. Frederick Scarf, "Voyager II; Uranus Fly By"; David Behrman and George Lewis, "Installation for Parc de la Villette"; Snapshot, "Evening Sounds in Albion, Michigan"; Gordon Monahan, "Speaker Swinging"; Charlemagne Palestine, "Carillon Concert"; Bernard Baschet, Michel Deneuve, and Alain Dumont, "Extrait de Resurgence"; Paul Panhuysen and Johan Goedhart, "Jan Huygens I"; Liz Phillips, "Interview" and "Windspun for Minneapolis"; Leif Brush, "Teleconstructs III"; Ron Konzak, "Interview" and "Giant Puget Sound Windharp"; Bart Hopkins, "Disorderly Tumbling Forth"; Susan Stone, "House with a View"; Jeffrey Bartone, "Sky Concert"; Ellen Fullman "Immigration"; Pauline Oliveros, Linda Montano, Tom Jaremba, and children, "No More Fear"; Carl Stone, "Kuk II Kwan"; John Cage, "Interview"; Robert Rutman, "Something to Reflect the

Misery of Our World Today"; Ellen Zweig, "She Traveled the Landscape"; Peter Richards, "Wave Organ"; Paul DeMarinis and David Behrman, "Sound Fountain"; Alvin Curran, "Maritime Rites"; Tony Schwartz, "Factory, Whistle Carols." Whew ... almost an entire new-music festival on one cassette. This is a very well organized collection, especially interesting for its many sound-installation pieces rarely issued on recordings. –BGT

○ **Source Magazine - Issue 4 / SOURCE MAGAZINE**
Two 10-inch discs. Record no. 1 contains Robert Ashley, "The Wolfman," and David Behrman, "Wave Train." Record no. 2 contains Larry Austin, "Accidents," and Allan Bryant, "Pitch Out." A total of six issues were published bi-annually from 1967 to 1969. This magazine presented the most significant collection of scores, interviews, and commentary on new-music since the *New Music Quarterly* (1927-1958; recordings issued 1934-1949; refer to *Henry Cowell's New Music 1925-1936* by Rita Mead, UMI Research Press 1981). –BGT

○ **String Quartets / DGG**
Fundamental statements of new ideas about the string-quartet form by composers Cage, Lutoslawski, Pendrecki and Mayuzumi. Includes sensitive performances by the LaSalle Quartet. –BGT

○ **Tango / TELLUS**
Retakes on the idea and spirit of the tango. Includes works by Carlos Gardel, David Garland with Cinnie Cole and Zeena Parkins, Chris DeBlasio, Keith Keeler, B. Hutchinson with Gerry Lindahl, A. Tomlinson, Elodie Lauten, Jo Basile and Orchestra, "Blue" Gene Tyranny, Molly Elder, Mathew Nash, Christopher Berg, Fast Forward, and Mader. –BGT

☆ **Thomas Buckner, Full Spectrum Voice / LOVELY MUSIC**
An edition of premiere inspirations, beautifully sung, for voice, instruments, and electronics. Includes Robert Ashley, "Odalisque"; Jon Gibson, "Rainforest/Brazil (He Was Not Disappointed)"; Nils Vigeland, "March, Hymn and Waltz"; Peter Gena, "Mother Jones"; Annea Lockwood, "Night and Fog"; and Roscoe Mitchell, "because it's," "this," and "dim" — three songs on poems of e.e. cummings. –BGT

○ **Upper Air Observation / LOVELY MUSIC** 1991
Selections: Nils Vigeland, "Vara" (1979); Alvin Lucier, "Self Portrait" (1979/1990); Yasunao Tone, "Trio for Flute Player" and "Lyrictron"; Barbara Held, "Upper Air Observation." Remarkable musicality on originally commissioned works, producing new possibilities for flute and electronics. Lucier's "Self-Portrait" uses a wind anemometer activated by streams of air from the flutist's lips, which causes a light beamed through its blades to gradually reveal parts of the player's body. Haiku poems are generated by a computer that detects the pitches of the flute in Yasunao Tone's beautiful "Lyrictron." Held's "Upper Air Observation" uses recordings of a radio sonde weather balloon launching and other sounds. With Barbara Held (flute). –BGT

○ **Utopia Americana / NEW TONE** 1992
A wonderful view of what is "American" in contemporary American Music from an Italian producer's perspective. This is an interesting collection of new recordings and reissues of tracks from out-of-print or hard-to-get vinyls containing primarily rhythm-based music and soundtext rhythms from ordinary speech (Ginsberg's works), with some dreamy electronic music by Pauline Oliveros and solo jazz by Steve Lacy. Nice cover photo of Joey's Navajo Cafe and Dining Room, framed by the grills of several pickup trucks parked outside. Contains: Allen Ginsberg, "Hum Bomb" (1992) and "Father Death Blues"; Steve Reich, "Music for 18 Musicians" (live, 1976); Michael Galasso, "Baroque" (live, 1992); Ben Neill, "Bal"; John Cage, "Third Construction" (from a 1983 Italian studio recording); David Behrman, "A Traveler's Dream Journal (EWR-LAX)" (1992); Pauline Oliveros, "A Woman Sees How the World Goes with No Eyes" (from the Lovely Music LCD 1903, Crone Music); Steve Lacy, "Pannonica"; John Zorn and Andrea Centazzo, "First Environment for Sextet" (recorded in New York, WKCR Radio, 1978, from "Environment for Sextet," Ictus 0017). –BGT

Voice of the Computer / DECCA 1968
Bell Labs computer music from the 60s. Contains James Tenney, "Stochastic Quartet"; Max Mathews, "Masquerades," "Slider," and "Swan Song"; J. C. Risset, "Computer Suite from Little Boy"; J. R. Pierce, "Eight-Tone Canon." –BGT

○ **Wergo Collection: Music of Our Century / WERGO** 1988
An excellent sampler of 15 works, providing a quick taste of Henck, Cage, Ligeti, Penderecki, Henze, Stockhausen, and others. –BGT

CHILDREN'S

If children's music can be defined as musically amplifying thoughts, ideas, and concepts in young minds (minds that are themselves expanding at a great rate) then the first children's music may have been the initial fetal sounds heard by the first well-developed human womb-dweller. Perhaps a mother's sonorous voice. Certainly a mother's heartbeat. Since then, music for children (and indeed families) has developed right along with the rest of the human condition. But what, you may rightly ask, makes some of this music more worthy than the rest? How does one decide what to expose a child to (and yourself — over and over again) and what to leave alone?

There seem to be many answers to that question — almost as many as there are people to answer. Here, however, are some general thoughts that seem to recur as criteria to use in selecting music and related products for children:

1. Try to find age-appropriate music for your child. The 2-year-old and the 4-year-old are ships passing in the night, so different are they in the cumulative milestones of child development.

2. As a general rule, steer clear of the grossly exploitive. Though children's music has come a long, long way, there are still marketers whose sole thought is to get in quick, exploit at all costs, and get out. This product will almost always be evident to the individual caregiver if he/she simply looks and listens. Sometimes, purely exploitive music is the kids' market "flavor of the month" and will be asked for in plain terms by a child. If for no other reason, it seems worth resisting because of the aural torture you, the caregiver, can save yourself.

3. Under no circumstances purchase a recording that "looks down its nose" at children. Kids know it instantly and they'll turn off. There is no subject too sophisticated for a child to grasp on some level. Challenge the children a little. They'll love it.

4. The great children's music, that which will last and grow, is almost always that which has some appeal to big people as well as little people. "Clever" is a good key word here. So is "melody." So is "non-cutesy."

5. If you can help it, don't buy purely by price. The budget stuff may be good, but it also may be garbage.

6. If you're not sure about an artist or a recording, don't assume the record store clerk knows any more than you do. He or she may know (especially if it's a small, owner-operated retailer) about the world of children's music, but odds aren't good. If possible, listen to some of the music yourself. Make your own judgments. Awards won by particular recordings (*Parent's* Choice, American Library Association, Notable Recording, etc.) will pretty much guarantee the recording isn't junk, but unfortunately it is no guarantee beyond that.

7. Go with your children to concerts and other events that expose them and you to children's music. You'll find out fast what they really like.

8. Make a commitment to use music to expand your children, not simply to placate; to teach, not just babysit; to be proactive, not to create mini-couch potatoes. This requires some forethought and the use of suggestions 1-7, but if you're truly into parenting, the rewards outweigh the effort a thousandfold.

9. Don't get discouraged. You'll find the right recording.

10. It's OK to admit you really like this music too.

That brings us to the listings. We've tried to be as inclusive as possible, but the children's audio field is growing so rapidly right now that I apologize in advance for any omissions. We'll get you next time. Many of the artists putting out the best audio are not nationally known or released. To that end, we've done the best we could to provide a list of sources at the chapter's end to allow access by the reader to all the music we've run into. A few artists have not been reachable, but we've given all the information we had.

The video section is incomplete. Some video releasing companies didn't respond to our questionnaire, some did so partially. Further, much children's video is not essentially musical. We used our best judgment. Again, the second edition will exhibit a higher percentage of the total.

Finally, childhood and parenthood will be made richer, more texturally varied, and — last but not least — more fun if a dose of children's and family music is added. The big people and little people will know each other better, and both will benefit from the knowing.

Our overall goal is to make "totally adult" an obsolete concept.

— Bob Hinkle

AFRICAN SONGS & RHYTHMS

○ **African Songs & Rhythms / SMITHSONIAN-FOLKWAYS**
Properly set up by parent or caregiver, these can be exciting as well as eye-opening. It's music every child, regardless of culture, should know something about. Ages 4-10. –BH

ALICE IN WONDERLAND

☆ **Alice in Wonderland - Story/Songs / DISNEY**
This classic belongs in your collection. Boys and girls 3-6. –BH

AN AMERICAN TAIL

○ **A Musical Adventure with Fivel / MCA**
A good story and OK music. Kids seem to like these characters. Ages 3-6. –BH

ANNIE & THE NATURAL WONDER BAND

○ **The Honeybee Show / CASTLE OF DREAMS**
Environmentally oriented kid pop. Well-meaning but not there yet. A bit too silly and doesn't assume enough of kids. Ages 2-4.–BH
Wet & Wild: Wonders of Water / CASTLE OF DREAMS

BRENDA WONG AOKI

○ **Dreams and Illusions / ROUNDER**
Dreams and Illusions - Tales of the Pacific Rim has good artistic potential, largely unrealized. Ages 2-5. –BH

ARIEL

○ **Ariel & the Mysterious World Above / DISNEY**
Ariel & the Secret Grotto / DISNEY
For ages 3-5. –BH

ARISTOCATS

○ **Aristocats - Story/Songs / DISNEY / BB 137**
One of the better story soundtracks in Disney's catalog for ages 3-6. –BH

LOUIS ARMSTRONG

☆ **Disney Songs the Satchmo Way / DISNEY**
Satchmo and kids are a wonderful mix. Ages 3-10. –BH

LINDA ARNOLD

Happiness Cake / A&M
The Rainbow Palace / A&M
Peppermint Wings / A&M
○ **Make Believe / A&M**   1986
A top-notch performer for younger children. Her recordings are consistently good. Ages 3-5. –BH

AUDIO ALL STARS

● **Boomer Esiason - Story and Songs / DISNEY**
These three are potential role models. The voices are surprisingly good. The stories are OK. This is for older children, ages 6-10. –BH
○ **Isiah Thomas - Story and Songs / DISNEY**
For ages 6-10. –BH
○ **Joe Montana - Story and Songs / DISNEY**
For ages 6-10. –BH

BABY GAMES

○ **Baby Games / KIMBO**
For very young children. This is very basic, not particularly exciting or original. Ages 2-4. –BH

THE BABY SITTERS

○ **The Best of the Baby Sitters / VANGUARD**   1975
Former Weaver Lee Hays and then-future acting star Alan Arkin led this folk quartet, whose music is a kind of children's version of the Weavers. They are playing originals, Woody Guthrie songs, and traditional material for an audience ideally aged from one to five. –WR

BABYSONGS

○ **John Lithgow's Kid-Size Concert / MEDIA HOME ENT.**
Lithgow's warmth of personality and sincere love of children shine through on this minimal production. Ages 3-5. –BH
More Babysongs / HIGH TOP
For ages 2-4. –BH
Even More Babysongs / MEDIA HOME ENT.
For ages 2-4. –BH
Turn on the Music / MEDIA HOME ENT.
For ages 2-4. –BH

BAMBI

☆ **Bambi - Story/Songs / DISNEY**
Bambi is virtually a metaphor for some of the fears and joys of childhood. A must, for 4- to 6-year-olds especially. A classic. Should be seen and heard by every child. Ages 3-10. –BH

BANANA SLUG STRING BAND

○ **Songs for the Earth / MUSIC FOR LITTLE PEOPLE**
Environmentally correct silliness plus great bluegrass music, especially for 5- to 6-year-olds. Ages 5-7. –BH
Adventures ... / MUSIC FOR LITTLE PEOPLE
Adventures on the Air Cycle. For ages 5-7. –BH
Slugs at Sea / MUSIC FOR LITTLE PEOPLE
For ages 4-7. –BH
Dirt Made My Lunch / MUSIC FOR LITTLE PEOPLE
For ages 4-7. –BH

BARBIE

○ **Barbie - The Look / RHINO-RINCON**   1991
Good pop songs easily understood. The perennial favorite goes rock & roll. Ages 2-9. –BH

DAVID BARNETT & RIC LOUCHARD

○ **Winter Light / MUSIC FOR LITTLE PEOPLE**

BAROLK FOLK

○ **Come Out to Play / MUSIC FOR LITTLE PEOPLE**
Girls & Boys Come Out to Play has wonderful interactive music. Ages 3-7. –BH

JOANIE BARTELS

● **Lullaby Magic 1 / DISCOVERY**
Joanie's recordings are called the *Magic Series*. They are consistently good for young children. Joanie is a gentle person but also has enthusiasm. *Lullaby Magic 1* and *2* are both excellent. –BH
Morning Magic / DISCOVERY
For ages 2-5. –BH
Lullaby Magic 2 / DISCOVERY
For ages 2-5. –BH
Travelin' Magic / DISCOVERY
For ages 2-6. –BH
○ **Sillytime Magic / DISCOVERY**
One of Joanie's most popular. Recommended for ages 2-6. –BH
Bathtime Magic / DISCOVERY
For ages 2-4. –BH
Christmas Magic / DISCOVERY
For ages 2-6. –BH
○ **Dancin' Magic / DISCOVERY**
A good selection of well-arranged rock and pop songs. For ages 2-5. –BH

BEAN BAG ACTIVITIES

○ **Bean Bag Activities (Games Dances & Songs) / KIMBO**
For ages 2-4. –BH

BEAN BAG FUN

○ **Bean Bag Fun - Original Music and Sing Along / KIMBO**
For ages 2-4. –BH

BEAUTY AND THE BEAST

☆ **Beauty and the Beast - Story and Songs / DISNEY**
The Disney classic. Ages 3-6. –BH

SANDRA BEECH

○ **Yes, I Can / CHILDREN'S GROUP**
Sandra specializes in positive childhood values, with an

emphasis on self-esteem. Productionwise and vocally, not up to current standards, but there's much charm for younger children. Ages 3-6. –BH

Sidewalk Shuffle / CHILDREN'S GROUP
For ages 3-6. –BH
Inch by Inch / CHILDREN'S GROUP
For ages 3-6. –BH
Chickery Chick / CHILDREN'S GROUP
For ages 3-5. –BH

ANDY BELLING

○ **Imagine That! / RHINO-RINCON**
For ages 3-7. –BH

TALE OF BENJAMIN BUNNY

Story Cassette / BUMBLEBEEZ
For ages 3-6. –BH

GLENN BENNETT

○ **Let's Go on Safari / ZOOM EXPRESS**
Glenn is one of the great treasures of children's entertainment. Clever, funny rock & roll for early and middle childhood. Glenn refuses not to be loved. Ages 3-10. –BH
○ **I Must Be Growing / ZOOM EXPRESS**
More clever Glenn songs with good, clever pop arrangements and great vocals. Ages 3-10. –BH
★ **I Like My Music with a Beat / ZOOM EXPRESS**
Glenn's latest. The second side has a wonderful piece about an orchestra, which educates kids about orchestras and about life. Excellent. Ages 3-10. –BH

MIMI BESSETTE

○ **Lullabies of Broadway / MUSIC FOR LITTLE PEOPLE**
For ages 3-9. –BH

BIG BIRD

○ **The Best of Big Bird / GOLDEN**
If you like Big Bird, you'll love this. Ages 2-6. –BH

BILLY B.

○ **Stay Cool in School / DO DREAMS**
Billy B. is a folky pop artist. Clever lyrics and pretty good recordings. Especially good on environment. –BH
Romp in the Swamp / DO DREAMS
For ages 4-7. –BH

HEATHER BISHOP

○ **Duck in New York / CHILDREN'S GROUP**
The voice is an acquired taste to these ears, and the approach a bit old-fashioned. Not bad, but not great. Ages 3-6. –BH
Purple People Eater / CHILDREN'S GROUP
Belly Button / CHILDREN'S GROUP   1982

RORY BLOCK

○ **Color Me Wild / ALACAZAM**   1990
Rory has a wonderful sense of communication with children, particularly mid-childhood. Ages 4-5. –BH

MARIA BOSTICK

○ **There's a Dinosaur … / MUSIC FOR LITTLE PEOPLE**
There's a Dinosaur in My Bed. For ages 3-5. –BH

LIONA BOYD

○ **Paddle-to-the-Sea / CHILDREN'S GROUP**
Nice, but not geared to its audience. Ages 3-6. –BH

KIM AND JERRY BRODEY

○ **Out of This World / CHILDREN'S GROUP**
Kim and Jerry communicate well. Musically they've kept up with the times, doing an exceptional job of teaching positive values, self-esteem, and the wonders of common and uncommon occurrences in childhood. They sing and blend beautifully. Ages 3-7. –BH
Simple Magic / CHILDREN'S GROUP   1984
For ages 3-7. –BH
● **Family Pie / CHILDREN'S GROUP**   1986
My personal favorite from the Brodeys. Ages 3-7. –BH

LINDA SAXON BROWN

○ **Music from the Heart / LSB**
A respectable, knowing effort — not quite successful. For ages 3-6. –BH

BRYAN AND JAYO

○ **Floating Free / LAUNCH PAD**
A local Massachusetts phenomenon. This album shows promise, but it's not there yet. Ages 3-5. –BH

RACHEL BUCHMAN

○ **Hello Rachel, Hello Children / ROUNDER**
For ages 3-5. –BH

THE BUMBLEBEEZ

Rainy Day/Sunny Day / BUMBLEBEEZ
Good young children's material. Ages 2-4. –BH

MICHAEL CAINE w/WYNTON MARSALIS

○ **King Midas & the Golden Touch / RHINO-RINCON**
Well read, with wonderful Marsalis music. My problem with many of these celebrity readers is they don't know enough about children and don't take enough time to find out. This is one. Ages 4-6. –BH

FRANK CAPPELLI

○ **Look Both Ways / A&M**
Here is some clever material that seems to be aimed at mid-childhood. Production should be better. Good vocals. His albums have a sameness. Ages 4-7. –BH
Goes on Vacation / A&M
For ages 3-7. –BH
Says Be Good / A&M
For ages 3-6. –BH
You Wanna Be a Duck / A&M   1987
For ages 3-5. –BH
Pass the Coconut / A&M   1991
For ages 3-6. –BH

CAR SONGS

○ **Car Songs / KIMBO**
For ages 2-4. –BH

CARE BEARS

○ **Care Bears to the Rescue / CARE BEAR**
If your kids are into the Care Bears, these are good. Otherwise, these will age parents by the listening. Ages 2-4. –BH
Care Bears Sing-A-Long / CARE BEAR
For ages 2-4. –BH
Care Bears Best Loved Lullabies / CARE BEAR
For ages 2-4. –BH
Care Bears Nursery Rhymes / CARE BEAR
For ages 2-4. –BH
Care Bears Christmas / CARE BEAR
For ages 2-4. –BH

CARMEN CHAMPAGNE

○ **Un Voix Pour Les Enfants / CHILDREN'S GROUP**
For ages 5-7. –BH

CHANUKAH AT HOME

○ **Chanukah at Home / ROUNDER**
A musical explanation of Chanukah, presented in a clear way with music and spirit. Ages 4-10. –BE

TOM CHAPIN

○ **Moonboat / A&M**
More clever songs and arrangements. Chapin's voice seems particularly accessible on this one. "Don't Play with Bruno" is spectacular. Ages 4-10. –BH
Mother Earth / A&M
Also good, but aimed more at the environment. Ages 4-10. –BH
☆ **Family Tree / A&M**   1988
Chapin is one of the most professional and literate children's performers. His recordings, which include "Family Tree" and "Shovlin'," are among the wittiest and most appropriate for children (and big people love them too). Tom's recordings are among the best produced for children. This one is my favorite. Ages 3-10. –BH & CR

CHARLES THE CLOWN

○ **Charles the Clown / A&M**
For ages 2-4. –BH

CHARLIE BROWN

○ **Happy Anniversary, Charlie Brown / UNI**
The understated humor, character interaction, and great jazz music make these classics. Adults love them too. Ages 4-9. –BH
A Charlie Brown Christmas / UNI
For ages 4-9. –BH
A Boy Named Charlie Brown / UNI
For ages 4-9. –BH

STEVE CHARNEY

○ **The Riddle King's Riddle Songs / STEVE CHARNEY**
Steve and his friend Harry the dummy are corny and silly, but this works for me somehow. I think it's the way Steve and Harry fence with each other. Ages 3-6. –BH

THE CHENILLE SISTERS

○ **1-2-3 for Kids / RDHS**   1990
This is a really good and musical album. Recommended. For ages 3-7. –BH

CHER w/PATRICK BALL

○ **Ugly Duckling / WINDHAM HILL**
If you can't resist Cher, why not? Not for me. Ages 4-7. –BH

A CHILD'S GIFT OF LULLABYES

○ **A Child's Gift of Lullabyes / JAB RECORDS**
A beautiful record for very young children, including lullabies with vocals on side one and singalongs without vocals on the second side. A Grammy Award winner. Ages 2-4. –BH

CHILDREN OF SELMA

○ **Children of Selma / ROUNDER**
These kids speak for themselves clearly. The production allows them to. This wonderful record is from mostly older Black kids from Alabama. It is fun and very musical, but the message communicated by the very existence of the recording is important in and of itself. Ages 4-10. –BH

CHILDREN OF THE WORLD

○ **Children of the World: Rhythmic Activities / KIMBO**
For ages 2-4. –BH

CHILDREN'S ALL-TIME FAVORITE DANCES

○ **Children's All-Time Favorite Dances / KIMBO**
For ages 2-4. –BH

CHILDREN'S FAVORITE SILLY SONGS

○ **Children's Favorite Silly Songs / DISNEY**
For ages 2-5. –BH

CHILDREN'S FAVORITES

○ **Children's Favorites 1 (Disney) / DISNEY**
Disney's collections are uneven in general. One doesn't stand out to me as best. Familiar characters and songs can make them successful for kids, but you can do better. They're spineless. Ages 3-5. –BH
Children's Favorites 2 (Disney) / DISNEY
For ages 3-5. –BH
Children's Favorites 3 (Disney) / DISNEY
For ages 3-5. –BH
Children's Favorites 4 (Disney) / DISNEY
For ages 3-5. –BH

CHILDREN'S GAMES

○ **Children's Games / KIMBO**
For ages 2-4. –BH

CHIP 'N DALE RESCUE RANGERS

○ **Rootin' Tootin' Rangers / DISNEY**
For ages 3-5. –BH

THE CHIPMUNKS

Chipmunk Songbook / PETER PAN
For ages 2-4. –BH
○ **Let's All Sing with the Chipmunks / LIBERTY / BB 4**
1959
May be out of print, but the TV/music tie-in presented on this album was later used for the Monkees and the Partridge Family. Ages 2-4. –LL
The Chipmunks Sing the Beatles Hits / LIBERTY / BB 14
1964
The best Fab Four parody of all. Ages 2-5. –LL
Chipmunk Punk / EXCELSIOR   1980
Alvin, Simon, and Theodore enter the current pop mainstream. Covers of Billy Joel, Tom Petty, Blondie, and more. Ages 2-5. –LL

CINDERELLA

Story / BUMBLEBEEZ
For ages 2-5. –BH
Cinderella / SCORE PRODUCTIONS
For ages 2-5. –BH
○ **Story/Songs / DISNEY**
The Disney version is the best of them. Ages 2-5. –BH

THE CLASSICAL KIDS

The Classical Kids - Collection / CHILDREN'S GROUP
This collection includes the individual recordings reviewed herein. The collection is well worth the investment, if you're interested in giving a child a positive leg up on loving the classics. Ages 3-10+. –BH
★ **The Collection / CHILDREN'S GROUP**
Without question, the best way to introduce young children to the major classical composers and their music. Adults learn a lot too. Ages 3-10+. –BH
○ **Mozart's *Magic Flute* / CHILDREN'S GROUP**
This one's a bit frenetic but has some wonderful moments. A young girl gets mysteriously caught as an extra character in the opera. Ages 3-10+. –BH

○ **Vivaldi's Ring of Mystery / CHILDREN'S GROUP**
A fanciful stay in old Vienna. Ages 3-10+. –BH

☆ **Beethoven Lives Upstairs / CHILDREN'S GROUP**   1990
This is the best of the series by far. A classic. Ages 3-10+. –BH

○ **Mr. Bach Comes to Call / CHILDREN'S GROUP**   1990
The ghost of Johann Sebastian visits a young pianist. Ages 3-10+. –BH

GLENN CLOSE w/LIZ STORY

○ **The Legend of Sleepy Hollow / WINDHAM HILL**
Though the "celebrity descends from heaven, reads for the kiddies, and leaves" formula is generally not my cup of tea, this is quite good. Ages 5-8. –BH

GLENN CLOSE w/MARK ISHAM

○ **The Emperor's Nightingale / WINDHAM HILL**
For ages 4-6. –BH

JUDY COLLINS

Baby's Bedtime / LIGHT YEAR
For ages 2-3. –BH

○ **Baby's Morningtime / LIGHT YEAR**
Judy's voice is the main good point with both of these — but that's a very good point. Ages 2-3. –BH

PETER COMBE

○ **Spaghetti Bolognaise / ZOOM EXPRESS**
Australia's version of the Pied Piper, this is very clever material, with Combe's own unique delivery. Ages 3-9. –BH
Songs for Little Kids / ZOOM EXPRESS
Great Aussie-flavored songs for young children. Ages 2-5. –BH

★ **Chopsticks / ZOOM EXPRESS**
The best Combe, especially the title track. Ages 2-10. –BH
Toffee Apple / ZOOM EXPRESS
For ages 3-8. –BH

○ **Newspaper Mama / ZOOM EXPRESS**
For ages 3-8. –BH
... Very Best of Peter Combe ... / ZOOM EXPRESS
The Absolutely Very Best of Peter Combe (So Far). Recorded in concert. Ages 3-9. –BH

DAN CONLEY

☆ **Yes, Yes, Yes / COCO**
Conley is extremely tuned to the young child's point of view. His songs stretch children's imaginations. Big things can be expected from Dan. Ages 3-9. –BH

COOKIE MONSTER & GROVER

○ **True Blue / GOLDEN**
For ages 2-5. –BH

DON COOPER

○ **Recycled Songs / RANDOM HOUSE**
This is the best recording from this artist. Good teaching songs, such as what kids can do about recycling. –BH
Hanukkah Songs and Games / RANDOM HOUSE
Merry Christmas Songs and Games / RANDOM HOUSE
Songs of America / RANDOM HOUSE
For ages 3-6. –BH

STEWART COPELAND w/JAMES EARL JONES

○ **Noah's Ark / LIGHT YEAR**
James Earl Jones's voice carries the day on this well-told tale. Ages 5-8. –BH

STEVE COUCH

○ **The World Is a Rainbow / RAINBOW ENTERPRISES**
A little-known and hard-to-find record, but very good. For ages 4-8. –BH

CRAIG & COMPANY

○ **Morning 'N' Night / SWEET LOUISE**
A little cute, but good for very young children. It nearly underestimates its audience. Ages 3-5. –BH

CARRIE CROMPTON

○ **Come Let Us Be Merry / MUSIC FOR LITTLE PEOPLE**
Come Out to Play / MUSIC FOR LITTLE PEOPLE
For ages 2-5. –BH

DAN CROW

○ **Oops! / ROUNDER**
Dan's sweet heart and genuine love for children shine through. It's fun but thin (musically and in production). Ages 2-4. –BH

PATTI DALLAS & LAURA BARON

○ **Nitey-Nite / GOLDEN GLOW**
The *Golden Glow* series is an instrumentally rich, well-conceived series for very young children. Ages 2-5. –BH
Good Morning Sunshine / GOLDEN GLOW
For ages 2-5. –BH
The Golden Glow / GOLDEN GLOW
For ages 2-5. –BH
Playtime Parade / GOLDEN GLOW
For ages 2-5. –BH

DARKWING DUCK

○ **Story and Songs / DISNEY**
For ages 3-6. –BH

LYDIA ADAMS DAVIS

Gift of Story / THREE FEATHERS
Good stories for very young children. It's liable to lose anyone above age 6. –BH

○ **Time's Running Out / THREE FEATHERS**
Pleasing vocals in unevenly produced recordings. A good live artist who communicates well with children. Ages 3-6. –BH

LOU DELBIANCO

○ **The Storymaker, Tunes and Tales / CL RECORDS**
A good storyteller for very young kids. Not for repeated listening by big people. Ages 3-5. –BH

DENNIS

Music for Children by Dennis / BERNER
A little-known artist. These hard-to-find recordings are quite good for ages 3-6. –BH

○ **Dennis Sings Again / BERNER**
Hard recordings to find, but quite good for ages 3-6. –BH

DIAMONDZ

○ **Outer Space / ASTRO**
A lovable, wonderful eccentric. One of the best visual performers for children. She's *just* crazy enough. Ages 3-8. –BH

DIAPER GYM

○ **Diaper Gym / KIMBO**
For ages 2-4. –BH

DICK TRACY

○ **Big Boy Turns Up the Heat / DISNEY**
If you're already into Dick Tracy, these will feed the fire. If not, you can do better. Ages 4-7. –BH
Everything Comes Up Blank / DISNEY
For ages 4-8. –BH

DISNEY

○ **Silly Songs / DISNEY**
Disney Afternoon - Story & Songs / DISNEY
For ages 3-5. –BH
Disney Babies - Wake Up / DISNEY
For ages 2-4. –BH
Disney Babies - Lullaby / DISNEY
For ages 2-4. –BH
Disney Babies - Baby's Day / DISNEY
For ages 2-4. –BH
Disney Babies - Animal Friends / DISNEY
For ages 2-4. –BH
Disney Children's Favorites 2 / DISNEY
For ages 2-5. –BH
Disney Children's Favorites 3 / DISNEY
For ages 2-5. –BH
Disney Children's Favorites 4 / DISNEY
For ages 2-5. –BH
Disney Collection - Best Loved Songs #2 / DISNEY
For ages 2-5. –BH
Disney Collection - Best Loved Songs #3 / DISNEY
For ages 2-5. –BH
Disney - the Official Album of Disneyland / DISNEY
For ages 3-6. –BH

○ **Mousercise Songs / DISNEY**
A workout for children, conducted by that omnipresent mouse and friends. Mickey, can you see your toes? My limited experiments showed kids will get moving around with this one, but it also fades, and doesn't stand many workouts. For ages 3-6. –BH
Music of Disneyland: Songs / DISNEY
For ages 3-5. –BH

MICKEY DOLENZ

○ **Lullabies / RHINO-RINCON**
A surprisingly good effort from this former Monkee. For ages 3-5. –BH

● **Puts You to Sleep / RHINO**
Monkee Dolenz makes his solo debut with this children's album. His covers of 60s standards by the Beatles, Hollies, Paul Simon, and Neil Young won't erase the originals from anyone's mind, but they're pleasant enough. –JT

FLOYD DOMINO

○ **White Album / JTG**
For ages 5-8. –BH

DOUG & GARY

○ **Surfin' / PLAYTIME**
This duo from Rochester, NY, is consistently good. Particularly good vocals for ages 3-7. Humor and cleverness without condescension. –BH
I'm a Happy Pirate / PLAYTIME
For ages 3-7. –BH

DR. MIKE

○ **Put on a Happy Face & Sing with Dr. Mike / AMEE LU**
Dr. Mike is a real dentist. The recording is good for a first effort. Here's an artist to watch. Ages 3-5. –BH

DUMBO

○ **Dumbo - Story and Songs / DISNEY**
Much-loved music — especially "When I See an Elephant Fly," which is one of the great 3- to 7-year-old mind-stretcher word-game songs. –BH

SHELLY DUVALL

○ **Animal Express / MCA**
Shelly is a staple in a good collection of children's recordings. Ages 3-5. –BH
Huggables / RHINO-RINCON
For ages 3-5. –BH
○ **Sweet Dreams / RHINO-RINCON**
For ages 3-5. –BH

EARLY EARS

☆ **Early Ears Zero / ZOOM EXPRESS**
This series is a way to put music for a particular age (0-6) in the hands of children of that age. The titles are self-explanatory. This is a personal favorite — especially since I created it! *Zero* is for pregnant moms and dads and for infants under 12 months. *One* is still somewhat for parents and for infants 12-23 months and so on, up to *Six* for first graders. The series is based loosely on the milestones in child development occurring during each year of childhood up to six. *Zero* is very soft and a bit ethereal; beautiful music and sentiments. It contains one of the most beautiful pieces ever written for kids: "Mother and Child Suite for Horn and Harp," by composer Paul Riggio. Also toe-counting, first steps, and loving. –BH

○ **Early Ears One / ZOOM EXPRESS**
Low-key, this has some activity. Age 1. –BH
○ **Early Ears Two / ZOOM EXPRESS**
Two-year-olds are active, establishing their separate identities. The recording is more upbeat, with more songs directed at the child: toddling, puddle-jumping, learning colors in Spanish, feeling happy. Age 2. –BH
○ **Early Ears Three / ZOOM EXPRESS**
More active than earlier ones, speaking more directly to the children. More cleverness: giving up "blankie," skating on the moon, playing double kazoo, going on safari, and hugging. Age 3. –BH
○ **Early Ears Four / ZOOM EXPRESS**
Extremely active. Participation abounds. Very clever; funny and silly too. Singing dog duets, dancing, getting the best of the bogeyman, learning space words, making friends, fooling parents. Age 4. –BH
○ **Early Ears Five / ZOOM EXPRESS**
A bit more sophisticated than some in this series. It includes a fair amount about friends and socialization, with songs that include a still-active school bus as monster, wishing to fly, a grandpa best friends, and a rock & roll dog. Age 5. –BH
○ **Early Ears Six / ZOOM EXPRESS**
The most sophisticated. Becoming aware of the opposite sex, food song ("Fish is Delish"), brotherhood (in the larger sense), one-person-can-make-a-difference song, reggae song. Upbeat, happy, and thoughtful. Age 6. –BH

EIGHT DAYS OF HANUKAH

☆ **Eight Days of Hanukah / HIGH TOP**
Wonderful songs written by George David Weiss. He is a masterful writer. All kids' voices, and a fun way to learn about the Maccabees, etc. Recommended. Ages 4-10. –BH

FANTASIA

☆ **Fantasia / DISNEY**
Food for fantasy for three generations, this is a must. Ages 3-forever. –BH

MIA FARROW

○ **Beauty & the Beast / LIGHT YEAR**
Well told by Ms. Farrow. Not as exciting as the recent movie, it is nonetheless a valid reading. Ages 4-7. –BH
Pegasus / LIGHT YEAR
This story is a bit confusing, perhaps, for younger children, but well read. The music is not very meaningful. Ages 5-7. –BH

FAVORITE SONGS FOR LITTLE PEOPLE

○ **Favorite Songs for Little People / KIMBO**
For ages 2-4. –BH

CATHY FINK

Help Yourself / ROUNDER
A how-to-take-care-of-yourself recording, with Marcy Marxer. I usually find such albums a bit preachy, but this one is much less so. Ages 4-7. –BH
● **Grandma Slid Down the Mountain / ROUNDER**   1984
Cathy sings, plays, and produces up a storm. Imaginative songs imparting good general positive values. Ages 4-7. –BH
○ **When the Rain Comes Down / ROUNDER**   1987
Another good Cathy, especially the title cut. Ages 3-7. –BH

THE FLYERS

○ **Family Hug / HOOTENTOOT**
This regionally popular (upper Midwest) group makes recordings with at least two or three wonderful original tunes and some chestnuts. Well produced and well conceived, this is a worthy addition for 3- to 8-year-olds. –BH

FOLK DANCE FUN

○ **Folk Dance Fun / KIMBO**
For ages 2-5. –BH

NORMAN FOOTE

☆ **Foote Prints / DISNEY**
Creative and imaginative both on record and video, Norman is one of Disney's best contributions to children's entertainment. His show uses mime, music, and comedy, all to great effect. Ages 3-8. –BH

FOR OUR CHILDREN

☆ **For Our Children / DISNEY**
Very famous artists (Little Richard, James Taylor, among others). Some proceeds from the sales go to the Pediatric AIDS Society. Ages 3-10. –BH

JODIE FOSTER w/VAN DYKE PARKS

○ **The Fisherman & His Wife / WINDHAM HILL**
Good in its genre. Ages 4-7. –BH

FOX & THE HOUND

○ **Story / DISNEY**
For ages 3-5. –BH

GARFIELD

○ **Am I Cool or What! / GRP**
Yes, Garfield, you are — you and all your friends from the world of jazz. Here's some great music done with great spirit (even if the cat is a bit lazy and cynical). If you and your child like Garfield, you'll like these. Ages 4-8. –BH
Here Comes Garfield / UNI

GEMINI

Pulling Together / GEMINI   1987
Received a *Parents* Choice Honors Award. Combination of traditional and original materials. –JME

○ **Growing Up Together! / GEMINI**   1989
Aside from their children-and-family music, identical twins Sandor and Laszlo Slomovitz have recorded twelve albums of international folk dance music for the High/Scope Educational Research Foundation, to teach movement and dance to young children. These well-known singer/songwriters are superb vocalists, and both play a variety of instruments very well. For ages 4-10 and family listening. *Growing Up Together!* received a *Parents* Choice Award and was cited by the American Library Association as a notable children's recording. –JME
Two of a Kind / GEMINI   1991
Uptempo, exuberant songs of family celebration. Also storytelling. Recommended. –JME

BOB GIBSON

○ **A Child's Happy Birthday / BIG RECORDS**
Longtime folkie Gibson gives us a gentle record for younger kids (3-5) to celebrate with. A nice birthday present. –BH

JOHN GIELGUD w/MARK ISHAM

○ **The Emperor's New Clothes / WINDHAM HILL**   1989
Sir John (brilliant as he is) is not the ultimate children's reader for US ears, but somehow it works. Ages 4-7. –BH

DANNY GLOVER w/TAJ MAHAL

○ **Brer Rabbit / WINDHAM HILL**
Truly wonderful. I recommend it. Ages 3-8. –BH

DANNY GLOVER w/LADYSMITH BLACK MAMBAZO

○ **How the Leopard Got His Spots / WINDHAM HILL**
I like this one. With a wonderful story, narration by Danny Glover, and perfect music backing from Ladysmith Black Mambazo, it is one of the few times when the "celebrity" formula actually works well for kids. Ages 3-8. –BH

BOBBY GOLDSBORO

○ **Easter Egg Mornin' / RHINO-RINCON**
This series is positive for younger children 3 to 6. It's a little cutesy, though. –BH
Stinger, King of the Bees / RHINO-RINCON
For ages 3-6. –BH
Snuffy, the Elf Who Saved Christmas / RHINO-RINCON
For ages 3-6. –BH
Lumpkin, the Pumpkin / RHINO-RINCON
For ages 3-6. –BH

RED GRAMMER

○ **Can You Sound Just like Me? / CHILDREN'S GROUP**
For very young children. Gets them participating. This one's a good addition to a collection. Ages 2-5. –BH
★ **Teaching Peace / CHILDREN'S GROUP**   1986
Teaching Peace is one of the top five children's recordings of all time. Red's fantastic tenor voice would be successful in any musical genre. A man with a very big heart. Ages 3-10. –BH

GREAT MOUSE DETECTIVE

○ **Great Mouse Detective - Story/Songs / DISNEY**
For ages 4-7. –BH

GREG & STEVE

● **We Live Together / YOUNGHEART**
Chances are, more young children than adults know about this duo because they've crisscrossed the country playing in schools for years. Positive values, self-esteem, and fun characterize these recordings. The *We Live Together* recordings are a good bet. Ages 3-6. –BH
We Live Together #2 / YOUNGHEART
For ages 3-6. –BH

We Live Together #3 / YOUNGHEART
For ages 3-6. –BH
We Live Together #4 / YOUNGHEART
For ages 4-6. –BH
○ **Kidding Around / YOUNGHEART**
For ages 4-6. –BH
On the Move / YOUNGHEART
For ages 4-6. –BH
Quiet Moments / YOUNGHEART
For ages 3-6. –BH
○ **Kids in Motion / YOUNGHEART**
From the same-name video. Good songs. For ages 3-7. –BH
Holidays & Special Times / YOUNGHEART

DAVID GROVER

○ **One World, Songs from America & Other Places / BQB**
These songs are all a bit too synthesized (and same-sounding) for big people to get the multicultural effect, but it's perhaps a good start for kids. Ages 4-7. –BH

JACK GRUNSKY

● **Imaginary Window / CHILDREN'S GROUP**
Jack's first record. Both listed here are current products, consistently good for ages 3-8. –BH
○ **Children of the Morning / CHILDREN'S GROUP**
One of Canada's new contributions to children, providing gentle music with a positive outlook. Ages 3-8. –BH

VINCE GUARALDI

○ **Oh! Good Grief / UNI**
More Charlie Brown sound. Wonderful. Ages 4-9. –BH
Jazz Impressions of a Boy Named Charlie Brown / UNI
Still the original Charlie Brown good light jazz sound. –BH

GUMBY

○ **Green Album / DISNEY**
Various rock bands. Very cute. Listenable for parents as well, at least those into pop music. Ages 3-10. –BH

ARLO GUTHRIE

○ **Baby's Storytime / LIGHT YEAR**
If the parents are Arlo fans, this one will work well. If not, it may be trying. Ages 3-6. –BH

WOODY GUTHRIE

Nursery Days / SMITHSONIAN-FOLKWAYS
For ages 2-5. –BH
The Science of Sound / SMITHSONIAN-FOLKWAYS
○ **For Mother and Child / FOLKWAYS**   1956
Some of the last songs written and recorded by Woody Guthrie were his children's songs. Their strength, shown in *Songs to Grow on for Mother and Child*, is an unusually strong identification with actually being a child, in all its simplicity and charm, along with the ability to win over listeners. Good examples on here are "Rattle My Rattle" and "I Want My Milk." Woody Guthrie is an acquired sonic taste worth acquiring. Ages 3-5. –WR & BH
Nursery Days / FOLKWAYS   1964
In *Songs to Grow On - Vol. 1 (Nursery Days)*, Guthrie once again effectively evokes the child's point of view with such simple, yet exciting songs as "Car Song" (with its chorus "Goin' for a ride in the car car") and "Put Your Finger in the Air." Ages 3-5. –WR

HALLOWEEN FUN

○ **Halloween Fun / KIMBO**
For ages 2-4. –BH

HANSEL AND GRETEL

○ **Hansel and Gretel - Story / BUMBLEBEEZ**
For ages 3-5. –BH

BILL HARLEY

○ **Monsters in My Room / ROUND RIVER**
Clever and assertive, Bill takes the child's point of view bravely and unswervingly. Parents also recognize their own foibles in Bill's songs. Ages 3-8. –BH
Grownups Are Strange / ROUND RIVER
Ages 3-8. –BH
Come On Out & Play / RED ROVER
Ages 3-8. –BH
I'm Going to Let It Shine / ROUND RIVER
Ages 3-8. –BH
○ **Fifty Ways to Fool Your Mother / ROUND RIVER**   1986
For ages 3-9. –BH
Cool in School / ROUND RIVER   1987
Cool in School - Tales from the Sixth Grade is for ages 6-10. –BH
Dinosaurs Never Say Please / ROUND RIVER   1987
For ages 4-9. –BH
★ **You're in Trouble / A&M**   1989
My favorite. Wonderful songs. Ages 3-9. –BH

HEEL TOE AWAY WE GO (K-3)

○ **Heel, Toe, Away We Go (K-3) / KIMBO**
For ages 4-6. –BH

PRISCILLA HERDMAN

○ **Star Dreamer - Nightsongs & Lullabies / ALACAZAM**
Folk music for kids. Very nice vocals and stories. –CR

ROSALIND HINMAN

○ **Three Hairs from the Devil's Chin / BAMME**
For ages 4-8. –BH

DAVID HOLT

○ **Tailybone & Other Strange Stories / HIGH WINDY**
For ages 5-10. –BH

HOMEMADE GAMES AND ACTIVITIES

○ **Homemade Games and Activities / KIMBO**
For ages 2-4. –BH

HOLLY HUNTER w/ART LANDE

○ **3 Billy Goats Gruff/3 Little Pigs / WINDHAM HILL**
Surprisingly good Holly, especially the goats. Ages 3-7. –BH

WILLIAM HURT w/MARK ISHAM

○ **The Boy Who Drew Cats / RHINO-RINCON**
For ages 3-7. –BH

JEREMY IRONS w/MARK ISHAM

○ **Steadfast Tin Soldier / WINDHAM HILL**
A very good, comprehensible reading by Jeremy. Ages 3-8. –BH

IT'S A SMALL WORLD

○ **It's a Small World - Story/Songs / DISNEY**
For ages 3-6. –BH

BURL IVES

○ **Best of Burl's for Boys and Girls / MCA**
The voice has been singing folksy songs to all ages for three generations. It's not modern and not well produced or flashy, but it still works after all this time. Ages 2-6. –BH

JACK & THE BEANSTALK

○ **Jack & the Beanstalk / SCORE PRODUCTIONS**
A credible version of the classic. Ages 3-5. –BH

ELLA JENKINS

☆ **This-A-Way That-A-Way / SMITHSONIAN-FOLKWAYS**
The great lady of music for young children. Having a serious children's music collection without Ella is like collecting rock & roll without Chuck Berry. Different people like different titles. Shop around, look at titles, and listen if you can. –BH
My Street Begins ... / SMITHSONIAN-FOLKWAYS
My Street Begins at My House. –ED
... America's Children / SMITHSONIAN-FOLKWAYS
We Are America's Children. –ED
Adventures in Rhythm / SMITHSONIAN-FOLKWAYS
Come Dance by the Ocean / SMITHSONIAN-FOLKWAYS
Early Childhood Songs / SMITHSONIAN-FOLKWAYS
Nursery Rhymes / SMITHSONIAN-FOLKWAYS
Little Johnny Brown ... / SMITHSONIAN-FOLKWAYS
Little Johnny Brown & Other Songs. –ED
Rhythm and Game Songs / SMITHSONIAN-FOLKWAYS
This Is Rhythm / SMITHSONIAN-FOLKWAYS
★ **You'll Sing a Song ... / FOLKWAYS**   1966
You'll Sing a Song and I'll Sing a Song. Born in St. Louis, raised in Chicago, Jenkins has been a folksinger since 1956. Concentrating on educating music teachers through her now-famous "Adventures in Rhythm" workshops, she demonstrated new group-singing and rhythm-building techniques. Author of two books and any number of albums, Jenkins is possibly *the* major talent in children's music. Her talent is so great that, once heard, she is never forgotten. This is how kids' songs should sound. No family should be without at least one album, and this classic is the place to start. –JME
Counting Games ... / SMITHSONIAN-FOLKWAYS   1967
Counting Games & Rhythms. –ED
Call & Response / SMITHSONIAN-FOLKWAYS   1968
And One & Two / SMITHSONIAN-FOLKWAYS   1969
Growing Up with ... / SMITHSONIAN-FOLKWAYS   1969
Growing Up with Rhythm Songs. –ED
... Call and Response Songs & Chants / FOLKWAYS 1970
Jambo & Other Call and Response Songs and Chants. –ED
Play Your Instruments ... / FOLKWAYS   1975
Play Your Instruments (& Make a Pretty Sound). –ED
Rhythms of Childhood / FOLKWAYS   1979
Seasons for Singing / SMITHSONIAN-FOLKWAYS   1979

IAN JOHNSTONE

○ **Dear Mr. Johnstone / DANDELION**
For ages 3-7. –BH
Love & Warm Fuzzies / DANDELION
For ages 3-7. –BH

BESSIE JONES

○ **Step It Down / ROUNDER**
For ages 3-7. –BH

JUNGLE BOOK

○ **Jungle Book - Story/Songs / DISNEY**
This film and record have defined the personalities of animals for two generations because of the wonderful voice-overs and music. Ages 3-8. –BH

JUNIOR JUG BAND

○ **Songs to Sing / CHILDREN'S GROUP**
Clever, understated, and mostly just plain fun. Ages 4-8. –BH

CONNIE KALDOR

○ **Lullaby Berceuse / MUSIC FOR LITTLE PEOPLE**
For ages 1-4. –BH

KATHY KALLICK

○ **What Do You Dream About? / KAL**
For ages 3-5. –BH

KAMOTION

○ **Jumpin' in a Puddle /**
For ages 2-5. –BH
Stayin' Up / KAMOTION
For ages 2-5. –BH

KARAN & THE MUSICAL MEDICINE SHOW

Comin' to Your Town / MEDICINE SHOW
These recordings sound like the Mamas and the Papas of children's music. Rich harmonies, well-produced and well-written songs, and Karan's expressive voice. Ages 3-9. –BH
☆ **Warm Fuzzies / MEDICINE SHOW**
"Story of the Star Spangled Banner" and "One Hand, One Heart" are sentiments every child should be exposed to. Other songs are also excellent. Highly recommended. Ages 3-9. –BH

KAREN & TOMMY

○ **The Dinosaur & More / BEANSTALK**
Excellent writing in various musical styles. Very good voices and good blend. Recommended. Ages 3-6. –BH

DANNY KAYE

☆ **Hans Christian Andersen / MCA**
For pre-MTV kids, this is a must. If Hans Christian Andersen had been around in the 50s, he'd have been Danny Kaye. For ages 2-6. –BH

KIDDIN' AROUND

Kiddin' Around / MUSIC FOR LITTLE PEOPLE
For ages 3-8. –BH

KIDS OF WIDNEY HIGH

○ **Kids of Widney High / ROUNDER**   1989
Kids of Widney High - Special Music from Special Kids is for ages 3-7. –BH

BEN KINGSLEY w/RAVI SHANKAR

○ **The Tiger & the Brahmin / RHINO-RINCON**
A taste of India — a very good taste. Recommended for ages 4-8. –BH

DAVE KINNOIN

Fun-A-Rooey / SONG WIZARD
Wonderful voice. The songs are uneven, but the production is good. Worth a second look. Ages 3-6. –BH
○ **Daring Dewey / SONG WIZARD**
Consistent songs, same great voice. Ages 3-6. –BH

FRED KOCH

○ **Children's Record / RED ROVER**
Chicago's teacher extraordinaire gives us two diverse and wonderful recordings, especially "Daddy Plays Drums." For ages 4-8. –BH
This Lil' Cow / RED ROVER
For ages 4-8. –BH

LADY & THE TRAMP

○ **Lady & the Tramp - Story/Songs / DISNEY**
The story spans generations. Children love it. Ages 3-6. –BH

LOIS LAFOND

Creatures of Summer / BOULDER'S CHILDREN'S PROD.
While Creatures of Summer Sleep includes stories and songs
that are also for very young children. Ages 2-4. –BH

○ **I Am Who I Am / BOULDER'S CHILDREN'S PROD.** 1985
Lois and her band the Rockadiles (from Colorado) stretch
children's imaginations with great music and outstanding
vocals. For moms and the very young. Ages 2-5. –BH

Something New / BOULDER'S CHILDREN'S PROD. 1987
A very good, eclectic collection of songs from several cultures
for infants, parents, and very young children. Ages 4-10. –BH

★ **One World / BOULDER'S CHILDREN'S PROD.** 1989
This is a classic for kids and parents. A world music,
multicultural record with wonderful songs and great vocals.
It is in this writer's Top Ten. Ages 3-10, maybe beyond. –BH

GARY LAPOW

○ **I Like Noodles / SPRING BOARD** 1987
Good for very young kids but, I think, intended for a bit older.
Another "nice guy, nice music" record. Thank goodness there
are fewer than there used to be. Ages 2-5. –BH

SHARI LEWIS

○ **Lamb Chop in the Land of No Manners / A&M**
Excellent. Shari is one of the very few whose act has been
universally well presented, consistent, and truly funny. And
not just to kids. Lamb Chop frequently says and does things
kids see themselves doing or wish they could. Ages 4-10. –BH

SYD LIEBERMAN

○ **Joseph the Tailor ... / SYD LIEBERMAN**
Joseph the Tailor & Other Jewish Tales. Anyone (young or old)
who appreciates the subtleties, twists, turns, and universal
humor and pathos in stories will like this one. Ages 5-10. –BH

THE LITTLE MERMAID

★ **The Little Mermaid - Story/Songs / DISNEY**
The original soundtrack is a wonderful recording. One of the
best of the 90s. This recording has the story too. –BH

The Little Mermaid Collection / DISNEY
Little Mermaid Collection - Read-Along Special Edition is for
ages 3-10. –BH

☆ **Sebastian - Songs / DISNEY**
The crab from Disney's the *Little Mermaid*, Sebastian is the
children's music answer to the party band. It is almost
impossible to sit still for a whole side. Caribbean rhythms
abound. –BH

LITTLE RED RIDING HOOD

○ **Little Red Riding Hood - Story / BUMBLEBEEZ**
For ages 3-6. –BH

RIC LOUCHARD

○ **G'morning Johann / MUSIC FOR LITTLE PEOPLE**
For ages 4-8. –BH

G'night Wolfgang / MUSIC FOR LITTLE PEOPLE
For ages 4-8. –BH

TAJ MAJAL

☆ **Shake It to the One ... / MUSIC FOR LITTLE PEOPLE**
Shake It to the One You Love the Best. The only blues hero
doing real children's music. Parents will like this music almost
as much as their children will. Ages 3-8. –BH

Shake Sugaree / MLP
A little simpler. A worthwhile recording. –BH

MAKAROVA/ROSENBERGER

○ **Prince Ivan & the Frog Princess / DLS**
For ages 4-8. –BH

Snow Queen / DLS
For ages 3-8. –BH

MAKE THE RIGHT CHOICE

○ **Make the Right Choice / KIMBO**
Make the Right Choice (Issues Kids Are Confronted With) is for
ages 4-9. –BH

MARREL OF BONKEYS MAND

○ **Over in the Meadow / MUSIC FOR LITTLE PEOPLE**
For ages 3-8. –BH

MARCY MARXER

○ **Jump Children / ROUNDER** 1986
Marcy has a gentle, smart approach to children's music. She's
best when concentrating on fun and mind-stretching — like
here. For ages 3-6. –BH

MARY POPPINS

○ **Mary Poppins - Soundtrack / DISNEY**
A wonderful, classic story with timeless songs. Ages 3-10. –BH

JOHN MCCUTCHEON

○ **Howjadoo / ROUNDER** 1983
John's first album for kids. Quite good. Ages 3-7. –BH

● **Mail Myself to You / ROUNDER** 1988
Clever songs, great playing, good vocals. Just plain enjoyable
for big and little people alike. Ages 3-8. –BH

SEONA MCDOWELL

○ **Citizens of the World / SMD**
A good recording with uneven production. Seona has a good
touch for kids and teaches some big ideas well. Ages 3-6. –BH

MCGEE & ME!

○ **Hits / GEFFEN**

KELLY MCGILLIS w/MARK ISHAM

○ **Thumbelina / WINDHAM HILL**
For ages 4-8. –BH

ME AND MY BEAN BAG (BEAN BAG GAMES)

○ **Me and My Bean Bag (Bean Bag Games) / KIMBO**
For ages 2-4. –BH

MICKEY'S ROCK AROUND THE MOUSE SONGS

○ **Mickey's Rock Around the Mouse Songs / DISNEY**
Babysitting music. It's lively and all that, but that's where it
stops. Ages 3-5. –BH

KATHI MILENKO & FRIENDS

○ **On the Way / MUSIC FOR LITTLE PEOPLE**
On the Way to Somewhere is for ages 2-5. –BH

Good Morning / MUSIC FOR LITTLE PEOPLE 1987
Good Morning, Good Night is for ages 2-6. –BH

GERALD MILNES

○ **Granny, Will Your Dog Bite? / RANDOM HOUSE**
For ages 3-5. –BH

MINNIE 'N ME

○ **When We Grow Up / DISNEY**
Seems like the Minnie Mouse emphasis a while back just
might have been a bit of a Disney nod toward women:
progress. Minnie's recordings, however, tend to be
sugarcoated and without substance. Not that everything has
to be fraught with message, but this stuff just disappears as it
plays. For ages 3-5. –BH

Magical Zoo / DISNEY
For ages 3-5. −BH
Minnie 'n Me - Songs / DISNEY
For ages 3-4. −BH
Vacation Adventure / DISNEY
For ages 3-4. −BH

MISCHIEF CITY

○ **Mischief City / CHILDREN'S GROUP**
Originally a play mounted in Toronto, this one's really fun.
Good songs, well done. The title says it. Ages 4-7. −BH

MISS MOLLY

○ **Every Cowboy Needs a Horse / MZM**
Texas swing for kids by a singer from Western Canada. A great
band. Mostly very familiar songs. This is a good door for kids
into "Western" music. Ages 4-8. −BH

LISA MONET

○ **Circle Time / MUSIC FOR LITTLE PEOPLE**
For ages 4-8. −BH
My Best Friend / MUSIC FOR LITTLE PEOPLE
For ages 3-7. −BH

MOTHER GOOSE

The Tarts / BUMBLEBEEZ
For ages 3-4. −BH
Jack Sprat / BUMBLEBEEZ
For ages 2-3. −BH
○ **Humpty Dumpty / BUMBLEBEEZ**
For ages 2-4. −BH
Hot Cross Buns / BUMBLEBEEZ
For ages 2-4. −BH
The Cat and the Fiddle / BUMBLEBEEZ
For ages 2-3. −BH
If Wishes Were Horses / BUMBLEBEEZ
For ages 2-4. −BH
Rain, Rain / BUMBLEBEEZ
For ages 2-4. −BH
Banbury Cross / BUMBLEBEEZ
For ages 2-3. −BH

MOTHER GOOSE (DELUXE)

○ **Mother Goose - (Deluxe) Red / SMARTY PANTS**
These recordings are generally OK, but just OK. You can do
better. They're meant for very young kids. For ages 2-4. −BH
Yellow / SMARTY PANTS
For ages 2-4. −BH
Blue / SMARTY PANTS
For ages 2-4. −BH
Green / SMARTY PANTS
For ages 2-4. −BH

MOTHER GOOSE RHYMES

Mother Goose Rhymes - Story/Songs / DISNEY
For ages 1-4. −BH

MARIA MULDAUR

☆ **On the Sunny Side / MUSIC FOR LITTLE PEOPLE**
Marie's voice works surprisingly well for kids. Great
arrangements, wonderful song choices. A well-thought-out,
very successful recording. Recommended. Ages 4-8. −BH

MUSICAL PLAYTIME FUN

○ **Musical Playtime Fun / KIMBO**
For ages 2-4. −BH

MUSICAL TREASURE CHEST

○ **Musical Treasure Chest - Vol. 2 / DISNEY**
For ages 3-5. −BH
Musical Treasure Chest - Vol. 3 / DISNEY
For ages 3-5. −BH

MY TEDDY BEAR AND ME

○ **My Teddy Bear and Me / KIMBO**
For ages 1-3. −BH

ERIC NAGLER

○ **Improvise with Eric Nagler / ROUNDER**   1989
Eric Nagler is a mainstay on Sharon, Lois, and Bram's
"Elephant Show." A good singer, good player. Creative and
interactive. Ages 3-7. −BH

NEW TROUBADOURS

○ **Festival of Light / MUSIC FOR LITTLE PEOPLE**
For ages 3-6. −BH

JACK NICHOLSON w/BOBBY MCFERRIN

○ **Elephant's Child / WINDHAM HILL**
I love Bobby McFerrin — there is no exception. Jack does
well, but he's essentially not a young kid's reader. Ages 4-9. −BH
How the Rhinoceros Got His Skin / WINDHAM HILL

TIM NOAH

○ **Kaddywompas / A&M**   1982
This may be good for very young children, but it comes close
to underestimating its audience. Too close. Ages 3-5. −BH
In Search of the Wow Wow Wibble / A&M   1983
The same thing as the first recording, but for me it's a pass.
Ages 3-5. −BH

NURSERY RHYMES FOR LITTLE PEOPLE

○ **Nursery Rhymes for Little People / KIMBO**
For ages 1-3. −BH

OLD MACDONALD HAD A FARM

○ **Old MacDonald Had a Farm / SCORE PRODUCTIONS**
For ages 1-3. −BH

OLD WORLD LULLABIES

○ **Old World Lullabies / RHINO-RINCON**
Wonderful old lullabies recorded in their original environs
with old instruments. A great idea that's well executed. For
ages 1-4. −BH

OLIVER & COMPANY

○ **Oliver & Company - Story/Songs / DISNEY**
Not what Dickens had in mind, but it's a typical Disney
shaggy-dog story that works, if a bit fluffy. Ages 3-5. −BH

101 DALMATIONS

○ **101 Dalmations - Story/Songs / DISNEY**
The famous Disney dog story. A good one, worth having. For
ages 3-6. −BH

OVER THE MOON

☆ **Over the Moon / OVER THE MOON**
This duo has made a wonderful tape that sounds sometimes
like The Byrds, sometimes like early rock & roll, but always
like two mommies singing and playing their hearts out. A
rough-sounding recording, but the energy and honesty are
unmistakable. Ages 3-10. −BH

MICHAEL PALIN w/STEWART COPELAND

○ **Jack & the Beanstalk / REV**
For ages 3-7. –BH

HAP PALMER

○ **Homemade Band / RANDOM HOUSE**
Hap is considered by many to be a big figure in children's music. He communicates very well with children and sings directly to them. These recordings have integrity. Ages 3-7. –BH
We're On Our Way / RHINO-RINCON

PARACHUTE EXPRESS

○ **Circle of Friends / DISNEY**
This group tends to play bluegrass-style music for children. "Enthusiastic," "well-meaning," and "child-appropriate" apply; however, something is missing. The albums don't quite click — not any of them. Ages 3-5. –BH
Feel the Music / DISNEY
For ages 3-5. –BH
Sunny Side Up / DISNEY
For ages 3-5. –BH
Happy To Be Here / DISNEY
For ages 3-5. –BH

PATRIOTIC SONGS AND MARCHES

○ **Patriotic Songs and Marches / KIMBO**
For ages 3-5. –BH

TOM PAXTON

○ **A Child's Christmas / FLYING FISH**
Tom proves that clever lyrics deftly sung are not ever lost on children. Ages 3-8. –BH
Peanut Butter Pie / FLYING FISH
The newest one. Very clever. Tom's voice clicks with kids. Mom and Dad probably already know it. Ages 3-6. –BH
★ **Marvelous Toy ... / FLYING FISH** 1984
The Marvelous Toy & Other Gallimaufry. Paxton's humor and winning performing style (plus such songs as the title track, a long-time concert favorite) make him a natural children's performer, but it was only 25 years into his career that he made an album for kids. The result is a charming collection, full of rabbits and elephants and, of course, that famous toy that makes all the funny noises. For ages 3-8. –WR
Balloon-Alloon-Aloon / PAX 1987
Fish, crows, monkeys, and less familiar folk, such as "The Woolly Booger" and "The Thing That Isn't There," populate Paxton's second delightful collection of children's music, part of a series called "the kid stuff tapes." (78 Park Place, East Hampton, New York 11937.) –WR

SUNI PAZ

○ **Alerta Sings / SMITHSONIAN-FOLKWAYS**
For ages 4-8. –BH
Canciones Para El Recreo / SMITHSONIAN-FOLKWAYS
For ages 4-8. –BH

PEACE IS ...

○ **Peace Is ... / MUSIC FOR LITTLE PEOPLE**
Peace Is the World Smiling is for ages 3-7. –BH

PEANUTS

● **Flashbeagle / UNI**
Snoopy music. How can a dog that doesn't talk, bark, or sing get away with making music? The imagination is a wonderful thing. Ages 3-10. –BH
○ **Peanuts - Snoopy Come Home / UNI**
Our favorite beagle on the lam. It's good. Ages 3-10. –BH

PEGGOSUS

○ **Jubilee! / BOSTON SKYLINE**
To my knowledge, this is the only band for children and families that sounds like the Grateful Dead. Even though the lead vocalist, Peggy, is clearly a woman, it somehow still reads as Dead-like. Good playing, good songs. Worth having. For ages 3-8. –BH

FRED PENNER

● **Fred Penner's Place / A&M** 1920
This artist is much better than "Fred Penner's Place" would indicate. The TV show would suffocate a lesser artist. Fred is a good singer and player who knows how to communicate with children. I like Fred better than the recording. Ages 3-6. –BH
○ **Collections / A&M** 1921
This one's better. –BH

PETER PAN

○ **Peter Pan - Story / BUMBLEBEEZ**
Take the Disney version if you're needing a Peter Pan of this sort. The original or *Hook* might be better. Ages 2-6. –BH
Peter Pan - Story/Songs / DISNEY

THE TALE OF PETER RABBIT

○ **Story / BUMBLEBEEZ**
For ages 2-5. –BH
Book and Cassette / SMARTY PANTS
For ages 2-5. –BH

PINOCCHIO

○ **Pinocchio - Story / BUMBLEBEEZ**
Disney wins again. Ages 3-5. –BH
Pinocchio - Story/Songs / DISNEY
For ages 3-7. –BH

DAVID POLANSKY

● **A-Z Alphabet Animal / PERFECT SCORE SONG MUSIC**
There are many animal alphabet recordings. This is one of the very best. Ages 4-7. –BH
○ **I Like Dessert / PERFECT SCORE SONG MUSIC** 1987
I Like Dessert is hard to find but well worth the search. David is a wonderful writer, especially of songs depicting the daily drama of child-parent relationships. Ages 3-8. –BH

BARRY LOUIS POLISAR

Naughty Songs / RAINBOW MORNING
Naughty Songs for Boys and Girls is for ages 4-5. –BH
Well-Behaved Children / RAINBOW MORNING
Songs for Well-Behaved Children is for ages 4-5. –BH
Stanley Stole My Shoelace / RAINBOW MORNING
Stanley Stole My Shoelace and Rubbed It in His Armpit is for ages 3-6. –BH
Juggling Babies and a Career / RAINBOW MORNING
○ **I Eat Kids & Other Songs / RAINBOW MORNING** 1975
Barry is an acquired taste. Parents are generally left out, and Barry sings extremely silly songs to younger children. Parents, on the other hand, do get to watch their children laugh wildly at songs about full diapers, nose picking, and other not-quite-so-graphic subjects. There's no great attempt to educate or stretch a young mind. It's lowest-common-denominator fun. You can tell by the titles that these recordings bear a strong relationship to each other. –BH
My Brother Thinks ... / RAINBOW MORNING 1977
My Brother Thinks He's a Banana is for ages 3-5. –BH
Captured Live ... / RAINBOW MORNING 1978
Captured Live and in the Act is for ages 4-5. –BH
Off-Color Songs for Kids / RAINBOW MORNING 1983
For age 5. –BH

BEATRIX POTTER

○ **Sing-a-Long / BUMBLEBEEZ**
For ages 2-4. –BH

PRELEARNING SKILLS

○ **Prelearning Skills / KIMBO**
For ages 1-2. –BH

PRESCHOOL ACTION TIME

○ **Preschool Action Time / KIMBO**
For ages 1-3. –BH

THE PRINCE & THE PAUPER

○ **The Prince & the Pauper - Story/Songs / DISNEY**
For ages 2-5. –BH

THE PROFESSOR (UNCLE WILTON)

○ **Multiplication Facts from 1-12 / UNCLE WILTON**
Singing and Rapping the Multiplication Facts from 1-12.
Anyone listening to this "Rap the Facts" series will be hard-pressed not to know their basic math when they're finished. Wilton's love and concern for kids is plain throughout the series. I wish someone had released it when I was learning the multiplication tables. Ages 5-10. –BH
Addition Facts from 1-12 / UNCLE WILTON
Singing and Rapping the Addition Facts from 1-12 is for ages 5-10. –BH
Division Facts from 1-12 / UNCLE WILTON
Singing and Rapping the Division Facts from 1-12 is for ages 5-10. –BH
Subtraction Facts from 1-12 / UNCLE WILTON
Singing and Rapping the Subtraction Facts from 1-12 is for ages 5-10. –BH

RADUM SCADUM

○ **Radum Scadum / ABC**
This mostly instrumental Australian music is interesting, fun, and electric. Ages 7-9. –BH

RAFFI

○ **In Concert / MCA**
Here is the first really major figure in modern children's music. He blazed the trail for many to follow. Every recording is recommended. Raffi is Canada's gift to children everywhere. Ages 2-6. –BH
○ **More Singable Songs / MCA**
Not much letdown here. Still excellent. Ages 3-7. –BH
○ **Everything Grows / MCA**
For ages 3-7. –BH
○ **One Light One Sun / MCA**
For ages 3-8. –BH
○ **Rise & Shine / MCA**
Apparently this is to be Raffi's last recording mostly for children. He's since turned his attention to the environment and somewhat away from children's recordings. This is a fine album. Ages 3-8. –BH
Evergreen Everblue / MCA
Raffi's first environmental statement. This is not really a children's recording, and apparently Raffi didn't intend it to be. However, since some of the most ferocious recyclers I know are children, and since these kids will inherit our mess, I think older children would benefit from it. Ages 10+. –BH
★ **Singable Songs for the Very Young / MCA** 1976
This is the one that started it all. Still one of the most popular recordings for children. Ages 4-10. –BH
○ **Corner Grocery Store ... / A&M** 1979
Raffi is something of an heir to the children's music of such folkies as Pete Seeger and the Babysitters. In *Corner Grocery*

Store and Other Singable Songs, he is especially interested in adapting some familiar folksongs — "Pick a Bale o' Cotton," "Goodnight Irene" — as children's songs, along with such traditional material as "Frère Jacques." He has a light, bouncy singing style that is irresistible to children and parents alike. Ages 3-7. –WR
☆ **Baby Beluga / MCA** 1980
This is probably the world's most popular whale. This record is a delight. Ages 3-8. –BH
○ **One Light One Sun / A&M** 1985
Raffi turns more to his own originals on this, his best collection, but also turns in excellent versions of traditional songs such as "Apples and Bananas" and claims some nominally adult songs such as "Octopus's Garden" for the children's market. For ages 4-9. –WR

PHYLICIA RASHAD & JASON MILES

○ **Baby's Nursery Rhymes / LIGHT YEAR**
Cosby's TV wife does synth-backed nursery rhymes — a lot of them. I love Ms. Rashad's voice, but that is where this album stops. Ages 1-3. –BH

RESCUERS

Rescuers - Story/Songs / DISNEY
Rescuers and *Rescuers Down Under* both originate with the animated feature films of the same name. They are exciting stories for younger children. –BH
○ **Rescuers Down Under - Story/Songs / DISNEY**
For ages 3-6. –BH

RHYTHMS FOR BASIC MOTOR SKILLS

○ **Rhythms for Basic Motor Skills / KIMBO**
For ages 1-2. –BH

RIDERS IN THE SKY

○ **Saddle Pals / ROUNDER**
The Riders introduce children to Western music in a really fun way. If one becomes enthralled with the music, these are a real find. Ages 3-6. –BH
Harmony Ranch / ROUNDER
For ages 3-6. –BH

LEE RITENOUR & RAUL JULIA

○ **The Monkey People / RHINO-RINCON**
For ages 4-8. –BH

ROBIN HOOD

○ **Story/Songs / DISNEY**
For ages 3-7. –BH

THE ROCK-A-BYE COLLECTION

○ **The Rock-A-Bye Collection / JAB RECORDS**
This is the second recording from the people who brought you *A Child's Gift of Lullabies*. Ages 1-2. –BH

SALLY ROGERS

Piggyback Planet / ROUND RIVER
Sally has a really beautiful and expressive soprano voice that is capable of a whole range of emotions, including love, mischief, mystery, and constructive silliness. Very good songs, but the production doesn't live up to the voice. Ages 3-6. –BH
○ **Peace by Peace / FLYING FISH** 1988
A more peace- and issue-oriented recording. Sally still sounds wonderful. The songs are even better; the production is better too. Ages 3-7. –BH

RORY

I'm Just a Kid / ROAR
Adults trying to turn into kids on record make my caution-

light come on. This is a very good-sounding production, with a few really good songs ("Bubble Bath Is Even Better"). This would be more believable if the artist would do almost the same thing as more of an adult. There is a spark about this recording that I like. Ages 3-5. –BH

Make Believe Day / ROAR
A more adult-like record makes the vocals more believable. The songs, though, are not as good as those on the first recording. Ages 3-6. –BH

○ **Little Broadway / ROAR**
Broadway for children is a great idea. The songs here are well and cleverly chosen. The delivery is a little obvious and should be cleverer. Nevertheless, children can learn a bit about theatrical music here. Ages 4-6. –BH

ROSENSHONTZ

Sing a Happy Song / RANDOM HOUSE
For eight recordings and a number of years, Bill and Gary have helped to define fun for children across the US. Ages 3-6. –BH

Quiet Time / RANDOM HOUSE
A simple, quiet, mostly acoustic recording. Good for young children. Ages 2-5. –BH

Uh Oh / RS
Also very good. Ages 3-5. –BH

Tickles You! / RS   1980
A little more rambunctious. Ages 2-5. –BH

Share It / RS   1982
A bit more sophisticated. A good value-teacher. Ages 2-6. –BH

It's the Truth / RS   1984
The guys start to go rock & roll. Very good. Ages 3-7. –BH

Rock 'n Roll Teddy Bear / RS   1986
More rock. The fun continues. Ages 2-6. –BH

○ **Family Vacation / RS**   1988
This personifies Rosenshontz. It's well produced, with good songs, and is more adventurous than their other records. If you can only have one Rosenshontz, this is it. Ages 2-8. –BH

KEVIN ROTH

The Secret Journey / MARLBORO
For ages 3-6. –BH

After the Rain / MARLBORO
For ages 3-6. –BH

● **The Sandman ... / MARLBORO**
The Sandman, Lullabies & Other Night Time Songs is a truly lovely lullaby-type album. Recommended. Ages 1-3. –BH

The Toy Maker's Christmas / MARLBORO
For ages 2-4. –BH

Dinosaurs, Dragons & Other Songs / MARLBORO
For ages 3-5. –BH

○ **Unbearable Bears / MARLBORO**   1986
Kevin's accessible voice and super playing make his recordings a positive for any collection. This one's really all bears all the time. Ages 2-6. –BH

ROUNDER KIDS

○ **Rounder Kids / ROUNDER**
For ages 3-7. –BH

MEG RYAN w/ART LANDE

○ **Red Riding Hood & Goldilocks / WINDHAM HILL**
For ages 3-7. –BH

TOMMY SANDS

○ **Down Bendy's Lane / GREEN LINNET**
A delightful children's album featuring songs and stories Sands has picked up since childhood. "The Boy with No Story" will have you on the edge of your seat. "Moya Is My Darling," about his daughter, is priceless. Even an adult can enjoy this one. –CR

SAVE THE EARTH SAVE THE ANIMALS

○ **Save the Animals, Save the Earth / KIMBO**
For ages 4-7. –BH

SAXON & CROSS

○ **Steppin' to the Music / LSB**
For ages 3-6. –BH

BOB SCHNEIDER

○ **In a Child's Heart / GOLDEN**
For ages 2-6. –BH

JOE SCRUGGS

○ **Traffic Jams / RABBIT SHADOW**
Great writing, a sense of humor, and consistency characterize Joe's work. As a vocalist and communicator in general, he is eminently likable. Ages 3-8. –BH

Deep in the Jungle / RABBIT SHADOW
For ages 3-8. –BH

Even Trolls Have Moms / RABBIT SHADOW
A personal favorite. Ages 3-8. –BH

Abracadabra / RABBIT SHADOW
For ages 3-8. –BH

Late Last Night / RABBIT SHOW
For ages 3-8. –BH

SEBASTIAN

○ **Party Gras! / DISNEY**
For ages 2-6. –BH

MIKE AND PEGGY SEEGER

○ **American Folk Songs for Children / ROUNDER**
For ages 3-7. –BH

PETE SEEGER

A Fish That's a Song / SMITHSONIAN-FOLKWAYS
For ages 3-7. –BH

Folk Songs for Young People / SMITHSONIAN-FOLKWAYS
For ages 3-7. –BH

Activity Songs / SMITHSONIAN-FOLKWAYS
American Game & Activity Songs is for ages 2-5. –BH

Song and Play Time / SMITHSONIAN-FOLKWAYS
For ages 2-4. –BH

American Folk Songs / FOLKWAYS   1954
American Folk Songs for Children is for ages 3-7. –BH

○ **Bugs & Little Fish / SMITHSONIAN-FOLKWAYS**   1955
These two recordings, *Birds Beasts Bugs & Little Fish* and *Birds Beasts Bugs & Bigger Fish* are the heart of what Pete has to say to children. They still work — especially for younger ones. For ages 3-7. –BH

Bugs & Bigger Fish / SMITHSONIAN-FOLKWAYS   1955
For ages 3-7. –BH

★ **Abiyoyo ... / SMITHSONIAN-FOLKWAYS**   1967
What can one say about the father of it all? Pete has been a staple in this music for a long, long time. His voice and banjo — and his life — stand for positive values for people in general, especially on this album, *Abiyoyo & Other Story Songs.* For ages 3-7. –BH

SESAME STREET

Bert & Ernie: Side b Side / GOLDEN
Sesame Street products are generally kid-friendly (this one too) and educationally worthy. The production is a bit behind the times but the voices are familiar. This is particularly good. Ages 3-6. –BH

The Best of Ernie / GOLDEN
If you like Ernie, you'll like this. Ages 3-5. –BH

○ **Bob McGrath's Favorite Street Songs / A&M**
Bob from Sesame Street sings well-arranged, well-orchestrated, and well-produced songs. His positive approach, gentle manner, and "rose-colored glasses" style make one tend to forget his vocal weaknesses. Ages 3-6. –BH

☆ **Put Down the Duckie / GOLDEN**
Sesame Street, hipper than usual. *Put Down the Duckie - New Hits from Sesame Street* is one of the most musical of the CTW records. Recommended. Ages 3-6. –BH

★ **The Best of Sesame Street / GOLDEN**
Exactly what it implies, a compilation. It's quite good. For ages 3-6. –BH

○ **Alphabet Album / GOLDEN / BB 189**
There are better alphabet recordings, but this one has those lovable characters. Ages 3-6. –BH

In Harmony / WARNER
For ages 3-7. –BH

SHARON LOIS AND BRAM

Stay Tuned / ELEPHANT
Children's music's "arena" act. SL & B are more than Nickelodeon's "Elephant Show." They are so well loved, by virtue of their wit, perceptiveness, and ability, that children want to be like them. These recordings could be purchased according to desired subject matter. They do tend to be a bit alike. Pick up the package and have a look. Ages 2-4. –BH

Live in Concert / ELEPHANT
For ages 3-5. –BH

Elephant Show / ELEPHANT
For ages 2-5. –BH

Happy Birthday / ELEPHANT
For ages 2-5. –BH

One Elephant / ELEPHANT	1978
For ages 2-5. –BH	
Smorgasbord / ELEPHANT	1979
For ages 2-5. –BH	
Singing 'n Swinging / ELEPHANT	1980
For ages 3-5. –BH	
In the Schoolyard / ELEPHANT	1981
For ages 3-5. –BH	
○ **Mainly Mother Goose / ELEPHANT**	1984
For ages 2-4. –BH	

PATRICIA SHIH

○ **Big Ideas / FRAGILE GLASS**
As one of the few Asian-American singers and writers for children and families, Patricia has made a very strong recording. One flaw — the production isn't up to the songs or vocals. Otherwise, this is a "voice" that should be heard. "Color Song" and "Eating Is Fun ..." are worth the cost all by themselves. Ages 4-7. –BH

MAX SHOWALTER

○ **Bremen Town Musicians / AMME**
For ages 3-7. –BH

Gold Dog / AMME
For ages 3-6. –BH

ANITA SILVERT

○ **Rainbow Earth / LOCAL FOLKEL**
This shows promise. Wait until the next one. She's good, but new to the market as a writer and producer. Ages 3-6. –BH

LAURA SIMMS

○ **There's a Horse in My Pocket / GENTLE WIND**
Laura is one of the truly great storytellers. She could hold a

brick spellbound. Her stories know no limits in time and space. I think she might be magic! None of these will disappoint. Ages 2-10. –BH

An Incredible Journey / GENTLE WIND
For ages 3-8. –BH

Stories Just for Kids / GENTLE WIND
For ages 3-8. –BH

SIMPLE FOLK DANCES

○ **Simple Folk Dances / KIMBO**
For ages 3-5. –BH

SINGABLE NURSERY RHYMES

○ **Singable Nursery Rhymes / KIMBO**
For ages 2-4. –BH

SINGAMAJIG

○ **We Are Singamajig / S**
For ages 3-4. –BH

SINGING GAMES FOR LITTLE PEOPLE

○ **Singing Games for Little People / KIMBO**
For ages 3-4. –BH

SLEEPING BEAUTY

○ **Sleeping Beauty - Story / BUMBLEBEEZ**
The classic. Ages 3-5. –BH

Sleeping Beauty - Story/Songs / DISNEY
For ages 3-6. –BH

SLEEPYTIME ON SESAME STREET

○ **Sleepytime on Sesame Street / GOLDEN**
The inclusion of the characters makes it desirable. Otherwise, it's just OK. Ages 2-5. –BH

THE SMOTHERS BROTHERS

○ **Aesop's Fables / MUSIC FOR LITTLE PEOPLE**
These two could read the phone book and I'd laugh. I think kids will get it too. Ages 3-7. –BH

SNEAKERS

○ **Sneakers - Music for Sophisticated Kids / SMI**
Enthusiasm and good basic values taught with songs that range from OK to very good. The vocals are uneven. Production will get better as they go along. Ages 4-8. –BH

RONDAL SNODGRASS

○ **Coyote Tails / MUSIC FOR LITTLE PEOPLE**

SNOW WHITE & THE SEVEN DWARFS

○ **Snow White & The Seven Dwarfs - Story/Songs / DISNEY**
Disney wins this one. This one has life, the other one kind of sits there. Ages 3-6. –BH

Story / BUMBLEBEEZ
For ages 3-6. –BH

DON SPENCER

○ **Feathers, Fur or Fins / ABC**
If you want children to know about Australia, this is your guy. Folksy, down under fun, particularly *Australia for Kids* and *Australian Animal Songs*. Ages 4-8. –BH

Australian Animal Songs / ABC
For ages 4-8. –BH

Let's Have Fun / ABC
For ages 3-6. –BH

Australia for Kids / ABC
For ages 4-9. –BH

LYNNE STONES

○ **Bananas in His Eyebrows / BANANA**
For ages 3-6. –BH

MERYL STREEP w/LYLE MAYS

○ **Tale of Peter Rabbit / RHINO-RINCON**
For ages 3-6. –BH

MERYL STREEP w/THE CHIEFTAINS

○ **Tailor of Gloucester / RHINO-RINCON**
What a great combination — Meryl and the Chieftains make the recording fly by. Ages 4-7. –BH

SWEET DREAMS

Sweet Dreams / KIMBO
For ages 2-4. –BH

SWEET HONEY IN THE ROCK

○ **All for Freedom / MUSIC FOR LITTLE PEOPLE**   1989
Children need to know about freedom hard won and about music coming directly from someone's soul to their ears. This recording can do that. Ages 4-10. –BH

MAX VON SYDOW

○ **East Of Sun-Norelco / RHINO**

THE TALE OF SQUIRREL NUTKIN

○ **Story Book and Cassette (SP) GBD 8006 / BUMBLEBEEZ**
For ages 2-4. –BH

TALE SPIN

○ **Drumming Up Business / DISNEY**
For ages 3-5. –BH
Seeds of Victory / DISNEY
For ages 3-6. –BH

TBA

○ **Finn McCoul / RHINO-RINCON**

TEDDY RUXPIN

○ **Teddy Ruxpin & Friends / RHINO-RINCON**
For ages 2-4. –BH
Teddy Sings Lullabies / RHINO-RINCON
For ages 1-4. –BH
I Am Proud to Be Me / RHINO-RINCON
For ages 3-4. –BH

MARLO THOMAS

☆ **Free to Be You & Me / ARISTA**   1972
A real groundbreaker, this recording caught the fancy of hundreds of thousands well before modern children's music. The values it imparts are still important, particularly in the area of equality of males and females. Ages 3-10. –BH
Free to Be a Family / A&M   1988
More of the above. Ages 3-10. –BH

THE THREE LITTLE PIGS

○ **The Three Little Pigs / SCORE PRODUCTIONS**
For ages 3-5. –BH
Story and Songs / DISNEY
The Disney version is the better of the choices. Ages 3-5. –BH

TICKLE TUNE TYPHOON

○ **Hearts and Hands / MUSIC FOR LITTLE PEOPLE**
For ages 3-5. –BH

Keep the Spirit / MUSIC FOR LITTLE PEOPLE
For ages 3-6. –BH
Circle Around / MUSIC FOR LITTLE PEOPLE   1983
For ages 3-5. –BH
Hug the Earth / MUSIC FOR LITTLE PEOPLE   1985
For ages 3-7. –BH
All of Us Will Shine / MUSIC FOR LITTLE PEOPLE   1987
For ages 3-7. –BH

TALE OF MRS. TIGGY-WINKLE

○ **Story Book and Cassette (SP) GDB 8004 / BUMBLEBEEZ**
For ages 2-5. –BH

TALE OF TIMMY TIPTOES

○ **Story Book and Cassette (SP) GDB 8008 / BUMBLEBEEZ**
For ages 2-4. –BH

TOES UP TOES DOWN

○ **Toes Up, Toes Down / KIMBO**
For ages 2-4. –BH

JACKIE TORRENCE

○ **Classic Children's Tales / ROUNDER**
Jackie's stories bring her characters absolutely to life. Her delivery usually gets the attention of even the most rambunctious kid. Some of her tales capture the African-American oral tradition as well as any. Ages 4-10. –BH
Jump Tales / ROUNDER
For ages 4-10. –BH

TOTALLY MINNIE

○ **Totally Minnie / DISNEY**
Disney finally emphasizes a female character, and it only took 50+ years. Children should know that female mice can be popular too. Ages 2-5. –BH

TURNER w/TANGERINE DREAM

○ **Rumpelstiltskin / RHINO-RINCON**
For ages 3-7. –BH

UGLY DUCKLING

○ **Story / SCORE PRODUCTIONS**

LIV ULLMANN w/JEAN-LUC PONTY

○ **Puss in Boots / RHINO-RINCON**
For ages 4-10. –BH

UNCLE FRED

○ **Let Your Inside Out / UNCLE FRED-PINWHEEL**
These songs are terrific. The recordings sound very fresh and clever. Fred is the Randy Newman of the genre. Ages 3-7. –BH

PETER USTINOV

○ **Orchestra / MARU**
For ages 3-7. –BH

MICHELE VALERI & MICHAEL STEIN

○ **Dinosaur Rock / CAEDMON**   1983
For ages 3-8. –BH

JIM VALLEY

Dinosaur Ride / RAINBOW PLANET
Jim cowrites most of his songs with children, giving the songs a particular kind of energy and thrust. Each title is remarkably consistent as well as imaginative. *Dinosaur Ride* is a good place to start. For ages 3-7. –BH

Imagine That / RAINBOW PLANET
For ages 3-7. −BH
Friendship Train / RAINBOW PLANET
For ages 3-7. −BH
○ **Rainbow Planet / RAINBOW PLANET**   1984
For ages 3-7. −BH

DAVE VAN RONK

○ **Peter & the Wolf / ALACAZAM**
I confess to being a bit jaded and overexposed to this piece. As Snoopy said in the comics upon being exposed to it for the umpteenth time, "I hope the wolf eats him." However, new ears tend to like our friend Peter. Never has there been a wolfier voice than Van Ronk's. Ages 3-8. −BH

VELVETEEN RABBIT

○ **Story / BUMBLEBEEZ**
For ages 4-8. −BH
Book and Cassette / SMARTY PANTS
For ages 4-8. −BH

VITAMIN L

Walk a Mile / LOVABLE CREATURES
12 singers (children and adults), who captivate with a positive world vision. Ages 3-8. −BH
○ **Everybody's Invited / LOVABLE CREATURES**
This second recording shows development and further promise. A group to watch. Ages 3-8. −BH

MAX VON SYDOW w/LYLE MAYS

East of the Sun, West of the Moon / RHINO-RINCON
For ages 4-8. −BH

WASHINGTON w/UB40

○ **Anansi / RHINO-RINCON**
For ages 3-9. −BH

WEAVER w/JASON MILES

○ **Snow Queen / LIGHT YEAR**
For ages 4-8. −BH

WEAVER w/RYUICHI SAKAMOTO

Peachboy / RHINO-RINCON
For ages 4-8. −BH

WEE SING

○ **Wee Sing / PRICE STERN SLOAN**
At the risk of going counter to a substantial-selling, long-standing, and extensive catalog for very young children, I find many of these albums underestimate their listeners, under-think their stories, and manage to do all of this at a very reasonable price. Many people obviously disagree with this assessment. Low price should not by definition rule out quality products. Ages 2-4. −BH
Wee Sing and Play / PRICE STERN SLOAN
For ages 2-4. −BH
Nursery Rhymes and Lullabies / PRICE STERN SLOAN
For ages 2-4. −BH
Wee Sing King Cole's Party / PRICE STERN SLOAN
For ages 2-4. −BH
Around the Campfire / PRICE STERN SLOAN
For ages 2-4. −BH
Australia / PRICE STERN SLOAN
For ages 2-4. −BH

Wee Sing America / PRICE STERN SLOAN
For ages 2-4. −BH
Bible Songs / PRICE STERN SLOAN
For ages 2-4. −BH
Wee Sing for Christmas / PRICE STERN SLOAN
For ages 2-4. −BH
Dinosaurs / PRICE STERN SLOAN
For ages 2-4. −BH
Fun-n-Folk / PRICE STERN SLOAN
For ages 2-4. −BH
Over in the Meadow / PRICE STERN SLOAN
For ages 2-4. −BH
Silly Songs / PRICE STERN SLOAN
For ages 2-4. −BH

BILL WELLINGTON

○ **WOOF Radio / WELL IN TUNE**
Though I think this artist will grow a lot more, I still like this one: a radio station as broadcast through the in-class "announcements" wall speakers. Quite original. Ages 4-8. −BH

WHAT'S IN THE SEA?

○ **What's in the Sea? Songs about Marine Life / KIMBO**
For ages 3-5. −BH

ROBIN WILLIAMS w/RY COODER

☆ **Pecos Bill / WINDHAM HILL**
A Grammy-winning recording. I usually don't recommend the "stars tell the story" as a guarantee for a great product; this one, as it turns out, is brilliant. Ages 3-10. −BH

ROBIN WILLIAMSON

○ **Songs for Children of All Ages / FLY**
For ages 3-7. −BH

MACHEIS WIND

○ **Doughey, the Pancake Man / MOLE END**
One terrific pancake. He takes kids away to fight pirates, with butter and syrup dripping from his rounded self. Ages 3-7. −BH

WINNIE THE POOH

☆ **Honey Tree / DISNEY**
Here is Pooh at his best. Recommended. I think these stories should live on and on. Ages 2-6. −BH
A Blustery Day / DISNEY
For ages 2-6. −BH
Tigger Too / DISNEY
For ages 2-6. −BH
A Day for Eeyore / DISNEY
For ages 2-6. −BH

GEORGE WINSTON w/MERYL STREEP

○ **The Velveteen Rabbit / RABBIT EARS**
This one made quite a splash and is indeed very good. For ages 4-9. −BH

JONATHAN WINTERS w/LEO KOTTKE

○ **Paul Bunyan / WINDHAM HILL**
Yes, Winters can communicate well indeed with children. He's a wonderful kind of silly. Ages 3-10. −BH

WIZARD OF OZ

○ **Story/Songs / DISNEY**
For ages 3-8. −BH

CHILDREN'S COLLECTIONS

All of Us Will Shine / MUSIC FOR LITTLE PEOPLE
For ages 3-8. –BH

○ **American Children / ALACAZAR**
Various interesting singers contribute songs to this slightly eccentric but wonderful collection. Peter Schickele, John Sebastian, Maria Muldaur, and more. Ages 3-8. –BH

Babysongs / HIGH TOP
For ages 1-3. –BH

Babysongs Presents Baby Rock / M
For ages 2-5. –BH

The Children's Musical Companion / SAN
For ages 3-7. –BH

Disney Children's Favorites 1 / DISNEY
All of these are about equal in quality. Just look for the songs you like. Nothing new, inventive, or earth-shattering here. Ages 2-6. –BH

Disney Collection - Best Loved Songs #1 / DISNEY
Of these three collections, I like #1 best, just for the integrity of the sequencing, song selection, and such. Chestnuts abound. Ages 3-7. –BH

Family Folk Festival / MUSIC FOR LITTLE PEOPLE
For ages 3-8. –BH

Hug the Earth / MUSIC FOR LITTLE PEOPLE
For ages 4-8. –BH

Keep the Spirit / MUSIC FOR LITTLE PEOPLE
For ages 3-8. –BH

○ **Laugh-Along Songs / RANDOM HOUSE-KIMBO**
Most Kimbo recordings are essentially educational. Not that they're flat or dull — just that their first priority seems to be education, not entertainment. Ages 2-5. –BH

○ **Moonbeams & Gentle Dreams / MUSIC FOR LITTLE PEOPLE**
Various artists. For ages 1-4. –BH

○ **One Wide River - Songs & Stories / AMERICAN MELODY**
A nice collection of folk ballads, folk songs, and stories that can be enjoyed by adults and children alike. Jonathan Edwards and Dave Mallett offer up their usual strong performances. Tom Callinan, Phil Rosenthal, and Phil Bloch do a great version of "The Ragglin' Bog." This is not the kind of music that will wind up your children at bedtime. –CR

Sing with Me Animal Songs / RANDOM HOUSE
For ages 3-5. –BH

Sing with Me Christmas Songs / RANDOM HOUSE
For ages 3-5. –BH

Sing with Me Lullabies / RANDOM HOUSE
For ages 1-3. –BH

Sing with Me Mother Goose / RANDOM HOUSE
For ages 2-3. –BH

Sing with Me ... & Counting Songs / RANDOM HOUSE
For ages 2-3. –BH

Sing-Along Take Along Library / RANDOM HOUSE
For ages 2-3. –BH

○ **Time Can Be So Magic / NORTHSTAR**   1988
Produced by Bill Thomas. A collection of songs from "The Captain Kangaroo Show" featuring Noel Paul Stookey, Dave Mallett, Cheryl Wheeler, Paul Geremia, and Peter, Paul & Mary. A thoroughly enjoyable and classy recording. –CR

CHILDREN'S VIDEO

○ **Abel's Island / RANDOM HOUSE**
Great story. The art is wonderful and the narration is quirky and appealing. Children's Circle is the originating company of this tape. Their stuff is generally very high quality — you can't easily go wrong. –BH

○ **Adventures of Scrabble ... / VESTRON VIDEO**
The Adventures of Scrabble People in a Pumpkin. Full of nonsense. –BH

○ **Babar Comes to America / VESTRON VIDEO**
If you're a Babar fan, these will probably satisfy. I prefer Babar as a book. –BH

○ **Baby Songs - John Lithgow's ... / MEDIA HOME ENT.**
I like *Baby Songs - John Lithgow's Kid-Size Concert* in spite of itself. It's Lithgow that makes it work. It would be infinitely better with a bit more production value applied with a bit more thought. –BH

○ **Baby Songs (W/ Hap Palmer) / MEDIA HOME ENT.**
Hap Palmer's famous series. Much positive interaction between the children and parents means a real "feel good" series. –BH

○ **Glenn Bennett - Musical Chairs ... / ZOOM EXPRESS**
Glenn Bennett - Musical Chairs Concert Series. Concert-music video for children as it ought to be. A great artist and band, wonderful songs, and a turned-on audience. Super production. I love it — rock & roll for big and little people. I'm biased — it's on my label, but it's wonderful. –BH

○ **The Berenstein Bears' Christmas / RANDOM HOUSE**
Famous bears for young children. Good stories that translate well to video. –BH

○ **Bucky O'Hare: Kreation Konspiracy / FAMILY HOME**
If you like the character, this will be satisfactory. It's not a music video. –BH

○ **The Care Bears Movie / VESTRON**
Not for me. –BH

○ **It's the Great Pumpkin, Charlie Brown / HIGH TOP-**
If you love Peanuts, these will be familiar from TV. –BH

○ **Clifford's Fun with Letters / FAMILY HOME ENT.**
These are for young children. Very popular. –BH

○ **Judy Collins - Baby's Bedtime / LIGHT YEAR**
No one can sing a lullaby like Judy Collins. Attractive art. For very young children. –BH

○ **Judy Collins - Baby's Morningtime / LIGHT YEAR**
As much as I love the music (especially Judy's wonderful voice), this one worked better as audio only. As a video it's really stretched too far. –BH

○ **Dickens Collection: A Christmas Carol / VESTRON**
This is one way to introduce Charles. I'd rather children waited and read the books. –BH

○ **Doug & Garry / SURF PRODUCTIONS VIDEO**
This live concert for families, *Doug & Garry - Adventures of the Happy Pirates*, has much to recommend it. It's silly, musical, very interactive, but most of all, it's fun. If big people can get past Gary's role as an oversized eight-year-old, they'll like it too. –BH

○ **Dr. Seuss - The Shape of Me & Others / RANDOM HOUSE**
The books are better but these are fun. –BH

○ **Fairy Tale Classics - Vol. 1 / VESTRON**
Fairy tales should be more exciting. –BH

○ **Fisher-Price : Little Red Riding Hood/ MEDIA HOME**
Good — but only for very young children. –BH

Gemini - Fancy That! / GEMINI VIDEO   1990

○ **Live in Concert / YOUNGHEART MUSIC**
These two are personalities many young kids have been aware of through school for quite a while. Positive values, helping kids feel good about themselves, and fun music make this a worthwhile record. –BH

○ **Gumby Celebration / FAMILY HOME ENTERTAINMENT**
I love Gumby, and this stretches the imagination. –BH

○ **Arlo Guthrie: Baby's Storytime / LIGHT YEAR**
Arlo's understated narration and music make these classic stories easy to listen to. –BH

○ **I'm a 3-Toed, Triple-Eyed ... / RMM**
I'm a 3-Toed, Triple-Eyed, Double Jointed Dinosaur. Lowest-

common-denominator stuff. Full diapers and throwing up. The voice isn't very good by my standards and the playing is only adequate. There's nothing especially to recommend the video production. Still, kids do laugh at this stuff. –BH

○ **Ella Jenkins (For the Family) / FOLKWAYS**
Although I prefer Jenkins live, on audio, or in the studio, her great understanding of children and her ability to teach while entertaining shines through on this video. For very young children. –BH

○ **Lamb Chop in the Land of No Manners / A&M**
If you like Lamb Chop, you'll love this. –BH

○ **Tim Noah: In Search of the Wow Wow Wibble ... / A&M**
In Search of the Wow Wow Wibble Woggle Wazzie Woodle Woo! is a story about space, monsters, and such in the closet, which is where this tape should stay. –BH

○ **Pegasus (Stories to Remember) / LIGHT YEAR**
Mia Farrow's narration is quite good. The animation is very basic, and the characters look a bit like Saturday morning cartoons. –BH

○ **The Point / VESTRON**
Harry Nilsson's classic about finding one's own place and overcoming ostracism. Wonderful music and narration.

Though the animation is a bit basic, it is quite clever. This one's a must — if you can find it. –BH

○ **Rosenshontz: Feel Better Friends / GOLDEN MUSIC**
Bill and Gary are better on audio. –BH

○ **Richard Scarry - Best ABC Video / RANDOM HOUSE**
Richard Scarry's stories are better as books but do make it fairly well onto video. –BH

○ **Sesame Street Dance Along Songs / RANDOM HOUSE**
Sesame Street videos are pretty consistent. They look like the TV show. Buy according to content. –BH

○ **Sharon, Lois and Bram / A&M**
Sharon, Lois and Bram - Elephant Show/Soap Box Derby. This is are the only "arena" act in the children's business. It's all because of the "Elephant Show" and, of course, because these three are very good at what they do. These videos can be seen as episodes of the show. –BH

○ **TMNT - Attack of the Big Macc / FAMILY HOME ENT.**
With the Teenage Mutant Ninja Turtles and many other character-oriented videos, take your child's pulse to be sure they're still popular before you spend the money. –BH

○ **Wee Sing Mountain / PRICE STERN SLOAN**
Not for me. Harmless, but that's where they stop. –BH

Children's Music Sources

2 M Records, Box 364, Stn G, Calgary, Alberta, Canada T3A 2G3

A Gentle Wind Productions, Box 3103, Albany, NY 12203

Alkazar, PO Box 429, Waterbury, VT 05676

Amee Lu Records

Astro Records, 8033 Sunset Blvd. Ste 685, Los Angeles, CA 90046

Australian Broadcasting Corporation, Polygram

Banana Records, Station A Box 405, White Rock, B.C. V4B 5G3

Beanstalk Productions, 160 Madison Avenue, 6th Fl., New York, NY 10016

Berner Publishing Co., 6320 Cartwright Drive, New Orleans, LA 70122

Big Bear Music, PO Box 532, N. Egremont, MA 01252

Big Records, 1812 W. Hood, Chicago, IL 60660

Boston Skyline, Paul, Peggo (603) 623-1458, (603) 225-8986

Bumblebeez, 21535 Claretta Ave., Lakewood, CA 90715

Caedmon Records, 1995 Broadway, New York, NY 10023

Care Bears, Score Productions, 3414 Peachtree Rd., Atlanta, GA 30326

Castle of Dreams Music, PO Box 147, Bedford Hills, NY 10507-0147

Children's Circle, Weston, CT 06883

The Children's Group, 561 Bloor St. W, #300 Toronto, Ontario, Canada M5S 1Y6

Coco Records, Dan Conley, 10 Weavers Hill, Greenwich, CT 06831

Dandelion Music, 275 King St. E., Ste 22, Toronto Ontario, Canada M5A 1K2

DBV Walt Disney Records, 500 S. Buena Vista St., Burbank, CA 91521

Discovery Music, 4130 Greenbush Avenue, Sherman Oaks, CA 91423

Do Dreams Music, 2770 S.171 St., PO Box 248, New Berlin, WI 53151-0248

Easy Street Records, 2 Easy Street, Woodbury CT 06798

Educational Activities, Box 392, Freeport, NY 11520

Elephant Records, PO Box 101 Station Z, Toronto, Ontario, Canada M5N 2Z3

Ellen Feldman, BMI, PO Box 17561, West Hartford, CT 06117

Family Home Entertainment, 15400 Sherman Way, Box 10124, Van Nuys, CA 91410

Fragile Glass Music Publishing, PO Box 1554, Huntington, NY 11743

Gemini, 2000 Penncraft Court, Ann Arbor, MI, 48103

Golden Glow, 800 Livermore St., Yellow Springs, OH 45387

Golden/Western Publishing, 1220 Mound Ave., Racine, Wisconsin 53404

High Top/Media Home Entertainment, 5959 Triumph Street, Commerce, CA 90040-1688

High WindyRecords, Fairview, NC 28730

Imagine If Productions, 41 Brookside Ave., Valley Cottage, NY 10989

J. Aaron Brown, 1508 16th Avenue South, Nashville, TN 37212

Kamotion Music, PO Box 844, Bala Cynwyd, PA 19004

Kimbo Educational, Box 477, Long Branch, NJ 07740

Launch Pad Records, 16 Stacey St., Randolf, MA 02368

Laura Simms/Gentle Wind Productions, Box 3103,
Albany, NY 12203

Light Year/Media Home Entertainment, 5959 Triumph
Street, Commerce, CA 90040-1688

Local Folkel, Box 17196, Rochester, NY 14617

Lois LaFond, Boulder Children's Productions, PO Box 4712,
Boulder, CO 80306

Lovable Creatures Music, 105 King Street, Ithaca, NY 14850

Magic Dragon, PO Box 1952, London, Ontario N6A 5J4

Marlboro Records, 845 Marlboro Spring Road,
Kennett Square, PA 19348

Media Home Entertainment, 5959 Triumph Street,
Commerce, CA 90040-1688

Medicine Show Music, PO Box 389, Hughsonville, NY 12537

Moles End Music, RD #3, Box 118, Hampton, NJ 08827

Music For Little People, PO Box 1460, Redway, CA 95560

Musical Munchkins, PO Box 356, Pound Ridge, NY 10576

Over the Moon, (201) 659-8369

Pax Records, 78 Park Place, East Hampton, NY 11937

Perfect Score Music, PO Box 5061, Cochituate, MA 01778

Peter Pan Records, 88 St. Francis Street, Newark, NJ 07105

Playtime Music, 282 Wimbledon Rd., Rochester, NY 14617

Price Stern Sloan, 410 N. Cienega Blvd.,
Los Angeles, CA 90048

Rabbit Ears, 2225 Colorado Avenue,
Santa Monica, CA 90404-3555

Rabbit Shadow Records, PO Box 180476, Austin, TX 78718

Rainbow Enterprises, PO Box 733, Clinton, IA 52732

Rainbow Morning Music, 2121 Fairland Road,
Silver Spring, MD 20904

Rainbow Planet, PO Box 735, Edmonds, WA 98020

Random House, 400 Hahn Rd., Westminster, MD 21157

Red Rover Records, PO Box 6490, Evanston, IL 60202

Rhino/Rincon Recordings, 2225 Colorado, Ave.,
Santa Monica, CA 90404-3555

Roar Records, 2 Wisconsin Circle, Ste #800,
Chevy Chase, MD 20815

Rosenshontz, RS Records, Box 651, Brattleboro, VT 05302

Round River Records, c/o Debbie Block, 301 Jacob St,
Seekonk, MA 02771

Score Productions, Atlanta, GA

Seatofourpants Productions, 1250 Riverbed,
Cleveland, OH 44113

Sid Leiberman, 2522 Ashland, Evanston, IL 60201

Singamajig, PO Box 147, Madison, NJ 07940

Smarty Pants, 15104 Detroit Ave., Ste 2,
Lakewood, OH 44107

Song Trek, 2600 Hillegass, Berkley, CA 94704

Song Wizard, PO Box 93242, Los Angeles, CA 90093

Spring Board Records, 2140 Shattuck Ave., Box 2317,
Berkeley, CA 94704

Steve Charney, 2199-8 Stoll Rd., Saugerties, NY 12477

Storymaker Records, 18 Village Green,
Port Chester, NY 10573

Surf Productions, 282 Wimbleton Rd., Rochester, NY 14617

Three Feathers Music, 311 Sixth Avenue,
Brooklyn, NY 11215

Timeless Tunes, PO Box 240, Roslyn, NY 11576

Uncle Fred Records/Pinwheel Productions, 211 W. 56th St,
Ste 8J, New York, NY 10019

Uncle Wilton Productions, Wilton Banks, PO Box 490,
Desoto, TX 75115

United Media, 200 Park Avenue, New York, NY 10166

Well in Tune Productions, 301 Thompson St.,
Staunton, VA 24401

Youngheart Music, 2413 1/2 Hyperion Avenue,
Los Angeles, CA 90027

Zoom Express, 568 Broadway, Suite 1104,
New York, NY 100120

WORLD MUSIC

Any book with a single chapter on "world music" runs straight into a very basic problem. You can tell it like it really is, from the perspective of the proverbial "musical Martian," giving a balanced picture of styles (99% of which are totally unknown to Americans,) or you can wildly distort reality and produce something your public can relate to. The latter course is the only reasonable one in a book like this, but the result is a little like a supermarket with three shelves: "soup," "pretzels," and "everything else."

Even if you simply divide the world into *The West* and *The Rest*, ignoring the fact that a good deal of Western music ends up in the World category, we're looking at one chapter devoted to at least 85% of the world's music. Obscure stuff, of course — like Chinese music, which is relevant to a mere one-fifth of the world's population (a bit more than that, if you count the millions of overseas Chinese). Or Indian music, with not one but two major classical traditions, three "universal" religions, and many more regional ones. Latin America: 33 nations, two major languages, and styles that have transformed the whole rhythmic basis of popular music in the United States. And if international influence rather than numbers is the issue, there's Cuba: an island of 10.5 million people whose sounds beat the US out for enduring influence on other cultures.

Just as no chapter (and no book and no ten-volume series) can really offer more than a drop in the ocean of world music, there's no way I can pretend to sum things up in a few hundred words. Instead I've decided to point out a few hidden confusions and traps in the American (and therefore this chapter's) concept of the subject.

Much the most important of these is the very major difference between what I like to call "other people's music" and the intercultural experiments of Western musicians, whether it's Yehudi Menuhin playing with Ravi Shankar, Art Blakey playing with Solomon Ilori, or Annabaoula mixing various Middle Eastern styles with various Western idioms. Though these mixes have recently come to be called "world beat," they're really Western styles with non-Western elements, just as willow-pattern Delft china was Dutch plates with Chinese motifs.

This would be a lot more obvious if almost every music in the world didn't stem from a mix of other music, very frequently from different cultures. There may be a couple of Amazonian nose-flute players and a didjeridu virtuoso in central Australia who was never influenced from outside, but that really isn't the way most music works, and the richest cultures are usually the most mixed (United States, Balkans, Latin America, India). On this level, pretty much all music is crossover music.

"Other people's music" is in fact most of the music that exists. This would be more obvious if the US weren't so large, so geographically isolated, and so musically deprived. I know somebody who did a survey of recordings on sale in an open-air market in Abidjan, the capital of Ivory Coast. There were local recordings. There were recordings from other African countries. There was soul. There was jazz. There was French pop. There were the Beatles. There was US country music (lots of it, though stressing Jim Reeves). There was New York salsa. There were several sorts of Cuban music. There was more, which I've forgotten. All of this in a stall next to a woman selling yams. I defy anybody to find an equivalent range of music in your average US mall.

We also tend to overestimate our influence on the rest of the world. So it comes as a bit of a surprise to learn that, while the rest of the world has consumed US music quite freely for the last half century, Cuba and Argentina have been overwhelmingly more influential internationally over the last 75 years or so. Over the long term, the powerhouse has been the Middle East, which gave both Asia and the West most of their musical instruments.

One reason for listening to "world music" is because it's most of the music there is. The second reason — and most important — is because it's enriching beyond belief. World beat can be nifty, but the real thing can strike like lightning — it can raise the hair on the nape of your neck. It wasn't some worldbeat recording (or Xavier Cugat) that really launched the Latin takeover in the US in 1930; it was a recording of "The Peanut Vendor" by a genuine Cuban band. And the same is true for individuals. I've known people whose entire lives have been changed by the revelation of Cuban or Indian music (or, in my case, calypso-and-blues-and-flamenco-and-Arabic music all at once).

So, welcome to "other people's music" in all its many-splendored glory.

— John Storm Roberts

INTERNATIONAL COLLECTIONS

☆ **Compact Real World / ATLANTIC**　1989
Here is a superb sampler of Real World releases, some of which do not appear on the artist's individual albums. A great

way to get to know Baaba Maal, Guo Bros., Remmy Ongala, Nusrat Fateh Ali Khan, Tabu Ley (Rochereau), and others. –MB

○ **Globestyle Worldwide Tour Guide / GLOBESTYLE**
This sampler CD is a real ear-opener, and essential listening for those curious about this innovative label's bag of worldly goodies. –MYLES BOISEN, ROOTS & RHYTHM

○ **Horizons Sampler / MOTW**　1992
Includes tracks from *Asian Journal, Malaga to Cairo, Piano*

Crossroads, Basic Tendencies, and Ramama, and features new recordings with Jim Bowie (banjo) and Anders Rosen (saxophone quartet). Great sounds in a modern world music sampler. –MUSIC OF THE WORLD

☆ **Memory of the Peoples / UNESCO** 1990
This budget-priced import sampler of 28 selections really covers the globe, and is worth tracking down. –MB

Voices - World's Greatest Choir / RHINO 1991
This multi-disc box assembles a joyful variety of international vocal groups — from Bulgarian choirs to Buddist monks to Pygmy polyphony to the Mormon Tabernacle! –MB

○ **Welcome to Our World - 1990 / RYKODISC** 1990
New and traditional music from scattered regions. Beautifully recorded. –MB

AFRICA

ALGERIA

HOURIA AICHI

Neo-traditional.
Chants de l'Aurès / AUVIDIS
Music of the Aurès mountains south of Constantine, recorded in a vein now regarded as old-fashioned (for which read traditional or even classic), with flute and percussion backing. Wonderful. –JSR

CHABA FADELA

Rai. One of the Rai Rebels from Algeria. –MGN
○ **Hana Hana / MANGO** 1978
On this album, backed by a more modern sythesizer sound and pristine French production, the Queen and King (her husband Cheb Sahraoui is here also) of rai unite for a series of solid duets. –BT

○ **You Are Mine / MANGO** 1988
"N'sel Fik" by Fadela and her husband Cheb Sahraoui is the biggest Algerian hit in the country's history. The rest of the tracks here aren't bad either. See the *Rai Rebels* listing. –JP

CHEB KADER

Rai. The Elvis of rai music. Potent hybrid — emotional Arabic vocals and melodies set against contemporary rock percussion and production. –HD
○ **From Oran to Paris / SHANACHIE**
An odd hybrid of emotional Arabic vocals and melodies set against contemporary rock production. –HD

CHEB KHALED

Rai. Many got their first exposure to Algerian rai music through Cheb Khaled, who set the pace for most of the young Chebs with his youthful good looks and rebellious, streetwise stance. With noted producer Rachid Baba behind him, Khaled brought the sensuous rhythms and high-tech gloss of pop-rai to the English-speaking world, leaving an indelible mark with his soaring vocals and tales of debauchery. –MB
○ **Kutche / CAPITOL-INTUITION** 1989
Though its heart-of-hearts is in the right place, even the best Algerian rai usually suffers from a less than state-of-the-art synthesizer sound. Not so here. Collaboration between Paris-based keyboard whiz Safy Boutella and one of rai's most powerful voices sets tough standards for other discs. –BT

MOHAMED KHAZNADJI

Classical andalus.
○ **Nouba du Mode Maya / ESPERANCE**
Half of what was once a double-LP set by one of the best contemporary classical vocalists in the andalus style that goes back to the idiom brought by refugees from the collapse of Muslim Spain. Here he sings a nouba (vocal suite) in Maya mode, whose title in English is "Wedding Morning," backed by string and percussion orchestra. Thorough French notes accompany the release. –JSR

CHEB MAMI

Rai. Mami was one of the first "Chebs" to be heard in the West when rai music came out into the open in 1985-1986. Known as the Prince of Rai, he presented a clean-cut, fashionable image consistent with the Paris scene, but maintained a rootsy stance on his first few recordings. –MB
Prince of Rai / SHANACHIE 1989
Unlike most rai, this disc features live musicians, including a wailing Arabic fiddle guaranteed to raise goose bumps. –JP

BELLEMOU MESSAOUD

Rai.
○ **Le Père du Rai / WORLD CIRCUIT**
Messaoud was not only an early pop-rai luminary but a man with the bizarre but ultimately successful notion of using a trumpet in Maghrebi music. This release, with new vocalist Cheb Ourrad Houarri, has a basically acoustic band consisting of accordion, guitar, keyboards, and rhythm. –JSR

CHEIKHA REMITTI

Rai.
○ **Ghir el Baroud / MICHEL LEVY**
A stunning new recording by the Bessie Smith of rai. Aside from the sheer splendor of the performance, its flute-and-percussion backing is the "missing link" between urban styles like chaabi and the electronic rai of the new generation. The controlled emotional charge of this antiestablishment music comes with a subdued humor, but the overriding effect is of power. –JSR

ALGERIA COLLECTIONS

Algeria (Sahara) / EMI
Strong tribal music. –DLM
○ **Folklore Kabyle / CLUB DU DISQUE ARABE**
The Kabylie mountain dwellers of Algeria maintain a fierce cultural independence. The backbone of the resistance against the French, they have since proven a thorn in the side of the independent government. Musically, they have contrived both to preserve their tradition and to refresh it. These recordings include several by the great Kabylie women singers, Hanifa, Djamila, as well as the superb younger Daughters of Djudjura, plus examples of traditional double reeds and drumming. Much of the music is not so much traditional as popular-infused-by-traditional. Adequate English notes. –JSR
☆ **Rai Rebels / VIRGIN** 1988
Virgin's collection goes beyond the obvious rai heavies, though it includes Fadela's "N'sel Fik" yet again. Here are the great Chaba Zahouania and a particularly fine newcomer, Houari Benchenet, who gets a great deal of mileage out of mixing the older harmonium sound with his electronics — plus, natch, Sahraoui, Khaled, and Hamid. Adequate sound, rather ragged editing, wonderful music. –JSR
☆ **Rai Rebels - Vol. 2 - Pop Rai & Rachid Style / ATLANTIC**
The anthology includes selections from Cheb Zahouzni, Cheb Khaled, Chaba Zahouania, etc. An excellent intro to the East African pop sound of rai. –RW
Sahara: Music of Gourara / AUVIDIS
Gourara, an area of oases, was once prosperous and wealthy, and though some of its music is common to the whole Sahara, some of the most ancient reflects a strong cultural individuality. There's a wide range of music here, some religious, some secular, but mostly reflecting a classic sacred/secular unity-in-duality. The singing is mostly choral with a strong solo lead, and much of it is underpinned with

percussion, but there's also some fine reed flute and spike fiddle. —JSR

BURUNDI COLLECTIONS

Burundi: Traditional Music / OCORA
○ **The Master Drummers of Burundi / ARION**

Why do some tiny countries produce more kinds of soul-snaring music than others ten times their size? The most striking music on the Ocora recording is the eerily beautiful whispered singing that accompanies the inanga zither. But even the more common East African sounds — the delicacy of the sanza, the almost-human musical bow, the crisp acridity of the spike-fiddle — seem to reach a peak of eloquence in this moon-mountain land. The master drummers were once royal musicians and they preserve a courtly tradition that has vanished in too many African countries. —JSR

CAMEROON

FRANCIS BEBEY

Neo-traditional. A composer, guitarist, and novelist from Cameroon, Bebey has combined Latin American, Western (pop and classical), and African elements into his compositions. —JP

○ **Akwaaba / ORIGINAL MUSIC**   1984
These compositions for sanza (thumb piano), drums, and claves are accompanied by singing, including a technique called double voice, a method of singing two notes at the same time. The music is peaceful, eerie, and spiritual. —JP

MONI BILE

Makossa.
○ **Moni Bile / MB**
Cameroonian makossa has more drive that Zairian zoukous, and a larger dollop of local traditional rhythms. Bile is an absolute top makossa artist, and this excellent album shows why, with drive, fine solos, and variety in arrangements. —JSR

LES TETES BRULÉES

Bikutsi. Africa's first "punk" band appears on stage in tribal paint, wearing shades and outrageous costumes, and plays a blistering guitar pop that's almost heavy metal in its attack. The first African guitar band to radiate "attitude" with a capital A, with the musicianship to back up their aggressive stance. Their style has been dubbed "Bikutsi" and expands on many of the current melodic and rhythmic formulas of West African pop. —JP &MB

☆ **Hot Heads / SHANACHIE**   1989
Exciting, electric "new wave" band from Cameroon. Funky and punky. —MB
Bikutsi Rock / SHANACHIE   1992
Cameroon's "hot heads" sweeten their sound with the Mory Kante Group's horn section and multilayered vocals by Charlotte Mbango. This comes across less like African punk than like a Gold Coast funk and soukous experiment. —BT

CHARLOTTE MBANGO

Makossa.
○ **Maloko / ENERGY**
Mbango is a very nifty singer in a vein reminiscent of Mbilia Bel, whose backings mix zouk influences and Cameroonian instrumental sound. Mix and match maybe, but a mix that does indeed match. Nothing blindingly innovative, just warmth, charm, bounce. Toto Guillaume, Joe Mboule, Naimro zouk it to 'em on keyboards. Outrageously short, but that's all too standard in makossa/soukous/zouk. —JSR

African Music

There's no way to write coherently about the music of a continent covering 52 independent nations, between 800 and 1600 languages (depending on your definition), and at least five major cultural groupings. The confusions inherent in this kind of diversity are many, but a few stand out. Some of the confusion stems from the fact that African music has been both influential and influenced. The direct or indirect influence on new-world popular music has been varying, but all of it, "White," "Black," or "Latin," has at least a touch of Africa. And the compliment has been returned. African music has always been (and remains) essentially local, but African musicians have always drawn from elsewhere: over a thousand years from Islam, over a couple of hundred from Europe, over half a century from the Americas, somewhat (and increasingly) from US African-American styles and reggae, greatly in the past from US country music, and enormously from Cuba and Latin New York.

More confusion results from the Western stereotype that associates drums with African traditional music. In reality, western Nigeria (for example) has a dozen or so 20th-century urban styles for voices and percussion alone, and at least one of these outshines in popularity all the Nigerian musicians known to the West.

There's another confusion of much greater immediate importance to this listing of African recordings. Different circumstances have led to noticeably different levels of "Africanness" in contemporary pop styles. At the most "African" level, there's what happens when a whole culture falls in love with an overseas influence, as the Congolese did with Cuban music. Sophisticated individual bands sometimes develop styles with an abnormally high proportion of overseas influence (Fela Kuti, Manu Dibango). When expatriate musicians form bands to play the music of their homeland, as did Osibisa in London, they come under different influences and produce a different mix. Different yet again are groups combining expatriate African musicians with Europeans, like the Germano-Ghanaian "Burger-Highlife" bands in Germany. Lastly, famous musicians with a local or expatriate African audience (N'Dour, Ade, many others) have recently been trying to "cross over" internationally, with still different results.

All this tends to mislead newcomers to African music. At first, naturally enough, people tend to like music that's not too foreign, which means very American-influenced. So we latch onto individual musicians with a strong American element and assume, usually incorrectly, that Africans think as much of them as we do. The result is that Fela or Manu Dibango get described as "African superstar" when they are not by any means the superstars of their own countries and are pretty much unknown elsewhere in Africa. (In fact, the only musicians with a real pan-African appeal are the big names of soukous, and even they don't have any noticeable following in South Africa.)

All of which means that if you want to explore African music, albums by Fela or the recent big-label recordings of Youssou N'Dour make handy vehicles for starting the journey. But if that's as far as you go, you haven't even landed yet.

— John Storm Roberts

SAM FAN THOMAS

Makossi.
☆ **Makassi / TAMWO** 1984
This French album features "African Typic Collection," the tune that made Thomas a worldwide star with its fusion of zouk, soukous, and other West African beats. –JP
Makassi Again / CELLULOID 1990
This is high-energy dance music, but fairly generic compared to earlier efforts. –JP

CAMEROON COLLECTIONS

Cameroon: Musiques du Cameroun / OCORA
Music of the Bakweri, Bamileke, Bamoun, and Beti peoples are featured on this recording. –DLM
Music of the Baka Pygmies / AUVIDIS
My favorite music from the Cameroons. There is one particular track that features young girls singing and slapping the water. –DLM

CAPE VERDE COLLECTIONS

○ **Cape Verde Islands: The Roots / PLAYA SOUND**
A 1990 recording of the Afro-Lusitanian tradition of Cape Verde, which leans heavily toward the Portuguese end of the Verdean spectrum; mornas and coladeiras for cavaquinho and viola (guitar family), and funanas for accordion and metal scraper — all radiating the nostalgic melancholy the Portuguese call saudade. Of special interest, on the more Afro end, is a song for the rare cimboa spike fiddle. –JSR

CENTRAL AFRICAN REPUBLIC COLLECTIONS

Banda Polyphony / PHILIPS
Fascinating polyphonic horn and flute ensembles and vocal ensembles. –DLM
Bobe Ceremony / OCORA
A wonderful recording of the soundscape of these Pygmy people from their ritual to honor the forest.) –DLM
Drum Chant & Instrumental Music / NONESUCH
Drum Chant & Instrumental Music - Niger, Mali & Upper Volta includes strong and interesting drumming, chants, lutes, and flute. –DLM
Musical Anthology of the Aka Pygmies / OCORA
Central Africa: Musical Anthology of the Aka Pygmies is one of the finest recordings ever done of a traditional soundscape. The recordings were done by Simha Arom, who pioneered the recording of polyphonies. –DLM
Musique Centrafricaine / AUVIDIS
This is the best overview of various tribal musics throughout the Central African Republic. It includes music from the following peoples: Azande, Babinga, Bagandou, Bianda, Bofi, Broto, Dakpa, Isongo, Linda, and Ndokpa. –DLM

CHAD COLLECTIONS

Chad: Music from Tibesti / CHANT DU MONDE
My favorite recording of traditional music from Chad that is currently available on CD. –DLM

DAHOMEY COLLECTIONS

○ **The Fulani / AUVIDIS**
The six million or so Fulani are scattered through several Sahelian countries, but these recordings are all from two groups, one living in North Dahomey and the other in Niger. This re-release from the old UNESCO World Atlas series is simply splendid: varied, superbly played, well recorded, and well documented. A lot of fine flute playing, praise songs to lute and other instruments, and various ritual and work songs — as well as an unduly substantial example of jaw harp, the recording's only longueur. –JSR

ETHIOPIA

MAHMOUD AHMED

Pop. Mahmoud Ahmed is a well-dressed elder statesman of Ethiopian popular music, leading the field for over 20 years at home, and even making concert appearances in the US. He is a master vocalist in the highly ornamented East African style and is known for inducing the uninhibited shaking of "eskeukta" on the dance floor. –MB
☆ **Ere Mela Mela / HANNIBAL** 1986
Ere Mela Mela: Modern Music from Ethiopia is a dark and brooding mix of 60s San Francisco rock ambience with Ethiopian modality. Driven by bluesy sax riffs and Ahmed's passionate vocals. –BT

ASTER AWEKE

Pop. Washington, DC, singer who combines Ethiopian melismatic singing with contemporary dance beats. –ED
○ **Aster / COLUMBIA** 1989
If Aretha Franklin had been born in Ethiopia, she might have grown up to be Aster Aweke. The singer mixes jazz, soul, funk, and Ethiopian strains to produce a form that's made her a superstar back home and a fast-rising talent in the US. American soul music has been a force in Ethiopia since the 60s, so Aweke's fervent vocalizing should ring a bell with most listeners. –JP
Kabu / COLUMBIA
This one is more Western, with jazzier arrangements, but Aweke's voice sounds even earthier and more passionate than on her debut album. –JP

SELESHE DAMESSAE

Traditional.
Tesfaye: Vocal & String Music of Ethiopia / MOTW 1986
Seleshe Damessae, an accomplished singer and musician from Ethiopia, offers a wonderful selection of compositions rendered in complex vocal stylings and sung in Amharic, his native language. He accompanies himself on the krar, a six-string lyre, which dates back to the ancient civilizations of the Nile. –MUSIC OF THE WORLD

MINDANOO MISTIRU

Traditional.
○ **Mindanoo Mistiru - Vol. 1 / LYRICHORD**
A good introduction. Avoids restrictive definitions and offers contemporary barroom music for accordion and percussion as well as some of Africa's most ancient idioms. –JSR

ETHIOPIA COLLECTIONS

○ **Jewish Liturgies of Ethiopia / INEDIT**
Though their own legends make the Falasha, or Ethiopian Jews, descendants of the Queen of Sheba, the oldest solid records go back to the 14th century AD, and the oldest scholarly guesstimate I've seen goes to the 4th. Whatever, their liturgical music is very different from both local secular forms and Ethiopian Orthodox Christian liturgy. Here are parts of Sabbath offices, wedding prayers, and circumcision songs. –JSR
○ **Music of Ethiopia - Vol. 3 / MUSICAPHON**
The baganna, the magnificent "harp of David," here on *Music of Ethiopia - Three Chordophone Traditions*, plays its essential role as accompaniment to songs of meditation. The krar, known as the devil's instrument, is used to accompany love and topical songs. The masinqo, a spike fiddle of a type common in Africa, as well as the Middle East and the Balkans, is heard in music for weddings and other social gatherings. All are played on this album by exceptional musicians. –JSR
○ **Musiques Ethiopiennes / OCORA**
An excellent overview. –DLM

GAMBIA

ALHAJI BAI KONTE

Kora. Traditional kora player from the Gambia, an elder of the West African pop generation, and father of Dembo Konte. –MB

○ **Kora Melodies / ROUNDER**
Kora player Alhaji Bai Konte was a virtuoso of the older style of the instrument, and this recording brings out its rich delicacy. Comparison with the second album, by two cousins of a younger generation of Konte, offers a rare opportunity to hear how traditional African music changes over time. Good recording quality. The notes to the first album are particularly valuable because they give a strong feeling of the music's physical environment, not merely its technicalities. –JSR

FODAY MUSA SUSO

Kora. Foday Musa Suso is a master musician with one foot on the dance floor and one foot in the villages of Africa. Suso was born in Gambia to a distinguished family of griots (musician storytellers) that can trace their line back almost a thousand years. He has been tireless in his efforts to spread African music and culture to all corners of the globe. On his solo recordings, and as a member of his Mandingo Griot Society, he plays traditional African folk music. On his Mandingo records he leads an electro funk fusion band that can rock the house with the best rap, funk, and house groups. He's played extensively with Herbie Hancock (that's his kora on "Rockit") and frequently collaborates with Bill Laswell on various Afro-fusion experiments. –JP

○ **Hand Power / FLYING FISH**   1969
A solo album of traditional Gambian acoustic music. –JP

New World Power / CELLULOID
On this album Suso continues his Afro-funk experiments with Bill Laswell and other members of New York's Downtown Art/Rock Mafia. –JP

GAMBIA COLLECTIONS

African Journey / VANGUARD
African Journey: Roots of the Blues in Africa features very interesting brass band music, Christian choral singing, kora, and mandingo drumming. –DLM

Ancient Heart / MANGO-AXIOM
Traditional music from musicians of the Mandinka and Fulani ethnic groups featuring kora (African harp) and balafon (wooden marimba). An excellent example of Africa's folkloric roots recorded in the field by Foday Musa Suso. Some of this stuff sounds like it could be the rhythmic ancestor of house music. –JP

GENERAL AFRICA COLLECTIONS

☆ **Africa Dances / AUTHENTIC**   1972
This groundbreaking pan-African anthology was the first and is still the only continent-wide survey, also the only one to compare and contrast pan-African developments during the crucial 50s-70s period. The CD has music from 13 countries, two more than the LP/cassette versions. –JSR

○ **Africa on Mango / MANGO**   1988
Pleasant collection of very accessible contemporary pop-oriented music from Africa. Some sung in English and some in native tongues. Rhythmic, "happy," generally uptempo, easy on the ears. Features the Bhondu Boys, Salif Keita, Mbougeni Ngema, and others. –NJF

○ **African Acoustic / ORIGINAL MUSIC**   1988
More of Africa's enchanting acoustic guitar styles: 1981 recordings by both adults and kids. The only name known even to megabuffs is the late Losta Abelo, once a friendly rival of Mwenda Jean Bosco. The most bewitching cuts of all, in my view, are by a Tanzanian who plays only for friends; one song is briefly and unintentionally accompanied by the clattering of crockery. The kids include a group of blind school children

African Musical Terms

Afrobeat — West African dance music with strong Afro-American influences, symbolized by Fela Anikulapo-Kuti of Nigeria.

Apala — 20th century Islamic-influenced street music with vocals and percussion.

Bátá — Nigerian lap drums (three double-headed drums played together) used for religious purposes in Cuba.

Benga — Guitar music originating with the Luo people of Western Kenya but now widely popular throughout the country.

Fuji — Post World War II Western Nigerian percussion and vocal music.

Griot — A traditional bard of the Mandingo people, revered and respected as an essential member of their community, performing at all ritual functions.

Highlife — A complex of dance styles from English-speaking West Africa, developed around the turn of the century. Guitar band music heard with jazz-like horn sections or in rural areas with just multiple guitars.

Jit — Music from Zimbabwe that features percussion and vocals. The Bhundu Boys and James Chimombe were among those who adopted more modern styles.

Juju — Talking drums, multiple guitar lines, and call and response vocals are prime lements of this music, with links to the traditional drumming of the Yoruba tribe of western Nigeria. Ebenezer Obey, I. K. Dairo, and King Sunny Ade are the grand masters of juju music.

Kora — A 21-string harp-lute linked to Mandingo culture, and frequently played in Mali, the Gambia, Guinea, and Senegal.

Kwassa kwassa — Zairean dance fad popular in the late 80s.

Kwela — South African pennywhistle street music developed in the 50s.

Makossa — Cameroon's major contemporary dance rhythm, combining soukous with traditionally local elements.

Mbalax — A Senegalese percussion music. Also the modern dance style of Youssou N'Dour and others.

Mbaqanga — South African township music first popular in the mid 60s.

Mbira — The Zimbabwean name for the finger piano widespread throughout sub-Saharian Africa.

Mbube — A choral music style from South Africa with roots in the glorious local traditions and Afro-American gospel.

Milo jazz — The namesake of Milo malt drink, this is a Sierra Leone street dance.

Palm wine guitar — An older West African acoustic guitar music named after the drink.

Rai — Although an older form, contemporary rai is a teenage rebel music, mixing electronics with Algerian street idioms.

Soukous — A popular teenage dance music from 70s Zaire. From the French word for "shake," it is the generic name for an influential music of Zaire and the Congo that has spread across Africa. Combining local musical ingredients with Cuban/Caribbean rhythms and elements of 30s and 40s American country music (the guitar sound of Jimmie Rodgers, for example).

Taarab — Afro-Arab urban music of the East African coast in the Swahili language. This is listening, not dance music, typically heard at wedding parties.

making very adept music with homemade instruments, and a hell-for-leather cut for high-pitched voices and tomato-can banjo. −JSR

○ **African Moves - Vol. 1 / ROUNDER**   1987
This CD has soukous from Tabu Ley Rochereau, juju from Ebenezer Obey, and highlife from African Brothers as well as other artists. −JP

○ **African Moves - Vol. 2 / ROUNDER**   1987
A sampler featuring crossover artists, musicians that mix African and Western styles, especially funk and reggae, for a sound pleasing to Europeans as well as the folks back home. Solid work by Salif Keita, Papa Wemba, and Aster Aweke, among others. −JP

Music of Africa / KALEIDOPHONE
The most outstanding contribution to documenting African musics is the *Sound of Africa* series by Hugh Tracey. That entire collection can be found only in particular college libraries and homes of collectors, but the ten-volume *Music of Africa* is available on the Kaleidophone label: *Musical Instruments 1, Strings; Musical Instruments 2, Reeds (Mbira); Musical Instruments 3, Drums; Musical Instruments 4, Flutes & Horns; Musical Instruments 5, Xylophones; Musical Instruments 6, Guitars 1; Musical Instruments 7, Guitars 2; Rhodesia 1; Tanzania 1;* and *Uganda 1.* −DLM

○ **Out of Africa / RYKODISC**   1988
A good continental selection that includes Senegal's Youssou N'Dour, South Africa's Mahotella Queens, Nigeria's juju master Ebenezer Obey, and Rochereau. −JP

○ **Sound d'Afrique - Vol. 1 / MANGO**   1981
The first compilation of African dance music to be issued in North America by a major label and still one of the best. −JP

○ **Sound d'Afrique - Vol. 2 / MANGO**   1982
Soukous and soukous-influenced sounds from other West African countries. Highly recommended. −JP

○ **Sounds Eastern & Southern / ORIGINAL MUSIC**   1988
Acoustic guitar styles of many African nations: 20 examples of African acoustic guitar from nine different countries: Kenya, Somalia, Tanzania, Zaire, Zambia, Malawi, Zimbabwe, Mozambique, and South Africa. In most cases, contrasting tracks give an idea of the range of acoustic idioms in any one country. (Four CD cuts are drawn from existing albums.) −JSR

GHANA

MUSTAPHA TETTEY ADDY

Percussion.

○ **Master Drummer from Ghana / LYRICHORD**
Addy, a Ga from Accra, spent many years learning the major traditions of other groups as well as such recent developments as kpanlogo, a style developed by Accra teenagers in the 60s. Good technical quality; adequate notes. −JSR

A. B. CRENTSIL

Highlife.

Moses / AFRICAN MUSIC   1982
Aided by a denunciation from the Christian Council of Ghana, *Moses* brought Crentsil new stardom after his career slumped somewhat when the Sweet Talks collapsed. −JSR

○ **Reminiscin' in Tempo / AFRICAN MUSIC**   1991
A. B. Crentsil & the Sweet Talks were major figures in the highlife renaissance of the 70s. This 1978 "Hollywood Highlife Party" recording, the band's last, is one of the best 70s highlife offerings I know. −JSR

KAKRABA LOBI

Neo-traditional. Kakraba Lobi, who comes from a family of xylophonic virtuosi, is one of a large and growing number of African musicians who expand traditional music from within besides teaching it at university level. −DLM

Xylophone Player from Ghana / TANGENT
On this deeply satisfying recording, Lobi plays mostly his own

compositions and arrangements of traditional material, supported by percussionist Mustapha Tettey Addy. −DLM

E. T. MENSAH & TEMPOS DANCE BAND

Highlife. Mensah has had the longest reign of any of African music's self-crowned kings. The King of Highlife made his first records in 1952 and was an instant success with his Latin and Caribbean-inspired danceband style. He played in England in 1953 and toured West Africa steadily in the 50s and 60s. In the 70s, the sweet and swinging sounds of highlife were drowned out by a profusion of new styles, but Mensah's influence was still strongly felt. −MB

○ **All for You / RETRO**   1986
This highlife pioneer from Ghana merged the rhythms of calypso, Latin, and local tradition to establish the first African supergroup. −JP

Day by Day / RETRO   1987
Here is another stunning collection from Mensah and the Tempos. −JP

OBOADE

Percussion.

○ **Kpanlogo Party / LYRICHORD**
Contrary to the notions of many Westerners, African percussion musics are by no means all traditional. Kpanlogo, which surfaced in Accra during the 60s, was a new music created by teenagers hanging out, and it met the usual disapproving reaction from the older generation. Oboade, a family group led by master drummer Mustapha Tettey Addy, played it superbly. −JSR

GHANA COLLECTIONS

Ancient Ceremonies / NONESUCH
Ancient Ceremonies: Songs & Dance Music is a Nonesuch re-release of music recorded in the 70s, and the best general introduction to Ghanian traditional music that I've met, in that there's variety in singing styles, types of music, and instrumentation, along with excellent playing and very fine recording quality. −JSR

○ **Giants of Danceband Highlife / ORIGINAL MUSIC**   1990
In their palmy days, E. T. Mensah's 50s Tempos were the most influential band in West Africa. Here are four of their most charming early hits. The Ramblers — one of the hottest bands of the 60s — and the Uhurus were both jazz-oriented. The Ramblers stuck to straightahead dance music; Uhuru experimented, with phenomenal results, in the early 70s. This was the cutting edge of highlife in its time, and its extinction was a real loss. −JSR

Master Drummers of Dagbon - Vol. 2 / ROUNDER   1988
Some years back, John Miller Chernoff introduced Americans to the drumming traditions of the North Ghanaian Dagbamba, as he comments in the notes to this fine followup, as rich and diverse as those of better-known West African groups. −JSR

○ **Music of the Northern Tribes / LYRICHORD**
Reissue of an admirable mid-70s set of recordings by ethnic groups from Ghana's northern savannah. Much of this music shows the influence of Islam in its tight tone and vocal shake. There's a lot of variety here in styles and instrumentation (the Dagarti, for example, are noted xylophonists), and a sharp contrast with the better-known sounds of the southern forests. −JSR

GUINEA

BEMBEYA JAZZ NATIONAL

Sahelian.

○ **Wa Kele / SONODISC**
Bembeya Jazz National, one of the oldest and greatest of all Sahelian bands, was the inspiration for more famous groups (Les Ambassadeurs among them). Like any working band,

they keep up with the trends (at times too much so). But the great guitars, the punch and flow, are all their own. Particularly intriguing here is a version of the old Creole/calypso number, "Mammy Water." –JSR

SONA DIABATE

Sahelian pop. Sona Diabate comes from an extensive family of hereditary griot musicians from Guinea that includes many of the biggest names in traditional West African music. She is a particularly gifted singer who, as part of her occupation, must memorize vast amounts of oral history and compose "praise songs" to important figures and benefactors. She has also performed as a singer and guitarist with the band Les Amazones de Guinea. –MB

○ **Girls of Guinea / SHANACHIE**   1988

Two female vocalists and a pair of intertwining acoustic guitars weave in and out of the deep recesses of the heart in an urgent appeal to traditional values. Recorded live to two-track tape with acoustic guitar backing by guitar master Sekou Diabate and background singing from Les Amazones, this stirring set of vaguely Western-sounding songs bristles with passion and immediacy. –BT & MB

JALI MUSA JAWARA

Sahelian. Jali Musa Jawara, the half-brother of African pop star Mory Kante, performs traditional Manding songs of West Africa, praising important citizens and delivering well-intentioned advice. His glittering kora (multi-stringed gourd harp) is the centerpiece of gentle folk groups that include the marimba-like balafon, guitar, and a characteristic West African vocal chorus. –MB

☆ **Yasimika / HANNIBAL**

This new US release was first issued in France in 1983. Two koras, a balafon, and a splendid female chorus backing Jawara's lead make for a deserved bestseller among Africans in France. This is contemporary-traditional Mandingo music, purely and wonderfully performed and admirably recorded. A treasure, in fact. –JSR

Soubindoor / MANGO   1988

Guinean pop musician Jawara returns to his roots with a folk ensemble built around kora (Mandikan harp), balafon (marimba), guitar, and soaring high-energy vocals. –BT

GUINEA COLLECTIONS

Musics of Fouta-Djalon / PLAYA SOUND

Fouta-Djalon, in North Guinea, is home to groups with a strong griot tradition. This collection includes string and flute ensembles, a rare type of transverse flute, balafon, and of course various forms of song. –DLM

○ **Musique d'Afrique Occidentale / VOGUE-OLYMPIC**

An excellent sampling from West Africa, with xylophones, women's chorus, flutes, drums, and musical bow. This particular recording has had a profound effect on many of my friends as an introduction to African music. Out of print, but worth searching for. –DLM

IVORY COAST

ADAMA DRAME

Neo-traditional.

○ **Percussion: Adama Drame / AUVIDIS**

A master drummer. –DLM

IVORY COAST COLLECTIONS

Senufo-Fodonon Funerary Vigil / AUVIDIS

An interesting recording from the Ivory Coast. Music for Senufo funeral services is provided by orchestras of one-string harps and gourd rattles, which play continuously under the various vocal parts of the traditional liturgy. –DLM

KENYA

ABANA BA NASERY

Omutibo. A delightful trio of Shem Tube and Justo Osala Omufila on guitars and Enos Okola on Fanta bottle percussion. The three, also known as the Nursery Boys, have performed since the late 60s in the omutibo style, which is based on the Kenyan "dry guitar" tradition. –MB

○ **Abana Ba Nasery / GLOBESTYLE**   1989

Shem Tube and Justo Osala play acoustic guitars, Enos Okola is a percussionist who rubs the grooves on an empty Fanta bottle with a nail, and all three sing. An import collection of various Nasery singles from the 60s and early 70s. The style is called omutibo and sounds like a mix of Hawaiian folk music, early Delta blues, and acoustic soukous. An amazing record. –JP

MAULIDI AND MUSICAL PARTY

Taarab.

○ **Mombasa Wedding Special / GLOBESTYLE**   1990

Charming urban-Kenyan version of Swahili taarab, so freewheeling and laidback it's a wonder the music doesn't whirl apart. Recorded live at a women-only wedding celebration. –BT

DANIEL OWINO MISIANI

Benga. D. O. Misiani, the king of Kenya's "Benga" pop music, is an energetic and varied guitarist. His band Shirati Jazz is also featured on *The Nairobi Beat* (Rounder 5030) with other important Benga groups, and it's good to see him getting his due in the world music explosion of the 80s. –MB

○ **Shirati Jazz / GLOBESTYLE**

The Shirati Jazz release is a really outstanding collection of the benga heavies' early recordings, with founder Misiani. There's no date given here, but we'd guess mid 70s from the sound. The album consists of yet more recordings from a fine and influential band, these recently made. –JSR

☆ **Benga Blast / ATLANTIC**   1990

This features classic dance music from this Kenyan pioneer. Wild guitar! –MB

ORCHESTRA VIRUNGA

Soukous. Samba Mapangala left Zaire and settled in Kenya in the late 70s. He first led a soukous band of Zairian musicians called Les Kinois (Kinshasa Boys). When they broke up, he looked for local talent and formed Virunga, a group that takes soukous and adds Kenya's benga beat, as well as Western rock and blues influences. –JP

○ **Virunga Volcano / EARTHWORKS**   1990

This disc, with Samba Mapangala, compiles the band's early hits including "Malako," the tune that made them famous. –JP

ZEIN MUSICAL PARTY

Taarab.

○ **Zein Musical Party / GLOBESTYLE**   1990

The "men's taarab" on *Zein Musical Party - The Style of Mombasa* emphasizes the music's Arabic origins. The 'ud, violin, and hand-drum instrumentation is strictly traditional, but Zein isn't afraid to experiment, launching into spidery flamenco-influenced 'ud solos when the spirit strikes. –BT

KENYA COLLECTIONS

☆ **Guitar Paradise of East Africa / EARTHWORKS**   1990

The "other" guitar sound of Africa. Rootsier than soukous — with an emphasis on melody to match the propulsive rhythms — benga dance music from Kenya explodes in a sweet, energy-laden combination of fraternal vocal harmonies and chiming electric guitars. –BT

○ **Kenya Dance Mania / EARTHWORKS**   1991

A retrospective of rhumba and benga-influenced mega-hits

recorded during Nairobi's heyday as a trendsetting recording center in the late 70s and early 80s. Astonishing guitar breakouts, bottomless bass lines, and homespun homilies vie for center stage. –BT

○ **The Nairobi Beat / ROUNDER**   1989
A must-have release: a slew of Kenya's major benga bands, including the Maroon Commandos, Super Bunyoure, Shirati Jazz, and the splendid Kalambya Sisters. These aren't brand-new (1964, though you wouldn't know it from the otherwise excellent notes), but they're typical of many versions of the Kenyan sound documented on Original CDs. –JSR

○ **The Nairobi Sound / ORIGINAL MUSIC**   1982
This is still the only release covering the 60s pre-benga electric guitar, and the acoustic material fills the gap between Kenya Dry and the more recent British releases. Both the acoustic and electric sounds back then — before soukous took over the world — were strongly local and idiosyncratic, and this set offers a side of each (including the original version of "Malaika," which Miriam Makeba once turned into an international hit). –JSR

○ **Songs the Swahili Sing / ORIGINAL MUSIC**   1982
The first compilation of the Muslim music of East Africa's coast. With Indian film music and occasional rock and salsa influences grafted onto its basic Afro-Arab stock, this is a totally unexpected monument to the diversity of the Black experience. This, incidentally, was the release that brought taarab to the attention of the outside world, and it's still the most varied introduction, with fine singers male and female in idioms that range from near-Arab to one of the world's most improbable cha cha chas. –JSR

MADAGASCAR

RAKOTOFRAH

Popular.
○ **Flute Master of Madagascar / GLOBESTYLE**
Among the European styles reworked in Africa and the Caribbean was military fife-and-drum music and its civilian pipe-and-tabor equivalent, both of which fit nicely with various African equivalents. This is an enchanting (though awfully short) example of the sort of thing that resulted: a new music with clear European as well as local roots. The results sound very Caribbean — unless you know the older sega of Mauritius, Reunion, and the Seychelles. –JSR

RAKOTOZAFY

Traditional.
○ **Valiha Malaza / GLOBESTYLE**
The tube-zither valiha is one of the pinnacles of Malagasy music, typical in its mix of Southeast Asian and African ingredients. This re-release of the 60s recordings of the instrument's best-known master is much the best of Globestyle's Malagasy issues, and a worthy substitute for the vanished Ocora valiha album (which also, incidentally, included cuts by Rakotozafy). –JSR

ROSSY

Afro-pop.
○ **Island of Ghosts / REAL WORLD**   1991
The soundtrack from a British documentary about Madagascar, created by one of the island's most popular and innovative musicians. –JP

MADAGASCAR COLLECTIONS

○ **Madagasikara One / GLOBESTYLE**   1986
Madagasikara One: Current Traditional Music of Madagascar features the rapid, tumbling accordion styles and the sound of the valiha box-harp that typify the airy music of the Malgasy Republic. Also contains selections by master flutist Rakotofrah and the out-of-place military-band troupe Tsimialona Volambita. –BT

☆ **Madagasikara Two / GLOBESTYLE**   1986
Madagasikara Two: Current Popular Music of Madagascar. Island-accented township jive, Trio FA's irresistible accordion jam, and a pair of African outreach cuts by rising star Rossy testify to the richness of island culture. The diversity of material here, and its uniqueness is impressive. –BT

MALI

AMBASSADEURS INTERNATIONAUX

Sahelian.
☆ **Ambassadeurs Internationaux / ROUNDER**   1984
The Ambassadeurs go back a long way, but the period just after Salif Keita and Kante Manfila had moved the group to Ivory Coast and before they split up was certainly one of their great periods. This fine anthology presents the group at its best, playing for Africans and with none of the hit-hunting encumbrances that made the much-hyped Soro so disappointing. –JSR

FANTA DAMBA

Traditional.
○ **Mamadou Magadji / ESPERANCE**
Fanta Damba is a peerless singer in the classical Malian vein, a vocalist of power, restraint, and subtlety with centuries of Afro-Islamic tradition behind her. –JSR

ZANI DIABATE

African rock.
○ **Zani Diabate and the Super Djata Band / MANGO**   1988
Malian beats roil and boil beneath Diabate's sheets of electric guitar à la Jimi Hendrix, Freddie King, and a touch of the Doors. Psychedelic solo fever resembling nothing else in African music. –BT

NAHAWA DOUMBIA

Sahelian.
○ **Didadi / SHANACHIE**
Fine album from a young female vocalist. Her first album has a somewhat over-hip backing in places, but mostly it works well, and Doumbia herself is gorgeous. –JSR

IVORY'S

Kora. Folk trio from Mali plays acoustic music from the Manding Ethnic Group on kora (harp) and balafons (wooden xylophones). Simple, powerfully moving music. –JP
○ **Bala / WW**   1991
Two balafons and a kora played by members of the traditional Manding musicians' caste. Among all the kora music available, it is a too rare pleasure to hear the balafons at length. –DLM

MORY KANTE

Sahelian pop. Along with Salif Keita, Mory Kante was an early member of the seminal Rail Band of Bamako, joining as a singer when he was in his teens. After a stint as lead vocalist, he left the band to form his own theatrical troupe, which included dozens of performers and his brother Jali Musa Jawara. In the 80s he became an international pop star, exploring neo-traditional Manding music on the kora, as well as club-ready dance mixes. His "Yeke Yeke" became the biggest-selling African release to hit the European pop charts in 1987. –MB
○ **Akwaba Beach / BARCLAY**   1987
The first single from *Akwaba Beach*, "Yeke Yeke," was a major European dance hit for Kante in 1987. Dismissed by some for his heavy dance beat, Kante's crossover sound is a perfect way to ease your ears into the joys of African pop. –JP

SALIF KEITA

Afro-pop. Salif Keita was born in Mali into a family that can trace their roots back to Soundjata Keita, the warrior king who founded the Malian Empire in 1240. Keita was born an albino (a bad omen), and his family frowned upon his choice of a musical career. When he refused to follow a traditional path of study, Salif's father disowned him and he was left to wander the streets of Bamako, Mali's capitol. After years of singing on street corners and in small clubs, Keita landed a job as vocalist for the Super Rail Band, a government-sponsored group that was gaining national fame with their mixture of traditional and Western (especially Cuban) music. Mali is one of the northernmost states in Black Africa, and has always been a cultural melting pot, with Arabic, French, Spanish, and regional ethnic groups contributing to a unique musical and cultural mixture. In the Rail Band, Keita met guitarist Kante Manfila, another musician with an international pop vision, and together they pursued their vision of a Cuban/Zairean/Malian fusion. In 1973, the duo left the Rail Band and joined Les Ambassadeurs Internationaux, where their stylistic hybrid began to earn them an international reputation. As Les Ambassadeurs became more successful, they also became more aware of their roots and, as the Arabic influences of their culture crept back into the music, they developed one of Africa's most unique and hypnotic sounds.

In 1987 Keita left the Ambassadeurs to pursue a solo career in Paris. With the cream of that city's African session players, he recorded *Soro*, the international hit that brought him to the attention of Island Records, who now record his music for international distribution. –JP

Ko-Yan / MANGO   1989
A cabaret touch invades this Parisian production; which blends straightahead Afro-pop and punk with lacy electronic ornamentation. –BT

Soro / MANGO   1991
The album that propelled Keita into the front ranks of the international scene. –JP

○ **Amen / ISLAND**   1991
Produced by Joe Zawinul (Weather Report), this set is more international in scope, with guest shots by Carlos Santana and Wayne Shorter adding to its commercial appeal. –JP

KANTE MANFILA

Sahelian.
○ **Kankan Blues / AFRICAN MUSIC**   1991
A stunning record. Ace Afro-Frankfurter Gunter Gretz went to Manfila's hometown of Kankan and recorded him and various relatives, including balafonist Balla Balla. As you'd expect of a family of griots, there's magnificent traditional singing here, along with acoustic and electric guitar and superb balafon. Gretz's notes are both eccentric and very revealing, with a long account of the sundry hazards of field recording. –JSR

OUSMANE SACKO SACKO w/YAKARE DIABATE

Traditional.
The Night of the Griots / OCORA
My favorite recording of traditional music from Mali would have to be this one. –DLM

OUMOU SANGARE

Sahelian.
Moussolou / WORLD CIRCUIT   1989
This traditional recording (produced by Ibrahim Sylla, who turned the knobs for Salif Keita's international breakthrough *Soro*) was West Africa's biggest-seller in 1989. Sparkling kora (African harp), driving percussion, and a stunning multi-tracked voice that often recalls an African version of the Shirelles makes this one a winner. –JP

ALI FARKA TOURE

Guitar. Often hyped as "the African John Lee Hooker," Ali Farka Toure has a relationship to blues music much deeper

than this derivative label would suggest. The blues came to America with the slave trade, on ships loaded in West Africa. Farka Toure's music reclaims these forms by bringing the country blues back to its ancestral home. –MB

☆ **Ali Farka Toure / MANGO**   1988
At first blush you think you're hearing American Delta blues — then the Malian-language vocals kick in. Starkly beautiful acoustic guitar with tasty calabash and bongo percussion. –BT

○ **The River / MAKOSSA**   1990
Toure's second release expands his adventuresome blues-based approach, with a harmonica, sax, and native violin beefing up the sound on several cuts. –BT

African Blues / SHANACHIE   1990
A compilation of formative import recordings from this West African bluesman. –MB

MALI COLLECTIONS

Ancient Strings / BARENREITER MUSICAPHON
A particularly fine set of Malian traditional music released by the country's Ministry of Information. –DLM
First Anthology of the Music of Mali / MUSICAPHON
Wassolou Sound / STERNS
This documents great female vocalists from the southern part of Mali. –DLM

MAURITANIA

KHALIFA OULD EIDE w/DIMI MINT ABBA

Sahelian.
○ **Moorish Music from Mauritania / WORLD CIRCUIT**
Mauritanian music has been unavailable for so long, this would be an important release even if it were not also an absolutely gorgeous example of the enormously rich brew of Afro-Islamic nexus. The two women singers featured (the country's most famous) sing in a contemporary-traditional idiom like those of Fanta Sacko and other Malians. A total must-have. –JSR

MAURITANIA COLLECTIONS

Music and Songs of Mauritania / AUVIDIS
My favorite recording from Mauritania, performed by the great female vocalist Dimi Mint Abba is now available on CD. –DLM

MAURITIUS

JEAN-CLAUDE

Sega.
Pat Patoua / PIROS
Attractive mainline sega — a pop sound, but a strictly local one. Most of Jean-Claude's numbers have the familiar backwards 6/8 rhythm, but others are underpinned by a more traditional-sounding beat. The backings are basic small-group, with insistent but not aggressive rhythm, and the lead instrument is a feisty electric guitar. Nice stuff! –JSR

MAURITIUS COLLECTIONS

Segas de l'Ile Maurice / PIROS DISQUES
At last a new sega collection with the idiosyncrasy, tacky lilt, and small-town bounce of the style at its best. The singers are of Indian background, but that fact makes no odds stylistically. Tune after tune is backed by the typical sega backwards-waltz beat. Irresistible after all these years. –JSR

MOROCCO

A. BELKAYAT & A. DOUKALI

Moroccan pop. Abdelhadi Belkayat and Abdelwahab Doukali, leaders of the first wave of big-time Moroccan pop music, both began singing in the 60s. Both were inevitably influenced by Egypt, and indeed spent time there. But neither simply "went Egyptian," and both in fact ended up international stars. In very broad terms, Belkayat is reminiscent of Egypt's Abdel Hali Hafez. Doukali is a more dramatic singer with lusher and slightly more adventurous backings. –JSR

☆ **A. Belkayat & A. Doukali / DISQUE ARABE**
They make a terrific pairing on a super CD. –JSR

NASS EL-GHIWAN

Neo-traditional.
○ **Gnawa Songs / BUDA**
The Gnawa are Afro-Moroccan descendants of slaves from the south. Their mystical brotherhoods and their music combine North and Black African elements very differently from Sahelian music. Nass El-Ghiwan is a hugely popular young traditionalist group. The beautiful, and splendidly recorded, vocals and instrumentals mostly involve percussion and a remarkable three-stringed bass, the guembri, as well as occasional flute. –JSR

HASSAN ERRAJI

Traditional.
○ **Traditional Arabic Music / SAYDISC**   1991
Erraji excels on 'ud, darbouka, bandir, nay, and vocals in performances with his trio. –LK

NAJAT ATABOU

Berber.
○ **The Voice of the Atlas / GLOBESTYLE**   1991
She's mad as hell and she's not going to take traditional, restrictive views of women anymore. Searing, snarling vocals set fire to Berber drumming and wickedly sharp 'ud accompaniment. A mesmerizing recasting of North Moroccan folk music. –BT

CHEIKH SALAH

Classical.
☆ **Arabo-Andalusian Music / BUDA**
The late Cheikh Salah led one of the finest modern orchestras, playing North African classical music based on forms brought by refugees from the great music school of Cordoba at the collapse of Muslim Spain. This is pure and authentic style, superbly sung and backed by a small ensemble of local instruments. Dismal notes, short measure for a steep price, but the superb music more than compensates. –JSR

MOROCCO COLLECTIONS

○ **Gnawa Music of Marrakesh / AXIOM**   1990
Gnawa Music of Marrakesh: Night Spirit Masters — the great lost Led Zeppelin all-acoustic tapes? Naw! Primal rock from Morocco's Gnawa people — used in trance rituals and therapeutic practices — with layered percussion and ecstatic vocals. Could be the authentic roots of a sound heard round the world. Excellent contemporary recording of one of the many traditional Moroccan, drum-based styles. Heavily atmospheric moods. –BT & MB
☆ **The Master Musicians of Jajouka / ADELPHI**   1972
A field recording of hypnotic Moroccan oboe, string, and drum ensembles made famous by Brian Jones (Rolling Stones guitarist). –MB
○ **Pan-Islamic Tradition / LYRICHORD**
Pan-Islamic Tradition - Music of Morocco, features powerful music-flutes, double-reed oboe, drums, and chanting. –DLM
Rwayes Anthology - Berber Songs ... / INEDIT
Rwayes Anthology - Berber Songs and Instrumental Music from the Sous Region is included in a large and highly recommended series from Morocco on the Inedit series of recordings put out in France by the Maison des Cultures du Monde. –DLM
Sacred & Secular Music of the Middle-Atlas / OCORA
The French have a special gift for making recordings both

totally authentic and immediately attractive, as is this collection of vocal and instrumental pieces, mostly for flute and drum but including some lute-playing. Not only truly beautiful, it is also fairly unusual, since double-reed pipes are more common in the Maghreb region (and in Sufi music) than flutes. –JSR

MOZAMBIQUE

EDUARDO DURAO w/ORQUESTIA DURAO

Chopi.
○ **Timbila / GLOBESTYLE**
Timbila — New Chopi Music from Mozambique is highly recommended. –DLM

MAMA MOSAMBIKI EYUPHURO

African.
○ **Mama Mosambiki Eyuphuro / REAL WORLD**
Another highly recommended CD. –DLM

ORCHESTRA MARRABENTA STAR

Popular.
○ **Independance / PIRANHA**
Almost the hardest of all African music to find is the Portuguese-influenced idiom of Angola and Mozambique. This is no street music but the country's top band, using local rhythms and elements ranging from South Africa to the US via Youssou N'Dour (with a good dollop of Portuguese here and there). The results are quite varied, and fresh as well as polished. –JSR

NIGER COLLECTIONS

Nomades du Niger / OCORA
This very important early Ocora recording is devoted to the Touareg and the Bororo. It has just come out on CD. –DLM

NIGERIA

KING SUNNY ADE & HIS AFRICAN BEATS

Juju. Ade was born to a royal family in the Yoruba tribe, but like many musicians, he dropped out of (grammar) school and left home in search of fame and fortune. Ade's first gig was with the highlife band Moses Olaiya and his Rhythm Dandies, but he was increasingly drawn to juju, which traces its roots back to various forms of traditional Yoruba guitar playing that includes but is not limited to Christian "Aladura" church music and a Nigerian "blues" form. In the 20s, as cheap gramophones became available in Nigeria, players added elements drawn from American country music, Hawaiian and Cuban folk music, and the British music hall tradition. I. K. Dairo is known as the father of modern juju; he added electric guitars, accordion, and bass guitar to the music's folky style, while Ebenezer Obey added pedal steel and other African and modern touches.

Ade formed his first juju group, the Green Spots, in 1967. In 1974, tired of the hassles common to the Nigerian music industry, Ade formed his own record company and has since released over 40 albums and countless singles and EPs for both the home and international markets. Island Records promoted him in the States as the "African Bob Marley," but after pumping millions into Ade's organization they admitted defeat and dropped him from the label in 1984.

Ade's juju is heavy on the guitars (usually six guitars, each playing different lead lines), and the band produces a shimmering tidal wave of rhythm (live gigs use seven or more percussionists) and melody that's soothing and energetic at the same time. –JP

Return of the Juju King / POLYGRAM
More contemporary grooves from Ade's own label. –MB
☆ **Juju Music / MANGO-ANTILLES**   1982
The first of Ade's international releases on Mango, the record

that made North American and British fans aware of the richness of African music. A classic. —JP

Synchro System / MANGO   1983
High-tech sound and some electronic instruments give this an international appeal. —MB

Aura / MANGO   1984
A dense album tailor-made for international consumption with electronic percussion, high-tech production, and help from Stevie Wonder and Herbie Hancock. Surprisingly successful. —BT

Live Juju Live / RYKODISC   1988
An entire set (70+ minutes) that captures some of the live power of Ade and his band; recorded in 1988. —JP

SEGUN ADEWALE & HIS SUPERSTARS

Juju. Adewale was a willing participant in the juju boom of the early 80s, with an eclectic mix of Nigerian and Western styles he dubbed "yo-pop." He never quite made the splash that Obey or King Sunny did, but he produced a couple of exciting, distinctive albums in his heyday. —MB

○ **Play for Me / ROUNDER**   1988
Adewale's juju style is less guitar-centered than that of other, more popular Nigerian groups. The vocal harmonies are a major attraction here, as are the tracks in apala style, with just vocals and throbbing drums. Some English lyrics. —MB

AKANNI ANIMASHAUN & APALA GROUP

Traditional. Traditional Nigerian drum ensemble. —MB

☆ **Akanni De Alawiye Orin / SHANACHIE**   1984
A very important introduction to Yoruba percussion. —MB

BARRISTER

Fuji.

○ **More Fuji Garbage / GLOBESTYLE**   1991
Take Nigerian juju, strip it down to its rhythmic essentials, discarding everything else but atmospheric bursts of Hawaiian guitar and Barrister's incantory voice, and you've got the meanest, leanest sound this side of rap. —BT

I. K. DAIRO & HIS BLUE SPOTS

Juju. Considered by many to be the "father of juju" for his many innovations, Isaiah Kehinde Dairo was born in Kwara State, Nigeria, in 1931. One story has it that his lifelong love of music stemmed from a drum that his father, a carpenter, made for him in his youth and that accompanied him wherever he went. In early adulthood, Dairo tried earning a living as a barber, a construction worker, a cloth merchant, and with other jobs. Dairo sat in with early juju bands at night, led by musical pioneers Ojoge Daniel and Oladele Oro. In the mid 50s he formed his own group, the ten-member Morning Star Orchestra, which gained fame later as the Blue Spots.
Though highlife was the most popular form of band music in West Africa at the time, Dairo and his band released a long succession of influential singles that, by the end of the Nigerian Civil War in 1970, helped establish juju as the premier Nigerian sound. Dairo changed the tenor of juju by introducing the accordion and talking drums to the orchestra and singing in a variety of regional dialects, which widened the rural appeal of the music. When his appeal began to wane at the end of the 70s, he gave up performing, turning first to managing clubs and a hotel in Lagos, then to a ministry in the Cherubim and Seraphim church movement. In 1990 he recorded his first album in 15 years with a re-formed Blue Spots band. —BT

○ **I Remember / MOTW**   1991
One of the founding fathers of Nigerian juju returns after a 15-year retirement from the music business. The accordion anchor to his sound is a charming antidote to over-produced, technology-heavy pop. —BT

African Pop

The roots of popular US music can be traced to Africa. The guitar, the world's favorite folk instrument, is a North African lute that was modified by the Spanish during the Moorish conquest. The origins of the blues, which led to rhythm & blues, rock & roll, soul, heavy metal, disco, new-wave, rap, and every other youth music of the past several hundred years, can be traced back to the rhythms of West Africa brought to the new world by slaves. Jazz was born in New Orleans, a city where Africans mixed their music with that of their English, French, and Spanish neighbors. Salsa is a combination of African drumming and Spanish folk music with the rhythms of the native peoples of Cuba and the Dominican Republic; soca is African with a dose of English and Latin folk music; zouk is what happened when Africans, native Islanders, and French people mixed in Guadeloupe — the permutations are endless. Despite the racism and economic exploitation of European incursions, African rhythms have emerged triumphant whenever outsiders came in contact with Africans.

Attempting to compile a basic library of African music is a difficult task. Imagine for a moment that someone had never heard any (North) American music. Where would you send that person to begin an investigation? Mississippi blues? Miami or New York salsa? Tex-Mex accordion music? Zydeco? Rock? Disco? Polka? And the US is only one country. Africa is a continent that includes several Arabic nations as well as thousands of Black ethnic groups, each with their own music, language, and culture. There are some obvious starting points. The impact of artists like Franco, Fela, Kuti, Mahlathini, Ladysmith Black Mambazo, Salif Keita, and Youssou N'Dour on our planet's growing international consciousness has been increasing and will continue to do so, but they don't begin to tell the story. While the listings here merely scratch the surface, they should provide you with a starting place. With a few exceptions, these are confined to current recordings that should be easy to track down in any large record store.

— J. Poet

○ **The Glory Years / ORIGINAL MUSIC**   1991
I. K. Dairo, the most influential juju master ever, created its gorgeous vocal sound by borrowing the harmonies of the local Church of the Cherubim and Seraphim, besides widening its appeal beyond the Yoruba core audience. These are the early 60s recordings that made him the king overnight (and won him the MBE the Beatles also got). Splendid guitar, soaring vocals, great percussion, plus the jaunty accordion playing he also introduced. The major Dutch music magazine called it the "re-release van het jaar" (re-release of the year). Savvy chaps! —JSR

FELA ANIKULAPO KUTI   ♭1938

Afro-beat. Fela Kuti was born the son of a strict minister father and a mother named Funmilayo, who went on to become one of Nigeria's leading feminists. Fela was a problem child in grammar school, and by the age of 16 he was singing in a highlife band, much to the chagrin of his parents. Upon the death of his father, Fela convinced his mother to send him abroad to study music. He landed in London in 1957 where he studied trumpet, got married, and formed his first band, Koola Lobitos. In 1963, Fela and the band moved back to Nigeria and began experimenting with various stylistic innovations ranging from highlife to jazz to soul. In 1968, after hearing the music of James Brown (through cover versions played by the band of Geraldo Pino from Sierra Leone), Fela added funk to his mixture and called it "Afrobeat."

In 1969 he took his band on an extended US tour, where a month's residence in Los Angeles brought him in contact with the Black Panthers and other American Black Nationalist groups. He attended consciousness-raising groups, read widely in Black and African history, and returned to Nigeria with a militant gleam in his eye. Between 1970 and 1977 Fela released over 30 albums of incendiary African agit-pop that took the Nigerian government to task for corruption, brutality, and mismanagement. In 1977 the government responded by burning Fela's living quarters and nightclub to the ground; Fela was jailed and tortured. On his release, he continued to make records that made the government squirm as much as they made the common folk dance. As his reputation grew, Fela added more and more musicians and dancers, until his troupe grew to a revue of some 80 people. Although most of his recent music has been rather perfunctory in nature, his 70s classics stood out in the African pop landscape. –JP

Best of Volumes 1 & 2 / CELLULOID
A nice overview of Kuti's incendiary recordings for the Celluloid label. –MB

○ **Fela's London Scene / MAKOSSA**
A superb early-70s album of funky Afro-pop, one of his most successful efforts at blending Nigerian music with James Brown-style soul grooves. –MB

Volumes 1 & 2 / EMI   1977
A two-album anthology on EMI (France) of Kuti's Nigerian hits from the early to mid 70s, when he was at the height of his lyrical and musical powers. –JP

☆ **Original Sufferhead / SHANACHIE**   1981
A CD version of one of Kuti's best albums (*Black President*) along with the title track of the *Original Sufferhead* album. If you only buy one Kuti album, this is the one you want. –JP

O.D.O.O. ... / SHANACHIE   1989
O.D.O.O. (Overtake Don Overtake Overtake) is an epic piece with Kuti's large band Egypt '80. –MB

LIJADU SISTERS

African. Kehinde and Taiwo Lijadu are a rarity in the African music scene — liberated twin sisters, who share the spotlight on smooth close harmonies and command a sharp, inventive backing band. –MB

☆ **Double Trouble / SHANACHIE**   1984
Apala is just one of many Yoruba street-popular styles for voices and percussion. Among the others is a women's equivalent called waka. And waka is the strong local root that makes the Lijadu Sisters' pop style blossom. Not only is their singing rich with its glorious choral sound, but the electric bass line and guitars are equally balanced by Yoruba percussion. All of which makes this a very fine recording, outclassing many of those with more famous names. –JSR

PRINCE NICO MBARGA

Panco. With his band, Rocafil Jazz, Prince Nico scored the biggest African hit ever. His 1976 triumph was a song called "Sweet Mother" and its appeal (13 million copies sold) was largely due to Mbarga's pan-African mix of Cameroonian, Nigerian, and Zairian styles. Despite his multi-instrumental talents and ownership of his own record label, Prince Nico has not been able to sustain his success, and seems fated to go down in history as a one-hit wonder. –MB

○ **Aki Special / ROUNDER**   1987
Mbarga plays panco, a style from East Nigeria that borrows from reggae, funk, soukous, highlife, and more. This CD collects most of the tracks from Mbarga's two Rounder albums *Sweet Mother* and *Free Education.* –JP

EBENEZER OBEY

Juju. Chief Commander Ebenezer Obey has been a Nigerian superstar since the 60s, producing dozens of classic juju recordings. His "miliki" style differs from King Sunny Ade's (his only competition as a star bandleader) in its Christian messages and traditional orientation (except for the occasional Euro-disco-tainted release). –MB

Get Yer Jujus Out / RYKODISC
This is how juju music should be — live and full of "juice." Drum heaven. More than 75 minutes of juju's polyrhythmic madness by one of the genre's inventors. –MB & JP

○ **Je Ka Jo / VIRGIN**   1983
His first international release on Virgin UK, a shimmering masterpiece of hypnotic polyrhythmic madness. –JP

☆ **Juju Jubilee / SHANACHIE**   1985
Obey and Sunny Ade are the kings of juju, and for 20 years each has tried to top the other by adding more guitars, more singers, pedal steel licks, and so forth. This compilation, Obey's first US release, collects Obey's best-selling singles and album tracks from the early 80s. –JP

BABATUNDE OLATUNJI

Traditional drumming. Olatunji came to the US in the early 60s to study medicine, but when a group of African expatriates he put together to combat homesickness took off, he became one of the first African musicians to make a major impact on the American market. –JP

☆ **Drums of Passion / COLUMBIA**   1959
This set came out on vinyl in 1959 and stayed on the charts for several years, an amazing feat for a record of traditional chanting and drumming. Olatunji's success allegedly sparked John Coltrane's interest in African culture, and the music has lost none of its power over the years. –JP

ORIENTAL BROTHERS

Highlife.

○ **Heavy on the Highlife! / ORIGINAL MUSIC**   1991
Two of the top bands playing the kicking, East Nigerian brand of highlife. This has developed into a tough style, with ferocious guitar and hoarse, urgent vocals. This album includes both Sir Doctor Warrior and Dan Satch's versions of the band in 70 minutes of music covering 1973-1988. One reviewer called this "the dance groove of the year." If all you have heard is the Ghanian version, you ain't heard nothing. This one would sear steak. –JSR

NIGERIA COLLECTIONS

○ **Azagas & Archibogs / ORIGINAL MUSIC**   1991
Nigerian dance-band highlife had a wild-edged jauntiness and a go-for-the-jugular instinct for mixing local rhythms and melodies with jazz-tinged horn solos and Congo-inflected guitar work. They even had the percussion jams we tend to associate strictly with juju. This collection covers nine bands. Some were stars throughout West Africa; others were strictly local. The variety is incredible: only the quality is consistent — they'd all blow your socks off. Killed by the Biafra war and totally forgotten today, this was one of the greatest of African urban dance-band traditions. –JSR

The Benues - Rise Up Africa / WORLD RECORDS
The Tiv of Benue State are a highly musical people whose culture is unknown outside Nigeria (despite Charles Keil's excellent book *Tiv Song*). The music here is for voices, percussion, and the swange shawm, and is essentially traditional material performed by a largely young group. The notes give some background and track detail, but not where it was recorded. –DLM

○ **The Igede of Nigeria / MOTW**   1989
The Igede of Nigeria: Drumming, Chanting and Exotic Percussion is an exceptional recording of tribal musicians from Nigeria's Benue state. Ensembles from many different

villages sing and play a variety of drums and percussion instruments in accordance with sacred ceremonies and rites of passage. In addition to polyphonic singing, featured instruments include talking drums, clay pots, and calabash trumpets. A very powerful recording. −MUSIC OF THE WORLD

○ **Juju Roots: 1930s-1950s / ROUNDER**   1985
The earliest juju music evolved from the West African palmwine guitar style and went through many changes before emerging as a potent world music phenomenon in the hands of Sunny Ade. This is a superb "roots" collection, as well as one of a very few non-import compilations of African 78 RPM recordings. Scholarly notes are a plus. −MB

Musiques du Nigeria Central / OCORA
This collection features Idoma, Alago, Lindiri, Eggon, Chamba, and Junkun. −DLM

○ **Yoruba Street Percussion / ORIGINAL MUSIC**   1992
The true stars of West Nigerian pop music are the percussionists, who mix Islamic singing, local drumming, and Afro-Cuban feedback in endless permutations of voices and drums. Here are five different styles, all 20th century, all true street music, all different, all recorded for the local market in the 60s. Percussive offshoots of juju are joined by very early fuji, apala, sakara, the Latin-tinged agidigbo, and waka, the women's music. −JSR

SENEGAL

PASCAL DIATTA w/SONA MANE

Acoustic guitar.
○ **Simnade / ROGUE**
An outstanding recording by a fine woman singer and a man who developed his own acoustic guitar style, avoiding any conscious influence from outside. (Unconscious influences, of course, are a different issue.) This is the real thing, by a local hero of the southern Casamance recorded (extremely well) on location. Altogether exceptional acoustic guitar, and more evidence that African acoustic guitar is alive and highly creative, even if the local record industries have blinders. −JSR

LAMINE KONTE

Kora.
○ **The Kora of Senegal - Vol. 1 / ARION**
Beautiful music by the great kora master. −DLM

A Minstrel of Senegal / JVC
Another highly recommended work. −DLM

DJIMO KOUYATE

Kora.
West African Kora Music / MOTW   1983
The kora is a 21-string harp from West Africa played by oral historians, who pass on their traditions from generation to generation. Djimo Kouyate from Senegal sings and plays kora and drums on this recording. "His playing is gentle, the sounds haunting, and the final effect vital and original" *New York Times.* −MUSIC OF THE WORLD

ISMAEL LO

Mbalax.
○ **Ismael Lo / MANGO**   1992
Moody guitar finger-picking and Dylanesque harmonica playing kick off this attractive pop amalgam of American and Manding folk styles, which untimately shifts into straightahead mbalax. −BT

BAABA MAAL

Pop. One of the most accomplished performers in the high-pitched vocal tradition of West Africa, Senegal's Baaba Maal is also one of his country's biggest international stars, right up there with Youssou N'Dour. −MB

☆ **Baaba Maal, M. Seck & Djam Leelii / MANGO**   1989

Baaba Maal and Mansour (Thione) Seck, two of Senegal's biggest pop stars, return to their roots (and the roots of the blues, from the sound of it) on this beautifully hypnotic picking session, which also features Djam Leelii. Two guitars, accented by a bit of African percussion and some tasty electric fills by Aziz Dieng, produce pure magic. −JP

YOUSSOU N'DOUR

Mbalax. N'Dour was born in Senegal to musician parents, and was performing ceremonial music at circumcisions and baptisms before he was a teen. His first single, "M'Ba," was released before his 14th birthday, and by 16 he was the featured vocalist with the Star Band. In 1977 he left the Star Band with six other musicians to form Étoile de Dakar. Their first record, *Xalis Money*, was a major hit, earning them enough money to move to Paris, where N'Dour reorganized them as Super Étoile de Dakar in 1979. After seeing a concert by Toure Kunda in 1981, N'Dour decided to combine more international rhythms — reggae, funk, soca — into his traditional mbalax style. His early-80s albums for Virgin International (*Set, Immigrés, The Lion*) and high-profile collaborations with Peter Gabriel cemented N'Dour's place as *the* African singer to watch in the 90s. −JP

Immigrés / VIRGIN   1988
Senegalese hard rock. This is the album that got Peter Gabriel hooked on African Music. −JP

The Lion / VIRGIN   1989
N'Dour's big crossover album, with several English-language songs. Good, but not great work. −JP

☆ **Set / VIRGIN**   1990
The title tune became the anthem of Senegalese youth in 1990. This is the first album N'Dour hasn't re-recorded for the international market. It's very African, and his best recorded work to date. −JP

ORCHESTRE BAOBAB

Sahelian.
○ **Pirate's Choice / WORLD CIRCUIT**   1982
Too many current releases are hit-hunting hybrids truly deserving of the vile "Afro-pop" label, which overshadow the superb music made in Africa by Africans for Africans. This charming recording from 1982 is the real thing, driving, delicate, and wholly African. It is to much of the Afro-Parisian stuff on the market as fresh-squeezed orange juice is to lukewarm Kool-aid. −JSR

TOURE KUNDA

Djabdong. Toure Kunda was formed in Senegal by Amadou Tilo Toure to provide singing and drumming accompaniment to the djabadong ceremonies of their native region. To some, djabadong sounds much like reggae, so when Amadou Tilo and his three brothers moved to Paris in the 70s, it seemed natural for them to experiment with a djabadong/reggae fusion. As their popularity increased, the brothers Toure added electric guitars, keys, and more percussion, finally hiring on more musicians from Africa and the French Caribbean. After the death of Amadou Tilo the band reorganized and went on to become one of the top commercial attractions in France with their winning mix of reggae, rock, funk, and traditional Senegalese rhythms. −JP

Casamance au Clair de Lune / CELLULOID   1984
An acoustic set of traditional tunes from Senegal. −JP

○ **Live / CELLULOID**   1984
One of the few live albums that lives up to its name, worth its hefty import (French) price. All their early hits in extended versions recorded before an adoring crowd that pushes the musicians to their limits. Also available as a single CD. −JP

SEYCHELLES COLLECTIONS

Forgotten Music/Kamtole / OCORA
Both ends of the musical continuum of the islands: the Afro-

Malagasy, with part-French melodies accompanied by various instruments including percussion, in lullabies, canoe songs, topical songs, drummed dance music, and even a dance-drama; and the Afro-French Indian Ocean music, with fiddles and percussion playing waltzes, schottisches, and the like in a style that kept much of the 19th-century delicacy of the originals while beefing them up with percussion. –JSR

SIERRA LEONE

SOOLIMAN E. ROGIE

Afro-pop.
African Lady / ROGIEPHONE   1975
Rogie is a palm-wine guitarist from Sierra Leone. His style, which sounds like a low-key, acoustic version of calypso, is marked by his lilting tenor and playful way with a lyric. This album, recorded in California with African and American musicians, is a delight. –JP
○ **The Sixties Sounds of S. E. Rogie / ROGIEPHONE**   1986
Rogie wisely retained the rights to his early compositions, and this compilation of his early hits is magical. Early African rock ("Twist with the Morningstars") and palm-wine hits ("My Lovely Elizabeth") from a true innovator. –JP

SIERRA LEONE COLLECTIONS

○ **African Elegant / ORIGINAL MUSIC**   1992
Freetown, Sierra Leone's capital, early developed a charming, calypso-like Creole-language palm-wine guitar music. The style's undisputed king was Ebeneezer Calendar, whose Maringar band (acoustic guitar, tuba, percussion) ruled the roost for 30 years. His gentle, extraordinarily catchy hits, on the order of "Jollof Rice" and "Arriah Baby," dominate this unique collection. Also present are several recordings by the Kru seamen who first developed the guitar style that was to travel via Ghana to the world, as well as some Mandingo and Mende groups with wonderfully eccentric brass playing. –JSR

SOMALIA COLLECTIONS

○ **Jamiila ... / ORIGINAL MUSIC**   1987
Jamiila: Songs from a Somali City. Somali popular music has almost never been recorded, yet it has a rich musical culture whose Afro-Islamic ingredients have Swahili, Italian, and Indian garnishes. These delightful performances from 1984 include songs for the 'ud; 'ud and flute; acoustic guitar; and guitar with slightly batty electronic organ (replacing the old portable harmonium). An authentic grassroots sound, with its unselfconcious mix of tradition and gadgetry, and the street-corner hipness of a music that's strictly a neighborhood affair. –JSR

SOUTH AFRICA

BOYOYO BOYS

Township jive.
○ **Back in Town / ROUNDER**   1987
Rollicking sax-centered jive by premiere South African instrumental combo, who guested on Paul Simon's *Graceland*. This disc is hot, but short at 30 minutes. –BT

JOHNNY CLEGG (JULUKA/SAVUKA)

Mbaqanga. Johnny Clegg was the founder and chief songwriter of Juluka, South Africa's first interracial and intercultural rock & roll band. For the first year and a half, Juluka played mostly in Black areas where Whites didn't see them, but as they became more popular they often risked their lives (literally) to play the kind of music they loved.
Clegg met Sipho (See-poe) Mchunu, a "formidable guitarist," when they were both 17. They formed a strong musical and personal bond and in 1976 cut an album of Zulu ethnic songs under the name of Juluka ("sweat"). The next albums added elements of South African folk, rock, funk, and Zulu street

guitar. By 1979 they had a Zulu/rock, South African folk/fusion band with six members (three White and three Black) and a platinum album. Juluka's success helped break down the racial barriers that separated musical styles, and before they disbanded in 1985 they even had a Top 40 hit in Europe with "Scatterlings of Africa," a poignant tribute to the African diaspora.
As the political situation heated up in the late 80s, Clegg returned with another interracial band called Savuka ("we have arisen"), this time writing and singing highly political material. After a tumultuous tour of South Africa and western Europe, Savuka inked a worldwide deal with EMI International (Capitol in the US). –JP
African Litany / RHYTHM SAFARI   1982
Juluka's second release with Johnny Clegg, the first album by an integrated rock band in South Africa, went gold in three months. This first single "Impi" was based on a Zulu war chant and was considered a call to revolution by people in the know. –JP
Ubuhle Bemvelo / RHYTHM SAFARI   1982
Juluka's followup to *African Litany*, a selection of traditional Zulu folk songs done in a rock & roll style. –JP
Scatterlings / WARNER   1982
A good Juluka set featuring "Scatterlings of Africa" and "Simple Things." –SWB
☆ **The Best of Juluka / PRIORITY**   1983
A good summary of Clegg's work with Juluka. –SWB
○ **Third World Child / EMI**   1987
"Asimbonanga (Mandela)" is an anthem already adopted by Joan Baez and others, while the title tune devastatingly discusses what it's like to be asked to "walk in the dreams of the foreigner." –WR
Cruel Crazy Beautiful World / CAPITOL   1989
By his third album with Savuka, Clegg had adopted some Los Angeles production techniques, such as those booming drums, perhaps in an attempt to meet the marketplace. But the message is still there: "Woman Be My Country" brilliantly examines Clegg's conflicting feelings about his homeland, while the title song expresses his alternating realism and optimism: "It's your world, so live in it!" –WR

LADYSMITH BLACK MAMBAZO

Mbube. Ladysmith Black Mambazo was founded by Joseph Shabalala in 1974. They've cut 29 albums over the past 14 years, but the group did not become well known outside of South Africa until Paul Simon asked them to perform on *Graceland*.
Shabalala was born into a poor family that lived on a White man's farm near the town of Ladysmith. There were eight children in the Shabalala family, and, as the oldest boy, it was Joseph's duty to take care of the family after his father died.
Shabalala's first musical experience, save for a bit of fooling around on the guitar, came with a choral group called the Blacks. Shabalala eventually took over leadership of the group and became its main composer.
The Blacks won most of the local vocal competitions and became the most popular Zulu vocal group, but Shabalala felt that something was missing. "I had been hearing a voice inside me," Shabalala said. "I didn't know it, but it was the voice of God." When the voice told him to fast, Shabalala obeyed, and on his fast, he had a vision of a new kind of vocal music. Shortly thereafter he became a Christian. Taking the choral music he heard in the Christian church, he combined it with the Zulu tradition to create his own style.
When the Blacks refused to take part in Shabalala's experiments, he formed Ladysmith Black Mambazo. The group consists of seven bass voices, an alto, a tenor, and Shabalala singing lead. Even if you don't speak Zulu, when they hit a low rumbling note, you can literally feel the power of their voices in your body.
"In Zulu singing there are three major sounds," Shabalala

explains. "A high keening ululation; a grunting, puffing sound that we make when we stomp our feet; and a certain way of singing melody. Before Black Mambazo you didn't hear these three sounds in the same songs. So it is new to combine them, although it is still done in a traditional style. We are just asking God to allow us to polish it, to help keep our voices in order so we can praise Him and uplift the people." –JP

Induku Kethu / SHANACHIE   1984
This group can be heard at its most direct and unadorned on this collection, with Joseph Shabalala leading the ensemble through some swooping vocal harmonies and the group's unique stop-and-start call-and-response sequences. (In Zulu.) (Also recommended: The religious collection *Ulwandle Oluncgwele*.) –WR

○ **Shaka Zulu / WARNER**   1987
In the wake of their participation on his *Graceland* album, Paul Simon produced this Ladysmith album, their most accessible work for Western ears, which is pristinely recorded and sung partially in English. –WR

● **Classic Tracks / SHANACHIE**   1991
A selection of tunes from Ladysmith's many South African albums. –JP

SIPHO MABUSE

Zulu pop.
○ **Sipho Mabuse / VIRGIN**   1987
One of the first African pop records to get wide US distribution. Contains "Burn Out" and several other tracks from the South African album of the same name, but the market wasn't ready. –JP

Chant of the Marching / VIRGIN   1989
Another South African take on funk, rock, and Zulu pop, with many tracks in English. –JP

MAHLATHINI   b 1937

Mbaqanga.. Simon Nkabinde Mahlathini (nicknamed "the Lion of Soweto") came to international attention via the 1985 sampler *The Indestructible Beat of Soweto*. He began to tour internationally with female singers the Mahotella Queens, although he has been playing and singing his brand of mbaqanga (Zulu pop music, heavily influenced by traditional singing styles) since the early 60s.
Mahlathini started singing on street corners, graduated to men's choral music, and went on to form his own smaller group in the mid 60s. When he "went electric" in the mid 70s, his new sound caused a sensation, and much controversy. With the Mahotella Queens supplying their dynamic backing vocals and fancy dance routines (think of a South African version of the Supremes) and Mahlathini's primal groaning filling the air, you don't have to understand the language to get the message, although the group has occasionally recorded in English.
Another part of Mahlathini's success is the backing supplied by West Nkosi and the Makgona Tsohle Band. "Makgona Tsohle means 'Jack-of-all-trades,'" says Nkosi. "Our mbaqanga is a blend of traditional styles with modern instruments, a music anyone can relate to." –JP & WR

○ **The Lion of Soweto / EARTHWORKS**   1987
The compilation that introduced Mahlathini to the rest of the world. Primal, growling mbaqanga (with backing vocals by the Mahotella Queens) that prompted many critics to call Mahlathini the "Howlin' Wolf of South Africa." –JP

Thokozile / VIRGIN   1988
Another exemplary outing from Mahlathini and the Mahotella Queens, with a kwela-like swing to the arrangements. –JP

○ **Rhythm & Art / SHANACHIE**   1990
More Zulu and accordion jive from Mahlathini and the Queens, with several songs in English. –JP

The Lion Roars / SHANACHIE   1991
Mbaqanga was in disfavor when Paul Simon's *Graceland*

rekindled interest in the form. This is a late-80s reunion album that shows Mahlathini and the Queens have lost none of their fire. –JP

MAHOTELLA QUEENS

Mbaqanga. The Queens, often heard in concert and on record with deep-voiced "groaner" Simon Mahlathini, represent the South African township style with absolute perfection. Established in 1964 as a session harmony group, they came to prominence in the 70s with their tough vocal style and rock-solid mbaqanga backing band. Some of the original Queens have toured the States with Mahlathini recently, displaying their sprightly dancing and gutsy harmonies to appreciative Western audiences. They are also heard to great effect on the collection album *Soweto Never Sleeps — Classic Female Zulu Jive* (Shanachie 43041) with other sister groups. –MB

Marriage Is a Problem / SHANACHIE
The Queens often steal the show away from Mahlathini, and this solo disc lets you know why. This is a worthy followup in the vein of the *Izibani* album. –JP & MB

☆ **Izibani Zomgqashiyo / SHANACHIE**   1986
Gutsy, liberated songs from one of the world's most dynamic female groups. Multipart harmonies abound. –MB

MIRIAM MAKEBA   b 1934

Pop. Born in Johannesburg, South Africa, she played with the Black Mountain Brothers from 1954 to 1957. In 1959 she met Harry Belafonte, who brought her to the States and groomed her career. Makeba's Black Nationalist position in the late 60s led to public backlash, which she did not overcome until the 80s. –BC

The World of Miriam Makeba / RCA   1986
Fine mix of social commentary, folk, and African styles. –BC

○ **Sangoma / WARNER**   1988
Makeba's comeback album, her first US release in almost a decade. A beautiful collection of traditional South African songs with spare production values that highlight the power of Makeba's vocals. An excellent set of Xhosa folk songs Miriam learned as a child. –JP & BC

Miriam Makeba / RCA   1989
The first American album from Makeba, this is a long-out-of-print classic. –JP

DOROTHY MASUKA

Marabi.
○ **Pata Pata / MANGO**   1991
Though this disc reprises the cream of her decades-long career, nostalgia is never an issue. Smooth South African jazz called marabi meets Masuka's sweetly urging voice. –BT

MBONGENI NGEMA

Pop. Ngema wrote and performed *Woza Albert*, an anti-apartheid comedy/drama that got rave reviews when it toured the US in 1984. Along with Hugh Masakela, Ngema wrote *Sarafina*, a musical drama that told the story of a day in the life of a South African Township as seen through the eyes of a group of high school children. –JP

☆ **Sarafina - Original Cast Album / RCA**   1988
The songs express the conflicting feelings of hope, terror, love, and struggle of life under the gun. –JP

Time to Unite / MANGO   1988
More songs of struggle and liberation; featuring the cast of *Sarafina*. –JP

DUDU PUKWANA   b 1938

Township jazz.
○ **Diamond Express / ARISTA**
An early-70s recording of this saxophonist, with the late trumpeter Mongezi Feza, in their last meeting before Feza

died of pneumonia. Squeaky sax and ensemble in an unabashed mood. South African free-jazz. −MGN

In the Townships / EARTHWORKS   1973
An excellent recording with Feza, Louis Moholo, and Harry Miller. −MGN

Zila / JIKA   1981
A live date at the 100 Club in London, with a larger ensemble and great soloists. −MGN

SOUL BROTHERS

Mbaqanga. One of South Africa's most popular dance bands, a prime mover in the mbaqanga revolution of the 60s. −JP

○ **Jive Explosion / VIRGIN**   1988

PHILIP TABANE w/MALOMBO

Jazz.

○ **Man Phily / AFRICAN**
This rich anthology ranges over 17 years and a stylistic range with room for hand piano as well as electric guitar, for kwela and marabi and blues. −JSR

SOUTH AFRICA COLLECTIONS

★ **Indestructible Beat of Soweto / SHANACHIE** 1986
This anthology of South African artists surprised everyone by becoming a best-seller. It introduced worldbeatniks to Ladysmith Black Mambazo, Mahlathini, and Moses Mchunu and paved the way for Paul Simon's *Graceland.* Winner of *The Village Voice*'s Jazz and Pop Poll for Best Record of 1987. An essential sampler of modern African stylings. A revelation and a joy. −JP & HD

☆ **Freedom Fire / EARTHWORKS**   1990
The third of the Earthworks *Indestructible Beat* series (distributed by Virgin) series is as good as, if not better than Vol. 1. −JP

○ **Mbube Roots / ROUNDER**   1987
Historical vocal group recordings from the 30s on, in the style currently associated with Ladysmith Black Mambazo on Paul Simon's *Graceland.* Includes "The Lion Sleeps Tonight." Good notes. −BLP

☆ **Noise Khanyile - The Art of Noise / GLOBESTYLE**
Dynamite Zulu fiddling, with township bands and more rural groups, by a man who played with most of the big names of the time. This has to rank as one of the best reissues of down-home 70s sounds so far — one not to be missed. The notes are better than most, too, despite the misuse of the word traditional — an irritating inaccuracy that seems to be spreading. −JSR

Rhythms of Resistance / ATLANTIC
A broad survey of South African styles collected by filmmaker Jeremy Marre on a documentary shoot — good variety but not on a par with many collections released since then. −MB

○ **Singing in an Open Space / ROUNDER**   1990
This set of Zulu semi-rural music from 1962 to 1982 is emphatically the best South African release I've heard in the current glut. None of it is traditional (as the above-average notes rightly point out, the word is routinely misused). All of it — voices, guitars, fiddles, harmonicas — is far more intense than the usual city sounds. −JP

○ **Siya Hamba / ORIGINAL MUSIC**
Two faces of 50s Azanian music, from recordings by Hugh Tracey of the International Library of African Music. The first side covers a wide range of rural sounds, including some amazing harmonica (dances with vocals and strange hyperventilations, bluesy solos); concertina; an entirely unexpected piece backed by autoharp; and various wonderful country guitar styles. Side two is a session of smalltown dance music from the jazz- and jump-blues-influenced kwela period, with some terrific women singers. −JSR

Soweto Never Sleeps / SHANACHIE   1986
Subtitled *Classic Female Zulu Jive.* With the Mahotella Queens and others. −MB

Zulu Beats from South Africa / HANNIBAL
Fine dance music from various electric guitar bands. −BLP

SUDAN

HAMZA EL DIN

Neo-traditional. Hamza El Din is recognized worldwide as the musical ambassador from Sudan, and he is one of the greatest masters of the 'ud, a fretless lute popular throughout the Arab world. He is a celebrated concert performer and an evocative singer, keeping the musical traditions of the Nubian region alive. −MB

Music of Nubia / VANGUARD   1964
The debut session — eight songs from 1964. −MB

☆ **Escalay: The Water Wheel / NONESUCH**   1968
Extensive selections of a unique style of music personally developed by the soloist-vocalist on 'ud and tar. *Escalay: The Water Wheel - Oud Music of Nubia* is the recording that brought El Din's Nubian traditions to the attention of many in the West — an ethnomusicological classic. −MB & DLM

○ **Eclipse / RYKODISC**   1978
Meditatively paced traditional songs by a master of Sudanese music. Hamza's deep, smoky voice is accompanied by the 'ud — a precursor to the lute — and by compelling use of a simple Nubian frame drum called the tar. A beautiful, even lush recording of El Din's latest 'ud mastery. −BT & MB

ABDEL AZIZ EL MUBARAK

Popular.

○ **Straight from the Heart / WORLD CIRCUIT**
Mubarak was featured on an earlier World Circuit release with a small group, but this is a much better release: Mubarak as the Sudanese hear him, backed by a ten-piece group including accordion and saxophones. A fine live recording (made at a London concert) that shows off one of the most exciting and least known of the Afro-Arab pop idioms. −JSR

○ **Abdel Aziz el Mubarak / GLOBESTYLE**   1987
Mubarak is one of Sudan's most popular bandleaders, a man who combines Western influences (including reggae) with his country's age-old Muslim traditions. −JP

ABDEL GADIR SALIM

Merdoum.

○ **Nujum Al-Lail/Stars of the Night / GLOBESTYLE** 1989
Silky-voiced Sudanese bandleader delivers a strong set of swaying music highlighted by the gentle alto saxophone of Abdel Hadi. Contains "A'Abir Sikkah," a successful attempt to meld reggae with a local village rhythm. −BT

○ **Merdoum Kings Play Songs of Love / SHANACHIE** 1991
Backed by the All Stars, a seven-piece band with an understated but compelling orchestral sound, Abdel Gadir returns with more lush music from the Sudan. The complex layering of instruments and medium-boil tempos suggests the effortless flow of a juju all-nighter. −BT

SUDAN COLLECTIONS

○ **Sounds of Sudan / WORLD CIRCUIT**   1990
Arabic pop music by Abdel Aziz el Mubarak, Abdel Gadir Salim, and Mohamed Gubara. −JP

TANZANIA

MLIMANI PARK ORCHESTRA

○ **Sikinde / LINE**
A great compilation of 80s recordings. A big group and, thanks to the flexibility of cassette (Tanzania has no record industry), it lays out at length in fine style. Expensive, but not to be missed on any account — a rare-to-unique release with great horns, real-thing strength, and total absence of worldbeat slickness. −JSR

NYOTA

Taarab.
○ **Nyota / GLOBESTYLE**
Fine taarab (wedding music of the Swahili) by Black Star and
Lucky Star, two groups that helped keep the coastal style alive
by stylistic changes and the development of orchestras
featuring accordion and the like. A thrilling retrospective on
an all-but-forgotten genre. –DLM & BT

REMMY ONGALA

Popular.
○ **Nalilia Mwana / WOMAD**
Life gets very confusing in East Africa! Ongala is Congolese by
origin, and his group consists mostly of expatriate Zairians.
Not that the sound is soukous: it's a mix of truly Tanzanian
elements with early-70s boucher. The results are highly
individual — and, given that contemporary Tanzanian bands
just don't get recorded, not to be passed up. –JSR
Songs for the Poor Man / REAL WORLD   1990
This Tanzanian take on soukous is as restrained as the Zairian
form is hedonistic. Ongala's songs on social themes are
delivered with winning conviction. –BT
○ **Mambo / REAL WORLD**   1991
Backed by Orchestre Super Matimila, Ongala trades the
laidback soukous of his first US release for political songs —
in English and Swahili — whose directness recalls Nigeria's
Fela Anıkulapo Kuti and includes touches of contemporary
Latin music and a shot of rhythm and blues. –BT

ORCHESTRA SUPER MAZEMBE

Soukous.
○ **Kaivaska / VIRGIN**   1982
This Tanzanian band with a heavy Congolese influence can
really tear it up. Check out "Malamba d'Amour" ("Words of
Love") to see what Buddy Holly would have sounded like if
he'd been born in Africa. –JP

WATAFITI

Traditional. An all-acoustic, mostly percussion band. –JP
Umoja / KOCH   1990
Very energetic music rooted in the local traditions. –JP

HUKWE UBI ZAWOSE

Traditional.
Hukwe Ubi Zawose / JVC
Ilimba (66-key finger-piano) virtuoso Zawose is quite well
known to Womad audiences and featured largely on Triple
Earth releases. Zawose is essentially on the more traditional
end of a large and varied spectrum of African musicians
working to transmute traditional forms to keep them relevant
in changing times. –DLM
Mateso / TRIPLE EARTH
Perhaps the world is at last waking up to the fact that
musicians all over Africa are exploring various ways of
renewing traditional idioms without betraying or ossifying
them. –DLM

TANZANIA COLLECTIONS

○ **Music of Zanzibar - Taarab 2 / GLOBESTYLE**   1988
The vocal approach is borrowed from Indian film music, the
instrumentation from Arabic orchestras, and the rhythms
from Latin America — but the music's heart is as large as its
influences. Deliciously cornball in the best pop-music sense.
From Zanizibar (now part of Tanzania). –BT
○ **Music of Zanzibar - Taarab 3 / GLOBESTYLE**   1990
This is a collection of hits by some of Zanzibar's best taarab
bands, including supergroups Ikhwani Safaa Musical Club
and Culture Musical Club. –JP
○ **The Tanzania Sound / ORIGINAL MUSIC**   1987

In the 50s, Tanzania built its own blend of local Afro-Cuban
and Congolese ingredients into a new dance style. Here are its
50s and 60s classics — both the early bands, like the
legendary Kiko Kids with their strong Afro-Arab tinge, and
the groups of the classic era. The Tanzanian bands, more
driving than their Congolese models and more dance-
oriented than their Kenyan neighbors, used local rhythms
earlier than the proto-soukous bands themselves and
contained some splendid hornmen with very individual
sounds. They also had a melancholy vocal sound entirely
different from their Congolese models. –JSR

TUNISIA

ANOUAR BRAHEM

Traditional. This 33-year-old virtuoso of the Arabic lute is the
director for the official musical ensemble of Tunis. Brahem
incorporates many strains of North African music into a
modern blend of classicism and innovation and has worked
with West African pop star Manu Dibango and other
fusionists. –MB
☆ **Barzakh / POLYGRAM**   1991
This album offers profoundly beautiful settings for 'ud, violin,
and percussion, featuring Brahem's innovative Tunisian-style
'ud playing on 13 cuts. An excellent introduction to pan-
Arabic string music. –MB

HASSAN ELGHARBI w/MOHAMED ELAKKAD

Traditional.
○ **Enchanted Kanun / CDDA**
Elgharbi, Tunisia's leading player of the kanun zither, is a
major virtuoso. In 1976 he won the grand prize at Iran's
prestigious Shiraz Music Festival. Here he plays the piece that
gained him the prize, along with various other improvisations
on traditional modes and personal compositions (one backed
by a bassist!). The CD winds up with a couple of recordings by
an Egyptian virtuoso of the early 20th century. –JSR

UGANDA

SAMITE

Neo-traditional. Singer and multi-instrumentalist Samite is a
little like Francis Bebey in that he over-dubs both his own
voice and various African and Western instruments
(including the big East African litungu lyre, finger piano, and
flutes). While he has a slight, slight folky edge in places and is
not a strong solo singer, his overdubbed polyphonic vocals
and most of his instrumental work are gorgeous. –JSR
○ **Abaana Bakesa / SHANACHIE**   1992
Abaaba Bakesa - Dance, My Children, Dance offers joyful,
endearing, traditional-based songs performed on marimba,
kalimba (finger piano), and litungu (Ugandan harp). Samite's
mellifluous vocals exert a powerful charm. Recommended for
listeners with children. –BT

UGANDA COLLECTIONS

○ **The Kampala Sound / ORIGINAL MUSIC**   1988
A unique recording, since the national shipwreck caused by
Idi Amin's policies sank the Uganda dance-music scene
almost before it got going. These kicking, charming cuts from
1964-1968 are backed by Kenyan and Zairian as well as
Ugandan musicians. But the mellow vocal sound is unique,
and some of the numbers here deserve to be pan-African
classics. –JSR

ZAIRE

EMPIRE BAKUBA w/PEPE KALLE

Soukous.
○ **Massassi Calculé / ACMPI**
Inventors of the recent kouassa-kouassa dance craze, and

arguably the greatest contemporary hard-soukous band bar none, Bakuba is heavy on the guitars and with no time for horns or pop frills. Leader and lead vocalist Pepe Kalle has a voice a little similar to the late Franco, set off beautifully by the backup singers. Guitarist Boeing 737 (really!) is more adventuresome than the recently hyped Diblo Dibala, with a bare-feet-on-a-hot-road guitar style and very well integrated echoes of funk and rockabilly. Typical of soukous bands, though Bakuba is one of the monsters of the 80s and 90s, it has been recording since the late 60s. –JSR

MBILIA BEL

Soukous.

○ **Phénomène / MELODIE**
Bel sang for years with Rochereau and went out on her own in 1988. Bameli Soy presents her in the Rochereau days. The marvelous *Phénomène* was the first fruit of her artistic freedom and it's wonderful, with ace arranger Rigo Star's work framing her sensuous style without making it soupy. And given how well Bel's style and voice blended with the benign drive of Afrisa International, as Bameli Soy attests, her solo success was against considerable self-competition. –JSR

CHOC STARS

Soukous. A spin-off from Zaiko Langa Langa. One of the most energetic of the "new-wave" soukous bands. –JP
○ **Choc Shock Choc / GLOBESTYLE**   1986

DIBLO DIBALA

Soukous. Dibala began playing guitar when he was 12. By the time he ws 15 he almost beat Franco, Zaire's top guitarist and band leader, in a guitar duel, and Franco offered Diblo a job in his band. Dibala became Zaire's top session player and arranger, playing and composing material on over 60 albums by other artists. In 1979 Kanda Bongo Man lured Dibala away from Franco; the band relocated to Paris where their success can be traced in large part to the fiery solo work he has contributed to Bongo Man's albums. In 1986 Dibala left Kanda to form Loketo with singer Aurlus Mabele. –JP
○ **Super Soukous / SHANACHIE**   1989
This was the buzz-record, only patchily available, that drew the attention of US buffs to Dibala, a sparkling guitarist. On this, his first solo recording, he was backed by zouk keyboard heavy Ronald Rubinel as well as by Loketo itself. No-frills punch is the watchword. –JSR

FRANCO   d1990

Soukous. After World War II, Kinshasa (the capitol of what is now Zaire) became a bustling city where the popular music of Ghana (highlife), Cuba (rumba), and various local groups simmered down into the folkloric form of pop known as soukous. Franco, "the Sorcerer of the Guitar" was the leader of the TPOK Jazz Band, the most influential and popular band in Africa's modern history.
A natural guitar talent, Franco joined Ebengo Dewayon's Watam band while in his early teens, cutting his first guitar solo record "Bolingo Na Ngai Beatrice" at the tender age of 13. He formed the first edition of TPOK at the age of 15, and the group dominated the charts from that moment until Franco's death in 1990. –JP
20ème Anniversaire / AFRICAN   1976
A two-record (French import) set released to celebrate Franco's 20th year in the music business; a good buy if you can find it. –JP
○ **Franco & His All Powerful TPOK Jazz / MAKOSSA**   1984
One of the master's last big hits, "Très Impolie," has a catchy chorus, great guitar fireworks, and a relentless groove. –JP
Originalité / RETRO   1987
Remastered from original 78-inch singles cut between 1956 and 1959, these are the hits that established Franco (and TPOK Jazz Band) as Africa's reigning guitar god. –JP

KANDA BONGO MAN

Soukous. One of the biggest stars of the fashion-conscious Parisian soukous scene, Kanda Bongo Man issued his own records in Paris and Zaire before hitting it big internationally. His long-time lead guitarist Diblo Dibala is now a star bandleader in his own right. –MB
○ **Sai-Liza / HANNIBAL**
The recording that introduced the kouassa-kouassa dance has been a runaway smash in Paris and Africa. Unsure why this has been one of the biggest hits in quite a while? Try Dibala on lead guitar, Lokassa ya Mbongo backing him up, and Pablo Lubadika on bass guitar, all of them in top form. Add KBM's admirable liking for a small tight group — aside from those mentioned, there's only synth, drum, and a two-voice backup vocal group. Kanda Bongo Man is one musician who almost always deserves the semi-adulation Western buffs have given him. –JSR
☆ **Amour Fou (Crazy Love) / HANNIBAL**   1988
Sharp soukous from two Paris albums. Diblo Dibala's agile guitar is a real plus on this American debut. –MB
Kwassa Kwassa / HANNIBAL   1989
More dance-floor fun. Very uptempo and infectious Zairian pop. –MB
Zing Zong / HANNIBAL   1991
Kanda's latest ups the pleasure quotient a notch to achieve absolute delirium. Effervescent vocals ride the crest of lead guitarists Dally Kimoko and Nene Tchakou. –BT

LOKETO

Soukous. Loketo's Diblo Dibala may be Zaire's finest guitarist. Since forming the band with singer Aurlus Mabele in 1986, Diblo's amazingly sharp fretwork and melodic phrasing has made Loketo one of the top attractions on the Parisian and African music scene. Loketo is one of the best purveyors of "new-wave" soukous. –JP
Extra Ball / SHANACHIE   1991
Loketo's swansong as a group is their most highly charged, hook-filled release yet, with dazzling guitar pyrotechnics from Diblo Dibala and friends. –BT & JP

AURLUS MABELE

Soukous.
○ **King of Soukous / SOUND WAVE**   1991
Brief as an aerobics workout and just as stimulating, this 30-minute disc presents the voice of Loketo after the breakup of that massively popular band. Filled with can't-miss spiraling soukous rhythms, saucy backup vocalists, and great guitar by Dally Kimoko. –BT

SAM MANGWANA

Soukous. This former singer with Rochereau and Kanda Bongo Man has added elements of soca and zouk into his high-octane soukous style. –JP
○ **Aladji / SHANACHIE**   1978
This album contains hits from several African albums; one of the hottest African dance compilations of the late 80s. –JP

TSHALA MUANA

Soukous.
☆ **Nasi Nabali / ESPERA**
One of the best recordings by a singer whose reputation just keeps growing — and rightly so. The ingredients are familiar enough — what's done with them is what counts. Muana and her chorus work almost as one unit, and the backings balance fluid guitars, tough disco elements, and jaunty traps; punchy horns that blend R&B licks with older Afro/Carib references; and local traditional elements to subtle and splendid effect. She has the best voice of all the Zairian women singers. –JSR
○ **Soukous Siren / SHANACHIE**   1985

Forget soukous. Muana hits hardest when she throws herself into mutuash, a dizzying rural polyrhythm the Zairian singer/songwriter backs up with strong melodies and molten arrangements. –BT

DOCTEUR NICO

Soukous.

○ **W/ Orchestra African Fiesta / AFRICAN**   1966
Docteur Nico w/ Orchestra African Fiesta. Whatever any Zairian guitarist does (and therefore almost an African guitarist from anywhere), he is in some way echoing something created 20 years ago by the late Docteur Nico. A constant experimenter, Nico did for the guitar what Rochereau (his colleague in both African jazz and African fiesta) did for Congo music vocals, blending and reworking the idiom's Cuban and local strains into something brilliantly new. All these recordings, therefore, are basic to any soukous collection. The second listing here dates from around 1969, when the kiri-kire was hip but the rhumba still ruled. –JSR

TABU LEY ROCHEREAU

Soukous. Tabu Ley (Rochereau), with Franco, is the father of modern African pop. His band, Africa International, was a leading innovator and changed the way Congolese (and later Zairian music) music was played. In an interview with Ronnie Graham, later reprinted in Graham's *Guide to Contemporary African Music* (Da Capo, 1988), Tabu Ley spoke at length about his life and music.
"Tabu is my father's name; Ley is my father's father's name. Rochereau is a name I got in grammar school. During a French history lesson I was the only one who knew the names of Napoleon's generals; the rest of the class was punished because of it. They teased me and called me Rochereau, but I liked the sound of it and kept it as my artistic name."
Rochereau learned sacred and secular music at the Catholic grammar school he attended, although he'd been singing at home since he was a child. At the age of 14, he wrote his first hit, "Besama Muchacha," which was recorded by L'African Jazz, the band of Le Grande Kalle, the greatest bandleader of the 40s, 50s, and 60s. Because Rochereau was underage, the songwriting credit was taken by Kalle. When Rochereau finished high school, Kalle gave him a job as a singer with L'African Jazz, and the first tune he wrote for them, "Kelia," made Rochereau an instant success.
In 1965 Rochereau left Kalle to form African Fiesta with Docteur Nico, another Kalle alumnus. Since then, Rochereau has led the pack in musical innovations and creative drive. He's written more than 2000 songs for himself and other artists, and recorded more than a hundred albums, with almost every new release bringing a new facet of his creativity to the fore. He's added Latin, jazz, soul, and disco elements to his music. His organization is a fertile training ground for other musicians, who have gone on to fame and fortune (including Sam Mangwana and Mbilia Bel). –JP

○ **Omana Wapi / SHANACHIE**   1976
Picked by *The Village Voice's* Robert Christgau as one of the greatest albums of the 80s, this historic collaboration teams Rochereau with Franco, Zaire's greatest singer and guitarist, for one of the few "supersessions" worthy of the title. –JP

Man from Kinshasa / SHANACHIE   1991
In a nod to contemporary logic, the Zairian master gets behind a drum machine. With another nod to roots, he dares accordion-driven soukous on one of the many highlights here, including "Tour Eiffel." –BT

PAPA WEMBA

Soukous. Besides being a sartorial role-model who launches fashion after fashion, Wemba has come to symbolize the younger generation of soukous. He started with Zaiko Langa Langa and sticks to an updated version of the driving ZLL style. No heavy funk/R&B overlays, no horns: at most some

bluesy flashes in the scintillating guitar work. Just a sparkling, glittering interplay of guitars and drums and voices that doesn't let up. –JSR

☆ **L'Esclave / GITTA**
This recording was a massive hit for a full six months when it first came out and testifies to a driving Zairian style that other big names have neglected in favor of more laidback sounds. –JSR

○ **Amour Kilawu / ESPERANCE**
This collaboration with Viva La Musica (a band of ZLL alumni) is among his very best from the mid 80s. The collaboration with Modogo (full title: *Papa Wemba, Modogo Gian Franco Ferre and Viva la Musica: Nouvelle Generation à Paris.* Phew!) is an outstanding example of how they moved the basic sound forward a notch for the 90s. –JSR

○ **La Voyageur / EARTHBEAT!**   1992
American debut by one of the continent's most arresting vocalists, who is loathe to let a syllable escape his throat without first gift-wrapping it in brightly colored knots. Compositions hurl themselves from soukous to mbube, dashing against the rocks only during flirtations with mellow rock and jazz — but his amazing cockcrow of a voice continually triumphs. –BT

ZAIKO LANGA LANGA

Soukous. In the early 70s, the Zaikos hoisted the banner of change in Zairian music by stripping soukous down to its rhythm, guitar, and vocal essentials. The absence of horn players and their rebellious attitude established ZLL as the new wave of youth music, and a host of new bands came from their ranks. Offspring of the "Clan Langa Langa" include Papa Wemba, Bozi Boziana, and the groups Zaiko WaWa, Langa Langa Stars, Choc Stars, Anti-Choc, and many more. –MB

Langa Langa F.D. / CELLULOID   1990
One of the few non-import CDs available. –JP

ZAIRE COLLECTIONS

○ **Compact d'Afrique / GLOBESTYLE**   1986
New-wave soukous from Congo and Zaire: faster and hotter than the old style pioneered by Franco and Rochereau. Great cuts by Kanda Bongo Man, Papa Wemba, Choc Stars, and Les Quatres Étoiles. –JP

Heartbeat Soukous / EARTHWORKS   1987
A great collection that features collaborations between members of Kassav' and some of West Africa's most progressive pop musicians, a forward-looking fusion of soca, zouk, and soukous. Musicians include Pablo, Kanda Bongo Man, Bopol, Rigo Star, Pepe Kalle, and others. –JP

○ **Mbuti Pygmies of Ituri Rainforest / FOLKWAYS**   1992
This CD reissue combines two long-out-of-print recordings that were among Folkways' most popular African releases of the 50s. Anthropologist Colin Turnbull's field recordings may not match the sonics of today's digital productions, but their scope still impresses. Spotlights the gorgeous, free-flowing vocal style call hocketing, where singers pass short melodic lines from person to person in sort of a round that forms shimmering harmonic patterns. –BT

☆ **Merveilles du Passé / AFRICAN**
From the late 50s onward, the music of Zaire that came to be called soukous has been an overwhelmingly huge influence on all other Black African styles, with the exception of South Africa. This wonderful collection documents some of the gems of the early day, from the adolescence of the 50s through the 70s new-wave of Zaiko Langa Langa and such. Here — though not always at their super-peak — are most of the influential names in African music: Le Grand Kalle, Franco, Verckys, Bavon Marie-Marie, Rochereau, and on and on. If you want to know African music at any level, you have to know this stuff. –JSR

○ **Music of the Rainforest Pygmies / LYRICHORD**   1992
Another reissue of Colin Turnbull's field recordings, this one

from 1961. Song-types are more varied than his Folkways collection because selections include the Mbuti influence on music of neighboring peoples. Contains a delightfully baffling Twa pygmoid rendition of "(Oh, My Darling) Clementine," presented to Turnbull as a very old and sacred song. –BT

○ **Sound of Kinshasa / ORIGINAL MUSIC**   1982
Zairian classics from the acoustic 50s to the soukous 70s, from an example of the great Shaba acoustic tradition and a gorgeous biguine in a forgotten style, to biggies such as OK jazz and early-empire bakuba. Every cut is crème de la crème, and they're arranged chronologically so you can hear the style grow from acoustic birth to electric maturity two decades later — by which time it was profoundly influencing music all across Black Africa. –JSR

ZAMBIA COLLECTIONS

○ **From the Copperbelt / ORIGINAL MUSIC**   1989
If you're into country blues, Mwenda Jean Bosco, or roots in general, this is for you. The remarkable guitarists of the 50s Zambian copper mines were mostly wandering minstrels who roamed from mine to mine, crisscrossing the border between Zambia and Katanga and forming part of a guitar movement that has always been incorrectly credited to East Zaire alone. There's an enormous variety here, from rugged, rootsy stuff to the beginnings of an urban-influenced sound with US and South African as well as Congolese elements. –JSR

ZIMBABWE

BHUNDU BOYS

Jit. The Bhundus built up a national following in Zimbabwe by taking the more traditional guitar styles of chimurenga (made popular by Thomas Mapfumo), adding some English/American-style finger-picking and a heavy disco-like bass drum beat, and playing with a lilting, rhythmic swing that's part highlife and part soukous. They call their hybrid "jit." In 1986 the Bhundu Boys put out their first record; when Scottish booker Gordon Muir heard it, he called Zimbabwe and flew the Bhundu Boys to England for a tour that became a year-long residence. With music industry heavies like Elvis Costello and Madonna touting them to the press, the Bhundus were soon under contract to Warner Brothers International (Island in the US). Influenced by the Rolling Stones and soukous as well as the traditional music of their native Zimbabwe, the Bhundu Boys are one of Africa's most ass-kicking guitar bands. –JP

☆ **Shabini / DISQUE AFRIQUE**   1986
An earlier album with a relatively under-produced sound. Guitars, bass, keyboard, and percussion. Exciting music from Zimbabwe. –HD

Tsvimbodzemoto / DISQUE AFRIQUE
Their second album, another great recording that mines the roots of Zimbabwe and serves them up with plenty of dazzling rock guitar. –JP

○ **True Jit / MANGO-ANTILLES**
Their international debut is considered "watered down" by some purists, but it'll still knock your socks off. With a fuller sound and some English lyrics. –JP & HD

STELLA CHIWESHE

Neo-traditional. As a woman in a male-dominated field, Stella Chiweshe has faced many struggles to survive as a musician and keep her native traditions alive. But her persistence has paid off and, along with her own small mbira (also known as sanza or thumb-piano) groups, she has recorded numerous traditionally oriented import albums of Zimbabwean folk music. –MB

○ **Ambuya / SHANACHIE**
An earthy, deeply satisfying document of traditional and original Zimbabwean thumb-piano (mbira) music by this talented performer. –MB

○ **Ambuya/Ndizyozvo / GLOBESTYLE**   1988
As you can hear on the last four tracks of this CD, Chiweshe experiments with a fusion of rock and traditional Zimbabwean styles. (This import version includes material from the *Ndizyozvo* EP the Shanachie version lacks.) –JP

THOMAS MAPFUMO

Chimurenga. Thomas Mapfumo made revolutionary changes in Zimbabwe's pop-music scene by recording a song for which he'd written his own music. Before Mapfumo, songs in the traditional style were always based on tunes that had been handed down for generations.

Mapfumo's music, chimurenga ("music of struggle"), became popular during the civil war against White minority rule, but his popularity made the government unhappy. In 1977 he was sent to a prison camp for subversion. To obtain his release, Mapfumo agreed to perform for the ruling party, but at the concert he sang only his most revolutionary songs. "I told them that since I'd been in detention, I didn't have time to write new ones."

Mapfumo grew up in the country, went to a British colonial school, and worked as a herd boy, watching over the cattle. After hearing the Beatles and Wilson Pickett in the early 60s, Mapfumo taught himself guitar and started a band that played pop music from African countries as well as Beatles, Rolling Stones, funk, and soul.

Mapfumo left Western music behind to form the Acid Band. Their first album, *Hokoyo* ("Beware"), contained the songs that led to Mapfumo's detention.

After Zimbabwe's liberation in 1978, Mapfumo formed Blacks Unlimited and released *Gwindingwe Rine Shumba* (Lion in the Bush), a joyous celebration of his country's independence. Jumbo Van Renen, the president of Earthworks Records, arranged to put out Mapfumo's music in England; when Van Renen later became CEO of Island Records in the UK, he signed Mapfumo again, this time to an international recording contract. –JP

Shumba / EARTHWORKS
An anthology of Mapfumo's biggest hits from the late 70s and early 80s. Includes most of *Gwindingwe Rine Shumba*, an album released by Mapfumo to celebrate Zimbabwe's independence. –JP

☆ **Chimurenga Singles / SHANACHIE**   1984
The early hit singles by Mapfumo and Blacks Unlimited. These sides were recorded during the long civil war; their musical and lyrical content completely revamped the face of pop music in Zimbabwe. A classic. –JP

Ndangariro / CARTHAGE   1984
These were done shortly after the Zimbabwean independence and still have that youthful fire. –MB

Corruption / MANGO   1989
Mapfumo's first international release. This has more stunning guitar, and the title tune is sung in English to a calypso-like beat. A joyful mix of innovation and traditional roots. Great dance music. –JP & MB

Chamunorwa / MANGO   1991
Sidestepping his characteristic flinty sound, Mapfumo digs in deep with extended trance-inducing grooves propelled by thundering bass-drum heartbeats. –BT

DUMISANI MARAIRE

Neo-traditional.
Chaminuka: Music from Zimbabwe / MOTW   1988
This is an unparalleled recording that features the rhythms and melodies of Zimbabwe from the master musician Dumisani Maraire. Maraire sings and plays mbira and is joined on several selections by Minanzi III, a powerful marimba-and-percussion ensemble. Together, these two elements provide a fascinating glimpse into the music of Zimbabwe. –MUSIC OF THE WORLD

ZIMBABWE COLLECTIONS

○ **Take Cover / DISQUE AFRIQUE** 1986
Guitar pop from Zimbabwe by various artists, in the chimurenga style pioneered by Thomas Mapfumo. Pick hit: "Tarira Nguva," the African take on country & western, by the Family Singers. –JP

○ **Viva! Zimbabwe / EARTHWORKS** 1983
Post-liberation pop with generous samplings of jit, soukous, chimurenga, and other styles. –JP

ASIA

BURMA COLLECTIONS

Art Music / OCORA
Self-isolation since WWII has obscured Burma's major classical music tradition, a model of subtlety, delicacy, and grace. As a result, this two-CD collection is important for the rarity as well as the quality of its contents. One section each is devoted to the Burmese harp, flute, xylophone, and vocal music, and two sections are devoted to hsiang-waing orchestras playing the music of the traditional court. –JSR

CAMBODIA

MUSICIANS OF CAMBODIA NATIONAL

Traditional.
○ **Homrong / ATLANTIC** 1991
This classical performing troupe lacks refinement but is one of the few groups to survive the bloody Khmer Rouge revolution, and so is commendable for keeping the tradition alive. Classical vocals plus oboe, xylophone, flute, violin, percussion, and so forth. –MB

SAM-ANG SAM ENSEMBLE

Traditional.
○ **Music of Cambodia / WORLD MUSIC INSTITUTE**
Sam-Ang Sam is affiliated with Seattle's Cambodian Studies Center. He here leads various groupings of traditional musicians in wedding music and other songs traditional and contemporary. Good notes. This is part of the World Music Institute's New Americans series. –JSR

CAMBODIA COLLECTIONS

Royal Music of Cambodia / PHILIPS
A long piece by pinpeat orchestra, wooden-keyed xylophones predominating with gongs. Various smaller ensembles and mohori orchestra. –DLM

CHINA

LU-SENG ENSEMBLE

Chinese.
○ **Shantung ... / NONESUCH**
Shantung Folk & Traditional Instruments. Peaceful melodies from the Lu-Sheng Ensemble and excellent examples of folk and classical music played on sona (oboe), drum and cymbals, sheng, cheng, t'unti, nan'hu, and ti-tzu. Truly the people's music, not fussy or Westernized. –MB & DLM

LI XIANTANG

Traditional.
○ **Art of the Qin / OCORA**
Li's performance of compositions from 223 to 1937 highlights the transcendence of styles and eras typical of the seven-stringed qin zither (and indeed Chinese music as a whole). Bizarre, maybe, but as a bassist, I'm fascinated by the qin. Not only are some new basses like a vertical version of it, but Li's techniques provide a wonderful model, from the delicate,

breathy slides of the rare "Fisherman's Song" to the vigor of "Flowing Waters." –CARL HOYT, ORIGINAL MUSIC

CHINA COLLECTIONS

China / MUSICAPHON
A varied and very beautiful set, recorded in mainland China, of classical compositions for stringed instruments — pipa, qin, and zheng — plus one for xiao bamboo flute and qin. The pieces are all several hundred years old (dates are often disputed). The musicians are of different generations and reflect several approaches to their tradition. The notes and illustrations are, as always, admirable. –JSR

China - Music of the Pipa / NONESUCH
Folk and classical instrumentals on the four-string Chinese lute by master Lui Pui-Yuen. –MB

Chinese Turkestan/Xinjian Uighur Music / OCORA
Music from the Mideast/Asia interface. Though ruled by China, Uighur and Dolan are Muslim, and their music (despite Asian influences more obvious in the look of its instruments than in its sound or structure) is a highly individual descendant of the Arabo-Persian nexus. A superb recording of instrumental and vocal pieces, with very full notes. (144 minutes) –JSR

○ **Classical Instrumental Music / PLAYASOUND** 1986
These eleven ancient traditional pieces for cheng, pipa, and flute are played by senior members of the Hong Kong Orchestra. –ROOTS & RHYTHM

Hong Kong - Instrumental Music / AUVIDIS
A re-release of an old *Musical Atlas* album mostly devoted to solo music, notably (though not solely) to stringed instruments: pipa lute, butterfly harp, and ch'in zither are all represented along with various wind instruments, all in particularly fine performances. The term "classical" may be unsuited to the Chinese tradition, but this is art music, old and new, of high order. (48+ minutes) –JSR

○ **Living Classical Music / OCORA**
Music for pipa lute, banhu fiddle, diizi flute, and sheng mouth-organ, by a group of young musicians. They are part of what the notes call an evolutionary process, which appears to me to include elements of an international sensibility, less in material than in more indefinable interpretative attitudes. Good notes with illustrations of the instruments. –JSR

☆ **Spring Night on a Moonlit River / NONESUCH**
Spring Night on a Moonlit River - Music of the Chinese offers beautiful Chinese classical music, featuring the soulful sounds of the seven-string ch'in. –MB

GENERAL ASIA

MUSIC OF THE RAMAYANA

Classical.
Vol. 1: India / OCORA
A wonderful idea, and, like so many wonderful ideas, quite a simple one. This series shows the ways in which three musical cultures have treated a central Hindu legend. Most of the 71-minute Indian CD is devoted to a 1979 recording of the Kalakendra dance drama, "Ramlila," a Maharashtra song from the tournament episode, and a Carnatic kriti hymn by the great M. S. Subbulakshmi. –JSR

Vol. 2: Cambodia / OCORA
This album (50+ minutes) is a recording of a 1964 performance of the *Reamker* or *Khmer Ramayana* by the Cambodian Royal Ballet. –JSR

Vol. 3: Bali & Sunda / OCORA
The 15-minute extract from the Balinese *Wayang Wong* masked drama and the much-longer (47-minute) recording of the Sundanese marionette play *Wayang Golek* both come from the early 70s. –JSR

GENERAL ASIA COLLECTIONS

☆ **Islamic Music of Asia / INEDIT**

Muslim music from Pakistan, India, Malaysia, and Indonesia. Here are a call to prayer from Pakistan, a qawwal from India and one from Pakistan (Sabri Brothers); a Pakistani ghazal; a Malaysian maulidd, and a salawat dulang, a two-singer vocal contest special to Indonesia. Admirable idea, fine music. —JSR

☆ **Tuva - Voices from the Center of Asia / FOLKWAYS**
Not only have we here 33 examples of some of the most impressive vocal techniques in the world (including chordal throat-singing), with some almost equally remarkable instrumental work, but the notes, though cheaply produced, are extremely thorough. —JSR & MB

INDIA

NIKHIL BANERJEE

Classical.
The Hundred-Minute Raga / RAGA   1982
Two CDs. The Raga label specializes in concert recordings of classical Indian music, on the eminently logical ground that concert music is at its best in concert. This splendid performance by the late Nikhil Banerjee, one of the greatest of sitar players, was given in Berkeley in 1982. As the name suggests, it consists of the whole of one lengthy raga (except the start of the introductory alap, which was missed for reasons explained). The notes are adulatory but informative, and an interview with Banerjee is included. —JSR

Live: Berkeley 1982 / RAGA   1982
This extensive raga — "Misra Kafi" — shows Banerjee at his best (especially since it was recorded in the second part of the concert). Very fine digital recording. (78:52) —JSR

JAGDEEP SINGH BEDI

Classical.
Soft & True / MOTW   1989
Features the surbahar (bass sitar) and sitar of Jagdeep Singh Bedi, a virtuoso who creates a kaleidoscope of sound and melody with his instruments. Side 1 features solo surbahar with tanpura; Side 2, sitar and flute duets with tabla accompaniment. —MUSIC OF THE WORLD

JOTIN BHATTACHARYA

Classical.
Raga Lalita Gouri/Raga Bhagawati / ARK
Little-known in the West but a major musician, sarod-player Bhattacharya is the pupil of the great Ustad Allaudin Khan who is regarded as closest to the master's spirit and style, which reconciled the freedom of khyal and the intensity of drupad. —JSR

HARIPRASAD CHAURASIA

Classical.
○ **Rag Kaunsi Kanhra / NIMBUS**
Sensuous evening raga for the bamboo bansuri flute, with tabla by Sabir Khan. Lovely. —MB

Venu / RYKODISC
Classical flute master Chaurasia and one of India's leading young tabla players, Zakir Hussain, in a 1974 live recording, which was remixed a couple of years ago. The entire CD is devoted to one raga, "Rag Ahir Bhairav," a light-classical, early-morning raga that mixes a well-known classical piece, "Bhairav," with a folk melody called "Ahir." Superb music, finely recorded with good notes. —JSR

THE DAGAR BROTHERS

Classical.
Rag Kambhoji / MOTW   1989
Dhrupad is one of the oldest and most respected forms of classical Indian music, and the Dagar Brothers are its internationally acclaimed master vocalists. This outstanding release features Ustads N. Zahiruddin and N. Faiyazuddin Dagar singing "Rag Kambhoji." They are accompanied by Mohan Shyam Shara (pakhawaji drum) and Mussarat and Wasif Dagar (tanpuras). —MUSIC OF THE WORLD

K. S. GOPALKRISHNAN

Classical.
Carnatic Flute / WERGO
Gopalkrishnan is perhaps the leading flutist in the southern Indian tradition. On this release he plays mostly kirtis and bhajans accompanied by percussionists and a leading violinist. (74:15) —JSR

GANGUBAI HANGAL

Classical.
The Voice of Tradition / WERGO
At 75 years, Hangal may be the last representative of a generation that valued tradition and simplicity over show. She has been singing publicly since the late 20s and still performs with a group that includes her daughter and granddaughter. These performances of ragas from the "Kirana Gharana" are an important rarity amid the multiple recordings of familiar virtuosos. (70:07) —JSR

ANUP JALOTA

Popular/Traditional.
Farmaish / MUSIC INDIA
Devoted to the traditional Persian-derived lovesongs called "ghazals" which have recently re-entered Indian pop music with a vengeance. Jalota is mostly known for religious bhajans, but this is a really splendid set in a semi-classical vein, wonderfully sung to violin, harmonium, and percussion accompaniment. (61+ minutes) —JSR

VG JOG w/BRIJ KABRA

Classical.
Jugalbandi / CHHANDRA DARA
A fascinating example of naturalization: classical music of a high order played on two Western instruments — the violin, part of Indian music since the 18th century, and the guitar, adapted by Kabra himself — and both as appropriate to the style as is conceivable. "Raga Bagewari" is played in duet, "Raga Khamaji" by Jog, "Hansadwani" by Kabra, and "Raga Barwa" by Kichlu, a noted khyal singer. —JSR

KHAN FAMILY

Classical.
○ **Rag Jhinjoti/Rag Pilu / NIMBUS**
A good introduction to Indian music from these collective improvisations by Imrat Khan and his two sons. Note: "Rag Pilu" is a familiar Western musical scale. —MB

IMRAT KHAN

Classical.
Rag Madhur-Rhanjani / MOTW   1991
With Imrat Khan, sitar, and Shafaat Khan, tabla, Imrat Khan's newest recording is a passionate rendering of "Rag Madhur-Rhanjani" (which is a blend of "Rag Madhuvanti" and "Shivranjani"). The depth of feeling is expressed just a few minutes into the recording, which features a 30-minute alap. Audiophile sound quality. —MUSIC OF THE WORLD

SALAMAT ALI KHAN

East Indian.
○ **Raga Gunkali/Saraswati/Durga / NIMBUS**
Vocal ragas. —MB

○ **Salamat & Nazakat Ali Khan / HANNIBAL**   1988
Classical vocal duets in the uplifting Khayal tradition. —MB

USTAD ALI AKBAR KHAN

Classical. One of the greatest Indian musicians of the 20th century (many would argue *the* greatest), although his fame has always been eclipsed by that of his cousin Ravi Shankar. The reigning master of the fretless sarod, Ali Akbar Khan has done hundreds of recordings in India and runs an influential Indian music school in California. An important innovative force outside of India. –MB & JSR

☆ **Duet / RSM**
A near-perfect example of the classical duet. This superb live concert features star violinist L. Subramaniam and tabla drummer Zakir Hussein. –MB

○ **Signature Series - Vols. 1 & 2 / ALAM MADINA**
His long-unavailable 1967 recordings for the Connoisseur Society were the gateway to raga for many Americans. More than that, they are examples of one of the great schools of Hindustani classical music. Among the first of the Connoisseur series to be reissued, these and all his recordings are essential. Volume 1 has ragas "Chandranandan," "Gauri Manjari," "Jogiya Kalingra"; Volume 2, ragas "Medhavi," "Khammaj," "Bhairavi Bhatiyar w. Ragmala." –JSR

USTAD SABRI KHAN

Classical.
Raga Darbari/Raga Multani / AUVIDIS
Ustad Sabri Khan is one of the greatest living masters of the Indian violin. His most important contribution to the advance of the tradition (like many 20th-century masters) has been to give his instrument an important solo role, after a period in which it had fallen into disrepute. Here he plays two ragas associated with khayal, which express more tension than most chosen by contemporary musicians. (69:28) –JSR

Ustad Sabri Khan w/ Ghulam Sawar Sabri / ARCD
The sarangi is strongly associated with accompaniment, but even in solo — a recent development pioneered by Sabri Khan — the sarangi normally follows khayal and thumri forms. (59:41) –JSR

USTAD SULTAN KHAN

Classical. Along with his contemporary Ram Narayan, Ustad Sultan Khan is one of a handful of Indian classical musicians keeping the sound of the sarangi alive. This archaic instrument is bowed, with the performer sliding his fingernails along the melody strings; the many sympathetic strings vibrating in harmony produce a haunting drone accompaniment. –MB

☆ **Sarangi - Music of India / RYKODISC**
This shows many emotional sides of the living master of the sarangi, an ancient bowed string instrument. –MB

RAMNAD KRISHNAN

Carnatic. The Carnatic style is primarily a showcase for vocalists, who must present long composed pieces in addition to intense and demanding improvisations. Ramnad Krishnan began studying at the age of six and, after achieving celebrity status in both South and North India, went on to teach at Wesleyan University in Connecticut. –MB

☆ **Songs of the Carnatic Tradition / NONESUCH**
Ramnad Krishnan: Vidwan - Songs of the Carnatic Tradition features vocals with violin and mrdangam. Extended performances, lengthy alap. An essential record of the South Indian vocal art in all its complexity. –DLM & MB

S. AND R. MAHARAJAPURAM

Classical.
Carnatic Music / AUVIDIS
Sathanam and Ramachandran Maharajapuram, the father-and-son team, among the major singers of their respective age groups, are also the sixth and seventh generation of a major

The Music of India

The music of India has enjoyed a worldwide explosion since coming into vogue in the psychedelic 60s. Most Indian musicians come from musical families and begin study from an early age at the knee of a father or uncle. In the classical tradition (the majority of recordings available in the US are by North Indian classical musicians), music is a prestigious, life-long pursuit where sustained solo expression figures prominently. Centuries-old scales called ragas serve as the basis for extended improvisation in small groups, typically involving a tabla drummer and tambura player, whose ethereal drone reinforces the mood of the raga for the lead instrumentalist.

Popular lead instruments in the North Indian school are the multi-stringed sitar, sarod, sarangi, and santour, and woodwinds — bamboo flute and shehnai — a double-reed oboe sometimes heard in larger ensembles. The voice is also featured in both North and South Indian classical forms — in the South the dominant art music is the Carnatic style, which emphasizes highly ornamented improvisation based on long melodies of folk, sacred, and classical origin. Common instruments in the South are the stringed vina and violin, often used in larger groups with singers and a variety of percussion — the double-headed mridangam, clay-pot drum, and tambourine. In recent years, Western instruments — mandolin, guitar, clarinet, piano, and even the saxophone — have been embraced by younger innovators and incorporated into the classical tradition (though not without protest).

India also has a rich legacy of regional folk music; religious songs of various sects; theatrical epics involving mythology, dance, and music; pop forms; and of course an extremely prolific film-music industry, just beginning to be appreciated abroad. Recordings offered by American companies are just the tip of the iceberg — go to an Indian market in a major city and you will find a bewildering array of national styles, most on inexpensive cassettes.

— Myles Boisen

vocal dynasty. Their duet style is as beguiling as it is authentic. –JSR

BUDHADITYA MUKHERJEE

Classical.
Rag Bagesri/Rag Des / NIMBUS
Sitar ragas. –MB

○ **Rag Ramkali/Rag Jhinjoti / NIMBUS**
Sensitive sitar from one of the instrument's leading younger exponents, specializing in the vocal-derived gayaki style. –MB

MUSIC OF INDIA SERIES

Classical.
Southern Dance & Theatre Music / MUSICAPHON
Introduces some of the major strains of Indian classical and religious music. The theatrical dance forms covered are women's bharata natyam and men's kathakali. –JSR

Vedic Recitation & Song / MUSICAPHON
Vedic chant is thought to be the oldest extant form of psalmody, preserved unchanged over thousands of years by extremely strict and complex instruction. These recitations and incantations, the heart of Hindu ritual, have endured as an unchanging constant in all the richness and variety of Indian music as a whole. –JSR

RAM NARAYAN

Classical.
Rag Bhupal Tori/Rad Patdip / NIMBUS
Ragas on sarangi by the best-known contemporary practitioner. –MB

☆ **Rag Lalit / NIMBUS** 1989
Dark and dissonant — the most intense Indian music I've heard. Mostly solo sarangi (an ancient bowed instrument), with some tablas to break up the 73-minute length. –MB

TRICHY SANKARAN

Carnatic.
Laya Vinyas / MOTW 1989
Highlights the mrdangam (double-headed barrel drum) from South India. In addition to solo performances, this recording features kanjira (frame drum) and vina, one of the oldest stringed instruments of the Indian subcontinent. This is highly rhythmic and pulsating music — an excellent representation of the pure sound and complex nature of South Indian drumming. –MUSIC OF THE WORLD

SHRI EMANI SHANKARA SASTRY

Carnatic.
Art of the Vina / PLAYASOUND
The vina, an ancestor of the sitar, is the most important instrument of the South Indian Carnatic tradition. Shri Sastry is an heir to several generations of vina virtuosity. This 1974 recording (48+ minutes) contains lengthy ragas and shorter pieces. An outstanding performance with superb notes and photos. –JSR

ARUNA SAYEERAM

Carnatic.
Carnatic Song / AUVIDIS
Sayeeram sings a program with many kritis (religious songs somewhat like bhajans), accompanied by violin and the usual supporting instruments. (65:05) –JSR

LAKSHMI SHANKAR

Classical.
Songs of Devotion / AUVIDIS
Shankar sings mostly religious bhajans and semi-classical thumri in the khayal style, accompanying herself on the swaramandal zither — a relation to the santur. (65:33) –JSR

RAVI SHANKAR

Classical. Known worldwide as the ambassador of Indian classical music, thanks largely to Beatle George Harrison and fiery performances at important 60s rock festivals, Ravi Shankar is also one of the most proficient North Indian musicians. He is a particularly nimble and exciting performer on the many-stringed sitar, especially in duet situations. Albums and tapes of his many 60s and 70s recordings are almost always available at used-record stores and/or Indian grocery stores in metropolitan areas, and his recent works, often in the world music/fusion vein, are easy to find. –MB

Genius of Ravi Shankar / CBS
Another worthy effort from Shankar's period of worldwide fame. –MB

○ **Sounds of India / CBS**
Good notes and a spoken prolog by Shankar make this a fine introduction to North Indian classical music. –MB

Ravi Shankar / CAPITOL
One of the best recordings of this excellent sitar player. –DLM

☆ **Ragas / FANTASY** 1973
A less-than-perfect recording, but this double-album is an impeccable document of inspired raga duets by the masters Ravi Shankar and Ali Akbar Khan. –MB

Raga Parameshwari / CAPITOL 1976
A full raga cycle, with his best tabla drum accompanist, Alla Rakha. –MB

SHIVKUMAR SHARMA

Classical.
Colours of 100 Strings / EMI INDIA
Until Sharma brought it into the classical canon quite recently, India knew the santur largely as a Kashmiri folk instrument. On this recording he plays an extended "Rag Vachaspati" and a shorter piece, based on a Rajasthani folk form, that creeps into the classical canon. (67+ minutes) –JSR

K. SRIDHAR & K. SHIVAKUMAR

Classical.
○ **Shringar / REAL WORLD**
Ragas for sarod and violin in the southern Carnatic tradition, recorded in concert by two brothers (Shivakumar and Sridhar) from the younger generation of musicians. "Raga Bageshri" is a late-night raga, while the extremely popular "Bhairavi" is played at any time of the day. Here they are both given somewhat contemplative renderings that focus on spiritual depth rather than technique. –JSR

PARVEEN SULTANA & DILSHAD KHAN

Classical.
Khayal / ESPERANCE
Khayal developed (like the European romantic movement) to reassert the primacy of expressiveness over rules that are too rigid; lyricism, freedom, improvisation, and virtuosity are its hallmarks. Sultana and Khan, perhaps the most highly regarded of India's younger singers, perform both solos and duets in a recording that is, at times, breathtaking. –JSR

From Dawn to Dusk / AUVIDIS
Sultana and Khan perform in the expressive khayal style. –JSR

PANKAJ UDHAS

Popular-traditional.
Paimanas / MUSIC INDIA
Devoted to the traditional Persian-derived lovesongs called "ghazals" that have recently re-entered Indian pop music with a vengeance, the Udhas set is quite as good as their *Farmaish* but in a more pop vein, with backings that draw from an intriguing mix of Indian and overseas (including Greek and Spanish) influences. (Over 65 minutes) –JSR

INDIA COLLECTIONS

Carnatic Music / MUSICAPHON
A very fine recording involving vocals by Semmangudi Srinavasa Aiyar, the vina player K. S. Narayanaswami, and mridangam player Palghat Ragu. They perform two kritis by Muttuswami Dikshitar, one of the three founders of Carnatic music, along with two raga medleys. Major musicians (this series is bizarre in its reluctance to treat performers as individual artists rather than carriers of a style), excellent notes, and recording by John Levy. –JSR

○ **Festival of India / MOTW** 1990
The great masters of North India perform classical and folk music on this landmark production, *Festival of India: A Hindustani Sampler*. Featured artists include V. G. Jog (violin), Sultan Khan (sarangi), G. S. Sachdev (bamboo flute), Purna Das Baul (Bengali folk ensemble), and the Dagar Brothers (Dhrupad vocal music). An excellent introduction to North Indian music. –MUSIC OF THE WORLD

Folk Music of Uttar Pradesh / MUSICAPHON
Any collection from India's most populous state is clearly only going to scratch the surface, but this one is unusually impressive. It's basically an overview — a range of instrumental cuts (lots of percussion) followed by vocal music of all sorts. But this is an overview quite out of the ordinary

798

because of the incredibly detailed notes — 84 pages of English (a few credits aside). Moreover, the recording quality is superb. A fine start for Musicaphon's CD series. (74:54) –JSR

☆ **Golden Voices of the Silver Screen 2 / GLOBESTYLE**
Finally, recognition that Indian film music is a major popular form with both creativity and enormous influence! Ben Mandelson, who selected the cuts, is overly fond of the more manic sitar-to-polka-to-Indo/Dixieland-type mixes, to the detriment of the style's less flamboyant examples. Also, none of the younger generation of singers is included (though most of the greatest names are here). But it's a fine start, and to have notes to this stuff is a blessing in itself. –JSR

☆ **Indian Classical Music / CAPRICE**
This standout set of two LPs covers several different approaches to both of the major classical traditions. Young sitarist Debu Chaudhuri takes a strongly traditional approach. So does S. Balachander, the greatest Carnatic vina player of the older generation. Bhimsen Joshi, too, sings khayal and thumri with more austerity than vocalists like Parveen Sultana. Lastly, flutist Hariprasad Chaurasia and santurist Shivkumar Sharma play Vivaldi and Bach in performances that are airy and playful, while in no way less serious. –JSR

○ **North Indian Folk Music / AUVIDIS**
A really fine glimpse into an enormously rich musical culture. Aside from their very great instrinsic merits, many of these recordings — among them a bhajan by a wandering monk, a shahnai solo, an episode from the *Ramayana* — give a feeling for the popular equivalents of music more familiar in their classical aspect in the West. (50:30) –JSR

○ **Songs of the Madmen / CHANT DU MONDE**
The "madmen" are the Bauls, the wandering mystics of Bengal, who "proceed against the tide of habit, received ideas, and generalization." Not surprisingly, therefore, they set great store by singing, dancing, and ornamentation of the body, making this a very lively recording. The very thorough notes include English translations of the songs. –CARL HOYT, ORIGINAL MUSIC

INDIAN DIASPORA

BHANGRA POWER

Indo-British.
Bhangra Power / MULTITONE
Bhangra, a new fusion idiom built from a Punjabi folk form by Indo-Brit teenagers for their own communal purposes, is not quite like anything from India itself. Punjabi percussion, electronics, and vocals from all quarters blend splendidly with enormous vitality to form that quite rare phenomenon, a truly teenage music. The groups on this album span the style riotously. (57+ minutes) –JSR

SHEILA CHANDRA

Indo-British. Like Najma, Sheila Chandra has brought her Indian ancestry to the open ears of the British pop market, scoring with a series of dance records throughout the 80s. Her music relies mainly on Western harmonies and rhythms, typically in a beat-heavy dance mold, with her supple voice supplying a sheen of Eastern exoticism. –MB

☆ **Silk / SHANACHIE**   1991
A career retrospective of one of the innovators of the British Indi-pop style, this album contains moody and danceable hits collected from various 80s releases. *Silk* combines classical Indian music and Western pop. –BT & MB

NAJMA

Indo-British. Najma Ashtar, a beautiful and talented young woman born in England of Indian parentage, seems bound for stardom in our world-music-conscious age. She sings traditional lyrics of the Urdu-language poets primarily, backing the complex poetry with a very contemporary musical palette that includes pop, jazz, and popular Indian

The Music of Indonesia

One of the most populous regions of the world, Indonesia is also extremely culturally diverse, spread out across nearly 3000 islands. Although only the three larger islands of Java, Sumatra, and Bali are represented by current recordings, they comprise elements of many ethnic influences, including Hindu, Buddhist, Tao, Islamic, Christian, and animist religions. This diversity reflects the influences from their Indian and Asian neighbors as well as the European presence of the Dutch.

Perhaps the best known of Javanese and Balinese music is gamelan (orchestra) music. Gamelan is an ensemble of instruments consisting of gongs (kempul), hand drums (kendhang, ketipung), wooden and bronze xylophone-like instruments (gembang, saron), and bronze kettles, gongs, and bowls (bonang, kenong, kethuk) as well as bowed lutes, plucked zithers, and flutes. Derived from centuries of Indonesian bronzesmithing, the gamelan accompanies ceremonial rituals, dance-dramas, and the wayang (leather shadow puppet theater tracing its origins to the Indian epics *Mahabharata* and *Ramayana*). Some of these performances can last the better part of one day and well into the next morning. The percussive and metric melodies of gamelan music are beautifully ornate, embellished by various instruments in the ensemble. The effect is hypnotic; in fact, the music is used for trance-induction in certain rituals.

The musical tradition in Indonesia is so rich and varied, we don't have room here to describe all the many styles. Here are just a few. *Ketjak* (or monkey chant) is a ritual drama and trance-inducing dance in which a choir of singers chants the sound "Chak"). *Kroncong* is a style of solo vocal accompanied by small groups of European-style instruments, including ukelele (the word kroncong refers to a similar Indonesian instrument), violin, guitar, plucked three-string cello, or (on the Muslim northern coast) accordion. This urban folk-music style, popular from the 20s to the 60s, is now primarily nostalgic "oldies" music for middle-aged Indonesians. *Langgam jawa* (Javanese song) is a regional form of kroncong from Central Java, especially Surakarta, that is sung in Javanese.

Dangdut, another folk music, is the "country music of Indonesia," with songs about the misfortunes of ordinary people. Rhoma Irama is the principle figure in dangdut music and can be heard on the Smithsonian/Folkways recording *The Music of Indonesia - Vol. 2.*

Jaipongan is a contemporary dance and musical form created by producer and musical *auteur* Gugum Gumbira Tirasondjaja in the Sundanese section of West Java during the cultural revolution of the 60s.

Another contemporary style, called *pop Indonesia*, or simply pop, is cross-cultural mass-market music intended to appeal to a wide diversity and unite the various ethnic groups.

— Scott Bultman

music. Recently she has branched out to include qawwali, Indian ragas, and Western songs in her repertoire, always keeping her sensuous music close to its roots. –MB

☆ **Qareeb / SHANACHIE**   1989
Anglo-Indian female vocalist sings modernized medieval Persian love songs called "ghazals" in a traditional Indian-music setting of tabla and violin — plus the addition of smooth, jazz-inflected sax. –BT

INDONESIA

MUSIC OF INDONESIA

Popular.

Vol. 1 - Songs Before Dawn / SMITHSONIAN-FOLKWAYS
Though you wouldn't think it from the Western obsession with gamelan, Java has a wealth of "contemporary" and more or less syncretic popular styles, many of them with strong Muslim elements and influences from the Middle East and India. This is a splendid set in a lavish and altogether admirable vein. The first of the trio is devoted to gandrung banyuwangi, which has links with ancient religious beliefs, but is performed by professionals as party music with a female singer who also dances with the guests, backed here by two violins, gongs, and percussion. –JSR

○ **Vol. 2 - Indonesian Popular Music / SMITHSONIAN**
Vol. 2 includes commercial recordings of Muslim dangdut, kroncong, and langgam jawa. These slick and street-wise popular music groups demonstrate individualistic approaches influenced by Indian film music, European folk, and Western pop. –MB & JSR

Vol. 3 - From the Outskirts of Jakarta / SMITHSONIAN
The third, and my personal favorite, is real local street music of the capital, Jakarta — a mix of Chinese and Indonesian elements, which paradoxically sounds quite Muslim. –JSR

Vol. 4 - Nias & North Sumatra / SMITHSONIAN   1992
Another slap-in-the-face collection of startlingly bright music in the Smithsonian *Music of Indonesia* series, this one spotlighting the rich diversity of a small region of the westernmost archipelago. The frenetic Toba and Karo peoples' gong and vernacular oboe recordings are impressive enough. But the unaccompanied hoho vocal music of the men of the island of Nias steals the show, crafting deeply resonant wells of sound from a four-tone scale — simultaneously funereal and lusty. Meticulously recorded and documented. –BT

INDONESIA (BALI)

KUSUMA SARI

Gamelan.

Gamelan Batal Wayang Ramayana / CMP
Gamelan batel music from Sading, a village just north of Bali's capital, Denpasar. Kusuna Sari is a ten-piece group of part-time musicians, mostly farmers. Here they play mostly music to accompany the wayang kulit shadow theater. That this is just one of thousands of such groups on Bali is a staggering tribute to a deeply musical culture. (69 minutes) –JSR

INDONESIA (BALI) COLLECTIONS

Balinese Contemporary Music / MUSICAPHON
These early-to-mid-80s recordings give examples of the gamelan gong kebyar in the villages of Pinda and Sawan — both centers of the most widespread contemporary Balinese gamelan sound. Kebyar is one of those few forms that develop out of tradition with little or no outside influences (a much more common procedure than is sometimes realized). The music is splendid and the documentation and photos, as usual, outstanding. –JSR

Gamelan Music from Seloatu-Bali / ARCHIVE
A dramatic, shimmering, precise, and exciting gamelan. –DLM

Gamelan Semar Pegulingan / NONESUCH
Gamelan Semar Pegulingan: Gamelan of the Love God - Bali. An excellent recording of a full, rich, classical gamelan. –DLM

☆ **Golden Rain - Balinese Gamelan Music / NONESUCH**
An introduction to the exciting Balinese kebjar style, plus a long excerpt from the gripping ritual drama known as ketjak (monkey chant). –MB

☆ **Music from the Morning of the World / NONESUCH**
This combines two classic Nonesuch albums to offer a good

survey of gamelan music from Bali, along with the famous monkey chant ritual. –MB

○ **Music of Bali / NONESUCH**
A good contemporary survey of major traditional Balinese styles. Lots of variety. –MB

INDONESIA (BORNEO) COLLECTIONS

Musiques de l'Asie Traditionelle - Vol. 6 / PLAYA SOUND
This volume, *Musiques de l'Asie Traditionelle - Vol. 6 (Borneo)*, contains Hindu-influenced-music as well as gong-ensemble music. –DLM

INDONESIA (JAVA)

EUIS KOMARIAH

Jaipongan.

Jaipongan Java / GLOBESTYLE   1990
Euis's frail and plaintive vocals adrift in a landscape of jagged gamelan percussion and rhythms. Capricious, moody, inspired, and dosed with shots of wit. –BT

○ **The Sound of Sunda / GLOBESTYLE**   1990
Western vocal harmonies combine with music-box-style gamelan-derived instrumentation in a recording of torch songs in the popular degung genre. Playing the part of heart-wrenched lovers, the entwining yearnings of Euis and Yus Wiradiredja recall the best and most soulful American male-female pop duets. Highly recommended. –BT

NASIDARIA GROUP SEMARANG

Popular.

☆ **Keadilan / PIRANHA**
This is a truly wonderful recording. The all-woman Nasidaria is a supergroup by Javanese standards, with 32 cassette releases under their belts. This is yet another of the great Muslim crossover sounds, with Indian and Arabic (including contempo-Cairo) influences, but also a sound totally its own. Traditional Qasidah was epic poetry accompanied by percussion and response singing. Indonesian Muslims use the form as a kind of Islamic calypso of social and topical comment, and Nasidaria added synth, guitars, and so on, along with Indian drumming, *filmi* touches, and all the usual wonderful stuff. –JSR

SLAMET A. SJUKUR'S ANGKLUNG GROUP

Traditional.

Slamet A. Sjukur's Angklung Group / ARION
A recording made at a 1975 Dijon wine festival! The role of the bamboo angklung, which started life as a rhythm instrument, has been expanding its melodic role over the years. Sjukur's group exemplified this in a performance that also used a fairly wide range of vocal styles. The recording as a whole is a good example of the way in which young musicians all over the world have tried to adapt traditional styles to changing times. The frivolous will adore track four. (44:57) –JSR

INDONESIA (JAVA) COLLECTIONS

Flute & Gamelan of West Java / TANGENT
Recordings by the National University group of Jakarta, featuring Indonesia's best-known flute player, Sulaeman. The first side is devoted to music for bamboo flute accompanied by kacapi zither. The gamelan pieces are played by a group half-a-dozen strong, in the coastal style. –JSR

Java: Historic Gamelans / PHILIPS
This recording features ome old, rare, varied, and interesting types of gamelans. –DLM

○ **Java - Vocal Art / AUVIDIS**   1990
This is Javanese macapat poetry, which clearly shows the introspective and subtle character of much of Java's vocal music. –GINO ROBAIR, ROOTS & RHYTHM

○ **Java - Vol. 1 (Opera of Danuredjo 7) / OCORA**
World premiere recording of Langen Mandra Wanara, a once-popular form of Javanese opera. —PETER GARELLICK, ROOTS & RHYTHM

○ **Javanese Court Gamelan ... / NONESUCH**
Javanese Court Gamelan from the Pura Paku Aleman,
Jogjakarta offers some extended stately and beautiful pieces by a very traditional Central Javanese gamelan. —DLM & MB

☆ **Street Music of Java / ORIGINAL MUSIC**   1989
Three major street-popular idioms. Kroncong, a seductive music for fiddle, ukulele, and guitar, is thought to have originated under Portuguese influence as far back as the 17th century. Dangdut is a newer style, with strong Muslim influences (including Egyptian film music). The street versions here are based on the percussion that gives it its name. Langgan Jawa is a regional form of kroncong with stronger musical links to other local styles. Also included is some village ronggeng and a guitar-backed style called melayu that crosses local, Latin, and Indian influences. —JSR

○ **The Sultan's Pleasure / MOTW**
Recordings of courtly music from the Sultan's palace, where the classical tradition is maintained and developed. Made during the ceremonial performances associated with the Sultan's birthday, they include examples of several of the 18 different royal gamelan sets. —JSR

Sunda (West Java) / PHILIPS
Gamelan music and music for small kecapi suling ensemble is featured on this album. —DLM

JAPAN

JAPANESE KOTO CONSORT

Classical.

○ **Japanese Koto Consort / LYRICHORD**
Very fine recordings of sokyoku, instrumental music for koto, shamisen, and shakuhachi, two of them accompanying vocals. Though the instruments are a lot older, these ensembles took hold during the Edo period when a new mercantile class was having a profound effect on what had until then been mostly a courtly and religious tradition. The notes are sparse but fairly informative, the duration chintzy even for an LP reissue, but the music delightfully combines authenticity and accessibility. —JSR

SHOUKICHI KINA

Popular.

○ **The Music Power from Okinawa / GLOBESTYLE**   1991
Delirious, high-spirited ditties shelter a tough sense of nationalism, cultural identity, and opposition to colonialism — hence Bob Marley's admiration for Kina, captured here in a 1972 live recording, which is deliciously ragged. A pair of bonus studio tracks demonstrate the power of Okinawan pop at full hi-tech tilt. —BT

KODO

Japanese.

Heartbeat Drummers of Japan / SHL
Authentic Japanese Taiko-drum ensemble, who sometimes add modern and/or Western touches to their thunderous drumming repertoire. —MB

KOHACHIRO MIYATA

Traditional.

Shakuhachi - The Japanese Flute / NONESUCH   1976
Five solo pieces recorded in 1976 by one of Japan's leading shakuhachi players. All are parts of the standard repertoire, and most are meditative in nature. The music is magnificent, the recording excellent, and the notes exemplary in their combination of clarity and information. Short measure at 34+ minutes. —JSR

TADASHI TAJIMA

Shakuhachi.

Shingetsu / MOTW   1991
The shakuhachi, a notched bamboo flute, is the most important wind instrument of Japan. This recording features eight pieces for solo shakuhachi played in a distinctive style by Tadashi Tajima, one of Japan's finest traditional shakuhachi masters. Tajima's breath, phrasings, and use of long flutes combine in making this an exceptional recording.
—MUSIC OF THE WORLD

KINSHI TSURUTA

Traditional.

Satsuma-biwa / OCORA
The satsuma-biwa, a type of lute, has its own traditions and repertoire. The energetic and percussive style featured in the music composed for this instrument appeared in 16th-century South Kyusu, whose then-ruler wrote its first lyrics. Tsuruta, one of the major living interpreters of satsuma-biwa, sings three contrasting songs here. Exemplary music; brief but adequate notes. (60:20) —JSR

JAPAN COLLECTIONS

☆ **Bell Ringing in the Empty Sky / NONESUCH**
Haunting, quieting, evocative solo shakuhachi bamboo flute by Goro Yamaguchi. *Bell Ringing in the Empty Sky - Japan Shakuhachi Music* offers two lengthy selections. —DLM

☆ **Flower Dance - Japanese Folk Melodies / NONESUCH**
Ten ancient folk tunes — lullabies, drinking songs, dances, and so forth — featuring the Noday family performing on shamisen and koto (both stringed instruments), plus percussion and bamboo flute. —MB

Japan 11: Gagaku / BARENREITER
Dramatic and beautiful ensemble music for the court. —DLM

Japan - Semi-classical & Folk Music / EMI
Good recordings of nagauta, koto, and shakuhachi. Especially good selections of folk music. —DLM

○ **Kabuki & Traditional of Japan / ELEKTRA**
A nice recording of Japan's dramatic but austere theater music. —MB

○ **Kagura - Shinto Ritual Music / HUNGAROTON**
Kagura is the general word for Shinto practices associated with music and song. As this recording documents, that covers a wide range: an invocation from the ancient shamaness tradition; festival dances of various kinds; folk drama on mythological themes; court ceremony. A wide range of recordings is enhanced by admirable recording and very thorough notes. —JSR

○ **Koto Music of Japan / NONESUCH**
Stately art music for the resonant Japanese zither, played in solo or ensemble settings. —MB

Noh Play/Recitation to Biwa / MUSICAPHON
Lyrical Noh choral drama, developed in the late 14th century and largely unchanged since, consists largely of recitative and song. Includes *Hagoromo*, one of a class of plays concerning romantic and nature spirits. Also includes an example of a pre-Noh-play narrative tradition. —JSR

○ **O-Suwa-Daiko Drums / AUVIDIS**
Originally used in Shinto rituals, later also as military music, the complex percussion ensembles of the Suwa valley use other instruments only as garnishes. As privileged audiences in the US have recently discovered, this is one of the great percussion traditions of the world, overwhelming even on record. (41:51) —JSR

Shinto Music / MUSICAPHON
Traditional Music of Japan - Shinto Music. Shinto music goes back to the 4th century, but it was much reworked in the mid 19th century. Here are religious dance-songs and other music, including both wind and stringed instruments. —JSR

Traditional Vocal & Instrumentals / ELEKTRA
A nice variety of Japanese singing and instrumental styles from the traditional Ensemble Nipponia. –MB

KOREA

SAMULNORI

Neo-traditional.
Record of Changes / CMP
Contemporary-traditional ritual song and percussion. Salumnori is a young group that composes (or re-creates) compositions stemming from ancient Korean ceremonial music, arranged and played by 20th-century Koreans. As such, it is part of a quite widespread attempt to adapt tradition to modern life and beliefs. –JSR

PARK SANG-WON

Classical.
○ **The Kayagum - Korea - Vol. 1 / DISQUES ESPERANCE**
Park's technique on the 12-string kayagum is formidable. –MYLES BOISEN, ROOTS & RHYTHM

KOREA COLLECTIONS

Korean Music / PHILIPS
Prominent on this album are the oboe-like hyangpiri played in small court ensemble and the taegum flute, both expressive and virtuosic. –DLM
☆ **P'ansori / NONESUCH**
Although difficult for Westerners, the p'ansori vocal style featured on *P'ansori - Korea's Epic Vocal & Instrumental* is highly regarded in Korea, and singer Kim So-Hee is a national treasure. –MB

LAOS COLLECTIONS

Lam Saravane/Khen Music / OCORA
In the lam, performed at various important village occasions, male and female vocalists sing a kind of competitive love song in which he charms and she exposes the shallowness of his charming. A performance of delicate strength, backed by flute and khen (bamboo) mouth-organ. To this performance by one of the great women lam singers is added a number of solo pieces for khen. Fine performances, excellent recording, good notes. –JSR
Laos / MUSICAPHON
An admirable introduction to the varied classical and village idioms of this musically rich nation, with its ancient Indian as well as Chinese and Southeast Asian elements. Included are several varied pieces for the khene, a bamboo mouth organ that is the precursor to the Chinese cheng, and various classical orchestras, some dominated by strings, some by xylophones, one (in a *Ramayana* epic) by oboe and percussion. Fine photos, slighter notes than usual in this series. –JSR
Southern Laos: Traditional Music / PHILIPS
Music for khenes (mouth organ), singer, pi-phat orchestra, wedding orchestra, buffalo sacrifice, gong with singer. Exciting and interesting. –DLM

MALAYSIA COLLECTIONS

Fataleka & Baegu Music from Malaita / UNESCO
This is one of my favorite recordings of panpipe music and vocals. –DLM
Malaysia / MUSICAPHON
This album in Unesco's *Musical Anthology of the Orient* series includes several examples of gamelan, as well as pieces associated with various dance-dramas and the wayang-kulit shadow play, rabab, and other music. As always, fine illustrated notes. –JSR
Negrito of Malacca / MUSICAPHON
The Negrito of the Malacca Peninsula are among the aboriginal inhabitants of Malaya. Their music is entirely religious, and underlying its apparent simplicity is a sophisticated approach to timbre or tone-color. The first side of their album consists of shamanistic dance songs, the second of instruments, more shamanistic music, and a historic 1924 recording. –JSR
Protomalayans of Malacca / MUSICAPHON
The 17,000 proto-Malayans are in transition, but in 1963, when this album was recorded, they still preserved much of their old culture. Their music is tightly intertwined with communal/spiritual values. It is also quite rich, with a wide range of styles both ancient and contemporary. –JSR

MONGOLIA COLLECTIONS

Instrumental & Vocal Music of Mongolia / INEDIT
This album contains instrumental and vocal music of Mongolia. Recommended. –DLM
Mongolia / AUVIDIS
There are many incredible recordings of the traditional musics of Mongolia available now. This new recording is the best one available. –DLM
Mongolian Folk Music / HUNGAROTON
In a world with ever more fine recordings of once-unobtainable music, this two-CD collection of 1967 recordings by a Hungarian ethnomusicologist remains almost hors concours (even from Jean Jenkins's Tangent set). Superb recording quality does justice to a very wide selection of vocal and instrumental pieces that are remarkable in their beauty and variety (three different musical subcultures). One song is also remarkable in its almost spookily Scots-Irish sound. English notes. –JSR

PAKISTAN

NUSRAT FATEH ALI KHAN

Qawwali. Like the Sabri Brothers, Khan has captured the attention of the world music community with the vocal intensity of his qawwali music. But his performances have more of an individual focus, with emphasis on dramatic improvisational cascades and other flashy singing techniques. He has been recorded on a number of import labels, and has even done a pop-fusion album for Peter Gabriel's Real World label. –MB
Shahen-Shah / ATLANTIC
Four lengthy selections of Sufi devotional music with impassioned chorus and accompaniment. –MB
Live in Paris - Vols. 1 & 2 / OCORA
There is no single greatest singer of qawwalis, the ancient Sufi songs that have become central to popular religion and popular music in Pakistan. But if there were, his name would be Nusrat. Khan inherits a family tradition of qawwali singing going back several centuries, and in live performances like this concert he can be emotionally devastating. –DLM
Day, Night, Dawn, Dusk / SHANACHIE   1991
More passionate Pakistani devotional music. –MB
☆ **Shahbaaz / ATLANTIC**   1991
This shows Kahn taking chances with tradition, pushing his dynamic voice and ensemble to new expressive heights. –MB

THE SABRI BROTHERS

Qawwali. The Sabri Brothers are not brothers by birth but members of a mystical Islamic Sufi brotherhood. They were the first group to bring their devotional qawwali songs to the West from Pakistan, recording and giving concerts of this boisterous and highly rhythmic music outside of its religious setting. Their sound is full of interplay and group singing, in contrast to the style of soloist Nusrat Fateh Ali Khan. –MB
○ **The Music of the Qawal / AUDIVIS-UNESCO**
Excellent performances by the Sabri Brothers — heirs like Nusrat Fateh Ali Khan to generations of family virtuosity — in which they hew closer to Sufi tradition than in more recent recordings aimed at the Pakistani market. Superb. –JSR

Qawwali / NONESUCH 1978
The first Pakastani Sufi record issued in the US, and a fine example of full-throated qawwali. –MB
○ **Ya Habib / ATLANTIC** 1990

PAKISTAN COLLECTIONS

☆ **Treasures of Pakistan / PLAYASOUND**
Excellent examples of music for sarinda and sarangi fiddles as well as the rabab lute, extremely well recorded on location. As a nice touch, the producer is Kudzi Erguner, a Turkish musician, rather than the usual Western ethnomusicologist (not the first — I remember Deben Bhattacharya's recordings with nostalgia — but still too rare). Brief but cogent notes. (69 minutes) –JSR

PHILIPPINES

KULINTANG ARTS

Neo-traditional.
Ancient Rhythms/Urban Sounds / KULINTANG ARTS
Kulintang is South Philippine music for string, gongs, and percussion. This multimedia group of young Bay Area Philippinos plays a contemporary version of kulintang and also various offshoots, fusions, and parallels. The cassette has one side of kulintang, and one of a mixed bag of compositions ranging from jazz-oriented to a folky sound also common in the Philippines. –JSR

PHILIPPINES COLLECTIONS

○ **Gong Music from Lanao - Vols. 1 & 2 / LYRICHORD**
Unlike the mainstream musical culture of the Philippines, which shows heavy Hispanic elements, the Muslims of the southern island of Mindanao have stronger links with Malaysia and Indonesia. Kulintang gong music is related to Indonesian gamelan, though somewhat simpler and (to import a concept) hotter in feel. The kulintang itself is also invariably a women's instrument. A particularly accessible and attractive pair of recordings. –JSR
Music of the Magindanao / FOLKWAYS
Examples of gongs used in a gamelan-like ensemble; also with Jews' harps, flutes, vocal chants, boat lute, and percussion beams. –DLM

SRI LANKA

MAHA PIRIT - THE GREAT CHANT

Sri Lankan.
Maha Pirit - The Great Chant / JECKLIN
One part of a new series from Switzerland, this album is particularly important because most attention to Buddhist chant has focused on Tibetan and Zen traditions. In fact, I know of no other recording of Sri Lankan Buddhist music. The material comes from the 70s recordings of ethnomusicologist Wolfgang von Laade, founder of the Music of Man Archive. –DLM

SRI LANKA COLLECTIONS

Kolam - The Masked Play / MUSICAPHON
Music of Sri Lanka's majority ethnic group. Kolam, more like a masquerade than a drama in the European sense (involving dance, mime, and highly elaborate costumes), belongs mainly to three villages in southern Sri Lanka, and even there it is dying out. This recording includes songs and music for the dance sections, and comes with outstanding notes and photos of the intricately beautiful masks and costumes. –JSR
Singhalese Music ... / MUSICAPHON
Singhalese Music - Singing & Drumming is the music of Sri Lanka's majority ethnic group. The first recording is mostly religious folk, with a side devoted to unaccompanied vocals, including various agricultural songs. The second consists of

drumming with and without vocals: notable are part of the "heavenly elephant" dance and the fine drum duet. –JSR

THAILAND

SAMAN HONGSA & GROUP

Traditional.
○ **Isan Slete / GLOBESTYLE**
Modern songs and music from northeast Thailand, sung by a husband-and-wife team with traditional ties and instruments but a modern attitude (and an electronics shop). The instrumentals, including kaen, xylophone, panpipe, and lute, are played by traditionalists rather than village musicians. Exhilarating music; fine notes. –JSR

THAILAND COLLECTIONS

The La Hu Nyi of Thailand / MUSICAPHON
Music of a minority group of northern Thailand, Burma, Laos, and part of China's Yunnan province. Unlike in Thailand as a whole, the bamboo mouth organ is a major instrument here and heavily represented. The examples on this recording include music for a New Year's dance and for a lunar festival, mostly for mouth organ. Also here are love songs, some accompanied by lute. –JSR
Thailand: The Music of Chieng Mai / EM I
Three lengthy complete pieces by piphat orchestra, (ceremonial orchestra of monastery), an old Thai ensemble with fiddles, zither, flute, and percussion. –DLM

TIBET

ACHE LHAMO

Traditional.
Tibetan Musical Theatre / ESPERANCE
Ache Lhamo is a form of traditional theater that has been very popular at all Tibetan social levels since it developed in the 15th century, but pretty much unknown to the world at large. Members of the India-based Tibetan Institute of Performing Arts here perform scenes from an early libretto, accompanied by the traditional drums and cymbals. –JSR

KARMA KAGYU INSTITUTE

Ceremonial.
○ **Chenresik / KARMA KAGYU INSTITUTE**
An authentic version of the Tibetan Buddhist ritual to Chenresik, the Bodhisattva of Compassion. This complete version of the classic ritual chant practice also includes the remarkable "Calling the Guru from Afar" written by the First Jamgön Kongtrül Lodrö Thaye. Produced at the Karme Thegsum Choyang Studio with authentic personnel, this is the actual ritual as it has been practiced for hundreds of years in Tibet. –JME

TIBET COLLECTIONS

Music of Tibet: Tantric Ritual / ANTHOLOGY
Excellent example of a chord-like vocal phenomenon in this type of chanting. Extensive notes. –DLM
○ **Shartse College of Ganden Monastery / BRIDGE** 1978
Three extended pieces by monks of the Gelugpa (Dalai Lama) sect of Tibetan Buddhism, two a cappella, and one with a full ritual orchestra — cymbals, handbells, conch shells, long and short trumpets, drums, etc. One of these pieces is the song of the great Tibetan saint Tsongkhapa to the Buddha, and the other two involve the dharma protectors Setab and the fierce Yamantaka. –JME
○ **Tantras of Gyütö / NONESUCH** 1978
Two extended pieces by monks of the Gelugpa (Dalai Lama) sect of Tibetan Buddhism. These monks from the Gyütö Tantric college (some 40 monks) chant from two of the most profound Tibetan texts, the one dedicated to the deity Guhyasamaja (*Sangway Düpa*), which concerned with the

self-existing sacredness of the universe; and the other dedicated to the fierce dharma protector Mahakala — Tibetan Buddhism's chief protector. −JME

○ **Tibet: Musiques Sacrées / OCORA**
This album was recorded in Nepal at Tibetan Buddhist monasteries of the Gelugpa and Nyingmapa sects. Most of the cuts are Gelugpa, including part of the Chöd — a cleansing ritual. Other sections include the assembly call (with conch horns), prayer wheel, prostration rites, and more. A second group of tracks includes a ritual to Vajrayogini — a major female deity in Tibetan Buddhist practice. Various ritual instruments (thigh-bone trumpets, hand drums, cymbals, oboes, etc.) are heard. −JME

○ **Tibetan Ritual Music / AUVIDIS**
A rare recording of an entire Tibetan ritual from the Nyingmapa monastery of Dehra Dun. Divided into three parts, each of which has both chanting and music for metal horns and trumpets as well as oboes and drums. Nominally an invocation to the goddess Yeshiki Mamo, though the notes overstate the shamanistic elements involved. (44:51)
−CARL HOYT, ORIGINAL MUSIC

TIBET (LADAKH) COLLECTIONS

Ladakh Monastic/Village Music / CHANT DU MONDE
Ladakh is a large plateau, bordered by the Himalayas and the Karakorams, where China, India, and Pakistan meet. −DLM
Songs and Dances from Central Tibet / NONESUCH
Lovely folk songs and instrumentals from the highlands of central Tibet. −DLM

VIETNAM

TRAN QUANG HAI

Vietnamese.
Dreams & Reality / PLAYASOUND
Tran Quang Hai, a virtuoso of the dan tran zither as well as many other instruments, is also a well-known author and researcher. Singer Bach Yen started professional life as a Saigon pop singer before she went to Paris to study voice. Both have been working for years outside Vietnam: Bach Yen sings in Hebrew and several European languages as well as Vietnamese, and Tran Quang Hai's playing shows clear, though intermittent signs of influence by European harp playing. As you'd expect, their performances are colored by these experiences in a personal way that is rather different from the customary intercultural cross-fertilizations. −JSR
Landscape of the Highlands / MOTW   1985
Original compositions for the dan tranh, a sixteen-string zither from Vietnam. The mesmerizing sound of this instrument combined with the virtuosity of Tran Quang Hai make this a unique and very special recording. "Deliriously beautiful and highly rhythmic." *New Age Journal.*
−MUSIC OF THE WORLD

PHONG NGUYEN ENSEMBLE

Traditional.
○ **Music of Vietnam / WORLD MUSIC INST.**
As musician and ethnomusicologist, Phong Nguyen is one of the major international figures of Vietnamese music. Here he joins other expatriate musicians (including the 77-year-old master of the dan nguyet lute, Nguyen Cia Cam) to perform a wide range of traditional and contemporary music. (These recordings were made at two WMI concerts in New York City.) Excellent recording, notes, and production as always with the World Music Institute. −JSR

VIETNAM COLLECTIONS

Ca Tru & Quan Ho / AUVIDIS
Two traditional forms from North Vietnam. Ca Tru is a rather delicate women's art-music form based on codified modes,

rhythms, and ornamentations and accompanied by various combinations of lute, zither, flute, and percussion. The equally beguiling but notably more robust quan ho songs, a form for young men and women, also has a traditional repertory but is often improvised. In this recording, made in Hanoi in 1976, they are backed by wind and stringed instruments but without percussion. (46:47) −JSR
The Tradition of Hué / MUSICAPHON
Covers musicial idioms from central Vietnam. The *Hué* album devotes a side to several forms of court music, and another to ritual and entertainment music. Includes pieces for a wide range of wind, string, and percussion groups. Fine notes and photos. −JSR

CARIBBEAN

BAHAMAS

BLIND BLAKE

World Caribbean.
○ **Bahamian Songs - Vol. 1 / ART**   1951
A hard-to-find out-of-print album by Blake Higgs (no relation to the blues player of the same name). Higgs plays with a small acoustic folk group, but his timeless music makes an indelible impression. He wrote several tunes, including "Pretty Boy" and "Love Alone" (the story of King Edward's abdication), which became standards during the 60s folk revival. −JP

JOSEPH SPENCE   1910-1984

Folk. Born on the island of Andrus in the Bahamas, Spence created an idiosyncratic (and inimitable) guitar style rife with percussive and improvisatory vamps around staid hymns and such "square" standards as "Coming in on a Wing and a Prayer." He was a folk guitarist's Thelonious Monk and his growling vocal counterpoint and surprising inventions are one of folk music's great delights. −MH

☆ **The Complete Folkways Recordings / FOLKWAYS**   1958
Just when the aspiring folk guitarist thought mastering "Freight Train" was a feat, along came this mind-boggler! These are Spence's most influential recordings; field quality sound but stunning music. −MH
Happy All the Time / CARTHAGE   1964
Waxed for Elektra in 1964, this has better sound than the Folkways recordings and offers some of Spence's most percussive playing. −MH

CAYMAN ISLANDS COLLECTIONS

☆ **Under the Coconut Tree / ORIGINAL MUSIC**   1984
Music of Grand Cayman, off Jamaica, and Tortola in the British Virgin Islands. Cayman has a remarkable fiddle tradition, with US country as well as Scot-Irish roots, with Creole polka drumming under all! Tortola's funji groups mix guitar and mandolin with percussion and washtub bass. Add homegrown calypso plus roots music of all sorts — none ever recorded before — and you have some very special stuff. −JSR

DUTCH ANTILLES COLLECTIONS

○ **Tumba, Cuarta & Ka'l / ORIGINAL MUSIC**   1986
The only previous album of the music of Aruba, Bonaire, and Curaçao is long gone. Yet small though these islands are, they're musically remarkable: both because they've preserved more purely African styles and instruments than any other area, and because of the richness of the other influences on them: not only Dutch, but Venezuelan and Anglo-American. And here it is, from accordion- and guitar-led "tipiko" dance groups to signal-conches. −JSR

Caribbean Music Styles

Biguine — Throughout the long history of the biguine, the dominant sound has been that of the clarinet and trombone, both solo and as a duet, and, while the phrasing often recalls New Orleans jazz, the overall sound is unmistakably Caribbean. The signature sound of the biguine is the interplay between the clarinet and trombone, which can still be heard today throughout the Antilles musical milieu, from the most traditional music to the music of the cadence era or the pop sounds of today's zouk. Any contemporary music that uses biguine as its base, even that which ventures as far off as contemporary jazz, is considered "biguine moderne." The classic music of carnival in the Antilles is an uptempo version of the biguine rhythm, called "biguine vide."

Cadence —A constantly changing style that evolved primarily among the islands of Guadeloupe, Martinique, Dominica, and Haiti. The cadence era was exciting and extremely fertile, requiring musicians of only the highest calibre, who could master not only Antilles pop styles like biguine and Creole mazurka but also those of Haiti and the other neighboring islands. The cadence years saw the evolution of the pop influences that embellish the rootsier foundation of today's Antilles musicians, allowing for expression in an internationally familiar musical language: electric instruments, riffing horn sections, trapset drums, topical lyrics, and specific stylings of rock music, reggae, soca, American Black music, and more. In addition to Les Aiglons, this was the heyday of big bands like La Perfecta, Typical Combo, La Selecta, Les Maxels, Les Léopards, Les Vikings de la Guadeloupe (whose co-leader, Pierre-Edouard Decimus, went on to create Kassav' at the end of the decade), and Gordon Henderson's Exile One of Dominique. Recordings from this era, while fascinating and enjoyable, often suffer from out-of-tune instruments and sub-par recording quality. Cadence led directly into the early 80s and the rise of zouk, and it was the musicians schooled in cadence who were the first zouk stars. The major catalyst behind the emergence of zouk was the desire to produce a new Caribbean music that treated the multifaceted music of the Antilles to the state-of-the-art recording technology of the Paris studios.

Chouval bwa — A rural Martiniquan style of music that evolved as accompaniment to the "manege" (or carousel). Originally featuring a large drum like a bass drum, hand drums, and ti bwa, chouv' was led by melodic instruments like accordion, bamboo flute, and wax-paper/comb-type kazoos. One young artist, Claude Germany, is attempting to carry on the traditional form of chouval bwa, while others have updated it minimally (by the addition of electric bass) or dramatically (as in the case of zouk chouv', which features an array of electric instruments, including synthesizer). Chouval bwa is Creole for the French term "cheval bois," meaning "wooden horse."

Compas — Haitian dance music, started by Nemours Jean-Baptiste in the 50s, known first as compas-direct.

Gwo ka — The various indigenous rhythms of Guadeloupe are played on a two-drum family of hand drums called gwo ka. Gwo ka music is rhythm-driven by the two drums and is often accompanied by a mounted stick or bamboo log hit with sticks called a ti bwa. The drummers lead the way for dancers, and usually there is singing accompaniment. Gwo ka has been an underlying element of zouk from day one, and, in fact, Kassav's first album was entitled *Love and Ka Dance*. Anzala and Ti Celeste (or Ti Seles) are two gwo ka artists still recording today, the latter sticking to the roots while the former has electrified his sounds.

Road March — Chosen at the carnival in Trinidad, this is the most popular song of the year.

— Gene Scaramuzzo

FRENCH ANTILLES

LES AIGLONS

Zouk. A classic Guadeloupian band of the 70s cadence era who, like nearly all bands of the period, were heavily influenced by the Haitian music that literally overwhelmed the Antilles from the late 50s to the early 80s. Les Aiglons held the record for the most sales of a record (*Cuisse-La*) of any Antilles band until the overwhelming success of Kassav' with *Zouk-La Se Sel Medikamen Nou Ni* in 1985. The band broke up quietly after their 1987 release, *Bon'm La*, but two members resurfaced in the summer of 1988 as a more commercial project called Love Stars. –GS

Le Cerveau / HENRI DEBS	1983
Bidimbo/Ay Lopital / HENRI DEBS	1985
○ **Bon'm La / HENRI DEBS**	1987

ALPHONSO ET SON ORCHESTRE ANTILLAIS

Biguine. A biguine artist who represents the classic form of the biguine as it evolved through the war years. –GS

○ **Vive la Biguine / DISQUES FESTIVAL**	

ANZALA

Gwo ka. One of the preeminent stars of the Guadeloupian music called "gwo ka," featuring two-hand drums of the same name. In an effort to compete with the zouk market, Anzala has released a couple of successful records that add electric instruments to the basic drum and vocal gwo ka sound. –GS

○ **Se Roule Moin Ka Roule / HENRI DEBS**	1983

An early-80s effort featuring the rawer gwo ka for which he is most famous. –GS

BATAKO (PATRICK PAROLE)

Zouk. Band led by Guadeloupian guitarist Patrick Parole, who plays strongly in the Haitian mini-jazz-band guitar style. Because of this, Batako records continue to be among the more Haitian-sounding and thus stand apart from formula zouk efforts. –GS

Kontente Nou / MORADISC	1986
Patrick Parole & Jean Losio / MORADISC	1986
Bilou / MORADISC	1987
○ **Chiraj / HENRI DEBS**	1988

Parole's release was one of the best of what has, admittedly, not been a particularly inspiring period for zouk. It's mellow but not soupy, with a nice Creole tinge to some of the melodies, a lot of Haitian influence (what goes round comes round), and such passing felicities as a neat trumpet solo. Evidence that zouk's recent pop orientation doesn't necessarily mean triviality. –JSR

Poupourrit / HENRI DEBS	1990

JOCELYNE BEROARD

Zouk. Martiniquan lead singer for Kassav' whose popularity soared in 1986 because of her endearing stage personality and her convincing vocals on Kassav' classics like "Pa Bisouin Pale" and "Move Jou." –GS

☆ **Siwo / GEORGES DEBS**	1987

This lead female vocalist from Kassav' sings zouk love ballads better than anyone. Backed by the group Kassav'. Excellent. A zouk classic. Import. –RVR & GS

Milans / COLUMBIA 1991

Her second solo effort. A formula success pleasing all but those who wished to hear her break new ground. –GS

BLACK JACK (PIPO ET RONALD)

Zouk. A studio zouk project by Ronald Rubinel and Kassav's Jean-Philippe Marthely, that includes contributions by every major star imaginable. Featured is a kind of techno-zouk, heavy on programmed drums, that is the trend of zouk in the 90s. –GS

○ **Black Jack (Pipo et Ronald) / SONODISC** 1991

Nods to rap and raggamuffin reggae are accomplished with moderate success. The raggamuffin-style "Machand Poisson" was one of the huge hits of 1991. –GS

ERIC BROUTA

Zouk. A Guadeloupian singer/songwriter who is among an elite clique of studio musicians including Luc Leandry. Always with a crisp, highly percussive sound, but his quality of songwriting varies. –GS

Pa Ka Tenn / DEBS PRODUCTIONS

This drummer and vocalist from Henri Debs's studio became a star with this record. –RVR

○ **Telephone / HENRI DEBS** 1988

A particularly strong release. –GS

BWA CAN'NON

Cadence. An extremely interesting Martiniquan band in that their records present the complete range of music to be found in the Antilles repertoire: cadence, biguine, quadrille, Creole mazurka, calypso, merengue ... everything but zouk. –GS

○ **Amour Passion / SOLO GAMMES** 1986

CHAMPAGN'

Zouk. A zouk studio project by Zouk Allstar Frederic Caracas, always enlisting a star-studded cast of singers and musicians. Their consistently above-average songwriting leans toward "zouk love" but features the kind of strong instrumental accompaniment that would be expected of a member of the Zouk Allstars. –GS

Cocktail Lavax / MORADISC 1987
Lombraj / MORADISC 1988
○ **Hit ("Tire Baton La") / MORADISC** 1988

CHIKTAY

Zouk. One of the best of the Guadeloupian zouk vocal groups. They're consistently good, always employing a strong stable of studio musicians. –GS

○ **Balanse le Dam / BAMBOU** 1987
Douceur des Iles / AKATOTO 1989

MAX CILLA

Folklore. A Martiniquan bamboo flutist who is a favorite guest for live performances of traditional music. These two wonderful records have a strong foundation of hand drums and flute, with rhythms ranging from chouval bwa to bele to ti kannot. –GS

La Flute des Mornes - Vols. 1 & 2 / HIBISCUS 1988

GEORGES DECIMUS

Zouk. Two early solo efforts by one of the founders of Kassav'. After more than a decade with Kassav', Georges went off in 1990 to form his own band, called Volt-Face. –GS

☆ **La Vie / MORADISC** 1982

Recorded during the highly experimental phase of Kassav' and featuring the prototype formula soon adopted by the group and by zouk artists in general. –GS

★ **Nwel / LISO MUSIQUE** 1983

Another example of the experimental phase of Kassav'. A classic. –GS

JACOB DESVARIEUX

Zouk. One of the three founding members of Kassav', Desvarieux credits the title cut from *Banzawa* as being the spark that touched off the zouk explosion. –GS

☆ **Banzawa / GEORGES DEBS** 1983

After listening to the title cut (and the entire album), there will be no question in one's mind as to why this set off the zouk craze. –GS

○ **Yelele / GEORGES DEBS** 1984

As with all solo Kassav' efforts, these albums include participation by all members of the band. Among the more than two dozen Kassav'-related records released since 1979, *Yelele* and *Gorée*, duo efforts by Desvarieux and Georges Decimus, are among the absolute cream of the crop. –GS

Goré / GEORGES DEBS 1986

DJO DEZORMO

Biguine vide. One of the most unusual of all the contemporary artists of Martinique, Dezormo is best known for being one of the few singers of "angaje" (political/social-commentary) lyrics, always releasing his records at carnival time in order to add some spice to the festivities. From the separatist community of Rivière-Pilote, Dezormo is a political activist in a country not known for activism. His commentaries have included everything from local politics to French presidential candidate Jean-Marie Le Pen. His Carnival 1990 "Voici les Loups" (Here Come the Wolves), a huge success, pictured Europe as a wolf devouring Martinique, alluding to a European Community agreement that will soon allow citizens of any member country to buy land in any other member country, which includes by default Martinique and Guadeloupe. Brother of biguine moderne artist Michel Godzom, Dezormo also loves biguine, Creole mazurka, and waltz, always incorporating these styles into his music. –GS

Sa Pe Change / SOLO GAMMES 1988

The Creole lyrics are a barrier to understanding his clever messages, but fortunately the fine music carries the day. –GS

○ **Voici les Loups / HIBISCUS** 1990

ETHNIKOLOR

Traditional. One of the surprise hits of the 1991 carnival and indicative of the growing revival of interest in classic Antilles pop music. The brainstorm of Martiniquan "living legend" Ronald Rubinel, the Ethnikolor discs feature a Who's Who of Antilles artists ranging from Kassav' members to biguine moderne clarinetist Michel Godzom to chouval bwa stars Marce Pago and Dede St. Prix. –GS

Bel Biguine / NEW DEAL 1991

The Carnival 1991 release featured two long medleys, one a biguine, the other a Creole mazurka, much in the spirit of the early-80s Soukoue Ko Ou Carnival releases but with more of a live feeling. –GS

☆ **Vol. 2: La Fete Antillais Continue ... / NEW DEAL** 1992

The Carnival 1992 release was even better, covering an even wider range of Antilles sounds and including a rootsy, percussive tribute to the late Eugene Mona. –GS

EXPERIENCE 7

Zouk. A Guadeloupian band from the 70s cadence era, led by Guy Houllier and Yves Honore (who have the further distinction of directing the studio band at the Henri Debs studio in Point à Pitre, Guadeloupe). While the band can be heard lending their particular sound to countless successful projects involving the Debs studio, their own records as Experience 7 are usually uneven, due to an admirable willingness to experiment far beyond the zouk formula. –GS

Zouk

When zouk music from the French Antilles islands of Guadeloupe and Martinique exploded onto the international music scene in the mid 80s, attention was again focused on a part of the Caribbean that hadn't been heard from musically since the popularity of the biguine in the early 20th century. Created in the late 70s by a small clique of Guadeloupian musicians residing in Paris, zouk presented a mélange of global influences that touched millions in the French-speaking African diaspora, subsequently acting as a catalyst for an exciting mid-80s period of musical experimentation.

With the Paris recording studios as a common meeting ground, francophone musicians from Africa and the Caribbean gathered to exchange ideas and "zoukify" their respective pop music forms, placing an indelible mark on the soukous of Zaire/Congo, the makossa of Cameroon, and a host of others. Haitian musicians, themselves a major influence on the French Antilles music scene, were in turn deeply affected by zouk, as were eventually (to a much lesser degree) English-speaking Caribbean artists from the Virgin Islands to Montserrat to Antigua.

Zouk truly draws its power from the rich musical heritage of Africa and the Caribbean. In its bubbly, light, loping beat can be heard elements from Guadeloupe, Martinique, Dominica, and Haiti, with dashes thrown in from Paris, Zaire, Antigua, Trinidad, Cuba, Puerto Rico, the Dominican Republic, and more. With so many influences, it's not surprising that popular zouk can range from highly percussive, driving dance music to slow ballads that hover dangerously close to French disco and cabaret singing.

Since the late 80s, zouk has become somewhat locked into a restrictive formula not unlike soca, and from an international viewpoint, its popularity has waned. Ironically, this has obscured from view the fact that today the French Antilles are bubbling with exciting musical experimentations involving many classic types of Antilles music like the biguine, chouval bwa, bele (belair), and ti kannot (kalenda). Inspired by a renewed sense of identity (and a dramatically increased knowledge of recording technology) afforded by the success of zouk, older Antilles musicians are returning to the musical riches of their islands. As we move into the 90s, the overall musical output of the Antilles is bursting with rhythmically propulsive, melodic sounds like zouk, zouk chouv', biguine moderne, biguine vide, and more.

With zouk (and to a lesser extent the modernized forms of classic music), the Antilles music scene revolves around the studio rather than live performance. Only a dozen or so self-contained bands exist that actually tour outside of Paris and the islands. Like many forms of Caribbean music, the majority of Antilles recordings reflect studio projects involving certain cliques of musicians, and it's not unfair to say that looking at the musicians' names on the record jacket will give a fair idea of the music within, before the shrink wrap is ever peeled off. As for the lyrics, aside from a few rare exceptions, all projects are in Creole and avoid anything "angaje" (political or social commentary).

Records come out twice a year in the Antilles, timed either for summer vacation or for the Christmas holidays leading into carnival. Most recordings are done in Paris, with Henri Debs's studio in Guadeloupe running second, and J-P Mauriello's Hibiscus Studio in Martinique running a far-distant third. Excluding sure sellers like Kassav' and occasional huge successes, most releases are treated to only one pressing by Antilles record producers. This means records quickly become hard to find after their initial appearance.

Fortunately, compilations featuring collections of hits are becoming increasingly available and often represent the only means of hearing the music. Of even more interest is the recent appearance of a few anthologies of artists, like the superb Hibiscus Records releases of early music by Eugene Mona and other classic music from the defunct 3A label.

— Gene Scaramuzzo

Mwen Ke Devire / HENRI DEBS   1985
An early zouk record that features Eric Brouta and Tanya Stival. −RVR
Goudjoua / HENRI DEBS   1987
○ **Sundama / HENRI DEBS**   1989

FLAMME ABYMIENNE

Quadrille. Members of a Guadeloupian society for the preservation of the Creole form of the European dance called the quadrille. The band still plays occasional dances on the island and were coaxed into traveling to Louisiana in 1991 to perform at the Festival International de Louisiane alongside old-time Cajun accordion and fiddle bands. −GS
○ **Festival de Quadrille / HENRI DEBS** −GS   1979

GILLES FLORO

Zouk. One of the star crooners of the "zouk love" style, Floro produces hit after hit. Every album contains chartbusters, not only the ones listed below. −GS
○ **Rêve Bleu / LISO MUSIQUE**   1986
On Douce/Patade / NEW DEAL-CARRERE   1989
Spirituelle / LISO MUSIQUE   1991

MICHEL GODZOM

Biguine moderne. One of the great biguine moderne artists of Martinique (an all-encompassing term that includes any contemporary styles using biguine as the basis). Clarinetist Godzom is a great experimenter, exploring the limits of biguine, mazurka, quadrille, and waltz, usually hitting solidly on the mark as he did on the albums listed below. −GS
☆ **Hotel Diamant des Bains / GEORGES DEBS**   1984
Les Petits Trots / SM   1985
Larye Pei / AMA   1988
Waneke / DISC LAKAILLE   1991
10ème Anniversaire / SOLO GAMMES   1991

BOD GUIBERT

Zouk. Unlike most Antilles artists of the zouk era that have basically copied Zairian soukous, producing a not overly interesting sound I've dubbed "zoukous," Guibert has managed to produce quality zouk combining equal amounts of both African and Antillais. The unique sound captured on his albums has made them collector's items. −GS
○ **Ma Mail La / DEG SA**
Totally unique Afro-zouk of unsurpassed quality. A collector's item. −GS
Normalement (Bibiche) / BG   1989
Features a mélange of elements African and Antillais. Hard to find. −GS

SIMON JURAD

Zouk. Simon Jurad is one of the few Martiniquan musicians

who can be found playing live somewhere on the island almost every night of the week, his gigs including everything from tourist bar/lounge performances to hip zouk shows. His career began in the cadence era, so as both singer and musician he has a wealth of experience under his belt. Jurad's biggest strength is his consistent ability to write catchy, musically interesting songs, although contractual complications have prevented him in recent years from being able to credit himself as songwriter on his albums. –GS

Faut Pas Faire / MELODIE	1986
☆ Mama / GEORGES DEBS	1989
Glorye La Te A / AKATOTO	1991

KALI

Folklore. Kali began his professional music career in what many consider to have been Martinique's finest reggae band, Sixième Continent, which hit big with a 12-inch single called "Reggae Dom-Tom." In the late 80s Kali picked up a century-old family heirloom, a banjo, and began exploring roots music of a different nature ... music of the Martiniquan capital St. Pierre that was destroyed at the beginning of the century by the eruption of Mount Pelée. He can often be heard contributing his banjo to zouk and traditional projects alike, from recordings by Pier Rosier and Ze Top to Max Ransay and the latest by Malavoi. –GS

○ **Racines - Vols. 1 & 2 / HIBISCUS**   1989
A re-exploration of the classic forms of Antilles music. This vocalist and banjo player performs neo-traditional biguine moderne. Charming. –GS & RVR

Live au New Morning / HIBISCUS   1991
A live recording of classic Antilles music, which helped put Kali on top of the list of Martiniquan roots music artists. –GS

☆ **Roots / PHILIPS**   1991
The best cuts from Kali's first three albums. –GS

KASSAV'

Zouk. The zouk scene evolved from a studio project by Guadeloupian Pierre-Edouard Decimus, who had moved to Paris in the late 70s following an extremely successful career as co-leader of the legendary cadence band Les Vikings de la Guadeloupe. Enlisting the services of his brother Georges and Paris studio wizard Jacob Desvarieux, himself a Guadeloupian, Decimus began to forge a new sound that treated Antilles musical traditions to the state of the art recording technology available in Paris. By 1984 the three had settled on a stable lineup of musicians and singers (now representing both Guadeloupe and Martinique), had made their first live performance (in Guadeloupe), and had achieved their first massive radio success with "Banzawa" from a Desvarieux solo album.

Parties in the Antilles are called "zouks," and since Kassav's new records were the music of choice at the zouks, their music came to be called "zouk music." By 1985 nearly every Antilles musician was jumping on the zoukwagon and a whole new style of music was born.

Supported by a horn section, two dancers, extra keyboard, drummer, and percussion, the core of Kassav' is Jocelyne Beroard, Jacob Desvarieux, Jean-Philippe Marthely, Patrick St. Eloi, Jean-Claude Naimro, and until recently, Georges Decimus (who recently quit the band to pursue a career with a new group; Pierre-Edouard comes and goes at whim, never performing live but often resurfacing as a songwriter). Through the release of *Majestik Zouk*, the band has released ten studio albums and one live album. Each bonafide member of the band has also released solo albums that include support by the entire band. In fact, since 1987, all re-pressings of the back catalog of solo releases has had the name Kassav' added to the cover in bold letters. Add various carnival projects under the pseudonyms Soukoue Ko Ou and Turbo II, and the total number of Kassav'-related albums approaches 30.

The early releases were certainly experimental in nature as

Desvarieux and the Decimus brothers searched for the right mix of musicians and musical elements. The best of the solo and carnival efforts can be found under the discography entries for the particular band member or carnival project. It's indisputable that much of the most dramatic groundbreaking occurred on the early- to mid-80s solo releases. Of the official Kassav' albums, all are interesting in that they provide a view into the development of what became the zouk sound. The formula from which the whole Antilles zouk scene evolved had kicked in by the sixth release, so from there on specific preferences are merely a matter of personal taste. –GS

Love and Ka Dance / CELLULOID	1979
Lague Moin / CELLULOID	1980
#3 / 3A	1981
○ Eva / 3A	1982

This, their fourth album, was the first with the touch of total greatness. –GS

| #5 / LISO MUSIQUE-CELLULOID | 1982 |
| Passeport / SONODISC | 1983 |

This is precisely the sound that made zouk so influential — a modified Haitian beat, Stevie-Wonder-style keyboards, and heaps of traditional gwo ka percussion — surprising when you consider the techno-monster the style has become. Includes two songs from *Oh Madiana*. –CARL HOYT, ORIGINAL MUSIC

Aye / GEORGES DEBS	1984
○ An-Ba-Chen'n La / GEORGES DEBS	1985
Vini Pou / CBS	1987

Ironically, the first to receive widespread distribution in the States was one of their weaker efforts. –GS

Kassav' Aux Zenith / GEORGES DEBS   1987
I've always found Kassav' to be a variable band, capable of great music but too prone to lapse into an overslick funk typical of any pickup group of session-men (which is how they began life). These tending to be studio-oriented faults, it's perhaps not surprising that this live concert recording was one of the most genuinely exciting Kassav' sessions ever recorded. –JSR

| ○ Majestik Zouk / COLUMBIA | 1989 |
| ☆ Zouk Is ... / GREENSLEEVES | 1989 |

Zouk Is the Only Medicine We Need. A superb greatest-hits collection from the top band. –RVR

EDITH LEFEL

Zouk. A Martiniquan zouk singer whose sparkling strong voice graced many records by Lazair, Simon Jurad, Kassav', and others before she attempted her own record. –GS

○ **La Klé / GEORGES DEBS**   1988
A huge success even though (or because) Lefel opted to sing in the weak, rather wimpy vocal style that was the rage of late-80s zouk-love. –GS

LOVE STARS

Zouk. A Guadeloupian "zouk love" studio project involving three singers, two of whom were original members of Les Aiglons. As with many Henri Debs productions, it includes a star-studded cast. –GS

Ipokrit / HENRI DEBS   1988
This album is, in fact, excellent, and particularly notable for fine solo sax rather than the usual ensemble riffs, as well as for a pleasingly batty edge and plenty of verve. –JSR

| ○ Yo Malade/Jane / HENRI DEBS | 1989 |
| De Plus Belle / HENRI DEBS | 1992 |

LA MAAFIA

Compas. A Martiniquan band led by drummer, singer, and songwriter Jean-Michel Cabrimol, and one of a handful, including Diapason, Filpak, and Nouvelle Galaxie, that specializes in playing a Martiniquan version of classic Haitian mini-jazz. La Maafia's albums are typically a balance of uptempo dance numbers and slow ballads graced by flute. It's certainly not formula zouk but very popular, nonetheless, because of the long-time Antillean love of Haitian music. –GS

Mama l'Anmou / JAPP

☆ **Mama Afrika / JMC**   1988
Exquisite Antilles funk jazz (a Martinquan version of Haitian compas) featuring flute, sax, trumpet, and conga. –RVR

Domi Bien Propre / JMC   1989

MALAVOI

Folklore. Led by Martiniquan pianist Paulo Rosine, Malavoi has been recording since the late 60s. The original band featured a horn section and consisted mainly of Latin music enthusiasts. The band added a string section in the late 70s and recorded a superb album of charanga-style music that included percussion by Dede St. Prix. Only this one album captured the brief period when Malavoi had both a horn section and a string section; the horns left soon afterward. An anthology of hits from this era is now available on the Hibiscus label release *L'Autre Style*.

The albums listed below are among the best of the band as it exists today, presenting a varied repertoire of "Creolized" European dance forms like the quadrille, mazurka, and waltz along with strong elements of biguine and charanga. Pipo Gertrude, who replaced long-time Malavoi vocalist Ralph Thamar in late 1987, appears on *Jou Ouve* and *Souche* (which is not listed because it's not among their best), as well as the group's latest. The *Live au Zenith* album features Thamar. –GS

Gram e Gram / GEORGES DEBS   1982

Zouel / GEORGES DEBS   1983
Wow! Phoosh! When it comes to string-band arranging, this one has the kitchen with faucets. I mean, lush!! And lush is the word — the calorie count has to be enormous, but the cream is real and rich, the chocolate dark and gorgeous. Ralph Thamar sings. Vocalist Marijosc Alic, who has been listening to the Brazilians with good results, is featured on one cut. Seriously, the uptempo numbers swing mightily, the traditional ones operate perfectly (great quadrille!), and the slow ones, by the very splendor of their richness, simply obliterate the usual sub-bolero plod. Oh, yes, demon bass and dynamite piano too. –JSR

Marinelle / GEORGES DEBS   1985

La Case à Lucie / BLUE SILVER   1987

Jou Ouve / FLARENASCH   1988

○ **Live au Zenith / BLUE SILVER**   1989
A classic 1987 concert from this large orchestra. "String Creole music" featuring Edith Lefel on vocals. –RVR

○ **Malavoi - L'Autre Style / HIBISCUS**   1992

☆ **Matebis / BMG-DECLIC**   1992

MARCE ET TOUMPAK

Chouval bwa. Drummer Marce Pago, along with Dede St. Prix, took the torch first lit by Eugène Mona in the 70s and ran with it to bridge the gap between the growing early-80s zouk scene and a rural percussive form of Martiniquan music called chouval bwa. Dispensing with chouval bwa's large bass-drum-like tambour, but adding electric instrumentation to the basic lineup of rhythmic vocals, hand drums, bamboo flute, and occasional accordion, both Marce and St. Prix took chouval bwa to a level of popularity right alongside zouk. Marce coined the term for this new form, "zouk chouv'," with his 1987 album of the same name. His early albums, prior to *Zouk Chouv'*, are not strong on electric instruments and are, in fact, in many ways more in keeping with the return-to-roots trend of the 90s. –GS

Ca Ca Ye / DEESE

○ **Pawol Deye / GEORGES DEBS**   1984

☆ **He Binzot / GEORGES DEBS**   1985

Zouk Chouv' / GLOBESTYLE   1987
Neo-traditional with heavy roots percussion and great horn riffs. –RVR

The French Antilles (Martinique & Guadeloupe)

These two Caribbean islands are technically part of France, with Martinique being more developed and Guadeloupe the poorer sister island. The creole culture has seen a wide mix of peoples and, therefore, music. The beguine was the first Antilles popular music to reach international audiences and was influential in jazz, Brazilian, and African music. As it faded in the late 50s, cadence became popular, being similar to the popularity of Haitian compas in the 60s and 70s.

As people were listening to other Caribbean music, traditional African-derived "gwo ka" drumming and chanting survived. Ti Celeste and Marce' et Tumpak have become popular, playing such traditional music. Exile One merged music from Haiti, Trinidad, and the Antilles into a new popular music called "cadence-lypso." They helped revive the local music scene and influenced other Caribbean musicians as they toured extensively.

As many Antilleans moved to France (especially Paris) in search of work, a collective of musicians named Kassav' began blending cadence, compas, and other Caribbean styles into a new dance music called zouk. They quickly became an international phenomenon in the 80s as they took their high-energy dance music to the world.

Recorded and live music experienced an unprecedented boom for Antilles music. Countless zouk artists emerged, and *le zouk* could be heard all over Paris, the French Caribbean, Francophone Africa, and dance floors the world round. At the same time, other traditional or neo-traditional music thrived, including the creole string music of Malavoi, the chouval bwa of Dede Saint Prix, and the Haitian compas of J. M. Cabrimol et La Maafia. Musically, these little islands have become massive.

— Robert Leaver

Titine / RYTHMODISC   1991

EUGENE MONA

Traditional.

Témoignage / HIBISCUS   1989
This live album features raw roots music. –GS

○ **Blan manje / HIBISCUS**   1991
Recorded nearly five years after *Témoignage*, *Blan Manje* is a percussive/electric treat. –GS

● **Mona - Vols. 1 & 2 / HIBISCUS**   1992
This anthology of Mona's 70s music is a must for any fans of Dede and Marce. –GS

DOMINIQUE PANOL

Zouk.

○ **Bolotte / GEORGES DEBS**   1987
Panol, a perennial sideman himself, features Decimus, Maimro (on acoustic piano!), St. Eloi, and Alibo, and still comes up original. His fortes are tough beat propelled by his own bass, and a total lack of moderation: more machine-like drum machines, more synthetic synth, larger and richer backup vocals, even a Malavoi-like string quartet. As campy as hell. Also terrific. –JSR

PLASTIC SYSTEM BAND

Biguine vide. An approximately 80-piece carnival street band that consists of horns, stiltwalkers, and dozens of percussionists playing on plastic drums and ti bwa. In the Martiniquan carnival tradition, their recordings are medleys of everything from French nursery songs to popular zouk songs to the myriad of Antilles carnival songs. These recordings give a superb introduction to Martiniquan carnival music. *Bel Je* includes both songs found on the "Kalot Kannaval" 12-inch single. –GS

Kalot Kannaval / SOLO GAMMES	1988
☆ **Bel Je / PLASTIC SYSTEM BAND**	1991

MAX RANSAY

Zouk. This original member of the 70s Martiniquan cadence band Les Léopards made a stunning reappearance in 1988 with the first biguine to make Radio Caraibe DJ Balthazar's Creole Hit Parade in nearly a decade. The followup album is a fine collection of biguine, zouk, and ti kannot (kelenda). Earlier 80s efforts by Ransay are also worth hearing. –GS

Folklore Martiniquais Traditionnel / RN

Ransay and Michel Thimon; two original Les Léopards members team up. –GS

La Route Chanflo / HIBISCUS	1988
☆ **Au Secours en Mwe! / HIBISCUS**	1989

PIER' ROSIER

Zouk. A Martiniquan singer of traditional music who went the zouk route in 1985 with a first-rate group of Paris-based musicians calling themselves Gazoline. Artistic differences between Rosier and the band led to their breakup in late 1987, so Rosier went on to form his own handpicked band of underlings, which he named Gazolinn'. His entire catalog, with both bands, is worth hearing, strong on chouval-bwa-influenced rhythms and providing some of the most serious hard-edged "zouk chire" this side of Kassav' (in terms of technical and songwriting excellence). The Shanachie Records anthology is a fine introduction and includes many of the best of Rosier's collaborations with the original Gazoline. –GS

Carrément Nous / MORADISC	1985
Déchire / MORADISC	1986
Console Mwen / MORADISC	1987
Tchie Moin Pa Pare / RHYTHMODISC	1988
○ **Le Bidongaz / CYCLONN'**	1989
☆ **Zouk Obsession / SHANACHIE**	1990

Among the top Zouk groups on the worldbeat circuit. This 1990 release of their greatest hits spotlights the great Pier' Rosier. –RW

RONALD RUBINEL

Zouk. Aside from Michel Alibo, there is no Antilles musician with a longer list of musical credentials, both live and on record, than Ronald Rubinel. He was a staple of touring Haitian bands in the 70s, who was heard adding rare keyboard parts to soukous recordings by Loketo and the other superstar Zairian bands. In the Antilles, he was a cadence star in the 70s and a zouk star in the 80s through to today. He is also the catalyst behind Martinique's most exciting carnival creation of the past two years, Ethnikolor. Besides playing on nearly as many zouk releases as the members of the Zouk Allstars, he has released a handful of his own recordings, always featuring a Who's Who of Antilles stars. *Bal Boutche* may be the best introduction. –GS

Zoulou / GEORGES DEBS	1987
Tilda / GEORGES DEBS	1987
○ **Bal Boutche / GEORGE DEBS**	1989

DEDE ST. PRIX

Chouval bwa. A hand drummer, bamboo flutist, and songwriter, St. Prix is one of the rootsmen of Martinique. After stints as percussionist in many local bands (including E+, Malavoi, and Pakatak), he formed his own band, Avan Van, in the early 80s and has never looked back. His pioneer

efforts were in the melding of zouk sounds with a rural musical tradition called chouval bwa. As a songwriter he has lent his efforts to a variety of projects, reaching a pinnacle with an extremely funky cut called "Amazon" that appeared on Joelle Ursull's *Black French* album. *Mi Se Sa*, re-issued on Mango Records, is the most electric and not the most indicative of the total recorded output of St. Prix, even though it's likely to be the easiest to find. –GS

Ian Mou / GEORGES DEBS	1983
Avan Van Tombe d'Amour / GEORGES DEBS	1984
Mi Se Sa / MANGO-ANTILLES	1988

Altogether successful at putting over a classical chouval bwa, freshened but not threatened by the contemporary touches. (33:39). –JSR

Kannel/Wis Way / NEW DEAL-CARRERE	1989
☆ **Leve/Arrête Ton Delire / KARAC**	1991

TANYA ST. VAL

Zouk. The darling of the French Antilles music scene, St. Val's records benefit from strong support by the best the islands have to offer. Her voice is hefty, much in the way of Grace Slick, and her interpretations are always convincing. She is definitely deserving of her star status. –GS

○ **Tamboo / HENRI DEBS**	1987
Zouk a Go Go ("Mi Yo La") / HENRI DEBS	1989

SARTANA

Zouk. This prolific Guadeloupian zouk star uses gwo ka as the basis of his sound. Some may find Sartana's very unusual voice unpleasing, although in some ways it adds a sense of authority and demands attention much like Peter Tosh. Early albums include collaboration by most members of Kassav', although ironically his later releases are more zoukish. –GS

Un Message Peut en Cacher ... / MORADISC	1986
○ **Bom'me Lacrimogène / TROPIC PROD.**	1988
Observe e Medite / MORADISC	1989

SOUKOUE KO OU

Biguine vide. This is the best of four carnival/Christmas medleys put out in the early 80s by Kassav' founder and Guadeloupian Pierre-Edouard Decimus, utilizing the same core of musicians used on the early Kassav' records. The unsophisticated use of programmed drum machine kills the joy of most of these discs, but the superb songs on *Vacances* cannot be beaten down. See the listings for Pierre-Edouard Decimus for an earlier such effort. –GS

○ **Vacances / NR**	

SOUSKAY

Zouk.

Libertine / JE PRODUCTIONS

Souskay have let 'er rip electronically this time. They always were ones for the Godzilla drum machines, but this time it's let joy be unconfined. I like the woman singer, Patsy Geremy, who's all over Side 2. Play that first and you'll feel benign about Side 1. –JSR

○ **Mr. Sho / MORADISC**	1988

A big hit — ultra fast. –RVR

STELLIO

Biguine.

☆ **Et Son Orchestre Antillais / MUSIC MEMORIA**

Classic biguine was a manically charming dance style with a front line consisting of clarinet and trombone. Clarinetist and bandleader Stellio was the great name of between-the-wars biguine, a major composer and leader of the most popular and influential band of the era, both in Paris and back in the islands. These biguines, mazurkas, and so forth cover his prime, from the late 20s to late 30s. A bedrock-indispensable part of a Caribbean (or just plain any) collection. (70:09). –JSR

TATIANA & ZOUTI

Zouk.

○ **Tatiana & Zouti / DEBS PRODUCTIONS**   1988
Tatiana and Zouti came on the scene a year or so ago, with this
sleeper second album. The sound is familiar enough, but zouk
(especially lovers' zouk) is in the ascendant. Lead singer
Tatiana and her equally young group have an oomph that
several bigger names are beginning to lose. –JSR

RALPH THAMAR

Zouk. A longtime lead singer for Malavoi, who went his
separate way in 1987. Thamar is known for very hard-edged,
techno-zouk, creative songwriting, and rather classical-style
singing. –GS
Exil / GEORGES DEBS   1987
○ **Caraibes / DECLIC**   1991

TI EMILE

Belair. One of the best opportunities to hear traditional
Martiniquan bele (belair) drumming and singing. –GS
○ **25 Ans de Bel-air / 3A**   1977

TI RAOUL (GRIVALLIERS)

Belair. A very raw, exciting example of Martiniquan belair
singing and drumming. –GS
○ **La Rivye Leza / APAL**   1988

TI SELES (CELESTE)

Gwo ka. Basic gwo ka drums and singing but a real standout
because of Seles's authoritative voice, beautiful singing, and
occasional use of very melodic sax. –GS
○ **Virus La / WIREM**
Singer Ti Seles has the reputation variously of a gwo ka
traditionalist and a modernizer of the form, both of which
theories are true. His "Hommage à Robert" (a gwo ka legend)
is rootsy drumming, and his voice is always deep and rural.
But for several tracks he adds synth and piano, very
successfully, in a quite effective adaptation of zouk to the far
more local Guadeloupian sound of gwo ka. –JSR
○ **Ou Pa Kare / HENRI DEBS**   1985
☆ **Ses Plus Grands Succes / HENRI DEBS**   1991

JOELLE URSULL

Zouk. An original member of the Guadeloupian female vocal
trio Zouk Machine until she was manipulated out of the band,
Ursull went on to become a solo star with the help of an
incredible musical cast on *Miyel* and later with a crossover
masterpiece, *Black French.* –GS
☆ **Miyel / CBS**   1988
Black French / CBS   1990
Includes a collaboration with none other than French bad boy
Serge Gainsbourg. The Gainsbourg/Ursull duet "White and
Black Blues" took Europe by storm in summer of 1990, but it's
the Dede St. Prix composition, "Amazon," that makes the
album worth buying. –GS

GUY VADELEUX

Zouk. This hardworking Martiniquan artist, recording since
the cadence days, got his start as a bassist for Pierre Rassin's
authentic biguine band, where he was properly schooled in all
the musical traditions of the Antilles. It's for this reason that
Vadeleux's albums of the zouk era are unusual and popular,
containing familiar references to biguine, cadence, and Creole
mazurka, while never failing to hit the zouk bull's-eye.
Vadeleux can be seen most nights of the week playing solo
and group gigs in tourist spots, although those hoping to hear
a sound similar to his records will be disappointed. –GS
Ambiance Bo Kaille / 3A   1984
○ **Mazouk' Potpourri / SOLO GAMMES**   1991

Compas

Haitian bandleader Nemours Jean-Baptiste coined the phrase
"compas direct" in the 50s to refer to his style of music.
"Compas" means musical measure in Spanish, and "direct"
refers to the absence of a third chord. Although similar to
merengue, compas has a more driving rhythm; its moderate
tempo is paced by a steady bass, which anchors the drum
and cowbell percussion.

The instrumentation changed from a big band with a full
horn section to the smaller "mini-jazz" combos of the later
60s and 70s, who introduced electric guitars and trap drums
while retaining the solo saxophone (most typically, the alto
sax) and sometimes the accordion. Compas now had a less
direct meaning and became a generic term to refer to the
Haitian style or, more specifically, rhythm. New York City
became home to the top compas bands as the immigrant
community grew. Compas spread to Miami, Montreal, Paris,
and throughout the Caribbean, especially Guadeloupe and
Martinique. In exile, compas has been influenced by soul and
funk and more recently by zouk, a popular dance music
inspired by Haitian compas.

— Robert Leaver

FRANCKY VINCENT

Zouk. Probably the best way to get acquainted with this
master of suggestive lyrics is through the recent anthology on
Declic Records, although the other one listed may still be in
print. Vincent's album jackets and music are often downright
hilarious, although the clever wordplay will be lost on non-
Creole-speaking listeners. The reason his records are listed as
of high interest is the irony that instrumentally his music is
superb, featuring sparkling production, ringing instruments,
and creative songwriting. One of the true talents of the
Antilles. –GS
15 Ans Déjà ... (Braguette d'Or) / BLEU CARAIBES 1989
○ **Coquinement Zouk / DECLIC**   1991

ZAZA

Zouk. One of Martinique's carnival stars, who often releases
her work only on 45 RPM records. –GS
○ **The Best of Zaza / HIBISCUS**   1989
This recent anthology provides a rare opportunity to
experience her music. –GS

ZE TOP

Zouk. This first-class gathering of musicians casts a witty,
irreverent look at zouk and Antilles music in general. –GS
○ **Ka Dance / HIBISCUS**   1991
This record came out at carnival time 1991 and is already one
of the classics. It will probably remain available for years to
come. –GS

ZOUK ALLSTARS

Zouk. The Zouk Allstars are Dominique Gengoul, Jean-Luc
Alger, Frederic Caracas, and Charles Maurinier, four young
musicians who have made an indelible mark on Antilles
music of the 80s and early 90s. To call them prolific is a gross
understatement; pick up any ten zouk albums, and it's likely
that one or more of their names will appear on at least seven
as producers and/or instrumentalists. Solo projects include
studio groups like Karata, Mazout', Champagn', and Lazair.
The crystal clarity of their production, the funkiness of their
playing, and their ceaseless creativity are the reasons behind
their popularity. –GS

○ **An Nou Swe / MORADISC** 1987
☆ **Vol. 2 / MORADISC** 1988
Top Niveau / MORADISC 1989

ZOUK MACHINE

Zouk. A Guadeloupian female vocal trio who incorporate many American Black music elements into their music, a trait that has made them extremely popular in Paris and the Antilles but has left most Americans cold. It was erroneously thought by many Antilleans that Zouk Machine, along with backup provided by Experience 7, would be the zouk band to break the American market. The 1986 release includes Joelle Ursull, who was replaced shortly afterward by Jane Fostin. –GS
Zouk Machine / HENRI DEBS 1986
Includes the hit "Pisime Zouk." –RVR
○ **Maldon / HENRI DEBS** 1988
Kreol / BMG 1991

FRENCH ANTILLES COLLECTIONS

Antilles d'Aujourd'hui / FESTIVAL 1978
Undoubtedly the best, and probably only, collection of Antilles music circa mid to late 70s. Includes cuts from many of the biggest names of the era, usually their most popular songs. This collection confirms what was said earlier about the diverse talents of Antilles musicians, presenting everything from cadence and Haitian compas to biguine, Creole mazurka, and calypso. Still occasionally surfaces in Paris record stores. –GS
☆ **Dance! Cadence! / GLOBESTYLE** 1985
A wonderful look at cadence, biguine moderne, ti kannot, (kalenda), and early zouk by the likes of Eugène Mona, Georges Decimus, and Michel Godzom. A classic. –GS
○ **Generation Zouk - Vols. 1-3 / NEW DEAL-CARRERE**
Arguably the best of the collections of radio hits, but please refer to the *Planète Zouk* record entry to read more on this. The New Deal/Carrere label features some of the best music made in the Antilles, and whoever was responsible for compiling these collections (which feature artists from all labels) showed typical good taste. –GS
Le Grand Merchant Zouk / SONODISC 1990
A live concert featuring all the top zouk musicians — Kassav', F. Caracas — playing together. –RVR
☆ **Hurricane Zouk / ATLANTIC**
A collection of recent material spotlighting zouk and modern African music. Not as comprehensive or well produced as some other anthologies; skewed toward acts and artists who record in Paris. –RW
○ **Planète Zouk - Vols. 1 & 2 / DECLIC100%** 1991
An abridged version of Vol. 1 was reissued as *Planet Zouk: The World of Antilles Music (Rhythm Safari),* and there are plans to do the same soon with Vol. 2. These are compilations of radio hits from a variety of record labels circa 1988-1991 from Paris and the French Antilles. The cuts feature samples from a Who's Who of Antilles greats, from Kassav', Dede St. Prix, Malavoi, and Ronald Rubinel to lesser known but also accomplished artists like Edith Lefel, Ralph Thamar, Eric Virgal, and Experience 7. Many good songs can be found here, from the biguine tinges of Thamar's "Polisson" to the underlying soukous feeling of Experience 7's "Goudjoua." Eric Virgal's "Pa Fe Mwen la Pen" is a fine example of zouk-love, while Edith Lefel's lead vocal on her cocomposition with Ronald Rubinel ("Sensation") shows the best melding of zouk with American soul sounds, an oft-made attempt that is rarely successful. The fact that these are all radio hits implies a common thread that runs throughout the set of music: strong on formula, weak on experimentation. This is a "safe" set of music, which features good songs but few surprises and few moments of pure zouk ecstasy. –GS
Les Rois du Zouk / RIAHI
Desvarieux, Grammacks, Jeff Joseph, Panol, and a couple of others, plus instrumentals. It could have been a disaster, but

zouk is in the details, and the details here are mostly real tasty. This is no groundbreaker, but it's a real cute listen. The major cuts are "An Nou Alle" (Desvarieux); "Creole Mix" (K. Rodney); "Sensations" (Panol); "Hot Music" (Jeff Joseph); "Laisse Moin Vive" (Sylvie Drai); "Reggae Boulevard" (Grammacks); "Debar Debar" (Jeff Joseph); "Reminiscence" (Kassav'). –JSR
☆ **Zouk Attack / ROUNDER** 1992
The first zouk compilation to be put together by an American label, this set reflects an outsider's view of what is good about Antilles music rather than being a collection of radio hits. Brings together interesting non-formula artists like Patrick Parole (Batako), Pier Rosier with the original Gazoline, and the cadence-era band Typical along with zouk stalwarts Frédéric Caracas, Tanya St. Val, and Ramon Pyrmée. –GS
○ **Zoukollection - Vols. 1-3 / HIBISCUS** 1988
Although much the same argument can be made for these compilations (released 1988-1990) as for the above *Planète Zouk* discs, the difference is that these are mostly all artists from the Hibiscus label, a stable of unusual artists who are much more involved in experimentation and a return to classic forms like biguine, ti kannot, etc. –GS

GENERAL CARIBBEAN COLLECTIONS

○ **Calypsos: Afro-Limonese Music / LYRICHORD**
Like Panama, Costa Rica has a substantial minority of English-speaking inhabitants. These pieces — mostly calypsos, after a terrific percussion comparsa — were recorded in the Costa Rican port city of Puerto Limón. They have a spread from wonderful to tentative, but this is street-music pure, presenting a range of singers and styles mostly old and unaffected by commercial recordings. Very unspecific notes, disgracefully short measure even for an LP, let alone CD, but very rare music that is never less than charming. –JSR
Caribbean Island Music / NONESUCH
I recorded this material on my first field trip in 1971. Many of these recordings are still unique: Jamaican country mento, digging songs, and nine-night songs; a Haitian acoustic merengue group; Dominican merengues, salves, tonadas, drum groups, and the English-language Mummies later featured in the British "Repercussions" TV/video series. Enjoy! –JSR
○ **Music of the West Indies / NONESUCH**
Here's a treat: until now these 1969-1971 recordings have only been available on cassette. It's a fine and varied set that moves from Trinidad to the Dominican Republic, including some smaller islands, and has mazurkas, reels, merengues, tamboo bamboo, calypso, shango rites, baptist hymns, and even a Hindu epic from Guadeloupe! –CARL HOYT, ORIGINAL MUSIC

HAITI

BOSSA COMBO

Compas.
Accolade / MINI RECORDS
Bossa Combo has always been one of my favorite bands for its original arranging style. Here, after the rather subdued first cut, they'd sear steak. –JSR

CARIBBEAN SEXTET

Haitian.
En Gala / MINI RECORDS
The Caribbean Sextet, one of my favorite Haitian bands, opens here a bit heavily into the synth. But after a dreamy opening, the second cut kicks into a righteous Creole number, and joy reigns. Fine sax here, too, with a slight R&B edge, flute (rare in Haitian music), and a fine trumpeter. –JSR

FRANTZ CASSEUS & MARC RIBOT

Instrumental.
Haitian Suite / MOTW 1989
Frantz Casseus, the genius of contemporary Haitian guitar

music, was the first classical guitar composer to draw inspiration from the African-derived music of his homeland. Marc Ribot, a highly accomplished guitarist, interprets these timeless and haunting beautiful melodies. —MUSIC OF THE WORLD

COUPÉ CLOUÉ

Haitian. An enigmatic guitarist and singer, Coupé Cloué acquired this nickname (translated as "kickout") from his prowess on the soccer field. He is famous, or rather notorious, for his lyrics containing sexual double-entendre, long "raps" ranging from risqué to romantic, and social satire. His "compas mamba" (peanut compas) seems very African, with a guitar style resembling West African highlife and the use of Cuban bongo drums and bamboo tubes played with sticks in addition to the standard conga and drum kit.

Appearing on many album covers wearing African clothing, Coupé Cloué with his shaved head cuts a striking figure. This may explain why he was given the title "Le Roi" (the king) when he played in the Ivory Coast, West Africa, in 1975. Of all the electric Caribbean bands, Coupé Cloué has the strongest African sound, which shows the strength of his roots, for he claims he never heard African music before his 1975 trip. —RL

L'Essentiel Coupé Cloué / MINI RECORDS
Gesner Henry (Coupé Cloué) runs one of the prettiest guitar bands on either side of the Altantic, though Tabou Combo's hit-hunting has kept C.C. out of the international spotlight. Here are the interlocking guitars, roosty percussion, and chatty vocals which make Coupé in general, and this mid-70s collection in particular, one of our undisputed faves. (50:46) —CARL HOYT, ORIGINAL MUSIC

The Preacher / MINI RECORDS
Eight classic 70s cuts and "Myan Myan." —RVR

DJET-X

Compas.
Egal Ego / MINI RECORDS
Djet-X leader Gerard Daniel was Shleu Shleu's last saxist before it transmogrified into Ska Shah #1. Great band. This 1990 recording combines contempo keyboards and oddments like a smattering of rap with your basic mini-jazz guitar band bounce and (not surprisingly) neat horns. (35:15) —JSR

BOUKMAN EKSPERYANS

Haitian.
○ **Vodou Adjae / MANGO-ANTILLES**
Exciting blend of traditional drum rhythms and modern Caribbean pop attack. —BT

ENSEMBLE NEMOURS JEAN-BAPTISTE

Compas.
☆ **A Musical Tour of Haiti / ANSONIA**
Inventor of compas; most records out of print. This CD includes 17 cuts of classics from the early 60s. —RVR

GM CONNECTION

Haitian.
You and I / MINI RECORDS
GM is salsa-oriented, with longer horn lines, a more stretched-out swing, more fine sax solos, and some strings on the order of Martinique's great Malavoi. —JSR

LES GYPSIES DE PETION-VILLE

Haitian.
Courage / MACAYA
70s style from Haiti, not New York City. —RVR

MINI ALL STARS

Haitian.
15 Titres d'Or de Jean-Baptiste Nemours / MRS   1981
A set of Nemour's classics updated. —RVR

ORCHESTRA TROPICANA

Haitian.
25ème Printemps / LOUIS   1990
From Cap Haitien. Huge classic compas orchestra. —RVR

RARA MACHINE

Compas.
○ **Break the Chain / SHANACHIE**   1991
Undoubted winner of the 1991 award for the most startlingly rapid improvement. Rara Machine's first album was amiable enough but exceedingly bland — and on the whole, Haitian recordings for non-Haitian companies have a poor track record. So imagine my surprise when I let this one loose and discovered an altogether outstanding set with a really good mix of Creole singing, percussion roots, mini-jazz arrangements, and just enough zouk in the trimmings. Such surprises bless the day. —JSR

LES SHLEU SHLEU

Mini jazz. Shleu-Shleu, the Haitian forerunner of what in NYC became Ska-Shah, was one of the great bands. Their combination of swing and delicacy was one reason, but from this distance what stands out from that pre-funk era is their strong Creole flavor, not just in the melodies but in the wonderful solo sax, a style no longer heard. Here's a question: given the Congo touch in the guitars, who was influencing whom? —JSR

☆ **Ace Frape / MINI RECORDS**
Early/mid 70s. —RVR

Tête Chauve / MINI RECORDS
Includes a mambo instrumental. —RVR

Ce La ou Ye / MINI RECORDS   1990
Early-70s classic mini-jazz. —RVR

Pionniers / MELODIE MAKERS   1991
A new, different band. Modern sound with soukous-like guitar and full horn section. —RVR

SKA-SHAH #1

Haitian. See Les Shleu Shleu. —ED
For Ever / MINI RECORDS
Ska-Shah has great swing, kicking alto and tenor sax solos, flashes of soukous-like guitar, and a general hell-for-leather exuberance that makes me want to laugh aloud. —JSR

Ska-Shah #1 / SKA-SHAH
Mid-70s album with one of Ska-Shah's biggest songs. —RVR

L'Ex Shleu-sleu /

TABOU COMBO

Haitian. Formed in the Port-Au-Prince suburb of Petion-Ville by the Chancy brothers, Albert on bass and Adolphe on guitar, this young band won the Radio Haiti mini-jazz competition in 1968. They relocated to Brooklyn in 1971, and their song "New York City," which spoke of the difficulty of life in exile, reached #1 on the Paris pop charts in August 1975. They competed with Ska-Shah for top band honors in the 70s and 80s and fought "musical duels" similar to the Weber Sicot/Jean-Baptiste Nemours battles of the 50s and 60s.

An irresistible live band, Tabou Combo takes Haitian compas to the widest of audiences. From their regular appearances in the 80s at the famous Zenith Theatre in Paris, to an audience of 20,000 in New York's Central Park, to the Jazz and Heritage Festival in New Orleans, in football stadiums throughout the Caribbean, and on the turntables of the top DJs, this band makes people dance.

Influenced by funk and soul in their adopted home, Tabou took on the likeness of the Commodores on the covers of their late-70s releases. They even made a demo tape with hopes of a Motown contract. Their desire to reach the Black US market remains unsatisfied, but they should be proud that popular musicians such as Kassav' from the Antilles/Paris and Wilfrido Vargas from the Dominican Republic have absorbed their music. –RL

8ème Sacrement / MINI RECORDS　　　　　　1974
The CD is from 1974, which some regard as the band's golden age. Back then it was essentially a guitar band (with accordion to link back to Nemours!), with a perfect blend of drive and simplicity. "New York City," the biggest Haitian hit of all time, is featured on this live album. –JSR

Live au Zenith / ESPERANACE　　　　　　1989
The band's relative recent success outside its core community led to hit-hunting that marred its 1989 release. Happily, however, there's little of it in this Zenith set, recorded at a gig in Paris. This double album (also available on video) has plenty of zouk influence, but on the whole it's a return to the band's 80s sound at its best. –JSR

Any Antilles / TC　　　　　　1989
New sound. Ultimate Haitian dance music. –RVR

TOTO BISSAINTHE

Haitian.
○ **Chante Haiti / ARION**
With Marie-Claude Benoit and Mariann Matheus. Slave songs from Jodou cult. Powerful, beautiful, and haunting. –RVR

WAWA

Ceremonial.
Bonsoi Couzin Zaka / GERONIMO
A studio recording, made in Port au Prince by a group apparently led by Wawa, whose name crops up on many of the best vaudou recordings (he's only credited with production and mixing but may be the lead singer). The choir, as always, is a little under-recorded, but the recording as a whole is okay technically and the music splendid. –JSR

HAITI COLLECTIONS

○ **Caribbean Revels / SMITHSONIAN**
Caribbean Revels: Haitian Rara & Dominican Gaga. Rara and Gaga are basically the same thing — vaudou-related Easter parade music using (traditionally) African-derived single-note shawms, and — quite often these days — trumpets and saxes as well as percussion. Gaga is distinct from rara to the extent that the Haitian minority in the Dominican Republic has developed its own traditions. Both branches are exuberantly documented here through street recordings of both traditional and trumpet-led examples. Joyous stuff from a beleaguered people. –JSR

Generation Kompa - Vol. 1 / MELODIE MAKERS　1991
Compilation of very electronic dance crossover from the "nouvel jenerayson," largely in Miami, including Loubert-Chancy, Skanpal, and Shleu Shleu. –RVR

☆ **Konbit Burning Rhythms of Haiti / A&M**
Filmmaker Jonathan Demme compiled this sharp package of classic (and rarely heard) Haitian music from 1957 to the present, with most tracks coming from the last half of the 80s and containing potent political sentiments, not to mention potent dance rhythms. –MB

JAMAICA

JOLLY BOYS

Mento.
○ **Pop'n'Mento / FIRST WARNING**　　　　　1989
Mento is one of the rhythms that went into the mix that became reggae. The Jolly Boys (the youngest of whom is 50 plus) have been playing their acoustic brand of double entendre, crowd-pleasing mento for decades. Includes traditional faves like "Big Bamboo," "Shaving Cream," "River Come Down," and "Back to Back (Belly to Belly)." –JP

JAMAICA COLLECTIONS

Bongo Bakra & Coolie / FOLKWAYS
Bongo Bakra & Coolie - Jamaican Roots - Vol. 1 contains magico-religious songs and Jamaican East Indian music. –DLM
○ **From Kongo to Zion / HEARTBEAT**
Vocal and percussion music from Jamaica's four major local religious traditions: Central African-based Kumina, Afro-Christian, Revival Zion, and Rastafari. Splendid music in its own right, this dramatically underlines the diversity of neo-African adaptations in the Caribbean and is, of course, a main root of reggae. The notes are unusually good. –JSR
John Crow Say... / SMITHSONIAN-FOLKWAYS
Contains an entire quadrille for harmonica and drum, a couple of kids' songs, some very rare Revival Zion sings, recorded by yours truly. But perhaps the greatest treasure is a four-part version of "Adam Where Art Thou," a song very obviously of British origin but "lost" without trace in the UK. Also the title song in a fine version by Valerie Walker. –JSR

TRINIDAD

ALLROUNDER

Soca.
○ **Whey Going On! / CROSBYS**　　　　　　1989
One of the more hilarious tunes of 1989 was Allrounder's tongue-in-cheek defense of Jimmy Swaggert in "Innocent Jimmy" from this EP. –GS

ARROW

Soca. From Montserrat, Arrow got his start as a first-class calypsonian in the traditional Trinidadian style but soon began exploring ways to bring the music to an international level. Always an innovator, he played around with mixing elements of cadence, salsa, and American R&R guitar into his music. In 1983 he experienced his first pan-Caribbean success, "Hot Hot Hot" (a song that later became an international hit). Since then he has branched out to include a wider array of world-music elements, from hip-hop to the sounds of various African nations, while concentrating on lyrics that act predominantly as a vehicle to drive the music to a higher frenzy. A late-80s contract with Island/Mango Records has made him the soca artist most widely distributed and most easily available in the States. His 1992 release, *Zombie Soca,* was notable for including three songs with social commentary lyrics. Unlike those of most calypsonians, Arrow's early releases, including those preceding the Island/Mango albums, are still easily available. –GS
○ **Instant Knockout / CHARLIE'S**　　　　　1980
From his heavily cadence-flavored period, featuring the original version of the social commentary "Bills." –GS
○ **Hot Hot Hot / ARROW**　　　　　　1983
An exciting album not only for the title cut; every song is great. Still featuring social commentary. –GS
Soca Savage / ARROW　　　　　　1984
Early Arrow album with two major dance hits, "Party Mix" and "Columbia Rock," one of soca's best Latin fusion tunes. –JP
Knock Dem Dead / MANGO　　　　　　1988
This disc continues Arrow's fusion experiments and includes Zulu soca, Latin soca, and heavy metal soca courtesy of guitar ace Chris Newland. –JP
O'la Soca / MANGO　　　　　　1989
Hot tracks and exuberant, though sometimes irritating vocals. A remix of his 1989 *Massive* album. –RW
Soca Dance Party / MANGO　　　　　1990
Arrow's latest exploration of Caribbean rhythms includes an excursion to Guadaloupe entitled "Zouk Me." –JP
☆ **Hot Soca Hot / ARROW**　　　　　　1990
Outstanding anthology of hits. Unlike other Arrow anthologies, this one was put together by the man himself, and therefore features what he knows is the best. –GS

Zombie Soca / ARROW   1992
An outstanding album by Arrow, this includes the superb dance hall soca "Wine Yuh Body." Complete with several re-mixes, social commentaries, and a total of 70 minutes of music, it is the best Arrow album to come along in a while. –GS

BALLY

Soca. An extremely consistent young calypsonian who has already won the Jr. Calypso Monarchy Crown and usually places in the finals for the National Calypso Monarchy competition. More often than not, his hits have meaningful lyrics. –GS

Lucifer in Powder Form / B'S   1986
Party Time/The Magicians / B'S   1987
○ **Bally with Love / LOVE PEOPLE RECORDS**   1988
Features "Shaka Shaka" and "Bacchanal Start." –GS
Pleasure / LOVE PEOPLE RECORDS   1989
Contains the dancehall soca hit "Maxi Dub." –GS

BARON

Soca. Known for his sweet voice, dark skin, and multitudes of gold jewelry, Baron is one of the favorites among the ladies. His topics are rarely political, sticking more to love songs, tales of risqué encounters, and global messages about peace. Every album is good. –GS

○ **Full of Fire / B'S**   1987
One of his biggest years, including the suggestive "Say Say." –GS
Party Fusion / JW PRODUCTIONS   1989
"Somebody" was possibly his biggest hit ever. –GS

BECKET

Soca.
○ **Gal Ah Rush Me / COCOA**   1990
From the island of St. Vincent, Becket often hits hard with party soca, but "Gal Ah Rush Me" and "Teaser" from this album were huge hits. –GS

BLACK STALIN

Soca. Stalin is the master of socially conscious lyrics combined with infectious soca dance music, and is a revered legend in T&T (the Trinidad & Tobago style). Song topics range from local concerns like support for the steel drums and calypsonians to concerns of African and Caribbean unification, with occasional global topics like the litany against world leaders in "Burn Dem." Between 1967 and 1992 Stalin has been a finalist contender for the coveted National Calypso Monarchy crown 15 times, winning it four times. –GS

○ **Caribbean Man / MAKOSSA**   1979
The album that brought him his first Calypso Monarchy crown with "Caribbean Unity" and "Play One." –GS
Wait Dorothy Wait / CHARLIE'S   1985
12-inch single backed with "Ism Schism;" these two songs brought him his second crown. –GS
I Time / B'S   1987
Includes "Burn Dem," the most internationally known of any Stalin composition. Brought him his third crown. –GS
☆ **Roots Rock Soca / ROUNDER**   1991
A crucial anthology of most of Stalin's award-winning compositions as well as most of the cuts from his landmark *Caribbean Man*. Essential. –GS
The Bright Side / STRAKER'S   1991
A great album that will go down in history for including his first hit with party lyrics, "Ah Feel to Party." The song brought him his fourth crown. Excellent from beginning to end. –GS

BLUEBOY (SUPERBLUE)

Soca. Blueboy may very well be the most loved of T&T's calypsonians. After dominating the Road March competition in the early 80s, a difficult bout with personal problems

removed him for a while from the big leagues. His triumphant return in 1991 as Superblue was met with overwhelmingly positive response by a public that had been truly empathetic during his "lost years." In both 1991 and 1992 Superblue was so far ahead in the Road March competition that his ultimate victories were pronounced long before Carnival Tuesday. –GS

○ **Soca in the Shaolin Temple / CHARLIE'S**   1980
Classic early-80s album. –JP
Thundering Soca / CCP   1984
Soca with a hard rock edge. –JP
Caribbean Magic / B'S   1988
The still-embattled Blueboy managed to come through with hints of his past grandeur with this album, which includes "Ding Ding" and "Look the Devil Deh." –GS
10th Anniversary / CHARLIE'S   1991
A soca masterpiece. Contains the 1991 Road March, "Get Something and Wave." –GS
☆ **Jab Jab /**   1992

BROTHER RESISTANCE

Soca. Main artist in a dub-poetry style of soca called rapso. Eloquent in interviews and in lyrics, he is an artist who would be of great interest outside of T&T if only better known. In his homeland, he often must struggle to find a spot in a calypso tent and only infrequently releases a record. –GS

Tonight Is de Nite /   1988
○ **Heart of the Rapso Nation /**   1992

BURNING FLAMES

Soca. From Antigua, this band represents the epitome of the high-energy, multiple-influenced, synthesizer-driven soca bands of some of the other soca islands. Years of tourist gigs and a stint as backup band to Montserrat calypsonian Arrow laid the groundwork for their solo debut ... total domination of the Antigua carnival in 1986 with "Stiley Tight." Elements of rock, funk, reggae, cadence, zouk, and more, put to frenetic tempos of amphetamine-like proportion, were the trademark of this band until 1989's "Workey Workey," a funky, zoukish second-line that was an international sensation. They zouked it out further in 1990 with "Chook and Dig" and shortly afterward were anthologized on a Mango release, *Dig*, although the re-mixing done for the record worked to the detriment of each cut. –GS

Stiley Tight/Go Go / A&B   1986
○ **Me Na Freard / BF**   1989
Many songs from this album, including "Workey Workey," were selected and re-mixed for Mango's *Dig* anthology. –GS
Mek E Bark / BF   1990
More hit songs selected and re-mixed for *Dig*, this time including "Chook and Dig." –GS
Dig / MANGO   1991
Re-mixes of some of the band's best late-80s output, surprisingly de-emphasizing the frenzied tempos that first made them famous. –GS

CALYPSO ROSE

Soca. Rose has won more national and international awards than any other calypsonian save for Sparrow and Kitch. The National Calypso King Competition had to be changed in name to the National Calypso Monarchy Competition as a result of her being the first female to ever take the crown (in 1978). Her material is often feminist in nature, and the music is much in the style of Antigua's Swallow ... heavy on the cowbell and horn section. It is no exaggeration to say that every album by Rose is worth hearing. –GS

○ **Trouble / STRAKER'S**   1984
One of calypso's small number of women performers and the only female Carnival "King," Rose has a strong message of Black pride and feminist consciousness, often turning in scathing criticisms of the way men treat women. This album is one of her best. –JP

● **Pan in Town / STRAKER'S**   1985
This one is among her best; includes "Huttam Pullam," "Put It on the Table" and "Turn On the Pressure." –GS

Stepping Out / STRAKER'S   1986
The songs that appear on this album were documented in the outstanding calypso film *One Hand Don't Clap*. –GS

Soca Explosion / STRAKER'S   1988
This above-average album from one of soca's top singers is especially notable for a really fine Indo-calypso (an old calypso tradition that has produced many fine songs) in "Indian Baccanal," and a rare and welcome bonus: lots of solo horn to freshen the backings. –JSR

Jump with Power / STRAKER'S   1991
Includes "Pray Brother John Pray" and "Can't Take the Jamming." –GS

CHALKDUST

Soca. An extremely dedicated social commentator, schoolteacher Chalkdust predominantly limits his lyrics to local concerns, with a point of view that often forces Trinidadians to look within themselves for the causes and answers to the country's problems. He's won the Monarchy crown four times since 1976. A kaiso legend, but probably not very accessible to those with a passing interest in calypso. –GS

○ **Total Kaiso / STRAKER'S**   1989
"Chauffeur Wanted" is a scathing indictment against the prime minister of the time, a song that brought Chalkdust the National Calypso Monarchy Crown in 1989. –GS

CHARLIE'S ROOTS

Soca. A T&T brass band that had been popular for many years prior to the emergence of one of their lead singers, David Rudder, as a solo calypsonian in 1986. In that year Rudder won both the Road March and the National Calypso Monarchy crown. In 1988 another Charlie's Roots lead singer, Chris "Tambu" Herbert, began a three-year domination of the Road March as a solo artist. Despite the solo careers of the two, they remain to this day as singers for Charlie's Roots, although as of 1988 they began to release albums under their own names, with the band listed as backup artists. Albums are still released occasionally under the group's name. Sire Records reissues Rudder's music with Charlie's Roots in nice packages that are more easily available than the original Charlie's releases. Their tendency to mix songs from different years may confuse those who really wish to familiarize themselves with Rudder as a developing artist. –GS

☆ **The Hammer / CHARLIE'S**   1986
The legendary album featuring Rudder's triumphs, "Bahia Gyal" and "The Hammer." –GS

10th Anniversary / CHARLIE'S   1987
Featuring Rudder again, this time with "Dedication" and "Calypso Music." This album, along with the previous year's "Bahia Gyal," was reissued on Sire Records as *This Is Soca - Vol. 1.* –GS

☆ **Total Party / CHARLIE'S**   1992
This album, which features Rudder on "Savannah Party," was one of the finest releases from Carnival 1992. –GS

CRAZY

Soca. As #2 he certainly tries harder. There is perhaps no artist in T&T who more consistently composes a party masterpiece aimed at the Road March and yet loses time and again, usually placing second. Best known internationally for his Indian soca success, "Nani Wine," he has actually been responsible for many huge hits, including "Ain't Bong for You" (from 1984), "Drive It" (1988), "Gimme More" (from 1990), and "Penelope/Party Now Start" (from 1992). Only once, in 1985, did he win the Road March, with "(Suck Me) Soucouyant." For all-out party soca, any record by Crazy will do. –GS

New Directions /   1984

Contains two great songs for the road, "Ain't Bong for You" and "Soca Tarzan." –GS

Soucouyant / TRINITY-CRAZY LTD   1985
Another three-song "LP" from Crazy. A soucouyant is a Trinidadian spirit that can suck the life out of you, but Crazy is so pumped up on soca energy that he taunts the apparition with one of the great double entendre lines of the 80s, "Suck Me, Soucouyant." –JP

☆ **Nani Wine / TRINITY**   1989
This only has three songs, but the title track is a classic. –JP

○ **Crazymania / JW PRODUCTIONS**   1992

CRO-CRO

Soca. Little known outside T&T, Cro-Cro is responsible for some of the most scathing calypso diatribes against corruption and political chicanery. Because his topics are of local interest, he rarely tours internationally, even in the years when he has won the National Calypso Monarchy crown. Another legend, like Chalkdust, whose records will probably be fairly inaccessible to those with only a general interest in calypso. –GS

○ **Still de Best / STRAKER'S**   1991
Probably the most accessible of his albums. –GS

DESIGNER

Soca.

My Burning Desire / CHARLIE'S   1983
An up-and-coming singer drops rock and funk rhythms into the mix for a style that appeals to Islanders living in the USA as well as Trinidad. "Rockin' Fever" is a perfect example of rock done calypso style. –JP

○ **Ra-Ti-Ray / JW PRODUCTIONS**   1992
Infectious melody and chorus with throwaway lyrics; one of the biggest party hits of 1992. –GS

DRUPATEE (RAMGOONAI)

Soca. East Indian singer who nearly took the Road March in 1988 with "(Roll Up the Tassa) Mr. Bissessar," an Indian soca that was the motivation behind the following year's "Nani Wine" response by Crazy. –GS

☆ **Mr. Bissessar / KPS**   1988
A classic 12-inch single. –GS

Pepper Pepper/Hotter Than Ah Chulha / AKASH   1989
This 1989 effort was almost as popular as the previous year's hit, and was the last offering by Drupatee that played a major part in carnival. –GS

Throw Me Down / AKASH   1990
Cooler than ah Carib or Stag. –GS

DUKE (MIGHTY)

Soca. A legendary calypsonian for his unduplicated feat of winning the calypso Monarchy four years in a row. Considered one of the major figures in calypso, Duke releases albums that are always of interest. He never fails to deliver a party soca for the Road March competition but has only once captured it (in 1987 with "Is Thunder"). His topics range from party lyrics to global concerns, addressing only on rare occasions something of local concern. –GS

○ **Calypso Forever / STRAKER'S**   1983
Duke (aka Mighty Duke) is one of calypso's founding fathers; this is one of his best efforts from the early 80s. –JP

● **Yesterday, Today and Tomorrow / LEM'S**   1987
Containing the 1987 Road March, "Is Thunder." –GS

Party for Yuh Life! / JW PRODUCTIONS   1989
"Yahhhhhhh" was among the hottest songs of 1989. –GS

The Phung-Uh-Nung Sweet / STRAKER'S   1992
Title cut and "Rocket in Yuh Pocket" are worth hearing. –GS

EXPLAINER

Soca. A severely underrated calypsonian who rarely makes it

Calypso and Steelband Music of the Caribbean

The musical output of Trinidad & Tobago — calypso, steelband music, and now, soca — is centered around the carnival season that begins shortly after Christmas and culminates with "Carnival Tuesday," the day before the Catholic feast of Ash Wednesday. The island calypsonians compose (or buy) at least two new songs annually, which they then perform nightly throughout carnival season at the "calypso tents." Of course, all those who can arrange it will also produce recordings of their songs that will be released sometime between Thanksgiving and a few weeks before Carnival Tuesday.

The annual music crop is highly affected by two major music contests in which the vast majority of calypsonians compete during carnival season, the National Calypso Monarchy (best calypsonian of the year) and the Road March (best party song of the year), as well as by a host of other smaller competitions like Junior Monarch, Calypso Queen, and Extempo Monarch. Most compositions are a reflection of attempts of calypsonians to win these competitions. Consequently, they fall into two camps: party songs vying for Road March and lyrically strong calypsos vying for the Monarchy by addressing a wide range of social and political topics.

Recordings of calypso (whose more uptempo contemporary form is called "soca," from the words Soul and Calypso) feature a fairly standard formula of programmed drums and rhythm section, calypso guitar, occasional lead or tenor pans (steel drums), horns, and a syncopated bass guitar that gives the music its true soul. While the lyrical content and cleverness will differ dramatically from song to song, a calypso album will typically include some songs strong on lyrics and some that put lyrics secondary to a strong dance beat. The best of the lot are undoubtedly those that combine infectious dance beats with thoughtful or timely messages.

Although on a much smaller scale, similar competitions exist on most of the other soca islands (Antigua, Barbados, Virgin Islands, Aruba, etc.), influencing their calypsonians to produce records in much the same way as in Trinidad and Tobago.

The strongest trend both in Trinbago and the other soca islands is the greater visibility of brass bands (the name given to self-contained bands with horns). In days past, the main function of the brass bands was to play covers of the hits of the day, but since 1986 and the emergence of David Rudder from the Charlie's Roots brass band, these bands are beginning to be responsible for many of the original hits of carnival. In T&T, the lead singers of these bands are beginning to be looked upon as bonafide calypsonians (not without controversy), but this facet of brass-band emergence is not happening on the other islands. Instead, the strong trend in non-Trinidadian brass bands is a group effort to produce a supercharged soca with frenetic tempos and touches of outside influences like rock, funk, rap, dancehall reggae, and more. These wild forms of soca are coming from the Burning Flames of Antigua, Jam Band of St. Thomas, WCK of Dominique, the Humanoids of St. Thomas, Arrow of Montserrat, and many others.

A discussion of Trinidad & Tobago calypso/soca wouldn't be complete without mention of the steel drum (simply called a "pan" in the islands). For decades, the steel bands, large and small, waited to hear the annual crop of new music and then selected their favorite to arrange and perform during carnival. Since the mid 80s, however, there has been a growing trend for steelband arrangers to write an original song and record it as soca, with a calypsonian singing. This has added exciting new music to carnival that very often features virtuoso lead or tenor panplaying. In Carnival '92 there was a remarkable dozen popular tunes written by steelband arrangers.

In searching for interesting calypso records, a good rule of thumb is to select those that enjoyed a high measure of success during a given carnival season, be it Trinidad & Tobago or any of the other calypso/soca islands like Antigua, Barbados, the Virgin Islands, and St. Vincent. This practice will provide the opportunity to experience a wider range of artists than just those internationally known, like the Mighty Sparrow, Lord Kitchener, Shadow, David Rudder, and Calypso Rose. At the same time it will introduce the listener to the cream of the crop as seen through the eyes of the islanders, an important lesson considering that past success does not guarantee popularity at every carnival: the biggest sensations of one year's carnival could be the kiss of boredom the next.

Likewise, the age of CDs is bringing to us for the first time a host of easily available compilations and anthologies, another excellent way of getting a broader taste. Aside from the CDs, don't expect to find many liner notes on albums, but do look for the names of the three major arrangers, Frankie McIntosh, Leston Paul, and Pelham Goddard, in order to experience their somewhat differing approaches to the calypso/soca art form. The major labels as we move into the 90s are Charlie's, Lypsoland, Charlo's, Straker's, and JW's.

— Gene Scaramuzzo

---

to the Monarchy finals but who nearly always releases an album of interest. His albums are always a talented mix of social commentary and (often risqué) party tunes. –GS

○ **The Awakening / B'S**   1984
"Caribbean Change" was one of the best commentaries on the unrest being caused by foreign intervention in the Caribbean (Grenada, Cuba, etc.). A gem. –GS

Dedicated to You / B'S   1985
Explainer is very political, and one of the few soca singers who can tell a tale from the women's perspective. Features "Lunch Time," an amusing celebration of oral sex. –JP

Tongue / CHARLIE'S   1991
Especially good; includes the party hit "Curfew Jam" as well as one of the first soca tunes ever written about a love affair between a calypsonian and his hand. –GS

☆ **Positive Vibrations / VISTA**   1991
One of the few calypsonians to date to have his past work anthologized, this disc provides a taste of all the styles of lyrical commentary that make Explainer great. –GS

FRANCINE (SINGING)

Soca. A calypsonian who rarely plays a major role in carnival but who often makes a good commentary on some local issue. 1988's "Carnival Controversy" and 1989's "Sing for the Judges" show her to be unafraid to speak out against the T&T government, and these in fact represent two albums that would provide a good introduction to her music. –GS

She/Chinaman /   1984
A 12-inch single with funky soca featuring steel drum lead that livened up Carnival '84. –GS

○ **Reaching Out / STRAKER'S**   1988
"Cultural Controversy" was a major commentary of 1988. –GS

Dedication / STRAKER'S   1989
"Sing for the Judges" was mentioned above, but "Soca Do That" is also a fine tune from 1989, although admittedly it was not among the biggest hits. –GS

GABBY (MIGHTY)

Soca.

○ **Boots / ICE**   1984
By Gabby of Barbados, a hard-hitting anti-war commentary deploring the use of tax money for a costly acquisition of boots for the military. It had a particularly strong impact coming as it did in the same year as the invasion of nearby Caribbean island Grenada. –GS

GYPSY

Soca. Gypsy is one of the outstanding calypsonians of T&T who annually since 1988 has won the National Extempo Calypso crown, a competition in which contestants must compose lyrics on the spot. He has had a roller-coaster career that has reached the extremes of peaks and valleys. His "Sinking Ship: SS Trinidad" from his classic 1986 release was considered by most to be the crowning blow that brought on the downfall of the PNM government, which had been in power for nearly 30 years. Despite his triumph, he lost out that year to David Rudder's "Bahia Gyal/The Hammer." Somewhat bitter (a 1987 calypso, "Sing Ram Bam," sarcastically refers to the "inane" lyrics of Rudder's "Bahia Gyal"), and further embattled by other career setbacks, he has nonetheless gone on to compose outstanding calypsos each year. Any album by Gypsy is recommended. –GS

☆ **The Action Too High / MRS PRODUCTIONS**   1986
A classic featuring the aforementioned "The Sinking Ship." The title cut is also one of the most danceable commentaries ever written in soca style concerning the drug problem. –GS

We Need More Love / J&M-MRS PRODUCTIONS   1987
One of the best albums from the sometimes uninspired second half of the 80s. Gypsy, who is consistently good and consistently underrated, devotes one side to party and topical lyrics. The title track is a tearaway, but my own favorite cut is "Sing Ram Bam," which has a classic calypso melody and nice acid guitar punctuations. –JSR

I Believe in You / MRS PRODUCTIONS   1990
A true calypsonian who comments on the issues of the times, Gypsy sings on the previous year's incident, in which toilet paper was thrown at him during a live performance, and on the terrible new Value Added Tax, in "No VAT." He boogies down in "Gimme the Thing." Another great album. –GS

Bad Behavior / MRS PRODUCTIONS   1992
Another first-rate offering. –GS

HUMANOIDS

Soca.

○ **Humanoids / ETIENNE PRODUCTIONS**   1990
The band hails from St. Thomas, V.I. With Georges "Soul" Thomas of the legendary group Gramacks, and Herrie Etienne of Swinging Stars, both of Dominique, this album is a wonderful blend of soca sounds with 70s-era cadence music. Worth hunting down. –GS

JAM BAND

Soca.

○ **We Run Things / PARROT FISH**   1988
Another high-energy band à la Burning Flames, this time from St. Thomas, V.I. This band has dominated the St. Thomas Road March competition in recent years. –GS

KAISO GENIUS

Calypso.

○ **Going Back to Africa / MAKOSSA**   1980
Older, pre-soca-style calypsos, which deal with the usual topics: sex, romance, politics, and Black pride. –JP

JOHNNY KING

Soca. A policeman who annually releases a 12-inch single or EP with meaningful lyrics backed by an uptempo dance tune. Some years, such as 1985, it was the meaningful melody that caught on, although he has hit very big in other years with serious Road March contenders. 1988 was probably his highest party moment with "Wet Me Down." –GS

Appreciation/Ah Want It / KING PRODUCTIONS   1985

○ **Wet Me Down/War Mongers / HIBISCUS**   1988

Don't Rub Me/Pan Victory / M. CHANKA PROD.   1989

KITCH (LORD KITCHENER)

Soca. Kitch is, along with the Mighty Sparrow, the most well-known of any calypsonian of T&T. With a career spanning over two decades, he has an extremely large catalog of annual releases, complicated further by an unknown number of anthologies and reissues. Amazingly, none are bad. Several anthologies of pre-soca-era material are listed below as starters, along with a handful of the best annual releases from the soca era, beginning with the early 80s release, *Kitchener Goes Soca*, in which he dramatically demonstrated that he was more than capable of keeping abreast of any latest musical fashion. –GS

○ **King of Calypso / MELODISC**
One of the pioneers of calypso. This collection reaches back to the hits of the 40s and early 50s for classics like "Black & White," "Life Begins at 40," and "Short Skirts." –JP

Spicy Delight / MELODISC
More early Kitch, leaning toward the bawdy tunes that first made him popular. –JP

Kitchener Goes Soca / CHARLIE'S   1981
There is no denying that Kitch is the master here as he picks up the tempos and delivers some of the best soca tunes of the day. Includes "Soca Jean" and "Kitchener It Bon Down." –GS

☆ **Roots of Soca / CHARLIE'S**   1984
This album doesn't have a single second-rate song on it. One of the high points of Carnival 1984. –GS

○ **Master at Work / KALICO**   1985
"Soca Misinterpretation" may very well be the best party song Kitch has written in the 80s, aided by a fantastic echoed mix courtesy of arranger Leston Paul. –GS

The Grand Master / B'S   1987
"Pan in A Minor" was a huge 1987 hit among the steelbands and more than enough reason to search out this album. –GS

The Honey in Kitch / MC PROD.   1992
The popularity of "Bee's Melody" among the steelbands in 1992 may have even surpassed their enthusiasm in 1987 for Kitch's "Pan in A Minor." –GS

LLOYD LOVINDEER

Soca.

Soca Babylon Boops / TSOJ   1986
Simultaneous to hitting big in Jamaica with a reggae version of "Babylon Boops," Jamaican Lovindeer released this soca version famous for the slack B-side in which he goes into great detail as to how he's going to defend the lady in trouble. –GS

○ **Soca Nights / TSOJ**   1987
Hot on the heels of "Soca Babylon Boops" came this album famous for "Big Panty Lady" with its request to "show me your panty size." Plenty slack and a big hit. –GS

MAESTRO

Soca. One of the founding fathers of soca music, Maestro was tragically killed in the late 70s. –GS

○ **Anatomy of Soca / CHARLIE'S**   1978
This one and *Soca Explosion* by Lord Shorty are the two albums that most dramatically re-defined T&B music. –GS

MELODY (LORD)

Calypso. Another of the legends of calypso who died just at the end of the 80s. Responsible for many classic songs. –GS

○ **Through the Looking Glass / COOK**
Melody gained fortune, if not fame, by writing hits for Harry Belafonte, including "Momma Look at Boo Boo." This early 60s album contains some of his biggest hits, including "Sí Senior," an early Latin-influenced calypso, which Belafonte recast as "Sweetheart from Venezuela." –JP

I Man / CHARLIE'S   1979
This was Melody's first crack at soca, just a year after Maestro and Shorty started the ball rolling. A classic that still sounds great. –GS

Lola / B'S   1982
A strong soca effort from 1982, which shows Mel rocking just as hard as the young turks. –JP

MERCHANT

Soca.

Ah Coming Too / STRAKER'S   1987
A strong album from Merchant's large catalog of releases. "Ah Coming Too," a feminist tale, was the hit, but "Tumble Down" was another great tune done in a funk fashion. –GS

MARCIA MIRANDA

Soca.

○ **Come Fly with Me / STRAKER'S**   1991
In her first year on the scene as a solo artist, Miranda hit very hard with this album, which is good from start to finish. One of the great albums of Carnival '91. –GS

NELSON

Soca. A New York-based calypsonian who was one of the earliest to experiment with synthesizers and disco sounds, Nelson has always been somewhat of an innovator. He's been responsible for some outstanding party soca, which doesn't mean he's not also a lyricist, penning some fine social commentary. –GS

○ **Hotter Than Hot / B'S**   1984
The subject is sex, the music is hot, and Nelson's self-effacing humor is delightful. –JP

Love You Forever / JOKER   1988
Some of the singer's best compositions played by a session band that smokes. –JP

When the World Turns Around / SHANACHIE   1990
A member of calypso's greatest generation (Sparrow, Kitch, Melody, etc.), still going strong and growing musically at sixty plus. He currently uses rap, R&B, reggae, and other rhythms to spice up his soca rhymes. –JP

Bring Back the Voodoo / SHANACHIE   1991
Nelson re-records a few older hits ("Mi Lover," "Down by the Seaside") and offers some new material, much of it more political than ever before, especially the ballad "We Can Overcome." –JP

OBSTINATE (KING)

Soca. One of Antigua's best calypsonians, a frequent winner of the Monarchy competition. –GS

○ **Obstinate / GREENBAY**   1987
Includes two uptempo party tunes, "Voyier y Montez" (zouk style) and "Jam Band Beat" (a Road March contender). –GS

ORGANIZER

Soca.

○ **That's Ah Bandit / WRECKER**   1989
This social commentary was one of the runaway hits of Carnival '89, describing the many different ways that the people of T&T had been ripped off. The melody is really pretty on this, also. –GS

OUR BOYS STEEL ORCHESTRA

Steel drum.

○ **Our Boys Steel Orchestra / MANGO**

PENGUIN

Soca. Penguin has consistently produced first-rate records during his career but has never repeated the level of popularity he enjoyed in the early 80s. –GS

○ **Touch It / B'S**   1984
In 1984, with this album, he dominated the Road March competition with "Sorf Man" (although he lost out to Sparrow) and took the Monarchy crown with "We Livin' in Jail" and "Sorf Man." –GS

KEN "PROFESSOR" PHILMORE

Soca. The arranger for Fonclaire Steel Band, Philmore has begun to produce outstanding soca music driven by pan, and often, as in these two albums below, with singing by calypsonian Designer. –GS

☆ **Pan by Storm / STRAKER'S**   1990
One of the true gems of Carnival '90. If you like pan, you must find this one. –GS

Pan Ecstasy / STRAKER'S   1991
Not as exciting as last year's tune, but still a pan treat. –GS

DENYSE PLUMMER

Soca. Enlisted by Phase II Pan Groove steelband arranger Len "Boogsie" Sharpe in 1986 to sing his band's Panorama entry, Plummer began making a name for herself as a calypsonian. In 1988, with yet another Len "Boogsie" Sharpe pan tune, "Woman Is Boss," she arrived at the National Calypso Monarchy finals and also won the Calypso Queen crown. Since then she has taken the Calypso Queen crown a total of four times and has won the World Calypso Crown three times. Blessed with a strong voice and always an outstanding composition, Plummer makes records that are fresh and exciting. –GS

☆ **The Boss / WELDON'S**   1988
Includes "A Nation Forges On" and "Woman Is Boss." –GS

Still the Boss / BOSS PRODUCTIONS   1989
With "Together Right Here" and "The Champ." –GS

Victory / OSCAR'S   1990
A 12-inch EP with "DJ Fever" and "The Message," which brought Plummer her third Calypso Queen crown. "DJ Fever" was a much-welcomed tribute to the DJs worldwide who push soca. –GS

Carnival Killer / VP   1991
The title track brought her yet another Calypso Queen Crown, her fourth. –GS

POSER

Soca.

Heavy Action / STRAKER'S   1987
A particularly good year for Poser, with "Tonight" and the social commentary "Ah Never Thought." –GS

○ **The Bus Conductor / WRECKER**   1990
"Bus Conductor" was a surprise party hit that took off early in the season and continued strong in popularity right through carnival. A classic from 1990. –GS

PROTECTOR

Soca. Among the top of the list of underrated calypsonians, Protector has yet to release a bad record. He delivers plenty of good party soca but is also very skilled at social commentary (local and global) and has several times made it to the Monarchy finals. Any Protector album is recommended. –GS

Simply Beautiful / CHARLIE'S 1985
An EP that lives up to its name, featuring the killer "Spanish Party" and the slow, funky tale of unrequited love, "Charmaine." –GS

Going Places / STRAKER'S 1989
Includes the excellent commentary on today's youth, "Young-Restless." –GS

○ **Total Protection / STRAKER'S** 1990
The superb "Crossover Sweet" is enough reason to look for this album, but the whole package is another fine offering from this talented calypsonian who is not that well known outside T&T. –GS

DAVID RUDDER b 1953

Soca. Rudder has become perhaps soca's most visible performer, and one of the few on a major American label. Rudder began singing in 1965 as a member of a group called the Solutions. He began heading his own group in 1970, doing pop and soul songs, then turned to soca in the late 70s, working with the great Kitchener before joining Charlie's Roots in 1980 as a replacement for lead vocalist Chris "Tambu" Herbert. Rudder finished third in the Road March competition for Carnival '85, then in 1986 became one of the few performers to win the Young King and Calypso Monarch titles. Rudder has gotten heavy criticism from calypso traditionalists for his incorporation of R&B, blues, funk, and rock elements into his soca compositions, but his popularity has increased so that he now appears at international jazz and blues festivals as well as carnival and soca events. –RW

☆ **Haiti / LYPSOLAND-SIRE** 1988
In terms of Road March power, 1988 was Rudder's finest moment, with "Bacchanal Woman" and the superb social commentary, "Panama." The title cut was a remarkable ode to Caribbean unity. Sire reissued this album with cuts from the previous two years under the same title, *Haiti*. –GS

☆ **1990 / LYPSOLAND-SIRE** 1990
A concept album from the king of contemporary soca, which details the international struggle against racism with particular emphasis on South Africa. –JP

Frenzy / LYPSOLAND-SIRE 1992
"Knock Them Down" and "Stiff Waist Man" were popular, but "De Long Time Band," with its unusual percussion and old-time sound, is a song that will long be remembered. –GS

SCORCHER

Soca.
○ **The Hoper / STRAKER'S**
Excellent album that mixes a nonstop party vibe with militant Afrocentric lyrics. –JP

SCRUNTER

Soca. Another calypsonian who presents a problem in deciding which of his records to list. He's so consistently good that all are recommended. He often presents social commentary, but his party music is what really stands out. –GS

Doh Jam Dis / 2 GUYS 1985
A killer 12-inch single from 1985. –GS

○ **Every Shadow / CHARLIE'S** 1986
Every song on this record is great, and plenty are risqué. "Ah See You" was a party hit, "Every Shadow" a commentary on crime, "Nanny" and "John Dick" not very subtle odes to sex, and "Me No Want No Man" a great story from a woman's perspective. –GS

Soca Bacchanal / HIBISCUS 1987
"She Want Me to Sing in She Party" was the big hit on this 12-inch single, but "Lost Tenor" is a fantastic pan tune. –GS

SHADOW

Soca. There are many calypso lovers who await Shadow's annual release more than that of any other calypsonian. Like Stalin and just a handful of others, Shadow is a totally unique calypsonian; there is no other like Shadow. Since 1974 and his landmark composition "De Bassman," he has never failed to deliver some of the toughest basslines, most infectious grooves, and most original compositions of anyone in the Caribbean. On top of all this, he has a low, authoritative voice that lends an air of truth and finality to all he sings. His social and political commentaries are delivered in such a clever way (and propelled as they are by his unique soca beat) that the messages often sink in subliminally, a testimony to his unique lyrical skills. With this in mind, how does one narrow down his nearly 20 records to a handful of recommendations? –GS

○ **De Bassman /** 1974
The legendary album that brought Shadow to fame. –GS

If I Coulda I Woulda I Shoulda / CHARLIE'S 1979
A particularly outstanding album from this era of Shadow's career, featuring a raw sound worth hearing. Quite different from the Shadow of today. –GS

Return of De Bassman / STRAKER'S 1984
The end of an era for a particular raw sound to Shadow's music. As always, a killer mix of hits like "More Music," "Snakes," and the title cut. –GS

○ **High Tension / STRAKER'S** 1988
This represents the epitome of Shadow's late 80s recorded output. "Tension" was a killer in the Road March arena, yet was in serious competition with two other songs from this same album, "Bad Boy Peter" and "Garden Want Water" (with sexual tension in all three). "Crazy Computer" was a favorite in the tents, giving Shadow four hit songs in one year. –GS

☆ **Columbus Lied / SHANACHIE** 1991
Shadow is one of the few calypsonians who has been anthologized on an American label. This recent release presents eight of the best of his songs from 1988 through 1990, a landmark period in his career. –GS

Winston Bailey Is the Shadow / KISSKIDEE 1992
A decidedly different approach on this album. Only one song on this album, "Hard Head," was Road March bound. Neither "Soucouyant," the superb commentary on AIDS, nor the late-bloomer "Music" (aka "Dingolay") were typical uptempo grooves, showing that Shadow can hit no matter how far he strays from formula. –GS

SHANDILEER (BRASS BAND)

Soca. A T&T brass band that consistently produces party hits, although some years the songs tend to sound alike. You can't go wrong with the two listed below, but any others are worth hearing. –GS

○ **Happy /** 1988
A serious Road March contender in 1988. –GS

Do What You Want / SORRELL 1991
Another highlight in their bid for Road March; includes "Do What You Want" and "We Pushin'." –GS

SHORTY (LORD)

Soca. The founding father of soca music who, along with Maestro, brought a new image to calypso at the end of the 70s. He still occasionally releases records as Ras Shorty I. –GS

○ **Soca Explosion / CHARLIE'S** 1978
The ultimate classic. –GS

The Collection (Best Of) / CAROTTE
A wonderful anthology covering Shorty's scandalous early career of extremely suggestive calypsos, including a handful

of cuts from *Soca Explosion*. Sound quality is rather poor, unfortunately. –GS

SPARROW (MIGHTY)

Calypso. There are few people in the world who haven't heard of the Mighty Sparrow. He's won the National Calypso Monarchy crown more often than any other calypsonian and trails behind only one man, Lord Kitchener, in the number of Road March victories. His nearly 40-year career is filled with expertly crafted political and social commentary; he is a master of lyricism. At the same time he has an international reputation for his risqué, often overtly obscene, calypso tales. His charisma on stage is undeniable, and he continues as strong today as when he first hit the scene in the mid 50s. As with Kitch, there are countless anthologies of his music in addition to his 30 or more annual releases. In the late 80s, Sparrow released two volumes of his early, calypso-era hits, redone in a soca style. –GS

○ **25th Anniversary / CHARLIE'S**   1980
A double-record set released to celebrate 25 years of calypso classics. Features "Wanted: Dead or Alive" a worldwide pop hit later covered by the Manhattan Transfer. –JP

The Greatest / CHARLIE'S   1983
There are no bad Sparrow records, but some are better than others, including this masterpiece from 1983. Includes a critique of inflation, "Capitalism Gone Mad," as well as "Phillip My Dear," a nasty account of what "really" happened when that stranger crept into Queen Elizabeth's bedroom. –JP

Party Classics 1 & 2 / CHARLIE'S   1985
The aforementioned two volumes of 50s through 70s hits by Sparrow, redone in a soca style. Titles like "Jean & Dinah" and "Mr. Walker," which appear on Volume I, are surely known by most of the world. The biggest hit, though, "Congo Man," was on Volume 2. –GS

SQUIBBY

Soca.
Pan Running Wild / B'S   1984
An absolutely thrilling, breathtaking soca featuring double tenor pans on lead. –GS

SUGAR ALOES

Soca. Sounds like ... wears lots of gold like ... moves onstage like ... Baron. Nonetheless an entity unto himself who, in three years, has consistently reached the Monarchy finals with a biting political commentary, while at the same time aiming at the Road March with great party tunes. –GS

○ **Solid As a Rock / WRECKER**   1990
○ **Pure Sugar / WRECKER**   1991
○ **Special Assignment / WRECKER**   1992

SWALLOW

Soca. Antigua's undisputed party master who pleases everyone from the Caribbean to NYC to Toronto with cowbell- and horn-driven soca. Talented beyond compare, able year after year to compose infectious hooks with catchy lyrics. There's not a bad release by Swallow throughout his long career. –GS

Subway Jam, Pace Yourself / CHARLIE'S   1981
Swallow specializes in party jams, usually without any social or sexual message beyond "Have a good time." "Subway Jam," the title tune, is an all-time soca anthem. –JP

Party in Space / CHARLIE'S   1983
The title track has Sally Ride jammin' to the soca beat with her fellow astronauts and a saucerful of aliens. A great party album. –JP

○ **First Take / CHARLIE'S**   1984
This one will leave you breathless. Includes "Flagwoman," "Town Mash Down," and "Satan Comin' Down." –GS

Hit Man / CHARLIE'S   1987
Here is one of the best albums from the second half of the 80s.

Swallow's 1987 "Hit Man" is notable for a very fine kick-em-up about the Brooklyn carnival. –JSR

☆ **Swallow on the Streets of Brooklyn / CHARLIE'S**   1988
"Fire in the Backseat" had everyone moving in 1988. –GS

Steam / CHARLIE'S   1990
The title cut was another gem. –GS

TAMBU (CHRIS HERBERT)

Soca. This Charlie's Roots singer began his solo career after fellow Charlie's Roots singer David Rudder's successful attempt in 1986. Tambu succeeded in capturing the Road March title three years in a row with basically the same song recycled, as well as making it to the Monarchy finals each of those years. Tambu is a good singer and, despite the fact that he recycles song ideas, he's capable of writing very catchy choruses. –GS

○ **Culture / LYPSOLAND-SIRE**   1988
The title cut was somewhat of an anthem during Carnival '88, calling for the preservation of T&T's unique cultural achievements like steelband, limbo, calypso, and East Indian tassa drumming, although it was "This Party Is It" that captured the Road March. A great album from 1988. –GS

The Journey / LYPSOLAND   1989
Road March #2 was "Free Up" from this album. –GS

The Cry / LYPSOLAND   1990
"No No We Eh Going Home" and "Let's Do It" brought Tambu his third Road March victory and again brought him to the Monarchy finals. –GS

Reach Out / LYPSOLAND   1991
Ironically, "Rant and Rave" and "Not Me Is the Music" from this album were two of Tambu's better songs, but they were crushed in the Road March competition by Superblue's "Get Something & Wave." –GS

TAXI (BRASS BAND)

Soca.
○ **Made in Trinidad / RAINBOW**   1991
This features the legendary sex-on-the-dance-floor romp, "Dollah," a Caribbean anthem on a par in popularity with Arrow's "Hot Hot Hot," and "Workey Workey" by Burning Flames. –GS

WCK

Soca.
○ **Culture Shock / CHARLO**   1991
This Dominiquan band was a surprise hit during T&T's 1991 Carnival with the title cut. A splendid mix of zouk, cadence, and soca, in a genre similar to Burning Flames but leaning much more heavily toward the French Antilles. –GS

TRINIDAD COLLECTIONS

☆ **Calypso Breakaway / ROUNDER**   1990
This new set of classics from 1927 to 1941 brings more gems from Atilla the Hun, Tiger, Executor, Caresser, Beginner, and other great names. I've never bought the anti-soca line of many old-hand calypso buffs: there were plenty of feeble calypsos back then too. But the vocal and instrumental verve of the best calypsos have never been equalled. –JSR

○ **Calypso Pioneers - 1912-1937 / ROUNDER**   1989
Another anthology covering the early period of calypso, with selections from the 20s and 30s. Some artist duplication with *Calypso Breakaway*. A marvelous release that highlights prime calypso innovators. –RW

○ **Calypso Season / MANGO**   1989
A fine collection full of unintended ironies. Most of it is in fact soca, balanced between names (Baron, Tambu, Sparrow) and unknowns (All Rounder). But there are two old-calypso cuts with acoustic guitar by Roaring Lion, and one by classic steelband the Desperados — and all three strike like a cool breeze in a crowded dancehall. Still and all, the soca cuts are

just fine in their own affably shallow way. Whoever selected this lot had fine ears (pity Mango couldn't have spared the time or the bucks for at least some kind of notes, fer crine out loud). –JSR

○ **Calypsos from Trinidad / ROUNDER**
The subhead of this CD is a lot more to the point than the title: *Politics, Intrigue and Violence in the 1930s, Including the Butler Calypsos*. This is a dynamite collection of political comment — not just about Butler's union activities and their aftermath, but Mussolini in Abyssinia and Depression at home. The lyrics make current soca sound tame, and the melodies, singing, and backup playing have a delicate fire that would make you want to ban electric sockets from the market. This, all in all, is probably the best of the several superb classic calypso sets now available. A terrific 24-page booklet adds to it all. –JSR

○ **Carnival Jump-Up / DELOS**
Anthology featuring various steel-bands from Trinidad and Tobago. All recordings were made on location, and it includes songs by Amoco Renegades, Carib Tokyo, Neal and Massy Trinidad All-Stars, etc. Sterling sound. –RW

○ **Heart of Steel: Steelbands of T&T / FLYING FISH**
Modern steelbands from Trinidad and Tobago. Little duplication with other anthologies, and it's also better produced. More instructive than inspirational. –RW

☆ **Heat in de Place: Soca from Trinidad / ROUNDER**   1990
A wonderful collection of modern soca tunes, with a good mix of topical and socio-political selections. –RW

○ **Jazz n' Steel from Trinidad & Tobago / DELOS**
Another anthology, this one featuring the Rudy Smith Trio & Annise Hadeed Quartet. It features steelbands that combine improvisational flair and eclectic approach. –RW

☆ **Pan Classics / BLUE RHYTHM**
For decades now, steelbands have been playing arrangements of popular classical and semi-classical pieces, and that — augumented by piano from time to time — is what is featured here. Four of Trinidad's most popular steelbands play Handel, Johann Strauss, Vivaldi, and even Wagner! I frankly hate this stuff and deeply regret the much less grandiose steelband of the early days. Still, it's an authentic local phenomenon, and the groups here — Samaroo Jets, Solo Harmonites, Tropical Angel Harps, and Trinidad Cement Ltd Skiffle Bunch Steel Orchestra (!) — are no flash-in-the-pan (sorry ...). –JSR

○ **Rebel Soca: When the Time Comes / SHANACHIE**
Unlike reggae, soca plays not a Messianic-rebellious role in Trinbago society, but a pragmatic reformist one. The three weakest tracks here seem attempts to justify a basically inappropriate concept. The rest, ranging from good to terrific, are from mainstream soca commentators from Stalin and Nelson to Ras Iley and Red Plastic Bay. –JSR

☆ **This Is Soca / SIRE**   1987
This two-record set makes for a fine introduction to soca/calypso. Record #1 is David Rudder's strong 1987 effort, while record #2 is a compilation of hits, including Stalin's "Burn Dem." –JP

☆ **Say What? Double Entendre Soca / ROUNDER**   1990
Anthology featuring contemporary soca and calypso musicians from Trinidad who specialize in songs containing sexual innuendos and explicit/implicit messages. The roster includes Shadow, Bally, Monarch, Poser, etc. –RW

○ **Trinidad Carnival / DELOS**   1989
Various steelbands recorded live at the 1989 Trinidad Carnival. Fine sound. –RW

○ **Wind Your Waist / SHANACHIE**   1991
Fine selection of soca dance hits by Arrow, Shadow, and Kitch; includes Tambu's 1987 anthem, "This Party Is It." –JP

US VIRGIN ISLANDS

BLINKY & THE ROADMASTERS

Scratch.
○ **Crucian Scratch Band Music / ROUNDER**   1990
A treasure: admirably recorded music from the US Virgin

Islands, well annotated. The Rounder release is dedicated to a semi-professional scratch band with a charming old-Creole sound. Varied, exhilarating, and authentic: What more can one expect? –JSR

EUROPE

ALBANIA COLLECTIONS

Folk Music of Albania / TOPIC
Sandwiched between Yugoslavia and Greece, part Christian, part Muslim, Albania is a tiny land with a rich and ancient musical culture. Fine recordings by A. L. Lloyd of songs, dances, and instrumentals, among them bagpipe, flutes, and lutes. Given the country's beleaguered history, the vocals include many epic ballads old and new. –JSR

Marcel Cellier Presents Albanian Folklore / CELLIER
Another great project by the man who brought us the *Mystère des Voix Bulgares*. Twelve traditional selections for solo and group voices, flute, clarinet, and folk orchestras, with many interesting similarities to the music of Greece and neighboring Baltic countries. Recommended. –ROOTS & RHYTHM

Vocal & Instrumental Polyphony / CHANT DU MONDE
An absolutely stunning recording. Albanian singing (unlike Bulgarian, which is gorgeous but in the South Slav mainstream) really is mysterious. Very ancient — it's thought to trace right back to ancient Illyria — and individual, though with Islamic elements and occasional reminders of the Epirot idiom of North Greece (all the examples here are from the south). –JSR

ARMENIA

DJIVAN GASPERIAN

Traditional. Djivan Gasperian is a master performer on the duduk, a wooden reed instrument used in Eastern Europe and Turkey. His expressiveness and warm, rich tone have brought him international fame, and he has been honored as "People's Artist of the Republic" in Armenia. –MB

☆ **I Will Not Be Sad in This World / OPAL**
These singularly beautiful pieces backed by a second duduk acting as a drone are, so to speak, meditations on folk themes rather than traditional performances. –JSR

ELIA PEHLIVANIAN

Traditional.
○ **Traditional Music of Armenia - Kanon / BUDA**
The kanon is a 72-string plucked zither which functions as a piano throughout the Arab world. –ROOTS & RHYTHM

ARMENIA COLLECTIONS

Armenia 1 ... / OCORA
Armenia 1 - Liturgical Songs & Instrumental Music. Reissue of two Ocora albums of Armenian music. The first half is devoted to stark Christian hymns from the medieval period. The initial eight selections feature early male choir works with haunting two-part melodies that are profoundly affective, but the following six solo voice pieces are less pleasing. After the final contemporary mixed chorus piece we move on to the instrumental portion of the disc, which showcases ten solo, duo, and small-group settings of modern social music on traditional instruments. As is the case with the music of neighboring Iran and Turkey, a rich confluence of Arabic, Oriental, and eastern European influences is extant here, and the variety of styles is astounding. My particular favorites are the introspective duets for fiddle and recorder, but all tracks are worthwhile, making the second half a satisfying conclusion to this eclectic 72-minute program. –MYLES BOISEN, ROOTS & RHYTHM

AUSTRIA COLLECTIONS

Austrian Folk Music - Vols. 1 & 2 / ARHOOLIE
Austrian Zither / PLAYASOUND
Twenty-two zither zingers with a distinctive alpine flavor, including Anton Karas's "Harry Lime Theme" played by J. C. Ollier-Urfer. –MYLES BOISEN, ROOTS & RHYTHM
Bavarian Yodeling Songs & Polkas / OLYMPIC
○ **Lieder u. Jodler aus den Bergen / KOCH**
Alpine yodeling is one of humanity's most remarkable vocal techniques, and commercial "Jodlerlieder" are worthy of much more attention than they get. Some of the best stuff is on ill-documented collections like this one, which mixes some outstanding "Jodler" with pretty zither playing. –JSR
○ **Zither-Perlen / KOCH**
Why does the Austrian zither get so little respect? It's not raunchy, but neither is the Finnish kantele. Its players don't improvise, but the world is full of non-improvised traditional music. Is it *The Third Man*? or those leather shorts? Anyway, here for the contrarian is a disc-full of a neglected European instrumental tradition. (37:53) –JSR

BOSNIA HERCEGOVINA

KALESIJSKI ZVUCI

Bosnian.
○ **Bosnian Breakdown / GLOBESTYLE**   1991
A wild mix of Turkish, Gypsy, shepherd, and polka music with violin, accordion, and folk guitar. Electric bass and drum kit update adds to the off-kilter feel of traditional festival songs with roots in an ancient civilization. –BT

BULGARIA

MYSTÈRE DES VOIX BULGARES   d

Bulgarian. The Mysterious Voices of Bulgaria belong to the National Radio and Television Chorus, the premier women's choir popularized worldwide through the efforts of ethnomusicologist Marcel Cellier. His recordings, issued on various import labels before appearing on Nonesuch, made a big splash in Western Europe and the US, cultivating vast new audiences for the group's dramatic adaptations of folk singing styles. Their spine-chilling harmonies, punctuated by whoops and quavers, are presented in full choral arrangements and smaller groups — duos and trios — with and without instrumental backing. –MB
○ **Mystère des Voix Bulgares / NONESUCH**
This is the record that started the boom. An excellent introduction to this thrilling Bulgarian women's choir. –MB

MYSTÉRE DES VOIX BULGARES

Bulgarian.
Volume 2 / NONESUCH
Equal to the haunting beauty of the first volume. –MB
Volume 3 / POLYGRAM   1991
Still more ethereal choir work. All three volumes are consistently good. –MB
Bulgarian Polyphony - Vols. 1 & 2 / JVC
A two-part collection of sublime recordings by the *Mystère des Voix Bulgares* choir. –MB

IVO PAPASOV & HIS ORCHESTRA

Bulgarian. This very popular Bulgarian bandleader is a fierce clarinetist known for brilliant improvisations and blazing interpretations of all manner of Balkan melodies. His Bulgarian Wedding Band has caused a sensation, particularly among younger Bulgarians, with its blending of traditional music and high-octane Western rock, delivered at the upper limits of speed and volume. –MB
Orpheus Ascending / HANNIBAL   1989
An energetic debut of this thrilling Bulgarian clarinetist and wedding band leader. –MB

Bulgarian Music

Although the Bulgarian Mysterious Voices get all the publicity, there is a profusion of highly developed vocal and instrumental groups within the borders of Bulgaria. A number of ethnically and geographically distinct regions — Piron/Macedonia, Thrace, Rhodope, Shope, and others — boast their own village groups, heard on various compilations. And with heightened interest in the usual national folklore ensembles, plus the opening of borders in Eastern Europe, a new wave of recordings can be expected. Already many female and male choirs have entered the market, and classic recordings of the Philip Koutev folklore ensemble are being reissued. Wedding Band clarinetist Ivo Papasov (an ethnic Turk) has toured the US twice with his red-hot Wedding Band and his wife, a stunning vocalist in the traditional Thracian style. Complex rhythms and exotic instruments like the gaida (bagpipe), the gadulka (a primitive violin with droning strings), breathy kaval and ravalcheta flutes, the clarinet, accordion, and more, add to the appeal of the richly varied Bulgarian expression.

— Myles Boisen

☆ **Balkanology / HANNIBAL**   1991
This surpasses the *Orpheus Ascending* album on every count. Simply amazing. –MB

PIRIN ENSEMBLE

Traditional.
State Ens. for Folk Dances / BALKANTON   1990
Excellent one-hour CD of authentic Bulgarian music by the leading traditional folk music ensemble, led by long-time director and scholar Kiril Stefanov. Most of the 19 selections are vocal settings with instrumental accompaniment by kaval (flute), zurna (oboe), stringed instruments, etc. A must-have for pure folk enthusiasts. –MYLES BOISEN, ROOTS & RHYTHM

TRIO BULGARKA

Bulgarian.
○ **The Forest Is Crying / HANNIBAL**
Three women from the *Mystère des Voix Bulgares* choir singing their hearts out in varied groupings. –MB

BULGARIA COLLECTIONS

○ **Balkan - Mysterious Voices of Bulgaria / ATLANTIC**
Film soundtrack recordings, mostly original music, offering a departure from the *Mystère des Voix Bulgares* repertoire. –MB
○ **Bulgarian Musical Folklore / BALKANTON**
The Hungarians aside (most of the time), Eastern European record companies are vague to hopeless about distinguishing between genuine village music, more-or-less tarted-up People's Ensembles, and semi-folknik groups — which, of course, means that recordings like this are normally a very mixed bag. The balance on this particular CD is mostly tipped toward authenticity, and the variety is fine. There's some really super bagpipe and double-reed playing, and, though the singers are often a bit too professional, they all out-sing the overly hyped and wimpy Trio Bulgarka to a faretheewell. The notes are rotten on detail but somewhat informative in general. –JSR
○ **Bulgarian Village Singing ... / ROUNDER**   1990
In *Bulgarian Village Singing - Two Girls Started to Sing*, the roots of the commercially acclaimed Bulgarian "mystery" vocals are explored in this field recording of harvest, wedding, and ritual songs of remote villages. A vibrant document of a

vanishing musical form. Features extensive helpful liner notes. –BT

Folk Music of Bulgaria / TOPIC 1966
This release nicely complements the *Village Music of Bulgaria* album on Nonesuch Records and includes some other far-flung regions. –MB

In the Shadow of the Mountain ... / NONESUCH
In the Shadow of the Mountain: Bulgarian Folk Music - Pirin, Macedonia features excellent folk ensemble playing, dance music, and strong women singers. –DLM

○ **Macedonian Songs & Dances / NONESUCH**
A nice variety of singing, from solo to choirs, from the Turkish-influenced region of Pirin-Macedonia. –MB

○ **Music of Bulgaria - Balkana / HANNIBAL** 1987
Ten of Bulgaria's leading professional musicians illustrate the breadth of Bulgarian traditional music. Includes the unmistakable vocal sound of Trio Bulgarka and the exhilarating flute-and-bagpipe romps of Trakiiskata Troika (the Thracian Trio). –BT

☆ **Village & Folk Music of Bulgaria / NONESUCH**
Combining two of the best Nonesuch collections into one unbeatable folk music document. –MB

Village Music of Bulgaria ... / NONESUCH 1968
Recordings from four major Bulgarian regions, each with its own captivating style of singing and accompaniment, are featured on this album, *Village Music of Bulgaria - A Harvest, a Shepherd, a Bride*. This is the real thing. –MB

BYELORUSSIA COLLECTIONS

Byelorussia / AUVIDIS
This wonderful recording covers a relatively small area, but a particularly rich one. The extraordinary Slavic contrapuntal choral music is there in pure form, along with other songs, plus fiddle, pipe, and other instrumentals. –JSR

CYRPUS COLLECTIONS

○ **Folk Music of Cyprus / LYRICHORD**
Music of the Greek, Turkish, and Maronite communities. The major traditions, Greek and Turkish, exist separately in Cyprus, each with links to its metropole. But each has distinctly Cypriot elements and a considerable amount of common ground (as indeed is true of Greece and Turkey). Fine recordings by Wolf Dietrich, with scruffily reproduced but adequate notes. –JSR

CZECHOSLOVAKIA COLLECTIONS

Czechoslovakia / PLANETT
Kind of a generic release, as you'll gather from the fact that it really has no discernible title. But the music is nice enough. What you get is a series of regional groups and singers that smack overmuch of your standard over-arranged National Folk Ensemble but which contain some signs of local roots. Among them are some more-than-just-agreeable performances. It badly needs a few rude boors to give it more zip and vulgarity, but it's very amiable. (55:12). –JSR

Songs & Dances from Czechoslovakia / ARGO ZFB
Panpipes, fiddles, string orchestras, and vocals — interesting selection. –DLM

FINLAND

KONSTA JYLHA

Finland.
Master Fiddler / FINNISH FOLKMUSIC INSTITUTE
Jylha became an icon of the Finnish folk revival. A fiddler whose groups also played popular music for village hops, he was both authentic and versatile. Side 1 is devoted to superlative traditional playing backed by accordion. Side 2, a 1971 concert, has fine but more familiar playing. –JSR

PIIRPAUKE

Finland.
○ **Algazara / ROCKADILLO**
An excellent group performing imaginative arrangements of a wide variety of tunes stemming from different ethnic sources. –ROOTS & RHYTHM

FORMER SOVIET REPUBLICS COLLECTIONS

Journey to the USSR / CHANT DU MONDE
Unparalleled in their scope, the six CDs in this collection cover both instrumental and vocal music in, respectively (and at times illogically), Russia, Ukraine, and Bielorussia; Uzbekistan (!); Kirghizistan, Azerbaijan, and Turmenistan; North Caucasus; the Volga/Urals region; and Siberia. The musical range is just as wide: from wonderful, authentic music to the kind of pseudo-folk ensemble ruined by unsuitable arrangements from some party hack of a third-rate composer. Worth it, though, for the good stuff. –JSR

☆ **Musics of the Soviet Union / SMITHSONIAN**
A superb sampler of traditional regional styles covering many of the significant republics. The uniformly genuine quality makes this highly commendable. A fine overview with good non-academic notes. –MB & DLM

FRANCE COLLECTIONS

☆ **Chansons de la Belle Époque / MUSIC MEMORIA**
France's Cafe Concert style under its various names was as rooted in the urban working class as in English music hall, but it reached further into cafe society and produced international stars as the London music hall never did. Here are some great early moments — major stars like Yvette Guilbert and Mistinguett and huge hits like Bruant's original "Auprès de Ma Blonde," but mostly earlier and more obscure names like Paul Lack, who influenced Chevalier and Felix Mayol (a song about the *maxixe*, a Brazilian dance introduced at the same time as the tango but without the staying power). Rotten notes. (57:39) –JSR

○ **Corsica - Religious Music ... / AUVIDIS** 1989
Among the most neglected of idioms are the oral religious traditions of Europe, and particularly western Europe. *Corsica - Religious Music of the Oral Tradition* offers recordings of an ancient polyphonic church style from the remote village of Rusiu that are probably unique: certainly I know nothing quite like them (some Sardinian singing is loosely similar). The outstanding a cappella music is backed by outstanding notes. –JSR

Grand Bal Folk / HEXAGONE
A wonderful collection of traditional French dance music performed by four of France's best folk groups in the 70s — La Bamboche, Malicorne, Le Grand Rouge, and La Chiffonie. A delightful collection of bourrées, branles, marches, waltzes, among others, played on guitars, accordions, hurdy gurdies, bagpipes, dulcimer, fiddle, etc. –FRANK SCOTT, ROOTS & RHYTHM

Songs & Dances of Corrèze / ARION
Corrèze lies in the isolated Massif Central, and its dances are typical of heartland French tradition. The dance-oriented notes (French only) include an illustration of the basic steps of the bourrée as well as descriptions of the polka piquée, the demi-valse, various bourrées, and many other dances played by a local bagpipe and fiddle band that has the real sound. –JSR

GEORGIA

RUSTAVI CHOIR

Georgian choir. The Rustavi Choir is an all-male vocal group, the best known of the many ensembles now active in the Georgian Republic (formerly USSR). Their traditional repertoire encompasses many Georgian regions and is largely polyphonic, with rich intertwining melodic lines and dramatic vocal effects. —MB

○ **Georgian Voices / ELEKTRA** 1989
A soulful representation of the distinctive Georgian vocal chorus sound. Similar to Bulgarian music, with a different sense of drama. —MB

GEORGIA COLLECTIONS

Georgia 1 / BARENREITER
Polyphonic religious music with surprising and strange harmonies: "yodeling." Beautiful music. —DLM

Georgia Work Songs and Religious Songs / OCORA
Georgia is home to ancient polyphonic traditions and an epicenter where ancient Asian and southern European cultures met. It has also benefited from considerable isolation: one amazing, hocketed piece here is sung only in one village! This is an essential and often eerily beautiful recording. —DLM

The Marvels of Polyphony in Sakartvelo / JVC
I picked up this CD upon a friend's insistence that the finest vocal music in the world comes from Soviet Georgia (in the Caucasus mountain range, bordering on Turkey and the Black Sea). Inside the vague Japanese packaging, I was most pleased to find 15 live recordings of truly unforgettable choral music. The first half presents nicely varied female ensemble pieces, some in Western hymn style, others in a more Eastern European "mysterious voices" mode. More remarkable are the male choir works which follow — a potent combination of modern and ancient harmonies, uniquely layered rhythms, and some very robust singing. Incorporated in many of these pieces is an unparalleled yodeling style; also heard is a small amount of applause and noise from the audience, who are unable to control their enthusiasm at a few points. Get this one and you may have a few uncontrolled outbursts of your own! CD only, 48 minutes long. —MYLES BOISEN, ROOTS & RHYTHM

GERMANY COLLECTIONS

German Drinking Songs / BESCOL
Octoberfest / PRO ARTE

GREECE

SOTIRIA BELLOU

Rembetiko.
☆ **Sotiria Bellou / MARGO**
Fourteen vintage recordings by one of the most highly regarded female rembetiko singers. A+ rating. —ROOTS & RHYTHM

40 Sotiria Bellou / LYRA 1988
Nineteen selections by this rembetika star, commemorating her 40 years as a renowned singer. The sound is very good, which leads me to believe that these must be recent, instead of "vintage," recordings. Compared to her more impassioned early songs the material is a little on the light and delicate side, but even if this CD doesn't persuade you to make a marathon run to the bottom of a bottle of ouzo it's still a great rembetika without the scratches and grit. An important contribution to the small world of authentic Greek music on CD. —MYLES BOISEN, ROOTS & RHYTHM

GEORGE DALARAS

Rembetiko.
Fifty Years of Rembetika Songs / MINOS
Recent recordings of 19 rembetika songs, totaling 68 minutes. Although the title implies that Mr. Dalaras is a venerable rembete, his clear and supple voice leads one to believe that he is a newcomer, providing us with updated versions of a half century of classic pieces by Tsitsanis, Tountas, and others. As a "revivalist" work it is quite good (although I'm sure that purists hate this sort of thing), conveying much of the feeling and form of the old songs by way of the clean and simple studio recording. The arrangements are played expertly in the lilting, yet mournful Greek manner, and Dalaras's voice is

European Music

As the small list here suggests (even allowing for the fact that Great Britain and Ireland are taken care of in the Celtic and British Isles section), the reaction against Euro-centrism can go too far. True, Eastern Europe has recently been "discovered," with much harrumphing from the marketing departments, but even here the proportion of derivative to authentic is notably out of whack. But the traditional music of western Europe is not only extraordinarily varied (perhaps most startlingly so in the case of Italy), but much of it formed the other major root of New World styles of all kinds. Spain isn't so badly off, though the focus is exclusively on flamenco. Portugal is beginning to surface. Greece is beginning to take an interest in its roots. But the rest is — almost everywhere — silence. While there are plenty of revivalists, less than a dozen recordings of true traditional French singers ever existed and all but two are now deleted. Germany is not so badly off, thanks only to an active regional commercial industry: German ethnomusicologists no sooner hatch than they fly south to Africa and beyond, like so many geese in winter.

— John Storm Roberts

plaintive and technically precise. His only shortcoming is that he fails to deliver the soulful passion that the "golden age" singers possessed, in this praiseworthy effort to keep their music alive. —MYLES BOISEN, ROOTS & RHYTHM

KALAMATIANA/SYRTA

Traditional.
☆ **Kalamatiana/Syrta / EMI**
EMI's huge Demotic Anthology was a treasury and it's wonderful to see a CD version starting. These were not village recordings but very fine performances by professionals close to the roots, with traditional backings. Among those splendidly present are singers Iota Lidia, Rosa Abatsi, Yoryos Nakos (superb, underrated), Papasideres, and clarinetists Karakostas and Malliaras. —JSR

IOTA LIDIA

Popular.
○ **Mega Souxe / EMI**
Lidia was at her considerable peak in the urban music called laika and the country-based dimotika, which varied as much as anything in their instrumentation (bouzouki + accordion equals laika, clarinet + fiddle equals dimotika, in a justified oversimplification). The songs here, of whatever idiom, are gems of the point where Europe and the Middle East intersected. I have a passion for the more Eastern rhythms of Lidia. A superb CD. —JSR

IORGOS MANGAS

Traditional.
○ **Iorgos Mangas / GLOBESTYLE**
Mangas is a fine clarinetist in the dimotiki tradition, which long since left the villages to play a role more like US "country" music. His first solo album is a fusion music with accordion from the urban laika style, various traditional instruments, electric guitar from the pop idiom, and rembetika touches. It's not a new mix, but this band does it well. —JSR

POLY PANOU

○ **Mega Souxe / EMI**
By Panou's time, the earlier styles of laika and dimotiki had

coalesced into something mainstream but still very Greek. Panou out-sings Lidia by a hair on this superb CD. –JSR

BASSILES PERPINIADES

Rembetiko.

○ **Bassiles Perpiniades / MARGO**
Fourteen selections by a bouzouki performer, on the acclaimed Margo rembetiko series. –ROOTS & RHYTHM

MIKIS THEODORAKIS

Traditional.

Canto General / MINOS
Large-scale work by Theodorakis, which sets the poems of Pablo Neruda to an orchestral score. Complete version, recorded live in Germany with the Stockholm Orchestra, St. Jakob's Chorus, and featured vocalists Maria Farandouri and Petros Pandis. –MYLES BOISEN, ROOTS & RHYTHM

VASILLIS TSITSANIS

Traditional.

Concert at Herakleio Crete / MINOS
Thirty-two songs recorded live (no date given) by a legendary and popular singer. –MYLES BOISEN, ROOTS & RHYTHM

IORDANIS TSOMIDIS

Traditional.

Bouzoukee: The Music of Greece / NONESUCH
Flashy fretwork with an old-fashioned group. –MB

THEODORE VASSILIKOS & ENSEMBLE

Sacred.

Great Epochs of Sacred Byzantine Chant / OCORA
The exquisite vocal blending of Theodore Vassilikos's male choir brings ancient Greek Orthodox hymns to life again, and the effect is unforgettable. Vassilikos has taken great care in researching Byzantine sacred music of the 14th to 18th centuries, successfully re-creating not only the authentic sound but also the undying spiritual potency residing within the eight chants on this maximum-length CD. While the use of limited intervals and monody (single melody lines) invites comparison to Gregorian chant, the liberal use of ornamentation is distinctively Greek. This decoration of melody gives the music a complex internal structure that captivates the ear and leads the willing listener into a trance-like state. Ocora continues to impress me with the quality and scope of their releases, and this work of solemn beauty is among their finest. Superb digital recording, with informative booklet. –MYLES BOISEN, ROOTS & RHYTHM

S. XARCHAKOS & N. GATSOS

Rembetiko.

Rembetiko / CBS
CD contains 13 of the songs issued on the Greek import two-LP set. Excellent contemporary Greek music. –ROOTS & RHYTHM

Y. XINTARIS & Y. SARRIS

Rembetiko.

Songs from the "Dawn Song in the Minor" / MINOS
Contemporary rembetika from this Greek TV series — 23 selections by Tsisanis, Vamvakaris, and others, performed by modern ensemble. –MYLES BOISEN, ROOTS & RHYTHM

GREECE COLLECTIONS

☆ **Folk Music of Greece / TOPIC**
Rural Greek music is commonly divided into the Mountains and the Islands. This collection opens with a variety of mainland music, including some splendid clarinet as well as the usual impassioned and highly decorated vocals. The second side focuses on the very different styles of the Aegean

Isles, stressing fiddle and lute as well as the ancient Balkan bagpipe. Good notes; great music. –JSR

Greece: Chansons et Danses Populaires / VDE   1991
A lovely collection of traditional music from various parts of Greece, recorded between 1930 and 1959 by ethnomusicologist Samuel Baud-Bovy. There are six performances recorded in 1930 in the Dodecanese Islands including lyra and lauto instrumental duets, a couple of gorgeous duet vocals, and a couple of solo vocals. There are 16 performances recorded in Crete in 1954, featuring a wide range of vocal and instrumental music. Finally there are seven tracks recorded in continental Greece between 1930 and 1959, including solo vocals and instrumental performances on flute, clarinet, and lute. Sound is excellent, even on the earliest recordings. The booklet, with notes in English and French, has extensive information on the source of the recordings, background to the music, and a discussion of every track, and there are a handful of wonderful photos. –ROOTS & RHYTHM

Greece Is ... Magic / FALIREAS BROTHERS   1989
Ok, so this looks like a tacky "tourist" item, there's hardly any English info on the thing, and it's expensive. But in spite of being a merchandising failure, this CD contains 13 examples of *the* most soulful modern Greek music I've ever heard — the kind of passionate tunes that make you want to soak up ouzo like a sponge and smash glasses 'til dawn. The heartfelt sounds of violin, accordion, 'ud, bouzouki, and an abundance of mournful clarinet dominate the instrumental landscape, with just one powerful vocal number starting off the program. I believe these recordings (all done in the studio) come from the Greek AF label; clarinet legend Yiorgos Mangas is included, as well as samples from a gorgeous AF record of Byzantine music. I'm not sure about the origin of the rest, but every one is a gem, the variety of styles is captivating, and I'll bet my last drachma that you'll be yelling for more when this hour-long disc is done. –MYLES BOISEN, ROOTS & RHYTHM

☆ **Greek-Oriental Rembetika / FOLKLYRIC**
A wonderful introduction to one of the great 20th-century urban musics. Not only does it include both famous names (Papasideris and Abatsi, who are widely reissued elsewhere) and names otherwise entirely obscure, but it has excellent notes in English. It's even more important now that the Greek EMI recordings have become so hard to find. –JSR

Kassatina / EMI
Greece has spawned a huge variety of rich musical expression, making the term "Greek music" (like African, Asian, or American music) an almost useless generalization. This Greek import disc graciously leads the listener into a rewarding in-depth examination of many traditional musics heard in Greece, still presenting only a fraction of the multitude of regional and historical styles. The respected scholar Alain Danielou has assembled 14 top-quality selections recorded in seven isolated areas where the native traditions have been preserved more-or-less intact. Follow him to Epirus, Macedonia, the Peloponnese, Thrace, the island of Crete, and farther east into present-day Turkey, in search of some of the most distinctive instrumental work and plaintive singing heard anywhere in the Mediterranean. Good recordings, and the notes, though not long-winded, are extremely informative. Essential. –ROOTS & RHYTHM

Clarinet Virtuosi of Greece / DISQUES CELLIER   1980
Traditional clarinet field recordings. –MB

☆ **Rembetica / ROUNDER**
A welcome collection, especially since the Folklyric LP is now history. I do have some musical and conceptual cavils, but each is more than balanced by a strength. Some of the cuts are far from their singers' best, and the Papaioannis piece is plain unworthy. But there's a great deal of fine music from unfamiliar as well as familiar artists (including the first recorded bousouki solo — check out the "Moonlight Sonata" piano!). Anyway, how many CDs are 100% flawless? Buy it, enjoy. (65+ minutes) –JSR

○ **Rembetiko 1930-60 / MARGO**

Greek Music

The folk music of Greece is some of the most varied and sophisticated of any in the world, enriched by a multitude of modern and Hellenic cultures. Musical notation was used in Greece centuries before the birth of Christ, and these pieces have been dramatically revived on a French album entitled *Musique de la Grece Antique* (Hamonia Mundi 1015). From the dawn of the recording era, Greek folklore was documented on 78 RPM records. The most sought-after recordings from the period between the wars are in the *rembetiko* style. Rembetiko was the music of the rembetes, a poverty-stricken subculture who carried knives, ran afoul of the law, and took solace in drink, hashish, and soulful songs about their origins in western Turkey, across the Aegean Sea. This was the blues of Greece, sung in passionate, melancholy scales by men and women alike, accompanied by the 8-string bouqouki and sometimes a violin or other stringed instrument.

Like the blues music of the US, the character of rembetiko changed after WWII (outstanding early rembetiko collections have just come out on the Rounder and Arhoolie labels). It had become popular, even respectable, and was presented in the tavernas instead of the hash dens. This mass acceptance was followed inevitably by lighter renditions of the music at faster tempos; gradually the music of the underworld became slick, glitzy folk-pop, known as "laiki." In tavernas today (even in the US, where tight-knit communities abound), you can still hear echoes of rembetiko in the slow "zembekiko" dance, done usually by a lone man from the audience who turns slowly, lost in introspection, arms outstretched.

In this country, tavernas and the rare Greek gift-shop/grocery provide your best chances to learn about the music first-hand. The best folk-music recordings (or pop, for that matter) are not produced for English language consumers and are rarely found in mainstream stores. Used-record stores might yield the occasional gem, but beware of generic-looking albums with pictures of the Parthenon or polyester-clad bouzouki players on the cover. The American labels Nonesuch, Folkways, Peters/PI, and Olympic have issued good folk collections; recommended Greek labels include Intersound, AF, EMI, Columbia, Margo, Lyra, and Venus. If there is English writing, look for the words "Demotika" or "Ahmotika." Bouzouki collections often feature a mixture of rembetika, pop, and folk, with flashy fretwork guaranteed on at least a few cuts.

Genuine folk recordings often focus on a particular region, instrument, or dance style. Some of my favorite instruments are bagpipes, the bouzouki and other members of the string family, the accordion, and especially the clarinet (clarino), which takes on a fluid, vocal quality with dramatic leaps added for effect. Of course the vocalist's art is highly developed here; Greek singers have been breaking hearts for thousands of years! The proximity of Greece to Arabic and Balkan cultures endows even the roughest village music with the best of many worlds. Intense emotion, virtuosity, improvisation, swirling melodies, and unusual rhythms are plentiful.

Another musical resource is folk-dancing clubs, which can still be found scattered around college towns and major cities. Go there on Greek-dance nights to hear and learn the hassapiko (butcher's dance), zembekiko, tsifteteli (relative of the belly dance), syrtaki (from *Zorba the Greek*), the athletic tsamiko, and tricky odd-meter dances from the north, also common in Albania, Yugoslavia, and Bulgaria. And if all else fails, ask a Greek friend, or meet one — I have always found Greek people to be very friendly and more than willing to talk music with genuinely interested Americans.

Vitality, pride, and love of music seem to be part of the national character and can be found in abundance in even the most average Greek recordings, so don't be afraid to go shopping or take a chance — you'll be glad you did.

— Myles Boisen

Fourteen various rembetiko performers on an excellent reissue label. —ROOTS & RHYTHM
Rembetiko 1950-60 / MARGO
Fourteen more rembetiko songs. —ROOTS & RHYTHM
Soul Dances of the Greeks / PETERS
A sampler of favorite folk dance styles by a solid group. —MB
This Is the Best of Bouzouki / EMI   1981
Popular masters of the 8-string bouzouki. —MB

HUNGARY

KARIKAS EGYUTTES

Traditional. This six-person band combines strong throaty female vocals, often in unison duet, over a background of tamburas, citterns, and string bass, with lots of fiddle and some clarinet and Hungarian end-blown flute. The result is a powerful yet poignant sound, with a rhythmic drive that characterizes folk dance music. —ROOTS & RHYTHM
Ez A Vilag Olyan Vilag / RADIOTON
Highly recommended traditional album. —ROOTS & RHYTHM

KALYI JAG

Traditional.
Gypsy Folk Songs from Hungary / HUNGAROTON
Interesting and very listenable record of Hungarian Gypsy songs adapted for performance by the four young members of Kalyi Jag. Their approach to the Gypsy legacy is analogous to the treatment of folk material during the American folk music boom of the early 60s — to quote the liner notes, "the music they play is traditional, yet not quite: once folk music has been uprooted from the medium that produced and fosters it, once it is performed as an artistic production rather than used, it automatically alters, adjusting to its new (stage) function and setting." The end result is an album of 19 lovely vocal pieces, including energetic renditions of uniquely Gypsy singing techniques, with understated strings and percussion accompaniment. Compared to the field recordings I'm used to, these three men and one woman sound almost too polished, but this fine studio recording is sure to delight many of you, especially fans of European folk song. —ROOTS & RHYTHM

KOLINDA

Hungarian.
○ **Kolinda / HEXAGONE**   1978
A CD reissue of a 1978 album by a fine progressive Hungarian group. —ROOTS & RHYTHM
Kolinda / PAN   1987
A recent album. —ED

MUZSIKAS (MARTA SEBESTYEN)

Traditional. The diminutive Marta Sebestyen is a giant of Hungarian music leading the folk revival field, and also experimenting with pop forms. Her strong and expressive voice is often backed by the Muzsikas, a young group who have revived interest in a number of Hungarian ethnic styles with their energetic, traditional performances. Marta also records with other folkloric ensembles such as Vujicsics. –MB

Blues for Transylvania / HANNIBAL
Their second domestic release, also with Sebestyen, is part celebration and part commemoration of a troubled history. This recording explores the traditional music of the Romanian region of Transylvania (taken from Hungary after WWI). Even the fast and furious songs have a meditative quality. Another outstanding release from one of Europe's premier folk ensembles. –BT & MB

○ **Marta Sebestyen with Muzsikas / HANNIBAL**
A lovely solo effort by the premier Hungarian singer, once again with her performing group Muzsikas. –MB

☆ **Prisoner's Song / HANNIBAL** 1988
Dark and powerful statement of life in a Cold War climate, explored through traditional Hungarian songs and instruments. Marta Sebestyen's amazingly evocative voice connects with the medieval sound of the hurdy gurdy and the sting of Mihaly Sipos's Gypsy violin. –BT

VUJICSICS

Hungarian. Named after a popular Hungarian musicologist, Vujicsics is a group of schooled and professional musicial folklorists who concentrate on preserving the traditions of Serbia and Croatia (southern Hungary and Yugoslavia). They are highly regarded for their broad repertoire of collected songs and spirited performances with a variety of singers, including Marta Sebestyen. –MB

☆ **Vujicsics / HANNIBAL** 1988
Stunning instrumental wizardry and undiluted Slavic songs from southern Hungary. *Vujicsics* features Marta Sebestyen and others. –MB

Serbian Music ... / HANNIBAL 1989
Serbian Music from Southern Hungary is another landmark recording of vibrant Hungarian music from the Hannibal label. Vujicsics is a traditional music ensemble with roots in the leading Hungarian conservatories, but they sure don't sound like a bunch of scholars — this collection of songs and dance tunes will have you whirling so fast you just might lose your borscht if you're not careful. Technically their repertoire is not Hungarian but Serbian, belonging to a distinct ethnographic area spanning Hungary and Yugoslavia, with a slightly crazed sound relying on rapid tempos and odd rhythms. The presence of singer Marta Sebestyen (also with Muzsikas) is a bonus — add this to your must-have list! Twelve selections for concertina, accordion, bass, clarinet, flute, violin, guitar, vocals, and more. –ROOTS & RHYTHM

HUNGARY COLLECTIONS

Bukovinai Szekelyek ... / HUNGAROTON 1989
Bukovinai Szekelyek Magyarorszagon is a collection of Hungarian folk songs of the much-displaced Bukovinian Szekelys. These are not professional performances but field recordings of seven different women, most of them housewives, singing unaccompanied songs of lamentation, regret, disappointment, and displacement that date back almost two centuries. The performances are stark (solo voice) but conscientious, broken up only by occasional interludes by fiddler Laszlo Laszlo. The melodies and especially the lyrics are quite beautiful. A booklet is included containing background info, lyrics with translations, and written music of each song. –RUSS SCHOENWETTER, ROOTS & RHYTHM

Sandor Dioszegi: Valahol A Szivem Melyen / QUALITON
Various artists perform the popular songs and operetta selections of Hungarian composer Sandor Dioszegi on this tribute album. –ROOTS & RHYTHM

Gypsy Folk Songs / HUNGAROTON
Flamenco aside, genuine Gypsy music has not been much recorded, so this CD reissue of a wonderful — and long-vanished — double album is welcome indeed. This is Gypsy-to-Gypsy a cappella singing, as opposed to semi-pro village-hop, let alone Budapest-restaurant "Gypsy" groups. Particularly remarkable are examples with a specialized form of "double-bassing" mouth-music under a solo vocal. One hundred minutes of music are enriched by a thorough booklet of notes. –JSR

Sixth Hungarian Dance-House ... / HUNGAROTON 1989
Sixth Hungarian Dance-House Festival is a beautiful collection of Hungarian music recorded in 1987, featuring mostly young folk revivalists along with some traditional performers. Lots of that distinctive fiddle and bowed bass sound that is so appealing in Hungarian music plus some fine bagpipe playing, flute, and some wonderful singing, including a powerful performance by Balazs Nagy with the Taltos Ensemble and an unaccompanied lullaby by the incomparable Marta Sebestyen. –ROOTS & RHYTHM

☆ **Szatmári Bandák / HUNGAROTON**
Four local Gypsy string bands from Hungary's northeastern Szatmár region, an area with a particularly rich but rapidly disappearing musical tradition. Perhaps the most fascinating cuts are old Hungarian Jewish tunes preserved by the Gypsies, but all of this is outstanding in the semi-professional vein of many Gypsy musicians — musically skilled but down-to-earth and locally rooted. Very thorough notes in English. (53+ minutes) –JSR

ITALY

I GIULLARI DI PIAZZA

Traditional.
Dea Fortuna / SHANACHIE
Subtitled "Traditional Italian Folk Music and Theatre." A company of musicians, actors, singers, and dancers reviving theatrical and musical traditions of southern Italy, attempting to recreate the atmosphere of the Italian town square. Here they lead us through an enticing program of traditional and adapted antique rituals, love songs, chants, and exorcisms dating back as far as the 13th century and beyond. This recording is quaint, and slightly menacing. –RUSS SCHOENWETTER, ROOTS & RHYTHM

RITMIA

Progressive folk.
Perhaps the Sea / SHANACHIE
Fantastic! Ritmia is an enormously talented new quartet from Italy, whose music is firmly rooted in pan-European instrumental folk music but also strikingly progressive in the most positive sense. Using mostly acoustic instruments (guitars, reeds, small drums, accordion) and tastefully understated pop technology (electric bass and guitar, and very subtle synthesizer) they have constructed four intricate suites, which are completely spell-binding, full of heart and humor, and refreshingly original without ever sounding contrived or trendy. Atop this lush soundscape are set four impressionistic short poems (in Italian), which add texture to the music, but never intrude or distract. This is one of those rare finds that commands your attention as soon as the needle drops and satisfies all the way through; a seamless debut album with profound depth, promising many rewarding listenings to come. –ROOTS & RHYTHM

ITALY COLLECTIONS

The Bagpipe in Italy / LYRICHORD
Bagpipes, of course, are extraordinarily widespread throughout the world. But Italy, it's fair to say, is not one of the areas most buffs would identify as pipes heaven. Wrong, as this album licensed from the superb Italian Albatros collection reveals. Here are pipes small and pipes huge, mostly from the Mezzogiorno, but including two examples from the

north and one from Zardinia. Also included are low-tech but thorough photocopied notes, a big plus. −JSR

☆ **Folk Music of Calabria / MUSICAPHON**
The new Musicaphon CDs are all remarkable for the quality of their documentation (here, a 70-page English booklet filled with photos as well as admirable text). This one is also the most remarkable so far for the quality of its material. Italian traditional music, with its range of influences from French to Berber, is staggeringly rich and varied. That Calabria — the toe of the Italian boot — is as rich as any, the music here amply proves. Extraordinary bagpipe music, ancient and magnificent polyphonic singing, accordion, shepherd's pipe, on and stunningly on. (68+ minutes) −JSR

Italian Folk Music - Vol. 1 ... / FOLKWAYS
Italian Folk Music - Vol. 1 (Piedmont, Emelia, Lombardy) features nice songs and small instrumental ensembles with clarinets, accordion. −DLM

○ **Polyphonies of Sardinia / CHANT DU MONDE**
If Italian traditional music is the richest in western Europe, Sardinian is some of the most extraordinary, with Arabic and ancient Berber as well as mainland influences. Except for one track, the music here is an amazing four-voice a cappella polyphonic idiom with an improvising lead on a two-voice bass of extraordinary deep vocalizations unlike anything I have heard from Europe or the Mediterranean. The last track is a more orthodox song to guitar and jaw-harp. The effect of this interpolation is a little odd: I could have used either more variety or a total concentration on the one form. −JSR

Sicily / ARGO ZFB
Short selections but great variety of folk music, some surprising and raucous, some plaintive and charming. −DLM

LATVIA

THE LATVIAN WOMEN'S CHOIR

Choral.
○ **Dzintars: Songs of Amber / RYKODISC**   1983
Gorgeous-sounding 76-member choir performs unexpectedly avant-garde compositions as well as traditional Latvian, Russian, and Yiddish songs. Stately rather than rootsy. Produced by the Grateful Dead's Mickey Hart. −BT

NORWAY

VIOLA LEE

Traditional.
Old Time Dance Music from Norway / BENJAR

SVEN NYHUS

Traditional.
Norwegian Fiddling / SHANACHIE

MARI BOINE PERSEN

Traditional. Persen began her musical career singing about the trials of the Lappish people, who have been rapidly assimilated into other Scandinavian cultures. She still gives voice to protest, keeping homeland issues and music alive with a fusion of traditional and contemporary folk music popular throughout the region. −MB

☆ **Gula Gula / REAL WORLD**   1989
Bone-chilling vocals power this contemporary adaptation of traditional songs from Lapland. Stark, but seductive. −MB

POLAND

KURPIANKA

Polish.
Kurpianka / POLSKIE NAGRANIA
Polish folk songs for weddings and dances. −ROOTS & RHYTHM

RENATA & GIRLS

Polish.
○ **Tickled Pink / ALEATORIC**
Renata Romanek and her all-woman band does old-fashioned polkas American-style. −ROOTS & RHYTHM

SLASK STATE FOLK BALLET ENSEMBLE

Traditional.
Christmas in Poland / MONITOR
Slask State Folk Ballet - Vols. 1 & 2 / MONITOR

WOJTASIAK & KMIECIK ORCHESTRA

Traditional.
Journey into Poland / MONITOR

POLAND COLLECTIONS
Evening at a Polish Tavern / APON
Polkas, waltzes, songs. −ED

PORTUGAL

FRANCISCO FIALHO

Fado.
Best of Fado / ARC MUSIC
It isn't that, of course, but Fialho is a really fine singer in the somewhat starker Coimbra vein, and the duo backing (Alfredo Marceneiro and Fernando Farinha) are also right on the money. Lots of saudade and all the fixings, in fact. −JSR

FERNANDA MARIA

Fado.
Fado ... Fados! / ARION
One of the younger artists in the pure Lisbon fado vein, Fernanda Maria adds to the traditional saudade a predilection for more uptempo numbers, sometimes accompanied by accordion and/or triangle as well as the classic guitars of fado itself. Ever less Lisbon fado being available, this is one to celebrate. −JSR

CARLOS PAREDES

Instrumental. The Portuguese guitar is a 12-string instrument with double courses (string pairs) and a small body, similar in tone to the mandolin or Greek bouzouki. Its penetrating sound is championed by Carlos Paredes, a sensitive, even shy performer who balances tradition and spontaneous invention. His original approach was likened to the freshness of Ornette Coleman by bassist Charlie Haden, who is himself a minor cultural hero in Portugal. −MB

Guitarra Portuguesa / ELEKTRA
The old-fashioned crystalline beauty of this instrument has made Paredes an overnight sensation. −MB

○ **Dialogues / ANTILLES**   1990
A collaboration with jazz bassist Charlie Haden. A marvel of sensitive string playing. −MB

AMALIA RODRIGUES

Fado.
☆ **Fados e Guitarradas / FESTIVAL**
Almost all of Amalia Rodrigues's greatest recordings were made during the 78 RPM era when she was a purely national treasure. Many have disappeared, but some of the best are available on a French release with gorgeous packaging but no notes beyond the titles, lengths, and composers. The CD version consists of only one of the LPs in the vinyl set. Still, here are some of the great moments in 20th century urban popular music. −JSR

FERNANDO MACHADO SOARES

Fado.
Coimbra Fado / OCORA
Coimbra fado, for centuries the heritage of that city's university students, has a pure and impassioned classicism unique in my experience. Vocals and guitar backings are both ravishing beyond my power to describe or even suggest. The fact that this is the only example available is, to my mind, proof positive of the doctrine of the Cosmic Fall. (57:04) –JSR

PORTUGAL COLLECTIONS

Anthology of Portuguese Music / FOLKWAYS
Nice, simple, and heartfelt songs sung by various women, as well as instrumental music –DLM
Portuguese String Music / HERITAGE
Lovely instrumental music from various string bands emerging from the Portuguese traditions of choros, fados, and Cape Verde Creole music. The earliest selections are four splendid choros from the Bahia region of Brazil, from 1908, with two featuring charming flute, guitar, and cavaquinho (or ukelele), and two lively "tangos" on mandolin and guitar. The eight Portuguese tunes are instrumental variations on popular fados from 1926 to 1929, played on guitar and lute, with those of João de Mates, Eduardo Alves, and Ricardo Borges de Sousa especially lilting and sensuous. Finally, four fiery fiddle, guitar, and cavaquinho pieces from Cape Verde Creoles recorded in the US in the 30s round out this eye-opening and very welcome release. Now for some Portuguese vocal music. –JOHN MCCORD, ROOTS & RHYTHM
Portuguese Traditional Music / AUVIDIS
Seventeen selections from four different areas of Portugal — the provinces of Beira Baixa, Alentejo, and Douro Littoral, and fados from Lisbon. –ROOTS & RHYTHM

ROMANIA

DUMITRU FARCAS & MARCEL CELLIER

Instrumental.
Taragot and Organ / CELLIER
Excellent album of pastoral improvisations on Romanian themes, featuring the elegant sounds of the taragot, an archaic cousin of the clarinet and oboe, accompanied by pipe organ. Superb recording — nine pieces. –ROOTS & RHYTHM

SANDOR FODOR

Popular.
○ **Hungarian Folk from Transylvania / HUNGAROTON**
The toughest thing to find is music falling between the pure field-recording and the neo-folk music of Muszikas and their ilk. Fodor is a superb example of a regional semi-professional, a man of regional fame with far more technical skill than village musicians. He and his string band play wonderful dance music, with Romanian, Hungarian, and Gypsy influences. –JSR

SZÁZCSÁVÁS BAND

Traditional.
○ **Folk Music from Transylvania / QUINTANA**
The Szászcsávás Band is a Gypsy orchestra from a village of some 900 souls. This group plays local dance music of a high order, but still the kind of small string band that plays the village hops. Wonderful music, the rich result of Romanian, Hungarian and Gypsy interpenetration. (64+ minutes) –JSR

THE TARAF OF CLEJANI

Romanian Gypsy.
○ **Roumania - Music of the Tziganes / OCORA**
Superlative CD featuring Gypsy sextet of Tziganes from Clejani in Romanian Wallachia. –MYLES BOISEN, ROOTS & RHYTHM

TINTERETULUI DIN BUCHUESTI/JULII SIBIULUI

Romania.
Folk Ensemble / VIVACE
Not village music, but firmly based on it — Tinteretului Din Buchuesti Ensemble, the first group here, which has most of this compact disc to itself, is a hell-for-leather ensemble with a lot of demon accordion and pipe-playing; it will, in the old Romanian expression, knock your socks off. The Julii Sibiului group is only marginally more polished and less high-energy. I have no idea what place these people have in the Romanian musical scheme, but I'm for it. No notes. (48:09) –JSR

ROMANIA COLLECTIONS

○ **Reflections of Romania ... / NONESUCH**
Reflections of Romania - Village & Urban Folk Traditions combines the best this musically rich country has to offer — rough Gypsy peasant songs contrasted with polished ensemble work. –MB
Romania: Transylvania / OCORA
A wide-ranging survey of musical folklore from the Transylvanian region of Romania, collected during the 70s. Every one of these selections is a genuine, and often surprisingly primitive, example of peasant music. The emphasis here is on solo vocals, vocal ensembles, flute music, and tarafs — small ensembles, primarily of Gypsy origin, which feature violin as the lead instrument. Although the recording quality is inconsistent and somewhat distracting from one cut to the next, the variety and potency of the pieces are more than sufficient to hold one's attention throughout the 20-track, 50-minute program. A must for those who lust after the pure untainted folk sound from Drac's backyard. –MYLES BOISEN, ROOTS & RHYTHM
Romania: Village Music - Oltenia / VDE   1991
Rough but potent folkloric recordings from the Constantin Brailoiu collection, recorded by Braliloiu and his assistants between 1933 and 1943. Featured are 23 selections of authentic peasant music from the province of Oltenia, where Gypsy traditions enrich the performance of ancient long songs, dance music, and ceremonial music. Many vocal selections, and some remarkable work on flute and string instruments. –MYLES BOISEN, ROOTS & RHYTHM
○ **Roumanian Songs and Dances / PLAYASOUND**
This album is a well-rounded and truly inspired compilation of traditional music. –MYLES BOISEN, ROOTS & RHYTHM
○ **Transylvanian Folk Music / FONTI MUSICALI**
Like many relatively isolated out-groups, the Hungarian minority of Romania preserved forms often lost in Hungary itself. This is a rich, varied, admirably recorded collection of music ranging from solo voice to small dance band. The standard of playing is remarkable. What isn't clear is the provenance of the performers, though (given that one of the singers is Marta Sebestyen) it's pretty clear these weren't recordings made in situ. –JSR

RUSSIA

VALIA DIMITRIEVITCH & ALIOCHA

Gypsy.
○ **The Russian Gypsies / DISC AZ**
Russian Gypsy music — 12 by Valia and Aliocha, and 8 from the Matrioschka Ensemble. –ROOTS & RHYTHM

DMITRI POKROVSKY ENSEMBLE

Traditional.
The Wild Field / REAL WORLD
A thrilling project, with an interesting story behind it. Pokrovsky's group is referred to here as a "living laboratory" — a hub of musicians and scientists who tested their theories about the dynamics of village life by touring outlying towns in the Russian countryside. A portion of the entrancing vocal

polyphony they picked up is enthusiastically performed here, without a hint of academic reserve. Robust men's choirs are followed by equally gutsy female solos, interspersed with small vocal groups and extracts of crazily swirling flute ensembles. A raucous mixed chorus ends this all-too-brief treasure chest on a high note, with a total of ten unique village songs. —MYLES BOISEN, ROOTS & RHYTHM

THE TEREM QUARTET

Neo-traditional.
○ **Terem / REAL WORLD**   1992
Quotes from Tchaikovsky share equal space with Gypsy melodies in this highly literate set of compositions by an ensemble of Russian folk instruments. The Quartet's eccentric approach transforms everything it touches into shades of humor and delight. —BT

RUSSIA COLLECTIONS

Music of the Tundra & Taiga / INEDIT
A rare collection of the music of Russian Asian groups, bordering on Mongolia: notably the Burait, but also Tungus, Yakuts, Nenets, and Nganasans. Some of the vocal styles are extremely impressive, but the most extraordinary cuts are of jaw-harp playing, almost a parody of electronic music. This has been a very elusive release, but we hope less so in the future. (62:37) —JSR

Women's Songs from Old Russia / INEDIT
Songs, in fact, from the women's choirs of three villages, one in the far north, a second a little south of Moscow, and the third (settled by exiles) near Lake Baikal. As obvious as the common roots of this ancient idiom are the differences between the three groups. But, whatever the level of complexity, all are grassroots versions of the great Slavic choral sound. (54:57)   JSR

SCANDINAVIA COLLECTIONS

Nordic Folk Instruments / CAPRICE
The Nordic countries are — by northern European standards — remarkably rich in instrumental music. No fewer than 24 instruments, indigenous and naturalized, are presented in this admirable album, from the simple birchbark through flutes, fiddles, zithers, to accordions and guitar. A lavish illustrated booklet has an English translation. —JSR

SLOVENIA

SLAVKO AVSENIK

Traditional.
○ **Freude and Musik Mit ... / KOCH**
Avsenik's music — all of which is self-composed — is quite polished (though not too fancy), but I find the mix of accordion, clarinet, and oompah irresistible. A tuba does weird and wonderful things to a waltz. —JSR

SPAIN

JACINTO ALMADEN

Flamenco.
Cante Flamenco / FANDANGO   1989
Excellent singer (1899-1968), born Jacinto Antolin Gallego in Almaden, in the Cuidad Real mining province north of Cordoba. An admirer of Antonio Chacon, his strong suit was the Andalusian (non-Gypsy) cantes, especially malaguenas, tientos, marinetes, and mining cantes. With fine accompaniment from Pepe Badajoz and Melchor De Marchena, these 30s recordings have a haunting intensity that makes them extremely attractive. —JOHN MCCORD, ROOTS & RHYTHM

MANOLO CARACOL

Flamenco.
Manolo Caracol / FANDANGO   1989
Fine 30s and 40s recordings from this flamboyant Gypsy

singer, whose passionate voice led him to great popularity. Born Manuel Ortega in 1909 in Seville to a famed musical and bullfighting family, he won his first contest at 12, going on to fabulous and often extravagant success. A major contributor to the popularizing of "opera flamenco," he could still be one of the most intense singers of cante grande — the deepest form of flamenco singing — as these recordings show, as do his 1958 recordings with Melchor De Marchena (reissued on Le Chant Du Monde). Backed by Paco Aguilera, his treatment of seguriyas, alegrias, and bulerias is stunning. —JOHN MCCORD, ROOTS & RHYTHM

FERNANDA AND BERNARDA DE UTRERA

Flamenco.
Cante Flamenco / OCORA
Fernanda de Utrera emerged from the Andalucian heartland in 1959, acclaimed by many sound critics as the finest pure flamenco singer of her generation. Her younger sister, Bernarda, is regarded at least as highly. —DLM

THE GIPSY KINGS

Flamenco pop. The very popular Gipsy Kings developed out of the family group Los Reyes, led by patriarch José Reyes in the 70s and 80s. In 1983, they brought the sound of Spanish gypsy guitarists to the world as the Gipsy Kings, keeping their traditions intact on the first few releases. —MB

☆ **Gipsy Kings / ELEKTRA**   1988
Their US debut is an especially dynamic introduction to the sound of the Spanish Gypsy ensemble. —MB

Allegria / ELEKTRA   1989
This album features raw, early recordings from this Gypsy family. Very authentic. —MB

Luna de Fuego / PHILLIPS   1989
The Gipsy Kings had major crossover success last year with their splendid and innovative third album, which used drums, bass, percussion, and synthesizer to beef up the sound. This French import is their first album from 1983, and it is a much more traditional affair, with only acoustic guitars, voices, and hand claps. I feel that it shows that artistically the sound did not need to be beefed up; the music is still wonderful. How can an array of seven guitars and full-throated passion not be wonderful? Commercially, I can see how the additions to their sound helped break the Gipsy Kings through to a larger audience, but now that their name is known, I think it should be possible for more people to go back and appreciate this album. It is in no way crude or unpolished, and the artistry and playing are of an equally high quality. —ROOTS & RHYTHM

PEPE HABICHUELA

Flamenco.
○ **A Mandeli / HANNIBAL**
Guitarist Habichuela, born into a well-known flamenco clan in 1944, wears two hats. Under one, he is an eminent traditionally oriented guitarist. Under the other, he has recorded with Don Cherry and with North African musicians. Several tracks on this album are traditional: on others he works with electric bass, percussion, and even lute. Either way, he's dazzling. —JSR

KETAMA

Popular. This Spanish group consists of the brothers Carmona, their cousin Jose Miguel (son of the great flamenco artist, Pepe Habichuela) and Jose Soto, a leader of the "new flamenco" movement. —SWB

○ **Ketama / HANNIBAL**
The funk-fusion-flamenco of Ketama is by now a very well-established style. To the Andalucian root, this young trio adds Cuban and vaguely disco touches, but also what sound remarkably like Indian passages (presumably from lute, since there's no Indian instrument in the credits). I find the results

interesting but less than 100% successful — mostly because the flamenco underpinnings are hardly virtuosic. –JSR

CARMEN LINARES

Flamenco.

○ **La Luna en el Rio / AUVIDIS**
Example of "new flamenco." Linares, an important figure in the field, works with young new-wave flamenco musicians to mix fairly traditional singing with contemporary approaches to playing style, and at times lyrics from major poets living and dead. –JSR

LOS GITANILLOS DE CADIZ

Flamenco.

Los Gitanillos De Cadiz / FESTIVAL
An excellent troupe of young singers and dancers who reflect the transition from ethnic to popular music. Particularly interesting because they include lesser known traditional material along with the classic fandangos, seguidillas, etc., and also because they open (under the name rumba gitana), with one of the Cuban tunes that so influence younger flamenco artists. –JSR

ANTONIO MAIRENA

Flamenco.

Antonio Mairena / CHANT DU MONDE
Mairena, a member of Carmen Amaya's troupe, was also a traditionalist who fought to preserve the pure cante jondo form and even revived dying forms. If he lacked the fire of some of the great at their greatest, he had all their power and more than their consistency. Greatness, in fact, takes many forms. (60:40) –JSR

LA NIÑA DE PUEBLA   *b* 1909

Flamenco. Born in La Puebla de Cazalla, near Seville and named Dolores Jimenez Alcantara, Niña was blinded as a youth, turned to singing and made her debut in 1931.
–JOHN MCCORD, ROOTS & RHYTHM

Cante Flamenco / FANDANGO   1989
She specialized in cante chico styles like fandangos and zambras, some with popular influences, but all, like "Y No Llores como un Niño" and "Hiciste Sangre en Mis Labios," are quite intense, featuring her strong voice and trilling ululations, and fine backing by Manolo de Badajoz, Antonio Delgado, and Luis Yance. –JOHN MCCORD, ROOTS & RHYTHM

PASTORA PAVÓN

Flamenco.

☆ **La Niña de los Peines / CHANT DU MONDE**
○ **La Niña de los Peines / FANDANGO**   1989
Able to chant the most intense siguiriyas or bulerias or a frivolous cante chico with equal beauty and sublime originality, she casts a spell on these 30s recordings, aided by the guitars of Manalo de Badajoz and Melchor de Marchena, that is unforgettable. With no duplication of the Chant du Monde set and excellent sound, this is essential. –JOHN MCCORD, ROOTS & RHYTHM

PACO PENA

Flamenco.

Flamenco / POLYGRAM   1978
This 1971 recording shows instrumental flamenco in full and wonderful flower. (50:18). –JSR

PEPE PINTO

Flamenco.

Pepe Pinto / FANDANGO   1989
Pepe Pinto, born in 1903 in Seville, had a mellow singing voice which, along with his extensive repertoire and sense of

theater, made him quite popular, though a bit commercial in the 40s and 50s. Married to the great La Niña de los Peines, he performs here in a pure style, accompanied mostly by guitarist Melchor de Marchena, on these fine recordings from 1930-1946. –JOHN MCCORD, ROOTS & RHYTHM

NIÑO DE RICARDO

Flamenco.

Niño de Ricardo / CHANT DU MONDE
The superb guitarist I knew as Niño Ricardo without the "de" backed La Niña de los Peines (who sings on the last cut here) and other great singers of the 30s. This set was almost all recorded in the mid 50s when he took up solo playing late in life, when guitarists began to move out from under the vocals. (59:25) –JSR

RUMBA POP

Pop.

Bailaras Con Alegria / POLYGRAM
Two men, two women, and a lot of chutzpah make up Rumba Pop, which might also be called Hispa-rock. Some of these songs were once salsa, others Spanish, others who knows? A group setting scratch against flamenco clapping, not to mention guitar rock and guitar Spanish, and melodies Spanish, rock, *and* Colombian, is well worth the boggle! –JSR

JUANITO VAREA

Flamenco.

Juanito Varea / FANDANGO   1989
Born in Castellon province north of Valencia in 1908, he grew up near Barcelona with Gypsies, from whom he learned the intense style of singing that he sang until his death in 1985. Performing in the "flamenco opera" companies of Angelillo and Pepe Marchena, he sometimes performed in their more popular styles, but these 30s recordings are mostly excellent examples of pure, breathtaking cante flamenco, as the alegria "Mariquita Mia" or the solea "A una Gitarilla una Tarde." With Niño Ricardo, Paco Aguilera, and occasional orchestra. –JOHN MCCORD, ROOTS & RHYTHM

ANTONIA GILIBERT VARGAS

Flamenco.

○ **La Perla de Cádiz / CHANT DU MONDE**
Cadiz singer Antonia Gilibert Vargas, "La Perla de Cádiz," was the daughter of a major singer, married to another, and is regarded as the finest singer of *bulerías* of her generation. This is outstanding classic flamenco — *cante hondo* enough to please all but the most picky, by a singer of power and unusual joy: one of the greatest of singers from a city with a major flamenco tradition of its own. (52+ minutes) –JSR

SPAIN COLLECTIONS

Basque Songs & Dances / LYRICHORD
Choral songs. Music for flute and drums. An unexpected sound from Spain. –DLM

The Best of Sevillanas: Vols. 1-4 / ORO   1990
These four volumes, culled from a mid-70s LP series, showcase the popular flamenco-based Sevillanas, the joyful carnival music that fills the springtime air in Seville and surrounding Andalusia. It's a catchy sound, undeniably Spanish, with energetic brass and group vocals driven by clattering castanets, guitars, and a variety of innovative drums, pianos, and strings. Artists interspersed among the discs include Los Hermanos Reyes (early Gipsy Kings), El Pali, Los Marismenos, Amigos de Gines, Los Romeros de la Puebla, and more. Recommended for those of us who like to keep up on world music currents, as well as fans of Spanish flamenco and the Gypsy music of the Andalusian region. –MYLES BOISEN, ROOTS & RHYTHM

Cante Gitano - Gypsy Flamenco ... / NIMBUS
Cante Gitano - Gypsy Flamenco from Andalusia is a digital

recording of an authentic late-night gypsy flamenco session, featuring singers José de la Tomasa, Maria la Burra, and Maria Solea. This is the real thing, folks, the heart and soul of flamenco laid bare on eight intoxicating selections. The first seven pieces feature the individual singers, including two by the mighty Maria Solea, my favorite of the bunch. The last piece, a collection of bulerias with all singers contributing, is a 22-minute epic of rarely heard intensity that caps off this lively maximum-length disc. Thrilling guitar accompaniment throughout by brothers Paco del Gastor and Juan del Gastor. —MYLES BOISEN, ROOTS & RHYTHM

Early Cante Flamenco (1934-1939) / FOLKLYRIC
Includes the classic "La Niña de los Peines." These are historic recordings. —DLM

Riches Heures du Flamenco / CHANT DU MONDE 1990
Flamenco recital with singers Pepe de la Matrona and El Niño de Almaden, dancer La Joselito, and Pedro Soler on guitar. Ten selections. —ROOTS & RHYTHM

☆ **Young Flamencos / HANNIBAL**
Devoted to various of the young fusion flamenco types: Pata Negra, Ketama, and some less-known groups. Purist buffs become hypertensive over this stuff. Personally, I find it interesting, not necessarily good (most of the singing is plain weak), but then some really lousy performances form part of important stylistic change. —JSR

SWEDEN

FILARFOLKET

Traditional.
Smuggel / AMALTHEA
Filarfolket continue to use Swedish folk music as a starting point for their own blend of music. "Tuffepolskan," "Karnevalspolska," "Polska Lucumi," "Tartan," "Rockan," and others. —ROOTS & RHYTHM

1980-1990 / AMALTHEA
A 19-cut retrospective taken from this eclectic unit's recordings on the Amalthea label. —ROOTS & RHYTHM

NORRLATAT

Traditional.
Korpens Tecken (1974-1987) / MANIFIEST
An entertaining selection of 17 songs and tunes drawn from six albums recorded by this popular Swedish group between 1974 and 1987. The music is consistently varied and imaginative and ranges from the lovely traditional twin fiddle sound to a more electric group sound. Instrumentation includes fiddles, soprano sax, trombone, accordion, bass, piano, guitar, and synthesizer, among others, and there are several fine vocals by Hans Alatalo. Well worth a listen. —FRANK SCOTT, ROOTS & RHYTHM

SWEDEN COLLECTIONS

Accordion Music from Angermanland / CAPRICE
The northeast Swedish province of Angermanland is an accordion stronghold, where old melodeons as well as contemporary instruments can be heard. The music here is played on a large number of different types (plus one harmonica), with an extraordinary range of sound quality. The results are equally varied, and highly beguiling. English notes included. —JSR

America Swedish Spelmans Trio / ROUNDER
Folk Fiddling from Sweden / NONESUCH
○ **Harmonica & Accordion / CAPRICE**
Accordion and harmonica playing from all over Sweden: polskas, polkas, waltzes, and other dances on a wide variety of instruments, finely recorded in the homes of local musicians. Excellent illustrated notes in English as well as

Swedish. An extraordinarily varied recording of a tradition virtually unknown outside its homeland. —JSR

○ **Have You Heard the Terrible News? / CAPRICE**
From "Sir Patrick Spens" to "Frankie and Johnny," the recounting of crime and tragedy has been central to traditional music; and in Sweden as well as Britain, street-singers hawking the printed versions that have come to be called broadside ballads spread their material through the land with remarkable speed. Here, typically, are Lincoln's assassination and an accidental shooting of purely local fame, the tragedy of Elvira Madigan and the murder of a pregnant maidservant. The notes' tracing of roots and procedures is outstandingly good, as are the illustrations. —JSR

○ **Master Fiddlers from Närke & Västmanland / CAPRICE**
A wonderful collection of cylinder recordings, including music for fiddle, nyckelharpa (keyed fiddle), clarinet, and jaw harp. The inherent value of recordings made before the international folk movement (which influenced as well as preserved traditional styles) is obvious. But these performances are also beautiful — and the sound quality, despite underlying crackle, amazing. —JSR

Older Musicians 1913-1920 / CAPRICE
Another wonderful set of cylinder recordings, featuring the same set of instruments as the above listing. —JSR

○ **Singing Tornedalen / CAPRICE**
The Tornedalen region of northeastern Sweden borders on Finland. It is Finnish- and Lappish- as well as Swedish-speaking, and very different from the rest of Sweden in its singing style (instrumental music was, for religious reasons, unknown until recently). Most of the examples here are in Finnish, the rest in Swedish and Lappish. Wonderful notes and photos. —JSR

○ **So Makaroni ... / CAPRICE**
So Makaroni: Living Children's Tradition in Sweden. Children's songs and games are extraordinary in the way they preserve ancient elements while changing constantly. One rhyme here seems to come from the pre-Reformation Latin missal; another uses Hitler as material. Crucial even though, alas, only the general parts of the notes are translated. —JSR

○ **Visor I Skillingtryck / CAPRICE**
Skillingtryck were cheap booklets of songs. Like the British broadside ballad, the great era of the skillingtryck was the 18th and 19th centuries, but both have remained fresh in traditional singers' memories. Both often told of drama and murder and moralistic mayhem. Some derived from very ancient themes. One sung here is well known in English and Appalachian balladry. —JSR

SWITZERLAND COLLECTIONS

Folk Music of White Swiss Mountains / CMS-SUM.
Jüüzli: Muotatal Jodel / CHANT DU MONDE
One of the very few available recordings of the true mountain jodel (as opposed to commercial recordings of jodler, which are regional popular songs). As such, it is essential to a European collection. —JSR

Mountain Songs and Yodeling of the Alps / FOLKWAYS
Swiss Folksongs & Dances
Swiss Folklore 1 (Trad. Folksongs & Dances) / BRIDGE
Swiss Folklore 2 (Souvenirs of Switzerland) / BRIDGE
Zauerli: Yodel of Appenzell / AUVIDIS
A wonderful recording done by Hugo Zemp. —DLM

UKRAINE COLLECTIONS

Eastern Carpathian Traditional Music / QUINTANA
These recordings made in Ukrainian areas that were once part of Hungary have the strengths and weaknesses of a seriously imperiled tradition. The music (including Gypsy and Jewish material) is enormously rare and precious. The performances

are sometimes limited, though some of the instrumentals are charming. –JSR

Music of the Tatar People / TANGENT
Music of both the Muslim majority and Orthodox minority of Tatars, mostly unaccompanied vocals (including remarkable duets and trios), but with examples of a local copper pipe, jaw harp, and violin. A remarkable documentation of one of the obscure frontiers between Europe and Asia that are home to so much superlative music. –JSR

Ukraine / AUVIDIS
Like just about all of the series, this reissue of the old UNESCO *Musical Atlas* (which was designed specifically for non-academic listeners) has an unusually fine balance of authenticity and variety. The multifarious splendors of Slavic choral singing are very well represented, but there's also plenty of splendid instrumental work. –JSR

Ukrainian-American Fiddle & Dance ... / FOLKLYRIC
Ukrainian-American Fiddle & Dance Music - 1926-1934 - Vol. 1 contains reissues of historic recordings. Lively music. –DLM

YUGOSLAVIA

JOVA "BESIR" STOJILKOVIC'

Serbia.
○ **Blow "Besir" Blow / GLOBESTYLE**   1988
True "heavy metal" music delivered by Stojilkovic' and his raucous brass band, Brass Orkestar. Incredibly dynamic performances of festival and wedding standards that seem constantly on the verge of dissolving into chaos. Cheery and invigorating. –BT

YUGOSLAVIA COLLECTIONS

Folk Music of Yugoslavia / TOPIC
Given Yugoslavia's ethnic diversity and geographical position, the variety of its music is hardly surprising. Here are open-throated singing in the magnificent Slavonic choral style, decorated vocals of Balkan-Turkish ilk, ancient diaphonic duets, Gypsy songs, clarinet/violin duos, and solos for bagpipes, one-string fiddle, flute, and other ancient instruments — all of it superb. –JSR

Islamic Ritual Music from Yugoslavia ... / PHILIPS
Islamic Ritual Music from Yugoslavia - Zikr of the Rufai Brotherhood offers strange, ecstatic, trance-like music. –DLM

○ **Serbia: Pastoral Dances and Melodies / AUVIDIS**
A splendid recording of non-vocal music recorded in the 70s, divided by instrument: violin trio, bagpipes small and large, ditto flutes, and one of those irresistible local brass bands — a very fine one, both lyrical and marginally comic. The notes are very thorough (sometimes to the point of irrelevance), the recording quality is remarkable by any standards, but the music is simply superlative. *All* of it, which is far from always the case. (75 minutes) –JSR

Songs & Dances of Yugoslavia / PLAYASOUND
Serbian, Macedonian, and Bosnian folk songs, mostly played by the Rakija ensemble. Not particularly inspired performances, but they do present a wealth of traditional melodies in a sort of polished folk style. –ROOTS & RHYTHM

LATIN CONTINUUM

ARGENTINA

CARLOS GARDEL

Latin. Carlos Gardel was one of the biggest stars of the Argentine tango in its classic period between the wars. He was a handsome, passionate singer backed by the leading "orquestras típicas," and also enjoyed considerable fame in Paris when tango and other Latin American music was all the rage. His most popular songs are issued on RCA International,

and a comprehensive reissue series has come out on the import El Bandoneon label. –MB

○ **16 Hits - Vol. 1 / CAPITOL**
An appearance in 1917 at the Teatro Colon in Buenos Aires made Gardel a star the like of which has rarely been seen, and launched the tango as a vocal form. This collection is often grotty (some cuts must have come from 78s and/or soundtracks), but technical issues pale before the wonderful mix of early guitar- and orchestra-backed material. –JSR

○ **Classic Gardel / ORIGINAL MUSIC**   1985

ASTOR PIAZZOLLA   *d*1992

Tango. Often referred to as the originator of the "nuevo tango," Piazzolla was an Argentine visionary who endured the wrath of many of his countrymen for adapting their national dance to his own modern ends. A soulful and accomplished performer on the accordion-like bandoneon, Piazzolla's many recordings have placed him as a leading international composer. Besides his own hand-picked groups, he recorded with a mix of jazz and classical players in the US. –MB

Concierto para Bandoneon / NONESUCH
This recording with a classical orchestra is Piazzolla's apotheosis. For years he has been turning a dance form into an art music. Here he essentially crosses into the regional conservatory style called national music. –JSR

Maria de Buenos Aires / MILA
Recent "opera tango." –MB

☆ **Tango: Zero Hour / MCA**
Astor says it's his best — I agree. The perfect haunting, passionate recording from the master of the new tango, with his best group. –MB

Love Tanguedia / TROPICAL STORM-SOUND WAVE
Soundtrack recordings, with some vocals by singer Roberto Goyeneche. –MB

Rough Dancer & the Cyclical Night / AMERICAN CLAVE
Along with *Tango: Zero Hour*, one of his crowning achievements, nostalgic yet uncompromisingly modern. –MB

TIERRA DEL FUEGO

Tango.
Tierra del Fuego / ADDA
Well! Roll over Piazzolla! If Astor's tango is nuevo, these guys play avant nuevo! But it's tough to place them at all, what with tango/danza references, a tendency to carry the classical elements already inherent in the style to extremes, and jazz touches. They work with various combinations of flute (and bass flute), cello, guitar, piano, double-bass (plucked and bowed), and percussion. After an initial boggle or two I decided I really like this one. –JSR

BOLIVIA COLLECTIONS

Instruments and Music of Bolivia / FOLKWAYS
Raucous, strong, sometimes discordant music, but with great dignity and charm. –DLM

BRAZIL

ALCIONE   *b*1947

Brazilian. A former schoolteacher from the northern state of Maranhao, Alcione Nazar is strongly identified with samba but excels at regional styles and ballads as well. –TH

○ **Personalidade / POLYGRAM**
An exciting sampling of her work, including "Etelvina Minha Nega" (composed by her father João Carlos), the dreamy ballad "Amantes da Noite," and the anthemic "Não Deixe o Samba Morrer." –TH

LENY ANDRADE

Samba. A carioca (native of Rio de Janeiro), Andrade has been called Brazil's First Lady of Jazz, but she is a masterful interpreter of the great Brazilian composers, classic and contemporary. –TH

○ **Cartola 80 Años / PAN**   1987
In this 1987 recording, Andrade's husky contralto and the beautiful songs of the samba composer Cartola make an inspired pairing. The arrangment on this album was done by keyboardist Gilson Peranzzetta. –TH

JACOB DO BANDOLIM

Forro.
Mandolin Master of Brazil / ACOUSTIC DISC
Mandolin, no: he plays an instrument that is its big brother. But the "master" bit is right. This is choro, a rough parallel to ragtime, and a particularly fine string-band sound. The recordings here date mostly from the 50s and include some mellow accordion on three cuts. This is true but polished music from the magic (and very rare) moment when a viruoso develops an idiom out of a street sound without doing it in. (67:08) –JSR

JORGE BEN   b 1940

Samba. Born in 1940, this carioca singer and guitarist devised an ingenious synthesis of samba and pop rhythms that helped earn him many worldwide hits, notably the oft-covered "Mas Que Nada." –TH
Benjor / WEA LATINA
Ben's most recent outing lacks the punch of his Brazilian-label releases. –RW
☆ **Personalidade (Best of Brazil) / POLYGRAM**
Truly a best-of collection, including "Mas Que Nada," "País Tropical," "Oba, Lá Vem Ela," and "Taj Mahal," which years later was transmogrified into Rod Stewart's megahit "Do Ya Think I'm Sexy?" –TH

MARIA BETHANIA   b 1946

Tropicalia/MPB. Possessed of a magisterial yet sensuous contralto, Bethania has been at the forefront of Brazilian music for 25 years and is one of Brazil's biggest international stars. –TH
Memoria de Pele / VERVE
Bethania, of course, is one of the great names. Above all, she is a fine, smoky ballad singer with a gorgeous voice, as this 1989 release of songs by composers from João Bosco to Djavan amply testifies. The best cut, among many great ones, is simply gorgeous song to fado-style guitars. –JSR
☆ **Alibi / POLYGRAM**   1978
On this breakthrough million-selling 1978 album, Bethania sang romantic ballads by some of Brazil's best young composers: Chico Buarque, Gilberto Gil, and her brother Caetano Veloso. –TH

LUIZ BONFÁ   b 1922

Bossa nova. From Rio de Janeiro, Bonfá was already well-established as a composer and guitarist when he was invited to contribute to *Black Orpheus*. He was both progenitor and popularizer of the bossa-nova style. Famous for writing "Manhade Carnival" and "Sambsade-Orfeu," he worked with Stan Getz on bossa-nova recordings of 60s. –TH & MGN
Non-Stop to Brazil / CHESKY
Recent but classic jazz-bossa by one of its defining spirits. The elusive Bonfá, an important influence on US jazz-bossa who has pretty much vanished, is superbly evanescent in style. The recording expresses the close links of bossa nova and jazz. Bonfá is joined for a trio of tracks by NY guitarist Gene Bertoncini. (46:55) –JSR
○ **The Bonfá Magic / CAJU**   1991
A sublime 1991 recording, his first in Brazil in 30 years, of Bonfá compositions old and new. Guaranteed to transport the listener to a Rio café, complete with tropical breeze and caipirinha. –TH

Brazilian Music

For many Americans, Brazilian music means bossa nova and "The Girl from Ipanema" or perhaps summons up a vague image of Carmen Miranda in an extravagant tropical headdress. The truth is that Brazil's popular music has more diversity, more vitality, and more impact in the world arena than that of any other country except the United States.

The last decade has seen Brazilian music enjoying a resurgence of popularity beyond its home borders: many artists have been able to record for US labels and tour in North America, Europe, and Japan. But in fact an ongoing Brazilian-American cultural exchange of significant proportions has been in progress at least since the bossa nova explosion of the early 60s.

There are many parallels between the two countries' histories and many affinities between the two melting-pot cultures. Brazil was colonized by a European power (Portugal) that decimated native Indian populations and instituted African slavery. Regional styles of music — such as baiao, frevo, chorinho, forro, afoxe, carimbo — arose as European, Indian, and African elements collided, converged, blended.

Samba, which originated in a Black urban setting in Rio de Janeiro, is at the root of it all. It is fundamental in Brazilian music, just as the blues — born in the Black rural American South — informs most American popular music.

Out of samba came the cool, captivating syncopation of bossa-nova, whose creators and popularizers — João Gilberto, Antonio Carlos Jobim, Luiz Bonfá, Vinícius de Moraes, Nara Leão, Baden Powell — found themselves part of a giant wave that would break on distant shores. Bossa-nova proved irresistible to the rest of the world, and so too has much of the music that has followed in its wake.

In the late 60s, the rock-influenced tripicalismo movement was spearheaded in Salvador, Bahia, by Gilberto Gil, Caetano Veloso, Gal Costa, and Maira Bethania, all of whom are still active and successful recording artists. MPB, or Musica Popular Brasileira, was a loose confederation of post-bossa-nova singer/songwriters who emerged in the 70s and whose ranks included Milton Nascimento, Chico Buarque, João Bosco, Djavan, and Ivan Lins. It was an exciting, unusually fertile period, which that represented an apogee of artistic development for these individuals and for Brazilian music overall.

The music of Brazil is generally distinguished by an unrivaled integration of melodic and harmonic sophistication with rhythmic invention and richly poetic lyrics. Whatever the style, it is invariably imbued with saudade, a yearning for a person or place or thing that conveys itself as a sadness or melancholy. (Music, of course, is the celebration that helps to matar, or alleviate, saudades.) The inscription "Disco e cultura" (Records are culture) that appears on many Brazilian albums demonstrates an awareness on the part of Brazilians that their music is an authentic expression of who they are, that it is an uplifting, unifying force. It is at the same time a universal language understood everywhere, enriching all who listen.

— Terri Hinte

JOÃO BOSCO   b 1946

MPB. A virtuosic guitarist and galvanic performer Bosco was born in the state of Minas Gerais. He emerged in the 70s as a leading MPB (Musica Popular Brasileira) composer, whose urban sambas have been recorded by many top artists. –TH

○ **Gagabiró / BARCLAY**   1984
Bosco's lengthy and productive partnership with lyricist Aldir Blanc reached a creative peak on this 1984 recording, a dazzling, highly sophisticated fusion of African and Brazilian rhythms and styles. –TH

CHICO BUARQUE   b 1944

Samba. Chico Buarque de Hollanda is widely considered to be the most gifted poet in the Portuguese language. He is also a superb composer, and many of his songs are popular standards. –TH

Francisco / RCA
Buarque, of course, is a name to conjure with. He is also fairly mainstream in his musical tastes, setting his activist lyrics to eclectic arrangements including a string section, though one cut, "Bancarota Blues," uses a cute muted trumpet line. –JSR

☆ **Chico Buarque / BARCLAY**   1984
This marvelous 1984 collection of Buarque originals, including sambas ("Vai Passar," "Pelas Tabelas"), film themes ("Mil Perdoes," "Samba do Grande Amor"), ballads, and boleros, grows richer with each listening. –TH

DORI CAYMMI   b 1943

Brazilian. Dori, son of Dorival Caymmi, has worked extensively as a producer and arranger in both Brazil and the US. He is a major artist in his own right, a singer, guitarist, and composer whose songs have been widely covered. –TH

○ **Brasilian Serenata / QWEST**   1988
His second American release is a lush, impressionistic work of great beauty. He sings his own material (in English and Portuguese) and two of his father's classics ("Você Já Foi à Bahia," "Pescaria"). –TH

Dori Caymmi / ELEKTRA   1988
If you like *Brasilian Serenata*, you'll want this one too. –MGN

DORIVAL CAYMMI   b 1914

Brazilian. Called Brazil's greatest living composer by no less than Tom Jobim, Caymmi has vividly and lovingly depicted his native Bahia in songs, much as Jorge Amando has done in his novels. –TH

○ **Caymmi's Grandes Amigos / EMI**   1986
The master and his remarkable offspring (Dori, Nana, and Danilo Caymmi) sing each other's compositions together and separately. Their sonorous vocal blends and obvious affinities make this album uncommonly satisfying. –TH

NANA CAYMMI

Pop. A singer of exceptional sophistication and emotional power, specializing in ballads and boleros (some by her father and brothers) and with a fine ear for new composers. –TH

○ **Nana Caymmi / EMI**   1979
Caymmi is backed on this 1979 date by top musicians such as João Donato, Robertinho Silva, and Toninho Horta. With her brothers also on hand as writers and sidemen, she invites listeners into her magic inner circle. –TH

ROBERTO CORREA

Neo-traditional.
Viola Caipira / MUSICAPHON
This is not strictly traditional music (though played on a traditional Brazilian guitar) but compositions by a young player with classical training as well as traditional roots. As such, they lack the fire of their source but retain an elegance

reminiscent of classic Coimbra fado guitar. The notes are so all-encompassing as to be confusing. (68:20) –JSR

GAL COSTA   b 1946

Latin pop. Maria de Graa Costa Penna Burgos, an artist of extrordinary range, went on from early associations with fellow baianos Veloso, Gil, and Bethania to sustain a career as Brazil's top female singer. –TH

Bem Bom / RCA
Bem Bom was tropicalista Costa's bid for superstardom in the mid 80s, with the involvement of everybody who is anybody (well, almost). The jazz and R&B touches are more mainstream than before — but the Brazilian pop avant-garde has long drawn heavily on US sources, besides being more sympathetic to lushness than its US counterparts. In vinyl, this album is now a rarity. –JSR

☆ **Gal Canta Caymmi / POLYGRAM**   1975
In this 1975 release, Costa sings ten of Dorival Caymmi's musical vignettes of life in Salvador, Bahia, about which she knows a great deal (it's her hometown). –TH

Fantasia / POLYGRAM   1981
A huge record for Costa in 1981, containing songs by Ivan Lins ("Roda Baiaña"), Caetano Veloso ("Meu Bem, Meu Mal"), and Djavan ("Faltando um Pedao"). –TH

MARIA D'APPARECIDA

Latin pop.
Maria D'Apparecida/Baden Powell / ADDA
Apparecida started out as a classical singer and switched to popular music after a car accident in France, where she lives permanently. Despite her background, she's not just technically good, but amazingly authentic. And of course any recording with Baden Powell is basically a must. –JSR

MARTINHO DA VILA

Samba.
○ **Samba Enredo / RCA**
Martinho's somewhat languorous vocal delivery contrasts intriguingly with the busy rhythms percolating behind him on these dozen sambas-enredo (the "theme song" performed by each samba school during Carnival). –TH

VINÍCIUS DE MORAES

MPB.
○ **Toquinho e Vinícius/Personalidade / POLYGRAM**
Guitarist and composer Toquinho (b 1946) and Vinícius recorded as a duo during the 70s (until Vinícius's death). Together they created exuberant, joyful music that was also very popular — in Brazil and abroad. –TH

DJAVAN   b 1950

Brazilian. A Brazilian composer/vocalist hailing from the northeastern state of Alagoas, he has fashioned an appealing and influential blend of Brazilian, African, and rock rhythms that have been called "South American global pop." –TH

Flor de Lis / WEA LATINA
Recordings newly available in America. –RW

☆ **Seduzir / WORLD PACIFIC**   1981
Djavan's third album (1981) has all the hallmarks of his unique style, which includes asymmetrical melodies and captivating rhythms, and some of his most memorable tunes ("PedroBrasil," "Luanda," "Seduzir"). –TH

GILBERTO GIL   b 1942

Bossa nova. An important Brazilian vocalist, composer, and political activist who has been on the cutting edge of Afro-Latin music over at least three decades. Gil was a pioneer in utilizing everything from reggae to rock in his music. He is idolized by many American rockers and was one of a wave of musicians signed by US labels in an attempt to reap the worldbeat harvest. Gil is an outstanding and charismatic vocalist. –RW

☆ **Realce / ELEKTRA**   1978
A good example of how Gil mixes it all up: recorded in Los Angeles with a Brazilian/American cast, this 1978 session combines Gil's unique samba-rock-funk fare with a Portuguese version of Bob Marley's "No Woman, No Cry." –TH

JOÃO GILBERTO   b 1932

Bossa nova. Vocals, guitar, composer. One of the greatest Brazilian singers of all time. It would be difficult to overestimate the influence of João Gilberto on Brazilian music. "Everything he did, and does," Caetano Veloso has remarked, "illuminates the past and the future of the music in Brazil."
Born in Bahia in 1932, Gilberto electrified the country with his 1958 recording of Jobim's "Chega de Saudade." Just a few years later the colossal hit "The Girl from Ipanema," which he recorded with then-wife Astrud and saxophonist Stan Getz, precipitated the worldwide bossa-nova phenomenon.
Gilberto is generally recognized as the architect of bossa nova: he condenses samba polyrhythms into his syncopated, thoroughly original guitar style, while his cool, caressing, utterly free vocals define intimacy and swing. –TH

☆ **João Gilberto / POLYGRAM**
Minimalist João (guitar and percussion) for maximal intimacy. "As always," comments Arto Lindsay in his notes, "his music is defined as much by what it leaves out as by what is there." –TH

Amoroso / WARNER   1977
This 1977 classic is to swoon over: Gilberto singing in Portuguese, Spanish ("Besame Mucho!"), Italian, and English, with strings arranged and conducted by Claus Ogerman. Qué beleza ... –TH

The Legendary João Gilberto / WORLD PACIFIC   1990
A 1990 compilation of Gilberto's alluring bossa-nova recordings (1958-1961), containing a generous 75 minutes of music. At the time of its original release, it changed the musical landscape of Brazil and beyond. –TH

João / POLYGRAM   1991
Recent but classic jazz-bossa by one of its defining spirits. Vocally, Gilberto is in fine muttering form, communicating intensely with somebody in his breast pocket, and his guitar is as delicate as ever. This recording expresses the close links of bossa nova and jazz. *João* has Clare Fisher arranging and on some cuts playing keyboards, along with one of those saccharin string-sections even the most avant-garde Brazilians love. (50 +) –JSR

EGBERTO GISMONTI

Latin jazz. This brilliant, prolific composer, guitarist, and multi-instrumentalist has in effect created his own genre of music, with elements from the entire spectrum of Brazilian styles as well as classical and jazz influences. –TH

Academia de Danças / EMI
An ensemble with strings enhances the beauty of Gismonti's improvisations. –MGN

● **Dança das Cabeças / ECM**   1976
The initial American release features extended pieces for guitarist and percussionist Nana Vasconcelos. Side 1 is a tour de force, with the pieces segueing together beautifully. –MGN

○ **Sol Do Meio Dia / POLYGRAM**   1977
This is also an excellent record. Gismonti plays an eight-string guitar. –MGN

Sanfona / ECM   1981
A two-disc set that describes itself as "a trip through Brazilian rhythms, musical forms, and popular festivals." Egberto performs solo on one disc, is backed on the other by a trio featuring drummer Nenê. –TH

Works / ECM   1983
Excellent compilation. Looking for a Volume II. –MGN

Cuban Music

You can't imagine American music in the 20th century without the influence of Cuban music. Period. In the 19th century, the port cities of New Orleans and Havana traded licks across the shipping route between them. Later, the synocopated basslines of Cuban son helped the rhythm of jazz move from a foursquare chunk to something hipper. Many rock standards use typically Cuban beats, transplanted and disguised. And then there's salsa, which is Cuban music mixed with Puerto Rican and other influences.

Cuban music has seen many styles in this century: the 20s son; the danzon-playing charangas of the 30s; the blazing-trumpet conjuntos of the 40s; the cha cha cha of the 50s; the ever-present rumba; and, of course, in back of it all, African religious music. Cuban musicologists — and common people as well — know not only what the Afro-Cuban religious music is, but where in Africa it comes from. They know what is Yoruba, what is Dahomeyan, what is Kongo, what is Abacua. I know a salsa musician in New York who says, "If you want to know about Africa, go to Cuba."

Cuban music is alive and kicking. The rhythms are still rooted in the land and the people, and the popular beats continue to evolve.

— Ned Sublette

○ **Infancia / ECM**   1991
A stunning effort by Egberto and his current (1991) working group: guitarist/synthesist Nando Carneiro, bassist Zeca Assumpao, and cellist Jacques Morelen-baum. –TH

ANTONIO CARLOS JOBIM   b 1927

Brazilian. One of the greatest 20th-century composers of popular music. The extraordinary body of work created by Antonio Carlos Brasileiro de Almeida Jobim has had an incalculable influence on Brazilian and American music.
His music, he has said, comes from nature. It is romantic, urbane, lyrical, rhythmically and harmonically sophisticated, and very, very beautiful. Tom Ze, the singer, pianist, and arranger, is one of the finest interpreters of Jobim's songs, but they've held strong appeal for an incredible array of international artists over the last 35 years.
"Wave," "Corcovado," "Aguas de Marco," "Felicidade," "Once I Loved," "Dindi" "The Girl from Ipanema," "One Note Samba," "Desafinado," "Triste" — these are just a few of the carioca composer's classic. –TH

☆ **Elis e Tom / VERVE**   1974
A perfect record: Brazil's beloved cantora Elis Regina singing an all-Jobim program, accompanied by the composer, who also joins her for several duets, notably his masterpiece "Aguas de Maro." –TH

Urubu / WARNER   1976
This beautiful 1976 session features Claus Ogerman's incomparable string arrangements. In fact, half the album is orchestral-only; on the other half, Jobim sings such gems as "Correnteza," cowritten by Bonfá. –TH

Terra Brasilis / WARNER   1980
Once again teaming with arranger Claus Ogerman on this 1980 double album, Jobim reworks many of his classic compositions, including "Dindi," "One Note Samba," and of course "The Girl from Ipanema." –TH

Passarim / VERVE   1987
Jobim's "Banda Nova" is a family affair (including wife Ana, daughter Elizabeth, and son Paulo Jobim), which has been touring the world since the mid 80s. Danilo Caymmi is a featured band member. –TH

NARA LEÃO
1942-1989

Bossa nova. Nara Leão was known as "the muse of bossa nova," but she also recorded samba de morro ("from the hills," i.e., the real thing) and was later an integral part of Tropicalia (with Gil, Gal, Bethnia, Caetano). –TH

○ **Personalidade (Best of Brazil) / POLYGRAM**
Practically a bossa sampler: Leão's gentle voice caresses some of the classics of the genre, such as "Sabe Você" (by Carlos Lyra and Vinícius), "Telefone" (Roberto Menescal), and several by Jobim and Buarque. –TH

IVAN LINS
♭1945

Brazilian. The carioca singer, composer, and pianist got his first break with Elis Regina's 1970 hit of his "Madalena." Since then he's had a distinguished solo career; American jazz musicians are especially enamored of Lins. –TH

○ **A Noite / ODEON**
1979
This album contains impassioned performances of some of Lins's best-known songs — "Antes Que SejaTarde," "Comear de Novo" ("The Island"), and "Velas" (a Grammy winner as recorded by Quincy Jones). –TH

EDU LOBO
♭1943

Brazilian. Although no longer active in popular music, this singer, composer, and guitarist had enduring contributions in the post-bossa era. His "Arrastão" (written with Vinícius) helped launch the career of Elis Regina. –TH

○ **A Arte de Edu Lobo / FONTANA**
Lobo's warm vocal style and intricate northeastern-flavored guitar work make this two-LP compilation a must. "Upa Neguinho" and "Casa Forte" are among the highlights; the Tamba Trio backs him on seven tracks. –TH

MARISA MONTE

Rock Brasileira.
Mais / WORLD PACIFIC
Despite a few NYC credits (notably John Zorn and a couple of recording studios), this is Brazilian with extensions rather than worldbeat. There's muito rock in this, which gives it an attack harder than the familiar bossa-nova mega-mellowness, but there aren't enough Americanisms to swamp the basic Brasileirismo. Fresh and interesting. (64:34) –JSR

MILTON NASCIMENTO
♭1942

MPB. Milton Nascimento grew up in the small town of Tres Pontas in Minas Gerais, and retains a strong indentity as a mineiro (i.e., resident of Minas).
Since making his recording debut in 1967, Nascimento has enjoyed broad international acclaim as a singer and composer; he's also been a favored collaborator of many American artists, notably Wayne Shorter, Pat Metheny, and Paul Simon.
Nascimento's songs incorporate influences as diverse as the Beatles, Gregorian chants, American jazz, African rhythms, bossa nova, and mineiro folk music, and address both the personal and political. A singer of uncommon emotional power whose plaintive tenor can soar to an otherworldly falsetto, he is "the Voice of Brazil" for audiences around the world. –TH

Minas / A&M
1975
Although several of Nascimento's most familiar songs are contained in this debut American release, *Minas* (referring to his home state of Minas Gerais) is a remarkably cohesive piece of work that stands as one of his finest. Includes famous tunes "Carvo e Canela" and "Nada Sera como Antes." –TH & MGN

Geraes / ODEON
1976
Stylistically and emotionally a counterpart to *Minas*, *Geraes* (an obsolete spelling of "Gerais") includes some of Nascimento's most haunting melodies, as well as a powerful duet with Chico Buarque, "O Que Ser (A Flor da Pele)." –TH

☆ **Sentinela / ARIOLA**
1980
Folk themes with sacred overtones: this 1980 session is one of the most spectacular examples of how Nascimento weaves many threads into his music. The title track is an unforgettable duet with Nana Caymmi. –TH

Missa dos Quilombos / POLYGRAM
1982
Quilombos were settlements established by runaway slaves during the Portuguese colonial period. Nascimento's mass (recorded in 1982) "celebrates the death and resurrection of the Negro people in the death and resurrection of Christ." It was banned by the Vatican. –TH

OS CARETAS

Samba.
☆ **Cem Anos de Samba / POLYDOR**
1971
A best-selling 1971 recording, this three-LP set purports to document "100 Years of Samba," and succeeds while having a thoroughly good time. All the classic samba composers and their hits are here. –TH

HERMETO PASCOAL

Brazilian. This Brazilian multi-instrumentalist is of paramount influence on Airto and Flora Purim. He improvises heavily in contemporary high-energy orchestra-like fusion settings. –MGN

○ **Hermeto / BUDDAH**
Legendary Brazilian composer and multi-instrumentalist with a large ensemble in the early 70s. Wildly creative music in a jazz/rock vein. Rare and good to find. –MGN

QUARTETO NEGRO

Latin jazz.
Quarteto Negro / AUVIDIS
The Quarteto Negro consists of singer Zeze Motta, reedsman Paulo Moura, guitarist/bassist Jorge Degas, and percussionist Djalma Correa. Moura, who here plays splendid soprano sax and clarinet, has one foot in jazz and the other in classical music. So did Correa. Motta started out as an actress and film star before starting to sing professionally in the mid 70s. Degas, by contrast, came up from the popular dance halls and has played behind samba-based singers such as Martinho de Vila and Elba Ramalho, as well as Gal Costa and Alcione. The whole thing comes together because nobody tries to be what he or she isn't. The result is strong Latin jazz with lots of Brazilian in the mix, flowing and mellow and generally righteous. (58:33) –JSR

ELIS REGINA
1945-1982

Brazilian. Arguably the greatest female singer Brazil has ever produced, Elis Regina was born in the southernmost state of Rio Grande do Sul. A drug overdose in 1982 took her life at the height of her popularity and artistic powers. –TH
Arte de Elis Regina / FONTANA
1975
This 1975 best-of is a well-rounded portrayal of Regina's rich artistry, including hits like "Madalena" and "Arrastao" and her definitive performances of songs by many of Brazil's most important composers. –TH

☆ **Essa Mulher / WARNER**
1979
A beautifully produced and conceived collection of songs (by João Bosco, Danilo Caymmi, Cartola, Baden Powell, Joyce) on which Regina arrasou (outdid herself, that is to say). –TH

BOLA SETE

Bossa Nova. Sete ranks among the better Brazilian and Latin-jazz acoustic guitarists. He came to America in 1960 and has worked with Dizzy Gillespie, Paul Horn, and Vince Guaraldi among others. Sete has made solo releases, straight jazz dates, and bossa-nova records, and is equally accomplished playing in flamenco or Latin settings. –RW

☆ **Bossa Nova / FANTASY**
Tremendous guitar solos, authentic Brazilian fare done in a mainstream jazz context. −RW

○ **Incomparable Bola Sete / FANTASY**
His finest instrumental playing. −RW

☆ **Autentico / FANTASY**
Brilliant recordings with his New Brazilian Trio. −RW

SIMONE

Brazilian.

○ **Amar / COLUMBIA**   1982
One of Simone's most satisfying albums, with masterful versions of tunes by Buarque, Jobim, Nascimento (including the title track), and the baiano Moraes Moreira ("Pao e Poesia"). −TH

TAMBA TRIO

Bossa nova.

○ **Tamba Trio / RCA**   1975
Though recorded past the group's heyday, this 1975 album captures them in their finest bossa form. They're joined by guests Toninho Horta, Danilo Caymmi, João Bosco, and Ivan Lins, who each contributed songs. −TH

ALCEU VALENÇA

MPB.

Alceu Valença / RCA
Valença is less well known than many MPB stalwarts, but quite as good. Musically, in fact, he is more individual than many big wheels in this rather text-oriented genre. He has a liking for harder rock influences than most of his compatriots, but also at times turns to a very pretty classic Luso-Brazilian acoustic guitar sound. −JSR

NANA VASCONCELOS

Latin jazz. Renowned Brazilian percussionist who has always maintained a broad world music focus in his jazz-based recordings with Don Cherry, Ron Carter, Pat Metheny, Egberto Gismonti, and others. −MB

○ **Saudades / ECM**   1979
Afro-experimentalist Vasconcelos's finest. It presents his various facets — berimbao playing, intricate overlaid vocals, fine percussion, even gorgeous guitar — simply and with the almost overwhelming sonic clarity that is an ECM trademark. With guitarist Egberto Gismonti and Radio Symphony Orchestra of Stuttgart. The extended pieces are best. A unique idea to combine classical background with expertly conceived Brazilian sounds. −JSR & MGN

Bush Dance / POLYGRAM   1986
Vasconcelos vocalizes, plays DMX keyboard and percussion. Guests are rock guitarist Arto Lindsay, keyboardist Peter Scherer, and guitarist Maria Toledo. World fusion at its zenith; perhaps a bit too dense but good to listen to closely. −MGN

VELHA GUARDA DA PORTELA

Latin jazz.

Grandes Sambistas / AUVIDIS
Fine examples of the (by now fairly familiar) escola de samba style, from the musicians of one of the major competitors in the Rio carnival. Here the group (which includes two seriously important composers, Wilson Moreira and Nelson Sargento) plays a Saturday-night string-band style with the cavaquinho and guitars very audible. There's also some nice jazz trombone in places. (67:10) −JSR

CAETANO VELOSO   b 1942

MPB. From his emergence as one of the aesthetic revolutionaries in the tropicalismo movement, Caetano has been a risk-taker-groundbreaker who has contributed immeasurably as singer, composer, and social conscience. −TH

○ **Cores Nomes / PHILIPS**   1982
The compositions on this 1982 recording by Djavan, João Donato, Dorival Caymmi, and of course, Veloso, are exquisitely matched to Caetano's refined vocal style (which owes much to fellow Bahian João Gilberto). −TH

TOM ZE

Latin pop.

○ **The Best of Tom Ze / WARNER**
A cofounder of the tropicalista movement with Veloso, Gil, Bethania, et al., Ze has faded into obscurity as his music becomes more and more experimental and eccentric. This is by far the best Brazilian recording I've ever heard (caveat emptor!), partly because of the gentleness of Ze's weirdness and partly because he sounds so Brazilian even as the other tropicalistas come to associate "avant-garde" with increasingly Pan American pop-soup. (42:42) −CARL HOYT, ORIGINAL MUSIC

BRAZIL COLLECTIONS

Afro-Brazilian Religious Songs / LYRICHORD
The album is an outstanding overview of the music of the Fon/Yoruba-derived religions of Salvador in northeastern Brazil, a religious center nicknamed "The Rome of the Africans." The pieces were recorded over eight years during the ceremonies themselves. −JSR

Amazonia ... / LYRICHORD
Amazonia: Cult Music of Northern Brazil features the Afro-Brazilian religious music of Amazonia, which is very different from that of the Bahian version mostly because it mixes Amerindian ingredients with its Yoruba elements. Though most of the music on the album is religious, there are also a couple of splendid sambas by a local band. −JSR

☆ **Black Orpheus ... / FONTANA**
Black Orpheus - Original Soundtrack Recording. The prodigious talents of Antonio Carlos Jobim and Vinícius de Moraes ("Felicidade") and Luiz Bonfá ("Manha de Carnaval") were introduced to the world on this unforgettable soundtrack. −TH

☆ **Bossa Nova Brasil / POLYGRAM**   1991
A good various-artists sampler of the modern Brazilian sound, including cuts from contemporary artists like Jorge Ben and Gilberto Gil. −RW

Bossa Nova Trinta Anos Depois / VERVE
A collection of early Brazilian recordings that is not just a great listen, but a salutary reminder about a music that has attracted a lot of nonsense talk. Bossa nova — the authentic, real, genuine stuff — was from the start strongly jazz-oriented and heavily pop in musical aesthetic. Here to prove it are Velosa, Regina, Gilberto, Toquinho, and all sorts of other legends semi- and total. −JSR

Brazil ... / AUVIDIS
This recording may be an indicator of the future of world music. *Brazil: The Sound World of the Bororo Indians* has field recordings from a small tribal group, which up until recently may have been regarded as "primitive." They have a remarkably rich mythology and cosmology, with which their music is intimately connected. This digital recording covers both specifically religious and more secular songs and dances. What grabs me is the attention to music and nature being intertwined. −DLM

☆ **Brazil Classics - Beleza Tropical / WARNER**   1977
The first of a three-volume set, compiled by David Byrne, that gives gringos a chance to pick up on the salacious sounds that've been going on in Brazil. Fans of Talking Heads' later work or Paul Simon's African excavations will enjoy these well-done sets. −JF

○ **Brazil Classics - O Samba / WARNER**   1985
The second volume in the *Brazil Classics* series. −ED

○ **Brazil Classics - Forro / WARNER**   1985
The third volume in the *Brazil Classics* series. −ED

☆ **Brazil Forro / ROUNDER** 1989
Brazil Forro - Music for Maids and Taxi Drivers is a textbook intro to forro sounds; well packaged and well produced, with excellent sound and a nice cross-section. Featured artists include José Orlando and Toinho de Alagoas. –RW

○ **Brazil Today - Vol. 2 / POLYGRAM** 1985
A sampler focusing on Brazilian music in the mid 80s. The second of a two-part series originally issued in 1985. –RW

☆ **Brazil-Roots-Samba / ROUNDER** 1989
Examples of classic and vintage samba, with cuts from Wilson Moriera, Nelson Sargento, Velha Guarda Da Portela, etc. –RW

Bresil 88 / BUDA MUSIQUE
An attractive anthology with a largely samba-based feel. Some cuts are by artists known in the US — Jorge Ben, Milton Nascimento, Elis Regina, Gilberto Gil — but more who are at least as good though less famous here: Jovelina Perola Negra, Maria Creuza, Marcos Valle, Wando, Filo, and more. –JSR

Bresil - Musiques du Haut Xingu / OCORA
Interesting long horns, animal songs, and flutes. Fascinating people fast disappearing. –DLM

In Praise of Oxala & Other Gods ... / NONESUCH
In Praise of Oxala & Other Gods - Black Music of South America is festive music from Colombia, Ecuador, and Brazil. –DLM

Creadores de Lambada / TH-RODVEN
In its origins, the lambada (like bossa nova, though on a much smaller scale) was something authentic. The first version of the enormous Brazilian hit "Chorando Si Foi," which is included here in its Spanish-language version, was stupendous in its drive and its echoes of Bolivian flutes. The other cuts on this satisfying CD are samba with a lot of fine jazz-tinged soloing. –JSR

Music of Mato Grosso - Brazil / FOLKWAYS
Especially interesting for animal calls and eight-foot long flutes. From the Xingu area. –DLM

CHILE COLLECTIONS

Amerindian Ceremonial Music of Chile / PHILIPS
Music for panpipes; curing ceremony of a shamaness. Lengthy selections. –DLM

☆ **Hispano-Chilean Metisse ... / AUVIDIS**
Hispano-Chilean Metisse Traditional Music. is from the re-released *UNESCO World Atlas* series, and is almost the only recording of Hispano-Chilean traditional music. Included are religious music, including parade-dances influenced by the Andean Indians, various types of guitar-accompanied ballads, harp-backed cuecas, and more. Thorough notes, though the English translation is eccentric and in a couple of places positively cryptic. –JSR

Traditional Music of Chile / ABC-COMMAND
Music for guitarron, accordion, guitars, and singers — mestizo music. –DLM

COLOMBIA

JOE ARROYO w/LA VERDAD
Salsa.
Fuego / FUENTES
Arroyo had become a major favorite among European salsa buffs, and a considerable success on the Latin concert circuit. Novelty aside, I think the reason is that while he hews to a tight but pretty standard salsa sound, he uses all sorts of Colombian rhythms (including cumbia), thus giving his universality strong local roots. –JSR

EMBAJADORES VALLENATOS
Vallenato.
○ **Embajadores Vallenatos / FUENTES**
Down-home accordion from a charming quartet that, here at least, dumps the cumbia in favor of a quiverful of pasoes, which are just as rural and equally jaunty but a little less gimpy of rhythm. Lisandro "Nonpareil" Meza aside, I particularly like groups like this, which contrive to stay faithful to the típico sound's plain-man affability, using their undoubted chops to do the job right, rather than flashing things up. –JSR

LISANDRO MEZA
Vallenato.
Cancion para Una Muerte Anunciada / TOBOGA
This riff on a famous novel is just part of what makes Meza the finest vallenato musician extant. He takes the Marques story and re-works it back into a small-town drama with brilliance, setting it to a melody that is amazingly sophisticated without ever going beyond tradition. This is, in fact, not your average rural accordionist, but a man who manages to be both sophisticated and true to what is still very much a roots music. It's amazing how many changes he can ring on what is, theoretically, a fairly simple idiom. An unacknowledged classic, this. –JSR

TOTO LA MOMPOSINA
Afro-Colombian.
Music of the Atlantic Coast / ASPIC
Tota la Momposina sings the music of the Atlantic coast backed by a percussion group that includes a marimbula or bass finger-piano and sometimes a cane flute. These days, she is an international performer very popular in France, but this is the nearest thing available to Afro-Colombian roots music, and a pleasure. This and the collection album *La Ceiba* are non-vallenato releases for a change. –DLM

PEREGOYO Y SU COMBO VACANA
Salsa-cumbia.
Peregoyo y Su Combo Vacana / TROPICALISIMO
Reissue of an early-70s release by a band alas long defunct. The style is your basic salsa-cumbia (salsa-currulao, salsa-porro, etc.). But Peregoyo's group stood out for a splendid mix of originality and down-home típico, plus an improvised solo trumpet lead to the frontline that gave the whole thing far more flair than the usual arranged horns. –JSR

SONORA DINAMITA
Pop cumbia.
De Nuevo 16 Exitos / SONOTONE LATINO
Fine batty dance-band cumbia with a mess of singers male and female, all good. This is jovial double-entendre country music by and large, from the opening "No Provoques me Pichiche" (giggle giggle) on down. Everything is real crisp, real easy, and real good. –JSR

LINDA CONJUNTO VERA w/CARMEN RIVERO
Cumbia.
A Bailar la Cumbia / CBS
Re-release of a very fine band from the 50s. Vera is a fine singer in the semi-plaintive, semi-humorous cumbia vein, and the mambo-inflected band (two trumpets, two saxes) is with her all the way. Fine though some of the new Colombian salsa groups are, the cumbia bands have much more regional flavor, and this one is a classic. –JSR

COLOMBIA COLLECTIONS

La Ceiba / ASPIC
New versions of several of Toto la Momposina's performances, along with several other groups playing gaitas, porros, bullerengues, and even a fandango. –DLM

☆ **Cumbia Cumbia / WORLD CIRCUIT**
Running from the 50s to the 80s, these cuts perfectly showcase the most charming of Latin American music — a kind of musical equivalent to the poetry of Edward Lear.
—CARL HOYT, ORIGINAL MUSIC

○ **Fiesta Vallenata / SHANACHIE**   1986
Fiesta Vallenata: Colombian Dance Music is a non-stop orgy of uptempo accordions. A sure cure for the blues. –MB

Mejores Duetos / SONOLUX
One of a slew of compilations devoted to the old duet style of Colombian popular music, mostly accompanied by guitars but occasionally running to a piano (or even an organ) or other small-scale instrumentation. Most of this stuff must go back a long way, before the salsa influences became unavoidable. It's simple, often sentimental, sometimes courtly, and most enchanting. –JSR

○ **Sacred & Profane Music of the Ika / FOLKWAYS**
Music of the mountain Indians of North Colombia. Dance music played on accordion with rasp. Recordings of Puerto Rican mountain music include the great Ramito, Jibarito, and La Callandria, all major discoveries. –DLM

CUBA

CHOCOLATE ARMENTEROS & CHAPPOTTIN

Conjunto.
○ **Estrellas de Cuba / ANTILLA**
Chappottin and Chocolate were perhaps the two greatest names of the generation that developed Cuba's jazz-oriented conjunto trumpet sound. Chocolate still records in New York. Chappottin, his equal, was nicknamed the Louis Armstrong of Cuba; he's now forgotten by all but the buffs. The music here is from one of 20th-century popular music's greatest Golden Ages. –JSR

DON AZPIAZU & HIS HAVANA CASINO ORCH.

Traditional. Don Azpiazu was until recently a forgotten giant. This was the band whose 1930 "Peanut Vendor" not only became a huge national hit, launching a decade of rumbamania, it was also the first US recording of an authentic national Latin style (in other words, Latin music, not US music to a Latin rhythm, like the 20s tangos). Equally important, Azpiazu's "Peanut Vendor" introduced to the US all those Cuban percussion instruments we now take for granted. His second recording, "Green Eyes," was the first example of true crossover with a North American vocalist. More important yet, this was simply a very fine band indeed, by the standards of its own or any other day. –JSR

○ **Don Azpiazu & His Havana Casino Orch. / HARLEQUIN**

DON BARRETO

Rumba.
Don Barreto 1932-1935 / HARLEQUIN
Singer and guitarist Emilio "Don" Barreto was one of many expatriate Cuban musicians who kept the rumba going in Europe, and indeed his group was an important missionary of the genre. His band already shows influences from Martinique, and in fact a lot of the cuts here are biguines. The whole thing is very mellow and charming, with admirable clarinet (a Martiniquan element that was pretty much dying out in Cuba), as well as fine Cuban flute, guitar, and singing. (59:15) –JSR

CARIDAD CUERVO

Guarachera.
Sonaron 12 Companas / AREITO
One of the great Afro-Cuban guaracheras. The voice is still redolent of power and grace. The backing is one of those splendid everything-bands that Cuba has gone in for recently, with mule-kick trombones, rock-ish keyboards and guitar, strings, you name it. This is the sort of group that can even more or less carry off the boleros that reduce most salsa groups to banality. –JSR

CONJUNTO CASINO

Conjunto.
15 Exitos Originales / KUBANEY
The Conjunto Casino was one of the greatest bands of Cuba's 40s and 50s Golden Age. This CD has zilch notes — who plays the super piano on some cuts, I don't know — and the sound is a bit muffled. But the music is so good and so rare as to turn the flaws into minor irritants. –JSR

CONJUNTO RUMBAVANA

Conjunto.
Dejale Que Baile Sola / VITRAL
Rumbavana, one of the great conjuntos of the 40s, is still playing the righteous típico sound in Cuba, using occasional modernisms (a bass riff here, a trumpet phrase there, more percussion than in the old days) to keep themselves classic rather than dated. It's a style, and a band, of perfect balance, of power and delicacy. The real thing never ages; in fact, it just matures. –JSR

CELIA CRUZ & LA SONORA MATANCERA

Guarachera.
○ **Celia Cruz y la Sonora Matancera / TH-RODVEN**
Buy anthing you find; it will be good. Any of their titles on Palladium Records are fine — here are a few: *Canta Celia Cruz, La Tierna, Conmovedora, Bamboleadora, ¬La Dinamica!* On Seeco Records, try *Homenaje a los Santos - Vol. 2,* which emphasizes the Afro side of Afro-Cuban. There are also a number of Celia Cruz records made in the US with various salsa artists. She's never bad, but if you get *The Mambo Kings* soundtrack instead of the Palladium reissues, you're making a mistake. –NS

PELLO EL AFROKAN

Mozambique.
Un Sabor Que Canta / VITRAL
The mozambique was the first and perhaps only Afro-Cuban creation of the Castro era (when Eddie Palmieri recorded one in New York, he got death threats!). Its creator was Pello el Afrokan. This is deep Afro — a contemporary trombone-led sound but very heavy on the percussion, and with vocals far more African than standard salsa singing. Arguably the most original happening in Cuban típico since the 50s. And stunning stuff. –JSR

HENRY FIOL

Salsa.
○ **Sonero / EARTHWORKS**   1983
In the mid 80s Fiol recorded on his own Corazon label some of the most consistently elegant recordings in Cuban-tipico vein. As this British compilation from Corazon shows, he's a terrific singer, light and throwaway for a sonero. And his band's mix of classic elements with versatile tenor sax punctuations works a treat. Elegant is the word; alas, too short are two more equally valid ones. –JSR

CELINA GONZALEZ

Lucumí.
A Santa Barbara / SUARITOS
You may have come across the British issue of an 80s Celina Gonzalez album. But her great days were much earlier, when she was singing with her late husband, Reutilio. They specialized in what may seem to an outsider a slightly odd form: Afro-Cuban religious pop songs backed by a group of guitar (Reutilio), rhythm, and (excellent and distinctive) piano. Celina was a more restrained singer than Celia Cruz, but this is magnificent music from a magnificent period. –JSR

○ **Que Viva Chango! / QBADISK**
The queen of campesino, or Cuban country music, in a one-

hour anthology of her Cuban albums. The music is rootsy, light, and moves forward with tremendous momentum. –NS

IRAKERE

Cuban. Irakere, led by piano monster Jesus "Chucho" Valdes (son of bandleader Bebo Valdes), is generally conceded to be the heaviest collection of players in Cuba. They are very intense. Sometimes their records catch it, sometimes not. They're two bands in one: a jazz band and a dance band. –NS

Misa Negra / MESSIDOR MUSIC

○ **Homenaje a Beny More / MESSIDOR**

This record shows off their pop-dance side. Worth having for the incendiary "Bacalao con Pan" alone. –NS

ISRAEL "CACHAO" LOPEZ

Latin jazz.

○ **Cuban Jam Sessions in Miniature Descargas / PANART**

There are a number of albums with this title, not all of them by Cachao. Descarga means "jam"; the original session was a defining moment in Cuban jazz. Cuba's best, in a studio in Havana in the 50s with nothing written down. –NS

LOS MUÑEQUITOS DE MANTANZAS

Guaguancó.

○ **Cantar Maravilloso / GLOBESTYLE**

Recorded in a good studio in London on their first trip ever outside of Cuba (in 1989!), Cuba's most famous rumba group. (The classic sides, recorded for Puchito in 1952, are out of print now.) –NS

Rumba Caliente / QBADISK

A coupling of cuts from two albums recorded 12 years apart — one in 1989, the other produced by musicologist Maria Teresa Linares in 1977. Real street rumba — nothing on Muñequitos's records but voices and percussion. –NS

○ **Los Muñequitos de Mantanzas / VITRAL**

Much harder to find than the religious drumming of Cuba is the secular street rumba generally known as guaguancó — a rowdy, dance-party music that retains all the complexity and precision of its religious cousins, and yet adds touches not generally approved of by the pious, including a good dose of humor. Mostly guaguancós with one columbia, one yambu, and one abakua. Absolutely terrific and a great excuse for a party! –CARL HOYT, ORIGINAL MUSIC

LOS PAPINES

Guaguancó.

Homenaje a Mis Colegas / VITRAL

There are only three great voices-and-percussion guaguancó or rumba callejera groups left, and their recordings come and go confusingly. Here one of them, Los Papines, has added musicians, including ex-Irakere trumpeter Arturo Sandoval. The effect varies between rumbon with horns, and conjunto with amplified percussion. –JSR

Guaguancó / BRAVO

The vocals of this set are not their best, but the drumming is well up to speed. A year or two ago it was well nigh impossible to find secular Afro-Cuban music like this, but paradoxically enough the CD-driven decline of the LP has also led to the cassette reissue of all sorts of very rare recordings. –JSR

BENY MORE

Sonero. Venerated by buffs of the 50s Cuban sound, Beny More was, like New York's Tito Rodriguez, not only a dynamic sonero but a fine, fine bolero singer. He was also a big deal as a bandleader fronting full-throated mambo bands. The first Cuban artist to have his own TV show, he was, as far as I know, the only Cuban singer to have an entire book written about him. –JSR

☆ **The Most from Beny More / RCA**   1976

Even though this reissue lacks documentation except for

titles, his biggest 50s hits are a basic item for your collection. Worth every cent and more. –NS & JSR

ORQUESTA ARAGON

Charanga.

○ **That Cuban Cha-Cha-Cha / RCA**

This group — which still exists — was world famous in the 50s. This is as good an introduction to them as you'll find. –NS

ORQUESTA CASINO DE LA PLAYA

Rumba.

○ **Memories of Cuba / TUMBAO**

It doesn't get any better than this. The great Miguelito Valdes — the man who made "Babalu" famous — sang with this orchestra. You hear a little of him in virtually every important Cuban singer who came after. –NS

ORQUESTA REVÉ

Latin pop.

○ **La Explosion del Momento! / REAL WORLD**

This is maybe the best widely available contemporary Cuban album, selected from three Cuban releases. Elio Revé, now in his 60s, still plays to an audience of teenagers. This is good-humored, whimsical, rootsy dance music. –NS

ORQUESTA REVÉ

Afro-cuban dance. A Latin-jazz/pop dance band that cooks as good as any. –MGN

○ **Suave Suave + 3 / DISCOS HABANOS**

One of Cuba's three or four finest modern bands in a fine example of the hot mix of flute-and-fiddle charanga with trombones — in this case heavier on the trombones than shared by several contemporary Cuban bands. Revé is hot enough to sear steak, and a super mix of classic and new (the singing style re-creates the high nasality of the golden age). The band's also notable for a brilliant pianist. Fire-and-filigree, in an idiom that's one of the most amazing survivals-by-adaptation in New World dance music. –JSR

ISAAC OVIEDO

Son.

○ **Routes of Rhythm - Vol. 3 / ROUNDER**   1992

Ninety-year-old Oviedo is a master of the ultra-Cuban tres guitar, melodic heart of the classical *sones* at the heart of Cuban music. This one-of-a-kind recording presents him jamming on various occasions with a tight musical clan of family and friends. A recording that for once deserves the now-clichéd title of "roots." –JSR

RITMO ORIENTAL

Charanga.

○ **La Ritmo Oriental Te Esta Llamando / GLOBESTYLE**

Recordings licensed from Cuba by a classic charanga. This group's heyday was in the late 60s and 70s, and their best sides have yet to come out here; this record is not definitive, but not bad either. –NS

ARSENIO RODRIGUEZ   1911-1971

Conjunto. Rodriguez was blinded at age three when kicked in the face by a horse. The Marvelous Blind One, as he was fondly referred to, changed the course of Afro-Cuban dance music when he became the first to utilize the conga drum in a dance band in 1937. His son montuno sound was first heard in 1944, four years after he formed his trumpet conjunto. Considered one of Cuba's best composers and tres guitarist, he left Cuba in 1952 for New York City. –MS

○ **Arsenio Rodriguez y Su Conjunto / ANSONIA**

This CD version of two albums from his New York period brings together just about all of his material currently available. –JSR

Salsa

In 1974 Salsa became a household word in the Hispanic communities. It was first heard when Cuba's Ignacio Pineiro's Sexteto Nacional introduced his tune "Echale Salsita" at the 1932 Chicago World's Fair. Salsa, the Spanish word for spicy sauce, was uttered when dancers urged bandleaders to swing the music. The word lay dormant until 1962 when Seeco Records released Joe Cuba's *Stepping Out* album, in which vocalist Jimmy Sabater's tune "Salsa y Bembe" appeared for the first time after 30 years. Salsa's thrust to national recognition occurred after Cal Tjader's 1964 recording of "Soul Sauce" (Salsa del Alma), which received airplay on jazz, R&B, and Latin-music programs across the United States. It achieved international acceptance after the fiery music of the Fania All-Stars and the bands of Larry Harlow, Johnny Pacheco, Ray Barretto, Eddie Palmieri, Orchestra Broadway, La Sonora Poncena, Willie Rosario, El Gran Combo, the Willie Colon/Ruben Blades combination, and Tito Puente modernized the Afro-Cuban sound in the 70s.

The roots of salsa sprouted with the Cuban *son*, a rhythm created in Santiago De Cuba by Theodora Ginez. El son began its rhythmic change in 1791 after hundreds of White Frenchmen and Haitians fled the revolution and relocated in Cuba. During the 18th century, the Cuban government forbade the playing of el son, in that its lyrics protested the inhuman slavery conditions, causing riots. Soldiers from as far away as Havana were sent to Oriente. Those who were musicians returned home with the new rhythm, and it soon found its way throughout Cuba.

In 1920, during a carnival in Havana Guillermo Castillo's Grupo Tipica, Oriental played el son. After the carnival, the group became El Sexteto Habañero, and the era of the trumpet conjunto and the popular el son rhythm began.

In April 1930, the Cuban orchestra of Don Aspiazu started the New York salsa era when it overwhelmed its audiences with its version of "The Peanut Vendor." From the RKO Palace in midtown Manhattan, the tune's infectious melodies filtered to all of New York. RCA Victor recorded it on May 13, 1930, and released it five months later. "El Manisero" was the background music for the 1931 movie *Cuban Love Song*. By the mid 30s, every Latin music aggregation included el son in its repertoire. The most popular groups were those of Vicente Sigler, Nilo Melendez, Alberto Socarras, Rafael Hernandez's Grupo Victoria, Augusto Coen, Xavier Cugat, Montecino's Happy Boys, and Alberto Iznaga's La Siboney. In Cuba during the late 30s, Afro-Cuban rhythms were demonstrating further innovations. Orestes Lopez, a revered musician of Antonio Arcano's charanga (a piano, flute, strings, and rhythm section) invented the danzon mambo rhythm in 1938. The mambo became the standard third part of the danzon, adding an overwhelming excitement that has not yet been improved upon. During the 40s, the Cuban guaracha rhythm joined el son in popularity; the best recordings were by Miguelito Valdes, Machito and the Afro-Cubans, Anselmo Sacassas, Noro Morales, José Curbelo, and Marcelino Guerra.

The next innovation occurred in 1943 at La Conga Club in midtown Manhattan. On Sunday evening, May 28, 1943, the Machito orchestra finished playing a tune. While the next number was being searched for, pianist Luis Varona began to play the introduction to the tune "El Bottellero" (The Bottlemaker). All of a sudden, bassist Julio Andino joined in, plucking the same notes. At a rehearsal the following evening, Mario Bauza (trumpeter and Machito's musical director) told Varona and Andino to play the same introduction while he sang out the broken chords he wanted saxophonists and trumpeters to repeat. Bauza then wrote a melody for the band to play on top of the broken chords. Thus the tune "Tanga" was conceived, and Afro-Cuban jazz (now Latin jazz) was created.

In 1949, Perez Prado's "Mambo #5" became a monstrous hit and officially kicked off the mambo era. Among the then-new bandleaders who revised Prado's sound for New York dancers were Tito Puente and Tito Rodriguez, whose orchestrations were the model for the Palladium mambo. In addition to the two Titos, the most popular bands of the 50s included Machito, Miguelito Valdes, Pupi Campo, Joe Loco Quintet, Alfredito, La Playa Sextet, Cal Tjader, and Noro Morales, along with the Cuban bands of Arsenio Rodriguez, Orquesta Aragon, Enrique Jorrin, Felix Chappotin, Jose Fajardo, Roberto Faz, Bebo Valdes, Cachao y Su Descargo, and Beny More.

The pop dance bands of the 60s were Johnny Pacheco, Charlie Palmieri, Eddie Palmieri, Joe Quijano, Orlando Marin, Joe Cuba Sextet, Ricardo Ray, Pete Rodriguez, and Lou Perez, along with the boogaloo bands of Johnny Colon, King Nando, Joey Pastrana, the Le Bron Brothers, and Joe Bataan. The 70s was an exciting decade because of Gerald Masucci, president of Fania Records. Mr. Masucci spent thousands of dollars in the 60s and 70s promoting unknown musicians who today are superstars earning great sums of money. Masucci bought three hours of air time in every large Hispanic-populated city, including San Juan, Puerto Rico. He flew artists all over the world until they became well known. Eddie Palmieri was the superstar of the 70s. Ray Barretto's tune "Cocinando" was the best of the 70s. The most popular bands were those of Larry Harlow, Johnny Pacheco, Ray Barretto, Bobby Valentine, Willie Colon, Willie Rosario, Tipica Novel, Bobby Rodriguez y La Compania, Angel Canales, La Sonora Poncena, El Gran Combo, Mongo Santamaria, and the sizzling Orchestra Broadway, who never failed to pack ballrooms.

The 80s saw the comeback of Tito Puente among the top bands, with great Concord Jazz label recordings. Joining Puente were Orchestra Broadway, Oscar DeLeon, Louis Ramirez, Willie Rosario, Ray Barretto, Eddie Palmieri, Luis "Perico" Ortiz, Roberto Torres, Papaito Munoz, Charanga America, Conjunto Candela, Grupo Fascinación, Santiago Ceron, Wayne Gorbea, Libre, and the red-hot Conjunto Clásico. So far the 90s have included Poncho Sanchez, Bongologic, Shades of Jade, José Alberto, Tito Nieves, Columbia's Joe Acosta, Santo Domingo's Cuco Valoy, and Japan's Orquesta de la Luz. Salsa would never have achieved its heights of popularity without music arrangers, the music-makers who create hit records — for example, Marty Sheller, Louie Ramirez, Papo Lucca, Oscar Hernandez, Isidro Infante, Alfredito Valdes Jr, Hector Rivera, Rene Hernandez, Lou Perez, Israel "Cachao" Lopez, Arturo "Chico" O'Farrill, Ray Santos, Joe Loco, and Tito Puente.

— Max Salazar

SEXTETO HABAÑERO

Son.

○ **Sexteto Habañero / TUMBAO**
Tumbao is a Swiss label that's turned up this year with some previously unavailable classic sides. This is one of the greatest of the great son groups of the 20s. –NS

SINTESIS

Fusion.

○ **Ancestros / QBADISK**
The most important progressive rock album in Cuba, ever. Authentic Afro-Cuban religious ritual melodies, sung passionately and with great fidelity to the originals, arranged for contemporary instrumentation with electric guitar and synthesizer. People fall in love with this album. –NS

TRIO MATAMOROS

Son.

☆ **20 Exitos Inolvidables / KUBANEY**
If I had to live with only one popular recording for all eternity, this might well be it. "Son de la Loma," "Lagrimas Negras," "El Que Siembra Su Maiz," "Santiaguera," the great Matamoros wrote them all, and here they all are. True, the luscious "Olvido" is missing, but there's probably such a thing as too much bliss. –JSR

LOS VAN VAN

Charanga-plus.

Dancing Wet (Bailando Mojao) / WORLD PACIFIC
An anthology of killer tracks from the 80s through 1990, including a very hot live cut. –NS

Los Van Van / VITRAL
A heavy CD from one of Havana's heaviest contemporary groups. Van Van, a cross between a charanga and a trombone conjunto, is perhaps less adventurous than Irakere, but it doesn't recycle familiar material nearly as much and is more consistently terrific. It also has one of the finest pianists in the whole Latin field. –JSR

CARLOS VARELA

Cuban.

○ **Jalisco Park / ELIGEME**
Good luck trying to find this one; it's on a tiny Spanish label, but it's worth the trouble. At 28 years of age, Varela is an independent voice; his lyrics register as daring in the political context of Cuba. He's the poet of young Havana in the early 90s. This album, recorded in Spain with Spanish sidemen, is an impressive debut by someone who will likely be a major artist in years to come. –NS

CUBA COLLECTIONS

○ **Cuba Classics 1: Canciones Urgentes / WARNER**
An anthology, compiled by David Byrne, of various tracks by Silvio Rodriquez, one of the leaders of Cuba's nueva trova (new song) movement. –NS

☆ **Cuba Classics 2 / WARNER** 1988
I'm biased, I admit: I helped compile *Cuba Classics 2 - Dancing with the Enemy*. At the burrito joint where I eat lunch, they play it every day, and Peter Watrous at *The New York Times* gave it #2 on his Ten Best of 1991 list. These are obscure recordings mostly, the majority from the 60s and 70s. Damn good, if I do say so. –NS

○ **Cuba Classics 3 / WARNER** 1992
This album is more forward-looking. Buy with confidence. –NS

☆ **Cuban Counterpoint / ROUNDER**
A number of reissues of the wonderful groups from Cuba during the golden age are now available. Here is one album that must be mentioned. From the 20s through the 60s, it

traces the development of the son montuno, perhaps the best example of the mixed genre of Cuban popular music. –DLM

○ **Cuban & Puerto Rican Music / MOTW** 1987
Side 1: Orlando Puntilla Rios and Nueva Generacion perform sacred Yoruba santeria music sung and played on Afro-Cuban drums and percussion. Side 2 features Puerto Rican jibaro music by Israel Berrios and El Sexteto Criollo, and bomba and pleña by Los Pleneros de la 21. A great introduction to the Afro-Carribbean tradition. –MUSIC OF THE WORLD

☆ **Dances of the Gods / OCORA**
Here's something crucial for percussion buffs: field recordings covering all the major religious traditions (lucumi, arara, palo monte, tambor yuka, abakwa, transplanted Haitian), along with a couple of street rumbas (guaguancó and columbia). More of the latter would have been nice, and the notes are a bit confused on relationships between denominations. But this is still essential stuff. –JSR

○ **Joyas Tropicales / ANSONIA**
Most of this gem is devoted to cuarteto and septeto music, including many cuts by the Trio Matamoros and Guaracheros de Orients. Others in this vein include the Cuarteto Marcano, the Puerto Rican Cuarteto Borniquen, and others less well known. Most of the rest is from the Sonora Matancera. Pretty much all of it is gold, a most long-buried treasure trove. –JSR

Routes of Rhythm - Vols. 1 & 2 / ROUNDER 1988
Volume 1 is subtitled *Carnival of Cuban Music* and the second volume is subtitled *Cuban Dance Party*. (See Isaac Oviedo for Volume 3.) –ED

○ **Sabroso!: Havana Hits / EARTHWORKS**
Probably the standout in this various-artists compilation is Los Van Van's original recording of "Muevete." –NS

☆ **Salt & Tabasco / MANGO**
A good anthology that blends soca, reggae, Afro-Cuban, and Latin selections. Includes the Cuban group Los Van Van, plus Arrow and others. –RW

DOMINICAN REPUBLIC

BELKIS CONCEPCION

Merengue.

○ **Con lo Mio No Te Metas / KUBANEY**
Belkis Concepcion started out with an all-woman group, Las Chicas del Can, and has carved a career for herself out of a belting voice, a tough-cookie joke, and a general atmosphere of riotous assembly. A kicking group in the great manic merengue mainstream, as contemporary as all get-out, but with lots of roots underpinning the fun and games — not to say talent. Accept no imitations. –JSR

CONJUNTO QUISQUEYA

Merengue.

Conjunto Quisqueya / VIVA
Conjunto Quisqueya shot smartly into the charts last year as part of the remarkable return of the merengue, based on an unusual vocal sound and charming old-style-merengue solo sax, a combination whose end result is considerable freshness. I love salsa-merengue, but there's no denying an occasional glibness that this group conspicuously lacks, to its benefit. –JSR

JOSSIE/PATRULLA ESTEBAN

Merengue.

15 Exitasos / TTH
Esteban has had less publicity than Vargas (of whom he was a protégé like practically all the younger merengueros), Belkis, or Villalona. But he's chalked up some hefty hits over the last few years on a mix of tearaway vocals, humor, and a tight, tight band. Heard again in this best-of, most of them stand up just fine. –JSR

LA INDIA CANELA

Merengue.

Que Siga la Fiesta / JOSE LUIS
Yet another female accordionist to add to Maria Díaz and the unparalleled Fefita la Grande. This one, known to her buddies as Mery Hernandez, is no Fefita, but she's less shaky than Maria Díaz can sometimes be, in the same effective and mellow style, with the mania being (in traditional fashion) provided by the saxist. (53:47). −JSR

LOS GRANDES DEL MERENGUE TIPICO

Merengue.

☆ **Los Grandes del Merengue Típico / JOSE LUIS**
This album is a selection of the young Turks who have brought the country-style accordion sound roaring back from the trashcan of history, updating it into a splendidly happening sound. Fefita La Grande, Francisco Ulloa, and the older Ciego de Nagua are here, but so are a bunch of younger up-and-comers. Most add a sax in the jovial lunacy called perico ripiao. The whole thing is as much re-creation as revival, and wonderfully so. −JSR

MILLY & JOCELYN & LOS VECINOS

Merengue.

7+1 - Vecinos / MP RECORDS
Milly comes out as if she's looking to bite somebody, but she's marginally mellower here than in previous albums, though consistently ebullient (and a lifestyle away from cutesy types like Las Chicas del Can, Belkis, or for that matter her sister Jocelyn). Aside from that, the usual originality in both vocal and instrumental arrangements. −JSR

○ **14 Grandes Exitos / CAPITOL**
It doesn't fool with any crossover elements (Debbie Gibson covers for example), just pushes ahead with an oomph higher and mightier than I would have believed possible. I listen to a lot of merengue, now I listen to 56 minutes more. −CARL HOYT, ORIGINAL MUSIC

TEODORO REYES

Bachata-merengue.

El Cieguito Sabio / GUITARRA
Before the accordion hit the Cibao a century ago, the merengue was backed by string-picking. Reyes obviously doesn't play 19th-century guitar, and there are other modern carryings-on. But with its rural vocals, simple basslines, and classic tambora throb, it provides a contemporary take on something virtually extinct: Dominican country picking. A gem and a rarity. −JSR

WILFRIDO VARGAS

Merengue.

○ **Wilfrido 86 / KAREN**
Vargas was the most creative head of 80s merengue, and in fact pretty much masterminded the entire merengue renaissance of the period. Virtually every Dominican band or singer of the 80s either started out with him or was encouraged by him. He had hit after hit, and used his popularity as license for experiments. A list of the external novelties — harmonica, highly original guitar licks, what sounds like harp (though none's credited), ditto harpsichord — no way does justice to the general air of jovially manic creativity. −JSR

JOHNNY VENTURA

Merengue.

○ **Y Su Combo / KUBANEY**
With the rise of the merengue new-wave, Ventura, once the hippest of the salsa-merengueros, has become something of a Grand Old Man — an elder statesman à la Tito Puente. Here

are the original versions of some of his greatest hits going back a couple of decades, including "El Pinguino," and "El Problema de Ramon." This stuff holds up. −JSR

ANGEL VILORIA

Merengue.

○ **Y Su Conjunto Cibaeno / ANSONIA**
This was the band that set off the first New York merengue craze, 20 years or more ago. The Cibao is merengue heartland, and this group had it all, including lots of the loopy C-melody sax that is a basic part of the sound (as well, of course, as great accordion and vocals, metal scraper, and tambora). −JSR

DOMINICAN REPUBLIC COLLECTIONS

Bachatazos - Vol. 1 / JOSE LUIS
Bachata Rosa, though pretty enough, was basically the pop sound you'd expect from a big hit. The music in this first-of-its-kind compilation is the real bachata, the small-town guitar-based music that grew from Dominican backyard barbecues of the same name. It's mostly bolero-based, but its influences (other than local) are enormously varied: from classic trios to Mexican to Puerto Rican. Delicious. −JSR

ECUADOR

LOS REBELDES

Cumbia.

Cumbia Rebelde / DISCOLANDO
At first blush, Los Rebeldes are just another affable keyboard-centered mid-70s band. But there's a reason they were picked up by a New York label. At the simplest level, they're a fine band with an uncomplicated kick and a sax player who augments the whole without getting too clever for the rest of the guys. Their mix of local rhythms, cumbia, boogalu, and Dominican merengue is far from standard. And some of their songs ("El Problema Electrico" in this album) have a pleña-like topical twist. −JSR

ECUADOR COLLECTIONS

Music of the Jivaro / FOLKWAYS
Music of a very interesting jungle tribal people. −DLM

EL SALVADOR COLLECTIONS

Recordando Nuestra Patria - Vol. 2 / DISCOLANDO
Some of the cuts here are basically somewhat eccentric salsa. Some have strong cumbia influences. Many have that particularly haunting quality of something almost, but not quite, familiar. Only one heartthrob comes near to being a dud — and that only in that he's your standard balladmonger. −JSR

GENERAL LATIN

NANDO BOOM & THE EXPLOTION BAND

Hispa-rap.

○ **Nando Boom & the Explotion Band / ARIOLA**
A very satisfying recording in the Spanish-reggae vein — the music is straightahead dancehall with no surprises, but Nando has a fabulous voice and knows exactly how to work it. He reminds me a lot of the English toasters in style, especially Smiley Culture, and he even does a Spanish-English translation rap like Smiley's "Cockney Translation." A special bonus is a Spanish reggae version of then-Cat Stevens's "Wild World" — also a fine soca. −CARL HOYT, ORIGINAL MUSIC

EL GENERAL

Latin pop.

○ **Muevelo Con ... / BMG**
Listening to the dancehall basslines and the tongue-twister Spanish rap of the Panamanian El General ... I daydream of

driving a Jeep with a "local motion" competitive sound-system through the streets of Brooklyn ... loud enough so my license plates would rattle and buzz to the beat. In the spring of 1991, his hit "Tu Pun Pun" (which is only hinted at here), blared forth from a zillion Brooklyn restaurant-kitchens. Gastro-funk. (39:17) —RAISSA ST. PIERRE, ORIGINAL MUSIC

GENERAL LATIN COLLECTIONS

Indian Harps / PLAYASOUND
The Indios took to the Spanish harp with enthusiasm and creativity, building a dozen regional variants and styles. This particularly beguiling release covers Mexico, Venezuela, Colombia, Paraguay, and Peru. The range is from wonderfully fiery street groups to virtuoso concert performers. —DLM
Music from Mexico & Colombia / MOTW   1987
Los Pregoneros del Puerto sing and play traditional Veracruz melodies using harp, jarana, and requinto. Side two presents Aires Colombianos who perform music from the mountains and plains of Columbia with vocals, string, and percussion instruments. Also featured are Mexican-American songs by the legendary Lydia Mendoza. —MUSIC OF THE WORLD
Musica de la Tierra - Vol. 1 / MOTW   1988
Talented musicians from all over Latin America present a wonderful selection of instrumental music from South America, Mexico, and the Caribbean. Featured artists: Pepe Santana, Atahualpa Poalasin, Gonzalo Mata, Sukay, Marc Ribot/Frantz Casseus, Los Troveros Cuyanos, Aires Comombianos, and El Sexteto Criollo. An excellent instrumental sampler. —MUSIC OF THE WORLD
Musica de la Tierra - Vol. 2 / MOTW   1988
Presents a sampling of instrumental and vocal melodies from Brazil, Ecuador, Colombia, Argentina, Peru, Mexico, and Haiti. Artists include Tico Da Costa, Tahuantinsuyo, Los Troveros Cuyanos, Atahualpa Poalasin, Los Pregoneros del Puerto, and Aires Colombianos. A dynamic cross-section of Latin American music. —MUSIC OF THE WORLD

GUATEMALA COLLECTIONS

La Guelaguetza-Vol. 3 / SON-ART
An unusually attractive marimba recording, somewhere at the town-square end of the pop spectrum, with a kit-drummer who moves between Andean Indian and banda norteña. As a bonus, at least one cut includes a rather intimidated-sounding accordionist. Rackety, in fact, and on the verge of the anarachic; in all, much better than most of its ilk. —JSR

MEXICO

ALEGRES DE TERAN

Norteño.
Triunfadores del Norte / CBS LATINO
A hugely popular norteño group introduced to Anglos by Chris Strachwitz's reissues. The basic sound here is the gentle older duo/trio style, in which accordion and bajo sexto are underpinned by electric bass, but not traps. As in most of the Alegres's many recordings, however, the core unit is joined on-and-off by mariachi backings. —JSR

LOLA BELTRAN

Ranchera.
La Grande ... / PEERLESS
Lola Beltran has claims to be the greatest woman singer in the high-octane pop-ranchera style. The Beltran CD has a wide range of superb songs. Perhaps the finest is one, somewhat out of her main line, called "Pelea de Gallos"; there's also a "Caballo Blanco" which is worth comparing with Jimenez's original. —JSR

CONJUNTO LINDO VERA CRUZ

Conjunto.
Alegria Jarocha / CAPITOL
This old (from internal evidence, 60s) Mexican Capitol release

is by far the finest Vera Cruzan group I've yet heard on record. This is the real thing, for harp, jarana, and guitar, and hotter'n jalapeño. —JSR

HERMANAS HUERTA

Ranchera.
Más Exitos / CBS DISCOS
This duo in its time was a very big deal in commercial ranchera, for many excellent reasons. Though rich in power and elegance, the duo tended to be a little less high-octane than solo singers like Lola Beltran. Whether backed by mariachi, clarinet duo, or accordion, the Huerta Sisters are gorgeous. —JSR

JOSE ALFREDO JIMENEZ

Ranchera.
○ **Homenaje a Jose Alfredo Jimenez / SONY DISCOS**
One of a zillion recyclings. Contains his three greatest songs: "Caballo Blanco," "Camino de Guanajuato," and "El Jinete," which I find so moving I can't listen to it. Undoubtedly the greatest ranchera composer, and to my mind among the finest singers. Ranchera is, to my mind, the ultimate evidence that bigtime film-musical-type music can achieve greatness. —JSR

MARIACHI COCULENSE DE CIRILO MARMOLEJO

Mariachi.
Mariachi Coculense de Cirilo Marmolejo / FOLKLYRIC
Despite tourist stereotypes, mariachis are an enduring part of Mexican tradition, going back more than a century in the western Mexican states. These lovely recordings are from one of the 30s groups that made mariachi a national style. —JSR

PREGONEROS DEL PUERTO

Son.
Sones Jarochos / ROUNDER   1990
A lovely record. The sones of the harp-led groups of Vera Cruz are a lot more complex than norteño music both rhythmically and in playing style, and arguably even more impassioned. Los Pregoneros del Puerto are an old-established professional group with a regional base, so they are both authentic and virtuoso, which is by no means always the case. Superb music; very full notes with lyrics and translations. Four stars at least. —JSR

LUCHA REYES

Ranchera.
Lucha Reyes / RCA
I know nothing about Reyes except what I hear; a powerful ranchera singer with a fresh and natural style nearer to the grassroots than most later singers. The original copyright of this collection is 1964 but she both sounds and looks earlier. I imagine she was, like most, a singer/filmstar, but both her singing and the instrumental backing date from a simpler time. —JSR

RITA Y JOSÉ

Popular.
Adios Morena / CBS DISCOS
This was another highly successful duo in the commercial ranchera style in much the same way that the Hermanas Huerta (see above) were. Rita y José had the added dimension of a wonderfully raffish group, including what I can only call reverent tuba-playing — odd, but enchanting. Never mind intellectual rigor: they sing, I melt. QED. —JSR

MEXICO COLLECTIONS

Fiestas of Chiapas & Oaxaca / NONESUCH
An excellent selection ranging from church music to brass band, small string ensemble, solo singer, and guitar. David

Lewiston must be highly commended for this brilliant recording. Now available on CD. –DLM

Indian Music of Northwest Mexico / CANYON
Indian Music of Northwest Mexico: Tarahumara - Warihio - Mayo features lovely, gentle music, including matachin dance with five violins, pascola with harp, violin, and rattles. –DLM

Mexique - Musique Traditionnelles / OCORA
A good introduction to traditional music from Mexico. –DLM

Modern Maya: Indian Music of Chiapas / FOLKWAYS
Soulful and plaintive music, recorded at various fiestas, with violins, harps, and guitars. –DLM

Music of the Tarascan Indians / FOLKWAYS
Some fine guitar and violin music, chirimias and flutes from one of the most musically interesting areas of Mexico. –DLM

PANAMA COLLECTIONS

○ **Street Music of Panama / ORIGINAL MUSIC**   1988
Panamanian music is among the most exciting in the whole Afro-Latin area. On the Afro end are the voices-and-drums tamboritos, sung and played superbly here by groups of young women. The fiddle-and-percussion cumbia and guitar-backed mejorana are both real Creole idioms, whose Spanish and African elements are both crucial. Then there's the carnival music of the diablitos, and oddest of all, the howling gritos of the midnight hours. This is the real thing, taped before the tradition began to fade. It is also the only album devoted to this wonderful idiom, and capped by a charming piece of Choco Indian flute playing. –JSR

PARAGUAY COLLECTIONS

Los Chiriguanos of Paraguay / NONESUCH
Bright, lively music played on guarani harps, sometimes with singing. –DLM

PERU

LEANDRO APAZA w/BENJAMIN CLARA

Traditional.
Peruvian Harp & Mandolin / MOTW   1984
This selection of traditional Peruvian folk songs was recorded in the ancient Incan city of Cuzco. The artists (blind street-musicians) play 33-string harp and 10-string armadillo-shell mandolin, and they sing in Quechua and Spanish. These beautiful love songs and haunting melodies represent the strongest musical tradition in the Americas. –MUSIC OF THE WORLD

EL CHOLO BERROCAL

Popular.
○ **El Cholo Berrocal / ANSONIA**
Polkas, boleros, waltzes, and a Festejo Peruano. What makes El Cholo click despite his middle-class politeness are a clear, unaffected voice and superb guitar playing. Where there is no harp, guitars take up the swift, brittle, unmistakably Andean runs. –CARL HOYT, ORIGINAL MUSIC

INTI-ILLIMANI

Peruvian pop. A six-piece South American folk group with ethnic instrumentation. –MGN
De Canto Y Baile / REDWOOD
Good companion to *Imagination*. –MGN
Palimpsesto / REDWOOD
Also a good representation of their work. –MGN
○ **Imagination / REDWOOD**   1984
Andean folkloric instrumental music; 14 tracks with the emphasis on joy and light. –MGN

PERU COLLECTIONS

Fiestas of Peru: Music of the High Andes / NONESUCH
Flutes, harps, guitars — festive music. –DLM

Flutes and Strings of the Andes / MOTW
An outstanding recording from an area almost entirely represented on record by imitators rather than source musicians. It casts a fairly wide net, with examples for voices, flutes, strings, and percussion from three provinces. Track by track, the music is marvelous, and the cassette is admirably programmed for diversity as well as authenticity. Good notes, too, for a cassette. –JSR

☆ **Huayno Music of Peru - Vol. 1 / ARHOOLIE**
The popular huaynos of Peru go back hundreds of years and come in all sorts of forms, from village square to (relatively) bigtime pop. Part Spanish, part Indian, they are almost nothing like the better-known Latin forms in feeling or rhythm. As this superlative collection shows, the truly popular versions are almost hypnotically beguiling. Stunning. –DLM

Mountain Music of Peru - Vol. 1 / SMITHSONIAN   1986
What makes a satisfactory national compilation is obviously to some extent a question of ideology. For my money, this one is superb as an overview and introduction. It ranges from shepherd pipe, solo voice, and carnival music, to popular huaynos from the towns. Unlike the plethora of middle-class groups with a political agenda that beclutter the field, this one does music that is real and superb, as are John Cohen's notes. Some was released in 1966, but 15 minutes' worth has been added for this re-release. (68:17) –JSR

Paucartambo: Festival Music ... / MOTW   1987
The selections on *Paucartambo: Festival Music from the Central Andes* were recorded live at the festival of La Mamacha Carmen in Paucartambo, Peru. This fiesta is one of the most deeply rooted mestizo celebrations in the entire Andean region. Flutes, strings, accordions, brass, and percussion instruments are used, and several selections are sung in Quechua and Spanish. –MUSIC OF THE WORLD

PUERTO RICO

CANARIO Y SUS PLENEROS

Pleña.
☆ **Canario y Sus Pleneros / ANSONIA**
The pleña is to Afro-Rican music what the calypso is to Trinidad — dance music, oral history, and Op-Ed page in song. Canario was perhaps the greatest composer of plenas ever, and this brand-new CD version of his only reasonably available recording contains many of his best-known recordings, among them "Cartaron a Elena" and the classic "Santa Maria." –JSR

CORTIJO

Salsa.
○ **16 Exitos / FUENTES**
Cortijo was not the only Puerto Rican salsero to give his music strongly Puerto Rican roots, but he was arguably both the most thorough-going and the most creative. He came out of the Afro-Rican village of Loiza Aldea, and very early on, he brought the bomba drum dance into salsa with a slew of wonderful recordings, many of which (along with equally classic plenas) are included here. An important re-release and (given the label) not guaranteed to be around for ever, so be warned. –JSR

GRAN COMBO

Salsa.
○ **Nuestra Música / COMBO**
El Gran Combo is a perennial sellout on pure tight mainstream salsa alone — mainstream in the contemporary sense, which includes a lot of Puerto Rican tinge. Here they carry the Boricua sound especially far, with an album rich in pleña, bomba, and even jibaro riffs and rhythms. They're also pretty funny guys: the jibaro-style "No Hay Cama Pa' Tanta Gente" rings a very cute change on the standard let's-mention-everybody. –JSR

Boogaloos Con ... / GEMA

Coming from the band's very early days, this is the genuine 60s Real Thing. The album has a lot of straight salsa in the Combo's typical down-home sound. Arranged by pianist/leader Ralph Ithier and featuring Andy Montanez on lead vocals. −JSR

Latin-up / COMBO

The title cut of the band's newest release is a kind of a sort of a boogalu in spots. As was and is customary, this album has a lot of straight salsa as is typical of the Combo's sound. Arranged by Ralph Ithier. −JSR

EL JIBARITO DE LARES

Jíbaro.

Volume 2 / ANSONIA

Since I first heard it almost 20 years ago, the impact of this incredible voice has never faded. This was a kid of around 15 years old, singing the pure mountain sound with unbelievable raw beauty. This second album is, if possible, even finer than the first: better songs, and more of the wonderful traditional cuatro-conjunto backings. −JSR

LA CALANDRIA

Jíbaro.

☆ **La Calandria / ANSONIA**

Navidad / ANSONIA   SALP

La Calandria is the greatest woman singer of the Puerto Rican jíbaro mountain style. Backings includes gorgeous cuatro by the great Nieves Quintero. This (obviously) is a Christmas collection, but it is not restricted either to aguinaldos nor to Christmas themes. A fine example of the tradition at large and of her own art. −JSR

LOS TRES HERMANOS

Jíbaro.

Los Tres Hermanos / ANSONIA

Euro-Rican jíbaro mountain music is some of the greatest as well as the most neglected of US music, equally superb vocally and instrumentally. The three brothers on this new CD of an old LP are Ramito, one of the greatest of all male jíbaro singers, Luisito, and Moralito. This is among the finest of many classic recordings of Puerto Rican seises, aguinaldos, decimas, and mapeye. The splendid singing is enhanced (as is only right and traditional) by very fine cuatro-picking. −JSR

LUIS MIRANDA w/NIEVES QUINTERO

Jíbaro.

Mi Musica Borincana / ANSONIA

Miranda's style and material are typical of the older generation. Quintero, a cuatro-player the equal of any, is wonderful on the album: he's at his best working within the constraints of backing a singer. Miranda, incidentally, provides a bonus in the form of a controversia — a theoretically improvised musical bicker using the ancient and complex decima form — with Joaquin Mouliert. −JSR

WILLIE ROSARIO   b 1930

Salsa. Arriving in New York City from Puerto Rico in 1948, Rosario was moved by Tito Puente's drumming ability at the Palladium Ballroom. He began his percussion studies and made his pro debut with Johnny Sequi's band in 1953. When Sequi moved to Puerto Rico, Rosario took over the band and today it is among the most popular salsa and Latin jazz aggregations in Latin America. −MS

Roaring Fifties / SONOTONE LATINO

Percussionist Rosario moved back to Puerto Rico in the 70s, but he came up in NYC. He once told me his influences were the likes of Tito Rodriguez and Herbie Mann, not the Cubans. He also said, "I like clean music, music that has definition." Put those two elements together and you have a dynamite big-

band sound: crisp, elegant, and driving. I'd call it timelessly classic, but this band plays as freshly as if they'd only just invented the sound! −JSR

EDDIE SANTIAGO

Salsa.

○ **Atrevido y Diferente / TH-RODVEN**

The biggest name in the newish salsa-romantica vein, which combines lushness and swing. This was Santiago's first real smash — something like a year in the Top Three! — and in retrospect it was, I think, his best recording. Part of his effect comes from a tendency to move more readily than traditional salsa singers from a low register to a fine, clear high one — a simple but effective way of gaining emotional clout. Almost as important was a dynamite band, crisp and tight, with a particularly fine pianist. −JSR

LA SONORA PONCEÑA

Salsa. One of Puerto Rico's most popular orchestras, which was founded by Quique Lucca in 1954 in Ponce, Puerto Rico. La Ponceña is directed by Lucca's son, the brilliant composer, arranger, and keyboardist, Papo, born in 1950. Papo Lucca's career started in 1964 when he became the band's pianist. At the moment, La Ponceña is among the top five salsa and Latin jazz bands in Latin music. −MS

○ **Into the 90s / INCA**

Sonora Ponceña, always a tight, fresh avant-mainstream group, has arguably become one of the great bands. With this recent release they're adding things around the edges — an effective touch of soul, an entirely out-of-idiom piano intro, a gravely beautiful bowed-bass break, and all sorts of other unexpected doings. All of which makes the title a little more substantial than such slogans usually are. −JSR

On the Right Track / INCA

Sonora Ponceña is one of the best bands around — and not just in Puerto Rico, though that's where it's based. With the possible exception of pianist Papo Lucca, these aren't names — just a very tight, fresh group with the ability to make a tradition-based sound brand new. Listen to the sudden trumpet duet in "Odiame" and rejoice! −JSR

PUERTO RICO COLLECTIONS

○ **Music of Puerto Rico 1929-1946 / HARLEQUIN**

A very fine set of recordings, mostly string groups, mostly from the mid 30s. Many of them are by New York-Puerto Rican groups in the fashionable Cuban idioms of the time — boleros, sones, and so forth — by major composers like Pedro Berrios and Rafael Hernandez. These have a lot of charm, but the gems are a handful of truly Puerto Rican forms: seises, aguinaldos, and plenas. A major bonus is a two-clarinet-lead danza. The only bummer: the greatest of all early pleneros, Canario, appears just once, playing a commercial bolero! −JSR

UNITED STATES

BAD STREET BOYS

New York salsa.

○ **Looking for Trouble / JAP**

The most interesting group to come out of Latin New York's English-language salsa substyle for decades — a joyous early-80s update of the boogalu traditions, trombones, chutzpah, and all. Who could resist a group that moves from urbane rap through "The Lady Is a Tramp" to "When Sunny Gets Blue" done boogalu? −JSR

BATACUMBELE

New York salsa. A hot Afro-Cuban outfit that rivals any today. Their name comes from the batá drum from Africa plus the "cumbia" rhythms of montuno and mambo, which evolved from tribal dance. −MGN

Con un Poco de Songo / DISCO HIT 1981

A recording by one of the most adventurous, interesting, and — more simply — best bands extant. The story is told by the instrumentation, which includes one trumpet, baritone sax, flute, clarinet, batá drums, and cuatro. Which translates into a sound drawing from a very wide range of traditions, mixing charanga and conjunto and the rest in a more varied way than the standard orquesta sound. –JSR

○ **In Concert ... / MONTUNO** 1988

In Concert at the University of Puerto Rico features hot and heavy Latin/Afro/Cuban music from this stellar 20-plus-piece band. Mostly includes traditional themes extended with improvisation. This is one you cannot live without. –MGN

RUBEN BLADES

New York salsa. The Panamanian-born Blades is one of salsa's leading artists and the first to incorporate rock consistently into his boiling sound. He has remained a prominent voice of leftist Latino politics through his topical songwriting and his active/activist role in Panama's political system. He has recorded a slew of albums, but his American output has been more sparse. The following is the best of that output. –JF

Antecedente / ELEKTRA

Although sung in his native tongue, his return to exuberant, dance-oriented salsa breaks through all language barriers. –JF

☆ **Ruben Blades y Son del Solar ... Live! / ELEKTRA**

A smoldering set, recorded live with his 11-piece band, Son del Solar, who romp and stomp for over an hour. Perfect for parties. –JF

Bohemio y Poeta / FANIA 1979

This release was a transition between Blades's post-Willie Colon sound and the 80s *Seis del Solar*. The salsa sounds predominate much of the time, and there's a Cuban classic in among his own compositions. But keyboards and vibes (presumably from Louie Ramirez, who did some of the arranging) point to a new dispensation in the offing, with their (here, at least, very successful) fusion edge. –JSR

○ **Buscando America / ELEKTRA** 1984

A masterful concept album (the title means "searching for America") that spins hard-hitting tales of Latino strife and American injustice. This album includes some of his most gorgeous ballads. –JF

CARABALI

Salsa quintet.

○ **Carabali / MANGO** 1981

A super young band working in the great vibes-led Latin-jazz-inflected quintet sound of the 50s and early 60s! You've heard Cal Tjader and, I hope, stopped sneering at George Shearing. But the great groups in this vein — the TNT Band and the like, even Joe Cuba, were filled with New York Latinos and cut much closer to the salsa bone. Carabali has the whole thing down pat, including the change-of-pace English language songs and terrific vibist Valerie Naranjo working off Oscar Hernandez's piano just like the hippest of mellow old times. Joy cometh in the morning ... –JSR

MILTON CARDONA

New York salsa.

○ **Bembe / AMERICAN CLAVE** 1985

Cardona, one of New York salsa's finest percussionists, is an initiate in the lucumi faith that traveled from West Africa to the New World. This New York recording of the songs for various orisha is part of a widespread religious practice whose local differences are mostly superficial. (Worth comparing with the Afro-Cuban anthology issued by Areito.) –JSR

WILLY CHIRINO

Miami Sound.

○ **Acuarela Del Caribe / SONY LATINO**

Like his great *Zarabanda* album, Chirino's new one superbly exploits the riches of the Miami sound, which stem from a true verbal and musical bilingualism. The opener is just staggering: a kind of mad medley veering between típico and rock; between (literally) Sergeant Pepper and "Purple Haze" and "Son de la Loma." –JSR

14 Exitos / TH-RODVEN

Chirino is a leader of the Miami-Latin sound, which draws from disco and other Anglo forms, Cuban music, and New York salsa. Alas, his best-ever song "San Zarabanda" isn't included. But it's good to see a break in the usual neglect of this creative and individualistic Florida idiom. –JSR

WILLIE COLON   b 1950

New York salsa. Born to Puerto Rican parents, Colon began music studies in 1964 while he directed his group. He signed with Fania Records in 1967 and immediately established his name with the tracks "Jazzy" and "I Wish I Had a Watermelon." Colon is idolized outside the US. He's a cultural hero in Latin America. He improves with every recording. –MS

○ **Metiendo Mano / FANIA**

Salsa history in the making: the album in which Willie Colon introduced Ruben Blades to the wider world! An obvious classic, given Blades's subsequent history, but also a gorgeous album with Yomo Toro on two tracks (one playing guitar), the great pianist Sonny Bravo on two cuts, and ace percussion with Milton Cardona and Nicky Marrero. –JSR

☆ **The Big Break/La Gran Fuga / FANIA**

Colon's third album and clearest early sign of his individuality, with a Ghanaian children's song, the first of his Panamanian-influenced numbers, and a prophetic venture into Brazilian rhythms. –JSR

Asalto Navideño / FANIA

A groundbreaking early-70s recording, *Asalto Navideño* was a Christmas album, and Christmas is the time when the old jibaro mountain sound comes briefly into its own. Colon hired cuatro player Yomo Toro and gave him a leading role, launching him on a new career. A major album, which includes one of Colon's finest Panamanian-flavored early hits, "La Murga." –JSR

Tiempo Pa' Matar / FANIA

Colon, one of the most creative heads of the 60s, has retained the same restlessness and inquiring mind, and the same ability to come up with music both beguiling and intelligent. (Check out the use of the female *coro* in "Volo" on this album.) Fine vocals, fine musicians, and who would dare claim to spot all the stylistic sideglances under the surface of this subtle and enchanting album? –JSR

○ **El Malo / FANIA**

El Malo was Colon and Hector Lavoe's first-ever recording, made in 1967 when Colon was a mere 17 years old. Every number's a killer: "Jazzy," "Juana Pena," "Borinquen," "El Malo." *Plus* boogalu! –CARL HOYT, ORIGINAL MUSIC

☆ **The Good, the Bad, the Ugly / FANIA** 1975

A classic recording by one of the most creative heads in New York salsa. In 1975 *The Good...*, a New Directions release after Colon got fed up with the two-trombone sound, was the evidence that he could reach beyond his youthful sound into an idiom both wider and deeper. It was also the last album with Hector Lavoe, who had decided to stay with being a teen idol. *The Big Break*, *Asalto Navideño*, and this album in their different ways were pinnacles of early to mid-70s salsa. –JSR

JOE CUBA   b 1931

New York salsa. Cuba's music career started with La Alfarona X in 1950. In 1955 the Joe Cuba Sextet came into being and his vibraharp sound caught on. In 1962, when the group recorded "To Be with You" for Seeco Records, the band began to soar to popularity because of Nick Jimenez's arrangements and the vocals of Cheo Feliciano and Jimmy Sabater. When the boogaloo era arrived, the majority of the popular New York bands were put out of work. The Cuba sound changed with its recordings of "El Pito" and "Bang Bang"; it not only sold millions but enabled the Cuba sextet to enjoy the #1 spot in the Latin music world along with the Eddie Palmieri Orchestra. –MS

○ **Joe Cuba Sextet / TICO**
The 50s/60s cusp saw a last flowering of the bilingual, Cubop-inflected, often vibraphone-led quintet sound. Puente was one of its heavies, but in New York at least, the tradition was maintained into the pachanga and even boogalu era of the 60s by Joe Cuba. Jaunty mambo, soupy English-lyric boleros, Latin-jazz or neo-típico; this was an archetypal Latin New York sound. –JSR

PACO DE LUCIA

Latin jazz, flamenco.
○ **Siroco / VERVE**
At times, flamenco phenomenon De Lucia has branched out into jazz, bossa nova, and Cuban mixes. Here, however, he plays essentially solo compositions based on pure flamenco, though with a virtuosity and reach that belong in a concert hall rather than in the traditional settings. –JSR

● **Entre Dos Aguas / POLYGRAM**
Any and all of his albums have a great blend of traditional elements and virtuoso playing. –RW

Live ... One Summer Night / POLYGRAM
Ranges from sentimental to animated. –RW

Fabulosa Guitarra De Paco De Lucia / POLYGRAM   1991
Amazing solos and playing throughout. –RW

MACHITO   1908-1984

Cubop. Machito left Cuba for New York in October 1937. He sang with several groups before organizing his orchestra in 1940. The Decca 78s "Sopa De Pichon," "La Paella," "Nague," "Tingo Talango," and "Chacumbele" enabled the band to enjoy top billing status by 1943. It was the WOR radio remotes from La Conga Club in midtown Manhattan that enabled the band to be heard coast to coast. During its 44 years, the Machito band recorded for major labels. –MS

Mucho Macho / PABLO
Finally in CD, Pablo's old compilation of some of Machito's finest Cubop classics, by what was perhaps the finest of all his bands. "Asia Minor," "Babarabatiri," "Tea for Two," "St. Louis Blues," even (!) "Donkey Serenade." Fine notes; great old photos. If I don't say more about this ultra-classic, it's because words will not ... etc., etc. –JSR

Cubop City / TUMBAO
More amazing Latin jazz from Machito and his Afro-Cubans, recorded live in 1949-1950, featuring bop players Howard McGhee, Brew Moore, and Flip Phillips, plus Ella Fitzgerald scatting on one cut. –JOHN MCCORD, ROOTS & RHYTHM

○ **Machito & His Salsa Big Band / IMPULSE**
This was the recording that won Machito a Grammy in 1983. A dynamite band with Chocolate Armenteros in the trumpet section and Macho's daughter as lead female vocalist, and a fine mix of well-known and less-familiar numbers including "El Manicero" and a Machito warhorse, "Quimbombo." A worthy memorial indeed. –JSR

NORO MORALES   1911-1964

New York salsa. Morales was in New York in 1935, played briefly with the bands of Alberto Socarras and Augusto Coen before establishing the Brothers Morales (Noro-Humberto-Esy) orchestra in 1939. The 1942 Decca 78 "Serenata Ritmica" gave Morales instant recognition. During the decade of the 40s his and Machito's band was the most popular in NYC. –MS

○ **His Piano and Rhythm / ANSONIA**
Like so many of the big names of the 40s, Morales went from enormous popularity to total oblivion. Which is a major pity, since he was very important in the early days of New York salsa as a main creator of a quintet style that blended jazz with

classic Cuban piano. This late-period album documents both the brillance and the prolixity of a musician long overdue for a reassessment. –JSR

CHARLIE PALMIERI   b 1936

New York salsa. Palmieri began piano studies at 6, was sitting in with bands at dances at 14, and was a full-time musician at 16. He formed his group, El Conjunto Pin Pin, in 1948. He played piano for Pupi Campo, Tito Puente, Tito Rodriquez, Bicentico Valdes, and Pete Terrace before forming his Charanga Dubonney group in 1958. –MS

○ **Adelante Gigante / ALEGRE**
Eddie Palmieri always said his elder brother was the better player, and by the time of his death, Charlie Palmieri was well enough known outside the barrio to get an obituary in the *New York Times*. This classic mid-70s album has all his usual taste, talent, classic piano (and in a couple of places organ) along with his favorite lead singer, Vitin Aviles, and a tight band. –JSR

EDDIE PALMIERI   b 1936

Salsa. Palmieri started out as a vocalist and was influenced by elder brother Charlie to study piano. Eddie Palmieri is the only Latin bandleader to win five Grammies and is a tremendous record seller. He started with the neighborhood band of Orlando Marin and made his professional debut in 1955 with Johnny Sequi's orchestra. After stints with Vicentico Valdes, Pete Terrace, and Tito Rodriquez he formed Conjunto La Perfecta in 1962. –MS

El Rey De Las Blancas Y Las Negras / SONY
Any release from this great salsa/Latin-jazz master is mandatory. –RW

Sueño / INTUITION
The 80s *Sueño*, produced by poly-buff Kip Hanrahan, went nowhere much, perhaps because Capitol didn't know what to do with it. But it's another example of what made Palmieri one of the great salsa bandleaders. –JSR

○ **Sentido / MUSICAL PRODUCTIONS**
The Coco-Records-era *Sentido*, regarded by some as his greatest album ever. "Puerto Rico" alone would put it hors concours, even without the version of that piano intro in "Adoracion" and the bi-cultural funk of "Condiciones." A one-man avant-garde who did it all while still preserving his street cred! What a family! Pa and Ma Palmieri, we thank you! –JSR

Mozambique / TICO   1965
Palmieri first hit in the 60s with his classic two-trombone sound. This is one of his finest albums; unassuming, joyous, punchy, and sharp, with the outstanding Ismael Quintana on vocals and Manny Oquendo on timbales. –JSR

☆ **Sun of Latin Music / COCO**   1973
This album almost perfectly combines Palmieri's experimentalism with the devastating swing that kept him ahead on the street. The "Un Dia Bonito" suite got most attention, but "Una Rosa Española," a one-cut mini-history of salsa, is enchanting. –JSR

DANIEL PONCE

Latin jazz. Latin percussionist whose presence and magnetism is inspirational of its own accord. Primarily a conga player who leads contemporary Latin-jazz dance oriented bands. A premier, in-demand sideman. –MGN

○ **Arawe / POLYGRAM**
Superb conga playing throughout; decent-to-strong arrangements. –RW

NY Now! / CELLULOID   1982
First album. Musicians include Paquito (sax), Olufemi (keyboards), Ignacio Berroa (drums), Bill Laswell (bass), and Michael Beinhorn (keyboards). Seven pieces are by conga man Ponce. There is a bit of a contemporary edge, but all is in the Latin spirit. –MGN

● **Chango Te Llama / MANGO-ANTILLES**   1991
The large ensemble is burning hot. This is an excellent companion to *Arawe*. Ponce wrote three selections. There is lots of vocalist Tito Allen and saxophonists Mario Rivera and Dave Snachez. –MGN

TITO PUENTE   ♭1923

New York salsa. Puente mastered percussion and piano during his early teens; he dropped out of high school at age 16 to become a full-time musician. Since 1939 he has compiled an enviable record of acomplishments. Dr. Puente proficiently plays five instruments, is a composer and arranger, won four Grammies, and is the only Latin bandleader to have recorded over 100 albums. To list the best of Puente would take pages. –MS

Hits Candentes / RIN
Some of his best-known cuts. –RW

● **Salsa Meets Jazz / CONCORD**
Excellent, maybe his best on the label. Phil Woods (alto sax) joins the party and soars. –RW

Puente Goes Jazz / RCA   1956
Birdland series. Orchestra plays jazz and Latin musics. "What Is This Thing Called Love?" and "Birdland after Dark" are great. –MGN

○ **Top Percussion / RCA**   1957
A stunner from Puente's golden age, this 1957 recording brought together Tito, Mongo, Willie Bobo, Aguabella, and Julito Collazo on percussion with vocalists that included Mercedita Valdez, in seven wonderful cuts of traditional and (then) contemporary Afro-Cuban skin-on-skin. Then as an unexpected gift, there is a seven-minute Latin-jazz suite featuring Puente's considerable jazz-arranger head and a powerful band with (Ripley, though should still be living at this hour) Doc Severinson on lead trumpet. –JSR

○ **Dance Mania / RCA-BMG**   1958
What a treasure! We'd long despaired of finding anything from the days of Puente's young prime, and here's his two best albums reissued in CD! This was Puente's big band at the height of its powers, one of the great documents of New York Latin music and the sort of thing that established the man's claim to be one of the creators of big-band mambo. –JSR

○ **On Broadway / CONCORD**   1982
Always impressive Puente percussion; good arrangements. Not among his most rhythmically ambitious. –RW

○ **Un Poco Loco / CONCORD**   1987
One of his best for the label. Puente's playing in both large and small contexts. –RW

○ **The Mambo King / SONY-RMM**   1991
Puente's 100th album is a celebration of that fact, with a procession of vocalists, most of whom — like Celia Cruz — were professionally associated with him at one time or another. That doesn't make for a very tight concept, but recordings by musicians of Tito's generation didn't have concepts, they had music. So does this one, including a minor riot with Celia Cruz riding a big, burly mambo arrangement by a band full of just everybody, and a wonderful "El Bribon del Aguacero" with Chocolate Armenteros on trumpet. –JSR

Mamborama! / TICO-CHARLY   1991
A blistering reissue of Tito Puente's Tico label recordings. 24 spicy numbers, rarely deviating much from the upbeat to furious tempos demanded by the ostentatious mambo dancers. If you want anything hotter than this you better fireproof your stereo first. –MYLES BOISEN, ROOTS & RHYTHM

RICARDO RAY   ♭1945

New York salsa. Ray organized his octet in 1963. He was considered a virtuoso pianist, music arranger, and composer, whose band enjoyed tremendous drawing power and was among the best sellers in the 60s and 70s. –MS

○ **Jala, Jala Boogaloo - Vol. 2 / ALEGRE**
Glue your hat on your head, because this stuff'll blow it right

Latin American Terms

Berimbau — Originally an African instrument brought to Brazil, this bow-shaped instrument has one steel string and a gourd resonator.

Bossa nova — Syncopated Brazilian dance music that developed out of a mixture of samba and cool jazz from the late 50s and early 60s.

Charanga — A delicately fiery Cuban ensemble featuring violins, solo flute, timbales, piano, and unison singing. The cha cha cha originated from a charanga group.

Conjunto — A small group, itrumpet-led in Cuban music and accordion-led in Mexico. It additionally features vocals, piano, bass, conga, and bongos.

Cuatro — Puerto Rican ten-stringed guitar used in "jibaro" music.

Cumbia — An accordion-led "vallenato" style combining Andean Indian, African, and European elements. Hugely popular in Colombia.

Danzón — An older Cuban ballroom-dance style played by charanga orchestras.

Forró — Down-to-earth, jaunty music of Northeastern Brazil, comprising accordions, triangles, and a shallow drum called a zabumba.

Güiro — A percussion instrument, it is shaped like a gourd, has carved ridges, and is scraped with a stick.

Jíbaro music — Puerto Rican mountain music featuring guitar, cuatro, maracas, guiro, and voice. Its beginnings are found in Spanish-derived traditions of verse.

Lambada — Extremely popular in Europe in 1989, this close dance is done to Afro-Brazilian-Caribbean rhythms.

Mambo — Hugely popular Cuban big-band music that swept the US in the 50s. Also the name of the instrumental section in contemporary salsa.

Merengue — The "national" music of the Dominican Republic. Played with a tambora drum and güiro in both accordion-led and big-band styles.

Méringue — An older Haitian dance rhythm, related to the Dominican rhythm.

MPB — An acronym for Musica Popular Brasileira, it is a common term for a recent, text-oriented Brazilian popular music (of Milton Nascimento and others), which followed the bossa-nova.

Partido alto — A form of the samba featuring a slow tempo.

Plena — Puerto Rican street music lyrically similar to Trinidadian calypso and played on panderetas (hand-held frame drums), güiro, harmonica, and accordion.

Rumba — A US misnomer for the son, which became an international dance craze in the 30s. Afro-Cuban percussion music with various offshoots.

off. Ricardo Ray was one of the great names of 60s Latin boogaloo, the ultra-Latin-New York mix of salsa, jazz, and R&B. A ballad with an elegant neo-classical backing is also wonderful, but the rest has a kick like a dancing mule. –JSR

MON RIVERA

New York salsa.

○ **Karakatis-ki / ANSONIA**
Rivera was probably the true originator of the trombone conjunto sound associated with early Eddie Palmieri and Willie Colon. But he was also an important figure in the period when Puerto Rican influences in general and the plena and bomba in particular were at their peak in New York salsa.

And most basically he was a fine (and at times comic) singer with a smoking band. —JSR

TITO RODRIGUEZ   1923-1972

New York salsa. Rodriguez came to New York in 1939, where he sang with the orchestras of his brother Johnny Rodriguez, Enric Madriguera, Caney, Xavier Cugat, Noro Morales, and José Curbelo. Rodriguez formed a quintet in 1947 and enlarged it in 1948 to a trumpet conjunto. In 1963 his recording of "Inolvidable" in Argentina sold 1,000,500 copies throughout Latin America. —MS

○ **Un Retrato de ... / TR RECORDS**
The great TR was, of course, part of the New York mambo troika of which Puente and Machito were the other members. A fine singer of both mambo and romantic material, he ran a band as fiery as any. Here are "Mama Guela" and "Yambu" in the former vein, and the monster hit "Cuando Cuando" in the latter, as well as much more. A major re-release. —JSR

○ **Uptempo / TICO**
An interesting cut-out of relatively unfamiliar Rodriguez mambos, cha cha chas, and such, including his version of "El Manicero." Rodriguez was a major heart-throb, and his albums always had plenty of schmaltz. Not being into big-band bolero, which seems to me a major waste of a rhythm section, I'm happy to have the hotter stuff unsullied. —JSR

PONCHO SANCHEZ   b1951

New York salsa. Born to Mexican parents, Sanchez studied flute and guitar in junior high school and later took up percussion. He gigged with Gary Foster, Mark Levine, Willie Bobo, and Luis Gasca until he joined Cal Tjader's Combo on Dec 31, 1975. When Cal Tjader died, Sanchez inherited the group. The Sanchez aggregation is hot property — it is always in demand, has great drawing power, and is a top record seller. —MS

○ **Gauiota / DISCOVERY**   1980
Some first-rate sessions with Clare Fischer on piano. —RW

● **Fuerte / CONCORD**   1987
An octet recording, with standouts pianist and composer Charlie Otwell (who wrote the title track and two other cookers) and saxophonist Ken Goldberg (who wrote two others). Because of them, this stands as a prime Sanchez album, in addition to the group's hot playing. —MGN

Chile Con Soul / CONCORD   1989
The CD version has two bonus cuts. —RW

○ **A Night at Kimball's East / CONCORD**   1990
Sanchez is best live, and this set proves it. Eleven numbers vary from swing-era tunes to James Brown numbers with a Latin beat. This very entertaining and musically worthwhile album, featuring an eight-piece band, is also available on video. —MGN

Cambios / CONCORD   1990
Two bonus cuts on CD. —RW

MONGO SANTAMARIA   b1927

New York salsa. Santamaria directs one of a few bands that play mambos, Latin jazz, and Latin rock. He left Cuba for Mexico in 1948 and worked with Perez Prado before moving to New York City in 1949. He performed with the bands of Johnny Sequi and Jose Luis Monero, and with Gilberto Vales's Danzon Orchestra, and Marcelino Guerra before joining Tito Puente in 1951. Seven years later he was playing conga for Cal Tjader, but he left in 1960 to direct his own group. Santamaria has won one Grammy. —MS

● **Skins / MILESTONE**   1962
Two sessions: 1962 and 1964. Afro-Latin cuts with amazing solos, plus great Chick Corea piano. —RW

○ **Mongo at the Village Gate / OJC**   1963
A jumping live date, recently reissued. —RW

Sofrito, 5 on the Color Side / VAYA   1976

A much-sought-after 1976 release, which links Mongo's once groundbreaking Latin-jazz funk to the somewhat spacy fusion-jazz of the era. The jazz names aren't really "names," the heavies being Pretty Purdie, Gaugua Rivera, and arranger Marty Sheller. But the absence of stars may be one reason for the very cohesive effect of the whole affair. The sound is very much of its time, but in no way dated. (48:46) —JSR

○ **Live at Jazz Alley / CONCORD**   1990
Good group. —RW

UNITED STATES COLLECTIONS

○ **Caliente=Hot / NEW WORLD**
Five fine NYC roots groups re-create classic idioms from Afro-Cuban drumming through pleña to the pure conjunto and sones sound: the Pleneros de la 110th Street, Julito Collazo, Hector Rivera y Su Conjunto, Sexteto Criollo Puertorriqueño, and the Sepeto Son de la Loma. —JSR

○ **Salsa Greats - Vol. 2 / FANIA**
This fine compilation dates back to 1978, but most of it not only stands up but is still jumping. Present, and more than correct, are classics like Eddie Palmieri's great "Azucar," Puente's "Para los Rumberos," Barretto's "Mirame de Frente," Larry Harlow's "Aresnio," Willie Colon's "Che Che Cole," and less familiar numbers by Pacheco, Roberto Roena, Ricardo Ray, Bobby Valentin, and the Sonora Poncera. —JSR

○ **Sixties Gold / MUSICA LATINA**
The Gran Manzana of the 60s, the era of the boogaloo and Latin soul, was an enormously creative and rackety time. This was the era of East Harlem Black-Latin crossover. It brought forth names still famous — Barretto, Pacheco, Colon — and names forgotten — Pagan, Bataan, Colon. (Buy the record! Educate yourself!) Here are Ray's original "El Watusi," Joe Cuba's "Bang Bang," Mongo's "Watermelon Man," and a dozen other pearls of musical mayhem in a purely neoyorquino style the looming típico revolution was about to kill stone dead, to the great loss of the scene. —JSR

VENEZUELA

BILLO & HIS CARACAS BOYS

Popular.
Viejo Pero Sabroso / DISCOLANDO
Despite all the competition from Cuban and US bands, Billo and the lads were popular well beyond the borders of Venezuela in the 60s and 70s. The sound was mainstream mambo-era big band but with the variations you might expect from a South American group, particularly but not only in the group's excursions into cumbia. —JSR

JULIO JARAMILLO

Popular.
Colección de Pasillos / DISCOLANDO
A mid-70s recording. This is elegant, delicate, charming, and very Venezuelan singing with guitar-led backings (bass, a touch of harp) to match. Jaramillo had an international name at times, but this is far more local than the pan-Latin trio music of groups like Los Panchos. It would be nice to see this kind of classic sound rediscovered. —JSR

PASTOR LOPEZ w/LOS MAYORALES

Popular.
En Mexico / DISCOLANDO
Lopez became a big-time exponent on the heartthrob end of contemporary cumbia, but he started real rootsy. The band here has horns along with its accordion, but this is still a great small-town sound, and Lopez himself is super. —JSR

MARIA RODRIGUEZ

Traditional.
La Tremenda / WORLD CIRCUIT

Rodriguez came out of the Venezuelan street comparsa, became a Cuban-style pop singer in the 40s, and then went home to teach and sing the traditional comparsas and joropos. On this admirable first album by a new British label she is backed by a classic quartet of mandolin, cuatro, guitar, and maraccas, and a few more beautiful sounds. –JSR

VENEZUELA COLLECTIONS

Folk Music from Venezuela / REPORTAGE
Side 1 of this cassette is devoted to a semi-pro revivalist — or at least preservationist group, which performs fulias and other forms from all over Venezuela in a pretty authentic style. Side 2 is given over to field recordings of all three types of Venezuelan music — Euro-Venezuelan, Afro-Venezuelan, and Indian. Particularly fine is some of the drumming, but the string groups playing for joropos are also a rarity. Outstanding notes, for a cassette. –JSR

○ **Los Grandes del Cuatro / LEON**
A tremendous recording of a little-known member of the American guitar family, the four-string Venezuelan cuatro, fronting five small guitar-and-percussion combos in a variety of styles: mainly Venezuelan folkloric, but including the occasional bossa and jazz number. The playing is even more manically virtuosic than flamenco, echoes of which surface here. Andean touches are also prevalent. (53:21) –CARL HOYT, ORIGINAL MUSIC

○ **Music of Venezuela / ZU-ZAZZ**
A very fine set of recent recordings by amateur and semi-professional groups, with a focus on stringed instruments — violin as well as members of the huge family of Latin guitars and mandolins. Many of the styles included are available on commercial recordings, but not on the whole in such grassroots idioms, nor with such excellent notes. This album is also available in the US on the High Water label. –JSR & MB

YAQUI COLLECTIONS

Anthology of ... / FOLKWAYS
Anthology of Central & South American Indians. A good sampling from Yaquis in the north all the way to Tierra del Fuego. –DLM

Yaqui Dances / FOLKWAYS
Haunting, enchanting, and beautiful music, with violin and guitar. –DLM

MIDDLE EAST

AFGHANISTAN COLLECTIONS

Afghanistan Folk Music - Vol. 2 / LYRICHORD
Very interesting selection of vocal and instrumental folk music –DLM

Music of Afghanistan / ARGO
Fine selection of vocal and instrumental music. –DLM

The Music of Afghanistan / MUSICAPHON
Cultural crossroads, Afghanistan's music has elements from India as well as Iran, Turkey, and even Russia and ancient Greece. Here are a piece in Farsee, of clear Persian inspiration; pieces with apparent links to ancient Europe; Indian-style drumming. Here are vocals, percussions, varied pipes, and lutes. One of Musicaphon's finest recordings. –JSR

AZERBAIJAN

HAJI BABA HUSEYNOV

Traditional.
Maqam of Azerbaijan / INEDIT
One cultural benefit of recent events is that the former Soviet Middle East is no longer an inaccessible mystery land. This means, for example, that Azeri classical music can reclaim its position as a major tradition within the Persian-Turkish-Arabic nexus. A fine recording by leading exponents of vocal

style, tar lute, and kemantche fiddle. Splendid music; informative notes. (54:47) –JSR

ALEM KASSIMOV

Traditional.
Two Mugam / INEDIT
Azeri art music is one of the lesser known of major idioms within the Mideastern/Islamic tradition. Of the two mugam (loosely, modes) for tar lute, spike fiddle, and daf frame drum performed here, the 51-minute "Mugam rast" is overwhelmingly the major work with its 19 vocal and instrumental sections. Excellent performance; fine recording; passable notes. (61:58) –JSR

BAHRAM MANSUROV

Traditional.
Azerbaijani Mugam: Bahram Mansurov / PHILIPS
Virtuosic performances by Bahram Mansurov of several rnugams on the stringed tar. –DLM

AZERBAIJAN COLLECTIONS

○ **Azerbaijan - Trad. Music / CHANT DU MONDE**   1991
A great collection that details the wonders of musical cross-pollination. –MYLES BOISEN, ROOTS & RHYTHM

EGYPT

MOHAMED ABDEL WAHAB

Popular. As singer and as influence on Egyptian music during its renaissance, Abdel Wahab was equaled only by Umm Kulthum. But while she was a traditionalist to the core, Abdel Wahab believed in learning from Western music. Yet he too was a musical nationalist, renewing rather than diluting Egyptian tradition. Starting from a highly traditional sound as a teenager, he gradually moved into a highly varied (and internationally popular) film-based repertoire. But besides contributing to the pop world, he introduced more fundamental elements, such as long instrumental passages, a major element in his work. –JSR

Vol. 1 (1920-1925) / ARTISTES ARABES ASSOC.
This set of Wahab's earliest recordings is an event of supreme importance. It's also superb — and as a double bonus, it has fine notes (translated into English) by a man who knew him most of his artistic life. Major, major stuff. –JSR

○ **Vol. 10 (1939) / ARTISTES ARABES ASSOC.**
The most recent in this ongoing series dedicated to Egypt's greatest 20th-century singer/composer. Consists of music from a film, *Youm Said.* Whether or not it was his first, I have no idea. But both Abdel Wahab's singing and the accompaniments (despite a little accordion and piano here and there) were mostly far more traditional than his later movies. A significant transition period. –JSR

AMINA

Pop.
○ **Yalil / MANGO**   1989
Egyptian motifs tangle with hot Parisian production styles in the service of pouty-voiced diva Amina, who knows the power of sexy exotica over the feet of continental clubgoers. An intriguing experiment in widening North African pop. –BT

ASMAHAN

Popular.
☆ **Asmahan & Farid / BAIDAPHON**
Farid al Atrache is one of the great names in 20th-century Egyptian popular music. Asmahan had one of the greatest voices of 30s and 40s pop. Both were stars of Egypt's musical cinema. This set of their 40s hits charmingly recalls an era of experiment and eccentricity. –JSR

Aleik Salat Allah / ARISTES ARABES
This recording — which atypically has English notes —

Middle Eastern Music

Though ethnic sounds from throughout the world have been gaining popularity in recent years, Middle Eastern recordings remain the most challenging to American and European ears. Many people, in fact, initially find it uncomfortable to listen to the intricate, microtonal melodies and passionate rhythms of Arabic music. Once you get used to the exotic intensity of these highly evolved styles, however, there's no turning back. The simplistic melodic structures and heavy-handed beats of Western music can seem naive, reserved, and even downright stodgy by comparison. Still, there are several barriers to appreciating Middle Eastern music, most notably the lack of recordings available in the West. Even when you can obtain a few intriguing releases, chances are the liner notes don't include any information about the artists or the music. This is especially true of companies that import albums directly from Near Eastern countries.

The situation has improved somewhat over the last five years through the efforts of Western labels that have started to license and repackage albums by Middle Eastern pop stars, particularly Algerian rai artists who combine the melismatic fervor of their heritage with the glitz and drive of Western rock. Labels like Lyrichord, CMP, Playasound, and Rykodisc, on the other hand, have released their own high-quality recordings of traditional and classically oriented styles. These albums offer an excellent introduction to the Middle Eastern aesthetic, not only because they provide easy-to-grasp explanations of the music in the liner notes, but because the labels choose to present musicians on the basis of consummate artistry, high production standards, and relative accessibility. Many of the younger artists, in fact, temper their mastery of ancestral styles with their appreciation of and exposure to modern Western techniques. Turkish ney (flute) player Kudsi Erguner, Galilee-born oud virtuoso Simon Shaheen, and Lebanese multi-instrumentalist Ali Jihad Racy are three "rising stars" in the West who walk that fine line between tradition and innovation in some satisfying new ways.

"The idea of incorporating Western elements is something that Middle Eastern musicians have valued in the last 50 years or so," explains Racy, who moved to the US in 1968 and currently serves as Professor of Ethnomusicology at UCLA. "I have tried to experiment with my own Arab instruments and see how I can use them to create effects and new sounds to convey certain feelings and ideas. Electronic instruments have been really taking over in our music, for better or worse, and you find that the traditional resources have shrunk. Many musicians are using a more limited number of rhythmic patters and modes. Short, danceable rhythms are important. They make the music more accessible to people in the West. But there are still people who are developing new techniques and taking traditional instruments in some (admirable) new directions. It's an exciting time."

Though their approaches may be quite different, many of these revolutionary artists have retained the sense of ecstasy that Middle Eastern music treasures. From Turkish Sufi meditations to Arabic classical styles and more modern aproaches, the idea of mixing the sublime with the sensual has long been a powerful element. Religious writings in this part of world, in fact, often include amorous poetry in which feelings of earthly love and yearning are used as metaphors for the ultimate love of God. "In our music, the idea of creating ecstatic effects is very important," says Racy. "Mysticism and passion are not incompatible. Rather they work together to create a total experience. The players are skillful and the music is complex, not for the sake of technique, but rather to perfect the ability to emotionally tranform the listener."

This, indeed, is what Middle Eastern music does best. Ultimately, you don't have to understand the forms, modes, and rhythmic cycles to grasp the appeal. At the hands of an accomplished artist, the emotion behind the music comes through loud and clear.

— Linda Kohanov

---

covers rather the same ground as *Asmahan & Farid*, though with more of Asmahan's early classic or neo-traditional recordings along with the crossover film material. –JSR

FARID AL ATRACHE

Middle Eastern pop.
○ **Addi Errabi / VOICE OF LEBANON**
In a career that took him from young traditional singer to major film-star and concert artist, Atrache was at the center of Egyptian music for a very long time. This 1973 live recording is typical of his concerts in its progression from solo 'ud to Atrache's tenderly stark vocals, all punctuated by passionate audience response. –JSR

AZIZA GALAL

Popular.
Wal Tekeina Netkabel Sawa / EMI
Behind her spectacles, Moroccan-born, Cairo-based Galal clearly has no truck with pop-star glitz in her appearance or her art, but she is one of the finest living singers in the Egyptian vein. She seeks flexibility rather than flash and purity rather than richness of tone, and her accompaniments impeccably vary the now classic string sound with unobtrusive modern touches. –JSR

ABDEL HALIM HAFEZ

Popular.
Kariat al-Fengan / SOUTELPHAN
Concert recording by a major star of the post-WWII generation. Like Lebanon's Fairuz, Hafez fronts settings that range from the now-traditional chorus and strings-and-percussion orchestra to various groups with heavy overseas influences. But his own style and the melodies he sings are both quintessentially Egyptian. –JSR
Ala Hasb Weddad / SOUTELPHAN

HANAN

Popular.
Haluwa / SLAM
Hanan is one of the finest singers on the younger Egyptian scene. There's less Euro-pop on this than on the earlier Slam releases, more strongly Egyptian material, plus a few splendid oddities, such as an intro that sounds vaguely like Astor Piazzolla. –JSR

ALI HASSAN KUBAN

Nubian pop. Ali Hassan Kuban is a master singer and popularizer of Nubian music, a typically vocal expression native to the border region of Egypt and Sudan. In the mid 50s, Kuban added electric guitars, keys, a horn section, and percussion to his music, fusing traditional songs of love with uptempo pop instruments in a Western-influenced mix. His group appeals to old and young alike. –MB & JP

☆ **From Nubia to Cairo / SHANACHIE**   1980
Traditional wedding and love songs of southern Egypt, with propulsive drumming, clapping, and strings, R&B influenced horn charts, and Farfisa-like electric organ underpinning Kuban's arid vocals. A masterpiece. –MB & JP

UMM KULTHUM

Traditional. Umm Kulthum (also known in the West as Oum Kalsoum) is among the greatest singers of the 20th century. She has been called the Bessie Smith of Egypt, and for stark passion she was all of that. But she was also more. She found a way of moving traditional music into the contemporary mainstream without dilution, and, without compromising, Kulthum achieved a popularity unparalleled by any singer anywhere. –JSR

Umm Kulthum - Vol. 1: 1926 / ARTISTS ARABES
Hajrik / SONO CAIRO
Her incredible first recordings recordings are backed by the traditional small groups that later grew into positive orchestras. Notes in English are a rare bonus. *Hajrik* is typical of Kulthum at her prime, shortly after the album form allowed live performances to be recorded at length and in depth, both vocally and instrumentally. –JSR

☆ **El Atlaal / SONO CAIRO**
El Atlaal is typical of Kulthum at her prime, shortly after the LP form allowed her to record songs the way she sang them live. –JSR

Rubayaat el-Khayyam / SONO CAIRO
On the second CD, Kulthum sings Omar — though not, of course, the Fitzgerald version. This is another of the best-known recordings of Kulthum's late-classic period from the 40s to the 50s. –JSR

Faat el-Mi'ad / SONO CAIRO
On this concert recording from Kulthum's later years, she didn't change her own style but acknowledged contemporary Egyptian musical developments in accompaniments, with far from classic but fascinating elements: notably sensational taqassim for saxophone. –JSR

MUSICIANS OF THE NILE

Egyptian. The Musicians of the Nile are an international performing troupe of professional musicians from the Luxor area. Using only folk instruments, this group keeps the traditions of Upper Egypt alive. –MB

☆ **From Luxor to Isna / REAL WORLD**   1989
A first-class collection of Arabic folk music from Egypt from the country's premier touring group. Strictly traditional drums, strings, reeds, and songs from the desert. –MB & JP

IHAB TAWFI

Popular.
Ikmini / SLAM
This is the cassette from which Island extracted the cut "Masakeen." Tawfi's a fine singer, with a sound locally enough rooted (along with the hip version of local rhythms) to subdue and turn to good purpose the international-pop garnishes. At its best, the newer Egyptian sounds approach rai in intensity, and surpass it in variety. –JSR

EGYPT COLLECTIONS

Cairo Tradition / AUVIDIS
All the music on *Cairo Tradition: Taqasim & Layali* is played by members of the Takht ensemble under the aegis of the Cairo conservatory. There's a lot of excellent kanun zither playing, both solo and under the layali, vocal improvisations

on a maqam. There are also admirable 'ud and nay solos. A core recording, all in all. –DLM

○ **Golden Age ... / CLUB DISQUE ARABE**
Golden Age of Egyptian Music. Superb recordings from 1905 to 1930, during the Arabic cultural renaissance, covering a wide range of instrumental and vocal idioms. This is an extraordinary recording musically speaking (despite the limited time available on 78 RPM recordings). It is also phenomenal technically: amazing how well the old acoustic horn could handle instruments operating in a limited dynamic range. –JSR

Music of Egypt - Upper & Lower / RYKODISC
The Grateful Dead's Mickey Hart recorded these pieces in 1978, having happened across the music during a tour. The first four are from the Aswan area, the last two are fine instrumentals, one for a mizmar oboe group, the other for tar with a darabukka backing. –DLM

Musicians of the Nile - Vols. 1 & 2 / OCORA
The music of contemporary Egypt has come a long way from the villages of the Egyptian Nile. But its roots are in the flutes, the oboes, the two-stringed fiddles, and impassioned vocalism and drumming of a peasant culture with strong Gypsy roots, in which popular and classical met. –DLM

☆ **Yalla - Hit List Egypt / MANGO-ANTILLES**
Hard-hitting overview of a variety of gritty, hardworking Egyptian pop that mixes elements of bazaar culture with Eurodisco technocraft. Disc is divided equally between uptown and street styles. Contains "Elli Shatr Enhaa Tgannen," the naughty newlywed rap that had Cairo's elders blushing. –BT & MB

GENERAL MIDDLE EAST

MUSIC IN THE WORLD OF ISLAM

Traditional.
The Human Voice - Vol. 1 / TANGENT
A magnificent collection of recordings, *Music in the World of Islam* covers almost the entire sweep of the Islamic musical world, from Algeria to Malaysia by the way of the Gulf, Ethiopia, you name it. Now we have the boxed set of six albums — and what a set. Vol. 1 covers the human voice, whose solo possibilities the Islamic tradition developed to a peak. Truly a breathtaking series. –JSR

Lutes - Vol. 2 / TANGENT
Strings - Vol. 3 / TANGENT
Strings other than lute. –JSR

Flutes & Trumpets - Vol. 4 / TANGENT
Flutes and shawms. –JSR

Reeds & Bagpipes - Vol. 5 / TANGENT
Drums & Rhythms - Vol. 6 / TANGENT
This volume is devoted to drums and other percussion. –JSR

ALI JIHAD RACY   b 1943

Traditional. An accomplished multi-instrumentalist, Racy has done much to promote an appreciation for Middle Eastern music in the West. Born in Lebanon, Racy came to the US in 1968, where he earned his Masters and Doctorate degrees from the University of Illinois before accepting a position as Professor of Ethnimusicology at UCLA. His recordings for various labels provide a showcase for his mastery of the flute-like nay and the clarinet-like mijwiz, as well as the stringed instruments 'ud and buzuq, both important to Middle Eastern styles. Racy is currently working on a book tentatively titled *The Art of Ecstasy in Arab Music.* –LK

Ancient Egypt - A Tribute / LYRICHORD
Contemporary compositions in the style of ancient Egypt by noted performer/ethnomusicologist Racy. –ROOTS & RHYTHM

○ **Taqasim / LYRICHORD**
Taqasim (the plural of taqsim) are extended, non-metrical instrumental improvisations. This collection of three such

pieces features Simon Shaheen on 'ud and Racy on buzuq, offering a rare opportunity to hear the sublime, at times feverish, interactions of two virtuoso performers. −LK

○ **Jazayer / EARTHBEAT!**   1989
Originally recorded by the Grateful Dead's Mickey Hart in 1979, this collection features traditional and contemporary Middle Eastern dance music performed with great spirit and skill by Racy in collaboration with the members of Jazayer, an American ensemble of Middle Eastern music enthusiasts. −LK

SIMON SHAHEEN   b1955

Arabic classical. A virtuoso on the 'ud as well as the violin, Shaheen is equally adept at performing traditional Arabic music and Western classical styles. Born in the village of Tarshiha in northern Galilee, he learned his craft initially from his father. At the same time, Shaheen also studied Western classical music, graduating from the Jerusalem Music Academy in 1978. Two years later, he moved to New York where he continued his studies at the Manhattan School of Music. In addition to his performances worldwide, Shaheen teaches 'ud and violin, composes for theatrical productions, and produces recordings. −LK

○ **Turath / CMP**   1992
On his most recent album, Shaheen explores his Turath, or "heritage," through a masterly presentation of both traditional Middle Eastern selections as well as some impressive original compositions. Playing violin, 'ud, and bass 'ud, he is joined by Faruk Tekbilek on nay, Hassan Ishkut on the dulcimer-like qanun, and Samir Khalil on percussion instruments like the riq and tar. The pristine production quality is a rarity among Middle Eastern recordings and adds to the appeal of Shaheen's finely crafted performances. −LK

GENERAL MIDDLE EAST COLLECTIONS

Arabian Music: Maquam / PHILIPS
Very fine performances on 'ud. −DLM
○ **Desert Nomads / PLAYASOUND**
Highly recommended. −DLM
☆ **Holy Quran: Surat Yusuf / ORIENT**
Orthodox Islam has always viewed music with ambivalence, if not downright disapproval. Yet the recitation of the Koran and the call to prayer form the aesthetic bedrock of all the music of the Islamic world. The late Sheikh Mahmoud Khalil El Houssary, a former head of the Al Azhar Mosque in Cairo, recites Surat Yusuf, the Koranic story of Joseph (no coat of many colors, but the pit, the fat and lean kine are there). −JSR
Sung Poetry / AUVIDIS
In most cultures the distinction between recitation and song, poem and lyric, is not nearly as distinct as in the West. Many great poems of the Middle East are still sung, and cantatas or song-cycles with particular structures are the backbone of the Andalus classical tradition, whether in Syria or the Maghreb. The examples here are in Turkish, Farsi, and Arabic. −DLM

IRAN

ENSEMBLE MOSHTAQ

Classical.
○ **Dashti-Mahur / BUDA**
Classical music by a Paris-based quartet (singer, setar lute, kamantche fiddle, and percussion) dedicated to the pure form of one of the world's most important and influential musical traditions. Most striking here is the magnificent singing by a young woman vocalist, Homa; the notes describe her singing as both powerful and subtle — an understatement for a change. The instrumental backings provide support of classic simplicity, with a power only half-masked by their restraint. The music consists of two extended vocal suites. Adequate notes. −JSR

KARIMI/MUSAVI

Traditional.
Masters of Traditional Music - Vol. 2 / OCORA
Reissue of 1979 recording. The CD is entirely devoted to a fine recording of duets by singer Mohammad Karimi and Musavi on nay. Extremely good technically. (70 minutes) −JSR

FARAMARZ PAYVAR

Traditional. Faramarz Payvar is an important composer and conservator of Persian classical music, leading his touring ensemble on the 72-string santur (hammer dulcimer). Various other string instruments are featured in this group, as well as the zarb drum and soloist Khatereh Parvaneh, a prominent female vocalist. −MB
○ **Faramarz Payvar Ensemble / NONESUCH**   1974
Iran has arguably been the world's most important musical culture. It links us with ancient Greece, and is at the root of both Arabian and Indian (and thence Southeast Asian) classical idioms. Santurist Payvar's ensemble brought together some of Iran's finest classical musicians in the group and solo performances for santur zither, kamancheh fiddle, tar lute, zarb percussion, with — a rare treat — a fine woman singer, Khatereh Parvaneh. −JSR

MANOOCHEHR SADEGHI

Traditional.
Sounds of the Santur / IER RECORDS
The Iranian santur is the progenitor of a great sweep of instrumentals from China to southcentral Europe, and a major classical instrument in its own right. Sadeghi is one of the recognized younger leaders of the renaissance in the instrument, whose tradition was being gradually lost. Here he plays two dastgahs (essentially, suites), one of them also played on the nay by Hossein Omoumi. −JSR

DARIUSH TALA'I w/MOHAMMAD MUSAVI

Traditional.
Masters of Traditional Music - Vol. 1 / OCORA   1979
Reissue of classic 1979 recording is devoted to instrumentals for tar (Dariush Tala'i), nay (Mohammad Musavi), and santur (Majid Kiani). All are outstanding, but the nay playing, for my money, is simply breathtaking. Superb music; notes that give plenty of general background but are totally lacking in properly attributed track information. Extremely good technically. (70:58) −JSR

IRAN COLLECTIONS

☆ **Classical Music of Iran ... / FOLKWAYS**   1991
The *Classical Music of Iran: The Dastgah Systems* collection of classical Iranian music performances was recorded before the 1979 Iranian revolution drove many accomplished players into exile. Extensive liner notes add to the appeal of this historic document. −LK
Music of Iran - Vol. 1 / MUSICAPHON
This recording is of music for solo kamantche, voice with tar, and solo sehtar. −JSR
○ **Music of Iran - Vol. 2 / MUSICAPHON**
A good range of music from renowned musicians of several generations: dumbek solo; piece for santur; mathnavi mystical poem in a mode like one used in Indian devotional chant; nay flute solo; and tar and kamantche duet. −JSR

IRAQ

NAZEM AL-GHAZALI

Traditional.
○ **Nazem Al-Ghazali / DUNIAPHON**
Perhaps the greatest modern singer in a traditional style close to Arabic classical music. The accompaniments are a mix, with string sections influenced by Egypt and some endearing

tries at Western crossover, but strongly local backup singing and percussion. (63+ minutes) –JSR

MUNIR BACHIR w/MOHAMED ELKASSABGI

Classical.
Munir Bachir & Mohamed Elkassabgi / CDDA
'Ud virtuosi of two generations and two traditions. Munir Bachir is perhaps the finest living player in the great Iraqi school. In the Geneva concert featured in this record, he plays both traditional modes and looser, more personal improvisations of marked Spanish influence. The great Egyptian player Elkassabgi both composed for and accompanied Umm Kulthum in her early glory days: his solos here, mostly from the 30s, are drawn from 78s originals. –JSR

ISRAEL

THEODORE BIKEL

Yiddish.
○ **Sings Yiddish Theatre ... / BAINBRIDGE**   1991
Sings Yiddish Theatre & Folk Songs was originally released in the 60s on Elektra. This 1991 reissue features the original liner notes, complete with Yiddish lyrics and English translations for all 16 tracks by one of the Yiddish theater's best-known actors. This also features the arrangements of master maestro Dov Seltzer. –PF

DIASPORA YESHIVAH BAND

Chassidic.
○ **Land of Our Fathers / TAMBUR**   1981
This group changed the face of modern Chassidic music with their compositions, which combine Jewish spirituality with rockabilly sensibilities. This release finds the band at their peak of songwriting and performing. –PF

GLORA FEIDMAN

Klezmer.
○ **Jewish Soul Music: 20 Jewish Tunes / HED ARZI**   1989
This release features both live and studio recordings from the early 70s, digitally remastered on CD. A virtual greatest-hits by this greatest of Klezmers. –PF

DAVID "DUDU" FISHER

Yiddish. One of Israel's leading male vocalists, Fisher has recorded numerous albums in Hebrew, ranging from showtunes (he played Jean Valjean in the Tel Aviv production of *Les Miserables*) to Chassidic and Hebrew versions of 60s classic rock tunes. –PF
○ **Mamma Loshen (Mother Tongue) / HELICON**   1992
Fisher sings 22 of the greatest Yiddish songs ever written. –PF

MOSHE GANCHOFF

Cantorial.
○ **Cantorial Masterworks - Pt. 1 / MUSIQUE INT'L**   1991
This cassette release only features recordings originally made in 1942, many of which have not been previously issued. –PF

GIDI GOV

Israeli.
○ **Derech Eretz / HED ARZI**   1987
Among Israel's hottest rock stars, Gov teams on this debut album with one of Israel's most famous songwriters, Ychuda Poliker. One of the hardest-rocking albums ever to come out of Israel. –PF

OFRA HAZA

Israeli pop. By the early 80s, Ofra Haza was already a popular teen singer/songwriter in Israel, before she exploded onto the international scene with a glossy album of ancient Yemenite songs updated for the nightclub set. Since then, pop sensibilities have overshadowed the Jewish traditions in her music, and she has even applied her gorgeous, sensual singing to English-language chart attempts. –MB

50 Gates of Wisdom / SHANACHIE   1984
Like the Berber songs of Algeria's Markunda Aures, Haza's contemporary versions of Yemeni Jewish songs feature tradition-based singing with pop backings. Her gorgeous voice carries all before it, but the arrangements are over-slick at times. Still, this was Haza as kibbutz pop-star, unlike her later worldbeat wanderings. –JSR

Shaday / TELEDEC   1988
This CD made Haza a household name throughout Europe because it was her first to sell literally millions of copies there, earning her the nickname "the Israeli Madonna." She combines Hebrew, Yemenite, and English in prayers and original compositions with a driving European dance beat. Includes the international hits "Im Nin Alu" and "Galbi" (later made famous after rap stars Eric B. & Rakeem sampled it for one of their hits). Also available domestically on Sire with bonus remixes of the above tracks. –PF

KLEVELAND KLEZMORIM

Klezmer.
○ **Casbah / WKSU-FM**   1989
This CD by a regional Klezmer band combines authentic European Klezmer with original modern compositions performed in a Klezmer style. –PF

AARON LEBEDEFF

Yiddish.
○ **Sings 14 Yiddish ... / GREATER RECORDING CO.**   1964
Sings 14 Yiddish Favorites. As the title implies, this features the legendary Yiddish vocalist on 14 of the best-known Yiddish songs, including the all-time favorite, "Roumania, Roumania." –PF

LONDON SCHOOL OF JEWISH SONG

Chassidic.
○ **London School ... / HOLYLAND MUSIC**   1991
London School of Jewish Song. One of the finest recordings of Chassidic music, performed by a boys choir and conducted by Yigal Calek. –PF

THE MAZLETONES

Klezmer.
○ **Meshugge for You / GLOBAL VILLAGE**   1989
Updated arrangements of Klezmer favorites on this CD release. –PF

MEGAMA

American Jewish pop. American Shalom Levine and Canadian Moshe Yess moved to Israel and formed this group, releasing the two most definitive English-language/Jewish-content albums of the past 20 years. Unfortunately the group split following the release of their second album. –PF
○ **Megama / CBS**   1980
Their debut features folksy lyrics and catchy tunes as well as the moving "My Zadie," one of the most popular English-language Jewish songs ever written. –PF
G-d Is Alive and Well and in Jerusalem / CBS   1982
Just as listenable and entertaining as their first album. –PF

ALBERTO MIZRAHI

Cantorial.
○ **The Voice of a People / ANSHE EMET SYNAGOGUE** 1992
This CD captures one of America's finest living cantors in digital excellence. –PF

EFFI NETZER SINGERS

Popular.

○ **Effi Netzer Singers / OLYMPIC**
A collection by what must surely be one of Israel's most recorded groups. Included are "Hinneh Ma Tov," "Vitbarach Shimcha," "Yevarechecha," "Ssissu Vessimchu," "Essa Ainy," "Kol Rina Vishu'ah," "Yedid Nefesh," "Ssissu et Jerusalem," "Uveyom Sabat," and "Av Harachaman." Notes consist of titles and lyrics in English and (a nice change) Hebrew. –JSR

PIAMENTAS

Chassidic.

○ **Piamenta 1990 / HOLYLAND**   1990
The first CD release from Avi and Yossi Piamenta, two brothers who are former New York studio musicians who now compose and perform Jewish music with a grinding guitar and an elegant flute sound combined with a rock & roll backbeat. This features "Asher Boro," a prayer sung at Jewish weddings, set here to the tune of Men At Work's "Down Under." –PF

MOLLY PICON

Yiddish.

○ **At the Yiddish ... / GREATER RECORDING CO.**   1971
At the Yiddish Theatre captures the late Yiddish star's greatest hits from her days in the Yiddish theater, many of which were written and produced by her husband Yonkel Kalich. –PF

SAFAM

American Jewish pop. Safam is Hebrew for mustache and the name of this leading English language Jewish group in America today, with numerous recordings available on CD. –PF

○ **Bittersweet / SAFAM**   1983
Easily the most even of their albums to date, combining original English compositions, new tunes for old prayers, and the Israeli classic "Al Kol Eileh." –PF

TOFA'AH

Contemporary inspirational.
Contemporary Jewish Music / TOFA'AH

VOICE OF THE TURTLE

Ladino.
Flowers Appear on the Earth / TOR
The fourth in a series of recordings from this Massachusetts-based group. This excellent-sounding CD features prayers and even comedy performed entirely in Ladino, the native language of Sephardic (Spanish and North African) Jews. –PF

CHRISTOBEL WEERASINGHE

Traditional.
Israel - Its Music and Its People / DESTO
Folk songs and dances, religious and cantorial music, with a narrative by Weerasinghe. –ROOTS & RHYTHM

ISRAEL COLLECTIONS

○ **Hassidic Tunes of Dancing and Rejoicing / FOLKWAYS**
A delicious album that includes music for clarinets and percussion; a charming dance for clarinet, trumpet, and accordion; a great deal for voices, including some fine "mouth music." Strong Balkan and eastern European, of course, but also a few reminiscent of the western European ballad tradition. These field recordings are backed by extensive notes and photos. –JSR

○ **Israel - Forty Years / ATOLL**
An anthology doubly welcome for its wide view of Israeli popular music. Here are rock/disco-influenced idioms (very interesting); straight rock; the more traditional but equally fine Central European sound of the Effi Netzer Singers; the sonic chicken soup of the Kibbutz Folk Singers; and several other styles to boot. Very varied, very unfamiliar, and mostly very good. –JSR

○ **Israeli Chassidic Song Festival / HED-ARZI-CBS**
These "cast" recordings have been released annually on cassette and vinyl since the first festival in 1968. Many of the tunes first released on these albums have passed into the public's consciousness as though they had been written hundreds of years ago. –PF

Jewish Music / PHILIPS
Religious chants from the Mediterranean-Middle Eastern area from Gibraltar and Morocco to Turkey and Yemen. –DLM

○ **Le Folklore Israelien / ATOLL**
Not field recordings, but a mix of traditional and traditional-style songs of which the best-known is perhaps "Hava Nagila." Many are performed by the Effi Netzer Singers. Also featured here are Ianit, Lahakat Hanachal, Luci Arnon, and Danny Granot. –JSR

○ **Let's Sing with Effi Netzer / HATAKIT**
On these 17 tracks, Netzer compels the audience to join him and share the lead vocals on some of Israel's best-loved folk songs. –PF

○ **A Time for Music - Pt. 5 / HASC**   1992
A live two-CD recording featuring the king of American Chassidic music, Mordechai Ben David, as well as performances by other greats in the American Chassidic music field. –PF

○ **Treasury of Immortal Performances / RCA**   1966
A set of three albums each by a different cantor (Josef Rosenblatt, Samuel Vigoda, and Moshe Koussevitsky). Released in 1966, this boxed set repackaged recordings from as early as 1928 and includes a booklet on the cantors. The Koussevitsky portion has been re-released on CD (Israel Music ICD 5002) with two additional tracks, while the Rosenblatt portion (Israel Music ICD 5001) has three bonus tracks. –PF

○ **The Very Best of Israel / CBS**   1990
This compilation covers material from CBS Israel's vaults, spanning 40 years of Israeli folk and light popular music. –PF

KURDISTAN COLLECTIONS

○ **Kurdish Music / MUSICAPHON**
Ethnically and culturally united though they are, the Kurds of the mountainous region that is split between Iran, Iraq, Turkey, and the Soviet Union are also a part of the great Islamic Middle-Eastern cultural block. The music here — all superbly performed — includes flute solos and duets (the Kurds, a pastoral mountain people, have no stringed instruments) and songs epic and romantic, as well as a Soviet Kurdish dance piece. –JSR

Kurdish Music (Philips) / PHILIPS
Dramatic, exciting music. Excellent recording. –DLM

Kurdistan / AUVIDIS
Though they are spread across several Middle Eastern countries, the Kurds are very much a cultural entity and their music a recognizable subset of the general regional idiom, with strong links to Persian tradition and a particular liking for the Dorian mode. The Kurds are also traditionally nomadic: they have relied largely on shepherd's pipes and the human voice (though they have adopted stringed instruments from their neighbors over time). –JSR

KUWAIT COLLECTIONS

○ **Stars of Kuwait - Vol. 1 / BUZAIDPHONE**
In the late 80s, Kuwait developed a whole new take on mainstream Arabic pop, in which a bunch of fresh new singers fronted groups not only with the standard string sections but also with novelties ranging from Greek bouzouki to the only Arab piano playing to use the bottom half of the

keyboard. Most of the important names are here: Rabab, Nawaal, Adul Karim Kader, and seven others. Lots of range stylistically, from at least a couple of mini-generations. Beside singing, the Kuwaitis are into a lot of intriguing instrumental stuff including occasional gorgeous solo fiddle. –JSR

LEBANON

MAJIDA EL ROUMI

Arabic pop.

☆ **Kalimaat / MUSIC MASTER**
A wonderful example of the everything-goes experimentalism of much Arabic pop. El Roumi sounds a little like Fairuz, though with more honey and less smoke. Gorgeous, in a word. In places she shows very strong Indian *filmi* influences, not just in the arrangements but in her singing. One song has a loopy sub-Dixieland backing. Yet others are somewhat more orthodoxly splendid. I love it! –JSR

FAIRUZ

Popular.

○ **Kifak Inta / RELAX-IN**
I've rewritten this a hundred times trying to convey my passion for the most beautiful voice in the world (only Billie Holiday comes close). Make no mistake, this is big-time Arabic pop that owes much to US styles, yet the arranging by son-and-musical-director Ziad Rahbany is subtle and sophisticated, and together he and Fairuz have the ability to make a style, however incongruous (Earth Wind & Fairuz), all their own. –JSR

☆ **The Very Best of Fairuz / EMI**
For beauty of voice, brilliance in ballad singing, indefinability of genre, and general gorgeousness of art, Fairuz might be compared with Sarah Vaughan. Like Vaughan, too, she has had her share of fairly unredeemable numbers to sing. Both these CDs assemble several albums, both contain a certain amount of Euro-schmaltz — but the bulk of the songs in each are straight Lebanese pop. Ironically, the silliest arrangements at times inspire her finest vocals. And after all, Sarah Vaughan also transformed some clunkers in her time. –JSR

LEBANON COLLECTIONS

Prayer and Religious Incantation / MUSICAPHON
A particularly fine recording of prayers, muwashaat (hymns), and other religious material. Druze, Sunni, and Shiite: music of the mosque, not of the mystical sects. Despite the ambivalence and intermittent hostility of Islam to music, this is not only beauty of a high order but the sound that underlies all other vocal idioms of the whole Islamic world. –JSR

SAUDI ARABIA

MOHAMED ABDU

Saudi pop.

○ **Mohamed Abdu / SAUT EL JAZIRA**
Currently one of the big names of Saudi popular music, Abdu is squarely in the mainstream. You get here three long songs from a concert appearance. Vocally he reminds me a little of Abdel Halim Hafez, though his voice is more sinewy. Instrumentally there are touches of updating — occasional keyboards, electric guitar, and the like. But the orchestra, and particularly the strongly Egyptian string sound, would mostly fit fine behind Umm Kulthum in her later days. –JSR

ETTAB

Pop.

○ **The Very Best of Ettab / RELAX-IN**
Afro-Saudi Ettab is, in my book, terrific. Like most Saudi singers she doesn't get as contemporary as, say, the Egyptians. But she's a vocalist of power and charm both. Moreover, her

backings add to the mainstream strings all sorts of effective garnishes, from accordion to keyboards, that contrive to be at once goofy and effective. (64:35) –JSR

SYRIA

SOUHEIL ARAFEH

Pop.

Magic Touch / BYBLOS
Arafeh uses a mix of highly traditional instruments and styles with occasional modernisms (drum rhythm, electric organ), in what amounts to an instrumental suite evocative of various provincial towns and other places in Syria. The result is a kind of program music building on tradition, which is relatively unfashionable in modern Arabic music but really very attractive. –JSR

OMAYA ORCHESTRA/CHORALE

Andalus classical.

Raska al Samah/Waslat Mouachahat / BYBLOS
Syrian andalus classical music differs from its Maghrebi cousin not just in that it has ancient Byzantine elements but because Syrian orchestras have been more willing to borrow ensemble string voicings from the West. These two vocal suites are typical and splendid, opening with a fine kanoun solo and sung magnificently throughout. –JSR

TURKEY

KUDSI ERGUNER   b 1952

Traditional. Fans of traditional Turkish music know Kudsi Erguner as a master of the end-blown nay flute and a contributor to the film scores of *The Last Temptation of Christ* and *The Mahabharata*. He is also a scholar of traditional music and a highly respected member of the Erguner family, who have kept the Mevlevi Sufi (Whirling Dervish) traditions intact through many generations of cultural upheaval. –MB

○ **Turkey: Art of the Ottoman Tanbur / VDE-GALLO**   1989
Kudsi Erguner recorded this album featuring alternating solo performances by two modern masters of the tanbur, Abdi Coskun and Fahreddin Cimenli. The tanbur is the most commonly used lute-like instrument in Turkish art music. The musicians here fully exploit the rich, sonorous timbre of the instrument, which can be either plucked or bowed. –LK

○ **Sufi Music of Turkey / CMP**   1990
A powerful recording of Middle Eastern music. Kudsi plays nay with Mahmoud Tabrizi Zadeh adding the scintillating sounds of the santur (a type of hammer dulcimer) and the sensual melodies of the kemantche (a bowed string instrument). Bruno Caillat also plays zarb and tabla. –LK

Whirling Dervishes from Turkey / ARION   1991
Another fine performance of Sufi music from Kudsi, collaborating this time with some traditional singers and instrumentalists who perform a Mevlevi Whirling Dervish ceremony. –LK

THE ERKOSE ENSEMBLE

Popular.

○ **Tzigane - Gypsy Music of Turkey / CMP**   1992
I fell instantly in love with the Ekrose's first recording on Ocora, and I'm surprised that this is only the second one available in the West. This CD has the same format as the (now out-of-print) LP: a prodigiously virtuosic Gypsy dance suite followed by improvisations for the various members: kanun, violin, 'ud, and my favorite, clarinet. The Erkoses are, strangely enough, the only Turkish Gypsies on record, and yet, according to the notes by Kudsi Erguner, play a variation of tzigane closer to its roots in North India than the more familiar eastern European version. –CARL HOYT, ORIGINAL MUSIC

TALIP OZKAN

Saz.

○ **Mysteries of Turkey / MOTW**   1988
The mysterious and exotic sound of the saz, a long-necked lute, is the focus of this recording. Talip Ozkan, a master musician from Turkey, presents traditional songs and dances from his homeland with this unique instrument. Both solo saz and accompanying vocal selections are featured on this recording. −MUSIC OF THE WORLD

The Dark Fire / AXIOM   1992
Buzzing, stinging forays into medieval Turkish music by Ozkan, master of the saz — a member of the lute family played with a cherrywood plectrum — accompanied by stark frame-drum and wooden spoon percussion. Fierce performances brimming with slurred runs, angular melodies, and fractal-shaped riffs. −BT

NESRIN SIPAHI

Sharki.

○ **Sharki: Love Songs of Istanbul / CMP**   1992
First-ever collection of sharki music recorded with traditional instruments. Dating back to the 18th century, sharki is a dark and bluesy offshoot from Turkish classical music lamenting the decline of the Ottoman Empire, and the shivery-voiced Sipahi conveys deep recesses of collective sorrow with her subdued vocal delivery. The eight-piece Kudsi Erguner ensemble adds colorful accompaniment. Tightly focused, starkly arranged, and emotionally compelling. −BT & LK

BAYRAM BILGE TOKER

Traditional.

Bayram / MOTW   1991
The baglama is the most popular stringed instrument of Turkey. In the hands of a skilled musician like Bayram Bilge Toker, its beautiful, mysterious sound makes for an immediately appealing and refreshing recording. Representing many different styles from all over Turkey. −MUSIC OF THE WORLD

TURKEY COLLECTIONS

Asik / INEDIT
The Asik form an ancient Anatolian popular tradition of songs amatory and philosophical, here wonderfully performed by a young woman singer and middle-aged master of the genre, backed by equally fine saz. Like much of this kind of music, it has the subtlety of the classical tradition while being more forthright in overall manner. (63:59) −JSR

○ **The Best of Turkey / ATOLL**   1991
Actually Turkish pop. Seven popular Turkish artists are included, here, with each contributing two pieces. −GINO ROBAIR, ROOTS & RHYTHM

○ **Masters of Turkish Music / ROUNDER**   1990
Scholarly (though very entertaining) collection of Turkish 78s, divided evenly between classical vocal music and various instrumental recordings, all demonstrating sophisticated musicianship. −MB

Turkey: Art of the Ottoman Tanbur / VDE
Turkey: Ceremony of the Kadiri Dervishes / VDE   1991
Sufi chanting ceremonies of the Kadiri dervishes. Four selections, over an hour long. −ROOTS & RHYTHM

UNITED ARAB EMIRATES

ABDALLAH BELKHAIR

Traditional.

Abdallah Belkhair / AL-SHAB
A fine singer from Dubai in a strongly traditional style, backed by strings and percussion of that mixed Egyptian/Bedouin descent that has become mainstream. In

contrast with the "new sound" singers of Egypt, and Kuwaitis like Nawaal, it is quite devoid of interpop or overt Westernisms. −JSR

UZBEKISTAN

SHASHMAQAM

Jewish.

○ **Music of Bukharan Jewish Ensemble / FOLKWAYS** 1991
A wide variety of passionate music by expatriate members of the Central Asian city of Bukhara mixes a dramatic Hassidic vocal style with Indian and Islamic instrumentals. An intriguing collection of ancient folksongs, ghazals (allegorical love poems), wedding songs, instrumentals, and more from the Jewish repertoire of this fertile region. −MB & BT

YEMEN

ABDEL RAB IDRIS

Pop.

Ta'er / FARASAN
An extremely attractive singer/songsmith with a fine singing style and an excellent taste in backings. Idris has the ability to move from the mainstream string sound and somewhat traditional choruses into the more synthesized world of the younger generation, without losing a sense of individuality or falling into the pastiche that often bedevils other young artists. −JSR

YEMEN COLLECTIONS

North Yemen / AUVIDIS   1989
This is a reissue of a long out-of-print Unesco album surveying the diversity of ceremonial music in North Yemen. −MYLES BOISEN, ROOTS & RHYTHM

NORTH AMERICA

NATIVE AMERICAN COLLECTIONS

○ **Arctic Circle / OCORA**
This is very important recording, done by the scholar Jean Malaurie. Includes Inuit chants and drums from Thule to the Bering Strait. −DLM

Canada: Vocal Games of the Inuits / OCORA
As for Native American traditions from the North, this is my favorite recording. Included are Caribou, Netsillik, and Igloolik. These examples of voice imitating sounds of nature are mind-blowing. −DLM

○ **Inuit Games and Songs / AUVIDIS**
A recording like this was my introduction to ethnic music, and the sonic complexity and communal nature of the breath games has had a tremendous impact on my musical thinking. In addition to the games, this CD contains goose imitations, a shamanic song, and a very rare piece for Inuit violin. Good, if not too extensive, notes. (45:01) −CARL HOYT, ORIGINAL MUSIC

☆ **Navajo Songs ... / NEW WORLD**   1991
Navajo Songs from Canyon de Chelly. Award-winning contemporary field recordings of Navajo social songs and ceremonies, including the exciting Enemy Way chant. −MB

Night and Daylight Yeibichei / INDIAN HOUSE
My all-time favorite recording of Navajo elders singing healing songs that make the walls of your home tremble. −DLM

Pow Wow Songs / NEW WORLD   1975
This 1975 collection of social and ceremonial music of the Great Plains Indians mostly focuses on intertribal music from southern groups, mostly Oklahoman, although there are five cuts of northern plains music. Most of the selections involve groups singing at a powwow in Skiatook, OK. Here are war dance songs, contest songs for straight dancers and fancy

dancers, a Sioux flag song, a Vietnam song, and grass dance songs. –JSR

○ **Songs of Earth, Water, Fire & Sky / NEW WORLD**   1991
Nine ceremonial dances from various tribes of the American Southwest, plus East and West Coast tribes. Clear and vibrant field recordings from 1975. –MB

UNITED STATES

DAVE TARRAS

Klezmer.

○ **Yiddish-American Klezmer Music / YAZOO**
As this delicious compilation makes very clear, clarinetist Tarras was a big deal in US klezmer music for three decades. In fact this is a wonderful release on several counts: simple musical quality, variety, and the inclusion of vocal cuts of music right up to the mid 50s, and of evocative radio announcements and jingles. –JSR

PACIFIC

AUSTRALIA COLLECTIONS

Aboriginal Sound Instruments / AIAS
More than a mere demonstration, because almost all the tracks are performances, with singing where relevant. All are, of course, musicologically important. Most involving for non-academics are the eerily beautiful didjeridu tracks. The booklet includes the cultural background, thorough notes on individual tracks, and transcriptions of all examples. –JSR

☆ **Djambidj: An Aboriginal Song Series / AIAS**
Clan-song series like *Djambidj* constitutes an important musico-poetic form with strong spiritual and ritual significance. Two singers are accompanied by didjeridu and percussion. This, along with *Goyulan: The Morning Star*, are the only recordings of complete Aboriginal song series. The accompanying very substantial monographs include transcriptions and translations as well as detailed background notes. Crucially for its quality, it is a real collaboration between the main singer and an ethnomusicologist. –JSR

Goyulan: The Morning Star / AIAS
This and *Djambidj: An Aboriginal Song Series* are the only recordings of complete Aboriginal song series. –JSR

Music of the Torres Strait / AIAS
Like Native Americans, Aborigines have developed a range of new music as well as drawing on an expansion of their own resources (including intertribal styles) borrowing from other traditions. The two cassettes covering traditional and modern idioms illustrate the process and its results in changing old styles or evolving new ones. Excellent booklet of notes. –JSR

Songs from North Queensland / AIAS
One in a series of three sets in the outstanding collection issued by the Australian Institute of Aboriginal Studies. Contains examples of both traditional music and more syncretic styles from a town in North Queensland. Comes with substantial booklet. –JSR

Songs from the Kimberleys / AIAS
One in a series of three sets in the outstanding collection issued by the Australian Institute of Aboriginal Studies. The Kimberleys area of Western Australia offers a quite different tradition. Comes with substantial booklet. –JSR

Songs from Yarrabah / AIAS
One in a series of three sets in the outstanding collection issued by the Australian Institute of Aboriginal Studies. Contains examples of traditional music and more syncretic styles from a town in North Queensland, offering in greater detail one stylistic area in the region covered more generally by the North Queensland album. Comes with substantial booklet. –JSR

Hawaiian Music

In the early days of recording history, Hawaiian music was not like the music we associate with tourist hotels and slow hula dances today. Vintage island sounds, passed on to us by a number of outstanding 78 RPM reissues, were hot and peppy, featuring flashy slide guitarists like Sol Hoopii, King Benny Nawahi, and mainlander Roy Smeck. Island guitarists, inspired by hot jazz and blues, traveled to the states regularly, where they enjoyed great popularity and in turn influenced the emerging bottleneck blues style. Country musicians were also fascinated by the Hawaiian-style slide, and the pedal steel is a direct descendant. With the advent of amplification, the guitar had more sustaining ability, and guitarists tended to slow down to a more leisurely pace. The characteristic soaring vocal harmonies of the male and female groups also became more languid, bringing the golden age to a slow, syrupy halt. After decades of kitschy commercialization, the music of the islands has revitalized and returned to its roots, with slack-key guitarists Gabby Pahinui and Raymond Kane again finding favor on this continent, and slide enthusiast Bob Brozman bringing back not only the classic sounds but the surviving members of the celebrated Tau Moe family.

— Myles Boisen

Songs of Aboriginal Australia / FOLKWAYS
Vocal songs and didjeridu music. –DLM

Songs of the Northern Territory / AIAS
Camp and corroboree singing recorded in 1962-1963 in a wide range of locations in Australia's vast Northern Territory. Most of the music is ceremonial. These tapes are a remarkably thorough exploration of a series of interlocking cultures. The 60-page accompanying illustrated booklet goes into great detail about the individual tracks and background. –JSR

HAWAII

SOL HOOPII

Hawaiian. The most celebrated steel guitarist of the Hawaiian golden age was undoubtedly Sol Hoopii, who first came to the mainland as a stowaway in 1919. I believe he is the only performer to appear on every Hawaiian slide compilation, where liner notes typically describe him with a single word — "hot." Most of his 78s (over 200!!) were recorded in Los Angeles, where he enjoyed great popularity in such clubs as the Hula Hutt and Seven Seas. He appeared in many movies, toured the country advancing his highly rhythmic slide techniques, and left his stamp on an entire generation of lap steel and pedal steel guitarists in the emerging country & western style. –MB

Vol. 1 - Master of Hawaiian Guitar / ROUNDER   1987
All late-20s recordings showing his early technique on steel guitar. Masterful. –MB

☆ **Vol. 2 - Master of Hawaiian Guitar / ROUNDER**   1988
A retrospective from throughout Sol's influential career. Lots of hot Hawaiian slide here. –MB

KALAMA'S QUARTETTE

Vocal.

○ **Hawaiian Classics / ARHOOLIE**
Vintage late-20s Hawaiian music, with an emphasis on sweet vocal harmonies. –MB

RAYMOND KANE

Hawaiian.
○ **Master of the Slack Key Guitar / ROUNDER**   1988
A contemporary recording of this traditional, old-style guitarist/singer. −MB

THE MELENLANI SERENADERS

Traditional.
Kaulana 'O Ni'ihau / HULA
Music from the island of Niihau, Hawaii. −ROOTS & RHYTHM

NA MELE O NA OPIO

Traditional.
○ **It's a Small World / PUMEHANA**
Twenty-nine-member youth group performs a variety of Hawaiian styles. −ROOTS & RHYTHM

OHTA-SAN

Instrumental.
○ **Contemporary Hawaiian Mood / POKI**
Ukelele master with modern Hawaiian music. −ROOTS & RHYTHM

HAWAII COLLECTIONS

Hawaiian Guitar Hot Shots / YAZOO
The most agile dazzlers of the 78 RPM era. A slide guitarist's dream come true. −MB
Hawaiian Steel Guitar 1920s-50s / ARHOOLIE   1976
Hawaiian Steel Guitar Classics - 1920s-50s features Hawaiian, cowboy, and vaudeville slide experts. −MB
Hawaiian Steel Guitar - Vol. 2 / ARHOOLIE   1981
Hawaiian Steel Guitar Classics - Vol. 2 (1927-1934) is a Bob Brozman compilation of all-authentic Hawaiian acts, both popular and obscure. −MB
☆ **Hula Blues / ROUNDER**   1971
Another great sampling of top Hawaiian and stateside sliders, some with a country beat. −MB
Na Mele O Paniolo / HAWAII STATE FOUNDATION
The local cowboys and their 19th-century predecessors from Mexico were major catalysts in Hawaiian music. This recent project (recorded in the mid and late 80s by the Hawaii State Foundation of Culture & the Arts) offers performances of traditional material performed by several groups from several islands, most of them with ranch connections. Very fine recordings; excellent booklet. −DLM
Vintage Hawaiian Music - Vol. 1 / ROUNDER   1989
Vintage Hawaiian Music - Steel Guitar Masters (1928-34) contains the earliest Hawaiian 78 RPM recordings. With its companion volume of singers, they are important historical documents. Both volumes are treasures. −MB
☆ **Vintage Hawaiian Music - Vol. 2 / ROUNDER**   1989
Very early Hawaiian 78 RPM recordings, *Vintage Hawaiian Music - Great Singers 1928-34* has a companion volume of steel guitar. An important historical document. Both volumes are treasures. −MB
○ **Vintage Original Hawaiian Classics / VINTAGE**   1990
A lovely collection of 20s and 30s Hawaiian tunes, put together lovingly by Noel McMillan. −JOHN MCCORD, ROOTS & RHYTHM

NEW CALEDONIA COLLECTIONS

Kanak Songs - Feast & Lullabies / CHANT DU MONDE
The culture of the New Caledonian Kanaks east of Australia varies from island to island and community to community (the 60,000 Kanaks speak at least 20 languages), yet the music has a good deal of underlying cohesion. The examples here, including a remarkable recitative speech and many swirling songs to percussion, were mostly recorded on the main island of Grande Terre. The music comes with the usual thorough notes. (45:34) −JSR

NEW ZEALAND

INIA TE WIATA

Traditional.
Waiata Maori / WAIKIKI
The Maori people are known for their joyous communal singalongs known as waiata. −ED

PACIFIC ISLANDS COLLECTIONS

Island Music of the South Pacific / NONESUCH

PAPUA NEW GUINEA COLLECTIONS

Kaluli Weeping and Song / MUSICAPHON
Music of Middle Sepik / MUSICAPHON
Thanks in part to geography, Papula/Nugini is surely the territory with the most musical variety per head of population. The recordings (mostly Iatmul), made from the early 60s to early 70s, include fine flute music for solo and ensembles, as well as other wind music and a little percussion. −JSR
Music of the Abelam / MUSICAPHON
This album is more vocally oriented than *Music of Middle Sepik* and is devoted to music for socio-religious events: building and consecrating a ceremonial house, yam festivals, and rites of passage. Its focus is much more vocal. −JSR
Music of the Iatmul / MUSICAPHON
The set was recorded in the early 70s and covers a good deal of the same musical ground as *Music of Middle Sepik*. −JSR
Voices of the Rainforest / RYKODISC
This recording deserves a place of its own. Steve Feld's new recordings from Kaluli territory set it in a sonic context reflecting the reality that the rainforest is a "dense, layered aural tapestry to which the Kaluli lend their voices." The arrangement is that of a day in the life of the Kaluli and the rainforest. Its powerful effect is enhanced by outstanding recording technique and admirable notes. −DLM

SAMOA COLLECTIONS

Samoan Songs: Historical Collection / MUSICAPHON
An outstanding recording bringing together Samoan recordings of great rarity. Three were recorded before WWI, three in 1940, and the rest in the mid and late 60s. They include dance songs, war songs, and topical songs of various sorts, including political ones. Music of enormous importance is underpinned by Musicaphon's thorough notes. −JSR

SOLOMON ISLANDS COLLECTIONS

Fataleka & Baegu Music / PHILIPS
Fataleka & Baegu Music: Malaita, Solomon Islands is a very interesting and beautiful collection of vocal polyphonies and panpipes. −DLM
Polyphonies of Solomon Islands / CHANT DU MONDE
Polyphony — for both voices and panpipes — is crucial to Solomon Islands music. This recording is from Gaudalcanal and Savo. This re-release of classic 1974 recordings by Hug Zemp contains fine examples of both (including one amazingly like a shape-note sol-fa), with very thorough notes and photos. −JSR

TAHITI COLLECTIONS

Bastille Celebrations in Polynesia / ARION
Recorded in Polynesia by Gérard Krémer. −ED
Dream Island (traditional) / PLAYASOUND
The Gauguin Years (Songs & Dances) / NONESUCH
Love Songs of Tahiti / WAIKIKI
Paumotu Style / WAIKIKI
1st US Tour / MONITOR

WORLDBEAT

3 MUSTAPHAS 3

Worldbeat. The 3 Mustaphas 3 pratfell onto the burgeoning worldbeat scene from out of nowhere in 1986 — or from Szegerely, somewhere in the Balkans, if you believe their press releases. According to Mustapha mythology, the Balkan Beat Boys first sharpened their musical teeth at the Crazy Loquat Club under the guidance of Uncle Patrel Mustapha Bin Mustapha. Then, seeking broader horizons, they stole away one night, accompanied by their favorite refrigeration equipment, to seek world success from a UK base.
The Mustapha's humor has been a double-edged scimitar, however. In the beginning it allowed them to introduce difficult music to unsuspecting audiences new to the worldbeat sound. But the burlesque that initially forwarded their agenda also worked against them by threatening to consign the group to the purgatory of novelty act. An increasing emphasis on solid musicianship, plus their collaboration with revered African performers like Stella Chiweshe, have begun to win the band the critical respect they deserve. And no one else makes a crash course in world music so much fun. –BT

☆ **Soup of the Century / RYKODISC**   1990
Stung by allegations that they're nothing but a "joke band," the Mustaphas cook up their hardest set yet, recorded live in the studio with minimal overdubbing. Look for mindboggling genre fusions plus molten clarinet and electric bazouki breakouts. –BT

○ **Friends, Fiends & Fronds / FLYING FISH**   1991
A portrait of the artists as an evolving concept is presented in this collection of singles, B-sides, and remixes. Worth its weight in premium goat's cheese for the two versions of their masterpiece "Linda Linda" and a pair of brand new songs. –BT

ANCIENT FUTURE

Worldbeat.
○ **World without Walls / SONA GAIA**   1990
Squeaky clean acoustic romp by San Francisco quartet through African and Asian rhythms, with a dose of jazz and a dollop of Zakir Hussain sitting in on Indian percussion. –BT

ANNABOUBOULA

Worldbeat. Lead singer Anna Paidoussi sounds like the Cowboy Junkies' Margo Timmins on speed. Their hit "I'd Rather Set Myself on Fire" illustrates their hybrid sound — traditional Greek harmonies and instrumental work, set against a modern rock production. Challenging and unusual music. –HD

In the Baths of Constantinople / SHANACHIE   1989
More than a world music fusion, a noisy cultural collision between traditional Greek rembitiko music and Western dance styles. Guess which side wins? Raucously inventive. –BT
○ **Greek Fire / SHANACHIE**   1990
The rough edges of the Greek/house-music merger have been sanded off. Good news if you like your dance music seamless, bad if you crave the unexpected dash of grit and spice. –BT

BAHIA BLACK

Worldbeat.
○ **Ritual Beating System / AXIOM**   1991
Collision between Brazilian drum troupe Olodum, American jazz artists (Herbie Hancock, Wayne Shorter, Henry Threadgill), bucket drummers (Larry Wright, David Chapman), rap, samba, funk, rock, and more — produced by Bill Laswell. Whatever kind of music this is, I want to hear more of it. –BT

BOILED IN LEAD

Worldbeat.
○ **Orb / ATOMIC THEORY-FLYING FISH**   1990
Worldbeat with a twist the 3 Mustapha 3 way — and with an undercurrent of punk aggressiveness. Nothing intimidates these Minnesotans, neither Serbian kolos, Romanian klezmer, Scottish ballads, nor traditional Armenian fare. Produced by Hijaz Mustapha himself. –BT

BRATSCH

Worldbeat.
○ **Transports en Commun / GRIFFE**   1991
French troupe of purported Gypsy musicians display astonishing virtuosity throughout a wide range of styles: Bulgarian, klezmer, flamenco, jazz, classical touches. –BT

DAN DEL SANTO

Worldbeat. Del Santo lives in Austin, TX, where he has assembled a mighty group of players who can leap from reggae to juju to rock and back again without breaking into a sweat. He coined the term "worldbeat" to describe his music, a mix of Western and African pop that draws from many influences without ever sounding watered down or "commercial." –JP
○ **Off Your Nyash / FLYING FISH**   1990
Del Santo's politically aware lyrics give you plenty to think about while the band's rhythms motivate your feet. –JP

DIGA RHYTHM BAND

Worldbeat.
○ **Diga / RYKODISC**   1976
Grateful Dead drummer Mickey Hart has long been a proponent and student of world music. He produced this 1976 all-percussion outing, which is a compelling and powerful recording that draws in the listener with its spellbinding rhythms. –JT

EARTH ISLAND ORCHESTRA

Worldbeat.
○ **Earth Island Orchestra / I WANNA RECORDS**   1992
Detroit's Arab and Indian community contribute pieces to this wild jigsaw puzzle of international influences. –BT

HASSAN HAKMOUN w/ADAM RUDOLPH

Worldbeat.
○ **Gift of the Gnawa / FLYING FISH**   1991
Moroccan musician Hakmoun's compelling vocals and sintar (lute) playing rides the tide of Adam Rudolph's fierce tabla foundation. Joined by Don Cherry's trumpet and Richard Horwitz on nay (flute), they produce an intensely evocative fusion. –BT

MICKEY HART   b 1943

Worldbeat. Mickey Hart is a drummer, an ethnomusicologist, and an author. He joined the Grateful Dead as its second percussionist in 1967. In 1970 Hart left the band and cut the solo album *Rolling Thunder* in 1972, featuring various members of the Dead. Hart returned to the band in 1974.
Hart's musical activities outside the Dead have been extensive. In 1976, the Dead's Round Records label released *Diga* by the Diga Rhythm Band, an early experiment in worldbeat fusion put together by Hart. His interaction with drummers from around the world sparked an abiding interest in the role of the drum in other cultures — and a steadily expanding curiosity about non-Western musics. 1979 and 1980 saw the release of two albums of music from the film *Apocalypse Now*, much of it contributed by Hart. In 1983 Hart released albums under the heading *The World*. These began with a reissue of *Diga*

Rhythm Band (an album by Babatunde Olatunji produced by Hart). Then came a series of albums of music Hart had recorded around the world. In 1989 Hart released *Music to Be Born By*, an album based on the heartbeat of his son in the womb, and 1990 saw the simultaneous release of Hart's first book, *Drumming at the Edge of Magic*, and an album, *At the Edge*. In 1991 another book and disc, both called *Planet Drum*, appeared. Both albums made the upper reaches of new-age and world-music charts. –WR & BT

The Apocalypse Now Sessions / ROUNDER   1980
Hart's soundtrack work for *Apocalypse Now* expanded into these free-ranging, rather abstract tracks with fellow Grateful Dead drummer Billy Kreutzmann. –BT

○ **Däfos / RYKODISC**   1983
An established audiophile classic for its thrilling, nearly overpowering sonics, this percussion-based journey to a mythical country features Brazilian percussionist Airto Moreira and vocalist Flora Purim. –BT

○ **Planet Drum / ROUNDER**   1991
A dazzling all-percussion workout with plenty of muscle and deep grooves featuring many of the world musicians from *At the Edge*. Loosely tied to Hart's book of the same name. –BT

HENRY KAISER w/DAVID LINDLEY
Worldbeat.

○ **A World out of Time / SHANACHIE**   1992
A series of five CDs highlighting the best musicians of Madagascar collaborating here with avant-garde rock musicians Kaiser and Lindley. Features Madagascar's rising pop star Rossy and 72-year-old flute master Rakotofrah. –BT

ANGELIQUE KIDJO
Worldbeat.

○ **Logozo / MANGO**   1991
State-of-the-art production and mainstreamed African dance beats are poised to propel this talented singer from Benin to international pop stardom. Branford Marsalis, Ray Lema, and Manu Dibango contribute. –BT

DEMBO KONTE
Kora.

○ **Jali Roll / WORLD CIRCUIT**   1990
In their own right, these masters of the West African kora harp captivate. Backed by bass, drum, guitars, and accordion, courtesy of the 3 Mustaphas 3, they achieve a new dimension without sacrificing subtleties. Many brilliant, beautiful moments with Kausa Kuyateh. –BT

KOTOJA
Worldbeat.
Freedom Is What Everybody Needs / RHINO
This band, made up of Nigerian and American musicians, is based in Berkeley, CA. They mix soca, Latin, funk, and Nigerian elements into their dance-happy sound. The group includes bassist Ken Okulolo (with King Sunny Ade) and trumpet ace Babatunde Williams from Fela's Africa '70 band. –JP

RAY LEMA
Worldbeat.
Nangadeef / MANGO   1990
If Herbie Hancock's "Rock-It" had been recorded by the Zairian diaspora in Paris, it might have sounded something like this. Though the low spots are pretty generic, the frequent thunderclaps on this forward-looking disc are worthy of Youssou N'Dour at his best. –BT

Gaia / MANGO   1991
Kraftwerk meets the rain forest as Lema refines his vision of Africa as reference point for the rest of the world. May be the source of the most mind-boggling computer-rhythms ever

committed to disc. An organic approach to synthesis laden with insight and wit. –BT

BENJAMIN LEW & STEVEN BROWN
Worldbeat. Brown was a founder of the West Coast group, Tuxedomoon; Lew is a Belgian composer/filmmaker. –JSR

Twelfth Day / ORIGINAL MUSIC   1984
Their first recording's acoustic/electronic mix had African overtones with echoes witty or wistful of idioms ranging from the Orient to baroque Germany and 30s French cabaret. The result is both original and all of a piece — one of those recordings that doesn't really fit into any neat definitional box, and thus has remained the preserve of a too-small number of passionate devotees. –JSR

CARLOS LOMAS
Worldbeat.
From Malaga to Cairo / MOTW   1986
Carlos Lomas is a masterly interpreter of the flamenco guitar and an exciting composer. Together with his friends who play Indian sitar, Middle Eastern drums, flutes, banjo, and violin, he creates a very special type of world music with a flamenco flavor. –MUSIC OF THE WORLD

MANDINGO GRIOT SOCIETY
Worldbeat. Foday Musa Suso is a Mandingo (West African tribe) griot (hereditary musician and cultural curator) who can trace his hereditary lineage back to the first performer on the 21-string kora lute. After a traditional apprenticeship in Africa, he came to the US in 1977 and formed the Mandingo Griot Society to bring his native sounds to a new, receptive audience. The group included Adam Rudolph (who recently appeared on Hassan Hakmoun's *Gift of the Gnawa* CD) and had featured jazz trumpeter Don Cherry as a guest, anticipating world music fusion many years before the worldbeat era. –MB

○ **Watta Sitta / CELLULOID**
This is another great kora electrification project. Watta Sitta bravely attempts to mold an international dance music sound around Muso's African harp, while Herbie Hancock provides moral support. –BT

MOUTH MUSIC
Worldbeat.

○ **Mouth Music / ROUNDER**   1991
Intriguing blend of puirt a beul (traditional Gaelic vocal music intended for dancing) with African and other drumming styles plus the requisite drum machine and synths, resulting in the world's first Irish-roots house music. –BT

OUTBACK
Worldbeat. Outback is a four-piece band that plays a unique brand of world/fusion music. The backbone of their music is Graham Wiggins (didjeridu) and Martin Craddick (acoustic guitar). Sagar N'Gom delivers a nice West African percussion sound, with Ian Campbell on drums and Paddy LeMercier on French fiddle. –CR

○ **Baka / HANNIBAL**   1990
Acoustic guitarist Martin Craddick makes a strong team with Graham Wiggins, whose axe of choice is the Australian aboriginal instrument, the didjeridu. Wiggins's unorthodox techniques on this instrument — which generate percussive patterns as well as animal barks — finds their equal in Craddick's narrative instrumental style. –BT

MIKE RICHMOND
Worldbeat.
Basic Tendencies / MOTW   1988
Mike Richmond is one of the most talented and exciting bass players of our time. Features rhythms and flavors of distant

lands, and brings them together within a framework of acoustic double bass. With Glen Velez, Joe Passaro, and Badal Roy (percussion); Lois Colin (harp); and Simon Shaheen ('ud). –MUSIC OF THE WORLD

SONGHAI

Worldbeat.

☆ **Songhai / HANNIBAL**
Unique multicultural supergroup: Toumani Diabate (Mali) on kora, Danny Thompson (UK) on bass, and the Gypsy guitar group Ketama from Spain, plus guests. –MB

GLEN VELEZ

Worldbeat.
Handdance: Fame Drum Music / MOTW   1984
Glen Velez is an internationally recognized authority on

tambourine history and playing techniques from around the world. On this recording [with Layne Redmond] he plays tambourines and mbira (African thumb piano), and utilizes harmonic singing. "A multi-fingered rain forest of percussion." *Washington Post.* –MUSIC OF THE WORLD
Ramana / MOTW   1990
A remarkable hand percussionist, Glen Velez specializes in frame drums from all over the world. Glen plays frame drums, unbira, and steel drums, and is joined by Layne Redmond (percussion) and Howard Levy (harmonica). "Magic happens when he begins to play." *The Village Voice.* –MUSIC OF THE WORLD

ENVIRONMENTAL

ROBERT RICH

Rainforest / HEARTS OF SPACE 1989
A polyrhythmic, electro-acoustic trip into the lush green beauty of the tropical soundspace — in the natural harmonics of just intonation, a tuning system that uses pure musical intervals. –ED

THE ATMOSPHERE COLLECTION

○ **Sunset Surf - a Day on Cape Cod / RYKODISC** 1986
Relax to the gentle swells of the Cape Cod surf. –ED
Summer Rain - A Day on Cape Cod / RYKODISC 1986
A background of white noise from the steady downpour of a New England rainshower. You can even hear the sounds of the water draining from the eaves trough. –ED
Early Cape Morning / RYKODISC 1986
A mix of light breezes and birdsongs from the Cape Cod countryside that will fill your room with soothing nature sounds. –ED
Babbling Brook - A Day on Cape Cod / RYKODISC 1986
Gently trickling water from a meadow stream. –ED
Waterfall - A Week in Hawaii / RYKODISC 1987
An hour of water-induced white noise provides aural effervescence to sooth and relax the listener. –ED
Island Jungle - A Week in Hawaii / RYKODISC 1987
This 60-minute recording was taken from the east coast of the island of Hawaii, revealing the ocean and its surrounding wildlife. –ED
○ **Midnight Rainshower / RYKODISC** 1987
Sixty minutes of a soothing tropical rainshower, several miles inland on the coast of Hawaii, in the Kalopa Park nature reserve. The noise of the rain is interspersed with animal sounds of the rainforest. –ED
Tropical Surf - A Week in Hawaii / RYKODISC 1987

EARTH SOUNDS

Tennessee Nightwalk / EARTH SOUNDS 1976
Recorded by Gordon Hempton in the heart of Appalachia, frogs and toads join their songs in this 60-minute piece. –ED
Ebb & Flow / EARTH SOUNDS 1989
This album features over 22 minutes of ocean surf, and over 35 minutes more of tide pools, rocky coves, sand dunes, and sandspits. Recorded by Gordon Hempton. –ED
Dawn Chorus / EARTH SOUNDS 1990
Recorder Gordon Hempton captures 20 North American songbird habitats on this hour-long recording. –ED

ENVIRONMENTS

Disc 1 / ATLANTIC 1971
Classic enviromental recordings from the 70s, this series helped establish the environmental recordings genre. Many are now available on CD or cassette. This disc is subtitled *Psychologically Ultimate Seashore.*–ED

Disc 2 (Tintinnabulation) / ATLANTIC 1972
Disc 3 (Dawn/Dusk at New Hope) / ATLANTIC 1974
Disc 4 (Ultimate Thunderstorm) / ATLANTIC 1975
Ultimate Thunderstorm/Gentle Rain in a Pine Forest. –ED
Disc 5 (Ultimate Heartbeat) / ATLANTIC 1981
Disc 6 - (Dawn/Dusk in Okefenokee) / ATLANTIC 1982
Intonation (Meditation Sound) / ATLANTIC 1987
Summer Cornfield / ATLANTIC 1987
Wind in the Trees / ATLANTIC 1987
English Meadow / ATLANTIC 1988

GENTLE PERSUASION

○ **Sounds of Nature / SPECIAL MUSIC PRODUCTS (CAMCO)**
This is a boxed set containing five CDs: "The Cry of the Loon," "Sounds and songs of the Humpback Whales," "Sounds of the Tropical Rain Forest," "Peaceful Ocean Surf," and "Electrifying Thunderstorms." All natural sounds — digital recordings. –ED

INTUITIVE AUDIO

Sonoma Surf / INTUITIVE AUDIO
Nothing but mesmerising and refreshing ocean sounds in this exceptionally relaxing release. A great sleep aid. –ED

LULLABY FROM THE WOMB

○ **Lullaby from the Womb / CAPITOL**
"Mother sounds for the newborn baby," including the sound of the main artery of the mother, heartbeat, and other sounds from the womb. Combined with gentle classical music. –ED

NATURE RECORDINGS

Dawn/Dusk in Vendanta Wilderness / TAPE MASTERS

SONG OF THE NIGHTINGALE

Song of the Nightingale / WERGO 1988
Field recordings by Walter Tilgner from 1983. –ED

SONGS OF THE HUMPBACK WHALE

○ **Songs of the Humpback Whale / EARTH MUSIC** 1991
Classic recordings of the "Bel Canto" age of whale singing. The 10-minute track "Solo Whale" was recorded at a depth of 1500 feet by deep-water microphones that were claimed by the sea, making this a one of a kind. –ED

SOUNDS OF THE S. AMERICAN RAIN FOREST

Sounds of the S. American Rain Forest / FOLKWAYS

TIMBERWOLF IN THE TALL PINES

○ **Timberwolf in the Tall Pines / RYKODISC**
The North woods and wilderness come alive on this 60-minute recording of a wolf pack (with cubs), black bears, and coyotes. Animal sounds combine with a backdrop of insects and wind. –ED

Celtic & British Isles

There is in me (faint memory of a smile)
The soul of a shivery old cat —
Let the wood-grey body be wounded, beaten,
Whatever be at it, it will live.

These words, written in the 14th century by the Welsh bard Dafydd ap Gwylim, express the unquashable endurance of the Celtic cultures of Europe. Through centuries of oppression, of systematic attempts by foreign occupiers to destroy Celtic cultural identity, their expressive arts have continued to develop and to spawn new and emergent forms. It is a supreme and fitting irony that we consider English folk music under the rubric of "Celtic and British Isles" music.

The term "Celtic" in its most rigid sense refers to languages: to Irish, Manx, and Scots Gaelic, and to Welsh, Cornish, and Breton Brythonic. However, what we think of as Celtic music is performed by both Celtic speakers and speakers of English and French, in the Celtic homelands in the British Isles, Ireland, Brittany and a diaspora that spans the globe from Australia to America. It is defined here as music that has sprung from the ancient, ever-developing musical tradition of the Celtic homelands.

There are various levels of "professionalism" and "traditionality" among performers of this music. The tradition continues of amateur musicians and singers who watch and listen to their elders, gradually learning to express themselves within the medium of traditional musical performance. On the other hand, a revival of interest in traditional music since the 60s has created an international demand for newer groups influenced by classical, folk, jazz, and pop music. The result is a musical system with many genres and styles, ranging from unaccompanied singing or solo playing to highly structured arrangements of folk ensembles and to rock & roll bands belting out jigs and reels with a vicious backbeat.

The standard of musicianship in this music is extraordinarily high. This is due partly to the important role of music in the cultural and national identities of the countries and ethnic groups in question, partly to vigorous systems of musical competition leading to national championships for each instrument. The high standard of performance, combined with the multifarious genres and styles considered in this section, lead to a problem of sorts: there are a huge number of good records to buy and limited space for us to guide you to them. This section concentrates somewhat on the newer, revival acts, which have a broader appeal than strictly traditional approaches. Many of these groups list their traditional sources in the notes to their albums, giving the interested listener leads for further listening.

This, then, is but a tip of the old cat's tail, a vantage point from which to begin your own explorations of the rich realms of Celtic and English folk music.

— Stephen Winick

THE ALBION BAND

English. Originally formed to accompany Shirley Collins, they later broke off on their own. They use both acoustic and electric instruments to create a sound much like Fairport Convention. They have existed as the Albion Band, the Albion Country Band, and the Albion Dance Band. –sw

○ **Battle of the Field / CARTHAGE**　　　　　　1976
Recorded in 1973, released in 1976, this lovely album was the band's debut as a separate entity. –sw

Rise up Like the Sun / CARTHAGE　　　　　　1978
Traditional and modern songs with a less folky sound. –sw

Christmas Present from the Albion Band / FUN
Carols, songs, and recitations pertaining to the holiday, featuring the lovely singing of Cathy LeSurf. –sw

ALTAN

Irish. Ireland's most electrifying current group features fiddles, flute, bouzouki, and guitar in driving and precise arrangements of dance tunes, along with songs in Gaelic and English by the stunning Mairead Ni Mhoainaigh. –sw

The Red Crow / GREEN LINNET　　　　　　1973
Superb. The band really nails down its sound on this one. –sw

○ **Harvest Storm / GREEN LINNET**　　　　　　1992
Their latest and best. A true necessity. –sw

ALISTAIR ANDERSON

English. A pioneering force in Northumbrian folk music, Anderson plays Northumbrian pipes and concertina. –sw

Plays English Concertina / TRAILER　　　　　1972
And he plays it well, on his first solo album. Features several of the Boys of the Lough as guests. –sw

The Concertina Workshop/Topic / FREE REED　1974
The title says it all. –sw

○ **Steel Skies / FLYING FISH**　　　　　　　　1982
Anderson and band perform recently composed tunes. –sw

WILLIAM ANDREWS w/LIAM WALSH

Irish. Andrews and Walsh, two very different pipers, were both born in the 19th century. Andrews was winning contests before WWI, and both men had direct contact with the giants of the older tradition. –sw

○ **Classics of Irish Piping / TOPIC**
Virtually all of these recordings date from the late 20s, and these reels, airs, hornpipes, and jigs represent a highly important link with the past. –JSR

DAN AR BRAS

Breton. A truly great acoustic and electric guitarist, and a good singer as well, Ar Bras was the guitar wizard in many of Alan

Stivell's arrangements. He has also had a long and productive solo career. –sw

Douar Nevez / HEXAGONE 1977
A Breton rock concept album relating the story of Ys, the Breton equivalent of Atlantis. –sw

○ **Acoustic / GREEN LINNET** 1985
Highly personal compositions with a Celtic feel. –sw

ARCADY

Irish. A Galway band featuring several former members of De Danann, as well as fine singing by Frances Black. –sw

○ **After the Ball / SHANACHIE** 1991
Features traditional Irish tunes, sentimental ditties, and one French song from Brittany. –sw

AR LOG

Welsh. A premier Wales folk group, formed in 1976, featuring singing in Welsh with harps, fiddle, and guitar. –sw

Ar Log / DINGLE'S 1978
This debut is full of great singing and playing, if still a little rough. –sw

○ **Ar Log 2 / DINGLE'S** 1980
Smooth vocal harmonies and powerful virtuoso playing. Their best. –sw

FRANKIE ARMSTRONG

English. One of the most powerful voices in English folksong, Armstrong has been part of Ewan MacColl's Critic's Group. Her solo albums are all worth listening to. –sw

Out of Love, Hope and Suffering / BAY 1971
Serious, humorous, and bawdy songs and ballads. –sw

○ **Songs and Ballads / ANTILLES** 1975
Classic old ballads. –sw

I Heard a Woman Singing / FLYING FISH 1984
The traditional and original songs on this album address women's issues. –sw

THE BATTLEFIELD BAND

Scottish. Scotland's foremost folk-revival band, based in Glasgow. Their older albums are quite traditional in style and content, but their newer ones are tinged with pop. –sw

○ **At the Front / TOPIC** 1978
A brilliant older album, featuring the singing of Jamie McMenamy (later of Kornog) and Pat Kilbride. –sw

The Story So Far / FLYING FISH 1982
A compilation of some of their older material, including rare tracks. –sw

Home Ground / TEMPLE 1989
The band captured live in the highlands, performing old favorites and new. –sw

New Spring / TEMPLE 1991
A new lineup, producing equally fine music. –sw

DEREK BELL

Irish. Best known as the harpist with the Chieftains, Derek Bell periodically records solo albums that allow his instrumentals to take center stage, backed by his fellow Chieftains on whistle, bodhran, and fiddle. –BE

○ **Carolan's Favorite / SHANACHIE**
Probably Bell's best and most mystical album, a subdued and varied account of Turlough Carolan's music. –BE

Carolan's Receipt / SHANACHIE
Bell's tribute to 17th-century harpist Turlough Carolan, backed by the New Irish Chamber Orchestra. –BE

Derek Bell's Musical Ireland / SHANACHIE
A more general look at Irish music spanning numerous periods in various styles. –BE

PETER BELLAMY

English. Bellamy was one of the English folk revival's greatest voices. He was born in Norfolk in 1944. In the early days of 1965 he moved to London, where he met up with Royston Wood and Heather Wood, and the three got a regular gig at a club whose name they would eventually adopt — The Young Tradition. In flamboyant costumes, with witty presentation, and with the startling power of Bellamy's voice backed by his companions, they entertained a lot of audiences, recorded a pair of albums, gained a reputation for excellence, and were still unable to make a living as performers. So, in 1969, they broke up. As Bellamy would later point out, they became important and influential, even legendary, after they had ceased to exist.

In 1970 the idea first struck Bellamy to set the poems of Kipling to music. This fascination with Kipling continued until Bellamy's death, resulting in no fewer than five albums of Kipling songs. Also in the 70s, Bellamy composed *The Transports*, a ballad opera in the mold of Ewan MacColl's work, and recruited such people as Martin Carthy, Nic Jones, A. L. Lloyd, and Cyril Tawney to record it. It was released as an album in 1977 and also had several stage runs in England. During the 70s and 80s, Bellamy was trying to find an audience wider than the traditional folk crowd, so he cut back on the traditional songs in his shows, turning them into multimedia historical presentations. But traditional singing was in Bellamy's blood, and the beginning of the 90s found him back to performing mostly a traditional repertoire once again, with the exuberant enthusiasm he has always been known for. Bellamy felt there was a lack of appreciation for the music to which he had devoted his life. More than once he has commented on how countless performers have ditched traditional music for other forms of "folk" music. Some, he felt, did it for money, something he no doubt understood but regretted. More often, though, he expressed regret that interest in traditional song was simply on the wane, not only with audiences, but with performers as well. He always acknowledged that his own unwillingness or perhaps his inability to compromise had led to the demise of the Young Tradition. Perhaps, some 22 years later, it helped lead to his own; in September 1991, Peter Bellamy took his own life. All Peter Bellamy recordings are recommended. –sw

Barrack-Room Ballads / GREEN LINNET 1976
Bellamy performs songs of Rudyard Kipling. –sw

★ **The Transports / FREE REED** 1977
Bellamy's masterpiece ballad opera, starring himself and other influential folk singers. –sw

○ **Songs an' Rummy Conjurin' Tricks / FELLSIDE** 1991
Recorded live a scant nine months before his death, this album is an excellent example of Bellamy's charm as a live performer. –sw

BLEIZI RUZ

Breton. One of Brittany's top bands, blending traditional accordion and bombarde playing with the newer sounds of electric guitars, bass, and drums –sw

En Concert / ESCALIBUR 1991
A live album featuring innovative instrumentals and traditional and original songs. –sw

○ **Coz Lizoriou-Klask Ar Plac'h / PLURIEL**
Two albums on one CD. A lot of good, solid, instrumental music, and one song. –sw

BLOWZABELLA

English. A highly electric band featuring Andy Cutting (melodeons, percussion), Nigel Eaton (hurdy-gurdies, cello, percussion), Jo Freya (vocals, tenor saxophone, clarinet), Paul James (saxophone, bagpipes, rauschfeife, percussion), and Jon Swayne (saxophone, bagpipes). Their music has been highly influenced by Middle Eastern, Irish, and Bulgarian music. –CR

○ **Vanilla / GREEN LINNET**
You'll hear all types of European influences on this CD. Not for the faint of heart; only fans of the eclectic need apply. –CR

THE BOTHY BAND

Irish. This groundbreaking band of the 70s folk revival includes pipes, flute, fiddle, guitar, and more, plus the unbelievable singing voice of Triona Ni Dhomhnaill. –sw

○ **The Bothy Band / GREEN LINNET**   1975
Brilliant 1975 debut, featuring fiddler Tommy Peoples. –sw

Old Hag You Have Killed Me / GREEN LINNET   1976
A great title for a great album. –sw

★ **Best of the Bothy Band / GREEN LINNET**   1988
Intricate arrangements, lovely singing, powerful rhythms. An absolute must. –sw

LA BOTTINE SOURIANTE

Canadian. Quebec's traditional music is a blend of French and Irish styles. This is Quebec's top folk ensemble, incorporating fiddle, accordion, guitar, and more. –sw

○ **La Traversée de l'Atlantique / GREEN LINNET**   1988
Their most Irish-sounding album, with a bodhran player adding to the distinctly Canadian percussion of heavy boot-tapping. –sw

Je Voudrais Changer d'Chapeau / ROUNDER
The most progressive their albums, consistently upbeat and fun. –sw

THE BOYS OF THE LOUGH

Celtic/English. A folk-revival group featuring members from England, Ireland, and Scotland, led by the great Shetland fiddler Aly Bain. –sw

○ **The Boys of the Lough / SHANACHIE**   1973
This debut album is particularly brilliant because of Robin Morton and Dick Gaughan's contributions. –sw

Live at Passim's / PHILO   1975
A great early album, still with Morton. –sw

To Welcome Paddy Home / SHANACHIE   1985
The tragic death of guitarist Tich Richardson left the band short and shocked for a while, but they bounced back beautifully on this album. –sw

Sweet Rural Shade / SHANACHIE   1987
Includes their top three releases. –CR

Farewell and Remember Me / SHANACHIE   1987
One of their finest records. –CR

Second Album / ROUNDER   1990
Live album. Good sound quality. –CR

Live at Carnegie Hall / SAG
A good live album. The crowd is into the show. –CR

Far from Home / SHANACHIE
Highly recommended. –CR

ANNE BRIGGS

English. Both a singer of traditional songs and a songwriter, Briggs was an influence on many important revival singers — June Tabor, Maddy Prior, Sandy Denny, Jacqui McShee, Christy Moore, and others — before she gave up performing for a quieter life. Her lovely voice and accompaniments on guitar and bouzouki still sound fresh and vital. –sw

The Time Has Come / CBS   1971
Quiet, introspective original songs. –sw

★ **Classic Anne Briggs / FELLSIDE**   1990
This CD re-release captures all of her recordings for Topic between 1964 and 1971. Almost every folk song she recorded is here. An absolute must! –sw

JOE BURKE

Irish. One of Ireland's best-known accordion players, Burke comes out of the great Galway squeezebox tradition. –sw

The Tailor's Choice / GREEN LINNET   1983
Burke mostly plays a boxwood flute. Maire Ni Chathasaigh joins him on harp. –sw

Happy to Meet & Sorry to Part / GREEN LINNET   1986
Trio album with Michael Cooney and Terry Corcoran featuring pipes, accordion, guitar, and singing. –sw

○ **Traditional Music of Ireland / GREEN LINNET**
Recorded in 1972 and 1973, this album was released in this country in 1983. A truly classic accordion album with impressive lift and verve. –sw

KEVIN BURKE

Irish. The most fluid and mesmeric fiddler playing Irish music, Burke has been a member of Patrick Street and the Bothy Band. –sw

If the Cap Fits / GREEN LINNET   1978
A showcase of Burke's amazing talents. –sw

Promenade / GREEN LINNET   1979
With Michael O Dhomhnaill. Not to be missed. –sw

● **Eavesdropper / GREEN LINNET**   1981
Kevin and Jackie Daly show amazing empathy for one another's playing — a true musical union. –sw

○ **Portland / GREEN LINNET**   1982
Another fine display, with Michael O Domhnaill. –sw

○ **Up Close / GREEN LINNET**   1984
A gem, featuring guests like Matt Molloy, Joe Burke, and the Murphy family of harmonica players. –sw

BUTTONS & BOWS

Irish. This group is made up of Jackie Daly, along with brothers Seamus and Manus McGuire on fiddles. –sw

○ **Buttons & Bows / GREEN LINNET**   1984
Dance tunes from the Celtic lands as well as Scandinavia, in impressive arrangements. –sw

The First Month of Summer / GREEN LINNET   1987
More of a good thing. –sw

IAN CAMPBELL

Scottish. Ian Campbell & The Ian Campbell Folk Group were Britain's favorite folk performers, bar none, during the 60s. Based in Birmingham, they featured singers Ian and Lorna Campbell of Aberdeen as well as Dave Swarbrick and Dave Pegg, later of Fairport Convention. Their arrangements are somewhat dated today, but with their rousing guitar, banjo, and fiddle accompaniments, some songs still sound fresh, and Swarbrick in particular was ahead of his time. –sw

Across the Hills / TRANSATLANTIC   1964
A good general Campbell album. –sw

○ **Coaldust Ballads / TRANSATLANTIC**   1965
Mining songs, mostly from the Northeast. –sw

The Singing Campbells / TOPIC   1965
Ian and Lorna, plus their sister Winnie, their parents Dave and Betty, and their friend Bob Cooney. All unaccompanied traditional songs, including old ballads and modern street songs. Wonderful! –sw

Tam O'Shanter / XTRA
Ian Campbell alone, performing songs by Robert Burns. –sw

CAPERCAILLIE

Scottish. Featuring accordion, fiddle, whistles, and guitar along with an array of electronics, Capercaillie makes new Scottish folk music. –sw

Crosswinds / GREEN LINNET   1986
Still a bit tentative, but a good album. –sw

○ **Sidewalk / GREEN LINNET**   1989
Donal Lunny's production and the band's skill make this collection of driving, syncopated tunes and songs very exciting indeed. –sw

LIZ CARROLL

Irish. A fantastic Irish fiddler from Chicago. –sw

Irish Fiddle and Piano / SHANACHIE   1978
Her first solo album, full of good traditional material. –sw

Kiss Me Kate / SHANACHIE   1978
Carroll is joined by accordionist Tommy Maguire for another fine album. –sw

○ **Liz Carroll / GREEN LINNET**   1988
Powerhouse tunes, some of which she wrote herself. Accompanied by guitarist Daithi Sproule. –sw

★ **Trian / FLYING FISH**   1992
Utterly brilliant. Carroll and Billy McComiskey play as one, and Daithi Sproule's accompaniment and singing are as good as it gets. –sw

MARTIN CARTHY

English. A key player in England's folksong revival of the early 60s, singer/guitarist Martin Carthy (who also played a short stint in the electric folk band Steeleye Span in the 70s) specializes in retrieving and refreshing traditional British folk material with new embellishments, although he also occasionally throws a number of his own into his albums and sets. As much a scholar as a stylist, Carthy also played a key (though indirect) role in the US folk-rock boom (where he introduced a visiting Paul Simon to a traditional song called "Scarborough Fair"). Most of Carthy's solo work has been recorded with help from fiddle virtuoso Dave Swarbrick. –BE

Crown of Horn / ROUNDER   1971
A solid, representative album, more polished than Carthy's early-60s solo work, but with the hearty earthiness one would expect from this veteran. His albums *Sweet Wivelsfield*, *Because It's There*, and *Out of the Cut* (all on Rounder) are also worth hearing, but serious listeners should also try to find his early-60s albums. –BE

○ **Life & Limb / GREEN LINNET**
Singer/guitarist Martin Carthy and fiddler Dave Swarbrick, stars of the British folk circuit in the 60s, are reunited on a fine 90s set. Fleet and passionate playing. –MH

THE CHIEFTAINS

Folk. The Chieftains evolved directly out of Ceoltoiri Cualann, a group created in 1960 by composer Sean O'Riada. O'Riada's visionary innovation was to produce an Irish ensemble based on traditional instruments and classical orchestral principles. With piper Paddy Moloney at the helm, and such important musicians as Matt Molloy, Martin Fay, and Derek Bell aboard, the Chieftains have evolved beyond O'Riada's original concept, but their music still maintains strong affinities to classical music. –sw

Chieftains 1 / SHANACHIE   1965
A rather tame debut album, exploring what was truly unknown territory during the mid 60s. Better things would follow. –BE

Chieftains 2 / SHANACHIE   1969
More fully developed and secure sound, with Moloney stepping out in front and the rest of the group forming up nicely. –BE

Chieftains 3 / SHANACHIE   1971
The group's first great record, a haunting trip through an Ireland of song, story, and legend. –BE

○ **Chieftains 4 / SHANACHIE**   1973
The record that broke the group with college audiences in the mid 70s — this is elegant, wistful, and ethereal in equal measures. –BE

Bonaparte's Retreat / SHANACHIE   1976
The group's attempt to merge their traditional sound with a progressive form, and only partly successful — overdone and overambitious, but still worth hearing. –BE

The Chieftains Live! / SHANACHIE   1977
An older lineup performs a rousing live set. –sw

The Chieftains 7 / COLUMBIA   1978
A boisterous and exuberant traditional album. –sw

Ballad of the Irish Horse / SHANACHIE   1985
Quite a concept album — songs devoted to the Irish horse and its importance and role in legend and history. –BE

★ **The Chieftains 10: Cotton-Eyed Joe / SHANACHIE**   1988
More great traditional sounds. –sw

Irish Heartbeat / MERCURY   1988
Van Morrison sings traditional Irish songs with the Chieftains. –sw

Reel Music: The Film Scores / RCA   1991
The collected film tracks by the group, which constitute their most famous work to the public at large. A generous collection. –BE

○ **The Bells of Dublin / BMG**   1991
Guests include Elvis Costello, Nanci Griffith, and Marianne Faithfull. A Celtic Christmas album. –sw

An Irish Evening / BMG   1992
Guests are Nanci Griffith and Roger Daltrey. –sw

THE CLANCY BROTHERS

Irish. This singing family from Carrick-on-Suir, County Tipperary, are the most famous Irish folksingers in the world. They usually have a lead singer from outside the family. (They have sung with Tommy Makem, who comes from a singing family in Keady, County Armagh.) –sw

○ **Live! / VANGUARD**   1982
With nephew Robbie O'Connell, from Waterford City. Another indication of their skill at handling the audience. –sw

By the Rising of the Moon / TRADITION
Their first album, recorded in Kenneth S. Goldstein's kitchen with Tommy Makem. Free from some of the hokeyness of later efforts. –sw

The Clancy Brothers Greatest Hits / VANGUARD
A set with Lou Killen, a famous singer of Northumberland folksongs and sea shanties. Killen and the Clancys make an interesting combination, and a record worth getting. More Scottish material than is common for the Clancys. –sw

CLANNAD

Irish. Made up of three siblings and their twin uncles, this family band went on to great fame as a pop group. Their pre-pop days, however, produced albums far more exciting to Celtic music fans, with Celtic harp, flutes, and other instruments backing up lovely Gaelic singing. –sw

● **Clannad 2 / SHANACHIE**   1974
Crisp and subtle arrangements. –sw

Dulaman / SHANACHIE   1976
Heavier, more driving arrangements, and a jazzier sound. –sw

Clannad in Concert / SHANACHIE   1978
Live set featuring long jazz solos during some songs. –sw

○ **Past Present / RCA**   1988
A hits package with a good sampling of tracks from their later albums, *Macalla* and *Sirius*. –swb

JACK AND CHARLIE COEN

Irish. These two musicians, formerly of Woodford, County Galway, emigrated to New York in the 50s. Both have played whistle and flute, though Jack now concentrates on flute and Charlie on concertina. Charlie Coen, also a fine singer, is known in Irish music circles simply as "Father Charlie," since his day job is serving the Church as a priest. –sw

○ **The Branch Line / GREEN LINNET**   1977
A 1992 re-release of a classic 1977 Topic album. Reels, jigs, hornpipes, flings, and polkas, by each musician solo and by the pair of them. Real traditional Irish music at its best. –sw

SHIRLEY COLLINS

English. One of the most important singers and collectors of the early revival, Collins was a source from whom groups like Pentangle got many of their songs. Her sweet, sweet voice and Sussex accent made her quite popular for a time, but she gave up recording years ago. –sw

○ **Folk Roots, New Routes / DECCA**   1964
Collins with Davy Graham, a fantastic guitarist. –sw

The Sweet Primeroses / TOPIC   1967
Her sister, Dolly Collins, adds portative pipe organ to Shirley's voice and banjo. –sw

No Roses / PEGASUS   1971
Features a truly impressive folk/rock backing band, later to become the Albion Band. –sw

COPPER FAMILY

English. Farmers, shepherds, carters, and innkeepers, the Coppers have sung for at least 200 years in the same Sussex village, in a style reflecting the tradition of pub bard on Saturday, church choir on Sunday. –JSR

○ **Coppersongs / EFDSS**
Four generations of this most important of English singing families continue, delightfully, an unusually pure example of living tradition. –JSR

THE CRITIC'S GROUP

English/Scottish. This discussion group led by Ewan MacColl eventually began recording albums as singers. They included some later-well-known people like Frankie Armstrong and John Faulkner. All are well worth hearing. –sw

The Female Frolic / ARGO   1968
Songs addressing women's issues. –sw

○ **Waterloo-Peterloo / ARGO**   1968
Songs of laborers and soldiers. –sw

As We Were a-Sailin' / ARGO   1970
Sea songs, featuring MacColl himself. –sw

TONY CUFFE

Scottish. Tony's voice, whistle, and guitar are as wonderfully expressive alone as they were when he sang with Ossian. –sw

○ **When First I Went to Caledonia / IONA**   1988
Beautiful selections, beautifully done. –sw

JOHN AND PHIL CUNNINGHAM

Scottish. John, an outstanding Scottish fiddler, was a founding member of Silly Wizard. Phil, an equally impressive accordionist, joined after the group lost its original accordion player. Though known best for their work with the Wizard, John and Phil have a few other records available. –sw

● **Against the Storm / SHANACHIE**   1980
Scottish pipe tunes, Irish reels, and haunting slow airs fill this lovely album. –sw

Thoughts from Another World / SHANACHIE   1981
John's first solo album, and an impressive debut, including Celtic and American tunes. –sw

○ **Fair Warning / GREEN LINNET**   1983
Great fun from John Cunningham. Quicksteps and reels rub shoulders with slower, more haunting pieces. –sw

○ **Airs & Graces / GREEN LINNET**   1984
A Phil Cunningham solo outing. Not only accordion, but great whistle playing and moody synthesizer sounds make this an outstanding recording. –sw

The Palomino Waltz / GREEN LINNET   1989
Another Phil Cunningham solo album, and a nice followup to his other work. –sw

DE DANANN

Irish. One of the wave of Irish folk ensembles to follow in the wake of the Chieftains' rise to international fame, this variably-sized band (whose members, especially the support singer, have come and gone with dizzying regularity) has built

up a name for itself with a sound that compromises between the pipe-dominated instrumental sound of the Chieftains and the more vocal-dominated sound of Planxty. They aren't afraid to go into all manner of variations on Irish history, including the American branch.
This group produces vibrant modern arrangements of music in the style of Galway and Kerry, two of Ireland's most musically rich counties. –BE & SW

De Danann / BOOT   1975
Their debut, featuring singer Dolores Keane. –sw

The Star-Spangled Molly / SHANACHIE   1978
A rousing and boisterous — and utterly unique — tribute to the Irish-American repertory, all treated with lots of passion and great vigor. –BE

○ **The Mist Covered Mountain / SHANACHIE**   1980
One of their strongest albums instrumentally. –sw

★ **Best of De Danann / SHANACHIE**   1991
Probably as good a way as any to start off, with the most popular cuts from the group's albums. –BE

1/2 Set in Harlem / GREEN LINNET   1991
They blend their traditional music with gospel, klezmer, and other styles. –sw

○ **Song for Ireland / SUGAR HILL**
Mary Black contributes the stunning vocals that have made her famous, and the instrumentals have even more energy than usual. –sw

MICKEY DOHERTY

Irish. For some perspective on all the revivalist "Celtic" music around, here is an undisputed grand master of Irish tradition. Mickey Doherty was one of the great names of Donegal fiddling and storytelling. –JSR

○ **Gravel Walks / IRISH FOLKLORE COMMISSION**   1949
These superb recordings, his first, were made pretty much by happenstance during a 1949 field trip. –JSR

JOHNNY DORAN

Irish. An undisputed grand master of Irish tradition. Doran, a traveler from Clare, was heir to a major family tradition of pipers and a true original (he was a major influence on Willy Clancy, among others). –JSR

○ **The Bunch of Keys / IRISH FOLKLORE COMMISSION**
This tape includes the handful of recordings he made for the Irish Folklore Commission in the mid 40s. –JSR

SEAMUS EGAN

Irish. A young virtuoso from Philadelphia, Egan has won the all-Ireland championship on four different instruments. –sw

○ **A Week in January / SHANACHIE**   1990
Seamus Egan's fine flute and banjo playing make for an exciting album. –sw

Traditional Music of Ireland / SHANACHIE
Seamus and his sisters, Siobhan and Rory Ann, rip through some fine tunes. –sw

SEAMUS ENNIS

Irish. A folklorist, singer, storyteller, and performer on Uillean pipes and tin whistle, Ennis was one of the pioneering figures in Irish folklore. His fluency in English and every dialect of Irish and Scottish Gaelic made him an excellent cultural ambassador, telling translated Gaelic tales and playing venerable tunes to English audiences with a flair that revealed the genius hidden in their music. –sw

○ **Feidlim Tonn Ri's Castle / CLADDAGH**   1977
On *Feidlim Tonn Ri's Castle, or the King of Ireland's Son*, Ennis tells a long Gaelic heroic folktale in English, with music on his pipes and whistle. Literally wonderful. –sw

Forty Years of Irish Piping / GREEN LINNET   1977
A musical biography of Ennis, plotting the development of his playing. Compiled by Pat Sky. –sw

The Wandering Minstrel / TOPIC 1977
Solo piping by Ennis. –sw

FIGGY DUFF

Canadian. In Newfoundland, the proximity of traditional performance to American rock & roll produced naturally what Fairport and Steeleye produced consciously in England: a hybrid of traditional English and Celtic music with rock. Figgy Duff is the most important exponent of this Newfoundland music, featuring the haunting voice of Pamela Morgan combined with a strident rock & roll approach. –sw

○ **Figgy Duff / HAGDOWN** 1980
Their debut, and their folkiest outing. –sw

After the Tempest / CELTIC MUSIC 1988
Their second album, featuring a lot of great music, traditional and new. –sw

Weather out the Storm / HYPNOTIC
Powerful pop music with Celtic roots. –sw

ARCHIE FISHER

Scottish. See the biography for the Fisher Family. –ED
Archie Fisher / CELTIC MUSIC 1968
Released in 1968, this first album shows off Fisher's gentle voice and guitar accompaniments. –sw

○ **The Man with a Rhyme / FOLK-LEGACY** 1976
More gentle singing and guitar. His best. –sw

Off the Map / SNOW GOOSE 1986
Archie Fisher's singing and guitar wedded to Garnet Rogers's fiddle and flute. –sw

CILLA FISHER

Scottish. See the biography for the Fisher Family. –ED
For Foul Day and Fair / FOLK-LEGACY 1978
The album is the first and only US release for Cilla Fisher and Artie Tresize. –sw

○ **Cilla and Artie / TOPIC** 1979
Riveting arrangements of excellent traditional and contemporary songs, with Artie Tresize. –sw

THE FISHER FAMILY

Scottish. Children of a Gaelic speaker and occasional singer from the isle of Barra and a Glasgow police inspector who sang choral music, opera, and music-hall songs, the Fishers have become respected traditional and contemporary folksingers. Archie Fisher sings the old songs, as well as writing his own, Ray sings the old ballads in a magnificent voice, and Cilla, with her husband Artie Tresize, performs both traditional and contemporary music as well as a large repertoire of children's music. The siblings occasionally unite for tours or special appearances, but most of their recorded material is separate. –sw

○ **The Fisher Family / TOPIC** 1965
In 1965, when this was recorded, Cilla was barely a teenager. Still, she makes valuable contributions along with Archie, Ray, and her other sisters Joyce, Audrey, and Cindy. The guitar accompaniments by Archie are little more than simple strumming, but the singing is all wonderful. This is a real collector's item. –sw

RAY FISHER

Scottish. See the biography for the Fisher Family. –ED
Bonny Birdy / TRAILER 1972
Superbly passionate renderings of ballads, backed by an all-star cast of folk revival musicians including members of Steeleye Span and the High Level Ranters. –sw

Willie's Lady / FOLK-LEGACY 1982
This one's more sparsely arranged than *Bonnie Birdy*, but no less gorgeous. –sw

★ **Traditional Songs of Scotland / SAYDISC** 1991

This proves that a voice can get even better over time. A brilliant 18-track achievement. –sw

FIVE HAND REEL

Scottish. A great 70s folk/rock group from Scotland, featuring Dick Gaughan. –sw
Five Hand Reel / BLACK CROW 1976
Magnificent electrified traditional songs. –sw

○ **For A' That / BLACK CROW** 1977
Five Hand Reel's best recording, featuring a rare occurrence: Gaughan singing in Gaelic. –sw

Earl o' Moray / RCA 1978
Their third album, recorded in 1978. A fine effort, though not as good as the first two. –sw

GEORGE FORMBY

English. Formby was one of the greatest stars of that most English urban genre, the music hall. He was famous for his banjolele, but also for comic songs like "When I'm Cleaning Windows" ("For a nosy parker it's an interesting job"), "The Lancashire Hot Pot Swingers" (Not that — we're talking the 1930s here!), "Grand-dad's Flannelette Nightshirt," and the charming "Leaning on a Lamp-Post," which was featured in the recent revival of "Me and My Girl," though it wasn't part of the original show. –JSR

○ **When I'm Cleaning Windows / ASV**

DICK GAUGHAN

Scottish. Gaughan is one of the finest singers and guitarists on the Scottish scene, and has put his talents to both traditional music and contemporary political material. –sw
No More Forever / LEADER 1972
His first album, all traditional and wonderful. –sw

Coppers and Brass / GREEN LINNET 1977
Originally released in 1977, this is a brilliant all-instrumental set of guitar tunes. –sw

★ **A Handful of Earth / GREEN LINNET** 1981
Another fine album. "Song for Ireland" is a classic. Features Brian McNeill, Phil Cunningham, and Stewart Isbister. Voted Album of the Decade of the 80s by *Folk Roots* magazine, *A Handful of Earth* is Gaughan's best blend of traditional and contemporary songs. –CR & SW

○ **Gaughan / TOPIC** 1992
This CD re-release features all of the excellent 1978 album *Gaughan*, plus four sets from *Coppers and Brass* and two from his guest spots on the High Level Ranters album *Bonnie Pit Laddie*. –sw

A Different Kind of Love Song / FOLK FREAK
The sound of this import CD is stellar. There is a chilling song, "Prisoner 562," a song to make you "think again." I can't fault a thing on this one. Buy it. –CR

THE GREEN FIELDS OF AMERICA

Irish. Mostly a touring ensemble, Green Fields has included many of the very finest musicians on the Irish-American scene. –sw

○ **Live in Concert / GREEN LINNET** 1989
A fine showcase of a lot of talent, including Mick Moloney, Seamus Egan, Eileen Ivers, Robbie O'Connell, and Jimmy Keane. –sw

GWERZ

Breton. Erik Marchand's startling voice and Soòg Siberil's guitar work helped Gwerz become one of Brittany's best-known bands, and deservedly so. –sw
Musiques Bretonnes de Toujours / DASTUM 1985
Interesting arrangements, but not as masterful as the second album. –sw

○ **Au Delê / ESCALIBUR** 1987

Their best album. −sw

TIM HART & MADDY PRIOR

English. A young duo from St. Albans who founded Steeleye Span with Ashley Hutchings and Gay and Terry Woods. Most of their influence on the music scene has been with that band, but their solo albums are also classics. −sw

Folk Songs of Olde England / ADRHYTHM   1968
Simple accompaniments with guitar, banjo, and dulcimer grace two volumes of top-flight renditions of traditional songs. −sw

○ **Summer Solstice / SHANACHIE**   1971
An album that features fuller, more mature arrangements. −sw

FRANK HARTE

Irish. A source of traditional songs among folk-revival singers, Harte has collected thousands of songs and has published a book and several albums of Dublin street songs. −sw

Dublin Street Songs / TOPIC   1967
Includes classic ballads as well as humorous pieces. With Alf Edwards on concertina. −sw

○ **And Listen to My Song / RAM**
Broadside ballads of old Dublin, with Donal Lunny on bouzouki and Bertram Levy on concertina. −sw

Through Dublin City / TOPIC
Just Harte, unaccompanied. −sw

JOE HEANEY

Irish. A magnificent singer in both Gaelic and English, Heaney sings in *sean-nos*, the highly ornamented style of traditional Irish song. −sw

○ **Joe and the Gabe / GREEN LINNET**   1979
Heaney's remarkable voice is joined by the flute, whistle, and fiddle playing of Gabe O'Sullivan, for a fine cross-section of Galway music and song. −sw

O Mo Dhuchas / GAEL-LINN
All unaccompanied, all Gaelic. For really hardcore fans. −sw

THE HIGH LEVEL RANTERS

English. A Northumbrian group, formed in the late 60s and featuring Alistair Anderson, Tom Gilfellon, Johnny Handle, and Colin Ross. The High Level Ranters were very regionally oriented, with lovely songs in broad Geordie dialect and tunes identified with the region. −sw

High Level / TRAILER   1971
They first perfected their arrangements on this album. −sw

○ **A Mile to Ride / TRAILER**   1973
Beautiful singing from Handle and Gilfellon, subtle but rousing work on the tunes. Highly recommended. −sw

● **Bonny Pit Laddie / TOPIC**   1975
A double album of songs about the lives of coal miners. Very well done, with guest appearances by Dick Gaughan and Harry Boardman. −sw

HORSLIPS

Irish. The first group in Ireland to mix electric rock with traditional music. Their early albums are the most interesting for Celtic music fans. −sw

○ **Happy to Meet, Sorry to Part / ATCO**   1972
Raw and raunchy folk/rock with fiddle, banjo, and flute along with electric guitars, bass, and drums. Traditional songs and Tull-like rockers. −sw

● **The Tain / ATCO**   1974
A concept album relating the story of Tain Bo Cuailgne, Ireland's great medieval epic. −sw

PAUL HUELLOU

Breton. Paul Huellou is well known in his native Brittany where he has become one of the foremost singers of the Breton music tradition. −MUSIC OF THE WORLD

Musical Instruments of England and the Celtic Countries

Bagpipes — Bagpipes are found all over the world. In its simplest form, a bagpipe consists of an air reservoir (or bag), a chanter (a pipe fitted with a double reed), and a means of inflating the bag. It may also be fitted with one or more drones (pipes that sound a single continuous note). Scottish Highland pipes, called "warpipes" in Ireland, have a mouth pipe to inflate the bag, three drones, and a nine-note fingered chanter. In the lowlands of Scotland and the north of England, mellow-toned, bellows-blown smallpipes are the norm. In Ireland, the Uillean pipe, the world's most complex bagpipe, reigns supreme. It consists of bellows, a bag, a two-octave chanter, three drones, and three regulators (keyed drones controlled by the player's wrist) that can play short rhythmic bursts of any of a number of chords as accompaniment to the chanter.

Free Reeds — Named after their metal reeds, which are free to vibrate on three sides, these instruments include the harmonica and various squeezeboxes. The harmonica (or "moothie" in Scotland) is popular all over Britain and Ireland, owing to its affordability and small size. The melodeon (or diatonic accordion) is a squeezebox with one, two, or three rows of buttons tuned to different diatonic scales. The accordion can be the familiar piano-keyed instrument or a melodeon whose rows are tuned a half-step apart, creating a chromatic instrument. In general, chromatic-button accordions are the most popular in Ireland, melodeons are the most popular in England, and piano accordions are the most popular in Scotland, but all forms are played in all countries. The concertina is a squeezebox of hexagonal cross-section, whose buttons are spread over both ends.

Woodwinds — The whistle is a metal tube with either a wooden fipple or a plastic mouthpiece, with fingerholes like a recorder. The flute, either wooden or metal, was popular originally in Ireland but is beginning to find popularity elsewhere as well. The bombarde, a high, piercing oboe, is one of the national instruments of Brittany.

Strings — The fiddle, or violin, is popular everywhere in Europe. The harp is a very important instrument, historically speaking, to the Celtic countries; it is still the national symbol of Ireland. Celtic harps are smaller and have fewer strings than the familiar concert harp, and have no pedals. Fretted, plucked, and strummed strings like guitars, banjos, and mandolins have become important to the folk revival, both as accompaniment to singing and as solo instruments. The bouzouki, a Greek instrument imported to Irish music, and the cittern, a revived Renaissance instrument, as well as mandolas and mandocellos, also grace the music frequently.

Percussion — Anything handy may be knocked together as percussion, but the most common are spoons and bones, which can become amazingly precise, rhythmically speaking, in the right person's hands. In Ireland, the bodhran, a goatskin on a wooden frame, is the drum of choice, and this has spread all over the Celtic lands. In Scotland, side drums and snare drums are used, mostly in military music.

— Stephen Winick

Songs from Brittany / MUSIC OF THE WORLD
This recording features Mr. Huellou (vocals), J. Pol Huellou (flutes), Paddy Keenan (pipes), Brendan Fahy (guitar), and Pascal Segart (violin). —MUSIC OF THE WORLD

THE IRISH ROVERS

Irish. This quintet started out in the late 50s (curiously, by the way of Canada) and by the mid 60s were a popular folk ensemble on television on two continents. Although their work, exuberant and boisterous, with relatively little scholarship, and lacking a traditional sound, became less fashionable with the ascent of groups like the Chieftains, the Irish Rovers continue to have a devoted core following. —BE

○ **Irish Rovers' Greatest Hits / MCA**   1981
The record to start with to get to know the Irish Rovers. It isn't representative of their full range of material. —BE

The Unicorn / MCA / BB# 24
The single most popular record that the Irish Rovers ever made, their cover of Shel Silverstein's slyly written "The Unicorn" stands apart from the more straightforward material on this album, which is devoted to good times, family, and religious differences, and other significant elements of Irish song. —BE

THE IRISH TRADITION

Irish. Baltimore-area trio featuring Billy McComiskey's accordion and Brendan Mulvihill's fiddle, as well as the sweet singing and skillful guitar of Andy O'Brien. —SW

The Corner House / GREEN LINNET   1978
Impressive second album. —SW

○ **The Times We've Had / GREEN LINNET**   1985
A thoughtfully performed album, varied in material but consistent in quality. —SW

ANDY IRVINE

Irish. Irvine has been the lead singer for Planxty and Patrick Street, as well as a solo artist. —SW

○ **Andy Irvine and Paul Brady / GREEN LINNET**   1981
Irvine and Paul Brady (former Planxty members) team up for one of the greatest albums ever of traditional Irish songs. Their unique sound will stay with you long after the music has stopped. —SW & CR

Andy Irvine and Dick Gaughan / GREEN LINNET   1983
On *Andy Irvine and Dick Gaughan: Parallel Lines*, Irvine and Gaughan make a formidable duo, performing both traditional and contemporary material. Nicely balanced. --SW & CR

Rude Awakenings / GREEN LINNET   1992
An album of songs Irvine wrote about his heroes, from Raoul Wallenberg to Woody Guthrie. —SW

NIC JONES

English. Jones, one of the best English singers and guitarists in folk music, had a relatively short career before being paralyzed in an auto accident. His albums are all worth buying. —SW

● **Ballads and Songs / TRAILER**   1970
Debut album that established him as one of the best. —SW

Nic Jones / TRAILER   1971
Beautiful followup to *Ballads and Songs*. —SW

The Noah's Ark Trap / SHANACHIE   1977
A few guests join him to fill out the arrangements. —SW

○ **Penguin Eggs / SHANACHIE**   1980
Even better than *The Noah's Ark Trap*. Many critics consider this his best. —SW

RON KAVANA

Irish. Kavana is a songwriter, singer, and musician who appreciates traditional music as well as rock & roll. A somewhat controversial figure, he is often the topic of discussion among British and Irish folk fans. —SW

○ **Home Fire / SPECIAL DELIVERY**   1991
Mostly original songs, performed on acoustic instruments. Captures the spontaneity sometimes lost in Celtic music recordings. —SW

DOLORES KEANE & JOHN FAULKNER

Irish/English. An English husband and Irish wife in a harmonious (though temporary) partnership. She sings with an angel's voice; he also sings and plays guitar, bouzouki, and fiddle. —SW

○ **Brokenhearted I'll Wander / GREEN LINNET**   1981
Features Reel Union, a band including pipes and fiddle, as backup. A truly gorgeous album, this is Keane and Faulkner's best work. —SW

Farewell to Eireann / GREEN LINNET   1981
Poignant emigration ballads, including the lovely "Galway Bay." —SW

Sail Og Rua / GREEN LINNET   1984
Mostly Gaelic songs, with guests that include Keane's aunt Sarah, a well-known traditional singer. —SW

PAT KILBRIDE

Irish. Virtuoso guitarist, cittern player, and singer, and one of the most dynamic solo performers in Irish music. —SW

○ **Rock and More Roses / TEMPLE (US)**   1989
This extra-length CD and cassette includes the entirety of Kilbride's 1980 *Rock and Roses* album, along with six tracks of instrumental music recorded in 1986 and 1987. Brilliant and a bargain to boot. —SW

JOHN KIRKPATRICK

English. A fine melodeon player, Kirkpatrick has been a member of Steeleye Span. He is a champion of English music and dance and also heads a Morris dance team. —SW

The Rose of Britain's Isle / TOPIC   1974
Lovely material, lovely performances with Sue Harris. Harris, Kirkpatrick's wife, sings and plays the oboe, and also heads a dance team. —SW

Shreds and Patches / TOPIC   1977
Excellent followup with Sue Harris. —SW

○ **Going Spare / FREE REED**   1978
All-original songs and tunes, some of them weird and hilarious. —SW

KORNOG

Breton/Scottish. Brittany's greatest instrumentalists team up with Scottish singer and instrumentalist Jamie McMenamy (previously of the Battlefield Band) for an unbeatable combination. —SW

Kornog / ESCALIBUR   1983
Debut album. Overlaps in material with *Première*, but still worth having. —SW

○ **Première / GREEN LINNET**   1984
Live in Michigan. The ambiance of a live album, plus some great Scottish ballads, make this Kornog's best album. —SW

Ar Seizh Avel / GREEN LINNET   1985
This is a pretty album of traditional and original tunes and songs. —SW

LA BOTTINE SOURIANTE

Canadian. Quebec's traditional music is a blend of French and Irish styles. This is Quebec's top folk ensemble, incorporating fiddle, accordion, guitar, and more. —SW

Les Epousailles / GAMMA   1981
Their second album, with a lot of good material. —SW

SAM LARNER   1878-1965

English. The fens, farms, and fishing ports of East Anglia were among the richest lodes of southern English traditional songs, and Larner one of the finest East Anglian source singers. He was a fisherman from the age of 12, but his repertoire went far beyond sea songs or the standard broadside ballad fare. –JSR

○ **A Garland for Sam / TOPIC**
Splendid notes amplify splendid music. –JSR

EWAN MACCOLL   1915-1989

Scottish. Ewan MacColl may well have been the most influential person in the current British folksong revival. From his early manhood until his death in 1989, he remained passionately committed to folksong, though not exclusively; he was also a poet, playwright, organizer, activist, songwriter, husband, and father. MacColl was born in Scotland in 1915. His father was a lowland man who spoke Scots English, his mother a highlander who spoke Gaelic. Both of his parents were singers. MacColl left school at fourteen to busk and act in the streets and was quickly discovered by the BBC. Soon he was not only singing, but also writing programs for the radio. He founded the first folk club in England, the Ballads and Blues Club, as well as the Critic's Group, an influential early singing group that included such singers as Frankie Armstrong, Anne Briggs, and John Faulkner. He himself was one of the foremost interpreters of traditional songs ever recorded. The most ambitious project he undertook was to record a representative sampling of Professor Francis James Child's English and Scottish popular ballads.

While his early repertoire was mainly of street songs and traditional material, he has always also been an important songwriter. Most impressive was his competence in producing expressions that had appeal for all levels of society; his songs have been covered by performers as diverse as Dick Gaughan, the Pogues, Roberta Flack, and Elvis Presley, and many have been collected in several versions from the oral tradition. They range from savage political satire to tender love songs and are supremely effective at producing the desired emotions. Beyond his activities as a singer and songwriter, MacColl was an actor and a playwright. In 1947, George Bernard Shaw commented, "Apart from myself, MacColl is the only man of genius writing for the theatre in England today." His playwrighting and songwriting joined seamlessly in his "radio ballads," radio plays that bordered on ballad operas. Many of his most lovely and best-remembered songs were written for these plays, some of which have been released in album form. MacColl was married to Peggy Seeger, herself a singer of folk songs (and half-sister to American icon Pete Seeger). Together MacColl and Seeger, sometimes accompanied by their children, who are also skilled musicians and singers, have recorded quite a few albums as well. Many of MacColl's albums are out-of-print products of long-defunct record companies. Some, however, are readily available. All, like MacColl himself, are important factors in the history of the folk revival, to be cherished by all who encounter them. This great singer made many, many albums over many years. All of them are recommended for fans of great singing, though some may be a bit specialized (i.e., unaccompanied singing in broad Scots dialect) for some listeners. –SW

○ **English/Scottish Popular Ballads / RIVERSIDE**   1956
English and Scottish Popular Ballads (The Child Ballads), a nine-album set, edited by Kenneth S. Goldstein and performed by MacColl and A. L. Lloyd, is the first systematic attempt to record a representative sampling of the Child canon of ballads in a traditional British singing style. It is important for academic reasons, but more so for those who simply love the English-language ballad. Exquisite performances by MacColl and Lloyd. –SW

The Wanton Muse / ARGO   1968
Bawdy and sexually suggestive songs. –SW

★ **Black and White / GREEN LINNET**   1991
A compilation of twenty important tracks that will lead you to further listening. –SW

The Angry Muse / ARGO
Protest songs. –SW

Scots Street Songs / RIVERSIDE
Urban folksong at its best. –SW

DOUGIE MACLEAN

Scottish. This singer, guitarist, songwriter, and fiddler has been a member of the Tannahill Weavers and Silly Wizard. He now owns his own studio and record label in his hometown of Dunkeld. –SW

Singing Land / DUNKELD   1985
Mostly original songs. –SW

Real Estate / DUNKELD   1988
Same story. His songs revolve around ideas of home, land, and love. –SW

○ **Indigenous / DUNKELD**   1992
His latest and best album. Also mostly originals, with two by Robert Burns. –SW

MALICORNE

French. Although not strictly Celtic, this group was heavily influenced by the Celtic revival. Lead singer/guitarist Gabriel Yacoub got his start in Alan Stivell's famed Breton band. Later the group's music resembled that of British bands. Malicorne creates a synthesis of French folk music and rock & roll, much as Steeleye Span does with English and Celtic music. –SW

Malicorne / HEXAGONE   1974
Their debut. More acoustic and folky than their later works, and just as terrific. –SW

○ **Almanach / HEXAGONE**   1976
Beautifully packaged album consisting of seasonal songs and music from around France. Malicorne's most consistently excellent album. –SW

L'Extraordinaire Tour de France d'Adelard Rousseau / ELEKTRA   1978
Concept album following a Compagn, the French equivalent of a Freemason, through his rite of passage, a tour of France. Dan Ar Bras guests. –SW

BILLY MCCOMISKEY

Irish. Simply the best Irish accordion player in America, and one of the best in the world. –SW

○ **Makin' the Rounds / GREEN LINNET**   1981
Billy is joined by a few friends, including the late great accordionist Sean McGlynn, for a rousing and expertly arranged album of dance music. –SW

SEAMUS AND MANUS MCGUIRE

Irish. The McGuire brothers are two of Ireland's great fiddle players who rarely tour internationally. They can be heard on several grand recordings, though, including those by Buttons and Bows. Daithi Sproule is a distinguished Gaelic singer and guitarist now living in the US. He, too, has played with several great bands, including Skara Brae and Altan. –SW

○ **Carousel (with Daithi Sproule) / GAEL-LINN**   1984
They breeze through reels, waltzes, and jigs, and Sproule sings three lovely songs in Gaelic. –SW

MATT MOLLOY

Irish. This supremely talented flute player has been a member of some of the most influential Irish groups: Planxty, the Bothy Band, and the Chieftains. –SW

Matt Molloy with Donal Lunny / GREEN LINNET   1984
Molloy plays reels and airs like no one else can. –SW

○ **W/ Tommy Peoples & Paul Brady / GR. LINNET**   1985
A 1985 release of 1977 studio sessions, with fiddler Peoples and guitarist and singer Brady joining Molloy for unbelievably fiery trio playing. –SW

Stony Steps / GREEN LINNET   1987
Molloy again demonstrates his amazing virtuosity. –SW

MICK MOLONEY

Irish. Moloney is one of the most active members of the Irish-American musical community. In the 60s he played with the Johnstons, one of the most important early revival bands. A singer, instrumentalist, and folklorist, Moloney hails from Limerick but now lives in Philadelphia, where he recently earned his Ph.D. in folklore with a brilliant dissertation on Irish music in America. –sw

We Have Met Together / TRANSATLANTIC   1973
Interesting first solo album, including traditional and modern songs and tunes. –sw

● **With Eugene O'Donnell / GREEN LINNET**   1978
A beautiful album, with lovely songs and tune arrangements. Derry-born O'Donnell is king of slow airs and set dances on the fiddle. –sw

○ **Strings Attached / GREEN LINNET**   1980
Mick's only all-instrumental recording, featuring his mastery of tenor banjo and mandolin as well as guitar and bouzouki accompaniments. –sw

Uncommon Bonds / GREEN LINNET   1984
Classic Irish and Irish-American material with Eugene O'Donnell. –sw

MOLONEY, O'CONNELL & KEANE

Irish. Dr. Mick Moloney occasionally joins forces with Robbie O'Connell and accordion player Jimmy Keane to tour and record. –sw

There Were Roses / GREEN LINNET   1986
Also a brilliant title track. Fiddler Liz Carroll guests. –sw

○ **Kilkelly / GREEN LINNET**   1988
The title track is an absolute classic. –sw

CHRISTY MOORE

Irish. Founder of Planxty and Moving Hearts, Moore has also had an important solo career and has played both traditional music and folk-tinged pop music. –sw

Live in Dublin / TARA   1964
Christy at his best on this better-than-average live album. –cr

Prosperous / TARA   1972
Guests include Andy Irvine, Liam O'Flynn, Donal Lunny, and Kevin Conneff. A collector's item, mainly because it was the album that spawned Planxty. –sw

The Iron Behind the Velvet / TARA   1978
His band on this one includes Moore's brother Barry, aka Luka Bloom. –sw

The Time Has Come / WEA IRELAND   1983
Great solo effort featuring traditional and political songs. –sw

Nice 'n Easy / POLYGRAM   1984
This import contains "Sacco & Vanzetti," "Nancy Spain," and "Lanigan's Ball." –cr

● **Ride On / GREEN LINNET**   1984
A powerful CD featuring "Ride On," "City of Chicago," "Lisdoonvarna," and "Among the Wicklow Hills." This one is so good it can make his other good ones seem weak. –cr

Ordinary Man / GREEN LINNET   1985
A notch below *Ride On.* Featuring "Delirium Tremens," "Reel in the Flickering Light," and "Quiet Desperation." –cr

Unfinished Revolution / WARNER   1987
Very good. Contains "Biko Drum," "A Pair of Brown Eyes," and the title track. Produced by Donal Lunny. –cr

Voyage / ATLANTIC   1989
Produced by Donal Lunny. Not as strong as his others. –cr

The Christy Moore Folk Collection / TARA
A hard-to-find collection of Moore's early works. Buy it if you see it. –cr

● **Christy Moore / POLYDOR**
Terrific album of traditional songs and ballads. –sw

NA FILI

Irish. This important trio set an early high standard for group playing on pipes, fiddle, and whistle. –sw

○ **An Ghaoth Aniar: The West Wind / MERCIER**   1969
Playing is augmented by explanations of the tunes and songs right on the record. –sw

Farewell to Connacht / OUTLET   1971
Another fine Na Fili album. –sw

Na Fili 3 / OUTLET   1972
Features several religious songs sung in Gaelic. –sw

MAIRE NI CHATHASAIGH

Irish. Considered one of Ireland's finest clarsach (harp) players, Ni Chathasaigh is also a fine singer in Gaelic and English. –sw

○ **The New-Strung Harp / TEMPLE**   1985
Ni Chathasaigh shows off all her talents, particularly that of arranging dance tunes on the harp. –sw

Out of Court / OLD BRIDGE MUSIC   1991
With Ni Chathasaigh's husband, Chris Newman, an eclectic talent on the guitar. Together, they make lovely and lively instrumental music. –sw

MAIREAD NI DHOMHNAILL

Irish. As the sister of Triona, and a member of Skara Brae, Mairead Ni Dhomhnaill is also a wonderful bilingual singer. –sw

○ **Mairead Ni Dhomhnaill / GAEL-LINN**   1976
As fine as her sister's solo album. –sw

TRIONA NI DHOMHNAILL

Irish. A member of Skara Brae and the Bothy Band, Ni Dhomhnaill always seems to be part of an interesting musical outing. Her clear singing voice and harpsichord playing are an asset to any lineup. –sw

○ **Triona / GREEN LINNET**   1975
Solo album that features some of her loveliest recorded songs, some in English and some in Gaelic, with accompaniment by some of Ireland's greatest players. –sw

ROBBIE O'CONNELL

Irish. This nephew of the world-famous Clancy Brothers is also a fine folksinger and a respected songwriter. –sw

○ **Close to the Bone / GREEN LINNET**   1982
O'Connell's gentle voice and guitar perform traditional songs. Quite a treat. –sw

Love of the Land / GREEN LINNET   1989
Mostly original songs that prove he's a fine songwriter. –sw

OSSIAN

Scottish. Formed in the mid 70s, Ossian became famous for lush arrangements including harp, bagpipes, flute, guitar, fiddle, cello, cittern, whistles, and synthesizers, not to mention excellent singing. –sw

St. Kilda Wedding / IONA   1978
Features Billy Ross singing in English and Gaelic. –sw

Seal's Song / IONA   1981
Another lovely, lovely album. Singer Tony Cuffe shines. –sw

○ **Borders / IONA**   1984
A masterpiece; every tune and song is gorgeous. –sw

PATRICK STREET

Irish. Veterans of a lot of old, great bands like Planxty, the Bothy Band, and De Danann got together in the mid 80s to form Patrick Street. The most consistent members are Kevin Burke, Jackie Daly, Andy Irvine, and Arty McGlynn. –sw

Patrick Street / GREEN LINNET   1986
Much lighter, airier, and less intense than a lot of Irish music.
It's a style that fits the artists well. –sw

No. 2 Patrick Street / GREEN LINNET   1988
Another thoroughly enjoyable album. –sw

○ **Irish Times / GREEN LINNET**   1990
The addition of pipes and another fiddle makes for a fuller
sound. Their best work. –sw

PLANXTY

Irish. Irish Andy Irvine, Liam O'Flynn, Donal Lunny, and
Christy Moore were pioneers of the Irish folk revival. Their
Planxty albums stand as some of the finest available. –sw

★ **Planxty / SHANACHIE**   1973
Stunning 1973 debut featuring arrangements of traditional
songs and tunes with both punch and subtlety. –sw

○ **Cold Blow and the Rainy Night / SHANACHIE**   1974
Lunny is replaced by Johnny Moynihan of Sweeny's Men and
De Danann fame. –sw

The Well Below the Valley / SHANACHIE   1974
Not quite as compelling, perhaps, as the debut album, but still
a treasure. –sw

Collection / SHANACHIE   1976
Just a notch below *Well Below the Valley*. Well produced. –cr

After the Break / TARA   1979
Brilliant tunes and songs featuring Matt Molloy. –sw

The Woman I Loved So Well / TARA   1980
Some of the fire is gone from their arrangements, but a few of
the songs are their best ever. –sw

After the Break / TARA   1982
Has a real fun feel to it. –cr

JEAN REDPATH   b 1937

Scottish. Known throughout the US for her many appearances
on "A Prairie Home Companion," Redpath is one of Scotland's
best-loved singers of folksongs. Her older albums are more
pleasing to fans of traditional music than her later ones, on
which she has developed a nearly operatic vibrato. –sw

○ **First Flight / ROUNDER**   1989
Compilation of material from her first few albums. –sw

The Jean Redpath Scottish Ballad Book / ELEKTRA
Scottish ballads, beautifully done. –sw

Laddie Lie Near Me / ELEKTRA
More of the same. –sw

The Songs of Robert Burns / PHILO
Ambitious multi-volume set aims at recording all of Burns's
songs, with authentic accompaniment. –sw

BOB ROBERTS

English. The accordion was an important British folk and
popular instrument from the mid 19th century on, and also
very much a sailors' instrument. Roberts, who worked on
sailing cargo wherries much of his life, was a fine melodeon
player and a singer with a very wide repertory: a hilarious epic
about a North Sea oil rig; "The Grey Hawk," of Renaissance
origin; "The Foggy Dew" in an eastern English version;
shanties and more. –jsr

○ **Songs from the Sailing Barges / TOPIC**

TOMMY SANDS

Irish.

○ **Beyond the Shadows / SPRING**   1992
Tommy's "We Will Rise Again" and "1999" are songs of hope.
"Red Wine" and "Make Me Want to Stay" are finely written
love songs. "When the Boys Come Rolling Home" is an
infectious, good-time song. This CD is my pick for Top Ten of
1992. Keep up the good work, Tommy! –cr

★ **Singing of the Times / GREEN LINNET**
Jam-packed with great songs and emotions, "There Were

Roses" is a classic, dealing with the senseless killing in
Northern Ireland. "I'm Going Back on the Bicycle" and "Don't
Wake Me Early in the Morning" are fun songs. "Humpty
Dumpty Was Pushed" questions us, and "Your Daughters &
Your Sons" has been used as an anthem throughout the world.
Highly, highly recommended! –cr

Down Bendy's Lane / GREEN LINNET
A delightful children's album featuring songs and stories he
picked up since childhood. "The Boy with No Story" will have
you on the edge of your seat. "Moya Is My Darling," about his
daughter, is priceless. Even an adult can enjoy this one. –cr

SCARTAGLEN

Irish. Scartaglen is a four-piece Kansas City band that plays
traditional Irish music. The members of the band include
Connie Dover (vocals, keyboards), Michael Dugger (vocals,
fiddle, guitar, banjo), Roger Landes (bouzouki, mandolin,
guitar, bodhran), Kirk Lynch (Uillean pipes, tinwhistle, guitar,
bouzouki), and Rebecca Pringle (fiddle). –cr

The Middle Path / CASTLE ISLAND   1986
A very good album featuring great vocals — a totally
satisfying sound. –cr

○ **Last Night's Fun / CITY SPARK**   1992
Their finest release to date. Everything about their music has
matured to the point that I feel Scartaglen is one of the finest
Celtic bands on the scene to date. Highly, highly
recommended. –cr

SILEAS

Scottish. Fabulous harp players and singers, Patsy Seddon and
Mary McMaster are one of the few harp duos playing. Seddon
plays gut-strung harp and McMaster plays wire-strung and
electric instruments, creating a good deal of tonal variety.
Their playing and singing complement each other for a
beautiful act. –sw

○ **Delighted with Harps / GREEN LINNET**   1987
A pretty collection of traditional melodies and songs. –sw

Beating Harps / GREEN LINNET   1987
More fine tracks. One original composition by Seddon. –sw

SILLY SISTERS

English. Steeleye Span's Maddy Prior and folk diva June Tabor
teamed up in 1976 for the first Silly Sisters album. It was more
than a decade before they followed it up with a second, but
both recordings feature a gorgeous melding of Prior's clear,
brassy soprano with Tabor's darker tones. –mpd

★ **Silly Sisters / SHANACHIE**   1976
Maddy Prior and the then little-known June Tabor team to
keen a delightful lark of an album. An enduring minor piece
with many, many of the English folk revival's best players.
Whimsical and spirited. –mh

○ **No More to the Dance / SHANACHIE**
A long-awaited second collaboration between June Tabor and
Steeleye Span's Maddy Prior. –mpd

SILLY WIZARD

Scottish. Generally considered the world's finest performers of
traditional and contemporary Scottish music — and with
good reason. Silly Wizard's music is at once driving and
sensitive, powerful and poignant, at times hypnotic, often
humorous, with sensitive group interplay and virtuoso-level
musicianship, particularly from brothers Phil (accordion,
keyboards, whistles, guitar, vocals) and Johnny (fiddle)
Cunningham. Their repertoire includes centuries-old
instrumental dance music along with traditional and
contemporary narrative ballads: tales of joy and woe, of men
and women, of time and travel, of love and loss. Silly Wizard is
not just another folk music group; they rank with the greatest
creators and performers from any country from any time.
Several members of the group, particularly the Cunningham
brothers and vocalist Andy Stewart, have made solo and duo

recordings and have performed and recorded with other artists, primarily Scottish traditionalists. These recordings are also well worth investigating, but get the Silly Wizard stuff first. −NJF

Caledonia's Hardy Sons / SHANACHIE   1978
A wonderful early album; Stewart's voice is sweeter and more innocent than on later works. −SW

So Many Partings / SHANACHIE   1980
Another great early set. −SW

Best of Silly Wizard / SHANACHIE   1985
Really only the best of their Shanachie releases; still, it's a great compilation. −SW

★ **Live Wizardry / GREEN LINNET**
This two-for-one bargain captures the group live in 1988, at the culmination of their career. A brilliant set. −SW

SKARA BRAE

Irish. A vocal quartet featuring Michael O Dhomhnaill and his sisters Triona and Mairead Ni Dhomhnaill of Rann na Feirste in Donegal and Daithi Sproule from Derry city. −SW

○ **Skara Brae / SHANACHIE**
Michael and Triona went on to form the Bothy Band, and Daithi became a fine solo artist and a member of groups like Altan, but this was their first recorded effort, made in the early 70s, of beautifully performed Gaelic songs. The four vocalists are skillfully backed by guitar from Micheal and Daithi and harpsichord from Triona. −SW

J. SCOTT SKINNER

Scottish. James Scott Skinner, born in 1843, was already playing by 1855. Skinner was no folk artist, but a virtuoso of a drawing-room style that drew from both the folk and classical traditions. −JSR

○ **The Strathspey King / TOPIC**
These extraordinary recordings link us with a style first formed about 150 years ago, and a musical idiom not just dead but unjustly forgotten. −JSR

SKYLARK

Irish. An excellent group featuring Len Graham of Antrim, one of Ireland's great singers, along with Gerry O'Connor's fiddle and Garry O'Briain's mandocello and guitar. −SW

Skylark / SHANACHIE / BB# 12   1979
Skylark's first album, featuring Andrew McNamara's accordion. This is dance music, along with singing in Graham's rich voice. −SW

○ **All of It / GREEN LINNET**   1979
Several guests add fullness to the arrangements; otherwise, it's more of the same good thing. −SW

ANDY M. STEWART

Scottish. The lead singer of Silly Wizard, Stewart has also had an impressive career on his own and with Manus Lunny, who backs his vocals with expert playing of bouzouki and guitar. −SW

● **Dublin Lady / GREEN LINNET**   1987
A masterpiece, and a must for Celtic music fans. With Manus Lunny. −SW

At It Again / GREEN LINNET   1990
With Manus Lunny. Not as fantastic as *Dublin Lady*, but still a fine record. −SW

○ **By the Hush / GREEN LINNET**
Excellent solo album, winner of *Melody Maker*'s Folk Album of the Year award in 1983. −SW

ALAN STIVELL

Breton. Probably the best-known artist from Brittany, and the most influential. He began by performing traditional Celtic music on the Breton harp, an instrument his father

reinvented. Later, he delved into folk/rock music with a band that included Brittany's best musicians and original compositions, playing bagpipes and singing as well as playing the harp. −SW

From Celtic Roots / FONTANA   1973
Features Irish, Scottish, and Welsh music as well as Breton, with an electric folk/rock band. −SW

○ **E Langonned / FONTANA**   1974
Stivell's finest acoustic band performing traditional and original material. −SW

DAVE SWARBRICK

English/Celtic. This fiddler is best known for his partnership with Martin Carthy and his participation in groups like the Ian Campbell Group and Fairport Convention. He also has many excellent solo albums to his credit. −SW

○ **Swarbrick / TRANSATLANTIC**   1976
Swarb's first solo album, featuring old buddies from his Ceilidh band days as well as Martin Carthy and Fairport Convention. A lot of good dance music, plus a few slower tunes. −SW

Swarbrick 2 / TRANSATLANTIC   1977
Really a continuation of *Swarbrick*, with the same personnel and produce, Swarbrick even wears the same shirt for the cover photo! −SW

Lift the Lid and Listen / SONET   1978
Continues the trend started on his first two albums. −SW

SWEENY'S MEN

Irish. An early and important Irish group that influenced both the acoustic and the electric folk revival. It featured Andy Irvine, later of Planxty and Patrick Street, Johnny Moynihan, later of Planxty and De Danann, and Terry Woods, later of Steeleye Span and the Pog. −SW

○ **1968 / TRANSATLANTIC**   1968
Mostly traditional songs. A great collector's item. −SW

The Legend of Sweeny's Men / DEMON   1988
Best of Sweeny's Men. −SW

JUNE TABOR

English. One of the folk revival's greatest voices, Tabor has sung with the duo Silly Sisters as well as with the Oyster Band. She also has several solo recordings. −SW

○ **Airs and Graces / SHANACHIE**   1976
This album features mostly traditional songs, as well as Eric Bogle's now-classic "... and the Band Played "Waltzing Matilda'" in its first recorded version. −SW

Ashes and Diamonds / GREEN LINNET   1977
American CD re-release of this 1977 album. The overall sound is a bit dated, but lovely singing from Tabor and Nic Jones's guitar make this a treat. −SW

● **A Cut Above / TOPIC**
This one features Martin Simpson on guitar. More brilliant renditions of traditional songs. −SW

SCAN TESTER   1887-1972

English. Accordionist Scan Tester was that great rarity, a southern English traditional instrumentalist who was repeatedly recorded. −JSR

○ **I Never Played to Many Posh Dances / TOPIC**
The music here, all from the late 50s to mid 60s, includes solos (including some traditional Sussex fiddle), duets, and group numbers. Wonderful music, a very thorough job, and a unique record of the range and style of a pub-cum-village-hop musician. Not to be missed by any lover of English traditional music. −JSR

KATHRYN TICKELL

English. A young virtuoso on the Northumbrian bagpipes and fiddle, Tickell was named official piper to the Lord Mayor of Newcastle-upon-Tyne in 1984. She is the first person to hold that title in over 150 years. –sw

○ **On Kielder Side / SAYDISC**   1984
An excellent collection of English and Celtic tunes from Tickell and her small band. –sw

TRI YANN

Breton. A band whose music over the years has ranged from punchy acoustic arrangements of traditional songs to original rock & roll that is based on the tradition. –sw

Suite Gallaise / MARZELLE   1974
Their best acoustic album, full of bouncy energy. –sw

Les Filles des Forges / MARZELLE   1977
Early double-album compilation. –sw

○ **Si Mort a Mors / PHILIPS**   1982
Excellent double album compilation that covers the first ten years or so, without overlapping *Les Filles des Forges.* –sw

JOHN WHELAN & EILEEN IVERS

Irish. A great button accordion player, Whelan has won the all-Ireland championship on the instrument six times, and the all-Britain seven. His playing is exciting and fresh, if not strictly traditional. Ivers is his match, having won all-Ireland fiddle titles seven times herself. –sw

○ **Fresh Takes / GREEN LINNET**
Accompanied by Mark Simos and Triona Ni Dhomhnaill, Whelan and Ivers tear into some wonderful tunes, using consistently fresh and newfangled arrangements to keep the album interesting. –sw

THE YOUNG TRADITION

English. A vocal group started in the mid 60s by Peter Bellamy, Heather Wood, and Royston Wood, the Young Tradition were known for flamboyant costumes and witty presentation as well as for wonderful singing. –sw

○ **The Young Tradition / VANGUARD**   1966
Magnificent three-part harmonies. –sw

Galleries / VANGUARD   1968
More of the same. –sw

CELTIC & BRITISH ISLES COLLECTIONS

○ **The Best of the Irish Folk Festivals / GREEN LINNET**
The Best of the Irish Folk Festivals - The Seventies features over 60 minutes of live music from DeDanann, Clannad, Liam O'Flynn, Mick Hanly, Dolores Keane, John Faulkner, Jackie Daly, and Eddie and Finbar Furey. The recordings are from the Irish Folk Festivals held in West Germany. –cr

○ **The Big Squeeze / GREEN LINNET**   1988
Nine of the finest accordion players are presented on *The Big Squeeze: Masters of Celtic Accordion* collaboration featuring Joe Burke, Phil Cunningham, Jackie Daly, James Keane, Jimmy Keane, Billy McComiskey, Sean McGlynn, Paddy O'Brie, and John Whelan. –cr

Bonny North Tyne / TOPIC
Perhaps because it borders on Scotland, Northumberland has a stronger instrumental tradition than most of England, including a small, delicate-sounding local bagpipe. The musicians here — farmers, many of them — play fiddle, harmonica, whistle, Northumbrian pipes, and accordion. These are all nonvocals and mostly dance pieces. –jsr

Boscastle Breakdown / TOPIC
Recordings of southern English traditional instrumental music are as rare as hens' teeth. This fine album includes rare recordings of accordion and string bands as well as solo players, and covers the south coast tradition and the (marginally) better-known Cornish bands. There's even a hint at the origins of Caribbean polka drumming! –jsr

Bothy Ballads / TANGENT
Recording from the School of Scottish Studies of Edinburgh University, with solid documentation. The bothies of northeastern Scotland were basically dormitories for unmarried farm labor, which became music incubators. Here are instrumental jigs, diddling (mouthmusic), ballads old and new on themes heroic and pretty, all in the Anglophone lowland tradition. –jsr

★ **A Celebration of Scottish Music / TEMPLE**   1988
A compilation featuring the Battlefield Band, Cilla Fisher, and other great players and singers. –sw

○ **Celtic Folk Festival / CALIG**   1982
Live in concert. Features the Welsh music of Ar Log as well as the Breton band Bleizi Ruz. –sw

○ **The Celts Rise Again / GREEN LINNET**   1990
Green Linnet shows off its stable of Celtic artists, and it's our gain — featuring 18 tracks by Altan, Capercaillie, John & Phil Cunningham, Andy Irvin, Matt Molloy, and Robbie O'Connell. Great sampler. –cr

○ **Dans / IGUANE**   1988
The best in Breton dance music, this should lead you to new explorations of the Breton scene. –sw

○ **Feed the Folk / TEMPLE**
Featuring tracks by the Chieftains, the Battlefield Band, Fairport Convention, Steeleye Span, Martin Carthy, Paul Brady, and others. All proceeds go to charity. –sw

The Fiddler and His Art / TANGENT
This presents examples of five regional styles played by seven of Scotland's finest musicians in recordings ranging from the 30s on. An enormously valuable recording enhanced by admirable notes and delightful packaging. –jsr

★ **Flight of the Green Linnet / GREEN LINNET**
Flight of the Green Linnet - The Next Generation is a first-class collection of Scottish, Irish, and British music featuring Relativity, Silly Wizard, Capercaillie, the Chieftains, Patrick Street, the Tannahill Weavers, and many more. 70 minutes of excellent music and song. A favorite. –cr & sw

Volume 3: Jack of All Trades / TOPIC
Volume 4: The Child Ballads / TOPIC
Volume 5: The Child Ballads 2 / TOPIC
Volume 6: Sailormen & Servingmaids / TOPIC
Volume 7: Fair Game & Foul / TOPIC
Volume 8: A Soldier's Life for Me / TOPIC   1977
Volume 9: Songs of Ceremony / TOPIC
Volume 10: Animals & Other Marvels / TOPIC

○ **Folk Songs of Britain: Songs of Courtship / TOPIC**
How to sum up this stunning set? Ten volumes, organized by themes, of a huge body of field recordings by Peter Kennedy, Alan Lomax, Hamish Henderson, and several other collectors over a period of some 15 years (and originally issued, though long deleted, on the Caedmon label). Some performers (the Copper brothers of Sussex, Jeannie Robertson, and Sean Ennis) are familiar source singers; others are totally unknown. All are outstanding and authentic artists. Together they present an unprecedentedly full picture of a rich but, cohesive tradition. –jsr

Gaelic Psalms from Lewis / TANGENT
The superb psalm style of Lewis is a truly Celtic flowering. –jsr

○ **The Gathering / GREENHAYS**   1981
Features the likes of Donal Lunny, Matt Molloy, Paul Brady, and Andy Irvine. –sw

Grand Airs of Connemara / TOPIC
Much Irish and Scots music is part of a general northwest European tradition rather than particularly Celtic. Nor is the Gaelic material necessarily particularly ancient (several songs on this album mention emigration to the States). But the decorated solo ballads collected here are indeed quite specifically Irish in origin and performing style. –jsr

★ **Heart of the Gaels / GREEN LINNET**   1992
A follow up to *The Celts Will Rise Again*, this 18-track sampler of Celtic music features over 70 minutes of Altan, Patrick Street, the Tannahill Weavers, Dick Gaughan, Matt Malloy, Sean Keane, Andy Irvine, and others. –swb

○ **High Kings of Tara / TARA**   1980
Features Planxty, Christy Moore, Andy Irvine, and more. –sw

Irish Dance Music / FOLKWAYS
A historic collection. –dlm

The Irish Pipes of Finbar Furey / NONESUCH
A modern piper, sometimes with guitar or flute. –dlm

Irish-American Dance Music & Songs / FOLKLYRIC
Historic recordings from the late 20s. –dlm

Melodeon Greats / TOPIC
Features pre-1920 recordings of Scots polkas, reels, jigs, marches, and the like in early 20th century urban popular style, mostly with piano accompaniment. –jsr

The Muckle Sangs / TANGENT
The *muckle sangs* — the great ballads (sung unaccompanied in the true style) are the backbone of the Scots-English idiom, and of much Anglo-American music as well. –jsr

★ **Music and Song of Scotland / GREENTRAX**
A CD sampler from a great company in Scotland, featuring music that should point you in new, exciting directions. –sw

Music from the Western Isles / TANGENT
The Western Isles are among the few areas in which Scots Gaelic is not extinct. –jsr

○ **My Love Is in America / GREEN LINNET**
A toe-tappin' collection guaranteed to get you on your feet, featuring some of the finest Irish fiddlers. This CD was recorded at a concert at Boston College, Mar 25, 1990, featuring Kevin Burke, Seamus Connolly, Eileen Ivers, and many more. A good way to get into Irish fiddle music. –cr

○ **Playing with Fire / GREEN LINNET**   1989
With 16 Celtic fiddlers on *Playing with Fire: The Celtic Fiddle*

Collection, this well-thought-out album is long overdue. Don't fiddle around — pick it up! –cr

○ **The Rights of Man / GREEN LINNET**   1991
The Rights of Man: The Concert for Joseph Doherty is a great collection of music from the Feb 24, 1990, benefit in NYC for political prisoner Joseph Doherty. Celtic Thunder, Cherish the Ladies, Seamus Connolly, Seamus Egan, Eileen Ivers, Jimmy Keane, Pat Kilbride, Donal Lunny, Robbie O'Connell, and John Whelan are featured. Highly recommended. –cr

○ **Sandy Bell's Ceilidh / GREENTRAX**   1977
A good overview of the Edinburgh folk scene, all live at a landmark pub. Includes Dick Gaughan. –sw

Scottish Tradition 2 ... / TANGENT
Scottish Tradition 2-Music from the Western Isles. Some "waulking" songs by women, with bagpipes and flutes. Good notes. –dlm

Shetland Fiddle Music / TANGENT
Shetlanders are also great fiddlers, virtuosi in a tradition still richly individual. –jsr

Traditional Concertina Styles / TOPIC-FREE REED
County Clare is the Irish concertina heartland, and five of the musicians here hail from there. Though these charming 1974 recordings feature three generations, all adhere to the old solo tradition and the small British instrument. Their jigs, reels, hornpipes, and the rest are linked to both Irish pipe-playing and the English concertina tradition typified by William Kimber. –jsr

Vol. 2: Songs of Seduction / TOPIC

Waulking Songs / TANGENT
Besides the Gaelic waulking (cloth-fulling) songs, there are pipe reels, mouth music, laments, pibroch, a hymn, and even a Fenian song. –jsr

With Shawm & Bagpipe / MHS
A living tradition that carries the thread from medieval Europe. *With Shawm & Bagpipe - The Traditional Music of Brittany* is very interesting. –dlm

REGGAE

"Reggae music is boring; it all sounds the same."

Those are fighting words in the torpid back alleys of Kingston, because nowhere on the face of the earth is there more recorded output per capita than on this Isle of Springs, where literally hundreds of 7-inch singles are released each week, in a staggering variety of styles. It started as the 60s dawned, when steamy-hot and ripe-for-revolution JA was about to oust its British master, and the music (ska) drove the engine of change — double-time, frenetic, and as unyielding as a fully loaded cane truck on a hairpin turn. Ska turned to the half-time lope of rock steady for a couple of years, producing some of the most lyrical and lasting musical mementos of the century, songs of freedom that will be chanted by sufferers I-ternally. Then reggae burst on the scene in 1968, and the world has never stopped listening.

Reggae is as close to a universal music as this receding century has — with superstars like Bob Marley, Peter Tosh, Jimmy Cliff, Toots and the Maytals, and other touring pioneers; with the cult classic movie "The Harder They Come" and a soundtrack that has never stopped selling; with the success of the annual Sunsplash extravaganzas in Montego Bay and their touring counterparts from Japan, Europe, and North America; and with major American labels turning gold and platinum with artists such as Ziggy Marley and Shabba Ranks.

Check it! Maori, Tongan, and Fiji Islanders put aside age-old battles to form a reggae band called Herbs; a Japanese boy toasts (raps) in the rattle-blasted patter of a Kingston speed-rapper; Havasupai Indians at the foot of the Grand Canyon regard Marley as a prophet and display his picture in their homes; Poland's top ethnic fiddler joins a Twinkle Brother for a Polski hoedown/dub showdown, while at the shipyards in Gdansk, 10,000 people (most in red, gold, and green clothing) cheer an eight-hour reggae festival; and Aboriginals form a protest group whose chosen rhythm of resistance is reggae, calling themselves No Fixed Address. Reggae is triumphant, the irresistible heartbeat call to consciousness, the call of the LA rioters — "No Justice, No Peace!"

It is a call that can be as deep and spooky as a bad dream; as lopey and leering as Red Foxx after hours; ethereal and eternal — the true new Psalms; as understated as a pause and as robust as a rocket. This is the music of the Movement of Jah People, future folk who know God is a living man and paradise is right here right now. It is Jah love made manifest, not fe de weakheart, and definitely not boring.

— Roger M. Steffens

ABYSSINIANS

Reggae. Dreadly serious purveyors of praise-filled Rastafarian religious music, this superb trio began by writing and recording "Satta Massagana" in 1969. The song became a heavily covered standard. Although their output has been spotty, the group is still active. –RMS

○ **Forward / ALLIGATOR**   1982
"Satta" and other hymns for the hearticle. –RMS

LILLIAN ALLEN

Dub poetry. Canada's preeminent dub poet, whose all-female band kicks as hard as Dennis Bovell's, with equal genre-bending. Brilliant language that snaps like gum, with perfectly matched musical beds. –RMS

○ **Revolutionary Tea Party / REDWOOD**   1988
A masterpiece of conscious female passion. –RMS

BOB ANDY

Reggae. An early member of the mid-60s Paragons of "Tide Is High" fame, Bob Andy has written some of Jamaica's most lasting songs such as "Desperate Lover" and "Feeling Soul." With Marcia Griffiths, he hit the UK Top Ten in the early 70s. Andy is strong, lyrical singer of powerful love songs and incisive social statements. His "Fire Burning" became one of 1992's most-used rhythms. –RMS

● **Retrospective / HEARTBEAT**   1986
A fine overview of a sorely overlooked reggae vocalist, composer, arranger, and session singer. –RW

○ **Song Book / STUDIO ONE**   1988
Among Coxsone Dodd's most important albums ever, virtually every cut a classic. –RMS

ASWAD

Reggae. These three longtime UK singers and musicians started hard in the 70s but failed to break through commercially. By the end of the 80s, their sweet-soul/pop/reggae soared in the UK charts, but they lost their roots authenticity in the process. Their earliest work, however, reverberates still. –RMS

Aswad / MANGO   1976
Their leadoff album that established the group's sound. –RW

Hulet / MANGO   1979
A late-70s session that never gets going. –RW

Showcase / MANGO   1981
Mainly album re-mixes. –RW

New Chapter of Dub / MANGO   1982
Fine dubs of songs from the *New Chapter* album. –RW

Live and Direct / MANGO   1983
This compiles several group favorites. A solid live outing. –RW

Rebel Souls / MANGO 1984
Good covers of Marvin Gaye and Toots Hibbert classics. –RW

To the Top / SIMBA 1986
Contains the wonderful single "Bubbling" and good vocal harmonies. –RW

Distant Thunder / MANGO 1988
A crossover album geared toward a non-reggae audience. –RW

○ **Crucial Tracks - The Best of Aswad / MANGO** 1989
The best collection for both fans and novices. –RW

Too Wicked / MANGO 1990
A standard, par-for-the-course session. –RW

BIG YOUTH

DJ. In the early 70s, no toaster (the Jamaican word for rapper) was bigger than Big Youth. His choice of cuts over which to chat was always impeccable, and he had multiple entries in the Jamaican Top Ten. From a whisper to a scream, hearing him even once explains why he was Bob Marley's favorite DJ. –RMS

Screaming Target / TROJAN 1973
Excellent toasts and fine instrumental versions of reggae classics by Dennis Brown, Gregory Isaacs, and others. –RW

Hit the Road Jack / TROJAN 1976
One to own. –MGN

★ **Natty Cultural Dread / TROJAN** 1976
A definitive early-period album from this reggae toaster. A must for every reggae lover. –MGN

Dreadlocks Dread / CAROLINE 1979
An outstanding set of early material, with the spotlight on their compositional prowess. –RW

○ **Excellent Skank / TROJAN** 1980
A tremendous anthology containing early, out-of-print singles and album cuts. –RW

Live at Reggae Sunsplash / SUNSPLASH 1983
High-energy live performances of Big Youth's greatest hits, backed by the Soul Syndicate. –RMS

A Luta Continua / HEARTBEAT 1984
Featuring songs of the 80s worldwide struggle — sung, not toasted. –RMS

BLACK UHURU

Reggae. By 1992, Black Uhuru (Black Sounds of Freedom) had gone through six distinct incarnations, the only common factor being Duckie Simpson, their dreadly serious harmonist and sometime composer. Founded in the mid 70s, the group hit its key period in the early 80s with a charismatically scowling lead singer named Michael Rose, who remade his classic "Dreadlocks Coming ..." as "Guess Who's Coming to Dinner." A fearsome prowler onstage with a Far East style of roots warbling, Rose was often touted as the "next Bob Marley," an observation that has ruined the career of many a lesser performer. The militancy of the group was enhanced by an African-American woman with a Master's degree from Columbia University, Puma Jones, whose wavy-armed dancing and high, chromatic harmonies echoed the communal gatherings she had witnessed while working in Mama Africa. Add to this the essential underpinnings of rhythm twins Sly & Robbie, who were considered equal members of the group while Rose was aboard, and you have the quintessential reggae lineup of the post-Marley era and reggae's first-ever Grammy winners. However, internal problems and dissatisfaction with their record label broke up that lineup. But 1986's *Brutal*, featuring new lead singer Junior Reid, revealed a surprisingly strong resolve to continue. Eventually, visa problems sidelined Reid and Puma died of cancer, and in full circle the three original members came together to take the group to a new level. The current lineup , composed of solo star Don Carlos (whose style is hauntingly similar to Reid's and Rose's), Duckie Simpson, and former Wailing Soul Garth Dennis, shows that the concept could be successfully molded to fit almost anyone willing to give voice to these sounds of freedom and righteous indignation. –RMS

Love Dub / ROHIT
Nice studio techniques, otherwise average. –RW

☆ **Sinsemilla / MANGO** 1980
An outstanding set that helped break them in the States. –RW

Black Sounds of Freedom / SHANACHIE 1981
A reissued remix of the early *Love Crisis* album. –RW

Guess Who's Coming to Dinner / HEARTBEAT 1981
A reissue'of a fine album, *Showcase*. –RW

★ **Red / MANGO** 1981
This album is a landmark release, one of the great reggae sessions of the 80s. –RW

Chill Out / MANGO / BB# 146 1982
Featuring superb Sly & Robbie backing — dark, haunting, and bare. –RMS

Tear It Up / MANGO 1982
A strong live date, though an overly familiar selection. –RW

The Dub Factor / MANGO 1983
A great dub date. –RW

Reggae Greats / MANGO 1985
An adequate collection of past hits. –RW

Brutal / RAS 1986
The debut of a new lead singer, Junior Reid. –RW

Brutal Dub / RAS 1986
A dub-variation version of *Brutal*. –RW

Positive / RAS 1987
Yet another unveiling of a revised lineup. –RW

Live in New York City / ROHIT 1988
For completists only. –RW

Positive Dub / RELATIVITY 1988
Another dub of a prior release. –RW

Now / MESA-BLUE MOON 1990
A more recent session. –RW

Now Dub / MESA-BLUE MOON 1990
Dub one more time. –RW

Iron Storm / MESA-BLUE MOON 1991
The latest from this anthemic ensemble. –RW

ALPHA BLONDY

Reggae. An Ivory Coast native, his name means "First Bandit." One of Africa's biggest stars in the 80s, his initial album *Jah Glory* sold a million copies in Africa. He dresses as a Rasta, wears a star of David, carries a Bible and Koran. He sings in Arabic in Israel and in Hebrew in the Arab world. Wailers-like music with African accents. –RMS

Jah Glory / CELLULOID 1985
A dynamic early 80s album with Blondy establishing his sound and style. It hasn't yet been released on a US label. –RW

Jerusalem / SHANACHIE 1987
Blondy sings in Arabic, Hebrew, French, English, and many African languages in an effort to reach as many people as possible. On this disc, one of his most popular titles, he's backed by the Wailers (sans Bob Marley) for a simmering, roots-heavy session. –JP

Cocody Rock!!! / SHANACHIE 1988
Blondy's best-selling African album. –JP

The Prophets / CAPITOL 1989
Blondy's first international release under a new worldwide contract with EMI. It's as soulful and militant as past efforts, with an added gloss to the production that may win new listeners. –JP

Apartheid Is Nazism / SHANACHIE 1990
This is Blondy's most militant statement, and a continent-wide hit. –JP

○ **Best of Alpha Blondy / SHANACHIE** 1990
This disc lives up to its title with hits like "Jerusalem," "Cocody Rock," and "Apartheid Is Nazism." –JP

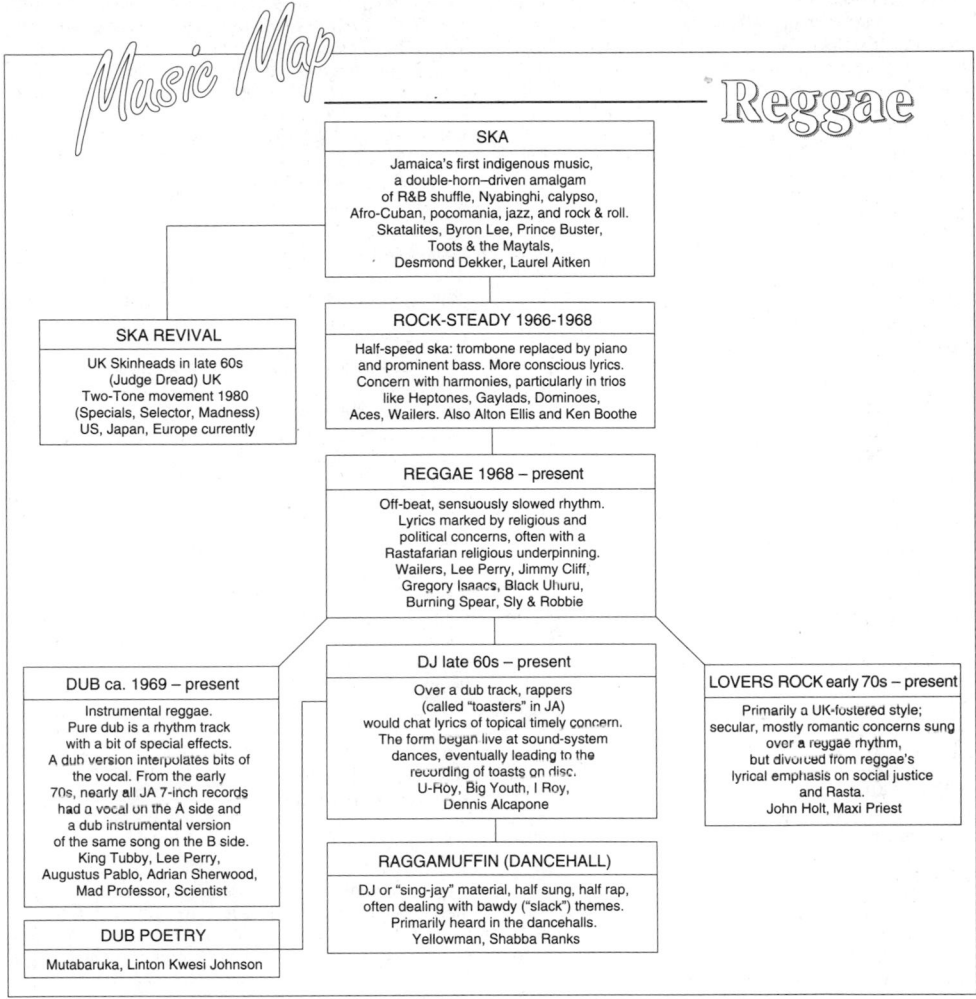

SKA

Jamaica's first indigenous music,
a double–horn–driven amalgam
of R&B shuffle, Nyabinghi, calypso,
Afro–Cuban, pocomania, jazz, and rock & roll.
Skatalites, Byron Lee, Prince Buster,
Toots & the Maytals,
Desmond Dekker, Laurel Aitken

SKA REVIVAL

UK Skinheads in late 60s
(Judge Dread) UK
Two-Tone movement 1980
(Specials, Selector, Madness)
US, Japan, Europe currently

ROCK-STEADY 1966-1968

Half-speed ska: trombone replaced by piano
and prominent bass. More conscious lyrics.
Concern with harmonies, particularly in trios
like Heptones, Gaylads, Dominoes,
Aces, Wailers. Also Alton Ellis and Ken Boothe

REGGAE 1968 – present

Off-beat, sensuously slowed rhythm.
Lyrics marked by religious and
political concerns, often with a
Rastafarian religious underpinning.
Wailers, Lee Perry, Jimmy Cliff,
Gregory Isaacs, Black Uhuru,
Burning Spear, Sly & Robbie

DUB ca. 1969 – present

Instrumental reggae.
Pure dub is a rhythm track
with a bit of special effects.
A dub version interpolates bits of
the vocal. From the early
70s, nearly all JA 7-inch records
had a vocal on the A side and
a dub instrumental version
of the same song on the B side.
King Tubby, Lee Perry,
Augustus Pablo, Adrian Sherwood,
Mad Professor, Scientist

DJ late 60s – present

Over a dub track, rappers
(called "toasters" in JA)
would chat lyrics of topical timely concern.
The form began live at sound-system
dances, eventually leading to the
recording of toasts on disc.
U-Roy, Big Youth, I Roy,
Dennis Alcapone

LOVERS ROCK early 70s – present

Primarily a UK-fostered style;
secular, mostly romantic concerns sung
over a reggae rhythm,
but divorced from reggae's
lyrical emphasis on social justice
and Rasta.
John Holt, Maxi Priest

RAGGAMUFFIN (DANCEHALL)

DJ or "sing-jay" material, half sung, half rap,
often dealing with bawdy ("slack") themes.
Primarily heard in the dancehalls.
Yellowman, Shabba Ranks

DUB POETRY

Mutabaruka, Linton Kwesi Johnson

CEDELLA MARLEY BOOKER

Reggae. Bob Marley's mother. Hear this big-voiced one-of-a-kind gospel-reggae singer, and you'll know instantly where Bob got his power. –RMS

○ **Awake Zion / RYKODISC**   1990
An offbeat album backed by the Wailers, with covers of, and tributes to, her son. –RMS

KEN BOOTHE

Reggae. Legendary producer Coxsone Dodd dubbed Boothe "Mr. Rock Steady" in the mid 60s and this hard-belting crooner had some of that genre's biggest hits. His career has spanned the past 30 years, in a style rooted in the Jamaican fundamentalism called "pocomania" and mixed with a touch of Otis Redding. His cover of Bread's "Everything I Own" hit #1 on the UK pop charts. –RMS

Call Me / ROHIT
One of reggae and Jamaican music's finest pure singers. –RW

○ **Live Good / LIBERTY**   1978
Coxsone sessions including the hits "Moving Away," "Live Good," and "Thinking." –RMS

Talk to Me / VP
He's always worth hearing, even on haphazard or predictable material. –RW

BRIGADIER JERRY

DJ. A speed-rapping pioneer, "Briggy" was the featured toaster of the Jah Love sound system run by an uptown Rasta organization called the Twelve Tribes, which counted Bob Marley among its membership. His raps are invariably cultural, not slack (bawdy), and he ruled the mid-80s DJ clashes in Jamaica. –RMS

○ **Jamaica Jamaica / RAS**   1985
His first album, featuring some of his best-known toasts. –RMS

PETER BROGGS

Reggae. An 80s rootsman, better known in the US than home in Jamaica, Broggs has become a convincing singer thanks to strong support from his US label, RAS. –RMS

○ **Reasoning / RAS**   1990
A fine, aware collection. Brogg's is backed by the Wailers and Roots Radics. –RMS

DENNIS BROWN

Reggae. Often referred to as "Emmanuel, the Crown Prince of Reggae," Dennis Brown was Bob Marley's favorite singer. He was 13 when his career began, recording initially (and typically) for Coxsone Dodd, scoring big with a 1968 cover of

"No Man Is an Island" (the Impressions) in 1968. In the 70s he made a series of exciting albums for Joe Gibbs and had a UK hit with his classic "Money in My Pocket." From 1977 to 1982 he recorded for Joe Gibbs, in his peak period producing such classics as "Revolution," "Have You Ever Been Lonely (Have You Ever Been Blue)," "The Promised Land," and "Sitting and Watching." A live album was cut in Montreux in 1979, a year after he was featured in the film *Heartland Reggae*. With a no-nonsense, straight-ahead style, Brown is capable of wrapping a love song in a crooning caress or inciting a crowd (as he did memorably at the 1983 Sunsplash in Montego Bay) to heights of uncontrolled hysteria. He continues to be one of Jamaica's classiest and most riveting performers. –RMS

Visions / SHANACHIE 1978
Wonderful work from Brown. –RW

Words of Wisdom / SHANACHIE 1979
Outstanding. –RW

Brown Sugar / RAS 1986
Soulful, frequently emphatic, and energized. –RW

History / LIVE & LOVE 1986
Despite some pro-forma nods to Jah, Brown was one of the first of the post-Rasta wave. In this album he used a mellow late-reggae style to put over the new word of dancehall music: "We Should Make Love," "Dance All Night," and the rest of the party-time ethos. –JOHN STORM ROBERTS, ORIGINAL MUSIC

Slow Down / SHANACHIE 1987
Good-to-great leads. –RW

Greatest Hits / ROHIT 1988
An arguable title, but no problems otherwise. –RW

○ **Inseparable / VP** 1988
Simply stunning. –RW

Unchallenged / VP 1989
The songs, production, and arrangements on this album are all first-rate. –RW

My Time / ROHIT 1989
Keeps things at a generally high level. –RW

Good Vibrations / ROHIT 1989
A harder edge and tone. –RW

Over Proof / SHANACHIE 1991
Uniformly excellent. Exuberant, passionate vocals. –RW

Go Now / ROHIT 1991
Another fine session. –RW

Victory Is Mine / RAS
Mixes contexts and styles well. –RW

BURNING SPEAR

Reggae. Winston Rodney took his stage name from Jomo Kenyatta, hero of Kenyan independence. The Spear, as he is called, first recorded in 1969 for Coxsone Dodd. Those productions, collected six years later on a pair of Studio One albums, were lean, mysterious, and way ahead of their time: a similar sound would sweep Jamaica in the late 70s and be dubbed the "Rockers" style. Not meeting much initial success, Spear retreated to his rural home in St. Ann's, in the hills of North Coast Jamaica. Eventually he returned in 1975 as part of a self-named trio for producer Jack Ruby. This time the world woke up, and Spear was recognized as a major figure. After two albums Spear dismissed his backing trio, journeyed to London, and cut one of the most astonishing live reggae sets ever for Island, for whom he recorded until 1980. That same year, he was featured unforgettably in an a cappella performance of "Jah No Dead" in the reggae movie *Rockers*. Since then he has skipped through several major and minor labels, returning in 1990 to Island.

Spear is one of those artists whose style is so immediately recognizable that those who like him from the start seem to have followed his every move with joy. He is similar to a trance singer, especially in his horn-lofted live performances, whirling around the stage with arms outstretched, a dreadlocked dervish chanting of dark carnal nights of captivity and imminent deliverance. By the end of his best shows he has often repeated phrases in delicious delirium, reaching the higher heights (irie ites) that is reggae and Rasta's promised land. Without question, Spear is one of reggae's greats. –RMS

Garvey's Ghost / MANGO 1976
A pulsating dub version of his album "Marcus Garvey." –JF

Man in the Hills / MANGO 1976
Nearly repeating the success of his debut, through a wide-ranging array of topics and a sturdy groove. –JF

★ **Marcus Garvey / MANGO** 1976
A reggae cornerstone. The most focused and musically exhilarating tribute to Marcus Garvey, a recurring theme in his music. –JF

☆ **Live / MANGO** 1977
Aswad back's Spear's solo debut, one of Reggae's greatest live sets ever. –RMS

☆ **Harder than the Best / MANGO** 1979
A magnificent career overview that includes every highlight from Spear's canon. The best songs from otherwise turgid albums. –JF

Farover / HEARTBEAT 1982
Some superb compositions and searing vocals. –RW

Fittest of the Fittest / HEARTBEAT 1983
Taut production, memorable leads from Winston Rodney. –RW

Resistance / HEARTBEAT 1984
A great pairing of Rodney vocals and horn section. A Grammy nominee, this boasts the added bonus of a wonderful non-political piece "Love to You." –RW

People of the World / SLASH 1989
A nice debut on a major label not known for reggae. This release also includes eclectic material and a female horn section. –RW

Mek We Dweet / MANGO 1990
Spear makes a triumphant return to the label where he started his career, at least from a worldwide perspective. –RW

JOHNNY CLARKE

Reggae. A crucial 70s vocalist, Clarke made some of his biggest marks for producer Bunny Lee, especially "Enter into His Gates with Praise." His numerous cover versions often outstripped the originals, and he is acknowledged as one of the great unknown masters of Jamaican singing. –RMS

○ **Authorised Rockers / CAROLINE**
Another great pure singer, adept at soul, reggae, or lovers-rock styles. –RW

Enter into His Gates with Praise / ATTACK 1989
Mid 70s tracks, mixed by virtuoso King Tubby. Gripping. –RMS

Reggae Archives / GONG SOUNDS 1991
An up-to-the-second production that brings well-deserved exposure to the mellifluous Mr. C. A real winner with 16 cuts. –RMS

JIMMY CLIFF b 1948

Reggae. The first artist in Lesley Kong's groundbreaking Beverly's label stable in 1962, Jimmy Cliff has been a figure of major influence in the internationalization of Jamaican music for thirty years. Bob Dylan called Cliff's late-60s hit "Vietnam" the best protest song he ever heard. Hearing that same tune led Paul Simon to travel to Kingston, book the same rhythm section, engineer, and studio, and record "Mother and Child Reunion," the first Yankee reggae song ever.

Despite a number of ska hits and an Island Records contract in 1967, it wasn't until he was recruited to act in Perry Henzell's rollickingly hypnotic film *The Harder They Come* that Cliff achieved true stardom. He sang a number of his own compositions in the movie, including "Many Rivers to Cross," "Sitting in Limbo," and the title track, three standards that helped make the soundtrack album one of the biggest sellers in reggae history. The followup albums, however, were generally unfocused, their spotty material spoiling Cliff's bid to become reggae's main exponent, a gap rushed into and filled brilliantly by Bob Marley. By 1976, Cliff had regrouped and enlisted Wailers tutor Joe Higgs to be his bandleader. A yearly stream of albums followed, with songs as good as anything he ever recorded ("Beyond the Boundaries," "Bongo Man"); and Cliff became a mainstay on the international festival and touring circuit, achieving huge fame in places like Nigeria, where he keeps a second home.

Cliff's style is a high, almost gospel plaint, with a keen rhythmic sense that echoes Africa as well as R&B. A concert film, *Bongo Man*, was released around 1980, as Cliff looked unsuccessfully for the proper vehicle to follow up the worldwide penetration of *The Harder They Come*. Cliff, a father figure to several generations of young musicians, can still be counted on to deliver thoroughly professional shows and recordings. –RMS

Wonderful World, Beautiful People / A&M   1970
Contains the Cliff anthem "Vietnam." –WR

☆ **The Harder They Come / MANGO / BB# 140**   1972
Jimmy Cliff starred in this gritty film about street life in Kingston, Jamaica. The album is a brilliant compilation of early reggae music, and Cliff's own songs. "You Can Get It If You Really Want It," "Many Rivers to Cross," "The Harder They Come," and "Sitting in Limbo," are among the best of a very good lot. –WR

Reggae Greats / MANGO   1985
This is a good overview of his hits, including "Vietnam," "The Harder They Come," "Many Rivers to Cross," and "Struggling Man." –SWB

Hanging Fire / CBS   1988
Cliff has long since been eclipsed by other reggae stars, but this later release shows him effectively mixing his own quick-step version of the music with general pop trends. –WR

CULTURE

Reggae. The gritty vocal textures and poetic invocations that characterize lead singer Joseph "Culture" Hill's genius are evident on all his work. Like Burning Spear, he mixes prophecy with his personal experiences. He managed to close down the entire country of Jamaica when the "Two Sevens Clashed" on 7-7-77. "Fussing and Fighting" became an anthem for the ghetto peace movement in Kingston the following year. It's as if Elijah, the Old Testament prophet, came back with a trio. –RMS

☆ **Two Sevens Clash / SHANACHIE**   1977
The landmark debut, with gorgeous vocals, concise rhythms, and tough and properly impassioned heart makes this a cornerstone of any reggae collection. –JF

Cumbolo / SHANACHIE   1978
A classic, almost on par with *Two Sevens*, utilizing similar themes and sung with similar amounts of passion. –JF

International Herb / SHANACHIE   1979
The politics have subsided just a notch, but this is still a beauty. –JF

Too Long in Slavery / CAROLINE   1980
Here is a decently compiled collection of their output up to *Cumbolo*. –JF

Lion Rock / HEARTBEAT   1982
An exemplary 80s session with Hill in top form. –RW

Nuff Crisis / SHANACHIE   1988
Topical, passionate, and, as always, beautifully sung. –RW

JUNIOR DELGADO

Reggae. The feeling soul of gruff-edged vocalist Junior Delgado has been heard on record since he was 14. Producer Lee Perry discovered him in 1969. Delgado has also sung for Joe Gibbs, Coxsone Dodd and Randy's. His songs of whiplash emotions and armed robberies are balanced by the Hallmark

sentimentalism of his lovers rock and an occasional masterpiece, such as the 1986 *Raggamuffin Year*. –RMS

○ **Raggamuffin Year / MANGO**   1986
Rasta, "ragga," love, and rage are the topics in this A. Pablo production. –RMS

LUCKY DUBE

African. Of the many reggae artists at one time or another dubbed "the next Bob Marley," South Africa's Lucky Dube seems a likely candidate for the crown. Not only is he the biggest-selling recording artist in his country, but his first release (*Prisoner*, 1989) was also the top-selling South African album of all time. Partly his success is due to charismatic live performances revealing unmatched energy from vocal verve to Zulu-inspired choreography. For the international fans who know him simply through his recordings, Dube's combination of a strong melodic gift and his straightforward approach to social-issue songwriting recall many of Jamaica's greatest at top form. Even when the message of his music is the most serious, a buoyancy and spirit of unity make the heavy reasonings go down easy. –BT

○ **Captured Live / SHANACHIE**
This intense live recording captures Lucky Dube's charismatic force as none of his studio discs do — plus he's backed by a hot horn section. –BT

Slave / SHANACHIE   1983
Another strong statement of militant "sufferation," liberation, and love. –JP

● **Prisoner / SHANACHIE**   1991
One of the best efforts from a South African reggae superstar whose vocal style owes much to Peter Tosh. Dube is one of the finest post-Marley singer/songwriters in the reggae field. –JP

House of Exile / SHANACHIE   1992
The latest refinement of Dube's sound features his toughest songwriting yet and several numbers with the expanded version of his band, the Slaves. –BT

EEK-A-MOUSE

Reggae. Born Ripton Hylton, this "six-foot-six above sea level" toaster was named after a race horse. The Mouse's Far Eastern "bong-gong-giddy-mem-giddy-hoy" style set the pace for many early-80s imitators. His sing-jay lyrics run the gamut from wildly funny to terrifying and touching. A master of stagecraft, his witty costumes range from Mexican caballero to Samurai warrior and help keep him touring successfully into the 90s. –RMS

○ **Wa-Do-Dem / SHANACHIE**   1982
Classic innovative title track and autobiographical material make this a major debut. –RMS

ALTON ELLIS

Reggae. One of Jamaica's first singers, the silken-smooth Alton Ellis made his first hit "Muriel" in 1959 as part of a duo with Eddie Perkins. Producer Coxsone Dodd oversaw a string of subsequent successes. Eventually Ellis, seeing little financial remuneration, left for Coxsone's archrival Duke Reid and his Treasure Isle label. Tunes like "Dance Crasher," "Cry Tough," and "Girl, I've Got a Date" gave Reid his first chance to pass Dodd in the popular mind as Jamaica's heaviest studio and sound system.

By 1966 the red-hot double-time ska beat had given birth virtually overnight to a much slower, hiccupping rhythm dubbed "rock-steady," and it was Alton who was to be its midwife. "One evening in the studio," Alton recalls, "the bass man didn't show up. So Jackie Mittoo, the keyboardist, had to play the bass pattern on the piano with his left hand, but he couldn't hold it steady, and we all thought the line was so fresh and nice. When the bass player turned up next time, Jackie insisted that he play what Jackie was playing with his left hand. That's how rock-steady was born; we called it so that night."

Coxsone lured Alton back, and by 1968 Alton was the undisputed King of Rock-Steady with shots like "Willow Tree," "I'm Just a Guy," and "Sitting in the Park," often highlighted with his trademark yelp of "Looka here now!" Again, the money failed to follow the hits, and somewhat disillusioned, Alton spent several years in the US and Canada before pulling up stakes and moving permanently to England in 1973. Scores of songs were issued steadily, cementing his reputation as one of the most consistent reggae artists around. By 1984 he was celebrated internationally for his 25 years in show business, making a pair of critically acclaimed appearances at Jamaica's Sunsplash festival in 1983 and 1985. From 1989 on, he has been releasing compilations on his own Alltone label of his early masterpieces, and he even recorded *Man from Studio One*, a new 12-inch for Coxsone in 1991. One of the real gentlemen of reggae, Alton is a satisfying and scintillating singer, one of Jamaica's extraordinary gifts to the world, right up there with Bob Marley. –RMS

☆ **Best of Alton Ellis / COXSONE**   1988
A great cross-section of mid-60s covers that sound far better than the originals, along with self-penned classics. –RMS

Legendary Alton Ellis / ALLTONE   1990
Ska, rock-steady, and early reggae singles, including the essential "Cry Tough" and "Dance Crasher." –RMS

Alton and Hortense / HEARTBEAT   1990
Brother Alton and sister Hortense duet on several unreleased tracks, offering more 60s classics from Coxsone's master tapes. –RMS

ETHIOPIANS

Reggae. A duo founded in 1966, the Ethiopians featured Leonard "Jack Sparrow" Dillon leading songs like "Owe Me No Pay Me," "Train to Skaville," and "The Whip." Their biggest hit, "Everything Crash" in 1968, spoke of the quotidian realities of life in the ghetto, a common concern of their literally hundreds of singles. This is classic roots music by one of the most critically acclaimed Jamaican groups ever. –RMS

○ **Ethiopians / TROJAN**   1986
These 21 songs from 1966 to 1972 give the best available overview of a major Jamaican duo. –RMS

MAJEK FASHEK

African. Nigerian Majekodunmi Fasheke, otherwise known as Majek Fashek, is (along with South Africa's Lucky Dube) Africa's prime proponent of reggae. But while Dube keeps the music close to its Jamaican source, Fashek lights a polyrhythmic fire under the familiar reggae beat, with ferocious talking drum volleys and multilayered percussion. Though influenced by Jimmy Cliff and Bob Marley, Fashek's initial love (and the music he first sang) was Indian film music. He began playing guitar while in secondary school in Benin, forming a band called Jah Stix, which made the club circuit in Lagos. In 1988, he struck out on his own. The African release of his first reggae album, *Prisoner of Conscience*, sold 200,000 copies and spawned two singles that rode high on the Nigerian charts for over a year. –BT

Prison of Conscience / MANGO   1988
Heavily influenced by Marley — Fashek sounds more like the reggae avatar than Ziggy — this batch of Nigerian-flavored "skanking" is startlingly redeemed by the brilliant "Send Down the Rain," which took on near-incantatory intensity on Fashek's tours across the drought-stricken continent. –BT

○ **Spirit of Love / INTERSCOPE**   1991
Seamlessly blending elements of juju with reggae, Fashek turns from imitator to innovator in a disc with so much clear-eyed enthusiasm and vision you'd think reggae was his personal invention. "Majek Beware" is the most powerful reggae song in years, awash in talking drums, jungle chants, and shamanistic lead vocals. –BT

GENERAL TREES

DJ. A mid-80s speed-rapper with timely topical lyrics and high-energy performances, he won the JBC's 1986 Song of the Year award for "Mini Bus." –RMS

○ **Nuff Respect / SHANACHIE**   1987
A good collection of most of his earliest Jamaican hits, including "Mini Bus." –RMS

ALBERT GRIFFITHS & THE GLADIATORS

Reggae. A harmony group fronted by Griffiths, whose high-pitched, slightly nasal voice gave them an instantly identifiable sound influenced by the Wailers and the Techniques in the 60s. Still active after 25 years. –RMS

○ **Trenchtown Mixup / VIRGIN**   1976
Captured at their peak, with some of their most representative compositions, such as "Hello Carol" and "Thief in the Night." –RMS

On the Right Track / HEARTBEAT   1989
Their best 80s effort, with assistance from members of the I-Tones. –RW

MARCIA GRIFFITHS

Reggae. Jamaica's longest-running and perhaps biggest female vocalist ever. Griffiths began as a teenager in Coxsone's Studio One, racking up hit after hit, then joined with paramour Bob Andy as Bob & Marcia for the Top Five UK pop hit "Young, Gifted and Black." She formed the I Threes to back Bob Marley's international tours and recordings from 1974-1980 and scored a massive international hit with "Electric Boogie" in the 80s. Despite a few 70s Rasta tunes like "Stepping out of Babylon," she is known primarily for her strong, smooth-as-mousse love songs and captivating live performances. –RMS

Carousel / POLYGRAM
It's always worth hearing her sing, but the album is not essential. –RW

Marcia / RAS
Nice songs, and even better vocals. –RW

● **Naturally / SKY NOTE**   1978
Ten of her greatest early hits, seven written by Bob Andy. –RMS

○ **Steppin' / SHANACHIE**   1979
Stirring leads from a wonderful singer. –RW

HEPTONES

Reggae. Bigger in the mid 60s than the Wailers, the Heptones were led by Studio One bassist and singer Leroy Sibbles, one of Jamaica's most compelling vocalists. The belting Sibbles lead, with the harmonies of Earl Morgan and Barry Llewellyn, made the Heptones a model for trios through the late 70s, when Sibbles left. Now fronted by Naggo Morris, the Heptones 80s material never recaptured the majesty of the earlier era. Sibbles continues as a highly popular international touring artist. –RMS

★ **Book of Rules / ISLAND**   1976
The title track is transcendent poetry. This album includes brilliant updates of classics such as "Fatty Fatty," "I've Got the Handle," and "Mama Say." –RMS

Night Food / MANGO   1976
Wonderful harmonies. –RW

○ **Party Time / MANGO**   1977
Sizzling. One of the first reggae vocal groups to hook Americans. –RW

Better Days / ROHIT   1981
Top-flight singing. –RW

On the Run / SHANACHIE   1982
A reggae institution. –RW

TOOTS HIBBERT & THE MAYTALS

Reggae. Toots Hibbert sings as if he's determined to summon the ghost of Otis Redding. Since his arrival on the ska scene in the early 60s, Hibbert and the Maytals have provided the clearest evidence of the link between American soul and the hometown bop of Jamaica. Some of his albums have been spotty, but his enthusiastic vocals make everything he's cut worth hearing (and not just for reggae aficionados). –JF

☆ **Funky Kingston / MANGO**
This is the album that brought Toots's soul-infused testifying to American audiences. Forget about this being a great reggae album; this set transcends categorization. –JF

Reggae Greats / MANGO
It's skimpy, but this one offers an adequate smattering of essentials, including their first hit, "54-46 Was My Number," "Funky Kingston," and "Sweet and Dandy." –JF

Toots in Memphis / MANGO   1988
Recorded with a slew of Memphis studio pros, Toots pays homage to the power of Southern soul with sterling covers of "I Can't Stand the Rain," "Knock on Wood," "Love and Happiness," "Hard to Handle," and six others. An amazing return to form. –JF

Do the Reggae / ATTACK
Sixteen cuts from their early days, when the Maytals were perfecting their sound. Includes some seminal and rare early material. –JF

JOE HIGGS

Reggae. The "godfather of reggae music," teacher of Bob Marley and the Wailers, the Wailing Souls, and dozens of other Trenchtown youths, Higgs is also known as the "Jazz Connection" for Jamaican music. He became one of Jamaica's first indigenous stars in the late 50s, helping turn R&B covers into a new kind of music called ska. In the mid 70s, he was Jimmy Cliff's bandleader on worldwide tours. His career continues into its fourth decade with regularly released albums showcasing his sharp-shock style and vocal daring. –RMS

● **Life of Contradiction / MICRON**   1975
Remakes of big 60s hits including "There's a Reward" and "Song My Enemy Sings." Passion personified. –RMS

Triumph / ALLIGATOR   1979
Smashing, defiant vocals from a legendary figure, done during the brief time Alligator was involved in reggae. –RW

○ **Blackman Know Yourself / SHANACHIE**   1990
Wonderful in every aspect. –RW

JUSTIN HINDS & DOMINOES

Reggae. This sugarcane-sweet country/gospel trio (begun in 1964) spotlighted the inimitable round warmth of leader Justin Hinds. Their music is marked by themes of righteousness often cloaked in hoary folk sayings. The ska revival in the UK in 1980 renewed interest in the group, although Hinds remains a recluse in the North Coast bush and rarely leaves Jamaica. –RMS

Jezebel / MANGO   1976
Well sung and well produced. –RW

Just in Time / MANGO   1979
Hot leads, piercing harmonies. –RW

○ **Travel with Love / NIGHTHAWK**   1984
Eight perfectly beautiful mid-tempo country croonings. –RMS

JOHN HOLT

Lovers rock. The father of lovers rock (non-Rasta, non-political reggae rhythm in service of the ultimate emotion), Holt is a founder of the Paragons and the songwriter of some of the biggest hits of the 60s in Jamaica, such as "On the Beach" and "Wear You to the Ball," as well as a consistently interesting smooth-voiced coverer of US and UK pop hits. Still active, he finally got his payday when Blondie covered his "Tide Is High." –RMS

Love I Can Feel / TROJAN
Fine Coxsone productions from the early 70s. –RMS

Sweetie Come Brush Me / VOLCANO
This mid-80s career reviver includes "Ghetto Queen," backed by the Radics. –RMS

I ROY

DJ. A reggae toaster and original rapper, I Roy uses quick wit and sharp rhythms to make modern poetry in a stylish roots-skank mode. –MGN

○ **Truth & Rights / GROUNATION**   1975
Horns, organ, and a rhythm section by Sly & Robbie. Top-drawer toasting. –MGN

Musical Shark Attack / VIRUS   1976
This album features "Semi-classical Natty Dread" and "Tribute to Marcus Garvey." –MGN

IJAHMAN

Reggae. Folk poet Trevor Sutherland, under the nom de chanteur Ijahman Levi, has since the late 70s issued yearly compilations of (generally) acoustic, lengthy mediations of Jah, repatriation, and the healing power of love, occasionally abetted by his wife Madge. Soft, subtle, sensuous — he's a one-of-a-kind balladeer in an otherwise electrified music. –RMS

○ **Haile I Hymn (Chapter 1) / MANGO**
Four extended tracks that epitomize spiritual longing; includes "Jah Heavy Load" and "I'm a Levi." –RMS

● **Are We a Warrior / MANGO**   1979
The title track and "Moulding" are two of reggae's most haunting meditations ever. –RMS

INNER CIRCLE

Reggae. Jacob Miller's backup band struggled on after their lead singer's untimely death in 1980, finally topping the reggae charts with the "Cops" TV theme "Bad Boys" a decade later. They continue to tour with new vocalist Carlton Coffie, mixing rock-oriented messages for the masses. –RMS

○ **One Way / RAS**   1987
"Bad Boys" highlights a return to form. –RMS

GREGORY ISAACS

Reggae. Nobody sings a love song quite like Gregory Isaacs, reggae music's "Cool Ruler." His voice is languidness personified, insinuating itself around snatches of rhythm like a duppy through a canefield. There's no insistence here, more an intimation. His is the voice of lullabies and laments and loneliness, of indignation and sufferation, of soothing and seething. Few singers in Jamaica have had as many hits as he, few his impressive durability. A recent issue of the *Reggae Directory* was devoted entirely to a discography of Isaacs, listing more than 400 releases in the past twenty years. Recording initially in the late 60s as part of the Concordes, he cut his first solo disc, "Another Heartache," for WIRL, the label founded by onetime Jamaican prime minister Edward Seaga. Almost immediately, Gregory decided to establish his own labels, Cash and Carry and African Museum, and produce himself. On his third album, *Extra Classics*, he found his own voice on such laidback laments as "Mr. Cop" and "Rasta Business," and most especially "Loving Pauper." The followup, *Mr. Isaacs*, joined him with Sly & Robbie and the Heptones and gave the world the four Ss: "Sacrifice," "Slavemaster," "Smile," and "Storm." As an example of the respect other artists accord Gregory, on the *Soon Forward* album he is backed by the voices of Junior Delgado, Dennis Brown, and Leroy Sibbles. The *Cool Ruler* collection continued the streak of classics, which culminated in 1983's *Night Nurse*, one of his all-time best-sellers. Throughout the 80s, Gregory released more music than any other artist of the time, sometimes offering six singles in the space of a week. Many of them were critically and commercially successful, such as "Rumours" and "Private Beach Party." Throughout his career, though, he has had frequent and well-publicized run-ins with the law, contributing to his image as the ultimate rude-boy artist, with his head in the clouds and his feet in the street. Ultimately, though, as Gregory says, "Only love can win the war!" –RMS

Feature Attraction / VP
Any of his albums on VP are worth hearing. –RW

Heartbreaker / ROHIT
A superb title track. –RW

Past & Future / VP
Hot, anguished leads. –RW

The Best of Gregory Isaacs / TASSA 1977
Misleading, since his output can't be compiled on a single (or even double) album. –RW

Extra Classic / ROHIT 1981
Outstanding. –RW

Mr. Isaacs / SHANACHIE 1982
Heartfelt, exuberant. –RW

Out Deh / MANGO 1983
Almost as brilliant vocally as *Night Nurse*, despite its erratic songs. –RW

○ **Night Nurse / MANGO** 1983
A classic. –RW

All I Have Is Love / TAD'S 1983
First-rate vocals, and great co-production by Isaacs and Alvin Ranglin. –RW

Private Beach Party / RAS 1985
Enchanting, if sometimes off-center, vocals. –RW

Victim / VP 1987
Excellent, with a harder edge. –RW

Watchman of the City / ROHIT 1987
Fine song selection. –RW

Red Rose for Gregory / RAS 1988
Some torrid and tepid moments. –RW

Sly & Robbie Present Gregory Isaacs / RAS 1988
A smart compilation. –RW

Call Me Collect / RAS 1990
Tart, and sometimes exemplary. –RW

● **Cool Ruler; Soon Forward Select / CAROLINE** 1990
A good twin set, pairing past releases. –RW

Dancing Floor / HEARTBEAT 1990
The excellent digital production fully captures his vocal quality. –RW

My Number One / HEARTBEAT 1990
A thorough compilation of past hits, plus rare cuts and remixes. –RW

Once Ago / CAROLINE 1990
As good as it gets, though after a while Isaacs falters. –RW

Come Again Dub / ROIR 1991
A good dub version of *Come Again*. –RW

Love Is Overdue / HEARTBEAT 1991
Soulful and vibrant. –RW

ISRAEL VIBRATION

Reggae. Israel Vibration consists of three young men who met in a polio rehab center. Their voices are among the holiest of Jamaican trinities. Dr. Dread of RAS Records arranged their reunion following a mid-80s period of breakup, and reggae fans have been thanking him ever since. Ever soulful, ever sure, their voices are so close to the roots you can hear the earth itself in their blending. Roots exemplaire. –RMS

○ **Forever / RAS** 1991
The flowing "Reggae on the River" celebrates some of America's most famous reggae locales; a satisfying and sultry collection. –RMS

Why You So Craven / RAS-ARRIVAL
Contains "Highway Robbery" and a great title track. A formative album produced by Junjo and engineered by Scientist. –RMS

THE ITALS

Reggae. Keith Porter and Ronnie Davis, joined by either Lloyd Ricketts or David Isaacs, are lead singers with big voices capable of filling a club without a mike. The result is often stunning as this powerful trio takes on songs with consciousness at their core, delivered with meltdown intensity. –RMS

○ **Brutal Out Deh / NIGHTHAWK** 1982
A powerhouse reggae trio. –RW

Give Me Power! / NIGHTHAWK 1983
Intense and energized. –RW

Easy to Catch / PRIORITY 1991
Good, but not vital. –RW

Cool & Dread / NIGHTHAWK
Nicely sung. A fine set of compositions. –RW

Early Recordings 1971-1979 / NIGHTHAWK
Groundbreaking records that brought this trio initial recognition. –RW

WINSTON JARRETT

Reggae. He came to Kingston to sing with his idol, Alton Ellis, whose voice is very similar to Jarrett's. Joining the Flames in the mid 60s to back Ellis, he soon branched out on his own to record a series of albums which often feature Marley and Ellis covers, and self-penned ghetto plaints as evocative as Bosch paintings. –RMS

○ **Kingston Vibrations / RAS** 1991
Strong, forceful, and rootical. –RMS

LINTON KWESI JOHNSON

Dub poetry. "I coined the phrase dub poetry because I was trying to argue that what the DJs in Jamaica were actually doing is poetry — improvised, spontaneous, oral poetry." Johnson's initial recorded work, *Dread Beat an' Blood* (recorded in the UK in 1978), provided an entirely different way to look at Caribbean rhythms and life, and had a major impact on Jamaican poet/performers like Mutabaruka, Michael Smith, and Oku Onuora. Johnson had emigrated with his family to England in 1963, eventually receiving an honors degree in sociology from the University of London. He joined the British arm of the Black Panthers in 1970, where he began writing poetry and reciting it publicly. His topics were revolutionary in both content and style — using Jamaican patois to reflect the realities of immigrant life in the ghettos of Britain. *Forces of Victory*, his second album, was a musical novel about oppression and confrontation, backed by the machine-gun force of Dennis Bovell's Dub Band. The followup *Bass Culture* expanded Johnson's themes to include meditations on the relationship of art to its audience, and was followed by *LKJ in Dub*, an instrumental version of his most powerful sessions. *Making History*, released in the Orwellian year of 1984, broadened his rhythmic horizons and added a pan-Caribbean flavor to his sound. A live album, summing up his career to date, came out the following year, after which Johnson claimed he had retired. But in 1991, he made a well-received return to the scene with *Tings and Times*, another multi-rhythm outing of indignant rhymes. Taking stage in a porkpie hat and modest demeanor, Johnson's understated performances belie the power of his carefully observed imagery and uncompromising calls for change. He is one of the true internationalizers of the form, a musical Marxist with upheaval on his mind. –RMS

Dread Beat an' Blood / CAROLINE 1978
Debut album with political statements about racism and inequality. A powerful forum. –MGN

★ **Forces of Victory / MANGO**   1979
Johnson's best studio date. Many of his finest numbers, recorded for the first time. –MGN

Bass Culture / MANGO   1980
A studio date, with this rapper at his best. –MGN

In Concert with the Dub Band / SHANACHIE   1984
A fine live show and a good introduction. –MGN

○ **LKJ in Dub / MANGO**   1989
Desert-island dub. Johnson's better early material, with vocals deleted. All instrumental, all outstanding. –MGN

Tings an' Times / SHANACHIE   1991
A wonderful reunion between Johnson and Bovell, plus several brilliant compositions. –RW

INI KAMOZE

Reggae. Ini Kamoze burst full-grown on the scene in 1983 with one of the touchstone albums of the 80s, the self-titled *Ini Kamoze.* Produced by Sly and Robbie at their creative peak, its half-dozen tracks are all essential. In 1985 *Settle with Me* continued with the jarring "Call the Police" and "Taxi for Me." His output has been erratic lately, but it's always compelling. –RMS

☆ **Ini Kamoze / ISLAND**   1983
Essential to the understanding of early-80s roots. Simply brilliant. –RMS

BARRINGTON LEVY

Reggae. A sweet midrange lovers rocker, Levy goes from strength to strength as he matures and internationalizes. From the late-70s *Bounty Hunter* to the recent US release *Here I Come,* Barrington is as satisfying as dancehall reggae gets. –RMS

Teach Me Culture / LIVE AND LEARN
First-rate vocals, good production. –RW

○ **Broader than Broadway: The Best of ... / PROFILE**   1990
A fine collection of his best hits of the 80s. –RMS

J. C. LODGE

Reggae. With her classic girlish pop voice, J. C. Lodge helped bankrupt producer Joe Gibbs when he failed to pay songwriter's royalties to Charley Pride for J. C.'s million-selling cover of "Someone Loves You, Honey." In the late 80s, her "Telephone Love" became a massive, long-lasting international hit penetrating the dancehalls as well as radio stations. She seems poised for a genuine breakthrough in the 90s by piecing rock, reggae, and soul into a highly seductive mosaic. –RMS

○ **Revealed / RAS**   1985
A remade "Can't Hurry Love" and other dancehall faves. –RMS

Tropic of Love / TOMMY BOY   1992
Her debut for a major label has both high and low points. Contains the smash "Telephone Love." –RW

MAD PROFESSOR

Dub. Neil Frazer built his own studio in London in the late 70s, encouraged by the inspired lunacy of Jamaica's Lee Perry. Although ridiculed at first by an unenthusiastic public, Frazer (the "Mad Professor") grew quickly to become the premier UK-based Perry-style producer for such artists as Pato Banton and Macka B. –RMS

At Checkpoint Charlie / ROIR
MP meets the German reggae band Puls der Zeit for crazy times. –MB

Escape to the Asylum of Dub / RAS   1983
These 1983 sessions are his most traditional dub, but they point the way to the craziness to come. Many female vocalists are heard here. –MB

☆ **Who Knows the Secret of the Mad Professor / RAS**
More creative instrumentation and plenty of dub madness

make this album a unique offering in a sometimes overdone field. –MB

Captures Pato Banton / RAS
Collaboration with Jamaican singer Pato Banton. Typically mind-expanding, with more pop intent and extending vocal tracks. –MB

Science & the Witchdoctor / RAS   1989
The professor's treatment of reggae backing-tracks is most inspired on Side Two. Lots of wild keyboards. –MB

Recaptures Pato Banton / ARIWA   1989
This collaboration with Jamaican singer Pato Banton is typically mind-expanding with more pop intent and extending vocal tracks. –MB

Psychedelic Dub / RAS   1990
More craziness, with guest appearances by singer Macka B and the legendary trombonist Rico. –MB

Hi-Jacked to Jamaica / RAS
Part II of the "Dub Me Crazy" series was actually done in Jamaica, rather than in the Professor's England home. –MB

BOB MARLEY   1945-1981

Reggae. Born of a middle-age white father and a teenage Black mother, Robert Nesta Marley transcended the humility of his rural beginnings to become not only a million-selling artist and stadium-filling entertainer but — more importantly — a nearly religious figure whose pleas for brotherhood and justice achieved universal anthemic status.

He began singing professionally at 16 with his self-penned "Judge Not!" It and its followup were not successful, and he returned to his ghetto neighborhood of Trenchtown to be tutored by Joe Higgs, a recording artist who coached promising youngsters like Marley, Bunny Livingstone, and Peter Tosh (who would become the Wailers). Signed in 1963 to Coxsone Dodd's influential, pace-setting Studio One, the Wailers saw their first release, "Simmer Down," become an instant #1. During the next two-and-a-half years, the group recorded over a hundred songs, and at one point in 1965 held five of the top ten slots on the Jamaican charts.

Forming their own label, Wail 'n Soul 'm, in 1966, the Wailers continued a series of local hits, with little financial remuneration. Following an album with Leslie Kong (*Best of the Wailers*), they hooked up with the seminal oddball producer, Lee Perry, and produced an amazing series of singles that are collected under a variety of names and remain their finest hour.

In 1972, Island Records prez Chris Blackwell signed the Wailers, but after two albums the group broke up, leaving Marley at the head of the band, to which he added a female backing trio, the I Threes. By 1975, Marley had gone clear as a revolutionary standard bearer, the inheritor of the 60s activist energy and hippie ganja enlightenment. Almost assassinated in 1976 in Kingston, Marley was given the UN Peace Medal on behalf of 500 million Africans in 1978 for his humanitarian achievements. He headlined a Peace Concert that same year in Jamaica, uniting the warring factions in the Kingston slums. But his greatest honor came when he was invited to headline the Zimbabwe Independence Celebrations in 1980. He outdrew the Pope in Milan, fathered eleven children by seven women, sold tens of millions of records worldwide, left a $30 million estate, wrote "the new Psalms," and died at 36 of melanoma (cancer). –RMS

The Best of the Wailers / BEVERLY'S   1969
Pressed under dozens of subsequent names, this is the Leslie Kong collection, reggae's first real album project. Includes "Soul Shakedown Party," "Soon Come," and "Stop the Train." A moving pep talk to themselves. –RMS

○ **Soul Rebels / TROJAN**   1970
Bare, haunting Lee Perry productions with the Wailers, echoing into eternity. –RMS

☆ **Catch a Fire / ISLAND / BB# 171**   1973
This was the first Wailers album on Island, their first with a real budget, their first international success. It is very nearly the birth of international reggae music — songs include Peter Tosh's "Stop That Train" and Marley's "Concrete Jungle," "Kinky Reggae," and "Stir It Up." –WR

☆ **Burnin' / ISLAND / BB# 151**   1973
Another extraordinary collection of songs with the Wailers, strongly featuring the vocal blend of Marley, Peter Tosh, and Bunny Livingstone on such songs as "Get Up, Stand Up," "I Shot the Sheriff," and "Burnin' and Lootin.'" The last album to feature the original group. –WR

☆ **African Herbsman / TROJAN**   1974
Sixteen Perry tracks, brilliant late-60s classics that may be the best work of the Wailers trio ever. "Put It On," "Sun Is Shining," "Small Axe," and "Brain Washing" are standouts. –RMS

☆ **Natty Dread / ISLAND / BB# 92**   1974
Adding a female vocal trio, Marley proved himself up to the task of carrying on without Tosh and Livingstone, delivering the memorable songs "Lively Up Yourself," "No Woman, No Cry," and "Them Belly Full (But We Hungry)." –WR

☆ **Live! / ISLAND / BB# 90**   1975
One of the great live albums of all time, this collection demonstrated not only Marley's charismatic presence as a leader, but also the power and subtlety of the Wailers as a band. It's one live recording that captures the feel of the concert perfectly. –WR

○ **Rastaman Vibration / ISLAND / BB# 8**   1976
Marley's breakthrough American album finds him discovering new polyrhythms while continuing to turn out powerful new songs, among them the title tune, "Who the Cap Fit," and "War." –WR

Exodus / ISLAND   1977
Kaya / ISLAND / BB# 50   1978
Laid-back ganja meditations, love songs, plus "Running Away," which tells the critics he hasn't gone soft. –RMS

☆ **Babylon by Bus / ISLAND / BB# 12**   1978
Double album. Arguably the most powerful live album in reggae's history, recorded with the Wailers at various international stops over a three-year period. Demonstrates how Marley remade his music constantly, especially in performance. –RMS

Survival / ISLAND / BB# 70   1979
Perhaps Marley's most militant statement, its bare-boned production put many off at first, but it returned him to the political realm in powerful fashion. "One Drop," "So Much Trouble," and "Babylon System" are among his best. –RMS

Uprising / ISLAND / BB# 45   1980
The last album Marley released in his lifetime, this collection is one of his most impassioned, especially the acoustic folk song that closes it, "Redemption Song." –WR

Confrontation / TUFF GONG / BB# 55   1983
Posthumous collection of singles and newly created tracks based on work tapes Marley left behind. Includes "Buffalo Soldier." –RMS

★ **Legend / ISLAND / BB# 54**   1984
This well-chosen 14-track greatest hits collection serves as an excellent introduction to the definitive reggae musician. Songs like "No Woman, No Cry" and "I Shot the Sheriff" remain among Marley's most moving efforts. Start here. –WR

○ **Soul Revolution 1 & 2 / TRLD**   1988
Thoughtful repackaging of 14 of the best Perry vocal sessions plus the only "legitimate" Wailers dub album ever, with four bonus tracks. –RMS

○ **Reggae Greats / MANGO**   1989
A good, although not formidable, compilation. –RW

All the Hits / ROHIT   1990
A great, but disgracefully packaged, 20-cut collection of works from 1969 to 1972, mostly Lee Perry productions. Includes the

only available copies of rarities like "Satisfy My Soul Jah Jah," abetted by ten dub tracks, eight of which have never appeared before. –RMS

Talkin' Blues / ISLAND   1990
Valuable, previously unissued sessions (1973-1975) including a rare radio interview. –RW

○ **One Love at Studio One / HEARTBEAT**   1991
The only Studio One collection pressed from the unaltered master tapes. There are 40 tracks, many never before available, including a 1965 rehearsal and several alternates. Essential 1963-1966 Bunny, Bob, and Peter. –RMS

RITA MARLEY

Reggae. Rita Anderson was the leader of the Soulettes, a Studio One trio in 1964, when she met her husband-to-be Bob Marley. She recorded with two separate lineups of her group in the 60s, backed several early Wailers recordings, then became a solo artist before helping form the I Threes in 1974 (along with Marcia Griffith and Judy Mowatt) to back Bob on his world-spanning tours through 1980. Following her husband's passing in 1981, she had the biggest hit of her career, a frothy pro-ganja delight called "One Draw." She devoted the 80s to guiding her children's careers in the Melody Makers, and now that the Marley estate's legal battles have been mostly settled, she continues to showcase her teenage-high voice again. –RMS

○ **Who Feels It Knows It / SHANACHIE**   1981
"One Draw" and several of Rita's greatest hits of the 70s. –RMS

ZIGGY MARLEY & THE MELODY MAKERS

Reggae. Raised in the studio, these four children of Bob and Rita Marley (Ziggy, Stephen, Sharon, and Cedella) are third-generation professionals. Their debut album was named after a song Bob wrote for them years earlier ("Children Playing in the Streets"), and now all four have become composers. "We are here to complete Bob's mission," says Ziggy, and they have had stupendous early success, becoming the first reggae group to top the US R&B singles chart with "Tumbling Down" and already winning two Grammies. Their material is revivifying modern roots music, with an occasional nod to dancehall in Stephen's attitude-rich speed-rapping. –RMS

Play the Game Right / CAPITOL   1985
An interesting concept, but underdeveloped potential. –RW

Hey World / CAPITOL   1986
Establishing a style, sound, concept, and direction. –RW

○ **Conscious Party / VIRGIN**   1988
A pivotal release, with special guest Keith Richards. –RW

Time Has Come - The Best of ... / CAPITOL   1988
A compilation of his formative material. –RW

One Bright Day / VIRGIN / BB# 26   1989
An excellent followup album that helped cement Ziggy's popularity. –RW

Jahmekya / ATLANTIC   1991
Possibly his best overall release, it didn't enjoy the same impact as other material. –RW

FREDDIE MCGREGOR

Reggae. "Little Freddie" joined the Clarendonians at the age of seven in 1963 and hasn't stopped singing since, first for Coxsone Dodd's Studio One, through the Soul Syndicate in the late 70s, then as his own producer in the 80s. *Bobby Bobylon* became one of the finest productions in Dodd's history, compiling a decade's worth of unreleased tracks into Freddie's masterpiece. Equally at home in lovers rock or Rasta roots, composer/singer McGregor is consistently satisfying. –RMS

Across the Border / RAS   1984
Another set of invigorating performances. –RW

All in the Same Boat / RAS   1986
Outstanding singing. –RW

Come On Over / RAS   1986
Super vocals. –RW

Big Ship / SHANACHIE   1988
A fine reissue of a classic session. –RW

Reggae Rockers / ROHIT   1989
More exciting, enthused vocals. –RW

Now / VP   1991
Always in good voice, here with unexceptional material. –RW

☆ **Bobby Bobylon / HEARTBEAT**
Freddie's overall best, the product of a decade's work, sung over nothing but classic Coxsone rhythms. –RMS

Live at the Town & Country Club / VP
A good choice of live settings. –RW

THE MEDITATIONS

Reggae. An early reggae trio whose smooth vocal stylings were tuned mainly to Rasta consciousness. "Tricked," "Woman Is like a Shadow," and "Running from Jamaica" are examples of harmony at its most effective. –RMS

○ **Greatest Hits / SHANACHIE**   1984
Just as it says, two sides of pleasing meditations. –RMS

MELODIANS

Rock-steady. This rock-steady vocal trio is led by soulful Brent Dowe. "Rivers of Babylon," featured on the crucial soundtrack of the *The Harder They Come* film, is a world-class standard, often covered but never duplicated. –RMS

○ **Pre-Meditation / SKY NOTE**   1986
"Swing and Dine" and "Don't Get Weary" make this an exemplary collection of the rock-steady style. –RMS

MIGHTY DIAMONDS

Reggae. The most consistent and long-running vocal trio in Jamaican musical history, consisting of the judge (Judge), the jester (Bunny), and the prophet (Tabby, the lead singer). Possessing one of the most achingly pure voices on earth, Tabby croons mini morality plays, limning life on the island of suffering with the precision of a microscope. –RMS

☆ **Right Time / SHANACHIE**   1976
The right album at the right time, with the right musicians, the right mix, and the right things to say. Eternal. –RMS

Reggae Street / SHANACHIE   1981
A fine, funky knockout. –RW

Indestructible / ALLIGATOR   1982
The only release that was issued and licensed on Alligator Records. –RW

Roots Is There / SHANACHIE   1982
Well done. –RW

Struggling / LIVE & LEARN   1985
A host of stirring numbers. –RW

The Real Enemy / ROHIT   1987
The title track is another memorable message piece. –RW

Get Ready / ROHIT   1988
Nice harmonies, but the leads vary in energy and quality. –RW

Go Seek Your Rights / FRONT LINE   1990
The title cut is among the best message tracks. –RW

JACOB MILLER

Reggae. One of reggae's brightest lights, Miller was abruptly snuffed out in a car crash in 1980, at which time he had become more popular than Marley among the in-crowd. Huge, bubbling, and boyish, Jacob blew spliff smoke in the face of authority (literally) and demanded that "we jam all night until daylight." His songs are timeless testaments to Jah and the healing power of herb. His loss is immense. –RMS

Jacob "Killer" Miller / RAS-TOP RANKING   1978
"Shaky Girl" and "Forward Ever," backed by the Fatman riddim section of the Lewis Brothers, peg Jacob's stuttering style for all time. –RMS

Natty Christmas / TOP RANKING   1978
Along with DJ Ray I, Jacob sends up Xmas; "Deck the Halls with Boughs of Collie" sets the pace. –RMS

○ **Reggae Greats / MANGO**   1984
The true greatest hits. –RMS

SUGAR MINOTT

Ragamuffin. Penning hit after hit for two decades, Minott is not only one of dancehall reggae's all-timers, but also a mentor to two generations of young stars developed by his Youth Promotions organization. Timely and touching, Minott at his best is utterly irresistible, as enticing as his nickname. –RMS

○ **Slice of the Cake / HEARTBEAT**   1984
"Buy out the Bar," "Level Vibes," "No Vacancy." All killer, no filler. –RMS

Extra Hot / RAS   1986
"Herbman Hustling" and other 80s standouts. –RMS

PABLO MOSES

Reggae. Moses possesses a nasal, untutored voice that seems perfectly matched to his ghetto-aware lyrical concerns. His masterpiece, *A Song*, juxtaposed that voice against avant-Euro-disco arrangements for a one-of-a-kind triumph. –RMS

☆ **A Song / MANGO**   1980
A masterpiece of forward-looking sophistication from a roots perspective. –RMS

In the Future / ALLIGATOR   1983
Reliable and dependable — frequently electrifying. –RW

Reggae Greats / MANGO   1984
A decent collection. –RW

Tension / ALLIGATOR   1985
This second album on Alligator Records tops the first. –RW

Live to Love / ROHIT   1988
A capable production, first-rate vocals. –RW

We Refuse / PROFILE   1990
Updated, forthright, and to the point. –RW

JUDY MOWATT

Reggae. Starting as lead singer for the Gaylettes in the mid 60s, Judy Mowatt has been one of reggae's leading female vocalists for a quarter century with no signs of diminishment. Originally planning to become a preacher, Mowatt posesses one of the most sweetly powerful voices in Jamaica, an instrument she places in the service of Rastafarian and feminist causes above all else.

After a series of local hits for her group or under the temporary pseudonym of Juliann, Mowatt became an international celebrity by helping form the I Threes, Bob Marley's backup singers, in 1974. When Marley built Tuff Gong, his own studio in Kingston, in 1977, Mowatt's seminal album *Black Woman* was the first to be recorded there. Considered by many critics to be the finest female album ever made in Jamaica, Mowatt wrote nearly all its tracks (Freddie McGregor and Bob Marley wrote the others). The title track and "Sisters Chant" are two ethereally beautiful cuts that encapsulate women's concerns everywhere and have achieved the status of anthems.

Following Bob Marley's death, Mowatt has carved out a successful solo career, releasing a series of carefully crafted albums of canny originals and clever covers ("Grooving" and "Sing Our Own Song") that have solidified her forefront position in reggae's pantheon. –RMS

☆ **Black Woman / SHANACHIE**   1979
The debut by this former Bob Marley backup vocalist blends touching romanticism with impassioned feminism and religious Rastafarian fervor. –JF

Only a Woman / SHANACHIE 1982
Wonderful vocals, fine production, and a quiet but discernible edge. –RW

JUNIOR MURVIN

Reggae. A high-pitched alto verging on falsetto distinguishes this languid singer from his peers. "Police and Thieves," produced by the wacky genius Lee Perry, is a prophetic standard which Murvin himself has rewritten several times in various versions. –RMS

○ **Police and Thieves / MANGO** 1977
A mid-70s golden age of reggae masterwork. –RMS

MUSICAL YOUTH

Reggae. One-hit wonders, these five UK-based boys conquered the world's charts in 1982 with the four-million seller "Pass the Dutchie." Too cute to last despite a massive promotional push, they fell apart within three years due to serious illness and poor material. –RMS

○ **Youth of Today / MCA / BB# 23** 1982
"Pass the Dutchie" and other juvenile concerns in assured studio productions. –RMS

MUTABARUKA

Dub Poetry. Jamaican dub poet Mutabaruka seems to have chosen recitation as his idiom because his message is too hot for any melody to hold. Unlike America's angry rappers, Mutabaruka's outrage is delivered at slow burn. Wit is as much a part of his repertoire as scathing social commentary, especially when indictments of hypocrisy wind so tightly around the wheel of contradiction. The result becomes an ontological question both larger and more absurd than geopolitical verities. The limitations of words themselves as a means of conveying objective truth is a favorite topic, but his frustrations at the subjectivity of language are tinged with playfulness. In addition to his recordings, Mutabaruka has published several volumes of his poetry. He operates a natural food store in Jamaica and lives in a mountain home. –BT

○ **Check It! / ALLIGATOR** 1983
Brilliant debut for Jamaica's hardest dub poet. Essential. –RMS

Outcry / SHANACHIE 1984
More militant poetry with a rock-hard beat. –RMS

The Mystery Unfolds / SHANACHIE 1986
Poems with more highly orchestrated backing. –RMS

Any Which Way ... Freedom / SHANACHIE 1989
His first release in three years was as potent, abrasive, and defiant as any of the prior dates. –RW

Blakk Wi Blak ... Kkk / SHANACHIE 1991
Strong, assertive, but nothing new. –RW

SONNY OKOSUNS

African. With 16 African album releases to his credit — many of them gold — Nigeria's Sonny Okosuns is one of the continent's most enduringly popular performers. Okosuns initially caught the pop music bug via Elvis and the Beatles, forming his first band, the Postmen, in 1964. In the early 70s, he helped usher in a back-to-African-roots trend with a stylistic mix of Western pop and local highlife he called "ozzidi." He later broadened it to include the rapidly spreading gospel of reggae. His diversity has kept him from being pigeonholed. He was featured in *Black Star Liner*, a 1983 anthology of African reggae, and more recently appeared on the anti-apartheid *Sun City* EP produced by Steve Van Zandt. His albums typically feature vocals in English as well as the Nigerian Ishan language. –BT

○ **3rd World / OTI**
This is one of his best African records. –JP

African Soldiers / PROFILE 1991
Okosuns expands his music, moving away from a predominantly reggae-based music by adding highlife, funk, soca, and some punchy horn chants. –JP

JOHNNY OSBOURNE

Reggae. A twenty-five-year career that shows no sign of letting up, from soulful reggae to a massive dancehall catalog. With his warm voice filled with conviction and yearning, he's one of the island's best, especially on standards like "Ice Cream Love," "Water Pumping," and countless rub-a-dub singles. –RMS

Rougher Than Them / VP
A standout, whether singing fast or slow. –RW

Cool Down / VP
An expert with reggae, soul, or even quasi-pop. –RW

☆ **Truth and Rights / STUDIO ONE**
With backup from Freddie McGregor and Jennifer Lara, one of Coxsone Dodd's most righteous and impressive outings. –RMS

AUGUSTUS PABLO

Reggae. The name hasn't gained the international recognition of Bob Marley's, but Augustus Pablo (Horace Swaby) is one of reggae's legitimate legends, a pioneer who flipped the genre completely upside down. Along with producer King Tubby, Pablo almost singlehandedly invented dub, where reggae's fat bass and popping drums are twisted and contorted until they crack like bullwhips and rumble like syncopated earthquakes. This is instrumental music: voices will emerge from the supple rhythms only to trickle into an echo-shrouded void, forsaking their contribution to the bedrock grooves. And Pablo's haunting splashes of melodica (which at times conjure images of Ennio Morricone's Sergio Leone soundtracks) give his music a sound that is immediately identifiable and as singular as anything Marley managed. As a youngster, Swaby hung around Kingston's jostling recording studios, watching the masters. There he met the original Augustus Pablo — the Upsetters keyboardist Glen Adams — who invented the name and played the melodica, the odd instrument that gave reggae its "Far East" sound. Adams moved to the States in 1971 and left the concept to Swaby, who began recording in 1972. Pablo released a string of brilliant singles over the next five or so years on his Rockers label. The best of those singles are collected on *Original Rockers*; his best early album is *King Tubby Meets Rockers Uptown* (1976). His more recent work has only occasionally matched the breathtaking innovation of the old stuff. Only the 1981 *East of the River Nile* has equaled his early triumphs. But he's still at it, occasionally striking a balance between the technical wizardry of his Tubby years and the slick production style of modern reggae. The results aren't always great but they are always interesting. –JF & RMS

Rebel Rock Reggae - This Is Augustus Pablo / HEARTBEAT 1972
Augustus Pablo formed his mysterious dub style on these early sessions, with Lee Perry producing and the best reggae session players backing. –MB

○ **King Tubby Meets Rockers Uptown / MESSAGE** 1976
A personal favorite, with Robbie Shakespeare and members of Bob Marley's band. –MB

Original Rockers / SHANACHIE 1979
Yet another heavy early work. –MB

★ **East of the River Nile / MESSAGE** 1981
Many regard this as Pablo's masterpiece, a superlative blending of earthy dub techniques with floating melodic lines in an exotic, oriental mode. –MB

Meet King Tubby Inna Fire House / SHANACHIE 1981
Another early gem, *Rockers Meet King Tubby Inna Fire House* shows the influence of dub pioneer King Tubby. –MB

Earth's Rightful Ruler / SHANACHIE   1983
Top session players and some vocal assistance from Hugh
Mundell, Delroy Williams, and others makes this an early
classic. –MB

Rising Sun / SHANACHIE   1985
This 1985 effort is a little slicker than others, but still
worthwhile. –MB

Eastman Dub / RAS   1988
Pablo extends his musical arsenal to include xylophone and
various keyboards in addition to his trademark melodica. –MB

Blowing with the Wind / SHANACHIE   1990
One of his newest recordings, with a Far Eastern sound
reminiscent of *East of the River Nile*. –MB

Rockers International Showcase / RYKODISC   1991
This compilation of Pablo tracks gives a nice cross-section of
his work. –MB

FRANKIE PAUL

Reggae. Nearly blind from birth, young Frankie Paul is one of
the most dependable dancehall singers of the 80s. With a
pleasant midrange voice, he eschews slackness in his well-
regarded live performances. Consistent and exemplary. –RMS

○ **Pass the Tu-Sheng-Peng / GREENSLEEVES**   1984
Frankie goes to the dance and lives to sing about it. Lots of
fun. –RMS

Get Closer / PROFILE   1990
Stalwart dancehall numbers. Good leads and production. –RW

LEE "SCRATCH" PERRY

Reggae. The "bumpity riddim" of Lee Scratch Perry, Jamaica's
most outrageous producer, percolates like an aural gallop
through a minefield in a hailstorm. Why is he named
"Scratch"? "Because," he cackles, "all things start from
Scratch. So check it out — who am I?"
Whenever a dub track is shattered by an earthshaking shriek
from the ninth dimension, whenever a glossolalia-quick burst
of word salad blurts over an acid-tinged assault of bass and
drums, whenever a "Croaking Lizard" grunts toward some
"Roast Fish and Cornbread" — chances are great that the
diminutive Mr. Perry has had his flexible fingers in it.
Starting as an assistant to Coxsone Dodd as he struggled to
begin his seminal Studio One in the mid 50s, Perry soon was
mixing, arranging, and engineering sessions. Shortly after, he
was producing and singing as well. By the late 60s he had
established a series of labels under the Upsetter umbrella and
forged one of the most critical links in the chain of reggae's
worldwide successes by joining his studio band with Bob
Marley, Peter Tosh, and Bunny Livingston (the Wailers). The
result was a pair of crucial albums that have never stopped
selling since 1970 — *Soul Rebels* and *African Herbsman* — re-
released all over the world in dozens of different titles, most
notably Trojan's recent vocal and dub triumph called *Soul
Revolution Vol. I and II*, an absolutely essential Wailers
compilation and a triumph of early reggae minimalism.
Perry suffers from a combination of glossolalia (speaking in
tongues) with phrases like "wizzy wizzy" for "wisdom," and
"graphalalia" (filling every available surface with writing).
He's a beat poet times ten, the original speed-rapper whose
Black Ark studio became home to a myriad noteworthy 70s
artists who were discovered by, or whose careers were
revivified by, Perry's take-no-prisoners production
techniques. These singers included the Heptones (the
essential "Party Time" album), Big Youth, the Mighty
Diamonds, Max Romeo ("War Ina Babylon"), Gregory Isaacs,
Delroy Wilson, U-Roy, I Roy, Junior Murvin ("Police and
Thieves"), and Dillinger, to name a tiny fraction. As the 80s
dawned, artists from Paul McCartney to the Clash beat a path
to the graffiti-scrawled door of Perry's Black Ark in Kingston.
During periods of controlled madness in the past decade,
Perry toured Europe with a stage lineup similar to Marley's,

right down to the three female backup singers. Recently, he
married an allegedly titled Swiss woman and began spending
half of each year in the Alps. His music is unmistakable still:
wacky, wondrously histrionic, and persistent as a jackhammer
to the brain. Long may he rave! –RMS

● **Reggae Greats / MANGO**
Perry productions featuring the Heptones, Junior Murvin,
Max Romeo, Prince Jazzbo, and the upsetter himself — fairly
straightforward but brilliant song settings. –MB

Chicken Scratch / HEARTBEAT   1980
Mid-60s material with the Upsetter from Studio One — Perry
is the featured vocalist on singles with the Wailers, Rita
Marley, the Skatalites, and more. –MB

Lord God Muzick / HEARTBEAT   1981
Recent dementia, recorded with the Upsetters after a
European tour and dedicated to his new European and
American fans ... hmm! –MB

○ **Roast Fish Collie Weed & Corn / VP**   1982
A fairly typical all-Jamaican effort done at Perry's Black Ark
studio (before he burned it down). –MB

Scratch Attack / RAS   1985
Two albums on one CD — the imaginative *Chapter 1* and the
dubbed-out *Blackboard Jungle Dub* session, from Perry's own
Black Ark studio. –MB

From the Secret Laboratory / MANGO   1990
Produced by modern dub master Adrian Sherwood, with
Perry presiding regally over a crew of Jamaican, English, and
American players. –MB

○ **Some of the Best / HEARTBEAT**   1991
Odds and ends from the reggae/rockers era (1968-72), with
Bob Marley and the Wailers, Junior Byles, Linval Thompson,
and the ever-creative Upsetters. –MB

MAXI PRIEST

Lovers rock. Britain-based lovers rocker Maxi Priest is one of
the 80s great crossover success stories, making chart-toppers
on both sides of the Atlantic. A pleasant, easygoing vocal
manner coupled with a sexy stage presence have yielded
consistent hits — the outlook is good for a long international
career. –RMS

○ **Bonafide / CHARISMA**   1990
Priest scored a #1 pop hit with "I Just Want to Be Close to You"
from this album, which is more pop/R&B with a reggae touch
than it is real reggae. –RW

Maxi Priest / ATLANTIC
This bends the reggae/pop equation back toward the
crossover side. –RW

PRINCE FAR I

DJ. With a voice deeper and more darkly shaded than a mid-
ocean trench, Prince Far I rapped tales of eccentrics like
Bedward, "the Flying Preacher," and prophesied the
holocausts of these "last days," before being murdered in his
bed at the close of the 80s. –RMS

☆ **Black Man Land / CAROLINE**
A reissue of his penetrating vocal raps on the Virgin/Caroline
label. –MB

Dubwise / CAROLINE
More Virgin/Caroline recordings reissued, with an emphasis
on spacey dub mixes. –MB

Musical Revue / ROIR   1982
A rare live recording from 1982, with his celestial band, the
Suns of Arqa. –MB

Cry Tuff Dub Encounter IV / ROIR   1983
A heavily dubwise adventure with the Arabs. One of the first
Jamaican efforts to use English avant-garde musicians. –MB

Voice of Thunder / TROJAN   1983
This showcases his earthshaking vocals, conscious lyrics, and
sharp backing tracks. –MB

SHABBA RANKS

Reggae. The 1992 reggae Grammy winner, this dancemaster is noted for his lewd and leering lyrics that represent the polar opposite of reggae's spiritual and unifying concerns. Hugely popular, with major label support, Ranks is Jamaica's DJ emissary to the weird world of the 90s. –RMS

○ **As Raw As Ever / CBS**   1991
This is an X-rated hip-hop reggae crossover that won a Grammy. –RMS

RAS MICHAEL & THE SONS OF NEGUS

Reggae. Negus is a title of Ethiopian Emperor Haile Selassie, the Almighty God of the Rastafarian movement, and none pays him more eloquent homage than Ras Michael and his group. This is the beat of the heart, based on the original "instrument of ten strings," the hand-beaten drum. On *Dadawah* in 1975, Michael took a religious ceremonial gathering as the basis for an album of elegant poetry and raw, visceral power. Later, eschewing minimalism, such works as *Promised Land Sounds* added electronics and produced a primeval psychedelia without compare in Jamaican history. This is the sound of the Roots Church in the 21st century, highly charged hymns for humanity's future survival. –RMS

★ **Dadawah / TROJAN**
The best Rasta testament from the 70s. Spin it and become a "Man in the Hills." –RMS

○ **Rastafari / TOP RANKING**
More Rasta gospel music, including the essential "None a Jah Jah Children No Cry" and "Mr. Brown." –RMS

Promised Land Sounds / LIONS GATE   1980
Four extended Nyabinghi jams; the Grateful Dread meets 2001. –RMS

Rally Round / SHANACHIE   1985
More Rasta standards from their primary musical spokesman. –RMS

RASTAFARI ELDERS

Reggae. Doctor Dread, head of DC's RAS Records, brought a touring group of Rastafarian men and women into the studio in 1990 (people with names like Ras Headful and Bongo Shep) and came out with one of the only recordings ever of a legitimate "grounation." This Rastafarian religious gathering is replete with preaching, testimony, and timeless music, the essential heartbeat "riddim" upon which all Jamaican music of the past 30 years has been based. –RMS

○ **Rastafari Elders / RAS**   1990
The single best place to begin a study of Rastafarian wisdom and beliefs, set to truly heartfelt music. –RMS

MAX ROMEO & THE UPSETTERS

Reggae. His leering 60s UK smash "Wet Dream" was really (said Max) about "a leaky roof." In the 70s he made several roots reggae standards, most notably for producer Lee Perry. Although still active, he's had no material in the 80s that equals his talent and sweet intensity. –RMS

○ **War Ina Babylon / MANGO**   1976
One of Lee Perry's most perfect 70s productions, especially on the chilling title track and "One Step Forward." –RMS

ROOTS RADICS

Reggae. The key studio band of the 80s in Jamaica, they've recorded with everyone from Gregory Isaacs (his greatest, *Night Nurse*) to Bunny Wailer (*Rock & Groove*). With Dwight Pinkney on finger-picked guitar, Flabba Hold on wicked punchy bass, Style Scott on hard metronomic drums, and Bingy Bunny on precise rhythm guitar, along with Steelie on scintillating keyboards, they set the standard for a decade of increasing, unceasing, international penetration of Jamaican music. –RMS

○ **World Peace Three / HEARTBEAT**   1992
Includes the great Garvey song, "International Hero." The culmination of two decades' work in the studios. –RMS

SCIENTIST

Dub. The premier UK dub master of the rockers style, Scientist produced a super series of great Greensleeves dub outings in the early 80s. His was the last gasp of critical versioning prior to the digital onslaught of the Mad Professor and other synthesists. –RMS

★ **Tribute to King Tubby Dub / ROIR**
Top-notch knob twisting and echo-chamber overload from this early dub stylist. –MB

Vampires / GREENSLEEVES
Classic Radics tracks from producer Junjo Lawes, with monstrous overdubs. –RMS

○ **Heavyweight Dub Champion / GREENSLEEVES**   1980
Bone-crushing, psychedelic, heart-stopping romps with surprisingly radical effects. –RMS

Scientist Encounters Pac-Man / GREENSLEEVES   1982
One of the most futuristic of Scientist's many Greensleeves albums, now all out of print. –MB

ROY SHIRLEY

Reggae. Perhaps the quirkiest, most unique voice in Jamaica, Roy Shirley twists, contorts, whines, and prowls his way through three octaves in his course of musical mayhem. "Hold Them" may be the tune that birthed rock-steady — it is indubitably a classic. His output is often hysterically funny and nearly always compelling in a "My God how can he get away with that" fashion. Though it's difficult to find, it's worth every effort. –RGS

○ **Return of the High Priest / WEED BEAT**   1982
The Jamaican Frank Zappa at the roots of the outrageous. –RMS

SKATALITES

Reggae. Ska was Jamaica's first indigenous creation, a compelling mix of fast R&B, Rastafarian African rhythms, and Afro-Cuban percussion highlight. This double-time delight ruled Jamaica from 1962 to 1966, and none played it more convincingly than its creators, the Skatalites. Led by a mentally disturbed world-class trombonist named Don Drummond, the Skatalites were composed of the top instrumentalists on the island at the time: Tommy McCook, Roland Alphonso, and "Ska" Campbell on tenor sax; Lester Stering on alto; Karl Bryan on baritone; "Dizzy Johnny" Moore and Baba Brooks on trumpet; Lloyd Brevett on bass; Lloyd Knibbs on drums; Jackie Mittoo on piano; and Lyn Tait and Jah Jerry on guitar. This is a roster of Jamaica's musical gods, the foundation of all that would come out of this tiny land of two million people to influence the entire world of music for the next 30 years. Rock-steady, reggae, rockers, dub — all are merely tempo reworkings of the skipping ska beat.

It is remarkable, then, to note that the Skatalites existed for a mere 14 months. As 1965 dawned, Drummond murdered his wife, and was put away in "de Bellevue" mental hospital, where he died a couple years later. The band then broke up into several different lineups, most notably Tommy McCook and the Supersonics, and the Soul Brothers. Their rhythm slowed in 1966 to the rock-steady, a twin result of Drummond's loss and a torpid steamy summer during which people no longer wanted to dance as frenetically as they had before. But ska underwent period revivals, most notably among British skinheads in the late 60s; Northern British two-tone skanksters in 1980; and massive movements in the 80s in places as far afield as Brussels, Tokyo, and California. Today, ska has achieved a permanent place in the world's beats, as alive, fresh and exciting as rock & roll. Yet even now no interpretation sounds more compelling than the original Studio One recordings made by ska's masters, the Skatalites. –RMS

○ **Ska Authentic / STUDIO ONE**
Early 60s ravers, including "Lee Oswald" and "Bridge View" (any Studio One Skatalites collection is worth owning). –RMS

● **Scattered Lights / ALLIGATOR**   1984
Recorded from 1962 to 1965 for Justin Yap's Top Deck, and featuring some of the final shots of Don Drummond. Admirable. –RMS

SLY & ROBBIE

Dub. The Rhythm Twins — Sly Dunbar (drums) and Robbie Shakespeare (bass) — have provided the rhythm section for many records since the mid 70s. They were one of the major creators of the Rockers sound with the Revolutionaries band. Featuring lots of high-hat, and a massive rhythmic barrage, Sly's drumming style has had great influence on others, popularizing the use of syndrums in the late 70s. Sly & Robbie helped combine hip-hop and Jamaican "riddims." Members of Black Uhuru at its peak Grammy-winning period, they have backed Bob Dylan, Carly Simon, Peter Tosh, and Grace Jones, as well as collaborating with Bill Laswell and Bootsy Collins on their solo albums. –RMS & ED

Reggae Greats / MANGO   1984
A good sampling of dub from this in-demand rhythm duo on this installment of Island/Mango's *Reggae Greats* series. –SWB

Language Barrier / ISLAND   1985
Sly & Robbie team with producer Bill Laswell for an edgy dub set. Guests include Herbie Hancock, Bob Dylan, Afika Bambaataa, and Manu DiBango. –SWB

○ **Rhythm Killers / ISLAND**   1987
Another session with Bill Laswell. The all-star guest lineup includes Bootsy Collins, Bernie Worrell, Bernard Fowler, Henry Threadgill, Nicky Skopelitis, Shinehead, and Pat Thrall. Features a killer version of the Ohio Players hit "Fire," with funky Bootsy Collins grooves throughout the album. –SWB

SLIM SMITH

Reggae. In the 60s, Slim Smith was one of the lead singers of the seminal Techniques, then went on to form (with Jimmy Riley) the Uniques. Often compared to Curtis Mayfield (his major influence), Smith never achieved the financial rewards his extensive, big-selling output deserved. He died tragically in the early 70s when he punched his fist through a glass door in frustration and bled to death before he could summon help. One of Jamaica's most venerated and gifted interpreters, virtually everything he cut is worth owning, particularly if your tastes run to Impressions-style harmonics. –RMS

○ **Born to Love / HEARTBEAT**   1991
Includes the eternal "You Don't Care" and the oft-versioned "Rougher Yet." –RMS

TAMLINS

Reggae. Carlton Smith, Junior Moore, and Derrick Lara (the Tamlins) are among the most widely respected backup singers in reggae, especially for their years of international touring in support of Peter Tosh. They have backed John Holt, Delroy Wilson, Pat Kelly, Marcia Griffiths, and a host of others, as well as recording on their own. Lara's ethereally high lead vocals bring to mind the best of 70s Philly soul music, a style they have often covered. –RMS

○ **Love Devine / HEARTBEAT**
Soothing, often enjoyable, but not substantive. –RW

THIRD WORLD

Reggae. Third World's cover of "Now That We Found Love" is an R&B radio staple, along with the reggae classic "96 Degrees in the Shade." Comprised of well-educated and -connected uptown Jamaicans, Third World blends a sophistication in instrumentation (note guitarist Cat Coore's live cello

excursions) with a pop consciousness that seems ironically unable to penetrate the mainstream market despite years of major label attempts. –RMS

○ **96 Degrees in the Shade / MANGO**   1977
The album that cemented their stateside popularity. –RW

Rock the World / CBS / BB# 186   1981
Well-meaning, this juggles R&B, pop, and reggae. –RW

All the Way Strong / CBS / BB# 137   1983
Teetering on the pop tightrope. –RW

Reggae Greats / MANGO   1985
A decent place to start on reggae's longest-lasting pop ensemble. –RW

Sense of Purpose / CBS   1985
A-1 production and arrangements. –RW

Hold On to Love / CBS   1987
Solid vocals and production on a weak musical menu. –RW

You've Got the Power / COLUMBIA / BB# 63   1989
Some above-average ballads and social cuts. –RW

TIGER

Dancehall. Gruff-voiced 80s DJ Tiger leaped to prominence in the Jamaican dancehalls with an anti-fat rap called "No Wanga Gut." A scintillating live performer, Tiger overcame an extended period of substance abuse to return in the early 90s and regain his growly crown. –RMS

○ **Me Name Tiger / RAS**   1986
"No Wanga Gut" and "Puppy Love" anchor his US debut. –RMS

ANDREW TOSH

Reggae. Eldest son of the late Wailer Peter Tosh, Andrew made his debut at his father's funeral in 1987, wowing the mourners with his physical and vocal similarities to Peter. Two promising albums later, Andrew is looked upon as one of conscious reggae's greatest hopes. A tour with the Wailers in 1991 solidified his live reputation. With strong material, he could fill his famous father's shoes in a manner similar to that of Ziggy Marley. –RMS

Original Man / ATTACK   1988
Niney-produced debut, with lots of fine covers of Tosh's dad Peter. –RMS

○ **Make Place for the Youth / TOMATO**   1989
Self-penned mini-dramas showcase Andrew's promising growth. –RMS

PETER TOSH   1944-1987

Reggae. In the early Wailers lineup, Winston Hubert McIntosh (Peter Tosh) stood apart from the other members not only because of his six-foot-plus height but because of his boasty-boy attitude. He was known as the "stepping razor" after a song Joe Higgs had written, and his knife-sharp temper could whittle many a bad man down to size. But he had a soft, extremely humorous side as well, as evidenced in his frequent word play: he complained about the "crime ministers who shit in the House of Represent-a-Thief" and called America "A-sada-ca, because there is nothing merry about it."
Tosh joined up with Bunny Wailer and Bob Marley in 1962, and they rehearsed nearly two years before they made their Studio One debut with "Simmer Down." Tosh played guitar, melodica, piano, and organ on many of their early tracks, and even played behind American pop star Johnny Nash's Columbia Records sessions in the late 60s, when Nash had hired the Wailers as songwriters. By 1973, Tosh felt the need to pursue a solo career because of the mass of material he had written and his dissatisfaction with Island Records boss Chris Blackwell. *Legalize It* was his debut in 1976, remaking many of his earlier Jamaican recordings and giving the marijuana movement its most potent anthem in the title track, which Tosh would perform not once but twice in his 70s live concerts.

A firm opponent of the hypocritical "shitstem," Tosh was a favorite target of Babylon's legal forces. Police in Jamaica beat him nearly to death on at least three occasions, and he bore the scars till his death. *Equal Rights*, 1977's followup, provided a key line that echoed 15 years later in the mouths of LA rioters: "I don't want no peace, I want equal rights and justice!" The Rolling Stones, impressed by Tosh's ferocious and unflinching posture, signed him to their fledgling label and released *Bush Doctor* in 1978, another series of hymns and harrangues. *Mystic Man* (1979) and *Wanted: Dread & Alive* (1981) kept a militant attitude while trying to cross over to the mainstream that Marley had conquered, without achieving anything near Marley's success. Following 1983's *Mama Africa* and a live album from that tour, Tosh disappeared for four years, seeking advice from traditional medicine men in Africa and trying to extricate himself from various recording agreements when he found his records released in South Africa against provisions in his contracts. In 1987, shortly after the release of *No Nuclear War*, Tosh was assassinated at his home in Kingston. Only one of the three gunmen responsible was arrested; he was sentenced to hang after a brief trial. Like Marley, Tosh left at least ten children and no will. A brilliant documentary *Peter Tosh: Red X-Stepping Razor* was released in 1992, and there is hope that at least one more album will come out of the vaults. –RMS

Legalize It / CBS 1976
Tosh cut this album after leaving the Wailers, but used virtually the entire Wailers band (minus Bob Marley) to do it. His "Legalize It," a plea about marijuana with a twist ("I'll advertise it"), is still winning. –WR

★ **Equal Rights / CBS** 1977
Tosh's most political album includes his own version of "Get Up, Stand Up," as well as the chilling "Stepping Razor." The music, anchored by Sly & Robbie, is as tough as the lyrics. –WR

Bush Doctor / ROLLING STONES 1978
"Creation" is Genesis set to music; "Moses" continues the story; "Don't Look Back" teams Tosh with Jagger. An appealing collection. –RMS

Wanted Dread & Alive / CAPITOL 1981
Great Binghi roots-rave on "Rastafari Is," plus the gorgeous ballad "Fools Die" and other mixed pleasures. –RMS

○ **Mama Africa / CAPITOL** 1983
A strong collection with the hit "Johnny B. Goode" and remakes of "Maga Dog" and "Stop That Train." –RMS

No Nuclear War / CAPITOL 1987
His valedictory album, with "Lesson in My Life," strangely foreshadowed his murder by a "friend." –RMS

THE TWINKLE BROTHERS

Reggae. Norman Grant is the unifying factor in the various lineups of the Twinkles over the past 20 years. Possessing a rootical North Coast sensibility, as opposed to the harder-edged Kingston vibe, the Twinkle Brothers' music is Rastafarian belting at its best. Grant is even a big star in reggae-loving Poland, where he has cut five albums for that market. –RMS

○ **Live at Reggae Sunsplash / SUNSPLASH** 1984
Superb vocals and a representative live set. –RW

★ **Free Africa / FRONT LINE** 1990
Grab anything you can find by this tremendous outfit. –RW

U-ROY

DJ. In the late 60s, Ewart Beckford (U-Roy) almost single-handedly invented the modern DJ rap style in Jamaica by toasting on the sound system of pioneer King Tubby, who was the first engineer to mix reverb and echo effects on deconstructed rhythm tracks. This led directly to the Jamaican peculiarity of having only one song per 7-inch single (the A-side being the vocal, the B-side being the "dub version" or rhythm bed that any local toaster could "skank" over with

the events of the day). But U-Roy remains the most trickily tasteful exemplar of the style, due largely to his uncanny choice in tracks over which to toast, creating ad hoc dialogs with the singer, commenting on and responding to the lyrics in such classics of the form as "On the Beach," "Wear You to the Ball," and "Tide Is High," not to mention the royalty-ridiculing 70s scat "Chalice in the Palace," on which he invites the Queen herself to suck on the ganja pipe (chalice). Still active, living in Los Angeles, he is now referred to respectfully as Daddy U-Roy. –RMS

○ **Dread in Babylon / FRONT LINE** 1983
It's this veteran rapper's best album, comparable to any in this idiom. –MGN

BUNNY WAILER

Reggae. Born Neville O'Reilly Livingston and dubbed Bunny Wailer, this crucial Jamaican singer and songwriter was raised as Bob Marley's brother from the age of nine. As co-founder of the Wailers (along with Peter Tosh), Bunny gave high chromatic shadings to some of the most exhilarating harmonies ever pressed on wax, the equal of the finest work done by their contemporaries, the Impressions. Bunny's "Pass It On" was one of the standout tracks on the final album the Wailers did together as a trio, 1973's *Burning*. Three years later, Bunny released his first solo project, one of reggae's most majestic achievements, the roots classic *Blackheart Man*, which included hymnlike chants with titles like "Dreamland," "Bide Up," and "Rastaman." Bunny's baritone has been showcased in as many as three albums a year, most notably *Struggle* (1980); *Bunny Wailer Sings the Wailers* (1980's collection of covers); *Rock & Groove* (1981 dancehall classics); *Live* (recorded at his first solo concert in Kingston in December 1982); and *Liberation* (1988's consciousness-raiser that is the acknowledged peer of his spectacular debut album *Blackheart Man*). He won a Grammy in 1991 for *Time Will Tell*, a tribute collection of covers of Bob Marley songs. He has toured abroad twice, trying to overcome his reputation as reggae's most reclusive artist, backed by members of the original Skatalites, Sly & Robbie, and the Roots Radics. A spectacular show at NY's Madison Square Garden (1986) has been released on video. Today Bunny is obsessed with reaching the teenage dancehall crowd, attempting to wean them away from the predominant slackness of the form and back to a recognition of the truth and rights that were reggae's original concerns. He also feels the need to continue the work of his late partners, Tosh and Marley, bringing to oppressed people everywhere the twin messages of hope and the faith to carry on. –RMS

Gumption / SHANACHIE

★ **Blackheart Man / MANGO** 1976
Maybe his best, certainly a classic. –RW

Protest / MANGO 1977
Inspirational. –RW

Bunny Wailer Sings the Wailers / MANGO 1980
As poignant a tribute as you'll ever hear. –RW

Struggle / MANGO 1980
The title cut is anthemic; everything else is superb. –RW

○ **Live / SOLOMONIC** 1983
Tough to find, but worth the effort. –RW

Roots Radics Rockers Reggae / SHANACHIE 1983
A reggae original runs the genre's gamut. –RW

Marketplace / SHANACHIE 1985
Entertaining and enriching. –RW

Rootsman Skanking / SHANACHIE 1987
Emphatic vocals. –RW

Rule Dance Hall / SHANACHIE 1987
Controversial content, but outstanding. –RW

Liberation / SHANACHIE 1989
A textbook Wailer outing. –RW

Time Will Tell / SHANACHIE 1991
Heartwarming, Grammy-winning remakes of Marley compositions. –RMS

WAILING SOULS

Reggae. If lead singer Winston "Pipe" Matthews sounds like a slightly higher-pitched version of Bob Marley, it may be because he was tutored by the same teacher (Joe Higgs) in the same yard that produced the Wailers. The Souls have gone through many different lineups, but Pipe and his partner Lloyd "Bread" McDonald have survived as a duo, and currently record for Columbia Records. Through most of their history, however, they were one of reggae's only quartets with shimmering harmonies that gave voice to Jamaican folk-sayings and righteous religious rumblings. –RMS

★ **Wild Suspense / MANGO** 1979
Brilliant quartet triumphs, echoing the harmonic heights of the early Wailers. Virtually their greatest hits, backed by Sly and Robbie. –RMS

Firehouse Rock / SHANACHIE-GREENSLEEVES 1981
Junjo-produced, with the Radics mixed by Scientist at King Tubby's. What's not to like? –RMS

○ **The Best of the Wailing Soul / EMPIRE** 1984
Channel One classics produced by Jo Jo Hookim and backed by the Revolutionaries. –RMS

○ **All Over the World / CHAOS-COLUMBIA** 1992
A genre-busting all-star duo debut; guest shots from L. Shankar to U- Roy. –RMS

YABBY YOU

Reggae. Yabby You (Vivian Jackson) is the odd-man-out in roots reggae, professing deep conviction in traditional Christian beliefs while sporting a mane of dreadlocks. His seventeen albums are spare, dark, and meditative, a turgid view of the "downpression" of ghetto living, chanted in ominous fugues. –RMS

Conquering Lion / PROPHET 1977
Debut beauties, deliciously menacing and admonitory. –RMS

○ **Deliver Me from My Enemies / PROPHET** 1977
Timeless social commentary and Rasta prophecy. –RMS

● **One Love, One Heart / SHANACHIE** 1983
An anthology of some of his greatest hits: what to bring when you summer in the Cave of the Dead Sea Scrolls. –RMS

YELLOWMAN

Dancehall. DJ Winston "Yellowman" Foster, a tall, lanky Jamaican albino, became the biggest star in the wake of Bob Marley's death in 1981. He released over four dozen records in 1982 alone and was the undisputed star of that year's Sunsplash in Montego Bay. Yellowman knows how to work a crowd to a frenzy, although he is highly controversial because of his homophobic, anti-feminist lyrics and his extremely "slack" style of toasting, which have made him as many fans as detractors. He continues to perform internationally, but his recorded output has diminished to a trickle in the 90s. –RMS

○ **One in a Million / SHANACHIE** 1989
One of the few non-slack albums in his career, this boasts Yellowman's signature rap "Mad Over Me" and serious scenarios of guns and fire. –RMS

REGGAE COLLECTIONS

○ **Best of Reggae Dance Hall - Vol. 1 / ROHIT**
An outstanding retrospective, with many unknown or obscure artists. –RW

Best of Reggae Dance Hall - Vol. 2 / ROHIT

○ **The Best of Reggae Sunsplash / SUNSPLASH**
Second-level production, first-level vocals, and an energetic audience response. –RW

☆ **Best of Studio One - Vol. 1 / HEARTBEAT**
A stunning series devoted to the voluminous output of Clement Dodd's Jamaican studio. The first two volumes cover the best stuff from the 60s and 70s, from shimmying ska to the rock-steady period. –JF

Best of Studio One - Vol. 2 / HEARTBEAT

Best of Studio One - Vol. 3 / HEARTBEAT
This third installment features a scalding set of instrumentals, full of crashing cymbals, twisting bass lines, and razor-sharp guitars. –JF

○ **Black Star Liner / HEARTBEAT**
Subtitled *Reggae from Africa*, this makes a welcome antidote to most of the computerized dancehall beats that are making Jamaican reggae so bland. Includes the smash hit "Fire in Soweto" by Sonny Okosuns as well as work by Victor Uwaifo, Cloud 7, and Bongos Ikwue. –JP

○ **Calling Rastafari / NIGHTHAWK**
An excellent anthology, with gems from Culture, Itals, and others. –RW

○ **Club Ska '67 / MANGO**
This decent assortment of latter-day ska tracks serves as a nice complement to the label's *Intensified* series. –JF

Country Man (Soundtrack) / MANGO 1983
A double album of fab remakes of Toots and Marley and a dozen other early-80s performers. –RMS

○ **Dance Hall Ensemble - Vol. 1 / COSMIC FORCE**
Good variety. A nice cross-section of modern reggae. –RW

○ **Dance Hall Session / RAS**
This is an excellent retrospective featuring red-hot dancehall tunes. –RW

Dance Hall Sizzling - Vol. 1 / VP
A trio of burners, many unheard in America except in dance halls. –RW

Dance Hall Sizzling - Vol. 2 / VP

Dance Hall Sizzling - Vol. 3 / VP

○ **Dance Hall Stylee - Best of Reggae Dancehall / PROFILE**
A comprehensive collection geared toward American audiences. –RW

Dance Hall Superstars - 90s / ROHIT
A comprehensive set, although production and technical qualities vary. –RW

○ **Fresh Reggae Hits / POW WOW**
Everything from sultry soul to funky and funny contemporary material. –RW

Fresh Reggae Hits - Vol. 2 / POW WOW
More of the same. –RW

○ **Great British Reggae Roll Call 1989 / I.R.S.**
Part of a series that highlights songs and "toasts" of top reggae Brits from Papa Levi to Dee Sharpe. –RW

Greensleeves Sampler / SHANACHIE
This is rare and hard-to-get reggae. –RW

Greensleeves Sampler 2 / SHANACHIE
An extra helping of some superb and seminal cuts. –RW

☆ **Groove Yard / MANGO**
If you're looking for a crash course in reggae, this is the place. The biggest names from Island Records with their biggest hits on this generous 70-minute set. Includes key songs from Jimmy Cliff, the Melodians, Augustus Pablo, Junior Murvin, and 15 others. –JF

○ **Heartbeat Reggae / HEARTBEAT**
A tremendous collection, culled from labels on the Heartbeat roster. –RW

Intensified! - Original Ska 1962-66 / MANGO
In-depth two-disc overview of some seminal reggae, highlighted by choice cuts by the Maytals, the Skatalites, and Justin Hines. –JF

More Intensified! - Vol. 2 (1963-1967) / MANGO 1988
○ **Legends of Reggae Music / ROHIT**
An authoritative collection of top reggae stars and cuts. −RW
○ **Raggadubbin' U.K. / ROIR**
A good overview of the British scene, with obscure sounds and names. −RW
○ **Ram Dancehall / MANGO**
Focusing on current dancehall hits. −RW
☆ **RAS Tapes - Reggae Jamdown / RYKODISC**
An essential set that compiles authentic and hard-to-find reggae. −RW
RAS Tapes - Vol. 2 (Nice Up Dancee) / RYKODISC
More topflight cuts. −RW
○ **Reggae Classics / DCC**
A good collection, but most of the selections are available elsewhere. −RW
○ **Reggae Dance Party / RAS**
These cuts focus on modern-day dance and "computerized" reggae. −RW
Reggae Dancehall Classics - Vol. 1 / ROHIT
Strictly for dances. −RW
○ **Reggae Greats - Strictly for Lovers / MANGO**
A high-caliber review of artists who popularized the "lovers" style. −RW
☆ **Reggae Greats - Strictly for Rockers / MANGO**
Here is another well-done overview, this time for "rockers" artists. −RW
○ **Reggae House Music - Vol. 3 / VP**
A good set that highlights the reggae/house confluence. −RW
Reggae It's Fresh / TAD'S
Good, but not state-of-the-art. −RW
Reggae Legends / ROHIT
More from the prolific vaults of Rohit. −RW
○ **Reggae Sunsplash '81 / ELEKTRA**
Tribute to Bob M. A heartfelt tribute to a departed genius, although the performances don't always match the passion of the occasion. −RW
○ **Reggae Superstars - Vol. 2 / ROHIT**
A good addition to Rohit's anthology line. −RW

Rockers (Soundtrack) / MANGO 1980
A super soundtrack to the 1980 film. −RMS
☆ **Ska Beats / ROIR**
An excellent cassette sampler of vital songs done in early Jamaican ska style, a reggae forerunner. −RW
☆ **Ska Bonanza / HEARTBEAT**
A brilliant collection from ace compiler Chris Wilson containing 41 Studio One ska chestnuts. −RMS
○ **Street Reggae / KTEL-QWIL**
A decent place for the novice to get an introduction to the music of present-day reggae stars like Shelley Thunder, as well as veterans. −RW
Strictly the Best / VP
A possibly deceptive title, but great music throughout. −RW
○ **Studio 1 Presents Rare Reggae / HEARTBEAT**
Culled from the fruitful Coxsone Dodd lab. −RW
○ **This Is Lovers Reggae / ARIWA**
"Lovers reggae," second-generation style. −RW
☆ **This Is Reggae Music - Vol. 1 / ISLAND**
First of five essential volumes. You can't have one without the others. −RW
☆ **This Is Reggae Music - Vol. 2 / ISLAND** 1975
A compilation with Scotty & Lorna Bennett, Arthur Louis, and Desi Young. −MGN
☆ **This Is Reggae Music - Vol. 3 / ISLAND** 1976
A compilation with Junior Murvin, Prince Jazzbo, and Bunny Wailer. −MGN
○ **Towering Dub Inferno - Roir Tapes / RYKODISC**
A powerhouse compilation, with Lee Remy, Scientist, and others. −RW
☆ **Twenty Reggae Classics - Vol. 4 / TROJAN**
Never pass anything from the fertile Trojan vaults and collections. −RW
○ **Wiser Dread / NIGHTHAWK**
A marvelously annotated collection of vintage 70s tributes to Rastafarianism. Not many big names here, but everything from the Bunny Wailer cuts to "Cut Them Down" by the Morwells comes on like a classic. −JF

JAZZ

Jazz is a music with a history and a heart. Born in the rich melting pot of New Orleans after the turn of the century, jazz has grown into a vast and deep current of American musical culture. Historically and culturally, it is a music that had to happen. Though it is undoubtedly Black America's gift to the world, it is culturally a profound integration of musical factors: African rhythms and tonalities, the sensibilities of Blues and Gospel expression, European styles and instrumentation, and the creative energy of America's expansive and tumultuous early 20th century. Important battles against racism were won in the jazz era as bands and audiences began to integrate by virtue of sharing the music. Thus jazz is both historically and musically a very deep expression of American culture. We achieved in this music what we couldn't - and have yet to - achieve in our social environment: a true and harmonious integration of the diverse streams of human culture that converged in America. Even more than rhythm & blues or rock & roll, jazz has become a melting pot, absorbing and integrating the musical styles of the whole world, which is in fact our cultural legacy. The types of jazz are many, ranging from blues-based styles drenched in feeling to the more airy styles of jazz that are almost indistinguishable from modern classical music. Your own favorite kind of jazz is in there somewhere; you just have to find it. What is important is to hear the different styles of jazz and find ones that work for you.

And chances are you that may already be somewhat of a jazz expert. If you like movies or watch TV, you are already hearing all-kinds of jazz. Many soundtracks and almost all the background music used for movies and many TV shows is popular jazz. Whether its a Woody Woodpecker cartoon, an old Laurel & Hardy bit, or the latest full-length movie, jazz is the predominant music behind the video that we watch.

For all this cultural significance, jazz is remarkably easy to listen to, with an unpretentious, spontaneous feeling, and a wide emotional range. It has tremendous diversity in its styles and historical eras, and the richness of recorded jazz (recorded music started about the same time as jazz itself) makes it a wonderful project for long-term enjoyment and learning. Most of us who listen to jazz have found one or two favorite types of jazz that we can really get into. We work outward from there.

Jazz is synonymous with improvisation - the spontaneous and unrehearsed expression of musical ideas. Once common in classical European music (Bach and Mozart were awesome, among others) improvisation was gradually eliminated from music education. Jazz brought it back to us with a vengeance. Although jazz is largely instrumental, jazz melody and rhythm are deeply influenced by vocal music, especially by the early tradition of African-American vocal music. In turn, many jazz vocalists have been heavily influenced by instrumental jazz.

— Michael G. Nastos, JME, DNM

AHMED ABDUL-MALIK   b1927

Post-bop, world fusion.   Brooklyn-born bassist, whose father is from Sudan, also plays oud. He played with Art Blakey, Randy Weston, and had a particularly fruitful two years (1957-1958) with Thelonious Monk. –MGN

○ **East Meets West / RCA VICTOR**   i 1959
Thelonious Monk's bass player established early fusion of jazz and eastern music. –MGN

AHMED ABDULLAH   b1947

Post-bop, early free. New-York based trumpeter, best known for working in the 70s loft jazz scene. In the 80s, he led a group known as the Solomonic Quintet, and he has also worked with Chico Freeman, Malachi Favors of the Art Ensemble, and Charles Brackeen, and for many years with Sun Ra. An aggressive, striking soloist, Abdullah has recorded for independent labels like Silkheart and Cadence Jazz. –RW

● **Live at Ali's Alley / CADENCE**   1978
Live date. W/ Chico Freeman (ts). Extended and potent. –MGN

○ **Life's Force / ABOUT TIME**   1978
Progressive trumpeter with sextet in an all-original program. Includes Jay Hoggard on vibes and Vincent Chancey (French horn). –MGN

JOHN ABERCROMBIE   b1944

Post-bop, jazz-rock, neo bop, modern creative. One of the most sensitive and virtuosic of the fusion guitarists, he absorbed solid mainstream jazz influences such as Jim Hall, Bill Evans, and tenor sax giants Sonny Rollins and John Coltrane. Early organ trio work with Johnny Hammond gave him a solid grounding in blues-based styles. He soon became associated with many top players in 70s progressive jazz and fusion, such as Jack DeJohnette, Gato Barbieri, Billy Cobham, and Gil Evans. Abercrombie's recording career shows him in a variety of creative settings. His Gateway Trio work with Dave Holland and DeJohnette was a high point, achieving a powerful rhythmic sound while retaining a chamber jazz aesthetic with great spontaneity. Generally his recorded work exemplifies the "ECM sound," a coloristic wash of sounds played by well-trained musicians with eclectic influences. He uses electronic effects from the rock world; more importantly, he absorbs sounds, techniques, and musical ideas from the virtuoso rock solo styles. *Sargasso Sea* with Ralph Towner is a gem of guitar duet work. His more recent recordings have emphasized electric guitar synthesizer explorations. –DNM

★ **Timeless / ECM**   1974
Abercrombie (g), Jan Hammer (organ), J. DeJohnette (d). Quintessential early new-age. –MGN

899

○ **Gateway / ECM / DB 5**   1975
W/ Dave Holland (b), Jack DeJohnette (d).
☆ **Sargasso Sea / ECM / DB 5**   1976
Excellent duets. W/ Ralph Towner (g). An album that is worth
looking for. −DNM
Five Years Later /   1981
W/Ralph Towner (g). Abercrombie is more electric in this
duet setting. Three pieces cowritten by the duo. Two vastly
different sounds mesh nicely. −MGN
Getting There / POLYGRAM
W/ Michael Brecker (ts).
○ **Night / POLYGRAM**
Spirited original featuring Jan Hammer (k). Favorable group
setting for guitarist Abercrombie and timeless trio. Michael
Brecker (ts). Definitive. −MGN

PAUL ABLER

Post-bop, neo bop. Abler is a guitarist influenced by
Joe Henderson. He plays nice modal, mainstream, and post-
bop jazz. Abler was a former Heritage Jazz Competition
winner. −MGN
○ **Goin' Up / RED CAR**   ca. 1991
Quartet for guitarist who wrote five of the seven selections.
Straightahead mainstream modes. W/ Henry Gibson (p), Rod
Hicks (b), and Bobby Battle (d). Very pleasant. −MGN

MUHAL RICHARD ABRAMS   b 1930

Early free, progressive big band, modern creative. Abrams was a
founding member of the Association for the Advancement of
Creative Musicians (AACM), and a premier player, arranger,
conductor, and writer. He formed the Experimental Band in
1961, with a lineup including Eddie Harris, Donald Garrett,
and Roscoe Mitchell. A cooperative intended to help Chicago
musicians promote and present their own music, it evolved
into a major force within the Chicago Black music community,
with festivals, concerts, and a school for young musicians. As
a pianist, Abrams's style incorporates everything from stride
and ragtime to bop and free, and his compositions seamlessly
blend vintage and current idioms. He has influenced countless
musicians, been a confidant to such players as George Lewis
and Joseph Jarman, and gained some measure of long-
deserved recognition in the last few years thanks to a series of
outstanding albums issued by the Black Saint/Soul Note
family, plus CD reissues of his landmark Delmark 60s
sessions. −RW
○ **Levels & Degrees of Light / DELMARK**   1967
Seminal early date, Abrams featured on clarinet. W/ Anthony
Braxton (as), Leroy Jenkins (violin). −RW
○ **Young at Heart, Wise in Time / DELMARK / DB 5**   1969
On the surface, this is typical period free jazz, but its
individuality is revealed in the detail work ... Muhal's swirling
but lean piano avoids obvious models. −KEVIN WHITEHEAD, CADENCE
Sightsong / BLACK SAINT   1975
Fine duets with Malachi Favors (b); first Black Saint date. −RW
1-OQA+19 / BLACK SAINT   1977
W/ Anthony Braxton (as). An album of potent, creative
ensemble music. −MGN
○ **Life a B line c / NOVUS**   1978
This pianist is a champion of avant-garde. W/ Joseph Jarman
(reeds), A. C. Myers (p). −MGN
Mama and Daddy / BLACK SAINT   1980
Funky, inventive group sessions. −RW
Duet / BLACK SAINT   1981
Great duo with Anthony Braxton (as). −RW
○ **Rejoicing with the Light / BLACK SAINT**   1983
Tremendous big-band date. −RW
● **Colours in Thirty-Third / BLACK SAINT**   i 1986
This is a daring sextet with violinist John Blake. W/ Fred
Hopkins (b), Andrew Cyrille (d), Dave Holland (b) in the
rhythm section. −RW

The Hearinga Suite / BLACK SAINT / DB 5   r 1990
Cut to the chase. Stated simply, a masterwork — the latest
chapter in a career marked by leadership and fierce
determination. −WILLARD JENKINS, JAZZ TIMES

GEORGE ADAMS   b 1940

Post-bop, neo bop, modern creative. Tenor sax, flute, bass
clarinet. A dynamic, aggressive player whose style reflects
both sizable blues/R&B influence and the vocal effects and
spiraling solo tendencies of avant-garde players. Adams
played with such notables as Howlin' Wolf, Lightnin' Hopkins,
and Bill Doggett, plus backed singers like Sam Cooke and
Hank Ballard. Adams came to New York from Georgia in 1968.
He established his jazz reputation through a stint with Art
Blakey, then later played with Roy Haynes and Gil Evans.
Major gigs came with Charles Mingus in the 70s. With pianist
Don Pullen, he then co-led the George Adams-Don Pullen
quartet, one of the top small combos of the 70s and 80s. His
last group was Phalanx with Blood Ulmer in the mid 80s. (*also
see* Don Pullen) −RW
● **Suite for Swingers / HORO**   1976
Extended compositions, w/ Don Pullen. One of the great jazz
quartets of the last two decades. All albums worthwhile. −MGN
○ **Don't Lose Control / SOUL NOTE**   1979
Excitable saxophonist / flutist. Must-buy. With Don
Pullen (p). −MGN

PEPPER ADAMS   1930-1986

Bop, hard-bop, post-bop. Baritone sax. Born Park Adams in
Highland Park, MI. He came to prominence in the late 50s as a
hard-bop baritone saxophonist with a big sound and multi-
noted attack. Co-leader of a group with Detroit trumpeter
Donald Byrd (late 50s-early 60s). Member of the first Thad
Jones-Mel Lewis Band beginning in late 1965. Active in New
York studio work and with many freelance jazz groups until
the mid 70s when he devoted himself full-time to jazz. Many
recordings as a leader and sideman. Among his best are
Ephemera (Spotlite), *Encounter* (Prestige), *Plays Charles
Mingus* (Workshop), *Urban Dreams* (Palo Alto), and *The
Master* (Muse). −BP
Pepper Adams / MODE   1957
The first and one of the finest from this baritone master. −DS
● **10 to 4 at the 5-Spot / OJC**   1958
The best example of the bebop baritone saxophonist from
Detroit. Includes a young Donald Byrd (tpt) and pianist Bobby
Timmons. −DS
Pepper-Knepper Quintet / METROJAZZ   i 1958
○ **Plays Compositions of Mingus / JAZZ WORKSHOP**   1963
Adventurous outing, which builds on Adams's bebop base. −DS
Encounter! / PRESTIGE   1968
Solid effort, w/ Zoot Sims (ts), Tommy Flanagan (p). −DS
Julian / INNER CITY   1975
A live set by the ever-reliable saxophonist. −DS
○ **Reflectory / MUSE**   1978
Excellent hard-bop vehicle. −RW
Conjuration — At Fat Tuesdays / RESERVOIR   1983
Contains three previously unissued selections from the week-
long engagement .... Adams symbolized everything positive
about jazz and his presence is already much missed. −LARRY
HOLLIS, CADENCE

CANNONBALL ADDERLEY   1928-1975

Bop, hard-bop, post-bop, cool, soul jazz, jazz-rock. Few
saxophonists were able to combine popularity and artistry
better than Cannonball Adderley. A music teacher from Fort
Lauderdale, Adderley moved to New York in 1955. Arriving
very shortly after the death of Charlie Parker, he forged a
sound that displayed not only aspects of Bird but also the
influence of Benny Carter, Louis Jordan, and Eddie
"Cleanhead" Vinson. Adderley had a full, rounded tone, and
could play beautiful ballads or swirling, blistering tempos. In

later years Adderley's band became very popular through his incorporation of blues, R&B, and gospel elements, but above all else he was a champion of melody and one of the greatest ballad stylists ever. He had his own band with his brother Nat from 1956-1957, then joined Miles Davis from 1957-1959, appearing on some of Davis's greatest masterpieces of the era, among them *Kind of Blue* and *Milestones*. From 1959 until his death, he once again led groups with his brother. His groups included such distinguished alumni as Yusef Lateef, Charles Lloyd, Sam Jones, Joe Zawinul, and George Duke. The 1967 song "Mercy, Mercy, Mercy" was a sizable pop hit. –RW

Spontaneous Combustion / SAVOY / DB 5   1955
These are Cannonball's first recordings. W/ Donald Byrd (tpt), Horace Silver (p), Paul Chambers (b), Kenny Clarke (d), Nat Adderley (cnt), and Jerome Richardson (ts, fl). –JME

★ **Somethin' Else / BLUE NOTE**   1958
Quintet. Absolutely essential. W/ Art Blakey (d), Miles Davis (tpt), Hank Jones (p), and Sam Jones (b). Great "Autumn Leaves." –MGN

○ **Portrait of Cannonball / OJC**   1958
Adderley's first album for Riverside, recorded while he was working as a sideman in Miles Davis's classic sextet. W/ Blue Mitchell (tpt), Bill Evans (p), Sam Jones (b), and Philly Jo Jones (d). –JME

○ **Things Are Getting Better / OJC**   1958
First pairing of Milt Jackson with Cannonball for an all-star blowin' session. This one works. W/ Wynton Kelly (p), Milt Jackson (vib), Percy Heath (b), and Art Blakey (d). Recorded while Adderley was a sideman with the classic Miles Davis Sextet. –JME

○ **In San Francisco / OJC**   1959
Live date with Bobby Timmons (p), Nat Adderley (cnt), Sam Jones (b), and Louis Hayes (d). Contains the classic and soulful "This Here." –HD

Them Dirty Blues / LANDMARK   1960
W/ Bobby Timmons (p), Nat Adderley (cnt), Barry Harris (p), Sam Jones (b), and Louis Hayes (d). The first studio recording by Cannonball's new quintet. Features two takes of Nat's new tune "Work Song" — soon to be a jazz classic. –JME

○ **Poll Winners / LANDMARK**   1960
Cannonball's only recording date with Wes Montgomery (discovered by Adderley less than a year prior). Also, the first recording of Victor Feldman on piano (hired as a vibes player) with Adderley. W/ Ray Brown (b), and Louis Hayes (d). –JME

Know What I Mean? / OJC   1961
Great album. W/ Bill Evans (p), Percy Heath (b), and Connie Kay (d). –JME

Quintet Plus / OJC   1961
Recorded just after Adderley's group returned from a very successful European tour. The band is tight. The "Plus" is Wynton Kelly (p). Also Victor Feldman (p, vib), Nat Adderley (cnt), Sam Jones (b), Ron Carter (b), and Louis Hayes (d). –JME

In New York / OJC   1962
Live date at The Village Vanguard in NYC. W/ Nat Adderley (cnt), Yusef Lateef (ts, fl), Joe Zawinul (p), Sam Jones (b), and Louis Hayes (d). –JME

In Europe / LANDMARK   1962
Live concert at the International Jazz Festival, Comblain-La-Tour, Belgium — over 30,000 people. W/ Nat Adderley (cnt), Yusef Lateef (ts, fl), Joe Zawinul (p), Sam Jones (b), and Louis Hayes (d). –JME

Jazz Workshop Revisited. / LANDMARK   1962
Return to San Francisco for the second live "Lighthouse" recording with Cannonball's (now-seasoned) sextet. This album reached #11 on the charts! W/ Nat Adderley (cnt), Yusef Lateef (ts, fl), Joe Zawinul (p), Sam Jones (b), and Louis Hayes (d). –JME

Nippon Soul / OJC   1963
First live jazz album. Recorded in Tokyo by Cannonball Adderley, with Yusef Lateef (ts). –MGN

○ **Mercy, Mercy, Mercy! / EMI (JAPAN)**   1966
Quintet. This is a great live performance with Nat Adderley (cnt), Victor Gaskin (b), Roy McCurdy (d), and Joe Zawinul (p) at The Club in Chicago. "Mercy, Mercy, Mercy" was a pop hit. –JME

Cannonball in Japan / CAPITOL   1966
Companion to *Nippon Soul*. –MGN

○ **Black Messiah / CAPITOL**   1970
Superb two-record live set from late 70s. –RW

● **Best of the Capitol Years / CAPITOL**   i 1975
Contains "Mercy, Mercy, Mercy" and Adderley's most successful jazz/gospel/pop fusion work with Joe Zawinul (k). –HD

NAT ADDERLEY   b 1931

Bop, hard-bop, post-bop, cool, soul jazz, jazz-rock. Nat is the lesser-known brother of Julian "Cannonball" Adderley. He was a trumpeter before switching to cornet. He had some success playing with Lionel Hampton prior to joining Cannonball for a short stint in the 50s, then rejoined Hampton in 1959 after periods with Woody Herman and J. J. Johnson. From 1959 to 1975, when Cannonball died, the Adderleys were the dominant soul-jazz group, making records that had popular appeal yet retained a jazz/improvisational base and integrity. Nat has led various bands since the mid 70s, with some success. –RW

● **Work Song / OJC**   1960
With Wes Montgomery (g) and Bobby Timmons (p). Features Nat's "Work Song." Also "Sack of Woe." –MGN

In the Bag / OJC   1962
Interesting album with New Orleans musicians Nat Perrilliat (reeds), Ellis Marsalis (p). –MGN

○ **A Little New York Midtown Music / GALAXY**   1978
Excellent quintet date. First-rate Johnny Griffin (ts) solos. –RW

AIR

Early free, modern creative. This fine trio formed in Chicago during the early 70s. The group consisted of multi-saxophonist Henry Threadgill, bassist Fred Hopkins, and percussionist Steve McCall. The three had absorbed the lessons of spontaneous creation, theatrical flair, and a gritty blues underpinning from their years as members of the Association for the Advancement of Creative Musicians (AACM). They moved to New York in 1975 and made a stunning first album in 1977. The group continued until McCall left in 1983 and they went on to make other good albums as New Air from 1983 to 1986. Threadgill continues heading his own group and often works with Hopkins. McCall died several years ago. –RW

Live Air / BLACK SAINT / DB 5   1977
1976 New York/1977 Ann Arbor. Bass, drums, and sax. –MGN

★ **Air Time / NESSA**   1977
Their finest album. –RW

Open Air Suite / ARISTA-NOVUS / DB 5   1978
Live. Some great tenor solos from Threadgill. –RW

○ **Air Lore / RCA / DB 5**   1979
Avant trio plays traditional themes. Essential. –MGN

AIRTO   b 1941

Latin, jazz-rock, world fusion. The greatest Brazilian percussionist to make an impact in jazz, Airto showed the value of incorporating Latin American rhythms and instrumentation into both a jazz-rock and a mainstream context. Leaving Brazil with wife Flora Purim in 1968 to come to the USA, he began working with Miles Davis in 1970. He made an enormous splash and appeared with everyone from Stan Getz to the early edition of Weather Report. He is still an active session percussionist. –RW

○ **Free / CBS**   i 1972
Includes first version of "Return To Forever." With Chick Corea

(k), Keith Jarrett (p), Stanley Clarke (b), and Joe Farrell (ts). A great album. –MGN

Fingers / CTI 1973
Vocals by Flora Purim. Potent, uplifting music. Many familiar themes. –MGN

TOSHIKO AKIYOSHI b 1929

Bop, post-bop, progressive big band. Japanese-born, Bud Powell-influenced jazz pianist. Progressive-minded composer and arranger, mostly in a big band format, but also works with a trio. Uses heritage to create expansive, orchestral voicings. A most influential presence for modern jazz in the 70s and 80s.–MGN

○ **Long Yellow Road / RCA / DB 5** 1974
An excellent big-band studio date. –RW

● **Road Time / RCA** 1976
Definitive live date from potent, creative, modern big band. A must-buy. –MGN

Dedications / INNER CITY 1976
One of his trio recordings. –JME

○ **Finesse / CONCORD** 1978
Great trio jazz. Featuring Edvard Grieg's "Solvegg's Song." –MGN

MANNY ALBAM b 1922

Progressive big band. Manny Albam has been a writer and player in several bands during the 40s, 50s, 60s, and 70s. Albam came to America as an infant. He played alto and baritone sax in a number of bands during the 40s, among them the groups of Muggsy Spanier, Boyd Raeburn, Bobby Sherwood, Sam Donahue, and Charlie Barnet. He was also a prominent arranger and bandleader in the 50s, and also did extensive film and television work.

The Drum Suite / RCA VICTOR i 1956
W/ Ernie Wilkins (sax).

○ **Jazz Greats of Our Time - Vol. 1 & 2 / CORAL** i 1958

JOE ALBANY 1924-1988

Bop, post-bop. Pianist. Albany is a solid bop soloist and accompanist with a fine blues sensibility. He was a prolific player in the pre-bop era, then made the transition despite a strong personality that led to creative differences with many players (notably Charlie Parker). Albany continued from the 50s through the 80s, doing a variety of things from backing singers to trios to solo dates. –RW

○ **Right Combination / OJC** 1957
The only early documentation of the swinging bebop pianist. Features Warne Marsh (ts). –DS

Bird Lives / STORYVILLE 1979
Interplay; fine Parker tribute. –RW

Portrait of an Artist / ELEKTRA 1982
A good recent example of Albany's hard-driving and infectious style. –DS

HOWARD ALDEN b 1963

Swing, post-bop. Among the best swing-influenced small combos of the 80s, the Howard Alden Trio was anchored by this guitarist, one of a group of young 70s and 80s players whose muse wasn't bop but swing. First date was the 1989 Howard Alden Trio effort on Concord with Lynn Seaton and the late Mel Lewis. Alden's own prominent career on Concord has seen him record with quartets and strings and co-leading the Howard Alden-Dan Barrett (tb) Quintet. –RW

Salutes Buck Clayton / CONCORD 1989
Snowy Morning Blues / CONCORD 1990
Trio. A good introduction to guitarist Alden. –MGN

○ **13 Strings with George Van Eps / CONCORD**
Alden's 6-string and Van Eps's 7-string make the 13. Long overdue for George Van Eps. Excellent. –MGN

MONTY ALEXANDER b 1944

Post-bop, soul jazz, Latin, world fusion. An outstanding pianist, one of a group from the Caribbean (others include Wynton Kelly and Andrew Hill) who utilized their background and interspersed it through a jazz focus. Alexander came to Florida in 1962, then went to New York five years later. He's been a prolific contributor throughout the 70s, 80s, and 90s, though his best albums are solos or trios. –RW

Facets / CONCORD 1979
Good exchanges w/ Ray Brown (b), Jeff Hamilton (d). –RW

Ivory & Steel / CONCORD 1980
Includes steel drummer Othello Molineaux. –MGN

★ **Triple Treat I / CONCORD** 1982
Definitive recordings from a virtuosic jazz trio of Alexander with Ray Brown (b) and Herb Ellis (g). –MGN

Overseas Special / CONCORD 1982
A very good live recording. –MGN

Duke Ellington Songbook / POLYGRAM 1983
Outstanding rendition of Ellington standards. –ED

○ **The River / CONCORD** 1985
Some emphatic, moving solos in this set. Disc bonus cut. –RW

☆ **Triple Treat II & III / CONCORD** 1987
More definitive recordings from the virtuosic jazz trio of Alexander with Ray Brown (b) and Herb Ellis (g). –MGN

Trio / CONCORD

LOREZ ALEXANDRIA b 1929

Ballads. Veteran vocalist who specializes in ballads and blues. Her hallmark is her ability to master the subtle and understated. –MGN

Lorez Sings Prez / KING r 1958
Tribute to Lester Young. Formerly rare, now reissued in original form. –HD

☆ **Great & More of the Great Alexandria / MCA** 1964
1964-1965. Twofer. Fine jazz vocal stylings. Combines two Impulse albums. –HD

May I Come In? / MUSE 198?
Recent sides with Houston Person on sax. –HD

Sings Johnny Mercer - Vol. 1 & 2 / TREND 198?
Excellent recent work. Jazz vocals. Classy material with solid four-piece backing. –HD

Lorez Sings / KING
Very collectible (pricey) album now available on CD. –HD

ALIVE

Post-bop, ballads, Latin. All-female quintet from San Francisco area. Hard swinging, with Latin leanings. As they said in a song, "for lack of a better word, call it jazz." –MGN

○ **Alive / URANA** 1979
All-female group swung like mad and held no punches. All original contents include three by lead singer Rhiannon and one from Michelle Rosewoman. "City Life" is an absolute knockout. Features Barbara Borden on drums, Carolyn Brandy (per), Janet Small on piano, Suzanne Vincenza on bass. Where are they now when we need them? –MGN

GERI ALLEN

Post-bop, modern creative. Pianist, composer. One of the prime stars of the 80s and 90s, Allen contributed to Steve Coleman's controversial M-Base movement in Brooklyn. She emerged in the free, mainstream, hard-bop, or R&B/funk arena in the early 80s as a sparkling soloist whose style was eclectic yet compelling. She has worked with Paul Motian, Charlie Haden, and Coleman, and led her own groups, recording mainly on JMT and Blue Note. She is a player to watch in the 90s, as a composer/player and bandleader. –RW

★ **The Printmakers / MINOR MUSIC** 1984
Pianist's first album is a beauty. W/ Anthony Cox (b), Andrew Cyrille (d). Essential modern piano. –MGN

○ **In the Middle / POLYGRAM**   1987
Some interesting work. –RW
● **In the Year of the Dragon / POLYGRAM**   i 1990
Allen's extraordinary trio recording. W/ Charlie Haden (b),
Paul Motian (d). A solid record, all tracks right in there.
Consensus album of the year for 1990. –MGN
○ **Twylight / POLYGRAM / DB 5**   r 1990
Many excellent original compositions. Fine rhythm section of
Tani Tabbal (d), Jaribu Shahid (b). –MGN
The Nurturer / CAPITOL   r 1991
Most recent release; strong playing by Kenny Garrett (sax),
Marcus Belgrave (tpt). –RW

HENRY ALLEN   1908-1967

Trad, Dixieland, swing. The son of the leader of the Allen Brass
Band of Algiers, LA, "Red" Allen is often characterized as a
"swing" trumpeter in the Armstrong mode. He first played
with his father's band, and worked with several other brass
bands in New Orleans before joining King Oliver's Dixie
Syncopators in St. Louis in 1927. He built a reputation as a
featured soloist, gradually becoming one of the most
influential trumpeters in the big band field. He played with
the Luis Russell band in 1937 (which was then backing Louis
Armstrong), and after 1940 made recordings with Jelly Roll
Morton and Sidney Bechet. After 1943, he gravitated once
again toward the mainstream, forming bands which included
sidemen such as Coleman Hawkins, Buster Bailey, and Pee
Wee Russell. "Red" Allen's stylistic proficiency tended to lead
to comparisons with Louis Armstrong, and like Armstrong,
he adapted his playing to suit the particular bands and
periods in which he participated. True to his New Orleans
roots, he liked to keep his audiences guessing, wondering
what he might come up with next. As a soloist and singer,
Allen was a consummate entertainer who knew how to have
fun with his music and how to communicate that spirit to the
audience. –BR
Henry Allen & Coleman Hawkins / HEP   1933
Driving swing-era favorites mixed with popular songs of the
day, delivered by two masters. –BR
Original 1933-1941 Recordings / TAX   1933
"Red" in various contexts, providing a good sampler of his
early recordings. A memorable solo by Allen on "Body and
Soul." –BR
☆ **World on a String / RCA**   i 1957
Red Allen with J. C. Higginbotham (tb), Coleman Hawkins
(sax), Buster Bailey (cl), and others — a collaboration which
shines on "I Cover the Waterfront," tickles on "Ride, Red,
Ride." –BR

ALLIANCE HALL DIXIELAND BAND

Dixieland. Preservation Hall spinoff led by ex-Basie
trumpeter Wallace Davenport, trombonist Freddie Lonzo, and
banjo player Don Vappie. –MGN
○ **A Closer Walk / PRO ARTE**
Energized. Good title cut. –RW
New Orleans / PRO ARTE-PRO JAZZ
Fairly formulaic traditional material. –RW

MOSE ALLISON   b 1927

Post-bop, cool, blues-jazz. Among the most understated yet
distinctive pianists and vocalists in either jazz or blues, Mose
Allison combines wry humor, exceptional timing, and a
marvelous vocal approach. He's managed to fuse the rhythmic
intensity of an improvising singer with the storytelling
acumen of the country blues artists. Moving to New York in
1956, he worked with Stan Getz, Gerry Mulligan, Al Cohn, and
Zoot Sims, and then formed his own trios and played both in
New York and overseas in Paris, Stockholm, and Copenhagen.
From the 60s on, he has toured frequently. –RW

Music Map

Jazz Drums

African, Caribbean Drummers

Millitary Marches

Early Jazz Drummers
Baby Dodds (1898- 1959)

Chicago & New York : The 20s
Ben Pollack (1903-1971) — Dave Tough (1907-1948)
Barrett Deems (1914)

Swing Era
Sonny Greer (1895-1982) — Cozy Cole (1906-1981)
Dave Tough (1907-1948) — Gene Krupa (1909-1973)
Chick Webb (1909-1939) — Big Sid Catlett (1910-1951)
Jo Jones (1911-1985) — Buddy Rich (1917-1987)

Swing Era / Big Band
Cuba Austin w/ McKinney's Cotton Pickers
Walter Johnson w/ F. Henderson (1904-1977)
J. C. Heard (1917-1989)

Bop Drumming
Art Blakey (1919) – Philly Joe Jones (1923-1985)
Max Roach (1924) — Roy Haynes (1926)
Kenny Clarke (1929-1985) – Dannie Richmond (1935-1988)

Post Bop
Elvin Jones (1927) — Arthur Taylor (1929)
Alan Dawson (1929) — Jimmy Cobb (1929)
Billy Higgins (1936) — Pete La Roca (1938)

Avant Garde
Ed Blackwell (1929 — Rashied Ali (1935)
Sunny Murray (1937) — Andrew Cyrille (1939)
Famoudou Don Moye (1946)

Jazz Rock
Bobby Colomby (1944) — Billy Cobham (1944)
Tony Williams (1945) — Ronald Shannon Jackson (1940)

Post Bop
Roy Brooks (1938) — Dennis Charles (1933)
Jerome Cooper (1946)

Major Influence 60s to now
Jack DeJohnette (1942)

80s-90s
Jeff Watts (19) — Adam Nussbaum (1955)
Tani Tabbal — John Vidacovich

Back Country Suite / OJC / DB 5   1957
A wonderful date mixing his country blue warblings, dynamic
piano playing, and cabaret-from-the-backwoods styles. –RW
Mose Allison Sings / PRESTIGE   1957
Reissue of two fine Allison albums, *Back Country Suite* (1957)
and *Local Color* (1957). –JME
Mose Allison Plays for Lovers / PRESTIGE   1957
Selections from five albums ranging from 1957 to 1959. –JME

JAZZ STYLES

Ragtime — A piano-based music style that is classically derived and rhythmically bouncy. Main proponents: Scott Joplin, Eubie Blake, Joe Lamb.

New Orleans Traditional — The original jazz style; band music for celebrations and funerals. Tuba and clarinet are prominent. Main proponents: the Dodds Brothers, Louis Armstrong, King Oliver, Preservation Hall Jazz Band(s), Papa Celestin, Sidney Bechet, Jelly Roll Morton, Jimmy Noone, Buddy Bolden.

Dixieland — Riverboat shuffles, emphasizing banjo and brass; uptempo, happy music. Major proponents: Bob Scobey, Al Hirt, Pete Fountain, Dukes of Dixieland, World's Greatest Jazz Band, Bix Beiderbecke.

Harlem Stride — Piano music. More heavily rhythmic than ragtime, and more nimble. Major proponents: Fats Waller, Meade Lux-Lewis, Albert Ammons, James P. Johnson, Willie "The Lion" Smith.

Boogie & Blues Piano — Rollicking, no-holds-barred music, with train rhythms prevalent. Major proponents: Pete Johnson, Jimmy Yancey, Little Brother Montgomery, Roosevelt Sykes, Tuts Washington, Professor Longhair, James Booker, Mr. B.

Swing Era — American popular songs played instrumentally. Musical films of this era were a great promoter for these songs and bands. It was immensely popular concert music as well. Major proponents: Bobby Hackett, Jack Teagarden, the Quintet of The Hot Club of France, Benny Goodman, Lester Young, Coleman Hawkins, Buck Clayton, Art Hodes, Earl Hines.

Big Band Era — Jazz orchestras playing swing-oriented music. Used for dancing primarily; very popular on radio. Major proponents: Artie Shaw, the Dorsey Brothers, Jimmie Lunceford, Fletcher Henderson, Glenn Miller, Duke Ellington, Boyd Raeburn, Erskine Hawkins, Cab Calloway, Billy Eckstine, Count Basie.

Bop — The artistic evolution of swing produced this quick, harmonically intricate, virtuoso music. Bop marked the departure of jazz from mainstream pop music, as many didn't like or understand it, but it was the source of (or at least influence on) all later jazz styles. Major proponents: Thelonious Monk, Dizzy Gillespie, Charlie Parker, Kenny Clarke, Bud Powell, Max Roach, Miles Davis, Fats Navarro, Billy Eckstine, Sonny Stitt.

Hard-Bop — A return to a bluesier, earthier sound than bop, while retaining and evolving its highly virtuosic instrumental styles. Major proponents: Lee Morgan, Art Blakey, Jackie McLean, John Coltrane, Miles Davis, Clifford Brown, Sonny Rollins.

Post-Bop— Less reliance on popular-song forms and more open-ended harmonies brought new possibilities for extended improvisation. Early exploration of world music influences. "Modal Jazz" is also used to describe much of this music. Major proponents: John Coltrane, Donald Byrd, Gigi Gryce, Max Roach, Wayne Shorter, McCoy Tyner, Kenny Dorham.

Cool-Jazz — A reaction to the hyper-kinetics of bop which emphasized a restrained feel, softer colors, and purposefully limited dynamics. Originating in the famous "Birth of the Cool" sessions, it developed as primarily a West Coast phenomenon. Major proponents: Chet Baker, Gerry Mulligan, Miles Davis, Paul Desmond, Stan Getz.

Blues/Jazz — Blues rhythms incorporated into a swinging context. Also the vestiges of rhythm & blues. Major proponents: Louis Jordan, Big Jay McNeeley, Dave Bartholomew, Slim Gaillard, Mose Allison, Jay McShann, Ray Bryant.

Ballads & Blues Vocals — Classic singers interpreting American popular songs and new originals. Major proponents: Lena Horne, Billie Holiday, June Christy, Anita O'Day, Dinah Washington, Joe Williams, Billy Eckstine, Mel Torme, Eddie Jefferson, Sarah Vaughan, Ella Fitzgerald, Sheila Jordan.

Soul Jazz/Original Funk — Blues-based but with modern harmonies, usually with a back beat. Strong Gospel influence. Organ and guitars are prevalent. Major proponents: Horace Silver, Jimmy Smith, Ramsey Lewis, Lee Morgan, Jack McDuff, Jimmy McGriff, Grant Green, the

---

Local Color / OJC	1957

Another fine date. This one's more strictly jazz style. –RW

☆ **I Love the Life I Live / COLUMBIA**   i 1960

Mose Alive / ATLANTIC   1965
Flashy piano and funny, inventive vocals. –RW

○ **Western Man / ATLANTIC / DB 5**   1971
A first-rate set. –RW

Mose in Your Ear / ATLANTIC   1972
Super on both ends: singing and playing. –RW

● **Your Mind Is on Vacation / ATLANTIC**   1976
The title cut is a classic. –RW

○ **Middle Class White Boy / ELEKTRA**   1982
Tremendous writing, fine performances. –RW

Lessons in Living / ELEKTRA   1982
Lou Donaldson (as) brings a welcome blues and soul-jazz flavor to an already impressive cast and musical menu. –RW

Ever Since the World Ended / BLUE NOTE / DB 5   1988
A wonderful update of his sound, with dauntless work by Mose. W/ Arthur Blythe (as), and Kenny Burrell (g). –RW

○ **Best of Mose Allison / ATLANTIC**   COMP
Contains 20 songs. A retrospective of Allison's Atlantic years. –RW

LAURINDO ALMEIDA   b 1917

Cool, Latin. Acoustic guitar, composer. Almeida is another Brazilian instrumentalist who migrated to America and became a significant figure on the US jazz scene. He arrived in America in 1947. After a stint with Stan Kenton, he formed his own trio. He has worked often with Bud Shank, recorded with West Coast players, made successful Latin-jazz and classical albums, and won a Grammy award. He was one of the best during the 60s bossa-nova craze. *See* the L.A. Four. –RW

○ **Brazilliance - Vols. 1 & 2 / CAPITOL / DB 5**   r 1962
W/ Bud Shank (as, fl) on both albums. W/ Gary Peacock (b) and Chuck FLores (d) on the second album. It is almost possible to hear the birth of the Bosa Nove in these albums. –JME

Artistry in Rhythm / CONCORD   i 1972
W/ Bob Magnusson (b), Milt Holland (per). This is lovely easy-listening music, in the best sense of that term. –JME

Jazz Origin - Brazilliance / PA-USA   i 1973

Music of the Brazilian Masters / CONCORD   i 1973

Concierto De Aranjuez / INNER CITY   1978
This album includes songs from *Black Orpheus* and a Gershwin medley. –JME

1st Concerto for Guitar and Orchestra / CONCORD   1979

Latin Odyssey / CONCORD   1982
W/ Charlie Bryd (g).

Brazilian Masters / CONCORD   1989

BARRY ALTSCHUL   b 1943

Post-bop, early free. Barry Altschul has been among the better

Adderley Brothers, Lou Donaldson, Hank Crawford, Stanley Turrentine, Shirley Scott.

Early Free Jazz — The original improvisers who changed the face of jazz in the late 50s to late 60s, doing away with fixed harmonic and rhythmic structures in lieu of spontaneous feelings. Major proponents: Ornette Coleman, Cecil Taylor, Archie Shepp, Bill Dixon, Sam Rivers, John Coltrane, Don Cherry, Pharoah Sanders, the A.A.C.M., Bobby Bradford, John Carter, Albert Ayler, Sonny Sharrock, the Art Ensemble of Chicago.

Progressive Big Band — This is music for listening, with denser, more modernistic arrangements than the earlier, more dance-oriented big-band styles, and more room to improvise. Major proponents: Gil Evans, Stan Kenton, Toshiko Akiyoshi, Cal Massey, Frank Foster, Carla Bley, George Gruntz, David Amram, Sun Ra, Duke Ellington.

Latin-Jazz — Latin rhythms melded to jazz melodies, with heavy emphasis on hot beats, horn charts, and choral lyrics in Spanish. Major proponents: Dizzy Gillespie, Machito, Chano Pozo, Tito Rodriguez, Noro Moralez, Tito Puente, Ray Barretto, Mario Bauza, Eddie Palmieri, Poncho Sanchez, Cal Tjader, Mongo Santamaria.

Early Jazz/Rock Fusion — A melding of rock rhythms with jazz solo techniques, prevalent in 1968-1974. Major proponents: Miles Davis, Larry Coryell, John McLaughlin, Herbie Hancock ("Mwandishi"), Chick Corea (Return to Forever), Passport, Frank Zappa, Weather Report, Santana, Brand X, Bill Bruford, Gong, National Health, Jean-Luc Ponty.

World Fusion — Combining a wide variety of world music rhythms and melodies into improvisation-based instrumental music. Major proponents: John McLaughlin ("Shakti"), Oregon, Airto, Flora Purim, Don Cherry, David Amram, Ronald Shannon Jackson, M'Boom, Abdullah Ibrahim.

New-Age — Atmospheric, cerebral, spiritual, and earthy music used for meditation, relaxation. Major proponents: Windham Hill artists, George Winston, Andreas Vollenweider, Eno, Tangerine Dream, Paul Winter, Suzanne Ciani, Terry Riley.

Instrumental Pop — Commercial music with minimal improvisation or creative risks. Generic, short in duration, simple themes. Major proponents: Herb Alpert, Chuck Mangione, Kenny G, Acker Bilk, Boots Randolph, George Benson.

Neo-Bop — A new generation of young players taking bop and other influences and creating traditional acoustic jazz. Sidestepping rock/fusion/electric influences, they are diligent students of earlier styles, often with spectacular results. They may not all be innovators, but often try to stretch the parameters. Major proponents: Wynton Marsalis, Kenny Garrett, Bob Berg, Terrence Blanchard, Brian Lynch, Courtney Pine, Roy Hargrove, Benny Green.

Contemporary Funk — Dance-oriented 4/4 music, slow or mid-tempo. No swing, little blues. Major proponents: Grover Washington Jr, David Sanborn, Joe Sample and the Crusaders, Bob James, George Howard, Gerald Albright.

M-Base/Avant Fusion — Combining some creative music precepts with funky dance rhythms. Major proponents: Steve Coleman, Greg Osby, Charnett Moffitt, Jamaaladeen Tacuma, Geri Allen.

Modern Creative — Continuing the tradition of the 50s-to-60s Free-jazz mode. Musicians may incorporate free playing into structured modes, or play ... well, anything. Major proponents: John Zorn, Henry Kaiser, Eugene Chadbourne, Tim Berne, Bill Frisell, Steve Lacy, Cecil Taylor, Ornette Coleman, Ray Anderson.

— Michael G. Nastos

---

percussionists and drummers in both free and mainstream circles since the 60s, when he was a member of the Jazz Composers Guild. Studying with Charlie Persip, he worked with Carmell Jones, Leo Wright, and Johnny Griffin. Altschul was a member from 1970-1972 of the premier group Circle, with pianist Chick Corea, bassist Dave Holland, and multi-saxophonist Anthony Braxton. Since then, he's worked often with Braxton as well as other free and avant-garde musicians such as saxophonist Sam Rivers, as well as heading his own band and playing with more conventional jazz musicians such as Art Pepper. He's studied African, Indian, Afro-Latin, and Caribbean music and integrated aspects from all these styles into his music. −RW

☆ **You Can't Name Your Own Tune / MUSE / DB 5**　1977
Creative drummer leads ensemble in a progressive mode. W/ Sam Rivers (ts), Muhal Richard Abrams (p). −MGN

Another Time, Another Place / MUSE　1978
Good followup. −RW

Brahma / SACKVILLE　1980
W/ Ray Anderson (tb). −MGN

FRANCO AMBROSETTI　1941-1990

Post-bop, neo bop, modern creative. Trumpet, flugelhorn, composer. Ambrosetti is a good brass player from Switzerland whose father played with Charlie Parker at the 1949 Jazz Festival. A onetime classical pianist, Ambrosetti switched to trumpet in the early 60s and taught himself. A fiery, well-regarded soloist, he has led both Europeans and Americans in groups and has worked with his father, George Gruntz, and Daniel Humair in the George Gruntz Concert Jazz Band since the early 70s. Appearances at various festivals, plus occasional recordings, keep his profile visible to US jazz critics and fans. −RW

○ **Movies Too / CAPITOL-RHINO**　r 1988
Brilliant playing from Swiss-born trumpet/flugelhorn player. W/ Geri Allen (p) and all-star cast. "Superman," "Angel Eyes," "Peter Gunn." −MGN

Sunday Walk / I GRANDI DEL JAZZ
Italian import made with brother saxophonist Flavio. Great hard bop. −MGN

AMERICAN JAZZ ORCHESTRA

Big band, progressive big band. A distinguished collection of jazz musicians organized by critic Gary Giddins and composer, pianist, and conductor John Lewis to function as a repertory group playing the compositions of the music's giants. They have given concerts since the late 80s and have issued recordings of Ellington and Jimmie Lunceford works. −RW

● **Ellington Masterpieces / ATLANTIC / DB 5**　r 1990
A group assembled by critic Gary Giddins & pianist John Lewis. Exemplary readings of Duke Ellington classics. −RW

○ **Jimmie Lunceford / MUSICMASTERS**　1992

ALBERT AMMONS　1907-1949

Stride. A founding father of boogie-woogie, Albert Ammons was a remarkable soloist and a driving, galvanizing performer. He became a national figure when the boogie-woogie rage dominated the country in the late 30s. Ammons worked in Chicago clubs during the 20s, then played with territory bands and orchestras in the early 30s, before heading his own group in Chicago from 1934-1938. In 1939 Ammons moved to New York for a Carnegie Hall concert, then made regular appearances at Cafe Society, sometimes with Pete Johnson, and other times in a trio with Meade Lux Lewis. He continued performing and recording into the 40s. −RW

☆ **Complete Blue Note Albert Ammons / MOSAIC**   1939
W/ Meade Lux Lewis.

○ **Boogie Woogie Trio - Vol. 3 / STORYVILLE**
Albert Ammons, Meade Lux Lewis (p), and Peter Johnson (p).
Not a trio, but separate cuts (one duo) from 1939-1949. –JME

GENE AMMONS   1925-1974

Bop, hard-bop, blues-jazz, soul jazz. Son of boogie-woogie
pianist Albert Ammons, Gene Ammons came to prominence
as teenage tenor saxophonist with Billy Eckstine's big band
(1944-1946), later with Woody Herman (1949). He had his
own combos from 1947-1955 featuring Sonny Stitt as co-
leader (1950-1952), and his recordings for Mercury (1947-
1949) include the big hit "My Foolish Heart." Ammons began
recording with Prestige in 1950 and (except for 1952/1953)
continued with this label until his death in 1974. Highlights
include: tenor battles with Stitt ("Blues Up And Down") and
small combo singles to 1955; hi-fi jam sessions and album
contests from 1955-1958; small group with occasional guests
from 1960-1962. Later recordings (1969-1974) resumed after
a lengthy prison sentence for narcotics violations and involve
a whole spectrum of settings.
Always a popular jazz artist, Ammons recorded dozens of
albums. His most creative period was the early 60s when
almost anything he recorded is worth hearing. There have
been album collections of his complete Mercury output,
complete Chess recordings, and a whole spate of Prestige
reissues. His work is highlighted by a hard-driving mixture of
bebop and R&B devices delivered with a tone as big as a
house. One of the great ballad players of any era, he has been
widely hailed as a great interpreter. –BP

○ **All Star Sessions / OJC**   1950
Four sessions from 1950 to 1955. W/ Sonny Stitt (ts), Duke
Jordan (p), Jo Jones (d), Junior Mance (p). –JME

Red Top / SAVOY   1953
○ **Happy Blues / OJC**   1956
Scintillating Ammons blues. –RW

Funky / OJC   1957
A blues-oriented bop album that is not "funky" in the soul-
jazz sense of that word. An exception is the title cut, a bluesy
tune with Kenny Burrell (g). W/ Jackie McLean (as), Art
Farmer (tpt), Mal Waldron (p). –JME

Jammin' in Hi Fi / OJC   1957
This has some hot Ammons solos. –RW

Big Sound / OJC   1958
John Coltrane (ts) and Pepper Adams (bar sax) included in
backing group; weighty Ammons solos. –RW

● **Blue Gene / OJC**   1958
This is a wonderful blues date, with great support from
Pepper Adams (bar sax), Mal Waldron (p), Art Taylor (d),
Doug Watkins (b), Idrees Sulieman (tpt), and Ray Barretto
(conga). –RW

Boss Tenor / OJC   1960
Outstanding quintet session. Tommy Flanagan plays great
piano. W/ Doug Watkins (b), Art Taylor (d), and Ray Barretto
(conga). –RW

Gene Ammons Story: Organ Combos / PRESTIGE   1960
1960 & 1961. Includes two albums: *Angel Eyes* and *Twisting
The Jug*. –JME

Gene Ammons Story: Gentle Jug / PRESTIGE   1961
Two classic albums from 1961/1962: *Nice N' Cool* and *Gene
Ammons* –JME

○ **Boss Tenors / POLYGRAM**   1961
There are perhaps no better tenors, no better jazz. Definitive.
W/ Sonny Stitt. –MGN

Soul Summit / PRESTIGE   1962
W/ Sonny Stitt.

Jug and Dodo / PRESTIGE   1962
A very good team. Dodo Marmarosa was a tasty pianist and a
highly underrated player. –RW

The Boss Is Back / PRESTIGE   1969
Some cuts from *Brother Jug* album. –JME

Brother Jug / PRESTIGE   1969
Live! in Chicago / OJC   r 1970
Nice live date. –RW

Black Cat / PRESTIGE   1970
W/ Harold Mabern (p) and Ron Carter (b).

You Talk That Talk / PRESTIGE   1971

DAVID AMRAM   b 1930

Early free, progressive big band, Latin, world fusion. A multi-
instrumentalist most prominent on French horn. Originally
from Philadelphia. Classically trained. He played in the 50s
with Charles Mingus, Sonny Rollins, Lionel Hampton, and
Oscar Pettiford. He scored for TV and Broadway in the 60s,
and carved a singular identity by combining world rhythms,
especially those found in Cuban music. A fine orchestrator,
most notably with Benny Carter. –MGN

☆ **Havana/New York / FLYING FISH**   1977
Historic US/Cuban exchange of 1977. Important document.
W/ Pepper Adams (bar sax), Thad Jones (cnt), Candido
(conga), and members of Irakere. –MGN

No More Walls / FLYING FISH   1978
Variety of different settings. Large ensemble orchestra. W/
Lynn Sheffield (v). Eclectic and tuneful. 70s reissue. –MGN

At Home/Around the World / FLYING FISH   1980

ERNESTINE ANDERSON   b 1911

Ballads, blues. Ernestine Anderson is a tremendous singer in
the jazz vein. She has been active since the 40s and had a hit
in 1947 with K. C. Lover while a member of Shifty Henry's
band. Anderson was the *DOWN BEAT* Critic's Poll New Star
winner in 1959, then basically dropped out of sight ten years
later, after singing a number for the soundtrack of Sidney
Poitier's film *The Lost Man*. She did selected dates in the
Northwest until bassist Ray Brown became her manager in
the mid 70s and secured her a Concord Records post in 1976.
She's been quite busy ever since. –RW

Hot Cargo / MERCURY / BB 15   i 1958
Moanin', Moanin', Moanin' / MERCURY   r 1961
Live from Concord to London / CONCORD   1976
A nice live jazz date. –RW

Hello Like Before / CONCORD   1976
A wonderful session marking Anderson's return to the scene
in 1976. Classy, brassy, and delightful swing and vocals. –RW

Sunshine / CONCORD   1977
More toward the contemporary, flashy side, but a nice basic
jazz set. –RW

Never Make Your Move Too Soon / CONCORD   1980
A great mix of old and new. A little toward blues/pop side,
especially the title cut. –RW

○ **Big City / CONCORD**   1983
With sublime Hank Jones (p) and fine vocals. Solid, swinging
arrangements. –RW

● **Be Mine Tonight / CONCORD**   198?
The best of her 80s albums, sparked by hot Benny Carter alto
sax. –RW

Live at the Alley Cat / CONCORD
Standard big-band arrangements and solos, but Anderson (v)
makes welcome appearances. –RW

RAY ANDERSON   b 1952

Neo bop, modern creative. Trombone, cornet, tuba, slide
trumpet. One of the best contemporary players, Anderson is
also knowledgeable about earlier traditional and swing styles.
An active player since childhood, he began attending AACM
concerts and blues shows in Chicago as a teenager. He played
in funk bands during the early 70s and came to New York in
1972. Early stints with Mingus led to gigs with Barry Altschul

and Anthony Braxton, plus many session dates in Latin-jazz bands. He has been a bandleader since the late 70s and won the 1981 *DOWN BEAT* Critic's Poll in the category of Talent Deserving Wider Recognition. –RW

Old Bottles — New Wine / RHINO / DB 5   r 1987
Highly recommended. His best is yet to come. –MGN

○ **Blues Bred in the Bone / RHINO / DB 5**   r 1989
A 1990 reissue of a good contemporary session. –RW

Wishbone / RHINO   r 1991
Highly recommended. –MGN

ANDY & THE BEY SISTERS

Ballads, soul jazz. Pop, blues, and light jazz vocalizing, most times with a solid social message to boot. –MGN

○ **Now Hear / PRESTIGE**   i 1965
Expressive vocalists hook up w/ Jerome Richardson (sax and fl), Kenny Burrell (g) for expansive treatments of jazz. –MGN

RAY ANTHONY   b 1922

Big band, instr. pop. Trumpet, bandleader. Ray Anthony played two years with Glenn Miller and ten with Jimmy Dorsey before forming his own band. Anthony led a group in the Pacific during WWII, then had a highly popular dance band. He probably has as much fame, if not more, as the writer of the theme for *Dragnet*, the novelty tune "The Bunny Hop," and the hit single "Dancing in the Dark." He also had plenty of film and TV work in the 50s, including an appearance in the film *Daddy Long Legs.* –RW

○ **Original Big Band Recordings / HINDSIGHT**   COMP
Very, very pop and "sweet" cuts. –RW

PETER APFELBAUM

Progressive big band, world fusion, modern creative. Leader of his Hieroglyphics Ensemble, saxophonist/composer. Uses jazz, ethnic influences, large ensemble arrangements in a modern/creative format. –MGN

○ **Signs of Life / POLYGRAM**   1989
Good modern large ensemble. Multi-cultural jazz. –MGN

LOUIS ARMSTRONG   1901-1971

Trad, Dixieland, swing. Trumpet, bandleader, vocals. Known variously as "Pops" to most musicians and "Satchmo" to the public, Louis Armstrong is considered by many critics to be the most important and influential figure in jazz history. Any writer who deals with Armstrong soon realizes that all the superlatives that might be applied to his musical contributions have long ago been exhausted, but the current trend is to assign equal importance to his dual roles as artist and entertainer, thus opening up the entirety of his extensive recorded output to serious consideration. From his *Hot Five* rendition of "Heebie Jeebies" (often identified as the first recorded example of "scat" singing) to the All Stars "Hello Dolly" (which displaced the Beatles at the top of the charts in 1964), there is literally something for everyone in the Armstrong discography. Small wonder that his "What A Wonderful World" is currently being used to advertise a variety of products — its appeal is truly universal.

Attempts to explain Armstrong's virtuosity on cornet and trumpet in terms of influences usually focus on Joe "King" Oliver (and sometimes Bunk Johnson), but it is more likely that he drew on the entire range of styles available to him while a precocious youth in New Orleans (including Buddy Petit, Chris Kelly, Henry "Kid" Rena, Manuel Perez, as well as Oliver and Johnson), creating a synthesis which was intensely personal and compelling. Historians now credit him as the pioneer figure in the development of extended solo improvisation with his *Hot Five* recordings, effectively transcending the collective improvisational techniques which were the hallmark of the early New Orleans jazz bands. His singing style was no less creative, setting the standard for virtually every major jazz vocalist who followed him.

Throughout his long career, Armstrong maintained a "down to earth" quality which made him accessible to his audiences; considering his meteoric rise from the Waif's Home to superstar status by the mid 20s, this was a remarkable achievement in its own right. As a symbol for the aspirations of African-Americans, "Pops" offered the world vision of harmony which was more than strictly musical. This fact was not lost upon the State Department: Armstrong's All Stars became the group of choice for "good will" tours designed to win over Third World countries with the escalation of the Cold War in the 50s.

During the course of his recording career, Louis Armstrong was affiliated with virtually every major label in the United States, and a complete sampling of his oeuvre requires a dedicated sense of commitment from the listener because of the sheer enormity of the undertaking. For those who are up to the task, what soon becomes apparent is Armstrong's adaptability — he followed (or led) every trend from the "hot" jazz of the 20s through the swing era, but eventually drew the line at "modern" jazz (bebop), at which point he returned to a "traditional" format with the formation of the All Stars in 1946. In a sense, he came full circle, returning to his roots and the intimacy of a small-band setting populated with a succession of close musical friends. What held all these bands together, what gives Armstrong's work continuity, is his personality, a gift which he offered modestly and sincerely. The sweat-soaked handkerchief and the "Satchmo" smile said it all: It's easy to work hard when you love what you do. This simple message to a complex world is precisely what Louis Armstrong was all about. –BR

○ **The Genius of Louis Armstrong /**   1923
This two-album set, which despite the title, contains recordings made between 1924 and 1932, is out-of-print, but that's the only reason it is denied the highest possible recommedation. Containing 29 tracks, it traces Armstrong's evolution from sideman to his Hot Fives and Hot Sevens and is the best one-album look at this early years. –WR

★ **Hot Fives - Vol. 1 / CBS / DB 5**   1925
Classic early Armstrong as he defines the role of the jazz soloist and vocalist in his initial efforts as a leader. "Heebie Jeebies," "Cornet Chop Suey," "My Heart" are wonderful. –BR

☆ **Hot 5's & Hot 7's - Vol. 2 / CBS / DB 5**   1926
1926-1927. Joined by Kid Ory (tb), Johnny Dodds (cl), Johnny St. Cyr (g), and Lil Hardin Armstrong (p/vcl), Louis keeps the ball rolling with "Wild Man Blues," "Keyhole Blues," "Potato Head Blues." The artist emerging! –BR

Hot 5's & Hot 7's - Vol. 3 / CBS   1927
Earl Hines (p) makes his presence felt and Baby Dodds (d) joins the hit parade, yielding "A Monday Date," "Struttin" With Some Barbecue," "S.O.L. Blues," "Savoy Blues," and "Hotter Than That." A brilliant collaboration and soloing. –BR

☆ **Louis Armstrong & Earl Hines / CBS / DB 5**   1927
A dazzling mesh of talents in "Weather Bird," "West End Blues," "Muggles," and "Basin Street Blues." –BR

Louis Armstrong of New Orleans / MCA   1927
1927-1950. An eclectic overview of Armstrong's career including Johnny Dodds's Black Bottom Stompers, Lil's Hot Shots, the Armstrong-Bechet Quartet, various Armstrong Orchestras, and the All Stars. A great sampler! –BR

Louis & the Big Bands / DRG   192?
Fine late-20s and early-30s cuts. –RW

Stardust / PORTRAIT   1930
Beautiful 1930-1932 sessions. Portrait label didn't last long, but put out some great stuff while it was active, both old and new. –RW

Rare Louis Armstrong / JAZZ ANTHOLOGY (TIS)   1934
Memorable swing versions of "St. Louis Blues" and "Tiger Rag" recorded during a European tour (1934), plus Louis with the Fats Waller sextet (1938). –BR

Best of Decca Years - Vol. 2 / MCA   1935
Vol. 2 : Armstrong the Composer. These recordings range from

a take of "Old Man Mose" recorded in 1935 to a version of "Hobo, You Can't Ride This Train" recorded with Sy Oliver's Orchestra in 1957, and the focus, as the subtitle indicates, is on Armstrong as songwriter, so you get such standards as "Potato Head Blues" and "Struttin' With Some Barbecue," albeit not in their original recordings. This is a 1990 CD compilation. –WR

Pops / RCA   1946
Super reissue of his fine 1946-47 big-band cuts. Probably his last really creative aggregation. –RW

Pops: 1940's Small-Band Sides / RCA   1946
Live and studio dates emphasizing novelties but also revealing the shift toward the All Star format. Duet with Jack Teagarden (tb) on "Rockin' Chair" is a special treat. –BR

At Pasadena Civic Auditorium / GNP-CRESCENDO   1951
Louis and All Stars Joe Darensbourg (cl), Edmond Hall (cl), Trummy Young (tb), and Teddy Buckner (tpt) performing "Sleepytime Down South," "Tin Roof Blues," "Ole Miss," "Perdido," and other favorites. –BR

At Pasadena Civic - Vol. 2 / GNP-CRESCENDO   1951
1987 release. Followup to nice set of 1951-1956 live concerts. –RW

☆ **Plays Fats / CBS**   1955
Mack the Knife / PABLO   1957
1990 reissue of wonderful sessions with longtime favorites Trummy Young (tb) and Edmund Hall (cl). –RW

Meets Oscar Peterson / POLYGRAM   1957
Fantastic meeting of the minds. CD has four bonus cuts from this excellent session. –RW

What a Wonderful World / MCA   1967
1967 & 1968. Pops in the company of Clark Terry (tpt), Urbie Green (tb), J. J. Johnson (tb), Hank Jones (p), and other stars, pleasing and playing on "What a Wonderful World," "Cabaret," "Dream a Little Dream of Me," and the like. –BR

○ **Complete Sessions / CAPITOL**   196?
An album with Duke Ellington. This is a joyful collaboration by two of the greatest names in jazz. Tunes include "Mood Indigo," "Black and Tan Fantasy," and other Ellington pieces. Sideman Barney Bigard (cl) adds particular charm to "It Don't Mean a Thing." –BR

What a Wonderful World / RCA   1970
Title track plus "Mood Indigo," "Give Peace A Chance," "We Shall Overcome," "Boy From New Orleans," with Louis backed by a large string orchestra. –BR

Best of Louis Armstrong / MCA
Mid-60s reissue that contained his Decca cuts in cursory fashion. –RW

Best of Louis Armstrong / VANGUARD-CLASSICAL
Cursory compilation of similar material. –RW

Compact Jazz / POLYGRAM
Louis Armstrong with the Russell Garcia Orchestra and the Oscar Peterson Quartet, the latter including Herb Ellis (g), Ray Brown (b), and Louie Bellson (d), hitting the standards. –BR

○ **Ella and Louis / POLYGRAM / BB 12**
The master and one of his greatest pupil/trainees, Ella Fitzgerald. –RW

Essential / VANGUARD-CLASSICAL
Very nice 1965 two-record set of traditional-style sessions done in Paris. –RW

Jazz 'Round Midnight / POLYGRAM
Good session. –RW

Louis in New York - Vol. 5 / CBS
Super music, part of Columbia's effort to reissue their complete Armstrong output. –RW

Plays W. C. Handy / CBS
Magnificent tributes to Handy by Armstrong. Glittering solos and vocals. –RW

Porgy & Bess / POLYGRAM
The best version of this available in a jazz context. –RW

Rhythm Saved the World / GRP
○ **Satch Plays Fats / CBS / BB 10**
A broad range of moods and melodies as the All Stars explore a nice selection of Waller tunes, including "Blue Turning Grey over You," "Keepin' out of Mischief Now," "Ain't Misbehavin'," and more. –BR

St. Louis Blues - Vol. 6 / CBS
Soaring solos and vocals. –RW

Together/Great Reunion / ULTRADISC
W/ Duke Ellington. Excellent release of their return engagement. Some shaky moments, also some fine moments. –RW

Essence of Louis Armstrong / CBS   COMP
Another anthology. Good, but one record of any type cannot communicate the essence of such a great musician. –RW

ART ENSEMBLE OF CHICAGO

Early free, modern creative. The most famous group to emerge from the AACM (Association for the Advancement of Creative Musicians), formed in the Windy City in 1965, this quintet consists of Lester Bowie (trumpet and other brass instruments), Joseph Jarman and Roscoe Mitchell (reed instruments), Malachi Favors (b), and Don Moye (d). In addition to these main instruments, all five also double on a variety of sound-producing devices, ranging from vibes and banjo to whistles, conch shells, sirens, etc. The AEC started in Paris in 1969 (Moye joined in 1970) and made 11 albums in Europe. After returning home in 1971, the members of the AEC have been involved in many other ventures, singly or together, but the group has remained intact for concert, festivals, and other major engagements. Their motto, "Great Black Music — Ancient to The Future," describes their eclectic approach, based in free jazz but ranging widely over the spectrum of jazz and contemporary improvised music. Costumes, masks, makeup, pantomime, and other forms of theatrics have been an AEC trademark from the start. The group performs its own music exclusively; after more than two decades together, its members have reached a remarkable degree of spontaneous yet disciplined interaction. –DM

Certain Blacks / INNER CITY   1970
○ **Bap-Tizum / ATLANTIC**   1972
Recorded at Ann Arbor Blues & Jazz Festival. Essential. Improvised music. –MGN

○ **Fanfare for the Warriors / ATLANTIC / DB 5**   1973
Joined by Muhal Richard Abrams (p). A great album. –MGN

☆ **Nice Guys / POLYGRAM**   1978
A classic. –RW

● **Full Force / POLYGRAM**   1980
One of their best of the last several years. –MGN

Urban Bushmen / ECM   1980
This is arguably the greatest avant-garde jazz band of the 60s and 70s. –RW

Third Decade / POLYGRAM   1984
Good set; extensive compositions. –RW

DOROTHY ASHBY   ♭1932

Post-bop. Detroit jazz harp player Ashby took blues and gospel roots, classical notions, and swinging rhythms to their height on an unlikely instrument. She sometimes ventured into syrup and original funk, but for the most part she played purely jazz. –MGN

○ **Jazz Harpist / REGENT**   i 1957
Her first and best album. W/ Frank Wess on flute. –MGN

Dorothy Plays for Beautiful People / PRESTIGE   1958
☆ **Hip Harp / PRESTIGE**   i 1958
Fantastic Jazz Harp / ATLANTIC   1965
Detroiter Ashby is the premier player on her instrument. With horns and percussion from Richard Davis (b), Grady Tate (d), Willie Bobo (per). –MGN

Afro Harping / CHESS

AUSTRALIAN JAZZ QUARTET

Swing. 50s and 60s band modeled on the Modern Jazz Quartet. With vibraphonist Jack Brokensha. –MGN

○ **Australian Jazz Quartet / BETHLEHEM**   i 1955
    Australian Jazz Quartet / BETHLEHEM   i 1956

ROY AYERS   b 1940

Post-bop, Latin, contemporary funk. A very talented vibist, Ayers was among the top jazz players of the 60s. He had speed, technique, and the good fortune to appear on some high-profile albums with Herbie Mann. He turned more and more to R&B and funk in the 70s. His group Ubiquity began with prototype jazz-based R&B, then moved more into straight R&B/funk through the 70s. By the late 70s and early 80s, Ayers was essentially an R&B bandleader, with eight albums making the Billboard charts in 1976-1979. –RW

● **West Coast Vibes / UNITED ARTISTS**   i 1964
    Daddy Bug & Friends / ATLANTIC   1969
    Pop-soul & funk touches, but fine vibes solos. –RW
    Ubiquity / POLYDOR   r 1971
    Start of Ubiquity phase; best of funk with R&B-jazz. –RW
○ **Mystic Voyage / POLYDOR / BB 90**   1975
    Africa, Center of the World / POLYDOR   i 1981

ALBERT AYLER   1936-1970

Post-bop, Latin, contemporary funk. Albert Ayler is remembered by many as the epitome of the fire-breathing 60s saxophonists. He was a quirky, genre-crossing tenorist whose raw, bluesy tone combined the archaic vibrato of the early New Orleans jazzmen with the reed-splitting multiphonics of the R&B screamers. In his day he was dismissed as a primitive, a fake, a destroyer of jazz, and, paradoxically, a sell-out when, on his final albums, he shifted his attention to blues and rock grooves (anticipating Miles Davis's more successful fusion efforts). He got his start touring as a teenager with blues harpist Little Walter, and later traveled to California and then to Europe, trying in vain to find musicians and an audience for his evolving ideas. His first recordings were made in Scandinavia in 1962-1963, using local musicians, and during those years he did receive encouragement from Cecil Taylor, Don Cherry, Sonny Rollins, and John Coltrane. What little literature there is often assigns a mentor role to Coltrane, and while Coltrane may have been responsible for getting Ayler a contract with Impulse Records, the musical evidence suggests a mutual relationship, with Coltrane benefiting mainly from the liberating influence of their association.
During Ayler's most fertile period (1964-1966), he made several records in the states for Debut, ESP, and Impulse, and he toured Europe, with many live recordings resulting. His mid-sized ensembles followed a simple, almost formulaic approach — concise sing-along melodies reminiscent of nursery rhymes, hymns, and brass band material would segue abruptly into wild collective improvisation, with Albert's evocative tenor playing the role of a Pied Piper gone mad. This was the time for music of emancipation and catharsis, and Ayler's fresh conception, freed of jazz clichés and delivered with sweat-drenched intensity, was certainly timely. In the late 60s his output decreased, although he seemed more willing than ever to experiment — singing, playing bagpipes, and adding White rock musicians and soul singers to his band. One of these vocalists was his companion Mary Parks (aka Mary Maria), who seemed to dominate the last few efforts before his death by drowning in 1970. Few figures have generated as much controversy and mystified speculation as Ayler, but whatever label you choose to apply — conservative, radical, folk musician, or jazz revolutionary — he created his own unique sound, and that sound is still revelant today. In the CD era, unissued material is still coming out, and his best albums are also being reissued, sparking a long overdue critical reappraisal of his importance. –MB

Albert Ayler, The First Recordings / G.N.P.   1962
His initial album, cut in Stockholm with local bassist and drummer, is mainly of historical importance, but does show the influence of Sonny Rollins and John Coltrane. –MB
    Spiritual Unity / ESP-DIS   1964
☆ **New York Eye and Ear Control / ESP**   1964
A summit meeting of the NYC jazz avant-garde. W/ Don Cherry (tpt), John Tchicai (as), Roswell Rud (tb), Gary Peacock (b). –MB
    Vibrations / ARISTA   1964
Another frequently reissued work with trumpeter Don Cherry has two versions of his memorable "Ghosts." –MB
    Spirits Rejoice / ESP-DIS   1965
    Bells / ESP   1965
Album-length live piece, with a quintet including Charles Tyler (as). Dan Morgenster's insightful notes give a contemporary account of this ensemble archaic sound and wild humor. –MB
☆ **Live in Greenwich Village / MCA / DB 5**   1967
His most-often reissued album presents singalong melodies and free jazz energy from length concert recordings. –MB
● **Love Cry / GRP**   1967
Ayler's second album on Impulse gives a clear view of his folky simplicity in short, well-defined thematic improvisations. –MB
    Music is the Healing Force of the Universe / 9191   1969
At a peak of experimentation, Ayler used bagpipes, blues instrumentals, and vocals to expand his challenging sound and keep his music at the center of controversy. –MB
    Live Lorrach/Paris / HAT ART   1982
Definitive 2-record set of Ayler's touring group featuring his brother Donald (tpt) and Michael Sampson (violin). Clean live recordings enhance the complexity of this band at its peak, ranging from town band melodies to pure sural assault. –MB

AZIMUTH

Jazz. A trio that comprises English vocalist Norma Winstone, her husband, pianist John Taylor, and trumpeter Kenny Wheeler. Winstone formed this trio in the late 70s after playing at Ronnie Scott's club in England with Taylor. She is among England's most revered singers, and a true vocal improviser. Penning songs for Wheeler, pianist Bill Evans, guitarist Egberto Gismonti, and others, she is also a top composer. Taylor has recorded on his own with Wheeler and bassist Dave Holland. –RW

○ **Azimuth / ECM**   1977
John Taylor (p, synth), Kenny Wheeler (tpt), Norma Winstone (v). Deep improvisations, communicative and spiritual. Compositions by Taylor, lyrics by Winstone. –MGN
    The Touchstone / ECM   1978
Taylor adds organ. More atmospheric. –MGN
    1985 / ECM   1985
Some lyrics by Jane White. An acquired taste, but if you do, you'll not let go. –MGN

AZYMUTH

Contemporary funk. Prolific Brazilian jazz trio active for two decades. The originals were Jose Roberto Bertrami on keyboards, Ivan Conti on percussion, and Alex Malheiros on bass. Bertrami met Conti playing in a rock band in 1967. The duo later found Malheiros playing in a bowling alley. They blended Brazilian rhythms and jazz-tinged funk. Their first album was the soundtrack from the film *O Fabuloso Fittipaldi* in 1973. A 1977 Montreux Festival date gave them visibility. –RW

○ **Flame / MILESTONE**   r 1984
The one to get. Flora Purim (v) joins them and things move up a notch. –RW
    Azymuth '85 / POLYGRAM   1985
Prolific Brazilian group makes pleasant, lightweight Afro-Latin mood music. –RW

Crazy Rhythm / MILESTONE 1987
Another good one, featuring Joe Pass (g). –RW

EDDIE BACCUS b 1936

Soul jazz. Baccus is a legendary Cleveland organist — the bridge between Jimmy Smith and Larry Young. –MGN
○ **Feel Real / SMASH** 1962
Studio date. Rare find, but worth the search. –MGN

BENNY BAILEY b 1925

Swing, cool. Trumpeter Bailey played with Teddy Edwards toured with Jay McShann. He later worked with Dizzy Gillespie and Lionel Hampton. He made his home in Europe in 1953, and over the years has recorded with Stan Getz, Eric Dolphy, Les McCann, George Gruntz. An exciting soloist. –JME
○ **Big Brass / CANDID** 1960
Septet w/ trumpeter/leader. Phil Woods (as, bass cl), Julius Watkins (French horn), Les Spann (fl, g), and Tommy Flanagan (p) Trio. Well-known standards and two originals. Extensions from Quincy Jones Big Band, i.e., large sound from 7 pieces. Fine document. –MGN

MILDRED BAILEY 1907-1951

Ballads. Many critics deem Bailey the finest pure jazz singer among White female vocalists. She had a marvelous sense of swing, great timing, and could be rousing, alluring, bawdy, or compelling. She had one of the highest-pitched ranges in jazz history, and also had excellent phrasing. Her brother Al was in Paul Whiteman's Rhythm Boys trio with Bing Crosby, and she worked with Whiteman in the 20s and 30s. She co-led a superior band with her husband Red Norvo from 1936-1939, a group that was billed as featuring "Mr. and Mrs. Swing." After working in 1939 with Benny Goodman, Bailey went solo in the 40s and had her own radio program in 1944-1945. –RW
○ **Mildred Bailey 1944 / HINDSIGHT**
Her Greatest Performances / CBS COMP
A beautiful 3-disc compilation covering the years 1929-1946. –JME

CHET BAKER 1929-1988

Bop, cool, ballads. Baker came to prominence as a trumpet player with Charlie Parker (briefly), then Gerry Mulligan in Los Angeles 1952. He began to record as a leader in 1953 and formed his first quartet with pianist Russ Freeman. Baker's first vocal recordings also date from 1953, and his early recordings for Pacific Jazz are his essence. A light, middle-range-dominant trumpet player and a singer of similar characteristics, his early recordings have an innocence about them rarely captured in his later, more technically assured work. The Prestige albums from 1965 are also fine examples of small combo playing without vocals. Dogged by a narcotics habit throughout his adult life, he spent much of his professional career in Europe. The recordings from Europe vary widely in quality but, in general, the earlier the better. The subject of a film, *Let's Get Lost*, he recorded right up until his death in 1988. –BP
☆ **Complete Pacific Jazz Studio / MOSAIC** 1953
Studio recordings. 1953-1957. W/ Chet Baker Quartet and Russ Freeman. Chet Baker at the height of his powers. –MK
○ **Chet Baker with Strings / COLUMBIA** 1954
Wonderful playing; intelligent orchestrations. –RW
○ **Complete Pacific Jazz Live Recordings / MOSAIC** 1954
W/ Chet Baker Quartet and Russ Freeman. Chet Baker at his peak. –MK
○ **Chet Baker in New York / RIVERSIDE** 1958
Outstanding lineup includes Johnny Griffin (ts), Al Haig (p), Paul Chambers (b), and Philly Joe Jones (d). –RW
Introduces Johnny Pace / OJC 1958
Some interesting guests, among them Herbie Mann (fl), Philly Joe Jones (d). –RW

Playboys / PACIFIC JAZZ r 1958
● **Chet / OJC** 1959
Chet's romantic best, done with Pepper Adams (bar sax), Kenny Burrell (g). –MGN
Plays Lerner & Loewe / OJC r 1959
Some stalwart Baker renditions of Lerner & Lowe greats. –ED
Let's Get Lost / NOVUS i 1989
Songs from the rarely seen movie about Baker. –MGN
The Route / CAPITOL 1991
Live at Ronnie Scotts / POLYGRAM
New Blue Horns / OJC
A rare meeting with Kenny Dorham (tpt). –RW

BURT BALES 1916-1989

Trad, Dixieland. Known primarily as a pianist, Burt Bales was also accomplished on mellophone and baritone horn. He began his career with dance bands in the 30s, but soon responded to the "traditional" revival of New Orleans jazz that hit the Bay Area in the early 40s. He played with Bunk Johnson during the trumpeter's triumphal visit to San Francisco in 1944 and led his own band in 1945-1949, while also maintaining a working relationship with Lu Watters and Turk Murphy, then later with Bob Scobey and Marty Marsala in the 50s. His love of ragtime and early jazz piano style (especially Jelly Roll Morton) was clearly evident throughout his career, but most reviewers felt that Bales added a sensitivity and subtlety to the music that was all his own. Often described as playing with a "rocking" style, Burt Bales was a specialist at bringing "old" music back to life. –BR
○ **They Tore My Playhouse Down / GOOD TIME JAZZ** 1953
Burt Bale's testament to Jelly Roll Morton, with numbers such as "Wild Man Blues," "New Orleans Joys," and "Midnight Mama," backed with Paul Lingle's mixed bag of W.C. Handy and Jelly Roll blues and stomps, including "Memphis Blues" and "Black Bottom Stomp" (1953). –BR

AMIRI BARAKA b 1934

Post-bop, modern creative, spoken word. A poet/activist who occasionally reads his powerful works with musicians, Baraka is a premier Black spokesperson. –MGN
☆ **New Music, New Poetry / INDIA NAVIGATION** 1980
Inciendiary poet reads in performance with David Murray (ts) and Steve McCall (d). –MGN

PAUL BARBARIN 1899-1969

Trad. A member of one of New Orleans' most renowned musical dynasties, Paul Barbarin developed his drumming style on the streets of the Crescent City playing with bands like Buddy Petit's Young Olympians while still a teenager. In 1917 he left home to find work in the stockyards of Chicago but soon found more conducive employment playing with transplanted homeboys like King Oliver and Jimmie Noone, as well as a number of Chicago outfits. He maintained a strong association with New Orleans artists, working with Oliver's Dixie Syncopators in the mid 20s before joining Luis Russell's Orchestra in 1928, a move which afforded opportunities to play with Jelly Roll Morton and Louis Armstrong in the 30s. By 1939 Barbarin was back in New Orleans, but he returned to Chicago in 1942-43 to join Henry "Red" Allen's Sextet and in the following year Sidney Bechet. After World War II he stayed in his hometown, performing with a variety of small combos and brass bands, including the Onward Brass Band (formed in 1960 and named after the original Onward which his father Isidore had led at the turn of the century). In the last decade of his life he became affiliated with many of the musicians who worked at Preservation Hall, such as Sweet Emma Barrett, with whom he recorded. During this period he also made several recordings under his own leadership, for Atlantic, Nobility, and Southland. His death in 1969 occured while he was leading the Onward for a street parade, ending his career as he first began it. –BR

☆ **New Orleans Jazz / ATLANTIC**   1955
Fine traditional New Orleans cuts, one of the rare sessions of this type on Atlantic label. −RW

Jazz at Preservation Hall - Vol. 3 / ATL   1962
This album offers a mixed bag featuring Paul Barbarin's Band/Punch Miller's Bunch & George Lewis (cl). Worth acquiring for Barbarin composition "The Second Line" alone, but offers much more. −BR

New Orleans Jazz Band / GOOD TIME   1962
Arguably their best on this label. −RW

CHRIS BARBER   b 1930

Big band, blues-jazz, progressive big band. British big band leader and trombonist; he has few domestic recordings or US tours since the 60s. He has worked in New Orleans and blues styles with Dr. John. −MGN

○ **Live in East Berlin / BLACK LION**   1968

GATO BARBIERI   b 1934

Early free, Latin, jazz-rock, contemporary funk. Tenor sax, composer. Barbieri ranks among the most popular Latin-jazz players ever. He has had a complete career turnaround since the mid 60s when he was a screaming avant-garde player under the influence of Pharoah Sanders. Born in Argentina, Barbieri made an early impact in Lalo Schfrin's band in 1953. He traveled through Europe, meeting Don Cherry in Paris in 1956 and recording with him in New York in 1966. Barbieri made a splash in 1969 by mixing Latin American rhythms with free-music influences and techniques. During the early 70s, he made some substantial records with sweeping, blazing solos, but he switched to a lush, romantic style in 1972 with the Grammy-winning *Last Tango in Paris* soundtrack. Despite cutting adventurous albums with Latin musicians during the 70s, his sensual sessions with strings are now viewed as his legacy. −RW

In Search of Mystery / ESP   1967
Gato Barbieri is on the edge in this animated, though uneven date. −RW

The Third World / FLYING DUTCHMAN   1969
Frenetic tenor solos, daring Afro-Latin concept. −RW

★ **Fennix / FLYING DUTCHMAN**   1971
The manic album that won him fame on college campuses in early 70s. Still his greatest record on all levels. Nana Vasconcelos is tremendous on percussion. −RW

El Pampero / FLYING DUTCHMAN   1971
Live. Some of his fiercest playing on record. −RW

Under Fire / FLYING DUTCHMAN   1971
Superb solos, great bass work from Stanley Clarke. −RW

○ **Last Tango in Paris / UNITED ARTISTS**   1972
An incredibly popular soundtrack, dreamy and lush. Still sounds great 20 years later. Grammy winning, sensual soundtrack to the controversial film. −RW

○ **Chapter 1: Latin America / MCA / DB 5**   r 1973
One of the four chapters. You may wish to hear them all. Early to mid 70s. Definitive work from this Argentinian saxophonist. −MGN

Chapter 3: Viva Emiliano Zapata / GRP   1974
After disappointing sequel, the third volume in the series again had the fire and energy of the first. −RW

Chapter 4: Alive in New York / ABC-IMPULSE   1975
Satisfactory conclusion to Latin America series. −RW

○ **Caliente / A&M / BB 75**   1976
His best Latin jazz/pop recording. −RW

Third World Revisited / BLUEBIRD   r 1988
Driving solos, nice arrangements. −RW

A. SPENCER BAREFIELD   b 1953

Modern creative. Acoustic guitarist whose creative improvised stance allows him a unique sound and approach, yet with a

---

Music Map **Jazz Piano**

> **Keyboards from Europe**

> **Ragtime**
> Scott Joplin (1868-1917) — Joe Lamb (1887-1960)

> **Early Jazz Piano**
> Eubie Blake (1883-1983)
> ● Jelly Roll Morton (1890-1941) — Earl Hines (1903-1983)

> **Stride Piano**
> Lucky Roberts (1887-1968) — Willie "the Lion" Smith (1897-1973)
> James P. Johnson (1894-1955) — Fats Waller (1904-1943)

> **Boogie-Woogie**
> Jimmy Yancey (1898-1951) — Pine Top Smith (1904-1929)
> Pete Johnson (1904-1967) — Meade "Lux" Lewis (1905-1964)
> Little Brother Montgomery (1906-1985)
> ● Albert Ammons (1907-1949) — Memphis Slim (1915)

> **Major Influence**
> Art Tatum (1909-1956)

> **Swing Piano**
> Count Basie (1904-1986) — Jess Stacy (1904)
> Art Hodes (1904) — ● Teddy Wilson (1912-1986)
> Erroll Garner (1921-1977) — Ralph Sutton (1922)

> **Transition to Bop**
> ● Thelonious Monk (1917-1982)

> **Bop Piano**
> Mary Lou Williams (1910-1981) — Lennie Tristano (1919-1978)
> ● Bud Powell (1924-1966) — Al Haig (1924)
> Oscar Peterson (1925) — Barry Harris (1929)

> **Cool Piano**
> Lennie Tristano (1919-1978)
> John Lewis (1920) — Bill Evans (1929-1980)

> **Post Bop**
> Herbie Nichols (1919-1963) — Red Garland (1923-1984)
> Randy Weston (1926) — ● Horace Silver (1928)
> Phineas Newborn (1931) — Jaki Byard (1922)
> Tommy Flanagan (1930) — ● Wynton Kelly (1931-1971)
> Bobby Timmons (1935-1974) — ● McCoy Tyner (1938)

> **Free-Style**
> Sun Ra (1915) — ● Cecil Taylor (1929)
> Muhal Richard Abrams (1930)

> **Electric / Contemporary**
> Joe Zawinul (1932) — ● Herbie Hancock (1940)
> ● Chick Corea (1941) — Keith Jarrett (1945)

> **Revival**
> Jim Dapogny — Judy Carmichael — Mr. B
> Dick Wellstood (1927-1987) — Dick Hyman (1927)

> **New Players**
> Mulgrew Miller (1955) — Renee Rosnes — Geri Allen
> Marcus Roberts — Kenny Kirkland (1955) — Benny Green

haunting melodicism and angular ideas that reflect Monk influence. –MGN

○ **Trans-Dimensional ... / TRANS-AFRICAN** 1981
Trans-Dimensional Space Window. Progressive but listenable venture for unique guitar sound of innovator Barefield. With Anthony Holland (sax) and Tani Tabbal (per). "In Between Song" is exceptional. –MGN

DANNY BARKER b 1909

Trad, Dixieland, swing. Guitar, banjo, vocals, composer. Legendary New Orleans guitarist. Transcends all early eras and styles of jazz while staying true to tradition. A most knowledgable and witty player. –MGN

○ **Save the Bones / ORLEANS** 1988

GEORGE BARNES 1921-1977

Swing. Jazz guitar pioneer. One of the first to plug in, Barnes actually recorded on electric guitar before Charlie Christian, as a sideman to blues singers. His unmistakably bright sound and attack, clarinet-like lines, and masterful nuances revealed the instrument's potential to a generation of 40s guitarists who heard him on the radio. It was Barnes, as much as anyone, who demonstrated that the guitar could achieve equal footing with the horns as a melodic instrument. He made the instrument sing as few jazz guitarists have done. In 1963, after having spent many years as a studio musician, Barnes teamed with guitarist Carl Kress for a series of excellent recordings. In the 70s, he played duets with guitarist Bucky Pizzarelli, before forming a quartet with cornetist Ruby Braff. –RL

Uncollected George Barnes / HINDSIGHT 1946
W/ Octet. Unusual arrangements by Barnes, featured here with NBC studio musicians. –RL

Blues Going Up / CONCORD r 1977
Live date, Barnes's last. A nice introduction to his style. –RL

○ **Guitars Anyone / CARNEY**
Grab this album if you are lucky enough to find a copy. One of the great guitar duos. Carl Kress's rich rhythm guitar playing and chorded solos perfectly complement by Barnes's lead work. –RL

CHARLIE BARNET 1913-1991

Swing, big band. Bandleader, vocals, saxophone. Barnet was a fine swing-era bandleader and player of musical and political importance. He headed bands from age 16 until his death at 78. He was a master talent evaluator, spotting Lena Horne, Buddy De Franco, and Dodo Marmarosa, among many others, in their early stages. He had some big hits in the 30s and 40s, particularly "Cherokee" in 1939. He was also among the first White bandleaders to hire Black musicians in the 30s, without the fanfare given to some others. –RW

○ **Barnet - Vol. 1 (1935-1939) / EPM** 1935
An excellent reissue of late and mid-30s swing cuts. –RW

● **Clap Hands, Here Comes Charlie / RCA** 1939
Cuts from 1939-1941. Classic swing with rare Lena Horne vocals. First-rate mastering. –RW

Charlie Barnet - Vol. 1 / RCA 1939
Tremendous recordings from 1939-1942. –RW

Orchestra - 1941 / CIRCLE 1941
Top-drawer 1941 recordings. –RW

Orchestra - 1945 / CIRCLE 1945
More exciting big-band recordings. –RW

Big Band 1967 / MOBILE FIDELITY 1966
An example of late Barnet. A surprisingly good set. Wonderful recording. –RW

RAY BARRETTO b 1929

Soul jazz, progressive big band, Latin, salsa. Barretto ranks among the greatest, most influential percussionists of all time. He brought Latin rhythms into the jazz mainstream and has been exhaustively recorded since the early 50s. He has also

done numerous R&B and rock dates and many salsa sessions. Born in Brooklyn, Barretto played with jazz musicians in New York. He made his way up the ladder and eventually replaced Mongo Santamaria in Tito Puente's band, working with him for four years. Barretto made his first Latin-jazz album for Riverside in 1965 and has been active ever since as a player, session man, and producer. He rivals Mongo and Puente as the best-known Latin-jazz instrumentalist. –RW

○ **Carnaval / FANTASY** 1973

KENNY BARRON b 1943

Post-bop. His professional career as a pianist began at 15 with an R&B band in his native Philadelphia. He then worked with Philly Joe Jones, Yuseff Lateef, and Jimmy Heath. Barron came to New York in 1961 and joined Dizzy Gillespie's group a year later, staying until 1966. Stints with Freddie Hubbard, Stanley Turrentine, Buddy Rich, Ron Carter, and many others followed. He became one of the most in demand recording artists in jazz. Barron made his first album as a leader in 1974, a year after he'd been appointed to the faculty of Rutgers University (where he's a tenured professor). He co-led the group Sphere (dedicated to the music of Thelonious Monk) and has fronted his own trios and quintets. In the early 90s, Barron hooked up with saxophonist Stan Getz, who made his final live recording (*People Time*) with just the pianist. A marvelously musical player with his own distinctive touch, Barron can adapt to any situation and could be described as a latter-day Hank Jones. –RW

Sunset at Dawn / MUSE 1973
A fine early date. –RW

Peruvian Blue / MUSE 1974
Golden Lotus / MUSE 1980
Spiral / EASTWIND 1982
Autumn in New York / UPTOWN 1986
Lemuria-Seascape / CANDID 1991

● **Quickstep / RHINO** r 1991
Composer Barron's best group effort. "Big Girls" is a big composition. –MGN

Rhythm-A-Ning / CANYON r 1991
A pair of superb pianists trade, swap, and complement each other. –RW

○ **Live at Maybeck Recital Hall / CONCORD**
Wonderful Kenny Barron solo set. Bonus cuts in disc. –RW

GARY BARTZ b 1940

Hard-bop, post-bop. Baltimore-born saxophonist whose tart/sweet sound makes him distinctive. He can play straight or out, or both. –MGN

● **Libra / MILESTONE** 1969
Excellent compositions and playing in mainstream mode. Features Kenny Barron on piano and Jimmy Owens on Trumpet. This is the more lyrical side of Bartz. –MGN

○ **West 42nd Street / CANDID** 1990
There Goes the Neighborhood / CANDID 1991

PAUL BASCOMB b 1910

Trad, Dixieland. Originally from Alabama, the brother of Dud Bascomb. A tenor saxophonist, he worked extensively with Erskine Hawkins Orchestra and led his own bands in Chicago and Detroit in the 50s. –MGN

○ **Bad Bascomb! / DELMARK** 1951

COUNT BASIE 1904-1984

Swing, big band. One of the towering figures in big-band jazz, Basie was a leader from 1935 until his death. His lean piano style was like a signature, and he was a master at setting tempos and making a rhythm section swing. Born in New Jersey, Bill Basie learned his piano craft from James P. Johnson and Fats Waller and was touring on the vaudeville circuit while still a teenager. Stranded in Kansas City in 1927, he settled there, joined Walter Page's Blue Devils (the hottest KC band), and then Bennie Moten's Orchestra (the most successful KC band). He took over when Moten died suddenly in 1935, but then scaled down to a smaller band, the Barons of Rhythm, at the Reno Club in KC. Talent spotter John Hammond heard the band on his car radio and zoomed out to hear them live, got them a record deal, and made Basie expand to go on a national tour. With such soloists as Lester Young and Herschel Evans on tenors, Buck Clayton and (a bit later) Harry Edison on trumpets, and a rhythm section of Freddie Green, guitar, former boss Walter Page, bass, and Jo Jones, drums, the streamlined swing of Basie & Co. captivated both jazz fans and dancers and made the band part of jazz royalty. Though he briefly was forced to lead a sextet (1950-1951), Basie soon was back at the helm of a 16-piece crew; this "new testament" band (as it was dubbed by Basie biographer Albert Murray) became a jazz institution, notably after singer Joe Williams joined, and continues today as the Count Basie Band led by Frank Foster, one of Count's most distinguished post-1952 alumni. In the history of jazz, no name is more synonymous with swinging big-band jazz. —DM

Best of Count Basie / MCA   1937
Nice two-record set of his 1937-1939 material on Decca. —RW

Essential Count Basie - Vols. 1 & 2 / CBS   1939
1987 reissue of majestic cuts from his powerhouse band, along with septet cuts. The Basie band in glorious form. —RW

The Complete Decca Recordings / GRP   193?
All of Basie's best sides from 1937-1939. —MGN

Brand New Wagon / RCA   1947
1990 reissue of cuts with his 1947 band that still packs a sizeable punch. CD has four bonus cuts. —RW

Essential Count Basie - Vol. 3 / CBS   194?
More super 40s cuts. These three volumes are first in a full series of reissues covering Basie's Columbia output. —RW

Greatest! Basie Swings, Williams Sings / VERVE   1955
Good compilation of big hits. —RW

○ **Swings with Joe Williams / POLYGRAM**   1955
Simply glorious after all these years. Williams was the greatest singer in this style in 1955, at least among males. —RW

At Newport / POLYGRAM   1957
Wonderful date, rocking sides. —RW

Atomic Mr. Basie / ROULETTE   1957
Romping, swinging cuts. Neal Hefti compositions. —RW

★ **April in Paris / POLYGRAM**   1959
Basie's best without a doubt. A classic among classics. W/ Thad Jones (tpt), Joe Newman (tpt), Frank Foster (ts), Frank Wess (ts), Freddie Green (g), and Sonny Payne (d). —MGN

○ **Basie Swings, Bennett Sings / ROULETTE JAZZ**   1959
Dynamic meeting of the great singer and great band. —RW

○ **Sing Along with Basie / CAPITOL**   1959
Brilliant date with Lambert, Hendricks & Ross doing their take on Basie. —RW

Basie in London / POLYGRAM / DB 5   195?
1988 reissue of some superb 50s cuts with Joe Williams (v) on the case. CD has a few bonus cuts. —RW

Hits of the 50's and 60's / REPRISE   1960
Good renditions of established hits. —RW

Kansas City Suite / CAPITOL   1960
1990 reissue of this beautiful set with Benny Carter's compositions. Nice lineup. —RW

Count Basie Story / ROULETTE   1961
Nice anthology for its time frame. —RW

☆ **Basie & Kansas City 7 / MCA**   1962
1986 reissue of masterful 60s date that's been undervalued in Basie legacy. Tasteful, restrained, yet it still swings. —RW

On the Sunny Side of the Street / VERVE   1963
Tremendous dates with Ella Fitzgerald (v). Quincy Jones arranged. —RW

Sinatra-Basie / REPRISE / BB 5   1963
Just a wonderful collaboration. Sinatra still sounds interested and dynamic. —RW

Fun Time / PABLO   1975
This is a 1991 reissue of good set. Jovial, relaxed, and very well done. —RW

Basie Jam - Vols. 1-3 / PABLO   1976
Nice big-band sets, but not on level of his greatest groups. —RW

Yessir, That's My Baby / PABLO   1978
1987 reissue of a fine set. —RW

High Voltage / POLYGRAM   197?
Good early-70's material. —RW

Ella & Basie / POLYGRAM   1991

1975 Jam Session at Montreux / POL / DB 5
Very solid, enjoyable sessions. —RW

Afrique / DR. JAZZ
Arrangements by Oliver Nelson. —MGN

Basie in Sweden / CAPITOL
First-rate 1991 reissue of Basie in Sweden with good group including Frank Wess, Frank Foster. The CD version has two bonus cuts. —RW

Basie & Zoot / PABLO / DB 5

Blues by Basie / CBS
Interesting concept: great selections from various Basie orchestras, 1939-50. Some glittering solos and vocals. —RW

Count Basie Meets Oscar Peterson / PABLO

For the First Time / PABLO
Outstanding trio recordings. Count shows off his piano savvy alongside Ray Brown (b) and Louis Bellson (d). —RW

Legend — The Legacy / POLYGRAM
Nice playing, familiar cuts. —RW

Long Live the Chief / POLYGRAM
Solid modern recordings, nothing flashy or fancy. —RW

Loose Walk / PABLO
Loose and entertaining pairing. —RW

○ **One O'clock Jump / MCA**
This a 1990 reissue of prime Basie cuts. His powerhouse 30's/40's orchestra with Lester Young (sax), Jimmy Rushing (v), etc. —RW

Satch & Josh / PABLO
Oscar Peterson (p) makes a fine partner. —RW

Satch & Josh Again / PA2
W/ Oscar Peterson (p). The duo revive their act with excellent results. —RW

○ **Sixteen Men Swinging / VERVE**

MICKEY BASS   b1943

Jazz. Bass Player from Pittsburgh. —MGN

○ **Another Way Out / EARLY BIRD REC.**
Bassist Bass as leader. Might be hard to find, but worth the search. —MGN

BILLY BAUER   b1915

Swing, bop.. Swing to Bop guitarist whose ability to play free within structures sets him apart from strict chordal players. Innovative for his time. —MGN

○ **Let's Have a Session / AD LIB**   i1955
Plectrist / NORGRAN   i1956

BAY CITY JAZZ BAND

Trad, Dixieland. 50s traditional jazz band (an octet). —RW

○ **Golden Days! / GOOD TIME JAZZ**   195?

BEBOP & BEYOND

Post-bop. A quality West Coast ensemble led by Mel Martin, they issued several good hard-bop and mainstream albums in the late 80s and 90s, most with a balance between originals and standards. Their best is a recent collaboration with Dizzy Gillespie, where Diz's Latin-jazz background and still-impressive trumpet mastery are in evidence. —RW

Plays Dizzy Gillespie / RHINO   r 1991
Bebop & Beyond / CONCORD
○ **Plays Thelonious Monk, Plays Dizzy Gillespie / RHINO**
These are two excellent albums. Led by saxophonist Mel
Martin. –MGN

SIDNEY BECHET   1897-1959

Trad, Dixieland, swing. Clarinet, soprano saxophone. Born in
New Orleans, Bechet was a prodigy who turned pro at 13 and
left home three years later. By 1919, he was in Europe with
composer Will Marion Cook's Southern Syncopated Orchestra.
Back home in 1924, he made his first records, showing that he
had no peers when it came to soloing; soon he was teamed on
disc with another New Orleanian, Louis Armstrong, the only
player then who could hold his own with him. Soon Bechet
was off to Europe again, touring as far afield as Russia, where
he was lionized. The 30s found him back home; his 1932 sides
with his New Orleans Feetwarmers are classics. After some
years in Noble Sissle's Society Dance Band, Bechet was
rediscovered and became a fountainhead of the traditional
jazz revival. After World War II, he re- turned to Europe;
settling in France in 1951, he became one of that country's
biggest stars. Though he never abandoned the clarinet, from
1920 on Bechet concentrated on the soprano sax, of which he
was the first and greatest master. His tone was as powerful as
a trumpet's, and he took the lead in any group he played with.
His autobiography, *Treat It Gentle*, is one of the most moving
books about jazz. –DM

And the Blues Singers - Vol. 1 / FAT CAT'S JAZZ   1923
Early Bechet with Clarence Williams's Blue Five, Sara Martin,
Eva Taylor, and Margaret Johnson. Bechet as accompanist. –BR
○ **And Bechet in New York / SMITHSONIAN**   1923
1923-1925. A good set that's better than what's available
elsewhere. –RW
Wild Cat Blues / MUSIC MEMORIA   1923
New set covering the years 1923-1937. The first of a series
documenting the complete Bechet legacy. Some duplication
with other available sets. –RW
Sidney Bechet, 1924-38 / BBC CD   1924
A compendium of Bechet sides with the Blue Five, Red Onion
Jazz Babies, Noble Sissle & His International Orchestra, and
Noble Sissle's Swingsters, providing good coverage of the
clarinetist in differing musical formats (especially on
sarrusophone on "Mandy, Make Up Your Mind!"). –BR
Jazz Heritage - Blackstick (1931-1938) / MCA   1931
★ **The Legendary / RCA**   1932
Duplicates some of the cuts on *Master Takes* — good
collection more suitable for initial sampling. –BR
☆ **Master Takes 1932-1943 / RCA / DB 5**   1932
Three-disc set containing the bulk of Bechet's recordings
made in the US, covering seventeen different combinations of
musicians (including the renowned one-man band session in
which Bechet accompanied himself in 1941!). The epitome of
passion by one of New Orleans's greatest clarinet/soprano
masters. –BR
Port at Harlem Jazzmen / MOSAIC   1939
Super date from 1939. –RW
☆ **Complete Blue Note Recordings / MOSAIC**   i 1939
Fantastic six-disc set covering all 13 Blue Note recording
sessions. –RW
And Friends / POLYGRAM
At Storyville / BLACK LION

JOE BECK   b 1945

Jazz-rock, contemporary funk. Studio and session guitarist best
known for hits when backing vocalist Esther Phillips on Kudu
in the 70s. During the 80s he made a series of competent
fusion and pop/jazz recordings for DMP, and had a big hit
recording with Dave Sanborn on CTI in 1975. –RW
○ **Beck & Sanborn / CBS**   1970

BIX BEIDERBECKE   1903-1931

Dixieland, swing. Dead at 28 of alcohol abuse, Bix Beiderbecke
is one of jazz's great romantic legends — an icon of the "jazz
age." In fact, Bix was an enormously gifted "natural" who took
to the new musical language of jazz as if to the manner born.
His cornet sound ("like a girl saying 'yes'," in Eddie Condon's
words) was a thing of beauty, and it survives on a few dozen
records, none of which give him much room. But Bix could tell
a story in eight or sixteen bars. Also an accomplished pianist,
he recorded his most famous composition, "In a Mist," on that
instrument. He reached the peak of his career as a member of
Paul Whiteman's orchestra (1927-1929), then at the pinnacle
of the popular music world, but though Whiteman loved his
playing, he had to let him go. The whole sad story of Bix's
short life is told in rich detail by Dick Sudhalter et al., in *Bix:
Man & Legend.* –DM
Bix Lives! / RCA   1927
This album includes Jean Goldkette and Whiteman material.
A nice compliment to the Columbia Records compilations
(Vols. 1 & 2). –RL
○ **And the Chicago Cornets / MILESTONE**
Essential early Beiderbecke, but terrible sound quality. –RW
At the Jazz Band Ball - Vol. 2 / CBS
1990 reissue, followup to material on *Singin' the Blues.* –RW
☆ **Singin' the Blues - Vol. 1 / CBS**
With Frankie Trumbauer (sax), Eddie Lang (g), and
others. –RL

RICHIE BEIRACH   b 1947

Post-bop, early free, jazz-rock, neo bop, modern creative. A good
modern pianist who is equally adept at acoustic or electric
piano and synthesizer, Beirach's forte is duet sessions in which
his ability to anticipate and react are most beneficial. His best
releases thus far are duets with John Abercrombie and George
Coleman and a 1989 combo tribute to Chet Baker. –RW
● **Forgotten Fantasies / A&M**   ca. 1975
This features brilliant duets with longtime partner David
Liebman (fl/sax), on the creative side. Beirach wrote three of
the six cuts, and shows his original approach to jazz. –MGN
Elegy for Bill Evans / PAJ   1981
This tribute to Beirach's good friend and influence, has trio
jazz with Al Foster on drums and George Mraz on bass.
Includes three songs cowritten by Evans and Miles Davis, two
other standards, and Evans's immortal "Peace Piece." –MGN
○ **Convergence / TRIPLE X**
Great communications. Pianist Richard Beirach and tenor
saxophonist George Coleman. –MGN

BOB BELDEN

Progressive big band, neo bop. Known for Gil Evans-influenced
larger ensemble music, themes for ESPN programs. Uses
updated sounds as vehicle for improvisation. Spirited. –MGN
○ **Treasure Island / SUNNYSIDE**   r 1990
Compositional jazz in the tradition of George Russell and Gil
Evans. A very good effort. –MGN

MARCUS BELGRAVE   b 1936

Post-bop, post-bop, soul jazz, progressive big band. Veteran
trumpeter whose major credits include work with Ray
Charles, Charles Mingus, McCoy Tyner, and George Gruntz. A
major inventive contributor to the jazz language. –MGN
○ **Gemini II / TRIBE**   1974
Nonet with master trumpeter. Sometimes funky, spacy, or
swinging, but always potent. With Roy Brooks, Wendell
Harrison, Harold McKinney, and Phil Ranelin. The band
sounds twice its size due to the expansive compositional
stance of the leader. –MGN

LOUIE BELLSON   b 1924

Swing, big band, post-bop, progressive big band. Drummer and bandleader, primarily West Coast. Occasionally he heads his own big band or plays as a sideman. Collaborates frequently with other drummers. Technically brilliant, he plays swing-oriented music primarily, but is adept at blues or rock. A popular figure. –MGN

Thunderbird / JASMINE   1963
Torrid playing in spots, excellent arrangements. –RW

● **150 M.P.H. / COJ**   1974
Good big-band work. –RW

Explosion / CONCORD   1975
Fine mid-70's sessions. –RW

Louie Bellson's 7 / PABLO   1976
Nice septet cuts, some strong drum solos. –RW

Ecue Ritmos Cubanos / OJC   1977
Raincheck / COJ   1978
Nice combo recordings. –RW

Side Track / COJ   1979
Fine small-combo recordings. –RW

Jazz Giants / MUSICMATES   1989
Excellent 1989 set with some major names; w/ a good Buddy Rich (d) vs. Bellson track. –RW

○ **Airmail Special / MUSICMASTERS**
A Salute to the Big Band Masters. Powerhouse salute to big-band masters. –RW

TEX BENEKE   b 1914

Big band. Very popular big band entertainer, singer, tenor saxophonist. He sang with the Glenn Miller Orchestra (1938-1942), then led his own group. Beneke sang and toured with the Modernaires and appeared on recordings such as "Chattanooga Choo Choo." He continued to perform into the 80s. –MGN

○ **Palladium Patrol / AEROSPACE**
Big band.

SATHIMA BEA BENJAMIN

Ballads, modern creative. Benjamin is a good, expressive singer who has found a balance between African and jazz vocal styles. Her most recent date was a 1990 session with Ricky Ford, and she also appears on some of her husband Abdullah Ibrahim's releases. –RW

● **Windsong / BLACK HAWK**   1985
Jazz standards with the Kenny Barron (p) Trio. –MGN

○ **Love Light / CAPITOL-RHINO**   r 1990
A fine set. Carlos Ward almost steals the show on alto sax. –RW

GEORGE BENSON   b 1943

Cool, soul jazz, instr-pop, contemporary funk. George Benson ranks among the most talented jazz guitarists and vocalists currently active, although he has enjoyed his greatest commercial success making his least (artistically) impressive music. His initial recognition was as a vocalist, making some recordings at 11 for a tiny R&B label. He began studying guitar shortly after and, as a teen, joined Jack McDuff's group, staying with him from 1962-1965. Benson led his own band with organist Lonnie Smith, then won fame for his participation in a 1967 Spirituals To Swing anniversary concert. He began to move into lighter, pop-influenced crossover material in the late 60s on A&M, which was enjoying success with Wes Montgomery in a similiar vein. He hit the bigtime in 1976 with *Breezin'* (a Top Ten hit), a collection of easy-listening, orchestrated numbers centered around a vocal rendition of Leon Russell's "Masquerade." After a string of hit albums all patterned on the same formula, Benson returned to jazz in 1990, cutting a date with the Count Basie orchestra. His fluidity, relaxed yet dynamic vocal presence, and overall skills make almost anything Benson records at least interesting, and he periodically flashes his real skills in either live performance or special recording sessions. –RW

○ **New Boss Guitar / OJC**   r 1964
Definitive early album. W/ Brother Jack McDuff (organ). –MGN

○ **Cookbook / COLUMBIA**   1966
Simmering interplay, fueled by guitarist Benson and baritone saxophonist Ronnie Cuber make this early-60s effort one to savor. Six Benson originals, four standards. Produced by John Hammond. Lonnie Smith (organ), Bennie Green (tb). –MGN

The Other Side of Abbey Road / A&M   r 1970
Important for signs of external change in direction. –RW

○ **Beyond the Blue Horizon / CBS**   1971
Very worthwhile. Originally on CTI. –MGN

○ **White Rabbit / CBS**   1971
This is the best collaboration between Benson and guitarist Earl Klugh (g). –RW

● **Best Of George Benson / CBS**   1971
This is a 1989 compilation covers Benson's tenure at CTI Records, 1971-1975, and presents his best as a pure jazz guitarist, prior to his move to singing and the pop-jazz approach found in "Breezin'" and later albums. –WR

Bad Benson / CBS / BB 78   1974
A good overview of soul-jazz period. –RW

○ **Good King Bad / CBS**   1976
This is a good place to hear Benson playing at his jazz best, rather than his commercial best. –JME

● **Breezin' / WARNER / BB 1**   1976
This was the definitive Benson album commercially; counterpart to Wes Montgomery's pop works of the 60s. Platinum Album. –RW

GEORGE BENSON (SAXOPHONIST)   b 1929

Swing, bop. Veteran saxophonist plays alto and tenor from Detroit. A smooth, lyrical, melodic player somewhat similar to Johnny Hodges and Paul Desmond. A small group player. –MGN

● **The Detroit Jazz Tradition - Alive & Well / PARKWOOD** 1983
The Detroit saxophonist is with All Stars J. C. Heard (d), Claude Black (p), and Dave Young (b). All standards save two are Heard bluesy swing numbers. A solid album through and through. –MGN

○ **Swings & Swings & Swings / PARKWOOD**   1986
Detroit's premier alto and tenor saxophonist sings and swings on his instruments here. Includes two Benson originals and five standards, with a particularly nice "Record-A-Me." Canadian Reg Schwager is on guitar, with Dave Young on bass and Archie Alleyne on drums. –MGN

BOB BERG   b 1951

Post-bop, neo bop. Bob Berg is one of many modern sax players (tenor and soprano) whose career has been affected by his time with Miles Davis. A free-jazz player with energy and style in the 60s, Berg became an orthodox hard-bop soloist in the 70s, then joined Miles in the mid 80s and got the fusion/electric conversion. He's very solid technically — a big sound. Lately his releases have balanced traditional and contemporary elements. –RW

○ **New Birth / XANADU**   1978
Tenor man's best effort. Originals, swinging. With Tom Harrell (tp). –MGN

Short Stories / DENON   r 1988
Includes the hit "Friday Night at the Cadillac Club." –MGN

KARL BERGER   b 1945

Post-bop, early free, world fusion, modern creative. One of the more prolific players during the 60s and 70s, Karl Berger has been more prominent as an educator than as a musician in recent years. But he's one of the greatest vibes players ever, and was a daring, explosive soloist and ambitious composer who worked with and/or led some of the more interesting and intriguing bands from the mid 60s on through the 70s. Berger earned a doctorate in musicology and sociology from the University of Heidelberg in 1963, switching from piano to vibes on the advice of French vibist Michel Hausser, with whom he played in Germany and France. Berger moved to Paris in 1965, where he met trumpeter Don Cherry and played with him for 18 months. He then worked for a month with soprano saxophonist Steve Lacy in 1966, before leaving for New York with Cherry. During the late 60s and early 70s, Berger played with (among others) trombonist Roswell Rudd and saxophonist Marion Brown. Berger founded the Creative Music Foundation with Ornette Coleman in 1971, then moved to Woodstock, NY in 1973 where he established the Creative Music Studio and set up full-time classes in various musical departments. Berger has still found time to tour, perform, aand record. –RW

● **Live at the Donaueschingen Festival / MPS**   1979
Definitive Berger originals done live in Germany with the Woodstock Workshop Orchestra, a combination of Creative Music Studio students and instructors. –MGN

○ **Transit / BLACK SAINT**   r 1988
Essential. Trio with Ed Blackwell (d), David Holland (b). –MGN

JERRY BERGONZI   b 1947

Post-bop, post-bop, neo bop. Excellent tenor saxophonist of Michael Brecker school. Blows neo-bop hard and strong. Original ideas within highly stylized sound. –MGN

○ **Jerry Bergonzi Featuring Bruce Gertz / NOTFAT**   1986
Essential album. Bruce Gertz plays bass. –MGN

Standard Gonz / BLUE NOTE   1991

BUNNY BERIGAN   1908-1942

Swing, big band. Trumpet, vocals. Berigan was a tragic figure, right alongside model and fellow early-jazz White trumpet star Bix Beiderbecke. A wonderful player, Berigan was noticed in the late 20s while playing in a college band. He joined the CBS studio band in 1931, then became a member of Paul Whiteman's group as a late replacement for Beiderbecke, but left to join Benny Goodman in 1935. Berigan made the definitive version of "I Can't Get Started." –RW

. **Bunny Berigan / SWG**   COMP
Recent anthology of Berigan material. –RW

○ **Complete Bunny Berigan - Vols. 1-3 / BLUEBIRD**   COMP
First-rate anthology of his memorable cuts. –RW

TIM BERNE   b 1954

Modern creative. This dynamic alto saxophonist is right near the top of the current generation. He is very eclectic; among the few in the 70s and 80s still experimenting rather than being content to mine the hard-bop vaults. He has been a bandleader and a member of many exciting ensembles and also worked in the NYC "downtown" environment. His best work has been on JMT. –RW

○ **Fulton Street Maul / COLUMBIA**   1986
Avant saxophonist at the height of his powers. His other albums are also challenging. –MGN

Fractured Fairy Tales / POLYGRAM / DB 5   r 1990
Dynamic and uneven, but ambitious. –RW

Pace Yourself / POLYGRAM
Some outstanding playing; erratic songs. –RW

BILL BERRY   b 1930

Swing, big band. Born in Benton Harbor, MI; now lives in Los Angeles. Plays trumpet and vibes. Worked with Woody Herman and Duke Ellington. Leads a swing to bop West Coast big band. –MGN

○ **Hello Rev / CONCORD**   1976
Stylized big-band cuts, good production. –RW

CHU BERRY   1910-1941

Swing, bop. Easily one of the best tenor saxophonists of all

time. Berry played with Teddy Hill, Fletcher Henderson, Lionel Hampton, Cab Calloway in the 30s, but died in 1941 in an auto accident. He was known for a full, round tone. –MGN

○ **Indispensable / RCA**   1936
1936-1939. A wide variety of sessions from an immortal stylist. W/ Gene Krupa (d), Lionel Hampton (vib), Cab Calloway (v), Fletcher Henderson (leader), and Wingy Manone's bands. –MGN

● **Memorial / COMMODORE**   i 1954
Very worthwhile document and compilation. –MGN

○ **Chu Berry / COMMODORE**   i 1959
Giants of Tenor Sax / COMMODORE

EDDIE BERT   b 1922

Swing, big band, bop, progressive big band. Veteran bop and post-bop trombonist. Excellent ensemble mate. Played with Stan Kenton and Benny Goodman in 40s and many big bands thereafter. –MGN

Eddie Bert / DISCOVERY   1952
Bert's first, which features guitarist Sal Salvador. –DS

Musician of the Year / SAVOY   r 1955
This is a solid example of straightahead bebop, with Hank Jones (p). –DS

● **Let's Dig Bert / TRANSWORLD**   r 1956
Brilliant bebop session by neglected trombonist. Includes the equally neglected saxophonist Dave Schildkraut. –DS

○ **Like Cool / SOMERSET**   1958
Recently reissued. Trombonist with sextet. –MGN

ED BICKERT   b 1932

Swing, bop, cool. Canadian Ed Bickert is a sleeper in the world of jazz — little known, but quite simply one of the finest guitarists there is. He has been a steady presence in the studio and club scenes in Toronto since the 50s. His first major recording was with clarinetist Phil Nimmons in 1961. An affinity for working with horn players shows up in his recordings with Rob McConnell's Boss Brass and Paul Desmond. Bickert thrives on a kind of hard-swinging traditionalist jazz that sidesteps the angularity of the bop movement altogether, while at the same time employing a modern and sophisticated harmonic sense. As a chordal player, Bickert has few if any equals. His relaxed sense of melody and gentle tone, joined with his evident rapport in ensembles, makes for some very accessible and listenable music — virtuoso jazz without the pretenses. –DNM

○ **Bickert at Toronto's Bourbon Street / CONCORD**   r 1983
Guitarist's definitive live date. –MGN

Bye Bye Baby / CONCORD   r 1984

I Wished on the Moon / CONCORD   r 1986
Definitive studio date. –MGN

BIRD-TRANE-SCO-NOW!

M-base, modern creative. Teenage improvisers led by Donald Washington. Spawned saxophonist James Carter and bassist Rodney Whitaker. –MGN

○ **Bird-Trane-Sco-Now! /**   1986
Recording from young improvisers directed by Dr. Donald Washington. Five pieces, two from D. Washington. The first recording for firebrand saxophonist James Carter. Also features Koli Gives (tpt) and Cassius Richmond (fl/p). –MGN

WALTER BISHOP JR.   b 1927

Bop, hard-bop, post-bop. Bishop is an underrated pianist with Caribbean roots. He has mainly been a classic-bop player, famous for utilizing the right-hand cording technique of Erroll Garner. He has been under-recorded, which has only made him more obscure. –RW

Speak Low / MUSE   1961
Bishop's first as a leader. –DS

○ **Hot House / MUSE** 1977
Excellent bebop session by this pianist, assisted by Junior
Cook (ts) and Bill Hardman (tpt). –DS

BLACKBYRDS

Instr-pop, contemporary funk. Donald Byrd put together this
R&B/fusion instrumental crew of students in the early 70s.
Their albums were big hits in urban contemporary circles, but
had little improvisatory thrust, rhythmic energy, or harmonic
distinction. The group finally ran its course, and Byrd
ultimately returned to a less-commercial form of jazz. –RW
○ **City Life / FANTASY / BB 16** 1975
This was a gold album. –ED
Greatest Hits / FANTASY COMP

EUBIE BLAKE 1883-1983

Ragtime, trad. Blake was one of ragtime's most noted
performers and an American institution. As a child, he
started playing hymns, but heard the sounds of the then-new
form all around him in Baltimore, from brass bands to
saloons to dance halls. Blake picked up his technique by
playing for everything from medicine shows to backing
vocalists in gaming houses, writing his first
major number "The Charleston Rag" in 1899. He teamed with
Noble Sissle in 1915 for a vaudeville appearance, and the duo
eventually made it to Broadway in 1921 with the musical
Shuffle Along. Blake subsequently became a prolific composer
for shows, among them the famous *Blackbirds Review*, then
left the field to study the Schillinger system at New York
University after World War II. He became a celebrity on the
strength of a 1969 album, *86 Years of Eubie Blake*, and made
an acclaimed appearance at the 1970 New Orleans Jazz
Festival. He was awarded the James P. Johnson award in 1970
and the Duke Ellington Medal in 1972, and collaborated with
Terry Waldo on the comprehensive book *This Is Ragtime* in
1976. The 1976 Broadway show *Eubie* was a memorable
overview of his career, which was capped off by his receiving
the Presidential Medal of Honor in 1981. –RW
The 86 Years of Eubie Blake / CBS 1969
Produced by John Hammond. –JME
○ **Memories of You / BIOGRAPH** 1990

JOHN BLAKE

Jazz-rock, modern creative. This strong violinist began his
career in two wildly divergent 70s groups. He played on
several Alice Coltrane albums and also toured with the Isaac
Hayes movement. His style uses slurs, smears, broken lines,
and strumming. He has divided his time between jazz and
R&B ever since and made some fine contributions to a McCoy
Tyner session in the 80s. –RW
○ **A New Beginning / RHINO**
A reissue of an uneven session featuring violinist Blake. –RW

RAN BLAKE *b* 1935

Early free. While many musicians have either avoided the
"Third Stream" school or deplored it, Ran Blake has long been
one of its champions. His style blends some devices from
contemporary classical music, the rhythms of the church, and
influences from film scoring. During the late 50s and early 60s
he teamed with vocalist Jeanne Lee for a series of duets that
were mainly vocal and piano improvisation, with little or no
structure in classic jazz sense. He became a staff member at
the New England Conservatory of Music in the late 60s, and
in 1973 was named the head of the Third Stream Department.
He's also worked extensively with saxophonist Ricky Ford and
vocalist Eleni Odoni. –RW
Film Noir / ARISTA NOVUS 1980
Intriguing third-stream arrangements, all-star lineup. Blake's
most hypnotic concept statement. –RW
○ **You Stepped Out of a Cloud / CAPITOL-RHINO** r 1991
Pianist Blake and vocalist Jeanne Lee's first record since the
mid 60s. –MGN

ART BLAKEY 1919-1991

Bop, post-bop, post-bop. As much as any one person can be
called the creator of a style, Art Blakey looms as one of hard-
bop's founders. His emphatic playing manner, with its
bombastic snare drum licks, slashing beats, and amazing
array of rhythms behind soloists, was always easily
identifiable and at the core of numerous brilliant units. Blakey
actually began as a pianist and was heading his own band at
15. When Erroll Garner proved a more substantial pianist,
Blakey switched to drums. He was part of Mary Lou
Williams's first New York group in the early 40s, then played
with Fletcher Henderson and Billy Eckstine's pioneering big
band. He had an early aggregation he called the 17
Messengers and made an intriguing album for Blue Note in
1947. He also worked with Thelonious Monk, Charlie Parker,
Miles Davis, Horace Silver, Lucky Millinder, Buddy DeFranco,
and the Tadd Dameron-Fats Navarro band in the late 40s and
early 50s. A 1954 studio date that was supposed to spotlight
Horace Silver eventually led to the creation of the Jazz
Messengers, featuring Blakey, Silver, trumpeter Kenny
Dorham, saxophonist Hank Mobley, and bassist Doug
Watkins. By 1956, the Messengers had become the signature
name for all Blakey units, and it ranked as jazz's premier
repertory and talent development unit until Blakey's death.
The group was the vehicle for countless up-and-coming jazz
musicians, the place where they honed their skills under fire
and then left the nest, to be replaced by other talented but
green novices. The alumni list includes Johnny Griffin, Wayne
Shorter, Jackie McLean, Lee Morgan, Curtis Fuller, Slide
Hampton, Bobby Timmons, Cedar Walton, and John Gilmore,
to cite only a few, as well as both Branford and Wynton
Marsalis and three super Memphis pianists, Mulgrew Miller,
James Williams, and Donald Brown.
Blakey made some impressive contributions outside the
Messengers arena throughout his career, among them seminal
dates with Sonny Rollins, Milt Jackson, Cannonball Adderley,
Hank Mobley, James Williams, and a year-long stint with the
Giants of Jazz in 1971-1972. –RW
Night at Birdland #1 / BLUE NOTE 1954
1987 CD reissue of early editions of the group. How can you
overlook the sets with Horace Silver (p) and others? Many feel
they are his best live dates. I agree. –MGN
At the Cafe Bohemia - Vols. 1 & 2 / BLUE NOTE 1955
Mid-80's reissue of live Jazz Messengers from 1955. CD
version. –RW
○ **Jazz Messengers / BLUE NOTE** 1955
Important document. –MGN
Jazz Messenger / CBS 1956
Early period (mid-50s) recordings. Excellent. W/ Jackie
McLean (as). –MGN
Once upon a Groove / BLUE NOTE 1957
Jazz Messengers / ATLANTIC 1957
W/ Thelonious Monk (p) cuts. This is an essential reissue
from 1973. –RW
Theory of Art / RCA 1957
This is an outstanding session with Jackie McLean (as),
Johnny Griffin (ts). –RW
★ **Moanin' / BLUE NOTE** 1958
Here is a superb session. W/ Lee Morgan (tpt) and Bobby
Timmons (p). –HD
1958 Olympia / POLYGRAM 1958
Prototype Blakey on 88 reissue. Lee Morgan (tpt), Benny
Golson (ts), and Bobby Timmons (p) all superb. –MGN
Paris Concert / PORTRAIT 1959
Big Beat / BLUE NOTE 1960
Brilliant drumming and prime ensemble pieces. –MGN
○ **Mosaic / BLUE NOTE** 1961
Prime hard-bop statement. –RW
Three Blind Mice - Vols. 1 & 2 / BLUE NOTE 1962
Super two-record set with arguably his best three-horn front

line (Wayne Shorter, Freddie Hubbard, Curtis Fuller) plus consistently fine piano from Cedar Walton. –RW

○ **Caravan / OJC** 1962
Same band as *Ugetsu*. Shorter writes "Sweet 'N Sour" and "This Is for Albert," two of his lesser known but great compositions. His best work. –MGN

● **Ugetsu / RIVERSIDE** 1963
Blakey's best sextet with Wayne Shorter (sax), Freddie Hubbard (tpt), and Curtis Fuller (tb). Cedar Walton is prominent as music director, arranger, and composer. Live at Birdland, NYC. Famous tunes "One by One," "On the Ginza," and title track. Among his best work. –MGN

○ **A Jazz Message / MCA** 1963
Not the Jazz Messengers, but featuring McCoy Tyner (p), Sonny Stitt (ts). Extraordinary version of "Cafe." –MGN

Free for All / BLUE NOTE 1964
1988 reissue of prime 60s set with Wayne Shorter (sax), Freddie Hubbard (tpt), and Curtis Fuller (tb). –RW

○ **Kyoto / OJC** 1964
His best work. –MGN

Indestructible / BLUE NOTE 1964
Bonus cut on 1986 reissue of a very hot date. –RW

Percussion Discussion / MCA r 1976
Double-album, one each for Blakey and Max Roach (d). –RW

In This Korner / CONCORD 1978
This is one of the Keystone Korner recordings with the Marsalis brothers. –MGN

Night in Tunisia / BLUE NOTE 1979
Rates with his best. –MGN

Album of the Year / TIMELESS / DB 5 1981
1988 reissue, one of the best from Marsalis period. –RW

Straight Ahead / CONCORD / DB 5 1981
This is one of the Keystone Korner recordings with the Marsalis brothers. It is good early-80s Blakley. Also spry piano by James Williams. –MGN

○ **Keystone 3 / CONCORD / DB 5** 1982
Another of the Keystone Korner recordings featuring the Marsalis brothers. –MGN

○ **Oh, by the Way / TIMELESS** 1982
Featuring Johnny O'Neal (p). –MGN

One for All / A&M 1990
Last Jazz Messengers edition. Shouldn't be omitted. –MGN

TERENCE BLANCHARD   b 1962

Post-bop, neo bop. Trumpeter Blanchard was one of several fine New Orleans prodigies to emerge in the 80s. He became a star member of Art Blakey's Messengers in the early 80s and was a musical partner with fellow Crescent City musician Donald Harrison for a long period. The duo made a string of glittering, though musically conservative, releases for Concord and CBS before going their separate ways. Blanchard has it all: range, tone, ideas, facility, and confidence. *See:* Donald Harrison. –RW

New York Second Line / CONCORD 1984
Blanchard-Harrison. The 1984 set that helped cement their status in the emerging crop of 80s young lions. –RW

○ **Crystal Stair / CBS** 1987
Blanchard-Harrison. Good set. –RW

● **Black Pearl / CBS** 1988
Blanchard-Harrison. The best by trumpeter Blanchard and saxophonist Donald Harrison, especially the title track. –MGN

Fire Waltz Live #1 / PRO ARTE-PRO JAZZ 1991

○ **Terence Blanchard / CBS** 1991
Blanchard steps out as a leader. Impressive release. –RW

BLAZING REDHEADS

Latin. All female septet from California who play upbeat Latin-jazz on the funky side. SF Bay area darlings. P.S. None are actually redheads. –MGN

○ **Blazing Redheads / REFERENCE** r 1988
Worth getting. Latin-jazz, funky, get-down music. –MGN

Crazed Women / REFERENCE r 1991

CARLA BLEY   b 1938

Early free, progressive big band, jazz-rock, neo bop, modern creative. A wonderful composer, pianist, madcap personality, and arranger, she married pianist Paul Bley in 1957 and built a career as a songwriter and an active participant in the 60s free movement. She cofounded the Jazz Composers' Guild, the Jazz Composers' Orchestra, and the Jazz Composers' Orchestra Association. Later she started Watt records, divorced Bley, and married Michael Mantler. Her output has been huge, and her influence considerable, most notably as a bandleader and composer. She is a quirky, unorthodox piano player whose wit and charisma communicate a genuine depth of musicality. –RW

○ **A Genuine Tong Funeral / RCA** 1967
Masterpiece with Gary Burton (vib). –MGN

● **Escalator over the Hill / POLYGRAM / DB 5** r 1972
Erratic but has some arresting compositions. –RW

Dinner Music / POLYGRAM r 1977
First excursion on a funky trail, executed immaculately. Near essential. –MGN

☆ **European Tour 1977 / POLYGRAM** 1977
Great compositions, concepts, and execution. Bley's followers love her for her originality. Essential. –MGN

○ **Musique Mecanique / POLYGRAM** r 1979
Creative larger ensemble. Fun. –MGN

Social Studies / POLYGRAM r 1981
Excellent throughout. Great instrumental compositions. –MGN

○ **Duets / POLYGRAM** r 1989
With Steve Swallow on bass; their tremendous musical rapport and precise wit are really beautiful. Highly recommended. –DNM

○ **Very Big Carla Bley Band / POLYGRAM** r 1991
Her best of the last decade, it's a Latin-tinged *Lo Ultimo*. –MGN

PAUL BLEY   b 1932

Post-bop, early free, modern creative. A fine supportive pianist who's always been better in a cooperative rather than individual spotlight situation. He left Montreal for New York, went back to Canada briefly, then returned to New York full-time in 1954. His first recordings came as a member of a trio with Charles Mingus and Art Blakey. He has since worked with cutting-edge avant-gardists like Ornette Coleman, and he's always moving ahead. His best bands and recordings are trio dates with an emphasis on interaction. At times, his music has a spacey quality, but it never loses its guts or edge. –RW

Improvisations: Introducing Paul Bley / OJC 1953
W/ Charles Mingus (b), Art Blakey (d). Most intriguing trio. Highly recommended. –MGN

● **Floater / SAVOY** 1962
1962 & 1963. Trio sessions were with Steve Swallow (b) and Pete La Roca (d). Paul and Carla Bley and Ornette Coleman wrote the music for this dense and wide-ranging trio. –MGN

○ **Paul Bley with Gary Peacock / POLYGRAM** 1963
Good 60s session with bassist Peacock, Paul Motian on drums. –RW

○ **Syndrome / SAVOY** 1963
The followup to *Floater* features more music from Carla Bley. The Savoy albums really introduced her work (through her then husband) to the world. –MGN

○ **Paul Bley Quartet / POLYGRAM** 1964
One of his stronger groups. John Surman (sax) and Bill Frisell (g) especially sharp. –RW

Open, to Love / POLYGRAM / DB 5 1972
Paul and Carla Bley and Annette Peacock share the writing on this beautifully recorded album. –MGN

Paul Bley & Scorpio / MILESTONE / DB 5   1972
Life of a Trio - Saturday/Sunday / RHINO   r 1991
W/ Jimmy Giuffre (cl) and Steve Swallow (b).

JANE IRA BLOOM

Neo bop, M-base, modern creative. A progressive and original composer, she plays soprano saxophone and uses electronics live. Has composed music for NASA. Highly rhythmic, and can be simple or complex. For the challenged listener.–MGN

● **Modern Drama / CBS**   1987
Brilliant soprano saxophonist improviser. With live electronics and heavy percussion. –MGN

○ **Slalom / COLUMBIA**   1988
1988 followup. Also potent listening. Best is "Ice Dancing (For Torvil & Dean)." –MGN

BLUESIANA TRIANGLE

Blues-jazz. A group formed by Dr. John (k, g, v), David Newman (sax, fl), and Art Blakey (d). –BP

○ **Bluesiana Triangle / WINDHAM HILL**   r 1990
A collaboration by Dr. John (k, g, v), David Newman (sax, fl), and Art Blakey (d). The music is an above-average mixture of jazz, blues, and funk. –BP

Dr. John & Friends / WINDHAM HILL
Bluesiana 2. More of what was on *Bluesiana Triangle*, with drummer Will Calhoun replacing Blakey and Ray Anderson added on trombone. –BP

HAMIET BLUIETT

Modern creative. A premier player, and one of the finest improvisers to emerge during the 70s and 80s. Bluiett has a deep, robust tone, facility, and imagination, and has combined the swing savvy of a Harry Carney with the range and fluidity of a Pepper Adams or Serge Chaloff. He's a charter member of the World Saxophone Quartet, and was also a member of Clarinet Summit, and has recorded several albums as a leader. –RW

○ **Endangered Species / INDIA NAVIGATION**   1976
Avant baritone saxophonist live at Ladies' Fort, NYC, with trumpeter Olu Dara. Meaty improvisations. –MGN

S.O.S. / INDIA NAVIGATION   1977
Explosive live quartet set that includes slashing piano from Don Pullen. –RW

Orchestra Duo and Septet / CHIAROSCURO   1977
Array of pieces by Bluiett. Excellent duet with Pullen, good sextet numbers, interesting orchestral piece. –RW

ARTHUR BLYTHE   b 1940

Post-bop, early free, modern creative. Alto sax, soprano sax. Misinformation, false perceptions, and hype have hurt the career of Arthur Blythe, who has always been an excellent player. In the 70s he was nicknamed "Black Arthur," leading to the exaggerated notion that he was a Black nationalist/activist. He joined Columbia in the 70s after relocating to NYC from LA and was the victim of a senseless hype campaign calling him the "greatest saxophonist in the world." From his days with Stanley Cowell and Chico Hamilton to his present involvement with the World Sax Quartet and his groups, his work has been consistently high-caliber and thoughtful. Blythe is a superb uptempo improviser who has become equally adept at ballads and composition over the years. –RW

The Grip / INDIA NAVIGATION   1977
Great album, done the same day as *Metamorphosis*, with sextet. –RW

○ **Metamorphosis / INDIA NAVIGATION**   1977
A superb album that was done at the same session as *The Grip*. Fine sextet. –RW

Jazz Bass & Double Bass

| **1890s Ragtime Orchestras & String Bands** |
| Tub & Stick |
| Billy Marrero — Henry Kimball |

| **Early Jazz Bass** |
| Classic Jazz Era |
| Bill Johnson (1872-1972) — John Lindsay (1894-1950) |
| Wellman Braud (1891-1966) |

| **Early Rhythm Section** |
| Pops Foster (1892-1969) — Al Morgan (1908-1974) |
| Billy Taylor (1906-1986) — Hayes Alvis (1907-1972) |
| Grachan Moncur II (1915) — George Kelly (1915-1985) |

| **1930s Players** |
| Walter Page (1900-1957) — John Kirby (1908-1952) |
| ●Jimmy Blanton — ● Oscar Pettiford (1922-1960) |

| **1940s Players** |
| Ray Brown (1926) — Milt Hinton (1910) |
| Tommy Potter (1918-1988) — Red Callender (1916) |
| ●Charles Mingus (1922-1979) — Slam Stewart (1914-1987) |

| **1950s Players** |
| Ray Brown (1926) — Charles Mingus (1922-1979) |
| Red Mitchell (1927) — Scott LaFaro (1936-1961) |

| **Mainstream** |
| ●Paul Chambers (1935-1969) — Ron Carter (1937) |
| Walter Booker Jr. (1933) — Jimmy Garrison (1934-1976) |
| ● George Mraz (1944) |

| **Major Players** |
| Charlie Haden (1937) — Dave Holland (1946) |
| Eddie Gomez (1944) — Cecil McBee (1935) |

| **Electric Bass** |
| Steve Swallow (1940) — Eberhard Weber (1940) |
| Stanley Clarke (1951) — Jaco Pastorius (1951-1987) |

| **80s-90s** |
| Mark Johnson — Ratso Harris — Robert Hurst |
| Rodney Whitaker — Ray Drummond — Rufus Reid (1944) |
| Sirone (1940) — Malachi Favors — Fred Hopkins |

★ **Lenox Avenue Breakdown / CBS**   1979
Alto saxophonist with septet. Quintessential. Track this one down — it's vital. –MGN

Basic Blythe / COLUMBIA   1987
Hipmotism / RHINO   1991
Long time coming for this extremely gifted saxophonist. Originals too. The ultimate. –MGN

CLAUDE BOLLING   b 1930

Instr-pop. More a light classical player than a jazz musician, Bolling has had some luck with a couple of recordings with a blend of jazz and classical material. –RW

California Suite / CBS
Suite for Cello & Jazz Trio / CBS   1981
Original Ragtime / COLUMBIA
Expertly presented, nicely played. –RW

○ **Suite for Flute & Jazz Piano / CBS**
This was a very popular album of jazz/classical fusion, continuing in the vein of Dave Brubeck's 50s works. –MB

JOE BONNER   b 1948
Post-bop. Good contemporary pianist and composer, particularly as a soloist. Bonner has had several strong releases on independent labels. –RW
Angel Eyes / MUSE   1974
○ **The Lifesaver / MUSE**   1974
Solo piano. Pretty playing, but never predictable. –MGN
● **Impressions of Copenhagen / THERESA**   1978
1978-79 recording for modern pianist from San Francisco with strings and horns. A beautiful album. –MGN

BESS BONNIER
Swing, bop, post-bop, cool. A classic jazz pianist with classical and bop overtones, Bonnier is one of Detroit's premier players of all time. –MGN
○ **And Other Jazz Birds / NOTEWORKS**   1985
Premier bop and swing pianist from Detroit joined by Pepper Adams, Sir Roland Hanna, Carol Sloane, Larry Nozero and the Detroit Rhythm Section. There is one Bonnier original on this spirited, well-organized, and realized album. –MGN

BERYL BOOKER   b 1922
Post-bop, cool. Pianist whose limited recording career showed her a most able composer and interpreter, mostly in cool to post-bop mode. –MGN
Beryl Booker Trio / DISCOVERY   i 1953
● **Beryl Booker with Don Byas / DISCOVERY**   i 1953
○ **Girl Met a Piano / EMARCY**   i 1954
Beryl Booker / CADENCE   i 1955

JAMES BOOKER   1940-1983
Boogie. Certainly one of the most flamboyant New Orleans pianists in recent memory, James Carroll Booker III was a major influence on the local rhythm and blues scene in the 50s and 60s. By the time he was out of high school he had recorded on several occasions, including his own first release, "Doing the Hambone," in 1953. In 1960 he made the national charts with "Gonzo," an organ instrumental, and over the course of the next two decades played and recorded with artists as varied as Lloyd Price, Aretha Franklin, Ringo Starr, The Doobie Brothers, and B. B. King. A prison term on drug charges interrupted his career, but the rediscovery of "roots" music by college students during the 70s (focusing primarily on "Fess" — Professor Longhair) provided the opportunity for a comeback by 1974. Booker's performances at the New Orleans Jazz & Heritage Festivals took on the trappings of legendary "happenings," and he often spent his festival earnings to arrive in style, pulling up to the stage in a rented Rolls Royce and attired in costumes befitting the "Piano Prince of New Orleans," complete with a cape. He might easily plant some Chopin into a blues tune or launch into a jeremiad on the CIA with all the fervor of a "Reverend Ike-meets-Moms Mabley" tag team match.
He successfully amalgamated the jazz and rhythm & blues idioms of New Orleans, with more than a touch of gospel thrown in for good measure. Booker had a plaintive and seering vocal style which was equally comfortable with gospel, jazz standards, blues, or popular songs. Despite his personal eccentricities, he had the respect of New Orleans's best musicians, and elements of his influence are still very much apparent in the playing of pianists like Henry Butler and Harry Connick Jr. –BR
○ **Classified / ROUNDER**   r 1984
Booker solo and with a combo featuring saxophonist Red Tyler. High points are a medley of Professor Longhair pieces and the Little Willie John hit, "All Around the World (Grits Ain't Groceries)." –BR

● **New Orleans Piano Wizard: Live! / ROUNDER**
A typical Booker set recorded at the Boogie-Woogie and Ragtime Piano Contest in Zurich, Switzerland, with all his quirks intact. His vocal on Percy Mayfield's "Please Send Me Someone to Love" is a masterpiece." –BR

RON BOUSTEAD   b 1951
Post-bop, ballads. Jazz vocalist whose sound is reminiscent of Mark Murphy. –MGN
○ **First Light / MO PRO**   r 1984
Pittsburgh native has very good chops and diction. With the Steve Schmidt Trio. Worthwhile. –MGN

LESTER BOWIE   b 1941
Progressive big band, neo bop, modern creative. Trumpet, flugelhorn, composer. A maverick player, humorist, and charter member of the Art Ensemble of Chicago, Lester Bowie has shown it's possible to be on the edge musically without being solemn or pompous. His solos are alternately complex and simple, crisp or full of blues licks and tricks. His constant shifting between outside and inside reflects his eclectic background. He has played with the Art Ensemble, backed his ex-wife Fontella Bass in gospel, and led jazz-rock and trumpet repertory and experimental duos. Comparisons are made to Cootie Williams due to his use of growls, slurs, and high-octane solos. –RW
Fast Last / MUSE   1974
Rope-A-Dope / MUSE   r 1975
☆ **The 5th Power / BLACK SAINT**   1978
1978 quintet w/ Arthur Blythe (as), Amina Myers (p). Creative jazz and a progressive gospel segment. Bowie at his eclectic best. Essential. –MGN
Great Pretender / POLYGRAM   1981
A highlight. –MGN
All the Magic! / POLYGRAM   1982
Avant Pop / POLYGRAM   1986
B+ Lester, highlight "The Emperor." –MGN
○ **Twilight Dreams / ATLANTIC**   1987
Best album for the Brass Fantasy. –MGN
● **Works / POLYGRAM**   COMP
Excellent collection. –MGN

CHARLES BRACKEEN   b 1940
Early free, modern creative. Tenor sax, trumpet. Explosive soloist and composer whose best recordings were done for the Strata-East label in the 70s. For a time was married to pianist Joanne Brackeen. –RW
○ **Rhythm X / STRATA EAST**   1973
Avant saxophonist on early date. Wild, uninhibited. –MGN
Attainment / SILKHEART   1987
Slightly larger and smaller instrumentation as on *Rhythm X.* Equally well done. –MGN
Bannar / SILKHEART   1987
Quartet. Outward bound. –MGN

JOANNE BRACKEEN   b 1938
Post-bop, early free, neo bop, modern creative. A pianist and composer who usually works in trio format. A unique player in the creative mode, she also interprets standards with wit and verve. One of the most innovative piano voices of the past twenty years, her work is always substantive.–MGN
○ **Tring-a-Ling / CHOICE**   1977
Brilliant pianist/composer with powerful modern modal music (all originals). With Michael Brecker on sax plus two bassists. –MGN
Mythical Magic / MPS   1978
Solo piano. All originals; perky and pungent. –MGN
Fi-Fi Goes to Heaven / CONCORD / DB 5   r 1987
CD version features this energized, capable pianist at her best,

with some sharp assistance from Branford Marsalis (ts) and Terence Blanchard (tpt). −RW

Live at Maybeck Recital Hall / CONCORD   r 1990
She shows her mettle in live solo context. −RW

● **Where Legends Dwell / KEN**
Extraordinary trio with Eddie Gomez on bass and Jack DeJohnette on drums, this is her best work of the past decade. Twelve tracks are all originals. Over 70 minutes of incredibly ingenious jazz included. This is easy to dig into. −MGN

RUBY BRAFF   b 1927

Swing. Cornetist. When Braff came to New York from his native Boston in 1953, he was considered an oddball because he modeled his playing on Louis Armstrong and Lester Young rather than bebop. But he was received with open ears by the older mainstream jazzmen and soon was recording prolifically and working with Benny Goodman and other luminaries. There was a long association with the Newport All Stars and, later, an interesting quartet co-led with guitarist George Barnes. More recently, Braff's done fruitful work with pianist Dick Hyman — their duets are special. As a stylist, Braff is an original; his exploration of the cornet's lower register and his approach to melody make his work stand out. He's gone from young iconoclast to revered elder statesman. −DM

Hustlin' & Bustlin' / BLACK LION   1956
○ **With the Newport All Stars / BLACK LION**   1967
W/ Buddy Tate (ts), George Wein (p), Jack Lesberg (b), and Don Lamond (d). Both Tate and Braff are in top form on this one. −JME

Plays Gershwin / CONCORD   ca. 1974
Salutes Rodgers & Hart / CONCORD   ca. 1974
Bravura Eloquence / CONCORD   r 1990
A wonderful set from a great cornetist. W/ Howard Alden (g), Jack Lesberg (b). −JME

GEORGE BRAITH   b 1939

Post-bop. Played the "Braithaphone," two saxophones welded to each other, creating the option for harmonic invention. Precursor to Rahsaan Roland Kirk. His last name was shortened from Braithwaite. −MGN

Soul Stream / BLUE NOTE   i 1964
○ **Two Souls in One / BLUE NOTE**   i 1964

ANTHONY BRAXTON   b 1945

Early free, progressive big band, modern creative. After jazz achieved total freedom of expression in the mid 60s, where could it go next? Saxophonist Anthony Braxton devised a brilliant solution beginning with his first album on Delmark (1968). Working closely with members of the Art Ensemble of Chicago and the Association for the Advancement of Creative Musicians (AACM), Braxton staged his own quiet revolution with written structures that could accommodate compositional complexity alongside improvisational liberation. In essence, his debut *Three Compositions of New Jazz* turned the oft-publicized extremes of free-jazz inside out, favoring silence and quiet sounds, purposefully excluding the usual rhythm section, and substituting small and unusual instruments to reinforce his frameworks of spacious tension. At the same time, he was building an impressive repertoire of solo alto sax works and, like many of his Chicago peers, reintroducing forgotten members of the saxophone and clarinet family to jazz audiences. His early influences included both cold and hot reedmen — Paul Desmond, Warne Marsh, Charlie Parker, John Coltrane, Ornette Coleman, Eric Dolphy — as well as advanced European composers like Stockhausen. But the most obvious inspiration for Braxton's highly theoretical approach came from the senior members of the AACM cooperative, many of whom, like Muhal Richard Abrams, Leroy Jenkins, Roscoe Mitchell, Steve McCall, and Joseph Jarman, were his earliest collaborators.

After a period of European self-exile and work with the Circle Trio (with Dave Holland and Chick Corea) in the early 70s, Braxton's music has taken off in manifold directions, incorporating the best of American jazz, free improvisation, and the European vanguard. He has played consistently with his own quartets or quintets, performing his labyrinthine "creative music" compositions in standard jazz instrumentation, as well as expanding his multi-instrumental mastery in solo and ensemble settings. Improvised duos with diverse and challenging partners have been a staple over the years, and more recently, Anthony has taken to recording entire albums of jazz standards. As a player his scope and facility are unsurpassed; as a composer he is as prolific as he is imaginative. His compositions, all bearing graphic titles instead of names, run into the hundreds and cover almost every musical ensemble imaginable from solos to large orchestras. His more adventuresome pieces involve theater, dance, opera, and multiple orchestras performing simultaneously in different locations — even on different planets! Many of his best recordings are on import labels and can be found in major record stores along with out-of-print copies of his many US Arista label albums from the 70s. −MB

○ **For Alto / DELMARK / DB 5**   1968
○ **In the Tradition - Vol. 2 / INNER CITY**   r 1975
● **Creative Orchestra Music 1976 / RCA / DB 5**   1976
Most startling orchestral recording of the last three decades. Challenging listening. −MGN

Six Compositions: (Quartet) / POLYGRAM   1984
○ **Seven Standards 1985 - Vol. 1 / MAGENTA**   1985
Saxophonist plays straightahead with the Hank Jones (p) Trio. Very enjoyable. Vol. 2 also excellent. −MGN

JOSHUA BREAKSTONE   b 1955

Post-bop. This Canadian guitarist's steady style and pleasant solos have been heard on a series of milestone recordings. Not flashy or exciting, but reliable, Breakstone has a clean sound and reflects the basic full-toned jazz-guitar approach that has passed from Charlie Christian on down. −RW

Wonderful / SONORA   1983
This studio date for the guitarist with the Barry Harris Trio features two Breakstone tunes and five standards from Tristano, Dameron, Gershwin, and Django. This was a good portent of things to come. −MGN

○ **4/4 = 1 / SONORA**   1984
With the Kenny Barron (p) Trio, this one features two more from Breakstone, Frank Lacy's great "Theme for Ernie," and four standards. −MGN

● **9 to 3 / CONTEMPORARY**   ca. 1990
Includes seven trio tracks with Dennis Irwin on bass, Kenny Washington on drums. Includes lots of Monk. Breakstone is starting here to break out of a formulaic mold. −MGN

LENNY BREAU   1941-1984

Post-bop, neo bop. An outstanding finger-style jazz guitarist who performed on both acoustic and electric guitars. Breau's right hand drew on classical, flamenco, and country (Travis/Atkins) finger-picking techniques. He was among the first guitarists to digest the impressionistic, post-bop chord voicings of pianist Bill Evans. Breau developed the ability to simultaneously comp chords and improvise single-string melodies, creating the illusion of two guitarists playing together. His facility with artificial harmonics remains the envy of many guitarists. Late in his career, Breau began using a seven-string guitar that extended the instrument's range in the upper register. Breau's early RCA recordings are eclectic and technically dazzling. His later work is less flashy, but communicates on a deeper level. −RL

○ **5 O'Clock Bells / ADELPHI**   1977
1977 & 1978. Solo guitar and vocals. This includes five Breau originals, two standards, and McCoy Tyner's "Visions." Guitar students, this is your homework — find this album. −MGN

● **Mo' Breau / ADELPHI**   1977
1977 & 1978. The companion to *5 O'Clock Bells* features solo versions of four of Breau's originals, one melded to McCoy Tyner's "Ebony Queen" and three nice standards, including "Emily." –MGN

Trio / ADELPHI   r 1979
Two of guitarist's originals, Coltrane's "Mr. Knight," two pop songs. Virtuoso player, with bassist and pianist Don Thompson and drummer Claude Ranger. –MGN

Quietude / ELECTRIC MUSE   1983
These were recordings in Toronto with bassist Dave Young. The album includes four standards, one Breau piece, and a reprise (11 minutes plus) on "Visions." Features pristine playing by two virtuosos. –MGN

Last Sessions / ADELPHI   1984

BRECKER BROTHERS

Post-bop, jazz-rock, neo bop, contemporary funk. Randy plays trumpet, Michael plays tenor sax. Teamed in the group Dreams in the late 60s, they later formed this pioneering jazz-funk fusion group. A good vehicle for their solid improvisations. Many other groups followed their lead. Also leaders in neo-bop contemporary jazz. –MGN

○ **Brecker Brothers / ARISTA**   1975
First date for brothers from 1975. Side one is solid jazz/funk/fusion. They called it "skunk-funk." With David Sanborn (as) and Don Grolnick (k). –MGN

○ **Return of the Brecker Brothers / GRP**   1992
Their latest effort, and a good one. Michael Brecker reflects some his experience with African music while on tour with Paul Simon. –JME

● **Brecker Brothers Collection / NOVUS**   COMP
Vols. 1 & 2. Randy and Michael Brecker. Compilation from five of their albums. –JME

MICHAEL BRECKER   b 1949

Post-bop, jazz-rock, neo bop. Versatility has been saxophonist Michael Brecker's strong suit, as he's forged a career in both jazz and rock. His father was a pianist; Brecker studied under Vince Trombetta and Joe Allard in the mid 60s. After one year at Indiana University in 1970, Brecker joined his brother Randy in New York. His style, a mix of intense Coltrane-influenced licks and blues/funk tinges, has become among the most recognizable of his generation. He started with organist/vocalist Edwin Birdsong in 1970, then was in the excellent but commercially ill-fated band Dreams. The two Breckers formed their own band in the mid 70s, a top-flight jazz/rock ensemble musically that managed to inject some quality into songs that were often predictable and stilted. Prior to that, Michael Brecker had worked with James Taylor, Horace Silver, Billy Cobham, and Yoko Ono. After the Brecker Brothers disbanded, he joined Steps, which later became Steps Ahead.
In 1986, Brecker's belated debut album as a leader, "Michael Brecker," topped the jazz charts for months, finally establishing him as a solo star. On that and subsequent albums, Brecker used both conventional horn and the EWI (Electronic Wind Instrument), a synthesizer activated by blowing. His use of the EWI has helped establish it and other synthesized instruments as valid jazz tools. In 1980, Brecker embarked on a world tour with Paul Simon, and he had a featured solo spot in each show. –RW
& WR

Michael Brecker / MCA / DB 5   1986
The highlight of this very good album is "Nothing Personal." With Pat Metheny (g), Charlie Haden (b), and Jack DeJohnette (d). –MGN

○ **Don't Try This at Home / MCA**   r 1989
● **Now You See It.... / GRP**   r 1990
His best work leading a group. Used as the Weather Channel bridges. –MGN

RANDY BRECKER   b 1945

Post-bop, jazz-rock, neo bop. This trumpeter has played jazz, funk, fusion, and rock with the likes of Horace Silver, Dreams, Jack DeJohnette, and Frank Zappa. He collaborates frequently with his wife, Brazilian keyboardist Eliane Elias. Also a very capable straightahead player, one of the best. –MGN

☆ **In the Idiom / DENON**   1986
Straightahead and excellent. A shining hour with Joe Henderson (sax). –MGN

DEE DEE BRIDGEWATER   b 1950

Post-bop, ballads. Dee Dee Bridgewater is a supremely talented jazz singer whose records have not always been indicative of her skills. Her best work came with the Thad Jones-Mel Lewis big band. She can sing loud or soft, do brassy upbeat tunes, blues, or sentimental ballads, and she became popular overseas in the late 70s for her one-woman show, "Lady Day." She is always on the edge of superstardom. –RW

○ **Live in Paris / MCA**   1987
A topnotch date reissued in 1989. Bridgewater soars and struts throughout. A definitive work — her best album. –RW

NICK BRIGNOLA   b 1936

Bop, post-bop. A great baritone saxophonist, Brignola is also an adept multi-instrumentalist and composer. –MGN

○ **Baritone Madness / BEEHIVE**   1977
Studio date with Pepper Adams (bar sax) and Ted Curson (tpt). Incredible playing. –MGN

BOB BROOKMEYER   b 1929

Post-bop, progressive big band. Though well known as a premier valve trombonist, Bob Brookmeyer actually began professionally as a pianist in the early 50s. He established himself on valve trombone in later years, particularly in the 70s, when his blend of swing phrasing and sound variations plus humor proved appealing. He started in the bands of Stan Getz, Gerry Mulligan, and Jimmy Giuffre. He co-led a fine early-60s group with Clark Terry and was a founding member of the Lewis-Jones big band. A prolific session player and arranger throughout the 70s, he is still active. –RW

● **And Friends / COLUMBIA**   1964
W/ Stan Getz (ts), Herbie Hancock (p), Ron Carter (b), Gary Burton (vib), and Elvin Jones (d).

○ **Small Band 1 & 2 / GRYPHON**   1978
Live at Sandy's in Beverly, MA in 1978. With Michael Moore (b), Jack Wilkins (g), Joe LaBarbera (d). Mostly standards, some music of Andy Laverne. Two Brookmeyer originals. All arrangements by Brookmeyer. Fine group effort. –MGN

CECIL BROOKS III   b 1961

Post-bop, neo bop. This developing young drummer's initial releases merged bop expertise with the swaggering energy of youth, thanks to saxophonists Greg Osby and Gary Thomas. It is a little early to judge whether he'll be a long-term factor, but he's off to a promising start. –RW

○ **The Collective / MUSE**   1989
This is an auspicious debut for top-rate drummer, w/ Geri Allen (p). –MGN

ROY BROOKS   b 1938

Hard-bop, post-bop, post-bop, soul jazz, world fusion, modern creative. Jazz drummer/percussionist who was a "drumist" (his description) in early-60s Horace Silver bands and charter member of M'Boom. He leads the Artistic Truth combo, and the Aboriginal Percussion Choir, and also plays solo. –MGN

○ **The Free Slave / MUSE**   1970
Recorded at Left Bank Jazz Society in Baltimore, Maryland, this All Star quintet features George Coleman (ts), Woody Shaw (tpt), Hugh Lawson (p), Cecil McBee (b), and Brooks (d/per). There are four originals, all extended, with room to stretch for musicians. Wild club date. –MGN

Live at Town Hall / BAYSTATE   1974
NYC. With Marcus Belgrave (tpt), Sonny Fortune (as), Sonny
Red (as), and Eddie Jefferson (v). There are three standards
and Brooks's famous "Prophet" and "Blues for the Carpenter's
Saw." –MGN

TINA BROOKS   1932-1974
Hard-bop, post-bop, soul jazz. Tenor sax. Brooks evolved from
an interesting R&B player with Sonny Thompson and Amos
Milburn into a solid, engaging soloist and writer. His tenure
with Jimmy Smith was especially noteworthy, where his
warm, robust sound filling in spaces was striking. His albums
mixed soul-jazz rhythmic foundations and ambitious
compositions. All his albums are available in a Mosaic
boxed set. –RW

☆ **Blue Note Recordings / MOSAIC / DB 5**   1958
1958-1961. Tenor saxophonist with four different bands,
including Lee Morgan, Freddie Hubbard, Blue Mitchell, and
Johnny Coles (trumpets). Also Jackie McLean. Trios led by
pianists Sonny Clark, Duke Jordan, and Kenny Drew. 15
Brooks originals, seven standards. Brooks was an unsung
hero. His work deserves your investigation. –MGN

CLIFFORD BROWN   1930-1956
Bop, hard-bop, post-bop. One of the greatest trumpet players
of all time. The bulk of his work is for Emarcy 1954-1956 and
can be found in a definitive ten-CD set *Complete Emarcy
Recordings* in which there is a preference for studio group
sessions co-led with Max Roach of the wonderful *Clifford
Brown with Strings* material. Studio jam sessions and live
jams for this label yield much excellent Brown but bog-down
somewhat in lengthy solos by lesser lights.
While there is no Clifford Brown not recommended, one to
avoid because of very poor audio is the double Columbia
album *Live at the Bee Hive* (Columbia), while *Daahoud*
(Mainstream) is a pirate release of Emarcy material despite
what the album notes say. Other domestic recordings can be
found on Prestige, which also includes Swedish recordings
from 1953, 1954 concert recordings on GNP, Blue Note and
Pacific Jazz combined in the recommended five-album box
The Complete Blue Note/Pacific Jazz Clifford Brown (Mosaic)
which feature him in a sideman's role for the most part. The
French Vogue recordings from 1953 have been issued on a
number of US labels — Prestige and GNP among others. One
convenient way to have them is a three-album box *Clifford
Brown/Paris Collection* (Japanese Vogue).
There are bits and pieces of live jams in Ingo, Hall of Fame
Elektra/Musician, and Xanadu but the quintessential Clifford
Brown is the album *The Beginning and the End* (Columbia),
which combines his earliest work as an R&B band sideman
with three lengthy jams recorded shortly before his death. His
solo on "Donna Lee" from this session is probably the single
greatest modern jazz trumpet solo. –BP

Alternate Takes / BLUE NOTE   1953
With three groups: Lou Donaldson (tpt), J. J. Johnson (tb), and
Clifford Brown Sextet. –JME

Big Band in Paris / OJC   1953
Though the big band was of dubious quality, Brown was in
peak form on all 'volumes. –RW

Quartet in Paris - Vols. 1 & 2 / PRESTIGE / DB 5   1953
☆ **Complete Blue Note/Pacific Jazz / MOSAIC**   1953
Classic sessions. –JME

Study in Brown / POLYGRAM   r 1954
Clifford Brown All Stars / POLYGRAM   r 1954
Excellent Brown playing. –RW

Jazz Immortal / PACIFIC JAZZ   r 1954
This album includes some takes and Brown material
unavailable elsewhere. –RW

Brown-Roach Inc. / POLYGRAM   r 1955

★ **Brownie / POLYGRAM / DB 5**
The complete Emarcy recordings. The definitive record for a
one-of-a-kind band. A must-own with Max Roach (d). –MGN

○ **The Beginning and the End / COLUMBIA**   COMP
Side one has his earliest recordings of some Caribbean-
influenced R&B material; side two is a live recording of his last
performance, the night before he died. Includes the famous
"Donna Lee" solo. A touching tribute album. –DNM

DONALD BROWN   b 1954
Post-bop, neo bop, modern creative. This Memphis-born pianist
is one of the top players and writers on the current scene. Like
many Memphis pianists, he wound up in Art Blakey's band.
His knowledge of blues and soul reflects both his background
working in the Stax scene of the 70s and his love for all styles.
A fluid, often exuberant soloist, Brown has a busy career as a
producer (Kenny Garrett, Donald Byrd) and performer and is
also a professor of music at the University of Tennessee at
Knoxville. –RW

● **Early Bird / SUNNYSIDE**   1987
Sextet recording. Thoroughly satisfying. –MGN

○ **Sources of Inspiration / MUSE**   r 1991
Quirky but interesting album from Memphis pianist, formerly
w/ Art Blakey (d). –MGN

People Music / MUSE   1992

LES BROWN   b 1914
Swing, big band. A very popular bandleader in the 40s and
early 50s. His orchestra was strictly a dance group, with
lightweight arrangements and novelty tunes like the 1941 hit
"Joe Dimmaggio." Later Brown had a steady career in radio
and television, working with Bob Hope, Steve Allen, and Dean
Martin. –RW

○ **And His Orchestra / HINDSIGHT**
Top-rate big-band swing from the man who backed Bob Hope
and discovered Doris Day. –DS

Anything Goes / USA MUSIC GROUP
Smooth. Good sound quality. –RW

Digital Swing / FANTASY
Recent updated pieces. –RW

● **Best of the Big Bands / CBS**   COMP
His biggest hits, part of an overall big-band series. –RW

Sentimental Journey / POLYGRAM   COMP
Recent overview of his most popular material. –RW

MARION BROWN   b 1935
Post-bop, early free. Though he's best known as a free or avant-
garde player, saxophonist Marion Brown's roots are in swing
and blues. He played with Johnny Hodges in the 50s before
moving to New York, where he worked with Archie Shepp and
the Jazz Composers Orchestra before starting his own group
in 1965. He appeared on many landmark 60s releases,
including *Ascension*, and then in the 70s had a duo with
trumpeter Leo Smith. Pungent lines, sometimes frenetic solos
balanced by tender melodies, and expressive lines are Brown's
trademark on alto. His 70s releases have reflected his interest
in and absorption with African and African-American folk
music and traditional rhythms and songs. –RW

☆ **Three for Shepp / IMPULSE**   1966
○ **Geechee Recollections / IMPULSE**   1973
● **Vista / IMPULSE**   1975
Great progressive saxophonist with pianists Stanley Cowell
and Anthony Davis. A beauty. –MGN

Back to Paris / FREELANCE   1980
At La Dreher in Paris. Quartet with pianist Hilton Ruiz.
Excellent, moving music. –MGN

RAY BROWN ♭1926

Swing, big band, bop, hard-bop, post-bop, cool, progressive big band. Long considered to be the finest bass player in jazz. Thousands of recording sessions as a sideman. His own albums begin with Verve in 1956 and continue on an occasional basis through 1965 for a total of six albums including two co-led with Milt Jackson. Several of these are orchestral and are less dependent on Brown's own contribution than on the writing of the arrangers. Of the small band items, *This Is Ray Brown* (Verve) is a relaxed session involving Oscar Peterson and Herb Ellis, while *Much In Common* (Verve) has Kenny Burrell and Hank Jones as well as gospel singer Marion Williams on some titles as well as Jackson. Of the big-band albums, *Ray Brown with the All Star Big Band* (Verve) involves arrangements by Al Cohn and Ernie Wilkins and a New York personnel which truly lives up to the album title. Began recording for Concord Records in 1975, again on an occasional basis, often in the company of pianists Jimmy Rowles, Monty Alexander, or Gene Harris. He continues to contribute to dozens of recordings on this label today. If the quality of some sessions is less than others it is never Brown's fault. One recording apart from the Concord work that demands mention is *Super Bass* (Capri), which features Brown with his protégé and most likely successor, John Clayton. This is masterful bass playing throughout and an ideal example to demonstrate the lasting brilliance of Ray Brown. –BP

Brown's Bag / CONCORD	1975
Red Hot Ray Brown Trio / CONCORD	1975
● **Something for Lester / OJC / DB 5**	1977

Tribute to Lester Young — from the heart! –MGN

Ray Brown 3 / CONCORD	1982
Soular Energy / CONCORD	r 1986
Moore Makes 4 / CONCORD	1991
Don't Forget the Blues / CONCORD	

All blues is good news for virtuoso bassist Brown. –MGN

○ **Live at the Loa-Summer Wind / CONCORD**

Brown's trio with Gene Harris (k) and Jeff Hamilton (d). Perhaps Brown's very best. –MGN

RUTH BROWN ♭1928

Blues-jazz, ballads. Jazz/R&B Vocalist Ruth Brown was one of the early hitmakers for Atlantic, netting a slew of Black chart hits in the early 50s: "Teardrops from My Eyes," "5-10-15 Hours," and "Mama He Treats Your Daughter Mean." She has recorded prolifically over the years and enjoyed a comeback in the late 80s thanks to a successful Broadway show. –JF

☆ **Miss Rhythm / ATLANTIC** 195?

This two-disc set contains all the highly influential early-50s smashes of this legendary R&B vocalist. Great support from Atlantic's studio aces, including saxophonists Willis Jackson and King Curtis. –BD

Have a Good Time / FANTASY r 1989

Nice recent material, with Brown showing she's still got some power. –RW

○ **Blues on Broadway / FANTASY** r 1990

A great mix of show business panache with a bluesy undergirding. –RW

Fine & Mellow / FANTASY 1991

A very good recent album, heavy on the blues side of her personality. –RW

DAVE BRUBECK ♭1920

Cool. Pianist, bandleader. The master of odd time signatures, Dave Brubeck began at age 13, playing with bands in Concord, CA. His studies with Milhaud and Schoenberg were a lasting influence on the construction of his solos and compositions. During the 50s and 60s, his groups were the most popular in the world, especially on college campuses. He was the most popular "cool" stylist ever from an exposure standpoint. He and alto saxophonist Paul Desmond were precise, sparing players whose every note seemed measured, and they seldom pushed or rushed any tempos. Brubeck employed a host of things from the classical world — block chording, counterpoint, and fugues — and made them palatable. He's been a huge seller since 1954 and remains immensely popular. –RW

○ **Fantasy Years 1949-1954 / FANTASY / DB 5** 1949

A nice overview of his material in the years before he crossed over and became a celebrity. –RW

○ **Jazz at the College of the Pacific / OJC** 1953

Wonderful exchanges and dialogs between Brubeck and Paul Desmond (sax). –RW

○ **Jazz Goes to College / CBS / DB 5** 1954

The early live material that set the stage for the quartet's subsequent breakout nationally. A 1989 CD reissue. –RW

Jazz: Red, Hot & Cool / SONY SP / BB 7	1955
Dave Brubeck Octet / OJC	195?

Early post "Birth of the Cool" Brubeck. –MGN

★ **Time Out / CBS / BB 2** 1960

With "Take Five," the best bet. Still definitive after all these years. Gold album. –MGN

○ **All the Things We Are / ATLANTIC** 1961

Has cuts with Braxton (sax), Lee Konitz (sax), and others. Very different from regular Brubeck. –RW

○ **Jazz Impressions of New York / COLUMBIA** r 1965

Some of his most engaging, appealing playing. –RW

Last Set at Newport / ATLANTIC	1971
Duets / A&M	1975

Studio date. Lilting, memorable melodies. –MGN

Blue Rondo / CONCORD 1976

Some of his best and liveliest playing. –RW

Moscow Nights / CONCORD r 1988

CD issue of historic Russian concerts in 1987. Bonus cut. –RW

Tritonis / CONCORD

One of Brubeck's most intriguing contemporary releases, with Jerry Bergonzi (ts). –MGN

24 Classic Original Recordings / FANTASY COMP

BILL BRUFORD

Jazz-rock. British drummer influenced by Art Blakey and Max Roach; he developed that style into a powerful personal expression. A great experimenter with extensions of rock and jazz, using electronics as an enhancement, not as a slave-device. He also uses African polyrhythms frequently. Played with the bands Yes and King Crimson; now leads his own ensemble, Earthworks. –MGN

Feels Good to Me / CAROLINE 1977

With Dave Stewart, Jeff Berlin, Kenny Wheeler, Annette Peacock, and Allan Holdsworth. This is electric music without droning, whining, or overt funk. –MGN

○ **One of a Kind / CAROLINE** 1979

This is Bruford's best group and music. The title track (parts I and II) is absolutely astounding. Features Jeff Berlin, Allan Holdsworth, and Dave Stewart. –MGN

Earthworks / CAROLINE 1986

Features Django Bates on keys and Iain Ballamy on saxes. This is more jazz oriented than previous efforts. Sounding like a seasoned band playing together, this is loaded with good sounds. –MGN

● **Master Strokes, 1978-1985 / CAROLINE** COMP

This is a very good compilation and can be recommended with no reservation. –MGN

RAINER BRUNINGHAUS

Jazz-rock, new-age. Scandinavian keyboardist well known for

ECM records with Eberhard Weber. An atmospheric, modal, minimalist player. −MGN

○ **Freigeweht (Set Free by the Wind) / ECM**   1980
Keyboardist from Eberhard Weber's band, with Kenny Wheeler (tpt) and Jon Christensen (d). Airy, minimalist compositions from a 1980 session in an Oslo studio. Title track and "Steps" (in 7/4) show this band's empathy. −MGN

RAY BRYANT   b1931

Bop, hard-bop, post-bop, cool, blues-jazz, soul jazz. One of the greatest pianists of the post-WWII period. Professional career started with Tiny Grimes in the late 40s. Worked in Philadelphia with singers and visiting soloists until the mid 50s. Became favorite sideman of many small combo leaders. Dozens of albums as sideman from mid to late 50s. Own recordings for Epic, Prestige, New Jazz, and Signature in either solo or trio context. His 60s associations with Columbia (1960-1962), Sue (1963-1965), and Cadet (1966-1969) are variable. There are commercial attempts mixed in with straight jazz dates, but in general the quality is solid. The Columbia period produced his biggest hit, "Madison Time," a dance featuring calls by a Baltimore DJ over tasty mainstream jazz, with players such as Al Grey, Sweets Edison, and Buddy Tate involved! The Atlantic (1970-1972) period produced a fine solo album, *At Montreux* (Atlantic), but the remaining items are failed commercial attempts. A return to Cadet was disappointing but an album recorded for French Black & Blue, *Hot Turkey*, in 1975, is recommended. Late-70s recordings for Pablo are all fine as are late-80s recordings for Emarcy. −BP

Alone with the Blues / OJC   1958
● **Con Alma / CBS**   r1960
This is definitive early Ray Bryant album, and includes "Cubano Chant." −MGN
Me & the Blues / PRESTIGE   r1974
Solo Flight / PABLO   1976
○ **Trio Today / POLYGRAM**   r1987
Loaded with standards and two Bryant classics: "Tonk" and "Slow Freight." Recommended. −MGN
Blue Moods / POLYGRAM   1987
○ **Ray Bryant Plays Basie & Ellington / EMARCY**   1987
Tremendous renditions of swing and jazz anthems. −RW
Golden Earrings / EMARCY   1988

RUSTY BRYANT   b1929

Post-bop, soul jazz. Among the finest funky and soul-jazz tenors of the 70s, Bryant is noted for his thick tone, robust sound, and jam-session-style albums. −RW
Rusty Bryant Returns / PRESTIGE   1969
This is great funk music! Rusty Bryant on amplified alto-sax (Conn Multi-Vider) — his only album on alto! Take-off album for Prestige. W/ Grant Green, playing some nice funk guitar. Sonny Phillips on Hammond organ fills out that classic small-group sound. −JME
○ **Soul Liberation / FANTASY**   1970
Soul-jazz classic. His most popular composition. −RW

MILT BUCKNER   1915-1977

Swing, soul jazz. Milt Buckner was among the innovators and popularizers of the organ, as well as an excellent arranger and the younger brother of alto saxophonist Ted (not Teddy) Buckner. He played and arranged for several Detroit bands in the 30s, notably McKinney's Cotton Pickers, then became a star with swirling, dashing riffs and phrases during two stints in the 40s and 50s with Lionel Hampton. Between Hampton periods, Buckner had his own 17-piece (later 10-piece) group, which he eventually paired down to a trio in the early 50s. He teamed with saxophonist Illinois Jacquet in the 70s. −RW
○ **Rockin' Hammond / CAPITOL**   1956
Classic organ combo with a master. From blues to ballads. A fine representation of Buckner's brilliance. −MGN

Midnight Slows - Vol. 3 / BLACK & BLUE   1973
Straightahead jazz with Gatemouth Brown (g), Arnett Cobb (sax), and Candy Johnson (sax). −MGN
Green Onions / INNER CITY-CLASSIC JAZZ   1975
With French rhythm section, guitarist Roy Gaines, drummer Panama Francis. Funky and groove-laden. −MGN

TED BUCKNER   b1913

Swing, big band, cool. A St. Louis alto saxophonist, brother of organist Milt Buckner. He worked extensively with the Jimmy Lunceford Orchestra and led his own group in Detroit in the 50s. −MGN
○ **T.B. & the All-Stars / GNP CRESCENDO**

MONTY BUDWIG   b1929

Post-bop, cool. Veteran West Coast bassist is primarily a session player. Credits include work with Benny Goodman, the Lighthouse All Stars, and serving as house bassist for Concord Records. −MGN
○ **Dig / CONCORD**

HIRAM BULLOCK

Contemporary funk, fusion. Osaka, Japan native Hiram Bullock is a guitar pyrotechnician whose three Atlantic albums land him firmly in fusion-funk territory. He can play all kinds of music, from the blues to speed-metal, and enlivens his shows with friendly mugging, virtuoso technique, and undeniable enthusiasm. Influenced by the Mahavishnu Orchestra and taught by Pat Metheny, the athletic Bullock has worked with the likes of Phyllis Hyman, David Sanborn, Steely Dan, James Taylor, and Carla Bley and was a member of David Letterman's studio band. −CTW
○ **Give It What U Got / ATLANTIC**
High-caliber studio funk. −RW

JOHN BUNCH   b1921

Swing, cool. Mainstream pianist and Concord/Famous Door recording artist who works best in small-combo, light-bop, or swing-oriented settings. −RW
○ **Best Thing for You / CONCORD**   r1988
Well-played, swing-influenced mainstream. −RW

DAVE BURRELL   b1940

Post-bop, early free, modern creative. Pianist Dave Burrell has been active in musical, educational, and cultural circles, particularly in the 70s. He received degrees from both Berklee and the Boston Conservatory, and later taught for two years at Queens College. He's among the more percussive, dynamic pianists and an underrated soloist and composer. His first release was on the Douglas label in the mid 60s, and he later recorded for Affinity and other European and Japanese labels. −RW
High Won — High Two / ARISTA-FREEDOM   1968
Creative pianist does it all on 2-fer from 1968 recordings. Wonderful ideas. −MGN
○ **Jelly Roll Joys / GAZELL**
Modern and traditional piano. −MGN

KENNY BURRELL   b1931

Bop, hard-bop, post-bop, cool, blues-jazz. Burrell came to New York in 1956 from his native Detroit as part of the wave of important musicians from the Motor City. Soon he was in demand for record dates with practically everybody in modern jazz (but also with such veterans as Buck Clayton and Benny Goodman) and as leader of his own studio and working groups. One of the most musical and versatile of jazz guitar stylists, Burrell has never flirted with rock or pop but always remained a pure jazz guitarist. He can be heard on literally hundreds of albums. −DM

Sunup to Sundown / CONTEMPORARY
His latest album shows that Burrell is still as good as ever. –JME
For Charlie Christian & Benny Goodman / VERVE 1956
Nice tributes. –RW
All Night Long / JCI &ASSOCIATED 1956
W/Donald Byrd (tpt). Outstanding blues, mid-tempo set with soul/jazz leanings. More Burrell's influence than Byrd's. A pair of fine bonus CD cuts; good help from Hank Mobley (ts), Mal Waldron (p), Jerome Richardson (reeds). –RW
All Day Long / OJC 1957
A tight, nicely played, welcome reissue. –RW
Kenny Burrell / OJC 1957
His first Prestige recording with an all-Detroit crew (plus baritone sax) in New York. Burrell as we love him — clear, bluesy, with a touch of funk. –JME
Two Guitars / OJC 1957
Excellent guitar exchanges. Good reissue and remastering. W/ Jimmy Raney (g), Jackie McLean (as), Mal Waldron (p), Art Taylor (d). –RW
● **Kenny Burrell & John Coltrane / OJC / DB 5** 1957
Definitive teamwork in music. A must-buy. –MGN
○ **Blue Lights - Vols. 1 & 2 / CAPITOL** 1958
I would certainly not overlook this pair of small-combo gems. Burrell deftly juggles blues, ballads, and soul-jazz. Tina Brooks (sax), Art Blakey (d), Junior Cook (ts), and others shine on both sets. These are 1989 CD reissues. –RW
At the Five Spot Cafe / BLUE NOTE 1959
○ **A Night at the Vanguard / MCA** 1959
A wonderful live set. CD reissue has two bonus cuts. –RW
● **Midnight Blue / BLUE NOTE** 1963
Best of the Blue Note period, with Stanley Turrentine (ts), Major Holley (b). Solid album. –MGN
Guitar Forms / POLYGRAM / DB 5 1964
An experimental "artsy" record arranged by Gil Evans that has become a classic. However, don't look for the usual bluesy format. –JME
God Bless the Child / CBS 1971
Despite a murky backdrop, Burrell's guitar solos are fluid and hypnotic. –RW
☆ **Ellington Is Forever - Vols. 1 & 2 / FANTASY** 1975
Group sessions. Burrell's best of the 70s. Every collection must have both albums. –MGN
Tin Tin Deo / CONCORD 1977
Live at the Village Vanguard / MUSE 1978
For Duke / FANTASY r 1981
Moonglow / PRESTIGE r 1982
Another great team. W/ Coleman Hawkins (sax). –MGN
Generations / BLUE NOTE 1986
A good blend of modern and classic sensibilities. –RW
Guiding Spirit / CONTEMPORARY r 1990
Fluid, expressive Burrell. –RW

GARY BURTON   b 1943

Early free, jazz-rock, neo bop. A world-class vibraphonist and developer of the four-mallet technique. Well-known as a jazz theoretician and instructor. Worked in early period fusion groups, then attained his own group sound. Can play atmospheric, lilting ballads or steady rolling jazz. An important presence in the past 30 years.–MGN
○ **Duster / RCA / DB 5** 1967
Prophetic session with references to everything from country to rock. Suggested new directions for jazz musicians. –RW
○ **Gary Burton and Keith Jarrett / ATLANTIC / DB 5** 1971
What might seem a mismatched pair proved a good duo. –RW
☆ **Crystal Silence / ECM / DB 5** 1972
Debut on ECM with Corea (k). The first of many successful pairings of the two. –RW
New Quartet / POLYGRAM 1973
Prelude to *Passengers* with Mick Goodrich (g). –MGN

Ring / POLYGRAM / DB 5 1974
W/ Eberhard Weber. These nice arrangements are a bit more energetic than standard ECM. –RW
Dreams So Real / POLYGRAM 1975
All Carla Bley tunes; w/ Pat Metheny (g). –MGN
○ **Passengers / POLYGRAM** 1976
Includes some stirring originals w/ Pat Metheny (g), Eberhard Weber (b). –MGN
Reunion (with Pat Metheny) / GRP r 1990
The leader reunites with his prize student. –RW
Works / POLYGRAM
Excellent solos — a good session. –RW

BILLY BUTLER   1925-1990

Blues-jazz. R&B/jazz guitarist. As part of organist Bill Doggett's combo, Butler brought a strong Charlie Christian jazz influence to 50s R&B grooves. Coaxing a warm fat tone from a hollow-bodied electric guitar, he laid down tasty and deceptively simple solos and fills that have become staples of the R&B guitar vocabulary. Doggett's "Honky Tonk," featuring Butler, is perhaps the classic R&B guitar instrumental. "Ram-Bunk'-Shush" and "Big Boy" are other highlights of his work with Doggett. Butler also did fine work on Charles Brown's 1986 recordings for Alligator Records. –RL
○ **This Is Billy Butler / PRESTIGE** r 1969
The best of Butler's three Prestige albums. –RL
Don't Be That Way / BLACK AND BLUE 1976
W/ Wild Bill Davis (organ), Oliver Jackson (d), and "Lockjaw" Davis (ts). –RL
● **Guitar Soul / OJC** 1976

FRANK BUTLER   1928-1984

Bop, hard-bop, post-bop. A Los Angeles drummer who played with Miles Davis and countless West Coast players, Butler is truly an unsung hero. –MGN
○ **The Stepper / XANADU** 1977
Quartet. Solid and swinging. One to discover. –MGN

HENRY BUTLER

Ballads & blues, neo bop, modern creative. A New Orleans pianist and vocalist who's better known for his fusion-oriented releases than for his playing prowess, which mixes second line-beats, blues influences, and gospel nuances. –RW
Fivin' Around / MCA r 1986
☆ **The Village / MCA-IMPULSE** 1987
New Orleans pianist. 2-fer (all originals). Can't do without this one. –MGN

JAKI BYARD   b 1922

Stride, big band, bop, hard-bop, post-bop, early free. An inventive pianist who is capable of any style from stride to avant-garde, Byard is a most ingenious composer. –MGN
Blues for Smoke / CANDID 1960
○ **With Strings / PRESTIGE** 1968
Top-notch recording for the brilliant pianist with George Benson (g), Ray Nance (tpt), Ron Carter (b), Richard Davis (b), and Alan Dawson (d). –MGN
There'll Be Some Changes Made / MUSE 1972
● **Family Man / MUSE** 1978
W/ Major Holley on bass. Includes excerpts from "Family Suite." Challenging listening. –MGN
Phantasies / SOULNOTE 1985
W/ Apollo Stompers Big Band in NYC. Mostly standards and lots of Ellington. –MGN

DON BYAS   1912-1972

Swing, bop, blues-jazz. Byas is a classic example of a superb tenor saxophone stylist who was influential but not innovative. He played in the swing bands of Don Redman,

Lucky Millinder, Andy Kirk, and Count Basie. Byas knew all the tricks of the trade: overblowing effects, a huge tone, an incredible blues and ballad player. Some view him as a transitional figure between swing and bop, but his later releases were neatly balanced between those styles, and he had no problem fitting in with new players like Monk and Max Roach. He left America for Holland in the 50s and died there in 1972. –RW

Midnight at Minton's / ONYX VINYL   ca. 1941
Torrid uptempo cuts and lovely ballads. Very rare album. –RW

○ **Savoy Jam Party / SAVOY**   194?
Fun session with a variety of bands, from the mid 40s –MGN

A Tribute to Cannonball / CBS / DB 5   1961
Extraordinary. W/ pianist Bud Powell. –MGN

● **Don Byas in Paris / PRESTIGE**   i 1982

A Night in Tunisia / BLACK LION

○ **On Blue Star / POLYGRAM**   COMP

CHARLIE BYRD   b 1925

Cool, Latin. A guitarist best known for his mastery of Latin forms, Byrd started out as a very fine classical and light jazz player. His studies with Segovia in the 50s taught him the rudiments of the instrument as well as an awareness of its romantic, sentimental qualities. Byrd played with Woody Herman in 1959, then toured Latin America for the State Department. He and Stan Getz helped launch the samba/bossa-nova craze in the 60s when he suggested they record Antonio Carlos Jobim tunes. He has been busy ever since and made many nice recordings with Bud Shank. –RW

At the Village Vanguard / OJC   1961

Bossa Nova Pelos Passaros / OJC   1962
Nice excursion into bossa nova. –RW

○ **Byrd at the Gate / OJC**   1963
Delightful solos, solid set. Guest appearance by Clark Terry (tpt). –RW

● **Brazilian Byrd / CBS**   1965
One of his finest, a session that cemented his reputation. –RW

Sugarloaf Suite / CONCORD   1979
This trio date has fine Byrd guitar. –RW

Brazilville / CONCORD   1981
A good quartet date with Bud Shank (as). Shank adds spice to Charlie Byrd's cool Afro-Latin setting. –RW

Isn't It Romantic / CONCORD   1984
Sentimental and wonderfully played. –RW

It's a Wonderful World / CONCORD   1989
Includes one bonus cut on CD version. –RW

Latin Byrd / MILESTONE

DONALD BYRD   b 1932

Bop, hard-bop, post-bop, cool, soul jazz, contemporary funk. Donald Byrd has been among the finest trumpeters of his generation. During the 60s he was especially strong as a soloist, playing with great confidence and passion and displaying a fine range and ideas. He gained his initial fame as a member of Art Blakey's Jazz Messengers in the late 50s. His 60s Blue Note albums were striking, especially the two volumes recorded live at the Half Note, and others like *A New Perspective* that featured a jazz hymn. Byrd began moving into murky waters in the 70s, first working with a 12-piece band, then gradually getting away almost totally from his jazz base and doing straight R&B with his Blackbirds band. His albums in the 80s and 90s have returned to the improvisational thrust that characterized his best work. –RW

First Flight / DELMARK   1955
An instructive session; you can hear Byrd's trumpet conception taking form. Backing groups include Yusef Lateef (sax), Barry Harris (p). Prototype 80s Detroit/Chicago jazz sound. –RW

All Night Long / OJC   1956

Jazz Eyes / SAVOY   1957
Biting collaboration with alto saxophonist John Jenkins. –RW

September Afternoon / DISCOVERY   1957
Interesting rare session with orchestrations; w/ Clare Fischer (p). –RW

Byrd in Paris - Vols. 1 & 2 / POLYGRAM   1958
Two-volume set of early hard bop done in Paris. Presence of Bobby Jaspar (fl, ts), well-regarded but little-known international musician, increases importance. These two dates helped Jaspar establish his reputation. Walter Davis (p), Doug Watkins (b), and Art Taylor (d) make a fine rhythm section. –RW

Fuego / BLUE NOTE   1959
A good one for this Detroit trumpeter, with Jackie McLean (as) and Duke Pearson (p). –MGN

At the Half Note Cafe - Vols. 1 & 2 / BLUE NOTE   1960
The album has two bonus cuts; good though rather standard early-60s hard bop with Pepper Adams (bar sax) and Duke Pearson (p). –RW

Free Form / BLUE NOTE   1961
Nice date; w/ bonus CD track. –RW

New Perspective / BLUE NOTE   1963
Includes remarkable "Christo Redentor," a Duke Pearson hymn. Excellent merger of gospel, choral, and jazz sensibility and arrangements. –RW

● **Blackjack / BLUENOTE**   1967
Perhaps his very best of many recordings with Sonny Red (as), Hank Mobley, (ts), and Cedar Walton (p). –MGN

Byrd in Hand / BLUE NOTE   1969
A good straightahead release, available in 1975 reissue package. –RW

○ **Electric Byrd / BLUE NOTE**   1970
Pivotal release with Byrd using 12-piece group. Duke Pearson on electric piano. The arrangements and mood are harbingers of Byrd's shift into pop, funk, and R&B. –RW

Ethiopian Knights / BLUE NOTE   1971
Interesting jam-session feel. Top jazz players manage to retain credibility in essentially R&B setting. Album cited by many as reflective of label's trend away from its roots in the 70s. Concept was brainchild of George Butler, now Dr. George Butler of Columbia. –RW

GEORGE CABLES   b 1944

Post-bop. A favorite pianist of saxophonists from Art Pepper to Frank Morgan, Cables has been in demand as a session regular since the mid 60s. After studying at Mannes College, he worked with premier drummers Max Roach and Art Blakey in both the 60s and the 70s. Cables was Sonny Rollins's pianist in 1969, and spent two years with Joe Henderson, two with Dexter Gordon, and six in two stints with Freddie Hubbard. He made two acclaimed duet works with Art Pepper and worked with him in the final three years of Pepper's career. Cables is an exciting, very rhythmically potent player, a first-rate accompanist, and a delightful soloist. –RW

Cables' Vision / CONTEMPORARY   1979

● **Circle / CONTEMPORARY**   1979
Aggressive date with robust solos from Joe Farrell (ts), decisive playing by Cables. –RW

○ **Phantom of the City / CONTEMPORARY**   r 1986
Fine straightahead mainstream session. –RW

○ **By George / CONTEMPORARY**   r 1987
Cables's unique arrangements of Gershwin standards. Outstanding playing. "My Man's Gone Now." Piano trio jazz of the highest order. –MGN

CADENCE ALL-STARS

Post-bop, neo bop. A one-shot sextet asembled by Cadence Magazine's Bob Rusch. Featured Ernie Krivda (ts), Glenn Wilson (bar sax), Rory Stuart (g), plus rhythm section. They played thoroughly modern, hard-driving jazz with guts and passion. –MGN

○ **Lee's Keys Please / TIMELESS**   1987
Sextet with Ernie Krivda (sax), Rory Stuart (g), Glenn Wilson (bar sax), and Jon Hazilla (d). Excellent. A great group. –MGN

JOEY CALDERAZZO   *b*1966

Post-bop, neo bop. A good, if derivitive pianist, whose recent Blue Note album is distinguished by the presence of Branford Marsalis. –RW

○ **In the Door / CAPITOL**   1991
A wonderful debut album with a cast of great sidemen, including Michael Brecker (sax), Branford Marsalis (tpt), and Jerry Bergonzi (ts). Very modern chord changes. –PK

HADLEY CALIMAN   *b*1932

Post-bop, neo bop. West Coast saxophonist and flutist best known for his rousing solos on Santana's *Caravanserai* release. He has also contributed to other dates by Todd Cochran and other fusion/jazz-rock/rock players. He's also issued a few albums of varying distinction. –RW

Iapetus / MAINSTREAM   1972
His second album. Progressive and hip. –MGN

○ **Celebration / CATALYST**   1977
San Francisco tenor sax and flutist's best album of four; w/ Elvin Jones (d). Straightahead. –MGN

RED CALLENDER   *b*1918

Swing, big band, bop, cool. Legendary West Coast session bassist. Also played tuba. A most dependable musician, who could do it in his sleep. A true unsung hero worldwide. –MGN

○ **Swingin' Suite / MODERN**   i 1956
W/ Buddy Collette (sax).

Callender Speaks Low / CROWN   i 1957
W/ Buddy Collette (sax).

The Lowest / METROJAZZ   i 1959
W/ Buddy Collette (sax).

CAB CALLOWAY   *b*1907

Swing, big band, ballads. Cab Calloway is a vocalist and bandleader. An incredibly energetic performer, best known as the zoot-suited, hip-talking, scat-singing "Highness of Hi-De-Ho," Calloway's influence on all Black performers who came after him is incalculable. He started in Baltimore, eventually coming to New York and forming his first band. He followed Duke Ellington as the house band into the legendary Cotton Club and it was there that he made his reputation as the hippest musician in all of Harlem, becoming a national phenomenon with radio broadcasts done live from the club. With an act chock full of wild physical energy, his long black hair flying, he made "hi-de-ho" a national catchphrase when "Minnie the Moocher" became a hit in 1930. Hollywood beckoned and Cab's manic, visual style and excellent orchestra were put to good effect in such films as *Stormy Weather*, *Manhattan Merry-Go-Round*, *The Big Broadcast of 1932*, among others. He kept performing in his familiar, affable style throughout the intervening decades, coming to the attention of a whole new audience with his appearance in *The Blues Brothers* in 1980. He still actively performs today and shows no signs of slowing down. –CK

○ **Jazz Heritage — Mr. Hi-De-Ho (1930-1931) / MCA**   1930
A budget compilation of Calloway's early-30s cuts. A good starter set despite the uneven sound. –RW

Cab Calloway & Co. / RCA (FRANCE)   1933
Prime recording of his 30s and 40s material. –RW

Jumpin' Five / ZETA   193?
An excellent collection of prime late-30s and 40s material. –RW

★ **Hi-De-Ho Man / CBS**   1958
Two album best-of retrospective that's the perfect place to start, featuring the hits and high points. In and out of print

for years and may actually be on CD by the time this is published. –CK

Hi-De-Ho-Man / RCA
1958
Updated, fiery Calloway cuts. –RW

Best of the Big Bands / CBS
COMP
Nice collection of his material from the 30s. –RW

○ **Kicking the Gong Around / ASV**
COMP
Cab's naughtier side, with the virtues of substance use imbuing the lyrical text of several tunes included here. If you thought drug songs didn't start until the late 60s in rock music, be prepared for a shock. –CK

On Film 1934-1950 / HARLEQUIN
COMP
Solid collection of performances taken from soundtracks of his many film appearances. High energy makes up for spotty sound on certain tracks. –CK

MICHEL CAMILO   *b*1952

Latin, neo bop, modern creative. Hottest Latin-jazz pianist to come on the scene in years. Plays mostly with trio, sometimes with horns. Potential for big things. –MGN

Michel Camilo / CBS
Debut US album has all the ingredients to cook. –MGN

○ **On Fire / CBS**
Burning Latin-jazz piano trio. Recommended. –MGN

CONTE CANDOLI   *b*1927

Swing, big band, bop, cool, progressive big band. Trumpeter Conte Candoli, well known for his work on the "Tonight Show" with Doc Severinsen, played with other fine leaders including Woody Herman, Stan Kenton, Charlie Barnet, and Howard Rumsey's LightHouse All Stars. He also worked with Shelly Manne and was a member of Supersax. –JME

Conte Candoli / BETHLEHEM   1956
A fine session by this mainstream/bop trumpeter. –DS

○ **Quartet / MODE**   1957
Excellent West Coast swinging bop. –DS

VALERIE CAPERS

Post-bop. A pianist/composer who plays soul, Latin, and mainstream to progressive jazz adeptly, Capers is mostly known as an instructor. –MGN

○ **Portrait in Soul / ATLANTIC**   1966
Rare septet, all Capers originals. Worth searching for. –MGN

Affirmation / K-M-ARTS   1982
All standards, and well played. A good one to find. –MGN

FRANKIE CAPP   *b*1931

Swing, bop. West Coast drummer leads small combos or big band with pianist Nat Pierce in swing to bop setting. –MGN

Juggernaut / CONCORD   1976
Here is a good lineup of big-band pros. CD issue has two bonus cuts. –RW

○ **Live at the Century / CONCORD**   1978
Great big band from West Coast. W/ vocal cameo by Joe Williams. –MGN

○ **Presents Rickey Woodard / CONCORD**   An impressive
session that spotlights top-flight saxophonist Woodard. –RW

LARRY CARLTON   *b*1949

Jazz-rock, instr-pop. Carlton is a steady, well-respected session guitarist who has been a major figure in the Los Angeles studio scene and also issued a fair number of albums under his own name. His best work came with the Crusaders in the 70s. –RW

On Solid Ground / MCA   1969
Here are some good arrangements and playing. –RW
○ **Larry Carlton / WARNER**   1972
His best. –MGN
Friends / MCA   1973
Larry Carlton / MCA   1975
Fine technique, less interesting material. –RW

JUDY CARMICHAEL   b 1952

Trad, stride, boogie, swing. Early period jazz preserver,
excellent technical pianist capable of great improvisations in
this traditional setting. A keeper. –MGN
○ **Jazz Piano / PROGRESSIVE**   1983
Solo piano from a lady who knows this music well. Interprets
music from Earl Hines, Fats Waller, James P. Johnson, and the
like. She is one of a kind, and is a very good player. –MGN
Old Friends / C&D   1983
Live session with Warren Vache (cnt) and Howard Alden (g)
in 1983 and 1985. More Fats, James P. Johnson, and Jelly Roll
Morton. 13 tracks. A very good representation of her
capabilities. –MGN
Pearls / STATIRAS   1985
With quartet including Warren Vache (cnt), Howard Alden (g),
Red Callender (b). All oldish standards, played with
considerable wit. –MGN
Trio / C&D   ca. 1989
With Michael Hashim (sax), Chris Flory (g). There are 11
cuts without a bass, but based in early piano swing. Fats
Waller, James P. Johnson, Ellington, and Basie repertoire
featured. –MGN

BARBARA CARROLL   b 1925

Ballads. As a pianist, Carroll is a student of Bud Powell, but
she headed for the more pretty side, bordering on pop. She is
still a good example of the quiet and introspective. –MGN
○ **Live at the Carlyle / DRG**   1990

JOE CARROLL   1919-1981

Bop, ballads. A bop and ballad singer closely associated
with Dizzy Gillespie, Carroll was one of the first to tackle
vocalese. –MGN
Joe Carroll / EPIC   i 1956
W/ Ray Bryant (p).
○ **Man with a Happy Sound / CHARLIE PARKER**   r 1962
A date with guitarist Grant Green. Lots of fun as Carroll scats
on his favorite themes. Rare. –MGN

BENNY CARTER   b 1907

Swing, big band, bop, cool, progressive big band. Billed in the 40s
as "The Amazing Man of Music," alto saxophonist Benny
Carter is that even more so today — vitally active as a player,
writer, and leader in his eighth decade of musical activity.
Born and raised in New York City, Carter led his own first big
band in 1928. After working with Charlie Johnson and other
leaders, he then joined Fletcher Henderson. He had his own
band again in 1933-1935, then spent three years in Europe,
where he wrote for the BBC in London, led an integrated band
in Holland, and made history in the Paris recording studios.
Back home, Benny introduced a new band at Harlem's Savoy
Ballroom; he continued to lead big bands until the late 40s,
but from 1943 on he also became active in the Hollywood
studios, scoring for many feature films as well as appearing
on screen; later he also wrote for TV. While he continued to
play in the 50s and 60s, including tours abroad with Jazz at the
Philharmonic and the direction of many fine albums, he
became fully active as a leader and player again from the mid
70s on. Carter was one of the pace setters of jazz at the dawn
of the swing era, both as an alto sax stylist (rivaled only by
Johnny Hodges) and as an arranger (his scoring for

saxophones, especially, was — and is — state of the art). And
he is still at the top today — truly an amazing man. –DM
Benny Carter - 1933 / PRESTIGE   1933
Uncollected Benny Carter... / HINDSIGHT   1944
Carter with Eddie "Lockjaw" Davis (ts) and Harry "Sweets"
Edison (tpt) show the youngsters what jazz phrasing, taste,
and sophistication are all about. –RW
● **On Keynote / POLYGRAM**   194?
Here's a fine representative sampling of prime Carter 40s cuts.
With Arnold Ross Quintet, his own LA group at the time. –RW
Jazz Giant / OJC   1957
The title says it all. –MGN
○ **Swingin' the 20's / OJC**   1958
Brilliant tribute to the foundation of the music. Earl Hines (p)
and Carter make a wondrous team. –RW
☆ **Further Definitions / MCA**   1961
This is classic, a masterpiece of arranging, playing, and
composing. Carter duplicated the instrumental setting and
included some cuts from a landmark session he'd done back
in Paris during the 30s. Still sounds wonderful 31 years later,
though the vinyl album is superior to MCA reissue. –RW
Birdology - Vol. 1 / POLYGRAM   ca. 1971
Great jam session; tart solos from Jackie McLean (as). –RW
My Man Benny My Man Phil / MUSICMASTERS   ca. 1971
W/ Phil Woods (as). A pair of old friends, these alto sax giants
make a great team. –RW
The King / PABLO   1976
A slightly pretentious title but wonderful lineup. Sidemen
Tommy Flanagan (p), Milt Jackson (vib), and Joe Pass (g) are
superb. –RW
Live & Well in Japan / PABLO   1977
Carter has a good workout on this live set. Ray Bryant (p) is
impressive. –RW
Benny Carter 4 / PABLO   1977
A stately live date. –RW
Montreux 1977 / PABLO   1977
● **A Gentleman and His Music / CONCORD**   1985
Best late-period studio work from a master musician. Must-
buy.–MGN
In the Mood for Swing / MUM   1987
He can still play ballads with zeal and cook on the uptempo
tunes. Dizzy Gillespie (tpt) takes some nice turns. –RW
Over the Rainbow / MUSICMASTERS   1988
Some beautiful solos by Carter. A good release, though not
essential. –RW
Cookin' at Carlos 1 / MUSICMASTERS   1988
Fine playing from Carter. Ordinary compositions, but the
group romps through them with style. –RW
All That Jazz — Live / MUSICMASTERS   1990
At Princeton. Carter in typically accomplished form. Guests
including Clark Terry (tpt) and Kenny Barron (p). –RW
○ **Additions to Further Definitions / IMPULSE**
Followup to the seminal *Further Definitions.* –RW
All of Me / RCA
Recent reissue of authoritative Carter compositions
and sessions. –RW
Birdology - Vol. 2 / POLYGRAM
Good tribute date, loose jam-session feel. –RW
3-4-5 — Verve Small Group / POLYGRAM   COMP
Verve small-group sessions. Very nice reissue of some prime
Carter combo, small-group sessions. –RW
Three Great Swing Saxophonists / BLUEBIRD   COMP
These are some superb cuts with Carter and fellow jazz
statesmen Ben Webster (ts) and Coleman Hawkins (ts).
Though main body of songs can be found elsewhere, the CD
has six bonus cuts. –RW

BETTY CARTER   b 1930

Bop, ballads. Betty Carter is among the few genuine jazz singers and vocal improvisers. She has her own style and communicative approach, is an amazing interpreter, and does several of her own arrangements. She turned professional in 1946 after studying piano at the Detroit Conservatory, then winning an amateur contest. Using the moniker "Be-Bop" in the first phase of her career, she toured with Lionel Hampton, Miles Davis, Sonny Rollins, and others before forming a trio that became a college fixture in the 70s. The distinctiveness and individuality of her albums (few short songs, scatting) and her refusal to compromise have led to the inability to secure recording dates on major labels, and she has issued and distributed her own recordings since the 70s. A new pact with Verve in the late 80s has given her widespread fresh exposure, as has an appearance on "The Cosby Show." –RW

Meet Betty Carter / EPIC   1955
Social Call / CSP / DB 5   1956
1955-1956. Hitting her stride with Roy Bryant Quartet or Gigi Gryce's 14-piece band. Truly excellent. –MGN

Out There / PEACOCK   1958
W/ Gigi Gryce (as), Melba Liston (tb), and Benny Golson (ts). Rare and wonderful. –MGN

○ **Modern Sound of Betty Carter / ABC**   1960
Some spectacular cuts. Find it in used record shops. –RW

☆ **Ray Charles & Betty Carter / ABC / BB 52**   1961
This album still has its charm, though it's not a favorite of Carter's. –RW

Inside Betty Carter / UNITED ARTISTS   1964
Finally / CAPITOL   1969
A long-awaited reissue of Carter's 1969 album that was a jazz-vocal fan's bonanza. –RW

○ **Round Midnight / CAPITOL**   1969
Excellent album. –RW

Betty Carter 1 & 2 / BET-CAR   1970
She put these out herself to get the music out in the marketplace. You can get them directly from her. –RW

The Betty Carter Album / POLYGRAM   1972
Excellent vocals and a fine rhythm section. –RW

○ **What a Little Moonlight Can Do / IMPULSE**   1976
1958 & 1960. 2-fer of studio recordings showing her versitility and depth. This is loaded with great musicians of the 50s and 60s. –MGN

★ **Audience With / POLYGRAM / DB 5**   1979
Definitive 2-fer live set w/ John Hicks Trio. A must-buy. –MGN

Whatever Happened to Love / POLYGRAM   1982
Rangy, adventurous, appealing vocals. –RW

Look What I Got / POLYGRAM / DB 5   1988
A fine recent session with Winard Harper (d) and Benny Green (p). –RW

Droppin' Things / POLYGRAM   1990
Extraordinary players, but Carter holds the spotlight. –RW

JOHN CARTER   1929-1991

Early free, modern creative. An ambitious composer and superb clarinet player who was never able to get the widespread exposure he deserved, even in jazz circles, Carter played with Ornette Coleman and Charles Moffett in the 40s and 50s. He formed a critically acclaimed quartet with Bobby Bradford in 1965, then led his own groups from 1973 until he joined James Newton's woodwind quintet in 1980. He was also a vital member of the original Clarinet Summit in the mid 80s. –RW

● **Dauwhe / BLACK SAINT**   1982
Unequaled player shows range of technical prowess. –RW

○ **Castles of Ghana / RHINO / DB 5**   1985
Ambitious part of series showcasing Black achievement. –RW

Dance of the Love Ghosts / RHINO / DB 5   1987
Experimental, daring concept work with Andrew Cyrille (d)

and Fred Hopkins (b). Excellent clarinet solos and arrangements by Carter. –RW

Fields / RHINO   1988
A 1989 reissue of part of his impressive series spotlighting African-American musical achievement. –RW

Shadows on a Wall / RHINO / DB 5   r 1990
Clarinetist's avant-garde magnum opus, "Roots & Folklore: Episodes in the Development of American Folk Music." –MGN

RON CARTER   b 1937

Bop, hard-bop, post-bop, cool, jazz-rock. Bassist. An extremely talented individual whose musical skills extend to violin, clarinet, trombone, and tuba, Ron Carter started on cello at ten and soon giving concerts. He switched to bass in high school in Detroit, and later graduated from the Eastman School of Music in 1959. Carter played and recorded with the Eastman Philharmonic Orchestra before joining Chico Hamilton in 1959. From 1960 until the present, the list of greats Carter has worked with includes Eric Dolphy, Miles Davis, McCoy Tyner, Lena Horne, the New York Bass Choir, the New York Jazz Quartet, and many others. His huge tone, sense of time, rhythmic pulse, imagination, and ability to provide whatever's necessary in any musical situation have enabled Carter to do everything from solos to duos to trios, and even work with rappers. He formed his own quartet in 1976, and his exchanges with fellow bassist Buster Williams, plus his use of the piccolo bass, were breathtaking. Carter's legacy runs over 500 albums. –RW

Where? / OJC   1961
Essential session with Carter on both bass and cello. Awesome solos by Eric Dolphy (sax) — stunning pieces. –RW

● **Uptown Conversation / ATLANTIC**   1969
Arguably his best release. A 1989 reissue of Embryo album that featured some rangy, vibrant Carter solos. –RW

Blues Farm / CBS / DB 5   1973
One of his best dates as a leader. A good set with Bob James (k), Richard Tee (k), and Hubert Laws (fl) — revealing jazz chops they've seldom shown otherwise. –RW

Spanish Blue / CBS   1974
Interesting concept with good solos by Carter and Hubert Laws (fl). –RW

Yellow & Green / CBS   1976
W/ Billy Cobham (d) and Don Grolnick (k). A sleeper. –MGN

Pastels / FANTASY   1976
Some tremendous playing by Carter, Kenny Barron (p), and Hugh McCracken (g), though the strings get intrusive. –RW

☆ **Piccolo / MILESTONE**   1977
Live 2-fer. Quartet with Carter on piccolo-bass, Buster Williams on contrabass. Carter's shining hour. –MGN

○ **Third Plane / MILESTONE**   1977
Trio behind mid-60s "Miles Steps Out." Rare date. –MGN

A Song for You / MILESTONE   1978
1 + 3 / FANTASY   1978
Parade / MILESTONE   1979
☆ **Telephone / CONCORD**   1984
W/ Jim Hall (g). One of the top bass/guitar duos ever. –RW

All Alone / POLYGRAM   1988
Nice showcase for Carter's impeccable bass skills. –RW

Ron Carter / MILESTONE
Well-played if unambitious mainstream/bop fare. –RW

Standard Bearers / OJC
An overlooked date. Carter with some first-rate players including Red Garland (p), McCoy Tyner (p), Herbie Hancock (k), and many others, work their way through a program of jazz classics. CD has a bonus cut. –RW

MICHAEL CARVIN   b 1944

Hard-bop, post-bop. Drummer Carvin came to fame playing with Jackie McLean in the 70s and has gone on to make some good, if conservative recordings in the hard-bop mold. –RW

The Camel / INNER CITY   1975
His debut as a leader, with Sonny Fortune (as). Find this one
— it's a keeper. −MGN

First Time / MUSE   1986
Excellent ensemble jazz. −MGN

○ **Between Me and You / MUSE**   1988
Incredible playing on mostly originals. A solid album. −MGN

AL CASEY   b 1915

Swing, blues-jazz. A guitarist prominent with Fats Waller in
the 40s and 50s. He also worked with Teddy Wilson and King
Curtis, and led his own bands. A solid, if not prolific, early
period jazz master. −MGN

Al Casey Quartet / MOODSVILLE   i 1960
Companion to *Buck Jumpin'*. −MGN

○ **Buck Jumpin' / OJC**   1960
Quintet sides w/ Herman Foster Trio and reedman Rudy
Powell. Nine tracks, mostly old timey and bluesy, sweet and
mellow. Two previously unreleased tracks. −MGN

Genius of Jazz Guitar / JSP   1982
Side one w/ pianist Gene Rogers Trio, side two w/ Jay
McShann or Mike Carr's Trio. Swing, blues, and gospel
standards. −MGN

OSCAR CASTRO-NEVES   b 1940

Latin, new-age. Guitarist. Largely classical in style, with tinges
of his South American heritage, especially samba and bossa
nova. −MGN

Oscar! / LIVING MUSIC   1987
Excellent production, good arrangements. Paul Winter (sax)
and Eugene Friesen (b) bring a new-age feel. Castro-Neves
adds Latin tinge. −RW

○ **Maracuja' / MCA-GRP**   i 1989
His best from a Latin jazz standpoint. −RW

DORI CAYMMI   b 1943

Latin, world fusion. Dori, who has worked extensively as a
producer/arranger both in Brazil and the US, is a major artist
in his own right: singer, guitarist, and composer whose songs
have been widely covered. −TH

● **Brasilian Serenata / WAR**   1990
Guitarist takes the work of Egberto Gismonti into an
even more lush, romantic environment. Orchestral and
ensemble work. −MGN

○ **Dori Caymmi / ELEKTRA**
You'll want this one too. −MGN

SERGE CHALOFF   1923-1957

Swing, big band, bop, cool. Few have better exploited the
richness and depth of the baritone sax than Serge Chaloff,
who began playing with big bands as a teenager. He worked
with Boyd Raeburn, Georgie Auld, and Jimmy Dorsey before
he joined Woody Herman in 1947. He spent two years with
Herman and another with Basie before returning to Boston.
Chaloff also made a few releases as a leader. Despite a rather
slim discography, his commanding style and formidable
sound have seldom been equalled on his instrument. −RW

Fable of Mable / BLACK LION   1954

Boston Blow-Up / CAPITOL   1955
Another swinging, boppish session from a musician who was
once a mainstay of Woody Herman's band. −DS

○ **Blue Serge / CAPITOL**   1956
An indispensable session from one of the great underrated
baritone sax players, featuring Sonny Clark (p) and Philly
Joe Jones (d). −DS

JOE CHAMBERS   b 1942

Post-bop, early free, neo bop. Drummer Chambers has the
ability to be both commanding and sensitive, on top of the
beat or slightly behind it. He moved to New York in 1963,
where he became a regular on the scene, working with, among
others, Eric Dolphy, Freddie Hubbard, and Andrew Hill. He
spent five years with Bobby Hutcherson from 1965-1970 and
has worked since 1970 with Max Roach's M'Boom, as well as
doing several sessions as a freelancer. −RW

○ **The Almoravid / MUSE**   1973
1971 and 1973 recordings for pianist/percussionist. A
great album. −MGN

● **Double Exposure / MUSE**   1977
Definitive duets with Joe Chambers and organist Larry
Young. −MGN

PAUL CHAMBERS   1935-1969

Hard-bop, post-bop, cool. One of the great bass players of the
50s and 60s. A member of Miles Davis's working groups,
1955-63, after which he formed a cooperative trio with pianist
Wynton Kelly and drummer Jimmy Cobb. This group
appeared frequently with Wes Montgomery in the mid 60s
and recorded with him and also with guitarist Kenny Burrell
for Verve. While these albums are solid items — and the
Montgomery *Smokin' at the Half Note* much more than that —
the best Chambers as a leader is on Blue Note. Any Blue Note
album is highly recommended by this artist and his Vee Jay
sessions are just a slight cut beneath the Blue Notes. As a
soloist Chambers is noted for his bowed solos and is heard to
great advantage in the trio of pianist Red Garland on many
Prestige and Prestige Moodsville albums, 1955-1959. An
active freelance recording musician around New York, he is
present on dozens of albums and his presence adds a little
extra quality to any setting. −BP

High Step / BLUE NOTE   1955
Complete all-star group sessions from mid 50s that include
John Coltrane contributions. Rare two-record set that was part
of mid-70s Blue Note reissue line. −RW

Whims of Chambers / BLUE NOTE   1956

○ **Bass on Top / BLUE NOTE**   1957
Extraordinary bassist. Highly recommended. A definition for
modal-jazz expression. −MGN

Chambers' Music / BLUE NOTE   r 1958
Also recommended −MGN

Ease It / AFFINITY   1959

Go / VEE JAY   1959

Just Friends / VEE-JAY   1959
Rare 1959 and 1960 sessions Chambers led for Vee Jay label.
These were once available as poorly remastered bootleg; they
are tough to locate. −RW

1st Bassman / CHAMELEON   1960

TEDDY CHARLES   b 1928

Bop, hard-bop, post-bop, cool, progressive big band. Vibes,
composer. Teddy Charles's conception and approach have
changed considerably from his early days of working with big
bands led by Benny Goodman, Chubby Jackson, Artie Shaw,
and Buddy DeFranco. In the 50s, both in his own groups and
playing with others, Charles began to play aggressively and try
newer things, especially as a producer. He created groups for
recordings with three trumpets and a rhythm section or a
tenor and two baritones; his 50s solos on vibes were far-
reaching and a precursor to the things being done currently
by Jay Hoggard or Steve Nelson. −RW

Evolution / OJC   1953
Two dates. One w/ Jimmy Giuffre (sax/cl), Shelly Manne (d);
the other with Charles Mingus (b). −JME

○ **Tentet (Jazzlore 48) / ATLANTIC**   1956
Good album, showing Charles as an original thinker. −MGN

On Campus / FRESH SOUNDS   1960
Very rare album with the adventurous Charles finding a way
to mesh with Zoot Sims (ts). On the Fresh Sounds import
label; the Bethlehem original is long gone. −RW

○ **Live/Verona / SOULNOTE** 1988
Concert date with Harold Danko trio. Highlight is the Mingus composition "Nostalgia in Times Square." –MGN

DOC CHEATHAM b 1905

Trad, swing. Trumpeter. A jazz legend and elder statesman, Cheatham remained a formidable, exciting soloist and performer at 87. His ability to hit high notes, play with fire and zip, excel at ballads, blues, or bop, and still be a dominating figure on the bandstand has been exemplary for over five decades. Cheatham came to Chicago in the mid 20s and played and recorded with Ma Rainey. He played with Wilbur de Paris's orchestra in 1927-1928, then went to Europe the next year with Sam Wooding's ensemble. Cheatham played with Cab Calloway for six years in the 30s, taking time off at various times to work with Teddy Wilson and Benny Carter. He later spent two years in Fletcher Henderson's Orchestra, then played later in the 40s with Eddie Heywood and Marcelino Guerra. Cheatham displayed his proficiency in Afro-Latin and Latin jazz in the 50s, spending a year with Perez Prado, and touring in the summers with Calloway's band. He reunited with de Paris in the 50s, then led his own band in New York City at International on Broadway from 1960-1965. Cheatham spent a year with Benny Goodman's group in 1966, and during the 70s and 80s has made several delightful records for mainly independent labels. –RM

○ **Black Beauty / SACKVILLE** 1979
A Salute to Black American Songwriters. Classic music duet w/ pianist Sammy Price. Mostly pre-40s music. Trumpet and piano in perfect harmony — truly a great album to start a collection with. –MGN

It's a Good Life / PARKWOOD 1982
W/ Chuck Folds Trio. Well recorded and played. A solid effort from all. –MGN

The Fabulous / PARKWOOD 1983
W/ Dick Wellstood Trio. Old-timey standards that are timeless as the day they were written. Cheatham's personal spark is clearly evident. –MGN

JEANNIE AND JIMMY CHEATHAM

Swing, blues-jazz, ballads. A husband-wife duo who've had moderate success with a series of big-band and blues recordings on the Concord label. Their releases blend elements of Kansas City swing, down-home blues, soul, and traditional jazz. –RW

Sweet Baby Blues / CONCORD 1984
Homeward Bound / CONCORD 1987
Nice blues/jazz mix. –RW

○ **Back to the Neighborhood / CONCORD** 1988
Best of their albums thus far. CD version. –RW

Luv in the Afternoon / CONCORD 1990
Good set from 1990. –RW

DON CHERRY b 1936

Post-bop, early free, jazz-rock, world fusion, modern creative. Don Cherry began as an experimental trumpeter and gradually expanded his interest and involvement with ethnic and international music until it's become his primary mode. He played piano in an R&B band with drummer Billy Higgins in his teens, then the two joined up with Ornette Coleman in the late 50s. Cherry's pungent, rippling trumpet made the ideal contrast to Coleman's sprawling, bluesy, and then greatly misunderstood alto sax leads. Cherry and Coleman spent the summer of 1959 at the Lenox School of Music, he then made a controversial debut in New York that autumn with bassist Charlie Haden and Higgins. Cherry stayed two years with Coleman, then freelanced with John Coltrane, Steve Lacy, and Sonny Rollins before becoming a founding member of the short-lived but invigorating New York Contemporary Five. Cherry, Archie Shepp, John Tchicai, and others toured and recorded in Europe, then disbanded in 1964. Cherry

continued working with Albert Ayler, Gato Barbieri, and George Russell, then gradually became immersed in world music. He lived in Sweden in the 70s, then returned to New York. In 1976 he started working with a group of Coleman alumni that blossomed into the group Old and New Dreams. The band featured a lot of Coleman classics, but also worked in compositions from Cherry and Haden. –RW

● **The Avant-Garde / ATLANTIC** 1960
Misleading title, but substantial session that was really Cherry's, though John Coltrane (ts) plays with fire.–RW

○ **Complete Communion / BLUE NOTE** 1965
Dynamic, raw, and experimental mid-60s material. Gato Barbieri (ts) in his Pharoah Sanders soundalike period. –RW

Symphony for Improvisers / BLUE NOTE 1966
Chaotic, rousing, and free. Barbieri (ts) and Sanders (ts) take things out and beyond. –RW

Brooklyn Is Now / BLUE NOTE 1966
Pharoah Sanders (ts) explodes; Don Cherry is almost as daring. –RW

Eternal Rhythm / BLUE NOTE / DB 5 1968
Beginning of expansion beyond jazz. Cherry is sparkling on cornet, and switches to a variety of flutes and other instruments. Albert Mangelsdorff (tb) and Sonny Sharrock (g) join the party. –RW

MU — First Part & Second Part / ACTUEL 1969
Electrifying duets with Ed Blackwell (d). This music has been released both as one set and as two separate albums. –RW

☆ **Don Cherry / A&M** 1971
Cherry is accessible and full of surprises. Percussive, slightly electric, and always potent. Easy to recommend. –MGN

Relativity Suite / JCOA / DB 5 1973
With Jazz Composers Orchestra. Cutting edge music. Features many of Cherry's familiar themes. –MGN

Brown Rice / A&M 1975
A bit more funky and loose than some Cherry sessions. –RW

Hear & Now / ATLANTIC 1976

○ **El Corazon w/ Ed Blackwell / POLYGRAM** 1982
Great duets, much spirit. –MGN

○ **Art Deco / A & M / DB 5** 1988
With a premier progressive trumpeter and James Clay on tenor sax. Satisfying throughout. –MGN

DAVID CHESKY

Progressive big band. Chesky is a pop, funk, jazz, and big band arranger/producer. Plays keyboards. Leans more toward commercial than traditional. Works with excellent sidemen. –MGN

○ **New York Chorinhos / CHESKY** 1990
Interesting fusion based on Brazilian chorinhos (crying songs). Piano and guitar. Nice background music. –JME

BUDDY CHILDERS b 1926

Trad, swing, progressive big band. Self-taught trumpeter Marion "Buddy" Childers played in the Stan Kenton band and also worked with Benny Carter, Les Brown, Woody Herman, and Tommy Dorsey. Recorded two albums as a leader. –DS

○ **Quartet / LIBERTY** 1956
A swinging, driving session by this former Stan Kenton trumpeter. –DS

BILLY CHILDS

Post-bop, neo bop, M-base. Pianist. Capable player and composer, one of the rare mainstream/hard-bop types who've recorded for Windham Hill. –RW

○ **Take for Example This.... / WINDHAM HILL** 1988
Brilliant debut album with exceptional playing and compositions. –PK

Twilight Is upon Us / WINDHAM HILL 1989
Followup album w/ Bob Sheppard and Jimmy Johnson (d). –PK

His April Touch / WINDHAM HILL   1991
There is intriguing playing and strong melodic songwriting on this, his third solo album. A modern jazz style with great production. –PK

LEONID CHIZHIK   b1947

Post-bop, cool. Russian jazz musician recently featured on the Mobile Fidelity reissue of a 1988 date in Chicago. –RW

○ **In Concert (Piano) / MOBILE FIDELITY-BBC/CAFE**

CHARLIE CHRISTIAN   1916-1942

Swing, bop. He made his first records in the fall of 1939 and was hospitalized for TB in the summer of 1941; though he didn't live to see another spring, the music he had recorded — live and in the studio — immortalized Charlie Christian and influenced everyone who picked up a guitar in his wake. The Texas-born genius was a pioneer of amplified guitar and set the style for playing jazz on what was, in effect, a new instrument. A master of the blues and of sophisticated harmonic "changes," he was a tireless and creative improviser who loved to play in jam sessions. Recommended to John Hammond by Mary Lou Williams, he was brought to Benny Goodman's attention by Hammond, hired after a single hearing, and featured in a new Goodman Sextet. His solos were of necessity short on the 78 discs of the day. Fortunately, he was also captured jamming in Harlem (at Minton's and Monroe's), so we can hear him "stretching out." Every note he left us is a gem. –DM

○ **Genius of the Electric Guitar / COLUMBIA**   1939
The great Benny Goodman Sextet sides. Fifty years have passed, but no one has swung harder. –RL

JODIE CHRISTIAN   b1932

Post-bop, neo bop, modern creative. This Chicago pianist can play blues, swing, bop, or ballads, and is particularly potent as a creative improviser. One of the better of the "hometown" pianists who choose to stay put instead of going to New York City. –MGN

○ **Experience / DELMARK**   ca. 1992
Brilliant progressive and traditional Chicago pianist finally records with trio. Four of ten tracks written by Christian. Good bassist in Larry Gray. –MGN

PETE CHRISTLIEB   b1945

Bop, hard-bop, post-bop. A West Coast tenor saxophonist and "Tonight Show" veteran, Christlieb is a former Top Fuel Dragster driver. –MGN

○ **Apogee / WARNER / DB 5**   1978
Pete Christlieb and Warne Marsh. Tenors, a pair, produced by Steely Dan. A must-buy. –MGN

● **Mosaic / CAPRI**   1990
Recorded at Portland Inn. Christlieb and Bob Cooper swing dual tenors. –MGN

CIRCLE

Early free. One of the great free bands of the 70s. This unit had Anthony Braxton on reeds, Chick Corea on keyboards, Dave Holland on bass, and Barry Altschul on drums. It was an explosive, fiery, and experimental group, far ahead of its time, and totally unmarketable for the labels they were on (ECM and Blue Note). –RW

○ **Paris Concert / POLYGRAM**   1971
Chick Corea (the pure improviser) with Dave Holland (b), Anthony Braxton (sax), and Barry Altschul (d). Definitive improvisational music. For special tastes only. –MGN

SONNY CLARK   1931-1963

Post-bop, soul jazz. Pianist. A wonderful accompanist and gifted writer, Clark was admired especially for his amazing right-hand lines and incredible rhythmic drive. He started recording in 1953 with Wardell Gray, then replaced Kenny Drew in Buddy DeFranco's band. He moved to New York in 1957 and became a familiar name on Blue Note dates. Note: *See* Grant Green. –RW

Sonny Clark Trio / BLUE NOTE   1957
Uptempo. Straightahead mainstream jazz. The CD has three alternate takes. –JME

○ **Sonny's Crib / BLUE NOTE**   1957
Striking sextet performances. Memorable efforts from John Coltrane (ts), Curtis Fuller (tb), and Donald Byrd (tpt). 1987 CD reissue has three fine bonus cuts. –RW

Trio / BLUE NOTE   1957
Captivating trio date. W/ Paul Chambers (b) and Philly Joe Jones (d). Three bonus cuts on CD. –RW

Cool Struttin' / BLUE NOTE   1958
Vols. I & II provide an excellent forum for Clark's brilliant composing and bandleading talents. –MGN

● **Leapin' and Lopin' / BLUE NOTE**   1961
Mainstream, mostly uptempo jazz with a slight taste of funk. One of Clark's best albums as a leader. The CD has two extra tracks. –JME

Voodoo / BLACK SAINT   1985
Voodoo: Sonny Clark Memorial Quartet. This is not an album by Sonny Clark, but a tribute to him by John Zorn. Essential Clark repertoire played by progressivists, with John Zorn on alto sax and Wayne Horvits on piano. –MGN

KENNY CLARKE   1914-1985

Bop, hard-bop, post-bop, progressive big band. Drummer. A good argument can be made over whether Kenny Clarke or Max Roach should be deemed the founder of bop playing. Clarke was surely among the instituters of the style, with his steady work on the snare and bass, plus his unflappable beats and pulse. He was also among the few equally capable of spearheading a large group or a small combo. He got his national start with Roy Eldridge in 1935, and later joined the Edgar Hayes group in 1937. He cut some records as leader, then worked with Claude Hopkins and Teddy Hill in the early 40s.

As part of the Minton's house band, Clarke was among the experimenters whose jam sessions and woodshedding culminated in the modern jazz revolution of the mid and late 40s. Clarke worked with the Gillespie big band in 1946 and 1948, going with them to Europe in 1948. He stayed in Paris a few months, then joined Tadd Dameron in 1948, going with him to Paris in 1949. Working with Billy Eckstine and Milt Jackson in 1951, Clarke was also featured that year backing Charlie Parker and in a trio with pianist John Lewis. He was an original member of the Modern Jazz Quartet before he left in 1955. Clarke settled in France in 1956 and was a busy studio and session musician there for the remainder of his life. –RW

Kenny Clarke All-Stars / SAVOY   1954
An explosive debut as a leader by one of the originators of bebop. With Frank Morgan (sax) and Milt Jackson (vib). –DS

Bohemia after Dark / SAVOY   1955
All-star bop with Nat (cnt) and Cannonball Adderley (as) and Horace Silver (p). –DS

○ **Klook's Clique / SAVOY**   1956
An indispensable session by the bop pioneer, with John LaPorta (sax) and Donald Byrd (tpt). –DS

● **Kenny Clarke Meets the Detroit Jazzmen / SAVOY**   1956
Plays Andre Hodeir / EPIC   1957
The best example of this drummer's work in France, featuring Martial Solal (p). –DS

○ **Pieces of Time / SOUL NOTE**   1983
Standout session late in his career, with fellow drummers Andrew Cyrille, Milford Graves, and Don Moye. –RW

Live at Ronnie Scott's / MPS
Representative live date. Crisp percussion and drumming by Clarke. –RW

STANLEY CLARKE   b 1951

Jazz-rock, contemporary funk. Many of the now-established techniques of contemporary bassists were pioneered by Stanley Clarke in the 70s. A one-time violinist and cellist from Philadelphia, Clarke approached bass like a guitar, with dazzling, rapid patterns his specialty. Clarke's rock background and amazing skill made him a favorite on both acoustic and electric bass. He was initially a prolific contributor in hard-bop circles, then a pivotal member of Return to Forever (in each phase) with Chick Corea. He finally hit the R&B bigtime with the George Duke Project and reaped rock dividends with Jeff Beck and the New Barbarians. One of the greats of his generation. –RW

Children of Forever / POLYDOR   1973
○ **Stanley Clarke / CBS / DB 5**   1974
Definitive early-period funk/fusion. Clarke's finger-pop bass is up front. –MGN

School Days / CBS / BB 34   1976
Crossover appeal. –RW

The Clarke-Duke Project / CBS   1983
A big hit among the fusion/Quiet Storm crowd. –RW

If This Bass Could Only Talk / CBS   1988
One of a few of his contemporary releases with some good music and an indication of his prodigious talent. –RW

CLASSIC JAZZ ENSEMBLE

Trad, Dixieland. Armen Vou Der Heydt's traditional jazz revival group. They have played a lot in Chicago clubs, but scarcely recorded. A good-time, sweet-swinging group. –MGN
○ **Twice in a While / DELMARK**   1991
Top-drawer traditional/early period jazz from Chicago. –MGN

THOMAS CLAUSEN   b 1949

Neo bop. Scandinavian pianist (sideman on occasion) leads jazz trio in contemporary format reminiscent of Keith Jarrett. Introspective. –MGN
○ **She Touched Me / MAMOU**   1988
European pianist's most available domestic release. Very good jazz trio. Search for imports of this. –MGN

JAMES CLAY   b 1935

Bop, hard-bop, post-bop, cool, soul jazz. James Clay is an underrated tenor saxophonist suddenly enjoying a publicity burst in the 90s. He played honking sax and blues in the Southwest during the 50s and was an early partner of Ornette Coleman. During the 60s Clay was a featured member of the Ray Charles Orchestra and cut a superb album with Fathead Newman before dropping out of sight. He resurfacing on Antilles and Caravan of Dreams recordings. –RW

Tenorman / JAZZ WEST   i 1956
W/ drummer Lawrence Marable as a co-leader. Five standards, three by Sonny Clark. Also includes some sessions with Bobby Timmons. –MGN
● **Sound of the Wide Open Spaces / OJC**   1960
Dueling Texas tenors on an album recorded by Cannonball Adderley. Definitive music. –MGN

A Double Dose of Soul / OJC   1961
Bluesy, hypnotic, and essential. W/ Nat Adderley (cnt), Victor Feldman (vib), and the Gene Harris Trio. –RW
○ **I Let a Song Go Out of My Heart / POLYGRAM**   1989
His first album in years. Excellent collection of standards, most in ballad mode. W/ Cedar Walton Trio. –MGN

Cookin' at the Continental / ANTILLES   1991
W/ Fathead Newman (sax), Roy Hargrove (tpt). Three old standards, six more from Horace Silver, Bobby Timmons, Charlie Parker, and Babs Gonzalez. An up mode. –MGN

CLAYTON BROTHERS

Post-bop, cool. Bassist John and saxophonist Jeff play mainstream jazz. Classically trained John is a virtuoso; Jeff, who also doubles on oboe, is reminiscent of Lester Young on tenor. –MGN
○ **It's All in the Family / CONCORD**   1980
Jeff and John Clayton. Guitarist Emily Remler provides extra punch. –RW

BUCK CLAYTON   1911-1991

Swing, big band. Clayton was an emphatic swing-era trumpeter who began heading a band in the 30s. He enjoyed seven stellar years with Count Basie in the 30s and 40s and was a keen arranger for Basie, Goodman, Harry James, and others in swing's peak period. He then led small combos throughout the 50s until his death in 1991. He was a striking trumpeter — a truly great muted player — and was thoroughly versed in vintage Kansas City stomping jam-mode. –RW

Classic Swing of Buck Clayton / OJC   1946
A swing-era mainstay performs vintage Kansas City early jazz material with a wonderful roster. Tiny Grimes (g), Trummy Young (tb), and a host of others make it a worthy romp. Authoritative 1990 reissue of important 1946 date. –RW

Big Band at the Savoy Ballroom / RCA   1957
Elegant and lusty, Clayton wrote and played up a storm. –RW

Goin' to Kansas City / OJC   1960
○ **Olympia Concert 22 April 61 / VOGUE**   1961
A splendid set with vintage sensibility and a jam session atmosphere. Buddy Tate (ts) and Sir Charles Thompson (p) are on the money. –RW

Jam Sessions from the Vault / COLUMBIA   196?
Limited edition. Hot set with guests ranging from the familiar (Dicky Wells) to the eyebrow-raising (Tommy Newsom). –RW

Jam Session / CHI-SOUND   1975
Good dates for Chiaroscuro. –RW

Kansas City Night / PRESTIGE   r 1975
A Swingin' Dream / STASH   ca. 1988
Clayton is nearing end of the line, but still playing with exquisite taste and good arrangements. Mel Lewis drives the date on drums. –RW

Buck Meets Ruby / VANGUARD   198?
W/ Ruby Braff (cnt). A pair of spry, individualistic trumpet masters meet to a good end. –RW

Heart & Soul / CAPITOL
Nice repertory/big band date. Orchestra contains both spotlight soloists and tremendous session players. –RW

JAY CLAYTON

Ballads, modern creative. A wordless and lyric vocalist in the progresssive vein, Clayton shapes sounds in innovative ways. –MGN
○ **All Out / ANIMA**   1980
This is a studio date for a most creative female improviser. Highly recommended. With soprano saxophonist Jane Ira Bloom. –MGN

CLAYTON/HAMILTON ORCHESTRA

Swing, big band, bop. A big band vehicle for West Coast session men and their friends. Features John Clayton (b) and Jeff Hamilton (d). This is a good modern-day equivalent to the Thad Jones/Mel Lewis or the early Quincy Jones orchestras. –MGN
○ **Heart & Soul / CAPRI**   ca. 1991
Nineteen-piece big band plays five standards, four compositions by bassist John Clayton. Great solos from younger and older musicians. Jeff Hamilton (co-leader), Ricky Woodward (ts), Shooley Young, Oscar Brashear, George Bohannon on brass, and Bill Cunliffe (p). –MGN

ARNETT COBB   ♭1918

Swing, big band, bop, hard-bop, post-bop, blues-jazz, soul jazz, progressive . One of the original "honking" tenor saxophonists, Cobb was a contemporary of Illinois Jacquet, and assumed the star tenor's chair when Jacquet left Lionel Hampton's band in 1942. These reedsmen had many interesting parallels — both spent early years in Houston, played in trumpeter Milton Larkins's "territory bands" in the 30s, and went on to form their own orchestras in the late 40s. In the heady post-war period, tenor "battles" and extroverted showmanship were all the rage, ushering in the uninhibited music (and uncontrollable capacity crowds) of the R&B/ rock & roll era. These were Cobb's best years, before health problems knocked him from the top of the heap. Sporadic but generally top-notch recordings of his straight-ahead jazz blowing have been made and sporadically reissued since the 50s (mostly for Prestige/ OJC). Cobb's contributions to the superb *Atlantic Honkers* compilation (Atlantic) reveal his truly great stature, as do the albums listed here. –MB

The Complete Apollo Sessions / JAZZ LEGACY   1947
The fiery tenor leading his own small swing band. –MB

● **Smooth Sailing / OJC / DB 5**   1959
Noteworthy appearance from undervalued Buster Cooper (tb). Textbook soul power; exemplary sax technique from Cobb. –RW

Very Saxy / PRESTIGE   1959
Some early prototype Cobb material. –RW

Party Time / OJC   1959
A straight jazz date with pianist Ray Bryant, includes the classic "Flying Home." –MB

Wild Man from Texas / CLASSIC JAZZ   1971
Not all that wild, actually, but wonderful nonetheless! –RW

Again with Milt Buckner / BLACK & BLUE   1973
Import. A tough, bluesy session with organist Milt Buckner.–MB

Jazz at Town Hall / CLASSIC JAZZ   1973
This is a sensational pairing with fellow tenor player Illinois Jacquet. –RW

○ **Arnett Cobb Is Back / PROGRESSIVE**   1978
Faulty distribution kept this solid release from getting its due in the jazz community. –RW

Live at Sandy's! - Vols. 1 & 2 / MUSE   1978
'A stalwart night of ripping tenor exchanges with Cobb, Eddie "Cleanhead" Vinson, and Buddy Tate. –RW

○ **Go Power! / PRESTIGE**   198?
Madcap exchanges with Eddie "Lockjaw" Davis (ts). If you find it, savor the purchase. –RW

Funky Butt / PROGRESSIVE   1980
Real funky jazz; not instrumental pop fodder. –RW

Keep On Pushin' / BEEHIVE   1984
Overlooked soul-jazz, blues, and bop date with sparkling piano by Junior Mance and fine drumming from Panama Francis. –RW

Showtime / FANTASY   1987
W/ Dizzy Gillespie & Jewel Brown. Singer Brown isn't everyone's cup of tea. Cobb & Dizzy (tpt) are just what you'd expect. –RW

BILLY COBHAM   ♭1946

Latin, jazz-rock, contemporary funk. From the age of eight, when he sat in with his pianist father, Billy Cobham has been a prime drummer. He spent time in the army during the 60s, where he met Billy Taylor. He made a shift from a standard timekeeper in a hard-bop context to a dashing, flamboyant anchor with Miles Davis, Dreams, and the Mahavishnu Orchestra, where he became a rock idol. At one time his combination of bombastic power and rhythmic clarity made him THE drummer, and his barrages accented John McLaughlin's equally brilliant guitar on the 70s jazz-rock

scene. His 1976 group Spectrum had George Duke and John Scofield. Cobham became an active educator in the late 70s and 80s, doing clinics and living in Switzerland. –RW

○ **Spectrum / ATLANTIC / BB 26**   1973
Early period Cobham is the best. –MGN

Crosswinds / ATLANTIC / BB 23   1974
Last of the orchestral Cobham. –MGN

CODONA

Early free, world fusion. Name derived from the letters of the name of *Co*llin Walcott (tabla, sitar), *Do*n Cherry (tpt, p, hunter's guitar), and *Na*na Vasconcelos (per). Multi-ethnic improvisational music, mostly stemming from Walcott's interest in Eastern Indian rhythms and Vasconcelos's Brazilian heritage. Cherry's experience with folk music of Scandinavia, Morocco, and Africa makes for a unique, major-league fusion. –MGN

Codona 2 / POLYGRAM   1980
Walcott adds tympani, cherry melodica, Nana talking-drum. More Ornette and Walcott compositions, a traditional African piece "Godumaduma," and Cherry's vital "Malinye." Absolutely uplifting. –MGN

○ **Codona / POLYGRAM**   1980
Their definitive debut. Walcot adds dulcimer and sanza, Nana Berimbau and cuica, Cherry on ethnic flutes. Side 2 is solid with Walcott's chant-like "Mumakata " and "New Light." Side 1 has an Ornette Coleman/Stevie Wonder medley. These three communicate! –MGN

Codona 3 / POLYGRAM   1982
Walcott's final recording before passing away in an automobile accident in Germany. –MGN

JIMMY COE   ♭1921

Swing, bop. Alto sax, tenor sax, clarinet. From Indianapolis, Coe plays swing and big band to bop. He's an underground icon. –MGN

○ **After Hours Joint / DELMARK**   1953
Stirring jazz and blues. –MGN

BASIL COETZEE

Post-bop, neo bop, modern creative. South African modern-to-creative saxophonist who has worked frequently as a sideman for Abdullah Ibrahim. Powerful soloist. –MGN

○ **Sabenza / PRO ARTE-PRO JAZZ**   i 1987
A pop/jazz outing with a township flavor from this South African saxophonist. –MB

AL COHN   1925-1988

Swing, big band, bop, hard-bop, post-bop, cool, progressive big band. A veteran tenor saxophonist and member of Woody Herman's bands in the 40s. Teamed with fellow tenor Zoot Sims to form a most formidable tandem. Solidly rooted in the swing to bop tradition.–MGN

○ **Natural Rhythm / RCA**   1955
Wonderful mid-50s date with Freddie Green (g) stepping outside Basie's orchestra; Joe Newman accenting things on trumpet. –RW

From A to Z / RCA   1956
Sterling Cohn with Zoot Sims (ts) pairing. Nice reissue. –RW

Be Loose / BIOGRAPH   1956
Unusual lineup. Milt Jackson (vib) out of his MJQ arena. –RW

○ **Al & Zoot / MCA**   1957
All Cohn/ Zoot Sims (ts) dates here are memorable, though you can't say the same thing for MCA's mixes and remastering. –RW

The Progressive Al Cohn / SAVOY   195?
Worthy reissue of some crackling 50s sessions. Horace Silver (p) spurs and spars with Cohn. –RW

● **Body & Soul / MUSE / DB 5**   1973

Immortal tenor pair with Jaki Byard (p), plus George Duvivier (b) and Mel Lewis (d). Can't miss. –MGN

Play It Now / XANADU 1975
Again the Cohn/ Barry Harris (p) team clicks. –RW

○ **True Blue / EPM** 1976
Excellent reissue of mid-70s duo, quintet, and septet sessions. High-quality pairing of Cohn with Dexter Gordon (ts). –RW

America / XANADU / DB 5 1976
Steady tenor, nice piano from Barry Harris. –RW

Heavy Love / XANADU 1977
Exquisite duets with pianist Jimmy Rowles. –RW

Nonpareil / CONCORD 1981
Stately, pleasant, and occasionally arresting, though Cohn has been in better combos. –RW

Tour de Force / CONCORD 1981
W/ Buddy Tate (ts), Scott Hamilton (ts). A wonderful meeting between Hamilton, Buddy Tate, and Al Cohn. –RW

Overtones / CONCORD 1982
Tasty Cohn solos with precise, dignified support from Hank Jones (p) and George Duvivier (b). –RW

○ **Standards of Excellence / CONCORD** 1983
Accurate title. Confident veterans going through their paces with a minimum of flash and a maximum of talent. Herb Ellis (g) shines. –RW

East-Coast West-Coast Scene / FRESH SOUNDS ca. 198?
Fruitful meeting of Cohn and Shorty Rogers (tpt). Only available currently on high-priced import. –RW

EDDIE COLE

Swing, blues-jazz. A vocalist whose style blends elements of jazz, R&B, and blues. He's best known for his sessions with the Three Peppers. –RW

○ **That's Right / CBS**
Nice jive, jazzy vocal, and traditional cuts — typical budget-collectibles sound fashion. –RW

RICHIE COLE   *b* 1948

Bop, hard-bop. Alto, tenor, and baritone sax. Cole's studies as a teen with Phil Woods have never been forgotten. He is as much under his influence as some have accused Woods of being under Charlie Parker's. At times, Cole's phrasing and tone are identical to Woods's, though he has labored to create his own sound. His playing never lacks passion or energy. His releases are seldom poor, but have yet to get beyond the (admittedly highly virtuosic) norm of the Parker-Woods influence. –RW

Battle of Saxes - Vol. 1 / MUSE 1976
Entertaining, stimulating match of alto sax styles of Cole and Eric Kloss. –RW

○ **New York Afternoon-Alto Madnes / MUSE** 1976
Perhaps Cole's and vocal master Eddie Jefferson's best work together. Very worthwhile. –MGN

Pure Imagination / CONCORD 1986
Fine standards, uptempo cuts. –RW

Bossa International / MILESTONE 1987
Cole and Hank Crawford (sax) make an effective team. –RW

Signature / MILESTONE 1988
One of his stronger, more emphatic sessions. –RW

EARL COLEMAN   *b* 1925

Swing, big band, ballads. A vocalist originally from Port Huron, Michigan. A most effective ballad and blues singer. Out of the crooning tradition. Favorably compared to Al Hibbler and Billy Eckstine.–MGN

○ **Earl Coleman Returns / PRESTIGE** 1956
Great jazz singer. Sympathetic setting from the late 50s. –MGN

GEORGE COLEMAN   *b* 1935

Hard-bop, post-bop. Coleman is one of the premier tenor

saxophonists of all time and one of many originally from Memphis. –MGN

○ **Amsterdam after Dark / TIMELESS** 1978
Legendary tenor saxophonist blows up a storm with the Hilton Ruiz Trio. This has been reissued on CD. Best cut is "New Arrival." –MGN

ORNETTE COLEMAN   *b* 1930

Post-bop, early free, progressive big band, jazz-rock, neo bop, modern creative. Alto saxophonist Ornette Coleman is a soft-spoken, unassuming man whose music reflects playful, almost child-like simplicity and fascination with melody. Contrary to his sweet nature, Coleman has provoked more critical schizophrenia and outright hatred than almost any other jazz figure. Anecdotes about his formative years are the stuff of tragicomic legend — getting physical threats on the bandstand, having his horn confiscated and destroyed by an angry mob, or being left behind in Los Angeles after an ill-fated tour out West with bluesman Pee Wee Crayton. Legends aside, it is true that a progressive underground existed in Los Angeles when Ornette arrived, and in 1958 he made his first record there for Contemporary. This was the beginning of the free-jazz movement, and immediately the critics were split into two warring camps. Some proclaimed him to be the most important stylist since Charlie Parker, to whom he was indebted stylistically (and perhaps also for his use of a plastic alto); others found his music unlistenable, boring, or dismissed it as a novelty. With the help of admirer John Lewis of the Modern Jazz Quartet, Coleman soon found himself recording for Atlantic Records and playing an extended engagement at the prestigious Five Spot in New York.

Ornette's most sympathetic bandmates during these years were also his students back in Los Angeles, where he first devised his revolutionary concept of melodic and harmonic improvisation without the use of prearranged chord changes. Trumpeter Don Cherry, bassist Charlie Haden, drummer Billy Higgins, and (later) bassist Scott La Faro and drummer Ed Blackwell have contributed to many of his best performances over the past three decades. All of the aforementioned, plus multi-reedist Eric Dolphy and trumpeter Freddie Hubbard, recorded the landmark *Free Jazz* album in December 1960; this album-length piece documented the "Double Quartet" improvising collectively in the studio without written music. Many forward-thinking musicians seized on the free-jazz concept, and this influential work sounds tame today when compared to the many varieties and extremes of freedom it propagated. But after *Free Jazz* and a handful of other records on Atlantic, Ornette's career faltered, and his output of the next few years was inconsistent.

There were more advances and outrages in the mid 60s — new ensembles, pieces for classical chamber groups, challenging film soundtracks, recordings with his preteen son Denardo, and unschooled solos on trumpet and violin. Ornette seemed to pick up steam again in the late 60s, reuniting with his former bandmates and discovering a sympathetic new voice in tenorist Dewey Redman, who joined him on two Blue Note sessions with Coltrane alumni Elvin Jones and Jimmy Garrison. His classical ensemble writing continued to thrive into the 70s — his orchestral masterpiece *Skies of America* was premiered at the Newport Jazz Festival on the 4th of July, 1972. This triumph was followed by more years of relative inactivity and the emergence of Coleman's theories of harmonic, melodic, and rhythmic improvisation, called "harmolodics." The exact meaning of harmolodics varies from one interpreter to the next, but this approach to pan-tonal collective improvisation has been a major feature of Ornette's music since the mid 70s. Various incarnations of the Prime Time band, typically an electric rock sextet of drums/bass/guitar pairings, ply their high-density harmolodics on hip young audiences, further polarizing both fans and critics. But despite the endless debate, or because of it, his music lives on — in his own occasional projects, in the acoustic jazz homages of Old and New Dreams, through younger sidemen like Ronald Shannon Jackson, Jamaaladeen Tacuma, and James Blood Ulmer, and in the efforts of Coleman converts like Pat Metheny. –MB

Music of Ornette Coleman: Something Else!!! / OJC 1958
Coleman's first studio recording was just what the title promised, and the only one with a pianist (Walter Norris). In attendance were long-time bandmates Don Cherry (tpt) and Billy Higgins (d), playing relatively tame straight jazz and Latin numbers. Originally issued on Contemporary. –MB

● **Tomorrow Is the Question / OJC** 1959
More early explorations of his second Contemporary label date. The affinity between Coleman and Don Cherry (tpt) is more obvious here, but the music is still hampered by a less-than-ideal rhythm section. –MB

○ **Shape of Jazz to Come / ATLANTIC** 1959
Another phrophetic title, and Coleman's first recording with his own band, including Charlie Haden (b). This New York session marks the beginning of his most innovative period, and contains the jarring "Congeniality." –MB

Twins / ATLANTIC 1959
Later release of early Coleman. Features the first take of his classic "Free Jazz." –JME

○ **Change of the Century / ATLANTIC** 1959
Coleman's roots in New Orleans jazz ("Ramblin'") and Charlie Parker ("Bird Food") are still audible here, with the title cut indicating the way of the future. Drummer Ed Blackwell enlives the whole affair. –MB

● **Art of the Improvisers / ATLANTIC / DB 5** 1959
1959-1961. From six early Atlantic sessions. Close-to-definitive group interplay. Extraordinary musicianship. –MGN

This Is Our Music / ATLANTIC 1960
The classic quartet, poised at the edge of total freedom. –MB

☆ **Free Jazz (a Collective Improvisation) / ATLANTIC** 1960
An across-the-board definitive album. Must-buy. Only for open ears. –MGN

○ **Ornette on Tenor / ATLANTIC** 1961
Coltrane bassist Jimmy Garrision joins Ed Blackwell (d), Don Cherry (tpt) and Coleman. A fascinating date, and his only one on the tenor sax — "Cross Breeding" is an 11-minute tour de force. –MB

Town Hall Concert / ESP-DIS 1962
More new ideas were brewing, as Coleman combined his latest trio (David Izenzon and Charles Moffet) with a string quartet, signaling from the start an ongoing flirtation with classical music forms. –MB

○ **At the "Golden Circle" / BLUE NOTE / DB 5** 1965
Vol. 1 & 2. At Stockholm. More trio recordings (without the string quartet) — very edgy and uncompromising, with energy to spare. Ornette's violin and trumpet make fine appearances here. –MB

Forms & Sounds / RCA 1967
Some of it works, some of it doesn't, but all of it demands your attention. –RW

New York Is Now / BLUE NOTE / DB 5 1968
Another excellent representation of Coleman's creative brilliance. With Dewey Redman (ts), Jimmy Garrison (b), and Elvin Jones (d). –MGN

Dancing in Your Head / A & M / DB 5 1973
○ **In All Languages / CARAVAN OF DREAMS** 1987
Album features Ornette's late-50s and early-60s quartet with Charlie Haden (b), Don Cherry (tpt), and Billy Higgins (d). Their work is still vital. This recording also features Coleman's electric Prime Time Double Trio. The utterly no-nonsense approach and high intensity make this a recording challenged music listeners must have. –MGN

Ornette! / ATLANTIC r 1987
The followup to *Free Jazz* enlists Scott LaFaro on bass, and is the rarest of the Atlantic releases. –MB

Virgin Beauty / CBS / DB 5 r 1988

STEVE COLEMAN

M-base. Saxophone, composer. Coleman is a Brooklyn-based theorist whose ideas about merging jazz, funk, reggae, and R&B into a seamless mix lead some to sing his praises and others to proclaim him a charlatan. Coleman has talked for years about a multiple musical approach (M-Base), and his Five Elements work includes many top players from the current generation. His own playing, while rooted in funk and blues, is also solidly in the hard-bop tradition, something that shows up more when he makes guest appearances. –RW

Motherland Pulse / POLYGRAM 1985
This shows the jazz side of Coleman. W/ Geri Allen (p), Lonnie Plaxico (b), Graham Haynes (tpt). –JME

○ **World Expansion / POLYGRAM** 1986
W/ Geri Allen (k), Robin Eubanks (tb). Not his jazziest release, but a lot of good clean funk. –JME

Black Science / NOVUS 1990
Rhythm People / NOVUS r 1990
Rhythm People (the Resurrection of Creative Black Civilization. Funky, creative improvisations along the lines of Ornette Coleman's harmedelic music. W/ Dave Holland (b), Robin Eubanks (tbn). –JME

On the Edge of Tomorrow / POLYGRAM
Modern soul music. This is real contemporary funk, most of it danceable. W/ Geri Allen (synth) and Cassandra Wilson (v). –JME

JOHNNY COLES   b 1926

Bop, hard-bop, post-bop, cool, progressive big band. Trumpet, flugelhorn. A mostly self-taught, sparing stylist who's always eschewed high-note antics or bending, twisting maneuvers. His forte is squeezing the most into a few notes, reminiscent of Miles Davis. He has worked with Philly Joe Jones, James Moody, Gil Evans, George Coleman, Herbie Hancock, Ray Charles, Charles Mingus, and Duke Ellington. –RW

○ **Little Johnny / BLUE NOTE** 1962
The best of this hard-bop trumpeter, w/ Leo Wright (as) and Joe Henderson (sax). –DS

New Morning / CRISS CROSS 1982
Excellent recent work by infrequently recorded trumpeter. –DS

BUDDY COLLETTE   b 1921

Bop, cool. Saxophone, clarinet, flute, composer. Veteran West Coast bop and big-band saxophonist. Taught Eric Dolphy and James Newton. Unsung hero! –MGN

○ **Man of Many Parts / OJC** 1956
Compiled from three recording sessions. –JME

Jazz Loves Paris / SPECIALTY 1958

AL JAZZBEAU COLLINS

Bop, post-bop, ballads. This ex-DJ recites entertaining prose and has recorded humor and jazz albums with Slim Gaillard and Steve Allen. –MGN

○ **Steve Allen's Hip Fables / DR. JAZZ** 1983
This is an album by Al "Jazzbeau" Collins and Slim Gaillard could be the funniest jazz of all time. A must-buy. Includes "3 Little Pigs," "Little Red Riding Hood," and "Jack & the Beanstalk." –MGN

CAL COLLINS   b 1953

Swing, bop, cool. Guitarist from Cincinnati plays softly hued chords and lines. In the tradition of Herb Ellis, Barney Kessel, Tal Farlow; he follows their cues. –MGN

○ **Crack'd Rib / MO PRO** 1984
Finest hour for unsung guitarist with Steve Schmidt Trio. Thoroughly swinging date. –MGN

ALICE COLTRANE   b 1937

Early free, progressive big band, modern creative. Piano, vibes, harp. Jazz had its own Yoko Ono/John Lennon controversy in the 60s, when some blamed the former Alice McLeod with breaking up (or influencing her husband to break up) the famed John Coltrane Quartet. They married in 1966. Her background was as a member of the Terry Gibbs Quartet, plus backing vibist Terry Pollard. She and drummer Rashied Ali changed the sound and scope of Coltrane's band, shifting the focus totally onto Coltrane and Pharoah Sanders's energized dialogs. After Coltrane's death, Alice led bands in the late 60s and the 70s. Her ethereal harp playing was the most striking part of her repertoire. –RW

○ **Ptah the El Daoud / IMPULSE**   1970
With Joe Henderson (sax) and Pharoah Sanders (sax). A great one to savor. –MGN

Journey in Satchidananda / MCA   1970
Harp and strings with jazz and Indian influences. Extraordinarily beautiful. –MGN

JOHN COLTRANE   1926-1967

Bop, hard-bop, post-bop, cool, early free, progressive big band.
Few musicians of the post-bebop era have enjoyed such fame and endured such controversy as John William Coltrane, the major saxophone stylist of an age when the saxophone reigned supreme. During the late 40s and early 50s he developed his urgent tenor style with the rhythm & blues bands of Eddie "Cleanhead" Vinson and Earl Bostic, as well as jazz heavyweights Dizzy Gillespie (where he had his recording debut, on alto) and Johnny Hodges. Like all young players of his generation, Coltrane profited from the advances of Charlie Parker, but showed little direct influence of Bird in his mature style — this is an important difference between his playing and that of his major contemporary (and friendly rival) Sonny Rollins. It was in the acclaimed Miles Davis Quintet of 1955 that "Trane" really came into his own as a pure-toned sideman and independent, often brash soloist. Soon afterward he became a sought-after session participant and, inevitably, a leader in his own right, featured on dozens of recordings for the leading jazz labels Prestige and Blue Note during the last half of the 50s. He worked off and on with Davis up through 1960, perfecting his cascading "sheets of sound" technique and exploring the modal structures of pieces like Miles's classic "So What" as a foundation for future innovations. During this period he also honed his chops with three of the most challenging and idiosyncratic pianists of the day, Thelonious Monk, Mal Waldron, and Cecil Taylor, and threw down the gauntlet in good-natured "cutting contests" with saxophone stars Johnny Griffin, Hank Mobley, Sonny Rollins, and others.
Besides being a top-notch technician and superb at ballads, John was always seeking new levels of expression, practicing obsessively and listening attentively to the insurgent efforts of the new jazzmen. Around 1960 he was associating with Los Angeles renegades Ornette Coleman, Don Cherry, and Eric Dolphy, and his final recordings with Miles demonstrate, in lengthy volcanic phrases, that Coltrane had moved beyond the hard-bop conventions he had helped to establish a few short years before. At the beginning of the most turbulent decade in jazz, Coltrane was winning *DOWN BEAT* polls and alienating conservative critics at the same time; he had also begun assembling the quartet that accompanied him throughout the first half of the 60s — pianist McCoy Tyner, bassist Jimmy Garrison, and drummer Elvin Jones.
On the Atlantic and Impulse labels, the classic Coltrane quartet ushered in a new era of musical freedom, typically along modal lines (although not as controlled and austere as Miles Davis) with dense, interwoven harmonic and rhythmic webs underpinning lengthy solo statements. These were the years of albums with side-long compositions, exotic Afro-centric themes, the introspective spirituality of *A Love Supreme*, the resurrection of the soprano sax as a lead instrument, and what many regard as the greatest performances of his productive and multi-faceted career. Never content to rest on his laurels, Coltrane kept pushing on, recording with the newest of the New York revolutionaries and

bringing some of them into his band, prompting the eventual departure of Tyner and Jones. Jimmy Garrison stayed with Coltrane as he pursued the emotive and often frenzied extremes of his final free-jazz phase, spurred on by saxophonist Pharoah Sanders, pianist Alice Coltrane (his second wife), and drummer Rashied Ali. The Coltrane-Ali duo album *Interstellar Space* indicated yet another new direction in Coltrane's unceasing development, but liver cancer overtook him soon afterward, and he died in July 1967. Ornette Coleman and Albert Ayler played at his funeral, and since that day, musicians of all persuasions have paid tribute to the diverse and significant achievements John Coltrane brought to the most volatile epoch of jazz. –MB

Wheelin' / PRESTIGE   1957
Dakar / OJC   1957
With baritone saxophonists Pepper Adams and Cecil Payne. Lowdown and sultry jazz. Great collection. –MGN
Cattin' with Coltrane & Quinichette / OJC   1957
○ **Lush Life / OJC / DB 5**   1957
★ **Blue Train / BLUE NOTE**   1957
A landmark album — stunning. This is Coltrane's only Blue Note recording as a leader. W/ Curtis Fuller on Trombone. –JME
○ **Soultrane / OJC / DB 5**   1958
● **Black Pearls / OJC**   1958
W/ Donald Byrd (tpt), Red Garland (p), Paul Chambers (b), and Art Taylor (d). –JME
Dial Africa / SAVOY   1958
Stardust / PRESTIGE   1958
W/ Wilbur Hardin (tpt), Red Garland (p), Art Taylor (d).
Coltrane Time / BLUE NOTE   1958
W/ Cecil Taylor (p).
Bahia / OJC   1958
☆ **Bags & Trane / ATLANTIC**   1959
W/ Milt Jackson (vib), Hank Jones (p), Paul Chambers (b), and Connie Kay (d). A classic collaboration between two giants. –MGN
☆ **Giant Steps / ATLANTIC**   1959
With his best-known tunes and musicians. A must-buy. –MGN
○ **Avant-Garde / ATLANTIC**   1960
W/ Don Cherry (tpt). This meeting of the titans doesn't sound so "out" nowadays. Influenced by Ornette Coleman. –MGN
★ **My Favorite Things / ATLANTIC / DB 5**   1960
Classic early Coltrane. The title cut is most beautiful, and contains unforgettable piano by McCoy Tyner. –JME
Coltrane Plays the Blues / ATLANTIC   1960
Single session. Great tunes like "Mr. Day" and "Mr. Knight." A much neglected, but important Coltrane album. –MGN
○ **Live at the Village Vanguard / MCA**   1961
Ballads / MCA   1961
A very sweet album, but never syrupy. –MGN
● **Africa/Brass - Vols. 1 & 2 / MCA**   1961
This two-volume recording features the orchestral Coltrane. Important recordings, available on one CD. –MGN
○ **Olé Coltrane / ATLANTIC**   1961
Great Trane/ Eric Dolphy (sax) combo, with extended compositions. –MGN
Live at Birdland / MCA   1962
From air-checks on two different sessions. –JME
○ **Impressions / MCA / DB 5**   1962
Lively and upbeat. –MGN
○ **John Coltrane & Johnny Hartman / MCA**   1963
Definitive vocals: Hartman w/ sensitive accompaniment. –MGN
Crescent / MCA   1964
First recording of "Wise One." –MGN
★ **A Love Supreme / MCA / DB 5**   1964
A most powerful statement. His most acclaimed and definitive recording. –MGN
Coltrane's Sound / ATLANTIC   r 1964

Ascension / IMPULSE / DB 5 1965
Coltrane's first album considered tonally "Free." –JME

New Thing at Newport / GRP r 1965
One of the earliest examples of Coltrane moving in a newer, freer direction. Archie Shepp (sax) made an immediate impression. –MGN

Live in Seattle / IMPULSE 1965
A two-record live set that should be approached only by the truly converted, and absorbed in spurts. –MGN

Om / MCA 1965
Perhaps Coltrane's only major release of questionable quality, this was reportedly recorded on his first (and only) LSD trip. Featuring screechy playing and moaning vocals, this is for true believers and historical interest only. –DNM

Meditations / MCA 1965
A perfect companion to *A Love Supreme*. As powerful and pure in spiritual content and intent. Long, extended, embellished passages in hymn-like prayer session. W/ Pharoah Sanders (ts), Elvin Jones (d), Rashied Ali (d), McCoy Tyner (p), Jimmy Garrison (b). –MGN

Sun Ship / IMPULSE 1965
Wonderful, compelling quartet sessions that languished for years in the ABC vaults. –MGN

Transition / IMPULSE 1965
On this album, Coltrane switches musical gears to amazing effect. –MGN

At the Village Vanguard Again / IMPULSE / DB 5 1966
Live. Shattering, piercing, and unforgettable. Coltrane and Sanders (ts) blast off to places unforeseen. –MGN

Cosmic Music / IMPULSE 1966
Emphatic, surging, and sometimes unfathomable late-period Coltrane. –MGN

Expression / IMPULSE / DB 5 1967
His final recording session. Features more flute than any other of his recordings. –MGN

Interstellar Space / GRP / DB 5 1967
First Meditations / IMPLULSE i 1970
Recorded before *Meditations*, but released in 1970, reissued in 1978 and 1992. CD version has original version of "Joy." "Compassion" is a standout Coltrane anthem. –MGN

○ **Gentle Side of John Coltrane / GRP**
Excellent 2-fer that was recently reissued on CD. –MGN

Live in Japan / GRP

Best of John Coltrane - Vol. 2 / MCA COMP
Good to go. –MGN

His Greatest Years - Vol. 1 / MCA COMP
A good record to have. –MGN

● **The Prestige Recordings / PRESTIGE** COMP
Coltrane was THE major sax stylist in a decade when the tenor saxophone reigned supreme, and his 1955-1958 recordings for Prestige live on as marvels of jazz invention .... The complete set of 31 albums he made as leader and sideman — that's 125 slices of jazz genius on 16 CDs. The Rudy Van Gelder studio recordings are warm and clear, simply state of the art. –MB, ROOTS & RHYTHM

CONCORD ALL STARS

Swing, bop. All-stars from the Concord jazz label record at Concord Jazz Festival, includes tenor saxophonist Scott Hamilton and cornetist Warren Vache. –MGN

○ **Ow! / CONCORD** 1987
Jam session date with standout playing by Red Holloway (sax) and Scott Hamilton (ts). CD issue has a bonus cut. –MGN

Take 8 / CONCORD 1988
The eighth in the line of all-star dates. –MGN

CONCORD SUPER BAND

Swing, bop, progressive big band. More all-stars, like guitarist

Cal Collins, pianist Dave McKenna, bassist Phil Flanagan, drummer Jake Hanna. –MGN

In Tokyo / CONCORD 1978
Good mainstream outing. –MGN

○ **Concord Super Band 2 / CONCORD** 1979
A top lineup of youthful and veteran swing/mainstream types doing a conservative recording of jazz standards. –MGN

EDDIE CONDON   1905-1973

Swing, big band. Banjo, guitar. Eddie Condon was a self-taught musician, first on ukelele, then on banjo and guitar, and helped define what is often referred to as "classic Chicago style" jazz in the McKenzie-Condon Chicagoans, a recording group cofounded with Red McKenzie in 1927. Moving to New York in 1929, he fell in with several musicians with whom he maintained long associations, including Max Kaminsky, Jack Teagarden, Sid Catlett, Pee Wee Russell, and Bud Freeman. In 1938 he helped to launch Milt Gabler's Commodore label with a series of small-band recordings. He worked during the 40s with such players as George Wettling, Billy Butterfield, and Bobby Hackett, using them at various gigs around New York City and on the famous Town Hall concerts which were broadcast to servicemen in World War II. Condon also started his own nightclub in the Village in 1945, where he continued to promote integration of the bandstand — an idea to which he was fully committed. He continued to perform, albeit infrequently, at Condon's in the 50s and also made tours to Europe and the Orient, 1957-1964.

As a promoter and entrepreneur of small-band jazz, he effectively used his music and his wit to expand appreciation of the music that he loved. In addition to the groups which he led, Condon performed as a sideman with a wide array of jazz talents, including Fats Waller, Artie Shaw, Red Nichols, Miff Mole, and Wild Bill Davison. –RR

Jammin at Commodore / COMMODORE 1938
1938-1944. The Windy City Seven date that launched the Commodore label, plus a Bud Freeman-led combo. Musicians include Pee Wee Russell, Bobby Hackett, George Brunies, Dave Tough, Jess Stacy, and others. –BR

And His Jazz Concert / STASH 1944
A who's who of the Condon clique, including Bobby Hackett (cnt), Pee Wee Russell (cl), Ernie Caceres, Billy Butterfield, as well as Edmond Hall. Tunes include "Ballin' the Jack," "Ja-Da," "That's A Plenty," "Royal Garden Blues," and "Muskrat Ramble," among others. –BR

Definitive - Vol. 1 / STASH 194?
Prime Condon on this 40s reissue with Pee Wee Russell (cl), Hot Lips Page (tpt), and Bobby Hackett (cnt). –RW

○ **In Japan / CHI-SOUND** 1964
Relaxed and often brilliant soloing from Condonites Buck Clayton, Vic Dickenson, and Pee Wee Russell, with three vocals by Jimmy Rushing. "Stompin' At the Savoy," "Three Little Words," "Rose Room," and more. –BR

Live at the New School / CHI-SOUND 1972
Excellent 1989 reissue of a brilliant swing-tinged concert. –MGN

★ **Ballin' the Jack / COMMODORE**
Dixieland Jam / CBS
If you like traditional jazz, you'll love any and all Eddie Condon. –RW

CHRIS CONNOR   b 1927

Swing, big band, cool, ballads. The prime "torch" singer of the 50s. Connor first studied clarinet, but began singing at the University of Missouri with a band led by Bob Brookmeyer. She was a member of Claude Thornhill's vocal quintet The Snowflakes before going solo. Later she was in the Kenton big band, where she became known for a cool, tantalizing style that had its romantic and alluring side but was far from bawdy or bluesy. She was a star in the 50s and 60s, then made a comeback in the late 70s and stayed active through the 80s. –RW

Lullabies for Lovers / BETHLEHEM		1954
Chris / BETHLEHEM		1956
Chris Connor / ATLANTIC		1956

First date for Atlantic upon leaving Bethlehem in a huff. Nice arrangements; Zoot Sims (ts) has good solos. –RW

Lullabies at Birdland / BETHLEHEM 1956
By turns soft, silky, and sultry. –RW

● **Sings Gershwin / ATLANTIC** ca. 1957
First-rate two-record set, one of her best. –RW

☆ **Chris Craft / ATLANTIC** 1958
More upbeat, daring. –RW

Ballads of the Sad Cafe / ATLANTIC 1959
Poor concept, fine vocals. –RW

Chris in Person / ATLANTIC 1959
Chris Connor with Helen Forrest / STASH 195?
A pair of prime "torch" stylists from the 50s. One classic album from each. –RW

○ **Cocktails and Dusk / BETHLEHEM** 195?
Fine album. Unsung vocalist of the 50s. Lots of Cole Porter, with J.J. & Kai (tb), Ralph Sharon (p), Matt Hiaton (b). –MGN

Double Exposure (Jazzlore #21) / ATLANTIC 1960
With Maynard Ferguson (tpt) and an early-60s big band. Very good. –MGN

○ **A Portrait of Chris / ATLANTIC** i 1960
Free Spirits / ATLANTIC 1962
Looser, more feeling. –RW

Chris Connor at the Village Gate / FM 1963
Sings Gentle Bossa Nova / ABC-PARAMOUNT 1965
Her turn at the bossa-nova craze. –RW

Sweet & Swinging / PROGRESSIVE 1978
One of her 70s comeback recordings. –RW

Classic / CONTEMPORARY 1986
Good though mannered set from longtime "torch" favorite. Fine lineup, including Paquito D'Rivera (as). –RW

New Again / CONTEMPORARY 1987
A very proficient 1987 date. –RW

BILL CONNORS ♭1949

Early free, jazz-rock. This is the guitarist who replaced Al Di Meola in Return to Forever. He was able to demonstrate rock influences (flashy licks, sustained tones, feedback, and the wah-wah pedal) yet reveal his jazz ties as well. –RW

● **Theme to the Guardian / POLYGRAM** 1975
An album of terrific solo acoustic guitar from a former member of Return to Forever. –PK

Of Mist and Melting / ECM 1978
An atmospheric jazz album with Jack DeJohnette (d), Gary Peacock (b), and Jan Garbarek (ts). –PK

○ **Swimming with a Hole in My Body / ECM** 1980
Brilliant solo acoustic guitar with some overdubs. Required listening. –PK

○ **Step It! / PATHFINDER** 1984
Superb instrumental fusion album with Connors on electric guitar. Strong compositions. A must! –PK

Double-Up / PATHFINDER 1986
Electric trio album, with K. Plainfield replacing Dave Weckl on drums. –PK

Assembler / PATHFINDER 1987
His third electric release, in an Alan Holdsworth style. All his electric albums are highly recommended. –PK

JUNIOR COOK ♭1934

Bop, hard-bop, post-bop, soul jazz. Cook is a very good, steady tenor saxophonist who's often been overlooked because he wasn't a groundbreaking soloist or top composer. He spent ten years with two groups, the Horace Silver and Blue Mitchell

quintets, which intermingled several members. Later he co-led two fine 70s groups with Louis Hayes and Bill Hardman. Cook is the kind of forthright jazz musician who has never yet become a hero, yet is invaluable. –RW

Junior's Cookin' / JAZZLAND 1961
A hard-driving first session as a leader. –DS

Good Cookin' / MUSE 1979
All-star hard-bop cast, including Bill Hardman (tpt) and Slide Hampton (tb). –DS

○ **Something's Cookin' / MUSE** 1981
Excellent playing by this neglected hard bopper. –DS

BOB COOPER ♭1925

Big band, bop, hard-bop, progressive big band. Veteran West Coast tenor saxophonist. Member of Lighthouse All Stars. Outstanding soloist/arranger/composer. More cool than Trane-like. –MGN

Shifting Winds / CAPITOL-AFFINITY 1955
Worthy reissue of an intriguing session with Cooper on unusual instruments (oboe and English horn), plus tenor. –RW

● **Coop! The Music of Bob Cooper / OJC** 1958
Excellent aggregation with delightful work from Cooper and friends. –RW

Tenor Sax Jazz Impressions / TREND-DISCOVERY 1979
Well-done material from late 70s. –RW

Bob Cooper Plays Michel Legrand / DISCOVERY 1980
Cooper extends and expands music of Legrand. –RW

○ **In a Mellotone / CONTEMPORARY**
Enchanting mid-80s collaboration. Snooky Young (tpt) sounds energized. –RW

JEROME COOPER ♭1946

Early free, modern creative. A progressive percussionist and former Revolutionary Ensemble member, Cooper is a tour de force solo performer. –MGN

○ **Unpredictability of Predictability / ABOUT TIME** 1979
Progressive percussion solos. Potent and extended. –MGN

JIM COOPER

Post-bop, neo bop. The Chicago vibraphonist plays post-bop. Not a truly distinctive sound, but a very good player of standards and originals. Deserving wider recognition. –MGN

○ **Tough Town / DELMARK**
Chicago vibist with Ira Sullivan. Very good throughout. –MGN

CHICK COREA ♭1941

Post-bop, early free, progressive big band, Latin, jazz-rock, neo bop. An electric and acoustic pianist, composer, and bandleader, Corea played free-jazz and Latin-jazz early in his career. He carved his identity as a premier fusion innovator with the group Return to Forever. He plays lovely acoustic piano when the mood strikes. A melodic genius. Some later fusion is not as potent. His work is, in general, of good quality. A true heir of improvised-based music. A good starting point for the novice. –MGN

● **Tones for Joan's Bones / VORTEX** 1966
Youthful Corea makes quick splash. This is an extremely rare album. –RW

○ **Now He Sings, Now He Sobs / CAPITOL** 1968
Solid trio from early period. The CD has extra tracks. Highly recommended. –MGN

Song of Singing / BLUE NOTE 1970
Corea in avant-garde free/experimental mode, cutting loose with Dave Holland (b) and Barry Altschul (d). This 1989 reissue contains three bonus cuts. –RW

Circling In / BLUE NOTE 1970
This is one of many great trio sessions. Corea would later reunite with rhythm mates Miroslav Vitous (b) and Roy Haynes (d). –RW

○ **Paris Concert / ECM**   1971
The forward-looking Circle trio, plus the striking Anthony Braxton (sax). –RW

Piano Improvisations - Vol. 1 & 2 / ECM / DB 5   1971
Here is good, infrequently compelling solo piano. This is beautifully recorded, played with a high degree of technical proficiency. –RW

★ **Return to Forever / POLYGRAM**   1972
The first and by far the best and most appealing edition. Flara Purim sings wistfully; Stanley Clark dominates on bass; Corea is a sharp, creative pianist. –RW

○ **Light As A Feather / POLYGRAM**   1972
W/ Flora Purim on vocals and Airto (per). –MGN

☆ **Crystal Silence / POLYGRAM**   1972
W/ Gary Burton on vibes; a wonderful collaboration between two superb musicians. –RW

Hymn of 7th Galaxy / POLYGRAM   1973
Return to Forever's best electric set as a whole package. –RW

Where Have I Known You Before / POLYGRAM   1974
Crackling electric Return to Forever. Includes one killer composition, but arks the beginning of the end if you are looking for a jazz influence.. –RW

My Spanish Heart / POLYGRAM / BB 55   1976
Two-record set that rambles and flounders but also has some impressive segments. –RW

○ **Romantic Warrior / COLUMBIA**   1977
W/ Return to Forever.

Evening With / POLYGRAM   1978
W/ Herbie Hancock. Overall fine pairing; as good as duo piano ever gets. –RW

Friends / POLYGRAM / BB 86   1978
This quartet date features good contributions from Joe Farrell (ts). –RW

Trio Music / POLYGRAM / DB 5   1981
Great live dates. –MGN

Children's Songs / POLYGRAM   1983
Fine solo piano. –KW

● **Trio Music Live in Europe / POLYGRAM / DB 5**   1984
An expert trio date that includes impeccable ensemble interaction and solos from Corea, Miroslav Vitous (b), and Roy Haynes (d). –RW

Akoustic Band / GRP   r 1989

○ **Inner Space / ATLANTIC**   COMP
Formative dates from late 60s reissued as a comprehensive CD anthology. Hubert Laws (fl) at his most ambitious. Woody Shaw (tpt), Joe Farrell (ts), and Ron Carter (b) also are on hand. –RW

JAYNE CORTEZ

Early free, modern creative, ballads, spoken word. A visionary and socially conscious poetess with feminist leanings, Cortez is as wise a person as is out there. She was married to Ornette Coleman. –MGN

○ **Celebrations & Solitudes / STRAT EAST**   1974
Fiery poetry with bassist Richard Davis. Strong stuff. –MGN

Unsubmissive Blues / BOLA PRESS   1979
With larger band and electric guitarist Bern Nix; includes "You Know." –MGN

Maintain Control / BOLA PRESS   1986
Quite topical. Includes "Deadly Radiation Blues" and "Chocolate." –MGN

● **Everywhere Drums / BOLA PRESS**   1990
"Firespitters" and "Make Ifa" show the power. "What's Happening" and "Nelson Mandela Is Coming" make the statements the government and apathetic public do not want to hear. Truth rings out in 11 tracks with avant-funk backdrop. Excellent recent album for Cortez. –MGN

LARRY CORYELL   ♭1943

Early free, jazz-rock, neo bop. Guitar. A former journalism student at the University of Washington, Coryell has a long background in rock and jazz. He was on the ground floor of the jazz-rock tradition with the Gary Burton Quartet and band Free Spirits, and his solos with Chico Hamilton in 1965 suggested the coming of a new era. Later groups Foreplay and Eleventh House squeezed all the creative juice out of that form. Coryell is superb on both acoustic and electric guitar and has made striking acoustic and classical statements. At his best, he's unforgettable. –RW

Spaces / VANGUARD   1970
His best early album. –MGN

○ **Barefoot Boy / FLYING DUTCHMAN**   1971
Tremendous interaction between Steve Marcus (ts, sop sax) and Coryell. Roy Haynes stars on drums. –RW

Eleventh House / VANGUARD   1972

○ **Just Like Being Born / FLYING FISH**   1984
W/ Brian Keane (g). Soothing acoustic guitar duets by two excellent players. –PK

Comin' Home / MUSE   1985
Fine mid-80s set that signaled a change in direction back toward conventional jazz. –RW

Dragon Gate / SHANACHIE   1990
Nice set with impressionistic, soaring solos by Coryell. –RW

Twelve Frets to One Octave / SHANACHIE   199?

● **Essential Larry Coryell / VANGUARD**   COMP
His best work of the 60s and early 70s. –MGN

EDDIE COSTA   1930-1962

Swing, bop. Vibes, piano. Costa was among the first to pursue an aggressively percussive piano style. He was known for using the lower half of the keyboard for his rippling lines, and you can hear some Cecil Taylor antecedents. After playing with Joe Venuti in 1949, he came to fame through dates with Kai Winding and finally Tal Farlow and Woody Herman in the 50s, before forming his own trio. –RW

Trio / JUBILEE   1956
A solid session with Vinnie Burke (b). –DS

☆ **Quintet / MODE**   1957
A classic bop session with Art Farmer (tpt) and Phil Woods (as). –DS

House of Blue Lights / DOT   1959
Adventurous date which borders on the avant-garde. With Paul Motian (d). –DS

CURTIS COUNCE   1926-1963

Bop, hard-bop, post-bop, cool. A first-rate accompanist and great proponent of the "walking" bass style — a floating, yet propulsive way of articulating and phrasing notes to create the effect of the bassline walking along underneath the soloist and the other players. Counce worked with many of the best West Coast players of the 50s, among them Wardell Gray and Shorty Rogers, and also did a lot of film work and private teaching. He led some fine groups as well. –RW

○ **Landslide / OJC**   1956
This is the same lineup as *Sonority*, and the music swings just as hard. –RW

● **Sonority / CONTEMPORARY**   1956
A relaxed, yet vibrant date, with Harold Land (ts) and Carl Perkins (p) as standouts. –RW

You Get More Bounce with Curtis Counce / OJC   1956
Excellent bassist from the West Coast. Slightly naughty artwork. Worth looking for. –MGN

○ **Carl's Blues / OJC**   1957
Top-rate West Coast jazz, with pianist Carl Perkins. –MGN

STANLEY COWELL   ♭1941

Post-bop, early free, jazz-rock, neo bop, modern creative.

Originally from Toledo, Ohio, he was classically trained in piano at the University of Michigan, becoming a leader in jazz and creative improvised music. An outstanding composer and arranger, he also worked with the Heath Brothers. Cowell sometimes leads piano/choir ensembles, but mostly plays in a trio or solo format. He his noted for pretty and probing melodies. One of the best. –MGN

● **Blues for the Viet Cong / ARISTA-FREEDOM**   1969
Trio. Attractive originals. –MGN

Illusion Suite / ECM   1972
Trio w/ Stanley Clarke (b). More of Cowell's original repertoire. Prime. –MGN

Regeneration / STRATA EAST   1975
Larger ensemble. Afro-American stance. Excellent. –MGN

○ **Back to the Beautiful / CONCORD**   1989
A good session, with Steve Coleman (reeds) in an unusual mainstream role. –RW

Live at Maybeck Recital Hall - Vol.5 / CONCORD   1990
This is part of an outstanding solo piano series. Cowell displays impressive technique and holds his own in the solo setting. –RW

IDA COX   1896-1967

Swing, ballads, blues-jazz. Blues and jazz vocalist. A stalwart performer whose career began in minstrel shows, Ida Cox was a bawdy, free-wheeling performer with a love for "blue" jokes and double-entendre vocals. During the 20s she made memorable cuts with first-rate jazz musicians and was a tent-show star in the 30s. She was one of the earliest, biggest stars on the Black circuit. She made a final triumphant recording for Riverside, backed by the Coleman Hawkins group in 1961. –RW

○ **Blues for Rampart Street / OJC**   1961
This is latter-period Cox, w/ jazz all-stars. Some of her best tunes. –MGN

HANK CRAWFORD   b 1934

Hard-bop, blues-jazz, soul jazz. Alto sax, baritone sax, piano, composer. This Memphis-born musician's initial fame came as a member of the Ray Charles groups of the late 50s. He ascended through the ranks to musical director before leaving in 1963. Blues-drenched, soulful jazz has been Crawford's specialty ever since. His Atlantic albums were generally great, his CTI 70s sessions were commercial fusion. He made a good comeback in the late 70s, 80s, and 90s on Milestone. –RW

Soul of the Ballad / ATLANTIC   r 1963
Lots of blues, mellow numbers, and funky cuts. –RW

True Blue / ATLANTIC   1964
First album to establish his reputation as a leader outside the Ray Charles orchestra. –RW

○ **After Hours / ATLANTIC**   r 1966
Soul-jazz and blues with ensembles of varying size from trio up to octet. Detroiters Ali Jackson and Wendell Harrison appear, as well as stalwarts Howard Johnson, Wilbert Hogan, and Joe Dukes (drums), and John Hunt and Fielder Floyd (trumpet). Four standards including the title track. Originals by Bennie Golson, Ben Tucker, Stanley Turrentine, and the leader. –MGN

Midnight Ramble / MILESTONE   1981
Fine blues, bop, and ballads menu. –RW

Night Beat / MILESTONE   1983

Roadhouse Symphony / MILESTONE   1985
An earthy date. –RW

Soul Survivors / MILESTONE   1986
W/ Jimmy McGriff (organ), George Benson (g), Mel Lewis (d).

Mr. Chips / MILESTONE   1986
The funk is more notable on this 1986 set. –RW

Steppin' Up / MILESTONE   1987
W/ Jimmy McGriff (organ), Jimmy Ponder (g). Solid, exuberant soul-jazz. CD version has a bonus cut. –RW

Indigo Blue / FANTASY   198?
W/ Dr. John (p, organ), David "Fathead" Newman (ts). Good session with soul-jazz leanings. –RW

On the Blue Side / MILESTONE   r 1990
Funky, mellow, and gritty. –RW

Portrait / MILESTONE   ca. 199?
Here is Crawford's latest collection of funky cuts and mellow ballads. –RW

SONNY CRISS   1927-1977

Bop, hard-bop, post-bop, soul jazz. Although alto saxophonist Sonny Criss was a devoted Charlie Parker disciple, he also found a way to vary and ultimately overcome Parker's influence and build his own vibrant, intense style. He moved from Memphis to the West Coast in the 40s and was a key figure in the California Black jazz scene of the 50s. He had a three-year gig with Buddy Rich in the 60s and spent time in Europe. During the 70s, Criss toured Europe again. –RW

California Bopping / FRESH SOUND   1947
A session done early in Criss's career that shows formative style and moving solos. –RW

Intermission Riff / PABLO   1951
A fine session reissued on Pablo in 1988. –RW

This Is Criss! / OJC   1966
Early-period recording from this unsung hero. Highly recommended. –MGN

Portrait of Sonny Criss / OJC   1967
Valuable reissue of a stalwart date. Criss is in piercing form; high-caliber rhythm section work. –RW

Sonny's Dream / PRESTIGE   1968

Crisscraft / MUSE / DB 5   1975
Highly recommended, without reservation. –MGN

Out of Nowhere / MUSE   1975
Tremendous date that reactivated the memory of Criss among longtime jazz fans who had overlooked him. –RW

Memorial Album / XANADU   COMP
Good teamup with Hampton Hawes (p). Includes cuts done from 1947-1965. –RW

Sonny Criss 1949-1957 / FRESH SOUNDS   COMP
There is some duplication with Xanadu label; better sound quality. –RW

BOB CROSBY   b 1913

Swing, big band. Vocals, bandleader. An arch-conservative Dixieland stylist, Bob Crosby's roots as a singer date back to the 30s. He went from his role as frontman for a group led by Gil Rodin to heading a group known as Bob Crosby's Band Plus the Bobcats. Crosby got on-the-job training for a seven-year period, and became a confident presenter and serviceable vocalist, though far from being in his brother Bing's class. After 1942, Bob went solo and later became a radio and TV star. –RW

Bob Crosby & Orchestra & Bob Cats / EPM   193?
New reissue of prototype late 30s recordings. –RW

○ **Plays 22 Original Big Band Records / HINDSIGHT** 195?
Recent 1988 reissue of early-50s cuts. –RW

CRUSADERS

Soul jazz, contemporary funk. A once proud soul-jazz combo, the former Jazz Crusaders of the 60s and 70s are commercial fusion session players today. Wilton Felder, Wayne Henderson, Joe Sample, and Stix Hooper were longtime friends and musical associates who forged a group sound out of the blues, soul, and small-combo jazz they loved. Their Gulf Coast Sound has a funk foundation and jazzy melodic fervor. –RW

○ **Southern Comfort / MCA / BB 31**
This has good jam-session touches. Gold album. –RW

Scratch / MCA / BB 73   1975
One of their best. This is a prime example of the Crusaders doing the soul-jazz they invented and perfected. –RW

Street Life / MCA / BB 18   1979
This album contains their single biggest hit with the title cut. Gold album. –RW

☆ **Second Crusade / CHISA**
Another fine two-record set. Prototype of their "Gulf Coast" sound. –RW

RONNIE CUBER   b 1941

Bop, hard-bop, post-bop, progressive big band. Baritone saxophone. One of New York's busiest baritone session players in the 70s and 80s, Cuber was equally versed in Latin-jazz and mainstream. Thick, booming sound and a knowledge of salsa and Latin styles made him a perennial favorite of Latin-jazz bandleaders. When not in the Latin groove, he'd cut nice hard-bop and mainstream sessions. –RW

○ **Cuber Libre / XANADU**   1976
Explosive baritone from Cuber. Steady Barry Harris keeps grooves in place on the piano. –RW

Eleventh Day of Aquarius / XANADU   1978
A quintet with Tom Harrell (tpt) and the Mickey Tucker Trio playing Latin and jazz. –MGN

Passion Fruit / PRO ARTE-PRO JAZZ   1985
George Benson (g) makes a guest appearance on this well-engineered recording. –RW

Two Brothers / PRO ARTE-PRO JAZZ   1985
Live at the Blue Note / PRO-ARTE   1986
Best of Ronnie Cuber / PRO ARTE-PRO JAZZ   COMP

XAVIER CUGAT   b 1900

Big band, Latin, instr-pop. Best known for being a popularizer of the Afro-Latin sound, and also for being married to Abbe Lane and scoring a hit with the original version of "Babalu" in 1944, Xavier Cugat's musical importance often gets obscured. He was a prime mover in bringing Latin rhythms and beats to the attention of mass audiences, and while his groups had plenty of show biz antics, they were often excellent musicians. Cugat moved to Cuba as a child, studied violin, and played in the Havana opera company. He later studied in Berlin and worked with the Berlin Orchestra before coming to America. He organized his first Latin dance band in the late 20s, then became a film star in the 30s, appearing in the movie *Gay Madrid* — the first of many to which he made a noteworthy contribution. Cugat was particularly prominent during the 40s and was featured in many MGM musicals. He had many hits in the 30s and 40s and made appearances with Bing Crosby and Desi Arnaz. He officially retired in 1970, turning his band over to Tito Puente. Cugat returned to Spain in 1980. –RW

1933-1940 / SUNBEAM   1933
Some seminal early numbers. Extremely hard to find. –RW

1944-1945 / CIRCLE   1944
More great early material. –RW

○ **Best of / MCA**   COMP
Recent domestic reissue of his prime material. –RW

CURRENT EVENTS

Contemporary funk, M-base. Keyboardist Darrell Grant's fusion band. Dedicated to a world with no limits. –MGN

○ **Current Events / POLYGRAM**
One of the more intriguing later-period contemporary fusion bands. –MGN

TED CURSON   b 1935

Post-bop, early free. Trumpet, piccolo trumpet, flugelhorn. After attending Granoff Music Conservatory and taking private lessons with Jimmy Heath, Ted Curson moved from Philadelphia to New York, where he worked with Mal Waldron, Red Garland, Philly Joe Jones, and Cecil Taylor, then Charles Mingus with Eric Dolphy. His first recordings came with Mingus; then he co-led a band with Bill Barron, played with

Max Roach, and led his own groups. He spent the late 60s and 70s in Europe much of the time. Curson is an ambitious, always combative and challenging player whose recordings never have broken him out to a general audience. –RW

Plays Fire Down Below / OJC   1962
Good 1990 reissue by Prestige of a dashing session. –RW

Flip Top / ARISTA-FREEDOM   1964
This is a Paris date from one of the music's best trumpeters, with tenor saxophonist Bill Barron. Some of his better originals. –MGN

○ **Tears for Dolphy / ARISTA / DB 5**   1964
A poignant, biting tribute to a fallen comrade. –RW

○ **The New Thing, the Blue Thing / ATLANTIC**   1965
Incendiary, rollicking hard bop. –RW

Ode to Booker Ervin / EMI   1970
Curson's eulogy for Ervin. –RW

Ted Curson & Co. / INDIA NAVIGATION   1976
Sharp, stark quartet date. –RW

★ **Jubilant Power / INNER CITY**   1976
Slashing, dynamite exchanges, and an intense approach make this the Curson to grab. –RW

KING CURTIS   1934-1971

Post-bop, blues-jazz, ballads, soul jazz. King Curtis was the last of the great R&B tenor sax giants. He came to prominence in the mid 50s as a session musician in New York, recording, at one time or another, for most East Coast R&B labels. A long association with Atlantic/Atco began in 1958, especially on lockrecordings by The Coasters. He recorded singles for many small labels in the 50s — his own Atco sessions (1958-1959), then Prestige/New Jazz and Prestige/TruSound for jazz and R&B albums (1960-1961). Curtis also had a #1 R&B single with "Soul Twist" on Enjoy Records (1962). He was signed by Capitol (1963-1964), where he cut mostly singles, including "Soul Serenade." Returning to Atlantic in 1965, he remained there for the rest of his life. He had solid R&B single success with "Memphis Soul Stew" and "Ode to Billie Joe" (1967). Beginning in 1967, Curtis started to take a more active studio role at Atlantic — leading and contracting sessions for other artists, producing with Jerry Wexler and later on his own. He also became the leader of Aretha Franklin's backing unit, The Kingpins. He compiled several albums of singles during this period. All aspects of his career were in full swing at the time he was murdered in 1971. –BP

Trouble in Mind / ORIGINAL BLUES   r 1961
The King sings, a lot. Very good. –MGN

○ **Soul Meeting / PRESTIGE**   r 1962
W/ Nat Adderley (tpt). Sparkling soul-jazz with hot solos. –RW

Soul Twist / COLLECTIBLES   196?
1960-1964 hits. The title cut was a 1962 smash, and this album is worthwhile for that alone. –RW

Blues at Montreux / ATLANTIC / DB 5   r 1973
Quintessential King Curtis sax and Jack Dupree piano. –MGN

Jazz Groove / PRESTIGE   r 1974
Best of King Curtis / PRESTIGE
Authoritative soul-jazz date. –RW

King Soul / PRESTIGE
A fine pairing with Nat Adderley (cnt). –RW

Enjoy the Best of King Curtis / COLLECTABLES   COMP
That's Alright / RED LIGHTNIN   COMP
Collects mostly vocal cuts from various albums. Some duplication with Prestige albums. –RW

MEREDITH D'AMBROSIO   b 1941

Cool, ballads. A soft, dusky-toned vocalist who specializes in ballads. –MGN

South to a Warmer Place / SUNNYSIDE   ca. 1989
Eddie Higgins Trio joined by trumpeter Lou Columbo. Two lyrics by singer. Sweetness and light. –MGN

○ **Love Is Not a Game / SUNNYSIDE**   ca. 1990
With husband Eddie Higgins Trio. Dreamy, soft-voiced
D'Ambrosio makes a definitive emotional statement. Fifteen
tracks, nine standards (three adapted or modified by
D'Ambrosio). Five written by her. Nice twisting on "I Love
You/You I Love," "Oh, Look At Me Now/But Now Look At Me,"
and "Lament/This Lament." –MGN

PAQUITO D'RIVERA   b 1948

Post-bop, Latin, jazz-rock, contemporary funk. Flamboyant alto
saxophonist who gained his initial fame as a member of the
Cuban band Irakere. He departed Cuba in the 80s while on
tour, leaving his family behind. D'Rivera's rubbery, frenetic
alto solos are the high point of his albums. –RW

● **Blowin' / CBS**   ca. 1981
Alto saxophonist at his zenith. "Chucho" is Paquito at his
best. –MGN

○ **Mariel / CBS**   ca. 1983
With pianists Hilton Ruiz and Jorge Dalto. Becoming more
funky. Also includes "Moment's Notice." –MGN

Manhattan Burn / CBS   1986
1987 release, some torrid solos. –RW

Celebration / CBS   1987
1988 release, some high-flying moments. Claudio Roditi (tpt)
is great. –RW

Tico! Tico! / CHESKY   1989
Nice date, good Latin grooves. Excellent solos all around. –RW

Reunion / MESSAGE   r 1991
Excellent session done for German label, distributed
domestically by Rounder. D'Rivera at top of his game. –RW

Mariel / CBS
Funk and jazz from Cuban fire-spitter. –MGN

TONY DAGRADI   b 1953

World fusion, neo bop. A strong contemporary New Orleans
saxophonist who hasn't left for NYC and become a champion
of hard-bop or turned to fusion. Instead he has stayed in
Crescent City and worked with both New Orleans regulars and
touring pros. –RW

○ **Oasis / GRAMAVISION**   1980
An all-original, creative jazz program with Kenny Werner (p)
and Gary Valente (tb); this was a hard-blowing date. A nice
cross-section between improvisational and ethnic ideals. –MGN

Dreams of Love / ROUNDER   1987
Beautiful statement from New Orleans saxophonist. Multicultural influences. –MGN

ALBERT DAILEY   b 1938

Post-bop. Dailey was a pianist, and an outstanding
contributor to several 70s jazz-combos and also released a
couple of fine albums as a leader. He never attained
widespread attention, but was a favorite accompanist and
session man for many musicians, including Stan Getz. Dailey
died in the late 70s. –RW

○ **Textures / MUSE**   1981

JORGE DALTO

Latin, jazz-rock, instr-pop. Light pop, fusion, and Afro-Latin
keyboardist best known for his contributions to some of
George Benson's biggest hit releases. He also did some
recording as leader, notably working with a group called the
Interamerican Band. –RW

○ **Urban Oasis / CONCORD**   1985
His finest, most Latin jazz date with Interamerican band. –RW

TADD DAMERON   1917-1965

Post-bop, cool, progressive big band. Pianist and
composer/arranger Dameron was the master melodist of the
bebop era. He was an arranger for many groups but is best
known for his Royal Roost quintet of 1948 which featured Fats

Navarro, Allen Eager, Curly Russell, and Kenny Clarke. Several
recordings by this group have been reissued under Navarro's
name on Blue Note, Savoy, and Riverside/Jazzland while
others for Prestige have been reissued by sidemen such as
Clifford Brown or John Coltrane. His orchestral approach is
best displayed on his Capitol recordings from 1949 and a 1956
Prestige album *Fontainebleau*, although more personnel
would have helped each session. A big band recording for
Riverside in 1962 suffers from a lack of rehearsal time. While
not highly regarded as an instrumentalist, Dameron's
compositions are held in the highest regard by the entire
bebop fraternity. His arrangements for vocalists such as
Carmen McRae (Decca) and Sarah Vaughan (Musicraft) are
models of their kind. –BP

● **Fontainebleau / OJC**   1956
One of his best. Highly recommended. –MGN

○ **Mating Call / OJC**   1956
Super quartet session with John Coltrane (ts). –RW

Magic Touch / RIVERSIDE   1962
Some wonderful arrangements, plus Bill Evans (p). –RW

EDDIE DANIELS   b 1941

Post-bop, neo bop. A technically wondrous contemporary
clarinetist who has emerged as a fusion star, thanks to GRP
recordings. While his solos are faultless and his skills very
evident, Daniels has actually been more impressive in a light-
classical setting than when doing jazz. –RW

○ **To Bird with Love / GRP / DB 5**   r 1987
This clarinetist's best solid and swinging studio date, w/ Fred
Hirsch (p) and Al Foster (d). –MGN

This Is Now / GRP   r 1991

JAMES DAPOGNY   b 1940

Trad, Dixieland, stride, swing, big band. Early period jazz
expert. Historian, author, pianist, educator — Jelly Roll
Morton to Ellingtonia. –MGN

○ **Piano Music of J. R. Morton / SMITHSONIAN**   ca. 1976
Recorded in the actual Library of Congress in Washington,
D.C., this album includes twelve of Jelly Roll Morton's best-
known blues and stomps, played precisely by pianist.
Dapogny wrote a book on Morton, so he should know this
material cold — he does. –MGN

Chicago Jazz Band / JAZZOLOGY   ca. 1982
Recorded in a St. Louis studio with an octet. Nine cuts ranging
from early Dixieland. Dapogny wrote "Dreamer's Blues." The
band plays in an up mode. Paul Klinger (cnt), Peter Ferran,
and Russell Whitman (reeds), Hal Smith (d) stand out. A fine
display of traditional jazz. –MGN

● **How Could We Be Blue? / STOMP OFF**   ca. 1988
Recorded in Ann Arbor, MI. Duets on twin pianos with
Dapogny and Butch Thompson. Great idea to team these two.
12 cuts. "Today's Blues" written by participants. Material by
Morton, Waller, Ellington, Sidney Bechet, and others.
Thompson plays clarinet on two tracks. –MGN

KENNY DAVERN   b 1935

Swing. Soprano saxophonist and clarinetist. Played
extensively with fellow soprano sax/clarinetist Bob Wilber. He
is tried and true to tradition. Davern is a current-day leader
on his instruments and for early period jazz. –MGN

○ **Soprano Summit / CONCORD**   1976
Live at the Concord Festival with Bob Wilber and quintet. Two
Wilber originals, one by guitarist Marty Grosz. A fine
representation of two artists in Dixie-early-swing mode with
blues and a touch of Ellington. –MGN

El Rado Schuffle / KENNETH   1980
A tribute to Jimmy Noone. With Swedish sextet. (Two Noone
tunes, the rest are played nicely.) –MGN

The Very Thought of You / MILTON KEYNES   1984
An award-winning, distinctive session. –RW

Live Hot Jazz / STATIRAS   i 1986
Trio with Dick Wellstood (p), Chuck Riggs (d). Standards played without bass. Davern sticks to clarinet with no clichés. Fine concept and execution. —MGN

I'll See You in My Dreams / MUSICMASTERS   1988
Outstanding, musically conservative date, with fine playing from Davern and Howard Alden (g). —RW

One Hour Tonight / MUSICMASTERS   1988
Quartet with Howard Alden (g). Top flight. All jazz and very well done. One Davern original. —MGN

Stretchin' Out / JAZZOLOGY
A fine swing/traditional date with Dick Wellstood (p) and Chuck Riggs (d). —RW

ANTHONY DAVIS   b 1951

Early free, modern creative. Pianist and composer whose music is as singular as any. Very dense passages, free improvisations, textures are unlike any other. An acquired taste, but one that reaps great rewards. Solo piano recordings and group efforts; also writes for dancers. Dream motifs are a great inspiration. For the intellectual and open-minded. —MGN

Past Lives / RED VPA   1978
Engaging and appealing; it could be his best "jazz" piano playing. —RW

● **Of Blues and Dreams / SACKVILLE**   1978
On the cutting edge of avant-garde. W/ violinist Leroy Jenkins and cellist Abdul Wadud. —MGN

○ **Song for the Old World / INDIA NAVIGATION**   1978
Quartet showcases this brilliant pianist's compositions. —MGN

Hidden Voices / INDIA NAVIGATION   1979
This quintet album has great teamwork w/ George Lewis (tb), James Newton (fl). —MGN

Lady of the Mirrors / INNOVATIVE   1980
New reissue of a stunning late-70s set has one bonus cut. —RW

Episteme / GRAMAVISION / DB 5   . 1981
Masterful compositions and arrangements. —RW

I've Known Rivers / CAPITOL-RHINO   1982
Precious document. Top-notch improvisers team up. Sparks fly! W/ James Newton (fl), Abdul Wadud on cello. —MGN

Hemispheres / RHINO / DB 5   1983
A 1990 reissue of one of Davis's more advanced works. —RW

Middle Passage / GRAMAVISION   1984

Trio / CAPITOL-RHINO   r 1990
Invigorating followup. Has classical as well as improvisational influence and elements. —RW

Ghost Factory / RHINO

EDDIE "LOCKJAW" DAVIS   1922-1986

Big band, bop, blues-jazz, soul jazz, progressive big band. Eddie "Lockjaw" Davis was a popular tenor sax star for his entire professional career. He made his first recordings with Cootie Williams (1944); also played with Andy Kirk, Lucky Millinder, and other big bands. Popular in Harlem, he worked regularly in clubs there throughout the 40s and 50s. Davis recorded for many small labels in the 40s. His 50s recordings for Roost, King, Roulette, and Prestige often included an organist (Bill Doggett, Doc Bagby, or, most frequently, Shirley Scott). The Davis trio with Shirley Scott was the first of many organ/tenor sax combos in the 50s and 60s. He was a unique tenor sax stylist, employing rasps and squeals often associated with R&B players but filtered through his own highly original harmonic conception. In 1952 he joined the Count Basie Orchestra and retained a long relationship with that band, being in and out of it for the next 20 years. His longest unbroken tenure with Basie was from 1966-1973. He also co-led a quintet with saxophonist Johnny Griffin (1960-1962) and actually retired from music for a period in 1963 when he worked as a booking agent. Davis was a prolific recording artist throughout his career and was often present in all-star jam sessions. During the 70s he was often featured in a group

with trumpeter Harry Edison. He also recorded frequently in Europe where he was always popular. Davis's recordings are rarely dull but rarely inspired. His "Cookbook" series for Prestige with Shirley Scott is worthy of note and the best collaboration with Griffin is the live material from Minton's, also on Prestige. —BP

● **The Cookbook - Vols. 1 & 2 / OJC**   1958
A pair of new reissues featuring the late 50s group, with Davis and Shirley Scott (organ) riding herd on the band. —RW

Jaws / OJC   1958
W/ Shirley Scott (organ). This is an excellent reissue of this quartet session. —RW

Griff & Lock / OJC   1958
Here is the hot, combative team of Eddie Davis and Johnny Griffin (ts). —RW

Jaws in Orbit / OJC   1959
Includes Shirley Scott on the Hammond organ. This is early Scott, not yet all that funky. Traditional swinging, uptempo music. —JME

○ **Live at Minton's / PRESTIGE**   1961
This exciting live date with Johnny Griffin (ts) is tough to find. Two discs. —RW

Afro-Jaws / RIVERSIDE   1961
1989 reissue of a wild, dashing date with Clark Terry (tpt) and Ernie Royal (tpt). —RW

Trane Whistle / OJC   r 1962
A reissue of invigorating big-band pieces. —RW

Very Saxy / OJC   1964
Red-hot jam session. Summit meeting of mainstream veterans. —RW

Love Calls / RCA   ca. 196?
Paul Gonsalves (ts) matches fours and spirit with Davis. —RW

● **Tough Tenors / VERVE**   1970
A rugged workout with Johnny Griffin (ts); w/ Francy Boland (p) and Kenny Clarke (d) in the rhythm section. —RW

Tough Tenors Again 'n Again / PA-USA   1970
Includes robust duet/duels with longtime comrade Johnny Griffin (ts). —RW

Sweet & Lovely / CLASSIC JAZZ   1975
A very inviting blues, ballads, and bop date. —RW

Straight Ahead / OJC   1976
This is a new reissue. Tommy Flanagan is incredible on the piano. —RW

Heavy Hitter / MUSE   1979
Emphatic and mellow mainstream session. —RW

Jaw's Blues / CAPITOL-RHINO   1981
Hard-to-find session is now generally available on CD. Horace Parlan makes an all-too-infrequent guest spot as pianist. —RW

Best of Eddie 'Lockjaw' Davis / PA2   COMP
A grab-bag set of Pablo cuts. —RW

WALTER DAVIS JR   1932-1990

Bop, hard-bop, post-bop. Walter Davis Jr was an always-enjoyable pianist whose proficiency was apparent from his early sessions in the 50s and some top trio dates in the 60s. He worked with Max Roach, Sonny Rollins, and Art Blakey frequently. He didn't make many records on American labels and didn't have a wide profile outside the jazz community, but was a particularly invigorating solo pianist. —RW

○ **Davis Cup / BLUE NOTE**   1959
Propulsive hard bop with Donald Byrd (tpt) and Jackie McLean (as). —DS

Blues Walk / RED   1979
A solid effort by this imaginative pianist. —DS

MILES DAVIS   1926-1991

Bop, hard-pop, post-bop, cool, progressive big band, jazz-rock, world fusion,. Trumpeter. Miles Davis was the master of understatement, and one of the rare jazz musicians to enjoy widespread acclaim and recognition across the spectrum of popular music. Davis defied clichés, trends, and norms and refused to remain static or stagnant at any point in his life or career. He often scandalized or angered fans who preferred he remain in a particular phase rather than forge ahead. Receiving a trumpet from his father for his thirteenth birthday, he later played (in the early 40s) in his high school band and, as a student, with Eddie Randall's Blue Devils — a St. Louis R&B group. He had early encounters with Clark Terry, Dizzy Gillespie, and Charlie Parker before he went to New York in 1944 to study at the Juilliard School of Music. Davis left there shortly to learn in a less formal setting: the laboratory of 52nd Street. He became a member of Charlie Parker's group before he was 20 and worked with them from 1946 to 1948. He later helped assemble an innovative unit that offered a stylistic alternative to the bop approach. The idea for a nonet, culled from discussions that had been held in Gil Evans's apartment in New York, resulted in the *Birth of the Cool* sessions as well as a short-lived band featuring Davis, Gerry Mulligan, Lee Konitz, Evans, and others. Davis endured hard times personally and professionally from 1949 (following a stint at the Paris Jazz Festival) until 1954, when he reemerged and began to forge the remarkable sound and style that would stamp him forever as a musical giant. During the 50s Davis's crisp, concise, and often unforgettable solos showed one could make an impact through intelligent use of space and time as much as speed and flash. His work with arranger Gil Evans was equally influential in its ability to blend a dynamic ensemble around Davis — a captivating lead player. Davis introduced the metal Harmon mute (minus the stem) and utilized the flugelhorn as a legitimate alternative brass instrument.

His great combos of the mid and late 50s, with pianists Red Garland or Bill Evans, saxophonists John Coltrane and Cannonball Adderley, bassist Paul Chambers, and drummers Philly Joe Jones or Jimmy Cobb were seminal in their impact inside and outside jazz. The *Kind of Blue* album in 1959 popularized modal jazz, with its improvisations based on a series of scales rather than chord sequences, a technique that generated more thought and creativity along melodic lines. During the 60s and 70s, Davis continued to break ground, with his mid-60s band being among the most fluid and revolutionary of its era. This band, with pianist Herbie Hancock, bassist Ron Carter, and drummer Tony Williams, plus saxophonist Wayne Shorter, worked with written themes but no prearranged harmonies. This allowed both the soloist and the answering rhythm-section players to choose whatever notes or chords they desired after the initial theme statement. From the late 60s and on into the 70s, Davis opted for longer pieces without composed structures. He used rock as the rhythmic foundation, employed Indian and Asian instrumentation along with standard jazz pieces, and went electric, yet his trumpet solos remained as definitive and clear as in earlier, acoustic periods. But a debilitating illness, plus other personal problems, resulted in Davis taking a break from 1975 to 1980. Through the 80s, Davis's playing seemed to get stronger and more interesting, especially his use of the middle and lower registers, but controversy raged around his albums. He steadily moved more and more into funk and R&B, although he also made an appearance at the 1991 Montreux Jazz Festival and had allegedly talked about doing a reunion Birth of the Cool date. The most recent posthumous Davis release features his always expressive trumpet work over hip-hop arrangements. —RW

☆ **Birth of the Cool / BLUE NOTE**   1949
Definitive late-40s Miles. A must-buy. Recently reissued on CD by Blue Note (1990). These seminal "cool" sessions have been reissued extensively. This is the most recent and still sounds great 40 years later. —RW

And Horns / OJC   1951
Instructive early-50s sessions. Miles emerges out of a "cool"

bag, Sonny Rollins (ts) is strong, and Al Cohn (ts) and Zoot Sims (ts) participate. —RW

Conception / OJC   1951
Some thrilling playing. Limited-edition reissue. —RW

Dig / OJC   1951
Standout dates with sublime Miles, challenging Sonny Rollins (ts). —RW

Volume 1 / BLUE NOTE   1952
Overlooked, solid Miles Davis sessions for Blue Note. —RW

Collector's Items / OJC   1953
A good bunch of early Miles sessions. Includes cuts with Charlie Parker (as) and Sonny Rollins (ts). —RW

Volume 2 / BLUE NOTE   1953
Some undervalued dates with Jimmy Heath (sax) and J. J. Johnson (tb). —RW

At Last / OJC   1953
A rare meeting of Miles and the Lighthouse crew. Bob Cooper (sax), Chet Baker (tpt), and a steady Max Roach (d) are standouts. —RW

Tune Up / PRESTIGE   1953
From four sessions from 1953 to 1954. —ED

Blue Haze / OJC   1953
Fine 50s Davis. Presence of seldom-heard David Schildkraut (as) enhances its value. Supporting cast, which includes Charles Mingus (b), John Lewis (p), Horace Silver (p), et al, isn't too shabby either! —RW

Walkin' / OJC   1954
This may well be his best single Prestige date. A wonderful session with Lucky Thompson (sax), Horace Silver (p), Percy Heath (b). —RW

And the Modern Jazz Giants / OJC   1954
Worthy 50s material. Miles works with established greats and shows he belongs in their league. Monk (p), Horace Silver (p), Sonny Rollins (ts), and Milt Jackson (vib) all take turns. —RW

○ **Bags' Groove / OJC**   1954
Sterling sessions with Miles and Monk (p), Milt Jackson (vib), Sonny Rollins (ts), and Horace Silver (p). —RW

Musings of Miles / PRESTIGE   1955
An arresting quartet date with Oscar Pettiford dominant in the bass chair. —RW

Green Haze / PRESTIGE   1955
Blue Moods / OJC / DB 5   1955
A bit different in lineup and intentions. Rare vinyl meeting between Miles and jazz rebel Teddy Charles (vib). W/ Charles Mingus (b). —RW

☆ **'Round About Midnight / CBS / DB 5**   1955
A masterpiece with Miles's great 50s quintet. —RW

Circle in the Round / CBS   1955
Interesting vault items w/ various Miles' groups. —RW

New Miles Davis Quintet / PRESTIGE   1955
Stirring work from the then-emerging group, with John Coltrane (ts) coming of age. —RW

Plays for Lovers / PRESTIGE   1955
○ **Steamin' with the Miles Davis Quintet / PRESTIGE**   1956
This is a landmark 50s work. Both vinyl and CD reissue are topflight. —RW

○ **Cookin' / OJC / DB 5**   1956
Miles's great early-50s group. —MGN

○ **Workin' with the Miles Davis Quintet / OJC / DB 5**   1956
○ **Relaxin' with the Miles Davis Quintet / OJC / DB 5**   1956
His great early-50s group. —MGN

○ **Miles Ahead / CBS / DB 5**   1957
A stunning collaboration with Gil Evans, it is the only album with lots of Davis on flugelhorn. The remastered CD version has problems; get the vinyl album if you can find it. —RW

Ascenseur pour l'Echafaud / POLYGRAM   1957
English translation is "Lift to the Scaffold." An interesting mid-50s sound-track album. —MB

1958 Miles / CBS   1958
Some recorded May 26, 1958. Rare sessions, never available before. Well worth it. –MGN

○ **Milestones / CBS**   1958
A heart-stopping session — wonderful Miles, Coltrane (ts), and Cannonball Adderley (as). Again, get the vinyl if you can find it, though this CD reissue isn't as bad as some others. –RW

Miles & Monk at Newport / CBS   1958
This is not the two artists playing together — one side is Miles, the other is Monk (p) w/ Pee Wee Russell (cl). –MGN

○ **Porgy & Bess / CBS / DB 5**   1958
Vital playing, amazing arrangements by Gil Evans. –RW

○ **Miles & Coltrane / CBS**   1958
You can't get any better. A must-buy. –MGN

★ **Kind of Blue / CBS**   1959
This could be the most influential and popular jazz album of all time. What, you say you don't own a copy? –MGN

☆ **Sketches of Spain / CBS / DB 5**   1959
Arguably his most popular single album. The playing and arrangements are unmatched. –RW

Someday My Prince Will Come / COL   1961
Great mid-60s group. –MGN

Friday Night at the Blackhawk / CBS / BB 68   1961
Vol. 1. If possible, find the complete two-disc set. –RW

Saturday Night at the Blackhawk / CBS / BB 68   1961
Vol. 2. This concert is available in a complete two-disc set and is best heard that way. Hearing only half or part distorts impact and understanding. –RW

At Carnegie Hall 1961 / CBS / BB 59   1961
Transitional early-60s sessions. Hank Mobley (sax) tries hard, but doesn't really fill Coltrane's shoes. W/ good Gil Evans orchestra cuts. –RW

Facets / COLUMBIA   1962

○ **Quiet Nights / CBS / BB 93**   1962
Beautiful orchestrations, delightful playing from Miles. –RW

Seven Steps to Heaven / CBS / DB 5   1963
Emphatic session. –RW

○ **Four & More - Live / CBS**   1964
Good material from mid-60s period. Herbie Hancock (p) has fine solos. –RW

○ **My Funny Valentine/Miles Davis in Concert / CBS**   1964
Herbie Hancock (p) is captivating. –RW

● **E.S.P. / CBS**   1965
One of numerous mid-60s standout albums by the great band w/ Wayne Shorter (sax), Herbie Hancock (p), Ron Carter (b), Tony Williams (d). Get the vinyl album if at all possible; Columbia's new reissue leaves a lot to be desired. –RW

Cookin' at the Plugged Nickel / COLUMBIA   1965
Tremendous live set that's been poorly treated in the past. A prime 60s group in smashing form. –RW

Miles Smiles / CBS   1966
More excellent mid-60s Miles. –MGN

Nefertiti / CBS   1967
This tremendous late-60s cut gives you transcendent Wayne Shorter (sax). Can't say the same about lackluster Columbia remastering of the new reissue. –RW

Sorcerer / CBS / DB 5   1967
This vigorous 1967 session has nonmusical significance: Miles put Cicely Tyson's face on the album cover, which scored points for visual impact and the image of black women. –RW

Filles de Kilimanjaro / CBS / DB 5   1968
Another good pre-*Bitches Brew* album. –MGN

Miles in the Sky / CBS   1968
This suggestive, prophetic date is clearly inching toward *In a Silent Way* and *Bitches Brew* territory. –RW

☆ **In a Silent Way / CBS**   1969
Exceptional. W/ John McLaughlin (g). A prelude to *Bitches Brew*. –MGN

★ **Bitches Brew / CBS / BB 35**   1969
The pivotal jazz-fusion album. A must-buy. Gold album. –MGN

Live - Evil / COLUMBIA   1970
Here is more transitional early-70s material. Davis is increasing his R&B and rock content and approach. He plays plenty of organ and wah-wah electric trumpet. Includes fierce solos by Gary Bartz (sax). –RW

● **Tribute to Jack Johnson / COLUMBIA**   1970
Superior soundtrack/tribute. Arguably better than any pop/R&B/rock-tinged set, even *Bitches Brew*. Recently reissued on disc. W/ John McLaughlin (g), Herbie Hancock (k), Steve Grossman (sop sax), Billy Cobham (d), and Michael Henderson (b). –RW

At the Fillmore / CBS   1970
Raucous, roughhouse live set; Miles is totally plugged in. Steve Grossman (sop sax) and multiple keyboards — roaring, spewing, and exploding. –RW

On the Corner / COLUMBIA   1972
First-rate for what it is: rock/R&B-laced instrumentals. –RW

Agharta / CBS / DB 5   1975
CD reissue of a pivotal rock-oriented date. W/ rambling, extensive solos with a loose feel. Miles plays keyboards as well as trumpet. Funk backings with torrid sax by Sonny Fortune and explosive guitar by Pete Cosey. Jazz purists were scandalized. –RW

Pangaea / CBS / DB 5   1975
Finally, the domestic reissue of the incredible live set done in Japan. Sonny Fortune (sax) and Pete Cosey (g) are in the stratosphere. –RW

Aura / CBS   1985
This is a very different type of Miles record: A ten-part suite in which he weaves in and out. The moods, feel, and sound keep shifting, thanks to Palle Mikkelborg's compositions and arrangements. –RW

Tutu / WARNER   1986
Pretty dismal compositions, but good playing by Miles. –RW

Amandla / WARNER   1989
Although nearing the end of his life, Miles plays surprisingly well here. Standard fusion/pop textures provided by Marcus Miller. –RW

○ **Miles in Paris / WARNER**

Siesta / WARNER
Music from *Siesta*. –ED

Ballads / CBS   COMP
These are beautiful, timeless pieces, but should really be heard in their original, intact sessions. This is aimed at the casual Davis listener, novices, or new fans. –RW

Basic Miles / COLUMBIA / DB 5   COMP
Great pieces. These too should really be heard in their original sessions. Also aimed at the casual Davis listener. –RW

○ **Chronicle / PRESTIGE / DB 5**   COMP
The complete Prestige recordings. This is an unbelievable eight-disc set of 93 performances containing everything on the Prestige label. –RW

Columbia Years 1955-1985 / CBS   COMP
Boxed set of rare and unreleased material, as well as well-known tracks from all his periods. –MGN

RICHARD DAVIS   b 1930

Post-bop, early free, modern creative. Bassist. Multi-talented African-American instrumentalist could have been a symphonic rather than jazz player. Richard Davis has combined both worlds, playing in symphony orchestras as well as jazz combos and groups through the 50s, 60s, 70s, and beyond. His mastery of the bass is self-evident; he can drive or break up the beat, plays marvelously with both bow and fingers, uses the full instrument, and varies his approach constantly. Davis began with Ahmad Jamal and Don Shirley, later played with Charlie Ventura, Sarah Vaughan, Kenny

Burrell, Eric Dolphy, Jaki Byard, and the Jones-Lewis big band. He has also done session work in both classical and jazz veins. Not a prolific bandleader, his catalog is small. –RW

Now's the Time (recorded live at Jazz City) / MUSE   1970
Fine set with stirring Clifford Jordan (ts). CD issue. –RW

○ **Harvest / MUSE**   1977
Premier bassist with groups of varying size. Most interesting listening for the adventurous jazz lover. –MGN

With Understanding / MUSE   r 1978
Chick Corea (k) center stage with fine Davis support. –RW

Heavy Sounds / IMPULSE
A top teamup with Elvin Jones (d). –RW

WILD BILL DAVISON   b 1906

Swing. Cornetist. A traditional mainstay, Wild Bill Davison became a fixture on the jazz scene in the late 20s and had his own band by 1931. He overcame a lip injury in 1939 and came to New York in 1941. A re-creation of the Original Jazz Band for the Katherine Dunham Show resulted in a 1944 recording session and paved the way for a switch from a Chicago-style approach to a New Orleans-traditional approach. He joined Eddie Condon in 1945 and became a fine lead player and charismatic personality. His skills were and are centered in a very active style, with lots of grunts, grimaces, long tones, and crackling leads. –RW

That's A Plenty / COMMODORE   ca. 1943
Lots of Pee Wee Russell (cl) and George Brunis (tb) from old 78s. Nice album to find. –MGN

This Is Jazz - Vol. 1 / STORYVILLE   1947
Sessions with the All-Star Stompers, including George Brunis, Albert Nicholas, Ralph Sutton, Danny Barker, Pops Foster, Baby Dodds, and James P. Johnson. –MGN

Ringside at Condon's / SAVOY   1951
1951 and 1952. Another great swinger with Hall, Cutshall, Drootin, Condon, Cliff Leeman, and others. –MGN

● **Individualism of.... / SAVOY**   1951
1951 sessions at Eddie Condon's in Boston. Features Cutty Cutshall (tb), Ed Hall (cl), George Wein (p), Buzzy Drootin (d). Sextet and septet recordings with two different groups. Dixie to swing standards the master cornetist. 23 cuts. –MGN

Live at the Rainbow Room / CHAROSCURO   196?
60s date with Dorothy Dodgion (d), Claude Hopkins (p), and George Duvivier (b) in septet. –MGN

Plays Hoagy Carmichael / REAL TIME   1981
Good record introducing guitarist Howard Alden. Great work from tenor saxophonist Eddie Miller. –MGN

○ **Jazz A-Plenty / COMMODORE**
Forthright, dynamic traditional jazz/swing player. –RW

BLOSSOM DEARIE   b 1926

Ballads. A tiny-voices song stylist with a unique sound. A true icon of American popular music. An acquired taste, on the cabaret side. –MGN

○ **Blossom Dearie / POLYGRAM**   i 1956
Very stylized and effective. –RW

My Gentleman Friend / VERVE   i 1959
May I Come In? / DAFFODIL   1964
Sessions from 1964. –MGN

Needlepoint Magic / DAFFODIL   1979
With vocalist Bob Dorough. –MGN

Simply / DAFFODIL   1983
Available on vinyl only, this features Bob Dorough on vocals and Jay Berliner on guitar. –MGN

Et Tu Bruce / DAFFODIL   1984
A live performance from 1984. –MGN

Songs of Chelsea / DAFFODIL   ca. 1987
Includes ten cuts, with trio. –MGN

JOEY DEFRANCESCO   b 1971

Post-bop, soul jazz, neo bop. Like Charles Earland, Jimmy McGriff, and countless other Hammond B-3 organists, the young DeFrancesco hails from Philadelphia. He's got their chops, but he's less than half their age, and his material is more jazz-oriented. His recordings for Columbia have already thrust him upon the scene as one of the new young jazz players to watch in the coming years. This Miles Davis protégé, who's in his early 20s but began playing when he was just four, has a maturity and dexterity in his playing that goes far beyond his years. –RS

○ **All of Me / CBS**   1989
Young lion organist shows promise on debut. –RW

Where Were You? / CBS   1989
Nice mix-and-match quartet sessions. The lineup is split between esteemed veterans like Illinois Jacquet (sax) and Milt Hinton (b) and the younger Wallace Roney (tpt) and Kirk Whalum (ts). –RW

Part III / CBS
Substantial fluctuation in material quality and performances. Defrancesco has a good flair for soul jazz and hard bop but gets bogged down at times in pop-tinged pablum. –RW

BUDDY DEFRANCO   b 1923

Swing, big band, bop, cool. Clarinet, bass clarinet, alto sax. Multi-reed player DeFranco had extensive training and nurturing while playing with Charlie Barnet, Tommy Dorsey, Gene Krupa, and Count Basie in the 40s and early 50s, before establishing his own group. In the Basie band in the 50s, he was not allowed to be shown in a filmed short with the otherwise all-Black band. He has been slammed repeatedly by critics for his peerless, but allegedly soulless, technique and lack of blues or earthy grounding. –RW

Blues Bag / AFFINITY   1964
This is a reissue of a hot date with Lee Morgan (tpt), Curtis Fuller (tb), and a slashing Art Blakey (d). –RW

○ **Like Someone in Love / MOSAIC**   1977
Simply incredible in every way! Sonny Clark offers moving, heated piano, and this is some of DeFranco's most sumptious, engaging, and accomplished playing. With majestic Tal Farlow guitar work. –RW

Mr. Lucky / PABLO / DB 5   ca. 1984
W/ good solos by DeFranco. –RW

Holiday for Swing / CONTEMPORARY   1988
An often intriguing teamup with Terry Gibbs (vib). –RW

HAROLD DEJAN'S OLYMPIA BRASS BAND   b 1909

Trad. Founded by saxophonist Harold Dejan in 1958, the Olympia Brass Band has continued to satisfy New Orleans audiences at funerals, Mardi Gras parades, and concerts in the French Market (as well as on sundry other occasions), making it one of the most enduring of all such units. The Olympia, which usually consists of about a dozen traditional band instruments, has made trips to Europe on several occasions and appeared in the James Bond movie, *Live and Let Die.* In comparison to more recent brass bands like the Dirty Dozen, Dejan's Olympia maintains "traditional" repertoire consisting of hymns, marches, and New Orleans-style jazz standards. –BR

Basin Street Blues / PRO ARTE-PRO JAZZ
Continuing a tradition more than a century old, Dejan's Olympia Brass Band here shows the potency of the traditional brass band approach. –BR

○ **New Orleans-Mardi Gras / PRO ARTE-PRO JAZZ**
Music of the streets of New Orleans at festival time. You'll be ready for Lent after a Fat Tuesday musical blow-out like this one. –BR

On Bourbon Street / PRO ARTE-PRO JAZZ
Good cuts, nice playing. –RW

JACK DEJOHNETTE   b 1942

Post-bop, early free, jazz-rock, neo bop, M-base, modern creative. Drums, piano, melodica. A classical piano student for over a decade and an American Music Conservatory graduate, it is drums rather than keyboards that have become Jack DeJohnette's instrument of choice. His background in R&B, free, and everything else got him regular work in Chicago before he moved to New York in 1966. His playing with the Charles Lloyd Quartet in the late 60s provided a final break after prior stints with John Patton, Jackie McLean, Abbey Lincoln, and Betty Carter. DeJohnette is unmatched as a timekeeper and anchor, and has led jazz-rock, hard-bop, and all other styles of groups. –RW

DeJohnette Complex / OJC   1968
Early session has some appealing cuts. Outstanding personnel; Jack occasionally doubles on melodica. New reissue. –RW

○ **Have You Heard? / EPIC / DB 5**   1970
A high-level Japanese session. –RW

Sorcery / PRESTIGE   1974
Dynamic Bennie Maupin (sax), fiery DeJohnette. –RW

Cosmic Chicken / PRESTIGE   1975
Funk suggestiveness, improvisatory energy. –RW

★ **Special Edition / POLYGRAM / DB 5**   1979
First and best, with David Murray (ts), Arthur Blythe (as). A must-buy. *DOWN BEAT* Critics' Choice for that year. –MGN

New Directions in Europe / ECM   1979
1988 reissue of his other great 70s group, recorded live and on fire. W/Lester Bowie (tpt), John Abercrombie (g), and Eddie Gomez (b). –RW

Inflation Blues / ECM   1982
The best of two early-80s sets with Chico Freeman (d). –RW

Album Album / POLYGRAM / DB 5   1984
Interesting title, often illuminating set. –RW

Piano Album / LANDMARK   1985
DeJohnette on piano, not drums. Very well done! –MGN

Irresistible Force / MCA-IMPULSE   1986
One of the few substantial albums to emerge from the hyped MCA revival of the Impulse line. –RW

Parallel Realities / MCA / DB 5   r 1990
An overlooked session with Pat Metheny (g) in definite jazz phase. Herbie Hancock shows his steadfast piano form. –RW

THE DELTA RHYTHM BOYS

Blues-jazz. Though not a jazz vocal ensemble in the classic sense, this was a busy backup band. They made appearances backing Ruth Brown, Lavern Baker, and other Atlantic stars. They are good harmonizers — a highly effective studio unit. –RW

○ **The Delta Rhythm Boys / MERCURY MG-25153**

BARBARA DENNERLEIN   b 1964

Post-bop, M-base. A fast-rising organist whose methodology combines the best of soul-jazz and the more outside, ambitious style of Larry Young. In recent years, Dennerlein has become something of a favorite of the critics. –RW

○ **Straight Ahead / CAPITOL-RHINO**   1988
Organ-fired and guitar-laced modern jazz from this up-and-coming keyboardist. A solid album throughout. –MGN

Hot Stuff / RHINO   r 1991
Emerging organ star comes out with adventurous session. –RW

JOHNNY DESMOND   1920-1985

Cool, ballads. Johnny Desmond's ultra-smooth vocals earned him the nickname of "The Creamer." He enjoyed success in Detroit during the 30s before forming a foursome known as the Downbeats, which joined Bob Crosby's band, the Bob-O-Links. Desmond joined Gene Krupa's band as a lead singer in

1941, later worked with Glenn Miller's Air Force Band, and was known as "The G.I. Sinatra." He later was a featured member of Don McNeill's Breakfast Club in Chicago and recorded for RCA, Coral, MGM. He was also featured on 50s television staples "Hit Parade" and "Face the Music." –RW

○ **Memories of World War II / COMPOSE**
Nice nostalgia material. –RW

PAUL DESMOND   1924-1977

Cool. Alto sax. No one's done more with the short-breath approach than Paul Desmond. Desmond studied clarinet in high school and college and joined Dave Brubeck's octet in 1948, where he stayed until 1950. He left, and then came back to the regular group from 1951-1967, returning often in the last decade of his life for tours. Desmond was emphatic and appealing in his own way and could swing, despite the shortness of his lines. He was among the top players on alto in the early 50s, using the upper harmonics of the instrument. Desmond, who is a superb improviser, is a prime example of the "cool" sax approach of Lester Young and Benny Carter. He has a lovely luminous tone. His best recordings are with Gerry Mulligan and Jim Hall. –RW
   & JME

● **Paul Desmond/Gerry Mulligan Quartet / FANTASY**   1952
Lovely. Four dates, from 1952 to 1954. –JME

Blues in Time / FANTASY   1957
An evocative, effective set w/ Gerry Mulligan (bar sax). –RW

East of the Sun / DISCOVERY   1959
First-rate quartet session. Jim Hall (g), Percy Heath (b), and Connie Kay (d) are super. –RW

☆ **Paul Desmond - Jim Hall Recordings / MOSAIC**   1959
Incredible music! A 6-disc boxed set of recordings from 1959-1965 featuring Desmond with Jim Hall. Desmond plays flawless sax, and Jim Hall likewise on guitar. In brief, these are classic cuts; the best. Whether a beginning listener or a jazz expert, this is satisfying music. Mosaic does it again. –JME

Late Lament / RCA   1961
Good early material on an 1987 reissue. –RW

Two of a Mind, w/ Gerry Mulligan / BLUEBIRD   1962
Old pros of one mind. It's hardly challenging, yet quite attractive. Another Desmond/ Gerry Mulligan (bar sax) winner. –RW

Easy Living / RCA   1965
A wonderful reissue of a timeless, captivating set with Jim Hall (g), Percy Heath (b), and Connie Kay (d). –RW

From the Hot Afternoon / A & M   1969
A 1989 reissue of a satisfying, if unsubstantial, Desmond release. –RW

○ **Bridge over Troubled Water / A&M / DB 5**   1969
Beautiful Desmond with fine Herbie Hancock on electric piano, but occasionally annoying orchestrations. –RW

In Concert at Town Hall / DRG   1971
This delightful collaboration with MJQ has been reissued several times. This is one of the better editions. –RW

Skylark / CBS / DB 5   1973
Very glossy, with some beautiful moments. –RW

Pure Desmond / CBS / DB 5   1974
Undemanding but nicely played set (1987 reissue). –RW

○ **The Paul Desmond Quartet Live / A&M HORIZON**   1975
Concert in Toronto. Best album of Desmond's last years. –MGN

Best of Paul Desmond / CBS   COMP
Cool saxophonist. Some feel his best work is with Brubeck. –MGN

DETROIT JAZZ COMPOSERS LTD.

Progressive big band. Progressive big band of Detroiters; they're mostly horn players, post-Coltrane, post-bop. –MGN

○ **Hastings Street Jazz Experience / MIDNITE**
This is a 12 voice, 30 instrument big band from Detroit in modernist, self-determining stance. Notables include vocalist

Kim Weston; saxophonists Lou Barnett, Ted Buckner, Ted Harris Jr., Ernie Rodgers, Charlie Gabriel, and Miller Brisker; trumpeters Herbie Williams and Eddie Jones; trombonists Jimmy Wilkins and Phil Ranelin; bassist Duke Billingslea. –MGN

AL DI MEOLA   b 1954

Jazz-rock. Guitarist. Di Meola earned his early fame as a member of Return to Forever, but he's a versatile player equally capable of playing jazz, blues, rock, Latin, or classical. He started as a nine-year-old, then picked up the steel-string guitar at fifteen. Di Meola attended Berklee in Boston in the mid 70s, then joined Return to Forever in 1974. After that experience, Di Meola has led his own band, the Al Di Meola Project, and has toured and recorded with John McLaughlin and Paco De Lucia. He's a superb electric and acoustic stylist. –RW

Elegant Gypsy / CBS / BB 58   1976
The frenetic, slashing stylist shows his sentimental, restrained, and romantic side. Gold album. –RW

Land of the Midnight Sun / CBS / DB 5   1976
A jazz-rock/fusion set of distinction. –RW

○ **Splendido Hotel / CBS**   1979
A 1990 reissue of an intriguing set, spiced by the appearance of Les Paul (g). –RW

Friday Night in San Francisco / CBS / BB 97   1980
W/ John McLaughlin (g), Paco De Lucia (g). The other of two good triple-threat sessions. –RW

● **Passion Grace & Fire / CBS**   1983
W/ John McLaughlin (g), Paco De Lucia (g). Spectacular triple guitar threat — fireworks! –MGN

Tirami Su / BLUE NOTE   ca. 1990
Guitar work is aggressive and often superb. –RW

○ **World Sinfonia / CAPITOL-RHINO**   1991
This ia an outstanding venture into the international/Latin arena. –RW

GARRY DIAL

Hard-bop, post-bop. A contemporary trio led by New Jersey pianist Garry Dial. Dial is a good mainstream player and soloist. –RW

Dial & Oates / DMP   1988
Never Is Now / CONTINUUM

WALT DICKERSON   b 1931

Post-bop, cool. A premier vibist, Dickerson hardens his mallets with a special solution. His styles span post-bop to progressive jazz. –MGN

A Sense of Direction / NEW JAZZ   i 1962
W/ Austin Crowe Trio. Three standards, five of Dickerson's boldly tinged originals. A fresh approach to vibes. –MGN

○ **Lawrence of Arabia / DAUNTLESS**   1963
Jazz Impressions: Lawrence Of Arabia. This effort from the vibraphonist stretches the parameters of Maurice Jarre's themes. Rare, but great to have. –MGN

DIRTY DOZEN BRASS BAND

Trad, post-bop, progressive big band, neo bop. The appearance of the Dirty Dozen Brass Band in 1975 (emerging, like a phoenix, from the kazoo and drum corps of "second-liners") signalled a new phase of development in traditional New Orleans music, which was at once popular and controversial. While they kept parts of the traditional repertoire, they also added titles associated with modern jazz and rhythm and blues — a departure which did not always sit well with other brass bandsmen. But the public loved it! From modest beginnings at neighborhood bars, the members of the Dirty Dozen soon became local celebrities, opening doors which have since led to international celebrity on the festival circuit. The band's success ushered in a renaissance in the New Orleans brass band field, attracting young musicians who formed bands of their own, such as the Rebirth. In retrospect, the Dirty Dozen has done more to revitalize the New Orleans brass band tradition than to endanger it. Their music is vibrantly attractive for its often stunning virtuosity and the sort of infectious street rhythms that compel dancing. –BR

○ **My Feet Can't Fail Me Now / CONCORD**   1984
The Dozen on the rise — the title track is still the band's "flag waver" and never fails to stir things up. –BR

Live: Mardi Gras Montreux / ROUNDER / DB 5   r 1985
Dance music in a conceptually revolutionary jazz package — "The Flintstones Meets the President (Meets the Dirty Dozen)" illustrates the band's sense of humor effectively. –BR

Voodoo / CBS   r 1989
Guest stars Dizzy Gillespie (tpt), Dr. John (p), and Branford Marsalis (ts) fit right in with the band's masterful ensemble work. –BR

New Orleans Album / CBS   r 1990
This time, veteran Orleanians Danny Barker, Eddie Bo, and Dave Bartholomew join in, plus Elvis Costello — the fun quotient runs off the meter with plenty of solos and absolutely infectious rhythms. –BR

JOHNNY DODDS   1892-1940

Trad, Dixieland, swing. Clarinet. In the early years of recorded jazz music, ensemble work was the main measure of a band's merit. Solo statements were often confined to short unaccompanied breaks, and bandleaders were not always known for producing exciting (or even competent) melodic improvisation. Louis Armstrong was one of jazzdom's first brilliant soloists; clarinetist Johnny Dodds was another. His birthplace — New Orleans — was the birthplace of jazz, and in that city the clarinet has always reigned supreme, due at least in part to his formative work with Kid Ory, and 20s sessions with King Oliver, Jelly Roll Morton, Armstrong, and many more. Dodds was not a technical giant on the clarinet, but his audience wasn't concerned with embouchure and fingering patterns — they were amazed (as are listeners to this day) at his freedom of spirit, impressive soaring lines and confident, even brash, expression. Many early jazz players made ends meet by accompanying vocalists; and Dodds's work with blues singers Ida Cox, Lovie Austin, and others was time well spent. He was an excellent blues player, and his wide creole vibrato, throaty tone, and commanding aural presence (that has all the hallmarks of the ranking female blues vocal) with a jazz clarinet was not revolutionary, but his ability to make the instrument sing was, and jazz hasn't been the same since. Note: Affinity 1023 is a three-CD box just released (U.K.) that has many of Dodd's landmark recordings from 1926-27. This is volume one; more are anticipated to trace his career up to his death in 1940. –MB

☆ **South Side Chicago Jazz / MCA**   1927
1927-1929. Dodds in various combinations, from his Trio through the Black Bottom Stompers to Jimmy Blythe's Washboard Wizards and the Beale Street Washboard Band. "Wild Man Blues" shows one of many reasons Dodds was one of most individual and celebrated clarinetists from New Orleans. –BR

Blue Clarinet Stomp / RCA   1927
1927-1929. Classic jazz at its best — Dodds with Jelly Roll Morton's Trio, with his own orchestra, his Washboard Band, and the Dixieland Jug Blowers. Alternate takes show improvisational character of Dodd's approach. CD has four bonus cuts –BR

PIERRE DOERGE   b 1946

Post-bop, progressive big band, neo bop, modern creative. This Scandinavian guitarist combines South African jazz with progressive arrangements. He plays mostly with the large New Jungle Orchestra. –MGN

Even the Moon Is Dancing / STEEPLECHASE   1985

Incorporates African free-jazz and ethnic Scandinavian themes. –MGN

○ **Johnny Lives / STEEPLECHASE**
For the late bassist Johnny Dyani. Diverse, improvisational big band. Definitive and creative music. –MGN

NIELS LAN DOKY   b 1963

Post-bop, neo bop. This pianist from Copenhagen is of Vietnamese parentage. His styles are contemporary and neo-bop, leaning toward the latter. –MGN

● **The Truth / STORYVILLE**   1987
Brilliant live CD featuring Bob Berg (ts), Bo Stief (b), and Terri Lyne Carrington (d). Exceptional solos by all sidemen and excellent live sound quality. –PK

○ **Dreams / MILESTONE**
Young pianist from Copenhagen in a contemporary setting. Very good — more to come. With Randy Brecker (tpt), Bob Berg, and John Scofield (g). –MGN

Friendship / MILESTONE
This CD comprises two sessions, one in New York and the other in Copenhagen. Personnel include B. Evans, R. Brecker, R. Margitza, C. Minh Doky, A. Nussbaum, and more. An excellent followup to his *Dreams* CD. –PK

BO DOLLIS AND THE WILD MAGNOLIAS

Zydeco, trad. A striking feature of New Orleans musical life is the ritual observance of Mardi Gras and St. Joseph's Day by the so-called Mardi Gras Indians. The Mardi Gras Indians are not unlike the various marching clubs that parade annually in New Orleans, but their outfits and musical style are unique. Chanting a traditional repertoire sung in a patois tracing to the Haitian origins of many black New Orleanians, the Indians use only percussion for musical accompaniment — drums, tamborines, cowbells, and rattles — as they play the streets of their designated neighborhoods. Competition between the tribes is now friendly, but the ritual is taken very seriously: individual members can spend upwards of a thousand dollars on their costumes, which take a full year's work to prepare. The Wild Magnolias are one of many tribes, divided into "uptown" and "downtown" factions. They were the first band of this sort to release a recording, "Handa Wanda," as early as 1970, but the street music played by the Indians does not follow the same instrumentation or interpretation heard on such recordings, which are specially made for the popular market. Even so, the music of the Wild Magnolias, whether on the street or on disc, defies the listener to keep still. As with most New Orleans music, it is made for dancing. The spirit of the Mardi Gras Indians has influenced New Orleans musicians from Jelly Roll Morton through Professor Longhair and is one of the enduring elements that has shaped this wonderfully distinctive and regional culture. –BR

○ **I'm Back at Carnival TIme / ROUNDER**
Original New Orleans funk and street party music. Absolutely addictive, with Snooks Eaglin, George Porter Jr. of the Meters, and the Rebirth Brass Band lending support to Indian standards like "Iko Iko," "Big Chief," and "Meet de Boys on the Battlefront." –BR

DOLPHINS

Neo bop. Post-fusion, contemporary band featuring keyboardist Andy LaVerne and Brubeck brothers Dan (drums) and Chris (bass, trombone). –MGN

○ **Malayan Breeze / DMP**
Contemporary-fusion with drummer Dan Brubeck (son of Dave Brubeck). –MGN

ERIC DOLPHY   1928-1964

Post-bop, early free. Alto sax, bass clarinet, flute. Like many 60s jazz innovators, Eric Dolphy spent his formative years in the creative cauldron of 50s Los Angeles, nourished on a diet of Charlie Parker and other bop visionaries. Also like so many others, his career was cut short by the rigors and self-neglect of the jazz life. He apprenticed with an R&B band, drummer Roy Porter's big band, and navy bands, and had numerous opportunities to try out his ideas in jam sessions with many prominent Los Angeles progressives. His associations with major figures like John Coltrane, Charles Mingus, Oliver Nelson, George Russell, Ornette Coleman, Booker Little, Max Roach, Gunther Schuller, and many others were always satisfying, vitalized by Eric's relentless search to expand the role of the alto sax, the flute, and the somewhat obscure bass clarinet. In Dolphy's hands each of these instruments gained new personalities and produced absolutely stunning unaccompanied solos; in ensembles his playing had the controlled invention of Parker, but with all the smooth edges broken off and discarded. Dolphy is remembered as an iconoclast, but his performances with Chico Hamilton's easygoing 1958-1959 group, various Latin jazz dates, Oliver Nelson's blues-flavored projects, bebop jams, and the third-stream constructions of Schuller and John Lewis demonstrate the versatility and traditional grounding of this gentle multi-instrumentalist. It is tragic that Dolphy, a well-loved figure throughout the modern jazz community, had to endure the "anti-jazz" epithets of reactionary critics and pursue his career with pick-up bands in Europe, where he died of diabetes in 1964. His *Out to Lunch* still stands as a definitive statement of the mid-60s "new thing" avant-gardists. –MB

○ **Outward Bound / OJC / DB 5**   1960
His first session as a leader, with hints at the bold ideas to come, while showcasing Dolphy's early talents. –MGN

Status / PRESTIGE   1960
Four sessions from 1960-1961. –MGN

Other Aspects / BLUE NOTE   1960
A posthumous compilation of private recordings, many with a classical music feel. –MB

○ **Out There / OJC**   1960
An unusual quartet, with bass and cello, carries out Eric's new concepts, with a nod to Mingus. –MB

○ **Far Cry / OJC**   1960
Booker Little was under recorded, which makes this significant. The album marks Dolphy's departure from standard jazz repertoire playing, with originals and exciting Parker-inspired material. –ED

Looking Ahead / FANTASY   1960
Good exchanges and nice pairing of Dolphy with obscure multi-saxophonist Ken McIntyre. –RW

Candid Dolphy / CANDID   1960
From 1960-1961. This is an excellent collection of small-combo sessions with numerous luminaries such as Ted Curson (tpt), Kenny Dorham (tpt), Abbey Lincoln (v). –RW

★ **At the Five Spot - Vol. 1 / OJC**   1961
The first of the immortal Dolphy live dates, with incredible interaction between Dolphy and Booker Little (tpt). Awesome alto sax and bass clarinet, with feverish tempos. –RW

☆ **At the Five Spot - Vol. 2 / OJC**   1961
Just as vital as its predecessor. Wondrous solos and compositions. 1987 reissues of a landmark concert. –RW

☆ **Great Concert of Eric Dolphy / PRESTIGE / DB 5**   1961
The complete Five Spot concert recordings in a three-album package. It may be unavailable now. –RW

Berlin Concerts / RHINO   1961
Tremendous Dolphy with good assistance from Jamil Nasser (b) and Benny Bailey (tpt). –RW

Eric Dolphy, in Europe - Vols. 1-3 / PRESTIGE   1961
Live recordings from two dates, spread over three albums. All feature excellent soloing and capable, if reserved, backing from a Danish trio. –MB

Copenhagen Concert / PRESTIGE   1961
Stockholm Sessions / RHINO   1961
Dolphy is typically amazing. Borderline European players and material. 1990 CD issue has a bonus cut. –RW

Memorial Album / OJC   1963

This is not essential, but it contains excellent material. –RW

Iron Man / CELLULOID   1963

Unheralded, sometimes chaotic set of recordings that includes much of value. Prince Lasha (vib) gets second star. –RW

Conversations / CELLULOID   1963

For those who want all the Dolphy out there. Often brilliant material, but haphazardly compiled. –RW

★ **Out to Lunch / BLUE NOTE**   1964

His classic. Daring structures and startling solos from a quintet who would all go on to star status. W/ Freddie Hubbard (tpt), Bobby Hutcherson (vib). –MB

○ **Last Date / POLYGRAM / DB 5**   1964

Done in Europe with an incredible band. Dolphy at his career high-point. –MGN

Remembered / PRO ARTE-PRO JAZZ   r 1988

Not Dolphy. Tribute from trumpeter Terence Blanchard, Donald Harrison (sax) with Dolphy's rhythm section. –MGN

Latin Jazz Quintet / VA

Unusual, uneven, but compelling. In Afro-Latin setting. –RW

Magic / PRESTIGE / DB 5

The Essential / FANTASY   COMP

This is strictly for the budget-conscious. It does have some valuable material, but no anthology can accurately assess Dolphy's importance. –RW

Vintage Dolphy / GM   COMP

A collection of early-60s Dolphy recordings that veer everywhere stylistically. Worth having. –RW

LOU DONALDSON   b 1926

Post-bop, blues-jazz, soul jazz. Alto saxophonist. Donaldson came to prominence in the early 50s via Blue Note recordings of his own as well as sessions with Art Blakey and Jimmy Smith. He has been a bandleader based in New York from that point until today. Originally associated with bebop, he combines a thorough knowledge of bebop harmony, a fondness for little known songs, and a genuine feeling for the blues. His work was on Blue Note until 1964, when he began a six-album contract with Chess/Cadet. He returned to Blue Note in 1967 and achieved some of his greatest success in the late 60s. His 70s work features an electric saxophone, and his Blue Note and Atlantic/Cotillion releases from this period are commercial departures from what he does best. In general his 50s work is either in the hard-bop vein — though Donaldson is not a hard bopper — or comfortable mainstream/modern albums where he is usually the only horn. His 60s work features organ more often than not, and Donaldson becomes a talent scout here, providing major breaks for the likes of Grant Green, John Patton, Charles Earland, and Melvin Sparks. A return to straightahead jazz marked his 80s work, and he recorded frequently in Europe and Japan, where he is a major star. His work has often featured blind pianist Herman Foster in recent years. One Muse album *Sweet Poppa Lou* is recommended, while his 90s Milestone releases are his most recent domestic output. He is still touring nationally and internationally. –BP

● **Blues Walk / BLUE NOTE**   1958

This is a great album, great alto saxophonist. Highly recommended. –MGN

Here 'Tis / BLUE NOTE   1961

Robust, earthy soul-jazz and blues with overlooked organist Baby Face Willette. –RW

Natural Soul / BLUE NOTE   1962

Pure soul-jazz. –RW

Good Gracious / BLUE NOTE   1963

Look out for smoking Big John Patton on organ. –RW

Rough House Blues / ARGO   1964

Best and most ambitious of mid-60s Argo albums. Oliver Nelson supplied the arrangements for this nine-piece band. –RW

○ **Lush Life / BLUE NOTE**   1967

Smooth, moody, suggestive, and enlightening. –RW

Alligator Boogaloo / BLUE NOTE   1967

Prototype funk, soul-jazz, blues, boogie, and ballads from a stalwart alto master. –RW

Forgotten Man / TIMELESS   1981

Donaldson breaks into the 80s with verve, contributing an interesting vocal on "Whiskey Drinkin' Woman." –RW

Back Street / MUSE   1982

Stately, yet still funky. –RW

Play the Right Thing / MILESTONE   r 1991

This is the latest in a long line of sumptious soul-jazz/funky workouts. –RW

Quartet/Quintet/Sextet / BLUE NOTE

Both soul-jazz and more mainstream/hard-pop sessions. Elmo Hope (p), Horace Silver (p), Blue Mitchell (tpt), Kenny Dorham (tpt), and cast of all-stars. –RW

KENNY DORHAM   1924-1972

Bop, hard-bop, post-bop. Trumpet, composer. A youthful prodigy who played piano at seven, Kenny Dorham combined a seemingly fragile, brittle style with subtlety, melodic dexterity, and a creative, sparse approach. He was also among the rare jazz musicians to be a published critic. He was a superb blues player whose lyricism enlivened the most trite ballad. He began with Billy Eckstine, Lionel Hampton, and Dizzy Gillespie in the 40s and replaced Miles Davis in the Charlie Parker quintet in 1948. A charter member of Art Blakey's Jazz Messengers in the 50s, he was very prolific in the 50s and 60s. Dorham was also a brilliant composer. –RW

Kenny Dorham Quintet / OJC   1953

Wonderful session originally on Debut. Outstanding Jimmy Heath (sax). –RW

○ **Afro-Cuban / BLUE NOTE**   1955

Shows Dorham's love for Latin music. –MGN

Round Midnight - Vol. 1 & 2 / BLUE NOTE   1956

Vol. 1 is tremendous live set at Cafe Bohemia and includes some of Dorham's greatest solos on any record. Vol. 2 is equally strong. –RW

Jazz Contrasts / OJC   1957

Solid session with Sonny Rollins (ts), Max Roach (d), and fellow greats. –RW

○ **2 Horns, 2 Rhythm / OJC**   1957

Includes the brilliant Ernie Henry (as), who has been sadly overlooked, plus more excellent Dorham. –RW

This is the Moment / PRESTIGE   1958

Contains two Dorham vocals, but good luck finding it. –RW

Blue Spring / OJC   1959

Cannonball Adderley (as) shines. Very moving Dorham, top lineup. –RW

Quiet Kenny / PRESTIGE   1959

Emphatic, remarkable quartet session reissued in 1987. Immaculate Tommy Flanagan (p). –RW

Whistle Stop / BLUE NOTE   1961

Remarkable Dorham solos, excellent compositions. –RW

Ease It! / MUSE   1961

Date with saxophonist Rocky Boyd. Quite spirited. –MGN

Matador/Inta Somethin' / BLUE NOTE   1962

1961-1962. Reissue combines two fine Dorham albums. –RW

○ **Una Mas / BLUE NOTE**   1963

1987 reissue of excellent session. Super Dorham solos. –RW

★ **Trompeta Toccata / BLUE NOTE**   1964

The composer/trumpeter's finest hour. A quintet with Joe Henderson (ts). –MGN

Kenny Dorham Sextet / CADET   1970

A still blossoming Muhal Richard Abrams on piano joins Dorham. –RW

BOB DOROUGH   b 1923

Bop, cool, ballads. Remember "Multiplication Rock"? That was

Dorough, whose goofy, cutesy scat is immediately recognizable. A fine interpreter of bop and blues. The bridge between Babs Gonzales and Mark Murphy. −MGN

Devil May Care / BETHLEHEM   i 1955

● **Yardbird Suite / BETHLEHEM**   1956
Bird-influenced vocalist performs twelve standards and two he wrote with Bill Takas on bass. The title and "Devil May Care" are classics. For some, Dorough's cutesy voice is an acquired taste. −RW

○ **Just About Everything / INNER CITY**   ca. 1966
NYC studio sessions included Al Schackmann on guitar, Ben Tucker on bass, and Percy Brice on drums playing four Dorough tunes. Classics include the song, "Crawdad Song," and the pristine "Tis Autumn." −MGN

Skabadabba / PINNACLE   ca. 1987
Contains seven cuts where the latter-period Dorough still sounds in control. Bill Takas (b) and trumpeter Lee Katzman workout. The vocalist Dorough wrote three of these bop-inflected numbers. −MGN

JIMMY DORSEY   1904-1957

Big band. Clarinet, alto sax, trumpet. The younger brother who was a featured member in his older sibling's group in the 30s, Dorsey had worked before in many bands, including Paul Whiteman's. During the famous 1934 fight over the tempo of a song, Jimmy replaced his brother and took over the leadership. After that, Jimmy Dorsey had many successful bands, though at the end of WWII, the swing era took its toll. He reunited with his brother in 1953 and took over the band again for a brief time upon Tommy's death. −RW

Greatest Hits / MCA   COMP
Good attempt to present his best material. −RW

○ **Greatest Hits / CUR**   COMP
A 1991 compilation. −ED

TOMMY DORSEY   1905-1956

Big band. Trombone, bandleader. Tommy worked with his younger brother from the 20s until the 1934 argument that split them. After that, he took over Joe Haymes's orchestra. His efforts to woo big stars with huge (for the era) salaries helped his orchestra become prominent. The best-known member was a singer named Frank Sinatra. Dorsey kept up with changes by adding a string section in 1942 and Charlie Shavers in 1945. A 1947 film *The Fabulous Dorseys* fancified their lives. They reunited in 1953. He billed himself "The Sentimental Gentleman of Swing." −RW

This Is Tommy Dorsey - Vol. 1 & 2 / RCA
Solid two-record set of prime sessions. −RW

Best Of / RCA   193?
An anthology of 30s material. −RW

All-Time Greatest Hits - Vols. 1 - 4 / RCA 1940
When RCA decided to issue its early 40s Tommy Dorsey recordings containing Frank Sinatra vocals on compact disc, it abandoned the chronological sequencing found on the Grammy-winning album series *The Dorsey/Sinatra Sessions* and instead jumped back and forth through the catalog. This first volume of four contains some of the biggest hits, notably "I'll Never Smile Again" and "I'll Be Seeing You," and thus is the best selection for beginners. But be sure to move on to Vol. 2 and Vol. 3 and, especially, Vol. 4, which contains Sinatra's first solo session. −WR

Best Of / MCA   COMP
A fair anthology of Decca material. −RW

Best of the Big Bands / CBS   COMP
Nice selection of his best-known material. −RW

Sessions - Vols. 1-3 / RCA   COMP
Excellent set from the period when this was one of the most popular group in the music world. −RW

Seventeen Number Ones / RCA   COMP

Good 1990 overview of their biggest selling popular music standards. −RW

Yes, Indeed! / RCA / DB 5   COMP
Nice 1990 anthology of their best material. −RW

KENNY DREW   b 1928

Bop, hard-bop, post-bop, cool. Pianist. From his formative years as an accompanist for Lester Young and Buddy DeFranco, Kenny Drew has developed into a first-line soloist and accompanist. A keyboard master with a specialty of long lines in the right hand; he is a dynamic soloist. −RW

Talkin' & Walkin' / BLUE NOTE   r 1955
Prototype hard-bop/mainstream Blue Note, with Drew immense on piano. −RW

Kenny Drew Trio / RIVERSIDE   1956
State-of-the-art trio material. −RW

● **This Is New / OJC**   1957
Certainly impressive. −RW

Trio-Quartet-Quintet / OJC   ca. 1957
A wonderful collection of first-rate pianists in varied contexts, w/ Donald Byrd (tpt), Paul Chambers (b), and Philly Joe Jones (d) on the job. −RW

○ **Undercurrent / BLUE NOTE**   1960
Underrated pianist. One of many superlative Blue Note offerings. −MGN

Home Is Where the Soul Is / XANADU   1978
Brilliant, tasty, and exciting piano and compositions. −RW

For Sure / XANADU   1978
Robust and dynamic session from the late 70s. −RW

And Far Away / SOUL NOTE   1983
He can still drive a group and play with class, elegance, and beauty. −RW

EDDY DUCHIN   1910-1951

Big band. Bandleader, piano. "Sweet" bands were often more pop than jazz, and Duchin's was no different. His band was hugely popular in the 30s, making not only lots of records but radio and film appearances. His career waned in the 40s due to a combination of military service and illness. Duchin was not a virtuoso pianist, playing the simplest of styles. −RW

I'll See You in My Dreams / CBS
Excellent presentation. −RW

○ **Best of the Big Bands / COLUMBIA**   COMP
Nice overview of his work. −RW

Dream Along / CSP   COMP
A good collection of Duchin's material. −RW

DUKES OF DIXIELAND

Dixieland. The story of this band is a chapter in the saga of one of New Orleans's many musical dynasties, that of the Assunto family, which has at least three generations of musicians. Jac Assunto was one of the first jazzmen to record in New Orleans, and The Dukes was formed by his two sons, Freddie and Frank, in 1959. During the 50s it rose to national prominence, first as a feature of the Bourbon Street scene, then as a touring act when it traveled to Chicago and Las Vegas. By this time, "Papa" Jac had joined the band, and the following year they made Las Vegas their headquarters as they prepared to take the country, and the world, by storm. Between 1956 and 1966 the band made numerous recordings, including several with Louis Armstrong, and did extensive international touring. The death of Freddie Assunto in 1966 brought the Dukes back to New Orleans in 1967; six years later Frank passed away, ending the predominance of the family in the band. The Dukes continued with a new lineup, and in the late 70s established itself as a tourist attraction once again in its own nightclub atop the Montleone Hotel in the French Quarter, and is holding forth to this day at Lulu White's Mahogany Hall, on Bourbon Street. In all its manifestations, the Dukes of Dixieland has offered listeners a snappy, toe-tapping style of jazz which is at once musically and visually entertaining. –BR

○ **Best Of / CBS / BB 10**   1962
A collection of the Assunto's most popular material, delivered with vim and vigor. –BR

Best Of / PRO ARTE-PRO JAZZ   i 1987
The tradition continues with a modern version of the Dukes — still on Bourbon Street! –BR

Dukes of Dixieland / HINDSIGHT
Straightforward, often enjoyable cuts. –RW

Hearing Is Believing / LEI
A bit more upbeat than usual. –RW

FIONNA DUNCAN

Trad, swing, ballads. Scottish jazz and old-time pop-vocalist Fionna Duncan's vocal style is part silk and part sandpaper. She is a hidden treasure with a delightful persona. –MGN

○ **Fiona's Fellas / FATT**   ca. 1982
This Scottish jazz singer in an early period, traditional vein. Loads of fun. –MGN

Come & Get It / VELOCE   ca. 1985
Teamed with reed man Eggy Ley's Hot Shots. Duncan's gutsy voice shines on this set. –MGN

EDDIE DURAN   b 1925

Latin. A solid mainstream jazz player best known for his 70s and 80s recordings on Concord. His most interesting release conceptually, *Jazz Guitarist* from 1957, has recently been reissued. –RW

Jazz Guitarist / OJC   1957
○ **Ginza / CONCORD**   1979
Tasteful, restrained mainstream material. –RW

JOHNNY DYANI   1945-1986

Post-bop, early free, progressive big band, world fusion modern creative. This South African bassist, pianist, and composer was a highly influential figure in the progressive jazz of the 70s and 80s. –MGN

Song for Biko / STEEPLECHASE   1978
W/ Don Cherry (cnt). Very enjoyable progressive music. –MGN

○ **Afrika / STEEPLECHASE**   1983
The South African bassist/pianist/composer with septet. Well-respected as a musician worldwide. A unique amalgam of styles. –MGN

ALLEN EAGER   b 1927

Bop, hard-bop. Tenor saxophonist Eager began as a swing-era player with Tommy Dorsey as a teen, but he made the switch to bop in the 40s and remained proficient at swing as well. He worked with Buddy Rich and Tadd Dameron in the late 40s and 50s, then made infrequent appearances through the mid and late 50s both abroad and in America. He made a brief jazz return in the 80s. –RW

○ **Tenor Sax / SAVOY**   1947
A lyrical, swinging session by this saxophonist. –DS

New Trends in Jazz / SAVOY   i 1953
Renaissance / UPTOWN   1982
A notable return of the driving, tenor saxophonist. –DS

JON EARDLEY   b 1928

Bop, hard-bop, post-bop. Trumpeter of the 50s post-bop era. Played with Buddy Rich and Gerry Mulligan. –MGN

○ **From Hollywood to New York / OJC**   1954
This has an interesting East/West Coast combative quality, with nice work by J. R. Monterose (ts). –RW

In Hollywood / NEW JAZZ   i 1954
Hey There / PRESTIGE   i 1955
Jon Eardley Seven / PRESTIGE   1956

A good septet date, but uneven compositions. –RW

CHARLES EARLAND   b 1941

Post-bop, blues-jazz, soul jazz. Originally a saxophonist from Philadelphia, Earland started out working with Jimmy McGriff and was leading his own band by the early 60s. Unable to keep organists in his group, he switched to the Hammond organ in 1963 and later played that instrument with Lou Donaldson. Forming his own organ trio, he recorded *Black Talk* in 1969, a commercial success. A groove player, Earland went on to make many albums in the soul-jazz vein. –JME

★ **Black Talk / OJC**   1969
This is hot sixties organ-combo work. Earland derives his reputation from cuts like "The Mighty Burner," "More Today Than Yesterday".... in fact, this whole album. Soul-jazz with a kicker. –JME

Living Black / PRESTIGE   1970
Funky taste of soul done at the Key Club in Newark. W/ Grover Washington, Jr. –RW

Charles III / PRESTIGE   1972
Sparkling vocals by Joe Lee Wilson. –RW

☆ **Leaving This Planet / PRESTIGE**   1973
Great stints by Joe Henderson (sax), Eddie Henderson (tpt), and Freddie Hubbard (tpt). His most ambitious album. –RW

Smokin' / MUSE   1977
Mama Roots / MUSE   1977
Impressive reunion with George Coleman (ts). –RW

Pleasant Afternoon / MUSE   1978
○ **Front Burner / MILESTONE**   1988
Comeback for veteran organist. "Mom & Dad" (in 10/4 time) is infectious. –MGN

Third Degree Burn / MILESTONE   1989
Sparkling funky tenor from David "Fathead" Newman and solid organ from Earland. –RW

BILL EASLEY

Post-bop, neo bop. One of the most versatile reed players among the current crew, Easley plays alto, tenor, baritone, clarinet, and flute with equal clarity and skill. During the 60s, he moved to Memphis from the East Coast and attended MSU. He played in Stax and Isaac Hayes bands in the 70s. Since the mid 70s, he has been a busy session man and periodic bandleader. –RW

○ **Wind Inventions / SUNNYSIDE**   r 1988
Premier clarinetist in a neo-contemporary setting. Very attractive music. –MGN

First Call / MILESTONE   1990
Blues and bop from versatile saxophonist. Includes notable appearances by old and new Memphis jazz stars from George Caldwell to Bill Mobley. –RW

BILLY ECKSTINE   b 1914

Big band, bop, ballads. He could have been a great trombonist; instead, Billy Eckstine parlayed his rich, deep voice and suave personality and looks into a career as a romantic idol. He had a revolutionary big band in the 40s, which he had to disband due to economics. A careful shift from a strict jazz-based style, where the instrumentalist may surpass the singer, to lush MOR ballads made him a superstar, and he has remained among the most popular for sentimental fare. –RW

★ **Mister B. & the Band / SAVOY**   1945
1945-1946. Landmark recordings from whence bop partly (maybe fully) emerged. Album has incredible personnel and great vocals. –RW

Mister B. Sings / SAVOY   194?
More from the same period as *Mister B. and the Band*. –RW

○ **At Basin Street East / MERCURY**   ca. 1962
A 1990 reissue of a fine live date with Quincy Jones leading the orchestra and writing the tracks. –RW

○ **Sings with Benny Carter / POLYGRAM** 1987
A super Grammy-nominated set that showed neither Eckstine nor Carter (as) was ready for the rocking chair. –RW

○ **Everything I Have Is Yours / POLYGRAM** COMP
1947-1957. Sessions with various big bands (Sonny Bucke, Hugo Winterhalter, Russ Case, Pete Rugolo, Woody Herman, Nelson Riddle, Metronome All Stars) plus two cuts with Sarah Vaughan. Mostly ballads. –MGN

HARRY EDISON   b1915

Swing, big band, bop. Trumpeter. Few players deserve the description of being "natural" players, but Harry "Sweets" Edison merits it. An early Louis Armstrong disciple, Edison began in territory bands before coming to New York in the 30s. He joined Basie in 1938 and stayed until 1950. He worked in the studios and, in the early 50s, began an association with Frank Sinatra. Through the 50s, 60s, and 70s, he stayed busy on all fronts: touring, bandleading, and recording. Edison was once a mercurial, rampaging trumpeter, but later was a reserved, elegant stylist. He revolutionized the use of the mute and perfected lengthy solos without losing creativity or ideas. –RW

● **The Swinger / VERVE** r1959
Both torrid and mellow — this is striking Edison. –RW

The Inventive Mr. Edison / PACIFIC r1961
Crisp, crackling, and declarative Edison trumpet. –RW

○ **Jawbreakers / OJC** 1962
Solid, inviting duo work, matching Edison with Eddie "Lockjaw" Davis (ts). –RW

Opus Funk / STORYVILLE 1976
Nice straightahead date. –RW

Blues for Basie / PABLO 1977
Just delightful mid and uptempo blues and ballads. –RW

Just Friends / PABLO 1978
Super pairing with Zoot Sims (ts). –RW

Jazz at the Philharmonic / PABLO 1983
Great exchanges with Al Grey (tb) and Eddie "Lockjaw" Davis (ts). Fine solos. –RW

○ **For My Pals / PABLO** 1988
Trumpeter Edison never sounded better than on this studio date. Highly recommended. –MGN

TEDDY EDWARDS   b1924

Big band, bop, hard-bop, post-bop, cool. Tenor saxophonist Edwards is known as a West Coast player, but he was born in Jackson, MS, and stayed there until 1944, when he moved to Los Angeles. The deep-blues and jump-shuffle influences in his solos show his Southern and Southwestern roots. Edwards switched from alto to tenor when he worked with Howard McGhee in the 40s. He did battle with Dexter Gordon and later played with Red Callender, Benny Carter, Gerald Wilson, and the Max Roach-Clifford Brown quintet. Edwards has been a bandleader since 1958 and has done a little session work. –RW

The Foremost / ONYX ca.1947
Breakout, formative sessions by Delta saxist turned West Coast player. Reissue. –RW

Central Avenue Breakdown / ONYX 1948
Definitive portrait of emerging Black jazz scene on the West Coast. Not exactly "cool" or "hot." Fine playing by Hampton Hawes (p), Red Callender (b), and Benny Bailey (tpt). –RW

Teddy's Ready / CONTEMPORARY 1960
This is one of four worthy albums Edwards cut in an early-60s run. –RW

● **Together Again! / OJC** 1961
Dynamite pairing with Howard McGhee (tpt). Incredible piano by Phineas Newborn Jr. (p) –RW

Good Gravy! / OJC 1961
Earthy at times and sentimental in other places. –RW

Heart and Soul / OJC 1962

A welcome reissue. Warm, appealing, and engaging mainstream fare. –RW

Nothing But the Truth / PRESTIGE 1966
Taut, tough, but almost impossible to find. –RW

It's Alright / PRESTIGE 1967
Fine New York sessions, breezy tenor. –RW

○ **Feelin's / MUSE** 1974
This session finds Edwards in good swinging company. All originals (except "Georgia On My Mind"). Forthright and well done. –RW

Inimitable / XANADU / DB 5 1976
Steady, high-standard mainstream. –RW

Out of This World / STEEPLECHASE 1980
Representative of his output in style and tone. –RW

MARTY EHRLICH

Modern creative. A former member of the St. Louis-based Black Artist Group (BAG), Ehrlich epitomizes the contemporary African-American improviser with socio-political and musical concerns. He is a gifted saxophonist whose work tries mightily to embrace many idioms and appeal across the board. He's not a fusion player, though he welcomes fans from all genres. –RW

Emergency Peace / NEW WORLD 1990
A fascinating blend of improvisation and original structures. –MB

Traveller's Tale / RHINO / DB 5 r1990

○ **Falling Man / MUSE**

EITHER/ORCHESTRA

Post-bop, progressive big band, jazz-rock, neo bop, modern creative. Boston-bred ten-piece group led by saxophonist, composer, and arranger Russ Gershon. Plays a wide range of music, from Ellingtonia and Basie to mutated Bennie Moten and Fletcher Henderson, Sun Ra and South African township music, distorted rock motifs inspired by Miles Davis, and creative originals that borrow heavily from Oliver Lake and Julius Hemphill to Robert Fripp and the blues. About as diverse as music gets. –MGN

Dial E / ACCURATE 1986
First album features two Russ Gershon originals and one each by Thelonious Monk, Sonny Rollins, and Roland Kirk. It's a fine debut, as they feel their way around new jazz music. –MGN

Radium / ACCURATE 1987
Includes three standards and five originals. Trombonist Curtis Hasselbring and baritone saxophonist Charles Kohlhase stand out as soloists. "Born in a Suitcase" and Roscoe Mitchell's "Odwalla" are the best tracks. –MGN

○ **The Half-life of Desire / ACCURATE** ca.1989
Led by saxophonist/composer Russ Gershon, this shows progressive sensibilities with jazz aesthetics. Recorded at Van Gelder's, this album features great originals and interesting twists on "Temptation," "Circle in the Round/I Got it Bad and That Ain't Good," and King Crimson's "Red." –MGN

ROY ELDRIDGE   b1911

Swing, big band, bop, cool. Dubbed "Little Jazz," the compact bundle of energy that was Roy Eldridge was all jazz. No one loved playing or was more competitive. He took the innovations of Louis Armstrong a step higher and faster, and added harmonic daring that captured the ear of young Dizzy illespie, whose idol Roy became. As a soloist in many big bands, including those of Teddy Hill (with whom he made his first important records in 1935) and Fletcher Henderson, and on many great small-group sides with Billie Holiday and Teddy Wilson (1935-1941), Roy's style was studied by every trumpeter of the day, but it was his sensational flights with his own swinging little band in 1937 that really showed what this "Wizard of the Trumpet" could do. In 1941, he became the first Black musician to join an otherwise White band (Gene Krupa's) not just as a featured attraction or singer, but as a regular member of the section. He played the same role with Artie Shaw a few years later. After 1945, he strictly led his own bands, big or small, though he joined other stars in *Jazz at the Philharmonic*, of which he was a mainstay from the 40s through the 70s. In JATP, he was often teamed with Coleman Hawkins; these two giants also worked a lot together on their own. A 1980 heart attack put an end to Roy's trumpeting, but he was a fine singer and continued to perform occasionally in that role until his death. He was one of the most exciting players in the history of the music. –DM

★ **After You've Gone / GRP**   1930
Excellent reissue of Decca material with mannerly solos from John Kirby (b) and Buster Bailey (cl), and some soul from Big Sid Catlett. A gorgeous collection. –RW

The Early Years / COLUMBIA   193?
A fine collection of 30s and 40s material, now deleted. –RW

○ **Little Jazz / CBS / DB 5**   193?
A 1989 Columbia reissue of 30s material; the top-notch trumpeter swings sweetly. –MGN

Uptown / CBS   1941
1941-1942. An outstanding compilation of some prime Eldridge cuts with Anita O'Day (v) & Krupa (d). Nice for those who only want a limited amount of his material. –RW

○ **On Keynote / POL**   194?
A very good collection of 40s Eldridge done for Keynote. The Coleman Hawkins quintet sides are particularly tasty. –RW

Roy Eldridge & the Swing Trumpets / VERVE   194?
A wonderful two-disc set with 40s Eldridge sessions. –RW

○ **Mexican Bandit Meets.... / FANTASY**   1973
Mexican Bandit Meets Pittsburgh Pirate. Interesting title for this wonderful collaboration between Eldridge and Paul Gonsalves (ts); a delightful date. –RW

Jazz Maturity.... Where It's Coming From / PA2   1975
Two trumpeters in an upbeat mode. –MGN

Trumpet Kings at Montreux / PABLO   1975
W/ Dizzy Gillespie and Clark Terry. Good workout between these jazz immortals. –RW

Montreux 1977 / OJC / DB 5   1977
A session that is nice and hot. Fine Eldridge and excellent Oscar Peterson (p). –RW

Roy Eldridge Four / PABLO   1977
A good reissue of a live date from Montreux. –RW

Happy Time / OJC   1978
This is a 1991 reissue of a pleasant session with Oscar Peterson (p). –RW

ELEMENTS

Jazz-rock. Duo of Mark Egan and Danny Gottlieb who've recorded several albums on Antilles and Novus, working with such guest players as saxophonist Bill Evans and guitarist Steve Khan. –RW

○ **Spirit River / NOVUS**   r 1990
Airto (per) and Flora Purim (v) give session distinction. –RW
Illumination / NOVUS
Interesting group; Bill Evans on sax is the best improviser. –RW

THE ELEVENTH HOUSE

Jazz-rock. Early jazz-fusion rock. Guitarist Larry Coryell's pioneering fusion band of the early to mid 70s. Hard-edged sound — penetrating and loud. A great vehicle for Coryell. First three albums show most potential. Includes drummer Alphonse Mouzon, keyboardist Mike Mandel. –MGN

○ **Introducing the Eleventh House / VANGUARD**   1972
One of the quintessential fusion albums. –MGN

ELIANE ELIAS   b 1960

Latin, neo bop. Pianist Elias has found a niche doing updated Afro-Latin music. She's not as striking or sensual in her

delivery as numerous Portuguese and Latin vocalists. Her Blue Note releases have featured better jazz songs than Brazilian cuts. Married to trumpeter Randy Brecker –RW

○ **Cross Currents / DENON**   r 1989
This Brazilian pianist's best album to date, though it only scratches the surface of her immense talents. –MGN

So Far So Close / CAPITOL   1989
W/ backing from the Brecker brothers. –RW

A Long Story / CAPITOL
Her latest has more jazz content and more punch. –RW

DUKE ELLINGTON   1899-1974

Stride, swing, big band, cool, progressive big band. One of the greatest composers of the 20th Century and leader for 50 years of a band that became the greatest of all jazz orchestras, Ellington is, alongside Louis Armstrong, the dominant figure in jazz history. He began his career in his native Washington, D.C., and came to New York in 1924. His first group was a sextet; by the time his became the resident band at New York's Cotton Club in late 1927, it had grown to 11 pieces; by 1933, when it made its first visit to Europe, it had stabilized at 14 men. By that year, Ellington had reached his first peak as creator of the most original and personal big-band music in jazz. Throughout the 30s and into the first two years of the next decade the band enjoyed remarkable stability of personnel, enabling Ellington to use it as his "instrument." A remarkable group of soloists interpreted the music he wrote for them: trumpeter Cootie Williams; cornetist Rex Stewart; trombonists Lawrence Brown and "Tricky Sam" Nanton; clarinetist Barney Bigard; alto saxist Johnny Hodges; baritone saxist Harry Carney; and Duke himself at the piano. In 1939, tenorist Ben Webster and the sensational young bassist Jimmy Blanton joined. The 1940-1942 band is considered by some to have been Ellington's greatest; co-arranger and composer (and sometime pianist) Billy Strayhorn had also come on board by then. But Ellington continued to write great music and lead great bands until the final days. Such works as, for example, the suite *Such Sweet Thunder* (1957) equal anything in Ellingtonia. Among the musicians who starred in later editions of the band, trumpeter Clark Terry, cornetist and violinist Ray Nance, tenorist Paul Gonsalves, and clarinetist, arranger, and sometime tenorist Jimmy Hamilton must be noted. Key rhythm section players included pioneers Sonny Greer (drums) and Wellman Braud (bass), and, later Louis Bellson and Sam Woodyard (drums) and Oscar Pettiford (bass). Ellington's output was extraordinary, ranging from short pieces to suites, film scores, so-called "Sacred Concerts," and all-time hits like "Mood Indigo," "Solitude," "Sophisticated Lady," and "Satin Doll." Ellington made more records, including wonderful small-group things and piano features, than any other single performer in jazz, and treasures continue to be uncovered. –DM

Jungle Nights in Harlem / RCA   1927
Material from 1927-1932; 1991 reissue, good period cuts. CD has two bonus tracks. –RW

Early Ellington (1927-1934) / RCA   1927
Yet another collection of seminal early tracks. It really depends on individual preference which anthology you pick. –RW

Brunswick Era - Vol. I (1926-29) / MCA   192?
Nice 1990 reissue of his mid/late-20s cuts. The sessions have been reissued often. This version is nicely remastered. –RW

○ **Okeh Ellington / CBS**   192?
1991 reissue of tremendous material on Okeh label. –RW

Jungle Band 1929-1931 / MCA   192?
Companion volume to 1990 reissue, second set of late-20s and early-30s cuts. –RW

☆ **Braggin' in Brass / CBS**   1938
Wonderful two-record set of some essential sessions. –RW

Duke Ellington - 1938 / SMITHSONIAN   1938
Another superb look at a vital year. –RW

Duke Ellington - 1939 / SMITHSONIAN   1939
Marvelous anthology covering a prime year in his career. –RW
Blanton-Webster Band / RCA   1939
1939-1942. Important material, but there's some question about the sound quality and production of this set. –RW
○ **Back Room Romp / CBS**   193?
Fine late-30s small-band cuts, many of them hard to find. –RW
At Fargo / BOOK-OF-THE-MONTH / DB 5   1940
Amazing three-volume set. Available only via mail-order. –RW
★ **Carnegie Hall Concerts: 1943-1947 / PRESTIGE**   1943
• Here is a more in-depth presentation of Black Brown, & Beige concerts. A series of four two-record sets covering each year completely. –RW
● **Black Brown & Beige / RCA / DB 5**   194?
Outstanding three-disc set that collects his somewhat controversial mid- and late-40s concert recordings into one nice package. –RW
Back to Back / POLYGRAM   195?
Nice late-50s cuts. –RW
Great Times / RIVERSIDE   r 1950
Overlooked pairing of Duke and his greatest pupil/cohort, Billy Strayhorn. –RW
1953 - Pasadena Concert / GNP-CRESCENDO   1953
1986 reissue of a great live concert. –RW
1954 - Los Angeles Concert / GNP-CRESCENDO   1954
1987 reissue of excellent date. –RW
● **Drum Is a Woman / COLUMBIA / DB 5**   1956
Incredible concept album. –RW
At Newport / CBS / BB 14   1956
1987 reissue of his landmark concert. –RW
○ **Duke Ellington - Vols. 1 -10 / ATLANTIC**   1956
1956-1970. This essential series came from his private collection; many brilliant cuts and well worth having. Hard to separate any of the individual volumes. Studio and dance sessions/suites. –RW
☆ **Ellington Indigos / CBS**   1957
1989 reissue of some excellent recordings. –RW
○ **Anatomy of a Murder / RYKO**   1959
This movie soundtrack makes most intriguing listening. –MGN
Live - Newport Jazz Festival 1959 / POLYGRAM   1959
Prime cuts from his Newport sessions. –RW
Jazz Party / CBS   195?
Nice mid-50s date, which has been reissued as part of masterpieces series. –RW
○ **Side by Side / POLYGRAM**   195?
Joyous 1986 reissue of magnificent late-50s small-group material. –RW
Uptown / CBS   195?
Collection of two good 50s sets. –RW
Blues in Orbit / CBS   1960
1988 reissue of nice album. –RW
○ **Money Jungle / BLUE NOTE**   1962
Trio with Charles Mingus, Duke Ellington (p), and Max Roach (d). Great music, easy to listen to. –MK
● **Duke Ellington & John Coltrane / MCA**   1962
Jazz immortals collaborate. Mostly pristine music. –MGN
Featuring Paul Gonsalves / OJC   1962
Excellent session; reissued in 1991. –RW
○ **First Time! Count Meets Duke / CBS**   r 1962
Nice collaboration between longtime contemporaries. –RW
● **Duke Ellington Meets Coleman Hawkins / MCA**   r 1963
A landmark meeting, still among the most hypnotic albums ever on Impulse. This is a 1986 reissue of marvelous small-combo work. –RW
New Mood Indigo / DOCTOR JAZZ   1964
1989 reissue of some good material. –RW
Never-Before-Released Recordings / MUM   1965

1965-1972. Some interesting newly discovered material. –RW
Far East Suite / RCA / DB 5   1966
A definitive work. –MGN
★ **His Mother Called Him Bill / RCA**   1967
Acclaimed work w/ Billy Strayhorn. Desert island music. –MGN
Latin American Suite / OJC / DB 5   1968
Recommended. –MGN
○ **Soul Call / VERVE**   1968
1968 live recording from the Antibes Jazz Festival with an extended "La Plus Belle Africaine." Extraordinary late-period Ellington. –MGN
Yale Concert / OJC / DB 5   1968
Prime 1991 reissue of a superb concert. –RW
☆ **Great Paris Concert / ATLANTIC**   196?
Sensational recordings done in Paris during 60s, not issued in America till 70s, reissued on CD recently. –RW
Hot Summer Dance / CBS   196?
1991 reissue. Some interesting recordings for a 60s dance. –RW
Intimacy of the Blues / OJC   196?
1991 release of some fine late-60s, early-70s cuts. –RW
Up in Duke's Workshop / OJC   196?
Nice 1991 reissue of late-60s, early-70s material. –RW
○ **Second Sacred Concert / PRESTIGE / DB 5**   1970
The first and second volumes are a must-buy. –MGN
☆ **New Orleans Suite / ATLANTIC / DB 5**   1970
Amazing 70s set, w/ the final appearance on record of Johnny Hodges. –RW
Afro-Eurasian Eclipse / OJC   r 1971
Fine 70s material. –RW
Duke's Big 4 / PABLO   r 1976
Wonderful quartet date. –RW
This One's for Blanton / PABLO / DB 5   r 1976
These are sublime duets. Some of Ray Brown's best bass work on record. –RW
Symphony in Black / SMITHSONIAN   r 1982
Great Ellington compositions done by Smithsonian Jazz Repertory Ensemble. –RW
Digital Duke / MCA-GRP   r 1987
Recent material, with the band led by Duke's son Mercer. –RW
○ **All Star Road Band - Vols. 1 & 2 / CBS**
Newly discovered and super Ellington dates. –RW
Ellington Suites / OJC
Recommended. –MGN
Essence of Duke Ellington / CBS
Greatest Jazz Concert in the World / PA2
A fine three-record set. The title is pretentious, but the album does offer plenty of great music and a cross-section of swing, mainstream, and blues. –RW
Happy Reunion / CBS
1991 recordings of recently issued material. –RW
Harlem / PA2
Good live dates. –RW
In the Uncommon Market / PABLO
1987 live set of then rediscovered trio cuts. –RW
Indigos / CBS
Fine reissue of some loose sessions. –RW
Memories of Duke / ATLANTIC
Music Is My Mistress / MUM
The Pianist / COLUMBIA
Some of his greatest piano solos on record. –RW
☆ **The Piano Album / CAPITOL**
Rare example of his piano prowess, 1989 reissue. –RW
Piano Duets-Great Times! / OJC
Essential Duke and Swe' Pea. –MGN
Recollections of the Big Band Era / ATLANTIC
Superb recordings. –RW
Small Groups - Vol. 1 / CBS

Solos, Duets & Trios / RCA
A 1990 reissue of amazing and ahead-of-their-time cuts. Ellington shows his keyboard skills; Jimmy Blanton his bass prowess. –RW

Three Suites / CBS
Recommended. –MGN

Best of Duke Ellington / PA2   COMP
Misleading title but a very good anthology covering 40s-70s tracks. –RW

Best of Duke Ellington / CBS   COMP
1989 compilation of recently discovered material. –RW

Duke's Men: Small Groups - Vol. 1 / CBS   COMP
Fine 1991 reissue of great combos led by Ellingtonians, a few also with the Duke. –RW

○ **Sophisticated Ellington / RCA**   COMP
This is a wonderful two-record set of material ranging from the 20s to the 60s. –RW

DON ELLIS   1934-1978

Hard-bop, post-bop, progressive big band. Innovative composer/trombonist/trumpeter. Early period 50s recordings show progressive bent. Albums in the 60s on the electric side. A fine improviser, but most well known for inventing split meter time signatures. Works in progressive big band format for the most part. –MGN

How Time Passes / CANDID   1960
Some of his better straight jazz playing. –RW

Out of Nowhere / CANDID   1961

○ **New Ideas / OJC / DB 5**   1961
The original thinking-jazz-lover's music. –MGN

Live in 3 2/3/4 Time / PACIFIC   1966
Unorthodox playing in varying time and musical contexts, done live at Monterey in the mid 60s. –RW

Electric Bath / COLUMBIA / DB 5   ca. 1968
Intriguing experiments with time and musical settings. –RW

At the Fillmore / COLUMBIA   1970
The release that helped break him into a mass audience. It is live, daring, loud, annoying, and distinctive all at once. –RW

Haiku / BASF   1973
Striking, surging, and unpredictable. –RW

Live at Montreux / ATLANTIC   1977
Six pieces with big band and strings (21 pieces in all). John McLaughlin-influenced "The Sporting Dance" is a highlight. Lots of interplay, excellent solos from saxophonists Ann Patterson and Ted Nash, and Ellis on quarter-tone trumpet and the superbone. –MGN

HERB ELLIS   b 1921

Swing, big band, bop, cool. Ellis began as a banjo player in his childhood and learned the rudiments of guitar on his own before attending North Texas State College with Jimmy Giuffre and Gene Roland. He got his start in the mid 40s with the Casa Loma Orchestra and Jimmy Dorsey band. In 1947 he formed the Soft Winds trio, a unit that echoed the influence of the Nat King Cole trio right down to Ellis's guitar lines underneath pianist Lou Carter's leads and bassist John Frigo's accompaniment. The trio stayed together until 1952 and had the successful song "Detour Ahead" recorded by Billie Holiday. Ellis replaced Barney Kessel in Oscar Peterson's group in 1953 and attained stature and stardom. He has worked extensively with Ray Brown since the 70s. Exhaustive studio and session and recording work hasn't dulled his passion. He is a prototype jazz guitarist in the Charlie Christian tradition. –RW

Windflower / CONCORD
With fellow guitarist Remo Palmier and quartet. More light swing. –MGN

Nothing But the Blues / VERVE / DB 5   1957
Wonderful, elegant, with a dose of funk blues and ballads. –RW

○ **Herb Ellis Meets Jimmy Giuffre / VERVE**   1959

Unusual team; Giuffre (sax) fits in effectively. –RW

Thank You Charlie Christian / VERVE   ca. 1961
60s date in tribute to the early jazz-guitar great. Ellis does Christian proud. –MGN

Herb Ellis & Stuff Smith / COLUMBIA   1963
Smith soars on violin; Ellis proves able to work alongside. –RW

Herb Ellis & Charlie Byrd / COLUMBIA   1963
Lush, romantic, and intriguing. –RW

Jazz at Concord / CONCORD   1973
A wonderful collaboration with his old friend Joe Pass (g) on a standard, though nicely played, mainstream date. –RW

● **Seven Come Eleven / CONCORD / DB 5**   1973
Concord's second record. Titans clash. Great music. Good on CD. First-rate band doing prototype arrangements. –RW

Two for the Road / PABLO   1974
W/ Joe Pass. Exemplary two-guitar date. –RW

Soft Shoe / CONCORD / DB 5   1974
"Sweets" Edison (tpt) brings some fire to this Ellis/Ray Brown (b) set. –RW

Hot Tracks / CONCORD   1975
W/ Ray Brown Sextet. 1989 reissue of this session with Ray Brown (b) sharing the spotlight. –RW

Pair to Draw / CONCORD   1976
Nice and breezy. –RW

Wildflower / CONCORD   1977
Typically restrained, quietly swinging set. –RW

Soft & Mellow / CONCORD   1978
On-the-money title. Ellis shows the difference between restraint and detachment. W/ Ross Tompkins (p). –RW

Herb Ellis at Montreux / CONCORD   1979
Tasteful session at the famed Montreux festival. These old pros acquit themselves nicely. –RW

Herb Mix / CONCORD   1981
A good 80s date. –RW

○ **Doggin' Around / CONCORD**   1988
W/ "Far Side" artwork; Red Mitchell on bass. The CD has two bonus cuts. –MGN

RON ENGLISH   b 1941

Hard-bop, post-bop, early free, jazz-rock, contemporary funk. Veteran guitarist who plays in a variety of modes — progressive and creative, or more commercial. A completely original approach. –MGN

○ **From Now to Then / HOT DOC**   1981
The Detroit guitarist plays standards, modern, and contemporary with a distinctive flair. Steve Wood is quite noticeable on the sax and flute. Bob Allison plays vibes, with Dan Spencer on drums, and John Dana and Don Mayberry playing exceptional bass. –MGN

BOBBY ENRIQUEZ   b 1943

Post-bop, Latin. "The Madman from Mindinao." Philippine pianist is an absolutely wired player, on all the time — virtuosic beyond belief. Plays standards and powerfully, a great inventor. Not a pussycat. Mostly plays with a trio. His live performances are electrifying. –MGN

Live in Tokyo - Vols. 1 & 2 / GNP CRESCENDO   1982
Twin set of above-average Enriquez sessions. –RW

Prodigious Piano / GNP CRESCENDO   1982
Excellent trio date. –MGN

Live at Concerts by the Sea - Vol. 1 & 2 / GNP   1985
Much more exuberant than the prototype fusion dates this label churns out religiously. –RW

○ **Wild Piano / CBS**   1987
Filipino "Wild man from Mindanao" plays fiercely probing trio jazz. Look for GNP albums too. –MGN

PETER ERSKINE   b 1954

Progressive big band, jazz-rock, neo bop. A drummer who started with bands of Stan Kenton and Maynard Ferguson, then joined Weather Report. Ability is unquestioned — can swing hard or play dance rhythms. One of the most well-rounded drummers in contemporary music. Solo albums range from neo-bop to futuristic-fusion. –MGN

○ **Peter Erskine / OJC**   1982
First release by a first-rate drummer and lots of New York friends. "All's Well that Ends" is a winning track, as is "Leroy St." –MGN

Transition / DENON   1986
Some fine, if erratic, compositions. –RW

Motion Poet / DENON   1988
An excellent percussionist makes an uneven, but ambitious statement. –RW

BOOKER ERVIN   1931-1970

Hard-bop, post-bop. A marvelous robust tenor saxophonist and a prime example of the huge "Texas Tenor" style, Ervin played trombone as a child and later studied tenor and music theory at Berklee. He played in the Air Force Band in 1951-1952, then toured from 1954 to 1958 in Ernie Fields's R&B band. From the late 50s and often throughout the 60s, Ervin worked with Charles Mingus's Jazz Workshop groups, where his honking, funky sound was ideal for those compositions that featured a pronounced gospel or blues tone. Ervin also worked with Randy Weston, Dexter Gordon, Horace Parlan, and Ted Curson in the 60s, while making a number of marvelous albums as a leader. –RW

○ **The Book Cooks / AFFINITY / DB 5**   1960
Robust, earthy Ervin throughout. This tremendous combo date was originally on Bethlehem. –RW

Down in the Dumps / SAVOY   1960
An explosive set from Ervin's prime period, reissued on disc with additional material from the following year (1961), with trombonist Dr. Billy Howell. –RW

That's It / CANDID   1961
This is an outstanding date, but hard to find. –RW

○ **Back from the Gig / BLUE NOTE / DB 5**   1963
1963 and 1968 tracks from the extraordinary tenor saxophonist. –MGN

★ **Freedom and Space Sessions / PRESTIGE**   1963
paris blu*The Freedom Book* (1963) and *The Space Book* (1964). Two albums covering some prime Ervin cuts on Prestige. –RW

Song Book / PRESTIGE   1964
Blues Book / PRESTIGE   1964
Setting the Pace / PRESTIGE   1965
This is an earthy, booming workout with Dexter Gordon (ts) aboard. –RW

The Trance / PRESTIGE   1965
This one's both soulful and thoughtful. –RW

Heavy! / PRESTIGE   1966
Some soul, some funk, and lots of power. –RW

Groovin' High / PRESTIGE   r 1966
Booker and Brass / PACIFIC   1967
Stirring Ervin tenor in a big-band setting. –RW

The In Between / BLUE NOTE   1968
For the more adventurous. With Bobby Few on piano and Richard Williams on trumpet, Ervin veers between inside and outside jazz. –RW

RON ESCHETE   b 1951

Post-bop, neo bop. This West Coast guitarist is able to pop off bop phrases or fusion licks. He prefers a modern approach. Excellent studio musician. –MGN

○ **Stump Jumper / BAINBRIDGE**   1984

Music Map

Jazz Clarinet

First Used in Brass Bands
New Orleans Players
John Casimir — Polo Barnes — George Lewis

Sammy Rimington

Creole Musicians
Lorenzo Tio Family (1893-1933) — Alphonse Picou (1878-1961)

Major Clarinetists
Sidney Bechet (1897-1959) — Barney Bigard (1906-1927)
Albert Nicholas (1900-1973) — Edmond Hall 1901-1967)
Pee Wee Russell (1906-1969) — Frank Teschemacher (1906-1932)
Artie Shaw (1910) — Jimmy Noone (1895-1944)
Benny Goodman (1909-1986)

The rise of the saxophone limits clarinet use.

Benny Goodman Tradition
Peanuts Hucko (1918) — Aaron Sachs (1923) — Bob Wilber (1928)

Bass Clarinet
Eric Dolphy (1928-1964) — Bennie Maupin (1940)
Howard Johnson (1941) — David Muray (1955)

Modernists
John Carter (1929) — Perry Robinson (1938)
Anthony Braxton (1945) — John LaPorta (1920)
Jimmy Giuffre (1921) — Tony Scott (1921)
Buddy De Franco (1923) — Bill Smith (1926)
Rahsaan Roland Kirk (1936-1977)

1980s John Carter's clarinet quartet

1980s-1990s
Eddie Daniels (1941) — Wendell Harrison

CHRISTIAN ESCOUDE   b 1947

World fusion, modern creative. Gypsy guitarist uses unusual harmonic technique in creative/modern/fusion idioms. Elusive personality, hard to pin down, but a virtuoso any way you hear him. –MGN

○ **Gipsy Waltz / POLYGRAM**   1989
Mainstream/fusion fare with a tilt toward the international market. –RW

PETE ESCOVEDO

Latin, jazz-rock. A veteran Latin session percussionist and bandleader who's unfortunately better known as being the father of one-time Prince protégé and confidante Sheila E, than as a fine rhythmmaker and player. He made a pair of excellent albums for Concord in the late 80s, working with a 12-to-16-piece band. –RW

○ **Yesterday's Memories / CROSSOVER**   1985
Yesterday's Memories — Tomorrow's Dreams. Some fusion mixed in with Latin jazz by Escovedo's 12-piece group. –RW

Mister E / CONCORD   1987
This is a little on the erratic side. Pete Escovedo leads a 16-piece group. –RW

AYDIN ESEN   b 1962

Post-bop, neo bop. Turkish-born modern jazz pianist who favors both fusion and New York neo-bop. Good young player whose best years lie ahead. −MGN

○ **Aydin Esen / RHINO**
Turkish jazz pianist in a trio context. Very good. Bassist is Eddie Gomez. −MGN

ETERNAL WIND

World fusion. Post-*Bitches Brew* band using dense rhythmic textures and jungle melodies. Features trumpeter Charles Moore, percussionists Adam Rudolph and Hank Drake. World music extensions with jazz background. −MGN

Eternal Wind / FLYING FISH

KEVIN EUBANKS　　　　　　　　　　　　　　b 1957

Instr-pop, neo bop, M-base. Fusion guitarist who has concentrated on funk, but is also capable of playing excellent jazz. An adept neo-classicist as well. Early albums show great potential, good improviser, readily identifiable sound. −MGN

Guitarist / ELEKTRA　　　　　　　　　　　　　　1982
Produced by Michael Gibbs. Acoustic guitar solos and group works, with Ralph Moore (ts), Roy Haynes (d), Charles David (p), and Robin Eubanks (tb). This is a fine debut album. −MGN

● **Opening Nights / GRP　　　　　　　　　　　　　1985**
By far his best. Accept no substitute. −MGN

Promise of Tomorrow / GRP　　　　　　　　　　r 1990
Good, has real jazz content. −RW

ROBIN EUBANKS

Neo bop, M-base, modern creative. Trombone-playing brother of Kevin. Use of multi-phonics, overdubbing, or teaming with other trombonists shows willingness to experiment. Promising young contemporary jazz player should do great things. −MGN

○ **Dedication / POLYGRAM**
W/ Steve Turre. Two trombonists live up to their reputations with much vital music. −MGN

● **Different Perspectives / JMT (JAZZ MUSIC TODAY)**
Exceptional first album from this trombonist. A great listening album w/ many components, mostly in a progressive vein. −MGN

Karma / POLYGRAM
A noteworthy experimental session with both pop and improvisational elements. −RW

BILL EVANS　　　　　　　　　　　　　　　1929-1980

Cool. Arguably the most lyrical and expressionistic of all jazz pianists, Bill Evans was an extraordinary player and soloist from his first album as a leader in 1956 until his death. He did his best work by far in the trio mode, where his touch, technique, facility, phrasing, and imagination were at their peak. He was a member of the pivotal Miles Davis unit that helped popularize modal jazz, and even his detractors had to admire Evans's skill while they bemoaned the alleged lack of energy and vitality in his solos. Evans worked for a time with Tony Scott and also spent eight months with Miles Davis but otherwise led his own groups. He did have important collaborations during his career with Charles Mingus, Philly Joe Jones, and George Russell; still, his solo and trio releases are his most intriguing and memorable. His interplay with bassists Scott LaFaro and later Eddie Gomez were very distinctive, especially the range that Evans would display and the answering lines and directions that LaFaro and Gomez would craft. He also proved a wonderful partner to singer Tony Bennett and guitarist Jim Hall and made some Grammy-winning releases through clever incorporation of multi-tracking. His complete Riverside and Fantasy recordings have been compiled and released in two huge boxed sets. −RW

New Jazz Conceptions / OJC　　　　　　　　　1956

This was his first — a stirring debut. −RW

Everybody Digs Bill Evans / OJC　　　　　　　1958
A worthy session with the great Philly Joe Jones drumming. Bonus cut on the CD issue. −RW

○ **Undercurrent / CAPITOL　　　　　　　　　　1959**
A must-have reissue of brilliant date with Jim Hall (g). −RW

Portrait in Jazz / OJC / DB 5　　　　　　　　1959
Here is an excellent reissue of a solid concert, with some typically stunning Scott LaFaro on bass. −RW

Explorations / OJC　　　　　　　　　　　　　1961
In this wonderful date, Paul Motian opens up new fields as a drummer. −RW

● **Sunday at the Village Vanguard / RIVERSIDE　1961**
Crisp, constantly changing, and delightful. −RW

Waltz for Debby / OJC　　　　　　　　　　　1961
Highly recommended. −MGN

Village Vanguard Sessions / MILESTONE　　　1961
This is a collection of several fine 60s cuts that are all available elsewhere. Aimed at the budget-conscious. −RW

How My Heart Sings / OJC　　　　　　　　　1962
More from the Evans-Chuck Israels- Paul Motian lineup. −RW

Moon Beams / RIVERSIDE　　　　　　　　　1962
Top trio again features Evans, Israels (b), and Motian (d). −RW

Interplay / OJC　　　　　　　　　　　　　　1962
A dazzling small-group date with top-flight Freddie Hubbard (tpt). 1987 reissue. −RW

Solo Sessions - Vol. 1 & 2 / MILESTONE　　　1963
Fine, decisive Evans. −RW

Conversations with Myself / POLYGRAM / DB 5　1963
These stunning multiple-tracked piano solos won a Grammy in a rare acknowledgment of amazing achievement. Great playing and admirable use of multi-track technology. −RW

Bill Evans Trio at Shelly's Manne-Hole / OJC　1963
On this 1987 reissue of a super trio date, Chuck Israels is vastly different from Scott LaFaro on bass, yet equally effective. −RW

Trio 1964 / POLYGRAM　　　　　　　　　　1963
This is among his most captivating trio dates. −RW

☆ **Bill Evans at Town Hall / POLYGRAM　　　　1966**
Excellent and appealing, a wonderful live set. −RW

○ **Intermodulation / VERVE　　　　　　　　　1966**
A beautiful return engagement with Jim Hall (g). −RW

○ **At the Montreux Jazz Festival / VERVE　　　1968**
A superb trio date. Eddie Gomez (b) and Jack DeJohnette (d) are brilliant in accompanying roles. −RW

Alone / VERVE　　　　　　　　　　　　　　1968
Just what the title says, and beautifully done. −RW

Bill Evans Album / CBS　　　　　　　　　　1971
Displays his typically strong playing from that period. −RW

The Tokyo Concert / OJC / DB 5　　　　　　1973
Highly recommended. −MGN

Since We Met / OJC　　　　　　　　　　　1974
A new reissue of a worthy trio date. −RW

Intuition / OJC　　　　　　　　　　　　　1974
This is a wonderful pairing of musically attuned comrades Bill Evans and Eddie Gomez (b). −RW

Montreux 3 / OJC / DB 5　　　　　　　　　1975
The third time is certainly a charm for Evans. −RW

Quintessence / FANTASY　　　　　　　　　1976
This fine quintet set has a great lineup of first-rate horn players. −RW

Eloquence / FANTASY　　　　　　　　　　1976
Aptly titled and nicely done. −RW

○ **You Must Believe in Spring / WARNER　　　1977**
Highly recommended. −MGN

Affinity / WARNER　　　　　　　　　　　　1978

W/ Toots Thielemans (harmonica). A good date from his late-70s period. −RW

Paris Concert / ELEKTRA / DB 5 1979
Edition 1 & 2. The old master shows his new tricks. −RW

★ **Complete Fantasy Recordings / FANTASY** 197?
This gorgeous boxed set is a collection of his 70s selections. It covers everything in all contexts and is a must-have for piano fans. −RW

At the Village Vanguard / FANTASY
Simply uncanny; influential performances. −RW

Blue in Green / MILESTONE
Highly recommended. −MGN

Nirvana / ATLANTIC
W/ Dave Pile (vibes), Herbie Mann (fl). A nice date from a surprising team. −RW

Time Remembered / MILESTONE
Topflight mid-60s date. −RW

★ **Riverside Recordings / RIVERSIDE / DB 5** COMP
12 CDs. Fantasy/1985. All the marvelous Evans one could ever want is on this incredible 18-disc boxed set. It is a wonderful, comprehensive collection of superb performances, with some of his most majestic trio and solo dates. −RW

GIL EVANS 1912-1988

Progressive big band. Best known for his marvelous collaborations with Miles Davis, the self-taught arranger and reluctant pianist formed his first own band in Stockton, California at 21. In 1938, singer Skinnay Ennis fronted the band and Claude Thornhill came in as pianist and co-arranger. When Claude started his own band in 1941, he hired Gil. By the late 40s, Evans had started to incorporate the ideas of Charlie Parker and Dizzy Gillespie into his scores, and was one of the leading thinkers behind the *Birth of the Cool* recordings of Miles Davis, with whom he forged a lifelong friendship. When Miles signed with Columbia, he was able to bring Gil into the studios with a large ensemble, and the resultant albums — *Miles Ahead* (1957), *Porgy and Bess* (1958), *Sketches of Spain* (1959) — became milestones in the careers of both men. Because he was a perfectionist, with little regard for record company budgets, Evans did not work as much as he might have, but there were some fine albums in the 60s, and occasional club and concert work with a big band. In the next decades, Evans became more consistently visible and was able to keep fairly stable personnel together for long stretches of time; musicians wanted to work with him even when jobs and money were skimpy. Evans experimented with electronics and free-jazz improvisatory principles; he toured Europe with the band, and in his last years of life did some film scoring, was reunited with Miles in the studios, and visited Brazil. Insatiably curious about new musical ideas until the end, Gil Evans was a man who followed his own star. Miles Davis's final public appearance was in a tribute to Gil. −DM

Gil Evans & Ten / OJC 1957
Excellent arrangements, with a lineup and compositions that are of high quality. −RW

Great Jazz Standards / BLUE NOTE / DB 5 1959
1988 reissue of a brilliant album. −RW

○ **Out of the Cool / MCA / DB 5** 1960
You may want to find the companion album, *Into the Hot.* Challenging music. −MGN

Blues in Orbit / RHINO 1969
Plays the Music of Jimi Hendrix / RCA / DB 5 1974
Svengali / ATLANTIC / DB 5 1974
Priestess / POLYGRAM 1977
● **Live at Sweet Basil - Vols. 1 & 2 / CAPITOL-RHINO** 1984
Definitive live sets that are must-buys. Progressive orchestra zenith. −MGN

Rhythm-A-Ning / EMARCY 1987
A joint effort, nicely done. −RW

Paris Blues / RHINO / DB 5 r 1988
A new summit of a great arranger and an unorthodox, distinctive soprano saxophonist, Steve Lacy. −RW

JON FADDIS b 1953

Hard-bop, post-bop. The charge of being a Dizzy Gillespie clone has dogged Jon Faddis during much of his career. He began trumpet studies at eight and was a regular with R&B bands at thirteen. After some early-70s stints with Lionel Hampton, Gil Evans, Charles Mingus, and the Jones-Lewis big band, he began guesting with Gillespie in 1974, recording and playing with him and Oscar Peterson. Faddis's upper-register fireworks and a tendency to construct solos and play in a manner similar to Gillespie generated controversy for many years. Faddis retreated into the studios for a while in the 80s, then reappeared as an active player in 1985 at the Chicago Jazz Festival. −RW

○ **Youngblood / PABLO** 1976
This date with Kenny Barron Trio is an ode to Dizzy. −MGN

Good & Plenty / DCC 1978
Some bright, exciting trumpet solos. −RW

○ **Legacy / CONCORD** 1985
A tremendous mainstream session to which Harold Land (ts) and Kenny Barron (p) make excellent contributions. −RW

Into the Faddisphere / CBS 1989
Check out "Ciribiribin" for a taste of Faddis and his trumpet acrobatics. Also has pianist Renee Rosnes and drummer Ralph Peterson. −MGN

● **Hornucopia / CBS** 1990
This is his best release. He works with his idol Dizzy Gillespie (tpt), and makes a case for his own voice and style as well. −RW

MIKE FAHN

Neo bop. Valve trombonist from the West Coast. Plays a nice combination of Ellingtonia, West Coast cool, post-bop, and contemporary. A player to watch in the years ahead. −MGN

○ **Steppin' Out / CEXTON** 1989

CHARLES FAMBROUGH b 1950

Hard-bop, post-bop, progressive big band, neo bop. New Orleans-born bassist was prominent in 70s with McCoy Tyner and Art Blakey. He is a solid musician and composer, mostly in modern mainstream style, though he has played some fusion. −MGN

○ **Proper Angle / CTI**

GEORGIE FAME b 1943

Ballads. Known for pop-jazz hit maker in the 60s, "Yeah, Yeah," Based on the vocalese of Eddie Jefferson.

○ **Cool Cat Blues / RHINO**
Better known for rock/pop, Fame makes a good, sometimes worthy, jazz statement. −RW

TAL FARLOW b 1921

Bop, cool. A leading early bop guitarist, Tal Farlow helped define the modern jazz guitar with his great speed, technique, and flow of ideas. A self-taught, non-reading musician, he took up the instrument at a fairly late age and learned Charlie Christian solos by heart from records. Early performances with Red Norvo and Artie Shaw earned him acclaim as an inventive player; he won the *DOWN BEAT* critics "New Star Award" in 1954. Tal uses a special shorter fingerboard for looser tuning and softer sound. He was also an early explorer of artificial harmonics. In what may well be a positive testimony on his character, he never much liked the business side of the music world and the life on the road. Returning to his native North Carolina and working as a sign painter, he has been rather reclusive for many years, emerging only occasionally for recording and performances. −DNM

☆ **Tal / POLYGRAM** 1956

The great guitarist's best effort of the 50s. –MGN

Fuerst Set / XANADU 1956
Outstanding guitar and high-caliber work from Farlow and Eddie Costa (p). –RW

Second Set / XANADU / DB 5 1956
This is a fine reprise of material from Farlow and Eddie Costa (p). –RW

Poppin' and Burnin' / VERVE 195?
This is a fine two-record set of some cracking 50s sides. –RW

Tal Farlow Returns / OJC 1969
This exceptional release spotlights an often stunning guitar master. –RW

On Stage / CONCORD 1976
Farlow's reunion w/ Red Norvo (vib), plus Hank Jones (p) and Ray Brown (b). –RW

A Sign of the Times / CONCORD 1976
An album with excellent playing, with Ray Brown (b) and Hank Jones (p). –MGN

Tal Farlow 1978 / CONCORD 1977
Farlow tends to dominate this good trio date. –RW

Chromatic Palette / CONCORD 1981
Superior interaction with Tommy Flanagan (p). –RW

Cookin' on All Burners / CONCORD 1982
Excellent piano from James Williams, plus outstanding guitar by Farlow. –RW

The Legendary / CONCORD 1984
A good set. –RW

Guitar Player / PRESTIGE COMP
This fine compilation of Farlow's 60s Prestige material is hard to find. –RW

ART FARMER   b 1928

Bop, post-bop, cool, progressive big band. Farmer is a fine trumpeter who has become better known as a flugelhorn specialist. With his twin brother, Addison, he moved to Los Angeles from Phoenix in 1945 and got plenty of R&B experience in the Johnny Otis and Roy Porter bands while playing jazz with Gerald Wilson, Benny Carter, and Jay McShann. He really made his name in the 50s with Wardell Gray, Lionel Hampton, Gigi Gryce, Horace Silver, and Gerry Mulligan. Farmer relocated to New York in the 50s, then co-founded the Jazztet with Benny Golson in 1959. He later led a quartet with Jim Hall, then with Steve Kuhn. He is one of the finest interpreters and ballad players ever, and the flugelhorn was perfectly suited for his less aggressive, warm, and behind-the-beat phrasing. –RW

Art Farmer Quintet / OJC 1954
Good mainstream date. –RW

When Farmer Met Gryce / OJC 1954
A well-done teaming of Farmer and Gigi Gryce (as). –RW

Two Trumpets, with Donald Byrd / OJC 1956
This nice date puts two top trumpets together. –RW

★ **Farmer's Market / OJC** 1956
A top release from the 50s, with precise, deftly-played solos, compositions, and arrangements. It has a wonderful all-star lineup and is one of the rare occasions where Farmer worked on record with his brother Addison. –RW

Portrait of / OJC 1958
Exemplary session, with Roy Haynes dynamic on drums. –RW

Modern Art / BLUE NOTE 1958
An outstanding reissue of late-50s sessions with Bill Evans (p) and Benny Golson (ts). –RW

○ **Meet the Jazztet / MCA** 1960
W/ Benny Golson. The first Jazztet recording and definitive ensemble jazz. Featuring McCoy Tyner (p) and Curtis Fuller (tb). –MGN

Live at the Half Note / ATLANTIC 1963
This is a good date. –RW

On the Road / OJC 1976
A wonderful pairing of Farmer with Art Pepper (as). –RW

Big Blues / CBS 1978
Subdued, but has some good work with Jim Hall (g). –RW

Work of Art / CONCORD 1981
This is a crisp, no-nonsense session. –RW

☆ **Maiden Voyage / POLYGRAM** 1983
This is Farmer's first release on the CTI label. –RW

Back to the City / CONTEMPORARY 1986
This fine update of vintage Jazztet format has high-quality help from Curtis Fuller (tb). –RW

Something to Live For / CONTEMPORARY / DB 5 1987
The music of Billy Strayhorn. This is a beautiful tribute to Billy Strayhorn. Clifford Jordan (ts) and James Williams (p) are sublime. The CD has a bonus cut. –RW

○ **Blame It on My Youth / CONTEMPORARY** 1988
A great group effort: Farmer's best of the past decade. Featuring Clifford Jordan on tenor and soprano sax. –MGN

PH.D. / CONTEMPORARY 1989
The followup to *Blame It on My Youth*, with Clifford Jordan (sax) and James Williams (p). –MGN

Central Avenue Reunion / CONTEMPORARY 1989
This is an outstanding update of the overlooked West Coast sound by Black jazz players. –RW

In Concert with Lionel Hampton / RHINO 198?
Both have been represented on record with better results, but this is still a good mid-80s release. –RW

○ **Gentle Rain / MAINSTREAM**
Beautiful playing with the Vienna orchestra. –RW

ALLEN FARNHAM   b 1961

Post-bop, neo bop. Cleveland native pianist, heavily influenced by Chick Corea & McCoy Tyner. Fine technician. A bright future for a talented musician. –MGN

○ **Fifth House / CONCORD** 1989
Good effort from this powerful Cleveland pianist. Good potential for the future. Check out "Tones for Joan's Bones." CD version has two bonus cuts. –MGN

JOE FARRELL   1937-1986

Post-bop, progressive big band, Latin, jazz-rock. Tenor sax, flute. A top player on all instruments, Joe Farrell was an excellent soloist and reliable musician who squeezed in work as a big-band performer, octet contributor, and small-combo session man, plus jazz-rock and R&B dates. He began with Ira Sullivan in Chicago, then moved to New York in 1960 and joined Maynard Ferguson. His biggest break was as a founding member of the Jones-Lewis big band and also as part of the Elvin Jones 70s groups. During the 70s, Farrell's flute solos enhanced the first edition and the last version of "Return to Forever." He returned to mainstream in his final years. Farrell was both a superb uptempo player and a thoughtful, capable soloist who could play with precision and passion and also condense his statements. –RW

○ **Follow Your Heart / CTI** 1970
A superior release, with Farrell in top form. Reissue. –RW

● **Joe Farrell Quartet / CBS** 1970
Early CTI recordings for this West Coast transplant. Farrell's flute and sax are well represented. This must-buy also includes John McLaughlin (g) and Chick Corea (p). Includes "Follow Your Heart." –MGN

○ **Moon Germs / CBS** 1972
Another early CTI recording. Farrell's flute and sax are well represented. A must-buy, though a bit electric. –MGN

Skateboard Park / XANADU 1979
A solid date with Chick Corea (p). –RW

PIERRE FAVRE   b 1937

Modern creative. Favre is among the better European percussionists. He started as a teen and was in many bands by 17 and the Basel Radio orchestra at 19. His work with the American Jazz Ensemble in Rome in 1961 won high praise. He played with numerous Europeans and Americans through the 60s and 70s. Lately he has been a familiar figure on ECM and European label sessions and has done solo and theatrical concerts and conducted many rhythm workshops in his native Switzerland and around the world. –RW

○ **Singing Drums / POLYGRAM**   1985
One of the few domestic albums from this brilliant European percussionist. For special tastes. –MGN

LEONARD FEATHER   b 1914

Swing, bop. A famous jazz writer, songwriter, and piano/vibes player, Feather emmigrated from England to NYC in 1939 after being a critic and promoter. He was an early advocate for woman artists and recorded many for the first time. He introduced an all-women's group led by Mary Lou Williams and gave Dinah Washington her first shot as a solo artist. As a writer, his many accomplishments include establishing the *Esquire* magazine jazz poll in the 40s, originating the Blindfold test in *DOWN BEAT*, penning many encyclopedias of jazz, and writing a syndicated column in the *Los Angeles Times.*

○ **Swinging on the Vibories / MGM**   1956
This all-star bop date includes Sonny Clark (p), Kenny Drew (p), Frank Wess (fl), and jazz journalist/sometimes vibe player and pianist Leonard Feather. –DS

All-Stars / MAINSTREAM
Here is an example of this noted jazz critic's songwriting abilities, though it doesn't match the tunes he penned for Dinah Washington and others in the 40s and 50s. –RW

VICTOR FELDMAN   1934-1987

Post-bop, cool, Latin, instr-pop. Feldman was a British pianist/vibist who found a home in the USA, coming in 1955 to join Woody Herman. A prodigy who started playing at age eight, he'd been active on the English scene before leaving there. He was prolific through the 50s and 60s, most creatively with Cannonball Adderley and Miles Davis, for whom he wrote "Seven Steps to Heaven." He refused Davis's offer of a permanent gig in order to stay with his wife, becoming a busy studio musician in the 70s and 80s. Rockers may remember his contributions to Steely Dan records from the mid 70s to 1980. –RW

Suite Sixteen / OJC   1955
A limited edition new reissue of an excellent large group session. –RW

With Mallets a Fore Thought / V.S.O.P.   1957
This very early release, with Feldman's vibes technique emerging, is almost impossible to find. –RW

● **Arrival of Victor Feldman / OJC**   1958
A reissue of early recording that gained him recognition in the jazz world, this is great playing from the pianist/vibist w/ Scott LaFaro on bass. –MGN

Latinville / CONTEMPORARY   1959
This is an intriguing ten-piece band date with an Afro-Latin flavor. –RW

Merry Olde Soul / OJC   1960
This is an interesting concept; a fine session. –RW

○ **Artful Dodger / CONCORD**   1977
Later recording. Feldman deserves wider recognition. –MGN

To Chopin with Love / PALO ALTO   1983
Impressionistic; outstanding playing. –RW

Fiesta / TBA   1984
Good arrangements. Feldman plays with some vigor, though not as strongly as on his more jazz-oriented releases. –RW

Best of Feldman & the Generation Band / NOVA   COMP
An overview of Feldman's pop/fusion material. –RW

MAYNARD FERGUSON   b 1928

Big band, progressive big band, instr-pop, contemporary funk. A dazzling stylist with incredible range, Ferguson got notoriety through stints with Boyd Raeburn and Stan Kenton in the late 40s and early 50s. He had his own band from 1957-1965, then began a gradual shift into jazz-rock and pop with the M. F. Horn group. He would first increase then shrink his band, do rock and big-selling film soundtracks, then return to jazz. At his best, he can blow paint off the roof, then make you sit up and notice his ballad skills. –RW

○ **Maynard 1961 / CAPITOL**   1961
A 1990 reissue of earlier work. Straight jazz duties. –RW

M. F. Horn/M. F. Horn Two / COLUMBIA   1970
1970-1972. A combination of two of Ferguson's biggest hit albums, with minimal jazz content. –RW

Carnival / CBS   1978
Popular. A big seller, but weak from the jazz standpoint. –RW

Best of Maynard Ferguson / CBS   COMP
Good compilation. –MGN

FIREHOUSE FIVE + TWO

Trad. One of the most prolific and accomplished traditional jazz bands. The original Firehouse Five dates back to the 40s, while the Firehouse Five + Two made several good albums for the Good Time Jazz label in the 50s and 60s. –RW

○ **16 Dixieland Favorites / GOOD TIME JAZZ**   195?
Very fine material. –RW

Dixieland Favorites / GOOD TIME JAZZ   195?
One of the great traditional groups in top form. –RW

FIRST HOUSE

Jazz-rock. British fusion band featuring keyboardist Django Bates and saxophonist Iain Ballamy, now of Bill Bruford's Earthworks ensemble. –MGN

○ **Erendira / ECM**   1985
Progressive British fusioneers. Led by pianist Django Bates. Ken Stubbs (sax) wrote six; Bates three. Good aesthetic. –MGN

Cantilena / POLYGRAM   1989

CLARE FISCHER   b 1928

Cool, progressive big band, Latin, instr-pop. Keyboardist, graduate of Michigan State University. Well-versed in Latin music, also a skilled arranger and composer. Now on the LA scene. –MGN

○ **Machacha / DISCOVERY**   1981
Salsa picante at its instrumental best. Latin jazz-hots with Rick Zunigar (g), Gary Foster on saxophone and flute, and Alex Acuna and Poncho Sanchez on percussion. –MGN

ELLA FITZGERALD   b 1918

Swing, big band, ballads. Ella Fitzgerald ranks as perhaps the most accomplished jazz singer alive and certainly among the best of the century. After winning an amateur contest in 1934, she was hired by bandleader Chick Webb, and began scoring hits by 1936. In 1938, her recording of "A-Tisket, A-Tasket" topped the charts for ten weeks, becoming one of the first records to sell really well since the start of the Depression. In 1939, after Webb's death, Fitzgerald took over leadership of the Webb orchestra, then went solo in 1942. Among her major hits in the 40s were "I'm Making Believe" and "Into Each Life Some Rain Must Fall," the latter with the Ink Spots. In the 50s, Fitzgerald began issuing a series of two-record "songbooks," each devoted to a different songwriter or songwriting team. The first was *Ella Fitzgerald Sings the Cole Porter Song Book*, and others were devoted to Rodgers and Hart, and George and Ira Gershwin. Fitzgerald's flawless performances were marked by clear enunciation and a light, warm tone that made her renditions near-definitive. She has continued to perform regularly into the 90s. –WR

○ **Cole Porter Songbook / POLYGRAM / BB 15**   1956
Ella at her finest. −RW

○ **Ella & Louis Again / POLYGRAM**   r 1956
W/ Louis Armstrong. This is excellent material and wonderful vocals. −RW

With Louis Armstrong / POLYGRAM   ca. 1956
Wondrous. −RW

Porgy and Bess / VERVE / DB 5   1957

○ **Rodgers & Hart Songbook / POLYGRAM / BB 11**   1957
Vols. 1 & 2. You should grab the full two-disc set to get the genuine feel of the session. −RW

● **The Irving Berlin Songbook / POLYGRAM**   1958
Brilliant and beautiful. Berlin never sounded so good! −RW

At the Opera House / VERVE / DB 5   r 1958
A pair of electric JATP concerts with Ella backed by the crown jewels of swing: Coleman Hawkins (ts), Lester Young (ts), Roy Eldridge (tpt). −RW

★ **Duke Ellington Songbook / POLYGRAM / DB 5**   r 1958
Vols. 1 & 2. Vol. 1 is w/ Ellington's orchestra, Vol. 2 is w/ smaller groups led by Ben Webster, Paul Smith, and Oscar Peterson. Outstanding recordings, worthwhile both as documents of a fertile period for Ella, and simply as the great music they are. −MGN

○ **Ella in Rome - The Birthday Concert / POLYGRAM**   1958
This concert was either lost or forgotten and was reissued in 1988. Ella is in fighting form. CD has four bonus cuts. −RW

Ella Sings Gershwin / MCA   i 1958
Marvelously. −RW

Gershwin Songbook / POLYGRAM   1958
Contains some majestic interpretations. She makes the songs sound fresh. −RW

In Berlin / POLYGRAM / BB 11   ca. 1960
In Berlin — Mack the Knife. Fine, very stylish vocals and nice arrangements. −RW

Clap Hands, Here Comes Charlie! / POLYGRAM   r 1962
A bit to the cutesy side. CD has three bonus cuts. −RW

○ **Jerome Kern Songbook / POLYGRAM**   1963
A 1988 reissue of the definitive set. −RW

These Are the Blues / VERVE   1963
A 1986 reissue of a set that showed Ella did indeed know the blues. −RW

● **Johnny Mercer Songbook / POLYGRAM**   1964
Glittering. A landmark of popular song. −RW

Stockholm / PABLO   1966
Good backing, with excellent vocals. −RW

Harold Arlen Songbook - Vol 1 & 2 / POLYGRAM   196?
W/ Billy May Orchestra and strings on some cuts. Arlen's immaculate material is in good hands here. 26 cuts. −MGN

Ella 'A Nice / OJC   1971
W/ some spry Tommy Flanagan piano. −RW

Take Love Easy / PABLO   1973
With Joe Pass (g). Nice and smooth. −RW

Fine and Mellow / PABLO   1974
A good title cut, strictly by the book. −RW

Ella and Oscar Peterson / PABLO   1974
Outstanding all around. −RW

Ella in London / PABLO   1974
Good latter-day Ella, with plenty of ballads, uptempo cuts, standards, and scat. −RW

Montreux '75 / PABLO   1975
Pretty much formulaic, though nicely done. −RW

Again / PA2   1976
A worthy album. −RW

Lady Time / PABLO   r 1978
Some fine moments. Mostly set pieces. −RW

○ **A Classy Pair / PABLO**   1979

W/ Count Basie. They certainly are, and they show it in great form. −RW

Live - Digital 3 at Montreux / PA2   1979
W/ Count Basie and Joe Pass (g). Pass takes the instrumental honors. −RW

Perfect Match / PA2   1979
W/ Count Basie. A relaxed, great date, though both are on the other side of the mountain. −RW

Nice Work If You Can Get It / PA2   r 1984
Andre Previn (p) sounds great with Ella. −RW

All That Jazz / PABLO   1989

Best Is Yet to Come / PABLO
Not a high point lyrically, but her singing is always fine. −RW

Intimate Ella / POLYGRAM
An accurate title. Some lush and lovely ballads. −RW

Jazz 'Round Midnight / POLYGRAM
Plenty of scat — lots of everything she's known for. −RW

Lady Be Good! / POLYGRAM
Stomping, surging live cuts from a JATP session. −RW

Thirty by Ella / CAPITOL
Good idea for those who'd like one representative date. −RW

For the Love of Ella / POLYGRAM   COMP
1956-1966.

Silver Collection - The Songbooks / POLYGRAM   COMP
For once, a decent idea. The songbooks are condensed into an acceptable compilation. −RW

TOMMY FLANAGAN   ♭1930

Bop, hard-bop, post-bop, cool. Pianist. A marvelous, often undervalued artist who established his reputation quickly as a Detroit teenager. He first recorded in 1945 with Dexter Gordon, moved to New York in 1956 and later worked with Ella Fitzgerald. His tenure with her and Tony Bennett established the standard for backing vocalists without losing your playing identity. Flanagan is not only one of jazz's finest accompanists but an equally amazing soloist, with bop, blues, and a delicate touch that is immediately identifiable. −RW

● **Cats, with John Coltrane & Kenny Burrell / OJC**   1957
Detroiters get down to mainstream jazz heaven with John Coltrane (sax), Kenny Burrell (g). A must-buy. −MGN

Lonely Town / BLUE NOTE   1959
Beautiful compositions and playing. −RW

Tommy Flanagan Trio / OJC   1960
Sensational trio recordings. −RW

Tokyo Festival / PABLO   1975
Excellent live set. −RW

Eclypso / ENJA   1977

○ **Montreux 1977 / PABLO**   1977
A very good live trio recording. −MGN

○ **Alone Too Long / DENON**   1977
Wonderful solo piano. −RW

○ **Our Delights / GALAXY / DB 5**   1978
Precious duets w/ Hank Jones (p). Two ex-Detroiters. −MGN

○ **More Delights, w/ Hank Jones / GALAXY**   1978
A followup to the album *Our Delights.* −MGN

Something Borrowed, Something Blue / OJC   1978
A nice date from the late 70s. −RW

Plays Music of Harold Arlen / INNER CITY   1978
A great pianist's wonderful tribute to a great songwriter. −RW

Ballads & Blues / INNER CITY   1978
Includes fine duets with George Mraz (b). −RW

Super Jazz Trio / RCA   1978
An excellent date that has been poorly publicized. −RW

Together, w/ Kenny Barron / POLYGRAM   1978
A fine, well-produced album by two piano masters. −MGN

You're Me / PHONTASTIC   1980
A dose of blues and funk with bassist Red Mitchell. −RW

Magnificent Tommy Flanagan / PROGRESSIVE 1981
A highly accurate title: outstanding piano. –RW
Giant Steps / RHINO 1982
Flanagan perfectly plays Coltrane. A beautiful tribute. –MGN
★ **Thelonica / RHINO** 1982
Simply amazing Flanagan piano solos. –RW
Blues in the Closet / BAYBRIDGE 1983
This includes nice blues, ballads, and bop material. –RW

BOB FLORENCE b 1932

Big band, progressive big band. West Coast studio musician and big-band leader, one of the few able to still record and tour in the 80s and 90s. He's issued recent releases on the Trend and Discovery labels. –RW
○ **State of the Art / USA** 1988
Five standards, four Florence originals. W/ 20-piece big band. Cool as a breeze for these West Coast veterans. –MGN

CHUCK FLORES b 1935

Swing, bop. West Coast jazz drummer, studied with Shelly Manne, worked with Woody Herman, Art Pepper, Carmen McRae. Leads quintet in mainstream jazz. –MGN
Flores Azules / DOBRE 1975
Swinging, straightahead Latin-based date w/ Bobby Shew (tpt), Bob Hardaway (sax). –DS
○ **Drum Flower / CONCORD** 1977
Solid followup to *Flores Azules* with the same personnel (except for bassist Bob Magnusson) but less Latin flavor. –DS

RICKY FORD b 1954

Post-bop, neo bop. There was no young-lion hype for tenor player Ricky Ford to exploit in the 70s when, as a 20-year-old, he was making his debut with Gunther Schuller and working with Jaki Byard and Ran Blake. His style, which blended swing-era volume, bop discipline, and harmonic knowledge, matured with the Charles Mingus group in the late 70s. During the 80s, he penned charts for Lionel Hampton and the Mingus Dynasty, toured and recorded as a leader, and was part of a wonderful Afro-jazz group led by Abdullah Ibrahim. Ford continues to be a highly valuable asset on the jazz scene. –RW
Loxodonta Africana / NEW WORLD 1977
Flying Colors / MUSE 1980
A tight, tart, and intense quartet date. –RW
● **Tenor for the Times / MUSE** 1981
Among Ford's best. Fine piano by the late Albert Dailey. –RW
Interpretations / MUSE 1982
Brilliant lineup, aggressive hard-bop/mainstream format. –RW
Shorter Ideas / MUSE 1984
A good tribute to one of his mentors, Wayne Shorter. –RW
Looking Ahead / MUSE / DB 5 1986
An outstanding session, with a first-rate supporting cast. –RW
Saxotic Stomp / MUSE 1987
Nice multi-sax outing. CD bonus track. –RW
○ **Ebony Rhapsody / CANDID** 1990
Ford's best of the past decade. He is a hard-swinging and melodic tenor saxophonist. –MGN

BRUCE FORMAN b 1956

Bop, cool, neo bop. Fusion and contemporary jazz guitarist, also has done good solo work. Plays mostly electric, potent melodic content. Always in the wings. –MGN
The Bash / MUSE 1982
○ **Full Circle / CONCORD** 1984
San Francisco guitarist plays pristine mainstream jazz with vibist Bobby Hutcherson. –MGN
Dynamics with George Cables / CONCORD 1985
This is Forman's best all-round album: good material and outstanding playing. –RW

There Are Times / CONCORD / DB 5 1986
Bruce Foreman Quartet: Pardon Me / CONCORD 1988
W/ Billy Childs Trio. CD edition has a bonus cut. –MGN
Still of the Night / KAMEI
Jazz with a shimmering edge. –MGN

MICHAEL FORMANEK b 1958

Neo bop. Excellent bassist, logical heir to Charlie Haden. He's been around the block, and starting to be recognized. He plays post-bop to fusion. –MGN
○ **Wide Open Spaces / RHINO** r 1991
Bassist plays urban landscape/contemporary jazz. Highly original. –MGN

JIMMY FORREST 1920-1980

Big band, blues-jazz, soul jazz. Tenor saxophonist. He didn't invent the term or the style, but he was among the greatest honking-sax/soul-jazz players ever. Forrest worked with many St. Louis bands as a teen and joined Jay McShann in 1942. He later played with Andy Kirk and Duke Ellington before heading his own group and later working with the Harry Edison quintet. He was with Count Basie in the late 70s. Forrest had an immortal version of "Night Train" that actually fuses the Ellington tunes "That's the Blues, Old Man" and "Happy-Go-Lucky Local." Techniques such as smears and slurs, expert projection of lines, and a great, thick tone made Forrest a soul-jazz master. –RW
★ **Night Train / DELMARK** 1951
This is tremendous early-50s material from Forrest's days on the pioneering United label. The label was owned by a Black postman and was one of the earliest Black-owned record companies in the nation. The title cut was a huge jukebox and R&B hit. –RW
○ **All the Gin Is Gone / DELMARK** 1959
Straight bop. Grant Green's (g) first recording session — he was flown in from St. Louis by Forrest. W/ Harold Mabern (p), Elvin Jones (d). –JME
○ **Black Forrest / DELMARK** 1959
Bop. From the same session as *All the Gin Is Gone*. Includes the lovely "But Beautiful," featuring Grant Green (g), with Forrest sitting this tune out. –JME
○ **Forrest Fire / OJC** 1960
An exceptional date, with some instructive early Larry Young (organ) solos. –RW
Out of the Forrest / OJC 1961
A stirring date. Forrest is more straightahead than usual. Joe Zawinul provides great piano. –RW
Sit Down & Relax / PRESTIGE 1961
W/ Hugh Lawson on piano. Worth the search. –MGN
Most Much / OJC 1961
A well-done mainstream/soul-jazz set. –RW
O. D. (Out 'Dere) / GREYFORREST 1980
W/ trombonist Al Grey and organist Don Patterson. –MGN

SONNY FORTUNE b 1939

Post-bop, jazz-rock, neo bop. This Coltrane-influenced saxophonist and flutist has forged his own personal, lyrical sound. He is one of the best. –MGN
Long Before Our Mothers Cried / STRATA EAST 1974
A large-ensemble recording. A fully realized creative album and very listenable as well. W/ Charles Sullivan (tpt) and Stanley Cowell (p). –MGN
○ **Serengetti Minstrel / ATLANTIC** 1977
Studio date from this virile Philadelphia saxophonist/flutist, who tackles the Coltrane legacy in fine fashion with Woody Shaw (tpt) and Kenny Barron (p). –MGN

FRANK FOSTER b 1928

Big band, bop, progressive big band. Foster's writing and

arranging skills have been so keen, some people have forgotten what a sharp, animated, and complete saxophone soloist he has been. He played with Wardell Gray and Elvin Jones in the 40s. After two years in the army during the 50s, he joined Count Basie for 11 memorable years. He was highly active in the 60s and 70s as an arranger, a member of the Elvin Jones and Jones-Lewis groups, and a bandleader. He co-led an 80s group with Frank Wess and took over the Basie band in 1986. His best-known composition is "Shiny Stockings." –RW

★ **Two Franks Please! / SAVOY**   1957
High-quality hard-bop set with trumpeter Donald Byrd. –RW
Manhattan Fever / BLUE NOTE   1968
Excellent sextet with trumpeter Marvin Stamm. –MGN
○ **Loud Minority / MAINSTREAM**   1974
Progressive big-band music. Impressive. –MGN
Manhattan Fever / DENON   1977
Another album with same title; w/ big band. Progressive and tasty. Recommended. –MGN
Twelve Shades of Black / LEO   1978
Topflight large-group sessions. –RW
Roots, Branches and Dances / BEEHIVE   1978
Wonderful arrangements, slashing playing. –RW
Two for the Blues / PABLO   1983
Excellent duo set. –RW
○ **Frankly Speaking / CONCORD**   1984
One of Foster's many sparkling collaborations with his longtime friend, fellow Basie bandmate Frank Wess. Outstanding rhythm section as well. –RW
Non-Electric Company / CONCORD
Foster here is an equally accomplished leader and player. –RW

PETE FOUNTAIN   b1930

Dixieland. Clarinetist Fountain goes back to the 40s in New Orleans music, where he worked with Monk Hazel, the Junior Dixieland Band, Phil Zito, and others. He spent four years with the Basin Street Six, then hit the jackpot with Lawrence Welk. Records and television appearances followed. From the 60s on, many people identified New Orleans music with either Fountain or Al Hirt. He has undeniable gifts, especially his tone. –RW

Mr. New Orleans/Pete Fountain / MCA
Two recent sets combined. –RW
○ **Best of Pete Fountain - Vols. 1 & 2 / MCA**   COMP
Good overview of recent cuts. –RW

BRUCE FOWLER   b1947

Post-bop, jazz-rock, neo bop. Son of famous jazz educator Dr. William L. Fowler, Bruce is an extraordinary trombonist whose jazz credits are based in L.A. studios. Played well with Frank Zappa, and as a member of the raucous Fowler Brothers Band. –MGN

○ **Ants Can Count / TERRA NOVA**

T. J. FOWLER   b1910

Big band, blues-jazz, ballads, R&B. This Detroit bandleader of the 40s and 50s played jazz and jump blues. –MGN
○ **T. J. Fowler & His Rockin' Jump Band / SAVOY**   1948
1948-1953. A great jazz/R&B band from Detroit. –MGN

AL FRANCIS

Post-bop. Francis was a vibist in the 50s-60s who struck out in a modern post-bop style and discovered a different voice on his chosen instrument. He is one to seek and study. –MGN
○ **Jazz Bohemia Revisited / LCU**   1986
Legendary vibist Francis joins John Neves (b), Joe Hunt (d), for one standard, one by Jaki Byard, and six Francis originals. Inventive modern music. This is a great album to find in a lonely cut-out bin — grab it! –MGN

PANAMA FRANCIS   b1918

Swing, big band. Among the last of the top swing drummers, Francis learned his craft playing in his church in Miami at revivals before joining George Kelly's band. He moved to New York in 1938, and in 1939 he became part of Roy Eldridge's band. He got his nickname from wearing a Panama hat. The glory years came with Lucky Millinder's band at the Savoy. His bombastic style, complete with riveted Chinese cymbal, galvanized audiences through the mid 40s, and Francis keeps re-forming various editions of the Savoy Sultans. He later had a lucrative studio career as an R&B session player, laying down similar beats and keeping the groove going. By the 70s he'd gotten back into some jazz as well as backing vocalists, and he has once again formed a version of his beloved Savoy Sultans. –RW

○ **All-Stars 1949 / CBS**   1949
Sizzling swing set propelled by a truly fine drummer. –RW
Francis & the Savoy Sultans / CLASSIC JAZZ   1979

BUD FREEMAN   1906-1992

Swing, bop. Tenor saxophonist. A master of vintage Chicago-style jazz, Freeman was an innovator in his genre. His lush, witty style was absorbed by generations of White tenor players. Freeman began in the 20s with C-melody sax, then switched to tenor in 1925. He spent nine years with the cream of Chicago-based leaders, including Red Nichols and Eddie Condon. He moved to New York and joined Ray Noble in the 30s, then attained super popularity with Tommy Dorsey. In the late 30s he appeared on Broadway in a musical with Louis Armstrong and Maxine Sullivan. From the 40s on, through associations with Condon or on his own, Freeman kept the cause of traditional jazz alive, though his playing never calcified or lost its charm. He was a founder of the World's Greatest Jazz Band in 1968 and returned to Chicago in 1970. –RW

The Commodore Years 1938-1939 / COMMODORE   1938
An anthology/overview of his most influential material from the late 30s. –RW
And His Summa Cum Laude Trio / DOT   i1958
○ **Featuring Shorty Baker / OJC**   1960
Freeman is a neglected but great tenor saxophonist. –MGN
Song of the Tenor / PHILIPS   197?
A mid-70s session with Roy Williams on trombone. –MGN

CHICO FREEMAN   b1949

Post-bop, early free, modern creative. The son of venerable Chicago tenor saxophonist Von Freeman, Chico took up tenor while at Northwestern University. His studies with Muhal Richard Abrams and Joe Daley, plus a Masters in composition, resulted in both formal and practical training. He settled in New York in the 70s and became known as a player whose sound had power, appeal, and flexibility. He was grounded in swing and bop but is also able to use an avant-garde framework creatively. –RW

Morning Prayer / INDIA NAVIGATION   1976
A tremendous quintet date. Wonderful solos by Freeman, plus a strong supporting cast w/ Muhal Richard Abrams (p). –RW
○ **Beyond the Rain / OJC**   1977
With the Hilton Ruiz Trio, featuring the compositions of M. R. Abrams and Freeman's hard-charging playing. –MGN
● **Chico / INDIA NAVIGATION**   1977
A standard for creative tenor saxophonists to live up to. –MGN
The Outside Within / INDIA NAVIGATION   1978
A sterling quartet session. –RW
○ **Spirit Sensitive / INDIA NAVIGATION**   1979
Beautiful album of ballads. The CD has extra tracks. –MGN
Destiny's Dance / CONTEMPORARY   1981
An excellent, ambitious early-80s release. –RW
Freeman and Freeman / INDIA NAVIGATION   1981

Father and son make a wonderful team on this release with Von and Chico Freeman. –RW

Tradition in Transition / ELEKTRA / DB 5 1982
Superior production values and sound, with excellent playing by Freeman. –RW

Pied Piper / BLACKHAWK 1984
Tangents / ELEKTRA 1984
Tales of Ellington / BLACKHAWK 1987
A gorgeous homage. A sleeper. –MGN

GEORGE FREEMAN

Swing, bop. Brother of Von from Chicago. Also plays a bluesy-based tenor with raucous, R&B tendencies. An underappreciated master. –MGN
○ **All in the Game / LRC JAZZ CLASSICS**

RUSS FREEMAN   b 1926

Swing, bop. Pianist Russ Freeman played with West Coast bop groups in the late 40s, including Howard McGhee, Dexter Gordon, Art Pepper, Wardell Gray, and Shorty Rogers. He worked with Chet Baker in 1954, and began his longtime association with Shelly Mann in 1955. From the mid 60s onward, he has worked in television and Hollywood as a music director, and pianist. –JME
○ **Trio with Richard Twardzik / BLUE NOTE** 1953

VON FREEMAN   b 1922

Hard-bop, post-bop. A masterful veteran and another in the long line of jazz greats who attended Du Sable High School in Chicago and studied under Capt. Walter Dyett. His huge, quickly recognizable tone, articulation, proficiency on ballads, and great timing have made Von Freeman an admired player. His insistence on spending most of his career in Chicago has certainly kept him from gaining wider recognition. Freeman played with Horace Henderson, Sun Ra, and Charlie Parker and recorded in the early 50s with Andrew Hill. His infrequent (but always enjoyable) albums have had a great mix of blues, ballads, and bop. He finally got some degree of the spotlight in 1981 when he recorded on Columbia with his son Chico for half of the delightful *Fathers and Sons* work. –RW
○ **Serenade & Blues / NESSA** 1975
On-the-edge ballads and blues from Chico's dad. –MGN

DON FRIEDMAN   b 1935

Bop, post-bop. Veteran pianist and composer from San Francisco. Mostly heard as a sideman. Played bop with the masters; also played with Clark Terry Big Band. A true original. –MGN
○ **Day in the City / OJC** 1961
A limited-edition reissue of an intriguing concept piece. –RW

DAVID FRIESEN   b 1942

Early free, world fusion, neo bop. Friesen is a talented bassist who has worked in both straight jazz and more chamber-like settings with equal ease. His most exciting playing came in sessions with Mal Waldron and Ted Curson, where his skills were extended and he had to be a forceful contributor to the rhythm section. –RW
Star Dance / INNER CITY / DB 5 1976
● **Amber Skies / PALO ALTO** 1983
Encounters / MUSE 1984
Solid date. Superb contributions from Mal Waldron (p). –RW
Departure / RHINO 1990
Good combination of Afro-Latin-jazz and chamber music with guests Airto (per) and Flora Purim (v). –RW

BILL FRISELL   b 1951

Neo bop, modern creative. Guitarist. Frisell studied with Jim

Hall and at the Berklee College of Music. His influences include Jim Hall, Wes Montgomery, and Jimi Hendrix. His many recordings for ECM have made him a sort of house guitarist for that label, doing successful work with Jan Garbarek and percussionist Paul Motian. He has also recorded duets with Tim Berne and John Scofield. Frisell blends jazz, rock, and avant-garde influences in an exuberant and unpredictable style. Perhaps his most distinctive quality as a guitarist is creative and tasteful use of synthesizers and electronic effects, creating sonorities like wind instruments and organs. –DNM
In Line / POLYGRAM 1982
Intense, though erratic conceptually. –RW
● **Smash & Scatteration / RYKODISC** 1984
W/ Vernon Reid (g). This is one of the best 80s guitar duo dates. It has everything from far-out to far-in, and lots in the middle — jazz, rock, blues, and pop. –RW
○ **Rambler / POLYGRAM** r 1985
Reissue of a fine date. An excellent rhythmic foundation laid by Paul Motian (d). –RW
○ **Lookout for Hope / POLYGRAM** 1987
"Country and Eastern" music with Frisell's distinct guitar sound. Constantly challenging listening. –MGN
Before We Were Born / ELEKTRA / DB 5 r 1989
Outstanding example of this guitarist's versatility. There are some sparkling exchanges with the sax section led by Julius Hemphill. –RW
Is That You? / ELEKTRA / DB 5 r 1990
Works / POLYGRAM
Good representations of creative impulses. Not definitive, but a good point of reference. –MGN

DAVID FRISHBERG   b 1933

Cool, ballads. This singer and pianist is best known for writing and singing funny, witty songs with a distictive delivery. A special individual, with a one-of-a-kind style. Baseball fan. Astute observer of society. –MGN
You're A Lucky Guy / CONCORD 1978
Al Cohn (ts) elevates the entire set. –RW
○ **Live at Vine Street / FANTASY / DB 5** 1984
Arguably his best of the 80s batch. –RW
Can't Take You Nowhere / FANTASY 1986
Let's Eat Home / CONCORD 1989
● **Dave Frishberg Classics / CONCORD** COMP
This hits collection reissued almost all of his most well-known tunes. A must-buy. –MGN

TONY FRUSCELLA   b 1927

Cool. Trumpeter who worked with Gerry Mulligan, Lester Young, and Stan Getz in the 50s. He recorded with his own group in 1955, and with trumpeter Don Joseph after that time. –JME
○ **Tony Fruscella / ATLANTIC** 1956
A brilliantly bopish session by this little-recorded trumpeter, with Allen Eager (ts). –DS

CURTIS FULLER   b 1934

Bop, post-bop. Fuller ranks near the top among bop trombonists. One of the class of the 50s in Detroit jazz circles, he studied music in high school and played with Cannonball Adderley in the US Army Band. Fuller moved to New York in 1957. He is almost as fast and technically flawless as his main influence, J. J. Johnson, though not so fond of vocal effects and less flamboyant. A master at slow, lyrical pieces and not quite so creative or imaginative on faster tunes; he's never behind or ahead of the beat. –RW
New Trombone / OJC 1957
Wonderful robust trombone from Fuller. Sonny Red sparkles on sax. –RW

With Hampton Hawes / PRESTIGE   1957
This is an unorthodox, intriguing date, with Hawes excellent on piano, Julius Watkins and David Amram on French horns. It's hard to find. −RW

● **All-Star Sextets / SAVOY**   1959
Combos led by trombonist Fuller, members of the Jazztet and Coltrane ensembles. Essential jazz/post-bop. Seminal material from a brilliant trombonist. Features Lee Morgan (tpt), Wynton Kelly (p), McCoy Tyner (p), and others. −RW

Blues-Ette / SAVOY   1959
A powerhouse session with Fuller leading a stalwart group. Benny Golson (ts) and Tommy Flanagan (p) are sublime. −RW

○ **Crankin' & Smokin' / MAINSTREAM**   r 1972
At the time, this was his most adventurous playing in quite a while. −RW

○ **Four on the Outside / TIMELESS**   1978
A strong cast. Frequently exceptional playing. −RW

GIL FULLER   b 1920

Big band, progressive big band. Arranger of large ensembles and big bands. Prolific composer; best-known tune was "Things to come." Worked extensively with Dizzy Gillespie. −MGN

○ **And Monterey Festival Orchestra / PACIFIC JAZZ** i 1965
W/ Dizzy Gillespie (tpt). −PR

CHARLIE GABRIEL   b 1932

Trad, swing, cool. A member of the famous Gabriel family from New Orleans. He plays saxes and clarinets, from early traditional to romantic and cool. −MGN

○ **And Friends in Asia / POLYDOR**   1987
A mellow album from the Detroit saxophonist, at times with a soulful edge. With New Orleans musicians Ed Frank and Leroy Jones. Special guests also include El Dee Young, Red Holt and Chicago pianist Wallace Burton. This is a nice LP with three Gabriel originals. −MGN

SLIM GAILLARD   b 1916

Swing, cool, ballads. The guitarist and singer-songwriter who invented "vout," a silly way of interpolating vocalese. Slim Gaillard is a most entertaining ex-Detroiter. −MGN

Cement Mixer, Putti, Putti / FOLKLYRIC   1945
1945-1949.

☆ **Opera En Vout / VERVE**   1946
A variety of sessions from 1946, 1947, 1951 and 1952 from Gaillard. A perfect representation of Gaillard's musical and comedic mastery. −MGN

Dot Sessions / MCA   195?
An essential compilation of Gaillard's 50s material. −RW

ERIC GALE   b 1938

Jazz-rock, instr-pop. A first-rate technician, guitarist Eric Gale has played many bluesy, nicely constructed, and funky solos for various soul and jazz acts over the years. Gale has fluidity, blues acumen, and the flair to accompany anyone. −RW

○ **In a Jazz Tradition / POLYGRAM**   1987
A rare foray into jazz terrain. −RW

LARRY GALES   b 1936

Bop, hard-bop, post-bop. The bassist for several years in the 50s and 60s with Thelonious Monk, he now leads his own groups playing Monk-style jazz. Quite a personality. −MGN

○ **A Message from Monk / CANDID**

HAL GALPER   b 1938

Post-bop, neo bop. Pianist. Influenced by fellow virtuosos McCoy Tyner and Oscar Peterson. Worked with many of NYC's finest modern ensembles — primarily bop and post-bop.

Was a member of the Phil Woods Quintet for ten years. Galper's bands are great, displaying him at his best. −MGN

○ **Speak with a Single Voice / ENJA**   1978
First quintet recording, with the Brecker Brothers, at Rosie's in New Orleans. Essential. −MGN

Redux 1978 / CONCORD   1978
A followup recording to the *Speak With A Single Voice* album. An important document of this great band. CD has two bonus cuts. −MGN

Live at Maybeck - Vol. 6 / CONCORD   1990
First-rate, stately solo piano. −RW

Invitation to a Concert / CONCORD   r 199?
This is one of his most recent. The pianist dominates the session. −RW

GANELIN TRIO

Modern creative. Russian free-jazz improvisers; they are the premier band of this style. They constantly switch instruments, on occasion playing each others'. −MGN

Poi Segue / EAST WIND   1981
More seamless, no-holds-barred free music. −MGN

○ **Concerto Grosso / MELODYA**   r 1982
Russian trio of wildly pure improvisers. A must-buy for the challengable listener. −MGN

JAN GARBAREK   b 1947

Early free, modern creative. Tenor saxophonist. A Norwegian jazz artist, Garbarek's early influences included John Coltrane, and he played with and studied the tonal system of George Russell. He also played with Terje Rypdal, Keith Jarrett, and Don Cherry. His music combines elements of free-jazz, jazz/rock, folk music, and European avant-garde, all within a very introspective and personal improvisation process. An ECM recording artist, his contemplative sound epitomizes that label's style of high-quality improvisational art music. His recordings range from extremely avant-garde to spacious mood music, and include highly successful collaborations with artists such as Keith Jarrett (*Nude Ants*). Garbarek has also composed for TV, theater, and film. His European stylistic influences range from traditional church and folk harmonies to the acerbic minimal gestures of 20th-century classicism. His music is often slower, more moody, and more spacious than the dense textures of urban jazz, but his powerful tone and fluid technique, influenced by the intense and "searching" sound of Coltrane, places him squarely in the jazz tradition. Garbarek practices what is truly an international jazz style, yet without contradiction it can be said to be completely personal as well. −DNM

○ **Afric Pepperbird / POLYGRAM / DB 5**   1970
His best, most exciting date from 1970. −RW

Sart / POLYGRAM   1971

● **Witchi-Tai-To / POLYGRAM / DB 5**   r 1973
One of the albums that defined the ECM Records sound. A must-buy. −MGN

Folk Songs / POLYGRAM   1979

Paths, Prints / POLYGRAM   1981
One of the better, more exciting releases — thanks to Bill Frisell (g). −RW

Wayfarer / POLYGRAM   1983
Bill Frisell (g) enlivens things considerably. −RW

JAN GARBER   1897-1977

Big band. Violinist Jan Garber was able to flit between smooth, sweet big-band styles and hotter, more aggressive arrangements during his career. Garber attended the Univerity of North Carolina and later became the violinist in the Philadelphia Symphony Orchestra before forming the Garber-Davis Orchestra with pianist Milt Davis. He then took over the leadership reins of Freddy Large's Canadian band and became a regular on Burns and Allen's radio show. He later moved back to a stronger, swing-oriented approach in 1942, and hired the sister of Benny Goodman's vocalist Martha, Liz Tilton. –RW

1946-1947 / HINDSIGHT   1946
And his Orchestra / HINDSIGHT
Great Jan Garber / HINDSIGHT
○ **Plays 22 Original Big Band Records / HINDSIGHT**

LASZLO GARDONY

Post-bop, neo bop. Hungarian born modern-jazz pianist in the acoustic style of Corea, Hancock, and Jarrett. Mostly plays with a trio. –MGN

○ **The Secret / POLYGRAM**   1986
A Hungarian pianist with a modern approach. –MGN

Legend of Tsumi / POLYGRAM   1988
Not quite as good as *Secret*, but still potent. –MGN

RED GARLAND   1923-1984

Bop, post-bop, cool. Pianist. Influenced by Count Basie and Nat King Cole, as well as by modernists such as Bud Powell and Art Tatum, Red played with the great horn players of his era, including Charlie Parker, Coleman Hawkins, and Lester Young. His greatest recognition came as part of the famous Miles Davis rhythm section with Paul Chambers and Philly Joe Jones. He led his own trio but functioned mostly as a sideman, exemplifying the many fine jazz musicians who never became huge stars in their own right but played with all the greats. Red was a fine ensemble player. –DNM

Garland of Red / OJC   1956
Expertly played late-50s session. –RW

Red Garland's Piano / OJC   1957
A fine reissue. –RW

Groovy / OJC / DB 5   1957
This is state-of-the-art languid Garland. –RW

All Mornin' Long / OJC   1957
Loose, with elements of funk and soul-jazz, plus the usual excellence from Byrd (tpt), Coltrane (ts), and Garland. –RW

● **Soul Junction / OJC**   1957
More Donald Byrd (tpt), John Coltrane (ts), Red Garland. Solos from Coltrane and Byrd are better than on *High Pressure*. –RW

Dig It! / OJC / DB 5   1957
1989 reissue contains more from the mammoth Garland late-50s output, with Donald Byrd (tpt), John Coltrane (ts), Paul Chambers (b), Art Taylor (d), and the underrated George Joyner (tpt). –RW

Manteca / OJC   1958
Afro-Latin flavoring from Ray Barretto (per) spices up an otherwise proficient but musically standard trio date. –RW

Red Garland Trio / OJC   1958
First-rate interaction from Garland, Paul Chambers (b), and Art Taylor (d). –RW

All Kinds of Weather / OJC   1958
Smooth, high-level Garland, with Art Taylor (d), and Paul Chambers (b). –RW

● **Red in Bluesville / OJC**   1959
Prototypical late-50s set: lean, lush, and enticing. –RW

Moodsville - Vol. 1 / OJC   1959
As exacting and demanding as any from the combo of Garland, Art Taylor (d), and Paul Chambers (b). –RW

Alone with the Blues / MOODSVILLE   1960
An album that shows that Garland was a technical, harmonic, and rhythmic marvel. Hard to find but worth the effort. –RW

○ **Red Alone / MOODSVILLE**   1960

Immense solo piano, one of two memorable sessions from that year. –RW

Bright and Breezy / OJC   1961
This 1987 reissue is from a good, though unexceptional, trio date. –RW

Red's Good Groove / JAZZLAND   1962
Large doses of funk & soul-jazz, plus fine baritone from Pepper Adams and Blue Mitchell on trumpet. –RW

○ **When There Are Grey Skies / PRESTIGE**   1962
Red Alert / OJC   1977
A 1991 issue of an excellent album date with superb Garland piano and top contributions by Nat Adderley (cnt), Harold Land (ts), and Ira Sullivan (tpt). –RW

○ **Crossings / OJC**   1977
Tremendous update. An example of Garland's ability to heave and create in a trio setting, this time with Ron Carter (b) and Philly Joe Jones (d). –RW

I Left My Heart... / MUSE   1978
Strike up the Band / GALAXY   1979
Some stunning solos from George Coleman (ts). Garland is still an impressive player in the final stages of his career, though not as much the driving force as in the past. –RW

ERROLL GARNER   1921-1977

Swing, bop, cool. One of the most original piano stylists in all of jazz, Garner never learned to read music but conceived of the piano as a big, swinging band in which he was both the melody voice and the rhythm section. He used his left hand almost like Count Basie's sterling guitarist Freddie Green, and in the trio setting he preferred (with bass and drums just keeping steady time), he could outswing most bands and combos at the middle and up tempos he mastered. On ballads, he adopted a heavily arpeggiated, romantic approach that contrasted with the impish humor he brought to his swinging style. Garner also liked to keep his listeners in suspense with elaborate solo introductions that were little masterpieces in themselves. Though he never said a word on stage, he could hold the largest audience spellbound just with his music, which was filled with joy and life. Like Louis Armstrong, he transcended the jazz category and had fans of all ages and musical persuasions. Also like Armstrong, he was one of the first (and few) jazz performers to establish himself as a concert attraction. A prolific recording artist, he left behind a legacy from which treasures continue to be culled. His most famous composition, of course, is "Misty." –DM

○ **The Elf / SAVOY**   1949
Brilliant 40s material that helped establish Garner immediately as a remarkable improviser. –RW

Yesterdays / SAVOY   194?
More shimmering, striking 40s dates from Garner. –RW

Long Ago & Far Away / CBS   1950
1950-1951. This is great Garner. Unfortunately, the remastering is not as great. –JME

★ **Concert by the Sea / CBS / BB 12**   1955
The most popular jazz album since Brubeck's *Time Out.* –MGN

Mambo Moves Garner / POLYGRAM   r 1955
A 1988 reissue of a fine session where Garner applied his unforgettable skills to the Afro-Latin arena. –RW

Other Voices / CBS / BB 16   1956
Among his more pop (and popular) releases when it was issued in 1956. This reissue isn't of the highest caliber; it's merely a decent one. Find the original if possible. –RW

○ **Erroll Garner Plays Misty / POLYGRAM**   195?
A classic. –MGN

○ **Original Misty / POLYGRAM**   195?
This is a reissue of the first Garner version of Misty made in the early 50s. –RW

Easy to Love - Vol. 1 / POLYGRAM   1961

1961-1965. This is feathery at times, tenacious at others. –RW

A New Kind of Love / MERCURY   1963
Beautiful Garner, plus a 35-piece orchestra. –RW

Errol Garner Plays Gershwin & Kern / POLYGRAM 1964
1964-1968. A wonderful reissue of some immaculate renditions from Garner at the top of his game. –RW

A Night at the Movies / MGM   r 1965
Takes you into, through, and around the cinema via Garner's adept, crackling riffs and rhythms. –RW

That's My Kick / MGM   1967
Hot piano and excellent bass by Milt Hinton, with a guest stint by Johnny Pacheco (fl, v, per). –RW

Up in Erroll's Room / MPS   r 1968
A delightful, clever, and slashing workout. –RW

Gemini / MPS   1969
Garner takes a turn on the harpsichord. –RW

Greatest Garner / ATLANTIC   COMP
Some strong solos and material, but the title is deceptive since he didn't exactly make his best or his most popular work for this company. –RW

Too Marvelous for Words - Vol. 3 / POLYGRAM   COMP
The third in the Polygram series of overviews. Plenty of majestic performances. –RW

CARLOS GARNETT   b 1938

Hard-bop, post-bop. Garnett was a saxophonist, one-time member of Pharoah Sanders's group, and bandleader who made some good albums for Muse in the 70s. –RW
○ **Journey to Enlightenment / MUSE**

LARRY GELB   b 1948

Post-bop, neo bop. This pianist's main fame is as an accompanist, mostly with Charlie and Chan Parker's daughter (and Phil Woods's step daughter) Kim. –MGN
○ **New Souls / ESSENE**   1979
With vocalist Kim Parker. –MGN

HERB GELLER   b 1928

Bop, progressive big band. Alto sax. Geller got his start in the swing era with Joe Venuti. He later moved to NY from California and played with Claude Thornhill and Billy May. When he returned to LA in 1951, he became a busy combo leader. –RW
○ **American in Hamburg / View from Here / NOVA** 1975
Rhyme & Reason / DISCOVERY   1975
Good quintet sessions, plus (for those who value him) Mark Murphy (v). –RW

Jazz Song Book / RHINO   1988
This is much better than you'd expect from the low-key publicity. Geller deserves a wider profile, having been an active player since the 40s. Walter Morris is a prominent figure on the piano. –RW

Quartet / FRESH SOUNDS
An outstanding quartet date, with Kenny Drew sharp on the piano. –RW

GEORGE GERSHWIN   1898-1937

Ballads. Perhaps the greatest American composer of the 20th century, George Gershwin wrote both memorable popular songs for stage and screen, starting with his first big hit, "Swanee." Others include opera *Porgy and Bess* and classical works such as *Rhapsody in Blue. See* classical section. –RW
○ **Gershwin Performs Gershwin / MUSICMASTERS** 1931
1931-1934. A rare treasure, this CD contains two 15-minute episodes of the 1934 "Music by Gershwin" radio program (complete with laxative commercials!), a radio appearance with Rudy Vallee, and rehearsals for the *Second Rhapsody* and *Porgy and Bess* conducted by Gershwin himself. Gives great

insight into the personality of one of the century's major composers. –WR

The George and Ira Gershwin Songbook / RCA   COMP
The Gershwins' continuing appeal is demonstrated on this 20-track collection of recordings from the 50s and 60s, which features Benny Goodman, Julie Andrews, Perry Como, the Ames Brothers, and other stars of the era. –WR

The Song Is.... Gershwin / LIVING ERA   COMP
In recordings from the 20s and 30s, a variety of stage performers (Al Jolson, Fred Astaire, Gertrude Lawrence) and recording artists (Fats Waller, Paul Whiteman) sing and play some of Gershwin's best theater music. And the versions of "My One and Only" and "When Do We Dance?" are by George Gershwin himself. –WR

STAN GETZ   1927-1991

Bop, cool, Latin. At 16, he went on the road with Jack Teagarden's band and never looked back. The most gifted and famous of the Brothers — tenormen who emulated Lester Young and most of whom were alumni of Woody Herman's Second Herd — Getz established himself with a beautiful solo on Herman's "Early Autumn" (1948). Though his personal life had its ups and downs, his music was consistently brilliant. Highlights include the association with guitarist Jimmy Raney; his great success with the bossa nova (in the 60s, when there was no other instrumental music on the hit charts); his wonderful collaboration with Eddie Sauter on *Focus*, a unique composition created for Stan; and his final triumph over a debilitating illness in the duets with pianist Kenny Barron (*People Time*). Getz was above all a supreme melodist, who could make even a mediocre song sparkle, but he was also a marvelous improviser and master of high-speed invention. As a saxophonist, he was without peers. –DM

The Brothers, w/ Zoot Sims / OJC   1949
From 1949 & 1952. Seminal material with Getz alongside his musical comrades, including fellow tenor players Zoot Sims and Al Cohn, as well as Allen Eager (ts) and others. –RW

Early Stan / OJC   1949
With Jimmy Raney (g). This is a 1991 reissue of formative material from 1949-1953. Red Mitchell (b) and Shorty Rogers (tpt) occasionally steal the spotlight from the then-emerging Getz. –RW

Stan Getz at Storyville - Vols. 1 & 2 / CAPITOL   1951
Some fierce live Getz. W/ Jimmy Raney (g), Al Haig (p), Teddy Kotick (b), and Tiny Kahn (d). –RW

Roost Quartets / CAPITOL   1951
A new reissue of Blue Note material. Worth having. –RW

Plays / POLYGRAM   1952
A good, though musically unadventurous, date on Mercury. The CD has four bonus cuts. –RW

○ **Diz & Getz / POLYGRAM**   1953
1953 & 1956. W/ Dizzy Gillespie (tpt). Two jazz giants make great music together. –MGN

The Steamer / VERVE   1956
Very rare and hard to find, but one of his first superstar releases. –RW

○ **Diz & Getz / VERVE**   ca. 1956
This is prime material with two giants playing bop and old time standards with characteristic verve and wit. John Lewis (p) and the Oscar Peterson quartet join the masters. –MGN

And the Oscar Peterson Trio / VERVE   1957
Getz shines while Peterson (p) keeps the trio whipped to a frenzy behind him. –RW

W/ J. J. Johnson: Opera House / POLYGRAM / DB 5 1957
Powerhouse pairing. Explosive music, though the two principals are actually featured in separate concerts. –RW

Stan with Cal Tjader / OJC   1958
1987 reissue, super Latin-jazz summit. Billy Higgins fits in nicely on drums. –RW

○ **Focus / POLYGRAM / DB 5**   1961

Essential, and one of his more influential recordings. Amazing arrangements by Eddie Sauter and brilliant Getz solos. −RW

○ **Jazz Samba / VERVE / BB 1** 1962
This recording was not just a laidback treasure, but a really major milestone: the 1962 album that introduced the bossa nova to the US. Byrd conceived it, Getz got a Grammy off one cut, "Desafinado." So much silliness ensued that the whole idiom's importance has been downplayed, but it was the beginning of a permanent Brazilian tinge in jazz −JSR

Big Band Bossa Nova / POLYGRAM / BB 13 1962
This is an essential part of his bossa nova period. W/ Gary McFarland; this album was one of his biggest sellers. −RW

☆ **Bossa Nova Years (Girl from Ipanema) / VERVE** 1962
1962-1964. The five Getz Bossa albums in a boxed set: *Jazz Samba, Big-Band Bossa Nova, Jazz Samba Encore, Getz/Gilberto,* and *Getz/Almeida.* In a word: great music for young and old, even non-jazz buffs. Each of these discs is jam-packed with classic Getz tracks. Highest recommendation. −JME

Jazz Samba Encore / VERVE / BB 88 1963
Wonderful pairing of Stan Getz and Luiz Bonfa (g). −RW

● **Getz/Gilberto / VERVE / BB 2** 1963
Getz/Gilberto & Antonio Carlos Jobim. The huge hit with Getz, Joao (g), and Astrud Gilberto (v). "The Girl from Ipenema" was an international smash. Gold album. −RW

Getz/Almeida / POLYGRAM 1963
W/ Laurindo Almeida (g). Music that is lush, beautiful, and substantial. −RW

Stan Getz & Bill Evans / VERVE 1964
As musically serene and amazing as you'd expect. Getz and Evans are incredible, while Ron Carter (b), Richard Davis (b), and Elvin Jones (d) aren't too bad either. −RW

Getz Au-Go-Go / POLYGRAM / BB 24 1964
W/ Joao Gilberto. Landmark release. Getz completed a run in 1964 of hit albums that were both popular and influential. Astrud Gilberto (v) was sensual, dynamic, and unforgettable while with Getz. −RW

Song After Sundown / BLUEBIRD 1966
Getz plays with his usual brilliance on this date, reissued in 1987. W/ Arthur Fiedler and the Boston Pops. RCA does an excellent remastering job. −RW

○ **Sweet Rain / POLYGRAM / DB 5** 1967
From someone who made so many classics, this might be his best romantic work overall. −RW

Dynasty / POLYGRAM 1971
Amazing playing from Getz in this date cut in London, partly at Ronnie Scott's. −RW

○ **Captain Marvel / COLUMBIA** 1972
This brilliant mainstream date w/ Chick Corea (p), Stanley Clarke (b), Tony Williams (d), and Airto (per) got lost in publicity fever over the rise of jazz-rock. It came out three years after it was done in 1972. −RW

Best of Two Worlds / CBS 1975
An outstanding set, with Getz doing both mainstream and bop work, then backing Joao Gilberto. −RW

The Peacocks / COLUMBIA / DB 5 1975
Stan Getz is masterly and pianist Jimmy Rowles equally impressive. −RW

The Master / COLUMBIA 1975
Wonderful Getz. Delightful piano playing by Albert Dailey. −RW

Brothers & Other Mothers - Vol. 1 / SAVOY r 1976
W/ Al Cohn (ts), Serge Chaloff (sax), Brew Moore (ts), and Allen Eager (ts).

Live at Montmartre / STEEPLECHASE 1977
Superb Getz, plus some of Joanne Brackeen's finer playing on piano. −RW

Another World / COLUMBIA 1977

Andy Laverne makes a good impression on piano. Getz again is amazing. −RW

Gold / INNER CITY 1977
Recorded for Stan's 50th birthday in 1977 with JoAnne Brackeen on piano and Billy Hart on drums, this album includes two from Getz, Wayne Shorter (sax), and several other single standards. Recorded live at Cafe Monmaitre, Copenhagen. 2-fer. −MGN

The Dolphin / CONCORD 1981
An underrated date. Getz is superb, with a sympathetic trio backing him. −RW

Pure Getz / CONCORD / DB 5 1982
A wonderful quartet date with Getz stretching out and Marc Johnson (b) taking second star. −RW

Poetry / ELEKTRA / DB 5 1983
A sorely overlooked duet with Albert Dailey (p). −RW

Line for Lyons / STORYVILLE 1983
A good collaboration with Chet Baker (tpt) on limited-availability release. −RW

○ **Anniversary! / POLYGRAM** 1990
A brilliant, rousing date, with Kenny Barron (p) in peak form. Getz is enthused, animated, and intense. −RW

Billy Highstreet Samba / POLYGRAM 1990
Another high-quality Getz date. −RW

Serenity / POLYGRAM r 1991
One of his last recordings, this album has beautiful solos from Getz. Kenny Barron is immense on piano. −RW

For Musicians Only / POLYGRAM
This has plenty of great players and lots of amazing music. Getz, Dizzy Gillespie (tpt), and Sonny Stitt (as) are great, as are John Lewis (p) and Herb Ellis (g). −RW

People Time / POLYGRAM
A worthy posthumous set. Two discs of breathtaking songs done with pianist Kenny Barron in the final months of Getz's life. −RW

Stan the Man / VERVE COMP
ca. 1952-1957. A wide variety of musicians all play straightahead. Features Duke Jordan, Jimmy Rowles, Bob Brookmeyer, Lionel Hampton, Oscar Peterson, Mose Allison, Gerry Mulligan, J. J. Johnson, Victor Feldman, Steve Kuhn, Swedish musicians, and more. A 2-fer. All standards. −MGN

GIANTS OF JAZZ

Swing, bop. A 70s group featuring Dizzy Gillespie, Thelonious Monk, Kai Winding, Sonny Stitt, Al McKibbon, and Art Blakey. They made two albums for Mercury. −RW

○ **In Berlin 1971 / POLYGRAM**
Fine supergroup pairing with Dizzy Gillespie, Monk, Sonny Stitt, Kai Winding, Art Blakey, and Al McKibbon. The all-star lineup unites and makes quality music. −RW

MIKE GIBBS ♭ 1937

Progressive big band. Progressive arranger, conductor, composer, pianist, and trombonist. Good at organizing great talent to play his original music, this native of Zimbabwe studied in UK and Boston. He was a disciple of Herb Pomeroy, and worked with Carla Bley. −MGN

○ **Big Music / CAROLINE** r 1990
A session more striking by the presence of a big lineup. −RW

TERRY GIBBS ♭ 1924

Swing, big band, post-bop, cool, Latin, jazz-rock. Vibist Gibbs won a radio amateur contest at 12 and was a professional drummer before joining the army in WWII. He apprenticed with Tommy Dorsey, Chubby Jackson, Buddy Rich, and Woody Herman in the 40s, then with Louie Bellson and Benny Goodman in the 50s, before getting his own group. Gibbs didn't play with the vitality or inspired flair of Milt Jackson, but he could provide highly charged solos or accompaniment in a more swing-era mode than straight bop. Many feel his 40s big band, which often had Mel Lewis on drums, was a forerunner to the Thad Jones/Mel Lewis big band. –RW

Dream Band - Vol. 1 / CONTEMPORARY 1959
Reissue of a session with Gibbs leading a fine big band. –RW

Dream Band - Vol. 2 / CONTEMPORARY 1959
The Sundown Sessions. A 1987 reissue of big-band dates. Nicely played, with excellent arrangements but a low energy level. –RW

Dream Band - Vol. 3 / CONTEMPORARY 1959
Flying Home. The third in the series. –RW

Dream Band - Vol. 5 / CONTEMPORARY 1959
The Big Cat. The last of the quintet, and one of the better volumes in the series. –RW

○ **El Nutto / LIMELIGHT** 1964
From the vibist and quartet with pianist Alice McLeod, featuring all originals. –MGN

Latin Connection / CONTEMPORARY 1986
Fine playing by Frank Morgan (sax) and Tito Puente (per). Gibbs handles Afro-Latin rhythms expertly. –RW

Chicago Fire / CONTEMPORARY 1987

ASTRUD GILBERTO b 1940

Ballads, Latin. Vocals. Before 1963, it's doubtful anyone outside her native city of Rio had ever heard of Astrud Gilberto. Then, in response to a request to sing the English lyrics to a song titled "The Girl from Ipanema," history was made. Despite (or perhaps, in part, because of) a deadpan and childlike vocal style, she and the song were a smash. Gilberto toured frequently through the years with Getz; the 1964 album *Getz A-Go-Go* was a chart-topper and has just been reissued. –RW

○ **Look at the Rainbow / POLYGRAM** 1966
Good 1986 reissue of sessions arranged and conducted by Gil Evans. –RW

Plus James Last Orchestra / POLYGRAM 1986
1987 release. Gilberto still has alluring sound. –RW

Silver Collection / POLYGRAM COMP
Collection of her bossa-nova material. –RW

DIZZY GILLESPIE b 1917

Bop, soul jazz, progressive big band, world fusion. This year (1992) marks the 75th anniversary of a musical legend, personality, and innovator — John Birks "Dizzy" Gillespie. Though his father died when he was 10, he had an enormous influence on Dizzy through his mastery of multiple instruments — he played bass, mandolin, drums, and piano. Dizzy began on trombone at 12, then picked up the trumpet a year later.

The Gillespie approach, which flowered in the 40s, represented the next phase from Armstrong in terms of individual virtuosity on trumpet. From the incredible leaps across intervals, the smears and slurs, riveting work in the upper register, amazing angular runs, and pinpoint swing ability, Dizzy Gillespie's solos were seldom less than works of art. This solo style began to emerge in 1937, when he replaced his idol Roy Eldridge in the Teddy Hill band. He stayed with them two years, during which he recorded his first solos. He later became a star with Cab Calloway from 1939-1941, learning to write big band arrangements and also making friends with Charlie Parker. Gillespie was a participant in jam sessions at Minton's Playhouse, working out fresh, then-radical ideas about harmony and playing. Gillespie worked two years with various big bands from 1941-1943, among them Benny Carter, Charlie Barnet, and Earl Hines; he later worked in small combos on 52nd Street in 1944, then joined Billy Eckstine's band. He left Eckstine in 1945, then formed and toured with his own big band following a short period when he headed a small group called the Three Deuces. His

band, which included Parker on alto sax, bassist Curley Russell, and drummer Sid Catlett, played this new music and astonished the jazz world. Later Gillespie recruited some new members and took a sextet to California for eight weeks in December 1945.

He re-formed a big band in 1946 and disbanded it in 1950. Since 1950, Gillespie has led countless small combos and served as a larger-than-life spokesman for jazz, the Bahai faith, and music in general. Gillespie has penned many anthems, among them "A Night in Tunisia" and "Salt Peanuts," and his contributions to Latin and Afro-Latin music have often been underrated or undervalued. He's an excellent conga player, had Chano Pozo in his band in the late 40s, and has been a surrogate father and mentor for such current stars as Jon Faddis and Arturo Sandoval. He's also been one of the most vibrant and cheerful onstage performers, sometimes drawing fire for alleged comical excesses in concert. –RW

○ **Dizziest / RCA** 1946
An interesting reissue of 1946-1949 material. Bopish scat vocals and explosive Gillespie solos. Johnny Hartman (v) is suave and smooth. –RW

At Salle Pleyel (Paris, France - 1948) / PRESTIGE 1948

○ **Development of an American Artist / SMITH.** 194?
A thorough compilation of Gillespie's formative 40s dates. Available by mail-order only from the Smithsonian. –RW

● **Groovin' High / MUSICRAFT** 194?
A nice repacking and reissue of seminal mid-40s Gillespie small bands. –RW

Legendary Big Band Concerts / VOGUE 194?
Formative material from the late 40s. Gillespie's solos are full of force, ideas, and energy. The sound quality fluctuates. –RW

One Bass Hit / MUSICRAFT 194?
A good reissue spotlighting Gillespie's prime orchestra in the mid 40s. –RW

Dizzy Gillespie / DEE GEE i 1951
W/ Joe Carroll (v).

★ **Greatest Jazz Concert Ever / PRESTIGE** 1953
Despite a debatable title, this was a summit meeting of jazz legends at Massey Hall in the early 50s. Gillespie and Charlie Parker are transcendent, while Bud Powell makes some slashing statements on piano. Mingus (b) and Max Roach (d) complete the brilliant lineup. –RW

Dizzy Gillespie with Roy Eldridge / VERVE 1954
1954 & 1955 sessions. This spry, sparkling collection pairs Gillespie with a fellow giant. A sparkling collaboration, with Oscar Peterson (p) assisting. –RW

One Night in Washington / ELEKTRA 1955
A superb live date that Elektra reissued for a short while, then deleted. –RW

Duets: Sonny Rollins & Sonny Stitt / POLYGRAM 1957
Includes sax greats Rollins and Stitt. Incendiary, robust material. –RW

Sonny Side Up / POLYGRAM 1957
W/ Sonny Rollins and Sonny Stitt (sax). The dynamic threesome hit some impressive heights, with Stitt at his peak. –RW

○ **Dee Gee Days / SAVOY** 195?
This is an essential compilation of 50s sides on Savoy, including prime early Coltrane on alto sax. –RW

S'Wonderful / VOGUE 195?
This is an excellent reissue of outstanding early-50s big-band dates. –RW

Portrait of Duke Ellington / POLYDOR r 1961
A reverential tribute. –RW

Dizzy on the French Riviera / PHILIPS 1962
A 1986 reissue of a sterling concert. The European players are good-to-boring, but Gillespie is frequently riveting. –RW

Something Old, Something New / PHILLIPS 1963

A great quintet, with James Moody (sax) in peak form. −RW

○ **Swing Low Sweet Cadillac / MCA**   1967
Very entertaining Diz. −MGN

Portrait of Jennie / PERCEPTION   1970
This little-known but beautifully-played combo session from the 70s seems to have totally vanished from the face of the earth. −RW

○ **Afro-Cuban Jazz Moods / OJC / DB 5**   1975
W/ Machito (per). A revolutionary album. A must-buy! −MGN

Jam Montreux 1977 / OJC   1977
This is frequently explosive, exciting Gillespie, though everything else seems pretty conservative and standard. −RW

New Faces / GRP   1984
Branford Marsalis (ts) and Kenny Kirkland (p) help out the venerable trumpet giant. −RW

Live at Royal Festival Hall / RHINO   1989
This is a recent all-star effort, with Gillespie exciting and enjoyable. Pacquito D'Rivera burns on alto sax, while longtime friends James Moody (sax) and Slide Hampton (tb) are part of the orchestra. −RW

And Stan Getz / POLYGRAM

Dizzy's Party / PABLO
Excellent straight bop/mainstream date with a festive air. −RW

Trumpet Kings Meet Turner / PA2
This is an excellent collaboration by three established, outstanding trumpeters, plus rollicking Joe Turner (v) near the end of a wonderful career. W/ Roy Eldridge (tpt) & Harry Edision (tpt). −RW

JOHN GILMORE   b 1931

Hard-bop, post-bop, early free, progressive big band, modern creative. John Gilmore was among the most versatile and dynamic tenor saxophonists of all time, though he spent most of his career contributing to the Sun Ra Arkestra. He was extremely effective performing both hard-bop, fluid solos and doing freer, high-energy material with upper register effects and fireworks. He was also the Arkestra's auxiliary drummer. Gilmore played tenor and clarinet in high school during the 40s, and later in an army band. He spent one year with the Earl Hines band in 1952, then began working almost exclusively with Sun Ra from 1953 until his death, with the exception of one year in the mid 60s with Art Blakey. −RW

○ **Blowing in from Chicago / BLUE NOTE**   i 1957
W/ Clifford Jordan (ts).

JIMMY GIUFFRE   b 1921

Swing, big band, bop, early free, progressive big band. Composer, clarinet, tenor sax, baritone sax. A genuine multi-talent, Jimmy Giuffre has never failed to turn in a quality performance, no matter what the context or instrument. From his student days at North Texas State, Giuffre moved to the big bands of Jimmy Dorsey, Buddy Rich, and Woody Herman, where he penned the immortal "Four Brothers" and the fine "For Others." He ventured into experimental circles in the 50s but fell somewhere between avant-garde and total chaos. His work in the 70s and 80s saw him emphasize supreme tonal quality on all instruments. At times he incorporated the swing style of his youth, at other times he again employed unconventional devices. −RW

Four Brothers and Tangents in Jazz / AFFINITY   1954
This is Giuffre's first major album as a leader for Capitol. −RW

○ **Jimmy Giuffre 3 / ATLANTIC / DB 5**   1956
Wonderful recording with guitarist Jim Hall that features the classic "The Train And the River." −MGN

Princess / FINI   1958
An exceptional date with Jim Hall (g). −RW

● **Lee Konitz Meets Jimmy Giuffre / VERVE**   1959
A simply amazing collaboration. Extra spice comes from Hal McKusick (as), Warne Marsh (ts), and Bill Evans (p). −RW

The Easy Way / VERVE   1959

A compelling trio date with Jim Hall (g). −RW

Free Fall / COLUMBIA   1962
Fine trio pieces with Paul Bley (p) and Steve Swallow (b). −RW

Quiet Song / COLUMBIA   1974
Exceptional trio output with Paul Bley (p) and Bill Connors (g). −RW

IAI Festival / IMPROVISING ARTISTS   1978
First-rate quartet with Lee Konitz (as), Paul Bley (p), and Bill Connors (g). −RW

○ **Dragonfly / SOUL NOTE**   1983
Giuffre enters the 80s with a bang. −RW

Liquid Dancers / SOUL NOTE   ca. 1991
Giuffre's most recent effort. −RW

DON GOLDIE   b 1930

Big band, bop, instr-pop. Trumpeter enamored with Louis Armstrong. Played his share of pop, studio sessions, and older period jazz. A virtuoso musician. −MGN

Brilliant / ARGO   i 1960
W/ Eddie Higgins.

LARRY GOLDINGS   b 1968

Post-bop, instr-pop, neo bop. Contemporary jazz bassist who is currently recording on the Verve label. −RW

○ **Intimacy of the Blues / POLYGRAM**
W/ Fathead Newman (sax) and Bill Stewart (b). −RW

VINNY GOLIA   b 1956

Progressive big band, modern creative. A prolific avant-gardist, Golia plays a vast array (nay, battalion) of reed instruments. Perhaps a reaction/response to the political climate of conservative Los Angeles (his home) brings out the fire in his sound, also partially due to his native New Jersey. Has led very large orchestras (arguably his best work) or scaled down small groups. Plays solo on occasion. −MGN

○ **Spirits in Fellowship / NINE WINDS**   1977
His first album, quartet recordings w/ John Carter (cl). "Haiku" is Balinese or Tibetan-like, "The Human Beings" for Louis Armstrong, and "Duke Ellington & the American Indian" are Golia's passion and compass for freedom. Boldly inventive. −MGN

BENNY GOLSON   b 1929

Bop, hard-bop, post-bop, cool, soul jazz, progressive big band. Tenor saxophonist, composer, arranger. Golson is another jazz veteran with strong R&B ties. He began with Bull Moose Jackson in the early 50s, then worked with Lionel Hampton and Johnny Hodges and later with Earl Bostic. A two-year period with Dizzy Gillespie helped his arranging and composing skills flower, and he became an in-demand writer. Along with Art Farmer, he cofounded the Jazztet in 1959 and kept it going until 1962. After the Jazztet folded, Golson decided to be a writer exclusively and spent the remainder of the decade writing for recording sessions, television series, and commercials. He began playing again in the late 70s and re-formed the Jazztet in 1982 for periodic engagements. A good if derivative soloist with a big-tone and warm sound. His best-known composition is "Killer Joe." −RW

Benny Golson's New York Scene / OJC   1957
This was one of the first albums to establish Golson's reputation as a soloist and composer. −RW

● **Other Side of Benny Golson / OJC**   1958
Golson's on top of the game. Excellent band and sound. −MGN

Groovin' with Golson / OJC   1959
A mainstream date with traces of soul-jazz. Golson is solidly in the pocket on tenor. −RW

Blues on Down / MILESTONE   195?
A good pairing of two fine albums that cemented his sound and concept. −RW

Take a Number from 1 to 10 / ARGO   1960

An often surprising session, with Golson veering between conventional arrangements and pop/soul-jazz influences. –RW

Turning Point / MERCURY 1962
A quartet session that is surging and frequently electric. –RW

Free / ARGO / DB 5 1962
Includes some of Golson's hottest, most expressive solos. –RW

Killer Joe / COLUMBIA 1977
This album broke Golson's long hiatus in America and reintroduced him to the domestic jazz audience, but it wasn't quite the hit for him as for Quincy Jones. –RW

○ **California Message / TIMELESS** 1980
This fine small-combo effort was one of many for the Timeless label in the early 80s. –RW

Stardust / DENON 1987
A high-caliber session, with Golson and Freddie Hubbard (tpt) more than capably splitting the leadership duties. –RW

EDDIE GOMEZ   b 1944

Post-bop, Latin, jazz-rock, neo bop, modern creative. Bassist. This Puerto Rican player is able to do everything from free to fusion jazz and is especially good in trio settings and when backing pianists. Gomez was raised in New York and joined the Newport Jazz Festival Band at 14. His early experiences with Rufus Jones, Marian McPartland, and Gary MacFarland were instructive, but his year-long stint with Paul Bley was monumental — he began to expand his ideas about the range and style of his playing. Gomez's repertoire truly grew during an 11-year stay with pianist Bill Evans. He became known for his forays into the bass's upper register and for his melodic adventurousness. He later brought that same flashy technique to the electric bass, though he mostly preferred playing amplified acoustic in fusion sessions. Since 1977 he has been very busy, and he helped found the group Steps (later Steps Ahead) in 1979. –RW

○ **Gomez / POLYGRAM** 1984
Nice, mainstream fare. –RW

Street Smart / CBS 1990
A session with a balance between radio-oriented fusion and more ambitious traditional material. –RW

PAUL GONSALVES   1970-1974

Big band, cool. Among the most expressive, frenetic tenor players in jazz history. Indeed, his exciting, polyrhythmic technique enabled Gonsalves to get away with a rather fragile, thin tone. He played with Shabby Lewis and Count Basie in the 40s and with Dizzy Gillespie briefly in 1949-1950, but it was his 24 years with Duke Ellington that cemented Gonsalves's fame. Gonsalves was a competitor who seldom lost in jam-session battles. His incredible, 20-plus chorus solo on "Diminuendo and Crescendo in Blue" at the 1956 Newport Jazz Festival is a musical high point and helped get the Ellington band on the cover of *Time* magazine. –RW

○ **Cookin' / ARGO** r 1957
With Clark Terry (tpt). –MGN

Gettin' Together / OJC 1960
W/ Nat Adderley (cnt). –RW

Salt & Pepper / JASMINE 1963
This is probably unavailable in the US now. It's a very good collaboration with Sonny Stitt (as). –RW

Tell It the Way It Is / IMPULSE ca. 1963
With Johnny Hodges (as). –MGN

Buenos Aires Session / CATALYST 1968
Music that is lush and sentimental. Effortless bluesy tenor from Gonsalves. –RW

● **Just A-Sittin' and A-Rockin' / BLACK LION** 1970
It's hard to find better or more enjoyable small-group blues, swing, and jazz. –RW

○ **Mexican Bandit / FANTASY** 1973

Here is a sumptuous pairing with Roy Eldridge (tpt). Both are super. –RW

VIRGIL GONSALVES   b 1931

Post-bop, cool. California-based sax player who played with Alvino Rey, Jack Fina, and Tex Beneke before forming his own group. Recorded three albums as a leader. –DS

○ **Jazz San Francisco Style / LIBERTY** 1955
A cool and bouncy sound from this neglected saxist. –DS

BABS GONZALES   1919-1980

Bop, ballads. Vocals. A be-bop vocalese wacko of another kind. Comedic extension of Joe Carroll and Eddie Jefferson. Delightfully out-to-lunch. –MGN

Voila! / HOPE i 1958
W/ Johnny Griffin (ts).

Tales of Manhattan / JARO i 1959
W/ Les Spann (g).

Sundays at Small's Paradise / DAUNTLESS i 1963

○ **Weird Lullaby / BLUE NOTE** COMP
Long unavailable sessions from 1947, 1949, 1956, and 1958. 20 tracks, including three-bips-and-a-bop sessions with Todd Dameron, the first Sonny Rollins recording. Also with Don Redman, Ray Nance, Herbie Stewart, Jimmy Smith (organ), Art Pepper (sax), and countless others. A prize. –MGN

DENNIS GONZALEZ   b 1954

Post-bop, modern creative. This Dallas multi-instrumentalist is a prolific, progressive composer, concentrating on trumpet and percussion. –MGN

Little Toot / DAAGNIM 1985
Octet recording with an emphasis on horns and improvisation. Gonzalez has many other fine recordings. If you like creative music, seek them out. –MGN

○ **Stefan / SILKHEART** 1986
Creative trumpeter and percussionist leads ensemble. All originals and a fresh unconventional sound. –MGN

JERRY GONZALEZ   b 1949

Bop, post-bop, progressive big band, Latin, neo bop. A first-rate conga player and trumpeter, Jerry Gonzalez heads one of the best contemporary Latin-jazz groups, the Fort Apache Band. A New Yorker, his music merges traditional Afro-Cuban rhythms, urban sensibility, and jazz ambition. –RW

● **River Is Deep / RHINO** 1986
Powerhouse group; strong material. A sparkling session that helped cement Gonzalez's status among the new crop of Latin-jazz stars. –RW

Rumba Para Monk / SUNNYSIDE 1988
Great production by Jim Anderson on eight Monk standards. Stripped to quintet with Carter Jefferson, the tenor sax foil. Very intriguing concept, melding Latin rhythms to Monk's off minorisms. –MGN

☆ **Obatala / ENJA** 1988
Live in Zurich. Killers with killin' repertoire includes "Nefertiti" (sounds crossed with Bass Desires's "Samauri Hee Haw"), Monk's "Evidence" and "Jackie-ing," Miles and Ron Carter's "81," plus two chants. Outstanding band with Larry Willis, Pop Vasquez (tb), Edgardo Miranda (g), and percussionists J. Gonzalez, Steve Bevrios, Flaco Hernandez, and the immortal Nicky Marrero and Milton Cardona. Saxophonist John Stubblefield is also on it for good reason — he is a great lyrical improviser. –MGN

Earthdance / SUNNYSIDE 1990
Red-hot modern Afro-Latin and Latin-jazz, with driving grooves, great playing, and up-to-the-minute rhythms. –RW

Earthdance / SUNNYSIDE 1990
Split between jazz and Latin-jazz. Sextet with Joe Ford (alto/soprano sax) joining. Studio version of the 1981 number one hit by Monk, Larry Willis (the gorgeous "Night Fall"),

Wayne Shorter, I. Gonzalez, and Eddie Heyman's "When I Fall In Love." –MGN

BENNY GOODMAN   1909-1986

Swing, big band, instr-pop. By the time he formed his first big band in 1934, Goodman had been a pro for a decade. Born into a large and poor family in Chicago (of which he became the main support after his father's death in 1926), he joined drummer Ben Pollack's band at 16, came to New York with it in 1928, and soon was one of the Big Apple's most in-demand recording and radio studio musicians. His clarinet style, influenced at first by Jimmie Noone and Frank Teschemacher, was fluent and swinging and was widely imitated during the Swing Era, which he helped ring in. As a bandleader, Goodman was a demanding taskmaster. He lived for music and expected others to be as dedicated; this often caused friction, but the personnel of his bands, which he led full-time until 1948 and sporadically thereafter, nevertheless was quite stable. Dubbed "King of Swing," a title he neither invented nor invited but felt no need to refuse, Goodman helped break down racial barriers in popular music by hiring pianist Teddy Wilson, vibist Lionel Hampton, guitarist Charlie Christian, trumpeter Cootie Williams, and other Black stars-to-be, first for his small "bands-within-the-band," then for the full orchestra. His choice of arrangers, chief among them Fletcher Henderson (though Jimmy Mundy was the most productive), also bespoke his admiration for Black musical creativity. Goodman helped launch the band — leading the careers of Gene Krupa, Harry James, and Hampton, among others. He liked to perform classical music and commissioned compositions from Béla Bartók, Paul Hindemith, Aaron Copland, and Leonard Bernstein. Though he periodically went into semi-retirement, Goodman could never stay away from his beloved clarinet for long; at the very end of his life, he was once again leading a big band that specialized in Fletcher Henderson arrangements. Until the end, the number of his fans was legion. DM

Clarinet à La King - Vol. 2 / CBS   193?
1988 reissue, more superb cuts from the late 30s and early 40s. –RW

○ **Legendary Performer / RCA**   193?
A valuable collection of mid-30s sides, now available in new, better mastered collections. –RW

★ **Sing, Sing, Sing / RCA**   193?
Prime 30s material reissued. –RW

Complete Benny Goodman - Vols. 1-8 / RCA   1935
1935-1939. The value of this series has now dipped somewhat, with new, better remastered lines. Still, it is his RCA/Bluebird cuts issued in chronological order. –RW

○ **Carnegie Hall Concert / CBS**   1938
Sensational 1987 reissue that features excellent material from his great appearance at Carnegie Hall. –RW

Live at Carnegie Hall / POLYGRAM   1938
Live and explosive. Features seven incredible performances from his Trio and Quartet. –CK

☆ **Featuring Charlie Christian / CBS**   1939
1939-1941. The cream of his sessions with the great guitarist Charlie Christian. –RW

From Spirituals to Swing / VANGUARD   1939
Carnegie Hall concerts featuring five great early Goodman Sextet performances plus a host of jazz greats. –CK

Sextet / CBS   193?
1989 reissue with gorgeous performances from his vital late-30s, early-40s sextet with Charlie Christian (g) and Lionel Hampton (vib). –RW

Best of Big Bands / CBS   193?
Some nice late-30s and 40s material. –RW

Roll 'Em Live: 1941 / VINTAGE JAZZ   1941
Good collaboration with Big Sid Catlett (d). Not-so-good sound quality. –RW

Small Groups: 1941-1945 / CBS   1941
Tremendous 40s cuts with various Goodman bands. –RW

Slipped Disc, 1945-46 / CBS   1945
1988 reissue of some nice 40s cuts. –RW

All the Cats Join In - Vol. 3 / CBS   194?
1988 reissue, fine early-40s material. –RW

B. G. In Hi-Fi / CAPITOL / BB 7   195?
Tremendous 1989 reissue of some fine 50s Goodman. –RW

○ **Together Again! / RCA**   1963
W/ Lionel Hampton (vib), Gene Krupa (d), Teddy Wilson (p). Excellent 1987 reissue of wonderful release that reunited surviving members of his landmark late-30s and early-40s small group. –RW

Live in Stockholm 1970 / POLYGRAM   1970
1988 reissue. –RW

☆ **After You've Gone - Vol. 1 / RCA-BLUEBIRD**   COMP
The Original Benny Goodman Trio and Quartet. The complete Trio and Quartet sides for Victor. Great sound. –CK

Airplay / CBS   COMP
1989 reissue covering previously unreleased material from live broadcasts. –RW

Avalon - Vol. 2 / RCA   COMP
Some nice small-combo material. –RW

Collector's Edition / CBS   COMP
Some wonderful sessions. Part of Masterpieces series. –RW

Greatest Hits / CBS   COMP
Highly misleading title, but some valuable material. –RW

Roll 'Em - Vol. 1 / CBS   COMP
1987 reissue, sparkling big-band cuts. –RW

This Is Benny Goodman - Vol. 1 & 2 / RCA   COMP
First volume in attempted overview series. –RW

○ **Yale Recordings - Vols. 1-6 / MUM**   COMP
This complete set consists of unreleased recordings and cuts from his private collection that were given to the Yale Archives after his death in 1986. They cover the gamut of studio and live dates. Any and all of them are worth having. –RW

MICK GOODRICK

Jazz-rock. A technical genius on the guitar, his music is well worth study. He is a fine teacher as well. His limited recordings show an individuality that defies easy description, though a "post-fusion" label might work. A true champion of improvised music. –MGN

○ **Biorhythms / CMP**
Fusion. –MGN

BOB GORDON   1928-1955

Post-bop, cool. Brilliant California baritone-sax player who recorded with Chet Baker, Herbie Harper, Shelly Manne, and Bill Holman. Tragically, he died in a car crash on route to a gig. Recorded one album as a leader. –DS

○ **Meet Mr. Gordon / PACIFIC JAZZ**   1954
A brilliant testimony to the baritone-sax player who helped define the cool and bouncy West Coast sound. W/ Jack Montrose (ts). –DS

DEXTER GORDON   1923-1990

Bop, hard-bop, post-bop, cool. The leading tenor stylist of bebop, Gordon's personal amalgam of Lester Young, Charlie Parker, and himself set the tenor pace until the maturity of Sonny Rollins, who was influenced by Dexter. Even more so was John Coltrane, whose earliest recorded solos are pure Gordon. Dexter — six feet, three inches, filled with charm — had periodic bouts with drugs that interrupted his career (which took off after early work with the bands of Lionel Hampton, Louis Armstrong, and Billy Eckstine). In 1962 he settled in Denmark. There he found steady work and a stable lifestyle, and when he returned to the US in 1976, he was at the top of his playing form and enjoyed the greatest success of his career. In 1986, he starred in the French film *Round Midnight*, for which he got an Oscar nomination. At his best, Gordon could play chorus upon chorus without repeating himself, notably on the blues or rhythm changes; he was also a master of the ballad. –DM

Long Tall Dexter / SAVOY   1945
1945-1947. Brilliant, compelling early Gordon dates. –RW

Hunt / SAVOY / DB 5   1947
Sparkling, torrid tenor sax workouts with Gordon and the much underrated Wardell Gray (ts). –RW

Dexter Calling.... / BLUE NOTE   1951
A standout among Gordon's many exceptional Blue Note albums. –RW

Dexter Blows Hot & Cool / DUOTONE-BOPLICITY 1955
Wonderful and inventive Dexter. –RW

Doin' Alright / BLUE NOTE   1961
A high-quality Blue Note date with touches of soul-jazz and African-American slang influence in the title. –RW

Go! / BLUE NOTE / DB 5   1962
With the Sonny Clark (p) Trio. Classic Dexter repertoire included, like "Cheese Cake" and "Love For Sale." Rhythm section a monster. –MGN

Swingin' Affair / BLUE NOTE / DB 5   1962
Brilliant session. Gordon is at his razor-sharp best. –RW

● **Our Man in Paris / BLUE NOTE**   1963
This is a tremendous album done in Paris w/ Bud Powell (p), Kenny Clarke (d), and Pierre Michelot (b). 1987 reissue, CD version. –RW

One Flight Up / BLUE NOTE   1964
A fine session, done in France. –RW

Clubhouse / BLUE NOTE   1965
A sterling reissue of an outstanding release. –RW

Gettin' Around / BLUE NOTE   1965
A solid date. –RW

Montmartre Collection / BLACK LION   1967
This excellent two-disc sampler is from Gordon's extensive sessions at the famed Montmartre Club. –RW

Day in Copenhagen / POLYDOR   1969
W/ Slide Hampton (tb). A superior collaboration between longtime comrades. –RW

○ **Tower of Power / OJC**   1969
An exceptional late-60s album with Gordon meeting the challenge supplied by James Moody (ts). A super rhythm section as well. –RW

The Panther / PRESTIGE / DB 5   1970
Here is outstanding Gordon, backed by knockout piano from Tommy Flanagan. –RW

The Chase / PRESTIGE   1970
A two-tenor workout with Gene Ammons. –RW

Jumpin' Blues / PRESTIGE   1970
Amazing piano from Wynton Kelly, fine Gordon. –RW

★ **Homecoming / CBS / DB 5**   1976
Live at the Village Vanguard. His return to the US. Landmark album for the music (which is extraordinary) and the media attention it garnered. May have been the turning point for the popularity of jazz, but give Gordon and his mates their due for being the virtuosos that pulled it off. W/ Woody Shaw (tpt). Ten prime cuts. –MGN

Nights at the Keystone - Vols. 1-3 / BLUE NOTE   1978
1978 & 1979. This is a series of solid late-70s live dates done at the Keystone. George Cables nearly steals the show on piano. 1990 reissue. –RW

Gotham City / CBS   1981
A good session, though George Benson (g) sometimes sounds a bit lost. Art Blakey (d) makes a rare appearance outside Messengers. –RW

Other Side of Round Midnight / BLUE NOTE   1985

Outtakes and alternate cuts from the soundtrack of the film that got him an Oscar nomination. –RW

JOE GORDON   1928-1963

Big band, bop, hard-bop, post-bop, cool. A veteran jazz trumpeter with a style that has swing era roots, but also flexible enough to play in a mainstream or bop setting. Gordon has a very small discography; currently there are only a couple of early 60s sessions in print. –RW

○ **Lookin' Good! / OJC**   1961
This trumpeter is in good form. A chance to discover an uncrowned king. –MGN

DANNY GOTTLIEB   b 1953

Jazz-rock, neo bop. Veteran contemporary drummer and clinician. Overwhelming technique harnessed into concise, driving propulsion. Much in demand, quite musical. –MGN

○ **Aquamarine / ATLANTIC**
The debut album from this former Pat Metheny Group drummer, featuring guitarist John Abercrombie. –PK

Whirlwind / ATLANTIC
Great followup album, with an incredible list of sidemen, featuring John Abercrombie (g). –PK

JIMMY GOURLEY   b 1926

Bop, blues-jazz. Guitarist. A veteran of the jazz wars! Played bop in Paris, and has done his share of blues and rock. He is an on-call studio cat who truly can do it all. –MGN

○ **The Left Bank of New York / UPTOWN**   1986

SANDY GRAHAM

Trad, swing, cool. Contemporary jazz and pop-tinged vocalist whose last release was done in 1989 for the Muse label. –RW

○ **Sandy Graham / MUSE**   1989
1991 release. Graham is a very straightforward performer. Good supporting cast with Kenny Burrell (g) particularly strong. –RW

STEPHANE GRAPPELLI   b 1908

Swing. The sole survivor of the first generation of accomplished European jazz musicians, Grappelli in his 80s is as elegant and smooth on the fiddle as ever. A chance encounter with the great Gypsy guitarist Django Reinhardt led to the formation of the unique Quintet du Hot Club de France in 1934. Despite extreme differences in temperament and character, the musical partnership continued until 1939, when Grappelli decided to stay in Great Britain for the duration of World War II. After the war, they worked together again for about a year, but then went their separate ways. Grappelli's international career blossomed in the 70s, the decade during which he established his popularity in the US with many festival, club, and concert appearances, and on records with his collaborations with Yehudi Menuhin. Grappelli has a beautiful tone, perfect intonation, and a flair for making a melody swing and sing. –DM

○ **Violins No End / PABLO**   1957
With Stuff Smith (violin), and the Oscar Petersen Trio. No disappointments; a great session. All standards except two improvised blues. –MGN

Feeling + Finesse Equals Jazz / ATLANTIC   1962

★ **Duke Ellington's Jazz Violin Summit / ATLANTIC** 1963
The Duke assembles Grappelli, Svend Asmussen (violin), and Ray Nance (violin), to maximum effect. –RW

Afternoon in Paris / VERVE   1971
A stately, often saucy, session. –RW

Homage to Django / CLASSIC JAZZ   1972
A nice two-record set, though Grappelli towers over the British session pros. –RW

Parisian Thoroughfare / BLACK LION / DB 5   1973

Thoughtful at times, funky in spots. Gary Burton (vib) proves a fine partner. −RW

The Reunion, w/ George Shearing / POLYGRAM 1976
A high-caliber reissue of a delightful date with George Shearing (p). −RW

Tea for Two / EMI 1977
This is the best of Grappelli's dates with Yehudi Menuhin (violin). −RW

Live at Carnegie Hall / CBS / DB 5 1978
This is an entertaining set on Bob Thiele's short-lived Signature label. −RW

Young Django / POLYGRAM 1979
Outstanding selections. Grappelli gets intense support from Larry Coryell (g) and Phillip Catherine (g). −RW

Tivoli Gardens, w/ Joe Pass / OJC 1979
This is a 1990 reissue of an excellent set — sterling work all around. −RW

○ **A Two-Fer! / MUSE** 1979
A wonderful release, with Hank Jones the dominant second voice on piano. −RW

Happy Reunion, w/ Martial Solal / RHINO 1980
A 1991 reissue of a super collaboration between Grappelli and pianist Martial Solal. −RW

At the Winery / CONCORD 1980
A fine date, with good work from John Etheridge (g). −RW

Plays Jerome Kern / GRP 1987
Tasteful orchestrations and exuberant interpretations make this much better than the usual GRP outing. CD version has two bonus cuts. −RW

Olympia 1988 / ATLANTIC 1988
The CD issue has six bonus cuts plus some riveting piano from Martial Solal. Svend Asmussen comes aboard for some tasty violin duets. −RW

One on One, w/ McCoy Tyner / MILESTONE · 1990
This unlikely pair works well. Very interesting harmonic combinations. −MGN

In Tokyo / DENON 1990
Live at Bunkamura Cocoon in Tokyo. Grappelli also plays some piano. One of the violin legend's better albums of the past decade. −MGN

Shades of Django / POLYGRAM
A solid tribute piece, one of several that recount the impact and influence of Reinhardt. −RW

GLEN GRAY   1906-1963

Big band. Alto saxophonist, bandleader. During the 30s, Glen Gray formed a band from an orchestra contracted to Jean Goldkette (called the Orange Blossoms) and named it after a hotel that never opened. Through savvy talent-recruiting and immensely popular records, the Casa Loma Band became a sensation in 1931-1935. This was precision, drilled music with virtually no rhythmic fervor or blues feeling, but the Casa Loma Band maintained its popularity through the 30s and into the 40s. Gray retired in 1950 but kept working with the band until his death in 1963. Alumni include Herb Ellis, Red Nichols, and Bobby Hackett. −RW

○ **Casa Loma in Hi-Fi / CAPITOL / BB 18**
Studio recreation of the original Casa Loma band, which recorded sparingly. Includes both jazz and sweet aspects of Glen Gray. −DS

Best of the Big Bands / CBS COMP
Nice overview of orchestra. −RW

WARDELL GRAY   1921-1955

Big band, bop, hard-bop. Tenor saxophonist. Wardell Gray was on his way to being a jazz giant when he died under mysterious, still-unresolved circumstances. He toured with

the Earl Hines band from 1943 to 1945 after working locally in Detroit. He then settled on the West Coast and had his first session as a leader in 1946. Later he worked twice with Benny Carter and had brief stints with Benny Goodman, Count Basie, and Tadd Dameron in 1948, with subsequent second stays with Goodman and Basie in 1949 and 1950-1951. But it was his remarkable recording sessions in 1946-1950, especially those with Dexter Gordon, that made his reputation. He had the same combination of lyricism, blues fervor, and facility as Lester Young, a major influence, but was also able to incorporate bop techniques, resulting in a sound that was his own and quite striking. −RW

The Chase and the Steeplechase / MCA 1952
1951 & 1952. Exuberant romps with fellow tenors Dexter Gordon and Paul Quinichette. Almost impossible to find. −RW

Live at the Haig / FRESH SOUND 1990
A hot 1952 session with an excellent lineup. Previously issued on Xanadu and Straight Ahead with different titles. −RW

○ **Central Avenue / PRESTIGE** COMP
Excellent sessions in NYC, Detroit, and Los Angeles in 1949, 1950, 1952, 1953. A handful of trio and sax sides, larger bands featuring Dexter Gordon, Art Farmer, Clark Terry, and Sonny Criss, Frank Morgan, and Sonny Clark. Gray's tenor is unmatched. −MGN

GREAT JAZZ TRIO

Post-bop, cool. Hank Jones on piano, Ron Carter on bass, and Tony Williams on drums. Post-bop group that recorded in the 70s. All-stars who make all world mainstream jazz. −MGN

Love for Sale / INNER CITY 1976
Buster Williams joins in bass. Includes six standards. −MGN

Kindness, Joy, Love & Happiness / INNER CITY 1977
Carter rejoins for seven more cuts, including his "Doom," Jones's "Ah, Qui," and an exalted "Freedom Jazz Dance." −MGN

Milestones / INNER CITY 1978
A mix of selections written by Hank Jones, Ron Carter, and Tony Williams (one apiece) and standards; includes a great "81" and "Lush Life." −MGN

○ **New Wine in Old Bottles / INNER CITY** ca. 1978
With "Appointment in Ghana, Again." Features "Little Melonae Again" by McLean and four standards. Hank Jones (p), Ron Carter (b), and Tony Williams (d) join alto-sax master Jackie Mclean. This is a great album by four jazz geniuses. −MGN

● **At the Village Vanguard / INNER CITY**
Album cover features classic photos of playoffs in pro baseball (Roger Moret and Roy White for Red Sox and Yankees). Four boppish numbers. −MGN

Club New Yorker / DENON
Exquisite, creative, and enjoyable trio material from a fine group. −RW

Standard Collection / DENON
Three masters tackle established anthems with zest. −RW

BENNIE GREEN   1923-1977

Swing, big band, bop. Chicago trombonist, influenced by Dizzy Gillespie, worked with Earl Hines in the early and late 40s, early 50s, and saxophonists Coleman Hawkins, Gene Ammons and Charlie Ventura. Bop to post-bop leader. −MGN

Bennie Green Blows His Horn / PRESTIGE 1955
A nice, mainstream showcase for Green's trombone. Charlie Rouse (ts) sparkles outside Monk's group. −RW

○ **Walkin' Down / OJC** 1956
A fine reissue from this trombonist's group. −MGN

BENNY GREEN   b 1964

Post-bop, neo bop. Young jazz pianist, worked with Art Blakey, leads a trio. Influenced by Thelonious Monk, Bud Powell,

McCoy Tyner. Loads of potential; bound to be a premier jazz musician into the year 2000. –MGN

○ **Lineage / CAPITOL**   1990
His best so far. A young pianist influenced by McCoy Tyner (p). Check out "Trust." –MGN

Greens / CAPITOL   r 1991
This is the second release from this fine pianist who is destined to be a major keyboard figure. –RW

BUNKY GREEN   b 1935

Post-bop, neo bop. Green is a good saxophonist, though not an innovator. He has done lots of session work and made some recordings as a leader. He has good tools and is a nice blues and ballads player and a reliable improviser. –RW

● **Places We've Never Been / VANGUARD**   1979
With Randy Brecker (tpt), Al Dailey Trio. Modal "East & West" shows alto saxophonist at his improvisational best. –MGN

In Love Again / MARK   ca. 1987
Quintet with trumpeter Willie Thomas. Three by saxophonist Green, one by Thomas, one cowritten by the pair, one standard ("You Stepped Out Of a Dream"). –MGN

○ **Healing the Pain / DELOS / DB 5**   1990
A fine, understated and underpublicized session from a veteran who's never achieved mass recognition. –RW

FREDDIE GREEN   b 1911

Big band, cool. Freddie Green was the consummate rhythm guitarist, a player who proved you could be as vital to a band's success as any frontline brass or reed soloist. He didn't even use an amplifier and never stepped out front, yet his lines, phrases, and riffs were always a vital ingredient in the Basie orchestra mix. John Hammond heard him at the Black Cat Club in Greenwich Village, and later recommended him to Basie as a replacement for Claude Williams. He auditioned for Basie in his dressing room at the Roseland Ballroom in 1937, and remained with the band until his death. Many consider the rhythm section of Green on guitar, bassist Walter Page, and drummer "Papa" Jo Jones to be the greatest trio in big-band and swing history. –RW

○ **Natural Rhythm / RCA**   1955
Green's *Mr. Rhythm* & Al Cohn's *Natural Seven* albums combined. A wonderful collaboration between Freddie Green (away from the Basie band) and Al Cohn (ts). –RW

GRANT GREEN   1931-1979

Bop, hard-bop, post-bop, cool, blues-jazz, soul jazz. Grant Green is one of the great unsong heroes of jazz guitar. Green always claimed that he listened to horn players and not other guitar players, and it shows. No other player has this kind of single-note linearity (he avoids chordal playing). There is very little of the intellectual element to Green's playing, and his technique is always at the service of his music. And it is music, plain and simple, that makes Green unique. Green recorded during the late 50s and early 60s with players like Jimmy Forrest, Lou Donaldson, and with many organ combos, including those of Jack McDuff and Larry Young. Although he shared time and space with the very popular Wes Montgomery, Grant Green remained his own man. His music is immediately recognizable — perhaps more than any other guitarist. The greatest example of Green's work can be found in the Blue Note boxed set — a treasure. Green has been almost systematically ignored by jazz buffs with a bent toward the cool side, and he has only recently begun to be appreciated for his incredible musicality. Perhaps no guitarist has ever handled standards and ballads with the brilliance of Grant Green. Note: Also see Ike Quebec, Larry Young. –JME

Grantstand / BLUE NOTE   1961
This is his third album for Blue Note. A quartet session with Yusef Lateef (ts, fl) and vintage Jack McDuff on the Hammond organ. The 15-minute "Blues in Maude's Flat" is very nice

indeed, and "My Funny Valentine" (with Lateef on flute) is just plain lovely. No one does standards like Green. –JME

● **Born to Be Blue / BLUE NOTE**   1961
Marvelous 1961/1962 dates, with splendid playing by Ike Quebec (sax), Sonny Clark (p), and Green. CD has three bonus cuts. –RW

☆ **Complete Blue Note with Sonny Clark / MOSAIC**   1961
1961-1962. Includes Blue Note albums *Gooden's Corner, Nigeria, Oleo, Born To Be Blue* (w/ Ike Quebec), plus unissued tracks. Some of the best bluesy jazz in existence, with the guitarist at the top of his form. Great liner notes. Just incredible music. –JME

Nigeria / BLUE NOTE   1962
Annotator Ben Sidran perceptively characterizes Green as "kind of corny at times, but very hip." The guitarist's blues-imbued style retains something of a country twang, and even exploiting the sustain and reflex capacities of his hollow-body electric, he sounds perfectly natural. The familiar tunes all elicit winning solos from Green, but on the sanctified "Necessarily" he is especially good. –FRANCIS DAVIS, CADENCE

Feelin' the Spirit / BLUE NOTE   1962
An entire album of spirituals — all jazz instrumentals. Green, already a bluesy guitarist, lets himself out in the gospel format. The result is an album that remains true to both the jazz and gospel genres. Unique. –JME

Idle Moments / BLUE NOTE   1963
Excellent album, with Green in good form. Bobbi Hutcherson (vib) in the group produces a somewhat different sound than the usual Green album, so make a note of that. Joe Henderson (ts) is hot. –JME

Solid / BLUE NOTE   1964
Green's solos are crisp and clean single-note executions, and Joe Henderson (ts) comes through with some fine moments ... What one gets is the by-now standard Blue Note recording of that era: solid, straightahead jazz with no frills. –CARL BRAUER, CADENCE

○ **Matador / BLUE NOTE**   1965
With Coletrane sidemen McCoy Tyner (p) and Elvin Jones (d) — still with Coltrane at the time. Green tackles the Coltrane hit "My Favorite Things" and pulls it off in his own style. This is a fine album. –JME

GREENE STRING QUARTET

New-age, modern creative. Richard Greene (ex-Seatrain) leads bluegrass-jazz inflected instrumental music influenced by David Grisman. Heavy on rhythm. –MGN

○ **Molly on the Shore / HANNIBAL**
Moving neo-classical cum bluegrass improvisations. –MGN

SONNY GREENWICH   b 1936

Post-bop, modern creative. A Canadian guitarist whose technique, style, and sound set him apart. Greenwich is a remarkable musician. –MGN

Bird of Paradise / JUSTINTIME   1986
Studio date for the eclectic electric guitarist and hermit from Canada. Four originals, two standards. A unique voice on his instrument. –MGN

○ **Live at Sweet Basil / JUSTINTIME**   1987
Live club date in New York City. Three originals and one standard with quartet. This man is an unsung hero, revered by guitarists. –MGN

AL GREY   b 1925

Swing, big band, bop, hard-bop. A crowd-pleasing trombone stylist who became a major name in the late 50s due to his role in the Count Basie orchestra. He became so identifiable there, few remember he also played with Benny Carter, Lucky Millinder, Jimmie Lunceford, Arnett Cobb, Lionel Hampton, and Dizzy Gillespie, plus a navy band, all before Basie. Grey's use of the mute, humor, swing, and rhythmic verve, plus his teamwork in the Basie section and exchanges with Eddie "Lockjaw" Davis made him a world-class hero until he left in the early 60s. Grey did lots of studio work, *Jazz at the Philharmonic*, and George Wein All-Star dates in the 60s. He toured regularly in the 70s with Jimmy Forrest, and in the 80s, after Forrest's death, he worked often with Buddy Tate. He has also returned often for guest stints, records, and appearances with the Basie band. —RW

The Al Grey/Billy Mitchell Sextet / ARGO   i 1961
○ **Having a Ball / ARGO**   i 1963
W/ Dave Burns (tpt).
Grey's Mood / CLASSIC JAZZ   1973
1973 & 1976 sessions.

JANET GRICE

World fusion. One of the few bassoon players in contemporary music. Former Creative Music Studio student. Recordings reflect a love for contemporary Brazilian music. Interesting fusion of classical and South American techniques as a base to improvise from. —MGN

○ **Song for Andy / OPTIMISM**
Bassoonist Grice plays Brazilian themes. —MGN

JOHNNY GRIFFIN   b 1928

Bop, hard-bop, post-bop, cool, progressive big band. Griffin is an amazingly fast, extremely aggressive tenor saxophonist, whose style and technique weld the fervor of swing, the lowdown grit of blues, and the harmonic mastery of the bop era, with a nod toward the freewheeling tendencies of avant-garde, though he's never ventured too far out of the mainstream. A member of Lionel Hampton's Orchestra at 17, Griffin then became a mainstay on the R&B circuit with a breakaway group headed by trumpeter Joe Morris. He had brief stints with Arnett Cobb and Jo Jones in the early 50s, and spent three years in Hawaii, returning to his Chicago hometown in the mid 50s. He led his own group, plus had career-turning tenures with Thelonious Monk and Art Blakey. During the 60s and 70s, Griffin led his own smashing two-tenor group with Eddie "Lockjaw" Davis and was a featured soloist in the Kenny Clarke-Francy Boland big band. He remains active. —RW

Introducing Johnny Griffin / BLUE NOTE   1956
A seminal date that shows Griffin's speed, technique, and power. —RW
○ **A Blowing Session / BLUE NOTE**   1957
Half of this session features Griffin. The other half with fellow tenors Coltrane, Eddie "Lockjaw" Davis, Clifford Jordan, and John Gilmore. —MGN
The Congregation / BLUE NOTE   1957
Sassy, frenetic, brilliant. With implied inspirational fervor. —RW
Way Out! / PRESTIGE   1958
Explosive quartet material. —RW
The Little Giant / OJC   1959
Smashing sextet performances. —RW
The Jams Are Coming / INNER CITY   1975
A nice straightahead date. —RW
● **Live in Tokyo / INNER CITY**   1976
Arguably Griffin's hottest and coolest live-session playing on an album. Horace Parlan (p) is equally incredible. —RW
○ **Return of the Griffin / GALAXY / DB 5**   1978
Griffin's first US album as a leader since the 60s; wonderful solos. —RW
Paris Reunion Band / SONET   1986
Includes some smoking exchanges w/ Woody Shaw (tpt); steady material. —RW
The Cat / POLYGRAM   1990
His latest — a tasty, often impressive, outing. —RW

TINY GRIMES   b 1916

Swing, big band, bop, cool, blues-jazz. Guitarist Grimes is a unique musician's musician, a veteran performer on the 4-string tenor guitar whose playing touches on the best of blues, vintage R&B, and small-group swing jazz. He has been an accomplished sessionman throughout his life (including many recordings with Charlie Parker), a frequent jam-session participant, and a danceband leader in the 40s and 50s, whose popular Rocking Highlanders wore kilts and tams onstage! —MB

Callin' the Blues / OJC   1958
Long, informal, laid-back jams. Good guitar, as always, in a jazzier vein than his early work. —MB
Tiny Grimes & Friends / COLLECTABLES   195?
Fine 50s and 60s music; very bad production and remastering, though. —RW
Tiny in Swingsville / SWINGSVILLE   i 1960
W/ Jerome Richardson on reeds. —ED
○ **Profoundly Blue / MUSE / DB 5**   1973
Just a brilliant, restrained, and bluesy date. —RW
Some Groovy Fours / CLASSIC JAZZ   1974
Tasty date with Lloyd Glenn (p). —RW
★ **Volume 1 & 2 / COLLECTABLES**   COMP
Amazing high-octane R&B from the golden age, with Red Prysock's honkin' tenor sax and Screamin' Jay Hawkins's earliest vocals. —MB

GRIOT GALAXY

M-base, modern creative. "The Sci-Fi Band," Detroit's premier creative improvised band. With three horns and two on rhythm. They're not afraid to cut loose. —MGN

○ **Kins / BLACK & WHITE**   1981
Detroit's powerful creative music innovators, 3 saxes, bass and drums. On a par with WSQ or AEC. David McMurray, Anthony Holland and Faruq Z. Bey (saxes), Tani Tabbal (d), and Jaribu Shahid (b). —MGN

DON GROLNICK

Post-bop, neo bop. Clever composer, very able pianist and an excellent producer. Very inspirational to NYC's neo-bop/contemporary instrumentalists. Capable jazz and fusion presence. Limited recordings, but ones that are out are worthwhile. —MGN

Hearts and Numbers / WINDHAM HILL   ca. 1985
A very attractive contemporary project. "Pointing at the Moon" and "More Pointing" make for sprightly music. —MGN
○ **Weaver of Dreams / CAPITOL / DB 5**   1989
NYC studio keyboardist swings solidly. "Or Come Fog" is a gem. —MGN

GEORGE GRUNTZ   b 1932

Progressive big band. Swiss-born pianist, composer/arranger, and bandleader. Has worked mostly with extremely large all-star progressive big bands. Complex melodic statements, but harmonic content is most impressive. Able to bring the best out of his cohorts. Musically a contemporary of Gil Evans. —MGN

○ **GG-CJB / MPS**   ca. 1978
GG-CJB (George Gruntz Concert Jazz Band). 21-piece band. Stunning music by ensemble. Soloists include Elvin Jones (d), John Scofield (g), Lew Tabackin (sax). Other players, like Woody Shaw (tpt), Jimmy Knepper (tb), and Bennie Wallace (ts), make this band special. —MGN
Theatre / POLYGRAM   1983
This is a 1983 studio date with 18-piece group. Sheila Jordan singing "No One Can Explain It" is a waterfall of emotion. Lots of Dino Saluzzi on bandoneon, brass heavy. Operatic and soaring. —MGN
The Band / MPS
Live at Schauspielhaus. 21-piece co-led by Ambrosetti

Brothers, drummer Daniel Humair, and Gruntz. "Epitaph" for Ake Persson. No holds barred. –MGN

First Prize / RHINO
Live in Zurich. Pianist Gruntz with four compositions, originals by saxophonist Larry Schneider, trumpeters Franco Ambrosetti and Kenny Wheeler, and trombonist Ray Anderson. Standout is Gruntz's "Gorby-Chief." 18-piece band, horn and brass-heavy, with dynamite rhythm section of Gruntz, Mike Richmond (b), Adam Nussbaum (d). –MGN

DAVE GRUSIN   ♭1934

Instr-pop. Pianist, arranger, composer. Though he's had extensive experience as a session pianist and Grammy-winning arranger, Dave Grusin is probably best known among today's jazz audience for film scores, conducting, and for a string of commercial fusion records. He has also done plenty of computerized and synthesized dates and increasingly moved away from improvisation, specializing in composition and heading sessions. –RW

Subways Are for Sleeping / EPIC   i 1962
○ **Discovered Again / SHEFFIELD LAB**   r 1977
A good recording. –MGN
Migration / GRP   1988
This one's better than usual, thanks to Branford Marsalis. CD has three bonus cuts. –RW
Gershwin Collection / MCA-GRP   1991
Grusin's only GRP release that could be recommended to a jazz fan. –RW

GIGI GRYCE   1927-1983

Bop, post-bop, progressive big band. Alto sax, arranger, composer. A first-rate writer whose passionate, fiery playing was gradually eclipsed by his compositions, even in the jazz world. Following early studies in Boston during the 40s, Gryce had a concert in Hartford with a 33-piece group. Among the participants was young Horace Silver. Gryce got a scholarship to Paris in the early 50s, then returned and worked with Max Roach, Tadd Dameron, and Lionel Hampton. From 1953, Gryce became a prolific composer and combo leader, attracting wide attention with his pieces for Oscar Pettiford's band and the Jazz Lab group he co-led with Donald Byrd. He led other groups in the late 50s and early 60s and played on a strong Monk date. –RW

Gigi Gryce & the Jazz Lab Quintet / OJC   1957
1991 reissue of an intriguing work. Donald Byrd (tpt) and Wade Legge (p) step to the front in this limited-edition offering. –RW
Gigi Gryce Quartet / METROJAZZ   1958
A fine mainstream date, but probably long gone. –RW
The Hap'nin's / PRESTIGE   1960
A solid, tasteful date, with soul-jazz and hip influences. –RW
○ **Rat Race Blues / OJC**   1960
In his prime, compositionally and improvisationally. –MGN
Reminiscin' / MERCURY   1961
This is alternately reflective, dashing, and sentimental. –RW

VINCE GUARALDI   1928-1976

Cool, instr-pop. Guaraldi was a good pianist and a frequent contributor to West Coast sessions in the 50s and 60s. Unfortunately, he became more identified with concept projects like *Impressions* and *Black Orpheus* in the 60s and the recent Charlie Brown/"Peanuts" releases. Although he's well-versed in bop, mainstream, show tunes, and Latin, Guaraldi's style is most evident in trio recordings, where his solo playing and phrases are clean, creative, and nicely constructed. His best work came in the 50s and 60s on Fantasy. –RW

Modern Music from San Francisco / OJC   1955
An entertaining, stimulating meeting of Guaraldi with the Ron Crotty Trio and the Jerry Dodgion Quartet. –RW
Vince Guaraldi Trio / OJC   1956

Straightforward trio material. –RW
A Flower Is a Lovesome Thing / OJC   1957
Spry playing and interesting, unusual arrangements. –RW
Jazz Impressions of Black Orpheus / OJC / BB 24   1962
Guaraldi blends jazz improvisation with Afro-Latin and bossa-nova stylings. –RW
○ **Boy Named Charlie Brown / FANTASY**   1964
A most delightful album. –MGN
Live at El Matador / OJC   1966
A hotter-than-normal Guaraldi set, with Bola Sete (g) bringing a whole new ethos to the date. –RW
Oh, Good Grief / WARNER
Solid jazz, familiar themes, pure joy. –MGN

TRILOK GURTU

World fusion, modern creative. Multiple percussion wizard; born in India. Has credits in his native folk music, creative improvised music, as well as fusion. Recently a member of Oregon and the John McLaughlin Trio. Should win a Nobel Peace Prize for his ability to bring cultures together. –MGN

Usfret / CMP   1987
1987 & 1988. Includes Mother Shabha Gurtu (v), Don Cherry (tpt), Ralph Towner (g, k), L. Shakar (violin), Jonas Helborg (b). –MGN
○ **Living Magic / CMP**   1990
1990 & 1991. W/ Jan Garbarek (saxes), Nana (per), Danial Goyone (k). Septet. Indian, Turkish, Scandinavian, and Brazilian world-fusion, very well conceived. One of Garbarek's better recent efforts, as collaborator or leader. –MGN

H.M.A. SALSA-JAZZ ORCHESTRA

Latin. Jazz orchestra. Hispanic Musician Association of Los Angeles Big Band: Repertory orchestra plays hip Afro-Cuban music. New to national audiences. Worth your attention. –MGN

○ **California Salsa / SEA BREEZE**   r 1991
Fine West Coast band with an excellent feel for what this music brings to jazz and vice versa. A group/collective to watch and listen to. –MGN

CLIFF HABIAN

Neo bop. Cleveland keyboardist in multi-directional format. Monkish post-bop more potent than funk or fusion. Good composer. –MGN

○ **Tonal Paintings / MILESTONE**   1987
A good effort from this Cleveland pianist. Much potential. A mix of progressive and contemporary. –MGN

BOBBY HACKETT   1915-1976

Dixieland, swing. Cornetist, arranger, bandleader. A master accompanist, Hackett had a wonderful, immediately recognizable sound and such knowledge of harmony he could truly be said to have never played a bad note. Elegant, tasteful, and striking, Hackett managed to make memorable music, playing in lightweight 40s bands like Glenn Miller and the Casa Loma Orchestra. He became a staff player at ABC in the late 40s and a regular at Eddie Condon's club, and he was the musical director for Louis Armstrong's historic 1947 Town Hall concert, plus the second cornetist. He became famous in the 50s for contributions to Jackie Gleason albums and dates with Jack Teagarden and his Hudson Hotel band. During the 60s, he worked with Benny Goodman, Ray McKinley, and Tony Bennett. Late in his career, Hackett did guest stints with the World's Greatest Jazz Band and with Dave McKenna. –RW

○ **Hackett Horn / COLUMBIA**   1930
Nice compilation of late-30s, early-40s cuts. –RW
Live at the Rustic Lodge / JAZZ   1949
A spry, hot jam session with Tony Parenti (cl). –RW
Bobby Hackett and his Orchestra / JAZZOLOGY   194?
An excellent collection of 40s Hackett big-band cuts. –RW

Horn a Plenty / COMMODORE   i 1951
Coast Concert / CAPITOL   1955
This exciting octet date is difficult to find. −RW
Jazz Ultimate / CAPITOL   r 1958
Sparkling exchanges with Jack Teagarden (tb). −RW
Live from Mannasas / JAZZOLOGY   1969
Sublime teamup with V. C. Dickenson (tb). −RW
Live at Roosevelt Grill / CHIAROSCURO / DB 5   1970
Vols. 1-4. As a full set, a great example of traditional style moving into the 70s. Also swing element, even some bop. W/ Vic Dickenson reigning on trombone. −RW
Jazz in New York / COMMODORE
Solid traditional date. −RW

CHARLIE HADEN   b 1937

Early free, progressive big band, modern creative. Bass. Charlie Haden's name will always be linked to Ornette Coleman due to this magnificient bassist's pivotal role on Ornette's classic Atlantic albums and his continued association with the alto saxophone rebel. But Haden is not just an important sideman; he is an important and inimitable stylist who is credited with shaping the sound of Pat Metheny, Keith Jarrett, Old & New Dreams, Geri Allen, and more, as well as leading his own Liberation Music Orchestra and Quartet West. His upright-bass technique is deceptively simple, sometimes characterized as a "folk" approach, using pedal tones and insistent double-stop chording much like a country or blues guitarist. Haden is often cited for the economy of his playing and for making each note function as a foundation for the ensemble — no small feat, considering the freely improvisational and often atonal settings he works in. Haden's status as an in-demand studio player (especially for ECM) and critic's favorite would seem to be at odds with his eclectic modernist leanings. But in many ways his playing thrives on very traditional merits — he is almost always rhythmically steady, tonally centered, and adept at carrying a tune. He is to be commended for carrying the acoustic bass (literally and figuratively) into the 90s, while the vast majority of bassists have gone electric. Charlie is also involved in progressive political causes, with a special interest in Latin and South American issues, inspiring his leadership of the Liberation Music Orchestra projects. −MB

★ **Liberation Music Orchestra / IMPULSE**   1969
A definitive 1970 progressive orchestra collaboration with Carla Bley (p). Passionate. A must-buy. −MGN
○ **Closeness / A&M / DB 5**   1976
This one is absolutely essential. One duet apiece with Ornette Coleman (sax), Alice Coltrane (p), Keith Jarrett (p), Paul Motian (d). −MGN
Golden Number / A & M   1976
Gitane / ALL LIFE   1978
The American bassist meets Gypsy guitarist Christian Escoude. −MGN
Magico / POLYGRAM   1979
Outstanding trio work on this reunion of the group that made the superb "Folk Songs" in 1979. −RW
○ **Quartet West / POLYGRAM**   1986
Fine quartet material, with Ernie Watts (d) far more aggressive and animated than usual. −RW
In Angel City / POLYGRAM   1988
This is a solid session, w/ the undervalued Lawrence Marable on drums. Ernie Watts (reeds) does his best playing with Haden. −RW
Dream Keeper / CAPITOL   1990
Consensus Album of the Year, with the Liberation Music Orchestra. −RW
Dialogues / POLYGRAM
Jazz bassist Haden meets Portuguese guitarist. Stangely beautiful. −MGN

JIM HALL   b 1930

Bop, cool, neo bop. Guitar. Admired — even revered — by guitarists and jazz sophisticates for his purity of tone, imagination, and elegant taste in melody and harmony, Jim Hall remains as respected a presence in jazz today as when he emerged in the 50s. His early work with Chico Hamilton and Jimmy Giuffre led to many fine small-group recordings with the likes of Bill Evans, Sonny Rollins, and Paul Desmond. *Intermodulation* with Evans stands out as a gem of the empathetic duet playing of two masters in their prime, while the sessions with Paul Desmond show him in quartet work at his best. His recordings often have a chamber-music-like feel, but his deep immersion in the blues and swing make his music pure jazz. Later recordings with Ron Carter, George Shearing, and even classical violinist Itzhak Perlman point out his effectiveness in small groups. His recordings with younger players such as Don Thompson and Terry Clarke show him moving in a more modern direction while keeping his strong sense of melodic beauty. Highly influential on a whole generation of guitarists, Hall's presence in the world of jazz has been a bit like one of his solos: understated, gentle, and expressing real musical values. −DNM

● **Jazz Guitar / BLUE NOTE**   1957
Topflight session. Features a brilliant Carl Perkins (p). Hall is a marvel on guitar. −RW
Good Friday / PACIFIC   1960
Some early, less-restrained Hall material. −RW
Guitar Workshop / PA-USA   1967
Includes standout solos and accompaniment. A technical masterpiece. −RW
Where Would I Be? / OJC   1971
Fine quartet recordings, nicely reissued. −RW
☆ **Alone Together / OJC / DB 5**   1972
Best bass/guitar duets. A must buy. −MGN
Concierto / CBS / DB 5   1975
A beautiful session, one of the few CTI albums to have a lasting impact. The title cut is a masterpiece. Chet Baker (tpt), Paul Desmond (as), Sir Roland Hanna (p), and Hall are majestic. −RW
○ **Live / A&M**   1975
Live at Bourbon Street, Toronto. W/ Don Thompson (b), and Terry Clarke (d) who are absolutely empathetic company for Hall. They stretch out on five standards, as the players combine a tight/loose aesthetic with some startling pure improvisation in a pristine manner. −MGN
Commitment / A & M   1976
A sterling reissue of a beautiful album, with only pianist Don Thompson. −RW
Jim Hall & Red Mitchell / ARTIST HOUSE / DB 5   1978
Simply irresistible. −RW
Circles / CONCORD   1981
An impressive session, with solid bass by Rufus Reid. −RW
Jim Hall's Three / CONCORD   1986
Though Hall dominates, this is a nice trio session. −RW
These Rooms / POLYGRAM   1988
W/ a sparkling Tom Harrell (tpt) on three cuts. −RW
Live at Town Hall - Vols. 1 & 2 / MUSICMASTERS   1990
Jim Hall and friends. A recent live date with outstanding personnel. −RW

LIN HALLIDAY   b 1936

Hard-bop, post-bop, cool. This veteran Chicago saxophonist plays standards and ballads with verve and savvy, and is woefully underrecorded. −MGN

○ **Delayed Exposure / DELMARK**   1991
Halliday got his start with Maynard Ferguson's band in 1958. From there he went on to play with Louie Bellson and Philly Joe Jones, moved around a lot, did studio work ... all in all a

standard jazz life. It seems a shame that he never got to make an album of his own in the late 50s hard-bop heyday. Here it is, better late than never. W/ Ira Sullivan (tpt) and George Fludas (d). A refreshing mainstream set that echoes the classic era without sounding derivative. —MYLES BOISON, ROOTS & RYHTHM

CHICO HAMILTON   b 1921

Post-bop, jazz-rock, neo bop. Drummer. A former clarinet player, Hamilton got a headstart to musical glory in high school in Los Angeles, where he played with fellow students Dexter Gordon, Charles Mingus, Ernie Royal, and Buddy Collette. He subsequently worked with Floyd Ray, Lionel Hampton, and Slim Galliard, then spent four years in the army, where he studied (among other things) drums with Jo Jones. Brief encounters with Lester Young, Jimmy Mundy, and Count Basie led to his first established gig, a seven-year stint with Lena Horne, during which he toured often. He also worked in the early 50s with Gerry Mulligan before forming his own quintet. The self-styled chamber-jazz unit used flute, clarinet, and cello. It had an intimate sound and elements of "cool" and symphonic music. Never so aggressive as many drummers, Hamilton has nevertheless been among the best at spotting and debuting new talent. The list of major names who started with him includes Buddy Collette, Jim Hall, Paul Horn, Eric Dolphy, Ron Carter, Charles Lloyd, Gabor Szabo, John Abercrombie, and Arthur Blythe. Hamilton is still active and recently released a new album. —RW

Gongs East / DISCOVERY   1958
These groundbreaking sets have a chamber-jazz influence and some of the earliest Eric Dolphy (sax). —RW

Drumfusion / COLUMBIA   i 1962
W/ Charles Lloyd (reeds).

Man from Two Worlds / IMPULSE   1963
An arresting date with Charles Lloyd on reeds and Gabor Szabo (g). —RW

● **Passin' Thru / IMPULSE**   r 1963
One of Hamilton's best groups, with Charles Lloyd (reeds) and Gabor Szabo (g). —RW

Chic Chic Chico / IMPULSE   i 1965
W/ Harold Land (ts).

El Chico / IMPULSE   i 1965
W/ Jimmy Cheatham.

The Further Adventures of El Chico / IMPULSE   1966
Sometimes super and sometimes ragged cuts with Charlie Mariano (as). —RW

○ **The Dealer / MCA**   1966
This groundbreaking session heralded the coming of jazz-rock in 1966 and introduced Larry Coryell (g) to the jazz world. —RW

Arroyo / SOULNOTE   ca. 1990
An excellent recent release for this drummer and the quartet Euphoria, including two standards and four of Hamilton's earthy and electric numbers on the eight cuts. This is easily recomended. —MGN

JEFF HAMILTON   b 1953

Post-bop, cool, progressive big band. West Coast drummer, preferred by Ray Brown and Monty Alexander. Co-leads big band with John Clayton. Swing to bop; total pro. —MGN
○ **Indiana / CONCORD**   1982
This ia a mainstream date; Mark Murphy (v) shares star billing. —RW

JIMMY HAMILTON   b 1917

Swing, big band. Talented clarinetist, most closely associated with Duke Ellington. Sports a swinging, laugh-laden tone. The logical extension of Benny Goodman. —MGN
○ **Swing Low Sweet Clarinet / EVEREST**   i 1960
W/ Paul Gonsalves (ts).

SCOTT HAMILTON   b 1954

Swing, bop. Tenor sax. Hamilton was a prototypical young traditionalist, though his preference was for the swing-era rather than hard bop. He became famous in New England circles in the 70s, then moved to New York and was recommended to Benny Goodman by John Bunch. He met a frequent collaborator, cornetist Warren Vache, in a club. His tenure with Goodman led to a contract with Concord Records and widespread (overdone) publicity that he was leader of a swing revival. Hamilton has persevered, gradually developing his own stirring, distinctive sound. He still reflects the timbre, tone, and vocabulary of swing-era greats Coleman Hawkins, Ben Webster, Lester Young, and Don Byas, but his solos and phrases are now his, not just theirs recycled. —RW

Back to Back / CONCORD   1978
A tasty workout with Buddy Tate (ts). —RW

Skyscrapers / CONCORD   1979
A bright, sometimes brassy collaboration with Warren Vache (cnt). —RW

● **Scott's Buddy / CONCORD**   1980
A good two-tenor workout with Buddy Tate. —RW

Apples & Oranges / CONCORD   1981
A nice date that spotlights Hamilton's flexibility. Various units and teams are paired. Jimmy Rowles (p) is the highlight. —RW

Close Up / CONCORD   1982
A solid swing/mainstream date. —RW

Scott Hamilton Quintet in Concert / CONCORD   1983
A nice live set. CD has bonus cut. —RW

Second Set / CONCORD   1983
A solid, consistent set. —RW

Major League / CONCORD   1986
A baseball motif underlines this good set in which Dave McKenna (p) and Jake Hanna (d) share the spotlight with Hamilton. —RW

○ **Scott Hamilton Plays Ballads / CONCORD**   1989
Lush, romantic, and wonderfully played. CD version has three bonus cuts. —RW

Radio City / CONCORD   1990
W/ fine contributions from Dennis Irwin (b). The CD version has two bonus tracks. —RW

All-Star Tenor Spectacular / PROGRESSIVE
A superior jam session set. —RW

JAN HAMMER   b 1948

Jazz-rock, instr-pop. A pianist and drummer as a child, Jan Hammer played in a trio with Alan and Miroslav Vitous during his high school years in Prague, Czechoslovakia. He studied classical composition and piano at the Prague Conservatory and won a 1966 international music competition and a scholarship to Berklee. Hammer left his homeland for the USA in 1968, following the Soviet invasion. During the early 70s, he worked with Sarah Vaughn and Jeremy Steig, before meeting John McLaughlin. His work with the Mahavishnu Orchestra and Billy Cobham's Spectrum established him as an excellent acoustic and electric pianist, one of the rare synthesizer players able to present the instrument as a musical asset rather than electronic bombast. The first Mahavishnu Orchestra suggested the possibility of a fertile form emerging that truly blended rock dynamics and jazz sensibility. Hammer enjoyed new fame in the 80s as the first composer for the "Miami Vice" TV show. —RW

Make Love / MPS   1968
An album with a wonderful title and an excellent example of real jazz-rock. —RW

Like Children / NEMPEROR   ca. 1974
The keyboardist and violinist Jerry Goodman away from Mahavishnu. They play all instruments (overdubbed). "Country and Eastern Music" and "Steppings Tones" were high water marks for this new breed (at the time). —MGN

Early Years / CBS   1974
1974-1979. A comprehensive compilation of Hammer's best cuts from the 70s. −RW

○ **Oh Yeah / NEMPEROR**   1976
This is an album of fusion at its best. "Magical Dog" and "Red & Orange" are definitive statements. This was the first exposure for violinist Steve Kindler. David Earle Johnson is on congas. −MGN

Live / COLUMBIA / BB 23   1977
A great teamup with Jeff Beck (g). −RW

Here to Stay / COLUMBIA   1983
Fine interaction with Neal Schon (g). −RW

JOHNNY HAMMOND   b 1933

Soul jazz. Organist. He is also known as Johnny "Hammond" Smith to distinguish him from the more famous record producer, executive, and critic and/or his son. An organist in the soul-jazz mode, he had a brief moment in the spotlight with the 70s album *Breakout*, where his version of "It's Too Late" with Grover Washington Jr and Hank Crawford was a huge East Coast radio hit. Hammond is a competent, sometimes funky player. −RW

○ **Breakout / KUDU-COL**
His best CTI work, spiced by Hank Crawford (as) and Grover Washington Jr.(ts) −RW

LIONEL HAMPTON   b 1909

Swing, big band, progressive big band. Vibist. Lionel Hampton's musical preferences have always been straightahead, celebratory, and rousing. In his early years he formed the Chicago Defender Newsboys Band in Chicago and learned tympani and marimba under Major N. Clark Smith. He worked in several territory and regional bands before joining Les Hite in backing Louis Armstrong at the Los Angeles Cotton Club in the 30s. He chose to play vibes as a means of spotlighting himself in a special manner. During Hampton's 1936 residency at the Paradise Cafe in Los Angeles, Benny Goodman saw Hampton and subsequently ended up on stage playing with him, along with Gene Krupa on drums and pianist Teddy Wilson. This quartet became a prolific unit, recording several sides and working together through the end of the 30s. Hampton stayed with Goodman until 1940, then formed his own big band, which he's led in some fashion ever since. Hampton, like Art Blakey, was good at spotting new talent, and His discoveries over the years include Charles Mingus, Art Farmer, Dinah Washington, Joe Williams, Dexter Gordon, and Ernie Royal for starters. Lionel Hampton has remained an active, entertaining, and captivating showman and bandleader. −RW

Small Groups - Vol. 2 / MUSIC MEMORIA   1930
A reissue of some sublime late-30s cuts. Some duplication with RCA Bluebird material. −RW

Hot Mallets - Vol. 1 / BLUEBIRD   193?
Here is sensational late-30s material that forecasts the development of Hampton into a vibes genius. Wonderful swing-era work from Chu Berry (ts), Dizzy Gillespie (tpt), Benny Carter (as), and others, on a great remastering job. −RW

○ **Jumpin' Jive - Vol. 2 / RCA**   193?
The All-Star Groups. The second volume of topflight late-30s material, with exuberant solos from Johnny Hodges (as), Benny Carter (as), and Dizzy Gillespie (tpt). −RW

● **Flying Home 1942-45 / MCA**   1942
An excellent compilation of similar material. A great big band, plus some driving vibes solos. −RW

The Blues Ain't News to Me / VERVE   1951
1951-1958. Despite his long tenure on Verve, one of the very few Hampton albums available on that label. −RW

Hamp and Getz / POLYGRAM   r 1956

A superb match: swinging Hampton and impressionistic Getz (ts). −RW

In Paris 1956 / DISQUES SWING   1956
A good, sometimes insightful pairing of Hampton with Claude Bolling (p). −RW

Just Jazz / MCA   195?
An erratic but frequently spirited late-50s reissue. −RW

Where Could I Be? / FANTASY-OJC   1971
A new reissue of this fine date, with some supple, bombastic vibes from Hampton. −RW

Live — 50th Anniversary Concert / PAIR   1978
This rousing celebratory session is more important for its recognition of his achievement than for its music. −RW

All-Star Band at Newport / TIMELESS   1978
Here is an overlooked live date with ageless Hampton swing and drive. −RW

Sentimental Journey / ATLANTIC   1985
An often-entertaining set. The vocals are more good-natured than anything else. −RW

Mostly Blues / MUSICMASTERS   1988
A spry update on the old Hampton swing/drive feeling. A good set of blues cuts. −RW

Mostly Ballads / MUSICMASTERS   1990
An elegant session. Hampton still swings in his 80s. −RW

Live at the Blue Note / TELARC
Hot playing, and solid professionalism enliven some familiar material. −RW

SLIDE HAMPTON   b 1932

Progressive big band, post-bop. Hampton's notoriety not only springs from the fact he's one of the rare left-handed trombonists, but because he's among the fastest, most fluid players in the modern era. Hampton played in the 50s with Lionel Hampton and Maynard Ferguson, as well as Buddy Johnson, before forming his own octet in 1959. He worked for R&B and blues singer Lloyd Price as musical director and did freelance arranging in the 60s, joining Woody Herman in 1968. He toured Europe and re-settled there. Hampton returned to New York in 1977 and began heading his 12-piece band, the World of Trombones. He's been an activist in jazz education in the 80s, and still does occasional recording sessions. −RW

○ **World of Trombones / BLACK LION**   1979

HERBIE HANCOCK   b 1940

Post-bop, jazz-rock, contemporary funk. Herbie Hancock is a jazz keyboardist who has succeeded in a variety of styles, from the free-jazz of the 60s, when he played with Miles Davis and made a variety of groundbreaking albums for Blue Note, to the fusion of the 70s and beyond, which have seen him invading the pop charts regularly.

Hancock moved from Chicago to New York in 1961 and worked with a variety of jazz stars before joining Davis's quintet in 1965, a unit that also included Ron Carter, Tony Williams, and Wayne Shorter and is now remembered as among the best bands Davis ever led. In addition to the memorable music turned out by this group (some of it written by Hancock), the pianist also contracted to Blue Note for a series of solo albums, starting with *Takin' Off* in 1962. In 1966 Hancock scored the film *Blowup*, which made the pop charts. Leaving Davis in 1968, Hancock eventually began to divide his time between acoustic-piano work and electric playing, the result being that he became a major star in both genres. His "straight" jazz dates included the V.S.O.P. group (which was the old Davis quintet with Freddie Hubbard substituting for Davis) and albums with fellow keyboardist Chick Corea. His fusion albums included the gold-selling 1974 release *Head Hunters*. In all, he charted 11 albums during the 70s, amazing for a jazz musician.

Of course, there are few who like all of his work. This became even more true when Hancock scored on the dance floor and the singles chart with "Rockit," a hip-hop track with a successful video that went gold in 1983. Since then, Hancock has continued to move back and forth between the worlds of purist-jazz and outright pop. –WR

Takin' Off / BLUE NOTE 1962
A prophetic title for this session with Dexter Gordon (ts) and Freddie Hubbard (tpt). –RW

My Point of View / BLUE NOTE 1963
Tremendous compositions and playing in an all-star date that helped make Hancock a star. –RW

Inventions & Dimensions / BLUE NOTE 1963
First-rate early work. Willie Bobo makes a scintillating percussive contribution. –RW

Empyrean Isles / BLUE NOTE 1964
1985 reissue of one of Hancock's seminal releases. Freddie Hubbard (tpt) is daring and aggressive. Ron Carter (b) and Tony Williams (d) are squarely in the pocket. –RW

★ **Maiden Voyage / BLUE NOTE / DB 5** 1965
The definitive Blue Note Herbie with an ensemble. You can't go wrong with this one. –MGN

Speak Like A Child / BLUE NOTE 1968
A simply beautiful title cut, plus wondrous arrangements and playing throughout. –RW

The Prisoner / BLUE NOTE / DB 5 1969

○ **Fat Albert Rotunda / WARNER** 1969
Herbie plays Fender Rhodes with Joe Henderson (ts). Featuring "Tell Me A Bedtime Story." –MGN

● **Mwandishi / WARNER** 1970
A forerunner of Africentric sentiment. One of Hancock's finest electric, jazz/rock outings. –RW

Crossings / WARNER 1971
An explosive, experimental, far-ranging session. –RW

○ **Headhunters / COLUMBIA / BB 13** 1973
Platinum album.

Thrust / CBS / BB 13 1974
This is among Hancock's better R&B/funk/rock works. –RW

V.S.O.P. Quintet / CBS / BB 79 1976
This often stunning quintet set was done live at Newport. Hancock again confounds cynics who insist he's lost his jazz roots. –RW

Evening with Chick Corea / COLUMBIA 1978
Quartet / CBS 1981
A fine mainstream set that showed detractors Hancock hadn't lost his jazz chops. Wynton Marsalis (tpt) (then reaping a wave of prodigy/discovery headlines) is in the group. –RW

Village Life / COLUMBIA
An arresting mix of Hancock's jazz concept with African Foday Suso's rhythmic innovations. –RW

● **Best of Herbie Hancock / BLUE NOTE** COMP
The Blue Note years. A good compilation to start with. Many of his best works. –MGN

JOHN HANDY   b 1933

Post-bop, ballads, world fusion. Alto saxophonist. Not to be confused with "Captain" John Handy, the traditional jazz player, John Handy is a self-taught reed specialist who later took theory in college. He moved from Dallas to New York in 1958 and joined Mingus in 1959. His flexible, bluesy, and hard-edged alto style, which was a cross between classic bop and free, emerged in his work with Mingus and his own band in the late 50s and 60s. His 1965 quintet with violinist Michael White was another of those bands whose work suggested the coming jazz/rock marriage. They were a huge hit at Monterey that year. Handy had another ahead-of-its-time group in 1968 with Mike Nock, White, and Ron McClure, who later became Fourth Way. During the 70s and 80s, Handy repeatedly experimented with jazz/Indian collaborations and symphony

compositions, been an educator, and played numerous festivals. He had a hit in the late 70s with the album *Hard Work*, then in 1989 he resurfaced heading an otherwise-all-woman group. –RW

○ **Live at Monterey / COLUMBIA** 1965
An album of red hot, animated work from Handy — some of his best. –RW

New View / COLUMBIA r 1967
Some shimmering alto sax. Music in the spirit of the impending jazz-rock fusion. –RW

Hard Work / IMPULSE / BB 43 1976
The title cut was a moderate hit on R&B radio. –RW

SIR ROLAND HANNA   b 1932

Post-bop, cool, bop. Pianist. One of the most elegant, impressive soloists ever, Hanna wis an excellent accompanist as well. He played in Detroit regularly in the early 50s before joining Benny Goodman in 1958, then Charles Mingus in 1959. He was a longtime member of the Thad Jones-Mel Lewis orchestra and a founding member of the New York Jazz Quartet. His best work has come as head of his own trios and duos since 1959. –RW

Destry Rides Again / ATCO i 1959
Easy to Love / ATCO i 1960
○ **Perugia / BLACK LION-FREEDOM** 1974
Excellent piano solos — some of Hanna's sharpest. –RW

This Must Be Love / AUDIOPHILE 1978
Enchanting pieces and wonderful playing. –RW

Bird Tracks / PROGRESSIVE 1978
Tingling versions of songs by and about Charlie Parker. –RW

Duke Ellington Piano Solos / MUM 1991
Includes some exquisite solo work — a moving tribute to Duke Ellington. –RW

KIP HANRAHAN   b 1937

Progressive big band, jazz-rock, world fusion, modern creative. He leads the band, and doesn't really play, but Hanrahan is an incredible organizer of all-star progressive bands and a forward thinker. –MGN

○ **Desire Develops an Edge / AMERICAN / DB 5** r 1984
Multi-faceted musician organizes an all-star band of progressive romanticists with Jack Bruce (b), Ricky Ford (ts), and Jerry Gonzalez (tpt). Highly recommended. –MGN

Vertical's Currency / PANAGEA / DB 5 r 1985
More of the same, with Jack Bruce (b) prominent. Seek out the other albums like *Coup de Tete* and *Conjure* for some fabulous music. –MGN

BILL HARDMAN   b 1933

Bop, hard-bop, post-bop. Trumpeter, flugelhornist. Hardman is an example of a player who became better over time, while working with demanding bandleaders like Charles Mingus, Art Blakey, Horace Silver, and Lou Donaldson. By the mid 60s Hardman had become a confident, vibrant soloist. His longest stint has been with Lou Donaldson (seven years), though he had four different periods with Art Blakey. Hardman led his own group, the Brass Company, in the late 60s and was with Junior Cook in the late 70s and early 80s. –RW

○ **Jackie's Pal / PRESTIGE** 1956
Great modal-jazz w/ Jackie McLean (as). Highly recommended album. –MGN

Saying Something / SAVOY 1961
An album with topflight blowing from Sonny Red (sax). This is perhaps Hardman's best date; among his most memorable. –RW

Home / MUSE 1978
Beautiful, evocative playing. –RW

Politely / MUSE 1981
A terse, searing date. –RW

ROY HARGROVE
b 1970

Post-bop, neo bop. Hargrove is among the high-profile young lions. This 20-something trumpeter has just released his third RCA album. He has been in the spotlight since his late teens, when word surfaced about a dynamic, exciting player from the East Coast. Hargrove's sound and technique are still emerging. His tone has improved, and he could always range over his instrument. He is now maturing, playing with more thought and expressiveness and not relying on just speed or power. –RW

○ **Diamond in the Rough / RCA-JIVE/NOVUS** 1989
Young trumpeter sounds good, especially on originals. –MGN

Public Eye / NOVUS 1990
Hargrove's second album displays great promise, though things sometimes get ragged. CD has a bonus cut. –RW

BILLY HARPER
b 1943

Post-bop, early free. A premier tenor saxophonist, progressivist, and a logical extension of Coltrane, Harper is a fine, lyrical player in modal jazz. –MGN

○ **Black Saint / BLACK SAINT** 1975
An important document and the first album for the Italian Black Saint label. A potent quartet, with Harper's most familiar themes. This is essential listening in the modal jazz idiom. –MGN

Trying to Make Heaven My Home / MPS 1979
A quintet recording for this incendiary tenor saxophonist. An extended, hard-blowing session. –MGN

HARPER BROTHERS

Post-bop, neo bop. Winard and Phillip Harper have a new album out and are in the vanguard of the young-lion/hard-bop movement. A trumpet/drums duo whose group sound reflects a huge influence from Art Blakey's Messengers, they are critically respected and admired for their decision to stick to genuine jazz. Their newest album includes more blues nuances, plus the presence of vocalists, as they try to broaden their audience without losing their integrity. –RW

Harper Brothers / POLYGRAM 1988
○ **Remembrance — Village Vanguard / POLYGRAM** 1989
A solid live album from young cats. –MGN
Artistry / POLYGRAM

HERBIE HARPER
b 1920

Swing, big band, cool, progressive big band. Trombonist; a bit obscure but very talented. Excellent arranger for years with NBC Orchestra. Extraordinary technical player. –MGN

Quintet / TAMPA 1954
A well-played date. –RW

○ **Herbie Harper / LIBERTY** 1956
A swinging session with Bud Shank (as) and Bob Gordon (bar sax) from this ex-big-band trombonist. W/ Charlie Mariano (sax) –DS

Sextet / MODE 1957
An exellent example of the lyrical West Coast bounce of the 50s. W/ Jay Corre –DS

Revisited / SEABREEZE 1981

TOM HARRELL
b 1946

Post-bop, neo bop. Brilliant post-bop trumpeter, with occasional contemporary overtones. Sideman with Phil Woods, Bob Berg, Joe Lovano. Also plays sweet serene flugelhorn. Easily in the top five today on his instrument. –MGN

Aurora/Total / ADAMO-PINNACLE 1976
Harrell's first album features choice material and Bob Berg (ts). –MGN

○ **Sail Away / CONTEMPORARY / DB 5** 1989

Spirited originals and his best effort to date. Featuring Dave Liebman (sop sax) and Joe Levano (ts). A must-buy. –MGN

Form / CONTEMPORARY 1990
On this top quintet session, Joe Lovano (ts) enhances his sizable reputation. CD has a bonus cut. –RW

Visions / CONTEMPORARY ca. 1991
This latest session has an all-star lineup, with large-group pieces. –RW

JOE HARRIOTT
1928-1973

Post-bop, world fusion. Until Courtney Pine emerged, Joe Harriott had the distinction of being the most prominent Jamaican jazz figure in British history. He came to England in 1951, having played in dance bands and studied clarinet at a boys school. He worked in various combos during the 50s, touring with the Modern Jazz Quartet in 1959. Harriott became famous in the 60s for forging a sound that merged elements of Indian and Asian music with jazz. –RW

Free Forms / JAZZLAND i 1961
Southern Horizons / JAZZLAND i 1961

BARRY HARRIS
b 1929

Bop, cool. One of the finest of all bebop pianists and a first-class interpreter of Bud Powell and Thelonious Monk. His national reputation began in Cannonball Adderley's group in 1960, and he moved to New York, working frequently with Coleman Hawkins, Yusef Lateef, and Charles McPherson, as well as working his own groups. He made many sideman appearances in the 60s and 70s, with the first recordings of his own for Riverside and Prestige (60s). He was recorded frequently by Xanadu in the 70s, with one-shot album appearances for a variety of labels. There are no bad albums by this artist, but in general his later work is his most interesting, with the Xanadu albums being his finest. –BP

Barry Harris at the Jazz Workshop / OJC 1960
Reissue of a superb date with Sam Jones (b) and Louis Hayes (d). –RW

Preminado / OJC 1960
A fine 1991 reissue of high-quality trio performances. –RW

Listen to Barry Harris / RIVERSIDE 1961
Striking solo piano. –RW

Luminescence / PRESTIGE 1967
Brilliant, driving piano solos and fine compositions. –RW

Barry Harris Plays Tadd Dameron / XANADU 1975
A criminally underrated arranger/composer gets showcase treatment from an equally overlooked pianist. –RW

○ **Live in Tokyo / XANADU / DB 5** 1976
Wonderful Harris plus guest stints from Charles McPherson (sax) and Jimmy Raney (g). –RW

Barry Harris Plays Barry Harris / XANADU 1978
The always dynamic Harris spotlights his own songs. –RW

● **Live at Maybeck Recital Hall / CONCORD**
Harris as a solo pianist has no equal. –MGN

BEAVER HARRIS
1936-1992

Early free, progressive big band, modern creative. Harris played baseball in the Negro Leagues and blended sports and music for a while. He played in the army band, then moved to New York in 1963. He freelanced with Sonny Rollins, Thelonious Monk, Joe Henderson, and Freddie Hubbard before joining Archie Shepp in 1966. He spent time with Shepp, Sonny Stitt, Dexter Gordon, and Clark Terry before forming a cooperative band with trombonist Grachan Moncur III in 1969. The 360 Degree Experience did free music with zest and flair, anchored by Harris's rollicking, inspired, but always steady drumming. Harris continued to work with Shepp in the 70s and appeared in the pit band for some plays. He toured Japan with a Newport Jazz Festival Tour in the mid 70s, and also recorded in the 70s with Steve Lacy, Pharoah Sanders, Gato Barbieri, and Albert Ayler. –RW

○ **In: Sanity / BLACK SAINT**   1976
Recording with 360-Degree Music Experience. Improvisational music with world-music touches from percussionist Harris and pianist Dave Burrell. An essential purchase for the adventurous listener. −MGN

Live at Nyon / CADENCE   1979
An ambitious, swinging quintet date, with a welcome appearance from Grachan Moncur III (tb). −RW

Negcaumongus / CADENCE   1979
Brilliant septet cuts. Ricky Ford (ts) and Don Pullen (p) are magnificent. −RW

Well Kept Secret with Don Pullen / HANNIBAL   r 1985

BILL HARRIS   1916-1973

Big band, bop, blues-jazz. Veteran guitarist played blues/jazz in DC night clubs. −MGN

○ **Bill Harris and Friends / OJC**   1957
A good big-band/swing date w/ trombonist Harris, better known for his stint in the Woody Herman orchestra. −RW

CRAIG HARRIS   b 1954

Neo bop, modern creative. Craig Harris is a strong contemporary trombonist who is knowledgeable in every style from New Orleans and "tailgate" to bop and free. He has been prominent on the jazz scene through the 80s and 90s as a session man, bandleader, and composer. As one of the younger players seeking some option besides hard-bop, he has done updated versions of James Brown tunes with a group of like-minded players, done songs on an instrument from Australia similar to the trombone, blended in Afro-Latin cuts, and played straight hard-bop as well. −RW

Aboriginal Affairs / INDIA NAVIGATION   1983
A fine set featuring top players who seldom record — like Ken McIntyre (as) and Donald Smith (k). −RW

Shelter / JMT   1984
This is an aggressive, never-dull session that operates in the stylistic middle ground between jazz, R&B, blues, and rock. −RW

○ **Blackout in the Square Root of Soul / POLYGRAM**   1987
A first-rate example of a fresh direction in jazz that blends improvisatory zeal, funk, and R&B references. −RW

EDDIE HARRIS   b 1934

Post-bop, soul jazz, jazz-rock. A popular tenor saxophonist of the 60s and 70s, Harris burst into national prominence with his version of "Exodus" which reached Top 40 pop single status in 1961. His Vee Jay recordings from 1961-1964 displayed his light-toned saxophone over a gently funky rhythm section, usually featuring guitar. He seemed to have found a popular group sound. He came to Atlantic in 1965 and, after a couple of straightahead jazz albums, turned to the electronic saxophone and a more funk-oriented approach. This resulted in "Listen Here," a pop/R&B success from 1968, and a hit album *The Electrifying Eddie Harris.* From this point forward, his work became more commercial and more involved with a variety of electronics, to the point where his mid-70s work was virtually devoid of any jazz content. His album, co-led with pianist/vocalist Les McCann (*Swiss Movement*), provided a jazz hit with "Compared to What" in 1970. After an almost endless series of commercial attempts, Harris returned to jazz and made some fine straightahead jazz albums in the 80s. −BP

○ **Exodus to Jazz / CHAMELEON / BB 2**   1961
An outstanding session, done when Harris was emerging as a dashing tenor player. −RW

Electrifying Eddie Harris / ATLANTIC / BB 36   1967
The birth and fruition of Harris's use of varitone and electronics on tenor as a legitimate technique. −RW

★ **Swiss Movement / ATLANTIC / BB 29**   1969
W/ Less McCann. Evergreen! Contains the monster hit "Compared to What." A must-buy, if you don't have it already. −MGN

Free Speech / ATLANTIC   1970
This is not political, but a fiery tract nonetheless. −RW

○ **Second Movement / ATLANTIC / BB 41**   r 1971
W/ Less McCann. The followup to *Swiss Movement* didn't sell so well, but still has plenty of fine music. −RW

Live at Newport / ATLANTIC   1972
Harris's robust playing makes the critics stand up and take notice. −RW

Playing with Myself / RCA   1979
The title notwithstanding, this is an intelligent, attention-grabbing solo album. −RW

Steps Up / STEEPLECHASE   1981
Some torrid interchanges and dialogs with pianist Tete Montoliu. −RW

Homecoming / SPI / DB 5   1985
A very nice, underrated teaming of Eddie Harris and Ellis Marsalis (p). It's understated, bluesy, mellow, and sometimes challenging. −RW

Live in Berlin / TIMELESS   1988
Recent, exemplary Harris material. −RW

There Was a Time / RHINO   1990
This is a fine retrospective and mainstream date. CD bonus cut. −RW

Excursions / ATLANTIC
A very underrated, two-record live set with some of Harris's best acoustic and electric sax solos. −RW

● **Best of Eddie Harris / ATLANTIC**   COMP
A skeletal anthology of some of Harris' Atlantic cuts. It leans toward hits, but does contain "Listen Here" and "Theme from Exodus." A good introductory album to his work. −RW

GENE HARRIS   b 1933

Post-bop, soul jazz, progressive big band. Pianist. Gene Harris is one of those players who is undervalued because of a lack of flash, hype, or reputation. A tasty, blues-influenced pianist, he formed the Sounds in 1957 and was an immediate hit, with a string of good albums on Blue Note and Verve. The group became the Three Sounds pretty quickly in 1958 and were a precursor to other, more lightweight groups like the Ramsey Lewis Trio, doing standards, pop/R&B, and soft/jazz. Harris had credentials outside the Three Sounds, recording with Nat Adderley, Lou Donaldson, and Stanley Turrentine. In the 80s he has done trio and small-combo dates for Concord. Harris is always an inventive, resourceful, and tasteful player, a fine accompanist and above-average soloist. −RW

● **Feelin' Good / BLUE NOTE**   ca. 1959
Prototypical Three Sounds release. Elements of funk, soul-jazz, and blues merge into a workable jazz concept. −RW

Anita O'Day and the Three Sounds / VERVE   1963
Classy vocals with good trio backing. −RW

○ **Live at Otter Crest / BOSCO**   1981
Underrated latter-period Harris on piano with trio. Great extended "Battle Hymn," Basie's repertoire represented in "Shiny Stockings" and "Ate" and your reliable Harris's "A Little Blues There" included. −MGN

Plus One / CONCORD   1985
On this solid release, the always enjoyable Harris trio is augmented by hot tenor from Stanley Turrentine. −RW

Tribute to Count Basie / CONCORD   1987
An emphatic big-band tribute to the swing master. −RW

At Last / CONCORD   1990
A wonderful teamup of Gene Harris with Scott Hamilton's band. CD version has two bonus cuts. −RW

Live at Town Hall NYC / CONCORD   1990
A fine, traditional big-band outing. −RW

World Tour 1990 / CONCORD   1990
This is a fine big-band showcase, with three bonus cuts on CD issue. −RW

Listen Here! / CONCORD
A solid mainstream date with light soul-jazz flavor. CD version has two bonus cuts. −RW

JEROME HARRIS   b 1953

Neo bop, modern creative. Electric bassist and guitarist known for his work as a sideman, studio musician, and collaborator with Sonny Rollins in the 80s. Works in many idioms — jazz, funk, creative improvised. Albums as a leader show considerable mettle as an original composer. −MGN

○ **Algorithms / MINOR MUSIC**   1986
Bassist and guitarist in sympathetic progressive setting. Similiar to Michael Gregory Jackson's *Gifts*, as a companion album with similiar personnel. Highly recommended. −MGN

In Passing / MUSE   1989
An engaging session. −RW

TED HARRIS

Swing, bop. A swing-to-bop saxophone veteran from New Jersey, Harris is an under-appreciated master. −MGN

○ **More Giants of Jazz / H&D**   1982
A larger group for this mainstream tenor/baritone saxophonist with Richard Williams (tpt) and Kiane Zawadi (tb). −MGN

Supernova / H&D   1989
Mainstream saxophonist. Good band, with trumpeter Irvin Stokes. −MGN

DONALD HARRISON   b 1960

Post-bop, neo bop. One of the genuine stalwarts and talents among the heralded "young lions" jazz class, saxophonist Donald Harrison emerged in the early 80s while a member of Art Blakey's Jazz Messengers. Harrison studied under both Ellis Marsalis and Alvin Batiste in New Orleans, then went to Berklee in 1979. He played with Roy Haynes from 1980-1981 and Jack McDuff in 1981, then spent four years with Art Blakey from 1982-1986. Harrison worked in tandem with fellow New Orleans musician trumpeter Terence Blanchard from the mid 80s until 1991. His best instrument is alto sax, but he's also become proficient on soprano. −RW

● **Crystal Stair / CBS**   1987
W/ Terrance Blanchard (tpt).

Black Pearl / CBS   r 1988
W/ Terrance Blanchard (tpt).

For Art's Sake / CANDID

WENDELL HARRISON   b 1942

Post-bop, soul jazz, instr-pop, neo bop. As of late, this clarinetist is moving up in the polls with straightahead jazz albums. He's also an excellent clinician, who plays tenor in funk and more commercial settings. −MGN

Fly by Night / WEN-HA
These mostly quintet recordings include three standards and four Harrison originals. With Cecil McBee and Jaribu Shahid (b), Kirk Lightsey and Pam Wise (p), Doug Hammond (d), and Rob Pipho (vibes). −MGN

○ **Forever Duke / WEN-HA**   1990
Clarinetist leads modern ensemble through five Duke tunes and two originals. Guests include Charles Tolliver (tpt) and Harold McKinney (p). There is a brief appearance by a 5-piece clarinet ensemble. −MGN

Live in Concert / WEN-HA   1992
This 1992 performance in Detroit's Museum of African American history includes a big band and Clarinet Ensemble. Unique music, mostly modern, with three standards. −MGN

NANCY HARROW

Ballads. A sweet song stylist whose debt to Helen Merrill seems obvious. She has a bit of a daring edge, but is most effective with ballads and torch songs. −MGN

○ **Wild Women Don't Have the Blues / CANDID**   r 1961

BILLY HART   b 1940

Post-bop, progressive big band, neo bop. This Washington, DC, drummer leads his own groups and has played with early fusion and progressive combos. He backs singers. −MGN

Enchance / A & M   1977
A recording just at the edge of all-out. Powerful, pretty, and potent. All originals. An important document. −MGN

Oshumare / GRAMAVISION   1985
○ **Rah / GRAMAVISION**   1987
Excellent original compositions. This is very listenable, time after time. Many great soloists and ensemble players. Highly recommended. −MGN

JOHNNY HARTMAN   1923-1983

Ballads. A classic love-ballad/standards singer and heartthrob vocalist, Hartman studied piano and sang as a child and earned a vocal scholarship in 1939. He got his first fame in the 40s with Earl Hines, then worked with Dizzy Gillespie before becoming a solo star. He never attained the notoriety of similar types like Billy Eckstine or Arthur Prysock, though his glorious voice was equal to theirs. His amazing early-60s collaboration with John Coltrane didn't get the fame it merited at the time. −RW

Songs from the Heart / BETHLEHEM   1956
○ **I Just Dropped by to Say Hello / MCA**   1963
Definitive vocal-ballad artistry. −MGN

John Coltrane and Johnny Hartman / IMPULSE   1963
Marvelous love songs, superior playing. Sadly, the reissues have been sonic nightmares, so seek out the original. −RW

The Voice That Is / IMPULSE   r 1965

HAMPTON HAWES   1928-1977

Bop, hard-bop, post-bop. Pianist Hampton Hawes was a major member of the 50s West Coast movement, though he was no "cool" player. Hawes had his initial R&B experience with Big Jay McNeely as a teen, plus a brief time with Charlie Parker. He was emerging as a prime player in a 50s trio with Red Mitchell, where his combination of crisp, precise solos and gospel-blues riffs and patterns paralleled the rise of funk sound in hard-bop. In the early 70s he took up electric piano and actually got more attention in session endeavors and tours with people like Joan Baez than among the jazz audience. −RW

Piano: East/West / OJC   1953
Hawes and Freddie Redd (p) split an album, revealing their differing, yet mutually appealing, stylistic tendencies. −RW

The Trio - Vols. 1-3 / CONTEMPORARY   ca. 1955
An essential set of powerhouse mid-50s trio works with Hawes, Red Mitchell (b), and Chuck Thompson (d). −RW

Everybody Likes.... - Vol. 3 / CONTEMPORARY   1956
The trio. −ED

All Night Session - Vols. 1-3 / OJC   1956
Some wondrous, invigorating playing from everyone included, especially Hawes and Jim Hall (g). −RW

● **All Night Sessions / CONTEMPORARY / DB 5**   1956
The original recording of the first in a series of smashing 50s concerts. −RW

Four! / OJC   1958
This is an outstanding date, with excellent Barney Kessel guitar. −RW

The Sermon / CONTEMPORARY   1958
A 1988 reissue of a tight, tough trio work. −RW

Green Leaves of Summer / OJC   ca. 1964
Frequently amazing piano work from Hawes. −RW

Here & Now / OJC   1965

Adept and nimble work from Hawes. Chuck Israels roams and booms on bass. −RW

○ **The Seance / OJC**   1966
Another sparkling trio date. −RW

○ **The Challenge / STORYVILLE**   1968
Stunning solo piano. −RW

○ **Key for Two / AFFINITY**   1969
A stomping workout with fellow pianist Martial Solal. −RW

A Little Copenhagen Night Music / ARISTA   1971
An album where Hawes adds electric piano and synthesizer to his arsenal. −RW

○ **Blues for Walls / PRESTIGE**   ca. 1972

● **Live at the Jazz Showcase in Chicago / ENJA**   1973
Vol. 1. As fine as any trio set Hawes ever made, with Cecil McBee (b) and Roy Haynes (d). −RW

At the Great American Music Hall / CONCORD   1975
A fine showcase for some brilliant playing by Hawes, in a live setting. Tremendous sound on this recording. −RW

Hampton Hawes at the Piano / CONTEMPORARY   1976
Killing Me Softly ... / CONTEMPORARY   1976
The swan song for the Hawes trio sessions, with top contributions by Ray Brown (b) and Shelly Manne (d). −RW

COLEMAN HAWKINS   1904-1969

Swing, big band, bop, cool, progressive big band. After starting on piano and cello, Hawkins took up the saxophone at nine; seven years later, singer Mamie Smith picked him from a Kansas City theater-pit band to join her touring Jazz Hounds, with whom he made his first records. In New York he was part of a group of freelance musicians who chose Fletcher Henderson to front them for an audition in 1923; they landed the job, and Hawkins stayed with Fletcher for a decade, becoming the leading stylist on his instrument in jazz — the first to create a viable vocabulary for the tenor. In 1934 British bandleader and promoter Jack Hylton invited him to Europe; he stayed until the late summer of 1939 and influenced a generation of European musicians. Back home, he recorded his two-chorus variations on "Body and Soul" and immediately reestablished his supremacy, which had been challenged by such comers as Chu Berry, Hershel Evans, and, notably, Lester Young. Hawk, or "Bean," as he was nicknamed, formed his own big band, but it was not a success and he soon reverted to small groups. Among the musicians he hired on 52nd Street before there was such a term as "bebop" were Thelonious Monk, Howard McGhee, and Dizzy Gillespie. Hawkins was the premier champion of the young modernists among established players, and they in turn admired and respected him. He was an early and permanent member of *Jazz at the Philharmonic* and often teamed with another JATP regular, Roy Eldridge, during the last two decades of his life. Not until his health began to deteriorate in the late 60s was Hawk ever less than a commanding presence on the bandstand, his tone alone a thing to marvel at, his harmonic knowledge unbeatable. −DM

Dutch Treat / XANADU   193?
Late-30s seminal cuts; Hawkins now an established star. −RW

In Paris / DRG   193?
A wonderful collection of prime material featuring Hawkins and Benny Carter (as) overseas during the 30s and 40s. −RW

★ **Coleman Hawkins on Keynote / VERVE**   1944
Classic tenor sax. A must-buy. −MGN

☆ **The Big Three / CBS**   194?
An album with Lester Young and Ben Webster. This is a 1990 reissue that spotlights classic 40s cuts of the three featured tenor stars. −RW

Hollywood Stampede / CAPITOL   194?
Pivotal 40s and 50s cuts, with Hawkins featured in several settings. An interesting array of characters. −RW

Hawk Flies High / OJC   1957

A robust swing/mainstream and blues session. −RW

Encounters Ben Webster / POLYGRAM   1957
These aren't encounters in the confrontational sense, but a merger of great musical minds. −RW

Genius of Coleman Hawkins / POLYGRAM   1957
A 1986 reissue. A master aided by an all-star lineup that includes Oscar Peterson (p) and Herb Ellis (g). −RW

The Real Thing / PRESTIGE / DB 5   1958
From three sessions, in 1958, 1959, and 1969. −JME

Soul / OJC   i 1958
Soothing, charming late-50s Hawkins. −RW

Hawk Eyes / OJC   1959
On this top date Hawkins was ably assisted by Charlie Shavers (tpt), Tiny Grimes (g), and others. −RW

Coleman Hawkins & Confreres / POLYGRAM   i 1959
Ben Webster (ts), Roy Eldridge (tpt), and Hawkins head things up. This is one of the few worthwhile releases in this special Alpha series. −RW

High & Mighty Hawk / POLYGRAM / DB 5   r 1959
On this delightful mainstream date, Hawkins mixes it up with Buck Clayton (tpt), Hank Jones (p), and company. −RW

With Red Garland Trio / OJC   1959
Just as smooth and wonderful as you'd expect from this gathering. −RW

Standards and Warhorses / JASS   195?
Bombastic cuts with Red Allen (tpt) and Hawkins. −RW

Coleman Hawkins All Stars / OJC   1960
Jam-session flavor. Guest stint by Vic Dickenson (tb). −RW

At Ease With / OJC   1960
A nice 1988 reissue of this relaxed, joyous date with Hawkins, Tommy Flanagan (p), and company. −RW

Bean Stalkin' / PABLO   1960
He's not at the top of his game, but Hawkins still makes a few solid statements. −RW

Night Hawk / OJC   1961
Another Eddie Davis (ts) /Hawkins summit meeting. −RW

○ **Desafinado / MCA**   1962
A great record! Coleman Hawkins shows us Stan Getz wasn't the only one who could handle the bossa nova. Lush reissue of this classic. −RW

Wrapped Tight / GRP   1965
Recent CD reissue from an Impulse recording. −MGN

Giants of Tenor Sax / COMMODORE
A nice link between Hawkins and Frank Wess (fl), a swing and big-band veteran. −RW

○ **In a Mellow Tone / OJC**
A superior session with Hawkins, Eddie "Lockjaw" Davis (ts), and others. −RW

Jazz at the Philharmonic / POLYGRAM
These are prime, exciting live dates, with Coleman Hawkins dazzling. −RW

Three Great Swing Saxophones / RCA
An album with Ben Webster (ts), Benny Carter (as). A textbook example of swing sax technique from three of the founding fathers. −RW

☆ **Body & Soul / RCA**   COMP
1939-1965. Five discs; Hawkins plays his most famous number (the title track), among others. −MGN

Classic Tenors / CBS / DB 5   COMP
A good compilation of formative swing work from Hawkins and Lester Young (ts). −RW

ERSKINE HAWKINS   b 1914

Big band. Trumpeter, bandleader of one of the greatest Southern swing bands. Erskine Hawkins, who began playing trumpet at 13 and was an immediate Louis Armstrong devotee, formed a band from a college group based at Alabama State Teacher's College. The orchestra, which came to New York in 1934 and eventually replaced Chick Webb's band at the Savoy after Webb's death, was a textbook romping, stomping swing aggregation, with crowd-pleasing songs and top performances. During the 40s, they traveled all over the South from their New York base, and they recorded for Vocation from the mid 30s. Their big hits included "Tuxedo Junction," "Tippin' In," and "Somebody's Rocking My Dreamboat." Hawkins, a ferocious, accomplished trumpeter himself, kept going as a combo leader and player into the late 70s. –RW

Original Tuxedo Junction / RCA   1938
1938-1942. Nice 1989 release of a rather overlooked big band. Title cut was a huge hit. –RW

○ **Tuxedo Junction / MCA**   1950
This includes 1950 big-band and 1960 quintet recordings. Contrast the title track between the two groups. –MGN

LOUIS HAYES   b 1937

Hard-bop, post-bop. This Detroit drummer and hard swinger has been prominent with the Adderley Brothers, Woody Shaw, and his own bands. –MGN

Louis Hayes / VEE JAY   i 1960
Breath of Life / MUSE   1974
Ichi-Ban / TIMELESS   1976
Tight, tough duo work with Junior Cook (ts). –RW

○ **The Real Thing / MUSE**   1977
His best band, with Woody Shaw (tpt), Rene McLean (sax), and Slide Hampton (tb). All originals, all excellent. –MGN

Light & Lively / STEEPLECHASE   1989
Another good one, with Charles Tolliver (tpt) and Bobby Watson (as). –MGN

The Crawl / CANDID   1989
Live at Birdland, with Charles Tolliver (tpt) and Gary Bartz (sax). Very good. –MGN

TUBBY HAYES   1935-1973

Swing, bop. Tenor saxophonist Tubby Hayes was among the finest European jazz musicians of all time. He was a professional at 15, working in various big bands led by Kenny Baker, Vic Lewis, and Jack Parnell, among others. Hayes led his own octet in the mid 50s, with which he toured England. He started playing vibes a year later and co-led the Jazz Couriers with Ronnie Scott from 1957-1959. During the early and mid 60s, he became a featured soloist at several clubs in America, while also having a regular television show in England from 1961-1963. A superior soloist and arranger, Hayes made two recordings heading American bands that included the likes of Clark Terry, Rahsaan Roland Kirk, and James Moody. –RW

○ **New York Sessions / CBS**   1961
Tubby Hayes (UK tenor man) blows strong with Clark Terry (tpt). A sleeper. –MGN

GRAHAM HAYNES

M-base. Graham Haynes, a trumpeter, is the son of noted jazz drummer Roy Haynes. His band No Image has been tabbed as one of the more influential ensembles mixing improvisational arrangements with funk, rock, and reggae nuances. Deemed one of the leaders of a sound some call "acid-jazz," Haynes has been profiled in British and international jazz magazines. He's also collaborated with members of the Black Rock Coalition and M-Base. –RW

○ **What Time It Be! / MUSE**   1990
One of the rising stars among acid-jazz. This release has jazz, reggae, and rock elements, yet retains its improvisational thrust. –RW

ROY HAYNES   b 1926

Bop, hard-bop, post-bop, early free. Sometimes a light sound can be as attention-grabbing and definitive as a bombastic one, and that's been Roy Haynes's trademark as a drummer.

Music Map

Jazz Violin

Soloist Claude Williams (1908)

Great Soloists
Joe Venuti (1903-1978) w/ Eddie Lang
Stephane Grappelli (1908) w/ Django Reinhardt
Stuff Smith (1909-1967)

Swing-Era Violinists
Svend Asmussen (1916)
Eddie South (1904-1962) – recorded w/ Grappelli/Reinhardt
Ray Nance w/ Duke Ellington

Experimental, Free-Jazz Players
Leroy Jenkins (1932) — Zbigniew Seifert (1946-1979)
John Blake — Didier Lockwood (1956)

Late 1960s Violin
Irène Aebi w/ Steve Lacy

Though he's every bit as inventive, steady, and capable as any other percussionist, Roy Haynes has not played with the volume or power of other well-known bop stars such as Max Roach or Art Blakey. Haynes worked in Boston with the Shabby Lewis band, as well as Frankie Newton and Pete Brown in the 40s, before touring with Luis Russell from 1945-1947 and the Lester Young sextet from 1947-1949. After stints with Kai Winding and Bud Powell, Haynes joined Charlie Parker's band from 1949-1950 and later worked with Wardell Gray and Stan Getz. He was Sarah Vaughan's regular drummer for a five-year period in the mid 50s, then spent time with Miles Davis, Lee Konitz, and Thelonious Monk before heading his own bands. In the 60s, Haynes split time between his groups and periods with George Shearing, Lennie Tristano, Kenny Burrell, Getz, John Coltrane, and Gary Burton. Perhaps his most heralded band in recent years was the wonderful Hip Ensemble of the early 70s, whose roster included George Adams on tenor sax and Hannibal Marvin Peterson on trumpet. –RW

○ **We Three / OJC**   1958
A wonderful session, with spectacular piano by Phineas Newborn and great bass from Paul Chambers. –RW

○ **Out of the Afternoon / IMPULSE**   1962
Definitive creative music with Roland Kirk (reeds) and Tommy Flanagan (p). –MGN

Cracklin' / NEW JAZZ   1963
A fine date, with Booker Ervin center stage on tenor sax. –RW

★ **Hip Ensemble / MAINSTREAM / DB 5**   1971
This explosive session helped cement the reputations of George Adams (ts) and Hannibal Marvin Peterson (tpt). –RW

Senyah / MAINSTREAM   1973
The energetic material continues here, with great Haynes drum support. –RW

Thank You, Thank You / GALAXY   1977
An excellent hard-bop session. –RW

Equipoise / MAINSTREAM   197?
A good mainstream set from the 70s, reissued. –RW

True or False / FREELANCE   1986
This live session in Paris with Ralph Moore (ts) is proof that Haynes is a premier jazz drummer. –MGN

JON HAZILLA

Post-bop, neo bop. This Boston drummer has been used as a

sideman and leads his own trio. He was a charter member of The Cadence All Stars. −MGN

○ **Chicplacity / CADENCE**   1986

A trio that includes pianist John Hicks and bassist Ray Drummond. Half standards, half originals. Spirited playing. An excellent recording. −MGN

J. C. HEARD   b 1917

Swing, big band, bop, progressive big band. Swing to bop big-band drummer. Most extensively documented on record of the mid-period jazz drummers. Heard in JATP bands and with almost all the great artists of the 40s and 50s. Lived in Japan for years before going home to his native Detroit. −MGN

○ **This is Me J. C. / ARGO**   i 1958

● **Some of This, Some of That / HIROKO**   1986

Master drummer leads 13-piece band. Loads of blues and modern jazz along with some goofy fun and solid musicianship. Fine "Nica's Dream" and "Sweet Love of Mine, Sweet Samantha." Heard vocalizes frequently on this album which features trumpeter Walt Szymanski. −MGN

ALBERT HEATH   b 1935

Bop, hard-bop, post-bop, progressive big band. The drummer of the Heath brothers is an absolute virtuoso. He can kick it out or cry in whispers of diaspora that perfectly reflect his jazz/African heritage. −MGN

Kawaida / TRIP   1969

An adventurous octet date with Don Cherry (tpt) and Herbie Hancock (p). −RW

○ **Kwanza (The First) / MUSE**   1973

Excellent recording from the Heath Brother's drummer, with brothers Percy (b) and Jimmy (sax), Curtis Fuller (tb), Ted Dunbar (g), and Kenny Barron (p). −MGN

HEATH BROTHERS

Bop, soul jazz, early free, contemporary funk. This group, composed of Percy on bass, Jimmy on sax, Albert on drums, plus Stanley Cowell at the piano, and Tony Purrone on guitar can and will do it all, from bop to funk to horn charts and string sections as backup. Philadelphia's most famous musical family, all very influential. −RW

○ **Marchin' On / STRATA EAST**   1975

This studio date is their best; w/ Stanley Cowell (p). Features "The Smilin' Billy Suite" for Billy Higgins. A treasure. −MGN

Live at the Public Theater / COLUMBIA   1979

Their first date without Albert on drums. Akira Tana (d) joins the fold. −RW

In Motion / COLUMBIA   1979

A stalwart session spiced by Keith Copeland (tpt). −RW

Expressions of Life / COLUMBIA   1980

Their last work on Columbia. −RW

Brotherly Love / POLYGRAM / DB 5   1981

A welcome reissue of an album that had consistently good compositions and excellent solos from Jimmy Heath. Stanley Cowell (p) and Tony Purrone (g) are first-rate. −RW

Brothers & Others / POLYGRAM   1983

A solid blend of typically sharp Heath Brothers material, with guest contributions by Slide Hampton (tb). A 1991 reissue of a session previously available on Columbia. −RW

JIMMY HEATH   b 1926

Bop, hard-bop, post-bop. Saxophonist. His nickname "Little Bird" is a tip-off to Jimmy Heath's array of talents. A superb soloist whose facility rivals his creativity, Heath actually stopped playing alto for much of his career to establish a reputation and style on tenor, where he's one of the great hard bop players. Yet he played alto with Nat Towles and Howard McGhee in the 40s, led his own big band in Philadelphia in 1948-1949, and joined Dizzy Gillespie in 1949-1950. A gifted writer and arranger, Heath penned tunes for Miles Davis, Chet

Baker, and Art Blakey in the 50s, then later arranged for Milt Jackson, Davis, Kenny Dorham, Art Farmer, and Gil Evans in the late 50s and 60s. In addition, he cut his own dates. In the 70s he formed the Heath Brothers group with bassist Percy and drummer Albert. −RW

Really Big / MILESTONE   1960

This is one of Heath's earliest as a leader and showcases his savvy as both a leader and a player. −RW

Swamp Seed / MILESTONE   1963

An early version of the Heath Brothers, with Albert (d) and Percy (b) on board. −RW

On the Trail / MILESTONE   1964

This is a worthy quartet vehicle with Albert and Paul Chambers (b). −RW

○ **The Gap Sealer / COBBLESTONE / DB 5**   1972

Some of Heath's finest, most aggressive playing. He is a standout on soprano, flute, and tenor. −RW

Jimmy / MUSE   1972

Love and Understanding / MUSE   1973

An outstanding group buttressed by trombonist Curtis Fuller and Billy Higgins (d). −RW

Picture of Health / XANADU   1975

A fine quartet. Super playing by Barry Harris (p), Heath, and Higgins (d). −RW

New Picture / LANDMARK   1985

One of Heath's most recent. An assured, consistently productive, and appealing mainstream date, with Tommy Flanagan on piano as a bonus. −RW

○ **Peer Pleasure / LANDMARK**   1987

A smooth session with sharp work from Heath. As usual, it has fine compositions. The CD has a bonus cut. −RW

● **Nice People / OJC**   COMP

A compilation of Riverside albums. Well programmed. −MGN

TED HEATH   1900-1969

Big band. One of Britain's best-known bandleaders, Heath headed an orchestra for BBC after leading other groups from 1944 to 1964. His group always had strong arrangements and was a topflight aggregation throughout its career. Tadd Dameron was staff arranger and composer in the mid 60s. The group's albums did well on the overseas market, though the material was resolutely swing and standards. −RW

○ **At the London Palladium / LONDON**   195?

ca. 1953/1954. American breakthrough by British bandleader who led a swing band including such jazz artists as Ronnie Scott (ts) and Johnny Dankworth (reeds). −DS

BILL HEID   b 1948

Blues-jazz, ballads, soul jazz. This Pittsburgh-born pianist is well suited to blues or jazz, with a virtuosic technique. He has recorded with Koko Taylor, Fenton Robinson, Henry Johnson, and records film soundtracks. He also tours Japan regularly. −MGN

○ **Blues on the Road / CORONA**

Blues and piano a là Mose Allison from Heid. Vocals on all cuts. Music varies from pop to classic blues, R&B, and modern jazz as they display phenomenal techniques. Five-piece horn section led by trumpeter Walt Szymanski. Includes bassist Chris Giles and Ken Kellett, drummers Ike Allen and Randy Gelispie, guitarist Perry Hughes, and percussionist David Koether. Four of the eleven cuts are Heid originals. −MGN

MARK HELIAS   b 1950

Neo bop, modern creative. This fine bassist was initially considered part of the "free" movement, but has since moved a bit toward the mainstream. Later he became part of the early jazz-rock scene, playing with Miles Davis and other mainstream-jazz combos. He doesn't have an extensive catalog or legacy of recordings and seldom works as a bandleader. −RW

● **The Current Set / ENJA**   ca. 1987
Septet w/ Tim Berne (as), Robin Eubanks (tb), Greg Osby (as), Herb Robertson, Victor Lewis, and Nana Vasoncelos (per). Six originals by leader and bassist, all in strong improvisatory flavor, while keeping rhythm intact. "Greetings from L. C." a fave. –MGN

Split Image / ENJA   ca. 1987
With Dewey Redman (ts), Tim Berne (as), Herb Robertson (tpt), and Gerry Hemingway. Six more Helias originals. –MGN

○ **Desert Blue / RHINO**   1989

JONAS HELLBORG

M-base. Electric bass guitarist known for work with John McLaughlin. A wild improviser, Hellborg leans more toward rock than jazz. No doubt a virtuoso. –MGN

○ **The Word / POLYGRAM**   1990
An intriguing, eclectic venture into the world between free-form jazz and heavy metal. Tony Williams is immense on drums. –RW

JULIUS HEMPHILL   b 1940

Early free, progressive big band, modern creative. A topflight alto saxophonist from Fort Worth, TX. Hemphill got his start in St. Louis in the late 60s, where he was a member of the Black Artists Group (BAG). During the 70s, he played with Anthony Braxton and became known for a pungent, soaring alto style with equal parts blues, free, bop, and soul. He was a cofounder of the World Saxophone Quartet in 1977 and has done other types of recording in eclectic formats. His big band has many top players and jumps all over the stylistic board in a manner similar to most Hemphill sessions. –RW

○ **Dogon A. D. / ARISTA-FREEDOM**   1972
Early-period recording for St. Louis avant-garde saxophonist. "Out there" and captivating. With Abdul Wadud on cello and Barkida Carroll on trumpet. –MGN

● **Coon Bid'ness / ARISTA-FREEDOM**   1975
Remainder of St. Louis 1972 sides and 1975 New York City. Includes the 20-minute cut "Hard Blues." –MGN

● **Roi Boye & the Gotham Minstrels / SACKVILLE**   1977
Psycho-theater drama in the form of the free African-American creative-jazz movement at its height. –MGN

Flat Out Jump Suite / BLACK SAINT   1980
Quartet with Abdul Wadud (cello), Olu Dara on trumpet, and Warren Smith on percussion. Unabashed free music, at times funky. –MGN

○ **Julius Hemphill Big Band / ELEKTRA**   1988
Some roaring, delightful big-band and large group recordings done in updated, brassy style. –RW

BILL HENDERSON   b 1930

Ballads. For a long time he was one of the best ballad and blues singers. Smooth as any. Can swing with the best. Underappreciated. –MGN

Live at the Times / DISCOVERY   1975
Stylized. Some good moments with Joyce Collins (v). –RW

Tribute to Johnny Mercer / DISCOVERY   1981
Great songs sung by a great voice. –MGN

○ **Bill Henderson / Oscar Peterson Trio / POLYGRAM**
Exceptional release from an unsung hero of jazz vocals. Highly recommended. –MGN

Something's Gotta Give / DISCOVERY
Nice session, with Joyce Collins (v) present. –RW

FLETCHER HENDERSON   1897-1952

Big band. Though he came to New York from Georgia to do graduate work in chemistry, Henderson's aptitude at the piano led him into a musical career, first as house-band leader for Black Swan (the first African-American-owned record label), then as accompanist for singer Ethel Waters. He was chosen by a group of recording musicians to front them for an audition; his good looks and pleasant manner made him a likely leader, but he had no flair for business. Nevertheless, he presided over an array of musical talent that remained unmatched for the 20s: Louis Armstrong, Coleman Hawkins, Benny Carter, Don Redman, Jimmy Harrison, Buster Bailey, Rex Stewart, and many others graced his band, which made its home at the Roseland Ballroom in Manhattan and recorded hundreds of sides. Though his main reputation is as an arranger, Fletcher did not begin to write until the early 30s; before that, Redman and Carter, among others, created the band's book. Once he took pen in hand, however, Fletcher quickly mastered the new idiom of swing and had a major role in the success of Benny Goodman's newly formed band. (In 1934, when Goodman started, Fletcher's men deserted him, and he was without a regular band for six months.) Though his arrangements were noted for their difficult keys, they were phrased in a manner that practically made the notes swing. Fletcher's last great band, in 1936, had much of its book written by his younger brother Horace, who also was a better pianist. It included such new stars as Roy Eldridge, Chu Berry, and Sid Catlett. By 1939 Fletcher was staff arranger and band pianist for Goodman, who helped him start another band in 1941; he hung in until the end of the decade. By 1949 Fletcher led a sextet. In his best charts, such as "King Porter Stomp" and "Sometimes I'm Happy," Fletcher Henderson gave big-band swing a very special lilt. –DM

Fletcher Henderson's Orchestra / BIOGRAPH   1923
1923-1927. Includes great early cuts from the Henderson Orchestra. –RW

★ **A Study in Frustration / COLUMBIA / DB 5**   1923
1923-1938. Definitive collection. 4-disc set that truly displays the greatness of this orchestra and Fletcher Henderson. –RW

○ **First Impressions / MCA**   1924
1924-1931. Arrangements are by Don Redman and F. Henderson. With Louis Armstrong, Buster Bailey, Coleman Hawkins, Benny Morton, Russell Procope, John Kirby on tuba, and Edgar Sampson on alto sax and violin. –MGN

And the Dixie Stompers / SWING   192?
Wonderful reissue of some great 20s cuts. –RW

Hocus Pocus / RCA   192?
Superb 20s and 30s cuts that spotlight Henderson's compositional, conducting, and bandleading skills. Amazing personnel as well, Coleman Hawkins (ts), Roy Eldridge (tpt), and others. –RW

Crown King of Swing / SAVOY   1931
Excellent set of superb Henderson recordings. –RW

● **Complete / RCA BLUEBIRD**   COMP
1927-1936. With 34 different tracks, this is a field day for Henderson lovers. Here are more definitive sides from the most influential big band next to Ellington. –MGN

JOE HENDERSON   b 1937

Bop, hard-bop, post-bop, Latin, jazz-rock. 1992 has been the year for tenor saxophonist Joe Henderson, long admired by musicians but generally unknown outside the jazz sphere. His looping lines, mournful, passionate ballad playing, and often fiery solos with strategic wails and cries are always done tastefully and with swing and verve. Henderson's initial fame came when he headed a band with trumpeter Kenny Dorham from 1962-1963. He was then part of Horace Silver's band from 1964-1966 and co-led the Jazz Communicators with Freddie Hubbard from 1967-1968. Henderson was in Herbie Hancock's sextet from 1969-1970 and then had a highly publicized but short-lived stint with Blood, Sweat & Tears in 1971. Since then he's mainly headed his own bands and also has been active as an educator. He was part of the group who helped re-launch Blue Note Records in 1985, but his 1992 album *Lush Life* has thrust him into the spotlight. –RW

○ **Page One / BLUE NOTE**   1963

A 1988 reissue of an outstanding date. Kenny Dorham (tpt) and McCoy Tyner (p) soar; Henderson is frenetic. –RW

Our Thing / BLUE NOTE   1963
A wonderful 1986 reissue of a prime 1963 date. The lineup is amazing, with Andrew Hill (p) and Kenny Dorham (tpt). CD has a bonus cut. –RW

In 'N Out / BLUE NOTE   1964

● **Inner Urge / BLUE NOTE**   1964
This is his best work. The other Blue Notes are also worth having. –MGN

☆ **Mode for Joe / BLUE NOTE**   1966
An early masterpiece. CD has bonus cut. –RW

The Kicker / OJC   1967
A stormy, dynamic date that teeters on the avant-garde edge, yet holds the bop center. –RW

Tetragon / MILESTONE   1967

Power to the People / MILESTONE   1969
An album with Afrocentric flavoring — frenetic and introspective at times. –RW

In Pursuit of Blackness / MILESTONE / DB 5   1970

If You're Not Part of the Problem.... / MILESTONE   1970
Fiery, smashing Henderson solos. Excellent lineup. –RW

Live at the Lighthouse / MILESTONE   1970
Firehouse playing from the wonderful team of Henderson and Woody Shaw (tpt). –RW

Joe Henderson in Japan / MILESTONE   1971
Masterly playing by Henderson. –RW

Black Is the Color / MILESTONE   1972
Includes dips, swoops, honks, screams, and tenor-sax pyrotechnics. –RW

Multiple / MILESTONE   1973

○ **The Elements / MILESTONE**   1973
Ambitious concept work gets an ethereal feeling via Alice Coltrane's harp. –RW

Canyon Lady / MILESTONE   1973
Some Afro-Latin flavor and shuddering Henderson sax. –RW

Relaxin' at Camarillo / CONTEMPORARY   1979
An album of easy and confident yet blistering tenor sax by Henderson. –RW

State of the Tenor - Vols. 1-2 / BLUE NOTE   1985
Recorded live at the Village Vanguard. First-rate; an overlooked hard-blowing set of recordings by the individualistic player. –RW

☆ **Lush Life / VERVE**   i 1992
It won Jazz Album of the Year in 1992. A brilliant, memorable tribute by Henderson to Billy Strayhorn. –RW

Best of the Blue Note Years / BLUE NOTE   COMP
Good compilation. –MGN

SCOTT HENDERSON

World fusion. Jazz guitarist Scott Henderson has performed with Jeff Berlin, Jean-Luc Ponty, Chick Corea and Joe Zawinul as well as others. –PK

Spears / RELATIVITY-COMBAT   1986
The debut release featuring Henderson's exceptional guitar tones in a small-group setting. Well worth a listen. –PK

○ **Dr. Hee / RELATIVITY**   1987
Exceptional album of jazz, rock, and fusion compositions. A must for guitarists. –PK

Nomad / RELATIVITY   1990
Jazz/fusion similar to Weather Report at times. A brilliant guitarist and composer. –PK

JON HENDRICKS   b 1921

Big band, bop, ballads. Vocalist. Self-taught drummer Jon Hendricks used the radio as an early inspiration and reference. He sang on broadcasts in Toledo as an 11-year-old. One of 17 children in his family, he studied law for a time after

high school but turned full-time professional musician at the urging of Charlie Parker. He moved to New York in 1952 and had his song "I Want You to Be My Baby" recorded by Louis Jordan. He put lyrics to "Four Brothers," "Cloudburst," and some George Russell songs on his *New York, New York* album in the late 50s. His backup group was the Dave Lambert Singers and ultimately Lambert, Hendricks, and Annie Ross. This trio was a dominant jazz vocalese unit from the late 50s to the mid 60s, adding lyrics to a host of tunes by Count Basie, Horace Silver, Miles Davis, and Art Blakey. –RW

● **The Swingers! / AFFINITY**   1959
Tremendous vocals and harmonies by Hendricks with Lambert and Ross. The trio in their prime. –RW

Fast Livin' Blues / COLUMBIA   1961
Jive and blues vocals. Some poignant cuts, some merely enjoyable. –RW

In Person at the Trident / SMASH   r 1965
Dynamic, forceful singing and scatting. –RW

Recorded in Person at the Trident / POLYGRAM   1965

Cloudburst / ENJA   1972
Expressive. Takes some chances. –RW

○ **Tell Me the Truth / ARISTA**   1976
This is one of Hendricks's toughest, most social-oriented releases. –RW

Blues for Pablo / ARISTA   197?
Strong, assertive leads. –RW

Love / MUS   1981
Good though erratic 1981-1982 sessions. –RW

● **Freddie Freeloader / POLYGRAM**
Tour-de-force recording with Bobby McFerrin (v), George Benson (g), Al Jarreau (v), and Manhattan Transfer (v). –MGN

Salute to João Gilberto / REPRISE
This is a fine homage to the distinguished Brazilian musical figure. –RW

☆ **Sing Along with Basie / ROULETTE**
A wonderful followup to *Sing a Song of Basie*. This time the trio cut with the full Basie Orchestra. –RW

MICHELE HENDRICKS

Bop, cool, ballads. The daughter of the great lyricist and vocalist Jon Hendricks, Michele hasn't achieved the fame or status thus far of her legendary father, but she has released a pair of good albums in the mainstream setting. Her father was a guest on her 1989 album *Keepin' Me Satisfied*. –RW

○ **Carryin' On / MUS**   1987
A satisfying, topical jazz date. Stan Getz (ts), Ray Drummond (p), and "Smitty" Smith contribute greatly. –RW

Keepin' Me Satisfied / MUSE   1989
A set with her famous father Jon as a guest star. It's unambitious, but professionally done. –RW

ERNIE HENRY   1926-1957

Post-bop. Henry was a tremendous performer on alto, despite a short career. Though he only played about a decade, his work with Tadd Dameron, Dizzy Gillespie, Charles Mingus, and Thelonious Monk (along with a few sessions with Illinois Jacquet) cemented his importance. He was a searing, attention-getting saxophonist, whose phrasing and intensity were matched by his ideas and expressiveness. –RW

● **Presenting Ernie Henry / OJC**   1956
His first album. As good as *Last Chorus*. –MGN

Seven Standards & A Blues / OJC   1957
Exemplary playing and interpretations from an alto saxophonist who might have become a pivotal figure, with a normal lifespan and career. –RW

○ **Last Chorus / OJC**   1957
Here is the legendary saxophonist at zenith. Excellent musicianship. –MGN

WOODY HERMAN   1913-1987

Swing, big band. The greatest and most innovative and influential of the White big-band leaders, Woody Herman headed a band from the 30s until his death in 1987. A child singer and vaudevillian, Herman began playing the sax at 11 and was working in bands at 15. When Isham Jones retired from his band in the mid 30s, the other members picked Herman to be his successor. Herman kept things going until 1946. After briefly working as a vocalist, Herman re-formed a big band from 1947-1949, then a small group, then another big band in 1950. His Herds became famous for their precision as an orchestra, enhanced by his ability to recruit and spotlight top soloists, arrangers, and writers. He was also able to incorporate musical changes over decades, yet keep a standard sound and maintain a feeling of unity, similiar in his way to how Count Basie and Duke Ellington operated. He wasn't a spectacular clarinetist like Benny Goodman, but his simple statements were effective and often declarative. He was a marginal alto player and added soprano in his later years for another voice. His greatest band, the Four Brothers aggregation of the late 40s, included Stan Getz, Zoot Sims, Serge Chaloff, and Jimmy Giuffre. It was both a marvelous horn section and an array of singular talents. Still, the song that was the Herman orchestra's signature tune was "At the Woodchoppers' Ball," which they played from the 40s until the end. They were also great at the traditional swing-era stompers that defined the big-band sound. Herman did a 40th Anniversary concert in 1976 and a 50th Anniversary concert in 1986. –RW

○ **Blues on Parade / MCA-GRP**   1930
This is a thorough 1991 release of his late-30s/40s Decca material. –RW

Best of the Decca Years / MCA   1939
1939-1944. 1988 issue has some fine cuts. Somewhat supplanted by recent reissue. –RW

☆ **Thundering Herds / CBS**   1945
1945-1947. 1988 reissue has some prime cuts from a productive period. –RW

Memorial Album / XANADU   1957
Misleading title, but a sturdy session. –RW

Live at Monterey / ATLANTIC   1959
Fine concert recording. –RW

○ **Concerto for Herd / VERVE**   1967
Fine set with Bill Holman's marvelous title composition. –RW

The Raven Speaks / OJC   1972
Outstanding early-70s cuts. –RW

○ **Giant Steps / OJC / DB 5**   1973
This is arguably the best release from his 70s and 80s material. Herman tackles contemporary and bop material with vigor. –RW

● **40th Anniversary Carnegie Hall / RCA**   1976
Excellent set w/ sax greats Stan Getz, Al Cohn, and Jimmy Giuffre. –RW

○ **Woody & Friends / CONCORD**   1979
1992 reissue of a fine set with Herman featuring people he seldom played with, such as Woody Shaw (tpt) and Slide Hampton (tb). –RW

Presents: Concord Jam - Vols. 1-3 / CONCORD   1980
The best of his 80s output. –RW

Live at Concord Jazz Festival 1981 / CONCORD   1981
Nice late-period set with sax-alumni Al Cohn, Stan Getz. –RW

World Class / CONCORD   1982
Good release of Woody in small-combo mould. –RW

○ **50th Anniversary Tour / CONCORD**   1986
Good spirit, nice tributes. –RW

Woody's Gold Star / CONCORD   1987
Nice date with a 15-piece, stripped-down band and top Latin percussionists. –RW

Early Autumn / RCA-BLUEBIRD
Wonderful sessions. A youthful, stunning Stan Getz (ts). –RW

On Keynote / POLYGRAM
Outstanding collection of cuts featuring Woody Herman's "Small Herds" on Keynote. –RW

Best of the Big Bands / CBS   COMP
Sampler containing his best-known big-band material. –RW

Greatest Hits / CBS   COMP
This is a good attempt to put his Columbia period in perspective. –RW

VINCENT HERRING   b1964

Post-bop, neo-bop. Alto sax, composer. Here's another new name on the horizon. Vince Herring has already earned praise for good, hard-bop compositions and a loose, animated alto-sax style that recalls the traditional references of many modern altoists, such as Cannonball and Parker. He has two fine sessions under his own name, plus appearances on other albums, and is gaining stature as a player and leader. –RW

An American Experience / MUSICMASTERS   1986
The emerging alto saxophonist reveals his debt to Cannonball Adderley and Charlie Parker. Good tone, lots of potential. –RW

○ **Evidence / LANDMARK**
A much sharper, clearer statement than his other release. The compositions are better and the music is more dynamic. –RW

FRED HERSCH

Post-bop, neo-bop. Cincinnati pianist with original voice. Plays much original contemporary music. Excellent accompanist for singers. –MGN

Horizons / CONCORD   1984
This session has an adventurous quality and sensibility. –RW

○ **Forward Motion / CHESKY**   i 1991
This is a release that has components of jazz, chamber, and new-age. –RW

CONRAD HERWIG   b1959

Post-bop, progressive big band, neo bop. Trombonist known as a premier sideman. Member of the Toshiko Akiyoshi Orchestra, and a bandleader of late. Works well with standards, post-bop and modal music. Plays lean and quick. –MGN

New York Hardball / KEN MUSIC   1989
One of the better underpublicized trombonists on the contemporary scene. –RW

○ **With Every Breath / KEN MUSIC**
Topnotch trombonist plays modern jazz with no frills. Highly recommended. Reissued on CD (originally on Seabreeze Records). –MGN

EDDIE HEYWOOD   b1915

Swing, big band, instr-pop. Eddie Heywood enjoyed stardom in the 40s as a musician and in the 50s as a writer. Heywood played in his father's 81 Theater orchestra for a time, then joined Clarence Love's band, coming with them to New York in 1937. He worked with Benny Carter, Zutty Singleton, and Georgie Auld before forming his own group in the early 40s. This band made a series of landmark recordings in 1943 with such vocalists as Bing Crosby, Billie Holiday, Ella Fitzgerald, and the Andrews Sisters, among them the song "Begin the Beguine." Heywood enjoyed major success in the 50s as a composer, with such hits as "Canadian Sunset," "Soft Summer Breeze," and "Land of Dreams." Heywood stopped playing again in the late 60s, returned in 1972, and has produced some swing-era revival albums for Time-Life. –RW

○ **Jazz at Cafe Society 1940s / COMMODORE**   194?
Stately, timeless swing-era session. –RW

Canadian Sunset / RCA / BB 16
Authentic, with fine playing throughout. –RW

JOHN HICKS
b 1941

Post-bopmodal-jazz, cool. Hicks is a busy modern pianist whose initial reputation was built on probing trio sessions and accompaniment for Betty Carter. He has done traditional trio and small-combo dates, played in the Power Trio doing more adventurous rock and free improvisation, made a dazzling solo record, and made some critically acclaimed recordings for the DIW label. His playing approach has some elements of McCoy Tyner, but he's far from an imitator — he is a dynamic interpreter and a striking soloist in complete command of the instrument. –RW

○ **After the Morning / WEST 54**   1979
This first album is a real keeper. Great piano playing throughout. –MGN

Some Other Time / THERESA   1981
A standout vehicle, with languid solos. –RW

Power Trio / NOVUS   1990
You can't go wrong with this one. Virtuosos all. –MGN

Live at Maybeck Recital Hall - Vol. 7 / CONCORD   1990
Rollicking, thoughtful, unpredictable, and eclectic solo piano. CD version has two bonus cuts. –RW

● **Eastside Blues / DIW**   i 1991
His most recent excursion into the trio vein, this album is explosive and substantive, with Curtis Lundy and Victor Lewis. –RW

Is That So? / TIMELESS
A new trio set, with rangy and spiraling phrases. –RW

John Hicks in Concert / THERESA
An excellent example of Hicks at his best, live. –RW

Naima's Love Song / DIW
Hicks moves into overdrive. Wonderful alto sax from Bobby Watson. –RW

BILLY HIGGINS
1936-1973

Bop, hard-bop, post-bop, early free. "Smilin' Billy" is, next to J. C. Heard and Art Taylor, the most recorded jazz drummer of the last 40 years. His unflagging time, consistent virtuosity, and innate ability to listen and contribute to a group sound keep him in demand. Truly one of the all-time greats. –MGN

Soweto / RED   1979
A superior quartet session, with some of Bob Berg's best tenor-sax work. –RW

The Soldier / TIMELESS   1979
This recording with Cedar Walton (p) presents post-bop standards, well-played. –MGN

○ **Bridgework / CONTEMPORARY**   1980
A rare Higgins album, with conservative arrangements and compositions, plus outstanding technique and percussive foundations. –RW

● **Mr. Billy Higgins / RIZA**   1984
His best as a leader. A peerless drummer. Excellent compositions include "Morning Awakening" with Gary Bias on saxophone and William Henderson on piano. –MGN

EDDIE HIGGINS
b 1932

Swing, bop, cool, soul jazz, neo bop. Swing to bop pianist whose startling technical facility does not get in the way of his soulfulness or ability to interpret. Absolutely convincing in live performance. A good research project. –MGN

○ **Eddie Higgins / VEE JAY**   i 1961
W/ Frank Foster (sax). –ED

Soulero / ATLANTIC   i 1965

DAVE HILDINGER

Post-bop. Canadian pianist whose limited recording and obscurity keep him out of the limelight. His recordings are almost impossible to find. –MGN

○ **The Young Moderns / BATON**   i 1957

ANDREW HILL
b 1937

Post-bop, early free, modern creative. A visionary, percussive pianist who evolved from R&B and mainstream roots into one of the more advanced theorists and players on the 60s scene. Hill worked with everyone in Chicago, from Paul Williams and Dinah Washington to Von Freeman and Gene Ammons, before moving first to Los Angeles, then to New York in the 60s. He has varied his approach and his harmonic and rhythmic tendencies, has utilized Caribbean textures, and has played very outside at times and at other times quite conventionally. His 60s Blue Note albums and his playing with Joe Henderson were models of balance between composition and freedom, complexity and simplicity. His latest albums have seen him again carefully mixing experimental and traditional elements. –RW

○ **Black Fire / BLUE NOTE / DB 5**   1963
Haiti's gift to jazz piano of the 50s and now. For adventurous listeners. –MGN

Smoke Stack / BLUE NOTE   1963
This is an early example of Hill's percussive, Afro-Caribbean sound. –RW

☆ **Point of Departure / BLUE NOTE**   1964
A 1989 reissue of a remarkable session that still has avant-garde quality today. Eric Dolphy (sax) and Joe Henderson (sax) break barriers with their splendid solos. –RW

○ **Compulsion / BLUE NOTE**   1965
Exacting, dynamic compositions, with intense playing. –RW

Involution / BLUE NOTE   1966
Hill splits this two-record set with Sam Rivers (sax). Both are incredible. –RW

Lift Every Voice / BLUE NOTE   1969
Andrew Hill incorporates vocals into his concept with ease and skill. –RW

● **One for One / BLUE NOTE**   1969
These are previously unreleased sessions from 1969 & 1970. Group efforts, at times with a string quartet. Hefty solos from B. Maupin, P. Patrick, J. Henderson, F. Hubbard, and C. Tolliver. –MGN

Invitation / STEEPLECHASE   1974
Dashing pieces, first-rate piano. –RW

Spiral / ARISTA   1974
This is a wonderful quintet w/ Ted Curson (tpt), Lee Konitz (sax). –RW

Live at Montreux / ARISTA   1975
Beautiful, authoritative solo playing. –RW

○ **From California with Love / ARTIST'S HOUSE**   1978
Overlooked and low-selling, but a certified masterpiece. –RW

Strange Serenade / SOUL NOTE   1980
Hill enters the 80s on a stirring trio note. –RW

Shades / SOUL NOTE / DB 5   1986
Both Hill and Clifford Jordan (ts) are impressive. –RW

Eternal Spirit / CAPITOL   1989
This newer material showcases Hill's influence on young lion Greg Osby (as) and includes a reunion with Bobby Hutcherson (vib). –RW

But Not Farewell / CAPITOL   r 1991
A latter-day set with the smouldering Greg Osby on alto sax. Hill updates his sound. –RW

BUCK HILL
b 1928

Swing, bop. Hill is a good mainstream tenor saxophonist who has gotten lots of mileage out of the fact he's also a mailman. He has recorded infrequently but made a splash with some fiery works in the 80s and 90s. His tenor-sax phrasing and tone exemplify the best qualities of the sturdy, robust style of Booker Ervin — never far from blues and a very solid ballad and standards player. –RW

○ **Scope / STEEPLECHASE** 1979
A studio date with the Kenny Barron Trio. Hill is a DC postman by day, a great tenor saxophonist by night. –MGN

● **Plays Europe / TURNING POINT** 1982
This live concert in Holland is worth finding. –MGN

Capital Hill / MUSE 1989
Lusty soul-jazz and funk ingredients, plus lots of blues. –RW

I'm Beginning to See the Light / MUSE ca. 199?
The latest entry from this mailman turned jazz soloist. Hill's style has soul-jazz seasoning and a bluesy bite. –RW

EARL HINES 1903-1983

Stride, swing, big band, cool. Known as "Fatha," Hines is the progenitor of modern jazz piano style; he took the instrument on a new road when he applied the discoveries, rhythmic and harmonics, of Louis Armstrong (his closest musical associate in Chicago in 1927-1928) and his own daring ideas to the keyboard. He was the first to give the piano a real voice within a band, with his ringing right-hand clusters and uncanny sense of timing. After his seminal collaborations with Armstrong, Hines formed his own big band in 1929; its stay at Chicago's Grand Terrace Ballroom lasted ten years. Among the band's notable alumni in that first decade were Omer Simeon, Budd Johnson, Trummy Young, Ray Nance, and Billy Eckstine; in 1943 Hines had both Dizzy Gillespie and Charlie Parker in his ranks, as well as Sarah Vaughan. By 1947 Hines threw in the towel; the next year he'd joined his old friend Armstrong's All Stars. But he soon was on his own again, eventually settling in San Francisco and nearly forgotten by the jazz audience until two New York concerts (coproduced by this writer) launched him on a new and vital career as a soloist, mainly fronting trios but adding a horn and a singer when the budget allowed, and making tons of records, many of them superb examples of his undimmed vitality and inventiveness. –DM

★ **Piano Man / RCA** 1939
A 1989 reissue of glittering 1939-1942 dates with the Earl Hines Orchestra. CD has six bonus cuts. –RW

Harlem Lament / CBS 193?
A first-rate compilation of superb 30s cuts with Jimmy Mundy (ts) and Orner Simeon (cl). Stride, rag, and blues elements merge seamlessly. –RW

South Side Swing / MCA 193?
A comprehensive reissue of mid-30s Hines material. –RW

○ **A Monday Date / OJC / DB 5** 1961
Topflight, bluesy, and impressive piano. –RW

Up to Date / RCA 1964
A 1988 reissue of some priceless Hines sessions done with Ray Nance (tpt) and Budd Johnson (ts). –RW

Legendary Little Theater Concert / MUSE 1964
Vols. 1 & 2. A stunning concert from 1964, with Hines displaying the total piano package. –RW

At the Village Vanguard / EPM 1965
A solid pairing with Roy Eldridge (tpt). –RW

Blues So Low / STASH 1966
Pulsating, driving tributes to Fats Waller. –RW

Earl Hines at Home / DELMARK / DB 5 ca. 1970
Solid, stately, and immaculate. –RW

Comes in Handy / AUDIOPHILE 1972
Expressive tributes to W. C. Handy. –RW

○ **Hines Does Hoagy / AUDIOPHILE / DB 5** 1972
1972-1973. A wondrous homage to Louis Armstrong. –RW

Tour De Force / BLACK LION / DB 5 1972
A wonderful reissue of a prime session. –RW

○ **Live at the New School 1973 / CHI-SOUND** 1973
A 1989 reissue of a solid live date. Hines could still pound the keyboard. –RW

○ **Partners in Jazz / MPS**

W/ Jaki Byard (p). Piano duets from masters of two styles and generations. Definitive. –MGN

Solo Walk in Tokyo / BIOGRAPH
Hines in explosive, fiery form. –RW

The Father Jumps / RCA COMP
A good compilation from 1939-1945. The music is now available in other, better remastered reissues. –RW

TERUMASA HINO b 1942

Post-bop, neo bop, jazz-rock. A top trumpeter in the prototypical hard-bop mold, Hino is one of the best Japanese jazz players. He was a prolific player in Japan during the 50s and early 60s and was a member of the Japanese group Shiraki. He became a very visible, popular figure on Japanese television and played on film soundtracks and with his own band. He came to America in 1975, working with Gil Evans, Jackie McLean, and Dave Liebman. A superb technician, Hino made a conscious effort in the 80s to trim the amount of notes he played in his solos, to make better use of space, and to vary his moods. He can play with ease in any style. –RW

Bluestruck / CAPITOL 1989
A capable though derivative trumpeter leads a standard hard-bop date. –RW

○ **Bluestuck / BLUE NOTE** 1989
His best album as a jazz player. Eight-piece band with John Scofield (g), Bob Watson (as), and Bob Hurst as principals. Hino wrote six of the eight tracks. –MGN

From the Heart / BLUE NOTE ca. 1991
Smaller group with Alan Gumbs Trio and guests. "Free Mandela" and "Lava Dance" stand out. Six by Hino, one by Gumbs, one standard. –MGN

AL HIRT b 1922

Dixieland. A classically-trained trumpeter, Al Hirt (best known as "Jumbo" to his friends in New Orleans) picked up jazz licks by listening to the recordings of Harry James and Roy Eldridge in the 40s. He began his professional career working with the swing bands of Tommy and Jimmy Dorsey, but when he returned to New Orleans in the latter 40s he gravitated toward the "traditional" jazz format. In 1955 he formed a combo that included Pete Fountain, and over the next five years worked on attracting national recognition. His greatest popularity, however, came in the mid 60s, when he had back-to-back hits with "Java," and "Cotton Candy," tunes that were perhaps closer to a popularized country-music style than to Dixieland. During the 70s, he operated his own nightclub on Bourbon Street. After a hiatus of several years, in the early 90s he returned to Bourbon Street, where he is still active. Al Hirt's substantial popularity stems from his genuine technical virtuosity and powerful delivery. –BR

Super Jazz - Vol. 1 / CBS
Al Hirt's and Pete Fountain's bands playing separately and together. This gives an illustration of why these players remain popular and continue to attract new converts to New Orleans jazz. –BR

○ **That's a Plenty / PROARTE**
Jumbo with Peanuts Hocko, Bobby Breaux, Dalton Hagler, and others pouncing on New Orleans favorites like "Royal Garden Blues," "Bourbon Street Parade," and "Saints." –BR

All-Time Greatest Hits / RCA COMP
His best-sellers and biggest pop hits. –RW

Best of Al Hirt / RCA / BB 13 COMP
Compilation of familiar cuts. –RW

ART HODES b 1904

Trad, stride, swing, blues-jazz. One of the last great traditional jazz and blues pianists, Art Hodes came to America when he was six months old and grew up in Chicago. His rollicking style was honed playing dances at Hull House and working with Chicago bands, as well as playing in New York on 52nd Street in the late 30s. Hodes made his debut on record in 1928 with Wingy Manone and has recorded periodically ever since. Most of his releases are solo, but his activities in music are not limited to the performing arena. –RW

○ **Albert Nicholas / DELMARK**   1959
Bucket's Got a Hole / DELMARK   1968

JOHNNY HODGES   1907-1970

Swing, big band, blues-jazz, progressive big band. Perhaps the most influential alto saxophonist until Charlie Parker arrived, and one of the most beloved musicians ever, Johnny Hodges brought a lyrical beauty and relaxed majesty to the instrument that has seldom been equalled and never surpassed. Hodges grew up on Hammond Street in Boston with such neighbors as Harry Carney, Toots Mondello, and Charlie Holmes. He was privileged to get saxophone lessons from the great Sidney Bechet, who taught him the soprano. He later worked at the Club Bechet in New York and played some duets with the master. Duke Ellington signed him in 1928 to replace Otto Hardwicke, and he became the saxophone section's director for the next 22 years. Hodges eventually stopped playing soprano because Ellington was penning so many pieces that accented his alto, which he played with a flawless tone and impressive, yet seemingly easy technique. For a time Johnny Hodges and His Orchestra were a small-group unit within the Ellington combine. Such masterpieces as "Jeep's Blues," "The Jeep Is Jumpin'," "Empty Ballroom Blues," and "Warm Valley" were showcase pieces for Hodges. He finally left the Ellington nest in 1951 and headed his own group until 1955, when he returned to Ellington's orchestra to stay. –RW

The Jeep is Jumpin' / VERVE   1951
1951-1958. Both hot and smooth Hodges sessions. –RW

○ **The Big Sound / VERVE / DB 5**   i 1958
An excellent showpiece for Hodges's divine alto. –RW

A Smooth One / VERVE   1959
1959 & 1960 dates. Lean, languid, and fluid Hodges alto sax solos. –RW

Back to Back / VERVE   i 1959
An album with the spotlight is on Hodges, though Duke is omnipresent. –RW

Side by Side / VERVE
Some fine small dates with Hodges up-front and Duke around the corner. –RW

At the Berlin Sportpalast / PABLO   1961
Norman Granz session in the vault until recently. –RW

Everybody Knows / IMPULSE   1964
This is among his lesser-known RCA albums. –RW

In a Mellotone, w/ Bill Davis / RCA   1966
A 1990 reissue of a Hodges/Davis set that doesn't insult either the music or the listener. –RW

Triple Play / RCA   1967
1987 reissue. W/ Ray Nance (tpt) and Tiny Grimes (g). Small-group Ellingtonia, the first from 1955, the second from 1967. The earlier one has longer and superior performances with Harry Carney, Lawrence Brown, and Jimmy Hamilton also featured, while the latter (in stereo) falls just short of the mark. The RCA version will likely appeal to diehard Hodges fans. –RW

Don't Sleep in the Subway / VERVE
The orchestrations are uneven, but Johnny Hodges is uniformly sharp. –RW

● **On Keynote with Rex Stewart / POLYGRAM**
A thorough collection of sides from Keynote, spotlighting Ellingtonians Hodges and Rex Stewart (cnt). –RW

Used to Be Duke / POLYGRAM
Sentimental, mellow, and engaging. –RW

HOLLY HOFMANN

Post-bop, cool, neo bop. A classical flute player gone jazz. A

reserved tone and style suit her well, and she can swing just fine (without the stiffness of some former classical musicians). She has good potential for the future. –MGN

○ **Further Adventures / CAPRI**   1989

JAY HOGGARD   b 1954

Post-bop, early free, world fusion, neo bop, modern creative. During the 70s and most of the 80s, Jay Hoggard seemed like one of the emerging important voices on vibes. His use of counterpoint and his ambitious compositions, solo ability, and participation in some cutting-edge sessions stamped him as a prime jazz figure. Lately he has recorded less. He issued a disappointing fusion date and has taken a much lower profile. –RW

Rain Forest / CONTEMPORARY   1980
Riverside Dance / INDIA NAVIGATION   1985
Overview / MUSE   1989
Very good, with Geri Allen (p). –MGN

● **The Little Tiger / MUSE**   1990
An album with the vibist at his best. The title track is worth the price alone. –MGN

○ **Mystic Winds, Tropical Breezes / INDIA NAVIGATION**

BILLIE HOLIDAY   1915-1959

Swing, big band, ballads. Perhaps the greatest of all female jazz singers, "Lady Day," as her friend Lester Young dubbed her, was raised in poverty. She started to sing by default — her dancing was no good. She was heard in a small Harlem club by talent-spotter John Hammond, who got her a record date with Benny Goodman in 1933. A bit later, again with Hammond behind her, she began a series of wonderful recordings with select small groups, whether led by pianist Teddy Wilson or herself. These established Holiday as a unique stylist. Her voice wasn't much of an instrument (limited range, little power) but conveyed tremendous feeling, and her phrasing came straight from Louis Armstrong and Bessie Smith, her idols. Among the musicians who recorded with her was Lester Young, who also was on Count Basie's band, which Billie joined as vocalist in 1937. Pres (she named him that) and Billie made music unmatched for symbiotic empathy. By the decade's end she also sang briefly with Artie Shaw's otherwise white band (not a happy experience), she was a successful single act, and she gradually drifted away from the joyful interaction with jazz hornplayers that had characterized her early work.

For the most part, Holiday's 30s recordings were made for Vocalian, Brunswick, Columbia, or OKeh, all labels now found on Columbia (CBS or Sony Music). But she had to go to Commodore in 1939 to find someone interested in letting her cut the controversial "Strange Fruit." In the 40s she recorded for Decca (now MCA or GRP), and in the 50s Verve (now Polygram), though there are a couple of Columbia dates, notable "Lady In Satin," from near the end of her life. –DM & WR

Billie Holiday / COMMODORE   1934
Includes Commodore cuts from 1934 & 1939. These are vintage performances. –HD

○ **Billie Holiday 1939-1949 /**   1939
A European import containing "Strange Fruit" and other recordings made around the same time. –WR

Billie's Blues / CAPITOL   1942
1942 Capitol session and 1951 Aladdin session. Billie is a bit rough on the 1951 date. –HD

★ **Complete Decca Recordings / GRP**   1944
Two CDs, 50 tracks, new songs, alternate takes. Classic songs with lush and full orchestration. 1944-1950. –HD

Lady's Decca Days - Vols. 1 & 2 / MCA   1944
A 1988 reissue of some good 1944-1950 material which is now compiled in a far superior 1991 package. –RW

Lady Sings the Blues / POLYGRAM / DB 5   1954
Immaculate 1954 and 1956 recordings with an all-star lineup

and smashing Holiday cuts. One of her last great dates. CD has three bonus cuts. –RW

All or Nothing at All / POLYGRAM   1955
Some good 1955-1956 cuts. –RW

Embraceable You / POLYGRAM   1957
Two sessions in 1957. A good two-record set that leans toward ballads and moody material. It's been eclipsed a bit by recent anthologies. –RW

Songs for Distingue Lovers / POLYGRAM   1957
Six tracks from a jazz-based session with Ben Webster (ts) and Barney Kessell (g). –HD

☆ **Lady in Satin / CBS**   1958
An unforgettable date, with Holiday clearly at the end of the line, yet still sounding hypnotic. –RW

Last Recording / POLYGRAM   1959
In many ways, a sad event. 1988 reissue of an album with Ray Ellis and his orchestra. It's poignant in a tragic way. –RW

Story / MCA   1959
Set that tried to give an overview of her years on Decca. –RW

Billie Holiday Songbook / POLYGRAM   195?
Excellent play on the songbook trend, with Holiday doing her own material. –RW

Essential ... Carnegie Hall Concert / VERVE   195?
An excellent live set. Holiday in wonderful form. –RW

First Verve Sessions / POLYGRAM   195?
Early-50s cuts — some great, some erratic. –RW

Stormy Blues / POLYGRAM   195?

God Bless the Child / CBS
Holiday's best-known single cut. –RW

I'll Be Seeing You / COMMODORE
Some fine Commodore cuts. –RW

Sound of Jazz / CSP
Billie Holiday, w/ Red Allen (tpt), Pee Wee Russell (cl), Jimmy Giuffre (reeds).

○ **Billie's Blues / COLUMBIA**   COMP
If you're going to overlook other anthologies or boxed sets, this is a compilation of 1936-1958 material. –RW

○ **The Complete Billy Holiday on Verve / VERVE**   COMP
A 10-disc set that has it all from 1946-1959. –RW

The Golden Years - Vols. 1-2 / CBS / DB 5   COMP
A pair of three-album boxed sets that at one time were the standard for Holiday reissues. They've since been eclipsed by CD sets, but are still fine. –RW

Greatest Hits / CBS   COMP
An impossible task. These are some of her best single cuts from the Columbia years, but only for those who prefer a completely condensed approach. –RW

Lady Day / COLUMBIA / DB 5   COMP
A fine single-disc compilation that has five cuts with Lester Young (ts). –RW

★ **Legacy 1933-1958 / CBS**   COMP
Most welcome; the best overview of her many fine Columbia sessions, from the very first to the last. Great sound quality, high-caliber booklet. –RW

○ **Quintessential - Vol. 1 - 9 / CBS**   COMP
In-depth material on Columbia. Nine CDs. Excellent. –JME

Silver Collection / POLYGRAM   COMP
Fourteen tracks with a jazz emphasis. W/ Ben Webster (tpt) and Sweets Edison (tpt). –HD

JOE HOLIDAY   b 1925

Post-bop, Latin. Saxophonist who loved his mambo and post-bop. Nurtured a combination of the two long before most, which makes him a maverick of sorts. –MGN

○ **Mambo Jazz / PRESTIGE**   i 1953
W/ Billy Taylor (p).

DAVE HOLLAND   b 1946

Early free, jazz-rock, neo-bop, M-base, modern creative. It seems ironic that Dave Holland, one of today's most respected and virtuosic acoustic bassists, got his big break playing in Miles Davis's *Bitches Brew*-era electric fusion band. After backing Miles, Chick Corea, Anthony Braxton, and other boundary-extending jazzmen, Holland came out with his brilliant "Conference of the Birds" album. On this highly regarded debut he achieved a rare mixture of spontaneity, structure, and widely varied moods, setting the tone for his many ECM recordings to come. Over the years he has evolved as a writer and a technician, known for tricky composing in small groups which display his jaw-dropping solo talents alongside equally proficient young players. Though Holland has always kept in touch with the iconoclastic sentiments of the European free improvisers he grew up with, his music usually avoids the extremes of the avant-garde. He is at the most exploratory on his very satisfying solo albums (on bass as well as cello), and also contributed unconventional bass techniques to various small-label recordings with tenor saxophonist Sam Rivers in the 70s. But he also knows the tradition inside and out and, like Charlie Haden, has been a major contributor to the diverse offerings on the ECM label, among others. –MB

★ **Conference of the Birds / POLYGRAM / DB 5**   1972
This English bassist's finest hour. Definitive progressive music, with Sam Rivers (ts), Anthony Braxton (reeds), and Barry Altschul (d). –MGN

○ **Emerald Tears / ECM**   1977
Bass solos. Holland is a rare virtuoso who makes solo performance a varied and joyous proposition. –MB

Life Cycle / POLYGRAM   1982
Wholly original cello solos in jazz and folk flavors. –MB

Jumpin' In / POLYGRAM / DB 5   1983
The first quintet project, with Steve Coleman (sax), Kenny Wheeler (tpt), and Julian Priester (tb) displaying structures, freedom, and far-ranging vocals. –MB

Seeds of Time / POLYGRAM / DB 5   1984
A substantial release of this evolving quintet's knotty, brassy compositions. –MB

○ **Razor's Edge / POLYGRAM**   1987
An outing of fascinating group structures featuring NYC saxophonist Steve Coleman in a stronger role. –MB

Triplicate / POLYGRAM   1988
The best setting for hearing Holland's bass mastery and compositional logic at work. –MB

Extensions / POLYGRAM / DB 5   r 1990
W/ Kevin Eubanks (g). This was the 1990 *DOWN BEAT* Critic's Album of the Year. Very good band/album music. Percussionist Smitty Smith is unreal. Recommended. –MGN

RICK HOLLANDER   b 1956

Post-bop, neo bop. A drummer with chops and musicality to burn. European expatriatism has helped hone his craft. –MGN

○ **Out Here / TIMELESS**
A nice mix of two standards and six originals. The drummer leads the band in high voltage and alternately moody "The Healer." Here is an up-and-coming bandleader with technique to burn. –MGN

Private Ear / VPM
1988 session in Holland from perky drummer and band with Tim Armacost (sax). Seven originals all penned by Hollander, in modern to post-bop mode. –MGN

RED HOLLOWAY   b 1927

Bop, blues-jazz, soul jazz. A veteran alto and tenor saxophonist and top sideman and session man, Holloway plays swing to bop, soul jazz with an R&B edge, and blues as well as any, better than most. Legendary collaborator with Sonny Stitt. –MGN

Cookin' Together / OJC   1964

A 1988 reissue of a textbook soul-jazz date. –RW

Red Holloway & Company / CONCORD   1987
A fine session that juggles blues, swing feeling, and soul-jazz sensibility. –RW

○ **Locksmith Blues / CONCORD**   1989
Raucous jazz and blues from trumpeter Clark Terry and saxophonist Red Holloway. –MGN

CHRISTOPHER HOLLYDAY   b 1970

Bop, post-bop, neo bop. Saxophonist. Along with his brother Richard, Hollyday has been a much-discussed figure among East Coast jazz fans for years. He emerged as a confident, impressive saxophonist while a teen, playing in Boston and New York clubs. He made some recordings for tiny labels, then debuted on RCA/Novus in 1989. He has made two other records since. Still in his 20s, his sound and style seem much older in both structure and quality. He is a first-rate bop/hard-bop stylist. –RW

○ **Christopher Hollyday / RCA-JIVE/NOVUS**   1989
This young alto saxophonist's best so far. Capable of great things. –MGN

On Course / NOVUS   1990
Some rough spots, but also many fine moments. –RW

The Natural Moment / NOVUS   1991
The progress on this album is evident. –MGN

BILL HOLMAN   b 1927

Post-bop, progressive big band. West Coast tenor saxophonist/big-band leader. A visionary of post-bop expression in 50s. Still going strong. Phenomenal soloist. –MGN

○ **The Bill Holman Band / MCA-GRP**
A very good contemporary recording of modern big-band music. It swings nicely. –MGN

RICHARD "GROOVE" HOLMES   1931-1991

Post-bop, soul jazz. One of the great jazz organists, Holmes first recorded for Pacific Jazz (1961-1963) and had successful albums featuring guests such as Les McCann, Ben Webster, Gene Ammons, and Clifford Scott (as Joe Splink). While these early efforts resulted in some fine music, the guests more than Holmes are the reason for the interest. His Prestige period (1965-1968) found him in more trio settings and better recorded. Foremost among the albums of this time is *The Soul Message*, featuring a huge hit single in "Misty." Other Prestige albums tend to have solid jazz content and represent Groove at his best. A return to Pacific Jazz in 1969 resulted in no hit albums and none that are especially well remembered musically. Work for Groove Merchant in the 70s was good — including two meetings with Jimmy McGriff in two organ battles! Muse recordings begun in 1977 and continued on an occasional basis until 1989 have fine Holmes work, frequently with Houston Person on tenor sax. Apart from these entries, beware! Like so many of his contemporaries, Groove experimented with various electronic keyboards during the 70s. These efforts all fall short of his best work. –BP

Groove / CAPITOL   1961
A 1990 reissue of an interesting meeting between Groove Holmes and Ben Webster (ts). Webster shows he's capable of adapting his robust soul into a soul-jazz context. –RW

Groovin' with Jug / CAPITOL   1961
Recorded live at The Black Orchid and at the Pacific Jazz Studio earlier that afternoon. Ammons at his peak of popularity, Holmes just about to become well-known — the only date they ever played together. Both players are on. Holmes, also a bassist and famous for his organ bass lines, can be heard to good advantage on "Morris the Minor." –JME

● **Soul Message / OJC**   1965
Torrid soul-jazz with Holmes blazing away at the organ. Contains his biggest hit "Misty." –RW

○ **That Healin' Feelin' / PRESTIGE**   ca. 1969

Rusty Bryant smokes on tenor, as does Richard "Groove" Holmes on organ. –RW

Comin' on Home / BLUE NOTE   1974
Funky and nice. –RW

Shippin' Out / MUSE   1977
There is a lot of fine music here — all of it funky, spacious, clear. This album feels good. It has some of that soul-jazz magic. –JME

Good Vibrations / MUSE   1977
An album of uptempo cookers from his middle period. W/ Houston Person (ts). –JME

Broadway / MUSE   1980
W/ Houston Person (ts). Tight band. Later, uptempo but slick. It lacks the space that his early small-combo funk albums have. –JME

Blues All Day Long / MUSE   1988
W/ Houston Person (ts), Jimmy Ponder (g). Respectable, and enjoyable later effort by Holmes. Slightly uptempo, but funky. Very nice album. –JME

Hot Tat / MUS   1989
One of the last recordings of "Groove" Holmes. W/ Houston Person (ts), Cecil Bridgewater (tpt), and Jimmy Ponder (g). The album is bit uneven, but its good to know that someone is still playing this old-style funk. There is some good guitar by Jimmy Ponder. –JME

ELMO HOPE   1923-1967

Post-bop. An excellent pianist in the bop tradition, with fast, rippling runs, exemplary harmonic knowledge, and a keen rhythmic sense, Hope was also a good composer, well grounded in the vocabulary of R&B and blues plus jazz. He started in the Joe Morris R&B band in the late 40s, then worked with Sonny Rollins and Clifford Brown before forming his own group. He relocated to Los Angeles in 1957 and spent three years there playing with Harold Land and Lionel Hampton. –RW

The Elmo Hope Trio / CONTEMPORARY / DB 5   1953
Dense, intense piano, some of Hope's best trio work. –RW

Trio & Quintet / BLUE NOTE   1953
Three early sessions: 1953, 1954, & 1957. –JME

○ **Hope Meets Foster / OJC**   1954
Pianist Hope meets saxophonist Frank Foster. The result is some of the finest group jazz of the 50s. –MGN

Meditations / OJC   1955
Expert piano from Hope, with support from John Ore (b) and Willie Jones (d). –RW

All-Star Session / MILESTONE   1956
Includes two sessions, in 1956 & 1961. A gathering of greats, supervised and sparked by Hope on piano. The list includes Coltrane (ts), Donald Byrd (tpt), and Jimmy Heath (sax). –RW

From Riker's Island / CHIAROSCURO   1963
A tense, moody, and explosive date, done at Riker's Island Prison. –RW

Final Sessions - Vols. 1-2 / OJC   1966
A 1991 reissue of the excellent two-record set that marked the last work of pianist Elmo Hope. –RW

SHIRLEY HORN   b 1934

Ballads. Vocals, piano, bandleader. Shirley Horn has been a star in Washington, DC since the 80s and is gradually becoming known around the nation. She studied at Howard University and got help early in her career from Miles Davis and Quincy Jones. She is one of the few whose vocal and piano skills are equal. She is a fine singer in the cabaret mode and prefers intimate ballads, show tunes, and standards. Horn is a first-rate pianist whose solo and accompanying skills are masterful. Her late 80s and 90s records are getting critical raves. –RW

Live at the Village Vanguard / CAM-AM INTL 1961

This one is very hard to find. Her first album, it established her skills. –RW

Loads of Love / MERCURY   i 1963
W/ Billy Taylor (p).

Travelin' Light / ABC PARAMOUNT   i 1965
An album with Frank Wess, Jerome Richardson contributing on reeds. –ED

A Lazy Afternoon / STEEPLECHASE   1978
Brisk, inviting, and well played. –RW

Garden of the Blues / STEEPLECHASE   1984
Tremendous piano, fine compositions. –RW

○ **I Thought About You / POLYGRAM**   1987
Live At Vine Street, Hollywood. –MGN

Close Enough for Love / POLYGRAM   1988
A wonderful release from a surely underrated singer/pianist. CD has two bonus cuts. –RW

● **You Won't Forget Me / POLYGRAM**   1991
The set that finally got her some attention. Miles Davis (tpt) and Wynton (tpt) and Branford Marsalis (ts) are part of the guest cast. Great piano and delightful vocals. –RW

FREDDIE HUBBARD   b 1938

Hard-bop, post-bop, contemporary funk. Only occasional lapses in taste and material mar the otherwise glorious reputation and record of Freddie Hubbard, a perennial jazz giant. Hubbard got his start playing with the Montgomery Brothers in Indianapolis and at a Chicago club with Bunky Green, Frank Strozier, and Booker Little. Hubbard moved to New York in the late 50s and roomed with Eric Dolphy for 18 months. He worked with Sonny Rollins, Slide Hampton, J. J. Johnson, and Quincy Jones from 1959-1961, when he joined Art Blakey's Jazz Messengers. This stint earned Hubbard widespread recognition, a *DOWN BEAT* New Star Award in 1961, and validation of his driving, high-note, and often acrobatic trumpet style. His work with Blakey, his freelance appearances on a host of 60s gems from Ornette Coleman's *Free Jazz* to Coltrane's *Ascension*, and his own releases showed Hubbard's other trumpet gifts. These included a wonderful full tone, extensive range in the upper register and overblowing effects, the ability to play with distinction in structured or free situations, and a dynamic, individualistic approach. Hubbard became a crossover star of sorts in the 70s: his albums *Red Clay* and *Straight Life* sold well outside the jazz world and his 1972 album *First Light* won a Grammy. Hubbard flirted for a while with fusion and jazz/rock but was largely unsuccessful from both an artistic and a financial standpoint. Hubbard reunited with Herbie Hancock, Wayne Shorter, Ron Carter, and Tony Williams in 1977. Calling themselves VSOP, the band had an acclaimed worldwide tour and an equally praised recording. Hubbard was also part of the relaunching of Blue Note Records in 1985. The bulk of his releases in the late 70s and throughout the 80s and 90s have been in the mainstream or hard-bop tradition, though they haven't been on the cutting edge the way his 60s releases were. –RW

Hub Cap / BLUE NOTE   1961
Right there. –MGN

Open Sesame / BLUE NOTE   1961
Another good one. –MGN

○ **Artistry of Freddie Hubbard / MCA**   1962
A misleading title, but a good attempt to compile Hubbard's best cuts from his 60s stint on Impulse. –RW

○ **Hub-Tones / BLUE NOTE**   1962
Ranks in the top five.–MGN

Here to Stay / BLUE NOTE / DB 5   1962
Some crackling Hubbard solos. –RW

Breaking Point / BLUE NOTE   1964
A 1991 reissue. This is prototype Blue Note, with James Spaulding (as) in full gear. –RW

Blue Spirits / BLUE NOTE   1965

One of his better mid-period albums. –MGN

The Night of the Cookers - Vols. 1 & 2 / BLUE NOTE 1965
This is an album with Hubbard in the midst of his freewheeling Blue Note phase. –RW

Backlash / ATLANTIC   1966
A 1986 reissue of a fine Atlantic date, with none of his stylistic excesses. James Spaulding (as) is fine. –RW

☆ **Red Clay / CBS**   1970
With his most well-known composition, it stands the test of time. Done with Joe Henderson (ts). –MGN

○ **Straight Life / CTI**   1970
The second of his two best early-70s releases. Joe Henderson (ts) is amazing and Hubbard is in top form, plus George Benson (g). –RW

Sing Me a Song of Songmy / ATLANTIC / DB 5   1971
Intriguing, experimental, sometimes pedantic. Protest lyrics, choir, strings, and electronics. –RW

First Light / CBS   1971
This is over-arranged (as is usual with CTI), but has wonderful Hubbard solos. –RW

Live at the Northsea Jazz Festival / PABLO   1980
Triumphant, rousing playing despite lifeless sound production on the recording. –RW

A Little Night Music / FANTASY   1981
This is the best of three sets made at Keystone Korner with Bobby Hutcherson (vib) and Joe Henderson (ts). –RW

Born to Be Blue / PABLO   1981
A spirited sextet session with Harold Land (ts). –RW

Face to Face / PA2   1982
A fine collaboration with Oscar Peterson (p). Neither allows his stylistic excesses to ruin the music. –RW

● **Sweet Return / ATLANTIC**   1983
A good lineup, especially pianist Joanne Backeen. W/ Lew Tabackin (sax). –RW

○ **Double Take / BLUE NOTE / DB 5**   1985
Dynamic date with Woody Shaw (tpt). –MGN

Life Flight / BLUE NOTE   1987
A nice date with old and new stars and good Hubbard. –RW

○ **Bolivia / MUSICMASTERS**   1991
A set with good contributions by Ralph Moore (ts), Cedar Walton (p), and Billy Higgins (d). –RW

Back to Birdland / REAL TIME
Hubbard awakens from his fusion stint. –RW

Eternal Triangle, w/ Woody Shaw / BLUE NOTE
Good album. –MGN

LANGSTON HUGHES   b 1902

Spoken word. Pre-eminent statesperson of the African-American movement, before Martin Luther King. His expression was directly related to jazz and blues. A quintessential figure. –MGN

○ **Jazz for Children and Young People / FOLKWAYS**   i 1954
The full title is *The Story of Jazz for Children and Young People and Others.* –MGN

The Weary Blues / MGM   i 1958
W/ Charlie Mingus (b) and Red Allen (tpt).

HELEN HUMES   1913-1981

Blues-jazz, ballads. Though she often swore she wasn't a blues player, there was plenty of low-down soul in Helen Humes's best vocals. She had four songs cut by Okeh when she was 14 and was working steadily in the 30s with Stuff Smith and Jonah Jones, Vernon Andrade, and Al Sears. When Count Basie selected her in 1938 to replace Billie Holiday, she spent three years with him, then became a popular part of 40s package shows. A move to the West Coast and associations with Norman Granz and John Hammond helped her shift to the R&B circuit. She became a powerhouse vocalist in that style, while keeping her jazz roots by working with Red Norvo. Humes lived in Australia during the early 60s, returned when her mother got sick in 1967, and resurfaced in triumph at the 1973 Newport Jazz Festival. She enjoyed great success for a long spell in the 70s. –RW

☆ **E-Baba-Le-Ba / SAVOY**   1944
The rhythm and blues years. 1986 reissue of 1944 & 1950 sessions. Stomping, lusty cuts with Humes at her most down-and-dirty. Though she said she didn't sing blues, this is sure close to it. –RW

Tain't Nobody's Biz-Ness If I Do / OJC   1959
A super session, with great players and Humes in fine, sassy, and swinging form. –RW

Songs I Like to Sing / OJC   1960
Helen Humes / AUDIOPHILE   1974
Classy, vigorious, and emphatic. –RW

On the Sunny Side of the Street / JZM   1974
Black Lion 1983 reissue. A booming, authoritative live date from the Montreux Festival. –RW

Helen Humes & the Muse All Stars / MUSE   1979
Solid, swinging material with Arnett Cobb (ts), Buddy Tate (ts), and "Cleanhead" Vinson (as). –RW

Helen / MUSE   1980
A first-rate jump and jazz swing. W/ Buddy Tate (ts). –RW

PERCY HUMPHREY AND HIS CRESCENT CITY JOYMAKERS   b 1905

Trad. Percy is a New Orleans trumpeter, the brother of clarinetist Willie and trombonist Earl. He is an original member of the Preservation Hall Jazz Band. He also works in the Humphrey Brothers Band, the Eureka Brass Band, and his own Crescent City Joymakers. –MGN

○ **Climax Rag / PEARL**

BOBBY HUTCHERSON   b 1941

Post-bop, Latin. As an early devotee of Milt Jackson, it's only fitting that Bobby Hutcherson has emerged as one of the few vibists besides Jackson to forge an independent direction on the instrument. Hutcherson started playing piano as a child, then switched to vibes, for which one of his early teachers was Dave Pike. He worked with Curtis Amy and Charles Lloyd, then joined the Billy Mitchell-Al Grey band and went to New York with them in 1961, where they played at Birdland. Hutcherson earned his jazz spurs appearing on the album *Out to Lunch* in 1964. He worked with several New York players in 1965, among them Archie Shepp, Hank Mobley, Charles Tolliver, and Jackie McLean, before he returned to the West Coast. In 1968 he formed a group with Harold Land, and until 1971 they were among jazz's finest small combos. –RW

● **Dialogue / BLUE NOTE**   1965
An album that was a landmark work in its time, this still has an edgy, avant-garde feeling, thanks to Sam Rivers (ts) and Andrew Hill (p). –RW

Happenings / BLUE NOTE / DB 5   1966
Reissue of a fine Blue Note recording when Hutcherson was a dominant force on his instrument. –RW

Total Eclipse / BLUE NOTE   1967
A 1985 reissue of a great album. This is an example of the empathy he shared with Harold Land (ts). –RW

Oblique / BLUE NOTE   1967
A Blue Note date reissued. Interesting dialogs with Herbie Hancock (k). –RW

Blow Up / JAZZ MUSIC YESTERDAY   1969
This wonderful concert recording of the Hutcherson/Land group never surfaced until now. –RW

Now / CADET   1969
Prime Hutcherson/Harold Land quintet material. –RW

Head On / CADET   1971

Another super work, among the last for the Hutcherson/Land unit. –RW

○ **In San Francisco / BLUE NOTE**   1971
This studio date with saxophonist Harold Land and Joe Sample (p) is one in a series of excellent records from this premier jazz quintet. –MGN

Natural Illusions / BLUE NOTE   1972
A good quintet, augmented by strings and flutes. –RW

☆ **Cirrus / BLUE NOTE**   1974
Harold Land returns, to good effect. –RW

Dance of the Sun / TIMELESS   1977
Topflight compositions and vibes solos. –RW

○ **Knucklebean / BLUE NOTE**   1977
With sidemen Freddie Hubbard (tpt), Hadley Caliman (ts). Great tunes. –MGN

Highway One / COLUMBIA   1978
Hutcherson makes a label switch, to good result. –RW

Un Poco Loco / COLUMBIA   1979
Fine Hutcherson exchanges with George Cables (p). –RW

Solo/Quartet / OJC / DB 5   1981
A 1990 reissue of some 1981 and 1982 sessions. McCoy Tyner (p) is on the mark as usual. –RW

Four Seasons / TIMELESS   1983
A good recent quartet date. –RW

Good Bait / LANDMARK   1984
An excellent date with the cream of old and new players. Branford Marsalis (ts) is in top form. –RW

Color Schemes / LANDMARK   1986
An excellent date. Hutcherson glides on vibes. –RW

In the Vanguard / LANDMARK   1986
A smooth, relaxed date. Kenny Barron (p) clicks with Hutcherson. –RW

Cruisin' the Bird / LANDMARK   1988
Both reverential and intense. –RW

Ambos Mundos / LANDMARK   1989
A fine venture into Afro-Latin and Latin jazz. Hutcherson is tops on vibes and marimba, joined here by three percussionists. –RW

Mirage / LANDMARK
This is a recent date. Nothing new, but everything sounds glorious. –RW

DICK HYMAN   b 1927

Trad, stride, swing. Dick Hyman has done valuable work on behalf of jazz in several capacities. He collaborated with critic/journalist Leonard Feather on a series of "History of Jazz" concerts and did a series of major historical concerts with the New York Jazz Repertory Company, re-creating the music of Louis Armstrong, James P. Johnson, Jelly Roll Morton, and Scott Joplin in the 70s. He's done several technically wondrous albums in the 80s of vintage and classic jazz piano, and has recorded programs for British television. Hyman was an early advocate of expanding the role of synthesizers in jazz and *The Electric Eclectics of Dick Hyman* was a 60s sensation. –RW

● **Manhattan Jazz / MUM**   1985
A wonderful, if very dated, example of vintage swing-era material. It's not traditional, simply a classic approach. –RW

Dick Hyman Plays Fats Waller / REFERENCE   1989
A classy tribute to Waller, though Hyman lacks his humorous bite and rhythmic edge. Depending on the version, this is either direct-to-disc or direct-to-CD. –RW

○ **Blues in the Night / MUM**
Excellent playing, regardless of how you feel about the rigidity of the rhythms. –RW

ABDULLAH (DOLLAR BRAND) IBRAHIM   b 1934

Progressive big band, modern creative. Although this pianist/

composer's recordings are plentiful (on Enja primarily, and also Black Lion, Japo, Sackville, Plane and others), he is not always easy to find in stores. One reason for this is that he started performing and recording as Dollar Brand (born Adolph Johannes Brand), and, to make matters worse for record store clerks, he is a South African artist who usually includes African references in his album titles. But once located, his works are uniformly satisfying and consistently jazz-based, with unconcealed affinity for the music of Duke Ellington and Thelonious Monk.

Ibrahim left South Africa in 1962, but before expatriation he left a legacy of lasting impact, in the form of recordings with Hugh Masekela, Kippy Moeketsi and other forward-looking jazzmen. And he has never neglected his roots, maintaining the trademark "marabi" township sound in an ever-changing mix of solo, small group, large-band, straight jazz and his own original compositions. His eclecticism and 60s influences often get him lumped in with the avant-garde, but his style is consistently melodious, and in recent years he has gravitated toward simpler African forms and mellow reflection, with breathy flute as his second instrument. Abdullah is the subject of a video entitled "A Brother With Perfect Timing," offering an engaging look into his personal blend of politics, spirituality and world music. −MB

African Sketchbook / ENJA   1963
Amazing solo piano. −RW

Ellington Presents Abdullah Ibrahim / REPRISE   1963
Immaculate, stunning trio work. Ellington knew music and recognized Ibrahim's potential. −RW

Anatomy of a South African Village / POLYDOR   1965
A sublime, transcendent date. −RW

The Dream / ARISTA-FREEDOM   1965
Poignant, memorable piano. −RW

African Piano / POLYGRAM   1969
Early piano solos show his fascination with Monk, along with African themes. −MB

African Portraits / SACKVILLE   1973
Tremendous solos and rhythms. −RW

Banyana - Children of Africa / CAPITOL-RHINO   1976
1990 reissue. Sharp trio playing on a varied program. −MB

Journey / CHIAROSCURO   1977
An excellent nonette with Hamiet Bluiett (baritone sax) and Don Cherry (tpt). −RW

○ **Echoes from Africa with Johnny Dyani / RHINO**   1979
Touching bass and piano duets from the South African soil. Nice vocals, too. −MB

● **African Marketplace / ELEKTRA**   1979
More 12-piece works. −RW

African Dawn / RHINO   1982
These are solo versions of his greatest originals, plus Monk tributes. −MB

○ **Zimbabwe / RHINO**   1983
Excellent quartet with Carlos Ward on sax and flute. −MGN

☆ **Ekaya / EKAPA / DB 5**   1983
This studio date with septet is a must-buy. Extraordinary ensemble music. −MGN

Water from an Ancient Well / BLACKHAWK   1986
This is among Ibrahim's most beautiful releases ever. −RW

African River / RHINO   1989
Seamless, breathtaking blend of jazz and traditional African rhythms featuring Ibrahim and his group, Ekaya. −RW

☆ **Mantra Mode / RHINO**
The newest group recording with fellow South African players. Very listenable. Recommended. −MGN

JACKIE & ROY

Ballads. Vocal team; sings harmonies in style of 50s crooners.

They stand alone in terms of their contributions to vocal jazz. −MGN

Jackie Cain and Roy Kral / BRUNSWICK   i 1955
Presents Jackie and Roy / STORYVILLE   i 1956
Sing Baby Sing / STORYVILLE   i 1956
Jackie Cain and Roy Kral / REGENT   i 1957
Star Sounds / CONCORD   1979
A Stephen Sondheim Collection / STET   1982
An excellent live date with solid vocals throughout. −RW

○ **We've Got It / DISCOVERY**   1984
The Music Of Cy Coleman. Expertly done tributes to Cy Coleman. −RW

An Alec Wilder Collection / AUDIOPHILE
These tributes are wonderfully sung. −RW

Stephen Sondheim Collection / DRG
Excellent interpretations of Sondheim's stage music by Jackie and Roy. −RW

FRANZ JACKSON   b 1912

Trad, swing. An 80-year young veteran saxophonist and clarinetist of traditional jazz. Later period recordings only scratch the surface of his rich and full life in music. −MGN

○ **Snag It / DELMARK**   ca. 1990
With Jim Beebe's Chicago Jazz Band. 14 swing-era-styled songs, with Jackson's reed work and vocals shown. Beebe plays trombone with sextet. Excellent sound of band and recording. About time we heard Jackson on a recording — he's 80! −MGN

MICHAEL GREGORY JACKSON   b 1953

Ballads, M-base, modern creative. Formerly known as Michael Gregory Jackson, Jackson was an ambitious guitarist who was recording with some of the more experimental, ambitious modern jazz players in the late 70s and early 80s. As an acoustic and electric stylist, he was interested not only in comping behind singers and doing conventional single-line solos, but in sounds, rhythms, and textures. Then he shifted gears abruptly and began doing fusion and R&B songs with quasi-relevant lyrics and lost his jazz focus. −RW

○ **Gifts / NOVUS**   1979
Quintessential group recording for creative guitarist. An important progressive music album, with Jerome Harris, Marty Ehrlich, Baikida Carroll and Pheeroan Aklaff. −MGN

MILT JACKSON   b 1923

Bop, post-bop, cool. Arguably the greatest vibes player of the modern jazz era, Milt Jackson has become the epitome of class, skill, and mastery on his instrument by varying his approach on vibes, emphasizing longer notes, and playing in a subtle, careful fashion opened up by Charlie Christian and passed down through numerous players from Kenny Burrell to Wes Montgomery. *See* Modern Jazz Quartet. −RW

In the Beginning / OJC   1947

Music Map

Jazz Harmonica

A Few Early Jazz Harmonica Players

Some Jazz, with Classical & Popular Music
Larry Adler (1914)

Major Player
Toots Thieleman (1922)

W/ Sonny Stitt (sax). This is a 1991 reissue of superb recordings. Both principals are in top form. Limited-edition recordings. –RW

● **Milt Jackson / BLUE NOTE**
W/ Thelonious Monk Quartet, this is the best early Milt away from the Modern Jazz Quartet. –MGN

Opus De Funk / PRESTIGE   1954
His first album with Horace Silver (p). –RW

Milt Jackson Quartet / OJC   1955
Solid date, available in limited-edition form. –RW

Bags & Flute / SAVOY   1957
With Bobby Jaspar (ts) and Frank Wess (sax). This album is top notch. –MGN

☆ **Soul Brothers / ATLANTIC**   1958
Both this and Milt Jackson/Ray Charles releases are essential. The perfect marriage of blues, jazz, soul, and elegance. –RW

☆ **Bags & Trane / ATLANTIC**   1959
Exceptional meeting of minds between Jackson and John Coltrane (ts). –RW

That's the Way It Is / MCA   1960
Mellow, sometimes bluesy date. Reissued. –RW

Bags Meets Wes / PRESTIGE   1961
His Riverside debut album was a stunner. Wonderful Wes Montgomery Guitar. –RW

Big Bags / OJC   1962
Good reissue of a fine big-band session. –RW

Live at the Village Gate / OJC   1963
This is a 1988 reissue of smoking concert with Jimmy Heath (sax). –RW

Olinga / CBS / DB 5   r 1974
One of few Jackson CTI dates where his playing had fire. –RW

At the Kosei Nenkin / PABLO   1976
Live in Japan with Teddy Edwards (ts) and Cedar Walton (p). Great concert. –MGN

Live-Montreux 1977 / OJC   1977
W/ Ray Brown (b). Live collaboration between two veterans who were truly in sync. –RW

Ellington Album / OJC   1980
Outstanding tribute by classy band of pros. –RW

It Don't Mean A Thing ... / OJC   1984
It Don't Mean A Thing If You Can't Tap Your Foot To It. The group sounds so cohesive, it's hard to believe they're not a regular working band. –RW

Brother Jim / PABLO   1985
An underrated set with Jackson and a great lineup going easy through mainstream material. –RW

Bebop / ATLANTIC   1988
An excellent example of his recent work. –MGN

○ **The Harem / MUSICMASTERS**
Fine newer release. His best of the last decade. –MGN

Mostly Duke / PABLO
Superb tribute to Ellington, wonderful solos. –RW

RONALD SHANNON JACKSON   b 1940

Early free, jazz-rock. Ronald Jackson is in the top echelon of contemporary drummers. He was in bands as a teen in Dallas, playing with legendary figures James Clay and Leroy Cooper. Later he got a music scholarship in New York, cut freestyle records with Charles Tyler, and played with Albert Ayler, Betty Carter, and others. By the mid 70s, Jackson was at the center of a pulsating, cutting-edge, "harmolodic" band, playing drums in Ornette Coleman's group. He also played with Cecil Taylor and later "Blood" Ulmer, then formed Last Exit with Sonny Sharrock and Bill Laswell. He is a master at holding together seemingly chaotic sessions with his crisp, attacking drumming, varying the beat and the pulse. –RW

● **Mandance / POLYGRAM**   1982

W/ The Decoding Society. This drummer's best music and group. Raucous. Jazz/Rock taken to the limit. –MGN

○ **Barbeque Dog / ANTILLES**   1983
Erratic, powerful, and explosive. –RW

Pulse / CELLULOID   1984

○ **Red Warrior / POLYGRAM**   1990
Sprawling drums and guitar highlight this recent session. Produced by Bill Laswell. –RW

Taboo / CAROLINE   ca. 1990
Some dynamic adventures with Vernon Reid (g) venturing outside Living Colour arena. –RW

WILLIS JACKSON   1932-1987

Post-bop, soul jazz. Saxophonist Willis Jackson is a soul-jazz giant. He invented the "gator" horn, a long sax with a ball-shaped bell and a small opening that had a sound between alto and soprano. An established professional at 14, Jackson got his nickname when he cut his original "Gator Tail" while playing with Cootie Williams. From the 50s to the 80s, he was superb at a funky, blues-based, and soulful style with lots of honks, moans, and vocal effects — never outside or fancy, but very popular and appealing. Jackson also had a busy schedule of R&B dates in the 80s and was married for a time to Ruth Brown. Soul-jazz was his menu from the 60s on. –RW

On My Own / MUSE   1950
1950-1955. Frenetic soul-jazz; w/ torrid organ from Charles Earland. –RW

Please Mr.Jackson / OJC   1959
1988 reissue of fine soul-jazz date. –RW

Cool Gator / OJC   1959
Red-hot jazz sax. –RW

● **Thunderbird / PRESTIGE**   1962
Great Jackson, robust Freddy Roach organ. –RW

○ **Shuckin' / PRESTIGE**   1962
His second great album that year. All-star lineup included Kenny Burrell (g), Tommy Flanagan (p). –RW

Gator Tails / VERVE   1964
Hot soul-jazz tenor with orchestral backing. –RW

Smokin' with Willis / CADET   1965
Scorching sextet session. –RW

West Africa / MUSE   1973
Exuberant title cut. –RW

Headed & Gutted / MUSE   1974
Brilliant soul-jazz date. –RW

Ya Understand Me? / MUSE   1980
With "Groove" Holmes on organ duties, and some tart tenor from Jackson. –RW

ILLINOIS JACQUET   b 1922

Swing, big band, bop, blues-jazz. Jean Baptiste Illinois Jacquet, one of the great tenor saxophonists of all time, was raised in Houston and began his professional career while in high school, with the Milt Larkin band. He moved to Los Angeles in 1939, and came to prominence in the Lionel Hampton band. With Hampton, he recorded the "Flying Home" solo (1942), among the most famous tenor sax solos ever. He did more big-band work with Cab Calloway (1943-1944) and Count Basie (1944-1946) and was active in the California jam session scene that resulted in the first *Jazz at the Philharmonic* concert (July 1944), which was recorded. Though the records took almost two years to be issued, they created a sensation via Jacquet's screaming tenor work. The records were the first live jazz on record. Of his JATP solos, "Blues Part 2" was the most famous. He made national tours with JATP (1946-1948, 1951 and 1955-1957) and was a frequent participant on JATP recordings (PERDIDO). His own small band was formed in the mid 40s, and he recorded for Apollo, Alladin, and RCA (1945-1950). Of these, the Apollos have a slight edge on the Alladins, with the RCAs some distance behind, but all contain his driving, sensual tenor work in combos of varying size, utilizing a swing/bob/jump combination typical of the 40s. He began recording for Mercury/Clef (later Verve) in 1951. "Port of Rico" is a big hit featuring tenor/organ sound. Albums begin in 1955, and there are many good ones on Verve, Roulette, Epic, and Prestige (*Bottoms Up*, *The Blues*, *That's Me* are especially good). European and Japanese recordings from the 70s and 80s are variable, but his best in many, many years is *Jacquet's Got It* (Atlantic), devoted to his big band (formed in 1983) and showing him still in top form. –BP

Black Velvet Band / RCA   1947
Prime 8- & 10-piece group cuts from 1947-50, plus one cut from 1967 Newport festival. –RW

The Kid and the Brute / VERVE   r 1956
Delightful. W/ Jacquet and tenor comrade Ben Webster. –RW

Swing's the Thing / VERVE   1957
A nice session with prime Roy Eldridge (tpt). –RW

Flies Again / CAPITOL   1959
1991 reissue. Incendiary set. Explosive Jacquet. –RW

Banned in Boston / CBS   1962
Very nice reissue that didn't get much attention. –RW

Illinois Jacquet / ARGO   1963
Stirring cuts, plus rare bassoon songs. –RW

Bottoms Up / OJC   1968
This is a 1991 reissue of a sterling blues, soul-jazz, and swing date. –RW

How High the Moon / PRESTIGE   1968
A worthy compilation of the best Prestige 60s cuts. –RW

Soul Explosion / OJC   1969
An excellent recent reissue of big-band dates. –RW

Blues-That's Me! / OJC   1969
1991 reissue. A welcome return of this fine blues date, with torrid, lusty Jacquet solos. –RW

Genius at Work / JZM   1971
Expert playing; smooth and cool — sometimes hot. –RW

Illinois Jacquet w/ Wild Bill Davis / CLASSIC JAZZ 1973
Powerhouse, rough-edged, and blistering on all counts. –RW

○ **Blues from Louisiana / CLASSIC JAZZ**   1973
A fine concert with Jacquet and Panama Francis (d). –RW

Jacquet's Street / CLASSIC JAZZ   1976
A bit smoother, and still plenty of sparks. –RW

Jacquet's Got It! / ATLANTIC   1988
A fine, underrated big-band date that the label let die on the vine. –RW

Flying Home / RCA
Jacquet's most famous solo. –RW

● **The Cool Rage / VERVE**   COMP
A comprehensive anthology of Jacquet's hottest, stomping Verve dates 1951-58. –RW

AHMAD JAMAL   b 1930

Post-bop, cool, instr-pop. Pianist Jamal was amazingly influential, though far from being a Tatum or Powell. His left-hand voicings and teasing right-hand contrasts, plus a liberal inclusion of block chords, got an enormous boost through the embrace and utilization of other Jamal techniques by Miles Davis. Jamal formed his first band in 1949 after leaving the George Hudson group and scored a hit with a new arrangement of "Billy Boy." He adopted his textbook trio formula in the 50s when he replaced the guitar with drums and upgraded bassist Israel Crosby's role. He pre-dated other popular trios like Ramsey Lewis, though a superior stylist. –RW

● **Poinciana / MCA**   1952
Includes his big hit, the studio-recorded title track. –MGN

○ **At the Pershing/But Not for Me / MCA**   1958
A 2-fer. Third album (includes hit "Poinciana") was the

turning point in his career. His liberal use of silence influenced many jazz musicians, including Miles Davis. –JME

★ **But Not for Me / ARGO**   1958
Arguably his greatest album, a smash hit. –RW

Ahmad Jamal - Vol. 4 / ARGO   1958
One of his most popular albums ever in its original issue. Fine, if a bit to the pop side. –RW

Jamal at the Penthouse / ARGO   1959
W/ string section; another huge hit. –RW

Live at the Alhambra / VOGUE   1961
Fine reissue of premier recording. –RW

Cry Young / CADET   ca. 1967
Fine, enjoyable date from his peak period of popularity. –RW

Tranquility / IMPULSE   1969
His stunning debut on new label. –RW

The Awakening / MCA   1970
This is a 1986 reissue of some of his most beloved trio performances. –RW

Free Flight / IMPULSE   1971
Jamal turns electric on some cuts. –RW

Outertimeinnerspace / IMPULSE   1972
His last for Impulse, a wonderful finale. –RW

Genetic Walk / 20TH CENTURY   1978
Last of his albums to enjoy crossover chart activity. Used horn section on some cuts. –RW

Live in Concert / BLACK LABEL   1981
Nice live set from Cannes. –RW

Digital Works / ATLANTIC   1985
Later Jamal, experimenting with digital sound electronics. He remains a gripping player. –RW

Live at Montreal Jazz Festival / ATLANTIC   1985
Shimmering, attacking style at times. Still the master of space and pauses. –RW

Rossiter Road / ATLANTIC   1986
W/ sharp Jamal playing, but not-so-sharp support. –RW

Crystal / ATLANTIC   1987
Jamal is still an inventive, entrancing pianist. –RW

Pittsburgh / ATLANTIC   1989
One of his best works with a large symphony orchestra. –RW

○ **What's New / TELSTAR**   COMP
Giants of Jazz series. 17 hits from a variety of his original Chess recordings. Includes "Poinciana." –JME

BOB JAMES   b 1939

Instr-pop. Pianist, composer. This extremely intelligent, well-educated player took a turn toward fusion in the early 70s and never returned to straight jazz. In the 60s, James worked for Maynard Ferguson, then spent five years with Sarah Vaughan. He amassed a lot of studio credits as a composer/arranger until 1973, when he hit the jackpot with CTI/Kudu. Since then he has specialized in making instrumental pop albums with catchy melodies, heavy beats, and little jazz content. –RW

Bold Conceptions / MERCURY   i 1963
Explosions / ESP   i 1965
One / CBS / BB 85   r 1974
Two / TAPPAN ZEE-COLUMBIA / BB 75   r 1975
○ **Grand Piano Canyon / WARNER**
James displays his forgotten jazz roots. –RW

H / CBS / BB 47
Prototype fusion. –RW

HARRY JAMES   1916-1983

Swing, big band. In 1942, Harry James had the most popular band in the US, broke Benny Goodman's attendance record at New York's Paramount Theater, and made more money than any living musician. He was married to Betty Grable, the #1 pin-up of the Armed Forces, and appeared in feature films himself. It was this great fame, little remembered today, that enabled James to carry on as leader of a big band long after most others had quit — indeed, only Count Basie, Duke Ellington, Woody Herman, and Stan Kenton joined him in that select circle. James came to stardom with Benny Goodman's band, which he joined at 20. The son of a circus band leader and a sometime contortionist, he was raised under the big top; his first instrument was drums. At ten, he took up trumpet and soon was winning contests; at 17, he hit the road. His idol was Louis Armstrong, but it was with a piece of "schmaltz," *You Made Me Love You,* that his struggling big band finally hit the jackpot. From then on, he had to provide liberal doses of sweet stuff, but remained loyal to his jazz muse. (He also was Mr. Nice, letting the unknown singer he'd been first to hire, Frank Sinatra, go on to bigger bucks with rival Tommy Dorsey).

Harry had integrated bands; altoist Willie Smith of Lunceford fame was with him for decades. He liked good drummers: Buddy Rich and Louis Bellson both spent time with him. And he loved the Count Basie sound, hiring Ernie Wilkins and Thad Jones and Neal Hefti to write for him. When he wanted to, Harry could play jazz trumpet with the best of them, and more often than not, he did. –DM

○ **Harry James and Dick Haymes / CIRCLE**   194?
Pivotal, exceptional material. –RW
Hits of Harry James / CAPITOL   195?
Some of his most popular cuts. –RW
Man with Horn / COLUMBIA   195?
Nice solos and sessions. –RW
More Harry James in Hi-Fi / PASVA   195?
Nice reissue of prime James from 50s. –RW
Golden Trumpet of Harry James / POLYGRAM
Some fine cuts from sessions on London. –RW
Best of Big Bands / CBS   COMP
1990 reissue spotlights his big-band cuts. –RW
Big Band Recordings / HINDSIGHT   COMP
1987 release of familiar material. –RW

DAVID JANEWAY   b 1955

Post-bop, Latin, neo bop. Janeway plays electric and acoustic piano in Latin and modern jazz idioms. A fine composer and arranger. –MGN

○ **Entry Point / NEW DIRECTIONS**
The pianist cooks on acoustic and Fender Rhodes. Side A with NY friends Bob Berg (ts), Steve Berrios (d). Side B features Detroiters Marcus Belgrave (tpt), Vincent York & Phil Lasley (saxes), and George Davidson (d). Every cut worthwhile. –MGN

JOSEPH JARMAN   b 1937

Early free. Jarman was a founding member of the Art Ensemble of Chicago and an early participant with Muhal Richard Abrams and Roscoe Mitchell in an experimental band that led to the formation of the Association for the Advancement of Creative Musicians (AACM). He studied drums in high school, then learned sax and clarinet while in the army, before taking additional courses at Chicago Conservatory. He and Mitchell were members of Abrams's experimental band, later teaming up with trumpeter Lester Bowie, bassist Malachi Favors, and drummer Don Moye to form the Art Ensemble of Chicago, a band that performed everything from meticulously structured pieces to freewheeling statements, incorporating aspects of theater and makeup into their performances. Jarman also headed his own bands in the late 60s, including poetry and programmed selections during his performances, as well as premiering theatrical pieces. –RW

○ **Song For / DELMARK**   1966
As If It Were the Seasons / DELMARK / DB 5   1968
Together Alone / DELMARK   1971
W/ Anthony Braxton (sax).

KEITH JARRETT   b 1945

Cool, early free, modern creative. This popular pianist plays a highly individual style. A progressive idealist, he plays jazz and jazz extensions. Group works show immense power as well. Jarrett tends to hum/moan distractingly during melodic passages. A most unique improviser and personality, enigmatic and fascinating. –MGN

Somewhere Before / ATLANTIC   1968
A 1968 live trio recording at Shelly's Manne Hole in Hollywood, w/ Charlie Haden (b), Paul Motian (d). Rare and excellent. –MGN
With Gary Burton / ATLANTIC   1968
An overlooked, yet very stimulating date. –RW
Birth / ATLANTIC   1971
Very early example of his quirky style, technique. Jarrett is an excellent pianist, but a horrible recorder/soprano saxist. W/ first-rate personnel: Charlie Haden (b), Paul Motian (d), and Dewey Redman (ts). –RW
Facing You / POLYGRAM / DB 5   1971
This is a very good solo piano album. A prelude to the Köln concert. –MGN
Ruta and Dayta / ECM   1972
Piercing duets with Jack DeJohnette (d). –RW
○ **Expectations / CBS**   1972
Two-record set with lots of experimental, high energy moments. 1991 reissue. –RW
In the Light / POLYGRAM / DB 5   1973
1988 release; for hardcore Jarrett fans. –RW
○ **Fort Yawuh / MCA**   1973
Sprawling, edgy set from 1973. Again, Jarrett and his group keep things interesting. –RW
Treasure Island / MCA   1974
One of many fine sessions from his prolific quartet of the mid 70s. –RW
○ **Backhand / IMPULSE**   1974
Landmark quintet with Dewey Redman (ts), Charlie Haden (b), Paul Motian (d), Guilherme Franco (per). Any recording by this band is worthwhile. –MGN
○ **Belonging / POLYGRAM**   1974
This quartet album is a fine first collaboration between Jarrett and Jan Garbarek (ts). –MGN
★ **Köln Concert / POLYGRAM / DB 5**   1975
Quintessential live solo piano. A must-buy on CD. –MGN
Mysteries / MCA   1975
W/ prime Jarrett group. –RW
Shades / IMPULSE / BB 4   1975
Another great gem by the mid-70s quintet. –MGN
Survivor's Suite / POLYGRAM / DB 5   1976
1987 reissue of first-rate quartet date. –RW
Eyes of the Heart / ECM   1976
Excellent music from a great quartet. Dewey Redman (ts) challenges Jarrett for solo honors. –RW
Staircase / POLYGRAM   1976
1987 reissue of fine solo date. –RW
Sun Bear Concerts / POLYGRAM / DB 5   1976
Monstrous 10-disc set. If you're a glutton for punishment, go ahead! –RW
My Song / POLYGRAM   1977
Good quartet performances, though the European lineup doesn't match the caliber of the Redman/Haden/Motian ensemble. –RW
● **Nude Ants / POLYGRAM / DB 5**   1979
A live 2-fer quartet recording at the Village Vanguard with Jan Garbarek (ts). –MGN
Concerts / POLYGRAM   1981

1988 reissue of solo concerts. Moments of glory, moments of boredom. –RW

Changes / POLYGRAM   1983
This is a recording of erratic, but often compelling trio material. Gary Peacock (b), Jack DeJohnette (d) cover up some sins. –RW

Standards - Vols. 1 & 2 / ECM   1983
A pair of studio sets with trio cutting jazz anthems. –RW

Spirits 1 & 2 / POLYGRAM   1985
More a technical showcase than a musically worthy enterprise. Jarrett plays 18 instruments, using multi-tracking to strut his stuff. –RW

Standards Live / POLYGRAM   1985
1987 release of 1985 live concert with trio executing established standards nicely. –RW

Still Live / POLYGRAM   1986
Another trio date, little different from many others. CD has bonus cut. –RW

Paris Concert / POLYGRAM   r 1990
Arguably his best work outside strict jazz quartet. –RW

BOBBY JASPAR   1926-1963

Post-bop. Tenor sax, flute. Jaspar is a topflight European musician, especially on flute. He made his reputation playing at US Army bases and in Europe during the early 50s. Moved to New York in the mid 50s with his wife, Blossom Dearie, and had a long string of fine dates with J. J. Johnson, Miles Davis, Donald Byrd, Bill Evans, and Chris Connor before a final tour in the 60s with Rene Thomas. A good but derivative tenor player, Jaspar's long lines and fluid melodies and solos on flute were often magnificent. –RW

○ **Bobby Jaspar in Paris / DISQUES SWING**   1956
Wonderful 1986 reissue of prime Jaspar small-combo dates from mid 50's. Tommy Flanagan (p), Elvin Jones (d), Milt Hinton (b) among the crew. –RW

With George Wallington, Idrees Sulieman / OJC   ca. 1957
Sturdy, nicely played date with Jaspar in top form. –RW

Memory of Dick / POLYGRAM
Nice session from underrecorded Belgian musician. –RW

Phenil Isopropil Amine / POLYGRAM
Ungainly title, excellent date fueled by Kenny Clarke (d). –RW

With Friends / FRESH SOUND
Sterling mainstream date. –RW

JATP

Swing, bop. Jazz At The Philharmonic. Norman Granz's idea to bring players in the swing and bebop eras together to present all-star concerts of incredible magnitude. A treat for audiences of the 40s to 50s. Some of the participants include Charlie Parker, Coleman Hawkins, Oscar Peterson, Lester Young, Dizzy Gillespie, Ron Webster, Herb Ellis, Nat Cole, J. C. Heard, and countless others. –MGN

JATP: Ella Fitzgerald / POLYGRAM
Ella Fitgerald Set. Mellow, wonderful Ella vocals. –RW

○ **JATP: Historic Recordings / VERVE**   1944
1944 & 1946. W/ Nat Cole (p) Trio, Les Paul (g), Illinois Jacquet (sax); plus lots of Billy Holiday. Recorded in Los Angeles. –MGN

☆ **JATP: Bird & Pres / POLYGRAM**   1946
Jazz At The Philharmonic (JATP). Bird/Pres 1946 concert. Great session with Charlie Parker (as), Dizzy Gillespie (tpt), and Lester Young (ts). Ultimate melding of swing era and bop musicians. –MGN

JATP: Bird & Pres / POLYGRAM   1949
Bird/Pres 1949.

○ **Hartford — 1953 / PABLO LIVE**   1953
Includes a fifteen-minute jam on "Cottontail," an Oscar Peterson Quartet set with Lester Young (ts). J. C. Heard and Gene Krupa are on drums with Ben Webster (ts), Flip

Phillips (ts), Benny Carter (as/tpt), and Roy Eldridge (tpt) as jammers. –MGN

JATP: Tokyo — Live / PA2   1953
In Tokyo-Live 1953. A good two-record set. –RW

JATP: London / PA2   1969
London 1969. This is a nice two-record set. More intensity than usual. –RW

JATP: Tokyo — Return To Happiness / PA2   1983
A good three-record set with nice Ella Fitsgerald (v), Oscar Peterson (p), and Zoot Sims (ts). –RW

○ **Stockholm 1955 / PABLO**

JAZZ COMPOSER'S ORCHESTRA

Early free, progressive big band. This cooperative venture was begun in 1964 by Carla Bley and Michael Mantler as an attempt to give free players a chance to record and work in an orchestral setting. It blossomed into a record label as well and stands as one of the few musician-driven cooperative ventures to enjoy some degree of success. –RW

○ **Communications / ECM**
Outstanding large group recording with both swing and avant-garde influences. Sprawling and experimental. –RW

JAZZ MODES

Bop, hard-bop, post-bop. Underrated swinging bop group earmarked by the distinctive sound of Julius Watkins on french horn. Also included Monk sax player Charlie Rouse, pianist Gildo Mahones, bassist Ron Jefferson, and sometimes percussionist Chino Pozo. Recorded five albums between 1956 and 1958. –DS

○ **Jazzville 1956 / DAWN**   1956
Swinging, soaring jazz led by Charlie Rouse (ts) and french hornist Julius Watkins. –DS

Les Jazz Modes / DAWN   i 1956
W/ Paul Chambers (b). –ED

Smart Jazz for the Smart Set / SEECO   i 1960

JAZZTET

Hard-bop, post-bop. This group, formed in 1959, was co-led by Benny Golson and Art Farmer, with McCoy Tyner on piano. It survived until 1962 in its first incarnation, then resurfaced in 1985 with Farmer and Golson once again at the helm. The group was — and remains — famous for nicely structured, precise, yet soulful pieces and a swinging style. Both Golson and Farmer know how to play without excess, yet retain energy and impact. –RW

★ **Meet The Jazztet / CHESS**   1960
The first band known as the Jazztet led by trumpeter Art Farmer and tenor saxophonist Benny Golson. Includes the original versions of "Killer Joe," "Blues March," and "I Remember Clifford," all written by Golson. The band also includes Curtis Fuller (tb), McCoy Tyner (p). –MGN

○ **Real Time / CONTEMPORARY**
Return of one of the early 60s finest combos w/ originals Benny Golson (ts), Art Farmer (tpt), and Curtis Fuller (tb). Well done, enjoyable. –RW

EDDIE JEFFERSON   1918-1979

Bop, ballads. A real vocal improviser, who created lyrics to fit songs like Jon Hendricks rather than specializing in scatting. Jefferson and King Pleasure virtually appeared at the same time in 1952, a few months apart. Jefferson was a big member of James Moody's group in the late 50s. Supplanted in popularity by Lambert, Henricks, and Ross in the late 50s, Jefferson spent a decade in obscurity before returning in 1967 as a dancer and rejoining Moody in 1968. This reignited his career, and he co-led the group Artistic Truth in 1974 and 1975, then worked his last few years with Richie Cole. –RW

☆ **Letter from Home / OJC**   1961
1961 & 1962. Definitive vocalese from the man! –MGN

○ **Body & Soul / OJC** 1968
1989 reissue of highly delightful session, with James Moody (sax), Barry Harris (p). –RW

Come Along with Me / OJC 1969
1991 reissue of another solid Jefferson date. –RW

Things Are Getting Better / MUSE r 1975
Overly optimistic title reflects Jefferson's boundless enthusiasm, energy, wit. –RW

Godfather of Vocalese / MUSE 1976
1990 reissue of sturdy set. CD version has bonus cut. –RW

Still on the Planet / MUSE 1976
Super vocals, hot Richie Cole on alto. –RW

Main Man / INNER CITY 1977
Swan song for a remarkable figure. –RW

Jazz Singer / INNER CITY COMP
Good compilation of lesser-known cuts from 1959-1961. –RW

● **There I Go Again / PRESTIGE** COMP
1953-1969. More greatness from E.J. –MGN

GORDON JENKINS 1910-1984

Swing, cool. Gordon Jenkins enjoyed sizable fame as an arranger, conductor, composer, and bandleader from the 30s through the 60s. He began as a multi-instrumentalist freelancing on radio, then became a prolific arranger, contributing to sessions by Isham Jones, Benny Goodman, Lennie Hayton, and others. He conducted *The Show Is On* in 1935 on Broadway. After a stint with Paramount, he worked for NBC in Hollywood from 1938-1944 and was Dick Haymes's arranger for four years after that. He became the managing director for Decca and had several hits for the label in the late 40s and 50s. He's noted for spotting the Weavers folk group in the Village Vanguard in the early 50s, getting them a recording session and later backing them. He supported other stars such as Louis Armstrong, the Andrews Sisters, and Haymes in the 50s. Later he was Judy Garland's conductor for an English concert, and then Nat King Cole's arranger and conductor for a time. Jenkins won a Grammy in 1967 for the Frank Sinatra album *September of My Years*. –RW

The Manhattan Tower / CAPITOL / BB 13 1956
Sophisticated / PAIR
Nice, though derivative music. –RW

JOHN JENKINS b 1931

Hard-bop, post-bop. A good saxophonist who enjoyed some recognition in the 50s and 60s by working with such players as Jackie Mclean and Bobby Timmons. Some of his Prestige sessions have been reissued on disc. –RW

○ **Jenkins, Jordan & Timmons / OJC** 1957
1987 reissue of prototype jam session/blowing date with Clifford Jordan (ts), John Jenkins, Bobby Timmons (p). –RW

LEROY JENKINS b 1932

Early free. A former school teacher, Leroy Jenkins in one sense took the violin and viola away from their usual classical settings and made them a sawing, percussive, aggressive component of the avant-garde. Another graduate of DuSable High School in Chicago, Jenkins gave up the alto sax for the violin in the early 60s and worked in both Alabama and Chicago. He became involved with the AACM in the 60s and went to Europe in 1969 with Anthony Braxton and Leo Smith. He was back in the USA in 1970 and moved to New York with Braxton later that year. During the 70s, Jenkins worked with many free-jazz luminaries. In 1971, he formed the invigorating Revolutionary Ensemble with Sirone on bass and trombone and Jerome Cooper on drums and piano. They stayed together six years, a marvelous band that had every conceivable style. They mixed classical and improvisational, structured and free, serene and chaotic. Jenkins later toured with Andrew Cyrille and Anthony Davis. –RW

○ **Solo Concert / INDIA NAVIGATION** 1977

About as adventurous and experimental as violin playing gets. Despite far-out tendencies, Jenkins knows when to come back in and how. –RW

Space Minds, New Worlds... / TOMATO / DB 5 1978
Space Minds, New Worlds, Survival of America. Music that is dynamic, and invigorating, far from hard bop, swing, or traditional styles. –RW

BILL JENNINGS b 1919

Swing, blues-jazz, R&B. Jenning's sound has been compared to Tiny Grimes with a hint of early Charlie Christian. A peer of Billy Butler, Jennings played with Louis Jordan in the late 40s and early 50s. He also recorded R&B sides with Leo Parker and Bill Doggett. –MGN

○ **Stompin' with Bill / COLLECTABLES** 195?
Five titles circa mid-50s by guitarist Jennings originally from Gotham label. Disc also has five Ray Bryant Trio, two Tiny Grimes (g), one Billy Davis, and one Gay Crosse from the same period and the same source. Quality varies but all the music is rare, and there are interesting moments in much of it. –BP

BUDD JOHNSON 1910-1984

Swing, big band, bop. This tenor sax player is a jazz mainstay who played both swing and bop. His roots date back to a Texas group led by Terrence Holder, then Louis Armstrong's 30s band in Chicago, followed by nine years with Earl Hines. Johnson was a busy arranger and participant in various swing bands through the 40s, then became part of the rock revolution in the 50s, arranging and producing several records as well as publishing songs and helping Alan Freed by putting together huge bands for his shows. Toward the end of the 50s, Johnson's playing picked up again, and he worked with Benny Goodman, Gil Evans, Quincy Jones, and Count Basie. He reunited with Earl Hines often in the 60s and later formed his own group with Hines's personnel. In the 70s, he did repertory work, plus guest work and many tours. Throughout his career, Johnson was among the warmest, most humorous, and most enticing ballad and blues players around, as well as a great interpreter. –RW

Blues A La Mode / RIVERSIDE 1958
Rare Johnson septet date. –RW

○ **Let's Swing / OJC** 1960
Stout, robust vehicle with standard Johnson solos. –RW

And the Four Brass Giants / RIVERSIDE 1960
1985 reissue. –RW

And the Four Brass Giants / RIVERSIDE i 1960
W/ trumpeters Nat Adderley, Harry Edison, Clark Terry, and Ray Nance. –ED

Ya Ya / ARGO r 1964
Colorado Jazz Party / MPS ca. 197?
Robust, often hot session. –RW

BUNK JOHNSON 1889-1949

Trad. One of the seminal trumpeters in the classic New Orleans traditional style, Bunk Johnson as a youngster played with such heralded players as Adam Olivier, Bob Russell, and Buddy Bolden. He became known as a superb second trumpet player, someone especially keen at playing behind the beat, while also being a marvelous blues stylist and interpreter. Johnson left New Orleans in 1915, then toured the South working in every type of traveling show and theatrical troupe. Johnson had a flurry of activity from 1942-1945, making nearly 100 sides while recording sessions produced mainly by David Stuart. These records helped spur a trad-jazz resurgence and garnered Johnson a little national acclaim, though it didn't exactly make him a star. Harold Drob, a former GI, helped Johnson assemble another band near the end of his life, one that recorded in 1947 and gave him some final attention as a genuine early jazz marvel. –RW

○ **Bunk & Lu / GOOD TIME JAZZ** 1941

1941 & 1944; w/ Lu Watters (tpt). Tremendous traditional jazz and blues. −RW

CANDY JOHNSON

Swing, big band, bop, blues-jazz. Saxophonist who went through swing, bop and R&B in the 50s. With a soulful, refined voice, Johnson also was an excellent teacher. −MGN

○ **Live - BGSU /**   1974
Rare recording, for legendary saxophonist. With Ted and Milt Buckner, Dave Wilborn. All Swing Era and American Popular Song standards. −MGN

DICK JOHNSON   ♭1925

Swing, big band. Clarinetist who has led Artie Shaw Orhestra. Excellent swing player, perhaps unsung. −MGN

○ **Plays Alto Sax / CONCORD**   1979
Conservative but enjoyable swing-influenced set. −RW

Swing Shift / CONCORD   1981
Ranges from sentimental to jovial to upbeat, though little you haven't heard before. −RW

EDDIE JOHNSON   ♭1921

Post-bop, cool. This Chicago tenor saxophonist plays smooth ballads and blues in swing to bop styles. −MGN

○ **Indian Summer / NESSA**   1981
From the Chicago tenor saxophonist, with Paul Serrano on trumpet and the John Young Trio. −MGN

ELLA JOHNSON   ♭1923

Ballads, R&B. Ella Johnson made her mark as the vocalist with Buddy Johnson's big band during the 40s and 50s, and it is in that context she really shines. Her later solo sides for Mercury are pale imitations of her work with the band. Although many of Ella's hits are uptempo (e.g. "I Don't Want Nobody"), it is on ballads and torchy blues that she really brings it together. In fact, her earliest work for Decca during the mid 40s (much of which is not yet reissued) is uncannily good. At her best, Ella sounds like a pouty, vulnerable, and very sexy young girl. Like so much of her life, it was no affectation. The comparison to Billie Holiday is inevitable, but Ella is her own singer. −HD

○ **Swing Me / POLYGRAM**   195?
Hot 50s sessions, although they're more R&B than jazz. −RW

FRED JOHNSON   1904-1961

Blues-jazz, ballads, Latin. Sings soulful jazz, bop, pop, and Brazilian music. Reminiscent of a more reserved Jon Hendricks, but still his own man. −MGN

○ **Live at B. B. Joe's / OFFSHORE**   1984
Sweet vocal stylings from a unique interpreter. Three standards, two blues, a Nascimento tune with pop inflections. Excellent back-up led by Kamau Kenyatta. −MGN

J. J. JOHNSON   ♭1924

Swing, bop, hard-bop, post-bop, cool. Indianapolis trombonist whose technical facility is unmatched. The premier bebop player on his tricky instrument. A great role model to study. Recent years have kept him in the studio as opposed to live performing, but that does mean more of his recordings are available. −MGN

Mad Bebop / SAVOY   1946
Seminal material from 1946-1954. Pivotal dates pairing Johnson with movers and shakers like Sonny Rollins (ts), Charles Mingus (b), Bud Powell (p). −RW

☆ **Eminent Jay Jay Johnson / BLUE NOTE**   1953
Vols. 1 & 2. Standout hard bop with Clifford Brown (tpt). −RW

Four Trombones / PRESTIGE   1953
W/ Kai Winding (tb), Bennie Green (tb). Outstanding 1990 reissue of superb 1953 four-trombone summit. −RW

Jay & Kai at Newport / COLUMBIA   1956
W/ Kai Winding. Dynamite two-trombone live set. −RW

At the Cafe Bohemia / FRESH SOUND   1957
Glittering date with Bobby Jaspar (ts). −RW

J.J. Inc. / COLUMBIA   1960
Fine effort with several Johnson tunes, plus great work by Clifford Jordan (ts), Freddie Hubbard (tpt). −RW

○ **Great Kai & J.J. / MCA**   1960
Definitive work for two trombonists, plus Bill Evans (p), Paul Chambers (b), Art Taylor (d). −RW

Perceptions / VERVE   1961
Ambitious six-part composition with 21-piece band. −RW

Proof Positive / IMPULSE   1964
Dashing, impressive solos. −RW

Say When / RCA   1964
1964-1966. This is a 1987 reissue of excellent big-band recordings. −RW

Yokohama Concert / PABLO   1977
Tremendous date with Nat Adderley (tpt). −RW

Pinnacles / MILESTONE   1979
Johnson makes solid statement. −RW

Concepts in Blue / PABLO   1980
Wonderful session with Clark Terry (tpt). −RW

Things Are Getting Better All the Time / PABLO   1983
Good date in J.J./Kai Winding vein with Al Grey on second trombone. −RW

○ **Quintergy — Live / POLYGRAM**   1988
Live At Village Vanguard. This live album is excellent — top-notch J. J. Highly recommended. −MGN

○ **Blue Trombone / COLUMBIA**
Sensational solos, fine arrangements, compositions. −RW

● **Jay & Kai Octet / COLUMBIA**
W/ Kai Winding. Wonderful six-trombone showcase. −RW

Standards: Live at the Village / POLYGRAM
Fine recent outing with same band from *Quintergy*. −RW

Trombone Master / CBS   COMP
1989 compilation of good 1957-1960 Johnson cuts. Mastering is uneven. −RW

JAMES P. JOHNSON   1894-1955

Stride, boogie. The "father of stride piano," James P. Johnson was an extensively trained player who still became a great stylist doing the popular music of the era: rags, blues, reels, novelty tunes, and originals. His neatly crafted bass lines, prominent but not rigid rhythms, and sweeping right-hand lines are still masterful. He was a regular in New York by 1912 and was cutting piano rolls in 1916 and recording by 1917. In the 20s he played with a host of famous names, composed scores for a Broadway show, and directed music for Bessie Smith's film short *St. Louis Blues.* He wrote plays and composed a symphony in the 30s. He went back on the circuit playing with bands from 1939 until he became an intermission pianist at Condon's and Pied Piper in Greenwich Village in 1946. −RW

Parlor Piano Solos / BIOGRAPH   1917
Wonderful piano rolls from 1917-1921. −RW

Rare Piano Roll Solos - Vol. 1 & 2 / BIOGRAPH   1917
Vol. 1 1917-1921, Vol. 2 1917.

○ **Carolina Shout / BIOGRAPH**   ca. 192?
Landmark solos from Johnson's early days. −RW

Piano Solos / SMI
Barrelhouse, stride, blues, & majestic technique. −RW

Plays Fats Waller/Art Tatum Masterpieces / MCA

Ragtime - Vol. 2 / BIOGRAPH
Let it rag, let it roll! −RW

● **Snowy Morning Blues / GRP**

Good record to start your collection. Some brilliant piano musings. –MGN

☆ **Father of the Stride Piano / COLUMBIA**   COMP
Seminal recordings. –RW

MARC JOHNSON

Post-bop, neo bop. An excellent session bassist and bandleader who currently heads the group Bass Desires. He has also worked with Gary Burton. –RW

○ **Bass Desires / ECM**   1985
Prime contemporary fusion with guitarists Bill Frisell and John Scofield. A worthy purchase. –MGN

Second Sight / POLYGRAM   1987
Fine release from Bass Desires. A top modern unit that blends improvisatory, pop, and rock components. –RW

2 by 4 / POLYGRAM   1991
Better than average tunes, excellent playing from Gary Burton (vib), Toots Thielemans (harmonica). –RW

PLAS JOHNSON   ♭1931

Post-bop, cool, soul jazz. Plas Johnson was best known as a prolific R&B and R&R tenor saxophonist in the 50s. He was actually a well-grounded player who could do more than honk and play snippets during breaks. Johnson began to move in a more conscious jazz direction in the 70s after spending the 60s doing studio work with Henry Mancini and playing in Merv Griffin's studio band. During the 70s and 80s he has cut straight mainstream dates for Concord, where his full, big tone and lush sound get more time in the spotlight. –RW

○ **The Blues / CONCORD**   1975
Here is the veteran honking sax star in more conventional jazz setting. –RW

Positively / CONCORD   1976
Good mainstream date with soul-jazz feel. –RW

BOBBY JONES   1928-1980

Hard-bop, post-bop. This legendary ex-Mingus tenor saxophonist and flute player was an original thinker who died far too young and scarcely recorded. –MGN

○ **The Arrival of Bobby Jones / COBBLESTONE**   1972
This is a studio session from this highly original reed/flute player, plus Charles McPherson (as), Jaki Byard (p); a must-buy. –MGN

CARMELL JONES   ♭1936

Hard-bop, post-bop. Kansas City trumpeter, prominent w/ Horace Silver in the 60s before expatriating to Germany. A bright, solid-toned player. –MGN

○ **The Remarkable / PACIFIC JAZZ**   i 1961
W/ Harold Land (ts).

ELVIN JONES   ♭1927

Post-bop, early free. Drums. The youngest of the famed Jones brothers (which include pianist Hank and trumpeter Thad), Elvin became a member of the jazz "who's who" during his influential half-decade with the John Coltrane Quartet. Jones's status is further underlined by his earlier work with Coltrane's rival in the Sonny Rollins Trio. With Coltrane (from 1960 to 1965) he did not make himself conspicuous with volume or flashiness; instead he pursued a subtle percussive density that balanced pianist McCoy Tyner's web of sound and Coltrane's long solo lines. He obscured the beat with carefully placed accents, but rarely abandoned pulse, and in so doing inspired the coming generation of free-jazz percussionists. After leaving Coltrane (an unfortunate departure provoked by the addition of second drummer Rashied Ali), Elvin's career has been hit-and-miss. Most of his many albums as leader (on Blue Note, Impulse, Enja, and others) lack the edge and excitement of his earlier years, but his two albums under Ornette Coleman's leadership worked very well. And

just recently he teamed up with former bandmate Pharoah Sanders and guitarist Sonny Sharrock for the excellent *Ask the Ages* recording (Axiom 422 848 957), proving that there are still many good things to come from this drumming master. –MB

Elvin! / OJC   1961
1987 reissue of fine Riverside set with Thad Jones (cnt), Frank Foster (ts). –RW

● **Illumination / IMPULSE**   1963
Sextet w/ Jimmy Garrison (b), Prince Lasha (as), Sonny Simmons (as), Charles Davis (bar sax), and McCoy Tyner (p). All originals in progressive stance. A jewel. Must-find. –MGN

○ **Dear John C / IMPULSE**   1965
Superb quartet work with Charlie Mariano (as). –RW

Puttin' It Together / BLUE NOTE / DB 5   1968
Solid pianoless trio date, Joe Farrell handles heavy reed load. Jimmy Garrison on bass. –RW

Heavy Sounds / MCA   1968
One of Elvin Jones lesser-touted albums. A good session co-led by strong bassist Richard Davis. –RW

Poly-Currents / BLUE NOTE   1969
1986 reissue of Blue Note release. W/ horn players Joe Farrell, Pepper Adams, George Coleman. Farrell plays English horn on one cut. –RW

Merry-Go-Round / BLUE NOTE   1971
A big 11-piece dynamic sound. –RW

Genesis / BLUE NOTE   1971
Often magnificent; three horn frontline. –MGN

Live at the Lighthouse - Vol. 1 & 2 / BLUE NOTE   1972
Originally solid twin-record set reissued in separate versions. Strong quartet with saxmen Steve Grossman, Dave Liebman. CD has two bonus cuts. –RW

Live at the Village Vanguard / ENJA   1973
Excellent tenor by George Coleman. –RW

Summit Meeting / VANGUARD   1976
These are some top-shelf sessions w/ James Moody (sax), Clark Terry (tpt). –RW

Remembrance / MPS   1978
Quintet with saxophonists Michael Stuart and Pat La Barbera. This is an excellent album of mostly La Barbera originals. –MGN

Very R.A.R.E. / TRIO   1979
A 12-inch 45 RPM with six tunes. R.A.R.E. is an acronym made up of the first letter of the first names of Richard Davis (b), Art Pepper (as), Roland Hanna (p), and Elvin Jones. A wonderful date. –MGN

Heart to Heart / DENON   1980
Exemplary material, superb Tommy Flanagan (p). –RW

Brother John / QSV   1982
Reissue of good 1982 session from Palo Alto. –MGN

Reunited / BLACKHAWK   1986
McCoy Tyner (p) and Elvin together again; Pharoah Sanders (sax) plus intriguing guitar from Jean-Paul Bourelly. –RW

HANK JONES   ♭1918

Swing, bop, cool. The elder brother of Thad and Elvin Jones, Hank is one of the founding members of the extraordinary "school" of Detroit pianists. He has a very reserved, almost careful approach that doesn't mean he's not a brilliant player. He is a first-rate accompanist and a very effective soloist. He moved to NY in 1944, where he worked with Hot Lips Page, Andy Kirk, Coleman Hawkins, and Ella Fitzgerald in the 40s and 50s. Since the early 50s, he has made multiple records as a leader and has been in countless settings (solo, trio, combo, backup for vocalists, etc.). –RW

● **Trio / SAVOY**   1955
Seminal stuff from Hank Jones, with Kenny Clarke (d), Wendell Marshall (b). –RW

Bluebird / SAVOY   ca. 1955

Formative 50s cuts. –RW

Relaxin' at Camarillo / SAVOY   1956
Both steady and appealing, with excellent Bobby Jaspar. –RW

Songs from Porgy & Bess / CAPITOL   1960
Unforgettable versions of well-known Gershwin. –RW

○ **Bop Redux / MUSE**   1977
Trio date shows this pianist in fine form. –MGN

At the Village Vanguard / VANGUARD / DB 5   1977
Great Jazz Trio at the Village Vanguard. Stunning and gripping solos, accompaniment. –RW

Just for Fun / OJC   1977
Includes some good working by this always-insightful, creative soloist. –MGN

Tiptoe Tapdance / GALAXY   1977
Finely crafted solo piano. –RW

Groovin' High / MUSE   1978
Nicely phrased and played, mellow and memorable. –RW

Ain't Misbehavin' / GALAXY   1978
Mostly Jones paying his tribute to Waller. –RW

In Japan / AAJ   1979
1991 reissue of excellent live trio take. –MGN

Lazy Afternoon / CONCORD   1989
Strong mainstream date, some spry Jones solos. –RW

○ **The Oracle / POLYGRAM**   r 1991
Includes three different generations of jazzmen. A very nice album. –MGN

I'm All Smiles / VERVE
Expressive, charming duets with Tommy Flanagan (p). –RW

JO JONES   1911-1985

Swing, big band. "Papa" Jo Jones is considered by many to be the finest swing-era drummer of all, superior to even Gene Krupa and Buddy Rich, but he didn't compare to them in power, flash, or speed. Instead, he was the preeminent timekeeper, quite fast enough but especially skilled at driving the beat and punctuating the pulse. He had a lengthy apprenticeship with various territory bands but became a star with Count Basie in 1934. Jones spent 12 years with Basie in two different stints and helped establish the percussive vocabulary for swing drummers and beyond. He did plenty of session work in the 50s but was taken out of the mainstream by the changing tastes of the 60s. –RW

Jo Jones Special / VANGUARD / DB 5   1955
This is a first-rate, swing-influenced set, later combined with a second album into the *Essential Jo Jones* package on Vogue. –RW

○ **The Main Man / PABLO**   1976
This date w/ Harry Edison (tpt), Roy Eldridge (tpt), Vic Dickerson (tb) and others is sterling silver. –MGN

OLIVER JONES   b 1934

Post-bop, cool, blues-jazz. Oliver Jones is an effective Canadian pianist who is getting more attention, thanks to his recent recordings on the Justin Time label. He works regularly with drummer Ed Thigpen and has also backed Canadian vocalist Ranee Lee. –RW

○ **Cookin' at Sweet Basil / JUSTIN TIME**   1987
This brilliant Canadian pianist caught live. Excellent. –MGN

PHILLY JOE JONES   1923-1985

Bop, hard-bop, post-bop, cool. Among the most influential drummers ever in the bop genre. His technique of "rim" shots, use of wire brushes, and accompaniment behind soloists have become a part of the modern jazz vocabulary. Jones got his nickname from the many years he worked in Philadelphia, his hometown, before leaving to tour with Joe Morris's R&B band. After a short stint with Ben Webster in 1949, he moved to New York and was an active freelancer until 1953. During the mid 70s he became part of the Miles Davis

group and worked with him in 1952-1955, 1955-1957, 1958, and 1962. In the 60s he worked extensively with both Gil and Bill Evans, then moved to England in 1967 and worked and taught all over Europe until returning to Philadelphia in the mid 70s. His last extended engagement was heading the repertory band Dameronia, playing Tadd Dameron's compositions from 1981-1985. Jones's final group was Pieces of Time for a few months in 1985. –RW

○ **Blues for Dracula / OJC**   1958
One of his earliest dates as a leader. –RW

Drums Around the World / RIVERSIDE   1959
Exciting, dynamic percussion package. –RW

Showcase / OJC   1959
Fine sextet and septet material. –RW

Round Midnight / LOTUS   1969
Excellent Italian set with sorely neglected Dizzy Reece on trumpet. –RW

Advance! / GALAXY   1978
Steady and consistently high caliber. –RW

○ **Drum Song / GALAXY**   1978
W/ Blue Mitchell (tpt) and Slide Hampton (tb). –MGN

○ **To Tadd with Love / UPTOWN**   1982
Debut of repertory band Dameronia, which gave the work of Tadd Dameron some needed exposure. –RW

Look Stop Listen / UPTOWN / DB 5   1983
First-rate playing from Cecil Payne (bar sax), Walter Davis Jr. (p), and others. –RW

QUINCY JONES   b 3/14

Progressive big band, instr-pop, contemporary funk. Trumpet, composer, arranger. He's such a big name in pop circles today that Quincy Jones's jazz background has almost been forgotten. But in the 50s Jones was a major figure among jazz musicians, spending two-and-a-half years in the early 50s with Lionel Hampton, who recorded several Jones pieces. Later he was Dizzy Gillespie's musical director. He spent 18 months in France and Scandinavia, studying composition and working for Barclay Records in 1957-1958, and formed his own all-star big band for the European opening of the show *Free and Easy.* This band played for two years, while Jones also wrote for albums by Count Basie and recorded arrangements for Sarah Vaughan, Dinah Washington, and Billy Eckstine. A fine trumpeter particularly known for his use of chords built in fourths, Jones was also a terrific arranger and writer. He expanded into film soundtracks in the 60s and was also an executive at Mercury Records, where he enlarged his interests and reach into the pop market. –RW

Sweden — American All Stars / PRESTIGE   i 1953
W/ Arne Domnerus (as) and Lars Gullin (bar sax). –ED

★ **The Birth of a Band / EM ARCY**   1959
His best music by far. A must-buy — don't think twice. –MGN

Birth of a Band - Vol. 2 / MERCURY   1959
Continuation of strong big-band sessions. –RW

I Dig Dancers / MERCURY   i 1960
W/ Jerome Richardson (reeds).

Great Wide World of ... : Live! / POLYGRAM / DB 5   1961
A 1985 reissue of exemplary sessions with a host of great players. –RW

The Quintessence / MCA   1961
A 1986 reissue of a solid big-band set. –RW

Live at Newport / TRIP   1961
Jones's formative period: shaping his sound. –RW

○ **Walking in Space / A&M**   1969
A Grammy-winning work that marked the beginning of Jones's shift into R&B and pop. –RW

Gula Matari / A & M   1970
A superb followup that might have been better than *Walkin' in Space* overall. –RW

Smackwater Jack / MOBILE FIDELITY   1971

Grammy winner. Near end of Jones's jazz phase. —RW

Body Heat / A&M   1973
Transitional album marking his gradual move toward complete R&B sound, minor jazz influence. —RW

Mellow Madness / A & M   1975
The first appearance of Brothers Johnson, with Quincy now a bigtime R&B star. —RW

Roots / A & M   1977
Monumental soundtrack for a landmark TV show that eclipses Jones's past film and television work in symbolic impact. —RW

Sounds & Stuff Like That / POLYGRAM   1977
Pretty straight R&B. —RW

The Dude / A & M   1981
A wonderful production that leans more toward soul pop than jazz. —RW

25th Anniversary Series - Vol. 3 / A&M   COMP
A good overview and compilation from an R&B/pop perspective. —RW

SAM JONES   1924-1981

Hard-bop, post-bop, cool, blues-jazz, soul jazz, progressive big band. A wonderful accompanist equally skilled at bass or cello, Jones made being in the rhythm section an artform. He moved from Florida to New York in the 50s, working first with Tiny Bradshaw, then with Illinois Jacquet and Kenny Dorham. His first major impact was as a member of Cannonball Adderley's early quintet from 1956-1957, followed by time with Dizzy Gillespie and Thelonious Monk. Jones stayed in the re-formed Adderley group from 1959-1966, then spent three years in the Oscar Peterson trio. For the rest of his career, Jones was an active session player, plus he led a 12-piece band part-time. —RW

★ **The Soul Society / RIVERSIDE**   1960
A great soul-jazz romp with wonderful Bobby Timmons on piano. —RW

○ **Down Home / RIVERSIDE**   1962
A dynamic duo with Ron Carter (b). —RW

Cello Again / XANADU   1976
An excellent quintet set in mainstream mold. —RW

Something in Common / MUSE   1977
A fine sextet plus Cedar Walton on piano and Billy Higgins on drums. —RW

Changes and Things / XANADU   1977
Louis Hayes on drums shakes the rafters. Excellent Jones on bass. —RW

The Bassist / DISCOVERY / DB 5   1979
A solid trio date with Kenny Barron (p). —RW

Something New / SEABREEZE   1979
An intense 12-piece session. —RW

Right Down Front / OJC
Some nice large group sessions with a host of stars. —RW

SPIKE JONES   1911-1965

Swing, big band, comedy. Born Lindley Armstrong Jones, this bandleader and drummer started as a Dixieland drummer and radio session player working with Al Jolson, among others. He formed Spike Jones & the City Slickers in the early 40s. Although the accent was primarily on comedy (using bells, whistles, gunshots, broken glass, etc.), the quality of musicianship in his band was higher than in most big bands of the day playing straight music. Jones scored several Top 10 hits from 1942-1949, with sendups of current chart toppers, and it became the badge of honor with pop musicians that you really hadn't tasted true success until Spike & the City Slickers destroyed your song. A tenacious bandleader, Jones molded his various sidemen into a crackerjack unit, with split-second timing and an ability to cover many styles successfully. His stage show (later transferred to movies and TV with great

popularity) was no less mind-boggling, needing a full railroad car just to carry the props, and it was all presented without electronic gimmickry of any kind. Though parodies of pop music continue to proliferate, Spike Jones & the City Slickers did it better than anyone before or since. —CK

○ **1946 / HINDSIGHT**   1946
Best Of - Vols. 1 & 2 / RCA   COMP
A good selection of his work. —JME

THAD JONES   1923-1986

Big band, bop, hard-bop, post-bop, cool, progressive big band. An excellent arranger and bandleader whose considerable lead-trumpet abilities were overshadowed by his skill at composing songs and penning charts for bands. Both his arrangements and his playing emphasized technical acumen and creative imagination. His playing was fresh, fiery, and assertive, always distinctive, and never recycling clichés, gimmicks, or excessive notes. Thad Jones worked with his famous brothers Elvin and Hank in Detroit in the late 30s. After serving in the army during WWII, he cut an album on Charles Mingus's Debut label. Later he did more recording with Mingus while joining Count Basie's band for a memorable nine-year period. After departing the Basie band, he became a prolific freelance arranger and player, doing albums for Harry James and playing with everyone from George Russell to Thelonious Monk and Gerry Mulligan. He was also on staff at CBS in 1964. In 1965 (with Pepper Adams), he co-led a quintet whose personnel included drummer Mel Lewis. That association blossomed into the two deciding to head an 18-piece big band, with Jones writing most of the arrangements. The Thad Jones-Mel Lewis big band was among the dominant large groups of the 60s and 70s, becoming a fixture on Monday nights at the Village Vanguard and releasing several critically acclaimed albums. —RW

○ **Magnificent Thad Jones / BLUE NOTE**   1956
An excellent reissue. Subtle, harmonic ensemble jazz. —MGN

● **Fabulous Thad Jones / OJC**   195?
A 1991 reissue of super cuts from Debut label. —RW

○ **Mean What You Say / OJC**   1966
A great reissue with Pepper Adams (bar sax). —MGN

Three and One / STEEPLECHASE   1985
An excellent quartet session. —RW

SCOTT JOPLIN   1868-1917

Ragtime. Ragtime's finest composer, Scott Joplin has nonetheless been a source of controversy and scorn in some jazz sectors, mainly by those who've taken issue with his emphasis (some might say obsession) with making ragtime a "serious" music. For much of his life, Joplin battled to get his opera *Treemonisha* performed, and was highly depressed when it was performed in Harlem in 1911 and was a commercial flop. He was also a stickler about having his rags played at the proper speed, hating to hear them being speeded up. Joplin played cornet in the Queen City Negro Band of Sedalia, MO, in the 1890s, and even played at the 1893 World's Fair. He began selling his compositions in 1895, receiving a royalty from publisher John Stark for "Maple Leaf Rag," the idiom's biggest hit. He moved to St. Louis in 1900 and wrote the 20-minute "Ragtime Dance" ballet in 1902. He wanted to establish a "classic rag" and composed a second opera, *The Guest of Honor*, but it was never published. He composed fifty piano rags, and both "The Entertainer" and *Treemonisha* have received widespread exposure and publicity. —RW

King of Ragtime Writers / BIOGRAPH
Taken from classic piano rolls. —JME

Complete Scott Joplin / GREENER PASTURES
Vols. 1 & 2. Played by Scott Kirby. —JME

○ **Elite Syncopations / BIOGRAPH**
Scott Joplin's Rag Time / GREENER PASTURES
Played by Scott Kirby. —JME

CLIFFORD JORDAN b 1931

Hard-bop, post-bop, early free. Tenor saxophonist Jordan was a mainstay in the Chicago jazz school, along with friends and classmates Johnny Griffin and Richard Davis. Jordan switched from piano to tenor sax at 14. He started his career playing in local R&B bands before hitting the road in jazz groups led by Max Roach and Horace Silver. He briefly replaced Sonny Rollins in Roach's 1957 group. He was also a member of J. J. Johnson and Kenny Dorham's ensembles before he reunited with Roach for three more years in the mid 60s. After a short period with Charles Mingus, Jordan spent several years as a soloist and arranger in Europe before becoming an established figure in New York during the 70s. His style, with its big tone and full sound, mixes blues references and total harmonic and melodic control. He's never adopted any of the nuances of the free or avant-garde stylists, yet has recorded many memorable solos over the years. He is an excellent player solidly in the mainstream school. –RW

Starting Time / OJC 1961
A fine set. –RW

Bearcat / OJC ca. 1961
A 1991 reissue of formative material. –RW

These Are My Roots / ATLANTIC 1965
An intriguing concept: Jordan arranging and doing Leadbelly songs. –RW

In the World / STRATA EAST r 1969
Dynamic, adventurous playing. –RW

○ **Glass Bead Game / STRATA EAST** 1973
Outstanding in both concept and playing. –RW

Night of the Mark VII / MUSE 1975
An expressive, demonstrative set. –RW

Firm Roots / STEEPLECHASE 1975
One of Jordan's best releases with the Magic Triangle ensemble of Cedar Walton (p), Sam Jones (b), and Billy Higgins (d). –RW

The Highest Mountain / STEEPLECHASE 1975
The fifth of five sets by the Triangle group. –RW

The Adventurer / MUSE 1978
Steady, with consistently interesting and gripping solos. –RW

Repetition / SOUL NOTE / DB 5 1984
Strong leads and good compositions. –RW

Royal Ballads / CRISS CROSS 1986
Brilliant interpretations. –RW

● **Down through the Years / MILESTONE** 1992
With an extraordinary big band. –MGN

DUKE JORDAN b 1922

Bop, hard-bop, post-bop, cool. Consistency has not been Jordan's strong suit, but whenever he's been active, he's been a solid, enjoyable pianist. He played with a sextet that won an amateur competition at the 1939 World's Fair and he worked with both swing and bop groups during the 40s, playing with Coleman Hawkins and the original Savoy Sultans at one time, then later with Charlie Parker. He spent nine months in a group led by Stan Getz in 1952. Jordan was among the rare pianists in the 40s and 50s able to display a personalized approach different from the dominant one created by Bud Powell. He was neither as fast nor as complex in his solo structure as Powell, but his phrasing and statements were just as convincing and emphatic. During the 50s Jordan was quite active in recording sessions. Then he went to Europe in 1959, where he wrote music for the French film *Les Liaisons Dangereuses*, using the name Jack Murray. –RW

● **Flight to Jordan / BLUE NOTE** 1960
The release that established Jordan as a prime player. –RW

○ **Brooklyn Brothers / MUSE** 1973
A nice session with fellow reed player Cecil Payne. –RW

Flight to Denmark / STEEPLECHASE 1973
Aggressive, dynamic solos. –RW

Duke's Delight / STEEPLECHASE 1975
Lovely ballads and fine uptempo pieces. –RW

Lover Man / STEEPLECHASE 1975
Jordan shows his blues side. –RW

Duke's Artistry / STEEPLECHASE 1978
Masterful tones. –RW

The Great Session / STEEPLECHASE 1978
Aptly titled — wonderful Jordan playing. –RW

Midnight Moonlight / STEEPLECHASE 1979
Duke in the spotlight. –RW

LOUIS JORDAN 1908-1975

Blues-jazz, ballads, R&B. In his youth, Louis Jordan made a reputation among musicians as a great jazz clarinetist, but it was as a singer and showman that he climbed to the very top of showbusiness, with several million-selling records to his credit when that kind of figure still meant something. In 1938, Jordan left Chick Webb's big band and debuted a sextet, Louis Jordan and his Tympany Five (his drummer featured tympany), at a small Harlem club, the Elk's Rendezvous. This swinging little group mixed jazz and jive in a manner that appealed to both dancers and listeners and communicated well on records (Jordan had a Decca contract from the start and recorded steadily). Its big hits didn't come until the early 40s. Much of the group's success came from Jordan's terrific sense of time and pacing; he could put on a show with the best of them. On records, he could almost make you see him as he preached mock sermons ("Beware"), told funny stories ("Five Guys Named Mo"), or just sang the blues with a message that all could absorb ("Early in the Morning") . Sometimes the story took both sides of a 78 to tell ("Saturday Night Fish Fry"), and sometimes the story was even romantic ("Don't Let the Sun Catch You Cryin'"). Nat Cole, Ray Charles, B. B. King — they all learned from Louis Jordan. Not forgotten, Jordan has been celebrated on records and on stage, most recently with *Five Guys Named Mo*, first in London, then on Broadway in 1992. –DM

○ **Louis Jordan and his Tympany Five / CIRCLE** 1940
Wondrous cuts that combined hip vocals, robust solos, and inventive lyrics into a sound that was later called R&B. These are also available in other collections on Charly and Jukebox Lil. –RW

Jordan and Barber / BLACK LION
W/ Chris Barber (tb). Jordan returned to his jazz-swing roots with this batch of nice cuts. This album was recorded with British players. –RW

Rock N' Roll / MERCURY
Later-period Jordan, when he was an established R&B star. He recut some big hits with a huge orchestra. Quincy Jones arranged and conducted the sessions. –RW

★ **Best of Louis Jordan / MCA** COMP
Seminal 40s R&B bandleader's hottest Decca sides, which influenced almost all who heard them, especially Chuck Berry and Louis Prima. The CD deletes the album's excellent liner notes. –JF

○ **Look out! / CHARLY** COMP
Super cuts from Jordan's prime period. –RW

MARLON JORDAN b 1972

Post-bop, neo bop. Another in the increasing line of Crescent City players who've migrated to New York in the 80s and 90s and quickly gained fame and attention. The trumpeter was discovered by a Columbia Recording executive, Dr. George Butler, playing in a New Orleans club and was eventually signed to a deal. He's the brother of New Orleans flutist Kent Jordan, who has also recorded for Columbia. As a trumpeter, Marlon has been linked to both Wynton Marsalis and Terence Blanchard but has yet to make the impact they have made. He is a promising player, extremely good on ballads and still building a following. –RW

For You Only / CBS   1988
An erratic but worthy 1990 release of this latest New Orleans prodigy's debut. –RW

○ **Learson's Return / CBS**   r 1991
A more confident, strønger release. –RW

SHEILA JORDAN   b 1928

Bop, post-bop, ballads, early free, modern creative. Vocals. There's something at once esoteric, yet eminently accessible about Jordan. She sounds so unlike anyone else that it can be hard to get a handle on her at first listening. She is one of the idiom's most personal, intense, and emotionally direct vocalists. Her singing is infused with intelligence, musicianship, and deep feeling. A jazz singer from the word go, she eschews all the trappings of show biz glitz without becoming aloof to her audience. You'll never hear a glib or facile lick thrown on to demonstrate how hip, soulful, or technically adept she is. Yet, she has plenty of chops. She is not afraid to take chances, especially in her scat singing, which she infuses with a whimsical humor. Jordan's current partnership with bassist Harvie Swartz has yielded some of her finest moments. A greatly under-appreciated artist. –RL

● **Portrait of Sheila Jordan / BLUE NOTE**   r 1963
Innovative date w/ Barry Galbraith (g), Steve Swallow (b), and Denzil Best (d). The one to get –RL

. **Sheila / STEEPLECHASE / DB 5**   1977
Rousing, striking, and declarative. –RW

● **Playground / ECM**   1979
A studio date with the Steve Kuhn Trio. The most distinctive voice in modern jazz. Some of Jordan's best work. –MGN

Old Time Feeling / MUSE   1982
Wonderful leads. Good duo date with Harvie Swartz (b). –RW

The Crossing / BLACKHAWK / DB 5   1984
Outstanding sessions with brilliant — often breathtaking — lead vocals. –RW

Lost and Found / MUSE   1989
Superb singer who — sadly — doesn't record very often. –RW

○ **Last Year's Waltz / ECM**
Live at Fat Tuesdays in NYC with the Steve Kuhn Trio. Sheila at her best. –MGN

STANLEY JORDAN   b 1959

Instr-pop, neo bop, contemporary funk. Guitarist Jordan was an 80s sensation. His background as a pianist has certainly played a role in his revolutionary guitar technique. He is famous for the "hammering-on" technique, a method in which he plays the guitar like a keyboard, with both hands playing melody lines by tapping the strings rather than strumming or using a pick. He also uses different tuning, getting a much different sound, one that his detractors say sounds too much like a thin piano instead of a guitar, although they acknowledge he's been able to do some amazing things like playing melodies in the right hand and doing chords and bass lines in the left. Though he was discovered playing guitar on the streets, no one should confuse Jordan with a vagrant prodigy. He began playing piano at age six, was playing guitar at eleven, and earned a music degree from Princeton. He also spent parts of those years practicing and playing in clubs. He moved to New York in 1984 and, shortly after, got an invitation to play the Kool Jazz Festival. That was followed by an appearance at Montreux and a recording contract. –RW

Touch Sensitive / TANGENT   1982
Rare independent release on which he first featured the two-handed touch style which he has perfected. –PK

○ **Magic Touch / BLUE NOTE / DB 5**   1985
The debut album by a musician who helped to redefine how a guitar is played. A must! –PK

Standards - Vol 1 / BLUE NOTE   1986
A stunning collection of jazz standards done to perfection by a superb guitarist. –PK

Stolen Moments / CAPITOL

VIC JURIS   b 1953

Post-bop, neo bop. This stunning session guitarist is adept at blues-rock, funk, and straight-ahead jazz. No doubt a master. –MGN

○ **Roadsong / MUSE**   1977

RICHIE KAMUCA   1930-1977

Big band, bop, hard-bop, cool. Tenor player was born in Philly, lived in Los Angeles. Prominent soloist with Big Bands of Stan Kenton, Woody Herman, Maynard Ferguson. –MGN

The Brothers / RCA VICTOR   i 1956
W/ sax artists Al Cohn and Bill Perkins. –ED

Jazz Erotica / HI FI   i 1959

○ **West Coast Jazz in Hi Fi / OJC**   1959
A worthy reissue. A good West Coast-style effort. Limited-edition release. –RW

GEORGE KAWAGUCHI

Hard-bop, post-bop, neo bop. A slick, technically proficient big band leader that records for Projazz. His band's arrangements and ensemble interaction are sharp, their solos and compositions uneven. Their albums are well recorded, if unambitious. –RW

○ **Maiden Voyage / PRO ARTE-PRO JAZZ**   1987
A recent set from this Japanese bandleader. Among the better examples of the effectiveness of Terrence Blanchard (tpt) and Donald Harrison (sax). –RW

LEWIS KEEL

Hard-bop, post-bop. Memphis-based alto saxophonist has limited recordings. A fine exponent of Charlie Parker's style, he is the southern equivalent of Frank Foster. –MGN

○ **Coming Out Swinging / MUSE**

GEOFF KEEZER   b 1970

Post-bop, neo bop. Keezer is an emerging piano star on the East Coast. His speed, facility, creativity, and flash have already stunned several East Coast critics, and he's certainly become a prime young lion. He's had one solo album to his credit and has also played with Roy Hargrove, Antonio Hart, and many others. –RW

○ **Here & Now / CAPITOL**
Best album from Wisconsin pianist. More to come from Keezer. With Steve Nelson on vibes. Excellent version of Harold Mabern's "There But for the Grace of ..." –MGN

ROGER KELLAWAY   b 1939

Cool. Well known as an accompanist. Played piano with swing to bop stars Jimmy McPortland, Kai Winding, Al Cohn and Zoot Sims. Works with his own trio now. Also toured with pop stars Joni Mitchell and Tom Scott. –MGN

Roger Kellaway Trio / PRESTIGE / DB 5   1965
This superb session date includes originals and a Beatles tune. Creative work. –HD

Stride! / WORLD PACIFIC   1966
Deepest look at stride influence in all of Kellaway's work. –HD

Spirit Feel / PACIFIC JAZZ   1967
Traces of soul in his solos. –RW

Roger Kellaway Cello Quartet / A&M   r 1971
Reissue of a quirky set with music written for a cello-driven quartet. –RW

● **Ain't Misbehavin' / CHOICE**   1986
Rare reissue of an authentic stride-piano session. –RW

○ **Live at Maybeck Recital Hall / CONCORD**   198?
Recent view of Kellaway's style. Melodic yet driving. Strong stride-piano influence. –HD

Fifty-Fifty / STASH
A solid 1987 duo with Red Mitchell (b). –RW

WYNTON KELLY   1931-1971

Hard-bop, post-bop, soul jazz. One of the great pianists of the post-WWII era. Originally influenced by Nat Cole, Kelly began in small bands around New York in the late 40s. Working with Lester Young and Dizzy Gillespie, he soon became the favorite session pianist in New York, featured with Miles Davis (1959-1963), in a cooperative trio with Paul Chambers and Jimmy Cobb (1964-1967), and often with Wes Montgomery. He is present as a sideman on dozens of recordings (the albums from the 50s and early 60s are good), though the mantle of leadership is not worn easily by Kelly. His Verve recordings from the mid-60s tend to be more commercial. Any time he recorded with Chambers and a good drummer (Cobb, Blakey, PJ Jones, ect.) as a rhythm section, is a listener's delight. –BP

Piano Interpretations / BLUE NOTE   1951
Trio. His first solo recording sessions. Even the uptempo pieces have a gentle quality. Very nice mainstream jazz. –JME

Piano / OJC   1958
Expansive, wonderfully played sessions with Kenny Burrell (g), Paul Chambers (b), and Philly Joe Jones (d). CD has a bonus cut. –RW

● **Wynton Kelly / RIVERSIDE**   1958
Mostly uptempo bop. Crisp, tight, and clear. Not funky. –JME

○ **Kelly Blue / OJC**   1959
Small Group. Classic Kelly. Bluesy, bright, nice. There is magic in this album. –JME

Trio & Sextet / RIVERSIDE   1959
Super trio session. Sextet workouts are good, if a bit unchallenging. –RW

Whisper Not / RIVERSIDE   i 1962
Outstanding interpretations. –RW

Blues on Purpose / XANADU   1965
Kelly's later-period material, calmer and more reflective. –RW

☆ **Smokin' at the Half Note / VERVE**   1965
Wynton Kelly Trio w/ Wes Montgomery (g). Slow to mid-tempos — very listenable. Both Wynton and Wes are in fine form. A rare chance to hear Montgomery in a small-group setting. –JME

Full View / MILESTONE   1966
Trio work; solid and authoritative. –RW

In Concert / VEE JAY   1988
Nearing the end. Ron McClure brings new sound and fresh direction on bass. –RW

HAL KEMP   1905-1940

Trad. Hal Kemp was among the most popular and commercially-successful bandleaders of the 30s, scoring a huge number of dance hits. Kemp played in a band at the University of North Carolina from 1924-1926, with his Carolina Club Orchestra recording for Okeh. He worked with Bunny Berigan in 1930 and toured Europe with his group. Kemp's band was famous for a sentimental, "sweet" but substantial style; his arranger John Trotter did some innovative things for the era with instrumentation and contrast of brass and horn section parts. Lead vocalist Bob Allen was also an audience favorite on ballads. After Trotter left to join Bing Crosby, Art Mooney became the arranger, and the band continued to sparkle. They were boosted by assistance from a vocal trio called the Smoothies, and from appearances on radio and in film. Their last hit was a novelty-song version of "I'm Looking Over a Four Leaf Clover." –RW

○ **Best of Big Bands / CBS**   COMP
Compiles his hits. –RW

STAN KENTON   1911-1979

Progressive big band. Pianist, arranger, composer. Controversy followed Stan Kenton throughout his career, from accusations of pretentiousness to charges of racism. Kenton started playing piano as a teenager and was touring at 18. He formed his own band in California in the early 40s, after working with the orchestras of Gus Arnheim and Vido Musso. He started doing conventional dance-oriented swing, but started to experiment with time signatures and tempo with the arrival of such players as Shelly Manne and Art Pepper. In the early 50s, he composed avant-garde pieces and expanded to a 40-piece group with 16 strings, something that earned him ridicule in both classical and jazz quarters. Following this, he cut back to a more standard swing/big band, though from time to time he again experimented with comedy numbers or odd symphonic/jazz unions. Kenton won a Grammy in 1956 and in 1962. –RW

And His Orchestra - Vol 5 / HINDSIGHT   1945
1945-1947. For fans only. –RW

○ **New Concepts of Artistry in Rhythm / CAPITOL**   1952
Still intriguing conceptually. 1990 reissue. –RW

Sketches on Standards / CREATIVE WORLD   1953
Some ambitious renditions. –RW

● **Cuban Fire / CAPITOL / BB 17**   1956
Kenton's hottest music. –MGN

Viva Kenton / CREATIVE WORLD   1959
Nice Latin influence. –RW

West Side Story / CREATIVE WORLD / BB 16   1961
Another Grammy winner. –RW

Adventurers in Jazz / CREATIVE WORLD   r 1963
A Grammy winner. –RW

Adventures in Blues / CREATIVE WORLD   r 1964
Prototype Kenton. –RW

○ **Road Show / CAPITOL**   1966
Fine live recording from 1959. June Christy is a bit below par due to a cold on the day of the recording. –KMC

Stan Kenton Today / PHASE FOUR   1972
The last Kenton release of any real musical value. Done in London. –RW

○ **Comprehensive Kenton / CAPITOL**   COMP
Extensive set with probably all the Kenton most people would ever want. –RW

○ **Stan Kenton / MOSAIC**   COMP
The Holman and Russo Charts. Four-CD set contains all 72 works that Russo and Holman wrote and/or arranged for Kenton. Long unavailable. This is the highwater mark of Kenton's career as one of the chief innovators in experimental big-band jazz. –JME

KAMAU KENYATTA   b 1955

Post-bop, Latin, world fusion, neo bop, M-base. Saxophonist, pianist, and composer using contemporary and modal themes in alliance with inspiration from Black poets and writers. –MGN

Strongmen / OMNI-ARTS   1982
Dedicated to Sterling A. Brown, this album features the same band as *Bigger*, except that Tony Holland is on sax, which is also played by Kenyatta. More of a contemporary stance. –MGN

○ **Bigger / OMNI-ARTS**   1984
Instrumentals for contemporary and post-bop ilk. Vocals on occasion by Fred Johnson. "Detroit 1970" and "American Hunger Blues" definitive — inspired by Black writers. In a class by itself. Kenyatta plays piano and synthesizers, composed all but one story. With Walt Szymanski (tpt), Bob Allison (vib), Vincent Bowens (sax), Shahid & Tabbal (rhythm).

BARNEY KESSEL   b 1923

Bop, post-bop, cool. Influential jazz guitarist. Kessel picked up the torch from Charlie Christian and became a major presence on the electric guitar by the mid 40s. Prior to Kessel, most jazz guitarists had specialized in either single-string or chord-melody solos. Kessel became a complete jazz guitarist by incorporating both approaches into his aggressive, hard-swinging, bluesy style. As a sideman, Kessel gained a reputation through his work with Artie Shaw's Gramercy Five, the Oscar Petersen Trio, and with Charlie Parker, among others. His 50s albums with bassist Ray Brown and drummer Shelly Manne put the guitar trio format on the map, revealing the electric guitar as a fully-formed jazz voice. −RL

Easy Like / OJC   1953
Fluid, superbly played standards. A nice tribute cut to Charlie Christian. CD has two bonus cuts. −RW

Kessel Plays Standards / OJC   1954
Excellent, prototype jazz guitar date. −RW

● **Poll Winners, w/ Ray Brown & Shelly Manne / OJC** 1957
Definitive West Coast jazz virtuosos in an absolutely perfect setting. −MGN

Let's Cook / CONTEMPORARY   1957
A good reissue of prime cuts originally on a 10-inch album. Two cuts with Ben Webster (ts). −RW

Kessel Plays Carmen / OJC   1958
A good 1987 reissue with an interesting concept. −RW

○ **Poll Winners Ride Again / OJC**   1958
Super playing, familiar material. −RW

○ **Some Like It Hot / OJC**   1959
First-rate, with excellent solos by Art Pepper (as). −RW

Exploring the Scene / CONTEMPORARY   1960
Includes Ornette's "The Blessing." With Ray Brown (b) and Shelly Manne (d). −MGN

Guitar Workshop / SABA   1967
Live at the Berlin Festival. Stunning cuts, some with Jim Hall (g). −RW

Blue Soul / BLACK LION   1967
Outstanding guitar in a trio context. −RW

Reflections in Rome / RCA (ITALY)   1969
Kessel plays 12-string and electric guitar. −RW

Feeling Free / OJC   1969
Fine, vintage Kessel treatments. −RW

Barney Plays Kessel / CONCORD   1975
A good, career-summation, retrospective vehicle. −RW

☆ **Straight Ahead / CONTEMPORARY**   1975
W/ Shelly Manne (d) and Ray Brown (b). −JME

Poor Butterfly / CONCORD   1976
Fine playing but a low energy level. −RW

Soaring / CONCORD   1976
Jake Hanna (d) lays down a nice foundation. −RW

Jellybeans / CONCORD   1981
Supple solos and straightforward accompaniment. −RW

Solo / CONCORD   1981
Superb — some of Kessel's best playing in the 80s. −RW

To Swing or Not to Swing / OJC   r 1984
High-caliber interpretations. −RW

Spontaneous Combustion / CONTEMPORARY   1987
Excellent piano from Monty Alexander. −RW

○ **Red White & Hot / CONTEMPORARY**
With Bobby Hutcherson (vib) and the Kenny Barron trio. Three original tunes. −MGN

Artistry of Barney Kessel / FANTASY   COMP
A recent compilation available only on CD. A good starter set. −RW

STEVE KHAN   ♭1947

Jazz-rock, neo bop. Steve Khan is a well-known session guitarist who has amassed a large number of credits doing mainly fusion-style material, though he's a good straightahead jazz player. He has been ranked alongside Cornell Dupree and Eric Gale as the most versatile studio players but doesn't have the blues facility of the other two. He has made some records as a leader, but has done better as accompanist to a host of pop/R&B big names, among them

Sheila Jordon, Chaka Khan, Bob James, and Grover Washington Jr. −RW

Evidence / NOVUS   1970
A 1990 reissue of a fusion/jazz-rock set. −RW

Casa Loco / POLYGRAM   1983
○ **Let's Call This / RHINO**
Monk's music done solidly by electric guitarist and a trio. −MGN

ANDY KIRK   ♭1898

Big band. Born in Denver, Kirk led a great Midwestern territorial big band in the 30s, mostly around Kansas City. Pianist Mary Lou Williams was his main soloist and arranger. The band spawned Don Byas, Fats Navarro, and Howard McGhee, among others. −MGN

○ **1944 / HINDSIGHT**
A Mellow Bit of Rhythm / RCA VICTOR   i 1957
W/ Al Cohn (ts) and Ernie Royal (tpt). −ED

RAHSAAN ROLAND KIRK   1936-1977

Post-bop, soul jazz, early free, progressive big band. His incredible musicianship, vibrant onstage personality, and fondness for creating sometimes-outlandish instruments led some in the jazz world to mistakenly downplay Rahsaan Roland Kirk's immense skills. But Kirk was an amazing improviser, a musician completely knowledgeable of the entire jazz spectrum, and a cultural advocate who was displeased that both he and the music he loved were often viewed with disdain or ignored. He could swing, play fiercely or with serenity, handle blues, bop, or free, interpret the anthems, or make up his own songs and lyrics on demand. Kirk was blinded shortly after birth and studied at the Ohio State School for the Blind. He was playing sax and clarinet at 12 and was heading his own dance band in 1951, while doing freelance work with other groups as well. He began his technique of playing three instruments at once at 16, going into a music store and finding two long-forgotten saxophones that had been used in turn-of-the-century Spanish marching bands: the manzello and the stritch. He found a way to play these two plus the tenor at the same time, and generated some unforgettable moments on record and in concert over the years. Kirk was also a master of circular breathing, a means of holding notes and sustaining them while still finding a way to breathe. Kirk's 1956 debut release didn't get much attention, but when Ramsey Lewis got him a date with the Cadet label, detractors dismissed him as a showman and charlatan. In 1961 he played on the Mingus album *Oh Yeah*, obliterating much of the early criticism. He toured with Mingus as well, going with his band to Europe and appearing at a festival in West Germany. From 1963 until his death, Kirk headed his own bands and was never unwilling to buck the odds or sound off in print or on television about the plight of jazz and African-American musicians. −RW

Early Roots / BETHLEHEM / DB 5   1956
Vital formative cuts. −RW

Introducing Roland Kirk / MCA   1960
A taste of what would come, with Ira Sullivan (tpt). −MGN

Kirk's Work / OJC   1961
THis is a fine reissue of Kirk in a soul-jazz and mainstream vein. −RW

○ **We Free Kings / POLYGRAM**   1961
The date that helped establish Kirk's reputation. −RW

Reeds and Deeds / MERCURY   1963
A great title and wonderful playing. −RW

I Talk to the Spirits / LIMELIGHT   1964
Entrancing flute solos. −RW

Rip, Rig & Panic/Now Please Don't ... / EMARCY   1965
1965 & 1967. Also: *Now Please Don't You Cry, Beautiful Edith.* A couple of Kirk's more popular 60s albums combined. −RW

Inflated Tear / ATLANTIC   1967
Beautiful solos. −RW

Left and Right / ATLANTIC   1968
Large orchestra and string works. −RW

○ **Volunteered Slavery / ATLANTIC / DB 5**   1968
The title cut became the Black nationalist jazz anthem. −RW

○ **Rahsaan/Rahsaan / ATLANTIC**   1970
The beginning of a new phase in Kirk's career. −RW

National Black Inventions / ATLANTIC   1971
Tour de force for his instrumental inventions. −RW

Blacknuss / ATLANTIC   1971
Kirk's most effective socio-political jazz date. −RW

Prepare Thyself to Deal ... / ATLANTIC / DB 5 1972
Prepare Thyself to Deal with a Miracle. Some intriguing solos
and raps. −RW

A Meeting of the Times / ATLANTIC   1972
Great vocals by Al Hibbler. −RW

★ **Bright Moments / ATLANTIC**   1973
Definitive, live club date on a 2-fer from Keystone Korner.
Desert island music, with Rahn Burton on piano and Robert
Sky on drums. Lots of Kirk talk. −MGN

Case of the 3-Sided Dream / ATLANTIC / DB 5   1975
Inspired concept, with fine playing throughout. −RW

Kirkatron / WARNER   1976
Nearing the end. Still some vital cuts. −RW

Man Who Cried Fire / ATLANTIC   197?
This is an interesting collection of live, previously unissued,
material. −RW

☆ **Rahsaan — Complete on Mercury / POLYGRAM**   COMP
Definitive. Expensive, but worth it. −MGN

● **The Vibration Continues / ATLANTIC**   COMP
This is a compilation from 1968-1974. Excellent introduction
to a virtuoso. −MGN

KENNY KIRKLAND   b 1955

Post-bop, neo bop, M-base. Though he's not as widely known
or lavishly praised as some other 80s stars, pianist Kenny
Kirkland deserves just as much attention and critical acclaim
for his slashing, stirring playing. Kirkland, who began piano
lessons at six and studied classical piano performance and
theory at the Manhattan School of Music, made his first
impact as a member of violinist Michael Urbaniak's group in
the late 70s in Europe and Scandinavia. In 1979-1981, he
worked with Angela Bofill, Don Alias, and Terumasa Hino,
and he met Wynton Marsalis in 1981 when Marsalis was
touring Japan. That began an association that saw him
featured on several Marsalis albums in the 80s. −RW

○ **Kenny Kirkland / GRP**   r 1991
This is a good set with Afro-Latin and hard-bop influences
mixed. −RW

EIJI KITAMURA   b 1929

Swing. Japanese clarinetist who led swing-styled ensembles
from the 50s to the present. Benny Goodman-Woody Herman
influenced. −MGN

○ **Seven Stars / CONCORD**   1981
Mainstream date w/ nice vocals by Ernestine Anderson. −RW

Swing Eiji / CONCORD   r 1981
Nice swing cuts. −RW

JOHN KLEMMER   b 1946

Early free, jazz-rock, instr-pop. A saxophonist who has seemed
on the verge of stardom since the early 70s, Klemmer has
never been able to make the definitive album that would
establish his credibility. Very much influenced by Coltrane in
his early years, Klemmer experimented with the echoplex on
some Impulse 70s recordings. The mid-70s release
"Waterfalls" remains his finest work. −RW

○ **Waterfalls / MCA / DB 5**   r 1973
A stunning, explosive date. By far his best material. −RW

Touch / MOBILE FIDELITY / BB 90   r 1976
Better solos and higher energy level than most of Klemmer's
albums. This is the best-sounding version. −RW

ERIC KLOSS   b 1949

Bop, hard-bop, post-bop, neo bop. A blind alto saxophonist with
an exuberant, intense style and biting tone. He's never been a
superstar but has made some arresting records for
independent labels, particularly Muse. −RW

One, Two, Free / MUSE   1972

● **Battle of the Saxes / MUSE**   1976

○ **Celebration / MUSE**   1979

EARL KLUGH   b 1954

Jazz-rock, new-age, instr-pop, neo bop, contemporary funk. Self-
taught guitarist Earl Klugh claims to have been inspired by
Chet Atkins, George Van Eps, and Laurindo Almeida and was
recording with Yusef Lateef at the age of 15. He worked with
George Benson and Chick Corea's Return To Forever, and was
selected by George Shearing for one of his famous tours.
Klugh plays acoustic nylon-stringed guitar, and has resisted
efforts to go electric. Although not strictly jazz, almost all of
his albums have found commercial success in the pop-
instrumental market. He is noted for his deft solos and subtle
phrasing. −JME

Finger Paintings / CAPITOL
An nice-sounding electronic/contemporary date reissued on
CD. −RW

Key Notes / CAPITOL
The greatest hits of his first fusion period. −RW

Living Inside Your Love / CAPITOL
He scored an adult contemporary hit with the title cut, which
was popular on urban stations. −RW

○ **Earl Klugh / CAPITOL**   1976
The session that portended his light-touch, fusion-pop
approach. −RW

Soda Fountain Shuffle / WARNER   1985
Synthesizer, drum machine backgrounds. Easy-listening
programmed light jazz with a touch of space music. One of his
most popular. −JME

Solo Guitar / WARNER   1989
Nice guitar work, minus the fusion touches. Stretches of
impressive technique. −RW

Whispers & Promises / WARNER   1989
Standard fusion. Pleasant, lightweight material. −RW

● **Trio - Vol. 1 / WARNER**

JIMMY KNEPPER   b 1927

Bop, hard-bop, post-bop, progressive big band. Among the rare
trombonists able to forge a direction blending elements of
both modern and vintage jazz, Jimmy Knepper has combined
a fluid, rapid-pace technique with the slurs, growls, and
smears of so-called "tailgate" players. Knepper began playing
professionally in the 40s with a band co-led by Dean Benedetti
and Chuck Cascales. He toured with Freddie Slack in 1947 and
alto saxophonist Johnny Bothwell in 1948, then worked in Roy
Porter's band alongside Eric Dolphy in 1948-1949. He worked
in other big bands in the 50s before relocating to New York,
where he replaced Willie Dennis in Charles Mingus's Jazz
Workshop band in 1957-1958. Knepper had a lengthy but
often turbulent relationship with Mingus, working with him
in the late 50s and early 60s, then reuniting with him in 1976
and 1977. Knepper became a member of the Thad Jones-Mel
Lewis big band in 1967 and remained with them until 1973,
then joined Lee Konitz's nonet from 1975-1979. He's been
involved with the Mingus Dynasty as both a player and
musical director since 1979 and has also issued recordings as
a leader on various independent labels. −RW

● **Idol of the Flies / BETHLEHEM**   1957
Arguably Knepper's best record as a leader. Great drums by
Dannie Richmond. −RW

○ **Pepper-Knepper Quintet / MGM** · 1958
A smooth, humorous, and mellow meeting with Pepper Adams (bar sax). −RW

○ **Cunningbird / STEEPLECHASE** · 1976
Quintet w/ Al Cohn (ts), Sir Roland Hanna (p), George Mraz (b), Dannie Richmond (d). A tremendous date. −RW

Jimmy Knepper in L.A. / INNER CITY · 1977
A well-played session. −RW

I Dream Too Much / SOUL NOTE · 1984
W/ John Clark (french horn), John Eckert (tpt). All brass front line. Includes three Knepper compositions, 2 standards, 1 by Hanna. −MGN

LEE KONITZ · b 1927

Bop, post-bop, cool, early free. Born in Chicago, young Lee there met the unique and Svengali-like pianist teacher Lennie Tristano, with whom he studied. He made his recording debut with Claude Thornhill's band (featured on Gil Evans's bop arrangements) and participated in the famous *Birth of the Cool* sessions. During these activities, he also worked with Tristano's groups, notably the sextet including tenorist Warne Marsh, with whom he fashioned unique, sinuous lines in unison and counterpoint. Tristano also pioneered a kind of aleatory group improvisation (*Intuition*, 1949). On his own early recording dates, Konitz used Miles Davis and played music by George Russell.
From 1952 to 1954, Konitz toured with Stan Kenton's band, in which he was a very effective voice, then led his own groups, also working with Gerry Mulligan and Gil Evans. Unlike most altoists of his generation, Konitz did not attempt to play like Charlie Parker (whom he admired) but fashioned his own unique style, rooted in a firm belief in improvisation. From the 60s on, Konitz spent much time in Europe, also in Japan, and made many records in a wide variety of playing situations, from duets to his own nonet. In 1992 he was awarded the prestigious Danish Jazzpar prize, and he continues to fearlessly explore the musical horizon. −DM

Subconscious-Lee / OJC · 1949
1949-1950. Intriguing material with oracle Lennie Tristano (p), plus Warne Marsh (ts). −RW

● **Inside Hi-Fi / ATLANTIC** · 1956
This is among Konitz's first classic album statements. −RW

Lee Konitz Meets Jimmy Giuffre / VERVE · 1959
Two distinctive stylists make an effective team. −RW

○ **Motion / VERVE** · 1961
5 standards played with non-standard passion. W/ Elvin Jones (d), Sonny Dallas (b). −MGN

Modern Jazz Compositions from Haiti / GRP · 1966
About as unorthodox as it gets. −RW

Duets / MILESTONE / DB 5 · 1967
Tour de force with Konitz playing multiple saxes and occasional electric alto. −RW

Lee Konitz Duets / OJC · 1967

○ **Altissimo / PHILLIPS (JAPAN)** · 1973
A great four-alto summit meeting. −RW

Alto Summit / POLYGRAM / DB 5 · r 1973
Swinging alto jam session/blowing date theatrics. −RW

I Concentrate on You / STEEPLECHASE · 1974
A nice duo with Red Mitchell (b). −RW

Satori / MILESTONE · 1974
Exemplary solos and compositions. −RW

Windows / STEEPLECHASE · 1975
Another good duo, this time with Hal Galper (p). −RW

Lee Konitz Meets Warne Marsh Again / PA-USA · 1976
The once and future duo reunite. −RW

Lee Konitz Quintet / VERVE · 1977
Both tough and introspective compositions. −RW

Lee Konitz Nonet / CHIAROSCURO / DB 5 · 1977
Super concept, lineup, and execution. −RW

Live at Laren / SOUL NOTE · 1979
1979 version of his nonet. Extended examples of Corea's "Matrix" and "Times Lie." −MGN

○ **Seasons Change / CIRCLE** · 1979
W/ vibist Karl Berger. −MGN

Idea Scene / SOUL NOTE · ca. 1986
Latter-day Konitz can still play with fire. −RW

○ **Konitz Meets Mulligan / BLUE NOTE**
A simply wonderful pairing of idiosyncratic talents. −RW

Ezz-Thetic / PRESTIGE · COMP

WAYNE KRANTZ

M-base. Fiery fusion guitarist. Krantz is an excellent multi-dimensional player, as likely to rock like Hendrix, or play duets with Leni Stern. −MGN

○ **Signals / RHINO** · 1990

ERNIE KRIVDA · b 1945

Bop, hard-bop, post-bop, neo bop. This powerhouse tenor saxophonist from Cleveland has a post-Coltrane, unique approach and is an inexhaustable soloist. −MGN

The Glory Strut / INNER CITY · 1979
Original music from Cleveland's innovative, relentless post-Coltrane disciple. Pretty melodies forcefully maneuvered. A solid album. −MGN

○ **Tough Tenor, Red Hot / CADENCE** · 1985
Live date at Cleveland State University. Originals and standards from this brilliant tenor saxophonist. −MGN

KARIN KROG · b 1937

Ballads. This Norwegian vocalist, who has been featured with Archie Shepp and Dexter Gordon, sings words and wordless, other worldly, material. −MGN

○ **Hi-Fly / COMPENDIUM-FIDARDO**
A recording of this most unique vocalist with Archie Shepp (sax). All standards interpreted innovatively. −MGN

GENE KRUPA · 1909-1973

Swing, big band. One of the great swing era drummers, Krupa came to prominence with Benny Goodman (1935-1938), playing in the big band as well as trios and quartets from within the band. His flashy solo style focused attention on the drummer for the first time. Krupa led his big band off and on from 1938-1951, and his own combos after that. He was often featured on *Jazz at the Philharmonic*. His 30s and 40s big-band recordings reveal an exciting, thoroughly musical organization at all times. Early stars included Sam Donahue, Roy Eldridge, and vocalist Anita O'Day, while his mid-40s band gave major exposure to Red Rodney, Charlie Ventura, and arranger Gerry Mulligan. Columbias are mostly very good while the RCAs (1950-1951) should be avoided. Small groups for Mercury/Clef, beginning in 1952, are fine until the late 50s when the quality of the soloists begins to drop off. A reunion with Ventura from 1964 is an exception. Several studio big-band projects for Verve (1956-1961) of which *Drummin' Man* and *Plays Gerry Mulligan Arrangements* are recommended. −BP

○ **Drummer Man / POLYGRAM** · 1956
Big-band remakes from 1956 of Krupa favorites of the 40s. Brilliant hi-fidelity and splendid Quincy Jones arrangements, plus wonderful playing by Roy Eldridge and singing by Anita O'Day. Highly recommended. −BP

Gene Krupa Story (Soundtrack) / VERVE · i 1959
W/ Benny Carter (as) −ED

Gene Krupa and Buddy Rich / POLYGRAM · ?zz
Studio recordings from each drummer with several joint appearances. The small-group titles are better than the big-band selections, featuring as they do the likes of horn giants Flip Phillips, Illinois Jacquet, Dizzy Gillespie, and Roy Eldridge. −BP

Drum Battle - Jazz at the Philharmonic / POLYGRAM
Jazz at the Philharmonic appearances by various performers (together on the title track), with emphasis on drum solos. Certain to excite drum fanatics. –BP

MARTY KRYSTALL

Post-bop, neo bop, modern creative. This progressive saxophonist has an approach similar to Monk's angularity. He takes Coltrane's teachings a step ahead. –MGN

○ **Ready for the 1990s / K2B2**   1980
1980 release with this progressive-edge saxophonist leading the way. Very well-done music for special tastes. Featuring Buell Neidlinger (b), Cecil Taylor (p) and Warren Gale. –MGN

Our Night Together / K2B2   1981
Very potent music. Easy to enjoy. –MGN

JOACHIM KUHN   b 1944

Jazz-rock, neo bop, modern creative. German-born progressive jazz pianist. Brother is clarinetist Rolf. Quirky melodic player, along the lines of Thelonious Monk. Usually heard with a trio. Had done fusion in the 70s. –MGN

○ **From Time to Time Free / CMP**   1988
Has intense improvisations from the German veteran pianist. Kuhn evokes images of Monk, Nichols, Taylor, and Tyner. J. F. Jenny Clarke is on bass, Daniel Humair on drums. This trio knows each other well. Standouts are "Spy vs. Spy" and "Para." Also a nice version of Coltrane's "India." –MGN

Live 1989 / CMP   1989
Here's more of the same from the trio on *From Time to Time Free.* Only one repeat ('Para') from the studio date. Recorded live in Paris, this album includes two standards and four Kuhn originals. –MGN

ROLF KUHN   b 1929

Post-bop, jazz-rock, neo bop. This marvelous clarinetist from Europe is equally comfortable in mainstream, fusion, or creative modes. –MGN

○ **As Time Goes By / BLUE FLAME**

STEVE KUHN   b 1938

Post-bop, cool, early free, neo bop. Steve Kuhn often gets more attention for being one of the pianists to precede McCoy Tyner in John Coltrane's group than for his own fine playing and writing abilities. Kuhn began taking lessons at five, and by 1959 he was accomplished enough to earn stints with Coltrane, Kenny Dorham, and Stan Getz. He was a member of the Art Farmer Quartet from 1964-1966. Kuhn moved to Sweden in 1967, living there until 1971 and heading his trio throughout Europe from his Stockhom base. He returned to New York that year, heading a quartet and since then recording and touring frequently, appearing at festivals throughout America and Europe. –RW

○ **Playground / ECM**   ca. 1979
With Sheila Jordan (v), Harvie Swartz (b), Bob Moses (d). Intense group interplay with Jordan's deep tones. Very emotional music, especially "The Zoo" and "Deep Tango." A record for the ages. –MGN

Last Year's Waltz / ECM   1981
Live at Fat Tuesday's in New York City. "Turn To Gold" an absolute tearjerker. –MGN

Life's Magic / BLACKHAWK   ca. 1986
Live at New York City's Village Vanguard. With Ron Carter (b), Al Foster (d). Four Kuhn originals, three standards. Pristine quality of Kuhn's playing shines. –MGN

Easy to Read / RHINO
Fine playing all around. Material varies in quality. –RW

Looking Back / CONCORD
Superior playing and meager compositions. CD version has two bonus cuts. –RW

Oceans in the Sky / OWL

Excellent piano solos, but otherwise routine. –RW

STEVE KUJALA

Jazz-rock, new-age, neo bop. An atmospheric flutist in a contemporary, fusion, and new-age mode, and an adept composer whose best work is in the future. –MGN

○ **Fresh Flute / COLUMBIA**

SERGEI KURIOKHIN

Modern creative. Flighty, free-spirited pianist and percussionist whose "noise with toys" approach brands him a revolutionary. –MGN

○ **Popular Science / RYK 20118**   r 1989
Russian pianist with American guitarist Henry Kaiser in free improvised mode. Expect the unexpected. –MGN

CHARLES KYNARD   b 1933

Soul jazz. Organ, electric bass. Kynard is an organist whose jazz-funk leanings rival his predecessors and peers, though not eclipsing them. Solid, though never flashy. He also plays electric bass. –MGN

● **Charles Kynard / WORLD PACIFIC**   1964
Kynard's best combo effort. Shows him in a more favorable light as a soul-jazz proprietor. –MGN

○ **Reelin' with the Feelin' / PRESTIGE**   1969

L.A. FOUR

Cool. A group composed of Laurendo Almeida (g), Ray Brown (b), Shelly Manne (d), and Bud Shank (sax/fl), which functions as a vehicle for the neo-classical/swing ideas of the four. –MGN

○ **L.A. Four / CONCORD**   ca. 1975
A solid effort by jazz veterans Bud Shank (sax, fl), Laurindo Almeida (g), Ray Brown (b), and Jeff Hamilton (d). An interesting mix of West Coast jazz and Latin beats. –DS

Live at Montreux / CONCORD   1979
There's a little more fire than usual in this date. –RW

Executive Suite / CONCORD   1982
An accomplished ensemble that seldom excites, but never fails to play with technical excellence. –RW

PETE LA ROCA   b 1938

Hard-bop, post-bop. A New York jazz drummer whose staggering technique made him in demand in the 50s. La Roca played w/ Sonny Rollins, Tony Scott, Jackie McLean, Slide Hampton, and Chick Corea. He is now a lawyer. –MGN

○ **Basra / BLUE NOTE**   i 1965
W/ Joe Henderson (ts).

STEVE LACY   b 1934

Post-bop, early free, modern creative. Other than Sidney Bechet and arguably Wayne Shorter and John Coltrane, no musician has been more singlehandedly identified with the soprano sax than Steve Lacy. Though he began on piano and later played clarinet, Lacy's squeaks, tortured lines, squiggly solos, and vocal effects have been a jazz delight since the late 50s. He also went from one extreme to another, getting his initial inspiration from traditional jazz but ultimately turning into a champion of spontaneous improvisation. Lacy studied with Cecil Scott and attended both the Schillinger School of Music (now Berklee) and the Manhattan School of Music. After his early immersion into vintage New Orleans music, Lacy began working and playing with Cecil Taylor, a shift that took him to the far reaches of composition and playing. Lacy worked for a while in the late 50s with Gil Evans, Mal Waldron, and Jimmy Giuffre and began studying the works of Thelonious Monk. He spent four months in Monk's quartet in 1960, then formed his own group with trombonist Roswell Rudd and drummer Dennis Charles, playing almost exclusively Monk material. Lacy left that group in 1965, working in Denmark with pianist

Kenny Drew, then formed a group in Italy with trumpeter Enrico Rava and toured South America. He subsequently returned to New York and started another group, though Rava remained a member. Finally in 1967, Lacy returned to Europe to live with his wife, Irene Aebi. He spent three years in Rome, studying electronics extensively and sound. He moved to Paris in 1970 and two years later started giving solo soprano sax recitals. Throughout the 70s and 80s, he worked with some of Europe's most individualistic players, such as guitarist Derek Bailey and saxophonist Steve Potts. –RW

The Complete Steve Lacy / FRESCO   1954
2-fer of "progressive" Dixieland with Dick Sutton sextet. Lacy on soprano and clarinet. Interesting, considering where Lacy's music was headed. –MGN

○ **Soprano Saxophone / OJC**   1957
A brilliant set. Lacy stakes out his claim as king of soprano sax, years before Coltrane popularizes it. –RW

☆ **Reflections: Plays Thelonious / OJC**   1958
Includes some wonderful interpretations. An always-vibrant improviser. –RW

☆ **Straight Horn of Steve Lacy / CANDID**   ca. 1960
Wonderful cuts, marvelous solos. –RW

○ **Evidence / NEW JAZZ-PRESTIGE**   1961
Quartet with Don Cherry (cnt). Transitional period, eschewing echoes of Monk, Ellington, and Cecil Taylor. A pivotal recording and an important document. –MGN

School Days / EMANEM   1963
Rough, skittery, and inspired. –RW

Saxophone Special / EMANEM   1974
This is a chaotic meeting. Some of Europe's best avant-gardists. –RW

Trickles / BLACK SAINT   1976
The reunion with trombonist Roswell Rudd. –RW

Raps / ADELPHI   1977
This is a quirky, explosive date with co-conspirator Steve Potts (as). –RW

Troubles / BLACK SAINT   1979
Lacy and Steve Potts (as) at their best and most frenetic. –RW

● **Regeneration / SOULNOTE**   ca. 1982
The consensus album of the year in 1983, it includes one side of Monk and the other by Herbie Nichols's music. Includes Roswell Rudd (tb), Misha Mengleberg (p), Kent Carter (b), and Hans Bennik (d). –MGN

Change of Season / SOULNOTE   1984
This is the followup to *Regeneration*, this features George Lewis (tb) and Anjen Garter (b). All material by Herbie Nichols. –MGN

The Condor / SOUL NOTE   1985
A good sextet date. –RW

One Fell Swoop / SILK   1986
An overlooked quartet romp with Charles Tyler (sax). –RW

Forest & the Zoo / ESP-DIS   1986
The Gleam / SILKLEAF   1986
Another good sextet date. –RW

○ **Momentum / RCA-NOVUS**   1987
Lacy has put out several hundred albums. This, with a sextet, is not only his most accessible, but contains his best group playing. Highly recommended. –MGN

Only Monk / SOUL NOTE   1987
Lacy mines Monk's lode with a vengeance. –RW

The Door / NOVUS   1988
Taut duo and trio cuts. Two bonus tracks on CD. –RW

Hot House / NOVUS   1990
A 1991 reissue of some fine duets. –RW

Anthem / NOVUS   r 1990
Some of Lacy's most recent material. The playing equals his past standards. –RW

○ **Live at Sweet Basil / NOVUS**   ca. 1991

Recorded live in a New York club with a sextet. Includes many familiar themes. –MGN

BIRELI LAGRENE   b 1966

Jazz-rock, new-age, neo bop. Gypsy guitarist leans toward fusion and rock more than jazz, but capable of all three. Unquestioned technical ability. –MGN

○ **Foreign Affairs / CAPITOL**   r 1989
Some excellent solos and better songwriting than usual. CD has two bonus cuts. –RW

RICK LAIRD   b 1941

Post-bop, jazz-rock. This electric bassist who played with the Mahavishnu of the 70s is a well-traveled sideman. He is also an exceptional professional photographer. –MGN

○ **Soft Focus / TIMELESS**   1976
From ex-Mahavishnu bassist and featuring Joe Henderson (sax). Lively, creative, and intriguing mix of standards and originals. –MGN

OLIVER LAKE   b 1944

Early free, neo bop, contemporary funk, M-base, modern creative. Alto sax, soprano sax, flute, synthesizer. A founding member of the Black Artists Group (BAG), a St. Louis ensemble similar in scope to the Chicago-based AACM, Lake has always found a way to combine bop, free, funk, and blues influences into a coherent, seamless sax and compositional style. He has worked in bands like Jump Up, which have pronounced rhythmic pieces, and the adventurous World Saxophone Quartet. An explosive, spirited saxophonist, fully knowledgeable in bop and hard-bop, Lake is able to go outside easily, then return and play standards with authority. –RW

Heavy Spirits / ARISTA-FREEDOM   1975
Bubbling, soaring solos and engaging compositions. –RW

Holding Together / BLACK SAINT   1976
Driving solos, surging pieces. –RW

○ **Shine / ARISTA-NOVUS**   1978
One side neo-classical w/ strings. Hauntingly beautiful. –MGN

Clevont Fitzhubert / BLACK SAINT   1981
Animated, aggressive, and vital. –RW

Jump Up / GRAMAVISION   1981
Lake steps back to dance music with mixed results. –RW

○ **Expandable Language / BLACK SAINT**   1984
Ranges from powerful to thoughtful. –RW

● **Gallery / GRAMAVISION**   1986
This quartet recording features pianist Geri Allen. An A+ album of angular saxophony. The cover artwork is as fascinating as the music. –MGN

LAMBERT HENDRICKS & ROSS

Bop, ballads. The finest jazz vocal trio of the late 50s, early 60s, consisting of Jon Hendricks, Dave Lambert, and Annie Ross. For seven years they were sensations, improvising vocally and harmonizing on lyrics to solos written by Hendricks. Their version of "Four Brothers" stands as a jazz singing anthem. –RW

☆ **Sing a Song of Basie / ABC**   1957
Arguably the best and most influential of the Lambert, Hendricks & Ross recordings. Hendricks writes lyrics for strings and solos. –RW

Everybody's Boppin' / CBS   1959
1959, 1960, & 1961. Excellent, stylish harmonies. –RW

○ **The Swingers / CAPITOL**   i 1959
First-rate stuff. –RW

● **Lambert, Hendricks, and Ross / COLUMBIA**   1960
The prototype Lambert, Hendricks & Ross effort. –RW

Sings Ellington / COL.SPEC. PROD   r 1960
Swingin' Till the Girls Come Home / RCA   1962
1962 & 1963. Erratic, with some great stuff. –RW

○ **High Flyin' with ... / COLUMBIA**   r 1962
Very nice set. –RW
○ **Best Of / CBS**   COMP
Excellent compilation. –MGN

BYARD LANCASTER   b 1942

Early free, modern creative. This Philadelphia progressive saxophonist and flutist has been living in Jamaica as of late. He has a powerful voice on his instruments. –MGN
○ **It's Not up to Us / VORTEX**   1968
A rare recording. Two standards, six originals. –MGN

HAROLD LAND   b 1928

Hard-bop, post-bop. A steady, always invigorating player, Harold Land has been a jazz mainstay since 1949 when he made his first recording. Land moved to Los Angeles in 1954 and for a time was part of the landmark Max Roach-Clfford Brown Quartet, though he had the misfortune of leaving before the band became a sensation (he was replaced by Sonny Rollins). He was part of Curtis Counce's group from 1956-1958 and also played with Gerald Wilson and Shorty Rogers's group, before co-founding a band with bassist Red Mitchell in 1961-1962. There were sessions with Wes Montgomery and Kenny Dorham and dates of his own in the 60s, but the group that did get Land some overdue recognition was one he co-led with vibist Bobby Hutcherson from 1969-1971. It was among the finest small combos of the period and served to introduce his son Harold Land Jr on piano. Land reunited with Hutcherson in 1983 for a European tour. –RW

Harold in the Land of Jazz / OJC   1958
Steady and entertaining, if predictable. –RW
● **The Fox / OJC / DB 5**   1959
This is one of Land's best. While Elmo Hope (p) swings, Land is bluesy and emphatic. –RW
Grooveyard / CONTEMPORARY   i 1959
West Coast Blues! / OJC   1960
Recorded with Wes Montgomery (g), this is another of many excellent Land albums. –MGN
Eastward Ho! / OJC   1960
An exemplary date, w/ Kenny Dorham (tpt) in top form. –RW
○ **Mapenzi / CONCORD**   1977
W/ Kirk Lightsey (p), Blue Mitchell (tpt). Near essential album. –MGN
Xocia's Dance (Sue-Sha's Dance) / MUSE   1981
Damisi / MAINSTREAM
An excellent date with a touch of funk. Listen to the elegant "Pakistan." –MGN

ART LANDE   b 1958

Post-bop, new-age, neo bop. Lande is a pianist who plays originals, standards, and modern modal or improvisational music. A truly complete musician who rivals any of the masters. –MGN
○ **Rubisa Patrol / ECM**   ca. 1976
Some stunning compositions, four by Lande. "Corinthian Melodies" is a thing of beauty! Trumpeter Mark Isham and Lande w/ quartet. Contemporary improvised music with relaxed, well-paced programming. –MGN
Desert Maranders / ECM   ca. 1977
The group's second album. W/ Bill Douglass (b/fl), and Kurt Wortman (d). This is solid, improvising music; a touch laid back. –MGN
We Begin / ECM   ca. 1987
An album of keyboard and trumpet duets, with synthesizers tossed in. –MGN

EDDIE LANG   1902-1933

Swing. If you struggled to learn to play jazz or pop music on guitar in the 20s or early 30s, Eddie Lang was the man you listened to. Lang was an exciting, propulsive rhythm player and a superb, imaginative accompanist with a knowledge of the fingerboard that was unheard of at that time. As a soloist, he was the first to express the era's harmonic and melodic vocabulary on the guitar. During his brief career, Lang recorded with countless vocalists, dance bands, and small jazz combos. He is prominent on many recordings by Bing Crosby, the Boswell Sisters, Red Nichols, and with the Jean Goldkette and Paul Whiteman bands. His most celebrated recordings are his collaborations with violinist Joe Venuti, and a small number of band dates with Bix Beiderbecke and Frankie Trumbauer. One should also hear Lang's duets with Lonnie Johnson. Lang's full, pianistic guitar accompaniments provide the perfect foil for the blues guitarist's fluid solo lines. –RL
○ **Jazz Guitar Virtuoso / YAZOO**   ca. 192?
Lang's solo features, plus duets with guitarists Lonnie Johnson and Carl Kress. To get the complete picture of Lang this recording should be heard in conjunction with the Joe Venuti/Eddie Lang duets (*see* Joe Venuti). –RL

ELLIS LARKINS   b 1923

Swing, bop. The pianist of choice among many vocalists, Ellis Larkins is also an excellent soloist, and he has made some good albums with instrumentalists as well as singers. Larkins studied at Juilliard in the 40s, then worked in many New York clubs before playing with Coleman Hawkins and Dicky Wells. He began to make his mark accompanying Mildred Bailey; he's subsequently worked with Larry Adler, Joe Williams, Ella Fitzgerald, Chris Connor, Ruby Braff, Tony Middleton, and Sylvia Sims, among others. –RW
Blues in the Night / DECCA   i 1951

PRINCE LASHA   b 1929

Early free. Progressive multiple saxophonist; leanings toward Eric Dolphy aesthetic, which he succeded in extending via his group "The Firebirds." –MGN
○ **The Cry / CONTEMPORARY**   i 1963

LAST POETS

Early free, spoken word. A New York group of street poets whose raw, declarative, and nationalist material has been viewed in some quarters as a precursor to rap. The poets' messages were angry, witty, and striking in cadence, presentation, and impact. They also included in their rhymes praises for and tributes to jazz and jazz musicians, especially in the cut "Jazzoetry." Their early 70s debut work and their later albums have been reissued on disc by Celluloid. –RW
○ **Delights of the Garden / DOUGLAS**   1977
Reactionist/revolutionist/humanist poets on fire. Highly recommended. With drummer Bernard Purdie. –MGN
Oh, My People / CELLULOID
Updated sound, same powerful message. –MGN

BILL LASWELL

Jazz-rock, contemporary funk, modern creative. A busy producer and bassist, famous for working with cutting-edge groups like Material, Massacre, and Curlew, Laswell has also played with more on-the-edge musicians like drummer Ronald Shannon Jackson and guitarist Sonny Sharrock. Laswell's productions have typically juggled rock, reggae, and improvisational foundations. He's had the occasional hit like Herbie Hancock's synth-R&B chart topper "Rockit" in 1983. He has also worked with pop stars Mick Jagger, Yoko Ono, and Nona Hendryx. He has been quoted as giving preference to noise in the studio rather than songs or rhythms. –RW
Hear No Evil / ATLANTIC   r 1988
A wonderful producer and bassist whose albums are more rock and instrumental pop than jazz. –RW

YUSEF LATEEF   b 1920

Hard-bop, post-bop, soul jazz, early free, world fusion. Reeds, composer. Before there was something called "worldbeat," Yusef Lateef was experimenting with instruments from China and Africa, playing Indian scales, and integrating jazz with the music of other cultures. Lateef began on alto in high school, then moved to tenor, oboe, and other flutes and began making his own instruments. He played with Lucky Millinder and Dizzy Gillespie in the 40s and began his own group in the mid 50s. He left Detroit for New York in the 60s and worked there with Charles Mingus, Olatunji, and Cannonball Adderley for two years. Lateef was never comfortable with the tag "jazz musician" and was seeking a fuller concept in the early 60s. As a saxophonist, he's basically a prototype hard-blowing, bop-centered soloist; his flute work and his use of oboe, argol, and other more non-Western instruments have been more exciting, with long lines and enticing melodies and vocal effects. –RW

Yusef Lateef Plays for Lovers / PRESTIGE   1957
Four sessions from 1959-1961. –JME

Gong / SAVOY   1957
Quintet of Detroiters, w/ trumpet by Wilbur Harden. –MGN

● **Morning / SAVOY**   1957
This is prime 50s material w/ Curtis Fuller excelling on trombone. –RW

○ **Angel Eyes / SAVOY**   1959
Recorded with pianist Terry Pollard, this is a 2-fer loaded with modern post-bop expression. –MGN

○ **Cry!-Tender / OJC**   1959
First-rate 50s works cover a diversity of jazz standards, European folk, and blues, with Yusef on tenor, flute, and oboe fronting a mid-sized group. –MB

Other Sounds / OJC   1959
These recordings are among his early African/Middle Eastern fusion efforts, with many exotic instruments. –MB

○ **Eastern Sounds / OJC**   1961
This is a 1991 reissue. Important session demonstates Lateef's embrace of new sounds from the international marketplace. –RW

● **Into Something / PRESTIGE**   1961
Lateef at his pre-international best. –RW

A Flat, G Flat & C / IMPULSE / DB 5   r 1966
Mid-60s date with Hugh Lawson Trio. –MGN

○ **The Golden Flute / IMPULSE**   1966
Superb flute playing. –RW

○ **The Blue Yusef Lateef / ATLANTIC**   r 1969
A new reissue of a Lateef gem. –RW

Blues for the Orient / PRESTIGE / DB 5   r 1974
Gentle Giant / ATLANTIC   1974
An overlooked date, with Kenny Barron (p). –RW

In Nigeria / LANDMARK   1983
Lateef's mid-80s comeback features top-notch African musicians and a genuine world-jazz focus. –MB

Nocturnes / ATLANTIC   1989
Introspective. –MB

Meditations / ATLANTIC
More recent and introspective works. –MB

ANDY LAVERNE   b 1947

Progressive big band, jazz-rock, neo bop. Electric and acoustic pianist comfortable with fusion and contemporary jazz. Plays some standards. Reminiscent of Chick Corea. –MGN

○ **Liquid Silver / DMP**   1984

HUBERT LAWS   b 1939

Post-bop, Latin, jazz-rock, instr-pop. Flute, tenor sax. From his beginnings as a member of the Jazz Crusaders at 15, Hubert Laws went full circle as a flutist and tenor saxophonist, gradually becoming the voice of light-classical and Third Stream music. He also played some classical as a teen, but during the 60s was mostly working with Mongo Santamaria, Lena Horne, Sergio Mendes, Benny Golson, Jim Hall, and many others, plus some dates with Gunther Schuller's Orchestra USA. Laws became one of the few Black members of the Metropolitan Orchestra in the 60s and worked with the New York Philharmonic in the early 70s, while also heading his own groups. A dazzling flute player with unlimited range, Laws scored a hit album with *Afro-Classic* in 1973. –RW

○ **Afro Classic / CBS / DB 5**   1970
This is by far the best solo work Laws has on record. He sets the standard for classical-influenced modern jazz. –RW

Rite of Spring / CBS   1971
A good follow-up to *Afro Classic*. –RW

● **Wild Flower / ATLANTIC / DB 5**   r 1973
A nice date from an earlier Laws period with a harder tone and more traditional jazz direction. –RW

San Francisco Concert / CBS   1975
Solid playing, but an otherwise humdrum release, though with occasional moments of glory. –RW

Best of Hubert Laws / CBS   COMP
A debatable title, this culls cuts from his 70s albums. –RW

RONNIE LAWS   b 1950

Instr-pop. Had this tenor sax player come along in the 40s rather than the 60s, he would have gotten a grounding in early R&B rather than fusion and would have had a good career playing it and jazz as well. Instead, he's come along in an era that's seen both R&B and jazz decline in terms of profitability, and thus he's increasingly turned toward more commercially viable material. Laws got his first major fame playing with Earth, Wind & Fire in the 70s and has never really made any substantial noise in jazz circles. Still, he possesses sizable talent, including the big sound traditionally found in Texas tenors. –RW

○ **Pressure Cooker / BLUE NOTE**

JANET LAWSON   b 1940

Post-bop, ballads, neo bop. Intriguing vocalist who creates new nuances that others will not attempt. She can swoop and soar, or sing a straight lyric with her pliant, resounding voice. –MGN

○ **Quartet / INNERCITY**   ca. 1980
Features the same band as *Dreams Can Be.* Tunes are by Fats Waller, Bob Dorough, Thelonious Monk, Blossom Dearie, and Sam Brown. Lawson's creative voice comes through and the band mates are locked in. This is artistry on such a high level that it may take some getting used to. –MGN

Dreams Can Be / OMNI-SOUND   1983
W/ Bill O'Connell (p), Ratso Harris (b), Jimmy Madison (d), and Roger Rosenberg (sax and fl.). Here she does Ellington, Mingus, Dameron, and more.

YANK LAWSON   b 1911

Trad, Dixieland, swing. Another sterling veteran whose roots date back to the 30s, Yank Lawson began playing trumpet as a teenager and played with college bands before joining first Wingy Manone and then Ben Pollack. He left Pollack's band in 1935 after Pollack refused to spotlight Lawson's girlfriend. He came to New York and eventually joined Bob Crosby's band, staying there from 1935-1938. He worked a time with Benny Goodman, then became a staple in the New York studios and clubs from 1942-1968. Ragged lines, marvelous mute technique, and a moving blues and swing feel are always exemplified in Lawson's solos. He helped form the great trad group The World's Greatest Jazz Band in 1968, and his work with comrades such as Bob Haggart or Billy Butterfield had a classic sound, but a modern warmth and appeal. –RW

○ **World's Greatest Jazz Band / ATLANTIC**

LEEANN LEDGERWOOD

Neo bop. Keyboardist (electric and acoustic). Influenced by Monk melodies, tends to try new things, take risks; playful. –MGN

○ **You Wish / TRILOKA**
Debut album from pianist, with husband and flutist Jeremy Steig. Good originals, and more to come. –MGN

JEANNE LEE   *b* 1939

Post-bop, ballads, soul jazz, modern creative. Among the most breathtaking and unpredictable vocal improvisers in jazz history, Lee is best known for upper-register percussive singing with pianist Ran Blake or clarinetist Gunther Hampel. She can do straight singing but is far more provocative and compelling with her array of loops, screams, yells, and other devices. –RW

○ **Legendary Duets / RCA**   1961
It's an appropriate title. A must-buy for creative music listeners. Jeanne Lee does vocals; Ran Blake is on piano. –RW

RANEE LEE

Ballads. Canadian jazz song stylist, influenced by Billie Holiday. –MGN

○ **Deep Song / RHINO**
A nice jazz vocalist still developing a sound. –RW

MICHEL LEGRAND   *b* 1932

Instr-pop. Well-known composer of pop music, works with symphonies, not much connection to jazz, but jazz players appreciate his melodies. –MGN

○ **Legrand Jazz / POLYGRAM / DB 5**   1958
A wonderful reissue of a late-50s album that includes Miles Davis (tpt), John Coltrane (ts), and others. –RW

● **At Shelly's Manne-Holc / POLYGRAM**   r 1969
A good upbeat mainstream session. Legrand shines as an improviser. –RW

Le Jazz Grand / DCC   1978
A surprisingly nice session. –RW

Le Grand Piano / CBS   r 1981
A repackaging of "I Love Pants." –RW

After the Rain / PABLO   1982

Compact Jazz - Michel Legrand / POLYGRAM   COMP
A sampler of Legrand's best jazz tunes. –RW

PETER LEITCH

Post-bop, neo bop. Canadian guitarist, also prominent critic. Stance extends post-bop traditions of Monk, Pat Martino, John Coltrane. Solid improviser. –MGN

Exhilaration / UPTOWN   1984
W/ Pepper Adams (bar sax). Leitch and Thelonious Monk share compositions. Formidable John Hicks Trio as backing. No frills bop and hard, swinging music. –MGN

● **Red Zone / RESERVOIR**   1985
W/ Kirk Lightsey Trio. Two originals, great rendition of Thelonious Monk's "Off Minor." Two by Wayne Shorter. A fine effort by all involved. –MGN

On a Misty Night / CRISS CROSS   1986
W/ trio. Well crafted. –MGN

○ **Mean What You Say / CONCORD**   1990
A nice mainstream date. Very conservative in tone and style. CD version has a bonus cut. –RW

TOM LELLIS

Post-bop, ballads, neo bop. This extraordinary vocalist ranges from Las Vegas showtunes to progressive and political mainstream. He is also a good pianist. –MGN

And in This Corner / INNER CITY   1979
The debut album for this vocalist/pianist, with Jeremy Steig on flute and Ron Busch on vibes. –MGN

○ **Double Entendre / BEAMTIDE**
Extraordinary originality and the mood shifts are stunning. A gem. –MGN

JAY LEONHART   *b* 1940

Swing, bop, neo bop. A bass guitarist in a light jazz, mainstream, and fusion mold, Leonhart has recorded for Sunnyside, Nesak, and DMP. –RW

○ **Salamander Pie / DMP**   1983
A well-played session. –RW

Life Out on the Road / NESAK INTERNATIONAL   1990
A nice set. –RW

MILCHO LEVIEV   *b* 1937

Jazz-rock, neo bop. Afro-Latin, Latin jazz bandleader, composer, arranger, and keyboardist, Leviev currently records for Optimism. –RW

○ **Plays the Music of Irving Berlin / DISCOVERY**   1982

MARK LEVINE   *b* 1938

Post-bop. Keyboardist who can play standards or post-bop with equal skill. His style is hard to pin down, but there is no doubt about his immense talent. –MGN

○ **Smiley & Me / CONCORD**   1985
Pianist Levine with left-handed drummer Smiley Winters. Worth searching for. –MGN

GEORGE LEWIS   1900-1968

Trad, Dixieland. This self-taught clarinetist made a name for himself in the 20s, working with some of the most popular Black bands in New Orleans. Throughout the decade he also performed on the streets of the city with the Eureka Brass Bands. By the early-30s he was with trumpeter Evan Thomas's Band. Later, during the New Orleans revival, Lewis traveled with Bunk Johnson's band to New York. On returning to New Orleans, he formed the George Lewis Ragtime Band with several of Johnson's former sidemen. By 1950 he was considered by many to be the central figure in the "traditional" jazz revival, and over the course of the next two decades he performed successfully on his own and with the Preservation Hall Jazz Band, touring the nation and making several international trips. Lewis was known for his fluent and highly individual style, which could match emotional intensity with lyrical grace and poingancy. Of the clarinetists identified with the New Orleans revival, Lewis's influence has been the most pervasive, inspiring players like Sammy Rimington, Tommy Sancton, and Woody Allen, among others. –BR

○ **With Kid Shots / AMERICAN MUSIC**   ca. 1944
Vintage Lewis in the company of trumpeters "Kid Shots" Madison and Willie "Bunk" Johnson, providing an interesting study in contrast between two masters of home-spun New Orleans music and his ability to adapt to each. –BR

George Lewis of New Orleans / OJC   1946
Some great New Orleans standards from the Original Zenith Brass Band and the Eclipse Alley Five, featuring Lewis in good company — Isidore Barbarin (Paul's father), Peter Bocage, Jim Robinson, Baby Dodds, and others. –BR

★ **At Herbert Otto's Party - 1949 / JAZZOLOGY**   1949
George Lewis at his peak, captured while performing for a private party in New Orleans. Excellent example of "Burgundy Street Blues," his signature piece. –BR

Hot Creole Jazz-1953 / DCC   1953
Outstanding CD reissue. –RW

Oxford Series - Vol. 1 / AMERICAN MUSIC   1954
Concert performances given at Miami University of Oxford, Ohio, which document Lewis in a particularly relaxed and spontaneous mood. –BR

Doctor Jazz / DELMARK   r 1957
Romping, stomping, jovial traditional sessions. –RW

On Parade / DELMARK   r 1958
Super traditional with great trombone solos. −RW
Perennial George Lewis / VERVE   r 1958
Outstanding session. −RW
Jazz in the Classic New Orleans Tradition / OJC   195?
Excellent reissue of tremendous set on Riverside. −RW
Jazz at Preservation Hall / ATLANTIC   1963
First-rate traditional, glittering solos. −RW
Reunion with Don Ewell / DELMARK   1966
Very fine collaboration with Don Ewell (p). −RW
☆ **Complete Blue Note Recordings / MOSAIC**   COMP
A centerpiece for the dedicated New Orleans collector,
beginning with Lewis's "Climax" session in 1943 and ranging
through a variety of studio and concert performances over a
twelve-year period — definitely some of the clarinetist's best
work (1943-1944, 1954-1955). −BR

JOHN LEWIS   b 1920

Bop, cool, early free, progressive big band. Piano, composer,
arranger. John Lewis has been said to be one of the few people
who really understand the similarities between jazz and
classical and who helps bridge gaps between these disciplines.
Lewis was Kenny Clarke's recommendation to replace
Thelonious Monk in Dizzy Gillespie's band in the late 40s.
After the band's demise, Lewis and Clarke stayed in Paris.
Lewis was a steady freelance player and arranger in the late
40s and early 50s, working with Illinois Jacquet, Charlie
Parker, Miles Davis, and Lester Young. The longtime Modern
Jazz Quartet had its beginnings in the Milt Jackson quartet of
the early 50s. The MJQ came in 1954 and was augmented in
1955 when Connie Kay replaced Kenny Clarke. That's been the
main vehicle for Lewis ever since, though he's done film
soundtrack work, been a professor of music at City College
since 1977, and been the cofounder and conductor of the
American Jazz Orchestra since the late 80s. What either
delights or irritates fans about Lewis is the sparseness of his
playing; there's none of the volume, power, or rhythmic
intensity normally associated with jazz. Instead he ambles
along, seeming to prefer subtlety and suggestion to energy or
verve. But some of his compositions (notably "Django") are
legend, and his contrast with Milt Jackson's bluesy, often
funky, vibes make the MJQ sound a jazz staple. −RW
European Encounter / ATLANTIC   1962
A 1986 reissue of a sublime meeting between Lewis and
violinist Svend Asmussen. −RW
Wonderful World of Jazz / ATLANTIC   1969
A 1989 reissue of a fine date. −RW
● **Kansas City Breaks / FINESSE**   1982
Has the interesting instrumentation of a flute, violin, guitar,
and piano trio. All selections are Lewis originals, including
the especially famous "Django," "Milano," and "Sacha's Mardi."
A sweet session. −MGN
Bach Preludes/Fugues / POLYGRAM   1984
Vols. 2 & 3. Sublime playing in a third-stream mold. −RW
Garden of Delight / POLYGRAM   r 1989
Garden Of Delight - Delauney's Dilemma. This is excellent —
both compositions and playing. −RW
○ **The Chess Game - Vols. 1 & 2 / POLYGRAM**
Wonderful technique. More third stream than jazz. −RW
Grand Encounter / CAPITOL
A 1988 reissue of a topflight date. Chamber jazz meets third
stream with Chico Hamilton (d), Jim Hall (g), Percy Heath (b),
and Bill Perkins (sax). −RW
Midnight in Paris / POLYGRAM
A marvelous session. −RW

MEADE LUX LEWIS   1905-1964

Stride, boogie. The greatest boogie-woogie pianist ever. He
and Albert Ammons, the father of Gene Ammons, played

around Chicago in the 20s and sorted out their ideas on a
piano owned by the taxi firm that employed them. The 1928
composition "Honky Tonk Train Blues" eventually was heard
by record producer John Hammond who started looking for
Lewis. Hammond found Ammons, then Lewis, and eventually
hooked these two up with Pete Johnson in the immortal 1938
"Spirituals to Swing Carnegie Hall" concert that made them
international stars. The exciting, pounding boogie style has
never been done with more artistry and craft than by Meade
Lux Lewis. −RW
☆ **Complete Blue Note Recordings / MOSAIC**   1939
W/ Meade Lux Lewis. 1939-1944. A wonderful, comprehensive
compilation of stamping, romping boogie-woogie piano by
the masters. −RW
Cat House Piano / VERVE REISSUE   194?
Smoking solos. −RW
Blues Piano Artistry of Meade Lux Lewis / RIVERSIDE
Immaculate and amazing. −RW

MEL LEWIS   b 1929

Big band, bop, post-bop, progressive big band. The son of a
professional drummer, Mel Lewis was a full-time player at 15.
He did combo work with Frank Rosolino and Hampton Hawes
in the 50s and played in big bands led by Boyd Raeburn and
Stan Kenton in the 40s and 50s. He started his own band in
1958, then worked in the Los Angeles studios during the early
60s, while also touring with Gerry Mulligan, Benny Goodman,
and Dizzy Gillespie. He moved back to his New York
hometown in 1963, and two years later co-formed a band of
top East Coast studio pros with trumpeter Thad Jones. The
Jones-Lewis orchestra began as a once-a-week venture and
became a staple on the jazz scene from 1965 on through the
70s, continuing even after Jones left in 1978. Lewis also did
some session work in the late 70s and 80s, continuing to shine
in his role as the anchor of any situation. A star at spurring
and heading a big band, and very underrated as a soloist and
small group leader. −RW
Greetings and Salutations / BIOGRAPH   1975
Recordings with Swedish Radio Jazz Group. −RW
○ **Suite for Pops / A&M**   ca. 1975
An album of spry, invigorating, and memorable Jones-Lewis
recordings. −RW
● **Mel Lewis & Friends / A&M**   1976
An outstanding combo with top players led by Lewis. −RW
Naturally / TELARC   1979
Topnotch recording with Lewis on the case as leader and
drummer. −RW
Live at Village Vanguard / DCC   1980
A 1991 reissue of prime sessions, with Lewis at the helm of his
longtime big band. High-octane solos and energetic
compositions. −RW
○ **Mel Lewis Plays Herbie Hancock / MPS**   1980
Live at Montreux. A first-rate big-band date. −RW
20 Years at the Village Vanguard / ATLANTIC   1985
A portrait of his orchestra with fresh faces and sounds. −RW
Soft Lights & Hot Music / MUSICMASTERS   1988
Here are some excellent big-band tracks, with fine solos by Joe
Lovano (ts). −RW
Definitive Thad Jones - Vol. 1 & 2 / MUM   1988
The band playing from the book of longtime co-leader Thad
Jones. −RW
● **The Lost Art / MUM / DB 5**   1989
This is the definitive small-group album, with pianist Ken
Werner. −MGN
Central Park North / SOLID STATE
Another big-band showcase. −RW
Consummation / BLUE NOTE
Sprawling, exciting — the orchestra is in prime form. −RW
Live in Munich / A&M
Second notable work on the short-lived Horizon label. −RW

Monday Night / SOLID STATE
Exciting powerhouse performances. –RW
To You: A Tribute to Mel Lewis / MUM
Fine recent big-band tracks. –RW

RAMSEY LEWIS   b 1935

Soul jazz, jazz-rock, instr-pop. Pianist, keyboards, synthesizer, composer. Led one of the most popular instrumental groups of the 50s and 60s, the Ramsey Lewis Trio. Lewis and friends (bassist Eldee Young and drummer Red Holt) had played in teenage bands. They started in 1956 recording for Argo. Though he's also worked with Sonny Stitt, Max Roach, and Clark Terry, the trio format served Lewis well. He was originally a good (though not great) soloist in the traditional bop mode, but he gradually trimmed down his stylistic flair, opting for simple melodic statements with occasional flourishes or fancy phrases. The trio hit it big in 1965 with "The In Crowd," a re-making of a Dobie Gray pop song. Since then, some 30 Lewis albums have charted, and he had two Top 20 albums and 13 singles on the Top 100 in the 60s alone. He also scored well in the 70s with duets where he backed Earth, Wind & Fire and Nancy Wilson. The original trio members Young and Holt left in 1966 and were replaced by Cleveland Eaton and Maurice White. White left in 1970 to lead Earth, Wind & Fire and was replaced by Maurice Jennings. Lewis had a reunion with Holt and Young in 1982. He remains very popular on urban/R&B radio stations among those who like easy-listening jazz. –RW

○ **The In Crowd / MCA / BB 2**   1965
Lewis's most popular album ever. The title cut was a monster hit. –RW
Wade in the Water / GARLAND / BB 16   1966
A major hit in its time, but of dubious quality from a remastering standpoint. –RW
○ **Sun Goddess / CBS / BB 12**   ca. 1981
Lewis's most popular album since *The In Crowd.* Very good for what it is. Gold album. –RW
Live at the Savoy / COLUMBIA   1981
More jazz content and feel. –RW
The Two of Us / CBS   1984
This is great supper club/cabaret fare. Not for serious jazz fans or purists. –RW
Keys to the City / CBS   1987
A pop date. –RW
We Meet Again / CBS
Billy Taylor (p) takes the date, but Lewis shows chops he seldom taps these days. –RW
Best of Ramsey Lewis / JCI &ASSOCIATED   COMP
A sampler of his 70s cuts for Columbia. –RW
Electric Collection / CBS   COMP
A 1991 reissue of Lewis's most popular (and pop) songs. –RW
● **Greatest Hits of Ramsey Lewis / CBS**   COMP
Reissue of best of Chess label recordings. –MGN

DAVE LIEBMAN   b 1946

Post-bop, early free, jazz-rock, neo bop, modern creative. Tenor sax, soprano sax, flute, piano, drums. A well-educated and versatile player, saxophonist Dave Liebman had lessons from such musicians as Bob Moses, Joe Allard, Charles Lloyd, and Lennie Tristano while also getting a degree in history from NYU and a teaching diploma in the late 60s. He began in a rock/jazz band Ten Wheel Drive in 1970. He's since divided his time between jazz stints with Elvin Jones, playing with Miles Davis, leading his own critically acclaimed groups Lookout Farm and Open Sky, and working with two European and Japanese musicians. His eclectic background has made it easy for Liebman to play any and everything; rock, R&B, hard bop, free, and a variety of Eastern and African styles have been filtered through his work. A very animated, intense player, an emphatic soloist, and a good composer. –RW

Open Sky / PM   1972
Adventurous pieces. A triumphant exhibition of multi-reed versatility. Tremendous work in a small-combo format. –RW
○ **Lookout Farm / ECM**   1975
Liebman at the top-of-the-heap as an unabashed improviser. A high-water mark for this period. Completely original post-Tristano piano of Richard Beirach. –MGN
● **Forgotten Fantasies / HORIZON**   1975
Fine playing. Not quite as accomplished conceptually. –RW
Doin' It Again / TIMELESS   1979
Hot playing and exuberant solos. –RW
Quest / PAJ   1981
Quartet with Liebman, Beirach (p), George Mraz (b), and Al Foster (d). They hit hard and heavy, or at times mournfully wistful. An excellent document of this all-world group. –MGN
The Loneliness of a Long-Distance Runner / CMP   1985
Solo saxes, multi-track dubbing. CD has bonus cuts. –RW
● **Quest II / STORYVILLE**   1986
Quartet set with Liebman, Richie Beirach (p), Ron McClure (b), and Billy Hart (d). –RW
Homage to John Coltrane / RHINO   1987
1991 reissue. An intense tribute to one of Liebman's prime influences. –RW
Trio + One / OWL   ca. 1988
Soprano master doing various variation of familiar themes and out-and-out original material. With Dave Holland (b) and Jack DeJohnette (d). Very worthwhile new music. –MGN

LIGHTHOUSE ALL STARS

Swing, bop. Bassist Howard Rumsey (proprietor of the Lighthouse Jazz Club in Hermosa Beach, CA in the 50s) was the centerpiece for a tight, swinging house band that included trombonists Bob Eneroldsen or Frank Rosolino, the Candoli Brothers, Bud Shank, Shorty Rogers, and Shelly Manne or Lou Levey on drums. –MGN

○ **Sunday Jazz à la Lighthouse / OJC**   r 1953
Lots of Jimmy Giuffre (reeds) and Shorty Rogers (tpt). Frank Patchen on piano. Ten-piece all-stars. Live at the Lighthouse in Hermosa Beach. Top-notch version of group. –MGN
Music for Lighthousekeeping / CONTEMP.   ca. 1956
Sextet with Bob Cooper's tenor sax and Bill Holman's music (four selections) dominating. Excellent "Taxi War Dance" and Sonny Clark's "I-Deal." –MGN

KIRK LIGHTSEY   b 1937

Post-bop, neo bop. This Detroit pianists range, from neo-classical to post-bop, makes him distinctive. He plays in The Leaders and loves duets. –MGN
○ **Everything Is Changed / SUNNYSIDE**   1986
Quartet w/ Jerry Gonzalez (congas). –MGN

ABBEY LINCOLN   b 1930

Ballads, early free, modern creative. Vocalist Abbey Lincoln (later called Aminata Moseka) is enjoying a rebirth in her career these last few years, after being away from both the music and acting scenes for quite a while. Lincoln began singing in dance bands as a teenager in Chicago, then moved to the West Coast in 1951. Her sultry looks earned her some brief notoriety as the "Black Marilyn Monroe," and she even appeared in the 1957 film, *The Girl Can't Help It.* But after meeting drummer Max Roach, Lincoln changed her image and became a serious vocalist and political activist. Their *Freedom Now Suite,* released in 1960, was one of the harbingers of changing sentiments in the Black community. During the 50s and 60s, Lincoln made many superb releases with top jazz names like Sonny Rollins as well as Roach. She changed her name to Aminata Moseka in 1975. She had a period of inactivity in the early 80s but resurfaced with a vengeance in the 90s. Lincoln is an intuitive, often-compelling singer who manages to overcome occasional problems with intonation and range. She is among the most striking vocalists ever from the standpoint of delivery, and few can match her way with lyrics and moods. –RW

Affair / LIBERTY   1956
W/ Benny Carter. A great collaboration that long ago disappeared. EMI's French division had it out as an import for a while. –RW

That's Him / OJC   r 1958
Striking cuts from the late 50s. Sonny Rollins (ts) is a dynamic guest star. –RW

Abbey Is Blue / OJC / DB 5   195?
Simply amazing interpretations by a premier jazz vocalist coming into her own now in terms of public recognition. She's always deserved it. –RW

☆ **Freedom Now Suite / CANDID**   1960
Definitive social protest and jazz. Lincoln and her then-husband Max Roach were a great team. –RW

○ **Straight Ahead / CANDID**   1961
A date of powerful music from a great vocal expressionist with Coleman Hawkins (sax), Eric Dolphy (reeds), Booker Little (tpt), and Mal Waldron (p). Quintessential. –MGN

Sounds as a Roach / LOTUS   1968
Dynamic live set. –RW

○ **People in Me / INNER CITY**   1973
As good as she gets on this recording. A perennial favorite for many. W/ David Liebman (soprano/tenor and fl.), Al Foster (d), Mtume (per), and two Japanese musicians. "Living Room," "Africa," "Naturally," and the title track stand out. Proud music. –MGN

Talking to the Sun / RHINO   1983
A 1990 release of a session with Lincoln singing and accompanied by some prime young lions. –RW

Abbey Sings Billie / CAPITOL-RHINO   1987
Interesting concept. In many ways, Lincoln is much closer to Holiday than many think. –RW

World Is Falling Down / POLYGRAM / DB 5   1990
Very worthwhile. –MGN

● **You Gotta Pay the Band / VERVE**   ca. 1991
Studio date featuring Stan Getz one last time, and Hank Jones Trio. Maxine Roach on viola for two cuts. Six cuts feature either words and/or music written by Moseka. She has lost absolutely none of her brilliance or passion for singing, interpreting, and creating. –MGN

FRED LIPSIUS

Post-bop, jazz-rock, neo bop. This saxophonist and alumnus of the group Blood, Sweat, and Tears plays neo-bop New York style. He is also an adept studio player. His scant recordings are overdue. –MGN

○ **Distant Lover(s) / ITI**   1984
The alto saxophonist with the Larry Willis Trio. A gem! –MGN

MELBA LISTON   b 1926

Big band, hard-bop, post-bop, progressive big band. Kansas City trombonist, and a brilliant arranger. Worked extensively w/ Gerald Wilson, Quincy Jones, and Randy Weston. –MGN

○ **And Her Bones / METROJAZZ**   i 1958
W/ Slide Hampton (tb).

BOOKER LITTLE   1938-1961

Hard-bop, post-bop. His premature death kept Booker Little from being one of the most consistently arresting players of the 60s, but his short ouput was still riveting and attention-grabbing. Little had one of the sharpest, most vibrant sounds of any trumpeter and could stretch and bend the fabric of a composition without destroying the harmonic framework or losing clarity or tone. He grew up in Memphis but began to make his mark after moving to Chicago in 1957. He joined

drummer Max Roach in 1958 and stayed with him for most of his remaining career, though he's best known for some incendiary sessions with Eric Dolphy at the Five Spot in 1961. He also played with Mal Waldron and John Coltrane. Little died of uremia, a rare blood disorder. –RW

☆ **Booker Little 4 & Max Roach / BAINBRIDGE**   r 1960
1991 reissue. Trumpeter Little's rare legacy. This is a must-buy. –MGN

Out Front / CANDID   1961
W/ Max Roach (d) and Eric Dolphy (reeds). An important album. –MGN

○ **Victory and Sorrow / BETHLEHEM / DB 5**   1961
Sizzling release. This is a mournful and moving work by Little. Great lineup with George Coleman (ts) and Julian Priester (tb). –RW

CHARLES LLOYD   b 1938

Cool, early free, jazz-rock, new-age, neo bop. Among the more engaging tenor saxophonists and daring flutists, Charles Lloyd played in R&B and blues bands with B. B. King and Bobby "Blue" Bland before moving to the West Coast in 1956. He later worked with Chico Hamilton and Gerald Wilson and toured with Cannonball Adderley before forming his own group in the mid 60s. His late-60s group (that also included pianist Keith Jarrett) enjoyed both jazz and pop notoriety, thanks to a 1967 concert his quartet played at the Fillmore. His tenor has the warm, bluesy sound associated with Southern and Southwestern stylists, although Lloyd also weaves vocal effects, honks, and upper-register careening into his solos. His flute lines, wavery phrases, and over-blowing are more energetic. –RW

☆ **Forest Flower / ATLANTIC**   1966
Live at Monterey. W/ Keith Jarrett trio. Definitive Lloyd. –MGN

In the Soviet Union / ATLANTIC   1967
A historic visit to the Soviet Union. Tremendous playing by Lloyd. –RW

Love-In / ATLANTIC   1967
An album where the menu is uneven, but the tenor sax solos are entrancing. –RW

Montreaux 1982 / ELEKTRA   1982
A recent live recording with Michel Petrucciani (p). –RW

Fish out of Water / POLYGRAM   1989
Upbeat Lloyd solos. –RW

Dream Weaver / ATLANTIC   1996
Sweeping flute, craggy tenor sax solos, and fine piano by Keith Jarrett. –RW

JOE LO DUCA

Post-bop, jazz-rock, neo bop. Acoustic and electric guitarist who wrote the theme for "Late Night America" and a number of movie soundtracks. His sound is influenced by John McLaughlin and Ralph Towner. –MGN

○ **Glisten / CORNUCOPIA**   1982
Contemporary guitarist swings and gets cerebral. With Ralph Armstrong (b) and Ralph Towner (g, p). All originals from a brilliant musician, known for film scores and TV themes. Excellent improviser. –MGN

DIDIER LOCKWOOD   b 1956

Jazz-rock. French violinist in jazz/fusion mold a là Jean-Luc Ponty. Very good musician. More funky than swinging. –MGN

○ **Surya / INNER CITY**   r 1981

CHUCK LOEB

Jazz-rock. Guitarist plays electric and acoustic. Concentrates mostly on contemporary fusion. Capable of playing jazz but does not venture onto that path. –MGN

○ **Magic Fingers / DMP**   1989
A good duet and an excellent recording. –RW

Life Colors / DMP
A fusion/mainstream date, well recorded. –RW

LOUNGE LIZARDS

Jazz-rock. Sleaze jazz and progressive fusion/avant garde visionaries. Onnette/Dolphy/Monk are their models, with French art leanings. –MGN

Live 1979-1981 / ROI   1979
Erratic, but the live venue makes this the most interesting of their sets. –RW

○ **Lounge Lizards / CAROLINE**   1980
First album. The best. Influenced by Ornette Coleman. –MGN

Big Heart-Live in Tokyo / ISLAND
Good recording. Interesting rock-oriented material. –RW

No Pain for Cakes / POLYGRAM
This 1991 reissue has instrumental character and uneven material. –RW

JOE LOVANO   b 1952

Post-bop, neo bop, modern creative. A fast-emerging tenor sax star, Joe Lovano has recently recorded with several top jazz figures, among them John Scofield, Bill Frisell, and Marc Johnson's Bass Desires, plus his own group. A versatile player equally at home in rock-influenced or fusion material, hard-bop, ballads, or blues. –RW

○ **Village Rhythm / SOUL NOTE**   1988
Quintet w/ Tom Harrell (tpt) and Ken Werner (p). This Cleveland saxophonist at his best. –MGN

Landmarks / CAPITOL   r 1991
Swinging and contemporary. Very good. –MGN

MUNDELL LOWE   b 1922

Swing, bop. Mundel is a West Coast guitar veteran. Primarily, he is a studio musician in LA. Writes for films, TV shows. Plays swing to bop. –MGN

○ **Mundell Lowe Quartet / OJC**   1955
A 1991 reissue. A good date on a limited-edition release. –RW

New Music of Alec Wilder / RIVERSIDE   1956
A nice vehicle for an 11-piece group. Joe Wilder is at the helm of the brass section. –RW

California Guitar / FAMOUS DOOR   1974
Classy, sophisticated fare with some funk supplied by Irving Ashby (g). –RW

TONY LUJAN

Post-bop, neo bop. West Coast trumpeter whose lyrical and swinging playing hold him in good stead. Fine, obscure jazz interpreter. –MGN

○ **Magic Circle / CAPRI**   r 1991
A good album. –MGN

JIMMIE LUNCEFORD   1902-1947

Swing, big band. Jimmie Lunceford has gotten less glory than any of the great big-band figures, even less than Fletcher Henderson or Bennie Moten. Lunceford led a marvelous band that mixed showmanship and discipline, precision and looseness, in a manner rivaled only by the finest ensembles led by Basie and Ellington. Lunceford studied music and worked with bands led by Elmer Snowden and Wilbur Sweatman, among others. He formed a school dance band there that included some master players. The group became a sensation in 1933 at the Lafayette Theater in New York, winning an invitation to the Cotton Club. They became a national hit in 1934, thanks to some road appearances. They had tremendous arrangers in Sy Oliver and Ed Wilcox, plus a host of first-rate players like trombonist Trummy Young, tenor saxophonist Joe Thomas, and alto saxophonist Willie Smith. –RW

Jimmie Lunceford / MASTERS OF JAZZ   1927
1927-1934. A new release covering early material. –RW

Music Map

Jazz Conga & Bongo

Afro-Cuban Jazz Roots

Chano Pozo (1915-1948) — Congas & bongos w/ Dizzy Gillespie (1947)

Jack Costanzo (1922) — Bongos w/ Stan Kenton (late 1940s)

Mongo Santamaria (1922) — Congas & bongos

Machito (1912-1984) Congas & bongos

Best Known Conga Players Ray Barretto (1929) — Big Black Candido Camero (1921) — Sabu Martinez (1930-1979) Armando Peraza (1924) — Carlos "Potato" Valdez (1926)

Bongo Players Armondo Peraza (1924)

Modern Players Daniel Ponce (1953) — Sammy Figueroa

● **Rhythm is Our Business / MCA**   1934
Recorded 1934-1935. The arrangements are by Sy Oliver and Ed Wilcox. Willie Smith and Lafonet Dent play sax up front. –MGN

Jimmie Lunceford and Orchestra (1940) / CIRCLE 1940
Sublime recordings of a fine big band. –RW

Jubilee / JOYCE   1940
1940 radio broadcasts with Bubbles Whitman as MC. Vocals by Maxine Sullivan and Joe Thomas. Also w/ Art Tatum, the Eddie South Trio, and the Golden Gate Quartet. –MGN

○ **The Last Sparks / MCA**   1941
Recorded 1941-1942. Arrangements here are by Ed Wilcox, Horace Henderson, Roger Segure, Tadd Dameron, Pee Wee Jackson, and Billy Moore Jr. These are another twelve great tracks. –MGN

Original Session / MUSIDISC   1942
Twelve tracks feature the notable soloists Russel Green, Freddy Webster, Joe Thomas, Willie Smith, Alphonso King, and Omer Simeon. –MGN

And His Harlem Express-Live / HINDSIGHT
Very fine recordings. –RW

Margie / SAVOY
A fine reissue of Lunceford material. –RW

OLEG LUNDSTREM   b 1916

Big band, progressive big band, instr-pop. Lundstrem's group is featured on a Mobile Fidelity reissue of a 1988 session. –RW

○ **In Swing Time / MOBILE FIDELITY**   1986
Wonderfully conservative. –RW

EVAN LURIE

Jazz-rock, modern creative. A sometime member of the Lounge Lizards, Lurie is also a part-time jazz artist who recently released an album of jazz-tinged rock and fusion on Antilles. –RW

○ **Selling Water by the Side of the ... / POLYGRAM**
Classical-oriented project. –MGN

BOBBY LYLE

Post-bop, instr-pop. A keyboard and synthesizer artist, Lyle is more in the fusion/pop camp than in jazz. He had an R&B hit a few years ago with the song "What You Won't Do for Love." He now records for Atlantic. –RW

Ivory Dreams / ATLANTIC i 1989
Far more R&B-tinged mood music than jazz. –RW

BRIAN LYNCH

Post-bop, neo bop. Excellent trumpeter, formerly with Art Blakey. Works effectively in Latin/jazz and modern post-bop bands. An excellent soloist. Good blend of all his influences. Starting to find himself as a composer. Much potential. –MGN

Peer Pressure / CRISS CROSS 1986
Debut album for a fine trumpeter w/ Jim Snidero (sax), Ralph Moore (ts) and Kirk Lightsey (p). –MGN

○ **In Progress / KEN MUSIC**
Lynch leads a conventional hard-bop outing. –RW

GLORIA LYNNE ♭ 1931

Ballads. Another vocalist whose style and songs blur the distinctions among popular singing, jazz, and blues, Lynne made both straight jazz and jazz-oriented material during the 50s and 60s and had some hits on the R&B scene. She has also done some acting and songwriting and has a good voice. Her strengths are expressiveness; she's a master at building tension in a song, telling a story, and punctuating a point. She has been doing more jazz-oriented work in recent years. –RW

A Time for Love / MUSE
The straight jazz and ballad side of Lynne. Fresh material, mellow vocals, good arrangements. –RW

○ **Golden Classics / COLLECTABLES** COMP
A nice batch of hits and signature songs from a vocalist who dabbles in pop, R&B, and jazz. –RW

JOHNNY LYTLE ♭ 1932

Post-bop, instr-pop. Nicknamed "Fast Hands," vibist Johnny Lytle plays in the mood-music/light-jazz mode formerly championed by Roy Ayers in his pre-Ubiquity days. Although his albums may not be startling or sensational, they are pleasant affairs. He's among the finest soloists from a speed perspective, but his solos are more rhythm and verve than creative or dazzling. –RW

○ **Nice and Easy / JAZZLAND** 1962
Probably the best effort by the funky vibist. This showcases jazz greats Johnny Griffin on sax and Bobby Timmons on piano. It's more boppish than many of Lytle's records. –DS

Village Caller! / OJC r 1964
The most popular date that encapsulates Lytle's funky groove, fueled by organist Milton Harris. –DS

Happy Ground / MUSE 1969
This underrated vibist seamlessly balances soul-jazz, mainstream, and R&B influences. –RW

Good Vibes / MUSE 1971
An album of blues, ballads, and funk. Robust tenor sax by Houston Person. –RW

Fast Hands / MUSE 1980
A more recent effort by the vibist, featuring Houston Person on sax. –DS

M'BOOM

Early free, world fusion, modern creative. A group of diverse percussionists and drummers started by Max Roach in the 70s. The lineup has grown as large as 14 at times, with the players alternating on conventional trap drums, congas, African talking drums, cowbells, marimbas, and other percussion instruments, playing mainly original, extended compositions. –RW

Re: Percussion / BAYSTATE 1973

Max Roach's percussion sextet. Two extended compositions by Joe Chambers. Excellent. –MGN

○ **M'Boom / COL**
Max Roach's percussion sextet. –MGN

HAROLD MABERN ♭ 1936

Bop, hard-bop, post-bop, cool, soul jazz. Veteran jazz pianist from Memphis. Straightahead swinger who has gotten down on his share of blues/funk or original soul. Primarily a sideman with MJT+3, Lionel Hampton, Miles Davis, Jazztet, J.J. Johnson, and many singers. Solid player. –MGN

○ **Rakin' & Scrapin' / OJC** 1968
Any old Mabern album is great. The Memphis pianist is now in NYC. –MGN

Live at Cafe Des Copains / SACKVILLE
Outstanding piano solos, sturdy compositions. –RW

TEO MACERO ♭ 1925

Post-bop, progressive big band. Producer for Miles Davis and progressive bandleader and arranger, Macero borders on 20th-century contemporary. He plays tenor sax. –MGN

Time + 7 / FINNADAR 1965
This album was way ahead of its time. A reissue with Art Farmer (tpt), John La Porta (reeds), Ed Shaughnessy (d), and Mal Waldron (p). –MGN

○ **Acoustical Suspension / DR.JAZZ** 1984
An avant-garde/big-band setting w/ Lionel Hampton (vib), Larry Coryell (g), and Dave Liebman (sax). –MGN

MACHITO ♭ 1912

Latin. Machito (Frank Grillo) is perhaps the best Latin-jazz bandleader of the 40s & 50s. Collaborated with Dizzy Gillespie. Set lofty standards for this fusion of American and Afro-Cuban rhythms. A most important figure. –MGN

☆ **Machito and His Afro-Cuban Salseros /** 1948
Recent reissue of amazing 1948 and 1949 cuts. –RW

Tremendo Cumban 1949-52 / TUMBAO 1949
Fresh reissue of inciendary late-40s, early-50s sessions. –RW

Afro Cuban Jazz / VERVE 194?
Late-40s and early-to-mid-50s, pivotal sessions with Chano Pozo, Chico O'Farril, Dizzy Gillespie (tpt), Charlie Parker (as), Mario Bauza, Flip Phillips (ts), and Buddy Rich (d). A must-buy. –MGN

○ **Latin Soul Plus Jazz / CHARLY** 1957
This band, under Machito's sizzling baton, blows up a storm that could wipe Cuba right off the map! Sitting in are jazz heavyweights Cannonball Adderley, Curtis Fuller, Joe Newman, Herbie Mann, Johnny Griffin, Candido Camero, and others, the year is 1957. Twelve sizzlin' sides, digitally remastered. –MYLES BOISEN, ROOTS & RHYTHM

● **At the Crescendo / GNP CRESCENDO** 1960
Gene Norman presents Machito at his club. –MGN

World's Greatest Latin Band / GNP CRESCENDO 1960
Strong reissue of a Hollywood session. –RW

Afro-Cuban Jazz Moods / PABLO 1975
Wonderful reunion with Dizzy Gillespie (tpt). –RW

Fire Works / TIMELESS 1977
Machito's son Mario Grillo is now music director. –RW

○ **Afro-Cuban Jazz/Machito / VERVE** 1977
Landmark sessions revealing the jazz/Afro-Latin rhythm connection. –RW

Dizzy Gillespie/Charlie Parker / VERVE 1977
A selection of prime Latin jazz cuts w/ both Parker and Diz plus Machito. –RW

Mucho Macho Machito / PABLO ca. 197?
Outstanding late-70s Machito Latin jazz and salsa. –RW

Machito! / TIMELESS 1982
One of his final sessions. –RW

Live at North Sea / TIMELESS 1982

Powerful, great live sessions. –RW

○ **1983 Grammy Award Winner / MCA**   1983
Showing the band is still vital, this live recording in Holland is hot. –MGN

Latin Soul Plus Jazz / TICO
Tremendous arrangements, driving solos, and good dance tunes. Originally issued as *Kenya*. –RW

FRASER MACPHERSON   b 1928

Swing, big band. Canadian tenor saxophonist from Winnipeg/Vancouver. Plays dixieland, Swing era and American popular songs. Delicate, deliberate, delightful. –MGN

○ **Live at the Planetarium / CONCORD**   1950
Another good, live, mainstream set. –RW

Indian Summer / CONCORD   1983
A mainstream set. –RW

MAHAVISHNU ORCHESTRA

Jazz-rock. The Mahavishnu Orchestra was a jazz/rock group formed in 1971 by British guitarist John McLaughlin and featuring drummer Billy Cobham, violinist Jerry Goodman, pianist Jan Hammer, and bassist Rick Laird; the name Mahavishnu was that given McLaughlin by his guru. The group featured dynamic, often quick-fingered playing and some fiery interaction between the players, and gained enormous success in 1972 and 1973 with the albums *The Inner Mounting Flame*, *Birds of Fire*, and *Between Nothingness & Eternity*. But the original unit only survived for those three records. Through 1976, McLaughlin recordings such as *Apocalypse*, *Visions of the Emerald Beyond*, and *Inner Worlds* continued to be credited to Mahavishnu, but other musicians were used. McLaughlin later renounced the Mahavishnu name, but in 1984 recorded an album that also featured Billy Cobham, again as "Mahavishnu." –WR

★ **Inner Mounting Flame / CBS / BB 89**   1971
Classic first album. Definitive fusion. –MGN

○ **Birds of Fire / CBS / BB 15**   ca. 1972
Classic second album. More definitive fusion. –MGN

Apocalypse / CBS / BB 43   r 1974
Live in Central Park. Excellent. –MGN

Visions of the Emerald Beyond / COLUMBIA   1974
Reached #68 on the Billboard charts. Orchestral concepts in ensemble format. –MGN

GILDO MAHONES   b 1929

Bop, hard-bop, post-bop. A legendary pianist of post-bop and hard bop. Mahones has a nice cross section of influences. He has few recordings. –MGN

○ **The Great Gildo/Soulful Piano / PRESTIGE**   1964
2-fer. Excellent jazz. A must-buy. –MGN

ADAM MAKOWICZ   b 1940

Swing, bop, neo bop. Pianist. He began playing professionally in 1962 in Cracow, then moved to Warsaw in 1965. He headed his own trio and toured extensively through Europe, Cuba, India, and around the world. Makowicz began writing both music and music criticism, as well as arranging in 1971. He joined violinist Michael Urbaniak's group the same year, spending three years with Urbaniak and his wife Urzula. He began working with the Tomasz Stanko trio and later formed a band with Stanko in 1975. Makowicz's reputation in Europe eventually spread to America, where critics began to recognize his fluency, rhythmic verve, and dazzling technique. –RW

○ **Adam / CBS**   1977
This solo debut album for this Czech pianist reminds one of Art Tatum. –RW

Classic Jazz Duets / STASH   1979

Name is Makowicz / SHL   1983
Shows technical prowess. –RW

● **Naughty Baby / NOVUS**   1987
An all-Gershwin program with two bassists, Dave Holland and Charlie Haden. Essential. –MGN

BOB MALACH

Post-bop, jazz-rock, neo bop. Michael Brecker-styled saxophonist, veteran studio player and sideman. Worked with fusion groups, Horace Silver, contemporary neo-bop combos. –MGN

○ **Mood Swing / RHINO**
A fine effort on the contemporary side from veteran sideman saxophonist. –MGN

TOM MALONE

Post-bop, jazz-rock, neo bop. A trombonist who has worked in classical, rock, and jazz. A very fluid, literate, real-time player. –MGN

○ **Standards of Living / BIG WORLD**

JUNIOR MANCE   b 1928

Post-bop, soul jazz. Junior Mance is among the funkier, more bluesy pianists around. He got his start in the Chicago scene of the late 40s, then moved to New York and joined Lester Young's group in 1949. He played with the Sonny Stitt/Gene Ammons band in 1950-1951, then spent three years in the army. Mance became Dinah Washington's accompanist for a year after that, then worked with Cannonball Adderley's first quintet in 1956-1957. Subsequently, Mance also worked with Dizzy Gillespie's group and the Eddie "Lockjaw" Davis/Johnny Griffin group. Mance then formed his own trio and since then has done mostly trio recordings, though he has also been quite prolific as a session player. Though some would lump him in with Ramsey Lewis or Ahmad Jamal, Mance's recordings have been more aggressive and less introspective than those of Jamal and have retained far more jazz integrity and content than most of Lewis's. –RW

● **At the Village Vanguard / JAZZ LAND**   1961
A solid date with Larry Gales (b) and Ben Riley (d). –RW

The Junior Mance Touch / POLYDOR   1973
Includes jazz originals from Mance, Martin Rivera, and Gil Fuller, a Leadbelly blues, and instrumentals of pop tunes from George Harrison, Johnny Nash, and Al Green. A nice approach without the schmaltz. –MGN

For Dancers Only / SACKVILLE   1983
Outstanding sets that includes some of Mance's flashiest recent playing. –RW

○ **Truckin' & Trakin' / BEEHIVE**   1983
Recorded by a quartet with pianist Mance and saxophonist David Newman. Produced by Bob Porter. Includes one Mance original, Hank Crawford's "Truckin'," and four standards. The group really comes together for the Blues/Jazz legend. –MGN

The Tender Touch / NILVA   1983
Produced by Alvin Queen, this album features duets between Mance and bassist Martin Rivera, a reprise of G. Harrison's "Something," and five standards. They create their own subtle rythms nicely. –MGN

MANDALA OCTET

Post-bop, progressive big band, modern creative. Ensemble led by bassist John Leaman from Boston. They play a minimalist modern-jazz with lots of room for improvisation. Careful listening of this group reveals hidden treasures. –MGN

The Notion of Obstacle / VOLITION   1988
Their first album. "It's Raining" is a minimalist jazz anthem. Very progressive improvisational notions. –MGN

○ **La Spada di San Galgano / ACCURATE**
Startling, delightful instrumentals in a progressive-minimalist mode. Members of either orchestra join leader/bassist John Leaman. Title track bears repeated listenings for the horn charts. Six originals. –MGN

ALBERT MANGELSDORFF   b 1928

Post-bop, early free, modern creative. Mangelsdorff is the master of multiphonics, the trombone technique of playing more than one note simultaneously. He's also among the prime veterans in the European free-improvisation school, though his roots date back to the late 40s, when he was playing bop. He appeared in America in 1958 as a member of the Newport International Band. He then played with a specially organized group called the European All Stars and toured Western Europe and Yugoslavia with his own band in the early 60s. He recorded with pianist John Lewis in 1962, then toured Asia in 1964. Enchanted by the sound of Indian music, Mangelsdorff began to work some ragas into his own music and recorded a song by Ravi Shankar. Later visits to Japan and Eastern and Western Europe, plus his involvement with the Globe Unity Orchestra beginning in the 60s, moved Mangelsdorff into free improvisation. Through the 70s, 80s, and 90s, Mangelsdorff has recorded with symphony orchestras, done solo concerts, worked with trios and duos, and been voted many times Europe's "Musician of the Year." –RW

The Wide Point / PA-USA   1975
Studio date with Elvin Jones (d). Heavy jazz. –MGN

○ **Trilogue / PA-USA**   1976
Live trio recording for virtuoso German trombonist. Startling sounds! With Jaco Pastorius (b). –MGN

CHUCK MANGIONE   b 1940

Post-bop, instr-pop. Trumpet, flugelhorn, bandleader. It would be stretching the term to call Chuck Mangione a jazz musician today. At one time, Mangione was a solid player with a bright tone on trumpet and a very mellow, appealing sound on flugelhorn. Mangione studied at the Eastman School of Music in Rochester and co-led a group called the Jazz Brothers with his own brother Gap from 1960 to 1964. He moved to NYC in 1965 and played with Woody Herman, Kai Winding, Maynard Ferguson, and Art Blakey's Jazz Messengers during the late 60s and early 70s. He also served as the director of the Eastman School's jazz ensemble from 1968-1972.

But things changed forever for Mangione in 1970, when a recording he made with the Rochester Philharmonic Orchestra, titled *Friends & Love*, became a crossover hit. Throughout the 70s and 80s, Mangione enjoyed substantial pop success by making lightweight, over-orchestrated mood music, though the arrangements were a bit more sophisticated than those employed for most pop instrumental music. His songs have been adopted for television commercials, used in the Los Angeles Summer Olympics, and recorded by everyone from Cannonball Adderley to Percy Faith. –RW

Children of Sanchez / POLYGRAM
Lots of radio air-play, but little jazz interest. Gold album. –RW

Live at the Village Gate 1 / FEEL SO GOOD
A recent release with no difference from Mangione's past efforts. –RW

Love Notes / CBS
Another very popular jazz-light set. –RW

● **Recuerdo / OJC**   1962
W/ Wynton Kelly (p), Sam Jones (b), Lou Hayes (d), and Joe Romano (fl, as). The is the real jazz Mangione. Recommended. –MGN

Land of Make Believe / POLYGRAM / DB 5   r 1973
Mangione's best from a jazz standpoint –RW

○ **Bellavia / POLYGRAM / BB 68**   1975
A less fluffy and more substantive Mangione. Bright and uplifting. –MGN

Feels So Good / POLYGRAM / BB 2   1977
Small group. Pop/jazz yes, but it is too pretty to not enjoy. Platinum album. –JME

Chase the Clouds Away / A&M   1987
A high pop quotient and low quality. Gold album. –RW

MANHATTAN JAZZ QUINTET

Post-bop, neo bop. Led by NYC studio veteran, trumpeter Lew Soloff and keyboardist David Matthews. Jazz with a Big Apple contemporary edge. George Young-tenor sax. –MGN

Manhattan Jazz Quintet / PROJAZZ   1984
Nicely played. –RW

Autumn Leaves / PRO-ARTE   1985
Classy, sophisticated, and conservative. –RW

○ **Live / PRO ARTE-PRO JAZZ**   1986
Their best from a playing standpoint; lively. –RW

My Favorite Things / PRO ARTE-PRO JAZZ   1987
Some wonderful playing of familiar items. –RW

Best of / PRO ARTE-PRO JAZZ   COMP
A compilation of their better cuts. –RW

MANHATTAN TRANSFER

Ballads, instr-pop. Vocal jazz/pop superstars. Modern commercial extension of Lambert, Hendricks & Ross. Cabaret darlings. Fusion leanings. –MGN

Manhattan Transfer / ATLANTIC / BB 33   1975
A nice set, more to the jazz side. Gold album. –RW

Extensions / ATLANTIC / BB 55   1979
A very stylized set. –RW

○ **Mecca for Moderns / ATLANTIC / BB 22**   1981
Manhattan Transfer's best from a jazz concept. –RW

Bop-Doo-Wop / ATLANTIC   1985
More of a jazz feel and style. –RW

● **Vocalese / ATLANTIC**   1985
Clearly their best. It's their roots. –MGN

Brasil / ATLANTIC   r 1988
Worth hearing. Milton Nascimento (v) and Stan Getz (ts) are on the date. Afro-Latin flavor. –RW

Best of Manhattan Transfer / ATLANTIC   COMP
A recent compilation of the group's hits. Gold album. –RW

HERBIE MANN   b 1930

Post-bop, soul jazz, Latin, jazz-rock, world fusion. No instrumentalist was more popular in the 60s and early 70s than Herbie Mann, nor more eclectic. Mann began to investigate and record bossa-nova music in 1961 and had his first hit single and album in 1962. Through the late 50s and early 60s, Mann had been a fairly conventional mainstream/bop saxophonist, but he switched to flute and became a superstar in the 60s. Mann's simple melodies and incorporation of international elements at times, or R&B, blues, and rock backbeats at other times, clicked with record buyers. He played in Brazil and Japan and regularly topped many listener/reader polls throughout the 60s. His late-60s release *Memphis Underground* was a monster smash and an early jazz/rock/fusion document. During the 70s Mann moved into reggae and disco, had his own label for a while, and produced sessions by Ron Carter, Miroslav Vitous, and Attila Zoller, among others. –RW

At the Village Gate / ATLANTIC / BB 30   1961
Reissue. Mann in a straight jazz vein. –RW

○ **Nirvana / ATLANTIC**   1961
W/ Bill Evans (p).

★ **Memphis Underground / ATLANTIC / BB 22**   1968
Mann's best pop/R&B recording has been enormously popular and is still somewhat influential. W/ Roy Ayers (vib), Larry Coryell (g), and Sonny Sharrock (g). –RW

Push Push / ATLANTIC   1971
Another popular release. Features Duane Allman (g). –RW

SHELLY MANNE   1920-1984

Swing, bop, post-bop. Born in NYC, lived in Los Angeles. A most melodic jazz drummer, influential on all who mixed company with him. Premier bandleader in the 50s. Played with Stan Kenton and Woody Herman in the 40s. Capable of hot swing to bop. Opened a nightclub — "Shelly's Manne Hole" — in Hollywood, in the 60s. Also a capable big-band drummer. Very smooth and agile. –MGN

West Coast Sound / OJC 1953
A nice larger group recording with Art Pepper (as) as a standout. –RW

Three & 'the Two' / OJC 1954
A first-rate reissue. Shorty Rogers (tpt) and Jimmy Giuffre (sax) are tremendous. –RW

Swinging Sounds - Vol 4 / OJC 1956
The fourth in a good series, though solidly in the style that by then was established. –RW

Shelly Manne & His Friends / DOCTOR JAZZ 1956
A festive, breezy quality. –RW

More Swinging Sounds / OJC 1956
1987 reissue. W/ strong alto sax by Charlie Mariano. –RW

My Fair Lady / OJC 1956
A bit to the polite side. Leroy Vinnegar brings some spunk on bass. –RW

● **At the Blackhawk - Vols. 1-5 / CONTEMPORARY** 1959
These live sessions are mainstream jazz at its most listenable. With Richie Kamuca on tenor sax, and Victor Feldman on piano. Great listening music! –JME

Mannekind / BBC-CAFE / DB 5 1972
○ **At the Manne-Hole / CONTEMPORARY**
Vols. 1 & 2.

RENEE MANNING

Ballads. A rising jazz singer who records on the Ken Music label. Manning has gotten good critical notices, and her albums showcase a strong voice and excellent range, though she's still maturing as a stylist. –RW

○ **As Is / KEN MUSIC** 1991
Spotlights an emerging jazz vocal star. –RW

KAREN MANTLER

Progressive big band, instr-pop. A good, unpredictable composer whose work very much reflects the influence of Carla Bley. Madcap themes, unorthodox arrangements, and somewhat skewed, though still arresting playing have typified her Watt albums. –RW

○ **My Cat Arnold / POLYGRAM** r 1990
Concept work, sometimes too cutesy. Has some interesting moments. –RW

MICHAEL MANTLER   b 1943

Early free, progressive big band, modern creative. Mantler has been among the few jazz musicians who have been active in the compositional, performing, and business ends of music. He studied at Berklee in Boston before relocating to New York in 1964. After playing with Cecil Taylor's group, Mantler was part of the group that formed the Jazz Composer's Guild to allow experimental musicians better opportunities. The Guild didn't last, but they were the forerunner of the Jazz Composers Orchestra Association (JCOA), which Mantler formed as a nonprofit cooperative to commission, perform, and record new compositions for jazz orchestras in the late 60s. Mantler and composer Carla Bley have had a long and fruitful relationship since the 60s, one that eventually resulted in their marriage. He and Bley formed Watt Works Records in 1973, a company devoted to their own music. –RW

No Answer / WATT 1973
Music by Mantler, Don Cherry, Carla Bley, and Jack Bruce with words from Samuel Beckett. –MGN

Alien / POLYGRAM 1985

Ambitious four-part composition that works at times and bombs at others. –RW

○ **Live / POLYGRAM** 1987
Performance art at its heights, with Jack Bruce (b), Don Preston (synth), and Pink Floyd drummer Nick Mason. –MGN

Many Have No Speech / POLYGRAM
An intriguing concept with 42-piece Danish Radio Concert Orchestra, rockers, and jazz elements. Not for all tastes. –RW

LAWRENCE MARABLE   b 1929

Bop, post-bop. A fine drummer and Blue Note session musician with a much smaller profile and reputation than most of that label's players in the 60s, Marable has only one album in print, having also recorded with Sonny Clark and Duke Jordan (among others). A very tasteful, resourceful percussionist, he has also worked quite often with James Clay, and at one time he played with Frank Morgan. –RW

○ **Tenorman / BLUE NOTE** r 1957
Exceptional album from drummer/leader, with James Clay on tenor sax. –MGN

RICK MARGITZA

Post-bop, neo bop. This is one of the new names in the Blue Note family. A Detroit tenor sax player, Margitza has made three recordings for Blue Note, two of them mixing fusion-oriented songs with hard-bop/mainstream stylings, while his most recent release was an album of standards. Margitza is a strong improviser with good tone and a command of the tenor. –RW

○ **Color / BLUE NOTE** 1989
A good tenor player still finding his identity. CD has a bonus cut. –RW

○ **Hope / BLUE NOTE** 1990
Varying material — pretty nice. –RW

TANIA MARIA   b 1948

Ballads, Latin. Maria is the singer who has supplanted Flora Purim in the 80s and 90s as the finest Brazilian and Afro-Latin singer working regularly in America (at least on a major label). Maria performs in both English and Portuguese, does jazz standards, originals, and Latin pieces, and has displayed a glorious voice, a charismatic personality, and vibrant sound. –RW

Piquant / CONCORD 1980
Good 1980 date, despite rather bland music. –RW

Taurus / CONCORD 1981
Fine vocals. –RW

○ **Come with Me / CONCORD** 1982
Maria remains impressive. –RW

Real Tania Maria: Wild / CONCORD 1984
Strong performances. –RW

Bela Vista / CAPITOL i 1990

Hope / BLUE NOTE ca. 1991
Her most recent effort. –RW

CHARLIE MARIANO   b 1923

Bop, post-bop, early free, jazz-rock, world fusion. Alto saxophonist Mariano began working in the Boston area with Jaki Byard, Sam Rivers, Herb Pomeroy, and others. Mariano spent two years with Stan Kenton in the 50s, then nearly three years working with Los Angeles players like Fran Rosolino, Shelly Manne, and others. He co-led a group with his then wife Toshiko Akiyoshi in the early 60s and also played briefly in 1962 with Mingus. During 1963 and 1964, Mariano lived in Japan with Akiyoshi, then returned to America in 1965. He also toured extensively with Astrud Gilberto. During the 70s and 80s, he lived in Europe and worked with many groups, while leading several bands. Mariano began as a bop advocate, though Johnny Hodges was also an early influence. In subsequent years, his sound has grown more lyrical and the impact of Asian and Eastern themes more identifiable. He's been among jazz's most powerful, penetrating soloists. −RW

● **Boston All Stars / OJC**   1953
Important document for this saxophonist. −RW

The Bethlehem Years / FRESH SOUND   ca. 1954
Prime 50s Mariano output. −RW

Reflektions / CATALYST / DB 5   1974
W/ Finnish musicians, particularly saxophonist Eero Koivistoinen. −MGN

○ **Helen 12 Trees / MPS**   1976
Lively date with Jan Hammer (synth), Zbigniew Seifert (violin), and Jack Bruce (b). Great. −RW

Crystal Bells / CREATIVE MUSIC   1979
Excellent set, w/ Don Alias first-rate as a percussionist. −RW

Jyothi / ECM   1983
Mariano wails, winds, and experiments with Karnataka College of Percussionists. −RW

The Charlie Mariano Group / MOOD
Outstanding group sessions. −RW

Standard Time - Vols. 1 & 2 / FRESH SOUND
Both volumes feature Charlie Mariano with the Tete Montoliu Trio. −RW

PHIL MARKOWITZ

Post-bop, neo bop. McCoy Tyner influenced pianist from Brooklyn & East Hampton. Worked with Chet Baker, Mellenis, and his own trio. BA from Eastman school. −MGN

○ **Sno' Peas / KEN MUSIC**
Excellent debut album from a pianist w/ trio. Modern to progressive. −MGN

HANK MARR

Post-bop, soul jazz. Unsung organist whose groove and place in history remains uncemented. Too bad — he is one of the masters of the Hammond B-3. −MGN

○ **Live at the Club / KING**   i 1964
W/ Rusty Bryant (sax).

BRANFORD MARSALIS   b 1960

Post-bop, neo bop. The current leader of the new "Tonight Show" band, Branford Marsalis hasn't been as controversial or as high-profile (until recently) as his brother Wynton. A member of jazz's most well-known family, Branford Marsalis began as an alto player, replacing Bobby Watson in Blakey's Jazz Messengers in 1981. He switched to tenor and soprano, then joined his brother's band in 1982, staying until 1985. The group toured extensively nationally and internationally and won critical applause, while selling vast numbers of recordings for jazz releases. But an alleged dispute over stylistic direction and a decision to join rocker Sting's tour purportedly led to the brothers' split in 1985-1986. A couple of years later, Marsalis was heading his own band and has since become a major player in his own right. His swooping, huge-tone, supple phrasing and witty licks have links to Wayne Shorter, Sonny Rollins, and even Coleman Hawkins or Ben Webster, but Marsalis has strived to develop his own voice and keeps developing in that regard. −RW

○ **Scenes in the City / CBS**   1983
The title track poem was once performed by Charles Mingus. A solid effort. −MGN

Romances for Saxophone / CBS   ca. 1986
Beautiful, exacting sax solos in a classical vein. −RW

Royal Garden Blues / CBS   1986
Quartet sessions that feature some outstanding piano by Kenny Kirkland. −RW

● **Renaissance / CBS**   1987
Marsalis's best ensemble with Kenny Kirkland (p), Bob Hurst,

and Tony Williams (d). Four standards, two of Tony's originals, and one of Branford's. A very solid album. −MGN

Random Abstract / CBS   r 1988
First-rate quartet performances and excellent solos. −RW

Trio Jeepy / CBS   r 1989
Fun and listenable, with Milt Hinton (b) and Jeff Watts. −MGN

Crazy People Music / CBS   1990
In these sessions, Branford moves farther out. −RW

Beautiful Ones Are Not Yet Born / CBS / DB 5   r 1991
An exciting pianoless session, plus a cut with guest star British tenor saxophonist Courtney Pine. −RW

ELLIS MARSALIS   b 1934

Trad, post-bop, cool. Pianist. The father of the Marsalis clan, Ellis is its lesser-known member but has begun to get notice lately for his own accomplishments. He is an excellent pianist, whose experiences include playing in a Marine Corps band, working with Al Hirt, and training a host of familiar names including Terence Blanchard, Donald Harrison, Harry Connick Jr, and Kent Jordan, as well as famous sons Branford and Wynton. Ellis is well-versed in traditional New Orleans music and blues, bop, and hard-bop. His style is precise, disciplined, yet engaging and swinging. He never rushes or hurries a tempo and plays with verve and feeling. −RW

○ **Father & Sons / CBS**   r 1982
The side with sons Wynton and Branford worth the price. They swing very hard. −MGN

Syndrome / ELM   r 1985
Solo piano. −MGN

Ellis Marsalis Trio / BLUE NOTE   1991
Spiraling piano at times on these trio sessions. −RW

● **Heart of Gold / CBS**   ca. 199?
Of his few recordings, this is a gem. With Ray Brown (b), Billy Higgins (d) — none finer for rhythm mates. All standards save one by Ellis, two by his son and producer Delfeayo. This album shows the pianist's depth in perception of the entire jazz spectrum. −MGN

○ **Piano in E-Solo Piano / ROUNDER**
Solid, sophisticated piano with a touch of the blues. −RW

WYNTON MARSALIS   b 1961

Post-bop, neo bop. Jazz's most honored trumpeter, multiple Grammy winner Wynton Marsalis is the top star and biggest celebrity in contemporary jazz circles. He has drawn lots of heat for not being an innovator but an imitator; his anti-rock and anti-rap diatribes and his jibes at eclecticism have also earned him derision in some sectors. But few dispute his obvious technical attributes; his crisp, crackling notes and full, pure sound have gotten warmer and tighter over the 80s and 90s, and he's proven, via forays into the blues, traditional jazz, and (lately) composition — that he's open to experimentation and change within the hard-bop format. Marsalis got his first trumpet at the age of six from fellow trumpeter Al Hirt, and began studying both jazz and classical music at 12, and joined Blakey's Jazz Messengers as an 18-year-old. Besides making several albums in the late 70s and early 80s with Blakey, he recorded with Herbie Hancock in 1981, then signed with Columbia a little over a year later. His subsequent Columbia debut won a Grammy, triggering a run of multiple awards, and in 1984 he became the first artist to ever win simultaneous Grammys for jazz and classical, repeating this feat in 1985. −RW

☆ **Wynton Marsalis / CBS**   1980
Best band, best music, best Wynton. −MGN

○ **Fathers and Sons / CBS**   1982
One side with the Marsalis family, the other with Von and Chico Freeman. A must-buy. −MGN

● **Think of One / CBS**   1983
Excellent. Well-produced. Title track is outstanding. −MGN

Hot House Flowers / CBS / BB 90   1984
Lots of fine solos, but not as strong in the material area. –RW
Black Codes (from the Underground) / CBS   1985
Very good music. Five stars from *DOWN BEAT*. –MGN
J Mood / CBS   1986
Good music –MGN
Live at Blues Alley / COLUMBIA   1986
Quartet. Fine live performances. –RW
Majesty of the Blues / COLUMBIA   1988
Good concept. Matisse artwork. –MGN
Standard Time - Vol. 2 (Intimacy Calling) / CBS   r 1990
Marsalis displays forte as a ballad stylist and interpreter. –RW
Standard Time - Vol. 3 / CBS / DB 5   r 1990
1987-1990. Subtitled: *The Resolution Of Romance*. Wynton, with his father Ellis, on the piano. Very traditional and very nice listening. –JME
Vol. 1 - Thick in the South / CBS
The best of the three-part series, with Joe Henderson (ts) dead center. –RW
Vol. 2 - Uptown Ruler / CBS
A good ensemble work. The solos thin out at times. –RW
Vol. 3 - Levee Low Moan / CBS
Marcus Roberts (p) plays with zest. –RW

WARNE MARSH   1927-1987

Bop, post-bop, cool. Tenor sax. Never a big name outside jazz circles, Warne Marsh was a creative, fluid saxophonist noted for surprising and often unorthodox phrases and vivid, rapid-paced solos. He started with the Hoagy Carmichael group in the mid 40s, then went into the army. He toured in 1948 with Buddy Rich, but met Lennie Tristano a year earlier while in the service. Tristano's influence remained with Marsh throughout his career, especially in the construction of his sax statements and in his writing. Marsh collaborated often with another Tristano disciple, Lee Konitz. During the 60s and 70s, Marsh made many vital recordings. –RW

Jazz of Two Cities / IMPERIAL   1956
An early example of Marsh's talent. –DS
○ **Music for Prancing / MODE**   1957
A swinging date by the master of cool. –DS
Winds of Marsh / IMPERIAL   1959
An excellent session by this tenor saxophonist. –DS
Jazz from the East Village / WAVE   1960
Another solid session. –DS
● **Live at Montmartre - Vols. 1-3 / STORYVILLE**   1975
State-of-the-art throughout. Blues, ballads, uptempo, and standards. –RW
Tenor Gladness / DISCO_MATE   1976
Brilliant and lively interplay between Marsh and the underrated Lew Tabackin (sax). –DS
All Music / NESSA / DB 5   1976
Rollicking, dynamite. –RW
Warne Out / INTERPLAY / DB 5   1977
An album where wit and inventiveness are the theme, from the title to the leads. –RW
Star Highs / CRISS CROSS   1982
A recent indication of this tenor's considerable and continued talent. With Hank Jones (p). –DS

MEL MARTIN

Post-bop, neo bop. This West Coast saxophonist is head of the group Bebop & Beyond, a dashing, hard-edged soloist and an underrated writer. Bebop & Beyond hasn't made a splash as yet, but a recent album with Dizzy Gillespie has generated a great deal of media attention. –RW

○ **Bebop & Beyond / CONCORD**   1984
A good band from San Francisco. The title says it all. –MGN

PAT MARTINO   ♭1944

Post-bop, jazz-rock, neo bop. A professional guitarist from an early age, Pat did a lot of performing on the "chitlin' circuit" with organists such as Jimmy Smith, Jack McDuff, and Jimmy McGriff. Moving to a more mainstream jazz style, he played with John Handy and led his own groups, which included Cedar Walton, Richard Davis, and Billy Higgins. A fluid and tasteful improviser with great speed and technique, Martino remains an important influence on advanced guitarists. –DNM

El Hombre / OJC   1967
1990 reissue of a solid date. –RW
● **East! / OJC**   r 1968
A beautiful recording with Far East themes. Worth searching for. –MGN
Desperado / OJC   1970
A fine set enlivened by Eric Kloss's wavery alto. –RW
○ **Consciousness / MUSE**   1974
Martino on the way up. Mostly quartet recordings for the brilliant guitarist. "Willow," a dark, understated gem. Contains seven tracks, three by Martino, three standards, and Joni Mitchell's "Both Sides Now." Guitar students should study this one. –MGN
Baiyina (Clear Evidence) / OJC / DB 5   r 1975
Tight, inventive Martino at his best. –RW
Exit / MUSE   1976
Expertly played. –RW
Strings! / OJC   1976
1991 reissue of a date w/ Martino in flashy form, plus Joe Farrell (ts) and Cedar Walton (p). –RW
The Return / MUSE   1987
Facile guitarist on a comeback with this live recording. –MGN

STEVE MASAKOWSKI

Post-bop, neo bop. This electric guitarist from New Orleans plays some heady fusion, but is also an adept modern mainstream sideman. –MGN

○ **Friends / NEBULA**   1984

HUGH MASEKELA   ♭1939

Soul jazz, world fusion. Trumpet, flugelhorn, vocals. Masekela is perhaps the best-known South African expatriate instrumentalist. Masekela heard both township music and vintage swing and bop in his teens, and the African/African-American mix has been retained in Masekela's own music. In the early 60s, he left South Africa after John Dankworth and Harry Belafonte got him a passport. During the 60s, Masekela had a steady career recording for Mercury, MGM, and later his own label, Chisa, while living in London and New York and on the West Coast. He even had a Number 1 pop hit with "Grazing in the Grass" in 1968. But a 1970 trip to Lagos and a concert with Fela Kuti rekindled his interest in African music, and he moved to London in 1972 to work and record with other expatriates. He returned to America in 1977 but went back to Africa in 1980, this time to Zimbabwe, then Botswana, and toured with his ex-wife Miriam Makeba on Paul Simon's Graceland tour in the late 80s. He has been able to find a middle ground between commercialized Afri-funk, Afri-jazz, and true township music. –RW

○ **Masekela / UNI**   1965
It all comes together here. Magic synthesis of trumpet-led African sounds, jazz, and R&B. –HD
The Promise of a Future / UNI / BB 17   1968
African and English vocals in an assertive and roughhewn, brassy setting. –HD
24 Karat Hits / VERVE   196?
Prime 60s cuts, including "Grazin' in the Grass." –RW
● **Grrr / MERCURY**   ca. 196?
Masekela as a young trumpeter from the mid 60s. Rare, but clearly his best format and playing. –MGN

○ **Home Is Where the Music Is / BLUE THUMB** 1972
An outstanding blend of Afro-pop and jazz with strong work
by Dudu Pukwana. (as) –RW
Uptownship / NOVUS 197?
Fine recordings in a driving Afro groove. –RW
Trumpet African / MERCURY
Striking early recordings. –RW

THE MASTERSOUNDS

Post-bop, cool. Softly swinging quartet anchored by
Montgomery brothers Buddy (vibes) and Monk (bass), and
propelled by pianist Richie Crabtree and drummer Benny
Barth. Compared to the Modern Jazz Quartet, the group
interpreted jazz and popular showtunes on 11 albums from
1957 to 1961. Their brother Wes Montgomery joins them on
"Kismet." –DS

● **Jazz Showcase / PACIFIC JAZZ** r 1958
The debut of this lightly swinging quartet that is distinguished
by the vibist Buddy Montgomery. Appeals to fans of the
Modern Jazz Quartet. –DS
Date with the Mastersounds / FANTASY 1961
The last studio date of the distinctive quartet. –DS
○ **Swinging with the Mastersounds / OJC** 1961
Exquisite, precise swinging jazz that delivers a light, unique
sound. –DS

RONNIE MATHEWS ♭1935

Post-bop, neo bop. Pianist. Well-known sideman in post-bop
tradition. Good with singers. Some compositions are recorded
by several artists; he is possibly better known as a writer. –MGN
○ **Doin' the Thang / PRESTIGE** i 1964
W/ Freddie Hubbard (tpt).

DAVID MATTHEWS ♭1911

Progressive big band. Big band arranger/composer. Pop-fusion
leanings, but also has excellent progressive big-band charts.
Fine pianist too. –MGN
Big Band Live at the Five Spot / MUSE 1975
Big band (12 pieces) going through Matthew's originals, two
standards, and a couple of neo-funk/hip compositions,
particularly Joe Beck's "Penny Arcade." –MGN
○ **Night Flight / MUSE** ca. 1976
12-piece studio sessions. Chick Corea's "Time Lie," two Miles
Davis standards are the highlights. Very good band. –MGN
Blue in Green / PRO ARTE-PRO JAZZ 1986

BENNIE MAUPIN ♭1940

Post-bop, early free, jazz-rock. This Detroit multi-reedist and
flutist is a member of Mwandishi. A sideman and studio
sessioneer, he plays flute and bass clarinet very well. –MGN
○ **The Jewel in the Lotus / ECM** 1974
Detroit multi-instrumentalist with other members of Herbie
Hancock's Mwandishi. Early-period progressive fusion. –MGN
Almanac / IAI
Hard-edged swing and improvisations with Mike Nock, Cecil
McBee, and Eddie Marshall. –MGN

BILLY MAY ♭1916

Big band, instr-pop. Billy May was among the top arrangers of
the 50s, working with Peggy Lee, George Shearing, Jeri
Southern, Nat King Cole, and Frank Sinatra, among others.
May wroter and arranged songs for the Charlie Barnet
orchestra from 1938-1940, then played trumpet solos in the
Glenn Miller Orchestra in the early 40s. May arranged,
conducted, and performed on radio shows in the 40s and later
served as musical director for Willie Smith. He formed his
own band in 1950, then sold it to Ray Anthony in 1954 and
joined Capitol as staff arranger. –RW
Leading the Good Life / PAIR

○ **Best of Billy May / AEROSPACE** COMP

BILL MAYS ♭1944

Post-bop, cool, neo bop. A session and studio pianist, Mays
recently recorded two fine duo albums with bassist Ray
Drummond. He also played with noted West Coast musicians
in the 70s and 80s. –RW
○ **One to One / DMP / DB 5** 1989
Topnotch duo work, expertly recorded. –RW
One to One 2 / DMP 1990
A fine followup to an excellent initial outing. –RW

LYLE MAYS ♭1953

Jazz-rock, M-base. Keyboards. Best known for a long musical
relationship with Pat Metheny, Mays won prior acclaim for
composing and notating an album for the North Texas State
University Lab Band, which in 1975 became the first by a
college band to get a Grammy nomination. That same year, he
met Pat Metheny, beginning their association. Through the
70s and early 80s, Mays worked exclusively with Metheny. His
background was in classic bop, and his occasional forays on
acoustic piano reveal those roots, but it's his array of colors,
sounds, textures, and electronic support on synthesizer that
has earned him respect with Metheny. Mays has released
recordings as a leader on ECM since the mid 80s. –RW
○ **Lyle Mays / MCA-GEFFEN** r 1986
His best as a leader. Contemporary multi-keyboardist, with an
original concept. –MGN
Street Dreams / GEFFEN
This is more to the fusion side, but has lots of exceptional
playing. –RW

PAUL MCCANDLESS ♭1947

Early free, new-age, world fusion. An Oboe/English horn
specialist and multi-reed player who is well known for
collaborations with Paul Winter, as a charter member of
Oregon. With a tone that can be both atmospheric and earthy,
he has always reached for new sounds. –MGN
All the Mornings Bring / ELEKTRA 1979
W/ strings and horns. Quite enjoyable. –MGN
○ **Navigator / LANDSLIDE** 1980
Group includes McCandless (on his usual soprano sax,
English horn, oboe, bass clarinet), vocalist Jay Clayton and
vibist David Samuels. His best album. –MGN
Heresay / WINDHAM HILL 1988
This is a studio date with Art Lande (p) and Trilok Gurtu
(per). Atmospheric without being dissipated. Very good
record. –MGN

LES MCCANN ♭1935

Blues-jazz, soul jazz. Pianist and vocalist. A prime player in
the soul-jazz and pop-jazz arenas, McCann got his first major
exposure as a member of the Gene McDaniels backing band
in 1959, following a stint in the navy. He formed his own trio
in 1960 and has been consistently popular ever since. A fine,
earthy singer who has also done well with romantic ballads
and occasional protest songs, McCann has done a lot with
limited instrumental gifts. A dependable player in terms of
establishing grooves or setting up rhythms, and is not
renowned as a great soloist or technician. Instead, he lets
others like the Jazz Crusaders, Eddie Harris, or Rahsaan
Roland Kirk do the work when they collaborate. –RW
○ **Les McCann Sings / PACIFIC JAZZ** 1961
A super set with Ben Webster (ts) and Groove Holmes on
organ. Soul-jazz and blues at their best. –RW
Les McCann Ltd. in New York / CAPITOL 1961
1989 reissue; w/ hot tenor from Stanley Turrentine. –RW
Les is More / ATLANTIC 1967
A tremendous soul-jazz date composed of cuts previously in
McCann's vaults. –RW

Live at Montreux / ATLANTIC   1972
A good two-disc date, with two hot stints by Rahsaan Roland Kirk (reeds). −RW

☆ **Invitation to Openness / ATLANTIC**   1972
A classic. −MGN

Hustle to Survive / ATLANTIC / DB 5   1975

RON MCCLURE   ♭1941

Post-bop, neo bop. Veteran bassist can play post-bop, impressionist, comtemporary or fusion-jazz. All-around, well-rounded team player. −MGN

○ **Tonight Only / STEEPLECHASE**   ca. 1991
After decades as a sideman, the bassist leads a truly first-rate album. W/ Randy Brecker (tpt), John Abercrombie (g), Adam Nussbaum (d). Five McClure originals, mostly in post-bop/neo-contemporary vein and three nice standards. A great record. −MGN

Inspiration / KEN MUSIC
Stellar trio with McClure, Richard Beirach (p), Adam Nussbaum (d). Strong statement. Good on repeated listenings. −MGN

ROB MCCONNELL   ♭1935

Big band, progressive big band. Canadian trombonist leads his Boss Brass Big Band. Capable soloist. Goes from swing to post-bop, some funk. −MGN

○ **Boss Brass & Woods / MCA**   1985
Potent solos by Phil Woods (as), excellent playing by Canada's premier big band. −MGN

Jive 5 / CONCORD   1990
A fine session in swing/traditional style. −RW

Brass is Back / CONCORD   1991
More emphasis on post-bop from composers Silver and Kai Winding. Tunes from Don Thompson, R. Wilkins, Roger Kellaway, and McConnell. Two standards. Lots of music (over an hour) on this CD (2 bonus cuts). −MGN

SUSANNAH MCCORKLE

Ballads, Latin. Vocalist. Susannah McCorkle has made a sizable impact in a relatively brief period. While in Paris, McCorkle heard the music of Billie Holiday and was captivated. She has earned a Grammy nomination and has also published several short stories and articles in the New Yorker. McCorkle has a clear and striking voice and never picks bad or unsuitable material. She has established herself as a topflight performer. −RW

○ **No More Blues / CONCORD**   1988
A good vocalist. Her records are solid, though seldom ambitious. CD version has two bonus cuts. −RW

Sabia / CONCORD   1990
Here are some good arrangements and cuts. CD version: three bonus cuts. −RW

I'll Take Romance / CONCORD   1992
Her latest. CD has two bonus cuts. −RW

STEPHEN MCCRAVEN

Post-bop, early free, modern creative. A drummer whose role as a leader is more pronounced after years as a side man, McCraven ventures into mainstream and avant-garde. −MGN

Wooley the Newt / SWEET EARTH   1979
Excellent modal-jazz vehicle for improvisation. −MGN

○ **Intertwining Spirits / FREELANCE**   1983
Extraordinary free-jazz album working within rhythmic parameters with McCraven as leader/percussionist and Sam Rivers (sax). −MGN

RON MCCROBY

Swing, bop, cool. Cincinnati flutist/clarinetist and especially

whistler. Novelty musician seen on "The Tonight Show." He swings in the bop, ballad, blues vein. −MGN

● **Plays Puccolo / CONCORD**   1982
The famous Cincinnati whistler does standards. Recommended. −MGN

○ **Other Whistler / CONCORD**   1984
Some intriguing pieces. −RW

JACK MCDUFF   ♭1926

Post-bop, soul jazz. One of the great jazz organists and combo leaders. McDuff began as a bassist and switched to organ in the mid 50s. He first gained attention via the Willis Jackson group (1958-1960). His recorded work with Jackson on Prestige is of the highest quality organ/tenor sax collaboration. His own first recordings are for Prestige, beginning in 1960. This early work finds him in a studio pickup group with tenor saxophonist Jimmy Forrest. Two albums were cut, *Tough Duff* and *The Honeydripper*, and they are both outstanding. He formed his own group in 1961 with saxophonist Harold Vick and drummer Joe Dukes. McDuff's big breakthrough came in summer 1963 with a quartet that included Dukes, tenor-sax man Red Holloway, and young guitarist George Benson. The group has a number of best selling albums (1963-1965) and any music made by this group is worth hearing. This is the best McDuff music. Later groups lack the fire of this one, and Atlantic (1966-1967) and Chess/Cadet (1968-1969) albums never quite reach the same level. More recordings for Verve and Cadet again had moments but generally were, at best, good. Much of the 70s found McDuff getting more involved with electronic keyboards and sacrificing much of his identity in the process. *Cap'n Jack* (Muse) from 1988 finds him back on the right track. A versatile organist, McDuff is also a capable arranger and bandleader whose groups are well rehearsed and thoroughly conversant with his methods. −BP

Tough 'Duff / OJC   1960
Funk, soul-jazz. Mcduff's second lead session for Prestige. Good small-group Hammond organ funk — provided you like vibes, which is not a usual funk instrument. The title cut is excellent. Jimmy Forrest (ts) is in top form here. W/ Lem Winchester (vib). −JME

Honeydripper / OJC   1961
Soul jazz-funk. This is first-rate jazz-funk, perhaps a little more bluesy than average — which is nice. His third album, w/ Grant Green (g). Excellent. −JME

● **Brother Jack Meets the Boss / PRESTIGE**   1962
W/ Gene Ammons. Exceptional organ/tenor sax meetings from the early 60s. A looser, more relaxed McDuff than his subsequent Prestige recordings, yet equally as good. w/ Harold Vick (ts). −BP

Mellow Gravy / PRESTIGE   1962
Smoking Gene Ammons (ts) and the great Hammond B-3 from McDuff. −RW

Screamin' 62 / PRESTIGE   1962
One of McDuff's most popular extended sets; w/ George Benson (g). −RW

Live! / PRESTIGE / BB 81   1963
Quite strong commercially. Vintage soul-jazz. −RW

Moon Rappin' / BLUE NOTE   1969
Some nice melodies and a capable organ. −RW

○ **The Heating System / CADET**   r 1972
Plenty of funk, sax-wallop, and organ soul. −RW

Re-Entry / MUS   1988
A late-80s return to the sound of earlier recordings, featuring Houston Person (ts). Not inspired, but a solid performance all around. −BP

GARY MCFARLAND   1933-1971

Progressive big band. Vibist McFarland was a skilled, influential arranger and composer, though he didn't learn to read music until he was nearly in his 30s. He studied at Berklee in 1959, then moved to New York and had two compositions included on a 1965 Gerry Mulligan album. John Lewis and Anita O'Day also cut his songs, while Mulligan began issuing albums under his own name. He had a big hit album with Stan Getz during the bossa-nova craze of the mid 60s and later made a series of albums for Impulse that blended complex arrangements and Afro-Latin themes. McFarland cofounded the Skye label in the late 60s, and their concert album *America the Beautiful* reached the charts in 1969. A competent vibes player, it was McFarland's sharp arrangements and compositions that won him fame. –RW

○ **Point of Departure / IMPULSE**   1966
Brilliant arrangements, intriguing compositions. –RW

Tijuana Jazz / IMPULSE   1966
A nice incorporation of Latin themes and influences into the jazz-arranging mode. –RW

America the Beautiful / DCC / DB 5   1969
1991 reissue; impressive concept work (from a lineup and production standpoint). –RW

BOBBY MCFERRIN   ♭1950

Ballads, jazz-rock, instr-pop. Bobby McFerrin is a true vocal improviser. His ability to stretch and strain his voice, produce rhythmic patterns, use his entire body like a drum, and make notes by breathing in and then out, has made McFerrin an 80s pop icon. Jon Hendricks saw McFerrin, encouraged him, and later sang some duets with him. He began doing solo performances in 1983. He later scored a huge pop hit with "Don't Worry, Be Happy" and became a huge attraction. Over the years, his song content and performance approach have veered away from jazz, but he's an awesome stylist and a compelling vocalist. –RW

McFerrin, Bobby / ELEKTRA   1982
McFerrin's debut, which shocked, rocked, and amazed everyone. He's more of a vocal improviser than a performer of strictly jazz. –RW

● **The Voice / ELEKTRA**   1984
Live sets; 1984 sessions. Pre-superstar days. Very adventurous vocal music. –HD

Spontaneous Inventions / CAPITOL   1986
More superb vocal gymnastics. Takes on everyone from the Beatles to Dizzy Gillespie. –HD

○ **Simple Pleasures / CAPITOL / BB 5**   1988
The breakthrough album. Contains the mega hit "Don't Worry, Be Happy" and other gems like "Drive My Car." Platinum album. –HD

Medicine Music / CAPITOL   1990
An album with a somewhat spiritual turn. Standout track is "The Garden." –HD

JIMMY MCGARY   ♭1926

Bop, hard-bop, post-bop, neo bop. Cincinnati's finest tenor saxophonist plays in the modern mainstream. With solid tone and feeling, he is a legend still due recognition. –MGN

○ **Palindrome / MO PRO**   1987
Cincinnati's premier tenor sax with the Fred Hersch Trio in a set of standards. Extraordinary artistry. A must-buy. –MGN

HOWARD MCGHEE   ♭1918

Bop, hard-bop, post-bop. Howard McGhee was among bop's finest pure trumpeters, gifted with great range, taste, sensitivity, harmonic knowledge, and skill. McGhee played with Lionel Hampton in 1941; then, through the rest of the decade, worked with Andy Kirk, Charlie Barnet, and Georgie Auld, before coming under the musical spell of bop. His debut as a leader with Charles Mingus in 1945 (for Modern) was an indication that McGhee's style had made the transition. He later recorded for Dial, Blue Note, Bethlehem, and Savoy, working with such players as Milt Jackson, Fats Navarro,

Pepper Adams, and Tina Brooks. He continued into the 60s and 70s. –RW

● **Maggie / SAVOY**   1948
Trumpeter in studio sessions from Chicago (1948) and Guam (1951-1952) with the Heath Brothers, Billy Eckstine (valve trombone), and Milt Jackson (vib). Great jazz. –MGN

○ **Maggie's Back in Town / CONTEMPORARY**   1961
Solid quartet dates with vibrant McGhee trumpet. –RW

Cookin' Time / ZIM   1966
Fine big-band arrangements and playing. –RW

Here Comes Freddy / SONET   1976
Illinois Jacquet (ts) swaps licks with McGhee. –RW

Jazzbrothers / STORYVILLE   1977
Charlie Rouse (ts) equals his stints with Monk. –RW

Home Run / JAZZCRAFT   1978
Expatriate Benny Bailey (tpt) blows up the rafters. –RW

Live at Emerson's / ZIM   1978
Triple-threat bop with tenors Rouse and Frank Wess. –RW

Young at Heart / STORYVILLE   1979
A welcome appearance by Teddy Edwards (ts). –RW

CHRIS MCGREGOR   ♭1936

Post-bop, early free, progressive big band, modern creative. Pianist and bandleader Chris McGregor has combined African rhythmic and classic swing principles in a special, distinctive fashion. He studied music four years at Cape Town College of Music, where he mixed classical training with nightly experience in local jazz clubs. He formed the Blue Notes in 1962 with Dudu Pukwana, Mongezi Feza, Nick Moyake, Johnny Dyani, and Louis Moholo. The group eventually ran afoul of apartheid laws that banned live performances by mixed groups. They left the country for good in 1964, when they were invited to play at the French Antibes festival. They were helped by compatriot Abdullah Ibrahim, who got them jobs in Europe. McGregor gradually incorporated elements of free music into his repertoire after hearing Albert Ayler, Archie Shepp, and Cecil Taylor while his group was working alongside them at the Montmarte in Copenhagen. In 1970, McGregor created a larger group, the Brotherhood of Breath, which became a favorite on the international circuit. –RW

☆ **And the Brotherhood of Breath / NEON-RCA**   1971
Studio release with excellent compositions, particularly "The Bride." –MGN

● **Live at Willisau / OGUN**   i 1974
The pianist/leader w/ an 11-piece band of South African expatriates and English free-jazz men. Explosive. –MGN

○ **Country Cooking / ATLANTIC**
A rare domestic release from a great Afro-jazz big band. –RW

Live at Toulouse / OGUN
More excellent compositions. –MGN

JIMMY MCGRIFF   ♭1936

Post-bop, soul jazz. McGriff is one of the great jazz organists. His first record, *I Got A Woman* (Sue Records), was a Top 20 hit in 1962. Followups *All About My Girl* and *Kiko* were also hits in 1963-1964. McGriff joined Solid State records in 1966, beginning a long relationship with producer Sonny Lester, who also recorded McGriff on Blue Note, Capitol, Groove Merchant, and LRC. "The Worm" was a hit in 1968-1969. McGriff's 60s work, while R&B-oriented, is top-quality organ jazz. Of special interest is *The Big Band* (Solid State), which is a marvelous tribute to Count Basie. McGriff's 70s work found him alternating between small-combo organ jazz (including a couple of organ battles with Richard "Groove" Holmes) and more commercial attempts utilizing a battery of electronic keyboards. In general, the earliest Groove Merchants are the best, and LRC titles should be avoided. 1980s recordings (JAM, Milestone) find him back in his jazz bag, and all of these can be recommended. Among them are three collaborations with Hank Crawford and *Blue to the Bone* with trombonist Al Grey. McGriff considers himself a blues organist, and he is the very best at that, but his jazz abilities are considerable and should not be overlooked. Two recordings from 1990 and 1991 (Headfirst Records) find him alternating between the electronics and organ jazz. *See* Hank Crawford. –BP

○ **I've Got a Woman / SUE / BB 22**   1962
McGriff makes a national impact with his debut on Sue. –RW

○ **At the Apollo / COLLECTIBLES**   r 1964
A nice set, done at the Apollo with a disturbing remastered sound. –RW

Blues for Mr. Jimmy / COLLECTIBLES   i 1965
His very popular soul-jazz. Remastered sound of dubious quality. –RW

The Worm / SOLID STATE   ca. 1968
A high point of soul-jazz and funk. Both commercial and substantial. –RW

Countdown / MILESTONE   1983
A nice early-80s set. –RW

Skywalk / MILESTONE   1984
McGriff sometimes veers away from his soul-jazz strength, but it's still a fine set overall. –RW

● **The Starting Five / MILESTONE**   1986
Best of the last decade for one of the better Hammond B-3 organists. –MGN

Blue to the Bone / MILESTONE   1988
A recent date — smooth, yet funky. –RW

● **Toast to Golden Classics / COLLECTABLES**   COMP
Horrendous reissued sound, but some top cuts. –RW

KEN MCINTYRE   b 1931

Post-bop, early free. Peer of Eric Dolphy, rivals Dolphy in terms of stretching parameters. Primarily an alto saxophonist, also plays piano. Teaches at S.U.N.Y. and New York City public schools. –MGN

○ **Looking Ahead / OJC**   1960
W/ Eric Dolphy. Boundary-stretching saxophonists. Definitive. –MGN

Year of the Iron Sheep / UNITED ARTISTS   i 1962
Way Way Out / UNITED ARTISTS   i 1963
Tribute / SERENE
A welcome set from an extremely underrated multi-sax performer. –RW

MAURICE MCINTYRE   b 1936

Early free. Also known as Kalaparusha, he is a creative improviser on saxophone, a member of the AACM. Fiercely independent and at times wildly outrageous, this is a one-of-a-kind player. –MGN

○ **Forces and Feelings / DELMARK**
Humility / DELMARK

DAVE MCKENNA   b 1930

Swing. A veteran pianist, McKenna is especially appealing in solo format due to his ability to utilize both classic and contemporary keyboard styles. McKenna can play "stride," blues, or conventional bop and is known for brisk, romping solos that include aggressive passages, strong right-hand rhythmic accompaniment, excellent statements, and quick, unpredictable harmonies. McKenna began working with Charlie Ventura in 1949, then spent 1950-1951 with Woody Herman. McKenna worked with Gene Krupa, Stan Getz, Zoot Sims, and Ventura during the 60s, then started a string of club dates in Cape Cod in 1967. He returned to the touring circuit in the 70s and began a run on Concord in the 80s. Since then he's worked with small combos, done several solo releases, and appeared with the label's big Superband. During the early 70s, McKenna led a quartet with Zoot Sims, Major Holley, and

Ray Mosca, whose 1974 album was reissued last year by the Chiaroscuro label. –RW

This is the Moment / CBS   1959
Glittering phrases and nice rhythms. –RW

Dave McKenna Quartet / CHI-SOUND   1974
A 1990 reissue of a delightful date that's hotter than usual, thanks to Zoot Sims (ts) and Major Holley (b). –RW

Giant Strides / CONCORD   1979
○ **No Bass Hit / CONCORD**   1979
An entertaining baseball motif. Fine ensemble work, with Scott Hamilton (ts) steady. –RW

● **Plays Harry Warren / CONCORD**   1981
Good concept work. –RW

Celebration of Hoagy Carmichael / CONCORD   1983
This is a wonderful tribute, though you've heard the solos before. –RW

Left Handed Compliment / CONCORD   1983
Sharp riffs, good solos. –RW

The Keyman / CONCORD   1984
A good solo date. –RW

Dancing in the Dark / CONCORD   1985
Superb solo piano. –RW

My Friend the Piano / CONCORD   1986
Nifty solo piano. CD version has two bonus cuts. –RW

No More Ouzo for Puzo / CONCORD   1988
This is a reliable quartet date from 1988. Bonus cut on CD version. –RW

Live at Maybeck Recital Hall - Vol. 2 / CONCORD   1989
Fine technique, wonderful melodies. –RW

Shadows 'N Dreams / CONCORD
As usual, McKenna's playing ranges from good to great. CD version has two bonus cuts. –RW

MCKINNEY'S COTTON PICKERS   1895-1969

Swing, big band. McKinney's Cotton Pickers, fronted by Bill McKinney, was the first modern big band of the swing era, directed by Don Redman. It hit Number One with "If I Could Be With You One Hour Tonight" in 1930. –WR

○ **Band Don Redman Built / RCA**   192?
One of the most overlooked early big bands from the 20s. Pivotal cuts cover 20s through early 30s. Benny Carter (as), Coleman Hawkins (ts), and Fats Waller (p) are all part of the group. –RW

JOHN MCLAUGHLIN   b 1942

Early free, jazz-rock, world fusion. By the time Miles Davis introduced John McLaughlin to American audiences, the guitarist was already dazzling the British jazz crowd with his fluid technique, suggesting a schooled jazz player, unafraid to reflect rock influences. McLaughlin prominently guested on Miles's first two transitional fusion albums, *In a Silent Way* and *Bitches Brew* (ultimately others as well), while hooking up with Davis's drummer, Tony Williams, in the highly volatile *Lifetime* band.

McLaughlin soon put together his own group, Mahavishnu Orchestra, an exciting combination of rock and jazz players, one of the few groups to live up to the potential of the fusion revolution. Unfortunately, that group was to be short-lived, and in its place came a ponderous outfit with the same name, who's main purpose seemed to be spreading McLaughlin's religious ideology. This group did not last long either. What came next was Shakti, where McLaughlin teamed with musicians from India, and featured a return to acoustic guitar. While Shakti lasted no longer than the previous outfits, McLaughlin would largely concentrate on the acoustic from this time on. Although, McLaughlin's popularity has never regained the stature he enjoyed with the original Mahavishnu Orchestra, he has continued to record many fine albums, and his trio efforts with Trilock Gurtu rank among the highlights of his career. —SA

★ **Extrapolation / POLYGRAM** 1969
His first electric group still stands the test of time. W/ saxophonist John Surman. —MGN

○ **Devotion / DOUGLAS** 1970
An early winner suggesting McLaughlin would be a jazz-rock innovator. Buddy Miles holds the fort on drums. —RW

★ **My Goals Beyond / RYKODISC** 1970
A reissue of an original Douglas/CBS album. A landmark recording. One side is solo guitar, the other is the first Mahavishnu Orchestra. A must-buy. —MGN

Between Nothingness & Eternity / CBS / BB 41 1973
Plenty of stinging McLaughlin. —RW

Shakti / CBS 1975
Ragas meet jazz. Extraordinary energy. —MGN

Electric Guitarist / CBS 1978
1990 reissue of a date with Carlos Santana (g), Chick Corea (k), and Jack Bruce (b). —RW

Passion, Grace, and Fire / COL 1982
Updated version of trailblazing solos McLaughlin made during the height of his jazz-rock (not fusion) era. —RW

Live at Royal Festival Hall / POLYGRAM 1989
Trio recording with Kai Eckhart (b) and Trilok Gurtu (per). His best of the last decade. —MGN

JACKIE MCLEAN   b 1932

Bop, hard-bop, post-bop. Alto sax. Jackie McLean got early exposure to the music world, as his father played guitar in Tiny Bradshaw's orchestra. McLean's neighbor was Bud Powell, and he played and studied with Powell and Sonny Rollins. Powell got him a spot in the Miles Davis band from 1951 to 1952, after which McLean went to North Carolina A&T College, then played with Paul Bley and George Wallington. He completed the 50s working in groups led by Charles Mingus and Art Blakey. His animated, intense, and frenetic alto solos highlighted several vital 60s albums, many of which steadily pushed the jazz muse toward the edge. He worked on occasion with Ornette Coleman and penned some definitive works, including "Dig," "Dr. Jackle," "Little Melonnae," and "Hip Strut." —RW

Lights Out / OJC 1956
Super quintet date. Elmo Hope is breezy and understated on piano and Donald Byrd is dynamic on trumpet. —RW

McLean's Scene / OJC 1956
This excellent McLean hard-bop date from the late 50s features the masterly Red Garland (p), Paul Chambers (b), and Arthur Taylor (d) in the rhythm section. —RW

Jackie Mclean & Co. / OJC 1957
Another solid session. —RW

Strange Blues / OJC 1957
This is an intriguing, unorthodox date includes Webster Young (a Miles Davis influence on trumpet), and Ray Draper on tuba. —RW

○ **Alto Madness / OJC** 1957
Two great post-Bird altoists. —MGN

Makin' the Changes / OJC 1957
A 1985 reissue of a sterling date, spiced by a rare appearance from Webster Young (tpt) — an often overlooked influence on Miles Davis. —RW

● **Jackie's Bag / BLUE NOTE** 1959
Just about the best sweet and sour sax in jazz. —MGN

New Soil / BLUE NOTE 1959
A fine session. —RW

A Long Drink of the Blues / OJC 195?
A 1987 reissue of sextet and quartet performances. —RW

Bluesnik / BLUE NOTE 1961
A 1989 reissue of McLean at his torrid peak. —RW

☆ **A Fickle Sonance / BLUE NOTE** 1961
A remarkable merger of new-thing/avant-garde leanings and hard-bop fluidity and feelings. —RW

Let Freedom Ring / BLUE NOTE / DB 5 1962
The outer limits of the music is in good hands. Also look for *Destination Out.* —MGN

Hipnosis / BLUE NOTE 1962
McLean steps away from the Parker influence and makes his own sound and statement in this gem. —RW

Tippin' the Scales / BLUE NOTE 1962
Slashing arrangements with outstanding McLean solos. —RW

One Step Beyond / BLUE NOTE 1963
Terse, extensive solos were part of McLean's free/avant-garde-influenced Blue Note sessions from the early and mid 60s. —RW

Action / BLUE NOTE 1964
Blistering sessions spiced by the tremendous bass playing of Cecil McBee. —RW

Right Now / BLUE NOTE 1965
With pronounced Black-liberation and civil-rights undercurrents, this album is not so strong musically as others in the same period. —RW

● **Jacknife / BLUE NOTE** 1966
A 2-fer w/ Lee Morgan (tpt), Charles Tolliver (tpt), Larry Willis (p) and Jack DeJohnette (d). Potent. —MGN

○ **New & Old Gospel / BLUE NOTE / DB 5** 1967
With Ornette Coleman on trumpet! —MGN

○ **The Meeting / STEEPLECHASE** 1973
This is one of two great dates pairing McLean with Dexter Gordon (ts). The style and quality are reminiscent of Gordon's sessions with Wardell Gray on the West Coast in the 50s. —RW

○ **The Source / STEEPLECHASE** 1973
McLean/Gordon pairing equal to that on *The Meeting.* —RW

New York Calling / STEEPLECHASE 1974
A wonderful session that helped introduce McLean's then-26-year-old son Rene to the jazz audience. —RW

Altissimo 1974 / PHILLIPS 1974
This is a great summit meeting with McLean and fellow horn players Lee Konitz, Gary Bartz, and Charlie Mariano, plus a piano trio. —RW

○ **New Wine, Old Bottles / INNER CITY / DB 5** 1978
A superb quartet date w/ Hank Jones (p), Ron Carter (b), and Tony Williams (d). —RW

Dynasty / TRIPLE X / DB 5 1988
This album marked McLean's return to the recording scene in the 90s after a lengthy sabbatical. It features him alongside his son Rene. —RW

RENE MCLEAN   b 1946

Post-bop, neo bop. Son of Jackie McLean, he also plays saxes, but a larger battery (alto, tenor, soprano, as well as flute) than his dad. Coming into his own as a player and composer. —MGN

○ **Watch Out / INNERCITY** 1975
Sextet with Jackie McLean's son Rene. Right there. —MGN

JILL MCMANUS

Post-bop, world fusion, modern creative. Pianist uses jazz and Hopi Indian themes in progressive context. Highly orginal ideas. NYC-based, a regular at Kansas City Women's Jazz Festival. —MGN

○ **Symbols of Hopi / CONCORD** 1983
Native-American music meets jazz piano. Excellent artistic statement. —MGN

BIG JAY MCNEELY   b 1928

Blues-jazz, R&B. Saxophone. A giant of the honking sax school, McNeely mixed flamboyant onstage antics with simplistic, volcanic sax style. His robust, huge tone, and vocal effects were an extension of the swing-era technique into the

R&B/blues market. His penchants for rolling on the floor, playing on his back, or walking out into the audience were crowd-pleasing maneuvers commonplace on the R&B scene in the 40s and 50s, but they were incorporated so flawlessly into his act some thought he invented them. McNeely remains active on the California oldies and R&B circuit and cut some new recordings on his own label in the late 80s. –RW

○ **Swingin' Cuts / CBS**
Discover Big Jay! Guaranteed good time. –MGN

The Deacon Rides Again / MARCONI   COMP
Hot tenor licks, sweltering vocals from Jesse Belvin, and bluesy inflections courtesy of Mercy Dee. –RW

From Harlem to Camden / ACE   COMP
An album of lusty, robust honking sax on standard R&B arrangements. –RW

Meets the Penguins / ACE   COMP
This reissue of raucous, upbeat R&B cuts also includes the doo-wop harmony ensemble The Penguins. –RW

JIM MCNEELY   b 1949

Post-bop, neo bop. Excellent modern pianist who is similarly comfortable in big bands or modern combos. Fine composer. Currently pianist for Phil Woods. –MGN

○ **The Plot Thickens / MUSE**   1979
W/ guitarist John Scofield. Good originals in contemporary light. –MGN

MARIAN MCPARTLAND   b 1920

Swing, bop, cool. Few have combined performing, writing, and broadcasting more effectively than Marian McPartland, who has been an active pianist since the 40s. She came to America from England in 1946, one year after marrying Jimmy McPartland, a trumpeter in the classic Chicago vein. The two had met in Belgium in 1944 and played for Eisenhower in 1946. McPartland formed her own trio in 1959 and was also a house pianist at several clubs in the 50s and 60s. She formed her own label in 1969 and made a triumphant return to active club and concert work in the 70s. She began her Peabody-award-winning show "Piano Jazz" in 1979. Since then she has made extensive radio and television appearances, served on jazz boards, written critically praised essays, and made some outstanding albums. –RW

Maestro and Friend / HALCYON   1974
Includes sparkling duos recorded in Nice with violinist Joe Venuti. –RW

Plays Alec Wilder / HALCYON   1974
McPartland plays sharp, arresting versions of songs by preeminent composer. –RW

From This Moment On / CONCORD   1978
Fine playing of unremarkable compositions. –RW

Let It Happen / RCA   1978
An immaculate piano quartet session with guests Dick Hyman, Hank Jones, and Roland Hanna . –RW

○ **At the Festival / CONCORD**   1979
This nice small-group session accents McPartland's fortes: touch, delicacy, and melodic interpretation. –RW

Live at the Carlyle / HALCYON   1979
Excellent, strong uptempo cuts and ballads, done in the club popularized by Bobby Short. –RW

Portrait of Marian McPartland / CONCORD   1979
A good outing. –RW

Personal Choice / CONCORD   1982
Good if derivative trio date. –RW

● **Willow Creek & Other Ballads / CONCORD**   r 1986
The exemplary solo playing on this album helped embellish her new-star status won through her "Piano Jazz" series on National Public Radio. –RW

Plays Billy Strayhorn / CONCORD   1987

This is a solid tribute to Strayhorn, whose compositions are a perfect fit for McPartland. –RW

○ **Plays Benny Carter Songbook / CONCORD**   r 1990
This is McPartland's finest work in quite some time and includes wonderful interpretations of great compositions by Benny Carter — a spry, exciting alto soloist, in his eighth decade as a player! CD has 2 bonus cuts. –RW

Live at Maybeck Recital Hall / CONCORD
Great solos, with strong rhythmic work and phrasing. CD version has two bonus cuts. –RW

CHARLES MCPHERSON   b 1939

Bop, post-bop. Primarily alto saxophonist; capable tenor player. Ex-Detroiter now living in San Diego is an astoundingly rapid improviser. Mainly a bebop player. –MGN

● **Be-Bop Revisited / PRESTIGE**   1964
This is one of his first strong dates as a leader outside the Charles Mingus Jazz Workshop fold. Includes fine contributions from Barry Harris on piano and Carmell Jones on trumpet. –RW

Con Alma / PRESTIGE   1965
Good followup to *Be-Bop Revisited*, though the playing is a step below. –RW

● **Quintet Live! / PRESTIGE**   1966
Some frenetic trumpet solos from Lonnie Hillyer, recorded live at the immortal Five Spot. –RW

Live in Tokyo / XANADU   1976
Includes some superb playing by McPherson and nice piano from Harris. –RW

○ **Free Bop! / XANADU**   1978
Entertaining hard-bop workout. This is perhaps his fiercest, most exciting playing as a leader. –RW

Siku Ya Bibi / MAINSTREAM

CARMEN MCRAE   b 1920

Ballads. Many consider Camen McRae the greatest pure jazz vocalist currently active. She has remarkable interpretive ability, a striking delivery, and the kind of timing and musicality one would expect from a former pianist. McRae wrote the song "Dream of Life" for Billie Holiday when she was 16. She worked with Benny Carter's band in 1944 and also had a brief period with Count Basie. She sang for a year with Mercer Ellington's band in 1946-1947 as Carmen Clarke, while she was married briefly to drummer Kenny Clarke. After a stint as an intermission pianist and singer at various clubs in the early 50s, McRae began making records in the mid 50s. She had two songs hit the pop charts in 1956 and 1957, and became internationally known through tours and festival appearances as well as several acclaimed records. Her trio has had such famous pianists as Ray Bryant, Norman Simmons, and Duke Pearson. Her 1990 album *Carmen Sings Monk*, an incredible recasting of Monk songs into amazing lyric performances, was nominated but failed to win a Grammy. –RW

By Special Request / DECCA   i 1955
W/ Mundell Lowe (g).

Live - Take Five / CSP   r 1965
A very good meeting of the minds. Dave Brubeck (p) gets comfortable behind McRae. –RW

Mrs. Magic / DCC   1971
A good compilation of obscure cuts from McRae in different contexts. –RW

☆ **Great American Songbook / ATLANTIC / DB 5**   1972
A wonderful two-disc set, with McRae showing her complete music vocabulary and interpretive talents. –RW

I Am Music / BLUE NOTE   r 1976
Very dynamic early McRae. –RW

You Can't Hide Love / PA-USA   1976
Expressive. A good eclectic menu. –RW

Two for the Road / CONCORD   1980

Shearing (p) is smooth. McRae's hot at times and reflective or probing at others. –RW

Live at Bubba's / WHO'S WHO 1981
A fine, rather informal set from Lionel Hampton's label. –RW

○ **You're Lookin' at Me / CONCORD** 1983
Another super tribute. This one's to Nat King Cole, but it came too early to catch the wave of Cole nostalgia. –RW

Duets with Carter / GREAT AMER. MUSIC HALL 1987
W/ Benny Carter (sax). The music is superb. The two find ways to link dissimilar styles. –RW

● **Carmen Sings Monk / NOVUS / DB 5** 1988
This is one of McRae's greatest albums ever. CD has two bonus cuts. –RW

Fine and Mellow / CONCORD 1988
An excellent live set. McRae handles uptempo and ballads with ease. CD has one bonus cut. –RW

Sarah: Dedicated to You / RCA-JIVE/NOVUS ?zz
Beautiful and masterly tribute to a dear friend. –RW

It Takes a Lot of Human Feelings / GROOVE
Solid and often impressive. Groove Merchant label.–RW

Just a Little Lovin' / ATLANTIC
Sophisticated yet exuberant. –RW

Setting Standards / PAIR

Sound of Jazz / MAS
Fine vocals, not such fine arrangements. –RW

Ultimate Carmen McRae / MAINSTREAM
A slightly misleading title, but very nice. –RW

JAY MCSHANN b1916

Boogie, big band, bop, blues-jazz. Pianis Jay McShann is one of the great personalities of jazz and the embodiment of the Kansas City style of jazz and blues. He came to prominence in the late 30s with the last of the Kansas City big bands. His sidemen included alto saxophonist Charlie Parker, bassist Gene Ramey, drummer Gus Johnson, and vocalist Walter Brown. His Decca recordings (1941-1943) show the excellence of the band, but the emphasis on blues material probably gives less than a true picture of the band's overall abilities. The big band broke up in 1944 and McShann spent the rest of the decade in Los Angeles leading small blues-based combos and recording for Philo/Alladin, Mercury, Capitol, and DownBeat/Swingtime, among others. Sadly, except for the latter group on a Black Lion album, none of McShann's Los Angeles recordings have been properly collected. He returned to Kansas City in 1950 and has been based there since. He recorded for Vee Jay (1955-1956) and backed Priscilla Bowman on her big hit, "Hands Off," for that label. He return to records in 1966, after a long hiatus, resulted in an excellent Capitol album *McShann's Piano*, and rekindled interest in his work at home, but especially in Europe, where he quickly became a star touring attraction. He has many European recordings, notably for French Black & Blue, Danish Storyville, and English JSP. His recordings for the Canadian Sackville label have presented him in unique settings and in solo and duo settings as well as a more customary band setting. This intermittent association began in 1971 and continued through the 80s. American albums of special interest are *Last Of The Blue Devils* (Atlantic) and *Goin' To Kansas City* (Master Jazz). McShann often appears in all-star groups and has also become a frequent and engaging vocalist over the past 25 years. *Paris All Star Blues* (Music Masters) finds him at the helm of a big band, revisiting much of his old book to good effect. –BP

○ **Early Bird / SPOTLIGHT REISSUE** 1940
1940-1943 airchecks. –JME

Jay McShann / DECCA i 1954
W/ Charlie Parker (as). –ED

The Big Apple Bash / ATLANTIC 1971
Featuring the McShann's jazz, with some blues thrown in. An all-star session W/ Herbie Mann (fl, ts, cl), Gerry Mullidan

(bar sax), Earl Warren (as), Doc Cheatham (tpt), John Scofield (g), Milt Hinton (b), and Connie Kay (d). –JME

● **Confessin' the Blues / CLASSIC JAZZ** 1971
A great session with T-Bone Walker (g). Recorded in Paris. –JME

Man from Muskogee / SACKVILLE 1972
One of McShann's finest recordings. W/ Claude Williams (violin). –JME

MYRA MELFORD

Post-bop, neo bop, modern creative. An introspective young pianist, she is just starting to make her mark. Her recordings are scarce at this point, though she has received very favorable notice by jazz critics. She lives in New York City. –MGN

○ **Jump / ENEMY**

GIL MELLE b1931

Post-bop. Baritone saxophonist, dubbed his music "primitive modern" in 1956. A searcher whose unique outlook brands him a maverick. Ellington and Bartok influenced. –MGN

○ **Patterns in Jazz / BLUE NOTE** 1956
This is the best recording of Melle on his debut label, which includes the first quartet and the intriguing trombone of Eddie Bert. –DS

Gil's Guests / OJC 1956
1956-1957. What would otherwise be a routine set gets spiced by wonderful stints from Kenny Dorham on trumpet, intriguing use of Julius Watkins on French horn, and great alto sax by Phil Woods. –RW

Primitive Modern/Quadrama / OJC 1956
1956-1957. Swinging quartet dates led by the baritone-sax player, featuring the seldom-heard guitar of Joe Cinderella. –DS

BRIAN MELVIN

Post-bop, neo bop. Drummer whose claim to fame is a collaboration with the late bassist Jaco Pastorias. Good mainstream player. –MGN

○ **Standards Zone / CAPITOL-RHINO**
Good jazz trio with Jaco Pastorius (b). –MGN

VINCE MENDOZA

Instr-pop. A highly gifted composer, arranger, and keyboardist. Musically he encompasses jazz in many different moods and styles. One of the best composers to surface in years; very high level of musicianship. –PK

○ **Start Here / CAPITOL** 1990
A very melodic album from a fantastic composer, featuring an excellent lineup of jazz players. –PK

Instructions Inside / CAPITOL 1991
A followup album with many jazz styles, with Bob Mintzer (sax) and Randy Brecker (tpt) . –PK

DON MENZA b1936

Swing, big band, bop. This West Coast tenor saxophonist is primarily a sideman in combos and big bands. With cool to bop ability, he is as literate as they come. –MGN

○ **Horn of Plenty / VOSS** 1987
W/ sextet. Excellent mainstream jazz. –MGN

HELEN MERRILL b1930

Ballads. Helen Merrill was a successful jazz singer in the 50s and 60s, then opted for a long break from the recording scene. She became a professional in 1945 and sang in Earl Hines's sextet in 1952. She had four prolific years in 1954-1958 and made one album featuring Quincy Jones arrangements and Clifford Brown's extraordinary trumpet solos. Merrill made an album for Atlantic in 1959 and went to England that same year. She became a big name overseas and moved to Japan in 1967. She returned to America in 1972 and has made infrequent albums ever since. She reunited with Gil Evans, whom she'd worked with in the 50s, for an album shortly before his death in 1988. Merrill has been a charmingly enjoyable singer with good articulation. –RW

Collaboration / POLYGRAM
A surprising collaboration remake with Gil Evans shortly before Evans died. –RW

Just Friends / POLYGRAM
Album includes some lush, moving sax solos by Getz. Merrill acquits herself well. –RW

Rodgers & Hammerstein Album / DRG

Shade of Difference / LANDMARK
Here is the 1986 reissue of a 1968 session that's got brilliant musical support from Thad Jones, Jim Hall, Ron Carter, and others. –RW

● **Helen Merrill / EMARCY**   ca. 1955
This has arrangements by Quincy Jones and trumpet by Clifford Brown. It was a wonderfully emotive session, perfect for Merrill's serenely confident tones. All are standards. –MGN

The Nearness of You / EMARCY   i 1957
With small-ensemble accompaniment. Soloists include Bill Evans (p), Oscar Pettiford (b), George Russel (g), Jo Jones (d), and John Frigo (b). –MGN

Helen Sings, Teddy Swings / CATALYST   197?
All standards. The combination works well. Some tracks have a Japanese rhythm section, but the bulk are with Teddy Wilson (p), Larry Ridley (b), and Lennie McBrown (d). –MGN

Duets / POLYGRAM
Carter's dense, sparkling bass accompaniment lifts and caresses Merrill's vocals. –RW

No Tears, No Goodbyes / RHINO
Some good material. –RW

Sings Cole Porter / PRO ARTE-PRO JAZZ
Tasteful, excellent interpretations and technique. –RW

Sings Irving Berlin / PRO ARTE-PRO JAZZ
Merrill handles this well technically. –RW

You've Got a Date with the Blues / POLYGRAM
These are not the most enticing or compelling blues versions around, but Merrill gives them a good shot. –RW

○ **Complete H. M. on Mercury / POLYGRAM**   COMP
1945-1958. For Helen Merrill fans, here is an exhaustive 4-disc set. –RW

PAT METHENY   b 1954

Early free, jazz-rock, neo bop. Only a few guitarists in every generation achieve the kind of popular and artistic success that Pat has seen. He was an impressive virtuoso at an early age, and formed a beneficial early association with vibraphone innovator Gary Burton. Methany studied and taught at Berkelee College of Music and University of Miami. He has had many successful albums from the beginning. He brings a bit of the mystique and allure of the rock star to his image, but his popularity centers on his compelling and polished performance style. Later collaborations, such as *Song X* (with Ornette Coleman) and *80/81* (with Charlie Haden and others), show a highly accomplished and versatile jazz artist. Though he has great instrumental technique and speed, he has developed a very accessible style, with great lyrical ability and a fine melodic sense, working for simplicity rather than flash. He was an early and tasteful explorer of electronic effects, such as chorus boxes, and one of the first to use guitar synthesizer effectively. He has also written music for films. Some later albums have tended toward a rather ethereal sort of Latin-influenced mood music. –DNM

Bright Size Life / ECM   1975
First album, with Jaco Pastorius (b) and Bob Moses (d). Excellent original material. –MGN

Watercolors / POLYGRAM   1977
Reissue. The group's second album; important since it shows Metheny breaking away from the style he'd honed with Gary Burton. –RW

☆ **Pat Metheny Group / ECM**   1978
This is a quartet session. Metheny's playing is becoming more focused and Lyle Mays establishes himself on keyboards. –RW

New Chautauqua / ECM / BB 44   1978
Among his formative albums: he was still trying to find the right blend of rock, pop, fusion, and jazz elements. –RW

American Garage / ECM / BB 53   1979
This is the session that marked Metheny's coming of age; better songs, more intense playing, and more variety in arrangements. –RW

As Falls Wichita, So Falls Wichita Falls / ECM   1980
Intelligent, thoughtful compositions, with excellent solos and ensemble work. Billboard #50 –RW

● **80/81 / POLYGRAM / BB 89**   1980
Metheny's crowning jewel. Wonderful music with Michael Brecker (ts), Jack DeJohnette (d), Dewey Redman (sax), and Charlie Haden (b). –MGN

Offramp / POLYGRAM / BB 50   1982
This 1982 date is the successor to *Wichita Falls* but lacks that album's charm and flair. –RW

● **Rejoicing / POLYGRAM**   1983
Definitive trio recordings. Nearly essential. –MGN

Travels / ECM / BB 62   1983
Deftly played and nicely recorded, but for fans only. –RW

First Circle / POLYGRAM / BB 91   1984
A good quintet date, but doesn't break any new ground. –RW

○ **Song X / MCA-GEFFEN / DB 5**   1986
Metheny pays tribute to a surprising influence, teaming with Ornette Coleman in a collaboration that shocked everyone with its musical effectiveness. –RW

Still Life (Talking) / MCA-GEFFEN   1987
A standard Metheny session from 1987; he now has the formula down pat. It is well-played and well recorded. –RW

○ **Question & Answer / MCA-GEFFEN**   r 1991
A great trio. Metheny stretches out. This is highly recommended. –MGN

GEORGE MGRDICHIAN

Post-bop, world fusion. Oud player, also at times a bassist. Mgrdichian has played a prominent role in David Amram's bands of the 60s and 70s. –MGN

One Man's Passion / SHANACHIE   1986

○ **New Sounds Of The Middle East / MONITOR**

MICROSCOPIC SEPTET

Post-bop, progressive big band, modern creative. Four saxophones plus rhythm section; this is a progressive ensemble but they never ignore the tradition. At time irreverant and wacky, always working hard to make distictive music. –MGN

○ **Take the Z Train / PRESS**   1982
1982 & 1983. Four saxophonists and a rhythm section in progressive settings. If you like Carla Bley or Charles Mingus, you'll gravitate towards the Micros! –MGN

Let's Flip / OSMOSIS   ca. 1984
Forrester and Johnson each wrote three compositions. Includes Billy Strayhorn's "Johnny Come Lately" on this fine disc. Danny Nigro on tenor sax. –MGN

Offbest Glory / OSMOSIS   1986
These oblique chants are mostly originals. Some Monk tunes as well. –MGN

● **Beauty Based on Science / STASH**   1988
More wacky, loveable instrumental jazz done creatively. Paul Shapiro joins the group on tenor sax. –MGN

BOB MILES

Post-bop, jazz-rock, instr-pop. Fusion/light-jazz composer and performer who currently records for Optimism label. –RW

○ **Windstorm / OPTIMISM**

GLENN MILLER   1904-1944

Swing, big band. Bandleader, trombone. Glenn Miller was the most popular bandleader of the last part of the swing era, starting in 1939 with "In the Mood" and other hits. He led a military band during the war and was lost over the English Channel on his way to Paris. More biographical details are included in the reviews below. –WR

Legendary Performer / RCA   1939
The 22 live performances found here, taken from 1939-1942 airchecks, demonstrate that, in performance, the Miller band's notorious precision could give way (slightly) to electric excitement. If any demonstration were needed for the band's success, these tracks provide it. –WR

Glenn Miller in Hollywood / POLYGRAM   1941
Recordings for two film projects. –RW

Army Air Force Band 1943-1944 / RCA   1943
40s recordings. –RW

Major Glenn Miller.... / BLUEBIRD   1943
Recorded 1943-1944. W/ The Army Air Force Band. At what turned out to be the end of his career, Glenn Miller led a very big band, playing martial arrangements of often military-oriented material at bond rallies around the country. This collection preserves the gaudy, uplifting style of Miller's last music. –WR

○ **Moonlight Serenade & Other Hits / RCA**
1990 release of familiar items. –RW

○ **Pure Gold / RCA**
1988 reissue of familiar recordings. –RW

○ **Chatanooga Choo Choo - #1 Hits / RCA**   COMP
1991 release that spotlights some of his biggest songs. –RW

Collectors Choice-Vintage Glen / CBS   COMP
An attempt to put his career in perspective. –RW

Complete Glenn Miller - Vols. 1-13 / RCA   COMP
The 13-disc boxed set. –RW

Memorial 1944-1969 / RCA   COMP
Two-record set from 80s. –RW

★ **Popular Recordings / RCA**   COMP
Of the many compilations of Glenn Miller hits, this three-disc set strikes the best balance between comprehensiveness and economy. More casual listeners might want to try *Pure Gold*, while true scholars will have to have the *Complete Glenn Miller*, but this 60-track collection contains the best of the most popular bandleader of the last part of the swing era. –WR

MULGREW MILLER   b1955

Post-bop, neo bop. Arguably the most prolific and accomplished pianist among the contemporary generation, Miller is an outstanding soloist, especially in the trio setting, and has been able to adapt his style to any context from big band to solo to sextet or quintet. After attending Memphis State University and moonlighting in Memphis clubs during the 70s, Miller worked with Johnny Griffin and Woody Shaw. He spent three years with Mercer Ellington and then another with Betty Carter. After working with Blakey's Messengers in the early 80s, Miller recorded with the Terence Blanchard/Donald Harrison group and has been a leader since the mid 80s. He continues to work with numerous other groups, notably Tony Williams. –RW

Keys to the City / LANDMARK   1985
Trio session. Marvin "Smitty" Smith's drumming and Miller's solos give this one some clout. –RW

○ **Work / LANDMARK**   1987
Memphis pianist Miller with trio (Teri Lyne Carrington on drums). Excellent. –MGN

The Countdown / LANDMARK   r1988
A sparkling release that boasts standout writing and exacting interaction between Joe Henderson (ts), Ron Carter (b), and Tony Williams (d). –RW

Wingspan / LANDMARK / DB 5   1988
Fine group jazz, with saxophonist Kenny Garrett. Bonus cut on CD. –MGN

From Day to Day / LANDMARK   1990
Miller takes center stage and shows his Memphis roots in blues and gospel throughout, plus a good touch on the occasional standard. –RW

LUCKY MILLINDER   1900-1966

Big band. A big-band leader of the 30s, whose bands spawned Sweets Edison, Tab Smith, Bill Doggett, Wynonie Harris, and countless others. Active until the early 50s. –MGN

○ **1942 / HINDSIGHT**   1942

PETE MINGER

Hard-bop, post-bop, neo bop. This Florida-based trumpeter and flugelhornist is a good big band player, comfortable in moden mainstream or hard bop settings. He is also an excellent lyrical balladeer. –MGN

○ **Minger Paintings / JAZZ ALLIANCE**

CHARLES MINGUS   1922-1979

Bop, hard-bop, post-bop, early free, progressive big band, Latin. Charles Mingus was arguably the greatest bass player in the history of jazz, both as a virtuoso and an innovator. He brought the bass from primarily a rhythm instrument to the forefront as a melodic instrument, not only for himself but for all bass players to follow. He looms equally large as a composer, combining composition and improvisation seamlessly to achieve a seminal new sound. He also strongly supports the European perception of jazz as modern classical music. Mingus had a reputation as a stern and even unreasonable leader, demanding that his musicians pay total attention to the music they were playing and that they sound "like themselves." Yet he consistently elicits performances from his musicians that surpass any of their efforts elsewhere. Almost any Mingus album is instantly recognizable as his, even if he is not himself playing at the time. This is not background music, and his music is not relaxing, but energizing and exciting. If you would like to glimpse the essentially kind, humorous, and big presence of Mingus, both the film *Mingus 1968* and his autobiography, *Beneath the Underdog*, are highly recommended.
There are many ways to categorize Mingus's music. A simple but useful way is to separate it into four categories: His formative years — anything up to *Pithecanthropus Erectus*; his standards — original studio versions of his live-performance repertoire; his live performance recordings; and his compositions — usually one-time performances of a Mingus composition and arrangement.
Any Mingus album is worth owning. If you have never listened to Mingus, I would recommend, as a great starting point, *Mingus at Antibes* (live performance). This is Mingus with perhaps his strongest group, at the height of his powers, and is certainly some of the hottest live jazz ever recorded. –MK

● **Pithecanthropus Erectus / ATLANTIC**   1956
Mingus's breakthrough album, when he found his true voice. First great compositional recording. –MK

○ **The Clown / ATLANTIC**   1957
A wonderful date that has bitter, reflective, and poignant Mingus compositions. The album marked the first appearance on vinyl of trombonist Jimmy Knepper. –RW

○ **New Tijuana Moods / BLUEBIRD**   1957
A theme composition of Mingus's. Evoking a trip to Tijuana during a down time. Wonderful. Same as *Tijuana Moods*, but with extra tracks. –MK

○ **Blues & Roots / ATLANTIC**   1959
A great Mingus album of gospel church music. Exciting, high-energy music. –MK

○ **Mingus Ah Um / CBS / DB 5**   1959
/any think this is Mingus's best studio album. All the

selections are top notch: there are no letdowns on this album. Similar in feel to *Blues and Roots*, but more fully realized. If you could have only two Mingus albums, this and *Mingus at Antibes* would be the two. −MK

★ **Mingus at Antibes / ATLANTIC** 1960
Mingus with perhaps his strongest group and at the height of his powers. The best live jazz album ever recorded? −MK

Mingus / CANDID 1960
Same material as the *Mosaic Candid Recordings*. −MK

Mingus Presents Mingus / CANDID 1960
Same material as the *Mosaic Candid Recordings*. The album in its original configuration. Great music! −MK

○ **Oh Yeah / ATLANTIC** 1961
This album has a bluesy, New Orleans feel. Mingus plays piano and sings (no bass). Roland Kirk is featured on the siren and other instruments. A spirited, fun album. Very droll. There is a bonus 25-minute interview of Mingus by Nesuhi Ertegun that makes this a must-have for the Mingus fan. −MK

○ **Black Saint & the Sinner Lady / MCA** 1963
A remarkable work that showcases both Mingus the composer and Mingus the bandleader. A six-piece suite, the session showed the influence and impact of Ellington on Mingus as an arranger. −RW

Mingus Plays Piano / MOBILE FIDELITY 1963
Mingus noodling on the piano. He is not technically so adept as he is on the bass, but this is a wonderful album. Mingus did compose his music on the piano. −MK

○ **Mingus, Mingus, Mingus / MCA** 1963
A live performance at the Club Bohemia in New York, one of the first Mingus recordings to feature mostly his own compositions. Some are his future standards. Here are his first attempts at future techniques such as combining two songs into one. His bass playing really stands out. −MK

Town Hall Concert / OJC 1964
The first of many live recordings made of Mingus's touring band of 1964, most in Europe. One of Mingus's strongest lineups: Eric Dolphy (reeds), Johnny Coles (tpt), Clifford Jordan (ts), Jaki Byard (p), and Dannie Richmond (d). Every performance on the tour is worth listening to. The only knock against this disc is its 45-minute length. −MK

The Great Concert, Paris 1964 / MU 1964
Same lineup as the *Town Hall Concert*, but two days later, still in Paris. Great performance. −MK

Right Now — Live at Jazz Workshop / OJC 1964
Funny, funky, and vibrant material, with sterling work from Clifford Jordan (ts), John Handy (as), Jane Getz (p), and Dannie Richmond (p). −RW

Mingus at Monterey / VDJ 1964
At the Monterey Jazz Festival. Has attained legendery status. Some of his other live performances seem stronger. Good performance of his and Ellington's material. −MK

Let My Children Hear Music / CBS 1971
Some of his strongest later compositions. Can get a little tedious at times ("The Chill of Death"), but Mingus merely follows his muse. If you weren't told this was jazz, you might think it was modern classical music. −MK

Shoes of the Fisherman's Wife.... / CBS 1971
The Shoes Of The Fisherman's Wife Are Some Jive Ass Slippers. Most of the *Mingus Dynasty*, which features the same lineup as *Mingus Ah Hum* and has a similar feel but is less driving. Inexplicable inclusion of "Shoes of the...." from *Let My Children Hear Music*, recorded twelve years later. All great music. −MK

○ **Changes One & Two / ATLANTIC** 1974
Spotlighting the last of his great small bands, heralding the forerunner of the George Adams/Don Pullen quartet that became a preeminent 80s jazz quartet. −RW

Cumbia & Jazz Fusion / AMCY 1976
Japanese issue. His strongest late recording. Somewhat of a

departure for him. Big ensemble, exotic sound effects. Worthwhile. −MK

○ **Epitaph / CBS** r 1990
A tribute. Memorial orchestra directed by Gunther Schuller playing the late bassist's works. A magnum opus. −MGN

Next Generation Performs ... / CBS
Next Generation Performs Charles Mingus's Brand New Compositions. Spirited repertoire and tribute efforts from past Mingus sidemen like George Adams (ts). Two Mingus siblings, Charles and Eric, are along as well. −RW

☆ **Complete Candid Recordings / MOSAIC** COMP
Studio sessions with a particularly strong group that had been playing at the same club together for a year. Mingus at his most avant-garde. Beautiful solo work by all throughout. Many Mingus standards. Incredible packaging (always the case with Mosaic). Limited edition, so BUY IT WHILE YOU CAN! −MK

○ **Complete Debut Recordings / FANTASY** COMP
1951-1958. Early recordings. All of the sessions on which Mingus played for the label he and Max Roach founded. If you are a Mingus fanatic, you need this set to trace his development. If not, you can get the highlights by getting *Mingus at the Bohemia* and *Jazz at Massey Hall*. −MK

BOB MINTZER

Jazz-rock, neo bop. Yet another Michael Brecker-influenced tenor saxophonist. Also competent big-band leader, on progressive/neo-bop/fusion side. A good one. −MGN

Camouflage / DMP 1986

Urban Contours / DMP 1989
This set mixes small and big-band sessions. −RW

Art of the Big Band / DMP 1990
A great technical recording, with good sidemen but unadventurous music. −RW

● **One World / DMP** ca. 1991
This saxophonist's best small-group work, with fellow Yellow Jackets. The best cuts are the title and "Look Around." Ventures funky and creative into neo-bop modes. −MGN

○ **Spectrum / DMP**
An all-star lineup of R. Brecker, P. Erstine, D. Grolnick, B. Malach, L. Gaines, and 14 other players. This is big-band jazz at its finest. The recording was made live to 2-track digital, and the music deserves it! Exceptional from start to finish. −PK

BILLY MITCHELL
b 1926

Bop, hard-bop, post-bop. Billy Mitchell is a fine, big-toned saxophonist whose big-band and swing background often shows up in his warm, fluid, and energetic solos. Mitchell studied in Detroit, then worked for short periods with Nat Towles, Lucky Millinder, and Woody Herman before making his first record with the Milt Bruckner band in 1949. He led various groups in the 50s before joining Dizzy Gillespie in 1956. Mitchell had two stints with Count Basie (1957-1961 and 1966-1967) and co-led a group with Al Grey in 1965-1964. Mitchell was Stevie Wonder's music director in the mid 60s and became an active educator in the 70s, as well as a session musician. −RW

○ **Colossus of Detroit / XANADU** 1978
Robust, fierce tenor sax solos and understated yet definitive piano from Barry Harris. −RW

De Lawd's Blues / XANADU 1980
Rare appearance from expatriate trumpeter Benny Bailey and declarative tenor sax by Mitchell. −RW

BLUE MITCHELL
1930-1979

Bop, hard-bop, post-bop, cool. Trumpet. Accurately nicknamed, Richard Allen Mitchell was an expressive, dynamic player whose style was easily adapted to either R&B or jazz. Mitchell worked with Paul Williams, Earl Bostic, and Red Prysock's R&B groups in 1951-1955. He became a major figure on the jazz scene during his five years with Horace Silver (1958-1964), where his pungent lines and assured, emphatic solos were a welcome part of the Silver hard-bop/gospel/Caribbean-rhythms axis. Mitchell used similar instrument and group concepts when he formed his own group in 1964, using Chick Corea to fill the role Silver had previously occupied. Mitchell's final years were spent back in an R&B and blues setting, as he worked first with Ray Charles and then John Mayall before doing lots of session work. −RW

Big Six / OJC   1958
An outstanding date, with above-average solos from Johnny Griffin (ts), Curtis Fuller (tb), and Mitchell. The rhythm section of Wynton Kelly (p), Wilbur Ware (b), and Philly Joe Jones (d) aren't slouches, either. −RW

Blue's Moods / OJC   1960
Smooth 1960 session that blends romantic pieces, soul-jazz, and mainstream. −RW

○ **The Thing to Do / BLUE NOTE**   1964
W/ Chick Corea, Jr. Cook (ts), and Al Foster (d). Recommended for jazz/trumpet lovers. −MGN

Down with It / BLUE NOTE   1965
One of Mitchell's least-recognized sessions, this has some fervent trumpet pieces, plus nice piano from a then still-emerging Chick Corea. −RW

Blue's Blues / MAINSTREAM   1972
A fine mainstream/bop date that includes some arresting Mitchell trumpet work on ballads. −RW

Blues on My Mind / OJC
An all-star lineup of mainstream/bop greats. Mitchell holds his own against sax greats Jimmy Heath, Benny Golson, and Johnny Griffin. −RW

● **Hear Ye! / ATLANTIC**
Definitive post-bop quintet. −MGN

GROVER MITCHELL   ♭ 1930

Big band, soul jazz, progressive big band. Journeyman saxophonist Grover Mitchell is the leader of an interesting big band. It includes a good mixture of veterans like Frank Wess and Cecil Bridgewater, plus new faces such as Byron Stripling and Marcus McLaurine. −RW

○ **Hip Shakin' / KEN MUSIC**   1990
Here is a nice recent big-band/orchestra date from a leader who doesn't record all that much. A good combination of veterans and young players in the band. −RW

RED MITCHELL   ♭ 1927

Bop, hard-bop, post-bop, cool. Though viewed more as a rhythm-section mainstay than an innovative player, Red Mitchell has been in the forefront of expanding the bass's potential as a lead instrument. He took a horn-like approach to playing bass, varying his technique and articulation and reaching notes and playing in a dashing, distinctive fashion. Mitchell actually began as a pianist with Chubby Jackson in 1949, then was a bassist with Charlie Ventura that same year. After two years with Woody Herman, Mitchell's personalized bass approach came to fruition during stints with Red Norvo and Gerry Mulligan. Mitchell became part of the Hampton Hawes trio for two years (1955-1957). He also had his own quartet for a year in 1957, then played with Andre Previn and Shelly Manne for four years while simultaneously becoming a busy studio musician. After co-leading a group with Harold Land in 1961-1962, he reunited with Hawes in 1965-1966. −RW

Presenting Red Mitchell / CONTEMPORARY   1957
One of the earliest sessions for this bassist, pianist, and singer from New York City; it helped launch his career. Recently reissued. −RW

○ **Talking / CAPRI**
This is a top-of-the-line trio, w/ Kenny Barron (p), Ben Riley (d). −MGN

ROSCOE MITCHELL   ♭ 1940

Early free, modern creative. Reed player and composer. Roscoe Mitchell has achieved recognition in two different (though not mutually exclusive) capacities within the jazz sphere. He's a founding member and major participant in the Art Ensemble of Chicago, and he's also issued several stunning releases as a leader. A versatile improviser and exceptional soloist, Mitchell has recorded with distinction on alto, soprano, and bass saxes and a wealth of percussion and miscellaneous instruments. He played in both high school and the army, then worked in a small combo with Henry Threadgill before joining Muhal Richard Abrams's experimental band that ultimately led to the creation of the Association for the Advancement of Creative Musicians (AACM) in the 60s. He's an underrated composer, whose writing has creatively explored interesting uses of sound, space, and rhythm. −RW

Sound / NESSA / DB 5   1966
Mitchell's first significant statement as a leader has ambitious pieces, amazing solos, and unorthodox arrangements. −RW

Congliptious / NESSA / DB 5   1968
Simply a standout quartet date. Mitchell honks, bleats, and dashes full steam ahead. Issued as Roscoe Mitchell and Ensemble. −RW

Solo Saxophone Concerts / NESSA / DB 5   1973
A highly unusual session, with most cuts featuring four saxophones. Mitchell does all the solos. This is not for the timid. −RW

Quartet / SACKVILLE
With pianist Muhal Abrahms, trombonist George Lewis, and guitarist A. Spencer Barefield. Very challenging listening. −MGN

○ **Nonaah / NESSA / DB 5**   1976
1976-1977. This is arguably Mitchell's best solo statement. It includes a full-side treatment of the title cut, solo works, duos, and an incredible alto number with Mitchell, Henry Threadgill (as), Joseph Jarman (reeds), and the undervalued Wallace McMillan (b). −RW

L-R-G/The Maze/SII Examples / NESSA   1978
Free improvisation. Definitive statement from Art Ensemble saxophonist and composer. One piece is all horns, another all percussion, and one is solo. This one is for open ears only. −MGN

● **Snurdy McGurdy and Her Dancing Shoes / NESSA**   1980
This album is more upbeat and humorous, less dense and intense than some past Mitchell dates, but the music's just as ferocious. −RW

The Flow of Things / BLACK SAINT / DB 5   1986
High-energy, kinetic pieces. Jodie Christian (p) opens the eyes of doubters −RW

SHERMAN MITCHELL   ♭ 1930

Swing, bop, post-bop, Latin. A trombonist, flutist, and alto saxophonist who guided Yusef Lateef to play the oboe. Mitchell has been a prolific composer and arranger. −MGN

○ **Far from Tranquil / LAMB**   1988
Jazz combo led by Flint trombonist, an extraordinary musician. Five Mitchell originals, and "Body & Soul." Latin and bossa-nova touches in a satisfying jazz program. −MGN

Once upon a Lifetime / SLIM   1991
Duets with pianist Todd Carlon. Soft, introspective side of trombonist and flutist. High caliber musicianship. −MGN

MITCHELL-RUFF

Hard-bop, post-bop. Dwike Mitchell (p) and Willie Ruff (b, french horn) play neo-classical to bop duets. −MGN

○ **Appearing Nightly / FORUM**
Standards with a neo-classical twist. Rare, but worth it for a clean copy. −MGN

MIXED BAG

Post-bop, Latin. All-star quintet from Detroit area, a project initiated by Bob James, supported Sonny Stitt when saxophonist lived in Saginaw in the last years of his life. Principals were David Koether & Lorenzo Brown (perc), Dan Spencer (d), Larry Nozero (Sax, fl), Eddie Russ (p), Ron Brooks (b), and Jerry Glassel or Bruce Dunlap (g). –MGN
○ **First Album / TRIBE** 1976
Upbeat contemporary jazz, Latin, and fusion. Liners by Bob James. –MGN

MJT PLUS 3

Post-bop, cool. This group was drummer Walter Perkins's vehicle for post-bop and neo-classical expression. Nice idea, taking MJQ style to new territory. –MGN
○ **Walter Perkins MJT Plus 3 / VEE JAY** i 1959
A date for drummer Walter Perkins as a leader. W/ Harold Mabern (p) and Frank Strozier (as). Good to find. –MGN
MJT Plus 3 / VEE JAY i 1960
W/ Frank Strozier (as). –ED

HANK MOBLEY 1930-1986

Bop, hard-bop, post-bop, soul jazz. The embodiment of a mainstream second-line tenor player, Mobley was famous for precise, clipped, and noteworthy solos delivered in a fashion close to, but never completely, deadpan. His fluidity and very introverted tone made him an immediately identifiable player. Mobley was an effective foil for dazzling, energetic trumpeters like Donald Byrd and Lee Morgan. Mobley started playing professionally with Paul Gayten's band in 1950-1951, then was spotted by Max Roach and played with him in 1951-1953. In 1954-1956, he worked with Tadd Dameron and Dizzy Gillespie and was part of the 1954 Horace Silver quartet that evolved into the original Jazz Messengers. He made many albums as a leader for Blue Note while maintaining ties and recording with Silver, Roach, and Art Blakey through the 50s and Lee Morgan, Kenny Dorham, and Elvin Jones in the 60s. Mobley had a stint with Miles Davis in 1961-1962 which was affected by creative differences. Mobley toured Europe in the late 60s and early 70s and co-led a band with Cedar Walton in 1970-1972. –RW
Hank Mobley Quartet / BLUE NOTE 1955
This debut of Mobley on Blue Note includes Horace Silver on piano and Doug Watkins on bass, plus someone named Art Blakey on drums. –RW
Hard Bop / SAVOY 1956
Three sessions in 1956. –JME
Message / PRESTIGE 1956
Some of Mobley's earliest work as a leader. –DS
Tenor Conclave / OJC 1956
A hard-blowing, straightahead jam session. –RW
And His All-Stars / BLUE NOTE 1957
This is great Mobley with Milt Jackson (vib) and Horace Silver (p). –DS
○ **Another Workout / BLUE NOTE / DB 5** 1957
A wonderful session that remained in the Blue Note vaults until 1985. –RW
Hank Mobley Quintet / BLUE NOTE 1957
A classic date with Art Farmer (tpt), Art Blakey (d), and Horace Silver (p). –DS
☆ **Peckin' Time / BLUE NOTE** 1958
One of the best by this prolific yet underrated tenor. With Lee Morgan (tpt) and Wynton Kelly (p). –DS
○ **Soul Station / BLUE NOTE** 1960
Another good Blue Note date that languished until its reissue in 1987. –RW
Roll Call / BLUE NOTE 1960
W/ Freddie Hubbard (tpt) and Art Blakey (d). –DS

Workout / BLUE NOTE 1961
Good session w/ Wynton Kelly (p) and Grant Green (g). –DS
● **Straight No Filter / BLUE NOTE** 1963
1963, 1965, and 1966 sessions. A surprisingly good date with a host of luminaries, including Lee Morgan (tpt), Freddie Hubbard (tpt), Donald Byrd (tpt), and McCoy Tyner (p). A 1986 reissue. –RW
No Room for Squares / BLUE NOTE 1963
This is an interesting session with Lee Morgan (tpt) and Andrew Hill (p). –DS
The Turnaround / BLUE NOTE 1965
Barry Harris (p) and Freddie Hubbard provide great back up. –DS
Dippin' / BLUE NOTE 1965
Excellent hard bop with Lee Morgan (tpt). –DS
A Caddy for Daddy / BLUE NOTE 1965
One of Mobley's best, w/ Lee Morgan (tpt) and Curtis Fuller (tb). –DS
Far Away Lands / BLUE NOTE 1967
W/ high-octane trumpet work by Donald Byrd and excellent tenor sax from Mobley. Cedar Walton (p), Ron Carter (b), and Billy Higgins (d) uphold rhythm section with distinction. –RW

Music Map

Jazz Flute

Little jazz flute before late 1920s.

Alberto Soccarras
Bennett's Swamplanders (1930)

First True Jazz Flutists
Wayman Carver w/ Benny Carter, Chick Webb (from 1932)
Henry Klee w/ Ray Linn (1944) — Jimmie Lunceford (1902-1947)

Flute important element in Latin American Music
Johnny Pacheco (1935)

1950s – Major Jazz Flutists Emerge
Frank Wess (1922) – Count Basie's band
Also:
Jerome Richardson (1920) — Buddy Collette (1921)
James Moody (1925) —Bud Shank (1926)
Frank Foster (1928) — Eric Dolphy (1928-1964)
Moe Koffman (1928) — Canada
Bobby Jaspar (1926-1963)

1956 *Down Beat* Award established for best flutist .

Jazz/Jazz-Rock
Herbie Mann (1930) — Jeremy Steig (1943)
Dave Valentin — Alexander Zonjic

Major Influences
Rahsaan Roland Kirk (1936-1977) — James Newton (1953)
Ira Sullivan (1931) — Chris Hinze (1938)
Hubert Laws (1939)

Ethnic Flutes
Yusef Lateef (1920) - wood/bamboo flutes
Roland Kirk (1936-1977) - nose flute
Don Cherry (1936) — Joseph Jarman (1937)
Douglas Ewart (1946)

Hi Voltage / BLUE NOTE 1967
Later Mobley, backed by Jackie McLean (as) and Blue Mitchell (tpt). –DS

MODERN JAZZ QUARTET

Cool. The Modern Jazz Quartet is the longest-lived small combo in jazz and one of the most important. The group was formed by pianist John Lewis, vibraphonist Milt Jackson, bassist Percy Heath, and drummer Kenny Clarke in January, 1952, although the four had played together in various configurations prior to that. From 1952 to 1955 they recorded for Prestige Records, turning out such records as *Concorde* and *Django*.
In 1955 Clarke left the MJQ and was replaced by Connie Kay, and the lineup has not changed since. The same year, the group switched affiliations to Atlantic Records. *Fontessa*, released in 1956, was the first of 27 albums recorded for the label over 32 years.
The MJQ's repertoire consisted mainly of Lewis compositions, and the pianist proved an ambitious writer, notably scoring the film *No Sun in Venice* (also called *One Never Knows*) in 1958, and in 1959 and 1960 taking the MJQ into the hybrid field of "third stream" music, a confluence of jazz and classical music, on *Third Stream Music* and *MJQ and Orchestra.*
The MJQ broke up officially in 1974, though it continued to play concerts on an irregular basis until an official reunion in 1981. Its most recent new album at this writing is the 1988 *For Ellington*, though Atlantic released a four-disc boxed set retrospective, *MJQ40*, in 1991. –WR

Django / PRESTIGE 1953
Their signature song and the last call for Kenny Clarke as the group's drummer. –RW

Concorde / OJC 1955
A bit of blues, a little third stream, and lots in between. The Gershwin medley is recommended. –RW

At Music Inn - Vol. 2 / ATLANTIC 1956
This is good for the inclusion of tracks from their 1956 date that were omitted from Volume one. It's another release that's lost significance with the boxed-set reissue. –RW

Fontessa / ATLANTIC 1956
An elegant date that shows their evolution into a comfortable, post-Clarke mode. –RW

Modern Jazz Quartet / ATLANTIC 1957
Despite the unassuming title, this features a fine rendition of "Night in Tunisia" and a standout "Bags Groove." –RW

○ **No Sun in Venice / ATLANTIC** 1957
An adventurous John Lewis score for the Roger Vadim film of the same name. –RW

Odds Against Tomorrow / CAPITOL / DB 5 1959
Reissue of a rare session on Blue Note. –RW

● **Modern Jazz Quartet / PRESTIGE** 1959
First works from early 50s with drummer Kenny Clark. Quintessential MJQ. Rare Prestige recordings. –MGN

Third Stream Music / ATLANTIC 1959
For adventurous listeners. –MGN

European Concert / ATLANTIC / DB 5 1960
This double-set pairing of two single albums marks the MJQ's visit to Europe. –RW

Comedy / ATLANTIC 1962
Not for all tastes. Includes one vocal from Diahann Carroll. Lacks improvisational punch, but has solid playing. –RW

Lonely Woman / ATLANTIC 1962
MJQ at its deepest. –RW

Blues at Carnegie Hall / ATLANTIC / DB 5 1966
A fine live set with first-rate Milt Jackson vibes solos and good ensemble pieces. –RW

Place Vendôme / POLYGRAM r 1966
This is a good departure for MJQ. Swingle Singers are a fine unit. –RW

Plastic Dreams / ATLANTIC 1971
It's sassy, bluesy cute at times. John Lewis is on harpsichord for a few tracks. –RW

○ **Complete Last Concert / ATLANTIC** 1974
At the time, this two-record set was viewed as the end of an era. Now it only represents the climax of phase one. It's an excellent set, though — among their best live efforts. –RW

Together Again at Montreux Jazz / PA2 1982
The session that marked the group's return to active touring and performing. –RW

Echoes — Together Again 1984 / PA2 / DB 5 1984
Their second "return" album has typically bright and glossy playing, but it lacks the quality and power of their Atlantic releases. –RW

Three Windows / ATLANTIC 1987
A date matching the MJQ with the New York Chamber Symphony. –RW

Topsy: This One's for Basie / PA2
Includes nice tributes to the Count. It's Kansas City swing done third-stream style. –RW

Art of the MJQ / ATLANTIC / DB 5 COMP
Good if not definitive anthology of their Atlantic music. It's been rendered moot by the 40-year boxed-set package. –RW

Best of / ATLANTIC COMP
Grab-bag single album set of their 50s and 60s cuts, worth very little now. –RW

☆ **MJQ 40 Years — Boxed Set / ATLANTIC** COMP
Recent set gathers a variety of styles from forty years of recording. –JME

Pyramid / ATLANTIC / DB 5 COMP
Compilation of various 50s cuts from multiple sessions. –RW

CHARNET MOFFETT

Post-bop, neo bop, M-base. This bassist and son of drummer and trumpeter Charles Moffett has emerged as a fine accompanist, bandleader, and composer, with occasional questionable tastes. His recordings have sometimes been uneven, bouncing between jazz and fusion. Moffett has recorded for Blue Note since 1987. –RW

Beauty Within / CAPITOL 1989
○ **Nettwork / CAPITOL**
This recent Moffett has better songs than its predecessors but is still not completely satisfying. Guest appearances from his father and sister. –RW

LOUIS MOHOLO b 1940

Post-bop, early free, progressive big band, modern creative. Drummer Louis Moholo has been among the most dynamic and prolific of the expatriate South African musicians. His vibrant, crisp rhythm work has fueled many pivotal ensembles, and he's been a contributor in a variety of styles from mainstream to outside to rock. Moholo taught himself the drums before founding a big band in 1956 called the Chordettes. He later joined the Blue Notes, a band led by pianist Chris McGregor. After playing at the Antibes Festival, they arrived in England in 1965, settling in London. Moholo spent a year on tour with saxophonist Steve Lacy in 1966, performing throughout South America. He also worked with trombonist Roswell Rudd and saxophonists Archie Shepp and John Tchicai. He returned to England in 1967, where he performed with McGregor's Brotherhood of Breath and many other groups, led by such European musicians as saxophonist Peter Brotzmann and Mike Osborne. During the late 60s and throughout the 70s and 80s, Moholo has done extensive freelancing and recording and has headed his own groups such as Moholo's Unit, Spirits Rejoice, Culture Shock, and the African Drum Ensemble. –RW

○ **Spirits Rejoice / OGUN** 1978
The South African drummer with the Blue Notes and

Brotherhood of Breath leads an octet. This is a great album — a must-buy. –MGN

Vive La Black / OGUN   1988
London studio date with a sextet featuring Sean Bergin and Steve Williamson on saxes. Excellent modern music. –MGN

GRACHAN MONCUR   b 1937

Post-bop, early free. A premier trombonist among the most fluid of his generation, Grachan Moncur III is the son of Grachan Moncur, a fine bassist who was a member of the original Savoy Sultans and recorded with (among others) Billie Holiday and Mildred Bailey. Grachan Moncur III studied formally at the Manhattan School of Music and Juilliard in the early 60s, before touring with Ray Charles from 1961-1963. He also spent a year with the Art Farmer-Benny Golson group in 1962. He settled in New York and became a familiar name on many records of the 60s, playing with Jackie McLean, Sonny Rollins, and Archie Shepp, and later becoming part of drummer Beaver Harris's 360 Degree Music Experience. He became a member of the Jazz Composers Orchestra Association in the 70s, writing the song "Echoes of Prayer" for the group. He returned to Newark later in the 70s and became an educator and activist, though he recorded with organist Big John Patton in 1983. He toured Europe with the second edition of the Paris Reunion Band in 1986. –RW

Evolution / BLUE NOTE   1963
Easily recommended Blue Note date from the 60s with Lee Morgan (tpt) and Jackie McLean (as). –MGN

○ **Some Other Stuff / BLUE NOTE**   1964
Red-hot dates, with Moncur and Wayne Shorter (sax) swapping licks and keying the session. –RW

New Africa / ACTUEL-BYG   1969
A majestic statement on freedom, liberation, and everything else. –RW

● **Echoes of Prayer / JCOA**   1974
The 1974 *Melody Maker Jazz Album of the Year*. Progressive and thought-provoking. A legendary recording, with the Jazz Composers Orchestra. –MGN

THELONIOUS MONK   1917-1982

Bop, hard-bop, post-bop, early free. Only Duke Ellington and arguably Charles Mingus are the equals of Thelonious Monk as a composer. His works forced musicians to exert themselves to their fullest, put a premium on surprise, and demonstrated a harmonic knowledge and musical sophistication that fooled those who'd tabbed him a witless recluse or just an eccentric personality. His piano playing was just as subtle and unpredictable, with odd phrases, unexpected pauses, tempo changes, and melodic quirks that always came together at the end to make a coherent, memorable statement. Monk began playing piano at 11, backing his mother's vocals in church, and he became a professional in the late 30s, gaining the job of house pianist at Minton's in 1939. He worked with many in the emerging bop generation, laying down what would become the vocabulary of the 40s. He was part of the group hired by Coleman Hawkins in 1944 to make some of the earliest bop recordings. But his career was plagued by personal and political problems. He made many superb recordings with Atlantic, Savoy, Verve, Blue Note, and Riverside but didn't debut on a so-called major label until 1962, when he was signed by Columbia. His stint there was a stormy one, and the label in fact didn't issue most of his finest live material until he died. Toward the end of his career, Monk became a celebrated elder statesman, and he was honored in 1978 at a Jazz Party held at the White House by President Jimmy Carter. Several Mosaic sets issued since his death chronicle his greatness, while artists from McCoy Tyner to NRBQ's Terry Adams hail his genius. –RW

● **Genius of Modern Music / BLUE NOTE / DB 5**   1947
Vol. 1. Early-period trios. Essential. –MGN

● **Genius of Modern Music / BLUE NOTE / DB 5**   1951
Vol. 2. Essential recordings. A must-buy. –MGN

Thelonious Monk Trio / PRESTIGE   1952
1952 & 1954. Wonderful trio recordings. The difference between the Max Roach (d) and Donal Bailey (d) cuts is quite instructive. These are some of Monk's more captivating solos from the 50s. –RW

○ **T. Monk & S. Rollins / OJC**   1953
1953 & 1954. Another great jazz collaboration. –MGN

Monk / OJC   1954
These fine 50s quintet dates include particularly strong solos from tenors Sonny Rollins and Frank Foster, plus typically unusual and odd Monk piano solos. –RW

● **Thelonious with John Coltrane / OJC / DB 5**   1955
Pivotal collaboration of two jazz giants. Quintessential. –MGN

Plays Duke Ellington / OJC   1955
One genius tackles the music of another. Superb trio recordings spiced by Oscar Pettiford (b) and Kenny Clarke (d). –RW

○ **Brilliant Corners / OJC / DB 5**   1956
A recording feat. Clark Terry (tpt), Sonny Rollins (ts), and Max Roach (d). Excellent version of the title tune. –HD

Unique Thelonious Monk / RIVERSIDE   1956
The trio with Oscar Pettiford (b) and Blakey (d). Plays standards, no originals. –HD

☆ **Complete Riverside Recordings / RIVERSIDE**   1956
1956-1960. Priceless Monk, 15 CDs and worth every cent. Essential. –JME

Thelonious Himself / RIVERSIDE / DB 5   1957
These are mostly solo; with one cut Coltrane (ts) and Wilbur Ware (b). –RW

Mulligan Meets Monk / OJC   1957
What seemed like a mismatch proved superb. The Wilbur Ware-Shadow Wilson (d) rhythm section clicked as well. –RW

○ **Monk's Music / OJC / DB 5**   1957
Superb septet with tenor greats Coltrane and Coleman Hawkins. A five-star album in *DOWN BEAT*. –HD

At Town Hall / OJC   1959
A great orchestral showpiece for Monk the composer, one of his best live dates. It also contains a complete version of "Thelonious" (on disc). –RW

5 by Monk by 5 / OJC   1959
The music proves as intriguing as the title. Excellent trumpet solos from Thad Jones. CD has bonus cuts. –RW

Alone in San Francisco / RIVERSIDE / DB 5   1959
Solo piano. Exacting, distinctive renditions of such Monk classics as "Blue Monk," "Pannonica," and "Reflections." Bonus CD cuts. –RW

Misterioso / OJC   1959
Additional sessions with the Johnny Griffin (sax), Ahmed Abdul-Malik (b), Roy Haynes (d) group. –RW

At the Blackhawk / OJC   1960
Special guests Harold Land (ts) and Joe Gordon (tpt) make this a great sextet. Monk's playing is daring and energized. The CD version includes the complete "Epistrophy." –HD

Monk in Italy / OJC   1961
A good quartet date, with tremendous work from Charlie Rouse (ts) and Monk. –RW

Monk's Dream / COLUMBIA / DB 5   1962
Quartet with Charlie Rouse (ts). Monk is in superb form on his debut Columbia album. –HD

Criss-Cross / COLUMBIA   ca. 1963
This is as fine a quartet recording of Monk's early-60s work as exists in the Columbia catalog. –RW

Tokyo Concerts / COLUMBIA   1963
Live quartet date with Charlie Rouse (ts). Excellent version of "Pannonica." –HD

Solo Monk / CBS   1965
A beautiful solo record. −MGN

Underground / CBS   ca. 1967
An excellent latter-period Monk group. "Green Chimneys" is a prime cut. Charlie Rouse is on tenor sax. −MGN

☆ **Complete Black Lion & Vogue / MOSAIC**   1971
Most from 1971, plus some from 1954. This is a priceless and comprehensive overview of brilliant Monk releases. −RW

And the Jazz Giants / FANTASY
Interesting dialogs between Monk and various greats among saxmen: Coltrane, Rollins, and Coleman Hawkins. −RW

Best of the Blue Note Years / CAPITOL   COMP
Worthwhile sampler of Monk's earliest work. −HD

☆ **Complete Blue Note Recordings / MOSAIC**   COMP
If you can find it, this is a wonderful chronicle of Monk's Blue Note days. −RW

The Composer / CBS   COMP
A good showcase for his compositions, but not one of his more-notable playing releases. −RW

● **Greatest Hits / CBS**   COMP
First-rate sampler of Monk's CBS days, as well as some of his finest compositions. −HD

Memorial Album / MILESTONE   COMP
An outstanding 1961 release, with a good cross-section of sessions from the 50s and early 60s. −RW

Standards / CBS   COMP
A sparkling solo and good quartet performances culled from Columbia dates. −RW

Straight, No Chaser / CBS   COMP
Charlie Rouse (ts) and Monk's magic is the highlight of this 1966 set. −RW

J. R. MONTEROSE   ♭ 1927

Bop, hard-bop, post-bop. A Detroit-born tenor saxophonist, Monterose worked a lot in the Catskills of upstate New York. Bop and post-bop innovator. (Not related to fellow Detroiter Jack Montrose, and not to be confused with him.) −MGN

● **J. R. Monterose / BLUE NOTE**   i 1956
W/ Ira Sullivan (tpt) and Horace Silver (p).

○ **The Message / JARO**   i 1959
W/ Tommy Flanagan (p).

In Action / BAINBRIDGE   1964

MONTGOMERY BROTHERS

Post-bop, cool, soul jazz. This trio was originally known as the Mastersounds in 1957-1960, then as the Montgomery Brothers in 1960-1962. The group consisted of Wes Montgomery on guitar, Monk Montgomery on bass, and Buddy Montgomery on vibes. They made several fine albums that blended easy-listening, standards, blues, and originals. −RW

● **Groove Yard / RIVERSIDE / DB 5**   r 1961
Indianapolis brothers in their heyday together. Essential listening. −MGN

Montgomery Brothers in Canada / FANTASY   r 1962
Top-rate playing throughout. On red vinyl. −MGN

BUDDY MONTGOMERY   ♭ 1930

Post-bop, soul jazz. Pianist, vibist. Buddy is probably the least known of the Montgomery brothers. Like Wes and Monk, Buddy grew up in Indianapolis and played with local groups around town. The three worked together in two aggregations in 1957-1962, making a number of good small-combo recordings. Monk later went to Las Vegas and became fairly successful in pit and stage bands. Buddy resurfaced in the late 80s as a pianist and made a stunning solo album that was part of the *Maybeck Recital Hall* series. On that album, his piano playing had more depth, harmonic variety, and

rhythmic variety than anything he ever did with Mastersounds or the Montgomery Brothers. −RW

Of Love / LANDMARK   1986
This one is very good. W/ Eddie Harris (sax) and Marlena Shaw (v). −MGN

○ **So Why Not? / LANDMARK**   1988
Rare record as a leader. Well-done, with some contemporary touches. −MGN

WES MONTGOMERY   1925-1968

Post-bop, cool, soul jazz. A highly respected, loved, and widely imitated musician, Wes Montgomery was acknowledged as the most influential jazz guitarist after Charlie Christian. He expanded the resources of guitar in all its main functions — chordal, melodic, and rhythmic. Originally from Indianapolis, he had a long musical association with his brothers Monk and Buddy. Wes played the guitar with his thumb instead of a pick, and achieved a warm, controlled sound with great rhythmic feel — very melodic and accessible. He also mastered the use of parallel-octave style in soloing, giving a thicker, more penetrating punch to his brilliantly straightforward and unerring melodic style. Unfortunately, some of his records were pop-jazz compromises under commercial pressure, but these brought him widespread acceptance and success, including a Grammy award in 1965 for *Goin' Out of My Head.* The recordings that have stood the test of time are his small group efforts with many of the jazz greats of his time, such as Tommy Flanagan, Hank Jones, Wynton Kelly, Paul Chambers, and Johnny Griffin. These recordings, which include albums such as *Full House* and *Movin' Along*, also feature his fine original compositions. Seemingly set for a long and celebrated career in the jazz world, Wes appeared on the cover of *DOWN BEAT* only a week before his premature death of a heart attack at 43. −DNM

Far Wes / CAPITOL   1958
1958 & 1959. With Harold Land (ts) and the Montgomery Brothers. −MGN

Wes Montgomery Trio / OJC   1959
Quite extraordinary. −MGN

● **Incredible Jazz Guitar / OJC / DB 5**   1960
A super date, with outstanding backing cast. Tommy Flanagan is excellent on piano. −RW

Movin' Along / OJC   1960
This is especially noteworthy for the presence of James Clay (ts). Solid Montgomery guitar. −RW

So Much Guitar / OJC   1961
High-quality blues and mainstream, with Ray Barretto (conga) bringing an Afro-Latin edge to the proceedings. Nice piano from Hank Jones. −RW

Full House / OJC   1962
This is for those who don't realize how good a mainstream and bop guitarist Montgomery was before turning to pop. He gets fine assistance from Johnny Griffin (sax) and a dynamite rhythm section. −RW

○ **Boss Guitar / OJC**   1963
Tart, stinging Montgomery guitar and good suppport from Jimmy Cobb on drums. −RW

Portrait of Wes / OJC   1963
Easy to enjoy. −MGN

Movin' Wes / POLYGRAM   1964
Mid-60s Verve transitional material that is not among his best from playing or production standards. −RW

Bumpin' / POLYGRAM   1965
It's light on the compositions, but plenty of substance in Montgomery's lines. −RW

★ **Smokin' at the Half Note / POLYGRAM**   1965
Live 2-fer. Can't get better. A must-buy. −MGN

Tequila / VERVE / BB 51   1966
Another pop date elevated by Montgomery's flair. −RW

A Day in the Life / A & M / BB 13   1967
One of Montgomery's biggest pop-hit albums. His playing is excellent. It's the inspiration behind similar George Benson efforts. Gold album. −RW

Down Here on the Ground / A & M / BB 38   1967
A successful pop date. Outstanding guitar, but little else. −RW

Guitar on the Go / OJC   1967
W/ Mel Rhyne (organ). −MGN

Road Song / A & M / BB 94   1968
Although it's pop-oriented, it still offers plenty of fine Montgomery. −RW

Alternative Wes Montgomery / MILESTONE   COMP
1960-1963. This is a nice two-record set of early-60s Montgomery with a host of great players including Milt Jackson (vib) and Johnny Griffin (ts). −RW

Plays the Blues / POLYGRAM   COMP
A grab-bag set from past efforts. It's good for its mix of sessions pitting Montgomery with Jimmy Smith (organ), but has somewhat of a slapdash quality. −RW

TETE MONTOLIU   b1933

Post-bop, cool, neo bop. A catalonian jazz pianist, Montoliu is equal parts Monk, Brahms, Bill Evans, and Debussy. Quite an original player and composer. −MGN

○ **Lunch in L.A. / CONTEMPORARY / DB 5**   1980

JACK MONTROSE   b1928

Hard-bop, post-bop. Post-bop saxophonist, not to be confused with J. R. Montrose. −MGN

○ **With Bob Gordon / ATLANTIC**   i1955

JAMES MOODY   b1925

Bop, post-bop, cool, soul jazz. Alto sax, tenor sax, flute. Moody was among the first tenor players to master the demanding vocabulary of bop, although he scored a huge hit on alto with the 1949 song "I'm in the Mood for Love." Moody was in the air force band in 1943-1946, then worked with Dizzy Gillespie in 1946-1948, touring Europe with him during that stint. He was in Paris in 1948-1951, even while "I'm in the Mood for Love" was burning up jukeboxes. The song was a hit again in 1952, when King Pleasure wrote words to fit his solo and turned it into "Moody's Mood for Love." Moody added flute to his arsenal in the 50s, co-led a septet in 1951-1962, and then was in a three-tenor union with Sonny Stitt and Gene Ammons in 1962. He rejoined Gillespie in 1963-1968. He's been a leader ever since and worked in Las Vegas in the late 70s. He is currently recording on Novus with a new band that includes young lion Todd Coleman and old pro Kenny Barron. −RW

Wail / ARGO   1955
A tremendous late-50s workout, featuring fine blues and expressive Moody. −RW

★ **Moody's Mood for Love / ARGO**   1956
A strong version of the "Moody's Mood for Love," with a vocal by the late Eddie Jefferson (v). −RW

James Moody's Moods / OJC   195?
An excellent reissue of mid-50s sessions, with some strong Moody solos. −RW

○ **Everything You've Always Wanted.... / CADET**   1964
Everything You've Always Wanted To Know About Sax. 2-fer date with Eddie Jefferson (v) on some tracks. Also with Tom McIntosh (tb), Howard McGhee (tpt), Hank Jones (p), and Kiane Zawadi (euphonium/tb). −MGN

○ **Don't Look Away Now / PRESTIGE**   1969
A hot quartet date. −RW

Too Heavy for Words / PA-USA   1971
Crackling exchanges with guest Al Cohn on tenor sax. −RW

Something Special / NOVUS   i1986
This is the 1986 release that welcomed him to the Novus/RCA family. −RW

Moving Forward / NOVUS   1988
Excellent Kenny Barron piano. It's decent major-label material, with a good menu of standards. −RW

Honey / NOVUS
The selections on this recent album are eratic, but he and veteran Kenny Barron (p) uphold things. It is certainly not a classic, but is worth having. −RW

BREW MOORE   1924-1973

Bop, post-bop. One of the better bop/post-bop tenor saxophonists of the 50s. Worked with Claude Thornhill Big Band in 40s. A neglected champion of the tenor. −MGN

○ **Brew Moore Quintet / OJC**   1956
Unsung tenor saxophonist with pianist and composer John Marabuto. A good bet. −MGN

Brew Moore / OJC   1964
A good late-50s hard-blowing session from an underrated saxophonist. −RW

RALPH MOORE   b1956

Post-bop, neo bop. This exemplary young-lion tenor saxophonist moved to the West Coast from England in the 80s. He is a driving, exciting soloist and a versatile stylist who has managed to find work in every setting from big band to small combo. He has recorded for Landmark since 1989 and has solo albums on the German Criss Cross label as well. −RW

Round Trip / RESERVOIR   1985
First date from British tenor saxophonist. Some great playing here, in the mainstream bag with Brian Lynch (tpt). −MGN

Images / LANDMARK   1988
This is a well-done 1988 set with Terence Blanchard (tpt) and Benny Green (tb). −RW

○ **Furthermore / LANDMARK**   1990
One of the best among the young-lion tenor saxophonists makes an aggressive, explosive statement. −RW

FRANCISCO MORA

Post-bop, Latin. This Detroit Latin-jazz drummer, and percussionist is a composer, now with Max Roach's M'boom. −MGN

○ **Mora / AACE**   1987
Fine Latin jazz from Mora. All originals. −MGN

JOE MORELLO   b1928

Post-bop, cool, neo bop. Quicksilver drummer, most closely associated with the classic Dave Brubeck Quartets. He is also a fine arranger, composer, and bandleader in his own right. −MGN

○ **Joe Morello Sextet / INTRO**   i1956
W/ Art Pepper (as) and Red Norvo (vib).

FRANK MORGAN   b1933

Bop, hard-bop, post-bop, cool. Currently a hero to many young lions, the alto saxophonist overcame severe drug problems and two stretches in prison to become a viable, popular performer. In his 20s, Morgan was one of the leading lights on the West Coast scene, but was imprisoned in the 50s, right at the peak of his powers. He moved to California at the age of 14, heard Charlie Parker for the first time as a teen, and began playing professionally in the early 50s. He made his first recordings in 1955, then went to jail for a year. Morgan was in and out of prison often in the 60s and 70s and was once in the same San Quentin band as Art Pepper. After going to Synanon in 1974, Morgan was sent back to prison, then got paroled. In solo structure, tone, phrasing, and approach, he's among the closest to Parker of any living alto player. −RW

○ **Frank Morgan / GNP CRESCENDO**   ca. 1955
A reissue of vintage Morgan that includes work with some of the West Coast's best. The guest list includes Wardell Gray (ts),

Carl Perkins (p), and James Clay (ts). Also has Morgan with Machito's rhythm section. –RW

Easy Living / CONTEMPORARY   1985
Solid hard bop, blues, and ballads from a great veteran. –RW

Double Image / CONTEMPORARY   1986
An excellent collaboration, pairing a great old veteran and a relatively youthful one on piano in Cables. –RW

● **Bebop Lives! / CONTEMPORARY**   1986
Live date at the Village Vanguard in NYC, with this veteran alto saxophonist on top of things. Prime bop, not to be missed. –MGN

Reflections / CONTEMPORARY   1988
Studio date with Joe Henderson (sax). Recommended. –MGN

Mood Indigo / POLYGRAM / DB 5   1989
A guest appearance from Wynton Marsalis (tpt), with spry Morgan licks. –RW

○ **Yardbird Suite / CONTEMPORARY**   1989
Excellent piano from Mulgrew Miller, bass from Ron Carter, and drums from Al Foster. Morgan is sharp and authoritative as a leader and player. –RW

○ **A Lovesome Thing / POLYGRAM**   1990
As always, Morgan's alto sings. –RW

LEE MORGAN   1938-1972

Bop, hard-bop, post-bop, soul jazz. This amazing trumpet firebrand was in the top echelon among hard-bop players. Besides his great range, Morgan's lines and solos were bristling and intense. He often utilized slurs or bent notes and delivered retorts and rhythmic phrases that were unforgettable. Morgan joined Dizzy Gillespie's big band as an 18-year-old in 1956. Then two years later he became one of Art Blakey's Jazz Messengers during a pivotal era, when Benny Golson was the music director. Morgan's elastic, exuberant solos made him a headline. He got some pop action with the 1964 hit "The Sidewinder," his most popular composition. He became a consistent attraction on Blue Note in the 60s and early 70s before being killed by an ex-girlfriend at a night club. –RW

Candy / BLUE NOTE   1958
A crisp, delightful Morgan leads throughout this set. –RW

○ **A-1 / SAVOY**   195?
A collection of cuts from the group Morgan co-led with Hank Mobley (sax) in the 50s. –RW

The Young Lions / VEE JAY   i 1960
W/ Frank Strozier (as) and Wayne Shorter (sax).

Take Twelve / OJC   1962

● **The Sidewinder / BLUE NOTE / BB 25**   1963
Contains his biggest hit. –MGN

☆ **Search for the New Land / BLUE NOTE**   1964
W/ Grant Green. Absolutely gorgeous compositional jazz. Near essential. –MGN

Tom Cat / BLUE NOTE   1964
Intriguing music not issued upon recording date. –MGN

Rumproller / BLUE NOTE   1965
Anything but standard, thanks to Joe Henderson (sax) plus dynamic drums by Billy Higgins. –RW

The Gigolo / BLUE NOTE   1965
Here is first-rate, outstanding tenor-sax work by Wayne Shorter, with a wonderful rhythm section. –RW

Cornbread / BLUE NOTE   1965
You can't go wrong with Morgan matching phrases with Jackie McLean (sax) and Hank Mobley (ts), plus Herbie Hancock on piano. –RW

Delightfulee / BLUE NOTE / DB 5   1966
This is a slightly below-par Blue Note date, though Morgan is on fire. –RW

The Rajah / BLUE NOTE   1966
Good, but pretty standard. –RW

The Procrastinator / BLUE NOTE   1967
Featuring Wayne Shorter (sax), George Coleman (ts), and Bobby Hutcherson (vib). –MGN

○ **Live at the Lighthouse / BLUE NOTE**   1970
2-fer of great live club date with extended versions and Bennie Maupin (sax), Harold Mabern (p), Jymie Merritt (b), and Mickey Roker (d). –MGN

Lee Morgan / BLUE NOTE   1971
Studio date. Some of his last sessions and going progressive. A great band featuring Harold Mabern (p), Billy Harper (ts), Jymie Merritt (b), and Freddie Waits (d). –MGN

Dizzy Atmosphere / OJC
This is an excellent match between Lee Morgan and Wynton Kelly (p), plus stirring tenor from Bill Mitchell and rollicking trombone from Al Grey. Bonus cuts on CD. –RW

● **Best of Lee Morgan / CAPITOL**   COMP
Very good compilation and good tune choices. –MGN

BUTCH MORRIS

Modern creative. Once a promising cornetist and familiar figure in the avant-garde, Morris had been almost exclusively a composer and conductor in the 70s, 80s, and 90s, working extensively with David Murray. He's done some playing in Murray's big band, but prefers conducting and premiering his works for large orchestra. A one-time member of the Black Artists Group in St. Louis, Morris was an acclaimed free-style player in the 70s before switching almost totally to conducting. –RW

○ **Dust to Dust / NEW WORLD**   1990
A fine large-group recording. The ensemble has several top players, including Wayne Horvitz (k), Marty Ehrlich (reeds), and John Purcell (reeds). Morris conducts and supervises with his usual skill. –RW

JAMES MORRISON   b 1962

Post-bop, neo bop. Morrison is an Australian trumpeter and trombonist who has made a sizable impression since his debut release in 1988. He was a prominent player in Australian circles, was subsequently signed to an Atlantic deal, and has made appearances at various jazz festivals and in concerts worldwide. A superb trumpet technician and competent trombonist, Morrison's career and skills are in bloom. –RW

○ **Swiss Encounter / ATLANTIC**   1988
Adam Makowicz takes solo honors on the piano. Morrison made a good impact on this 1988 release, sounding more inspired in a live setting. –RW

Snappy Doo / ATLANTIC   r 1991
This acclaimed Australian has good technique and a high-caliber backing band that includes Ray Brown (b) and Herb Ellis (g). Morrison is a fine technician still developing a personalized sound. One bonus cut on the CD version. –RW

JELLY ROLL MORTON   1890-1941

Trad. Piano, composer. Ferdinand "Jelly Roll" Morton is widely regarded as the first great composer in the jazz idiom, witnessed especially in his Red Hot Peppers recordings made for Victor in 1926-1930. A Creole-of-color pianist who was extremely proud of his French heritage, he earned the disapproval of his family by beginning his career in the bawdy houses of Storyville, the famed Red Light district of New Orleans, where he is said to have earned $100 a night entertaining the patrons of places such as the Hilma Burt House while still in his teens. Jelly's early years were spent traveling the nation solo and with various tent shows and vaudeville troupes. During World War I he settled in Chicago, where he began to assemble bands to record his compositions and other traditional New Orleans fare. In 1923 he participated in recording sessions with the New Orleans Rhythm Kings (NORK — a White outfit) for the Gennett label, located in Richmond, IN. At that time Indiana was the scene for a resurgence of Ku Klux Klan activity, and integrated recording sessions were risky business. According to NORK trombonist George Brunies, Jelly was passed off as a Spaniard — apparently accepted without question because of the diamond inlay which the pianist flashed with his broad smile. For the next five years Morton toured with various outfits from his home base in Chicago, including stints with Fate Marable, W. C. Handy, and The Alabamians. He also worked as a staff writer for the Melrose Publishing House, which covered many of his most famous compositions. For the Red Hot Peppers sessions he recruited a number of talented New Orleans sidemen, including Omer Simeon, Kid Ory, and the Dodds brothers. By 1930, however, it seemed that changing fashions (and a depressed recording market) had passed Jelly Roll by, and he was dropped from the Victor roster. As was the case for many of the older New Orleans players, the Depression years were unkind to Morton, and by the end of the decade he was living in obscurity in Washington, DC, waiting tables at a shoe-box nightclub called the Band Box. A series of oral history recordings made by Alan Lomax for the Archive of American Folksong at the Library of Congress in 1938 returned Jelly to national attention for a time (especially among a cadre of "hot" record collectors), but his death in 1941 ended his illustrious career before he was able to benefit from the New Orleans revival of the 40s.

Morton was certainly one of the most colorful characters in jazz history. His bravura and penchant for self-promotion (including the claim that he personally invented jazz) may have won him some friends, but also made him many enemies. As a solo pianist, he was capable of milking the instrument completely, with the ability to make a piano sound like an entire band. As a composer, arranger, and bandleader, he demanded absolute adherence to his vision of the principle of traditional collective improvisation. The Red Hot Peppers records especially drew on a wide variety of musical elements, simultaneously restating themes from ragtime and presaging the syncopated section work that later became the hallmark of the swing era. –BR

Jelly Roll Morton / MILESTONE / DB 5   1923
1923-1924. Morton's early band recordings, as well as first solo efforts. The best context for appreciating the evolution of Jelly Roll as a composer and bandleader as he approached his "Red Hot Pepper" period. –BR

Blues & Stomps: Rare Piano Rolls / BIOGRAPH   1924
1924-1926. These are just immaculate classic rolls, seminal piano cuts. –RW

☆ **Complete Victor Recordings / RCA**   1926
1926-1929. The ultimate Morton collection for the specialist, although all possible Victor takes are not included and some appear twice. Even so, a splendid range of Mortonia from the Red Hot Peppers through Jelly Roll Morton and his New Orleans Jazzmen. –BR

★ **Jelly Roll Morton / RCA**   192?
A more-manageable selection of Morton's Red Hot Peppers, well-suited to the beginner. –BR

Pianist & Composer - Vol. 1 / SMITHSONIAN   192?
Glittering 20s cuts, some with King Oliver (cnt). –RW

Library of Congress Recordings / SOLO ART   1938
A fascinating mixture of music and reminiscence. Jazz history from the Morton perspective. –BR

New Orleans Memories Plus Two / COMMODORE   1939
Piano solos from Jelly just before his death, some with vocals, make interesting comparisons to his first recordings. –BR

SAM MOST   b 1930

Post-bop, cool, neo bop. Saxophonist from West Coast cool school; also one of the few truly great jazz flute players. Perfect role model for future generations. Aside from those listed

below, any of his albums on the Xanadu label are worth hearing. –MGN

Introducing a New Star / PRESTIGE EP   i 1953
W/ Doug Mettome (tpt).

I'm Nuts About the Most / BETHLEHEM   i 1955
W/ Barry Galbraith (g).

○ **Mostly Flute / XANADU**   1976
W/ Duke Jordan Trio and Tal Farlow on guitar. Two Sam Most originals, five standards. Great interplay between Most and Farlow. –MGN

○ **From the Attick of My Mind / XANADU**   1978
Eight Sam Most originals. W/ Kenny Barron Trio. Given credit as a great flute player, this album displays his compositional worth. –MGN

● **Flute Talk / XANADU**   1979
W/ Joe Farrell. Two flutists speak volumes of jazz history on five Most originals, 3 standards, two of the bop. –MGN

BENNIE MOTEN   1894-1935

Swing, big band. Piano, bandleader. A prime personality in the 20s, Bennie Moten began as a trio leader playing ragtime and traditional New Orleans jazz. He built his band to six pieces by 1925, then added more members three years later to build the orchestra to a full group. Moten emphasized dance-oriented compositions and was a precursor to the classic 30s Kansas City swing bands. He built his orchestra by raiding Walter Page's Blue Devils, forcing Page to dismantle his band and join Moten. His early-30s bands included Ben Webster, Eddie Barefield, Herschel Evans, and Lester Young. His band reached its peak in popularity in 1935. At his death, Moten's band became the Count Basie Band. –RW

● **Complete - Vols. 1 & 2 / RCA**   1926
1926-1928. Chicago recordings for pianist's Kansas City orchestra. –MGN

☆ **Basie Beginnings (1929-32) / RCA**   1929
Early-jazz treasure. Essential. –MGN

PAUL MOTIAN   b 1931

Early free, jazz-rock, neo bop, modern creative. Not a bombastic or dazzling or powerful percussionist, Paul Motian has become a formidable drummer through his ability to interact with group members and vary or break up the beat, rather than keep a steady, throbbing pulse. His best work has been done in loose outside or free contexts, rather than conventional hard-bop, mainstream, or swing. He began recording in the mid 50s. He worked with vocalist Bob Dorough and Miles Davis in the 50s before joining Bill Evans in 1959. He stayed until 1963, then played with Paul Bley and many others before joining Keith Jarrett for two long stretches (1966-1969 and 1971-1975). Motian was part of the Jazz Composers Orchestra Association and worked in Charlie Haden's Liberation Orchestra as well. During the 70s and 80s, he led small combos, worked in solo and trio situations, and reunited with Paul Bley on two excellent late-80s releases. –RW

● **Conception Vessel / ECM**   1972
This is Motian's debut as a leader. It includes ambitious cuts with guitarist Sam Brown and also features pianist Keith Jarrett. –RW

Tribute / ECM   ca. 1974
Quintet with guitarist Sam Brown, Charlie Haden (b), early work of saxophonist Carlos Ward. Ornette's 'War Orphans" and Haden's immortal "Song for Che" are included. –MGN

○ **Dance / ECM**   1977
Excellent solos by saxophonist Charles Brackeen and above-average writing and ensemble work. –RW

Jack of Clubs / SOUL NOTE   1984
A quintet with Jim Pepper (ts), Joe Lovano (ts), Bill Frisell (g), and Ed Schuller (b) plays seven pieces, all by Motian. This is very intense yet lyrical. Pepper and Lovano are excellent sax foils. –MGN

It Should Have Happened ... / POLYGRAM   1984
It Should Have Happened a Long Time Ago. A capable trio set. Motian is both a good percussionist and a fine bandleader. –RW

○ **On Broadway - Vols. 1 & 2 / POLYGRAM**   1989
An interesting concept (first of two). –RW

☆ **Monk in Motian / POLYGRAM**   r 1989
A top tribute, with sterling work by Frisell (g) and Dewey Redman (ts). –RW

Bill Evans Tribute / POLYGRAM   1991
An excellent quartet date featuring sensational guitar by Bill Frisell and nice tenor sax from Joe Lovano. –RW

ALPHONSE MOUZON   b 1948

Jazz-rock, contemporary funk. Premier fusion/funk drummer whose flashy clothes and startling technique have made him a star. Well-used as a sideman too. –MGN

○ **Funky Snakefoot / BLUE NOTE**   1973
One of the few intelligent uses of funk and soul in a 70s instrumental setting (at least from a fusion standpoint). After this album, he became more pop oriented. –RW

Essence of Mystery / BLUE NOTE   r 1973
Some frenetic drumming and good jazz/rock arrangments lift this far above many of the later Mouzon releases. –RW

FAMOUDOU DON MOYE   b 1946

Early free, neo bop, modern creative. A member of the Art Ensemble of Chicago, Moye has been one of the drummers of choice among the 60s-and-beyond free generation, along with Ed Blackwell and Sunny Murray. He took percussion classes at Wayne State University in 1965-1966 and played with a group called Detroit Free Jazz, touring Europe with them in 1968. He worked with saxophonist Steve Lacy in Europe, also playing with the Gospel Messenger Sisters, guitarist Sonny Sharrock, pianist Dave Burrell, saxophonists Gato Barbieri and Pharoah Sanders, and trumpeter Alan Shorter before joining the Art Ensemble of Chicago in Paris in 1969. He's been a member of the Ensemble ever since and has also made some freewheeling, ambitious records as a leader. –RW

● **Sun Percussion - Vol. 1 / AECO**   1975
Quintessential solo recording (all percussion) from an Art Ensemble standout. –MGN

Earth Passage/Density / BLACK SAINT   1981
First-rate compositions, solos, and thematic execution. Moye is especially noteworthy in a fine rhythm section. –RW

○ **Black Paladins / BLACK SAINT**   r 1981
Adventurous concept pieces, excellent percussive foundations, and adept playing. –RW

THE MUFFINS

Jazz-rock, modern creative. This Maryland-based neo-fusion quintet rivals Soft Machine, 801, and National Health for originality and high spirit. –MGN

○ **Manna/Mirage / RANDOM RADAR**   1978
Progressive group music reminiscent of latter-period Soft Machine. A good one to find. –MGN

185 / RANDOM RADAR   1981
1981 followup. Not as potent, but still very good. –MGN

GERRY MULLIGAN   b 1927

Swing, big band, bop, cool, progressive big band. Now an elder statesman of the cool sound, Gerry Mulligan is arguably the best-known baritone saxophonist in jazz. He grew up in Philadelphia and got some early recognition as a writer. Mulligan's never had any problems with the cumbersome baritone sax — getting a rich, full sound, and displaying great range, tone, and ideas. He had songs recorded by Gene Krupa in 1947 and Claude Thornhill in 1948, and he also played in both bands on alto. He joined the Miles Davis band in 1948,

switched to baritone, and was one of the participants in the seminal cool recordings that proved extremely influential in forging an alternative to bop. He led groups similar to the Davis orchestra in 1951, 1953, and 1972, and spent a year writing for Stan Kenton in 1953. But he attained his reputation for his work with a number of quartets in the 50s, particularly his 1952-1953 group with trumpeter Chet Baker, plus other groups he led with Jon Eardley, Bob Brookmeyer, and Zoot Sims. Mulligan led a 12-piece unit for three years in the early 60s and spent four years with the Dave Brubeck band. As a composer and arranger, Mulligan was famous for writing pieces that didn't include the piano, and for leading ensembles that lacked either piano or guitar. His arrangements emphasized precision, swing, and a mild sound, with Mulligan usually opting for either two or three trumpets in his brass section, rather than the customary four. He's also made some extraordinary albums working with people he wouldn't normally be stylistically linked with, such as alto saxophonist Johnny Hodges and tenor saxophonist Ben Webster. –RW

● **Mulligan Plays Mulligan / OJC**   1951
A standout date, with Mulligan doing his own songs and top-echelon playing by Allen Eager (ts). –RW

Gerry/Paul / OJC   1952
1952 & 1954 dates. This is a sparkling blend of alto/baritone horns. –RW

Best Of: With Chet Baker / CAPITOL   1952
1952-1953. A good anthology presenting a sampling of cuts linking Chet Baker (tpt) and Mulligan, but far from being comprehensive. –RW

California Concerts - Vol. 1 & 2 / CAPITOL   1954
A top reissue of the opening volume of a Mulligan live date with Chico Hamilton (d) and Red Mitchell (b). The second volume has eight fresh tracks, with great cuts from tenor saxophonist Zoot Sims, Red Mitchell (b), and Bob Brookmeyer (tb). –RW

At Storyville / CAPITOL   1956
Six extra cuts flesh out the CD release of this live set. –RW

○ **Mulligan Meets Ben Webster / VERVE / DB 5**   1959
A wonderful pairing of individualistic giants. –RW

At the Village Vanguard / MOBILE FIDELITY   1960
An outstanding recording of an exuberant Mulligan concert release. –RW

Mulligan Meets Johnny Hodges / VERVE   1960
A mellow, mild, and wonderful collaboration with alto King Hodges. –RW

○ **Holliday with Mulligan / DRG**   1961
Judy Holliday has vocal duties. –RW

☆ **Jeru / COLUMBIA**   1962
A nice session. Excellent piano from Tommy Flanagan. –RW

Night Lights / POLYGRAM   1963
Has class and charm. Art Farmer shines on trumpet and meshes well with Mulligan. –RW

Age of Steam / A & M / DB 5   1972
This large orchestral work marked the start of Mulligan's post-Brubeck period. –RW

Walk on the Water / DRG   r 1981
Grammy-winning effort features high-caliber Mulligan. –RW

Soft Lights & Sweet Music / CONCORD   1986
Excellent teaming on a swinging date. –MGN

Symphonic Dreams / PRO ARTE-PRO JAZZ   1987
Mulligan plays with the Houston Symphony Orchestra. A nice production of marginal material. –RW

○ **Lonesome Boulevard / A&M**
Newest record. "Jeru" is on this one. –MGN

Meets the Saxophonists / POLYGRAM   COMP
A cross-section of cuts matching Mulligan with most of the great sax players, among them Ben Webster, Paul Desmond, Stan Getz, Johnny Hodges, and Zoot Sims. –RW

★ **Pacific Jazz and Capitol Recordings / MOSAIC**   COMP
Complete Pacific Jazz and Capitol Recordings of the Original Gerry Mulligan Quartet and Tentette with Chet Baker. Virtually the entire 50s output of the superb Mulligan/Baker small and large groups (except their Fantasy dates). –RW

MARK MURPHY   b 1932

Bop, cool, ballads. New York-born, California-based jazz vocalist, championed in the 50s by Steve Allen. Great singer of ballads, blues, and bop. Incredible scat singer. Distinctive voice used well in all ranges. Influenced by Charlie Parker and inspired by Jack Keroac. A hipster. –MGN

Rah / OJC   1961
Reissue. You can hear Murphy's style being cemented. –RW

● **That's How I Love the Blues / OJC**   1963
Good reissue. One of the few Murphy releases I treasure. –RW

○ **Artistry of Mark Murphy / MUSE**   1982
Includes a stunning medley of "Babe's Blue/Little Niles/Dat Dere." Recorded with Tom Harrell (tpt), Gene Bertoncini (g), and Ben Aranov (p) in a larger-group setting. –MGN

☆ **Bop for Kerouac / MUSE / DB 5**   r 1982
Murphy at the height of his inventive powers. There are too many standouts to mention them all, but check out the songs with Kerouac readings and the poignant "All the Sad Young Men." With sidemen Richie Cole (sax), Bruce Forman (g), and Bill Mays (p). –MGN

September Ballads / MILESTONE   1987
Includes some beautiful playing from Larry Coryell (g), Art Farmer (tpt). –RW

○ **Kerouac Then & Now / MUS**   r 1990
Lord Buckley and Kerouac readings. Exceptional. –MGN

What A Way to Go / MUSE   1990
A 1991 release. Up and down. –RW

○ **Beauty & the Beast / MUSE**
This is really good Murphy, arranged by Bill Mays. McCoy Tyner's 'Effendi' is a highlight, as is "Doxy" and "I Can't Get Started." –MGN

TURK MURPHY   1915-1987

Swing, big band. Trombone, bandleader. Along with Lu Watters, Turk Murphy was instrumental in the revival of New Orleans-style jazz in San Francisco during World War II. He was the trombonist with Watters's Yerba Buena Jazz Band until 1947, when he decided to forge out on his own. The Turk Murphy Jazz Band made numerous recordings from 1950 to 1980; headquartered in San Francisco at Earthquake McGoon's for many years, it became a major influence on the Bay Area traditonal jazz scene. In the mid 70s Murphy's band toured Australia and Europe, and in 1987 it performed at Carnegie Hall. Playing in a full-bodied tailgate style, like Ory, Murphy used the trombone to achieve a spectrum of emotional coloring from humor to pathos. One of the adjectives most often applied to his playing was "gutsy," and considering the fact that Turk Murphy continued to make music until the final days of his life (despite a long illness), in this case the music can be said to define the man. –BR

Volume 1 / GOOD TIME JAZZ   1949
1949 & 1950. Murphy with Bob Scobey (tpt), Burt Bales (p), Bob Helm (cl), and others doing what comes naturally on "Struttin' with Some Barbecue," "New Orleans Stomp," "1919 Rag," and other favorites. –BR

● **Turk Murphy's Jazz Band / GOOD TIME JAZZ**   1950
More Bay Area revival sounds from Turk, this time with Bill Napier, Don Kinch, Wally Rose, and George Bruns among the sidemen on "St. James Infirmary," "Canal Street Blues," "Down By the Riverside," and more. –BR

San Francisco Memories / MRY   1985
1985-1986. Murphy's final studio recordings — a fine testament to a lifetime's devotion to the music he loved. An excellent retrospective performance. –BR

Concert in the Park / MERRYMAKERS
A rarity — Turk Murphy recorded live. A classic performance of "Weary Blues" closes the set. –BR

○ **Favorites / GOOD TIME JAZZ**
A good introduction to the Turk Murphy style. –BR

THE MURPHY'S

Swing, bop, cool. Bassist Clifford Murphy leads this trio, which at times has included pianists Johnny O'Neal, Larry Fuller, and Claude Blade. A solid mainstream bop, post-bop, and cool combo. –MGN

Downtown / SOPHIA   1985
An album with young pianist Larry Fuller, C. Murphy, and George Goldsmith (d). Includes some off-tune vocals from Glenda Biddlestone, yet there are good instrumentals, and an especially cute cross of "All Blues" and "Outskirts of Town." –MGN

○ **Reunion / SOPHIA**   1986
Johnny O'Neal's piano is the focal point on this album which includes Clifford Murphy (b) and Kermit Walker (d). There are two vocals from Jan Spencer in this productive session. Two O'Neal originals, and two from O'Neal's ex-jazz Messenger mates Bill Pierce and Donald Harrison. –MGN

AMANI A.W. MURRAY   b 1977

Post-bop, neo bop. Young saxophonist just arriving on the national recording scene. Plays solid modern, swinging jazz in the tradition. –MGN

○ **Amani A.W. Murray / MCA-GRP**
Teenaged saxophonist does it right. –MGN

DAVID MURRAY   b 1955

Early free, progressive big band, modern creative. Tenor sax, bandleader. Simply put, David Murray has presented himself in a variety of settings with more success than any other saxophonist of his time. While suggesting a strong link to the work of Sonny Rollins, Murray's music is steeped in the church (check out the DIW release *Spirituals* if there are any doubts) and in R&B, yet Murray is one of jazz's most uninhibited improvisers.
While many of raves have come in favor of Murray's octet dates, emphasising Murray's considerable voicing skills, one should not neglect the many excellent small-group settings, particularly the more recent DIW sets. Murray's big-band outings rank among his most challenging work and are worth investigation. And did we mention Murray's work with the esteemed World Saxophone Quartet? Any of these attributes would be distinguished enough on their own, and Murray has so skillfully negotiated them as to give cause for strong argument that he could be one of the most formidable jazz musician of our era. –SA

Low Class Conspiracy / ADELPHI   1976
This is one of his earliest albums to make an impact on the general jazz audience. Fred Hopkins (b) and Phillip Wilson (d) excel. –RW

○ **Flowers for Albert / INDIA NAVIGATION**   1976
This a dynamic quartet date, with Murray in fierce, outside form. –RW

Lower Manhattan Ocean Club / INDIA NAVIGATION 1977
Vols. 1 & 2. Two live sets of powerhouse live jazz by a majestic, robust player. –RW

Interboogieology / BLACK SAINT   1978
More rousing quartet material. Murray emerges as a standout with singular style. –RW

Sweet Lovely / BLACK SAINT   1979
Pinpoint writing and emphatic solos. –RW

☆ **Ming / BLACK SAINT / DB 5**   1980
Arguably his best octet recording. –RW

● **Home / BLACK SAINT**   1981

Here are some of Murray's top compositions; equally super playing. –RW

☆ **Murray's Steps / BLACK SAINT** 1982
Octet with classic "Flowers For Albert." Out of his some 100 albums, the very best. –MGN

Morning Song / BLACK SAINT 1983

● **Live at Sweet Basil - Vol. 1 / BLACK SAINT** 1984
Declarative big-band sessions. –RW

The Healers / BLACK SAINT 1987
A stirring duo, with Randy Weston striking on piano. –RW

Ming's Samba / CBS ca. 1989
A wonderful late-80s quartet date, with great piano by John Hicks. –RW

Hope Scope / BLS
The usual striking Murray solos and aggressive pieces. –RW

SUNNY MURRAY ♭1937

Early free, modern creative. A rampaging, fiery drummer, Sunny Murray has propelled some of the hottest free and outside jazz dates of the 60s and 70s. A self-taught player, Murray went to New York in 1956 and worked with Henry Allen and Willie "The Lion" Smith, playing rather traditional jazz, until he moved on to Jackie McLean and Ted Curson. But his 1959 meeting with Cecil Taylor changed Murray's professional life. Taylor's percussive, attacking, and slashing musical style resulted in a change in Murray's approach to the drums. He went to Europe with Taylor in 1963, then joined a memorable trio with bassist Gary Peacock and saxophonist Albert Ayler, where his playing became even more energetic, loose, and frenetic than with Taylor. He later worked with (among others) Don Cherry, John Coltrane, and Ornette Coleman before returning to France in 1968, where he played for a time with Archie Shepp and Grachan Moncur III. He was featured on a number of wonderful but poorly distributed and recorded albums for BYG in the late 60s. His group, The Untouchable Factor, did some recording in the 70s and appeared at the Wildflowers Festival in 1976, probably the high-water mark for the "loft jazz" movement. –RW

Sunny Murray Quintet / ESP 1966
Dynamic, slashing, left-field jazz, both free-form and more traditional hard bop. –RW

Homage to Africa / BYG 1969
If you can find it, this is a celebratory blend of nationalism, avant-garde fire, and spectacular drumming. –RW

○ **Never Give a Sucker an Even Break / AFFINITY** 1969
Studio date in Paris from Philadelphian free-jazz drummer with quartet. Definitive. –MGN

● **Hard Cores / PHILLY JAZZ**
Perhaps his best group, paced by pianist Don Pullen. –RW

AMINA CLAUDINE MYERS ♭1943

blues-jazz, ballads, neo bop, contemporary funk, modern creative. This pianist and organist has an extremely lovely voice. She plays blues, gospel, and her own witty originals that look to avant-garde musings. –MGN

○ **Song for Mother E / LEO** 1979
Duets with percussionist Pheeroan Aklaff. Sounds like a bigger group. Excellent. –MGN

★ **Salutes Bessie Smith / LEO** 1980
Vocal perfection and landmark recording for this keyboardist and singer. Desert-island music. –MGN

\NAKED CITY

Modern creative. This is an intriguing free-form group led by John Zorn. They play a wild blend of avant-garde, hard-bop, rock, pop, and things in-between. The group also includes Bill Frisell, Fred Frith, Wayne Horvitz, and Joey Baron. They made a 1990 recording titled *Naked City*. –RW

○ **Torture Garden / SHILOH**

An intense, sometimes chaotic improvisational jazz session. Sometimes entertaining, sometimes chaotic. Approach at your own risk. –RW

VAUGHAN NARK ♭1956

Big band, post-bop, neo bop. A fierce trumpeter, a true innovator. Usually heard w/ USAF bands, and occasionally on his own in post-bop mode. A great soloist. –MGN

○ **El Tigre / PROGRESSIVE** 1983
High-flying trumpeter with Airmen of Note. Excellent swinging jazz from this virtuoso. –MGN

NASH BROTHERS

Swing, bop, cool, progressive big band. Ted (tenor sax and flute) and Dick (trombone) both played in big bands and television soundtracks in Los Angeles/Hollywood. Ted was a featured soloist w/ Les Brown in the mid 40s; Dick played prominently w/ Glen Gray and Billy May's Orchestras. Both have freelanced for years and continue to play studio sessions for TV and movies. Both are excellent jazzmen. –MGN

○ **Brothers Nash / LIBERTY** 1957
Ted (saxes) and Dick (trombone) Nash play standards with Jimmy Rowes on piano. Rare, but worth it. –MGN

TED NASH ♭1922

Post-bop, progressive big band. Nash is a Concord recording artist and pianist whose latest release is "Conception." A good mainstream player and composer, he has a rather low profile nationally. –RW

○ **Conception / CONCORD** 1979
Exellent mainstream jazz. –MGN

FATS NAVARRO 1923-1960

Bop, hard-bop. The trumpeter whose big, brawny tone set the tone (along with Dizzy Gillespie and Miles Davis) for the rise of bebop, Navarro is another great artist whose career was cut short by tuberculosis, edged on by narcotics usage. He did scant recording between the mid 40s and his death in 1950. He was notable for his quick attack and Spanish-tinged phrasings. –MGN

Fat Girl / SAVOY / DB 5 1947
Landmark Navarro Savoy sessions with Howard McGhee (tp), Ernie Henry (as), and others. –RW

● **Fats Navarro with Tadd Dameron / MILESTONE** 1947
1989 reissue. Simply sublime sessions spotlighting the radical innovations of the great Fats Navarro, plus Tadd Dameron's creative arrangements. –RW

○ **Fabulous Fats Navarro - Vols. 1 & 2 / BLUE NOTE** 1947
1947-1948. Here are brilliant trumpet solos from the sadly neglected trumpet master Navarro. Blue Note may have deleted this completely by now. It has six bonus cuts featuring the equally undervalued Tadd Dameron. –RW

○ **Prime Source / BLUE NOTE** 1947
1947, 1948, and 1949 recording dates. Navarro as featured soloist with the Tad Dameron Sextet and Septet, the Howard McGhee/Navarro Boptet, and Bud Powell's Modernists. Reissue compilation of Navarro's prime early work. –MGN

BUELL NEIDLINGER ♭1936

Post-bop, early free, neo bop. Bassist Buell Neidlinger has played with distinction in free-jazz, traditional jazz, and bluegrass bands. He studied piano, trumpet, and cello as a child, then in his early professional years played traditional and mainstream jazz in New York with Rex Stewart, Eddie Condon, and Vic Dickenson, among others. During the 50s he was part of Cecil Taylor's explosive group and worked with him from 1955-1960. In fact, the great album *New York City R&B* was actually a Neidlinger session for Candid that wasn't issued until 11 years after it was recorded, and then under

Taylor's name. Neidlinger also worked in the 50s with Steve Lacy, then later did session work on electric as an R&B player. He switched styles again in 1960, spending two years playing part-time with the Houston Symphony Orchestra while also doing some club work playing soul jazz with Arnett Cobb. Then came rock sessions and dates with Frank Zappa and jazz-rock/fusion with Jean-Luc Ponty. He eventually formed his own K2B2 label and made jazz and contemporary music recordings, while doing freelance bluegrass and classical work. –RW

● **New York City R&B / CANDID**   1961
This is actually Neidlinger's date. It is currently issued under Cecil Taylor's name. –RW

○ **Locomotive / SOUL NOTE**   1987
Virtuoso bassist and Marty Krystall on tenor sax. Fine music written by Monk and Ellington. –MGN

OLIVER NELSON   1932-1975

Post-bop, soul jazz, progressive big band. Composer, arranger, alto sax, tenor sax, flute. A superb arranger and composer as well as a highly underrated soloist, Oliver Nelson was an incisive, frequently compelling alto saxophonist and quite accomplished on other horns and flute as well. He came from a musical family and began playing publicly as a child. He worked in territory bands around St. Louis in the late 40s, then joined Louis Jordan's big band in 1951. After serving in the military and studying music formally, Nelson moved to New York. He had stints with Erskine Hawkins, Wild Bill Davis, and Louis Bellson in California, and was with Quincy Jones in 1960-1961. Nelson began to build his reputation with some visual recordings from the early-through-mid 60s, including his first big-band recording as well as small-group releases and works with Eric Dolphy. Nelson's arranging greatness became evident in the 60s as well, and he began arranging for Jimmy Smith, Billy Taylor, Wes Montgomery, and many others. By the mid 60s and until 1975, Nelson was quite busy with studio and television work, arrangements, recordings, and tours. –RW

Meet Oliver Nelson / OJC   1959
This dynamic session pairs Nelson with Kenny Dorham (tpt), Art Taylor (d), and others. –RW

Screamin' the Blues / OJC   1960
An exuberant romp with Eric Dolphy (sax) and Richard Williams (tpt). Outstanding alto sax by Nelson as well. –RW

○ **Soul Battle / PRESTIGE 7223**   1960
Oliver Nelson with King Curtis and Jimmy Forrest ... called a "Soul Battle," but it's really just a straightahead blowing date by three saxmen with distinct styles representative of different eras and/or genres. None of the saxes concede or compromise. This is King Curtis' most compelling jazz work ... and makes one wonder just how big his talent was ... a stimulating session. –BOB RUSCH, CADENCE

● **Blues & the Abstract Truth / MCA**   1961
Simply classic arrangements, breathtaking solos from an all-star ensemble that includes Freddie Hubbard (tpt), Eric Dolphy (sax), and Bill Evans (p). –RW

Straight Ahead / OJC   1961
Surging session with the Oliver Nelson & Eric Dolphy (sax) tandem. –RW

○ **Main Stem / PRESTIGE**   1961
This is a laudable small-group date with solid piano by Hank Jones . –RW

More Blues & the Abstract Truth / MCA   1964
An essential followup to a 1961 classic. –RW

Sound Pieces / GRP   1966
This is slightly mannered, but Nelson's biting phrases cut through to the quick. –RW

Musical Tribute to JFK / IMPULSE   1967
A masterly homage to the slain President. –RW

Jazz Albums

The year listed is that of the recording, unless otherwise indicated. Years marked with an "i" indicate the year when the recording was issued/released. Those marked with an "r" indicate the year the album was reviewed in *DOWN BEAT* or *Cadence*. Albums maked with a decade such as "195?" indicate the recording date has been narrowed to that particular decade.

Black Brown & Beautiful / RCA   1969
An exciting set. The reissue has three bonus cuts. –RW

Swiss Suite / FLYING DUTCHMAN   1971
Gato Barbieri (ts) almost steals the show on tenor; Eddie "Cleanhead" Vinson (sax) also sparkles in a guest stint. –RW

☆ **Stolen Moments / INNER CITY**   1975
If Oliver's work touched you elsewhere, then you'll want to hear this. –JERRY L. ATKINS, CADENCE

Live in Berlin / FLYING DUTCHMAN
Leon Thomas makes a soaring, impressive vocal contribution. Nelson's alto sax solos sizzle. –RW

NEW ORLEANS ALL STARS

Trad. A group of traditional-jazz players including the great Pops Foster, who recorded for the GHB traditional label. –RW

○ **Dixieland Band / PROARTE**

NEW YORK ART QUARTET

Early free. Progressive music quartet featuring stunning personal statements from the uncompromising percussionist Milford Graves, trombonist Roswell Rudd, saxophonist John Tchicai, and occasionally poet Amiri Baraka. –MGN

○ **New York Art Quartet / ESP**   i 1965

NEW YORK JAZZ QUARTET

Post-bop, cool, neo bop. Frank Wess and Roland Hanna's vehicle for group expression, this is a most-respected unit playing soul-jazz, neo-classical, and bop. –MGN

○ **In Concert in Japan / SALVATION SAL**   1975
Live concert in Tokyo, with Roland Hanna (p), Frank Wess (fl/sax), Ron Carter (b), and Ben Riley (d). –MGN

● **Surge / INNERCITY**   1977
Their best compositions in the studio. With Sir Roland Hanna on piano, Frank Wess on flute/sax and George Mraz on bass. A must-buy. –MGN

Blues for Sarka / INNERCITY   1978
Studio date with Roland Hanna, Frank Wess, George Mraz and drummer Grady Tate, featuring a 14-minute "All Blues." –MGN

PHINEAS NEWBORN   1931-1989

Hard-bop, post-bop, soul jazz. Though not mentioned often in the same breath with Art Tatum and Bud Powell, Phineas Newborn was certainly in their class as a pianist. His speed, facility, phrasing, and harmonic knowledge were astounding, and he was unmatched in his ability to inject blues and gospel elements into his work without destroying the improvisational nucleus. Newborn formed a quartet and moved to New York in 1956; he made a trio of marvelous records for Atlantic and RCA in the late 50s, and also made the great *Downhome Reunion* for United Artists with his brother Calvin. Phineas continued making superb dates in the 50s and 60s for Prestige, Roulette, and Contemporary. He made triumphant comeback records in the mid and late 70s on Atlantic and Pablo and for foreign labels. –RW

● **Great Jazz Piano / OJC**   1961
Hip music which thankfully moves past technique with logic
and adventure –BOB RUSCH, CADENCE

☆ **World of Piano / OJC**   1961
An A+ album from an A+ player. –MGN

Newborn Touch / OJC   1964
Outstanding trio sessions — a nice reissue of a Contemporary
set. –RW

Harlem Blues / OJC   1969
An album with wonderful solos and a nice blend of blues,
gospel, and jazz. –RW

○ **Back Home / CONTEMPORARY**   1976
A stunning date with Ray Brown (b) and Elvin Jones (d). –RW

Piano Artistry Of / ATLANTIC
Brilliant Memphis pianist with phenomenal technique. Can't
go wrong. –MGN

DAVID NEWMAN   b 1933

Blues-jazz, soul jazz, progressive big band. Tenor sax, flute.
David Newman picked up his "Fathead" nickname from a
childhood music teacher. He started in local groups around
Dallas, then worked in blues bands led by Lowell Fulson and
T-Bone Walker. In 1954 he joined Ray Charles and became the
personification of tasteful but expressive and bluesy sax
playing. He stayed until 1964, played with King Curtis in 1966,
rejoined Charles in 1970-1971, and worked with Herbie Mann
from 1972-1974. Throughout the 50s, 60s, and 70s, Newman's
Atlantic solo albums had lots of funk, some blues and ballads,
plus an occasional more-daring piece that showed Newman
could also play bop. He moved farther into the straight jazz
vein in the early 80s, but since 1985 has been doing more
soul-jazz and funk. He recently appeared on James Clay's
second Antilles album. –RW

○ **Return to the Wide Open Spaces / AMAZING**   1960
An all-star lineup including saxophonist James Clay. Reprise
of early-60s group. –MGN

House of David / ATLANTIC   1967
A solid session with soul and funk elements, plus typical
blues flavoring. –RW

○ **Lonely Avenue / ATLANTIC**   1971
Textbook soul-jazz; fine vibes from Roy Ayers. –RW

Resurgence / MUSE   1980
Newman shows bop talents heading a fine ensemble and
supported by Cedar Walton on piano. –RW

● **Still Hard Times / MUSE**   1982
Saxophonist in his prime. Tuneful and exuberant. –MGN

Fire! (Live at the Village Vanguard) / ATLANTIC   1988
A nice outing that matches Newman with Stanley Turrentine
(ts) and Hank Crawford (as). –RW

JOE NEWMAN   1922-1992

Swing, big band, bop. Trumpeter. A veteran of the New Orleans
scene, Joe Newman was born into a musical family. He took
lessons from David Jones, a noted multi-instrumentalist, then
joined the band at Alabama State College. That band later
toured under his leadership. Newman joined Lionel Hampton
in 1941, then joined Count Basie two years later and remained
until 1947. He played for five years with Illinois Jacquet and
then with J. C. Heard before rejoining Basie in 1952-1961. He
has made several excellent albums, written extended pieces,
and toured the international scene. –RW

Salute to Satch / RCA   1956
Newman makes a keen tribute to his mentor, featuring a tart
big band. –RW

Jive at Five / OJC   1960
A hot quintet date sparked by Newman's interaction with
Frank Wess (fl/sax). –RW

○ **Good N' Groovy / OJC**   1961
Unsung trumpet master on fire. –MGN

In a Mellow Mood / STASH   1962
Swinging trumpet and a tantalizing rhythm section. –RW

Hangin' Out / CONCORD / DB 5   1984
This relaxed, jovial session is co-led by Joe Wilder (tpt).
"Smitty" Smith adds fire on drums. –RW

NEWPORT JAZZ FESTIVAL ALL STARS

Swing, bop. Assorted musicians assembled by George Wein
for Concord recording dates in the late 80s and early 90s.
Personnel included saxophonist Scott Hamilton, cornetist
Warren Vache and, on one date, special guest saxophonist Al
Cohn. The 1990 release was a live concert done in Bern in
1989, while the 1988 release was a 1987 show recorded in
Switzerland. –RW

○ **European Tour / CONCORD**
A good group of musicians play hard and well despite the
sameness of the material. The veteran ensemble shifts into
high gear and lifts things above a jam-session context. –RW

JAMES NEWTON   b 1953

Post-bop, early free, new-age, neo bop, modern creative. James
Newton is the most gifted flutist to emerge since Hubert Laws,
and among the few able to play flawlessly, yet with soul and
passion. He began as a bassist playing in rock and R&B bands
while in high school, then moved to alto sax and bass clarinet
before finally choosing the flute. He studied music at
California State College, where he was inspired by the work of
fellow-flutist Eric Dolphy. He played in both jazz and classical
bands in college, then moved to New York with saxophonist
David Murray and drummer/writer Stanley Crouch in 1975
after he received his degree. He decided to concentrate on
flute in 1977 and, by using special fingerings, became a
virtuoso and master in playing the flute and using his voice
simultaneously. His ability to improvise a melody while also
singing it was a revelation to critics hearing it for the first
time. He's made a number of first-rate recordings, and also
composed and played classical music. –RW

From Inside / BVHAAST   1978
Sparkling flute work. –RW

○ **Mystery School / INDIA NAVIGATION**   1979
Arguably Newton's best ensemble session. He gets first-rate
aid from John Carter (cl). –RW

Axum / ECM   1981
This thrilling solo flute extends the instrument's scope and
range beyond expected frontiers. –RW

James Newton / GRAMAVISION / DB 5   1982
Features three Newton originals for pianists Anthony Davis
and Billy Strayhorn. W/ Jay Hoggard (vib) and Slide Hampton
(tb). Excellent, creative music. –MGN

Portraits / INDIA NAVIGATION   1982
High-level duet and trio cuts. –RW

● **The African Flower / BLUE NOTE / DB 5**   1985
Extraordinary album for this atmospheric flutist in a
completely realized setting. A program of Ellington and
Strayhorn. –MGN

Romance & Revolution / BLUE NOTE   r 1987

Echo Canyon / CELESTIAL HARMONIES
Excellent playing of Newton's compositions for solo flute. –RW

NICK NICHOLAS   b 1922

Bop, hard-bop, post-bop, cool. A Saginaw, MI tenor saxophonist
with a dry tone and bluesy feeling, Nicholas was very
influential on John Coltrane. –MGN

○ **Big Nick / INDIA NAVIGATION**   1985
Important document. –MGN

HERBIE NICHOLS   1919-1963

Post-bop, early free. Pianist and composer Herbie Nichols was
involved in the startup of the new bop music, but shied away

from the jazz scene itself. Instead, he worked through the 40s and middle 50s in swing and Dixieland bands. His recordings are very few. He recorded three times for Blue Note in 1955 and 1956, and the Mosaic set is the result of those sessions. Almost everything he recorded were his own compositions. This is remarkable music. It is very listenable and at the same time sounds a wake-up call. It has an internal consistency and integrity that reminds one of both Thelonious Monk and the modern European classical tradition, in particular the music of Erik Satie. This is not "cool" music. It has humor and warmth. Perhaps every generation has a couple of "sleepers" — great music that, not heard when it was played, suddenly is found. The exquisite music of Herbie Nichols fits this description. —JME

☆ **Complete Blue Note / MOSAIC**   1955
1955-1956. This is just great stuff ... desert island material. The notes are informative, the sound superb, but it is the music that will make you return time and again. This material is best described as intelligent yet emotional music. It has its roots in the blues and post-bop ... truly timeless.
—RICHARD B. KAMINS, CADENCE

● **The Third World / BLUE NOTE**   1955
1955 & 1956. Trio session. Many of his best numbers. Part of the Mosaic box. —MGN

Bethlehem Session / BETHLEHEM   1957
This latest reissue ... should open even more ears. In short, Nichols was an unrequited master who was pitifully underrecorded and overlooked while alive.
—WILLIARD JENKINS, CADENCE

LENNIE NIEHAUS   b 1929

Swing, big band, bop, progressive big band. Alto saxophonist and arranger Lennie Niehaus is probably best known by members of the current generation for his work with actor Clint Eastwood on a number of films, among them *Bird*, and Eastwood's newest Western film *Unforgiven*. But his playing and arranging credentials go back to the 50s, when he worked with Stan Kenton twice, in 1952 and from 1954-1959. A soloist, whose style links swing, bop, and cool sensibilities seamlessly. —RW

○ **The Quintets - Vol. 1 / OJC**   1954
Niehaus is terrific throughout. —BOB RUSCH, CADENCE

The Octet #2 - Vol 3 / OJC   1955
This music streches, squeezes, and in general turns figure eights on itself, and glides through the whole like a well-oiled eel. —BOB RUSCH, CADENCE

The Sextet / CONTEMPORARY   1956
Predecessor to octet recording. —RW

MIKE NOCK   b 1940

Post-bop, jazz-rock, new-age, neo bop. One of the more futuristic players around, Mike Nock was in the vanguard of jazz pianists who quickly recognized the coming of electronics. Originally from New Zealand, he became house pianist in a Boston club in 1962-1963, accompanying several visiting stars. He toured with Yusef Lateef, Booker Ervin, Stanley Turrentine, and John Handy in 1964-1967. In 1968 Nock formed the Fourth Way, a fine jazz/rock band that played improvisational, ambitious pieces with rock energy. They stayed together until 1971. —RW

○ **Ondas / POLYGRAM**   1981
A good trio date. Eddie Gomez on bass tends to be a more interesting improviser than Nock or Jon Christensen (d). —RW

KEN NORDINE

Spoken word, bop, early free. Originator of "word jazz" — setting poetry with effects to music: "The Voice of God." Nordine is also an acute political and social observer. —MGN

● **How Are Things in Your Town? / BLUE THUMB**   195?
2-fer compilation for "Mr. Word Jazz." Late-50s/early-60s poetry with social commentary. An utter delight. —MGN

Music Map

Jazz Guitar

The Beginning
Lonnie Johnson (1889-1970) – Blues
● Eddie Lang (1902-1933) – Classical

Early Jazz Guitar
● Django Reinhardt (1910-1953) — George Van Eps (1913)
Dick McDonough — Al Casey (1915)
Carl Kress — Snoozer Quinn

Pre-War Electric Guitar
● Charlie Christian (1916-1942)
Floyd Smith (1917-1982)— George Barnes (1921-1977)

Swing & Bop
Oscar Moore (1912-1981) — Tal Farlow (1921)
Herb Ellis (1921) — Barney Kessel (1923)
Freddie Greene (1911) — Mary Osbourne (1921)
Jim Hall (1930) — Joe Pass (1929)
Kenny Burrell (1931) — Jack Wilkins (1944)
Ed Bickert (1932)

1960s Guitar
● Wes Montgomery (1923-1968) — Jimmy Raney (1927)
Pat Martino (1944) — Howard Roberts (1929-1992)
● Grant Green (1931-1979)

Acoustic Jazz
Bill Harris (1925) — Ralph Towner (1940)
Lenny Breau (1941-1984) — John McLaughlin (1942)
Larry Coryell (1943)

Jazz-Fusion
Sonny Sharrock (1940) — ● John McLaughlin (1942)
Larry Coryell (1943) — John Abercrombie (1944)
Allan Holdsworth (1948) — ● John Scofield (1951)
Kazumi Watanabe (1953) — Pat Metheny (1954)
Al Di Meola (1954) — Kevin Eubanks (1957)
Mike Stern

Avant Garde
James "Blood" Ulmer (1942)
Sonny Sharrock (1940) — Derek Bailey (1932)
Eugene Chadbourne — Bill Frisell (1951)
Fred Frith

Colors / PHILIPS   196?
Twenty-four 90-second tone colors. —MGN

Stare with Your Ears / SNAIL   ca. 1979
A more-contemporary musical setting with keyboardist Manfredo Fest and harmonicist Peter 'Madcat' Ruth. —MGN

Twink / PHILIPS
Poems of Robert Shure, 1958-1967. —MGN

WALTER NORRIS   b 1931

Post-bop, early free. This slashing pianist resurfaced on the jazz scene in 1990 with a fine solo work on Concord. Norris played on the West Coast and with Ornette Coleman briefly in the 50s. He went to Europe in the 60s and hadn't done much recording except for a 1978 session for Progressive. His 1990 release revealed a demonstrative, impressive soloist with a keen touch and a strong rhythmic edge. He has since released a first-rate trio date. –RW

○ **Live at Maybeck Recital Hall - Vol. 4 / CONCORD** ca. 1972
Here is another solid entry in a solo series. Norris is an under-recorded, daring pianist who also writes distinctive pieces and is good on standards as well. The CD version has three bonus cuts. –RW

Lush Life / CONCORD
A fine trio date, with a particularly good version of the title cut. CD version has two bonus cuts. –RW

RED NORVO   b 1908

Swing, bop, cool. During the first part of his long career, Norvo employed the xylophone, an instrument commonly dismissed as "the woodpile," on which he made exquisite music, in particular at the helm of a "little" (12-piece) big band from 1936 to 1939, with arrangements by himself and Eddie Sauter and vocals by his then-wife, the fine singer Mildred Bailey (they were known as "Mr. & Mrs. Swing"). In 1943 Norvo switched to vibes, which he plays with some of the same delicacy as the xylophone. After stints with Benny Goodman and Woody Herman, he formed a trio with guitarist Tal Farlow and bassist Charles Mingus; it was a special kind of modern jazz chamber group. Since then Norvo has performed in a wide variety of settings, always in the best of taste, but health problems, including deterioration of his hearing, have caused him to be largely inactive in the 90s. –DM

○ **Featuring Mildred Bailey / PORTRAIT** 1933
1933-1938. This neglected gem features Norvo with Mildred Bailey (v), Bunny Berigan (tpt), and Charlie Barnet (sax) on superb 30s swing cuts with excellent mastering. It's probably deleted by now. –RW

● **Fabulous Jam Session / SPOTLITE** 1945
Cream-of-the-crop recordings pairing this vibes great with Charlie Parker (as), Dizzy Gillespie (tpt), and friends. A high-caliber reissue. –RW

Improvisations on Keynote / POLYGRAM 194?
As nice a cross-section of mid-40s Norvo cuts as is available. It was culled from the massive Keynote box. –RW

○ **Red Norvo Trio / SAVOY** 1950
This excellent two-record set highlights Norvo in peak playing form with Tal Farlow (g) and Mingus (b). Thoughtful yet aggressive playing. –RW

With Jimmy Raney & Red Mitchel / OJC 1954
A solid trio date, newly reissued with superior sound. –RW

Just a Mood / RCA 1957
Some first-rate small-group/combo sides compiled on a 1987 reissue. –RW

Forward Look / REFERENCE 195?
A good mid-50s session, reissued in 1985. The sound quality is spotty. –RW

LARRY NOZERO

Bop, hard-bop, post-bop, cool. Alto saxophonist and flutist influenced by bop and classical. He is reminiscent of Richie Cole and Frankie Wess, and clearly in their league. –MGN

○ **Island Fever / MSI** 1980
Extraordinary saxophonist with original ideas. Strong rhythm section w/ Ned Mann (d) and Jonathan Peretz (d). Nozero also plays excellent flute. Jazz with a contemporary (read swinging, not disco) edge. –MGN

Kaleidoscopin / DOMINIC 1988
W/ Paul Keller (b), Terry Lower (p), Jim Ryan (d), and David Koether (per). Spirit comparable to Phil Woods or Richie Cole. Fine effort. –MGN

NUCLEAR WHALES

Swing, cool. A six-member saxophone orchestra modeled after such groups as the World Saxophone Quartet and the Rova Saxophone Quartet.–RW

○ **Thar They Blow / WHALECO**

KIRK NUROCK

Early free, neo bop. A neo-classical and progressive pianist, Nurock is mostly a solo artist with some avant-garde leanings in the Keith Jarrett mode. –MGN

○ **Nurock / ADAMO** 1976
Progressive, jazz-piano solos. –MGN

ANITA O'DAY   b 1919

Big band, bop, ballads. Anita O'Day is a legitimate jazz legend and diva. She was in Chicago dance marathons as a teenager and sang with Max Miller's combo in 1939. Her sizzling delivery and sound, along with her unmatched phrasing and timing, stood out during her years with Gene Krupa in the 40s, though she wasn't so successful with Stan Kenton in 1944-1945. O'Day was dominant in the swing era, working with Benny Goodman, Duke Ellington, Will Bradley, Ralph Burns, Benny Carter, and many others, and scoring several hits. She was equally prolific in the 50s, heading her own combos, recording frequently, and still having smash hits. She began a comeback in the 70s with albums on her own label and others for small independent companies. O'Day is still active, albeit on a reduced schedule. –RW

Sings Jazz / VERVE 1952
Authoritative, commanding, excellent vocals. Later reissued under a different title. –RW

Songs by Anita / VERVE 1954
1954-1955. O'Day heads her own group, plus sings with power. Also reissued under different title. –RW

Anita / POLYGRAM 1956
1986 reissue of fine recording. –RW

☆ **Drummer Man / VERVE** 1956
Tremendous reunion date with Roy Eldridge (tpt) and Gene Krupa (d). –RW

Anita Sings the Most / POLYGRAM / DB 5 1957
1987 reissue of prime cuts, with Oscar Peterson (p) heading the backing combo. –RW

Sings the Winners / POLYGRAM 1958
Very good renditions, fine musical support from a combo led by Bud Shank (as). –RW

● **Cool Heat / VERVE** i 1959
Jimmy Giuffre (cl, sax) is first-rate, as is O'Day. –RW

Swings Cole Porter / POLYGRAM 1959
A most appropriate title, since that's just what she does on the Cole Porter menu. Nice reissue. –RW

○ **Anita O'Day and the Three Sounds / VERVE** 1962
Wonderful collaboration. –RW

In Berlin / PA-USA 1970
Great live set. –RW

Mello Day / G.N.P. 1979
A better production and performance than most of what O'Day put on her own label in 70s. –RW

S' Wonderful (Big Band Concert - 1985) / EMI-USA 1985
Fine big band; good Hank Jones (p), with nice leads by O'Day. –RW

CHICO O'FARRILL   b 1921

Progressive big band, Latin, salsa. The architect of the fully-flowered Latin-jazz charts of the Machito/Chano Pozo/Dizzy Gillespie ground breaking dates of the 40s and 50s. Also an adept pop arranger. –MGN

○ **Chico O'Farrill Jazz / CLEF** i 1953
Chico with Flip Phillips (ts), Nick Travis (tpt), and Roy Eldridge (tpt). –MGN

Jazz North and South of the Border / VERVE i 1957

JOHNNY O'NEAL   b 1956

Post-bop, soul jazz, neo bop. Younger jazz pianist from Detroit, roots in gospel, blues and jazz. Technical marvel. Ex-Blakey. Usually heard with a trio, swings fairly hard, extraordinary ballad player. –MGN

● **Soulful Swinging / PARKWOOD** 1985
Studio session, with bassist Dave Young and four tracks without drummer Terry Clarke. Prime. –MGN

○ **Coming Out / CONCORD**
His first album — gospel, blues, and jazz extensions. –MGN

OLD AND NEW DREAMS

Early free, modern creative. This is Ornette Coleman's 60s combo without Ornette — Dewey Redman (ts), Don Cherry (tpt, p), Charlie Haden (b), Ed Blackwell (d). Playing out of Ornette's harmolodic bag, they are tuneful but challenging, and never dull. A most important ensemble in the last two decades. –MGN

○ **Old and New Dreams / BLACK SAINT / DB 5** 1976
Debut. Fully realized. Quintessential. Modern jazz supreme from Don Cherry (cnt), Dewey Redman (ts), Charlie Haden (b), and Ed Blackwell (d). –MGN

● **Old and New Dreams / ECM** 1979
Great music from Ornette Coleman's band, playing with his verve and creative spirit. –MGN

Playing / POLYGRAM / DB 5 1980
Live in Zurich. Potent — did you expect anything else? –MGN

A Tribute to Blackwell / BLACK SAINT 1987
Soaring instrumental praises to a drum master, from a great combo. –RW

KING OLIVER   1885-1938

Trad. Cornet, bandleader. Joe "King" Oliver is often remembered today as the man who gave Louis Armstrong his first big break, but his tremendous influence on the development of early jazz as a cornetist and bandleader requires a deeper examination of his contributions. He is credited with pioneering the use of mutes to achieve vocal effects on cornet and with being the prime influence in the development of "hot" cornet styles, departing from the approach represented by Buddy Bolden and Freddie Keppard, which they described as closer to ragtime and "corny" by comparison. As a member of the Kid Ory band before relocating to Chicago in 1918, Oliver enjoyed widespread popularity and picked up tips on how to manage musicians to best effect from Manual "Hoss" Manetta, the straw boss of the band. Between 1918 and 1923 he built the Creole Jazz Band into one of the most celebrated "hit" units in jazz history, adding Armstrong and dual cornet breaks as a finishing touch. Also present were the Dodds brothers (Johnny on clarinet and "Baby" on drums), musicians who knew how to integrate virtuosity into a collectively improvised concept that demanded "playing for the band." After the band began to record in April 1923, the cooperative spirit within the group started to crumble, largely because several of the members felt that King Joe had become too dictatorial.
Oliver's next project was the Dixie Syncopators, a larger ensemble. But Oliver's fortunes were in decline, especially after he took the band to New York, where he passed up an offer to become the featured act at the Cotton Club (the job went to Duke Ellington instead). As his career continued to decline, the Depression wiped out his savings, his teeth were lost to gum disease, and he abandoned the band business in 1937, a forgotten hero. He died the following year in obscurity, just barely in advance of the onset of the New Orleans revival that renewed interest in the Creole Jazz Band recordings. The tragic implications of Oliver's life story have attracted considerable attention, but the music he made was buoyant and joyful, a triumph of sorts over the adversity that plagued his final years, and a testament to a spirit that never lost its musicality. –BR

★ **King Oliver - Louis Armstrong / MILESTONE** 1923
1923-1924. Classic renditions of "Snake Rag," "Dippermouth

Blues," and "Canal Street Blues" by the hottest band of its day - Oliver's Creole Jazz Band. Also includes Oliver duets with Jelly Roll Morton. –BR

Papa Joe / MCA 1926
Recorded from 1926-1928. Mid-20s jazz with Oliver leading a coterie of New Orleans stars like Omer Simeon (cl), Kid Ory (tb), Barney Bigard (cl), Luis Russell (p), and Paul Barbarin (d) on tunes such as "Snag It," "Sugar Foot Stomp," and "Farewell Blues." –BR

N.Y. Sessions / RCA 1929
1929 & 1930. The King in the final chapter of his recording career with an excellent selection of titles, showcasing his abilities as a bandleader more than as a soloist. –BR

○ **New York Sessions / RCA** 192?
Pivotal 20s cuts with Oliver helping cement the jazz vocabulary. –RW

ORANGE THEN BLUE

Post-bop, progressive big band, neo bop. A reportory band led by bassist Ed Schuller (Gunther Schuller's son) to play Mingus music and progressive little big band charts. –MGN

○ **Orange Then Blue / GM** 1985
Debut of this creative big-band music directed by Ed Schuller and John La Porta. In the spirit of Charles Mingus. Excellent. Several other albums are also worthwhile. –MGN

OREGON

Early free, world fusion. Paul McCandless (oboe, English horn, bass clarinet, saxophones) Glen Moore (bass, violin, piano flute) Ralph Towner (classical and 12-string guitars, piano, and brass instruments), Colin Walcott (percussion, especially tabla, sitar, clarinet). All of Oregon's members were members of the Paul Winter Consort; the group formed in 1970. Although usually categorized as jazz, Oregon breaks all the boundaries. The genuine virtuosity and versatility of group members helped the group achieve an unprecedented level of integration of cultural and stylistic influences, somehow managing to make their wide range of influences work artistically and reach a large audience. Influences include classical music (including 20th-century), world music (especially Indian music), jazz (including group improvisation concepts from free jazz), all within a very sensitive, melodic aesthetic. The group accomplished very highly disciplined ensemble recordings, including many fine compositions by Towner and other group members. The death of Collin Walcott in an accident in Europe in 1984 was a terrible blow, but Oregon re-formed with percussionist Trilok Gurtu and is still touring and recording. Considered a seminal influence for much of the eclectic, new-age, and world-music-influenced efforts to follow, Oregon has never been surpassed for artistic standards and integrity in that genre. –DNM

○ **Music of Another Present Era / VANGUARD** 1972
A 1989 reissue of an outstanding release that blows most similar ECM albums out of the water. –RW

○ **Distant Hills / VANGUARD** r 1974
This is one of the first releases to click from this group that knows how to make soothing, acoustic fare without becoming boring or wimpy. –RW

★ **Winter Light / VANGUARD** 1974
Here are some simply brilliant, feathery compositions. Marvelous playing. –RW

Out of the Woods / ELEKTRA / DB 5 1978
Many familiar themes. Excellent. –MGN

Moon and Mind / VANGUARD 1978
Wondrous duets. –RW

Oregon / ECM 1983
This is among the more memorable ECM releases, and one of their best from an ensemble-playing standpoint. –RW

Crossing / POLYGRAM 1984
Ethereal playing with tremendous solos from Ralph Towner (on guitar and piano) and Paul McCandless (oboe/sax). –RW

Ecotopia / POLYGRAM 1987
New percussionist Trilok Gurtu makes an impact within the group. –RW

45th Parallel / CBS r 1989
Pastiche of the group's winning acoustic/chamber and music/new age jazz formula. –RW

Essential / VANGUARD-CLASSICAL COMP
Much of their early-period works. Truly essential. –MGN

ANTHONY ORTEGA b 1928

Hard-bop, cool, progressive big band. California sax/flute/clarinet player who worked with Lionel Hampton, Luis Rivera, Dizzy Gillespie, and Quincy Jones. Began in a hard boppish style and drifted to more free-playing by the late 60s. Recorded in both small-combo and bigger-band context. –DS

● **Jazz for Young Moderns / BETHLEHEM** 1957
Big-band bop. –DS

○ **A Man and His Horn / HERALD** 1958
Classic bop with Hank Jones (p). Indispensible. –DS

Rain Dance / DISCOVERY 1978
Adventurous, bordering on avant-garde. –DS

KID ORY 1890-1973

Trad, Dixieland, swing. The dean of New Orleans Creole-of-color "tailgate" trombonists, Ory led the first Black jazz band to record for the Nordskog label in Los Angeles in June 1921. As a sideman with Armstrong's Hot Five and King Oliver's Dixie Syncopators in the mid 20s, Ory recorded extensively in Chicago before returning to the West Coast to re-form his own band. He reclaimed national attention in the mid-40s as a result of the New Orleans revival. Along with Bunk Johnson and George Lewis, he became widely regarded as an example of how jazz sounded in its earliest years. Observers of Ory in his New Orleans days recalled that he blew "the most foul" trombone ever heard (intended as a compliment). Of special interest are the songs he sings in Creole dialect — a rarity even among New Orleans artists. Members of Ory's generation were arguably the last to rigorously maintain creole customs — including the spoken patois — and these tunes provide an important glimpse of the kind of "good time" music that filled dancehalls in New Orleans so many years ago. His masterful style conveys the sense of playful fun and revelry associated with New Orleans dance music. Ironically, Ory's most famous composition, "Muskrat Ramble," became the basis for one of the most pervasive protest songs of the Vietnam era — Country Joe MacDonald's "Feel Like I'm Fixin' to Die." –BR

○ **Creole Jazz Band at Club Hangover / STORYVILLE** 1953
The Kid with Don Ewell (p), Albert Burbank (cl), Ed "Montudie" Garland (b), and others, captured in remote broadcast. Specialties include "South Rampart Street Parade," "High Society," and "Milneberg Joys." Ewell and Burbank offer some inspired soloing and ensemble work. –BR

● **Legendary Kid / GOOD TIME JAZZ** 1955
Ory's Creole Jazz Band delivering traditional favorites such as "Mahogany Hall Stomp," "Snag It," and "Pallet," with sidemen Alvin Alcorn (tpt), Phil Gomez, Wellman Braud (b), and Minor Hall (d). –BR

○ **Favorites! / GOOD TIME JAZZ** COMP
A compilation of various Ory bands, this CD gives a useful overview of the typical Creole Jazz Band repertoire. –BR

MARY OSBORNE b 1921

Swing, bop, cool. A female guitarist whose place in history is based not only on who she is, but on her facile, bright playing. –MGN

○ **Now's the Time / HALCYON** 1977
1977 concert in Rochester, NY for this guitarist with Marian McPartland (p), Vi Redd (sax) and Dottie Dodgion (d). Essential. –MGN

GREG OSBY

Neo bop, M-base. Osby is a highly regarded alto saxophonist and one of the few young lions in the 90s to take an alternative approach to the hard-bop revival. He has led his own band, has played with the Black Rock Coalition and with Steve Coleman's groups, and has done session work in R&B, funk, and jazz contexts. He currently appears on Andrew Hill and Jack DeJohnnette recordings and has been on the JMT label since 1987. –RW

○ **Greg Osby & Sound Theatre / POLYGRAM** 1987
This is Osby's most-accomplished ensemble, especially with Michele Rosewoman on piano. –RW

Season of Renewal / POLYGRAM 1989
Strong cuts, good concept, and excellent Osby solos. –RW

Man-Talk for Moderns - Vol. 10 / CAPITOL 1990
Osby is among the top players in the emerging new jazz movement. Hip-hop, funk, R&B, and bop intersect, not always smoothly but never predictably. –RW

OTB

Post-bop, neo bop. Out of the Blue. Originally formed by Blue Note records as an all-star band of "young lions" and a vehicle for promoting the label and straightahead jazz. Original members that have gone on to prominence are bassist Robert Hurst and drummer Ralph Peterson Jr. –MGN

○ **Inside Track / BLUE NOTE**
This album has fierce solos and good band interaction, but was a little weak in the songwriting department. –RW

Live at Mt. Fuji / BLUE NOTE
A solid session, though not groundbreaking, with faithful, neo-conservative material. –RW

● **Out Of The Blue / BLUE NOTE**
Judging by the talent displayed on this impressive date (an extension of hard bop that does not neglect the innovations of the last 20 years) there are some future giants on this recording. –SCOTT YANOW, CADENCE

Spiral Staircase / CAPITOL
Renee Rosnes at the piano puts fresh spark in the group's sound. –RW

HAROLD OUSLEY b 1929

Post-bop, contemporary funk. Ousley is a saxophonist and flutist whose progressive leanings were overshadowed somewhat by his abilities as a funk player. –MGN

○ **The People's Groove / MUSE** 1977
Saxophonist who worked with Dinah Washington. The all-star cast includes Ray McKinney (b), Bobby Rose (g), and Norman Simmons (p). –MGN

TONY OXLEY b 1938

Early free, progressive big band, jazz-rock, modern creative. British drummer on the progressive side who has played fusion with John McLaughlin and avant-garde with Cecil Taylor. Equally comfortable in trio or big bands. –MGN

○ **Live-Berlin 1985 /** 1985
16-piece free-jazz ensemble led by drummer Oxley. Three-pieces written by Oxley and played with wild abandon. W/ saxes G. Dudek, E. L. Petrowsky, and Larry Stabbins, Marcio Mattos (b), Barry Guy (b), and five drummers. –MGN

MAKOTO OZONE b 1961

New-age, neo bop. A premier jazz musician in Japan, Ozone has made a successful transition to America, where he became equally prominent in this nation's improvisational community. He began on organ at four, then took up piano as a teenager. He went to Berklee in 1980 and studied composing and arranging. He was noticed by Gary Burton and later recorded with him and was part of his band. Ozone's striking ability (especially on mid-tempo pieces) and impressive technique made him a big hit at the Kool Jazz Festival. His 1984 debut recording featured Burton and bassist Eddie Gomez. It was a stunning example of complete knowledge and mastery of the full jazz piano spectrum. Ozone later worked with European pianist Michel Petrucciani and spent extensive time studying classical music. −RW

● **Makoto Ozone / CBS**   1981
Produced by Gary Burton. Solo piano in light-jazz to edges of new-age. Bright, but not shining. −MGN

○ **Starlight / GRP**

PABLO ALL-STARS

Swing, bop. A lineup of veteran swing and mainstream stars who were assembled in 1977 at Montreaux for a special jam session. The lineup included Milt Jackson, Clark Terry, Oscar Peterson, and Joe Pass. −RW

○ **Pablo All-Stars Jam / OJC**   1977
This is a 1989 reissue of an entertaining session from the Montreux Festival, with top work from Milt Jackson (vib), Clark Terry (tpt), and Oscar Peterson (p). Previously titled *Pablo Live.* −RW

JOHNNY PACE

Ballads. A ballad and blues singer with limited recordings, Pace was overshadowed by Sinatra, but rivaled Johnny Desmond, Chet Baker, and Bobby Darin. −MGN

○ **Chet Baker Introduces Johnny Pace / OJC**   1958
W/ Chet Baker (tpt), Herbie Mann (fl). This vocal album will bring great joy to Chet Baker completists ... Baker takes a number of solos, but it's not enough to distract one away from Mr. Pace. −BOB RUSCH, CADENCE

MARTY PAICH   ♭1925

Big band, cool, progressive big band. An arranger, big-band leader, and composer who made his best jazz recordings in the 50s. At one time, Paich led a band that included Art Pepper and Russ Freeman. He later became a successful studio and session musician, and also did television and film soundtrack work. −RW

○ **Picasso of Big Band Jazz / CANDID**   1957
West Coast mainstream ... These arrangements create a light, airy feeling punctuated by a crisp (Mel Lewis) beat. −PAUL B. MATTHEWS, CADENCE

REMO PALMIER   ♭1923

Swing, bop, cool. Palmier is a swing-to-bop (not Latin, as many have assumed) guitarist who was a staff musician at CBS for almost 30 years. Also a member of the Great Guitars group with Herb Ellis and Barney Kessel, he is a smooth, solid player. −MGN

○ **Remo Palmier / CONCORD**   1978

MARY FETTIG PARK

Swing, post-bop, cool, neo bop. Alto Saxophonist from California, ex-Kenton member; big tone and original sound in the mainstream idiom. −MGN

○ **In Good Company / CONCORD**   1985
Only record as a leader. Worthwhile. Look for a followup. −MGN

CHARLIE PARKER   1920-1955

Bop, hard-bop. If any single person might be deemed the father of "modern" jazz, Charlie Parker could legitimately qualify. No saxophonist has been more influential, and Parker's legacy towers over jazz and modern music to this day. As a player, his skills were unsurpassed, especially his ability to constantly invent melodies in his solos, and he was also a harmonic genius. He was able to modulate from any key to another key, play in any register, and provide endless surprises whether doing originals, shopworn show tunes, ballads, or blues. At times, Parker and his cohort Dizzy

Gillespie would even turn practice compositions upside down and play them that way for relief. Sadly, a lifelong addiction to drugs, plus other personality problems, not only prevented him from living beyond 34 but certainly limited the amount of time he was effective on the bandstand. Despite all this, Parker's talent and greatness emerged on scores of records and through accounts from musicians and fans who heard him. Parker grew up in Kansas City and started on alto as a child. He played baritone in a school band but dropped out at 15, and shortly afterward he began his tragic involvement with drugs. His early influences were local players Buster Smith and Lester Young, and Parker got his first significant tenure in Jay McShann and Harlan Leonard's bands in the late 30s. He moved to New York in 1939 and spent three months washing dishes at a club where Art Tatum worked. During a job in Harlem, Parker began making his mark on the jazz scene, improvising on the upper intervals of the chords in the song "Cherokee" rather than the lower ones, creating a new harmonic framework. He later recorded with McShann in 1941, following his return to Kansas City for his father's funeral.

After leaving McShann and returning to New York, he began appearing at the historic jam sessions at Minton's, while also playing in the bands of Noble Sissle, Earl Hines, Cootie Williams, Andy Kirk, and Billy Eckstine. In 1944 he made some combo dates with Tiny Grimes, then worked a year later in a quintet with Dizzy Gillespie. He changed locales in late 1945, going to Los Angeles and playing with a band that included Gillespie, Milt Jackson, Al Haig, and others. But following a record session for Dial, Parker had a mental breakdown and was confined for six months in Camarillo State Hospital. He made some more recordings for Dial in 1947, then returned to New York, heading various groups and continuing to make incredible solo performances when he could physically appear at the date. During the 50s, Parker played Afro-latin jazz with Machito and Gillespie, made many remarkable dates for Verve, participated in a legendary concert in Canada at Massey Hall with several other notables, and also made a controversial recording with a string orchestra. During the 40s and 50s he also wrote a number of seminal tunes, among them "Ornithology," "Scrapple from the Apple," "Parker's Mood," and "Yardbird Suite." Continued abuse of drugs and alcohol, plus other drug-induced escapades, eventually resulted in his death. Still, some 37 years later, Charlie Parker's music remains immense. −RW

★ **Dial Masters 1 & 2 / STASH**
This is the best set. −MK

○ **Bird & Pres / VERVE**   ca. 1946
Jazz At The Philharmonic. More in LA from Lester and Lee Young, Dizzie Gillespie, Charlie Parker, Buck Clayton, Willie Smith, Mel Powell, Howard McGhee, and Charlie Ventura. It is the ultimate melding of swing era and bop musicians. −MGN

Bebop & Bird - Vols. 1 & 2 / RHINO   1946
Here's an intriguing concept, the first of two volumes that collect various cuts from 1946-1952 with Bird and bop elders Miles Davis (tpt), Max Roach (d), Errol Garner (p), and more. Great mastering and good selection. 1988 reissue. −RW

● **Bird at the Roost, Savoy Years / SAVOY / DB 5**   1948
Vols. 1-4. 1948-1949. Absolute must-buys, every volume. Live at the Royal Roost in the late 40s. −MGN

Charlie Parker / PRESTIGE (FANTASY)   1948
1948 & 1950 sessions. Shaky sound quality but good Parker solos from a two-record reissue on Milestone. −RW

Bird on 52nd Street / OJC   1948
An excellent 1948 date, with formative Miles Davis (tpt) solos, good Duke Jordan (p), and brilliant Parker. −RW

Bird at St. Nick's / OJC   1950
In this top-shelf session, Red Rodney shines on trumpet and Al Haig stars on piano. −RW

Bird & Diz / POLYGRAM   1950
Sharp date with T. Monk (p) and Buddy Rich (d) is a nice

introductory vehicle for Parker novices. It has three bonus cuts on disc. –RW

Swedish Schnapps / POLYGRAM   1950
W/ strings. These are tasty Parker performances from the 50s in Sweden. –RW

Verve Years (1950-1951) / VERVE   1950
1950-1951. This authoritative twin set nicely compiles and covers two prime Parker years. –RW

Inglewood Jam / TIME IS   1952
A first-rate, previously unreleased early-50s date linking Charlie Parker and Chet Baker (tpt). –RW

Now's the Time / POLYGRAM   1952
One of his most famous pieces and some brilliant alto solos. Expert rhythm-section playing. Textbook bop courtesy of Max Roach (d), Al Haig (p), and Percy Heath (b). –RW

Verve Years (1952-1954) / POLYGRAM   1952
1952-1954. This is the continuation of twin anthologies covering the Verve years. –RW

Jazz at Massey Hall / OJC   1953
This is a Charlie Parker (as) and Dizzy Gillespie (tpt) album, with Charles Mingus on bass. –MK

Charlie Parker at Storyville / BLUE NOTE   1953
This spirited session from Boston only appeared in 1985. It has fiery Parker alto, inspired piano by Red Garland, and some surprise guests, including Boston hero Herb Pomeroy (tpt). –RW

West Coast Time / BLACK LABEL   195?
A good set of 50s Parker. –RW

○ **Live at Carnegie Hall / POLYGRAM**   1965
10th Memorial concert. Not Parker himself. Immortal sessions with various artists celebrating the Bird. –MGN

Charlie Parker with Strings / POLYGRAM
A seminal release — his finest playing in an orchestral setting. The date was once controversial, but is now universally accepted. –RW

Cole Porter Songbook / POLYGRAM
Bird takes Porter's songs and extends them to glorious heights. A fine reissue. –RW

Early Bird / PAIR
The foundation cuts, although (unfortunately) they're done here by a label that skimps on production and remastering values. Get the UK/Spotlite *Early Bird* instead. –RW

Jazz 'Round Midnight / POLYGRAM
Parker soars but the session sputters. –RW

☆ **Bird: Complete on Verve / POLYGRAM**   COMP
If you want one good boxed set, get this one. It contains 51 unissued selections — over 11 hours of engrossing, majestic music thematically and chronologically assembled to reflect Parker's peak 1946-1954 period on Verve. An exhaustive 36-page booklet is included. –RW

☆ **Bird — The Savoy Recordings / SAVOY**   COMP
Master takes. Classic sessions from 1944-1948 in the studio. Miles Davis (tpt), Dizzy Gillespie (tpt), Max Roach (d), Doc West (d), Clyde Hart (p), Tommy Potter (b), and others make great bop with Bird. Should be available again soon. –MGN

The Verve Years / POLYGRAM   COMP
1946-1954. This good two-record set collects the first two years of Parker's Verve output. –RW

○ **Very Best Bird / WARNER BROTHERS**   COMP
Despite a confusing and misleading title, this is a good two-record set of Parker cuts, covering songs he is best known for. It's not comprehensive, but a good introduction. –RW

ERROLL PARKER

Early free, progressive big band, modern creative. An Algerian pianist, drummer, composer, and bandleader, Parker conducts a ten-piece band in a progressive, avant-garde style. He's a great performer. –MGN

○ **Tribute to Thelonius Monk / SAHARA**   1982
Solo piano, although no tunes by Monk. –MGN

○ **Tentet / SAHARA**   1983
Algerian-born pianist/percussionist in an original mode. Extraordinary creative music, live in 'rehearsal' at the Williamsburg Music Center in Brooklyn. –MGN

● **A Night in Tunisia / SAHARA**   ca. 1991
Tentet plays six Parker originals and two standards. Teamwork in playing leader's quirky Monk-like themes is most evident. A fine outing. –MGN

LEO PARKER   1925-1962

Post-bop, blues-jazz. This overlooked baritone saxophonist made some good hard-bop recordings in the 60s. He was a fluent, formidable soloist and a strong accompanist and bandleader, as well as an above-average composer. Parker has gotten fresh exposure, thanks to 80s and 90s reissues on Blue Note and Collectables. –RW

● **Back to Back Baritones / CBS**   1948
1948-1950 recordings. Baritone sax work in early R&B-honker style with some jazz leanings. Small-combo backing. Album's use of multiple and alternate takes will be of particular interest to musicians and collectors. –HD

○ **Baritone Great (1951-1953) / CHESS**   1951
His best, with Sahib Shihab (fl/sax) and Red Saunders (d). One to seek. –MGN

Let Me Tell You 'Bout It / CAPITOL   1961
A good 1990 release that provides notable Leo Parker baritone sax. –RW

Rollin' with Leo / CAPITOL   1961
A very good album for this sax great. –MGN

HORACE PARLAN   ♭1931

Post-bop. A pianist discovered by Charles Mingus, Parlan has overcome disability and made it an asset. His right hand was partially crippled by polio when he was a child, yet he has made kinetic, rhythmic right-hand phrases part of his attack, contrasting them with striking left-hand chords. Parlan filters blues and R&B influences through solos that are stark, sometimes somber, but never dull or lifeless. Parlan began playing in R&B bands during the 50s, then moved from Pittsburgh to New York and joined Mingus's group from 1957 to 1959. He worked with Booker Ervin in 1960-1961, then was a regular pianist with the Eddie "Lockjaw" Davis-Johnny Griffin quintet in 1962. He played with Rahsaan Roland Kirk from 1963 to 1966. Parlan had a string of strong Blue Note releases in the 60s, but encountered tough times near the end of the decade. He left America for Copenhagen in 1973, and during the 70s and 80s he gained international recognition for some superb releases on Copenhagen, including a pair of stunning duet sessions with Archie Shepp. –RW

Movin' & Groovin' / BLUE NOTE   1960
An album of wonderful trio work with Sam Jones (b), Al Harewood (d). –RW

Up & Down / BLUE NOTE   1961
Tremendous solos from Booker Ervin (ts) and Grant Green (g), with dynamic and bluesy Parlan piano. –RW

● **Back from the Gig / BLUE NOTE**   1963
This was later issued under Booker Ervin's name, but was truly Parlan's date. Ervin's lusty tenor and Parlan's shimmering piano are impressive. –RW

○ **Happy Frame of Mind / CAPITOL**   1963
Expatriate pianist on a reissue of one of his best albums, with Booker Ervin (ts). Search for others. –MGN

No Blues / STEEPLECHASE   1975
A sparkling trio date. –RW

Blue Parlan / STEEPLECHASE   1978
Parlan gets down in this striking trio outing. –RW

○ **Going Home / STEEPLECHASE** 1979
Evocative duets with Archie Shepp (sax). −RW

The Maestro / STEEPLECHASE 1979
Listen to moving and definitive solo piano. −RW

Glad I Found You / STEEPLECHASE 1984
Straightahead blowing date. Eddie Harris (ts) almost outdoes Parlan. −RW

JOE PASS   ♭1929

Bop, cool. Joe Pass emerged in the early 60s after years of drug problems, displaying an astounding technical ability and overall mastery of the guitar. He recorded and toured in the 60s with many major jazz artists such as George Shearing, Sara Vaughan, and Carmen McRae, but was not well known until his first solo album, *Virtuoso,* on Pablo in 1973. This set of personal improvisations on standard tunes, featuring bass lines, chord solos, and lightning-fast melodic soloing — often with several of the above happening at the same time — established a new level of guitar mastery in mainstream jazz. He went on to several successful collaborations with artists such as Oscar Peterson, Ella Fitzgerald, and Herb Ellis, and has released several solo recordings in addition to extensive live performing as a solo artist. Joe's many contributions to jazz guitar include bringing its contrapuntal resources into the mainstream in new ways and showing that high-energy bebop melodies can stand on their own in solo guitar settings. He is musically a traditionalist, and the power and energy of his spontaneous improvisations make for exciting listening.
−DNM

Virtuoso / PABLO / DB 5 1973
Superior solo performances of well-known standards. −RW

Portraits of Duke Ellington / PABLO 1974
A tremendous set, with Pass paying homage to Ellington. −RW

○ **Virtuoso No. 2 / PABLO / DB 5** 1976
Solo outing ... with impeccable tone and warm approach ... Particularly great late-night music. −W. JENKINS JR., CADENCE

● **I Remember Charlie Parker / PABLO** 1979
This is a worthy reissue of Pass's late-70s tribute to Charlie Parker. −RW

Quadrant Toasts Duke Ellington / OJC 1980
There's a bit more intensity here, thanks to the presence of Milt Jackson (vib), Ray Brown (b), and Mickey Roker (d). −RW

Whitestone / PABLO 1985
Here's nothing new or fresh, but still solid Pass. −RW

At Akron University / PABLO 1986
Brilliant solo guitar performances expertly recorded in a live concert. −RW

Blues for Fred / PABLO 1988
The Pass guitar is impressive as always, though the songs are erratic. −RW

One for My Baby / PABLO 1988
Plas Johnson (ts) sounds a bit out of place in a 1988 recording; Pass is uniformly excellent. −RW

Summer Nights / PABLO 1989
This recent Pass boasts impeccable guitar but sometimes undistinguished cuts. −RW

Best of Joe Pass / PABLO COMP
The title is a misnomer, but there are good 70s and early-80s cuts from his Pablo sessions. −RW

PASSPORT

Jazz-rock, contemporary funk. Pioneering fusion group led by German saxophonist Klaus Doldinger. Early efforts (mid-70s) show great original sound. −MGN

○ **Looking Thru / ATCO** r 1974
This mid-70s album introduced them to the U.S. −MGN

JACO PASTORIUS   1951-1987

Progressive big band, jazz-rock. Jaco Pastorius may have been the finest bassist to emerge in the last three decades. He expanded the instrument's melodic and rhythmic role far beyond previous expectations and played complex, long lines at amazing solos at remarkable speeds, doing things, both unaccompanied and in combos, that still astonish critics and fans alike. He played in Fort Lauderdale clubs with such performers as the Temptations, the Supremes, and Nancy Wilson, while also hearing area players like the legendary Ira Sullivan.

Pastorius began writing arrangements as a teenager. He got extensive experience playing all types of music, from country to reggae, jazz, and soul. Bobby Colomby, then the drummer for Blood, Sweat & Tears, arranged for Pastorius to make an album for Columbia in 1975. The impact was immediate, and a year later Pastorius had joined Weather Report and also played on Pat Metheny's first ECM album. Pastorius stayed with Weather Report until 1983. In addition, he made several recordings with musicians like Sullivan, Paul Bley, Joni Mitchell, and Bireli Lagrene, and worked festivals with a big band. −RW

● **Jaco Pastorius / CBS** 1976
Studio group date and first album from this late/great electric bass guitar genius. A must-buy. −MGN

○ **Word of Mouth / WARNER BROS** r 1981
Big band. Excellent. −MGN

Invitation / WARNER BROTHERS 1983
More big-band music live in Japan. Look for the CD with more tracks. −MGN

KENNETH PATCHEN   ♭1911

Spoken word, post-bop, progressive big band. A pre-beat poet of the 30s and 40s, Patchen's work in the 50s was recorded. A bit more down than Kerouac, not hyper like Lenny Bruce, Patchen spoke volumes of love, tragedy, sorrow, and hope. −MGN

○ **Reads with Allyn Ferguson / DISCOVERY** ca. 1957
Patchen's mournful poetry coincides with Ferguson's sextet in a chamber-jazz dirge-like frame of reference. "Lonesome Boy Blues" and "I Went to the City" are outstanding. Downhearted, yes. Despondant, no. Ferguson plays piano, percussion, and french horn. −MGN

DON PATTERSON   1936-1988

Hard-bop, post-bop, soul jazz. A legendary organist, and highly influential on other organists, Patterson has a unique sound and staggering technique. He's really the best. −MGN

● **The Exciting New Organ of / PRESTIGE** i 1964
With Booker Ervin (ts). −MGN

The Return Of... / MUSE 1972
Quartet with Eddie Daniels (ts), Ted Dunbar (g), and Freddie Waits (d). Any Don Patterson album is worthwhile. −MGN

○ **These Are Soulful Days / MUSE** 1973
Quartet with this great Hammond B-3 organist, Jimmy Heath (sax), Pat Martino (g) and A. Heath (d). −MGN

JOHN PATTON   ♭1935

Soul jazz. Veteran Hammond B-3 organist; a groover with progressive bent. −MGN

○ **Blue John / CAPITOL** 1963
Recording from "Big John," another Hammond heavyweight. With George Braithwaite (sax), Grant Green (g), and Tommy Turrentine (tpt). −MGN

CECIL PAYNE   ♭1922

Bop, hard-bop, post-bop, progressive big band. Baritone saxophonist Cecil Payne has simply been a consistently first-rate contributor to a number of fine jazz dates since making his debut on record in 1946 on alto playing with J. J. Johnson. Payne worked with Dizzy Gillespie in 1947-1948 and toured Europe with him. He later played with James Moody, Tadd

Dameron, and others before spending two years in the early 50s with Illnois Jacquet. He had some lean periods before he worked again with Randy Weston in the late 50s; He continued working regularly in the 60s, spending time with Woody Herman's Orchestra, plus Machito and Weston. He formed the Jazz Zodiac Quartet for a time, then joined the New York Jazz Repertory Orchestra in 1974, touring with them and recording an album with his vocalist sister Cavril. Payne also did some R&B session work in the 50s and has continued to record for Muse and Spotlite, though not as regularly as his talents merit. –RW

Night at the Five Spot / SIGNAL   i 1955
W/ Phil Woods (sax). –MGN
○ **Zodiac / STRATA-EAST**   1960
Outstanding quintet date featuring Kenny Dorham (tpt), but hard to find. –RW
● **Brooklyn Brothers / MUSE**   1973
W/ Duke Jordan (p) & Trio. Excellent mainstream jazz. –MGN
○ **Bird Gets the Worm / MUSE**   1976
Some of Payne's most vibrant, expressive playing. Good ensemble and compositions. –RW
Bright Moments / SPOTLITE   1979
A London session with topflight Payne playing. –RW

GARY PEACOCK   b 1935

Post-bop, early free. World-class improvising bassist with unusual approach. Highly individual sound, able to inspire great, creative collective music. –MGN
○ **Tales of Another / POLYGRAM**   1977
W/ Keith Jarrett (p) and Jack DeJohnette (d). Their playing interweaves tightly, with many lines going on at once. Each musician strengthens rather than just supports the other. –JERRY DE MUTH, CADENCE
Shift in the Wind / POLYGRAM   1980
W/ Art Lande (p), Elliot Zigmund (d). This recording is a beautiful example of three musicians blending together to create outstanding music. –CARL BRAUER, CADENCE

CURTIS PEAGLER

Big band, bop, post-bop. This mainstream/hard-bop group led by veteran soul-jazz and blues saxophonist Curtis Peagler includes Gildo Mahones, Herbie Lewis, and Billy Higgins. The group records for Pablo. Peagler, Lewis, and Higgins are also well-known session musicians, particularly Higgins, who is among the most in-demand drummers in jazz since the 50s. –RW
○ **I'll Be Around / PA2**   1986
With veteran West Coast saxophonist Peagler and pianist Gildo Mahones. –MGN

DUKE PEARSON   1932-1980

Post-bop, soul jazz, progressive big band. Pianist, composer, and arranger, as well as A&R man for Blue Note. From Atlanta. Also accompanied many singers. A musician's musician. Best when leading a mid-size ensemble, where his harmonic genius comes shining through. Classic post-bop jazz of the 60s. True group music. –MGN
○ **Dedication / PRESTIGE**   1961
This is among Pearson's finest 60s sessions. Includes sterling solos by Freddie Hubbard (tpt) and Pepper Adams (sax). –RW
● **Wahoo / CAPITOL**   1964
From this late pianist/composer/arranger and A&R man. Many others by him are as excellent. Find this one and as many others as you can. –MGN
☆ **Introducing / BLUE NOTE**   1967
With larger ensemble and great compositions. –MGN
○ **Now Hear This! / BLUE NOTE**   1968
A worthy blend of civil rights advocacy and hard-bop dialogs with Pepper Adams (sax), Frank Foster (ts), and a surprising Randy Brecker (tpt). –RW

DAVE PELL   b 1925

Big band, post-bop, progressive big band. Veteran saxophonist and band leader inspired by Lester Young. Leads big bands and an octet. A solidly swinging, satisfying musician. –MGN
● **Pres Conference / GNP CRESCENDO**   1978
Lester Young tribute. Prime material. –MGN
○ **Live at Alfonse's / HEADS UP**   1988
Pell has many older albums that are excellent, as is this one, his newest. –MGN

KEN PEPLOWSKI   b 1959

Swing, big band, cool. Cleveland saxophonist and clarinetist who is a revisionist of swing and light-bop traditions. Well known as a sessionman and sideman. –MGN
Sonny Side / CONCORD   1989
Another tasteful, restrained mainstream date, though Dave Frishberg (p) isn't for everyone. Extra cut on CD issue. –RW
○ **Mr. Gentle & Mr. Cool / CONCORD**   1990
This tasty swing/mainstream date has exciting piano by Hank Jones and excellent drumming from Alan Dawson. The CD boasts two bonus cuts. –RW
Illuminations / CONCORD   1990
A conservative but well-played small-combo set with swing influences. Junior Mance brings some blues fervor on piano. The CD has two bonus cuts. –RW

ART PEPPER   1925-1982

Hard-bop, post-bop. Though often lumped in with the cool school because of his status as a West Coast saxophonist, Art Pepper could burn with the hottest of the boppers. At his peak, Pepper played with a passion, harmonic élan, and zeal that echoed his devotion to Charlie Parker, while swinging with an ease and flow that also reflected a love and knowledge of Lester Young's style. Pepper played with Gus Arnheim's band as a teenager, but also spent lots of time working with Black bands on Central Avenue in Los Angeles. He had two stints with Stan Kenton in the early 50s, sandwiched around some time in the army. His 50s output included many superb dates with Chet Baker, Shorty Rogers, Carl Perkins, Hampton Hawes, Sonny Clark, Russ Freeman, and Warne Marsh, as well as the landmark 1957 album *Meets the Rhythm Section*, where Pepper worked with Miles Davis's great trio of pianist Red Garland, bassist Paul Chambers, and drummer Philly Joe Jones. He continued his run of fine releases in the early 60s, but finally ran afoul of the law due to his drug addiction. Pepper was off the recording scene through most of the 60s, then made a stirring comeback. During the 70s Pepper made several majestic releases. –RW
Modern Art / BLUE NOTE   1956
Complete Aladdin Recordings, Vol. 1. This 1988 reissue is slightly altered from the original Omega release. It has five cuts added from Omega sessions. –RW
● **Meets the Rhythm Section / OJC / DB 5**   1957
Arguably his best quartet session. Both Pepper and the Red Garland (p)-Paul Chambers (b)-Philly Joe Jones (d) rhythm section are in peak form. –RW
Plus Eleven / CONTEMPORARY / DB 5   1959
This is the original great album subsequently reissued by Modern Jazz Classics. –RW
○ **Smack Up / OJC**   r 1960
A nice set, reissued with two bonus cuts. –RW
Intensity / OJC   1960
Although not Pepper's greatest release from the standpoint of lineup, Dolo Coker has several good moments on piano. Pepper is at his usual best. –RW
Living Legend / OJC   1975
Despite the pretentious title, Pepper hits some high notes and has many exciting solos. Pianist Hampton Hawes and bassist

Charlie Haden make some excellent contributions. CD issue has one bonus cut. −RW

● **The Trip / OJC**   1976
With the George Cables Trio and Elvin Jones (d). One of his strongest quartet efforts in his final ten years. −MGN

More for Less / CONTEMPORARY   1977
This fourth volume of Village Vanguard sections is no leftover item. Pepper is masterly, as are George Cables (p), George Mraz (b), and Elvin Jones (d). −RW

No Limit / OJC   1977
A good session. CD reissue has a bonus cut. −RW

Birds and Ballads / GALAXY   1978
Good duels of three headliners. Pepper and Joe Henderson (sax) make an interesting contrast, but Joe Farrell (ts) is not so impressive. −RW

Today / OJC / DB 5   1978
A reissue of mid-70s work. −RW

Ballads by Four / GALAXY   1978
Art Pepper, John Klemmer (ts), Joe Henderson (ts), and Johnny Griffin (ts). −RW

New York Album / GALAXY   1979
Fine date; Hank Jones steps out on piano. −RW

Art of Pepper / VSOP   197?
A solid late-70s date, with some rousing solos — some breezy and some sentimental. −RW

○ **Straight Life / OJC**   1980
Authoritative, statesmanlike Pepper on alto, while Tommy Flanagan proves a distinguished second soloist on piano. −RW

The Way It Was / OJC   1980
Some late-50s and early-60s Pepper group material. CD reissue has two bonus cuts. −RW

11 Modern Jazz Classics / OJC   1980
Here is a sublime matchup of Pepper, bop classics, and a large supporting cast. Includes some blistering renditions of jazz anthems. The CD issue has three bonus cuts. −RW

◡ **Winter Moon / OJC**   1980
Beautiful Pepper solos and intelligent orchestrations make this an exceptional release. −RW

Gettin' Together / OJC   1980
Pepper is in hot form, with a superior Wynton Kelly (p), Paul Chambers (b), and Jimmy Cobb (d) rhythm section. −RW

Maiden Voyage Sessions / GALAXY   1981
Hardly vital, but contains some solid solos. −RW

Goin' Home / OJC   1982
Vibrant interaction between Pepper and George Cables (p), plus fine renditions of bop standards. CD has two extra cuts. −RW

The Art of Pepper / BLUE NOTE
This is the third in what was originally a set covering stinging Pepper performances on Aladdin. These are master takes of 12 selections leased to Omega. It's solid Pepper, but there's much better available elsewhere. −RW

Art with Warne / CONTEMPORARY
Marvelous work between Pepper and Warne Marsh (ts). −RW

☆ **Complete Galaxy Recordings / GALAXY / DB 5**   COMP
This massive 16-disc set covers almost everything in the last phase of Pepper's career. Exquisite piano throughout by George Cables; invaluable liner notes by Gary Giddins. It has 58 unissued tracks, plus alternate takes. −RW

JIM PEPPER

Post-bop, early free, world fusion, neo bop. Saxophonist/flutist with Kaw Indian heritage. Wrote famous "Witchi Tai Toe." Powerful improvisation. Limited record output. Anything you can find, you should grab. Recently passed away. −MGN

○ **Coming and Going / POLYGRAM**   1987
Art Pepper with the Kirk Lightsey Trio. A fine representation of this Native-American's recent work. He wrote "Witchi-Tai-Toe." −MGN

BILL PERKINS   ♭1924

Swing, big band, bop, cool. Tenor sax, bandleader. "Tonight Show" orchestra veteran. Plays sax, primarily tenor. Has recorded with own ensembles and big bands. Woody Herman devotee. −MGN

○ **Quietly There / OJC**   1966
A very-overlooked West Coast saxophonist in one of his better sessions. Reissue of 1966 album as compact disc. −RW

CARL PERKINS   1928-1958

Bop, hard-bop, post-bop. Legendary West Coast post- and hard-bop pianist whose influence on the cool and mainstream eras is still resounding. His advanced harmonic and rhythmic sense was astounding. −MGN

○ **Introducing / DOOTONE**   1956
Recorded two years before legendary West Coast pianist's death. W/ Leroy Vinnegar (b), Lawrence Marable (d). Six Perkins originals make this an important document. He was an important sideman. Here as a leader he shows his true worth. A must find/buy. −MGN

CHARLIE PERSIP   ♭1929

Big band, bop, hard-bop, post-bop, progressive big band. A drummer whose experience in jazz ensembles and big bands is second to none, Persip is also an excellent composer. −MGN

○ **And the Jazz Statesmen / BETHLEHEM**   r1961
Early-60s date for this drummer with Detroiters Marcus Belgrave (tpt), Ron Carter (b), and Freddie Hubbard (tpt) too. −MGN

HOUSTON PERSON   ♭1934

Post bop, soul jazz. This solid, big-toned tenor saxophonist has made many good sessions in the soul-jazz, blues, and ballads vein through the 70s, 80s, and 90s. He often works with vocalist Etta Jones. He doesn't play in relentless, experimental, or innovative fashion but offers nice, pleasing solos and interpretations. An 80s duet album with bassist Ron Carter opened some eyes to his ability to stretch out and go beyond the norm; he's still best in uptempo situations with funk, blues, or soul-jazz arrangements and foundation. −RW

○ **Goodness! / PRESTIGE**   1969
A 1988 reissue of one of Person's few releases available outside the Muse armada. Typical soul-jazz, blues, and standards, with nice help from Billy Butler and Sunny Phillips. −RW

Talk of the Town / MUSE   1971
Marvelous standards and ballads, with excellent trumpet solos by Cecil Bridgewater. −RW

Stolen Sweets / MUSE   1976

Suspicions / MUSE   1980
Some robust funk and fine soul licks, plus solid mainstream fare. −RW

Basics / MUSE   1987
A good session, with blues and bop leanings. −RW

Why Not! / MUSE   1990
Person's most-recent album includes hot contributions by young lions Phillip (d) and Winard Harper (tpt). −RW

Something in Common / MUSE
Person shows his more-adventurous side in duels with bass great Ron Carter. No funk or blues or soul-jazz licks to hide behind. −RW

EDWARD PETERSEN

Post-bop, neo bop. Young Chicago tenor saxophonist influenced by Coltrane and modernists. −MGN

○ **Upward Spiral / DELMARK**   1989
Young Chicago saxophonist shows much promise on his originals-laden debut album. −MGN

PETE PETERSEN

Big band, progressive big band. The leader of the Collection Jazz Orchestra, a big band that's issued a pair of light-jazz and middle-of-the-road dates for CMG Records. –RW

○ **Playin' in the Park / CHASE MUSIC GROUP**   1989
Good arrangements and playing, but unambitious compositions. –RW

HANNIBAL MARVIN PETERSON   *b* 1948

Hard-bop, post-bop, soul jazz, early free, neo bop. Exciting high-note trumpeter who first surfaced as a member of Roy Haynes's Hip Ensemble in the early 70s. He later worked with Pharoah Sanders and Gil Evans, and has also made some recordings as a leader. –RW

● **Hannibal / MPS**   1975
Studio date for a trumpeter on fire. All originals. –MGN

○ **On Antibes / INNERCITY**   1977
Live recording from the south of France. Two long compositions, with George Adams (sax). Burning. –MGN

OSCAR PETERSON   *b* 1925

Swing, bop, hard-bop, cool. Canadian virtuoso pianist Oscar Peterson started out on classical piano and by his teens was playing on a weekly radio show. In the mid-40s he was playing with the Johnny Holmes Orchestra in a style reminiscent of Teddy Wilson, Erroll Garner, and Art Tatum. He was discovered by Norman Grantz and invited to appear at a Jazz at the Philharmonic concert in Carnegie Hall in 1949. This was his real start.
He then formed a trio using piano, guitar, and bass after the style of Nat "King" Cole. His most famous trio, including Herb Ellis (g) and Ray Brown (b), was together from 1953 to 1958, and he worked with other trio members until 1965. After 1970, Peterson concentrated on solo piano performances, and has worked with symphony orchestras since the mid 70s.
Next to Art Tatum, Peterson is considered by musicians and critics as the greatest virtuoso jazz pianist. He has recorded extensively, issuing as many as six albums a year. –JME

Oscar Peterson & Dizzy Gillespie / PA2
Well-done. It's restrained but has moments of brilliance. –RW

Portrait of Sinatra / POLYGRAM   1959
Just as immaculate, polished, and emphatic as you would expect. Peterson is at his most stately. –RW

George Gershwin Songbook / POLYGRAM   1959
Peterson proves adept at reworking George Gershwin. –RW

○ **Peterson Plays Cole Porter Songbook / VERVE**   1959
Peterson reworks Cole Porter and says something original and distinctive. –RW

○ **Very Tall / POLYGRAM**   1961
Peterson and Milt Jackson (vib) stand tall. A must-buy. –MGN

☆ **The Trio / POLYGRAM**   ca. 1961
Outstanding early-60s session that includes some of Peterson's strongest playing from this time frame. –RW

West Side Story / POLYGRAM / DB 5   1962
Peterson does do a wonderful job of bringing a jazz edge to the show-tune arena. –RW

Bursting Out / POLYGRAM   1962
Peterson shows he can fit into the big-band context. The lineup includes Cannonball Adderly (as), James Moody (sax), and Ray Brown (b). –RW

○ **Night Train / POLYGRAM / DB 5**   1962
Very impressive. –MGN

● **We Get Requests / POLYGRAM**   ca. 1963
Classic Oscar Peterson. Essential. –MGN

Eloquence / POLYGRAM   1965
A good mid-60s set from Copenhagen, reissued in 1987. –RW

Blues Etude / POLYGRAM / DB 5   1965
Sparkling quartet sessions, wonderful Peterson piano. –RW

Tracks / POLYGRAM   1970
Don't overlook this if you enjoy solo piano — a good set. –RW

Good Life / OJC   1973
Unadventurous, though delightful. W/ Joe Pass (g) and N. H. O. Pedersen (b). –RW

At Salle Pleyel / PABLO   1975
Aggressive, animated solo piano. –RW

Live-Montreux 1977 / OJC   1977
A sparkling live set matches Peterson with Dizzy Gillespie (tpt), Clark Terry (tpt), Eddie "Lockjaw" Davis (sax), and others. CD issue has a nice bonus cut. –RW

Montreux 77 / OJC   1977
Peterson takes the harmonic and solo spotlight. Nice assistance by Ray Brown (b) and Niels-Henning Orsted Petersen (b). –RW

Silent Partner / PABLO   1979
A simply wonderful date, with special solos from Zoot Sims (ts), Clark Terry (tpt), Eddie Davis (sax), and company. –RW

Live / PA2   1980
Some excellent music. –RW

Nigerian Marketplace / PABLO   1981
An entertaining and unique album. –MGN

Tribute to My Friends / PABLO   1983
Standard Peterson. The solos are solid. –RW

Oscar Peterson & Harry Sweets / PA2   1986
W/ Eddie Cleanhead Vinson (as). A litany of swing and bop veterans, who converge for a marvelous, tasteful session. –RW

Saturday Night at the Blue Note / TELARC   1990
Excellent recording, superb playing. –RW

Live at the Blue Note / TELARC   1990
Outstanding live date. Peterson hasn't lost his chops. –RW

Tristeza on Piano / POLYGRAM
Beautiful and lush, though the jazz content varies. –RW

With Terry Clark / POLYGRAM
A pair of old friends and jazz masters makes beautiful music together. –RW

RALPH PETERSON

Post-bop, neo bop, modern creative. This top drummer is rapidly becoming a star in the 90s jazz scene. He's a stirring accompanist, aggressive soloist, and intriguing composer and bandleader, who has managed to attract some of the best players around to record with him and play in his groups. Signed to Blue Note in the late 80s, he has made trio, small-combo, and large-group sessions. His fotet (4 pieces) release in 1991 was among the year's best recordings. –RW

● **Volition / CAPITOL**
Excellent session; wondrous lineup. Pianist Geri Allen and trumpeter Terence Blanchard are masterly. –RW

○ **Triangular / CAPITOL**   1988
Potent, with Geri Allen (p). –MGN

Presents the Fotet / CAPITOL   1989
An album where this tremendous young drummer unveils a strong lineup of contemporary talent and turns it loose on a hard-bop menu. –RW

MICHEL PETRUCCIANI   *b* 1962

Cool, neo bop. Pianist Petrucciani has made a strong impact in the jazz world. At age 15, he was playing with Kenny Clarke and doing guest stints with Clark Terry. He toured France in the early 80s, following a visit to New York, and moved full-time to America in 1982. He was part of Charles Lloyd's comeback band in 1982, recording and touring Europe with him, then made a heralded appearance at the Kool Jazz Festival in 1984. He subsequently recorded with Wayne Shorter, Jim Hall, and Lloyd, and cut many albums as a leader. Petrucciani is an accomplished technician whose solos show a masterfly harmonic talent. –RW

Oracle's Destiny / RHINO   1982
Better pieces; more soulful playing. –RW

● **Live at the Village Vanguard / CONCORD**   1984
Clearly his best, playing and compositionally, with a solid jazz trio. –MGN

○ **Pianism / BLUE NOTE**   1985
Some tremendous examples of Petrucciani near his peak as a player. –RW

○ **Power of Three / BLUE NOTE**   1986
Brilliant trio work that is Petrucciani's best, thanks to Jim Hall and Wayne Shorter, plus the live context. –RW

Michel Plays Petrucciani / BLUE NOTE   r 1989
The frequently arresting player tackles his own work. His solos outstrip his writing. –RW

Playground / CAPITOL   ca. 199?
In his most recent set, he dominates as soloist. Omar Hakim provides welcome energy on drums. –RW

OSCAR PETTIFORD   1922-1960

Bop, hard-bop, post-bop, early free. Pettiford is one of the most exemplary bassists and cellists of the 50s. He was born on a Native American reservation and played in a family band with ten musical siblings that was quite popular in the Midwest. He worked with Charlie Barnet in 1942, then went to New York and joined Roy Eldridge in 1943. He did several sessions in the mid 40s with Coleman Hawkins, Earl Hines, and Ben Webster. He co-led a group with Dizzy Gillespie in 1944, then had his own combos and big band in 1945. Pettiford relocated on the West Coast to work with Hawkins in 1945, then spent three years with Duke Ellington's orchestra. After that, he usually led his own bands, with the exception of a year with Woody Herman in 1949 and another year with Charlie Shavers and Louie Bellson's band in 1950. Pettiford was a marvelous improviser and pioneered the art of playing the pizzicato style on cello. His technique and intonation have been absorbed by nearly every bassist from the early 50s on, and such pieces as "Bohemia After Dark" and "Laverne Walk" are modern masterpieces. –RW

● **Discoveries / SAVOY**   1952
1952-1957. A stunning early work by the bass and cello great. Has some duets with Charles Mingus (b), plus other examples of his stirring cello technique. –RW

○ **New Oscar Pettiford Trio / OJC**   1953
A wonderful set. Pettiford is in prime form as a bassist and composer. –RW

Vienna Blues / BLACK LION   1959

ESTHER PHILLIPS   1935-1984

Blues-jazz, ballads. Not technically or exclusively a jazz singer, Esther Phillips was nonetheless an amazing vocalist, versatile enough to be successful in the R&B, blues, jazz, and soul fields. Phillips became nationally known after joining the Johnny Otis band and cutting sassy, saucy R&B hits such as "Little Esther" in the 50s for Savoy and King/Federal. She sang the blues with vigor and authority and was a convincing ballad interpreter. She sparkled on uptempo arrangements, never being dominated or obscured by Otis's booming jump arrangements underneath. She made a wonderful comeback in 1962 with the cover of a country tune, "Release Me." Phillips enjoyed a second boom period in the 60s, doing everything from Beatles songs to a triumphant appearance at the 1966 Newport Jazz Festival. She made yet another return in the 70s with a sensational live album, and later in the disco era, she enjoyed a surprise hit with a disco version of "What a Difference a Day Makes." Through the 70s, Phillips made wonderful recordings in blues, jazz, soul, and disco modes. –RW

King/Federal Recordings / CHARLY   195?
More seminal cuts, this time from 50s King dates. –RW

● **Confessin' the Blues / ATLANTIC**   1966
Undoubtedly her best. A must-buy. –MGN

Live at Freddie Jett's Pied Piper / ATLANTIC   1970
The other half of a great live set, fully showcased on wax. –RW

From a Whisper to a Scream / CBS   1972
Her version of "Home Is Where the Hatred Is" became an anthem, plus proved tragically prophetic. –RW

What a Diff'rence a Day Makes / CBS   r 1975
Reached Billboard's #34 spot. The title cut was the last big hit of her distinguished career. She actually sang very little jazz, but was a great blues and R&B singer from childhood until her death. –RW

Way to Say Goodbye / MUSE
The last release in a great career. –RW

☆ **Complete Savoy Recordings / SAVOY**   COMP
Great formative 1949-1959 sessions. Smoking R&B. –RW

FLIP PHILLIPS   b 1915

Swing, big band, bop. Tenor sax. One of the legitimate living masters of swing, Phillips first played alto sax and clarinet in Brooklyn groups in the 30s, then clarinet exclusively for Frankie Newton in 1940-1941. He turned to tenor and worked with Benny Goodman, Wingy Manone, Red Norvo, and Woody Herman in the early and mid 40s. But it was a 10-year tenure on the *Jazz at the Philharmonic* tours that earned him his jazz spurs. Phillips was a prime crowd-pleaser in these jam sessions, playing with energy and flash and adding honks, squalls, and vocal effects, plus possessing rhythmic vitality and sizzle. But he was (and is) also an excellent ballad stylist, and his albums in later years spotlighted that aspect of his talents. After leaving the JATP circuit, he moved to Florida, where he worked with Bill Harris and Woody Herman, toured Europe with Benny Goodman in 1959, and headed his own groups for 15 years. He returned to New York in 1975 and made another European tour in 1982. –RW

A Melody from the Sky / DR. JAZZ   1944
An album of 1944-1945 sessions from NYC with a good, swinging sound. –MGN

Flipenstein / PROGRESSIVE   1981
A very overlooked hot date on a rather obscure label. –RW

● **A Sound Investment / CONCORD**   1987
W/ Scott Hamilton (ts). An excellent, sympathetic collaboration. A standout pairing of this top swing-era stylist and a modern disciple. –RW

○ **Real Swinger / CONCORD**   1988
W/ Howard Alden (g), Butch Miles (d) and this veteran saxophonist on his most recent album. Still swinging after all these years. Highly recommended. –MGN

PIANO CHOIR

Post-bop, neo bop. Piano Choir has eight keyboardists, electric and acoustic, led by Stanley Cowell, Harold Mabern, and Sonelius Smith. –RW

○ **Handscapes - Vol. 1 & 2 / STRATA EAST**   ca. 1972
Brilliant. Volume 1 is 2-fer of originals from seven pianists led by Stanley Cowell (p). Volume 2 is a 1974 session. –MGN

GREG PICCOLO

Blues-jazz, R&B. A saxophonist, former longtime member of Roomful of Blues, and currently a solo performer. Piccolo hearkens back stylistically to the honking tenors, representing the link between swing and first-generation R&B in his playing. –RW

○ **Heavy Juice / BLG**   1990
Stomping tenor sax instrumentals of jazz and R&B repertoire from 40s and 50s. Many Roomful of Blues alumni such as Duke Robillard (g) and Al Copley (p) contribute. It doesn't rock any harder than this! –BP

LOREN PICKFORD

Post-bop, neo bop. An alto saxophonist who leans toward contemporary music, but plays pretty much straight. –MGN

○ **Song for a Blue Planet / CEXTON**   1988
Well-traveled alto saxophonist w/ George Cables (p) Trio and George Roesler (g). Nice modern jazz. –MGN

Dancing in the Spirit / CEXTON   1990
Mostly standards played with a sextet. W/ Pickford on alto, plus three of his originals. –MGN

BILL PIERCE

Hard-bop, post-bop, neo bop. A multi-instrumentalist and session player who's recorded for Sunnyside. A hard-bop/mainstream soloist, not to be confused with traditional jazz artist Billie Pierce. –RW

○ **William the Conqueror / SUNNYSIDE**   1985
It is the powerful tenor of Billy Pierce that makes this a highly recommended album. –SCOTT YANOW, CADENCE

NAT PIERCE   b 1925

Swing, big band, progressive big band. Nat Pierce is the rhythmic force on piano that Freddie Green was on guitar; no one sets up the band or soloists better or is more effective at driving and assisting an orchestra in establishing a groove or pace. Pierce worked twice with the Woody Herman Orchestra, once in the 50s and again in the 60s, spending a combined eight years with Herman as his principal arranger, organizer, and pianist. He also served in similiar capacities with Count Basie and Louie Bellson, and aided bandleaders Claude Thornhill, Stan Kenton, and Basie when they became ill. Pierce has doubled as a bandleader, done extensive session work, been an educator, and appeared at many festivals around the world. His most recent duties have entailed being a coleader of the Capp-Pierce Juggernaut, which has recorded frequently on Concord. –RW

○ **Pierce-Collins Nonet / OJC**   1954
One side features the driving West Coast bop of saxist Charlie Mariano, and the other features trumpeter Dick Collins and his more expansive sound. –DS

COURTNEY PINE   b 1964

Post-bop, neo bop. Tenor sax, soprano sax. Arguably the greatest British jazz musician of his generation, Pine first worked in reggae bands and funk groups. He formed a 21-piece Jazz Warriors orchestra in 1985, as well as a support alliance to promote the arts in Britain. His 1986 debut attracted international attention, and subsequent releases include hard-bop, reggae, and funk-influenced compositions. Pine has extensive gifts: a robust tone, extensive knowledge of jazz history, and the ability to play in a frenzied, aggressive manner, especially on soprano. –RW

● **Journey to the Urge Within / POLYGRAM**   1986
First and so far the best album. Original ideas sounding original off the bat. –MGN

○ **Destiny's Song ... / POLYGRAM**   1988
Destiny's Song & The Image of Pusuance. English young lion Courtney Pine has heart and soul, but sometimes lacks ideas and taste. –RW

Vision's Tale / POLYGRAM   1989
Erratic, yet with moments of charm, fire, and appeal. –RW

Within the Realms of Our Dream / POLYGRAM   1990
Ambitious. –RW

BUCKY PIZZARELLI   b 1926

Swing, big band, ballads. Better-known as Bucky than John, Pizzarelli is a self-taught player and well known for using a seven-string guitar and emphasizing touch, delicacy, and restraint instead of speed, aggression, or high volume. Pizzarelli started with Joe Mooney's combo, then became a studio musician with NBC in 1954. He switched to ABC in 1966 and played on the "Dick Cavett Show." Then Pizzarelli expanded his horizons in the 70s, doing more jam-session and free-lance work and building his reputation as a versatile musician who could contribute in small-combo, duo, big-band, or work with strings and support vocalists. His recordings have also been eclectic, ranging from solo acoustic to quartet and duo dates. –RW

○ **Complete Guitar Duos / STASH**

JANET PLANET

Ballads, jazz-rock, modern creative. A unique vocalist who swoops and soars, with all emotions considered; Planet has progressive and fusion leanings. –MGN

○ **Sweet Thunder / SEA BREEZE**
A unique vocalist on the edge. For the open listener. –MGN

LONNIE PLAXICO   b 1960

Post-bop, neo bop, M-base. A busy contemporary bassist primarily known for his work with such bandleaders as Gary Thomas and Jack DeJohnette. Has a sterling reputation as a prime accompanist and outstanding soloist who interacts well in free, hard-bop, or jazz/rock/fusion context. –RW

○ **Plaxico / MUSE**   r 1991
This fine young bassist makes a good though derivative hard-bop and mainstream statement. –RW

KING PLEASURE   1922-1981

Bop, ballads. Born Clarence Beeks. An inventor of and first popularizer of vocalese, the process of setting lyrics to instrumental solos. His first hit was "Moody's Mood For Love" (Prestige) in 1952, and he followed that with "Red Top" (Prestige) in 1953. His Prestige work was collected on an album "Moody's Mood For Love." Later sessions for Jubilee (1955) and Alladin (1956) are collected on the Blue Note CD, *Moody's Mood For Love,* along with an album recorded in 1962 for Untitled Artists. One last recording session for HiFi Jazz (*Golden Days*) was done in 1960. Vocalese requires a bit of getting used to, but Pleasure's recordings are some of the very best in the idiom. Pleasure could also handle a straight lyric with equal ability. –BP

● **King Pleasure Sings with Annie Ross / OJC**   1950
1950-1952. Undoubtedly Annie's best. A must-buy. –MGN

☆ **Source / PRESTIGE (FANTASY)**   1952
1952-1960. A 2-fer of essential material from the essential master of vocalese. –MGN

Moody's Mood for Love / CBS   1960
Always good to have this album. –MGN

Golden Days / OJC   1960
The always-entertaining King Pleasure does vocalize, scat, and vocals with humor, warmth, and comic ease. W/ Teddy Edwards (ts) and Harold Land (ts). –RW

Mr. Jazz / HI FI JAZZ   i 1962

TERRY POLLARD   b 1931

Bop, hard-bop, post-bop. Vibist/pianist whose claim to fame was collaboration with Terry Gibbs and Yusef Lateef. Advanced harmonic ideas placed her right up there with Monk, Herbie Nichols, and George Wallington. –MGN

○ **Terry Pollard / BETHLEHEM**   i 1954

JIMMY PONDER   b 1946

Soul jazz. Longtime champion of soul-jazz guitar, peer of Grant Green. Goes even more funky at times. Good chops and concept; complimentary player. –MGN

○ **Jump / MUSE**   1988
Ponder is a good guitarist in the Grant Green school, a fine soul/blues player. –RW

Come on Down / MUSE   r 1991
Nice, occasionally hot, soul-jazz. –RW

JEAN-LUC PONTY   b 1942

Jazz-rock, contemporary funk. Ponty began his career as a classically trained violinist from France; influenced by Stephane Grappelli. Worked with Grappelli, George Duke, Frank Zappa, John McLaughlin in the 60s. Formed own band in fusion format in the mid 70s. Created four albums of original music before turning more toward instumental formula rock. Has been working with African percussionists as of late. –MGN

Ponty/Grappelli / POLYGRAM
This is a good combination. Two generations of jazz violin virtuosos. –MGN

○ **Violin Summit / POLYGRAM**   1966
A nice pairing that forces Ponty into high gear. Sparkling solos by Stephane Grappelli, plus collaborations with Svend Asmussen and others. –RW

● **Upon the Wings of Music / ATLANTIC**   1975
Easily his best band, compositions, and originality. –MGN

BADEN POWELL   1924-1966

Post-bop, Latin-jazz, world fusion. Among Brazil's finest, most expressive guitarists, perhaps the strongest rhythmic player to emerge from the blend of Iberian baroque and West African/Latin influences. Powell's albums have had authenticity, beauty, and transcendent elegance, and he's demonstrated complete command of guitar and knowledge of jazz, flamenco, and classical genres. –RW

○ **Tristeza on Guitar / POLYGRAM**   1966
A superb Brazilian guitarist and a superb jazz album without the usual pop trappings. –MB

○ **Estudos / POLYGRAM**   r 1975
Beautiful, expressionistic playing from a Latin player. –RW

BUD POWELL   1924-1966

Bop, hard-bop, post-bop. The greatest pianist to emerge from the bop tradition, Bud Powell was another instrumental genius plagued during his lifetime with personal demons. A superior composer, Powell played in a frenetic rhythmic fashion and was as remarkable a harmonic and melodic inventor as Charlie Parker was an alto saxist. Only Art Tatum and arguably Oscar Peterson have ever been more suited to the trio format, and his accompaniment behind the soloists was often better than what was being played upfront. Powell studied classical music in his youth, then became immersed in the bop revolution in the early 40s. He joined the Cootie Williams band in 1943-1944 and made his debut on records with them. He later worked with Charlie Parker on 52nd Street, before being hospitalized in 1945, allegedly as a result of police brutality. Later in the 50s, Powell would suffer attacks during performances and have to be helped off stage. When lucid, he was a marvel at the piano. He made memorable sessions for Blue Note in the 40s and 50s, as well as Verve, and was part of the immortal Massey Hall concert in 1953 with Charles Mingus, Max Roach, Dizzy Gillespie, and Charlie Parker. Influenced early on by Teddy Wilson, Nat King Cole, Tatum, and the underrated and undervalued Billy Kyle, Powell was a legitimate innovator, and his rhythmic right-hand lines are famous among pianists. –RW

Trio Plays / CAPITOL   1947
1947 & 1953. Powell sparkles, but the songs aren't always up to par. –RW

★ **Amazing Bud Powell - Vols. 1-3 / CAPITOL**   1949
1949-1953. Three volumes of the essential Bud Powell, pianist extraordinaire. –MGN

○ **Genius of Bud Powell - Vol 2 / POLYGRAM**   1950
1950 & 1951. The title says it all. –MGN

Jazz at Massey Hall - Vol. 2 / OJC   1953
It might be leftovers, but any Bud Powell is worth hearing. –RW

Scene Changes / BLUE NOTE   1958
This late-80s Blue Note reissue is uneven but has plenty of Powell fireworks. –RW

Time Waits / BLUE NOTE   1959
A bonus cut in the 1987 reissue. Good sound and exceptional Powell solos. –RW

Jazz Giant / POLYGRAM   195?
A 1988 reissue that finds the ferocious Powell teamed with Ray Brown (b), Curley Russell (b), and Max Roach (d). –RW

Bouncing with Bud / DLM   1962
1987 reissue of a good set. Delmark deserves kudos for putting this out again. –RW

Best of Bud Powell / CAPITOL   COMP
The title is misleading, but it does contain some memorable cuts. –RW

MEL POWELL   b 1923

Post-bop, world fusion. Pianist, composer. A Pulitzer Prize winner in 1991, Mel Powell exemplifies extraordinary achievement in both jazz and classical circles. Though he hasn't made many records, his incredible technique and masterly solo approach, along with his flexibility, put him in the forefront of modern keyboard artists. As a teen, he was in Muggsy Spanier's big band, and he auditioned for Benny Goodman in 1941. He became a staff musician at CBS in 1942, then worked with Glenn Miller in 1943 and 1944, coming with him to England and eventually being featured on the BBC's "Piano Party" show. After returning to America, Powell dropped out of the jazz world, going first to Hollywood to work in the studios, then going to Yale to study composition with Paul Hindemith and piano with Nadia Reisenberg. Powell later taught music theory at Queens College and composition at Yale and was awarded a Guggenheim fellowship in 1959. During the 70s and 80s, Powell split his time between being Dean of Music at the California Institute of Arts and doing occasional jazz dates on cruises and with Bobby Hackett. An exceptional 1989 release on Concord with Benny Carter alerted a new corps of listeners about Powell's amazing talents. –RW

○ **The World is Waiting / COMMODORE**   1942
Album features Powell with Joe Bushkin (p). Some torrid piano playing. –RW

Unavailable Mel Powell / PA-USA   194?
Late 40s. Some of his top compositions from a peak period as a jazz writer and player. –RW

Return of Mel Powell / CHI-SOUND   1987
This Pulitzer prize winner returns to his jazz roots. Benny Carter (as) makes this session shine. –RW

SPECS POWELL   b 1922

Swing, bop. A studio and session drummer who was popular in the bop era, but played with swing-era bands. –MGN

○ **Movin' In / ROULETTE**   i 1958
W/ Jimmy Cleveland (tb) and Sahib Shihab (sax). –MGN

PRESERVATION HALL JAZZ BAND

Trad. Preservation Hall was founded in 1961 under the guidance of art dealer Larry Borenstein, the result of several years of "pass the hat" sessions held at his Associated Artists Gallery in New Orleans's French Quarter. The potential for the Hall as a showcase for venerable New Orleans jazzmen was developed by the husband-and-wife team of Allan and Sandra Jaffe, who dedicated themselves to the concept of a sympathetic and non-commercial environment that would emphasize the survival of the music and its practitioners above all else. Eventually their efforts (and those of other supporters, like Bill Russell and Dick Allen) paid off, especially when the Jaffes began to arrange touring schedules for the roster of musicians who relied on the Hall for their livelihood. Today, Preservation Hall is a major tourist attraction — a shrine to the jazz traditions of New Orleans. Many famous jazzmen have been associated with Preservation Hall since its inception, and the name "Preservation Hall Jazz Band" has been used to describe a variety of bands over the last thirty years. While the music that these groups play is not the same as the earliest sounds to emerge from the Crescent City, the spirit evident at their performances incorporates the best of the New Orleans heritage, amazing audiences all over the world with the antics of these grandfatherly musicians. —BR

○ **New Orleans - Vol. 1 / CBS**
The most famous of all traditional bands, caught live in their home town. —RW

● **New Orleans - Vol. 2 / CBS**
Same personnel as Volume 1, with great versions of "Shake It and Break It" and "The Bucket's Got A Hole in It." —BR

New Orleans - Vol. 3 / CBS
Simple and direct, the band breathes new life into tunes like "Closer Walk" and "When the Saints Go Marchin' In," with a particularly fine solo by Frazier on the latter. —BR

New Orleans - Vol. 4 / CBS
An exemplary version of "Precious Lord," played with warmth and feeling, featuring pianist James "Sing" Miller on vocals. Great ensemble work on "Gettysburg March" and "Lonesome Road." —BR

○ **Best Of / CBS**   COMP
A good sampler for the uninitiated - pass it on after you collect volumes 1-4. —BR

THE PRESIDENT

Modern creative. A downtown NYC supergroup led by keyboardist Wayne Horvitz hybridizes jazz, rock, improv, and dashes of blues guitar from Elliot Sharp. —MB

○ **Bring Yr Camera / ELEKTRA / DB 5**   ca. 1989
Avant-garde jazz-fusion with ethno-noise. —MGN

PRESTIGE ALL-STARS

Swing, bop. Lineup of major jazz musicians under contract to Prestige in the 50s, who recorded sessions without any featured leader. The roster included at various times Art Farmer, Bill Evans, Kenny Burrell, Jimmy Cleveland, Tommy Flanagan, and Mal Waldron. —RW

○ **Earthy / OJC**   1957
Dazzling stints by Kenny Burrell (g), Art Farmer (tpt), and Mal Waldron (p) on otherwise standard cuts. Limited Edition release. —RW

○ **Roots / PRESTIGE**   1957
A nice gathering of stars such as Bill Evans (p), Pepper Adams (bar. sax), and Tommy Flanagan (p). —RW

ANDRE PREVIN   b 1929

Cool. Classical conductor and pianist who also plays jazz. A bit pristine and crystalline. Collaborates with top-notch players. —MGN

○ **Double Play! / OJC**   1957
Arguably his best jazz date from a playing standpoint. —RW

Gigi / OJC   r 1958
The Shelley Manne (d)/ Red Mitchell (b) duo helps lift the session's energy level. —RW

Pal Joey / OJC   r 1958
Shelley Manne (d) and Red Mitchell (b) put some snap into Previn's musical menu. —RW

Like Previn! / OJC   r 1960
Before he became a famous maestro, Previn was a decent, sometimes superior, jazz pianist. This is solid, occasionally excellent, mainstream material. —RW

After Hours / TELARC   1989
The noted symphonic conductor can also play jazz. —RW

Uptown / TELARC   1990
This recent Previn is nicely done but doesn't have the sparkle of his Prestige sessions. —RW

BOBBY PREVITE

Modern creative. This progressive/creative drummer and bandleader presents a most unique perspective in modern improvised music. Third World influences creep in, and he handles free music capably. —MGN

○ **Claude's Late Morning / RHINO**   r 1989
The daring drummer doesn't tailor his work to conventional jazz tastes. Excellent playing, erratic compositions. —RW

Empty Suits / RHINO / DB 5   r 1991
Technique and emotion. —RW

Music of the Moscow Circus / RHINO
If you like circus music, you'll enjoy Previte's spin. —RW

● **Weather Clear Track Fast / RHINO**
Excellent composition and concept. —MGN

RUTH PRICE

Ballads, blues-jazz. A prominent vocalist in the 60s, she sang with Charlie Ventura, Red Garland, Shelly Manne, and Harry James. —MGN

○ **Lucky to Be Me / ITI**   1983
This disk is so fine, in fact, that it makes me wish ... that Price hadn't waited some twenty years since her last LP. —ALAN BARGEBUHR, CADENCE

SAMMY PRICE   b 1908

Trad, stride, boogie, swing. Among the last of the vintage stomping barrelhouse, blues and boogie pianists, Sammy Price actually got his start professionally as a singer and dancer with Alphonso Trent's band in the late 20s. He arrived in Kansas City in 1930 and spent three years immersing himself in the swing sound of Count Basie and Pete Johnson before he moved to Chicago and later Detroit. Price moved to New York in 1938, becoming house pianist for American Decca and providing the pianistic foundation for great sessions featuring such vocalists as Trixie Smith and Sister Rosetta Tharpe. He subsequently worked on 52nd Street, appearing at such clubs as the Famous Door and Cafe Society. Price organized the first Black-supervised and -administered jazz festival in Philadelphia in 1946, and later appeared at the Nice Festival with Mezz Mezzrow. Price worked a decade with Allen, until the latter's death in 1967. —RW

● **Blues & Boogies / BLACK & BLUE**   ca. 1969
Price is heard here on solo piano and vocal, playing eight Price originals and "See See Rider." It is good to hear him alone on this rare solo album, recorded in France. —MGN

○ **Fire / CLASSIC JAZZ**   1975
The Texas blues and jazz pianist plays in good time and old time format with the basic trio of J. C. Heard (d), Carl Pruitt (b), and guests Ted Buckner (tpt), The Mighty Flea (Gene Connors, tb), and Doc Cheatham (tpt). Includes ten Price originals. —MGN

Just Right / BLACK & BLUE   1977
A sextet with George Kelly (sax) and Freddie Lonzo (tb) plays two of Price's tunes, five standards (two by W. C. Handy), and one by trumpeter Johnny Lettman. —MGN

● **Paradise Valley Duets / PARKWOOD**   1988
Recorded live in Windsor, with J. C. Heard (d). Precious Texas piano stomps & jazz. —MGN

○ **In Paris / BRUNSWICK**
With Sidney Bechet (sop sax), Price's "Bluesicians" hit on old time and good time standards — Bechet, as always, in good tune. —MGN

JULIAN PRIESTER   b 1935

Hard-bop, post-bop, early free, jazz-rock, neo bop. He's not as adventurous as a George Lewis, but Julian Priester has been among the rare trombonists with a bop background who have embraced the synthesizer technology of the 70s and beyond. He spent five productive years in the mid 50s working with Lionel Hampton, Dinah Washington, and others in Chicago before he moved to New York in 1958. Priester was in the bands of Max Roach and Slide Hampton for a time, and played with Eric Dolphy, Clifford Jordan, and Booker Little in Roach's fine early-60s group. He worked with numerous bands in the 60s, among them a six-month period in Ellington's orchestra. Priester got national attention for his stint with Herbie Hancock's group from 1970-1973. During that period, he began to include synthesized effects in his performances, something he continued upon leaving Hancock's band. Priester stayed active in the 80s, working with Dave Holland's band until 1985. He's continued doing session and studio work. –RW

● **Keep Swinging / RIVERSIDE**   1960
Quintet. W/ Jimmy Heath (sax), Tommy Flanagan (p), and Elvin Jones (d). Excellent. –MGN

Spiritsville / JAZZLAND   i 1960
W/ Charlie Davis on baritone sax. –MGN

○ **Love, Love / ECM**   1974
Trombonist Priester is electrified; setting is extended. Hardhitting. –MGN

Polarization / ECM   1977
More power to Priester. Ambitious music with Ray Obiedo (g) and Curtis Clark (p). –MGN

ARTHUR PRYSOCK   b 1929

Ballads, soul jazz. Vocalist. His commanding, robust, and deep baritone have made their impression through smash R&B, blues, and jazz-flavored recordings, as well as commercials and radio spots. Arthur Prysock became famous in Buddy Johnson's band in 1944-1952, having a number of big R&B hits, as did his sister Ella Johnson. He gained even more notoriety as a romantic ballad specialist in the 50s and 60s. During the 70s Prysock did mainly club dates, but resurfaced as a recording artist in 1985 with super recording. –RW

I Worry About You / OLD TOWN   r 1962
● **Arthur & Count / POLYGRAM**   1965
1985 reissue of wonderful 60s cuts in which Prysock came closest of any replacements to duplicating the Joe Williams sound in the Basie orchestra. –RW

Double Header / OLD TOWN   r 1965
This Is My Beloved / POLYGRAM   ca. 1969
1985 reissue of prime Verve material. –RW

○ **Rockin' Good Way / MILESTONE**   1985
Great comeback on records that helped reestablish Prysock among some who'd forgotten his 50s & 60s material. –RW

This Guy's in Love with You / MILESTONE   1986
Classy session, excellent mood, and love songs. –RW

Today's Love Songs Tomorrow's / MILESTONE   1987
1988 release of some lush 1987 and 1988 sessions. Arthur Prysock sings wonderful ballads, backed by brother Red's good band. –RW

Best Of / POLYGRAM   COMP
Good single-disc reissue of Verve hits. –RW

○ **Songs That Made Him Famous / DECCA**   COMP
Good compilation of R&B and jukebox hits from 40s and 50s, some featuring his sister Ella Johnson. –RW

TITO PUENTE   b 1923

Latin, salsa. First-rate Latin-jazz vibraphonist/timbales player/bandleader. Known for his showmanship. Incorporates many styles of Latin music melded with jazz standards. A stalwart in this idiom, he has been extensively recorded for the last four decades. –MGN

Puente Goes Jazz / RCA   1956

On this mid-50s reissue, the king of Latin music strays into the realm of straightahead big-band jazz. These guys swing hard! With the full dynamic range you'd expect from the best big-band. –LEN PATERSON, ROOTS & RHYTHM

Let's Cha Cha with Puente / RCA   1957
W/ orchestra. –MGN

On Broadway / CONCORD   1982
Always impressive Puente percussion, good arrangements. Not among his most rhythmically ambitious. –RW

Mambo Diablo / CONCORD   1985
Has both Latin-jazz & Latin dance elements. –RW

○ **Un Poco Loco / CONCORD**   1987
One of his best for the label. Puente's playing in both large and small contexts. –RW

Sensacion / CONCORD   1987
Good session. –RW

Goza Mi Timbal / CONCORD   1989
1990 release, extended timbales solos. –RW

Out of This World / CONCORD   i 1991
His most recent with a topflight large group. –RW

○ **El Rey / TICO**   El R
Vocals by Santos Colon. –MGN

Cuban Carnival / RIN
Good reissue of earlier material. –RW

● **Salsa Meets Jazz / CONCORD**
Excellent, maybe his best on the label. Phil Woods (as) joins the party and soars. –RW

Hits Candentes / RIN   COMP
Some of his best-known cuts. –RW

DON PULLEN   b 1944

Early free, jazz-rock, neo bop, modern creative. One of the most percussive pianists in jazz, Don Pullen's razor sharp phrasing and intense right-hand clusters were especially noteworthy during his tenure as coleader of the Pullen/Adams quartet of the late 70s and 80s. Pullen studied with Muhal Richard Abrams and Giuseppe Logan before making his recording debut in 1964. He had his own groups and also worked with drummer Milford Graves as well as playing organ in R&B groups. He worked a year with Nina Simone in 1970-1971 and briefly with Art Blakey in 1974. But it was his stint with Charles Mingus in 1973-1975 that got Pullen substantial attention, as well as his teaming with saxophonist George Adams, who was also in the group. He and Adams teamed up in 1979, following several European tours Pullen had made with his own bands. The Pullen/Adams group was a staple on the 80s jazz scene until they disbanded. He's recently recorded with saxophonist David Murray. –RW

New Beginnings / CAPITOL   1969
A slashing, exciting pianist on his own. –RW

● **Tomorrow's Promises / ATLANTIC**   1977
Effervescent compositions from a virtuoso pianist. A must-buy. –MGN

Decisions / TIMELESS   ca. 1984
W/ George Adams Quartet. Earthy, roaring hard bop from a superb, disciplined combo. Newly reissued on CD. –RW

○ **The Sixth Sense / BLACK SAINT / DB 5**   1985
Studio date with quintet. Another great Pullen album. –MGN

☆ **Breakthrough / BLUE NOTE / DB 5**   1986
Pianist Don Pullen and sax/flute/vocalist George Adams (both ex-Mingus players) with drummer Dan Richmond at their creative zenith. –MGN

Song Everlasting / BLUE NOTE   r 1987
Another in a series of exceptional Pullen/George Adams dates. This was a superb small combo, one of the best and most popular in the 80s. –RW

Random Thoughts / CAPITOL   1990
A percussive, attacking pianist. –RW

○ **Earth Beams with George Adams Quartet / TIMELESS**

This is one of his best, most exacting sets. Newly available on CD. –RW

FLORA PURIM   b 1942

Jazz-rock, world fusion. Vocals, guitar, percussion. Since the early 70s Purim has been the best-known female vocalist from Brazil, though she's been somewhat surpassed in recent years by newer, more invigorating and on-the-edge types like Margaret Menezes. Her tremendous vocal range, which at one time was six octaves, plus her skill at blending her voice with other instruments in both acoustic and electric situations, coupled with good articulation, timing, interpretative ability and delivery, won Purim early fame after she left Brazil with her husband Airto Moreira in the late 60s. Purim made a significant jazz impact during a 1968 European tour with Stan Getz. She did sessions with Gil Evans in 1971, then joined the first edition of Chick Corea's Return To Forever. She and Moreira started their own band in 1973, and a year later Purim began recording solo albums. –RW

○ **Butterfly Dreams / OJC**   i 1973
A wonderful release that she's seldom equalled since. Joe Henderson (sax), George Duke (p), and Airto (per). –RW
Stories to Tell / OJC   1974
Nice set; reissued in 1991. –RW
● **Open Your Eyes / MILESTONE / BB 59**   r 1976
Purim's finest hour includes the title track that is Flora at her soaring, swooping best. There is great instrumental backing from George Duke (p) and friends. –MGN
Nothing Will Be As It Was ... Tomorrow / WARNER   r 1977
With lots of string, synth, and vocal arrangements, this includes classics such as the title track, "You Love Me Only," and "Bridges" (written by Milton Nascimiento). Support comes from keyboardists Patrice Rushen and George Duke, and Airto (per). –MGN
Love Reborn / MILESTONE   197?
Good mid-70s cuts with Ron Carter (b) and Airto (per). –RW
Humble People / CONCORD   1985
An all-star band supports Flora and Airto Moreira (per) through jazz, funk, and Latin pop. Guests include David Sanborn (as), Joe Farrell (ts), Milton Cardona (per), and Jerry Gonzalez (per). This is one of Purim's better later-period albums. –MGN

IKE QUEBEC   1918-1963

Swing, post-bop, blues-jazz. Perhaps the greatest "populist" sax player ever, a longtime people's choice who was seldom recognized by the critics. Quebec began as a pianist in the early 40s, switched to tenor in 1942, and quickly became celebrated for a raw, rough, and forceful style that had roots in the swing era, but was ideal for the emerging honking sax, R&B, and soul-jazz sounds of 50s and 60s. Quebec worked in Chicago and New York during the remainder of the 40s, making his debut as leader on Blue Note in 1944. His song "Blue Harlem" was a huge hit. Quebec recorded sporadically for Blue Note in the 40s, played with Lucky Millinder and Cab Calloway from 1949-1953, then departed the business for a while due to a combination of personal problems and a lack of opportunity. Quebec was a close friend of Blue Note's Alfred Lion and urged him to give chances to many top players who would go on to make the label a premier jazz outlet in the 50s and 60s. Quebec was prolific from 1959-1962, working with Sonny Clark, Dodo Green, Jimmy Smith plus heading several wonderful sessions, several of which yielded singles that were breakout hits in the jukebox arena. For a number of years he doubled as Blue Note's musical director. –RW
☆ **Complete Blue Note 45 Sessions / MOSAIC / DB 5**   1959
A wonderful three-disc collection of Quebec's 1959-1962 songs that packed jazz punch, had R&B appeal, and were originally recorded for and designed as singles for jukeboxes. –RW
Congo Lament / BLUE NOTE   1962

Africa meets Harlem with soul in a rousing Quebec date. –RW
● **Blue and Sentimental / CAPITOL**   ca. 1962
Hot, lusty, and wonderful. Quebec was a rare jazz musician who never lost his appeal in the R&B community. W/ Sonny Clark (p), Grant Green (g), Paul Chambers (b), Philly Joe Jones (d). –RW
Easy Living / BLUE NOTE   1962
Outstanding soul-jazz, mainstream material. –RW
○ **Complete Blue Note Recordings / MOSAIC**   COMP
With litlle-know tenor sax player John Hardee, not tandem with Quebec but with separate small- and medium-sized groups. The Hardee sides are rare, but the Quebec groups are precious. Quebec from 1944 to 1946, Hardee in 1946, mostly with Tiny Grimes (g). Ike's sides with Grimes, J. C. Heard (d), Buck Clayton (tpt), and John Collins (g) among others. –MGN

ALVIN QUEEN   b 1950

Post-bop, early free, neo bop. A drummer, producer, and record label owner, Queen is an expatriate living in France. Capable of being either a powerhouse or subtle, he is also a fine composer. –MGN
○ **In Europe / NILVA**   1980
Quintet with drummer Queen at the helm. Mainstream, bordering on progressive. –MGN

PAUL QUINICHETTE   1916-1983

Swing, big band, bop. Tenor sax. An excellent player with a powerful, appealing tone and excellent technique, though he got pegged in some quarters as being little more than a Lester Young imitator, a reputation he managed to shed through years of recording and performing. Quinichette worked in territory bands in the 40s, among them Jay McShann, Nat Towles, and Ernie Fields. He was in Johnny Otis's band in 1945, then relocated to New York from West Coast and played with Louis Jordan, Lucky Millinder, Red Allen, and Hot Lips Page. From there, Quinichette played with Count Basie for a year and even briefer stints with Benny Goodman, Nat Pierce, and Billie Holiday, while heading his own bands. After taking a sabbatical from music that lasted from the 60s until 1973, he resurfaced playing vibrant, swing-influenced music with Sammy Price and Buddy Tate, among others. –RW
○ **On the Sunny Side / OJC**
● **Pres Meets Vice-Pres / EMARCY**   i 1954
Vice-Pres / EMARCY   i 1954
W/ Freddie Green (g). –MGN
○ **The Chase Is On / BETHLEHEM**   ca. 1957
With fellow tenor Charlie Rouse, and the Wynton Kelly Trio, this is a nice mix of standards, tunes by Rouse and Carmen McRae. Two tracks are with Hank Jones (p) and Freddie Green (g). –MGN
The Chase Is On / BETHLEHEM   i 1957
W/ Charlie Rouse (ts). –MGN
Cattin' / PRESTIGE   i 1958
W/ John Coltrane (ts). –MGN

JIMMY RANEY   b 1927

Post-bop. One of the most fluid, melodic, and enjoyable guitarists directly connected to the bop tradition, and a superior accompanist. Raney worked as a teen in local groups in both Chicago and New York, then joined Woody Herman for a short stay in 1948. Raney played with a host of groups in the late 40s and early 50s, among them Al Haig, Buddy DeFranco, Artie Shaw, and Terry Gibbs and was a member of Stan Getz's quintet in 1951-1952 and later replaced Tal Farlow in Red Norvo's trio in 1953-1954. Raney then spent six years with pianist Jimmy Lyon and rejoined Getz in 1962-1963. During the remainder of the 60s and 70s, Raney did various gigs, from backing vocalists to session work. Reissues from the late 80s spotlight Raney's ability to interact with players as diverse as Sonny Clark, Sam Jones, and Billy Higgins. –RW
Plays / PRESTIGE   i 1953

W/ Red Mitchell (b). −MGN
- **A / OJC**   1954
1954-1955. Incredibly talented guitarist on A+ record. Near essential. W/ Teddy Kotick (b) and Hall Overton (p). −MGN
   Quartet / NEW JAZZ   i 1954
   W/ Hall Overton (p). −MGN
- ○ **Two Jims & Zoot / MOBILE FIDELITY**   1964
W/ Jim Hall (g). Steamy exchanges between Raney and Zoot Sims (ts). −RW

JOHN RAPSON

Post-bop, neo bop, modern creative. A West Coast progressive trombonist, Rapson can growl or coo. −MGN
- ○ **Deeba Dah-Bwee / NINE WINDS**   1984
Sextet with progressive trombonist from the West Coast. A rival to Ray Anderson. A sleeper, worth the search. −MGN

ENRICO RAVA   b 1943

Post-bop, early free, neo bop, modern creative. Enrico Rava ranks among Europe's top players. His mother was a classical pianist, and Rava taught himself the trumpet by listening to jazz records, though he began on trombone. He later studied in New York with Carmine Caruso upon coming to America. He made his initial splash in 1964 with the Gato Barbieri quintet, then played three years with Steve Lacy, touring in Europe, South America, and the United States. From 1969-1972 he was a member of Roswell Rudd's group as well as the Jazz Composer's Orchestra Association (JCOA) and Bill Dixon. Rava formed his own band in 1975 and has continued to head his own groups ever since, working with many of America's and Europe's best players. He also performed with Gil Evans in 1982 and toured Europe with Cecil Taylor in 1984, plus headed big bands with European and American stars. −RW
- ○ **Il Giro Del Giorno in 80 Mondi / BLACK SAINT**   1972
A recording that is "out" and sometimes funky, with guitarist Bruce Johnson. −MGN
   The Pilgrim & the Stars / ECM   1975
   Same group as "The Plot." −MGN
- **The Plot / ECM**   1978
Italian trumpeter with quartet. Original ideas and compositions. With guitarist John Abercrombie. −MGN
   Quartet / ECM   1978
   W/ trombonist Roswell Rudd. Heavy-handed. −MGN

REBIRTH BRASS BAND

Trad, post-bop, progressive big band, neo bop. After the Dirty Dozen Brass Band, perhaps the best contemporary New Orleans ensemble working in vintage marching band style. The group has cut albums for Rounder and Arhoolie since the late 80s, and utilizes multiple trombone/trumpet/tuba instrumentation. They also play booming uptempo tunes, spirituals, rags, marching numbers, and originals, doing them all with a traditional feel and contemporary sensibility. −RW
- ○ **Do Whatcha Wanna / MARDI GRAS**
- ○ **Feel Like Funkin' It Up / ROUNDER**   1989
Young'uns play New Orleans street music. Try it. −MGN
- **Kickin' It Live! / ROUNDER**
Recommended. −MGN

SONNY RED   1932-1981

Post-bop. An alto saxophonist from Detroit, whose bluesy, intense style made him a popular figure in the 50s and 60s. His full name was Sylvester Red Kyner. −RW
   Out of the Blue / BLUE NOTE   i 1959
   W/ Wynton Kelly (p) and Paul Chambers (b). −MGN
- **Two Altos / BLUE NOTE**   i 1959
   W/ Art Pepper (as). −MGN
- ○ **Images / OJC**   1961

Detroit's late/great sax master. Unique concept. −MGN
- ○ **Sonny Red / MAINSTREAM**   197?
Early-70s recording with Cedar Walton (p). −MGN

FREDDIE REDD   b 1928

Post-bop, cool. Recently resurfaced pianist who had double impact in late 50s and 60s as musician and actor. A surging, demonstrative player and penetrating soloist, Redd was a member of the more progressive West Coast jazz community, and worked with Hampton Hawes, George Tucker, John Ore, and others during the 50s. After long absence, Redd returned to recording in 1990, with a fine live trio date. He's since issued a strong combo work. −RW
- ○ **Piano: East/West / OJC**   1952
The East piano is played by Freddie Redd, the West by Hampton Hawes. This album is split 50/50 between each pianist's small group. −MGN
- **San Francisco Suite / OJC**   1957
A fine reissue of a thorough date. Redd in top form. −RW
- ○ **The Complete Blue Note Freddie Redd / MOSAIC**   1960
1960-1961. Redd's Blue Note albums *The Connection*, *Shades of Red*, plus an unissued session with Tina Brooks. W/ Paul Chambers (b), Benny Bailey (tpt). Jackie McLean (as) is on all sessions. −JME
   The Connection / BLUE NOTE   1960
   Concept work that features Redd's playing. −RW
- ○ **Shades of Redd / BLUENOTE**   ca. 1960
Quintet with Tina Brooks on tenor sax and Jackie McLean on alto sax plays all Redd originals with flair and bluesy poignancy. −MGN
   Live at the Studio Grill / PETER PAN-COMPO   1988
   An enchanting session with Al McKibbon (b) and Billy Higgins (d). −RW

VI REDD   b 1928

Bop, hard-bop, post-bop. This Bird-influenced alto saxophonist has left scant recordings, as she has devoted much of her life to teaching. −MGN
- **Birdcall / UA**   1962
Prime material from this Charlie Parker-influenced saxophonist with Carmell Jones (tpt), Roy Ayers (vib), and Russ Freeman (p). −MGN
- ○ **Lady Soul / ATCO**   i 1963

DEWEY REDMAN   b 1931

Post-bop, early free, neo bop, modern creative. A rambling, often electrifying saxophonist and frequent companion of Ornette Coleman. Redman's splintering, swirling forays have been heard in the groups of Keith Jarrett, Coleman, and Old and New Dreams, a Coleman-influenced band. Redman played for the first time with Coleman as well as Charles Moffett and Prince Lasha in a high school marching band. He moved to the West Coast in 1959 after finishing his college education, working with Pharoah Sanders and Wes Montgomery, among others, before moving to New York in 1967. He spent the next seven years working with Coleman, then worked with Charlie Haden's Liberation Orchestra, Carla Bley, and Rosewell Rudd before joining Keith Jarrett's group in the late 70s. During the 80s, he worked extensively with Don Cherry in Old and New Dreams and also made a surprising record with Pat Metheny. −RW
- ○ **Look for the Black Star / ARISTA**   1966
A stark, inventive, and explosive set that shows him in blues and free settings. −RW
   Tarik / BYG   1969
   Spirited musette solos and daring compositions. −RW
- ○ **Ear of the Behearer / IMPULSE**   1973
This is an excellent set that has free leanings and smashing Redman. −RW
   Coincide / IMPULSE   1974

Debut for this exciting saxophonist in a progressive setting, leaning toward avant-garde. –MGN

Redman & Blackwell in Willisau / BLACK SAINT 1980
W/ Ed Blackwell (d). Pivotal, swinging Redman material. –RW

● **The Struggle Continues / ECM** 1982
Look out for Redman on ECM. Much more assertive than standard the ECM date. –RW

DIZZY REECE   ♭1931

Hard-bop, post-bop, cool, progressive big band. Until Courtney Pine began getting headlines a few years ago, Dizzy Reece had the distinction of being the best-known jazz musician with a Jamaican heritage. Reece came to Europe in 1948. He moved to London in 1954 and five years later came to America. During the late 50s, his strong trumpet solos were heard on albums with Ronnie Scott, Tubby Hayes, Hank Mobley, and Donald Byrd. In the 60s, Reece worked with Joe Farrell, Cecil Payne, and John Gilmore. He got some wider attention in the 70s with recordings pairing him with Clifford Jordan and Ted Curson. Reece played in the Paris Reunion Band in 1985. –RW

● **Asia Minor / NEW JAZZ** i 1958
W/ Cecil Payne (bar sax), Hank Jones (p) Trio. Fine document.
–MGN

○ **Blues in Trinity / BLUE NOTE** i 1958
W/ Tubby Hayes (ts). –MGN

ISHMAEL REED

Spoken word, blues-jazz, world fusion, neo bop. Vocals. This writer of Black Evolutionist prose and poetry collaborates with Kip Hanrahan, Taj Mahal, and other Latin and jazz musicians. –MGN

○ **Conjure / PANAGEA** 1983
1983 recording of this Black poet, with Kip Hanrahan organizing the musicians. –MGN

WAYMON REED   ♭1940

Swing, big band, bop. A famed trumpeter with Count Basie and Duke Ellington. Reed, who doubles on the flugelhorn, is another unsung hero and a swing-to-bop master. –MGN

○ **46th & 8th / ARTISTS HOUSE** 1977
Rare date for this veteran trumpeter, with Jimmy Forrest (sax). Nice studio session. –MGN

BILL REICHENBACH   ♭1949

Post-bop, jazz-rock, neo bop. This young trombonist is comfortable in pop or fusion, but steps out in bop to hard-bop ensembles. –MGN

○ **Quartet / SILVER SEVEN** 1984
Studio date for this mainstream trombonist and son of a famous Washington D.C. drummer. –MGN

RUFUS REID

Hard-bop, post-bop, neo bop. A prolific, busy bassist, one of the top session players, particularly for hard-bop and mainstream dates. He's also made some solid releases as a leader on the Sunnyside label. –RW

○ **Perpetual Stroll / THERESA / DB 5** ca. 1980
Delightful session that makes an impact without reeds and brass. –RW

● **Seven Minds / SUNNYSIDE** 1984
Live at William Patterson College, NJ. Premier bassist Reid with pianist Jim McNeely and drummer Teri Lyne Carrington. Extraordinary playing, approaching telepathic. –MGN

Corridor to the Limits / SUNNYSIDE 1989
Recent Reid, featuring Harold Land (ts) plus excellent Reid compositions and playing. –RW

○ **Yours and Mine / CONCORD** 1990
Rufus Reid (b) and Akira Tana (d). Effective session with

strong help from young lions Ralph Moore (ts), Jesse Davis (as). CD version has two bonus cuts. 1991 release. –RW

STEVE REID

Post-bop, early free, neo bop. This progressive bassist attempts to extend the post bop tradition into other modalities and colors. –MGN

○ **Rhythmatism / MUSTEVIC** 1975
NY drummer in a modal setting with Charles Tyler (sax) and Arthur Blythe (as). –MGN

DJANGO REINHARDT   1910-1953

Swing. Born in a Gypsy caravan in Belgium and raised on the outskirts of Paris, Django received his first informal lessons from an uncle who was a banjo virtuoso. At 12, he was playing with some of the best local bands in working-class bars and at dances; he made his first records in 1928, the year in which he was gravely injured in a fire, losing the use of two fingers on his fret hand. With tremendous determination, he taught himself a new system of fingering and took up guitar. Introduced to jazz via Louis Armstrong records in 1931, he was also influenced by Eddie Lang; he became the favorite accompanist of singer Jean Sablon and, after a chance backstage meeting during which they jammed on "Dinah," formed the Quintet of the Hot Club of France with violinist Stephane Grappelli. It consisted of violin, solo guitar, bass, and two rhythms guitars. A born improviser, with a rhythmic drive to rival the best American players and an exceptional melodic gift, Django was the greatest jazz guitarist before Charlie Christian, whom he influenced; others who listened carefully to his records were Wes Montgomery and B. B. King. His brief visit to the US in 1946, during which he performed in concert with Duke Ellington's orchestra, was not a success, but during World War II, he was the toast of Paris. After the war he picked up electric guitar and listened to Christian and the boppers, but his harmonic ear had always been ahead of the pack. His compositions, among them "Nuages," "Django's Castle," and the haunting "Bolero," show the introspective side of his mercurial personality. Django was a unique musical phenomenon whose records continue to intrigue and inspire guitarists and fans. –DM

○ **Djangologie/USA #2 / DISQUES SWING** 1930
A terrific 2-CD set of 30s sides. Django is heard in small groups with Rex Stewart (cnt), Benny Carter (as), Eddie South (violin), as well as with Stephane Grappelli (violin) and The Hot Club Quintet. –RL

● **Djangologie/USA #1 / DISQUES SWING** 1935
Some of the best early (1935-1938) material with Grappelli (violin) and the Hot Club. –RL

Swing De Paris / ARCO-NTI 1947
Django on electric guitar here. Import CD. –RL

Djangology 49 / RCA 1949
Django and Stephane Grappelli (violin) with an Italian rhythm section in 1949. A cooler, more harmonically advanced Django with a pronounced bop influence. — Rl

☆ **Quintette of the Hot Club of France / GNP / DB 5** 194?
A new set featuring his mid- and late-40s dates with Hot Club. Wondrous playing by Reinhardt and Grappelli (violin). –RW

Swingin' with Django / PROARTE
Fine Reinhardt, but not-so-fine sound quality. –RW

EMILY REMLER   1957-1990

Post-bop, neo bop. Guitarist. Her first interests were folk music and rock, but she was introduced to jazz via records by Charlie Christian and Wes Montgomery and graduated from Berklee at 18. Encouraged by Herb Ellis, she played with him at the Concord Jazz Festival in 1978 and the following year began to record for Concord Jazz, also forming her own group and accompanying Astrud Gilberto. She made her first album as a leader in 1981; by then she'd established herself as one of the most interesting new voices on her popular instrument. Her tasteful conception, exceptional swing, and attractive sound combined to make her special. She was also an excellent teacher. Her death during a tour of Australia robbed jazz of a more than promising talent. –DM

○ **Firefly / CONCORD**   1981
Emily Remler is a solid interpreter, sharp guitarist. All her albums have value. –RW

Take Two / CONCORD   1982
Tremendous solos and interpretations by a fine player. –RW

Transitions / CONCORD   1983
Nice, tasteful songs and solos. –RW

● **Catwalk / CONCORD**   1984
Originals from her best studio session. –MGN

East to West / CONCORD   1988
With the Hank Jones Trio. –MGN

Retrospective - Vol. 1 — Standards / CONCORD   COMP
Good overview. –RW

○ **Retrospective - Vol. 2 / CONCORD**   COMP
Compositions. Excellent compositions from this late guitarist. You don't want to miss this. –MGN

REVOLUTIONARY ENSEMBLE

Early free, modern creative. Primarily a free-jazz ensemble, with the unusual instrumentation of Leroy Jenkins (violin), Sirone (b), and Jerome Cooper (per). –MB

Vietnam / ESP DISK   1972
Featuring "47:10 Suite." –MGN

○ **The People's Republic / A&M-HORIZON**   1975
Definitive statement from the all-time best avant-garde band (next to the Art Ensemble). Open listeners only. This album is a must-buy. –MGN

The Psyche / RE   1975
Rare date with three long pieces. –MGN

MEL RHYNE

Post-bop, soul jazz. Organist who was a major foil for Wes Montgomery. The bridge between Jimmy Smith and Larry Young. Still plays in the Milwaukee area, but was originally from the legendary Indianapolis conclave. –MGN

○ **Organizing / JAZZLAND**   i 1960
W/ Johnny Griffin (ts) and Blue Mitchell (tpt). –MGN

MARC RIBOT

M-base. Guitarist who cannot be categorized definitely an improviser — a free spirit-ex-Lounge Lizard. Roots in rock, pop, rub, jazz, and Alan Ginsberg. –MGN

○ **Rootless Cosmopolitans / POLYGRAM**   r 1990
Ribot's uniquely quirky guitar takes center stage in instrumental structures with bandmates from Tom Waits's group and more. –MB

BUDDY RICH   b 1917

Bop, ballads, progressive big band. Virtuoso drummer Buddy Rich began his entertainment career (at 18 months of age) as Traps, the Drum Wonder in his parent's vaudeville act. At the age of six he became a headliner, and his parents dropped out of the act to manage his career. Buddy gained national attention as a drummer when he joined Bunny Berigan (1938), Artie Shaw (1939), and the volatile Tommy Dorsey Orchestra with Frank Sinatra and the Pied Pipers (1939-1942). After two years in the Marines, Buddy rejoined Dorsey until 1946, when he left to form the first of many bands he would lead throughout his career.
With the exception of Harry James, whom he would join, quit, and rejoin several times (the last time as the world's highest paid sideman), Buddy would alternate between leading his own small groups, recording, and touring with Norman Grant's Jazz at the Philharmonic. During this period he played with virtually every great jazz musician around, including Art

Tatum, Lionel Hampton, Dizzy Gillespie, Charlie Parker, Oscar Peterson, and Count Basie. In 1966, he put together a new big band which had great success in clubs, concerts, and college campuses. From that point on until his death, he would contine to successfull tour with his big band both nationally and broad. –BO

Sings Johnny Mercer / VERVE   1956
Great example of his seldom-cited vocal ability. –RW

● **This One's for Basie / POLYGRAM**   1956
A classic! Marty Paich, Buddy, and top Los Angeles studio musicians play Basie. –BO•

○ **Rich vs. Roach / POLYGRAM**   1959
A classic matchup: swing versus be-bop! Each has his own band. –BO

Buddy & Soul / PA-USA   1969
Nice soul-jazz from unlikely source. –RW

Different Drummer / RCA / DB 5   r 1971
One of his best contemporary dates. –RW

○ **Rich in London / RCA**   1972
Great live set from Ronnie Scott's. –RW

& His Orchestra / LASERLIGHT   1973
A good solid collection of Buddy's 1973 band. Great studio recordings. –BO

Sound of Jazz / CLCD   1977
A good, swinging, small-band set — with Lionel Hampton (vib). –RW

Best Band I Ever Had / DCC   1977
Great direct-to-disc recording of an exciting, driving, contemporary big band. No drum solos. –BO

Just Sings / VERVE
Another vocal showcase. –RW

Swinging Count / VERVE
Amazing collaboration with Basie small band. –RW

○ **Swings & Swings & Swings / RCA**

Live at King Street Cafe / PACIFIC JAZZ   COMP
Good 3-disc compilation of his 60s cuts for Pacific Jazz. –RW

Time Being / RCA   COMP
Album tracks 4-7 are the only "live" recordings of Buddy currently available and come closest to capturing his awesome energy. –BO

PATTY RICHARDS

Swing, bop, ballads. A big, brash, bossy, bluesy singer with a lustrous belting voice. Humor is not lost on her, and she loves to entertain. –MGN

○ **Jazz at Boarshead / BOARDSHEAD**   1987
Live recording w/ drumless trio. Peter Domingnez (b), Jeff Kressler (p). Ballads and blues swing softly, but frequently. Richards bawdy personality and blustery joviality shines through. –MGN

JEROME RICHARDSON   b 1920

Swing, big band, bop, hard-bop, post-bop, cool, progressive big band, jazz-ro. Famed studio musician and sideman. A peerless saxophonist and flute player. He is so much in demand for TV, radio, and movies that he rarely ventures out. An unsung hero in the strictest sense. –MGN

● **Midnight Oil / NEW JAZZ**   i 1958
W/ Jimmy Cleveland (tb). –MGN

○ **Roamin' with Richardson / NEW JAZZ**   i 1959
W/ Charlie Persip (d). –MGN

Going to the Movies / UNITED ARTISTS   i 1962

DANNIE RICHMOND   1935-1988

Hard-bop, post-bop, soul jazz, progressive big band, jazz-rock. Dannie Richmond was a marvelous drummer, accomplished at anchoring a song, interacting with the rhythm section or putting a flourish on a tune. He was best known for being the favorite drummer of Charles Mingus from 1956 until his departure. Though he played tenor sax as a teen, Richmond made his debut on drums with Mingus on Atlantic in early 1957, and also made some fine trio releases in the 50s, backing Hampton Hawes. Richmond was quite eclectic; when not working with Mingus, he recorded with Chet Baker, Jimmy Knepper, Herbie Nichols, the Mark-Almond Band, Joe Cocker, Elton John, and Johnnie Taylor, and published a celebrated drum method book in 1965 in Germany.

After Mingus's death, Richmond was musical director of the Mingus Dynasty repertory band, and later was a founding member of the Adams/Pullen quartet. He also made a number of fine albums as a leader, most of them in the 80s, though he also recorded under his own name in the 60s and 70s. –RW

○ **In Jazz for the Culture Set / IMPULSE**   1965
W/ pianist Jaki Byard and harmonicist Toots Thielemans. Andy Warhol soup can cover art. Great record. –MGN

○ **Ode to Mingus / SOUL NOTE**   1979
A super tribute to his longtime employer and musical comrade. The set should have made the jazz world notice Bill Saxton on tenor sax. –RW

● **Quintet / GATEMOUTH**   1980
W/ Mingus drummer with bandmates trumpeter Jack Walrath, saxophonist Ricky Ford. Great 2 & 1/2 minute version of "Cumbia & Jazz Fusion." Prime! –MGN

○ **Dionysius / RED**   1983
This is nicely done mainstream/hard bop. A nod to free influences. –RW

Gentleman's Agreement / SOUL NOTE   1983
Sizzling cuts, with old pros Jimmy Knepper on trombone and Hugh Lawson on piano taking care of business. –RW

KIM RICHMOND

Post-bop, neo bop. Studio saxophonist who has played more than his share of pop studio sessions. Also a very creative musician who, on his own records, gets to cut loose. Plays neo-bop. –MGN

○ **Looking in Looking Out / USA MUSIC GROUP**   1988
Studio saxophonist plays potent jazz. "Trains" is best cut. –MGN

THE RIPPINGTONS

Contemporary funk. A jazz/pop group composed of guitar bass, drums, keys, and vocals occasionally. Formed by guitarist Russ Freeman. Musically very pleasant to listen to. –PK

○ **Kilimanjaro / GRP**   1988
Well written, produced, and performed. Very enjoyable. –PK

LEE RITENOUR   b 1952

Contemporary funk. Guitar, banjo, mandolin. Ritenour taught classical guitar at USC and has been a premier Los Angeles studio player since the mid 70s. Ritenour's knowledge of jazz, international; and pop styles is impressive and his speed, facility, phrasing, and technique are always flawless. He sometimes has been criticized for his choice of material and a penchant for fusion and commercial music. He has issued rock-dominated releases, instrumental pop, light Brazilian and film soundtracks, plus one or two rare sets where he's been able to stretch out and play with flair, distinction, and individuality. –RW

Captain Fingers / CBS   1977
A great player shows how easily he can handle trite pop. Wonderful Mobile Fidelity mastering job. –RW

Color Rit / GRP   1978
Interesting. With some hot licks by Ritenour. –ED

Captain's Journey / ELEKTRA   1978
Feel The Night / ELEKTRA   1979
One of the albums that established the guitarist. –JME

○ **Rio / MCA-GRP**   1979
Ritenour on acoustic. Very nice music. –JME

○ **Rit / ELEKTRA**   1985
Fusion/rock fireworks. –RW

Portrait / GRP   1988
An album summit of fusion/pop types. –RW

Stolen Moments / GRP   1989
A 1990 session that's trademark GRP instrumental pop. –RW

THE RITZ

Ballads. A jazz vocal group consisting of mainly new or emerging artists. Personnel includes Daryl Bosteels, Melissa Hamilton, Van Hawk, Christopher Humphrey, Jeff Auger, Marty Ballou, Fred Haas, and Les Harris, Jr. They've made four albums thus far for Denon, one a Christmas release, with their most recent effort featuring a guest stint from Clark Terry. –RW

○ **The Ritz / DENON**   1988
This vocal jazz ensemble made their first big splash on this 1988 outing. –RW

JAMES RIVERS

Trad, post-bop, soul jazz, neo bop. New Orleans saxophonist plays well in a number of different idioms — gospel, traditional, N.O. funk, and R&B, and neo-bop. Only one record out, looking forward to more. –MGN

○ **Dallas Sessions / SPINDLETOP**   1985
Excellent debut from this New Orlean saxophonist and his straightahead friends. More to come we hope. –MGN

SAM RIVERS   b 1930

Early free, modern big band, jazz-rock, progressive creative. Arguably the greatest unknown saxophonist around, Sam Rivers has never gotten any exposure outside limited jazz circles, despite amassing some extremely impressive credentials. He's been associated with the free school exclusively, but his style actually reflects the entire jazz spectrum, while being one of the most individualistic around. He's at his best on tenor but is also an invigorating flute player and a good soprano and piano soloist. He began his career with area musicians like Herb Pomeroy, Jaki Byard, and Gigi Gryce. He also accompanied Billie Holiday on tour during 1955. Rivers returned to Boston in 1958, working with the Pomeroy big band and leading his own quartet with a then-unknown 13-year-old named Tony Williams on drums. Before going on a tour of Japan with Miles Davis in 1964, Rivers led a Boston band that backed guest artists coming to town in every genre from jazz to blues and R&B. He played with Cecil Taylor from 1968-1973.

Rivers also made several pivotal albums in the early 70s — extremely personal, ambitious, and powerful recordings — among them a pair of duets with Dave Holland, trios, combos, and even one big-band date. In 1975 he was guest soloist with the San Francisco Symphony Orchestra, and his music was presented in glorious fashion at Carnegie Hall for the 1978 Newport in New York festival. A year later, a Rivers work for 32 musicians was presented at New York's Public Theater. He's continued to record, though no major American label has featured him since the 70s. –RW

● **Fuchsia Swing Song / BLUE NOTE**   1964
Mid-60s date with Jaki Byard (p). All Rivers originals and his best period album. –MGN

○ **Contours / BLUE NOTE**   1965
Excellent, w/ Herbie Hancock (p), Freddie Hubbard (tpt). –MGN

Dimensions & Extentions / CAPITOL   1967
Here are stinging, expansive solos with one foot in avant-garde, one in hard bop. –RW

○ **Streams-Live at Montreux / MCA**   1973
Live performance of "Streams Suite." –MGN

● **Crystals / IMPULSE**   1974
Creative orchestra music. Out of this world. His best. –MGN

Sizzle / IMPULSE   1975
Trio with Barry Altschul (d) and Dave Holland (b). Funky with electric touches. Fierce. –MGN

○ **Sam Rivers & Dave Holland / IAI**   1976
Vols. 1 & 2. Excellent, experimental duets between a great bassist and a superior improviser. Unfortunately, it's hard to find. –RW

Paragon / FLUID   1977
With the trio as on "Sizzle." –MGN

Colours / BLACK SAINT / DB 5   1982
Stomping, swinging arrangements. Exuberant 11-piece orchestra supervised and spurred by Rivers. –RW

MAX ROACH   ♭1924

Bop, hard-bop, post-bop, early free, modern creative. Though he could rightfully sit back and bask in well-deserved glory as an elder statesman of bop, Max Roach can still offer riveting, blistering drum solos at 68. Roach began playing the drums at 12 and worked with Charlie Parker as a teenager. He was part of the Minton's (jazz club) bop laboratory, though he was at that time very much under the influence of fellow drummer Kenny Clarke. After a brief stint with Duke Ellington, Roach joined the Benny Carter band and later recorded with Coleman Hawkins. But his amazing timing and rhythmic style became the percussive centerpiece for the bop revolution. He recorded with both Miles Davis and Charlie Parker in the late 40s, going with Parker to Paris in 1949. He went to Europe with one of Norman Granz's *Jazz at the Philharmonic* shows in 1952, and two years later was part of Howard Rumsey's Lighthouse shows. He co-led a quintet with trumpeter Clifford Brown that was among the most popular and influential in jazz. Roach continued heading great groups with such players as Sonny Rollins and Kenny Dorham in the 50s, and he was also a partner in Charles Mingus's ill-fated Debut Records label. In the early 60s, Roach had another great group with a wonderful trumpeter who died prematurely, Booker Little. Roach and then wife Abbey Lincoln made a watershed album in the 60s, *Freedom Now Suite*, a work that got them lots of heat and controversy from right-wing types. He's also maintained a progressive musical front, recording with gospel choirs and string quartets, and renegades like Cecil Taylor and Anthony Braxton, as well as performing the bop he's well known for championing. –RW

Featuring Hank Mobley / OJC   1953
Last 78 and first album session. –JME

In Concert / GNP-CRESCENDO   1954
Excellent Max Roach/Clifford Brown (tpt) music. –RW

○ **Plus Four / EMARCY**   1956
This is great. Roach with Sonny Rollins (ts), Kenny Dorham (tpt), Hank Mobley (ts), and more. –RW

○ **Jazz in 3/4 Time / MERCURY**   1957
Simply sublime hard bop; Roach sparkles on drums. –RW

Deeds, Not Words / OJC   1959

Speak Brother Speak / OJC   1962
Prophetic, demanding, and striking 60s Roach material. –RW

Drums Unlimited / ATLANTIC   1965
Recorded in 1965 and 1966.

● **Force — Sweet Mao — Suid Africa '76 / BASE**   1976
Duets with Archie Shepp (sax). Extended pieces from two virtuosos. Quintessential. –MGN

The Loadstar / HORO   1977
Quartet 2-fer (one piece per album) with Billy Harper (ts), Cecil Bridgewater (tpt), Reggie Workman (b). This is powerful music. –MGN

Max & Dizzy-Paris 1989 / A&M / DB 5   1989
This recent summit meeting of founding bop fathers shows both are still in shape. –RW

☆ **To the Max! / RHINO**
An excellent newer release showcasing this drummer's work

with the percussion ensemble M'Boom, choir and orchestra, and his long-standing quartet. A must-buy item. –MGN

HANK ROBERTS

World fusion, neo bop, modern creative. Cellist plays creative improvised music, with an occasional foray into commercial funk. A singularly unique artist. –MGN

○ **Black Pastels / POLYGRAM**   1987
This is more daring than usual for Roberts. –RW

Birds of Prey / POLYDOR   ca. 1990
This music crosses pop/funk/jazz/third-world parameters. Roberts is an excellent cellist. The music is progressive at times and too commercial at others. His best work lies ahead. –MGN

HOWARD ROBERTS   1929-1992

Swing, bop, post-bop, cool. Howard Roberts led an intense musical life from an early age, jamming and gigging in funky nightclubs and devoting himself to serious practice and study. Breaking into the Los Angeles studio scene in 1950, he had played on thousands of jazz, rock, and pop records by the early 70s. In his own creative work, he mastered a style combining the "funky" feel of a blues-based organ trio sound with glittering melodic speed and an advanced harmonic imagination. This impressive and very listenable style is heard on such albums as *Howard Roberts is a Dirty Guitar Player*. For someone who made so many recordings, it is ironic that his own albums are so hard to find nowadays, but the best of those are worth the search. Roberts was also well known for his monthly column in *Guitar Player Magazine* and as cofounder of Guitar Institute of Technology (now the Musician's Institute). –DNM

○ **H.R. Is a Dirty Guitar Player / CAPITOL**
This is classic Roberts. A very nice album to have around. –JME

The Movin' Man / VERVE   1957
More mainstream than later organ/funky efforts. Sidemen are not at Robert's level, but it is a very listenable set, a fine glimpse of his early bop-style playing. –DMN

Color Him Funky / CAPITOL   1963
W/ organ trio; Howard is slick and soulful. Find this one on vinyl and you'll smile and tap your foot. Organ sounds a bit dated, but it's part of the charm. –DNM

● **The Real Howard Roberts / CONCORD**   1977
Nice, tasteful swing-inspired music. –RW

MARCUS ROBERTS

Trad, swing, bop, post-bop, neo bop. Exciting New Orleans pianist and former pivotal member of Wynton Marsalis's group. His keen piano solos, probing lines, and steady rhythmic contributions made a sizeable impact in Marsalis's unit when he replaced Kenny Kirkland. He now records as a leader, and recently has been exploring classic New Orleans, stride, and gospel via unaccompanied recordings, as well as bop and hard-bop. –RW

The Truth Is Spoken Here / NOVUS   1988
Stirring, strong piano. –RW

● **Deep in the Shed / NOVUS / DB 5**   1989
His best group date. –RW

○ **Alone with Three Giants / NOVUS**   1990
This is a somewhat controversial solo outing. Roberts, in my view, is an outstanding young player. –RW

Prayer for Peace / NOVUS

HERB ROBERTSON

Post-bop, modern creative. This trumpeter and flugelhornist uses modal to free formats to create a large ensemble sound. –MGN

○ **Shades of Bud Powell / POLYGRAM**   1988
Extraordinary date from this trumpeter and the All-Star

Sextet on an all-Powell program, creatively arranged. Excellent beyond words. –MGN

PERRY ROBINSON   b 1938

Neo bop, modern creative. A post-bop-to-progressive clarinetist with technique to burn and ideas to match, Robinson is a neglected kindred spirit to his instrument. –MGN

○ **Funk Dumpling / SAVOY**   1962
W/ Kenny Barron (p). Creative, loose, straightahead. –MGN

● **The Traveler / CHIAROSCURO**   1977
W/ progressive clarinetist and quartet. A very interesting album. –MGN

Kundalini / IAI   1978
W/ Badal Roy on tabla and Nana Vasconcelos on percussion. Captivating world fusion. –MGN

SPIKE ROBINSON   b 1930

Swing, bop. A contemporary composer and mainstream jazz musician, Robinson has recorded several albums on Capri and Discovery. His albums are well-produced, contain good renditions of jazz standards, and often feature good guest stints from jazz veterans. –RW

○ **Just a Bit O' Blues / CAPRI**   1988
Dazzling swing/traditional jazz coalition. –RW

BETTY ROCHE   b 1920

Swing, big band, ballads. Betty Roche sang prominently with Duke Ellington in 1944. She made several good records, showing a pristine voice. –MGN

○ **Singin' an Swingin' / OJC**   1961
Backed soulfully by a quintet ... her free use of tempos and warm, distinct sound is nicely captured on this record. –BOB RUSCH, CADENCE

CLAUDIO RODITI   b 1946

Post-bop, neo bop. Jazz and Latin-jazz trumpeter who's done session work both on East and West Coast and has issued some releases as a leader. Roditi plays clean, crisp solos. –RW

○ **Claudio / UPTOWN**   ca. 1985
The quintet showcases this straightahead trumpeter from Brazil on six standards played with bop flavor (Dorham, Stiff, and J. J. Johnson wrote three.) Slide Hampton plays trombone. This is a good, upbeat band. –MGN

○ **Gemini Man / MILESTONE**   1988
A good player makes an average bop/Afro-Latin release. –RW

● **Two of Swords / CANDID**

RED RODNEY   b 1927

Bop, hard-bop, post-bop. Trumpet. Rodney is one of last living links to Charlie Parker and the bop era. He got big-band experience as a teen playing with Gene Krupa, Claude Thornhill, and Woody Herman, and made his first recordings as a leader at 19. He was Parker's trumpeter from 1949-1951 and came under his spell in every way, absorbing Parker's love for music. He made some fine records in the late 40s and early 50s, including a sensational session with Ira Sullivan in 1955. Rodney made yet another triumphant comeback with superb 1973 album matching him with Charlie McPherson. He had series of fine releases in 70s and 80s, and toured in 1987 with Australian phenom James Morrison. Recognized as a prime bop stylist, Rodney's fiery licks, harmonic knowledge, and crackling solos put him in upper echelon among 50s players. –RW

○ **Early Bebop on Keynote / POLYGRAM**   194?
A good 20-track overview of Rodney's mid-40s cuts on Keynote. Both his own band and his stints with others are covered. –RW

Modern Music from Chicago / OJC   1955
This nice reissue features the famous white trumpeter who once passed for both Black and Native American! –RW

○ **The Red Arrow / ONYX**   1957
W/ Ira Sullivan (tpt/sax) and Tommy Flanagan Trio. Historic early meeting between Rodney and Sullivan. Two by Rodney, one by bassist Oscar Pettiford, three standards. –MGN

Bird Lives / MUSE   ca. 1973
Quintet w/ Roy Brooks (d), Charles McPherson (as), Barry Harris (p), Sam Jones (b). Three Bird compositions, Monk's rousing "52nd St. Theme," "Round Midnight," and one standard. This is one great band for Red to blow with. –MGN

● **Live at the Village Vanguard / MUSE**   1980
With Ira Sullivan (tpt/sax) and quintet. Three Jack Walrath originals, three standouts. This is one of the most together jazz bands of the 80s. A perfect vehicle for Red and Ira to blow. Sullivan plays saxs, flute, and flugelhorn. –MGN

Sprint / ELEKTRA   ca. 1982
Recorded live at NYC's Jazz Forum. Three by pianist Garry Dial, two standards. More hot stuff. The "Red-Sullivan" show shines. –MGN

Red Alert! / CONTINUUM REC.   1990
A delightful workout, with excellent Rodney solos. –RW

SHORTY ROGERS   b 1924

Big band, post-bop, cool, progressive big band. A fine writer and good trumpet player, Rogers began with Will Bradley, Red Norvo, and Woody Herman in the 40s, and penned "Keen and Peachy" for Herman's band, before joining Stan Kenton in 1950-1951. He become a prominent member of White West Coast school during 50s, recording and touring with Art Pepper, Jimmy Giuffre, Shelly Manne, and others. He wrote some invigorating arrangements for both big bands and small combos in the 50s and 60s, and turned increasingly to film and television, giving up playing completely from 60s to early 80s. His compositions and arrangements merged the best of cool era discipline, precision, and subdued tones with the swing period's organization and sound. His pieces for nonet were especially inspired. –RW

○ **Short Stops / RCA**   1953
1953-1954. A thorough reissue that covers his first three RCA albums. For some strange reason, the CD only has 20 of 32 cuts. –RW

Big Band - Vol 1 / TIME IS   1953
Fine big band doing West Coast material. –RW

● **Martians Stay Home / ATLANTIC**   ca. 1955
The quintet for this trumpeter, from the West Coast via Massachusetts and New York, includes Jimmy Giuffre (cl), Pete Jolly (p), Curtis Counce, Shelly Manne, (d) and others. There are six Shorty originals and three standards. These are nice groups with Rogers's sensitive trumpet leading in a non-threatening, mainstream groove. –MGN

Jazz Waltz / DISCOVERY   1962
This is a big band (28 different players at one time or another) of all-stars too numerous to mention. Songs are by Shorty and Duke Ellington, and there are four other standards. –MGN

Yesterday Today & Forever / CONCORD   1983
Nice mid-80s date pairs Rogers with Bud Shank (as/fl). –RW

Swings / RCA
New reissue with three bonus cuts. Original RCA album. –RW

SONNY ROLLINS   b 1929

Hard-bop, post-bop, soul jazz, Latin, jazz-rock. The man most often deemed the greatest living saxophonist, and with good reason. Sonny Rollins has been a dominant player since the early 50s, and has made, note-for-note, as many unforgettable solos and recordings as any musician active in any idiom. His tone is among jazz's most vivid and full ever; his ability to constantly create, recycle, and rework melodies and incorporate fragments into his solos is both instructive and amazing, while he's also the master of the calypso jazz mode. He switched from alto to tenor and made his first recordings with Babs Gonzales in 1948. He subsequently worked with J. J.

Johnson, Thelonious Monk, Art Blakey, Bud Powell, Tadd Dameron, and Miles Davis. Rollins's reputation soared when he joined the Clifford Brown/Max Roach quintet in 1955. When that group disbanded following Brown's death, Rollins began heading his own bands, which he's done ever since. He made numerous fantastic releases in the 50s and 60s, including the famous pianoless trio dates, plus sessions with Monk and a guest stint on a Modern Jazz Quartet release. He flirted in the mid 60s with free playing but returned to a mainstream framework shortly after, though he's always out on the edge in his playing. In the 70s he began playing soprano. –RW

With the Modern Jazz Quartet / OJC   1951
1951-1953. Fire meets cool in this excellent reissue of their early-50s collaboration. –RW

Moving Out / OJC   1954
A nice date. –RW

On Impulse / MCA   1955
Outstanding set with propulsive Rollins solos. –RW

Worktime / OJC   1955
A notable quartet date. –RW

Sonny Boy / OJC   1956
This includes a dynamic Rollins solo and impressive stints by Kenny Dorham (tpt), Kenny Drew (p), and Max Roach (p) (among others). –RW

Plus Four / OJC   1956
A wonderful outing that was among the last for the Clifford Brown/Max Roach group. –RW

☆ **Tenor Madness / OJC**   1956
Just a gigantic session with the Miles Davis rhythm section and a wonderful duet with Coltrane (ts) on the title cut. Rollins emerges as his own man in style. –RW

★ **Saxophone Colossus & More / OJC / DB 5**   1956
Superb. Reissue of a seminal late-50s Rollins session. Max Roach crackles on drums. –RW

Plays for Bird / OJC   1956
This is an emphatic tribute to one of his idols, influences, and mentors. –RW

Tour De Force / OJC   1956
A fine session with Kenny Drew (p) setting the rhythm section pace on piano. Good bonus cut. –RW

Volume One / CAPITOL   1956
A fine mid-80s reissue of 50s sessions on Blue Note. This is not classic, but it's well done. –RW

Alternate Takes / CONTEMPORARY   1957
Leftovers, albeit some shining Rollins solos. –RW

○ **Way Out West / OJC / DB 5**   1957
A remarkable masterpiece. Explosive Rollins gets steady support from Ray Brown (b) and Shelley Mann (d). –RW

○ **Volume Two / BLUE NOTE**   1957
W/ Thelonius Monk. This second volume is spiced by topflight funky piano from Horace Silver. –RW

The Sound of Sonny / RIVERSIDE   1957
Wonderful standards and originals, with funky, inventive piano from Sonny Clark (p). Great bonus cut on CD. –RW

○ **Newk's Time / CAPITOL**   1957
W/ Wynton Kelly (p) and Philly Joe Jones (d). Blue Note. Just a super quartet date; excellent reissue with original cover and notes. –RW

☆ **Night at the Village Vanguard - Vol 1 / BLUE NOTE** 1957
One of two incendiary live dates from Vanguard in the late 50s. The pianoless trio steps forth and claims its fame. –RW

○ **Night at the Village Vanguard - Vol II / BLUE NOTE** 1957
An excellent follow to a legendary album. –RW

● **Freedom Suite / OJC**   1958
The pianoless trio in action at its best. Rollins strikes a blow for artistic, racial, and personal liberation. –RW

And Contemporary Leaders / OJC   1958
An excellent reissue of a contemporary set. –RW

Brass Trio / POLYGRAM   1958
Exemplary Rollins but uneven brass and strings. –RW

Quartets Featuring Jim Hall / RCA / DB 5   1962
Includes the Rollins classic "The Bridge." –MGN

○ **The Bridge / RCA / DB 5**   1962
Rollins makes a shattering return from sabbatical. He's joined by the youthful Jim Hall (g), who makes a great partner. –RW

Sonny Meets Hawk! / RCA   1963
W/ Coleman Hawkins (ts). The grand master teams with the still relatively young master for a moving, evocative session. Available mainly in a 2-record reissue with *The Bridge* by French RCA. –RW

All the Things You Are / RCA / DB 5   1963
1963-1964. Super 1990 reissue. It includes stints by Coleman Hawkins (ts) and Herbie Hancock (k). –RW

Alfie / MCA / DB 5   1966
Extraordinary versions of ordinary songs. –RW

○ **East Broadway Run Down / MCA / DB 5**   1966
The title cut is exceptional. Freddie Hubbard (tpt) is also great, as are Elvin Jones (d) and Jimmy Garrison (b). –RW

Next Album / OJC / DB 5   1972
Rollins makes another incredible return in this 1972 album, now available in a 1988 reissue. –RW

Horn Culture / OJC   1973
A session that's good, though not essential, Rollins. –RW

In Japan / JVC   1973
A tremendous recording of great Japanese concerts. –RW

○ **The Cutting Edge / OJC**   1974
Concert at Montreux w/ Stanley Cowell (p). Very spirited. –MGN

Nucleus / OJC   1975
An average (for Rollins) session, newly reissued. –RW

Sunny Days, Starry Nights / MILESTONE   1984
Although there are lovely Sonny solos, the material is uneven, and the contributions from sidemen are rather standard. –RW

The Solo Album / MILESTONE   1985
Long moments of aimless noodling are balanced by stretches of awesome improvising. To get the full effect, listen to it all the way through. –RW

G-Man / MILESTONE   1986
The support teeters and totters, but Rollins is often remarkable. –RW

Falling in Love with Jazz / MILESTONE   1989
Wonderful Rollins. Undistinguished material. Tommy Flanagan (p) and Branford Marsalis (ts) are tough. –RW

Best of Sonny Rollins / CAPITOL   COMP
Title is wholly misleading. Everything here is wonderful, but it's impossible to collect his best songs on one set. –RW

○ **Complete Prestige Recordings / PRESTIGE**   COMP
Sonny Rollins on Prestige — a 7 CD boxed set covering the years 1949-1956 (90 selections). Includes his early work as a sideman plus all of his solo albums for Prestige. About every jazz great appears somewhere in this compilation, from Charlie Parker and Miles Davis to Clifford Brown and John Coltrane. The liner notes are superb. This set is a treasure. –JME

ALDO ROMANO   b 1941

Post-bop, early free, neo bop, modern creative. Veteran jazz drummer, also explores advanced rhythms in creative context. Ornette Coleman devotee. –MGN

○ **Ritual / RHINO**
A session by drummer Romano. His playing surpasses the quality of the material. –RW

● **To Be Ornette to Be / RHINO**
An excellent release, perhaps his best, from this Italian drummer playing the music of Ornette Coleman. –MGN

WALLACE RONEY   b 1960

Post-bop, neo bop. First-rate young lion trumpeter very much in basic hard-bop mode. Roney, still in his 20s, has made some vibrant sessions for Muse and showed his knowledge of jazz standards and command of the trumpet. Especially good at upper-register statements, also plays very commendable ballads. He's still growing as a composer and bandleader. –RW

Verses / MUSE   1987
Aggressive, attacking material with fiery exchanges between Gary Thomas (reeds) and Roney. –RW

Intuition / MUSE   ca. 1988
This is a stirring set from one of the best "young lion" trumpeters. Very dynamic hard-bop line with superior alto and tenor sax by Kenny Garret (as/ts) and Gary Thomas (ts). Roney is great. –RW

○ **Obsession / MUSE**
The latest from this trumpet whiz boasts excellent songs supplied by both Roney and pianist Donald Brown. –RW

Standard Bearer / MUSE
High-flying mainstream from strong young lion. –RW

TED ROSENTHAL   b 1959

Post-bop, neo bop. Piano. Won 1988 Thelonious Monk Jazz Piano Competition. He is an original composer with a BA in music. Rosenthal is coming on as a writer and arranger. One to watch. –MGN

○ **New Tunes New Traditions / KEN MUSIC**   1989
The songs and playing of band members Tom Harrel (tpt), Billy Higgins (d), and Ron Carter (b) take some of the spotlight away from the leader. –RW

MICHELE ROSEWOMAN

Post-bop, Latin, world fusion, neo bop, modern creative. Pianist plays a lot of music including modal, Monk-ish melodic, harmolodic, Latin jazz, and creative. Works mostly in small ensemble format or with New Yoruba Latin Band. –MGN

○ **Contrast High / RHINO**   1988
Pianist with intriguing compositions. –MGN

RENEE ROSNES   b 1962

Post-bop, neo bop. Excellent pianist from Canada who's established herself on New York scene. Rosnes has worked with Joe Henderson, O.T.B., and led her own group, showing equal skills on acoustic keyboard, electric, and synthesizer. A percussive, driving soloist, excellent accompanist, and emerging jazz star. –RW

○ **Renee Rosnes / CAPITOL**   1988
High-caliber duet and quartet sessions. Rosnes proves captivating in any context. Guests include Wayne Shorter (sax) and Branford Marsalis (sax). –RW

For the Moment / CAPITOL   1990
A first-rate pianist and improviser takes center stage. –RW

FRANK ROSOLINO   b 1926

Big band, bop, hard-bop, post-bop, cool, progressive big band. Brilliant Detroit-born trombonist, lived and worked in Los Angeles. Played with Gene Kupa, Stan Kenton, Lighthouse All Stars, many West Coast post-bop ensembles, and studio sessions. Occasional big-band member. Known for his natural lyrical sense; uncanny balladeer. –MGN

Kenton Presents / CAPITOL   i 1954
W/ Charlie Mariano (as). –MGN

● **Frankly Speaking / AFFINITY**   1955
Perhaps his greatest album as a leader. Immaculate trombone solos. –RW

○ **5 / VSOP- MODE**   1957
This brilliant trombonist, with a quintet including Richie Kamuca (sax) and Vince Guaraldi (p), plays three Rosolino originals and five standards including Bill Holman's "Fallout."

A beautiful charcoal portrait of Rosolino by Eve Diana is on the front cover. –MGN

○ **Free for All / OJC**   1958
Top Rosolino session with Harold Land (ts) and Leroy Vinnegar (b). Outstanding CD reissue is a limited edition. –RW

○ **Thinking About You / SACKVILLE**   1976
Recorded live at Bourbon Street in Toronto with Ed Bickert (g), Don Thompson (b), and Terry Clarke (d), this album includes four long standards. With room to stretch, the whole band is up to the task. This is on the mellow side. There is a cover painting of the trombonist by Jerry Lazare. –MGN

ANNIE ROSS   b 1930

Bop, ballads. One-third of jazz's most famous vocal trio. She returned to her native England in 1947 and worked there and in France as a singer. She returned to America in 1952, winning fame for writing lyrics to a brilliant tenor sax solo by Wardell Gray on the song "Twisted" and recording a vocalese version. Ross sang with Jack Parnell and Tony Crombie in England in mid 50s before hooking up with Dave Lambert and Jon Hendricks. This unit made intricate verbalizing, vocalizing in jazz mode seem easy and was enormously popular in late 50s and early 60s, before Ross was forced to quit due to illness. She did a variety of singing and acting work in England from 1962-1966 and also ran her own club for a period. –RW

○ **King Pleasure Sings/Annie Ross Sings / OJC**   1952
Top notch. –MGN

● **Sings a Song with Gerry Mulligan / BLUE NOTE**   r 1959
W/ Gerry Mulligan (sax). Expertly done all-around, a wonderful collaboration. –RW

○ **Gasser! / BLUE NOTE**   1960
1988 reissue, another tremendous joint effort between Ross and a top saxophonist, this time Zoot Sims. –RW

CHARLIE ROUSE   1924-1988

Post-bop. Tenor sax. A wonderful, underrated musician, Charlie Rouse's fame has nevertheless stemmed mainly from his longtime association with Thelonious Monk. Rouse worked with Billy Eckstine, Dizzy Gillespie, Tadd Dameron, and Fats Navarro in the 40s, and joined Duke Ellington in 1949-1950. For almost the entire decade of the 50s Rouse was a free-lancer, but he joined Monk in 1959 and remained with him until 1970. No saxophonist better anticipated Monk's quirks, twists, tempo shifts, and textures, and his own understated, quirky yet emphatic style filled in the gaps nicely. He formed a repertory band with Mal Waldron in the early 80s; the band Sphere gradually expanded their repertoire from just Monk to originals and other standards. Rouse gained a measure of well-deserved publicity and recognition near the end of his career; he was a marvelous soloist and accompanist. –RW

Takin' Care of Business / OJC   1960
Quintet with Blue Mitchell (tpt) and the Walter Bishop (p) Trio plays two numbers penned by Randy Weston, one apiece by Kenny Drew and Rouse, and two standards. This is a supremely confident group that plays strong music in a somewhat cool mood. –MGN

Unsung Hero / CBS   1960
1960-1961. This is a 1990 reissue of a fine Rouse set for Columbia. –RW

○ **Two is One / STRATA-EAST**   1974
Surprising set. Animated Rouse solos and a Latin flavor. –RW

Cinnamon Flower / RYKODISC   1976
A fine big-band date led by Rouse. A topflight reissue courtesy of Rykodisc. –RW

● **Moment's Notice / STORYVILLE**   ca. 1977
This quartet features pianist Hugh Lawson, bassist Bob Cranshaw, and drummer Ben Riley. Rouse, a model tenor saxaphonist, plays with melodic wit and sense of purpose throughout. –MGN

Social Call / UPTOWN 1984
Wonderful playing by Rouse. Appearances by Red Rodney (tpt), Cecil McBee (b), and Al Dailey (d). —RW

Epistrophy / LANDMARK 1988
An adventurous late-80s date, with Rouse stepping out and handling the challenge posed by Don Cherry (cnt), Buddy Montgomery (p), and George Cables (p). —RW

ROVA SAXOPHONE QUARTET

Early free, modern creative. When ROVA formed in 1978, the World Saxophone Quartet was the only other such group playing improvisational music. Today there's a saxophone quartet in almost every major city, but not can match Rova's tight ensemble work, dedication to creative musical growth, and busy touring schedule. Their collective identity is an acronym of the founding member's names (Jon *R*askin, Larry *O*chs, Andrew *V*oight, and Bruce *A*ckley, with Steve Adams replacing Voight in the late 80s). From the start, ROVA has developed their own brand of structured improvisation, giving equal importance to spontaneity and intricate compositional sections within a single piece. Over the years, ROVA has thrived on the strong support of European audiences. —MB

Cinema Rovate / METALANGUAGE 1978
Debut album of open-ended compositions — a response to the groups's perceived lack of discipline in contemporary free jazz. —MB

Daredevils / METALANGUAGE 1979
Second album documents an early collaboration with guitarist Henry Kaiser. —MB

● **Favorite Street / BLACK SAINT** 1984
ROVA plays (and deconstructs) the music of saxophonist Steve Lacy — a triumph of structural improv and a personal favorite. —MB

○ **The Aggregate / SOUND ASPECTS** 1987
Superb live set with Anthony Braxton (sax) as a fifth member; onc of the last recordings with Voight. —MB

★ **This Time We Are Both / NEW ALBION** 1989
Live recordings from their second USSR tour in 1989. This is a definitive statement from the second version of ROVA with Adams — gorgeous sound and stunning scores. —MB

Long on Logic / SOUND ASPECTS 1990
Music by ROVA, Henry Kaiser (g), and Fred Frith; an outgrowth of a successful local concert series. One of the few sax quartet albums that utilizes studio and sampling technology as an artistic tool. —MB

JIMMY ROWLES   *b* 1918

Swing, bop, cool. Jimmy Rowles has long been known as a steady, relaxed, and confident pianist and master accompanist for vocalists. His style includes elements of stride and boogie-woogie, and he's flexible enough to handle any situation from solo to duo to small combo to large orchestra. Rowles moved to Los Angeles from Spokane, Washington in 1940, and worked with Slim Gaillard, Lester Young, Benny Goodman, and Woody Herman before going into the army in 1942. After finishing his tenure there, Rowles worked again with Goodman and Herman as well as Les Brown and Tommy Dorsey, while cutting a number of records as a freelance studio player. Rowles moved to New York in 1973, and has been a busy contributor ever since, appearing on a host of excellent sessions in mainstream and swing-influenced mode. —RW

○ **The Special Magic of Jimmy Rowles / HALCYON** 1974
This album includes duets with Rusty Gilder on bass. Solo, Rowles shows he can do it alone, and with Gilder, sparks occasionally fly. Mostly, this is laid back. They play lots of Duke Ellington. There is a good version of Carl Perkin's "Grooveyard." —MGN

○ **Grandpaws / CHOICE** ca. 1976
The trio for this pianist includes Buster Williams on bass and Billy Hart on drums. They play two by Rowles, the others are standards. They do an exquisite medley of "Lush Life/ A Train/ I Love You/ I Hadn't Anyone 'Till You/ Margie/ Chicago/ Desert Fire." Rowles shows his ballad skills best. —MGN

● **Plays Ellington & Billy Strayhorn / COLUMBIA** 1981
If you must limit Rowles purchases to one record, get this elegant yet exuberant tribute to a pair of keyboard greats. —RW

With the Red Mitchell Trio / CONTEMPORARY 1985
Volume 2 / CONTEMPORARY 1985
Although done in 1985, this set wasn't released until 1988. It is well done by Rowles, Red Mitchell (b), Rowles's daughter Stacey, and Colin Bailey (d). —RW

Trio / CONTEMPORARY 1986
Excellent date; splendid Rowles trio material. —RW

STACY ROWLES   *b* 1955

Swing, cool. Trumpet. The daughter of Jimmy Rowles, Stacy has cut some nice combo recordings as a leader on trumpet, and also done dates with her famous father. —RW

○ **Tell It Like It Is / CONCORD** 1984
Famous father teams with talented daughter. —RW

MARSHALL ROYAL   *b* 1912

Swing, big band. Longtime session saxophonist with extensive background in studios and in swing bands. He's currently playing in the Concord Superband and also has cut his own albums with veterans like Jake Hanna and Monty Alexander. Not a striking or fiery soloist, but above-average technically, strong on standards, and ballads. A nice blues player. —RW

○ **First Chair / CONCORD** 1978
More of the same as on the *Royal Blue* album. —MGN

● **Royal Blue / CONCORD** r 1980
Basie style alto sax player with low-key jazz. A must-buy. —MGN

ROSWELL RUDD   *b* 1935

Post-bop, early free, modern big band, modern creative. An innovative trombonist and composer and stick-to-your-ribs progressive, with a dash of soul and humor, Rudd is the real thing. —MGN

○ **Everywhere / IMPULSE / DB 5** 1966
W/ legendary flutist/bass clarinetist Giuseppi Logan and two bass players. All originals. —MGN

Numatik Swing Band / JCOA 1973
Immortal sessions with the Jazz Composers Orchestra. —MGN

● **Flexible Flyer / ARISTA-FREEDOM** 1974
Date for creative trombonist who fell in the cracks when Ray Anderson arrived. A solid album, with Sheila Jordan (v). —MGN

Inside Job / ARISTA 1976
Solid quintet date w/ intense Dave Burrell on piano. —RW

○ **Regeneration / SOUL NOTE** 1982
One of many intriguing collaborations pairing Rudd and Steve Lacy (sop sax). —RW

HILTON RUIZ   *b* 1952

Post-bop, Latin, neo bop. Bop-influenced Latin pianist. Equally comfortable as a Latin or jazz player. In-demand sideman and solo pianist. Later-period recordings straying more into funk. Style reflects Tyner-Corea-Hancock. —MGN

● **Piano Man / INNERCITY** 1975
Piano trio date and his first as a leader. Reissued from the Steeplechase label. First rate. —MGN

○ **Cross Currents / STASH** 1984
These trio and quintet performances helped cement Ruiz's status in the Afro-Latin and jazz communities. —RW

Something Grand / NOVUS 1986
Fine Afro-Latin jazz excursion by this solid pianist.

Sensational trombone by Steve Turre. Sam Rivers (sax) is also in the ensemble. –RW

Strut / NOVUS   1989
Funky and brassy, plus great arrangements, make this date a success. –RW

HOWARD RUMSEY   b 1917

Swing, post-bop, cool. Rumsey began on piano, then switched to drums. He began work in Vido Musso's band with pianist Stan Kenton, and was later a founding member of Kenton's first big band. Rumsey did a lot of freelance work in West Coast groups in the 40s, and started some jam sessions at the Lighthouse in Hermosa Beach, California in 1949. The sessions evolved into a who's who of West Coast jazz, and Contemporary began recording a series of albums done at the Lighthouse. Rumsey was a steady presence and unifying figure able to get contrasting, sometimes vastly differing personalities to mesh smoothly in studio/jam environment. The All-Stars series was a profitable one for Contemporary in the 50s, and some six volumes have been reissued by Fantasy. Rumsey went on to head various combos and big bands and spearhead a *Concerts By The Sea* series in the 60s and 70s. –RW

○ **Sunday Jazz à la Jazzhouse / OJC**   1953
This is textbook West Coast style. Hampton Hawes brings some fire on piano. –RW

Oboe/Flute / OJC   1954
Sonny Clark (p) and Max Roach (d) are standouts. –RW

○ **In the Solo Spotlight / OJC**   1954
1954 & 1957. This large-group date has its moments, but not enough to make it fully successful. –RW

Lighthouse at Laguna / OJC   1955
Trombonist Frank Rosolino is a standout on this otherwise routine set. –RW

Music for Lighthousekeeping / OJC   1956
Pianist Sonny Clark takes honors here. –RW

In the Solo Spotlight - Vol. 5 / CONTEMPORARY   i 1956
Jazz Rolls-Royce / LIGHTHOUSE   i 1957
W/ Bob Cooper (ts). –MGN

● **Jazz Invention / CONTEMPORARY**   1989
Nice ensemble and compositions; standard playing. –RW

JIMMY RUSHING   1903-1972

Big band, blues-jazz, ballads. One of the great singers of the Swing Era. A member of the Count Basie band from 1935-1950 and vocalist on dozens of Basie recordings from this period. Among his classics with Basie are "Outskirts Of Town," "Sent For You Yesterday," "Evenin'," and "Boogie Woogie." His own recordings began in 1945 when he made his first album for Vanguard. Two subsequent Vanguard albums are complemented by five Columbia albums (1956-1960). All these, with the exception of the Columbia album with accompaniment by The Dave Brubeck Quartet, are highly recommended. Rushing was a master of Kansas City blues and jazz and the Vanguards have a strong blues emphasis. Later albums on Colpix and ABC Bluesway have good moments and his last recording from 1971, "The You And Me That Used To Be," (RCA) is excellent. –BP

○ **Essential Jimmy Rushing / VANGUARD**
Jimmy Rushing And The Smith Girls / COLUMBIA
○ **And the Big Brass / COLUMBIA**   r 1958
Super vocals, nice arrangements. –RW

Rushing Lullabies / COLUMBIA   1965
● **Blues and Things / MASTER JAZZ**   1967
Tremendous session with Earl Hines (p) quartet. –RW

Who Was It That ... / MASTER JAZZ / DB 5   r 1973
Who Was It That Sang That Song? Excellent lineup, strong vocals. –RW

And The Big Brass / COLUMBIA   1990
Jazz Odyssey / COLUMBIA / DB 5
Strong vocals, plus Rushing plays piano. –RW

The Smith Girls / COLUMBIA
Rushing does songs previously made famous by classic female blues singers. –RW

GENE RUSSELL   b 1932

Post-bop, Dixieland. Pop, jazz, and soul keyboardist who played acoustic and Fender Rhodes. –MGN

○ **Talk to My Lady / BLACKJAZZ**   r 1973
Quadrophonic album. Sextet with keyboardist/leader. Also features Henry Franklin (b) Ndugu (d). Soul, jazz, and pop here in eight cuts, with three originals from Russell. –MGN

GEORGE RUSSELL   b 1923

Post-bop, early free, progressive big band, jazz-rock, neo bop. Composer, piano, theorist. As his father was a professor of music at Oberlin University, it's not surprising that George Russell would become a prime educator and theorist. He sold his first big-band composition to Benny Carter and Dizzy Gillespie in 1945. Russell wrote for Earl Hines in the mid 40s and also for some shows in Chicago before moving to New York. After overcoming an illness, Russell penned "Cubana Be, Cubana Bop" for Gillespie and premiered it in Carnegie Hall in 1947 by his big band with Chano Pozo. Russell became a widely-published composer in the late 40s and 50s, having songs recorded by Buddy Defranco, Charlie Ventura, Artie Shaw, Claude Thornhill, Lee Konitz, Jimmy Giuffre, and Charles Mingus. He taught at the School of Jazz in Lennox, MA in 1959-1960, formed and led his own group from 1960-1965 and played at the landmark 1962 Washington DC Jazz Festival. He spent several years in Europe after 1964, and also made many remarkable big-band and large-group works after 1959 with *New York, New York* on through 60s, 70s, and 80s. His 1972 work *Living Time* featured a collaboration with Bill Evans, while his 1983 *The African Game* was one of the first releases on the newly revived Blue Note label. –RW

● **New York, N.Y. / MCA**   1959
This is a landmark of conceptual, arranging, production, and playing magnificence. John Coltrane (ts), Max Roach (d), Bill Evans (p), Jon Hendricks (v) all soar. –RW

Stratusphunk / OJC   1960
Intriguing, often entrancing, compositions. –RW

Jazz in the Space Age / DECCA   i 1960
W/ Bill Evans (p) and Dave Young (b). –MGN

☆ **Ezz-Thetics / OJC**   1961
Sextet. Extraordinary group jazz with highly creative edge. Featuring Eric Dolphy (reeds) and Steve Swallow (b). –MGN

Stratus Seekers / OJC   ca. 1962
Fine example of Russell's inside/outside arranging style. Dave Baker (tb) is impressive. –RW

Outer View / OJC / DB 5   1962
Ensemble with progressive pianist. Excellent reissue. –MGN

○ **Electronic Sonata ... / STRATA EAST**   1969
Electronic Sonata For Souls Loved By Nature. A wild piece. For the adventurous, with guitarist Terje Rypdal and saxophonist Jan Garbarek. –MGN

African Game / BLUE NOTE   1983
Fine recent material, Russell still an aggressive, dynamic arranger/composer. –RW

So What / BLUE NOTE   1986
Good session. –RW

Outer Thoughts / MILESTONE

PEE WEE RUSSELL   1906-1969

Swing, big band, bop, hard-bop. Born in Oklahoma, Russell played piano and violin before taking up clarinet; he was a pro at 15. In 1924, he worked with the legendary pianist Peck Keily in a band that also included Jack Teagarden, who became his lifelong friend. In 1925, he played with Bix Beiderbecke in Frank Trumbauer's band and in 1927 he settled in New York, recording frequently in all-star groups assembled by Red

Adolphe Sax Invents Instrument ca.1840

Beginnings in Jazz
Rudy Wiedoeft, C-melody sax in vaudeville performances (1916).

Most Significant Soloists
Coleman Hawkins (1904-1969) – tenor
Lester Young (1909-1959) – tenor
Charlie Parker 1920-1955) – alto
John Coltrane (1926-1967) – tenor and soprano
Sonny Rollins (1930) – tenor

The Tenor Saxophone

Early Tenor Sax Influences
Prince Robinson (1902-1960) — Happy Caldwell (1903-1978)
Stump Evans (1904-1928)

Coleman Hawkins (1901-1969) First Major Tenor Soloist
Major influence on:
Charlie Barnet (1913) — Chu Berry (1908-1941)
Ben Webster (1909-1973)

Arnett Cobb (1918) — Illinois Jacquet (1922)
Flip Phillips (1915) — Ike Quebec (1918-1963)
Buddy Tate (1915) — Don Byas (1912-1972)

Lester Young (1909-1959) Major Tenor Soloist
Influenced:
Bud Johnson (1910-1984) — Dexter Gordon (1923)
Charlie Parker (1920-1955)

Later influence on:
Gene Ammons — Al Cohn — John Coltrane — Allan Eager
Stan Getz — Wardell Gray — Lee Konitz — Jackie McLean
Warne Marsh — James Moody — Art Pepper — Sonny Rollins
Zoot Sims — Sonny Stitt

Sonny Rollins (1930) Major Tenor Soloist
Influenced:
Joe Henderson (1937) — Rahsaan Roland Kirk (1936)
Yusef Lateef (1920)

John Coltrane (1926-1967) Major Tenor Soloist
Influenced by:
Earl Bostic (1913-1965) — Big Nick Nichols (1922)
John Gilmore of Sun Ra's Band (1931)

John Coltrane Influenced:
George Coleman (1935) — Joe Farrell (1937-1986)
Charles Lloyd (1938) — Sonny Fortune (1939)
Dave Liebman (1946) — Mike Brecker (1949)
Bob Berg (1951) — Steve Grossman (1951)
Branford Marsalis (1961)

Wayne Shorter (1953) (Also: Soprano Sax)

Free-Jazz / Avant Garde
● Albert Ayler (1936-1970)

Other Free Jazz :
David Murray (1955) — Joseph Jarman (1937)
Pharoah Sanders (1940) — Archie Shepp (1937)
Frank Lowe (1943) — Willem Breuker (1944)
Rev. Frank Wright (1935) — Peter Brötzmann (1941)
Jan Garbarek (1947)

The Alto Saxophone

Early Alto Players
Otto Hardwick (1904-1970) w/ Duke Ellington
Johnny Hodges (1907-1970) w/ Duke Ellington

Alto Players of the 1920s
Jimmy Dorsey (1904-1957) — Frank Trumbauer (1901)

Alto Players of the 1930s
Hilton Jefferson (1903-1968) — Willie Smith (1910-1967)
Benny Carter (1907)

Bop Alto Sax Players
● Charlie Parker (1920-1955)

Influenced:
Sonny Stitt (1924-1982) — Lou Donaldson (1926)
Sonny Criss (1927-1977) — Eric Dolphy (1928-1964)
Cannonball Adderley (1928-1975) — Phil Woods (1931)
Jackie McLean (1932) — Charles McPherson (1939)

Free-Jazz Alto Saxophone Players
● Ornette Coleman (1930)

Influenced:
John Tchicai (1936) — Henry Threadgill (1944)
Anthony Braxton (1945)

Jimmy Lyons (1933-1986)

The Soprano Saxophone

Sidney Bechet (1897-1959) Soprano Pioneer

Influenced:
Johnny Hodges (1907-1970) — Don Redman (1900-1964)
Woody Herman (1913-1987) — Charlie Barnet (1913)

Major Soprano Innovators:
John Coltrane — Wayne Shorter

Free-Jazz Soprano Sax
Steve Lacy (1934) — Evan Parker (1944)

The Baritone Saxophone

Early Baritone Sax
Harry Carney (1910-1974) — Jack Washington (1910-1964)
Ernie Caceres (1911-1971)

1950s
Gerry Mulligan (1927) — Lars Gullin (1928-1976)

Also:
Serge Chaloff (1923-1957) — Leo Parker (1925-1962)
Cecil Payne (1922)

Major Influence
Pepper Adams (1930-1987)

Coltrane's Influence
Charles Davis — Hamiet Bluiett (1940) — John Surman (1944)

Nichols but also working in dance bands, doubling on tenor, alto, and soprano.
In 1935 he joined Louis Prima's band on 52nd Street and went to California with the trumpeter. Back in New York, he was a key member of the musical fraternity around Eddie Condon; with the guitarist, he was a fixture at Nick's and later at

Condon's own clubs, playing in a style that always was unclassifiable and totally original, with a tonal palette that ranged from whispers to raspy shouts. Near death in 1951, he recovered and began to lead his own groups, mostly made up of young musicians, such as Ruby Braff. In 1963, he formed a quartet with valve trombonist Marshall Brown that featured a repertoire including pieces by John Coltrane and Ornette Coleman; in that same year, he performed with Thelonious Monk at Newport and finally began to receive the critical attention he'd so long deserved. Late in life, he also took up painting, for which he showed as natural a gift as for music, though he didn't develop it. –DM

And Rhythmakers / PRESTIGE   1938
Top date with octet, now available as half of two-record set along with good Jack Teagarden (tb) session. –RW

○ **Portrait Pee-Wee / DCC**   1958
1991 reissue of fine session now available on CD. Bud Freeman (ts) is excellent. –RW

Ji Grandi Di Del Jazz / FABBRI EDITORI   1958
CBS recordings from 1958 and 1962. Package is stunning from an art work and liner note standpoint. Music shows clarinetist turning the corner. With Ruby Braff (cnt), Bud Freeman (ts), Vic Dickenson (tb), Nat Pierce (p). Liners by John Lewis. –MGN

○ **Individualism Of / SAVOY**   195?
W/ Red Richards (p), Ruby Braff (tpt). Amazing, highly distinctive 50s cuts with Ruby Braff. –RW

The Sound of Jazz / COLUMBIA   ca. 195?
Fine duet with Jimmy Giuffre (cl). –RW

Over the Rainbow / XANADU   1965
Fine quartet recording. –RW

● **Spirit of 1967 / IMPULSE**   1967
Top session, previously under another name. –RW

○ **Memorial Album / PRESTIGE**   ca. 1969
With quintet featuring Tommy Flanagan Trio and Buck Clayton (tpt). Two Pee Wee originals — "Englewood" and "Midnight Blue." –MGN

TERJE RYPDAL   b 1947

Jazz-rock. Guitar, flute, soprano sax, composer. Rypdal played rock, blues, and jazz, becoming a member of Jan Garbarek's group in the late 60s. He later played with George Russell's sextet and big band, closely studying and absorbing Russell's Lydian Chromatic Concept. After working with Lester Bowie in 1969, he was featured on Garbarek's first two ECM releases and formed his own trio and group. He had a band with Palle Mikkelborg and Jon Christensen from the late 70s into the 80s. Rypdal's rock background is reflected in his liberal use of electronics, distortion, and synthesized backgrounds, and also has written many compositions for jazz combos and large orchestras, plus many symphonic works. –RW

● **Odyssey / POLYGRAM**   1975
Magnificent effort that combines crushingly powerful rock-jazz ("Over Bierkerot" is a killer) with long, brooding electric ruminations. Originally a double album, one track has been left off the CD. –MPD

Waves / POLYGRAM   1977
Contains some of Rypdal's jazziest music — "Per Ulv" even verges on bebop, despite its chattering rhythm box — alongside the more characteristic free-fall rhapsodies. –MPD

Descendre / POLYGRAM   1979
The unusual trio form of guitar, trumpet, and drums makes for some gorgeous floating sounds. –MPD

Eos / ECM   1983
Probably Rypdal's most experimental release, a set of heavily electronic duets with cellist David Darling. –MPD

Undisonus / POLYGRAM   1990
None of Rypdal's haunting guitar here: this is an album of his purely orchestral compositions. –MPD

○ **Works / POLYGRAM**   COMP

Excellent sampler of Rypdal's music, including two cuts from his superb (but currently unavailable) early-70s albums. –MPD

RANDY SABIEN

Cool. Jazz violinist with folk and fusion inclinations. Wisconsin born, Grappelli and Jerry Goodman influenced. –MGN

○ **In a Fog / FLYING FISH**   r 1983
Violinist plays jazz in a classic manner. Very good. –MGN

SAL SALVADOR   b 1925

Swing, bop. A guitarist and educator who played with Stan Kenton and Maynard Ferguson in the 50s and 60s, Salvador later headed his own combos. He's a good player in a traditional jazz, Brazilian, Afro-Latin, or big-band context, well versed in the classic jazz guitar style of Django Reinhardt and Charlie Christian. –RW

○ **Sal Salvador & Crystal Image / STASH**
W/ Ted Macero (synth), Barbara Oakes (v). Very enjoyable and unusual in its instrumentation and approach. –SHIRLEY KLETT, CADENCE

JOE SAMPLE   b 1939

Soul jazz, instr-pop, contemporary funk. Pianist Sample formed a group with some Texas comrades in the late 50s that played an aggressive brand of funky blues, instrumental R&B with jazz touches that they called the "Gulf Coast Sound." When the group moved to Los Angeles in 1960 they changed their name to the Jazz Crusaders. Though he also worked with some other musicians in the 60s, among them Tom Scott and the Harold Land/Bobby Hutcherson group, the main unit (Sample on keyboards, Wayne Henderson on trombone, Wilton Felder on tenor sax, and Stix Hooper on drums) were unparalled at playing R&B-infused soul-jazz. The group dropped the Jazz surname in the 70s, became the Crusaders, and gradually began doing less ambitious, markedly lighter material without the strong blues and R&B backing. Sample got more involved in the production in 70s and 80s, and his most recent releases have been heavy on studio touches, weaker on content. –RW

○ **Carmel / MCA / BB 56**   r 1978
Acceptable, sometimes above average and far from an accurate barometer of his skills. –RW

● **Rainbow Seeker / MCA / BB 62**   r 1978
If only all his solo projects maintained both their blues roots and musical integrity. –RW

DAVID SANBORN   b 1945

Jazz-rock, world fusion, instr-pop, contemporary funk. Alto saxophonist David Sanborn has moved back and forth between the musical worlds of jazz and pop as if there were no difference between them. Since 1975, he has made a series of popular fusion albums under his own name, and he is also an in-demand session player. –WR

○ **Taking Off / WARNER BROS**   1975
His first album is a good one throughout. –MGN

David Sanborn / WARNER BROS   1977
The second album is as good as the first. –MGN

Heart to Heart / WARNER BROS   1978
Still potent compositionally. –MGN

● **Another Hand / ELEKTRA-ASYLUM**   1991
Return by Sanborn to his real, true love: unadorned (or only partly adorned) jazz. –RW

PHAROAH SANDERS   b 1940

Early free, jazz-rock, neo bop, modern creative. After his first solo album on the radical ESP label, tenor saxophonist Pharoah Sanders joined John Coltrane in 1965 for his ground-breaking *Ascension* album, playing alongside such dynamic young modernists as Archie Shepp, John Tchicai, Marion

Brown, Freddie Hubbard, and others. This was a time of great transition for John Coltrane, and the addition of Sanders to his newly enlarged recording and touring group signalled the leader's commitment to the musical freedom and egoless Eastern spirituality of his final phase. In the weighty soundmass of what was essentially a free-jazz unit, Pharoah alternated long linear solos or engaged his boss in fiercely heated horn duets that marked this group's most explosive climaxes. His was an equal voice to Coltrane's, and he often exhibited superior expressiveness on tenor as well as other wind instruments, going all the way out in shrieking and gutteral ranges, unfettered by the vestiges of bop and modal structures.

After Coltrane's death, Pharoah recorded a string of acclaimed records for Impulse, consistently developing his freedom of expression in a deeply spiritual and often introspective setting. Like many of his peers, he began incorporating African, Asian, and other musical forms into his work in the late 60s, and he maintains a global focus, recently including a Moroccan traditional musician in his group. Infrequent collaborations with Don Cherry, the Jazz Composer's Orchestra, Sonny Sharrock, and a few others are noteworthy, but by and large he has followed his muse in expansive small groups, ably furthering the legacy of the 60s on a handful of small record labels. –MB

Tauhid / IMPULSE   1964
The Sanders/Sharrock connection is amazing. –RW

Izipho Zam (My Gifts) / STRATA-EAST   1969
Wild, crazy, and frenzied. Sanders and Sonny Sharrock (g) explore. –RW

○ **Karma / MCA**   1969
A classic of avant-garde/energy jazz with Sanders, Leon Thomas (v). Immense. –RW

Thembi / MCA   1970
Classic Pharoah, includes "Astral Travelling." –MGN

Black Unity / IMPULSE   1971
Powerhouse solos, dense compositions, two bassists, drummers. –RW

○ **Love in Us All / ASD**   1973
With two extended tracks. Includes the revered "Love Is Everywhere." –MGN

Beyond a Dream / ARISTA   1978
Great live date. –RW

● **Journey to the One / THERESA**   1980
17 compositions. –RW

Rejoice / THERESA   1981
Nice date with Bobby Hutcherson (vib). –RW

Oh Lord, Let Me Do No Wrong / CBS   1987
Good use of reggae beat on title cut. Fair set that splits contemporary production with traditional energy. –RW

Quartet Africa / TIMELESS   1987
Return to eras past. –RW

Jewels of Thought / IMPULSE
Leon Thomas (v) rocks the cosmos. –RW

ARTURO SANDOVAL   b 1949

Post-bop, Latin, neo bop, contemporary funk. Former Irakere member and acknowledged as perhaps the premier trumpeter in Latin jazz and Afro-Cuban circles. Sandoval first attracted attention in the States when Irakere performed during a 1977 State Department-sponsored jazz concert in Cuba, where he caught the eye of Dizzy Gillespie. Sandoval later traveled internationally with Irakere, recorded by special arrangement with Gillespie overseas, and eventually defected. Releases he did for German Messidor label both on his own and with former Irakere cohort Paquito D'Rivera are sparkling ensembles of his brassy, flashy, high-register style. –RW

○ **To a Finland Station / PABLO**   1982
W/ Dizzy Gillespie (tpt) in Helsinki. Excellent interplay. Lots of good feeling on this session. –MGN

● **Breaking the Sound Barrier / CCAA**   1983

Live date in Chicago from Cuban trumpeter. Cuban trumpeter plays it straight in jazz and Latin veins. No funk. His best. –MGN

MONGO SANTAMARIA   b 1922

Soul jazz, Latin. Congos, bongos, percussion, bandleader. The greatest Cuban percussionist since Chano Pozo, and certainly the most dominant of his generation. Santamaria originally studied the violin but switched to drums and dropped out of school in Cuba to play the congas. He established himself playing in clubs during the years prior to Castro's takeover; he left Cuba for Mexico City in 1948 with his cousin Armando Peraza. They came to New York in 1950 and were billed as the Black Cuban Diamonds. Santamaria's first American gig came with Perez Prado; he stayed with him three years, then spent seven glorious years with Tito Puente, where their multiple percussion barrages and rhythmic assaults made Latin-jazz history. Santamaria helped bring traditional African and Afro-Cuban music to the forefront in the 50s by cutting a series of albums featuring songs derived from Afro-Cuban religious groups and ceremonies. He also played Latin-Jazz and switched to Cal Tjader's group in 1958, cutting several great albums with him while staying for three years. He did some work with Dizzy Gillespie and Jack McDuff, while also cutting his own albums in the late 50s and throughout the 60s, many of them for Latin labels. During the 70s and 80s Santamaria also began to do more pop-oriented and fusion releases. But during the 80s Santamaria also made some outstanding works in vintage Latin-jazz and Afro-Cuban style, including an 1987 date with Charlie Palmieri. –RW

Free Spirit / BUDDAH-TROPICAL   1985
Nice, extensive set. –RW

ED SARATH

Post-bop, neo bop, modern creative. Trumpeter/flugelhornist who teaches jazz at the University of Michigan. A modernist whose playing reflects an extension of Dizzy Gillespie, and whose compositions are more of the edge of the envelope of pure improvisation while keeping within rhythmic parameters. Orchestral timbres within a small group context. –MGN

○ **Voice of the Wind / RHINO**
Debut album as a leader for this trumpeter/flugelhornist. Very intriguing and progressive compositions. With Dave Liebman (fl) and JoAnne Brackeen (p). –MGN

AKIO SASAJIMA   b 1952

Post-bop, neo bop. This Japanese-born and Chicago-based guitarist can play bop, post-bop, progressive, and fusion. –MGN

○ **Akio with Joe Henderson / MUSE**   1987
Japanese guitarist w/ Joe Henderson (ts) in straightahead context. Akio is quite a sensitive player. Mostly originals. –MGN

MASAHIKO SATOH   b 1941

Post-bop, jazz-rock. Masahiko is a Chick Corea-influenced pianist who also plays electric keyboards. His compositional depth is not considered as strong as his playing. –MGN

○ **Amorphism / CBS**   1985
W/ Eddie Gomez (b) and Steve Gadd (d). Satoh mostly plays acoustic piano but sounds most original when he switches to synthesizers. His music encompasses some semi-free sections. –SCOTT YANOW, CADENCE

SAUTER-FINEGAN ORCHESTRA

Big band, progressive big band. Big-band (1952-1957) lead by Eddie Sauter and Bill Finnegan. Extension of their experience with Woody Herman, Artie Shaw, and The Dorsey's. –MGN

○ **Adventure in Time / RCA VICTOR**   i 1956
● **New Directions in Music / RCA**   COMP

1952-1958. 1988 reissue of marvelous sessions. Masterly arrangements. −RW

JERRY SAWICKI   b 1930

Swing, bop, cool. Baritone saxophonist allied to the sound of Jerry Mulligan, with a little Pepper Adams. Also plays tenor and soprano. −MGN

○ **Second Time Around / SOPHIA**   1989
A Toledo saxophonist that plays baritone on the mellow side. Swing Era and American Popular standards. Plays great title track, "Georgia on My Mind" and "Lover Man." A good outing, backed by The Murphy's with Johnny O'Neal on piano. −MGN

DAVID SCHNITTER   b 1948

Bop, hard-bop, post-bop, neo bop. This ex-Jazz Messenger plays tenor sax and can be ferocious at times. He is an excellent interpreter and a developed composer. −MGN

○ **Invitation / MUSE**   1976
Recording debut from East Coast tenor saxophonist. Top-notch. −MGN

LOREN SCHOENBERG   b 1958

Big band. Famed swing and big-band historian/radio personality/band leader. Benny Goodman/Fletcher Henderson influenced. −MGN

Solid Ground / MUSICMASTERS   1988
Good playing. −RW

Time Waits for No One / MUSICMASTERS   r 1989
Conservative menu, fine techniques. −RW

○ **Just A-Settin' & A-Rockin' / MUSICMASTERS**
More interesting and entertaining, familiar agenda. −RW

GUNTHER SCHULLER   b 1925

Ragtime, progressive big band. Gunther Schuller has written comprehensive, extensive works on early jazz and the swing era and is an authority on both jazz and classical. He's also a musician who played with Miles Davis in 1949-1950 and in many symphony orchestras around the nation. He was an early advocate of third-stream music, and recorded albums in that style for Columbia and Verve in the 50s and Atlantic in the 60s. The president of the New England Conservatory, Schuller also formed a ragtime ensemble, made a hit ragtime album in 1973, and formed the New England Conservatory Jazz Repertory Orchestra to play classic arrangements of vintage tunes by Ellington and other greats. −RW

☆ **John Lewis Presents / ATLANTIC**   i 1960
Jazz Abstractions. −MGN

BOB SCOBEY   b 1916

Trad. Bob Scobey was one of the champions of traditional jazz, a good entertainer, and lead trumpeter who kept playing in and heading vintage New Orleans-style groups long after bop and other sounds dominated the scene. Scobey got an early music education playing in dance orchestras and bands in the 30s, then met Lu Watters in 1938. He spent much of the 40s working with Watters in the Yerba Buena Jazz Band, taking out four years for a stretch in the army, then left in 1949 and formed his own group. There, Scobey became a traditional-jazz star for 15 years, recording for the Good Time Jazz label. −RW

Scobey & Clancy / GOOD TIME JAZZ   1955
1990 reissue of prime material. −RW

● **Scobey's Story - Vol. 1 & 2 / GOOD TIME JAZZ**   195?
First-rate traditional date with veterans like Albert Nicholas (cl) and George Probert (sax) in lineup. −RW

○ **Bob Scobey's Frisco Band / GOOD TIME JAZZ**
Fine session, lineup not quite as good as earlier dates. −RW

Favorites / GOOD TIME JAZZ
Good renditions of familiar material. −RW

JOHN SCOFIELD   b 1951

Post-bop, early free, jazz-rock, neo bop, M-base. Electric guitarist who has played with people as diverse as his influences — Charles Mingus, Jack DeJohnette, Jay McShann, and Miles Davis. Steely tone and fluid lines earmark his distinctive style. Early fusion good, later period neo-bop/contemporary improvised music even better. Hitting his stride these days. −MGN

Rough House / RHINO   1978
Nice, more fusion/mainstream approach on 1978 release. −RW

Who's Who? / NOVUS   1979
Excellent solos, uneven material. −RW

Shinola / RHINO   1981
Trio set reissued in 1991. Dense, prickly, and lots of space for guitar work. −RW

Blue Matter / RHINO / DB 5   1986
1989 reissue of fine, expansive Scofield outing. −RW

Still Warm / RHINO   r 1986
Funky date, thanks to Omar Hakim (d). 1989 reissue. −RW

Loud Jazz / RHINO   1987
Another 1989 reissue, more animated and aggressive. −RW

Pick Hits Live / RHINO   1987
1990 release, live Japanese concert, explosive guitar. −RW

Flat Out / RHINO   i 1989
Excellent solos and guitar work. Bonus cut on CD. −RW

● **Time on My Hands / CAPITOL / DB 5**   1990
His best contemporary album. Excellent playing and writing. A must-buy for jazz/contemporary music listeners. −MGN

○ **Meant to Be / CAPITOL**   r 1991
Just about as good as *Time On My Hands*, maybe a little better in terms of composition. −MGN

Slo Sco: Best of Ballads / RHINO   COMP
1990 reissue of slow cuts. Good showcase for the other side of Scofield as improviser. −RW

BOBBY SCOTT   b 1937

Ballads. Bobby Scott had significant impact on jazz as a performer, teacher, and bandleader. He studied music with Edvard Moritz and Debussy, then worked in his early years with Louis Prima, Tony Scott, and Gene Krupa. In the 50s and 60s Scott recorded trio, combo, and big band albums with Bethlehem, Verve, and Atlantic. A number he composed for a 1961 play *A Taste Of Honey* became a hit for several artists in the 60s. He continued composing, arranging, producing, and performing into the 70s and 80s. −RW

For Sentimental Reasons / MUSICMASTERS
Nat King Cole tribute date, the delivery is a bit on the limp side. −RW

○ **Slowly / MUSICMASTERS**
An album that is smooth, sometimes sentimental. For the supper-club crowd. −RW

HAZEL SCOTT   b 1920

Post-bop, cool. Piano, vocals. Scott has laid back piano trio sounds, but close listening reveals an advanced harmonic sense. −MGN

○ **Late Show / CAPITOL**   i 1952
W/ Red Callender (b). −MGN

● **Relaxed Piano Moods / OJC**   1955
Definitive piano trio with Charles Mingus (b) and Max Roach (d). A must-buy. 3 bonus tracks on the CD. −MGN

Afterthoughts / TIOCH   1980
Last-known recorded work of Hazel Scott, still an intriguing pianist. −RW

SHIRLEY SCOTT   b 1934

Post-bop, soul jazz. One of the top organists of the 50s and 60s. Scott came to prominence in the trio of saxophonist Eddie

"Lockjaw" Davis in 1955 and recorded with him for King, Roulette, and Prestige. Her own first recordings (1958) were for Prestige including many with bass and drums accompaniment. Beginning in 1961, she started a long series of recordings with saxophonist Stanley Turrentine. Their collaborations for Prestige, Blue Note, Impulse, and Atlantic were very consistant organ combo jazz. Many of these sessions are under Turrentine's name. After a marital breakup with Turrentine in 1971, Shirley Scott's recordings became less frequent. In general, her work over the past twenty years has not equalled the quality of her earlier work. –BP

○ **Great Scott/For Members Only / MCA**   1958
Compilation blends two prime Scott albums (1958 & 1963); some cuts arranged and conducted by Oliver Nelson. –RW

Soul Sisters / PRESTIGE   1960
Dauntless, swinging affair. –RW

Like Cozy / MOODSVILLE   i 1960

Shirley Scott Trio / MOODSVILLE   i 1960

Satin Doll / PRESTIGE   1961
A bit more prim, though Scott still burns. –RW

Hip Soul / PRESTIGE   1961
Slashing, aptly titled. –RW

Hip Twist / PRESTIGE   i 1961
W/ Stanley Turrentine (ts). –MGN

○ **Sweet Soul / PRESTIGE**   1962
Good blend of soul, funk, blues, and jazz. –RW

○ **Blue Flames / OJC**   1964
This is exactly the kind of straightahead funky music you would expect from the Scott/Turrentine combination. No disappointments. –JME

● **The Great Live Sessions / IMPULSE**   1964
Recorded live at the Front Room in Newark, NJ, the album includes 10 tracks with a quartet including Stanley Turrentine (ts). On a rare night for music, the band delivered on all counts. You can't go wrong here. –MGN

Soul Shoutin' / PRESTIGE   i 1964
W/ Stanley Turrentine (ts). –MGN

Blue Seven / PRESTIGE   ca. 1965
A quintet with Roy Brooks (d), Oliver Nelson (ts) and Joe Newman (tpt) plays one Scott original, the title song by Sonny Rollins, and an excellent "Wagon Wheels." –MGN

Shirley Scott and the Soul Saxes / ATLANTIC   1969
Steamy workout with Scott, Hank Crawford (as), King Curtis (ts), and David Neuman (ts). –RW

Girl Talk / IMPULSE   196?
Trio. Album includes one Scott original. The rest, including the classic title track, are standards. A bit sweet. –MGN

● **One for Me / STRATA EAST**   1974
The record is a beauty with Harold Vick, perhaps the most suited and sensitive horn player Ms. Scott has worked with ... among her best recordings ... thoroughly enjoyable album of bop stream music, and while it is nothing overly heavy or deep it's thoughtfully and sensitively produced and of its kind an almost perfect album. –BOB RUSCH, CADENCE

STEPHEN SCOTT   b 1969

Post-bop, neo bop. Another highly publicized young lion pianist from New York. He's recently worked with Joe Henderson on his acclaimed album *Lush Life* and also released his own debut session. A captivating soloist despite being only in his 20s, and his debut reveals considerable expertise as a composer. Certainly still in developmental stage, but someone to watch in the 90s. –RW

○ **Something to Consider / POLYGRAM**   r 1991
Young lion roars out of the box with impressive piano debut, aided by both old stars like Joe Henderson (sax) and fellow brats like Roy Hargrove (tpt). –RW

TOM SCOTT   b 1948

Instr-pop, fusion. Multi-reed player and composer, Scott was among the most high-profile pop and rock session players and bandleaders on the West Coast in the 70s and 80s. While still in his teens, Scott was playing with Oliver Nelson and Don Ellis and appearing in bands for television shows. At 19 he was a featured soloist in Roger Kellaway's quartet and in his early 20s Scott was writing extensively for film and television. An excellent technical player, with extensive range, superb tone and facility, plus the flexibility to fit into blues, rock, pop, and fusion contexts as well as standard jazz, Scott became a crossover success with the formation of the LA Express in the 70s. Scott's own albums have tended to be fusion/pop endeavors, and seldom aedquate showcases for his skills. He's done better in his stints doing solos for sessions by Carole King, Joni Mitchell, and others. –RW

Desire / ELEKTRA-ASYLUM
A bit hotter solos, production. Material leaves sonmething to be desired. –RW

Target / ATLANTIC
A little more energy, fire. –RW

○ **Tom Scott & the L.A. Express / EPIC**   r 1974
Scott's most famous group. –RW

Them Changes / GRP   1990
1990 release; fusion and R&B. –RW

Keep This Love Alive / GRP   1991
1991 session with nice vocals by Brenda Russell. –RW

Best Of Tom Scott / COLUMBIA   COMP
Collection of high profile fusion. –RW

TONY SCOTT   b 1921

Swing, big band, post-bop, early free, world fusion. One of the great technicians in modern clarinet history, as well as one of the more eclectic, Scott studied at Juilliard and spent three years in army bands from 1942-1945. After leaving the service, Scott worked with Tommy Dorsey, Charlie Ventura, Claude Thornhill, and Earl Bostic (among others) before heading his own groups. He worked with a number of great jazz singers as well, among them Billie Holiday, Carmen McRae, and Sarah Vaughan. He was Harry Belafonte's musical director in 1955, and during international tours he made in 1957 and from 1959-1965 Scott became quite knowledgeable about ethnic music, especially Asian and Indian styles. His recordings date back to a 1946 session on Gotham with Vaughan and include several notable 50s and 60s works. His *Music For Zen Meditation* and *Music For Yoga Meditation* in 1964 and 1967 respectively are seen in some quarters as percursors for the new-age sound of the 80s. In recent years, he's recorded with Indonesian groups, and done albums paying homage to Africa. –RW

● **Scott's Fling / RCA**   1955
Outstanding septet featuring Scott and Milt Hinton (vib). –RW

Modern Art of Jazz / SEECO   1957
Beautiful, accomplished, and distinctive solos from Scott. Very hard to find. –RW

○ **Golden Moments / MUSE**   1959
Invigorating and evocative, with excellent lineup. Bill Evans (p), Jimmy Garrison (b), etc. –RW

I'll Remember / MUSE   1959
A second-time-around for same lineup proves equally rewarding. –RW

Sung Heroes / SUNNYSIDE   1959
Nice 1959 date, with Scott taking turns on guitar and piano plus baritone. –RW

Music for Zen Meditation / POLYGRAM   1964
Not quite what you'd think, but well worth investigating. –RW

Prism / POLYDOR   1977
Scott teams with the Jan Akkerman quartet. –RW

● **African Bird / SOUL NOTE**　　　　　1984
Clarinetist as a world music pacemaker. Removed from his early jazz and meditative phases, while combining aspects of both with African rhythms and Charlie Parker inflections. "African Bird Suite" is a modal stunner. –MGN

○ **Complete Tony Scott / RCA**　　　　　COMP
Best from series of mid-50s recordings showcasing Scott in quartet, big band, and combo situations. –RW

BERT SEAGER

Post-bop, neo bop. Progressive pianist in post-modern and modal vein. Excellent composer of ensemble music. –MGN

○ **Time to Burn / POLYGRAM**　　　　　1986
First album, with saxophonist Jimmy Mosher and trumpeter Tim Hagans. –MGN

● **Because They Can / POLYGRAM**　　　　1987
Studio date with quintet from this hard-driving pianist. Solid and original jazz. –MGN

AL SEARS　　　　　　　　　　b 1910

Trad, swing, R&B. This saxophonist and composer worked with the Chick Webb, Andy Kirk, and Duke Ellington Orchestras. He led his own big band in Buffalo, NY in the 30s. –MGN

Dance Music with a Swing Beat / AUDIO LAB　　i 1959
W/ Joe Thomas (fl/sax). –MGN

○ **Swing's the Thing / SWINGSVILLE**　　　i 1960
W/ Wendell Marshall (b). –MGN

JIM SELF

Post-bop, neo bop. Tuba player in post-bop and some swing. Not dependent on technique, accents lush textures instead of speed. –MGN

○ **Tricky Lix / CONCORD**　　　　　　1990
Nice, conservative, mainstream. –RW

CHARLIE SEPULVEDA

Post-bop, Latin, neo bop. A rising star on the Latin-jazz circuit. His current release features prominent Latin players like Arturo Ortiz, Ruben Rodriquez, and Adam Cruz, as well as young-lion tenor-saxophonist Ralph Moore, and is spiced by excellent originals. –RW

○ **New Arrival / POLYGRAM**　　　　　r 1991
Jazz and Latin music from this trumpeter. A solid first effort. Easily recommended. –MGN

PAUL SERRANO　　　　　　　　b 1932

Post-bop, progressive big band. A Chicago trumpeter of the bop, post bop, and hard bop school, he is a nice extension of 40s and 50s role models, and is also his own man. –MGN

○ **Blues Holiday / RIVERSIDE**　　　　　1960
Produced by Cannonball Adderley, with Bunky Green on alto-sax and Jodie Christian on piano. –MGN

DOC SEVERINSEN　　　　　　　b 1927

Big band, instr-pop. Trumpeter. Longtime "Tonight Show" bandleader and Johnny Carson foil, who spent several years playing in bop groups and jazz clubs before attaining his high visibility, big paying television gig. During the 40s, he worked with Charlie Barnet, Sam Donahue, and Tommy Dorsey, and did several sessions in studios. His studio reputation got him a chance to work at NBC, and he played in the bands for Steve Allen shows and other programs. He became a member of the Tonight Show orchestra, and assembled a first-class aggregation that often included many top players from major swing and big bands. Severinsen in the 80s has led his own big band and small combo when away from the Tonight Show, and won a Grammy in 1986. He's often been a guest soloist and conductor with various symphony orchestras, and he can hit high notes and play ballads and standards with ease. –RW

○ **Once More, With Feeling! / AMHERST**
Very restrained big-band dates. –RW

BUD SHANK　　　　　　　　　　b 1926

Bop, hard-bop, post-bop, cool, progressive big band. Though he's a good, sometimes inspiring saxophonist, Bud Shank deserves more recognition and credit for enhancing and expanding the role of the flute in the jazz context. He was among the first bop players to utilize the instrument as a legitimate lead, rather than a supportive or decorative one, and to explore its range and present it in its fullest improvising capacity. Shank started on clarinet at 10, moved to sax at 14, and moved to the West Coast in 1947. He spent a year with Charlie Barnet, and later played with Stan Kenton from 1950-1951. He was a featured member of the Lighthouse All Stars group from 1953-1956, and began making albums as a leader in 1954. He became a prominent studio and session player in the 60s, then was a founding member of the LA 4 in 1974. He's made several tours of Europe, and played with Frank Morgan and Shorty Rogers (among others) in the 80s and 90s. –RW

Crystal Comments / CONCORD　　　　1979
Good trio outing, though no one takes it beyond a merely enjoyable level. –RW

California Concert / CONTEMPORARY　　1985
Interesting, sometimes engaging live set. –RW

○ **Serious Swingers / CONTEMPORARY**　　1986
Some intense cuts, smooth and bluesy. –RW

At Jazz Alley / CONTEMPORARY　　　1986
Relaxed, jovial mainstream date. –RW

● **That Old Feeling / CONTEMPORARY**　　1986
Stronger, more aggressive Shank solos. –RW

Tomorrow's Rainbow / CONTEMPORARY　1988
Familiar material. –RW

Drifting Timelessly / CAPRI　　　　1990
Often aggravating backgrounds, fine playing. –RW

○ **The Doctor Is In / CANDID**

LAKSHIMINARAYAN SHANKAR　　b 1950

Jazz-rock, world fusion. This violinist has found a comfortable style that melds and combines classical Indian influences and jazz devices. He moved to America in 1969, eventually earned a doctorate in ethnomusicology at Wesleyan, where he began meeting jazz musicians like Ornette Coleman, Jimmy Garrison, and John McLaughlin while working as a teaching assistant and concert master of the university chamber orchestra. He studied with McLaughlin in 1973, and two years later, they cofounded the group Shakti, which was active until 1978. During the 80s and beyond, Shankar has recorded periodically as a leader, doing both jazz-based material and Indian classical music. He's also worked with rockers Peter Gabriel, Phil Collins, and Frank Zappa. –RW

○ **Who's to Know / POLYGRAM**　　　　1980
This is more like it. Genuine Indian classical ragas, though the somber quality robs session of vitality. –RW

Vision / POLYGRAM　　　　　　　1983
Jan Garbarek (ts) has some good solos. –RW

Song for Everyone / POLYGRAM　　　1984
One of Shankar's best. –RW

Nobody Told Me / POLYGRAM　　　　r 1990
Exquisite recording, moments of beauty. –RW

SONNY SHARROCK　　　　　　　b 1940

Early free, modern creative. Sonny Sharrock has more than carved out his own unique niche in the world of jazz and jazz-based rock. Sharrock studied at Berklee at 21, took four months of composition, then in 1965 began playing with Olatunji, Pharoah Sanders, Sunny Murray, and Don Cherry. His amazing solos creatively included lots of feedback, distortion, clusters and raking, and shattering phrases and notes, but all of it done in a very coherent, rhythmically and harmonically consistent fashion. He achieved his greatest notoriety as a member of various groups led by Herbie Mann from 1967-1973. He formed his own group in 1973, and did some tours and recording with his wife Linda. Sharrock later joined the group Last Exit in 1985, and recently has made both avant-garde and rock/R&B releases as a leader. –RW

○ **Ask the Ages / POLYGRAM / DB 5**　　　　1991
Across-the-board acclaim for this splendid power-drunk band. Sharrock's guitar still exposes new and fresh sounds. With Pharoah Sanders (ts) and Elvin Jones (d). Six pieces written by Sharrock. Need wide-open ears, and they may implode. Revolutionary and revelationary. –MGN

Highlife / ENEMY　　　　1991
More rock, pop, and blues elements, but superbly crafted and employed. –RW

ARTIE SHAW　　　　♭1910

Swing, big band. One of the swing era's biggest stars, Shaw was a successful studio musician in New York but hardly known to the public until he performed a number with a string quartet at the first so-called Swing concert, in 1936. Later that year he formed his first band, incorporating the strings; it was a flop, and Shaw reorganized along conventional lines. His playing, however, was anything but conventional; like his arch-rival Benny Goodman he was a musical perfectionist, but he didn't emulate Benny — his sound and style on the instrument were his own. A huge hit record, *Begin the Beguine*, launched Shaw to stardom in 1938, but tired of the showbiz nonsense that came with fame, he suddenly disbanded in 1939. To fulfil his record contract, he made *Frenesi* with a studio-group in 1940 and scored another monster hit. He then reformed his own band, eventually hiring the great black trumpeter and singer Hot Lips Page and featuring strings once again. He enlisted in the Navy in 1942 and led a first-rate service band in the Pacific Theater; in late 1944 he started a new civilian band with Roy Eldridge, and a rhythm section with guitarist Barney Kessel and the gifted young pianist Dodo Marmarosa. By 1953, he was leading a sextet that had Hank Jones on piano and Tal Farlow's guitar, but the next year he gave up the clarinet for good. He had already written his autobiography, *The Trouble with Cinderella*, and went on to publish a novel; he also pursued various non-musical enterprises, including film distribution. In 1983, he again fronted a big band playing his vintage library and some new arrangements; it had Dick Johnson on clarinet, but Shaw was clearly the musical director. The band has performed on and off since then. A highly intelligent, mercurial man (who was married to, among others, Lana Turner and Ava Gardner), Shaw's bands were consistently interesting and often outstandingly so; his own clarinet playing places him at the top of the all-time poll. –DM

○ **Free for All / CBS**　　　　1937
1988 reissue of sterling sessions. –RW

1938 - Vol. 1 / HINDSIGHT　　　　1938
Fine music, poor sound quality. –RW •

☆ **Complete Artie Shaw - Vol. 1-7 / RCA**　　　　1938
For those who want it all, the full set. They're also available in separate two-disc packages by year from 1938-1945. Vol. 1 1938-1939, Vol. 2 1939, Vol. 3 1939-1940, Vol. 4 1940-1941, Vol. 5 1941-1942, Vol. 6 1942-1945, Vol. 7 1939-1945. –RW

Blues in the Night / RCA　　　　1941
1941-1945. First-rate reissue of his dates with both Hot Lips Page (tpt) and Roy Eldridge (tpt). A 1990 reissue. –RW

1949 / MUSICMASTERS　　　　1949
Good reissue of late-40s sessions. –RW

Begin the Beguine / MUSICRAFT　　　　194?
Excellent mid-40's dates with Mel Tormé (v) and the Mel-Tones. –RW

☆ **Complete Gramercy 5 Sessions / RCA**　　　　194?

Music Map

Jazz Trombone

Parade Bands — ca. 1900

1920s
Increase of Trombones in large bands
Fletcher Henderson & Duke Ellington

Early Trombonists
Ike Rodgers (recorded 1929-1934)
Jim Robinson (1892-1976) w/ Sam Morgan (1927)
George Lewis (1900-1968)

Major Early Players
Georg Brunis (1902-1974) — Kid Ory (1890-1973)

Mif Mole (1898-1961), First jazz trombonist (recorded w/ Red Nichols)
Influence on trombonists, bandleaders:
Glen Miller (1904-1944) — Jack Teagarden (1905-1964)
Tommy Dorsey 1905-1956) — Trummy Young (1912-1984)

Duke Ellington's Trombonists
Juan Tizol (1900-1984)
Tricky Sam Nanton (1904-1946) w/ Ellington from 1926
Lawrence Brown (1907) — Quentin Jackson (1909-1976)
Britt Woodman (1920) — Buster Cooper (1929)

Swing Era Trombonists
Tommy Dorsey (1905-1956) — Jack Teagarden (1905-1964)
Vic Dickenson (1906-1984) — J. C. Higginbotham (1906-1973)
Benny Morton 1907-1985) — Dicky Wells (1907-1985)

Bop Trombonists
Bill Harris (1916-1973) — Lou McGarity (1917-1971)
Kai Winding (1922-1983) — Bennie Green (1923-1977)
J. J. Johnson (1924) — Frank Rosolino (1926-1978)
Carl Fontana (1928) — Bill Watrous (1939)

Post-Bop
Bob Brookmeyer (1929) — valve trombone
Slide Hampton (1932)
Jimmy Knepper (1927) w/ Charles Mingus

Multiphonics
Dick Griffin — Ray Anderson (1952)
Albert Mangelsdorff (1928)

American Free-Jazz
Roswell Rudd (1935) — George Lewis (1952)
Craig Harris (1954)

Wonderful 40s dates. Shaw at his peak, plus Roy Eldridge (tpt), Barney Kessel (g), etc. –RW

For You, for Me, Forever / MUSICRAFT　　　　194?
More with Mel Tormé (v) and the Mel-Tones. –RW

With Strings / MUSICRAFT　　　　194?
Here is another excellent anthology, this time with orchestrations. –RW

Last Recordings / MUSICMASTERS
New set culled from private files. Some amazing cuts. –RW

● **This Is - Vol. 1 & 2 / RCA**
Fine introductory volume to his RCA/Bluebird output. –RW

Beat of the Big Bands / CBS　　　　　　COMP
Nice retrospective of vintage Shaw. −RW
Begin the Beguine / RCA　　　　　　　COMP
1987 reissue of more pop-oriented cuts with Helen Forrest
and Tony Pastor (v), though it also has amazing sessions with
Billie Holiday. −RW

GENE SHAW　　　　　　　　　　　　　　b 1926

Post-bop, cool. Detroit trumpeter who played solid post-bop,
then moved to Chicago and subsequently retired. Was a major
voice when active. Worked briefly with Charles Mingus. −MGN
○ **Breakthrough / ARGO**　　　　　　　　i 1962
W/ Sherman Morrison (ts). −MGN
● **Debut in Blues / ARGO**　　　　　　　i 1963
W/ Jay Peters (ts). −MGN
Carnival Sketches / ARGO　　　　　　i 1964
W/ Richard Evans (p). −MGN

MARLENA SHAW　　　　　　　　　　　b 1944

Blues-jazz, ballads. Pop and light jazz vocalist who achieved
some crossover fame in the late 70s, Shaw has also done some
television acting. She has moved more in quasi-jazz direction
recently with a session cut for Verve's *Vine Street Live* series.
−RW
○ **It Is Love / POLYGRAM**　　　　　　　1988
Nice live set at Vine St. Bar. −RW

WOODY SHAW　　　　　　　　　　　　b 1944

Hard-bop, post-bop. Woody Shaw was one of the great underpublicized and mistreated top players of the 60s, 70s, and 80s.
He was a dynamic soloist and outstanding melodic
interpreter, who interacted well in any group situation and
headed an outstanding late-70s combo. His first major work
came in a group with Chick Corea, Joe Farrell, and Willie
Bobo; then in the early 60s he worked with Eric Dolphy. Shaw
spent time in Europe, where he played with Bud Powell,
Johnny Griffin, and Kenny Clarke, among others. When he
returned, he played in bands led by Horace Silver, Corea, and
for a short time Art, and Blakey. But his stunning 1970 release
Blackstone Legacy stamped Shaw as a fine hard-bop player
and trumpeter with a personal, distinctive approach and
message. Shaw and his band made three brillant, critically
acclaimed releases for Columbia. He continued to record for
Red Record, Enja, Timeless, and Muse in the 80s. −RW
☆ **Blackstone Legacy / CONTEMPORARY**　　　1970
Stunning two-record set marking Shaw's debut as leader.
Affirmative solos from Gary Bartz (sax), Bennie Maupin (sax),
and twin basses on several cuts. −RW
Song of Songs / OJC　　　　　　　　　1972
W/ septet and extended compositions. −MGN
Love Dance / MUSE　　　　　　　　　1975
Fine session, solid trumpet. −RW
The Moontrane / MUSE / DB 5　　　　　1975
Beautiful playing; title cut became Shaw's anthem. −RW
● **Concert Ensemble at Berliner Jazztage / MUSE**　1976
Definitive live date showing this trumpeter at his best with a
septet. −MGN
The Iron Men / MUSE　　　　　　　　1977
Very early Shaw, with Anthony Braxton (sax), Arthur Blythe
(as). −RW
☆ **Rosewood / CBS / DB 5**　　　　　　　1977
Consensus album of the year. Highly recommended. −MGN
○ **Little Red's Fantasy / MUSE**　　　　　1978
Outstanding compositions, prototype hard bop. −RW
Stepping Stones / COLUMBIA　　　　　1978
This is as fine a major-label jazz album as possible in the late
70s. −RW
Woody III / COLUMBIA / DB 5　　　　　1979

Third consecutive wonderful album for Columbia, which
responded by cutting him loose. −RW
Lotus Flower / RHINO　　　　　　　　1982
Aggressive, dynamic cuts. −RW
○ **Night Music / ELEKTRA**　　　　　　　1984
Both beautiful and fiery. −RW
Imagination / MUSE　　　　　　　　　1987
Vibrant, entrancing player. −RW

GEORGE SHEARING　　　　　　　　　b 1919

Swing, cool, Latin. Among England's most distinguished jazz
pianists. Blind from birth, Shearing studied classical piano at
a school for the blind, and learned jazz from hearing records.
He started playing professionally in the late 30s with the
Ambrose dance band, then appeared at hotels and did radio
work while playing with Harry Parry and Stephane Grappelli
in the early 40s. Shearing left London for America in 1946,
and settled here permanently in 1947. He formed a quintet
using vibes/guitar/bass/drums/piano format in 1949 and it
became an extremely popular, extensively recorded group
until 1967. The Shearing style, which incorporates elements
of boogie-woogie, bop, Latin, even blues and gospel, plus a
tasteful use of block chords and unison lines, has retained its
popularity for many decades. During the 70s, 80s, and 90s
Shearing has led trios and duos and made some acclaimed
recordings with vocalists Carmen McRae and Mel Torme, with
his 1983 date winning a Grammy. Shearing's vintage sessions
with Nat King Cole, Dakota Staton, and Nancy Wilson have
begun reappearing via reissues. −RW
● **Lullaby of Birdland / POLYGRAM**　　　194?
His classic and best-known cuts, plus lots of other seminal
music in this 1986 reissue of late 40s and 50s material. −RW
So Rare / SAVOY　　　　　　　　　　194?
Excellent collection of late-40s pieces. −RW
○ **I Hear Music / METRO**　　　　　　　r 1952
Early-50s date with guitarist Chuck Wayne. −MGN
An Evening With / CONCORD　　　　　r 1954
Glittering phrases, dynamic technique. −RW
Latin Escapade / CAPITOL　　　　　　r 1956
Outstanding versions in Afro-Latin groove. −RW
Black Satin/White Satin / CAPITOL　　　1956
Albums from 1956 & 1959. 1991 reissue; prime Shearing. −RW
Burnished Brass / CAPITOL / BB 17　　　1958
Nice brass/piano interaction arrangements. −RW
The Swinging's Mutual / CAPITOL　　　i 1960
Nancy Wilson (v) is divine, Shearing a captivating
accompanist. −RW
☆ **And the Montgomery Brothers / OJC**　　1961
A classic combination. Can't be beat. −MGN
☆ **Nat King Cole Sings/Shearing Plays / CAPITOL**　i 1961
Wonderful duo. A glorious union. −RW
Music is to Hear: Joe Williams / SHEBA　1973
The Heart and Soul of Joe Williams. Impossible to find, but
well worth the hunt. −RW
My Ship / POLYGRAM　　　　　　　　1974
This time Verve provides the forum for exacting Shearing solo
dates. −RW
Blues Alley Jazz / CONCORD　　　　　1979
W/ Brian Torft (b). Shearing is immaculate as usual, but
material is slim. −RW
Two for the Road / CONCORD　　　　　1980
Fine duo effort. Carmen McRae's individualistic vocals are
matched by Shearing's shimmering phrases. −RW
On a Clear Day / CONCORD　　　　　　1980
Another Shearing/Brian Torff live; a bit restrained. −RW
○ **Alone Together / CONCORD**　　　　　1981

These are majestic duets. George Shearing w/ Marian McPartland (p). –RW

First Edition / COJ   1981
Essential duets between Shearing and Jim Hall (g). –RW

Top Drawer / CONCORD   1983
Grammy-winning combination with Mel Tormé (v), one of several sparkling cuts featuring the duo. –RW

Live at the Cafe Carlyle / CONCORD   1984
Typically clean, vibrant Shearing. –RW

Grand Piano / CONCORD / DB 5   1985
Exquisite solos and wonderful sound. –RW

Plays Music of Cole Porter / CONCORD   1986
Superb interpretations. –RW

○ **Breakin' Out / CONCORD**   1987
Marvin "Smitty" Smith's chuckling drums bring out fresh qualities, and rhythmic verve in old master Shearing. –RW

Dexterity / CONCORD   1987
This is a concert in Japan; usual brisk, delightful solos by Shearing, fine vocals by Ernestine Anderson. CD has three bonus cuts. –RW

More Grand Piano / CONCORD   1987
Solo again, this time from 1987. –RW

Spirit of '76 / CONCORD   1988
Another stunning collaboration. CD has three bonus cuts. –RW

Perfect Match / CONCORD   1988
Top-flight collaboration between Shearing and Ernestine Anderson (v). –RW

In Dixieland / CONCORD   1989
Authentic New Orleans-style; Kenny Davern (cl) nearly steals the show. Shearing is impressive. CD version has bonus solo piano cuts. –RW

Piano / CONCORD   1989
Excellent solo cuts. –RW

In the Mind / CAPITOL
Dakota Staton's bluesy growls assisted by Shearing. –RW

JACK SHELDON   b 1931

Big band, cool, ballads. West Coast trumpeter who was active in 50s scene. Due to his comic, flashy personality, some forget about his 50s recordings in which he displayed a vibrant, sometimes exciting approach and good technique, though not an adventurous soloist. –RW

A Jazz Profile of Ray Charles / REPRISE   i 1961
W/ Marty Paich (p). –MGN

Oooo, But it's Good / CAPITOL   i 1963

○ **Stand by for Jack Sheldon / CONCORD**   1983
The trumpeter plays ten standards with the Ross Tompkins Trio. There is some of Sheldon's goofy vocalizing, but mostly fine playing. This set was long overdue from "The Tonight Show" veteran. With Ray Brown (b) and Jake Hanna (d). –MGN

Hollywood Heroes / CONCORD   1987
A quintet of fairly undistinguished sidemen provides good support for Sheldon. Mostly they play early-period Swing Era music bordering on bop. –MGN

ARCHIE SHEPP   b 1937

Early free, modern creative. Once the embodiment of the free, experimental, and often enraged generation, Archie Shepp has evolved into one of the revered and respected elders of jazz. Shepp studied piano, clarinet, and alto as a child before switching to tenor and soprano. He worked as a teen in R&B bands, and many attribute his fondness for poetic inclusions and spoken monologs in his music to the fact that Shepp has a degree in drama. Shepp worked with Cecil Taylor in 1960, then got involved with Bill Dixon and a short-lived but excellent group called the New York Contemporary Five, with John Tchicai and Don Cherry. Shepp later worked and recorded with John Coltrane and had a series of albums in the 60s on Impulse that featured lengthy, spiraling solos, slashing rhythms, and Black Nationalist themes. In the 70s and 80s, Shepp's playing, which always had a swing/mainstream grounding, became warmer and often more engaging, though he could still offer furious lines and phrases when so moved. But his best work in the 70s and 80s has been in a bluesy or ballad setting, where his thick, lush tone, and sentimental side are best presented. His more stark Impulse releases are being slowly reissued. –RW

Archie Shepp in Europe / DELMARK   1963

☆ **Four for Trane / IMPULSE**   1964
This is a smashing, effective tribute with rolling, memorable songs. –RW

Fire Music / MCA   1965
His best group work. Open ears required. The title is apt. –MGN

New Thing at Newport / IMPULSE   1965
Avant-garde revisited, with John Coltrane (ts). –RW

Live in San Fransico / IMPULSE   1966
Includes some wonderful trombone by Roswell Redd, intense Shepp solos. –RW

Mama Too Tight / IMPULSE   1966
Unorthodox, appealing octet works. –RW

On This Night / IMPULSE   1966
Sentimental half the time, on-the-edge the other. –RW

○ **Magic of Ju-Ju / IMPULSE**   r 1968
Searing solos over a veneer of African rhythms. –RW

Yasmina: A Black Woman / AFFINITY   1969
Part love songs, part avant-garde wail. –RW

Blase / AFFINITY   1969
Experimental quality, often raging solos. –RW

Attica Blues / IMPULSE   1972
Great, funky title song. Blues/soul meets avant-garde. –RW

● **Kwanza / IMPULSE**   1974
Important document musically and for people who need information about the traditional African Holy Week. 24 major names make appearances. –MGN

There's a Trumpet in My Soul / ARISTA   1975
Alternately moving, bluesy, and defiant. –RW

A Sea of Faces / BLACK SAINT   1975
Dips, thrusts, and soulful laments. –RW

Montreux One/Two / ARISTA   1975
Solid live concert sessions. –RW

Steam / ENJA   1976
Great title track; rubbery, wavery soprano from Shepp. –RW

Ballads for Trane / DENON   1977
Updates, reworks "Four For Trane" theme. –RW

On Green Dolphin Street / DENON   1977
Recent Shepp forays into standards and blues. –RW

○ **Going Home / STEEPLECHASE**   1977
Unforgettable duos with Horace Parlan (p). –RW

○ **Attica Big Band / INNER CITY**   1979
Live in Paris. 16 excellent tracks: Loaded. A must-buy. –MGN

Soul Song / ENJA   198?
W/ Ken Werner (p), Santi Di Briano (b), Smitty Smith (d). Powerful statement. –MGN

○ **Trouble in Mind / STEEPLECHASE / DB 5**   1980
More wonderful duets with Shepp and Horace Parlan (p). –RW

Looking at Bird / STEEPLECHASE / DB 5   1980
Emphatic solos, nice tribute. –RW

Duet / POLYGRAM   1981
Excellent duos with traces of Afro-pop and free-jazz. –RW

Down Home New York / SOUL NOTE   1984
One of best in the 80s. –RW

Duo Reunion / L&R
W/ Horace Parlan. One of the better, more moving sax/piano duos of the 70s reunite effectively. –RW

Splashes / L&R
Bluesy, aggressive, typically expressive. –RW

ANDY SHEPPARD

Post-bop, neo bop. Saxophone, composer. English jazz and jazz/rock musician, considered part of new crop of European players able to work effectively in both mainstream/bop and pop-tinged situations. A good saxophonist and composer, who has recorded in big-band, small-combo situations. –RW

○ **Andy Sheppard / POLYGRAM** 1988
Young British star, with Randy Brecker (tpt) making guest appearance. –RW
Introductions in the Dark / POLYGRAM 1989
Contemporary date. –RW

BOBBY SHEW b1941

Swing, big band, bop, post-bop, progressive big band. The inventor of the two bell "Shewhorn" trumpet is a West Coast cool cat, but can burn with the best. –MGN
○ **'Round Midnight / MO PRO** 1984
All standards, all vital, from this trumpeter and the Steve Schmidt Trio. –MGN

SAHIB SHIHAB b1925

Hard-bop, post-bop, cool, progressive big band. A strong baritone player and above-averge alto soloist who's also added soprano and flute to his arsenal in recent years, Sahib got his intial experience working in territory bands, then went to Boston in 1941 from Georgia for formal music studies. He toured with Fletcher Henderson in 1944-1945 on alto, then was a member of the Roy Eldridge band in 1946. He came to New York in 1947, and worked with Art Blakey, Thelonious Monk, and Tadd Dameron for remainder of the 40s and the early 50s. Shihab resurfaced with Dizzy Gillespie in 1953 playing baritone, which proved his best instrument. His sturdy tone, facility in both the upper and lower register, and ability to play with speed, clarity, and distinction on uptempo and slow pieces distinguished him as a premier baritone stylist. During the 50s Shihab worked with Illinois Jacquet, Oscar Pettiford's big band, Dakota Staton, and Quincy Jones's orchestra, plus led his own group. He settled in Europe following a Jones tour in 1959-1960 and remained there 12 years, becoming a regular member of the Kenny Clarke-Francy Boland Big Band from 1961-1972. His prime recordings for Savoy and Chess have begun turning back up through reissues. –RW
Summer Dawn / MCA 1964
Good reissue of Sahib's 60s material. –RW
Sentiments / STORYVILLE
Robust solos, nice compositions. –RW

BOBBY SHORT b1926

Ballads. Vocals, piano. A one-of-a-kind performer, perhaps the finest male cabaret vocalist and performer. Short, who left home at 11 with his mother's permission to perform in Chicago, has made singing the material of Cole Porter, Rodgers and Hart, and other classic composers of the pre-rock era a genuine artform. His diction, delivery, performance style, personality, and act charm even those usually bored to tears by stiff, proper cabaret environment and attitudes. In the 40s he worked the midwest circuit, where he met the likes of Nat King Cole and Art Tatum, as well as prime influences Hildegarde and Mabel Mercer. He survived a slump in the club business during the mid 60s, then on a recommendation from the Erteguns at Atlantic, Short replaced pianist George Feyer at the Cafe Carlyle in 1968 and has become an institution there, working eight months a year. His finest, highly stylized releases for Atlantic are now all available on CD reissues, including a wonderful pairing with Mabel Mercer. –RW
● **Bobby Short Loves Cole Porter / ATLANTIC / DB 5** 1972
An album in which one of the great cabaret singers tackles a ready-made menu. –RW
Guess Who's in Town / ATLANTIC i 1988

Release in which Short interprets Andy Razat's lyrics. Outstanding arrangements and vocals. –RW
Bobby & Noel & Cole / ATLANTIC
Great pairing of material from pair of two-record sets devoted to Noël Coward and Cole Porter. Brilliant performances. –RW
○ **Celebrates Rodgers & Hart / ATLANTIC**
Textbook Short. –RW
○ **50 from Bobby / ATLANTIC** COMP
The premier collection from a giant of cabaret music. For those who'd like one, comprehensive batch of his music. –RW
Is K-Ra-Zy for Gershwin / ATLANTIC / DB 5 COMP
1956, 1957, and most from 1973. Frequently spectacular renditions. Wonderful –RW

DAMON SHORT

Neo-bop, modern creative. Chicago-based free-jazz'and modern mainstream drummer. A no-holds-barred type musician. –MGN
○ **Penguin Shuffle / BLUE ROOM** 1987
Chicago drummer and his progressive New Orleans friends. Delightful, creative, swinging jazz, especially "S.O.L" and the title track. –MGN

WAYNE SHORTER b1933

Post-bop, jazz-rock, contemporary funk. He's been praised as perhaps the greatest soprano saxophonist since Steve Lacy, but Wayne Shorter was once viewed as the next great voice on tenor sax. When he joined Art Blakey's Messengers in 1959 (following a two-year stint in the army and periods with Horace Silver and Maynard Ferguson), his tone, ideas, facility, and sound were being widely lauded. Shorter attained the position of musical director during his four years with Blakey, then became a superstar when he joined Miles Davis in 1964. Not only did he provide the group with a superb second solo voice, he picked up soprano while in the Davis group, and contributed some unforgettable music to late 60s and early 70s classics like *In A Silent Way* and *Bitches Brew.* He left Davis in 1970 and cofounded Weather Report with Joe Zawinul. For many years, Weather Report was the finest electric jazz/rock outfit around, a band that really did understand the connection between jazz improvisation and rock energy, and how to blend them without compromising either. While spending nearly 15 years with Weather Report, Shorter broadened his horizons in the 70s and 80s, playing Brazilian music with Milton Nascimento, and working with Airto, Chick Corea, Herbie Hancock, Joni Mitchell, Steely Dan, Jim Hall, and Bobby McFerrin, among others. –RW
○ **Blues à la Carte / AFFINITY** 1959
Wonderous early cuts. –RW
Second Genesis / VEE JAY (AFFINITY?) 1960
Essential early Vee-Jay recordings. –RW
Wayning Moments / VEE JAY 1962
Seminal early-60s cuts on Vee Jay. –RW
● **JuJu / BLUE NOTE** 1964
His best single album composition. The playing is extraordinary. With McCoy Tyner (p). –MGN
Night Dreamer / CAPITOL 1964
1988 reissue of prime 60s lineup: Lee Morgan (tpt), McCoy Tyner (p), Reggie Workman (b), Elvin Jones (d). –RW
○ **Speak No Evil / BLUE NOTE** 1964
Reissue of one of his best: playing and writing. –RW
The Soothsayer / CAPITOL 1965
1990 reissue of prime 1965 effort. –RW
○ **Adam's Apple / BLUE NOTE** 1966
This is a galloping romp, one of Shorter's best 60s dates. Great record. –RW
Schizophrenia / BLUE NOTE 1967
One of his last and best "pure" jazz dates. –RW
Super Nova / CAPITOL / DB 5 1969

1988 reissue of careening, eventful date; has Chick Corea (k), John McLaughlin (g), Jack DeJohnette (d). –RW

Moto Grosso Feio / BLUE NOTE / DB 5 1970
Wide-ranging affair with excellent pieces & playing. –RW

○ **Odyssey of Iska / CAPITOL** 1970
An album that is alternately daring and sentimental. Wonderful soprano solos. –RW

☆ **Native Dancer / CBS / DB 5** 1974
Shorter's legendary sessions with Milton Nascimento (v) (Brazil's premier musician). Essential. W/ Herbie Hancock (k), and Airto (per). –MGN

Joy Ryder / CBS 1988
Spotlights more jazz/rock/fusion lineup and material. –RW

● **Best of Wayne Shorter / BLUE NOTE** COMP
A very well-done compilation. Good for beginners and aficionados. –MGN

Wayne Shorter / GNP CRESCENDO COMP
Good cross-section of 1959-62 material. –RW

BEN SIDRAN

Cool, ballads, instr-pop, contemporary funk. A journalist and musician, Sidran's book *Black Talk* is one of the better overviews of the history of popular music and African-American culture. He's also made some albums as a leader, hosted shows on VH-1, and toured and recorded with rocker Steve Miller. Several of Sidran's 70s releases have been reissued on Antilles. –RW

Bop City / ANTILLES r 1984
○ **Cool Paradise / RHINO**
Theorist, critic, and VH-1 host Sidran in good session. –RW

DICK SIEGEL

Cool, blues-jazz, ballads. A good-time cynic (yep!). Siegel's original material (sung with panache) is socially relevant and politically biting. He speaks of love with a jaundiced eye. His influences come from jazz, blues, and folk sources. A true original. –MGN

○ **Snap / BOOKAY- SCHOOLKIDS** 197?
A CD reissue of a late-70s/early-80s album. Siegel embraces blues, jazz, and pop structures in an interesting, arresting, and clever manner reminiscent of Mose Allison. A four peice horn section backs up the vocal trio. The Kevin O'Connell Trio, George Bedard on guitar, and Mike Blanchard on tenor sax are featured. There are ten cuts, all Siegel originals. Standouts are "Razzle Dazzle," "Angelo's," and "What Would Brando Do?." –MGN

JANIS SIEGEL

Ballads, instr-pop. Long a member of Manhattan Transfer, Siegel also released one album as a leader in 1987. She's probably their most popular, or at least their best-known individual member. –RW

○ **At Home / ATLANTIC** 1987
Very uneven, but at her best Siegel has some good things to show vocally. –RW

SILENT WILL

Jazz-rock, modern creative. The brainchild and writer of all songs for Silent Will, Andrea Marcelli plays drums, percussion, synthesizers and clarinet. –PK

○ **Silent Will / POLYGRAM** 1991
A terrific debut release by keyboardist/drummer A. Marcelli. Modern jazz-fusion featuring Allan Holdsworth (g), Wayne Shorter (sax), Bob Berg (ts), Mike Stern (g), and John Patitucci (b). Essential listening! –PK

HORACE SILVER b 1928

Hard-bop, post-bop, soul jazz. Horace Silver has fused gospel and Caribbean influences into his style for an immediately recognizable, always captivating keyboard approach. His father was Portuguese and from the Cape Verde Islands. Silver got his start working with Stan Getz in 1950-1951, then spent five years with Art Blakey and was a founding member of the original Jazz Messengers. He formed his own quintet in 1956, and his solos, with their blues quotes and backbeats, were the precursor to what was later deemed the "funk" school. He had a pair of hit albums in the late 60s, *Cape Verdean Blues* and *Song For My Father*. Silver experimented with vocalists, electronics, and extended suites and lyrics in the 70s, and also did albums with interacting strings and multiple percussion. He formed his own labels in the 80s and 90s, one for reissues, and one for his current material. –RW

Horace Silver Trio / CAPITOL 1952
Most Silver albums are with a mid-60s combo (quintet, etc.). It is refreshing and clarifying to listen to his trio work. Includes the classic "Opus De Funk." –JME

● **With Jazz Messengers / BLUE NOTE** 1954
1954 & 1955. The first Blakey band. Arguably the best. A must-buy. –MGN

Silver's Blue / EPIC-SONY 1956
Their initial recording ... one of Silver's most obscure sessions, a set of mostly new boppish tunes with attractive chord changes ... his quintet is heard in the process of forming its own identity while the leader's piano was already quite distinctive. –SCOTT YANOW, CADENCE

○ **Six Pieces of Silver / CAPITOL** 1956
Hard-bop/gospel-tinged jazz gem. 1988 reissue, CD has three bonus cuts. –RW

Finger Poppin' / CAPITOL 1959
W/ The Horace Silver Quintet. State-of-the-art late-50s Silver gospel, Caribbean-influenced jazz. –RW

Blowin' the Blues Away / BLUE NOTE / DB 5 1959
Standout Silver jazz-cum-blues and gospel from late 50s, 1985 reissue. –RW

Horace-Scope / CAPITOL 1960
1990 reissue of another Silver masterpiece. Includes the famous piece "Nica's Dream." –RW

Doin' the Thing (at the Village Gate) / CAPITOL 1961
1989 reissue of standard live set with Silver super, Blue Mitchell (tpt), Junior Cook (ts) in the groove. –RW

● **Song for My Father / BLUE NOTE / BB 95** 1963
Silver's most successful and popular album. Includes three additional tracks. Two sessions, two different bands. Aside from famous title track, includes quintet and trio versions of "Que Pasa." Essential –JME

Horace Silver Live - 1964 / EMERALD 1964
Subsidary label established to reissue selected dates leads off with very nice hard-bop set. Joe Henderson (sax) solid. –RW

○ **Cape Verdean Blues / CAPITOL** 1965
Another fine date. –MGN

The Jody Grind / CAPITOL 1966
Prototype Silver. 1991 reissue. –RW

○ **Serenade to a Soul Sister / CAPITOL** 1968
Great combination of gospel-tinged sensibility, first-rate jazz technique. –RW

○ **In Pursuit of the 27th Man / BLUE NOTE / DB 5** 1969
1969/1970 recording with the Brecker Brothers (sax & tpt). Very good. –MGN

That Healin' Feelin' / BLUE NOTE 1970
Lyrics a bit to the pretentious side; music overcomes it. –RW

Silver 'N Brass / BLUE NOTE 1975
Nice arrangements; 14-piece group works. –RW

Silver 'N Voices / BLUE NOTE 1976
Followers of Horace Silver from the 50s aren't going to like this blowing quintet sharing time with voices singing poetic lyrics, but at least Horace has again assembled a good quintet ... Horace's piano playing has changed somewhat from the "funky" days. –JERRY ATKINS, CADENCE

Silver 'N Wood / BLUE NOTE 1976
Interesting four-part suites. –RW
○ **Silver 'N Percussion / BLUE NOTE** 1977
W/ Tom Harrell (tpt). African, Native American rhythms, dense and bluesy piano. –RW
Spiritualising the Senses / SILVETO 1983
Nice, characteristic hard bop on his own label. –RW
There's No Need to Struggle / SILVETO 1983
Good concept release with vocal parts. –RW
★ **Best of Horace Silver - Vols. 1 & 2 / CAPITOL** COMP
The Blue Note Years Vol 1 & 2. Excellent compilation on CD. Two volumes. –MGN

NORMAN SIMMONS
b 1929

Post-bop, cool. Pianist, arranger. A superior arranger and good accompanist most famous for providing the hit arrangement of "Wade In The Water" for the Ramsey Lewis group. Simmons worked in the 50s and 60s for several vocalists, among them Dakota Staton, Ernestine Anderson and Carmen McRae, and has been a regular pianist for Joe Williams since 1979. He worked in 1960 with the Johnny Griffin-Eddie "Lockjaw" Davis group. His own recordings aren't currently in print. –RW
Trio / ARGO i 1956
○ **13th Moon / MILESTONE** 1985
Psuedo-psychic sensibility, good solos. –RW

SONNY SIMMONS
b 1933

Early free, jazz-rock, modern creative. A solid saxophonist who made some interesting records in the late 60s, then seemed to disappear. Simmon's best date, *Burning Spirits*, has long since been deleted, but the equally good *Manhattan Egos* is now available on compact disc. For a time he was married to trumpeter Barbara Donald, and the two recorded together. –RW
○ **Manhattan Egos / ARHOOLIE** 1969
Similiar hard-edged, avant-garde-styled date. –RW
● **Music from the Spheres / ESP DISK** 1969
Free-jazz gem from this saxophonist with trumpeter Barbara Donald. –MGN
Burning / CONTEMPORARY
A 2-fer with Barbara Donald (tpt), Cecil McBee (b) and Richard Davis (d). Simmons is also known as "Huey Simmons." –MGN

FRED SIMON

Post-bop, jazz-rock. A Chicago keyboardist who has collaborated with heavies like Larry Coryell. Simon mostly leads his own ensembles in the fusion arena, taking an interesting approach to this music, where most fall into clichéd traps. –MGN
○ **Tear It Up / FLYING FISH** r 1983
Some good moments. –RW
○ **Usually Always / RCA-WINDHAM HILL** 1988
Chicago electric/acoustic keyboarist. Quite intriguing contemporary fusion, with Paul McCandless (reeds) and vocalist Bonnie Herman. –MGN
● **Open Book / COLUMBIA** 1991
Newest and best album from Chicago keyboardist. Contemporary sound on progressive, punchy originals. –MGN
Musaic / FLYING FISH
An overlooked worthy date with Larry Coryell (g). –RW

NANA SIMOPOULOS

World fusion, modern creative. This Greek guitarist plays modal, progressive music of earthy nature. She plays acoustic, which sounds like oud or mandolin. –MGN
○ **Pandora's Blues / BANANAS** 1983

Session with Los Angeles musicians. Four duets with guitarist Joe Dorio. Quintet enjoyable. –MGN
● **Wings & Air / ENJA** 1986
Studio date for this Greek guitarist, with Charlie Haden (b), Don Cherry (tpt), and Jim Pepper (sax/fl). Uplifting and highly recommended. –MGN

ZOOT SIMS
1925-1985

Swing, big band, bop. California-born Sims made his debut in 1941 and played with various "name" bands, including Benny Goodman's, until he was drafted. He briefly rejoined Goodman but made his mark with his next leader, Woody Herman; in this band, he struck up a friendship with fellow tenorist Al Cohn that would last for life and result in wonderful music whenever these got together, live or on records. Sims toured frequently with *Jazz at the Philharmonic*, was often hired by Goodman for various gigs, including the famous tour of the Soviet Union (1962), and freelanced in clubs and on records in a variety of settings. No matter what the surroundings, Sims was consistently swinging and inventive; the music just seemed to flow from him in the most natural way, and he never played a meretricious note. –DM
Quartets / OJC 1950
1950-1951. 1987 reissue of two stalwart early-50s Sims sessions. –RW
● **Zootcase / PRESTIGE** 1950
1950-1954. Formative early 50s sessions, first meeting on wax with Al Cohn (ts). W/ Art Blakey (d), John Lewis (p). –RW
○ **Brother on Swing / INNER CITY** 1950
This was a Jazz Legacy album in 1950. Recorded by a quartet with Gerald Wiggins on piano, Pierre Michelot on bass, and Kenny Clarke on drums. Great rhythm section stokes Sims fire. Album includes five Sims originals, some with alternate takes. It was recorded in Paris, and the liner notes by Herb Wong are very informative. –MGN
First Recordings! / PRESTIGE ca. 1950
Seminal early dates done in Europe. –RW
☆ **Zoot! / OJC** 1956
Hot, memorable 50s set. Excellent recording and session. –RW
Happy Over There / JASS 1957
1957-1958. Septet with Al Cohn on baritone sax, Jimmy Cleveland on trombone, and session leader Elliot Lawrence. All tunes are the music of Hoagy Carmichael. Cute album cover. Also with Milt Hinton (b), Osie Johnson (d). Arrangements by Bill Elton. –MGN
One to Blow On / BIOGRAPH 1958
Some beautiful solos. –RW
○ **Down Home / BETHLEHEM / DB 5** 1960
Remarkable, hard-edged, with solid swing foundation. –RW
Live at Ronnie Scotti's / FRESH SOUND 1961
Superb 60s cuts. –RW
Zoot Sims in Paris / DISQUES SWING r 1963
Typically robust, winning Sims. 1987 reissue. –RW
Suitably Zoot / PUMPKIN 1965
Robust date. –RW
Zoot Sims & the Gershwin Brothers / PABLO 1975
Marvelous Sims solos, great assistance from Oscar Peterson (p). Timeless Gershwin songs. –RW
Warm Tenor / PA2 / DB 5 1978
Lusty, exuberant tenor, equally solid Jimmie Rowles (p). –RW
○ **Just Friends / OJC** 1978
Top-flight pairing of old friends. –RW
If I'm Lucky / PABLO r 1978
Smooth, often memorable cuts. –RW
Passion Flower / PABLO / DB 5 1980
He plays Duke Ellington. Nice, sentimental/blues mix. –RW
Blues for Two / OJC r 1983
Delightful romp with Sims and Joe Pass (g); sublime! –RW
Quietly There / PABLO 1984

With the Mike Wofford Quartet. Easy does it program focusing on many great compositions of the legendary Johnny Mandel. For those special moments. –MGN

In a Sentimental Mood / SONET   1984
The final set. –RW

Basie and Zoot / PABLO
A perfect pair. –RW

For Lady Day / PABLO
Wonderful tribute from exuberant Sims. –RW

I Wish I Were Twins / PABLO
Rollicking, jovial affair. –RW

The Modern Art of Jazz / FRESH SOUND / DB 5
Solid set with Bob Brookmeyer (tb). –RW

Best Of / PABLO   COMP
Good compilation of Pablo cuts. –RW

SINGERS UNLIMITED

Cool, ballads. An a capella vocal group who recorded in the mid 80s for Verve. The personnel included Bonnie Herman, Don Shelton, Len Dresslar, and Gene Puerling. –RW

○ **A Capella 1 / POLYGRAM**
Good concept and performances. –RW

SIRONE   ♭1940

Early free, modern creative. Once a member of the Revolutionary Ensemble along with Leroy Jenkins and Jerome Cooper, Sirone is a first-rate bassist, either as an accompanist or soloist, playing with the bow or his fingers. He played with Cecil Taylor after the Ensemble disbanded. –RW

● **Artistry / OF THE COSMOS**   1978
Revolutionary Ensemble bassist with flutist James Newton. Very enjoyable. –MGN

○ **Live / SERIOUS**   1980
Trio at NYC's Public Theatre. Potent, creative music. –MGN

CAROL SLOANE   ♭1937

Ballads. Contemporary jazz vocalist and Concord recording artist. She began to attract some attention in the 70s, has blossomed in the 80s. Adept at standards, sings melody lines well, good interpreter; shies away from scat. Well worth hearing. –RW

○ **Love You Madly / CONTEMPORARY**   1988
Very good singing in swing/mainstream vein. –RW

Real Thing / CONTEMPORARY   1990
Fine arrangements, acceptable-to-good vocals. –RW

ALMA SMITH

Cool, ballads. Pianist and vocalist known as the Countess in "3 Counts & a Countess." Smith sings scaldingly soulful ballads and blues. –MGN

○ **Dreamin' / VALMA**   1984
An album for "The Countess" of Detroit jazz. The sweet style contrasts with the advice-giving, low-down attitude. A wise woman who features all originals bordering on cocktail jazz, but with some nice touches of pop and bop. –MGN

JIMMY SMITH   ♭1925

Post-bop, soul jazz. Hammond organ. One of the greatest instrumentalists in jazz history. Revolutionized the sound of the Hammond organ in 1955 and began recording for Blue Note the following year. His Blue Note period (1956-1963) is highly recommended although his jam-session recordings contain lengthy solos by players who are sometimes not up to the task. Any collaborations with Kenny Burrell are among his finest work. There are many trio recordings with guitar and drums and only the length of some tracks brings down the overall rating for Smith in this setting.
His Verve period (1963-1972) tends to find him with big-band backing more often than not, but these recordings were some

of the biggest-selling albums (regardless of the type of music) in the 60s. Especially memorable are the arrangements of Oliver Nelson for Smith. As with the Blue Note recordings, the Verve period is all recommended until 1968. After that, Smith begins to flirt with rock music and in general there is a long downhill slide throughout much of the 70s.
A return to Blue Note in 1985 brought a welcome return to jazz and those recordings plus his sessions for Milestone in 1991 can compare with some of his best work from the 50s and early 60s. –BP

At the Organ - Vol. 2 / BLUE NOTE   1957
W/ K. Burrell (g), Art Blakey (d), Donaldson (as). Bluesy, yet driving. –HD

Confirmation / BLUE NOTE   1957
Smith has the best playing companions. Art Blakey (d) contains himself ... playing a subdued and excellent supportive role. Kenny Burrell's solo work ... on "Cherokee" are heavy highlights ... Lee Morgan (tpt) makes this album essential.... Bop lovers have to have this. –JERRY L. ATKINS, CADENCE

Special Guests / BLUE NOTE   1957
Some nice jam session/blowing date cuts. –RW

○ **Groovin' at Small's Paradise / BLUE NOTE**   1957
Volume 1 & 2. Live album.

● **Sermon / BLUE NOTE**   1958
Small group. Studio jam sessions (also two from Aug 25, 1957) featuring Lou Donaldson (sax), Lee Morgan (tpt), Kenny Burrell (g) that produced this album, *Houseparty*, and *Confirmation*. –JME

Softly As a Summer Breeze / BLUE NOTE   1958
Nice title cut, some good moments. –RW

○ **Cool Blues / CAPITOL**   1958
W/ Tina Brooks (ts), Lou Donaldson (as). This is, for the most part, a relaxed mid-tempo blowing date (live from Small's Paradise, NY) ... this is real; real people, real blowing, real feeling, real jazz. Something special has been captured here. –BOB RUSCH, EDITOR CADENCE

Home Cookin' / BLUE NOTE   1958
Trio recording. Bluesy, intense. Nice title track, good soul-jazz set. –RW

○ **Crazy! Baby / CAPITOL**   1960
Classic Smith Trio. Includes hit single "When Johnny Comes Marching Home." –JME

Open House / BLUE NOTE   1960
Studio session featuring Blue Mitchell (tpt), Ike Quebec (ts), and Jackie McClean (as). This is essentially a jam session without Smith's regular sidemen. More mainstream than most, but very nice tracks — fast and slow. This is an excellent album. –JME

○ **Midnight Special / CAPITOL / BB 28**   1960
Small Group. This was recorded at the same session as *Back At The Chicken Shack*, and it is almost as fine — that is: magical! This is a must-have for jazz organ fans. W/ Stanley Turrentine (ts). –JME

★ **Back at the Chicken Shack / BLUE NOTE / BB 14**   1960
Small Group. 1960 date with Stanley Turrentine (his first on Blue Note). Desert island music for cookers. A must-buy. –MGN

Bashin' / POLYGRAM / BB 10   1962
Debut session for Verve, his first with big-band backing. Featuring Oliver Nelson, his orchestra and "Walk On The Wild Side" (a hit single). Smith's first album with a bass player! Three cuts are with small combo. –JME

○ **Prayer Meetin' / CAPITOL / BB 86**   1963
Fine Album. Small group. Smith's last Blue Note album until 1986 (*Go For Whatcha Know*). Also, last two cuts from Jun 13, 1960 were released in Japan on an album: *Special Guests*. –JME

Hobo Flats / VERVE / BB 11   1963
Big band. Oliver Nelson and orchestra. Dynamic cuts, swirling organ. –RW

Live at the Village Gate / METRO   1963

Smith in a trio setting. Plenty of fine playing. –RW

Blue Bash / VERVE   1963
Good 60s sessions. –RW

The Cat / POLYGRAM / BB 12   1964
Large band. Conducted and arranged by Lalo Schifrin. This is perhaps his best-known album featuring the big-band sound. A Grammy Award winner. –JME

Monster / VERVE / BB 35   1965
Large band. Oliver Nelson conducts his band with Smith. Blistering organ solos. –RW

In Hamburg Live / METRO   1965
Jimmy Smith with a trio as part of a European tour in 1965. Latter-day sessions, Smith still plays torrid organ. –RW

○ **Organ Grinder Swing / POLYGRAM / DB 5**   1965
W/ Kenny Burrell (g). Trio album by Smith after much big-band success. This is reminiscent of Smith's early small-combo work. In other words, he cooks on this one. –JME

Got My Mojo Workin' / VERVE / BB 28   1965
Smith in his large-band context. With Oliver Nelson and his orchestra. –JME

○ **The Dynamic Duo / VERVE**   1966
W/ Oliver Nelson conducting. Exciting first collaboration with Wes Montgomery (g). –RW

Further Adventures / VERVE   1966
Outstanding. W/ Wes Montgomery (g). –RW

Respect / VERVE / BB 60   1967
Superb solos, soul-jazz with class. Prototype Smith. –RW

The Boss / VERVE   1969
Lots of fine solos. George Benson (g) does best soul-jazz work since McDuff days. –RW

○ **Fourmost / MILESTONE**   r 1991
Recent material, Smith still wails on organ. Stanley Turrentine (ts), Kenny Burrell (g) in top form. –RW

It's Necessary / MERCURY
Straightforward soul jazz. –RW

● **Best Of / CAPITOL**   COMP
1958-1986. Small Group setting. Selections from some of Smith's best Blue Note albums, such as: *The Sermon, Go For Whatcha Know, Midnight Special, Back At The Chicken Shack, A New Sound*, and *At The Organ*. –JME

○ **Greatest Hits / BLUE NOTE**   COMP
Recent compilation of Smith Blue Note cuts. –RW

JOHNNY SMITH   b 1922

Swing, cool. A guitarist/instrumentalist best known for having a hit with the song "Moonlight in Vermont." Smith is not to be confused with the organist known as Johnny "Hammond" Smith. –RW

○ **Moonlight in Vermont / CAPITOL**   i 1956

LONNIE SMITH

Blues jazz, soul jazz. Dr. Lonnie Smith, is a Philadelphia based Hammond B-3 organist who preceded Lonnie Liston Smith. He was a longtime sideman for saxophonist Lou Donaldson. –NGB

● **Think / CAPITOL**   1923
W/ Lee Morgan (tpt). This is an excellent 1986 reissue of a fine soul-jazz Blue Note date by organist Lonnie Smith. –RW

○ **Mama Wailer / KUDO-CTI**   1975
W/ Grover Washington Jr. (sax). –MGN

LONNIE LISTON SMITH   b 1940

Early free, contemporary funk. Lonnie Liston Smith was among the more influential keyboard players of the 70s, with his cluster style and keyboard colorations being featured on albums by Pharoah Sanders and Gato Barbieri. Smith played with Betty Carter in 1963-1964 and with Rahsaan Roland Kirk the next year, and then worked with Art Blakey and Joe

Williams before joining Pharoah Sanders in 1969. He stayed with Sanders for four years, and wrote the title song for Sanders's album *Jewels of Thought*. He spent one year in the mid 70s with Miles Davis, then had a string of his own albums from the late 70s through the 80s, many of which had new-age sensibility in their lyrics and arrangements. –RW

● **Astral Traveling / FLYING DUTCHMAN**   r 1973
Still has solid jazz content in his material. –RW

○ **Expansions / FLYING DUTCHMAN / BB 85**   ca. 197?
The best of his post-Pharoah Sanders releases. –RW

LOUIS SMITH   b 1931

Swing, bop, hard-bop, post-bop, cool. This bop to post-bop trumpeter played briefly with Horace Silver in the 50s. He has spent most of his career teaching at the University of Michigan and Ann Arbor public schools. –MGN

● **Here Comes / BLUE NOTE**   i 1958
W/ Duke Jordan (p). –MGN

Smithville / BLUE NOTE   i 1958
W/ Charlie Rouse (ts) and Sonny Clark (p). –MGN

○ **Just Friends / STEEPLECHASE**   1978
Great date for master trumpeter with Memphis friends, including George Coleman on tenor sax. –MGN

☆ **Ballads for Lulu / STEEPLECHASE**

MARVIN SMITH   b 1961

Post-bop, neo bop. In the top rung of current jazz drummers and percussionists. A sometimes spectacular soloist and tremendous player capable of consistently driving a date, stepping back and just keeping time or even dominating the date, depending on the circumstances. He's made some fine sessions as a leader in hard-bop mode, and has backed both young lions and old vets on numerous dates. –RW

● **Keeper of the Drums / CONCORD**   r 1988
Drummer with septet at his best. Great group interplay. –MGN

○ **Road Less Traveled / CONCORD**   1989
This is an octet with James Williams (p). Right up there, no restrictions. –MGN

○ **Carryin' On / CONCORD**
Good, nicely played date with a harder edge than usual for Concord material. –RW

MIKE SMITH   b 1938

Post-bop, neo bop. Fine young alto saxophonist from Chicago, influenced by Cannonball Adderley. Extends post-bop compositions. –MGN

○ **Unit 7 / DELMARK**   r 1991
Very good debut effort. –MGN

PAUL SMITH   b 1922

Swing, cool. Classic jazz pianist, accompanist for years to Ella Fitzgerald. He plays mostly in a trio context. –MGN

○ **Art Tatum Touch - Vol. 1 / OUTSTANDING**
It would be easy to dismiss this record as no more than easy listening, if it were not for the honesty and the heavy influences of Teddy Wilson and Art Tatum combined with Smith's own individual, rather elegant style. –BOB RUSCH, CADENCE

TAB SMITH   1909-1971

Big band, blues-jazz. Alto, C-melody sax. A honking/R&B/swing sax master. Tab Smith began on the C-melody, then switched to alto and eventually became a giant within his genre. Smith had lots of experience in territory bands during the 30s, achieved his first real fame with Lucky Millinder from 1936-1939. Later came stints with Frankie Newton, Red Allen, Teddy Wilson and Eddie Durham, before he joined Count Basie in 1940. He returned to Millinder in 1942 and stayed until 1944, after which he led his own groups, sometimes with singer Wynonie Harris. His explosive, torrid solos were tailor-made for the swing-derived, jumping material that comprised vintage R&B, and during the 50s Smith cut many songs that were huge hits in the black community and on jukeboxes for tiny independent labels. –RW

○ **I Don't Want to Play ... / SAXOPHONOGRAPH**   1944
1944-1945. *I Don't Want To Play in the Kitchen.* Great honking sax, swing-inflected solos. –RW

Joy at the Savoy / SAXOPHONOGRAPH   194?
Stalwart 40s and 50s swing and honking sax cuts. –RW

○ **Because of You / DELMARK**   195?
Wonderful honking sax cuts, R&B prototype from 50s. –RW

● **Jump Time / DELMARK**   195?
Another great reissue of prime honking sax cuts. –RW

WILLIE SMITH   1910-1967

Trad, swing, big band, cool. Not to be confused with Willie "the Lion" Smith, he was one of the greatest Duke Ellington soloists. His alto sax style contrasts starkly with Charlie Parker's — where Bird was frantic, Smith was smooth. He also played baritone sax. –MGN

○ **Snooty Fruity / CBS**   1944
1944-1955. Nice collaboration with Harry James that has more form than many of James cuts. –RW

Alto Sax Artistry / MERCURY   i 1950
W/ Billy May (tpt). –MGN

● **Relaxin' After Hours / EMARCY**   i 1954

WILLIE "THE LION" SMITH   1897-1973

Trad, stride, boogie. Piano, composer, vocals. Though he was without question one of jazz's greatest exaggerators and self-promoters, Willie 'The Lion' Smith could back up almost all of what he said with his playing. Smith started in the ragtime era. He was an influence on Duke Ellington, and a cohort of James P. Johnson and Fats Waller. Smith played on the first blues record released by Mamie Smith in the 20s. From the 30s until his death in the 70s, Smith was a storytelling, entertaining, dueling piano madman and performer. He wrote over 70 songs, recorded with a host of groups and bands, did duets with Jess Stacy and Joe Bushkin. His approach seamlessly incorporated all keyboard developments from rag, boogie-woogie, and stride through swing up to bop, with plenty of blues mixed in as well. Not to be confused with alto saxophonist and singer Willie Smith. –RW

Reminiscing the Piano Greats / VOGUE   1949
Extremely rare date with Smith stomping and romping for Dial USA label. –RW

○ **'The Lion' Willie Smith / INNER CITY**   1949
Part of the Jazz Legacy series, these 1949-1950 sessions with Wallace Bishop on drums include some solos and some combo efforts with Buck Clayton on trumpet, Claude Luter on clarinet, and Bishop on drums. Ten Smith numbers and eight standards. Includes Smith's classic "Echoes of Spring." –MGN

Compositions of James P. Johnson / BLUE CIRCLE   1953
Tremendous solo album. –RW

Lion Roars / DOT   1957
Superior solos, spirited. –RW

○ **Legend of ... / GRAND AWARD**   1958
Impossible to find, wonderful release. –RW

● **Memoirs of Willie "The Lion" Smith / RCA**   1959
Great two-disc set. –RW

Songs We Taught Your Mother / PRESTIGE   1961
Lucille Hegamin shouts and moans; Smith rocks. –RW

Pork and Beans / BLACK LION   1966
Rollicking solo cuts. –RW

Grand Piano / SACKVILLE / DB 5   1967
Great duets with Don Ewell (p). –RW

Live at Blues Alley / CHIAROSCURO   1970
Excellent live set. –RW

Relaxin' / CHIAROSCURO   1970
Stalwart blues, ballads, and standards. –RW

JIM SNIDERO   b 1958

Post-bop, neo bop. Alto saxophonist influenced by Jackie McLean. Has carved individual sound in the post-bop genre. Just starting to be an effective bandleader/composer. Already a fine alto saxophone soloist. –MGN

○ **Storm Rising / KEN MUSIC**   1990
Mid-30s saxophonist proves his mettle. More to come from this up and coming musician. Very good album. –MGN

ELMER SNOWDEN   1900-1973

Swing. A great banjo player and versatile musician who could also play excellent sax and guitar, Elmer Snowden was a rarity in the early jazz era: a trained player who could read in any key and also a smart businessman. Snowden played banjo and guitar as a child, and worked with Eubie Blake in a dance school in 1915, then played in a trio with Duke Ellington in 1919. Snowden took a band to New York from Washington in 1923, planning to use Fats Waller. When that didn't materialize, Snowden sent for Ellington, and the group became the Washingtonians. Snowden ran several bands in the mid and late 20s and early 30s. He headed his own bands for three decades, before moving to California in 1963 to teach at Berkeley. He began touring Europe for George Wein in 1967. Snowden declined an offer to rejoin Ellington's orchestra in late 60s. A fine quartet album he recorded for Fantasy in 1960 has recently been reissued. –RW

○ **Harlem Banjo / OJC**   r 1960
The legendary banjo player, with the Cliff Jackson (p) Trio, plays standards with the emphasis on old time swing, including some Ellington. This is a unique album, one every jazz fan should get to know. –MGN

MARTIAL SOLAL   b 1927

Post-bop, cool. Piano, composer. Any player with remarkable prowess and technical talents prone to utilize and display them on record runs the risk of critical displeasure, and that's been the case with Martial Solal. His vast harmonic knowledge, tendency to literally assault the listener with rippling phrases and complex passages, and his sometimes relentless pacing, turn off as many people as they impress. Solal settled in Paris in the late 40s, and worked with expatriate American musicians like Kenny Clarke and Don Byas, while recording with Sidney Bechet, Lee Konitz, and Hampton Hawes. He's led his own trios, done extensive session work since 1959, and became internationally famous through a 1963 visit to New York and subsequent Newport festival appearances. –RW

Happy Reunion / VOGUE   1956
1990 reissue of session with Solal playing with group of one-time Stan Kenton luminaries. –RW

○ **Martial Solal / BLUE NOTE**   r 1961
Brilliant piano work combining bop, Tatum, and Peterson. –DS

● **Trio in Concert / LIBERTY**   1962
Paris concert by this Algerian pianist, with Guy Pederson on bass and Damiel Humaia on drums. An excellent album to find. –MGN

○ **Four Keys / PA-USA**   ca. 1979
Seven compositions by this pianist/leader, with Lee Konitz (as), John Scofield (g), N.H.O. Pedersen (b). Intriguing combination of musicians. –MGN

Bluesine / SOUL NOTE   1983
A solid recent solo work. –DS

Triptyque / ADDA   1991
Newest Solal date, features him with group of French jazz musicians. –RW

Big Band / GAUMONT

Good arrangements, slashing big band. –RW
○ **Martial Solal / IGRANDI DEL JAZZ**
Italian release with fabulous graphics and liner notes. The music is also first rate. –MGN
Trio / DATHE
Stunning piano technique, solos. –RW
○ **Live / STEFANOTIS**   COMP
Comprehensive four-disc set of his material from 1959-1985 in every context. –RW

LEW SOLOFF   b 1944

Post-bop, Latin, jazz-rock, neo bop. Although he's a brilliant, flexible trumpeter, Lew Soloff has probably garnered more fame for being a longtime member of the Gil Evans Orchestra and working with Blood, Sweat and Tears in the 70s than for being a first-rate soloist and accompanist. Soloff had formal studies at Julliard Preparatory from 1961-1965; he later completed his music education at Eastman School and had supplemental studies at Julliard in 1965-1966. He got experience doing Latin-jazz in 1967-1968, then did freelance sessions with Maynard Ferguson, Joe Henderson, Clark Terry, and many others before joining Blood, Sweat and Tears from 1968-1973. While Wynton Marsalis won many classical Grammys in the 80s, Soloff was a featured soloist on many classical pieces in the 70s. He joined the Evans orchestra in 1973, continuing with him extensively during that decade and beyond, plus forming a quintet with Jon Faddis in 1975. He headed a trio in 1977, then did sessions and worked with Evans in the 80s. –RW
○ **Speak Low / PRO ARTE-PRO JAZZ**   1987
Veteran NYC studio trumpeter steps out. –MGN

SOPRANO SUMMIT

Trad, swing. This group is the vehicle for saxophonists Bob Wilbur and Kenny Davern. They work with a swing and big band repertoire, along with odes to their main man — Sidney Bechet. –MGN
○ **Live at Concord 1977 / CONCORD**   1977
Never less than interesting and sometimes electrifying. –SHIRLEY KLETT, CADENCE

EDDIE SOUTH   1904-1962

Swing. Classically trained violinist Eddie South studied at the Chicago Musical College for many years and, in 1924, became the music director of Jimmy Wade's Syncopators. After traveling extensively in Europe after 1928, he returned to Chicago in 1931 and started a band with Milt Hinton that recorded with Victor. South subsequently made recordings with Stephane Grappelli and Django Reinhardt. He had incredible technique and a dark tone led to his nickname as the "dark angel." –JME
○ **In Paris / DRG**

MUGGSY SPANIER   1906-1967

Trad. Muggsy Spanier had personality and charisma and was a good performer in traditional style. He began on drums, then switched to cornet at 13. He joined the Ted Lewis orchestra in 1929, staying with him until 1936, when he joined Ben Pollack's band for two years. The Ragtimers, a short-lived band he formed in the late-30s for dates at the Sherman Hotel in Chicago and Nick's in New York, was among the most popular trad bands of its day. Spanier rejoined Lewis for a short time, then led his own big band from 1941-1943 that was modeled after the Bob Crosby Orchestra, in which he'd played in 1940-1941. He played with Lewis again in 1944, then led various small groups in the 50s and 60s, also working for a time with Earl Hines. –RW
Muggsy Spanier 1931 and 1939 / BBC CLASSICS   1931
Brand new reissues of super 30s dates with Spanier and Fats Waller (p), Benny Goodman (cl), and Joe Bushkin (p). –RW
○ **Columbia / MOBILE FIDELITY.**   195?

Columbia — The Gem Of The Ocean. Excellent recording of fine 50s date. –RW
Relaxin' at the Touro / JAZZOLOGY
First-rate traditional, nice solos. –RW

LES SPANN   b 1932

Hard-bop, post-bop, cool, blues-jazz. Interesting figure who plays guitar and doubles on flute. Popular blues and jazz sideman in the 50s. –MGN
Gemini / JAZZLAND   i 1961
W/ Tommy Flanagan (p). –MGN

JAMES SPAULDING   b 1937

Hard-bop, post-bop, early free. A tremendous alto sax and flute player with one of jazz's slimmest profiles. Spaulding came to prominence during the 60s and 70s as a stirring alto soloist with one foot in bop and one in the free, expressive style being pioneered by Ornette Coleman. He was also among the best flute players, able to play lengthy lines and swirling solos, play sweetly or with funk and bite. He dropped out of sight for while in the 80s, then has been a steady contributor to many sessions for small jazz companies in late 80s and 90s. –RW
● **Gotstabe a Better Way / MUSE**   1988
Veteran saxophonist in his best light. –MGN
○ **Brilliant Corners / MUSE**   1988
Sparkling late-80s session. –RW

SPHERE

Post-bop. Nice repertory group formed by longtime Monk saxophonist Charlie Rouse in the 80s with pianist Kenny Barron, bassist Buster Williams, and drummer Ben Riley. The quartet began doing almost totally Monk material, gradually expanded to other composers plus some originals. Their finest release ironically was an album of Charlie Parker tunes. –RW
○ **Four in One / ELEKTRA**   r 1982
Tremendous tribute effort, outstanding versions of Monk classics. –RW
● **Bird Songs / POLYGRAM**   1988
1988 lineup of all-star players Kenny Barron (p), Charlie Rouse (ts), Buster Williams (b), and Ben Riley (d) play only Charlie Parker tunes, except for the lengthy and brilliant "I Didn't Know What Time It Was." –MGN
○ **Four for All / POLYGRAM**   1988
Topflight Monk repertory effort. CD has two bonus cuts. –RW
Flight Path / ELEKTRA / DB 5   1989
More worthy solos, great ensemble work. –RW

PETER SPRAGUE   b 1955

Post-bop, jazz-rock, neo bop. Guitarist influenced by Coltrane and Third World. Works well in modal setting. Good improviser, sometimes raga-like. –MGN
○ **Napali Coast / CONCORD**   ca. 1985
Quartet with leader Sprague uses influences of Indian (East and West) music, Coltrane, and Corea to make unique music with the brilliant flutist Steve Kujala, Bob Magnusson on bass, and Peter Eskine on drums. One cut, "Coltrane," recorded with Sprague's younger brother Tripp on tenor sax. There are two Corea numbers, three by Sprague, and three standards. –MGN

SPYRO GYRA

Contemporary funk. Perhaps the best-selling and most popular fusion group ever. They were started in the mid 70s by saxophonist Jay Beckenstein and pianist Jeremy Wall. They were initially primarily a studio band cutting faceless instrumentals. Then their 1979 album *Morning Dance* went gold and they became an international success. During the 80s and 90s they've had a string of similar sounding recordings, have been derided repeatedly by many jazz critics, and become a staple on adult contemporary, new-age and easy listening stations. −RW

○ **Access All Areas / MCA**   1984
An excellent live double album that includes live versions of songs from early albums. −PK

Alternating Currents / MCA   1985
Great songwriting and playing, and nice work by keyboardist Tom Schuman. −PK

Breakout / MCA   1986
An album with more mid-tempo jazz-style tunes and nice arrangements, with Julio Fernandez. Synths programmed by Eddie Jobson. −PK

Stories without Words / MCA   1987
A nice mix of jazz, with tenor and soprano-sax melodies that really sing. −PK

● **Collection / GRP**   COMP
A compilation CD that includes songs from many of their albums. −PK

JESS STACY   ♭1904

Swing, big band. A superb pianist in vintage swing style, with one of the greatest right-hands ever. Stacy arrived in Chicago from Merge Point, Missouri in the mid 20s and worked for many groups in dance halls, clubs, and speakeasies, showing the skills he'd developed from playing around the area on riverboats with such visitors as Bix Beiderbecke and Tony Catalano. Through the efforts of John Hammond, Stacy joined Benny Goodman in 1935 and stayed with him until 1939, attaining jazz immortality by playing a brillant solo on the 1938 Carnegie Hall performance of "Sing Sing Sing." He spent three years from 1939-1942 with Bob Crosby. Stacy went to the West Coast and played in piano bars in the 50s and early 60s. He came back in 1973, doing the soundtrack for the film *The Great Gatsby,* then getting a standing ovation at the 1974 Newport Jazz Festival. He began recording again for Chiaroscuro in the mid and late 70s, and his classic 40s sessions are being reissued −RW

● **Piano Solos / SWAGGIE**   1935
1935-1956. Includes a nice cross-section of influential, fine Stacy cuts. −RW

○ **Jess Stacy & Friends / COMMODORE**   1938
Top-flight material from 1938-1944 with Lee Wiley (v). −RW

Blue Notion / JAZZOLOGY   194?
A good compilation of tracks from early 40s. −RW

Stacy Still Swings / CHIAROSCURO   1974
Pianist could still rock the house at 70. −RW

Stacy's Still Swinging / CHIAROSCURO   1977
Likewise at 73. −RW

HEINER STADLER   ♭1942

Early free, progressive big band. This bandleader and composer is part of the international avant-garde jazz movement. He has not made many recordings that are available domestically. Stadler has led groups that reflect influences of Ornette Coleman, Art Ensemble of Chicago, and late-period John Coltrane. −RW

● **Brains on Fire / LABOR**   ca. 1973
African themes and classical motifs filter through an excellent jazz ensemble under Stadler's direction. "The Fugue #2," "Heide," and "All Tones" are all extended pieces. With Joe Farrell, Don Friedman, Jimmy Owens, Tyrone Washington, Garnett Brown, Joe Chambers, and Barre Phillips. Sextet and quartet recordings, with Stadler on piano on quartet cuts only. For listeners willing to be challenged. −MGN

Jazz Alchemy / TOMATO
Nice, occasionally appealing date by Stadler. −RW

○ **Retrospection / TOMATO**
Sometimes fiery, enjoyable set. −RW

Music Map

Jazz Trumpet

Early Jazz (New Orleans)
● Buddy Bolden (1877-1931) — Freddie Keppard (1890-1933)
● King Oliver (1885-1938)

Major Player and Influence on Trumpet and all of Jazz
Louis Armstrong (1901-1971)

Major Players (20s & 30s)
Jabbo Smith (1908) — Henry "Red" Allen (1908-1967)
Hot Lips Page (1908-1954) — Wingy Manone (1900-1982)
Mugsy Spanier (1906-1967) — Bix Beiderbecke (1903-1931)
Jimmy McPartland (1907) — Max Kaminsky (1908)
Wild Bill Davison (1906) — Bobby Hackett (1915-1976)

Ellingtonians
Cootie Williams (1911-1985) — Rex Stewart (1914-1987)
Ray Nance (1913-1976) — Al Killian (1916-1950)
Clark Terry (1920)

Swing Era
Roy Eldridge (1911) — Buck Clayton (1911)
Charlie Shavers (1917-1971) — Cat Anderson (1916-1981)
Tommy Ladnier — Doc Cheatham (1905)

Bop
● Dizzy Gillespie (1917) — Fats Navarro (1923-1950)
● Cliford Brown (1930-1956)

Cool Jazz
Miles Davis (1926-1991) — Chet Baker (1929-1988)

Hard Bop
● Donald Byrd (1932) — ● Lee Morgan (1938-1972)
● Freddie Hubbard (1938) — Woody Shaw (1944)
Booker Little (1938-1961) — Kenny Dorham (1924-1972)

Free Jazz
Don Cherry (1936) — Bill Dixon (1925)
Michael Ray — Lester Bowie (1941)
Mike Mantler (1943) — Leo Smith (1941)
Ted Curson (1935) — Charles Tolliver (1942)
Olu Dara (1941)

Jazz Rock
Miles Davis (1926-1991) — Maynard Ferguson (1928)
Don Ellis (1934-1978) — Bill Chase

Young Players
● Wynton Marsalis (1961) — Roy Hargrove — Brad Goode

MARVIN STAMM   ♭1939

Post-bop, neo bop. Prolific trumpeter and busy session player noted especially for his range, talent in the upper register and flexibility. Has played in big bands and combos, recorded with

Gil Evans orchestra, also worked in pit bands for Broadway shows, television studios. –RW.

○ **Bop Boy / MUSICMASTERS**   1991
This trumpeter's first album in a long time as a leader. Spirited playing. –MGN

DAKOTA STATON   b 1931

Ballads. Good jazz and blues singer who made a big impact in the mid 50s and early 60s. Staton was named by *DOWN BEAT* as most promising newcomer in 1955; her releases, especially *The Late, Late Show*, were both popular and enhanced her reputation as a vocalist who could swing, interpret standards, and sing convincing, pulsating blues tunes. She recorded with George Shearing in 1958, and also did one of the most successful vocal versions of "Misty." –RW

● **The Late Late Show / CAPITOL**   i 1957
W/ Hank Jones (p). –MGN
Softly / CAPITOL   i 1960
W/ Benny Carter (as) –MGN
○ **Dakota at Storyville / CAPITOL**   i 1961
W/ Norman Simmons (p) –MGN
Moonglow / LRC JAZZ CLASSICS

JEREMY STEIG   b 1942

Post-bop, soul jazz, Latin, jazz-rock, neo bop. Steig was among the first to find a good midpoint between the emerging electronic breakthroughs of the 70s and traditional acoustic instrumentation and arrangements in jazz and pop. His father was a famous musician, and Steig began playing recorder at six, taking flute lessons at 11. He worked with Paul Bley and Gary Peacock in 1961, then in 1966, he was part of a jazz/rock band that included Tim Hardin. The next year he began leading his own groups. His band Jeremy and the Satyrs was among the early, innovative groups truly able to do either impressive jazz tunes or authentic rock pieces. Steig was also an early proponent of electronics, incorporating them into his band without gimmickry or faddism. Steig was a star in Europe in the 70s, and his flute solos were among the most accomplished in either jazz or rock. His album output diminished greatly after the 70s. –RW

○ **Flute Fever / COLUMBIA**   ca. 1963
Some truly awesome playing. –RW
Jeremy and the Satyrs / REPRISE   ca. 1967
Cute concept, inspired flute solos. –RW
Lend Me Your Ears / CMP   1978
Trio with Eddie Gomez (b) and Joe Chambers (d). Steig also plays Mutron. –MGN
● **Music for Flute & Double Bass / CMP**   1980
Exacting flute and bass material. –RW
○ **Rain Forest / CMP**   1980
Virtuoso flute player. An improvisational tradition of various groupings. With Eddie Gomez (b), Jack DeJohnette (d), Mike Nock (k), and Nana Vasconcelos (per). –MGN

STEPS AHEAD

Jazz-rock, contemporary funk. Fusion/contemporary/neo-bop band from NYC, w/ vibist Mike Mainieri and Michael Brecker (ts). All-star rhythm sections utilized. Earlier imports a potent reminder of why this is an important band. –MGN
Steps Ahead / ELEKTRA   1983
This is one of the early albums from Brecker and Mainieri. –JME
○ **Modern Times / ELEKTRA-ASYLUM**   1984
Good session from interesting New York group. –RW
N.Y.C. / INTUITION   1989

LENI STERN

Jazz-rock, neo bop. Electric guitarist works on the understated side of neo-bop. Compositions show much depth and understanding of her instrument. –MGN

● **Clairvoyant / PASSPORT**   1985
Sextet w/ Bill Frisell (g), Bob Berg (ts). A fresh approach, not as acerbic as her husband Mike. Larry Willis (p) Trio, a fine support group — Harvie Swartz (b), Paul Motian (d). Stern plays plaintive electric guitar. –MGN
The Next Day / PPJ   1987
Same group as *Clairvoyant*, minus Frisell. Have your jazz with a contemporary edge. –MGN
Secrets / RHINO   1988
○ **Closer to the Light / RHINO**   r 1990
Surprising release with David Sanborn (as) showing his real skills; fine arrangements. –RW

MIKE STERN

Jazz-rock, contemporary funk. Ex-Miles Davis electric guitarist looks more toward rock-edged tone. Also good in neo-bop setting. More steely and psychedelic. –MGN
Upside Downside / ATLANTIC   1986
Great bass from Jaco Pastorius. Lightweight material. –RW
Time in Place / ATLANTIC   1988
With Michael Brecker (sax) and Bob Berg (ts). "Gossip" a good opening track. –MGN
○ **Jigsaw / ATLANTIC**   1990
High-powered jazz/rock with the emphasis on rock. –MGN

JOHN STEVENS

Post-bop, jazz-rock, neo bop. British drummer whose work with jazz/rock band (like Soft Machine) is not as important as his many other projects, especially his own group, Away. He is right up there in the hierachy of top U.K. drummers such as Jon Hiseman, Bill Bruford, and Cozy Powell. –MGN
● **Away / VERTIGO**   1975
British jazz drummer cooks with Trevor Watts (sax). –MGN
○ **Chemistry / VINYL**   1975
Top-notch, with Trevor Watts (sax) and Kenny Wheeler (tpt). Tribute for Bud Powell and Ornette Coleman. –MGN
Longest Night - Vols. 1 & 2 / OGUN   ca. 1976
On-the-edge releases with the frenetic Evan Parker (sax). –RW

HERBIE STEWARD   b 1926

Swing, big band, bop. A tenor saxophonist best known for being part of Woody Herman's Second Herd section alongside Stan Getz, Zoot Sims, and Serge Chaloff. Steward had a nice tone, interacted well, and was an above-average soloist. He has few albums in print at present. –RW
So Pretty / AVA   i 1962
W/ Orchestra –MGN
One Brother / MOBILE FIDELITY
This is an excellent recording, good date, but fairly formulaic material. –RW

BOB STEWART   b 1945

Post-bop, neo bop, modern creative. Tuba Player Bob Stewart started in traditional jazz in Philadelpha, and moved to New York in 1968. He worked with Carla Bley, Fran Foster, Sam Rivers, Gill Evans, Arthur Blythe, David Murray, and Lester Bowie. Stewart went on to work with Charles Mingus, McCoy Tyner, and Henry Threadgill. –JME
○ **First Line / POLYGRAM**   1987
Rambling but superior lineup, fine playing by Stewart and Steve Turre (tb). –RW
○ **Goin' Home / POLYGRAM**   1988
Premier tuba player Bob Stewart with quintet. One side is originals and the other is standards and traditional fare. Highly recommended. –MGN

REX STEWART   1907-1967

Swing, big band, progressive big band. Cornet. The master of the "half-valve" technique, in which he pushed the cornet and/or trumpet valves halfway down and created a wealth of quarter tones and fresh sounds. Stewart developed this method in part to create alternative, individual sound and help him deal with the challenging music he faced when he replaced his idol Louis Armstrong in Fletcher Henderson's orchestra in the 20s. Though he also worked with Elmer Snowden prior to joining Henderson, and later played with McKinney's Cotton Pickers and Luis Russell, Stewart attained star status during a 12-year tenure with Duke Ellington from 1934-1945. While with Ellington, Stewart's solos became famous on a pair of masterpieces, "Trumpet In Spades" and "Boy Meets Horn." Later he led his own groups, toured Europe and Australia, lived in New Jersey for a while in the 50s, later organized and led a Fletcher Henderson reunion band, played at Eddie Condon's, and recorded there as well. He led various groups under the banner of the Ellingtonians on several labels from 1936-1941. −RW

● **Rex Stewart & Ellingtonians / OJC** 1940
1940/1946 dates. Here is a fine set with both past and near-present Ellington-band members. W/ Shelly Monroe, Joe Thomas (sax). −RW

Porgy & Bess Revisited / SWING 1958
Outstanding release, with Ellingtonians Cootie Williams (tpt), and Laurence Brown (tb). −RW

Irrepresible Rex Stewart / JAZZOLOGY 1971
Stately-elegant posthumous releases. −RW

Memorial Album / PRESTIGE r 1971
Sublime, striking cornet solos. −RW

Trumpet Jive / PRESTIGE 1971
Top collaboration with Wingy Manone (tpt). −RW

○ **With Henri Chase / POLYDOR**
Subtle, supple playing. −RW

SLAM STEWART b 1914

Swing, big band, bop, ballads. As with Clark Terry, Stewart's fondness for mugging on stage and his trademark technique of bowing a bass solo and humming along in unison sometimes blinded observers into considering him more an entertainer than a first-class musician. Stewart also had a long-running collaboration and act with vocalist Slim Gaillard, and the team of Slim and Slam had several delightful vocal hits, among them "Flat Foot Foogie" and "Buck Dance Rhythm." They also appeared in the film *Stormy Weather*, and they toured and recorded with Art Tatum and Benny Goodman as well as having their own trio. Stewart worked with many great musicians on his own, from the 40s until the 80s. They included Lester Young, Tatum, Rose Murphy, Goodman, and Beryl Booker. He also headed his own groups in the 70s. The 1981 release, *Shut Your Mouth*, paired him with Major Holley, doing the familiar hum/scat/humor routines Stewart had patented earlier with Gailliard. −RW

○ **Shut Yo' Mouth! / DELOS** 1981
W/ Major Holley. Two great bassists get together for a good time. Highly recommended. −MGN

SONNY STITT 1924-1982

Bop, hard-bop, post-bop, soul jazz. One of the most important saxophonists in jazz history. Began recording in 1946 after appearing with Tiny Bradshaw, Billy Eckstine, and Dizzy Gillespie. Early recordings are on Savoy and Galaxy (via Sensation). He switched from alto to tenor sax in 1949 and created a sensation with Prestige/New Jazz recordings featuring Bud Powell, John Lewis and J. J. Johnson, then joined forces with Gene Ammons in 1950 playing both saxes (and, occasionally, baritone sax as well). His Prestige recordings of 1950-1952 are all worth hearing as are his sessions for Roost, Argo, and Verve throughout the 50s.

Stitt was a freelance recording artist throughout much of his career, which accounts for the large number of recordings done for different labels during the same period. In the 60s, Stitt got into organ sessions with players such as Jack McDuff and Don Patterson. More often than not, the organ sessions lack the spirit of his more bop-oriented recordings. From 1966 to 1971, Stitt made use of electronic attachments for his saxophone which tended to dull his tone and dampen the fire of the music. Those should be avoided.

Stitt made well over a hundred albums in his career but those in his later years that are especially recommended are those on the Muse label. Sessions involving pianist Barry Harris are among the best of all Sonny Stitt recordings. −BP

Stitt/Powell/Johnson / OJC 1949
1949-1950. Steaming, exciting collaboration. −RW

Kaleidoscope / OJC 1950
Five dates from 1950-1952. Fine reissue that features early 50s Stitt. −RW

Symphony Hall Swing / SAVOY 1952
Fine 50s sessions. −RW

Sonny Stitt / MCA 1958
1990 reissue of some 1958 Argo cuts. Haphazard job by MCA. Stitt was mostly wonderful. −RW

Sits in with the Oscar Peterson / POLYGRAM 1959
Everyone cooks, especially Stitt and Oscar Peterson (p). −RW

Stitt and Top Brass / ATLANTIC 1962
Dynamite arrangements and solos. −RW

Autumn in New York / BLACK LION 1962
1962-1967. Some top 60s sessions with Kenny Clarke (d), Walter Bishop Jr. (p), and Tommy Potter (b). −RW

☆ **Stitt Plays Bird / ATLANTIC / DB 5** 1963
Best Stitt of the 60s. Classic cover art. −MGN

Soul People / PRESTIGE 1964
Another good soul-jazz set. −RW

Nuther Further / PRESTIGE r 1966
Fine soul jazz with Jack McDuff (organ). −RW

○ **Constellation / MUSE / DB 5** 1972
W/ Barry Harris (p). Shattering album that had everyone sitting up and taking notice in its initial release. −RW

○ **Tune-Up! / MUSE / DB 5** r 1972
Amazing quartet date that reignites Stitt as soloist in 70s. 1987 reissue. −RW

The Champ / MUSE 1973
1991 reissue of wonderful 1973 date. −RW

Mellow / MUSE 1975
Fine ballads, nice pairing with Jimmy Heath (sax). −RW

In Walked Sonny / SONET 1975
Freewheeling, adept session. −RW

● **My Buddy: Stitt Plays for Gene Ammons / MUSE** 1975
Brash, robust, and lusty. −RW

○ **Blues for Duke / MUSE** 1975
Great tribute to Ellington via Stitt's solos. −RW

Moonlight in Vermont / DENON 1977
Typically high-class playing, very familiar menu. −RW

○ **I Remember Bird / CATALYST** r 1977
W/ trombonist Frank Rosolino −MGN

Sonny's Back / MUSE 1980
High-flying, solid set. −RW

In Style / MUSE 1981
Nearing the end, but Stitt still has power and fire. −RW

Last Sessions / MUSE 1982
The end comes. −RW

With Art Blakey / GAZELL
Excellent meeting of minds. W/ Art Blakey (d). −RW

○ **Soul Classics / OJC** COMP
Fine playing, frequently galvanizing solos. 1988 reissue of cuts from 1962-1972. −RW

STRAIGHT AHEAD

Hard-bop, neo bop, M-base. This all-female quintet from Detroit play straight modern jazz, feminist funk, odd meters, or pop. Their motion is a forward one, and it never wavers. –MGN

○ **Look Straight Ahead / ATLANTIC**   ca. 1991
Label debut for quintet of Detroit ladies who play straightahead bluesy and contemporary jazz. They all vocalize on occasion. Standouts are violinist Regina Carter, who has the ability to quote phrases of standards in her improvs, and bassist Marion Hayden-Banfield, as solid a player as is out there today. –MGN

STRATA INSTITUTE

M-base, modern creative. Detroit rhythm mates Jaribu Shahid (b) and Tani Tabbal (d) meet M-Base New Yorkers Steve Coleman and Greg Osby. –MGN
○ **Cipher Syntax / POLYGRAM**   1988
W/ Greg Osby (sax) and Steve Coleman (sax) for "cyborg-funk." An acquired taste, but still excellent. –MGN

BILLY STRAYHORN   1915-1967

Big band, progressive big band. Piano, arranger, composer. Among the greatest jazz arrangers and composers in history, and from 1939-1967 the partner and confidant of Duke Ellington. Strayhorn met Ellington in 1938, after completing high school in Pittsburgh. He began writing lyrics for him a year later, after playing piano briefly in a band led by his son Mercer. In fact, Strayhorn actually composed his most famous song "Lush Life" before he joined Ellington. The two became so close some observers claimed it was impossible to distinguish between their styles, though some argue that Strayhorn was more conventional in his voicings and arrangements. His list of compositions includes such classics as "Day Dream," "Chelsea Bridge" and the signature song "Take the A-Train." Ellington later had some of his extended pieces published with 'Ellington-Strayhorn' joint credit. Strayhorn was also a fine instrumentalist, though he seldom appeared in public with the orchestra or any of the small combos. He cut duets with Ellington, made trio and septet recordings with Johnny Hodges and in 1963 directed the band in a lavish Ellington concept piece "My People." –RW
Trio / MERCER   i 1951
W/ Duke Ellington. –MGN
○ **Cue For Saxophone / POLYGRAM**   1959
Fine Strayhorn arrangements for session of top-flight Ellingtonians. Johnny Hodges (sax) takes honors. Reissue of 1959 date. –RW
Septet / FELSTED   i 1959
W/ Johnny Hodges (sax). –MGN
Peaceful Side Of / UNITED ARTISTS   ca. 1961
Superb arrangements, vocals, and orchestrations. Made in Paris. –RW

FRANK STRAZZERI   b 1930

Bop, hard-bop, post-bop, cool. A mainstream/contemporary pianist, Strazzeri has recorded on Glendale, Fresh Sound, and Sea Breeze labels. –RW
○ **Frank's Blues / NIGHT LIFE**

FRANK STROZIER   b 1937

Post-bop. One of many alto saxophonists in the 50s and 60s who forged ahead after initially being heavily influenced by Charlie Parker. The Memphis-born player moved to New York, recorded with likes of George Coleman, Harold Mabern, and other fellow Memphians who'd moved to the East Coast. Strozier subsequently moved to a looser, freer alto style; in recent years he has switched to piano. His finest recordings from the 50s and 60s are slowly reappearing in print. –RW

● **Fantastic / VEE JAY**   1960
Classic hard bop by this Chicago alto saxophonist, with help from Booker Little (tpt) and Wynton Kelly (p). –DS
Fantastic / VEE JAY   i 1960
W/ Booker Little (tpt). –PR
Long Night / JAZZLAND   1961
Driving bop with George Coleman (ts). –DS
Long Night / JAZZLAND   i 1961
W/ George Coleman (ts). –PR
○ **March of the Siamese Children / JAZZLAND**   1962
An outstanding session with Harold Mabern (p). –DS
Remember Me / STEEPLECHASE   1976
A rewarding recent Strozier in a sextet setting. –DS

STRUNZ & FARAH

World fusion. Puerto Rican and Iranian guitarists fuse elements of their respective cultures to form unique music. –MGN
○ **Mosaico / CAPITOL-RHINO**   r 1984
The first and still best record for this team of Iranian guitarist Andeshir Farah and guitarist Jorge Strunz. It includes seven originals with a multi-ethnicity that is truly global. Latin, African, and jazz influences most prominent. –MGN

DAVE STRYKER

Post-bop, neo bop. A modern guitarist who swings hard. Stryker is a rival to John Scofield but not as hard-edged. –MGN
○ **Guitar on Top / KEN**   ca. 1991
Features a quartet with Stryker, Mulgrew Miller on piano, Bob Hurst on bass, and Victor Lewis on drums. These are extra-special musicians playing seven Stryker originals in modern mainstream plus two standards. It is good to discover and holds many surprises. –MGN

RORY STUART   b 1956

Post-bop, neo bop. A guitarist whose single-line melodicism is a nice extension of Wes Montgomery. Fine linear player in the modern-to-abstract school, but rarely ventures avant. –MGN
● **Nightwork / CADENCE**   1983
Live at 7th Ave. South in NYC, with quartet. Extended originals. One to seek. –MGN
○ **Hurricane / SUNNYSIDE**   1986
Studio date with quartet. Also worthwhile. –MGN

JOHN STUBBLEFIELD   b 1945

Post-bop, early free, neo bop. Good modern saxophonist who's recorded mostly for foreign labels like Enja, but also has been featured on small domestic independents. A versatile player, his best instrument is soprano, but he also has recorded on flute, alto, and tenor. A hard bop/mainstream type; capable soloist. He has yet to release the definitive or breakout session that would give him widespread visibility and notoriety. –RW
● **Prelude / STORYVILLE**   1976
Septet. All originals. Excellent mainstream jazz. –MGN
○ **Bushman Song / RHINO**   1986
Veteran saxophonist on his game. –MGN

L. SUBRAMANIAM   b 1947

World fusion. His father was a famous violinist and educator in India, and L. Subramaniam has upheld the family tradition. He was a member with his older and younger brothers of the Violin Trio, and eventually obtained a degree in medicine from Madras Medical College, subsequently earning a master's degree in music when he came to America in the 70s, studying Western music and composition. Since the mid 70s Subramaniam has worked with Ravi Shankar, George Harrison, John Handy, and Ali Akbar Khan, and has managed a comfortable merger of classic Indian and traditional American rythmic and harmonic concepts. –RW

Music Map — Jazz Singers

Early Jazz Singers Ethel Waters (1896-1977) – First concert jazz singer Louis Armstrong (1901-1971) – First scat singer Wingy Manone (1900-1982) — Henry "Red" Allen (1908-1967) Roy Eldridge (1911) — Louis Prima (1911-1978)	**1940s Singers** Sarah Vaughan (1924-1991) Joe "Bebop" Carroll (1919-1981) with Dizzy Gillespie
Women Singers Mamie Smith (1883-1946) — Ma Rainey (1886-1939) Bessie Smith (1894-1937) — Alberta Hunter (1895-1984) Ida Cox (1896-1967) — Sippie Wallace (1898-1986) Maxine Sullivan (1911-1987) — Josephine Baker (1906-1975)	**Vocalese** 1940s Eddie Jefferson (1918-1979) — Babs Gonzalez (1919-1980) 1950s King Pleasure (1922-1981) — Lambert, Hendricks & Ross
1929-1930 – First White jazz singers Jack Teagarden (1905-1964) — Mildred Bailey (1907-1951) Lee Wiley (1915-1975)	**Big Band** Al Hibbler (1915) — Mel Torme (1925) Anita O'Day (1919-1990) — June Christy (1925) Chris Connor (1927)
Crooners Frank Sinatra (1915) — Al Hibbler (1915)	**Major Singers** Carmen McRae (1922) — Johnny Hartman (1923-1983) Dinah Washington (1924-1963) — Sarah Vaughan (1924-1991) Abbey Lincoln (Aminata Moseka) (1930) — Betty Carter (1930)
1930s – Most Influential Female Jazz Singer Billie Holiday (1915-1959) **1930s – Most Influential Male Jazz Singer** Billy Eckstine (1914)	**Blues/Jazz Icon** Mose Allison (1927)
Major Singer Ella Fitzgerald (1918) – also bop and scat singing	**60s-70s** Bob Dorough (1923) — Grady Tate (1932) Mark Murphy (1932) — Karin Krog (1937) Irene Kral (1932-1978) — Sheila Jordan (1928) Jackie & Roy (1928 & 1921) — Singers Unlimited Joe Lee Wilson (1935) — Al Jarreau (1940)
Blues Shouters Jimmy Rushing (1903-1972) — Joe Turner (1907) Eddie "Cleanhead" Vinson (1917-1988) Joe Williams (1918) — Jimmy Witherspoon (1923)	**80s-90s** Tom Lellis — Roseanna Vitro Cassandra Wilson — Luba Raushiek — Nancy King
Entertainers/Comics Cab Calloway (1907) — Spike Jones — Slim Gaillard (1916)	**Avant Garde** Jay Clayton — Karin Krog Tziana Ghigllioni — Irene Aebi — Jeanne Lee (1939)
Major Singer Nat King Cole (1917-1965)	**Pop Jazz** Manhattan Transfer — Bobby McFerrin (1950) N.Y. Voices — Diane Schuur

○ **Spanish Wave / MILESTONE** 1983
The earliest and most satisfying of his classical/jazz fusion albums for Milestone, with top jazz and Indian musicians mixing it up. –MB

Mani & Co. / MILESTONE 1986
W/ Tony WIlliams (d), Bud Shank (sax), Larry Coryell (g). More fusion of jazz and Indian currents. –MB

IDREES SULIEMAN b 1923

Bop, hard-bop, post-bop, progressive big band. Trumpeter. Idrees Sulieman has been a valuable member of several groups, most notably the Kenny Clarke-Francy Boland Big Band. He left America for Switzerland in the 60s and settled in Copenhagen, Denmark, in the 70s. His early career was spent working with the Carolina Cotton Pickers and the Earl Hines Band in the 40s. Sulieman worked with Thelonious Monk and Mary Lou Williams in the mid 40s, and was quick to recognize the

changes in the jazz world and embrace bop. He worked with Monk, Coleman Hawkins, and others in the late 40s and through the 50s, before departing from America. –RW

○ **Coolin' / NEW JAZZ** i 1958
W/ Teddy Charles (vib) –MGN

IRA SULLIVAN b 1931

Hard-bop, post-bop, neo-bop.. One of the great multi-instrumentalists of modern jazz. Long associated with the Chicago modern-jazz scene, Sullivan moved to Florida in the mid 60s and has remained there for most of his career. Fluent on trumpet, fluglehorn, flute, and all the saxophones, Sullivan's work has almost always been involved with small groups. Sullivan has made a dozen or so albums under his own leadership and all are challenging, inspired modern jazz. His work with Red Rodney in a co-led group delighted fans in the early and mid 80s and the albums they recorded for Muse and Elektra/Musician are well worth seeking out. −BP

Blue Stroll / DELMARK 1959
In Chicago with Johnny Griffin (sax) and Jodie Christian (p). Excellent. −MGN

○ **Ira Sullivan / A&M-HORIZON** 1976
Studio date with Joe Dorio (g) and Jaco Pastorius (b). Interesting music. −MGN

Ira Sullivan / FLYING FISH 1977
Session that should have made him a star at that time. −RW

Peace / GALAXY 1978
Quintet with Joe Dorio (g). −MGN

MAXINE SULLIVAN
1911-1987

Ballads. A popular vocalist who also played valve trombone and flugelhorn. Among the more subtle and stylized musicians, Maxine Sullivan enjoyed major success in several decades as a jazz vocalist. She sang in clubs and on radio in Pittsburgh, then enjoyed what became a signature hit with the 1937 song "Loch Lomond," which was arranged by Claude Thornhill. She got national exposure for two years on CBS radio singing with her husband John Kirby's band in the late 30s; the show "Flow Gently Sweet Rhythm" was the only Black show on the radio network at that time. After touring with Benny Carter in 1941, she retired for a while in 1942, then made a comeback a few years later. She retired once more in 1954 but returned again in 1958, this time singing and playing valve trombone and flugelhorn. She did several festival dates and recorded in the 60s and 70s with the World's Greatest Jazz Band, Earl Hines, Ike Isaacs, Bob Wilber, and Dick Hyman. In the 80s, her popularity and profile continued to rise, and she made concept albums of Harold Arlen, Ted Koehler, and Jules Styne songs, plus a good date with the Scott Hamilton quartet. −RW

● **Tribute to Andy Razaf / DCC** 1956
1991 reissue of a super tribute to the master lyricist. −RW

Maxine / AUDIOPHILE 1975
Good date, some excellent lead vocals. −RW

Good Morning, Life! / AUDIOPHILE 1983
Nice sessions with Loonis McGlohen quartet. −RW

It Was Great Fun / AUDIOPHILE ca. 1983
Solid vocals, nice arrangements. −RW

Swingin' Sweet / CONCORD 1986
Successful meeting with Scott Hamilton (ts) Quintet. −RW

○ **The Music of Burton Lane / MOBILE FIDELITY** i 1986
1986 release. Sullivan makes excellent tribute work. −RW

Together / ATLANTIC i 1987
1987 release. Fine merger between Sullivan and Keith Ingram's (p) group. −RW

○ **Maxine Sullivan / RIFF (DUTCH IMPORT)**
A solid date with Ted Easton's sextet. −MGN

Maxine Sullivan and John Kirby / CIRCLE
Sullivan working with great bass player John Kirby. −RW

Uptown / CONCORD
Good workout with Scott Hamilton (ts) Quintet. −RW

SUN RA
b 1915

Big band, post-bop, early free, progressive big band, modern creative. Piano, bandleader, composer. Celestial traveller and master of the swing tradition, Sun Ra remains the most wonderfully confounding figure in the entire spectrum of jazz (or, make that music in general). Rocketing out of Chicago in the mid 50s, the Arkestra created sounds that defied their time and place, with perhaps a closer kinship to the great Black orchestras of the prewar years, than the then-current bop stylings. Already notable were the excellent line of soloists, the long-term members like Marshall Allen, Pat Patrick, and John Gilmore, acknowledged as a substantial influence upon John Coltrane. There were also the lesser-

known players, such as the brilliant Hobart Dotson and alto player James Spaulding. Even Ra's own keyboard work is fascinating, with electric piano and even primitive synthesizers popping up in the mix.

By the time *The Magic City* was released at the turn of the 60s, Ra had cut his earthly ties and began operations in the free-jazz territories, a pattern for better than the next decade and a half. Strengthing his usage of African lore, the Arkestra can clearly be seen as a forerunner of later groups such as the Art Ensemble of Chicago. When some were shocked to find Ra's eventual return to swing, we could safely say that once again, Sun Ra was way ahead of the "New Traditionalists." With the exhaustive Saturn catalog finally being unravelled, the time for the discovery of Sun Ra is here and now. −SA

● **Sun Song / DELMARK** 1956
Excellent early-period Ra from the 50s. −MGN

☆ **The Nubians of Plutonia / IMPULSE (SATURN?)** 1959
Madcap concept, outrageous music. −RW

Atlantis / SATURN-IMPULSE 1960
Sizzling, rambling jams and solos. −RW

We Are in the Future / SAVOY 1961
Good compilation. −RW

○ **Heliocentric Worlds of Sun Ra / ESP-DIS** 1965
Vols. 1 & 2. Two-disc masterpiece. −RW

Picture of Infinity / BLACK LION 1968
Some fine piano admidst the rumble. −RW

Solar Myth - Approach / AFFINITY 1970
Brilliant compositions, explosive solos. −RW

Astro-Black / SATURN-IMPULSE / DB 5 1972
First-rate, inspired chaos. −RW

○ **Space Is the Place / BLUE THUMB** 1972
Classic late-60s studio date. −MGN

Live at Montreux / INNER CITY 1976
Sprawling live set. −RW

● **Unity / HORO** 1977
Live at the Storyville, NYC. The Arkestra's best live album. Loaded with standards. Incredible musicianship. −MGN

Visions / STEEPLECHASE 1978
Just a super duo date with Sun Ra on piano, Walt Dickerson on vibes. −RW

Lanquidity / PHILLY JAZZ 1978
Sweeping, often maddening. −RW

○ **Strange Celestial Road / ROUNDER** 1980
All Ra is good Ra. −MGN

Sunrise in Different Dimensions / HAT ART 1980
Wonderful two-record set. With vintage swing cuts. −RW

Reflections in Blue / BLACK SAINT 1986
Rousing tribute, funk-swing cuts. −RW

Hours After / BLACK SAINT 1986
Good date only recently available in the US. −RW

○ **Live at Pit-In / DIW** 1988
Prototypical rowdy, vibrant Ra from 1988 set. −RW

Out There a Minute / ENIGMA-RESTLESS r 1990
Spotty sound, outrageous lyrics, inspired music. −RW

SUN SOUNDS ORCHESTRA

Post-bop, progressive big band, jazz-rock, world fusion. This group plays ethnic charts of instrumental composers from South Africa and South America. A true world-music jazz orchestra. −MGN

○ **Open the Doors / EASTLAWN**
The Detroit based big band plays jazzy treatments of South African township, highlife, and pop music. There are eight cuts, one an original by baritone saxophonist Rick Steiger. There is some uplifting music here. −MGN

SUPERBLUE

Post-bop, neo bop. Named after Freddie Hubbard tune. All-star band led by trumpeted arranger Don Sickler. Plays mainstream, post-bop blue note-type material. –MGN

○ **Superblue / CAPITOL**   i 1989
Top-flight octet includes Bobby Watson (as), Roy Hargrove (tpt), Mulgrew Miller (p). This group should have gotten more mileage out of its fine 1989 release. –RW

Superblue 2 / CAPITOL   1989
Nice followup with revamped personnel features Wallace Roney (tpt), Ralph Moore (ts), Rene Rosnes (p), and holdovers Bobby Watson (as), Don Sickler (tpt, conductor) impressive. –RW

SUPERSAX

Bop, progressive big band, instr-pop. Repertory band formed in 1972 by Med Flory and Buddy Clark that played classic Charlie Parker tunes and solos in unison. Their first album *Supersax Plays Bird* won a Grammy in 1973. They went on to record several other acclaimed albums in thr 70s and 80s, some with the L.A. Voices, others with Chubby Jackson. List of great players who've toured and/or recorded with them includes Warne Marsh, Conte Candoli. –RW

○ **Supersax Plays Bird / BLUE NOTE / DB 5**   1973
Their best all-round; 1991 reissue of Grammy-winning 1973 release! –RW

○ **Dynamite / MPS - PA USA**   ca. 1978
A ten-piece band plays glorified horn chants in the spirit of Charlie Parker. Has good, not great, arrangements, but excellent playing. Lanny Morgan (as), Don Menza (ts), and Frank Rosolino (tb) are included. Features seven standards, two by arranger Ned Flory. –MGN

● **Chasin' the Bird / POLYGRAM**   r 1980
Fine repertory band does faithful recreations of Parker tunes in swing/mainstream vein. –RW

Stone Bird / CBS   1989
1989 date keeps Bird tributes going. –RW

The Joy of Sax / PAIR
Not the best sound quality, but outstanding ensemble work. Solos good, though not especially dynamic. –RW

JOHN SURMAN   b 1944

Early free, modern creative. A striking player of multi-reeds and synthesizer, whose range, and mastery of the lower register and knowledge of harmonics, as well as his flexibility and arranging and composing skills, have made him a heralded musician on both sides of the Atlantic. His earliest professional collaboration was with Mike Westbrook in 1962, and he also played in some of Alexis Korner's early blues-rock bands. Surman won the best soloist award at the 1968 Montreux festival and in 1969 got his first major international recognition for his playing on John McLaughlin's *Extrapolation*, where he sparkled on both baritone and soprano. He led his own groups throughout the 70s, with the band SOS being particularly popular in the mid 70s, as Surman gradually worked electronics and synthesizers into his musical mix. Surman was part of Miroslav Vitous's quartet from 1979-1982, and later toured Australia with him in 1983, and returned there with vocalist Karen Krog in 1985. –RW

Anglo Sax / DERAM DES   1969
Very fresh. With sextet and small orchestra. –MGN

○ **Westering Home / ISLAND**   1972
Solo work from multi-faceted creative saxophonist –MGN

● **Morning Glory / ISLAND**   1973
Excellent all around. –RW

○ **S.O.S. / OGUN**   1975
Stormy, good lineup. –RW

○ **Upon Reflection / POLYGRAM**   1979
Some of his best playing for ECM. –RW

Amazing Adventures of Simon Simon / POL   1981
Excellent duets. –MGN

Such Winters of Memory / ECM   1982
W/ vocalist Karin Krog and percussionist Pierre Favre. –MGN

Private City / POLYGRAM   1987
An album with great sound and some good solos. –RW

Road to Saint Ives / POLYGRAM
Good solos, variable material quality. –RW

RALPH SUTTON   b 1922

Stride, boogie, swing. Sutton is among the last of the great traditional pianists. His career dates back to the early 40s, when he began playing with Jack Teagarden while still a college student. He later worked in a trio with Albert Nicholas, and was the intermission pianist at Eddie Condon's for eight years. He worked with Bob Scobey for a time, then was featured in 1963 at the first Dick Gibson Jazz Party. That would lead five years later to the formation of the World's Greatest Jazz Band, of which he was a founding member. He made a number of good releases in the 70s and 80s. –RW

○ **Last of the Whorehouse Piano Players / CHI-SOUND**
Stomping, throbbing piano the way it used to be. –RW

NEIL SWAINSON   b 1955

Post-bop, neo bop. Canadian bassist; unquestioned virtuoso. Plays mostly as a sideman in post-bop idiom. Starting to emerge as a writer. –MGN

○ **49th Parallel / CONCORD**   1987
Canadian bassist swings hard with Woody Shaw (tpt) –MGN

STEVE SWALLOW   b 1940

Post-bop, jazz-rock, M-base, modern creative. Bass, composer. Swallow ranks as one of the innovators on the electric bass, someone who's redefined the instrument and actually approached it as a totally different animal from its acoustic counterpart. Swallow changed the fingering system and played it like a guitar, and also sought out situations and songs where the electric bass was the requisite instrument. He joined Paul Bley's trio in the 60s, then worked with George Russell, Jimmy Giuffre, and Art Farmer before joining Stan Getz's group from 1965-1967, then participating in Gary Burton's radical ensemble from 1967-1970. This quartet was a forerunner of true fusion group, playing jazz, rock, and country in seamless mix and emphasizing electric rather than acoustic context. This experience led Swallow to give up the acoustic bass. He's worked extensively with Mike Gibbs and Carla Bley in the 70s and 80s, and has also become a prolific composer, with works recorded by Bley, Burton, Gibbs, and Chick Corea, among others. –RW

Home / ECM / DB 5   ca. 1980
Interesting concept with poetry from Robert Creeley. –RW

Carla / WATT   ca. 1987
This is a sextet with a three-piece string ensemble playing eight cuts with a progressive focus. All are originals by Steve Swallow. –MGN

○ **Swallow / WATT**   ca. 1991
All nine cuts were written by this premier electric bass guitarist and performed by a sextet with guests Gary Burton (vib) and John Scofield (g). Swallow finally steps out as a leader in the progressive mode. –MGN

HARVIE SWARTZ   b 1948

Jazz-rock. Bandleader, composer, and bassist Swartz has worked with the group Urban Earth and recorded with Sheila Jordan, Mike Stern, and others. –RW

○ **Underneath It All / GRAMAVISION**   ca. 1980
This bassist's debut album is with Ben Aranov on piano and John D'Earth on trumpet. This is challenging music, approaching fusion. All selections are Swartz's originals. His later albums don't quite match up, but this is virtuoso. His best is on the way. –MGN

SWINGLE SINGERS

Jazz-pop. Vocal group started by Ward Lamar Swingle. Swingle, who also was a pianist and alto saxophonist, formed a group to improve his sightreading abilities; the Swingle Singers did fugues and madrigals and proved a surprise hit. Swingle worked with Christiane Legrand, the sister of composer/conductor Michel Legrand. −RW

○ **Folk Song Album / ATLANTIC**
One of their most interesting and intriguing albums. −RW

GABOR SZABO   b 1936

Early free, jazz-rock. Guitar, composer. Though he didn't come to America until he was nearly 20, Hungarian guitarist Gabor Szabo has still been a successful contributor to several jazz groups and sessions. He made his first impact as a member of Chico Hamiliton's groups and later worked with Gary McFarland and Charles Lloyd. He co-led a group with Cal Tjader and McFarland in 1968-1969, then did some recording in which Lena Horne was the featured vocalist. Szabo led other West Coast bands in the 70s, among them a fusion/jazz-rock unit Perfect Circle in 1975, and later recorded with Chick Corea. −RW

● **The Sorcerer / MCA**   ca. 1967
Excellent playing; gypsy influences; 1990 reissue. −RW
Jazz Mysticism/Exotica / DCC
Good sextet performances. W/ Chick Corea (k). −RW
○ **Greatest Hits / MCA**   COMP
Good collection of his better 60s cuts for Impulse. −RW

LEW TABACKIN   b 1940

Bop, post-bop, progressive big band. Tenor sax, flute. While certainly a good tenor saxophonist, Lew Tabackin is known more as one of jazz's finest flutists, an excellent soloist and strong accompanist. He moved to New York in 1965 and worked with Maynard Ferguson, Clark Terry, the Thad Jones-Mel Lewis big-band, Joe Henderson, and several combos before starting his own trio in 1968-1969. Following a tour of Switzerland, a jazz workshop in Hamburg, and a stint as featured soloist with the Danish Radio Orchestra, Tabackin married pianist Toshiko Akiyoshi and toured Japan with her in the early 70s. They moved to Los Angeles in 1972 and began a series of workshops. Their workshop big-band evolved into the Akiyoshi-Tabackin big-band, one of the decade's finest. Tabackin alternated big-band and session work in the 70s and early 80s, with he and Akiyoshi moving back to New York in 1982, the same year he won *DOWN BEAT*'s critics poll on flute. Later he and Akiyoshi began their own label, Ascent Records. Among his best recent releases was a 1983 session with Freddie Hubbard titled *Sweet Return.* −RW
Tabackin / INNER CITY   1974
Recorded in Japan with with bass and drums only, this album includes four standards and one apiece from leader, Toshiko Akiyoshi, and Sir Roland Hanna (p). Without a piano, Tabackin has more room to breathe. −MGN
● **Tenor Gladness / INNER CITY**   ca. 1976
Dueling tenors with Warne Marsh. Six originals were written by the principles or Toshiko Akiyoshi. It is a bit progressive, and a thoroughly satisfying date from two virtuosos. −MGN
○ **Dual Nature / INNER CITY**   ca. 1976
Tabackin on flute (he is unbelievable), alto, and tenor sax, with the Don Friedman Trio. Tunes are from Tabackin, Toshiko Akiyoshi, Bill Mays. Also included: three standards. Tabackin is on sax on one side and flute on the other. There is some astounding musicianship from all. −MGN
○ **Rites of Pan / INNER CITY**   1977
1977-1978. Tabackin here is on flute alone with the Toshiko Trio. This is deep harmonic music from the participant's pens as well as some from Dizzie Gillespie, Fats Waller, and Kurt Weill. The flute is startling, but for open ears. −MGN

Desert Lady / CONCORD   1989
Better-known as coleader of Akiyoshi/Tabackin big band; Lew Tabackin (sax) show's he's a fine soloist as well. 1989 session. CD version has two bonus cuts. −RW
Let the Tape Roll / RCA (JAPAN)
Excellent (very-hard-to-find) date with Donald Byrd (tpt) and Duke Pearson (p). −RW

JAMAALADEEN TACUMA   b 1956

Neo bop, modern creative. Premier electric bassist, who became most known for his stint with Ornette Coleman's Prime Time Band. Extremely influenced by the style and technique of Stanley Clarke and Jaco Pastorius, Tacuma is one of the fastest and cleanest players, able to rip off rapid-fire passages, and huge, thick accompanying lines, and essentially play like a guitarist. His releases outside of Ornette Coleman's band Prime Time have largely been disappointing. −RW
● **Show Stopper / GRAMAVISION**   1982
1982-1983. The five-piece electric band for electric bassist shows many positive and eclectic forces rooted in jazz but not stuck in the past. Includes "Bird of Paradise" with the Ebony String Quartet. Title track with Olu Dara and Julius Hemphill is a treat of all-out contempo-bop. Other cameos are by Blood Ulmer on guitar and Cornell Rochester on drums. This is a fun album. −MGN
○ **Music World / GRAMAVISION**   1986
This is more so-called "avant-pop," with oriental themes played by Latin musicians. It includes Pharoah Sanders's "The Creator Has a Master Plan" with Leon Thomas on vocals. It's modern to the max. −MGN

HORACE TAPSCOTT

Post-bop, early free, progressive big band, neo bop, modern creative. Los Angeles's cultural hero. Leader of the UGMAA (Underground Musicians and Artists Alliance). Post-bop and creative pianist, composer, arranger, and band leader (big and small). A delicate or dense improviser. −MGN
○ **The Dark Tree / HAT ART**   i 1989
An album of composer's solid music with Arthur Blythe (as). A reissue. −MGN

BUDDY TATE   b 1913

Swing, big band, bop, cool, blues-jazz. One of the living prototypes of Texas tenor saxophone, Buddy Tate earned his spurs playing in territory bands before joining Count Basie's Orchestra in 1939, replacing the legendary Herschel Evans. He spent nine years with Basie, then worked with Lucky Millinder, Hot Lips Page, and Jimmy Rushing's Savoy band before getting the chance to take up residency at the Celebrity Club in Harlem. While spending 21 years there, Tate did plenty of recording and touring with swing and bop veterans. He continues performing today, playing with the robust, booming tone, quiet swing, and excellent style that has made him a master saxophonist. −RW
○ **Swinging Like Tate / POLYGRAM**   1958
Dynamic, hot solos. Prototypical Kansas City stomping set with Papa Jo Jones on drums. −RW
○ **Wild Women Don't Get the Blues / CANDID**   1960
Nancy Harrow (v) romps while Tate shows how to play behind a singer. −RW
● **Tate-A-Tate / OJC**   r 1961
A quintet date with Clark Terry (tpt), Tommy Flanagan (p) Trio. −MGN
And His Buddies / CHIAROSCURO   1973
Fine 70s set with Tate and Swing-era legends. −RW
Kansas City Woman / BLACK LION   1974
Outstanding solos. −RW
Meets Dollar Brand / CHIAROSCURO   1977
Most unusual pairing that clicks nicely. −RW
○ **Hard Blowin' / MUSE**   1978

Straightahead, pounding cuts. –RW

Muse All-Stars / MUSE   1978
This is a great jumping set with Arnett Cobb (s), and Eddie Vinson (tpt). –RW

○ **Ballad Artistry / SACKVILLE**   1981
1981 date with the Ed Bickert (g) Trio. Sweet. –MGN

Ballad Artistry of Buddy Tate / SACKVILLE   1981
Accurate title. –RW

Great Buddy / CONCORD   1981
Versatile outing, with Tate also on baritone and clarinet. –RW

Scott's Buddy / CONCORD   1981
One of his mentors shows Scott Hamilton (ts) how you play the blues. –RW

For Sentimental Reasons / OPEN SKY   1982
More outside than usual, yet still lots of blues. –RW

ART TATUM   1910-1956

Swing, bop, hard-bop. The most prodigiously gifted pianist to turn his talent to jazz was born with gravely impaired eyesight and received his musical training at an institution for the blind in his native Toledo. Musicians who heard him there as early as 1924 claim he was as amazing then as when he became visible on the national jazz scene in the early 30s.
He made his first records as accompanist to singer Adelaide Hail, but that was his last job working for someone else: he was a soloist to the manner born. Playing on 52nd Street and in nightclubs throughout the US, he made his first and only trip abroad to England in 1938, but even there he performed not in concert but on the vaudeville circuit. In 1943 he formed a trio with Tiny Grimes on guitar, and Slam Stewart on bass — the format that brought him his greatest popular success. Even so, it wasn't until Norman Granz took him under his wing, just three years before his untimely death, that Tatum was recorded under proper auspices, with the care an artist of his stature deserved. Tatum's technique was staggering and rivalled that of the greatest classical virtuosos, but unlike them, he was able to give free rein to his imagination and fully exercise his phenomenal rhythmic sense. But even when he unleashed a torrent of notes, the melody was kept in focus. Tatum loved to "battle" with other pianists and was as likely as not to smother hornplayers who sat in with him. Yet he could be a marvelous accompanist when he wanted, to singers he liked or to a hornsman (like Ben Webster) who was not a technical whiz but a great melodist. And Tatum was a master of the blues. His audacious harmonic inventions had considerable influence on Charlie Parker, who listened to him with great attention during a New York stay in 1939. Tatum was a phenomenon. –RW

○ **Classic Piano Solos (1934-39) / GRP**   1934
Simply brilliant, remarkable playing. –RW

● **Solos (1940) / MCA**   1940
Incredible. Should be required listening for all pianists. –RW

Complete Capitol Recordings / CAPITOL   194?
Vols. 1 & 2. Masterful cuts from 40s, mostly solo with four trio tunes. –RW

20th Century Piano Genius / POLYGRAM / DB 5   1955
1986 release of immaculate solos. –RW

Get Happy / BLACK LION   195?
Nice, spry playing. –RW

At the Piano / GNP CRESCENDO
As usual, incredible solos. –RW

○ **God Is in the House / POLYDOR / DB 5**
As good as it gets with Tatum, which says a lot. –RW

★ **Pablo Group Masterpieces / PABLO**   COMP
This is an absolute essential. Since Tatum was well-recorded solo, his group efforts are all that much more important. All here are standards (80 cuts here), some of them alternate and previously unissued takes. Mates included Louis Bellson, Red Callender, Buddy DeFranco, Harry Edison, Roy Eldridge,

Lionel Hampton, Jo Jones, Barney Kessel, and Ben Webster. –MGN

ART TAYLOR   b 1929

Bop, hard-bop, post-bop. A first-rate drummer, able to absorb the classic timekeeping-style of swing, then adjust to changing roles instituted by coming of bop and hard-bop. Taylor's earliest jobs were with Howard McGhee and Coleman Hawkins in the 50s, and his first recording session came with Hawkins. He later toured with Buddy DeFranco, then worked with Bud Powell's trio twice and George Wallington's trio and quintet during the mid and late 50s. He also had stints in that decade with Miles Davis and the Donald Byrd/Gigi Gryce group, as well as Thelonious Monk. He became a familiar figure in recording sessions at Prestige, Blue Note, and other labels in the 60s, at one point recording with John Coltrane, Jackie McLean, Hank Mobley, and Lee Morgan. He moved to Europe in 1963, and worked with various expatriates and/or musicians on tour. –RW

● **Taylor's Wailers / PRESTIGE**   1956
First-rate set. –RW

○ **A.T.'s Delight / CAPITOL**   1960
Early-60s definitive sides from this drummer and group known as Taylor's Wailers. –MGN

BILLY TAYLOR   b 1921

Big band, bop, cool. Piano. Few people have served jazz more effectively, as a writer, broadcaster, performer, and composer, than Billy Taylor. His many other activities have tended to overshadow his solid playing, which reflects both the influence of being tutored at one time by Art Tatum and his knowledge of and love for the blues and gospel. A fluid two-handed player, Taylor's rhythms in his prime could almost bowl you over, while his sweeping left-hand statements were immaculate and impressive. Taylor met Tatum and other Harlem legends during trips as a teenager from his North Carolina home. He moved to New York in the early 40s, then worked with Ben Webster, Dizzy Gillespie, Stuff Smith, and several others. He led the house rhythm section at Birdland in 1951, then had his own trio throughout the remainder of the decade. –RW

Cross Section / OJC   1953
1953 & 1954. Beautiful playing, limited edition set. –RW

With Candido / OJC   1954
Excellent trio date. Candido provides Afro-Latin flair. –RW

○ **The Billy Taylor Touch / ATLANTIC**   i 1957

☆ **With Four Flutes / RIVERSIDE**   i 1959
W/ Frank Wess, Herbie Mann, Jerome Richardson, and Phil Bodner. –MGN

Sleeping Bee / PA-USA   ca. 1969
Recorded with Ben Tucker on bass and Grady Tate on drums, this album includes four Taylor originals and four standards. Taylor is always at the top of the heap. –MGN

● **Wish I Knew How ... / TOWER**   196?
Wish I Knew How it Would Feel to be Free. Recorded with a trio and features Taylor's immortal song bearing the title of the album, several pop and jazz standards, Clare Fischer's "Morning" and "Pensativa," Taylor's "CAG." Bandmates featured are Ben Tucker (b) and Grady Tates (d). –MGN

○ **Live at Storyville / WEST 54**   1977
Recorded in New York City with drummer Grady Tate and bassist Victor Gaskin, this album includes classic standards and three Taylor originals including "I Wish I Knew ..." It ranges from modern to bop to ballads. This is standard virtuosity from Taylor — you expect nothing less. –MGN

Solo / TAYLOR-MADE   1988
Noted authority and journalist shows he's a super soloist. –RW

White Nights & Jazz in Leningrad / TAYLOR-MADE   1988
Latter-day piano date, fine solos. –RW

You Tempt Me / TAYLOR-MADE

Not so good as some of his other material. Fine melodies, nice solos. –RW

CECIL TAYLOR   ♭1929

Early free, modern creative. To say that pianist Cecil Taylor is a revolutionary musician is an understatement. Since the late 50s he has changed the method by which jazz improvisation can be approached as much as John Cage has influenced contemporary sound and concept. In lieu of Taylor's free-flowing, take-no-prisoners style, he has a recognizable voice that emphasizes chord clusters, connected phrases, and bluesy, dense ruminations to form an endless string of original ideas.

For those perhaps intimidated with the music of a firebrand and maverick, try his early albums on Contemporary, or the *N.Y. City R&B* album. Later albums with his combo, the 'Unit,' or his revelatory solo albums impart much of his knowledge and uncanny sixth sense as a true original.

Taylor has also another weapon in his arsenal. He is a wonderful poet who uses words in ethnic tongues and dialects in performance, melded with martial arts dance movements to creat a lasting impression of visual imagery along with the very potent music he creates. –MGN

Jazz Advance / CAPITOL   1956
1991 reissue of super set, one of Taylor's best groups with Steve Lacy (sax). –RW

Looking Ahead / OJC   1958
Prophetic title; Taylor, Earl Griffith (vib), and comrades beckon to the future. –RW

○ **Unit Structures / CAPITOL / DB 5**   1966
The place to start checking out Taylor's amazing style. –RW

Conquistador / BLUE NOTE / DB 5   1966
Smashing piano, intense compositions. –RW

☆ **Great Concert of Cecil Taylor / PRESTIGE / DB 5**   1969
Boxed set with Taylor in searing live concert alongside Sam Rivers (sax) and Jimmy Lyons (as). Three discs of amazing playing. –RW

Akisakila / TRIO PA   1973
Powerhouse two-disc set, done live in Tokyo. –RW

● **Spring of 2 Blue Jays / UNIT CORE**   1973
Expansion of soaring trio into quartet. –RW

Silent Tongues / ARISTA   1974
Lambasting, attacking piano solos. –RW

Dark to Themselves / ENJA   1976
1990 reissue of pulsating set. –RW

Air Above Mountains ... / CANDID / DB 5   1976
Air Above Mountains (Buildings Within). Bursting, dynamic piano solos. –RW

3 Phasis / NEW WORLD / DB 5   1978
Lightning strikes on piano. –RW

Live in the Black Forest / MPS / DB 5   1978
Typically sweeping piano solos. –RW

● **One Too Many Salty Swift ... / HAT ART / DB 5**   1978
With one of his greatist groups in a powerful performance, this was the Unit at its peak. –MGN

○ **Unit / NEW WORLD**   ca. 1978
A sextet, this is as close to as definitive an ensemble as Taylor has launched. With Jimmy Lyons (sax), Raphe Malik (tpt), Ramsey Ameen (violin), Sirone (b), and R. Shannon Jackson (d). This runs 60 min. on vinyl, including a 30-min. "Holiday En Masque." This is the one folks. –MGN

○ **Historic Concerts / SOUL NOTE**   1979
Great duo with Max Roach (d). –RW

● **Fly, Fly, Fly, Fly, Fly / MPS - PALUSA**   ca. 1980
A solo piano album that defines Taylor's individuality and does indeed fly. Diamond Award Winner in 1981. –MGN

For Olim / SOUL NOTE   1986

One of his greatest solo works. –RW

In Florescence / A&M   1990
1990 set that welcomes him back to major label. –RW

MARTIN TAYLOR

Cool. British acoustic guitarist known for work with Stephane Grappelli, Neo-classicist and folk tendencies. –MGN

○ **Skye Boat / CONCORD**   1978
1978 mainstream/swing, pleasant. –RW

JACK TEAGARDEN   1905-1964

Swing, big band. A jazz immortal, superb trombonist, and one of the real class acts and humorists in the music's long history. No one had ever so easily and completely mastered the trombone prior to Teagarden, and precious few since have had his total control over the instrument. He played difficult phrases, tricky lines, incredible solos, and pithy licks with such ease that his excellent, charming vocal abilities were thoroughly overshadowed. Teagarden's reputation began to grow when he played in Peck Kelley's band in 1921. Teagarden then worked with Willard Robison, Doc Ross, and Ben Pollack, then spent five years with Paul Whiteman, becoming his principal soloist despite having little respect for most of what he was playing. Teagarden formed his own band in 1939 and spent the next seven years heading various groups, before joining Louis Armstrong's All Stars in 1946. He stayed until 1951, then for the rest of his life led different aggregations, and made many remarkable records. Many of Teagarden's innovations, among them varying the volume at which he played, using water-glass mutes, and revolutionizing the use of the slide, have become a mandatory part of the trombone vernacular. –RW

○ **King of the Blues Trombone / SONY SP**   1928
1928-1940.

● **Jack Teagarden & Pee Wee Russell / OJC**   1938
W/ Pee Wee Russell (cl). 1938 & 1940. Two titans of classic New Orleans style make great match. –RW

Varsity Drags / SAVOY   ca. 1940
Material not previously issued on album. Originally from Varsity Label 78s. Features vocalists David Allyn, Kitty Kallen, and Marianne Dunne. –MGN

☆ **Meet Me Where They Play the Blues / BETH**   ca. 1954
These ten tracks are from smaller-group sessions. Help here is from Kenny Davern (cl), Ed Hall (cl), Carl Kress (g), Walter Page (b), Jimmy McPartland (cnt), and Jo Jones (d). –MGN

100 Years from Today / GRU

Accent on Sound / FRESH SOUND

Jazz Original / BETHLEM

Tribute to Teagarden / PA-USA

● **The Indispensable / RCA-BLACK & WHITE**   COMP
1929-1933. With a wide variety of bands — Eddie Condon, Ben Pollack, Paul Whiteman, Budd Freeman, and others — this is a great overview of the trombonists carreer. There are several vocals on the 31 cuts and four alternate takes. –MGN

○ **That's a Serious Thing / RCA**   COMP
1929-1957.

CLARK TERRY   ♭1920

Swing, big band, bop, ballads, progressive big band. Trumpet, flugelhorn, vocals. A superior trumpeter and one of the first to introduce the flugelhorn as a legitimate second instrument for jazz brass players. Indeed, Terry's utilization of vocal effects on trumpet, plus his striking rhythmic abilities, have made him highly admired among his peers. He got his early experience playing in St. Louis bands, then in Navy bands during World War II, where he met and worked with Willie Smith. He spent a brief period with Lionel Hampton, then worked with Charlie Barnet, Count Basie, Duke Ellington, and Quincy Jones from the late 40s until 1960. He spent 12 years in the "Tonight Show" band, becoming one of the first Black musicians hired for that august group in the 60s. He's also done plenty of studio work, led a periodic big band, participated in many clinics and co-led a group with Bob Brookmeyer. –RW

● **Serenade to a Bus Seat / OJC** 1957
Topflight set with Johnny Griffin (ts) and the always memorable Wynton Kelly (p), Paul Chambers (b), Philly Joe Jones (d) as a rhythm section. –RW

Duke with a Difference / OJC 1957
Fine 70s tribute to Duke, wonderful solos. –RW

○ **In Orbit with Thelonious Monk / OJC** 1958
Terry shows he can fit into any setting, even with Monk's always arresting, unorthodox piano style. Date also has Sam Jones (b) and Philly Joe Jones (d). CD has bonus cut, 1988 reissue. –RW

Paris 1960 / SWING 1960
The inimitable Martial Solal on piano. –RW

Color Changes / CANDID 1960

○ **New York Sessions / FONTANA** 1961
Exciting 60s date, with Tubby Hayes (ts) immense. –RW

○ **Gingerbread Men / MAINSTREAM** 1966
W/ Bob Brookmeyer (tb) Quintet. This is a fine set, reissued recently. –RW

It's What's Happenin' / MCA 1967
Good mix of topicality, humor, and fine playing. MCA reissue a bit questionable. –RW

○ **Big B-A-D Band Live / VANGUARD** 1976
Live At Buddy's Place. Brassy, steamy sound. –RW

☆ **Live at Buddy's / VANGUARD** 1976
W/ 17-piece band, with the Wilkins Brothers. Terry's shining hour. –MGN

Out of Nowhere / VOGUE 1978
New release of more animated Terry session with Horace Parlan (p). –RW

Funk Dumplin's / MATRIX 1978
Humorous, yet has requisite jazz flavor. –RW

Mother ...! Mother ...! / PABLO 1979
This one is great, especially Zoot Sims (ts). –RW

Ain't Misbehavin' / PABLO 1979

Memories of Duke / OJC 1980
More homage to Duke Ellington. –RW

To Duke & Basie / RHINO 1986
Duos with Red Mitchell (b). –RW

Portraits / CHESKY 1989
Good playing, lesser lineup except for Lewis Nash (d). –RW

Having Fun / DELOS 1990
W/ saxophonist Red Holloway. The title says it all. –MGN

Live from the Village Gate / CHESKY i 1991
Some very fine recent Terry with excellent Jimmy Heath (d), good Pacquito D'Rivera (as). –RW

Live on 57th Street / BIG BEAR
More adventurous big-band cuts, very hard to find. –RW

Oscar Peterson Trio with Clark Terry / MERCURY
Kudos all around, especially Peterson (p) and Terry. –RW

BOB THIELE b 1922

Producer, songwriter. Bob Thiele was an amateur clarinetist and jazz radio annoucer before becoming the editor and publisher of *Jazz Magazine* from 1939 to 1941. From 1940-1948 he owned and operated the Signature record label, recording artists like Coleman Hawkins, Art Hodes, Pee Wee Russell, and James P. Johnson. He was a director for Coral Records in the 50s, and worked for both Dot Records and Roulette. In the late 60s, Thiel produced a number of albums on impulse, in particular those of John Coltrane, Oliver Nelson, Archie Shepp, and Pharoah Sanders. The studio group the Bob Thiel Collective was organized by veteran jazz producer Thiele. –JME

○ **Sunrise Sunset / CBS** 1991
Session linking several major level contemporary stars, notably David Murray (ts), John Hicks (p). Definitely has that studio flair, but is a solid date. –RW

JEAN "TOOTS" THIELEMANS b 1922

Swing, cool. Belgian harmonicist/guitarist. Influenced by Django Reinhardt, played with Benny Goodman and George Shearing. Composed the famous "Bluesette." Incredible bop-like facility on harmonica. Tendency towards sweet ballads. Also can play modally. –MGN

○ **Man Bites Harmonica / OJC** 1957
Early period. Definitive harmonicist from Belgium. –MGN

● **Captured Alive / CHOICE** 1975
Stunning interplay. W/ Joanne Brackeen (p) Trio. Find this one. - MGN

Apple Dimple / DENON 1986
Good date, Thielemans delightful. –RW

Aquarela Do Brasil / POLYGRAM 1987
Some Afro-Latin beats, nice solos. –RW

○ **Only Trust Your Heart / CONCORD** 1988
Bit to sentimental side, good playing. CD version has two prime cuts. –RW

Footprints / POLYGRAM 1989
1991 release. Mulgrew Miller (p) ups the stakes. –RW

Autumn Leaves / SOUL NOTE ca. 198?
More recent material, solid solos. –RW

Toots and Svend / A&M
Exquisite duets. –RW

○ **Silver Collection / POLYGRAM** COMP
Recent two-disc collection of his Verve cuts. –RW

GARY THOMAS b 1962

Neo bop, M-base. Strong young-lion saxophonist from Baltimore, whose reputation for aggressive, sprawling solos is becoming well known. Thomas is more in the hard-bop mainstream than some contemporaries, and has even recorded an album of standards. But his releases also include the use of synthesizers and sometimes veer into rock and funk. –RW

● **By Any Means Necessary / POLYGRAM** 1989
Aggressive, young-lion-led session with R&B, electronic elements. Thomas is an explosive, constantly growing improviser. –RW

Code Violations / RHINO 1989
Striking 1989 session; Thomas can be exciting one cut, exasperating the next. –RW

○ **While the Gate Is Open / POLYGRAM**
Despite some rough moments in his solos, this is worth checking out. Emblematic of new wave of 90s jazz types with one foot in other camps. –RW

LEON THOMAS b 1937

Big band, blues-jazz, ballads, soul jazz. Well-known, deep-throated vocalist who worked w/ Count Basie, Pharoah Sanders, and blues bands. Expert yodeler. –MGN

○ **Blues & the Soulful Truth / FLYING DUTCHMAN** r 1973
This is his best studio album. Contains many of his best numbers. –MGN

● **Facets / FLYING DUTCHMAN** COMP
A compilation of late-60s and early-70s material that is well put together. –MGN

RENE THOMAS b 1927

Post-bop. Highly revered as a techician and harmonic guitar genius. Limited recordings available domestically. A good model for study. –MGN

○ **Guitar Groove / JAZZLAND** i 1960

W/ J. R. Monterose (ts) –MGN

BARBARA THOMPSON
b 1944

Post-bop, early free. British saxophonist plays straightahead, neo-bop, fusion, or funk. Incredible soloist. Unrealized potential waiting for the right break. America would love her. –MGN

○ **Just Music / SPOTLITE** 1974
With Don Rendell 5. Rendell on clarinet, flute, soprano, and tenor sax. Thompson on flute, tenor, and soprano. With Peter Lemer Trio. Rendell writes the bulk of this. Nice interplay with bass and tenor saxophonists. Hard to peg — it's progressive and traditional at the same time. Nice album to find. –MGN

Pure Fantasy / VERA BRA ca. 1984
Quintet with husband John Hiseman (d). Goes from funk, Latin, and contemporary jazz, occasionally veering straightahead. "Mother Earth" suite fairly interesting. –MGN

● **Songs from the Center of the Earth / BLACK SUN** i 1991
1991 release, eyeopener from fine player and group. –RW

BOB THOMPSON

Post-bop, instr-pop. West Virginia pianist plays electric and acoustic in mostly dance/funk style. Also plays excellent modal a là McCoy Tyner. –MGN

○ **Morning Star / RAINBOW** ca. 1981
Shows this pianist in straightahead-to-modern program on three of his originals and three standards. "Juba" shows originality with a hat tip to McCoy Tyner. All trio cuts. –MGN

BUTCH THOMPSON
b 1943

Boogie, swing. Piano, clarinet. Butch Thompson is best known for his 12-year association with Garrison Keillor's "Prairie Home Companion" radio show from 1974, but his traditional jazz credentials as a pianist and clarinetist date from as far back as 1962, when he joined the Hall Brothers' New Orleans Jazz Band in Minneapolis/St. Paul. During his 20-year stint with this band he had the opportunity to play with many of New Orleans's most celebrated performers, including George Lewis, Kid Thomas Valentine, Pops Foster, Manuel Manetta, and Raymond Burke. In the 70s he toured with Boston's Black Eagle Jazz Band and worked with the New Orleans Ragtime Orchestra. More recently, Thompson has taken his King Oliver Centennial Band to festivals such as the Ascona in Europe and concentrated on making a series of recordings dedicated to the memory of New Orleans, Chicago, and Harlem jazz greats. –BR

Thompson's King Oliver Centennial Band / GHB 1988
Thompson has succeeded in creating a band that effectively celebrates the spirit of Oliver's Creole Jazz Band without indulging in note-for-note imitation. –BR

○ **Chicago Breakdown 88's / DARING** 1989
A tribute to Jelly Roll Morton and King Oliver during their Chicago "salad days," Thompson offers a dazzling selection of stomps, tangos, and blues ballads — his collaboration with Little Brother Montgomery (p) on "Sunday Rag" is a gem. –BR

Good Old New York 88's / DARING 1989
The Harlem stride style done to perfection. A judicious sampling of the work of Fats Waller, James P. Johnson, and Eubie Blake, done by a virtuoso. –BR

○ **New Orleans Joys - 88's / DARING** 1989
Thompson's Ode to Jelly Roll - masterful renditions of tunes associated with Morton in his early years, such as "The Naked Dance" and "The Crave." Butch's own "Ecuadorian Memories" and "Dink's Blues" complement this compliment to Jelly Roll Morton. –BR

DON THOMPSON
b 1940

Post-bop, cool, neo bop. Canadian bassist and pianist, well-known and respected sideman. Works frequently with Ed Bickert, Jim Hall, Terry Clarke, Barney Kessel. –MGN

○ **Country Place / PM** ca. 1975

A trio with Gene Perla (b) and Joe La Barbera (d) plays all Thompson originals. Sparks fly here. –MGN

Beautiful Friendship / CONCORD 1984
W/ John Abercrombie (g), Paul Chambers (b). Lush, expertly played. –RW

LUCKY THOMPSON
b 1916

Swing, bop, cool. Tenor sax, soprano sax.
Thompson got his stars playing with the Trenier Twins in the early 40s, then moved from Detroit to New York, where he had brief stints with many bands, among them Lionel Hampton's, Don Redman's, Billy Eckstine's, Lucky Millinder's, and Count Basie's, before he left for the West Coast in 1946. He recorded with Dizzy Gillespie and Charlie Parker, as well as Boyd Raeburn and the Stars of Swing band, before returning to Detroit in 1947, moving back to New York in 1948. Thompson got involved in R&B song publishing, recording, and writing, and also led a band at the Savoy before going back to full-time jazz playing in the mid 50s. He appeared on the classic Miles Davis *Walkin'*= session in 1954, later worked with Milt Jackson, Jo Jones, Quincy Jones, Oscar Pettiford, and several others. He *was a master at making definitive, searing statements, despite beginning with a softer tone than normal in the bop mode. A fine recording he made for Vanguard in 1954 has recently reappeared, entitled Quartet.* –RW

★ **Featuring Oscar Pettiford / JASMINE** 1956
Very neglected tenor on a super album, backed by great Pettiford (b). –RW

○ **Paris 1956 / SWING** 1956
Robust statement from a great player in overdrive. –RW

Brown Rose / XANADU ca. 195?
Both Thompson and Martial Solal (p) burn. –RW

○ **Lucky Strikes / OJC** 1963
Classic album from Detroit tenor saxophonist. –MGN

Body and Soul / NESSA 1970
One of his last recent releases and very valuable. –RW

MALACHI THOMPSON

Early free, neo bop, modern creative. Chicago trumpeter, extension of Lee Morgan or Freddie Hubbard. Known as a creative improviser, but plays tunefully. Member of Lester Bowie's Brass Fantasy, AACM, RA Ensemble. Not really a screamer, he plays bluesy tunes. –MGN

○ **The Seventh Son / RA** 1974
W/ larger ensemble. Varied approach with well-arranged compositional jazz. –MGN

● **Spirit / DELMARK**
Progressive Chicago trumpeter. Originals. A solid album. –MGN

SIR CHARLES THOMPSON
b 1918

Bop, hard-bop, post-bop. This pianist came up in the bop school of Bird and Diz, and he was able to keep up and even push his speed-demon compatriots. –MGN

● **Takin' Off / DELMARK** 1945
This is a reissue of the classic Apollo series. The 1945 and 1947 sessions feature legendary bands with Charlie Parker, Dexter Gordon, Buck Clayton, Danny Barker, J. C. Heard, Joe Newman, Freddie Green, Pete Brown, and Shadow Wilson playing sixteen cuts, seven previously unissued. This is prime bop. –MGN

○ **And His All Stars / APOLLO** i 1950
W/ Charlie Parker (as), Dexter Gordon (ts) and Leo Parker (bar sax). –MGN

CLAUDE THORNHILL
1909-1965

Big band, progressive big band. Piano, arranger. Among the more gifted and distinctive arrangers in jazz history, Claude Thornhill found a way to combine dance-based arrangements and improvisational elements, and also did some innovative things in utilizing different instrumentation (notably French horns) and space and time within his compositions. Thornhill had conservatory training but got his practical experience in Midwest territory bands before moving to New York in the 30s. He worked briefly for Paul Whiteman, Benny Goodman, and Ray Noble, then did extensive session work as an arranger, including doing songs for Billie Holiday and providing a hit setting for Maxine Sullivan with "Loch Lomond" in 1937. He later toured with Sullivan in 1937-1938, then took over a West Coast band that had been headed by Gil Evans, coleading it with vocalist Skinny Ennis. Thornhill had his own band from 1940-1942, with Evans rejoining him in 1941. He re-formed his band in 1946, this time with a group that included Lee Konitz and Red Rodney. In 1948 Thornhill, Evans, Konitz, Gerry Mulligan and Miles Davis among others, participated in the landmark "Birth of the Cool" sessions; these dates helped pave the way for whole West Coast school that took its lead from the softer, more-subtle Thornhill/Evans approach. Thornhill continued to head dance-oriented bands into the 50s and 60s. −RW

☆ **Claude Thornhill and His Orchestra / HINDSIGHT** 1947
One of the greatest bands. −MGN

● **Real Birth of the Cool / COLUMBIA** 194?
A formative date featuring Thornhill's band doing "cool" arrangements back in early- and mid-40s. Has never been widely available in America, even the import. −RW

Best of Big Bands / CBS COMP
Nice collection of his label cuts. −RW

Claude Thornhill / HEP COMP
Overview of his material. −RW

○ **Tapestries / AFFINITY** COMP
A comprehensive, two-disc set of his prime cuts, with 17 arranged by Gil Evans. −RW

CLIFFORD THORNTON b 1936

Post-bop, early free. Thornton plays trumpet and trombone in addition to being a composer and bandleader. A very staunch progressivist, and rarely recorded. −MGN

○ **Ketchaoua / BYG-ACTUEL / DB 5** 1969
Paris studio date with Fire-breathers Archie Shepp (sax), Grachan Moncur III (tb), Dave Burrell (p), and Sonny Murray (d). −MGN

Communications Network / THIRDWORLD 1972
Live at NYC's Festival of African-American Music. Two long pieces, one with L. Shankar (violin) and the other with poet Jayne Cortez. Potent. −MGN

● **The Gardens of Harlem / JCOA** 1974
Definitive, brilliant creative statement from visionary trombonist with the Jazz Composers Orchestra. A must-have for progressive music listeners. −MGN

HENRY THREADGILL b 1944

Early free, progressive big band, modern creative. Whether it's for arranging, writing, or playing, alto-saxophonist Henry Threadgill ranks among the best contemporary musicians operating in the improvisational sphere. He played in gospel and blues bands growing up, and then joined Muhal Richard Abrams's experimental band in the early 60s and was a founding member of the AACM. His trio Air was one of the greatest and most versatile bands of the 70s, doing free pieces, blues-tinged originals, and ballads. Since their demise, Threadgill has headed a combo and also worked with other musicians, notably Oliver Lake. He's a master at incorporating R&B, blues, gospel, and swing voicings into his pieces, and balancing freedom with discipline in his group's performances. −RW

X-75 - Vol. 1 / NOVUS ca. 1979
Four bassists predominate (Hopkins, Rufus Reid, Smith, and Leonard Jones) in this pre-sextet recording. Amina Myers (p) and Joseph Jarmen (reeds) also show. Unrestrained freedom and beauty. −MGN

○ **Just the Facts / ABOUT TIME / DB 5** r 1983
Just the Facts and Pass the Bucket. Incorporates wealth of black music influences under the improvisatory umbrella. −RW

○ **When Was That? / ABOUT TIME** r 1983
Alternately funny, funky, and ferocious. −RW

Subject to Change / ABOUT TIME / DB 5 1986
Both blistering ensemble work and dynamic solos. −RW

★ **You Know the Number / RCA-JIVE/NOVUS** 1986
A wonderful release with quirky, jerky cuts; resolute, superb solos. −RW

Easily Slip into Another World / NOVUS 1988
Captivating session. −RW

○ **Rag, Bush, & All / NOVUS** 1989
Threadgill takes things up a notch, plus some dazzling cello from Diedre Murray. −RW

○ **Spirit of Nuff ... Nuff / BLACK SAINT / DB 5** i 1991
The latest Threadgill armada proves every bit as appealing as his past brigades. −RW

THREE SOUNDS

Post-bop, ballads, soul jazz. A group formed by pianist Gene Harris in the late 50s that evolved from original Four Sounds, a 1957 quartet. The trio was enormously popular in late 50s, early and mid 60s, despite the fact much of its music was in light cocktail-lounge or soul-jazz mode. Actually Harris was a fine bluesy stylist, and revisionist looks at Three Sounds material, especially a 1963 release with Anita O'Day, have resulted in some observers admitting they overlooked or undervalued this group. −RW

○ **Introducing the Three Sounds / BLUE NOTE** 1958
Excellent debut. −MGN

Feelin' Good / BLUE NOTE i 1960
Here We Come / BLUE NOTE i 1960

● **Babe's Blues / BLUE NOTE** ca. 197?
Their best. Gene Harris(p), Andy Simpkins, (b) and Bill Dowdy (d). −MGN

STEVE TIBBETTS b 1954

Jazz-rock, world fusion. Minneapolis-based contemporary guitarist whose urban-landscape fusion is looked upon as a totally original approach to sound. Master multi-track recording artist. −MGN

○ **Yr / POLYGRAM / DB 5** 1980
Reissued on ECM from original independent label release in Minneapolis. A perfect study item in regards to recording techniques and musicality. Guitarist has no boundaries on this insistently creative set. −MGN

● **Northern Song / POLYGRAM** 1981
With percussionist Anderson, Tibbetts explores urban landscape, especially on "Nine Doors/Breathing Space." Tibbetts is reminiscent of Ralph Towner. −MGN

Safe Journey / ECM ca. 1983
Five-piece. Ten compositions. All very arresting. −MGN

Exploded View / ECM ca. 1986
With larger ensemble. Featuring folk singer Claudia Schmidt. Three voice, tabla, bass, Marc Anderson's percussion, and Tibbetts's guitars, mbira, and tape loops. −MGN

TIMELESS ALL STARS

Post-bop, neo bop. Pianist Cedar Walton's all-star friends play post-MJQ music. Sometimes heavy, deep, and solemn, sometimes brightly swinging. Includes Curtis Fuller (tb), Bobby Hutcherson (vib), Harold Land (ts), Billy Higgins (d). −MGN

● **It's Timeless / TIMELESS** 1982
Live from the Keystone Korner in San Francisco. Definitive group jazz of the 80s. −MGN

○ **Timeless Heart / TIMELESS** 1983
Their debut. Sextet with Curtis Fuller (tb), Harold Land (ts)

and Bobby Hutcherson (vib). Cedar Walton prominent on piano. –MGN

BOBBY TIMMONS   1935-1974

Post-bop, soul jazz. Perhaps the finest gospel-tinged pianist ever (with exception of Horace Silver), and a major mover in the funk school of jazz. A Philadelphia native, Timmons began to get noticed in the late 50s through his work with Kenny Dorham, Chet Baker, Sonny Stitt, Maynard Ferguson, then attained jazz stardom through two stints with Art Blakey's Jazz Messengers in 1958-1959 and 1960-1961, plus one year with Cannonball Adderley in 1959-1960. For the rest of his life, Timmons led either trios or small combos, where his merger of blues feeling, gospel chording, and jazz timing were extremely popular. His two most famous pieces in gospel/funk style were "Dis Here" and "Dat Dere," both of which he penned while with Cannonball. Timmons also picked up the vibes in the mid 60s. –RW

● **This Here Is Bobby Timmons / OJC**   1960
Trio with Sam Jones (b) and Jimmy Cobb (d). This pianist's single best album. –MGN

○ **Workin' Out / PRESTIGE**   1964
One of many excellent soul-jazz Prestige dates. –RW

The Soul Man / PRESTIGE   1966
Plenty of funk, blues, and soul-jazz, plus great piano. –RW

○ **Live at the Connecticut Jazz Party / EARLY BIRD**   1981
A great reissue of classic hard bop with gospel touches date. Sonny Red (as) wails, Timmons is vibrant. –RW

○ **Moanin' / MILESTONE**   COMP
Compilation of five different albums 1960-1963. Great collection and collectable. –MGN

KEITH AND JULIE TIPPETT   b 1947

Early free, progressive big band, jazz-rock, modern creative. A British husband-and-wife performing team who've recorded with both jazz and rock groups. Keith Tippett led a sextet in the 60s and wrote a piece "Septober Energy" that was ultimately performed by the 50-piece orchestra Centipede. He later led a free ensemble called Ovary Lodge, worked in piano duos with Stan Tracey and Howard Riley, and toured with a septet. Julie worked with Keith in Ovary Lodge, sang in Brian Auger's rock and jazz-rock group, and has recorded with John Stevens and Bobby Bradford as well as with Keith. –RW

● **Sunset Glow / UTOPIA**   1975
Exploratory vocalist at her best and most accessible. With English and South African musicians. –MGN

○ **Frames / OGUN**   1978
A tour-de-force project with Ark Big Band, strings, horns and vocals. –MGN

CAL TJADER   1925-1982

Post-bop, Latin. Vibist. Tjader may have been the finest non-Latin bandleader and player to ever achieve fame in Latin-jazz circles. His groups, particularly those of the early 60s with Willie Bobo or the late 50s with Mongo Santamaria, never failed to hit the right groove, and Tjader's solos were always solidly in the spirit. His mother was a pianist, and Tjader played in the late 40s and early 50s with Dave Brubeck, and joined George Shearing in 1953-1954. After meeting bassist Al McKibbon, who sparked his emerging interest in Latin music, Tjader began to immerse himself in this style. Throughout the 50s, 60s, and 70s, Tjader's groups made numerous excellent Latin-jazz releases, as well as an occasional mainstream outing. He continued that pattern into the 80s and, at the time of his death, had well over 40 albums in print. –RW

○ **Tjader Plays Mambo / OJC**   1954
First-rate example of Tjader's prowess with traditional Latin forms. –RW

Mambo with Tjader / OJC   1954
1987 reissue of super session. –RW

Mas Ritmo Caliente / FANTASY   1955
Great date w/ wonderful violinist/saxist Jose Silva. –RW

Latin Kick / OJC   1956
1991 reissue of prime session. First-rate Latin-jazz. –RW

Jazz at the Blackhawk / OJC   1957
Expressive playing, pretty basic Afro-Latin Tjader groove. W/ Vince Guaraldi (p), Gene Wright (b), and Al Torre (d). –RW

Concert by the Sea - Vols. 1 & 2 / FANTASY   1959

○ **Monterey Concerts / PRESTIGE**   1959
This is a wonderful pairing of 1959 concert-by-the-sea dates with Mongo Santamaria (conga) and Willie Bobo (per) sessions. –RW

☆ **Night at the Blackhawk / OJC**   1959
1987 reissue from great period, with Bobo (per) and Santamaria (conga). –RW

Sona Libre / POLYGRAM   r 1963
Fine 60s set from Verve years. –RW

★ **Soul Sauce / POLYGRAM**   1964
Hugely popular release with Bobo, Donald Byrd (tpt), and Kenny Burrell (g). –RW

● **El Sonido Nuevo/New Soul Sound / VERVE**   1966
Riveting Latin jazz, Eddie Palmeiri (k) in high gear. –RW

○ **Primo / FANTASY**   ca. 1970
The frenetic Charlie Palmieri (k) joins Tjader. –RW

Breathe Easy / FANTASY   1977
More straight jazz with Hank Jones (p). –RW

● **La Onda Va Bien / CONCORD**   1979
Good date. Grammy winner and deservedly so. –RW

Gozame! Pero Ya / CONCORD   1980
Nice session. –RW

Shining Sea / CONCORD   1981
Beautiful playing by Hank Jones (p), more straight jazz than Latin. –RW

Heat Wave / CONCORD   1982
Carmen McRae steals honors on vocals. Sparkling vocals and vibes. –RW

Good Vibes / CONCORD   1983
The final session, a fine adios. –RW

○ **Bamboleate / TICO**
Eddie Palmieri (p) is amazing. –RW

Latin + Jazz Equals / DCC
Wonderful performances with Armando Peraza (per), compiled on disc. –RW

Tambu / FANTASY
W/ Donald Bryd (tpt). Fine collaboration between two prominent Latin-jazz players. –RW

● **Greatest Hits - Vols. 1 & 2 / FANTASY**   COMP
Nice collection of his strongest Latin jams. –RW

CHARLES TOLLIVER   b 1942

Hard-bop, post-bop, early free, progressive big band, neo bop. High-powered and fleet-fingered trumpeter whose ability is second to none. Specializes in post-bop modal forms. One of a handful of great composers. –MGN

● **The Ringer / ARISTA - FREEDOM**   ca. 1969
Includes five Tolliver originals with the Stanley Cowell Trio. All the cuts are important, but "Plight" and "On the Nile" are particularly gripping. Cowell solos marvelously. –MGN

Music Inc. / STRATA EAST   1970
First document of progressive big band. 17 pieces. Famous works "Ruthie's Heart," "On the Nile" and "Departure." –MGN

○ **Grand Max / BLACK LION**   1972
A brilliant showcase for Charles Tolliver ... superb rhythm section ... makes one realise how underrated he has consistently been. –BOB RUSCH, CADENCE

○ **Live at Slugs I & II / STRATA EAST**   1972
Trumpeter in live club session. W/ Cecil McBee (b), Stanley

Cowell (p), and Jimmy Hopps (d). Modal jazz played with a real genuine honesty. Extended compositions let the band stretch out. –MGN

○ **Impact / STRATA EAST**   ca. 1976
Six spectacular performances from trumpeters. 23-piece plus eight-piece string section orchestra. Great solos from Tolliver and pianist Stanley Cowell on "Plight" and throughout by James Spaulding (as), George Coleman (ts), Charles McPherson (sax), and Harold Vick (ts). As powerful a record as you're likely to hear. –MGN

○ **Live in Berlin - Vol. I / STRATA EAST**   1988
A quartet recording from 1988, this features a stunning elongated version of "Ruthie's Heart" among four originals. There is great group interplay. –MGN

ROSS TOMPKINS   b 1938

Swing, big band, cool. Ex-Detroit pianist, "Tonight Show" veteran. Mostly Los Angeles studio-session man. His own groups reflect swing-to-bop mentality. –MGN

● **Scrimshaw / CONCORD**   1976
Topkins plays solo piano in this album of all standards. It features elegant classicism in a jazz framework. The worth of this is that we finally get to hear the voice normally submerged in the big-band context. This is a fine representation of Tompkins's worth. –MGN

○ **Live at Concord 1977 / CONCORD**   1977
Recorded at the Concord Jazz Festival in California with legendary violinist Joe Venuti, Scott Hamilton on tenor sax, Roy Brown on bass, and Jake Hanna on drums. Three generations of jazz men do seven standards with all the energy this music needs. –MGN

Festival Time / CONCORD   ca. 1979
Recorded with all-stars Ray Brown (b), Cal Collins (g), Jake Hanna (d), Marshall Royal (as), and Snooky Young (tpt) at the Concord Jazz Festival. This is mostly early period jazz with one Tompkins original, "Pavilion Blues." –MGN

SUMI TONOOKA

Post-bop, neo bop. Pianist. Her life experiences in Philadelphia and Detroit have stamped an identity that lies somewhere between McCoy Tyner and Hank Jones. –MGN

○ **Taking Time / CANDID**
Modern pianist leads quartet through eight originals, and one standard. Craig Handy (sax), Rufus Reid (b), Akira Tana (d). Scratching the surface — better work yet to come. –MGN

DAVID TORKANOWSKY   b 1956

Post-bop, neo bop, modern creative. New Orleans pianist, part of the Crescent City's new guard. A good soloist and decent composer, who was featured a couple of years ago in Rounder series chronicling New Orleans's jazz youngbloods. Better known within Crescent City than by the jazz audience as a whole. –RW

○ **Steppin' Out / ROUNDER**   1988
This is the debut for this modern pianist from New Orleans. It includes five originals by the band, one by drummer James Black and one by guitarist Steve Masakowski, who does a solo of "Spring Can Really Hang You Up The Most." There are cameos by Donald Byrd and Rick Margitza. This is a fine effort and a fresh approach. –MGN

MEL TORME   b 1925

Swing, big band, bop, ballads. At the age of three, he was singing in public; at four, he was on the radio; at nine, he was acting professionally, and at 15, he published his first composition — an instrumental. After playing drums and singing in Chico Marx's band (1942-1943), he formed a vocal ensemble, the Mel-Tones, for which he wrote exceptional arrangements; it performed with Artie Shaw's band. From the late 40s on, Tormé has pursued a career as solo singer with

consistent success, also acting in films and on television and writing songs ("The Christmas Song" and "Born To Be Blue" have become standards). He has published a novel, a reminiscence of Judy Garland, an autobiography, and a biography of his friend and frequent coworker, Buddy Rich. Tormé is clearly a man of exceptional gifts; his voice has remained an astonishingly consistent and accurate instrument, and his upper range — always a special feature of his style — remains intact in his seventh decade of performing. He has few peers as an interpreter of the great American songbooks. –DM

● **Gone with the Wind / MUSICRAFT**   1946
Momentous 1946 and 1947 cuts that indicate Tormé's something special. –RW

It Happened in Monterey / MUSICRAFT   ca. 1946
Brilliant harmonies, arrangements with the Mel-Tones. –RW

Sings His California Suite / DISCOVERY   1949
Seminal 1949 cuts. Tormé wrote all songs, harmonizes with the Mel-Tones. –RW

Sings Fred Astaire / AFFINITY   1956
Great tribute to Fred Astaire; two-record set. –RW

Live at the Crescendo / VERVE   1957
Outstanding live set, in two-record package. –RW

Sings About Love / AUDIOPHILE   1958
Nice session, good orchestrations. –RW

Tormé / POLYGRAM   1958
Outstanding session. Tormé singing expressively backed by Marty Paich (p) orchestra. –RW

Back in Town / POLYGRAM   1959
With the Mel-Tones. There's a new 1991 reissue version. –RW

☆ **Swings Shubert Alley / POLYGRAM**   ca. 1959
First-rate interpretations by Mel Tormé. –RW

○ **Ellington/Basie Songbook / POLYGRAM**   1960
W/ Count Basie. 1960 & 1961. Superb Tormé renditions of cuts by two jazz immortals. –RW

Comin' Home, Baby / ATLANTIC   i 1962
One of his biggest hits ever, though Tormé loathes both the song and his Atlantic Records period. –RW

Round Midnight / STASH   ca. 1962
Fine reissue of prime 50s and 60s cuts, done with Marty Paich (p) and Shorty Rogers (tpt) among others. –RW

At Maisonette / ATLANTIC / DB 5   r 1975
Super early-60s live set. Grammy nomination. –RW

Together Again - For the First Time / GRYPHON ca. 1978
Recorded with Buddy Rich (d) and Orchestra and special guests Steve Marcus (sax), Phil Woods (sax), and Hank Jones (p). "Blues in the Night" and "Bluesette" stand out. –MGN

☆ **Live at Marty's / FINESSE**   ca. 1981
Trio sessions with guests Cy Coleman (p), Gerry Mulligan (sax), and Jonathan Schwartz (p); these are Tormé's finest live dates, a 2-LP loaded with standards and fun. Everyone really enjoyed this one, and Tormé's voice is unfettered. –MGN

Evening with George Shearing / CONCORD   1982
Grammy winner, a wonderful collaborative effort. –RW

Evening at Charlie's / CONCORD   1983
Shimmering, relaxed, and steady. –RW

Top Drawer / CONCORD   1983
Another in their line of successful collaborations. –RW

Elegant Evening / CONCORD   1985
Leans toward the restrained side. –RW

And Rob McConnell's Boss Brass / CONCORD   ca. 1986
With Rob McConnell's Canadian big band. Pop to swing, including a monster Ellington medley and the spirited "Cow Cow Boogie." –MGN

And the Boss Brass / CONCORD   1986
Fine production, excellent vocals. –RW

Vintage Year / CONCORD   1987
They've got it down pat. –RW

Reunion / CONCORD 1988
Tight arrangements; Tormé is lush and enchanting. –RW

In Concert Tokyo / CONCORD 1989
Has sparkle and high energy level. –RW

Night at the Concord Pavilion / CONCORD 1990
Very smooth and well done. –RW

Mel & George 'Do' World War II / CONCORD i 1991
Tormé & George Shearing (p) train keeps rolling. –RW

Songs of New York / ATLANTIC
Good concept work. –RW

London Sessions / DCC COMP
Good compilation of cuts done in London. –RW

DAVID TORN

Fusion. Hard-edged fusion guitarist with aura of mystery. Influenced by Hendrix, Jimmy Page, Terje Rypdal, and Robert Fripp. –MGN

○ **Best Laid Plans / POLYGRAM** 1984
Some compelling moments. –RW

● **Cloud Above Mercury / POLYGRAM** 1986
Hardcore fusion with guitarist Torn. Mark Isham (k), Tony Levin (b), Bill Bruford (d) join. Six Torn originals. Lots of electronic accouterments. –MGN

CY TOUFF b 1927

Swing, big band. Chicago-based bass trumpeter whose big band to swing musings are as enjoyable as they are uncompromising in a pure jazz context. (His name is pronounced "Tough.") –MGN

○ **Octet & Quintet / PACIFIC JAZZ** i 1956
W/ Russ Freeman (p). –MGN

Havin' a Ball / WORLD PACIFIC i 1958
Touff Assignment / ARGO i 1959

TOUGH YOUNG TENORS

Post-bop, modern creative. Fine session in vintage jam session context featuring solos from rising saxophonists Herb Harris, James Carter, Walter Blanding Jr, Tim Warfield Jr, and Todd Williams. Since the release of this set, all the performers stock has risen, particularly Williams and Harris. –RW

○ **Tough Young Tenors / ANTILLES** ca. 1991
Firespitter James Carter join the Marcus Roberts Trio for 11 selections. Various tenors team up with the rhythm section to varying degrees of success. Carter's reading of "Chelsea Bridge" with the trio, and Blanding on "Ask Me Now" stand out. Interesting mish-mash. Would like to hear each tenor on his own. –MGN

RALPH TOWNER b 1940

Early free, world fusion, modern creative. This unique acoustic guitarist brought the craft and discipline of classical guitar into modern improvisational settings. Very active as composer and member of the well-known group Oregon. Raised in a musical family, he studied trumpet and piano and earned a degree in composition. Though he worked as a jazz pianist, his real love is the acoustic guitar: he studied classical guitar intensively with Karl Scheit in Vienna. After playing with the Paul Winter Ensemble, he cofounded the eclectic ensemble Oregon in 1971; his many compositions are mainstays of that popular and artistically successful group. Also an innovator on 12-string guitar, his fine solo on the Weather Report album *I Sing the Body Electric* contributed to his early recognition. An early solo album *Diary* and his duets with John Abercrombie on *Sargasso Sea* show the clarity and energy of his style. Towner's unusually meticulous approach to artistic and technical issues on the guitar, combined with his fine ability as a composer, make all periods of his recorded work well worth investigating. –DNM

☆ **Diary / POLYGRAM** 1973

Solo guitar and piano. Quintessential melodic content is like no other. –MGN

Trios/Solos / POLYGRAM r 1973
Multiple combination work, some beautiful cuts. –RW

● **Solstice / POLYGRAM / DB 5** 1974
Not only sounds wonderful, it has plenty of fine guitar plus Jan Garbarek (ts). –RW

○ **Matchbook / POLYGRAM / DB 5** 1975
Definitive duets with vibist Gary Burton and Ralph Towner (g). Buy it on CD. –MGN

Sounds & Shadows / POLYGRAM 1977
Another stunning group album. –MGN

Old Friends, New Friends / POLYGRAM 1979
Excellent group work with trumpeter Kenny Wheeler. –MGN

Solo Concert / POLYGRAM / DB 5 1979
Beautiful playing, sometimes amazing. I'm not sure you could call all of it jazz, but guitar fans will love it. –RW

Blue Sun / POLYGRAM 1982
1987 release of multi-instrumental workout. –RW

City of Eyes / ECM r 1989
Solo guitar and group offerings. A treat. –MGN

LENNIE TRISTANO 1919-1978

Post-bop, early free. Blind from age nine, the Chicago-born musician played clarinet and tenor sax professionally early in his career and had a working knowledge of almost every instrument in jazz; at 19, he led his first band. After graduating from the American Conservatory, he concentrated on piano and became seriously involved in teaching; among his first students were Lee Konitz and trombonist, composer, and arranger Bill Russo. He moved to New York in 1946 and formed a trio (with Billy Bauer on guitar, and Arnold Fishkind on bass) with which he made his first commercially-released records. Championed by critic Barry Ulanov, Tristano enjoyed his greatest fame in the years 1948-1950, leading a sextet with Konitz and tenorist Warne Marsh, recording with and arranging for the Metronome All Stars, and broadcasting with Charlie Parker and Dizzy Gillespie. But Tristano, while a modernist (he pioneered what later became known as "free jazz," to an extent), was not a bebopper. He had his own ideas about how jazz should be played. As the years went by, Tristano played less and less in public. Though his prowess as a pianist didn't decline — he was exceptionally agile and had a profound knowledge of harmony and structure — he concentrated on teaching. His best students almost always became disciples as well and were expected to follow the master's way. Less directly, however, he had an influence on pianists as disparate as Martial Solal, Bill Evans, and Cecil Taylor. His best records — both as pianist and leader — stand as a very special contribution to jazz. –DM

● **Lennie Tristano on Keynote / VERVE** 1946
1946-1947 on Keynote. Early period progressive pianist. Quite innovative. –MGN

Descent into the Maelstrom / INNER CITY 1953
Mono recordings 1952-1952, 1961, 1965, and 1966. Includes rehearsals from recording date. Quite revealing. –MGN

Requiem / ATLANTIC / DB 5 1955
At times it is clear that only Tristano knew for sure what was happening. –RW

Lennie Tristano Quartet / ATLANTIC / DB 5 COMP
Alternately brilliant and baffling. –RW

GIAN LUIGI TROVESI

Post-bop, modern creative. Italian creative improviser who plays all reeds, primarily tenor sax, but is quite good on bass clarinet. –MGN

○ **Dances / RED** 1985
W/ trio. Italian reed player with dancing, improvisational based jazz. Most potent on bass clarinet. –MGN

GUST WILLIAM TSILIS   b 1954

Neo bop, modern creative. Vibraphonist, a creative thinker, unique musical stance, fine bandleader. Emerging in the past few years as a composer and front liner. −MGN

○ **Possibilties / KEN MUSIC**   1988
A fine record. Teri Lyn Carrington shows her true jazz chops on drums. −RW

● **Pale Fire / ENJA**
W/ Arthur Blythe (as). Good players, aggressive solos. −RW

TUCK & PATTI

Cool, blues-jazz, ballads, new-age, instr-pop. Canadian husband and wife duo: he plays acoustic guitar, she sings in a jazz-tinged contralto; moody, romantic but serious music. −BC

● **Tears of Joy / WINDHAM HILL**   r 1989
Beloved by critics, this duo has charm. Seems more folk to me than jazz, but that's a matter of opinion. −RW

○ **Love Warriors / RCA-WINDHAM HILL**   1990
Tuck Andress (g) and Patti Cathcart (v). A fine acoustic set of slow, moving declarations. −BC

○ **Reckless Precision / WINDHAM HILL**   r 1990
Fine solo guitar playing by Tuck Andress. A harmonic treat for the ears. −PK

Dream / WINDHAM HILL
Folkie sound. −RW

EARL TURBINTON

Trad, post-bop, soul jazz. New Orleans saxophonist Earl Turbinton and brother pianist Willie. Refreshing modern approach to jazz, modally and in post-bop areas. Earl is a post-Coltrane sopranoist, playing bluesy or funky as the mood fits. −MGN

○ **Brothers for Life / ROUNDER**   1987
Rare date for legendary New Orleans saxophonist as a leader, with Willie Tee (k). Modern and swinging. −MGN

STEVE TURRE   b 1948

Post-bop, Latin, neo bop. Dynamic trombonist equally versed in hard-bop, mainstream, and Latin-jazz, and currently a member of the "Saturday Night Live" pit band. Turre got his start playing with Woody Shaw, in recent years has been an active bandleader and one of the premier trombone soloists among the contemporary generation. He's gaining recognition as a composer as well; can play brisk uptempo pieces, slow ballads, or funk and R&B-flavored tunes. −RW

● **Viewpoint / STASH**   1987
Virile playing from trombonist. Also on conch shells. Extra tracks on the CD. Latin and jazz. His best. −MGN

○ **Fire and Ice / STASH**   1988
Wide-ranging quartet, octet, and nonet sessions, plus excellent use of string quartet. CD has three bonus cuts. −RW

○ **Right There / POLYGRAM**   r 1991
Solid, ambitious date by premier trombonist. −RW

STANLEY TURRENTINE   b 1934

Post-bop, soul jazz, instr-pop. One of the greatest tenor saxophonists of the past thirty years. He made his first records with Max Roach after apprenticeship with Lowell Fulson, Earl Bostic, and others. His own recordings began on Blue Note 1960 and he is also a part of key Jimmy Smith albums (*Midnight Special, Back at the Chicken Shack,* and *Prayer Meeting*). He had a long association with Shirley Scott, with frequent recordings under his and her names throughout the 60s. He was one of the first key artists to join CTI in 1970 and established himself as a top-selling artist with that label (*Sugar, Salt Song*), Fantasy (*Pieces of Dreams*) from 1974-1978 and later with Elektra and Blue Note (again). He is equally at home in a commercial setting or with straightahead jazz accompaniment. Turrentine's work for Blue Note (60s) is

exemplary, as is his CTI work in the 70s. His work for other labels can be very good or rather dull, depending on the concept and it's execution. Still one of the true saxophone stars of today, Turrentine is almost always worth a listen. −BP

Look Out / BLUE NOTE   1960
Small group. 1987 reissue of excellent soul-jazz. −RW

○ **Blue Hour / CAPITOL**   1960
Small group. A beautiful album of relaxed, bluesy sound. −JME

○ **Comin' Your Way / CAPITOL**   1961
Small group. 1988 reissue of sumptuous 60s soul-jazz date. Horace Parlan (p) at his bluesy best. −RW

Z.T.'s Blues / CAPITOL   1961
Small group. 1985 reissue of good, steady material. −RW

That's Where It's At / CAPITOL   1962
Small group. Excellent soul-jazz with Les McCann (p). −RW

● **Jubilee Shout / CAPITOL**   1962
Small group. Nice release. Sonny Clark (p) soars, Turrentine red-hot. −RW

Joyride / BLUE NOTE   1965
Large group. Throbbing tenor solos, big-band backing. −RW

● **Let It Go / MCA-GRP**   1966
Small group. Some recorded on Sep 21, 1964. Husband and wife team Turrentine and Shirley Scott (organ) produce one lovely album — blues/jazz, funky. −JME

Rough 'N Tumble / BLUE NOTE   1966
One of his most popular, lightest soul-jazz releases. −RW

The Look of Love / BLUE NOTE   1968
Both romantic and lusty, nice sessions. −RW

○ **Sugar / CBS**   1970
Larger group. By far the best thing he ever made on CTI. Among the handful of genuine jazz albums that were cut on that label. −RW

The Sugar Man / CTI   1971
Cutesy title, good compilation. − RW

Straight Ahead / BLUE NOTE   1984
Small group. Same great combination of musicians as on earlier cookers, but here it does not come off. Pleasant enough, but lacks high spots. −JME

TOMMY TURRENTINE   b 1928

Hard-bop, post-bop, soul jazz. The brother of saxophonist Stanley Turrentine, and a good, if derivative trumpeter who played on a few Blue Note albums and cut his own date on Bainbridge in 1960. −RW

○ **Tommy Turrentine / BAINBRIDGE**   r 1960
A good bop date led by trumpeter Turrentine ... joined by brother Stanley on tenor, trombonist Julian Priester, pianist Horace Parlan, bassist Bob Boswell, and drummer Max Roach. −CARL BRAUER, CADENCE

TURTLE ISLAND STRING QUARTET

Post-bop, world fusion, modern creative. David Balakrishnan's world jazz vision set in musical terms. More neo-classical in scope. Fine group interplay. −MGN

○ **Skylife / WINDHAM HILL**   ca. 1990
Occasional moments of glory. −RW

RICHARD TWARDZIK   1902-1957

Cool. Danish bandleader Richard Twardzik started out as a classical musician. He recorded with both Charlie Parker and Charlie Mariano, and toured with Lionel Hampton and Chet Baker. −JME

○ **Trio / PACIFIC JAZZ**   1956
Needed for any collection of West Coast bop. Brilliant performance by this pianist who met an untimely death. −DS

TWENTY-NINTH ST. SAXOPHONE QUARTET

Post-bop, neo bop, modern creative. Another foursome featuring four lead players; Bobby Watson, Ed Jackson, Rich

Rothenberg, and Jim Hartog. They've released a recent album on Antilles. –RW
○ **Underground / POLYGRAM**   i 1991
Surging, challenging; one of the better sax groups. –RW

ALVIN TYLER   b 1925

Trad, post-bop, neo bop. New Orleans saxophone icon. Plays it all straightahead or modal, rhythm & blues or funky. An American treasure. –MGN
○ **Graciously / ROUNDER**   1986
With mates from New Orleans: Masakowski, Torkanowski, Singleton, Vidacovich, and trumpeter Clyde Kerr Jr. Six of eight are the Tyler tunes, two are standards. Tyler is a rival to Red Holloway or Stanley Turrentine in terms of sound. –MGN
Heritage / ROUNDER   i 1986
1986 release of first foray into straight jazz on record from longtime R&B session king Alvin "Red" Tyler. He plays crisply, with distinction, but is much more animated on vintage New Orleans R&B. –RW

MCCOY TYNER   b 1938

Post-bop, early free, neo bop. Pianist. It's hard to imagine what John Coltrane's classic 60s quartet would have sounded like without the presence of pianist McCoy Tyner. He was just a youngster, not yet 21, when he joined the acclaimed hard-bop Jazztet of Art Farmer and Benny Golson. His prodigous technique soon landed him a job with Coltrane, and from 1960 to 1966 Tyner occupied the piano bench in one of jazzdom's most spectacular and hard-working groups. His was an inventive, expansive sound that breathed excitement into Trane's lengthy modal improvisations, employing thunderous right-hand chords that served to anchor and propel the music at the same time. In many ways McCoy was the glue that held this explosive group together, providing a flexible foundation for the saxophonist's free flights while complementing drummer Elvin Jones and bassist Jimmy Garrison with his percussive dynamism.
Subsequent solo recordings for Blue Note, Milestone, Impulse, and others have not been so fiery as the early 60s were, but Tyner has shared Coltrane's penchant for African themes and has also gone to the music of Asia for thematic material and instrumentation. As a leader, he has had a consistent and well-rounded career, often applying his distinctive touch to straight jazz standards in piano-trio formats when he's not pursuing modal or avant-garde settings. McCoy is still a busy club and festival performer, collaborating with the biggest names in jazz and leading a variety of groups as he continues to hone his bold piano style. –MB
Inception / MCA   i 1962
1988 reissue, penetrating trio cuts. –RW
○ **Inception/Nights of Ballads & Blues / MCA**   1962
1962 & 1963 trio albums on one CD. Very well done. –MGN
Nights of Ballads & Blues / MCA   1963
Probing, dense, and electric interpretations. –RW
Today & Tomorrow / GRP   1963
1991 release, reissue from limited Jazz Masters Series of 70s reissues. Superb music throughout. –RW
○ **The Real McCoy / BLUE NOTE**   1967
W/ Joe Henderson (sax). –MGN
● **Tender Moments / BLUE NOTE**   1967
Small big band. Some extraordinary music. –JME
Time for Tyner / CAP   1968
1987 reissue of dense session. Tyner and Bobby Hutcherson (vib) have some sparkling exchanges and dialogs. –RW
Expansions / CAPITOL   1968
Elastic, shimmering pieces, fine playing. –RW
○ **Sahara / OJC**   1972
Remarkable date, both in playing and compositional clout. Vital. –RW

○ **Echoes of a Friend / OJC**   1972
Stunning solo piano. –RW
Song for My Lady / OJC   1972
1988 reissue of nice set. –RW
Song of the World / OJC   1973
Reissued in 1991. Large-group recordings. Tyner fits in as usual. –RW
Sama Layuca / MILESTONE / DB 5   1974
Atlantis / MILESTONE   1974
☆ **Trident / MILESTONE**   1975
Ranks with his most memorable trio dates. –RW
● **Fly with the Wind / MILESTONE**   1976
Surprising popularity among non-jazz crowd, good Hubert Laws (fl). –RW
Inner Voices / MILESTONE   1977
Some masterly piano solos. –RW
● **Supertrios / MILESTONE**   1977
Two trios on each of two discs. First with Ron Carter (b) and Tony William (d),and also with Eddie Gomez (b) and Jack DeJohnette (d). Great after repeated listenings. –ED
Passion Dance / MILESTONE   1978
Solid live date from Tokyo. –RW
○ **4 X 4 / MILESTONE**   1980
W/ Al Foster (d), Cecil McBee (b), Freddie Hubbard (tpt), John Abercrombie (electric mandolin), Bobby Hutcherson (vib), Arthur Blythe (as). Hub has guts, Abercrombie sky bound, Hutch more angular, Blythe earth-rooted and vibrant. –MGN
13th House / MILESTONE   1981
○ **La Leyenda De La Hora / CBS**   1981
A definitive album. In Afro-Cuban large ensemble setting. Spirited. –MGN
Dimensions / ELEKTRA   1983
It's About Time / BLUE NOTE   1985
Most productive pairing. –RW
Double Trios / DENON   i 1987
Smashing piano solos from Tyner. –RW
Revelations / CAPITOL   i 1989
Usual sturdy material. CD has three bonus cuts. –RW
● **Uptown-Downtown / MILESTONE**   1989
Live date at the Blue Note in NYC. Quintessential Tyner big band. You can't live without this one. –MGN
New York Reunion / CHS   1990
Quartet with Joe Henderson (sax). A great idea to bring them back together. –MGN
Plays Ellington / MCA   r 1990
Wondrous treatments of Duke anthems. –RW
Things Ain't What They Used to Be / CAPITOL   r 1990
Upbeat attitude, with struttin' solos from John Scofield (g), George Drams. –RW
Remembering John / RHINO   r 1991
Good tribute, familiar territory. –RW
44th St.Suite / CBS
Recent date, slashing solos from David Murray (ts), Arthur Blythe (as). Fine Tyner. –RW
Double Exposure / LRC JAZZ CL.

JAMES BLOOD ULMER   b 1942

Early free, jazz-rock, contemporary funk. Guitarist. Originally from South Carolina, Ulmer sang with a gospel group The Southern Sons until he was 13. Moving to Pittsburgh in the late 50s, he played in many popular dance groups and in concerts hosted by Dick Clark. He later played and toured with several bands, including with Dionne Warwick. He spent several years in the late 60s in Detroit, working with a jazz- and blues-oriented band and doing explorations in progressive jazz. Ulmer went to New York in 1971 and began the study of Harmolodic Theory with Ornette Coleman. In that period he also recorded with Rashid Ali and played with

Art Blakey's Jazz Messengers. He has recorded with many of the most respected figures in progressive jazz, including Ronald Shannon Jackson, David Murray, Oliver Lake, Olu Dara, and Ornette Coleman. His percussive harmolodic funk brings together funky soul roots with the no-frills wide-open feel of free jazz. Also a composer and vocalist, his poignant vocals on *Are You Glad to Be in America?* and *America, Do You Remember the Love?* bespeak the irony of the American dream in terms of the Black experience. –DNM

● **Are You Glad to Be in America? / ROUGH TRADE**   1980
Visionary guitarist with a unique sound. His best. Must hear first. –MGN

★ **Tales of Captain Black / ARTISTS HOUSE**   r 1980
The best Ulmer from total package perspective. Everything works. –RW

○ **Freelancing / CBS / DB 5**   1981
Studio session. Also mind expanding. –MGN

America: Do You Remember ... / BLUE NOTE   i 1987
America: Do You Remember The Love. 1987 release, uneven but lots of excitement. –RW

UPTOWN STRING QUARTET

Swing, big band, early free, neo bop, modern creative. Intriguing women's string group featuring the daughter of drummer Max Roach, Maxine Roach, plus Lesa Terry, Diane Monroe, and Eileen M. Folson. The quartet has backed Roach on his albums, plus his percussion ensemble M'Boom and issued one release as a unit. They're excellent players, well-schooled in classical and jazz, and their music indicates exciting possibilities for stringed instruments in improvisational setting equaled only in past by similiar groups like the String Trio. –RW

○ **Max Roach Presents... / PHILIPS**   r 1977
Neo-classical jazz flavors from string quartet. Very nice. –MGN

PHIL URSO   b 1925

Bop, hard-bop. A New Jersey saxophonist who came up in big bands in the 40s and 50s. He prefers smoother cool tenors but is a capable bopper. –MGN

● **Urso-Brookmeyer Quintet / SAVOY**   i 1954
W/ Bob Brookmeyer (tb). –MGN

Philosophy of Urso / SAVOY   i 1955

Sentimental Journey / REGENT   i 1956

UZEB

Jazz-rock, contemporary funk. A three-piece jazz/fusion group from Canada made up of bass, guitar, and synthesizers. All musicians are very talented players, making the music above average for this style. –PK

○ **Fast Emotion / CREAM**   1983
A French import album featuring Michael Brecker's sax on two cuts. –PK

Between the Lines / IOU   1986
An independent album release from this Canadian band, featuring vocals on one cut. –PK

Noisy Nights / NOVA   1989
Another album from this Canadian three-piece fusion band. Includes "Goodbye Pork Pie Hat." –PK

WARREN VACHE   b 1951

Swing, big band, cool. Relatively youthful cornetist and trumpeter who prefers the swing era sound, pre-rock standards to hard-bop. Very influenced by Bobby Hackett and Ruby Braff, Vache plays with the vibrato of a vocalist, has a beautiful sound and extensive range. Vache was a student of Pee Wee Ervin and Jim Fitzpatrick and began working with Benny Goodman after he earned his music degree, as well as playing at Eddie Condon's in New York with Vic Dickenson and Bob Wilber. He played with his father's group as well, before issuing his debut release in 1976. His albums, both

collaborations with like-minded players like Dan Barrett or with longtime veterans like Hank Jones and George Duvivier, are always nice, sometimes dazzling, and usually conservative from standpoint of material. –RW

○ **Polished Brass / CONCORD**   1979
Several glimmering solos, excellent production. –RW

Midtown Jazz / CONCORD   1982
Vache takes center stage. –RW

Easy Going / CONCORD   1986
Sophisticated, cool, swing-inflected mainstream. Sextet performances. –RW

○ **Warm Evenings / CONCORD**   r 1990
Wonderful sound quality, production, and solos. Good production and arrangements, strings kept in right balance with Vache's trumpet. –RW

DAVE VALENTIN

Latin, jazz-rock, instr-pop, contemporary funk. An Afro-Latin and Latin-jazz flutist who's recorded mainly for GRP. His albums have been nice, middle-of-the-road affairs, and one with Herbie Mann is quite substantial. –RW

○ **Live at the Blue Note / MCA-GRP**   1988
This 1988 date is the pick. –RW

Mind Time / GRP   1988
Earl Klugh plays nicely, as does Valentin on this session. –RW

Two Amigos / GRP
W/ Herbie Mann. –RW

ART VAN DAMME

Swing, cool. Jazz accordion-master, Van Damme plays much more than cool/accordion mush. In fact, he was an innovator during 60s post-bop. He is an unsung hero. –MGN

● **New Sound Of... / CBS**   196?
60s album with septet. Good combo with accordianist Van Damme as improvisor on standards and interesting originals, with no throwaways. –MGN

○ **Sound / CBS**
More good music from Norway (Michigan) native. Quintet with vibist Charlie Calzaretta. –MGN

RUDY VAN GELDER

Recording engineer. Rudy Van Gelder is the legendary sound engineer whose technical ingenuity and love of music forever influenced the way we listen to recorded jazz. Van Gelder was a practicing optometrist in the late 40s when he set up his first modest recording studio in the living room of his parent's home in Hackensack, NJ. In that room he would record most of the major East Coast jazz artists of the 50s, including virtually every session for Blue Note and Prestige Records, as well as many classical dates for Vox and other labels. In 1959, over a single weekend, Van Gelder moved his studio to his new home in the town in Englewood Cliffs, NJ, where it has remained. Van Gelder has kept pace with the technical advances that have occurred since that time and remains as active as ever. (Quoted with permission from Mosaic Records) Note: Rudy Van Gelder has recorded more hard-bop and original funk that any other engineer. And no one has recorded Hammond organ jazz like Van Gelder. If it's a Blue Note or Prestige album that has been recorded in Hackensack or Engleword Cliffs, NJ, then chances are it's a Van Gelder recording. –JME

EARL VAN RIPER   b 1922

Swing, bop, cool. Veteran Detroit pianist who played swing, big-band, bop, and R&B. A light, bright personality on his instrument, but has made few recordings. –MGN

○ **Detroit's Grand Piano Man / PARKWOOD**   1987
Studio session with Marcus Belgrave (tpt) and Dave Young (b). Standards by Cedar Walton, Belgrave, Thad Jones, J. Van

Heusen, Ellington, and Quincy Jones. Van Riper proves his mettle as a veteran pianist solidly in jazz tradition, on the mellow side. One to savor. −MGN

TOM VARNER

Post-bop, early free, neo bop, modern creative. French horn is his axe. Plays neo-bop or creative music, more swinging than free, but able to do both. Varner's recorded output thus far has substance and quality. −MGN

○ **Jazz French Horn / NEW NOTE**   1985
Debut with quintet. Contains the parody on "What Is This Thing Called Love" titled "What Is This Thing Called First Strike Capability." Uplifting jazz. −MGN

NANA VASCONCELOS

World fusion. Next to Airto, Nana Vasconcelos has been the premier Latin percussionist of the 70s and beyond. His father was a professional guitarist, and Vasconcelos joined his band at 12, playing bongos and maracas. He later started playing the trap drums and working in bossa-nova bands. Vasconcelos moved to Rio in the mid 60s and worked with Milton Nascimento. He earned a reputation throughout Brazil for his ability to handle odd rhythms and his proficiency with the berimbau, a Brazilian folk instrument. He made his first splash in America in 1971, when Gato Barbieri recruited him for an album date. He later toured Europe with Barbieri, staying over in Paris and remaining there two years. During that stint, he also worked with Don Cherry in Sweden and recorded with Egberto Gismonti. Vasconcelos returned to New York in 1976, and since then has toured and recorded with Gismonti, Pat Metheny, and the group Codona, whose personnel included Cherry and the late multi-instrumentalist Collin Walcott. −RW

● **Saudades / POLYGRAM**   1979
Excellent percussion, despite uneven qualitities. −RW

○ **Bush Dance / POLYGRAM**   r 1987
Best recorded example of Vasconcelos' rhythmic mastery. −RW

Rain Dance / POLYGRAM   i 1989
1989 release spotlighting Vasconcelos band the Bushdancers. Mixed results. −RW

SARAH VAUGHAN   1924-1990

Big band, bop, cool, ballads. She sang and played piano in church in her native Newark, but on a dare entered the famous Apollo Theater Amateur Hour contest and won, singing "Body and Soul." Billy Eckstine heard her, recognized her very special talent, and recommended her to his boss, Earl Hines. This was in 1943, when Charlie Parker and Dizzy Gillespie were in the Hines band; she followed them into Eckstine's new and revolutionary big band in late 1944. By 1946 she was out on her own and pursued a successful solo career until the end of her life. Sarah (or "Sassy," as her fans called her; she was also known as "The Divine One") had a voice that would have served for an operatic career (or that of a gospel singer), but to our good fortune she chose jazz, though she often "crossed over" into pop. Her ear was as good as any improvising horn player's, her range spanned three full octaves. At her best, Sarah Vaughan not only had the finest voice ever applied to jazz singing — she had the creative ideas to match it. −DM

Columbia Years 1949-1953 / CBS   1949
This is a very nice compilation of her formative cuts on Columbia. −RW

In Hi-Fi / COLUMBIA   1950

Great Jazz Years 1954-1956 - Vol. 1 / POLYGRAM   1954
Undeniably fine performances. −RW

Great Show on Stage / POLYGRAM   1954
1954-1956. Another concept work. These are excellent songs and lead vocals, available elsewhere in original context. −RW

Rodgers & Hart Songbook / POLYGRAM   1954
1954-1958. This is the reissued version to get. −RW

In the Land of Hi-Fi / POLYGRAM   i 1955

Super album from late 50s. Vaughan and orchestra/combo are marvelous. −RW

Linger Awhile / COLUMBIA / BB 20   r 1956
A big-hit album. −RW

★ **Gershwin Songbook / POLYGRAM**   1957
Wonderful interpretations of Gershwin classics. −RW

Gershwin Songbook #2 / POLYGRAM   1957
Nice follow-up disc. −RW

○ **Irving Berlin Songbook / POLYGRAM**   1957
Prime reissue of a masterpiece. −RW

At Mister Kelly's / POLYGRAM   i 1958
First-rate, long-unavailable live club date with great rhythm section. −RW

No Count Sarah / POLYGRAM   i 1959
Interesting title, great songs and lead vocals. −RW

Recorded Live / POLYGRAM   195?
Excellent cuts from 50s and 60s, culled to fit on this concept release. −RW

After Hours / CSP   195?
Excellent early-50s cuts that haven't always been available domestically. −RW

Vaughan & Voices / POLYGRAM   ca. 1962
Wonderful release. Also part of two-record/one-disc set. −RW

Sarah Slightly Classical / CAPITOL   1963
Again, its value is in relation to appreciation of the concept. She sings wonderfully. CD 1991 reissue, six bonus cuts. −RW

○ **Sassy Swings the Tivoli / POLYGRAM**   r 1963
Sassy at her live-in-concert best. −MGN

Misty / POLYGRAM   1964
Actually two great albums on one disc, the other being "Vaughan And Voices." −RW

Sassy Swings Again / POLYGRAM   r 1967
First rate in every way. −RW

Singles Sessions / CAPITOL   196?
1991 release of some super sessions from the early 60s. −RW

How Long Has This Been Going On / PABLO   ca. 1972
Good vocals, wildly uneven material. −RW

In Japan - Vol. 1 / MAINSTREAM   ca. 1973
This is the original great single-album version of her master 70s concert. −RW

Live in Japan - Vol. 2 / MAINSTREAM   1973
Top-flight followup. −RW

○ **Complete — Live in Japan / MOBILE FIDELITY**   r 1974
Welcome reissue of one of her best from 70s, reissued in superb remastered form. −RW

Duke Ellington Songbook - Vol. 1 / PA2   1979
Nice 70s update on Songbook concept. Some of her last truly great singing. −RW

Duke Ellington Songbook - Vol. 2 / PA2 / DB 5   1979
Excellent companion to first volume. −RW

Brazilian Romance / CBS
Nice cuts, good compositions. −RW

Crazy and Mixed Up / PA2
Rather uneven, though she's mostly enjoyable. −RW

Send in the Clowns / PA2
This collaboration with Basie orchestra isn't what it would have been in the 50s or 60s, but it's still nice. −RW

Sings Great American Songs / POLYGRAM
First-rate songs and superb vocals from a prime period. −RW

○ **With Clifford Brown / POLYGRAM**
They didn't do much together, but what they did was unforgettable. −RW

With Michel Legrand / MAINSTREAM
Legrand's orchestrations not withstanding, nice singing. −RW

★ **Best of Sarah Vaughan / PABLO**   COMP
Compilation of Pablo cuts. −RW

Roulette Years / CAPITOL   COMP

1991 compilation of some fine cuts. –RW

☆ **Sarah Vaughan on Mercury / MERCURY**   COMP
Complete on Mercury. Monumental six-disc set that covers her extensive and exhaustive Mercury career. Of course, the company has also hacked this up into multiple packages to get separate profits off each. You can get it either way; I prefer the boxed set. –RW

CHARLIE VENTURA   b 1916

Swing, bop. Swing to bop saxophone all-star. Deep understanding of instrument. Extensive experience with Gene Krupa in 40s and 50s. –MGN

Charlie Boy / PHOENIX   1946
Early session, with Barney Bigard (cl). –RW

In Chicago / ZIM   1947
Some hot work from Ventura, plus Kai Winding (tb), Shelley Manne (d). –RW

● **Euphoria / SAVOY**   1948
Two-disc set of powerhouse 40s cuts. –RW

○ **And His Sextet / IMPERIAL**   i 1950
W/ Red Rodney (tpt). –MGN

In a Jazz Mood / NORGRAN   i 1955
Charlie Ventura Quintet in Hi-Fi / HARLEQUIN   1956
Dynamite date. –RW

East of Suez / REGENT   i 1958
Chazz / FAMOUS DOOR   1977
Later-day swing, quite nice. RW

Concert / MCA
Good high-energy concert reissue with Jackie & Roy, Bennie Green (tb). –RW

In Concert / GNP CRESCENDO

JOE VENUTI   1903-1978

Swing. One of the greatest practical jokers in jazz history, the man who put jazz violin on the map was cagey about his date and place of birth. Was it Italy or Philadelphia? 1894 or 1903? We may never know for sure, but it is certain that Venuti went to school in Philly with the great guitarist Eddie Lang, and that the two friends formed a team that made the first chamber-jazz records (in 1926) and was in great demand in the recording and radio studios and on the musical stage. Joe and Eddie appeared as special attractions with Paul Whiteman, and Eddie became Bing Crosby's favorite accompanist. When Lang died suddenly in 1933, Venuti was at first inconsolable, but soon found his form again. He toured Europe in 1934, had his own big band at the height of the swing era, and in 1944 settled in Hollywood to do film work. Almost forgotten, he resurfaced in the 60s, making lots of records, touring world-wide, and surprising fellow musicians and audiences with his undiminished vitality and joy in making music. As a violinist, Venuti did not have a big tone but exceptional facility and a sense of swing that was superior to most players on the 20s scene. His style hardly changed (though he amplified his instrument from the 50s on), but he sounded as hip in the 70s as 50 years before. –DM

○ **Joe Venuti w/ Eddie Lang – Vols. 1 & 2 / JSP**   1926
1926-1927. The early duos and Blue Four sessions (in chronological order). Volume 1 is essential; Vol. 2 is also recommended. –RL

Stringin' the Blues / COLUMBIA   192?
1920-1930s. Classic, formative cuts on two-disc set. –RW

The Mad Fiddler from Philly / SHOESTRING   1952
1952-1953. Nice airchecks from Crosby broadcasts. –RW

● **Joe Venuti and Zoot Sims / CHIAROSCURO**   r 1974
Another strong 70s date, with George Duvivier (b), Cliff Leeman (d), Dick Wellstood. (p) –RL

○ **Joe and Zoot / VANGUARD / DB 5**   1975
Excellent 1989 reissue of high-caliber date with Venuti and Zoot Sims (ts) establishing complete musical rapport. –RW

The Joe Venuti Blue Four / CHIAROSCURO   r 1976
Hard-swinging Joe from his 70s comeback period, with Milt Hinton (b), Bucky Pizzarelli (g), and others. –RL

Sliding By / SONET   1977
Pungent violin solos. –RW

Joe in Chicago / FLYING FISH   1978
Good session, with Venuti in vigorous form. –RW

The Daddy of the Violin / MPS   ca. 197?
Super playing at late stage in his career. –RW

Hot Sonatas / CHIAROSCURO
Rippling dialogs between Venuti and Earl Hines (p). –RW

○ **Violin Jazz 1927-1934 / YAZOO**   COMP
A good compilation, heavier on the small groups than on the duos with Eddie Lang (g). Much duplication of material with records on the JSP label. –RL

EDWARD VESALA   b 1945

World fusion, modern creative. Finnish improvising percussionist. European classicist image transcended by cunning instincts and vast array of instruments. –MGN

○ **Nan Madol / JAPO**   ca. 1974
Leader plays percussion, flutes, harp. With Finnish friends in duo to large-ensemble contexts. Each cut features different instrumentation, one is solo Vesala. Charlie Mariano (as), Juhani Aaltonen (sax) stand out. –MGN

● **Heavylife / LEO**   ca. 1980
Finnish percussionist in nonet of heavies — Bob Stewart and Joe Daley (tuba), Reggie Workman (b), Howard Johnson (bar sax), T. Stanko (tpt), J. D. Parran (ts), Chico Freeman (ts), James Spaulding (reeds/flutes). Extraordinary free music with soul and passion. Very listenable. –MGN

Ode to the Death of Jazz / ECM   r 1991
Pretentious title, but some good playing. –RW

HAROLD VICK   b 1936

Post-bop, soul jazz, progressive big band. A saxophonist who can hit the note on many levels of jazz: soulful, funky, straightahead, or fusion. –MGN

○ **Steppin' Out / BLUE NOTE**   i 1963
W/ Grant Green (g) and Blue Mitchell (tpt). –MGN

VIENNA ART ORCHESTRA

Progressive big band, modern creative. Neo-classical creative improvising ensemble. Circus-like image. Free and unabashed. Features American vocalist Lauren Newton. –MGN

● **From No Time to Rag Time / HAT ART**   ca. 1982
Powerful atonal improvisors Lauren Newton, Mathies Ruegg leading and conducting the 13-piece group. The best soloists are Herbert Joos on flugelhorn, Harry Sokal on sax/flute, and Wolfgang Pusching on sax. This is a 2-fer with eight long pieces. The best cuts are "Variations About Silence (for Ornette)," and "Jelly Roll, but Mingus Rolls Better." –MGN

○ **Perpetuum Mobile / HAT ART**   ca. 1985
Includes eleven pieces from these Kurt Weill/Carla Bley influenced zanies. "'Round Midnight" shows up. The band splits the writing. –MGN

Blues for Brahms / POLYGRAM   ca. 1988

LEROY VINNEGAR   b 1928

Post-bop, cool. One of the popularizers of the "walking" bass technique, where the normal four-to-the-bar bass lines are embellished through big, thick tones and nimble playing. Vinnegar would pluck open strings with the left hand, providing a much heavier accent and impact on the composition. Vinnegar and pianist Carl Perkins went to school together in Indianapolis, then later became colleagues in Los Angeles after working in Chicago backing Charlie Parker and Sonny Stitt. He later worked with Stan Getz, Barney Kessel, Herb Geller, and Shelly Manne. Later, Vinnegar worked with the Teddy Edwards, Joe Castro, and Gerald Wilson bands, and did some classic recordings with Sonny Rollins, Phineas Newborn, the Jazz Crusaders, and Kenny Dorham, plus a heralded appearance at the 1969 Montreaux Festival with Les McCann, and led some sessions on his own. His finest releases from the late 50s and early 60s have been reissued. –RW

○ **Leroy Walks! / OJC**   1957
Here are textbook walking bass lines, solid late-50s West Coast jazz. –RW

● **Leroy Walks Again / OJC**   1962
1990 reissue of two dates (1962 & 1963) with sorely overlooked saxophonist Teddy Edwards. –RW

○ **Jazz's Great Walker / VEEJAY**   ca. 1965
A rare one for this bassist — if you can find it. –MGN

MIROSLAV VITOUS   b 1947

Jazz-rock, neo bop, modern creative. A virtuoso bassist and among the finest players ever to come to America from Europe. His father was a saxophonist, and he studied violin at six, then piano before starting on bass at 14. He played with Jan Hammer and his brother Alan in a junior trio at the Prague Conservatory. Vitous studied at Berklee from 1966-1967, then went to New York and worked with Art Farmer, Freddie Hubbard, and the Bob Brookmeyer-Clark Terry quintet. He worked for a brief time with Miles Davis, then had an extended stint with Herbie Mann from the late 60s until the end of 1970. Later, he was a founding member of Weather Report and remained with them from 1971-1973. Vitous heading his own groups in 1976 and continued to do that, plus extensive session work, throughout the 80s. –RW

☆ **Mountain in the Clouds / ATLANTIC**   1973
By far his best. An all-star lineup, great cuts. –RW

● **Miroslav / ARISTA**   1976
1976-1977 sessions with Don Alias and Armen Halburian on percussion. Vitous overdubs bass and keyboards. A stunning musical trip through Afro-jazz texture music. "Tiger in the Rain" is absolutely captivating. –MGN

○ **First Meeting / ECM**   1979
Seven pieces written by Vitous. With John Surman (sax, b, cl), a very young Kenny Kirkland (p), and stellar Jon Christenson (d). This is very listenable music, rooted in freedom of expression. –MGN

Journey's End / POLYGRAM   1982
Excellent in most facets, lacks individualistic character. –RW

Emergence / POLYGRAM   1985
Excellent bass playing, light on the jazz side. –RW

ROSEANNA VITRO   b 1951

Ballads, neo bop. Sizzling vocalist whose sound is close to perfection. Capable of scat, vocalese, harmonic variance, and improvising on written melodies. Can also faithfully interpret Brazilian music, and is a fine blues belter. Her strong suit is ballads, and she can also sing pop. Perhaps the best on the current scene. –MGN

● **Listen Here / TEXAS ROSE**   1982
A straightahead date with the Kenny Barron (p) Trio, Arnett Cobb (sax), Bliss Rodriguez (p). Vitro proves her mettle on every tune, without fail. –MGN

○ **A Quiet Place / SKYLINE**   r 1988
An absolutely romantic statement and a pure delight. Poppy but pure, with pianist Fred Hersch. Desert-island music, if you get to pick the island. –MGN

☆ **Reaching for the Moon / CHASE MUSIC GROUP**
A solid effort from a most expressive and emotional singer. Jazz, Brazilian, and pop flavored music with pianist Ken Werner. She is one of the best. Highly recommended. –MGN

PAUL VORNHAGEN

Post-bop, ballads, neo bop. Saxophonist and flutist whose style ranges from new-age to mainstream jazz. His vocal style is absolutely from Chet Baker. –MGN

○ **Variations / STRAWBERRY**   ca. 1991
All standards. Phil Kelly or Rick Roe (p), Kurt Krahnke (b), Pete Siero (d). Hard swingin' standards from saxophonist and flutist. Uses Chet Baker-type vocal approach on occasion. Some aggressive playing. –MGN

LARRY VUCKOVICH

Post-bop, neo bop. Balkan-born pianist takes sound of his folklore into modern modal jazz, featuring gypsy violin and unison melodies. Very good at playing straightahead jazz standards. Good arranger. –MGN

● **Blue Balkan / INNER CITY**   ca. 1980
With B. Hutcherson (vib), Eric Golub (violin), John Heard (b), Eddie Moore (d). Marimba, vibes, and violin in combination especially the title track make for a unique sound. Pianist/leader an unsung virtuoso. Seven originals and standards by Brubeck and Avery Parrish. –MGN

○ **City Sounds, Village Voices / PAJ**   ca. 1981
Sextet with Tom Harrell (tpt), Jerome Richardson (reeds), and Charles McPherson (sax) up front. Five standards, "Vukovich's Variation," "Besame Macho," and two others. Good group forces pianist's hand. –MGN

○ **Tres Palabras / CONCORD**   1989
Light Latin-tinged jazz. CD version, three bonus cuts. –RW

COLLIN WALCOTT   1945-1984

Early free, world fusion. Trained in classical percussion, Walcott's interest in Indian music led him to be one of the first and only Westerners to master both sitar and tabla (Indian hand drums). He studied sitar with Ravi Shankar and tabla with Alla Rakha. Walcott had early recordings with Tony Scott and Miles Davis and became a member of the Paul Winter Consort in 1970. He is probably best known for his work with the chamber jazz ensemble Oregon, which he cofounded with Ralph Towner, Paul McCandless, and Glen Moore. Oregon was unusually successful in creating artistically valuable music from eclectic influences, and Walcott's contribution on tabla and sitar was an important component of the group's tone and ambience. He also had an association with Don Cherry and Nana Vasconcelos in the group Codona. Collin died in an accident in East Germany while touring with Oregon. –DNM

● **Cloud Dance / ECM**   1975

○ **Grazing Dreams / POLYGRAM / DB 5**   1977
His glory. Group music based around Walcott's sitar and tabla work. –MGN

Codona 2 / POLYGRAM   1980
Excellent playing, varying quality of material. –RW

Codona / ECM   1980
Good compositions, fine sound and performances. –RW

Codona 3 / POLYGRAM   1982
No difference from prior releases. –RW

○ **Works / POLYGRAM**   COMP
Compilation of ECM work. –RW

MAL WALDRON   b 1926

Hard-bop, post-bop, early free, modern creative. Among the more quirky, unpredictable pianists, with a style equally suited to avant-garde or more conventional settings. Mal Waldron earned a degree in music from Queens College in the 50s, then worked with Big Nick Nicholas, Ike Quebec, Della Reese, and various R&B groups. He became a regular member of various Charles Mingus bands from 1954-1956 and also was Billie Holiday's accompanist from 1957-1959. He led his own bands in the 60s, including backing both John Coltrane and Eric Dolphy, appearing on the immortal "Live At The Five Spot" sessions in the early 60s. During the 70s and 80s, he worked often with soprano saxophonist Steve Lacy, also did hard-bop with Clifford Jordan and Philly Joe Jones. A wonderful soloist, adept accompanist, and fine songwriter. −RW

● **Mal — 1 & 2 / OJC**   1956
Two early albums from 1956 & 1957. Classic work from post-bop to progressive pianist. −MGN

Impressions / OJC   1959
Excellent late-50s work. −RW

Set Me Free / AFFINITY   1969
Forthright trio with Philly Joe Jones (d). −RW

Free at Last / POLYGRAM   1969
Outstanding trio date of early ECM release. 1989 reissue. −RW

Black Glory / ENJA   1971
One among many superb trio dates. Waldron's playing is alternately expressive, bluesy, and exacting. −RW

Blues for Lady Day / BLACK LION   1972
Great tribute to Billie Holiday. −RW

○ **Hard Talk / ENJA**   1974
Slashing, dynamic date with Steve Lacy (sax). −RW

Moods / RHINO   1978
1990 reissue of a solid set. Wonderful sextet with Steve Lacy (sax) and Cameron Brown (b). −RW

The Call / ECM (JAPAN)   1979
Outstanding trio date. −RW

Herbe de L'oubli / HAT ART   1981
One of two fiery live duet sets with Steve Lacy (sax) done in Paris. −RW

Snake-Out / HAT ART   1981
Second of the two Paris 80s encounters with Steve Lacy (sop sax). −RW

What It Is / ENJA   ca. 1981
Clifford Jordan (ts) at his best, dauntless piano. −RW

Encounters / MUSE   1984

Live at the Village Vanguard / SOUL NOTE   1986
This is a high-caliber quartet set, w/ Woody Shaw (tpt) triumphant. −RW

You & the Night & the Music / PRO ARTE   1986
High-caliber lineup. W/ Reggie Workman (b), Ed Blackwell (d). −RW

Our Colline's a Treasure / SOUL NOTE
Fine interpretations and solos. −RW

DAN WALL

Post-bop, neo bop. This Atlanta-based keyboardist prefers progressive music; he's on fire when playing the Hammond B-3 organ. He can groove or work in the stratosphere. −MGN

○ **Song for the Night / LANDSLIDE**   r 1981
Very different from *Route 2* but also very good. With Steve Grossman on sax, Mike Richmond on bass, and Jimmy Madison on drums. −MGN

● **Route 2 / LANDSLIDE**
Organ-fired modern post-bop/neo-bop with excellent percussive touches. Forward-moving music with John Abercrombie on guitar and David Earle Johnson on congas as coleaders, plus Joe Chambers (d) and Jeremy Steig (fl). The title song and "Frozen Moments" are the best. −MGN

BENNIE WALLACE   b 1946

Post-bop, modern creative. Tenor sax. Country and R&B are part of Bennie Wallace's background, and he's never lost his love for these styles, periodically working them into his jazz material where possible. Wallace juggled jazz, R&B, and country dates as a teen, working in area bands around his Chattanooga hometown. He studied clarinet at the University of Tennessee, then moved to New York in the 70s. He worked with Monty Alexander and Sheila Jordan before making his recording debut with Flip Phillips and Scott Hamilton in

1977. He's since made some good sessions as a leader, displaying a style rooted in swing and bop, well-suited to uptempo pieces but effective on blues and ballads. −RW

Free Will / RHINO   1980
1990 reissue, consistently strong playing by Wallace. −RW

○ **Big Jim's Tango / ENJA**   1982

○ **Sweeping through the City / RHINO / DB 5**   1984
Large group date: blues and gospel element. 1991 reissue. Unwieldy at times, but effective overall. −RW

Brilliant Corners / POLYGRAM   1986
A wonderful, overlooked 1986 session with the Japanese pianist Yosuke Yamashita. −RW

● **Art of the Saxophone / DENON**   1987
Incendiary Tennessean Wallace joins four other saxophonists — one at a time — on each track. Duelers include Oliver Lake (as), Jerry Bergonzi (ts), Harold Ashby (ts), and Lew Tabackin (ts). Six by Wallace, two by Ellington, one by Gillespie. Great playing and a unique idea fully realized. −MGN

○ **Border Town / BLUE NOTE**   r 1988
Top mix of blues and jazz. Dr. John (p) and John Scofield (g) are first rate. −RW

Mystic Bridge / RHINO
With Chick Corea's (k) trio. −MGN

FATS WALLER   1904-1943

Stride, boogie, swing. Huge in girth and filled with mirth, Fats Waller was not only one of jazz's greatest pianists, but one of the century's greatest entertainers. On records (he made hundreds), radio (he had his own programs at a time when Black artists were not often recognized), and in film (he appeared in only three feature films and a handful of shorts, but stole every scene), his marvelous sense of humor (he was a champion ad libber), his tremendous time (he was swing incarnate), and his sheer physical force impressed audiences of every stripe. A prodigious creator of melodies, he wrote (with his chief partner, lyricist Andy Razaf) such evergreens as "Ain't Misbehavin'," "Honeysuckle Rose," "Black and Blue," "The Jitterbug Waltz," and dozens of others. At the time of his death, he had a hit show running on Broadway and could be seen on screens throughout the land in *Stormy Weather*, his best movie. Too much food and drink — Fats consumed liquor by the gallon — and not enough rest did him in at 39. But Waller records haven't been out of print since and he still makes new fans — not least among piano players. −DM

In London / DRG   1922
1922, 1938, 1939. With British septet. Waller plays some organ and celeste. 18 tracks, including "The London Suite" in six parts. −MGN

Rare Piano Roll Solos - Vol. 1 / BIOGRAPH / DB 5   1923
1923-1924.

Rare Piano Roll Solos - Vol. 2 / BIOGRAPH   1924
1924-1931.

○ **Fats Waller & His Buddies / RCA BLUEBIRD**   1927
Dates with Morris's Hot Babies, the La Sugar Babies, and Waller's "Buddies" include many tracks that had not been previously issued with proper titles. The 21 precious cuts are loaded with good vibes and silliness. This is a prime target for those new to Fats. −MGN

★ **Complete Fats Waller - Vols. 1 - 4 / RCA**   1934
Vol. 1, 1934-1935; Vol. 2, 1935; Vol. 3, 1935-1936; Vol. 4, 1936.

Fine Arabian Stuff / MUSE   1939

His Piano & His Rhythm 1939 / VOGUE   1939

Rare Piano Roll Solos - Vol. 3 / BIOGRAPH   193?

● **Last Years / RCA**   1940
1940-1943.

Classic Jazz / BIOGRAPH

Fats Waller / LASERLIGHT

Joint Is Jumpin' / RCA   COMP

GEORGE WALLINGTON b 1924

Swing, bop. Swing-to-bop piano giant. Phenomenal technique. Mostly works in trios occasionally in small group. Prolific composer. −MGN

George Wallington Trios / OJC 1952
Charles Mingus (b) and Oscar Pettiford (b) soar in these 1952 and 1953 trio dates. Wallington plays well, though not in either's class as a soloist. −RW

○ **Jazz for the Carriage / OJC** 1956
Excellent set. Phil Woods (as) and Donald Byrd (tpt) among the luminaries. 1985 reissue, limited edition. −RW

George Wallington Trio & Sextet / SAVOY i 1956
W/ Brew Moore (ts). −MGN

● **Dance of the Infidels / SAVOY** 1957
His definitive recording, with Donald Byrd (tpt) and Phil Woods (as) super and Wallington at his best. −RW

JACK WALRATH b 1946

Post-bop, progressive big band, neo bop. Good trumpeter who was part of what was perhaps the last vibrant Mingus ensemble, where he played alongside Don Pullen and George Adams. He's been a session player and bandleader since the late 70s, and currently heads the Masters Of Suspense. −RW

● **Demons in Pursuit / GATEMOUTH**
Mingus trumpeter with progressive quintet on all originals. Great liner notes by Walrath. Seek this one. −MGN

A Plea for Sanity / STASH 1982
Drummerless trio with pianist Michael Cochran and bassist Anthony Cox. All originals. A delight. −MGN

Master of Suspense / BLUE NOTE 1987
Septet cuts, exceptional playing by Walrath, Steve Torre (tb), and James Williams (p). −RW

Gut Feelings / MUSE 1991
W/ Walrath's current group. Carter Jefferson (ts), Anthony Cox (b) are prime players. −RW

○ **Neohippus / CAPITOL**
John Abercrombie slashes away on guitar. Rick Margitza (reeds) is effective soloist. CD has two bonus cuts. −RW

CEDAR WALTON b 1934

Post-bop, jazz-rock. Another keyboard great better known as a superb accompanist than a soloist, although he's delivered many masterly statements over the years. Walton moved to New York from Dallas in the late 50s, and was part of J. J. Johnson's sextet from 1958-1960. Later he replaced McCoy Tyner in the Jazztet in 1960-1961, then spent three pivotal years with Art Blakey's Jazz Messengers, whom he rejoined briefly in 1973. During his Messengers tenure, Walton's long lines, keen harmonic sense, and ability to interact with Blakey and the horn frontline put him in the upper echelon among jazz pianists. He began to get plenty of work on Blue Note and Prestige sessions and also started to release his own albums. Walton went to Europe in 1970 and has since spent lots of time there. During the 70s he made several memorable releases with Clifford Jordan, George Coleman, Hank Mobley, and others, was part of two excellent small combos, and also did an excellent series on Timeless under the banner of Eastern Rebellion. −RW

Cedar! / PRESTIGE 1967
Excellent 1967 session with Kenny Dorham (tpt) and Junior Cook (ts). Released in 1991. Typically no-frills, emphatic pieces and solos. −RW

● **Plays Cedar Walton / OJC** 1967
1967-1969. 1988 reissue of Walton giving his own work a showcase. Host of great players, among them Kenny Dorham (tpt) and Clifford Jordan (ts). CD has bonus cut. −RW

○ **Breakthrough / MUSE** 1972
Quintet with Hank Mobley (ts). Irresistible. −MGN

○ **Night at Boomer's - Vol. 1 / MUSE / DB 5** 1973
Luminous, beautiful quartet date. −RW

○ **Night at Boomer's - Vol. 2 / MUSE / DB 5** 1973
Equally first-rate set from Boomer's. −RW

☆ **Eastern Rebellion / TIMELESS** 1975
George Coleman (ts) at his peak, brilliant playing. −RW

Among Friends / THERESA ca. 1990
Just immaculate mainstream/bop with comrades Billy Higgins (d), Buster Williams (b), and Bobby Hutcherson (vib). −RW

Up Front / TIMELESS
Delightful piano. −RW

CARLOS WARD b 1940

Post-bop, neo bop, modern creative. Jamaican-born saxophonist and flutist. He had done steady work w/ Carla Bley and Abdullah Ibrahim and is as reliable, consistent, and rich with ideas as any. −MGN

○ **Lito / LEO** 1988
Live date at the North Sea Jazz Festival for saxophonist/flutist with quartet featuring trumpeter Woody Shaw. Extended work. Excellent. −MGN

WILBUR WARE 1923-1979

Bop, hard-bop, post-bop. A wonderful, exciting bassist. Wilbur Ware managed to overcome some stylistic limitations by his ability to break up the beats, and substitute tones and notes in his solos. He could sometimes befuddle others on the bandstand by this method, but he always managed to link his statements thematically, and resolve things to the success of the composition. He had great touch and articulation, but didn't approach or roam over the instrument like some other players, preferring to emphasize the lower end in his playing. Ware was a self-taught banjo player and his foster father made him a bass. He played in string bands around Chicago, then worked in groups led by Stuff Smith, Roy Eldridge, and Sonny Stitt in the late 40s. During the 50s he periodically had his own bands, while working with Eddie "Cleanhead" Vinson, Art Blakey, Buddy DeFranco, Thelonious Monk, and J. R. Monterose. He returned to Chicago from New York in 1959, went back to New York in the late 60s, and reunited with Monk in 1970. The last part of his life he played with Clifford Jordan and Paul Jeffrey. He led a group that recorded on Fantasy in the late 50s, and included Johnny Griffin, John Jenkins and Junior Mance. −RW

☆ **Chicago Sound / OJC** 1957
Legendary bassist. With Johnny Griffin (ts) and John Jenkins (as). A classic. −MGN

EARLE WARREN b 1914

Swing, big band, ballads. The first outstanding alto saxophonist ever in Count Basie's band, and one of the few who took some attention away from the perennially popular tenors like Herschel Evans and Lester Young. Warren joined Basie in 1937. He spent nearly 13 years with Basie, playing and doing some vocals. He left in 1950, later was a manager for such performers as Johnny Otis, and had three stints with Buck Clayton. He continued to tour into the 70s and 80s. −RW

○ **The Count's Men / MUSE** 1985
A nice set of swinging jazz ... Some Basie standards and some ballads performed with feeling and panache. −RON WEINSTOCK, CADENCE

DINAH WASHINGTON 1924-1963

Blues-jazz, ballads. They called her "The Queen of the Blues," but as Dinah herself said, she could "sing anything — anything at all." At first, she sang gospel with the Sallie Martin Singers. In 1943, having been discovered by manager Joe Glaser, she was with Lionel Hampton's band, getting little exposure on records but a new name. By 1946, with a Mercury

Records contract, she was on her own. Her earliest hits were in the rhythm & blues field, but before long she "crossed over," with such material as "Harbor Lights" and, especially, "What a Difference a Day Makes." With a great gift for projecting lyrics, a sardonic sense of humor, and a voice that was made for blues and jazz, Dinah Washington was also a terrific performer. Her records in a jazz setting (her horn accompanists included trumpeters Clifford Brown, Clark Terry, and Maynard Ferguson; her pianist Wynton Kelly and a young Joe Zawinul) rate with the best of the period, and had she lived, there's no telling what she might have accomplished. Her many emulators include the late Esther Phillips and Nancy Wilson. –DM

○ **Mellow Mama / DELMARK**   1945
At last, these Apollo sessions are available. Seminal Dinah, plus Lucky Thompson takes spotlight on tenor sax. –RW

Dinah Jams / POLYGRAM   1954
Very nice big-band/jazz date. –RW

Slick Chick - R&B Years / POLYGRAM / DB 5   1954
Nice big-band date. –RW

○ **Jazz Sides / POLYGRAM**   1954
1954-1958. Great two-record set that accents her mid-50s jazz cuts. Until recently, that was about all the jazz of Dinah's that was in print. –RW

Dinah / POLYGRAM   1956
This is a fresh reissue of a sumptuous 50s date with three bonus cuts. –RW

In the Land of Hi-Fi / POLYGRAM   1956
Super cuts — fast and slow. Nice orchestrations also. –RW

Fats Waller Songbook / POLYGRAM / DB 5   1957
Brilliant interpretations and sound. –RW

○ **Bessie Smith Songbook / POLYGRAM**   1957
1957 & 1958. A wonderful revision of classic blues cuts. –RW

Two of Us / POLYGRAM   1960
Wonderful duets between Brook Benton (v) and Washington, plus solo cuts by both from 1960. –RW

What a Diff'rence a Day Made / POLYGRAM   1960
Title cut is one of her biggest hits ever. Everything else is a bit over-arranged, but she sounds great. Billboard #34. –RW

Dinah 1963 / CAPITOL   1963
1990 reissue of last crop of Washington material. –RW

In Love / CAPITOL (ROULETTE?)   r 1963
A beautiful reissue with some six bonus cuts. –RW

★ **Complete on Mercury - Vols. 1 - 7 / POLYGRAM**   COMP
If you buy one, you'll want them all. Important musical documents. –MGN

GROVER WASHINGTON JR.   b 1943

Soul jazz, jazz-rock, instr-pop, contemporary funk. One of the most commercially successful saxophonists in jazz history. A versatile reed specialist, Washington is equally at home on soprano, alto, or tenor sax, and has recorded on flute and baritone sax. A much more creative improviser than his hit-making saxophone competitors, Washington has had hits with almost everything he has done since his first album (*Inner City Blues*) for Kudu in 1971. His biggest albums, *Mr. Magic* (Kudu) and *Winelight* (Elektra), have also spawned hit singles. His recordings for Kudu, Motown, Elektra, and Columbia are mostly commercial in content but, given that, Washington's saxophone work is always first rate and a good distance in front of his closest fusion rivals. –BP

● **Inner City Blues / MOTOWN**   r 1972
Definitive early-70s soul-jazz date. Washington has seldom been more convincing. Ron Carter is stalwart on bass. W/ Bob James (p), Eric Gale (g), and Airto (per), and Thad Jones (tpt). –RW

○ **Mr. Magic / MOTOWN / BB 10**   1974
This is one of his best early albums. –JME

Feels So Good / MOT / BB 10   1975
Infrequent good solos, mostly instrumental pop. –RW

○ **A Secret Place / MOTOWN / BB 31**   1977
Secret Place/All the King's Horses / MOTOWN 1977
Two fusion albums combined on single disc. –RW

Live at the Bijou / MOTOWN   r 1978

○ **Winelight / ELEKTRA-ASYLUM / BB 5**   1980
Double-platinum album. Contains hit single "Just the Two of Us." Gold album. –JME

○ **Then & Now / CBS**   1988
At times Washington has strong solos. His best supporting lineup, includes Herbie Hancock (k), Tommy Flanagan (p), and Ron Carter (b). –RW

ROB WASSERMAN

World fusion, neo bop. Inventive bassist Rob Wasserman made a splash in 1988 with his *Duets* album, featuring Bobby McFerrin, Ricki Lee Jones, and others. He has accompanied Lou Reed and sometimes plays in a duo with Grateful Dead guitarist Bob Weir. Also known for his fine work with David Grisman. –WR

Solo / ROUNDER   r 1983
Some super playing. –RW

● **Duets / MCA**   1988
Some amazing duets and a great lineup that includes Aaron Neville (v), Stephane Grappelli (violin), Dan Hicks (v, g), and so on. The jazz community missed this one. –RW

KAZUMI WATANABE   b 1953

Contemporary funk.
Japanese guitarist and Gramavision recording artist. Watanabe's best-known works are *Mobo Club I & II* and *Mobo Splash.* –RW

○ **To Chi Ka / DENON**   1984
A great album featuring Kenny Kirkland (k), Mike Manieri (vib) and Warren Bernhardt (p).   PK

○ **Spice of Life / RHINO**   1987
This album is a fusion-lover's dream. Bill Bruford (d) and Jeff Berlin (b) drive Watanabe. –PK

Spice of Life Too / RHINO   1988
A continuation of *Spice of Life* with stronger compositions and a hint of softer tones. Very nice! –PK

Kilowatt / RHINO   1989
This release picks up where *Spice of Life Too* left off. Bunny Brunel's bass work shines. –PK

SADAO WATANABE   b 1933

Bop, hard-bop, post-bop, jazz-rock, instr-pop, contemporary funk. A Japanese alto and soprano saxophonist with three main strengths: commercially oriented jazz/funk, avant-garde leanings, or the bop roots of his main influence, Charlie Parker. –MGN

Jazz & Bossa / POLYGRAM   1966
Some nice Afro-Latin arrangements. –RW

○ **Dedicated to Charlie Parker / DENON**   1969
One of his best, due mainly to material. –RW

Round Trip / VANGUARD   1974
More-progressive setting with Chick Corea (k), Miroslav Vitous (b), and Jack DeJohnette (d). –MGN

Nabasada & Charlie / CATALYST   1977
An excellent date with fellow saxophonist Charlie Mariano. Standards played with verve. –MGN

○ **Bird of Paradise / INNER CITY**   1979
Recording with great jazz trio. Japanese alto saxophonist plays bop with conviction. –MGN

Parker's Mood / ELEKTRA-ASYLUM   1986
Close to his best, both on his merit and thanks to aid from James Williams (p) and Jeff Watts (d). 1986 date. –RW

Elis / ELEKTRA-ASYLUM   1988
Some good playing. –RW

BENNY WATERS   b 1902

Post-bop, blues-jazz. Alto sax, clarinet, arranger. One of the great jazz veterans, whose experience and grounding extends back to the 20s. Waters managed to retain the energy and drive of a youngster while continuing his career well into his 80s. But he's an exceptional alto saxophonist, capable of executing difficult passages at top speeds easily and demonstrating extensive harmonic knowledge and creativity as a soloist. Waters studied at the Boston Conservatory before playing with Charlie Johnson's band from 1925-1932 and also recording with Clarence Williams and King Oliver. He spent time with Hot Lips Page and Fletcher Henderson in the 30s, and then worked with Claude Hopkins and the Jimmie Lunceford orchestra in the years before World War II. He led his own groups in the 50s, then left America for Europe, joining Jacques Butler's band in 1955. He became a star in Europe for 15 years, making tours, recordings, and periodically coming back to America for a visit. −RW

○ **From Paradise (Small's) to Shangrila / MUSE**   1987
An always interesting player elevates ordinary material. −RW
Memories of the Twenties, Stomp Off / SOS
Nice tribute to past eras. −RW

ETHEL WATERS   1896-1977

Ballads. A well-known vaudville and Cotton Club diva, Waters became famous recording "St. Louis Blues," "Stormy Weather," and "Cabin in the Sky." She worked with Duke Ellington, Benny Goodman, and many Black theater troupes. −MGN

○ **On Stage and Screen / COLUMBIA**

DOUG WATKINS   b 1934

Hard-bop, post-bop. Popular Detroit bassist whose list of credits dwarfs all except his better-half, Paul Chambers. Bastion of the 50s, post-to-hard-bop legion. −MGN

○ **Watkins at Large / TRANSITION**   i 1956
W/ Hank Mobley (ts). −MGN
● **Soulnik / NEW JAZZ**   i 1960
W/ Yusef Lateef (ts). −MGN

JULIUS WATKINS   b 1921

Hard-bop, post-bop, progressive big band. The pre-eminent post-bop French horn player in jazz. Prolific arranger and composer. Another of the Detroit jazz legends of the 50s. −MGN

○ **Sextet - Vol. 2 / BLUE NOTE**   i 1954
● **Sextet / BLUE NOTE**   i 1954
W/ Frank Foster (ts). −MGN

MARY WATKINS

Ballads, progressive big band. Although best known as a pianist and feminist composer, she has also written her share of jazz for small to large ensembles. −MGN

● **Winds of Change / PAJ**   1981
Large ensemble/orchestral recording done at Herbst Theatre in San Francisco. Watkins plays piano in the spirit of, say, Duke Pearson and Melba Liston. A fine album to find. −MGN
○ **Spiritsong / RDW**   1985
Different, perhaps arty. Imaginative. Worth looking for. −MGN

MITCH WATKINS

Contemporary funk, M-base. Fusion guitarist with wild streak. Also capable sideman in the soul/jazz organ combo. A progressive musician, leaning toward rock, but influenced by many musicians. A comer. −MGN

○ **Curves / RHINO**   1990
Fusion/mainstream set. −RW

CLEVELAND WATKISS

Post-bop, neo bop. Good British vocalist, not strictly a jazz stylist, but works in improvisational vein. He's similiar to

Bobby McFerrin in that he experiments with overdubbing, vocalisms, and rhythms and moods, rather than simply interpreting songs. His 1990 debut on Antilles attracted widespread praise. −RW

○ **Green Chimneys / POLYGRAM**   r 1991
An arresting session from a new British jazz vocalist. −RW

BOBBY WATSON   b 1953

Hard-bop, post-bop, neo bop. Alto sax. Bobby Watson has steadily emerged as a top player and now must be considered among the premier alto saxophonists on the jazz scene. He has a bright, full tone, a vibrant sound, and is versatile enough to have recorded bop and contemporary R&B, yet has not turned to fusion or instrumental pop. He moved to New York in the mid 70s, and was a member of Art Blakey's Jazz Messengers from 1977-1981, attaining at one point the position of musical director for the group. During the 80s Watson played with several groups, among them George Coleman's octet, Charlie Persip's Superband, the Louis Hayes quartet, and the 29th Street Saxophone Band, as well as Sam Riuck's Winds of Manhattan, Philly Joe Jones, Dameronia, Panama Francis, and the Savoy Sultans. His current band is Horizon, and Watson recently released his first album for the Columbia label to unanimous praises. −RW

● **E.T.A / ROULETTE**   1977
Some of his best compositions. −MGN
○ **Advance / RHINO**   1984
1991 reissue that heralded arrival of former Jazz Messenger Bobby Watson as major figure in 1984. −RW
No Question About It / CAPITOL   1988
Watson heads two groups. Many of the best players around, including John Hicks (p) and Roy Hargrove (tpt). −RW
○ **Post-Motown Bop / CAPITOL**   1990
Despite the title, this is an excellent and traditional set. Watson is sparkling. −RW
The Inventor / CAPITOL   r 1990
High-quality hard bop from one of the best combos of 80s and 90s. −RW

LU WATTERS   1911-1989

Swing, big band. Trumpet, bandleader. A major leader of the San Francisco phase of the New Orleans revival, Lu Watters played trumpet and led a big band on the West Coast during the 30s, but ultimately became dissatisfied with swing and began to seek new sources of inspiration, which he found in the music of King Oliver's Creole Jazz Band recordings. In 1940 he formed the Yerba Buena Jazz Band in an effort to achieve greater freedom of expression in a collectively/improvised, small-band format. While he was in the Navy during World War II, musicians from the Yerba Buena participated in the 1943-1944 Bunk Johnson sessions sponsored by the Hot Jazz Society of San Francisco. In addition to presiding over the return to "authenticity" among Bay Area jazz musicians, Watters contributed original compositions, such as "Big Bear Stomp," and "Emperor Norton's Hunch," to the "traditionalist" repertoire, as well as writing special arrangements of vintage New Orleans-style tunes that are still extremely popular with groups dedicated to the genre. By 1946 he was recording the Yerba Buena in venues like the Avalon Ballroom in order to get an authentic dancehall sound. In 1950 he retired from music to pursue his favorite hobby, the collection and study of gemstones. The Yerba Buena was the first of the San Francisco revival groups, but it was far from the last; sidemen such as trombonist Turk Murphy and trumpeter Bob Scobey went on to form groups of their own, making the Yerba Buena important not only for its own sake but also as an incubator for further development of the revival sound. As Nesuhi Ertegun so aptly put it, Lu Watters might best be considered as a "Johnny Appleseed of Jazz." −BR

● **San Francisco Style / GOOD TIME JAZZ**   1946
The repertoire that turned San Francisco "trad crazy" —

Morton's "New Orleans Joys," Richard M. Jones's "Jazzin' Babies Blues," and "Ory's Creole Trombone," among others, done in revival style. —BR

○ **San Francisco - Vol. 2 / GOOD TIME JAZZ**
Especially notable for originals by Watters such as "Big Bear Stomp," "Emperor Norton's Hunch," and "Annie Street Rock," as well as Turk Murphy's "Trombone Rag." —BR

CHARLIE WATTS

Bop, progressive big band. Longtime Rolling Stones drummer is also a devoted jazz fan, and has led both big bands and small combos in England for several years. A couple of years ago he recorded a tribute album to Charlie Parker and toured with a big band. He recently issued another tribute album, this time dedicating it to Parker's famous album with strings, utilizing a combo format with a string section. —RW

○ **Live at Fulham Town Hall / CBS**   1986
Rolling Stones drummer makes a go with a big band and succeeds. —MGN

WEATHER REPORT

Jazz-rock. Weather Report fired some of the first shots in the fusion revolution, and for the majority of the decade and a half of its existence were its premier exponents. Founded by Joe Zawinul and Wayne Shorter, two key participants in Miles Davis's initial fusion breakthrough, the duo was joined by a host of rhythm section members throughout the band's duration. At the outset, Weather Report remained firmly within jazz structures while working with voicings borrowed from rock. Miroslav Vitous's upright bass quickly gave way to Alphonso Johnson's electric work. Zawinul's Rhodes piano would ultimately be replaced by polyphonic synthesizers, further altering the texture of the group's sound. The arrival of bassist Jaco Pastorius not only gave Weather Report a dazzling new voice, but also gave the group another excellent composer. It was during this period that the group enjoyed its greatest popularity, breaking from the often-impressionistic style of its earlier work to a more open, pop-influenced direction. Still, Weather Report always avoided the pitfalls of many of their contemporaries, never resorting to mundane funk workouts. The considerable skills and musicianship of Zawinul and Shorter kept Weather Report well above the rest. —SA

○ **I Sing the Body Electric / CBS**   1971
A great record from the days when they were still a serious jazz band. —RW

☆ **Weather Report / CBS**   i 1971
The 1971 release that heralded their coming. At the time they were a breath of fresh life, with sterling compositions and great solos from Wayne Shorter (sax), Joe Zawinul (k), and Miroslav Vitous (b). —RW

Sweetnighter / COLUMBIA   1973
Funkier, and more rock-directed. —JME

★ **Mysterious Traveller / CBS / BB 46**   1973
1973-1974. Their best. —MGN

Tale Spinnin' / COLUMBIA   1975
Black Market / CBS / DB 5   1976
A good one with Jaco Pastorius (b). —MGN

Mr. Gone / CBS / BB 52   1978
Formulaic, though Shorter (sax) and Zawinul (k) are always great. —RW

Weather Report / COL / BB 68   1981
Jaco Pastorius (b) ruled the day. —RW

Heavy Weather / COLUMBIA   1987
One of their best-selling albums. —JME

EBERHARD WEBER   ♭1940

Jazz-rock, modern creative. Among Europe's greatest jazz bassists. He worked with Wolfgang Dauner from 1962-1972, becoming a full-time musician in 1972, then working with

---

Jazz Accordian

First Jazz... well-known Joe Mooney Quartet... in 1946-47
Other swing accordionists included Mat Mathews
Dutch group, the Millers
Art Van Damme from Norway

Popular in Europe
Kamil Behounek – soloist 1936 — Toivo Kärki — Nisse Lind
Buddy Bertinat (with the Original Teddies)

1950s and early 60s included:
Mat Mathews — Art Van Damme — Leon Sash
Pete Joyy — Tommy Gumina

Dave Pike in 1972-1973, and Volker Kriegel's Spectrum in 1973-1974. These extensive experiences enabled Weber to become skilled in every phase of bass playing, both jazz and rock, and led him to create a new instrument in the early 70s he called an "electrobass," an upright with electric properties. Weber began recording prolifically for ECM, both as a leader and also with Gary Burton and Ralph Towner, before forming his group Colours in 1975 and heading it until 1982. He joined Jan Garbarek's band in 1982, then began to do solo concerts in 1985, while remaining part of the United Jazz and Rock Ensemble. —RW

● **Colours of Chloe / POLYGRAM**   1975
German electric bassist in his glory. Original material. —MGN

○ **Works / POLYGRAM**   COMP
Compilation of his material. —RW

BEN WEBSTER   1909-1973

Swing, big band, bop, blues-jazz. Originally a pianist. After working with a series of great mid-western bands, among them Bennie Moten's and Andy Kirk's, he joined Fletcher Henderson in 1934, in the chair of his idol, Coleman Hawkins and later worked with Cab Calloway and Teddy Wilson's fine, short-lived band. But it was when he joined Duke Ellington in 1939 that Webster truly came into his own with such famous solos as "Cottontail," "All Too Soon," and "Sepia Panorama." The warmth of his tone, the drive of his beat, and the majestic simplicity of his melodic conception all came together in the settings the Duke devised for him. All of this was a big influence on his younger contemporaries. After leaving Ellington in 1943, he mostly worked with his own small groups, recording prolifically. He also toured with Jazz at the Philharmonic, but didn't visit Europe until 1965; once there, however, he stayed for good, living mostly in Copenhagen and Amsterdam and becoming a beloved elder statesman of jazz. His ballad playing of the later years is among the true glories of jazz. —DM

○ **Ben Meets Don / POLYGRAM**   ca. 194?
1986 release. An album of timeless, wonderful solos. W/ Don Byas (ts). —RW

● **Complete Ben Webster on Emarcy / EMARCY**   1951
1951-1953. Top anthology covering pivotal Webster cuts. —RW

○ **Ballads / VERVE**   1954
1954-1955. A primer on how to execute ballads. —RW

Soulville / POLYGRAM   r 1958
Two-record set of just incredible Webster cuts. —RW

Meets Gerry Mulligan / VERVE   1959
Just a great pairing, despite different concepts. —RW

☆ **Ben Webster & Associates / POLYGRAM**   r 1959
You can't go wrong with Webster, Coleman Hawkins (sax), Budd Jones (b), and many other masters of ballads, blues, and standards. –RW

At the Renaissance / OJC   1960
1989 reissue of nice set. CD has four bonus cuts. –RW

Ben and Sweets / CBS   1962
1987 release of super date. Harry Edison (tpt) is dynamic, Webster his usual impressive self. –RW

See You at the Fair / JASMINE   1964
Excellent set. –RW

Soulmates / OJC   r 1964
This is some of Zawinul's (k) best playing outside of his work in Miles bands, Weather Report, or his days with the Adderleys. –RW

Did You Call / NESSA   1972
Luminous, beautiful playing. –RW

Webster Meets Oscar Peterson / POLYGRAM   i 1986
1986 release, consistently seamlessly excellent. –RW

Giants of Tenor Sax / COMMODORE
Excellent pairing. –RW

The Kid and the Brute / VERVE
Here is another excellent pairing, this time w/ Illinois Jacquet (ts). –RW

DAVE WECKL

M-base. Drummer Weckl currently performs with Chick Corea's Elektric and Akoustic Bands. He has also performed with guitarist Bill Connors. –PK

○ **Master Plan / GRP**   1990
The solo debut from this Chick Corea Elektric Band drummer. Jazz, with hints of rock. Includes a track with drummer Steve Gadd. –PK

KEN WERNER

Post-bop, neo-bop. A fascinating pianist/electronic keyboardist who is bound by few restrictions. An absolutely astounding trio pianist, he can back singers (notably Roseanna Vitro) with perfect empathy, and has done some interesting synthesizer programming. –MGN

○ **Introducing the Trio / SUNNYSIDE**   ca. 1989
Werner (p), Ratso Harris (b), Tommy Rainey (d). Contains four compositions by Werner, two by Harris, three standards. Nice tribute to Herbie Nichols. One of the finer trio dates of the last decade. –MGN

○ **Uncovered Heart / SUNNYSIDE**   ca. 1990
Werner also adds synths and Randy Brecker (tpt), Joe Lovano (sax), Eddie Gomez (b), and John Riley and Cafe (per). More compelling from an emotional standpoint, near-gripping. Werner is quite a player; here he shows he's quite a human being. –MGN

● **Press Enter / SUNNYSIDE**   1992

FRED WESLEY

Neo bop, R&B/jazz. Wesley has played with Count Basie's orchestra. During the 60s and 70s, he was a pivotal member of James Brown's bands, serving at times as musical director. His slippery riffs and pungent, precise solos, contrasting with those of saxophonist Maceo Parker, gave Brown's R&B, soul, and funk tunes their instrumental punch. He later left Brown and spent several years playing with George Clinton's various Parliament/Funkadelic projects, even recording a couple of albums as a spinoff group, The Horny Horns. He recently cut an album as a leader on Antilles, working with many young-lion types, who remember his music with Brown and are interested in finding common ground between improvisatory and funk/R&B territory. –RW

○ **New Friends / POLYGRAM**   1990
All-star lineup doing soul-jazz, funk, and blues. Has been highly popular, despite dubious value. –RW

● **Comme Ci Comme Ca / ANTILLES**   ca. 1991
This trombonist shines in a jazz context with an eight-piece. Hugh Ragin on trumpet, Karl Denson and Maceo Parker on sax, and the Peter Madsen Trio are featured on this album of two standards, two pop-styled tunes, and originals played with punch. The title track is especially right-on. –MGN

FRANK WESS   b 1922

Big band, post-bop, progressive big band. Kansas City born Frank Wess is a flute player, and saxophonist with few peers. He played with Count Basie in the 50s and 60s, and with Sir Roland Hanna in the New York Jazz Quartet in the 70s. A premier soloist with Toshika Akiyoshi Big Band in the 80s, he has been leading his own big band lately, with roots in the music he has always played — thoroughly swinging. –MGN

○ **I Hear Ya' Talkin' / SAVOY**   1959
A super session with Thad Jones (cnt), Hank Jones (p), and Curtis Fuller (tb). –RW

☆ **Flute Juice / PROGRESSIVE**   1981
Smooth at times, bluesy at others. –RW

● **Flute Talk / PROGRESSIVE**   ca. 1981
W/ Tommy Flanagan Trio and guitarist Chuck Wayne, Wess is unbelievable. Includes four standards and two Wess originals. This might be tricky to locate, but dig for it. It is a great album. –MGN

Two at the Top / UPTOWN   1983
With Johnny Coles on trumpet and the Kenny Barron Trio, these are all standards with the emphasis on hard- and cool-bop from Kenny Dorham (tpt), Gigi Gryce (as), and Benny Golson (ts). Wess plays alto and tenor sax only. The arrangements are by Don Sickler. –MGN

Dear Mr. Basie / CONCORD   1990
Nice tribute to swing master. –RW

Entre Nous / CONCORD   1990
Very nice 1990 date, with longtime swing veterans showing the way it's done. CD version has two bonus tracks. –RW

Wess to Memphis / ENTERPRISE
Very pop and blues, but some good flute playing. –RW

MIKE WESTBROOK   b 1936

Progressive big band. Progressive big-band leader from UK who loves Ellington, Weill, and Blake. Multi-faceted music and performance art. Politically charged. –MGN

● **Marching Song / DERAM**   1969
Anti-Vietnam War jazz symphony. With British free-jazz heavies. –MGN

○ **Off Abbey Road / RHINO**   1969

RANDY WESTON   b 1926

Post-bop, cool, soul jazz, progressive big band, world fusion neo bop, modern. Randy Weston has been among the most visionary artists in jazz, incorporating elements of African and Indian music into his work long before it was either fashionable or commonplace to do so. He's especially innovative as a composer in the area of rhythm, and his arrangements are equally compelling, whether for small combos or large orchestras. Weston worked with Art Blakey in the 40s, then began heading his own groups in the mid 50s. He's lived and studied in Africa for many years, and at one time ran a club in Tangiers. He's also been a label owner for a short time, while recording for United Artists, Jubilee, Dawn, Roulette, CTI, Verve, Atlantic, and recently for Antilles. –RW

Jazz à la Bohemia / OJC   1956
Live trio recording. Excellent. –MGN

How High the Moon / BIOGRAPH   1956

○ **Uhuru Africa/Highlife / CAPITOL**   1961
Futuristic exploration of link between Africa and jazz, done in 1961 and 1964. Great players, and both traditional jazz, African, and Latin percussionists. –RW

● **African Cookbook / ATLANTIC / DB 5**　　　r 1972
High-caliber arrangements, bombastic piano. –RW

● **Blue Moses / CTI / DB 5**　　　1972
Very rare date on CTI, one of the few that wasn't geared to pop/R&B public but was ambitious and aggressive. –RW

Carnival / FREEDOM-ARISTA　　　1974
African and Caribbean influences with jazz base. –RW

Blues to Africa / FREEDOM　　　1974
Superior compositions, excellent solos. –RW

African Nite / INNER CITY　　　r 1975

Portraits of Duke Ellington / POLYGRAM　　　r 1990
Topflight set by Weston, paying his homage to Duke in a very distinctive fashion. –RW

Portraits of Monk / POLYGRAM / DB 5　　　1990
Engaging, thoughtful playing. –RW

Self Portraits / POLYGRAM / DB 5　　　ca. 1990
Percussive, aggressive, and intense piano. –RW

☆ **Spirits of Our Ancestors / ANTILLES**　　　ca. 1991
Weston with eleven-piece band and guests Pharoah Sanders and Dizzy Gillespie. The stellar arrangements are by Melba Liston. Familiar themes are "The Healers," "Blue Moses," "African Cookbook," and "African Village/Bedford Stuyvesant." Most of the ten tracks are extended on this two-CD set. This has album of the year potential. –MGN

Zulu / MILESTONE　　　COMP
Good compilation of 60s Weston sessions. –RW

KENNY WHEELER　　　b 1930

Post-bop, jazz-rock, neo bop, modern creative. Canadian-born, British resident. Plays trumpet and flugelhorn. Has worked in traditional and progressive big bands and free-music ensembles. His own group has an atmospheric, introspective quality, accounting for his personal sound. Hard to categorize, he is an improviser and melodicist first. –MGN

● **Gnu High / POLYGRAM**　　　1975
This is longwinded and worthwhile, w/ the Keith Jarrett (p) Trio. –MGN

○ **Deer Wan / POLYGRAM**　　　1977
Earthy and ethereal jazz from veteran flugelhorn and trumpet player with Ralph Towner (g), Jan Garbarek (ts), and John Abercrombie (g). Extended compositions. –MGN

Double, Double You / POLYGRAM　　　1984
Quintet set. Some good playing by Mike Brecker (sax). –RW

Widow in the Window / POLYGRAM　　　1990
Among his best, thanks to John Abercrombie (g) and Peter Erskine (d). –RW

Music for Large & Small Ensembles / POLYGRAM　r 1991
Good compositions and arrangements. –RW

JIGGS WHIGHAM　　　b 1943

Swing, bop. Jiggs Whigham has enjoyed success in both the academic and performing worlds. He spent three years in the Glenn Miller Orchestra (1961-1964), serving as lead trombonist and soloist, and later worked with Stan Kenton. He left America for Cologne, West Germany in 1965, joining Kurt Edelhagen and touring Africa with him a year later. He became a prolific studio musician in Germany. –RW

○ **The Jiggs Up / CAPRI**　　　1989
W/ Bud Shank (as). Strong players and an interestingly varied program covering the usual mainstream modern bases make this album a winner. –DAVID FRANKLIN, CADENCE

ANDREW WHITE　　　b 1942

Post-bop, early free, neo bop, modern creative. Transcriber of John Coltrane, Charlie Parker, and Ornette Coleman. Also a progressive and entertaining performer. Truly a one-of-a-kind player. –MGN

○ **Maxine Spotts & Brown / ANDREW'S MUSIC**　　　1975
Live recording at Top O' the Foolery with quartet. Includes the lengthy "Dizzy Atmosphere." Very good. –MGN

Live in New York - Vols. 1 & 2 / ANDREWS MUSIC　　　1977
Uneven but frequently exciting sessions from jazz loft sessions. –RW

● **I Love Japan / ANDREW'S MUSIC**　　　1979
Live recording at the One Step Down with quartet and this D.C. historian/transcriber/progressive saxophonist. –MGN

Fonk Update / ANDREW'S MUSIC　　　1979
Another solid statement, including the delightfully delirious "Who Got De Fonk?" –MGN

MICHAEL WHITE　　　b 1933

Trad. New Orleans traditional. New Orleans clarinetist who stays within the early-period jazz of his home. Was a mainstay of Preservation Hall in the 70s to 80s. –MGN

○ **Crescent City Serenade / POLYGRAM**　　　1990
Early-period jazz from New Orleans clarinetist/historian. Excellent recording. –MGN

○ **Live at Vanguard, New Year's Eve / ANTILLES**
High-quality New Orleans jazz, excellent clarinet solos. –RW

PAUL WHITEMAN　　　1890-1967

Big band, instr-pop. Born in Denver, where his father was supervisor of school music, Whiteman played in the local symphony but became interested in the new dance rhythms and formed a band in San Francisco. A 1919 Atlantic City engagement brought a Victor Records contract, and the band scored a tremendous 1920 hit with "Whispering." Pianist and composer Ferde Grofé was mainly responsible for Whiteman's early style; instead of playing stock arrangements, the band had its own original scores, and it soon became the pacesetter for modern dance music. Always ambitious, Whiteman branched out into popular concert music and in 1924 presented his famous concert of "symphonic jazz" in New York. For that occasion he commissioned young George Gershwin to write "Rhapsody in Blue." Dubbed "The King of Jazz," Whiteman by now was the world's most famous and best-paid band leader; he toured Europe in 1926 and in the following year, aware that his ever-growing band was not strong in real jazz players, hired the stars of the bankrupt Jean Goldkette band. Among these were Bix Beiderbecke, Frank Trumbauer, and arranger Bill Challis. Eddie Lang, Joe Venuti, Red Nichols, and the Dorsey Brothers had already worked with Whiteman, and a young singer named Bing Crosby was creating a new style (he was also a member of the hip Whiteman Rhythm Boys trio). Later, Whiteman featured such jazz stars as Jack Teagarden and Bunny Berigan, but it was from 1927 to 1930, when Challis, Tom Satterfield, Lennie Hayton, and William Grant Still were among his arrangers, that Whiteman came even close to justifying his title. (It must be kept in mind that "jazz" in the 20s did not connote what it does today — it meant snappy dance music of the day, not the music of Louis Armstrong and Duke Ellington.) Whiteman's unfortunate royal title cost him much of the respect he well deserves as a force for higher standards in popular music and as a great talent spotter who paid generous wages and treated his musicians very well. Whiteman retired from bandleading by 1943 (one of his last record dates featured Billie Holiday) but was frequently heard and seen on radio and TV as a host of popular-music programs. He left his enormous library of arrangements to Williams College. –DM

○ **With Bing Crosby / COLUMBIA**　　　192?
Prime late-20s, early-30s cuts. Bing Crosby emerging as a superstar. –RW

Bix Beiderbecke Legend / RCA　　　ca. 196?
Really not his session, but some seminal early jazz. –RW

○ **Victor Masters / RCA**
Some fine sessions. –RW

MARK WHITFIELD
b 1966

Post-bop, neo bop. Young jazz guitarist, stays within the bop/post-bop tradition, grooves quite a bit. Mixes single lines and chords nicely. So far so good. –MGN

● **The Marksman / WARNER BROS** 1990
Good young guitarist swings hard in the tradition. –MGN

○ **Patrice / WARNER BROS** 1991
W/ Alvin Batiste (cl), Ron Carter (b), Kenny Barron (p), and Jack DeJohnette (d). More progressive. –MGN

MARGARET WHITING
b 1924

Big band, ballads. Margaret Whiting was a dominant pop singer in the 40s and 50s, though whether she's a jazz vocalist is often in question. She had a clear, striking voice and the kind of quasi-innocent sensibility that worked on such songs as "It Might As Well Be Spring" and "Moonlight in Vermont." Some would question if she was an improviser, or had the kind of timing, sense of swing, and fluidity that defines the genuine jazz or jazz-influenced singer. Whiting's run of hits began in the early 40s when she was featured on radio shows, singing with composer/vocalist Johnny Mercer. She was later a prominent vocalist with the bands of Freddie Slack, Billy Butterfield, and Paul Weston. She had three huge hits in 1948 with "Now Is the Hour," "A Tree in the Meadow," and "Far Away Places," then teamed with Jimmy Wakely for another top hit in 1949, "Slippin' Around." She and Wakely were a very successful team for a time. Whiting had a comeback of sorts in the early 70s, appearing on a Cavalcade of Bands tour with the groups of Bob Crosby and others. –RW

Maggie's Back in Town / PAIR
Good comeback set. –RW

Then and Now / DRG
Interesting old and new cuts. –RW

○ **Collectors Series / CAPITOL** COMP
The best of her old stuff. –RW

GERALD WIGGINS
b 1922

Post-bop, cool. Veteran pianist plays bop and post-bop. Well-traveled as a sideman for singers, i.e. Lena Horne, Eartha Kitt, Helen Humes, even The Supremes. –MGN

From Around the World in 80 Days / FANTASY 1957
New reissue of ambitious set. Limited edition. –RW

Wiggin' Out / HI FI JAZZ i 1961
W/ Harold Land (ts). –MGN

● **Relax and Enjoy It / CONTEMPORARY** r 1962
W/ Jackie Mills (d). Nice piano, good soul-jazz, blues. –RW

Around the World in 80 Days / SPEED 1969
Some tasty solos. –RW

○ **Live at Maybeck Recital Hall - Vol. 8 / CONCORD** 1990
Outstanding solo set, shows Wiggins in more straight jazz setting. CD version has three bonus cuts. –RW

BOB WILBER
b 1928

Swing. Along with Kenny Davern, one of a pair of tremendous soprano saxophonists, both steeped in traditional and swing jazz history and technique. Bob Wilber began playing clarinet at Scarsdale High School and later studied under both Sidney Bechet and Lennie Tristano while a teen. He formed a band known as The Six in the 50s that mixed old and new concepts, then joined Eddie Condon before playing clarinet and vibes for a year with Bobby Hackett. During the 60s he was both a frequent contributor to sessions and a founding member of the World's Greatest Jazz Band, a group that elevated the notion of trad and vintage New Orleans music by drawing on contemporary as well as classic sources. He founded Soprano Summit in 1973 with Kenny Davern, a player with a very similiar background. –RW

Soprano Summit — Live at Concord / CONCORD r 1974
High-quality live date by very appealing traditional jazz/swing band. –RW

○ **Soprano Summit — In Concert / CONCORD** i 1990
Strong traditional jazz/swing set, 1990 release. –RW

Summit Reunion / CHI-SOUND 1990
Date by a top-flight traditional jazz/swing ensemble. –RW

BARNEY WILEN
b 1937

Bop, post-bop. One of Europe's better, more modern saxophonists. Wilen, a self-taught player, worked with many major American jazz artists in the 50s. He collaborated with Miles Davis on the soundtrack *Lift to the Scaffold* in 1957 and, that same year, appeared with him in concert. Then, two years later, he worked on another soundtrack — *Les Liaisaons Dangereuses* — with Art Blakey. During the 60s, Wilen explored free jazz a bit, appearing at the 1967 Berlin Festival and engineering Archie Shepp's 1969 live performance at the Algiers Festival. –RW

○ **Un Temoin Dans La Ville / POLYGRAM** 1959
Contains two film soundtracks, the album title and *Jazz Sur Seine*, the first with a quintet with Kenny Dorham (tpt), Duke Jordan (p), Paul Roverer, Kenny Clarke (d). The second with Milt Jackson (vib), Percy Heath (b), Kenny Clarke (d), and Gana M'Bow. –JME

LEE WILEY
1915-1975

Swing, ballads. Lee Wiley numbers among the best jazz singers for articulation, phrasing, and charm. She was a brilliant interpretative artist, never failing to fully present or exploit a lyric or convey a song's sentiment or theme. Wiley sang in many bands from the 30s through the 50s, and made a comeback in the early 70s. She also wrote lyrics, adding words to Victor Young's music for the songs "Got the South in My Soul" and "Anytime, Anyday, Anywhere." She worked with Johnny Green, Leo Reisman, Young, and Eddie Condon in the 30s, was married for a time to pianist Jess Stacy, and toured with his band in the 40s. She also made a series of excellent recordings doing definitive versions of classic pop songs during the late 30s and throughout the 40s. –RW

○ **As Time Goes By / RCA**

ED WILKERSON

Progressive big band, modern creative. Chicago saxophonist w/ Ethnic Heritage, Shadow Vignettes, and 8 Bold Souls. Charter member of AACM. One of the best creative musicians going today. –MGN

○ **Birth of a Notion / SESSOMS** 1985
Date with almost 30-piece band led by this progressive Chicago saxophonist. At times comedic and serious. Wild and delightful. –MGN

JACK WILKINS
b 1944

Post-bop. Guitarist. An underrated and underpublicized master, Wilkins is considered by many to be the top mainstream-jazz guitar player on the New York scene, bar none. A New Yorker from birth, he studied with jazz education pioneer John Mehegan, and his musical training also included piano, vibes, and classical guitar. He has toured and recorded with Buddy Rich and played concerts with many top names like Stan Getz, Dizzy Gillespie, Morgana King, and Pearl Bailey. Later recordings feature him with Jack DeJohnette, Eddy Gomez, Randy Brecker, Phil Woods, and Harvie Swartz. His solo style is fluid and vivid, with great warmth and melodic integrity. He uses classical-guitar technique in his playing to achieve a piano-like approach to chordal work, but can also play the blues like no tomorrow. Without any gimmicks or media hype, Wilkins is just busy being who he is: a top jazz artist. –DNM

○ **Windows / MAINSTREAM** 1973
Trio with this guitarist at his jazziest. A virtuoso. –MGN

● **Call Him Reckless / MUSICMASTERS** 1988
Outstanding, a bit more contemporary. –MGN

Alien Army / MUSICMASTERS								1991
Good mainstream pieces, nice guitar solos. –RW

## BUSTER WILLIAMS								♭1942

Post-bop, jazz-rock, neo bop. Outstanding bassist who's played with many major jazz stars since the 60s. Has appeared on numerous albums but is probably best known for working in Ron Carter's two-bass group during the 70s. Carter played the piccolo bass while Williams played the conventional acoustic, and their duets were often spectacular. He's a favorite session contributor due to his tendency not to overwhelm or dominate a session. Has almost no albums as a leader, which reflects his preference for accompaniment to soloing, though he's a capable player. –RW

● **Crystal Reflections / MUSE / DB 5**					1976
Excellent set. No reed or brass soloist but Kenny Barron (p) and Jimmy Rowles (p) are super. One of the last times Roy Ayers plays vibes in jazz context on record. –RW

○ **Heartbeat / MUSE**							1978
A diverse session of jazz touches by pop guests on the four originals by bassist Williams, one standard, and one by Jimmie Rowles. Includes Rowles (p), Kenny Barron (p), Ben Riley (d), and vocalist Suzanne Klewan, and strings from Pat and Gayle Dixon. –MGN

## JAMES WILLIAMS								♭1951

Post-bop, neo bop. Another in the long line of Memphis piano players, Williams attended Memphis State in the 70s, then moved to New York and worked for a time in Art Blakey's Jazz Messengers. During the 80s and 90s he has recorded some exceptional trio and small-combo sessions and done extensive sessions. His style and technique include healthy doses of gospel and blues influence, as he was once a church organist and worked in several blues and R&B groups in Memphis. A first-rate soloist and fine composer, he is one of the few modern players who don't trace their approach directly to McCoy Tyner. Instead, Phineas Newborn is Williams's mentor, especially in his phrasing and voicings. –RW

Everything I Love / CONCORD						1979
Nice touch by Williams on everything. Billy Pierce (sax) front and center. –RW

Arioso Touch / CONCORD							1982
Wonderful 1982 date; great solos, blues influences. Buster Williams (b) and Billy Higgins (d) are great. –RW

● **Alter Ego / SUNNYSIDE**						1984
1984 sextet recording of all originals with brilliant Memphis pianist. –MGN

○ **Magical Trio 1 / POLYGRAM**						1987
W/ Art Blakey (d) and Ray Brown (b). –MGN

Meet the Magical Trio / POLYGRAM					1988
Vigorous solos, excellent composition. –RW

Magical Trio 2 / POLYGRAM						1989
Date that's just as great as predecessor. Elvin Jones (d) in driver's chair this time. –RW

○ **Progress Report / SUNNYSIDE**
Another excellent mid-80s set by Memphis pianist and comrades. –RW

## JESSICA WILLIAMS								♭1948

Post-bop, neo bop. West Coast pianist, an impressive composer, parallel to JoAnne Brackeen. Some quite startling melodic content, dense harmonies, rich improvisations. Modern without being avant-garde. Potent performer. –MGN

● **Orgonomic Music / CLEAN CUTS**					1979
Recording for original pianist. Up to seven pieces. Quintessential modern music. –MGN

○ **Nothin' But the Truth / DELOS**					1986

## MARY LOU WILLIAMS							1910-1981

Swing, big band, bop, cool. Married to saxophonist John Williams in her teens, she went on the road with his little band; when he joined Andy Kirk, she replaced the band's regular pianist at their first recording session (he overslept) and soon had his job for good. She already showed great promise as an arranger and composer ("Mess-a-Stomp," 1929), and her first solo record, from 1930, is impressive proof that she heard Earl Hines and James P. Johnson very well indeed. When the Kirk band hit its stride in 1936, Mary Lou was *The Lady Who Swings the Band*, setting the tasteful, swinging style for this relatively small (12-piece) big band. She also freelanced as a writer, contributing such hits as "Roll 'Em" to Benny Goodman's library. Leaving Kirk in 1942, she wrote for Duke Ellington, did radio and night-club work in New York (she debuted an all-female group in 1945), and wrote a major work for jazz group and strings, "The Zodiac Suite" (1946). Hospitable to the new ideas in jazz, she befriended Budd Powell, Thelonious Monk, and other young musicians and shared her knowledge with them. She worked with Goodman during his bop flirtation (1949) and spent time in Europe. By 1954, a convert to Roman Catholicism, she retired from playing and did charitable work, but a Jesuit priest convinced her that playing music was not sinful and that she should not neglect her gift. She wrote religious music (*Mary Lou's Mass*, 1970; performed at St. Patrick's Cathedral in New York) but also resumed playing in night clubs and at jazz festivals. In 1977 she accepted a faculty appointment at Duke University, where she taught until her death. As a pianist, arranger, and composer, Mary Lou Williams never needed to be tagged "female"; she simply was up there with the best, respected and admired by her colleagues. She was, as Duke Ellington put it, "never out of style." –DM

Asch Recordings / FOLKWAYS						1944
1944-1947. Swinging, exuberant solos. –RW

○ **Roll 'Em / AUDIOPHILE**						194?
Good 1988 reissue of Williams doing boogie, swing, and blues from 40s. –RW

Zodiac Suite / SMI							194?
Wonderful, robust solos from the 40s. –RW

In London / GNP							ca. 1953
Dynamic, propulsive piano. –RW

Black Christ of the Andes / MPS					1963
W/ Howard Roberts (g), Budd Johnson (ts), and vocal choir. Challenging. –MGN

Zoning / MARY							r 1970
First-rate playing. –RW

Free Spirits / STEEPLECHASE / DB 5					1975
Includes great trio cuts w/ Buster Williams (b) and Mickey Roker (d). –RW

★ **Live at the Cookery / CHI-SOUND**					1976
Live date with bassist Brian Torff. Her best. –MGN

○ **Embraced / PABLO**							ca. 1977
Stormy, combative, but highly valuable duets with Cecil Taylor (p). –RW

Solo Recital (Montreux Jazz Festival 1978) / PABLO			1978
My Mama Pinned a Rose on Me / PABLO / DB 5			r 1979
Fine swing, blues, and original compositions. –RW

First Lady of Piano / GIANTS OF JAZZ				r 1980
Exceptional pieces, with Coleman Hawkins (sax), Don Byas (ts), and other swing lords. –RW

Best Of / PA2								COMP
Deceptive title. Good overview of her work on Pablo. –RW

## RICHARD WILLIAMS							♭1931

Post-bop, hard-bop. Trumpeter who played with Eric Dolphy, Sun Ra, and Booker Ervin. Tart tone and tremendous ideas flowed from this fine artist. –MGN

○ **New Horn in Town / CANDID**   1960
Quintet featuring three originals by Williams. His day to shine. A must-buy. −MGN

ROD WILLIAMS   b 1954

Post-bop, neo bop. Detroit pianist, accompanist for vocalist Cassandra Wilson. Monk-like in approach, good chordal backup, plays occasional M-base funk. On the way up. −MGN
○ **Hanging in the Balance / MUSE**   1989
Debut for this Detroit pianist and sextet. This is exploratory jazz. −MGN

TONY WILLIAMS   b 1945

Post-bop, jazz-rock, neo bop, modern creative. Drums, bandleader. The arrival of Tony Williams into the Miles Davis group altered the trumpeter's course in a way no one had since the brief stay of Bill Evans. Where Miles's early-60s work fell off the pace of the previous decade, Williams kicked the old book into overdrive. The mid 60s brought him recognition as the decade's most important jazz drummer, rivaled only by Elvin Jones. The original Lifetime lineup was one of the most volatile ensembles anywhere, and a later version of the group with guitarist Alan Holdsworth remains sadly underrated. With the 80s came a return to acoustic jazz with a fine, long-running group, furthering William's reputation as a composer and bandleader. Through all of his various phases, Tony Williams remains one of the most astonishing and musical drummers ever. −SA
○ **Life Time / CAPITOL**   1964
One of his best solo albums of the 60s. 80s reissue. −RW
● **Spring / BLUE NOTE**   1965
Early-period Blue Note recording with Sam Rivers (sax). Powerful music. −MGN
☆ **Emergency / POLYGRAM**   1969
One of the anthems of jazz-rock in 1969. −RW
○ **Turn It Over / POLYDOR**   1970
Groundbreaking early fusion in the late-60s with Jack Bruce (b), Larry Young (organ), and John McLaughlin (g). −MGN
Believe It / CBS   1975
This is a hard-edged fusion quartet w/ guitarist Allan Holdsworth. −MGN
○ **The Joy of Flying / COLUMBIA**   1978
An excellent, wide-ranging set. Williams plays with mix of mainstream, fusion, and avant-garde soloists. −RW
● **Foreign Intrigue / BLUE NOTE**   1985
Mid-80s band. Great compositions. Williams is always right there. −MGN
Civilization / BLUE NOTE   1987
Good set, with Williams serving as mentor and leader for good crop of young lions. −RW
Third Plane / CARRERE (IMPORT)   1987
Super trio date with Herbie Hancock (k) and Ron Carter (b). Available only as French import. −RW
Native Heart / CAPITOL   1990
Leading his by-now familiar band with Wallace Roney (tpt), Bill Pierce (reeds), and Mulgrew Miller (p). −RW

STEVE WILLIAMSON   b 1965

Post-bop, neo bop. Young British saxophonist, plays post-bop. Too young to tell how far he will go or in what direction, Williamson is a solid jazzman. −MGN
○ **Waltz for Grace / POLYGRAM**   1990
Overlooked fine date with wondrous Abbey Lincoln (v), one of Britian's top jazz players in Julian Joseph (p). −RW

LARRY WILLIS   b 1940

Post-bop, soul jazz, progressive big band, Latin, jazz-rock, neo bop. A veteran sideman and one of the best jazz pianists of all time, Willis plays straight, modal, latin, and funk. −MGN

○ **Inner Crisis / GROOVE MERCHANT**   r 1973
Willis plays acoustic & electric. Two different ensembles. Good compositional jazz. −MGN
● **Just in Time / STEEPLECHASE**   1989
Here is trio jazz from a veteran pianist, one of the best in America. −MGN
○ **A New Kind of Soul / BRUNSWICK**
More funky. With viable jazz horn sound for support. Easy to like. Three flugelhorns (Joe Newman, Jimmy Owens, Marvin Stamm). −MGN

BERT WILSON

Hard-bop, modern creative. Wilson plays one of the meanest tenors in a creative improvised mode. A winner. −MGN
○ **The Next Rebirth / NINE WINDS**   1986
W/ Nancy Curtis (fl) and the Allen Youngblood (p) Trio. Saxophonist blows up a storm in progressive setting. Impressive musicianship. −MGN

CASSANDRA WILSON

Ballads, neo bop, M-base. Somewhat-controversial vocalist who splits her time between conventional jazz, free-form, R&B, rock, and soul. She's affiliated with Steve Coleman and his Brooklyn-based M-Base group and has a wondrous voice, with a sultry, appealing quality, and excellent timing and articulation. Some question her material, and others consider her the best modern singer working in jazz or related styles. −RW
Point Of View / POLYGRAM   1986
Bounces between jazz, R&B, funk, avant-garde, and rock. −RW
Days Aweigh / POLYGRAM   1987
On the cutting edge of new jazz/rock movement. −RW
● **Blue Skies / POLYGRAM**   r 1989
Innovative, contemporary vocalist interprets standards. Interesting approach to singing. −MGN
Jumpworld / POLYGRAM / DB 5   i 1990
1990 release; some taut music, vocals. −RW
○ **She Who Weeps / POLYGRAM**
Very good album, with Rod Williams on piano and Tani Tabbal on drums. −MGN

GERALD WILSON   b 1918

Big band, progressive big band. A master arranger and solid trumpeter. Wilson began on piano and learned trumpet while attending college in Detroit. He played with the Jimmie Lunceford band from 1939-1942, then moved to Los Angeles. He worked with Benny Carter and other groups before joining the Navy. He formed his own big band upon his discharge in 1944, and has since been a popular leader, arranger, and musical director. His finest records from a jazz standpoint were done for Pacific Jazz in the 60s, and they are beginning to resurface on reissues. −RW
● **Portraits / CAPITOL (PACIFIC JAZZ)**   r 1964
Wonderful large-group recordings made in the 60s for Pacific Jazz. A 1992 reissue. −RW
○ **The Golden Sword / DISCOVERY**   r 1966
First-rate arrangements and solos. −RW
Lomelin / DISCOVER   1981
Solid session with his orchestra of the 80s. −RW
Calafia / TREND   1981
High-caliber orchestra arrangements and solos. −RW
Jessica / TREND   r 1983
Super orchestra recordings. −RW

JACK WILSON   b 1936

Post-bop, cool, soul jazz. A West Coast pianist who plays with non-typical Eastern fire on many occasions. Will tackle a less conservative repertoire. −MGN
○ **2 Sides / ATLANTIC**   1964

Trio w/ Leroy Vinnegar on bass and Philly Joe Jones on drums. Good swinging stuff from West Coast piano legend. –MGN

TEDDY WILSON
1912-1986

Stride, swing, big band, cool. Swing era, big-band era. Texas-born pianist. Worked with big bands, of Louie Armstrong, Jimmie Noone, Erskine Tate, and Benny Carter. Accompanied Billie Holiday, joined Benny Goodman's famous integrated quartet. Played later period in trios and solos, displaying his voice as one based in swing, blues, and elegance. A jazz immortal. –MGN

☆ **And His All-Stars / COLUMBIA / DB 5**　　193?
Wondrous compilation of seminal 30s and 40s sessions. –RW

Sunny Morning / MUSICRAFT　　1946
Amazing solo piano. –RW

And His All-Stars / MUSICRAFT　　194?
Great 40s dates with Charlie Shavers (tpt) and Ben Webster (sax). –RW

Time After Time / MUSICRAFT　　194?
Exemplary cuts, with Sarah Vaughan glorious. –RW

For Quiet Lovers / VERVE　　ca. 1956
Top-shelf lovers and sentimental music. –RW

Impeccable Mr. Wilson / VERVE　　r 1958
Superior solos, arrangements. –RW

Gypsy and Mr. Wilson / COLUMBIA　　ca. 1959
Outstanding swing-tinged piano. –RW

Elegant Piano / HALCYON　　195?
Beautiful duets with Marian McPartland (d). –RW

○ **I Got Rhythm / VERVE**　　195?
Prototypical swing, small-combo jazz. –RW

Air Mail Special / BLACK LION　　ca. 1968
Trio in Europe / FANTASY　　ca. 1968
Nice, more bop and blues included in playing style. –RW

Stomping at the Savoy / BLACK LION　　1969
Solid set. –RW

● **Piano Solos / COMMODORE**　　1973
Glimmering, fine duets. –RW

Blues for Thomas ... / BLACK LION

Mr. Gershwin / COLUMBIA
These are wonderful interpretations. Reworkings of vintage Gershwin. –RW

Prez and Teddy / VERVE　　COMP
Dynamite small combo cuts, amazing Lester Young (sax). –RW

LEM WINCHESTER
♭1928

Post-bop, cool. A solid 50s and 60s tenor saxophonist whose best work was done for the Fantasy label. His finest release, *Winchester Special*, was recently reissued on the OJC label. –RW

Lem's Beat / OJC　　r 1960
W/ Oliver Nelson (sax).

○ **Winchester Special / OJC**　　1985
Solid set pairing Benny Golson (ts) and Lem Winchester. –RW

KAI WINDING
1922-1983

Swing, big band, bop, hard-bop, post-bop, cool, progressive big band. Kai Winding was both a top-flight trombone soloist and a pliable musician who was able to work in many contexts effectively. He was among the ranks of 50s trombonists whose skill and technique helped rescue the instrument from obscurity. Winding came to America at 12 and began to make his mark in the late 40s, playing with Stan Kenton, Charlie Ventura, and Tadd Dameron, among others. He participated in the landmark Birth-of-the-Cool session in 1948; then, from 1954 to 1956, he co-led with J. J. Johnson the influential two-trombone quintet that showed the instrument could do much more than reproduce vocal effects or be plugged into a nostalgic traditional jazz format. Winding expanded the trombone's role even more with a novel four-trombone sextet

he led from 1956 to 1961. After working with a supergroup called the Giants of Jazz in the early 70s, Winding essentially retired for a few years, before resurfacing with another two-trombone group in the 80s with Curtis Fuller. He also toured in 1979 with Lionel Hampton. –RW

Bones / BLACK AND BLUE　　1950
Superior two-trombone set with Curtis Fuller (tb). –RW

○ **With Strings / OJC**　　1954
This is an outstanding 3-trombone lineup, with understated arrangements. –RW

Brass Fever / IMPULSE　　ca. 1956
Best of his 50s four-trombone lineup. –RW

● **Incredible Trombones / IMPULSE**　　ca. 1961
Great four-trombone set. –RW

GARY WINDO

Progressive big band, M-base, rock. A British jazz musician and member of groups led by Carla Bley. –RW

○ **Deep Water / POLYGRAM**　　ca. 1985
Nice set by British jazz/session player. –RW

NORMA WINSTONE
♭1941

Modern creative. An excellent, versatile singer who's a true vocal improviser, extremely capable lyric interpreter and outstanding stylist. She studied piano and organ for three years, then began singing with jazz groups in 1965. She joined the New Jazz Orchestra in 1966, and later became a member of Michael Garrick's group. She later married and worked with John Taylor, and has since performed with many of Europe's leading groups, orchestras, and combos. She formed the group Azimuth in the 80s, and has continued to tour and sing throughout Europe. –RW

○ **Somewhere Called Home / POLYGRAM**　　1986
Atmospheric vocalist. A unique approach to improvised music, with John Taylor on piano and Tony Coe on reeds. –MGN

SMILEY WINTERS
♭1924

Bop, hard-bop, post-bop. Drummer from the Northwest. He plays inside or out. He is what they call a "cozy" drummer, comfortable with variety. –MGN

○ **Smiley, Etc. / ARHOOLIE**　　1969
W/ brilliant progressive saxophonist Bert Wilson and trumpeter Barbara Donald. This is essential. –MGN

PHIL WOODS
♭1931

Bop, hard-bop, post-bop. Charlie Parker truly lives in the work of Phil Woods and a handful of others who've taken his legacy of alto greatness and both extended it and found their own voice through it without being consumed by it. Woods has a dynamic, soaring tone, unlimited harmonic knowledge, and the wit and technique to execute anything he desires in a solo or on the bandstand. Woods's career began in earnest when he joined the small combo of Jimmy Raney in 1955. He then spent two years with George Wallington, dividing his time there with stints in Dizzy Gillespie's big band and a two-alto unit with Gene Quill in 1957. He was a member of Buddy Rich's big band, staying with him until 1961, and became a prolific studio and session musician in the 60s, working on film soundtracks, cutting his own records and working on dates by Benny Carter and others. Woods formed the European Rhythm Machine in 1968, which was among the world's best small groups until its demise in 1972. He formed another quartet in the mid 80s, expanding it to a quintet for a time with trumpeter Tom Harrell. His many recordings from the 50s until the present are almost uniformly excellent; he's resisted the lure of fusion, has also been among the fiercest critics of free music. –RW

Woodlore / OJC　　1955

Outstanding reissue of brilliant date. –RW
Altology / PRESTIGE   1956
1956 and 1957 dates.
Young Bloods / OJC   1956
Fine reissue taken from days when Woods, Donald Byrd (tpt), and Teddy Kotick (b) were rising stars. –RW
○ **Pairing Off / OJC**   1956
First-rate 80s reissue of an excellent 1956 date with lots of heavy hitters — Kenny Dorham (tpt), Donald Byrd (tpt), Tommy Flanagan (p), and Woods. –RW
● **Four Altos / OJC**   1957
Some very different alto players together; all excellent. –RW
☆ **Phil & Quill with Prestige / OJC**   1957
Cute title, excellent session. –RW
Bird Feathers / OJC   1957
High-flying blowing/jam session from the 50s. –RW
Warm Woods / CBS   r 1958
Brisk, bright date, though the material comes up short. –RW
○ **Rights of Swing / CANDID**   1960
Marvelous originals, vivid solos. –RW
○ **Musique Du Bois / MUSE / DB 5**   r 1975
Exemplary solos. –RW
Phil Woods Quartet, Live - Vol. 1 / CLEAN CUTS   ca. 1975
1991 release. An overlooked worthwhile set. –RW
Live from the Showboat / RCA / DB 5   1976
A two-disc masterpiece, dynamic playing. –RW
More Live / ADELPHI   1978
1978 and 1979. Additional outstanding live cuts. –RW
Three for All / RHINO   1981
1990 reissue. This is an excellent trio date. W/ Tommy Flannagin (p). –RW
At the Vanguard / PALO ALTO   1982
Once again, powerhouse alto solos in live context. –RW
Integrity / RED / DB 5   ca. 1984
Aptly titled, bop the way it ought to be. –RW
Bop Stew / CONCORD   1987
First in series of live dates from 1987 Concord Festival in Japan. Tom Harrell (tpt) and Woods emphatic. CD version has bonus track. –RW
Bouquet / CONCORD   1987
Nice set from 1987 festival. CD version has bonus cut. –RW
Evolution / COJ   1988
Strong swing, bop cuts from ensemble that's neither traditional big band or small combo. –RW
Here's to My Lady / CHESKY   1988
First-rate 1988 date released in 1989. Woods is invigorating, as is Tommy Flanagan (p). –RW
Flash / CONCORD   1990
W/ both Hal Galper (p) and Tom Harrell (tpt). –RW
Real Life / CHESKY / DB 5   1990
1991 release of good combo date. Larger group than on most of his recordings. –RW
All Bird's Children / CONCORD   1991
One of Parker's forthright disciples shows where he got his inspiration. CD version has two bonus cuts. –RW
Live / NOVUS   i 1991
1991 release of excellent Woods live concert. –RW
Live from New York / QUICKSILVER   1991
Poor recording but excellent solos, especially Woods and Hal Galper (p). –RW
Little Big Band / CONCORD

WORLD SAXOPHONE QUARTET

Early free, modern creative. One of the finest small combos to emerge in jazz during the 80s. A foursome of sax players who, until their last release, recorded and performed all their music without any other accompanists. The original quartet

consisted of David Murray, Julius Hemphill, Oliver Lake, and Hamiett Bluiett. Hemphill left last year and was replaced by Arthur Blythe. They began splitting the material between driving originals, avant-garde blowing, and more hard-bop and mainstream pieces. In recent years, they've expanded the repetoire to include an Ellington tribute, an album of classic R&B, and their latest effort, a date with African percussionists. –RW
Point of No Return / MOERS   1977
Their first recording. –RW
● **Steppin' With / BLACKSAINT**   1978
Contains their definitive work. –MGN
Live in Zurich / BLACKSAINT   1981
Concert in Switzerland. Cookin' stuff. –MGN
☆ **Plays Duke Ellington / ELEKTRA-NONESUCH**   1986
Brilliant adaption of Ellington catalog. –RW
Dances & Ballads / ELEKTRA ENTERTAINMENT   1988
The Quartet extends its reach and scope to include danceable material. –RW
Rhythm & Blues / ELEKTRA ENTERTAINMENT   1989
Smashing update of traditional R&B. –RW
Metamorphosis / ELEKTRA-NONESUCH   ca. 1991
Amazing mix of African rhythms, African-American harmonies and solos. –RW

WORLD'S GREATEST JAZZ BAND

Dixieland, swing. The finest trad/swing group of modern times. This unit grew out of jazz fan and millionaire Dick Gibson's annual jazz parties. After his sixth celebration in 1968, a group featuring Yank Lawson, Bob Haggart, Bob Wilber, Ralph Sutton, and Billy Butterfield were tagged by Gibson as "The World's Greatest Jazz Band." They played together ten years, stressed the collective style of vintage New Orleans music, but were distinguished by the caliber of players and their willingness not to stagnate and become a camp Dixieland outfit. Their albums surpassed anything else remotely associated with "trad" or Dixieland material. –RWD
Live / ATLANTIC   1970
Excellent 1989 reissue of outstanding 1970 concert. –RW
○ **At Massey Hall / WORLD JAZZ**   ca. 1972
Anything from this delightful traditional jazz group is worth hearing. –RW

FRANK WRIGHT

Post-bop, early free. An ordained minister, Wright played fiery tenor à la Shepp or Ayler. Whether modal or free, Rev. Wright gets down. –MGN
Trio / ESP DISK   1966
W/ Henry Grimes on bass, Tony Price on drums. Unafraid to explore new terrain. –MGN
Your Prayer / ESP DISK   1968
Quintet. More groundbreaking avant-garde music. Lengthy improvs and counterpoint. –MGN
○ **Stove Man, Love Is the Word / SANDRA**   1979
Live at The Loft in Munich, Germany, with sextet. Rev. Wright is on the edge. This is an extension of Dolphy. Must have open ears. –MGN

JOHN WRIGHT   b 1934

Post-bop. Chicago pianist; contemporary of John Young and Jodie Christian. Excellent ballad and blues interpreter. Well known in 50s and 60s. –MGN
○ **South Side Soul / OJC**   r 1961
Swinging Chicago pianist. –MGN

LEO WRIGHT   b 1933

Post-bop. Alto saxophonist/flutist/clarinetist from Wichita Falls, Texas. With Dizzy Gillespie 1959-1962. Worked extensively in Europe. A forgotten bop/post-bop star. –MGN

○ **Blues Shout / ATLANTIC** 1960
A visceral and emotional session with Junior Mance (p). −DS
Suddenly the Blues / ATLANTIC 1962
More driving than "Blues Shout," w/ Kenny Burrell (g). −DS

STOMU YAMASH'TA

World fusion. For a brief moment, Yamash'ta was enormously popular as harbinger of increased popularity in world/international music. −RW

○ **Red Buddha / VANGUARD-CLASSICAL**
A new-age/fusion precursor — sometimes artful percussion and rhythms. −RW

YOSUKE YAMASHITA   b1942

Modern creative. Japanese pianist very much in the Cecil Taylor school. Wildly unabashed improviser, dense chords and slam-bang pyrotechnics. Great rewards for the listener willing to be challenged. −MGN
Breath Take / WEST 54 1975
Solo piano. −MGN
○ **Chiasma / MPS** 1975
Trio recording. Influenced by Cecil Taylor. For special tastes only. −MGN
Sakura / POLYGRAM 1990
Most recent recording by avant-garde pianist from Japan. −MGN

THE YELLOWJACKETS

Fusion. Though now known for increasingly sophisticated and polished studio albums with diverse influences, including jazz, world music, and pop, the Yellowjackets started in 1981 as an R&B-oriented band with guitarist Robben Ford. Russel Ferrante (keyboards) and Jimmy Haslip (bass) are the remaining original members, joined by drummer William Kennedy in the most recent lineup. The original idea was that they were studio musicians who wanted to play "real music," and they have crafted a string of very listenable and successful releases. Despite some harping by critics who can't quite find the right label to stick on them, and at least one rather forgettable album (*Shades*), the band has enjoyed well-deserved success behind fine compositions (notably by Ferrante), excellent musicality in its members, and very professional production work in the studio. Their most recent album, *Greenhouse*, received 4 stars from *DOWN BEAT*, no small feat for a band in their genre. −DNM
Samurai Samba / WARNER BROS
Highly popular fusion. −RW
Shades / MCA 1986
1986 set, prototype fusion. −RW
Four Corners / MCA 1987
Highly popular album, short on jazz feel. −RW
Politics / MCA 1988
Features appealing sax of Marc Russo, compositions of Russel Ferrante. Unpretentious, melodic, memorable. Fine studio sound. −DNM
○ **The Spin / MCA** r1989
Clearly their best album. It swings! −MGN
Green House / GRP 1991
Guest sax by Bob Mintzer, with fine orchestration for a real live string ensemble by Vince Mendoza. High level of musicianship all around. Very accessible. −DNM

VINCENT YORK   b1952

Post-bop, neo bop. Alto saxophonist York is a logical extension of Charlie Parker but closer to Bobby Watson. This excellent flutist also plays tenor. A rising star to watch. −MGN
○ **Blending Forces /**
York blows mean alto and tenor on this album on which Marcus Belgrave plays trumpet. All originals; swung hard. Soulful "Hymn 427" is a favori

Soulful "Hymn 427" is a favorite, as is Lawrence Williams originals "#3" and Eugene Thorns "Caribbean Fantasy." −MGN

JOHN YOUNG   b1922

Post-bop, cool, neo bop. A veteran Chicago mainstay of the piano, Young likes modal or mainstream textures. He can play the blues. He evokes favorable comparisons to McCoy Tyner or Kenny Drew. −MGN
Young John Young / ARGO i1958
W/ Herbert Brown −MGN
Themes and Things / ARGO i1961
W/ William Yancey −MGN
A Touch of Pepper / ARGO i1962
○ **Trio / DELMARK** r1964
Great Chicago pianist on one of his only dates as a leader. Highly recommended. −MGN

LARRY YOUNG   b1940

Post-bop, soul jazz, jazz-rock. An excellent, but greatly overlooked organist whose approach to the organ was many years ahead of its time. Young offered an alternative to the soul-jazz, bass-pedal-heavy style dominant in the 60s, and played in a swirling, loose, and rock-influenced fashion that was most favorably showcased in Tony Williams's Lifetime trio of the late 60s and early 70s, and also in his work with Miles Davis. Young made some more conventional jazz dates for Blue Note, but even these displayed a technique that was quite different from any other organist of the period. A recent Mosaic box-set showcases Young's Blue Note material in a comprehensive manner; the Lifetime material has also been reissued. −RW
Testifying / NEW JAZZ i1960
W/ Joe Holiday (ts), Thornel Schwartz (g), and Jimmie Smith (d). −MGN
Young Blues / NEW JAZZ i1960
Groove Street / PRESTIGE i1962
W/ Bill Leslie. −MGN
○ **Into Somethin' / BLUE NOTE** 1964
First-rate set from dynamic organist. −RW
● **Unity / CAPITOL** 1965
Innovative, far reaching organist. −RW
Lawrence of Newark / PERCEPTION 1973
Featuring massive percussion group. Interesting. −MGN
☆ **Complete Blue Note / MOSAIC** COMP
Definitive boxed-set of visionary organist's work. A must-buy. Set includes the first three Grant Green (g) albums. −MGN

LESTER YOUNG   1909-1959

Swing, big band, bop. The man who brought a new sound to his chosen instrument and a new sensibility to jazz began as a drummer in the family band led by his father, then also learned violin and saxophone. He left the family band in 1928, worked with various leaders, including King Oliver (1933), and was picked by Fletcher Henderson to replace Coleman Hawkins. But Henderson's musicians couldn't accept Lester's lighter, airier sound and innovative phrasing, so after three months, Lester asked to leave, and joined Andy Kirk. It was in 1936, after he invited himself into Count Basie's little band in Kansas City, that doors began to open for Lester. His first record (*Shoe Shine Swing/Lady Be Good*) caused quite a stir, and when he came East with Basie and started to record with Billie Holiday, the stage was set for the return from Europe of Coleman Hawkins and the great tenor divide. Lester's approach became the inspiration for cool jazz — he was also a profound influence on young Charlie Parker. Pres, as he was now known (short for "President," the nickname was given him by Holiday), left Basie in 1940 and led his own little bands, for a while with his drummer brother, Lee. Back with Basie in 1943, he was drafted in 1944; his army experience was grim, for he was incarcerated for pot and barbiturate use.

Released in 1945, he made some wonderful records (*D. B. Blues*, *These Foolish Things*), toured with *Jazz at the Philharmonic*, visited Europe, and maintained his place in jazz despite the rise of bop. But his health got progressively worse, mainly due to alcoholism. He died just hours after returning from a Paris engagement in his New York hotel room at the age of 49. Lester (who also invented a spoken language of his own) was the creator of a musical vocabulary that was wholly original and profoundly influential. His was a horizontal approach to melody — not the vertical, chord-based one favored by Hawkins, for example — and his long, sinuous lines were filled with unexpected twists and turns, swinging to the hilt. He was one of jazz's great poets and storytellers, and a master of the blues. –DM

Master Takes / SAVOY 1944

☆ **Carnegie Blues / POLYGRAM** 1946
1946-1957. Top-level cuts done in JATP mode, not comprehensive, but great playing. –RW

Lester Swings / POLYGRAM 1951
Good two-record set. –RW

In Washington, D.C. 1956 / PA2 / DB 5 1956
Vol. 1. Tremendous late-period Young shows he wasn't through as a player by the mid-50s. –RW

Jazz Giants '56 / POLYGRAM / DB 5 1956
Very nice, some wonderful Young solos. –RW

Giants of Tenor Sax / COMMODORE r 1958
First-rate playing, but rather shoddy sound. –RW

And the Oscar Peterson Trio / POLYGRAM ca. 195?
Super swing/mainstream music. –RW

Lester Young & Piano Giants / PABLO
Dynamite Young encounters with Nat King Cole (p), Teddy Wilson (p), and others. –RW

Newly Discovered Performances / ESP-DIS

★ **Complete Lester Young on Keynote / MERCURY** COMP
This is an amazing compilation of powerhouse cuts from 40s. –RW

☆ **Lester Young Story / COLUMBIA / DB 5** COMP
Vols. 1-3. Tremendous set that compiles Young's top work for Columbia label. –RW

SNOOKY YOUNG
b 1919

Swing, big band, bop. Another prolific studio and session player, and a fine high-note trumpeter. Snooky Young has been playing trumpet since he was five years old and managed to be a member of the Wilberforce College Band in his teens without ever attending the university. He joined the Lunceford orchestra in 1939 after playing in territory bands, and stayed there until 1942, becoming famous for his solo on "Uptown Blues." He worked briefly with Count Basie in 1942, then had stints with Lee Young, Les Hite, Benny Carter, and Gerald Wilson, plus another short stay with Basie before he joined him again for two years, from 1945-1947. He had his own band for nearly a decade before he hooked up with Basie for a fourth stay, this time from 1957-1962. Since then he's been a steady studio player, has appeared with "The Tonight Show" band and occasionally issued an album under his own name. –RW

○ **Horn of Plenty / CONCORD** 1979
Nice, tasty, and sometimes funny swing/mainstream set. –RW

WEBSTER YOUNG

Post-bop, cool. Native of Columbia, SC. Young is a cornet and trumpet player, who played in army bands in DC, w/ Hampton Hawes in 1956, collaborated w/ John Coltrane in 1957. He plays in the style of Miles Davis, and was championed by Billie Holiday. His smooth, lyrical lines are a model for young brass students. –MGN

○ **For Lady / PRESTIGE** 1957
Five of Billie Holiday's most famous tunes done instrumentally, plus the title track written by oft-neglected

Young. W/ Paul Quinichette (ts), Joe Puma (g), and the Mal Waldron Trio. Every young brass player should study Young's absolute lyricism and straight, strong tone. –MGN

ZAMBOMBA

Latin, jazz-rock, neo bop, modern creative. This Latin-jazz and progressive ensemble is led by multi-percussionist Mark Holen. –MGN

○ **Zambomba / ZAMBOMBA** 1984
Date with percussionist Mark Holen leading an ensemble in free/jazz, Latin/polyrhythmic setting. Excellent concept. –MGN

JOE ZAWINUL
b 1932

Soul jazz, jazz-rock. No one has ever been able to get a more human, funky sound out of electric keyboards and synthesizers than Joe Zawinul, Vienna's gift to the improvisational world. Zawinul began playing the accordion at six, and started studying classical music a year later at the Vienna Conservatory. He worked with Austrian jazz saxophonist Hans Koller in 1952, then with various Austrian groups in the mid and late 50s, while also playing in France and Germany with his own trio. Zawinul won a scholarship to Berklee in 1959, and upon coming to America spent only a week at Berklee before joining Maynard Ferguson and touring with him for eight months. He became Dinah Washington's pianist after a brief stint with Slide Hampton in 1959 and stayed with her until 1961. After a month in Harry Edison's group, he joined Cannonball Adderley and remained with his band until 1970. There, Zawinul's skills flourished, and he became a sturdy blues player, good soloist, and excellent accompanist. In 1969 and then throughout 1970 he worked in Miles Davis's electric units, gradually moving away from acoustic and concentrating on electric instruments. He co-founded Weather Report in 1971 with Wayne Shorter, and through the 70s and 80s made many influential recordings. Weather Report, especially in its early years, was a true jazz-rock band, able to make appealing, seminal work that had loose, adventurous foundations and energetic solos. Zawinul's synthesizer solos were never dry or dependent on gimmicks, but showed it was possible to play with individuality and distinction on what many regarded as simply a technological tool. He and Shorter finally went their separate ways in 1986; since then Zawinul has worked with his own bands. –RW

Zawinul / ATLANTIC r 1971
This is an interesting dual-keyboard effort. W/ Herbie Hancock (k). –RW

○ **Immigrants / CBS** 1984
Again, a wildly-eclectic menu. Interest depends on how much you enjoy improvisatory music filtered through lots of styles rather than the straight-jazz approach. –RW

Black Water / CBS 1989
His recent band has some strong players. This session is uneven by design, with Zawinul and crew going through many styles. –RW

DENNY ZEITLIN
b 1938

Post-bop, cool, early free. Chicago-born pianist, formed trio in 1964 after receiving his M.D. in psychotherapy at Johns Hopkins. Early period groups are quite stimulating. Newer material is also intriguing, a little more free-floating. All are excellent documents of his search for individualistic expression. He succeeds on all fronts, modern and creative. –MGN

Carnival / COLUMBIA 1964

○ **Live at the Trident / COLUMBIA / DB 5** 1965
W/ Charlie Haden (b), Jerry Granelli (d). A great find. –MGN

Zeitgeist / CBS 1966
60s trio recordings. Rare and wonderful. –MGN

● **Time Remembers One Time Once / ECM** 1981
Live date at Keystone Korner in San Francisco with bassist

Charlie Haden. Extraordinary recording of compositions by Ornette Coleman, Coltrane, and the participants. –MGN

Trio / WINDHAM HILL　　　　　　　i 1988

1988 release containing five Zeitlin originals, plus standards by Mingus, Ornette Coleman, J.J. Johnson, and Kern/Hammerstein. Quite enjoyable. –MGN

JOHN ZORN　　　　　　　　　　　b 1953

Neo bop, modern creative. The term avant-garde truly fits John Zorn; he falls into no easily definable category or school of playing or composition. His splaying, screaming alto sax solos, use of duck calls, and fondness for film soundtracks and mixing of rock, free, pop, and bop settings confound foes and friends alike. He's been identified with the New York "downtown" crowd, a tag he disdains. Zorn's work began to get wide attention in the mid 80s, especially the *Cobra '86* album on Hat Art, with its molecular system for 13 players, plus Zorn's live act which has included him blowing a mouthpiece under water. He's also worked with rockers the Golden Palaminos, the Kronos Quartet, been featured on tribute albums to Thelonious Monk and Sonny Clark, done solo, trio, duo, and combo recordings, and utilized studio technology like multitrack dubbing quite creatively –RW

Pool / PARACHUTE　　　　　　　　　1980

An album that is anarchic, chaotic at times. Gripping and emphatic always. –RW

Archery / PARACHUTE　　　　　　　　1981

Some amazing cuts. –RW

Big Gundown / ELEKTRA-NONESUCH　　1984

Music of Ennio Morricone. 1984-1985. Ambitious, rambling, and reflective of Zorn's flirtations with rock, and the New York downtown scene. –RW

Yankees / OAO　　　　　　　　　　r 1984

Far, far afield with ear-splitting exchanges between Zorn, George Lewis (tb), and string-breaker Derek Bailey (g). –RW

Cobra / HAT ART　　　　　　　　　　1985

Not sure if this is "jazz" in strictest sense. Zorn leads 13-piece group through songs based on a "molecular" system and doesn't play himself. Still, it's as interesting as it sounds. –RW

The Big Gundown / ELEKTRA　　　　r 1987

● **News for Lulu / HAT ART / DB 5**　　r 1988

This is a great power trio w/ George Lewis (tb), and Bill Frisell (g). –RW

Spillane / ELEKTRA-ASYLUM　　　　r 1988

An album of nice, dense, and foreboding concept work, w/ everything from shuffle guitar by Albert Collins to the Kronos Quartet. –RW

○ **Spy Vs. Spy / ELEKTRA-ASYLUM**　　r 1989

Another superb concept album, this time a top-knotch group performs 17 Ornette Coleman cuts. Tim Berne (as) is a worthy partner in crime. –RW

○ **Naked City / ELEKTRA-ASYLUM**　　r 1990

His most intriguing, nicely conceived and executed date, with sparkling solos by Bill Frisell (g), Wayne Horowitz (k), and Joey Baron (d). CD has three bonus cuts. –RW

☆ **Voodoo / BLACK SAINT**

His best date. Zorn leads a quartet in tribute to Sonny Clark, doing all his tunes. –RW

BARRY ZWEIG　　　　　　　　　　b 1942

Swing, bop, cool, early free. This guitarist, writer, and educator plays it all without compromise. Mostly he plays in the progressive mainstream, but he can and does venture into different arenas. –MGN

○ **Desert Vision / JAZZ CHRONICLES**　　1978

The intriguing guitar of Zweig and trumpeter Bobby Shew. All originals. –MGN

JAZZ COLLECTIONS

1930s Big Bands / CBS

○ **1930s: The Singers / CBS**

A fine anthology that culls songs from a wide number of 30s jazz sides. –RW

1940s: Small Groups — New / CBS

Good examples of changes in the 40s among combos. –RW

1940s: The Singers / CBS

1950s: The Singers / CBS

☆ **Afro-Cuban Jazz / POLYGRAM**

A seminal collection of classic Afro-Cuban music. Charlie Parker (as), Dizzy Gillespie (tpt), Flip Phillips (ts), and Machito are all in top form. –RW

○ **Amarcord Nino Rota / HANNIBAL**

Atlantic Jazz: Avant Garde / ATLANTIC

Dynamic, challenging material. An area where they didn't do enough recording, but what they did was excellent. –RW

Atlantic Jazz: Bebop / ATLANTIC

A fine set with strong performances all around. –RW

Atlantic Jazz: Boxed Set / ATLANTIC

This entire series is worth having and can be purchased in one 12-volume disc set or one 15-LP/cassette set. In compiling the discs, Atlantic for some reason omitted some cuts, making the vinyl a better buy. Of course, the vinyl is now deleted. –RW

Atlantic Jazz: Introspection / ATLANTIC

1967 sessions, some good Charles Lloyd (ts) and Keith Jarrett (p). Some not-so-good Hubert Laws (fl). –RW

Atlantic Jazz: Kansas City / ATLANTIC

Excellent cuts by Joe Turner (v) and T-Bone Walker (v).　RW

Atlantic Jazz: Mainstream / ATLANTIC

A debatable title, but very nice music. –RW

Atlantic Jazz: New Orleans / ATLANTIC

Nice, mostly traditional recordings, since Atlantic hasn't been in New Orleans to get the contemporary sound. –RW

Atlantic Jazz: Piano / ATLANTIC

One of the best in the line. Extraordinary solos from almost everyone. Wide range of styles. –RW

Atlantic Jazz: Post Bebop / ATLANTIC

Challenging title. This is the label's foray into the avant-garde, plus good tracks by MJQ, Von Freeman (ts), and Sonny Rollins (ts). –RW

Atlantic Jazz: Singers / ATLANTIC

A tremendous cross-section with only a couple of ringers. –RW

Atlantic Jazz: Soul / ATLANTIC

Very nice. A good cross-section. –RW

Atlantic Jazz: West Coast / ATLANTIC

Nice cuts. As an individual entry, this is not as strong as some of the others in the series. –RW

Autobiography in Jazz / OJC

Some excellent material that was previously on Debut, including Max Roach (d), Thad Jones (tpt), and Lee Konitz (sax). ca. 1956 –RW

Bebop & Beyond / CONCORD

Bebop Era / CBS

Some nice examples of bop. –RW

Bebop Revolution / RCA

A 1990 reissue. Nice formative cuts from the 40s. –RW

○ **Best of Blue Note - Vol 1 & 2 / BLUE NOTE**

Japanese import. An incredible (just the best!) collection of the very best cuts from the Blue Note label. A perfect introduction to hard-bop and soul jazz, if you can find it. –JME

Best of Chess Jazz / MCA

This is actually a nice package of cuts pulled from various Argo sessions. –RW

○ **Best of Chess Jazz / CHESS**

Best of the Big Bands / MCA

This offers a nice cross-section of Decca sets, especially Woody Herman. −RW

Best of the Swing Bands / HINDSIGHT
A good cross-section, heavy on big names. −RW

Big Band Jazz: Various / DELMARK
First-class compilation covering transitional orchestras in the late 40s and early 50s. −RW

Big Bands Hits / CAPITOL
4-CD gift set. One of the better anthologies. Pretty thorough, and includes both Black and White bands. −RW

○ **Big Bands of the Swinging Year - Vol. 1 / CBS**
This is a pick for those who only want an idea of what the era was like. −RW

Bird Lives! / MILESTONE
Also see Joe Albany. Outstanding solos by Art Pepper (as) and Frank Morgan (sax). A nice tribute to Bird. −RW

○ **Black Swing Tradition / SAVOY**

Blue Note 50th Anniversary - Vol. 1 / BLUE NOTE
1939-1956. Boogie to bop. Parts of the 50th Anniversary boxed set. Formative label sessions with boogie-woogie piano up to hard bop. −RW

Blue Note 50th Anniversary - Vol. 2 / CAPITOL
1956-1965. Jazz Message. Dynamic cuts, hard bop, and avant-garde. −RW

Blue Note 50th Anniversary - Vol. 3 / CAPITOL
1956-1965. Funk and blues. The birth of soul-jazz. −RW

Blue Note 50th Anniversary - Vol. 4 / CAPITOL
1964-1989. Outside in. Avant-garde, explosive cuts. −RW

Blue Note 50th Anniversary - Vol. 5 / CAPITOL
1970-1989. Least important and least distingushed of the set. −RW

Blue Porter: Blue Note Plays Cole Porter / CAPITOL
A good concept sampler. Songs and performances are mostly good. −RW

Blues for Tomorrow / OJC
A good 1957 sampler with various groups, including Sonny Rollins (ts) and Bobby Jaspar (ts). −RW

● **Brothers & Other Mothers - Vol 2 / SAVOY**

Chicago Jazz Summit / ATLANTIC
A 1988 release of some nice cuts done by Chicago jazz veterans at the 1986 JUC festival. −RW

○ **Chocolate Dandies / DISQUES SWING**
1928-1933. Essential early jazz. Important document. −MGN

Clarinet Summit / INNOVATIVE
Wondrous performances by the outstanding Clarinet Summit at Public Theater. Includes the late John Carter (cl). −RW

Classic Female Jazz Artists / RCA
1939-1952. Despite a dubious title, this is a worthwhile anthology of both blues and jazz artists. −RW

☆ **Classic Jazz / SMITHSONIAN**
The Smithsonian Collection of Classic Jazz is itself somewhat of a classic, referred to in many books, and used as the main learning source in at least one. If you don't know what you like in jazz and are looking for a well-put-together introduction, this set is a good bet. It starts with ragtime's Scott Joplin, and proceeds through Bessie Smith, Louis Armstrong, Art Tatum, Duke Ellington ... all the way up to and including the free jazz of Ornette Coleman, and even the World Saxophone Quartet. Of course John Coltrane, Thelonious Monk, Miles Davis, and all the other big guns are there — even Horace Silver and Lennie Tristano. This 5-CD set (94 tracks) contains classic cuts in most cases. This set is a great place to begin. −JME

○ **Classic Jazz Piano / RCA**
1927-1957. An excellent compilation of some seminal players and styles. CD has three bonus cuts. −RW

Classic Piano: Various Jazz Artists / CBS   COMP
A super cross-section of timeless piano cuts. Valuable anthology that gets lost in major label fumbling. Erroll Garner, Earl Hines, James P. Johnson, Bob Hodes, and more. −RW

Classic Rags & Novelties / VANGUARD-CLASSICAL
Fine examples of the ragtime and novelty-song tradition. −RW

Columbia Jazz Masterpiece Series / CBS
A good starter collection spotlighting jazz in the period when it still had some pop influence. This is a recent cross-section of jazz-based, scat, and popular song stylists. −RW

Columbia Jazz Masterpiece Series: 1930s Big Band / CBS
An excellent single-disc overview of 30s bands, both big names and obscure groups. −RW

Columbia Jazz Masterpieces: 1940s - The Singers / CBS
Good entry in the line. Album features some spectacular vocals throughout. −RW

Columbia Jazz Masterpieces: Sampler - Vol. 1 / CBS
Nice performances, compiled and aimed at the rare jazz buyer who might only want one release with many artists. −RW

Columbia Jazz Masterpieces: Sampler - Vol. 2 / CBS
Like Volume 1, this is a collection of nice performances from many artists. −RW

Columbia Jazz Masterpieces: Sampler - Vol. 6 / CBS
Another batch of performances aimed at introducing the line to novices. −RW

Concord Jazz Festival: Live 1990 / CONCORD   1990
This is the first set. Nice, though predictable, swing/mainstream fare. −RW

Concord Jazz Guitar Collection - Vols. 1 & 2 / CONCORD
Outstanding guitar cuts. −RW

Decca Jazz Sampler: 1927-1949 / MCA
A good sampler of nuggets from the Decca vaults. −RW

○ **Dixieland's Greatest Hits / PRA**
Traditional anthology. −RW

○ **Early Black Swing: Birth of Big Band Jazz / RCA**
1927-1934. Valuable, classic tunes from jazz pioneers, swing, and classic New Orleans. First-rate examples of vintage swing from the 20s and 30s. Plenty of examples from the cream of the crop, including Armstrong, Ellington, Fletcher Henderson. Great introductory item. −RW

Early Bones / PRESTIGE

Fifty Years of Jazz Guitar / CSP
A worthwhile compilation of various guitar tracks. −RW

Fire / GARLAND
Various nice cuts from albums by Cannonball Adderley, Yusef Lateef, Gene Ammons, Lee Morgan, Wayne Shorter, Wynton Kelly, Eddie Harris, Paul Chambers, Frank Strozier, and Sonny Stitt — 11 in all. Vee-Jay classics. −JME

○ **Fun on the Frets: Early Jazz Guitar / YAZOO**
A companion volume to Yazoo Record's "Pioneers of the Jazz Guitar." This compilation (1939-1949) features George Van Eps, Carl Kress, and Tony Mottola. −RL

○ **Giants of Small Band Swing - Vol. 1 / OJC**
Fine combo dates, mostly bop, plus occasional classic New Orleans style. −RW

○ **Giants of Small Band Swing - Vol. 2 / OJC**
A companion volume to its predecessor. −RW

○ **Giants of the Blues and Funk Tenor Sax / PRESTIGE**
A great 2-disc introduction to both honking-blues and funk (soul jazz) tenor saxophone. Great for beginners, but should be in any collection. Over three hours of blues/funk greats like Arnett Cob, Eddie "Lockjaw" Davis, Sonny Stitt, Willis Jackson, Houston Person, Stanley Turrentine, Rusty Bryant, and Gene Ammons. A classic collection. −JME
A good concept work, aimed at one-time, casual, and novice buyers. It's a three-record set with both blues and funk players in the spotlight. −RW

○ **Great Blues Vocals in Jazz: How Blue Can You Get? / RCA**
Excellent reissue shows the links between jazz and blues. −RW

○ **Great Ladies of Jazz / KTEL-QWIL**
Horrid sound, but some good selections by Sarah Vaughan, Billie Holiday, Nancy Wilson, and Dinah Washington. −RW

Great Trumpets: Classic Jazz to Swing / RCA
Many brilliant solos. Good as an introductory item. –RW

○ **Greatest Jazz Concert Ever / PABLO**

○ **The Historic Recordings / VERVE**   1944
Recorded 1944 and 1946 with Nat Cole Trio and Les Paul (g). Backing soloists included J. J. Johnson (tb), Illinois Jacquet (sax), and Jack McVea (ts). Plus lots of Billie Holiday. Recorded in Los Angeles. –MGN

○ **Honkers & Bar Walkers - Vols. 1 & 2 / DLM**
1952. A blasting R&B sax-anthology consisting of early-50s tracks from the Regal and United labels. –MGN

I Like Jazz / CBS   1951
A 1951 sampler, probably produced by the sales division. –RW

Impulse Collection: Best Of - Vol. 1 / MCA
Cross-section of good performances from the larger set. –RW

Impulse! Jazz: 30 Year Collection / MCA-GRP   i 1991
A two-record set that has many fine cuts celebrating this distinguished label's three decades. –RW

Jazz Arranger - Vol. 1 (1928-40) / CBS
A good overview of early jazz sides and the arrangers who made them work for such groups as the Dorseys, Cab Calloway, and Ellington. –RW

Jazz Arranger - Vol. 2 (1946-63) / CBS
A good companion volume. This updates the line. –RW

Jazz at Santa Monica Civic '72 / PA2   i 1972
JATP-styled blowing date with well-known Pablo acts. A three-record set from 1972. –RW

Jazz Club: Alto Sax / POLYGRAM
A strong entry in a good line of compilations. The CD as two bonus cuts. –RW

Jazz Club: Alto Sax Clarinet & Flute / POLYGRAM
Good selections. –RW

Jazz Club: Bass / POLYGRAM
A fine addition in a rare worthwhile compilation series. CD has one bonus cut. –RW

Jazz Club: Big Band / POLYGRAM
A fine cross-section of dynamic big-band outings. One bonus cut on CD. –RW

Jazz Club: Drums / POLYGRAM
A nice cross-section of drummers and percussionists. Recommended. CD has two bonus cuts. –RW

Jazz Club: Guitar / POLYGRAM
Very nice selection of artists/cuts. CD has two bonus cuts. –RW

Jazz Club: Guitar & Bass / POLYGRAM
Similar to the others in the series. –RW

Jazz Club: Piano / POLYGRAM
A highly-recommended starter set for novice fans — great cross-section of players. CD has three bonus cuts. –RW

Jazz Club: Tenor & Baritone Sax / POLYGRAM
In the same vein as the other compilations in this series. –RW

Jazz Club: Tenor Sax / POLYGRAM
Plenty of great tenor performances from a host of giants. Excellent for novices. CD has three bonus cuts. –RW

Jazz Club: Trombone / POLYGRAM
Find selections, notable artists. CD has two bonus cuts. –RW

Jazz Club: Trumpet / POLYGRAM
Equal quality to the rest of the series. Two CD bonus cuts. –RW

Jazz Club: Vibraphone / POLYGRAM
A solid compilation. CD has two bonus cuts. –RW

Jazz in the Thirties / DISQUES SWING
A very nice anthology with lots of cuts from underrated performers. –RW

Jazz in the USSR / MOBILE FIDELITY
Wonderfully-recorded collection spotlights Soviet artists. –RW

Jazz Loves Paris / SPEED
A Buddy Collette session with wonderful arrangements and nice solos. It's available once more after a long absence. –RW

Jazz Piano / SMITHSONIAN
Four discs — 68 cuts and over 40 artists — all the way from

Jelly Roll Morton through Teddy Wilson, Art Tatum, Erroll Garner, Bud Powell, Thelonious Monk, Tommy Flanagan, Bill Evans ... up to Chick Corea, Keith Jarrett, and Herbie Hancock — a great survey of piano styles. This collection focuses on piano solos, and most are unaccompanied. Overall, a very nice collection. –JME

○ **Jazz Singers / PRESTIGE**
Good range of featured artists aimed at novices and new fans. Very fine two-record set with an extensive cross-section from early Armstrong to Flora Purim. This is worth having, regardless of your jazz knowledge. –RW

Jazz Trumpet: Classic Jazz to Swing / PRESTIGE
Vol. 1. An excellent anthology covering the rest of trumpet styles in the first phase of jazz. –RW

Keys to the Crescent City / ROUNDER
Outstanding current New Orleans jazz & blues cuts. –RW

Kingdom of Swing & Republic Of / MUM
Jazz in July at the 92nd. Nice swing and mainstream performances. –RW

Kings of Ragtime / PRO ARTE-PRO JAZZ
A good compilation. –RW

☆ **Laughing in Rhythm / STASH**

Legends of Guitar: Jazz-Vol 1 / CAPITOL-RHINO
A fine, extensive overview of jazz guitar, with a host of stylists. CD has four bonus cuts. –RW

Legends of Guitar: Jazz-Vol 2 / CAPITOL-RHINO
Excellent follow-up release. Comprehensive and intelligently compiled. CD has three bonus cuts. –RW

Live: Jazz 'Round Midnight / POLYGRAM
Some fine live cuts. –RW

Maybeck Recital Hall - Vols. 1-4 / CONCORD
Wonderful solo playing throughout this series. –RW

○ **Mercury 40th Anniversary / POLYGRAM**   1985
V.S.O.P. Album. Fine sampler with many prime artists. –RW

Modern New Orleans Masters / ROUNDER
Excellent current music by well-known New Orleans performers. –RW

Jazz Sampler / MUSICMASTERS

○ **New New Orleans Music: Jump Jazz / ROUNDER**

○ **New Orleans Brass Bands: Down Yonder / ROUNDER**
An eclectic sampler of some of New Orleans' best: the Dirty Dozen, Dejan's Olympia, the Rebirth, and the Chosen Few. –BR

Newport Rebels: Various / CANDID

Nipper's Greatest Hits - 30s Vol. 1 / RCA
A trip down the 30s memory lane. –RW

○ **Pioneers of the Jazz Guitar / YAZOO**
Terrific compilation of 20s & 30s acoustic jazz guitar music featuring Eddie Lang, Carl Kress, Lonnie Johnson, Dick McDonough, and others. Yes, Virginia, there was jazz guitar before Charlie Christian. This volume is preferable to Yazoo's companion — *Fun On The Frets.* –RL

☆ **Prestige Soul Masterpieces / OJC**
Fine intro to funk or soul jazz on the Hammond organ. 15 cuts from classic funk albums by Charles Earland, Billy Butler, Jack McDuff, Gene Ammons, Charles Kynard, Oliver Nelson, King Curtis, Jimmy Forrest, Rusty Bryant, Shirley Scott, Stanley Turrentine, Willis Jackson, Houston Person, Harold Mabern, Eddie Davis, Red Holloway, Arnett Cobb, Richard Holmes, and many featured soloists. This is the real stuff. –JME

Reefer Songs: Various / JASS

The Foundations of Modern Jazz / DCC
The title is questionable, but there are some good performances on the disc. –RW

○ **Tribute to Duke / CONCORD**
Various artists, including Tony Bennett, Bing Crosby, and Woody Herman pay homage to Ellington. –RW

Yazoo's History of Jazz / YAZOO

☆ **From Spiritual to Swing / VANGUARD-CLASSICAL** 1938
An essential document. –MGN

SOUND EFFECTS

80 SPECTACULAR SOUND EFX - CDFX SERIES

80 Spectacular Sound Efx- CDFX series / LDMI
All digital, this features the usual animals, airplanes, and machine noises but also includes some more esoteric sounds like a stapler, filing cabinet, postage meter, soap opera organ, computer printer, sci-fi movie voices, and harp glissando. Nice ambient tracks like office atmosphere and commuter traffic. (DDD) –ED

COMPLETE LIBRARY OF SOUND EFFECTS

Library of Sound Effects - Vol. 1 / SONY
Birds, lions, elephants, pinball machine, timpani, thunderstorms, freight trains, steam train, and others. –ED
Library of Sound Effects - Vol. 2 / SONY
Birds, dogs, chickens, trains, vibraphone, pneumatic drill, satellites, stone quarry, and others. –ED
Library of Sound Effects - Vol. 3 / SONY
Penny arcade, slot machine, subway, bus station, roller rink, and others. –ED
Library of Sound Effects - Vol. 4 / SONY
Crowds, cars, trains, street cars, soccer match, car wash, indoor tennis, chicken coop, cement mixer, and others. –ED
Library of Sound Effects - Vol. 5 / SONY
Big Ben, 17-year locusts, thunderstorms, ultrasonic explosion, roller coaster, printing press, and others. –ED
Library of Sound Effects - Vol. 6 / SONY
Atom bomb, offset printer, typewriter, telegraph, music box, breaking glass, helicopter, Carnival de Rio de Janeiro, and others. –ED
Library of Sound Effects - Vol. 7 / SONY
Police siren, ambulance, air conditioner, tire repair shop, electric razor, moviola splicing table, and others. –ED
Library of Sound Effects - Vol. 8 / SONY
Bulldozer, lawnmower, sprinklers, steel works, blast furnace, steel works, submarine sonar, shipyard, and others. –ED
Library of Sound Effects - Vol. 9 / SONY
Donkeys, bees, dogs, owl, tiger, pigeons, roosters, coyote, bull, military calls and signals, the farmers market of Florence, Italy, and others. –ED
Library of Sound Effects - Vol. 10 / SONY
Bells, cuckoo clock, hammer blows, crackling firewood, mine explosions, spaceships, robots, space missles, and others. –ED

HALLOWEEN HORRORS

Halloween Horror / A&M

HOLLYWOOD SOUND EFFECTS

○ **Hollywood Sound Effects / PETER PAN-COMPOSE** 1988
This CD features 99 separate tracks of sounds you might hear used in a movie. Includes airplanes, battle sounds, household noises, people, animals, bowling alley sounds, and nature noises. (AAD) –ED

LIVING SOUND EFFECTS

○ **Living Sound Effects - Vol. 1 / BAINBRIDGE** 1988
This multi-volume series (originally released as a seven-LP set), is now on CD and contains over 300 sounds. –ED
Living Sound Effects - Vol. 2 / BAINBRIDGE 1988
Living Sound Effects - Vol. 3 / BAINBRIDGE 1988
Living Sound Effects - Vol. 4 / BAINBRIDGE 1988

MUSIC FOR NIGHT

Various Scary Things / TOTAL RECORDING

OFFBEAT SOUND EFFECTS

○ **Offbeat Sound Effects from BBC Comedy / BBC**

OUT OF THIS WORLD (OUTER SPACE & SUPERNATURAL)

Out of This World (Outer Space & Supernatural) / BBC

SOUND EFFECTS FROM DR. WHO

○ **Sound Effects from Dr. Who / BBC**
Your favorite noise and sound effects from this British sci-fi show from the 70s and 80s. –ED

SOUND SENSATION - 100 SOUND EFFECTS

○ **Sound Sensation - 100 Sound Effects / LDMI (CANADA)**
More all-digital sound effects from this Canadian distributor. More unique sounds like jungle atmosphere, kung fu fighting, downhill skiing, taxi meter, zipper, two drunk men in a bar, earthquake, slot machine, a crowd on New Year's Eve, and others. Also includes the ubiquitous sounds of a toilet, animals, vehicles, and military noise. –ED

SOUNDS OF TRAINS

○ **Sounds of Trains - Vol. 1 / BAINBRIDGE**
If you love trains, you'll love this CD. Listen for the distinctive sounds of dozens of different steam and diesel trains. –ED
Sounds of Trains - Vol. 2 / BAINBRIDGE
Sounds of Trains - Vol. 3 / BAINBRIDGE

STETHOSCOPIC HEART RECORDINGS

Stethoscopic Heart Recordings / CSP

TERROR SOUND EFFECTS

Terror Sound Effects / PETER PAN-COMPOSE

MARCHES

BAND OF H.M. ROYAL MARINES (ENGLAND)
Band of H.M. Royal Marines / FIDELITY SOUND

BOSTON POPS ORCHESTRA
Great American Marches / RCA

CZECHOSLOVAK BRASS ORCHESTRA
Marches by John Philip Sousa / NONESUCH

ARTHUR FIEDLER
Greatest U.S. Marches / RCA

HENRY FILLMORE
Great Marches / PRO ARTE

GARDIENS DE LA PAIX
Military Fanfares, Marches & Choruses / NONESUCH

GOLDMAN BAND
Golden March Favorites / MCA
Marching Along Together / MCA
Sousa Marches in Hi-Fi / MCA

INDIANA UNIVERSITY MARCHING HUNDRED
Indiana Our Indiana / FIDELITY SOUND
Indiana Univ. Marching Hundred / FIDELITY SOUND

PHILIP JONES ENSEMBLE
Sousa Marches / LONDON

MICHIGAN STATE UNIVERSITY BAND
Michigan State University Band / FIDELITY SOUND
Michigan State Univ. Band - Vol. 2 / FIDELITY SOUND

MICHIGAN UNIVERSITY BAND
Kick Off, USA / VANGUARD

OHIO STATE UNIVERSITY MARCHING BAND
Saturday Afternoon at Columbus / FIDELITY SOUND
Stars, Stripes 'N Bass / FIDELITY SOUND
Across the Field / FIDELITY SOUND
Buckeye Bandstand / FIDELITY SOUND
Buckeye Battle Cry / FIDELITY SOUND
Hats off to Heine / FIDELITY SOUND

OLYMPIA BRASS BAND
On Bourbon Street / PRO ARTE

THE ROYAL SCOTS DRAGOON GUARD
Amazing Grace / RCA

REGIMENTAL BAND
Marches #1 - British / DENON

ROYAL HORSE GUARDS BAND
Pomp & Circumstance of Regimental Bands / ALSHIRE

SCOTS GUARDS REGIMENTAL BAND
Pipes & Dreams of the 1st Battalion / FIESTA

BOB SHARPLES
America on the March / POLYGRAM

FELIX SLATKIN
Charge!/Military Band / CAPITOL   1979

JOHN PHILIP SOUSA
New Sousa - Stars & Stripes / BAINBRIDGE
Hands Across the Sea / CAPITOL
Marching Along / BAINBRIDGE
Original All-American Marches / DELOS

STATSMUSIKKORPS DER BUNDESWEHR
Marschmusik / FIESTA RECORDS

U. S. C. TROJAN MARCHING BAND
U. S. C. Trojan Marching Band / FIDELITY SOUND

UNIVERSITY OF MICHIGAN BAND
Hail Sousa! / VANGUARD
Stars & Stripes Forever (Sousa Marches) / VANGUARD
Touchdown USA! - Big Ten Marches / VANGUARD 1980
Great Football Marches / VANGUARD   1980

JOHN T. WILLIAMS
I Love a Parade / CBS

MARCH COLLECTIONS
American Marches / LEGACY INTL.
French Military Marches / LEGACY INTL.
Greatest College Football Marches / VANGUARD
Music & Marches of Bullfight Ring / LEGACY INTL.
New Orleans Parade Music / GNP CRESCENDO
Touchdown! - Greatest College Fight Songs / PRO ARTE

Audio Equipment: Some Guidelines

by Karl W. Nehring

If you are new to audio equipment, or want to upgrade your system and take advantage of the greater dynamic range of CDs, you may want to consider buying new components. Too often, audio stores are staffed by salespersons cut from the same cloth as car salesmen. It can be hard to get a straight answer, and many shops will only push brands for which they get a large discount. Or, you may be pushed into a much more expensive system than you need. We have asked Karl W. Nehring, the editor of the prestigious audiophile magazine The $ensible Sound, for some guidelines in purchasing audio equipment. For more information, contact: The $ensible Sound, 403 Darwin Drive, Snyder, NY 14226; phone (716) 662-0073. Subscriptions to this quarterly are $20. — JME

CD PLAYERS

"Perfect Sound Forever" was the original rallying cry of the CD revolution. Well, we found out that it wasn't perfect and it probably won't be forever. New media will come along to replace CDs — who needs a little record spinning around being tracked by a mechanical arm assembly?! — but while it is here, we might as well enjoy the fact that it sounds pretty damn good and will be around for a pretty long time, non-geologically speaking As far as picking a CD player for your system, there is no need for neurosis. It really doesn't matter whether you have a single- or a three-beam laser (a three-beamer is just a single laser with a little smoke and mirrors!), and it doesn't not really matter whether your player is 16-bit, 18-bit, 20-bit, or 1-bit. A lot of advertising money is being spent to convince you otherwise, but if you are smart enough to be reading this, you are smart enough not to fall for all the hype.

So what kind of CD player should you get? Well, as long as you avoid the real cheapo machines, you will probably do okay.

PLAYERS IN THE $299-450 RANGE

The new Marantz CD-52 is a nice little player for $299, and unless you want a CD changer or you just want more finish and features than the Marantz offers, there is no real reason to spend much more. The current audiophile darling seems to be the Rotel RCD-955, a nice machine at $450, and if it is important to impress your audiophile friends, the Rotel is probably your cheapest bet (but the Marantz is more feature-laden for two-thirds the price, and sounds just as good).

PLAYERS IN THE $550-750 RANGE

If you would rather get something slicker and more heavy-duty, I would recommend one of the Onkyo Integra CD players for example, their new DX-706 at $550 or their new DX-708 at $750. Or if you want to have a real conversation piece, you might consider the Carver SD/A-490t at $700, which features the comforting orange glow of vacuum tubes emanating from the top of the unit.

And hey, folks, there is no need to spend any more than that. There is especially no need to worry about a separate D/A converter. Trust me, you don't need one. Remember what I said about advertising hype?

AMPS/PREAMPS

There is plenty of good stuff on the market and it is hard to go wrong. (I can hear the audiophiles groaning now. Let them groan; your laughter, when you head for the bank, will drown them out anyway!) Adcom, Audio by Van Alstine (AVA), B&K, Carver, Marantz, Onkyo, Parasound — these are some of the companies who make affordable components that sound good and give good service. It's hard to go wrong with any of them, but let me single out a few components that deserve special mention.

AMPS IN THE $550-750 RANGE

For an interesting listening experience, you might want to try one of the Carver preamplifiers that contains Sonic Holography circuitry. The C-16 ($700), for example, is a full-featured unit that has Carver's hologram circuitry built in; it can do wonders for many recordings. And if you are in the mood to do it yourself, Audio by Van Alstine sells a kit version ($550) of their nice-sounding SuperPAS Omega preamplifier, a tube unit with solid-state buffers that can also be purchased factory-assembled for $750.

POWER AMPS ($399-975)

If you are looking for plenty of clean power in a compact chassis, then it is hard to beat Carver's magnetic field power supply series of amplifiers, exemplified by the TFM-42 ($975), which offers a rating of 375 watts per channel into 8 ohms but weighs about the same as many 100-watt amps. And speaking of 100-watt amps (which should have plenty of power for most applications), both Carver's TFM-15 ($399) and Parasound's HCA-800 II ($425) offer exceptional value — both sport volume controls, meaning that they can be used directly with a CD player, thus eliminating the need for a preamplifier in systems where CD is the sole program source.

LOUDSPEAKERS

Here we get to the heart of the matter, the last link between you and the music (but don't forget your room — poor placement can make even the best speakers sound so-so.) Like cars, speakers have been getting better in the past few years; but unlike cars, with speakers you can still find good performance at relatively low prices.

There are many good loudspeakers out there and I won't even pretend that the speakers listed below exhaust the list of good recommendations. Rather, these are speakers that represent excellent value at their respective price points. Auditioning them might serve to introduce a novice listener to what can be done for a given amount of money so that he or she can become a more informed speaker/auditioner and ultimately a more satisfied speaker buyer.

SPEAKERS IN THE $200-$500 RANGE

If you can only afford $200 for a pair of speakers, you might try the Sound Dynamics 50Ti set. No, these speakers do not equal the more expensive models listed below, but they offer a taste of audiophile sound for a relatively modest price. If you can ante up another hundred bucks, the Signet SL 250 B/Us are a good choice. For $300, they offer good sound, lacking only bass and power handling when compared with their larger brothers. The Fried Q/4s, at $500 per pair, really get you into audiophile territory, with significantly better bottom-end performance than the speakers mentioned above.

SPEAKERS IN THE $600-800 RANGE

Probably the most hotly-contested price class is the range between about six and eight hundred dollars per pair. This is where it starts to get serious. You can buy cheaper speakers for less, but if you are serious about music to the point where you are reading a guide such as this one, then you should be serious enough to think about spending more than $600 on your speakers, because this is where the fun really begins. Of all the speakers in the $600-$800 range, there are several models that stand out from the pack, including three models selling for $700: the Amrita Logos, the Fried A/3a, and the Signet SL 280 B/U. The Amrita Logos is the speaker in this group that I would recommend to the listener who likes to rock out, but who still wants a semblance of neutrality. The Amrita has a lively, dynamic sound, with plenty of punch and drive. The Fried, on the other hand, is the classical music champion of this group, with a sweet top end (excellent on massed strings) and a relatively tight bottom end that will not shake walls, but will at least offer a semblance of concert-hall bass without exaggerated boominess. The Signet SL 280 B/U offers a carefully balanced sound that falls somewhere between the Fried and the Amrita, meaning that it might be the safest overall choice of the three, for those with widely ranging musical tastes.

At $800 per pair, special mention should be made of the Icon Acoustics Lumen. This is a speaker that is physically smaller than the three mentioned above, but which has a big sound that belies its small size. Wonderfully neutral and able to project a most convincing stereo soundstage, the Lumen lacks only the last octave or so of bass that the more expensive speakers offer.

SPEAKERS FOR $1000-PLUS

At right around $1,000 per pair, the Altair speaker by Bright Star Audio offers unique styling and unmatched stereo

imaging. Although the appearance of this speaker might not be suited to every taste, its sonic performance may well win the day.

For a few hundred dollars more, you can get better bass with similar imaging characteristics in the Vandersteen 2Ce set, one of the safest recommendations that an audio buff can make to his or her friends. These are speakers that sound good on all kinds of music, and rival the much more costly speakers in neutrality and imaging ability. Another interesting choice at approximately the same price range is the Shahinian Arc. Shahinian speakers are not the easiest models to find, but the search is worth it. The Arcs come in a small physical package that is much less intrusive than the Vandersteens, but which is capable of filling the listening room with glorious music. And the Fried R/4 is a real contender in this same price range, with many of the virtues of the A/3a, but with better bass and more ability to play loud.

AND BEYOND...

Although any of the speakers listed in the above paragraph can be considered full-range, there are those who will want more, especially on the bottom end. If you will be satisfied only by a speaker that can truly thunder, then perhaps the best overall choice is one of the Carver Amazing loudspeakers. These speakers feature a ribbon driver for most of the hearing range and multiple woofers to cover the bass frequencies. Given sufficient power, the Amazing Loudspeakers (which range in price from just over $2,000 for the smaller Silver Edition in oak finish to just under $3,000 for the Platinum Edition when finished in stunning black lacquer) can do justice to the most challenging recordings. From the talking drum to the Telarc drum, the Carver Amazings will pump out the power but they can still sound sweet when called upon to reproduce the delicate sound of the clavichord.

So we top this survey out at just under $3,000 per pair. Is there any reason to spend even more? Not that I can think of. Enjoy!

Mail-order Audio

Some of you may not have access to audio stores. In that case, here is a dependable mail-order firm:

CRUTCHFIELD

In terms of reliability, good information, and a decent selection of components, one company is outstanding: Crutchfield. Although not the place to get expensive high-end equipment, they do offer a range of popular receivers, tape decks, and CD players — Sony, Kenwood, JVC, Pioneer, Proton, etc. Their speakers include Advent, Sony, Infinity, NHT, EPI, and Cerwin Vega. Crutchfield's free 120-page catalog not only details the equipment, but includes introductory sections that explain component features, the types of speakers, room layout — many of the things you might want to know if you're new to systems. The Crutchfield sales staff know their equipment, and can talk with you about your particular set-up. And their discounted prices make them competitive with local shops. I know this sounds like an ad. It's not. If you can't find a good source of info and systems close to you (without all the hype), here is a dependable mail-order alternative. Call 800/336-5566 for a free catalog. — JME

MUSIC RESOURCES

Aside from the music itself, there are many fine resources available that make your music journey more comfortable and fun. There is no room here for a comprehensive review of all the music books, magazines, mail-order firms, and record companies out there, but here are some that we feel provide a real service.

Record Companies

MOSAIC RECORDS

It seems that every generation has a few record labels where there is real magic happening. Jazz is no exception. If Blue Note was the standard-bearer of the 60s, then, in our time, it has to be Mosaic Records. Mosaic is not your average record label. Instead of recording jazz artists, they are expert at picking up on jazz gems neglected by other major labels and obtaining a license to publish them in very limited editions. Mosaic offers complete, chronologically ordered recordings (many previously unavailable) by acknowledged jazz masters at the peak of their careers. The sets include thoroughly researched booklets, including discographies and many photos, which, with the recordings, constitute definitive research documents for the featured musician. The quality of these Mosaic packages sets a standard for our times. Scholarship aside, what makes Mosaic founders Charlie Lourie and Michael Cuscuna great is their ability to search out pockets of recorded jazz that have been overlooked or forgotten and reissuing them. A class act. Best of all, Mosaic has found some of the very best jazz recordings ever made, and made them available. Here is some incredible music, and Mosaic sets never seem to get far from my stereo system. These albums can be obtained only through the mail. A detailed catalog is available by writing to 35 Melrose Place, Stamford, CT 06902; or call 203/327-7111.— JME

SMITHSONIAN RECORDINGS

There are two different companies that share a legitimate tie to the Smithsonian; Smithsonian Recordings is the first. You won't see these recordings in stores (you may get a flyer in the mail if you have used your credit card lately). These are, for the most part, boxed sets (CDs and albums) on different music generes — folk, country, jazz, big band, classical, and others. Many of these sets are well conceived and serve as good introductions to a particular kind of music. — JME

SMITHSONIAN/FOLKWAYS RECORDINGS

Folkways Recordings, started by Moses Asch and Marian Distler in 1947, introduced baby boomers to real folk music. Folkways was *the* folk/world label back in the 60s. With 2,100-plus albums in their catalog, Folkways is the way many of us first heard the likes of the New Lost City Ramblers, The Country Gentlemen, Woody Guthrie, Cisco Houston, Leadbelly, and others, not to mention a wealth of indigenous world music. But for a while it looked like Folkways (a real national treasure) would be gone forever.

But since 1987, thanks to a special arrangement with Rounder Records, every original Folkways album is once again available under a new company called Smithsonian/Folkways. New and priceless recordings from the archives have been added to the catalog. — JME

The complete Folkways catalog is available by writing to:

> Smithsonian/Folkways Recordings
> Center for Folklife Programs
> Smithsonian Institution
> 955 L' Enfant Plaza, Suite 2600
> Washington DC 20560.

TIME-LIFE SERIES

The Time-Life Series is available only by mail order. You will find it advertised everywhere — on TV and in many magazines. Time-Life offers sets of recordings on R&B, country, the music of the 70s, hit parade (40s and 50s hits), classic rock & roll, the rock & roll era, and others. Each set consists of many separate albums, each one containing the big hits for a particular year. In the case of rock, there are often second and third albums for a given year featuring additional minor hits.

The bad news is that these CDs are expensive. By the time you pay the shipping and handling, each one costs about $20 a shot, which is just too much. For this reason, I wish I could suggest that you ignore the Time-Life Series, that they were poorly done or there was some other reason not to buy them. But the truth is that these CDs are, for the most part, well conceived and well executed. No other hits collection series is even near as comprehensive. Perhaps some of the early albums in the rock series are a little shabby; still, they are worth having.

Typically, there are from 20 to 24 hits per disc, with good liner notes (and complete discographies!) written by well-known music writers. I am not alone in this opinion. After talking with some of the other editors of the *All-Music Guide*, the word is: this series is expensive but a real value. The R&B series is especially nice. — JME

DUNHILL COMPACT CLASSICS (DCC)

Since its inception in 1986, Dunhill Compact Classics has specialized in audiophile-quality reissues. The key player in producing their exceptional sound is Steve Hoffman, who has set standards throughout the industry and whose remastering techniques involve first-generation masters only. DCC entered the Gold Disc Audiophile Field with the "24 Carat Gold" series, featuring classic releases by Bob Dylan, Cream, the Eagles, the Doors, and others. — RC

MOBILE FIDELITY

Since the late 70s, Mobile Fidelity has been a leader in audiophile remastering, releasing recordings covering a

Record Labels

There are many record companies besides those just mentioned. Here are addresses for some you may wish to contact.

Alcazar Inc.
P. O. Box 429
Waterbury, VT 05676
802/244-8657

American Gramaphone
9130 Mormon Bridge Rd.
Omaha, NE 68152
402/457-4341

Arhoolie
10341 San Pablo Ave.
El Cerrito, CA 94530
415/525-7471

Canyon Records
4143 N. 16th St.
Phoenix, AZ 85016
602/266-4823
602/266-4659

Chacra Alternative Music
35 Parklane Pl., Dept. 3
Dollard-des-Ormeaux
Québec, Canada H9G 1B8
514/624-0278

Crescendo/GNP-Crescendo
8400 Sunset Blvd.
Los Angeles, CA 90069
213/656-2614

Dancing Cat
P. O. Box 639
Santa Cruz, CA 95061
408/249-5085

Editions EG
c/o J. E. M
3619 Kennedy Rd.
S. Plainfield, NJ 07080
201/753-6100

Eurock
P. O. Box 13718
Portland, OR 97213
503/281-0247

Flying Fish
1304 W. Schubert St.
Chicago, IL 60614
312/528-5455

Fortuna
4549 E. Ft. Lowell
Tucson, AZ 85712
602/326-4400

Gaia
121 W. 27th St.
New York, NY 10001
212/645-5252

Gramavision
260 W. Broadway
New York, NY 10013
212/645-5252

Hannibal
P. O. Box 667
Rocky Hill, NJ 08553
609/466-9320

Hearts of Space
P. O. Box 31321
San Francisco, CA 94131
415/759-1130

Higher Octave Music
8964 Wonderland Park AVe.
Los Angeles, CA 90046
213/856-0039

Innovative Communications
c/o Chameleon Music Group
3355 W. El Segundo
Hawthorne, CA 90250
213/973-8282
800/423-6935 (outside California)

Kuckuck
P. O. Box 30122
Tucson, AZ 85751
602/326-4400

Ladyslipper
P. O. Box 3130
Durham, NC 27705
919/683-1570

Living Music
1047 Amsterdam Ave.
New York, NY 10014

Music of the World
P.O. Box 258
Brooklyn, NY 11209

Music West
2200 Larkspur Landing Circle, #100
Larkspur, CA 94939
415/925-9800
415/459-6000

New World
179 Water St.
Torrington, CT 06790
800/233-1337

Novus
c/o RCA Records
1133 Ave. of the Americas
New York, NY 10036
212/582-0028

Philio
(See Rounder)

Private Music
220 E. 23rd St
New York, NY 10010
212/684-2533

Redwood Records
6400 Hollis St., #8
Emeryville, CA 94608
415/428-9191

Rounder
1 Camp St.
Cambridge, MA 02140
617/354-0700

Shanachie Records
Dalebrook Park
Ho-Ho-Kus, NJ 07423
201/445-5561

Shining Star
200 Tamal Vista Blvd., #417
Corde Madera, CA 94925
800/825-4848

Sona Gaia
1845 N. Farwell Ave., 2nd Fl.
Milwaukee, WI 53202
414/272-6700

Sonic Atmospheres
14755 Ventura Blvd., #1776
Sherman Oaks, CA 91403
818/505-6022

Soundings of the Planet
P .O. Box 43512
Tucson, AZ 85733
602/883-1784

Sound Rx
P.O. Box 2644
San Anselmo, CA 94960
415/491-1930

Spring Hill Music
5216 Sunshine Canyon
Boulder, CO 80302
303/938-1188

Tape Masters
176 Forest Ave.
Pacific Grove, CA 93950

variety of styles — from classic rock artists such as Pink Floyd, the Who, Moody Blues, Rod Stewart, and the Allman Brothers, to titles by Frank Sinatra and Johnny Mathis. Mobile's remasters of jazz greats such as Miles Davis and classical music have been highly acclaimed. — RC

RYKODISC

Founded in 1984, Rykodisc was the first CD-only label ("ryko" is Japanese for "sound from a flash of light"). Since then, Ryko has expanded into all formats, including DAT. Their catalog is impressively eclectic, ranging from rock to world music, reggae, folk, and jazz. Of particular note is the acclaimed David Bowe "Sound and Vision" series. Rykodisc can be reached at 200 N. 3rd Ave., Minneapolis, MN 55401; or call 612/375-9162. — RC

ROUNDUP RECORDS

Roundup Records is a first-class act. They were the first to provide straight talk about recordings, new releases and classic albums alike. Roundup Records can be reached at P. O. Box 154, North Cambridge, MA 02140; or call 617/661-6308 (there is a toll-free order line for credit card purchases: 800/44-DISCS). — JME

RHINO RECORDS

From their inauspicious beginnings in 1973 as a used-records strore, Rhino Records has become the foremost reissue label in the industry, known for excellent packaging, sound, and liner notes. Bill Inglot's sparkling remastering work is especially noteworthy. For a catalog, send a dollar to Rhino Records, Inc., Dept. C-10, 2225 Colorado Ave., Santa Monica, CA 90404. — RC

World Music Resources

ORIGINAL MUSIC

418 Lasher Road
Tivoli, New Yoirk 12583
(919) 756-2767

MUSIC OF THE WORLD

P. O. Box 3667
Chapel Hill, NC 27515-3667
(919) 932-9600
(Free Catalog)

AFROPOP WORLDWIDE

Listener's Guide
National Public Radio
2025 M St. NW
Washington D.C. 20036
(202) 822-2323
A business-size, self-addressed envelope will get you a great overview of African and Caribbean music, complete with lists and maps. A real help.

CENTER FOR CUBAN STUDIES

124 W. 23rd St.
New York, NY 10011
Not a record store, but they do sell records and videos imported from — as opposed to licensed from — Cuba; the selection is unpredictable but worth checking out.

QBADISK

P. O. Box 1256
Old Chelsea Station
New York, NY 10011
This address is for mail-ordering Qbadisk albums.

ROUND WORLD MUSIC

491 Aguerro Street
San Francisco, CA 94110
415/255-8411

JACOB'S JUDAIC BOOK & GIFT CENTER

13896 Cedar Road
University Hights, OH 44118
216/321-7200
Contact Jay Steingroot. This and the following two listings are resources for recordings of Jewish music.

MUSIQUE INTERNATIONALE

3012 West Jarvis
Chicago, IL 60645
312/743-3012
This is a resource for Jewish cantorial music.

DOR (ISRAELI)

21 Edgewood
Tenafly, NJ 07670
800/762-4944
Contact Dubi Gerber.

Used CDs

AUDIO HOUSE CD CLUB

There is a brisk business in used CDs. In the early days, all kinds of things were possible — swap clubs, two-for-one swaps, three-for-two swaps, premiums paid on used CDs, and so on. One major company paid $6 apiece for any used CD! By now, reality has asserted itself and all this has settled down. The oldest and largest of these clubs is the Audio House CD Club. Their newsletter/list, which now contains some 15,000 used CDs, comes out every month or so, at $2 a copy — mention the *All-Music Guide*, and then it's free. Write or call Audio House CD Club, 4304 Brayan Drive, Swartz Creek, MI 48473;(313) 655-8639. —JME

Catalogs

It's hard to get away from the all the hype the various record labels spin out about their particular releases. And too often, this hype gets repeated in the magazine reviews, without qualification. Have you ever looked for expert help in sorting out the good from the bad and the ugly in recordings? Of course, that's what this book is all about. But we learned a lot from the following two mail-order companies, which are pioneers in providing straight talk about recordings. Both companies have a family approach to staffing their operations. Staff members are either active musicians or have real experience in recorded music. You can call them up and talk with someone about the music.
I only wish they would cover popular, classical music, and the full rock spectrum. But these are places to find out about folk, blues, gospel, country, bluegrass, R&B, vintage rock, doo wop, some traditional jazz, world beat, ethnic, and the folk music of Europe and the British isles. (Note: See free coupons at the back of this book for both companies.) These catalogs are also educational, introducing readers to the genre (reggae, blues, and so on). Get a copy of these fine newsletters. They're free and they're useful. — JME

RECORD ROUNDUP

This is the grandfather of companies offering music-by-mail-with-reviews. Started in 1979 as an offshoot of Rounder Records, Record Roundup issues a 70-page newsletter free of charge several times a year. Each issue is chock-full of reviews and comments about the quality of the recordings offered. Rounder Records can be reached at P. O. Box 154, North Cambridge, MA 02140; call 617/661-6308 (customer service) or 800/44-DISCS (credit card orders).— JME

ROOTS & RHYTHM (FORMERLY DOWN HOME MUSIC)

If Record Roundup started it all, then the Roots & Rhythm catalog (begun in 1978) has perfected the art of catalog/album reviews. Originally called *Down Home Music*, and affiliated with the Arhoolie record label, *Roots & Rhythm* reads more like a magazine of reviews than a catalog. Each issue is filled with expert opinion, comment, and reviews on the latest in domestic and imported releases. The latest catalog, between 60 and 100 pages, is free. In addition to providing information on domestic labels, Roots & Rhythm stocks and reviews a great number of imported albums that are available nowhere else. Certainly this company deserves some sort of award for the groundbreaking work they have done and the example they have set for catalogs with music reviews. *Roots & Rhythm* can be reached at 6921 Stockton Ave., El Cerrito, CA 94530; or call 510/525-1494. — JME

Magazines, Periodicals, and Newsletters

THE CD-REVIEW DIGEST

This is an indexing service and a reference work intended for libraries, that publishes (quarterly) abstracts of CD reviews from 30 to 40 magazines. *All-Music Guide* readers will be interested in the annual bound volumes, one for classical and one for jazz and popular music. Current versions of both books run almost 700 pages each. These volumes are not cumulative, meaning that each volume has material released during the preceeding year but no material from previous years. Often more than one review abstract is included for each album. The *CD-Review Digest* is the work of Janet Grimes, who is a real pioneer in the field of substantive album reviews. The only downside of this remarkable work is the price. Intended for institutions, the price for either the popular or classical editions is $59. You may want to check it out at your local library. These books are invaluable to the avid CD buff (sorry no LPs or cassettes). A smaller edition, *Best Rated CDs* (popular music), is available at $19.95. Covering the years 1983 to 1992, it includes only the top-rated CDs, some 10% of what is in the larger volume. A smaller version for classical was scheduled for 1992. Write to *CR-Review Digest*, P. O. Box 348, Hemlock Ridge, Voorheesville, NY 12186-0348. — JME

GOLDMINE

Published since 1974, *Goldmine* is just that — a goldmine of discographical information, extended articles, and great album reviews. Nowhere else will you find in-depth articles on individual artists and groups of this length and breadth. And almost every article is accompanied by a complete discography — almost every album ever made is listed. *Goldmine* is geared to the record collector. In fact, a good part of each issue is filled with the ads of collectors. Reading through these is an experience in itself. Those of us who don't collect may have little idea of the amount of activity in out-of-print and hard-to-find albums. Thanks to these folks, it is possible to find almost any hard-to-find album.

Goldmine has some of the best writers in the business — almost every major free-lance writer has written for them at one time or another. It is a tabloid-size magazine of about 170 pages published biweekly! There is a lot of information here. If you have never browsed through a copy, you have an experience in store for you. It's an eye-opener. Write to them and mention the *All-Music Guide* and you will receive a free sample issue. *Goldmine* can be reached at 700 E. State St., Iola, WI 54990; or call 715/445-2214. — JME

DISCOVERIES

DISCoveries, like *Goldmine*, is a tabloid-size magazine (published monthly) devoted to record collectors and record collecting. And also like *Goldmine*, it is filled with articles (and discographies) on artists and groups that will interest non-collectors. The two magazines differ somewhat in the music and forms they try to cover. *Goldmine* is geared to rock & roll, blues, R&B, both on vinyl and CDs, while *DISCoveries* is oriented more toward vinyl, focusing on earlier rock and even some traditional popular music. In addition, *DISCoveries* encourages readers to communicate with each other about various bits of music trivia and record questions through their mailbox. Write to them, mention the *All-Music Guide*, and receive a free sample issue. *DISCoveries* can be reached at P. O. Box 255, Port Townsend, WA 98368; or call 206/385-1200. — JME

CADENCE MAGAZINE

If you love jazz and also buy records and CDs, you will love *Cadence* magazine. Started in 1976 and located in upstate New York, this is the magazine for those who want straight-talk about jazz and lots of reviews! Edited by Bob Rusch, the magazine has reviewed some 26,000 jazz albums over the years (many not reviewed elsewhere), and all back issues are still available. This is also a great place to purchase hard-to-find jazz albums. Not available on many newsstands, this fine magazine is worth checking out. Their record catalog is yours for the asking, and $2.50 will get you a sample issue of *Cadence*. Write to The Cadence Building, Redwood, NY 13679-9612; or call 315/287-2852. — JME

DOWN BEAT

In publication since 1934 and distributed in 142 countries, *DOWN BEAT* is the largest (and oldest) jazz publication. You can probably get a copy at your local newstand. If not, write to *DOWN BEAT*, mention the *All-Music Guide*, and you will receive a free sample issue. *Down Beat's* address is 180 West Park Ave., Elmhurst, IL 60126. — JME

JAZZ TIMES

Another fine jazz magazine, started in 1970, *Jazz Times* distinguishes itself via special issues on a variety of topics, including musical instruments, exceptional features on woman in jazz, plus useful directories of jazz festivals, record companies, education programs, and more. Both jazz and blues albums are reviewed. Write to them, mention the *All-Music Guide*, and get a free sample issue: *Jazz Times*, 8055 13th St., Suite 312, Silver Spring, MD 20910-4803. — JME

BOTH SIDES NOW STEREO NEWSLETTER

This is the quarterly newsletter from which *Both Sides Now* is assembled. It covers both CDs and vinyl and includes interviews with the people who put together oldies reissue packages, previously unpublished discographies and all kinds of information. Write to *Both Sides Now*, Box 384, Fairfax Station, VA 22039. (*Both Sides Now* is also a book; see under "Books on Music" in this section.)— JME

REJOICE! THE GOSPEL MUSIC MAGAZINE

With very few publications devoted to gospel music, *Rejoice!* is a welcome find. Lots of articles, pictures, and more on your favorite gospel groups, Black and White. It is published bi-monthly by the Center for the Study of Southern Culture, The University of Mississippi, University, MS 38677. Write to the editors of *Rejoice!*, c/o The University of Mississippi, University, MS 38677. — JME

LIVING BLUES: A JOURNAL OF THE AFRICAN-AMERICAN BLUES

This is the principal magazine for the blues in this country. Started by blues expert Jim O'Neal, the magazine is now sponsored and published by the Center for the Study of Southern Culture (as is the gospel magazine *Rejoice!*). *Living Blues* is a high-quality magazine (glossy publication) with many illustrations and up-to-date articles on major blues figures. The Center for the Study of Southern Culture can be reached by writing to The University of Mississippi, University, MS 38677. — JME

DIRTY LINEN

"The Traditional Magazine of Folk, Electric Folk, Traditional and World Music," *Dirty Linen* extends the range of folk music with "a wild sense of dedication matched only by good humor and intelligence" (*Library Journal*). *Dirty Linen* covers acoustic to electric, traditional to progressive, artists, festivals, new releases, venues, news, reviews, interviews, and more. For more information, write to *Dirty Linen*, P. O. Box 66600, Baltimore, MD 21239-6600. — JME

CD INTERNATIONAL

This is the most complete catalog of CDs in print we have yet seen. The winter 1991/1992 edition has 73,116 album titles on 120,827 discs (popular music only). If available, the label and number are given for each release in the US, UK, Germany, Japan, and Canada. This is the catalog of choice among the music pros, and the only one that lets you see what is available in other countries at a glance. This 8 1/2 x 11catalog is 650 pages. Write CDI Publishing Corp., P. O. Box 22014, Milwaukie, OR 97222— JME

CD INTERNATIONAL (AMERICAN GUIDE)

CD International offers an additional volume that contains only American CDs— some 21,369 discs. Similar in format to the above and about 300 pages long. For many of these discs, individual track listings and playing times (track by track) are included. CDI Publishing Corporation can be reached at PO Box 22014, Milwaukie, OR 97222. — JME

THE BEAT

The Beat is a bimonthly publication of reggae, African, Caribbean, and world music, providing information, news, interviews, discographies, reviews, and cultural features to an international market of music fans. It features the work of top writers, artists, and photographers who chronicle this rapidly expanding area of music and the increasing popularity of its associated lifestyle. *The Beat* was founded by Roger Steffens in 1982 as an outgrowth of his popular reggae radio program on KCRW in Santa Monica, CA. Within two years, the publication grew from a single-page playlist of records featured on Steffens' show to a nationally distributed newsstand magazine, then called "The Reggae and African Beat." The scope of the magazine increased to include African music and Caribbean pop, though reggae remained the primary focus.

Today, *The Beat* is the most widely circulated magazine in the country dedicated exclusively to world music. While feature articles still emphasize Jamaican and African artists, recent issues have been devoted to Brazilian pop and music of the Indian subcontinent. But the magazine's real crackle lies with its host of opinionated reviewers, who leave no corner of the world unexplored in their quest for the latest trends or the most obscure sounds.

Regular columns in *The Beat* include "Reggae Update," "African Beat," "Haitian Fascination," "Brazil Beat," "The Other Caribbean" (covering francophone Caribbean pop), "Hey Mr. Music" (hot sounds on the London club scene),

"Musical Murder" (reggae singles), and world music columns "Land of a Thousand Dances" and "Technobeat." "National Beat" keeps track of the grass-roots music scene in cities across the US and Canada, while "News and Reviews" eyeballs books and videos and turns a critical ear to recordings.

While not as slick as *Spin*, *Rolling Stone*, or *Option*, *The Beat*'s newsprint format (black and white) gives it an immediacy these other publications lack, highlighting it as an excellent source of news today on the inevitable influences on mainstream pop in years to come. *The Beat* can be reached at P.O. Box 65856, Los Angeles, CA 90065. — BT

ROCK & ROLL DISC

There are many excellent magazines out there that include album reviews, but there is only one major magazine (excluding fanzines and newsletters) that I am aware of that is devoted to laying it on the line with no hype — *Rock & Roll Disc* (est. 1987). Editor Tom Graves has assembled a superb group of writers who share his vision of integrity and straight talk in record reviews, including well-known writers such as Dave Marsh, Rick Clark, Stanley Booth, and Ed Ward, plus a good dozen lesser-known but equally fine writers.

Graves has marketed *Rock & Roll Disc* on the philosophy that the cost of a subscription for one year more than pays for itself if the reviews save you from buying two bad CDs. It works for me. *Rock & Roll Disc* covers blues, R&B, limited jazz and world beat, and rock in all of its various formats. This is a great magazine. Write to P. O. Box 17601, Memphis, TN 38187-0601. — JME

CD-REVIEW

If *Rock & Roll Disc* is the best insider publication, then *CD-Review* is its mainstream counterpart. Originally titled *Digital Audio*, later renamed *CD-Review*, and created by Wayne Green (founder of *Byte Magazine*, *Kilobaud*, *80 Microcomputing*, and other magazines), *CD-Review* is the most successful general publication devoted to reviewing recorded music. Aside from some hardware (stereo equipment) reviews, the magazine is devoted to reviewing all categories of music, from classical to country to contemporary adult (new-age). *CD-Review* established early on a method of rating CDs both for performance quality and for sound. It provides articles, reviews, collectors lists, and other fun features. Though it lacks the fierce integrity of *Rock & Roll Disc*, this is a fine magazine, available at most newsstands — check it out. I still have the first issue I got. Write to *CD-Review*, Forest Road, Hancock, NH 03449. — JME

ADVENTURES IN MUSIC (AIM)

Available through Wayne Green Enterprises (publishers of *CD-Review*), *AIM* and the *Almost Free Samplers* (see next article) are an attempt to provide access to artists who do not record on the major labels. Here's how it works: *AIM* solicits recordings from all comers (from small independent companies in particular) and offers sampler disks on various themes: jazz, new-age, world beat, folk, and so on (a list of the first 30 is provided below). The price is right — merely a shipping and handling charge of $3.79 each; or you can subscribe to the next 25 or 40 issues and bring the handling charge down still further. For not much money, you can sample a wide range of new artists you might never hear otherwise. But at this price, don't expect "jewel boxes"; they come in acceptable cardboard slip-cases.

AIM samplers will also appeal to those of you on a budget who want to hear a wide variety of music. And variety is what you get — both in music styles and quality. *AIM* offers you a chance to step outside the major-label offerings and hear some different tunes. You will like some and hate some, but you will hear new sounds. If you like a track, *AIM* provides the name of an entire album and where you can get it.

I enjoyed listening to most of the AIM samplers and actually learned more about a number of categories I was uncertain of — such as world beat and new-age. More important, I found at least one new artist who has become one of my all-time favorites. As for *CD-Review*, contact *AIM* by writing to Forest Road, Hancock, NH 03449. — JME

AIM-1 / Contemporary Instrumental
AIM-2 / Jazz I
AIM-3 / Pop; Rock I
AIM-4 / Classical
AIM-5 / Christmas
AIM-6 / World Beat
AIM-7 / Folk
AIM-8 / Jazz II
AIM-9 / Pop; Rock II
AIM-10 / New Age
AIM-11 / Classical II
AIM-12 / Quiet Places
AIM-13 / Blues
AIM-14 / Perfect 10/10s
AIM-15 / Bluegrass, Country
AIM-16 / Jazz III
AIM-17 / Kidding Around
AIM-18 / New Age II
AIM-19 / Reggae Party
AIM-20 / Rock III
AIM-21 / Organ Extravaganza
AIM-22 / World Horizons
AIM-23 / Joys of Jazz
AIM-24 / Traditional Christmas
AIM-25 / Music for Kids
AIM-26 / Contemporary
AIM-27 / Gospel
AIM-28 / Cotton Patch Blues
AIM-29 / Classical
AIM-30 / Rhythm & Blues

Books on Music

The following are a few of the books that you will find on the shelves of record collectors and that were helpful in checking information listed in the *All-Music Guide*.

RECORD RESEARCH

Of particular interest to music lovers is the series of books by Joel Whitburn and his company, Record Research. These books are standard items on the shelves of most music collectors and DJs. Originally basing these books on the various chart and sales data (such as #1 hits) coming out of Billbroad magazine (the industry newsletter of the record business), Whitburn has (in recent years) continued to add more and more valuable information. A few of these books may turn up in your local bookstore, but many are known only to DJs and record collectors. We have room here to describe just a few volumes in the series, but it is well worth sending for a complete catalog. These books include (where possible) the complete Billboard chart statistics: the date an album entered the charts, its peak, and the number of weeks on the charts. Most also have the RIAA Platinum/Gold or million-seller album status. Great reference works.

Record Research Inc. can be contacted by writing to P. O. Box 200, Menomonee Falls, WI 53052-0200; or call 414/251-5408. The following six resources for pop, R & B, and country music are all from Record Research. — JME

TOP POP ALBUMS 1955-1985

Every album ever to appear on *Billboard*'s "Top Pop Albums" chart. Includes detailed descriptions of over 14,000 albums (with original label and record numbers), complete chart statistics, artist and title notes, plus other fascinating lists of key albums. This one should be in every record lover's library. 516 pages.

POP MEMORIES 1890-1954

While there are lots of books on rock's recent history, here is one of the few definitive works on the pop's origins. It includes all kinds of chart data and facts on vintage recordings and artists, starting from ragtime and ending in the roots of rock. 660 pages.

TOP POP SINGLES 1955-1990

This classic pop-music reference work is the only comprehensive artist-by-artist listing of each of the nearly 20,000 singles ever to peak on the "Hot 100." Besides chart data, there are artist bios, title notes, and all kinds of charts, photos, and related data. 848 pages.

POP SINGLES ANNUAL 1955-1990

This is the companion volume to the above, with the hits arranged in year-by-year order. You get all kinds of data: charts, data, pictures, lists. Watch the hits roll by through time. 736 pages.

TOP R&B SINGLES 1942-1988

Here is hard-to-find information on R&B, urban contemporary, soul, and Black music singles. Includes extensive artist biographies and interesting record notes. 623 pages.

TOP COUNTRY SINGLES 1944-1988

This is a hit-by-hit account of top country singles. It includes artist biographies, notes, and charted singles. 564 pages.

TROUSER PRESS RECORD GUIDE

Ira A. Robbins, 1991, 763 pages, Collier Books (formerly the *Trouser Press Guide to New Wave Records*, 1983). A reference guide to alternative music (and some fairly mainstream artists) by the people behind *Trouser Press* magazine. Chock-full of biographies and reviews of obscure, revolutionary, and downright strange musical acts from the late 60s to early 90s. Offshoot bands and solo efforts are combined with the source band to show their evolutionary path. The reviews are fair and informative, and it's obvious that these folks really love the music. This new edition is up-to-date (into 1991), dropping a few of the lesser-knowns from the last volume to make room for the newest groups. — SWB

THE NEW ROLLING STONE RECORD GUIDE

Dave Marsh and John Swenson, 1983, 648 pages, Random House. One of the classics. Although somewhat dated now, a new edition is in the works. — JME

BLUES WHO'S WHO

Sheldon, 1987, 775 pages, Da Capo Press. No blues enthusiast should be without this. It contains in-depth career highlights for known blues singers, plus much useful data. — JME

BOTH SIDES NOW

Interested in oldies on CD? Compilations of your favorite artist? Collections of various artists? Hard to wade through a mass of reissues to find the performances you listened to 20 years ago? Here is a book that lists 3,000 CDs, including track listings for almost 2,000 of these; stereo information on some 1,500; ratings on 1,000; also the SPARS code, playing time, and year the CD was released (when available).

Of special interest is the section on artist compilations and collections. This alone makes *Both Sides Now* invaluable and virtually unique in pop-music literature. The CDs are listed both by label and title and indexed by artist. Its author is a stickler for indicating which cuts are mono and which are stereo (just what we buyers need to know). This is a great find! (A *Both Sides Now* newsletter is available on a subscription basis by writing to Both Sides Now Stereo Newsletter, Box 384, Fairfax Station, VA 22039.) — JME

ROCK ON – VOLS. 1-3

Norm N. Nite, 1974, 676 pages, Thomas Y. Crowell Co. Standard reference works for the classic rock period. — JME

ROCK RECORD 4

Terry Hounsome, 1991, Record Researcher Publications. Indispensible reference work containing not only a huge number of albums but sidemen and instruments for most of these as well. — JME

ROCK MOVERS AND SHAKERS

Dafydd Rees and Luke Crampton, 1991, 585 pages, Billboard Books classic rock reference work. Contains details not available elsewhere. — JME

PENGUIN ENCYCLOPEDIA OF POPULAR MUSIC

Donald Clarke, 1990, 1378 pages, Penguin Books. A fine reference work providing biographical details plus a list of major albums and their release dates. Worth owning. — JME

COLLECTIBLE RECORD ALBUMS 1949-1989

Neal Umphred, 1991, 608 pages, Krause Publications. Many price guides offer prices only for general categories within a particular label. What makes Umphred's books (he has one on 45s and a new one on jazz albums) useful is that they privide prices for each album listed. A useful book even for non-collectors because it provides a thorough list of albums for each artist. — JME

BRING THE NOISE: A GUIDE TO RAP MUSIC AND HIP-HOP CULTURE

Havelock Nelson and Michael A. Gonzales, 1991, 298 pages, Harmony Books.

THE ROLLING STONE JAZZ RECORD GUIDE

John Swenson, 1985, 219 pages, Random House. Sadly outdated, but still useful. We hope an update is in the pipeline. — JME

THE DOWN HOME GUIDE TO THE BLUES

Frank Scott, 1991, 250 pages, A Cappella Books. A recent release that provides a list of blues albums in-print, along with rating comments. Worth having. — JME

THE NEW GROVE DICTIONARY OF JAZZ

Barry Kernfeld, 1988, 1360 pages, Macmillan Press Limited. If you can afford it (some $300), this huge two-volume set deserves to be on your bookshelf. It is the best single work on jazz that we have seen. — JME

GOLD AND PLATINUM RECORDS

Adam White, 1990, 308 pages, Billboard Books.

ENCYCLOPEDIA OF FOLK AND COUNTRY & WESTERN MUSIC

Stambler, Irwin, Landon, Grelun, 1984, 902 pages, St. Martin's Press.

The Weather Channel

Cable-TV's Weather Channel provides more than just the nation's weather — in the background they are playing more than just background music. If you have noticed this too and are wondering what albums are getting played, here is a partial list of the albums.

George Benson	*The Best of 1969-1970*	(A & M)
Stanley Clarke	*Time Exposure*	(Epic)
David Grisman	*Acousticity/Zebra*	(Acoustic)
George Howard	*Dancing in the Sun*	(TBA)
Bill Cobham	*Picture This*	(GRP)
Billy Cobham	*Power Play*	(GRP)
Pat Metheny	*Off Ramp*	(ECM)
Pat Metheny	*First Circle*	(ECM)
Wes Montgomery	*On the Gourb*	(A&M)
Joe Sample	*The Hunter*	(MCA)
Joe Sample	*Rainbow Seeker*	(MCA)
David Sanbourn	*A Change of Heart*	(Warner Bros.)
Cedar Walton	*Animation*	
Sadao Watanabe	*Rendevous*	(Electra)
The Yellow Jackets	*Four Corners*	(MCA)
Lee Ritenour	*On the Line*	(Electra)
McCoy Tyner	*New York*	(Reunion)

RECORD COLLECTING

BY NEAL UMPHRED

There have been record collectors as long as there have been records. Special performances of operas and "classical" vocals were prized — and bootlegged — before the First World War; Enrico Caruso was a household name in much of middle class and working class America (well, at least in the east coast cities with large immigrant populations). The hobby began to soar when a generation of teenagers were swept up in the swing of the big bands. As these fans grew to maturity, their interest remained and many a successful individual whiled away his or her free hours pursuing elusive V-discs or Benny Goodman or Artie Shaw.

78-rpm singles remained the object of pursuit through the early 50s, especially as another type of collector was searching for Son House, Robert Johnson, and the more obscure pre-War blues and country singers. But the biggest boost came from the new jazz aficionados seeking sides by Bird and Diz and Miles. Many of these fans openly embraced the new "LP" format. Today, many a collector dreams of the heady feeling that will follow tracking down an elusive Blue Note, although the business of collecting out-of-print albums by pioneering jazz artists of the post-bop era is relatively recent and remains clouded in obscurity.

Until the waning days of the 60s, the 45 obtained the bulk of the hobby's passion and attention (along with the biggest of the bucks), as the "little record with the big hole" defined the listening experience of the mature collectors of that period — those who had come of age in the 50s, digging the wondrous harmonies of Black vocal groups from New York or the crazy rhythms of the Southern rockabillies. While such luminaries as the Five Keys and Elvis all recorded albums during the Eisenhower years, it is their Aladdin and Sun singles that command the hefty prices.

By the early 70s, there was an explosion of interest in collecting albums, sparked in no small part by the new generation of fans coming into some spendable cash: those who had cut their teeth on the Beatles and the Stones. The enormous market enjoyed by rock &' roll of the 60s — often referred to as "Rock with a capital R" — now seems pitifully small compared to the multi-platinum success that even mediocre artists achieved during the excesses of the past 20 years. Still, it was large enough that, along with the worldwide esteem in which much of the music is held, it guarantees that the demand — ever growing as new generations of listeners become enamored of Pet Sounds or Music from Big Park — will continue to outweigh the dwindling supply. And that, essentially the true foundation of capitalism (and the much vaunted but disappearing "free market"), is what the business of record collecting is about: simple supply and demand.

While dealers love to tout what is supposed to be a "rarity," the lack of supply of an item is meaningless if there is a corresponding lack of interest (i.e., demand). If there are only a half-dozen known copies of a record on the entire planet and there are only three known collectors, there is a glut of that record on the market! On the other side of the spectrum, an album that sold hundreds of thousands of copies in 1966 can be highly valued if there are hundreds of thousands of interested collectors interested in that record today. Such is the case with the infamous "butch cover" variation of the Beatles' *Yesterday and Today* album. Arguably the "world's most collectable album," by Capitol's own estimation the number of copies initially printed and distributed (with and without the revised, second cover pasted over the offending photo) were as few as 60,000 and as many as 600,000!

Near-mint originals comfortably — and with regularity — sell in the four figures; at least three still sealed, "first state" stereo copies of *Yesterday and Today* (i.e., a jacket where the second cover had never been pasted over the original; thus the album is in its original or first state) have sold in excess of $10,000. Even relatively trashed copies (referred to as "peel jobs," which range from the expert to the wretched) can bring a hundred dollars. And while virtually every hard-working dealer can turn up a few copies a year, the demand escalates, with the value.

Now, for the novice, wondering where to start .... Easy: Start with the music you like. Joining the collecting community and discovering previously unseen used record shops in your hometown, attending conventions an hour away and scouring through collectors' publications like *Goldmine* — this puts you in touch with such desirable items as live performances recorded exclusively for syndicated radio programs such as the "King Biscuit Flower Hour." Find out what the artist you admire cites as his or her obvious influences and trace down original copies of those artists' work. If Prince is your main man, your shelves will see a steady supply of soul and funk on labels such as Atlantic, Tamla, and Stax. If R.E.M. is your idea of the ultimate contemporary rock/pop ensemble, you'll find yourself with a collection of the original Byrds albums and, most likely, a growing interest in Bob Dylan.

I stress originals for several reasons: the pressings are often superior to those of the reissues (assuring your listening enjoyment); and of course, we are talking about collecting as a hobby and investment. Originals escalate in value; reissues rarely do. Either way, you're hooked, and another collector has joined the fold!

INDEX

Using the *All-Music Guide* Coupons

The five mail-order companies featured on the adjacent coupon page are the best in the business. *Roots & Rhythm* and *Roundup Records* are famous among music lovers, and are described in our music resources starting on page 1140. The other three companies also deserve mention. *Stash-Daybreak* is the largest and most established mail-order company specializing in jazz recordings. *SKR Classical* is a well-known midwestern mail-order firm catering to the classical buff. *Bose Express Music* handles every kind of music, and is one of the largest mail-order music companies in the country. All five of the firms are tried and ̄e. You can depend on them. Each has agreed to offer readers five coupons, each worth $5 off the ̄se of a CD. See the coupons for details, or call them for a catalog.